D1397357

TEXAS TECH UNIVERSITY HEALTH SCIENCES CENTER

Textbook of Pediatric Infectious Diseases

FIFTH EDITION

Textbook of Pediatric Infectious Diseases

VOLUME 1

Ralph D. Feigin, M.D.

J. S. Abercrombie Professor and Chairman, Department of Pediatrics, and Distinguished Service Professor, Baylor College of Medicine
Physician-in-Chief, Texas Children's Hospital
Physician-in-Chief, Service of Pediatrics, Ben Taub General Hospital
Chief, Pediatric Service, The Methodist Hospital
Houston, Texas

James D. Cherry M.D., M.Sc.

Professor of Pediatrics
David Geffen School of Medicine at UCLA
Member, Division of Infectious Diseases
Mattel Children's Hospital at UCLA
Los Angeles, California

Gail J. Demmler, M.D.

Professor, Department of Pediatrics
Baylor College of Medicine
Director, Diagnostic Virology Laboratory
Texas Children's Hospital
Houston, Texas

Sheldon L. Kaplan, M.D.

Professor and Vice-Chairman of Clinical Affairs, Department of Pediatrics
Baylor College of Medicine
Chief, Infectious Disease Service
Texas Children's Hospital
Houston, Texas

SAUNDERS
An Imprint of Elsevier Science

SAUNDERS
An Imprint of Elsevier Science

The Curtis Center
Independence Square West
Philadelphia, Pennsylvania 19106

Volume 1: Part no. 9997620194
Volume 2: Part no. 9997620208
Two-volume set ISBN 0-7216-9329-6

TEXTBOOK OF PEDIATRIC INFECTIOUS DISEASES

Notice

Pharmacology is an ever-changing field. Standard safety precautions must be followed, but as new research and clinical experience broaden our knowledge, changes in treatment and drug therapy may become necessary or appropriate. Readers are advised to check the most current product information provided by the manufacturer of each drug to be administered to verify the recommended dose, the method and duration of administration, and contraindications. It is the responsibility of the treating physician, relying on experience and knowledge of the patient, to determine dosages and the best treatment for each individual patient. Neither the Publisher nor the editor assumes any liability for any injury and/or damage to persons or property arising from this publication.

The Publisher

Library of Congress Cataloging-in-Publication Data

Textbook of pediatric infectious diseases/[edited by] Ralph D. Feigin... [et al.].-- 5th ed.
p.; cm.
Includes bibliographical references and index.
ISBN 0-7216-9329-6
1. Communicable diseases in children. I. Feigin, Ralph D.
[DNLM: 1. Communicable diseases—Child. 2. Pediatrics—methods. WC 100 T355 2004]
RJ401 .T49 2004
618.92′9—dc21 2002026835

Acquisitions Editor: Judy Fletcher
Developmental Editor: Melissa Dudlick
Project Manager: Lee Ann Draud

Printed in the United States of America

Last digit is the print number: 9 8 7 6 5 4 3 2 1

To our spouses—
Judith Feigin, Jeanne Cherry, Richard Demmler, and Marsha Kaplan.

our children—
Susan Feigin Harris and Jonathan Harris, Michael and Barbara Feigin, Debra Feigin Sukin and Steven Sukin; James Cherry, Jeffrey Cherry and Kass Hogan, Susan Cherry, Kenneth Cherry and Jennifer Carbry; Emily, Matthew, Amy, and Anna Rose Demmler; and Lauren Kaplan, Mindy Kaplan Langland and Lance Langland

and our grandchildren—
Rebecca and Sarah Harris, Matthew and Rachel Feigin, Jacob Sukin, and Ferguson and Dennis Carbry

CONTRIBUTORS

John G. Aaskov, Ph.D., F.R.C.Path.
Senior Lecturer, School of Life Sciences, Queensland University of Technology, Brisbane, Australia
Ross River Virus Arthritis; Murray Valley Encephalitis

Susan M. Abdel-Rahman, Pharm.D.
Associate Professor, Department of Pediatrics, University of Missouri—Kansas City, School of Medicine; Director, Developmental Pharmacokinetic and Pharmacodynamic Core Lab, Pediatric Clinical Pharmacology and Medical Toxicology, Children's Mercy Hospital and Clinics, Kansas City, Missouri
The Pharmacokinetic-Pharmacodynamic Interface: Determinants of Anti-infective Drug Action and Efficacy in Pediatrics

Walid Abuhammour, M.D.
Associate Professor of Pediatrics, Department of Pediatric Infectious Diseases, Michigan State University College of Human Medicine; Associate Professor of Pediatrics, Department of Pediatric Infectious Diseases, Hurley Medical Center, East Lansing, Michigan
Antimicrobial Prophylaxis

Cristoph Aebi, M.D.
Head, Pediatric Infectious Diseases Unit, Department of Pediatrics and Institute for Infectious Diseases, University of Bern, Bern, Switzerland
Tick-Borne Encephalitis

Joshua J. Alexander, M.D.
Assistant Professor of Physician Medicine and Rehabilitation and Pediatrics, University of North Carolina at Chapel Hill School of Medicine, Chapel Hill, North Carolina
Otitis Externa

Marvin E. Ament, M.D.
Distinguished Professor of Pediatrics and Chief, Division of Gastroenterology and Nutrition, David Geffen School of Medicine at UCLA, Los Angeles, California
Esophagitis

Donald C. Anderson, M.D.
Adjunct Professor of Pediatrics, Baylor College of Medicine, Houston, Texas; Senior Vice President and Chief Scientific Officer, Adaptive Therapeutics, La Solla, California
Pneumocystis carinii Pneumonia

Marsha S. Anderson, M.D.
Assistant Professor, Department of Pediatrics, University of Colorado School of Medicine; Director of Inpatient Medicine, Children's Hospital, Denver, Colorado
Meningococcal Disease

Stephen S. Arnon, M.D.
Founder and Chief, Infant Botulism Treatment and Prevention Program, California Department of Health Services, Berkeley, California
Infant Botulism

Ann M. Arvin, M.D.
Lucille Packard Professor, Department of Pediatrics and Microbiology and Immunology, Stanford University School of Medicine; Chief, Infectious Disease Service, Lucille Packard Children's Hospital, Stanford, California
Herpes Simplex Viruses 1 and 2

Jane T. Atkins, M.D.
Department of Pediatrics, University of Texas—Houston Medical School, Houston, Texas
Cryptosporidiosis, Cyclospora Infection, Isosporiasis, and Microsporidiosis

Robert L. Atmar, M.D.
Associate Professor, Department of Medicine, Molecular Virology, and Microbiology, Baylor College of Medicine; Chairman, Infection Control, Ben Taub General Hospital, Houston, Texas
Rhinoviruses

Carol J. Baker, M.D.
Professor and Texas Children's Hospital Foundation Chair in Pediatric Infectious Diseases, Department of Pediatrics, Molecular Virology, and Microbiology, Baylor College of Medicine; Attending Physician, Infectious Diseases Section, Texas Children's Hospital; Medical Director of Infection Control, Women's Hospital of Texas, Houston, Texas
Cervical Lymphadenitis; Group B Streptococcal Infections

Stephen J. Barenkamp, M.D.
Professor of Pediatrics and Molecular Microbiology, Department of Pediatrics, St. Louis University School of Medicine; Director, Division of Pediatric Infectious Diseases, Cardinal Glennon Children's Hospital, St. Louis, Missouri
Other *Haemophilus* Species

Elizabeth D. Barnett, M.D.
Associate Professor of Pediatrics, Boston University School of Medicine; Department of Pediatrics, Boston Medical Center, Boston, Massachusetts
Malaria

Robert D. Basow, M.D.
Community Preceptor Attending, Department of Community Pediatrics, University of Massachusetts Medical Center, Worcester, Massachusetts
Streptobacillus moniliformis (Rat-Bite Fever); *Spirillum minus* (Rat-Bite Fever)

William R. Beisel, M.D., F.A.C.P.
Adjunct Professor (retired), W. Harry Feinstone Department of Molecular Mirobiology and Immunology, Johns Hopkins School of Hygiene and Public Health, Baltimore, Maryland
Metabolic Response of the Host to Infections

Beth P. Bell, M.D., M.P.H.
Chief, Epidemiology Branch, Division of Viral Hepatitis, National Center for Infectious Diseases, Centers for Disease Control and Prevention, Atlanta, Georgia
Hepatitis A Virus

Gil Benard, M.D., Ph.D.
Medical Researcher, Clinical and Experimental Allergy and Immunology Laboratory, Medical School of the University of São Paulo, São Paulo, Brazil
Paracoccidioidomycosis

David I. Bernstein, M.D.
Professor, Department of Pediatrics, University of Cincinnati; Director, Division of Infectious Diseases, Cincinnati Children's Hospital, Cincinnati, Ohio
Rotaviruses

Charles D. Bluestone, M.D.
Eberly Professor of Pediatric Otolaryngology, Department of Otolaryngology, University of Pittsburgh School of Medicine; Director, Department of Pediatric Otolaryngology, Children's Hospital of Pittsburgh, Pittsburgh, Pennsylvania
Otitis Media

Michael D. Blum, M.D.
Assistant Vice President, Global Safety Surveillance and Epidemiology, Wyeth Research, Collegeville, Pennsylvania
Aspergillus Infections

Jeffrey L. Blumer, Ph.D., M.D.
Professor, Department of Pediatrics and Pharmacology, Case Western Reserve University; Chief, Department of Pediatric Pharmacology and Critical Care, Rainbow Babies and Children's Hospital, Cleveland, Ohio
Antibiotic Resistance

Robert Bortolussi, M.D., F.R.C.P.C.
Professor of Pediatrics, Department of Pediatrics and Microbiology and Immunology, Dalhousie University Faculty of Medicine; Chief of Research, IWK Health Centre, Halifax, Nova Scotia, Canada
Listeriosis

Thomas G. Boyce, M.D., M.P.H.
Assistant Professor of Pediatrics, Mayo Medical School; Consultant, Pediatric Infectious Diseases, Mayo Clinic, Rochester, Minnesota
Miscellaneous Gram-Positive Cocci; *Erysipelothrix rhusiopathiae*; Miscellaneous Gram-Positive Bacilli; *Citrobacter; Enterobacter; Klebsiella; Morganella morganii; Proteus; Providencia; Serratia;* Miscellaneous Enterobacteria; *Vibrio vulnificus;* Miscellaneous Non-Enterobacteriaceae Fermentative Bacilli; *Achromobacter* (*Alcaligenes*); *Eikenella corrodens; Chryseobacterium (Flavobacterium)*

Kenneth M. Boyer, M.D.
Women's Board Professor of Pediatrics, Rush Medical College of Rush University; Chairman, Department of Pediatrics, Rush Children's Hospital, Chicago, Illinois
Nonbacterial Pneumonia; *Borrelia* (Relapsing Fever); Toxoplasmosis

John S. Bradley, M.D.
Director, Division of Infectious Diseases, Children's Hospital and Health Center, San Diego, California
Peritonitis and Intra-abdominal Abscess; Retroperitoneal Infections; Outpatient Intravenous Antibiotic Therapy for Serious Infections

Michael T. Brady, M.D.
Professor and Vice Chair for Clinical Affairs, Department of Pediatrics, Ohio State University College of Medicine and Public Health; Associate Medical Director, Department of Pediatrics, Children's Hospital, Columbus, Columbus, Ohio
Pseudomonas and Related Genera

Kathryn Brady-McCreery, M.D.
Assistant Professor, Baylor College of Medicine; Staff Pediatric Ophthalmologist, Texas Children's Hospital, Houston, Texas
Ocular Infectious Diseases

William J. Britt, M.D.
Charles A. Alford Professor of Pediatrics, Professor of Pediatrics, Microbiology, and Neurology, University of Alabama School of Medicine; Attending Physician, Children's Hospital of Alabama and University of Alabama Hospitals, Birmingham, Alabama
Transmissible Spongiform Encephalopathies (Creutzfeldt-Jakob Disease, Gertsmann-Sträussler-Scheinker Disease, Kuru, Fatal Familial Insomnia, New Variant Creutzfeldt-Jakob Disease)

Annemarie Broderick, M.B., B.Ch., M.R.C.P.I.
Fellow, Combined Program in Pediatric Gastroenterology and Nutrition, Department of Pediatrics, Harvard Medical School; Fellow, Combined Program in Pediatric Gastroenterology and Nutrition, Department of Pediatric Gastroenterology and Nutrition, Children's Hospital, Boston; Fellow, Combined Program in Pediatric Gastroenterology and Nutrition; Department of Pediatric Gastroenterology, Massachusetts General Hospital, Boston, Massachusetts
Hepatitis B and D Viruses

David A. Bruckner, Sc.D.
Chief, Division of Laboratory Medicine, Department of Pathology and Laboratory Medicine, David Geffen School of Medicine at UCLA; Chief Operating Officer, Clinical Laboratories, UCLA Hospital Systems, Los Angeles, California
Nomenclature for Aerobic and Anaerobic Bacteria

Carrie L. Byington, M.D.
Associate Professor, Department of Pediatrics and Infectious Diseases, University of Utah, Salt Lake City, Utah
Streptobacillus moniliformis (Rat-Bite Fever); *Spirillum minus* (Rat-Bite Fever)

Judith R. Campbell, M.D.
Associate Professor, Pediatrics/Infectious Diseases Section, Baylor College of Medicine; Attending Physician, Texas Children's Hospital, Houston, Texas
Parotitis; Peritonitis and Intra-abdominal Abscess

Thomas S. Carothers, M.D.
Pediatric Ophthalmology and Adult Strabismus, Virginia Eye Institute, Richmond, Virginia
Ocular Infectious Diseases

Mariam R. Chacko, M.D.
Associate Professor, Department of Pediatrics, and Medical Director, Baylor Teen Health Clinics, Baylor College of Medicine; Attending Physician, Texas Children's Hospital, Houston, Texas
Genital Infections in Childhood and Adolescence; *Calymmatobacterium granulomatis; Trichomonas* Infections

Louisa E. Chapman, M.D.
Assistant to the Director for Biological Therapeutics, Division of AIDS, STD, and TB Laboratory Research, National Center for Infectious Diseases, Centers for Disease Control and Prevention, Atlanta, Georgia
Hantaviruses

Rémi N. Charrel, M.D., Ph.D.
Unité des Virus Émergents, Faculté de Médecine, Université de la Mediterranée, Marseilles, France
Arenaviral Hemorrhagic Fevers; Filoviral Hemorrhagic Fever: Marburg and Ebola Virus Fevers

James D. Cherry, M.D., M.Sc.
Professor of Pediatrics, David Geffen School of Medicine at UCLA; Member, Division of Infectious Diseases, Mattel Children's Hospital at UCLA, Los Angeles, California
Epidemiology of Infectious Diseases; The Common Cold; Pharyngitis (Pharyngitis, Tonsillitis, Tonsillopharyngitis, and Nasopharyngitis); Herpangina; Pharyngoconjunctival Fever; Sinusitis; Mastoiditis; Epiglottitis (Supraglottitis); Croup (Laryngitis, Laryngotracheitis, Spasmodic Croup, Laryngotracheobronchitis, Bacterial Tracheitis, and Laryngotracheobronchopneumonitis); Acute Bronchitis; Aseptic Meningitis and Viral Meningitis; Encephalitis and Meningoencephalitis; Cutaneous Manifestations of Systemic Infections; Roseola Infantum (Exanthem Subitum); *Arcanobacterium haemolyticum;* Pertussis and Other *Bordetella* Infections; Tetanus; Human Parvoviruses B19; Adenoviruses; Smallpox (Variola Virus); Other Poxviruses; Enteroviruses and Parechoviruses; Reoviruses; Rubella Virus; Measles Virus; Mumps Virus; Severe Acute Respiratory Syndrome (SARS); *Mycoplasma* and *Ureaplasma* Infections; Use of the Diagnostic Virology Laboratory

P. Joan Chesney, M.D.
Professor of Pediatrics, Division of Infectious Diseases, University of Tennessee, Memphis, College of Medicine; Active Staff, Department of Pediatrics, Le Bonheur Children's Medical Center; Director, Office of Academic Programs, St. Jude Children's Research Hospital, Memphis, Tennessee
Toxic Shock Syndrome

Javier Chinen, M.D., Ph.D.
Staff Clinician, Genetic and Molecular Biology Branch, National Human Genome Research Institute—National Institutes of Health, Bethesda, Maryland
Primary Immunodeficiencies

Natascha Ching, M.D.
Clinical Instructor, Department of Pediatrics, David Geffen School of Medicine at UCLA; Attending Physician, Department of Pediatrics, Division of Pediatric Infectious Diseases, Mattel Children's Hospital at UCLA, Los Angeles, California
Mycoplasma and *Ureaplasma* Infections

H. Fred Clark, D.V.M., Ph.D.
Research Professor, Department of Pediatrics, University of Pennsylvania School of Medicine; Adjunct Professor, Wistar Institute, Philadelphia, Pennsylvania
Rabies Virus

John R. Clark, Jr., M.D.
Resident in Pediatrics, Department of Pediatrics, Baylor College of Medicine; Resident in Pediatrics, Department of Pediatrics, Texas Children's Hospital, Houston, Texas
Parotitis

Thomas G. Cleary, M.D.
Professor of Pediatrics, Department of Pediatrics, Pediatric Infectious Diseases Division, University of Texas—Houston Medical School; Professor of Pediatrics, Department of Pediatric Infectious Diseases, Memorial Hermann Children's Hospital, Houston, Texas
Approach to Patients with Gastrointestinal Tract Infections and Food Poisoning; *Bacillus cereus; Shigella; Salmonella; Vibrio parahaemolyticus; Campylobacter jejuni;* Cryptosporidiosis, *Cyclospora* Infection, Isosporiasis, and Microsporidiosis

David K. Coats, M.D.
Associate Professor of Ophthalmology and Pediatrics, Department of Ophthalmology, Baylor College of Medicine; Chief, Section of Pediatric Ophthalmology, Department of Pediatric Ophthalmology, Texas Children's Hospital, Houston, Texas
Ocular Infectious Diseases

Armando G. Correa, M.D.
Assistant Professor, Department of Pediatrics, Mayo Medical School; Senior Associate Consultant, Department of Pediatric and Adolescent Medicine, Mayo Clinic, Rochester, Minnesota
Coagulase-Positive Staphylococcal Infections *(Staphylococcus aureus); Acinetobacter;* Clostridial Intoxication and Infection

J. Thomas Cross, Jr., M.D., M.P.H.
Vice President, Education, MEDStudy Corporation, Colorado Springs, Colorado
Fungal Meningitis; Other Mycobacteria

Ronald Dagan, M.D.
Professor of Pediatrics and Infectious Diseases, Faculty of Health Sciences, Ben-Gurion University of the Negev; Director, Pediatric Infectious Disease Unit, Soroka University Medical Center, Beer-Sheva, Israel
Pneumococcal Infections

Adnan S. Dajani, M.D.
Professor Emeritus of Pediatrics, Wayne State University School of Medicine; Director Emeritus, Division of Infectious Diseases, Children's Hospital of Michigan, Detroit, Michigan
Antimicrobial Prophylaxis

Toni Darville, M.D.
Associate Professor of Pediatrics and Microbiology/Immunology, Department of Pediatrics, University of Arkansas for Medical Sciences, Little Rock, Arkansas
Nocardia

Jeffrey P. Davis, M.D.
Adjunct Professor, Departments of Pediatrics and Preventative Medicine, University of Wisconsin Medical School; Chief Medical Officer and State Epidemiologist for Communicable Diseases, Bureau of Public Health, Wisconsin Division of Health, Madison, Wisconsin
Toxic Shock Syndrome

Gail J. Demmler, M.D.
Professor, Department of Pediatrics, Baylor College of Medicine; Director, Diagnostic Virology Laboratory, Texas Children's Hospital, Houston, Texas
Hepatitis; Opportunistic Infections in Kidney Transplantation; Human Polyomaviruses and Papillomaviruses; Cytomegalovirus; Antiviral Agents

Penelope H. Dennehy, M.D.
Professor, Department of Pediatrics, Brown University School of Medicine; Associate Director, Department of Pediatric Infectious Diseases, Rhode Island Hospital, Providence, Rhode Island
Active Immunizing Agents

Jaime G. Deville, M.D
Assistant Clinical Professor, Department of Pediatrics, David Geffen School of Medicine at UCLA; Attending Physician, Department of Pediatrics, Mattel Children's Hospital at UCLA, Los Angeles, California
Sinusitis

Jan E. Drutz, M.D.
Professor, Department of Pediatrics, Baylor College of Medicine; Director, Residents' Primary Care Group Clinic, Department of Pediatrics, Texas Children's Hospital, Houston, Texas
Arthropods

Desmond F. Duff, M.B., F.R.C.P.I., F.A.A.P.
Consultant, Paediatric Cardiologist, Our Lady's Hospital for Sick Children, Dublin, Ireland
Myocarditis

Paul H. Edelstein, M.D.
Professor, Department of Pathology and Laboratory Medicine, University of Pennsylvania School of Medicine; Director of Clinical Microbiology, Hospital of the University of Pennsylvania, Philadelphia, Pennsylvania
Legionnaires' Disease, Pontiac Fever, and Related Illnesses

Kathryn M. Edwards, M.D.
Professor of Pediatrics, Department of Pediatrics, and Vice Chair for Clinical Research, Vanderbilt University School of Medicine; Attending Physician, Vanderbilt Children's Hospital, Nashville, Tennessee
Bartonella: Cat Scratch Disease

Morven S. Edwards, M.D.
Professor, Department of Pediatrics, Baylor College of Medicine; Attending Physician, Department of Pediatrics, Texas Children's Hospital and Ben Taub General Hospital, Houston, Texas
Mediastinitis; Anthrax; Rickettisal Diseases; Animal Bites

B. Keith English, M.D.
Professor, Department of Pediatrics, University of Tennessee Health Science Center and Children's Foundation Research Center; Division Chief, Department of Infectious Diseases, Le Bonheur Children's Medical Center, Memphis, Tennessee
Enterococcal and Viridans Streptococcal Infections

Leland L. Fan, M.D.
Professor, Department of Pediatrics, Baylor College of Medicine; Department of Pediatrics, Texas Children's Hospital, Houston, Texas
Chronic Interstitial Pneumonitis and Hypersensitivity Pneumonitis

Ralph D. Feigin, M.D.
J. S. Abercrombie Professor and Chairman, Department of Pediatrics, and Distinguished Service Professor, Baylor College of Medicine; Physician-in-Chief, Texas Children's Hospital; Physician-in-Chief, Service of Pediatrics, Ben Taub General Hospital; Chief, Pediatric Service, The Methodist Hospital, Houston Texas
Interaction of Infection and Nutrition; Otitis Externa; Bacterial Meningitis beyond the Neonatal Period; Fever without Source and Fever of Unknown Origin; Diphtheria; *Aeromonas;* Tularemia; Leptospirosis; Rickettsial Diseases

George D. Ferry, M.D.
Professor of Pediatrics, Department of Pediatrics, Baylor College of Medicine and Texas Children's Hospital; Department of Pediatrics, Ben Taub General Hospital, Houston, Texas
Antibiotic-Associated Colitis

Philip R. Fischer, M.D.
Profesor of Pediatrics and Consultant, Pediatric and Adolescent Medicine, Mayo Medical School and Mayo Clinic, Rochester, Minnesota
Schistosomiasis

Randall G. Fisher, M.D.
Assistant Professor of Pediatrics, Eastern Virginia Medical School; Medical Director, Division of Pediatric Infectious Diseases, and Attending Physician, Children's Hospital of the King's Daughters, Norfolk, Virginia
Miscellaneous Gram-Positive Cocci; *Erysipelothrix rhusiopathiae;* Miscellaneous Gram-Positive Bacilli; *Citrobacter; Enterobacter; Klebsiella; Morganella morganii; Proteus; Providencia; Serratia;* Miscellaneous Enterobacteria; *Vibrio vulnificus;* Miscellaneous Non-Enterobacteriaceae Fermentative Bacilli; *Achromobacter (Alcaligenes); Eikenella corrodens; Chryseobacterium (Flavobacterium)*

Patricia M. Flynn, M.D.
Professor, Departments of Pediatrics and Preventative Medicine, University of Tennessee, Memphis, College of Medicine; Member, Department of Infectious Diseases, St. Jude Children's Research Hospital, Memphis, Tennessee
Candidiasis

Thomas R. Flynn, D.M.D.
Assistant Professor of Oral and Maxillofacial Surgery, Department of Oral and Maxillofacial Surgery, and Director, Predoctoral Oral and Maxillofacial Surgery Education, Harvard School of Dental Medicine; Associate Visiting Surgeon, Department of Oral and Maxiollofacial Surgery, Massachusetts General Hospital; Associate Attending Physician, Department of Dentistry, Brigham and Women's Hospital, Boston, Massachusetts
Infections of the Oral Cavity

David W. Fraser, M.D.
Yardley, Pennsylvania
Public Health Considerations

Lisa M. Frenkel, M.D.
Associate Professor, Department of Pediatrics and Laboratory Medicine, University of Washington School of Medicine; Children's Hospital and Regional Medical Center, Seattle, Washington
Dientamoeba fragilis Infections

Richard A. Friedman, M.D., M.B.A.
Assistant Professor of Pediatrics, Baylor College of Medicine; Chief, Arrhythmia and Pacing Services, and Chief, Cardiology Clinic, Texas Children's Hospital, Houston, Texas
Infectious Pericarditis; Myocarditis

David R. Fulton, M.D.
Associate Professor of Pediatrics, Harvard Medical School; Chief, Cardiology Outpatient Services, and Senior Associate in Cardiology, Department of Cardiology, Children's Hospital, Boston, Boston, Massachusetts
Noninfectious Carditis

Lynne S. Garcia, M.S., M.T., F.A.A.M.
Director, LSG & Associates, Santa Monica, California
Classification and Nomenclature of Human Parasites

Michael A. Gerber, M.D.
Professor, Department of Pediatrics, University of Cincinnati College of Medicine; Attending Physician, Division of Infectious Diseases, Cincinnati Children's Hospital Medical Center, Cincinnati, Ohio
Group A, Group C, and Group G Beta-Hemolytic Streptococcal Infections

Anne A. Gershon, M.D.
Professor, Department of Pediatrics, Columbia University College of Physicians and Surgeons; Director, Division of Pediatric Infectious Diseases, Department of Pediatrics, Columbia University Medical Center, New York, New York
Varicella-Zoster Virus

Mark A. Gilger, M.D.
Associate Professor of Pediatrics, Department of Pediatrics—Gastroenterology, Baylor College of Medicine; Director, Gastrointestinal Procedures Suite, Texas Children's Hospital, Houston, Texas
Whipple Disease; *Helicobacter pylori*

Daniel G. Glaze, M.D.
Associate Professor, Department of Pediatrics and Neurology, and Medical Director, Blue Bird Circle Rett Center, Department of Pediatrics, Baylor College of Medicine; Medical Director, Texas Children's Hospital Sleep Disorders Center, Department of Neurophysiology, Texas Children's Hospital; Medical Director, The Methodist Hospital Sleep Disorders Center, Department of Neurophysiology, The Methodist Hospital, Houston, Texas
Guillain-Barré Syndrome

W. Paul Glezen, M.D.
Professor, Department of Molecular Virology and Microbiology, Department of Pediatrics, Baylor College of Medicine; Adjunct Professor, Department of Epidemiology, School of Public Health, University of Texas Health Science Center; Attending Pediatrician, Department of Pediatrics, Ben Taub General Hospital; Courtesy Staff, Infectious Diseases, Texas Children's Hospital, Houston, Texas
Influenza Viruses

Mary P. Glodé, M.D.
Professor of Pediatrics, University of Colorado Health Sciences Center; Vice-Chair, Department of Pediatrics, and Chief, Section of Pediatric Infectious Diseases, Children's Hospital and University of Colorado Health Sciences Center, Denver, Colorado
Meningococcal Disease

Donald A. Goldmann, M.D.
Professor of Pediatrics, Harvard Medical School; Hospital Epidemiologist, Division of Infectious Diseases, Children's Hospital, Boston, Boston, Massachusetts
Nosocomial Infections; Prevention and Control of Nosocomial Infections in Health Care Facilities That Serve Children

Ellie J. C. Goldstein, M.D.
Clinical Professor, David Geffen School of Medicine at UCLA, Los Angeles; Director, R. M. Alden Research Laboratory, Santa Monica, California
Human Bites

Maria D. Goldstein, M.D.
Associate Clinical Professor, Department of Pediatrics, University of New Mexico Medical School; District Health Officer, Public Health Division, New Mexico Department of Health, Albuquerque, New Mexico
Plague *(Yersinia pestis)*

Nira A. Goldstein, M.D.
Assistant Professor, Division of Pediatric Otolaryngology, State University of New York Downstate Medical Center; Attending Physician, Division of Pediatric Otolaryngology, University Hospital of Brooklyn, Long Island College Hospital, and Kings County Hospital Center, Brooklyn, New York
Peritonsillar, Retropharyngeal, and Parapharyngeal Abscesses

Edmond T. Gonzales, Jr., M.D.
Professor of Urology, Scott Department of Urology, Baylor College of Medicine; Head, Department of Surgery; Chief, Pediatric Urology Service, Texas Children's Hospital, Houston, Texas
Renal Abscess; Prostatitis

Blanca E. Gonzalez, M.D.
Postdoctoral Clinical Fellow, Department of Pediatrics, Section of Infectious Diseases, Baylor College of Medicine, Houston, Texas
Cholera

Howard P. Goodkin, M.D., Ph.D.
Assistant Professor of Neurology and Pediatrics, Department of Neurology, University of Virginia, Charlottesville, Virginia
Parameningeal Infections; Transverse Myelitis or Myelopathy

Simin Goral, M.D.
Associate Professor, Division of Nephrology, University of Pennsylvania Medical Center, Philadelphia, Pennsylvania
Bartonella: Cat-Scratch Disease

Michael Green, M.D., M.P.H.
Professor of Pediatrics and Surgery, Department of Pediatrics, University of Pittsburgh School of Medicine; Professor of Pediatrics and Surgery, Division of Allergy, Immunology, and Infectious Diseases, Children's Hospital of Pittsburgh, Pittsburgh, Pennsylvania
Opportunistic Infections in Liver Transplantation

David Greenberg, M.D.
Lecturer, Faculty of Health Sciences, Ben-Gurion University of the Negev; Senior Physician, Specialist in Pediatrics and Infectious Diseases, Soroka University Medical Center, Beer-Sheva, Israel
Pneumococcal Infections

Andreas H. Groll, M.D.
Head, Infectious Disease Research Program, Department of Pediatric Hematology/Oncology, University Children's Hospital, Muenster, Germany
Antifungal Agents

Charles Grose, M.D.
Professor, Departments of Pediatrics and Microbiology, University of Iowa College of Medicine; Professor and Director of Infectious Diseases, Department of Pediatrics, University of Iowa Hospital, Iowa City, Iowa
Pyomyositis and Bacterial Myositis; Human Herpesviruses 6, 7, and 8

William C. Gruber, M.D.
Vice President, Clinical Research, Wyeth Vaccines Research, Wyeth Research, Pearl River, New York
Miscellaneous Gram-Positive Cocci; *Erysipelothrix rhusiopathiae;* Miscellaneous Gram-Positive Bacilli; *Citrobacter; Enterobacter; Klebsiella; Morganella morganii; Proteus; Providencia; Serratia;* Miscellaneous Enterobacteria; *Vibrio vulnificus;* Miscellaneous Non-Enterobacteriaceae Fermentative Bacilli; *Achromobacter (Alcaligenes); Eikenella corrodens; Chryseobacterium (Flavobacterium)*

Duane J. Gubler, Sc.D.
Director, Division of Vector-Borne Infectious Diseases, Centers for Disease Control and Prevention, Fort Collins, Colorado
Yellow Fever

Roberto A. Guerrero, M.D.
Children's Gastroenterology of South Florida, P.A., West Palm Beach, Florida
Whipple Disease

Laura T. Gutman, M.D.
Duke University Medical Center, Durham, North Carolina
Syphilis

Caroline Breese Hall, M.D.
Professor of Pediatrics and Infectious Diseases in Medicine, Department of Pediatrics, University of Rochester, School of Medicine and Dentistry, Rochester, New York
Parainfluenza Viruses; Respiratory Syncytial Virus

Scott B. Halstead, M.D.
Adjunct Professor, Department of Preventive Medicine and Biometrics, Uniformed Services University of the Health Sciences, Bethesda, Maryland
Chikungunya; Dengue and Dengue Hemorrhagic Fever

Margaret R. Hammerschlag, M.D.
Professor, Department of Pediatrics and Medicine, and Director, Division of Pediatric Infectious Diseases, State University of New York Downstate Medical Center; Attending Physician, University Hospital of Brooklyn and Kings County Hospital Center, Brooklyn, New York
Peritonsillar, Retropharyngeal, and Parapharyngeal Abscesses; *Chlamydia* Infections

I. Celine Hanson, M.D.
Adjunct Professor, Department of Pediatrics, Baylor College of Medicine; Regional Medical Director, Texas Department of Health, Houston, Texas
Chronic Bronchitis; Lentiviruses (Human Immunodeficiency Virus Type I and the Acquired Immunodeficiency Syndrome)

Rick E. Harrison, M.D.
Professor of Clinical Pediatrics, Division of Critical Care, David Geffen School of Medicine at UCLA; Chief of Staff, UCLA Medical Center, Los Angeles, California
Tetanus

C. Mary Healy, M.D., M.R.C.P. (UK)
Clinical Postdoctoral Fellow, Department of Pediatrics, Section of Infectious Diseases, Baylor College of Medicine and Texas Children's Hospital, Houston, Texas
Cervical Lymphadenitis

Ulrich Heininger, M.D.
Professor of Pediatrics, University of Basel Medical School; Chair, Division of Pediatric Infectious Diseases and Vaccines, University Children's Hospital, Basel, Switzerland
Pertussis and Other *Bordetella* Infections

Gloria P. Heresi, M.D.
Associate Professor, Department of Pediatrics, Pediatric Infectious Diseases Division, University of Texas—Houston Medical School; Associate Professor, Department of Pediatrics, Memorial Hermann Children's Hospital, Houston, Texas
Campylobacter jejuni

Paula M. Hertel, M.D.
Postdoctoral Fellow, Department of Pediatric Gastroenterology and Nutrition, Baylor College of Medicine; Postdoctoral Fellow, Department of Pediatric Gastroenterology and Nutrition, Texas Children's Hospital, Houston, Texas
Diphtheria

Peter W. Hiatt, M.D.
Associate Professor, Department of Pediatrics, Baylor College of Medicine; Attending Faculty, Texas Children's Hospital, Houston, Texas
Cystic Fibrosis; Adult Respiratory Distress Syndrome in Children

Harry R. Hill, M.D.
Professor of Pathology, Pediatrics, and Medicine, Department of Pathology, University of Utah Salt Lake City, Salt Lake City, Utah
Immunomodulating Agents

Ellis K. L. Hon, M.B.B.S., F.A.A.P.
Assistant Professor, Department of Paediatrics, Chinese University of Hong Kong; Honorary Medical Officer, Prince of Wales Hospital, Shatin, Hong Kong, China
Severe Acute Respiratory Syndrome (SARS)

Margaret K. Hostetter, M.D.
Chair, Department of Pediatrics, and Professor of Pediatrics and Microbiology, Yale University School of Medicine; Physician-in-Chief, Yale–New Haven Children's Hospital, New Haven, Connecticut
Infectious Disease Problems of International Adoptees and Refugees

Peter J. Hotez, M.D., Ph.D.
Professor and Chair, Department of Microbiology and Tropical Medicine, George Washington University; Senior Fellow, Sabin Vaccine Institute, Washington, DC
Amebiasis; *Blastocystis hominis* Infection; *Entamoeba coli* Infection; *Balantidium coli* Infection; Parasitic Nematode Infections; Drugs for Parasitic Infections

Dexter H. Howard, Ph.D.
Professor Emeritus of Microbiology and Immunology, Department of Microbiology, Immunology, and Molecular Genetics, David Geffen School of Medicine at UCLA; Consultant in Medical Mycology, Department of Microbiology, UCLA Clinical Laboratories, Los Angeles, California
Classification of Fungi

Walter T. Hughes, M.D.
Professor, Department of Pediatrics, University of Tennessee, Memphis, College of Medicine; Emeritus Member, Department of Infectious Diseases, St. Jude Children's Research Hospital, Memphis, Tennessee
Candidiasis; Cryptococcosis; *Pneumocystis carinii* Pneumonia

David A. Hunstad, M.D.
Instructor, Departments of Pediatrics and Molecular Microbiology, Washington University School of Medicine; Attending Physician, Department of Pediatrics, St. Louis Children's Hospital, St. Louis, Missouri
Molecular Determinants of Microbial Pathogenesis

Eugene S. Hurwitz, M.D.
Clinical Assistant Professor, Department of Pediatrics, Emory University School of Medicine; Respiratory Disease Management Associates, LLC, Atlanta, Georgia
Reye Syndrome

W. Charles Huskins, M.D., M.Sc.
Assistant Professor, Department of Pediatrics, Mayo Medical School; Consultant, Department of Pediatric and Adolescent Medicine, Division of Pediatric Infectious Diseases, Mayo Clinic, Rochester, Minnesota
Nosocomial Infections; Prevention and Control of Nosocomial Infections in Health Care Facilities That Serve Children

Mary Anne Jackson, M.D.
Professor of Pediatrics, University of Missouri—Kansas City School of Medicine; Chief, Pediatric Infectious Diseases Section, Children's Mercy Hospitals and Clinics, Kansas City, Missouri
Skin Infections

Michael R. Jacobs, M.B., B.Ch., Ph.D.
Professor of Pathology, Case Western Reserve University; Director of Clinical Microbiology, University Hospitals of Cleveland, Cleveland, Ohio
Pneumococcal Infections

Richard F. Jacobs, M.D.
Horace C. Cabe Professor of Pediatrics, Department of Pediatrics, University of Arkansas for Medical Sciences; Chief, Pediatric Infectious Diseases, Arkansas Children's Hospital, Little Rock, Arkansas
Pleural Effusions and Empyema; Lung Abscess; Fungal Meningitis; Other Mycobacteria; *Nocardia; Actinobacillus actinomycetemcomitans;* Actinomycosis

Ravi Jhaveri, M.D.
Associate, Division of Infectious Diseases, Department of Pediatrics, Duke University Medical Center, Durham, North Carolina
Cutaneous Manifestations of Systemic Infections

Maureen M. Jonas, M.D.
Associate Professor, Department of Pediatrics, Harvard Medical School; Associate in Gastroenterology, Department of Medicine, Children's Hospital Boston, Boston, Massachusetts
Hepatitis B and D Viruses; Hepatitis C Virus

Edward L. Kaplan, M.D.
Professor of Pediatrics, Department of Pediatrics, University of Minnesota Medical School; Attending Physician, Department of Pediatrics, Fairview University Medical Center, Minneapolis, Minnesota
Group A, Group C, and Group G Beta-Hemolytic Streptococcal Infections

Sheldon L. Kaplan, M.D.
Professor and Vice-Chairman of Clinical Affairs, Department of Pediatrics, Baylor College of Medicine; Chief, Infectious Disease Service, Texas Children's Hospital, Houston, Texas
Infectious Pericarditis; Renal Abscess; Prostatitis; Pyogenic Liver Abscess; Bacteremia and Septic Shock; Infection in Pediatric Heart Transplant Recipients; Diarrhea- and Dysentery-Causing *Escherichia coli;* Public Health Considerations; Use of the Bacteriology, Mycology, and Parasitology Laboratories

Saul J. Karpen, M.D., Ph.D.
Associate Professor, Department of Pediatrics, Baylor College of Medicine; Director, Texas Children's Liver Center, Houston, Texas
Cholangitis and Cholecystitis

Michael Katz, M.D.
Reuben S. Carpentier Professor Emeritus of Pediatrics, Department of Pediatrics, Columbia University College of Physicians and Surgeons; Consulant Emeritus, Department of Pediatrics, New York–Presbyterian Hospital, New York; Senior Vice President for Research and Global Programs, March of Dimes Birth Defects Foundation, White Plains, New York
Parasitic Nematode Infections

Gregory L. Kearns, Pharm.D., Ph.D.
Professor, Department of Pediatrics and Pharmacology, University of Missouri—Kansas City, School of Medicine; Division Chief, Pediatric Clinical Pharmacology and Medical Toxicology, Children's Mercy Hospital and Clinics, Kansas City, Missouri
The Pharmacokinetic-Pharmacodynamic Interface: Determinants of Anti-infective Drug Action and Efficacy in Pediatrics

Margaret A. Keller, M.D.
Professor, Department of Pediatrics, University of California, Los Angeles, Harbor-UCLA Medical Center; Director, Program for Pediatric HIV/AIDS, and Attending Physician, Department of Pediatrics, Harbor-UCLA Medical Center; Acting Chief, Pediatric Infectious Diseases, Department of Pediatrics, Harbor-UCLA Medical Center, Torrance, California
Passive Immunization

Gerald T. Keusch, M.D.
Associate Director for International Research and Director, Fogarty International Center, National Institutes of Health, Bethesda, Maryland
Diarrhea- and Dysentery-Causing *Escherichia coli;* Cholera

Martin B. Kleiman, M.D.
Ryan White Professor of Pediatrics, Indiana University School of Medicine; Director, Pediatric Infectious Diseases, Department of Pediatrics, James Whitcomb Riley Hospital for Children, Indianapolis, Indiana
Histoplasmosis

Jerome O. Klein, M.D.
Professor of Pediatrics, Boston University School of Medicine; Vice-Chairman for Academic Affairs, Department of Pediatrics, Boston Medical Center, Boston, Massachusetts
Otitis Media; Bacterial Pneumonias

Mark W. Kline, M.D.
Professor of Pediatrics, Head, Section of Retrovirology, Baylor College of Medicine; Attending Physician, Texas Children's Hospital, Houston, Texas
Primary Immunodeficiences

Heidi M. Kokkinos, M.T. (ASCP), B.S.
Core Technologist, Mycology Laboratory, University of California, Los Angeles; Clinical Laboratory Scientist, Department of Pathology and Laboratory Medicine, UCLA Medical Center, Los Angeles, California
Classification of Fungi

Peter J. Krause, M.D.
Professor, Department of Pediatrics, University of Connecticut School of Medicine, Farmington; Director of Infectious Diseases, Department of Pediatrics, Connecticut Children's Medical Center, Hartford, Connecticut
Babeisosis

Leonard R. Krilov, M.D.
Professor of Pediatrics, Department of Pediatrics, State University of New York at Stony Brook School of Medicine, Stony Brook; Chief, Pediatric Infectious Diseases, Department of Pediatrics, Winthrop University Hospital, Mineola, New York
Chronic Fatigue Syndrome

Paul Krogstad, M.D.
Associate Professor, Departments of Pediatrics and Molecular and Medical Pharmacology, David Geffen School of Medicine at UCLA, Los Angeles, California
Osteomyelitis and Septic Arthritis

Thomas L. Kuhls, M.D.
Chief, Department of Pediatrics, Norman Regional Hospital, Norman, Oklahoma
Appendicitis and Pelvic Abscess; Pancreatitis; *Kingella* Species

Timothy R. La Pine, M.D.
Adjunct Professor of Pathology and Pediatrics, Department of Pathology, University of Utah School of Medicine, Salt Lake City, Utah
Immunomodulating Agents

Ching C. Lau, M.D., Ph.D.
Assistant Professor, Department of Pediatrics, Division of Hematology-Oncology, Baylor College of Medicine; Attending Physician, Texas Children's Cancer Center, Texas Children's Hospital, Houston, Texas
Tularemia

Charles T. Leach, M.D.
Professor, Department of Pediatrics, and Chief, Division of Infectious Diseases, University of Texas Health Science Center at San Antonio; Attending Physician, Department of Pediatrics, Christus Santa Rosa Children's Hospital and University Hospital, San Antonio, Texas
Epstein-Barr Virus

Robert J. Leggiadro, M.D.
Professor, Department of Pediatrics, University of Medicine and Dentistry of New Jersey, Robert Wood Johnson Medical School, Newark; Vice Chairman, Department of Pediatrics, Hackensack University Medical Center, Hackensack, New Jersey
Other *Campylobacter* Species; Bioterrorism

Diana Lennon, M.B., Ch.B., F.R.A.C.P.
Professor of Population Health, Child, and Youth, Department of Paediatrics, University of Auckland; Paediatrician in Infectious Diseases, Department of Paediatrics, Starship Children's Hospital, Auckland, New Zealand
Acute Rheumatic Fever

Chi Wai Leung, M.B.B.S., F.R.C.P.C.H., F.R.C.P. (Edin.)
Consultant Paediatrician, Department of Paediatrics and Adolescent Medicine, Princess Margaret Hospital; Honorary Clinical Associate Professor of Paediatrics, University of Hong Kong, Hong Kong, China
Severe Acute Respiratory Syndrome (SARS)

Karen Lewis, M.D.
Physician Trainer, Office of Bioterrorism, Arizona Department of Health Sciences, Phoenix, Arizona
Mastoiditis

Albert M. Li, M.B.Bch., M.R.C.P. (UK)
Assistant Professor, Department of Paediatrics, Chinese University of Hong Kong, Honorary Medical Officer, Prince of Wales Hospital, Shatin, Hong Kong, China
Severe Acute Respiratory Syndrome (SARS)

Martin I. Lorin, M.D.
Professor, Department of Pediatrics, Baylor College of Medicine; Attending Physician, Texas Children's Hospital, Houston, Texas
Fever: Pathogenesis and Treatment; Fever without Source and Fever of Unknown Origin

Jorge Luján-Zilbermann, M.D.
Assistant Professor, Department of Pediatrics, Division of Infectious Diseases, University of South Florida College of Medicine; Attending Physician, Division of Pediatric Infectious Diseases, Tampa General Hospital, Tampa; Attending Physician, Division of Infectious Diseases, All Children's Hospital, St. Petersburg, Florida
Opportunistic Infections in Hematopoietic Stem Cell Transplantation

Timothy Mailman, M.D., F.R.C.P.C.
Assistant Professor, Department of Pediatrics, Dalhousie University Faculty of Medicine; Director of Microbiology, Department of Pediatrics, IWK Health Centre, Halifax, Nova Scotia, Canada
Listeriosis

Susan A. Maloney, M.D., M.H.Sc.
Chief Epidemiologist and Special Studies, Division of Global Migration and Quarantine, Centers for Disease Control and Prevention, Atlanta, Georgia
International Travel Issues for Children

Harold S. Margolis, M.D.
Director, Division of Viral Hepatitis, Centers for Disease Control and Prevention, Atlanta, Georgia
Hepatitis A Virus

Edward O. Mason, Jr., Ph.D.
Professor, Department of Pediatrics and Department of Virology and Microbiology, Baylor College of Medicine; Director, Infectious Disease Laboratory, Texas Children's Hospital, Houston, Texas
Use of the Bacteriology, Mycology, and Parasitology Laboratories; Use of the Serology Laboratory

David O. Matson, M.D., Ph.D.
Professor, Department of Pediatrics, Eastern Virginia Medical School; Attending Physician, Department of Infectious Diseases, Children's Hospital of The King's Daughters; Head, Department of Infectious Diseases Section, Center for Pediatric Research, Norfolk, Virginia
Caliciviruses and Hepatitis E Virus

Alan N. Mayer, M.D., Ph.D.
Instructor, Department of Pediatrics, Harvard Medical School; Assistant, Division of Gastroenterology, Children's Hospital, Boston, Massachusetts
Hepatitis C Virus

Marc A. Mazade, M.D.
Consultant, Department of Infectious Diseases, PID Associates, Dallas, Texas
Infections Related to Craniofacial Surgical Procedures

George H. McCracken, Jr., M.D.
Professor of Pediatrics, The GlaxoSmithKline Distinguished Professor of Pediatric Infectious Disease, and The Sarah M. and Charles E. Seay Chair in Pediatric Infectious Disease, University of Texas Southwestern Medical Center at Dallas; Attending Physician, Children's Medical Center of Dallas, Dallas, Texas
Perinatal Bacterial Diseases; Antibacterial Therapeutic Agents

Kenneth McIntosh, M.D.
Professor, Department of Pediatrics, Harvard Medical School; Senior Associate in Medicine, Division of Infectious Diseases, Children's Hospital, Boston, Boston, Massachusetts
Coronaviruses and Toroviruses

James E. McJunkin, M.D.
Professor, Department of Pediatrics, Robert C. Byrd Health Sciences Center, Charleston Division; Attending Physician, Charleston Area Medical Center, Charleston, West Virginia
La Crosse Encephalitis and Other California Serogroup Viruses

Kelly T. McKee, Jr., M.D.
Managing Research Physician, Camber Corporation, U.S. Army Medical Research Institute of Infectious Diseases, Fort Detrick, Maryland
Hantaviruses

Rima L. McLeod, M.D.
Jules and Doris Stein RPB Professor, Department of Visual Sciences, Pathology, Committees of Molecular Medicine, Genetics, and Immunology, University of Chicago; Attending Physician, Department of Medicine, University of Chicago Hospitals; Attending Physician, Department of Ophthalmology, Michael Reese Hospital and Medical Center, Chicago, Illinois
Toxoplasmosis

Wayne M. Meyers, M.D., Ph.D., D.Sc. (Hon)
Research Affiliate, Tulane Primate Research Center, Tulane University, Covington, Louisiana; Chief, Mycobacteriology Branch, and Registrar, Leprosy Registry, American Registry of Pathology, Armed Forces Institute of Pathology, Washington, DC
Leprosy and Buruli Ulcer: The Major Cutaneous Mycobacterioses

Ian C. Michelow, M.B.B.Ch., D.T.M.&H., F.C.Paed.(SA)
Instructor, Department of Pediatrics, Harvard Medical School; Assistant in Pediatrics, Department of Infectious Diseases, Massachusetts General Hospital, Boston, Massachusetts
Antibacterial Therapeutic Agents

James N. Miller, Ph.D.
Professor Emeritus on Recall, Department of Microbiology, Immunology, and Molecular Genetics, David Geffen School of Medicine at UCLA, Los Angeles, California
Nonvenereal Treponematoses

Marjorie J. Miller, Dr.P.H.
Senior Specialist, Clinical Laboratories—Microbiology, University of California Medical Center, Los Angeles, Los Angeles, California
Classification and Nomenclature of Viruses; Use of the Diagnostic Virology Laboratory

Linda L. Minnich, M.S.
Adjunct Assistant Professor, Robert C. Byrd Health Sciences Center, Charleston Division; Virologist, Charleston Area Medical Center, Charleston, West Virginia
La Crosse Encephalitis and Other California Serogroup Viruses

Sudipta Misra, M.D.
Assistant Professor, Department of Pediatrics, and Chief, Division of Gastroenterology, University of Illinois College of Medicine at Peoria, Peoria, Illinois
Esophagitis

Lynne M. Mofenson, M.D.
Chief, Pediatric Adolescent and Maternal AIDS Branch, National Institute of Child Health and Human Development, National Institutes of Health, Bethesda, Maryland
Oncoviruses (Human T-Cell Lymphotropic Viruses Types I and II) and Lentiviruses (Human Immunodeficiency Virus Type 2)

Edward A. Mortimer, Jr., M.D.*
University Professor Emeritus, Department of Epidemiology and Biostatistics, Case Western Reserve University, Cleveland, Ohio
Epidemiology of Infectious Diseases
*Deceased

James R. Murphy, Ph.D.
Professor, Department of Pediatrics, Pediatric Infectious Diseases, University of Texas—Houston Medical School, Houston, Texas
Campylobacter jejuni

Edmund A. S. Nelson, M.B.Ch.B., F.R.C.P.C.H., F.R.C.P. (UK)
Associate Professor, Department of Paediatrics, and affiliated member of the School of Public Health, Chinese University of Hong Kong; Honorary Consultant, Prince of Wales Hospital, Shatin, Hong Kong, China
Severe Acute Respiratory Syndrome (SARS)

Karin A. Nielsen, M.D., M.P.H.
Assistant Clinical Professor, Department of Pediatrics—Division of Infectious Diseases, David Geffen School of Medicine at UCLA; Attending Physician, Department of Pediatric Infectious Diseases, Mattel Children's Hospital of UCLA; Attending Physician, Maternal Child Immunology Clinic—HIV Medicine, UCLA Care Clinic, Los Angeles, California
Herpangina; Aseptic Meningitis and Viral Meningitis

Michael D. Nissen, B.Med.Sc, M.B.B.S., F.R.A.C.P., F.R.C.P.A.
Senior Lecturer, Department of Paediatrics and Child Health, University of Queensland School of Medicine; Director, Department of Infectious Diseases, Royal Children's Hospital, Herston, Queensland, Australia
Human Metapneumovirus: *Paramyxoviridae*

Christopher M. Oermann, M.D.
Assistant Professor, Department of Pediatrics, Baylor College of Medicine; Attending Faculty, Pulmonary Medicine Service, Texas Children's Hospital, Houston, Texas
Adult Respiratory Distress Syndrome in Children

Christian C. Patrick, M.D., Ph.D.
Chief of Staff and Senior Vice President for Medical Affairs, Miami Children's Hospital, Miami, Florida
Opportunistic Infections in Hematopoietic Stem Cell Transplantation; Coagulase-Negative Staphylococcal Infections

Evelyn A. Paysse, M.D.
Assistant Professor of Ophthalmology and Pediatrics, Department of Ophthalmology, Baylor College of Medicine; Active Staff, Department of Pediatric Ophthalmology and Strabismus, Texas Children's Hospital, Houston, Texas
Ocular Infectious Diseases

Eric Pearlman, M.D., Ph.D.
Assistant Professor, Department of Pediatrics, Mercer University School of Medicine (Savannah Campus); Staff Physician, Savannah Neurology, Savannah, Georgia
Bacterial Meningitis beyond the Neonatal Period

Georges Peter, M.D.
Professor of Pediatrics and Vice Chair for Faculty Affairs, Department of Pediatrics, Brown University School of Medicine; Director, Division of Pediatric Infectious Diseases, Department of Pediatrics, Rhode Island Hospital and Hasbro Children's Hospital, Providence, Rhode Island
Active Immunizing Agents

C. J. Peters, M.D.
John Sealy Distinguished University Chair in Tropical and Emerging Virology, Department of Microbiology and Immunology/Pathology, University of Texas Medical Branch, Galveston, Texas
Hantaviruses

Larry K. Pickering, M.D., F.A.A.P.
Professor of Pediatrics, Department of Pediatrics, Emory University School of Medicine; Senior Advisor to the Director, National Immunization Program, Centers for Disease Control and Prevention, Atlanta, Georgia
Approach to Patients with Gastrointestinal Tract Infections and Food Poisoning

Joseph F. Piecuch, D.M.D., M.D.
Clinical Professor, Department of Oral and Maxillofacial Surgery, University of Connecticut School of Dental Medicine, Farmington; Director, Oral and Maxillofacial Surgery Section, Hartford Hospital, Hartford, Connecticut
Infections of the Oral Cavity

Francisco P. Pinheiro, M.D., Ph.D.
Department of Arborivus, Instituto Evandro Chagas, Belém, Brazil
Oropouche Fever

Stanley A. Plotkin, M.D.
Emeritus Professor, Department of Pediatrics, University of Pennsylvania School of Medicine, Philadelphia; Medical and Scientific Advisor, Aventis Pasteur, Swiftwater, Pennsylvania
Rabies Virus

Scott L. Pomeroy, M.D., Ph.D.
Associate Professor, Department of Neurology, Harvard Medical School; Senior Associate, Department of Neurology, Children's Hospital, Boston, Massachusetts
Parameningeal Infections; Transverse Myelitis or Myelopathy

Alice Pong, M.D.
Department of Pediatric Infectious Diseases, Children's Hospital and Health Center, San Diego, California
Retroperitoneal Infections

Joan S. Purcell, M.D., F.A.A.P.
Chair, Department of Pediatrics, The Woodlands Memorial Hospital; Vice President, Step Pediatrics, The Woodlands, Texas
Trichomonas Infections

Jack S. Remington, M.D.
Palo Alto Medical Foundation, Palo Alto, California
Toxoplasmosis

Angela Restrepo-Moreno, Ph.D.
Senior Researcher, Medical and Experimental Mycology Group, Corporación para Investigaciones Biológicas (CIB), Medellín, Colombia
Paracoccidioidomycosis

Carina A. Rodriguez, M.D.
Postdoctoral Fellow, University of Tennessee, Memphis, College of Medicine, and Department of Infectious Diseases, St. Jude Children's Research Hospital, Memphis, Tennessee
Coagulase-Negative Staphylococcal Infections

Judith L. Rowen, M.D.
Associate Professor, Department of Pediatrics, University of Texas Medical Branch, Galveston, Texas
Group B Streptococcal Infections; Miscellaneous Mycoses

Xavier Sáez-Llorens, M.D.
Professor of Pediatrics and Infectious Diseases, University of Panama School of Medicine; Vice-Chairman and Head of Infectious Diseases, Hospital del Niño, Panama City, Panama
Perinatal Bacterial Diseases

Lisa Saiman, M.D., M.P.H.
Associate Professor of Clinical Pediatrics, Department of Pediatrics, Columbia University College of Physicians and Surgeons; Associate Attending Pediatrician, Department of Pediatrics, and Hospital Epidemiologist, Department of Pediatrics and Epidemiology, Children's Hospital of New York, New York, New York
Cystic Fibrosis

Joseph W. St. Geme III, M.D.
Professor and Director of Pediatric Infectious Diseases, Department of Pediatrics and Molecular Microbiology, Washington University School of Medicine; Attending Physician, Department of Pediatrics, St. Louis Children's Hospital, St. Louis, Missouri
Molecular Determinants of Microbial Pathogenesis

Pablo J. Sánchez, M.D.
Professor, Department of Pediatrics, Division of Neonatal-Perinatal Medicine and Pediatric Infectious Diseases, University of Texas Southwestern Medical School; Professor of Pediatrics, Division of Neonatal-Perinatal Medicine and Pediatric Infectious Diseases, Parkland Health and Hospital Systems and Children's Medical Center of Dallas, Dallas, Texas
Viral Infections of the Fetus and Neonate; Syphilis

Carlos A. Sattler, M.D.
Associate Director, Biologics Clinical Research, Merck Research Laboratories, West Point, Pennsylvania
Coagulase-Positive Staphylococcal Infections *(Staphylococcus aureus); Stenotrophomonas (Xanthomonas) maltophilia*

Jane G. Schaller, M.D.
Karp Professor of Pediatrics Emerita, Department of Pediatrics, Tufts University School of Medicine; Chief, Division of Pediatric Rheumatology, Tufts–New England Medical Center, Boston, Massachusetts
Noninfectious Carditis

Kenneth O. Schowengerdt, Jr., M.D.
Associate Professor, Department of Pediatrics, University of Florida College of Medicine; Medical Director, Pediatric Heart Transplant Program, University of Florida and Shands Transplant Center, Gainesville, Florida
Myocarditis

Gordon E. Schutze, M.D.
Professor of Pediatrics and Pathology and Pediatric Program Director, Department of Pediatrics, University of Arkansas for Medical Sciences; Attending Physician, Arkansas Children's Hospital, Little Rock, Arkansas
Blastomycosis

James S. Seidel, M.D., Ph.D.*
Professor, Department of Pediatrics, David Geffen School of Medicine at UCLA, Los Angeles; Chief, Division of General and Emergency Pediatrics, Department of Emergency Medicine and Pediatrics, Harbor-UCLA Medical Center, Torrance, California
Giardiasis; *Naegleria, Acanthamoeba,* and *Balamuthia*
*Deceased

Alan M. Shapiro, M.D., Ph.D.
Fellow, Division of Pediatric Infectious Diseases, Department of Pediatrics, David Geffen School of Medicine at UCLA, Los Angeles, California
Arcanobacterium haemolyticum

Craig N. Shapiro, M.D.
Medical Epidemiologist, Division of Viral Hepatitis, National Center for Infectious Diseases, Centers for Disease Control and Prevention, Atlanta, Georgia
Hepatitis A Virus

Eugene D. Shapiro, M.D.
Professor of Pediatrics, Epidemiology, and Investigative Medicine, Departments of Pediatrics, Epidemiology, and Public Health and the Children's Clinical Research Center, Yale University School of Medicine; Attending Pediatrician, Children's Hospital at Yale–New Haven, New Haven, Connecticut
Epidemiology and Biostatistics

Nina L. Shapiro, M.D.
Assistant Professor, Division of Head and Neck Surgery, David Geffen School of Medicine at UCLA; Attending Physician, Division of Head and Neck Surgery, UCLA Medical Center, Los Angeles, California
Sinusitis; Mastoiditis

William T. Shearer, M.D., Ph.D.
Professor of Pediatrics and Immunology, Baylor College of Medicine; Chief, Allergy and Immunology Service, Texas Children's Hospital, Houston, Texas
Chronic Bronchitis; Primary Immunodeficiences; Lentiviruses (Human Immunodeficiency Virus Type I and the Acquired Immunodeficiency Syndrome)

Ziad M. Shehab, M.D.
Professor of Clinical Pediatrics and Pathology, University of Arizona College of Medicine; Section Chief, Pediatric Infectious Diseases, and Clerkship Director, Department of Pediatrics, University of Arizona Health Sciences Center; Department of Pediatrics, University Medical Center and Tucson Medical Center, Tucson; Department of Pediatrics, Maricopa Medical Center, Phoenix, Arizona
Coccidioidomycosis

Jerry L. Shenep, M.D.
Professor of Pediatrics, University of Tennessee Health Science Center; Member, Department of Infectious Diseases, St. Jude Children's Research Hospital, Memphis, Tennessee
Enterococcal and Viridans Streptococcal Infections

W. Donald Shields, M.D.
Chief of Pediatric Neurology, Department of Pediatrics, David Geffen School of Medicine at UCLA, Los Angeles, California
Encephalitis and Meningoencephalitis

Robert E. Shope, M.D.
Professor of Pathology, Center for Tropical Diseases, University of Texas Medical Branch, Galveston, Texas
Rift Valley Fever

Stanford T. Shulman, M.D.
Professor of Pediatrics, Department of Pediatrics, Feinberg School of Medicine, Northwestern University; Chief, Division of Infectious Diseases, Children's Memorial Hospital, Chicago, Illinois
Kawasaki Disease

Constantine Simos, D.M.D.
Visiting Assistant Professor, Department of Oral and Maxillofacial Surgery, Tufts University, Boston, Massachusetts; Active Staff, Department of Oral and Maxillofacial Surgery, Robert Wood Johnson University Hospital; Active Staff, Department of Oral and Maxillofacial Surgery, St. Peter's University Hospital, New Brunswick, New Jersey
Infections of the Oral Cavity

Arnold L. Smith, M.D.
Professor, Department of Pathobiology, University of Washington School of Public Health; Member, Department of Bacterial Pathogens, Seattle Biomedical Research Institute, Seattle, Washington
Meningococcal Disease

Kimberly C. Smith, M.D., M.P.H.
Associate Professor, Department of Pediatrics, University of Texas—Houston Medical School, Houston, Texas
Tuberculosis

Jason S. Soden, M.D.
Department of Pediatrics, Baylor College of Medicine, Houston, Texas
Cholangitis and Cholecystitis

Steven L. Solomon, M.D.
Chief, Healthcare Outcomes Branch, Division of Healthcare Quality Promotion, National Center for Infectious Diseases, Centers for Disease Control and Prevention, Atlanta, Georgia
Public Health Considerations

Mary A. Staat, M.D., M.P.H.
Associate Professor, Department of Pediatrics, University of Cincinnati College of Medicine; Associate Professor, Department of Pediatrics, Division of Infectious Diseases, Cincinnati Children's Hospital Medical Center, Cincinnati, Ohio
Genital Infections in Childhood and Adolescence

Jeffrey R. Starke, M.D.
Professor, Department of Pediatrics, Baylor College of Medicine; Chief, Department of Pediatrics, Ben Taub General Hospital, Houston, Texas
Infective Endocarditis; Tuberculosis

Barbara W. Stechenberg, M.D.
Professor, Department of Pediatrics, Tufts University School of Medicine, Boston; Vice Chair and Director, Pediatric Infectious Diseases, Department of Pediatrics, Baystate Medical Center Children's Hospital, Springfield, Massachusetts
Eosinophilic Meningitis; *Moraxella catarrhalis;* Diphtheria; *Pasteurella multocida;* Bartonellosis; *Borrelia* (Lyme Disease)

Leah A. Stephenson, M.D.
Department of Pediatrics, Baylor College of Medicine, Houston, Texas
Interaction of Infection and Nutrition

E. Richard Stiehm, M.D.
Professor of Pediatrics, Department of Pediatrics, David Geffen School of Medicine at UCLA; Attending Pediatrician, Mattel Children's Hospital at UCLA, Los Angeles, California
Passive Immunization

Alan D. Strickland, M.D.
Clute, Texas
Amebiasis

Ciro V. Sumaya, M.D., M.P.H.T.M.
Dean, School of Rural Public Health, Cox Endowed Chair in Medicine, and Professor, Department of Pediatrics, Texas A & M University System Health Science Center, College Station; Attending Physician, Scott and White Hospital and Clinic, Temple, Texas
Epstein-Barr Virus

Douglas S. Swanson, M.D.
Assistant Professor, Department of Pediatrics, University of Missouri—Kansas City School of Medicine; Pediatrician, Department of Pediatric Infectious Diseases, Children's Mercy Hospital and Clinics, Kansas City, Missouri
Indigenous Flora

Tina Tan, M.D.
Associate Professor, Department of Pediatrics, Feinberg School of Medicine, Northwestern University; Infectious Diseases Attending, Co-Director, Travel Medicine Clinic, and Director, International Adoptee Clinic, Children's Memorial Hospital, Chicago, Illinois
Infections Related to Prosthetic or Artificial Devices

Herbert B. Tanowitz, M.D., F.A.C.P.
Professor of Pathology and Medicine, Department of Pathology, Albert Einstein College of Medicine of Yeshiva University; Attending Physician, Department of Medicine, Weiler Hospital–Montefiore Medical Center; Attending Physician, Department of Medicine and Pathology, Jacobs Medical Center, Bronx, New York
Leishmaniasis; Trypanosomiasis

Robert B. Tesh, M.D.
George Dock Distinguished Professor of Pathology, Department of Pathology, University of Texas Medical Branch; Member, Center for Biodefense and Emerging Infectious Diseases, University of Texas Medical Branch, Galveston, Texas
Crimean-Congo Hemorrhagic Fever; Phlebotomus Fever (Sandfly Fever)

Philip Toltzis, M.D.
Associate Professor, Department of Pediatrics, Case Western Reserve University School of Medicine; Attending Physician, Division of Pediatric Pharmacology and Critical Care, Rainbow Babies and Children's Hospital, Cleveland, Ohio
Antibiotic Resistance

Richard G. Topazian, D.D.S.
Professor Emeritus, Department of Oral and Maxillofacial Surgery, University of Connecticut School of Dental Medicine, Farmington, Connecticut
Infections of the Oral Cavity

Michael F. Tosi, M.D.
Associate Professor of Pediatrics, Sections of Leukocyte Biology and Infectious Diseases, Baylor College of Medicine, Houston, Texas
Immunologic and Phagocytic Responses to Infection

Jeffrey A. Towbin, M.D.
Professor, Department of Pediatrics (Cardiology) and Molecular and Human Genetics, Baylor College of Medicine; Associate Chief, Pediatric Cardiology, Texas Children's Hospital; Medical Director, Pediatrics Heart Failure and Transplant Service, Texas Children's Hospital; Texas Children's Hospital Foundation Chair in Pediatric Cardiac Research, Texas Children's Hospital, Houston, Texas
Myocarditis

Amelia P. A. Travassos da Rosa, B.Sc.
Visiting Scientist, Department of Pathology, University of Texas Medical Branch, Galveston, Texas
Oropouche Fever

Theodore F. Tsai, M.D., M.P.H.
Senior Director of Medical Affairs, Vaccines Division, Wyeth, Collegeville, Pennsylvania
Orbiviruses and Coltiviruses; Eastern Equine Encephalitis; Western Equine Encephalitis; Venezuelan Equine Encephalitis; Other Alphaviral Infections; St. Louis Encephalitis; Japanese Encephalitis; Tick-Borne Encephalitis; Other Flaviviral Infections; La Crosse Encephalitis and Other California Serogroup Viruses

Jerrold A. Turner, M.D., F.A.C.P., D.T.M.&H.
Professor Emeritus of Clinical Medicine and Microbiology, Department of Immunology and Molecular Genetics, David Geffen School of Medicine at UCLA, Los Angeles; Director, Turner Parasitology, Carson, California
Cestodes; Trematodes

Xilla T. Ussery, M.D.
Associate Director, Clinical Development, Infectious Diseases, Pfizer Inc., New London, Connecticut
Other Anaerobic Infections

Jesus G. Vallejo, M.D.
Assistant Professor of Pediatrics and Medicine, Section of Infectious Disease and Winters Center for Heart Failure Research, Baylor College of Medicine; Attending Physician, Infectious Disease Service, Texas Children's Hospital, Houston, Texas
Myocarditis; Cholera

John A. Vanchiere, M.D., Ph.D.
Assistant Professor, Department of Pediatrics, Section of Infectious Diseases, Baylor College of Medicine, Houston, Texas
Human Polyomaviruses and Papillomaviruses

Pedro Fernando da C. Vasconcelos, M.D., Ph.D.
Chief, Department of Arbovirus, Instituto Evandro Chagas, Belém, Brazil
Oropouche Fever

Ellen R. Wald, M.D.
Professor of Pediatrics and Otolaryngology, Department of Pediatrics, University of Pittsburgh School of Medicine; Chief, Division of Allergy, Immunology, and Infectious Diseases, Department of Pediatrics, Children's Hospital, Pittsburgh, Pennsylvania
Uvulitis; Genitourinary Tract Infections; Infections in Daycare Environments

Thomas J. Walsh, M.D.
Senior Investigator and Chief, Immunocompromised Host Section, Pediatric Oncology Branch, National Cancer Institute, Bethesda, Maryland
Antifungal Agents

Joel I. Ward, M.D.
Professor, Department of Pediatrics, David Geffen School of Medicine at UCLA, Los Angeles; Director, UCLA Center for Vaccine Research, and Director, Hospital Infection Control, Department of Pediatrics, Harbor—UCLA Medical Center, Torrance, California
Haemophilus influenzae

Richard L. Ward, Ph.D.
Professor, Department of Infectious Diseases, Children's Hospital Medical Center, Cincinnati, Ohio
Rotaviruses

Michelle Weinberg, M.D., M.P.H.
Medical Epidemiologist, Division of Global Migration and Quarantine, Centers for Disease Control and Prevention, Atlanta, Georgia
International Travel Issues for Children

Robert C. Welliver, M.D.
Professor, Department of Pediatrics, State University of New York at Buffalo; Co-Director, Division of Infectious Diseases, Department of Pediatrics, Women's and Children's Hospital of Buffalo, Buffalo, New York
Bronchiolitis and Infectious Asthma

J. Gary Wheeler, M.D.
Professor of Pediatrics, Department of Pediatric Infectious Diseases, University of Arkansas for Medical Sciences; Attending Physician, Arkansas Children's Hospital, Little Rock, Arkansas
Pleural Effusions and Empyema; Lung Abscess

A. Clinton White, Jr., M.D.
Associate Professor, Infectious Disease Section, Department of Medicine, Baylor College of Medicine; Chief, Section of Infectious Diseases, Department of Medicine, Ben Taub General Hospital, Houston, Texas
Schistosomiasis

Suzanne Whitworth, M.D.
Department of Pediatric Infectious Diseases, Cook Children's Medical Center, Fort Worth, Texas
Actinobacillus actinomycetemcomitans; Actinomycosis

Bernhard L. Wiedermann, M.D.
Associate Professor and Vice Chair for Education, Department of Pediatrics, George Washington University School of Medicine and Health Sciences; Attending in Infectious Diseases and Director, Medical Education and Pediatric Residency Training Program, Children's National Medical Center, Washington, DC
Miscellaneous Causes of Myositis; *Aspergillus* Infections; Sporotrichosis; Zygomycosis

Murray Wittner, M.D.
Professor of Pathology and Parasitology, Department of Pathology, Albert Einstein College of Medicine of Yeshiva University; Attending Physician, Department of Medicine and Pathology, Montefiore Medical Center, Bronx, New York
Leishmaniasis; Trypanosomiasis

Charles R. Woods, Jr., M.D.
Associate Professor of Pediatrics, Wake Forest University School of Medicine; Attending Physician, Brenner Children's Hospital, Winston-Salem, North Carolina
Genital Infections in Childhood and Adolescence; Gonococcal Infections; Other *Yersinia* Species

Ram Yogev, M.D.
Professor, Department of Pediatrics, Feinberg School of Medicine, Northwestern University; Associate Division Head and Director, Section of Pediatric, Adolescent, and Maternal HIV Infection, Department of Infectious Diseases, Children's Memorial Hospital, Chicago, Illinois
Infections Related to Prosthetic or Artificial Devices

Edward J. Young, M.D.
Professor, Department of Medicine and Molecular Virology and Microbiology, Baylor College of Medicine; Staff Physician, Infectious Diseases Section, Veterans Affairs Medical Center, Houston, Texas
Brucellosis

PREFACE

Despite the dramatic reduction in morbidity and mortality rates related to infectious diseases that followed the introduction of antimicrobial therapy, as well as active and passive immunization efforts, infectious diseases remain the leading cause of morbidity in infants and children. Children continue to experience three to nine respiratory infections annually, requiring visits to physicians that outnumber the visits made for the purpose of well-child care. Infectious diseases also are the most common cause of school absenteeism. In more recent years, the emergence of resistance to multiple antibiotics by a large number of bacterial microorganisms as well as the identification of new infectious diseases such as severe acute respiratory syndrome (SARS) also have contributed to the morbidity and mortalities related to infectious disease processes.

The first edition of our text was written because we and many of our colleagues were concerned that no single reference text existed that comprehensively covered infectious diseases in children and adolescents. With each subsequent edition, including this one, our goal has been to provide comprehensive coverage of all subjects pertinent to the study of infectious diseases in these populations. Any attempt to summarize our present understanding of infectious diseases for serious students of the subject is a formidable task. In many areas, new information continues to accrue so rapidly that material becomes dated before it can appear in a text of this magnitude. Nonetheless, we have endeavored with the help of many of our colleagues to provide the most comprehensive and up-to-date discussion of this field.

To provide a text as comprehensive and authoritative as possible, we have enlisted contributions from a large number of individuals whose collective expertise is responsible for whatever success we may have had in meeting our objective. We offer our most profound appreciation to the 245 fellow contributors from 180 universities or institutions in 12 countries for their professional expertise and devoted scholarship. Their cooperation and willingness to work with us leave us deeply in their debt.

We also are pleased to have enlisted for this fifth edition of our text the help of two additional co-editors whose expertise and scholarship have enhanced this endeavor immeasurably.

Dr. Gail J. Demmler is Professor in the Department of Pediatrics at Baylor College of Medicine and Director of the Diagnostic Virology Laboratory at Texas Children's Hospital. Dr. Demmler is a nationally recognized pediatric virologist whose own area of clinical and research expertise has been in the fields of cytomegalovirus infections, influenza virus infections, and pediatric human immunodeficiency virus (HIV) infections. Dr. Demmler has served for many years on the Executive and Program Committees of the Pediatric Academic Societies and currently is President of the Society for Pediatric Research. She also holds fellowship status in the Infectious Disease Society of America.

Dr. Sheldon L. Kaplan currently serves as Professor and Vice Chair for Clinical Affairs in the Department of Pediatrics at Baylor College of Medicine and as Chief of the Infectious Disease Service at Texas Children's Hospital. A Fellow of the Infectious Disease Society of America, Dr. Kaplan also is President of the Pediatric Infectious Diseases Society. Dr. Kaplan has done extensive work in the field of bacterial infections with specific emphasis on treatment of infections caused by antibiotic-resistant microorganisms. He also has served as Editor of *Current Therapy in Pediatric Infectious Diseases*.

Once again, infectious diseases are discussed according to organ systems that may be affected, as well as individually by microorganisms. In all sections in which diseases related to specific agents are discussed, emphasis has been placed, to the greatest extent possible, on the specificity of clinical manifestations that may be related to the organism causing the disease. Detailed information regarding the best means to establish a diagnosis and explicit recommendations for therapy are provided.

The entire text has been revised extensively. This edition continues the format that we initiated in the fourth edition in that infections with specific microorganisms have been reorganized to provide appropriate emphasis on the common features that may relate specific microorganisms to each other. Thus, all gram-positive coccal organisms are presented sequentially and are followed by gram-negative cocci, gram-positive bacilli, enterobacteria, gram-negative coccobacilli, Treponemataceae, anaerobic bacteria, and so forth. In addition, special sections of the text have been devoted to discussions of each of the following: molecular determinants of microbial pathogenesis; immunologic and phagocytic responses to infection; metabolic response of the host to infections; interaction of infection and nutrition; pathogenesis and treatment of fever; indigenous flora; epidemiology of infectious diseases; congenital immune deficiency; acquired immunodeficiency syndrome (AIDS) and other acquired immunodeficiency diseases; Kawasaki disease; chronic fatigue syndrome; international travel issues for children; infectious disease problems of international adoptees and refugees; nosocomial infections; prevention and control of infections in hospitalized children; pharmacology and pharmacokinetics of antibacterial, antiviral, antifungal, and antiparasitic agents; public health considerations; infections in daycare environments; and use of the bacteriology, mycology, parasitology, virology, and serology laboratories. The section on opportunistic infections in the compromised host has been divided into multiple chapters as follows: opportunistic infections in children with bone marrow transplantation; infections in pediatric heart transplant recipients; opportunistic infections in children with liver transplantation; opportunistic infections in children with kidney transplantation; infections related to prosthetics or artificial devices; and infections related to craniofacial surgical procedures. This reorganization has been necessitated by the large number of individuals, particularly post-transplantation recipients, who now serve as the source of many infectious disease problems and constitute a large part of the consulting practice of many pediatric infectious disease physicians.

With some sadness, we have introduced into the text for the first time a section on bioterrorism, which was necessitated by the current state of world affairs. The section on immunomodulating agents and their potential use in the treatment of infectious diseases has been expanded because information on this subject has become more extensive since the publication of the last edition. Specific sections also have been devoted to human and animal bites. The subject of biostatistics as applicable to the subspecialty of infectious diseases also has been included. A section on human metapneumovirus has been added to the chapter on respiratory syncytial virus infection, and a section on SARS has been added to the chapter on coronaviruses.

This book could not have been brought to fruition without the help and assistance of many individuals whose names do not appear in the text. No words are sufficient to adequately convey our gratitude appropriately; we hope that they know they have our heartfelt thanks.

We would like to single out certain individuals for specific mention. We cannot adequately convey our appreciation for the thousands of hours devoted by Dr. Lee Ligon, who edited and also proofread every word of the text that was submitted, as well as the galleys and page proofs. We are equally indebted to Mary Campbell, who spent an equivalent amount of time and who was specifically responsible for the coordination of the editorial effort, correspondence with our contributors and with the publisher, and coordination of the manuscript preparation process. She also typed and retyped many sections of the text. We also appreciate the assistance provided to Mary Campbell and to the editors by Tracey Ramsey and Carrel Briley, as well as the help provided by Brooke Taylor, Anabel Alvarez, Vionna Cabal, and Margarita Santiago.

We also appreciate the help and support of Judith Fletcher, Melissa Dudlick, Jennifer Shreiner, and Lee Ann Draud at Saunders, as well as the continued editorial guidance of Lisette Bralow who has helped us with every edition of this text.

Finally, we would like to thank the Baylor College of Medicine and Texas Children's Hospital in Houston, Texas, and the David Geffen School of Medicine at UCLA and the Mattel UCLA Children's Hospital for providing an environment that is supportive of intellectual pursuits.

Ralph D. Feigin, M.D.
James D. Cherry, M.D.

CONTENTS

Color plates appear between pages 762–763, 1976–1977, and 2720–2721.

VOLUME 1

PART I

Host-Parasite Relationships and the Pathogenesis of Infectious Diseases

PART II

Infections of Specific Organ Systems

SECTION I

UPPER RESPIRATORY TRACT INFECTIONS

SECTION II

LOWER RESPIRATORY TRACT INFECTIONS

SECTION III

INFECTIONS OF THE HEART

SECTION IV

CENTRAL NERVOUS SYSTEM INFECTIONS

SECTION V

GENITOURINARY TRACT INFECTIONS

SUBSECTION 5

GRAM-NEGATIVE COCCOBACILLI

VOLUME 2

SECTION XVIII

CHLAMYDIA

SECTION XIX

RICKETTSIAL DISEASES

SECTION XX

MYCOPLASMA

SECTION XXI

FUNGAL DISEASES

SECTION XXII

PARASITIC DISEASES

SUBSECTION 1

PROTOZOA

A AMEBAE

B FLAGELLATES (INTESTINAL)

C CILIATES (INTESTINAL)

D COCCIDIA, INICNOSPORIDIA (INTESTINAL)

PART VI

Prevention of Infectious Diseases

SECTION XXV

OTHER PREVENTIVE CONSIDERATIONS

PART VII

Guides to the Diagnosis of Infection

PART VIII

Biostatistics Applicable to the Subspecialty of Infectious Diseases

PART I

Host-Parasite Relationships and the Pathogenesis of Infectious Diseases

Molecular Determinants of Microbial Pathogenesis

DAVID A. HUNSTAD ■ JOSEPH W. ST. GEME III

Despite the availability of antibiotics and expanding vaccination programs, infectious diseases remain a leading cause of morbidity and mortality worldwide. Many factors, including an increase in the prevalence of antimicrobial resistance, an increase in global travel, and an increase in the number of individuals with altered immunity, contribute to the continuing importance of infectious agents. Furthermore, in recent years, several microorganisms have been implicated in diseases previously considered noninfectious, and a variety of new pathogens have been discovered.

Pathogens are defined as microorganisms that are capable of causing disease. However, not all pathogens are equal with respect to their pathogenic potential (their virulence). Many pathogens are commensal organisms and live in harmony with their hosts under most conditions, causing disease only when normal immune mechanisms are disrupted or absent. Other pathogens produce disease even in the setting of intact immunity and almost always cause symptoms.

For a given pathogen, pathogenic potential is determined by the specific array of virulence-associated genes. Some species of bacteria are capable of natural transformation and readily acquire fragments of DNA from other organisms, thereby expanding or altering their genetic composition, occasionally with consequences related to virulence. Many microorganisms carry virulence-associated genes on mobile genetic elements, including plasmids, transposons, and bacteriophages. These elements may equip the organism with genetic information that facilitates rapid adaptation to an unfavorable or changing environment.

In recent years, comparison of genomes from pathogenic and nonpathogenic members of a single genus or species has led to the discovery of "pathogenicity islands," defined as large blocks of chromosomal DNA that are present in pathogens and absent from related nonpathogens. These blocks are flanked by insertion sequences or repeat elements and differ in nucleotide composition relative to the surrounding genome, suggesting acquisition by horizontal exchange. Pathogenicity islands contain clusters of virulence-associated genes that encode a variety of factors, including secretion systems, secreted effector molecules, adhesins, and regulatory proteins.

To be successful, a pathogen must enter the host, then find an appropriate niche, and then multiply. Often the pathogen induces damage to the host and then spreads to other tissues, either near the initial site of infection or more distant. Ideally, the pathogen stops short of causing death to the host and produces symptoms such as cough or diarrhea that facilitate spread to another host.

In this chapter, we address several key steps in the pathogenic process. In each case, we present examples that highlight pathogens and paradigms of relevance to infectious diseases in children. As a reflection of our personal bias, we focus primarily on bacterial pathogens.

Colonization

Most infectious diseases begin with microbial colonization of a host surface, typically the skin, the respiratory tract, the gastrointestinal tract, or the genitourinary tract. Although colonization is not sufficient for an organism to produce disease, it is a necessary prerequisite. The process of colonization requires specialized microbial factors, called adhesins, that promote adherence to host structures and enable the organism to overcome local defenses, such as mucociliary function, peristalsis, and urinary flow. The cognate receptors for these interactions generally are either carbohydrate or protein structures, in some cases expressed on host cells, in others present in mucosal secretions or in submucosal tissue.

PILUS ADHESINS

Perhaps most common among bacterial adhesins are hair-like fibers called pili (also called fimbriae). Pili are polymeric structures, the major structural subunit of which usually ranges in size from 15 to 25 kDa. Because of their size and morphology, most pili can be visualized by negative staining transmission electron microscopy.

The prototype example among adhesive pili is the P pilus (or Pap pilus), which is expressed by uropathogenic *Escherichia coli* (UPEC) and has been associated strongly with pyelonephritis, especially among young girls. P pili recognize globoseries glycolipids, host molecules that are characterized by a core structure consisting of Gal-α1,4-Gal. The globoseries glycolipids are especially abundant in renal epithelium, thus accounting for the predilection of P-piliated *E. coli* to adhere to kidney tissue and cause pyelonephritis.[14] As shown in Figure 1–1, P pili are composite structures and consist of two subassemblies, including a thick rod that emanates from the bacterial surface and a thin tip fibrillum that extends distally.[107, 176] The pilus rod is a right-handed helical cylinder and is composed of repeating PapA subunits, whereas the tip fibrillum has an open helical configuration and contains mostly repeating PapE subunits. The two subassemblies are joined to each other by the PapK adaptor protein. PapG contains the adhesive moiety and is located at the distal end of the tip fibrillum, joined to PapE by the PapF adaptor.[93]

P pili are assembled in a process that involves a periplasmic chaperone, called PapD, and an outer membrane usher, called PapC (see Fig. 1–1).[34, 108] The crystal structures of PapD alone and PapD interacting with the PapK pilin subunit have been solved, revealing significant insights into PapD interaction with Pap subunits and the mechanism of P pilus assembly.[175] PapD consists of two immunoglobulin-like (Ig) folds oriented in an L shape with an intervening cleft. The PapK subunit consists of a single Ig fold but lacks the seventh, C-terminal β-strand (strand G1). The absence of this strand leaves a deep groove along the surface of PapK and exposes its hydrophobic core, predisposing the subunit

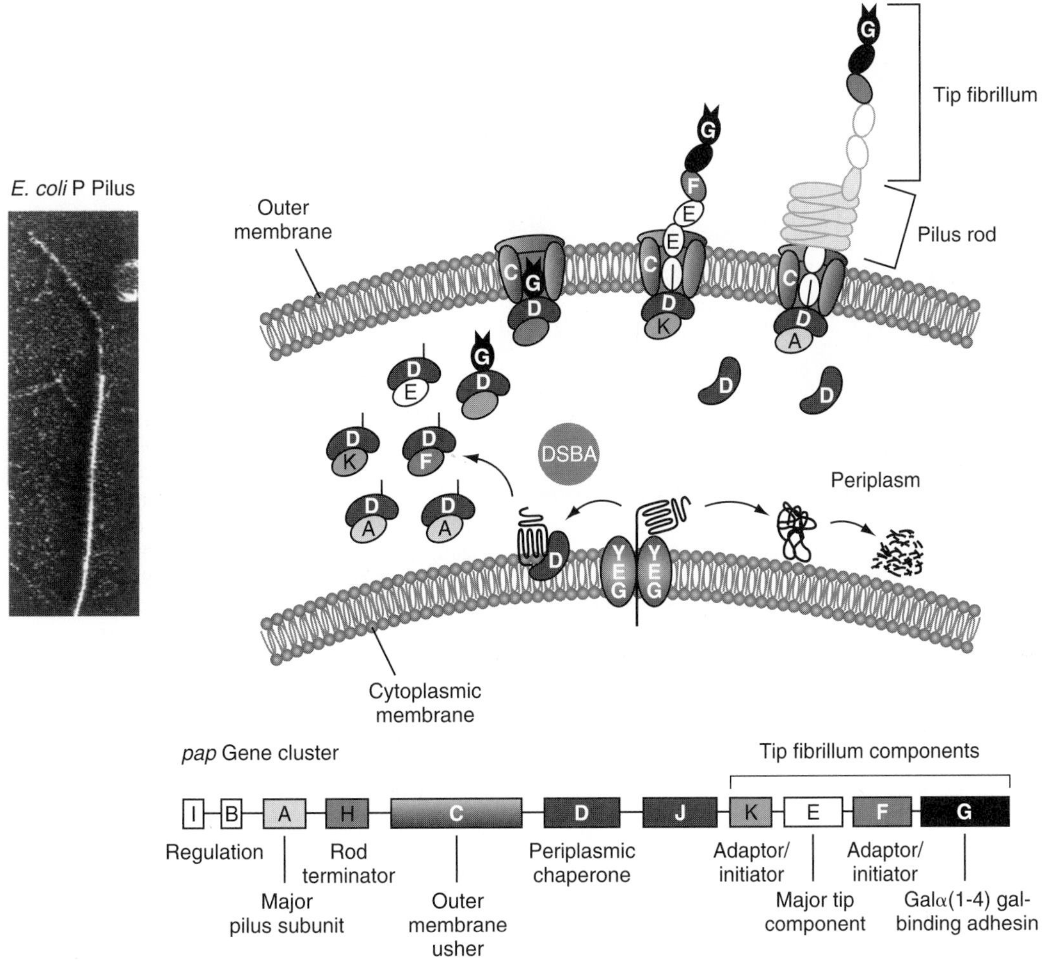

FIGURE 1–1 ■ Biogenesis and structure of *Escherichia coli* P pili. The *pap* gene cluster and the function of each of the gene products is indicated in the lower portion of the figure. Nascent pilin subunits are complexed with the PapD chaperone and added to the base of the developing pilus via the PapC usher. The mature pilus rod is composed of repeating units of PapA; the tip fibrillum contains the adhesin PapG. The ultrastructure of the pilus is shown in the electron micrograph at the left side of the figure. (Courtesy of S.J. Hultgren and F.G. Sauer.)

to aggregation and degradation. In the PapD-PapK complex, the G1 strand of PapD occupies the groove in PapK and completes the Ig fold, a phenomenon referred to as donor strand complementation (Fig. 1–2*A*). This interaction shields the hydrophobic core of the subunit and thus stabilizes the protein. Within the groove, the G1 strand of PapD interacts on one side with the C-terminal, F strand of PapK.[175] Ultimately, PapD delivers PapK and other Pap subunits to the PapC usher, which forms a multimer with a central pore approximately 2 nm in diameter. As the pilus is assembled on the bacterial surface, the N-terminal strand of a neighboring subunit (the one most recently added to the pilus base) replaces the G1 strand of PapD in a process called donor strand exchange. Thus, in the mature pilus, each subunit completes the Ig fold of its neighbor (see Fig. 1–2*B*).[87]

More than 30 different bacterial adhesive structures are assembled via the chaperone-usher pathway with a PapD-like chaperone and a PapC-like usher. These PapD-like chaperones can be divided into two distinct subfamilies based upon conserved structural differences that occur near the subunit binding site.[88] One subfamily is involved in the assembly of rodlike pili similar to P pili, and the second subfamily participates in the biogenesis of more atypical filamentous structures. Thus, the nature of the chaperone is linked directly to the architecture of the adhesive appendage.[184]

Type 4 pili represent a second class of pili, distinguished by a methylated first amino acid (usually phenylalanine), a short positively charged leader sequence, a conserved hydrophobic amino terminal domain, and a tendency to form bundle-like structures. Type 4 pili have been identified in numerous gram-negative bacterial pathogens, including *Neisseria gonorrhoeae*, *Neisseria meningitidis*, enteropathogenic *E. coli* (EPEC), *Vibrio cholerae*, *Pseudomonas aeruginosa*, *Kingella kingae*, *Eikenella corrodens*, *Moraxella* spp., and *Dichelobacter nodosus* (formerly *Bacteroides nodosus*).[41, 57, 124, 135, 160, 165, 178, 192, 200, 211]

Although the biogenesis of type 4 pili remains poorly understood, existing data suggest that the process is complex. For example, between 20 and 40 gene products are required for the assembly of *P. aeruginosa* type 4 pili, and at least 15 plasmid-encoded proteins are involved in the biogenesis of EPEC type 4 pili.[78, 190] Based on studies of *P. aeruginosa*, EPEC, *Neisseria*, and *V. cholerae*, the presence

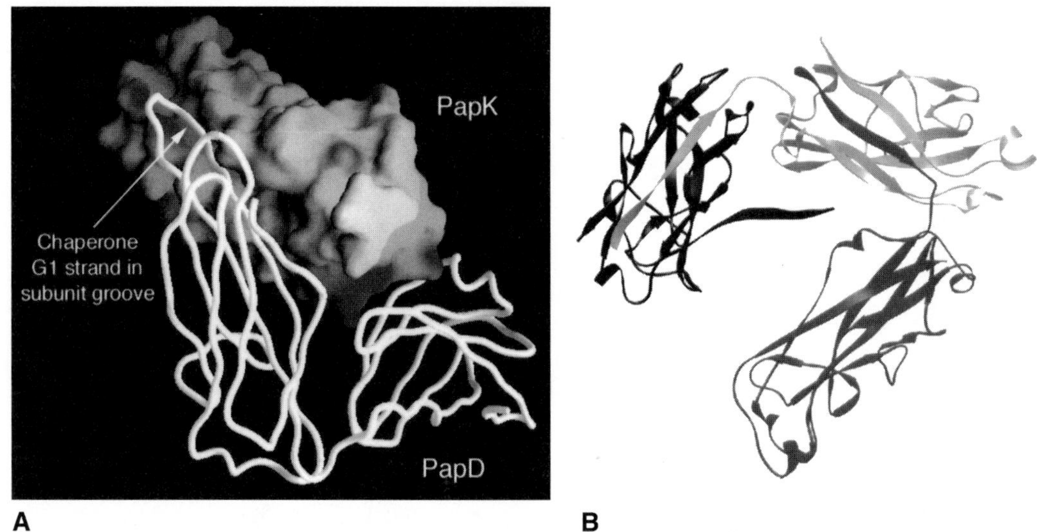

FIGURE 1–2 ■ *A,* The G1 strand of the PapD chaperone completes the immunoglobulin-like fold of the PapK pilin subunit (donor strand complementation). *B,* The mature P pilus rod comprises a helix (3.28 subunits per turn) of repeating PapA subunits; each subunit is completed by a strand donated by its neighbor. (Courtesy of S. J. Hultgren and F. G. Sauer.)

of an inner membrane prepilin peptidase appears to be a general prerequisite for type 4 pilus biogenesis.[97, 111, 144] The involvement of at least one protein with a canonical nucleotide-binding domain is another common feature. Many of the other proteins required for type 4 pilus assembly resemble proteins from filamentous phage biogenesis systems and DNA uptake and transfer systems, suggesting that similar transport and assembly mechanisms are used.[79, 171]

Despite marked differences in the assembly pathways for type 4 pili and P pili, examination by electron microscopy suggests that in some cases significant structural similarities may exist. For example, gonococcal type 4 pili are composed predominantly of the PilE structural subunit but also contain a minor phase-variable adhesive protein called PilC.[96] Based on immunoelectron microscopy, PilC appears to be located at the distal end of the pilus.[170] These observations suggest that *N. gonorrhoeae* pili may be composite structures with a tip-associated adhesin, analogous to P pili and other pili assembled by the chaperone-usher pathway.

Although adhesive pili are more prevalent in gram-negative bacteria, they also are found in some gram-positive species. One example is *Streptococcus parasanguis,* an oral pathogen and a member of the sanguis streptococcal family. This organism binds to calcium phosphate (the primary mineral component of tooth enamel) and also to other oral bacteria, epithelial cells, platelets, and fibronectin. Several adhesins, including pili referred to as long fimbriae, mediate these binding functions. Based on studies of *S. parasanguis* strain FW213, long fimbriae contain the protein Fap1, a 200-kDa protein that includes an unusually long signal sequence and a cell wall sorting signal typical of other gram-positive bacterial surface proteins.[221] Disruption of the *fap1* gene abrogates formation of long fimbriae, suggesting that Fap1 is the major structural subunit.[222] Interestingly, similar to gram-negative bacterial pili, long fimbriae appear to have a composite structure with a pilus tip. The tip contains an adhesin called FimA, which in purified form is capable of blocking bacterial adherence to saliva-coated hydroxyapatite.[43, 148] In work by Burnette-Curley and coworkers, deletion or interruption of the *fimA* gene resulted in 7- to 20-fold reduction in the incidence of endocarditis after intravenous inoculation of rats.[16]

NON-PILUS ADHESINS

Beyond pili, a variety of non-pilus adhesins exist. In most cases, non-pilus adhesins are proteinaceous and are monomeric or oligomeric surface structures, although isolated examples of carbohydrate and lipid-containing adhesive structures have been identified. In general, these molecules are difficult to visualize by electron microscopy, even with high-resolution techniques. Similar to pili, for the most part non-pilus adhesins can be classified according to their mechanism of secretion and presentation on the bacterial surface.

Among the best characterized bacterial non-pilus adhesins is filamentous hemagglutinin (FHA), a surface protein expressed by *Bordetella pertussis* and other *Bordetella* spp. FHA is synthesized as a large precursor protein with a calculated molecular mass of 367 kDa. A cleavage event occurs to eliminate the C-terminal one third of the protein and produce the mature 220-kDa species.[36] Our understanding of the structure of FHA stems from computer analysis of the amino acid sequence and examination of purified FHA by transmission electron microscopy and circular dichroism spectroscopy.[121] The FHA molecule is 50 nm in length and adopts the shape of a horseshoe nail. It has a globular head that appears to consist of two domains, a 37-nm long shaft, which averages 4 nm in width but tapers slightly from the head end, and a small flexible tail (Fig. 1–3). According to the most current model, FHA forms a hairpin, with the head composed of two regions of 19-residue repeats that generate amphipathic, hyperelongated β-sheets, and with the tail composed of the intervening sequence (see Fig. 1–3).

The export of FHA to the surface of the organism occurs via the so-called two-partner system and depends on an outer membrane protein called FhaC, which has β-barrel pore-forming properties and facilitates translocation of FHA across the outer membrane.[218] FhaC shares homology with a growing number of transport proteins, including proteins involved in the export of the *Serratia marcescens, Proteus mirabilis,* and *Haemophilus ducreyi* hemolysins, the *Haemophilus influenzae* heme:hemopexin binding protein (HxuA), and the *H. influenzae* HMW1 and HMW2 adhesins, among others.[4, 24, 151, 159, 202] Although experimental data are lacking, FhaC and other members of the FhaC family possibly

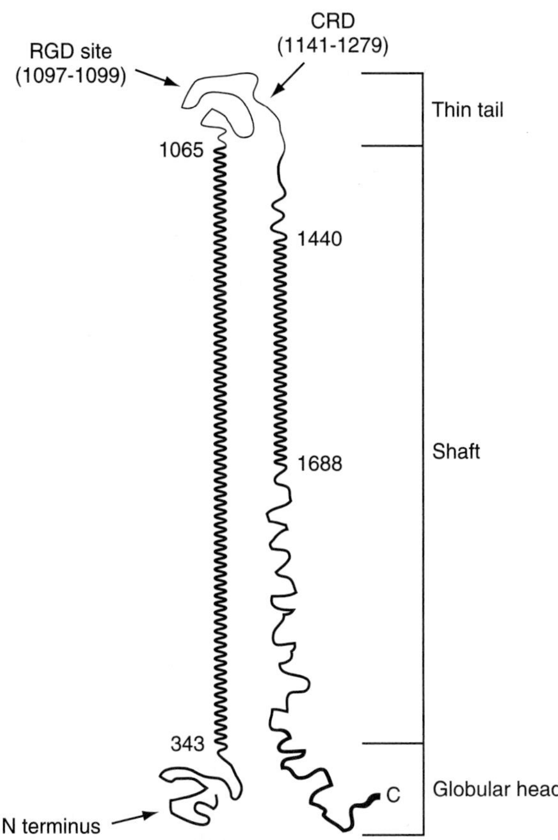

FIGURE 1–3 ■ Model for structure of filamentous hemagglutinin from *Bordetella pertussis*. (Reproduced with permission from St. Geme, J.W., III: Bacterial adhesins: Determinants of microbial colonization and pathogenicity. Adv. Pediatr. *44*:43–72, 1997.)

form multimeric structures with a central hydrophilic channel, analogous to the outer membrane ushers involved in assembly of pili.

Consistent with its large size, FHA contains at least four separate binding domains, three of which have been localized. The region involved in adherence to sulfated saccharides has been mapped to the N-terminus of the FHA molecule (see Fig. 1–3).[133] Sulfated saccharides such as heparin and heparin sulfate are a major component of mucus and extracellular matrix in the respiratory tract and also are found on the surface of epithelial cells.[126, 224] The region that recognizes lactosylceramides and promotes adherence to ciliated respiratory epithelial cells and macrophages has been localized to amino acids 1141 to 1279 (the carbohydrate recognition domain; see Fig. 1–3).[161] An arginine-glycine-aspartic acid (RGD) tripeptide is located at amino acids 1097 to 1099 and interacts with leukocyte response integrin–integrin associated protein (LRI-IAP), a leukocyte integrin that stimulates up-regulation of complement receptor type 3 (CR3).[92] Finally, FHA recognizes CR3 (CD11b/CD18), which is expressed by macrophages and allows for uptake by macrophages without stimulating an oxidative burst.[166, 220] The location of the CR3-binding domain is unknown.

A growing number of non-pilus adhesins belong to the so-called autotransporter family. These proteins are synthesized as precursor proteins with three functional domains: an N-terminal signal sequence, an internal passenger domain, and a C-terminal outer membrane domain (Fig. 1–4). The signal sequence directs the protein to the Sec machinery and facilitates transport from the cytoplasm to the periplasm. Subsequently, the C-terminal domain targets the protein to the outer membrane, inserting in the outer membrane and forming a β-barrel with a central hydrophilic channel. Next, the passenger domain is extruded across the outer membrane and appears to adopt its final native conformation on the surface of the organism.[71] One example of an autotransporter adhesin is the *H. influenzae* Hap protein, which was discovered based on its ability to promote adherence and low-level invasion in assays with cultured epithelial cells.[185] More recent evidence indicates that Hap also promotes bacterial aggregation and microcolony formation.[72] Examination of chimeric proteins and studies with purified protein have demonstrated that the adhesive activity responsible for Hap-mediated adherence, invasion, and microcolony formation resides in the passenger domain, referred to as Haps.[72] Other examples of autotransporter adhesins are listed in Table 1–1.

Another small group of non-pilus adhesins is typified by intimin, a protein expressed by EPEC, enterohemorrhagic *E. coli* (EHEC), *Hafnia alvei*, and *Citrobacter rodentium*.

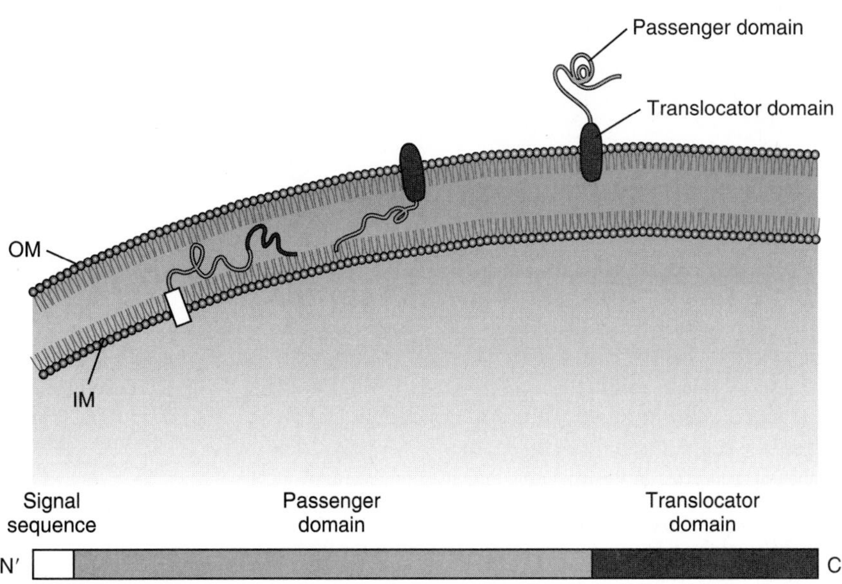

FIGURE 1–4 ■ Autotransporter protein secretion pathway. Autotransporter proteins are synthesized as preproteins with three functional domains, including an N-terminal signal sequence, an internal passenger domain, and a C-terminal outer membrane translocator domain. Among autotransporter adhesins, the passenger domain generally harbors adhesive activity. IM indicates inner membrane, and OM indicates outer membrane.

TABLE 1–1 ■ BACTERIAL ADHESINS THAT BELONG TO THE AUTOTRANSPORTER FAMILY OF PROTEINS

Organism	Protein
Escherichia coli	AIDA-I
	TibA
	Ag43
	Tsh
Haemophilus influenzae	Hap
	Hia
	Hsf
Bordetella species	Pertactin
	TcfA
Moraxella catarrhalis	UspA1
	UspA2H
Helicobacter pylori	BabA

Based on studies of EPEC, the amino-terminal region of intimin anchors the protein in the bacterial outer membrane and is predicted to form a pore. The C-terminal segment of intimin is extracellular and forms an elongated relatively rigid rod that consists of three Ig-like domains called D0, D1, and D2 and a C-type lectin-like domain called D3.[118] The D3 domain interacts with the intimin receptor, called Tir. Interestingly, Tir is synthesized by the bacterium, then inserted into the host cell membrane using the EPEC type III secretion system, which also translocates critical proteins called EspA and EspB.[99, 219] The interaction between intimin and Tir triggers a series of host cell events, resulting in dramatic rearrangement of the actin cytoskeleton and formation of a distinctive pedestal referred to as an attaching and effacing (A/E) lesion (Fig. 1–5).[99, 169] All of the genes essential for formation of A/E lesions are present within a 35-kb region of the EPEC chromosome called the locus of enterocyte effacement (LEE), an example of a pathogenicity island.[37, 127] This locus contains the genes that encode intimin, Tir, and the EPEC type III secretion system, with a total of 41 open reading frames overall.

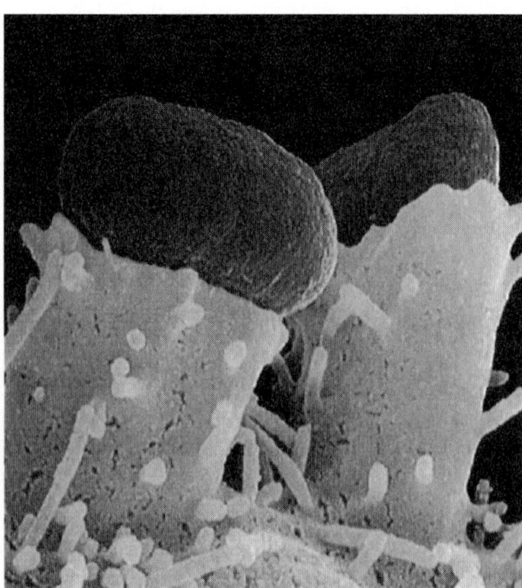

FIGURE 1–5 ■ Enteropathogenic *Escherichia coli* (EPEC) are perched on pedestals in the attaching and effacing lesion. (Courtesy of B.B. Finlay; reproduced with permission from Rosenshine, I., Ruschkowski, S., Stein, M., et al.: A pathogenic bacterium triggers epithelial signals to form a functional bacterial receptor that mediates actin pseudopod formation. EMBO J. *15*:2613–2624, 1996.)

During the past decade, investigators have identified a large family of non-pilus adhesins involved in adherence to extracellular matrix proteins, including fibronectin, laminin, vitronectin, collagen, fibrinogen, and a variety of proteoglycans. These adhesins have been referred to as "microbial surface components recognizing adhesive matrix molecules" (MSCRAMMs) and are especially prevalent among gram-positive bacteria.[155] In gram-positive organisms, they are covalently anchored to the cell wall peptidoglycan and have a characteristic primary amino acid sequence. In particular, the carboxy-terminus contains a segment rich in proline and glycine residues, an LPXTG motif (involved in sorting the protein to the cell wall), a hydrophobic membrane-spanning domain, and a short positively charged segment that resides in the cytoplasm and serves as a cell wall retention signal. Adhesive functions typically are located near the amino terminus.[45]

Staphylococcus aureus is a common gram-positive pathogen in children and is capable of producing a variety of MSCRAMMs, including collagen-binding protein (Cna), fibronectin-binding protein A (FnBPA), clumping factor (ClfA), and a distinct fibrinogen-binding protein. Strains recovered from patients with septic arthritis commonly express Cna, which mediates binding to cartilage in vitro and appears to play a key role in the pathogenesis of septic arthritis in experimental mice.[154, 156, 195] FnBPA shares homology with *S. pyogenes* protein F and mediates binding to both fibronectin and the γ chain of fibrinogen.[210] Accordingly, this protein likely is important in *S. aureus* infections of implanted biomaterials, which become coated with fibrinogen and fibrin soon after implantation. Clumping factor (ClfA) was named based on the observation that it mediates bacterial clumping in the presence of soluble fibrinogen.[128] Similar to FnBPA, ClfA mediates binding to fibrinogen-coated surfaces in vitro and probably contributes to infections of artificial surfaces. The active domain of ClfA is designated region A and is sufficient to mediate fibrinogen-dependent clumping when applied to latex beads.[129]

OTHER MECHANISMS OF ADHERENCE

Candida albicans is a common inhabitant of mucosal surfaces and an important cause of systemic disease, especially in patients with compromised immunity. *Candida* blastospores are capable of efficient adhesion to epithelial cells, leading to budding and division. In addition, germ tube formation occurs, facilitating penetration through the epithelial barrier and then dissemination to distant sites.[84] In recent years, several candidate *C. albicans* adhesins have been identified.[5, 83, 113, 225] Of particular interest is a protein called INT1, which shares functional homology with the vertebrate integrin family. Integrins normally are expressed by cells of the human immune system (neutrophils, monocytes, macrophages) and mediate cellular binding and shape-changing functions. Each integrin is a heterodimer of an α chain and a β chain. Numerous different α and β chains exist, and each combination displays a unique binding specificity. INT1 is an α-integrin–like protein that recognizes the RGD sequence of the C3 fragment iC3b on epithelial cells. In in vitro assays, short peptides encompassing the RGD sequence are capable of inhibiting *C. albicans* adherence by 50 percent, confirming that INT1 plays a significant role as an adhesin and suggesting that other adhesins also exist.[84] Beyond promoting adherence to epithelium, INT1 disguises organisms as leukocytes, allowing evasion of phagocytosis. Of note, expression of INT1 in *Saccharomyces cerevisiae* confers a capacity for adherence and also results in germ tube formation, indicating the importance of this protein in morphogenesis.[52, 53]

The adhesive properties of *C. albicans* are closely tied to its morphologic state. For example, adherence to buccal epithelial cells is greater by organisms bearing germ tubes than by yeast forms.[103] With this information in mind, Staab and coworkers searched a germ tube cDNA library and identified a putative adhesin called hyphal wall protein 1 (Hwp1), encoded by the *hwp1* gene. Examination of the predicted amino acid sequence of Hwp1 revealed similarity to proteins that are substrates for mammalian transglutaminase enzymes.[187] These enzymes form a cornified envelope on squamous epithelial cells (including buccal epithelial cells) by cross-linking relevant substrates.[188] Interestingly, the interactions of germ tubes with buccal epithelial cells resist stresses (e.g., heating or treatment with sodium dodecyl sulfate) capable of dissociating most typical microbe-host adhesive pairs, and elimination of expression of Hwp1 results in a marked reduction in adhesion to buccal epithelial cells.[12, 186] Together these observations support the notion that host transglutaminases act on Hwp1, cross-linking Hwp1 directly to surface proteins on buccal epithelial cells.

TISSUE TROPISM

Most microorganisms demonstrate restriction in the range of hosts, tissues, and cell types that they colonize. This restriction is referred to as tropism and generally reflects the specificity of the interaction between a given microbial adhesin and its cognate receptor. Accordingly, tropism is determined by the distribution of the relevant host receptor.

E. coli P pili serve as the platform for presentation of one of three different PapG variants, referred to as class I, class II, and class III PapG. All three variants recognize globoseries glycolipids, but each binds with a distinct specificity to the globoseries glycolipid isotypes. For example, class I PapG preferentially recognizes globotriosylceramide (GbO3, Gal-α1,4-Gal-β1,3-Glc-ceramide), class II PapG preferentially recognizes globoside (GbO4, GalNAc-β1,3-Gal-α1, 4-Gal-β1,3-Glc-ceramide), and class III PapG preferentially interacts with Forssman antigen (GbO5, GalNAc-α1, 3-GalNAc-β1,3-Gal-α1,4-Gal-β1,3-Glc-ceramide).[193] Globoside is the dominant globoseries glycolipid expressed in human kidney, and most human isolates of *E. coli* associated with pyelonephritis express class II PapG. In contrast, Forssman antigen is the most abundant globoseries glycolipid in dog kidney, and more than 50 percent of canine urinary isolates of *E. coli* express class III PapG.[223] *E. coli* expressing P pili with class II PapG are not found as a cause of urinary tract infection in dogs. Thus, the specificity of the PapG variant at the tip of the P pilus influences host range, favoring infection of either human or dog.

In recent work, Dodson and associates solved the crystal structure of class II PapG bound to Gal-α1,4-Gal, uncovering the structural basis of PapG binding specificity.[35] Of particular interest, the PapG receptor binding site is located on the side of the molecule and must be oriented with its N- to C-terminal axis parallel to the host cell membrane to allow docking to the receptor. This orientation may be facilitated by the flexibility inherent in the tip fibrillum. The PapG binding site consists of two regions. The first forms a β-barrel, and the second is composed of a central antiparallel β-sheet that is flanked on one side by two 2-stranded β-sheets and on the other side by an α-helix. When class II PapG interacts with GbO4, the arginine residue at position 170 in PapG makes contact with the GbO4 side chain. Interestingly, in class I PapG, a histidine residue occupies position 170, interfering with potential contact with the GbO4 side chain. Similarly, class II PapG and class III PapG differ in amino acids required for interaction with the GbO5 side chain.[35]

Group A streptococcus (*S. pyogenes*) is a common cause of infections of skin and soft tissue, including impetigo, cellulitis, and necrotizing fasciitis. Adherence to host cells by *S. pyogenes* is influenced by non-pilus proteins called M protein and protein F. M protein forms a fiber and consists of a C-terminal region that anchors the protein in the cell wall, a coiled-coil rod region extending approximately 50 nm from the cell wall, and a short nonhelical domain extending more distally.[44] Protein F is a 120-kDa protein that is notable for a tandem repeat element consisting of as many as six repeats of 32 to 44 amino acids adjacent to the C-terminus.[65, 150] Based on experiments with a series of isogenic strains that differ in expression of M protein or protein F or both, M protein clearly promotes adherence to human keratinocytes via interaction with the CD46 molecule (also called membrane cofactor protein or MCP), whereas protein F mediates adherence to epidermal Langerhans cells, which are located in the basal layer of the epidermis.[146, 147] Thus, both M protein and protein F contribute to group A streptococcal adherence to the skin, but each protein directs interaction with a different population of epidermal cells.

Early studies demonstrated that human immunodeficiency virus type 1 (HIV-1) infects $CD4^+$ cells and interacts with the CD4 molecule. More recent observations have established that numerous host cell chemokine receptors (e.g., CCR5 and CXCR4) serve as co-receptors for HIV-1 and are required for viral entry into $CD4^+$ target cells. These co-receptors appear to influence the cellular tropism displayed by different HIV-1 variants.[33] All HIV variants are able to replicate in primary T cells, but only some can replicate also in primary macrophages or in immortalized T-cell lines. Asymptomatic HIV-infected individuals carry predominantly macrophage-tropic (M-tropic) HIV-1 strains, which are restricted to CCR5 as a co-receptor and are non–syncytium-inducing in vitro. Rapid viral mutation caused by the error-prone HIV polymerase and HIV reverse transcriptase leads to the production of syncytium-inducing, T cell–tropic (T-tropic) HIV-1 strains, which predominate in the circulation of patients with acquired immunodeficiency syndrome (AIDS).[33] These variants generally are restricted to CXCR4 (expressed on T cells) as a co-receptor, although some primary syncytium-inducing variants can use both CCR5 and CXCR4.[38, 42, 181] T-tropic, syncytium-inducing strains are characterized by positively charged residues at fixed positions of the V3 loop and changes in charge and length of the V2 region of the viral envelope glycoprotein gp120, which binds to CD4 and co-receptors prior to viral entry into host cells.[46, 47, 61]

New HIV-1 infection is established selectively by M-tropic HIV-1 strains, even if the transmitting host harbors more pathogenic non–M-tropic strains as well.[206, 227] CCR5 also is expressed on the surface of rectal and vaginal epithelial cells, which may be sites of initial encounter between HIV-1 and the human host.[226] The importance of CCR5 in HIV-1 binding to $CD4^+$ cells is underscored by the observation that individuals homozygous for a 32-bp deletion in CCR5 (the Δ32 allele) are resistant to infection with HIV-1.[86, 114] Though Δ32 heterozygous cells are less susceptible to HIV-1 infection in vitro, the heterozygous state does not necessarily protect against HIV-1 acquisition. Recent evidence also suggests that CCR5 may be important in spread of HIV-1 infection to tissues lacking endogenous CCR5 expression.

In experiments by Mack and colleagues, the transfer of CCR5 from Chinese hamster ovary cells via membrane-derived microparticles to $CCR5^-$ (Δ32) monocytes rendered the latter cells susceptible to infection with HIV-1.[120] Finally, other co-receptors may determine the spectrum of tissue and organ involvement within the host. For example, the chemokine receptor CCR8 (TER1) may permit neurovirulent HIV-1 strains to enter brain cells.[95]

BIOFILMS

After attaching to a particular surface, many pathogens are capable of forming biofilms, defined as structured communities of microbial cells enclosed in a self-produced exopolysaccharide matrix.[162] Although most studies of biofilms have involved a single species, biofilms relevant to human infection likely often involve multiple species sharing the advantages of biofilm existence. Human infections associated with biofilms include dental caries, lower airway infection with *P. aeruginosa* in patients with cystic fibrosis, and foreign body infection in patients with prostheses and implanted devices. In addition, formation of biofilm may occur during osteomyelitis and endocarditis.[27]

P. aeruginosa is a model organism for the study of biofilms and forms pillars of stationary (sessile) bacteria held together by an extracellular polysaccharide called alginate. Interposed among these pillars are channels that facilitate the flow of nutrients and provide pathways for motile (planktonic) organisms to move about (Fig. 1–6). In experiments directed at defining the early steps of *P. aeruginosa* biofilm formation, O'Toole and Kolter established that flagella are required for initial bacterial attachment, presumably because these appendages promote movement toward the relevant surface. After attachment occurs, type 4 pili and pilus-mediated twitching motility promote formation of microcolonies.[149] In the context of microcolonies, transcription of *algC, algD,* and *algU* is activated, resulting in synthesis of alginate.[31] Of note, the alternative sigma factor σ^{22} positively regulates the *alg* genes and negatively regulates expression of flagella. Consistent with this observation, pulmonary isolates from patients with cystic fibrosis are highly mucoid (reflecting expression of alginate) and lack flagella.[50, 55]

Development of the complex community present within a biofilm requires intercellular communication. In the case of *P. aeruginosa*, this communication occurs via the LasR-LasI quorum sensing system, which involves the acyl-homoserine lactone called *N*-(3-oxododecanoyl)-L-homoserine lactone (3OC12-HSL).[32, 152] 3OC12-HSL is synthesized in a reaction catalyzed by LasI and accumulates with increases in population density. Ultimately 3OC12-HSL reaches a critical concentration and then interacts with LasR, serving to activate transcription of a number of genes. Organisms with a mutation in *lasI* are capable of attachment and microcolony formation, but the resulting microcolonies remain thin, undifferentiated, and sensitive to dispersion by a weak detergent. Addition of the missing signal to the *lasI* mutant restores development into structured, thick, biocide-resistant biofilms, analogous to those observed with wild-type organisms.

Biofilms constitute a protected mode of growth that allows survival in a hostile environment, such as in the presence of host immune mechanisms or antimicrobial agents.[27] Based on studies of *P. aeruginosa*, sessile bacteria release antigens and stimulate production of antibodies, but these antibodies are ineffective in killing organisms within biofilms.[21] Similarly, sessile *P. aeruginosa* stimulate a diminished oxidative burst and are relatively refractory to phagocytic uptake. In addition, organisms within biofilms are resistant to the effects of numerous antibiotics, in part because antibiotic agents are unable to diffuse through the biofilm, in part because these bacteria may exist in a slow-growing state and possibly because these organisms adopt a distinct and protected phenotype.[27] Understanding the mechanisms by which biofilms develop may yield novel approaches to antimicrobial therapy, aimed at disrupting biofilm formation or persistence.

Invasion, Intracellular Survival, and Cell-to-Cell Spread

After adhering to a host surface, many pathogenic organisms are able to invade and survive inside epithelial cells and other nonprofessional phagocytes (for instance, M cells in intestinal Peyer patches). In addition, some pathogens are able to survive inside professional phagocytes (macrophages and neutrophils). Invasion may represent a mechanism to breach host mucosal barriers and gain access to deeper or more distant tissues. Alternatively, invasion may provide the organism with a special niche, protected from host immune mechanisms. Generally, the process of invasion involves a class of molecules called invasins, which mediate microbial adherence and entry. Invasion is an active event that relies upon underlying host cell functions and is associated with rearrangement of the host cell cytoskeleton. Once inside the host cell, the invading or ingested organism usually is localized within a membrane-bound vacuole that contains lysosomal enzymes. In some cases, the pathogen

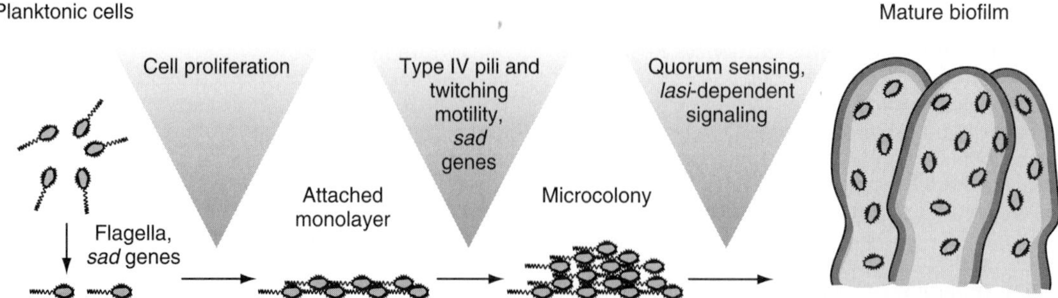

FIGURE 1–6 ■ Dynamics of the *Pseudomonas aeruginosa* biofilm. Keys to the formation of the biofilm include flagella-mediated attachment, type 4 pilus-based twitching motility, and a quorum sensing system. (Reproduced with permission from Costerton, J.W., Stewart, P.S., and Greenberg, E.P.: Bacterial biofilms: A common cause of persistent infections. Science *284*:1318–1322, 1999. Copyright 1999 American Association for the Advancement of Science.)

escapes from this vacuole and enters the cytoplasm, a more permissive environment. In others, the pathogen remains in the vacuole and neutralizes lysosomal enzymatic activity. The processes of invasion into cells, survival within cells, cell-to-cell spread, and entry into the circulation define the extent of infection and dissemination.

INVASION

In considering the molecular mechanism of microbial invasion, perhaps best characterized are the enteropathogenic *Yersinia* spp., namely, *Yersinia pseudotuberculosis* and *Yersinia enterocolitica*. These organisms usually are acquired by ingestion of contaminated food or water and typically cause self-limited enteritis or mesenteric adenitis. In infants and other individuals with compromised immunity, they sometimes produce systemic disease. The primary determinant of *Y. pseudotuberculosis* and *Y. enterocolitica* invasion is an adhesive outer membrane protein called invasin, which is encoded by a chromosomal locus called *inv* and binds tightly to a family of β_1-integrins expressed on host cells, including $\alpha_3\beta_1$ integrin on the surface of intestinal M cells.[91] The interaction between invasin and β_1-integrins initiates a cascade of signaling steps in the host cell, resulting in actin rearrangement and formation of large complexes of cytoskeletal elements (talin, vinculin, α-actinin, and others) called focal adhesions.[90] Bacterial entry into the host cell occurs via a "zipper-like" mechanism, with the plasma membrane zippering around the invading organism.

Beyond invasin, two additional proteins called Ail and YadA also influence invasion by enteropathogenic *Yersinia* spp. Ail is a 17-kDa outer membrane protein that also is encoded by a chromosomal locus (*ail*) and mediates high levels of adherence and low levels of invasion in assays with cultured epithelial cells. In addition, Ail mediates resistance to complement-mediated serum killing, independent of an effect on invasion.[10] YadA is a 45-kDa surface protein that is encoded by the 70-kb *Yersinia* virulence plasmid. Similar to invasin, YadA promotes invasion by binding to β_1-integrins on the host cell surface. YadA also mediates binding to extracellular matrix molecules. Based on studies using a mouse oral infection model, in *Y. enterocolitica,* YadA is essential for survival and multiplication in Peyer patches, whereas in *Y. pseudotuberculosis,* YadA is dispensable for full virulence.[11]

Similar to *Y. enterocolitica* and *Y. pseudotuberculosis*, *Listeria monocytogenes* invades epithelial cells via a zipper-like mechanism. Invasion is mediated by proteins called internalin A (InlA) and internalin B (InlB), which are required for virulence in animal models. InlA interacts with E-cadherin, a host cell transmembrane protein with an intracellular domain that interacts with the cytoskeleton.[132] InlB interacts with C1q on host cells and promotes invasion by activating the PI-3 kinase pathway.[13] Recent studies indicate that uropathogenic strains of *E. coli* also invade epithelial cells via a zipper-like mechanism, mediated by the FimH adhesin expressed on the tip of type 1 pili. In experiments with cultured bladder epithelial cells, FimH is both necessary and sufficient for entry, as demonstrated by examination of a *fimH* mutant and of latex beads coated with purified FimH.[125] Of note, based on animal data with mice and nonhuman primates, purified FimH represents a promising vaccine candidate and is currently in human trials.[109, 110]

Salmonella enterica serovar *typhimurium* (*S. typhimurium*) is an example of a pathogen that invades cells by a mechanism distinct from zippering. Upon contact with the epithelial cell surface, *S. typhimurium* triggers a dramatic host cell response characterized by actin rearrangement, calcium and inositol phosphate fluxes, and membrane ruffling. Bacterial entry into the cell occurs rapidly, with organisms appearing in membrane-bound vacuoles within a few minutes of initial contact with the host cell. The determinants of *S. typhimurium* invasion are encoded by a pathogenicity island called SPI-1, located at centisome 63 on the bacterial chromosome.[51] Especially important is a type III protein secretion system, which forms a needle-like complex on the bacterial surface and serves to translocate bacterial proteins directly into the host cell, ultimately disrupting the host cell cytoskeleton.[23] Studies of the structure of the needle-like complex have established that the base spans both the inner and outer membranes and is approximately 40 nm in diameter, whereas the needle itself is 8 nm in width and approximately 80 nm in length (Fig. 1–7). The base is composed of proteins called PrgH, PrgK, and InvG, with InvG playing a key role in pore formation in the bacterial outer membrane. The needle, in turn, is composed of PrgI, and its length is influenced by a protein called InvJ.[105, 106]

The proteins secreted through the *S. typhimurium* needle complex (and other type III secretion systems) and into the host cell are referred to as effector proteins. SopE is an effector protein that mediates the initial rearrangement of actin and ruffling of the host cell membrane. It functions as a guanyl-nucleotide exchange factor (GEF) and activates two host cell Rho GTPase proteins called Rac and Cdc42.[19, 64, 66] SptP is an effector protein that functions as an antagonist of SopE, mediating reversal of actin rearrangement by converting Rac and Cdc42 to the inactive forms (GDP forms). Consistent with these functions, SopE and SptP directly antagonize each other when co-injected into Ref52 cells.[49] Other effector proteins secreted by the *S. typhimurium* type III secretion system include SipB, SopB, AvrA, and SipC. SipB induces apoptosis in macrophages through a caspase-dependent mechanism.[74] The inositol phosphate phos-phorylase SopB disrupts normal host cell signaling mechanisms.[143] The functions of AvrA and SipC remain unknown.[23, 122]

Important accessory and regulatory genes also are present in SPI-1. As an example, the *sicA* gene is just upstream of the *sipB* and *sipC* genes and encodes an accessory protein with chaperone activity essential for stabilization and translocation of SipB, SipC, and SopE.[201] Other chaperones encoded by SPI-1 are involved in the stabilization and translocation of other effector proteins. The factors that regulate the expression of type III secretion machinery and secreted proteins also are beginning to be understood.[40]

INTRACELLULAR SURVIVAL

Once an organism invades a nonprofessional phagocyte or is ingested by a professional phagocyte, several potential outcomes exist. Often, the organism is killed. However, some pathogens have developed strategies to survive and replicate inside host cells, in some cases within a vacuole and in others by escaping from the vacuole.

The consensus is that *S. typhimurium* resides within a membrane-bound vacuole in both professional and nonprofessional phagocytes. However, the vacuole lacks several lysosomal markers typical of the main endocytic pathway (the mannose-6-phosphate receptor pathway) and appears to be distinct from this pathway. Insight into the molecular determinants of intravacuolar survival came in 1996, when two independent groups reported the discovery of a second *Salmonella* pathogenicity island, now called SPI-2.[73, 145] This island maps to centisome 31 and encodes another type

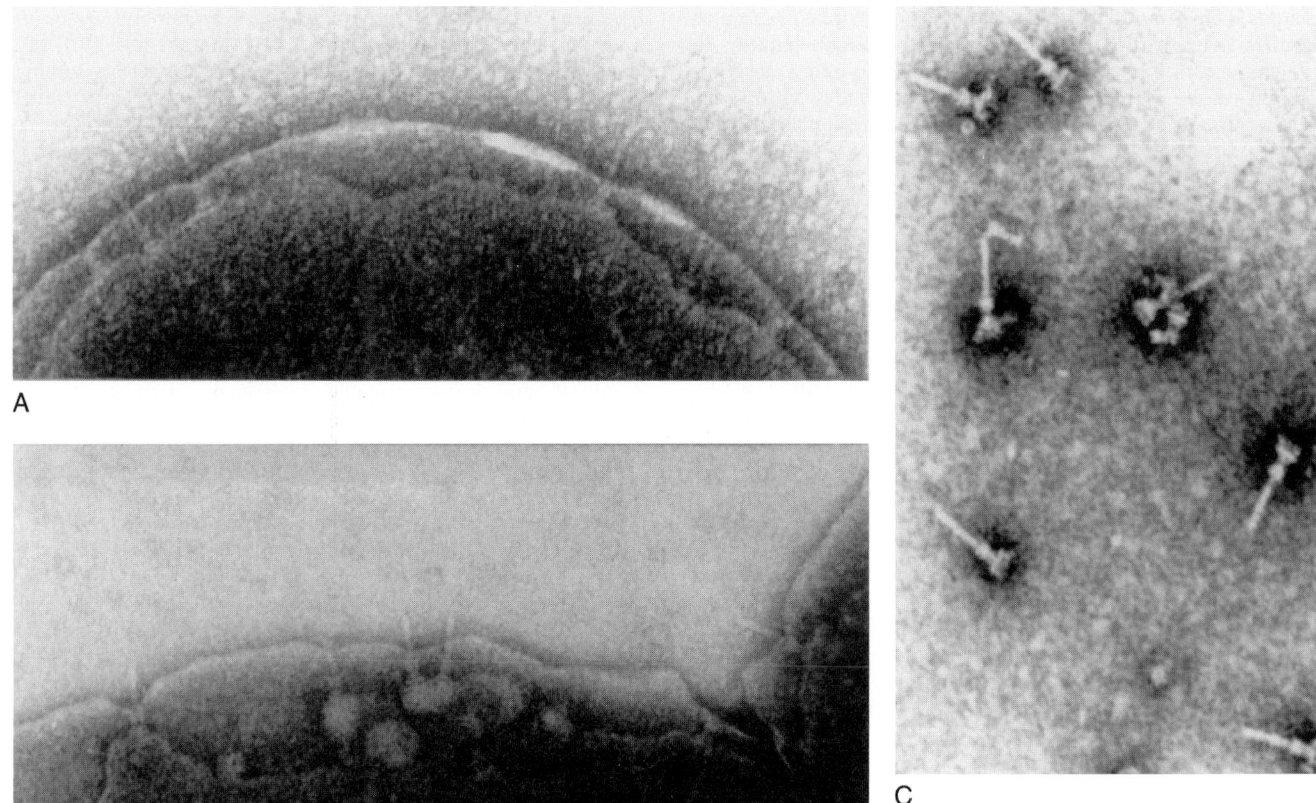

FIGURE 1–7 ■ *A* and *B*, Needle complexes of the *Salmonella* type III secretion system seen on the surface of nonflagellated *S. typhimurium* and (*C*) isolated in purified form. (Courtesy of J.E. Galán; reproduced with permission from Kubori, T., Matsushima, Y., Nakamura, D., et al.: Supramolecular structure of the *Salmonella typhimurium* type III protein secretion system. Science *280*:602–605, 1998. Copyright 1998 American Association for the Advancement of Science.)

III secretion system, including structural proteins (*ssa* locus),[73] effector proteins (*sse* locus), and accessory proteins (*ssc* locus). In addition, this region encodes a two-component regulatory system consisting of proteins called SsrA (formerly SpiR) and SsrB. SsrA is a membrane-located sensor kinase, and SsrB is a transcriptional regulator.[145] Expression of SPI-2 genes is up-regulated within the macrophage vacuole and is dependent at least partially on the acidic intravacuolar environment. Inhibition of macrophage vacuolar acidification using bafilomycin A1 (an inhibitor of the vacuolar proton ATPase) results in a sharp attenuation in transcription of SPI-2 genes. This effect is not reproduced by low pH alone outside the vacuole, suggesting that other environmental effects within the vacuole play a role.[20] Mutations in SPI-2 result in reduced survival inside macrophages, with no effect on adherence and invasion in assays with intestinal epithelial cells.[145] Furthermore, SPI-2 mutants demonstrate reduced virulence in experimental mice (up to a 10^4-fold reduction in 50% lethal dose), providing evidence that survival inside macrophages is a key factor in the pathogenesis of disease.[179]

A third *Salmonella* pathogenicity island called SPI-3 also influences survival inside macrophages. This island is located at centisome 82 and was discovered by examining the *Salmonella selC* locus, a tRNA gene where pathogenicity islands reside in some strains of *E. coli*.[7, 8] SPI-3 contains the *mgtB/C* operon, which permits *S. typhimurium* growth in environments with low concentrations of Mg^{2+}, including macrophages. In particular, mutation of the *mgtB/C* operon abolishes the ability of *S. typhimurium* to replicate in low-Mg^{2+} liquid media and in macrophages, and addition of Mg^{2+} to the medium after phagocytosis restores the ability to survive intracellularly. In addition, introduction of the *mgtB/C* genes into *E. coli* confers the ability to grow in low concentrations of Mg^{2+}. The *mgtB/C* genes are expressed preferentially after internalization into host cells under control of the PhoP/PhoQ two-component regulatory system, a complex that directs expression of a number of virulence determinants.[122]

The ability to survive within phagocytic cells may provide *Salmonella* with a means to exploit an intrinsic host pathway and disseminate to distant sites. In particular, certain phagocytes express the β_2-integrin CD18, which mediates leukocyte migration in response to various stimuli. During *S. typhimurium* infection, CD18-expressing phagocytes transfer organisms from the intestine to the spleen. On the one hand, this function facilitates initiation of a systemic immune response and benefits the host. However, at the same time, it provides bacteria with a mechanism of transit from the gut to organs of the reticuloendothelial system and elsewhere. In experiments comparing CD18-deficient mice and wild type mice after oral inoculation with *S. typhimurium*, Vazquez-Torres and coworkers found that CD18-deficient animals had relatively reduced numbers of bacteria in the liver and spleen.[207]

Mycobacterium tuberculosis, another intracellular pathogen, uses a variety of mechanisms to ensure intracellular survival. The *M. tuberculosis* vacuole lacks usual amounts of the vesicular proton ATPase responsible for mediating acidification and fails to acidify to normal levels.[194] In addition, *M. tuberculosis* blocks fusion of the vacuole with acidic lysosomes, further preventing acidification.[172] Similar to *Salmonella*, *M. tuberculosis* contains an *mgtC* gene, and mutation of this gene results in impaired virulence in cultured human macrophages and in mouse spleen and lung. Low Mg^{2+} concentration and mildly acidic pH inhibit the growth of the *mgtC* mutant, suggesting that the gene is important for survival in the phagosome, where such conditions may exist.[15] Another factor that influences *M. tuberculosis* survival inside macrophages is isocitrate lyase, an enzyme of the glycolytic shunt that is essential for metabolism of fatty acids. Expression of isocitrate lyase is up-regulated during infection of activated macrophages and is required for full virulence in a murine model of infection, independent of an effect on bacterial growth.[130] The structure of *M. tuberculosis* isocitrate lyase has been solved recently and may provide a target for new drug therapies against persistent infection, inasmuch as this enzyme is absent from vertebrates.[177]

During the course of interaction with macrophages, *M. tuberculosis* is capable of stimulating caspase-1 and inducing macrophage apoptosis. This process may be beneficial to the host, preventing spread of infection to other sites. At the same time, *M. tuberculosis* possesses at least two antiapoptotic mechanisms that further influence the outcome with macrophages. First, *M. tuberculosis* infection enhances host cell production of sTNFR2, a protein that inactivates TNF-α and interferes with apoptosis.[3] Increased sTNFR2 may be secondary to up-regulation of host cell production of IL-10. Second, *M. tuberculosis* infection activates production of NF-κB, which protects cells from apoptosis through mechanisms that still are being characterized.[54] Of interest, less virulent strains of *M. tuberculosis* are more potent inducers of apoptosis.[98]

Listeria monocytogenes is an example of an organism that escapes from the phagocytic vacuole in macrophages and epithelial cells and moves into the cytoplasm. This organism causes meningitis and focal brain abscesses in humans and has a predilection for the fetoplacental unit. In pregnant women, listeriosis results in fetal loss in 30 percent of cases. Escape from the vacuole is mediated by listeriolysin O, a hemolysin encoded by the *hly* gene. Listeriolysin O interacts with cholesterol in host cell membranes and forms pores, leading to lysis of the phagosome.[48] Mutants defective in *hly* fail to survive intracellularly and are avirulent in mice. Additional factors that contribute to escape from the phagosome include two phospholipase C molecules called PC-PLC (encoded by *plcB*) and PI-PLC (encoded by *plcA*). The relative contribution of PC-PLC and PI-PLC is dependent on host cell type. For example, PC-PLC seems more critical in epithelial cells, whereas PI-PLC is especially important in mouse bone-marrow macrophages.[123, 182]

CELL-TO-CELL SPREAD

Movement from one cell to another may help an organism gain a stronger foothold in host tissues. *L. monocytogenes* is one example of a pathogen capable of cell-to-cell spread. Once this organism is free in the cytoplasm, actin begins to polymerize on the bacterial surface. Eventually the condensed actin forms a polar tail or comet (Fig. 1–8), which propels the organism through the cytoplasm and into adjacent cells. The rate of bacterial movement within a cell correlates with actin tail length.[197] Actin accumulation and condensation is mediated by the *L. monocytogenes* ActA protein, which is tightly anchored to the bacterial surface and is expressed asymmetrically over the length of the organism.[183, 196] ActA is the sole *Listeria* factor required for actin polymerization, inasmuch as actin tails form in

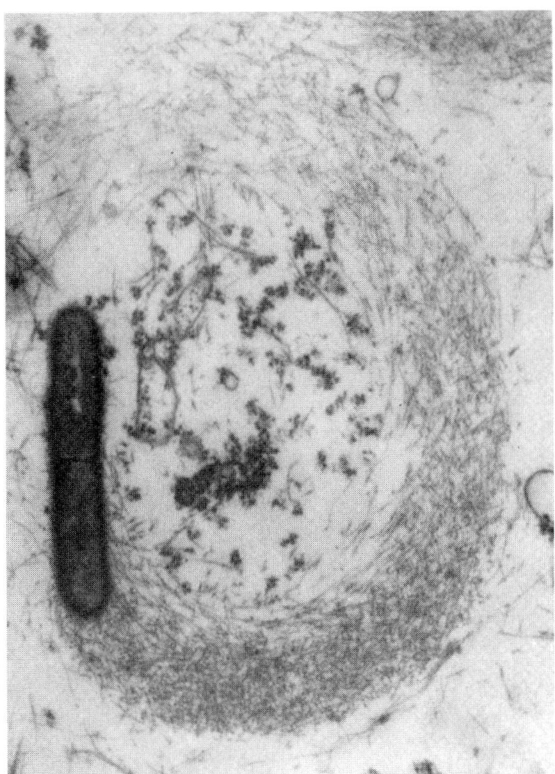

FIGURE 1–8 ■ Actin tail formation in *Listeria monocytogenes*. (Reproduced with permission from Theriot, J.A.: The cell biology of infection by intracellular bacterial pathogens. Annu. Rev. Cell Dev. Biol. *11*:213–239, 1995.)

Xenopus cytoplasmic extracts containing ActA-coated beads. However, in these experiments, motility occurs only when ActA is distributed asymmetrically on the beads.[17] ActA appears to interact directly with actin and also with a variety of other host cytoskeletal proteins.[48, 198] Cytochalasin D is an inhibitor of actin polymerization and inhibits the cell-to-cell spread of *L. monocytogenes* in epithelial monolayers.[30, 137]

On reaching the plasma membrane, bacteria protrude from the cell in filipodium-like structures (called listeriopods), which then are engulfed by neighboring cells. This engulfment may be part of a normal host process, inasmuch as MDCK cells demonstrate low-level endocytosis of adjacent cell membrane fragments even in the absence of bacteria.[168] The formation of listeriopods and the engulfment of these structures by neighboring cells are independent of listeriolysin O, PI-PLC and PC-PLC.[56] Once inside a nascently infected cell, *Listeria* escapes from the double-membrane vacuole via the action of PI-PLC, PC-PLC, and a metalloproteinase called Mpl.[48] On arrival in the cytosol, bacteria can enter another cycle of actin-based motility and cell-to-cell spread, although one or two bacterial generations may be necessary to regain motility.[168]

A second pathogen capable of actin-based motility and cell-to-cell spread is *Shigella flexneri*. In *Shigella*, a single protein called IcsA (also called VirG) is sufficient to induce formation of an actin tail, similar to that observed in *L. monocytogenes*. IcsA is an outer membrane protein that is encoded on the *Shigella* virulence plasmid and is distributed on the bacterial surface in a polarized fashion. Initially, IcsA is distributed over the entire bacterial surface, with a predominance at one pole. However, over time, a secreted bacterial protease called IcsP (also called SopA) cleaves roughly one half of the surface IcsA, mostly at the opposite pole, further polarizing distribution.[39, 189] Elimination of expression of IcsP leads to increased quantities of IcsA and increased actin-based motility, suggesting that IcsA (rather than host factors) is rate-limiting in the motility process.[180] Like ActA, IcsA is necessary and sufficient to induce polymerization of the actin tail, and the tail forms at the end where IcsA concentration is highest.[58] Despite the functional similarities between IcsA and ActA, no significant amino acid sequence homology exists between the two proteins. In contrast to ActA, no direct interaction between IcsA and actin has been demonstrated, and IcsA is found throughout the actin tail, not only at the bacterial pole–actin tail junction.

Rickettsia spp. also are capable of actin-based motility and cell-to-cell spread. Based on examination of *R. rickettsiae*, *Rickettsia* move through the cytoplasm of infected cells 2.5 to 3 times more slowly than do *L. monocytogenes* and *S. flexneri*. In *Rickettsia conorii*, the actin tails appear to be anchored to the bacterial body in a parallel manner, differing from the actin tails in *Listeria* and *Shigella*, which are composed of much shorter actin filaments organized in a random branching network.[60] Details of the bacterial determinants of movement of *Rickettsia* remain poorly defined.

PENETRATION BETWEEN CELLS (PARACYTOSIS)

Whereas some pathogens are capable of entry into cells and cell-to-cell spread, others are able to penetrate between cells. *H. influenzae* commonly is present in the lower respiratory tract in patients with chronic respiratory tract disease, including chronic bronchitis, bronchiectasis, and cystic fibrosis.[136] Examination of histopathologic samples from these patients reveals organisms between and beneath bronchial epithelial cells, suggesting that penetration between cells may facilitate chronic carriage, perhaps providing organisms with a niche protected from antibiotics and local immune mechanisms.[203] van Schilfgaarde and coworkers have developed an in vitro model for studying the process whereby *H. influenzae* penetrates between cells, referred to as paracytosis. Using cultured epithelial cells derived from lung and capable of forming tight junctions, these investigators have observed clusters of bacteria between cells.[204] In addition, they have discovered that more adherent strains are capable of higher levels of paracytosis. Recently, they identified two novel genes that likely play a role in this process.[205]

Damage to the Host

Damage to host cells and host tissues represents a fundamental mechanism by which a pathogen is able to survive at a given site and then spread within a host. Generally, damage is induced by microbial toxins. Most toxins are released extracellularly (exotoxins) and are capable of inducing damage at very low concentrations. Microbial attachment and invasion facilitate delivery of toxins to target cells and target tissues and serve to enhance toxicity.

Historically, microbial toxins have been classified according to a variety of criteria, including cellular target of action (e.g., enterotoxins, leukotoxins, neurotoxins), mechanism of action (e.g., ADP-ribosylating toxins, adenylate cyclase toxins, pore-forming toxins, proteolytic toxins), and major biologic effect (e.g., hemolytic toxins, edema-producing toxins). In recent years, the term *toxin* has been applied more broadly to include enzymes that mediate damaging effects via phospholipase or hyaluronidase activity.

WHOOPING COUGH AND *B. PERTUSSIS* TOXINS

Whooping cough (*B. pertussis* infection) is a classic example of a toxin-mediated disease and involves an interplay of multiple toxins.[100] The pathogenesis of whooping cough begins with *B. pertussis* colonization of the trachea, which is facilitated by a molecule called tracheal cytotoxin (TCT). TCT is a disaccharide tetrapeptide fragment of peptidoglycan and belongs to the family of muramyl peptides.[59] Many gram-negative organisms produce an analogous fragment during normal turnover of cell wall components, but significant extracellular release appears to occur only in *Bordetella* spp. and gonococci. In most species, an inner membrane protein called AmpG recycles this fragment back into the bacterial cell.[28] The toxic effects of TCT are conferred by its diaminopimelic acid side chains and not its disaccharide backbone, distinguishing it from other muramyl peptides.[115, 116] TCT is toxic to tracheal epithelial cells in vitro, stimulating nitric oxide synthase and local production of interleukin-1 and causing inhibition of ciliary motility, inhibition of DNA synthesis, and cell death.[68–70, 75] During natural infection, TCT likely paralyzes the mucociliary escalator and interferes with clearance of *B. pertussis* and respiratory mucus.

Beyond TCT, *B. pertussis* elaborates a toxin called adenylate cyclase toxin (CyaA), which has pore-forming activity and inhibits adenylate cyclase, resulting in accumulation of cyclic AMP (cAMP). In phagocytic cells, the elevated levels of cAMP inhibit oxidative activity and induce apoptosis, thus disabling this arm of the immune system.[101, 102, 158] In respiratory epithelial cells, the elevated levels of cAMP may result in increased fluid and mucus secretion, further impairing mucociliary function. Adenylate cyclase toxin has homology to numerous other bacterial calcium-dependent, pore-forming toxins known as RTX toxins (named because of a repeat found in each toxin), with the prototype being the *E. coli* HlyA hemolysin.[28] These toxins create pores in the host cell plasma membrane, ultimately leading to host cell lysis. Among the family of RTX toxins, the general mechanism of pore formation and the predicted amino acid sequences are conserved, but target cell specificities differ.

Pertussis toxin is thought to be a key determinant of the clinical manifestations of whooping cough. This toxin belongs to a family of bacterial ADP-ribosyltransferase enzymes. The target of pertussis toxin is host cell G proteins, resulting in disruption of normal signaling processes. Numerous biologic effects, including induction of lymphocytosis, stimulation of insulin release, sensitization to histamine, and disruption of phagocytic cell function, have been ascribed to pertussis toxin; however, the specific relationship between the effects of pertussis toxin and the symptoms of whooping cough remains unclear.[76] Of note, *Bordetella parapertussis* is related closely to *B. pertussis* and produces a similar cough illness but fails to produce pertussis toxin because of mutations in the *ptx* promoter region.[139]

HEMOLYTIC UREMIC SYNDROME AND SHIGA TOXINS

Numerous intestinal pathogens, including *Shigella dysenteriae*, enterohemorrhagic *E. coli* (including *E. coli* O157:H7), and *Citrobacter freundii*, among others, produce Shiga toxins. Shiga toxins are classic A-B toxins, consisting of an A subunit that has toxic activity and five B subunits arranged in a pentameric ringlike structure that promotes binding to host cells and delivery of the A subunit. The B subunits interact with host cell globoseries glycolipids, especially the

Pk trisaccharide moiety of globotriaosylceramide (GbO3). The A subunit is endocytosed by the host cell and traverses the cytoplasm in membrane-bound vesicles. Some of these vesicles fuse with lysosomes, resulting in degradation of toxin. Others travel in a retrograde fashion to the Golgi apparatus and then to the endoplasmic reticulum (ER).[174] Subsequently, toxin binds to host 28S ribosomal RNA and cleaves a single adenine residue via N-glycosidase activity. Ultimately, this depurination event results in inhibition of protein elongation and cell death.[173]

In humans, *E. coli* O157:H7 is an important cause of hemorrhagic colitis and sometimes produces hemolytic uremic syndrome (HUS). Infection begins with adherence to epithelial cells via intimin and other proteins encoded by the locus of enterocyte effacement (LEE), resulting in formation of attaching and effacing lesions analogous to those observed in EPEC infection.[127] Following adherence, the organism releases Shiga toxin, which traverses the intestinal epithelial cell and enters the bloodstream.[1] Toxin circulates to distant organs and mediates damage via toxicity to endothelium. Diarrhea likely results from damage to endothelium in small mesenteric vessels, leading to ischemia and sloughing of the intestinal mucosa. The renal effects observed in human HUS arise from microvascular and glomerular damage with luminal occlusion by fibrin and platelets.[228] Hemolysis and thrombocytopenia likely develop as a consequence of microangiopathy.

Shiga toxins can be divided into two antigenically distinct groups called STX-I and STX-II, which share 50 to 60 percent homology. Most isolates of *E. coli* O157:H7 recovered from patients with HUS express STX-II, and some express STX-I as well.[112] Wadolkowski and associates pretreated mice with antibodies against STX-I, STX-II, or both and then challenged these animals with an *E. coli* strain expressing STX-I and STX-II. Consistent with the importance of STX-II, mice pretreated with antibodies against STX-II (with or without antibodies against STX-I) were protected from severe disease, whereas 90 percent of mice pretreated with anti-STX-I alone or anticholera toxin died. However, pathologic examination of the kidneys demonstrated acute renal tubular necrosis and not glomerular injury, suggesting that this model has deficiencies in mimicking human disease.[208]

Understanding the interaction between Shiga toxins and human glycolipid receptors may lead to important therapeutic interventions to prevent HUS in children with enterohemorrhagic *E. coli* colitis.[67] As an example, Kitov and colleagues recently reported the construction of a multivalent "designer ligand" that binds to multiple B subunits of STX-I and STX-II and has inhibitory activity 10^6- to 10^7-fold higher than that of univalent synthetic ligands.[104] In addition, Paton and coworkers have pursued another novel approach, creating a nonpathogenic laboratory strain of *E. coli* expressing the Pk trisaccharide. In a mouse model, oral administration of this strain conferred complete protection against challenge with enterohemorrhagic *E. coli*.[153]

TISSUE-DEGRADING TOXINS

Numerous toxins have enzymatic activity and are capable of degrading tissue components. One example is hyaluronidase, which degrades hyaluronic acid, a repeating disaccharide glycosaminoglycan involved in cell motility, adhesion, and proliferation in normal hosts. Hyaluronic acid contains alternating N-acetylglucosamine and glucuronic acid moieties, connected by β linkages. It is prominent in extracellular matrix when cell turnover and tissue repair are prominent, for example in embryogenesis, wound healing, and carcinogenesis.[29] The primary host receptor for hyaluronic acid is CD44, which undergoes post-translational modification that varies according to host cell type. Interactions between hyaluronic acid and CD44 are critical to T and B cell stimulation, growth of certain lymphoid malignancies, and propagation of certain inflammatory responses.[134]

In *S. pyogenes*, hyaluronidase is a 96-kDa protein that is encoded by the *hylA* gene and is released extracellularly. It is proposed to promote invasion through cell layers and tissue planes and is considered one of several *S. pyogenes* spreading factors.[89] Interestingly, *S. pyogenes* also produces a thick "capsule" of hyaluronic acid that can interact with other host cellular and extracellular matrix proteins to contribute to tissue invasion by the organism. Other pathogens that produce a hyaluronidase include *S. agalactiae* (group B streptococcus), *Treponema pallidum*, *Candida*, *Entamoeba histolytica*, and *Ancylostoma braziliense*.[29]

Evasion of Immunity

In order to survive and replicate within the host, a pathogen must evade the host immune system. Initially, the organism must circumvent innate immune mechanisms, including mechanical forces, resident phagocytes, and complement activity. Over time, the organism also must overcome adaptive immunity, including the presence of specific antibodies.

ANTIPHAGOCYTIC FACTORS

As described earlier in this chapter, invasin-mediated entry into M cells plays an important role in the early stages of *Yersinia* infection. At the same time, evasion of phagocytosis is critical to the pathogenesis of *Yersinia* disease. The ability to avoid phagocytosis is dependent on the *Yersinia* virulence plasmid, which encodes numerous proteins called Yops.[26, 191] Both YopE and YopH interfere with ingestion by macrophages and neutrophils via slightly different mechanisms. YopE shares sequence homology with the *Salmonella typhimurium* SptP protein and down-regulates all three of the Rho GTPases (Rho, Cdc42, and Rac), thus inhibiting actin rearrangement and blocking formation of membrane ruffles (lamellipodia) and spikes (filopodia).[9] YopH is a protein tyrosine phosphorylase that appears to act on a host cell cytosolic protein called Cas, interfering with recruitment of Rho, Cdc42, and Rac and preventing formation of actin stress fibers, focal complexes, and focal adhesions.[6, 9] Other Yops that may have antiphagocytic activity are under active investigation. Elucidation of the Yop mechanisms may lead to development of Yop inhibitors that abolish the antiphagocytic properties of this pathogen.

Shigella employs another strategy to counter phagocytic function. This pathogen produces hemorrhagic enterocolitis and is an important cause of bloody diarrhea in children. Infection begins with ingestion of organisms, which attach to intestinal M cells and then cross the intestinal epithelium.[231] On entry into the subepithelial space, organisms are engulfed by resident macrophages and contained in membrane-bound vacuoles. However, they quickly escape from macrophage vacuoles and move to the cytosol of the cell, where they induce apoptosis.[230] The mechanism of apoptosis involves a protein called IpaB, which is encoded by the *Shigella* virulence plasmid and is injected into host cells by the *Shigella* type III secretion system. Work by Zychlinsky and coworkers has established that IpaB binds to cytosolic interleukin-1β converting enzyme (caspase-1), a cysteine protease that cleaves IL-1β to its active form.[77] Caspase-1 is homologous to many other enzymes involved in cell death pathways, including ced-3 of *Caenorhabditis elegans*. Interestingly, the *S. typhimurium* SipB protein shares homology with IpaB and also induces apoptosis by interacting with caspase-1.[74] The process of macrophage apoptosis is associated with release of interleukin-1β, which recruits neutrophils to the site of infection. The inflammatory response results in loss of tissue integrity and allows *Shigella* to spread to deeper sites.

EVASION OF COMPLEMENT ACTIVITY

S. pyogenes expresses at least three factors that interfere with host complement activity. Perhaps best known is M protein, which inhibits activation of the alternative complement pathway. This effect is mediated at least in part by the ability of M protein to bind complement factor H, a regulatory protein that inhibits assembly and accelerates decay of C3bBb. Recent studies indicate that serotype M1 and M57 strains express an extracellular protein called Sic (streptococcal inhibitor of complement-mediated lysis), which associates with human plasma proteins called clusterin and histidine-rich glycoprotein (HRG) and apparently blocks formation of the membrane attack complex (C5b-C9).[2] Studies of epidemic waves of M1 infection demonstrate that Sic undergoes significant variation over time, perhaps in response to the selective pressure associated with specific antibodies.[80, 81, 131] Of note, nonpolar inactivation of Sic results in reduced mucosal colonization of mice.[117] In addition, *S. pyogenes* produces a serine protease called C5a peptidase, which cleaves and inactivates C5a.[217] C5a is a cleavage product of C5 and serves as a powerful chemoattractant for neutrophils. Thus, C5a peptidase serves to attenuate the neutrophil response to streptococcal infection.

N. gonorrhoeae is a common cause of cervicitis, urethritis, and pelvic inflammatory disease and also is capable of producing disseminated disease. Interestingly, fresh clinical isolates of *N. gonorrhoeae* typically are resistant to complement-mediated killing, and resistance to complement is likely important in the pathogenesis of disease. Resistance is due in part to sialylation of lipooligosaccharide (LOS), which involves addition of host-derived cytidine monophospho-*N*-acetylneuraminic acid (CMP-NANA) by a bacterial sialyltransferase. Given the requirement for CMP-NANA, subcultivation in the absence of human serum or human neutrophils is associated with loss of sialylation and loss of resistance. Sialylated LOS binds factor H, resulting in down-regulation of activity of the alternative pathway C3 convertase. In addition, sialylated LOS interferes with neutrophil phagocytosis and with the normal oxidative burst in neutrophils.[167, 216] A second determinant of resistance to complement-mediated killing is Por1, an outer membrane porin protein that binds both factor H and C4b binding protein (C4b BP).[164] C4b BP binds C4b and serves to inhibit assembly and accelerate decay of C4b2a, the classical pathway C3 convertase. In recent work, Cardinale and Clark have identified a third factor that influences resistance to complement, namely an outer membrane protein called AniA that is induced under anaerobic conditions. The mechanism of the effect of AniA is under study.[18]

EVASION OF HUMORAL IMMUNITY

Numerous pathogens have evolved mechanisms to vary surface-exposed immunogenic molecules, thus facilitating evasion of a specific antibody response. Antigenic variation represents one such mechanism and is characterized by the emergence of modified molecules with novel antigenic properties. Phase variation represents a second such mechanism and is typified by the reversible loss or gain of a given molecule or structure.

N. gonorrhoeae is capable of producing recurrent infection, reflecting the fact that the antibody response to infection fails to provide lasting immunity. In this context, it is noteworthy that *N. gonorrhoeae* pili are an important target of serum antibody and undergo frequent antigenic variation. Gonococcal pilin expression is controlled by the *pilE* locus (the expression locus), which contains an intact pilin gene along with promoter sequences. In addition to *pilE*, the gonococcal chromosome contains numerous copies of variant *pil* sequences, called *pilS* loci.[63] These loci are transcriptionally inactive because they lack a promoter and 5′ coding sequence. However, they can be introduced into the expression locus by RecA-dependent recombination, resulting in an altered structural subunit and antigenically variant pili.[85] Because *N. gonorrhoeae* is naturally transformable, possibly horizontal exchange of species-related DNA also contributes to the generation of new *pil* sequences.

The African trypanosomes (including *Trypanosoma brucei*) cause sleeping sickness in sub-Saharan Africa and account for more than 50,000 deaths per year. These organisms are able to avoid humoral immunity by antigenic variation of a large family of proteins called variable surface glycoproteins (VSGs), which coat the entire surface of the trypanosome. VSGs are highly immunogenic and stimulate antibodies that lead to efficient and rapid clearing of parasites from the bloodstream. However, at any given point in time, the organism is able to express a new VSG, allowing some organisms to escape the antibody response against the previous VSG. Each parasite can express more than 100 different VSGs, with variation in expression occurring spontaneously at a rate of up to 10^{-2} per cell per generation. Overall, the genome of *T. brucei* contains more than 1000 *vsg* genes, including so-called expression sites (ESs) located near telomeres on minichromosomes and silent loci in nontelomeric sites on large chromosomes.[157, 199] In general, VSG antigenic variation occurs by two different mechanisms. The first is called in situ activation and involves the simultaneous activation of a new ES and inactivation of the old ES, occurring independent of DNA rearrangement. The second involves DNA recombination, either between the expressed *vsg* and another telomeric ES (reciprocal recombination) or between the expressed *vsg* and a silent *vsg* locus (gene conversion).[199]

In the case of *H. influenzae*, LOS likely is a key factor in facilitating colonization and is a major target of the antibody response to infection. Interestingly, *H. influenzae* LOS undergoes phase variation. LOS biosynthesis involves multiple enzymatic steps and numerous genes. Among these genes, *lic1A*, *lic2A*, *lic3A*, *lex-2*, and *lgtC* contain long stretches of tandem four-base pair repeats within their 5′-coding region. In studies of the *lic* loci, Weiser and coworkers observed that the number of repeats varies spontaneously, generating translational frame shifts with different ATG start codons falling in or out of frame.[212] Such frame shifts result in synthesis of a protein with a different N-terminus or eliminate protein production altogether (when no in-frame start codon exists). The mechanism of variation in repeat number is presumed to be slipped-strand mispairing, which occurs during DNA replication and involves a single repeat looping out on either the template or the replicating strand. Changes in *lic2A* and *lic3A* influence glycotransferase activity and alter reactivity with monoclonal antibodies directed against specific LOS oligosaccharide epitopes.[62] The *lic2A* gene product is responsible for the addition of a Gal-α1,4-Galβ moiety, which resembles the globoseries glycolipids and protects *H. influenzae* from antibody-mediated killing, possibly by molecular mimicry.[213] *lgtC* may be involved in formation of a Gal-β1, 4-Glu moiety.[82] Variation in the *lic1A* gene affects production of a choline kinase responsible for addition of phosphorylcholine (ChoP) to the LOS molecule, a physical change that enhances binding of C-reactive protein and results in susceptibility to serum bactericidal activity.[119, 214, 215]

ENCAPSULATION

Expression of an extracellular capsule represents a common strategy to evade phagocytosis, complement activity, and humoral immunity among pathogenic bacteria, fungi, and parasites. One example is *H. influenzae*, a common cause of childhood bacteremia and meningitis in underdeveloped countries. Among isolates of *H. influenzae*, six structurally and antigenically distinct capsular types are recognized and designated serotypes a to f. Serotype b isolates account for more than 95 percent of all *H. influenzae* invasive disease, reflecting the distinct virulence properties of the type b capsule, which is a polymer of ribose and ribitol-5-phosphate (PRP) and is encoded by the *cap*b locus.[138] In animal studies comparing derivatives of *H. influenzae* strain Rd expressing type a, b, c, d, e, or f capsule, the strain expressing the type b capsule was associated with the highest incidence of bacteremia after intranasal inoculation of infant rats. Similarly, this strain was associated with the highest magnitude of bacteremia and incidence of meningitis after intraperitoneal inoculation of experimental rats.[229]

In considering the mechanism by which the type b capsule promotes intravascular survival and invasive disease, in vitro studies using mouse peritoneal macrophages and human peripheral blood monocytes provide some insights. Based on work by Noel and colleagues, the type b capsule inhibits bacterial binding to macrophages in the absence of complement and a source of C3.[142] In addition, the type b capsule interferes with ingestion by macrophages when anti-PRP antibody is lacking.[141, 142] Furthermore, the type b capsule blocks complement deposition on the bacterial surface and resultant complement-mediated bacteriolysis. In almost all isolates of *H. influenzae* type b, the *cap*b locus is a tandem repeat of 18-kb *cap*b gene sequences.[140] As a consequence of this arrangement, the *cap*b locus serves as a template for further amplification of capsule gene sequences in vivo, resulting in increased capsule production. In a study by Corn and colleagues, 23 of 66 minimallypassaged invasive isolates had between 3 and 5 copies of the 18-kb repeat.[25] Further analysis demonstrated that amplification of the repeat results in augmented resistance to phagocytosis and complement-mediated bacterial killing.[140]

Given the importance of the type b capsule in the pathogenesis of disease, efforts to develop a vaccine effective against *H. influenzae* type b focused on the type b polysaccharide, initially as a plain polysaccharide vaccine and eventually as a conjugate vaccine with the polysaccharide linked to an immunogenic carrier protein. Since the implementation of routine immunization with conjugate vaccines in developed countries, the incidence of invasive *H. influenzae* type b disease in these countries has plummeted.

VIRAL LATENCY

Among viral pathogens, latency represents an important mechanism for viral persistence in the face of host immunity, especially in the case of viruses belonging to the herpes family. Herpes simplex virus (HSV) is one example, commonly establishing latency after both gingivostomatitis and genital tract infection. After infection of a host cell, HSV replication commences. Eventually, cell death occurs, resulting in cell lysis and release of viral particles, which then can infect adjacent cells. This so-called lytic replication is under control of a small number of *immediate early* (IE) genes, which must be transcribed in moderate amounts to allow expression of the remainder of the viral genome. IE gene expression is activated by VP16, a viral protein that binds to a sequence common to IE gene promoters.[163] After lysis of the host cell, new virions enter local nerve termini and travel up the long axon to sensory ganglia, where latency is established within days. In the latent state, viral DNA can be detected in the neuron, but infectious virions cannot be isolated. During latency, IE genes are repressed, and certain small fragments of DNA are transcribed at high levels, yielding latency-associated transcripts (LATs). Although the exact function of LATs is not known, one model proposes that these fragments are directly responsible for suppressing IE gene expression.[163] However, LAT-deficient mutants are still able to establish latency, suggesting that IE gene expression may be under multiple controls or may simply fail in some neurons.[209] The mechanism by which HSV is reactivated seems to require the viral thymidine kinase (TK) gene, as TK^- mutants are defective in lytic replication and ordinarily do not reactivate.[22, 94] However, a detailed understanding of reactivation is currently lacking.

Conclusion

With the explosion of molecular techniques in recent years, our understanding of the specific microbial and host factors involved in the pathogenesis of a variety of infectious diseases has expanded remarkably. As a consequence of this understanding, we have witnessed the development of numerous new vaccines, including the *H. influenzae* type b vaccine, the Lyme disease vaccine, and acellular pertussis vaccines, among others. In the coming years, we likely will benefit from novel approaches for treating and preventing human infections. Examples might include inhibitors of type III protein secretion systems, antagonists of periplasmic chaperones, and analogues of important host cell receptors. However, given the impressive adaptability of pathogenic organisms, as new therapeutic agents become available, we must remain vigilant for new microbial strategies allowing evasion of our interventions.

REFERENCES

1. Acheson, D. W., Moore, R., De Breucker, S., et al.: Translocation of Shiga toxin across polarized intestinal cells in tissue culture. Infect. Immun. *64*:3294–3300, 1996.
2. Åkesson, P., Sjoholm, A. G., and Bjorck, L.: Protein SIC, a novel extracellular protein of *Streptococcus pyogenes* interfering with complement function. J. Biol. Chem. *271*:1081–1088, 1996.
3. Balcewicz-Sablinska, M. K., Keane, J., Kornfeld, H., and Remold, H. G.: Pathogenic *Mycobacterium tuberculosis* evades apoptosis of host macrophages by release of TNF-R2, resulting in inactivation of TNF-alpha. J. Immunol. *161*:2636–2641, 1998.
4. Barenkamp, S. J., and St. Geme, J. W., III: Genes encoding high-molecular-weight adhesion proteins of nontypeable *Haemophilus influenzae* are part of gene clusters. Infect. Immun. *62*:3320–3328, 1994.
5. Barki, M., Koltin, Y., Yanko, M., et al.: Isolation of a *Candida albicans* DNA sequence conferring adhesion and aggregation on *Saccharomyces cerevisiae*. J. Bacteriol. *175*:5683–5689, 1993.
6. Black, D.S., and Bliska, J.B.: Identification of p130Cas as a substrate of *Yersinia* YopH (Yop51), a bacterial protein tyrosine phosphatase that translocates into mammalian cells and targets focal adhesions. EMBO J. *16*:2730–2744, 1997.

7. Blanc-Potard, A. B., and Groisman, E. A.: The *Salmonella selC* locus contains a pathogenicity island mediating intramacrophage survival. EMBO J. *16*:5376–5385, 1997.
8. Blanc-Potard, A. B., Solomon, F., Kayser, J., and Groisman, E. A.: The SPI-3 pathogenicity island of *Salmonella enterica*. J. Bacteriol. *181*:998–1004, 1999.
9. Bliska, J. B.: Yop effectors of *Yersinia* spp. and actin rearrangements. Trends Microbiol. *8*:205–208, 2000.
10. Bliska, J. B., and Falkow, S.: Bacterial resistance to complement killing mediated by the Ail protein of *Yersinia enterocolitica*. Proc. Natl. Acad. Sci. U. S. A. *89*:3561–3565, 1992.
11. Boyd, A. P., and Cornelis, G. R.: *Yersinia*. *In* Groisman, E.A. (ed.): Principles of Bacterial Pathogenesis. San Diego, Academic Press, 2001, pp. 227–264.
12. Bradway, S. D., and Levine, M. J.: Do proline-rich proteins modulate a transglutaminase catalyzed mechanism of candidal adhesion? Crit. Rev. Oral Biol. Med. *4*:293–299, 1993.
13. Braun, L., Nato, F., Payrastre, B., et al.: The 213-amino-acid leucine-rich repeat region of the *Listeria monocytogenes* InlB protein is sufficient for entry into mammalian cells, stimulation of PI-3 kinase and membrane ruffling. Mol. Microbiol. *34*:10–23, 1999.
14. Breimer, M.E., and Karlsson, K.A.: Chemical and immunological identification of glycolipid-based blood group ABH and Lewis antigens in human kidney. Biochim. Biophys. Acta *755*:170–177, 1983.
15. Buchmeier, N., Blanc-Potard, A., Ehrt, S., et al.: A parallel intraphagosomal survival strategy shared by *Mycobacterium tuberculosis* and *Salmonella enterica*. Mol. Microbiol. *35*:1375–1382, 2000.
16. Burnette-Curley, D., Wells, V., Viscount, H., et al.: FimA, a major virulence factor associated with *Streptococcus parasanguis* endocarditis. Infect. Immun. *63*:4669–4674, 1995.
17. Cameron, L. A., Footer, M. J., van Oudenaarden, A., and Theriot, J. A.: Motility of ActA protein-coated microspheres driven by actin polymerization. Proc. Natl. Acad. Sci. U. S. A. *96*:4908–4913, 1999.
18. Cardinale, J. A., and Clark, V. L.: Expression of AniA, the major anaerobically induced outer membrane protein of *Neisseria gonorrhoeae*, provides protection against killing by normal human sera. Infect. Immun. *68*:4368–4369, 2000.
19. Chen, L. M., Hobbie, S., and Galán, J. E.: Requirement of CDC42 for *Salmonella*-induced cytoskeletal and nuclear responses. Science *274*:2115–2118, 1996.
20. Cirillo, D. M., Valdivia, R. H., Monack, D. M., and Falkow, S.: Macrophage-dependent induction of the *Salmonella* pathogenicity island 2 type III secretion system and its role in intracellular survival. Mol. Microbiol. *30*:175–188, 1998.
21. Cochrane, D. M., Brown, M. R., Anwar, H., et al.: Antibody response to *Pseudomonas aeruginosa* surface protein antigens in a rat model of chronic lung infection. J. Med. Microbiol. *27*:255–261, 1988.
22. Coen, D. M., Kosz-Vnenchak, M., Jacobson, J. G., et al.: Thymidine kinase-negative herpes simplex virus mutants establish latency in mouse trigeminal ganglia but do not reactivate. Proc. Natl. Acad. Sci. U. S. A. *86*:4736–4740, 1989.
23. Collazo, C. M., and Galán, J. E.: The invasion-associated type III system of *Salmonella typhimurium* directs the translocation of Sip proteins into the host cell. Mol. Microbiol. *24*:747–756, 1997.
24. Cope, L. D., Yogev, R., Muller-Eberhard, U., and Hansen, E. J.: A gene cluster involved in the utilization of both free heme and heme:hemopexin by *Haemophilus influenzae* type b. J. Bacteriol. *177*:2644–2653, 1995.
25. Corn, P. G., Anders, J., Takala, A. K., et al.: Genes involved in *Haemophilus influenzae* type b capsule expression are frequently amplified. J. Infect. Dis. *167*:356–364, 1993.
26. Cornelis, G. R., Biot, T., Lambert de Rouvroit, C., et al.: The *Yersinia* yop regulon. Mol. Microbiol. *3*:1455–1459, 1989.
27. Costerton, J. W., Stewart, P. S., and Greenberg, E. P.: Bacterial biofilms: A common cause of persistent infections. Science *284*:1318–1322, 1999.
28. Cotter, P. A., and Miller, J. F.: Bordetella. *In* Groisman, E.A. (ed.): Principles of bacterial pathogenesis. San Diego, Academic Press, 2001, pp. 619–674.
29. Csóka, T. B., Frost, G. I., and Stern, R.: Hyaluronidases in tissue invasion. Invasion Metastasis *17*:297–311, 1997.
30. Dabiri, G. A., Sanger, J. M., Portnoy, D. A., and Southwick, F. S.: *Listeria monocytogenes* moves rapidly through the host-cell cytoplasm by inducing directional actin assembly. Proc. Natl. Acad. Sci. U. S. A. *87*:6068–6072, 1990.
31. Davies, D. G., and Geesey, G. G.: Regulation of the alginate biosynthesis gene algC in *Pseudomonas aeruginosa* during biofilm development in continuous culture. Appl. Environ. Microbiol. *61*:860–867, 1995.
32. Davies, D. G., Parsek, M. R., Pearson, J. P., et al.: The involvement of cell-to-cell signals in the development of a bacterial biofilm. Science *280*:295–298, 1998.
33. de Roda Husman, A. M., and Schuitemaker, H.: Chemokine receptors and the clinical course of HIV-1 infection. Trends Microbiol. *6*:244–249, 1998.
34. Dodson, K. W., Jacob-Dubuisson, F., Striker, R. T., and Hultgren, S. J.: Outer-membrane PapC molecular usher discriminately recognizes periplasmic chaperone-pilus subunit complexes. Proc. Natl. Acad. Sci. U. S. A. *90*:3670–3674, 1993.
35. Dodson, K. W., Pinkner, J. S., Rose, T., et al.: Structural basis of the interaction of the pyelonephritic *E. coli* adhesin to its human kidney receptor. Cell *105*:733–743, 2001.
36. Domenighini, M., Relman, D., Capiau, C., et al.: Genetic characterization of *Bordetella pertussis* filamentous haemagglutinin: A protein processed from an unusually large precursor. Mol. Microbiol. *4*:787–800, 1990.
37. Donnenberg, M. S., Kaper, J. B., and Finlay, B. B.: Interactions between enteropathogenic *Escherichia coli* and host epithelial cells. Trends Microbiol. *5*:109–114, 1997.
38. Doranz, B. J., Rucker, J., Yi, Y., et al.: A dual-tropic primary HIV-1 isolate that uses fusin and the beta-chemokine receptors CKR-5, CKR-3, and CKR-2b as fusion cofactors. Cell *85*:1149–1158, 1996.
39. Egile, C., d'Hauteville, H., Parsot, C., and Sansonetti, P. J.: SopA, the outer membrane protease responsible for polar localization of IcsA in *Shigella flexneri*. Mol. Microbiol. *23*:1063–1073, 1997.
40. Eichelberg, K., and Galán, J. E.: Differential regulation of *Salmonella typhimurium* type III secreted proteins by pathogenicity island 1 (SPI-1)-encoded transcriptional activators InvF and HilA. Infect. Immun. *67*:4099–4105, 1999.
41. Elleman, T. C., and Hoyne, P. A.: Nucleotide sequence of the gene encoding pilin of *Bacteroides nodosus*, the causal organism of ovine footrot. J. Bacteriol. *160*:1184–1187, 1984.
42. Feng, Y., Broder, C. C., Kennedy, P. E., and Berger, E. A.: HIV-1 entry cofactor: Functional cDNA cloning of a seven-transmembrane, G protein-coupled receptor. Science *272*:872–877, 1996.
43. Fenno, J. C., Shaikh, A., Spatafora, G., and Fives-Taylor, P.: The fimA locus of *Streptococcus parasanguis* encodes an ATP-binding membrane transport system. Mol. Microbiol. *15*:849–863, 1995.
44. Fischetti, V. A.: Streptococcal M protein: Molecular design and biological behavior. Clin. Microbiol. Rev. *2*:285–314, 1989.
45. Foster, T. J., and Höök, M.: Surface protein adhesins of *Staphylococcus aureus*. Trends Microbiol. *6*:484–488, 1998.
46. Fouchier, R. A., Broersen, S. M., Brouwer, M., et al.: Temporal relationship between elongation of the HIV type 1 glycoprotein 120 V2 domain and the conversion toward a syncytium-inducing phenotype. AIDS Res. Hum. Retroviruses *11*:1473–1478, 1995.
47. Fouchier, R. A., Groenink, M., Kootstra, N. A., et al.: Phenotype-associated sequence variation in the third variable domain of the human immunodeficiency virus type 1 gp120 molecule. J. Virol. *66*:3183–3187, 1992.
48. Fsihi, H., Steffen, P., and Cossart, P.: *Listeria monocytogenes*. *In* Groisman EA (ed.): Principles of bacterial pathogenesis. San Diego, Academic Press, 2001, pp. 751–803.
49. Fu, Y., and Galán, J. E.: A *Salmonella* protein antagonizes Rac-1 and Cdc42 to mediate host-cell recovery after bacterial invasion. Nature *401*:293–297, 1999.
50. Gacesa, P.: Bacterial alginate biosynthesis—recent progress and future prospects. Microbiology *144*:1133–1143, 1998.
51. Galán, J. E.: Molecular genetic bases of *Salmonella* entry into host cells. Mol. Microbiol. *20*:263–271, 1996.
52. Gale, C., Finkel, D., Tao, N., et al.: Cloning and expression of a gene encoding an integrin-like protein in *Candida albicans*. Proc. Natl. Acad. Sci. U. S. A. *93*:357–361, 1996.
53. Gale, C. A., Bendel, C. M., McClellan, M., et al.: Linkage of adhesion, filamentous growth, and virulence in *Candida albicans* to a single gene, INT1. Science *279*:1355–1358, 1998.
54. Gao, L., and Abu Kwaik, Y.: Hijacking of apoptotic pathways by bacterial pathogens. Microbes Infect. *2*:1705–1719, 2000.
55. Garrett, E. S., Perlegas, D., and Wozniak, D. J.: Negative control of flagellum synthesis in *Pseudomonas aeruginosa* is modulated by the alternative sigma factor AlgT (AlgU). J. Bacteriol. *181*:7401–7404, 1999.
56. Gedde, M. M., Higgins, D. E., Tilney, L. G., and Portnoy, D. A.: Role of listeriolysin O in cell-to-cell spread of *Listeria monocytogenes*. Infect. Immun. *68*:999–1003, 2000.
57. Giron, J. A., Ho, A. S., and Schoolnik, G. K.: An inducible bundle-forming pilus of enteropathogenic *Escherichia coli*. Science *254*:710–713, 1991.
58. Goldberg, M. B., Barzu, O., Parsot, C., and Sansonetti, P. J.: Unipolar localization and ATPase activity of IcsA, a *Shigella flexneri* protein involved in intracellular movement. Infect. Agents Dis. *2*:210–211, 1993.
59. Goldman, W. E., Klapper, D. G., and Baseman, J. B.: Detection, isolation, and analysis of a released *Bordetella pertussis* product toxic to cultured tracheal cells. Infect. Immun. *36*:782–794, 1982.
60. Gouin, E., Gantelet, H., Egile, C., et al.: A comparative study of the actin-based motilities of the pathogenic bacteria *Listeria monocytogenes*, *Shigella flexneri* and *Rickettsia conorii*. J. Cell Sci. *112*:1697–1708, 1999.
61. Groenink, M., Fouchier, R. A., Broersen, S., et al.: Relation of phenotype evolution of HIV-1 to envelope V2 configuration. Science *260*: 1513–1516, 1993.
62. Gulig, P. A., Patrick, C. C., Hermanstorfer, L., et al.: Conservation of epitopes in the oligosaccharide portion of the lipooligosaccharide of *Haemophilus influenzae* type b. Infect. Immun. *55*:513–520, 1987.
63. Hagblom, P., Segal, E., Billyard, E., and So, M.: Intragenic recombination leads to pilus antigenic variation in *Neisseria gonorrhoeae*. Nature *315*:156–158, 1985.

64. Hall, A.: Rho GTPases and the actin cytoskeleton. Science *279*:509–514, 1998.
65. Hanski, E., and Caparon, M.: Protein F, a fibronectin-binding protein, is an adhesin of the group A streptococcus *Streptococcus pyogenes*. Proc. Natl. Acad. Sci. U. S. A. *89*:6172–6176, 1992.
66. Hardt, W. D., Chen, L. M., Schuebel, K. E., et al.: *S. typhimurium* encodes an activator of Rho GTPases that induces membrane ruffling and nuclear responses in host cells. Cell *93*:815–826, 1998.
67. Haslam, D. B.: Molecular decoys: Novel approaches to the prevention of hemolytic uremic syndrome. Pediatr. Res. *48*:267–268, 2000.
68. Heiss, L. N., Flak, T. A., Lancaster, J. R., Jr., et al.: Nitric oxide mediates *Bordetella pertussis* tracheal cytotoxin damage to the respiratory epithelium. Infect. Agents Dis. *2*:173–177, 1993.
69. Heiss, L. N., Lancaster, J. R., Jr., Corbett, J. A., and Goldman, W. E.: Epithelial autotoxicity of nitric oxide: Role in the respiratory cytopathology of pertussis. Proc. Natl. Acad. Sci. U. S. A. *91*:267–270, 1994.
70. Heiss, L. N., Moser, S. A., Unanue, E. R., and Goldman, W. E.: Interleukin-1 is linked to the respiratory epithelial cytopathology of pertussis. Infect. Immun. *61*:3123–3128, 1993.
71. Henderson, I. R., and Nataro, J. P.: Virulence functions of autotransporter proteins. Infect. Immun. *69*:1231–1243, 2001.
72. Hendrixson, D. R., and St. Geme, J. W., III: The *Haemophilus influenzae* Hap serine protease promotes adherence and microcolony formation, potentiated by a soluble host protein. Mol. Cell *2*:841–850, 1998.
73. Hensel, M., Shea, J. E., Raupach, B., et al.: Functional analysis of *ssaJ* and the *ssaK/U* operon, 13 genes encoding components of the type III secretion apparatus of *Salmonella* pathogenicity island 2. Mol. Microbiol. *24*:155–167, 1997.
74. Hersh, D., Monack, D. M., Smith, M. R., et al.: The *Salmonella* invasin SipB induces macrophage apoptosis by binding to caspase-1. Proc. Natl. Acad. Sci. U. S. A. *96*:2396–2401, 1999.
75. Hewlett, E. L.: Pertussis: Current concepts of pathogenesis and prevention. Pediatr. Infect. Dis. J. *16*:S78–84, 1997.
76. Hewlett, E. L.: A commentary on the pathogenesis of pertussis. Clin. Infect. Dis. *28*:S94–98, 1999.
77. Hilbi, H., Moss, J. E., Hersh, D., et al.: *Shigella*-induced apoptosis is dependent on caspase-1 which binds to IpaB. J. Biol. Chem. *273*: 32895–32900, 1998.
78. Hobbs, M., Collie, E. S., Free, P. D., et al.: PilS and PilR, a two-component transcriptional regulatory system controlling expression of type 4 fimbriae in *Pseudomonas aeruginosa*. Mol. Microbiol. *7*:669–682, 1993.
79. Hobbs, M., and Mattick, J. S.: Common components in the assembly of type 4 fimbriae, DNA transfer systems, filamentous phage and protein-secretion apparatus: A general system for the formation of surface-associated protein complexes. Mol. Microbiol. *10*:233–243, 1993.
80. Hoe, N. P., Kordari, P., Cole, R., et al.: Human immune response to streptococcal inhibitor of complement, a serotype M1 group A *Streptococcus* extracellular protein involved in epidemics. J. Infect. Dis. *182*:1425–1436, 2000.
81. Hoe, N. P., Nakashima, K., Lukomski, S., et al.: Rapid selection of complement-inhibiting protein variants in group A *Streptococcus* epidemic waves. Nat. Med. *5*:924–929, 1999.
82. Hood, D. W., Deadman, M. E., Allen, T., et al.: Use of the complete genome sequence information of *Haemophilus influenzae* strain Rd to investigate lipopolysaccharide biosynthesis. Mol. Microbiol. *22*:951–965, 1996.
83. Hostetter, M. K.: Adhesins and ligands involved in the interaction of *Candida* spp. with epithelial and endothelial surfaces. Clin. Microbiol. Rev. *7*:29–42, 1994.
84. Hostetter, M. K.: Linkage of adhesion, morphogenesis, and virulence in *Candida albicans*. J. Lab. Clin. Med. *132*:258–263, 1998.
85. Howell-Adams, B., and Seifert, H. S.: Molecular models accounting for the gene conversion reactions mediating gonococcal pilin antigenic variation. Mol. Microbiol. *37*:1146–1158, 2000.
86. Huang, Y, Paxton, W. A., Wolinsky, S.M., et al.: The role of a mutant CCR5 allele in HIV-1 transmission and disease progression. Nat. Med. *2*:1240–1243, 1996.
87. Hung, D. L., and Hultgren, S. J.: Pilus biogenesis via the chaperone/usher pathway: An integration of structure and function. J. Struct. Biol. *124*:201–220, 1998.
88. Hung, D. L., Knight, S. D., Woods, R. M., et al.: Molecular basis of two subfamilies of immunoglobulin-like chaperones. EMBO J. *15*:3792–3805, 1996.
89. Hynes, W. L., Dixon, A. R., Walton, S. L. and Aridgides, L. J.: The extracellular hyaluronidase gene (*hylA*) of *Streptococcus pyogenes*. FEMS Microbiol. Lett. *184*:109–112, 2000.
90. Isberg, R. R.: Uptake of enteropathogenic *Yersinia* by mammalian cells. Curr. Top. Microbiol. Immunol. *209*:1–24, 1996.
91. Isberg, R. R., and Leong, J. M.: Multiple beta 1 chain integrins are receptors for invasin, a protein that promotes bacterial penetration into mammalian cells. Cell *60*:861–871, 1990.
92. Ishibashi, Y., Claus, S., and Relman, D. A.: *Bordetella pertussis* filamentous hemagglutinin interacts with a leukocyte signal transduction complex and stimulates bacterial adherence to monocyte CR3 (CD11b/CD18). J. Exp. Med. *180*:1225–1233, 1994.
93. Jacob-Dubuisson, F., Heuser, J., Dodson, K., et al.: Initiation of assembly and association of the structural elements of a bacterial pilus depend on two specialized tip proteins. EMBO J. *12*:837–847, 1993.
94. Jacobson, J. G., Ruffner, K. L., Kosz-Vnenchak, M., et al.: Herpes simplex virus thymidine kinase and specific stages of latency in murine trigeminal ganglia. J. Virol. *67*:6903–6908, 1993.
95. Jinno, A., Shimizu, N., Soda, Y., et al.: Identification of the chemokine receptor TER1/CCR8 expressed in brain-derived cells and T cells as a new coreceptor for HIV-1 infection. Biochem. Biophys. Res. Commun. *243*:497–502, 1998.
96. Jonsson, A. B., Nyberg, G., and Normark, S.: Phase variation of gonococcal pili by frameshift mutation in *pilC*, a novel gene for pilus assembly. EMBO J. *10*:477–488, 1991.
97. Kaufman, M. R., Seyer, J. M., and Taylor, R. K.: Processing of TCP pilin by TcpJ typifies a common step intrinsic to a newly recognized pathway of extracellular protein secretion by gram-negative bacteria. Genes Dev. *5*:1834–1846, 1991.
98. Keane, J., Balcewicz-Sablinska, M. K., Remold, H. G., et al.: Infection by *Mycobacterium tuberculosis* promotes human alveolar macrophage apoptosis. Infect. Immun. *65*:298–304, 1997.
99. Kenny, B., DeVinney, R., Stein, M., et al.: Enteropathogenic *E. coli* (EPEC) transfers its receptor for intimate adherence into mammalian cells. Cell *91*:511–520, 1997.
100. Kerr, J. R., and Matthews, R. C.: *Bordetella pertussis* infection: Pathogenesis, diagnosis, management, and the role of protective immunity. Eur. J. Clin. Microbiol. Infect. Dis. *19*:77–88, 2000.
101. Khelef, N., and Guiso, N.: Induction of macrophage apoptosis by *Bordetella pertussis* adenylate cyclase-hemolysin. FEMS Microbiol. Lett. *134*:27–32, 1995.
102. Khelef, N., Zychlinsky, A., and Guiso, N.: *Bordetella pertussis* induces apoptosis in macrophages: Role of adenylate cyclase-hemolysin. Infect. Immun. *61*:4064–4071, 1993.
103. Kimura, L. H., and Pearsall, N. N.: Relationship between germination of *Candida albicans* and increased adherence to human buccal epithelial cells. Infect. Immun. *28*:464–468, 1980.
104. Kitov, P. I., Sadowska, J. M., Mulvey, G., et al.: Shiga-like toxins are neutralized by tailored multivalent carbohydrate ligands. Nature *403*:669–672, 2000.
105. Kubori, T., Matsushima, Y., Nakamura, D., et al.: Supramolecular structure of the *Salmonella typhimurium* type III protein secretion system. Science *280*:602–605, 1998.
106. Kubori, T., Sukhan, A., Aizawa, S. I., and Galán, J. E.: Molecular characterization and assembly of the needle complex of the *Salmonella typhimurium* type III protein secretion system. Proc. Natl. Acad. Sci. U. S. A. *97*:10225–10230, 2000.
107. Kuehn, M. J., Heuser, J., Normark, S., and Hultgren, S. J.: P pili in uropathogenic *E. coli* are composite fibres with distinct fibrillar adhesive tips. Nature *356*:252–255, 1992.
108. Kuehn, M. J., Normark, S., and Hultgren, S. J.: Immunoglobulin-like PapD chaperone caps and uncaps interactive surfaces of nascently translocated pilus subunits. Proc. Natl. Acad. Sci. U. S. A. *88*:10586–10590, 1991.
109. Langermann, S., Mollby, R., Burlein, J. E., et al.: Vaccination with FimH adhesin protects cynomolgus monkeys from colonization and infection by uropathogenic *Escherichia coli*. J. Infect. Dis. *181*:774–778, 2000.
110. Langermann, S., Palaszynski, S., Barnhart, M., et al.: Prevention of mucosal *Escherichia coli* infection by FimH-adhesin-based systemic vaccination. Science *276*:607–611, 1997.
111. Lauer, P., Albertson, N. H., and Koomey, M.: Conservation of genes encoding components of a type IV pilus assembly/two-step protein export pathway in *Neisseria gonorrhoeae*. Mol. Microbiol. *8*:357–368, 1993.
112. Law, D.: Virulence factors of *Escherichia coli* O157 and other Shiga toxin-producing *E. coli*. J. Appl. Microbiol. *88*:729–745, 2000.
113. Li, R. K., and Cutler, J. E.: Chemical definition of an epitope/adhesin molecule on *Candida albicans*. J. Biol. Chem. *268*:18293–18299, 1993.
114. Liu, R., Paxton, W. A., Choe, S., et al.: Homozygous defect in HIV-1 coreceptor accounts for resistance of some multiply-exposed individuals to HIV-1 infection. Cell *86*:367–377, 1996.
115. Luker, K. E., Collier, J. L., Kolodziej, E. W., et al.: *Bordetella pertussis* tracheal cytotoxin and other muramyl peptides: distinct structure-activity relationships for respiratory epithelial cytopathology. Proc. Natl. Acad. Sci. U. S. A. *90*:2365–2369, 1993.
116. Luker, K. E., Tyler, A. N., Marshall, G. R., and Goldman, W. E.: Tracheal cytotoxin structural requirements for respiratory epithelial damage in pertussis. Mol. Microbiol. *16*:733–743, 1995.
117. Lukomski, S., Hoe, N. P., Abdi, I., et al.: Nonpolar inactivation of the hypervariable streptococcal inhibitor of complement gene (*sic*) in serotype M1 *Streptococcus pyogenes* significantly decreases mouse mucosal colonization. Infect. Immun. *68*:535–542, 2000.
118. Luo, Y., Frey, E. A., Pfuetzner, R. A., et al.: Crystal structure of enteropathogenic *Escherichia coli* intimin-receptor complex. Nature *405*:1073–1077, 2000.
119. Lysenko, E., Richards, J. C., Cox, A. D., et al.: The position of phosphorylcholine on the lipopolysaccharide of *Haemophilus influenzae* affects

binding and sensitivity to C-reactive protein-mediated killing. Mol. Microbiol. *35*:234–245, 2000.
120. Mack, M., Kleinschmidt, A., Bruhl, H., et al.: Transfer of the chemokine receptor CCR5 between cells by membrane-derived microparticles: A mechanism for cellular human immunodeficiency virus 1 infection. Nat. Med. *6*:769–775, 2000.
121. Makhov, A. M., Hannah, J. H., Brennan, M. J., et al.: Filamentous hemagglutinin of *Bordetella pertussis*. A bacterial adhesin formed as a 50-nm monomeric rigid rod based on a 19-residue repeat motif rich in beta strands and turns. J. Mol. Biol. *241*:110–124, 1994.
122. Marcus, S. L., Brumell, J. H., Pfeifer, C. G., and Finlay, B. B.: *Salmonella* pathogenicity islands: Big virulence in small packages. Microbes Infect. *2*:145–156, 2000.
123. Marquis, H., Doshi, V., and Portnoy, D. A.: The broad-range phospholipase C and a metalloprotease mediate listeriolysin O-independent escape of *Listeria monocytogenes* from a primary vacuole in human epithelial cells. Infect. Immun. *63*:4531–4534, 1995.
124. Marrs, C. F., Schoolnik, G., Koomey, J. M., et al.: Cloning and sequencing of a *Moraxella bovis* pilin gene. J. Bacteriol. *163*:132–139, 1985.
125. Martinez, J. J., Mulvey, M. A., Schilling, J. D., et al.: Type 1 pilus-mediated bacterial invasion of bladder epithelial cells. EMBO J. *19*:2803–2812, 2000.
126. Mawhinney, T. P., Adelstein, E., Morris, D. A., et al.: Structure determination of five sulfated oligosaccharides derived from tracheobronchial mucus glycoproteins. J. Biol. Chem. *262*:2994–3001, 1987.
127. McDaniel, T. K., Jarvis, K. G., Donnenberg, M. S., and Kaper, J. B.: A genetic locus of enterocyte effacement conserved among diverse enterobacterial pathogens. Proc. Natl. Acad. Sci. U. S. A. *92*:1664–1668, 1995.
128. McDevitt, D., Francois, P., Vaudaux, P., and Foster, T. J.: Molecular characterization of the clumping factor (fibrinogen receptor) of *Staphylococcus aureus*. Mol. Microbiol. *11*:237–248, 1994.
129. McDevitt, D., Francois, P., Vaudaux, P., and Foster, T. J.: Identification of the ligand-binding domain of the surface-located fibrinogen receptor (clumping factor) of *Staphylococcus aureus*. Mol. Microbiol. *16*: 895–907, 1995.
130. McKinney, J. D., Höner zu Bentrup, K., Munoz-Elias, E. J., et al.: Persistence of *Mycobacterium tuberculosis* in macrophages and mice requires the glyoxylate shunt enzyme isocitrate lyase. Nature *406*: 735–738, 2000.
131. Mejia, L. M., Stockbauer, K. E., Pan, X., et al.: Characterization of group A *Streptococcus* strains recovered from Mexican children with pharyngitis by automated DNA sequencing of virulence-related genes: Unexpectedly large variation in the gene (*sic*) encoding a complement-inhibiting protein. J. Clin. Microbiol. *35*:3220–3224, 1997.
132. Mengaud, J., Ohayon, H., Gounon, P., et al.: E-cadherin is the receptor for internalin, a surface protein required for entry of *L. monocytogenes* into epithelial cells. Cell *84*:923–932, 1996.
133. Menozzi, F. D., Mutombo, R., Renauld, G., et al.: Heparin-inhibitable lectin activity of the filamentous hemagglutinin adhesin of *Bordetella pertussis*. Infect. Immun. *62*:769–778, 1994.
134. Menzel, E. J., and Farr, C.: Hyaluronidase and its substrate hyaluronan: Biochemistry, biological activities and therapeutic uses. Cancer Lett. *131*:3–11, 1998.
135. Meyer, T. F., Billyard, E., Haas, R., et al.: Pilus genes of *Neisseria gonorrhoeae*: Chromosomal organization and DNA sequence. Proc. Natl. Acad. Sci. U. S. A. *81*:6110–6114, 1984.
136. Moller, L. V., Regelink, A. G., Grasselier, H., et al.: Multiple *Haemophilus influenzae* strains and strain variants coexist in the respiratory tract of patients with cystic fibrosis. J Infect Dis *172*:1388–1392, 1995.
137. Mounier, J., Ryter, A., Coquis-Rondon, M., and Sansonetti, P. J.: Intracellular and cell-to-cell spread of *Listeria monocytogenes* involves interaction with F-actin in the enterocytelike cell line Caco-2. Infect. Immun. *58*:1048–1058, 1990.
138. Moxon, E. R., and Kroll, J. S.: The role of bacterial polysaccharide capsules as virulence factors. Curr. Top. Microbiol. Immunol. *150*:65–85, 1990.
139. Nicosia, A., and Rappuoli, R.: Promoter of the pertussis toxin operon and production of pertussis toxin. J. Bacteriol. *169*:2843-2846, 1987.
140. Noel, G. J., Brittingham, A., Granato, A. A., and Mosser, D. M.: Effect of amplification of the Cap b locus on complement-mediated bacteriolysis and opsonization of type b *Haemophilus influenzae*. Infect. Immun. *64*:4769–4775, 1996.
141. Noel, G. J., Hoiseth, S. K., and Edelson, P. J.: Type b capsule inhibits ingestion of *Haemophilus influenzae* by murine macrophages: Studies with isogenic encapsulated and unencapsulated strains. J. Infect. Dis. *166*:178–182, 1992.
142. Noel, G. J., Mosser, D. M., and Edelson, P. J.: Role of complement in mouse macrophage binding of *Haemophilus influenzae* type b. J. Clin. Invest. *85*:208–218, 1990.
143. Norris, F. A., Wilson, M. P., Wallis, T. S., et al.: SopB, a protein required for virulence of *Salmonella dublin*, is an inositol phosphate phosphatase. Proc. Natl. Acad. Sci. U. S. A. *95*:14057–14059, 1998.
144. Nunn, D. N., and Lory, S.: Product of the *Pseudomonas aeruginosa* gene *pilD* is a prepilin leader peptidase. Proc. Natl. Acad. Sci. U. S. A. *88*:3281–3285, 1991.
145. Ochman, H., Soncini, F. C., Solomon, F., and Groisman, E. A.: Identification of a pathogenicity island required for *Salmonella* survival in host cells. Proc. Natl. Acad. Sci. U. S. A. *93*:7800–7804, 1996.
146. Okada, N., Liszewski, M. K., Atkinson, J. P., and Caparon, M.: Membrane cofactor protein (CD46) is a keratinocyte receptor for the M protein of the group A streptococcus. Proc. Natl. Acad. Sci. U. S. A. *92*:2489–2493, 1995.
147. Okada, N., Pentland, A. P., Falk, P., and Caparon, M. G.: M protein and protein F act as important determinants of cell-specific tropism of *Streptococcus pyogenes* in skin tissue. J. Clin. Invest. *94*:965–977, 1994.
148. Oligino, L., and Fives-Taylor, P.: Overexpression and purification of a fimbria-associated adhesin of *Streptococcus parasanguis*. Infect. Immun. *61*:1016–1022, 1993.
149. O'Toole, G. A., and Kolter, R.: Flagellar and twitching motility are necessary for *Pseudomonas aeruginosa* biofilm development. Mol. Microbiol. *30*:295–304, 1998.
150. Ozeri, V., Tovi, A., Burstein, I., et al.: A two-domain mechanism for group A streptococcal adherence through protein F to the extracellular matrix. EMBO J. *15*:989–998, 1996.
151. Palmer, K. L., and Munson, R. S., Jr.: Cloning and characterization of the genes encoding the hemolysin of *Haemophilus ducreyi*. Mol. Microbiol. *18*:821–830, 1995.
152. Parsek, M. R., and Greenberg, E. P.: Acyl-homoserine lactone quorum sensing in gram-negative bacteria: A signaling mechanism involved in associations with higher organisms. Proc. Natl. Acad. Sci. U. S. A. *97*:8789–8793, 2000.
153. Paton, A. W., Morona, R., and Paton, J. C.: A new biological agent for treatment of Shiga toxigenic *Escherichia coli* infections and dysentery in humans. Nat. Med. *6*:265–270, 2000.
154. Patti, J. M., Bremell, T., Krajewska-Pietrasik, D., et al.: The *Staphylococcus aureus* collagen adhesin is a virulence determinant in experimental septic arthritis. Infect. Immun. *62*:152–161, 1994.
155. Patti, J. M., and Höök, M.: Microbial adhesins recognizing extracellular matrix macromolecules. Curr. Opin. Cell Biol. *6*:752–758, 1994.
156. Patti, J. M., Jonsson, H., Guss, B., et al.: Molecular characterization and expression of a gene encoding a *Staphylococcus aureus* collagen adhesin. J. Biol. Chem. *267*:4766–4772, 1992.
157. Pays, E., and Nolan, D. P.: Expression and function of surface proteins in *Trypanosoma brucei*. Mol. Biochem. Parasitol. *91*:3–36, 1998.
158. Pearson, R. D., Symes, P., Conboy, M., et al.: Inhibition of monocyte oxidative responses by *Bordetella pertussis* adenylate cyclase toxin. J. Immunol. *139*:2749–2754, 1987.
159. Poole, K., Schiebel, E., and Braun, V.: Molecular characterization of the hemolysin determinant of *Serratia marcescens*. J. Bacteriol. *170*:3177–3188, 1988.
160. Potts, W. J., and Saunders, J. R.: Nucleotide sequence of the structural gene for class I pilin from *Neisseria meningitidis*: Homologies with the pilE locus of *Neisseria gonorrhoeae*. Mol. Microbiol. *2*:647–653, 1988.
161. Prasad, S. M., Yin, Y., Rodzinski, E., et al.: Identification of a carbohydrate recognition domain in filamentous hemagglutinin from *Bordetella pertussis*. Infect. Immun. *61*:2780–2785, 1993.
162. Pratt, L. A., and Kolter, R.: Genetic analyses of bacterial biofilm formation. Curr. Opin. Microbiol. *2*:598–603, 1999.
163. Preston, C. M.: Repression of viral transcription during herpes simplex virus latency. J. Gen. Virol. *81*:1–19, 2000.
164. Ram, S., Mackinnon, F. G., Gulati, S., et al.: The contrasting mechanisms of serum resistance of *Neisseria gonorrhoeae* and group B *Neisseria meningitidis*. Mol. Immunol. *36*:915–928, 1999.
165. Rao, V. K., and Progulske-Fox, A.: Cloning and sequencing of two type 4 (N-methylphenylalanine) pilin genes from *Eikenella corrodens*. J. Gen. Microbiol. *139*:651–660, 1993.
166. Relman, D., Tuomanen, E., Falkow, S., et al.: Recognition of a bacterial adhesion by an integrin: macrophage CR3 (alpha M beta 2, CD11b/CD18) binds filamentous hemagglutinin of *Bordetella pertussis*. Cell *61*:1375–1382, 1990.
167. Rest, R. F., and Frangipane, J. V.: Growth of *Neisseria gonorrhoeae* in CMP-N-acetylneuraminic acid inhibits nonopsonic (opacity-associated outer membrane protein-mediated) interactions with human neutrophils. Infect. Immun. *60*:989–997, 1992.
168. Robbins, J. R., Barth, A. I., Marquis, H., et al.: *Listeria monocytogenes* exploits normal host cell processes to spread from cell to cell. J. Cell. Biol. *146*:1333–1350, 1999.
169. Rosenshine, I., Ruschkowski, S., Stein, M., et al.: A pathogenic bacterium triggers epithelial signals to form a functional bacterial receptor that mediates actin pseudopod formation. EMBO J. *15*: 2613–2624, 1996.
170. Rudel, T., Scheurerpflug, I., and Meyer, T. F.: *Neisseria* PilC protein identified as type-4 pilus tip-located adhesin. Nature *373*:357–359, 1995.
171. Russel, M.: Phage assembly: A paradigm for bacterial virulence factor export? Science *265*:612–614, 1994.
172. Russell, D. G.: What does 'inhibition of phagosome-lysosome fusion' really mean? Trends Microbiol. *6*:212–214, 1998.
173. Sandvig, K., and van Deurs, B.: Endocytosis, intracellular transport, and cytotoxic action of Shiga toxin and ricin. Physiol. Rev. *76*:949–966, 1996.

174. Sandvig, K., and van Deurs, B.: Entry of ricin and Shiga toxin into cells: Molecular mechanisms and medical perspectives. EMBO J. *19*:5943–5950, 2000.
175. Sauer, F. G., Fütterer, K., Pinkner, J. S., et al.: Structural basis of chaperone function and pilus biogenesis. Science *285*:1058–1061, 1999.
176. Sauer, F. G., Knight, S. D., Waksman, G. J., and Hultgren, S. J.: PapD-like chaperones and pilus biogenesis. Semin. Cell Dev. Biol. *11*:27–34, 2000.
177. Sharma, V., Sharma, S., Höner zu Bentrup, K., et al.: Structure of isocitrate lyase, a persistence factor of *Mycobacterium tuberculosis*. Nat. Struct. Biol. 7:663–668, 2000.
178. Shaw, C. E., and Taylor, R. K.: Vibrio cholerae O395 tcpA pilin gene sequence and comparison of predicted protein structural features to those of type 4 pilins. Infect. Immun. *58*:3042–3049, 1990.
179. Shea, J. E., Hensel, M., Gleeson, C., and Holden, D. W.: Identification of a virulence locus encoding a second type III secretion system in *Salmonella typhimurium*. Proc. Natl. Acad. Sci. U. S. A. *93*:2593–2597, 1996.
180. Shere, K. D., Sallustio, S., Manessis, A., et al.: Disruption of IcsP, the major *Shigella* protease that cleaves IcsA, accelerates actin-based motility. Mol. Microbiol. *25*:451–462, 1997.
181. Simmons, G., Wilkinson, D., Reeves, J. D., et al.: Primary, syncytium-inducing human immunodeficiency virus type 1 isolates are dual-tropic and most can use either Lestr or CCR5 as coreceptors for virus entry. J. Virol. *70*:8355–8360, 1996.
182. Smith, G. A., Marquis, H., Jones, S., et al.: The two distinct phospholipases C of *Listeria monocytogenes* have overlapping roles in escape from a vacuole and cell-to-cell spread. Infect. Immun. *63*:4231–4237, 1995.
183. Smith, G. A., and Portnoy, D. A.: How the *Listeria monocytogenes* ActA protein converts actin polymerization into a motile force. Trends Microbiol. *5*:272–276, 1997.
184. St. Geme, J. W., III: Bacterial adhesins: Determinants of microbial colonization and pathogenicity. Adv. Pediatr. *44*:43–72, 1997.
185. St. Geme, J. W., III, de la Morena, M. L., and Falkow, S.: A *Haemophilus influenzae* IgA protease-like protein promotes intimate interaction with human epithelial cells. Mol. Microbiol. *14*:217–233, 1994.
186. Staab, J. F., Bradway, S. D., Fidel, P. L., and Sundstrom, P.: Adhesive and mammalian transglutaminase substrate properties of *Candida albicans* Hwp1. Science *283*:1535–1538, 1999.
187. Staab, J. F., Ferrer, C. A., and Sundstrom, P.: Developmental expression of a tandemly repeated, proline- and glutamine-rich amino acid motif on hyphal surfaces on *Candida albicans*. J. Biol. Chem. *271*: 6298–6305, 1996.
188. Steinert, P. M., Candi, E., Kartasova, T., and Marekov, L.: Small proline-rich proteins are cross-bridging proteins in the cornified cell envelopes of stratified squamous epithelia. J. Struct. Biol. *122*:76–85, 1998.
189. Steinhauer, J., Agha, R., Pham, T., et al.: The unipolar *Shigella* surface protein IcsA is targeted directly to the bacterial old pole: IcsP cleavage of IcsA occurs over the entire bacterial surface. Mol. Microbiol. *32*:367–377, 1999.
190. Stone, K. D., Zhang, H. Z., Carlson, L. K., and Donnenberg, M. S.: A cluster of fourteen genes from enteropathogenic *Escherichia coli* is sufficient for the biogenesis of a type IV pilus. Mol. Microbiol. *20*:325–337, 1996.
191. Straley, S. C., Skrzypek, E., Plano, G. V., and Bliska, J. B.: Yops of *Yersinia* spp. pathogenic for humans. Infect. Immun. *61*:3105–3110, 1993.
192. Strom, M. S., and Lory, S.: Cloning and expression of the pilin gene of *Pseudomonas aeruginosa* PAK in *Escherichia coli*. J. Bacteriol. *165*:367–372, 1986.
193. Stromberg, N., Marklund, B. I., Lund, B., et al.: Host-specificity of uropathogenic *Escherichia coli* depends on differences in binding specificity to Gal alpha 1-4Gal-containing isoreceptors. EMBO J. *9*:2001–2010, 1990.
194. Sturgill-Koszycki, S., Schlesinger, P. H., Chakraborty, P., et al.: Lack of acidification in *Mycobacterium* phagosomes produced by exclusion of the vesicular proton-ATPase. Science *263*:678–681, 1994.
195. Switalski, L. M., Patti, J. M., Butcher, W., et al.: A collagen receptor on *Staphylococcus aureus* strains isolated from patients with septic arthritis mediates adhesion to cartilage. Mol. Microbiol. *7*:99–107, 1993.
196. Theriot, J. A.: The cell biology of infection by intracellular bacterial pathogens. Annu. Rev. Cell Dev. Biol. *11*:213–239, 1995.
197. Theriot, J. A., Mitchison, T. J., Tilney, L. G., and Portnoy, D. A.: The rate of actin-based motility of intracellular *Listeria monocytogenes* equals the rate of actin polymerization. Nature *357*:257–260, 1992.
198. Theriot, J. A., Rosenblatt, J., Portnoy, D. A., et al.: Involvement of profilin in the actin-based motility of *L. monocytogenes* in cells and in cell-free extracts. Cell *76*:505–517, 1994.
199. Tomlinson, S., and Raper, J.: The lysis of *Trypanosoma brucei brucei* by human serum. Nat. Biotechnol. *14*:717–721, 1996.
200. Tonjum, T., Marrs, C. F., Rozsa, F., and Bovre, K.: The type 4 pilin of *Moraxella nonliquefaciens* exhibits unique similarities with the pilins of *Neisseria gonorrhoeae* and *Dichelobacter* (*Bacteroides*) *nodosus*. J. Gen. Microbiol. *137*:2483–2490, 1991.
201. Tucker, S. C., and Galán, J. E.: Complex function for SicA, a *Salmonella enterica* serovar typhimurium type III secretion-associated chaperone. J. Bacteriol. *182*:2262–2268, 2000.
202. Uphoff, T. S., and Welch, R. A.: Nucleotide sequencing of the *Proteus mirabilis* calcium-independent hemolysin genes (*hpmA* and *hpmB*) reveals sequence similarity with the *Serratia marcescens* hemolysin genes (*shlA* and *shlB*). J. Bacteriol. *172*:1206–1216, 1990.
203. van Schilfgaarde, M., Eijk, P., Regelink, A., et al.: *Haemophilus influenzae* localized in epithelial cell layers is shielded from antibiotics and antibody-mediated bactericidal activity. Microb. Pathog. *26*:249–262, 1999.
204. van Schilfgaarde, M., van Alphen, L., Eijk, P., et al.: Paracytosis of *Haemophilus influenzae* through cell layers of NCI-H292 lung epithelial cells. Infect. Immun. *63*:4729–4737, 1995.
205. van Schilfgaarde, M., van Ulsen, P., van Der Steeg, W., et al.: Cloning of genes of nontypeable *Haemophilus influenzae* involved in penetration between human lung epithelial cells. Infect. Immun. *68*: 4616–4623, 2000.
206. van't Wout, A. B., Kootstra, N. A., Mulder-Kampinga, G. A., et al.: Macrophage-tropic variants initiate human immunodeficiency virus type 1 infection after sexual, parenteral, and vertical transmission. J. Clin. Invest. *94*:2060–2067, 1994.
207. Vazquez-Torres, A., Jones-Carson, J., Baumler, A. J., et al.: Extraintestinal dissemination of *Salmonella* by CD18-expressing phagocytes. Nature *401*:804–808, 1999.
208. Wadolkowski, E. A., Sung, L. M., Burris, J. A., et al.: Acute renal tubular necrosis and death of mice orally infected with *Escherichia coli* strains that produce Shiga-like toxin type II. Infect. Immun. *58*:3959–3965, 1990.
209. Wagner, E. K., and Bloom, D. C.: Experimental investigation of herpes simplex virus latency. Clin. Microbiol. Rev. *10*:419–443, 1997.
210. Wann, E. R., Gurusiddappa, S., and Höök, M.: The fibronectin-binding MSCRAMM FnbpA of *Staphylococcus aureus* is a bifunctional protein that also binds to fibrinogen. J. Biol. Chem. *275*:13863–13871, 2000.
211. Weir, S., and Marrs, C. F.: Identification of type 4 pili in *Kingella denitrificans*. Infect. Immun. *60*:3437–3441, 1992.
212. Weiser, J. N., Maskell, D. J., Butler, P. D., et al.: Characterization of repetitive sequences controlling phase variation of *Haemophilus influenzae* lipopolysaccharide. J. Bacteriol. *172*:3304–3309, 1990.
213. Weiser, J. N., and Pan, N.: Adaptation of *Haemophilus influenzae* to acquired and innate humoral immunity based on phase variation of lipopolysaccharide. Mol. Microbiol. *30*:767–775, 1998.
214. Weiser, J. N., Pan, N., McGowan, K. L., et al.: Phosphorylcholine on the lipopolysaccharide of *Haemophilus influenzae* contributes to persistence in the respiratory tract and sensitivity to serum killing mediated by C-reactive protein. J. Exp. Med. *187*:631–640, 1998.
215. Weiser, J. N., Shchepetov, M., and Chong, S. T.: Decoration of lipopolysaccharide with phosphorylcholine: A phase-variable characteristic of *Haemophilus influenzae*. Infect. Immun. *65*:943–950, 1997.
216. Wetzler, L. M., Barry, K., Blake, M. S., and Gotschlich, E. C.: Gonococcal lipooligosaccharide sialylation prevents complement-dependent killing by immune sera. Infect. Immun. *60*:39–43, 1992.
217. Wexler, D. E., Chenoweth, D. E., and Cleary, P. P.: Mechanism of action of the group A streptococcal C5a inactivator. Proc. Natl. Acad. Sci. U. S. A. *82*:8144–8148, 1985.
218. Willems, R. J., Geuijen, C., van der Heide, H. G., et al.: Mutational analysis of the *Bordetella pertussis fim/fha* gene cluster: Identification of a gene with sequence similarities to haemolysin accessory genes involved in export of FHA. Mol. Microbiol. *11*:337–347, 1994.
219. Wolff, C., Nisan, I., Hanski, E., et al.: Protein translocation into host epithelial cells by infecting enteropathogenic *Escherichia coli*. Mol. Microbiol. *28*:143–155, 1998.
220. Wright, S. D., and Silverstein, S. C.: Receptors for C3b and C3bi promote phagocytosis but not the release of toxic oxygen from human phagocytes. J. Exp. Med. *158*:2016–2023, 1983.
221. Wu, H., and Fives-Taylor, P. M.: Identification of dipeptide repeats and a cell wall sorting signal in the fimbriae-associated adhesin, Fap1, of *Streptococcus parasanguis*. Mol. Microbiol. *34*:1070–1081, 1999.
222. Wu, H., Mintz, K. P., Ladha, M., and Fives-Taylor, P. M.: Isolation and characterization of Fap1, a fimbriae-associated adhesin of *Streptococcus parasanguis* FW213. Mol. Microbiol. *28*:487–500, 1998.
223. Xu, H., Storch, T., Yu, M., et al.: Characterization of the human Forssman synthetase gene. An evolving association between glycolipid synthesis and host-microbial interactions. J. Biol. Chem. *274*: 29390–29398, 1999.
224. Yanagishita, M., and Hascall, V. C.: Cell surface heparan sulfate proteoglycans. J. Biol. Chem. *267*:9451–9454, 1992.
225. Yu, L., Lee, K. K., Sheth, H. B., et al.: Fimbria-mediated adherence of *Candida albicans* to glycosphingolipid receptors on human buccal epithelial cells. Infect. Immun. *62*:2843–2848, 1994.
226. Zhang, L., He, T., Talal, A., et al.: In vivo distribution of the human immunodeficiency virus/simian immunodeficiency virus coreceptors: CXCR4, CCR3, and CCR5. J. Virol. *72*:5035–5045, 1998.
227. Zhu, T., Mo, H., Wang, N., et al.: Genotypic and phenotypic characterization of HIV-1 patients with primary infection. Science *261*: 1179–1181, 1993.

228. Zoja, A., and Remuzzi, G: The pivotal role of the endothelial cell in the pathogenesis of HUS. *In* Kaplan, B. S., Trompeter, R. S., and Moake, J. L. (eds.): Hemolytic uremic syndrome and thrombotic thrombocytopenic purpura. New York, Marcel Dekker, 1992, pp. 389–404.
229. Zwahlen, A., Kroll, J. S., Rubin, L. G., and Moxon, E. R.: The molecular basis of pathogenicity in *Haemophilus influenzae*: Comparative virulence of genetically-related capsular transformants and correlation with changes at the capsulation locus *cap*. Microb. Pathog. 7:225–235, 1989.
230. Zychlinsky, A., Prevost, M. C., and Sansonetti, P. J.: *Shigella flexneri* induces apoptosis in infected macrophages. Nature *358*: 167–169, 1992.
231. Zychlinsky, A., and Sansonetti, P. J.: Apoptosis as a proinflammatory event: What can we learn from bacteria-induced cell death? Trends Microbiol. *5*:201–204, 1997.

Immunologic and Phagocytic Responses to Infection

MICHAEL F. TOSI

This chapter provides an overview of the immunologic and phagocytic responses to infection by examining host interactions with pathogens, normal host defense mechanisms, immature host responses of neonates, specific immunodeficiency states, and components of the immunologic evaluation relevant to the practice of pediatric infectious diseases. It is intended to supply sufficient information to permit a working understanding of the basic mechanisms involved in the normal host response to infection, enable recognition of the usual clinical manifestations of common immunodeficiency disorders, and familiarize the reader with the general principles of immunologic evaluation and management of patients with immune disorders. For greater depth and detail, readers are encouraged to refer to the excellent reviews cited.

Host-Parasite Interactions

GENERAL FEATURES OF HOST-PARASITE INTERACTIONS

Humans constantly are exposed to a daunting number and diversity of microorganisms that can cause infection. Many organisms that usually coexist harmoniously with the human host on the skin or on mucous membranes of the oral cavity, upper airways, or lower gastrointestinal tract may invade and become pathogens only if the balance of the commensal relationship is disrupted. Other organisms are more invasive, and they overtly attack the host's normal surface barriers and internal defense mechanisms. The human host has evolved a complex array of protective mechanisms designed to defend itself against these continuous microbial challenges.[464] To understand the pathogenesis, pathology, and natural history of infectious diseases, one must be familiar with the features of infectious agents that confer virulence, which are addressed elsewhere in this book. However, equally important is an understanding of the elements of the host's response that contribute to containment, elimination, and protection against subsequent infection with these agents. Furthermore, recognizing that host responses to infections also may contribute to the pathophysiology of infectious diseases and may injure the host in other ways likewise is important.

The traditional view of the organization of the immune system is that it is composed of separate arms or compartments, such as complement, phagocytes, cell-mediated immunity, and humoral immunity.[118, 275] An alternative approach is to divide host responses into two larger categories: "innate immunity," which incorporates the more rapid and phylogenetically primitive, nonspecific responses to infection, such as surface defenses, complement activation, cytokine elaboration, and phagocytic responses, and "adaptive immunity," which involves more slowly developing, persistent, and highly evolved antigen-specific responses that exhibit extraordinarily diverse ranges of specificities such as antibody production and cell-mediated immunity. Although each of the various components of host defense may be studied and discussed separately, of vital importance is to recognize that the different arms of the immune system engage in numerous and complex interactions that are essential for optimal function of each individual compartment of the system and for the remarkable range of the immune response. For example, opsonization of encapsulated bacteria by complement proceeds most efficiently in the presence of specific anticapsular antibodies that can activate the classical pathway of complement.[55, 82] Opsonization itself is a prelude to the efficient attachment and engulfment of microorganisms by phagocytes expressing receptors for antibodies and opsonic complement fragments.[3, 55, 435] Mononuclear phagocytes can present processed peptide antigens to T cells.[285] T-cell help is essential for effective stimulation of production of antibodies against protein antigens, and they secrete cytokines that may influence the responses of B cells, phagocytes, and other cells profoundly.[285]

The characteristic features of specific infectious diseases are determined by the interactions of structural components and products released by microbial pathogens with host tissue, cells, and their products. Virulence tactics commonly used by organisms include adherence to host-cell surfaces, internalization within or invasion of host cells, production of toxins, elaboration of surface barriers such as bacterial polysaccharide capsules, usurpation of host synthetic mechanisms, and direct inhibition of specific defense mechanisms within host cells. The successful evolution of host strategies to protect against microbial attack has resulted in defenses designed to interfere with or to counteract many of these modes of microbial virulence. In recent years, some of humanity's oldest microbial adversaries (e.g., smallpox, poliomyelitis, measles) have been or are being systematically eradicated. In the meantime, previously unrecognized human pathogens such as human immunodeficiency virus type 1 (HIV-1) and Ebola virus have emerged as newer plagues on humankind. However, many of our oldest nemeses (e.g., tuberculosis, malaria) still have not been brought under control and remain serious problems worldwide. Continued study of the interactions between microbial pathogenesis and immunologic mechanisms is essential for the ongoing development of innovative approaches that can support and augment evolutionary adaptations of the human immune response to both old and new microbial challenges.

MAIN FEATURES OF HOST RESPONSES TO SPECIFIC CLASSES OF INFECTIOUS AGENTS

Viruses

Viruses are obligate intracellular parasites that consist of genetic material in the form of either DNA or RNA that usually is surrounded by a protein coat and may or may not be bound by a lipid envelope.[303] Diseases caused by viruses are remarkably diverse and range from mild and merely inconvenient to rapidly fatal and from acute or brief to chronic or lifelong. However, certain features are common to the pathogenesis of most viral infections. First, viruses must enter host cells to replicate. Entry is presumed to be initiated by attachment of a virus surface protein to a specific receptor molecule on the host cell. The specific viral ligands or their corresponding host-cell receptors have been identified in only a few viruses. For example, rhinovirus has evolved a capsid protein that binds to human intercellular adhesion molecule-1 (ICAM-1) on respiratory epithelium,[207] the envelope glycoproteins of HIV-1 interact with CD4 on T lymphocytes and distinct chemokine receptors on lymphocytes or macrophages,[131, 255, 463] and internalization of adenoviruses depends on interaction between a specific peptide sequence in the penton base complex of the viral capsid and α_v integrins on host cell surfaces.[458]

After the virus has entered the host cell, the cellular synthetic machinery is redirected to the synthesis of viral components. As with many native proteins made by the host cell, a portion of the viral protein is processed into peptides and presented on the infected cell surface by major histocompatibility complex (MHC) class I molecules (see later). The host mechanisms most important in defense against most viral pathogens include production of specific neutralizing antibodies against viral surface proteins, development of specific $CD8^+$ cytotoxic T-cell responses that eliminate infected cells, and production of interferons (IFNs) that disrupt viral replication.[285]

Other host defenses also may exhibit antiviral activity, although the importance of some of these mechanisms in protection against viral infection in humans has not been established as firmly. For example, natural killer (NK) cells possibly mediate the destruction of infected host cells,[285] and antibody-dependent cellular cytotoxicity (ADCC) may ensue after IgG antibodies bind to viral antigens on the infected cell and permit the subsequent attachment of NK cells or cytotoxic T cells via IgG Fc receptors.[169] IFNs and other cytokines may enhance NK and ADCC activity, and cytokines such as tumor necrosis factor–α (TNF-α) may exert cytotoxic actions on cells infected with certain viruses.[285] Furthermore, researchers have demonstrated that opsonic complement components bound to viral surfaces can interfere with cell attachment and that the late complement components of the membrane attack complex (MAC) can lyse enveloped viruses.[55]

Bacteria

The human host is colonized by a large variety of bacteria on the skin and mucous membrane surfaces.[325] The integrity of these mechanical barriers ordinarily prevents systemic invasion of local commensal bacteria.[93] The epithelial cells that constitute these barriers also may release defensins and other microbicidal molecules.[190] In addition, in healthy hosts, circulating polymorphonuclear leukocytes (PMNs) help keep the resident flora in check by leaving the bloodstream at mucosal sites containing the highest bacterial burdens, such as the oral cavity and the lower intestine.[26] This phenomenon helps account for the increased risk of development of local and systemic infection caused by oral and intestinal organisms in patients with severe neutropenia, including those who receive prolonged chemotherapy for malignancies, and in patients with phagocytic migratory function disorders such as leukocyte adhesion deficiency syndromes.[26] Important host defenses against most bacteria that invade the human host systemically include the complement system, specific antibodies that promote both the opsonic and the bacteriolytic functions of complement, and phagocytes.[3, 26, 55, 249, 435]

Fungi

Host defense mechanisms against fungi are less well understood than are those directed at bacteria and viruses. However, phagocytic activity and cell-mediated immunity appear to be most important.[158, 181] The relative importance of these factors appears to depend on the specific organisms involved, as demonstrated by clinical observations in patients with isolated defects in one or the other. Severe mucosal infections caused by *Candida* spp. are common occurrences in patients with acquired or primary cell-mediated immune deficits such as HIV infection, thymic aplasia (see later), chronic mucocutaneous candidiasis, and some forms of severe combined immune deficiency (SCID), as well as in patients with disorders of leukocyte migration.[26, 158] Disseminated candidiasis more often is attributed to iatrogenic factors such as prolonged antimicrobial therapy and indwelling vascular catheters. Patients with malignancies, complicated postsurgical courses, and burns also appear to be at increased risk. Although neutrophils from patients with myeloperoxidase (MPO) deficiency kill *Candida* organisms more slowly than do those from normal persons, *Candida* infections usually do not develop in these patients, thus suggesting that this aspect of neutrophil function is not critical.[26, 158]

In contrast to *Candida, Aspergillus* infections are not as great a problem for patients with cell-mediated immune defects as they are for those with defects in phagocytic host defenses, such as chemotherapy-induced neutropenia, or for those with genetic defects in phagocyte killing, such as chronic granulomatous disease (CGD).[53, 462] Fungi such as *Histoplasma* and *Cryptococcus,* like *Candida,* tend to cause severe infections in patients with defects in cell-mediated immunity, although phagocytes clearly are required for optimal clearance of these organisms.[145, 456] The main role of antibodies and complement in protection from fungi probably is to provide opsonic activity for enhancement of phagocyte function.[146]

Features of Normal Immune Function

The ability of the immune system to respond effectively to a remarkably broad range of microbial pathogens and their antigens depends on aggressive, early responses that may be nonspecific and relatively short-lived ("innate" immune responses) or more deliberate, long-lasting, specific, and designed to confer protection against subsequent exposure ("adaptive" immune responses). Although the arms of the immune system will be discussed separately, some of the complex interactions among the different components of the immune system previously noted will be addressed. A degree of redundancy is inherent in the system, so if one host mechanism fails or is inefficient in protecting against a particular pathogen, another may be able to help contain the microbe initially or provide long-term immunity, or do both.

CELL-MEDIATED IMMUNITY

Cell-mediated immunity provides several important functions in defense of the host against pathogenic microorganisms, including T-cell help for antibody production, cytokine production for stimulation and regulation of the immune responses, and cytotoxic T-cell activity against cells infected with viruses.[31, 149, 285, 344] The development of cell-mediated immunity requires complex interactions between T cells and antigen-presenting cells (APCs) via several types of surface molecules on the respective cell surfaces, including the interaction between an antigen-specific T-cell receptor (TCR) on the T lymphocyte and a peptide antigen presented by the APC (represented schematically in Fig. 2–1). Other respective pairs of accessory cell surface molecules (not depicted) that enhance interactions between T cells and APCs include CD40 ligand (CD40L)/CD40, lymphocyte function-associated antigen-1 (LFA-1)/ICAM-1, and CD28/B7. An additional molecule, cytotoxic T-lymphocyte antigen-4 (CTLA-4), expressed on activated T cells, also can bind to B7 molecules on APCs to generate a suppressive signal that may terminate T-cell activation.[285] The sustained physical interface between T cells and APCs at which these molecular interactions take place sometimes has been referred to as the "immunologic synapse."[204]

Antigen Presentation

For the immune system to respond specifically to microbial protein antigens, the antigens, either internalized by or synthesized within the APC, must be digested into smaller peptides.[285] These peptides are presented at the surface of the APC by class I or class II MHC molecules.[237] There they can be recognized and bound by T cells bearing receptors with the appropriate antigen specificity. Different mechanisms of foreign peptide antigen processing may be involved before presentation, depending on the type of APC and the type of infecting agent. A pathway for presentation of lipid and glycolipid microbial antigens by molecules of the CD1 family recently has been described.[351] The corresponding processes in the development of immune responses to polysaccharide antigens are understood less well.

CLASS I MAJOR HISTOCOMPATIBILITY COMPLEX

The class I MHC molecule presents antigenic peptides to $CD8^+$ T lymphocytes.[327, 421] It consists of a heavy chain that contains the peptide-binding domain, or cleft, and a transmembrane domain, and it exhibits genetic polymorphism. The class I MHC molecule also has a small extracellular subunit, β_2-microglobulin, which has an association with the heavy chain that is essential for effective antigen presentation.[65, 285, 362] The three major types of class I MHC heavy

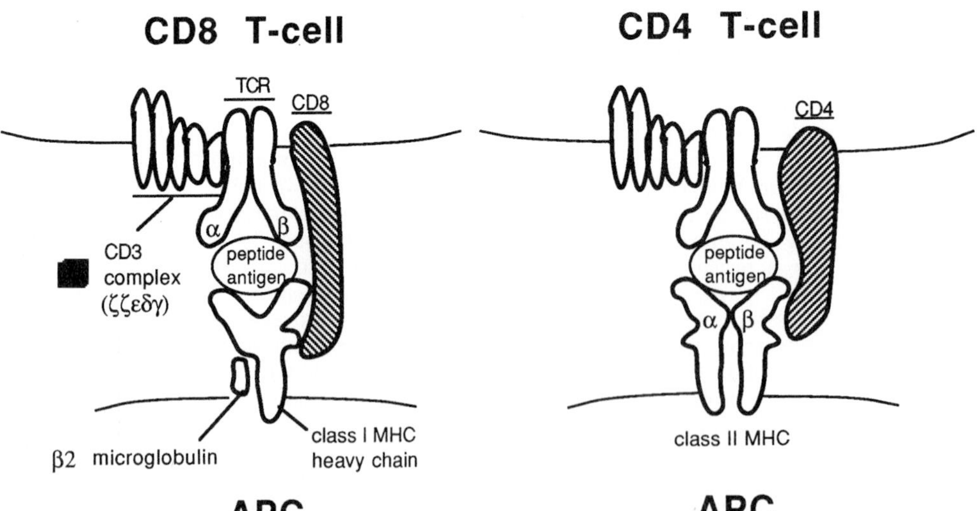

FIGURE 2–1 ■ Principal cell surface interactions between $CD8^+$ and $CD4^+$ T lymphocytes and peptide antigens complexed with major histocompatibility complex (MHC) class I and class II molecules, respectively. CD3 (composed of five subunits) is associated closely with the T-cell receptor (TCR), which recognizes a specific peptide presented on MHC molecules. Class I and class II MHC determinants are recognized by CD8 and CD4, respectively. Additional or accessory interactions are discussed in the text. (Adapted from Lewis, D. B., and Wilson, C. B.: Developmental immunology and role of host defenses in neonatal susceptibility to infection. *In* Remington, J. S., and Klein, J. O. [eds.]: Infectious Diseases of the Fetus and Newborn Infant. 4th ed. Philadelphia, W. B. Saunders, 1995, p. 22.)

chains in humans, HLA-A, HLA-B, and HLA-C, are encoded on chromosome 6 and have at least 22, 31, and 12 different alleles, respectively.[468] This polymorphism permits great diversity in the peptide-binding repertoire in individuals and within populations. A restricted degree of polymorphism would result in limitations in the ability to present a broad range of antigenic peptides and has been invoked as a possible explanation for the predisposition of certain populations with restricted MHC polymorphism, such as Native Americans, to the development of severe infections.[67]

Because class I MHC molecules ordinarily bind peptides derived from proteins recently synthesized de novo within the cell, under normal circumstances they provide an opportunity for cells to express their antigenic identity as "self."[168, 432] However, because viral pathogens use host-cell synthetic mechanisms, peptide antigens processed from newly synthesized viral proteins in infected cells also are presented by class I MHC.[167] With few exceptions, such as neurons, virtually all cells in the human host express class I MHC molecules, which they use to present peptide antigens at their surfaces.[129] A portion of the newly synthesized cellular proteins are processed into peptides by enzymes at an incompletely defined cytoplasmic site in the cell called the proteasome.[198] These peptides are transported actively into the endoplasmic reticulum, where they are bound in the peptide-binding cleft of MHC class I.[285] The characteristics of peptides that bind class I MHC are relatively restricted. Thus, not all peptide sequences exhibit antigenic potential. Suitable peptides usually are 8 to 10 amino acids in length, and they must contain certain amino acids at specific positions on the peptide to bind within the peptide-binding groove or cleft of the MHC class I molecule.[239, 285] Allelic variants of MHC class I require different amino acids at these "anchor" positions for binding to occur.[184]

The other amino acids of the peptide may be more variable and probably constitute the antigenic determinants that interact with specific TCRs on $CD8^+$ T cells.[66, 184, 285] The cytotoxicity of $CD8^+$ T cells for target cells expressing antigens via MHC class I requires the additional engagement of accessory molecule pairs for optimal activity, including LFA-1/ICAM-1. The signal via the TCR on $CD8^+$ cells (cytotoxic T lymphocyte [CTL]) leads to mobilization of Fas ligand to the cell surface, where it delivers a signal to the target cell for apoptosis, or cell death. Additionally, cytotoxic granules are mobilized to the CTL surface, where perforin and granzyme are released. Perforin creates a pore in the target cell membrane that allows the entry of granzyme, which also triggers target cell death.[285]

CLASS II MAJOR HISTOCOMPATIBILITY COMPLEX

The immune system includes several cell types that often are called professional APCs. They are bone marrow–derived cells, such as mononuclear phagocytes, B lymphocytes, and dendritic cells, and include specialized tissue-specific dendritic cells such as the Langerhans cells of the skin.[122] Dendritic cells, the most efficient APCs for primary activation of naive T cells, are macrophage-like cells of a distinct lineage that take up and process antigens in tissues and then migrate to local lymph nodes or to the spleen, where they are likely to come in contact with T cells specific for the presented antigens.[155, 213, 363, 421] One important feature of these professional APCs is their expression of class II MHC molecules in addition to class I MHC.[130] Class II MHC molecules are composed of an alpha and a beta chain, which together form the peptide-binding cleft.[83, 374]

Class II MHC molecules present peptides derived from proteins that are internalized during phagocytosis of microorganisms or endocytosis.[211, 240, 285] The peptide-binding cleft is configured to accommodate peptides from 13 to 17 amino acids in length, somewhat longer than those bound by class I MHC.[240, 374] The three major types of class II MHC alpha and beta chains, HLA-DR, HLA-DP, and HLA-DQ, each exhibit a high degree of polymorphism.[295] In uninflamed tissue, expression of class II MHC is restricted relatively to professional APCs. However, cytokines that may be present in an inflammatory milieu, such as IFN-γ and TNF-α, can induce MHC class II expression in a much broader distribution of cell types, including endothelial cells, epithelial cells of various organs, and eosinophils.[285] The peptide-binding function of MHC class II is highly dependent on its dissociation from a separate smaller molecule known as the invariant chain.[361, 425] Because the peptide-binding cleft of MHC class II in the endoplasmic reticulum is bound by the invariant chain, it cannot bind antigenic peptides in that compartment.[361, 425] In contrast, the endoplasmic reticulum appears to be a major site of peptide binding for MHC class I.[285, 361, 425] Available evidence suggests that after being processed through the Golgi, MHC class II enters an endosomal/lysosomal compartment, where dissociation of the invariant chain takes place and permits binding of antigenic peptides derived from internalized proteins.[361, 425] The class II MHC–peptide complex then moves to the cell surface, where it interacts principally with $CD4^+$ T cells.[156, 290]

Figure 2–2 depicts the essential features of the conventional peptide antigen presentation pathways that involve the class I and class II MHC molecules described earlier. Alternative mechanisms have been documented by which class I MHC may present peptides derived from internalized exogenous proteins and class II MHC may present peptides from newly synthesized proteins.[285] The importance of these unconventional pathways of antigen presentation in the immune response is not understood fully.

CD1 FAMILY OF ANTIGEN-PRESENTING MOLECULES

In humans, the CD1 family is composed of a group of four proteins with significant homology and structural similarity to the MHC class I heavy chain. All mammalian species express one or more members of the CD1 family, principally on professional APC cells (dendritic cells, some mononuclear phagocytes, B lymphocytes in lymphoid tissue). Five closely linked, nonpolymorphic human CD1 genes, CD1A to CD1E, are located on chromosome 1. Four human CD1 proteins, CD1a, CD1b, CD1c, and CD1d, have been identified. Like MHC class I, CD1 molecules are tightly associated with a β_2-microglobulin subunit. However, instead of presenting peptide antigens, CD1 molecules present lipid and glycolipid antigens. Mycolic acid, lipoarabinomannans, and other related components of mycobacteria are the best documented foreign antigens presented by CD1 molecules, and both internalized antigens and antigens synthesized within the APC by ingested mycobacteria may be presented via distinct trafficking patterns of the CD1-antigen complexes. Investigators have hypothesized that other antigens, such as the lipoteichoic acids of gram-positive bacteria, the complex capsular polysaccharides of *Haemophilus influenzae* and *Neisseria meningitidis,* and the glycophosphoinositol (GPI) components of GPI-linked proteins of malarial parasites and trypanosomes, also may be presented by CD1 molecules. Lipid antigens presented on APCs by CD1 molecules are recognized mainly by a specialized subset of T cells that lack CD4 and CD8, known as NK T cells. These cells, largely CD1 restricted, share characteristics of both NK cells and T cells, exhibit a very limited range of TCR specificity, and

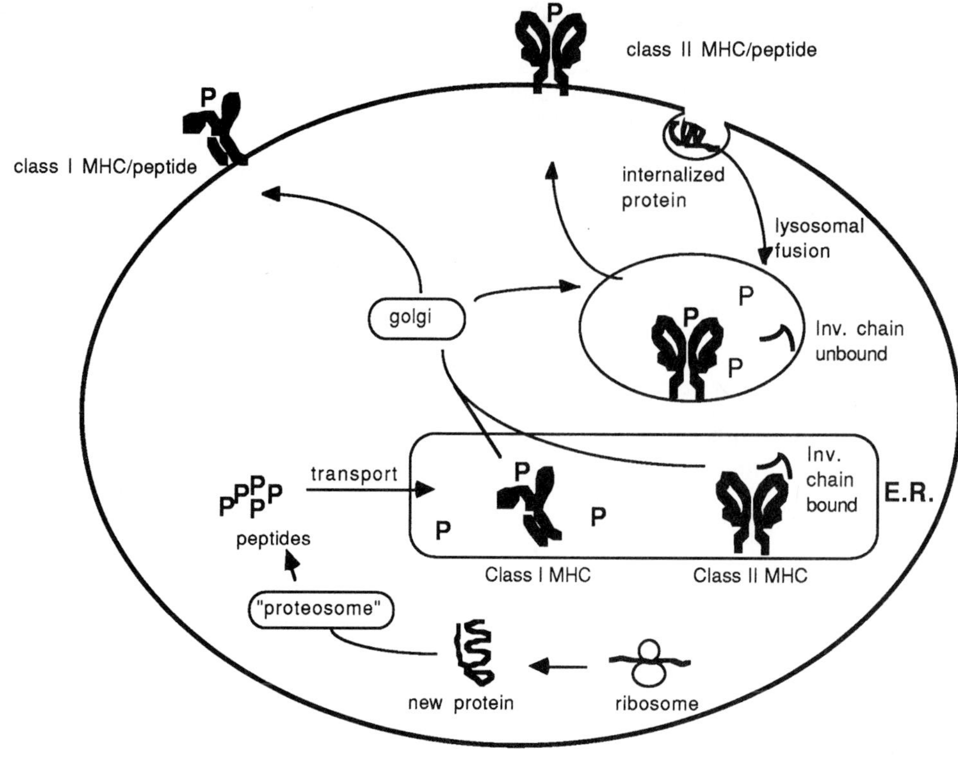

FIGURE 2–2 ■ Conventional pathways for peptide antigen presentation by class I and class II major histocompatibility (MHC) molecules. In the antigen-presenting cell, a proportion of newly synthesized proteins undergo proteolysis into peptides by enzymes that constitute the "proteasome." The peptides are transported actively into the endoplasmic reticulum (E.R.), where those with the appropriate length and sequence bind to MHC class I molecules. MHC class II molecules cannot bind peptides in the E.R. because of interference by the associated "invariant chain." The class I MHC/peptide complex is transported via the Golgi to the cell surface, where it may be recognized by $CD8^+$ lymphocytes. MHC class II molecules pass via the Golgi to a lysosomal compartment, where conditions favor release of the invariant chain. This release permits MHC class II molecules to bind peptides derived from internalized proteins that have entered the lysosomal compartment via fusion of endosomes or phagosomes with the lysosome. The lysosome translocates to the cell surface, where the class II MHC/peptide complex may be recognized by $CD4^+$ lymphocytes.

represent a sizable fraction of the T-cell compartment. Their function in the immune response is understood poorly. Greater detail regarding the structure, function, phylogeny, trafficking, expression, and T-cell interactions for members of the CD1 family may be found in an extensive recent review.[351]

T Lymphocytes

All lymphocytes have their origins in the pluripotent stem cells of the bone marrow. The development of T lymphocytes, or T cells, begins when the most immature cell committed to the T-cell lineage, the prothymocyte, leaves the marrow and enters the subcapsular region of the thymus.[154] This process initiates three stages of thymocyte development.[285] In stage I thymocytes, by mechanisms that are poorly understood, the thymic environment induces the rearrangement of TCR V (variable), D (diversity), and J (joining) gene segments (see later), with the eventual expression of mature alpha-beta TCRs complexed with CD3. This transition, along with the co-expression of both CD4 and CD8 and migration to the thymic cortex, marks the cell as a stage II thymocyte. Stage II thymocytes undergo processes of both positive and negative selection in which their TCR specificity is screened. The mechanism by which this screening takes place is the subject of intense investigation and theoretic controversy, and many excellent treatises and reviews on the subject exist.[112, 253, 298, 359] Thymocytes that do not pass this dual-screening procedure receive signals that induce programmed cell death (apoptosis).[318] Thymocytes that do pass this screening process probably are those for which TCR specificities and affinities are perceived as optimizing the repertoire for distinguishing self from nonself and eliminating TCR rearrangements that result in undesirably high self-reactivity. These cells, now stage III or medullary thymocytes, account for only approximately 5 percent of the original stage II thymocytes, and they express either CD4 or CD8, not both.[446] The next step in T-cell maturation is the release of these mature thymocytes into the periphery, where $CD4^+$ cells serve as the main source of interleukin-2 (IL-2) and provide help for B-cell antibody production and $CD8^+$ cells engage in cytotoxic activity.[285] The present and subsequent discussion of T cells and TCRs specifically relates to T cells that express TCRs composed of alpha and beta chains, or alpha-beta T cells. T cells of a distinct type, gamma-delta T cells, are far less numerous in most tissues (intestinal epithelium is a notable exception), exhibit much less TCR diversity than alpha-beta T cells do, may not require an intact thymus for development, and have been implicated in host responses to some intracellular bacterial pathogens, including *Listeria* and mycobacteria.[90, 251, 285]

The antigen specificity of alpha-beta T cells resides in their TCRs, which are integral membrane proteins that exhibit structural homology with immunoglobulins. TCR diversity results from rearrangement of the V, D, and J segments. These gene segments are dispersed widely on chromosome 7, and as many as 100 different V segments, 1 D segment, and as many as 100 different J segments exist in the complete germline configuration of the TCR genes.[460] Rearrangement of these gene segments into a mature VDJ sequence requires the action of a recombinase enzyme complex formed by two proteins, RAG-1 and RAG-2. This enzyme effects the deletion of intervening DNA so that a single VDJ sequence (or VJ in the case of the alpha chain) is formed.[336, 383] Thus, part of the TCR diversity is the result of all of the possible combinations of V, D, and J segments. However, because of the imprecise action of the recombinase enzyme complex, the degree of diversity is much greater. The variability in the number of nucleotides deleted during rearrangement results in a tremendous increase in diversity of the possible sequences of TCR antigen-binding domains.[174] Additionally, thymocytes undergoing TCR gene rearrangement express the enzyme "terminal deoxytransferase," which appears to add nucleotides at random to extend segments during rearrangement.[174, 395] Researchers have estimated that as many as 10^{15} different TCR specificities theoretically could result from the various mechanisms that influence TCR segment rearrangement.[134] As noted earlier, the basic structure of the TCR is similar to that of antibody molecules, and the mechanisms for generating diversity within the antigen-binding regions of antibodies are similar to those of the TCR.

T-CELL ACTIVATION BY SUPERANTIGENS

The term *superantigen* describes a class of protein antigens that includes numerous clinically important microbial exotoxins, including most staphylococcal enterotoxins, staphylococcal toxic shock syndrome toxin-1 (TSST-1), and related streptococcal TSST-1–like toxins. These bacterial toxins are potent pyrogens, can induce a potentially lethal toxic shock syndrome, and share binding domains for both TCR V regions and MHC class II molecules. Superantigens bypass normal antigen processing and presentation pathways by binding directly to class II MHC molecules on APCs and to specific variable regions on the beta chain of the T-cell antigen receptor. Through these interactions, superantigens induce polyclonal activation of T cells at orders of magnitude above antigen-specific activation. Such activation results in massive release of cytokines from T cells and APCs, including TNF-α and TNF-β, IL-1, IL-2, and INF-γ, which are thought to be responsible for the most severe features of toxic shock syndromes.[355]

NATURAL KILLER CELLS

NK cells represent a population of lymphoid cells that do not express clonally distributed receptors such as TCRs or surface immunoglobulin for specific antigens. They are found in the peripheral circulation and in the spleen and bone marrow. Like many other leukocytes, they can be recruited to sites of inflammation by chemokines and other chemoattractants. They appear to be important for the control of tumors in vivo and, by mechanisms that include ADCC, serve a critical function in host defense against some kinds of viral infection, especially those caused by herpesviruses.[169, 259, 315] NK cells are able to distinguish normal cells of self origin via receptors that recognize specific MHC class I determinants and thereby avoid undesirable NK cell–mediated injury to the host. Other receptors on NK cells, including the NK-specific receptors NKp46 and NKp30, as well as FcγRIII (CD16), contribute to NK cell cytotoxic activity.[169, 315]

B LYMPHOCYTES AND IMMUNOGLOBULIN

B Lymphocytes

B lymphocytes (B cells) are effectors of humoral immunity in that they are responsible for the production of immunoglobulin.[81, 285, 335] Like T cells, they are derived from pluripotent stem cells. The earliest recognizable precursors of B cells are pro-B cells, the surfaces of which bear the pan-B marker CD19. The next precursors are pre-B cells, which differ from pro-B cells in that they can produce mu heavy chain and are more numerous. Pre-B cells make up approximately 5 percent of bone marrow cells. Pre-B proliferation is stimulated by the IL-7 made by bone marrow stromal cells, and pre-B maturation into B cells capable of producing immunoglobulin depends on pre-B expression of a tyrosine kinase, *atk* or *btk*.[214, 433, 434, 443]

The transition from pre-B to mature B cells is marked by the expression of cell surface immunoglobulin and the resulting ability to recognize and bind antigen. B lymphocytes constitute approximately 20 percent of circulating lymphocytes and lymphocytes in peripheral lymphoid tissues, such as the lymph nodes, spleen, bone marrow, tonsils, and intestines.[81]

B cells can be identified via flow cytometry by the presence of surface immunoglobulin and the pan-B differentiation markers CD19 and CD20. Other surface markers vary among individual B cells but may include Fc receptors and the complement receptors CR1, CR2, and CR3.[81, 285]

B-cell activation is induced by recognition and binding of specific antigens to B-cell surface immunoglobulins. Activation leads to increased expression of receptors that bind cytokines (e.g., IL-2, IL-4, IL-6) or T cells and to B-cell clonal proliferation and differentiation into memory B cells and plasma cells. Some data suggest that B-cell differentiation into memory B cells is favored by exposure to CD40L on dendritic cells in lymphoid organs. In contrast, differentiation into plasma cells is favored by exposure to CD23, IL-1α, IL-6, and IL-10.[285, 288] Plasma cells differ from B cells in that they no longer have surface immunoglobulin expression and they are capable of secreting large amounts of antibody. In fact, they are responsible for most production of immunoglobulin. Plasma cells are found in the bone marrow, liver, peripheral lymph nodes, and lymphatic tissue in the respiratory and gastrointestinal tracts.

The B-lymphocyte response to some antigens, particularly polysaccharide antigens, proceeds largely without T-lymphocyte involvement and is called T-independent. The two types of T-independent antibody responses are thymus-independent type 1 (TI-1) and thymus-independent type 2 (TI-2). TI-1 antigens can bind to B cells and activate them directly without the help of T cells (e.g., fixed *Brucella abortus*). TI-2 antigens also can activate B cells directly, but antibody response to TI-2 antigens may be enhanced by the presence of T-cell help, and the isotype produced in response to TI-2 antigens depends on T-cell help. TI-2 antigens consist of repeating identical subunits, such as large polysaccharides (e.g., *H. influenzae* type b capsular polysaccharide).[218, 285]

The B-cell response to other kinds of antigens, particularly protein antigens such as tetanus and diphtheria toxoids, depends on T-cell help and, therefore, is called

T-dependent. B cells can efficiently process and present antigen to $CD4^+$ T cells that they encounter in the lymph nodes and spleen. B-cell surface immunoglobulin binds to the T-dependent antigen, the immunoglobulin-protein complex is internalized and processed, and then this complex is presented to the T cell bound to B-cell surface class II MHC molecules. Because antigen binding to B-cell surface immunoglobulin is of relatively high affinity, B cells possibly may permit T-cell activation by relatively small amounts of antigen. T cells appear to be stimulated more vigorously by B cells when the B cells present familiar, rather than new, antigens.[166, 186]

T-cell help is provided by both cell surface–associated signals and the release of soluble cytokines. T-cell surface CD40L, which is expressed transiently on activated T cells, binds CD40 on B cells and is important in the T-dependent B-cell response to protein antigens and isotype switching.[35, 326] The cytokine IL-4 stimulates switching to IgG1 and IgE, and IL-10 promotes switching to IgA.[138, 275, 353]

Immunoglobulin

Immunoglobulin molecules may be bound to the surface of B cells, as has been discussed, or may be free in the circulation, mucosal secretions, or tissues. Free immunoglobulin binds to specific antigens and functions in host defense against infection by opsonizing pathogens for ingestion and killing by phagocytes, fixing complement, neutralizing viruses and toxins, and participating in the formation of immune complexes.

Immunoglobulin molecules are composed of two identical heavy and two identical light chains as illustrated in Figure 2–3.[218, 285] The two heavy chains and the heavy and light chain pairs are bridged by disulfide bonds and noncovalent forces. The carboxyl terminus of the immunoglobulin

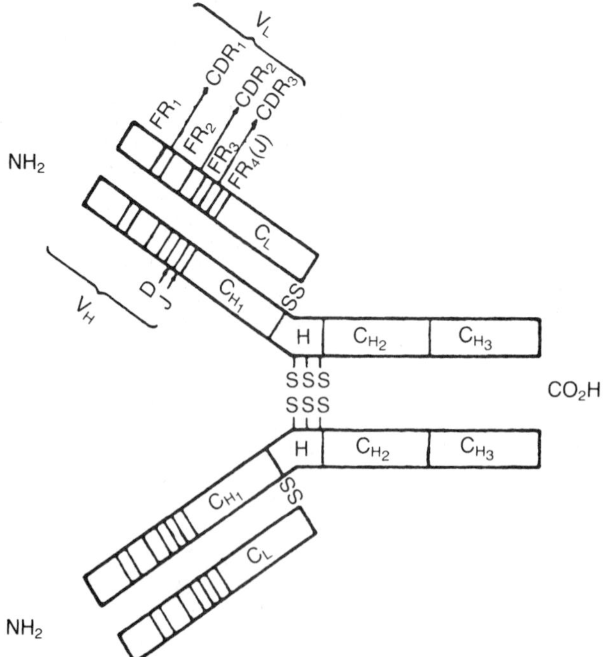

FIGURE 2–3 ■ Structure of an immunoglobulin molecule. That of IgG is shown. (From Lewis, D. B., and Wilson, C. B.: Developmental immunology and role of host defenses in neonatal susceptibility to infection. *In* Remington and J. S., Klein, J. O. [eds.]: Infectious Diseases of the Fetus and Newborn Infant. 4th ed. Philadelphia, W. B. Saunders, 1995, p. 37.)

molecule is the heavy chain constant, or Fc, region. The amino acid sequence of this region determines the nine immunoglobulin isotypes: IgM, IgG1, IgG2, IgG3, IgG4, IgA1, IgA2, IgD, and IgE. The constant region is encoded by the V, D, J, and constant (C) regions on chromosome 14.[58, 218, 285, 449] The Fc region is important in the phagocytosis of opsonized organisms because it can bind to leukocyte Fc receptors itself or it can participate in complement activation and help direct the deposition of complement on the organism's surface.

The two kinds of light chains, kappa and lambda, are determined by different constant regions; they are encoded by V, J, and C genes on chromosomes 2 and 22, respectively. Each immunoglobulin molecule has a pair of either kappa or lambda light chains.

The amino terminus is the variable, or Fab, region of the immunoglobulin molecule. It serves as the antigen recognition and binding site. Like the TCR, the Fab region consists of two identical heavy and light chain pairs. Diverse antigen specificity results from the variable nature of recombinase-mediated DNA rearrangements of the three hypervariable complementarity-determining regions (CDR1, CDR2, and CDR3) and the four framework regions.[283] The imprecision of the joining process leads to the generation of more than 10^{12} antigenic specificities, many of which are nonfunctional. Further variations in specificity result from differences in approximation of the three CDRs in relation to each other in the three-dimensional structure of the antigen recognition site, or the binding cleft.[312] Somatic mutation, particularly of the three hypervariable regions of the heavy and light chains, generates immunoglobulin with higher-affinity antigen-combining regions.[277, 328]

The ability of immunoglobulin molecules to recognize the three-dimensional structure of intact antigens such as microbial surface capsular polysaccharides or proteins differentiates them from most TCRs, which usually only recognize processed peptide antigens.

All immunoglobulin is derived from B cells expressing surface IgM. B cells change immunoglobulin isotype when they differentiate into plasma cells, which produce only one class or subclass of immunoglobulin each. Isotypes other than IgM are the result of isotype switching (e.g., from IgM to IgG) by replacing a part of the constant region of the immunoglobulin heavy chain with another isotype-specific segment. The Fab, or variable antigen-recognizing, region remains unchanged, and thus no change occurs in antigen specificity. As already noted, isotype switching primarily depends on cytokines and T cells. Specific cytokines have roles ranging from permitting (e.g., IL-4) or augmenting to preventing (e.g., IFN-γ) isotype switching.

IgG AND IgG SUBCLASSES

IgG is a monomeric molecule with a molecular weight of approximately 150,000,[218, 285] and it accounts for approximately 80 percent of the circulating immunoglobulin. IgG also is the predominant isotype in tissues because its monomeric structure permits it to penetrate much more readily than do polymeric immunoglobulins such as IgM and IgA. IgG is composed of the subclasses IgG1, IgG2, IgG3, and IgG4. The half-life of IgG1, IgG2, and IgG4 ordinarily is 23 days, and that of IgG3 is 9 days. In circumstances of hypoimmunoglobulinemia or hyperimmunoglobulinemia, the half-life of IgG often increases or decreases, respectively.

Initial exposure to most antigens induces an IgM and then an IgG response consisting of IgG1 and IgG3. IgG2 and IgG4 usually are produced during the secondary immune response. The formation of specific IgG can signal the formation of memory B cells and, thus, may reflect long-term, potentially lifelong immunity.

The functions of IgG in host defense against infection include opsonization, complement fixation, toxin and viral neutralization, and antibody-dependent cytolysis. IgG binds to antigen via its Fab region and to IgG receptors on phagocytes and some other cells via its Fc region. IgG1, IgG2, and IgG3, but not IgG4, can trigger complement activation by the classical pathway by binding to C1q. They also help localize complement deposition on the surface of organisms by directing it to specific antigens (e.g., capsules versus outer-membrane proteins or lipopolysaccharides).

Different subclasses of antibody are associated with defense against different kinds of organisms. For example, IgG1 is formed in response to protein antigens such as tetanus toxoid.[415] In adults, the main antibody response to polysaccharides is IgG2, whereas in infants and IgG2-deficient persons, it is IgG1 predominantly.[17] IgG3 appears to be an important subclass for viral neutralization.

IgM

Free IgM usually exists as a pentamer consisting of five monomeric paired heavy and light chains stabilized by a single J chain.[218, 285] Its half-life is approximately 7 days, and it has a molecular weight of 900,000. A hexameric IgM consisting of six monomeric heavy and light chains, but no J chain, exists in the circulation but is less abundant. Most IgM is found in the circulation.

The IgM response is the earliest of the isotype responses and appears within the first few days of infection, but it is transient. The formation of an IgM response in the absence of an IgG response to infection is not associated with the formation of memory B cells. Therefore, an isolated IgM response suggests transient immunity.

The main functions of IgM in host defense include fixing complement to opsonize organisms for ingestion by phagocytes, and agglutinating them for clearance by the reticuloendothelial system. Each of these activities is enhanced by the polymeric structure of the IgM molecule, which gives it more binding sites and permits more avid binding.

IgA

IgA exists in monomeric circulating and polymeric secretory forms and has a half-life of approximately 7 days.[125, 218, 285] Its molecular weight ranges from 160,000 for the serum form to 500,000 for secretory IgA. Both forms are produced mainly by plasma cells that have migrated to mucosal sites. The two subclasses of IgA, IgA1 and IgA2, differ in the composition of their heavy chains. Approximately 90 percent of IgA in the circulation is IgA1, whereas approximately 60 percent of IgA in secretions is IgA2. IgA1, but not IgA2, is cleaved by bacterial proteases.

Secretory IgA usually is composed of two IgA molecules joined by a stabilizing J segment that is secreted by plasma cells and a secretory component produced by mucosal epithelial cells. The secretory component permits delivery of IgA to mucosal surfaces. Secretory IgA is found in all mucosal secretions, and it provides host defense at mucosal surfaces by preventing adherence of bacteria and neutralizing viruses.

IgA can activate the alternative pathway of complement, but because it does not bind C1q, it cannot activate the classical pathway. It also can act as an opsonin or stimulate phagocyte superoxide production via IgA receptors and, in the presence of lysozyme and complement, may augment bactericidal activity.

IgE

The IgE molecule has a molecular weight of 200,000 and a half-life of only 2.3 days.[218, 285] Most IgE is produced by plasma cells in lymphoid tissue near gastrointestinal and respiratory mucosal surfaces and then released into the circulation. IgE also is found on mast cells and basophils. Serum IgE levels normally are low but tend to be higher in persons with a history of allergies.

The main function of IgE is to trigger immediate hypersensitivity reactions. Mast cells are activated when IgE bound to them by specific receptors is cross-linked by specific antigens. IgE-stimulated release of inflammatory mediators may permit an increased influx of other immune factors such as IgG, complement, and cells, including phagocytes, lymphocytes, and other eosinophils. IgE may aid in neutralizing toxin by enhancing the penetration of IgG antibody into the region. Persons with intestinal parasites have elevated serum levels of IgE, thus suggesting that it may play a role in protecting against parasitic disease. Potential functions of IgE could include directly damaging the parasites, preventing them from attaching and invading, or opsonizing them for phagocytosis and killing by macrophages with surfaces that contain Fc receptors specific for IgE. The IgE response to intestinal parasites also may protect by triggering release of the contents of mast cells to stimulate a local inflammatory response that results in expulsion of the parasite from the gastrointestinal tract.

IgD

IgD has a molecular weight of approximately 180,000 and a half-life of 2.8 days.[218, 285] It is present in most normal adult serum and secretions in low concentrations. Although some antigenic specificity for IgD has been demonstrated, its function in host defense is unclear. It cannot bind to phagocytes or fix complement. The most important function of IgD appears to be as an antigen receptor on the membrane of B lymphocytes, where it seems to be involved in regulating development of the normal B-cell antibody response.

COMPLEMENT

The complement system consists of more than 30 different free and membrane-bound activation and regulatory proteins. It plays multiple key roles in the clearance of invading microbes, including opsonization, recruitment of inflammatory cells, and lytic destruction of pathogens.[54, 141, 159, 160, 176, 246–248, 317] Complement and antibody often act synergistically in host defense against infection. Traditionally, they have been known as the heat-labile and heat-stable factors, respectively, and they contribute to serum opsonic and bactericidal activity. Activation of the complement response to the initial encounter with an organism usually occurs earlier than that of antibody because some components of complement activation are independent of antibodies and can be initiated before specific antibody can be produced. Once specific antibody is available, it serves to activate complement more efficiently and to direct complement binding to locations on the microbial surface that support the optimal execution of its effector functions, such as opsonization and killing.

Approximately 90 percent of complement proteins are synthesized in the liver, but some components can be produced locally at sites of infection by tissue mononuclear phagocytes and fibroblasts.[113, 345] In healthy persons, most complement is found in the circulation, less than 10 percent is in mucosal secretions, and little is detectable in cerebrospinal fluid. Circulating complement levels vary over the course of time, particularly in the presence of inflammation. The inflammatory response may lead to increases in levels of complement components that are acute-phase reactants, such as C3, or to decreases in individual components and total complement activity as a result of consumption.

The importance of normal complement component levels and activity in host defense has been well established and is based primarily on the increased susceptibility of patients with specific complement component deficiencies to recurrent and severe infections.[140, 141, 143, 159, 246, 247] Although the complement response to infection usually is beneficial to the host, it also may be associated with adverse clinical manifestations, such as septic shock and acute respiratory distress syndrome.[173, 451]

Complement Activation

Complement proteins are activated in cascade fashion via one of at least three pathways: the classical pathway, the alternative pathway, and the more recently described mannan-binding lectin (MBL) pathway as shown in Figure 2–4. These pathways converge at C3, and the complement cascade distal to C3 proceeds identically, irrespective of the pathway by which activation occurs. C3 convertases, C4b2a for the classical and MBL pathways and C3bBb for the alternative pathway, cleave the C3 molecule at exactly the same location and produce C3b, which binds to the target surface, and C3a, which is released into the fluid phase. Cleavage and activation of C3 lead to a conformational change in C3b that transiently renders its reactive thioester group capable of forming covalent ester or amide bonds with acceptor molecules on the target surface.[235, 274] If the acceptor molecules are situated on the surface of a microorganism, the bound C3b can act as an opsonin to promote phagocytosis, or it can bind with the classical and alternative pathway C3 convertases to form the C5 convertases C4b2a3b and C3bBb3b, respectively. C5 convertases bind and then cleave C5, with release of the C5a fragment into the fluid phase. The bound C5b fragment then can initiate formation of the MAC by sequential assembly of the remaining terminal components C6, C7, C8, and multiple molecules of C9. The MAC can insert into the outer membrane of target cells, such as erythrocytes or gram-negative bacteria, and cause cell lysis and death.[248]

THE CLASSICAL PATHWAY

Ordinarily, the classical pathway is activated by IgM or IgG bound to microbial antigenic targets or by other kinds of antigen-antibody complexes.[141] IgM activates complement more efficiently than IgG does because only one molecule of polymeric IgM is required versus at least two molecules of IgG.[120] Activation is initiated when C1q binds directly to an immunoglobulin molecule on the surface of an organism or, less often, to a surface molecule of the organism itself. C1r and C1s are activated and bound sequentially to C1q to form C1qrs. The enzymatic activity of this complex, which resides in the C1s molecule, can cleave multiple molecules of C4 and C2 into two fragments each. The C4a and C2b fragments are released into the environment, whereas C4b and C2a remain bound to each other on the surface of the target to form the classical pathway C3 convertase C4b2a. C4b2a can cleave and activate C3 and localize C3b binding to nearby sites on the target surface. As noted earlier, some C3b binds with C4b2a to form the classical pathway C5 convertase C4b2a3b.

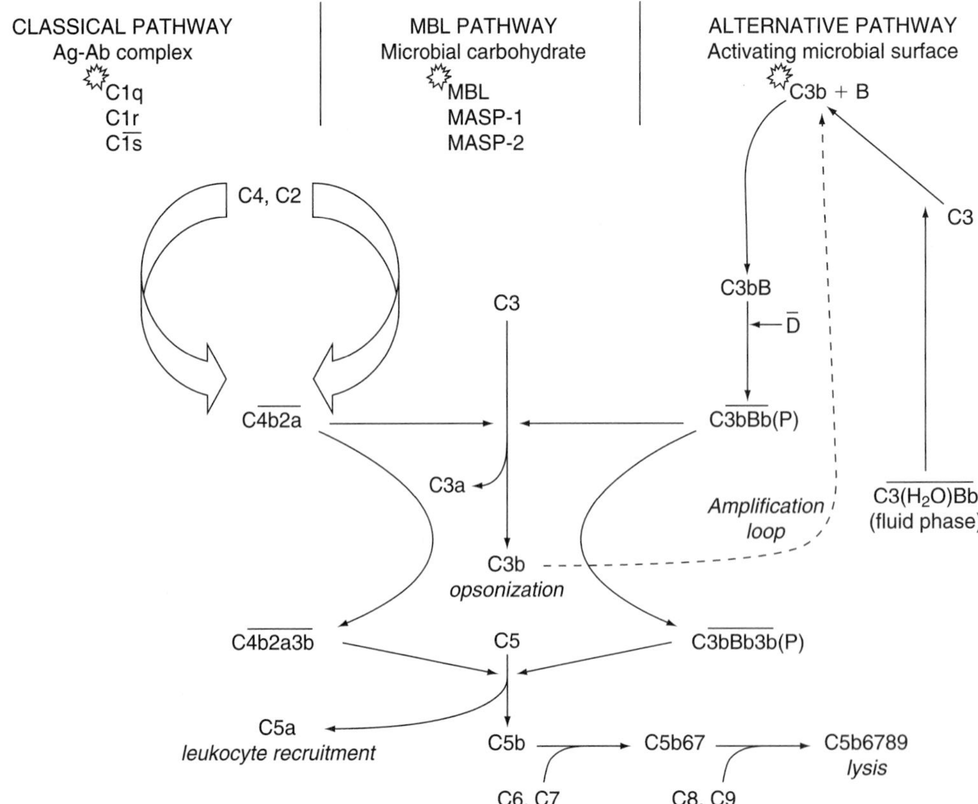

FIGURE 2–4 ■ The complement cascade. The initial binding events of the classical, mannan-binding lectin (MBL), and alternative pathways are indicated by a small *starburst*. These pathways intersect at the conversion of C3 to C3b. This step is followed by activation of the terminal components, beginning with binding and cleavage of C5 and release of C5a, with C5b left bound to initiate assembly of the remaining components to form the membrane attack complex (C5b, 6, 7, 8, 9). Enzymatically active proteases of the classical and alternative pathways that cleave and activate subsequent components are, by convention, shown with an *overbar*. The alternative pathway C3 and C5 convertases are shown associated with properdin (P), which increases their stability.

Classical pathway activation ordinarily is not initiated by complexes of antigens with IgG4, IgA, IgD, or IgE.

THE ALTERNATIVE PATHWAY

Because the classical and alternative pathways differ in their requirements for antibody, the classical pathway usually contributes substantially more to host defense in immune individuals. In contrast, the alternative pathway is more important in protection of nonimmune persons, such as premature infants who have low levels of transplacentally acquired antibody and older infants and young children who have maternal antibody that has waned but who have not yet produced their own specific antibodies. It can be initiated by microbial surface macromolecules (e.g., polysaccharide, lipopolysaccharide, teichoic acid), although as noted earlier, in some circumstances specific antibody increases alternative pathway efficiency and directs the location of C3b binding.[248]

A spontaneous low level of hydrolysis of the thioester of C3 in the fluid phase, a process sometimes referred to as C3 tick-over, results in an activated form of C3, C3(H_2O). This activated form of C3 can bind factor B, and the latter is cleaved by factor D to form the fluid-phase C3 convertase C3(H_2O)Bb. The constitutive presence of small amounts of this convertase in the fluid phase ensures that a small amount of C3b always is available to bind to microbial surfaces and initiate the alternative pathway.[342] The alternative pathway protein factor B has structural and functional similarities to C2, including the ability to bind to surface-bound C3b. Once bound to C3b, factor B undergoes proteolytic cleavage by factor D to release a small soluble fragment, Ba, with the larger fragment, Bb, left associated with C3b. C3bBb, the alternative pathway C3 convertase, is analogous to the classical pathway C3 convertase C4b2a. Properdin stabilizes the C3 convertase C3bBb, thereby permitting more efficient activation of C3 to form more C3b and creating the C3 amplification loop[170, 171] (see Fig. 2–4). Alternative pathway activation of C3 by this mechanism is several times less efficient than is activation via the classical pathway, but it is vital to host defense because it is the principal means by which a nonimmune person can activate C3 until a specific antibody response can be mounted.[142, 171]

The most important factor in determining whether a specific microbial pathogen will activate the alternative pathway is the biochemical nature of its surface. The surface biochemical features of a microorganism that characterize it as an activator are understood only partially. However, microorganisms that bear large amounts of surface sialic acid usually are known to be nonactivators. In fact, surface expression of sialic acid also is one of several means by which mammalian host cells are protected from complement-mediated lysis in vivo.[269] On surfaces rich in sialic acid, bound C3b is less able to bind factor B because another molecule, factor H, has a strong competitive advantage over factor B in these conditions. When bound by factor H, C3b becomes highly susceptible to further cleavage by factor I (C3b inactivator), and C3bi (or iC3b) is produced. This C3bi also can function as an opsonin, but it cannot bind factor B. Thus, no alternative pathway convertases can be formed, and no amplification loop is established.[54, 317] Organisms that have surfaces that do not support activation of the alternative pathway are some of the most successful pathogens in infants and young children. Such organisms include K1 *Escherichia coli,* groups A and B streptococci, *Streptococcus pneumoniae, N. meningitidis, H. influenzae* type b, and some salmonellae.[99, 248] Of note is that specific antibody against these organisms permits some activation of the alternative as well as the classical pathway of complement on their surfaces and correlates with protection.

THE MANNAN-BINDING LECTIN PATHWAY

Recently, a third complement activation pathway, the MBL pathway, has been described. MBL is a serum protein of the collectin family that has structural and functional similarities to C1q. However, it does not require antigen-antibody complexes to initiate its complement-activating function. MBL binds to mannose-containing carbohydrates on microbial surfaces, which leads to its association at the microbial surface with activated MBL-associated serine proteases (MASP-1 and MASP-2). These proteases appear to have structural and functional similarities to C1r and C1s and result in activation of C4, with sequential binding of C4b and C2a and the formation of C4b2a, the C3 convertase of the classical pathway. Further details of the MBL pathway and its possible role in infection and immune responses may be found in an excellent recent review.[346]

Effector Functions of Complement in Host Defense

Achieving any complement effector function in host defense against infection requires activation of the complement cascade through at least C3. The cascade needs to be activated only through C3 for effective opsonization, stimulation of leukocytosis, and immune regulation. Activation through C5 is required to produce a normal inflammatory response, including recruitment of phagocytes to sites of inflammation, and activation through C8 is needed for formation of the MAC. Complement may be activated and bound to cell surfaces but not be able to carry out its effector functions if it is bound in the wrong location.[82, 202, 234] For example, C3b bound to pneumococcal cell wall underneath a thick polysaccharide capsule is not accessible to CR1 on phagocytes and, therefore, does not promote effective opsonophagocytosis. Similarly, complement-mediated killing of some strains of *Salmonella* is prevented when the MAC is bound to long lipopolysaccharide molecules distant from the organism's cell membrane.[248, 249]

OPSONIC ACTIVITY

Complement opsonic activity is essential for effective removal of organisms from the circulation by macrophages in the liver and spleen and from other sites by neutrophils and tissue macrophages.[70] Opsonins facilitate recognition, binding, ingestion, and killing of microorganisms by phagocytes. Opsonization is particularly important for protection against gram-positive bacteria and fungi because their thick cell walls prevent them from being killed by the MAC.

As noted earlier, activation of C3 leads to a conformational change in C3b that permits its reactive thioester to bind covalently with acceptor molecules on microbial surfaces, where it can serve as an opsonin. C3b also can be cleaved by inactivators such as factor I and CR1 to form iC3b, which may be a more efficient opsonin than is C3b.[202, 235] Some organisms, including certain serotypes of pneumococci, have surfaces that support the degradation of differing amounts of surface-bound C3b to iC3b.[234] Surface-bound C3b and iC3b permit microbes to be recognized by circulating and tissue phagocytes by interacting with the phagocyte surface complement receptors CR1 (CD35) and CR3 (CD11b/CD18), respectively. These interactions lead to binding, ingestion, and intracellular killing of the organisms.[202, 235, 274]

Antibodies also are important opsonins in their own right, but they facilitate more rapid complement activation and more effective localization of C3b binding to the surface of the organism. In the absence of specific antibody to direct complement binding, complement deposition on the surface of the target will be determined principally by the nature of the surface, and effector functions such as opsonization may not be carried out as successfully. As noted earlier, this process is of particular importance for encapsulated organisms such as pneumococci because in the absence of specific anticapsular antibody, C3b will be deposited at the cell wall, where it is inaccessible to phagocyte receptors.[82, 234]

INFLAMMATION

The cleavage products of several complement proteins contribute to the development of an inflammatory response. C3a stimulates an increase in the number of circulating granulocytes, and C5a serves as a potent stimulus for monocyte, neutrophil, and eosinophil migration toward the source of C5a gradients being produced at infected tissue sites. C5a also up-regulates phagocytes' expression of CR1 and CR3 and stimulates them to release stored enzymes and other granular contents that also are important mediators of inflammation, aggregation, and production of microbicidal oxidants. C5a-induced neutrophil aggregation and stasis in the pulmonary circulation can be an important feature of the respiratory distress syndrome associated with sepsis.[451]

The anaphylatoxins C4a, C3a, and especially C5a induce the release of histamine from mast cells and basophils and, thereby, cause increased vascular dilatation and permeability, which in turn permit local influx of other inflammatory mediators.[238] In this way, they help produce the hallmark clinical manifestations of inflammation, swelling, and erythema. When large quantities of anaphylatoxins are released rapidly, they can contribute to septic shock.[173] Carboxypeptidase treatment of C4a, C3a, and C5a destroys their anaphylatoxin activity, but the C5a cleavage product $C5a_{des\ arg}$ maintains some chemoattractant- and phagocyte-activating activity.[254]

MICROBICIDAL ACTIVITY

Complement can act directly on certain bacteria to kill them. As noted earlier, C5b and the terminal complement proteins C6, C7, C8, and C9 form the MAC, which can kill and lyse target cells such as gram-negative bacteria by penetrating their outer membranes.[248] The C5b-C8 complex serves as a polymerization site for several molecules of C9. Although C9 is not essential to membrane penetration, its presence as poly-C9 allows penetration to proceed more efficiently.[424] Electron microscopy of the MAC demonstrates that it is composed of a ring-like structure at the outer surface of the target cell membrane and a perpendicular cylindric component that penetrates the cell membrane. As has been noted, the MAC cannot penetrate the thick cell walls of gram-positive bacteria and fungi and, therefore, cannot kill these organisms directly. The MAC can lyse some virus-infected host cells and some enveloped viruses themselves.[121] In addition, C1 and C4 can enhance neutralization of virus by antibody.

IMMUNE REGULATION

Complement is involved in the regulation of several facets of the immune response, both directly by binding to CR1, CR2, and CR3 on the surfaces of T cells, B cells, and other cells involved in antigen recognition and indirectly by stimulating the synthesis and release of cytokines.[165] For example, the C3b cleavage product C3dg, when covalently bound to antigen, brings the antigen close to B cells by binding to B-cell CR2 (CD21).[63, 75, 141, 332] Complement decreases the amount of antigen required to induce an immune response and increases the efficiency of the process by facilitating antigen presentation and localization. C3 also appears to be required for antigenic localization within germinal centers, and it is involved in anamnestic responses and isotype switching. The importance of complement in the immune response has been demonstrated by the finding that C1-, C2-, C4-, and C3-deficient animals have decreased antibody responses that can be restored by providing the missing protein. In addition, patients have been described who have complement deficiencies and low levels of IgG4 and IgG2.[63, 75, 141, 332]

PHAGOCYTES

Since Metchnikoff's earliest observations of host cells attacking foreign bodies in starfish,[304] phagocytes have been recognized as an important component in defense of the host. The most abundant phagocyte in the human host is the neutrophil, or PMN. Although some important differences exist between PMNs and other phagocytes, including monocytes, eosinophils, and tissue macrophages, the PMN is a worthy prototype for discussion of phagocyte function in general.

All phagocytes, including PMNs, have their origins in myeloid stem cells of the bone marrow. Differentiation into the various end-stage cells is regulated by specific growth factors and cytokines.[42, 286] The determinants of release of mature PMNs from bone marrow into the systemic circulation are understood poorly. One suggestion is that as granulocytes mature in the marrow, they gradually reduce the number of their surface receptors that bind bone marrow stromal components.[96] After a critical point during differentiation, stromal binding is reduced enough to permit release of the cells into the circulation.

Once in the circulation, the normal half-life of PMNs is approximately 8 to 12 hours.[448] In the absence of active infection, most PMNs leave the circulation via the gingival crevices and the lower gastrointestinal tract, sites at which the large populations of resident flora produce a continuous stimulation for recruitment of PMNs.[299] That necrotic gingivitis and ileocolitis develop in patients with neutropenia, such as that caused by chemotherapy for malignancies, is evidence of the importance of continuous vascular egress of PMNs at these mucosal sites for maintenance of the integrity of these tissues.

The professional circulating phagocyte has three main functions in defense of the human host: migration to the site of infection, recognition and ingestion of invading microorganisms, and killing and digestion of these organisms. When the normal barriers of the skin and mucous membranes are breached by microorganisms, interactions between microbial components and cellular and humoral constituents of the tissues result in the production of mediators that initiate the recruitment of PMNs into these tissues.

Phagocyte Recruitment

The first stage in the recruitment of phagocytes from the circulation into infected tissue is the activation of endothelial cells that line nearby capillaries and postcapillary venules.[94, 396] Various mediators, including cytokines, fragments of complement components, eicosanoid compounds, and microbial products, are elaborated as a result of interactions between the invading microbe and tissue proteins and resident cells. These mediators, including IL-1 and TNF-a, diffuse from the site of production and act on the nearby endothelial cells to up-regulate their expression of adhesion molecules that will interact with circulating phagocytes.[399] The first adhesion molecules to be up-regulated are members of the selectin family, P-selectin and E-selectin, which engage in carbohydrate-mediated interactions with their corresponding ligands on circulating PMNs.[62, 271] Expression of P-selectin is up-regulated in a matter of minutes because it resides presynthesized within the cell in rapidly translocatable membrane compartments, or Weibel-Palade bodies.[62] Within 3 to 6 hours of stimulation of endothelial cells, they begin to up-regulate expression of E-selectin via new synthesis.[62] The principal carbohydrate moiety responsible for binding to P-selectin and E-selectin is sialyl Lewis X, an oligosaccharide that is presented on several glycoproteins on PMNs, including L-selectin and a molecule on leukocytes that has been identified more recently, P-selectin glycoprotein ligand-1 (PSGL-1).[62, 271, 469] Circulating PMNs constitutively express L-selectin, and early selectin-mediated interactions, combined with capillary flow, result in a progressively slower, "rolling-like" behavior of leukocytes along the endothelial luminal surface. This phase is the first adhesive stage of leukocyte recruitment.[62, 94, 396]

Within 6 to 12 hours of endothelial stimulation, expression of adhesion molecules of the immunoglobulin supergene family becomes up-regulated. The most important of them is ICAM-1.[194, 396, 398] As the movement of PMNs along the endothelial surface becomes progressively slower, the PMNs themselves have time to become activated by locally produced mediators, especially chemokines such as IL-8. The source of IL-8 and other chemokines in this setting is the endothelial cells themselves. After chemokines are released from endothelial cells, they are bound at the endothelial cell surface by a variety of complex glycoproteins. These chemokines are more effective leukocyte activators in their bound form than as soluble molecules.[268]

As leukocytes are activated, they flatten on the endothelial surface, become polarized, and increase the expression or binding activity, or both, of the β_2 integrins (LFA-1 and macrophage antigen-1 [Mac-1]) that interact with ICAM-1 and related molecules on the endothelial cells.[290, 396, 398, 399, 412] Both LFA-1 and Mac-1 at the surface of the PMN undergo a conformational activation that increases their binding avidity.[144, 442] In addition, a large storage pool of Mac-1 is present inside the cell in at least two separate membrane compartments. This Mac-1 is translocated to the cell surface, where its expression rapidly is increased approximately 10-fold over baseline levels.[29, 34, 57, 72, 73] This second phase of adhesion mediated by integrin-ICAM interaction results in firm PMN adhesion to the endothelium and is required for transendothelial migration, or extravasation, of the PMNs.[29, 94, 398, 399] Platelet–endothelial cell adhesion molecule-1 (PECAM-1) on PMNs interacts with PECAM-1 on endothelial cells, further promoting transendothelial migration.[12] Cytokines such as TNF-α play some role in the activation of PMNs, but activation of PMNs for this second adhesive phase of recruitment occurs principally via chemoattractant agents, such as C5a, *N*-formyl bacterial oligopeptides, leukotrienes (e.g., LTB_4), and chemokines (e.g., IL-8), that may diffuse from the site of infection and bind to specific PMN receptors.[150, 319]

The receptors for most of these chemoattractants share a seven–transmembrane domain structure and similar intracellular G protein–dependent signaling mechanisms.[195, 319] They constitute the main sensory mechanisms of PMNs and are responsible for inducing increased adhesion and permitting spatial orientation and migration through the endothelium and extracellular matrix toward the source of a chemoattractant gradient. This migration of PMNs depends on the adhesive interactions described earlier, the ability of the cell to deform to permit passage between endothelial cells, the ability of the PMN to sense and orient itself within a chemoattractant gradient, and the active movement of adhesion sites in the plane of the membrane by the cytoskeletal contractile elements of the cell.[28, 29, 418] A scheme for PMN recruitment to infected tissue is presented in Figure 2–5. Molecular interactions that mediate PMN-endothelial adhesion during the recruitment process are depicted in greater detail in Figure 2–6.

Phagocytosis

After the migrating phagocyte reaches an infected site, its next task is to recognize and ingest, or phagocytose, the invading microbes. A process that greatly facilitates recognition and phagocytosis is opsonization, or coating of the microorganism with serum proteins, especially IgG antibodies and fragments of the third component of complement.[249, 427] PMNs and other phagocytes express specific receptors for the Fc portions of IgG and IgA and the two major opsonic fragments of C3, C3b, and iC3b.[55, 435] Phagocytosis can occur in the absence of opsonization, and some PMN surface molecules have been implicated in this process.[380] However, nonopsonic phagocytosis generally is inefficient in comparison to opsonin-dependent phagocytosis, and only the latter is addressed here.

OPSONIN RECEPTORS

CR1 is the main phagocyte receptor for C3b.[55, 172] It is expressed on most phagocytic cells, including PMNs. For circulating PMNs, only approximately 10 percent of the cells' CR1 is expressed on the cell surface. Most of the CR1 resides within the cells, stored in the membrane of small, irregular, low-density secretory vesicles.[54] When PMNs are activated by chemoattractants or other stimuli, these intracellular stores of CR1 are translocated rapidly to the cell surface.[54, 55, 57, 172] Internalization of the receptor also occurs,[54, 56] but the net effect of stimulation in the short term is to greatly increase the amount of CR1 available on the PMN surface for interaction with bound C3b on microorganisms.[54, 55] CR3 is the main PMN receptor for iC3b.[55] Like CR1, 90 percent or more of the cell content of CR3 is contained in intracellular membrane storage compartments that are translocated rapidly to the cell surface on cell activation.[26, 55, 57] A useful and interesting point to recall is that CR3 is identical to the adhesion-mediating integrin Mac-1 (CD11b/CD18).[26, 55] This integrin contains distinct extracellular binding domains for iC3b and its adhesion ligand ICAM-1.[26, 32] Thus, CR3 serves important functions relevant to both cell recruitment and phagocytosis. Although CR1 and CR3 clearly play important roles in phagocytosis, engagement of complement receptors alone results in relatively inefficient phagocytosis when compared with the combined effect of ligation of receptors for both complement fragments and opsonizing antibodies, especially IgG.[55, 249, 435]

Phagocytic cells may express as many as three different types of IgG Fc receptors, or FcγRs.[169, 435, 437] FcγRI (CD64) is a high-affinity receptor that is expressed mainly on mononuclear phagocytes, but PMNs exposed to IFN-γ may be induced to synthesize and express this receptor.[435] The two FcγRs ordinarily expressed on PMNs are FcγRII (CD32) and FcγRIII (CD16).[428, 435, 437] FcγRII is a 40-kd molecule conventionally anchored in the cell membrane. It exhibits polymorphisms that determine preferences for binding of certain IgG

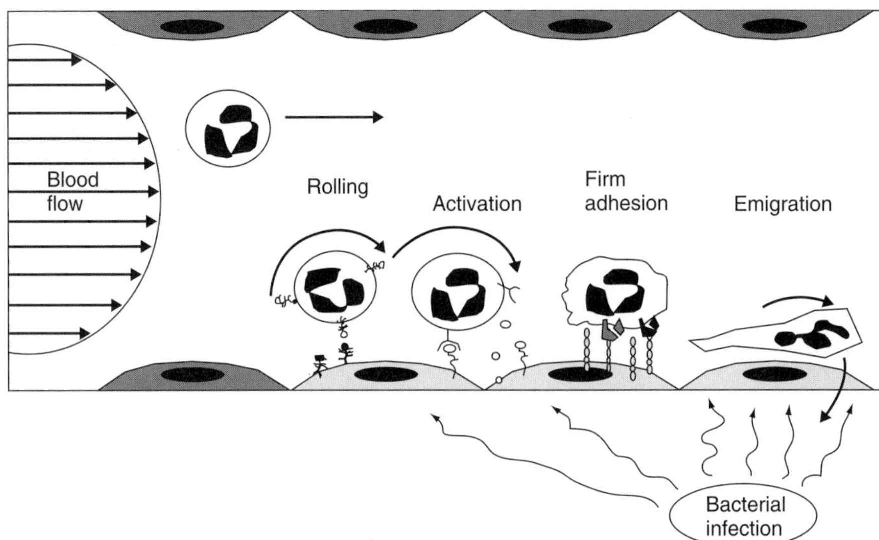

FIGURE 2–5 ■ Events that occur during leukocyte (PMN) recruitment to infected sites. Interactions between microorganisms in infected tissue and host cells and proteins result in elaboration of mediators that diffuse to the local microcirculation and stimulate endothelial cells. Such stimulation induces new surface expression of P-selectin and E-selectin, release of interleukin-8 and other chemokines, and new surface intercellular adhesion molecule-1 (ICAM-1). The endothelial selectins bind to constitutively expressed carbohydrate ligands on circulating PMNs and slow the passage of PMNs through the microvessels. As the PMNs slow further, they become activated by interaction with chemokines bound to complex glycopeptides on the endothelial surface. This activation of PMNs increases their expression and binding activity of the β_2 (CD11/CD18) integrins Mac-1 and LFA-1. Interactions between these integrins and ICAM-1 (and ICAM-2 in the case of LFA-1) lead to tight adhesion and spreading on the endothelial surface. These latter adhesive interactions also are used for migration between endothelial cells and through the subjacent extracellular matrix in response to the gradient of chemoattractants, such as C5a and bacterial peptides, released at the infected site. Homophilic interactions between the platelet–endothelial cell adhesion molecule PECAM-1 on PMNs and endothelial cells also appear to contribute to transendothelial migration.

subclasses.[435, 437] FcγRII appears to be important in direct activation of PMN oxidative burst activity.[428, 435] Its expression on PMNs is constitutive and relatively stable to proteolysis and most cell perturbations.[428, 430] FcγRIII is expressed on PMNs as a 50- to 70-kd glycolipid-anchored molecule, although it is anchored conventionally on NK cells and macrophages.[435] On the surface of circulating PMNs, it is approximately seven times more abundant than is FcγRII.[428]

In addition, an intracellular translocatable storage pool is present that contains approximately twice the amount of FcγRIII expressed on the surface of circulating PMNs.[430] When PMNs are activated, both shedding of this receptor from the cell surface and translocation of stored receptors from intracellular pools to the cell surface membrane occur.[430] FcγRIII appears to be more involved in binding of multivalent IgG than in direct generation of intracellular signals. However, binding of multivalent IgG ligand via FcγRIII appears to facilitate binding of ligand to FcγRII, thus suggesting a cooperative role for the former in producing cell activation by the latter.[379, 380, 428] FcγRIII also may play a more direct role in mediating IgG-dependent degranulation and phagocytosis.[379, 435]

Additional Fc receptors for IgA are expressed on phagocytes. Such receptors might be expected to play an important role at the mucosal surface, where IgA is prominent in secretions, although they also may play a role at other tissue sites. The best-characterized phagocyte IgA receptor, or FcαR, is the receptor for monomeric IgA (CD89).[313] This receptor is expressed on most classes of phagocytes and has been shown to promote phagocytosis and killing of IgA-opsonized bacteria.[236]

INGESTION

Engagement of phagocyte receptors with opsonins on microbes results in the local activation of cytoskeletal contractile elements, along with the simultaneous extension of pseudopods around the microbe and invagination of the membrane at the site of initial receptor engagement. This process in turn permits the ligation of additional opsonin-receptor pairs, with further cytoskeletal activation and eventual engulfment of the microbe. Engulfment is complete when the membrane compartment surrounding the organism is sealed to form a phagosome. This progressive engagement of opsonin-receptor pairs with eventual engulfment has been called the zipper hypothesis of phagocytosis[417] and is depicted schematically in Figure 2–7. One interesting exception to this conventional mode of ingestion of microorganisms is the progressive spiraling engulfment of *Legionella pneumophila* by mononuclear phagocytes, first described by Horwitz.[233]

Phagocyte Microbicidal Mechanisms

The PMN has a varied arsenal that it can use to kill microorganisms after they have been ingested. This intracellular killing usually occurs after the phagosome containing the ingested organism fuses with one or more types of lysosomal granules that carry these microbicidal weapons. The contents of the different types of PMN granules, which contain many of the PMN's microbicidal molecules either free within granules or anchored in the granular membrane, are listed in Table 2–1. The killing mechanisms of PMNs usually are categorized as either oxygen-dependent or oxygen-independent.[365] The oxygen-dependent microbicidal mechanisms of PMNs and other phagocytes depend fundamentally on the activity of a complex enzyme known as reduced nicotinamide adenine dinucleotide phosphate (NADPH) oxidase, the function of which is to convert molecular oxygen (O_2) into superoxide anion (O_2^-).[38, 107] This enzyme, in its active state, is assembled from six or more components that include a cytochrome (alpha and beta subunits, also designated gp91^{phox} and p22^{phox}, respectively), a flavoprotein, and a quinone, all of which are associated with the cell membrane and at least two cytoplasmic proteins (p47^{phox} and p67^{phox}; "phox" refers to phagocyte oxidase) and assemble with the membrane components to form the active enzyme complex.[37, 71, 107] The genetic absence or dysfunction of one or another of these oxidase subunits is what results in CGD of childhood (see later). The oxidative reactions that occur downstream from the formation of superoxide anion are summarized in Figure 2–8. Each of the oxidant products derived from these reactions exhibits some degree of microbicidal activity.[365] The spontaneous or catalyzed dismutation of superoxide anion results in the formation of hydrogen peroxide (H_2O_2), a compound commonly used in weak solutions to disinfect wounds. The subsequent interaction between H_2O_2 and a halide anion (usually Cl^-) in the presence of MPO results in the formation of hypochlorite (OCl^-), the basis of common household bleach and another compound with well-recognized microbicidal activity. These oxidants are relatively short-lived and, except for hypochlorite, have relatively weak microbicidal activity. However, hypochlorite interacts with ammonium (NH_4^+) and amino groups on peptides and proteins to form various chloramines (NH_3Cl, RNH_2Cl), which are much more stable compounds with potent microbicidal activity.[209] Additional reactions

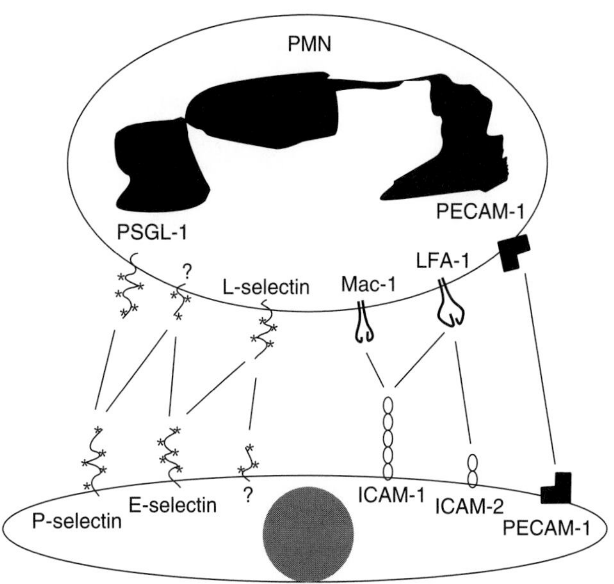

FIGURE 2–6 ■ Molecular interactions that mediate polymorphonuclear leukocyte (PMN)-endothelial adhesion. The selectins P-selectin and E-selectin on endothelium and L-selectin on leukocytes bind to oligosaccharide moieties, including sialyl Lewis X (sLeX), that decorate the selectins and other glycoproteins on the opposite cell, such as P-selectin glycoprotein ligand-1 (PSGL-1) on leukocytes. These interactions mediate the early adhesive phase of leukocyte recruitment. The β_2 integrins macrophage antigen-1 (Mac-1) (CD11b/CD18) and lymphocyte function-associated antigen-1 (LFA-1) (CD11a/CD18) on PMNs both bind intercellular adhesion molecule-1 (ICAM-1) on endothelial cells. LFA-1 also can bind ICAM-2, which is expressed constitutively on endothelium. Platelet–endothelial cell adhesion molecule-1 (PECAM-1) molecules interact with each other and are expressed on both PMNs and endothelial cells.

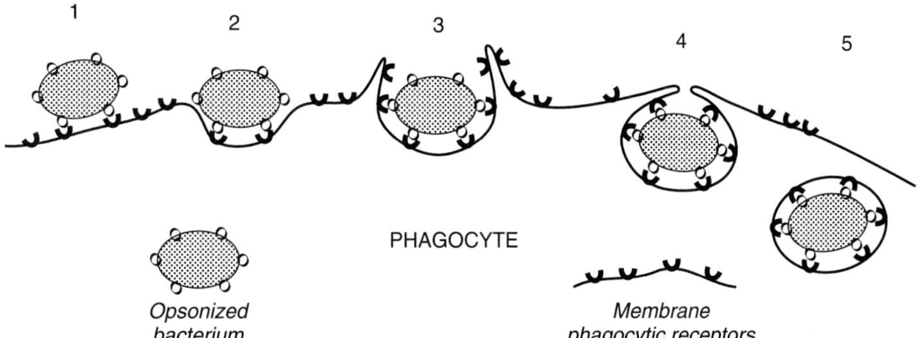

FIGURE 2–7 ■ Opsonin/receptor-mediated phagocytosis. Phagocytes such as PMNs that reach the site of bacterial infection are activated for enhanced recognition, attachment, and ingestion of bacteria that have been coated with opsonic C3 fragments, IgG, or both via specific receptors on the PMN surface. Binding of opsonized bacteria to opsonin receptors (1) activates contractile elements of the cytoskeleton to produce an invagination at the initial site of attachment (2), with subsequent extension of membrane pseudopods around the organism (3). This process, in turn, allows engagement of additional opsonin-receptor pairs as the organism becomes engulfed (4). Finally, the plasma membrane fuses completely around the bacterium to create a phagosome (5), which soon will fuse with lysosomal granules and expose the bacterium to the microbicidal components of the phagocyte.

TABLE 2–1 ■ STORED CONTENTS OF NEUTROPHIL GRANULES AND VESICLES

Primary (Azurophilic) Granules	Secondary (Specific) Granules[a]	Tertiary Granules[b]	Secretory Vesicles[c]
Elastase	Lactoferrin	Gelatinase	Alkaline phosphatase
Cathepsin G	Vitamin B_{12}-binding protein		
Myeloperoxidase	Lysozyme		
Defensins	Gelatinase		
Bactericidal/permeability-increasing protein			
"p15s"			
Other cationic proteins			
Lysozyme			

Selected membrane-bound proteins in intracellular granules and vesicles: f-met-leu-phe receptor[a,b,c]
type 1 complement receptor (CR1)[c]
CD11b/CD18 (CR3, Mac-1)[a,b,c]
cytochrome b_{558}[a,b,c]
type III Fcγ receptor (CD16)[?,c]

include a direct interaction between superoxide anion and H_2O_2 in the presence of catalytic iron to form hydroxyl radical (·OH) in the Haber-Weiss reaction.[365] Thus, PMNs can generate a diverse array of oxidant free radicals, many of which have potent antimicrobial activity.

The major sources of oxygen-independent microbicidal activity in PMNs are a group of proteins and peptides stored mainly within the primary (azurophilic) granules. Lysozyme is contained in both the primary and the secondary (specific) granules of PMNs.[411] It cleaves important carbohydrate linkages in the peptidoglycan structures of bacterial cell walls. The microbicidal activity of lysozyme is greatest when it is in concert with the complement MAC.[249] The primary granules contain several cationic proteins that exhibit well-documented microbicidal activity. A 59-kd protein, bactericidal/permeability-increasing protein, is active against only gram-negative bacteria.[453] Its action appears to require hydrophobic insertion of one segment of the protein into the bacterial outer membrane, which results in increased permeability and death of the organism. A group of arginine- and cysteine-rich 3- to 4-kd peptides known as defensins display microbicidal action against a wide range of pathogenic organisms, including both gram-negative and gram-positive bacteria, fungi, chlamydiae, and enveloped viruses.[190] Other groups of related microbicidal peptides or proteins have been identified in PMNs and include a group called p15s, a 37-kd cationic protein, and a class of propeptides called cathelicidins.[187, 189, 190, 280, 284] Although not all the mechanisms of these proteins and peptides have been elucidated fully, evidence suggests that some of them may interact with each other synergistically and markedly increase overall microbicidal activity.[283]

1. $2O_2 + NADPH \xrightarrow{\text{NADPH oxidase}} 2O_2^- + NADP^+ + H^+$

2. $2O_2^- + 2H^+ \xrightarrow[\text{catalyzed by dismutase}]{\text{Spontaneous or}} H_2O_2 + O_2$

3. $H_2O_2 + H^+ + Cl^- \xrightarrow{\text{Myeloperoxidase}} H^+ + OCl^- + H_2O$

4. $H^+ + OCl^- + RNH_2 \longrightarrow RNHCl + H_2O$

FIGURE 2–8 ■ Major reactions in the evolution of oxygen-dependent polymorphonuclear leukocyte microbicidal activity. The conversion of molecular oxygen to superoxide anion (O_2^-) by reduced nicotinamide adenine dinucleotide phosphate (NADPH) oxidase is the initial event in the sequence of the production of antimicrobial oxidants. Shown in order are the subsequent reactions for the production of hydrogen peroxide (H_2O_2), hypochlorite (OCl^-), and chloramines (RNH_2Cl).

ADDITIONAL IMPORTANT COMPONENTS OF INNATE IMMUNITY

Mononuclear Phagocytes and Toll-like Receptors

Mononuclear phagocytes, including circulating monocytes and tissue macrophages, and other phagocytic cells express a family of receptors that is highly homologous to the *Drosophila* receptor called Toll.[302] These receptors mediate a phylogenetically primitive, nonclonal mechanism of pathogen recognition based on binding to structurally conserved pathogen-associated molecular patterns, or PAMPs.[9, 467] Microbial components that can bind to human Toll-like receptors (TLRs) include gram-negative lipopolysaccharides, bacterial lipoproteins, lipoteichoic acids of gram-positive bacteria, bacterial cell wall peptidoglycans, and possibly unmethylated CpG dinucleotide motifs.[9] Binding of several types of these PAMPs also involves concomitant interaction with CD14 on the phagocytic cell surface. Signaling via TLRs occurs via a pathway that activates the important nuclear transcription factor NF-κB, which controls the genes for numerous proinflammatory products, including IL-1, IL-6, and IL-8. This mechanism serves as a means by which the host can mobilize an important form of innate immunity to mount an acute inflammatory response to bacterial pathogens independent of the specific antigen recognition mechanisms of adaptive immunity.[9, 467] Of added interest is that activation of TLRs also can induce expression of the co-stimulatory molecule B7 on APCs, which is required for activation of naive T cells.[302]

Antimicrobial Peptides of Epithelial Cells

The epithelial cells that line many of the hollow viscera in humans and other vertebrates serve both as a mechanical barrier to the invasion of microbial pathogens and as a source of important antimicrobial peptides that appear to play a significant role in local host defenses, especially in the respiratory and intestinal tracts. Distinct from the α-defensins stored in the primary granules of neutrophils, the human β-defensins HBD-1 and HBD-2 are not stored in granules but are released locally after synthesis by intestinal or airway epithelial cells, a process that can be stimulated by certain bacteria and cytokines such as TNF-α.[189, 190] Some epithelial cells also may secrete lysozyme, another antimicrobial product also found in neutrophil granules. Inactivation of defensins in the airway lumen in cystic fibrosis by high local salt concentrations has been hypothesized as a mechanism that permits initial colonization of the airways by *Pseudomonas* (see also later).[401]

CYTOKINES AND RELATED MEDIATORS THAT REGULATE HOST RESPONSES

A heterogeneous group of soluble small polypeptide or glycoprotein mediators, often collectively called cytokines, form part of a complex network that helps regulate the immune and inflammatory responses. Included in this group of mediators, whose molecular weight ranges from approximately 8 to 45 kd, are the interleukins, interferons, growth factors, and chemokines. Cells of the immune system, as well as many other cell types in the host, may release cytokines, respond to cytokines via specific cytokine receptors, or both, depending on the specific molecule in question. A list of cytokines and related molecules that play a role in immune function, along with selected characteristics, is provided in Table 2–2.[267, 285, 338, 349] New cytokines are being discovered and characterized regularly, and the range of sources and effects of cytokines and their interrelationships are of such complexity that they cannot be addressed here in great detail. Several excellent reviews are available,[131, 287, 367] and the use of cytokines as immunomodulating agents is discussed in Chapter 241. Two specific cytokines, IL-1 and TNF-α, are of such broad and fundamental importance in acute host responses to infection that they warrant specific discussion here.

IL-1 and TNF-α are small polypeptides, each with a molecular weight of approximately 17 kd, that exhibit a broad range of effects on immunologic responses, inflammation, metabolism, and hematopoiesis.[61, 338] Many of the well-characterized inflammatory and systemic responses of mammalian hosts to bacterial endotoxin or lipopolysaccharide are mediated by IL-1 and TNF-α.[61, 338] IL-1 has been known by various names in the past but originally was described as "endogenous pyrogen," which referred to its ability to produce fever in experimental animals.[338] TNF-α, originally named cachectin after the wasting syndrome that it produced when injected chronically in mice, induces some of the same effects produced by IL-1.[61, 338] Many of the physiologic changes associated with gram-negative sepsis can be reproduced by injecting experimental animals with these cytokines in the absence of microorganisms. Depending on

TABLE 2–2 ■ FEATURES OF SELECTED HUMAN CYTOKINES AND GROWTH FACTORS

	Main Cellular Sources	Biologic Effects
IL-1	Mo, TL, BL, NK, PMN, others	Broad range of cellular activation in inflammatory and immune responses
IL-2	TL, BL, NK	TL, BL proliferation and activation; enhances TL and NK cytotoxicity
IL-3	TL	General stimulation of hematopoiesis
IL-4	TL, BL, Mast, Mo	TL, BL proliferation; BL isotype switching; stimulates IgE synthesis; enhances MHC class II expression
IL-5	TL	Stimulation of Eo production
IL-6	TL, BL, Mo	Broad inflammatory activity; stimulates BL differentiation and megakaryocyte production
IL-7	Marrow and thymus stromal cells	TL, BL growth and differentiation
IL-8	Mac, Mo, Endo, Epi, PMN, Eo	Activation and chemotaxis of PMN, Eo
IL-9	TL	Mast cell growth and differentiation; growth of activated TL
IL-10	TL, BL, Mast, Mac	Broad anti-inflammatory actions; inhibits synthesis of several other cytokines (TNF, IL-2, IL-3, IFN-γ)
IL-11	Marrow stromal cells	General stimulation of hematopoiesis; BL growth and differentiation
IL-12	BL, Mo	Stimulation of TL growth; induction of IFN-γ production; enhancement of TL and NK cytotoxicity
IL-13	TL	BL proliferation and isotype switching; enhances MHC class II expression; inhibits production of cytokines by Mac
IL-14	TL, malignant BL	Induces BL growth
IL-15	Epi, Endo, Mo, Mac, Marrow stromal cells	Enhances NK growth, development, function; enhances TL growth/migration
IL-17	TL	Enhances TL growth; induces Mac cytokine release
IL-18	Kupffer cells, Epi, spleen, Mac	Promotes TL, BL, NK cytokine release; promotes TL, BL cytotoxicity
IFN-α	Mo, TL	Interference with viral replication; increases MHC class I expression
IFN-β	Epi, Fibro	Similar to IFN-α
IFN-γ	TL, NK	Similar to IFN-α, IFN-β; stimulates Mac inflammatory functions
TNF-α	Mo, Mac, TL, NK	Broad inflammatory effects; fever; cachexia; stimulates catabolism; activation of leukocytes and Endo
GM-CSF	TL, BL, Mo, PMN, Eo, Fibro, Mast, Endo	Growth of PMN, Eo, Mo, and Mac precursors; enhances leukocyte function
G-CSF	Mo, Epi, Fibro	Enhances production and function of granulocytes
M-CSF	Mo, TL, BL, Endo, Fibro	Promotes Mo production; stimulates Mo and Mac function

BL, B lymphocyte; Endo, endothelial cell; Eo, eosinophil; Epi, epithelial cell; Fibro, fibroblast; GM-CSF, granulocyte-macrophage colony-stimulating factor; IFN, interferon; IL, interleukin; Mac, macrophage; Mast, mast cell; MHC, major histocompatibility complex; Mo, monocyte; NK, natural killer cell; PMN, polymorphonuclear leukocyte; TL, T lymphocyte; TNF, tumor necrosis factor.

the doses injected, these effects may include fever, hypotension, and either neutrophilia or leukopenia.[61, 338] Both IL-1 and TNF-α, as well as lipopolysaccharide itself, stimulate inflammatory responses in infected tissue by inducing the expression of adhesion molecules on both endothelial cells and leukocytes; stimulating recruitment of leukocytes by inducing release of the chemokine IL-8; and, in the case of TNF-α, activating granulocytes for phagocytosis, degranulation, and oxidative burst activity.[61, 148] For some systemic actions, notably the production of hemodynamic shock, IL-1 and TNF-α are synergistic. Both IL-1 and TNF-α induce the production of IL-6, a somewhat less potent cytokine that exhibits some of the actions of IL-1 and TNF-α.[338]

IL-1 and TNF-α act on a wide range of cell types via specific receptors.[338] The importance of the effects mediated by IL-1 and TNF-α in the pathophysiology of septic shock has prompted much active research aimed at blocking their effects to reduce morbidity and mortality. Naturally occurring soluble antagonists of IL-1 and TNF-α include IL-1 receptor antagonist (IL-1ra) and soluble TNF-α receptor (sTNF-αR). Monoclonal antibodies against TNF-α have shown promise in vitro and in animal models of septic shock.[1, 41, 180, 338] However, one of the main impediments to the clinical success of such agents to date is that the processes that they inhibit often are well under way by the time that treatment can be initiated, and they are far more effective at preventing the effects of cytokines than reversing them. Additionally, because cytokines have beneficial effects in the host response, as well as pathologic effects, clearly discerning the overall effects of inhibiting their actions may be difficult.[338] More recent attempts to address the issue of the timing of intervention have been directed at the intracellular signaling mechanisms activated through the TNF-α receptor. One example is the administration of lipophilic inhibitors of protein tyrosine kinases, enzymes that propagate cellular signals via TNF-α receptors.[440] In experimental animals, one of these agents was found to enhance survival, even when the agent was administered 2 hours after systemic injection of endotoxin, whereas other strategies only showed benefit if used before or simultaneous with the administration of endotoxin.[440] The role of TNF-α and IL-1 in the inflammatory response in bacterial meningitis has prompted investigations aimed at better understanding and modifying this response, which appears to be responsible for some of the important sequelae of this disease.[447]

A specialized group of small cytokine-like polypeptides, chemokines, plays an increasingly complex role in the immune response as cellular activators that induce directed migration, mainly of immune and inflammatory cells. Chemokines all share the feature of being ligands for G protein–coupled, seven–transmembrane segment receptors.[195, 319, 372] Chemokines have been classified into four groups based on the motif displayed by the first two cysteine residues, and a corresponding set of four chemokine receptor families exists. Each of the CXC chemokines binds to one or more of the CXCRs (CXCR1 to CXCR5). Examples of CXC chemokines include IL-8 and Gro-α. Similarly, CC chemokines, such as MIP-1α, RANTES, and eotaxin-1 and eotaxin-2, bind to one or more of the CCRs (CCR1 to CCR9). A CX3C chemokine, fractalkine, or neurotaxin, binds to CX3CR1, currently the only receptor in its family. Similarly, lymphotaxin binds uniquely to XCR1. A new nomenclature has been proposed to designate each of the chemokines as a numbered ligand for its respective receptor family. Gro-α would become CXC ligand (L)-1 (CXCL-1), and IL-8 would become CXCL-8. Similarly, RANTES would become CCL-5.[372]

Clinical Conditions Associated with Deficient Host Responses to Infection

IMMATURE HOST RESPONSES OF THE NEWBORN INFANT

A mild febrile respiratory illness in a 10-month-old infant might prompt little more than gentle reassurance over the telephone from the child's pediatrician. However, if the patient is an infant in the first few weeks of life, the physician's response is likely to include an evaluation for systemic bacterial infection and administration of parenteral antibiotics in the hospital until a serious infection can be ruled out.[256] Similarly, the appearance of a few cutaneous perioral vesicles characteristic of herpes simplex virus in an older infant usually evokes little concern and no specific treatment. In contrast, the same condition in the first 3 weeks of life is likely to lead to prolonged hospitalization for administration of antiviral therapy because of the risk of development of serious central nervous system or disseminated infection.[457] Newborn infants are known to be much more susceptible to serious disease from many types of organisms than are older children and adults. This predisposition to infection is even more profound in infants born prematurely.[285] The basis for this special vulnerability of the neonate is complex and encompasses all arms of the immune system. It is of such importance that the clinical approach to infection in infants during the first month of life usually is far more aggressive than that in older children.

Cell-Mediated Immunity

Antigen presentation per se, via the mechanisms discussed earlier, appears to be relatively intact in a newborn infant. Expression of class I and class II MHC molecules has been documented in a broad range of fetal tissues by 12 weeks' gestation,[230, 337] and levels of expression are sufficient to mediate normal MHC class II–restricted antigen presentation by neonatal monocytes to maternal or paternal $CD4^+$ T cells, as well as induce vigorous rejection of allogeneic fetal tissue by $CD8^+$ cytotoxic T cells.[217, 229]

By approximately 20 weeks' gestation, the fetal repertoire of the diversity of TCRs has developed fully.[436] At the time of birth, although most basic functions of cell-mediated immunity are present, a high proportion of immature T cells, which can be identified by their co-expression of CD4 and CD8, is present in the peripheral circulation.[285] This phenotype typifies type II thymocytes, which usually are not found in the periphery in older persons.

Neonatal T cells appear to be relatively deficient in most of their major functions, including $CD8^+$ T-cell–mediated cytotoxicity, delayed hypersensitivity, and T-cell help for B-cell differentiation.[285] Diminished cytokine production by neonatal T cells probably accounts for much of this deficiency.[285] In turn, the relatively naive status of most neonatal T cells may account for the reduced cytokine production because memory T cells are much more efficient in all these functions.[285]

B Cells and Antibody

B CELLS

Pre-B cells are found in the fetal liver and omentum by 8 weeks' and in the fetal bone marrow by 13 weeks' gestation.[191, 285, 405] Pre-B cells with surface IgM have been detected as early as 10 weeks' gestation. After 30 weeks' gestation and delivery, pre-B cells are seen only in the bone marrow. Mature

B cells are present in the circulation by the 11th week of gestation and have reached adult levels in the bone marrow, blood, and spleen by the 22nd week of gestation.[136, 191, 405]

Fetal B cells express only IgM, whereas most adult B cells express both IgM and IgD. Neonatal B cells may express one of three immunoglobulin isotypes, IgG, IgA, or IgM, in combination with IgD on their surfaces.[191, 210] Data from experiments in mice suggest that exposing B cells with surface IgM, but not IgD, to antigens leads to anergy, or B-cell inactivation. Researchers have speculated that the absence of surface IgD on fetal B cells contributes to the induction of tolerance to self and, possibly, to maternal antigens in utero. In addition, the fetus has a higher proportion of the functionally immature $CD5^+$, or B1, cells than do adults. These cells produce autoantibodies and thus may play a role in the development of tolerance to self antigens, maternal antigens, or both.

Although germinal centers are not present in lymphoid tissue at birth, they begin to develop in the first few months of life, concomitant with the infant's exposure to antigens.[426] Despite conflicting in vitro data, neonatal T-cell help for B cells probably is comparable to that of adult T cells, as reflected by the excellent T-dependent antibody response of the newborn to immunization with protein antigens such as tetanus toxoid.[215] However, neonatal T-cell help is associated with the secretion of IgM alone, not other isotypes, possibly because neonatal T cells have diminished production of the cytokines critical for promoting isotype switching. Indeed, the addition of cytokines such as IL-2, IL-4, and IL-6 helps overcome neonatal B-cell dysfunction in vitro.[285] In contrast to adult B cells, neonatal B cells cannot respond to polysaccharides without T-cell help.

ANTIBODY

Maternal IgG accounts for the vast majority of the newborn's immunoglobulin because almost none is made by a healthy fetus and IgG is the only isotype of maternal immunoglobulin that crosses the placenta.[261, 296] Maternal transport of IgG can be detected as early as 8 weeks' gestation, and the newborn's IgG level is directly proportional to gestational age, with the level reaching 100 mg/dL by 17 to 20 weeks' gestation and 50 percent of the maternal level by 30 weeks' gestation[44, 285] (Fig. 2–9). By term, the infant has 5 to 10 percent more IgG than the mother does because maternal antibody is transported not only passively but also actively via trophoblast Fc receptors.[437] Trophoblast Fc receptors have higher affinity for IgG1 and IgG3 than for IgG2 and IgG4, so more of those subclasses are transported from the mother.[161, 279] Thus, newborns may have relatively higher levels of IgG1 and IgG3 than IgG2 and IgG4 than adults do, and term newborns' IgG1 levels may be higher than their mothers'.

By around 2 months of chronologic age, approximately one half of a term infant's quantitative IgG is of maternal and one half is of infant origin. The physiologic nadir of IgG in all infants occurs at approximately 3 to 4 months of age and ranges from less than 100 mg/dL in very low-birth-weight preterm infants to approximately 400 mg/dL in term infants[44, 416] (see Fig. 2–9 and Table 2–3). Maternal IgG essentially is gone by the age of approximately 12 months, at which time infant levels are approximately 60 percent of adult levels. Production of IgG1 and IgG3 matures more rapidly than does that of IgG2 and IgG4; adult levels of IgG1 and IgG3 are attained by approximately 8 years of age, versus 10 and 12 years of age for IgG2 and IgG4.[333]

Little IgM, IgA, IgE, or IgD is produced by the healthy fetus, and none is transported from the mother.[285] The presence of IgM levels greater than 20 mg/dL at birth suggests an intrauterine infection. Serum IgA levels at birth in both preterm and term infants usually are less than 5 mg/dL and consist of both IgA1 and IgA2. Secretory IgA is not detectable until after birth but generally is present within the first few weeks of life. IgM and IgA reach approximately 60 and 20 percent of adult levels, respectively, by the time the infant reaches 1 year of age (see Fig. 2–9). Secretory IgA reaches adult levels by the time children are 6 to 8 years of age.[285]

The IgG transferred from the mother to the fetus has been demonstrated to protect the newborn from many infectious agents, including viruses such as varicella, polio, measles, mumps, and rubella and bacteria such as tetanus, diphtheria, *H. influenzae* type b, and group

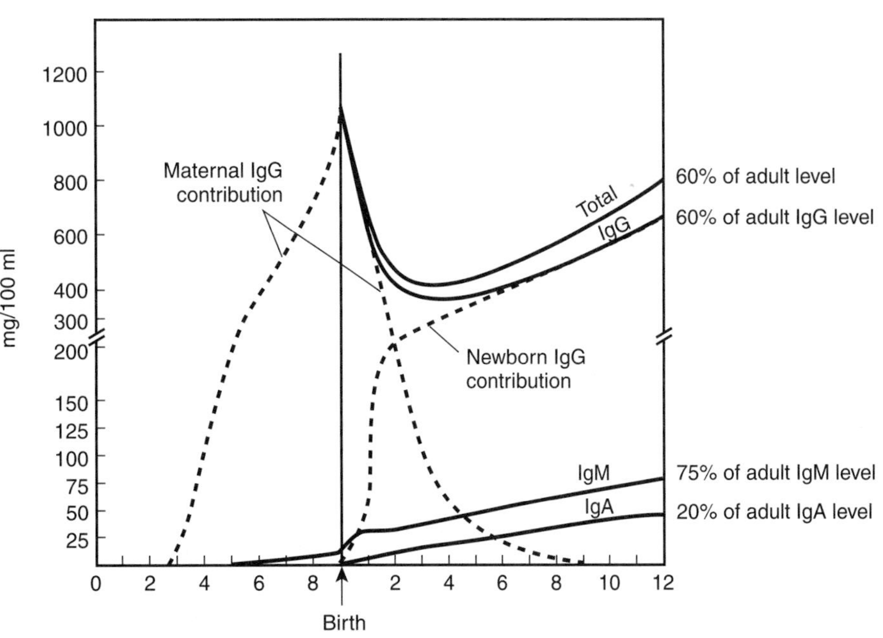

FIGURE 2–9 ■ Immunoglobulin (IgG, IgM, and IgA) levels in the fetus and infant in the first year of life. The IgG of the fetus and newborn infant is solely of maternal origin. Maternal IgG disappears by the time the infant is 9 months of age, by which time endogenous synthesis of IgG by the infant is well established. The IgM and IgA of the neonate are synthesized entirely endogenously, for maternal IgM and IgA do not cross the placenta. (After Braun, J., and Stiehm, E. R.: The B-lymphocyte system. *In* Stiehm, E. R. [ed.]: Immunologic Disorders in Infants and Children. 4th ed. Philadelphia, W. B. Saunders, 1996, p. 67.)

TABLE 2–3 ■ LEVELS OF IMMUNOGLOBULINS IN SERA OF NORMAL SUBJECTS, BY AGE

Age (mo)	IgG (mg/dL)	IgG (mg/dL)	IgG (mg/dL)	Total Immunoglobulin (mg/dL)
Newborn	1031 ± 200*	11 ± 5	2 ± 3	1044 ± 201
1-3	430 ± 119	30 ± 11	21 ± 13	481 ± 127
4-6	427 ± 186	43 ± 17	28 ± 18	498 ± 204
7-12	661 ± 219	54 ± 23	37 ± 18	752 ± 242
13-14	762 ± 209	58 ± 23	50 ± 24	870 ± 258
25-36	892 ± 183	61 ± 19	71 ± 37	1024 ± 205

*Values were derived from measurements made in 296 children and 30 adults. Levels were determined by the radial diffusion plate method using specific rabbit antisera to human immunoglobulins. Values are ± 1 SD.

Modified from Stiehm, E.R., and Fudenberg, H.H.: Serum levels of immune globulins in health and disease: A survey. Pediatrics *37*:715–727, 1966. Copyright American Academy of Pediatrics, 1966.

B *Streptococcus*.[115] However, the infant is not protected by the mother if she does not have specific IgG antibody, even if she is immune to a given organism. For example, the mother may have low or absent levels of circulating IgG antibody but good memory B cells capable of mounting a booster response. In this case, the mother is protected, but she cannot transfer protection to her infant. Similarly, because no IgM is transferred to the fetus, the mother cannot defend her newborn effectively against many gram-negative enteric organisms, even if she is immune.[118, 402]

The concept of passive transfer of protective IgG is being used to develop vaccines for maternal immunization before or during pregnancy so that passive transfer of vaccine-induced antibody will result in protection during the neonatal period. Examples of organisms for which such strategies are being investigated include group B *Streptococcus, H. influenzae* type b, meningococcus, pneumococcus, rotavirus, and respiratory syncytial virus.[43, 164, 241]

Researchers have documented that the fetus can respond to antigenic stimulation in the form of maternal immunization with tetanus toxoid vaccine and be primed for a secondary antibody response to repeat immunization after birth.[196, 197] Some, but not all, fetuses near term also can make IgM and IgA antibody to organisms such as the TORCH (toxoplasmosis, rubella, cytomegalovirus, herpes) agents.[162, 321] The amount of fetal antibody produced in response to intrauterine antigenic stimulation is proportional to gestational age.[137, 414]

The most hypervariable region of the immunoglobulin molecule, CDR3 ($>10^{14}$ peptides in adults), is shorter in the fetus than in adults. The result is that the diversity of the repertoire of fetal B-cell clones with different antigenic specificity is decreased markedly.[285] In the neonatal period, the repertoire for IgM and IgA, but not IgG, is more diverse because of the presence of more V, D, and J genes and longer CDR3 regions.[285]

Maternal antibody inhibits the ability of infants to respond to vaccines against certain organisms such as measles, but it does not prevent them from mounting protective immune responses to most normal childhood vaccine antigens, such as tetanus, diphtheria, polio, hepatitis B, and *H. influenzae* type b.[116] In general, neonates have protective responses to T-dependent antigens, even though they may produce less antibody to some antigens than do older infants and adults.[13, 132, 139, 177, 402, 403]

A newborn infant's response to TI-1 antigens is slightly decreased, and the response to TI-2 antigens is poor.[199] The antibody response to most TI-2 antigens, including the polysaccharide capsules of group B streptococci, pneumococci, and *H. influenzae* type b, is not mature until the infant is 18 to 24 months of age, although infants as young as 3 months can respond to group A meningococcal polysaccharide.[400] In contrast, in the first few weeks of life, infants mount excellent antibody responses to T-independent polysaccharide antigens that have been rendered T-dependent by covalent conjugation of the polysaccharide to a protein carrier (e.g., *H. influenzae* type b).[7]

Investigators have proposed that immunologic tolerance may be induced in infants by early exposure to some antigens. The subject remains controversial, but some data suggest that immunization to pertussis in the newborn period results in lower levels of antibody to subsequent doses of vaccine than does initial immunization at 1 month of age.[46, 352] No evidence, however, suggests that tolerance is induced by the administration of tetanus, diphtheria, or oral polio vaccines in the newborn period.[139, 385]

The response of premature infants to most routine childhood vaccines, including diphtheria, tetanus, pertussis, and oral and inactivated polio, is comparable to that of 2-month-old term infants.[8, 60, 98, 285, 403] Well documented, however, is that premature infants do not respond as well to hepatitis B vaccine for reasons that are unclear.[115, 273]

The data are conflicting, but small-for-gestational-age infants may have somewhat lower total levels of IgG at birth than do normally grown newborns,[161, 393, 465] possibly because of placental insufficiency. Their response to most routine vaccines is good, but it may be slightly decreased to inactivated polio vaccine.[101]

Complement

Complement proteins do not cross the placenta, but studies of mothers with congenital complement component deficiencies and mother-infant pairs discordant for variants of individual components, as well as studies of fetal tissues, have provided evidence for fetal synthesis of complement beginning as early as 5½ weeks' gestation. Most complement proteins are present by 10 weeks' gestation.[114, 260] Levels of complement activity and of individual complement components vary significantly among infants, but in general, the classical pathway hemolytic activity of term neonates ranges from 50 to 80 percent of maternal values (Table 2–4). Because serum complement levels are elevated during pregnancy, term neonates' levels are approximately 60 to 90 percent of normal adult values.[159, 246, 466] Alternative pathway hemolytic activity is decreased more consistently than is classical pathway activity and ranges from approximately 50 to 70 percent of normal adult values at term[6, 157, 329, 393] (see Table 2–4). Complement activity usually is lower in premature than in term infants, with the hemolytic activity of both pathways, as well as serum levels of most complement proteins, generally corresponding directly with gestational

TABLE 2–4 ■ SUMMARY OF PUBLISHED COMPLEMENT LEVELS IN NEONATES

Complement Component	Mean Percentage of Adult Levels	
	Term Neonate	Preterm Neonate
CH_{50}	56-90 (4)*	45-71 (3)
AP_{50}	49-65 (3)	40-51 (2)
Clq	65-90 (3)	27-58 (2)
C4	60-100 (4)	42-91 (3)
C2	76-100 (2)	96 (1)
C3	60-100 (5)	39-78 (4)
C5	75 (1)	—
C6	47 (1)	—
C7	67 (1)	—
C8	20 (1)	—
C9	<20 (2)	—
B	35-59 (8)	36-50 (3)
P	33-71 (5)	13-65 (2)
H	61 (1)	—
C3bi	55 (1)	—

*Number of studies.
Data from Lewis, D.B., and Wilson, C.B.: Developmental immunology and role of host defenses in neonatal susceptibility to infection. *In* Remington, J.S., and Klein, J.O. (eds.): Infectious Diseases of the Fetus and Newborn Infant. 4th ed. Philadelphia, W.B. Saunders, 1995, p. 65.

age.[157] However, complement levels are not proportional to weight in term infants. Small-for-gestational-age infants have complement levels comparable to those of babies of the same gestational age who have grown appropriately.[329, 393]

Some studies have found a correlation between infection and complement levels in the newborn period. One study from Japan demonstrated higher total serum hemolytic complement (CH_{50}) and Clq (C4 and C3) levels in infants of less than 34 weeks' gestation with amnionitis than in those without amnionitis.[95] Other studies have revealed lower complement levels in infected newborns as a result of increased complement activation.[157, 159]

The hemolytic activities of both the classical and the alternative pathways rise rapidly and reach adult levels by 3 to 6 and 6 to 18 months of age, respectively.

In addition to hemolytic activity, complement-mediated opsonic and bactericidal activity is decreased in newborn sera and generally correlates with C3 and factor B levels.[159] Studies of the opsonic and bactericidal activity of newborn sera have been reviewed in detail elsewhere.[159, 246, 247, 285] Levels of individual complement proteins do not always correlate with their functional activity.[192, 235] Zach and Hostetter[466] reported not only that total C3 levels were decreased as measured by enzyme-linked immunosorbent assay but also that C3 thioester reactivity was decreased and that it correlated with gestational age. Because the opsonic function of C3 is mediated by its thioester, such a defect may contribute to the newborn's deficiency in functional complement activity.

Although complement levels and activity are decreased substantially in most newborn infants, these abnormalities are relatively mild in comparison to those seen in hereditary complement deficiencies, and they do not predispose necessarily to the development of infection. For example, several studies have demonstrated that maternally derived type-specific antibodies are sufficient to overcome relative deficiencies in complement and other host defenses in the newborn. This phenomenon underscores the need to verify the information derived from in vitro studies with clinical observations before drawing firm conclusions about the importance of individual host defense mechanisms in protection against specific pathogens.

Phagocytes

The newborn infant exhibits both quantitative and qualitative deficits in phagocytic defense. Although the number of circulating PMNs usually does not differ greatly from those in older children and adults, under conditions of stress, including systemic infection, the release of marrow reserves of PMNs is impaired markedly.[104] In fact, whereas the ratio of marrow neutrophil reserves to circulating cells in older persons is nearly 15:1, in the newborn infant this ratio is between 2:1 and 3:1.[104, 294] Thus, neutropenia is more likely to develop during severe systemic infections in the newborn than in older children and adults.[103] The resulting deficiency in PMNs available for delivery to infected sites under conditions of stress is a stark disadvantage for the neonate in containing bacterial and fungal infections. Distinct from this quantitative deficiency in marrow reserves of PMNs are important functional impairments that also are fundamental in understanding neonatal phagocytic defenses.

The most important and best-documented functional impairments in neonatal PMNs are related to defective adherence and chemotaxis.[24–26, 265, 306] Many specific structural, functional, and biochemical abnormalities, any of which may contribute to the overall impairment in adhesion and migration of these cells, have been documented.[226] Impaired adhesion of neonatal PMNs to endothelial cells and other biologic substrates has been linked to deficiencies in expression or function of the β_2 integrins Mac-1 (CD11b/CD18) and LFA-1 (CD11a/CD18).[4, 26, 29, 84, 250, 300]

The most evident deficiency in this regard is the diminished level of surface expression of Mac-1 on stimulated neonatal PMNs, although expression on resting PMNs is similar to that in adults.[84, 250] The deficiency in stimulated Mac-1 surface expression can be explained principally by the observation that the total cell content of Mac-1 in PMNs from term neonates is only approximately 60 percent of that in adult PMNs.[4] The total PMN content of Mac-1 at the time of birth is related directly to gestational age, and PMNs from very early premature infants (less than 30 weeks' gestation) may contain less than 20 percent of the Mac-1 content of adult PMNs.[300] The PMN content of LFA-1, which is normal at term, appears to be reduced in infants born before 35 weeks' gestation.[300] Thus, the neonatal defect in PMN adherence and migration appears to be even more profound in very premature neonates.

Several other defects in neonatal PMNs that are likely to influence chemotaxis have been documented and include defective redistribution of surface adhesion sites,[24] impaired uropod formation during stimulated shape change,[25] reduced cell deformability,[307] impaired microtubule assembly,[25, 30] deficient F-actin polymerization,[212, 228, 376] reduced lactoferrin content and release,[23] reduced ability to induce membrane depolarization and intracellular calcium ion transients,[377] and impaired uptake of glucose during stimulation by chemoattractants.[5] The relative importance of each of these individual impairments to the overall deficiency in chemotaxis by neonatal PMNs remains to be determined.

Evidence suggests that the number and binding efficiency of receptors for chemoattractants, including C5a and synthetic bacterial peptides such as the formyl peptide *N*-f-met-leu-phe, are normal.[24, 377, 419] Phagocytosis and the microbicidal activity of neonatal PMNs have been found in several studies to be similar to those of adult PMNs.[305, 308] However, in some studies in which the assay conditions are designed to expose a potential defect in these functions (e.g., limiting concentrations of opsonins and high bacterial inocula), defects in phagocytosis and killing have been documented.[305, 308] Whether these potential deficiencies play a role in impaired neonatal phagocyte defenses in vivo is not clear.

PRIMARY OR HERITABLE IMMUNOLOGIC DEFICIENCIES

Physicians who care for children often are faced with the problem of a child who has a predilection for recurrent infections. Most of these children are normal infants or toddlers who have been exposed to a succession of common respiratory infections when they entered daycare or a similar setting for the first time.[118] Fortunately for most of these children, repeated exposure elicits relative immunity to many or most of the infectious agents. An important challenge for the physician is to identify infants and children who do not fit into the normal pattern but are unusually susceptible to infection with respect to frequency, severity, the type of causative agent, and response to appropriate treatment. This challenge usually falls to the pediatrician or family physician because, with few exceptions, the primary immune deficiencies are manifested during infancy and early childhood.[118]

As suggested earlier, an infant or toddler who experiences even six to eight presumed viral upper respiratory tract infections during the course of a winter season, without other complications, ordinarily would not be considered at high risk for having an immunodeficiency. In contrast, a child who had experienced five episodes of acute otitis media in the last 4 months, several episodes accompanied by sinusitis or pneumonia, has displayed reasonable cause for suspicion of a humoral immunodeficiency.[118] For certain organisms, infection in a healthy host is so decidedly uncommon that even a single episode should prompt a high suspicion of impaired host defenses. *Pneumocystis carinii* pneumonia strongly suggests a severe defect in T-cell number or function.[118] Similarly, lymphadenitis or osteomyelitis caused by gram-negative enteric bacilli points to a defect in phagocytic killing, such as CGD.[244] The discussion of specific immunologic defects and their infectious consequences will focus on well-characterized prototypic disorders within each class of primary defects but includes comments on other related disorders.

Antibody Deficiencies

Humoral immunity is provided by antibody and plays an important role in host defense against most pathogens, as illustrated by the finding that recurrent and sometimes life-threatening infections develop in patients with significant antibody deficiencies.[118, 125, 335] Such patients are particularly prone to otitis media, sinusitis, bronchitis, pneumonia, sepsis, and meningitis. Antibodies participate in complement-dependent and complement-independent opsonization, bactericidal activity, virus and toxin neutralization, and the formation of immune complexes that can be cleared by the reticuloendothelial system.[218, 285] The roles of different immunoglobulin isotypes and subclasses have been elucidated by the nature of infections found in patients with selective deficiencies and are outlined later.

X-LINKED AGAMMAGLOBULINEMIA

X-linked agammaglobulinemia (XLA), first described by Bruton, is a primary immunodeficiency disorder of the B-cell lineage and is the most serious disorder of humoral immunity.[85, 278, 335, 367] It is characterized by absent or severely decreased numbers of circulating B lymphocytes and absent or extremely low levels of all classes of circulating immunoglobulins. XLA is caused by several different mutations in the gene encoding for a B-cell–specific tyrosine kinase, *Btk,* which maps to the long arm of the X chromosome at Xq22.[433, 443] This abnormality in kinase activity results in an arrest in the development of B cells, usually at the pre-B stage, and thus few B cells or their progeny (e.g., plasma cells) are present in the circulation or lymphoid tissues.[201]

Chronic or recurrent pyogenic bacterial sinopulmonary or gastrointestinal infections develop in most persons with XLA, and they may have recurrent skin infections.[85, 278, 335, 367] Systemic disease, such as sepsis, and serious focal infections resulting from bacteremia, such as meningitis, osteomyelitis, and septic arthritis, do not occur as frequently as do respiratory and gastrointestinal infections, but they are more common and more severe than in normal hosts. The causative agents of most of these infections are *S. pneumoniae* and both type b and nontypeable *H. influenzae,* but *Staphylococcus aureus* and *Pseudomonas aeruginosa,* as well as other gram-negative organisms, may be implicated. The most troublesome gastrointestinal infections in XLA are caused by *Salmonella, Campylobacter,* and chronic infection with *Giardia lamblia.* Although they have no increased susceptibility to most viruses, these patients have been found to have unusually severe or chronic enterovirus infections that can be manifested by chronic meningoencephalitis, dermatomyositis, hepatitis, or a combination thereof, and vaccine-related paralytic poliomyelitis has developed in several patients with XLA after they received the live oral polio vaccine.[278]

The only abnormality on physical examination that is not related directly to infections is a paucity of normal B cell–containing lymphoid tissues, such as tonsils, adenoids, and peripheral lymph nodes.[335] Patients in whom XLA is diagnosed and treated early in life have normal physical examination findings, growth, and development.

Infants with XLA have normal levels of serum IgG at birth, and they are protected from infections during the first few weeks of life by passively transferred maternal antibodies. Most patients are seen initially at approximately 4 to 12 months of age, when maternal antibody levels have declined, but occasionally, the diagnosis is not established until the child is 5 years of age.

Older persons with XLA have low serum levels of IgG, IgM, IgA, and IgE. The diagnosis can be confirmed by studying lymphocyte markers.[335] They have a lack of circulating cells that stain for surface immunoglobulin or with B-cell–specific monoclonal antibodies against CD19, CD20, or both. The number and function of T lymphocytes are normal in XLA. Establishing the diagnosis in the newborn period may be difficult because maternally derived immunoglobulin bestows normal IgG levels. However, if the physician has other reasons to suspect this diagnosis, such as a newborn male with a documented family history, the diagnosis can be made by the striking decrease in circulating B cells.

Advances in genetic techniques have enabled detection of maternal carriers.[117] In contrast to carriers of some other X-linked genetic diseases, random X chromosome inactivation is not apparent in carriers of this disorder. Instead of two populations of B cells, one affected and one normal, the B lymphocytes of XLA carriers express only one population of B cells, those with the normal allele on the X chromosome, thus suggesting that B cells with the mutant allele are at a selective disadvantage and do not develop. Prenatal diagnosis is made by linkage analysis of amniotic fluid cells or by quantitation of fetal circulating B cells.

The prognosis for patients with XLA has improved markedly with earlier diagnosis, high-dose intravenous immunoglobulin (IVIG) therapy, and aggressive use of antibiotics.[335] Before the availability of IVIG, most patients who survived to the third decade of life had chronic lung disease from pulmonary infections and hearing loss from recurrent otitis media.[278]

IgG SUBCLASS DEFICIENCY

Persons with IgG subclass deficiencies have levels of one or more IgG subclasses that are more than 2 SD below normal for age, normal to slightly decreased total IgG, normal levels of other immunoglobulin isotypes, and, often, a poor antibody response to certain antigens.[59, 218, 220–222, 314, 335, 339, 340, 386–392] Patients with IgG subclass deficiency who also have IgM and IgA deficiencies may have another immunodeficiency disorder such as common variable immunodeficiency (CVI).

Patients with individual or combined deficiencies of IgG1, IgG2, and IgG3 may be at increased risk for acquiring infection, particularly if the deficiency is associated with an abnormal antibody response to antigenic stimulation.[59, 218, 220–222, 314, 335, 339, 340, 386–392] The most common kinds of infections in patients with IgG subclass deficiency are upper respiratory. Ordinarily, these patients do not have life-threatening systemic infections.

Deficiency of IgG1, because it accounts for approximately 60 percent of the total IgG, is most likely to be associated with hypogammaglobulinemia G, and it usually is accompanied by other subclass deficiencies.[17, 339, 389–391] IgG1-deficient persons may have recurrent pulmonary infections that can lead to chronic lung disease.

IgG2 deficiency is associated with normal total serum IgG levels and is more likely to be symptomatic if it is accompanied by IgG4 or IgA deficiency. As would be expected, patients with IgG2 deficiency have poor antibody responses to polysaccharide, but not protein antigens. Their infections primarily are localized to the respiratory tract, but some patients have been reported to have recurrent meningococcal meningitis or disseminated pneumococcal disease.

IgG3 deficiency has been associated with low total levels of serum IgG and recurrent respiratory infections, which also may lead to chronic pulmonary disease.[335]

IgG4 deficiency is difficult to diagnose because many normal persons have low serum levels of IgG4 and most normal infants have no detectable IgG4.[335] IgG4 deficiency appears to be of clinical significance, however, if it is associated with IgG2 and IgA deficiencies.

Treatment of children with IgG subclass deficiency usually is individualized according to the frequency and severity of symptoms. Noninvasive infections generally can be treated successfully with appropriate antibiotics. Patients with more severe manifestations may benefit from IVIG therapy, but those who also are IgA deficient should be monitored closely for the formation of anti-IgA antibodies and treated only with IgA-depleted IVIG preparations. Individuals with IgG2 deficiency should be immunized with vaccines consisting of polysaccharides conjugated to protein carriers, such as those for *H. influenzae* type b, pneumococcus, and, when available, meningococcus.

HYPER-IgM SYNDROME

Immunoglobulin deficiency with increased IgM is characterized by low levels of IgG, IgA, and IgE but normal to increased levels of IgM in the circulation and normal numbers of circulating B cells.[330, 335] The IgM is polyclonal and consists of both kappa and lambda light chains. The disorder is caused by an intrinsic T-cell abnormality that alters switching from IgM to other isotypes. The basis for the various genetic forms of this defect is the presence of one of several possible defects that involve interactions between CD40 on B cells and CD40L on T cells. In normal persons, CD40 on the surface of B cells interacts with CD40L on activated T cells to cause B-cell differentiation into memory B cells and switching from IgM to other isotypes. B cells from patients with the hyper-IgM syndrome make only IgM antibody, and their B cells express only surface IgM and IgD. The originally described and most common form of the defect is inherited in an X-linked recessive manner, and this form results from a mutation in the gene encoding CD40L, a protein expressed transiently on activated T cells.[14, 35] Autosomal recessive forms of this disorder described more recently involve mutations either in CD40 itself[175] or in a CD40-activated RNA editing enzyme, activation-induced cytidine deaminase (AID).[358] Other cells have surface CD40, and, therefore, immunologic abnormalities, such as the neutropenia and the increased incidence of *P. carinii* infection and malignancies in patients with hyper-IgM syndrome also may be the result of impaired cell interactions via CD40.

Clinically, hyper-IgM syndrome is manifested by recurrent bacterial infections, particularly respiratory ones, beginning after maternal immunoglobulin levels decline during the first few months of life.[329, 335] Such persons are susceptible to the same kinds of recurrent pyogenic infections that are associated with other immunoglobulin deficiencies, as well as infections with organisms encountered more commonly in patients with T-cell defects (e.g., *P. carinii*).[45] Some patients with this syndrome have recurrent diarrhea caused by *G. lamblia* and *Cryptosporidium* that is sufficiently severe to require parenteral nutrition. Life-threatening peritonsillar and peritracheal soft tissue infections also have been observed. In addition, approximately one half ofpatients have persistent or recurrent neutropenia. Those with autoantibodies may have thrombocytopenia, hemolytic anemia, nephritis, hypothyroidism, or arthritis, as noted earlier.

Physical examination usually is normal except for the sequelae of infections and lymphoid hyperplasia, which probably is caused by constant antigenic stimulation. Arthritis and arthralgia may be caused by chronic infection or the production of autoantibodies. Some patients have large verruca vulgaris lesions.

The diagnosis of X-linked hyper-IgM syndrome may be established by performing immunofluorescence to document absent expression of CD40L on activated T cells or absent CD40 expression on B cells or by demonstrating a mutation in one of the genes encoding CD40, CD40L, or the enzyme AID.

Treatment of hyper-IgM patients with IVIG usually results in marked clinical improvement.[45] Patients who have neutropenia despite receiving treatment with granulocyte colony-stimulating factor (G-CSF) and those with arthritis or other autoimmune symptoms also may require treatment with steroids. Hyper-IgM patients usually do not do as well as those with XLA because, in addition to their immunoglobulin deficiency, they have an increased incidence of neutropenia, autoimmune disease, and malignancy.

IgA DEFICIENCY

IgA deficiency, the most common immunodeficiency, occurs in approximately 1 in 400 to 1 in 800 people. All the functions of serum IgA can be performed by IgG and IgM.[125, 335] Thus, although deficiencies in secretory IgA may lead to recurrent respiratory or gastrointestinal tract infections, deficiencies in serum IgA usually are not associated with increased susceptibility to systemic infections.[22] IgA deficiency has been associated with many other conditions, including recurrent infections, IgG2 deficiency, a family history of immunodeficiency (e.g., relatives with CVI), autoimmune disorders, and malignancy.[21] Recurrent infections are most likely to occur in the subset of IgA-deficient patients who also have IgG2 deficiency.[125, 340] The infections usually are relatively mild and involve the upper respiratory and gastrointestinal tracts. Chronic gastrointestinal disease can be caused by *G. lamblia* infection, nodular lymphoid hyperplasia, lactose intolerance, malabsorption, ulcerative colitis, regional enteritis, or autoimmune disorders (e.g., chronic hepatitis, cirrhosis, pernicious anemia). Approximately 20 percent of IgA-deficient patients have allergies, and many have elevated levels of IgE.[125] Food allergy is a common finding and may be the result of abnormal processing of antigen at the mucosal surface. Other autoimmune diseases that are associated with IgA deficiency include rheumatoid arthritis, systemic lupus erythematosus, thyroiditis, Still disease, transfusion reactions, pulmonary hemosiderosis, myasthenia gravis, and vitiligo.[125]

IgA deficiency appears to be inherited sporadically, but familial cases have been described.[22, 125]

Serum IgA levels less than 5 mg/dL can be clinically significant because patients with levels this low who receive transfusions may make antibody against donor IgA and have severe reactions when transfused again.[384] IVIG reactions also may occur because IVIG preparations contain varying amounts of IgA. IgA-depleted preparations are available and generally are well tolerated, even in patients with high titers of anti-IgA antibodies.[126]

IgE DEFICIENCY

The clinical significance of selective IgE deficiency is unclear because it has been described in healthy persons. Some patients with profound antibody and cellular immunodeficiencies lack serum IgE, but several partial cellular immunodeficiency syndromes are characterized by elevated levels of IgE (e.g., DiGeorge syndrome, Wiskott-Aldrich syndrome, Hodgkin disease).[218, 335] The absence of IgE does not correlate with an enhanced susceptibility to infection in developed countries but has not been investigated in the developing world.

TRANSIENT HYPOGAMMAGLOBULINEMIA OF INFANCY

Hypogammaglobulinemia is a normal physiologic phenomenon that occurs in all infants beginning at approximately 3 to 4 months of age, when maternal antibody wanes and infant synthesis of immunoglobulin has not compensated yet.[218, 285, 335] The syndrome of transient hypogammaglobulinemia of infancy can be differentiated from physiologic hypogammaglobulinemia by the fact that immunoglobulin levels of normal infants begin to rise by the time that they are approximately 6 months of age, whereas those of infants with transient hypogammaglobulinemia of infancy do not begin to increase until the child is between 18 and 36 months of age.[218, 285, 335] Infants suspected of having this syndrome should be evaluated for XLA and CVI (see later) and monitored closely until their immunoglobulin levels rise to the normal range.

ANTIBODY DEFICIENCY WITH NORMAL OR ELEVATED LEVELS OF IMMUNOGLOBULINS

Some persons with normal levels of all circulating immunoglobulin isotypes have an increased risk for development of infection.[16, 18, 335] The cause of this disorder remains poorly defined but may be related to an inability to respond to specific antigens or the induction of tolerance by exposure to certain antigens too early in development, or it merely may reflect a delay in the development of the immune system in some persons. The most common infections in these patients are recurrent sinopulmonary infections and, occasionally, recurrent pneumococcal sepsis.[18] Such persons can be identified by their inability to make antibody in response to stimulation with specific antigens. They do not have abnormal total serum immunoglobulin classes or subclasses or B- or T-cell quantity or function. They can respond to some, but not all, antigenic stimulation. Therefore, testing them with a variety of stimuli is important. A good way to test for this syndrome is to immunize with protein antigens, such as tetanus and diphtheria toxoids, and with polysaccharide antigens, such as pneumococcal and *H. influenzae* type b capsular polysaccharide vaccines. Patients who can respond to protein but not polysaccharide antigens also respond to polysaccharide antigens that have been conjugated, or covalently coupled, to proteins.

Treatment with IVIG may help prevent recurrent infections in these patients, although the appropriate dose of IVIG is unclear because they have normal levels of immunoglobulin.

Defects in Cell-Mediated Immunity: DiGeorge Syndrome

The prototype of a pure T-cell defect, DiGeorge syndrome, is characterized clinically by congenital heart disease (usually involving the aortic arch), hypocalcemic tetany, unusual facial features, and recurrent infections.[147] In the classic or complete form of this disorder, the patient has an absence or hypoplasia of the thymus and parathyroid glands, cardiac or aortic arch deformities, and a stereotypic constellation of abnormal facial features.[147, 266, 423] Although the condition usually is considered to be associated with immune deficiency because of the thymic hypoplasia, only approximately 25 percent of patients actually exhibit an immunologic defect.[51] The term partial DiGeorge syndrome sometimes has been used to describe patients with the typical constellation of anatomic findings but without immune deficiency or similar patients with mild immunologic impairment.[232] The suggestion, in some sources, to designate this disorder as an "anomaly" rather than a syndrome stems from the observation that although the characteristic features of this disorder, either in complete or incomplete forms, stem from abnormal development of the same embryonic tissue (the branchial arches with contributions from cephalic neural crest tissue), the causes of this abnormal development are diverse, including disorders exhibiting classic mendelian inheritance patterns, teratogenic influences, and chromosomal abnormalities, especially specific deletions of chromosome 22 (22q11).[205, 206, 232, 270]

DiGeorge syndrome usually is recognized first by the presence of unusual but characteristic facial features, hypocalcemic tetany in the first 2 days of life, or the presence of serious cardiovascular manifestations, most commonly associated with an interrupted aortic arch or truncus arteriosus.[232, 289] Because of the serious nature of the cardiovascular defect, many patients with DiGeorge syndrome do not survive long enough for the immune defect to become a clinical problem.[232] However, with improvements in aggressive surgical approaches to the heart defects, more of these infants are surviving long enough to display manifestations of the immune deficiency, such as an increased frequency and severity of viral and fungal infections, as well as *P. carinii* pneumonia. In such patients, management often includes prophylaxis against pneumonia, periodic immunoglobulin infusions, and avoidance of live virus vaccines.[232] Transplantation of fetal or postnatal thymic tissue has corrected the immunologic problem for the long term in approximately one third of such attempts.[200, 232] More recently, HLA-matched bone marrow transplantation has been successful in a few cases.[74, 200, 232]

Combined Defects in Cellular and Humoral Immunity

SEVERE COMBINED IMMUNODEFICIENCY DISEASE

SCID describes a heterogeneous group of heritable immune deficiencies that involve serious impairments in both cellular and humoral immunity, with recurrent severe infections by a wide range of viral, bacterial, and fungal organisms. SCID has many different forms, which have been reviewed in detail elsewhere.[87, 232] Although the mode of inheritance has been determined in several of them, the specific nature of the defect has been defined in only a few forms. One autosomal recessive form of SCID for which the basis is well characterized is adenosine deaminase (ADA) deficiency. X-linked SCID, the most common form of SCID, now is known to be caused by a mutation in the common gamma chain of the receptor for IL-2 and several other cytokines (γ_c).[87, 282] A deficiency in Janus kinase-3 (Jak-3) is the basis for a more recently described autosomal recessive form of SCID.[87, 282] Long-term management of patients with SCID involves the modalities used in both T- and B-cell disorders, including prophylaxis against *P. carinii* pneumonia, avoidance of live viral vaccines, and immunoglobulin replacement therapy.[232] Bone marrow transplantation has corrected the defect in numerous cases. ADA deficiency is of historical interest in that it is the first heritable disorder for which gene therapy was attempted, although success was limited and difficult to assess because of concomitant administration of a conjugated form of exogenous supplemental ADA.[68, 282] Recent advances in gene therapy for X-linked SCID appear to be more promising.[178, 282]

COMMON VARIABLE IMMUNODEFICIENCY

CVI is described as a poorly defined group of combined immunodeficiencies that differ from most other primary immunodeficiencies in that they most often are manifested in the second or third decade of life, although they may occur at any age.[124, 219, 368] These patients have normal or only somewhat decreased numbers of circulating B cells; low, but not absent levels of IgG, IgM, and IgA; poor responsiveness to antigens; and abnormal T-lymphocyte function.[127]

Although both T- and B-cell abnormalities often can be demonstrated, the clinical findings usually are comparable to those in patients with humoral or B-cell defects (i.e., recurrent bacterial sinopulmonary infections).[124, 219, 368] Occasionally, however, in addition to having the organisms causing infections in patients with XLA, these patients also have infections with organisms more commonly found in persons with T-lymphocyte abnormalities, such as *P. carinii, Mycoplasma pneumoniae,* recurrent herpes simplex virus, and herpes zoster virus. Chronic gastrointestinal problems may be caused by *G. lamblia* or other intestinal pathogens. Patients with CVI are prone to the development of nodular lymphoid hyperplasia, autoimmune diseases, and malignancies. CVI occasionally has been reported to be familial, and it has been described in families with IgA deficiency.

Patients with CVI usually can benefit from therapy with IVIG. Chronic lung disease often develops in patients who go untreated.

Complement Deficiencies

Excellent reviews of complement deficiencies are available elsewhere.[140, 141, 143, 159, 246, 247, 371] Approximately 0.03 percent of the general population have complement deficiencies resulting from acquired or congenital abnormalities of single or multiple complement components or regulatory proteins.

The most common complement deficiencies are acquired and are transient. They include the relative complement deficiencies in infants (see earlier) and those that result from complement consumption in various inflammatory states, such as connective tissue disorders and acute or chronic infections.[140, 141, 143, 159, 246, 247] Acquired complement deficiencies usually are associated with low levels of more than one complement component.[141] These deficiencies are not generally absolute and are of questionable clinical significance in host defense against infection.

In contrast, congenital or hereditary deficiencies more often are manifested as an abnormality or absence of a single complement protein. Deficiencies of individual components may have profound clinical implications, however, because they have been well documented to predispose to the development of life-threatening infections. Most primary complement abnormalities (C1q dysfunction and C1rs, C2, C3, C4, C5, C6, C7, C8, and C9 deficiencies) are inherited as autosomal co-dominant traits.[141] Most secondary complement deficiencies are caused by complement consumption, decreased synthesis, or increased catabolism.

Activation plus binding of C3 is an absolute requirement for complement participation in host defense and immunoregulation by either the classical or the alternative pathway. Therefore, one is not surprised that the most serious complement deficiency state is the total absence of C3.[141] Patients with C3 deficiency have abnormal opsonization (including immune complex processing), inflammatory responses, leukocytosis, phagocyte recruitment to sites of microbial invasion, bactericidal activity, and immune regulation.

Congenital C3 deficiency is a rare event and results from decreased production of C3.[176, 371] Patients with deficiencies of factors H and I have low, but detectable, levels of C3. Absence of either of these regulatory factors allows continuous activation of the alternative pathway and uncontrolled C3 consumption. Similarly, complement nephritic factors permit continued C3 consumption by stabilizing the C3 convertases.

Patients with C3 deficiency caused by any of these mechanisms have an increased susceptibility to infections, particularly those caused by encapsulated bacteria such as pneumococci, meningococci, and *H. influenzae* type b. The infections usually are localized to the respiratory tract (otitis, sinusitis, bronchitis, and pneumonia), but C3-deficient patients also are predisposed to sepsis and meningitis.[141, 176, 371] The clinical manifestation of their infections is similar to that of patients with agammaglobulinemia.[141] In addition, collagen vascular disease develops in most C3-deficient persons.[141, 176, 371]

Patients with homozygous or heterozygous deficiency of the early classical pathway proteins C1, C2, and C4 are more prone to the development of collagen vascular disease than to infections. However, approximately 20 percent of patients with homozygous deficiency of the early components have problems with recurrent or severe infections that are similar to those seen in C3 deficiency.[141, 176, 371] As could be anticipated, these patients do not have as serious or as frequent problems with infections as do patients with alternative pathway deficiencies because they always can protect themselves via the alternative pathway regardless of whether they have specific antibody to the infecting organism. Their predilection to collagen vascular disease probably is caused, at least in part, by abnormal solubilization and removal of immune complexes. Although deficiency of one of the isotypes of C4 (C4B) has been reported to be associated with increased susceptibility to infection by encapsulated organisms, subsequent studies have not confirmed this finding.[64, 97]

Patients with C3, C4, C2, or CR3 deficiency have decreased antibody response and incomplete switching from IgM to IgG, whereas patients with deficiency of the terminal components have normal antibody responses.[332, 334]

Deficiencies of alternative pathway proteins predispose to the development of serious, often fatal infections because of the lack of ability to respond promptly to organisms not previously encountered.[141] Although the classical pathway is intact, patients with alternative pathway deficiencies often succumb before they have the opportunity to make the specific antibody required for its activation.

No homozygous factor B–deficient patients have been reported. Most cases of properdin deficiency are X-linked and have been associated with fulminant, usually fatal meningococcal infection.[143] Factor D deficiency occurs rarely but appears to predispose to recurrent neisserial infection.[258]

Patients with deficiency of the terminal complement proteins C5, C6, C7, and C8 also have an increased risk for development of systemic neisserial disease, both meningococcal and gonococcal (but particularly meningococcal).[140] Because C9 is not absolutely required for bacteriolysis (it simply makes it occur faster), C9 deficiency is associated with a relatively smaller increased risk for acquisition of infection than is deficiency of other terminal components. C9 deficiency is present in approximately 0.1 percent of the population in Japan. In a study performed there, the risk for development of meningococcal diseases was increased 5000-fold in C7-deficient and 700-fold in C9-deficient persons.[320]

The rate of infection is higher in patients with C5 deficiency than in those with deficiencies of other terminal proteins because C5 yields an important chemoattractant, C5a, and, thus, is critical for leukocyte recruitment to sites of microbial invasion, as well as for bactericidal activity.[140]

The incidence of collagen vascular disease also appears to be increased in patients with terminal component deficiencies, although one should note that because many patients have undergone complement testing because of collagen vascular disease, the denominator is not available.[141]

At least one episode of meningococcal disease occurs in approximately 60 percent of persons who have been identified as having C5, C6, C7, C8, or properdin deficiency, and 75 to 85 percent of documented bacterial infections in complement-deficient persons are meningococcal.[141, 176, 371] Of interest is that patterns of meningococcal disease are different in persons with complement component deficiencies and normal hosts. First, meningococcal disease occurs in individuals who are older (mean, 17 versus 3 years), and a higher proportion of disease is caused by groups Y, W-135, and X in complement-deficient than in normal persons.[141] Furthermore, the mortality rate is much lower than that for meningococcal disease in normal persons.

The presence of severe meningococcal infections in males, particularly in skipped generations, suggests X-linked properdin deficiency, whereas meningococcal disease in persons older than 10 years and caused by unusual serogroups (Y, W-135, and X) suggests terminal component deficiency (deficiency is detected in 5 to 10% and 31% with first or sporadic and recurrent episodes of disease, respectively).[140, 141]

Recently, mutations or variants in the gene for mannan-binding lectin, the initiator of the MBL pathway (see earlier), have been associated with an increased risk for development of recurrent infections.[223, 420] In particular, homozygosity for such mutations or variants was found to be associated with an increased risk for development of systemic meningococcal disease.[223]

Complement abnormalities may be quantitative or qualitative. Thus, determining both the total amount of individual complement proteins and their functional activity is important.[141] The test of complement function most commonly used measures total hemolytic complement (CH_{50}). This assay quantitates the activation of complement via the classical pathway by using antibody-coated sheep erythrocytes as the target cells for MAC cytolysis. A normal CH_{50} reflects a normal quantity and function of classical pathway proteins (C1, C4, C2), C3, and terminal components through C8. A normal CH_{50} is possible in the absence of C9. The alternative pathway proteins can be measured in a similar assay by using rabbit erythrocytes instead of antibody-coated sheep cells because the surface of rabbit erythrocytes, unlike that of sheep cells, does not contain sialic acid and, therefore, permits continuous activation of C3 by the alternative pathway amplification loop.

Indications for performing complement evaluations include recurrent serious bacterial infections, one episode of meningococcal disease, or recurrent systemic gonococcal infections.[141] Deficiencies in classical pathway components, C3, and terminal components can be detected by a CH_{50} that is a functional assay. Alternative pathway testing is not performed routinely and always should be done by reference laboratories. An important note is that quantitative C3 and C4 assays, which are available widely in routine laboratories, do not detect functional abnormalities or deficiencies of other complement proteins. In general, quantitation of individual proteins other than C3 or C4 should be performed in reference laboratories in consultation with an immunologist or expert on complement.

Replacement of missing complement proteins has been attempted with fresh-frozen plasma but usually has not been successful. It generally is not practical because of the short half-life of most of the components,[48, 133, 272, 373] and if a given protein is completely lacking, the patient has a risk of developing antibodies to it and thus having reactions to later therapy or transfusions.

Disorders of Phagocyte Function

GENERAL FEATURES OF PHAGOCYTE DISORDERS

Our most frequent reminder of the importance of an adequate supply of well-functioning phagocytes comes from patients in whom neutropenia develops after they have undergone chemotherapy for malignancies. The high risk of development of bacterial and fungal infections in these patients is mainly the result of a lack of circulating neutrophils available for delivery to infected tissue.[348] The qualitative disorders of phagocyte function discussed in this section result in similar susceptibilities to these infections, either because the circulating cells are unable to migrate to an infected site or because even after having migrated to the infected tissue, they are unable to engage in normal microbicidal function. Some overlap exists among the types of infectious complications associated with disorders of migration versus killing. However, as a rule, defects in neutrophil migration tend to be associated with infections at skin and mucous membrane sites. In contrast, killing defects are more likely to result in infections of soft tissues and internal organs, although skin infections are not uncommon occurrences.[225] Defects in circulating numbers of leukocytes, such as cyclic neutropenia, a relatively uncommon disorder involving periodic skin and mucosal infections that responds to G-CSF administration, and chemotherapy-induced neutropenia, are not addressed further here.

INTRINSIC DISORDERS OF CELL MIGRATION

Type 1 Leukocyte Adhesion Deficiency

In the late 1970s and the first half of the ensuing decade, several reports described patients with recurrent bacterial infections, diminished neutrophil motility, and delayed separation of the umbilical cord.[2, 27, 28, 33, 76, 123, 179, 216] The neutrophils of these patients were discovered to be markedly deficient in adherence to both natural and artificial surfaces, response to complement-opsonized particles, and expression of surface glycoproteins in the molecular weight range of 150 to 180 kd. The deficient glycoproteins were found to be members of a family of heterodimeric glycoproteins, LFA-1, Mac-1, and pl50,95, each defined by its own unique alpha subunit, CD11a, CD11b, and CD11c, respectively, but sharing a common 95-kd beta subunit designated CD18.[27, 28, 32, 413] These proteins, also called the β_2 leukocyte integrins, were identified as critical determinants of adhesion-dependent functions on neutrophils and other phagocytic cells, and their absence appeared to be directly responsible for the striking adherence-dependent defects that characterized the function of leukocytes from patients with this disorder.[27, 28, 32, 413] Variously called Mac-1 deficiency, MO1 deficiency, LFA-1 deficiency, CD11/CD18 deficiency, or CR3 deficiency, this disorder, now usually called type 1 leukocyte adhesion deficiency (LAD-1), is an autosomal recessive disorder localized to chromosome 21 and characterized by a defect in the β_2 integrin subunit CD18.[29, 32, 413] It has been identified in approximately 150 persons worldwide and encompasses a broad ethnic diversity.[29, 32] Patients may have a moderate or severe phenotype, depending on the extent of the defect in protein expression.[28, 29] The documented mutations of the β_2 subunit (CD18) that result in LAD-1 have been diverse and range from complete absence to truncations or extensions of the molecule, small deletions, and point mutations.[29, 32]

Recurrent necrotic skin and soft tissue infections with poor or absent pus formation develop in patients with LAD-1, and they exhibit poor wound healing.[28, 29] A severe generalized form of gingivitis or periodontitis develops, with patients often losing most or all of their primary and secondary dentition along with some of their alveolar bone.[28, 29] Enterocolitis, much like that seen in neutropenic patients, also may develop.[28, 29] Delayed separation of the umbilical cord, presumably secondary to an impaired inflammatory response, is a common feature of the more severe phenotype of this disorder,[28, 29] but this finding alone in infants without infectious complications or other characteristic features is of doubtful significance.[459] Pronounced leukocytosis is a frequent finding in patients with LAD-1, even in the absence of active infection.[28, 29] The reason for its presence is not understood completely. The fact that LAD-1 neutrophils are incapable of normal egress from the circulation to the oral cavity or lower intestinal tract long has been thought to provide the principal explanation for the high circulating neutrophil counts. However, recent studies in CD18-null LAD-1 mice have revealed abnormally high circulating G-CSF levels and suggest that a more likely explanation involves the absence of a negative feedback mechanism on G-CSF production that occurs during normal transendothelial migration of leukocytes and appears to involve IL-17. Absent transendothelial migration results in failure of this putative feedback mechanism and leads to elevated G-CSF levels and higher circulating granulocyte counts.[183]

Functional studies of neutrophils from patients with LAD-1 reveal a marked impairment in adherence-dependent functions that require the β_2 integrins, including attachment to various surfaces, orientation in a chemotactic gradient, chemotaxis through nitrocellulose filters or under agarose gels, aggregation, phagocytosis of iC3b-opsonized particles, degranulation or activation of the oxidative metabolic burst in response to such particles, and recruitment of PMNs in vivo to Rebuck skin windows or dermal suction blisters.[27–29, 91] In contrast, neutrophil functions that are independent of CD11/CD18-mediated interactions are normal and include degranulation or oxidative burst activation in response to soluble stimuli or polarized shape change in suspension in response to chemoattractants.[27–29] PMNs and NK cells from patients with LAD-1 exhibit impaired ADCC for virus-infected target cells, which suggests that CD11/CD18-mediated cell-cell adhesion is essential for normal killing of virus-infected cells by this mechanism[259] and that the increased severity of viral infections in a few of the most severely affected patients could be related to defective ADCC. The specific diagnosis of LAD usually is made by demonstrating absent or markedly deficient expression of the CD11/CD18 family of glycoproteins on circulating leukocytes by immunofluorescence, gel electrophoresis, or other techniques.[27–29, 32]

Careful attention to skin and oral hygiene, aggressive management of infections, and meticulous local care of wound sites are important factors in the care of patients with LAD-1 or any serious disorder of neutrophil migration. Prophylactic antibiotics, usually trimethoprim-sulfamethoxazole, have been used in many of these patients, but their efficacy has not been well established. Granulocyte transfusions have been used with some success to treat severe infections in a few patients with LAD-1.[29, 76] Bone marrow transplantation with HLA-matched allogeneic marrow has led to mixed results, from complete correction of the phagocyte defect to death from graft-versus-host disease 9 months after transplantation.[29, 179] The human CD18 gene has been cloned and sequenced, and human LAD-1 cells have been corrected successfully in vitro with the normal CD18 complementary DNA carried by retrovirus vectors, thus hinting at the future promise of gene therapy for patients with LAD-1.[224] The development of genetic knockout mice deficient in CD18 may provide a useful model for studying gene therapy in vivo, as well as for helping elucidate features of the underlying deficiency itself.[264]

Type 2 Leukocyte Adhesion Deficiency

In 1992, two unrelated patients were reported. Both patients were products of consanguineous matings, who exhibited clinical characteristics virtually identical to those described for LAD-1.[185] However, expression of the β_2 (CD18) integrins on leukocytes was normal. In addition to defects in neutrophil motility, these children had short stature, psychomotor retardation, and the Bombay (hh) erythrocyte phenotype (homozygous for absence of the H antigen). Phagocytosis by PMNs was normal. Recently, this defect has been documented to be caused by one or more mutations in a specific guanosine diphosphate (GDP)-fucose transporter,[291] and it results in the absence of fucosyl residues on sialyl Lewis X, the tetrasaccharide moiety that serves as an important ligand for members of the selectin family of adhesion molecules.[185, 271, 445] In vivo and in vitro studies comparing the adhesive functions of PMNs from patients with LAD-1 and this new disorder, now called LAD-2, have provided elegant validation of the distinct roles of selectins and integrins in the recruitment of leukocytes in vivo, with the initial selectin-mediated "rolling" stage (deficient in LAD-2) required first for the second integrin-mediated "firm adhesion and extravasation" stage (deficient in LAD-1) to occur.[446] A deficiency in either mechanism results in defective delivery of PMNs to infected sites and is manifested clinically as a form of LAD. The other somatic and neurologic features of LAD-2 may be related to more widespread consequences of the generalized defect in fucosylation of glycoproteins.[271] Because of the generalized nature of this deficiency, researchers have proposed to designate this disorder "type IIc congenital disorder of glycosylation," or CDG-IIc.[291]

Specific Granule Deficiency

Rare patients with hereditary specific granule deficiency have been reported, beginning with Spitznagel and colleagues' original description in 1972.[77, 188, 410] These persons exhibited recurrent and severe infections, primarily of the skin and mucous membranes but sometimes involving the lung and, in one patient, the mastoid. Normal human neutrophils contain both azurophilic (primary) and specific (secondary) granules, the contents of which have been summarized previously. Neutrophils from patients with this disorder exhibit bilobed nuclei and absent specific granules on Wright-stained blood smears. Lactoferrin released from specific granules reduces the negative surface charge of the plasma membrane and thereby contributes to nonspecific adhesiveness of the cell.[188] The specific granule membrane also contains some of the intracellular store of the important adhesion molecule Mac-1 (CD11b/CD18) that is mobilized to the plasma membrane after stimulation by chemoattractants or other stimuli that induce granule secretion.[55, 73] Thus, specific granule deficiency results in marked impairment of adhesion and migration of neutrophils, probably on the basis of both diminished intracellular pools of adhesive proteins and an inability to effect the change in surface charge by lactoferrin. This impairment, in turn, leads to the recurrent skin and mucous membrane infections caused by *S. aureus*, gram-negative bacilli, and *Candida* that characterize the natural history of patients with this disorder.[77, 188, 410] Neutrophils in this disorder also exhibit diminished microbicidal activity, presumably because of diminished amounts of the cytochrome b_{558} component of NADPH oxidase, which is stored in the membrane of specific granules.

Although the disorder probably is too rare to make such generalizations, specific granule deficiency most likely is autosomal recessive in its mode of inheritance because both males and females are represented equally. The recent documentation of a specific granule deficiency phenotype in mice rendered genetically null for an important myeloid cell transcription factor known as "CCAAT/enhancer binding protein ε" (C/EBPε) has led to studies in at least one patient with specific granule deficiency that confirmed a deletion in the C/EBPε gene with absent expression of this transcription factor.[281] Specific granule deficiency may be diagnosed in a person with recurrent skin and mucous membrane infections whose neutrophils exhibit the characteristic absence of specific granules on Wright stain, as well as a marked impairment in chemotaxis in vivo and in vitro.

Chédiak-Higashi Syndrome

Chédiak-Higashi syndrome is a complex, rare autosomal recessive disorder characterized by partial oculocutaneous albinism, recurrent pyogenic infections, peripheral neuropathy, and neutropenia.[69] The illness also may involve an accelerated lymphoproliferative phase.[69] Granular cells, including neutrophils, contain giant lysosomal granules that are the apparent result of spontaneous intracellular fusion of azurophilic granules and, to a lesser extent, specific granules.[69] Corresponding disorders in intracellular pigment granules and vesicle trafficking in axons account for the albinism and other manifestations of this disease.[69] Similar disorders have been described in Aleutian mink, beige mice, albino Hereford cattle, and albino whales.[69] The genetic basis of the defect now is known to involve either a nonsense or a frame shift mutation in the gene encoding a large protein called the "lysosomal trafficking regulator" (LYST), homologous to the "beige" gene in mice, with all mutations studied thus far resulting in a truncated protein.[47, 100]

Patients with Chédiak-Higashi syndrome are prone to development of the recurrent skin and mucosal infections, most often caused by *S. aureus,* that are characteristic of the infections observed in those with defects in phagocyte migration.[26, 69] These patients have a consistent defect in cell migration that appears to be related to abnormal regulation of microtubule polymerization after stimulation by chemoattractant agents.[69] A possible role of intracellular levels of cyclic adenosine monophosphate and guanylic acid in this microtubule abnormality has been suggested,[80] but the relationship between cyclic nucleotides and the microtubule dysfunction in Chédiak-Higashi syndrome has not been established. Ascorbic acid has been shown in at least one study to normalize both the elevated levels of cyclic adenosine monophosphate and the number of microtubules present within the cell.[80] Studies of two brothers with Chédiak-Higashi syndrome demonstrated abnormally increased tyrosinylation of the alpha subunit of tubulin.[69, 322] Phagocytosis is normal, but killing of ingested bacteria is defective or delayed. The reason for this deficient or delayed killing is uncertain but may involve defective phagolysosomal fusion or abnormalities in levels of microbicidal defensins, which also are stored in primary granules.[190] The diagnosis of Chédiak-Higashi syndrome usually is suspected clinically on the basis of partial oculocutaneous albinism and recurrent pyogenic infections. A Wright stain demonstrating giant lysosomal granules and laboratory studies showing defective cell migration are confirmatory.

Neutrophil Actin Dysfunction

Filamentous actin is the main contractile mechanism of neutrophils for migration and phagocytosis.[418] An extremely rare and apparently heterogeneous disorder, neutrophil actin dysfunction has been characterized by recurrent skin infections caused by *S. aureus* and *Candida albicans.* Biopsies of infected skin lesions in one child demonstrated necrotic tissue with a notable absence of neutrophils. In vivo and in vitro studies revealed severely impaired neutrophil chemotaxis and phagocytosis.[78] The capacity for polymerization of actin from cell extracts likewise was diminished markedly. Of interest is that PMNs from family members of this patient also were found to be variably deficient in the CD11/CD18 family of glycoproteins, which is the basis of LAD-1.[407, 408] The nature and significance of this association is uncertain. Another infant reported to have recurrent skin and mucosal infections and defective neutrophil chemotaxis was found to have abnormally high levels of a 47-kd protein, now identified as lymphocyte-specific protein-1 (LSP-1), that exhibits actin-binding activity.[110] More recently, a 12-year-old patient with recurrent infections, mental retardation, and abnormal neutrophil chemotaxis was reported to be heterozygous for a substitution of lysine for glutamic acid-364 in non-muscle β-actin.[331] This substitution lies in a region important for binding to profilin and other actin-regulatory molecules. This patient's neutrophils also exhibited reduced superoxide production, thus suggesting a possible role for normal actin function in assembly of the NADPH oxidase complex.

Glycogen Storage Disease Type 1B

Beaudet and colleagues[52] first reported the association of recurrent infection, neutropenia, and impaired neutrophil migration with glycogen storage disease (GSD) type 1B, a metabolic disorder characterized by defective microsomal transport of glucose-6-phosphate. In 1985, Ambruso and coworkers[19] reviewed the features of 21 patients with GSD type 1B, 15 of whom suffered from frequent infections, especially of the skin and subcutaneous tissues. Osteomyelitis, pneumonitis, sinusitis, and septicemia also were reported. Seventeen of these 21 patients were found to have serum inhibitors of myeloid stem cell proliferation, which was presumed to account for their chronic neutropenia. Impaired neutrophil motility was found in 8 of 11 patients in whom this finding was evaluated. Assays of neutrophil microbicidal capacity generally were normal. A specific relationship between the underlying metabolic defect in GSD type 1B and the mechanism of impaired cell motility has not been established. However, glucose has been found to be an important energy source for chemotaxis,[452] and an interesting note is that the uptake of glucose by PMNs in response to chemoattractant stimulation is impaired in GSD type 1B, as well as in neonates, both examples of patients with impaired PMN migration.[4, 49]

EXTRINSIC OR SECONDARY DEFECTS OF POLYMORPHONUCLEAR LEUKOCYTE MIGRATION

Defective Neutrophil Chemotaxis Associated with Serum Inhibitors of Cell Function

Many investigators have reported the presence of inhibitors of PMN chemotaxis in the serum of patients with recurrent infection.[263, 316, 397, 406, 439, 450] In most cases, the pathophysiologic mechanisms of these inhibitors are unknown. In many of the patients described, other associated immunologic disorders could account for at least part of the increased susceptibility to infection. However, in each case, the patient's neutrophils exhibited diminished chemotaxis in the presence of autologous serum or plasma, whereas identical assays in the presence of control serum or plasma resulted in a normal chemotactic response. Most such inhibitors appear to be immunoglobulins or immunoglobulin-like molecules.

Hyper-IgE Syndrome

In 1966, Davis and colleagues[135] described two young girls with coarse facial features, reddish hair, fair skin, severe eczema, dystrophic nails, staphylococcal skin abscesses, and recurrent sinopulmonary infections. The absence of classic signs of inflammation accompanying the staphylococcal abscesses led to their being characterized as cold abscesses. The term Job syndrome, referring to the similar biblical affliction, was suggested. Additional patients were described with a similar disorder, first associated by Buckley[86] with very high serum IgE levels, including a patient who exhibited a defect in neutrophil chemotaxis reported in 1973 by Clark and associates.[109]

Subsequent reports of similar patients have demonstrated that certain features are common to all the patients with the disease now called hyper-IgE syndrome. These consistent features include a history of staphylococcal infections of the skin and sinopulmonary tract beginning in infancy or early childhood and serum levels of IgE that are greater that 2000 IU/mL.[89, 152, 227] Other characteristic, but variable, features of this disorder include coarse facies, cold abscesses of the skin and subcutaneous tissues, a chronic eczematoid rash, eosinophilia, and mucocutaneous candidiasis.[152]

Comprehensive reviews have provided detailed characterizations of the abnormalities of patients with this poorly understood disorder.[88, 152, 193] Consistent abnormalities in cell-mediated immune function in patients with hyper-IgE syndrome suggest that the pathogenic basis involves a defect in T-cell regulation. Documented abnormalities include diminished reactivity to *Candida* and tetanus toxoid in delayed hypersensitivity skin testing, decreased in vitro lymphocyte proliferative responses to these antigens, and reduced numbers of T cells with the CD45RO memory T-cell phenotype.[88, 105, 152] A recent extensive study of 30 patients with hyper-IgE syndrome and 70 of their relatives concluded that this disorder is inherited as a single-locus autosomal dominant trait with variable expressivity.[208] The gene defect or defects responsible for this disorder remain elusive.

Some patients with hyper-IgE syndrome may have a defect in neutrophil chemotaxis.[152] The defect, if observed at all, usually is intermittent. In several cases, the presence of a serum inhibitor of chemotaxis has been recognized.[151] Donabedian and Gallin[151] demonstrated an inhibitor of granulocyte chemotaxis in supernatants of cultured peripheral blood monocytes from patients with hyper-IgE syndrome. The persistence of infectious complications in this disorder at times when chemotaxis has been found to be normal, as well as the presence of large purulent collections within cold abscesses, raises doubt about the significance of a chemotactic disorder in explaining the markedly increased susceptibility of these patients to recurrent infections.

Impaired Generation of Serum-Derived Chemotaxins

A deficiency in the host's ability to produce chemotaxins derived from serum components may have profound consequences for the recruitment of PMNs to an infected site. The most important serum-derived chemotaxin is a fragment of the fifth component of complement, C5a, and its des-arg form. Several kindreds have been described with either absent or defective C5.[370] The chemoattractant activity measured in activated normal serum is virtually absent in C5-deficient serum.[369] The risk of development of systemic *Neisseria* infections because of deficient activation of the lytic terminal complement sequence appears to be far more significant than any phagocytic recruitment defect caused by impaired production of chemotaxins.[55, 176] Patients with C3 deficiency also have impaired chemotaxigenesis because C5 cannot be activated. Host impairment usually is more severe because of the importance of C3 in opsonization, as well as its role in activation of the remainder of the complement cascade.[371] As noted earlier, newborn infants also are relatively deficient in chemotaxigenesis as a result of immature levels of many of the complement components.[260]

OTHER SECONDARY OR POORLY DEFINED DISORDERS OF POLYMORPHONUCLEAR LEUKOCYTE MIGRATION

Patients with protein-calorie malnutrition have defective PMN chemotaxis that appears to be based on systemic preactivation of circulating cells caused by the chronic low-level endotoxemia resulting from impaired intestinal mucosal integrity.[257] Shwachman-Diamond syndrome, in addition to pancreatic insufficiency, neutropenia, and growth retardation, is associated with defective PMN migration.[11] Two kindreds with congenital ichthyosis and an associated defect in PMN migration have been described.[309] An acquired form of specific granule deficiency characterized by impaired PMN migration beginning approximately 14 days after injury develops in patients with severe thermal injuries.[188] Children with juvenile periodontitis of various types may exhibit reduced PMN chemotaxis.[438] In some of these patients, this condition has been associated with gingival infections caused by *Capnocytophaga,* an anaerobic gram-negative organism with the ability to elaborate factors that markedly impair PMN migration in vitro.[394] However, in one such patient, the ultimate diagnosis was LAD-1, a finding that raises some uncertainty about the role of *Capnocytophaga* in such disorders (Tosi, M. F., Shurin, S. B., and Smith, C. W., unpublished data). Several reports have been published of a poorly defined disorder in neutrophil migration called lazy leukocyte syndrome.[10, 310] This syndrome is characterized by recurrent staphylococcal skin infections, rhinitis, gingivitis, stomatitis, neutropenia despite adequate marrow precursors, and diminished in vivo and in vitro migration of neutrophils.

DEFECTS IN PHAGOCYTE MICROBICIDAL ACTIVITY

As described earlier, the broad array of available phagocyte microbicidal mechanisms may be divided into oxygen-dependent and oxygen-independent mechanisms. To date, no isolated deficiency of a specific oxygen-independent microbicidal mechanism has been described. Thus, this section is concerned mainly with the known deficiencies in oxygen-dependent microbicidal mechanisms of phagocytes, especially CGD, the prototypic defect in this group. PMN migration usually is normal in these killing defects. Monocytes and the fixed phagocytes of the reticuloendothelial system generally share in the deficient microbicidal activity.

Chronic Granulomatous Disease

CGD was one of the earliest syndromes of phagocyte dysfunction to be characterized[354] and probably is the most extensively studied of the individual phagocyte defects. It is recognized now to be a family of biochemically and genetically heterogeneous disorders of distinct components of the phagocyte NADPH oxidase complex.[100, 128, 148] Thus, CGD results in an inability of phagocytes to generate superoxide anion and other reactive oxygen species.[148] Organisms that produce catalase pose a special problem for patients with CGD.[148, 153, 244, 276] Such organisms encompass a broad range of pathogens that include staphylococci, gram-negative enteric bacteria, *Pseudomonas* spp., yeast, fungi, *Nocardia,* and numerous other pathogenic species.[153, 244, 276, 462] Most microorganisms produce H_2O_2, which might be used by the CGD phagocyte as an effective microbicidal weapon because it feeds into the sequence of oxidant reactions downstream from the defective oxidase enzyme[365] (see Fig. 2–8). Organisms that produce catalase are able to survive within these deficient cells because catalase is an enzyme that degrades H_2O_2 to oxygen and water.[244, 365] Infections with catalase-negative bacteria, such as *S. pneumoniae, H. influenzae,* and *N. meningitidis,* do not occur with increased frequency in CGD patients,[462] and these organisms are killed normally in vitro by CGD phagocytes. Phagocyte functions not related directly to the oxidative mechanisms of intracellular killing, including adherence, chemotaxis, phagocytosis, and degranulation, usually are normal in CGD patients.[40, 311, 354, 404]

The genetic defect in CGD may be inherited by either X-linked recessive or autosomal recessive mechanisms.[108, 128] In female obligate carriers of X-linked CGD, the proportion of cells that express the defect usually is between 35 and 65 percent, depending on the proportion in which random inactivation of the normal versus the affected X chromosome occurs.[292] In most of the autosomal recessive forms of CGD, the quantity of cytochrome in cells is normal, but the individual has a deficiency in one of the two cytosolic proteins $p47^{phox}$ and $p67^{phox}$, each of which is a critical component of the fully assembled NADPH oxidase complex.[37, 107, 108] In the report of a recently created registry of 368 patients with CGD in the United States,[462] more than two thirds of patients had the X-linked recessive form with absent $gp91^{phox}$, the larger subunit of cytochrome b_{558}; approximately 12 percent had an autosomal recessive form with absent $p47^{phox}$; and less than 5 percent each had autosomal recessive disease with the absence of $p67^{phox}$ or the absence of $p22^{phox}$, the smaller subunit of cytochrome b_{558}. Approximately 12 percent had an unknown genetic form of the disease. These genetically diverse defects all result in defective function of the oxidase and the characteristic CGD phenotype. Included in the aforementioned registry were two rare adult women whose sons had X-linked disease and who exhibited clinical signs of the CGD phenotype because of dramatically skewed X chromosome inactivation with 5 percent or less of their phagocytes demonstrating oxidase activity. Overall, patients with X-linked disease have more severe courses and higher yearly death rates than do patients with autosomal recessive forms of the disease.[462]

Patients with CGD experience recurrent serious bacterial and fungal infections, usually beginning in the first few months of life. *S. aureus* and gram-negative bacilli, especially *Serratia* and *Burkholderia cepacia,* are the most common causes of infection in patients with CGD, but fungi, especially *Aspergillus* spp., also are prominent etiologic agents.[276, 357, 462] In fact, *Aspergillus* infection is the most common cause of death in patients with CGD.[462] Lymphadenopathy associated with lymphadenitis and chronic suppuration with poor healing is a common initial feature of CGD. The formation of granulomata at infected sites is one of the histologic hallmarks of this disorder.[244, 357] Pulmonary infections and their complications have been the reported cause of death in as many as 50 percent of patients with CGD in some series, and *Aspergillus* predominates.[462] These infections often are protracted and respond slowly to appropriate antibiotic therapy.[245, 357] Progression to lung abscess, empyema, or both occurs in approximately 20 percent of patients with CGD and pneumonia.[245] Liver abscesses develop in approximately one half of patients with CGD and may be recurrent.[106, 462] The hepatosplenomegaly that is a common finding in patients with CGD may result from these infections but probably is more likely to result from chronic infections at various sites with systemic lymphoid hyperplasia.[244, 357] Osteomyelitis occurs in approximately one third of patients with CGD.[244, 357, 462] In contrast to normal children, in whom this infection usually involves the metaphyseal area of long bones, infections of the small bones of the hands and feet more often develop in patients with CGD. In normal children, *S. aureus* is the most common etiologic agent, and this agent is responsible for a significant proportion of cases in patients with CGD. However, gram-negative bacilli and *Aspergillus* appear to be the predominant etiologies, and other agents, including *Nocardia,* also may be important etiologic agents of osteomyelitis in children with CGD.[422, 462] Skin infections in CGD may include pyoderma, purulent dermatitis, and cutaneous or subcutaneous abscesses and often are preceded by a chronic eczematoid rash.[357] However, skin infections are somewhat less of a problem in patients with CGD than in patients with leukocyte migration defects.

Although localized infections are the rule in patients with CGD, septicemia also may develop in these patients.[244, 357, 462] The most common cause of septicemia in most series has been *Salmonella,* but other gram-negative enteric bacilli also have been prominent.[244, 276] Of note, *S. aureus,* the single most common etiologic agent of localized infections in patients with CGD, is a proportionally less common cause of septicemia in these patients.[357, 462] Other infections sometimes seen in patients with CGD include recurrent urinary tract infections in approximately 6 to 8 percent of patients; ocular infections with conjunctivitis, blepharitis, or both in about 20 percent of patients; and rarely, chorioretinitis.[297, 357]

The formation of granulomata adjacent to hollow viscera in patients with CGD has been found to produce clinically significant obstruction. Reported examples of this problem include obstruction of the gastric outlet, esophagus, small intestine, and ureters.[20, 102, 153] This complication usually responds to treatment with corticosteroids.[102]

CGD should be suspected in patients with a history of recurrent indolent infections caused by catalase-positive organisms such as those described earlier, especially if granulomata are found in biopsy specimens of lymph nodes or other tissues. Confirmation of the diagnosis usually rests on the demonstration of an absent oxidative metabolic burst in the patient's phagocytes. It can be detected by the slide nitroblue tetrazolium test (Fig. 2–10) or by other measurements of oxidative burst activity, such as cytochrome reduction, lucigenin- or luminol-enhanced chemiluminescence, oxygen consumption, H_2O_2 production, and flow cytometry of cells loaded with oxidant-sensitive fluorescent dyes.[15, 38, 50, 301, 366, 429] Prenatal diagnosis has been achieved by use of the slide nitroblue tetrazolium test with blood from placental vessels obtained at fetoscopy.[324]

Management of patients with CGD traditionally has relied on antibiotic prophylaxis, usually with trimethoprim-sulfamethoxazole or an oral antistaphylococcal penicillin, and an aggressive approach to the specific diagnosis and treatment of acute infections.[357] Granulocyte transfusions have been reported to be at least partially beneficial in a few cases.[92, 111] Bone marrow transplantation has met with limited success, with only one successful long-term engraftment in four separate attempts in different patients.[203, 252, 356, 455] T-cell–depleted allogeneic peripheral blood stem cell transplantation without previous myeloablation has been somewhat more promising, but longer-term follow-up will be necessary to validate this procedure as an approach to treatment.

Definition of the molecular basis for CGD and cloning of the genes responsible for the various forms of this defect have led to correction of some forms of the defect in cultured cells and have been instrumental in the development of animal models of CGD in mice,[243, 350, 444] both of which are crucial steps in developing gene therapy for patients with this disorder in the future. Preclinical studies of gene therapy in CGD in mice have shown promise when bone marrow cells are transduced by retroviral vectors ex vivo and transplanted into irradiated syngeneic recipients.[148] Fifty to 80 percent of circulating neutrophils were oxidase-positive 12 to 14 weeks post-transplantation, and protection from respiratory challenge with *Aspergillus* was achieved.[148] Early human phase I trials using autologous peripheral blood stem cells retrovirally transduced ex vivo and then reinfused without previous marrow conditioning in both autosomal recessive ($p47^{phox}$) and X-linked CGD have yielded a maximum of 0.2 percent oxidase-corrected neutrophils in the circulation.[293] This advance is still far short of what probably must be achieved to produce a clinically meaningful correction.[148]

The most important recent development in the treatment of patients with CGD is the use of IFN-γ. A multicenter study demonstrated that daily subcutaneous injections of this agent reduced the requirement for hospitalization of patients with CGD for serious infections by approximately two thirds.[242] IFN-γ does not increase oxidase activity in neutrophils, and the mechanism by which IFN-γ exerts its beneficial effect in CGD has not been determined. This treatment carries some mild systemic side effects,[242] but it has become part of the standard regimen for managing most patients with CGD.

Deficiencies of Glucose-6-Phosphate Dehydrogenase and Glutathione Peroxidase

Normal activity of the NADPH oxidase enzyme complex depends on the continued availability of NADPH to reduce molecular oxygen to form superoxide anion.[36, 107, 365] The primary source of NADPH for this enzyme is the hexose monophosphate shunt. It is provided with the hexose substrate 6-phosphoglucose by the enzyme glucose-6-phosphate dehydrogenase, which also generates NADPH in a coupled reaction.[365] The reactions of the hexose monophosphate shunt itself are coupled to two other enzymes, glutathione reductase and glutathione peroxidase, which recycle oxidized and reduced glutathione.[365] Absence of any of these three enzymes results in a lack of available NADPH to drive the NADPH oxidase. Thus, deficiencies in any of these other

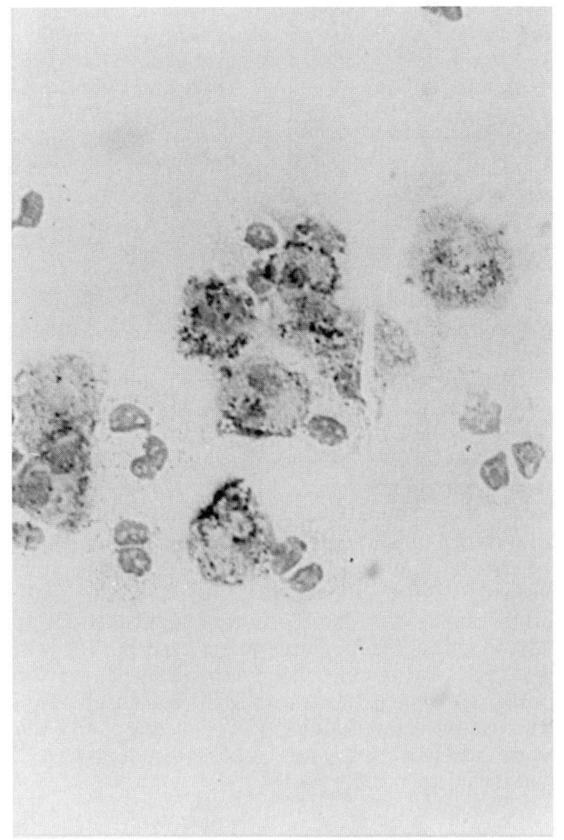

FIGURE 2–10 ■ Photomicrograph of a slide nitroblue tetrazolium (NBT) test of polymorphonuclear leukocytes (PMNs) isolated from the blood of a maternal carrier of X-linked recessive chronic granulomatous disease (CGD). Because of random inactivation of either the normal or the affected X chromosome in maternal carriers of this disorder, approximately half the PMNs exhibit the granular blue-black staining characteristic of the oxidative reduction of NBT by normal PMNs. In contrast, the remaining PMNs, which express the reduced nicotinamide adenine dinucleotide phosphate (NADPH) oxidase defect of CGD, are visible only by their nuclear counterstain.

three enzymes may result in a phagocyte killing defect similar to that with CGD. Patients with deficiencies of glucose-6-phosphate dehydrogenase or glutathione peroxidase have been described with functional oxidative metabolic defects and manifestations that are clinically indistinguishable from those of CGD.[39, 375] Glucose-6-phosphate dehydrogenase deficiency usually involves erythrocytes and is associated with hemolytic anemia, especially in conjunction with the administration of sulfonamides.[119] Only when the defect also involves myeloid cells and is severe or complete (<5% of normal enzyme levels) is the CGD-like disorder manifested.[39, 375] A partial deficiency of glutathione reductase has been reported in patients with hemolytic anemia and early cataracts, but no increased incidence of infection was noted.[364]

Glutathione Synthetase Deficiency

Glutathione, along with glutathione peroxidase and glutathione reductase, the two enzymes involved in its recycling between oxidized and reduced forms, constitutes a protective mechanism in PMNs against the membrane damage mediated by reactive oxygen intermediates formed during PMN activation.[364] Thus, synthesis of an adequate supply of glutathione is critical to these cells. Two brothers with glutathione synthetase deficiency and neutropenia, hemolytic anemia, acidosis, 5-oxyprolinuria, and recurrent infection were reported by Spielberg and colleagues.[79, 409] The PMNs from these patients exhibited elevated cytosolic H_2O_2 levels, diminished oxidative microbicidal activity, and impaired microtubule assembly. Antioxidant therapy with vitamin E normalized the in vitro abnormalities of the patients' PMNs, and they had no further difficulty with recurrent infections.[79] This finding suggested that vitamin E protected the cell membranes by scavenging the excess H_2O_2 produced during PMN activation and thus prevented or minimized oxidant-induced membrane damage.

Myeloperoxidase Deficiency

Congenital deficiency of neutrophil MPO, once thought to be a relatively rare disorder, has come to be recognized as the single most common heritable disorder in neutrophil function. However, its clinical significance remains in doubt. Population surveys made possible with the advent of automated flow cytochemical techniques have indicated an incidence of MPO deficiency of approximately 1 in 2000.[323, 343] Approximately one half of these patients have complete absence of this neutrophil enzyme, and the remainder have a partial deficiency. The precise mode of inheritance of this defect has not been established, but MPO is known to be a product of a single gene on chromosome 17.[441] The reaction of MPO with H_2O_2 and chloride, which causes the formation of hypochlorite, is one of the most effective microbicidal mechanisms of neutrophils, and cells from some patients with MPO deficiency have been found to exhibit delayed killing of *C. albicans* and *S. aureus.* However, MPO deficiency rarely has been associated with unusual infectious complications.

IMPORTANT EXAMPLES OF SECONDARY IMMUNODEFICIENCY (NOT INCLUDING HIV INFECTION)

Asplenia

Fulminant infections can occur in patients who have anatomic or functional asplenia.[381] The mortality rate from these infections in asplenic persons ranges from 40 to 80 percent.[461] The most common pathogens are encapsulated bacteria, including *S. pneumoniae* (50–70%), *H. influenzae,* and *N. meningitidis.*[461] They can cause fulminant, often fatal disease characterized by the rapid onset of shock. Malaria, babesiosis, and viral infections also are more severe in asplenic persons. Infections can occur at any time but most commonly within the first 2 years after a patient undergoes splenectomy.

Both the liver and the spleen are important in phagocytic clearance of bacteria from the circulation, and the spleen is an important site for production of antibody. The spleen is relatively more important than is the liver in processing antigen in naive hosts. The younger the person when splenic function is lost, the higher the risk for development of serious infection. Thus, young children who become asplenic are much more susceptible to fulminant infection than are adults because adults are more likely to have encountered antigens before undergoing splenectomy. Persons whose indication for splenectomy is thalassemia or Hodgkin disease have a higher risk of dying of overwhelming infection than do those who have functional asplenia from sickle-cell disease. Patients who undergo spleen removal for spherocytosis or idiopathic thrombocytopenia have a lower risk for development of infection. The lowest-risk group consists of adults whose spleens are removed surgically after trauma; such patients have little or no increased risk for development of infection.

Congenital asplenia usually is associated with complex congenital cardiac disease and occasionally with structural abnormalities of the gastrointestinal or genitourinary tract. Thus, asplenia should be suspected in any patient with congenital heart disease and sepsis caused by encapsulated organisms. Asplenia also should be suspected in patients with increased numbers of circulating pitted erythrocytes or erythrocytes that contain Howell-Jolly bodies.

Elective splenectomy for conditions such as hereditary spherocytosis should be delayed as long as possible, and splenic repair or subtotal splenectomy should be performed whenever feasible after trauma. Asplenic persons are managed with prophylactic antibiotics until at least 5 years of age.[116] They also should be immunized against encapsulated organisms at the appropriate ages (e.g., *H. influenzae* type b and pneumococcal conjugate vaccines beginning at 2 months and meningococcal polysaccharide vaccines at 2 years).[116] Patients should be warned about their increased risk for acquisition of serious infections caused by malaria and babesiosis.

Sickle-Cell Disease

The immunodeficiency in patients with sickle-cell disease is due, in large part, to their functional asplenia.[381] Part of the risk of infection stems from local infarction and tissue necrosis secondary to sickling, which causes sludging and resultant tissue hypoxia. The reticuloendothelial system also may be obstructed by having to deal with chronic hemolysis. Patients with sickle-cell disease are protected partially from *Plasmodium falciparum* malaria but have a high incidence of fulminant sepsis and meningitis caused by encapsulated organisms (e.g., *S. pneumoniae, H. influenzae* type b, *N. meningitidis*) and *Salmonella.*[182] The relative risk of pneumococcal meningitis occurring in children with sickle-cell disease is approximately 500 times that of normal children. *Salmonella* infections often are associated with osteomyelitis or meningitis.[163]

Patients with sickle-cell disease seem to have a normal antibody response to most antigens, including age-appropriate responses to vaccines. A deficiency in heat-labile opsonic activity has been reported and may be due to a defect in the alternative pathway of complement. Indeed, patients with sickle-cell disease who have deficiencies in factor B have been reported, but patients with sickle-cell disease have normal CH_{50} and normal levels of properdin, C3, and factor I.

Patients with sickle-cell disease should be managed with prophylactic antibiotics until at least 5 years of age and should be immunized against *H. influenzae* type b, pneumococci, and meningococci at the appropriate ages.[116]

Cystic Fibrosis

Cystic fibrosis is an autosomal recessive disorder caused by mutations in both alleles of the gene encoding the protein called cystic fibrosis transmembrane conductance regulator.[454] Chronic endobronchial infection with *P. aeruginosa* of the mucoid phenotype develops in most patients with cystic fibrosis. This infection is accompanied by an intense chronic airway inflammation with an exuberant influx of neutrophils that leads to destruction and fibrosis of lung and airway tissue.[262] No systemic disorder of immunity has been documented in cystic fibrosis, but local factors in the airway inflammatory milieu, especially neutrophil-derived proteases such as elastase, contribute to secondary impairments in opsonic and phagocytic host defenses by cleaving opsonic antibody and complement fragments, as well as important phagocytic receptors for these opsonins.[431]

Both the early pathogenesis of the unique chronic endobronchial infection in cystic fibrosis and its relationship to the underlying genetic defect have remained obscure. However, several possible explanations have been offered. A reduction in cell surface sialic acid on cystic fibrosis epithelial cells unmasks the glycoprotein asialo-G_{M1}, which appears to function as an epithelial receptor for adhesion by *P. aeruginosa* and may promote airway colonization.[378] Additionally, researchers have suggested that airway epithelial cells normally internalize *P. aeruginosa* before being sloughed and cleared by mucociliary action and that this internalization may be deficient in cystic fibrosis epithelial cells.[347] Finally, evidence suggests that microbicidal peptides of or related to the defensin family and released from airway epithelial cells as a local defense mechanism may be inactivated by abnormal salt concentrations at the airway epithelial surface, thereby thwarting an important first line of local antibacterial defense.[401] These proposed mechanisms are not mutually exclusive, and none has been proved conclusively to explain the pathogenesis of infection in the airways of cystic fibrosis patients. They remain subjects of intensive investigation.

Evaluation for Immunodeficiency in a Child with Recurrent or Severe Infections

Most immunodeficiency disorders can be diagnosed readily by using a methodical process that begins with careful analysis of the child's history and physical examination.[118, 125, 141, 231, 335, 381, 382] This information serves as the foundation for a rational laboratory evaluation. One should bear in mind that it is normal for children to have several infections every year. Normal children who are exposed to other children, particularly older school-age siblings or classmates, have approximately one infection per month. The overwhelming majority of infections in immunocompetent children are mild and localized to the gastrointestinal or upper respiratory tract, and they are either self-limited or respond rapidly to conventional therapy. Immunocompromised hosts tend to have more frequent, severe, and unusual infections that may not respond readily to appropriate therapy.

HISTORY

A detailed history alone is sufficient to determine whether an immunologic evaluation should be pursued in many children who have recurrent or severe infections. If tests for immunity are indicated, the history also serves as a guide to the types of studies that should be performed initially. Table 2–5 provides a list of historical information that is valuable in assessing the likelihood of immunodeficiency. Whenever possible, the child's complete medical records (including growth charts) should be obtained, particularly if several physicians have provided care, because the history often is complicated and incomplete or inaccurate information may be misleading.

The age at the onset of suspicious infections usually helps in defining the underlying problem. For example, children with isolated immunoglobulin deficiencies tend to do well during the first few months of life because they are protected by maternal antibody.[285] Serious infections generally start developing later in the first year of life. In those with cell-mediated or phagocytic disorders, infections may begin developing in the newborn period (see earlier). In contrast, healthy children who have been cared for at home by their mothers and who have no siblings often have relatively few infections in the first few years of life, but immunologic evaluation may be requested when recurrent infections begin to develop the first few weeks after entering daycare, nursery school, or kindergarten.

The number, nature, and severity of infections help in determining how aggressively to pursue an immunologic evaluation. Certain clinical manifestations of disease and causative organisms are associated with a high likelihood of an immunodeficiency. Antibody or complement deficiencies or functional asplenia should be suspected in children with

TABLE 2–5 ■ HISTORY IN THE EVALUATION OF A CHILD WITH RECURRENT OR SEVERE INFECTIONS

Age at onset of infections
Number, frequency, and periodicity of infections
Nature of infections
  Location on body
  Organism(s)
  Severity
  Duration
Nature and duration of therapy
Response to therapy
Hospitalizations
Surgery
Growth pattern
Periodontal disease
Allergies
Immunizations
Exposure history
  Contagious diseases in family, school, or community
  Number and ages of siblings
  Parents' occupations
  Babysitting or daycare arrangements
  Foreign travel
  Parental smoking
  Wood furnaces
Family history (especially in males)
  Immunodeficiency
  Recurrent, severe, or unusual infections
  Cause of early deaths
  Autoimmune disease
  Allergy
  Consanguinity
Days of school missed (and why)

recurrent or life-threatening infections such as sepsis and meningitis caused by encapsulated organisms (e.g., *S. pneumoniae, H. influenzae* type b).[85, 141, 247, 278, 335, 367] Complement deficiencies should be considered in persons with recurrent or severe neisserial disease.[143] CGD should be suspected in the presence of recurrent or unusual deep-tissue infections such as liver abscesses, lymphadenopathy, pneumonia, or osteomyelitis, especially when caused by unusual gram-negative bacteria such as *Serratia marcescens* or by *Aspergillus* spp.[462] *P. carinii* infection suggests a T-cell deficiency, either hereditary or caused by HIV infection. In contrast, recurrent or even severe infections with group A *Streptococcus* have not been associated with immunodeficiency. In addition, recurrent urinary tract infections usually are associated with anatomic abnormalities of the urinary tract and not immunodeficiency.

An essential part of the history is documentation of the child's growth pattern. Children who are thriving, particularly those older than 2 years, are much less likely to have serious immune disorders than are those with failure to thrive.

The immunization history should be documented carefully because it may prove useful in evaluating the child's ability to mount an antibody response to specific vaccine antigens. Any history of recent live viral immunization should be obtained in children who have clinical findings compatible with polio or measles because infection caused by the vaccine strains of these viruses is the first indication of immunodeficiency in some children.

Exposure to contagious diseases may lead to recurrent and, occasionally, even severe infections in persons with normal host defenses. Children who never leave the house may have recurrent infections with organisms brought home by older siblings, other relatives, or neighbors. Certainly, one must assume that children who attend daycare facilities or schools are being exposed constantly to common infections. Familiarity with community patterns of disease such as the prevalent clinical manifestations of enterovirus infection or the beginning of parainfluenza virus, respiratory syncytial virus, influenza, or rotavirus seasons can be used to reassure families of normal children with frequent mild infections. One also should bear in mind that environmental pollutants such as cigarette smoke and wood-burning stoves also have been associated with an increased risk for development of acute lower respiratory tract illnesses in children.[360]

Because many immunodeficiencies are hereditary, a detailed family history should be obtained that includes questions about the presence of immunodeficiency, recurrent or severe infections, contributing factors to any early deaths, the gender of affected persons, and consanguinity. A history of recurrent or severe infections in more than one male relative is highly suggestive of a familial immunodeficiency disorder. Autoimmune diseases may suggest a familial disorder of complement or cell-mediated immunity.[142]

A thorough history of school absenteeism and the reasons that the child stays home may be helpful in differentiating medical from psychosocial problems in older children being evaluated for recurrent infections, particularly when the symptoms are unusual or inconsistent with the physical findings. Prolonged absences for vague problems with no physical findings, particularly in those with normal growth, are less likely to be caused by infections than are those characterized by well-defined physical or laboratory findings and poor growth.

In general, recurrent severe infections beginning before the age of 1 year, failure to thrive, invasive disease caused by encapsulated or unusual organisms, or family histories of such infections should prompt an immunologic evaluation.

PHYSICAL EXAMINATION

Physical examination may provide valuable clues regarding the nature of the immune disorder. In certain cases, such as some patients with hyper-IgE syndrome[89, 227] and DiGeorge syndrome[147] who exhibit the characteristic facies, it may be highly suggestive.[89, 227]

As noted earlier, one of the most obvious signs that a child may have a serious underlying medical problem is failure to thrive. Every immunologic evaluation *must* include documentation of current growth parameters and a comparison with past growth.

Many immunodeficiency disorders have dermatologic manifestations. Eczematoid rashes are seen in patients with the hyper-IgE syndrome and CGD.[89, 227] CGD also is characterized by slow wound healing and the development of hypertrophic scars.[462] Patients with Chédiak-Higashi syndrome have partial albinism.[69] Severe gingival disease and early loss of teeth are prominent clinical features in disorders of neutrophil migration, such as LAD.[26]

The chest should be evaluated for physical signs of active disease, such as rales and rhonchi, as well as evidence of chronic infection, such as an increased anterior-posterior diameter. Pneumonia, bronchitis, bronchiectasis, and scarring can occur with most immunodeficiencies but are associated most frequently with immunoglobulin deficiencies.[85, 218, 335]

Cardiac abnormalities may suggest immunodeficiency disorders such as the DiGeorge syndrome,[147] and situs inversus should alert the clinician to the possibility of Kartagener syndrome.[118]

Although hepatosplenomegaly may be found in many types of immunodeficiency disease, it occurs more commonly in patients with disorders of phagocyte function.

LABORATORY STUDIES

The laboratory evaluation should be guided by the history and physical findings. Relatively simple and inexpensive screening tests often can help narrow the differential diagnosis and streamline the evaluation. One of the first tests that should be performed is a complete blood count with differential and evaluation of the blood smear. This simple test can detect several immunologic abnormalities, including neutropenia, lymphopenia associated with HIV-1 or forms of SCID, the abnormal neutrophil granules associated with Chédiak-Higashi syndrome, Howell-Jolly bodies found with asplenia, and some malignancies. Chest radiographs should be examined for thymic tissue, mediastinal lymphadenopathy, pneumonia, bronchiectasis, and other evidence of pulmonary infection. Consideration also should be given to performing a sweat chloride test to evaluate patients with chronic pulmonary disease for cystic fibrosis.

Quantitative immunoglobulin levels provide a useful screening test for evaluating patients with suspected humoral immune deficiency. One should remember, however, that IgG2 deficiency often is not reflected in the IgG level because it makes up such a relatively small proportion of total IgG. Thus, patients with suspected humoral immune deficiency usually should be tested for IgG subclasses, as well as quantitative IgG, IgA, and IgM. IgE levels may be helpful in establishing the diagnosis of hyper-IgE syndrome, although an elevated IgE level is found much more commonly in patients with allergies than in those with immunologic abnormalities. Immunoglobulin levels may be extremely elevated in children with HIV-1 infection.

Children who have normal quantitative immunoglobulin and IgG subclass levels but who continue to have frequent sinopulmonary infections that do not respond well to appropriate medical and surgical management (e.g., ventilation tubes) also can be evaluated by measuring antibody responses to specific antigens such as tetanus and diphtheria toxoids and *H. influenzae* type b, meningococcal, and pneumococcal capsular polysaccharides. Antibody levels can be measured before immunization and approximately 1 to 2 months after immunization to evaluate the child's ability to respond to different kinds of antigens (i.e., T-cell–dependent antigens such as diphtheria and tetanus toxoid or T-cell–independent antigens such as plain pneumococcal capsular polysaccharide vaccine).

The complement system should be evaluated in persons with recurrent or life-threatening neisserial disease, including systemic gonococcal infections and sporadic meningococcal disease. The best screening test for hemolytic complement is the CH_{50}. A normal CH_{50} reflects a normal quantity and function of classical pathway proteins (C1, C4, C2), C3, and the terminal components through C8, as noted earlier.[141] The alternative pathway proteins can be measured in a similar assay using rabbit erythrocytes instead of antibody-coated sheep cells. Alternative pathway deficiencies are extremely rare; therefore, demonstration of a normal CH_{50} generally is a sufficient indicator of normal complement activity. An abnormal CH_{50} should be repeated immediately, with care taken that the specimen is handled correctly. Complement abnormalities may be quantitative or qualitative. Thus, if the repeat CH_{50} remains low, determining both the serum levels of individual complement proteins and their functional activity is important, as has been discussed.

Delayed hypersensitivity skin testing with antigens such as *Candida* or mumps antigen may be useful to assess cell-mediated immunity, but the results are not always reliable. T-lymphocyte subset quantitation may be helpful in diagnosing such conditions as SCID and HIV, but more sophisticated testing of lymphocyte function such as mitogen and antigen stimulation should be performed in patients with recurrent or severe fungal infections. These studies should be directed by an immunologist.

Similarly, suspected phagocyte function disorders should be evaluated in consultation with experts in phagocyte function because lack of proper standardization and expertise often leads to misleading results from commercial laboratories. Phagocyte function studies should be directed toward adherence and migration in patients with recurrent skin and mucosal infections, poor or absent pus formation, and persistent leukocytosis indicative of a leukocyte adhesion defect. Tests of oxidative metabolic activity and killing should be performed in patients with recurrent staphylococcal or unusual gram-negative or fungal tissue infections suggestive of CGD.

Whenever clinical suspicion of an inherited immunodeficiency is confirmed by appropriate functional laboratory studies, arranging for a specific genetic diagnosis, when such testing is available, may be desirable to determine the precise nature of a patient's genetic mutation or variation. This testing may be of great assistance in subsequent genetic counseling and will add important information to the clinical database on patients with the specific disorder.

Management of Immunodeficiency Disorders

Proper management of immunodeficiency disorders (as described earlier) can enhance both the quality of life and life expectancy markedly. Although some children with immunodeficiency disorders have serious problems with autoimmune disease, malignancy, or both, the vast majority of morbidity and mortality results from infections. Therefore, this discussion is limited to the general principles of managing infectious complications of immunodeficiency.

EDUCATION

After thorough characterization of the immunologic abnormality, the first step in management is to educate the family and, when old enough, the patient regarding environmental risks, how to take medications, and precisely when and where to seek medical care. Families of patients with inherited disorders should receive genetic counseling and be offered the option of prenatal screening if it is available for the disease in question.

EVALUATION FOR INFECTION

Patients with known immunodeficiency disorders should be evaluated promptly and thoroughly for unexplained fever or any other indication of infection. Immunodeficient persons are susceptible to a wide variety of pathogens, their responses to appropriate therapy may be slow, and they often require prolonged treatment. Thus, every effort should be made to identify the infecting organism so that treatment can be specific. Unless the pathogen is known, extended courses of empiric broad-spectrum coverage may be required, and such treatment can lead to superinfection by multiply resistant pathogens.

TREATMENT

Many aspects of disease-specific therapy have been discussed already. In general, patients with immunodeficiency who are susceptible to bacterial infections should be treated empirically and aggressively with antibiotics at the first indication of infection. Antifungal therapy should be added empirically in patients with an increased risk for acquisition of fungal infection (e.g., patients with cell-mediated immune and neutrophil disorders) if they do not have a prompt response to antibacterial therapy. Once a definitive etiology has been established, treatment should be tailored to the pathogen. The duration of therapy must be individualized, but in general, patients with abnormal immune systems should be treated longer than normal hosts who have similar infections.

Bone marrow or stem cell transplants have been successful in a few patients with specific immunologic disorders, including SCID,[87] Wiskott-Aldrich syndrome,[341] and CGD.[232, 282, 455] Gene therapy suggests new possibilities for correcting certain immunologic defects, with early promise already demonstrated for X-linked SCID, as well as for CGD.[148, 282]

PREVENTION

Patients and household members should be immunized with appropriate vaccines as soon as possible after the diagnosis of immunodeficiency is made.[116] One should bear in mind that although many immunodeficient patients, such as those with XLA, cannot respond to immunizations, immunization of household members and other close contacts may reduce the patients' likelihood of developing infection. Patients with complement deficiencies, asplenia, and sickle-cell disease should be immunized with vaccines directed against encapsulated organisms such as meningococci, pneumococci, and *H. influenzae* type b. However, one should remember that these persons may not have a normal response to immunization, and, therefore, if possible, their antibody responses to these vaccines should be measured; if the response is low, these persons should receive extra doses of the vaccines.

Selected patients with recurrent or particularly severe bacterial or fungal infections may require prophylactic antibacterial or antifungal therapy. The benefits of long-term antimicrobial therapy must be weighed carefully, however, against the risk of emergence of multiply resistant organisms.

REFERENCES

1. Abraham, E., Wunderink, R., Silverman, H., et al.: Efficacy and safety of monoclonal antibody to human tumor necrosis factor-α in patients with sepsis syndrome. J. A. M. A. *273*:934–941, 1995.
2. Abramson, J. S., Mills, E. L., Sayer, M. K., et al.: Recurrent infections and delayed separation of the umbilical cord in an infant with abnormal phagocytic cell locomotion and oxidative response during opsonized particle phagocytosis. J. Pediatr. *99*:887–894, 1981.
3. Abramson, J. S., Wheeler, J. G., and Quie, P. G.: The polymorphonuclear leukocyte system. *In* Stiehm, E. R. (ed.): Immunologic Disorders in Infants and Children. 4th ed. Philadelphia, W. B. Saunders, 1996, pp. 94–112.
4. Abughali, N., Berger, M., and Tosi, M. F.: Deficient total cell content of CR3 (CD11b) in neonatal neutrophils. Blood *83*:1086–1092, 1994.
5. Abughali, N., Dubyak, G., and Tosi, M. F.: Impairment of chemoattractant-stimulated hexose uptake in neonatal neutrophils. Blood *82*:2182–2187, 1993.
6. Adamkin, D., Stitzel, A., Urmson, J., et al.: Activity of the alternative pathway of complement in the newborn infant. J. Pediatr. *93*:604–608, 1978.
7. Adderson, E. E., Schackelford, P. G., Quinn, A., et al.: Restricted Ig H chain V gene usage in the human antibody response to *Haemophilus influenzae* type b capsular polysaccharide. J. Immunol. *147*:1667–1674, 1991.
8. Adenyi-Jones, S. C. A., Faden, H., Ferdon, M. B., et al.: Systemic and local immune responses to enhanced-potency inactivated poliovirus vaccine in premature and term infants. J. Pediatr. *120*:686–689, 1992.
9. Aderem, A., and Ulevitch, R. J.: Toll-like receptors in the induction of the innate immune response. Nature *406*:782–787, 2000.
10. Aggarwal, J., Khan, A. J., Diamond, S., et al.: Lazy leukocyte syndrome in a black infant. J. Natl. Med. Assoc. *77*:928–931, 1985.
11. Aggett, P. J., Harries, J. T., Harvey, B. A. M., et al.: An inherited defect of neutrophil mobility in Shwachman syndrome. J. Pediatr. *94*:391–394, 1979.
12. Albelda, S. M., Muller, W. A., Buck, C. A., et al.: Molecular and cellular properties of PECAM-1 (endoCAM/CD31): A novel vascular cell-cell adhesion molecule. J. Cell Biol. *114*:1059–1068, 1991.
13. Alford, C. A., Stagno, S., and Reynolds, D. W.: Diagnosis of chronic perinatal infections. Am. J. Dis. Child. *129*:455–463, 1975.
14. Allen, R. C., Armitage, R. J., Conley, M. E., et al.: CD40 ligand gene defects responsible for X-linked hyper-IgM syndrome. Science *259*: 990–993, 1993.
15. Allen, R. C., and Loose, L. D.: Phagocytic activation of a luminol-dependent chemiluminescence in rabbit alveolar and peritoneal macrophages. Biochem. Biophys. Res. *69*:245–252, 1976.
16. Ambrosino, D. M., Siber, G. R., Chilmonczyk, B. A., et al.: An immunodeficiency characterized by impaired antibody responses to polysaccharides. N. Engl. J. Med. *316*:790–793, 1987.
17. Ambrosino, D. M., Sood, S. K., Lee, M. C., et al.: IgG1, IgG2, and IgM responses to two *Haemophilus influenzae* type b conjugate vaccines in young infants. Pediatr. Infect. Dis. J. *11*:855–859, 1992.
18. Ambrosino, D. M., Umetsu, D. T., Siber, G. R., et al.: Selective defect in the antibody response to *Haemophilus influenzae* type b in children with recurrent infections and normal serum IgG subclass levels. J. Allergy Clin. Immunol. *81*:1175–1179, 1988.
19. Ambruso, D. R., Edward, R. B., McCabe, M. D., et al.: Infectious and bleeding complications in patients with glycogenosis 1b: Relationship to neutrophil and platelet function. Am. J. Dis. Child. *139*:691–697, 1985.
20. Ament, M. E., Ochs, H. D., and Davis, S. D.: Structure and function of the gastrointestinal tract in primary immunodeficiency syndromes: A study of 39 patients. Medicine (Baltimore) *52*:227–248, 1973.
21. Ammann, A. J., and Hong, R.: Selective IgA deficiency and autoimmunity. Clin. Exp. Immunol. 7:833–838, 1970.
22. Ammann, A. J., and Hong, R.: Selective IgA deficiency: Presentation of 30 cases and a review of the literature. Medicine (Baltimore) *60*:223–236, 1971.
23. Anderson, D. C., Freeman, K. B., Hughes, B. J., et al.: Secretory determinants of impaired adherence and mobility of neonatal PMNs. Abstract. Pediatr. Res. *19*:257, 1985.
24. Anderson, D. C., Hughes, B. J., and Smith, C. W.: Abnormal mobility of neonatal polymorphonuclear leukocytes. Relationship to impaired redistribution of surface adhesion sites by chemotactic factor or colchicine. J. Clin. Invest. *68*:863–874, 1981.
25. Anderson, D. C., Hughes, B. J., Wible, L. J., et al.: Impaired motility of neonatal PMN leukocytes: Relationship to abnormalities of cell orientation and assembly of microtubules in chemotactic gradients. J. Leukoc. Biol. *36*:1–15, 1984.
26. Anderson, D. C., Rothlein, R., Martin, S. D., et al.: Impaired transendothelial migration of neonatal neutrophils: Abnormalities of MAC-I (CD11/CD18) dependent adherence reactions. Blood *76*:2613–2621, 1990.
27. Anderson, D. C., Schmalstieg, F. C., Arnaout, M. A., et al.: Abnormalities of polymorphonuclear leukocyte function associated with a heritable deficiency of high molecular weight surface glycoproteins (gp 138): Common relationship to diminished cell adherence. J. Clin. Invest. *74*:546–557, 1984.
28. Anderson, D. C., Schmalstieg, F., Finegold, M. J., et al.: The severe and moderate phenotypes of heritable MAC-1, LFA-1, P150,95 deficiency: Their quantitative definition and relation to leukocyte dysfunction and clinical features. J. Infect. Dis. *152*:668–689, 1985.
29. Anderson, D. C., Smith, C. W., and Springer, T. A.: Leukocyte adhesion deficiency and other disorders of leukocyte motility. *In* Scriver, C. R., Beaudet, A. L., Sly, W. S., et al. (eds.): The Metabolic Basis of Inherited Disease. New York, McGraw-Hill, 1989, pp. 2751–2777.
30. Anderson, D. C., Wibble, L. J., Hughes, B. J., et al.: Cytoplasmic microtubules in polymorphonuclear leukocytes: Effects of chemotactic stimulation and colchicine. Cell *31*:719–729, 1982.
31. Arai, K.-I., Lee, F., Miyajima, A., et al.: Cytokines: Coordinators of immune and inflammatory responses. Annu. Rev. Biochem. *59*:783–836, 1990.
32. Arnaout, M. A.: Structure and function of the leukocyte adhesion molecules CD11/CD18. Blood *75*:1037–1050, 1990.
33. Arnaout, M. A., Pitt, J., Cohen, H. J., et al.: Deficiency of a granulocyte membrane glycoprotein (gp 150) in a boy with recurrent bacterial infections. N. Engl. J. Med. *306*:693–699, 1982.
34. Arnaout, M. A., Wang, E. A., Clark, S. C., et al.: Human recombinant GM-CSF increases cell to cell adhesion and surface expression of adhesion-promoting surface glycoproteins on mature granulocytes. J. Clin. Invest. *78*:597–601, 1986.
35. Aruffo, A., Farrington, M., Hollenbaugh, D., et al.: The CD40 ligand, gp39, is defective in activated T cells from patients with X-linked hyper-IgM syndrome. Cell *72*:291–300, 1993.
36. Babior, B. M.: The nature of the NADPH oxidase. *In* Gallin, J. I., and Fauci, A. S. (eds.): Advances in Host Defense Mechanisms. New York, Raven Press, 1983, pp. 91–119.
37. Babior, B. M., Kipnes, R. S., and Curnutte, J. T.: Biological defense mechanisms: The production by leukocytes of superoxide, a potential bactericidal agent. J. Clin. Invest. *52*:741–744, 1973.
38. Babior, B. M., Rosin, R. E., McMurrich, B. J., et al.: Arrangement of the respiratory burst oxidase in the plasma membrane of the neutrophil. J. Clin. Invest. *67*:1724–1730, 1981.
39. Baehner, R. L., Johnston, R. B., and Nathan, D. G.: Comparative study of the metabolic and bactericidal characteristics of severely glucose-6-phosphate dehydrogenase–deficient polymorphonuclear leukocytes and leukocytes from children with chronic granulomatous disease. J. Reticul. Soc. *12*:150–160, 1972.
40. Baehner, R. L., Karnovsky, M. J., and Karnovsky, M. L.: Degranulation of leukocytes in chronic granulomatous disease. J. Clin. Invest. *48*:187–192, 1969.
41. Bagby, G. J., Plessala, K. J., Wilson, L. A., et al.: Divergent efficacy of antibody to tumor necrosis factor-α in intravascular and peritonitis models of sepsis. J. Infect. Dis. *163*:83–88, 1991.
42. Bainton, D. F.: Developmental biology of neutrophils and eosinophils. *In* Gallin, J. I., Goldstein, I. M., and Snyderman, R. (eds.): Inflammation: Basic Principles and Clinical Correlates. 2nd ed. New York, Raven Press, 1992, pp. 303–324.
43. Baker, C. J., and Edwards, M. S.: Group B streptococcal infections. *In* Remington, J. S., and Klein, J. O. (eds.): Infectious Diseases of the Fetus and Newborn Infant. 4th ed. Philadelphia, W. B. Saunders, 1995, pp. 980–1054.
44. Ballow, M., Cates, K. L., Rowe, J. C., et al.: Development of the immune system in very low birth weight (less than 1500 g) premature infants: Concentrations of plasma immunoglobulins and patterns of infections. Pediatr. Res. *20*:899–904, 1986.
45. Banatvala, N., Davies, J., Kanariou, M., et al.: Hypogammaglobulinaemia associated with normal or increased IgM (the hyper IgM syndrome): A case series review. Arch. Dis. Child. *71*:150–152, 1994.
46. Baraff, L. J., Leake, R. D., Burstyn, D. G., et al.: Immunologic response to early and routine DTP immunization in infants. Pediatrics *73*:37–42, 1984.
47. Barbosa, M. D., Nguyen, Q. A., Tchernev, V. T., et al.: Identification of the homologous beige and Chédiak-Higashi syndrome genes. Nature *382*: 262–265, 1996.

48. Barrett, D. J., and Boyle, M. D. P.: Restoration of complement function in vivo by plasma infusion in factor I (C3b inactivator) deficiency. J. Pediatr. *104*:76–81, 1984.
49. Bashan, N., Potashnik, R., Hagay, Y., et al.: Impaired glucose transport in polymorphonuclear leukocytes in glycogen storage disease 1b. Inherit. Metab. Dis. *10*:234–239, 1987.
50. Bass, D. A., Parce, J. W., Dechatelet, L. R., et al.: Flow cytometric studies of oxidative product formation by neutrophils: A graded response to membrane stimulation. J. Immunol. *130*:1910–1917, 1983.
51. Bastian, J., Law, S., Vogler, L., et al.: Prediction of persistent immunodeficiency in the DiGeorge anomaly. J. Pediatr. *115*:391–396, 1989.
52. Beaudet, A. L., Anderson, D. C., Michels, V. V., et al.: Neutropenia and impaired neutrophil migration in type 1B glycogen storage disease. J. Pediatr. *97*:906–910, 1980.
53. Bennett, J. E.: *Aspergillus* species. *In* Mandell, G. L., Bennett, J. E., and Dolin, R. (eds.): Principles and Practice of Infectious Diseases. 4th ed. New York, Churchill Livingstone, 1995, pp. 2306–2311.
54. Berger, M., and Frank, M. M.: The serum complement system. *In* Stiehm, E. R. (ed.): Immunologic Disorders in Infants and Children. 4th ed. Philadelphia, W. B. Saunders, 1996, pp. 133–158.
55. Berger, M., O'Shea, J., Cross, A. S., et al.: Human neutrophils increase expression of C3bi as well as C3b receptors upon activation. J. Clin. Invest. *74*:1566–1571, 1984.
56. Berger, M., Wetzler, E., August, J. T., et al.: Internalization of type 1 complement receptors and de novo multivesicular body formation during chemoattractant-induced endocytosis in human neutrophils. J. Clin. Invest. *94*:1113–1125, 1994.
57. Berger, M., Wetzler, E. M., and Wallis, R. S.: Tumor necrosis factor is the major monocyte product that increases complement receptor expression on mature human neutrophils. Blood *71*:151–158, 1988.
58. Berman, J. E., Mellis, S. J., Pollock, R., et al.: Content and organization of the human Ig V_H locus: Definition of three new V_H families and linkage to the Ig C_H locus. EMBO J. *7*:727–738, 1988.
59. Berman, S., Lee, B., Nuss, R., et al.: Immunoglobulin G, total and subclass, in children with or without recurrent otitis media. J. Pediatr. *121*:249–251, 1992.
60. Bernbaum, J. C., Daft, A., Anolik, R., et al.: Response of preterm infants to diphtheria-tetanus-pertussis immunizations. J. Pediatr. *107*:184–188, 1985.
61. Beutler, B., and Cerami, A.: The biology of cachectin/TNF-α primary mediator of the host response. Annu. Rev. Immunol. *7*:625–655, 1989.
62. Bevilacqua, M. P., and Nelson, R. M.: Selectins. J. Clin. Invest. *91*:379–387, 1993.
63. Bird, P., and Lachmann, P. J.: The regulation of IgG subclass production in man: Low serum IgG4 in inherited deficiencies of the classical pathway of C3 activation. J. Immunol. *18*:1217–1222, 1988.
64. Bishof, N. A., Welch, T. R., and Beischel, L. S.: C4B deficiency: A risk factor for bacteremia with encapsulated organisms. J. Infect. Dis. *162*:248–250, 1990.
65. Bjorkman, P. J., Saper, M. A., Samraoui, B., et al.: Structure of the human class I histocompatibility antigen, HLA-A2. Nature *329*:506–512, 1987.
66. Bjorkman, P. J., Saper, M. A., Samraoui, B., et al.: The foreign antigen binding site and T cell recognition regions of class I histocompatibility antigens. Nature *329*:512–518, 1987.
67. Black, F. L.: Why did they die? Science *258*:1739–1740, 1992.
68. Blaese, R. M.: Development of gene therapy for immunodeficiency: Adenosine deaminase deficiency. Pediatr. Res. *33* (Suppl.):49–55, 1993.
69. Blume, R. S., and Wolff, S. M.: The Chédiak-Higashi syndrome: Studies in four patients and a review of the literature. Medicine (Baltimore) *51*:247–280, 1972.
70. Bohnsack, J. F., and Brown, E. J.: The role of the spleen in resistance to infection. Annu. Rev. Med. *37*:49–59, 1986.
71. Borregaard, N., Heiple, J. M., Simons, E. R., et al.: Subcellular localization of the b-cytochrome component of the human neutrophil microbicidal oxidase: Translocation during activation. J. Cell Biol. *97*:52–61, 1983.
72. Borregaard, N., Kjeldsen, L., Lollike, K., et al.: Granules and vesicles of human neutrophils. The role of endomembranes as source of plasma membrane proteins. Eur. J. Haematol. *51*:318–322, 1993.
73. Borregaard, N., Kjeldsen, L., Sengelov, H., et al.: Changes in subcellular localization and surface expression of L-selectin, alkaline phosphatase, and Mac-1 in human neutrophils during stimulation with inflammatory mediators. J. Leukoc. Biol. *56*:80–87, 1994.
74. Borzy, M. S., Ridgway, D., Noya, F. J., et al.: Successful bone marrow transplantation with split lymphoid chimerism in DiGeorge syndrome. J. Clin. Immunol. *9*:386–392, 1989.
75. Bottger, E. C., and Bitter-Suermann, D.: Complement and the regulation of humoral immune responses. Immunol. Today *8*:261–264, 1987.
76. Bowens, T. S., Ochs, H. D., Altman, L. C., et al.: Severe recurrent bacterial infections associated with defective adherence and chemotaxis in two patients with neutrophils deficient in cell-associated glycoproteins. J. Pediatr. *101*:932–940, 1982.
77. Boxer, L. A., Coates, T. D., Haak, R. A., et al.: Lactoferrin deficiency associated with altered granulocyte function. N. Engl. J. Med. *307*:404–410, 1982.
78. Boxer, L. A., Hedley-Whyte, E. T., and Stossel, T. P.: Neutrophil actin dysfunction and abnormal neutrophil behavior. N. Engl. J. Med. *29*:1093–1099, 1974.
79. Boxer, L. A., Oliver, J. M., Spielberg, S. P., et al.: Protection of granulocytes by vitamin E in glutathione synthetase deficiency. N. Engl. J. Med. *301*:901–905, 1979.
80. Boxer, L. A., Watanabe, A. M., Rister, M., et al.: Correction of leukocyte function in Chédiak-Higashi syndrome by ascorbate. N. Engl. J. Med. *295*:1041–1045, 1976.
81. Braun, J., and Stiehm, E. R.: The B-lymphocyte system. *In* Stiehm, E. R. (ed.): Immunologic Disorders in Infants and Children. 4th ed. Philadelphia, W. B. Saunders, 1996, pp. 35–74.
82. Brown, E. J.: Interaction of gram-positive microorganisms with complement. Curr. Top. Microbiol. Immunol. *121*:159–197, 1985.
83. Brown, J. H., Jardetzky, T., Saper, M. A., et al.: A hypothetical model of the foreign antigen binding site of class II histocompatibility molecules. Nature *353*:845–850, 1988.
84. Bruce, M. C., Baley, J. E., Medvik, K. A., et al.: Impaired surface membrane expression of C3bi but not C3b receptors on neonatal neutrophils. Pediatr. Res. *21*:306–311, 1987.
85. Bruton, O. C.: Agammaglobulinemia. Pediatrics *9*:722–728, 1952.
86. Buckley, R. H.: Disorders of the IgE system. *In* Stiehm, E. R. (ed.): Immunologic Disorders in Infants and Children. 4th ed. Philadelphia, W. B. Saunders, 1996, pp. 409–422.
87. Buckley, R., Schiff, R. I., Schiff, S. E., et al.: Human severe combined immunodeficiency: Genetic, phenotypic, and functional diversity in one hundred eight infants. J. Pediatr. *130*:378–387, 1997.
88. Buckley, R. H., Schiff, S. E., and Hayward, A. R.: Reduced frequency of $CD45RO^+$ T lymphocytes in blood of hyper IgE syndrome patients. J. Allergy Clin. Immunol. *87*:313–321, 1991.
89. Buckley, R. H., Wray, B. B., and Belmaker, E. Z.: Extreme hyperimmunoglobulinemia E and undue susceptibility to infection. Pediatr. *49*:59–70, 1972.
90. Bucy, R. P., Chan, C.-L., and Cooper, M. D.: Tissue localization and CD8 accessory molecule expression of T$\gamma\delta$ cells in humans. J. Immunol. *142*:3045–3049, 1989.
91. Buescher, E. S., Gaither, T., Nath, J., et al.: Abnormal adherence-related function of neutrophils, monocytes, and EB virus–transformed B cells in a patient with C3bi receptor deficiency. Blood *65*:1382–1390, 1985.
92. Buescher, E. S., and Gallin, J. I.: Leukocyte transfusions in chronic granulomatous disease. N. Engl. J. Med. *307*:800–803, 1982.
93. Burnett, G. W., and Scherp, H. W.: Oral Microbiology and Infectious Disease. Baltimore, Williams & Wilkins, 1968.
94. Butcher, E. C.: Leukocyte–endothelial cell recognition: Three (or more) steps to specificity and diversity. Cell *67*:1033–1036, 1991.
95. Cabau, N., Levy, F. M., Zivy, D., et al.: Evolution of titre of serum IgG in newborn. Med. Microbiol. Immunol. *162*:251–258, 1974.
96. Campbell, A. D., Long, M. W., and Wicha, M. S.: Haemonectin, a bone marrow adhesion protein specific for cells of granulocyte lineage. Nature *329*:744, 1987.
97. Cates, K. L., Densen, P., Lockman, J. D., et al.: C4B deficiency is not associated with meningitis or bacteremia with encapsulated bacteria. J. Infect. Dis. *165*:942–944, 1992.
98. Cates, K. L., Goetz, C., Rosenberg, N., et al.: Longitudinal development of specific and functional antibody in very low birth weight premature infants. Pediatr. Res. *23*:14–22, 1988.
99. Cates, K. L., and Levine, R. P.: C3 binding to bacterial surfaces. *In* Cabello, F., and Pruzzo, C. (eds.): Bacteria, Complement, and the Phagocytic Cell. NATO ASI Series. New York, Springer-Verlag, 1988, pp. 109–128.
100. Certain, S., Barrat, F., Pastural, E., et al.: Protein truncation test of LYST reveals heterogeneous mutations in patients with Chédiak Higashi syndrome. Blood *95*:979–983, 2000.
101. Chandra, R. K.: Fetal malnutrition and postnatal immunocompetence. Am. J. Dis. Child. *29*:450–454, 1975.
102. Chin, T. W., Stiehm, E. R., Faloon, J., and Gallin, J. I.: Corticosteroids in treatment of obstructive lesions of chronic granulomatous disease. J. Pediatr. *111*:349–352, 1987.
103. Christensen, R. D.: Hematopoiesis in the fetus and neonate. Pediatr. Res. *26*:531–535, 1989.
104. Christensen, R. D., Shigeoka, A. O., Hill, H. R., et al.: Neutrophil and bone marrow exhaustion in human and experimental neonatal sepsis. Pediatr. Res. *14*:806–808, 1980.
105. Church, J. A., Frenkel, L. D., and Wright, D. G.: T lymphocyte dysfunction, hyperimmunoglobulinemia E, recurrent bacterial infections, and defective neutrophil chemotaxis in a negro child. J. Pediatr. *88*:982–984, 1976.
106. Chusid, M. J.: Pyogenic hepatic abscess in infancy and childhood. Pediatrics *62*:554–559, 1978.
107. Clark, R. A., Leidal, K. G., Pearson, D. W., et al.: NADPH oxidase of human neutrophils. J. Biol. Chem. *262*:4065–4074, 1987.
108. Clark, R. A., Malech, H. L., Gallin, J. I., et al.: Genetic variants of chronic granulomatous disease: Prevalence of deficiencies of two cytosolic components of the NADPH oxidase system. N. Engl. J. Med. *321*:647–652, 1989.

109. Clark, R. A., Root, R. K., Kimball, H. R., et al.: Defective neutrophil chemotaxis and cellular immunity in a child with recurrent infection. Ann. Intern. Med. *78*:515–519, 1973.
110. Coates T. D., Torkildson, J. C., Torres, M., et al.: An inherited defect of neutrophil motility and microfilamentous cytoskeleton associated with abnormalities in 47-Kd and 89-Kd proteins. Blood *78*:1338–1346, 1991.
111. Cohen, M. S., Isturiz, R. E., and Malech, H. L.: Fungal infection in chronic granulomatous disease: The importance of the phagocyte in defense against fungi. Am. J. Med. *71*:59–66, 1981.
112. Cohn, M.: The a priori principles which govern immune responsiveness. *In* Kaplan, J. G., Green, D. R., and Bleackley, R. C. (eds.): Cellular Basis of Immune Modulation. New York, Liss, 1989, pp. 11–44.
113. Colten, H. R.: Complement biosynthesis. Clin. Immunol. Allergy *5*:287–300, 1985.
114. Colten, H. R., and Goldberger, G.: Ontogeny of serum complement proteins. Pediatrics *64*(Suppl.):775–780, 1979.
115. Committee on Infectious Diseases: Update on timing of hepatitis B vaccination for premature infants and for children with lapsed immunization. Pediatrics *94*:403–404, 1994.
116. Committee on Infectious Diseases: 2000 Red Book: Report of the Committee on Infectious Diseases. 25th ed. Elk Grove Village, IL, American Academy of Pediatrics, 2000.
117. Conley, M. E., and Puck, J. M.: Carrier detection in typical and atypical X-linked agammaglobulinemia. J. Pediatr. *112*:688–694, 1988.
118. Conley, M. E., and Stiehm, E. R.: Immunodeficiency disorders: General considerations. *In* Stiehm, E. R. (ed.): Immunologic Disorders in Infants and Children. 4th ed. Philadelphia, W. B. Saunders, 1996, pp. 201–252.
119. Cooper, M. R., DeChatelet, L. R., and McCall, C. E.: Complete deficiency of leukocyte glucose-6-phosphate dehydrogenase with defective bactericidal activity. J. Clin. Invest. *51*:769–778, 1972.
120. Cooper, N. R.: The classical complement pathway: Activation and regulation of the first complement component. Adv. Immunol. *37*:151–216, 1985.
121. Cooper, N. R., and Nemerow, G. R.: Complement-dependent mechanisms of virus neutralization. *In* Ross, G. D. (ed.): Immunobiology of the Complement System. Orlando, FL, Academic Press, 1986, pp. 139–162.
122. Croft, M., Duncan, D. D., and Swain, S. L.: Response of naive antigen-specific $CD4^+$ T cells in vitro: Characteristics and antigen-presenting cell requirements. J. Exp. Med. *176*:1431–1437, 1992.
123. Crowley, C. A., Curnutte, J. T., Roskin, R. E., et al.: An inherited abnormality of neutrophil adhesion. Its genetic transmission and its association with a missing protein. N. Engl. J. Med. *302*:1163–1168, 1980.
124. Cunningham-Rundles, C.: Clinical and immunologic analyses of 103 patients with common variable immunodeficiency. J. Clin. Immunol. *9*:22–33, 1989.
125. Cunningham-Rundles, C.: Disorders of the IgA system. *In* Stiehm, E. R. (ed.): Immunologic Disorders in Infants and Children. 4th ed. Philadelphia, W. B. Saunders, 1996, pp. 423–442.
126. Cunningham-Rundles, C., Zhou, Z., Mankarious, S., et al.: Long-term use of IgA depleted intravenous immunoglobulin in immunodeficient subjects with anti-IgA antibodies. J. Clin. Immunol. *13*:272–278, 1993.
127. Cunningham-Rundles, S., Cunningham-Rundles, C., Ma, D. I., et al.: Impaired proliferative response to B lymphocyte activators in common variable immunodeficiency. J. Clin. Immunol. *1*:65–72, 1981.
128. Curnutte, J. T.: Classification of chronic granulomatous disease. Hematol. Oncol. Clin. North Am. *2*:241–252, 1988.
129. Daar, A. S., Fuggle, S. V., Fabre, J. W., et al.: The detailed distribution of HLA-A, B, C antigens in normal human organs. Transplantation *38*:287–292, 1984.
130. Daar, A. S., Fuggle, S. V., Fabre, J. W., et al.: The detailed distribution of MHC class II antigens in normal human organs. Transplantation *38*:293–298, 1984.
131. Dalgleish, A., Beverly, P., Clapham, P., et al.: The CD4 (T4) antigen is an essential component of the receptor for the AIDS retrovirus. Nature *312*:763–767, 1984.
132. Dancis, J., Osburn, J. J., and Kunz, H. W.: Studies of immunology of the newborn infant. IV. Antibody formation in the premature infant. Pediatrics *12*:151–156, 1953.
133. Davis, A. E., III: C1 inhibitor and hereditary angioneurotic edema. Annu. Rev. Immunol. *6*:595–628, 1988.
134. Davis, M. D., and Bjorkman, P. J.: T-cell antigen receptor genes and T-cell recognition. Nature *334*:395–402, 1988.
135. Davis, S. D., Schaller, J., and Wedgewood, R. J.: Job's syndrome: Recurrent "cold" staphylococcal abscesses. Lancet *1*:1013–1015, 1966.
136. DeBiagi, M., Andreani, M., and Centis, F.: Immune characterization of human fetal tissues with monoclonal antibodies. Prog. Clin. Biol. Res. *193*:89–94, 1985.
137. Decoster, A., Darcy, F., Caron, A., et al.: Anti-P30 IgA antibodies as prenatal markers of congenital *Toxoplasma* infection. Clin. Exp. Immunol. *87*:310–315, 1992.
138. Defrance, T., Vanbervliet, F., Briere, F., et al.: Interleukin 10 and transforming growth factor β cooperate to induce anti-CD40–activated naive human B cells to secrete immunoglobulin A. J. Exp. Med. *175*:671–682, 1992.
139. Dengrove, J., Lee, E. J., Heiner, D. C., et al.: IgG and IgG subclass specific antibody responses to diphtheria and tetanus toxoids in newborns and infants given DTP immunization. Pediatr. Res. *20*:735–739, 1986.
140. Densen, P.: Human complement deficiency states and infection. *In* Whaley, K., Loos, M., and Weiler, J. M. (eds.): Complement in Health and Disease. Dordrecht, The Netherlands, Kluwer Academic, 1993, pp. 173–197.
141. Densen, P.: Complement. *In* Mandell, G. L., Bennett, J. E., and Dolin, R. (eds.): Principles and Practice of Infectious Diseases. 4th ed. New York, Churchill Livingstone, 1995, pp. 58–78.
142. Densen, P., McRill, C., and Ross, S. C.: The contribution of the alternative and classical complement pathways to gonococcal killing and C3 fixation. *In* Poolman, J. T., Zanen, H. C., Meyer, T. F., et al. (eds.): Gonococci and Meningococci. Dordrecht, The Netherlands, Kluwer Academic, 1988, pp. 693–697.
143. Densen, P., Weiler, J. M., Griffiss, J. M., et al.: Familial properdin deficiency and fatal meningococcemia. Correction of the bactericidal defect by vaccination. N. Engl. J. Med. *316*:922–926, 1987.
144. Diamond, M. S., and Springer, T. A.: A subpopulation of Mac-1 (CD11b/CD18) molecules mediates neutrophil adhesion to ICAM-1 and fibrinogen. J. Cell. Biol. *120*:545–556, 1993.
145. Diamond, R. D.: *Cryptococcus neoformans*. *In* Mandell, G. L., Bennett, J. E., and Dolin, R. (eds.): Principles and Practice of Infectious Diseases. 4th ed. New York, Churchill Livingstone, 1995, pp. 2331–2340.
146. Diamond, R. D., Root, R. K., and Bennett, J. E.: Factors influencing killing of *Cryptococcus neoformans* by human leukocytes in vitro. J. Infect. Dis. *163*:1108–1113, 1972.
147. DiGeorge, A. M.: A new concept of the cellular basis of immunity (discussion). J. Pediatr. *67*:907–908, 1965.
148. Dinauer, M. C., Lekstrom-Himes, J. A., and Dale, D. C.: Inherited neutrophil disorders: Molecular basis and new therapies. Hematology (Am. Soc. Hematol. Educ. Program) 303–318, 2000.
149. Doherty, P. C., Allan, W., and Eichelberger, M.: Roles of αβγδ T cell subsets in viral immunity. Annu. Rev. Immunol. *10*:123–151, 1992.
150. Donabedian, H., and Gallin, J. I.: Deactivation of human neutrophil chemotaxis by chemoattractants: Effect on receptors for the chemotactic factor f-met-leu-phe. J. Immunol. *127*:839–844, 1981.
151. Donabedian, H., and Gallin, J. I.: Mononuclear cells from patients with the hyperimmunoglobulin E–recurrent infection syndrome produce an inhibitor of leukocyte chemotaxis. J. Clin. Invest. *69*:115–124, 1982.
152. Donabedian, H., and Gallin, J. I.: The hyperimmunoglobulin E recurrent infection (Job's) syndrome: A review of the NIH experience and the literature. Medicine (Baltimore) *62*:195–207, 1983.
153. Donowitz, G. R., and Mandell, G. L.: Clinical presentation and unusual infections in chronic granulomatous disease. *In* Gallin, J. I., and Fauci, A. S. (eds.): Advances in Host Defense Mechanisms. New York, Raven Press, 1983, pp. 55–75.
154. Donskoy, E., and Goldschneider, I.: Thymocytopoiesis is maintained by blood-borne precursors throughout postnatal life. A study of parabiotic mice. J. Immunol. *148*:1604–1612, 1992.
155. Douglas, S. D., and Yoder, M. C.: The mononuclear phagocyte and dendritic cell systems. *In* Stiehm, E. R. (ed.): Immunologic Disorders in Infants and Children. 4th ed. Philadelphia, W. B. Saunders, 1996, pp. 113–132.
156. Doyle, C., and Stominger, J. L.: Interaction between CD4 and class II MHC molecules mediates cell adhesion. Nature *330*:256–259, 1987.
157. Drew, J. H., and Arroyave, C. M.: The complement system of the newborn infant. Biol. Neonate *37*:209–217, 1980.
158. Edwards, J. E.: *Candida* species. *In* Mandell, G. L., Bennett, J. E., and Dolin, R. (eds.): Principles and Practice of Infectious Diseases. 4th ed. New York, Churchill Livingstone, 1995, pp. 2289–2306.
159. Edwards, M. S.: Complement in neonatal infections: An overview. Pediatr. Infect. Dis. *5*(Suppl.):168–170, 1986.
160. Eichenfield, L. F., and Johnston, R. B., Jr.: Secondary disorders of the complement system. Am. J. Dis. Child. *143*:595–602, 1989.
161. Einhorn, M. S., Granoff, D. M., Nahm, M. H., et al.: Concentrations of antibodies in paired maternal and infant sera: Relationship to IgG subclass. J. Pediatr. *111*:783–788, 1987.
162. Enders, G.: Serologic test combinations for safe detection of rubella infections. Rev. Infect. Dis. *7*(Suppl.):113–122, 1985.
163. Engh, C. A., Hughes, J. L., Abrams, R. C., et al.: Osteomyelitis in the patient with sickle-cell disease. J. Bone Joint Surg. Am. *53*:1–15, 1971.
164. Englund, J. A., Glezen, W. P., Turner C., et al.: Transplacental antibody transfer following maternal immunization with polysaccharide and conjugate *Haemophilus influenzae* type b vaccines. J. Infect. Dis. *171*:99–105, 1995.
165. Erdei, A., Fust, G., and Gergely, J.: The role of C3 in the immune response. Immunol. Today *12*:332–337, 1991.
166. Eynon, E. E., and Parker, D. C.: Small B cells as antigen-presenting cells in the induction of tolerance to soluble protein antigens. J. Exp. Med. *175*:131–138, 1992.
167. Falk, K., Rotzschke, O., Deres, K., et al.: Identification of naturally processed viral nonapeptides allows their quantification in infected cells and suggests an allele-specific T cell epitope forecast. J. Exp. Med. *174*:425–434, 1991.

168. Falk, K., Rotzschke, O., Stevanovic, S., et al.: Allele-specific motifs revealed by sequencing of self-peptides eluted from MHC molecules. Nature *351*:290–296, 1991.
169. Fanger, M., Shen, L., Graziano, R., and Guyre, P.: Cytotoxicity mediated by human Fc receptors for IgG. Immunol. Today *10*:92–99, 1989.
170. Fearon, D. T., and Austen, K. F.: Properdin: Binding to C3b and stabilization of the C3b-dependent C3 convertase. J. Exp. Med. *142*:856–863, 1975.
171. Fearon, D. T., and Austen, K. F.: The alternative pathway of complement—a system for host resistance to microbial infection. N. Engl. J. Med. *303*:259–263, 1980.
172. Fearon, D. T., and Collins, L. A.: Increased expression of C3b receptors on polymorphonuclear leukocytes induced by chemotactic factors and by purification procedures. J. Immunol. *130*:370–375, 1983.
173. Fearon, D. T., Ruddy, S., Schur, P. H., et al.: Activation of the properdin pathway of complement in patients with gram-negative bacteremia. N. Engl. J. Med. *292*:937–940, 1975.
174. Ferguson, S. E., and Thompson, C. B. A.: A new break in V(D) J recombination. Curr. Biol. *3*:51–53, 1993.
175. Ferrari, S., Giliani, S., Insalaco, A., et al.: Mutations of CD40 gene cause an autosomal recessive form of immunodeficiency with hyper-IgM. Proc. Natl. Acad. Sci. U. S. A. *98*:12614–12619, 2001.
176. Figueroa, J. E., and Densen, P.: Infectious diseases associated with complement deficiencies. Clin. Microbiol. Rev. *4*:359–395, 1991.
177. Fink, C. W., Miller, W. E., Dorward, B., et al.: The formation of macroglobulin antibodies. II. Studies on neonatal infants and older children. J. Clin. Invest. *41*:1422–1428, 1962.
178. Fischer, A., Hacein-Bey, S., Le Deist, F., et al.: Gene therapy of severe combined immunodeficiencies. Immunol. Rev. *178*:13–20, 2000.
179. Fisher, A., Trung, P. H., Descamps-Latsdra, B., et al.: Bone marrow-transplantation for inborn error of phagocytic cells associated with defective adherence, chemotaxis, and oxidative response during opsonized particle phagocytosis. Lancet *2*:473–475, 1983.
180. Fisher, C. L., Dhainaut, J. F., Opal, S. M., et al.: Recombinant human interleukin-1 receptor antagonist in the treatment of patients with severe sepsis. J. A. M. A. *271*:1836–1843, 1994.
181. Fleishmann, J., and Lehrer, R. I.: Phagocytic mechanism in host response. *In* Howard, D. H. (ed.): Fungi Pathogenic for Humans and Animals, Part B2. New York, Marcel Dekker, 1985, pp. 123–149.
182. Fleming, A. F., Storey, J., Molineaux, L., et al.: Abnormal haemoglobins in the Sudan savanna of Nigeria: I. Prevalence of haemoglobins and relationships between sickle cell trait, malaria, and survival. Ann. Trop. Med. Parasitol. *73*:161–172, 1979.
183. Forlow, S. B., Schurr, J. R., Kolls, J. K., et al.: Increased granulopoiesis through interleukin-17 and granulocyte colony-stimulating factor in leukocyte adhesion deficient mice. Blood *98*:3309–3314, 2001.
184. Fremont, D. H., Matsumura, M., Stura, E. A., et al.: Crystal structures of two viral peptides in complex with murine MHC class I H-$2K^b$. Science *257*:919–934, 1992.
185. Frydman, M., Etzioni, A., Eidlitz-Markus, T., et al.: Rambam-Hasharon syndrome of psychomotor retardation, short stature, defective neutrophil motility, and Bombay phenotype. Am. J. Med. Genet. *44*: 297–302, 1992.
186. Fuchs, E. J., and Matzinger, P. B.: Cells turn off virgin but not memory T cells. Science *258*:1156–1159, 1992.
187. Gabbay, J. E., and Almeida, R. P.: Antibiotic peptides and serine protease homologs in human polymorphonuclear leukocytes: Defensins and azurocidin. Curr. Opin. Immunol. *5*:97–102, 1993.
188 Gallin, J. I.: Neutrophil specific granule deficiency. Annu. Rev. Med. *36*:263–274, 1985.
189. Ganz, T., and Lehrer, R. I.: Antimicrobial peptides of vertebrates. Curr. Opin. Imunol. *10*:41–44, 1998.
190. Ganz, T., and Weiss J.: Antimicrobial peptides of phagocytes and epithelia. Semin. Hematol. *34*:343–354, 1997.
191. Gathings, W. E., Lawton, A. R., and Cooper, M. D.: Immunofluorescent studies of the development of pre-B cells, B lymphocytes and immunoglobulin isotype diversity in humans. Eur. J. Immunol. *7*:804–810, 1977.
192. Geelan, S. P. M., Bazemer, A. C., Gerards, L. J., et al.: Deficiencies in opsonic defense to pneumococci in the human newborn despite adequate levels of complement and specific IgG antibodies. Pediatr. Res. *27*:514–518, 1990.
193. Geha, R. S., Reinherz, E., Leung, D., et al.: Deficiency of suppressor T cells in the hyperimmunoglobulin E syndrome. J. Clin. Invest. *68*:783–791, 1981.
194. Gelfand, E. W., and Finkel, T. H.: The T-lymphocyte system. *In* Stiehm, E. R. (ed.): Immunologic Disorders in Infants and Children. 4th ed. Philadelphia, W. B. Saunders, 1996, pp. 14–34.
195. Gerard, C., and Gerard, N.: C5a anaphylatoxin and its seven transmembrane-segment receptors. Annu. Rev. Immunol. *12*:775–808, 1994.
196. Gill, T. J., III, Karasic, R. B., Antoncic, J., and Rabbin, B. S.: Long-term follow-up of children born to women immunized with tetanus toxoid during pregnancy. Am. J. Reprod. Immunol. *25*:69–71, 1991.
197. Gill, T. J., Repetti, C. F., Metlay, L. A., et al.: Transplacental immunization of the human fetus to tetanus by immunization of the mother. J. Clin. Invest. *72*:987–996, 1983.
198. Goldberg, A. L., and Rock, K. L.: Proteolysis, proteasomes and antigen presentation. Nature *357*:375–379, 1992.
199. Golding, B., Muchmore, A. V., and Blaese, R. M.: Newborn and Wiskott-Aldrich patient B cells can be activated by TNP-*Brucella abortus:* Evidence that TNP-*Brucella abortus* behaves as a T-independent type 1 antigen in humans. J. Immunol. *133*:2966–2971, 1984.
200. Goldsobel, A. B., Haas, A., and Stiehm, E. R.: Bone marrow transplantation in DiGeorge syndrome. J. Pediatr. *111*:40–44, 1987.
201. Good, R. A.: Studies on agammaglobulinemia: II. Failure of plasma cell formation in the bone marrow and lymph nodes of patients with agammaglobulinemia. J. Lab. Clin. Med. *46*:167–181, 1955.
202. Gordon, D. L., and Hostetter, M. K.: Complement and host defense against microorganisms. Pathology *18*:365–375, 1986.
203. Goudemand, J., Anssens, R., Delmas-Marsalet, Y., et al.: Essai de traitement d'un cas de granulomatose familiale chronique par greffe de moelle osseuse allogenique. Arch. Fr. Pediatr. *33*:121–129, 1976.
204. Grakoui, A., Bromley, S. K., Sumen, C., et al.: The immunological synapse: A molecular machine controlling T cell activation. Science *285*:221–227.
205. Greenberg, F., Crowder, W. E., Paschall, V., et al.: Familial DiGeorge syndrome and associated partial monosomy of chromosome 22. Hum. Genet. *65*:317–319, 1984.
206. Greenberg, F., Elder, F. F. B., Haffner, P., et al.: Cytogenic findings in a prospective series of patients with DiGeorge anomaly. Am. J. Hum. Genet. *43*:605–611, 1988.
207. Greve, J. M., Davis, G., Meyer, A. M., et al.: The major human rhinovirus receptor is ICAM-1. Cell *56*:839–847, 1989.
208. Grimbacher, B., Holland, S. M., Gallin, J. I., et al.: Hyper-IgE syndrome with recurrent infections—an autosomal dominant multisystem disorder. N. Engl. J. Med. *340*:692–702, 1999.
209. Grisham, M. B., Jefferson, M. M., Melton, D. F., and Thomas, E. L.: Chlorination of endogenous amines by isolated neutrophils. Ammonia-dependent bactericidal, cytotoxic, and cytolytic activities of the chloramines. J. Biol. Chem. *259*:10404–10413, 1984.
210. Gupta, S., Rahwa, R., O'Reilly, R., et al.: Ontogeny of lymphocyte subpopulations in human fetal liver. Proc. Natl. Acad. Sci. U. S. A. *73*:919–922, 1976.
211. Harding, C. V., Collins, D. S., Slot, J. W., et al.: Liposome-encapsulated antigens are processed in lysosomes, recycled, and presented to T cells. Cell *64*:393–401, 1991.
212. Harris, B. H., Shalit, M., and Southwick, F. S.: Diminished actin polymerization by neutrophils from newborn infants. Pediatr. Res. *33*:27–31, 1992.
213. Hart, D. N. J.: Dendritic cells: Unique leukocyte populations which control the primary immune response. Blood *90*:3245–3287, 1997.
214. Hayashi, S.-I., Kundisada, T., Ogawa, M., et al.: Stepwise progress of B lineage differentiation supported by interleukin 7 and other stromal cell molecules. J. Exp. Med. *171*:1683–1695, 1990.
215. Hayward, A. R.: Development of lymphocyte responses and interactions in the human fetus and newborn. Immunol. Rev. *57*:39–60, 1981.
216. Hayward, A. R., Leonard, J., Wood, C. B. S., et al.: Delayed separation of the umbilical cord, widespread infections and defective neutrophil mobility. Lancet *1*:1099–1101, 1979.
217. Heath, W. R., Kane, K. P., Mescher, M. F., et al.: Alloreactive T cells discriminate among a diverse set of endogenous peptides. Proc. Natl. Acad. Sci. U. S. A. *88*:5101–5105, 1991.
218. Heinzel, F.: Antibodies. *In* Mandell, G. L., Bennett, J. E., and Dolin, R. (eds.): Principles and Practice of Infectious Diseases. 4th ed. New York, Churchill Livingstone, 1995, pp. 36–57.
219. Hermaszewski, R. A., and Webster, A. D. B.: Primary hypogammaglobulinaemia: A survey of clinical manifestations and complications. Q. J. Med. *86*:31–42, 1993.
220. Herrod, H. G.: Management of the patient with IgG subclass deficiency and/or selective antibody deficiency. Ann. Allergy *70*:3–11, 1993.
221. Herrod, H. G.: Clinical significance of IgG subclasses. Curr. Opin. Pediatr. *5*:696–699, 1993.
222. Herrod, H. G., Gross, S., and Insel, R.: Selective antibody deficiency to *Haemophilus influenzae* type b capsular polysaccharide vaccination in children with recurrent respiratory tract infection. J. Clin. Immunol. *9*:429–434, 1989.
223. Hibberd, M. L., Sumiya, M., Summerfield, J. A., et al.: Association of variants of the gene for mannose-binding lectin with susceptibility to meningococcal disease. Lancet *353*:1049–1053, 1999.
224. Hibbs, M. L., Wardlaw, A. J., Stacker, S. A., et al.: Transfection of cells from patients with leukocyte adhesion deficiency with an intergrin B subunit (CD18) restores lymphocyte function-associated antigen-1 expression and function. J. Clin. Invest. *85*:674–681, 1990.
225. Hill, H. R.: Clinical disorders of leukocyte functions. *In* Snyderman, R. (ed.): Current Topics in Immunology. New York, Plenum Press, 1984, pp. 345–393.

226. Hill, H. R.: Biochemical, structural, and functional abnormalities of polymorphonuclear leukocytes in the neonate. Pediatr. Res. *22*:375–382, 1987.
227. Hill, H. R., and Quie, P. G.: Raised serum IgE levels and defective neutrophil chemotaxis in three children with eczema and recurrent bacterial infections. Lancet *1*:183–187, 1974.
228. Hilmo, A., and Howard, T. H.: F-actin content of neonate and adult neutrophils. Blood *69*:945–951, 1987.
229. Hoffman, A. A., Hayward, A. R., Kurnick, J. T., et al.: Presentation of antigen by human newborn monocytes to maternal tetanus toxoid-specific T-cell blasts. J. Clin. Immunol. *1*:217–221, 1981.
230. Hofman, F. M., Danilovs, J. A., and Taylor, C. R.: HLA-DR (Ia)-positive dendritic-like cells in human fetal nonlymphoid tissues. Transplantation *27*:590–594, 1984.
231. Holland, S. M., and Gallin, J. I.: Evaluation of the patient with suspected immunodeficiency. *In* Mandell, G. L., Bennett, J. E., and Dolin, R. (eds.): Principles and Practice of Infectious Diseases. 4th. ed. New York, Churchill Livingstone, 1995, pp. 149–158.
232. Hong, R.: Disorders of the T-cell system. *In* Stiehm, E. R. (ed.): Immunologic Disorders in Infants and Children. 4th ed. Philadelphia, W. B. Saunders, 1996, pp. 339–408.
233. Horwitz, M. A.: Interactions between *Legionella pneumophila* and human mononuclear phagocytes. *In* Thornsberry, C., Balows, A., Feeley, J. C., et al. (eds.): *Legionella.* Proceedings of the 2nd International Symposium. Washington, D. C., American Society for Microbiology, 1984, pp. 159–166.
234. Hostetter, M. K.: Serotypic variations among virulent pneumococci in deposition and degradation of covalently bound C3b: Implications for phagocytosis and antibody production. J. Infect. Dis. *153*:682–693, 1986.
235. Hostetter, M. K., Kreuger, R. A., and Schmeling, D. J.: The biochemistry of opsonization: Central role of the reactive thiol ester of the third component of complement. J. Infect. Dis. *150*:653–661, 1984.
236. Hostoffer, R. W., Krukovets, I., and Berger, M.: Enhancement by tumor necrosis factor-α of Fcα receptor expression and IgA-mediated superoxide generation and killing of *Pseudomonas aeruginosa* by polymorphonuclear leukocytes. J. Infect. Dis. *170*:82–87, 1994.
237. Hudson, A. W., and Ploegh, H. L.: The cell biology of antigen presentation. Exp. Cell Res. *272*:1–7, 2002.
238. Hugli, T. E.: Structure and function of the anaphylatoxins. Springer Semin. Immunopathol. *7*:193–220, 1984.
239. Hunt, D. F., Henderson, R. A., Shababowitz, J., et al.: Characterization of peptides bound to the class I MHC molecule HLA-A2.1 by mass spectrometry. Science *255*:1261–1263, 1992.
240. Hunt, D. F., Michel, H., Dickinson, T. A., et al.: Peptides presented to the immune system by the murine class II major histocompatibility complex molecule I-A^d. Science *256*:1817–1820, 1992.
241. Insel, R. A., Amstey, M., Woodin, K., et al.: Maternal immunization to prevent infectious diseases in the neonate or infant. Int. J. Technol. Assess. Health Care *10*:143–153, 1994.
242. International Chronic Granulomatous Disease Cooperative Study Group: A controlled trial of interferon gamma to prevent infection in chronic granulomatous diseases. N. Engl. J. Med. *324*:509–516, 1991.
243. Jackson, S. H., Gallin, J. I., and Holland, S. M.: The $p47_{phox}$ mouse knockout model of chronic granulomatous disease. J. Exp. Med. *182*:751–758, 1995.
244. Johnston, R. B., and Baehner, R. L.: Chronic granulomatous disease: Correlation between pathogenesis and clinical findings. Pediatrics *48*:730–737, 1971.
245. Johnston, R. B., and Newman, S. L.: Chronic granulomatous disease. Pediatr. Clin. North Am. *24*:365–376, 1977.
246. Johnston, R. B., Jr.: The complement system in host defense and inflammation: The cutting edges of a double edged sword. Pediatr. Infect. Dis. J. *12*:933–941, 1993.
247. Johnston, R. B., Jr.: Disorders of the complement system. *In* Stiehm, E. R. (ed.): Immunologic Disorders in Infants and Children. 4th ed. Philadelphia, W. B. Saunders, 1996, pp. 133–158.
248. Joiner, K. A.: Complement evasion by bacteria and parasites. Annu. Rev. Microbiol. *42*:201–230, 1988.
249. Joiner, K. A., Brown, E. J., and Frank, M. M.: Complement and bacteria: Chemistry and biology in host defense. Annu. Rev. Immunol. *2*:461–491, 1984.
250. Jones, D. H., Schmalsteig, F. C., Dempsey, K., et al.: Subcellular distribution and mobilization of Mac-1 (CD11b/CD18) in neonatal neutrophils. Blood *75*:488–498, 1990.
251. Kabelitz, D.: Function and specificity of human γδ-positive T cells. Crit. Rev. Immunol. *11*:281–303, 1992.
252. Kamani, N., August, C. S., Douglas, S. D., et al.: Transplantation in chronic granulomatous disease. J. Pediatr. *105*:42–46, 1984.
253. Kappler, J. W., Roehm, N., and Marrack, P.: T cell tolerance by clonal elimination in the thymus. Cell *49*:273–280, 1987.
254. Kew, R. R., and Wester, R. O.: Gc-globulin (vitamin D-binding protein) enhances the neutrophil chemotactic activity of C5a and C5a des arg. J. Clin. Invest. *82*:364–369, 1988.
255. Klatzman, D., Champagne, E., Chamaret, S., et al.: T-lymphocyte T4 molecule behaves as a receptor for human retrovirus LAV. Nature *312*:767–770, 1984.
256. Klein, J. O., and Marcy, S. M.: Bacterial sepsis and meningitis. *In* Remington, J. S., and Klein, J. O. (eds.): Infectious Diseases of the Fetus and Newborn Infant. 4th ed. Philadelphia, W. B. Saunders, 1995, pp. 835–890.
257. Klein, R. B., Fisher, T. J., Gard, S. E., et al.: Decreased mononuclear and polymorphonuclear chemotaxis in human newborn infants and young children. Pediatrics *60*:467–472, 1977.
258. Kluin-Nelemans, H. C., van Velzen-Blad, H., van Helden, H. P. T., et al.: Functional deficiency of complement factor D in a monozygous twin. Clin. Exp. Immunol. *58*:724–730, 1984.
259. Kohl, S., Springer, T. A., Shmalsteig, F. C., et al.: Defective natural killer cytotoxicity and polymorphonuclear leukocyte antibody-dependent cellular cytotoxicity in patients with LFA-1/OKM-1 deficiency. J. Immunol. *133*:2972–2981, 1984.
260. Kohler, P. F.: Maturation of the human complement system. I. Onset of the time and site of fetal C1q, C4, C3 and C5 synthesis. J. Clin. Invest. *52*:671–677, 1973.
261. Kohler, P. F., and Farr, R. S.: Elevation of cord over maternal IgG immunoglobulin—evidence for an active placental IgG transport. Nature *210*:1070–1071, 1966.
262. Konstan, M., and Berger, M.: Infection and inflammation in the lung in cystic fibrosis. *In* Davis, P. (ed.): Cystic Fibrosis. New York, Marcel Dekker, 1993, pp. 221–276.
263. Kramer, N., Perez, H. D., and Goldstein, I. M.: An immunoglobulin (IgG) inhibitor of polymorphonuclear leukocyte motility in a patient with recurrent infection. N. Engl. J. Med. *303*:1253–1258, 1980.
264. Kraus, J. C., Mayo-Bond, L., Rogers, C. E., et al.: An in vivo animal model of gene therapy for leukocyte adhesion deficiency. J. Clin. Invest. *88*:1412–1417, 1991.
265. Krause, P. J., Maderazo, E. G., and Scroggs, M.: Abnormalities of neutrophil adherence in newborns. Pediatrics *69*:184–187, 1982.
266. Kretschmer, R., Say, B., Brown, D., et al.: Congenital aplasia of the thymus gland (DiGeorge's syndrome). N. Engl. J. Med. *279*:1295–1301, 1968.
267. Kunkel, S. L., and Strieter, R. M.: Cytokine networking in lung inflammation. Hosp. Pract. *25*:63–76, 1990.
268. Kuschert, G. S., Coulin, F., Power, C. A., et al.: Glycosaminoglycans interact selectively with chemokines and modulate receptor binding and cellular responses. Biochemistry *38*:12959–12968, 1999.
269. Lachmann, P. J.: The control of homologous lysis. Immunol. Today *12*:312–315, 1991.
270. Lammer, E. J., and Opitz, J. M.: The DiGeorge anomaly as a developmental field defect. Am. J. Med. Genet. *2*(Suppl.):113–127, 1986.
271. Lasky, L. A.: Selectins: Interpreters of cell-specific carbohydrate information during inflammation. Science *258*:964–969, 1992.
272. Lassiter, H. A., Wilson, J. L., Feldhoff, R. C., et al.: Supplemental complement component C9 enhances the capacity of neonatal serum to kill multiple isolates of pathogenic *Escherichia coli.* Pediatr. Res. *35*:389–396, 1994.
273. Lau, Y.-L., Tam, A. Y. C., and Ng, K. W.: Clinical laboratory observations. Response of preterm infants to hepatitis B vaccine. J. Pediatr. *121*:962–965, 1992.
274. Law, S. K., Lichtenberg, N. A., and Levine, R. P.: Covalent binding and hemolytic activity of complement proteins. Proc. Natl. Acad. Sci. U. S. A. *77*:7194–7198, 1980.
275. Lawton, A. R., Cooper, M. D.: Development and function of the immune system. *In* Stiehm, E. R. (ed.): Immunologic Disorders in Infants and Children. 4th ed. Philadelphia, W. B. Saunders, 1996, pp. 1–13.
276. Lazarus, G. M., and Neu, H. C.: Agents responsible for infection in chronic granulomatous disease of childhood. J. Pediatr. *86*:415–417, 1975.
277. Lebecque, S. G., and Gearhart, P. J.: Boundaries of somatic mutation in rearranged immunoglobulin genes: 5' boundary is near the promoter, and 3′ boundary is > 1 kb from V(D)J gene. J. Exp. Med. *172*:1717–1727, 1990.
278. Lederman, H. M., and Winkelstein, J. A.: X-linked agammaglobulinemia: An analysis of 96 patients. Medicine (Baltimore) *64*:145–156, 1985.
279. Lee, S. I., Heiner, D. C., and Wara, D.: Development of serum IgG subclass levels in children. Monogr. Allergy *19*:108–121, 1986.
280. Lehrer, R. I., and Ganz, T.: Antimicrobial polypeptides of human neutrophils. Blood *76*:2169–2181, 1990.
281. Lekstrom-Himes, J. A., Dorman, S. E., Kopar, P., et al.: Neutrophil specific granule deficiency results from a novel mutation with loss of function of the transcription factor CCAAT/enhancer binding protein epsilon. J. Exp. Med. *189*:1847–1852, 1999.
282. Leonard, W. J.: X-linked severe combined immunodeficiency: From molecular cause to gene therapy within seven years. Mol. Med. Today *6*:403–407, 2000.
283. Levy, O., Ooi, C. E., Weiss, J., et al.: Individual and synergistic effects of rabbit granulocyte proteins on *Escherichia coli.* J. Clin. Invest. *94*:672–682, 1994.

284. Levy, O., Weiss, J., Zarember, K., et al.: Antibacterial 15-kDa protein isoforms (p15s) are members of a novel family of leukocyte proteins. J. Biol. Chem. *268*:6058–6063, 1993.
285. Lewis, D. B., and Wilson, C. B.: Developmental immunology and role of host defenses in fetal and neonatal susceptibility to infection. *In* Remington, J. S., and Klein, J. O. (eds.): Infectious Diseases of the Fetus and Newborn Infant. 5th ed. Philadelphia, W. B. Saunders, 2001, pp. 25–138.
286. Lieschke, G. J., and Burgess, A. W.: Granulocyte colony-stimulating factor and granulocyte-macrophage colony-stimulating factor, parts I and II. N. Engl. J. Med. *327*:28–35, 99–106, 1992.
287. Liles, W. C., and Van Voorhis, W. C.: Review: Nomenclature and biologic significance of cytokines involved in inflammation and the host immune response. J. Infect. Dis. *172*:1573–1580, 1995.
288. Liu, Y.-J., Cairns, J. A., Holder, M. J., et al.: Recombinant 25-kDa CD23 and interleukin 1α promote the survival of terminal center B cells: Evidence for bifurcation in the development of centrocytes rescued from apoptosis. Eur. J. Immunol. *21*:1107–1114, 1991.
289. Lodewyk, H. S., Van Mierop, M. D., and Kutsche, L. M.: Cardiovascular anomalies in DiGeorge syndrome and importance of neural crest as a possible pathogenic factor. Am. J. Cardiol. *58*:133–137, 1986.
290. Long, E. O.: Antigen processing for presentation to $CD4^+$ T cells. New Biol. *4*:274–282, 1992.
291. Lubke, T., Marquardt, T., Etzioni, A., et al.: Complementation cloning identifies CDG-IIc, a new type of congenital disorders of glycosylation, as a GDP-fucose transporter deficiency. Nat. Genet. *28*:73–76, 2001.
292. Lyon, M. F.: Some milestones in the history of X-chromosome inactivation. Annu. Rev. Genet. *26*:17–28, 1992.
293. Malech, H., Horwitz, M., Linton, G., et al.: Prolonged production of NADPH oxidase–corrected granulocytes after gene therapy of chronic granulomatous disease. Proc. Natl. Acad. Sci. U. S. A. *94*:12133–12138, 1997.
294. Manroe, B., Weinberg, A. G., Rosenfeld, C. R., et al.: The neonatal blood count in health and disease. I. Reference values for neutrophilic cells. J. Pediatr. *64*:60–64, 1979.
295. Marsh, S. G. E., and Bodmer, J. G.: HLA class II nucleotide sequences. Hum. Immunol. *31*:207–227, 1991.
296. Martensson, L., and Fudenberg, H. H.: Gm genes and gamma G-globulin synthesis in the human fetus. J. Immunol. *94*:514–520, 1965.
297. Martyn, L. J., Lischner, H. W., and Pileggi, A. J.: Chorioretinal lesions in familial chronic granulomatous disease of childhood. Trans. Am. Ophthalmol. Soc. *69*:84–112, 1971.
298. Matzinger, P.: Tolerance, danger and the extended family. Annu. Rev. Immunol. *12*:991–1045, 1994.
299. Mauer, A. M., Athens, J. W., Ashenbrucker, H., et al.: Leukokinetic studies. II. A method for labeling granulocytes in vitro with radioactive di-isopropylfluorophosphate (DFP32). J. Clin. Invest. *39*:1482–1489, 1960.
300. McEvoy, L. T., Zakem-Cloud, H., and Tosi, M. F.: Total cell content of CR3 (CD11b/CD18) and LFA-1 (CD11a/CD18) in neonatal neutrophils: Relationship to gestational age. Blood *87*:3929–3933, 1996.
301. McPhail, L. C., DeChatelet, L. R., and Shirley, P. S.: Deficiency of NADPH oxidase activity in chronic granulomatous disease. J. Pediatr. *90*:213–217, 1977.
302. Medzhitov, R., Preston-Hurlburt, P., and Janeway, C. A., Jr.: A human homologue of the *Drosophila* Toll protein signals activation of adaptive immunity. Nature *388*:394–397, 1997.
303. Melnick, J. L.: Nomenclature and classification of viruses. *In* Feigin, R. D., and Cherry, J. D. (eds.): Textbook of Pediatric Infectious Diseases. 3rd ed. Philadelphia, W. B. Saunders, 1992, pp. 1374–1389.
304. Metchnikoff, E.: Immunity in Infectious Diseases. (F. G. Binnie.) London, Cambridge University Press, 1905.
305. Miller, M. E.: Phagocytosis in the newborn infant: Humoral and cellular factors. J. Pediatr. *74*:255–259, 1969.
306. Miller, M. E.: Chemotactic function in the human neonate: Humoral and cellular aspects. Pediatr. Res. *5*:487–492, 1971.
307. Miller, M. E.: Developmental maturation of human neutrophil motility and its relationship to membrane deformity. *In* Bellanti, J. A., and Dayton, D. H. (eds.): Phagocytic Cell in Host Resistance. New York, Raven Press, 1975, pp. 295–314.
308. Miller, M. E.: Phagocytic function in the neonate: Selected aspects. Pediatrics *64*(Suppl.):709–712, 1979.
309. Miller, M. E., Norman, M. E., Koblenzer, P. J., et al.: A new familial defect of neutrophil movement. J. Lab. Clin. Med. *82*:1–8, 1973.
310. Miller, M. E., Oski, F. A., and Harris, M. B.: Lazy leukocyte syndrome: A new disorder of neutrophil function. Lancet *1*:665–669, 1971.
311. Mills, E. L., and Quie, P. G.: Congenital disorders of the functions of polymorphonuclear neutrophils. Rev. Infect. Dis. *2*:505–517, 1980.
312. Milstein, C.: From antibody structure to immunological diversification of immune response. Science *231*:1261–1268, 1986.
313. Monteiro, R. C., Cooper, M. D., and Kubagawa, H.: Molecular heterogeneity of Fcα receptors detected by receptor-specific monoclonal antibodies. J. Immunol. *148*:1764–1771, 1992.
314. Morell, A., Skvaril, F., and Hitzig, W. H.: IgG subclass: Development of the serum concentrations in "normal" infants and children. J. Pediatr. *80*:960–964, 1972.
315. Moretta, M., Bottino, C., Mingari, M. C., et al.: What is natural killer cell? Nat. Immunol. *3*:6–8, 2002.
316. Moy, J. N., Nelson, R. D., Richards, K. L., and Hostetter, M. K.: Identification of an IgA inhibitor of neutrophil chemotaxis and its membrane target for the metabolic burst. Immunology *69*:257–262, 1990.
317. Muller-Eberhard, H. J.: Complement: Chemistry and pathways. *In* Gallin, J. I., and Snyderman, R. (eds.): Inflammation: Basic Principles and Clinical Correlates. 2nd ed. New York, Raven Press, 1992, pp. 33–61.
318. Murphy, K. M., Heimberger, A. B., and Loh, D. Y.: Induction by antigen of intrathymic apoptosis of $CD4^+$ $CD8^+$ TCR^{lo} thymocytes in vivo. Science *250*:1720–1723, 1990.
319. Murphy, P. M.: The molecular biology of leukocyte chemoattractant receptors. Annu. Rev. Immunol. *12*:593–633, 1994.
320. Nagata, M., Hara, T., Aoki, T., et al. Inherited deficiency of ninth component of complement: An increased risk of meningococcal meningitis. J. Pediatr. *114*:260–264, 1989.
321. Naot, Y. D., Desmonts, G., and Remington, J. S.: IgM enzyme-linked immunosorbent assay test for the diagnosis of congenital *Toxoplasma* infection. J. Pediatr. *98*:32–36, 1981.
322. Nath, J., Flavin, M., and Gallin, J. I.: Tubulin tyrosinolation in human polymorphonuclear leukocytes: Studies in normal subjects and in patients with Chédiak-Higashi syndrome. J. Cell Biol. *95*:519–526, 1982.
323. Nauseef, W. M., Root, R. K., and Malech, H. L.: Biochemical and immunologic analysis of hereditary myeloperoxidase deficiency. J. Clin. Invest. *71*:1297–1307, 1983.
324. Newburger, P. E., Cohen, H. J., Rothchild, S. B., et al.: Prenatal diagnosis of chronic granulomatous disease. N. Engl. J. Med. *300*:178–181, 1979.
325. Noble, W. C.: Skin microbiology: Coming of age. J. Med. Microbiol. *17*:1–12, 1984.
326. Noelle, R. J., Ledbetter, J. A., and Aruffo, A.: CD40 and its ligand, an essential ligand-receptor pair for thymus-dependent B-cell activation. Immunol. Today *13*:431–433, 1992.
327. Norment, A. M., Salter, R. D., Parham, P., et al.: Cell-cell adhesion mediated by CD8 and MHC class I molecules. Nature *336*:79–81, 1988.
328. Nossal, G. J. V.: The molecular and cellular basis of affinity maturation in the antibody response. Cell *68*:1–2, 1992.
329. Notarangelo, L. D., Chirico, G., Chiara, A., et al.: Activity of classical and alternative pathways of complement in preterm and small for gestational age infants. Pediatr. Res. *18*:281–285, 1984.
330. Notarangelo, L. D., Duse, M., and Ugazio, A. G.: Immunodeficiency with hyper-IgM (HIM). Immunodefic. Rev. *3*:101–122, 1992.
331. Nunoi, H., Yamazaki, T., Tsuchiya, H., et al.: A heterozygous mutation of β-actin associated with neutrophil dysfunction and recurrent infection. Proc. Natl. Acad. Sci. U. S. A. *96*:8693–8698, 1999.
332. Ochs, H. D., Nonoyama, S., Zhu, Q., et al.: Regulation of antibody responses: The role of complement and adhesion molecules. Clin. Immunol. Immunopathol. *67*:S33–S40, 1993.
333. Ochs, H. D., and Wedgwood, R. J.: IgG subclass deficiencies. Annu. Rev. Med. *38*:325–340, 1987.
334. Ochs, H. D., Wedgwood, R. J., Heller, S. R., et al.: Complement, membrane glycoproteins and complement receptors: Their role in regulation of the immune response. Clin. Immunol. Immunopathol. *40*:94–104, 1986.
335. Ochs, H. D., and Winkelstein, J.: Disorders of the B-cell system. *In* Stiehm, E. R. (ed.): Immunologic Disorders in Infants and Children. 4th ed. Philadelphia, W. B. Saunders, 1996, pp. 296–338.
336. Oettinger, M. A., Schatz, D. G., Gorka, C., et al.: RAG-1 and RAG-2, adjacent genes that synergistically activate V(D)J recombination. Science *248*:1517–1523, 1990.
337. Oliver, A. M., Sewell, H. F., Abramovich, D. R., et al.: The distribution and differential expression of MHC class II antigens (HLA-DR, DP, and DQ) in human fetal adrenal, pancreas, thyroid and gut. Transplant Proc. *21*:651–652, 1989.
338. Oppenheim, J. J., and Feldman, M.: Introduction to the role of cytokines in innate host defense and adaptive immunity. *In* Oppenheim, J. J., Feldman, M., Durum, S. K., et al. (eds): Cytokine Reference. San Diego, Academic Press, 2001, pp 3–20.
339. Oxelius, V.-A.: IgG subclass levels in infancy and childhood. Acta Paediatr. Scand. *68*:23–27, 1979.
340. Oxelius, V.-A., Laurell, A. B., Linquist, B., et al.: IgG subclasses in selective IgA deficiency. N. Engl. J. Med. *304*:1476–1477, 1981.
341. Ozsahin, H., Le Deist, F., Benkerrou, M., et al.: Bone marrow transplantation in 26 patients with Wiskott-Aldrich syndrome from a single center. J. Pediatr. *129*:238–244, 1996.
342. Pangburn, M. K.: The alternative pathway. *In* Ross, G. D. (ed.): Immunobiology of the Complement System. Orlando, FL, Academic Press, 1986, pp. 45–62.
343. Parry, M. F., Root, R. K., Metcalf, J. A., et al.: Myeloperoxidase deficiency: Prevalence and clinical significance. Ann. Intern. Med. *95*:293–301, 1981.

344. Paul, W. E.: Pleiotropy and redundancy: T cell–derived lymphokines in the immune response. Cell *57*:521–524, 1989.
345. Perlmuter, D. H., and Colten, H. R.: Molecular immunobiology of complement biosynthesis: A model of single-cell control of effector-inhibitor balance. Annu. Rev. Immunol. *4*:231–251, 1986.
346. Peterson, S. V., Thiel, S., and Jensenius, J. C.: The mannan-binding lectin pathway of complement activation: Biology and disease association. Mol. Immunol. *38*:133–149, 2001.
347. Pier, G. B., Grout, M., Zaidi, T. S., et al.: Role of mutant CFTR in hypersusceptibility of cystic fibrosis patients to lung infections. Science *271*:64–67, 1996.
348. Pizzo, P. A., Robechaud, K. J., Gill, F. A., et al.: Empiric antibiotic and antifungal therapy for cancer patients with prolonged fever and granulocytopenia. Am. J. Med. *72*:101–111, 1982.
349. Plaeger, S. F.: Principal human cytokines. *In* Stiehm, E. R. (ed.): Immunologic Disorders in Infants and Children. 4th ed. Philadelphia, W. B. Saunders, 1996, pp. 1063–1065.
350. Pollack, J. D., Williams D. A., Gifford, M. A., et al.: Mouse model of X-linked chronic granulomatous disease, an inherited defect in phagocyte superoxide production. Nat. Genet. *9*:202–209, 1995.
351. Porcelli, S. A., and Modlin, R. L.: The CD1 system: Antigen-presenting molecules for T cell recognition of lipids and glycolipids. Annu. Rev. Immunol. *17*:297–329, 1999.
352. Provenzano, R. W., Wetterlow, L. H., and Sullivan, C. L.: Immunization and antibody response in the newborn infant. N. Engl. J. Med. *273*:959–965, 1965.
353. Purkerson, J., and Isakson, P.: A two-signal model for regulation of immunoglobulin isotype switching. FASEB J. *6*:3245–3252, 1992.
354. Quie, P. G., White, J. G., Holmes, B., et al.: In vitro bactericidal capacity of human polymorphonuclear leukocytes: Diminished activity in chronic granulomatous disease of childhood. J. Clin. Invest. *46*:668–679, 1967.
355. Rago, J. V., and Schlievert, P. M.: Mechanisms of pathogenesis of staphylococcal superantigens. Curr. Top. Microbiol. Immunol. *225*:81–97, 1998.
356. Rappeport, J. M., Newburger, P. E., Goldblum, R. M., et al.: Allogeneic bone marrow transplantation for chronic granulomatous disease. J. Pediatr. *101*:952–955, 1982.
357. Regelmann, W., Hays, N., and Quie, P. G.: Chronic granulomatous disease: Historical perspective and clinical experience at the University of Minnesota Hospitals. *In* Gallin, J. I., Fauci, A. S. (eds.): Advances in Host Defense Mechanisms. Vol. 3. New York, Raven Press, 1983, pp. 3–23.
358. Revy, P., Muto, T., Levy, Y., et al.: Activation-induced cytidine deaminase (AID) deficiency causes the autosomal recessive form of the hyper-IgM syndrome (HIGM2). Cell *102*:565–575, 2000.
359. Robey, E. A., Fowlkes, B. J., Gordon, J. W., et al.: Thymic selection in CD8 transgenic mice supports an instructive model for commitment to a CD4 or CD8 lineage. Cell *64*:99–107, 1991.
360. Robin, L. F., Lees, P. S. J., Winget, M., et al.: Wood-burning stoves and lower respiratory illnesses in Navajo children. Pediatr. Infect. Dis. J. *15*:859–865, 1996.
361. Roche, P. A., and Cresswell, P.: Invariant chain association with HLA-DR molecules inhibits immunogenic peptide binding. Nature *345*:615–618, 1990.
362. Rock, K. L., Gamble, S., Rothstein, L., et al.: Dissociation of β_2-microglobulin leads to the accumulation of a substantial pool of inactive class I MHC heavy chains on the cell surface. Cell *85*:611–620, 1991.
363. Romani, N., Koide, S., Crowley, M., et al.: Presentation of exogenous protein antigens by dendritic cells to T cell clones: Intact protein is presented best by immature, epidermal Langerhans cells. J. Exp. Med. *169*:1169–1178, 1989.
364. Roos, D., Weening, R. S., Voteman, A. A., et al.: Protection of phagocytic leukocytes by endogenous glutathione: Studies in a family with glutathione reductase deficiency. Blood *53*:851–857, 1979.
365. Root, R. K., and Cohen, M. S.: The microbicidal mechanisms of human neutrophils and eosinophils. Rev. Infect. Dis. *3*:565–598, 1981.
366. Root, R. K., Metcalf, J., Oshino, N., et al.: H_2O_2 release from human granulocytes during phagocytosis. I. Documentation, quantitation, and some regulating factors. J. Clin. Invest. *55*:945–955, 1975.
367. Rosen, F. S., Cooper, M. D., and Wedgwood, R. J.: The primary immunodeficiencies. N. Engl. J. Med. *311*:235–242, 1984.
368. Rosen, F. S., and Janeway, C. A.: The gamma globulins: III. The antibody deficiency syndromes. N. Engl. J. Med. *275*:769–775, 1966.
369. Rosenfield, S. I., Baum, J., Steigbigel, R. T., et al.: Hereditary deficiency of the fifth component of complement in man. II. Biological properties of C5-deficient human serum. J. Clin. Invest. *57*:1635–1643, 1976.
370. Rosenfield, S. I., Kelly, M. E., and Leddy, J. P.: Hereditary deficiency of the fifth component of complement in man. I. Clinical, immunochemical, and family studies. J. Clin. Invest. *57*:1626–1634, 1976.
371. Ross, S. C., and Densen, P.: Complement deficiency states and infection: Epidemiology, pathogenesis, and consequences of neisserial and other infections in an immune deficiency. Medicine (Baltimore) *63*:243–273, 1984.
372. Rossi, D., and Zlotnik, A.: The biology of chemokines and their receptors. Annu. Rev. Immunol. *18*:217–242, 2000.
373. Ruddy, S., Carpenter, C. B., Chin, K. W., et al.: Human complement metabolism: An analysis of 144 studies. Medicine (Baltimore) *54*:165–178, 1975.
374. Rudensky, A. Y., Preston-Hurlburt, P., Hong, S. C., et al.: Sequence analysis of peptides bound to MHC class II molecules. Nature *353*:622–627, 1991.
375. Rutenberg, W. D., Yang, M. C., Doberstyn, B., et al.: Multiple leukocyte abnormalities in chronic granulomatous disease: A familial study. Pediatr. Res. *11*:158–163, 1977.
376. Sacchi, F., Augustine, N. H., and Hill, H. R.: Abnormality in actin polymerization associated with defective chemotaxis in neutrophils from neonates. Int. Arch. Allergy Appl. Immunol. *84*:32–39, 1987.
377. Sacchi, F., and Hill, H. R.: Defective membrane potential changes in neutrophils from human neonates. J. Exp. Med. *160*:1247–1252, 1984.
378. Saiman, L., and Prince, A.: *Pseudomonas aeruginosa* pili bind to asialoGM1 which is increased on the surface of cystic fibrosis epithelial cells. J. Clin. Invest. *92*:1875–1880, 1993.
379. Salmon, J. E., Edberg, J. C., and Kimberly, R. P.: Fcγ receptor III on human neutrophils: Allelic variants have functionally distinct capacities. J. Clin. Invest. *85*:1287–1295, 1990.
380. Salmon, J. E., Kapur, S., and Kimberly, R. P.: Opsonin-independent ligation of Fcγ receptors; the 3G8-bearing receptors on neutrophils mediate the phagocytosis of concanavalin A–treated erythrocytes and non-opsonized *E. coli*. J. Exp. Med. *166*:1798–1813, 1987.
381. Sandberg, E. T., Kline, M. W., and Shearer, W. T.: The secondary immunodeficiencies. *In* Stiehm, E. R. (ed.): Immunologic Disorders in Infants and Children. 4th ed. Philadelphia, W. B. Saunders, 1996, pp. 553–601.
382. Schaffer, F. M., and Ballow, M.: Immunodeficiency: The office work-up. J. Respir. Dis. *16*:523–546, 1995.
383. Schatz, D. G., Oettinger, M. A., and Schlissel, M. S.: V (D) J recombination: Molecular biology and regulation. Annu. Rev. Immunol. *10*:359–384, 1992.
384. Schmidt, A. P., Taswell, H. F., and Gleich, G. J.: Anaphylactic transfusion reaction associated with anti-IgA antibody. N. Engl. J. Med. *280*:188–193, 1969.
385. Schoub, B. D., Johnson, S., McAnerney, J., et al.: Monovalent neonatal polio immunization—a strategy for the developing world. J. Infect. Dis. *147*:836–839, 1988.
386. Schur, P. H.: IgG subclasses. A historical perspective. Monogr. Allergy *23*:1–11, 1988.
387. Schur, P. H., Rosen, F., and Norman, M. E.: Immunoglobulin subclasses in normal children. Pediatr. Res. *13*:181–183, 1979.
388. Shackelford, P. G.: IgG subclasses: Importance in pediatric practice. Pediatr. Rev. *14*:291–296, 1993.
389. Shackelford, P. G., and Granoff, D. M.: IgG subclass composition of the antibody response of healthy adults, and normal or IgG2-deficient children and to immunization with *H. influenzae* type b polysaccharide vaccine or Hib PS-protein conjugate vaccines. Monogr. Allergy *23*:269–281, 1988.
390. Shackelford, P. G., Granoff, D. M., Madassery, J. V., et al: Clinical and immunologic characteristics of healthy children with subnormal serum concentrations of IgG2. Pediatr. Res. *27*:16–21, 1990.
391. Shackelford, P. G., Granoff, D. M., Polmar, S. H., et al.: Subnormal serum concentrations of IgG2 in children with frequent infections associated with varied patterns of immunologic dysfunction. J. Pediatr. *116*:529–538, 1990.
392. Shackelford, P. G., Polmar, S. H., Mayus, J. L., et al.: Spectrum of IgG2 subclass deficiency in children with recurrent infections: Prospective study. J. Pediatr. *108*:647–653, 1986.
393. Shapiro, R., Beatty, D. W., Woods, L. I., et al.: Serum complement and immunoglobulin values in small-for-gestational-age infants. J. Pediatr. *99*:139–141, 1981.
394. Shurin, S. B., Socransky, S. S., Sweeney, E., and Stossel, T. P.: A neutrophil disorder induced by *Capnocytophaga,* a dental micro-organism. N. Engl. J. Med. *301*:849–854, 1979.
395. Siu, G., Kronenberg, M., Strauss, E., et al.: The structure, rearrangement and expression of D_β gene segments of the murine T-cell antigen receptor. Nature *311*:344–350, 1984.
396. Smith, C. W.: Molecular determinants of neutrophil adhesion. Am. J. Respir. Cell. Mol. Biol. *2*:487–489, 1990.
397. Smith, C. W., Hollers, J. C., Dupree, E., et al.: A serum inhibitor of leukotaxis in a child with recurrent infections. J. Lab. Clin. Med. *79*:878–883, 1972.
398. Smith, C. W., Marlin, S. D., Rothlein, R., et al.: Cooperative interaction of LFA-1 and Mac-1 with intercellular adhesion molecule-1 in facilitating adherence and transendothelial migration of human neutrophils in vitro. J. Clin. Invest. *83*:2008–2017, 1989.
399. Smith, C. W., Rothlein, R., Hughes, B. J., et al.: Recognition of an endothelial determinant for CD18-dependent human neutrophil adherence and transendothelial migration. J. Clin. Invest. *82*:1746–1756, 1988.
400. Smith, D. H., Peter, G., Ingram, D. L., et al.: Responses of children immunized with the capsular polysaccharide of *Haemophilus influenzae.* Pediatrics *52*:637–644, 1973.

401. Smith, J. J., Travis, S. M., Greenberg, E. P., and Welsh, M. J.: Cystic fibrosis airway epithelia fail to kill bacteria because of abnormal airway surface fluid. Cell *86*:1–20, 1996.
402. Smith, R. T., Eitzman, D. V., Catlin, M. E., et al.: The development of the immune response. Pediatrics *33*:163–183, 1964.
403. Smolen, P., Bland, R., Heiligenstein, E., et al.: Antibody response to oral polio vaccine in premature infants. J. Pediatr. *103*:917–920, 1983.
404. Snyderman, R., Pike, M. C., and Altman, L. C.: Abnormalities of leukocyte chemotaxis in human disease. Ann. N. Y. Acad. Sci. *256*:386–388, 1975.
405. Solvason, N., and Kearney, J. F.: The human fetal omentum: A site of B cell generation. J. Exp. Med. *175*:397–404, 1992.
406. Soriano, R. B., South, M. A., Goldman, A. S., and Smith, C. W.: Defect of neutrophil motility in a child with recurrent bacterial infections and disseminated cytomegalovirus infection. J. Pediatr. *83*:951–955, 1973.
407. Southwick, F. S., Holbrook, T., Howard, T., et al.: Neutrophil actin dysfunction is associated with a deficiency of Mol. Abstract. Clin. Res. *34*:533, 1986.
408. Southwick, F. S., Howard, T. H., Holbrook, T., et al.: The relationship between CR3 deficiency and neutrophil actin assembly. Blood *73*:1973–1979, 1989.
409. Spielberg, S. P., Boxer, L. A., Oliver, J. M., et al.: Oxidative damage to neutrophils in glutathione synthetase deficiency. Br. J. Haematol. *42*:215–223, 1979.
410. Spitznagel, J. K., Cooper, M. R., McCall, A. E., et al.: Selective deficiency of granules associated with lysozyme and lactoferrin in human polymorphs with reduced microbicidal capacity. Abstract. J. Clin. Invest. *51*:93, 1972.
411. Spitznagel, J. K., Dalldorf, F. G., Leffell, M. S., et al.: Character of azurophil and specific granules purified from human polymorphonuclear leukocytes. Lab. Invest. *30*:774–785, 1974.
412. Springer, T. A., and Anderson, D. C.: The importance of adherence, chemotaxis, and migration into inflammatory sites: Insights from an experiment of nature. *In* Evered, D., Nugent, J., and O'Connor, M. (eds.): Biochemistry of Macrophages. Ciba Foundation Symposium. London, Pittman, 1986, pp. 102–126.
413. Springer, T. A., Thompson, W. S., Miller, J., et al.: Inherited deficiency of the Mac-1, LFA-1, P150,95 glycoprotein family and its molecular basis. J. Exp. Med. *160*:1901–1918, 1984.
414. Stepick-Biek, P., Thulliez, P., Araujo, F. G., et al.: IgA antibodies for diagnosis of acute congenital and acquired toxoplasmosis. J. Infect. Dis. *162*:270–273, 1990.
415. Stevens, R., Dichek, D., Keld, B., et al.: IgG_1 is the predominant subclass of in vivo– and in vitro–produced anti–tetanus toxoid antibodies and also serves as the membrane IgG molecule for delivering inhibitory signals to anti–tetanus toxoid antibody–producing B cells. J. Clin. Immunol. *3*:65–69, 1983.
416. Stiehm, E. R., and Fudenberg, H. H.: Serum levels of immune globulins in health and disease: A survey. Pediatrics *37*:715–727, 1966.
417. Stossel, T. P.: Phagocytosis: Recognition and ingestion. Semin. Hematol. *12*:83, 1975.
418. Stossel, T. P.: The mechanical responses of white blood cells. *In* Gallin, J. I., Goldstein, I. M., and Snyderman, R. (eds.): Basic Principles and Clinical Correlates. New York, Raven Press, 1992, pp. 459–475.
419. Strauss, R. G., and Snyder, E. L.: Chemotactic peptide binding by intact neutrophils from human neonates. Pediatr. Res. *18*:63–66, 1984.
420. Summerfield, J. A., Sumiya, M., Levin, M., and Turner, M. W.: Association of mutations in mannose binding protein gene with childhood in consecutive hospital series. B. M. J. *314*:1229–1232, 1997.
421. Swain, S.: T cell subsets and the recognition of MHC class. Immunol. Rev. *74*:129–142, 1983.
422. Tack, K. J., Rham, F. S., Brown, B., et al.: *Aspergillus* osteomyelitis: Report of four cases and review of the literature. Am. J. Med. *73*:295, 1982.
423. Taitz, L. S., Zarate-Salvador, C., and Schwartz, E.: Congenital absence of the parathyroid and thymus glands in an infant (III and IV pharyngeal pouch syndrome). Pediatrics *38*:412–418, 1966.
424. Taylor, P. W.: Bactericidal and bacteriolytic activity of serum against gram-negative bacteria. Microbiol. Rev. *47*:46–83, 1983.
425. Teyton, L., O'Sullivan, D., Dickson, P. W., et al.: Invariant chain distinguishes between the exogenous and endogenous antigen presentation pathways. Nature *348*:39–44, 1990.
426. Timens, W., Boes, A., Rozeboom-Uiterwijk, T., and Poppema, S.: Immaturity of the human splenic marginal zone in infancy. Possible contribution to the deficient infant immune response. J. Immunol. *143*:3200–3206, 1989.
427. Tosi, M. F., Anderson, D. C., Barrish, J., et al.: Effect of piliation on interactions of *Haemophilus influenzae* type b with human polymorphonuclear leukocytes. Infect. Immun. *47*:780–785, 1985.
428. Tosi, M., and Berger, M.: Functional differences between the 40 kDa and 50 to 70 IgG Fc receptors on human neutrophils revealed by elastase treatment and antireceptor antibodies. J. Immunol. *141*:2097–2103, 1988.
429. Tosi, M. F., and Hamedani, A.: A rapid, specific assay for superoxide release from phagocytes in small volumes of whole blood. Am. J. Clin. Pathol. *97*:566–573, 1992.
430. Tosi, M. F., and Zakem, H.: Surface expression of Fcγ receptor III (CD16) on chemoattractant-stimulated neutrophils is determined by both surface shedding and translocation from intracellular storage compartments. J. Clin. Invest. *90*:462–470, 1990.
431. Tosi, M. F., Zakem, H., and Berger, M.: Neutrophil elastase cleaves C3bi on opsonized *Pseudomonas* as well as CR1 on neutrophils to create a functionally important opsonin-receptor mismatch. J. Clin. Invest. *86*:300–308, 1990.
432. Townsend, A., and Bodmer, H.: Antigen recognition by class I–restricted T lymphocytes. Annu. Rev. Immunol. *7*:601–624, 1989.
433. Tsukada, S., Saffran, D. C., Rawlings, D. J., et al.: Deficient expression of a B cell cytoplasmic tyrosine kinase in human X-linked agammaglobulinemia. Cell *72*:279–290, 1993.
434. Uckun, F. M., Dibirdik, I., Smith R., et al.: Interleukin 7 receptor ligation stimulates tyrosine phosphorylation, inositol phospholipid turnover, and clonal proliferation of human B-cell precursors. Proc. Natl. Acad. Sci. U. S. A. *88*:3589–3593, 1991.
435. Unkeless, J. C., Shen, Z., Lin, C. W., and DeBeus, E.: Function of human Fc gamma RIIA and Fc gamma RIIIB. Semin. Immunol. *7*:37–44, 1995.
436. Vanderkerckhove, B. A. E., Baccala, R., Jones, D., et al.: Thymic selection of the human T-cell receptor Vβ repertoire in SCID-hu mice. J. Exp. Med. *176*:1619–1624, 1992.
437. van der Pol, W. -L., and van de Winkel, J. G. J.: IgG receptor polymorphisms: Risk factors for disease. Immunogenetics *48*:222–232, 1998.
438. Van Dyke, T. E., Horoszewicz, H. U., and Genco, R. J.: The polymorphonuclear leukocyte (PMNL) locomotor defect in juvenile periodontitis: Study of random migration, chemokinesis and chemotaxis. J. Peridontol. *53*:682, 1982.
439. Van Epps, D., Palmer, D. L., and Williams, R. C.: Characterization of serum inhibitors of neutrophil chemotaxis is associated with anergy. J. Immunol. *113*:189–200, 1974.
440. Vanichkin A., Patya, M., Gazit, A., et al.: Late administration of lipophilic tyrosine kinase inhibitor prevents lipopolysaccharide and *Escherichia coli*–induced lethal toxicity. J. Infect. Dis. *173*:927–933, 1996.
441. van Tuinen, P., Johnson, K. R., Ledbetter, S., et al.: Localization of myeloperoxidase to the long arm of human chromosome 17: Relationship to the 15:17 translocation of acute promyelocytic leukemia. Oncogene *1*:319–326, 1987.
442. Vedder, N. B., and Harlan, J. M.: Increased surface expression of CD11b/CD18 (Mac-1) is not required for stimulated neutrophil adherence to cultured endothelium. J. Clin. Invest. *81*:676–682, 1988.
443. Vetrie, D., Vorechovsky, I., Sideras, F., et al.: The gene involved in X-linked agammaglobulinemia is a member of the *src* family of protein-tyrosine kinases. Nature *361*:226–233, 1993.
444. Volpp, B. D., Nauseef, W. M., Donelson, J. E., et al.: Cloning of the cDNA and functional expression of the 47 kilodalton cytosolic component of the human neutrophil respiratory burst oxidase. Proc. Natl. Acad. Sci. U. S. A. *86*:7195–7199, 1989.
445. von Andrian, U. H., Berger, E. M., Ramezani, L., et al: In vivo behavior of neutrophils from two patients with distinct inherited leukocyte adhesion deficiency syndromes. J. Clin. Invest. *91*:2893–2897, 1993.
446. von Boehmer, H., Teh, H. S., and Kisielow, P.: The thymus selects the useful, neglects the useless and destroys the harmful. Immunol. Today *10*:57–61, 1989.
447. Waage, A., Halstensen, A., and Espevik, T.: Association between tumor necrosis factor in serum and fatal outcome in patients with meningococcal disease. Lancet *1*:355–357, 1987.
448. Walker, R. I., and Willemze, R.: Neutrophil kinetics and the regulation of granulopoiesis. Rev. Infect. Dis. *2*:282–292, 1980.
449. Walter, M. A., Surti, U., Hofker, M. H., et al.: The physical organization of the human immunoglobulin heavy chain gene complex. EMBO J. *9*:3303–3313, 1990.
450. Ward, P. A., and Schlegel, R. J.: Impaired leukotactic responsiveness in a child with recurrent infection. Lancet *2*:344–347, 1969.
451. Weaver, L. J., Craddock, P. R., and Jacob, H. S.: Association of complement activation and elevated plasma-C5a with adult respiratory distress syndrome. Pathophysiological relevance and possible prognostic value. Lancet *1*:947–949, 1980.
452. Weisdorf, D. J., Craddock, P. R., and Jacob, H. S.: Granulocytes utilize different energy sources for movement and phagocytosis. Inflammation *6*:245–251, 1982.
453. Weiss, J., Victor, M., and Elsbach, P.: Role of charge and hydrophobic interactions in the action of the bactericidal/permeability-increasing protein of neutrophils on gram-negative bacteria. J. Clin. Invest. *71*:540–549, 1983.
454. Welsh, M. J., and Smith, A. E.: Molecular mechanisms of CFTR chloride channel dysfunction in cystic fibrosis. Cell *73*:1251–1254, 1993.
455. Westminster Hospitals Bone-Marrow Transplant Team: Bone marrow transplant from an unrelated donor for chronic granulomatous disease. Lancet *1*:210–213, 1977.
456. Wheat, L. J., Connolly-Stringfield, P. A., and Baker, R. L.: Disseminated histoplasmosis in the acquired immune deficiency syndrome: Clinical findings, diagnosis and treatment, and review of the literature. Medicine (Baltimore) *69*:361–374, 1990.

457. Whitley, R. J., and Arvin, A. M.: Herpes simplex virus infections. *In* Remington, J. S., and Klein, J. O. (eds.): Infectious Diseases of the Fetus and Newborn Infant. 4th ed. Philadelphia, W. B. Saunders, 1995, pp. 354–376.
458. Wickham, T. J., Mathias, P., Cheresh, D. A., and Nemerow, G. R.: Integrins $\alpha_v\beta_3$ and $\alpha_v\beta_5$ promote adenovirus internalization but not virus attachment. Cell *73*:309–319, 1993.
459. Wilson, C. B., Ochs, H. D., Almquiest, J., et al.: When is umbilical cord separation delayed? J. Pediatr. *107*:292–293, 1985.
460. Wilson, R. K., Lai, E., Concannon, P., et al.: Structure, organization and polymorphism of murine and human T-cell receptors αβ chain gene families. Immunol. Rev. *101*:149–172, 1988.
461. Winkelstein, J. A., Lambert, G. H., and Swift, A.: Pneumococcal serum opsonizing activity in splenectomized children. J. Pediatr. *87*:430–433, 1975.
462. Winkelstein, J. A., Marino, M. C., Johnston, R. B., et al.: Chronic granulomatous disease: Report on a national registry of 368 patients. Medicine (Baltimore) *79*:155–169, 2000.
463. Wu, L., Gerard, N. P., Wyatt, R., et al.: CD4-induced interaction of primary HIV-1 gp120 glycoproteins with the chemokine receptor CCR-5. Nature *384*:179–183, 1996.
464. Yang, K. D., and Hill, H. R.: Immune responses to infectious diseases: An evolutionary perspective. Pediatr. Infect. Dis. J. *15*:355–364, 1996.
465. Yeung, C. Y., and Hobbs, J. R.: Serum-gamma G-globulin levels in normal, premature, post-mature and "small-for-dates" newborn babies. Lancet *1*:1167–1170, 1968.
466. Zach, T. L., and Hostetter, M. K.: Biochemical abnormalities of the third component of complement in neonates. Pediatr. Res. *26*:116–120, 1989.
467. Zarember, K. A., and Godowski, P. J.: Tissue expression of human toll-like receptors and differential regulation of toll-like receptor mRNAs in leukocytes in response to microbes, their products, and cytokines. J. Immunol. *168*:554–561, 2002.
468. Zemmour, J., and Parham, P.: HLA class I nucleotide sequences. Hum. Immunol. *31*:195–206, 1991.
469. Zimmerman, G. A.: Two by two: The pairings of P-selectin and P-selectin glycoprotein ligand-1. Proc. Natl. Acad. Sci. U. S. A. *98*:10023–10024, 2001.

CHAPTER 3

Metabolic Response of the Host to Infections

WILLIAM R. BEISEL

Although infectious microorganisms constitute a continuing threat at all ages of life, they are particularly dangerous in neonatal infants and young children. Despite the availability of modern sanitation, public health measures, vaccines, and antibiotics, most children suffer a sizable number of discrete episodes of acute infection before reaching adulthood. Depending upon their severity and duration, infectious illnesses can interrupt normal growth patterns. More importantly, if closely spaced in time, a series of infections can initiate a downhill health spiral, leading to malnutrition, chronic debilitation, immune system dysfunction, and death.[9, 10, 69, 70, 109] This possibility is of greatest concern in newborn infants and weanling children, especially those in Third World areas.

The human host normally protects itself against invading microorganisms by maintaining a broad array of general defensive mechanisms and immunologic responses. This array includes the initiation of acute-phase reactions triggered by the release of proinflammatory cytokines from macrophages, monocytes, and other cells.[8–10, 32] The resulting nonspecific defensive measures typically include fever and anorexia, slow-wave sleep, accelerated production of phagocytic cells, hormonal responses, and participation of many biochemical pathways and molecular mechanisms within body cells.[5–10, 141] The acute-phase reaction produces relatively stereotyped patterns of transient metabolic sequelae (diagrammed in Fig. 3–1), which accompany and follow most acute, generalized infectious illnesses and some localized ones.[60] A pediatrician should anticipate these metabolic changes in order to recognize dangerous complications, such as hypoglycemia and electrolyte imbalance, that may occur during an acute infection.

The array of metabolic changes depicted in Figure 3–1 typically is shared as a group of common responses during all generalized acute infectious diseases.[5–10, 141] Similar changes are seen during other types of disease or trauma when they are accompanied by fever or inflammatory reactions.[60] These common acute-phase responses are composed of a hypermetabolic admixture of anabolic and catabolic components. Each centigrade degree of fever causes basal cellular oxygen consumption to increase approximately 13 percent.[8] The resultant increase in cellular energy expenditure comes at a time when food intake and intestinal absorption are diminished by anorexia and, at times, by vomiting and diarrhea. In the absence of an adequate intake of nutrients, body energy needs are met, for the most part, by the oxidation of metabolic substrates that are derived from nutrient stores already contained within body tissues. The hypermetabolic effects of acute fever are fueled primarily by carbohydrates (some of which are derived from the metabolism of amino acids),[8] but if infectious illnesses become subacute or chronic, body fats then become the important sustaining fuel.

Generalized acute-phase metabolic responses may be modified by numerous factors, such as the severity of an infectious process, its duration, and its possible progression to a subacute or chronic disease.[5–10, 15] The age and sex of the patient, the presence of genetic resistance (or susceptibility) factors or partial immunity, the adequacy of nonspecific defensive mechanisms and de novo immune responsiveness, the preexisting nutritional status of the child, and the presence or absence of other diseases all combine to modify host metabolic responses through their diverse influences on the infectious process per se.

Superimposed on this general array of common host metabolic responses are additional metabolic changes that occur when an infectious process becomes localized within certain anatomic sites or organ systems. As examples, diarrhea during gastrointestinal infections can lead to depletion of fluids and electrolytes, hepatic infections can lead to derangements of carbohydrate and amino acid metabolism, and infections of the central nervous system that cause neuronal destruction are accompanied by muscle paralysis and atrophy. Other infections localized within the cranial vault

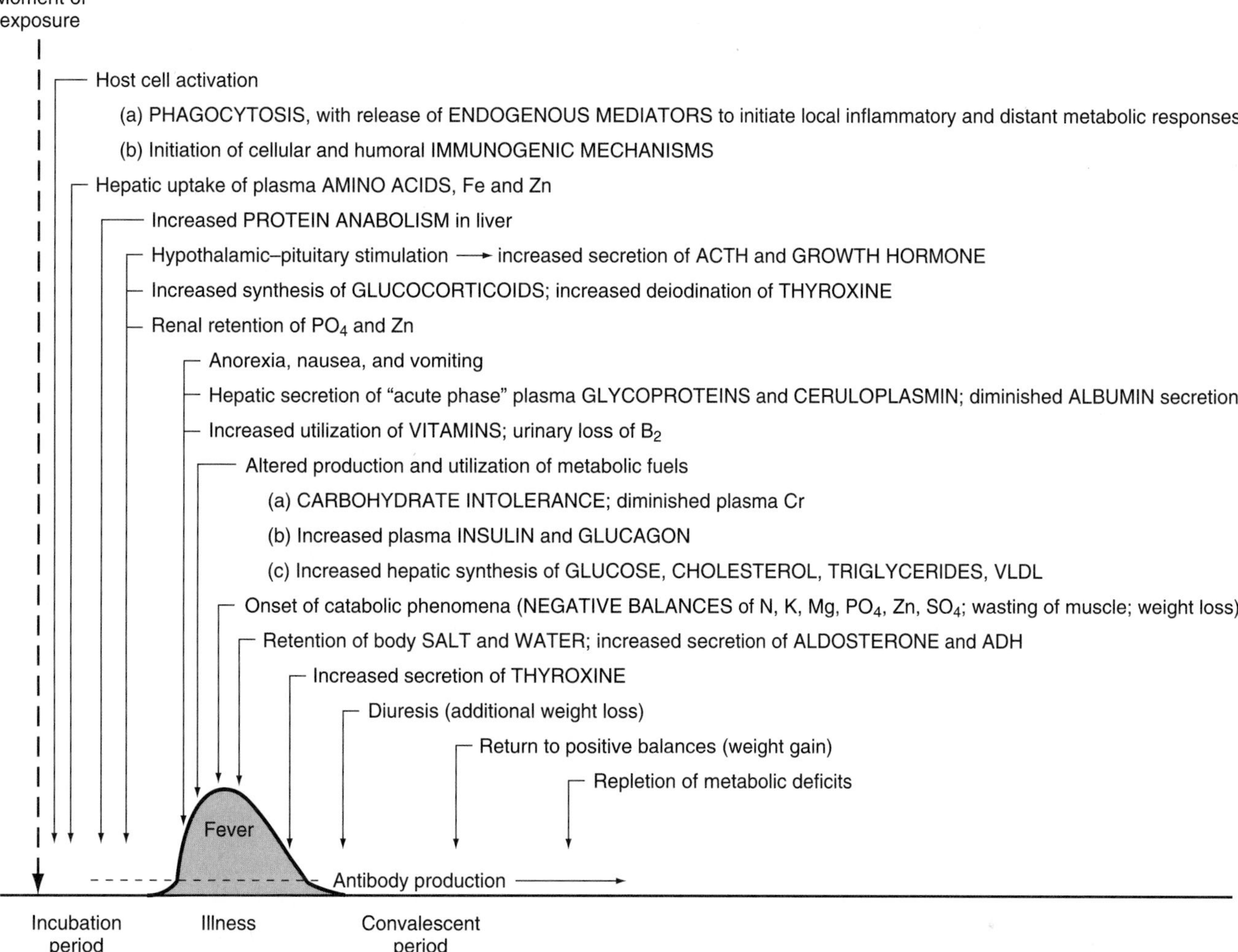

FIGURE 3–1 ■ Onset time of various host metabolic responses in relation to the sequential phases of a "model" acute, self-limited, generalized infectious illness. (From McKigney, J. I., and Munro, H. N. [eds.]: Nutrient Requirements in Adolescence. Cambridge, MA, MIT Press, 1976, p. 250.)

often produce an inappropriate secretion of antidiuretic hormone, leading to development of dangerous overhydration in children.[10] The development of shock syndromes during infectious diseases imposes additional metabolic derangements because of progressive stagnant hypoxia.[5, 115]

The total number of discrete metabolic responses known to occur during acute and chronic infectious illnesses continues to expand.[5] Accordingly, the most widely recognized of these multiple responses are grouped for discussion into major categories, which include changes in nitrogen, amino acid, carbohydrate, lipid, electrolyte, vitamin, and trace element metabolism. The important initiating and control mechanisms provided by cytokines, antioxidants, and the endocrine system also are discussed.

Importantly, each of the many individual metabolic changes that occur during infection must be interpreted in a manner that reflects its longitudinal development and progression over a period of time and its relationship to the evolving phases of the infectious process.[6] Thus, some metabolic changes may be detected during the incubation period, many other responses occur at the onset of fever, and still other phenomena develop during the recovery phase of illness or later during convalescence.

Nitrogen Metabolism

Fever and its accompanying hypermetabolic state, as induced by acute-phase responses during infectious illnesses, trigger a complex assortment of changes in protein, amino acid, and nitrogen metabolism.[15] Although the catabolic destruction of skeletal muscle protein is most obvious clinically, important anabolic events occur simultaneously. They involve the synthesis of new proteins and cells that are of special importance in host defense mechanisms. Increases in whole-body protein turnover involve both catabolic and anabolic events in chronic infections also, as demonstrated by recent leucine kinetic studies in patients with human immunodeficiency virus infections.[67]

NITROGEN BALANCE STUDIES

Because the ability of body cells to synthesize new proteins is a fundamental necessity for maintaining all known host defensive mechanisms, including the immunologic ones, understanding the changes that take place in the nitrogen metabolism of an infected person is important.[92] When the availability of free amino acids within body pools is restricted by diet or disease, the catabolism of certain existing body proteins (chiefly the contractile proteins of skeletal muscle) generates the free amino acids required to synthesize new body proteins with higher priorities in terms of the many new proteins needed for defensive purposes. Information about these metabolic responses has been gained through quantitative analyses of proteins and other nitrogen-containing compounds in tissues, body fluids, and excretions and through kinetic studies with tagged molecules.[67, 81, 88, 103, 129]

One useful approach has been the measurement of nitrogen balance throughout the sequential course of an infectious process.[5, 15, 92] Daily measurements of nitrogen intake and all nitrogen losses via different routes are obtained to determine whether the body is losing or retaining nitrogen. Other investigative techniques then are needed to provide specific information about the molecular mechanisms involved in producing any observed changes in nitrogen balance. Nonetheless, the use of balance techniques has provided information concerning the typical losses of body nitrogen and muscle mass during acute generalized infections (Fig. 3–2). Quantitation of these catabolic losses provides an important framework of reference for more detailed studies of changes in nitrogen metabolism.

A comprehensive series of nitrogen balance studies was obtained in young adult male volunteers subjected to different kinds of experimentally induced infections during the course of studies to test vaccine efficacy.[15] Extensive normal baseline data were obtained on each volunteer prior to the time of his or her inoculation with or exposure to infectious bacteria, viruses, or rickettsia. By making longitudinal serial measurements throughout the course of the infectious process, a comprehensive, prospective evaluation of metabolic balance changes in nitrogen and other elements was obtained.[15]

Nitrogen balances did not change from baseline values during the incubation periods of the infectious diseases studied (see Fig. 3–2). Only after symptoms and fever had begun did the body begin to lose nitrogen. These losses persisted for a period encompassing the acute illness. Then, in convalescence, the subjects began to retain nitrogen so that gradually, over a period of several weeks, body nitrogen losses were regained. Similar nitrogen balance studies were conducted in healthy control volunteers who were not infected.[11, 12, 15] Instead, these controls were subjected to (1) partial food deprivation to mimic the anorexia-induced reduction in dietary intake measured in the patients with infection; (2) a 24-hour exposure to artificially induced high environmental temperatures to produce an increase in body temperature comparable to that seen in patients with infection; (3) treatment with antibiotic therapy in courses identical to those given to patients with infections; or (4) treatment with oral hydrocortisone using sequentially changing daily doses to mimic the measured adrenal responses of infected subjects.

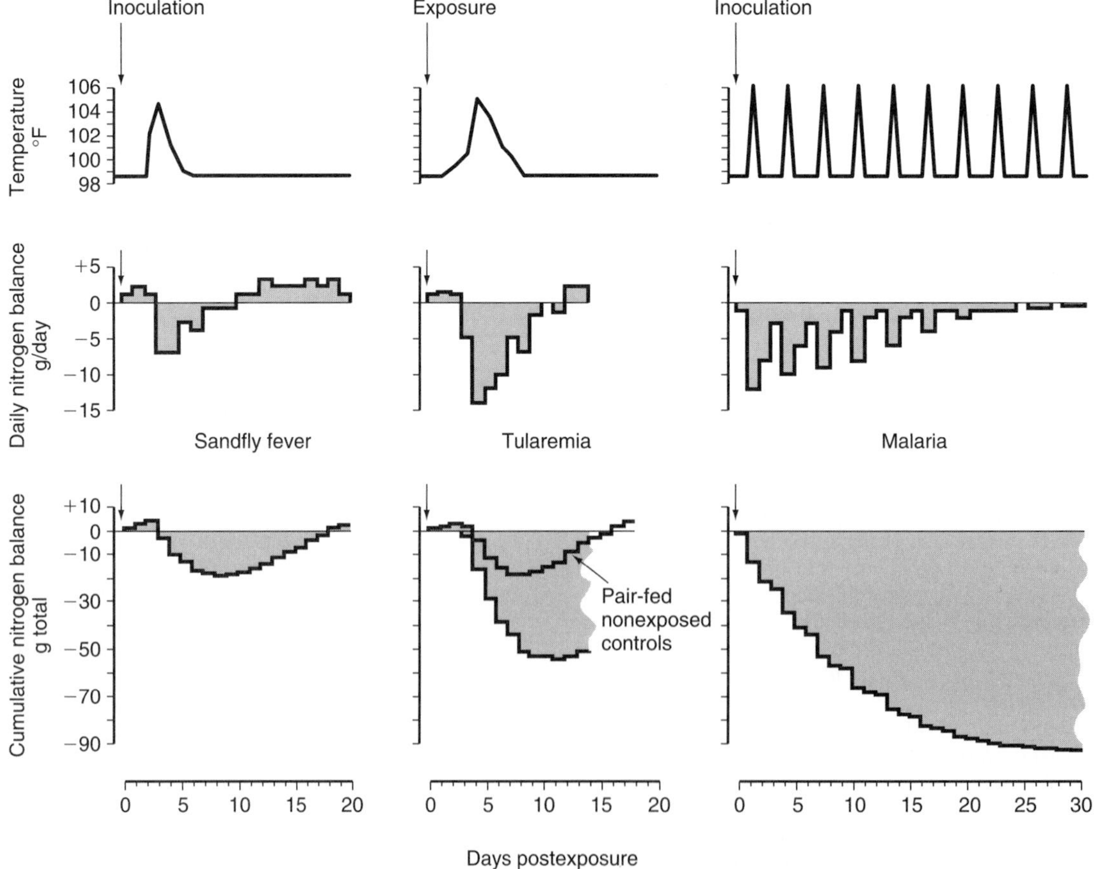

FIGURE 3–2 ■ Comparisons between the occurrence of fever (top) and changes in daily nitrogen balance (middle) and cumulative nitrogen (bottom) in patients with viral, bacterial, and generalized parasitic infections. Cumulative balance values for pair-fed healthy control subjects show the amounts of body nitrogen loss that can be ascribed to diminished food intake during infection. (From McKigney, J. I., and Munro, H. N. [eds.]: Nutrient Requirements in Adolescence. Cambridge, MA, MIT Press, 1976, p. 261.)

These balance studies showed that the major losses in body nitrogen resulted from the combined effects of a reduced intake of food plus a continued (or even increased) loss of nitrogen via the urine.[15] In contrast, simple starvation produced a prompt decrease in the daily losses of nitrogen via the urine. Thus, a patient with an acute infectious illness differed markedly from someone subjected to only simple dietary deprivation. Urinary nitrogen losses did not decline appreciably, or they increased in the presence of fever, whether the fever was caused by an active infection or an artificial increase in environmental temperatures.[12] The control studies also showed that the negative nitrogen balances that occurred during infection were not caused by adrenal glucocorticoid hormones or the antibiotics used in therapy.[11, 15] Rather, by terminating infection quickly, antibiotics helped to reverse the loss of body nitrogen, thereby allowing a more rapid restoration of nitrogen stores.

Because the loss of sizable quantities of nitrogen has important nutritional consequences, the same balance data were used to determine patterns of cumulative loss of body nitrogen.[5, 6, 15] As shown in Figure 3–2, total losses of body nitrogen grew progressively larger as the acute febrile phase of illness continued; the cumulative total loss of body nitrogen then persisted throughout early convalescence. When nitrogen balances finally became positive, nitrogen was recovered over a period of weeks as body stores were accumulated slowly.

Studies performed in adult patients suffering from infections such as tuberculosis and malaria suggested that the depletion of body stores of protein nitrogen did not continue unabated during subacute or chronic infections.[54] Rather, a new state of relative nitrogen equilibrium became established as chronically ill patients lapsed into a cachectic state. Total body nitrogen in such chronically ill patients was neither gained nor lost. Vital body processes continued to function for extended periods, despite the presence of cachexia and markedly depleted body nitrogen stores.[8] This state was hazardous at best and was comparable to the threat faced by infants and children with severe protein-energy malnutrition, who constantly face the additional threat of developing dangerous new or superimposed infectious diseases.[69, 70, 86, 109]

Only a limited amount of nitrogen balance data have been collected in children suffering from acute febrile infections. These data tend to reflect closely the patterns of change described in adults, with one major exception. Adults normally are in a state of nitrogen equilibrium, with neither a net gain nor a net loss over time, whereas healthy infants and children are consistently in positive balance because they must retain nitrogen to meet their needs for normal growth.

Few prospective measurements are available to document the changes in nitrogen balance throughout an entire infectious process in children. However, in 1926, Beck[4] in Germany reported a series of metabolic balance studies conducted in healthy infants inoculated with vaccinia virus. One study was begun in a child exposed to varicella 15 days before the onset of pustules; another study was begun in an infant exposed to measles virus 14 days before the onset of clinical illness. The grouped nitrogen balance data from the vaccinated infants are shown in Figure 3–3. Despite the development of a short-lived fever in this relatively mild infection, the infants maintained their usual food intake. Thus, the vaccinated infants did not go into negative nitrogen balance, and their rate of growth barely was slowed.[4] In measles or varicella, illness was of greater severity and a transient period of negative nitrogen balance was recorded. Similarly, Viteri and Béhar[127] measured nitrogen balance during childhood infections or after administration of live vaccines. Nitrogen loss varied with the severity of the illness. Wilson and colleagues[143] reported changes in nitrogen balances in hospitalized children who were convalescing from kwashiorkor when they developed varicella. A reduction in nitrogen retention occurred, and some children developed negative balances. Despite efforts to maintain a constant dietary intake, the children consumed less food during the course of the infection.

Acute nondiarrheal infections typically do not cause an increased loss of fecal nitrogen; however, if diarrhea is present during an illness, fecal losses of nitrogen and other nutrients can occur.[86, 107] Nitrogen losses also can occur through sweat, exudates, blood loss (from illness or from laboratory tests), sputum, gaseous exchanges, or sites of surgical drainage.[12, 15]

The absolute loss of body nitrogen, as measured by metabolic balance techniques during infection, also can be used as a guide for estimating the absolute losses from the body of other intracellular elements, such as potassium, magnesium, phosphate, and, to a lesser degree, sulfur and zinc.[5, 15] By using the ratios present in normal skeletal muscle of nitrogen to potassium and of nitrogen to magnesium, one can use measured losses of body nitrogen during infection to estimate concomitant losses of potassium and magnesium from the body. Similarly, a ratio of nitrogen to phosphorus in skeletal muscle can be used to estimate inorganic phosphate losses during infection, provided that corrections first are made to account for any phosphate losses originating from demineralized bone. Calculations such as these suggest that the absolute losses of body nitrogen during infection are derived primarily from intracellular sources because they

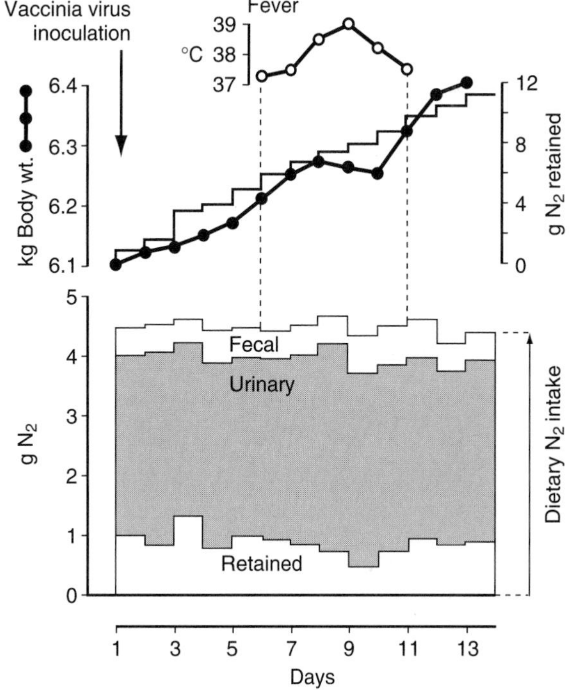

FIGURE 3–3 ■ Sequential measurements of body weight and cumulative nitrogen balance (top) and daily nitrogen balance (bottom) in a group of five healthy infants inoculated with vaccinia virus. Nitrogen intake values (plotted upward from baseline) and fecal and urinary losses (plotted downward from intake) reveal that the growing infants continued to retain nitrogen despite having brief periods of fever. (Drawn from numerical data published by Beck.[4])

correlate in both timing and magnitude with losses of the other principal intracellular elements.[15]

In contrast to infection-induced losses of intracellular elements, the losses of extracellular ions, sodium and chloride, follow an independent course during infection, and calcium losses are minimal in acute infection in the absence of long-term bed rest or paralysis with body immobilization.[15, 139]

URINARY EXCRETION OF NITROGEN-CONTAINING COMPOUNDS

The onset of fever typically is accompanied by an increased urinary loss of creatinine. This loss usually is followed within a day by increased losses of urea and ammonia.[15] Although alpha-amino nitrogen losses may increase transiently at the onset of fever in some infections, this excretion tends to be lower than baseline measurements during the remainder of illness and throughout convalescence. When measured prospectively, excretion of urinary alpha-amino nitrogen or most individual free amino acids did not change appreciably during sandfly fever, a mild virus infection.[130] In contrast, urinary losses of 3-methylhistidine and phenylalanine increased. The increased loss of phenylalanine appeared to reflect its increased concentrations in plasma.[131] Studies using radioactive compounds in rats suggested that most of the excess urea excreted during an acute infection was generated by the deamination of endogenous amino acids derived principally from skeletal muscle.[5]

Increased excretion of one of the amino acids, 3-methylhistidine, serves to indicate the extent of skeletal muscle catabolism. This amino acid cannot be reutilized after its release from contractile proteins.[65, 147]

Uric acid excretion may increase during febrile periods, but the greatest changes have been reported during infectious mononucleosis.[84] Uric acid losses are ascribed to an accelerated turnover of nucleic acids and enhanced purine degradation.

An increased excretion of urinary diazo reactants commonly occurs during most acute infectious illnesses, especially typhoid fever. These reactants include metabolites, such as kynurenine, 3-hydroxy-kynurenine, *o*-amino-hippuric acid, xanthurenic acid, and anthranilic acid, which are created during the accelerated hepatic metabolism of tryptophan via the kynurenine pathway.[99]

A sudden, dramatic increase in urinary nitrate excretion occurs during acute infections. This increase is a reflection of the cytokine-stimulated production of nitric oxide as a host defensive measure.[33, 119, 122, 128]

Metabolism of Free Amino Acids

The distribution, utilization, and metabolism of free amino acids undergo profound alterations during the course of acute infectious illness. Measurements in patients show patterns of change that can be explained by studies performed in experimental laboratory animals.[35, 94, 95, 132] As some proteins are produced, others are degraded, and many of the released amino acids are redistributed throughout the body before they are reutilized.

A diminution in the concentration of most free individual amino acids in plasma may begin even before the onset of symptoms. Hypoaminoacidemia generally persists throughout the febrile period of illness, the largest decreases occurring in the branched-chain amino acids, leucine, isoleucine, and valine.[81] The decline is caused primarily by an accelerated uptake of free amino acids by the liver. This increased flux from plasma to liver has been shown to occur in several species of animals during a variety of infections.[81] The amino acids that enter the liver are used for a variety of purposes. Amino acids may be metabolized to other compounds, oxidized, or reutilized for the synthesis of new proteins. Interleukin-6 appears to trigger many of the alterations in hepatic protein and amino acid metabolism during acute infection.[8, 113]

Amino acids become important sources of energy during the hypermetabolic phase of acute infections. Some amino acids are oxidized directly in muscle, whereas others are transformed progressively into glucose and glucagon. Gluconeogenic amino acids, such as alanine, are deaminated; their carbon skeletons are used as the principal substrate for producing glucose; and their nitrogen is used to create urea for excretion.

A complete spectrum of amino acids is required for the synthesis of new body proteins generated during infection, including hepatic enzymes,[100] such as tryptophan oxygenase and tyrosine transaminase, and the lipoproteins and glycoproteins released into the plasma.[5, 92, 93] This group of glycoproteins constitutes the "acute-phase reactants," which include alpha$_1$-antitrypsin, amyloid, alpha$_1$-acid glycoprotein, haptoglobin, C-reactive protein, fibrinogen (the third component of complement), and ceruloplasmin.

These acute-phase reactant proteins are produced in excess during infections, even in protein-deficient children who exhibit acute kwashiorkor.[90] Some of the potentially beneficial functions attributed to acute-phase reactants include an amplification of both humoral and cell-mediated immunity, antiproteinase effects that could limit or contain harmful enzymes liberated during inflammatory reactions, oxidase activities, and the detoxification of free hemoglobin.[92]

In addition to the accelerated synthesis of proteins within the liver, infection increases the production of phagocytic and lymphoid cells. A need for producing increased quantities of such diverse proteins as the cytokines, complement and kinin components, fibronectin, and the several classes of immunoglobulins also exists. All of these requirements involve the need for free amino acids.

Proinflammatory cytokines and interferon-γ stimulate the production of nitric oxide from arginine, its sole precursor.[33, 128] Among the many important biologic effects of nitric oxide are those resulting from its being a highly potent microbicidal, parasiticidal, and tumoricidal agent.[119] The importance of nitric oxide in these roles may rival those of free oxygen radicals in potency and effectiveness.[122] This newly recognized host defense agent is generated when cytokine-induced nitric oxide synthase initiates the oxygenation of one of arginine's guanido nitrogen groups to produce citrulline and nitric oxide.[119]

AMINO ACID AVAILABILITY

In the presence of anorexia and a diminished intake of food nutrients, the body in large measure must use endogenous sources to supply its increased amino acid needs. The principal sources of potentially available endogenous amino acids are the proteins of somatic tissues, including skeletal muscle and skin. The free amino acid pool contains the equivalent of approximately 12.5 g of protein in a normal adult man, an amount that represents only 0.1 percent of total body protein.[129] Because the normal turnover of protein in a healthy adult is approximately 200 to 250 g each day, the free amino acid pool must be resupplied continually from endogenous as well as exogenous sources. During infections, the absorption of individual amino acids from the intestine may be depressed and delayed[75] or increased,[28] depending on the infection. Protein synthesis is not stopped entirely within body somatic tissues during an infection but is slowed markedly. At the same time, the rates of degradation of somatic proteins are accelerated, so that a net loss of muscle, skin, and other somatic proteins occurs through catabolic wasting. Catabolic degradation of skeletal muscle protein can be initiated by interleukin-1,[3, 8, 25, 32] which triggers muscular proteases via the intracellular production of prostaglandin E_2. The body appears to sacrifice contractile proteins of skeletal muscle to obtain the free amino acids needed for higher priority requirements.

Some of the amino acids liberated during muscle protein catabolism are lost directly to the plasma. Others, such as the branched-chain group, are utilized in situ as sources of energy for muscle fibers; after oxidation, their amino groups are used to manufacture new glutamine and alanine, which can be used elsewhere for gluconeogenesis.[65] Because the branched-chain amino acids can be oxidized within skeletal muscle, their rate of release from muscle is decreased, which exaggerates the decline in their concentrations in plasma.[5, 81, 129] Some of the free amino acids liberated within muscle are retained within contractile cells and reutilized for the slowed but continuing process of muscle protein anabolism.

This catabolic breakdown of somatic protein to supply amino acids for use in other parts of the body is a highly visible clinical phenomenon. In this regard, the proteins of skin, skeletal muscle, and other somatic structures appear to constitute the principal body pool of "labile" nitrogen, which is called upon to maintain protein homeostasis and the physiologic functions of visceral tissues during periods of infectious illness or other stresses. Because infants and small children have very little muscle protein (and thus, a very small "bank" of readily available amino acids), the infection-induced need for free amino acids puts these youngsters at a special disadvantage.

To study the complex interrelationships involved in amino acid metabolism, workers have used isotopes to measure the simultaneous rates of anabolism and catabolism in the protein of skeletal muscle and other tissues of experimental animals during infection.[103] In addition, clinically useful estimates of skeletal muscle degradation can be obtained in patients through the quantitative daily measurement of 3-methylhistidine excretion into urine. More than 90 percent of the total body content of 3-methylhistidine is associated with the peptide chains of actin in all muscle and of myosin in white muscle fibers.[147] This unique amino acid is formed in situ through the transmethylation of histidine, but only after the histidine first has been incorporated into the amino acid structure of myofibrillar proteins. When released, 3-methylhistidine cannot be reutilized by the body and instead is lost via the urine. The increase in excretion of 3-methylhistidine during acute infections is in keeping with other estimates of skeletal muscle wasting. The extent to which proteolysis occurs during periods of severe surgical sepsis also has been quantified by measuring the differences between concentrations of glucose, lactate, free fatty acids, ketones, and alanine in femoral arterial and venous blood.[88] Neither free fatty acid nor ketone utilization was increased during occurrences of acute fevers, but an increased oxidation of glucose and of amino acids derived from protein was used to fuel cellular hypermetabolism. Although infection stimulates a sizable increase in the rates of body protein synthesis, the acceleration of protein catabolism is increased even further, and the body suffers a net loss of somatic proteins and even some visceral ones.[129]

Phenylalanine is one of the amino acids released by the accelerated catabolism of somatic proteins. However, only relatively limited amounts of phenylalanine can be utilized for the synthesis of new proteins or for its conversion into tyrosine.[129, 131] Accordingly, phenylalanine concentrations in the circulating free amino acid pool tend to rise rather than fall during periods of fever. These increases occur coincidentally with the typical declines in plasma values for tyrosine and most other free amino acids. The exaggerated phenylalanine-to-tyrosine ratio can be useful for evaluating these opposing changes during febrile illnesses. An increase in this ratio thus serves as a useful clinical index of the severity of infection-induced alterations in amino acid metabolism.[129] During occurrences of infections of great severity and those with hepatocellular dysfunction, hypoaminoacidemia may be replaced by an excessive accumulation of many other free amino acids in plasma.[5, 115, 141]

Free tryptophan, also liberated from degrading protein, undergoes an accelerated metabolism via several different metabolic pathways in the liver.[5, 78, 79, 94] In response to the increased hepatic availability of tryptophan or the increased synthesis of tryptophan oxygenase, or both, excess tryptophan enters the kynurenine pathways, where it is converted into different diazo-reactant compounds and pyrimidine nucleotides.[94] At the same time, tryptophan enters other pathways, leading possibly to increased synthesis of serotonin or indoleacetic acid.[99]

Carbohydrate Metabolism

During the febrile phase of infectious illnesses, carbohydrate metabolism provides much of the additional energy needed by body cells. An increased demand for metabolizable energy is met by a resetting of the endocrine control mechanisms to permit a marked acceleration of the synthesis and release of glucose from the liver.[29, 41, 142] Although some glucose is derived from hepatocellular glycogen, most additional requirements for glucose during acute infections are met by accelerated hepatic gluconeogenic mechanisms. Recycled lactate and amino acids, especially those with gluconeogenic potential, such as alanine, are the principal substrates used by the liver to increase its output of newly synthesized glucose; glycerol (derived from the metabolism of triglyceride lipids) and pyruvate also are used.[65]

Early in acute infectious illnesses, basal blood glucose concentrations tend to become somewhat elevated. Diabetic patients who require insulin often develop glycosuria at the onset of febrile infections, and more insulin must be given to maintain their control. The tendency for acute infections to be accompanied by an early modest hyperglycemia also is seen in laboratory animals. Modest hyperglycemia often is noted in animals after being injected with bacterial endotoxin.[19, 72]

Although an early hyperglycemic response appears to be the initial change in carbohydrate metabolism, the ability of the body to sustain an accelerated production of glucose may be lost. Hypoglycemia then may emerge as an important clinical problem. Hypoglycemia generally results from one of two major pathogenic mechanisms: a diminished availability of substrate molecules required for gluconeogenesis or a failure of the metabolic mechanisms needed to produce hepatic glucose. Carbohydrate pathway defects at the molecular level have not been found in overwhelming bacterial infections in laboratory animals.[48, 85] Therefore, carbohydrate depletion during overwhelming or terminal infections can be ascribed to nonavailability of substrate. However, if hepatic cells are injured during an infectious disease, such as viral hepatitis, hypoglycemia can result from a failure of gluconeogenic processes.[5, 36, 107]

The depletion of substrate for adequate gluconeogenesis occurs primarily as a dangerous clinical complication of neonatal sepsis. Infants are born with only minimal amounts of skeletal muscle protein. Because muscle contains the principal "labile nitrogen" pool for supplying amino acids that can be converted into glucose, neonatal infants lack a sufficient quantity of potential substrate molecules for sustaining long-term gluconeogenesis. Newborn infants especially are prone to develop severe hypoglycemia whenever a septic process becomes established.[146] On the other hand, hypoglycemia that results from a breakdown of hepatic gluconeogenic mechanisms occurs primarily when liver cells are damaged by an infectious or toxemic process. Thus, hypoglycemia can become an important complicating factor in severe viral hepatitis, yellow fever, or endotoxemia during gram-negative sepsis.[36, 72] These conditions can cause hepatocellular damage and a breakdown of enzyme-synthesizing mechanisms within the liver.[72]

A change in glucose tolerance can be detected within hours after the onset of a febrile infection.[102, 111] Baseline blood glucose values may be elevated somewhat, and disappearance of glucose is slowed moderately as a component aspect of a febrile illness. Under these circumstances, the pancreatic islets produce insulin in excess quantities. Despite an increase in plasma insulin concentrations, glucose disappearance rates are slowed; these combined metabolic changes resemble those caused by mild insulin resistance.

Bacterial and viral infections also cause increased secretion of pancreatic glucagon,[102, 105] which, together with release of catecholamines accompanying infection,[45, 47, 142] provides hormonal stimuli for accelerating gluconeogenesis within the liver. These hormonal stimuli initiate their hepatic effects during infection by activating adenylate cyclase.[29] The unusual simultaneous increase in basal concentrations of both insulin and glucagon in plasma results from direct cytokine stimulation of pancreatic islet cells.[8, 40, 145] Because of these hormonal changes and high plasma glucocorticoid values in patients with severe bacterial sepsis, infusions of glucose may fail to suppress hepatic gluconeogenesis.[65, 66] The resultant increase in glucose pool size helps to explain the apparent slowing of glucose disappearance and the occurrence of hyperinsulinemia during infections.

Certain viral infections in children seem prone to initiate acute juvenile-type, insulin-requiring diabetes mellitus. Although the evidence for a viral cause of diabetes has not been established fully in humans, epidemiologic findings indicate that juvenile diabetes may develop several months after onset of certain viral illnesses, especially mumps, coxsackievirus B (type 4) infection, rubella, or cytomegalovirus infection.[83] Additional epidemiologic evidence is based on a tendency for new cases of juvenile-type diabetes to appear in clusters.

Susceptibility to juvenile diabetes also may be influenced by genetic make-up. A high incidence of human leukocyte antigen types B8 and Bw15 has been detected in juvenile diabetics.[108] Studies in laboratory animals suggest that genetically susceptible species may have virus receptor sites on their insulin-producing beta cells. These receptors in species with high-risk haplotypes allow viruses to be adsorbed by the pancreatic beta cells, with subsequent destruction of insulin-producing cells.

The cytokine granulocyte colony-stimulating factor influences the uptake of glucose by phagocytic cells, as well as their mobilization during inflammatory reactions.[62] Availability of glucose contributes directly to the respiratory burst that accompanies phagocytosis, as well as to the production of the myeloperoxidase enzymes needed to kill engulfed organisms.

Lipid Metabolism

As Table 3–1 shows, numerous changes in lipid metabolism have been documented during infection. In contrast to the relatively stereotyped patterns of change in nitrogen and amino acid metabolism and in the accelerated production of glucose, responses involving body lipids are more variable from infection to infection. Plasma lipid changes also may be biphasic during the course of a single infection.

This complexity results in part from the multiple factors that control the metabolism of lipids during infectious illnesses,[5, 115] including the need for hepatic synthesis of serum lipoproteins, variations in the production and utilization of free fatty acids and ketones as sources of cellular energy, and variable changes in rates of uptake or release of lipids from body fat depots.[5, 115]

Lipids have another function that is of major importance during acute-phase reactions. This function involves the cytokine-stimulated use of polyunsaturated fatty acids localized within cell walls to serve as precursor molecules for various families of eicosanoids (prostaglandins, prostacyclines, thromboxanes, and lipoxines). These eicosanoid lipids,

TABLE 3–1 ■ BASIC MECHANISMS LEADING TO OBSERVED EFFECTS OF INFECTION ON LIPID METABOLISM OF THE HOST

Effects Associated with the Presence of Invading Microorganisms

1. Direct effects
   a. Microorganism use of host lipids for replication
   b. Disruption of host cell metabolism by intracellular microorganisms
   c. Localized destruction of fat cells by the infectious process
2. Indirect effects
   a. Alterations in host metabolism caused by bacterial exotoxins, endotoxins, or bacterial enzymes
   b. Activation of lipases and other lipid-affecting enzymes within host phagocytes

Effects Secondary to Development of Generalized Illness Due to Infection

1. Decreased dietary fat intake
2. Interference with intestinal digestion and absorption of lipids
3. Alterations in lipid transport
   a. Changing concentrations of lipid transport proteins
   b. Decreased lipoprotein lipase activity (caused by tumor necrosis factor), which allows triglycerides to accumulate in plasma
4. Altered lipid metabolism within host cells caused by proinflammatory cytokines
   a. Activation of cell wall phospholipases by proinflammatory cytokines
   b. Creation, from cell wall polyunsaturated fatty acids, of intracellular arachidonic and/or eicosapentanoic acids
   c. Transformation of arachidonic and eicosapentanoic acids into various eicosanoids (prostaglandins, prostacyclines, thromboxanes, and lipoxanes)
5. Other alterations of lipid metabolism within host cells
   a. Altered rates of hormone-mediated lipolysis within fat depots
   b. Accelerated fatty acid synthesis within the liver
   c. Depressed hepatic ketogenesis
   d. Altered rates of lipid uptake and use by peripheral tissues
6. Participation of newly formed eicosanoids in inflammatory and immunologic responses, as well as in the coagulation mechanisms
7. Effects related to the prior nutritional status of the patient
8. Terminal pathologic hyperlipidemic effects associated with gram-negative sepsis and hypotensive shock

in turn, trigger many of the diverse cellular responses seen during infection, inflammation, and immune responses.[58, 104]

PLASMA LIPIDS AND LIPOPROTEINS

Because the concentrations of individual lipid moieties in plasma depend on the algebraic summation of both input and removal rates, the mechanisms that control the release or uptake of individual lipids must be studied throughout the course of various kinds of infectious illnesses.

Concentrations of cholesterol have been reported to increase, to decrease, or to remain unchanged.[5] Mild virus infections often are associated with a transient decline in serum cholesterol values. When longitudinal studies were conducted during the course of experimentally induced sandfly fever in young adult male volunteers, plasma values for total and esterified cholesterol, phospholipids, and free fatty acids all declined in conjunction with, or immediately before, the onset of fever.[63] This decline in concentration included both the cholesterol and protein components of the low-density beta-lipoproteins. In contrast, the plasma triglyceride values showed a biphasic pattern of change: an initial decline was followed by a rise above baseline control concentrations during the early convalescent period. Depressions of total serum cholesterol values also have been reported to occur during pneumococcal pneumonia, cholera, tuberculosis, and malaria. However, when studied in rhesus monkeys experimentally infected with *Streptococcus pneumoniae* or *Salmonella typhimurium,* rates of [^{3}H] mevalonic acid incorporation into free cholesterol were accelerated,[37] and no evidence of an inhibition of squalene synthesis or its conversion to cholesterol was found. In contrast, the synthesis of cholesterol was blocked partially when monkeys with diet-induced hypercholesterolemia were subjected to a pneumococcal infection.[37]

Marked increases in the concentrations of total serum lipids and triglycerides are found consistently in patients with infections caused by gram-negative bacilli,[5, 55, 115] but this response is minimized or fails to occur in patients with viral or gram-positive coccal infections. A similar difference has been noted in monkeys with either *S. pneumoniae* or *S. typhimurium* infection.[56] Tumor necrosis factor, a proinflammatory cytokine with a unique additional function that inhibits the enzyme lipoprotein lipase, appears to be of central importance in accounting for these differences.[55]

Although a release of tumor necrosis factor from activated macrophages may occur in many infections, its release is stimulated markedly by bacterial endotoxins released during gram-negative infections.[8, 74] Hypertriglyceridemia occurring during periods of *S. typhimurium* infection in monkeys was generated by tumor necrosis factor–induced mechanisms that reduced both the clearance of lipids from plasma and the activity of heparin-sensitive plasma lipoprotein lipase. Hypertriglyceridemia that accompanied pneumococcal infections was far less severe than that observed with gram-negative infections. After endotoxin was administered,[55] hypertriglyceridemia developed chiefly as the result of an impaired lipid disposal mechanism, again, secondary to release of tumor necrosis factor from macrophages.[8] An acceleration in the rate of hepatic production of triglycerides from free fatty acid precursors also occurred.

LIPIDS AND ENERGY METABOLISM DURING INFECTION

Requirements for cellular energy during periods of chronic infections in laboratory animals appear to be met largely through the catabolism of stored body fat.[67] In contrast, fat wasting does not seem to be as prominent during rapidly lethal bacterial infections. Ketogenesis also seems to be blunted during periods of acute infections.[85] Concentrations of free fatty acid in plasma normally are increased by the actions of catecholamines, growth hormone, and glucagon, which are increased during infection.[5] On the other hand, concomitantly high concentrations of plasma insulin apparently serve to inhibit both lipolysis and ketogenesis.[5, 85] The contribution of free fatty acids to energy production during infection thus is influenced by the interplay of these hormones, the availability of glucose, and the functional capacity of the liver to take up fatty acids and convert them to triglycerides.[37, 38, 40, 41]

Finally, brown fat is thought to contribute importantly to heat production in newborn infants via sympathetic nerve activation of this tissue. Because numerous viruses are known to proliferate in brown fat,[116] fever that occurs during neonatal viral infections may involve brown fat thermogenesis.

Acute infectious illnesses produce surprisingly few effects upon the intestinal absorption of fat, although it may be reduced somewhat during intestinal infections and parasitemic or enterotoxemic illnesses.[91, 107] Lipid precursors needed for the replication of microorganisms within host tissues must be supplied from metabolic pools within the host. For example, malarial parasites obtain their structural lipids from red blood cell precursors; lipid-containing viruses appear to obtain the lipid components needed for their assembly from lipid-rich membranes already present within host cells.

LIPID METABOLISM AND HOST DEFENSIVE MEASURES

Rapid metabolic responses by cell wall lipids play a major role in initiating a panoply of intracellular events during acute-phase reactions. The attachment of proinflammatory cytokines to cell wall receptors triggers the conversion of polyunsaturated fatty acid in cell wall membranes to a variety of biologically active eicosanoids. Lipids of various eicosanoid families then become the messenger molecules that are responsible for many of the acute-phase metabolic and cellular responses[8, 32] that occur during infection. These short-lived eicosanoids are biopotent at nanomolar to picomolar concentrations. In addition to their importance within lymphocytes of the immune system, eicosanoid lipids transmit stimulatory or inhibitory signals between other cells and tissues in both health and disease.[58, 104] Although they do not initiate disease processes, various eicosanoid lipids (i.e., prostaglandins, leukotrienes, prostacycline, lipoxines, and thromboxanes) are important components of the pathogenic progression of infectious diseases.[58, 104]

Eicosanoids also have important effects on other white blood cells and platelets, as well as on such diverse organs as the brain, lungs, stomach, and kidneys. These eicosanoids appear to be components of complex, often overlapping, regulatory mechanisms that interconnect the immune system, the central nervous system, the endocrine glands, and the functions of many other organs and tissues. These homeostatic (and at times pathogenic) mechanisms are characterized by numerous duplications, amplifications, checks and balances, and feedback control loops.

Biochemical details now are well established concerning the intracellular synthesis of individual eicosanoids from both n-3 and n-6 polyunsaturated fatty acid precursors.[58, 104] After cytokines interact with cell wall receptors, they activate cell membrane phospholipase enzymes. These enzymes initiate the release (into the cell interior) of arachidonic acid from cell wall (n-6) polyunsaturated fatty acid or eicosapentanoic acid from (n-3) polyunsaturated fatty acid. These first steps of eicosanoid synthesis can be blocked by adrenocorticoid hormones. In target cells having cyclooxygenase enzymes, arachidonic acid is oxygenated into 4-series leukotrienes, 2-series prostaglandins, or thromboxanes and prostacyclin. On the other hand, if a cell possesses lipooxygenase enzymes, arachidonic acid is oxygenated into the sometimes less potent 5-series leukotrienes, 3-series prostaglandins, or lipoxins.[104] The highly active eicosanoid molecules are degraded rapidly. Importantly, synthesis of prostaglandins of both the 2- and 4-series can be blocked by certain nonsteroidal anti-inflammatory drugs, such as aspirin, indomethacin, and ibuprofen.[58, 104]

Other fatty acids may participate in defense mechanisms of the host and, on occasion, even may be involved in pathogenic events of a harmful nature. An increase in the fat content of vital organs is a common occurrence in patients dying of severe bacterial infections; fatty metamorphosis especially is prominent in the liver, kidney, and heart.[53] Hyperlipemia in gram-negative septicemia may be accompanied by fat embolization to the lungs. Other deleterious actions of body lipids involve the liberation of phospholipids from platelets and their subsequent participation in the activation of the blood-clotting cascade leading to disseminated intravascular coagulation.

Electrolyte and Acid-Base Metabolism

Many of the life-threatening medical emergencies faced by infants and children with acute infectious diseases involve problems in the areas of salt and water or acid-base balance. Some infections cause severe overhydration, and others produce dehydration with hypovolemic shock. Pathogenic mechanisms that come into play during various infections can lead to metabolic alkalosis or acidosis, to respiratory alkalosis or acidosis, or to complex admixtures of these pathophysiologic perturbations.[8, 16]

The onset of fever typically is accompanied by tachypnea and accelerated respiratory gas exchange, which leads in turn to an exaggerated loss of dissolved carbon dioxide from blood and a state of uncompensated respiratory alkalosis.[5] Alkalosis may persist as long as febrile tachypnea lasts and gas exchange within the alveoli remains unimpeded.

Conversely, infections that produce extensive pulmonary consolidation can impair carbon dioxide exchange and cause respiratory acidosis. Respiratory acidosis also is a complication in patients whose pulmonary musculature no longer can function effectively, as in those with poliomyelitis, tetanus, botulism, or respiratory distress syndrome.

Metabolic acidosis generally develops whenever an infectious disease process becomes severe. With the hypotension, vascular stasis, and cellular anoxia seen during gram-negative sepsis, the generation of excessive lactic acid and other acidic metabolic products exceeds the capacity of the body's buffering systems.[5, 115]

Diarrheal diseases can be accompanied by two other forms of metabolic acid-base derangement.[16, 107, 134] Toxigenic diarrhea characterized by high-volume stool loss, such as that seen in Asiatic cholera or *Escherichia coli* enterotoxemia, causes an excessive loss of fecal bicarbonate and an alkaline stool, with a resultant decline in blood pH. Bicarbonate is secreted actively in the lower ileum and cannot be reabsorbed completely by the colonic mucosa if high-volume losses of watery stool occur.[16] In contrast, diarrhea accompanied by only low-volume stool losses, as in rotavirus infections,[107] tends to be associated with an acid stool associated with an exaggerated loss of fecal potassium rather than bicarbonate. If fecal potassium losses persist chronically over a long period or occur rapidly as part of the massive fluid loss of acute secretory diarrheas, such as in pediatric cholera, body potassium can be depleted severely. The loss of cellular potassium then can produce metabolic alkalosis, cardiac arrhythmia, paralytic ileus, and weakness in children and the occurrence of hypokalemic vacuolization in cells of the myocardium and renal tubular epithelium. Even if balance of fluid is restored promptly in these patients, a prolonged state of metabolic alkalosis can persist until body potassium stores are replenished.

The importance of diarrheal diseases in infants and small children is great, with an estimated 2 to 3 million deaths occurring worldwide each year.[86] Life-threatening dehydration can result from the loss of body water and electrolytes during high-volume diarrhea. Because massive diarrhea produces an iso-osmotic loss of body water and electrolytes, the fluid losses come from the extracellular rather than the intracellular space.[134] The circulating blood becomes thick and viscous because of a relative increase in hematocrit values and a progressive concentration of serum proteins, which can increase to more than twice their normal values. Despite serious dehydration, concentrations of plasma sodium remain relatively normal, when expressed in terms of plasma water.[134] This type of acute, massive diarrhea can lead to the rapid onset of hypovolemic shock, renal failure, and death.

Dehydration usually does not become a problem in infectious diseases that lack protracted vomiting, diarrhea, or prominent sweat loss. Instead, severe generalized infections in children may be accompanied by some retention of body water and salt. Soon after the onset of a febrile illness, the adrenal secretion of aldosterone increases,[11, 14] and this mineralocorticoid stimulates the renal retention of sodium and chloride. These electrolytes virtually may disappear from the urine during a severe febrile illness. Retention of salt tends to be accompanied by a retention of body water throughout the period of illness.[5] Generalized edema is an infection-induced manifestation of kwashiorkor and also can be seen during severe infections in well-nourished children. Accumulations of excess water and salt typically are excreted after the acute phase of illness by a transient period of diuresis during the early convalescent period.

Some infections, particularly those that become localized within the central nervous system, also are complicated by an inappropriate secretion of antidiuretic hormone from the posterior pituitary.[34, 140] The ensuing retention of body water may dilute the sodium and chloride in plasma. Redistribution of sodium also may contribute to the development of hyponatremia during infections. Sodium may begin to accumulate within body cells, apparently because the sodium-pumping mechanisms in extracellular membranes may fail to maintain internal electrolyte homeostasis.[5] This form of sodium sequestration is evidence of severe illness. It is not reversed easily and may be a major complication in patients with severe infections, such as meningococcemia or Rocky Mountain spotted fever.

Vitamin Metabolism

Although few measurement data are available concerning infection-induced changes in vitamin metabolism, the consensus is that the utilization or metabolism of most vitamins is accelerated.[13, 126] Scattered reports suggest that infectious diseases in humans may be followed by classic scurvy, beriberi, pellagra, or xerophthalmia.[109]

Recent attention has focused on vitamin A, which once was termed the anti-infection vitamin. Declining concentrations of plasma vitamin A during episodes of childhood infections are accompanied or perhaps caused by a marked urinary loss of this vitamin.[1, 121] Not only does the heightened vitamin A deficiency induced by infection contribute to the subsequent development of ocular and conjunctival pathologies, but also subclinical deficiencies of vitamin A and their associated immunologic dysfunctions can heighten the mortality associated with childhood infections,[110] as shown most dramatically in measles.[118]

Depressed plasma concentrations of several other vitamins also have been reported.[5] In addition to the urinary losses of vitamin A,[1, 121] increased excretion of urinary riboflavin and vitamin C may occur in conjunction with negative nitrogen balance.[13]

Vitamins are known to participate in metabolic processes activated during host defensive mechanisms.[8] The rapid synthesis of steroid hormones by the adrenal cortex is accompanied by a decline in the adrenal content of vitamin C. The B-group vitamins, vitamin C, and folate all participate in the metabolism of activated phagocytic cells.

Controversy continues to exist over whether massive daily doses of vitamin C can suppress or prevent the common cold and other viral respiratory infections. More than two decades ago, the American Academy of Pediatrics Committee on Drugs failed to find sufficient scientific evidence to support Pauling's claim,[26] but new data subsequently were introduced.[50] Concentrations of vitamin C in neutrophils decline during infectious diseases. Vitamin C is recognized for its importance in the locomotive activity of phagocytic cells, as well as its contributions to the immune system.[2]

Intestinal parasites, such as tapeworms, may take up sufficient vitamin B_{12} from the succus entericus to diminish B_{12} absorption and lead to the development of megaloblastic anemia. The intestinal absorption of fat-soluble vitamins and folate also may be impaired for a time in children with enteric infections or parasitic diseases.[68]

The antioxidant role of several vitamins (A, C, and E) has been recognized recently. Antioxidants act to reduce oxidative stress within the body by serving as scavengers of singlet oxygen radicals. But the antioxidant functions of several other provitamin-A carotenoids are of still greater importance. They include betacarotene, lycopene (the red pigment found in tomatoes and other brightly colored fruits), lutein (from spinach), and zeoxanthin (from kale and other dark green collard greens). Lycopene is more abundant in plasma than is beta-carotene and twice as powerful in quenching free oxygen radicals. Lutein and zeoxanthin are retinal pigments, with lutein being found throughout the retina and zeoxanthin being concentrated in the macula. Antioxidants are thought to protect cell membranes, DNA, and arteries to augment the immune system and the function of natural killer cells and to help prevent heart attacks, macular degeneration, and various cancers, especially those of the prostate. Unfortunately, little is known about the probable role of antioxidants during infectious diseases of children.

Trace Element Metabolism

As Table 3–2 shows, infectious illnesses often are accompanied by changes in the concentration of several of the trace elements in plasma. The most consistent responses include a decrease in the concentrations of plasma iron and zinc and an increase in plasma copper.[5] This triad of trace-element changes has been reported in bacterial, viral, rickettsial, and parasitic infections. In acute viral hepatitis, however, serum iron values tend to increase in the second and third weeks of illness. Hepatitis also is associated with an unusual change in the binding of zinc to various ligands.[52] Soon after the acute onset of jaundice, plasma zinc is found to be bound almost entirely as microligands to small molecules, such as the amino acids. This phenomenon contrasts with the normal propensity for approximately 95 percent of plasma zinc to bind predominantly as a macroligand with either albumin or alpha$_2$-macroglobulin. In any event, plasma zinc is sequestered rapidly in the liver, where it becomes

TABLE 3–2 ■ INFECTION-RELATED CHANGES IN TRACE ELEMENTS

Trace Element	Observed Change during Infection	Suggested Pathophysiologic Mechanisms
Iron	Hyposideremia (common)	Flux of iron into liver and reticuloendothelial system cells
		Increased synthesis of ferritin
		Sequestration of iron in tissue stores
		Diminished iron absorption
	Anemia	Accelerated red blood cell destruction
		Direct blood loss
		Inhibition of erythropoiesis
	Reduced serum iron-binding capacity	Reduced synthesis of transferrin
	Hypersideremia (selective)	Hepatocyte damage during hepatitis
Zinc	Hypozincemia	Accelerated flux of zinc into liver
		Hepatic synthesis of additional metallothioneins
		Negative body balance of zinc
	Hyperzincuria	Hepatitis-induced inhibition of zinc binding to plasma proteins
Copper	Hypercupremia	Accelerated hepatic synthesis and release of ceruloplasmin
Chromium	Hypochromia	Unknown
Manganese	Hypermanganemia	Hepatocyte damage during hepatitis
Cobalt	Hypercobaltemia	Hepatocyte damage during hepatitis
	Macrocytic anemia	Intestinal parasitic competition for available vitamin B_{12}
Gallium	Hypergallemia	Hepatocyte damage during hepatitis
	Accumulation in sites of localized infection	Unknown
Iodine	Accelerated deiodination of thyroid hormones	Increased cellular metabolic rates
		Increased iodine availability for cellular bactericidal functions

tightly bound during acute infections to newly synthesized metallothioneins.[117]

CHANGES IN IRON METABOLISM

An abrupt depression in serum iron concentrations has been observed in virtually all infections in which iron values have been measured, except acute viral hepatitis, with pyogenic infections causing the greatest effects. This hypoferremia has been ascribed primarily to an accelerated flux of iron from plasma into the liver, where it becomes localized in reticuloendothelial cells and hepatocytes. There the iron becomes sequestered as intracellular hemosiderin molecules or as a complex with ferritin.[8] Tumor necrosis factor and interleukin-1 appear to trigger this sequestration of iron by inducing the formation of ferritin,[21] some of which may be found in plasma. Plasma ferritin values provide a valuable clue concerning the quantities of body iron available in storage depots. Once iron has become sequestered, it is not released readily until the infection is terminated.

During both acute and chronic infections, the normal mechanisms that allow for the continuing release from tissue stores of the iron needed for use in erythropoiesis appear to be inhibited. Thus, if an infection persists for a prolonged period, anemia may develop. Although the "anemia of infection" resembles iron deficiency anemia in its peripheral manifestations, it develops in the presence of adequate quantities of iron in storage sites and cannot be reversed by the therapeutic administration of iron.[8]

Other factors that influence iron metabolism during episodes of infection include an accelerated destruction of red blood cells and their direct loss in diseases in which hemolysis or bleeding is a factor. Excessive laboratory testing of blood samples can occur. In malaria, for example, serum iron values tend to decline, despite the unusually large amounts of hemoglobin released from parasitized red blood cells. The released hemoglobin rapidly complexes with haptoglobin and is taken up by reticuloendothelial cells.[82] As in other forms of hemolytic anemia, a depression of serum haptoglobin values in malaria can serve as an index of the severity of red blood cell destruction.

An inhibition of iron absorption in the intestinal tract also can contribute to an infection-induced depression of serum iron values.[137] Studies using radioactive iron showed that a febrile illness or the febrile response of infants or young children to immunization could depress intestinal iron absorption for several days.[18]

The abrupt fall in serum iron concentration, which can reach virtually undetectable values, takes place without any appreciable change in total serum iron-binding capacity. Although concentrations of serum transferrin decline along with those of albumin during states of severe protein deficiency, they decline only slowly, if at all, during occurrences of acute infections. The combination of a normal iron-binding capacity and a markedly depressed concentration of serum iron in previously well-nourished children results in an increase in the concentration of serum unsaturated transferrin.[8] Unsaturated transferrin may serve an important host defensive role by competing with siderophores of bacteria, which need to acquire iron for their growth and replication.[136] Because of its high affinity constant for iron, unsaturated transferrin serves as an important potential mechanism for inhibiting bacterial replication.

Increased concentrations of serum iron have been reported during bacillary dysentery, typhoidal infections, and, most commonly, acute viral hepatitis. The increase in concentrations of serum iron is delayed in hepatitis until several weeks after the initial appearance of jaundice; this increase may be large enough virtually to saturate the iron-binding capacity of serum. An impairment of mechanisms accounting for the normal daily hepatic removal of iron from serum has been thought to explain the hyperferremia noted during infections associated with liver cell dysfunction. An alternative hypothesis suggests that hepatitis-induced hyperferremia is caused by an escape of iron from the damaged hepatocytes. The latter explanation also is used to explain the reported increase in concentrations of serum manganese, gallium, and cobalt during acute hepatitis.[5]

CHANGES IN ZINC METABOLISM

Concentrations of zinc decline during periods of various infectious diseases, as they do with a large variety of other diseases characterized by the presence of an inflammatory process.[5, 93] Zinc values, however, rarely fall as low as do iron values. This difference apparently is because of the large amount of plasma zinc that is bound tightly to alpha$_2$-macroglobulin. This plasma protein remains relatively constant during periods of infection.[5]

Like iron, zinc appears to move into the liver at an accelerated rate during occurrences of acute infections. This increased flux of zinc from serum to liver appears to be triggered by the action of proinflammatory cytokines released from activated monocytes and macrophages.[5, 8] The hepatic uptake and sequestration of zinc are associated with an increased synthesis of zinc-binding metallothioneins within the hepatic cells.[117] The reason for this flux of zinc from serum to liver has not been explained in terms of host defense.

Body balances of zinc are thought to become negative during infectious diseases because of a combination of factors, including a reduction in dietary zinc intake, a diminished absorption from the intestinal tract, and a concomitant continuation (or increase) of zinc losses via the urine and possibly via the feces and sweat. During periods of acute infectious hepatitis, a marked increase in the urinary loss of zinc occurs. This loss is caused by enhanced glomerular filtration and excretion of zinc microligands.[52] The increased formation of zinc microligands with amino acids, such as histidine and cysteine, permits plasma zinc to be excreted from the body via the urine. Whether an increased binding of zinc to amino acid microligands occurs with infections other than acute hepatitis is not known; this phenomenon was not detected with sandfly fever.

CHANGES IN COPPER METABOLISM

Concentrations of plasma copper increase in virtually all infections. This increase appears to accompany the accelerated synthesis and release from the liver of ceruloplasmin, the copper-binding protein of plasma. The increase in plasma ceruloplasmin resembles that of other acute-phase reactant proteins produced by the liver during inflammatory states when triggered by interleukin-6 and other proinflammatory cytokines.[8] Increases in ceruloplasmin and copper occur somewhat later than do the abrupt depressions in serum iron and zinc. The increase in copper values tends to persist somewhat longer than do the changes in zinc and iron, apparently as a result of the relatively long in vivo half-disappearance time of ceruloplasmin from plasma. Body balances of copper have not been studied during an infectious illness.

Proinflammatory Cytokines

The generalized metabolic and physiologic responses to febrile infections are initiated and sustained by a unique control mechanism. This mechanism involves the secretion by various body cells of hormone-like cytokines (mainly monokines and lymphokines).[32] The cytokines include interleukins, interferons, colony-stimulating factors, and tumor necrosis factor. Cytokines also function during localized infections.[98]

Complex interactions of cytokines that occur during illness only now are being unraveled.[8, 32] Cytokines are not classified as hormones because they are produced by a variety of different cells located throughout the body, rather than by anatomically distinct glands; because cytokines are effective at far lower concentrations than are hormones; and because their interacting array of checks and balances is far more complex than that of hormones. Although cytokines are not components of either the central nervous or endocrine systems, they interact with and trigger responses by both of these major regulatory control systems.[8, 93]

Proinflammatory cytokines (which include interleukins-1, -6, and -8 and tumor necrosis factor) initiate and orchestrate the highly complex but relatively stereotyped admixture of concomitant anabolic and catabolic events that make up the generalized host response to febrile infections. Individual components of this generalized response form distinct patterns. Some metabolic responses begin during the incubation period, some at the onset of fever, some late in fever, and some during convalescence.[5–10] No matter which type of microorganism causes an acute, generalized, febrile infection, the onset of most metabolic, biochemical, or physiologic responses seems to occur at relatively consistent, predictable times. These many responses can be categorized temporally by their relationships to the time of onset of clinical symptoms and fever.[8] In fact, virtually every metabolic or biochemical process is influenced in some manner by the body's response to an acute infection. The duration and magnitude of individual components of the generalized response show some variability from infection to infection. More must be learned about how the cytokines influence this variability in host metabolic responses.

In today's terminology, this overall response is termed an acute-phase response, an acute-phase reaction, or the systemic inflammatory response syndrome. This acute-phase response may accompany other severe medical and surgical problems, in addition to infection.[60]

This complex response, which also activates complement and stimulates the immune system, appears to help defend the body.[8, 60] But on the darker side, acute-phase responses generate important nutritional costs,[5, 8, 106] costs that can produce severe, life-threatening malnutrition. In addition, acute-phase responses that become excessive or overly prolonged can lead to hypotensive shock, multiple organ dysfunction, and death.[32, 64, 88, 106]

Acute-phase responses are initiated and controlled by the proinflammatory cytokines.[32, 49, 51, 57, 64, 114, 120, 138] The cytokine interferon-α also can contribute to the wasting syndrome of acute infections.[27] The acute-phase reaction may be modified somewhat by bacterial endotoxins, which uniquely stimulate an exaggerated release of tumor necrosis factor, a cytokine that inhibits lipoprotein lipase enzymes, to account for the high concentrations of plasma triglycerides that develop during gram-negative sepsis.[8, 55]

The primary control mechanisms that initiate acute-phase responses normally exist in a standby mode but can be turned on whenever necessary by the activation of macrophages, blood monocytes, or other body cells and by the subsequent rapid release of proinflammatory cytokines.[8, 32, 74] Many diverse types of stimuli that can activate these cells include the phagocytosis of microorganisms, tissue debris, or other particulate matter; the effects of polynucleotides, certain drugs and chemicals, antigen-antibody complexes, and bacterial toxins; and the actions of other cytokines. During infectious illnesses, proinflammatory cytokines can be detected in body fluids, body secretions, urine, and stools.[42, 71, 98, 101]

After their release from producing cells, proinflammatory cytokines circulate via the plasma or diffuse through tissue fluids to stimulate cell populations in many locations throughout the body. These cytokines have multiple, often overlapping actions, and they stimulate the release of companion cytokines. Interleukin-1 previously was termed endogenous pyrogen, leukocytic endogenous mediator, and lymphocyte-activating factor,[32] and tumor necrosis factor once was called cachectin. Proinflammatory cytokines stimulate the hypothalamic temperature-regulating center to initiate fever,[8, 32] endocrine glands to secrete hormones, the liver to take up amino acids and trace elements and to synthesize many different proteins,[8, 93, 114] the pancreatic islets to release both insulin and glucagon,[40, 145] and the muscle cells to catabolize contractile proteins.[3, 25] These cytokines also stimulate the bone marrow to produce and release neutrophils[93] and synovial cells and fibroblasts to activate collagenase.[32] Marrow stimulation involves the effect of interleukin-1 on progenitor cells[80] as well as its ability to trigger the release of various colony-stimulating cytokines.[8, 46, 80] In this regard, interleukin-1 has been found to be identical with hematopoietin.[80] Importantly, the proinflammatory cytokines also activate the immune system and cause certain subsets of T lymphocytes to secrete interleukins-2, -3, -4, and -5.[8, 32]

Proinflammatory cytokines are thought to function, after attachment to their specific cell wall receptors, by activating phospholipase A_2 within the cell walls, thus leading to the intracellular release of arachidonic and/or eicosapentanoic acids from cell wall polyunsaturated fatty acid phospholipids.[32] Subsequent responses by the cytokine-stimulated cell then are determined by the intracellular enzymes that can metabolize these acids to one of many possible eicosanoids.

CONTROL MECHANISMS FOR PROINFLAMMATORY CYTOKINE ACTIONS

Like those of hormones, proinflammatory cytokine actions are regulated by numerous checks and balances. To act on a cell, a cytokine first must attach itself to a protein receptor on an exterior cell wall. However, cells produce other similar receptor proteins that then are released to float free in plasma.[61, 89] Freely circulating receptors can intercept and inactivate their matching cytokine.[39, 43] Other unique plasma protein molecules, receptor antagonists, also are produced.[124] They can attach to and block the cellular receptors for specific cytokines.[61, 89] Cytokine inhibitor proteins have been identified.[23, 125] Other cytokines, such as interleukins-4 and -10, can suppress the cellular production of proinflammatory cytokines.[30, 44, 61, 97, 123] Cytokine stimulation of cortisol release has complex feedback effects, for cortisol can block the intracellular formation of eicosanoids stimulated by the cytokines. On the other hand, cortisol and epinephrine also can stimulate the production of cytokines.[64]

CYTOKINE DETECTION IN BIOLOGIC FLUIDS

Individual components of this complex cytokine system of checks and balances now can be measured in body fluids, and their relationships can be studied throughout the course of an acute-phase reaction.[20, 22, 32, 57, 61, 120, 125] These cytokines and their free receptors can be found in mucosal fluids as well as in plasma.[87, 96, 101] Cytokine measurements may have diagnostic and prognostic value.[22, 114] As an example, identification of interleukin-8 in amniotic cord sera was reported to be a specific marker for preterm chorioamnionitis.[114]

Raqib and colleagues[101] described longitudinal measurements of cytokines and receptor antagonists in the plasma and stools of patients with acute shigellosis. Concentrations of tumor necrosis factor-α; interleukins-1β, -6, and -8; and interleukin-1 receptor antagonist in stools were quite high when patients with shigellosis first were seen and gradually returned to normal values during the next 2 weeks.[101] We still do not understand fully the pathogenic or physiologic effects of these interacting molecules in either systemic or localized diseases.

Hormonal Responses

Infectious illnesses are accompanied by a variety of endocrine responses, which especially include increased secretion of the hormones that regulate carbohydrate and energy metabolism and those that influence salt and water retention. These hormonal responses are secondary to and often are initiated by the primary release of proinflammatory cytokines from activated cells.

In addition to their participation in physiologic responses, endocrine functions also may be affected by pathologic complications of an infectious process that results in the direct destruction or dysfunction of hormone-producing cells. The adrenal glands may be destroyed if tubercle bacilli localize in these glands or if hemorrhagic necrosis becomes a complication of such infections as acute meningococcemia. Pancreatic islet cells may be destroyed during occurrences of viral infections of experimental animals, and the same pathogenic possibility may initiate insulin-requiring diabetes in children. Thyroid function may be impaired after occurrence of a viral infection that triggers an autoimmune thyroiditis, and gonadal tissues may be the site of localization and destruction by the mumps virus.

PITUITARY GLAND FUNCTIONS

Secretion of certain of the trophic hormones produced by the anterior pituitary is increased during periods of infection. An increase in adrenocorticotropic hormone production (stimulated by proinflammatory cytokines) triggers an increased secretion of several adrenocorticoids. Concentrations of plasma growth hormone generally are increased in acute infections in which this hormone has been measured,[17, 102] but the increases do not seem to correlate directly in timing or magnitude with the presence or severity of fever.[5, 6] This increase in plasma growth hormone may be due, in part, to its production by mononuclear leukocytes.[135] Concentrations of plasma growth hormone increase rapidly in a somewhat paradoxical manner if an intravenous infusion of glucose is given to patients or laboratory animals with an acute infection.[102] Thyroid-stimulating hormone, on the other hand, does not respond during the early phases of an acute febrile illness but may increase during the convalescent period. No increases in the gonadotropic hormones have been documented during infection. A release of several anterior pituitary hormones can be stimulated by fever-producing doses of bacterial endotoxin. Such responses have been used in the clinical testing of anterior pituitary function.[59, 77]

As described in the earlier discussion of salt and water imbalances, inappropriate secretion of antidiuretic hormone may occur in patients with severe infectious diseases.[34] Such a phenomenon also seems to be a characteristic response in patients whose infectious process becomes localized within the cranial vault.

ADRENAL FUNCTIONS

Although the adrenocortical hormones are known to influence the ability of a patient to respond to stressful situations, relatively few data define the duration and magnitude of the adrenal response or characterize the spectrum of specific steroid hormones produced in excess.[14, 76] Available data suggest that acute generalized infections typically are accompanied by a transient increase in the adrenal output of glucocorticoid hormones that is of short duration. Although these responses generally are limited in magnitude, they serve to maintain a relatively constant concentration of cortisol in plasma throughout the early periods of fever.[14] The usual diurnal decline in plasma 17-OH corticosteroid values fails to occur during the afternoon and evening hours if fever is present. Cortisol-binding proteins have not been observed to change in plasma during periods of acute infection.[11] Thus, the plasma concentrations of unbound, physiologically active cortisol are maintained at or somewhat higher than the normal peak early morning values throughout the initial period of a febrile illness.[11, 14] The total increase in glucocorticoid secretion rates during early illness ranges from two to five times normal values in infections that have been studied. Lesser degrees of increase have been noted in the adrenocortical output of pregnanetriol and the weak ketosteroid androgens.[14] If an infectious illness becomes chronic, adrenal output generally returns to or even falls below baseline values, and diminished adrenal responsiveness to adrenocorticotropic hormone may develop.

Extremely high concentrations of plasma 17-OH corticosteroids may develop during gram-negative septicemia or before death in patients with other severe acute infections.[73, 76] These high terminal values may be ascribed to failures in the hepatic clearance of cortisol from plasma and the metabolic pathways for converting cortisol to water-soluble metabolites; high plasma values are not the result of an extraordinary increase in adrenal secretion rates.[73] In a detailed study of adrenal function in children with meningitis, Migeon and coworkers[76] reported a maximum average increase in cortisol secretion rate of approximately threefold during uncomplicated aseptic or bacterial meningitis. This increase was accompanied by a threefold increase in the excretion of urinary 17-OH corticosteroids during the first few days of illness. On admission to the hospital, these children had concentrations of plasma cortisol that ranged from high normal to twice normal values. On the other hand, severely ill patients who were dying of adrenal hemorrhage generally had values that were depressed or absent.

Mechanisms by which relatively small increases in adrenal glucocorticoid secretion might serve to protect the host have not been defined. However, the ability of the liver to produce some of its proteins during periods of infection is known to be dependent on the permissive presence of glucocorticoid hormones.[14]

The increase in production of aldosterone appears to lag somewhat behind the increase in production of cortisol during periods of acute infections and then persists longer. Increases in aldosterone stimulate the intense retention of sodium and chloride by the kidney during periods of acute infections.[11]

The adrenomedullary secretion of catecholamines may increase in severe infectious diseases.[47, 142] High plasma epinephrine and norepinephrine values develop in gram-negative sepsis and bacterial meningitis. The catecholamine response contributes importantly to the acceleration of gluconeogenesis during periods of infection.

CARBOHYDRATE-REGULATING HORMONES

Hormones that serve in the normal regulation of carbohydrate metabolism also participate in the host response to infection. In addition to the heightened secretion of the glucocorticoids, catecholamines, and growth hormone, the major pancreatic hormones insulin and glucagon both circulate in increased concentrations in the plasma of patients with acute infectious diseases.[142] The combined effect of these hormonal actions is to accelerate the production of glucose within the liver and to stimulate the release of glucose from stored glycogen. These actions cause the glucose pool size to increase two- or threefold to provide an important source of metabolizable energy during the early febrile periods of acute infections.

Intravenous glucose tolerance tests performed early in the course of febrile infections in young adult subjects[102, 111] led to an exaggerated increase of concentrations of plasma insulin in both magnitude and duration, to an appropriate decline in elevated fasting concentrations of plasma glucagon, and to a paradoxical stimulation of growth hormone release. Extreme hyperinsulinism also was observed after glucose infusions were given to dogs with endotoxic shock.[19]

The modest increase in concentrations of fasting plasma insulin that occurs during periods of infection appears to account for an inhibition of both ketogenesis and fat depot lipolysis, two responses that would be expected to occur because of concomitant starvation or semistarvation. The simultaneous combination of high fasting plasma glucagon and insulin values and their effects on both the liver and peripheral fat depots and somatic tissues thus help to explain the observed differences between the anorexia-induced semistarvation associated with infectious illnesses and the starvation caused by food deprivation.

THYROID HORMONES

Thyroid hormones do not seem to initiate or sustain the hypermetabolic response to fever. Nevertheless, both thyroxine (T_4) and triiodothyronine (T_3) are deiodinated at accelerated rates within the body tissues, especially in the liver, during the early phases of infections studied in humans and experimental animals.[31, 133, 144] This acceleration in the metabolism of peripheral thyroid hormones accounts for an early decline in serum protein-bound iodine values.[112] Only after an infectious illness has progressed for several days does the thyroid gland hormone output appear to increase. This increase in thyroid secretion then persists into early convalescence, so that for a time the production of thyroid hormones exceeds apparent body requirements. As a result, protein-bound iodine values in serum are increased in the convalescent period. This sequence of events produces a biphasic response pattern with an initial decrease and a late increase in concentrations of thyroid hormones. Serum concentrations of "reverse T_3" (Rt_3) increase during febrile illnesses.[24] Because Rt_3 has an apparent role in regulating the peripheral cellular actions of T_4 and T_3, its function during acute infectious illness remains to be elucidated.

In studies of patients with falciparum malaria infection, serum T_3 values declined abruptly, whereas serum T_4 values were stable or increased slightly.[133] The decline in serum T_3 concentrations was accompanied by reciprocal increases in Rt_3. The slowing of T_4 turnover during periods of malaria may be caused by an impaired ability of hepatocytes to metabolize or deiodinate T_4. Hypothalamic suppression in early stages of malaria appears to result in a decreased release of thyroid-stimulating hormone from the anterior pituitary and a secondary decrease in T_4 and T_3 secretion from the thyroid gland.

REFERENCES

1. Alvarez, J. O., Salazar-Lindo, E., Kohatsu, J., et al.: Urinary excretion of retinol in children with acute diarrhea. Am. J. Clin. Nutr. *61:*1273–1276, 1995.
2. Anderson, R., Smit, M. J., Joone, G. K., et al.: Vitamin C and cellular immune functions. Ann. N.Y. Acad. Sci. *587:*34–48, 1990.
3. Baracos, V., Rodeman, H. P., Dinarello, C. A., et al.: Stimulation of muscle protein degradation and prostaglandin E_2 release by a leukocytic pyrogen: A mechanism for increased degradation of muscle protein during fever. N. Engl. J. Med. *308:*553–558, 1983.
4. Beck, O.: Weitere untersuchungen zum fieberstoffwechsel des säuglings: Die qualitätiven veranderungen des stickstoffwechsels im fieber. Jahrb. Kinderh. *112:*184–216, 1926.
5. Beisel, W. R.: Metabolic effects of infection. Prog. Food Nutr. Sci. *8:*43–75, 1984.
6. Beisel, W. R.: The influence of infection or injury on nutritional requirements during adolescence. *In* McKigney, J. I., and Munro, H. N. (eds.): Nutrient Requirements in Adolescence. Cambridge, MA, MIT Press, 1976.
7. Beisel, W. R.: Nutrition, infection, specific immune responses, and nonspecific host defenses: A complex interaction. *In* Watson, R. R. (ed.): Nutrition, Disease Resistance and Immune Function. New York, Marcel Dekker, 1984, pp. 3–34.
8. Beisel, W. R.: Nutrition and infection. *In* Linder, M. C. (ed.): Nutritional Biochemistry and Metabolism. 2nd ed. New York, Elsevier Science Publishing Co., 1991, pp. 508–542.
9. Beisel, W. R.: Infection-induced malnutrition: From cholera to cytokines. Am. J. Clin. Nutr. *62:*813–819, 1995.
10. Beisel, W. R., Blackburn, G. L., Feigin, R. D., et al.: Proceedings of a workshop: Impact of infection on nutritional status of the host. Am. J. Clin. Nutr. *30:*1203–1371, 1439–1566, 1977.
11. Beisel, W. R., Bruton, J., Anderson, K. D., et al.: Adrenocortical responses during tularemia in human subjects. J. Clin. Endocrinol. Metab. *27:*61–69, 1967.
12. Beisel, W. R., Goldman, R. F., and Joy, R. J. T.: Metabolic balance studies during induced hyperthermia in man. J. Appl. Physiol. *24:*1–10, 1968.
13. Beisel, W. R., Herman, Y. F., Sauberlich, H. E., et al.: Experimentally induced sandfly fever and vitamin metabolism in man. Am. J. Clin. Nutr. *25:*1165–1173, 1972.
14. Beisel, W. R., and Rapoport, M. I.: Inter-relations between adrenocortical functions and infectious illness. N. Engl. J. Med. *280:*541–546, 569–604, 1969.
15. Beisel, W. R., Sawyer, W. D., Ryll, E. D., et al.: Metabolic effects of intracellular infections in man. Ann. Intern. Med. *67:*744–779, 1967.
16. Beisel, W. R., Watten, R. H., Blackwell, Q., et al.: The role of bicarbonate pathophysiology and therapy in Asiatic cholera. Am. J. Med. *35:*58–66, 1963.
17. Beisel, W. R., Woeber, K. A., Bartelloni, P. J., et al.: Growth hormone response during sandfly fever. J. Clin. Endocrinol. Metab. *28:*1220–1223, 1968.
18. Beresford, C. H., Neale, R. J., and Brooks, O. G.: Iron absorption and pyrexia. Lancet *1:*568–575, 1971.
19. Blackard, W. G., Anderson, J. H., Jr., and Spitzer, J. J.: Hyperinsulinism in endotoxin shock dogs. Metabolism *25:*675–684, 1976.
20. Brown, C. C., Poli, G., Lubaki, N., et al.: Elevated levels of tumor necrosis factor-α in Zairian neonate plasmas: Implications for perinatal infection with the human immunodeficiency virus. J. Infect. Dis. *169:*975–980, 1994.
21. Campbell, C. H., Solgonick, R. M., and Linder, M. C.: Translational regulation of ferritin synthesis in rat spleen: Effects of iron and inflammation. Biochem. Biophys. Res. Commun. *160:*453–549, 1989.
22. Casey, L. C., Balk, R. A., and Bone, R. C.: Plasma cytokine and endotoxin levels correlate with survival in patients with sepsis syndrome. Ann. Intern. Med. *119:*771–778, 1993.
23. Chang, D.-M., and Shaio, M.-F.: Production of interleukin-1 (IL-1) and IL-1 inhibitor by human monocytes exposed to dengue virus. J. Infect. Dis. *170:*811–817, 1994.
24. Chopra, I. J., Chopra, U., Smith, S. R., et al.: Reciprocal changes in serum concentrations of 3,3N5N-triiodothyronine (reverse T_3) and 3,3N5-triiodothyronine (T_3) in systemic illnesses. J. Clin. Endocrinol. Metab. *41:*1043–1049, 1975.
25. Clowes, G. H. A., Jr., George, B. C., Villee, C. A., Jr., et al.: Muscle proteolysis induced by a circulating peptide in patients with sepsis or trauma. N. Engl. J. Med. *308:*545–552, 1983.
26. Committee on Drugs, American Academy of Pediatrics: Vitamin C and the common cold. Nutr. Rev. *32* (Suppl.)*:*39–40, 1974.

27. Constans, J., Pellegrin, I., Pellegrin, J. L., et al.: Plasma interferon-α and the wasting syndrome in patients with the human immunodeficiency virus. Clin. Infect. Dis. *20:*1069–1070, 1995.
28. Cook, G. C.: Increased glycine absorption rate associated with acute bacterial infections in man. Br. J. Nutr. *29:*377–386, 1973.
29. Curnow, R. T., Rayfield, E. J., George, D. T., et al.: Altered hepatic glycogen metabolism and glucoregulatory hormones during sepsis. Am. J. Physiol. *230:*1296–1301, 1976.
30. Derkx, B., Marchant, A., Goldman, M., et al.: High levels of interleukin-10 during the initial phase of fulminant meningococcal septic shock. J. Infect. Dis. *171:*229–232, 1995.
31. DeRubertis, F. R., and Woeber, K. A.: Accelerated cellular uptake and metabolism of L-thyroxine during acute *Salmonella typhimurium* sepsis. J. Clin. Invest. *52:*78–87, 1973.
32. Dinarello, C. A.: The proinflammatory cytokines interleukin-1 and tumor necrosis factor and treatment of the septic shock syndrome. J. Infect. Dis. *163*:1177–1184, 1991.
33. Drapier, J.-C., Wietzerbin, J., and Hibbs, J. B., Jr.: Interferon-gamma and tumor necrosis factor induct the L-arginine–dependent cytotoxic effector mechanism in murine macrophages. J. Immunol. *18:*1587–1592, 1988.
34. Feigin, R. D., and Kaplan, S.: Inappropriate secretion of antidiuretic hormone (ADH) in children with bacterial meningitis. Am. J. Clin. Nutr. *30:*1482–1484, 1977.
35. Feigin, R. D., Middelkamp, J. N., and Reed, C. A.: Murine myocarditis due to coxsackie B_3 virus: Blood amino acid, virologic, and histopathologic correlates. J. Infect. Dis. *126:*574–584, 1972.
36. Felig, P., Brown, W. V., Levine, R. A., et al.: Glucose homeostasis in viral hepatitis. N. Engl. J. Med. *283:*1436–1440, 1970.
37. Fiser, R. H., Denniston, J. C., and Beisel, W. R.: Infection with *Diplococcus pneumoniae* and *Salmonella typhimurium* in monkeys: Changes in plasma lipids and lipoproteins. J. Infect. Dis. *125:*54–60, 1972.
38. Fiser, R. H., Denniston, J. C., Kastello, M. D., et al.: Cholesterogenesis during acute infection in chronically hypercholesterolemic rhesus monkeys. Proc. Soc. Exp. Biol. Med. *140:*314–318, 1972.
39. Frieling, J. T. M., van Deuren, M., Wijdenes, J., et al.: Circulating interleukin-6 receptor in patients with sepsis syndrome. J. Infect. Dis. *171:*469–472, 1995.
40. George, D. T., Abeles, F. B., Mapes, C. A., et al.: Effect of leukocytic endogenous mediators on endocrine pancreas secretory responses. Am. J. Physiol. *233:*E240–E245, 1977.
41. George, D. T., Rayfield, E. J., and Wannemacher, R. W., Jr.: Altered glucoregulatory hormones during acute pneumococcal sepsis in the rhesus monkey. Diabetes *23:*544–549, 1974.
42. Girardin, E., Grau, G. E., Dayer, J.-M., et al.: Tumor necrosis factor and interleukin-1 in the serum of children with severe infectious purpura. N. Engl. J. Med. *319:*397–400, 1988.
43. Godfried, M. H., van der Poll, T., Weverling, G. J., et al.: Soluble receptors for tumor necrosis factor as predictors of progression to AIDS in asymptomatic human immunodeficiency virus type 1 infection. J. Infect. Dis. *169:*739–745, 1994.
44. Gömez-Jiménez, J., Martín, M. C., Sauri, R., et al.: Interleukin-10 and the monocyte/macrophage-induced inflammatory response in septic shock. J. Infect. Dis. *171:*472–475, 1995.
45. Griffiths, J., Groves, A. C., and Leung, F. Y.: Hypertriglyceridemia and hypoglycemia in gram-negative sepsis in the dog. Surg. Gynecol. Obstet. *136:*897–903, 1973.
46. Groofman, J. E., Molina, J.-M., and Scadden, D. T.: Hematopoietic growth factors. N. Engl. J. Med. *321:*1449–1459, 1989.
47. Groves, A. C., Griffiths, J., Leung, F., et al.: Plasma catecholamines in patients with serious postoperative infection. Ann. Surg. *178:*102–107, 1973.
48. Guckian, J. C.: Role of metabolism in pathogenesis of bacteremia due to *Diplococcus pneumoniae* in rabbits. J. Infect. Dis. *127:*1–8, 1973.
49. Halstensen, A., Ceska, M., Brandtzaeg, P., et al.: Interleukin-8 in serum and cerebrospinal fluid from patients with meningoccocal disease. J. Infect. Dis. *167:*471–475, 1993.
50. Hemiliä, H., and Herman, Z. S.: Vitamin C and the common cold: A retrospective analysis of Chalmer's review. J. Am. College Nutr. *14:*116–123, 1995.
51. Heney, D., Lewis, I. J., Evans, S. W., et al.: Interleukin-6 and its relationship to C-reactive protein and fever in children with febrile neutropenia. J. Infect. Dis. *165:*886–890, 1992.
52. Henkin, R. I., and Smith, F. R.: Zinc and copper metabolism in acute viral hepatitis. Am. J. Med. Sci. *264:*401–409, 1972.
53. Hirsch, R. L., MacKay, D. G., Travers, R. I., et al.: Hyperlipidemia, fatty liver, and bromsulfophthalein retention in rabbits injected intravenously with bacterial endotoxins. J. Lipid Res. *5:*563–568, 1964.
54. Howard, J. E., Bigham, Jr., R. S., and Mason, R. E.: Studies on convalescence. V. Observations on the altered protein metabolism during induced malarial infections. Trans. Assoc. Am. Physicians *59:*242–247, 1946.
55. Kaufmann, R. L., Matson, C. F., and Beisel, W. R.: Hypertriglyceridemia produced by endotoxin: Role of impaired triglyceride disposal mechanisms. J. Infect. Dis. *133:*548–555, 1976.
56. Kaufmann, R. L., Matson, C. F., Rowberg, A. H., et al.: Defective lipid disposal mechanisms during bacterial infection in rhesus monkeys. Metabolism *25:*615–624, 1976.
57. Keuter, M., Dharmana, E., Gasem, M. H., et al.: Patterns of proinflammatory cytokines and inhibitors during typhoid fever. J. Infect. Dis. *169:*1306–1311, 1994.
58. Kinsella, J. E., Lokesh, B., Broughton, S, et al.: Dietary polyunsaturated fatty acids and eicosanoids: Potential effects on the modulation of inflammatory and immune cells: an overview. Nutrition *6:*22–44, 1990.
59. Kohler, P. O., O'Malley, B. W., Rayford, P. L., et al.: Effect of pyrogen on blood levels of pituitary trophic hormones: Observations of the usefulness of the growth hormone response in the detection of pituitary disease. J. Clin. Endocrinol. Metab. *27:*219–226, 1967.
60. Koj, A.: The role of interleukin-6 as the hepatocyte stimulating factor in the network of inflammatory cytokines. Ann. N. Y. Acad. Sci. *557:*1–8, 1989.
61. Kuhns, D. B., Alvord, W. G., and Gallin, J. I.: Increased circulating cytokines, cytokine antagonists, and E-selectin after intravenous administration of endotoxin in humans. J. Infect. Dis. *171:*145–152, 1995.
62. Lang, C. H., Bagby, G. J., and Dobrescu, C.: Effect of granulocyte colony-stimulating factor on sepsis-induced changes in neutrophil accumulation and organ glucose uptake. J. Infect. Dis. *166:*336–342, 1992.
63. Lees, R. S., Fiser, R. H., Beisel, W. R., Jr., et al.: Effects of an experimental viral infection on plasma lipid and lipoprotein metabolism. Metabolism *21:*825–833, 1972.
64. Liao, J., Keiser, J. A., Scales, W. E., et al.: Role of epinephrine in TNF and IL-6 production from isolated rat liver. Am. J. Physiol. *268:*R896–R901, 1995.
65. Long, C. L., Haverberg, L. N., Young, V. R., et al.: Metabolism of 3-methylhistidine in man. Metabolism *24:*929–935, 1974.
66. Long, C. L., Kinney, J. M., and Geiger, J. W.: Nonsuppressibility of gluconeogenesis by glucose in septic patients. Metabolism *25:*193–201, 1976.
67. Macallan, D. C., McNurlan, M. A., Milne, E., et al.: Whole-body protein turnover from leucine kinetics and the response to nutrition in human immunodeficiency virus infection. Am. J. Clin. Nutr. *61:*818–826, 1995.
68. Mahalanabis, D., Jalan, K. N., Maitra, T. K., et al.: Vitamin A absorption in ascariasis. Am. J. Clin. Nutr. *29:*1372–1375, 1976.
69. Mata, L. J.: Malnutrition-infection interactions in the tropics. Am. J. Trop. Med. Hyg. *24:*564–574, 1975.
70. Mata, L. J., Kronmal, R. A., Urrutia, J. J., et al.: Antenatal events and postnatal growth and survival of children: Prospective observation in a rural Guatemalan village. *In* White, P. L., and Selvey, N. (eds.): Proc. Western Hemisphere Nutrition Congress IV. Acton, MA, Publishing Sciences Group, 1975.
71. Maury, C. P. J., Salo, E., and Pelekonen, P.: Circulating interleukin-1β in patients with Kawasaki disease. N. Engl. J. Med. *319:*1670–1671, 1988.
72. McCallum, R. E., Seale, T. W., and Stith, R. D.: Influence of endotoxin treatment on dexamethasone induction of hepatic phosphoenolpyruvate carboxykinase. Infect. Immun. *39:*213–219, 1983.
73. Melby, J. C., and Spink, W. W.: Comparative studies on adrenal cortical function and cortisol metabolism in healthy adults and in patients with shock due to infection. J. Clin. Invest. *37:*1791–1798, 1958.
74. Michie, H. R., Manogue, K. R., Spriggs, D. R., et al.: Detection of circulating tumor necrosis factor after endotoxin administration. N. Engl. J. Med. *318:*1481–1486, 1988.
75. Migasena, P., and Maegraith, B. G.: Intestinal absorption in malaria. I. The absorption of an amino acid (AIB-I ^{14}C) across the gut membrane in normal and in *Plasmodium knowlesi*–infected monkeys. Ann. Trop. Med. Parasitol. *63:*439–448, 1969.
76. Migeon, C. J., Kenny, F. M., Hung, W., et al.: Study of adrenal function in children with meningitis. Pediatrics *40:*163–183, 1967.
77. Moberg, G. P.: Site of action of endotoxins on hypothalamic-pituitary-adrenal axis. Am. J. Physiol. *220:*397–400, 1971.
78. Moon, R. J., Tremblay, E. S., and Morris, K. M.: Distribution and metabolism of ^{14}C-tryptophan in normal and endotoxic-poisoned mice. Infect. Immun. *8:*604–611, 1973.
79. Morris, K. M., and Moon, R. J.: Quantitative analysis of serotonin biosynthesis in endotoxemia. Infect. Immun. *10:*340–346, 1974.
80. Morrissey, P. J., and Mochizuki, D. Y.: Interleukin is identical to hematopoietin 1: Studies on its therapeutic effects of myelopoiesis and lymphopoiesis. Biotherapy *1:*263–271, 1989.
81. Moyer, E. D., and Powanda, M. C.: Amino acid metabolism during infectious illness. *In* Powanda, M. C., and Canonico, P. G. (eds.): Infection: The Physiologic and Metabolic Responses of the Host. Amsterdam, Elsevier/North Holland, 1981.
82. Murphy, S. G., Klainer, A. S., and Clyde, D. F.: Characterization and pathophysiology of serum glycoprotein alterations in malaria. J. Lab. Clin. Med. *79:*55–61, 1972.
83. Nelson, P. G., Pyke, D. A., and Gamble, D. R.: Viruses and the aetiology of diabetes: A study in identical twins. Br. Med. J. *4:*249–251, 1975.
84. Nessan, V. J., Geerken, R. C., and Ulvilla, J.: Uric acid excretion in infectious mononucleosis: A function of increased purine turnover. J. Clin. Endocrinol. Metab. *38:*652–654, 1974.
85. Neufeld, H. A., Pace, J. A., Kaminski, M. Y., et al.: A probable endocrine basis for the depression of ketone bodies during infections or inflammatory state in rats. Endocrinology *107:*596–601, 1980.

86. Nichols, B. L., and Soriano, H. A.: A critique of oral therapy of dehydration due to diarrheal syndromes. Am. J. Clin. Nutr. *30:*1457, 1977.
87. Noah, T. L., Henderson, F. W., Wortman, I. A., et al.: Nasal cytokine production in viral acute upper respiratory infection of childhood. J. Infect. Dis. *171:*584–592, 1995.
88. O'Donnell, T. F., Jr., Clowes, G. H. A., Jr., Blackburn, G. L., et al.: Proteolysis associated with a deficit of peripheral energy fuel substrates in septic man. Surgery *80:*192–200, 1976.
89. París, M. M., Friedland, I. R., Ehertt, S., et al.: Effect of interleukin-1 receptor antagonist and soluble tumor necrosis factor receptor in animal models of infection. J. Infect. Dis. *171:*161–169, 1995.
90. Patwardhan, V. N., Maghrabi, R. H., Mousa, W., et al.: Serum glycoproteins in protein-calorie deficiency disease. Am. J. Clin. Nutr. *24:*906–912, 1971.
91. Pawlowski, Z. S.: Implications of parasite-nutrition interactions from a world perspective. Fed. Proc. *43:*256–260, 1984.
92. Powanda, M. C.: Change in body balance of nitrogen and other key nutrients: Description and underlying mechanism. Am. J. Clin. Nutr. *30:*1254–1268, 1977.
93. Powanda, M. C., and Beisel, W. R.: Hypothesis: Leukocyte endogenous mediator/endogenous pyrogen/lymphocyte-activating factor modulates the development of nonspecific and specific immunity and affects nutritional status. Am. J. Clin. Nutr. *35:*762–768, 1982.
94. Powanda, M. C., Dinterman, R., Wannemacher, R. W., Jr., et al.: Tryptophan metabolism in relation to amino acid alterations during typhoid fever. Acta Vitaminol. Enzymol. *29:*164–168, 1975.
95. Powanda, M. C., Wannemacher, R. W., Jr., and Cockerell, G. L.: Nitrogen metabolism and protein synthesis during pneumococcal sepsis in rats. Infect. Immun. *6:*266–271, 1972.
96. Proud, D., Gwaltney, J. M., Jr., Hendley, J. O., et al.: Increased levels of interleukin-1 are detected in nasal secretions of volunteers during experimental rhinovirus colds. J. Infect. Dis. *169:*1007–1013, 1994.
97. Puccetti, P., Mencacci, A., Cenci, E., et al.: Cure of murine candidiasis by recombinant soluble interleukin-4 receptor. J. Infect. Dis. *169:*1325–1331, 1994.
98. Ramsey, K. H., Schneider, H., Cross, A. S., et al.: Inflammatory cytokines produced in response to experimental human gonorrhea. J. Infect. Dis. *172:*186–191, 1995.
99. Rapoport, M. I., and Beisel, W. R.: Studies of tryptophan metabolism in experimental animals and man during infectious illness. Am. J. Clin. Nutr. *24:*807–814, 1971.
100. Rapoport, M. I., Lust, G., and Beisel, W. R.: Host enzyme induction of bacterial infection. Arch. Intern. Med. *121:*11–16, 1968.
101. Raqib, R., Wretlind, B., Anderson, J., et al.: Cytokine secretion in acute shigellosis is correlated to disease activity and directed more to stool than to plasma. J. Infect. Dis. *171:*376–384, 1995.
102. Rayfield, E. J., Curnow, R. T., George, D. T., et al.: Impaired carbohydrate metabolism during a mild viral illness. N. Engl. J. Med. *289:* 618–621, 1973.
103. Reiss, E.: Protein metabolism in infection. I. Change in certain visceral proteins studies with glycin-N^{15}. Metabolism *8:*151–159, 1959.
104. Robinson D. R.: Lipid mediators of inflammation. Rheum. Dis. Clin. North Am. *13:*385–405, 1987.
105. Rocha, D. M., Santeusanio, F., Faloona, G. R., et al.: Abnormal pancreatic alpha-cell function in bacterial infections. N. Engl. J. Med. *288:*700–703, 1973.
106. Roubenoff, R., Roubenoff, R. A., Cannon, J. C., et al.: Rheumatoid cachexia: Cytokine-driven hypermetabolism accompanying reduced body cell mass in chronic inflammation. J. Clin. Invest. *93:*2379–2386, 1994.
107. Sack, D. A., Rhoads, M., Molla, A., et al.: Carbohydrate malabsorption in infants with rotavirus diarrhea. Am. J. Clin. Nutr. *36:*1112–1118, 1982.
108. Sasazuki, T., McDevitt, H. O., and Grumet, F. C.: The association between genes in the major histocompatibility complex and disease susceptibility. Ann. Rev. Med. *28:*425–452, 1977.
109. Scrimshaw, N. S., Taylor, C. E., and Gordon, J. E.: Interactions of Nutrition and Infection. Geneva, World Health Organization, 1968.
110. Semba, R. D.: Vitamin A, immunity, and infection. Clin. Infect. Dis. *19:*489–499, 1994.
111. Shambaugh, G. E., III, and Beisel, W. R.: Insulin response during tularemia in man. Diabetes *16:*369–376, 1967.
112. Shambaugh, G. E., III, and Beisel, W. R.: Early alterations in thyroid hormone physiology during acute infection in man. J. Clin. Endocrinol. Metab. *27:*1667–1673, 1967.
113. Shaw, A. R.: Molecular biology of cytokines: An introduction. *In* Thompson, A. W. (ed.): The Cytokine Handbook. New York, Academic Press, 1991, pp. 19–42.
114. Shimoya, K., Matsuzaki, N., Taniguchi, T., et al.: Interleukin-8 in cord sera: A sensitive and specific marker for the detection of preterm chorioamnionitis. J. Infec. Dis. *165:*957–969, 1992.
115. Siegel, J. H., Cerra, F. B., Coleman, B., et al.: Physiological and metabolic correlations in human sepsis. Surgery *86:*163–193, 1979.
116. Smith, R. E., and Horwitz, B. A.: Brown fat and thermogenesis. Physiol. Rev. *49:*330–425, 1969.
117. Sobocinski, P. Z., Canterbury, W. J., Mapes, C. A., et al.: Involvement of hepatic metallothioneins in hypozincemia associated with bacterial infection. Am. J. Physiol. *234:*E399–E406, 1978.
118. Sommer, A.: Vitamin A, infectious disease, and childhood mortality: A 2c solution? J. Infect. Dis. *167:*1003–1007, 1993.
119. Stamler, J. S., Singel, D. J., and Loscaizo, J.: Biochemistry of nitric oxide and its redox-activated forms. Science *258:*1891–1902, 1992.
120. Steinmetz, H. T., Herbertz, A., Bertram, M., et al.: Increase in interleukin-6 serum level preceding fever in granulocytopenia and correlation with death from sepsis. J. Infect. Dis. *171:*225–228, 1994.
121. Stephensen, C. B., Alvarez, J. O., Kohatsu, J., et al.: Vitamin A is excreted in the urine during acute infection. Am. J. Clin. Nutr. *60:*388–392, 1994.
122. Stuehr, D. J., and Nathan, C. F.: Nitric oxide: A macrophage product responsible for cytostasis and respiratory inhibition of tumor target cells. J. Exp. Med. *169:*1543–1555, 1989.
123. te Vede, M., Huijbens, R. J. F., Heije, K., et al.: Interleukin-4 (IL-4) inhibits secretion of IL-1 beta, tumor necrosis factor alpha, and IL-6 by human monocytes. Blood *76:*1392–1397, 1990.
124. van der Poll, T., van Deventer, S. J. H., ten Cate, H., et al.: Tumor necrosis factor is involved in the appearance of interleukin-1 receptor antagonist in endotoxemia. J. Infect. Dis. *169:*665–667, 1994.
125. van Deuren, M., van der Ven-Jongekrijg, J., and Demacker, P. M. N.: Differential expression of proinflammatory cytokines and their inhibitors during the course of meningococcal infections. J. Infect. Dis. *169:*157–161, 1993.
126. Vitale, J. J.: The impact of infection on vitamin metabolism: An unexplored area. Am. J. Clin. Nutr. *30:*1473–1477, 1977.
127. Viteri, F. E., and Béhar, M.: Efectos de diversas infecciones sobre la nutricion del prescolar especialmente el saramp i∴n. Bole. Ofic. Sanit. Panam. *78:*226–240, 1975.
128. Wagner, D. A., and Tannenbaum, S. R.: Enhancement of nitrate biosynthesis by *Escherichia coli* lipopolysaccharide. *In* McGee, P. N. (ed.): Nitrosamines and Human Cancer. Cold Spring, NY, Cold Spring Harbor Laboratories, 1982, pp. 437–441.
129. Wannemacher, R. W., Jr.: Key role of various individual amino acids in host response to infection. Am. J. Clin. Nutr. *30:*1269–1280, 1977.
130. Wannemacher, R. W., Jr., Dinterman, R. E., Pekarek, R. S., et al.: Urinary amino acid excretion during experimentally induced sandfly fever in man. Am. J. Clin. Nutr. *28:*110–118, 1975.
131. Wannemacher, R. W., Jr., Klainer, A. S., Dinterman, R. E., et al.: The significance and mechanism of an increased serum phenylalanine-tyrosine ratio during infection. Am. J. Clin. Nutr. *29:*997–1006, 1976.
132. Wannemacher, R. W., Jr., Powanda, M. C., and Dinterman, R. E.: Amino acid flux and protein synthesis after exposure of rats to either *Diplococcus pneumoniae* or *Salmonella typhimurium.* Infect. Immun. *10:*60–65, 1974.
133. Wartofsky, L., Burman, K. D., Dimond, R. C., et al.: Studies on the nature of thyroidal suppression during acute falciparum malaria: Integrity of pituitary response to TRH and alterations in serum T_3 and reverse T_3. J. Clin. Endocrinol. Metab. *44:*85–90, 1977.
134. Watten, R. H., Morgan, F. M., Songkhla, Y. N., et al.: Water and electrolyte studies in cholera. J. Clin. Invest. *38:*1879–1889, 1959.
135. Weigent, D. A., Baxter, J. B., Wear, W. E., et al.: Production of immunoreactive growth hormone by mononuclear leukocytes. FASEB J. *2:*2812–2818, 1988.
136. Weinberg, E. D.: Iron and susceptibility to infectious disease. Science *184:*952–956, 1974.
137. West, H. D., Jackson, A. H., Elliott, R. R., et al.: The utilization of ingested iron in disease. South. Med. J. *45:*629–633, 1952.
138. Westendorp, R. G. J., Langermans, J. A. M., de Bel, C. E., et al.: Release of tumor necrosis factor: An innate host characteristic that may contribute to the outcome of meningococcal disease. J. Infect. Dis. *171:*1057–1060, 1995.
139. Whedon, G. D., and Shorr, E.: Metabolic studies in paralytic acute anterior poliomyelitis. II. Alterations in calcium and phosphorus metabolism. J. Clin. Invest. *36:*966–981, 1957.
140. White, M. G., Carter, N. W., Rector, F. C., et al.: Pathophysiology of epidemic St. Louis encephalitis. Ann. Intern. Med. *71:*691–702, 1969.
141. Wiles, J. B., Cerra, F. B., Siegel, J. H., et al.: The systemic septic response: Does the organism matter? Crit. Care Med. *8:*55–60, 1980.
142. Wilmore, D. W., Long, J. M., Mason, A. D., Jr., et al.: Catecholamines: Mediator of the hypermetabolic response to thermal injury. Ann. Surg. *180:*653–669, 1974.
143. Wilson, D., Bressani, R., and Scrimshaw, N. S.: Infection and nutritional status. I. The effect of chicken pox on nitrogen metabolism in children. Am. J. Clin. Nutr. *9:*154–158, 1961.
144. Woeber, K. A.: Alterations in thyroid hormone economy during acute infection with *Diplococcus pneumoniae* in the rhesus monkey. J. Clin. Invest. *50:*378–387, 1971.
145. Yelish, M. R., and Filkins, J. P.: Mechanism of hyperinsulinemia in endotoxicosis. Am. J. Physiol. *239:*E156–E161, 1980.
146. Yeung, C. Y.: Hypoglycemia in neonatal sepsis. J. Pediatr. *77:*812–817, 1970.
147. Young, V. R., Alexis, S. D., Maliga, B. S., et al.: Metabolism of administered 3-methylhistidine: Lack of muscle transfer ribonucleic acid charging and quantitative excretion as 3-methylhistidine and its *N*-acetyl derivative. J. Biol. Chem. *247:*3592–3600, 1972.

Interaction of Infection and Nutrition

RALPH D. FEIGIN ■ LEAH A. STEPHENSON

The introduction to the World Health Organization (WHO) report on nutrition and infection, published in 1965, stated:

> *The concept that malnutrition could make man more susceptible to infectious disease and also alter the course and outcome of the resulting illness has long been current in the history of medicine and public health. Circumstantial evidence is plentiful, principally based on clinical experience. Well controlled observations have been few, and hence clear proof in support of the concept has been slow to accumulate. It has been much easier to demonstrate that infection is often directly responsible for lowering the state of nutrition.*[273]

Nonetheless, globally, infectious diseases are responsible for the deaths each year of 10 million children younger than 5 years of age, and more than one half of these deaths are associated with malnutrition.[36] This problem has been termed "silent genocide" by WHO officials and is the most underreported health problem facing humans.

The association of malnutrition with infection has been documented repeatedly. The devastating effects of long-term semistarvation in infants and small children were described with deep emotion by physicians trapped in the Jewish ghetto of Warsaw by the prolonged Nazi siege.[32, 271] They observed gross and microscopic evidence of lymphoid tissue atrophy and the disappearance of delayed hypersensitivity reactions and acute inflammation, as well as the disappearance of clinical allergies, blood eosinophils, and gastric acid in the severely malnourished. More recent data also support the concept that malnutrition renders people more susceptible to acquisition of infection. Metabolic, biochemical, and clinical evidence has accumulated that strongly supports the concept that nutrition affects profoundly the progress of infection within the host. The normal host response to infection is detailed in Chapter 3. Virtually every normal metabolic or endocrine function is altered in some manner by the presence of an infectious illness.

Traditionally, clinical inquiries into the interaction of nutrition and infection have focused on the patient with protein-calorie malnutrition. Nutrition is a critical determinant of immunocompetence and risk for development of illness. Young children with protein-calorie malnutrition exhibit increased morbidity and mortality rates due largely to infectious diseases.[50] These children often have isolated deficiencies of single nutrients, and both single-nutrient deficiencies and protein-calorie malnutrition are associated with impaired immune responses.

In light of the well-recognized biologic synergism between malnutrition and infection, of note is that malnutrition has not received comparable attention in child health and survival strategies. This oversight may occur partly because data on mortality gathered from health facilities in developing countries report only the proximate cause of death (usually infectious diseases), such that only the severe cases of nutritional deficiency are recorded as nutritional causes of death.[191]

Protein-Calorie Malnutrition

Protein-calorie malnutrition describes a wide range of clinical conditions resulting from mild to severe undernutrition. The WHO estimates that 174 million children younger than 5 years of age in the developing world are malnourished as indicated by low weight for age and that 230 million are stunted.[54] Mild protein-calorie malnutrition may be detected primarily by poor growth because, when energy consumption is low, amino acids from dietary protein are used for energy rather than for protein synthesis and growth. The conditions of kwashiorkor and marasmus represent manifestations of severe protein-calorie malnutrition. Both cases result from consumption of a diet deficient in both protein and calories, but infections also play an important role. An acute infection is incriminated frequently as the event precipitating kwashiorkor.[10, 93, 110, 244] Marasmus is characterized by severe wasting, whereas kwashiorkor is manifested by the presence of edema. In marasmus, the prognosis on refeeding is relatively good, whereas treatment of kwashiorkor is more difficult, and the prognosis often is poor.[98] African studies have estimated the mortality rate in kwashiorkor to be between 25 and 31 percent.[88, 156] In these children, infection was second only to electrolyte abnormalities as a leading cause of death. Inadequate diet, including insufficient intake of energy, protein, and micronutrients (such as iron, vitamins, and minerals), leads to weight loss, retarded growth rate, diminished immunity, and mucosal damage. These factors exacerbate the incidence, severity, and duration of infectious diseases, which, in turn, leads to the loss of nutrients, malabsorption, altered metabolism, and loss of appetite that leads to further inadequate dietary intake.[29]

That various infectious diseases interfere with or influence the responses of host defense is well known. Metabolic responses of the host to infection include increased utilization of proteins, carbohydrates, lipids, minerals, electrolytes, trace elements, vitamins, and hormones. The normal host responds to infection, however, by initiating an immediate and marked stimulus for protein anabolism. The chemical changes in protein-calorie malnutrition include low serum albumin, low concentrations of essential amino acids in serum, generalized amino aciduria, lower glycosylated hemoglobin levels, and decreased activity of many enzymes. Reduction in the activity of diphosphopyridine nucleotide, cytochrome *c* reductase, plasma esterase, and leukocyte pyruvate kinase has been documented. Thus, the patient with kwashiorkor, depleted of amino acids and protein, cannot initiate the necessary anabolic response when challenged by infection, which appears to alter the capacity of the host to resist the debilitating effects of infection. Decreased activity of the various enzymes that help to resist infection and the inability to synthesize new enzymes necessary for energy-producing reactions in the body impose an additional burden on the individual with protein-calorie malnutrition. If the diet does not sufficiently replace calories and protein, the individual becomes progressively depleted with each episode of infection. Repeated episodes of infection may be a major factor in precipitating frank kwashiorkor in children on a borderline diet with regard to protein and calories. In many instances, whether the malnutrition or the infection was the event that initiated the ultimate deterioration of the patient cannot be determined.

Postmortem studies have confirmed that acute bacterial infections are the major cause of death in severe protein-calorie malnutrition. Septicemia is the most dreaded infectious complication of protein-calorie malnutrition and has been reported in as many as 31 percent of hospitalized patients. Gram-negative enteric bacilli are the most common cause; less frequent agents include *Haemophilus influenzae, Shigella flexneri, Pseudomonas aeruginosa, Corynebacterium diphtheriae, Streptococcus* spp., *Staphylococcus aureus,* and *Neisseria* spp. Tuberculosis occurs more frequently, is more virulent, spreads faster, and reinfects more readily people with protein-calorie malnutrition. The rate of urinary tract infections in malnourished children is increased significantly, with gram-negative enteric bacilli encountered most frequently. Diarrhea is a common occurrence in malnourished children, the most common infectious cause being enteric pathogens such as *Salmonella enteritidis*, enteropathogenic *Escherichia coli*, and nontyphi *Salmonella* spp.[230] The occurrence of *Pneumocystis carinii* infection in malnourished individuals also has been highlighted.[110] Additionally, viral diseases such as measles, varicella, hepatitis, and herpes simplex are prevalent in patients with protein-calorie malnutrition.[10, 93, 244]

Almost all cases of severe protein-calorie malnutrition exhibit biochemical or clinical evidence of micronutrient deficiencies, such as vitamin A deficiency or iron-deficiency anemia. However, little evidence exists that any one micronutrient deficiency is the main cause of protein-calorie malnutrition or by itself is responsible for the edema of kwashiorkor.

Although protein is an essential and important nutrient, protein-calorie malnutrition is associated more often with deficient food intake than protein intake. When commonly consumed cereal-based diets meet caloric needs, they *usually* will meet protein needs, especially if the diet also provides modest amounts of legumes and vegetables. Control and prevention of protein-calorie malnutrition should focus on improving the quantity and quality of food consumed, immunization, providing oral rehydration therapy for diarrhea, early treatment of common diseases, regular deworming, and attention to the underlying causes of protein-calorie malnutrition, such as poverty and inequity.[141]

In Utero Effects of Malnutrition

The medical literature reports widespread occurrence of infant low birth weight throughout the nations of the world in which malnutrition is prevalent. Hytten,[113] discussing the relationship of maternal diet to the size of the infant body, called attention to the fact that dietary status in pregnancy is only part of the broad environmental picture. He emphasized that the mother's nutrition throughout life may be as important as nutrition during pregnancy in ensuring the birth of an infant of normal size. The well-fed mother deprived of food during pregnancy may have been able to lay down a sufficient energy reserve to protect the fetus during intrauterine life despite deficiencies in day-to-day intake. Short maternal stature, which is influenced by biosocial factors, large family size, malnutrition, and chronic disease, frequently becomes intergenerational. For example, women who were growth retarded as newborns tend to give birth to infants who also are growth retarded, which may be a reflection of poor maternal nutritional status during childhood and adolescence.[151] Clearly, however, severe nutritional deprivation during pregnancy may affect the size and vitality of the fetus. Abrams and Laros demonstrated that both underweight women and women with poor weight gain during pregnancy had an increased risk for delivering an infant weighing less than 2500 g.[1]

Maternal malnutrition results in impaired placental function and chronic vascular insufficiency, which, in turn, leads to symmetric growth retardation. As nutritional deprivation becomes more severe, first weight, then length, and finally brain mass are affected. Acute placental insufficiency results in asymmetric growth retardation. When the nutritional insult occurs late in pregnancy, when length velocity is declining and weight velocity is increasing, the amount of muscle, fat, and hepatic glycogen is affected adversely. This type of growth retardation is seen in postmature infants; in these infants, placental function no longer is adequate to meet fetal needs, and the fetus must mobilize its own fat and carbohydrate stores.[151]

Maternal malnutrition before or during pregnancy and maternal infection during pregnancy may act alone or in concert to influence the size, gestational age at birth, and vitality of the fetus. To the extent that the fetus is affected, one can conclude that the interaction of nutrition and infection begins in utero. This fact becomes significant because infection during pregnancy occurs commonly in the areas of the world where malnutrition is prevalent. In a prospective study in four Guatemalan villages, 12 percent of village women who were tested serologically throughout pregnancy for cytomegalovirus, herpes simplex, rubella, syphilis, and *Toxoplasma* species infection showed seroconversion during pregnancy to one of these agents.[160] These infections, as well as varicella, human immunodeficiency virus (HIV), malaria, and trypanosomiasis, are associated with intrauterine growth retardation.[25]

Infant size at birth correlates with neonatal survival to a greater extent than does the quality of extrauterine life. Village infants who are small for gestational age at birth have a greater risk for developing subsequent malnutrition and infection than do term infants with an adequate birth weight. Infants with low birth weight (predominantly small for gestational age) have higher rates of infection with *Shigella* spp., *Entamoeba histolytica*, and *Giardia* spp. in the first month of life and also exhibit higher occurrences of diarrhea and oral candidiasis in the first 6 months than do term infants. A case-control study in rural Africa suggests this susceptibility to infectious disease extends far beyond the first 6 months of life.[176] Even as late as adolescence, increased infectious mortality rates were seen in individuals who had been born during the "hungry season" compared with those born during the "harvest season." These findings suggest that nutritionally mediated growth retardation may permanently impair development of immune function. Animal models highlight these long-term effects of intrauterine malnutrition by demonstrating impaired T-cell–dependent immune responses in the first- and second-generation offspring of animals subjected to prenatal nutritional deprivation.[44]

Even in industrialized countries, the consequences of low birth weight can be extensive. Providing enteral nourishment to very-low-birth-weight infants can be very difficult because of systemic illnesses, such as respiratory distress syndrome and gastrointestinal tract immaturity. Many of these infants ultimately develop clinical and biochemical signs of malnutrition during the early postnatal period. This malnutrition may compromise an already inadequate immune system and alter host susceptibility to infection. Reductions in spleen, thymus, and body weights were noted in rats after intrauterine protein-calorie deprivation. After nutritional restoration in these animals, thymic tissue remained depleted of lymphocytes and significantly reduced in weight. Newborn infants may develop similar long-term immunologic defects after suffering in utero or early postnatal malnutrition. Low-birth-weight infants born to malnourished mothers demonstrate decreased thymus and spleen size as well as diminished cell-mediated immune responses, reduced transfer of maternal-fetal immunoglobulin G (IgG), and decreased number of T lymphocytes. Infants with fetal growth retardation have demonstrated diminished neutrophil chemotaxis, abnormal nitroblue tetrazolium oxidative reduction, and deficient microbicidal activity.[45, 97] After birth, nutritional deprivation may create the environment for frequent episodes of infection. Mechanisms responsible for the increased number and severity of infections in the malnourished host are detailed below.

Breast-feeding

The nutritional, immunologic, psychosocial, and child-spacing benefits of breast-feeding are recognized universally. According to numerous reports, breast-fed infants appear to be less susceptible than are bottle-fed infants to certain infections. The protective effect is most evident for upper respiratory infections, otitis media, and gastroenteritis and has been studied most extensively in developing countries; however, the impact of breast-feeding on other infections and in more developed countries also is under investigation. Many studies are investigating the specific agents present in human milk that may be important in imparting protection to the infant. In addition to its anti-infective properties, breast milk has been shown to exhibit other advantages over formula feeding; however, despite its many benefits, in certain situations, breast-feeding is contraindicated.

Epidemiologic studies of the association between infections and breast-feeding have come under great scrutiny. Strong evidence has shown that in developing countries, infant morbidity is reduced by breast-feeding. A pooled analysis[71] of studies performed in the Philippines, Brazil, and Pakistan indicates that breast-feeding offers protection against the risks of diarrhea and of mortality from acute respiratory infection. The greatest protection is offered early in infancy and then steadily declines. Breast-fed infants younger than 2 months old are 5.8 times more protected than are their formula-fed peers, but this difference decreases to 1.4 times more protection by 9 to 11 months of age. Studies in Mexico[149, 262] confirm that breast-fed infants have a decreased incidence, prevalence, and duration of both acute respiratory infection and diarrheal illness than do formula-fed infants. A population-based study of Navajo infants demonstrates that increased breast-feeding rates can decrease infant illness on a community level.[274] An intervention that increased breast-feeding rates from 16.4 to 54.6 percent was associated with 32.2 percent fewer children with pneumonia and 14.6 percent fewer children with gastroenteritis.

Many researchers consider that infants in more developed countries have similar benefits. In a longitudinal analysis of infants in the United States, the risk for developing otitis media or diarrhea increased as the amount of breast milk received decreased.[212] This study suggests protection from breast milk can be observed in a dose-dependent manner. The effect against otitis media may be the result of transmission of humoral or cellular immune components to the infant or the result of positioning during bottle feeding, which may predispose to otitis media. Data demonstrating general protection against infection are supplemented by studies that investigate the effects of breast milk on specific pathologic organisms. Formula-fed infants are more likely than are breast-fed infants to have colonization[106] or invasive disease[231] caused by *H. influenzae*. A case-control study of 467 North American children demonstrated that current breast-feeding was associated with a decreased risk for acquiring invasive pneumococcal disease (odds ratio of 0.27 compared with non–breast-fed controls).[144] Other studies have demonstrated decreased risk for developing meningococcal disease and human herpesvirus 7 infection with breast-feeding.[140, 174]

Despite studies such as these, the evidence in highly developed countries remains controversial. Bauchner and associates[16] presented a meta-analysis of the association between breast-feeding and infections in industrialized countries. Examination of 20 studies found only 6 that met strict methodologic standards. These investigators concluded that the evidence supports only a minimally protective effect of breast-feeding. In 1990, a group from Denmark reported their results after following 500 infants prospectively for the first year of life.[206] They were unable to document a protective effect of breast-feeding against infectious illness. These results conflict with earlier studies with larger sample sizes that supported an association between breast-feeding and fewer infectious episodes.[46, 56, 187, 265] These differences highlight the importance of environmental factors, such as socioeconomic status, parental education, exposure in daycare centers, and parental smoking, to the incidence of infectious disease in infants.

The antimicrobial system in human milk constitutes a complex group of biochemical agents that differ widely in structure but have a common effect at the mucosa. They include lysozyme, lactoperoxidase, lactoferrin, interferon, complement components, immunoglobulins, leukocytes, lipids, and retinol. These anti-infective factors transmitted by breast milk protect primarily by noninflammatory mechanisms and act to reduce the risk for development of mucosal infection in the gut. These proteins are thought to escape digestion in young infants as a result of low acid, reduced protease activity in gastric and pancreatic secretions, and the presence of protease inhibitors in breast milk. The component most important to the newborn infant may be secretory IgA, which is found in high concentrations in colostrum and early milk. Secretory IgA constitutes more than 90 percent of the immunoglobulins in human milk and is formed by intricate processes that may be regulated by cytokines and hormones produced late in pregnancy or during lactation. IgA possesses virus-neutralizing and antibacterial properties and is capable of activating the alternate complement pathway, thus providing local protection in the gastrointestinal tract. Lactoferrin is an iron-binding glycoprotein that competes with siderophilic bacteria for ferric iron and, thereby, interferes with the multiplication of organisms. Lactoferrin also may have a positive influence on cell growth and a negative effect on inflammation. Lysozyme is found in relatively high concentrations in external secretions, including human milk, and lyses susceptible bacteria by hydrolyzing β-1,4 linkages between *N*-acetylmuramic acid and 2-acetylamino-2-deoxy-D-glucose residues in cell walls. Lysozyme is relatively resistant to digestion by trypsin and denaturation caused by acid. Fibronectin is a high-molecular-weight protein found in breast milk that facilitates the uptake of particulates by phagocytic cells. Human milk also is rich in carbohydrate moieties that act as receptor homologues and inhibit attachment of pathogenic bacteria, such as *Vibrio cholerae, Streptococcus pneumoniae, H. influenzae*, and *E. coli*, onto epithelial cells.[58] Certain oligosaccharides in human milk promote the growth of *Bifidobacterium* spp. and lactobacilli in the lower intestinal tract, which, in turn, produce acetic acid and inhibit the multiplication of bacterial pathogens such as *E. coli* and *Salmonella* and *Shigella* spp. Additionally, lactadherin, a component of human milk, has been found to bind specifically to rotavirus and inhibit its replication in vitro.[182] A study of rotavirus infection in Nicaraguan children supports this finding by demonstrating an association between a longer duration of breast-feeding and decreased symptoms with rotavirus infection.[74]

Breast-feeding also has distinct advantages over bottle feeding, even in situations in which infection is not an important factor. In a study of 101 children with atopic asthma, only one breast-fed infant displayed clinical manifestations, compared with 11 children fed cow's milk or soy protein. Although evidence is inconclusive, breast-feeding is thought to provide protection against obesity, arteriosclerosis, celiac disease, and other metabolic disorders.[125] Colostrum and early milk contain hormones and growth factors such as epidermal growth factor, prostaglandins, insulin, and thyroid hormones that may benefit children whose gut integrity has been compromised by malnutrition and gastrointestinal disease.[196] However, whether these components are present in significant amounts to have any physiologic effect after the first few months of lactation is not clear. Breast milk also contains the digestive enzymes amylase, bile salt–stimulated lipase, and bile salt–stimulated esterase in measurable quantities after 6 months of lactation. Children whose digestive functions are compromised by malnutrition or small bowel overgrowth may benefit from the addition of breast milk enzymes.

In certain circumstances, however, breast-feeding is contraindicated. The most common of these situations is maternal HIV infection, a topic that has been the focus of much recent research. Recent studies estimate that one third to one half of mother-to-child transmissions of HIV occur through breast milk.[135, 250] Risk for transmission is approximately 14 percent in chronic maternal HIV infection and increases to 29 percent in acute infection. Other factors that may increase transmission of HIV through breast milk include longer duration of breast-feeding, mastitis in the mother, lower maternal CD4 counts, and mixed feedings (i.e., infants fed both breast milk and formula).[250] The mechanism by which mixed feedings increases transmission is currently under debate. Some researchers theorize that a subclinical mastitis caused by milk stasis is responsible, whereas others hypothesize that an inflammatory or immunologic response in the infant gut may play a role. A randomized clinical trial of 401 mother-infant pairs in Kenya[179] demonstrated that the risk for transmission in breast milk was 16.2 percent and that the use of formula feeding prevented 44 percent of infant infections. Currently, breast-feeding by HIV-infected women is contraindicated in areas where safe alternate sources of infant nutrition exist. Some researchers argue that in areas where environmental contamination precludes the safe use of other infant feeding regimens, exclusive breast-feeding should be promoted.

Breast-feeding also is contraindicated in mothers who are sputum-positive for *Mycobacterium tuberculosis* or who are carriers of hepatitis B virus. Breast milk also has been implicated in the transmission of rubella, cholera, Q fever, human T-cell lymphotropic virus 1, and cytomegalovirus in selected individuals. Human milk also can transmit environmental toxins, such as polychlorinated biphenyl compounds and dichlorodiphenyltrichloroethane. Toxic side effects can occur in nursing infants secondary to passive excretion of medicines taken by the mother.[70] On balance, breast milk clearly is preferable except in unusual circumstances and serves to help diminish the role of infection during infancy.

The Immune System and the Malnourished Host

MUCOSAL IMMUNITY

The first barrier to potential pathogens is the physical integrity of the skin and mucous membranes. The interstitial space in the submucosa of the respiratory and gastrointestinal tracts contains IgA-secreting plasma cells. Secretory IgA, a dimeric form, appears to be produced locally and not derived from intravascular sources; it can bind to the mucosa and serve as a proteolytic resistant "antiseptic paint." Diminished secretory IgA has been noted in malnutrition, which may increase host susceptibility to infection by permitting increased penetration of infectious agents into the circulation.[234, 242]

Furthermore, deficiencies in protein, vitamin A, B complex, ascorbic acid, and zinc are associated frequently with tissue changes that contribute to diminution in host resistance to infection. Severe protein malnutrition and xerophthalmia have been shown to suppress significantly the secretion of lysozyme in the tears of children,[266] which impairs host defense against the bacteria that are destroyed by lysozyme. Large visible epithelial lesions also may be caused by dietary deficiencies. Examples include the metaplastic hyperkeratosis caused by avitaminosis A; the dermatitis, cheilitis, and angular stomatitis from riboflavin and pyridoxine deficiency; the mucosal atrophy and dermatosis of pellagra; the spongy gums and subcutaneous hemorrhages of scurvy; and the atrophy of skin and gastrointestinal mucosa of severe protein deficiency.

As adjuncts to structural integrity and secretory IgA, mononuclear cells have an important role in mucosal immunity. In the gut, for example, Peyer patches contain antigen-primed lymphocytes that start to differentiate and proliferate after activation. These activated lymphocytes interact with T cells of perifollicular zones and subsequently enter the circulation to reach central immune organs, such as the spleen, bone marrow, and possibly thymus, where they experience further clonal expansion. Eventually, they become IgA-producing cells that re-enter the circulation and by a selective homing process deliver specific immunity to the mucosa of the gut, as well as to salivary, lacrimal, bronchial, and lactating mammary glands. Homing of these IgA-producing cells is a selective process that involves special corresponding binding sites on lymphocytes and endothelial venule cell membranes of lymph nodes and lymphoid mucosal tissue.[197] This common mucosal immune system normally provides a reservoir of antigen-committed lymphocytes; however, malnutrition compromises these defenses. Malnourished children have a reduced number of lymphocytes and plasma cells in the interstitial space. Migration of lymphoblasts from the mesentery also is decreased.[48]

HUMORAL IMMUNITY

Numerous studies of B-cell function have been performed in patients with protein-calorie malnutrition. Serum immunoglobulins may be normal or elevated.[235] Cohen and Hansen[55] showed that children with protein-calorie malnutrition who were infected synthesized gamma-globulin at three times the rate of uninfected malnourished individuals, thus documenting the fact that synthesis of gamma-globulin was not rate limited in malnutrition at the expense of other protein synthesis, such as that of albumin. In protein-calorie malnutrition, antibody affinity is decreased, which may explain the higher frequency of antigen–antibody complexes found in malnourished patients.

In protein-calorie malnutrition, the most dramatic change in humoral immunity concerns IgE. Serum IgE concentrations in healthy, well-nourished children are extremely low. Significant elevations of serum IgE in malnourished children have been reported in the absence of allergy or parasitic infections, possibly caused by imbalance in T-lymphocyte regulation of IgE-producing B-cell function. Possibly, the defect in cell-mediated immunity in patients with protein-calorie malnutrition could initiate an exaggerated IgE response during infections with respiratory pathogens, such as respiratory syncytial virus or parainfluenza virus, and also increase the risk for developing severe bronchiolitis.[128]

Antibody production after immunization with antigen remains the best functional measure of humoral immunity. Much of the data on specific serum antibody responses in human malnutrition are conflicting. The serum antibody response to many protein antigens is relatively well-preserved. Tetanus toxoid, for example, induces protective levels of antibody even in children with severe protein-calorie malnutrition. Antibody response to diphtheria toxoid also is normal; however, the responses to immunization with viral antigens are variable. Responses to yellow fever vaccine, hepatitis, and killed influenza A have been reported to be impaired in protein-calorie malnutrition. Chronic malnutrition also is associated with a poor response to measles vaccine.[263] A diminished antibody response to such polysaccharide antigens as killed typhoid vaccine (polysaccharide typhoid O antigen) is seen in protein-calorie malnutrition. The degree of malnutrition may be a critical host determinant; for example, mild protein-calorie malnutrition had no impact on the response to a meningococcal group C polysaccharide vaccine.[96] This diminished antibody response to polysaccharide antigens may be caused by a selective impact of protein-calorie malnutrition on the IgG subclasses that contain antibody to polysaccharide antigens, IgG2, and IgG4.[128] These effects of protein-calorie malnutrition on IgG subclasses potentially impair the patient's ability to resist encapsulated organisms. However, further studies investigating the relationship between IgG subclasses and protein-calorie malnutrition are needed.

The balance between T and B cells in the peripheral blood appears to be disturbed in malnutrition.[114] Several investigations have reported decreased numbers of spontaneous sheep erythrocyte rosette-forming cells (generally considered to be T lymphocytes) and normal to increased numbers of Fc and C3 rosette-forming cells (B lymphocytes). Because similar observations have been made in patients with chronic infections, determining whether these findings are manifestations of malnutrition per se or can be explained by chronic infection in the malnourished individual is impossible at present.

COMPLEMENT SYSTEM

The proteins of the complement system appear to be sensitive to nutritional stress. Seth and Chandra[224] noted low serum complement in patients with protein-calorie malnutrition. Sirisinha and associates[233] also reported low serum concentrations of all complement components (as best documented in reductions of C3, factor B, and total hemolytic activity),[52] except C4, in malnourished children. Patients with kwashiorkor had lower levels than did children with marasmus. These data are consistent with recent animal studies that show significantly decreased levels of C1, C2, C3, and C4 in malnourished rats compared with controls.[209] The etiology of hypocomplementemia is unclear. Electrophoretically distinct C3 breakdown products have been detected in one study, as have increased titers of immunocoagglutinin, an antibody directed to the C423b complex of activated complement. Alternatively, activation of the complement pathway may be a consequence of infection. Complement serum concentrations also may drop in the malnourished individual as a result of a consumption complementopathy. Complement-derived chemotactic factors, as well as opsonic factors, also are depressed. These functional deficits may contribute to an enhanced susceptibility to infection.

Despite these changes, complement may be less susceptible to nutritional stress than are other aspects of the immune system. In a study of malnourished patients hospitalized in Guatemala City, Sakamoto[207] found that during nutritional rehabilitation, the complement system (CH_{50} and C3 levels) recovered more rapidly than did delayed-type hypersensitivity skin testing. This finding suggests that the complement system is more effective in host defense during the early stage of nutritional recovery than is cellular immunity. Complement activity also appears to be preserved better in patients with severe protein-calorie malnutrition than is cell-mediated immunity, even though complement serum concentrations are maintained at lower levels than are those in well-nourished controls. In animal studies, both well-nourished and malnourished rats respond to injections of *S. aureus* with elevated serum complement concentrations. Despite a normal initial response, malnourished rats were unable to mount a second response during the later stages of *S. aureus* infection; however, this second complement response appeared as early as 1 week after initiation of nutritional rehabilitation in malnourished rats.[208] This finding may suggest a decreased ability to synthesize complement de novo in malnutrition; additional studies are needed to ascertain whether a similar response is noted in human malnutrition.

CELLULAR IMMUNITY

In patients with malnutrition, the cellular immune system (T-cell system) appears to be the component of the immune system affected most significantly. These children are much more susceptible to tuberculosis, measles, disseminated herpes simplex, hepatitis, and *P. carinii*, diseases whose prevention requires optimal function of the cellular immune system. Histologic studies of lymphoid tissues show severe depletion of T-cell areas in malnourished hosts.[164] Some studies suggest that the defect involves a failure of maturation of T cells. In malnutrition, a decrease in circulating lymphocytes bearing mature T-cell markers, normal numbers of B cells, and an increase in null cells are noted. These null cells, if incubated with thymic factors, further differentiate into T cells. Subsequent studies have shown decreased thymic factor activity in protein-calorie malnutrition as an important cause of this delayed T-cell differentiation. A decrease in the deoxynucleotidyl transferase activity also occurs, suggesting lymphocyte immaturity. Another study demonstrates elevated concentrations of adenosine deaminase in the serum of malnourished children compared with controls, a finding that may reflect increased lymphocyte adenosine deaminase activity due to immaturity.[171] The number of helper CD4 cells is decreased markedly, often to less than 40 percent of those in controls. Little change occurs in the number of suppressor T cells; thus, the helper-to-suppressor ratio is decreased significantly. Lymphocyte proliferation and synthesis of DNA also are reduced, especially in the presence of autologous plasma cell cultures, which may be related to inhibitory factors as well as to lack of essential nutrients in the plasma of malnourished patients.[52] McFarlane[162] reported that skin transplants in malnourished rats were rejected, suggesting that all aspects of cell-mediated immunity may not be impaired simultaneously or to the same extent.

Chandra[47] also observed that malnourished children had a decreased ability to respond to tuberculin antigen (purified protein derivative) after receiving bacille Calmette-Guérin (BCG) immunization, and, in most cases, they could not be sensitized to dinitrochlorobenzene. Smythe and associates[235] reported similar findings in malnourished children and also noted lymphocyte depletion in the thymus glands of 118 children at necropsy. At the time of death, 47 of these children had kwashiorkor, and 23 were marasmic. Another study of 69 children with protein-calorie malnutrition and 20 healthy controls demonstrated an association between all levels of protein-calorie malnutrition and decreased absolute lymphocyte count, but a decreased response to tuberculin antigen was found only in children with moderate or severe malnutrition.[171] Bhaskaram and coworkers[28] showed that malnutrition did not influence the ability of BCG-vaccinated children to localize tuberculosis infection; however, malnourished children who did not receive the vaccine had a significantly greater incidence of systemic tuberculosis infection than did BCG-vaccinated malnourished children.

Production of mediators (e.g., migration inhibition factor, lymphotoxin, interferon) by the lymphocytes of malnourished subjects has not been studied extensively. Schlesinger and associates[213] measured production of interferon by lymphocytes from nine marasmic infants and from three healthy control children. Production of interferon after stimulation with Newcastle disease virus was decreased significantly in the marasmic infants. Kramer and Good[134] reported that protein-deficient guinea pigs immunized with BCG vaccine produced equivalent amounts of migration inhibition factor compared with controls, even when dietary protein was reduced significantly.

Good and colleagues[91] have evaluated many aspects of the effect of nutritional status (including chronic protein deficiency) on cellular immune functions, including tumor immunity in animal models. Their results document an enhancement of cell-mediated immunity in chronic protein deficiency in the absence of infection. The mechanism for this enhancement is unclear; the stress of chronic protein deficiency may produce an adaptive response that includes increased output of thymic hormone, which may enhance differentiation of precursor cells into mature immunocompetent cells, or it may select populations of T cells that are more immunocompetent. The significance of these findings in humans is unclear.

THYMUS

The morphologic response of the thymus in malnutrition has been reviewed by Dourov.[68] As early as 1845, Simon recognized that the thymus was an "early critical barometer of nutrition." In protein-calorie malnutrition, the severe nutritional defect leads to thymic atrophy and fibrotic changes, with the cortex affected sooner than the medulla. In contrast to the atrophy of liver, kidney, or cardiac muscle, thymic atrophy is characterized more by a loss of cells than by a decrease in cell size. Histologically, corticomedullary differentiation is lost, and fewer lymphoid cells are present. Hassall bodies are enlarged, degenerated, and occasionally calcified. These changes are noted after 5 days of starvation and can be reversed after 6 days of refeeding. However, in contrast to other organs, thymic tissue does not regain normal size after refeeding. Histopathologic studies show an increase in the extracellular matrix-containing network in thymuses of 19 malnourished children at necropsy. The enhancement of thymic extracellular matrix in malnourished people corresponds positively with the degree of thymocyte depletion.[154]

The biochemical cause of thymic atrophy has yet to be elucidated fully. In general, stress-induced immunosuppression appears to be adrenal-mediated. The stress of malnutrition has been associated with an increase of serum glucocorticoids, and one hypothesis is that some of the thymic atrophy can be attributed to the action of glucocorticoids. In addition, the reduced serum protein in malnutrition leads to a lowered binding capacity for steroids and an increase in their metabolically active forms. Schlesinger and associates[214] found elevated levels of norepinephrine in the thymuses of rats with protein-calorie malnutrition that correlated with decreased immune response.

Functional changes resulting from thymic atrophy also are under investigation. Thymic factors, such as thymosin and thymopoietin, have been incubated with isolated T cells from malnourished children, resulting in a normalization of the maturational characteristics of the lymphocytes.[115, 185] These observations were confirmed when the results were controlled for infection and zinc content.[116] A study in Bolivian children hospitalized for severe protein-calorie malnutrition showed a high degree of T-lymphocyte immaturity that correlated with severe involution of the thymus. This high percentage of circulating immature T lymphocytes was concomitant with a decrease in mature T lymphocytes and a slight increase in cytotoxic T-cell subpopulations. After in vitro incubation with thymulin, the number of mature T lymphocytes increased, with a concomitant decrease in the number of immature T lymphocytes.[188]

PHAGOCYTOSIS

Phagocyte function can be divided into three main phases: (1) adherence and chemotaxis; (2) recognition, opsonization, and engulfment; and (3) postphagocytic events, which include formation of phagocytic vacuoles or phagosomes, followed by fusion of lysosomes with phagosomes and degranulation of lysosomal enzymes; microbicidal activity; and associated metabolic changes.[98] Phagocytosis and intracellular microbicidal activity of neutrophils and macrophages are critical host functions in the defense against pathogens. These functions depend on various components of the complement system, antibodies against surface microbial antigens, and possibly acute-phase reactants, such as C-reactive protein. Appropriate phagocytic function also requires adequate pool sizes of neutrophils and mononuclear phagocytes at inflammatory sites as well as adequate capacity of the bone marrow to mobilize these cells. Recent research suggests an association exists between low neutrophil count and decreased weight-for-height measurements in children.[257] Protein deprivation in mice results in a marked decrease in colony-forming units in the spleen, causing alterations in precursor cell pool sizes.[98]

In malnourished individuals, defects in phagocytosis and killing have been identified, but these deficits are subtle. Research has shown that neutrophils from malnourished children have enhanced baseline adhesion; however, after stimulation with chemotactic factors, the adherence response is decreased and neutrophil chemotaxis is diminished. After nutritional recovery, the abnormal adherence is reversed and chemotactic activity improves.[7, 98] Schopfer and Douglas[216] investigated the neutrophil function of 46 children with kwashiorkor. Chemotactic response was reduced at early intervals (30, 60, and 120 minutes) and reached values achieved by controls only after 180 minutes, which suggests an early migration defect. Of emphasis is that the intensity of the early cellular response may be of greater importance to the host than may the later response, which may approach that seen in normal individuals. Serum from malnourished patients is deficient in opsonic activity; therefore, the kinetics of microbial ingestion may be affected adversely. Studies of opsonization and phagocytosis of cells in malnourished animals and humans indicate that neutrophil membrane receptors for Fc-IgG and complement (C3b) are intact; however, kinetic studies show a defect in opsonization that likely is related to complement deficiencies in malnourished children.[97] No evidence has been found for any abnormalities in lysosomal fusion or degranulation in leukocytes of malnourished hosts.

Schopfer and Douglas[216] also noted that neutrophils from children with kwashiorkor did not kill *Candida albicans* intracellularly as well as did control cells. Similarly, Seth and Chandra[224] previously had noted that intracellular bactericidal killing was impaired in patients with kwashiorkor. De la Fuente and Munoz[64] showed a decrease in nitroblue tetrazolium reduction in stimulated (latex beads present) and nonstimulated (latex beads absent) macrophages from both young and old mice with protein-calorie malnutrition. Because the nitroblue tetrazolium dye reduction test in nonstimulated phagocytes indirectly measures intracellular hexose monophosphate shunt activity, protein-calorie malnutrition may interfere with this metabolic pathway. Additional studies from children with kwashiorkor show diminished neutrophil iodination during phagocytosis.[97] This observation suggests an abnormality in the myeloperoxidase-halide–mediated system in malnutrition. Fibronectin is a glycoprotein secreted by hepatocytes and macrophages; the levels of immunoreactive fibronectin are an indirect measure of opsonic activity. Starvation in rats, as well as protein-calorie malnutrition in infants, is associated with reduced levels of fibronectin. These levels of fibronectin increase to greater than normal values after nutritional rehabilitation.[97]

Single Nutrients

Many barriers to analyzing the clinical significance of single nutrients in maintaining normal immune function exist. First, nourishment is a combination event, and nutrient-nutrient interaction can be of major consequence. Competition for transport may affect absorption or excretion in both intracellular and extracellular environments. Second, a hierarchy exists for some nutrient requirements. If an element subserves several functions, as does iron, the prerequisite amount may vary with the function. Third, experimental animal models do not allow always for extrapolation to human medicine. For example, most species, with the notable exception of the guinea pig, make indigenous vitamin C, and no animal model exists for studying cobalamin deficiency. Finally, infection can affect body stores of essential nutrients. Chandra[49] has suggested a framework for micronutrient evaluation. Alterations in immune responses occur early in the course of reduced intake, and these alterations may predict the risk for developing infection and mortality. In the case of many nutrients, excessive intake also is associated with immune abnormalities.

Iron deficiency is the single most common nutritional deficiency in the world and results in systemic disease involving all cell systems. No evidence indicates that the function of iron is any less critical when the host is infected. On the other hand, iron may stimulate the growth of the pathogen with which the host is infected, may inhibit bactericidal proteins, and may enhance bacterial metabolism.[268] Iron in fluids such as plasma, milk, nasal secretions, and saliva is to a greater or lesser extent unavailable to many bacteria and fungi because of the presence of the iron-binding proteins transferrin and lactoferrin.[142, 150, 159, 251] The percentage of saturation of transferrin with iron in plasma correlates directly with the ability of the sera to support the growth of various microorganisms. When levels of saturation increase, sera can support additional bacterial growth. Microorganisms produce iron chelators known as *siderophores*. If the supply of iron in the host is so high that the physiologic processes to withhold it are exceeded, the invading microbes can obtain iron for growth.[228]

The administration of iron to animals by the intravenous, intramuscular, or intraperitoneal route reduces the LD_{50} for *P. aeruginosa, Salmonella typhosa,* streptococci, *Klebsiella pneumoniae, Salmonella typhimurium,* and *Listeria monocytogenes*.[268] Similarly, the administration of iron intramuscularly to children with kwashiorkor has resulted in overwhelming infection and death. Clinicians in these cases concluded that iron therapy should be deferred until transferrin synthesis was restored by protein nutrition. However, no evidence exists that gradual oral replenishment of iron predisposes children to infection.

Secondary bacterial infection occurs commonly in patients with bartonellosis and malaria,[143] and bacterial infection, particularly that caused by *S. pneumoniae* and *Salmonella* spp., occurs more frequently in individuals with sickle cell anemia.[14, 117, 143] This evidence has been cited by some investigators to support the concept that iron during infection is detrimental to the host. Clearly, this theory is not justified because patients with these diseases are known to have other deficits that intrinsically increase propensity for infection. Thus, the increased incidence of bacterial infection in these individuals cannot be attributed specifically to an increase in free iron.

Malaria frequently is cited as a situation in which iron-deficient states are protective to the host. Field researchers in malaria-endemic countries noted recently that treatment of iron deficiency, especially with parenteral iron, often was associated with an increase in the incidence of smear-positive malaria. Other studies have manipulated iron availability by using desferrioxamine, which is an iron chelator. Both in vitro and in vivo, desferrioxamine inhibits the growth of malaria parasites. The effect of desferrioxamine appears to be directly on parasitized erythrocytes, which behave as if they contain a chelation-labile iron pool.[127] However, in a recent study of Indian children, no statistical difference was found in the incidence or prevalence of malaria or in the severity of *Plasmodium falciparum* parasitemia at different hemoglobin or nutritional levels.[78]

Several studies[6, 153] of iron supplementation have reported fewer episodes of respiratory and gastrointestinal illnesses in iron-supplemented infants, but, because of difficulties defining and statistically evaluating infectious episodes, the significance of these findings is not compelling. In a study in Colombia[8] in which iron deficiency was severe, nutritional supplementation and medical care had no impact on the mortality caused by infectious diseases, but supplemented groups experienced an impressive reduction in enteric infections. The relative contributions of iron and other supplements in decreasing morbidity could not be ascertained.

Despite little evidence supporting the role of iron supplementation in controlling infection, numerous studies show the effects of iron deficiency on the immune system. Bactericidal capacity of leukocytes in iron deficiency is reduced, which may be caused by deficient function of iron-dependent myeloperoxidase and cytochrome enzymes.[51] Retention of iron in the reticuloendothelial system may enable macrophages to detoxify bacterial toxins. Iron in monocytes may enhance antibacterial activity of these cells.[160] Iron also may activate lysosomal hydrolases.[117] Thus, free iron may be detrimental to the host during bacterial infection, but iron within cells, particularly in selected tissue, appears to be beneficial to the host.

Cellular development of lymphoid tissues has been shown to be diminished in iron deficiency. Splenic and thymic tissue from iron-deficient rat pups showed histologic evidence of decreased lymphopoiesis. Lymphoid tissue from iron-deficient rats shows reduced cellularity and deranged histology, suggesting a reduced capacity for immunocompetence.[228]

Lymphocyte transformation is decreased in iron-deficient patients.[195] The production of migration inhibitory factor also is diminished in individuals with iron deficiency compared with those with normal serum iron concentrations.[123] Impairment of delayed cutaneous hypersensitivity responses, decreased in vitro lymphocyte response to mitogens, and reduced number of circulating T cells are found in humans with iron deficiency.[63] The rate at which granulocytes killed staphylococci also was decreased in 819 iron-deficient patients studied by Joynson and coworkers.[123] Natural killer cell activity is impaired significantly in both moderate and severe iron deficiency when compared with controls. Severely iron-deficient rats have an increased number of phagocytes in whole blood, but granulocytic activity as measured by nitroblue tetrazolium dye reduction is decreased significantly.[228] In iron-deficient patients studied by Macdougall and associates,[152] impaired leukocyte responsiveness, decreased bactericidal capacity, increased IgA, and increased C3 concentrations were observed. Restoration of normal bactericidal function 4 to 7 days after the initiation of iron therapy and before any increase in hemoglobin concentrations was noted, suggesting that tissue iron depletion rather than anemia was an etiologic factor in depressing bactericidal function.

Studies have shown that humoral immunity also is affected by iron deficiency. Five days after injection with sheep red blood cells, the production of IgM and IgG by splenocytes from experimental rats was significantly lower in severe and moderate iron deficiency. That plasma IgG was not affected by either severe or moderate iron deficiency, whereas plasma IgM was lower in severe but not moderate iron deficiency, also was shown. Although circulating plasma immunoglobulin may be normal in iron-deficiency anemia, iron deficiency may result in diminished antibody production. Interleukin-1 (IL-1) production is impaired in moderate and severe iron deficiency, which can affect cell-mediated immunity adversely and alter humoral immunity and bacterial killing by neutrophils, which is under partial control by IL-1.[216]

The interactions of iron, the host, and the microorganism clearly are important. Low levels of iron-binding protein as noted during malnutrition appear to be detrimental to the survival of the host during infection. Similarly, depletion of tissue levels of iron as noted in iron deficiency may be detrimental to optimal performance of the inflammatory and immune systems. To date, no studies have identified the point at which iron deprivation interferes with immunologic states. The suggestion that iron deficiency protects humans against infection cannot be supported. The diverse role of iron in multiple enzyme systems, both mammalian and bacterial, is understood best in a hierarchy of functions in which optimal activity of the different systems may be at different elemental concentrations.

Selenium has three major functions in the tissues and cells of the immune system: reduction of organic and inorganic peroxides, metabolism of hydroperoxides, and modulation of the respiratory burst. Glutathione peroxidase and phospholipid hydroperoxide glutathione peroxidase are selenium-containing enzymes that catalyze the reduction of peroxides formed from general metabolism, drugs, and other initiators of free radical chain reactions. Both of these enzymes also are involved in steps in the synthesis of thromboxane A_2, prostacyclin, and prostaglandins, as well as leukotrienes and lipoxins. Research has demonstrated reduction of eicosanoid biosynthesis in the absence of selenium and glutathione peroxidase. Selenium and the glutathione peroxidases also modulate the production of the oxidizing products of the respiratory burst: O^+_2, H_2O_2, CLO^+, and chloramines, which are used in the phagolysosome to lyse and destroy phagocytized cells. As predicted from these roles, selenium supplementation prevents oxidative stress-induced damage to immune cells. It also appears to boost cellular immunity by up-regulating the expression of the T-cell high-affinity IL-2 receptor, thereby enhancing T-cell response, and by altering platelet aggregation through a decreased ratio of thromboxane-to-leukotriene production.[163]

Selenium deficiency in experimental animals is associated with decreased glutathione peroxidase activity in phagocytic cells, release of increased amounts of H_2O_2 by macrophages and peritoneal granulocytes, and increased superoxide formation in macrophages.[49, 238] Splenic leukocytes from selenium-deficient rats proliferated less after mitogenic stimulation than did leukocytes from control rats.[194] This decreased proliferation may be related to an inability of leukocytes from selenium-deficient rats to internalize surface-bound transferrin, which depletes intracellular iron stores and compromises its ability to enter the S phase of the cell cycle.

Controversy still surrounds the role of selenium in the prevention of infections in humans. Deficiency has been associated with generalized immunosuppression affecting neutrophil function, antibody production, and lymphocyte proliferation. A recent study investigating selenium levels in 134 patients in intensive care units found that the mean plasma selenium concentration of these patients was 2 standard deviations below that of the general population.[84] This study also demonstrated a negative correlation between plasma selenium and severity of sepsis in these patients. The treatment of intensive care unit patients with supplemental selenium has not been investigated. In Keshan, China, selenium deficiency has been implicated in the pathogenesis of a dilated cardiomyopathy known as Keshan disease. The seasonal and annual incidences of Keshan disease were characteristic of an infectious disease, and screening of tissues from patients revealed the presence of numerous viruses, including coxsackieviruses. These findings are significant in light of Beck and Levander's[21] studies showing increased virulence of certain coxsackieviruses in selenium-deficient animals.

Zinc is a cofactor for more than 300 cellular enzymes, with functions ranging from signal transduction to transcription to replication. Zinc deficiency in humans has been associated with poor growth and development, impaired wound healing, and impaired sensory perception. The low levels of zinc in acrodermatitis enteropathica may be related to the thymic atrophy and high frequency of serious bacterial, viral, and fungal infections seen in these patients because pharmacologic zinc supplementation can reverse all of these symptoms.[178]

Multiple animal models demonstrate the association of zinc deficiency with altered humoral and cell-mediated immune responses.[219] Patients maintained on parenteral nutrition lacking in zinc showed reduced T-lymphocyte proliferation in response to mitogenic stimulation, which markedly increased after repletion of zinc.[229] Deficiencies in zinc also are associated with reduction in thymulin activity and slower neutrophil chemotaxis; these changes are reversed with the zinc supplementation.[49] Zinc deficiency also impairs the function of antigen-presenting cells.[217] Conversely, excessive supplementation with zinc has been shown to cause reduced chemotactic and phagocytic activities as well as a suppressive effect on lymphocyte proliferation.[57] The inhibition of T-cell proliferation appears to be caused by inhibition of an IL-1 receptor–associated protein kinase by zinc ions at higher concentrations.[269]

Recently, several randomized, double-blind, placebo-controlled trials of zinc supplementation have been performed with children in developing countries, most of whom exhibit some manifestations of malnutrition.[204, 205, 211, 258] These studies demonstrated the association of zinc supplementation with decreased incidence of and morbidity from respiratory infections as well as reduced morbidity from diarrhea in these malnourished children. Another trial in Indian children showed increased CD3 and CD4 cell counts and an increased CD4/CD8 ratio in zinc-supplemented children compared to controls.[210]

Copper facilitates absorption of iron from the gastrointestinal tract and is essential for the production of red blood cells. It also is critical for several oxidative enzyme systems. Copper deficiency has been shown to cause anemia of varying degrees and gross ataxia in neonates of many species, as well as defects in formation of connective tissue. Neutropenia has been documented in children with a copper-deficient diet. Copper deficiency is associated with depressed function of the reticuloendothelial system, reduced microbicidal activity of granulocytes, decreased response of splenic lymphocytes to T- and B-cell mitogens, and impaired natural killer cell cytotoxicity in animal models. This reduced microbicidal activity of granulocytes is attributed to the role of copper in superoxide dismutase and cytochrome *c* oxidase enzyme systems.[229] Copper-deficient patients are more susceptible to contracting bronchopneumonia and bacterial sepsis, especially with *E. coli*. Copper-deficient animals show increased mortality rates when exposed to *S. typhimurium*, *L. monocytogenes*, and coxsackievirus B.

The role of chromium in disease control remains undefined. Excess amounts adversely affect macrophage and lymphocyte cultures.[87, 264] Chromium acts as a cofactor for the potentiation of insulin at the cellular level, and deficiency is characterized by impaired glucose utilization.[165, 190] The role of chromium in impaired glucose homeostasis in kwashiorkor has been documented.[41]

Manganese is another essential trace element necessary for optimal growth. It affects the primary sites of chondroitin sulfate synthesis. In humans, manganese deficiency is characterized by weight loss, transient dermatitis, occasional nausea and vomiting, changes in hair color, hypocholesterolemia, and teratogenicity.

Lymphocyte and neutrophil functions in iodine deficiency are diminished. Iodide interacts with neutrophil peroxidases to form the halide-superoxide system, which is modulated by the amount of thyroid hormone, which supplies the iodide molecule. In hypothyroid patients, the bactericidal activity is decreased and restored after treatment with thyroid hormone.[49]

Three of the fat-soluble vitamins, A, D, and E, have recognized effects on immune system function. Before the discovery of antibiotics, researchers noted that urinary tract infections in children responded to vitamin A therapy. In the modern era, vitamin A deficiency is well documented to be a major determinant of respiratory and diarrheal disease in the Third World. Vitamin A levels in the serum have been used as markers of malnutrition; however, the independent effects of its deficiency are significant. Researchers have suggested that improving the vitamin A status of all children who are deficient will prevent approximately 1 to 3 million deaths each year, curtailing the incidence and severity of infectious episodes, especially respiratory and diarrheal infections.[111]

An important role of vitamin A is for the cellular differentiation of epithelial surfaces. In both animals and humans, vitamin A deficiency is associated with keratinizing metaplasia of mucus-secreting epithelial surfaces, particularly of the respiratory, gastrointestinal, and genitourinary tracts, as well as corneal tissues. This histopathologic alteration is conducive to an overgrowth of bacteria and secondary infections of loculated areas obstructed by keratinized debris. A classic example of this type of alteration is a Bitot spot, a triangular patch of xerotic conjunctiva characteristic of xerophthalmia, which is composed largely of keratin debris and a heavy growth of *Xerosis bacillus*, a saprophytic diphtheroid. Various studies also have shown that retinoids play a role in the regulation of cell-mediated and humoral immunity, cytokine production, and the functioning of neutrophils, natural killer cells, and macrophages.[222]

Immune changes in patients with vitamin A deficiency are characterized by disruption of the skin and epithelial barriers against microorganisms, reduced thymic weight, reduced immunoglobulin production, decreased T-helper cell activity, decreased lymphocyte proliferation, and increased bacterial binding to epithelial cells.[89] Vitamin A deficiency also is characterized by reduced phagocytosis and diminished nitroblue tetrazolium dye reduction. Lysozyme is a vitamin A–dependent glycoprotein; the activity of this protein is decreased markedly in vitamin A deficiency.[270]

Vitamin A deficiency in children appears to increase their susceptibility to various types of infection. In a malnutrition ward in Bangladesh, 78 percent of xerophthalmic children had bacteriuria determined by urine culture obtained by bladder tap, compared with 17 percent of nonxerophthalmic malnourished peers.[34] A case-control study of South African children showed a strong association between poor vitamin A status and increased severity of acute respiratory infections.[69] Vitamin A supplementation may reverse some of these susceptibilities. A double-blind, placebo-controlled trial in a malaria-endemic area of Papua New Guinea demonstrated that children supplemented with vitamin A had fewer febrile episodes, decreased spleen enlargement, and decreased parasite counts compared with unsupplemented controls.[226] The greatest difference was noted in children between 12 and 36 months of age. Finally, a meta-analysis of randomized trials of vitamin A supplementation in developing countries indicated a significant decrease in rates of respiratory and diarrheal disease mortality with vitamin A supplementation compared with placebo in children with no overt deficiency.[89]

Children in the Third World frequently are caught in a vicious cycle in which infection leads to vitamin A deficiency, which in turn increases the risk for subsequent development of infection. The impact that vitamin A supplementation will have on childhood morbidity and mortality depends on several factors, including the prevalence and severity of deficiency, aggravating conditions (e.g., protein-calorie malnutrition), associated nutrient defects, virulence of the infectious agents to which they are exposed, and adequacy of supplementation.[237] Carotenoids also have important immunoregulatory functions involving T and B lymphocytes, natural killer cells, and macrophages.[51]

Vitamin D serves both as an immunoregulatory hormone and as a lymphocyte-differentiating hormone in addition to its classic role of mineral homeostasis. 1,25-Dihydroxyvitamin D_3 functions in the manner of a steroid hormone in many different cell types. Receptors for 1,25-dihydroxyvitamin D_3 have been identified on the surface of T lymphocytes, monocytes, and macrophages,[260] and an extensive number of RNA polymerase II–transcribed genes that govern oncogene and lymphokine expression are regulated by this vitamin-hormone.[22] Although vitamin D must be present at a certain concentration for proper immune function, high-dose supplementation also may have detrimental effects. One study has demonstrated suppression of the delayed hypersensitivity response in patients with vitamin D deficiency as well as in those receiving high doses of vitamin D.[120] Activated vitamin D may inhibit T-lymphocyte proliferation and natural killer cell cytotoxicity as well as decrease concentrations of interferon-γ, IL-2, and IL-12, according to in vitro studies.[148] Additionally, the differentiation of immature dendritic cells into antigen-presenting cells is inhibited in culture by activated vitamin D.[192]

Vitamin E enhances immune responses and phagocytosis by acting as an antioxidant to prevent lipid peroxidation of cell membranes because rapidly proliferating cells of the stimulated immune and phagocytic systems are prone to peroxidative damage by free radicals, peroxides, and superoxides. In vitro studies of rat alveolar macrophages demonstrate that high levels of vitamin E suppress the release of reactive oxygen species after stimulation.[189] These findings suggest that vitamin E may reduce self-inflicted damage to macrophages and surrounding tissue during infection. The antioxidant effect of vitamin E also modulates the biosynthesis and activity of prostaglandins, thromboxane, and leukotrienes.[248] Several studies have shown that vitamin E deficiency impairs both cell-mediated and humoral immunity in different animal models. Some studies suggest that vitamin E deficiency may contribute to the decreased immune function of neonates, especially premature infants.[167] In humans, vitamin E deficiency impairs T-cell–mediated function, which is reversible by vitamin E supplementation. Supplementation in an amount 2 to 10 times greater than the present recommended dose significantly increased humoral and cell-mediated immune responses and phagocytic functions in laboratory animals and humans.[248] Vitamin E appears to interact with other micronutrients in immunomodulation. The heightened humoral response noted with vitamin E is synergistic with selenium[100] and copper.[248] In addition, zinc deficiency, even when marginal, can decrease markedly vitamin E serum concentrations.[201]

Concentrations of vitamins A, B_6, and C have been reported to be lower than normal during acute bacterial and viral infections, and reduced concentrations of folic acid in blood and serum have been found in infants with diarrhea or acute bacterial infection[161] as well as in adults with tuberculosis or malaria.[202] Severe xerophthalmia has been noted in vitamin A–deficient Indian children. The xerophthalmia often was preceded by diarrhea, measles, or a respiratory infection and may have been precipitated by a fall in serum vitamin A and retinol-binding protein concentrations during the course of the infection. A study in children with shigellosis showed increased urinary excretion of vitamin A during infection, which was attributed to impaired renal tubular absorption of low-molecular-weight proteins such as retinol-binding protein bound to retinol.[172] Infections may alter plasma retinol levels because activation of the acute-phase response may decrease the synthesis of the circulating proteins that transport retinol.[249]

Altered concentrations of circulating vitamins during infection also may be caused by several other mechanisms, including impaired absorption from the gastrointestinal tract, liver cell damage, and altered rates of vitamin excretion. Transient malabsorption of folic acid and vitamin B_{12} has been noted during and after recovery from acute intestinal infections, including cholera and salmonellosis.[146] The urinary excretion of the group B vitamins and vitamin C also has been observed to change during hepatitis and tuberculosis.[101, 121]

Vitamin B_6 deficiency impairs immunity by slowing the rate of production of one-carbon units necessary for nucleic acid synthesis in these rapidly proliferating cells. Animal models deficient in vitamin B_6 exhibit impaired antibody production, a delay in IgM-to-IgG class switching, and altered cell-mediated immunity with reduced delayed-type hypersensitivity responses.[252] Humans consuming a diet low in vitamin B_6 or being treated with deoxypyridoxine (vitamin B_6 antagonist) have a decreased number of circulating lymphocytes as well as reduced antibody production and a mild decrease in the percentage of helper T cells.[166] The thymus is smaller, and thymic hormone activity is decreased in vitamin B_6 deficiency.

Vitamin B_{12} also appears to affect immunity. Patients with vitamin B_{12} deficiency were found to have decreased numbers of lymphocytes, decreased CD8 cells, an altered CD8/CD4 ratio, and suppressed natural killer cell cytotoxicity.[245] All of these parameters improved with supplementation of vitamin B_{12}.

Osawa[186] first suggested that thiamine deficiency may predispose to the occurrence of tropical pyomyositis, a hematogenous pyogenic infection characterized by abscess formation in various muscle tissues. Muscle tissue generally is quite resistant to infection, but lack of thiamine may change the biochemical milieu of the muscle, rendering it more susceptible to infection.

Physiologic quantities of ascorbic acid are necessary for normal metabolism of lipids and iron. One of the major functions of vitamin C is as an antioxidant that protects the $alpha_1$ proteinase inhibitor from inactivation by free radical products of the respiratory burst. $Alpha_1$ proteinase inhibitor is present in plasma, where it reacts with elastase, thus protecting the extracellular space from escaped proteases from damaged cells. The concentration of intracellular vitamin C is approximately 50 times that found in plasma, which suggests that vitamin C may protect intracellular regions from oxidants that leak into the cytoplasm.

Host susceptibility to infection clearly is increased in scurvy. Vitamin C deficiency is associated with impaired phagocytic activity. Microtubule organization is responsible for phagocytosis and locomotion and depends on the redox state of the cell; vitamin C may modulate it by an antioxidant effect on tubulin tyrosinolation.[102] Macrophages from mice supplemented with vitamin C, vitamin E, or both demonstrated increased random migration, chemotaxis, ingestion, and superoxide anion production compared with controls.[65] Because vitamin C is associated with chemotactic activation of phagocytes, its use has been suggested in patients with disorders of phagocyte function, such as Chédiak-Higashi syndrome.[215]

The possibility that vitamin C may be important in preventing upper respiratory infections has received widespread publicity in both the medical and lay presses. Chalmers[43] reported, however, after reviewing 14 clinical trials of ascorbic acid in the prevention and treatment of the common cold, that differences between supplemented and nonsupplemented subjects were minor and insignificant. Nonetheless, in most studies, the severity of symptoms was worse in patients who received placebo. Miller and colleagues[168] performed a double-blind, co-twin controlled study on 44 monozygotic twins of school age. During the 5-month study period, no statistically significant difference in the number or severity of illness episodes was noted between the recipients of vitamin C and a placebo control group. Several studies have shown a consistent decrease in the duration of the common cold episodes; although most of the results are not statistically significant, all of them point consistently in the same direction.[102] Administration of ascorbic acid is not a panacea for upper respiratory infections. Also, whereas lack of vitamin C clearly is detrimental, excess intake is of no proven value.

Recent developments in the field of malnutrition and infection support the concept that malnutrition impairs the response of the host to infection; some of the mechanisms have been suggested. In vitro studies show alterations in immune cell function, and experimental animal models demonstrate an enhanced susceptibility to infection with extreme alterations in the levels of micronutrients. However, any deviation from optimal nutrition affects immune function, and combinations of less severe nutrient deficiencies must be studied to ascertain whether the effects are synergistic.

Considerations of Nutrition and Infection in Special Populations

Overall, the prevalence of malnutrition in industrialized nations is considerably less than that in developing countries; however, even in industrialized nations, certain populations are at increased risk for developing malnutrition. For instance, malnutrition is a common complication in individuals infected with HIV, regardless of their geographic location or economic situation. Critically ill patients have an increased risk for development of both malnutrition and infection. Recent research suggests that the route of nutrition in critically ill patients may influence susceptibility to infection, and numerous studies are investigating the role of specific enteral diets in reducing this risk. Finally, burn patients also have metabolic changes that highlight the interactions of infection and nutrition.

HUMAN IMMUNODEFICIENCY VIRUS AND MALNUTRITION

Acquired immunodeficiency syndrome (AIDS) has become one of the most pressing public health problems in the world. More than 1 million Americans are infected with HIV. Infection with HIV has a devastating effect on nutritional status. Malnutrition was one of the earliest recognized complications of AIDS, and unexplained weight loss remains one of the most common initial AIDS-defining diagnoses reported to public health authorities. Patients may lose 30 to 50 percent of their body mass before succumbing to their disease. The onset of depletion of body cell mass occurs early in HIV infection and may predate any significant immune deficiency, suggesting that the virus itself may be responsible.[132] However, most commonly, the malnutrition associated with HIV is multifactorial. Decreased caloric intake, malabsorption of nutrients, and elevated energy expenditure, especially during systemic opportunistic infections, all contribute to malnutrition in these patients. Protein-calorie malnutrition is encountered frequently, as are individual or combined micronutrient deficiencies. All of them contribute to the growth failure seen in children with HIV, emphasizing the need for early and intensive nutritional intervention and treatment in these patients.

Two major paradigms of weight loss that contribute to such in patients with HIV infection are starvation and cachexia.[13] Starvation refers to a voluntary or involuntary deprivation of food that leads to increased losses of body fat and extracellular water, with relative sparing of lean body mass. In contrast, cachexia is characterized by a disproportionate loss of lean body mass resulting from specific alterations in metabolism. These alterations during cachexia are caused by shifts in cytokine levels and may include changes in protein metabolism or energy expenditure, appetite changes, or derangement of the sleep–wake cycle. Investigation of energy metabolism in HIV-infected people has produced conflicting results. Some studies report increased resting energy expenditure, and others report that it was decreased. A study of 36 HIV-infected children between infancy and 10 years of age demonstrated that cardiac muscle mass and heart rate were correlated inversely with weight and skeletal muscle mass.[169] This finding is not consistent with the decreased energy expenditure of hypometabolic compensation that occurs in starvation; instead, it suggests that these children have cachexia and intrinsic metabolic changes.

Both animal and human studies have found correlations between cytokine levels and anorexia, cachexia, and altered lipid metabolism. Serum levels of interferon-α are increased in some patients with AIDS and are correlated significantly with elevated serum triglyceride levels. Adult patients with AIDS and with wasting were found to have higher plasma concentrations of tumor necrosis factor-α (TNF-α) and cholecystokinin octapeptide sulfate, an appetite neuropeptide, and lower levels of β-endorphins compared with well-nourished patients with AIDS and healthy controls.[9] These changes may pathologically inhibit appetite and contribute to weight loss.

Very different metabolic changes have been observed recently in patients with HIV who are receiving antiretroviral therapy. Lipodystrophy, or fat redistribution syndrome, seems to be associated more strongly with the administration of protease inhibitors than other antiretroviral agents. Patients with this condition develop a dorsocervical fat pad, abdominal adiposity, and facial, extremity, and buttocks wasting. Increased breast size also is seen in female patients. Other changes include hyperlipidemia with increased levels of total cholesterol and low-density lipoprotein and decreased levels of high-density lipoprotein. These patients also may develop insulin resistance with normal to elevated serum glucose, increased insulin levels, and abnormal glucose tolerance tests. The mechanism of this syndrome and its long-term consequences are unclear.

Involvement of the gastrointestinal tract in patients with HIV infections also undoubtedly plays a role in weight loss. Acute episodes of weight loss tend to occur in association with acute opportunistic infections, but more chronic weight loss often is related to gastrointestinal disease and malabsorption. The pathogenesis of malabsorption involves a combination of factors, including primary enterocyte injury with partial villus atrophy and crypt hyperplasia, ileal dysfunction with bile salt wasting and fat malabsorption, and exudative enteropathy.[133] Small intestine pathology or pancreatic insufficiency may lead to malabsorption of fat, weight loss, and depletion of fat-soluble vitamins.[139] Hypochlorhydria has been found in almost 75 percent of patients with AIDS and can allow for enteric infections as well as reduced absorption of micronutrients, such as folate and iron. Malabsorption of lactose is a common finding and is more severe in symptomatic than asymptomatic HIV-infected children.[276] Subclinical malabsorption may play a role in early HIV disease, whereas overt malabsorption is found more frequently in advanced HIV infection. Along with the direct effects of

HIV, immunosuppression leads to an increased frequency of gastrointestinal infections, which also exacerbate weight loss caused by diarrhea and malabsorption. Protozoal infections can disrupt mucosal architecture in the small intestine, resulting in severe malnutrition. Studies indicate that HIV-infected patients with diarrhea caused by enteric infections experience greater weight loss than do HIV-infected patients with diarrhea for which no pathogen can be identified.[40]

Protein-calorie malnutrition is a common occurrence in patients with AIDS and is considered a predominant cause of morbidity in AIDS. In the United States, between 30 and 50 percent of children followed in HIV programs have evidence of protein-calorie malnutrition.[170] The immune effects of protein-calorie malnutrition and HIV infection are similar: decreased CD4 cells, reversal of the helper-to-suppressor T-cell ratio, impairment of delayed hypersensitivity reactions, and abnormal humoral responses occur in both conditions. Thus, a child with both protein-calorie malnutrition and HIV infection is likely to have a worse outcome than will a child with either condition alone.

Low levels of vitamins A, E, B_6, B_{12}, and C and of carotenoids, selenium, and zinc are common findings in many HIV-infected populations. This deficiency may be caused by decreased dietary intake, diarrhea, malabsorption, impaired storage, or altered metabolism of micronutrients.[223] Some researchers attribute the low levels of zinc in HIV-infected patients to direct utilization of zinc by the virus for gene expression, multimerization, and integration into the host genome.[19] Recently, the prognostic significance of the status of selenium has received much attention. Several studies[17, 18, 39] have demonstrated that selenium deficiency is associated more strongly than are other micronutrient deficiencies with mortality in HIV-infected patients. Selenium-deficient HIV-infected patients had a 10- to 20-fold increase in mortality compared with those with adequate selenium levels. Among HIV-infected children who died, those with low selenium levels died at a younger age (mean age at death of 4.3 years versus 8 years), suggesting a more rapid disease progression in patients with selenium deficiency.[39] The relationship between selenium deficiency and early death in HIV may be associated with the role of selenium in preventing oxidative stress, which may be involved in maintaining viral latency in an infected cell. An in vitro study of HIV-infected monocytes and T lymphocytes emphasizes this role by showing that selenium supplementation partially suppresses the TNF-α–mediated replication of the virus.[107]

Controversy currently surrounds the role of maternal micronutrient status, particularly vitamin A, in the perinatal transmission of HIV. Various studies have produced conflicting results. Several studies[95, 221] demonstrate an increased risk for perinatal HIV transmission with maternal vitamin A deficiency, one of which[221] was able to demonstrate that the risk for perinatal transmission was correlated inversely with concentration of maternal serum retinol. However, two other studies showed no association between maternal vitamin A level and risk for transmission of HIV to the infant.[37, 38] Similarly, a randomized, double-blind, placebo-controlled trial of 1083 pregnant women in Tanzania[79] showed that neither multivitamin nor vitamin A supplementation had any effect on vertical transmission of HIV. Because of the conflicting nature of these studies, further research clearly is required before any conclusions can be drawn.

In children with HIV, the combination of diarrhea, malabsorption, protein-calorie malnutrition, and micronutrient deficiencies can have devastating effects on growth. HIV-infected infants may exhibit growth failure, failure to thrive, developmental delay, or frank malnutrition by as early as 4 months of age.[80] A retrospective, cross-sectional analysis of 54 children with perinatally acquired HIV demonstrated an early decline in the rate of linear growth (growth failure) with relative preservation of weight for age.[193] A prospective study of HIV-infected infants in Uganda[24] showed an association between mortality and the severity of growth failure. The exact nature of the relationship between growth failure and mortality in HIV infection remains unclear. Poor nutritional parameters may represent frequent opportunistic infections and debilitation in infants with already advanced disease; conversely, poor nutritional status may accelerate the progression from asymptomatic HIV infection to symptomatic AIDS.

Nutritional intervention is important for all HIV-infected patients, but it is particularly crucial in the management of infants and children with the virus. In June 2000, the American Dietetic Association and Dieticians of Canada recommended that children should be referred for a full nutrition evaluation as soon as possible after receiving the diagnosis of HIV.[80] Nutrition intervention should begin early in the course of HIV infection in the hopes of stabilizing weight loss and preventing growth failure. Evaluation should address stages of growth and development, anthropometrics, dietary intake assessment, and medical data, as well as any psychosocial or economic issues that may be barriers to establishing adequate nutrition. Specific dietary interventions include maximizing intake of high-calorie, nutrient-dense foods as well as vitamin and mineral supplements, especially vitamins A, B_6, B_{12}, E, and C and riboflavin, zinc, and selenium. In addition, dietary counseling should emphasize the importance of daily ingestion of a full complement of amino acids. If adequate nutritional status cannot be maintained orally, enteral supplementation should be used. To maximize absorption and minimize diarrhea, formulas that have low residue or low lactose and that contain peptides and medium-chain triglycerides should be used. If the patient has intractable diarrhea or impaired function of the gastrointestinal tract or if nutrient needs are not met by enteral nutrition, home total parenteral nutrition (TPN) may be considered for long-term use if the patient has a reasonable prognosis; however, parenteral nutrition therapy may be complicated by metabolic abnormalities (hypertriglyceridemia, hyperglycemia, fluid and electrolyte imbalance) and problems related to catheters, such as infection, hemorrhage, and pneumothorax. Standard nutritional recommendations for AIDS patients have not been established because of the heterogeneous nature of the complications of this disease.

ROUTE AND COMPOSITION OF NUTRITION IN CRITICALLY ILL PATIENTS

The effects of quality and quantity of nutrients on the immune system have been demonstrated, but the route of administration of nutrition also has been shown to affect host susceptibility to infection. The first experimental evidence that the route of nutrition plays a role in host defense came from Kudsk and associates[137] in the early 1980s. Before induction of hemoglobin–*E. coli* peritonitis, well-nourished rats were fed the same solution through either gastrostomy or central catheter for 12 days. The 48-hour survival after induction of hemoglobin–*E. coli* peritonitis was 60 percent in the group fed enterally, compared with 20 percent in the parenterally fed group. Improved survival also was observed in malnourished rats fed enterally compared with parenterally under similar experimental conditions.[136]

Analyses of infection rates in hospitalized patients appear to confirm an association between parenteral nutrition and susceptibility to infection. In a meta-analysis of data from eight prospective, randomized trials of early enteral versus parenteral feeding of high-risk surgical patients, Moore and colleagues[175] found a 35 percent risk for septic complications in patients receiving TPN, compared with an 18 percent risk in those fed enterally. Similar increases in infection rates have been observed in children. Several prospective cohort studies of patients in neonatal and pediatric intensive care units have demonstrated that TPN is the most significant risk factor for acquiring a nosocomial infection.[33, 90, 232]

Numerous hypotheses have been proposed to explain the increased risk for infection in parenterally fed patients. Intravenous nutrition may induce immunosuppression directly. In vitro studies of whole blood from infants receiving long-term parenteral nutrition demonstrated impaired phagocytosis and intracellular killing in response to challenge with coagulase-negative staphylococci, a model for bacteremia.[183, 184] The intracellular killing was correlated negatively with duration, but not amount, of parenteral feeding and was found to normalize after the addition of small enteral feeding.[183] Correction of this immune defect with enteral feeding implies the involvement of the gastrointestinal tract in the increased infection risk with parenteral feeding. Enteral feeding helps to maintain barrier function of the gut through increased gastric acidity, mucus production, and intact peristalsis.[5] Gastrointestinal tract "starvation" in animal models produces mucosal atrophy, bacterial overgrowth, decreased secretory IgA, increased intestinal permeability and translocation of bacteria or toxins, and atrophy of gut-associated lymphoid tissue (GALT).[5, 129] A recent study in mice demonstrated that parenteral feeding alters GALT, resulting in atrophy of T- and B-cell populations in the lamina propria, intraepithelial space, and Peyer patches.[145] Further human studies are necessary, but preliminary evidence suggests that enteral feeding may maintain immunologic integrity in the gut and result in increased resistance to infection.

The composition of enteral diets has been another area of recent investigation. Certain key nutrients are being recognized for their ability to modulate a variety of inflammatory, metabolic, and immune processes when ingested in increased amounts. Nutritional components such as dietary nucleotides, omega-3 fatty acids, glutamine, and arginine are being called "immune-enhancing agents" because of their potential roles in bolstering and maintaining host defenses against infection.

Nucleotides are thought to have immunomodulating properties because of their role as structural units for DNA, RNA, adenosine triphosphate, and cyclic adenosine monophosphate. The unaltered human gastrointestinal tract contains bacteria, the continuous turnover of which provides an adequate supply of nucleotides, but this flora may be altered in critically ill patients.[15] Periods of rapid growth or certain disease states also may create increased demands for nucleotides. Under these conditions, supplemental dietary nucleotides may spare the energy of de novo synthesis and optimize the function of rapidly proliferating cells of the immune system.[42] Numerous studies have shown the immunomodulating effects of nucleotides in vitro and in animal models.[124, 138] Recent studies in children also demonstrate these effects. Studies in infants showed that infants receiving nucleotide-supplemented formula had increased natural killer cell cytotoxicity, increased IL-2 production by stimulated mononuclear cells, and higher serum concentrations of IgM and IgA compared with those fed standard formulas.[42, 158]

Omega-3 fatty acids may regulate immune function by modulating formation of prostaglandins and regional blood flow. Some inflammatory mediators of shock and sepsis, including prostaglandins, leukotrienes, and platelet-activating factor, are metabolites of omega-6 fatty acids, the primary fat source in many nutritional formulations. Substitution of omega-3 fatty acids for omega-6 fatty acids has been shown to have anti-inflammatory effects.[15] Parenterally fed rats receiving supplemental omega-3 fatty acids had increased splanchnic blood flow in response to endotoxin challenge, compared with parenterally fed rats without supplementation.[199] They also had decreased viable bacteria in their mesenteric lymph nodes and liver, which may represent decreased bacterial translocation from the gastrointestinal tract or improved bactericidal activity.

Glutamine is the most abundant amino acid in human muscle and plasma and is utilized as a fuel source for lymphocytes, macrophages, and enterocytes. It also is a precursor of glutathione and nucleotide synthesis. Glutamine is a nonessential amino acid; however, during catabolic illness, glutamine uptake by small intestinal and immune cells may exceed synthesis and release from skeletal muscle, rendering it conditionally essential.[15] Studies of glutamine supplementation to enteral feeding solutions in adult trauma patients have shown significantly less pneumonia, bacteremia, and sepsis in supplemented groups compared with controls.[108] Glutamine has not been added routinely to formulas for critically ill neonates and is provided in only small quantities when enteral intake is low. A recent study, however, of 68 very-low-birth-weight infants[180] suggested that glutamine supplementation may be beneficial. Infants on standard premature formula were nearly four times more likely to develop sepsis than were infants fed glutamine-supplemented formula.

Arginine, a nonessential amino acid, has received considerable attention for its immune-enhancing properties. Arginine is a precursor for nitric oxide in vascular endothelial cells, macrophages, and neutrophils, and infusion of arginine stimulates release of growth hormone, glucagon, somatostatin, prolactin, and insulin.[15] A meta-analysis of 15 randomized, controlled trials comparing standard enteral nutrition with commercially available immune-enhancing enteral formulations containing arginine, with or without glutamine, nucleotides, and omega-3 fatty acids, was performed.[20] No effect on mortality was found, but patients receiving the immune-enhancing formulations demonstrated a decreased risk for developing infection (odds ratio, 0.67; 95% confidence interval [CI], 0.5 to 0.89) compared with controls. Their hospital stay also was a mean 2.9 days shorter than that for patients receiving standard enteral feedings.

These studies demonstrate promising effects of combinations of arginine, glutamine, omega-3 fatty acids, and dietary nucleotides on the immune system. Before these formulations are accepted as immune-enhancing, the significance of these components individually should be confirmed, and the specific mechanisms by which they "enhance" the immune system should be investigated more closely.

BURNS, INFECTION, AND NUTRITION

In the United States, approximately 2.5 million people seek medical care for burns each year. More than 100,000 people are hospitalized with burns each year, and 12,000 burn victims die of their injuries.[73] During the past 50 years, great strides have been made in the treatment and management of patients who have suffered thermal injuries. A marked decrease in burn mortality rates, particularly in patients younger than the age of 35 years, has occurred.

Infection always has been the predominant determinant of wound healing and outcome of burn patients. The incidence of infectious complications in burn patients increases in proportion to the fraction of the body surface injured. The direct effects of heat on skin and underlying tissue render the burn wound particularly susceptible to infection; the denatured protein in burn-injured tissue serves as a rich medium for microbial growth and proliferation. The thermal thrombosis that renders the eschar avascular further promotes infection by precluding delivery of the cellular components of the host defense system and limiting delivery of blood-borne antibiotics to the infected wound site. Further microbial proliferation occurs at the interface between viable tissue and the eschar, known as the *subeschar space.* If host defenses are adequate, the eschar is sloughed; however, microbial invasion of the viable tissue occurs if host defenses are deficient.

Infection remains the most common cause of morbidity and mortality in burn patients, even though the incidence of the burn wound infection has been reduced significantly since the introduction of topical antibiotics. Pneumonia is the most frequent infection occurring in burn patients. Other infectious complications, such as suppurative thrombophlebitis and septicemia, have been decreasing in incidence as a result of improvements in patient management, wound care, and infection control.[198]

Recently, a larger role in the development of sepsis has been attributed to the gastrointestinal tract. The gastrointestinal barrier normally is highly effective in containing its flora. However, the stress of thermal injury, as well as other stresses that can occur in burn patients, such as major trauma, surgery, malnutrition, or immunosuppression, can result in breakdown of the barrier followed by translocation of inert particles and microorganisms across the intestinal wall. This event may play a role in the colonization of burn wounds by gram-negative organisms, which are more likely to originate from the gastrointestinal tract hematogenously than from the skin. Alteration of the indigenous microbial flora, which may be caused by the stress of injury, antibiotics, or composition of enteral feedings, has been shown to increase translocation markedly.

Translocation of bacteria and their toxins from ischemic bowel in burn injury causes a massive release of cytokines and inflammatory mediators from macrophages in the splanchnic area. These factors include IL-1, IL-6, TNF, prostanoids, free radicals, endotoxins, catecholamines, cortisol, and glucagon.[62] The release of cytokines and inflammatory mediators after thermal injury results in the alteration of the immune system. Depressed cytotoxic activity of T cells, decreased ratio of helper-to-suppressor T lymphocytes, suppressed stimulation of lymphocyte proliferation by hemagglutinin, and suppressed mixed lymphocyte responses have been present after thermal injury. Phagocytes show depressed phagocytic activity, reduced intracellular killing, and increased superoxide formation. Decreased serum concentrations of immunoglobulins, activation of complement with release of anaphylatoxins, and formation of membrane attack complexes leading to inflammation and cytolysis are the sequelae of altered humoral immunity after burn injuries in children and adults.[99]

Major thermal injury is associated with extreme hypermetabolism and catabolism, which occur shortly after successful resuscitation from the shock phase of the burn injury. This hypermetabolic state is characterized by elevated cardiac output, increased energy expenditure, erosion of lean body mass, negative nitrogen balance, and production of abnormal substrate. In addition, gluconeogenesis, glucose oxidation, and plasma clearance of glucose are accelerated.[253]

The role of nutrition in maintaining immunocompetence and modulating hypermetabolism in burned patients has become increasingly important. The use of early enteral nutrition when combined with early excision of nonviable tissue has resulted in reduced energy requirements in burned children.[103] Providing proper nutrition by the enteral route when possible may satisfy caloric needs, regulate microflora, and maintain the integrity of the mucosa of the gut, but it also may blunt the hypermetabolic response after thermal injury.[119] Routine antimicrobial prophylaxis is not recommended, but short-term perioperative prophylaxis is used in many centers. Selective bowel decontamination with aztreonam has been shown to decrease colonization of burn wound with gram-negative bacteria.[157] Several studies have suggested that treatment with growth hormone accelerates healing of the donor site wound and promotes protein anabolism in severely burned children.[177] Many immunoprotective measures, such as intravenous immunoglobulins, specific tetravalent *Pseudomonas* spp. immunoglobulins, recombinant granulocyte colony-stimulating factor, neutrophil transfusions, plasmapheresis, and opsonin replacement using fresh-frozen plasma, have been described anecdotally; however, their efficacy has not been proved in larger clinical trials.[66, 99] The patient with thermal injury faces impaired metabolism, nutrition, and immunocompetence. Critical factors focusing on maintaining adequate nutrition, modulating hypermetabolism, restoring proper immune function, providing wound coverage, and controlling infection will need to be assessed continually to lessen the morbidity and mortality rates in these patients.

Obesity

In industrialized countries, the burden of morbidity and mortality continues to shift toward chronic diseases. Research has focused on the effects of surfeit nutrition, especially obesity.

A cross-sectional study of 1129 preadolescent children suggests that obesity in children may be a predisposing factor to acute respiratory disease.[118] The study demonstrated that children with a body mass index (BMI) greater than or equal to 20 experienced twice as high a risk for acquiring acute respiratory infections compared with children with a lower BMI (odds ratio, 2.02; 95% CI, 1.13, 3.59). In 1981, Chandra[47] examined the immunocompetence of obese children, adolescents, and adults. Approximately one third of the obese group showed a variable impairment of cell-mediated immune responses as well as a reduction of intracellular bacterial killing by neutrophils. The obese group had moderately low concentrations of serum zinc and iron, and therapy with these micronutrients for 4 weeks resulted in improvement in immunologic responses.

Obese adolescents and adults experience a greater risk for developing sepsis and wound infections after surgery than do lean control subjects.[77, 241] Obese people exhibit a slight impairment of delayed cutaneous hypersensitivity responses, decreased lymphocyte response to mitogens, reduced bactericidal capacity of neutrophils, and reduced helper T-cell populations. Humoral immunity also may be affected by obesity. A randomized clinical trial of immunogenicity of hepatitis B vaccine found obesity to be a risk factor for nonresponse to the vaccine.[12] Obese subjects were 2.1 times more likely to be nonresponders than were lean subjects.

Obesity also is implicated in altering cytokine responses. Animal studies have shown that elevated levels of TNF are associated with insulin resistance; however, Boeck and associates[30] reported that obese patients with significant insulin resistance had little or no detectable plasma TNF compared with control subjects. Genetically obese rodents have attenuated production of TNF as well as IL-6 in response to lipopolysaccharide when compared with their lean littermates.[147] These findings may reflect a refractive state in obesity in which production of TNF is down-regulated. Kolterman and colleagues[130] reported reduced release of migration inhibition factor by stimulated lymphocytes from moderately obese, nonhyperglycemic subjects to 36 percent of the level of normal weight controls.

A variety of cell-mediated immune responses have been evaluated in genetically obese animals. A study in rats demonstrated reduced T lymphocytes in peripheral blood, spleen, and thymus in genetically obese rats compared with nonobese littermates. The proliferative response of splenocytes to mitogens also was significantly lower in the obese rats, and a significant decrease in natural killer cell activity occurred.[246] When obese mice were immunized with lymphoma cells, the cytotoxic response of spleen cells was markedly lower than that of lean controls.[51] However, when lymphocytes from obese and lean mice were sensitized in vitro rather than in vivo, they performed similarly. This observation suggests that the microenvironment of obese animals, which includes hyperlipidemia, hyperglycemia, and altered levels of insulin, glucagon, cortisol, and adrenocorticotropic hormone, may be responsible for impaired cellular responses.

Recent studies indicate that leptin, a protein known to regulate appetite and energy expenditure, may play a role in the altered immune responses associated with obesity. Studies of rodents with genetic abnormalities of leptin or leptin receptor revealed obesity-related deficits in macrophage phagocytosis.[147] Leptin-deficient mice were unable to clear and kill circulating *E. coli* as efficiently as did normal mice. Treatment with leptin increased the phagocytic activity of macrophages harvested from normal mice or mice with homozygous leptin mutations, but not from animals with known mutations in the leptin receptor. Leptin receptors have been identified on macrophages, and treatment with recombinant leptin has been found to induce production of macrophage colony-stimulating factor by cultured macrophages.[86] These data are consistent with a direct leptin-mediated effect on macrophages.

According to animal studies, diet also may affect the ability to respond appropriately to infection. When dogs were fed a high-calorie diet, a greater susceptibility to distemper virus and a shorter survival time were noted than in control animals fed a normal diet.[181] When chickens on a high-protein diet were infected with Newcastle disease agent, mortality and morbidity were greater than those noted in control groups.[31] Swiss mice made obese by high-fat diets are less resistant to infection by *S. typhimurium* (which provokes both cellular and humoral responses) and *K. pneumoniae* (which provokes primarily a humoral response) when compared with Swiss mice fed a standard laboratory diet.[241] High-fat diets show consistently depressed host resistance to tuberculosis and malaria in rats and to pneumococcal infections in chickens.[155] Erickson and associates[72, 73] discovered that high levels of dietary fat, particularly polyunsaturated fat, suppressed the response of lymphocytes to T-cell mitogens. Animal models also have demonstrated the adverse effects of excess cholesterol. Fiser and coworkers[81] found that hypercholesterolemic monkeys developed altered humoral and cellular immune function. Hypercholesterolemia also has been found to increase mortality in mice infected with group B coxsackieviruses.[150] The specific effects of diet in humans is unclear, but these lines of evidence suggest that any deviation from normal nutritional status may enhance the susceptibility of the host to infection.

Effect of Malnutrition on Resistance to Infection

When malnutrition diminishes resistance to infection or when infection aggravates malnutrition, the relationship between the two can be described as synergistic. In other situations, malnutrition impedes the multiplication of the agent more than it diminishes resistance of the host. In this case, the interaction between infection and malnutrition can be considered somewhat antagonistic. Vitamin A–deficient patients have been reported to have a higher incidence of tuberculosis, bronchitis, otitis media, urinary tract infections, and bronchopneumonia. Protein deficiency leaves patients more susceptible to typhus, hepatitis, amebic dysentery, diarrheal disease, and tuberculosis. A reasonable assumption is that most deficiency states decrease host resistance to infection.

EXPERIMENTAL VIRAL INFECTION

The effects of malnutrition on experimental viral infection have been studied, but results have not been uniform. Many investigators have concluded that starved, fasted, or underfed animals are more resistant to viral infections than are normal animals and that the severity of viral infection is decreased.[23, 61, 200, 239, 240, 267] Most of these studies were published before 1950, and clinical criteria were utilized in evaluating the severity of viral infection. Despite reports by some investigators that the severity of viral infection is enhanced in protein-deficient animals, the concept that healthy animals are more susceptible than are their malnourished counterparts to experimental viral infection has gained broad acceptance.[218] This antagonistic effect of malnutrition on viral infection was attributed by some investigators to starvation of the virus at the cellular level, with restriction of viral replication.[26, 85]

The studies of Woodruff and Kilbourne[272] cast doubt on this prevailing concept and support the theory that protein-calorie malnutrition is as detrimental to the host response to viral infection as it is to bacterial infection. Their studies convincingly demonstrate an increased severity of infection with coxsackievirus B3 in male albino mice that were subjected to sustained postweaning undernutrition. Severity of infection was proportional to the magnitude of malnutrition. Virus persisted in the heart, spleen, pancreas, and liver of severely malnourished animals, and mortality was highest in these groups. If a quantitatively optimal diet was fed to previously malnourished mice at the time of infection, they were protected from further viremia and death. Further studies of coxsackievirus B in mice with specific nutrient deficiencies were performed by Beck and Levander.[21] In these studies, a normally benign strain of coxsackievirus B became virulent and induced cardiomyopathy in selenium- and vitamin E–deficient mice. The increased virulence in the selenium- and vitamin E–deficient host was caused by genotypic changes in the virus, so that the sequence of the normally benign virus now resembles that of more virulent strains. These viral genotypic changes may be secondary to a decreased immune response in the host, leading to increased viral replication and risk for mutation. Alternatively, the increased oxidative stress in a selenium- or vitamin E–deficient host may result in an increase in free radicals that could directly damage viral RNA and result in mutations. This study is the first example of a host diet having a direct effect on the genetic composition of a pathogen.

MEASLES

Measles may be the most extreme example of a childhood disease that is relatively benign in industrialized populations but associated with high mortality rates in developing nations. This difference can be attributed to many factors, including vaccination patterns, concurrent disease, and available medical care. However, one of the most important causes of this differential mortality is varying nutritional status. Measles influences the nutritional and immune status by several mechanisms. Like any other febrile illness, measles contributes to severe reduction in food intake, vomiting, and increased metabolic losses. Measles also can produce a viral enteritis that results in excessive nitrogen loss caused by a protein-losing enteropathy. Measles induces prolonged immunosuppression characterized by a decrease in the number of circulating T cells and impaired proliferation of T lymphocytes that has been shown to last for nearly 6 months.

A study in India revealed a close association between protein-calorie malnutrition and measles, with nearly 25 percent of children hospitalized for severe protein-calorie malnutrition reporting an episode of measles in the preceding 3 to 6 months.[29] In a prospective study performed in the urban slums of Hyderabad, measles was associated with a significant weight loss of 2 to 12 percent of the initial body weight in children younger than 5 years of age. These children also were shown to have retarded growth up to 6 months after the initial infection. Nearly 4 percent of children with measles developed clinical signs of kwashiorkor or marasmus within the next 3 to 6 months. All children manifesting clinical signs of severe protein-calorie malnutrition in the postmeasles period were undernourished before contracting the infection, which highlights the importance of nutritional status as a major determinant of the severity of nutritional deficiencies and growth failure that occur in the postmeasles period.[29]

In the malnourished host, the epithelial surfaces are affected severely by measles, with eye and mouth involvement, laryngitis, bronchopneumonia, and gastroenteritis. These children carry and transmit the virus three times longer than does a child with normal nutritional status, and they are more susceptible to viral and bacterial superinfection. A study in Nigeria found a mortality rate of 26 percent, with respiratory complications accounting for more than 90 percent of deaths.[75]

Vitamin A deficiency may cause some of the severe manifestations of measles that occur in malnourished hosts. As mentioned previously, vitamin A is essential for maintenance of epithelial surfaces and for the synthesis of the ground substance of the corneal stroma. The striking occurrence of postmeasles blindness in approximately 1 percent of all children with measles in developing countries demonstrates the critical role of vitamin A metabolism in the malnourished host. Vitamin A supplementation in patients with measles in developing countries is associated with significantly decreased morbidity and mortality rates.[89, 112] Vitamin A–supplemented patients demonstrated increased serum concentrations of IgG and faster resolution of virus-induced lymphopenia compared with controls, suggesting an increased immunoresponsiveness to the disease. Hyporetinemia is associated with increased severity of measles,[89] but the relationship between cause and effect is unclear. In the case of malnutrition, exhaustion of hepatic stores accounts for decreased retinol and may predispose to severe measles. Alternatively, hepatic stores of retinol may be mobilized inadequately during severe measles.

Vaccination is an extremely important tool in preventing measles and its associated infections. Often, tuberculosis and malnutrition are considered contraindications for administering measles vaccination. Unlike the natural measles infection, the attenuated virus has no immunosuppressive effect and, thus, is unlikely to activate latent tuberculosis.[29] Several studies in undernourished children have shown high rates of seroconversion to the measles vaccine, except in cases of severe protein-calorie malnutrition, thus indicating the efficacy of immunization against measles in undernourished children.[27, 60]

BACTERIAL INFECTION

Bacteremia, the most dreaded infective complication of severe malnutrition, varies in incidence between different studies from 2 to 31 percent. Most commonly, bacteremia is caused by gram-negative enteric bacilli, especially *Salmonella* spp. and *E. coli*, as well as the common organisms that infect normal hosts. Malnourished patients with bacteremia have an increased risk for organ failure and mortality compared with patients with adequate nutrition. Recent studies in rats[203] suggest that malnutrition leads to decreased antioxidant stores in the liver, causing an accelerated release of hepatic oxygen free radicals in response to insult. This finding may explain the mechanism of increased organ failure in malnourished patients with bacteremia. Malnutrition also may modify the response of the immune system to bacterial infections and increase the risk for development of long-term sequelae. In a study of Bangladeshi children with antecedent group A β-hemolytic streptococcal throat infections, poor nutritional status was associated with an increased risk for developing rheumatic fever.[275]

Recent research has examined the association between malnutrition and *Helicobacter pylori* infection. A study in Colombian children found an increased incidence of *H. pylori* infection in children with lower consumption of fruits and vegetables, vitamin C, and β-carotene.[92] Because *H. pylori* is associated with depressed gastric acid secretion and loss of the gastric acid barrier, it predisposes hosts to enteric infections and may exacerbate malnutrition. One study demonstrated decreased weight for age in infants with sustained *H. pylori* infections compared with uninfected controls.[59]

PARASITIC INFECTION

Parasitic disease in humans has been estimated to affect more than 1 billion people, particularly children who are living in developing countries in Africa, Asia, and Latin America, where protein-calorie malnutrition is endemic. Unfortunately, the same conditions of poverty, overcrowding, and inadequate sanitation that are associated with parasitic infections also are associated with people who are at the highest risk for malnutrition. A particularly vulnerable time for children appears to be from 4 months until approximately 5 years of age. During this period, the transition from breast-feeding to a home diet occurs, and the exposure to disease in the environment increases. Parasitic diseases may reduce intake, interfere with absorption from the intestine, or cause increased losses of nutrients from the body. Parasitic infection also can increase body nitrogen losses through increased intestinal losses of mucus or albumin, through blood loss, or by interference with protein absorption. Evidence suggests that parasitic infections in humans may reduce voluntary food intake by immunologic mechanisms that cause anorexia. Zwingenberger and associates[277] found elevated levels of TNF and cachectin in humans infected with *Schistosoma mansoni,* which normalized after treatment.

Schistosoma hematobium causes urinary schistosomiasis and is endemic in 52 African and eastern Mediterranean countries. *S. mansoni* and *Schistosoma japonicum* cause intestinal schistosomiasis. *S. mansoni* is endemic in Africa, the Middle East, and a few countries in South America and the Caribbean. Schistosomiasis is of major importance in tropical areas because it causes both reversible and irreversible damage to the urinary and intestinal tracts. Schistosomiasis has been implicated as a major contributor to the two most important forms of malnutrition in the Third World: protein-calorie malnutrition and iron-deficiency anemia. Both the larval and adult stages of the infection can alter nutritional status by reducing food and nutrient intake, by increasing nutrient excretion (mainly through blood loss, vomiting, diarrhea), or by altering nutrient metabolism within the body.

S. hematobium infection is characterized by hematuria and proteinuria. Infected subjects had mean hemoglobin levels 0.9 to 1.3 g/dL lower than those of uninfected controls from their areas. The daily urinary protein losses in urinary schistosomiasis are an average of 1 g/day when compared in multicultural studies. *S. hematobium* infection may cause splenomegaly and hepatomegaly. Splenomegaly may be related to increased destruction of erythrocytes and can predispose to anemia, whereas hepatomegaly may alter nutrient metabolism. Both hepatomegaly and splenomegaly are reversible with adequate treatment.[243]

S. mansoni infection is associated with blood loss in the stool. Farid and associates[76] estimated the daily fecal blood loss in seven chronically infected Egyptian patients to be equivalent to 3.3 mg/day of iron (range, 0.6 to 6.7 mg/day). These iron losses are sufficient to produce anemia if persistent and if the daily intake of iron is not adequate. Cross-cultural studies involving children with *S. mansoni* infection revealed no difference in anthropomorphic measurements between infected and uninfected children; however, severe infection resulted in significantly lower height for age and skin fold thickness than did milder or no infection. Some strategies for treating schistosomiasis address only the most heavily infected children and disregard those with mild infections; however, increasing evidence indicates that mild and moderate infections also have deleterious effects on childhood nutrition. A double-blind, placebo-controlled trial in Brazilian schoolchildren demonstrated that treatment of mild to moderate intensity *S. mansoni* infections was associated with improvement in height, weight, and BMI in boys.[11]

S. japonicum effects are similar to those of *S. mansoni*; however, they tend to be more severe because *S. japonicum* produces 10 times as many eggs per worm pair as does *S. mansoni*. Multiple cross-cultural studies in the Philippines and China report that the presence and intensity of *S. japonicum* infection are related directly to reduced arm circumference, skin fold thickness, height, weight, and weight-for-height ratios.[243]

Hookworms and *Trichuris* spp. are associated with significant intestinal blood losses. Foo[83] showed that children with hookworm infection were on average 1 kg lighter and 2.4 cm shorter than were their uninfected counterparts. These children also had hemoglobin levels 1.1 g/dL lower than those of hookworm-free children. *Ascaris lumbricoides* infection has been shown to interfere with the absorption of fat and is associated with reduced weight and height, decreased vitamin A and carotenoid concentrations, and reduced serum concentrations of albumin and vitamin C.[104] As well as reducing fat absorption, both *Giardia intestinalis* and *A. lumbricoides* reduce intestinal lactase activity, resulting in lactose intolerance. *Strongyloides stercoralis* infection is associated with a protein-losing enteropathy resulting in significant hypoalbuminemia. To a lesser degree, *Giardia lamblia* has been associated with a protein-losing enteropathy without hypoalbuminemia.[243] Several recent studies[53, 173] have demonstrated an association between infection with *Cryptosporidium parvum* and poor linear growth in children, with more marked and lasting effects seen with younger age at infection.

DIARRHEAL DISEASE

Disease of the intestinal tract is the most obvious link between the mutually aggravating conditions of infection and malnutrition. Historically, diarrhea has been a primary cause of childhood morbidity and mortality in developing countries. Poor nutrition increases susceptibility to diarrhea, and, in turn, diarrhea contributes to deteriorating nutrition. Overcrowding and poor sanitation, conditions that coexist with poverty, also act synergistically with malnutrition to enhance the risk for and morbidity of diarrhea. Steps to improve overall general nutrition and to provide oral rehydration therapy in acute situations can contribute to decreasing diarrheal disease and its effects.

The risk for developing diarrheal disease appears to increase proportionately with the degree of wasting. A study of children in the Sudan[131] demonstrated that mild to moderate wasting was associated with a 9 percent increased risk for diarrhea, severe wasting with a 34 percent increased risk, and very severe wasting with a 50 percent increased risk compared with normally nourished controls. Gracey[94] has suggested that protein-calorie malnutrition predisposes to chronic diarrhea in malnourished children by causing changes in the intestinal mucosa. The changes include thinning of the gut wall, flattening of the intestinal villi, inflammatory infiltration of the lamina propria, and alteration of the enterocytes from columnar to cuboidal or squamous. The gastric mucosa also is abnormal in malnourished states. Chronic gastritis has been noted in Indonesian children in association with a reduction of secretion of gastric acid. This condition, in turn, may lead to heavy bacterial infestation of the upper gut. The changes seen in the gastrointestinal tracts of children with malnutrition may account for their altered susceptibility to various pathogenic organisms. A cohort study of children in Bangladesh revealed that shigellosis and cholera were common causes of diarrhea in severely malnourished children, whereas rotavirus was seen more often in well-nourished children with diarrhea.[67] Lower socioeconomic status and increased exposure to bacterial pathogens in malnourished children also may play a role in this epidemiology.

The mechanisms of nutrient loss in diarrhea that lead to malnutrition include maldigestion resulting in insufficient breakdown of substrates, malabsorption characterized by inefficient uptake, and excessive wastage of nutrients from the body. Bile salt pool depletion and impaired micelle formation in malnutrition cause steatorrhea. Carbohydrate intolerance and malabsorption occur partly because of bacterial overgrowth. All of these mechanisms act synergistically with viral, bacterial, and parasitic agents to exacerbate the ill effects of malnutrition on the individual.[105, 236] Nutritional restitution is of vital importance and a key factor in survival. It may be initiated through oral feedings or by a modified parenteral route in those children who are unable to tolerate oral feedings. Ahmed and coworkers[4] recently tested a protocol for treating severely malnourished patients with diarrhea that emphasized oral rehydration, immediate refeeding, routine micronutrient supplementation, and broad-spectrum antibiotics. A 47 percent reduction in mortality rates was observed compared with treatment with the conventional protocol, which focused on immediate parenteral rehydration and delayed feeding without routine micronutrient supplementation.

Nonenteral infections, such as measles, pneumonia, septicemia, and meningitis, as well as severe dehydration and severe protein-calorie malnutrition, are major risk factors for mortality in diarrheal diseases. Measures such as correction of fluid and electrolyte imbalance, treatment of associated infections, and nutritional restitution have been shown to reduce the risk of mortality from diarrhea.[206] Several studies have suggested that breast-feeding and immunization against major pathogens (measles, rotavirus, cholera) serve a protective role in reducing the incidence of morbidity and mortality from diarrhea.[35, 109, 261] Important steps, such as improving water quality and availability, ensuring proper food and personal hygiene, controlling zoonotic reservoirs, and improving waste disposal and sanitation, will minimize transmission of pathogens to those individuals at risk.[105, 236]

RESPIRATORY INFECTION

In the underdeveloped world, acute respiratory infections rank with diarrheal disease as a leading cause of morbidity and mortality. In developing countries, acute respiratory infections account for approximately 28 percent of childhood deaths and are even more frequent than are diarrheal episodes. The annual incidence of pneumonia for children younger than 5 years of age in industrialized countries is 3 to 4 percent, compared with 10 to 20 percent in most developing countries. This increased incidence of lower respiratory infection likely relates to the increased incidence of malnutrition in these areas. Malnourished infants are 10 to 20 times as likely to contract pneumonia as are children of normal weight for age.[109] A prospective study of Kenyan children[227] demonstrated an association among poor nutritional status, decreased delayed-type hypersensitivity responsiveness, and increased risk for acquiring acute respiratory infection, which suggests that the effect of nutritional status on susceptibility to acute respiratory infection may be mediated by cellular immune function.

Severe complications, such as empyema and bronchiectasis, also are more likely to occur in the face of nutritional deficiencies. A community-based study in the Philippines clearly demonstrated that malnutrition was the most important determinant of mortality associated with respiratory disease.[254] Such evidence supports WHO recommendations that in areas of prevalent malnutrition the use of antibiotic therapy be determined on the basis of clinical signs that can be recognized by minimally trained health care workers.[247] The presentation of a child with cough, chest indrawing, inability to drink, or a respiratory rate of more than 50 breaths per minute meets the requirement for antimicrobial therapy.

The World Bank Health Sector Review on Acute Respiratory Infections suggested that the most cost-effective interventions to reduce mortality from respiratory infections are case management, promotion of breast-feeding, vaccination against childhood communicable diseases, reduction of malnutrition, and pneumococcal vaccination. Reduction in malnutrition probably is the most important preventive intervention because mortality correlates directly with nutritional status. Other studies also have stressed the importance of vitamin A supplementation in malnourished children, improving access to health care services, adequate housing, and proper waste management in reducing the transmission and development of acute respiratory diseases in children.[109, 255, 256, 259]

Prophylaxis and Immunization

The link between malnutrition and infection must be considered from both biologic and social viewpoints. Strategies for improving the control of disease in the developing world have been reviewed by Keusch and Scrimshaw.[126] Immediate interventions include immunizations, oral rehydration programs, promotion of breast-feeding, adequate weaning foods with increased protein, continued feeding during infection, nutrient fortification, and growth monitoring. Complex measures such as improved sanitation and general education are important long-term goals. Although data are far from complete, general information indicates that virtually every immunization program among populations with malnourished children has been successful.[114] Unfortunately, adequate studies to define the extent of immunization failure in malnourished populations have not been performed. Studies in Haiti have suggested that immunization schedules can be adjusted in less developed countries to maximize the beneficial effect.[105] Their observations confirmed that immunologic response is independent of nutritional status. The most important factor for seroconversion is the absence of passively acquired maternal antibodies.

Several studies were undertaken to find the effect of protein-calorie malnutrition on the immune response to immunization. Seth and associates[225] evaluated cell-mediated immune responses after BCG immunization in Indian school children with varying nutritional status. Demonstration of normal cell-mediated immune responses correlated positively with adequate nutrition. Cell-mediated immune responses to purified protein derivative waned more rapidly in malnourished than in normal individuals. These studies suggest that the timing of reimmunization with BCG must be planned on an individual basis in relation to the nutritional status of the child. Several investigators have concluded that the immune response to immunization remains unimpaired in balanced mild to moderate malnutrition; however, severe forms of protein-calorie malnutrition, especially when maintained for long periods, may affect negatively the ability to seroconvert after immunization.[2, 3, 60, 220] These results suggest that immunization of the mildly to moderately malnourished child may afford him or her degrees of protection comparable to those of the well-nourished child. The severely malnourished child, however, may have minimal, if any, response to immunization. Further research is needed to improve the immune response after vaccinations in children with severe protein-calorie malnutrition. Of even greater import, no data are available to answer important questions regarding the possible harmful effects of live viral vaccines in the malnourished child.

One form of immunologic reconstitution has been attempted in malnourished children to determine whether the frequency and severity of infectious episodes could be affected. Jose and associates[122] gave transfer factor to 40 Australian aboriginal children between 2 and 46 months of age who were hospitalized with acute infection. Many also suffered from protein-calorie malnutrition. These and a control group of 35 children were followed for at least 12 months. Children treated with transfer factor experienced significantly fewer episodes of diarrheal disease, but no protection against chest, middle ear, or skin infection could be demonstrated. Flo and associates[82] showed that malnourished rats, after oral immunization with cholera toxin, had diminished levels of total IgA in intestinal fluid as well as an impaired ability to neutralize cholera toxin in vitro when compared with well-nourished controls. This finding suggests that oral immunizations have a diminished capacity to evoke an immune response when compared with systemic immunizations in severe malnutrition.

Conclusion

Attempts to reduce the mortality and morbidity referable to infection in the malnourished individual must be predicated upon a more comprehensive understanding of this process than that presently available; the need for further research is clear. In the interim, every effort must be expended to control infection and improve nutrition throughout the world. To do so requires education, improvement in sanitation, improvement in prenatal care to reduce the incidence of prematurity, and either greater access to appropriate food supplies or education directed toward improving the utilization of food of appropriate nutritional quality when it already is available.

REFERENCES

1. Abrams, B. F., and Laros, R. K., Jr.: Prepregnancy weight, weight gain, and birth weight. Am. J. Obstet. Gynecol. *154*:503–509, 1986.
2. Adeiga, A., Akinosho, R. O., and Onyewuche, J.: Evaluation of immune response in infants with different nutritional status: Vaccinated against tuberculosis, measles, and poliomyelitis. J. Trop. Pediatr. *40*:345–350, 1994.
3. Ahmed, F., Jones, D. B., and Jackson, A.: Effect of under-nutrition on the immune response to rotavirus infection in mice. Ann. Nutr. Metab. *34*:21–31, 1990.
4. Ahmed, T., Ali, M., Ullah, M. M., et al.: Mortality in severely malnourished children with diarrhoea and use of a standardised management protocol. Lancet *353*:1919–1922, 1999.
5. Alverdy, J., Chi, H. S., and Sheldon, G. F.: The effect of parenteral nutrition on gastrointestinal immunity. The importance of enteral stimulation. Ann. Surg. *202*:681–684, 1985.
6. Andelman, M. B., and Sered, B. R.: Utilization of dietary iron by term infants: A study of 1048 infants from a low socioeconomic population. Am. J. Dis. Child. *111*:45–55, 1966.
7. Anderson, D. C., Krishna, G. S., Hughes, J. B., et al.: Impaired polymorphonuclear leukocyte motility in malnourished infants: Relationship to functional abnormalities of cell adherence. J. Lab. Clin. Med. *101*:881–895, 1983.
8. Arbeter, A., Echeverri, L., Franco, D., et al.: Nutrition and infection. Fed. Proc. *30*:1421–1428, 1971.
9. Arnalich, F., Martinez, P., Hernanz, A., et al.: Altered concentrations of appetite regulators may contribute to the development and maintenance of HIV-associated wasting. AIDS *11*:1129–1134, 1997.
10. Ascoli, W., Guzman, M. A., Scrimshaw, N. S., et al.: Nutrition and infection: Field study in Guatemalan villages, 1959–1964. IV. Death of infants and preschool children. Arch. Environ. Health *15*:439–449, 1967.
11. Assis, A. M., Barreto, M. L., Prado, M. S., et al.: *Schistosoma mansoni* infection and nutritional status in schoolchildren: A randomized, double-blind trial in northeastern Brazil. Am. J. Clin. Nutr. *68*:1247–1253, 1998.
12. Averhoff, F., Mahoney, F., Coleman, P., et al.: Immunogenicity of hepatitis B Vaccines. Implications for persons at occupational risk of hepatitis B virus infection. Am. J. Prev. Med. *15*:1–8, 1998.
13. Babameto, G., and Kotler, D. P.: Malnutrition in HIV infection. Gastroenterol. Clin. North Am. *26*:393–415, 1997.
14. Barrett-Connor, E.: Bacterial infection and sickle cell anemia: An analysis of 250 infections in 166 patients and a review of the literature. Medicine (Baltimore) *50*:97–112, 1971.
15. Barton, R. G.: Immune-enhancing enteral formulas: Are they beneficial in critically ill patients? Nutr. Clin. Pract. *12*:51–62, 1997.
16. Bauchner, H., Leventhal, J. M., and Shapiro, E. D.: Studies of breast-feeding and infections. J.A.M.A. *256*:887–892, 1986.
17. Baum, M. K., Shor-Posner, G., Lai, S., et al.: High risk of HIV-related mortality is associated with selenium deficiency. J. Acquir. Immune Defic. Syndr. Hum. Retrovirol. *15*:370–374, 1997.
18. Baum, M. K., and Shor-Posner, G.: Micronutrient status in relationship to mortality in HIV-1 disease. Nutr. Rev. *56*:S135–S139, 1998.
19. Baum, M. K., Shor-Posner, G., and Campa, A.: Zinc status in human immunodeficiency virus infection. J. Nutr. *130*(Suppl. 5):1421S–1423S, 2000.
20. Beale, R. J., Bryg, D. J., and Bihari, D. J.: Immunonutrition in the critically ill: A systematic review of clinical outcome. Crit. Care Med. *27*:2799–2805, 1999.
21. Beck, M. A., and Levander, O. A.: Host nutritional status and its effect on a viral pathogen. J. Infect. Dis. *182*(Suppl. 1):S93–S96, 2000.
22. Beisel, W. R.: Vitamins and the immune system. Ann. N. Y. Acad. Sci. *585*:5–8, 1990.
23. Bendinelli, M., Ruschi, A., and Santopadre, G.: Replicazione virale e produzione di interferone intopi a dieta carente infettai con virus mengo. Riv. Ital. Ig. *25*:191–204, 1965.
24. Berhane, R., Bagenda, D., Marum, L., et al.: Growth failure as a prognostic indicator of mortality in pediatric HIV infection. Pediatrics *100*:E7, 1997.
25. Bernstein, P. S., and Divon, M. Y.: Etiologies of fetal growth restriction. Clin. Obstet. Gynecol. *40*:723–729, 1997.
26. Beveridge, W. I. B.: Immunity to viruses. *In* Betts, A. O., and York, C. J. (eds.): Viral and Rickettsial Infections of Animals. Vol. 1. New York, Academic Press, 1967.
27. Bhaskaram, P., Madhusudan, J., Radhakrishna, K. V., et al.: Immunological response to measles vaccination in poor communities. Hum. Nutr. Clin. Nutr. *40C*:295–300, 1986.
28. Bhaskaram, P., Hemalatha, P., and Rao, K. V.: BCG vaccination in malnourished child population. Indian Pediatr. *29*:39–44, 1992.
29. Bhaskaram, P.: The vicious cycle of malnutrition-infection with special reference to diarrhea, measles, and tuberculosis. Natl. Inst. Nutr. Indian Council Med. Res. *29*:805–813, 1992.
30. Boeck, M. A., Chin, C., and Cunningham-Rundles, S.: Altered immune function in a morbidly obese pediatric population. Ann. N. Y. Acad. Sci. *587*:253–256, 1990.
31. Boyd, F. M., and Edwards, H. M., Jr.: The effect of dietary protein on the course of various infections in the chick. J. Infect. Dis. *112*:53–56, 1963.
32. Braude-Heller, A., Ratbalsam, I., and Elbinger, R.: Clinical aspects of hunger disease in children. *In* Winick, M. (ed.): Hunger Disease. New York, John Wiley & Sons, 1959, pp. 45–68.
33. Brodie, S. B., Sands, K. E., Gray, J. E., et al.: Occurrence of nosocomial bloodstream infections in six neonatal intensive care units. Pediatr. Infect. Dis. J. *19*:56–65, 2000.
34. Brown, K. H., Gaffar, A., and Alamgir, S. M.: Xerophthalmia, protein-calorie malnutrition, and infections in children. J. Pediatr. *95*:651–656, 1979.
35. Brown, K. R., Black, G., Lopez, R., et al.: Infant feeding practices and their relationship with diarrheal and other diseases in Huascar (Lima), Peru. Pediatrics *83*:31–40, 1989.
36. Brundtland, G. H.: Nutrition and infection: malnutrition and mortality in public health. Nutr. Rev. *58*:S1–S4, 2000.
37. Burger, H., Kovacs, A., Weiser, B., et al.: Maternal serum vitamin A levels are not associated with mother-to-child transmission of HIV-1 in the United States. J. Acquir. Immune Defic. Syndr. Hum. Retrovirol. *14*:321–326, 1997.
38. Burns, D. N., FitzGerald, G., Semba, R., et al.: Vitamin A deficiency and other nutritional indices during pregnancy in human immunodeficiency virus infection: Prevalence, clinical correlates, and outcome. Women and Infants Transmission Study Group. Clin. Infect. Dis. *29*:328–334, 1999.
39. Campa, A., Shor-Posner, G., Indacochea, F., et al.: Mortality risk in selenium-deficient HIV-positive children. J. Acquir. Immune Defic. Syndr. Hum. Retrovirol. *20*:508–513, 1999.
40. Carbonnel, F., Beaugerie, L., Abou Rached, A., et al.: Macronutrient intake and malabsorption in HIV infection: a comparison with other malabsorptive states. Gut *41*:805–810, 1997.
41. Carter, J. P., Kattab, A., Abd-el-hadi, K., et al.: Chromium (3) in hypoglycemia and in impaired glucose utilization in kwashiorkor. Am. J. Clin. Nutr. *21*:195–202, 1968.
42. Carver, J. D., Pimentel, B., Cox, W. I., et al.: Dietary nucleotide effects upon immune function in infants. Pediatrics *88*:359–363, 1991.

43. Chalmers, T. C.: Effects of ascorbic acid on the common cold. Am. J. Med. *58*:532–536, 1975.
44. Chandra, R. K.: Antibody formation in first and second generation offspring of nutritionally deprived rats. Science *190*:289–290, 1975.
45. Chandra, R. K.: Fetal malnutrition and postnatal immunocompetence. Am. J. Dis. Child. *129*:450–454, 1975.
46. Chandra, R. K.: Prospective studies of the effect of breastfeeding on incidence of infection and allergy. Acta Paediatr. Scand. *68*:691–694, 1979.
47. Chandra, R. K.: Immune response in overnutrition. Cancer Res. *41*:3795–3796, 1981.
48. Chandra, R. K., and Wadhwa, M.: Nutritional modulation of intestinal mucosal immunity. Immunol. Invest. *18*:119–126, 1989.
49. Chandra, R. K.: Micronutrients and immune functions. Ann. N. Y. Acad. Sci. *587*:9–16, 1990.
50. Chandra, R. K.: Immunocompetence is a sensitive and functional barometer of nutritional status. Acta Paediatr. Scand. *374*(Suppl.): S129–S132, 1991.
51. Chandra, R. K.: Nutrition and immunity: Lessons from the past and new insights into the future. Am. J. Clin. Nutr. *53*:1087–1101, 1991.
52. Chandra, R. K.: Nutrition and immunoregulation: Significance for host resistance to tumors and infectious diseases in humans and rodents. J. Nutr. *122*(Suppl. 3):754–757, 1992.
53. Checkley, W., Epstein, L. D., Gilman, R. H., et al.: Effects of *Cryptosporidium parvum* infection in Peruvian children: Growth faltering and subsequent catch-up growth. Am. J. Epidemiol. *148*:497–506, 1998.
54. Childhood Malnutrition. World Health Organization Fact Sheet No. 119, reviewed November 1996. Available at http://www.who.ch/
55. Cohen, S., and Hansen, J. D. L.: Metabolism of albumin and γ-globulin in kwashiorkor. Clin. Sci. *23*:351–359, 1962.
56. Cunningham, A. S.: Morbidity in breast fed and artificially fed infants. J. Pediatr. *95*:685–689, 1979.
57. Cunningham-Rundels, S., Bockman R. S., Lin, A. et al.: Physiological and pharmacological effects of zinc on immune response. Ann. N. Y. Acad. Sci. *587*:113–122, 1990.
58. Dai, D., and Walker, W. A.: Protective nutrients and bacterial colonization in the immature human gut. Adv. Pediatr. *46*:353–382, 1999.
59. Dale, A., Thomas, J. E., Darboe, M. K., et al.: *Helicobacter pylori* infection, gastric acid secretion, and infant growth. J. Pediatr. Gastroenterol. Nutr. *26*:393–397, 1998.
60. Dao, H., Delisle, H., and Fournier, P.: Anthropometric status, serum prealbumin level, and immune response to measles vaccination in Mali children. J. Trop. Pediatr. *38*:179–184, 1992.
61. Davies, W. L., Smith, S. C., Pond, W. L., et al.: Effect of dietary restriction on susceptibility of mice to infection with Theiler's GDVII virus. Proc. Soc. Exp. Med. *72*:528–531, 1949.
62. Deitch, E. A.: The management of burns. N. Engl. J. Med. *323*:1249–1253, 1990.
63. Delafuente, J. C.: Nutrients and immune response. Rheum. Dis. Clin. North Am. *17*:203–211, 1991.
64. De la Fuente, M., and Munoz, M. L.: Impairment of phagocytic process in macrophages from young and old mice by protein malnutrition. Ann. Nutr. Metab. *36*:41–47, 1992.
65. Del Rio, M., Ruedas, G., Medina, S., et al.: Improvement by several antioxidants of macrophage function in vitro. Life Sci. *63*:871–881, 1998.
66. Derganc, M.: Present trends in fluid therapy, metabolic care, and prevention of infection in burned children. Crit. Care Med. *21*:S395–S399, 1993.
67. Dewan, N., Faruque, A. S., and Fuchs, G. J.: Nutritional status and diarrhoeal pathogen in hospitalized children in Bangladesh. Acta Paediatr. *87*:627–630, 1998.
68. Dourov, N.: Thymic atrophy and immune deficiency in malnutrition. Curr. Top. Pathol. *75*:127–150, 1986.
69. Dudley, L., Hussey, G., Huskissen, J., et al.: Vitamin A status, other risk factors and acute respiratory infection morbidity in children. S. Afr. Med. J. *87*:65–70, 1997.
70. Edelman, R.: Infant nutrition and immunity. Ann. N. Y. Acad. Sci. *587*:232–235, 1990.
71. Effect of breastfeeding on infant and child mortality due to infectious diseases in less developed countries: a pooled analysis. WHO Collaborative Study Team on the Role of Breastfeeding on the Prevention of Infant Mortality. Lancet *355*:451–455, 2000.
72. Erickson, K. L.: Dietary fat modulation of immune response. Int. J. Immunopharmacol. *8*:529–543, 1986.
73. Erickson, K. L., Adams, D. A., and Scibienski, R. J.: Dietary fatty acid modulation of murine B-cell responsiveness. J. Nutr. *116*:1830–1840, 1986.
74. Espinoza, F., Paniagua, M., Hallander, H., et al.: Rotavirus infections in young Nicaraguan children. Pediatr. Infect. Dis. J. *16*:564–571, 1997.
75. Fagbule, D., and Orifunmishe, F.: Measles and childhood mortality in semi-urban Nigeria. Afr. J. Med. Sci. *17*:181–185, 1988.
76. Farid, Z., Bassily, S., Schulert, A. R., et al.: Blood loss in chronic *S. mansoni* infection in Egyptian farmers. Trans. R. Soc. Trop. Med. Hyg. *61*:289–314, 1967.
77. Fasol, R., Schindler, M., Schumacher, B., et al.: The influence of obesity on perioperative morbidity: Retrospective study of 502 aortocoronary bypass operations. Thorac. Cardiovasc. Surg. *40*:126–129, 1992.
78. Fawzi, W. W., Msamanga, G., Hunter, D., et al.: Influence of nutritional and haemoglobin status on malaria infection in children. Indian J. Pediatr. *62*:321–326, 1995.
79. Fawzi, W. W., Msamanga, G., Hunter, D., et al.: Randomized trial of vitamin supplements in relation to vertical transmission of HIV-1 in Tanzania. J. Acquir. Immune Defic. Syndr. *23*:246–254, 2000.
80. Fields-Gardner, C., and Ayoob, K. T.: Position of the American Dietetic Association and Dietitians of Canada: Nutrition intervention in the care of persons with human immunodeficiency virus infection. J. Am. Diet. Assoc. *100*:708–717, 2000.
81. Fiser, R. H., Jr., Denniston, J. C., McGann, V. G., et al.: Altered immune functions in hypercholesterolemic monkeys. Infect. Immunol. *8*:105–109, 1973.
82. Flo, J., Roux, M., and Massouh, E.: Deficient induction of the immune response to oral immunization with cholera toxin in malnourished rats during suckling. Infect. Immun. *62*:4948–4954, 1994.
83. Foo, L.: Hookworm infection and protein-energy malnutrition: Transverse evidence from two Malaysian ecological groups. Trop. Geogr. Med. *42*:8–12, 1990.
84. Forceville, X., Vitoux, D., Gauzit, R., et al.: Selenium, systemic immune response syndrome, sepsis, and outcome in critically ill patients. Crit. Care Med. *26*:1536–1544, 1998.
85. Foster, C., Jones, J. H., Henle, W., et al.: Comparative effects of vitamin B_1 deficiency and restriction of food intake on the response of mice to the Lansing strain of poliomyelitis virus, as determined by the paired feeding technique. J. Exp. Med. *80*:257–264, 1944.
86. Gainsford, T., Willson, T. A., Metcalf, D., et al.: Leptin can induce proliferation, differentiation, and functional activation of hemopoietic cells. Proc. Natl. Acad. Sci. U. S. A. *93*:14564–14568, 1996.
87. Gallagher, K., Matarazzo, W., and Gray, I.: Trace metal modification of lymphocyte transformation in vitro. Fed. Proc. *37*:377, 1978.
88. Gernaat, H. B., Dechering, W. H., and Voorhoeve, H. W.: Mortality in severe protein-energy malnutrition at Nchelenge, Zambia. J. Trop. Pediatr. *44*:211–217, 1998.
89. Gerster, H.: Vitamin A: Functions, dietary requirements and safety in humans. Int. J. Vitam. Nutr. Res. *67*:71–90, 1997.
90. Gilio, A. E., Stape, A., Pereira, C. R., et al.: Risk factors for nosocomial infections in a critically ill pediatric population: A 25-month prospective cohort study. Infect. Control Hosp. Epidemiol. *21*:340–342, 2000.
91. Good, R. A., Fernandes, E. J., Yunis, W. C., et al.: Nutritional deficiency, immunologic function and disease. Am. J. Pathol. *84*:599–614, 1976.
92. Goodman, K. J., Correa, P., Tengana Aux, H. J., et al.: Nutritional factors and *Helicobacter pylori* infection in Colombian children. J. Pediatr. Gastroenterol. Nutr. *25*:507–515, 1997.
93. Gordon, J. E., Ascoli, W., Mata, L. J., et al.: Nutrition and infection: Field study in Guatemalan villages, 1959–1964. Arch. Environ. Health *16*:424–437, 1968.
94. Gracey, M.: Chronic diarrhoea in protein-energy malnutrition. Paediatr. Indones. *21*:235–239, 1981.
95. Greenberg, B. L., Semba, R. D., Vink, P. E., et al.: Vitamin A deficiency and maternal-infant transmissions of HIV in two metropolitan areas in the United States. AIDS *11*:325–332, 1997.
96. Greenwood, B. M., Bradley, A. K., Blakebrough, I. S., et al.: The immune response to a meningococcal polysaccharide vaccine in an African village. Trans. R. Soc. Trop. Med Hyg. *74*:340–346, 1980.
97. Harris, M. C., and Douglas, S. D.: Nutritional influence on neonatal infections in animal models and man. Ann. N. Y. Acad. Sci. *587*:246–255, 1990.
98. Harris, M. C., and Douglas, S. D.: Nutritional modulation of phagocyte function with special emphasis on the newborn. Indian J. Pediatr. *57*:147–158, 1990.
99. Heideman, M., and Bengtsson, A.: The immunologic response to thermal injury. World J. Surg. *16*:53–56, 1992.
100. Heinzerling, R. H., Nockels, C. F., Quarles, C. L., et al.: Protection of chicks against *E. coli* infections by dietary supplementation with vitamin E. Proc. Soc. Exp. Biol. Med. *146*:279–283, 1974.
101. Heise, F. H., and Martin, G. J.: Ascorbic acid metabolism in tuberculosis. Proc. Soc. Exp. Biol. Med. *34*:642–644, 1936.
102. Hemila, H.: Vitamin C and the common cold. Br. J. Nutr. *67*:3–16, 1992.
103. Hildreth, M. A., Herndon, D. N., Desai, M. H., et al.: Current treatment reduces calories required to maintain weight in pediatric patients with burns. J. Burn Care Rehabil. *11*:405–409, 1990.
104. Hlaing, T.: Ascariasis and childhood malnutrition. Parasitology *107*:S125–S136, 1993.
105. Hodges, M.: Diarrhoeal disease in early childhood: Experiences from Sierra Leone. Parasitology *107*:S37–S51, 1993.
106. Hokama, T., Yara, A., Hirayama, K., et al.: Isolation of respiratory bacterial pathogens from the throats of healthy infants fed by different methods. J. Trop. Pediatr. *45*:173–176, 1999.
107. Hori, K., Hatfield, D., Maldarelli, F., et al.: Selenium supplementation suppresses tumor necrosis factor alpha-induced human immunodeficiency virus type 1 replication in vitro. AIDS Res. Hum. Retroviruses *13*:1325–1332, 1997.
108. Houdijk, A. P., Rijnsburger, E. R., Jansen, J., et al.: Randomised trial of glutamine-enriched enteral nutrition on infectious morbidity in patients with multiple trauma. Lancet *352*:772–776, 1998.

109. Huffman, S. L., and Martin, L.: Child nutrition, birth spacing, and child mortality. Ann. N. Y. Acad. Sci. *585*:236–247, 1990.
110. Hughes, W. T., Price, R. A., Sisko, F., et al.: Protein-calorie malnutrition. Am. J. Dis. Child. *128*:44–52, 1974.
111. Humphrey, J. H., West, K. P., Jr., and Sommer, A.: Vitamin A deficiency and attributable mortality among under-5-year-olds. Bull. W. H. O. *70*:225–232, 1992.
112. Hussey, G. D., and Klein, M.: A randomized, controlled trial of vitamin A in children with severe measles. N. Engl. J. Med. *323*:160–164, 1990.
113. Hytten, S. E.: Nutritional aspects of foetal growth. *In* Nutrition and Early Growth, Sixth International Congress of Nutrition. Edinburgh, Churchill Livingstone, 1964.
114. Immune response in the malnourished child. Subcommittee on Interactions of Nutrition and Infection. Committee on International Nutrition Programs. The National Health Research Council, National Academy of Science, May 1976.
115. Jackson, T. M., and Zaman, S. N.: The in vitro effect of the thymic thymopoietin on a subpopulation of lymphocytes from severely malnourished children. Clin. Exp. Immunol. *39*:717–721, 1980.
116. Jambon, B., Ziegler, O., Maire, B., et al.: Thymulin (facteur thymique serique) and zinc contents of the thymus glands of malnourished children. Am. J. Clin. Nutr. *48*:335–342, 1988.
117. Janoff, A.: The role of iron in macrophages. J. Theoret. Biol. *7*:168–170, 1964.
118. Jedrychowski, W., Maugeri, U., Flak, E., et al.: Predisposition to acute respiratory infections among overweight preadolescent children: An epidemiologic study in Poland. Public Health *112*:189–195, 1998.
119. Jenkins, M. E., Gottschlich, M. M., and Warden, G. D.: Enteral feeding during operative procedures in thermal injuries. J. Burn Care Rehabil. *15*:199–205, 1994.
120. Jones, G., Strugnell, S. A., and DeLuca, H. F.: Current understanding of the molecular actions of vitamin D. Physiol. Rev. *78*:1193–1231, 1998.
121. Jones, P. N., Mills, E. H., and Capps, R. B.: The effect of liver disease on serum vitamin B_{12} concentrations. J. Lab. Clin. Med. *49*:910–922, 1957.
122. Jose, D. G., Ford, G., Ford, W., et al.: Therapy with parent's lymphocyte transfer factor in children with infection and malnutrition. Lancet *1*:263–265, 1976.
123. Joynson, D. H., Walker, D. M., Jacobs, A., et al.: Defect of cell-mediated immunity in patients with iron-deficiency anaemia. Lancet *2*:1058–1059, 1972.
124. Jyonouchi, H.: Nucleotide actions on humoral immune responses. J. Nutr. *124*(Suppl. 1):138S–143S, 1994.
125. Kacew, S.: Adverse effects of drugs and chemicals in breast milk on the nursing infant. J. Clin. Pharmacol. *33*:213–221, 1993.
126. Keusch, G. T., and Scrimshaw, N. S.: Selective primary health care: Strategies for control of disease in the developing world. XXIII. Control of infection to reduce the prevalence of infantile and childhood malnutrition. Rev. Infect. Dis. *8*:273–287, 1986.
127. Keusch, G. T.: Micronutrients and susceptibility to infection. Ann. N. Y. Acad. Sci. *587*:181–187, 1990.
128. Keusch, G. T.: Nutritional effects of response of children in developing countries to respiratory tract pathogens: Implications for vaccine development. Rev. Infect. Dis. *13*(Suppl. 6):S486–S491, 1991.
129. King, B. K., and Kudsk, K. A.: Can an enteral diet decrease sepsis after trauma? Adv. Surg. *31*:53–78, 1997.
130. Kolterman, O. G., Olefsky, J. M., Kurahara, C., et al.: A defect in cell-mediated immune function in insulin-resistant diabetic and obese subjects. J. Lab. Clin. Med. *96*:535–543, 1980.
131. Kossmann, J., Nestel, P., Herrera, M. G., et al.: Undernutrition in relation to childhood infections: a prospective study in the Sudan. Eur. J. Clin. Nutr. *54*:463–472, 2000.
132. Kotler, D. P.: Management of nutritional alterations and issues concerning quality of life. J. Acquir. Immune Defic. Syndr. Hum. Retrovirol. *16*(Suppl. 1):S30–S35, 1997.
133. Kotler, D. P.: Human immunodeficiency virus-related wasting: malabsorption syndromes. Semin. Oncol. *25*(Suppl. 6):70–75, 1998.
134. Kramer, T. R., and Good, R. A.: Effects of protein insufficient diets on the ability of guinea pigs to produce antigen specific MIF. Fed. Proc. *34*:829, 1975.
135. Kreiss, J.: Breastfeeding and vertical transmission of HIV-1. Acta. Paediatr. Suppl. *421*:113–117, 1997.
136. Kudsk, K. A., Carpenter, G., Petersen, S., et al.: Effect of enteral and parenteral feeding in malnourished rats with *E. coli*-hemoglobin adjuvant peritonitis. J. Surg. Res. *31*:105–110, 1981.
137. Kudsk, K. A., Stone, J. M., Carpenter, G., et al.: Enteral and parenteral feeding influences mortality after hemoglobin-*E. coli* peritonitis in normal rats. J. Trauma *23*:605–609, 1983.
138. Kulkarni, A. D., Rudolph, F. B., and Van Buren, C. T.: The role of dietary sources of nucleotides in immune function: A review. J. Nutr. *124*(Suppl. 8):1442S–1446S, 1994.
139. Lake-Bakaar, G., Quadros, E., Beidas, S., et al.: Gastric secretory failure in patients with acquired immunodeficiency syndrome (AIDS). Ann. Intern. Med. *109*:502–504, 1988.
140. Lanphear, B. P., Hall, C. B., Black, J., et al.: Risk factors for the early acquisition of human herpesvirus 6 and human herpesvirus 7 infections in children. Pediatr. Infect. Dis. J. *17*:792–795, 1998.
141. Latham, M. C.: Protein-energy malnutrition: Its epidemiology and control. J. Environ. Pathol. Toxicol. Oncol. *10*:168–169, 1990.
142. Laurell, C. B.: Metal-binding plasma proteins and cation transport. *In* Putnam, F. W. (ed.): The Plasma Proteins, I. New York, Academic Press, 1960, pp. 229–264.
143. Lehmann, H., Huntsman, R. G., and Ager, J. A. M.: The hemoglobinopathies and thalassemia. *In* Stanbury, J. B., Wyngaarden, J. B., and Fredrickson, D. S. (eds.): The Metabolic Basis of Inherited Disease. 2nd ed. New York, McGraw-Hill, 1966, pp. 1100–1136.
144. Levine, O. S., Farley, M., Harrison, L. H., et al.: Risk factors for invasive pneumococcal disease in children: a population-based case-control study in North America. Pediatrics *103*:E28, 1999.
145. Li, J., Kudsk, K. A., Gocinski, B., et al.: Effects of parenteral and enteral nutrition on gut-associated lymphoid tissue. J. Trauma *39*:44–51, 1995.
146. Lindenbaum, J.: Malabsorption during and after recovery from acute intestinal infection. Br. Med. J. *2*:326–329, 1965.
147. Loffreda, S., Yang, S. Q., Lin, H. Z., et al.: Leptin regulates proinflammatory immune responses. FASEB J. *12*:57–65, 1998.
148. Long, K. Z., and Santos, J. I.: Vitamins and the regulation of the immune response. Pediatr. Infect. Dis. J. *18*:283–290, 1999.
149. Lopez-Alarcon, M., Villalpando, S., and Fajardo, A.: Breast-feeding lowers the frequency and duration of acute respiratory infection and diarrhea in infants under six months of age. J. Nutr. *127*:436–443, 1997.
150. Loria, R. M., Kibrick, S., and Madge, G. E.: Infection of hypercholesterolemic mice with coxsackievirus B. J. Infect. Dis. *133*:655–662, 1976.
151. Luke, B.: Nutritional influences on fetal growth. Clin. Obstet. Gynecol. *37*:538–549, 1994.
152. Macdougall, L. G., Anderson, R., McNab, G. M., et al.: The immune response in iron-deficient children: Impaired cellular defense mechanisms with altered humoral components. J. Pediatr. *86*:833–843, 1975.
153. MacKay, H. M.: Anaemia in infancy: Its prevalence and prevention. Arch. Dis. Child. *3*:117–144, 1928.
154. Madi, K., Maeda, C. T., and Savino, W.: Thymic extracellular matrix in human malnutrition. J. Pathol. *171*:231–236, 1993.
155. Maki, P. A., and Newberne, P. M.: Dietary lipids and immune function. J. Nutr. *122*(Suppl. 3):610–614, 1992.
156. Manary, M. J., and Brewster, D. R.: Intensive nursing care of kwashiorkor in Malawi. Acta Paediatr. *89*:203–207, 2000.
157. Manson, W. L., Dijkema, H., and Klasen, J.: Alteration of wound colonization by selective intestinal decontamination in thermally injured mice. Burns *16*:166–168, 1990.
158. Martinez-Augustin, O., Boza, J. J., Navarro, J., et al.: Dietary nucleotides may influence the humoral immunity in immunocompromised children. Nutrition *13*:465–469, 1997.
159. Masson, P. L., and Heremans, J. F.: Studies on lactoferrin, the iron-binding protein of secretions. *In* Peeters, H. (ed.): Protides of the Biological Fluids. Vol. 14. Amsterdam, Elsevier, 1967, pp. 115–124.
160. Mata, L. J.: Malnutrition-infection interactions in the tropics. Am. J. Trop. Med. Hyg. *24*:564–574, 1975.
161. Matoth, Y., Zamir, R., and Bar-shani, S.: Studies on folic acid in infancy. II. Folic and folinic acid blood levels in infants with diarrhea, malnutrition and infection. Pediatrics *33*:694–699, 1964.
162. McFarlane, H.: Cell-mediated immunity in protein-calorie malnutrition. Lancet *2*:1146–1147, 1971.
163. McKenzie, R. C., Rafferty, T. S., and Beckett, G. J.: Selenium: An essential element for immune function. Immunol. Today *19*:342–345, 1998.
164. McMurray, D. N.: Cell-mediated immunity in nutritional deficiency. Prog. Food Nutr. Sci. *8*:193–228, 1984.
165. Mertz, W.: Chromium occurrence and function in biological systems. Physiol. Rev. *49*:163–239, 1969.
166. Meydani, S. N., Hayek, M., and Coleman, L.: Influence of vitamins E and B_6 on immune response. Ann. N. Y. Acad. Sci. *585*:125–137, 1990.
167. Meydani, S. N., and Beharka, A. A.: Recent developments in vitamin E and immune response. Nutr. Rev. *56*:S49–S58, 1998.
168. Miller, J. Z., Nance, W. E., Norton, J. A., et al.: Therapeutic effect of vitamin C: A co-twin control study. J.A.M.A. *237*:248S–251S, 1977.
169. Miller, T. L., Orav, E. J., Colan, S. D., et al.: Nutritional status and cardiac mass and function in children infected with the human immunodeficiency virus. Am. J. Clin. Nutr. *66*:660–664, 1997.
170. Miller, T. L.: Nutrition in paediatric human immunodeficiency virus infection. Proc. Nutr. Soc. *59*:155–162, 2000.
171. Mishra, O. P., Agrawal, S., Ali, Z., et al.: Adenosine deaminase activity in protein-energy malnutrition. Acta Paediatr *87*:1116–1119, 1998.
172. Mitra, A. K., Alvarez, J. O., Guay-Woodford, L., et al.: Urinary retinol excretion and kidney function in children with shigellosis. Am. J. Clin. Nutr. *68*:1095–1103, 1998.
173. Molbak, K., Andersen, M., Aaby, P., et al.: Cryptosporidium infection in infancy as a cause of malnutrition: a community study from Guinea-Bissau, West Africa. Am. J. Clin. Nutr. *65*:149–152, 1997.
174. Moodley, J. R., Coetzee, N., and Hussey, G.: Risk factors for meningococcal disease in Cape Town. S. Afr. Med. J. *89*:56–59, 1999.

175. Moore, F. A., Feliciano, D. V., Andrassy, R. J., et al.: Early enteral feeding, compared with parenteral, reduces postoperative septic complications. The results of a meta-analysis. Ann. Surg. *216*:172–183, 1992.
176. Moore, S. E., Cole, T. J., Collinson, A. C., et al.: Prenatal or early postnatal events predict infectious deaths in young adulthood in rural Africa. Int. J. Epidemiol. *28*:1088–1095, 1999.
177. Muller, M. J., and Herndon, D. N.: The challenge of burns. Lancet *343*:216–220, 1994.
178. Neldner, K. H., and Hambidge, K. M.: Zinc therapy of acrodermatitis enteropathica. N. Engl. J. Med. *292*:879–882, 1975.
179. Nduati, R., John, G., Mbori-Ngacha, D., et al.: Effect of breastfeeding and formula feeding on transmission of HIV-1: A randomized clinical trial. J.A.M.A. *283*:1167–1174, 2000.
180. Neu, J., Roig, J. C., Meetze, W. H., et al.: Enteral glutamine supplementation for very low birth weight infants decreases morbidity. J. Pediatr. *131*:691–699, 1997.
181. Newberne, P. M.: Overnutrition on resistance of dogs to distemper virus. Fed. Proc. *25*:1701–1710, 1966.
182. Newburg, D. S., Peterson, J. A., Ruiz-Palacios, G. M., et al.: Role of human-milk lactadherin in protection against symptomatic rotavirus infection. Lancet *351*:1160–1164, 1998.
183. Okada, Y., Klein, N., van Saene, H. K., et al.: Small volumes of enteral feedings normalise immune function in infants receiving parenteral nutrition. J. Pediatr. Surg. *33*:16–19, 1998.
184. Okada, Y., Klein, N. J., van Saene, H. K., et al.: Bactericidal activity against coagulase-negative staphylococci is impaired in infants receiving long-term parenteral nutrition. Ann. Surg. *231*:276–281, 2000.
185. Olusi, S. O., Thurman, G. B., and Goldstein, A. L.: Effect of thymosin on T-lymphocyte rosette formation in children with kwashiorkor. Clin. Exp. Immunopathol. *15*:687–691, 1980.
186. Osawa, Y.: Ueber die Entstenung der Polymositis acuta purulenta in Japan. Beitr. Klin. Chirg. *146*:621–653, 1929.
187. Paine, R., and Coble, R. J.: Breast-feeding and infant health in a rural US community. Am. J. Dis. Child. *136*:36–38, 1980.
188. Parent, G., Chevalier, P., Zalles, L., et al.: In vitro lymphocyte-differentiating effects of thymulin (Zn-FTS) on lymphocyte subpopulations of severely malnourished children. Am. J. Clin. Nutr. *60*:274–278, 1994.
189. Pathania, V., Syal, N., Pathak, C. M., et al.: Vitamin E suppresses the induction of reactive oxygen species release by lipopolysaccharide, interleukin-1beta and tumor necrosis factor-alpha in rat alveolar macrophages. J. Nutr. Sci. Vitaminol. (Tokyo) *45*:675–686, 1999.
190. Pekarek, R. S., Hauer, E. C., Rayfield, E. J., et al.: Relationship between serum chromium concentrations and glucose utilization in normal and infected subjects. Diabetes *24*:350–353, 1975.
191. Pelletier, D. L., Frongillo, E. A., Jr., Schroeder, D. G., et al.: A methodology for estimating the contribution of malnutrition to child mortality in developing countries. J. Nutr. *124*(Suppl. 10):2106S–2122S, 1994.
192. Penna, G., and Adorini, L.: 1 Alpha,25-dihydroxyvitamin D3 inhibits differentiation, maturation, activation, and survival of dendritic cells leading to impaired alloreactive T cell activation. J. Immunol. *164*:2405–2411, 2000.
193. Peters, V. B., Rosh, J. R., Mugrditchian, L., et al.: Growth failure as the first expression of malnutrition in children with human immunodeficiency virus infection. Mt. Sinai J. Med. *65*:1–4, 1998.
194. Pighetti, G. M., Eskew, M. L., Reddy, C. C., et al.: Selenium and vitamin E deficiency impair transferrin receptor internalization but not IL-2, IL-2 receptor, or transferrin receptor expression. J. Leukoc. Biol. *63*:131–137, 1998.
195. Powanda, M. C., Cockerell, G. L., Moc, J. B., et al.: Induced metabolic sequelae of tularemia in the rat: Correlation with tissue damage. Am. J. Physiol. *229*:479–483, 1975.
196. Prentice, A.: Breast-feeding and the older infant. Acta Paediatr. Scand. Suppl. *374*:78–88, 1991.
197. Prindull, G., and Ahmad, M.: The ontogeny of the gut mucosal immune system and the susceptibility to infections in infants of developing countries. Eur. J. Pediatr. *152*:786–792, 1993.
198. Pruit, B. A., and MacManus, A. T.: The changing of epidemiology of infection in burn patients. World J. Surg. *16*:57–66, 1992.
199. Pscheidl, E., Schywalsky, M., Tschaikowsky, K., et al.: Fish oil-supplemented parenteral diets normalize splanchnic blood flow and improve killing of translocated bacteria in a low-dose endotoxin rat model. Crit. Care Med. *28*:1489–1496, 2000.
200. Rasmussen, A. F., Jr., Waisman, H. A., Elvehjem, C. A., et al.: Influence of the level of thiamine intake on the susceptibility of mice to poliomyelitis virus. J. Infect. Dis. *74*:41–47, 1944.
201. Rivlin, R. S.: The clinical significance of micro-nutrients in relation to immune functions. Ann. N. Y. Acad. Sci. *585*:55–57, 1990.
202. Roberts, P. D., Hoffbrand, A. V., and Mullin, D. L.: Iron and folate metabolism in tuberculosis. Br. Med. J. *2*:198–202, 1966.
203. Robinson, M. K., Rustum, R. R., Chambers, E. A., et al.: Starvation enhances hepatic free radical release following endotoxemia. J. Surg. Res. *69*:325–330, 1997.
204. Roy, S. K., Tomkins, A. M., Akramuzzaman, S. M., et al.: Randomised controlled trial of zinc supplementation in malnourished Bangladeshi children with acute diarrhoea. Arch. Dis. Child. *77*:196–200, 1997.
205. Roy, S. K., Tomkins, A. M., Haider, R., et al.: Impact of zinc supplementation on subsequent growth and morbidity in Bangladeshi children with acute diarrhoea. Eur. J. Clin. Nutr. *53*:529–534, 1999.
206. Rubin, D. H., Leventhal, J. M., Krasilnikoff, P. A., et al.: Relationship between infant feeding and infectious illness: A prospective study of infants during the first year of life. Pediatrics *85*:464–471, 1990.
207. Sakamoto, M.: The sequence of recovery of the complement systems and phytohemagglutinin skin reactivity in malnutrition. Nutr. Res. *2*:137–145, 1982.
208. Sakamoto, M., and Nishioka, K.: Complement system in nutritional deficiency. World Rev. Nutr. Diet *67*:114–139, 1992.
209. Sakamoto, M., Fujisawa, Y., and Nishioka, K.: Physiologic role of the complement system in host defense, disease, and malnutrition. Nutrition *14*:391–398, 1998.
210. Sazawal, S., Jalla, S., Mazumder, S., et al.: Effect of zinc supplementation on cell-mediated immunity and lymphocyte subsets in preschool children. Indian Pediatr. *34*:589–597, 1997.
211. Sazawal, S., Black, R. E., Jalla, S., et al.: Zinc supplementation reduces the incidence of acute lower respiratory infections in infants and preschool children: A double-blind, controlled trial. Pediatrics *102*:1–5, 1998.
212. Scariati, P. D., Grummer-Strawn, L. M., and Fein, S. B.: A longitudinal analysis of infant morbidity and the extent of breastfeeding in the United States. Pediatrics *99*:E5, 1997.
213. Schlesinger, L. A., Olbaum, L., Grez, L., et al.: Cell mediated immune studies in marasmic children from Chile: Delayed hypersensitivity, lymphocyte transformation and interferon production. *In* Suskind, R. M. (ed.): Malnutrition and the Immune Response. New York, Raven Press, 1977, pp. 91–98.
214. Schlesinger, L., Munoz, C., Arevalo, M., et al.: Depressed immune response in malnourished rats correlates with increased thymic noradrenaline level. Int. J. Neurosci. *77*:229–236, 1994.
215. Schmidt, K.: Interaction of antioxidative micronutrients with host defense mechanisms. A critical review. Int. J. Vitam. Nutr. Res. *67*:307–311, 1997.
216. Schopfer, K., and Douglas, S. D.: Neutrophil function in children with kwashiorkor. J. Lab. Clin. Med. *88*:450–461, 1976.
217. Scott, M. E., and Koski, K. G.: Zinc deficiency impairs immune responses against parasitic nematode infections at intestinal and systemic sites. J. Nutr. *130*(Suppl 5):1412S–1420S, 2000.
218. Scrimshaw, N. S.: Nutrition and infection. Prog. Food Nutr. Sci. *1*:393–420, 1975.
219. Scrimshaw, N. S., and SanGiovanni, J. P.: Synergism of nutrition, infection, and immunity: an overview. Am. J. Clin. Nutr. *66*:464S–477S, 1997.
220. Semba, R., Muhilal, Scott, A., et al.: Depressed immune response to tetanus in children with vitamin A deficiency. J. Nutr. *121*:101–107, 1992.
221. Semba, R. D., Miotti, P. G., Chiphangwi, J. D., et al.: Maternal vitamin A deficiency and mother-to-child transmission of HIV-1. Lancet *343*:1593–1597, 1994.
222. Semba, R. D.: The role of vitamin A and related retinoids in immune function. Nutr. Rev. *56*:S38–S48, 1998.
223. Semba, R.D., and Tang, A.M.: Micronutrients and the pathogenesis of human immunodeficiency virus infection. Br. J. Nutr. *81*:181–189, 1999.
224. Seth, V., and Chandra, R. K.: Opsonic activity, phagocytosis, and bactericidal capacity of polymorphs in undernutrition. Arch. Dis. Child. *47*:282–284, 1972.
225. Seth, V., Kukreja, R. K., Saundaram, K. R., et al.: Waning of cell mediated immune response in preschool children given BCG at birth. Indian J. Med. Res. *76*:710–715, 1982.
226. Shankar, A. H., Genton, B., Semba, R. D., et al.: Effect of vitamin A supplementation on morbidity due to *Plasmodium falciparum* in young children in Papua New Guinea: A randomised trial. Lancet *354*:203–209, 1999.
227. Shell-Duncan, B., and Wood, J. W.: The evaluation of delayed-type hypersensitivity responsiveness and nutritional status as predictors of gastro-intestinal and acute respiratory infection: a prospective field study among traditional nomadic Kenyan children. J. Trop. Pediatr. *43*:25–32, 1997.
228. Sherman, A. R.: Influence of iron on immunity and disease resistance. Ann. N. Y. Acad. Sci. *587*:140–146, 1990.
229. Sherman, A. R.: Zinc, copper, and iron nutriture and immunity. J. Nutr. *122*(Suppl. 3):604–609, 1992.
230. Shimeles, D., and Lulseged, S.: Clinical profile and pattern of infection in Ethiopian children with severe protein-energy malnutrition. East Afr. Med. J. *71*:264–267, 1994.
231. Silfverdal, S. A., Bodin, L., Hugosson, S., et al.: Protective effect of breastfeeding on invasive *Haemophilus influenzae* infection: A case-control study in Swedish preschool children. Int. J. Epidemiol. *26*:443–450, 1997.

232. Singh-Naz, N., Sprague, B. M., Patel, K. M., et al.: Risk assessment and standardized nosocomial infection rate in critically ill children. Crit. Care Med. *28*:2069–2075, 2000.
233. Sirisinha, S., Edelman, R., Suskind, R., et al.: Complement and C3-proactivator levels in children with protein-calorie malnutrition and effect of dietary treatment. Lancet *1*:1016–1020, 1973.
234. Sirisinha, S., Suskind, R., Edelman, R., et al.: Secretory and serum IgA in children with protein calorie malnutrition. Pediatrics *55*:166–170, 1975.
235. Smythe, P. M., Brereton-Stiles, G. G., Crace, H. J., et al.: Thymolymphatic deficiency and depression of cell-mediated immunity in protein-calorie malnutrition. Lancet *2*:939–943, 1971.
236. Solomons, N. W.: Pathways to the impairment of human nutritional status by gastrointestinal pathogens. Parasitology *107*:S19–S35, 1993.
237. Sommer, A: Vitamin A status, resistance to infection and childhood mortality. Ann. N. Y. Acad. Sci. *585*:17–23, 1990.
238. Spallholz, J. E., Boylan, L. M., and Larsen, H. S.: Advances in understanding selenium's role in the immune system. Ann. N. Y. Acad. Sci. *587*:123–139, 1990.
239. Sprunt, D. H.: Effect of undernourishment on the susceptibility of rabbit to infection with vaccinia. J. Exp. Med. *75*:297–304, 1942.
240. Squibb, R. L., and Grun, J.: Effect of nutritional status on resistance to infection in the avian species. Fed. Proc. *25*:1695–1700, 1966.
241. Stallone, D. D.: The influence of obesity and its treatment on the immune system. Nutr. Rev. *52*:37–50, 1994.
242. Steihm, E. D.: Humoral immunity in malnutrition. Fed. Proc. *39*:3093–3097, 1980.
243. Sullivan, P. B., Marsh, M. N., Phillips, M. B., et al.: Prevalence and treatment of giardiasis in chronic diarrhoea and malnutrition. Arch. Dis. Child. *65*:304–306, 1990.
244. Suskind, R. M., Olson, L. C., and Olson, R. E.: Protein calorie malnutrition and infection with hepatitis-associated antigen. Pediatrics *51*:525–530, 1973.
245. Tamura, J., Kubota, K., Murakami, H., et al.: Immunomodulation by vitamin B12: Augmentation of CD8+ T lymphocytes and natural killer (NK) cell activity in vitamin B12-deficient patients by methyl-B12 treatment. Clin. Exp. Immunol. *116*:28–32, 1999.
246. Tanaka, S. I., Isoda, F., Yamakawa, T., et al.: T lymphopenia in genetically obese rats. Clin. Immunol. Immunopathol. *86*:219–225, 1998.
247. Technical Advisory Group on Acute Respiratory Infections: A programme for controlling acute respiratory infections in children: A memorandum from a WHO meeting. Bull. W. H. O. *62*:47–58, 1984.
248. Tengerdy, R. P.: The role of vitamin E in immune response and disease resistance. Ann. N. Y. Acad. Sci. *585*:24–33, 1990.
249. Thurnham, D. I., and Northrop-Clewes, C. A.: Optimal nutrition: vitamin A and the carotenoids. Proc. Nutr. Soc. *58*:449–457, 1999.
250. Tomkins, A.: Malnutrition, morbidity and mortality in children and their mothers. Proc. Nutr. Soc. *59*:135–146, 2000.
251. Tracey, V. V., De, N. C., and Harper, J. R.: Obesity and respiratory infection in infants and young children. Br. Med. J. *1*:16–18, 1971.
252. Trakatellis, A., Dimitriadou, A., and Trakatelli, M.: Pyridoxine deficiency: New approaches in immunosuppression and chemotherapy. Postgrad. Med. J. *73*:617–622, 1997.
253. Tredget, E. E., and Yu, Y. M.: The metabolic effects of thermal injury. *16*:68–79, 1992.
254. Tupasi, T. E., Velmonte, M. E., Sanvictores, M. E., et al.: Determinants of morbidity and mortality due to acute respiratory infections: Implications for intervention. J. Infect. Dis. *157*:615–623, 1988.
255. Tupasi, T. E., deLeon, L. E., Lupsia, S., et al.: Community based studies of acute respiratory tract infections in young children. Rev. Infect. Dis. *12*:S940–S949, 1990.
256. Tupasi, T. E., Lucerno, M. G., Magdangal, D. M., et al.: Etiology of acute lower respiratory tract infection in children from Alabang. Metro Manila *12*:S929–S939, 1990.
257. Ulijaszek, S. J.: Immunology and growth faltering of Anga children, Papua New Guinea: Preliminary work. Am. J. Phys. Anthropol. *106*:515–520, 1998.
258. Umeta, M., West, C. E., Haidar, J., et al.: Zinc supplementation and stunted infants in Ethiopia: A randomised controlled trial. Lancet *355*:2021–2026, 2000.
259. Vathanophas, K., Sangchai, R., Raktham, S., et al.: A community-based study of acute respiratory tract infection in Thai children. Rev. Infect. Dis. *12*:S957–S965, 1990.
260. Veldman, C. M., Cantorna, M. T., and DeLuca, H. F.: Expression of 1, 25-dihydroxyvitamin D(3) receptor in the immune system. Arch. Biochem. Biophys. *374*:334–338, 2000.
261. Victora, C. G., Vaughan, J. P., Lombardi, C., et al.: Evidence for protection by breast-feeding against infant deaths from infectious diseases in Brazil. Lancet *2*:319–322, 1987.
262. Villalpando, S., and Lopez-Alarcon, M.: Growth faltering is prevented by breast-feeding in underprivileged infants from Mexico City. J. Nutr. *130*:546–552, 2000.
263. Waibale, P., Bowlin, S. J., Mortimer, E. A., Jr., et al.: The effect of human immunodeficiency virus-1 infection and stunting on measles immunoglobulin-G levels in children vaccinated against measles in Uganda. Int. J. Epidemiol. *28*:341–346, 1999.
264. Waters, M. D., Gardner, D. E., Arany, C., et al.: Metal toxicity for rabbit alveolar macrophages in vitro. Environ. Res. *9*:32–47, 1975.
265. Watkins-Leeder, S. R., and Corkhill, R. T.: The relationship between breast and bottle-feeding and respiratory illness in the first year of life. J. Epidemiol. Community Health *33*:180–182, 1979.
266. Watson, R. R.: Nutrition, disease resistance and age. Food Nutr. News *51*:1–6, 1979.
267. Weaver, H. M.: Resistance of cotton rats to virus of poliomyelitis as affected by intake of vitamin A, partial inanition and sex. J. Pediatr. *28*:14–23, 1946.
268. Weinberg, E. D.: Roles of iron in host-parasite infections. J. Infect. Dis. *124*:401–410, 1971.
269. Wellinghausen, N., Martin, M., and Rink, L.: Zinc inhibits interleukin-1-dependent T cell stimulation. Eur. J. Immunol. *27*:2529–2535, 1997.
270. West, C. E., Rombout, J. H. W. M., Zijpp, A. J. V. D., et al.: Vitamin A and immune function. Proc. Nutr. Soc. *50*:251–262, 1991.
271. Winick, M. (ed.): Hunger Disease: Studies by the Jewish Physicians in the Warsaw Ghetto. New York, John Wiley and Sons, 1959.
272. Woodruff, J. F., and Kilbourne, E. D.: The influence of quantitated post-weaning undernutrition on coxsackievirus B3 infection of adult mice. I. Viral persistence and increased severity of lesions. J. Infect. Dis. *121*:137–163, 1970.
273. World Health Organization: Nutrition and infection: Report of a WHO Expert Committee. W. H. O. Tech. Rep. Ser. *314*:5–30, 1965.
274. Wright, A. L., Bauer, M., Naylor, A., et al.: Increasing breastfeeding rates to reduce infant illness at the community level. Pediatrics *101*:837–844, 1998.
275. Zaman, M. M., Yoshiike, N., Chowdhury, A. H., et al.: Nutritional factors associated with rheumatic fever. J. Trop. Pediatr. *44*:142–147, 1998.
276. Zuin, G., Fontana, M., Monti, S., et al.: Malabsorption of different lactose loads in children with human immuno-deficiency virus infection. J. Pediatr. Gastroenterol. Nutr. *15*:408–412, 1992.
277. Zwingenberger, K., Irschick, E., Vergetti, S., et al.: Tumor necrosis factor in hepatosplenic schistosomiasis. Scand. J. Immunol. *31*:205–211, 1990.

CHAPTER 5 Fever: Pathogenesis and Treatment

MARTIN I. LORIN

Fever is defined as a centrally mediated elevation of body temperature in response to a stress or insult. Defining the limits of "normal" body temperature, however, is more difficult. Generally, the accepted range of rectal temperature is from 36.1° C to 37.8° C (97° F to 100° F).[32, 43] Children tend to have higher body temperatures than do adults. That young children can have rectal temperatures as high as 38.5° C (101° F) late in the afternoon (at the zenith of the circadian rhythm) or after physical activity is well recognized.[48] Clearly, a body temperature slightly above an arbitrary upper limit of 37.8° C (100° F) does not always imply a pathologic process. The important distinction between fever and heat illness is described later.

Temperature Regulation

Humans, like other mammals, are homeothermic, which means that body temperature normally is maintained within a relatively narrow range, despite significant fluctuations in energy intake and expenditure and despite widely varying environmental temperatures. Body temperature is controlled by an elaborate thermoregulatory system that modulates heat production and heat loss so that core temperature is maintained within normal limits. Numerous studies have confirmed that the thermoregulatory center is located in the preoptic region of the anterior hypothalamus (POAH).[14, 25, 63] In the laboratory animal, destruction of this region of the brain renders the animal incapable of properly controlling body temperature.[63] Profound changes in body temperature have been induced by injecting epinephrine, norepinephrine, and serotonin into the hypothalamus or lateral ventricles of the cat.[83] Separate, discrete anatomic regions or neurons within the POAH are thought to sense and compute core temperature (the *thermostat*), provide a reference point for normal temperature (the *set-point*), and control heat production and heat loss (the *heat gain center* and *heat loss center*, respectively).[12, 14]

Heat production is dependent on both metabolic and physical activity. Basal metabolic rates vary, with the highest rates occurring in the smallest individuals, whose surface area is great compared with body mass. A variety of factors such as age, thyroid status, environmental temperature, and ingestion of food influence basal metabolic rate. Physical activity and exercise markedly increase heat production by muscles. The release of catecholamines during exposure to cold increases oxygen consumption and heat production by 20 to 40 percent.[66] Shivering further increases heat production by muscles.

The newborn infant has a special heat-producing mechanism in the form of brown fat, which possesses a dense population of mitochondria and lipid vacuoles; the metabolic rate of this unique tissue exceeds that of the heart or liver,[26] and doubling of basal metabolic rate is possible without shivering (nonshivering thermogenesis).[74] The skin overlying brown fat frequently has a higher temperature than does the rectum.[34]

Heat is lost through radiation, evaporation, convection, and conduction. Generally, 60 percent of total-body heat loss occurs by radiation. Loss by radiation depends on differences in the temperature of the surfaces radiating toward each other and on the size of the surfaces involved.[66] The ratio of surface area to body mass is greatest during the neonatal period, resulting in relative temperature instability during this period of life. Skin temperature is affected by the rate of blood flow, and changes in perfusion of the skin represent the principal mechanism by which heat loss by radiation can be increased or decreased.

One of the most important methods of heat loss is evaporation. Insensible water loss from the skin and respiratory mucosa equals 750 to 800 mL/m^2 per 24 hours,[83] and considerable energy is lost during the process of evaporation. Evaporation of 1 mL of water requires 0.58 kcal of heat.[66] One fourth of all heat loss occurs by evaporation.[31, 63] Increased heat loss during exercise is accomplished primarily by radiation (cutaneous vasodilation) and by evaporation (sweating), which can dissipate as much as 1700 kcal/hr.[66] Evaporation is aided by convection because sweat must evaporate rather than fall from the skin to dissipate heat. Heat lost by convection depends on the movement of air across the body surface; the rate of heat loss is directly proportional to the velocity of air current and the amount of surface area exposed.

In the case of an individual who is standing, little heat is lost by conduction because only the feet are in contact with external objects. In contrast, for a child lying in contact with cold objects, loss by conduction is much greater. When a child is being bathed or sponged, conduction becomes the major mechanism of heat loss. Conduction also is a critical process by which heat within the body moves to the surface.[34]

Body temperatures tend to be higher in children than in adults. The decrease to adult levels begins at about 1 year of age and continues through puberty, stabilizing at 13 to 14 years of age in girls and at 17 to 18 years of age in boys.[4] The zenith of daily body temperature for most children occurs between 1700 and 1900 hours, whereas the nadir is noted in most individuals between 0 and 0600 hours. This circadian rhythm is not very evident in the first few months of life but is well established by the second birthday and tends to be more pronounced during childhood than during adulthood.

Pathogenesis of Fever

Fever, in contradistinction to heat illness, is a centrally regulated rise of body temperature in response to a pathologic stimulus. Considerable evidence suggests that the POAH acts as if the set-point had been raised, modulating the heat gain center upward and the heat loss center downward, until heat gain and heat loss are again in balance but at a higher body temperature.[22, 53, 58, 60]

The febrile response is mediated by a group of low-molecular-weight proteins (endogenous pyrogens), which are produced by polymorphonuclear leukocytes and most other phagocytic cells derived from bone marrow precursors.[2, 13, 37, 39] Numerous cytokines, especially interleukin-1, interleukin-6, and tumor necrosis factor, are thought to act as endogenous pyrogens directly in the POAH to elevate the set-point.[50, 70] In contrast, exogenous pyrogens, such as endotoxin, have no effect when injected directly into the POAH of animals. They are thought to produce fever by acting on circulating leukocytes, which, in turn, produce cytokines. The almost immediate febrile response to interleukin-1 injected intravenously and the delay in response of several hours to similar injections of endotoxins are compatible with this hypothesis.

The mechanisms of pyrogen production and release have been partially elucidated.[2, 92] Pyrogen-producing cells contain a nonpyrogenic precursor molecule that must be converted to a pyrogenically active form. Data indicate that mediators released by activated blood and tissue macrophages have a variety of diverse metabolic and physiologic actions that prepare the individual to handle stress or to combat infection.[6, 20, 27] In addition to fever, these responses include the production and release from the bone marrow of neutrophils, the hepatic synthesis of metal-binding proteins and the subsequent sequestration of iron and zinc, the production of acute-phase proteins, and the acceleration of skeletal muscle proteolysis that generates free amino acids needed for host defenses. The fact that some of these mediator-induced changes can be demonstrated in cultured cells or tissue preparations indicates that these effects are independent of the fever itself.

The mechanism of fever has been studied in few human diseases. Persistent fever in patients with typhoid fever has been attributed to endogenous pyrogen mobilized from various sites of inflammation.[41] The cause of fever in noninfectious diseases, such as sickle cell crises and inflammatory bowel disease, remains unclear. Because these disorders are associated with inflammation, fever in these patients probably also reflects a response to the release of cytokines from inflammatory cells.

A variety of disorders associated with antigen–antibody reactions can induce fever in humans. Antibodies to Rh-positive cells, for example, have been implicated as the cause of fever after transfusion of blood that is not compatible with that of the recipient. These reactions produce immune lysis of erythrocytes and may liberate antigen-antibody complexes, which, in turn, activate the production of endogenous pyrogens by host leukocytes.[76] Fever associated with hypersensitivity to penicillin also has been shown to be the result of the interaction of antigen-antibody complexes with leukocytes, which then release endogenous pyrogen.[18] Autoimmune destruction of host tissue has been suggested as the cause of fever in individuals afflicted with collagen vascular diseases.[67] The common denominator in all these conditions is thought to be the release of cytokines from activated macrophages in the blood or the reticuloendothelial system. Both cellular and humoral immune reactions appear capable of inducing the release of pyrogenic cytokines.[2]

Fever is a common finding in children with cancer. Pyrogenic substances are thought to be released from sites of tissue injury or from cells that have been stimulated by autoimmune factors induced by malignant cells.[2] In some cases, pyrogenic material may be secreted by the tumor itself because substances similar to the endogenous pyrogen originally described have been recovered from the urine of febrile patients with Hodgkin disease and from tissue extracts obtained from a human hypernephroma.[18]

In a few childhood disorders, cytokines appear to play no role in the production of fever. In children with familial dysautonomia (Riley-Day syndrome), fever primarily reflects an abnormality of the hypothalamic receptors or of the peripheral cutaneous nervous system as it modulates blood flow. In the child with thyroid storm or the rare youngster with a pheochromocytoma, fever is a direct result of peripheral activation of the thermoregulatory mechanisms that increase body temperature or reduce heat loss rather than an effect on the thermoregulatory center itself. Occasionally, whether these conditions should be classified as fever or as heat illness is unclear.

Distinction between Fever and Heat Illness

The distinction between fever and heat illness is important, not only with regard to understanding the pathophysiology of elevated body temperature but also because treatments of the two conditions are very different (Table 5–1). Although the term *fever* often is applied loosely to all types of elevated body temperature, its use is limited more precisely to those conditions in which the elevated temperature results from a thermoregulated response controlled by the POAH. That this response is controlled centrally has been amply documented.[23, 28, 81] The apparent upper limit of the febrile response is further evidence of its thermoregulated nature. Core temperatures above 41.1° C (106° F), even in severe, untreated infections, are seen only rarely,[33] and temperatures above this level often reflect involvement of the central nervous system or a component of heat illness.

The term *heat illness,* in contrast to *fever,* refers to situations in which either environmental stresses impair the ability of the central thermoregulatory mechanism to maintain normal body temperature or internal factors produce excessive heat or impair the body's ability to dissipate metabolic heat. The salient feature in heat illness is that body temperature is elevated despite a normal set-point in the POAH.[81] In victims of heat illness, core temperatures higher than 43.4° C (110° F) have been recorded.

Examples of heat illness include hyperthyroidism and malignant hyperthermia (increased heat production), anhidrotic ectodermal dysplasia (impairment of sweating and evaporative heat loss), and heat stroke (excess environmental heat). A variety of pharmacologic agents, both medical drugs (anticholinergics and phenothiazines) and street drugs (LSD and PCP), can cause heat illness by impairing the central or peripheral regulation of heat dissipation. Heat stroke and malignant hyperthermia are two especially dangerous forms of heat illness that carry a high mortality rate.

Although no data indicate that fever causes any permanent tissue or neurologic damage, the marked elevation of temperature accompanying heat illness clearly can have devastating effects on various tissues and organs.[80] Whereas the need to treat fever symptomatically can be debated, restoration of normal body temperature in heat illness is mandatory. Because the basic derangement in fever is an elevation of the set-point in the POAH, drugs such as acetaminophen and ibuprofen, which restore the set-point to normal, are rational and effective modes of therapy. In heat illness, in contrast, the set-point is normal, and administration of these agents is useless. The most effective therapy for heat illness is the prompt reduction of body temperature by external cooling. At the same time, all possible measures should be taken to correct the basic derangement itself. Time is of the essence in treating heat stroke and malignant hyperthermia. External cooling must be accomplished by such heroic measures as immersion in ice water or ice water sponging; cooling blankets and tepid sponges are inadequate.

TABLE 5–1 ■ CHARACTERISTICS OF FEVER COMPARED WITH HEAT ILLNESS

	Examples	Mechanism of Temperature Elevation	Need to Reduce Body Temperature to Normal	Treatment
Fever	Infection, malignancy, trauma	Centrally thermoregulated in response to elevation of set-point in POAH	Optional	Acetaminophen or ibuprofen
Heat illness	Hyperthyroidism, atropine poisoning, heat stroke, malignant hyperthermia	Increased heat production or decreased heat loss	Mandatory	External cooling

POAH, preoptic region of the anterior hypothalamus.

Measurement of Body Temperature

In ordinary clinical practice, core temperature is measured best by use of a rectal thermometer. Generally, rectal temperature is approximately 1° F higher than oral temperature and 2° F to 2.5° F higher than axillary temperature. Oral temperature can be influenced by the immediately prior ingestion of hot or cold liquids or solids and by tachypnea.[84] In the newborn infant, axillary temperature may be less reliable as a means of detecting fever than in the older child.[55]

Electronic thermometers achieve a steady-state reading in less than 30 seconds, compared with 2 to 4 minutes required for the mercury rectal thermometer. The electronic thermometer appears to be sufficiently accurate for routine clinical use, although the lack of calibration facilities on most models is worrisome. These instruments are practical for hospital, clinic, and office use; their role in the home remains to be defined. Devices that measure skin temperature by the use of temperature-sensitive liquid crystals are appealing but inaccurate. Studies have shown that these devices frequently underestimate core temperature,[64, 72] which is not surprising because skin temperature may be normal or even low in the early stages of fever when perfusion of the skin is decreased.

The infrared ear thermometer (IET) has been gaining popularity for hospital, office, and home use, despite considerable concern over the level of accuracy of these devices. These instruments *estimate* the temperature of the tympanic membrane, which is assumed to be in closer equilibrium with core temperature than is either oral or rectal temperature. Although some studies have shown sufficient correlation with rectal temperature to justify clinical use,[46] other studies have found the correlation to be inadequate.[36] Hooker[40] reported that the IET failed to identify 5 of 15 febrile patients, and Freed and Fraley[36] found poor correlation with rectal temperatures. Apparently, not all IETs are equally accurate; the very-low-priced models especially are suspect. One major problem in the clinical evaluation of IETs is the arbitrary use of rectal temperature as the gold standard. At times of rapid change in body temperature, rectal temperature clearly can lag behind core temperature. In these situations, tympanic membrane temperature may be a more accurate reflection of core temperature than is rectal measurement. When tympanic membrane temperature and rectal temperature disagree, one cannot always assume that the tympanic temperature is in error.

At this time, IET would seem to be ideal for situations in which measurement of rectal temperatures is inconvenient or contraindicated (e.g., major trauma, neutropenia, rectal inflammation) and the use of the oral thermometer is impractical. Use of the IET in other situations is a matter of personal preference. A wise decision is not to rely on the IET in neonates, very young infants, or other patients in whom small differences from rectal temperature would be important. Of importance is that personnel using IETs be familiar with the proper use of the instrument, especially with regard to any "offset" switches that allegedly convert the actual reading to a figure "equal" to oral or rectal temperature.

Symptomatic Therapy of Fever

If and when fever should be treated symptomatically are important but still incompletely answered questions. Unfortunately, despite the clinical frequency of fever and the ubiquity of fever in the laboratory animal and despite data indicating that fever is part of an integrated defense mechanism rather than an incidental biologic response, for the majority of clinical situations, we still do not know whether fever is beneficial, harmful, or neutral.[1, 2, 6, 27, 28, 32, 48] Clearly, conditions exist in which fever has a beneficial role and others in which it is detrimental. In most cases of acute, self-limited febrile illness in the otherwise well child, the most compelling reasons for treatment are relief of discomfort and alleviation of parental anxiety. Schmitt[71] aptly dubbed this parental attitude *fever phobia*.

POSSIBLE BENEFICIAL EFFECTS OF FEVER

In a few specific situations, the high temperature of fever may directly impair the reproduction or even the survival of an invading microorganism. Some species of gonococci and some treponema are killed by temperatures of 40° C (104° F) or higher.[7, 45] Before the antibiotic era, favorable effects of fever therapy were noted in cases of neurosyphilis and gonococcal urethritis, and data suggest that fever may impair the growth of some types of pneumococci and some viruses.[16, 75, 89] Kluger and associates[38, 49] have provided evidence that many pathogenic bacteria require more iron at higher temperatures and that in association with fever, both a decrease in serum iron and an increase in serum ferritin occur, diminishing the amount of free iron available to bacteria at the very time when they need it most. These investigators have proposed that the simultaneous rise in body temperature and decrease in free serum iron represent a coordinated host defense.

Modest elevation of body temperature has been associated with acceleration of a variety of immunologic responses, including phagocytosis, leukocyte migration, lymphocyte transformation, and increased interferon production.[3, 10, 65, 69] Whether these quantitatively small changes are clinically significant remains unclear. Several laboratory studies of bacterial infections in cold-blooded animals (goldfish and lizards) have shown improved survival with moderate elevation of body temperature.[11, 24] In a study of rabbits infected with *Pasteurella multocida*, Vaughn and Kluger[86] found that the best survival rates were associated with moderate elevations of body temperature in the range of about 4.5° F above baseline.

POSSIBLE ADVERSE EFFECTS OF FEVER

Although the above data indicate that fever, especially moderate fever, may enhance the immunologic response, other data suggest that fever, especially high fever, can impair the immunologic response. Ellingson and Clark[35] and Austin and Truant[3] reported that the in vitro phagocytosis of staphylococci by polymorphonuclear leukocytes decreased at temperatures of 40° C (104° F) or higher. Although Roberts and Steigbigel[65] found enhancement of lymphocyte transformation to mitogen at 38.5° C (101.3° F), they noted decreased cell viability and decreased function at 40° C (104° F). Several studies have found an increased mortality associated with fever in infected animals, especially those with endotoxin shock. In 1909, Ruata[68] reported that guinea pigs with gram-negative sepsis that were kept at an increased ambient temperature had a higher mortality rate than did animals similarly infected that were maintained at ordinary ambient temperatures. In a study of pneumococcal peritonitis in rabbits receiving suboptimal doses of penicillin, prevention of fever by shearing the animals' fur decreased the mortality rate.[47] In the Vaughn and Kluger[86] study with rabbits infected with *P. multocida* cited previously, body temperatures above 38.9° C (102° F) were associated with increased mortality rates.

Systematic studies of the effect of controlled euthermia during clinical infection in patients have not been performed. Metabolic studies during experimental human infection suggest that maintenance of euthermia rather than hyperthermia or hypothermia may be most beneficial.[5]

How can we reconcile the findings of worsened survival of infected animals if fever is prevented with the finding of improved survival associated with euthermia in septic shock? Perhaps fever is important in the early stages of infection, enhancing the immune response, but once shock develops, cardiorespiratory functions and tissue metabolic needs become more important than immunologic response in determining outcome. Actually, for the patient in shock, a heightened immunologic response with increased production of mediators and acute-phase reactants may well be counterproductive. Mackowiak[54] has proposed an evolutionary answer to this apparent paradox. He hypothesizes that the beneficial effects of fever on mild to moderate infection favor survival of the species when possible, whereas the deleterious effect of fever on severe infection hastens the demise of doomed animals, lessening the chance of epidemic spread among the species.

Although the metabolic effects of fever are well tolerated by the normal child, in certain clinical conditions, these metabolic changes may be deleterious. Fever increases the basal metabolic rate by 10 to 12 percent for each degree of centigrade temperature elevation and is accompanied by proportionate increases in oxygen consumption, carbon dioxide production, and fluid and caloric requirements. The need for free water is increased significantly because of increased insensible water loss from the skin and respiratory tract. Fever and the associated metabolic changes stress the cardiopulmonary system. Although fever appears to have little or no effect on normal pulmonary vasculature, in dogs it has been found to enhance hypoxia-induced pulmonary vasoconstriction.[8]

Fever can precipitate febrile seizures in the susceptible child between the ages of 6 months and 5 years. Researchers have estimated that as many as 2 to 4 percent of all children in this age group will experience at least one seizure in association with fever.[53] In addition, fever is associated with other neurologic manifestations—irritability, delirium, disorientation, and hallucinations. Finally, of note is that, although no data suggest that the temperature elevations usually associated with fever cause damage to the brain, experimental animal data indicate that fever can enhance the effects of injury on the brain. Clasen and associates[19] induced a standardized insult to the brains of monkeys in the laboratory. One half of the animals were kept at normal body temperature, the other half at a core temperature of 40° C (104° F) for 2 hours. The investigators found that the hyperthermic animals had increased edema and hemorrhage in the injured hemisphere.

Finally, one should note that in certain situations, reduction of fever renders evaluation of the patient easier. Disorientation, tachypnea, and tachycardia all may disappear with restoration of normal body temperature, alleviating concern about meningitis, pneumonia, and heart disease, respectively.

Treatment of Fever

The decision to treat fever symptomatically should be individualized for each patient. In general, there appears to be no compelling reason to treat all fevers or always to reduce body temperature completely to normal. A reasonable approach is to treat fever when it is making the patient uncomfortable and to treat fever in children who are susceptible to febrile seizures, either because of their age or because of a history of prior convulsions. Patients who are critically ill, as well as patients with presumed sepsis or septic shock, should be maintained in a euthermic state. Patients at risk for having cardiac or respiratory failure; patients with neurologic disease or injury; and patients with disturbed or precarious fluid, electrolyte, or metabolic status also benefit from reduction of fever. Finally, treating children with high fever—40° C (104° F) or greater—appears advisable.

Once the decision has been made to treat fever symptomatically, several options need to be considered with regard to the mode of treatment. Because fever is the result of an elevation of the set-point in the POAH, the most rational method of treating fever is to restore this set-point to normal, and, fortunately, drugs such as aspirin, acetaminophen, and ibuprofen accomplish exactly that. These agents lower the set-point to normal by interfering with the synthesis of prostaglandins in the POAH.

Aspirin and ibuprofen inhibit prostaglandin synthetase in a wide variety of tissues in addition to the central nervous system, and for this reason, these agents have a long list of side effects, even in therapeutic dosage. Gastritis and gastrointestinal upset,[57] gastrointestinal bleeding,[9] and impaired platelet aggregation[61, 85] have been well documented to occur with ordinary, short-term therapeutic administration of these medications. Bronchospasm occurs in almost one third of children with asthma after administration of a single dose of aspirin[62] and has been shown to be a direct pharmacologic effect rather than an allergic phenomenon.[90] In addition, therapeutic doses of aspirin have been shown—both in laboratory animals[15] and in patients[82]—to increase the leakage of pulmonary capillaries and to favor the formation of pulmonary edema. In vitro suppression of immunologic responses has been reported,[59] and ordinary doses of aspirin were shown to prolong the nasal shedding of rhinovirus in human subjects.[77] Because of the apparent relationship between aspirin and Reye syndrome,[78] aspirin no longer is recommended for antipyresis in children.

Acetaminophen, in contrast to aspirin and ibuprofen, is almost totally free of side effects when used in ordinary therapeutic doses.[21, 51] In addition, the excretion of acetaminophen is less rate-limited than is that of aspirin, and, hence, acetaminophen has less tendency to accumulate with moderate overdose.

Numerous studies have compared the efficacy of acetaminophen and ibuprofen. Most have been single-dose comparisons. Essentially all of the studies had the same finding: both acetaminophen and ibuprofen are effective antipyretic agents.[44, 73, 87, 91] For the first 2 hours after administration, no significant difference in temperature drop is seen between the two drugs. After 2 hours, patients receiving ibuprofen have a small but statistically significant lower temperature than do patients receiving acetaminophen. This difference is maximal (but still relatively small) at about 5 hours, leading to the often made, but not accurate, statement that acetaminophen lasts for 4 hours and ibuprofen for 6 hours. Despite the common thought that many patients who do not respond to acetaminophen respond to ibuprofen, no published studies exist that employ a rescue strategy, wherein children who fail to respond to acetaminophen are randomly maintained on acetaminophen or switched to ibuprofen. Only two studies compare multidose regimens[52, 88]; only one of these[88] looked at efficacy as well as toxicity and found no statistically significant difference between the two drugs.

Theoretically, ibuprofen shares most of the side effects of aspirin, other than an association with Reye syndrome. A large, multicenter study of ibuprofen versus acetaminophen in more than 700 pediatric and family medicine practices found no cases of Reye syndrome or acute renal failure with either drug and only a very low incidence (7.2 per 100,000 population) of gastrointestinal hemorrhage in the ibuprofen group.[52] No cases of hemorrhage were found in the group treated with acetaminophen, and none of the cases of gastrointestinal hemorrhage with ibuprofen required transfusion.

In view of the increased cost and potential toxicity of ibuprofen compared with acetaminophen and the questionable need to reduce fever maximally in most cases, acetaminophen remains the drug of choice for the routine treatment of fever. One potential advantage of ibuprofen is that in overdose it has less severe toxic effects than does acetaminophen. The major causes of morbidity and mortality in ibuprofen poisoning are acute renal failure and central nervous system changes, including apnea. All of them are managed more easily than is acute hepatic failure, which can occur with severe acetaminophen poisoning. However, current packaging has rendered serious acetaminophen poisoning an infrequent occurrence with the pediatric preparations of this drug.

Antipyretic agents often are prescribed on the basis of age, but weight-based dosage is preferable.[17, 29, 30] In the well-hydrated child with normal liver and renal function, acetaminophen appears safe in doses up to 15 mg/kg every 4 hours, although 10 mg/kg usually is adequate, and the package insert recommends a maximum of five doses per 24 hours. Because acetaminophen has a prolonged half-life in the newborn period and because few data regarding the kinetics of acetaminophen in the first few months of life exist, it should be used with caution in this age group, and then only in either reduced dosage or decreased frequency. The maximum dose for older children generally is presumed to be 600 mg every 4 hours.

The recommended dosage of ibuprofen is 5 to 10 mg/kg every 6 hours for temperatures higher than 38.9° C. No published data regarding either combined or alternating use of ibuprofen and acetaminophen exist, and, therefore, such practice cannot be recommended. However, trying ibuprofen for those patients whose response to acetaminophen is judged to be inadequate is reasonable.

Although restoration of the hypothalamic set-point by pharmacotherapy is the most rational way to treat fever, external cooling (as by sponging with cold, cool, or tepid water) can be effective in reducing fever and restoring body temperature to normal.[42, 79] Ice water sponging has a more rapid cooling effect than does tepid water sponging, but the associated discomfort renders it undesirable.[79] Water in the range of 29.4° C to 32° C (85° F to 90° F) generally is preferable. The addition of alcohol to the sponge water is contraindicated because absorption of alcohol through the skin and inhalation of fumes can result in central nervous system depression.[56] In the hospitalized patient, a cooling blanket may be more convenient. External cooling is especially effective in infants and young children because of their relatively large surface areas.

Because external cooling alone does not restore the POAH set-point to normal, its best use is in combination with the use of acetaminophen. The use of this combination may be the optimal approach in children with very high fevers or in cases in which reducing fever quickly is desirable. In a few situations, sponging alone may be indicated, for example, for very young infants, children with hepatic failure, and children with allergy to both acetaminophen and ibuprofen.

REFERENCES

1. Atkins, E.: Fever: New perspectives on an old phenomenon. N. Engl. J. Med. *308*:958–960, 1983.
2. Atkins, E., and Bodel, P.: Fever. N. Engl. J. Med. *286*:27–34, 1972.
3. Austin, T. W., and Truant, G.: Hyperthermia, antipyretics and function of polymorphonuclear leukocytes. Can. Med. Assoc. J. *118*:493–495, 1978.
4. Bayley, N., and Stolz, H. R.: Maturational changes in rectal temperatures of 61 infants from 1 to 36 months. Child Dev. *8*:195–206, 1937.
5. Beisel, W. R., Sawyer, W. D., Ryll, E. D., et al.: Metabolic effects of intracellular infections in man. Ann. Intern. Med. *67*:744–779, 1967.
6. Beisel, W. R.: Mediators of fever and muscle proteolysis. N. Engl. J. Med. *308*:586–588, 1983.
7. Bennett, I. L., Jr., and Nicastri, A.: Fever as a mechanism of resistance. Bacterial Rev. *24*:16–34, 1960.
8. Benumof, J. L., and Wahrenbock, E. A.: Dependency of hypoxic pulmonary vasoconstriction on temperature. J. Appl. Physiol. *42*:56–58, 1977.
9. Bergman, G. E., Philippidis, P., and Naiman, J. L.: Severe gastrointestinal hemorrhage and anemia after therapeutic doses of aspirin in normal children. J. Pediatr. *88*:501–503, 1976.
10. Bernheim, H. A., Bodel, P. T., Askenase, P. W., et al.: Effects of fever on host defense mechanisms after infection in the lizard, *Dipsosaurus dorsalis*. Br. J. Exp. Pathol. *59*:76–84, 1978.
11. Bernheim, H. A., and Kluger, M. J.: Fever: Effect of drug-induced antipyresis on survival. Science *193*:237–239, 1976.
12. Bligh, J.: Temperature Regulation in Mammals and Other Vertebrates. New York, American Elsevier Publishers, 1973, pp. 38–39.
13. Bodel, P., and Atkins, E.: Release of endogenous pyrogen by human monocytes. N. Engl. J. Med. *276*:1002–1008, 1967.
14. Boulant, J. A.: Role of preoptic-anterior hypothalamus in thermoregulation and fever. Clin. Infect. Dis. *31*[Suppl. 5]:S157–161, 2000.
15. Bowers, R. E., Brigham, K. L., and Owen, P. J.: Salicylate pulmonary edema: The mechanism in sheep and review of the clinical literature. Am. Rev. Respir. Dis. *115*:261–268, 1977.
16. Carmichael, L. E., Barnes, F. D., and Percy, D. H.: Temperature as a factor in resistance of young puppies to canine herpesvirus. J. Infect. Dis. *120*:669–678, 1969.
17. Cashman, T. M., Starns, R. J., Johnson, J., et al.: Comparative effects of naproxen and aspirin on fever in children. J. Pediatr. *95*:626–629, 1979.
18. Ciba Foundation Symposium: Pyrogens and Fever. *In* Wolstenholme, G. E. W., and Birch, J. (eds.): London, Churchill Livingstone, 1971.
19. Clasen, R. A., Pandolfi, S., Laing, I., et al.: Experimental study of relation of fever to cerebral edema. J. Neurosurg. *41*:576–581, 1974.
20. Clowes, G. H. A., Jr., George, B. C., Villee, C. A., Jr., et al.: Muscle proteolysis induced by a circulating peptide in patients with sepsis or trauma. N. Engl. J. Med. *308*:545–552, 1983.
21. Committee on Drugs, American Academy of Pediatrics: Commentary on acetaminophen. Pediatrics *61*:108–112, 1978.
22. Cooper, K. E., Cranston, W. I., and Snell, E. S.: Temperature regulation during fever in man. Clin. Sci. *27*:345–356, 1964.
23. Cooper, K. E.: The body temperature "set-point" in fever. *In* Bligh, J., and Moore, R. E. (eds.): Essays on Temperature Regulation. New York, American Elsevier Publishers, 1972, p. 150.
24. Covert, J. B., and Reynolds, W. W.: Survival value of fever in fish. Nature *267*:43–45, 1977.
25. Cranston, W. I.: Central mechanisms of fever. Fed. Proc. *38*:49–51, 1979.
26. Dawkins, M. J. R., and Hull, D.: Brown adipose tissue and the response of newborn rabbits to cold. J. Physiol. *172*:216–238, 1964.
27. Dinarello, C. A.: Interleukin-1 and the pathogenesis of the acute-phase response. N. Engl. J. Med. *311*:1413–1418, 1984.
28. Dinarello, C. A., Cannon, J. G., and Wolff, S. M.: New concepts on the pathogenesis of fever. Rev. Infect. Dis. *10*:168–189, 1988.
29. Done, A. K.: Treatment of fever in 1982: A review. Am. J. Med. *14A*: 27–35, 1983.
30. Done, A. K., Yaffe, S. J., and Clayton, J. M.: Aspirin dosage for infants and children. J. Pediatr. *95*:617–625, 1979.
31. DuBois, E. F.: Basal Metabolism in Health and Disease. 3rd ed. Philadelphia, Lea & Febiger, 1936.
32. DuBois, E. F.: Fever and the Regulation of Body Temperature. Springfield, IL, Charles C Thomas, 1948.
33. DuBois, E. F.: Why are fever temperatures over 106° F rare? Am. J. Med. Sci. *217*:361–368, 1949.
34. Eiler, D. M., and Stetson, J. B.: Fever: A physiological view. Int. Anesthesiol. Clin. *5*:359–379, 1967.
35. Ellingson, H. V., and Clark, P. F.: The influence of artificial fever on mechanisms of resistance. J. Immunol. *43*:65–83, 1942.
36. Freed, G. L., and Fraley, J. K.: Lack of agreements of tympanic membrane temperature assessments with conventional methods in a private practice setting. Pediatrics *89*:384–386, 1992.
37. Gander, G. W., and Goodale, F.: The role of granulocytes and mononuclear leucocytes in fever. *In* Lomax, P., Schonbaum, E., and Jacob, J. (eds.): Temperature Regulation and Drug Action. Basel, S. Karger, 1975, pp. 51–58.
38. Grieger, T. A., and Kluger, M. J.: Fever and survival: The role of serum iron. J. Physiol. (Lond.) *279*:187–196, 1978.

39. Hahn, H. H., Char, D. C., Postel, W. B., et al.: Studies on the pathogenesis of fever. XV. The production of endogenous pyrogen by peritoneal macrophages. J. Exp. Med. *126*:385–394, 1967.
40. Hooker, E. A.: Use of tympanic thermometers to screen for fever in patients in a pediatric emergency department. South. Med. J. *86*:856–858, 1993.
41. Hornick, R. B., Greisman, S. E., Woodward, T. E., et al.: Typhoid fever: Pathogenesis and immunologic control (first of two parts). N. Engl. J. Med. *283*:686–691, 1970.
42. Hunter, J.: Study of antipyretic therapy in current use. Arch. Dis. Child. *48*:313–315, 1973.
43. Ivy, A. C.: What is normal or normality? Q. Bull. Northwestern Univ. Med. Sch. *18*:22–32, 1944.
44. Kauffman, R. E., Sawyer, L. A., Scheinbaum, M. L.: Antipyretic efficacy of ibuprofen vs acetaminophen. Am. J. Dis. Child. *146*:622–625, 1992.
45. Kendell, H. W.: Fever Therapy. Springfield, IL, Charles C Thomas, 1935, pp. 67–83.
46. Kennedy, R. D., Fortenberry, J. D., Surratt, S. S., et al.: Evaluation of an infrared tympanic membrane thermometer in pediatric patients. Pediatrics *85*:854–858, 1990.
47. Klastersky, J., and Kass, E. H.: Effect of suppression of fever on mortality rate in experimental pneumococcal sepsis. Clin. Res. *17*:370, 1969.
48. Kluger, M. J.: Fever, Its Biology, Evolution and Function. Princeton, Princeton University Press, 1979, p. 31.
49. Kluger, M. J., and Rothenberg, B. A.: Fever and reduced iron: Their interaction as a host defense response to bacterial infection. Science *203*:374–376, 1979.
50. Kluger, M. J.: Fever revisited. Pediatrics *90*:846–850, 1992.
51. Koch-Weser, J.: Acetaminophen. N. Engl. J. Med. *295*:1297–1300, 1976.
52. Lesko, S. M., and Mitchell, A. A.: An assessment of the safety of pediatric ibuprofen: A practitioner-based randomized clinical trial. J. A. M. A. *273*:929–933, 1995.
53. Lorin, M. I.: The Febrile Child: Clinical Management of Fever and Other Types of Pyrexia. New York, John Wiley & Sons, 1982, pp. 153, 226–227.
54. Mackowiak, P.A.: Fever: Blessing or curse? A unifying hypothesis. Ann. Intern. Med. *19*:948–950, 1994.
55. Mayfield, S. R., Bhatia, J., Nakamara, K. T., et al.: Temperature measurement in term and preterm neonates. J. Pediatr, *104*:271–275, 1984.
56. McFadden, S. W., and Haddow, J. E.: Coma produced by topical application of isopropanol. Pediatrics *43*:622–623, 1969.
57. Miller, R. R., and Jack, H.: Acute toxicity of aspirin in hospitalized medical patients. Am. J. Med. Sci. *274*:271–279, 1977.
58. Nakayama, T. Thermosensitive neurons in the brain. Jpn. J. Physiol. *35*:375–389, 1985.
59. Opelz, G., and Terasaki, P. I.: Suppression of lymphocyte transformation by aspirin. Lancet *2*:478–480, 1973.
60. Palmes, E. D., and Park, C. R.: The regulation of body temperature during fever. Arch. Environ. Health. *11*:749–759, 1965.
61. Pearson, H.: Comparative effects of aspirin and acetaminophen on hemostasis. Pediatrics *62*(Suppl.):926–929, 1978.
62. Rachelefsky, G. S., Coulson, A., Siegel, S. C., et al.: Aspirin intolerance in chronic childhood asthma: Detected by oral challenge. Pediatrics *56*:443–448, 1975.
63. Reaves, T. A., and Hayward, J. N.: Hypothalamic and extrahypothalamic thermoregulatory centers. *In* Lomax, P., and Schonbaum, E. (eds.): Body Temperature. New York, Marcel Dekker, 1979, p. 58.
64. Reisinger, K. S., Kao, J., and Grant, D. M.: Inaccuracy of the Clinitemp skin thermometer. Pediatrics *64*:4–6, 1979.
65. Roberts, N. J., and Steigbigel, R. T.: Hyperthermia and human leukocyte function: Effects on response of lymphocytes to mitogen and antigen and bactericidal capacity of monocytes and neutrophils. Infect. Immunol. *18*:673–679, 1977.
66. Roe, C. F.: Fever and energy metabolism in surgical disease. Monogr. Surg. Sci. *3*:85–132, 1966.
67. Root, R. K., and Wolff, S. M.: Pathogenetic mechanisms in experimental immune fever. J. Exp. Med. *128*:309–323, 1968.
68. Ruata, G. Q.: L'influenza del caldo umido sulle infezioni. Bull. Sci. Med. Bologna *9*:59–110, 1909.
69. Ruiz-Gomez, J., and Isaacs, A.: Interferon production by different viruses. Virology *19*:8–12, 1963.
70. Saper, C. B., and Breder, C. D.: The neurologic basis of fever. N. Engl. J. Med. *330*:1880–1886, 1994.
71. Schmitt, B. D.: Fever phobia: Misconception of parents about fever. Am. J. Dis. Child. *134*:176–181, 1980.
72. Scholenfield, J. H., Gerber, M. A., and Dwyer, P.: Liquid crystal forehead temperature strips: A clinical appraisal. Am. J. Dis. Child. *136*:198–201, 1982.
73. Sidler, J., Frey, B., and Baerlocher, K: A double-blind comparison of ibuprofen and paracetamol in juvenile pyrexia. Br. J. Clin. Pract. *70*(Suppl):22–25, 1990.
74. Silverman, W. A., and Sinclair, J. C.: Temperature regulation in the newborn infant. N. Engl. J. Med. *274*:92–94, 1966.
75. Small, P. M., Tauber, M. G., Hackbarth, C. J., et al.: Influence of body temperature on bacterial growth rates in experimental pneumococcal meningitis in rabbits. Infect. Immunol. *52*:484–487, 1986.
76. Snell, E. S., and Atkins, E.: The mechanism of fever. *In* Bittar, E. E. (ed.): The Biological Basis of Medicine. Vol. 2. London, Academic Press, pp. 397–419, 1968.
77. Stanley, E. D., Jackson, G. G., Panusarn, C., et al.: Increased viral shedding with aspirin treatment of rhinovirus infection. J. A. M. A. *231*:1248–1251, 1975.
78. Starko, K. M., Ray, C. G., Dominguea, L. B., et al.: Reye's syndrome and salicylate use. Pediatrics *66*:859–864, 1980.
79. Steele, R. W., Tanaka, P. T., Lara, R. P., et al.: Evaluation of sponging and of oral antipyretic therapy to reduce fever. J. Pediatr. *77*:824–829, 1970.
80. Stine, R. J.: Heat illness. J. A. C. E. P. *8*:154–160, 1979.
81. Stitt, J. T.: Fever versus hyperthermia. Fed. Proc. *38*:39–43, 1979.
82. Sutcliffe, J.: Pulmonary oedema due to salicylates. Br. J. Radiol. *28*:314–316, 1955.
83. Talbot, N. B., Richie, R. H., and Crawford, J. D.: Metabolic Homeostasis: A Syllabus for Those Concerned with the Care of Patients. Cambridge, MA, Harvard University Press, 1959.
84. Tandberg, D., and Sklar, D.: Effect of tachypnea on the estimation of body temperature by an oral thermometer. N. Engl. J. Med. *308*:945–946, 1983.
85. Van Daele, M. C., and De Gaetano, G.: Purpura and acetylsalicylic acid therapy. Acta Paediatr. Scand. *60*:203–208, 1971.
86. Vaughn, L. K., and Kluger, M. J.: Fever and survival in rabbits infected with *Pasteurella multocida*. J. Physiol. (Lond.) *282*:243–251, 1978.
87. Walson, P. D., Galletta, G., Braden, N. J., and Alexander, L.: Ibuprofen, acetaminophen and placebo treatment of febrile children. Clin. Pharmacol. Ther. *46*:9–17, 1989.
88. Walson, P. D., Galletta, G., Chomile, F., et al.: Comparison of multidose ibuprofen and acetaminophen therapy in febrile children. Am. J. Dis. Child. *146*:626–632, 1992.
89. Walter, D. L., and Boring, W. D.: Factors influencing host-virus interactions. III. Further studies on the alteration of Coxsackie virus infection in adult mice by environmental temperature. J. Immunol. *80*:39–44, 1958.
90. Weinberger, M.: Analgesic sensitivity in children with asthma. Pediatrics *62*(Suppl.):910–915, 1978.
91. Wilson J. T., Brown, R. D., Kearns, G. L., et al.: Single dose, placebo-controlled comparative study of ibuprofen and acetaminophen antipyresis in children. Pediatrics *119*:803–811, 1991.
92. Wood, W. B., Jr.: The pathogenesis of fever. *In* Mudd, S. (ed.): Infectious Agents and Host Reactions. Philadelphia, W. B. Saunders, 1970, pp. 146–162.

CHAPTER 6

Indigenous Flora

DOUGLAS S. SWANSON

Indigenous flora and *normal flora* are terms used to describe the microorganisms that colonize the internal and external surfaces of healthy individuals.[103] *Colonization* is the presence of replicating microorganisms on or within a host, without evidence of the development of disease. The microbial agents that compose the normal flora are called *commensual*, *colonizing*, or *endogenous* organisms. They usually do not cause injury to the host and can be divided into categories of *resident* or *transient* flora.[24, 146] Resident flora are organisms that are present routinely in a specified anatomic location. For example, *Staphylococcus epidermidis* is a resident organism of the skin, and *Escherichia coli* is a resident organism of the gastrointestinal tract. Transient flora are organisms that are present only temporarily in a certain anatomic location, such as *Staphylococcus aureus* on the skin or *Pseudomonas aeruginosa* in the gastrointestinal tract. Blood, cerebrospinal fluid, urine, bile, and synovial fluid are considered sterile fluids and have no normal flora.

Environmental factors, host characteristics, and microbial properties all can influence the composition of the indigenous flora. Disruption of the balance among these various factors can have a profound impact on the normal flora and their subsequent potential for pathogenicity. Pathogens are microorganisms that are able to cause disease in the host. *Strict pathogens*, such as *Neisseria gonorrhoeae* and the rabies virus, always are associated with disease and are not considered part of the normal flora. Organisms such as *P. aeruginosa*, *S. epidermidis*, and *Serratia marcescens* are *opportunistic pathogens* and do not cause disease except in immunocompromised hosts or in special circumstances that support their dissemination. For example, central venous catheters can become contaminated with *S. epidermidis*, resulting in a bloodstream infection. Similarly, transient bacteremia after a dental procedure can cause viridans streptococcal endocarditis in a patient with an abnormal heart valve. *Facultative pathogens* fall somewhere between strict and opportunistic pathogens. They have the capacity to cause disease in healthy individuals and compose much of the indigenous flora found in the body (e.g., *Streptococcus pneumoniae*, *E. coli*, and *S. aureus*).[136, 146]

A useful tool for clinicians to have is a general understanding of the normal human microbial flora. First, familiarity with the organisms that compose the normal flora may help with the interpretation of culture reports, such as the isolation of diphtheroids from a peripheral blood culture. Second, when an infectious disease is present, knowledge of the indigenous flora can assist in determining the likely causative agents and provide a basis for determining the initial antimicrobial therapy. This knowledge is especially important because of the increasing number of immunocompromised individuals who are vulnerable to endogenous infections. Third, an understanding of the normal flora may assist in the decision to withhold antimicrobial therapy when a culture report identifies an organism considered to be a pathogen, but it is not for that patient's particular clinical presentation. For example, the isolation of *S. pneumoniae* from a throat culture of a patient with pharyngitis can be disregarded if one recognizes that this organism is a normal part of the nasopharyngeal microbial environment and an unlikely cause of pharyngitis. Finally, clinicians may prescribe broad-spectrum antimicrobial agents more judiciously if they have an appreciation for the role that indigenous flora perform as part of the host's defense system.[125]

Acquisition of Indigenous Flora by the Newborn

The fetus normally is in a sterile environment in the uterus. The newborn begins to acquire its indigenous microbial flora during delivery. Maternal flora provide the initial source of colonizing organisms. Exposure to organisms from other people and environmental sources contributes to the formation of the neonate's eventual normal flora.[126]

The gestational age, mode of delivery, and type of feeding all can affect the formation of the newborn's indigenous flora. Premature infants requiring prolonged hospitalization have a delay in bacterial colonization and more frequently are colonized with hospital flora, especially *Klebsiella*, *Enterobacter*, and *Citrobacter* spp., compared with healthy term newborns.[43, 49, 56] Infant-to-infant transmission by the hands of health care workers is an important factor contributing to gram-negative colonization of premature neonates.[49] Infants born by cesarean delivery have delayed intestinal colonization with anaerobic bacteria, and gut colonization can remain altered for as long as 6 months after birth.[18, 61, 96, 131] The intestinal flora also are influenced by the newborn's diet. *Bifidobacterium* spp. and a few other anaerobic bacteria dominate the intestinal flora of breast-fed newborns, whereas infants fed formula have a more complex intestinal microbial flora.[4, 11, 36, 99, 143, 171] As the infant gets older, the composition of the indigenous flora begins to resemble more closely that of an adult.

Mechanisms of Colonization

The normal flora differ substantially among the various anatomic sites because of local barriers to colonization. Environmental conditions, such as moisture, pH, oxygen tension, and nutritional supply, influence the ability of microorganisms to establish residence.[48, 103] In certain anatomic regions, mucociliary clearance, epithelial cell turnover, and the flow of secretions serve to restrict colonization to specific species of microbes.[103] Additional barriers include specific and nonspecific immune factors, the production of lysozyme, local attachment-blocking proteins, and microbial competition.[32]

The primary mechanisms of bacterial colonization are adherence to epithelial cells, colonization of mucus, and attachment to other colonizing organisms.[32] Adherence of bacteria to epithelial cells occurs primarily by specific binding between microbial surface antigens (adhesins) and epithelial receptor molecules.[10, 64, 86] For example, oral bacteria colonize specific sites within the mouth. *Streptococcus salivarius* binds to the epithelial cells of the tongue and buccal mucosa, whereas *Streptococcus mutans* and *Streptococcus sanguis* bind to tooth enamel.[125, 167] Normal flora also can be established by the colonization of the mucous layer without bacterial attachment to host cells, as demonstrated in the intestinal tract.[32] Finally, microbes can attach to colonizing organisms through adhesin-receptor binding. This means is established most clearly in the formation of dental plaque.[167]

Exogenous Influences on the Normal Flora

An individual's normal flora tends to remain relatively stable and consistent but can be affected by a variety of exogenous factors. Antibacterial soaps, topical antiseptics, and deodorants can suppress temporarily the skin flora.[12, 66, 84] Similarly, brushing teeth with fluoride toothpaste reduces dental microflora. Eating fresh fruits and vegetables may provide a source of transient intestinal colonization with *P. aeruginosa*.[87, 121] Viral infections can disrupt the normal flora and predispose the patient to development of bacterial superinfections.[27, 44, 46, 54, 62, 63, 97, 119, 148] For example, influenza virus infection increases susceptibility to bacterial pneumonia, otitis media, and bacteremia in part by facilitating the adherence of pathogenic bacteria to respiratory epithelial cells.[54, 133, 170]

Medications can influence the composition of the normal flora. Acid reduction therapy may permit bacterial overgrowth within the stomach and small intestine, resulting in deconjugation of bile salts and malabsorption.[37, 60, 83, 128, 151, 153, 168] Gastric acid suppression also may reduce the number of ingested pathogens needed to cause enteric disease.[168] Antimicrobial agents can alter significantly the indigenous flora and promote colonization with potential pathogens by eliminating susceptible commensuals.[8, 35, 53, 68, 74, 107, 112, 113] Such changes can lead to superinfections with overgrowing organisms.[3, 20, 98, 172] For instance, antibiotics can reduce the barrier effect of the normal intestinal flora, permitting *Clostridium difficile* to propagate and produce toxins, resulting in pseudomembranous colitis.[7] Antimicrobial effects on the indigenous flora depend on the type of antibiotic, route, dose, and duration of administration.

Severe or chronic illnesses alone can cause changes in an individual's indigenous flora.[71, 79, 80, 81, 93] Hospitalized patients with severe illness are much more likely to develop pharyngeal colonization with gram-negative bacilli than are hospitalized patients who are physiologically normal.[79, 80, 81] Furthermore, medical devices may alter the host's normal flora. Thomas and colleagues[152] demonstrated that patients requiring placement of nasogastric tubes had significantly greater nasopharyngeal colonization with aerobic gram-negative bacilli compared with patients in a control group.

Bacterial Composition at Specific Locations

SKIN

Because of the presence of moisture and sebum, most skin flora are associated with sweat glands (Table 6–1). Bacterial concentrations are highest on the face, neck, hands, and toe webs and in the axillae and groin.[105, 106] The organisms occupy the most superficial layers of the epidermis and are found primarily around the hair follicles, although some are located deeper within follicles.[9, 105, 111] Although soaps and other skin cleansers substantially reduce the number of most surface bacteria, organisms within hair follicles and sweat glands quickly reestablish the normal flora.[66, 84]

The normal skin flora are primarily of coagulase-negative *Staphylococcus* spp. (esp. *S. epidermidis*), *Proprionibacterium acnes*, *Corynebacterium* spp. (diphtheroids), and *Micrococcus* spp. *P. acnes* emerges at the onset of puberty, occupies hair follicles and sebaceous glands, and is a major contributing cause of acne. *S. aureus* and group A *Streptococcus* spp. are not usual residents of the skin but may cause transient colonization.[139] *Acinetobacter* spp. is a common resident of the toe webs. Other gram-negative organisms, such as *Klebsiella*, *Proteus*, and *Enterobacter* spp. and *E. coli,* are uncommon findings and only transient residents of the skin. The fungus *Pityrosporum* (*ovale* and *orbiculare*) normally inhabits the skin,[122, 123] but *Candida* spp. do not.[29] Many other microorganisms come in contact with the skin, but because of the skin's relative dryness and presence of organic fatty acids, they are present only briefly and do not propagate.

Newborns

Within hours, the normal full-term infant's skin becomes colonized with microbes. In addition to typical normal skin flora, potential pathogens (group B *Streptococcus* spp., *E. coli*, *Klebsiella* spp.) frequently are recovered from cultures of the external ear canal.[100, 115] However, obtaining routine surveillance cultures in an attempt to identify infants at risk for invasive disease is not recommended because their predictive value is limited.[77, 100, 115]

CONJUNCTIVAE

The mechanical actions of the eyelids and the washing effect of tears containing antimicrobial substances inhibit microbial colonization of the eye; however, normal flora do exist. The conjunctival flora probably originate from the eyelids and the nasolacrimal ducts. The organisms most commonly isolated are coagulase-negative *Staphylococcus, Corynebacteria, Micrococcus*, and *Proprionibacterium* spp. Other isolates include *S. aureus*, *Haemophilus* spp., viridans streptococci, *S. pneumoniae*, and *Bacillus* spp.[92, 117, 125, 164]

RESPIRATORY TRACT

The mouth and oropharynx contain several unique microbial habitats. Viridans (α and nonhemolytic) streptococci are the most prominent commensuals and include *S. mutans, S. sanguis, S. salivarius, Streptococcus milleri,* and *Streptococcus mitis*.[88, 125, 146] The flora of the gingival crevice include a diverse collection of facultative and anaerobic organisms. More common isolates include *S. mitis*, *S. mutans*, and *Actinomyces*, *Fusobacterium*, *Treponema*, *Veillonella*, *Peptostreptococcus*, and *Bacteroides* spp. *S. sanguis* and *S. mitis* are the initial colonizers of the tooth surface. Dental plaque forms when *S. mutans* and *Actinomyces*, *Fusobacterium*, *Treponema*, and *Veillonella* spp., along with other organisms, attach to the initial bacterial cell layer and each other.[167] The buccal mucosa, tongue, and saliva are colonized most heavily by *S. salivarius*, *S. mitis*, and *Veillonella* and *Lactobacillus* spp. Asymptomatic pharyngeal carrier rates of

TABLE 6–1 ■ COMMON INDIGENOUS FLORA AT VARIOUS ANATOMIC SITES

Body Site	Resident Flora	Transient Flora
Skin		
Opportunistic pathogens	*Corynebacterium, Staphylococcus epidermidis, Micrococcus, Peptococcus, Brevibacterium, Acinetobacter, Demodex folliculorum*	Viridans *Streptococcus, Enterococcus, Malassezia*
Facultative pathogens	*Propionibacterium acnes, Pityrosporum*	*Staphylococcus aureus, Enterobacter, Escherichia coli, Klebsiella, Proteus,* group A *Streptococcus, Candida, Trichophyton*
Eye		
Opportunistic pathogens	Coagulase-negative *Staphylococcus, Corynebacterium, Micrococcus*	*Bacillus,* viridans *Streptococcus, Propionibacterium*
Facultative pathogens	*Haemophilus*	*Staphylococcus aureus, Streptococcus pneumoniae*
Mouth and Oropharynx		
Opportunistic pathogens	Viridans *Streptococcus,* coagulase-negative *Staphylococcus, Haemophilus,* non–group A β-*Streptococcus, Treponema, Veillonella, Porphyromonas, Prevotella, Peptostreptococcus, Bacteroides,* non-meningococcal *Neisseria, Corynebacterium*	*Eikenella corrodens*
Facultative pathogens	*Fusobacterium, Streptococcus mutans*, Actinomyces**	Group A *Streptococcus, Lactobacillus,* Neisseria meningitidis, Kingella, Streptococcus pneumoniae, Moraxella, Candida,* cytomegalovirus, herpes simplex virus
Nose and Nasopharynx		
Opportunistic pathogens	Coagulase-negative *Staphylococcus,* viridans *Streptococcus, Corynebacterium*	Nonmeningococcal *Neisseria*
Facultative pathogens		*Staphylococcus aureus, Neisseria meningitidis, Streptococcus pneumoniae, Moraxella*
Stomach		
Opportunistic pathogens		*Streptococci, Lactobacillus*
Facultative pathogens		*Helicobacter pylori*
Small Intestine		
Opportunistic pathogens	*Lactobacillus, Streptococcus, Veillonella, Prevotella, Porphyromonas, Bifidobacterium*	*Candida, Entamoeba coli, Endolimax nana, Iodamoeba beutschlii, Trichomonas hominis, Chilomastix mesnili*
Facultative pathogens	*Bacteroides,* Enterobacteriaceae, *Clostridium*	*Blastocystis hominis*
Large Intestine		
Opportunistic pathogens	*Bifidobacterium, Peptostreptococcus, Lactobacillus, Veillonella, Eubacterium, Fusobacterium, Prevotella, Porphyromonas, Enterococcus*	*Candida, Corynebacterium, Pseudomonas, Mycobacterium avium* complex, *Entamoeba coli, Endolimax nana, Iodamoeba beutschlii, Trichomonas hominis, Chilomastix mesnili*
Facultative pathogens	*Bacteroides, Clostridium,* Enterobacteriaceae	*Aeromonas, Blastocystis hominis,* enterovirus
Anterior Urethra		
Opportunistic pathogens	*Corynebacterium,* coagulase-negative *Staphylococcus,* viridans *Streptococcus, Lactobacillus* (women)	*Mycobacterium smegmatis, Bacteroides, Fusobacterium*
Facultative pathogens		Enterobacteriaceae, *Enterococcus, Ureaplasma, Mycoplasma*
Vagina		
Opportunistic pathogens	*Lactobacillus, Streptococcus,* coagulase-negative *Staphylococcus*	*Enterococcus*
Facultative pathogens	*Gardnerella vaginalis, Mobiluncus, Prevotella, Actinomyces*	Group B *Streptococcus, Candida, Trichomonas vaginalis*

*Contribute to dental caries.

group A *Streptococcus* spp. in children range from 3 to 50 percent, with the highest prevalence rates associated with school outbreaks of pharyngitis.[30, 40, 47, 70, 118, 141, 144, 165, 169]

Compared with those of the mouth and oropharynx, the microbial flora of the nose and nasopharynx are less diverse. Coagulase-negative staphylococci, viridans streptococci, *Corynebacterium* spp., and *S. aureus* are the most prevalent strains isolated. Nasal carriage rates of *S. aureus* average from 20 to 35 percent, and the prevalence of methicillin-resistant *S. aureus* nasal colonization has been increasing, with estimates ranging from 0.2 to 2 percent.[1, 26, 69, 76, 137, 145, 157] Colonization of children with *Neisseria*, *Haemophilus*, and *Moraxella* spp. and *S. pneumoniae* is a relatively common occurrence.

Pneumococcal colonization of the nasopharynx generally is transient, averaging in length of duration from 1 to 4 months.[45, 59] Increased colonization is seen with younger age, overcrowding, attendance at a daycare center, winter season, and exposure to tobacco smoke. Nasopharyngeal carriage rates of *S. pneumoniae* average 40 to 50 percent in children and 20 to 30 percent in adults.[52] The prevalence of colonization with penicillin-nonsusceptible strains has not been well studied and varies by geographic location and population. Extrapolation of data from Wald and associates[160] suggests that approximately 35 percent of pneumococci colonizing children in the United States are not susceptible to penicillin. Despite the presence of potential pathogens in the nasopharynx, no convincing evidence supports the use of nasopharyngeal cultures to predict the etiology of acute otitis media, pneumonia, or sinusitis.[51, 161]

The sinuses and lower respiratory tract generally are assumed to be sterile. In actuality, bacteria from the mouth and nose probably reach these regions daily but are cleared promptly by local defense mechanisms.[125]

During the first week of life, the newborn's oropharynx usually is colonized by maternal vaginal flora, primarily *Lactobacillus* spp. and streptococcus viridans.[23, 109] These bacteria gradually are replaced by mouth flora from the mother and caretakers. *S. salivarius* and *S. mitis* predominate. Anaerobes, *S. mutans*, and *S. sanguis* are uncommon findings until eruption of teeth occurs.[88] *Ureaplasma* and *Mycoplasma* spp. from the maternal vagina readily colonize the newborn's respiratory tract.[147] They are a suspected, yet still undetermined, cause of chronic lung disease in premature infants.[67, 114, 163] Enteric bacilli can be recovered from more than one half of the throats of normal infants older than 2 months of age.[5]

GASTROINTESTINAL TRACT

The gastrointestinal tract consists of the esophagus, stomach, small intestine, and colon. The esophagus usually is sterile, and the stomach generally harbors only small numbers of bacteria. The digestive enzymes and acid in the stomach destroy most swallowed organisms, or they pass promptly into the small intestine. Among the microflora of the stomach are acid-tolerant organisms, such as lactobacilli and streptococci,[134] and *Helicobacter pylori*, which survives within the mucous layer overlaying the gastric mucosal epithelium.[19, 50, 82] The worldwide prevalence of *H. pylori* colonization in children ranges from 10 to 90 percent.[149] Factors associated with colonization include lower socioeconomic status, household crowding, ethnicity, and household contact to carriers.[58, 116, 155] When the gastric pH is raised, nasopharyngeal and fecal-type flora may colonize the stomach.[168]

Low concentrations of *Streptococcus*, *Lactobacillus*, *Veillonella*, and rare *Bacteroides* spp. can be found in the upper small intestine.[15, 25, 39] Higher concentrations of the same bacteria plus *Bifidobacterium*, *Clostridium*, and Enterobacteriaceae are present in the lower small intestine.[16, 104] Small bowel bacterial overgrowth can occur under conditions of gastric achlorhydria, a blind loop, or dysmotility. This syndrome may result in malabsorption and diarrhea.[85]

The colon contains a large and diverse population of microorganisms.[57, 138] More microbes occur in this location than anywhere else in the body. For many years, because of inadequate techniques available for culturing strict anaerobic bacteria, *E. coli* was thought to be the principal resident of the large intestine. What has become apparent is that the strict anaerobes outnumber the facultative microbes by as much as 1000 to 1, with hundreds of different anaerobic species being isolated from the colon.[134] *Bacteroides* and *Bifidobacterium* spp. comprise the largest percentage of fecal flora. Other major organisms in the colon include *Peptostreptococcus*, *Enterococcus*, Enterobacteriaceae, *Prevotella*, *Porphyromonas*, *Fusobacterium*, *Clostridium*, *Lactobacillus*, and *Eubacterium* spp.

Newborns

The newborn's intestinal flora usually are derived from organisms within the mother's birth canal and also from the baby's environment. Diet can influence the composition of the infant's intestinal flora.[32, 36, 96, 101] Full-term breast-fed infants are colonized predominantly with *Bifidobacterium* spp. Formula-fed infants have a more complex intestinal flora in which *Bifidobacterium*, *Bacteroides*, *Enterobacter*, *Clostridia*, and *Enterococcus* spp. are prevalent.[4, 11, 36, 99, 143, 171] Infants delivered by cesarean section have as much as 6 months' delay in colonization with anaerobic organisms.[18, 61, 96] At 12 months of age, after the introduction of solid foods, all infants have intestinal flora that more closely resembles those of an adult.[36]

Intestinal colonization of very-low-birth-weight infants is delayed, and the development of anaerobic flora is diminished. Anaerobes, especially *Bifidobacterium* and *Lactobacillus* spp., are thought to protect the host against invasion by pathogens. Paucity of these organisms permits bacterial overgrowth with potential pathogens, especially *E. coli* and *Klebsiella*, *Enterobacter*, and *Citrobacter* spp. Researchers suspect that this aberrant intestinal colonization of premature infants contributes to the pathogenesis of necrotizing enterocolitis.[28, 38, 91]

GENITOURINARY TRACT

The endogenous flora of the genitourinary tract normally are confined to the distal portion of the urethra and the vaginal mucosa. The anterior urethra in both men and women commonly are colonized with skin flora (coagulase-negative *Staphylococcus* and *Corynebacterium* spp. and streptococci) and may contain *Mycobacterium smegmatis* and *Bacteroides, Fusobacterium, Enterococcus,* and Enterobacteriaceae spp. The female anterior urethra also contains *Lactobacillus* spp. Asymptomatic colonization with *Ureaplasma urealyticum*, and to a lesser extent with *Mycoplasma hominus,* is not an uncommon event in sexually active individuals.[110, 150]

The microbial flora of the vagina is profoundly influenced by hormonal factors.[89, 90] During the first few weeks of life, estrogen from the maternal circulation creates a vaginal environment in the newborn girl conducive for the growth of *Lactobacillus* spp. This event is followed by development of a relatively scant vaginal flora, containing mostly coagulase-negative *Staphylococcus*, *Corynebacterium,* and occasionally Enterobacteriaceae and *Streptococcus* spp. With the onset of puberty, lactobacilli again become the predominate organisms isolated. Coagulase-negative *Staphylococcus* and *Corynebacterium* spp. and various anaerobic streptococci are also common.[6, 65, 120] *Enterococcus*, Enterobacteriaceae, and *Candida* spp. are found less frequently.[6] *U. urealyticum* is present in approximately one half of premenopausal women, and *M. hominis* is found in somewhat fewer numbers.[110, 150] The vaginal colonization rate of group B streptococci in pregnant women ranges from 5 to 35 percent.[2] Heavy colonization with *Gardnerella vaginalis*, *Trichomonas vaginalis,* and *Mobiluncus* and *Prevotella* spp. is associated with bacterial vaginosis.[140]

Beneficial Effects of the Indigenous Flora

Generally recognized is that pathogens first need to colonize the host before causing disease. The indigenous flora help to protect the host against infections through *colonization resistance*, also called *bacterial interference*.[22, 33, 72, 78, 95, 108, 132, 142, 158, 159] Colonization resistance is accomplished by several mechanisms, including competition for nutrients, competition for epithelial cell receptors, production of toxins and bacteriocins, and stimulation of the immune response.[17, 21, 22, 156, 166] Suppression of the normal flora with antimicrobial therapy correlates with an increased susceptibility to candidiasis,[135] *C. difficile* colitis,[7] and *Salmonella* infection.[73] Use of probiotic agents, live microbial food supplements (e.g., *Lactobacillus*, *Bifidobacterium* spp.), helps restore the normal intestinal microflora during antibiotic therapy and inhibits the growth of potential pathogens.[31, 130]

The endogenous intestinal flora appear to stimulate the cellular and humoral mucosal immune system.[14, 154, 162] In turn, this relationship influences the development of the newborn's immune system. Germ-free animals have underdeveloped, poorly differentiated lymphoidal tissues and low serum immunoglobulin concentrations. These animals have increased susceptibility to experimental challenges with pathogenic microbes.[42]

The normal flora provide some nutritional supplement for the host. The intestinal microflora ferment undigested carbohydrates into short-chain fatty acids. The short-chain fatty acids affect colonic epithelial cell transport and serve as an energy source for colonic epithelial cells, the liver, and muscle.[34, 124, 127, 129] The intestinal flora also participate in the enterohepatic recirculation of biliary metabolites and the degradation of toxins and carcinogens.[55, 104] In addition, normal flora microbes produce essential vitamins, such as vitamins K and B_{12}. However, whether humans use these vitamins in any substantial manner is uncertain.[41]

Adverse Effects of the Indigenous Flora

The indigenous flora can have unpleasant or even harmful affects on the host and are the source of intestinal gas and body odor. Oral flora are associated with dental caries and periodontal disease. In special circumstances, bacterial overgrowth of normal flora in the small intestine can result in malabsorption, diarrhea, and weight loss.[75, 85] Other clinical conditions can create the potential for bacterial translocation, the invasion of indigenous bowel flora across the intestinal mucosa.[13, 94] Intestinal toxins from endogenous bacteria may contribute to the encephalopathy, renal failure, and coagulopathy seen in hepatic failure.[32] Injury to the host from endotoxic shock may be caused to some extent by a hypersensitivity response induced by endotoxin from intestinal flora because germ-free animals are highly resistant to the effects of injected endotoxin.[146] Intestinal flora are speculated to cause cancer by metabolically activating carcinogens or by making carcinogenic products.[102] Finally, the intestinal normal flora may have a causative role in failure to thrive, arthritis, and autoimmune disorders.[32]

Summary

The indigenous flora of humans are unique to specific anatomic locations. They are influenced by intrinsic microbial properties, host characteristics, and exogenous factors. Indigenous flora provide clear benefits to the host as well as potential adverse affects. Familiarity with the normal flora should help clinicians provide improved care for their patients.

REFERENCES

1. Abudu, L., Blair, I., Fraise, A., et al.: Methicillin-resistant *Staphylococcus aureus* (MRSA): A community-based prevalence survey. Epidemiol. Infect. *126*:351–356, 2001.
2. American Academy of Pediatrics: Group B streptococcal infections. *In* Pickering, L. K. (ed.): 2000 Red Book: Report of the Committee on Infectious Diseases. 25th ed. Elk Grove Village, IL, American Academy of Pediatrics, 2000, pp. 537–544.
3. Asay, L. D., and Koch, R.: *Pseudomonas* infections in infants and children. N. Engl. J. Med. *262*:1062–1066, 1960.
4. Balmer, S. E., and Wharton, B. A.: Diet and faecal flora in the newborn: Breast milk and infant formula. Arch. Dis. Child. *64*:1672–1677.
5. Baltimore, R. S., Duncan, R. L., Shapiro, E. D., et al.: Epidemiology of pharyngeal colonization of infants with aerobic gram-negative rod bacteria. J. Clin. Microbiol. *27*:91–95, 1989.
6. Bartlett, J. G., and Polk, B. F.: Bacterial flora of the vagina: Quantitative study. Rev. Infect. Dis. *6*(Suppl. 1):S67–S72, 1984.
7. Bartlett, J. G., Chang, T. W., Gurwith, M., et al.: Antibiotic-associated pseudomembranous colitis due to toxin-producing clostridia. N. Engl. J. Med. *298*:531–534, 1978.
8. Barza, M., Giuliano, M., Jacobus, N. V., et al.: Effect of broad-spectrum parenteral antibiotics on "colonization resistance" of intestinal microflora of humans. Antimicrob. Agents Chemother. *31*:723–727, 1987.
9. Baxby, D., and Woodroffe, R. C. S.: The location of bacteria in the skin. J. Appl. Bacteriol. *28*:316–321, 1965.
10. Beachey, E. H.: Bacterial adherences: Adhesion-receptor interactions mediating the attachment of bacteria to mucosal surfaces. J. Infect. Dis. *143*:325–345, 1981.
11. Benno, Y., Sawada, K., and Mitsuoka, T.: The intestinal microflora of infants: Composition of fecal flora in breast-fed infants and bottle-fed infants. Microbiol. Immunol. *28*:975–986, 1984.
12. Benohanian, A.: Antiperspirants and deodorants. Clin. Dermatol. *19*:398–405, 2001.
13. Berg, R. D.: Bacterial translocation from the gastrointestinal tract. Trends Microbiol. *3*:149–154, 1995.
14. Berg, R. D., and Savage, D. C.: Immune responses of specific pathogen-free and gnotobiotic mice to antigens of indigenous and nonindigenous microorganisms. Infect. Immun. *11*:320–329, 1975.
15. Bernhardt, H., and Knoke, M.: Recent studies on the microbial ecology of the upper gastrointestinal tract. Infection *17*:259–263, 1989.
16. Bhat, P., Albert, M. J., Rajan, D., et al.: Bacterial flora of the jejunum: A comparison of luminal aspirate and mucosal biopsy. J. Med. Microbiol. *13*:247–256, 1980.
17. Bibel, D. J., Aly, R., Bayles, C., et al.: Competitive adherence as a mechanism of bacterial interference. Can. J. Microbiol. *29*:700–703, 1983.
18. Blakey, J. L., Lubitz, L., Barnes, G. L., et al.: Development of gut colonisation in pre-term neonates. J. Med. Microbiol. *15*:519–529, 1982.
19. Blaser, M. J.: Hypothesis: The changing relationships of *Helicobacter pylori* and humans. Implications for health and disease. J. Infect. Dis. *179*:1523–1530, 1999.
20. Bonhogg, M., Drake, B. L., and Miller, C. P.: Effect of streptomycin on susceptibility of intestinal tracts to experimental Salmonella infection. Proc. Soc. Exp. Biol. Med. *86*:132–137, 1954.
21. Borriello, S. P.: The influence of the normal flora on *Clostridium difficile* colonisation of the gut. Ann. Med. *22*:61–67, 1990.
22. Brook, I.: Bacterial interference. Crit. Rev. Microbiol. *25*:155–172, 1999.
23. Carlsson, J., Grahnen, H., Jonsson, G., et al.: Early establishment of *Streptococcus salivarius* in the mouths of infants. J. Dent. Res. *49*:415–418, 1970.
24. Casadevall, A., and Pirofski, L. A.: Host-pathogen interactions: Basic concepts of microbial commensalism, colonization, infection, and disease. Infect. Immun. *68*:6511–6518, 2000.
25. Challacombe, D. N., Richardson, J. M., and Anderson, C. M.: Bacterial microflora of the upper gastrointestinal tract in infants without diarrhea. Arch. Dis. Child. *49*:264–269, 1974.
26. Charlebois, E. D., Bangsberg, D. R., Moss, N. J., et al.: Population-based community prevalence of methicillin-resistant *Staphylococcus aureus* in the urban poor of San Francisco. Clin. Infect. Dis. *34*:425–433, 2002.
27. Chonmaitree, T., and Heikkinen, T.: Viruses and acute otitis media. Pediatr. Infect. Dis. J. *19*:1005–1007, 2000.
28. Claud, E. C., and Walker, W. A.: Hypothesis: Inappropriate colonization of the premature intestine can cause neonatal necrotizing enterocolitis. F. A. S. E. B. J. *15*:1398–1403, 2001.
29. Clayton, Y. M., and Noble, W. C.: Observations on the epidemiology of *Candida albicans*. J. Clin. Pathol. *19*:76–78, 1966.
30. Cockerill, F. R., MacDonald, K. L., Thompson, R. L., et al.: An outbreak of invasive group A streptococcal disease associated with high carriage rates of the invasive clone among school-aged children. J. A. M. A. *277*:38–43, 1997.

31. Collins, M. D., and Gibson, G. R.: Probiotics, prebiotics, and synbiotics: Approaches for modulating the microbial ecology of the gut. Am. J. Clin. Nutr. *69*:1052S–1057S, 1999.
32. Cooperstock, M. S.: Indigenous flora in host economy and pathogenesis. *In* Feigen, R. D., and Cherry, J. D. (eds.): Textbook of Pediatric Infectious Diseases. 3rd ed. Philadelphia, W. B. Saunders, 1992, pp. 91–119.
33. Crowe, C. C., Sanders, W. E., Jr., and Longley, S.: Bacterial interference II. Role of the normal throat flora in prevention of colonization by group A *Streptococcus*. J. Infect. Dis. *128*:527–532, 1973.
34. Cummings, J. H., and Macfarlane, G. T.: Role of intestinal bacteria in nutrient metabolism. J. Parenter. Enteral Nutr. *21*:357–365, 1997.
35. Dagan, R., Leibovitz, E., Cheletz, G., et al.: Antibiotic treatment in acute otitis media promotes superinfection with resistant *Streptococcus pneumoniae* carried before initiation of treatment. J. Infect. Dis. *183*:880–886, 2001.
36. Dai, D., and Walker, W. A.: Protective nutrients and bacterial colonization in the immature human gut. Adv. Pediatr. *46*:353–382, 1999.
37. Deane, S., Youngs, D., Poxon, V., et al.: Cimetidine and the gastric microflora. Br. J. Surg. *67*:371, 1980.
38. Deitch, E. A.: Role of bacterial translocation in necrotizing enterocolitis. Acta Paediatr. Suppl. *396*:33–36, 1994.
39. Dickman, M. D., Chappelka, A. R., and Schaedler, R. W.: The microbial ecology of the upper small bowel. Am. J. Gastroenterol. *65*:57–62, 1976.
40. Dierksen, K. P., Inglis, M., and Tagg, J. R.: High pharyngeal carriage rates of *Streptococcus pyogenes* in Dunedin school children with a low incidence of rheumatic fever. N. Z. Med. J. *113*:496–499, 2000.
41. Donaldson, R. M., Jr.: Normal bacterial populations of the intestine and their relation to intestinal function. N. Engl. J. Med. *270*:938–946, 994–1000, 1050–1056, 1964.
42. Dubos, R. J., and Schaedler, R. W.: The effect of the intestinal flora on the growth rate of mice, and on their susceptibility to experimental infections. J. Exp. Med. *111*:407–417, 1960.
43. Ehrenkranz, N. J.: Bacterial colonization of newborn infants and subsequent acquisition of hospital bacteria. J. Pediatr. *76*:839–847, 1970.
44. Eichenwald, H. F., Kotsevalov, O., and Fasso, L. A.: Some effects of viral infection on aerial dissemination of staphylococci and on susceptibility to bacterial colonization. Bacteriol. Rev. *25*:274–281, 1961.
45. Ekdahl, K., Ahlinder, I., Hansson, H. B., et al.: Duration of NP carriage of PRP: Experiences from the South Swedish Pneumococcal Intervention Project. Clin. Infect. Dis. *25*:1113–1117, 1997.
46. Elahmer, O. R., Raza, M. W., Ogilvie, M. M., et al.: The effect of respiratory virus infection on expression of cell surface antigens associated with binding of potentially pathogenic bacteria. Adv. Exp. Med. Biol. *408*:169–177, 1996.
47. Engelgau, M. M., Woernle, C. H., Schwartz, B., et al.: Invasive group A streptococcus carriage in a child care centre after a fatal case. Arch. Dis. Child. *71*:318–322, 1994.
48. Freter, R.: Interactions between mechanisms controlling the intestinal microflora. Am. J. Clin. Nutr. *27*:1409–1416, 1974.
49. Fryklund, B., Tullus, K., Berglund, B., et al.: Importance of the environment and the faecal flora of infants, nursing staff, and parents as sources of gram-negative bacteria colonizing newborns in three neonatal wards. Infection *20*:253–257, 1992.
50. Ganga-Zandzou, P. S., Michaud, L., Vincent, P., et al.: Natural outcome of *Helicobacter pylori* infection in asymptomatic children: a two-year follow-up study. Pediatrics *104*:216–221, 1999.
51. Gehanno, P., Lenoir, G., Barry, B., et al.: Evaluation of nasopharyngeal cultures for bacteriologic assessment of acute otitis media in children. Pediatr. Infect. Dis. J. *15*:329–332, 1996.
52. Ghaffar, F., Friedland, I. R., and McCracken, G. H.: Dynamics of nasopharyngeal colonization by *Streptococcus pneumoniae*. Pediatr. Infect. Dis. J. *18*:638–646, 1999.
53. Giuliano, M., Barza, M., Jacobus, N. V., et al.: Effect of broad-spectrum parenteral antibiotics on composition of intestinal microflora of humans. Antimicrob. Agents Chemother. *31*:202–206, 1987.
54. Glezen, W. P.: Prevention of acute otitis media by prophylaxis and treatment of influenza virus infections. Vaccine *19*(Suppl. 1):S56–S58, 2000.
55. Goldin, B. R.: Intestinal microflora: metabolism of drugs and carcinogens. Ann. Med. *22*:43–48, 1990.
56. Goldmann, D. A., Leclair, J., and Macone, A.: Bacterial colonization of neonates admitted to an intensive care environment. J. Pediatr. *93*:288–293, 1978.
57. Gorbach, S. L.: Intestinal microflora. Gastroenterology *60*:1110–1129, 1971.
58. Graham, D. Y., Malaty, H. M., Evans, D. J., et al.: Epidemiology of *Helicobacter pylori* in an asymptomatic population in the United States: Effect of age, race, and socioeconomic status. Gastroenterology *100*:1495–1501, 1991.
59. Gray, B. M., Converse, G. M. III, and Dillon, H. C., Jr.: Epidemiologic studies of *Streptococcus pneumoniae* in infants: Acquisition, carriage, and infection during the first 24 months of life. J. Infect. Dis. *142*:923–933, 1980.
60. Gray, J. D. A., and Shiner, M.: Influence of gastric pH on gastric and jejunal flora. Gut *8*:574–581, 1967.
61. Gronlund, M. M., Lehtonen, O. P., Eerola, E., et al.: Fecal microflora in healthy infants born by different methods of delivery: Permanent changes in intestinal flora after cesarean delivery. J. Pediatr. Gastroenterol. Nutr. *28*:19–25, 1999.
62. Gwaltney, J. M., Jr., Sande, M. A., Austrian, R., et al.: Spread of *Streptococcus pneumoniae* in families. II. Relation of transfer of *S. pneumoniae* to incidence of colds and serum antibody. J. Infect. Dis. *132*:62–68, 1975.
63. Hakansson, A., Kidd, A., Wadell, G., et al.: Adenovirus infection enhances *in vitro* adherence of *Streptococcus pneumoniae*. Infect. Immun. *62*:2707–2714, 1994.
64. Hamada, S., Amano, A., Kimura, S., et al.: The importance of fimbriae in the virulence and ecology of some oral bacteria. Oral Microbiol. Immunol. *13*:129–138, 1998.
65. Hammerschlag, M. R., Alpert, S., Onderdonk, A., et al.: Anaerobic microflora of the vagina in children. Am. J. Obstet. Gynecol. *131*:853–856, 1978.
66. Hartmann, A. A.: Daily bath and its effect on the normal human skin flora: Quantitative and qualitative investigations of the aerobic skin flora. Arch. Dermatol. Res. *265*:153–164, 1979.
67. Heggie, A. D., Bar-Shain, D., Boxerbaum, B., et al.: Identification and quantification of ureaplasma colonizing the respiratory tract and assessment of their role in the development of chronic lung disease in preterm infants. Pediatr. Infect. Dis. J. *20*:854–859, 2001.
68. Heikkinen, T., Saeed, K. A., McCormick, D. P., et al.: A single intramuscular dose of ceftriaxone changes nasopharyngeal bacterial flora in children with acute otitis media. Acta Paediatr. *89*:1316–1321, 2000.
69. Herold, B. C., Immergluck, L. C., Maranan, M. C., et al.: Community-acquired methicillin-resistant *Staphylococcus aureus* in children with no identified predisposing risk. J. A. M. A. *279*:593–598, 1998.
70. Hoffmann, S.: The throat carrier rate of group A and other beta hemolytic streptococci among patients in general practice. Acta Pathol. Microbiol. Immunol. Scand. *93*:347–351, 1985.
71. Holdeman, L. V., Good, I. J., and Moore, W. E. C.: Human fecal flora: Variation in bacterial composition within individuals and a possible effect of emotional stress. Appl. Environ. Microbiol. *31*:359–375, 1976.
72. Holm, S. E., and Grahn, E.: Bacterial interference in streptococcal tonsillitis. Scand. J. Infect. Dis. Suppl. *39*:73–78, 1983.
73. Holmberg, S. D., Osterholm, M. T., Senger, K. A., et al.: Drug-resistant *Salmonella* from animals fed antimicrobials. N. Engl. J. Med. *311*: 617–622.
74. Hooker, K. D., and Di Piro, J. T.: Effect of antimicrobial therapy on bowel flora. Clin. Pharm. *7*:878–888, 1988.
75. Husebye, E. Gastrointestinal motility disorders and bacterial overgrowth. J. Intern. Med. *237*:419–427, 1995.
76. Hussain, F. M., Boyle-Vavra, S., and Daum, R. S.: Community-acquired methicillin-resistant *Staphylococcus aureus* colonization in healthy children attending an outpatient pediatric clinic. Pediatr. Infect. Dis. J. *20*:763–767, 2001.
77. Jarvis, W. R.: The epidemiology of colonization. Infect. Control Hosp. Epidemiol. *17*:47–52, 1996.
78. Johanson, W. G., Jr., Blackstock, R., Pierce, A. K., et al.: The role of bacterial antagonism in pneumococcal colonization of the human pharynx. J. Lab. Clin. Med. *75*:946–952, 1970.
79. Johanson, W. G., Jr., Pierce, A. K., Sanford, J. P., et al.: Nosocomial respiratory infections with gram-negative bacilli: The significance of colonization of the respiratory tract. Ann. Intern. Med. *77*:701–706, 1972.
80. Johanson, W. G., Pierce, A. K., and Sanford, J. P.: Changing pharyngeal bacterial flora of hospitalized patients: Emergence of gram-negative bacilli. N. Engl. J. Med. *281*:1137–1140, 1969.
81. Johanson, W. G., Pierce, A. K., and Sanford, J. P.: Changing pharyngeal bacterial flora of hospitalized patients. N. Engl. J. Med. *281*:1137–1140, 1969.
82. Karlsson, K. A.: The human gastric colonizer *Helicobacter pylori*: A challenge for host-parasite glycobiology. Glycobiology *10*:761–771, 2000.
83. Karmeli, Y., Stalnikowitz, R., Eliakim, R., et al.: Conventional dose of omeprazole alters gastric flora. Dig. Dis. Sci. *40*:2070–2073, 1995.
84. Keswick, B. H., Berge, C. A., Bartolo, R. G., et al.: Antimicrobial soaps: Their role in personal hygiene. *In* Aly, R., Beutner, K. R., and Maibach, H. (eds.): Cutaneous Infection and Therapy. New York, Marcel Dekker, 1997, pp. 49–82.
85. Kirsch, M.: Bacterial overgrowth. Am. J. Gastroenterol. *85*:231–237, 1990.
86. Klemm, P., and Schembri, M. A.: Bacterial adhesins: Function and structure. Int. J. Med. Microbiol. *290*:27–35, 2000.
87. Kominos, S. D., Copeland, C. E., Grosiak, B., et al.: Introduction of *Pseudomonas aeruginosa* into a hospital via vegetables. Appl. Microbiol. *24*:567–570, 1972.
88. Kononen, E.: Development of oral bacterial flora in young children. Ann. Med. *32*:107–112, 2000.
89. Larsen, B., and Galask, R. P.: Vaginal microbiol flora: composition and influences of host physiology. Ann. Intern. Med. *96*:926–930, 1982.
90. Larsen, B., and Monif, G. R.: Understanding the bacterial flora of the female genital tract. Clin. Infect. Dis. *32*:69–77, 2001.

91. Lawrence, G., Bates, J., and Gaul, A.: Pathogenesis of neonatal necrotizing enterocolitis. Lancet *1*:137–139, 1982.
92. Levine, J., and Snyder, R. W.: Practical ophthalmic microbiology. J. Ophthalmic Nurs. Technol. *18*:50–59, 1999.
93. Li, L., Wu, Z., Ma, W., et al.: Changes in intestinal microflora in patients with chronic severe hepatitis. Chin. Med. J. *114*:869–872, 2001.
94. Lichtman, S. M.: Bacterial translocation in humans. J. Pediatr. Gastroenterol. Nutr. *33*:1–10, 2001.
95. Liljemark, W. F., and Gibbons, R. J.: Suppression of *Candida albicans* by human oral streptococci in gnotobiotic mice. Infect. Immun. *8*:846–849, 1973.
96. Long, S. S., and Swenson, R. M.: Development of anaerobic fecal flora in healthy newborn infants. J. Pediatr. *91*:298–301, 1977.
97. Loukides, S., Panagou, P., Kolokouris, D., et al.: Bacterial pneumonia as a suprainfection in young adults with measles. Eur. Respir. J. *13*:356–360, 1999.
98. Louria, D. B., and Kaminski, T.: The effects of four antimicrobial drug regimens on sputum superinfection in hospitalized patients. Am. Rev. Respir. Dis. *85*:649–665, 1962.
99. Lundquist, B., Nord, C. E., and Winberg, J.: The composition of the faecal microflora in breast fed and bottle fed infants from birth to eight weeks. Acta Paediatr. Scand. *74*:45–51, 1985.
100. MacGregor, R. R., and Tunnessen, W. W.: The incidence of pathogenic organisms in the normal flora of the neonate's external ear and nasopharynx. Clin. Pediatr. *12*:697–700, 1973.
101. Mackie, R. I., Sghir, A., and Gaskins, H. R.: Developmental microbial ecology of the neonatal gastrointestinal tract. Am. J. Clin. Nutr. *69*(Suppl.):1035S–1045S, 1999.
102. Mackowiak, P. A.: Microbial oncogenesis. Am. J. Med. *82*:79–97, 1987.
103. Mackowiak, P. A.: The normal microbial flora. N. Engl. J. Med. *307*:83–93, 1982.
104. Mallory, A., Kern, F., Smith, J., et al.: Patterns of bile acids and microflora in the human small intestine. I. Bile acids. Gastroenterology *64*:26–33, 1973.
105. Marples, M. J.: The normal flora of the human skin. Br. J. Dermatol. *81*(Suppl. 1):2–13, 1969.
106. Marples, R.: The normal flora of different sites in the young adult. Curr. Med. Res. Opin. 7(Suppl. 2): 67–70, 1982.
107. Marples, R. R., and Kligman, A. M.: Ecological effects of oral antibiotics on the microflora of human skin. Arch. Dermatol. *103*:148–153, 1971.
108. Martin, R. R., and White, A.: The reacquisition of staphylococci by treated carriers: A demonstration of bacterial interference. J. Lab. Clin. Med. *71*:791–797, 1968.
109. McCarthy, C., Snyder, M. L., and Parker, R. B.: The indigenous oral flora of man. I. The newborn to one year old infant. Arch. Oral. Biol. *10*:61–70, 1965.
110. McCormak, W. M., Rosner, B., Alpert, S., et al.: Vaginal colonization with *Mycoplasma hominis* and *Ureaplasma urealyticum*. Sex. Transm. Dis. *13*:67–70, 1986.
111. Montes, L. F., and Wilborn, W. H.: Location of bacterial skin flora. Br. J. Dermatol. *81*(Suppl. I):23–26, 1969.
112. Nord, C. E., Heimdahl, A., and Kager, L.: Antimicrobial induced alterations of the human oropharyngeal and intestinal microflora. Scand. J. Infect. Dis. Suppl. *49*:64–72, 1986.
113. Norrby, S. R.: Ecological consequences of broad spectrum versus narrow spectrum antibacterial therapy. Scand. J. Infect. Dis. Suppl. *49*:189–195, 1986.
114. Ollikainen, J., Heiskanen-Kosma, T., Korppi, M., et al.: Clinical relevance of *Ureasplasma urealyticum* colonization in preterm infants. Acta Paediatr. *87*:1075–1078, 1998.
115. Ostfeld, E., Segal, J., Segal, A., et al.: Bacterial colonization of the nose and external ear canal in newborn infants. Isr. J. Med. Sci. *19*:1046–1049, 1983.
116. Peek, R. M.: The biological impact of *Helicobacter pylori* colonization. Semin. Gastrointest. Dis. *12*:151–166, 2001.
117. Perkins, R. E., Kundsin, R. B., Pratt, M. V., et al.: Bacteriology of normal and infected conjunctiva. J. Clin. Microbiol. *1*:147–149, 1975.
118. Pichichero, M. E., Marsocci, S. M., Murphy, M. L., et al.: Incidence of streptococcal carriers in private pediatric practice. Arch. Pediatr. Adolesc. Med. *153*:624–628, 1999.
119. Ramirez-Ronda, C. H., Fuxench-Lopez, Z., and Nevarez, B. S. M. T.: Increased pharyngeal bacterial colonization during viral illness. Arch. Intern. Med. *141*:1599–1603, 1981.
120. Redondo-Lopez, V., Cook, R. L., and Sobel, J. D.: Emerging role of lactobacilli in the control and maintenance of the vaginal bacterial microflora. Rev. Infect. Dis. *12*:856–872, 1990.
121. Remington, J. S., and Schimpff, S. C.: Occasional notes. Please don't eat the salads. N. Engl. J. Med. *304*:433–435, 1981.
122. Roberts, S. O.: *Pityrosporum orbiculare*: Incidence and distribution on clinically normal skin. Br. J. Dermatol. *81*:264–269, 1969.
123. Roberts, S. O.: The mycology of the clinically normal scalp. Br. J. Dermatol. *81*:626–628, 1969.
124. Roediger, W. E. W.: Role of anaerobic bacteria in the metabolic welfare of the colonic mucosa in man. Gut *21*:793–798, 1980.
125. Roscoe, D. L., and Chow, A. W.: Normal flora and mucosal immunity of the head and neck. Infect. Dis. Clin. North Am. *2*:1–19, 1988.
126. Rotimi, V. O., and Duerden, B. I.: The development of the bacterial flora in normal neonates. J. Med. Microbiol. *14*:51–62, 1981.
127. Royall, D. R., Wolever, T. M. S., and Jeejeebhoy, K. N.: Clinical significance of colonic fermentation. Am. J. Gastroenterol. *80*:1307–1312, 1990.
128. Ruddell, W. S. J., Axon, A. T. R., Findlay, J. M., et al.: Effect of cimetidine of the gastric bacterial flora. Lancet *1*:672–674, 1980.
129. Ruppin, H., Bar-Meir, S., Soergel, K. H., et al.: Absorption of short chain fatty acids by the colon. Gastroenterology *78*:1500–1507, 1980.
130. Saavedra, J. M.: Clinical applications of probiotic agents. Am. J. Clin. Nutr. *73*:1147S–1151S, 2001.
131. Sakata, H., Yoshioka, H., and Fujita, K.: Development of the intestinal flora in very low birth weight infants compared to normal full-term infants. Eur. J. Pediatr. *144*:186–190, 1985.
132. Sanders, E.: Bacterial interference. I. Its occurrence among the respiratory tract flora and characterization of inhibition of group A streptococci by viridans streptococci. J. Infect. Dis. *120*:698–707, 1969.
133. Sanford, B. A., Shelokov, A., and Ramsay, M. A.: Bacterial adherence to virus-infected cells: A cell culture model of bacterial superinfection. J. Infect. Dis. *137*:176–181, 1978.
134. Savage, D. S.: Microbial ecology of the gastrointestinal tract. Annu. Rev. Microbiol. *31*:107–133, 1977.
135. Seelig, M. S.: The role of antibiotics in the pathogenesis of *Candida* infections. Am. J. Med. *40*:887–917, 1966.
136. Sharp, S. E.: Commensal and pathogenic microorganisms of humans. *In* Murray, P. A., Baron, E. J., Pfaller, M. A., et al. (eds.): Manual of Clinical Microbiology. 7th ed. Washington, D.C., ASM Press, 1999, pp. 23–32.
137. Shopsin, B., Mathema, B., Martinez, J., et al.: Prevalence of methicillin-resistant and methicillin-susceptible *Staphylococcus aureus* in the community. J. Infect. Dis. *182*:359–362, 2000.
138. Simon, G. L., and Gorbach, S. L.: Intestinal flora in health and disease. Gastroenterology *86*:174–193, 1984.
139. Somerville, D. A.: The normal flora of the skin in different age groups. Br. J. Dermatol. *81*:248–258, 1969.
140. Spiegel, C. A.: Bacterial vaginosis. Clin. Microbiol. Rev. *4*:485–502, 1991.
141. Spitzer, J., Hennessy, E., and Neville, L.: High group A streptococcal carriage in the Orthodox Jewish community of North Hackney. Br. J. Gen. Pract. *51*:101–105, 2001.
142. Sprunt, K., and Redman, W.: Evidence suggesting importance of role in interbacterial inhibition in maintaining balance of normal flora. Ann. Intern. Med. *68*:579–590, 1968.
143. Stark, P. L., and Lee, A.: The microbial ecology of the large bowel of breast-fed and formula-fed infants during the first year of life. J. Med. Microbiol. *15*:189–203, 1982.
144. Stromberg, A., Schwan, A., and Cars, O.: Throat carrier rates of beta-hemolytic streptococci among healthy adults and children. Scand. J. Infect. Dis. *20*:411–417, 1988.
145. Suggs, A. H., Maranan, M. C., Boyle-Vavra, S., et al.: Methicillin-resistant and borderline methicillin-resistant asymptomatic *Staphylococcus aureus* colonization in children without identifiable risk factors. Pediatr. Infect. Dis. J. *18*:410–414, 1999.
146. Swartz, M. N., Gibbons, R., and Socransky, S.: Indigenous bacteria: Oral microbiology. *In* Davis, B. D., Dulbecco, R., Eisen, H. N., et al. (eds.): Microbiology. 4th ed. Philadelphia, J. B. Lippincott, 1990, pp. 727–736.
147. Syringiannopoulos, G. A., Kapatais-Zoumbos, K., Decavalas, G. O., et al.: *Ureaplasma urealyticum* colonization of full term infants: Perinatal acquisition and persistence during early infancy. Pediatr. Infect. Dis. J. *9*:236–240, 1990.
148. Takase, H., Nitanai, H., Yamamura, E., et al.: Facilitated expansion of pneumococcal colonization from the nose to the lower respiratory tract in mice preinfected with influenza virus. Microbiol. Immunol. *43*:905–907, 1999.
149. Taylor, D. N., and Blaser, M. J. The epidemiology of *Helicobacter pylori* infection. Epidemiol. Rev. *13*:42–59, 1991.
150. Taylor-Robinson, D., and McCormack, W. M.: The genital mycoplasmas. N. Engl. J. Med. *302*:1003–1010, 1063–1067, 1980.
151. Theisen, J., Nehra, D., Citron, D., et al.: Suppression of gastric acid secretion in patients with gastroesophageal reflux disease results in gastric bacterial overgrowth and deconjugation of bile acids. J. Gastrointest. Surg. *4*:50–54, 2000.
152. Thomas, S., Raman, R., Idikula, J., et al.: Alterations in oropharyngeal flora in patients with a nasogastric tube: A cohort study. Crit. Care. Med. *20*:1677–1680, 1992.
153. Thorens, J., Froehlich, F., Schwizer, W., et al.: Bacterial overgrowth during treatment with omeprazole compared with cimetidine: A prospective randomised double blind study. Gut *39*:54–59, 1996.
154. Tlaskalova-Hogenova, H., Sterzl, J., Stepankova, R., et al. Development of immunological capacity under germfree and conventional conditions. Ann. N. Y. Acad. Sci. *409*:96–113.
155. Torres, J., Perez-Perez, G., Goodman, K. J., et al.: A comprehensive review of the natural history of *Helicobacter pylori* infection in children. Arch. Med. Res. *31*:431–469, 2000.

156. Tramont, E. C., and Hoover, D. L.: Innate (general or nonspecific) host defense mechanisms. *In* Mandell, G. L., Bennett, J. E., and Dolin, R. (eds.): Principles and Practice of Infectious Diseases. 5th ed. Philadelphia, Churchill Livingstone, 2000, pp. 31–38.
157. Vanden Bergh, M. F., Yzerman, E. P., van Belkum, A., et al.: Follow-up of *Staphylococcus aureus* nasal carriage after 8 years: Redefining the persistent carrier state. J. Clin. Microbiol. *37*:3133–3140, 1999.
158. van der Waaij, D., Berghuis de Vries, J. M., and Lekkerkerk van der Wees, J. E. C.: Colonization resistance of the digestive tract in conventional and antibiotic-treated mice. J. Hyg. *69*:405–411, 1971.
159. Vollaard, E. J., and Clasener, H. A.: Colonization resistance. Antimicrob. Agents Chemother. *38*:409–414, 1994.
160. Wald, E. R., Mason, E. O., Bradley, J. S., et al.: Acute otitis media caused by *Streptococcus pneumoniae* in children's hospitals between 1994 and 1997.Pediatr. Infect. Dis. J. *20*:34–39, 2001.
161. Wald, E. R., Milmoe, G. J., Bowen, A., et al.: Acute maxillary sinusitis in children. N. Engl. J. Med. *304*:749–754, 1981.
162. Walker, W. A.: Role of nutrients and bacterial colonization in the development of intestinal host defense. J. Pediatr. Gastroenterol. Nutr. *30*(Suppl. 2):S2–7, 2000.
163. Wang, E. E., Ohlsson, A., and Kellner, J. D.: Association of *Ureaplasma urealyticum* colonization with chronic lung disease of prematurity: Results of a metaanalysis. J. Pediatr. *127*:40–644, 1995.
164. Weiss, A., Brinser, J. H., and Nazar-Stewart, V.: Acute conjunctivitis in childhood. J. Pediatr. *122*:10–14, 1993.
165. Weiss, K., Laverdiere, M., Lovgren, M., et al.: Group A *Streptococcus* carriage among close contacts of patients with invasive infections. Am. J. Epidemiol. *149*:863–868, 1999.
166. Wells, C. L., Maddaus, M. A., Jechorek, R. P., et al.: Role of intestinal anaerobic flora in colonization resistance. Eur. J. Clin. Microbiol. Infect. Dis. 7:107, 1988.
167. Whittaker, C. J., Klier, C. M., and Kolenbrander, P. E.: Mechanisms of adhesion by oral bacteria. Annu. Rev. Microbiol. *50*:513–552, 1996.
168. Williams, C.: Occurrence and significance of gastric colonization during acid-inhibitory therapy. Best Pract. Res. Clin. Gastroenterol. *15*:511–521, 2001.
169. Yagupsky, P., Landau, D., Beck, A., et al.: Carriage of *Streptococcus pyogenes* among infants and toddlers attending day-care facilities in closed communities in southern Israel. Eur. J. Clin. Microbiol. Infect. Dis. *14*:54–58, 1995.
170. Young, L. S., LaForce, F. M., Head, J. J., et al.: A simultaneous outbreak of meningococcal and influenza infections. N. Engl. J. Med. *287*:5–9, 1972.
171. Yoshioka, H., Iseki, K., and Fujita, K.: Development and differences of intestinal flora in the neonatal period in breast-fed and bottle-fed infants. Pediatrics *72*:317–321, 1983.
172. Yow, M.: Development of *Proteus* and *Pseudomonas* infection during antimicrobial therapy. J. A. M. A. *149*:1184–1188, 1952.

Epidemiology of Infectious Diseases

EDWARD A. MORTIMER, JR.* ■ JAMES D. CHERRY

Epidemiology is concerned primarily with describing and explaining the occurrence of disease in populations. This chapter is a general review of epidemiology as it relates to infectious diseases of pediatric importance. Readers concerned with the epidemiology of a particular disease should consult the appropriate chapter for the available relevant information.

Physicians who engage in pediatric practice, teaching, or research in the area of pediatric infectious diseases or public health require competence in epidemiology to understand the mechanisms of infection, modes of transmission, and approaches to control. The principles and methods of epidemiology must be meshed with biostatistics (presented in detail in Chapter 251) and with more content-oriented sciences, including, but not limited to, clinical medicine, microbiology, pathophysiology, immunology, demography, and sociology.

Epidemiology may be considered to be of three types: descriptive, analytic or causative, and experimental. All three types are important in infectious disease.

Descriptive epidemiology provides accounts of the health experiences of populations, including morbidity and mortality. The data are of two types: incidence and prevalence. *Incidence* data consist of the numbers of new cases or deaths from a given disorder that occurs in a defined population for a period that may be measured from days to years. Sequential temporal comparisons often are used for assessing trends, and incidence data frequently are useful for setting public health priorities.

Prevalence data describe the existing number of cases of a disorder at a single moment in time. Prevalence data are applicable largely to chronic disorders such as diabetes mellitus, tuberculosis, or human immunodeficiency virus (HIV) infection and have no utility when applied to acute disorders such as measles. Additionally, in studies of infectious diseases, the prevalence of serologic markers may be used to estimate the immune status of a population or the proportion of a group that has had previous experience with an infectious agent. For certain infections such as tuberculosis and diphtheria, skin testing may serve as a substitute for serologic testing.

Analytic, or *causative*, epidemiology searches for clues to the cause of disease. It is based on the simple principle that disease does not occur at random in the population and classically considers time, person, and place. In other words, differences exist between those who acquire a given disorder and those who do not. Identification of these differences may lead to ascertainment of causation and to means of control. These differences may be inherent in the individuals themselves and include biologic characteristics (e.g., hereditary, such as race; acquired, such as immunity) and lifestyle. They may be external and largely consist of environmental risk factors for disease, including, in the instance of infectious diseases, various factors that influence the likelihood of exposure to an agent, such as geography, weather, contact with vectors (including other humans), and social and economic conditions. In studies of infectious diseases, considerable overlap exists between descriptive and analytic epidemiology for the simple reason that differences in the distribution of disease by person, place, and time often are obvious in descriptive data and provide clues for further study.

Analytic epidemiologic studies of infectious diseases, as well as those related to other types of conditions, generally fall into three categories. The least frequently used but

*Deceased

nonetheless useful category is the cross-sectional study. Such studies can be conducted in either of two ways. First, one might examine apparently comparable populations with differing prevalence rates of a given infection for characteristics that might explain these different rates. Alternatively, if a disorder is sufficiently common, one can determine rates of disease in those with and those without a suspected risk factor. A classic example is the relationship of sickle-cell trait to resistance to *Plasmodium falciparum* malaria, which was examined both ways.[1] In studies of variations in the prevalence of the sickle-cell gene in Africa, researchers noted that the trait appeared to be more prevalent in areas with a high incidence of malaria. Based on this observation, other studies were conducted and showed that in hyperendemic areas, individuals with the sickle-cell trait might have some resistance to malarial infection, thus permitting selective survival in malarial areas. This observation led to studies of the mechanism of this phenomenon and certain other erythrocyte characteristics that influence malarial infection, including blood subgroups.

The second type of causative or analytic epidemiologic study used in infectious diseases is the prospective study, sometimes called the cohort study. In this type of study, rates of infection and routes of transmission may be determined by examining subsequent rates of infection in groups of individuals with differences in exposure, which may be measured by timing, duration, intimacy of contact, or disparate sources or avenues of potential transmission. The classic studies of the transmission of group A streptococcal infection in military recruits are excellent examples. One particular finding was that transmission of infection from individuals with streptococcal pharyngitis to others in military barracks occurred at rates inversely related to distances between bunks, which established that transmission occurred largely by intimate respiratory contact with droplets containing hundreds or thousands of organisms rather than by airborne droplet nuclei.[73] In other studies, the same group showed that fomites, naturally contaminated with streptococci, did not participate in the transmission of infection.[62]

Studies of the transmission of staphylococci to newborn infants are other examples of prospective epidemiologic observation. In the 1950s, outbreaks of staphylococcal disease, sometimes severe, occurred in newborn nurseries. In an effort to determine how these organisms were transmitted to babies by personnel or other infants, nurseries with persistently high rates of colonization of infants were investigated.[56] Two types of prospective studies were conducted. One consisted of instituting measures that prevented transmission by all but one or two routes, thus permitting assessment of the importance of the unblocked routes in transmission. The other method was the reverse: one or another suspected route of transmission was blocked, and subsequent colonization of infants was monitored. These studies showed that transmission of organisms from personnel who were carriers or from previously colonized infants occurred primarily by the hands of personnel.

Another type of analytic epidemiologic study useful in infectious disease is the retrospective or case-control study. In the aforementioned prospective type of study, the investigator starts with individuals who are exposed to a given agent and, for comparison purposes, a similar group of unexposed individuals. The outcome measure of the study is infection or no infection. In contrast, in a retrospective study, the populations under study are composed of individuals who already have the disorder in question. For comparison, similar control subjects who do not have the disease are recruited. From all individuals in both groups, historical data about previous exposure, experience, and characteristics are obtained, usually by interview but sometimes by laboratory methods such as serology. Thus, in a retrospective study, the investigator starts with diseased individuals and searches for exposure; in a prospective study, the investigator starts with exposure and monitors for development of infection.

Retrospective studies are of particular utility when the disease is relatively uncommon because a prospective study might require an unwieldy number of subjects. A retrospective study obviously is preferable when no previous information about the probable cause or source of the disease exists. For this reason, retrospective studies sometimes are designated "fishing expeditions." A disadvantage of retrospective studies is that they do not provide an estimate of the true risk or rate of disease occurring after exposure (i.e., the proportion of exposed individuals in whom the disorder in question actually did develop). The reason is that the study addresses subjects who already have the disease and rarely, if ever, can an estimate be made of the size of the exposed population from which these subjects were drawn. Instead, a retrospective study provides only an odds ratio, which is the relative probability of exposed individuals acquiring the disease in comparison to those who have not been exposed. The odds ratio is, however, a reasonable approximation of the relative risk as determined by prospective studies.

The third type of epidemiologic study useful in infectious diseases is *experimental epidemiology* (the clinical trial). Clinical trials generally are used to determine the efficacy of preventive or therapeutic measures. As such, they often require previous information derived from analytic epidemiologic studies, as well as from other basic and clinical sciences. Sometimes, studies that are, in effect, clinical trials may provide useful information regarding the cause or routes of transmission of infection, as with studies of staphylococcal transmission in nurseries.

To assess the efficacy of therapeutic or preventive measures, experimental epidemiologic studies require comparison groups of individuals who do not receive the measure in question or, sometimes, are given an older or alternative modality.

Most clinical trials are not undertaken in situations in which the untreated group uniformly experiences an unambiguous outcome. Moreover, even when the outcome measure is a condition that is reasonably clear-cut, such as varicella, a trial of a preventive vaccine usually requires unimmunized controls because attack rates may vary from place to place and from year to year, intensities of exposure may be different, and some subjects already may be immune.[75]

In a controlled clinical trial, an important factor is that the treatment and control groups be as nearly similar as possible in terms of characteristics that may affect the outcome. Clinical trials designed to assess the efficacy of therapeutic or preventive measures must take into consideration many such factors, which usually include age, sex, socioeconomic status, general health, and likelihood of exposure. Therefore, in any trial, effort should be made to balance treated and untreated subjects in terms of recognized factors. However, not all variables that may inject bias into the results of a clinical trial are necessarily known or recognized in advance. Accordingly, to ensure insofar as possible that these characteristics are distributed approximately equally between the two groups, the process of randomization almost always is necessary. In addition, true randomization must occur; methods involving odd versus even record numbers or birth dates, alternate days of the week, and the like are inappropriate. The optimal method is a system of random numbers, as published in most textbooks of biostatistics.

Randomization avoids selection bias, best defined as underlying differences between the treatment and control groups, whether internal (inherent) or external, such as the likelihood of exposure. Avoidance of selection bias is of paramount importance for any type of comparative study, analytic as well as experimental epidemiologic studies.

Two other types of bias must be avoided: confounding bias and ascertainment bias. Confounding bias is defined best as a factor that appears more often in either the treated or control group and is likely to influence the outcome. Obviously, confounding bias in some instances is a form of selection bias. Nonetheless, specific forms of confounding bias may be found in clinical trials. If a study attempted to assess the value of steroids in the treatment of certain severe infections, the study might be confounded if the two groups received different antibiotics.

Very important is the potential for ascertainment bias. Put rather simply, ascertainment bias occurs in analytic epidemiologic studies and in experimental epidemiology. When ascertainment bias is derived from recounting of events by the study subjects, it usually is referred to as reporting or recall bias. Many examples exist. In a retrospective (case-control) epidemiologic study, affected individuals, for obvious reasons, may exert more diligence than healthy controls might in pursuing factors that they consider, or are led to think, might have had an effect on the development of their disorders or on the outcome. The potential for this type of recall bias was of particular concern in the studies that eventually pointed to salicylates as risk factors for development of Reye syndrome. Reporting bias also is a potential problem in experimental epidemiology, particularly when the outcome of the therapeutic or preventive measure under assessment depends on reporting of symptoms by subjects. If, for example, the study subjects anticipate a beneficial effect from a vaccine against the common cold, recipients may tend to ignore or fail to report minor symptoms after immunization (the placebo effect).

The other form of potential ascertainment bias involves observation by investigators. Those who pursue assessment of the efficacy of a new preventive or therapeutic measure in infectious disease as a rule would not do so unless they subscribe to the consensus that the measure in question might offer more benefit than can be realized with other approaches. Therefore, of importance is to ensure that the subtle, but nonetheless human, characteristic of anticipating the hoped-for outcome does not influence the observation of outcomes in analytic or experimental epidemiologic studies. In analytic studies that look for clues to causation, particularly retrospective studies, of paramount importance is that previous exposure of cases and controls be pursued with equal vigor.

For these reasons, comparative epidemiologic studies, whether analytic or experimental, usually require "blinding" of the investigators and subjects. Depending on the nature of the investigation, studies may be single-, double-, or triple-blind. In single-blind studies, the study subjects are unaware of their status as members of the treated or control groups. In double-blind studies, not only the subjects but also the investigators lack such knowledge. In triple-blind studies, those responsible for the analyses are blinded, as are the subjects and the researchers. Blinding of those who conduct the analyses, whether they are examining clinical or laboratory data, may have consequences when the data are subject to interpretation.

These principles apply to all epidemiologic studies, not just studies of infectious diseases. They are applicable to the study of cardiovascular disease, cancer, and all the other ills that affect humans. However, in infectious diseases, three additional factors contribute uniquely to who is and who is not affected: (1) the cause is a specific external agent (the infecting organism); (2) transmission of the organism to the host is required; and (3) certain host factors, such as immunity to infection or disease, may affect the outcome. Recognition of these factors (the infecting agent, transmission, and immunity) evolved gradually over many years. Before considering variations in person, place, and time, one should consider these special features of infectious disease causation.

Historical Perspectives

Epidemiology evolved from the study of great epidemic diseases such as plague, cholera, and smallpox. The periodic waves of these diseases, which were associated with high mortality rates, stimulated the first serious efforts to explain the occurrence of disease on the basis of other than supernatural or divine forces.

Fundamental to such explanations was the concept of contagion. This factor long had been implicit in attitudes toward victims of leprosy, as exemplified by such early Christian practices as conducting antemortem funerals for lepers, who then were given a bell and cup and forbidden further human contact or, more drastically, were buried alive or burned at the stake.[66] However, an Italian physician-poet, Girolamo Fracastoro (1478–1553), was the first to voice this concept formally, initially in a poem *(Syphilides, sine Morbi Gallici, libre tres)* in which he dubbed syphilis the "French disease" and later in the book *De Res Contagiosa* (published in 1546) in which he expressed the complete idea of infection transferred by minute, invisible particles.[68]

During the next 2 centuries, Fracastoro was forgotten, and views like those of Thomas Sydenham (1624–1689) prevailed.[21] This notable English physician, who introduced laudanum (derived from opium) as a pain killer and recognized the efficacy of Peruvian bark (quinine) in malaria, revived the hippocratic idea of "epidemic constitutions" (of atmospheric nature), which by grafting onto existing illness, gave all concurrent illnesses the character reflecting the then prevailing "constitution." These views persisted in colonial America, where they were expounded by such eminent persons as Noah Webster (of dictionary fame) and Dr. Benjamin Rush of Philadelphia.[78]

Nonetheless, by the mid-18th century, the theory of contagion had gained acceptance for particular diseases, including measles, syphilis, and smallpox. Indeed, it is alleged to have been exploited in an early act of biologic warfare: Massachusetts colonists reportedly presented the blankets of smallpox victims as gifts to the Indians, who then suffered a decimating epidemic.[25]

The true origin of the concept of immunity is uncertain, but it was applied first in relation to smallpox. Variolation (inoculation of young people with lesion material expected to induce modified, but immunizing disease) was practiced in China as early as the 11th or 12th century and in England and the American colonies in the early 18th century. Also popular in rural England at this time was the theory that cowpox, the minor disease acquired from afflicted cattle, induced immunity to smallpox. This theory was verified by Edward Jenner (reported in 1798) and resulted, years later, in general acceptance of cowpox vaccine (vaccinia) to protect against smallpox.

Implicit in the concept of contagion as formulated by Fracastoro in 1546 was the germ theory of disease. It was stated explicitly in 1855 by John Snow, an English anesthesiologist who took up cholera epidemiology as an avocation. Snow argued that the causative agent of cholera was a living cell that multiplied with great rapidity but was too small to be seen under the microscopes then in use.[70] Louis Pasteur (1822–1895) formally validated the germ theory by showing that the microorganisms responsible for fermentation were not generated spontaneously but came from the air.[60] On this basis, Joseph Lord Lister revolutionized surgery by using carbolic acid to combat atmospheric germs and minimize "putrification" in surgical procedures.[68]

In Pasteur's wake, bacteria were cultured with great frequency from ill persons and, all too often, were identified erroneously as causal agents. Robert Koch (1843–1910), who first isolated the bacterial causes of tuberculosis and cholera, also was the first to introduce scientific rigor into the proof of primary causation. His famed "postulates," to be satisfied before a causal relationship between a bacterium and a disease could be accepted, required that (1) the presence of the agent be demonstrated in every case by its recovery in pure culture; (2) the agent not be found in cases of other disease; (3) once isolated, the agent be capable of reproducing the disease in experimental animals; and (4) the agent be recovered in pure culture from such experimental disease.[33] Koch's postulates since have been modified, in large part to meet problems posed by viruses. As obligate intracellular parasites, viruses cannot be "cultivated in pure culture." In addition, they often are host-specific and will not produce disease in an animal model. Thus, other considerations that were invoked as elements of proof included the significance of recovery of the agent from diseased tissues, the demonstration of a rise in titer of specific antibody in temporal relation to the disease, and, most conclusive, the specific preventive effect of vaccines containing the viral antigen.[39] One further situation not recognized by Koch is that infections with true pathogens do not always cause disease. Indeed, we now recognize pathogenicity (defined as the proportion of infections that result in disease) as an important characteristic of infectious disease agents.

Cause of Disease

GENERAL CONCEPTS

Causation of infectious diseases is simple conceptually and relatively well understood. It is defined in terms of the primary cause and contributing factors (or secondary causes). The former is the specific microorganism (disease agent) without which the particular disease cannot occur. Contributing factors affect the likelihood that infection will occur and help determine that disease will result, given infection. Because identification of the causative agent in a comparatively few instances has led to the development of effective means for providing specific protective immunization (diphtheria and tetanus toxoids, vaccines against polio and measles), the importance of the primary cause often is overemphasized. An important note is that infection and disease are not synonymous, although infection obviously is necessary for disease to occur. *Infection* denotes colonization, multiplication, and, indeed, completion of the entire pathogenetic process of the organism in the host, usually including induction of an immune response but without producing recognizable pathologic and clinical manifestations. *Disease* is present when pathologic and clinical changes occur with infection. Many examples exist of infections that may or may not produce disease in the host, such as poliomyelitis and mumps; moreover, disease, when it occurs, varies in severity among infected people. Some infections, of course, produce full-blown disease in all infected susceptible persons; measles is an example. Simple *colonization,* in contrast to infection and disease, is a state in which the organism parasitizes the host at an appropriate site, replicates, and often persists but fails to proceed further with the processes of infection and disease, including induction of immunity. The *carrier state,* in which the organism persists over time and can be infective for others, may occur after colonization, infection, or disease.

Many contributing factors, largely related to the host and to the conditions of exposure, determine whether colonization takes place and whether the subsequent processes of infection and disease occur. These contributing or risk factors are many and various and from the standpoint of the host may include, but are not limited to, age, sex, race, immune status, genetic constitution, and the general state of health, including underlying diseases. Similarly, nonhost contributing factors may be multiple and include climate, the presence of vectors, sanitation, intimacy of exposure, and socioeconomic conditions. These contributing factors vary among infectious diseases and are discussed with the specific diseases.

AGENT FACTORS

Disease agents can be described collectively as invading, living parasites. They belong to one of four classes of organisms: (1) higher parasites (parasites, for short), which are multicellular animals (metazoa) including mites and helminths (worms), or single-celled animals (protozoa), such as amebae and the malarial parasites; (2) fungi; (3) bacteria, including two groups of obligate intracellular parasites (rickettsiae and chlamydiae); and (4) viruses. In other chapters, specific pathogens belonging to these groups are described with respect to their distinguishing characteristics and the diseases that they cause. Our interest here is in indicating what attributes of living parasites are significant epidemiologically. Properties directly important to the occurrence of disease are those that relate to perpetuation of the agent as a species, those that govern the type of contact required to infect humans, and those that determine the production of disease. Also important are characteristics useful in classification and specific identification of agents. Some of the important attributes are "intrinsic" in that they can be described after appropriate direct examination of the agent. Others can be described only on the basis of the behavior of the agents in the host; hence, they are "host related."

Intrinsic Properties

Classification of agents is important because knowledge of well-known agents, such as polioviruses, may help predict critical properties of similarly classified but less well studied agents, such as the numerous other enteroviruses. Precise identification of agents is basic to the specific recognition of infections and related disease. Both are dependent on intrinsic properties, including morphology (which alone provides the basis for identifying most higher parasites), chemical composition (the type of nucleic acid being important in viral classification), and antigenic character. The last is central to specific identification of agent isolates and antibodies induced by infection. Requirements for growth or replication provide keys to the identification of some bacteria (e.g., sugar fermentation) and many viruses that replicate optimally or only in cultures of certain types of cells incubated at specified temperatures. For example, rhinoviruses replicate best in human diploid cells incubated at 33° C.

Many infectious agents possess intrinsic markers that can distinguish strains within species. They also may assist in tracking down the source of infection. Thus, within poliovirus serotypes, strains from a common source can be identified by their distinctive antigenic character, for example, vaccine-like strains recovered from family contacts of vaccinated infants. More sophisticated techniques, such as nucleotide sequencing of wild polioviruses or outer-membrane serotyping of meningococci of the same group, permit epidemiologic tracing of various strains of the same organism worldwide. Similarly, sporadic cases of typhoid fever may be traced to a common carrier by the vulnerability of the isolated bacteria to lysis with a particular type of bacteriophage. Such markers also may be related to the pathogenicity of strains. Thus, infection with a temperate bacteriophage renders *Corynebacterium diphtheriae* toxigenic and, therefore, identifies pathogenic strains.

Several intrinsic properties relate to transmission and long-term survival of infectious agents. Persistence in the free state outside the host depends on requirements for replication (viruses replicate only within the cells of their host, whereas the nutrient requirements of bacteria often exist in food or milk) and on viability under natural conditions of temperature, moisture, and radiation. The ability of agents to persist determines whether transmission requires direct contact, as with influenza viruses, or can involve indirect mechanisms operating over longer periods. Examples include polioviruses, typhoid bacilli, and the bacterial cause of legionellosis.

The spectrum of animals and arthropods that an agent can parasitize (the host range) helps determine the possibilities for successful links in the transmission and reservoir mechanisms. The broader the range, the greater the possibilities. Agents that use arthropod vectors include St. Louis encephalitis virus and *Rickettsia prowazekii* (the cause of epidemic typhus). The former can infect many avian and mammalian species, as well as a wide range of mosquitoes, whereas the latter is restricted largely to the louse vector and the human host. Among agents requiring no vector, many infect only humans (diphtheria bacillus, measles virus), whereas others have multiple natural hosts (rabies virus, most of the *Salmonella* group of bacteria).

Elaboration of exotoxins is an intrinsic attribute of many bacteria and contributes in varying degrees to disease pathogenesis and, indirectly, to immunity in many infections. Another attribute, which can operate in two opposing ways, is susceptibility to chemotherapeutic agents or antibiotics. Successful treatment may shorten the period of communicability, as in streptococcal infections, but it may lead to relaxed precautions against infection; syphilis and gonorrhea are notable examples.

The instability of some intrinsic attributes as a result of the emergence of genetically different populations because of mutations, selective pressure, gene or plasmid transfer between bacteria, or genetic recombination can be of great importance. One example is the resistance to chemotherapeutic or antibiotic agents that may result from selective pressure (the probable explanation for the rapid acquisition of sulfanilamide resistance by gonococci) or plasmid transfer of resistance to antibiotics between enteric bacteria. Such resistance is currently of increasing importance, as exemplified by the appearance of multidrug-resistant *Mycobacterium tuberculosis* and penicillin-resistant pneumococci. Change in antigenic character can diminish the effectiveness of immunity and complicate specific recognition of infection. Influenza A virus is the classic example, with periodic major changes (shift) occurring in either or both critical surface antigens, hemagglutinin and neuraminidase, associated with pandemic disease and progressive minor change in hemagglutinin in the interpandemic period.

The major changes are thought to result from genetic recombination occurring when a human strain and an animal strain concurrently infect a single human or animal host. The resulting recombinant strain presumably possesses the infectivity of the human strain for humans and one or both surface antigens of the animal strain. The lesser interpandemic antigenic drift probably results from the selective pressure that occurs as the virus replicates in partially immune human hosts. Finally, the emergence of new diseases, such as St. Louis encephalitis, which first affected humans in Paris, Illinois, in 1932, or the appearance of a known disease in a new reservoir, possibly exemplified by sylvatic plague in the United States, can be the result of adaptation of the agent to a new host.

Host-Related Properties

As already noted, some epidemiologically important properties of infectious agents can be defined only with reference to specific hosts. Such properties include infectivity, pathogenicity, virulence, and immunogenicity.

Infectivity (ability to invade and multiply in a host) is measured conceptually in terms of the minimal number of infective particles required to establish an infection. This number, which can vary from one host to another and within the same host, depending on the portal of entry and host age, can be determined only experimentally. Hence, except for relatively benign agents such as rhinoviruses or vaccine strains of polioviruses with which challenge of human volunteers is permissible, the infectivity of agents for humans must be inferred from the facility with which they spread in populations or, more directly, from the frequency with which infection develops in exposed susceptible individuals within a reasonable incubation period (the *secondary attack rate*). By this latter measure, measles, varicella, and polioviruses are highly infective; rubella, mumps, and rhinoviruses are of intermediate infectivity; and typhoid and tubercle bacilli are of relatively low infectivity. However, of importance is to recognize that infectivity and, indeed, pathogenicity may vary among strains of the same organism. As examples, the infectivity of group A streptococci is related directly to the amount of M protein in the cell wall, and strains of *Staphylococcus aureus* that appear identical in the laboratory may differ strikingly in both infectivity and virulence. Additionally, some evidence indicates that strains of influenza A may vary in infectivity and virulence independent of preexisting immunity in the host.

Pathogenicity (ability to induce disease) is measured in terms of the proportion of infections that result in disease. It ordinarily can be determined readily by studies of the incidence and outcome of naturally occurring infections in humans. Although this proportion may be affected by the size of the infecting dose and numerous host factors, including age, commonly prevalent agents can be ordered in a gradient of pathogenicity on the basis of the usual outcome of infection. Highly pathogenic agents include typhoid bacilli, rabies, measles, varicella, and rhinoviruses. Those of intermediate pathogenicity include rubella, mumps, and adenoviruses; polioviruses and the tubercle bacillus are of low pathogenicity.

Virulence, offered as a synonym for pathogenicity in medical dictionaries, is defined more usefully as a measure of the severity of the disease that does occur. Various criteria may be used: days confined to bed, serious sequelae such as persisting paralysis, and death. The measure of virulence is the number of severe cases over the total number of cases, which when death is the criterion, becomes the familiar *case-fatality rate.* With this as our measure, the viral agents previously mentioned fall into a very different gradient from that based on pathogenicity. Rabies virus (with a case-fatality rate of 100%) qualifies as highly virulent, and poliovirus (with a case-fatality rate of 7 to 10% for paralytic disease) can be classed as moderately virulent. Measles, with an occasional death from encephalitis or pneumonia, is far down the scale but still ahead of mumps, varicella, nonfetal rubella, and rhinoviruses, for which the case-fatality rates are very low.

Immunogenicity (ability to induce specific immunity) is measured best in terms of the degree and duration of resistance conferred by infection. Although agents may differ with respect to the immunogenicity of their intrinsic "protective antigens," more important factors are the sites of primary infection and disease and the amount of antigen formed during infection to stimulate a host response. Superficial sites, such as the respiratory mucosa, are guarded chiefly by secretory antibody, which is poorly persistent; agents such as rhinoviruses, which replicate only at such sites, are relatively ineffective stimulants of the systemic immune response. The amounts of the respective toxins released during clinical tetanus and diphtheria usually do not induce satisfactory immunity. In contrast, systemic viral infections, as with measles and yellow fever viruses, induce solid and long-lasting immunity.

The Agent-Host Relationship

How the host contributes to survival of the agent as a species is of interest. At the minimum, the infected host provides a shelter in which the agent can multiply and from which it may spread. Key questions are how long the agent can persist in the host and over what period and by what avenues it can escape. We shall consider escape in relation to modes of transmission in a later section. Discussed here are the time relationships and descriptive terms of different phases of infection. They are suggested schematically in Figure 7–1.

When the agent is not readily recoverable but perhaps is hidden within host cells or at some other site, infection is termed *latent.* Conversely, when the agent is being shed, as in feces or respiratory secretions, or can be recovered from blood or tissues, infection is said to be *patent.* Infections are necessarily latent at first (the *latent period*) and become patent when the agent has multiplied sufficiently for shedding to begin. The *period of communicability* commonly begins soon after initial shedding and continues as long as the level of shedding is sufficient for transmission. The rapidity of spread of disease thus is related to the length of the latent period, which almost always is shorter (sometimes much shorter) than the better known *incubation period* (time until disease develops). Indeed, the period of communicability has no consistent relationship to either the occurrence or the duration of disease.

Persistence in the host is important to the agent for as long as escape remains possible. The period of persistence (see Fig. 7–1) varies widely among agents. Infection terminates completely within 2 to 3 weeks with many agents, such as most respiratory viruses, and after a few months with some, such as polioviruses or adenoviruses. Truly persistent lifelong infections may become permanently latent (some herpes group [Epstein-Barr virus, cytomegalovirus {CMV}] viral infections in some persons), may remain permanently patent (approximately 3% of typhoid cases, numerous hepatitis B virus infections), may be intermittently patent (herpes simplex virus infections), or after years of latency may recrudesce with both patency and associated disease (tuberculosis, Brill disease caused by *R. prowazekii,* herpes zoster caused by varicella-zoster virus [VZV]).

Reservoirs of Infectious Agents

Reservoir is defined here as the total mechanism responsible for perpetuation of an agent species. With the possible exception of agents such as tetanus spores, which virtually have indefinite potential for survival in the environment, the reservoir is a continuing chain of transmission from one host to another (host now including both vertebrate and invertebrate species). Chains with long links requiring infrequent transmission are especially favorable to survival of agent species.

Among agents for which humans are the only natural vertebrate host, many contrasting patterns exist. By far the most common is exemplified by infections with most respiratory viruses, which are characterized by short latent periods (1 to several days) and relatively short periods of communicability (rarely longer than 1 week). Thus, the links are short, and frequent transmission is necessary. At the other extreme are long-persisting infections associated with continuous (typhoid carriers, hepatitis B virus, HIV) or intermittent (herpes simplex virus) patency or shedding. The links in this case may be as long as the postinfection life of the host and render generation-to-generation transmission possible. Such transmission also may occur via congenital infection, as in mice infected with lymphocytic choriomeningitis virus. Examples in humans include CMV and hepatitis B virus infections. Long links also occur in persistent

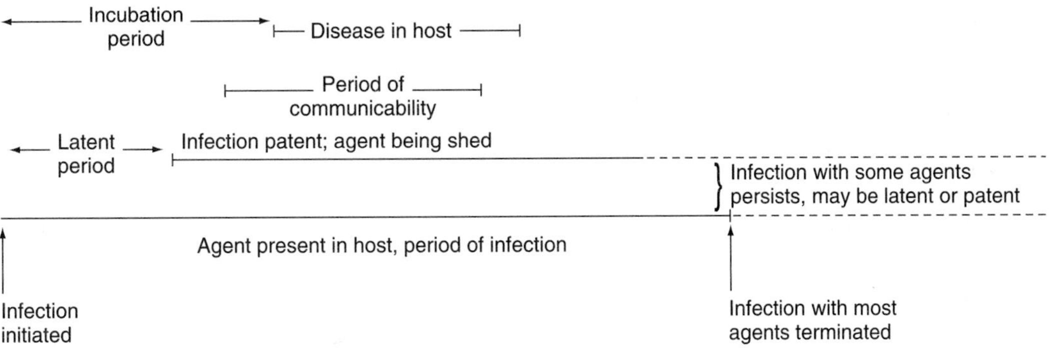

FIGURE 7–1 ■ Important phases of infection in vertebrate hosts.

infections that after many years of latency recrudesce to cause disease and renewed shedding (VZV and *R. prowazekii*). Basically similar patterns are known or presumed to exist in the case of zoonotic agents pathogenic for humans and their natural lower vertebrate hosts. Examples include *Brucella* and lymphocytic choriomeningitis virus and Machupo virus of Bolivian hemorrhagic fever.

When infection of invertebrate (vector) hosts is a link in the chain of transmission, a wide range of reservoir patterns is possible. The simplest involves agents for which humans are the only natural vertebrate hosts (malarial parasites, *R. prowazekii*, dengue virus), with the chain consisting of alternating links of human and vector infection. More commonly, the basic reservoir is a similar alternating chain primarily involving lower vertebrate hosts, with humans being an opportunistic and usually blind-end host. Examples include murine typhus rickettsiae and plague bacillus (both cycling primarily in rats and rat fleas), Lyme disease, and various arboviruses (yellow fever, St. Louis encephalitis). In the case of the latter, the relatively broad vertebrate (numerous avian and mammalian species) and invertebrate (various mosquito species) host range results in very complex patterns that in a given area are defined by the prevalent susceptible host species. With some interesting exceptions to be mentioned shortly, the links in these chains are defined temporally by the persistence of patent infection in the vertebrate host and the relatively short life span of the invertebrate host. In temperate regions, where vector abundance is highly seasonal, how many agents survive during winter remains an unanswered question.

Several aspects of infection of the invertebrate (vector) host are important. Typically, infection is acquired in a blood meal and endures for (and does not influence) the life span of the arthropod. Thus, hibernating arthropods may be the long link in the chain by which the agent survives the winter. In at least two instances, infection kills the vector: *R. prowazekii* in the body louse and plague bacilli in the rat flea. As with malaria, infection of the arthropod also may permit completion of an essential stage in the developmental cycle of the agent. Finally, transmission of infection from arthropod to arthropod may be alternate or necessary links in the chain. Transovarial transmission of *Rickettsia tsutsugamushi* (scrub typhus) in mites is essential because the individual mite feeds only once, during the larval stage, on vertebrate hosts. Transovarial transmission also occurs in ticks infected with *Rickettsia rickettsii* (Rocky Mountain spotted fever) and in *Aedes triseriatus* mosquitoes infected with La Crosse virus (California encephalitis), in both cases affording an overwintering mechanism. Venereal transmission of La Crosse virus between mosquitoes also has been demonstrated.[72]

Finally, the inanimate environment can play a role in the reservoir mechanism. Examples are bacteria that can multiply in the free state (salmonellae and staphylococci in food) and agents endowed with unusual survival capacity (tetanus bacillus and *Histoplasma capsulatum*, both of which form highly resistant spores). It also occurs when a brief sojourn under proper environmental conditions is required for a necessary stage in the life cycle (e.g., hookworm eggs from human feces must hatch into larvae to become infectious).

Mechanisms of Transmission

Transmission, in this context, is defined as the transport of an agent from one vertebrate host to another. It involves escape from the source host and conveyance to and entry into the recipient host. The basic interdependence of these sequential steps results in their usual correspondence, as illustrated in Table 7–1, which also presents specific disease examples. Although humans are the usual or only source for most agents of human disease, lower vertebrates serve as the major or only (rabies virus) source for some pathogens.

The basic concepts presented in Table 7–1 are fairly self-evident, but some definitions and special comments may be helpful. *Fomites* are intimate personal articles, such as handkerchiefs, playthings, and eating utensils. *Direct contact* includes not only physical contact (shaking hands, kissing, sexual intercourse) but also, in practice, short-range (within 10 ft) airborne transmission by heavy droplets containing hundreds or thousands of organisms that descend rapidly to the ground or floor. As an example, these heavy droplets are the primary route of transmission of group A streptococcal pharyngitis.[73]

Indirect transmission for respiratory and some other infections includes the acquisition of organisms from dust (such as tubercle bacilli), from fomites (inanimate objects in the environment such as bedding), and from airborne droplet nuclei (small droplets containing only one or a few organisms that promptly dry, float in the air for long periods, and may be wafted for moderately long distances, such as between rooms or floors in a hospital). Transmission by airborne droplet nuclei is limited to highly infectious agents such as varicella; because respiratory colonization with group A streptococci requires a large inoculum, airborne droplet nuclei play no role in their transmission. Other forms of indirect transmission include inanimate vectors such as food, milk, and water, which are frequent vehicles for spread, particularly of intestinal infections. Another source of indirect transmission is animate vectors, which either may function as a vehicle for transport (as with flies that carry organisms from feces to food) or actually may be infected. In the latter case, multiplication and transformation in the vector are required for transmission, as with African trypanosomiasis and the tsetse fly.

Conveyance ends when the agent reaches a portal of entry, which to be effective must provide ready access to a

TABLE 7–1 ■ TYPICAL CORRESPONDENCES AMONG ESCAPE FROM HOST, CONVEYANCE, AND PORTAL OF ENTRY

Agent Shed Via	How Conveyed	Portal of Entry	Disease Example
Respiratory secretions	Airborne droplets, fomites, direct contact	Respiratory	Common cold, influenza
Feces	Food, fomites, water, flies	Oral	Poliomyelitis, typhoid
Blood	Arthropod vector, transfusion, needle-stick	Skin, via insect bite, intravenous device	Typhus, dengue, malaria, human immunodeficiency virus, malaria B and C
Lesion exudate	Direct contact, sexual intercourse, fomites, flies	Skin, genital or ocular mucous membrane	Carbuncles, syphilis, trachoma, inclusion conjunctivitis

tissue in which the pathogen can lodge and multiply. For a given agent, a particular portal (nasal or genital mucosa, oral) often is obligatory or usual, but alternative portals may be possible. For instance, rhinoviruses replicate only in nasal mucosa, whereas typhus rickettsiae typically enter through skin broken by a louse bite but also can infect via ocular or respiratory mucous membranes.

HOST FACTORS

As suggested in considering why paralytic poliomyelitis occurs, many biologic and behavioral characteristics of the human host influence the occurrence of infection and subsequent disease. In this section, we consider biologic and behavioral factors separately and systematically. Although the host characteristics to be considered are of widely differing nature, they operate by influencing one or more of the following: degree of exposure, innate susceptibility to infection, and the likelihood of specific immunity. Although much of the discussion will focus on the individual human host, one should remember that factors that influence individuals also affect whole human populations.

Infection of the Host

Before considering specific factors, reviewing the initiation, course, and possible consequences of infection to the host is helpful. A key principle to be emphasized is the usual existence of a gradient of response to exposure and infection. Because of this gradient, the occurrence of characteristic overt disease is a notably unreliable measure of the extent of activity of a disease agent. Thus, given exposure, infection may not occur; given infection, disease may not result; and given disease, the consequences may range from trivial to the fully developed syndrome "characteristic" of the agent.

An inadequate challenge dose, an unsuitable portal of entry, or specific host immunity may explain failure of infection to develop. Whether infection causes disease and the extent, nature, and outcome of the resulting disease are determined partly by host-related properties of the agent (pathogenicity and virulence) and partly by host defense mechanisms, a variety of which confront an infectious agent that has reached a site of primary infection. Bacteria and other extracellular parasites stimulate an inflammatory response at the site in an effort to localize the invaders by a retaining fibrin network, and the invaders are destroyed by congregating numerous phagocytic cells. Organisms that escape are confronted with gauntlets of sinusoidal passages lined by phagocytic cells in regional (lymph nodes) and bloodstream (bone marrow, spleen, and liver) filters.

A further line of defense develops with the immune response to infection. Developing antibody combines with persisting extracellular organisms to render them more vulnerable to phagocytosis and digestion. The initial presence of specific antibody would, of course, have prevented or greatly limited invasion of the host. Viruses and other intracellular parasites are vulnerable to antibody while extracellular, as during invasion, but are unaffected once they have gained entrance into cells. Indeed, in the case of some viruses (lymphocytic choriomeningitis virus in the mouse is a model), the cell-mediated component of the immune response may play a role in the pathogenesis of disease rather than as an aid in defense.

Several aspects of the outcome of infection are important, the first being survival of the host. Death is an obviously unsatisfactory outcome not only for the host but also for the many agents for which survival as a species depends on the host. The remaining aspects relate to the surviving host. Was recovery from disease complete, or were permanent sequelae present? If the latter, were they stationary (as in paralysis resulting from polioviruses) or potentially progressive (rheumatic heart disease resulting from streptococcal infection, pulmonary tuberculosis)? Another aspect, persistence of the agent, was discussed previously under agent-host relationships. The final aspect is the state of postinfection resistance. If it is incomplete, the recovered host may experience reinfection, with or without disease, and again become a source of infection for others.

Biologic Factors

Biologic factors include characteristics such as age, sex, and race (ethnic group), which are so important and easily ascertained that determining their relation to occurrence of disease is a usual first step in an epidemiologic description. They also include other factors such as genetic make-up, general health status, and specific immunity.

The influence of *age* is illustrated best by means of common diseases such as varicella, measles, and mumps (before the advent of vaccines). All three diseases occur predominantly in young children, who are affected because of their usual lack of immunity and their high risk of exposure to their age peers, among whom most infections occur. Older people are very likely to be immune and, unless they are parents of young children, are unlikely to be exposed to infected individuals. Age also is related often to the outcome of infections in nonimmune individuals. Demonstration of this factor requires that all infections be recognized and classified according to the occurrence and severity of the resulting disease. When many or most infections are subclinical (as with polioviruses), the increase in case fatality with age is apparent immediately, but special studies are required to show that the proportion of infections that resulted in disease also increased with age. In contrast, the case-fatality rate for pertussis is highest in young infants. With measles and varicella viruses, infections at any age usually result in characteristic disease, but as exemplified by measles encephalitis, the frequency of serious disease rises with age.

That *sex* is a factor is indicated by the fact that with a few notable exceptions, such as acute respiratory disease and pertussis in women, diseases typically occur somewhat more frequently in males than females. The question, with respect to any particular disease, is whether these differences between sexes reflect innate differences in susceptibility to disease or can be attributed to sex-associated differences in play habits and occupation that affect the degree of exposure or host stress. Typical, for example, is the increased intrahousehold exposure of mothers and older girls who nurse ill family members. Antibody prevalence studies in the prevaccine era indicated that boys and girls had the same risk of acquiring infection with polioviruses, but the sex ratio for paralytic polio was 1.3:1.0 (male versus female). In those older than 20 years, this ratio was reversed. Possible explanations are the greater stress among boys (because of more strenuous play) and women (associated with child-bearing and rearing of children).

The incidence of many diseases varies greatly between groups defined by *race* or *ethnic group*. It is explained most often by socioeconomically determined differences in environmental factors related to the degree of exposure and resulting prevalence of immunity or, in more recent times, similarly determined differences in health awareness affecting acceptance of vaccines. However, ethnic groups share many genetically determined traits that may include heightened susceptibility or resistance to specific disease agents.

Thus, selective pressure may be invoked to explain the greater resistance of whites (exposed for countless centuries) to tuberculosis and the heightened resistance of blacks to malaria.

Genetically determined susceptibility or resistance also may be manifested by differences in occurrence of disease among families or kinships of the same ethnicity. However, before such differences can be attributed to genetic factors, adequate account must be taken of the many environmental influences that affect families as groups, including common exposures, diet, education, and economic status. The classic twin studies of Kallman and Reisner[42] clearly demonstrated a genetic contribution to the occurrence of tuberculosis. Similarly conclusive data for other infectious diseases are almost nonexistent, although the operation of genetic factors in humans must be presumed from observations in animal models, such as the classic work of Webster, who by selective inbreeding developed strains of mice susceptible or resistant to specific neurotropic viruses.[74] The genetic control of immune response, also demonstrated in the mouse model, provides a probable explanation. Its operation in humans is suggested strongly by studies showing a relationship of human leukocyte antigen specificity to chronic hepatitis B antigenemia.[37]

General health status includes the physiologic state, nutritional status, presence of intercurrent disease, and stress. The importance of such factors is, in many cases, commonly accepted but rarely documented by well-controlled studies. Infancy, during which immune mechanisms are immature, is a period of special vulnerability to many infectious diseases. Puberty, associated with rapid growth and change in endocrine balance, is a period of vulnerability to acne and tuberculosis. Pregnancy predisposes to both tuberculosis and paralytic poliomyelitis.

Gross protein malnutrition causes definite impairment in the cell-mediated immune response[43] and a correspondingly increased susceptibility to bacterial and parasitic infections and increased morbidity and mortality in many viral infections. Viral infections may depress cell-mediated immunity (and, thus, further increase susceptibility) to other concurrent infections. Current viral infection, by an interfering effect, may induce temporary resistance to a second virus. Diabetics are especially vulnerable to bacterial infections; measles and pertussis may reactivate quiescent tuberculosis; and, perhaps of greatest importance, otherwise benign respiratory viral infections, notably influenza, may pave the way for serious bacterial pneumonia. Furthermore, HIV infection enhances susceptibility to and the severity of tuberculosis, toxoplasmosis, and many other infections.

Finally, stress induced by widely divergent stimuli (including strong emotions, physical exertion, trauma, or excessive heat or cold), according to Selye,[67] may operate through a pituitary-adrenocortical hormonal path to decrease resistance to infections. Widely accepted examples include physical exertion, child-bearing, and rearing of children as factors predisposing to paralytic poliomyelitis and both pregnancy and rapid growth during puberty as causes of reactivation of quiescent tuberculosis.

Immunity and *immune response* are discussed elsewhere, but some general comments are appropriate here. In discussing infection in the host, immune response was considered a potential mechanism of defense and, thus, significant in relation to the course and outcome of infections. Though clearly important in recovery from bacterial infection, antibody response is of questionable significance in viral infections because viruses within cells are inaccessible to antibody and, by the time that antibody appears, many or most susceptible cells have been infected already. Nonetheless, the importance of antibody in viral infections is suggested by the great vulnerability of immunodeficient children to vaccine strains of poliovirus and by the sometimes beneficial effect of passive immunotherapy in progressive vaccinia. Cell-induced immune response may play a greater role in the pathogenesis of disease (tuberculosis, lymphocytic choriomeningitis virus infection in mice) than in recovery from infection.

Immunity to a specific agent usually develops after natural infection, may be induced by vaccine, or may be acquired passively, as by infants from mothers or via injected gammaglobulin, in which case it is of relatively short duration. A key point is that *immunity* is a relative term. At its maximum (exemplified by postinfection immunity to measles), protection against infection is virtually absolute. At the other extreme (exemplified by many respiratory viral infections), susceptibility to infection persists or wanes as with pertussis, although the severity of related disease may be reduced. In most instances, protection appears to be mediated by antibody, but the possible contribution of cell-mediated immunity has not been well evaluated.

To the extent that immunity protects the individual against infection or acts to minimize shedding of the agent when infection occurs, an immune host can play no part in the spread of an infectious agent in the population. This fact suggests that if a sufficient proportion of a population were immune, a contact-transmitted agent could not spread and any nonimmune members would be spared exposure. The obvious question, then, is what proportion must be immune to achieve effective *herd immunity?* Unfortunately, as explained in a review of this problem,[27] the question has no practical answer. The underlying concept is valid only in homogeneous, randomly mixing populations in which all possible pairs of individuals have the same probability of making effective contact. In real life, this situation does not exist and is approximated only in small, closed groups. Whether an agent can spread is not determined by the proportion of immune individuals but by the number (not the proportion) of susceptible individuals and the opportunity for contact among them. Thus, even though measles vaccine had been used extensively in the United States, outbreaks of measles continued to occur in segments of the population that failed to accept vaccine, often defined by race and low economic status. Indeed, a major outbreak of measles with approximately 30,000 cases occurred in 1989 and 1990 in the United States.[4]

Human Behavior

Governed largely by habits of the individual and the customs and culture of groups, human behavior greatly influences exposure to and modes of transmission of disease agents. Cultural factors also underlie attitudes toward preventive and curative practices. These relationships are so self-evident for the most part that no detailed discussion is needed.

Water is a potential vehicle for many agents. When commonly imbibed without boiling, as in the United States, community water systems constitute potential channels for transmission that, fortunately, usually are guarded well. Unfortunately, occasional operational failures occur, as exemplified by failure of a water quality monitoring device in a filtration plant that resulted in an outbreak of *Cryptosporidium* diarrhea affecting an estimated 403,000 persons in Milwaukee in 1993.[51] Foods and milk, especially items that are consumed raw or after minimal cooking, likewise are excellent vehicles for transmission of disease. Well-known examples include trichinosis from undercooked pork, fish tapeworm from raw fish (a delicacy in Scandinavia and parts of the Orient), and various forms of food poisoning caused by bacterial contamination during handling, poor refrigeration, and inadequate cooking. In recent years, outbreaks of bloody diarrhea caused by *Escherichia coli* O157:H7, often associated with hemolytic-uremic syndrome, have occurred as a result of improperly prepared products of bovine origin, particularly ground beef.[35] Of special interest to pediatricians is the fallacious belief that raw milk possesses nutritive values (and flavor) that are lost in pasteurization. The result is "certified" milk that, although produced under carefully controlled conditions, has been a frequent vehicle of streptococci, salmonellae, and other agents of serious disease, including *E. coli* O157:H7.

Closely related to water and foods is the disposal of human excreta. Casual defecation near habitations (as by young children) or in or near running water (a cultural compulsion in India) leads to dissemination of enteric pathogens by filth flies and by water. The use of human feces (night soil) in the Orient and elsewhere to fertilize crops commonly eaten raw, such as strawberries and lettuce, has an obvious similar potential.

Many more individual types of behavior also are important. Infrequent bathing and laundering of clothes favor infestation with body lice. Inadequate clothing increases exposure to arthropod vectors and, as in young children lightly clad for summer weather, facilitates the exchange of feces. Going barefoot provides exposure to hookworm larvae. Handwashing minimizes the role of hands in indirect transmission of both enteric (fecal) and respiratory (nasal secretion) pathogens. Rhinovirus infections result from inserting contaminated fingers into the nose and eyes.[36] Intimate personal contact (hand shaking, kissing, sexual intercourse, and play among young children) fosters the spread of a wide variety of agents. Even recreation, such as travel, picnics, and camping, may lead to unusual exposure to disease agents. Sexual behavior is associated with the transmission of numerous infections, including HIV, syphilis, gonorrhea, group B streptococci, and hepatitis B. Finally, education and individual temperament influence the utilization of health services and conscious avoidance of obvious health hazards.

ENVIRONMENTAL FACTORS

The environment in concept embraces all that is external to the individual human host. A convenient approach is to recognize three broad environmental areas: *physical,* which includes geologic and climatologic or meteorologic features; *biologic,* which consists of all flora and fauna, as well as all living microbial pathogens; and *socioeconomic,* which extends to encompass the interrelationships of humans. Identifying and evaluating the contribution of environmental factors often are difficult. Their multiplicity and the fact that they typically operate in an interrelated manner complicate the appraisal of their individual contributions. In addition, environmental factors often act through very indirect paths, and some have the potential to affect the agent, the host, and the agent-host relationship. Thus, solar radiation is lethal for many pathogens in the free state, helps humans synthesize vitamin D, and can provoke recrudescence of a latent herpes simplex virus infection and result in recurrent fever blisters. Finally, the capacity of people to modify adverse environmental conditions beneficially is another important factor.

The contribution of environmental factors to the occurrence of disease is complex. Here only a few selected examples will be used to illustrate how environmental factors influence the occurrence of infectious diseases.

Geographic and Geologic Factors

Dr. Jacques May was a pioneer in the field of geographic epidemiology, or medical geography.[53] Although many pathogens dependent on humans for their survival are active wherever people congregate in sufficient number, many others occur only in certain geographic areas. From a practical standpoint, knowledge of the geographic distribution of such diseases is important in preparing travelers to minimize exposure to agents prevalent at their destinations. However, Dr. May's greater interest was in factors that influenced the distribution of disease and how they acted.

Spread of disease agents on a global scale requires their transport, which obviously is influenced by distance alone and by geographic features—mountain ranges, oceans, rivers—that assist or impede travel. The importance of these factors declines as the extent and speed of travel increase, but it remains substantial, especially in developing countries. The minimal effect of geographic barriers in containing highly infective agents is exemplified by pandemic influenza, which in 1957 and again in 1968 emerged in the Orient and spread rapidly throughout the world.

More importantly, geography acts indirectly by determining other aspects of the environment. Climate is determined largely by latitude, longitude, altitude, and relation to bodies of water and mountain ranges and, in turn, greatly influences the biologic environment and human activity. Geography, together with geologic factors, also has an effect on the socioeconomic environment. The natural paths of travel (including waterways), natural harbors, and the location of mineral deposits help determine where populations will concentrate. Water supply, dependent in part on geologic formations, is a factor limiting population size and, together with fossil fuels and mineral deposits, influences the type, extent, and location of industrial development. Soil types vary greatly in their ability to hold and purify water and in their capacity to support vegetation, which in turn influences the type and abundance of animal life. Thus, soil is a determinant of the type and importance of agriculture and a major factor influencing the biologic environment.

Climate

The term *climate* describes the typical annual pattern, along with its seasonal variation, of climatologic conditions in a specified region. Such conditions (climatologic factors) include solar radiation, temperature, humidity, barometric pressure, winds, precipitation (and drought), and lightning. These factors can affect infectious disease agents directly. Many microbial agents in the free state are vulnerable to excessive heat and radiation and uncontrolled drying. The life cycles and reservoir mechanisms of many pathogens, including higher parasites, are dependent on appropriate temperature and humidity. Maturation and hatching of hookworm larvae from ova deposited in the soil require both warmth and reasonable humidity, and the multiplication of malarial parasites and arboviruses in their mosquito vectors and the very abundance of the vectors are favored by warm temperatures.

The usual seasonal variation in the incidence of specific infectious diseases suggests important influences of climatologic factors, but how they operate may be hard to determine. Overall, respiratory infections occur more frequently in the colder months, but within this period (roughly October through mid-May), the relative prevalence of the many respiratory pathogens is highly variable. Rhinoviruses, for example, peak in the early fall and spring, and influenza viruses are most active in midwinter. Parainfluenza virus type 1 and 2 infections usually peak in the fall. Increased congregation of people indoors clearly facilitates transmission, and fluctuations in temperature and humidity not only affect the viability of agents in airborne droplet nuclei or on fingers or fomites but also may affect host susceptibility to infection. Enterically transmitted infections occur most frequently in the warmer months, presumably largely because of season-related changes in host behavior. Thus, the outdoor play of scantily clad children facilitates the spread of skin infection and fecally shed agents such as enteroviruses. Rotavirus infections are an exception in that they occur most frequently in colder months. More completely understood are the seasonal patterns of infections spread by arthropod vectors; these patterns reflect seasonal variations in the abundance and activity of both the vectors and the various lower vertebrate host species, which together constitute the reservoir mechanisms of the specific disease agents. Indeed, climate overall, as a major determinant of the biologic environment, helps determine both the abundance and the particular species of flora and fauna in a given area.

Longer-term changes in climate have been associated with changes in patterns of infection. As an example, the hantavirus outbreak in the southwestern United States in 1993 has been attributed to unusually heavy precipitation in the spring of 1993 after 6 years of drought. This precipitation resulted in marked proliferation of the deer mouse population, the reservoir of the virus.[76]

Of current concern is the gradual increase in global temperature.[61] The geographic distribution of malaria is dependent on environmental temperature, and year-to-year variations have been associated with climatic changes in affected areas in Africa. In the Western Hemisphere, dengue and arboviral encephalitides, among other mosquito-born disorders, have shown year-to-year variation in incidence that is dependent on temperature and humidity. In another vein, the reproduction of toxin-producing marine algae and *Vibrio cholerae* is enhanced by warmer sea water, which may have been responsible for outbreaks of disorders attributable to these organisms. These short-term, climate-related variations in the distribution of infections may presage longer-term shifts in affected geographic areas as the atmosphere warms, as a result of which, for example, temperate areas may experience infections ordinarily associated with tropical or subtropical regions.

Biologic Environment

As living entities, microbial pathogens and higher parasites by definition are included in the biologic environment, as are the vertebrate and invertebrate species involved in the transmission and reservoir mechanisms of numerous agents. For some pathogens, including malarial parasites, dengue viruses, and epidemic typhus rickettsiae, humans are the only important vertebrate host, but transmission is by arthropod vectors. For others, referred to as zoonoses, the vertebrate reservoir hosts are subhuman. Some of them, including the rickettsiae of Rocky Mountain spotted fever and murine typhus, the plague bacillus, and the many arboviruses, require arthropod vectors for transmission, whereas others are spread directly from their natural vertebrate hosts (various salmonellae, rabies virus, and the agents of psittacosis and trichinosis).

Although bacterial and fungal pathogens are classified as plants (viruses are unassigned), the direct contribution of the biologic environment to occurrence of disease chiefly involves fauna. Plant and animal life also act in less direct and often interrelated ways. Human susceptibility to infection is affected by nutritional status, to which both flora and fauna contribute. The nature and abundance of plant life and their seasonal stages of development determine the number and species of wildlife present. Thus, grassy plains favor herbivores, and fruits and berries attract many birds. Arthropod vectors often depend on plants for breeding sites (tree holes, plant axils) and use foliage for shelter from predators and for resting in a suitable microclimate. The steel-belted radial automobile tire has changed the geographic distribution of at least one type of arthropod-borne viral disease: La Crosse encephalitis.[19] Used casings are difficult to recycle because of the steel belting and are discarded in waste dumps, often in large piles. Rain water accumulates in the casings and forms a favorable environment for breeding mosquitoes, which also serve as vehicles for transportation of infected larvae from one area to another. Animals provide them with blood meals that often contain infectious agents. The biologic environment also influences people's recreational activities (hunting, bird watching) and, by determining the type and importance of agriculture, their occupations and economy.

Socioeconomic Environment

This difficult-to-define sector depends on the density and distribution of populations; the available natural resources; the level of social, political, cultural, and scientific development; and most importantly, the interrelationships of people. Socioeconomic factors typically affect health by indirect means, and because they often are interrelated closely, evaluating the impact of individual factors is very difficult.

The relationship of population distribution and density to the occurrence of infectious diseases is substantial. Increasing density favors the spread of infectious agents to humans from both human and nonhuman sources and, hence, the occurrence of related disease and development of immunity. In large and dense populations, agents such as measles virus typically infect in early childhood and persist because a sufficient number of new susceptible individuals are added continuously by birth. In smaller populations, the agents are unable to persist and are reintroduced at unpredictable intervals, and as a result, manifestations of "childhood" diseases may be delayed for long periods. Populations of urban and rural areas differ not only in relative density but also in other important ways. Exposure to zoonotic agents, especially those prevalent in wildlife and livestock, is greater in rural areas, although rats and stray dogs may abound in city slums. Environmental sanitation (protection of water and milk supplies, safe disposal of sewage) often is a personal problem for rural residents but is handled by cooperative effort in urban populations. In addition, the relative importance of schools and school buses in facilitating exchange of infectious agents is greater in rural areas, where isolation of farm residents otherwise restricts contact between young children.

The basic population unit is the household, membership in which has similar implications for health in both rural and urban areas. Family members are similar genetically; share a common diet and economic status; are subject to the same cultural, religious, and educational influences; and are exposed to a common local physical and biologic environment. Most important for contact-transmitted diseases, intrafamilial contact is prolonged and increases in intimacy with household crowding. Prolonged contact is especially important for persisting infections such as herpes simplex and tuberculosis. Family size, regardless of the degree of crowding, is particularly important for acute infections because it determines the number of potential introducers who bring home infections acquired elsewhere. The likelihood of exposure in early childhood increases with family size. Except for early infancy, a period of special vulnerability to some agents (respiratory syncytial virus, pertussis), early exposure is beneficial because most resulting infections are less apt to have serious consequences.

A population with a highly developed *social and political structure,* through its capacity for cooperative action, enjoys many advantages that directly or indirectly benefit health, including provision of both preventive and curative health services, effective environmental sanitation, and well-developed educational facilities. Education, of course, closely relates to personal health practices that are based on understanding what individuals should do to minimize disease hazards. Schools, where the educational process begins, have been identified already as important factors in the exchange of disease agents among children, especially those spread by contact and airborne droplet nuclei. This matter is offset in part by the benefits derived from school-based immunization programs.

Economic status affects the occurrence of diseases indirectly through its relation to adequacy of housing, nutrition, level of education, and availability and use of health services. It also is related closely to occupation, which may be associated with exposure to specific infections such as Rocky Mountain spotted fever (forest workers and hikers in the south Atlantic coast states) and ornithosis (workers in poultry-processing plants).

Disease Occurrence in Populations

Patterns of occurrence of disease that are not random but instead reflect the influence of underlying causes (risk factors) not only help predict future occurrence of disease but also provide important clues to understanding causation.

Describing the pattern of occurrence of disease begins with definition and classification of disease in the individual so that cases can be identified and counted reliably. Next, we must develop ways to express the occurrence of disease in defined populations quantitatively. The full description results from the composite answers to three questions: Who is attacked? Where does disease occur? When does it occur?

INFECTION AND DISEASE IN THE INDIVIDUAL

Epidemiologic interest focuses on the specific etiologic identification of infection and disease, terms that, it must be stressed, are not synonyms. Technically, any deviation from normal function or state constitutes disease. Because virtually all infections cause at least some deviation from the normal state (such as a change in the white cell pattern in blood and mobilization of such cells at the site of infection), they do in fact cause disease. Practically, however, many infections result in no clinical evidence of disease and are important to the individual only for the reason that they induce immunity. Because subclinical infections help define the overall pattern of occurrence of infection and often play a significant role in its spread, their recognition is important epidemiologically. Unfortunately, subclinical infections go unrecognized except when healthy persons are observed for infection in longitudinal or case-control studies.

Thus, only infections resulting in disease usually come to our attention. To the extent that they are recognized etiologically, they provide the earliest and most available indicator of the pattern of infection in the population.

With few exceptions, such as measles and chickenpox, the resulting clinical syndromes are not pathognomonic and confront the clinician with the familiar problem of differential diagnosis. Basically, clinical manifestations depend more on the site or sites of disease than on the infecting agent. Because the number of possible disease targets in the body is small and the number of potential agents is large, reasonably distinct clinical entities may be caused by any of several agents. Notable examples include "common colds," some 40 percent of which are caused by rhinoviruses and 60 percent by any of many other viruses, and aseptic meningitis, which may be caused by mumps virus or by many enteroviruses. Moreover, infection with a specific agent may have several possible clinical outcomes. Infection with polioviruses usually is (perhaps 80%) subclinical but can result in brief febrile illness (approximately 15%), aseptic meningitis (4–5%), or classic paralytic disease (<1%). The response to agents with multiple potential targets varies even more widely. Group B coxsackieviruses, for example, can cause such disparate entities as acute upper respiratory disease, aseptic meningitis, polio-like paralytic disease, myocarditis (often fatal in infants), and epidemic pleurodynia (Bornholm disease).

Knowledge of the agents active in the community when a given illness occurs helps narrow the differential diagnosis, but a confirmed etiologic diagnosis requires laboratory assistance. It usually takes the form of identifying the agent by culture, by direct visualization in specimens related to the disease site, by antigen detection via polymerase chain reaction or other techniques, or by demonstration of a specific antibody response in tests of "acute" and "convalescent" serum pairs. The diagnosis is most secure when both approaches suggest infection with the same agent. Although demonstration of the agent in relation to the disease site carries special weight (for example, in a pharyngeal swab specimen from a respiratory illness), its presence could be the result of preexisting persisting infection unrelated to the current illness. Antibody response, indicative of newly acquired infection, excludes the latter possibility.

DESCRIBING INFECTION AND DISEASE IN POPULATIONS

At this point, before introducing and defining the terms and quantitative expressions commonly used in describing the occurrence of infection and disease in populations, we must briefly consider the availability and reliability of the relevant information.

Sources of Information

Many sources provide data regarding the incidence of infectious diseases, including U.S. Vital Statistics, which tabulates only fatal cases; the Centers for Disease Control and Prevention, which receives reports of specific notifiable diseases from state health departments and summarizes them in the *Morbidity and Mortality Weekly Report;* and state and local health departments. Unfortunately, these data vary in their completeness by source and by disease because of underreporting, subjects who are not seen, and errors in diagnosis.

Among the different states, reporting requirements vary, and indeed, adherence to these requirements by providers also varies. Reporting is most complete for uncommon but characteristic disorders of unusual interest, particularly if they are severe or fatal and require hospitalization, such as rabies, anthrax, trichinosis, plague, and diphtheria. Reporting is enhanced by outbreaks, as with measles and classic pertussis in recent years. Some notifiable infections, such as leptospirosis and atypical pertussis in partially immune persons, often are unrecognized and, therefore, not reported. Even after the advent of penicillin, until about 25 years ago, scarlet fever was a reportable disease in many areas. Because some health departments continued to subject affected households to useless or outmoded stringent control measures, such as quarantine or cremating the child's doll in the furnace, some physicians simply treated the patient with antibiotics and ignored reporting requirements. Today, physicians occasionally fail to report venereal diseases to avoid causing embarrassment to patients. Another source of data, often useful in certain areas, is state health department laboratories, which perform specific microbiologic or serologic tests for providers.

Infectious diseases that are not notifiable by law pose a difficult problem. Though necessarily limited in scale, longitudinal studies of defined populations of families have yielded valuable information. Examples include the Cleveland Family Study conducted by Dingle and colleagues[22]; the Tecumseh, Michigan, study of respiratory illnesses directed by Monto and associates[54, 55]; and the New York and Seattle Virus Watch studies.[18, 23, 28–32, 71] Finally, researchers now can use well-designed serosurveys to make reliable estimates of rates of previous infection with agents that induce long-persisting antibody.

International data on the incidence of infectious diseases are less precise except in well-developed countries such as the United Kingdom and Canada. For the developing world, the World Health Organization and the United Nations International Children's Emergency Fund provide estimates of the incidence of morbidity and mortality from various infectious diseases in different nations based on local reports, which are not necessarily collected systematically. Continuing collection of such data is important for monitoring the effects of the Expanded Program of Immunization, which is directed at controlling the major vaccine-preventable diseases of childhood. More difficult to develop are definitive data about the incidence and causation of the respiratory and diarrheal diseases that are estimated to kill as many as 6 million children annually in the developing world (approximately 5% of the yearly birth cohort).

Of maximal importance is arriving at a definition of disease that is as useful as possible, which means that the sensitivity and specificity of the definition should be so balanced that as many cases of the disease as possible are identified while avoiding the confusion that occurs when other disorders with overlapping manifestations meet criteria that are too nonspecific. Having an optimal definition of disease is particularly important in developing approaches to preventive measures, in searching for clues to causation of a new disease, in enabling comparisons among different studies, and in conducting clinical trials of prophylactic or therapeutic measures. A well-known example of a useful definition of disease is the Jones criteria for the diagnosis of rheumatic fever, established in 1944 at the request of the National Research Council in an effort to bring order out of chaos at a time when the disease was a major problem in both the civilian and military populations.[41] These criteria were modified in 1965 to enhance their specificity by making evidence of a previous group A streptococcal infection a sine qua non for the reason that too many cases of polyarthritis of other cause met the original criteria.[2]

Recognizing the importance of standardized diagnostic criteria for surveillance of infectious diseases of public health importance, in 1990 the Centers for Disease Control and Prevention published case definitions for reportable infections.[76] Optimal utilization of these criteria and reporting of confirmed and probable cases to the proper authorities are of particular importance currently, when for a variety of reasons, some formerly well-controlled contagious diseases are becoming recrudescent. All states mandate reporting contagious diseases of major public health importance, particularly those of childhood such as measles and poliomyelitis; for uncommon disorders such as listeriosis and for some common disorders that are differentiated less readily etiologically, such as influenza, requirements for reporting vary.[17]

Definitions of Terms and Rates

Two commonly used (and often misused) terms, *incidence* and *prevalence*, have significantly distinct meanings. *Incidence* refers to new occurrences of infection or disease in a population during a specified period, commonly a year, whereas *prevalence* refers to the state (infected, ill, immune) of individuals in a population at a specified point in time (point prevalence).

To describe variations in occurrence over limited periods within a single population such as a city or a state, a simple *numerical incidence* (number of cases or infections) often is used, for example, daily or weekly (during an epidemic), monthly (to reflect seasonal patterns), or annually (to compare successive years). However, comparisons among different populations or subgroups within a population or at widely separated times in the same population require use of the *incidence rate,* or *attack rate,* which is defined as follows:

$$\frac{\text{Number of new occurrences (cases, infections) within a specified period}}{\text{Population at midperiod}} \times 100, 1000, 10{,}000, \text{etc.}$$

Thus, if 10,000 cases of influenza occurred in a city of 200,000 people in a year, the incidence (or attack) rate would be expressed as 5 per 100 per year.

Unlike *incidence*, which is useful for determining both acute and persistent conditions, *prevalence* is applied usefully only in describing states of relatively long duration (months or years), such as immunity, persisting infection, and chronic disease. Hence, in relation to an acute disease such as influenza, we speak of the incidence of disease and the prevalence of immunity (reflected by antibody). Because most interest is in comparisons of different populations or population subgroups, prevalence is expressed customarily as the *prevalence rate,* which is defined as follows:

$$\frac{\text{Number of persons (infected, ill, or immune) at a given point in time}}{\text{Population at that time}} \times 100, 1000, 10{,}000, \text{etc.}$$

For infections transmitted by contact, the frequency with which infection or disease occurs among exposed susceptible persons provides a measure of the infectivity of the agent. This frequency, called the *secondary attack rate,* is defined as follows:

$$\frac{\text{Number of contacts becoming infected or ill within the maximal incubation period}}{\text{Total number of ``susceptibles'' exposed}} \times 100$$

The secondary attack rate is applied usefully only to relatively closed groups, households, or classrooms, where exposure safely can be presumed for all members. The first, or primary, case is the presumed source of exposure; other cases occurring within less than the minimal incubation period are called *co-primary cases*. In calculating the secondary attack rate, primary and co-primary cases are excluded from both the numerator and denominator. Cases occurring subsequently within the maximal incubation period constitute the secondary cases. Those developing later are excluded as being derived from outside sources or from tertiary spread. The exclusion of immune individuals from the denominator is feasible only for diseases (measles, chickenpox) sufficiently characteristic clinically that the history serves to identify them. Although immune individuals are not readily identifiable in the case of common respiratory diseases, the secondary attack rate based on all exposed members of the group still remains a useful tool. Its value decreases, however, when the period of communicability of the primary case (as with *Mycoplasma pneumoniae*) is longer than the incubation period because distinguishing between secondary and tertiary cases becomes difficult.

Finally, the occurrence of death caused by a specific disease is expressed in two different ways. One, the *cause-specific mortality rate,* is defined as follows:

$$\frac{\text{Number of deaths from the disease in a given year in a population}}{\text{Total population at midyear}} \times 100{,}000$$

It is a measure of the effect of the disease on the population. The potential significance of the disease to the affected individual is suggested by the *case-fatality rate* (or *ratio*), which is defined as follows:

$$\frac{\text{Number of deaths from the disease within a specified period}}{\text{Number of cases in the same period}} \times 100$$

RELATING INFECTION AND DISEASE TO PERSONAL CHARACTERISTICS

A multiplicity of attributes may serve to distinguish one person from another. Some factors are determined at conception: age, sex, ethnicity, genetic make-up, and birth order. Others, far more numerous, are acquired subsequently. They may be biologic (specific immunity, nutritional state), behavioral (smoking, dietary, recreational habits), or socioeconomic (occupation, educational level, marital status). As indicated in discussing host factors in causation of disease, many of these attributes relate to exposure to disease agents or to susceptibility or resistance to the effects of such agents and, hence, to the occurrence and severity of disease.

Relative Usefulness and Importance of Attributes

Personal attributes vary in both usefulness and importance in describing the occurrence of infection and disease. Usefulness depends chiefly on the ease and reliability with which the prevalence of an attribute in the population can be determined. Although almost any potentially relevant attribute of an individual patient can be identified, it is not very useful for purposes of description unless we can estimate how many people in the population also possess the attribute. From census data or other accessible records, numbers of people in groups defined by age, sex, race, occupation, or marital status can be estimated easily. However, special surveys would need to be conducted to estimate the prevalence of specific immunity or possibly significant exposure, such as to household pets.

The importance of personal characteristics to the description of a disease varies in two ways. One is in the degree of association that exists between an attribute and a specific disease. For example, age is associated strongly with disease caused by prevalent contagious agents, whereas sex usually is not. The second way is in the independence or relative interdependence of attributes as variables. Inherent characteristics such as age, sex, and ethnic origin are independent of one another, whereas acquired attributes rarely are. As examples, the nature of interpersonal contacts, degree of personal hygiene, and usual forms of recreation are associated closely with age or sex, or both. The common interdependence of attributes means that before making inference from a particular association, one should explore association with other, possibly correlated, attributes. Some examples will emerge in the following discussion of a few of the characteristics most commonly used.

Age Patterns

The occurrence of infection and disease in general is related so strongly to age that until possible differences in age distribution are taken into account, differences in occurrence among population subgroups defined by other attributes cannot be interpreted meaningfully. Fortunately, age as an attribute is ascertained easily and reliably for both affected individuals and the total membership of the relevant population. Description of the age pattern involves only computing a series of *age-specific rates* for sequential age groups, usually defined in intervals of 5 years or multiples thereof (0 to 4, 5 to 9, 10 to 19, etc.). For conditions of pediatric concern, the use of single-year intervals (<1, 1, 2, 3, and 4 years) to cover early childhood may be more informative. Affected persons in an age group form the numerator, and all persons in the population in that age group serve as the denominator. Rates so computed describe the age profile of immunity at a specified point in time (age-specific antibody prevalence rates), the age profile of new infections or disease (age-specific incidence rates), or the age profile of deaths caused by a disease (disease- and age-specific mortality rates).

Age-specific incidence rates for acute infectious diseases indicate the risk of disease occurring in each age group and, depending on the disease agent, more or less accurately reflect the underlying age-specific infection rates. Reasons that disease and infection rates may differ can be illustrated by comparing measles and polioviruses. Measles infection usually results in typical disease, and concordance between the two rates is very close. In the case of polioviruses (in the period before vaccines were available), the proportion of subclinical infections not only was high overall but also varied inversely with age.

Age Adjustment of Rates

The need to take age distribution into account when comparing disease in different populations is indicated when (1) the rates vary with age and (2) the distribution of the populations by age differs substantially. For example, from published U.S. mortality data for 1983 and 1984, one can compare pneumonia and influenza mortality rates for Alaska and Florida. During those years, 89 deaths were recorded among 986,000 Alaskans at risk, for an annual mortality rate of 9.0 per 100,000. In contrast, in sunny Florida, 4703 deaths occurred from pneumonia and influenza among the 21,792,000 residents at risk for those 2 years, for a rate of 21.6 per 100,000, nearly 2½ times that of Alaska. These rates are called *crude mortality rates.* However, in this instance, these rates are misleading for the reasons that the likelihood of death occurring from pneumonia and influenza increases with age and the age distributions of the populations of these two states differ strikingly. Indeed, national death rates from these infections are nearly 10-fold greater in people 65 to 74 years of age than in those 55 to 64 years of age. For those years, 17.5 percent and 3.0 percent of the Florida and Alaska populations, respectively, were 65 years or older. To make a valid comparison of the pneumonia and influenza mortality rates for these two states, one must perform an age adjustment, a relatively simple process that will not be detailed here because the method can be found in available texts of biostatistics and epidemiology. Rather simply, what is done is to determine mortality rates for specific age groups (usually 5 or 10 years) for the two populations and calculate the deaths that would be expected in a common (or standard) population for the same age groupings by using the age-specific rates of the populations being compared, in this instance those of Alaska and Florida. Summation of these expected deaths permits calculation of the rates that would have occurred in the standard population if the age-specific rates of Alaska applied and if those of Florida applied. In this example, the age-adjusted mortality rate for pneumonia and influenza for Alaska is 35.2 per 100,000 and that for Florida is 21.8, nearly the reverse of the crude rates. (The combined population of the two states was used as the standard.) One should note that these age-adjusted rates are not true rates; they are used for comparison. Though often applicable to infectious diseases, age-adjusted rates almost always are required for comparisons of morbidity and mortality from chronic diseases.

Sex Patterns

Because sex is a readily ascertained characteristic of the membership of populations, the occurrence of infections and disease in relation to sex is described easily. Its simplest form is the *sex ratio,* or the ratio of cases in males to cases in females. This ratio is meaningful only when, as in childhood, the population is divided approximately equally by sex. Although males exceed females at birth (106:100), the death rate for males exceeds that for females at all ages (average, 1.5:1). From approximately 20 years of age on, females outnumber males, the difference increasing with age, which means that when comparing sex-specific rates, age adjustment must be made, or better yet, the age profiles for the sexes should be compared directly so that important differences in the contour can be seen. This difference is illustrated in Table 7–2, which records the age- and sex-specific occurrence of epidemic neuromyasthenia, a disease of still unknown etiology, in Iceland in 1948 and 1949.[69] In this case, the male and female age distributions are sufficiently similar that the unadjusted sex-specific rates can be compared; the results suggested that the risk for females was about 1.6 times that for males. However, direct comparison of the corresponding age-specific rates reveals the additional, possibly important, fact that the female-male risk ratio for 20 years or older (2.05:1) was appreciably greater than that for the younger population (1.2:1).

TABLE 7–2 ■ EPIDEMIC NEUROMYASTHENIA IN AKUREYRI, ICELAND, 1948 TO 1949, BY AGE AND SEX

	Population		Rate per 100	
Age Group (yr)	Male	Female	Male	Female
0–4	425	395	0.24	1.26
5–9	313	310	2.88	2.90
10–19	673	687	11.74	13.25
20–29	534	559	5.06	11.99
30–39	455	499	5.49	10.82
40+	939	1098	2.88	5.37
Total	3339	3548	5.12	8.29

Adapted from Sigurdsson, B., Sigurjonsson, J., Sigurdsson, J.H., et al.: A disease epidemic in Iceland simulating poliomyelitis. Am. J. Hyg. *52*:222–238, 1950.

Ethnic or Racial Patterns

A third attribute by which members of the population can be grouped in describing occurrence of disease is race or ethnic origin, the usefulness of which has decreased with the increasing frequency of mixed marriages. The U.S. census classification is based on information collected regarding race and native origin. People of mixed racial parentage are classified by the race of the nonwhite parent or, if both are nonwhite, by that of the father. People of foreign birth are classified by country. Native-born children of foreign-born parents are identified as "foreign stock" and grouped according to parental origin. Thus, census data provide estimates of population subgroups belonging to several "races" (white, black, Native American, Chinese, Japanese) or "foreign stocks" (including both foreign born and first generation).

Among such population subgroups, differences in the occurrence of many infections and other diseases have been noted. Knowledge of such differences is useful in case finding and organizing the application of specific preventive measures. Explanation of the differences is essential to understand causation of disease but often leads to controversy. Subgroups defined by ethnicity possess some similarity in genetic constitution that may determine susceptibility or resistance to specific agents. They also may be affected distinctively by environmental factors because of voluntary or involuntary differences in behavior and patterns of living. The excess occurrence of tuberculosis in black Americans, potentially explainable on the basis of genetic or environmental factors, is a typically controversial phenomenon.

Disease Patterns in Kinships

Genetically determined susceptibility and resistance to specific infectious agents have not yet been associated clearly with recognized genetic markers that could serve as a basis for defining population subgroups, such as human leukocyte antigen type. Hence, most efforts to look for genetic influences have been studies of occurrence of diseases in people of differing degrees of relationship within kinships or in the total memberships of different kinships. An example of the former is the classic study of Kallman and Reisner,[42] who found that within the immediate families of patients with tuberculosis who were one of a pair of twins, disease prevalence was related directly to the degree of genetic similarity, highest in monozygotic co-twins, next in siblings (including dizygotic co-twins), and least in spouses. The latter approach is illustrated incompletely by a study in South Bend, Indiana, in which researchers found that the frequency of paralytic poliomyelitis in the preceding 5 years was significantly greater in the close kinships of current-year patients with polio than in the community at large.[64] Unfortunately, the investigator ignored the probability that the close relatives were subject to the same influences related to socioeconomic status and standards of hygiene that helped select the propositi patients from the community population in the first place.[34] To complete the study, the close kinships of healthy control propositi (matched with the patients for age, sex, and socioeconomic status) should have been observed similarly.

Family Episodes of Infection and Disease

With respect to contact-transmitted infectious diseases, the family is more important as the basic epidemiologic subgroup of a population than for its shared genes. Indeed, as described elsewhere in some detail,[26] the continuing observation of family units for episodes of infection and related illness has contributed significantly to knowledge of the epidemiology of widely prevalent disease agents. In the earliest family studies, illness (typically acute upper respiratory tract conditions) provided the only indication of infection, and all illnesses constituting an apparent family episode were assumed to be caused by the same, albeit unknown agent. In more recent studies, such as the Virus Watch programs in New York and Seattle,[18, 23, 28–32, 71] the available methodology allowed for monitoring family members for specific infections revealed by virus isolation or antibody response (or both), regardless of whether they were related to the illness.

The situation in all family studies begins with one member's infection, acquired from outside the house. That member then exposes the other family members. The introductory infection and any infections in those exposed constitute a family episode that is described basically in terms of the times of onset of the related infections and the identities (age, sex, position in the family) of the introducer and both the infected and uninfected contacts. Analysis of cumulated episodes of common respiratory illness, observed in the early studies, identified children as the most frequent introducers (hence, important in community spread). The age of the introducers varied with the setting: school age in rural England,[48] 6 years or younger in Cleveland,[22] and preschool age in London.[7] Analysis also yielded estimates of the risk of cross-infection occurring within the family, expressed in terms of secondary attack rates among specified members (for example, younger children) exposed to specified introducers (for example, a schoolchild or a parent). In general, the risk in contacts was related inversely to age overall, as a result of the influence of immunity, and to intimacy of within-family contact (ready exchange between spouses and between children nearest in age). Finally, the relationship of time between the onset of illness in the introducer and onset in those exposed serves to define the range of incubation periods.

Studies of the Virus Watch type make it possible to identify and analyze family episodes caused by specific viruses (influenza A) or groups of viruses (adenoviruses or rhinoviruses), including both subclinical and overt infections. Analysis of the episodes can yield additional information concerning such critical aspects as mode and duration of the agent's shedding; the spectrum of clinical response to infection, including the proportion that is subclinical; and the significance of previous immunity in the face of close exposure, as measured by the frequency and clinical consequences of the reinfections that result. The results of the analysis of adenovirus episodes are illustrative.[29] Virus appears regularly in the feces and less often (approximately 50%) in the pharynx, and shedding may be abortive (a few days only) or continue intermittently for many months. Overall, 50 percent of infections are subclinical, and illness, typically febrile and respiratory, occurs more commonly with pharyngeal excretion (65%) than with only fecal shedding (31%). Immunity is 85 percent protective against infection; reinfections that do occur usually are subclinical. Young children and especially infants younger than 2 years of age are the usual introducers, and within-family spread depends more on duration than on the mode of virus excretion by the introducer.

Socioeconomic Patterns

The foregoing discussion illustrates the use and usefulness of several family-related attributes and immunity. The use of other acquired attributes in describing the occurrence of disease is either quite limited or self-evident. A partial exception is *socioeconomic status,* which covers a complex of attributes, including levels of education and income and, less tangibly, "social standing." The problem is to discover a useful single indicator. One possibility is area of residence as classified by median income or measures that reflect housing standards, such as type of plumbing and average number of persons per room. Relevant data are available for census tracts, which have proved useful when the tracts are reasonably homogeneous.

However, occupation of the head of a household appears to be the one attribute most closely reflecting socioeconomic status. On this basis, the British have defined five broad social classes that directly apply to employed adults and can be extended to cover their dependents. These classes, in descending order, are professional, intermediate, skilled, partly skilled, and unskilled occupations. For use in the United States, based on census-recorded occupations, these terms have been translated as follows:

Professional workers
Non-farm technical, administrative, and managerial workers
Clerical, sales, and skilled workers
Semiskilled workers
Non-farm laborers
Farm workers of whatever level are included in a sixth group as agricultural workers.

RELATING INFECTION AND DISEASE TO PLACE

Place is of interest, epidemiologically, when occupied by humans and, unless indicated as relating to work, recreation, or travel, refers here to residence. Place usually is classified geographically (hemisphere, continent, nation) but also can be classified usefully by environmental characteristics, such as climate, altitude, stage of economic development, population density, and urban or rural nature. Variations in occurrence of disease with place reflect parallel variations in the operation of causative factors and raise an important general question. Are these factors to be found in the characteristics of the physical and biologic environment inherent to the place or in the characteristics of the inhabitants? The former is suggested when the age-adjusted risk of disease increases for immigrants and decreases for emigrants, when risk does not vary among the ethnic groups present, and when similar ethnic groups in other places enjoy a lower risk. As a cautionary note, in seeking to explain variation of disease with place, one must consider possible differences in reliability and completeness of recognition and reporting of disease.

Global Variation

On the global scale, the World Health Organization collects and publishes information concerning the occurrences of diseases derived from statistics compiled routinely within nations for morbidity from notifiable infectious diseases and for causes of death. Unfortunately, the great variations among nations in the quality and availability of medical care and other health services result in corresponding variations in the reliability and completeness of the data collected by the World Health Organization. Generally speaking, basic demographic data and the quality and availability of health services are equally good in well-developed countries, so specific disease rates can be compared. In less-developed countries, demographic data often are inaccurate and medical services are inconsistent in quality and concentrated in urban populations, within which their availability varies with economic status. Thus, many illnesses and deaths are unattended medically, especially in rural areas, and births commonly are attended by midwives. Because infant deaths are reported more completely than births are, infant mortality rates are notably unreliable.

Fortunately, with respect to infectious and parasitic diseases, knowledge of the frequency of disease is less important than is qualitative knowledge of the distribution and spread of disease. Such knowledge guides the application and enforcement of international control measures and is the basis for advice given by physicians to prospective foreign travelers. Important diseases such as yellow fever, plague, and cholera, because of their case-fatality rate and characteristic clinical picture, almost certainly will come to attention when substantial numbers of cases occur. However, such knowledge may not be publicized or may not be promptly available. For example, some countries, hopeful that a new outbreak (perhaps of cholera) will be controlled soon, may withhold information to avoid discouraging economically important tourists.

Two additional considerations are relevant to evaluating the disease hazards of foreign travel. One is the fact that recognized occurrence of disease in the indigenous population may be an inaccurate index of risk to a newcomer. Particular agents, such as polioviruses in the past and hepatitis A virus at present, may be so prevalent that infections in natives occur so early in life that they are usually subclinical. The second consideration is the nature of the proposed travel. The usual tourist or business traveler chiefly visits larger population centers and popular tourist attractions, where the most important hazards are pathogens transmitted by food or water. Those whose activities will bring them into more intimate contact with the people and the biologic environment (Peace Corps workers, military personnel) may encounter additional hazards such as rabies and the locally prevalent arthropod-transmitted pathogens.

As suggested in considering geographic influences on occurrence of disease, the distribution of many diseases is influenced by relevant environmental factors rather than political boundaries. Hence, in depicting (or predicting) the global distribution of a particular disease, identifying regions defined by the presence of factors thought to be important to disease occurrence is useful.

For the great majority of agents pathogenic for humans, the chief environmental requisite is a susceptible human population, and most such agents already exist wherever population size and density are sufficient for them to persist. Thus, concern about global spread is limited to a few important pathogens such as the cholera vibrio and influenza virus. Cholera is a special case in that its spread also depends on poor sanitation. Accordingly, neither persistence nor even limited spread should occur after its introduction into highly developed areas. However, although no recognized persistence has occurred after recent invasions of southern Europe, endemic cholera has existed since at least 1973 in the Louisiana and Texas bayou regions, with inadequately cooked shellfish being the source of reported cases.[5] Influenza A virus continues to be a major and thus far unstoppable threat by virtue of its ability to emerge at irregular intervals in a new antigenic coat, which largely negates the preexisting widespread immunity. Pandemics emerged in 1957, 1968, and 1977 in the Far East and rapidly spread in both directions around the world.

Variations within Nations

Our concern here is nations large enough to have substantial variations in environmental factors inherent in place. We will assume (as may be done safely in the case of developed nations such as the United States) that data for different parts of the country can be compared. Because they pose somewhat different problems, we will consider separately what might be called "diseases in nature" communicable to humans and diseases and disease agents that persist in humans alone.

Among the more important diseases in nature encountered in the United States are rabies, Lyme disease, rickettsial diseases, hantavirus infection, and encephalitis caused by several arboviruses. On the national level, of most interest are variations in the relative, rather than absolute, risks of acquiring infection; simple numerical incidence rather than rate often is used to depict the distribution of disease. This importance is particularly well illustrated for rabies, which is more important in the United States for the threat that it poses (and the extensive treatment required when exposure is suspected) than for the very few human cases that occur.

Data on rabies in animals and humans in the United States are collected by the Centers for Disease Control and Prevention. During the 20 years from 1975 to 1994, more than a threefold increase in animal rabies occurred, from 2627 to 8147 cases annually.[10, 11] This increase was limited to wild animals, which accounted for nearly 95 percent of animal rabies. The small number of cases in domestic animals, which usually result from contact with wild animals, constitutes a hazard to humans because of close contact. At present in the United States, most human cases result from contact with either bats or domestic animals. In recent years, an increase in instances of raccoon rabies has occurred, which accounted for more than one half of all animal rabies in 1993.[45]

The rickettsiae causing Rocky Mountain spotted fever exist in nearly every state, but the frequency of disease is dictated more by the number and density of humans living in suburban and rural areas, where the agent persists in a tick–lower vertebrate reservoir, than by the level of infection among the tick vectors. Of the 465 cases reported in 1994, 48 percent occurred in the south Atlantic coastal states (Maryland through Florida) and 14 percent in the west south central area (Arkansas, Louisiana, Oklahoma, and Texas).[10, 11] Only 13 cases were reported from the Mountain region for which the disease was named, in spite of the prevalence of infected ticks.

Six viruses—St. Louis encephalitis, West Nile encephalitis, Powassan encephalitis, California encephalitis, and western and eastern equine encephalitis—account for all cases of arbovirus encephalitis in the United States. The yearly number of cases that occurred between 1964 and 1983 varied widely, from 70 in 1972 and 1979 to 2113 in 1975 (mean, 285), and similar variations occurred in cases of St. Louis encephalitis (range, 5 in 1973 to 1815 in 1975; mean, 181) and western equine encephalitis (range, 0 in 1980 to 172 in 1965; mean, 28). Eastern equine encephalitis was less variable (range, 0 to 14; mean, 5), and California encephalitis was least so (range, 30 to 160; mean, 69). Geographic patterns also exhibit some yearly variations, but St. Louis encephalitis is distributed most widely and overlaps significantly with western equine encephalitis in the West and with eastern equine encephalitis in the Southeast. California encephalitis is concentrated in the upper Midwest.

West Nile virus, an African arbovirus, first appeared in the United States in the summer of 1999 and was responsible for an outbreak of encephalitis in New York City.[3] The activity of this virus increased during the subsequent 2 years such that its presence was noted in 359 counties in 27 states in 2001.[13]

Infections entirely dependent on humans also do not occur uniformly throughout the United States. The differences are largely temporal. For example, the periodic waves of influenza often are evident first along the East Coast, whereas in the prevaccine era, the 2- to 3-year cycling of measles in metropolitan areas was not synchronized nationally but determined in each area by the local build-up of susceptible individuals. Significant regional differences exist in the long-term frequency of diseases such as poliomyelitis in the prevaccination era (higher in the North than in the South) and viral hepatitis.

Figure 7–2 shows the incidence rates for hepatitis A and B by states and territories for 1994.[10, 11] For hepatitis A, striking geographic differences exist that are not explained entirely. The different geographic rates for hepatitis B are explained largely by intravenous drug use and male homosexual activity.

Local Patterns of Infection and Disease

"Local" units of population for which demographic data are readily available in the United States include "large" units, such as counties, metropolitan areas, and large cities, which contain smaller units (smaller cities and towns [within counties] and census tracts [within metropolitan areas and large cities]). The smaller units, including unincorporated areas within counties, often can be characterized by variables (urban or rural nature, population density, socioeconomic status, racial or ethnic group) that may help explain observed differences in the occurrence of specific infections and related diseases.

Particularly in relation to outbreaks of acute infectious diseases, spot maps commonly are used to show the local distribution of individual cases. Placing of new pins (a different color each week) to mark the residences of newly reported cases serves to visualize the outbreak's geographic progression. The final distribution of the pins may help identify a major source of infection. A classic example is the 1854 outbreak of cholera in the Golden Square district of London, in which the clustering of residences of fatal cases helped Snow incriminate the Broad Street pump as the source.[70] Sometimes, place of work is a better guide to the source of infection than is place of residence. In another classic study, that of endemic typhus in Montgomery, Alabama, in the early 1920s, the residences of cases (Fig. 7–3) were scattered widely, whereas the workplaces (Fig. 7–4) were concentrated in relation to feed stores and food-handling businesses, all heavily rat-infested. This finding led Maxcy to perform studies demonstrating the basic role of rats and rat fleas in this disease.[52]

Figure 7–5 shows the spot map technique in conjunction with census tract information to illustrate and interpret the change in pattern of poliomyelitis in Kansas City, Missouri, related to the introduction of Salk vaccine in 1955.[14] Cases in the 1946 and 1952 epidemics were scattered widely and, especially in 1952, involved many in the higher-income population in the southwestern part of the city. Vaccine acceptance by the white population was much greater than by the black population, among whom cases in the 1959 epidemic were concentrated sharply. Census tract information also was used to explain the occurrence of cases of St. Louis encephalitis in the 1964 epidemic in Houston, Texas.[50] Cases tended to cluster in the central area, and the incidence per 100,000 was highest (36.0) in the nonwhite areas; elsewhere, it varied inversely with the socioeconomic level of areas: upper, 11.3; middle, 21.0; and lower, 30.1. However, when census tracts were divided into a central zone and four concentric surrounding zones, incidence rates by zone dropped sharply with increasing distance from the center (from 78.7 in the central zone to 5.4 in the most peripheral), whereas rates within each zone did not vary appreciably between tracts grouped by socioeconomic level. Thus, distance of residence from the city center (where environmental conditions favored an abundance of vector mosquitoes), rather than race or social class, proved to be the critical determinant.

TEMPORAL PATTERNS OF INFECTION AND DISEASE

In discussing variations in occurrence of infection and disease with person and place, time was specified or implied. Similarly, in considering variations with time, the populations involved must be defined by place, at the least. Because temporal variations in observed effect must reflect parallel variations in the activity of causes, time is another important variable in seeking to identify causative factors.

Definitions

The unit of time used can vary from hours to decades to centuries. In describing acute outbreaks, the units are short—hours for food poisoning, days or weeks for most infectious diseases—whereas long-term time trends are described in longer units of years or decades. Comparisons extending over the course of 1 or more decades may be complicated by changes in diagnostic standards and reporting, as occurred with reporting poliomyelitis in the United States, which was extended in the 1940s to include both minor paralysis and nonparalytic disease.

Finally, the meanings of two words commonly used to describe the occurrence of disease over the course of time in a given area should be stated clearly. *Endemic* refers to diseases regularly present. The usual frequency, including expected seasonal variations, is called the *endemic level.* The term *epidemic* often is applied indiscriminately (and sometimes incorrectly) to any large clustering of cases in time and place. More precisely, it applies to any number of cases, small or large, representing a significant excess over the usual, or endemic, level.

This principle underlies the familiar monitoring of influenza in the United States by the Centers for Disease Control and Prevention on the basis of deaths caused by influenza and pneumonia. Such monitoring is illustrated in Figure 7–6, in which the weekly ratios of deaths caused by pneumonia and influenza to the total deaths observed from September 1980 to August 1983 are compared with the ratios expected from use of the time series method* and "epidemic threshold," which depicts the upper 95 percent confidence limit. When the observed value exceeds the expected one for 2 successive weeks, an influenza epidemic is indicated. On this basis, epidemics began in week 50 of 1980 and week 3 of 1983.

In practice, especially at the local level, health authorities use the term *outbreak* rather than *epidemic* (unless the number of cases is very large) to minimize public alarm. The term *pandemic* is used to describe excess disease occurring in many countries, as influenza did in 1957 and 1968.

---

*This method, which replaced the regression method of Serfling in 1980, is described in some detail by Choi and Thacker.[10, 11]

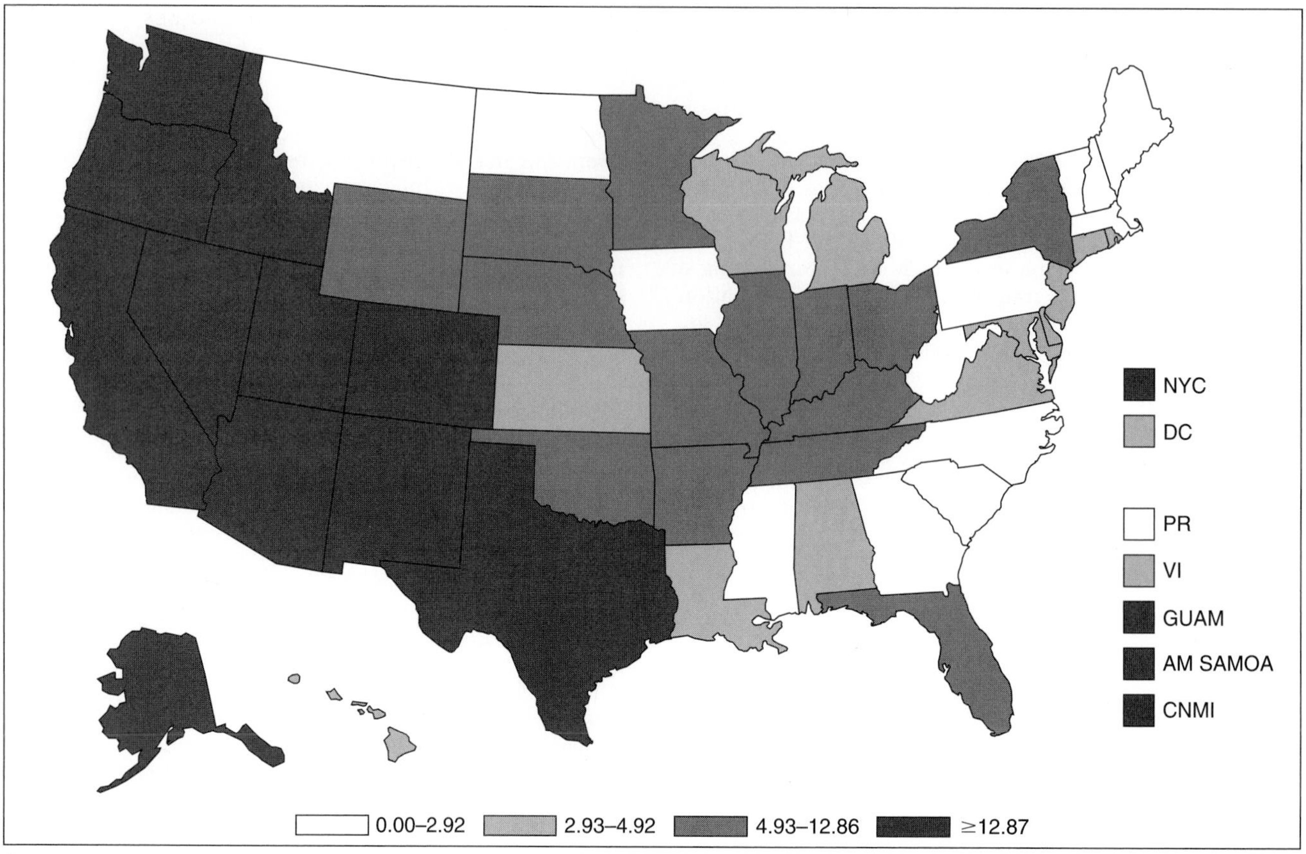

A

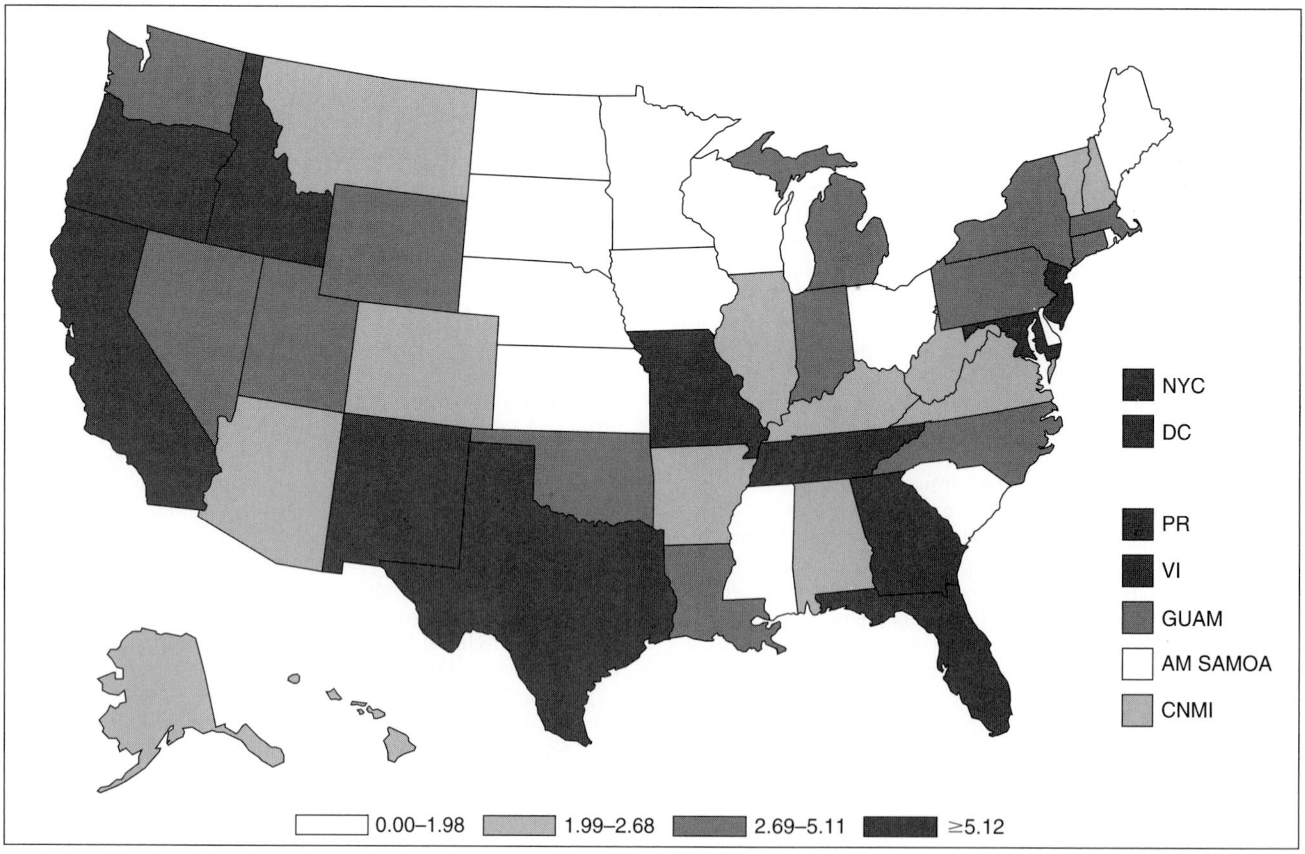

B

FIGURE 7–2 ■ Cases of hepatitis A and B per 100,000 population for each state and territory, United States, 1994. (From Summary of notifiable diseases, United States, 1994. M. M. W. R. Morb. Mortal. Wkly. Rep. *43*[53]:1–80, 1994.)

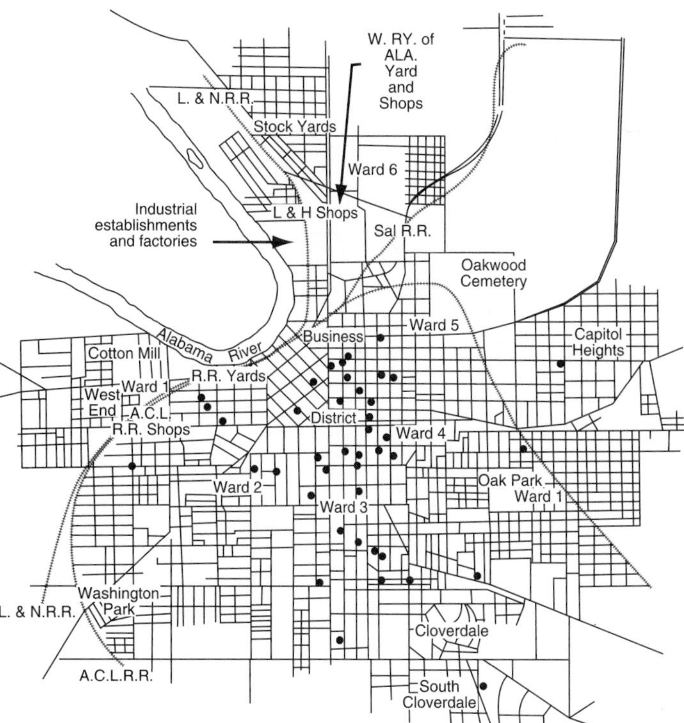

FIGURE 7–3 ■ Cases of mild typhus (Brill disease) in Montgomery, Alabama, 1922 to 1925, spotted according to residence. (From Maxcy, K. F.: An epidemiological study of endemic typhus [Brill disease] in the southeastern United States. Public Health Rep. *41*:2967–2995, 1926.)

Time Clusters

Concern here is with the recognition and interpretation of events (infections and disease) occurring with some frequency within a limited period, or clustering in time. A selected series of examples will serve to illustrate the more important possibilities.

An important determinant of clustering of infections is the incubation (or latent) period. Infection resulting from a known exposure is manifested within a predictable range of time by the initiation of shedding of the agent and the onset of disease (if it occurs). For simplicity, we will speak only of disease hereafter because it provides the only readily recognizable indication of infection. Although the average incubation period of a given disease is remarkably constant, the usual range broadens as the incubation period increases. This range can be estimated by accumulating cases for which the time of exposure is known precisely or approximately

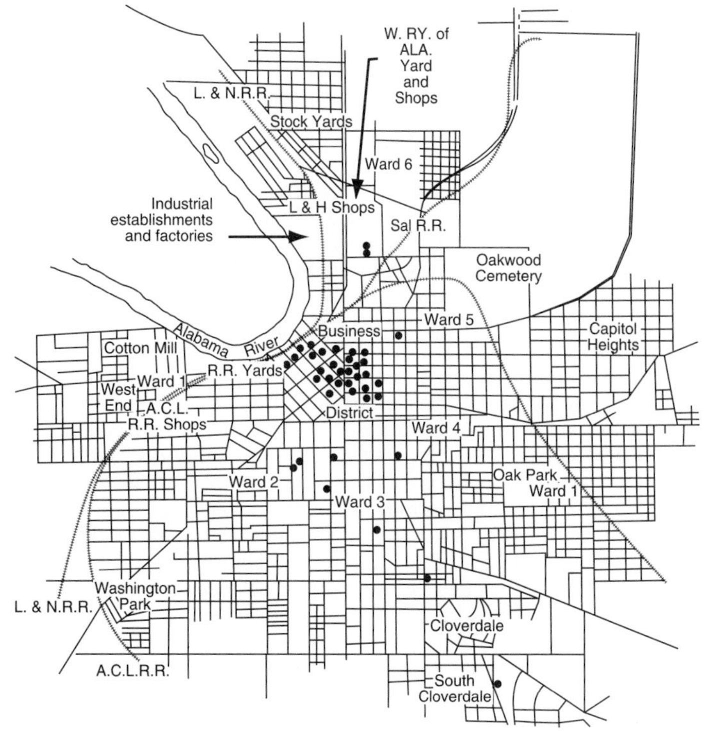

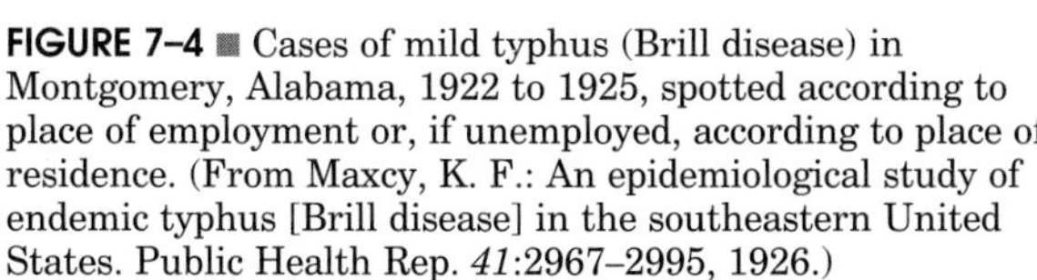

FIGURE 7–4 ■ Cases of mild typhus (Brill disease) in Montgomery, Alabama, 1922 to 1925, spotted according to place of employment or, if unemployed, according to place of residence. (From Maxcy, K. F.: An epidemiological study of endemic typhus [Brill disease] in the southeastern United States. Public Health Rep. *41*:2967–2995, 1926.)

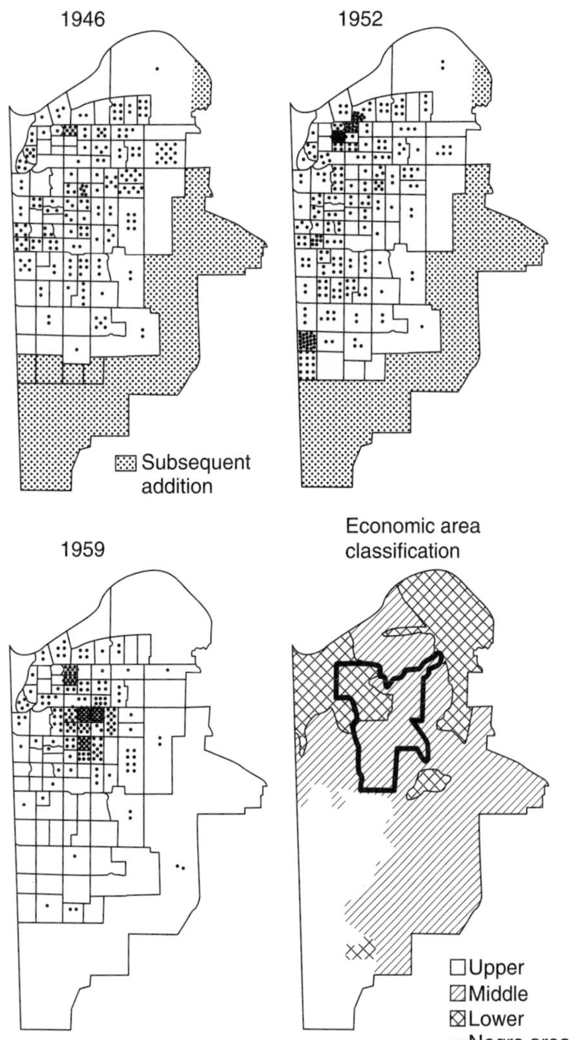

FIGURE 7–5 ■ Distribution of reported poliomyelitis cases, by census tract, Kansas City, Missouri, epidemic years 1946, 1952, and 1959. (From Chin, T. D. Y., and Marine, W. W.: The changing patterns of poliomyelitis observed in two urban epidemics, Kansas City and Des Moines, 1959. Public Health Rep. *76*:533–563, 1961.)

and, with this point as day 0 on the time axis, plotting the day of onset of each case. The width of the resulting cluster provides an estimate of the range of the incubation period. The best estimate is obtained by using only cases with single, clearly timed exposure, such as when contact with the source case occurred only once, as during a playmate's birthday party.

A more readily obtained but less precise estimate is that derived from the cumulative analysis of family episodes of a disease based on the assumption that the initial or primary case is the source of subsequent disease in family contacts. Because the primary case is infectious for several days, on any of which effective exposure may occur, the onset of secondary cases will cluster over a range that in theory may reflect the true range plus the period of infectivity of the primary case.

Knowledge of the range of incubation periods has several practical implications. For contagious diseases, it can be used to distinguish true secondary cases that occur in families from others arising as a result of extrafamilial sources (those with onset too soon after that of the primary case are called *co-primary cases)* or representing a second generation of spread within the family *(tertiary cases).* It also determines for how long after known exposure contacts should be observed or possibly held in quarantine for the subsequent development of disease. For poorly contagious diseases, such as typhoid fever, or for noncontagious diseases, such as food poisoning, the distribution of onset in an outbreak can be used to distinguish between "point" epidemics (common time and place of exposure) and outbreaks reflecting exposure to a possibly continuing source. In the former case, onset will fall within the usual range of incubation periods. Furthermore, when the point source is not obvious, investigation can be focused on the interval defined by subtracting the shortest incubation period from the date of onset of the first case and the longest period from the date of onset of the last case.

An example is the occurrence in 1939 of 13 cases of typhoid fever in Schenectady, New York. The onset of the first and last cases was June 5 and June 29, respectively. Assuming the usual range of incubation periods to be 5 to 30 days, the critical period was calculated to be May 29 to May 31, within which occurred a church-sponsored Memorial Day picnic at which, researchers discovered, salad prepared by an unrecognized typhoid carrier was served.

The concept of an incubation period has additional useful applications. By taking the onset of paralytic poliomyelitis as day 0 and looking backward on the time axis, "provoking" factors, such as irritant inoculations, were identified by the clustering of their times of occurrence. Similarly, by setting the time of vaccination at day 0, the cumulated experience of those vaccinated can be (and has been) analyzed for identification of adverse effects of specific vaccines, recognized as such because they cluster in time. Such evidence, for example, led to the recognition of poliomyelitis disease caused by both inactivated (Salk) and live virus (Sabin) polio vaccine and, in 1976, was an important point in linking swine influenza vaccine to Guillain-Barré syndrome.[46]

Short-Term Patterns

EPIDEMICS. "Point" epidemics, as noted, have a duration limited by the range of the period of incubation of the particular disease because no secondary spread of the agents occurs. Concern here is with the much more common outbreaks or epidemics that extend over longer periods of time. On the basis of the agents and the mechanisms of transmission, three distinct types can be recognized.

The first type typically consists of outbreaks of poorly contagious or noncontagious disease; such outbreaks reflect the new but persisting activity of a source that must be identified and terminated quickly. One example of such a "continuing source" type of outbreak was a community-wide outbreak of salmonellosis in Madeira, California, in 1965, which was traced quickly to the water supply.[65] Unrecognized typhoid carriers working as food handlers and shellfish harvested from sewage-polluted waters and contaminated with hepatitis A virus have provided many other examples of outbreaks requiring prompt and careful epidemiologic investigation to identify the source.

The element of contagion distinguishes the second type of epidemic, in which disease spreads from person to person. Such epidemics generally are self-limited, and the curve describing them often resembles the bell-shaped curve of a normal distribution. Modification of this curve, as in an abrupt decline from the peak, is the expected result of successful control efforts, evaluation of which often is controversial. As discussed in more detail elsewhere,[27] epidemics of contagious disease arise when the persisting or newly introduced agent exists in a population containing

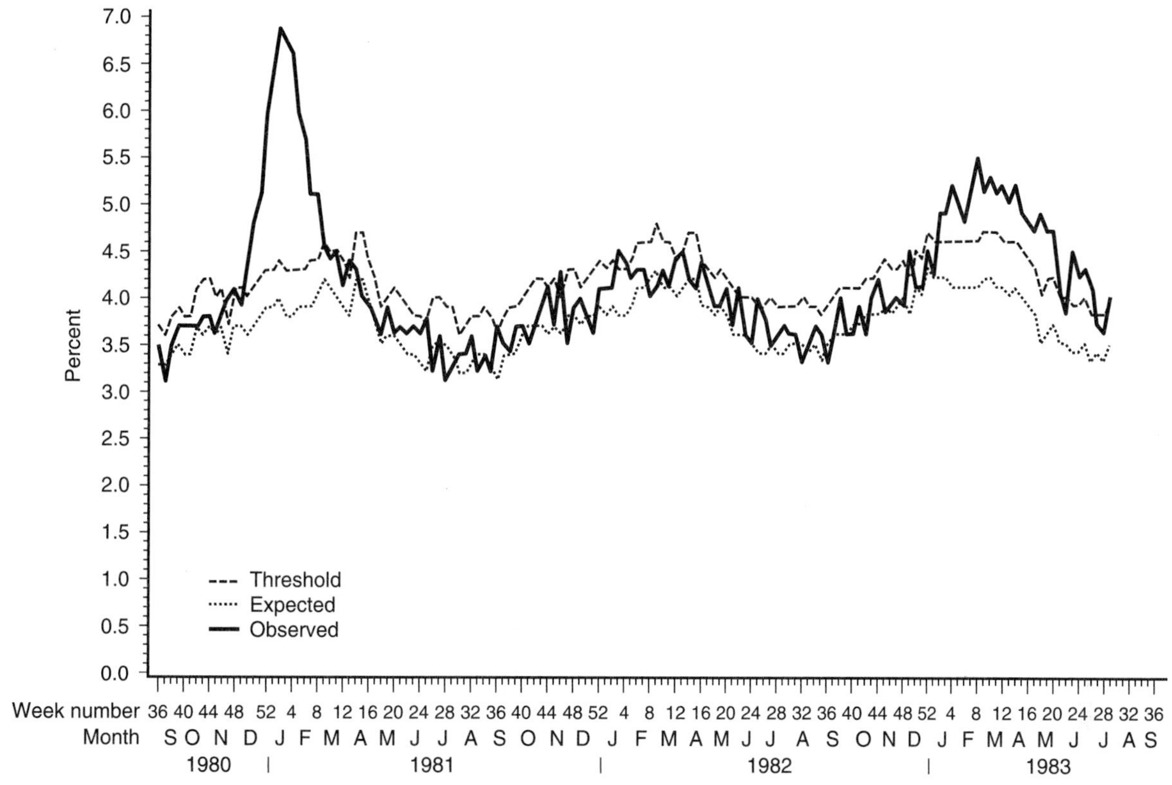

FIGURE 7–6 ■ Percentage of deaths attributable to pneumonia and influenza in 121 United States cities, 1980 to 1983. (From Annual summary 1982. Reported morbidity & mortality in the United States. M. M. W. R. Morb. Mortal. Wkly. Rep. *31*[54]:1–149, 1983.)

sufficient susceptible individuals who render contact with one another adequate to permit transfer of infection from each new case to, on average, more than one susceptible individual. When this average falls below 1, the curve declines, and when the probability of successful transfer of infection approaches 0, the epidemic terminates (typically, well before the supply of susceptible individuals has been exhausted).

Many reasons that underlie this decline and termination of transmission include seasonal changes in environmental factors affecting agent viability, such as temperature and humidity, and in host behavior affecting the intimacy of contact, such as indoor school versus outdoor play, as well as the progressive conversion of susceptible individuals to immune individuals. If one assumes constant units on the time axis, the slope of the ascending limb of the epidemic curve is determined by the incubation period (interval between successive cases) and factors influencing transmission (infectivity of the agent, frequency of adequate contact between susceptible persons). In the absence of effective control measures, the duration of epidemics of a particular disease depends on the size of the susceptible population and the persistence of favorable environmental factors.

Epidemics of "diseases in nature" constitute the third type. Because susceptible individuals usually are abundant in the exposed human population, these epidemics typically reflect increases in the number of sources of infection in nature. With zoonoses such as arbovirus encephalitis, the initiation, slope of the curve, and duration of the epidemic are determined by the number of susceptible lower vertebrate hosts, the seasonally determined abundance of the vector mosquitoes, and the length of the extrinsic incubation period in the vector. Thus, epidemics caused by western equine encephalitis virus tend to begin earlier and progress more rapidly than do those caused by St. Louis encephalitis virus, even when both agents use the same host and vector species, as in California. This difference occurs at least in part because the extrinsic incubation period is much shorter for western equine encephalitis than for St. Louis encephalitis.

SEASONAL AND CYCLIC VARIATIONS. Predictable periodic variations in disease take two forms, seasonal and cyclic, neither of which is understood completely in the case of agents infecting only humans.

Seasonal variations presumably reflect the influence of changes in temperature, precipitation, and length of days on the activity of the agent. It is understood readily with respect to diseases in nature that depend on lower vertebrate hosts and arthropod vectors, the abundance and activity of which are determined seasonally. Similarly, the increased occurrence of bacterial enteric infections (spread by indirect means) in the warmer months is explainable largely by more rapid bacterial growth in unrefrigerated milk and food, the increase in abundance of filth flies, and lowered sanitary precautions associated with summer recreational activities.

However, the mode of transmission is only a partial determinant of the seasonal pattern. Thus, although the enteroviruses (including polio), the rotaviruses causing acute gastroenteritis, and hepatitis A virus all are spread chiefly by fecal-oral mechanisms (both direct and indirect), the seasonal patterns are distinctly different (late summer and fall for enteroviruses and late winter for rotaviruses and hepatitis A virus). Similarly, although infections with agents present in respiratory secretions and spread by airborne mechanisms or contaminated fomites occur infrequently in the summer, when contact among susceptible children often is out of doors, their seasonal peaks occur at significantly different times. The season of respiratory diseases coincides roughly with the school year. Rhinoviruses are most active in the early fall and late spring, and parainfluenza virus types 1 and 2 peak in the fall. The annual peaks of respiratory syncytial virus vary among fall, winter, and spring. Mumps peaks in late fall, influenza in late winter or early spring, and measles typically in the spring. As suggested by London and Yorke,[49, 80] differences in incubation periods and infectivity are responsible, at least partly, for these differences in pattern.

Plotting variation over a series of years will reveal a roughly regular cyclic variation for some diseases. In larger metropolitan areas, the usual biennial measles epidemic appears as an enlarged annual wave. Before 1950, deaths caused by meningococcal meningitis occurred on a nationwide basis in cycles of 7 to 9 years, a phenomenon presumably terminated by the advent of sulfonamides and antibiotics. Cyclic patterns are thought to result in part from the fact that the degree of depletion of susceptible individuals during annual waves is inconstant, for reasons that with respect to measles are discussed in considerable detail by London and Yorke.[49, 80] Pandemic influenza A, which provides the most dramatic example of cycling, is explainable on a very different basis, namely, a major change in the antigenic character of the agent, the probable mechanism for which was discussed previously.

Long-Term Trends

Except for poliomyelitis during the first half of the 20th century, clearly defined long-term trends in the occurrence of infectious diseases in the United States usually have been downward, and in no case has description or understanding of the mechanisms posed a major difficulty. In the case of poliomyelitis, the increase in the rate of paralytic disease beginning about 1880 is attributable to numerous factors, including improved sanitation, which resulted in an expanding proportion of older children and young adults without previous exposure to the causative viruses. In young infants, the vast majority of poliovirus infections are benign but produce long-lasting immunity; the older an individual when infected, the more likely for that individual to have paralysis. Thus, the incidence of paralytic disease is related inversely to the level of sanitation as long as an opportunity exists for introduction of the virus into an area. In the United States, the increase in paralytic disease with epidemics continued unabated (with an apparent sharp increase around 1940 because of changes in reporting criteria) until the widespread use of poliovirus vaccines. The post-1955 decline in poliomyelitis, the much earlier decline in pertussis and diphtheria, the disappearance of smallpox, and the more recent marked decline in measles and rubella all are attributable chiefly to widespread use of effective specific vaccines. Similarly, the disappearance of indigenous malaria and the decline of rabies to a negligible level in humans reflect the application of a variety of effective control measures.

Since 1900, infectious disease mortality rates have decreased markedly in the United States.[57] For example, mortality caused by infection in infants decreased approximately 95 percent between 1900 and 1973, and that in children 1 to 14 years of age decreased 99 percent.[57] In adults, infectious disease mortality rates declined markedly as well. Much of this decline can be attributable to nonmedical measures (socioeconomic changes, improved sanitation, smaller families, and the like). With some exceptions, such as bacterial meningitis, smallpox, and poliomyelitis, newer measures such as antibiotics and vaccines played a lesser role in reducing mortality rates (though not morbidity; measles and pertussis mortality rates, for example, declined strikingly before the advent of the vaccines, but their incidence rates did not).

However, for reasons that are not entirely clear, strong evidence has indicated a recent increase in mortality rates from infectious diseases in the United States.[63] Data obtained from the National Center for Health Statistics for the years 1980 to 1992 showed a 39 percent increase in age-adjusted infectious disease mortality during that period. The increase in crude mortality rates, which better reflects the burden on the health care system, was 58 percent. The most important contributors to this increase were respiratory infections, acquired immunodeficiency syndrome (AIDS), and sepsis. Mortality rates in children younger than 5 years of age decreased. A more than sixfold increase in mortality in the 25- to 44-year-old population (presumably attributable in large part to AIDS) and a 25 percent increase in those 65 years or older occurred. Although these data are subject to the well-known physician-related inaccuracies of death certificates, no doubt a considerable increase in mortality from infectious diseases has occurred. Infectious diseases are not disappearing despite earlier trends, and these data reinforce the need for surveillance.

These phenomena warrant three unrelated final comments. First, as successful vaccines become available and are used widely, the disease under attack is reported far more completely. In the case of measles, researchers estimated that before vaccine was available, only approximately 10 percent of cases were reported. No recent national estimates are available, but as of 1984, probably less than 5 percent were reported. In New York City, 56 percent of approximately 1000 patients seen at or admitted to 12 hospitals were reported during a widely publicized 1991 epidemic.[20] Second, the widespread use of effective vaccines may alter the epidemiology of their target infections in ways that may not be anticipated if, in contrast to smallpox, the disease is not eradicated. Third, although age-adjusted incidence rates typically (and necessarily) are used in describing changes in occurrence of disease over long periods of time, they have little meaning as disease becomes very infrequent, possibly verging on disappearance. At this point, interest focuses on the actual number and distribution of cases, each of which requires explanation (as with paralytic poliomyelitis) or institution of rigorous, localized control measures (as would result with malaria, yellow fever, or smallpox).

Emerging Infections

Although 2 decades ago one might have said that most infectious disorders had been explored thoroughly epidemiologically and that little was left to do, this conclusion is no longer the case. Indeed, infectious disease epidemiology has become increasingly challenging, and in many ways the problems are more complex and necessitate greater cooperation with additional disciplines such as microbiology and molecular biology. In part, this concern exists because of so-called *emerging infections,* a term that has come into vogue in recent years and refers to two different groups of disorders. The first is associated with the appearance of previously unrecognized or possibly heretofore nonexistent infections in humans. Well-known examples are legionellosis, AIDS, Lyme disease, hemorrhagic colitis caused by *E. coli* O157:H7, Ebola virus infection, and hantavirus infection. The other group includes previously recognized human infections that exhibit changes in epidemiologic behavior or biologic characteristics that enhance their transmission or virulence. These changes usually can be attributed to external influences, such as altered demographics, including increasing population and rural-urban migration, international travel, new technology or technologic failure, changes in land use, adaptation of infecting organisms to various influences, and inadequate or underused public health measures.[47] To this list should be added changes in host factors such as immune defenses. Obviously, no clear dividing line exists between new infections and old ones with new behavior. However, examples of those with new behavior include multidrug-resistant tuberculosis, penicillin-resistant pneumococcal infections, invasive group A streptococcal (popularly known as flesh-eating bacteria) infections, staphylococcal toxic shock syndrome, cryptosporidiosis, and numerous infections that are fostered by immunosuppression or various therapeutic measures such as antibiotics and catheters.

These emerging infections are not minor threats. Although in some instances, relatively small populations have been affected to date, the potential for widespread disease of epidemic or even pandemic proportions exists. This potential can be expected to increase because the demographic and other conditions that have predisposed to the emergence of these infections continue to grow and intensify. Accordingly, maximal efforts must be made to reverse this process. To achieve this goal requires worldwide collaborative effort among various disciplines, including epidemiology, microbiology, entomology, immunology, clinical medicine, demography, nutrition, sanitation, and even political science, to list only a few.

In recent years, infectious disease epidemiologic surveillance has been enhanced by the development of sophisticated techniques for so-called *molecular epidemiology*. These techniques enable researchers to identify subtypes of specific organisms. Each of the three well-known strains of poliovirus can be subtyped on the basis of genetic variations, thereby providing a means of tracing the spread of infection with remarkable precision.[44] For example, a 1992 outbreak of type 3 poliovirus infection in a religious group opposed to vaccination in the Netherlands was shown to be most likely caused by a strain of virus from the Indian subcontinent.[59] In addition, the identical strain produced illness in religious groups of the same denomination in Alberta, Canada, undoubtedly because of travel-related contact. These techniques also are used to distinguish wild poliovirus strains from those of vaccine origin.[79] Parenthetically, of note is that immune responses to poliovirus vaccine are not affected by these molecular variations. Other well-known recent applications of molecular epidemiology include characterization of the hantavirus that produced illness in the southwestern United States,[58] the worldwide epidemiology of variants of HIV,[38] and the spread of animal species-specific strains of rabies virus in the United States.[45]

The responsibilities of epidemiologists regarding emerging infections may be described in three categories. The first is that of surveillance, including recognition of the appearance of a previously unrecognized infection or a new variant of an existing disease. Optimal surveillance requires systematic observations and specific diagnostic criteria to ensure precision. Recent examples of such criteria include those for AIDS,[9] streptococcal toxic shock syndrome,[6] and the recognition of drug-resistant pneumococci.[40] An important part of surveillance is to determine who, when, and where: who is affected (e.g., age and other personal characteristics, contact with others who are ill), when the disorder occurs (e.g., year-to-year variations, season, temporal course of the outbreak), and where it occurs (geographic locations, urban or rural, local ecology, etc.). Second, an important task is to use surveillance and other data to develop an understanding of the epidemiology of the infection, which often provides leads to the etiology and pathogenesis and approaches to control. The third role of epidemiology is that of monitoring the effects of various control measures, including, for example, assessment of the safety and efficacy of anticipated new vaccines such as those for rotavirus enteritis, malaria, and AIDS.

The increasing magnitude and speed of international travel enhance the likelihood of global spread of disease and complicate approaches to prevent or contain epidemic infections. Moreover, many of the emerging infections are not limited geographically by their ecologic requirements, as largely is the case with schistosomiasis. Thus, the nations of the world are increasingly dependent on each other for surveillance, a task that is not accomplished easily given the logistics; costs (in the face of other needs and priorities, particularly of many developing countries); and the required standardization, collaboration, communication, coordination, and centralized resource for assembly and analysis of surveillance. Although the World Health Organization, the Pan American Health Organization, the U.S. military and Public Health Service, and various other organizations do maintain surveillance systems and laboratories in various parts of the world, these efforts at present are considered to be inadequate except for some infections and in some areas. Accordingly, the development of comprehensive national and worldwide surveillance systems has been urged strongly.[12, 47]

REFERENCES

1. Allison, A. C.: Protection afforded by sickle-cell trait against subtertian malarial infection. B. M. J. *1*:290–294, 1953.
2. American Heart Association: Committee Report: Jones criteria (revised) for guidance in the diagnosis of rheumatic fever. Circulation *32*:664–668, 1965.
3. Asnis, D. S., Conetta, R., Teixeira, A. A., et al.: The West Nile virus Outbreak of 1999 in New York: The Flushing Hospital Experience. Clin. Infect. Dis. *30*:413-418, 2000.
4. Atkinson, W. L., Orenstein, W. A., and Knugman, S.: The resurgence of measles in the United States, 1989–1990. Annu. Rev. Med. *43*:451–163, 1992.
5. Blake, P. A., Allegra, D. T., Snyder, J. D., et al.: Cholera: A possible endemic focus in the United States. N. Engl. J. Med. *302*:305–309, 1980.
6. Breiman, R. F., Davis, J. P., Facklam, R. R., et al.: The Working Group on Severe Streptococcal Infections: Defining the group A streptococcal toxic shock syndrome. J. A. M. A. *269*:390–391, 1993.
7. Brimblecombe, F. S. W., Cruickshank, R., Masters, P. L., et al.: Family studies of respiratory infections. B. M. J. *1*:119–128, 1958.
8. Centers for Disease Control: Annual summary 1982. Reported morbidity & mortality in the United States. M. M. W. R. Morb. Mortal. Wkly. Rep. *31*(54):1–149, 1983.
9. Centers for Disease Control and Prevention: 1993 Revised classification system for HIV infection and expanded case definition for AIDS among adolescents and adults. M. M. W. R. Recomm. Rep. *41*(RR-17):1–19, 1992.
10. Centers for Disease Control and Prevention: Summary of notifiable diseases, United States, 1994. M. M. W. R. Morb. Mortal. Wkly. Rep. *43*(53):1–80, 1995.
11. Centers for Disease Control and Prevention: Summary of notifiable diseases, United States, 1995. M. M. W. R. Morb. Mortal. Wkly. Rep. *44*(53):1–87, 1996.
12. Centers for Disease Control and Prevention: Addressing Emerging Infectious Disease Threats: A Prevention Strategy for the United States. Atlanta, U.S. Department of Health and Human Services, Public Health Service, 1994.
13. Centers for Disease Control and Prevention: West Nile virus activity—United States, 2001. M. M. W. R. Morb. Mortal. Wkly. Rep. *51*(23): 497–501, 2002.
14. Chin, T. D. Y., and Marine, W. W.: The changing patterns of poliomyelitis observed in two urban epidemics, Kansas City and Des Moines, 1959. Public Health Rep. *76*:553–563, 1961.
15. Choi, K., and Thacker, S. B.: An evaluation of influenza mortality surveillance, 1962–1979. I. Time series forecasts of expected pneumonia and influenza deaths. Am. J. Epidemiol. *113*:216–226, 1981.
16. Choi, K., and Thacker, S. B.: An evaluation of influenza mortality surveillance, 1962–1979. II. Percentage of pneumonia and influenza deaths as an indicator of influenza activity. Am. J. Epidemiol. *113*:227–235, 1981.

17. Chorba, T. L., Berkelman, R. L., Safford, S. K., et al.: Mandatory reporting of infectious diseases by clinicians. J. A. M. A. *262*:3018–3026, 1989.
18. Cooney, M. K., Hall, C. E., and Fox, J. P.: The Seattle Virus Watch. III. Evaluation of isolation methods and summary of infections, detected by virus isolations. Am. J. Epidemiol. *96*:286–305, 1972.
19. Craig, G. B., Jr.: Biology of *Aedes triseriatus:* Some factors affecting control. *In* Calisher, C. H., and Thompson, W. H. (eds.): California Serogroup Viruses. Proceedings of an International Symposium. New York, Alan R. Liss, 1983, pp. 329–341.
20. Davis, S.: Unpublished data presented to Advisory Committee on Immunization Practices. Centers for Disease Control, June 3, 1991.
21. Dewhurst, K.: Dr. Thomas Sydenham (1624–1689). Berkeley and Los Angeles, University of California Press, 1966.
22. Dingle, J. H., Badger, G. R., and Jordan, W. S., Jr.: Illness in the Home. Cleveland, OH, The Press of Western Reserve University, 1964.
23. Elveback, L. R., Fox, J. P., Ketler, A., et al.: The Virus Watch Program: A continuing surveillance of viral infections in metropolitan New York families. III. Preliminary report on association of infections with disease. Am. J. Epidemiol. *83*:436–454, 1966.
24. Eng, T. R., Hamaker, T. A., Dobbins, J. G., et al.: Rabies surveillance, United States, 1988. M. M. W. R. CDC Surveill. Summ. *38*(1):1–21, 1989.
25. Fothergill, L. C.: Biological warfare and its defense. Public Health Rep. *72*:865–871, 1957.
26. Fox, J. P.: Family-based epidemiology studies. The Second Wade Hampton Frost Lecture. Am. J. Epidemiol. *99*:165–179, 1974.
27. Fox, J. P., and Elveback, L. R.: Herd immunity: Changing concepts. *In* Notkins, A. L. (ed.): Viral Immunology and Immunopathology. New York, Academic Press, 1975, pp. 273–290.
28. Fox, J. P., Elveback, L. R., Spigland, I., et al.: The Virus Watch Program: A continuing surveillance of viral infections in metropolitan New York families. I. Overall plan, methods of collecting and handling information, and a summary report of specimens collected and illnesses observed. Am. J. Epidemiol. *83*:289–412, 1966.
29. Fox, J. P., Hall, C. E., and Cooney, M. K.: The Seattle Virus Watch. VII. Observations of adenovirus infections. Am. J. Epidemiol. *105*:362–386, 1977.
30. Fox, J. P., Hall, C. E., Cooney, M. K., et al.: The Seattle Virus Watch. II. Objectives, study population and its observation, data processing and summary of illnesses. Am. J. Epidemiol. *96*:270–285, 1972.
31. Fox, J. P., Hall, C. E., Cooney, M. K., et al.: Influenza virus infections in Seattle families, 1975–1979. I. Study design, methods and the occurrence of infections by time and age. Am. J. Epidemiol. *116*:212–227, 1982.
32. Fox, J. P., Hall, C. E., Cooney, M. K., et al.: Influenza virus infections in Seattle families, 1975–1979. II. Pattern of infection in invaded households and relation of age and prior antibody to occurrence of infection and related illness. Am. J. Epidemiol. *116*:228–242, 1982.
33. Frobisher, M.: Fundamentals of Microbiology. 7th ed. Philadelphia, W. B. Saunders, 1962, p. 354.
34. Gelfand, H. M.: Inheritance of susceptibility to poliomyelitis. N. Engl. J. Med. *258*:964–965, 1958.
35. Griffin, P. M., and Tauxe, R. V.: The epidemiology of infections caused by *Escherichia coli* O157:H7, other enterohemorrhagic *E. coli* and the associated hemolytic-uremic syndrome. Epidemiol. Rev. *13*:60–98, 1991.
36. Gwaltney, J. M., Jr., and Hendley, J. O.: Rhinovirus transmission: One if by air, two if by hand. Am. J. Epidemiol. *107*:357–361, 1978.
37. Hillis, W. D., Hillis, A., Bias, W. B., et al.: Association of hepatitis B surface antigenemia with HLA locus B specificities. N. Engl. J. Med. *296*:1310–1314, 1977.
38. Hu, D. J., Dondero, T. J., Rayfield, M. A., et al.: The emerging genetic diversity of HIV: The importance of global surveillance for diagnostics, research, and prevention. J. A. M. A. *275*:210–215, 1996.
39. Huebner, R. J.: The virologist's dilemma. Ann. N. Y. Acad. Sci. *67*:430–438, 1957.
40. Jernigan, D. B., Cetron, M. S., and Breiman, R. F.: Minimizing the impact of drug-resistant *Streptococcus pneumoniae* (DRSP). J. A. M. A. *275*:206–209, 1996.
41. Jones, T. D.: Diagnosis of rheumatic fever. J. A. M. A. *126*:481–484, 1944.
42. Kallman, F. J., and Reisner, D.: Twin studies on the significance of genetic factors in tuberculosis. Am. Rev. Tuberc. *47*:549–574, 1943.
43. Katz, M., and Stiehm, E. R.: Host defense in malnutrition. Pediatrics *59*:490–495, 1977.
44. Kew, O. M., Mulders, M. N., Lipskaya, G. Y., et al.: Molecular epidemiology of polioviruses. Semin. Virol. *6*:401–414, 1995.
45. Krebs, J. W., Strine, T. W., Smith, J. S., et al.: Rabies surveillance in the United States during 1993. J. Am. Vet. Med. Assoc. *205*:1695–1709, 1994.
46. Langmuir, A. D., Bregman, D. J., Kurland, L. T., et al.: An epidemiologic and clinical evaluation of Guillain-Barré syndrome reported in association with the administration of swine influenza vaccines. Am. J. Epidemiol. *119*:841–879, 1984.
47. Lederberg, J., Shope, R. E., and Oaks, S. C., Jr., (eds.): Emerging Infections: Microbial Threats to Health in the United States. Washington, DC, National Academy Press, 1992.
48. Lidwell, O. M., and Sommerville, T.: Observations on the incidence and distribution of the common cold in a rural community during 1948 and 1949. J. Hyg. Camb. *59*:365–381, 1961.
49. London, W. P., and Yorke, J. A.: Recurrent outbreaks of measles, chickenpox and mumps. I. Seasonal variation in contact rates. Am. J. Epidemiol. *98*:453–468, 1973.
50. Luby, J. P., Miller, G., Gardner, P., et al.: The epidemiology of St. Louis encephalitis in Houston, Texas, 1964. Am. J. Epidemiol. *86*:584–597, 1967.
51. MacKenzie, W. R., Hoxie, N. J., Proctor, M. E., et al.: A massive outbreak in Milwaukee of *Cryptosporidium* infection transmitted through the public water supply. N. Engl. J. Med. *331*:161–167, 1994.
52. Maxcy, K. F.: An epidemiological study of endemic typhus (Brill's disease) in the southeastern United States. Public Health Rep. *41*:2967–2995, 1926.
53. May, J. M.: The ecology of human disease. *In* Studies in Medical Geography, No. 1. New York, MD Publications, 1958.
54. Monto, A. S., and Cavallaro, J. J.: The Tecumseh study of respiratory illness. II. Patterns of occurrence of infection with respiratory pathogens, 1965–1969. Am. J. Epidemiol. *94*:280–289, 1971.
55. Monto, A. S., Napier, J. A., and Metzner, H. L.: The Tecumseh study of respiratory illness. I. Plan of study and observations on syndromes of acute respiratory disease. Am. J. Epidemiol. *94*:269–279, 1971.
56. Mortimer, E. A., Jr.: Hospital staphylococcal infections: Interruption of transmission as a means of control. Med. Clin. North Am. *47*:1247–1256, 1963.
57. Mortimer, E. A., Jr.: Immunization against infectious disease. Science *200*:902–907, 1978.
58. Nichol, S. T., Spiropoulou, C. F., Morzunov, S., et al.: Genetic identification of a hantavirus associated with an outbreak of acute respiratory illness. Science *262*:914–917, 1993.
59. Oostvogel, P. M., van Wijngaarden, J. K., van der Avoort, H. G. A. M., et al.: Poliomyelitis outbreak in an unvaccinated community in the Netherlands, 1992–1993. Lancet *344*:665–670, 1994.
60. Pasteur, L.: The physiological theory of fermentation. *In* Eliot, C. (ed.): Scientific Papers. New York, P. F. Collier and Sons, 1910, pp. 289–381.
61. Patz, J. A., Epstein, P. R., Burke, T. A., et al.: Global climate change and emerging infectious diseases. J. A. M. A. *275*:217–223, 1996.
62. Perry, W. D., Siegel, A. C., Rammelkamp, C. H., Jr., et al.: Transmission of group A streptococci. I. The role of contaminated bedding. Am. J. Hyg. *66*:85–101, 1957.
63. Pinner, R. W., Teutsch, S. M., Simonsen, L., et al.: Trends in infectious disease mortality in the United States. J. A. M. A. *275*:189–193, 1996.
64. Reedy, J. J.: Recessive inheritance of susceptibility to poliomyelitis in fifty pedigrees. J. Hered. *48*:37–44, 1957.
65. Renteln, H. A., and Hinman, A. R.: A waterborne epidemic of gastroenteritis in Madeira, California. Am. J. Epidemiol. *86*:1–10, 1967.
66. Rosen, G.: A History of Public Health. New York, MD Publications, 1958, pp. 62–64.
67. Selye, H.: The Physiology and Pathology of Exposure to Stress. Montreal, Acta, 1950.
68. Sigerist, H. E.: The Great Doctors. New York, W. W. Norton, 1933, pp. 100–108, 375–379.
69. Sigurdsson, B., Sigurjonsson, J., Sigurdsson, J. H., et al.: A disease epidemic in Iceland simulating poliomyelitis. Am. J. Hyg. *52*:222–238, 1950.
70. Snow on Cholera, being a reprint of two papers by John Snow, M. D., together with a biographical memoir by B. W. Richardson and an introduction by Wade Hampton Frost. New York, Commonwealth Fund, 1936.
71. Spigland, I., Fox, J. P., Elveback, L. R., et al.: The Virus Watch Program: A continuing surveillance of viral infections in metropolitan New York families. II. Laboratory methods and a preliminary report on infections revealed by virus isolation. Am. J. Epidemiol. *83*:413–435, 1966.
72. Thompson, W. H., and Beaty, B. J.: Venereal transmission of La Crosse (California encephalitis) arbovirus in *Aedes triseriatus* mosquitoes. Science *196*:530–531, 1977.
73. Wannamaker, L. W.: The epidemiology of streptococcal infections. *In* McCarty, M. (ed.): Streptococcal Infections. New York, Columbia University Press, 1954, p. 157.
74. Webster, L. T.: Experimental epidemiology. Medicine (Baltimore) *25*:77–109, 1946.
75. Weibel, R. E., Neff, B. J., Kuter, B. J., et al.: Live attenuated varicella virus vaccine: Efficacy trial in healthy children. N. Engl. J. Med. *310*:1409–1415, 1984.
76. Wenzel, R. P.: A new hantavirus infection in North America. N. Engl. J. Med. *330*:1004–1005, 1994.
77. Wharton, M., Chorba, T. L., Vogt, R. L., et al.: Case definitions for public health surveillance. M. M. W. R. Recomm. Rep. *39*(RR-13):1–43, 1990.
78. Winslow, C. E. A.: The Colonial era and the first years of the Republic (1606–1799): The pestilence that walketh in darkness, No. 1. *In* Top, F. H. (ed.): The History of American Epidemiology. St. Louis, C. V. Mosby, 1954, pp. 31–44.
79. Yang, D.-F., De, L., Holloway, B. P., et al.: Detection and identification of vaccine-related polioviruses by the polymerase chain reaction. Virus Res. *20*:159–179, 1991.
80. Yorke, J. A., and London, W. P.: Recurrent outbreaks of measles, chickenpox and mumps. II. Systematic differences in contact rates and stochastic effects. Am. J. Epidemiol. *98*:469–482, 1973.

PART II

Infections of Specific Organ Systems

SECTION I

Upper Respiratory Tract Infections

The Common Cold

JAMES D. CHERRY

The common cold is an acute, communicable, viral disease characterized by nasal stuffiness, sneezing, coryza, throat irritation, and no or minimal fever. Although the terms *upper respiratory infection* (URI) and *nasopharyngitis* are used frequently as synonyms for *the common cold* by physicians and other health workers, the practice should be discouraged; the term URI is much too broad, and pharyngitis is not present in most colds. To add to the confusion regarding terminology, "a cold" frequently has an even more inclusive connotation to the lay person.

History

Although the common cold undoubtedly has had an impact on the events of history, the specific symptom complex in ancient times was overshadowed by more severe contagious problems (influenza, plague, smallpox) and by septic diseases (otitis, mastoiditis, pneumonia) that were complications of upper respiratory viral infections. The name *common cold* most certainly arose from the fact that the onset of symptoms included the feeling of chilliness on exposure to cold. This association was perceived as a cause-and-effect relationship. Of interest is that more than 200 years ago, Benjamin Franklin pointed out that colds were caught from other people rather than by exposure to cold.[96]

In 1914, Kruse[78] demonstrated that colds could be transmitted by the nasal instillation in healthy adults of Berkefeld-filtered nasal washings from ill persons and that the causative agent was smaller than common bacteria. These findings were confirmed clearly in 1930 by Dochez and associates.[35] The way was paved for more extensive study of respiratory viral infections when in 1933 Smith and colleagues[109] reported the isolation and cultivation of an influenza A virus from a human.

The greatest contribution to our present understanding of the common cold has been the use of human volunteers under carefully controlled conditions. The Common Cold Research Unit at Salisbury, England, was established in 1946,[4, 124] and volunteer studies at this institution and those performed in the United States* are responsible for our present understanding of colds in adults.

Although studies of respiratory illness in children also have been extensive, controlled virus challenge trials have not been performed. Pediatric studies have been most useful in delineating the spectrum of clinical manifestations by age group and seasonal prevalence rates of the different respiratory viruses.

*See references 1, 15, 27, 30–33, 52–54, 57–60, 68, 72, 76, 85, 88, 116, 119–122.

Etiologic Agents

Initial investigations into the etiology of the common cold were based on the hypothesis that only one etiologic agent needed to be discovered. Subsequent studies revealed that many different groups of viruses were involved etiologically and that within each group frequently many types existed. The agents associated with colds are presented in Table 8–1. Each of these agents is covered more fully in other chapters; in this chapter, only an overview is presented. As a group, rhinoviruses are the most common cause of colds in children and adults. Also of major importance in the etiology of colds are reinfections with parainfluenza viruses and respiratory syncytial virus. Although the quantitative contribution of coronaviruses to colds in children is not known as yet, they probably are significant contributors.

Enteroviruses and adenoviruses have been implicated frequently in upper respiratory illnesses, but in most instances, the illnesses do not conform to those of strictly defined colds. Reoviruses cause colds, but their contribution to the overall incidence is unknown. *Mycoplasma pneumoniae*, *Chlamydia pneumoniae*, *Streptococcus pneumoniae*, and *Haemophilus influenzae* infections have been identified serologically in young adults with colds, but in many instances, concomitant

TABLE 8–1 ■ INFECTIOUS AGENTS ASSOCIATED WITH THE COMMON COLD

Category	Agents
Common viruses that usually cause the common cold	Rhinoviruses Parainfluenza viruses Respiratory syncytial virus Coronaviruses
Common infectious agents that occasionally cause illness with common cold symptoms	Adenoviruses Enteroviruses Influenza viruses Reoviruses *Mycoplasma pneumoniae* *Chlamydia pneumoniae*
Illnesses with initial symptoms suggestive of the common cold	*Coccidioides immitis* *Histoplasma capsulatum* *Bordetella pertussis* *Chlamydia psittaci* *Coxiella burnetii*

TABLE 8–2 ■ COMPARATIVE INCIDENCE OF UPPER RESPIRATORY INFECTION BY AGE: LONDON, 1952–1953; SEATTLE, 1965–1969; AND CLEVELAND, 1948–1950

London		Seattle		Cleveland	
Age (yr)	Illnesses/Person/Year	Age (yr)	Illnesses/Person/Year	Age (yr)	Illnesses/Person/Year
0-4	5.0	<1	3.5	<1	6.9
5-9	3.6	1	3.8	1	8.3
10-16	4.1	2-5	3.7	2-5	8.3
Adult	2.9	6-9	2.7	6-9	6.1
		10-19	1.6	10-11+	5.5
		Adult	2.9	Adult	4.8

Data modified from Brlmblecombe et al.,[13] Fox et al.,[44] and Badger et al.[7]

viral infectious also were noted.[84] Other agents, such as *Coccidioides immitis, Histoplasma capsulatum, Bordetella pertussis, Chlamydia psittaci,* and *Coxiella burnetii,* also have been associated with illnesses with initial coldlike symptoms.

Epidemiology

The common cold is an exceedingly frequent illness in childhood. Although more than 100 serologically different viral types cause this illness, a general predictability of incidence and seasonal occurrence exists. Numerous epidemiologic studies have been conducted on the occurrence of respiratory illnesses, but calculating a precise incidence of the common cold is difficult because criteria of disease classification have been different. The findings in three carefully done studies are presented in Table 8–2. In a wide range of family life settings, the average number of colds per year in children is three to eight.[7–10, 13, 44] In the family setting, adults have on the average approximately one half the number of colds as do their children. The conventional spread of colds has its initial focus in the school.[7, 10, 13] School-age children become infected and introduce secondary infections into the home. Under these conditions, the secondary attack rate is highest in other school-age children and preschool-age children. Generally, the secondary attack rate in adult family members is approximately one half that of the children. The introduction of infection into the family by adults is an unusual occurrence. The present trend toward the use of daycare centers and preschool programs has increased the number of primary infections in these younger children and has made them the source from which secondary family infections frequently occur.[90] Close personal contact between children is necessary for the transmission of viruses that cause colds. In the typical pediatric practice office setting, no increased risk for the acquisition of respiratory illnesses by well babies has been demonstrated.[82]

Among children, boys tend to have more colds than do girls.[7, 13] On the other hand, in the conventional family setting, mothers tend to have at least one more cold a year than do their spouses.[7, 13, 44, 45] The usual incubation period of colds is 1 to 5 days.

In all nonisolated populations, colds occur more frequently during the winter months than during the summertime.[34, 46, 84, 124] This seasonal discrepancy in incidence is as apparent in areas of relatively high wintertime mean temperatures as it is in locations with extremely low temperatures. In the tropics, colds are more prevalent during the rainy season.

Colds occur throughout the world. However, in isolated populations in which the number of people is few (such as members of Antarctic exploration teams and isolated island communities), colds do not occur unless introduced by a visiting person.[66]

Although colds can be produced regularly in volunteers, the method of transmission of viruses, which results in colds under natural circumstances, is far from clear.* In people infected with respiratory viruses that cause colds, the greatest concentration of virus is in the nasal secretions. Children tend to have greater concentrations of virus than do adults, and they tend to shed virus for longer periods. Neither secretions related to coughing nor saliva contain appreciable amounts of virus and, therefore, are unlikely sources of contagion. During the process of talking, little virus is disseminated into the air. The greatest amount of virus from an infected individual is contributed to the surrounding environment by sneezing, nose blowing, and the general contamination of external surfaces (including the sufferer's hands) with nasal secretions. The route of acquisition of virus is by the nose and possibly the conjunctiva. With these facts in mind, one can easily see that a susceptible individual can become infected by the inhalation of virus in droplet nuclei (small particles) resulting from a sneeze, by the direct nasal hit of virus containing large droplets from a sneeze, by nose blowing, or by the inoculation of virus (usually by the fingers of the recipient) from nasal secretions from disseminators that have been transmitted directly or indirectly. In children, most likely the spread either involves close contact with large droplets of nasal secretions containing virus that are applied to the nose from the hands of the future host or occurs by close-range airborne acquisition.

As all readers of this chapter are aware, considerable folklore is related to the catching of a cold. However, all available evidence to date indicates that cold weather per se, chilling, wet feet, and drafts neither cause nor increase the susceptibility of persons to colds.[36, 72] In adults, risk factors for increased susceptibility to colds include stress, smoking, high basal levels of catecholamines, infrequent exercise, low intake of vitamin C, low sleep efficiencies, and lack of diverse social networks.[26, 113]

Pathophysiology

The pathophysiology of human infections with viruses that cause colds is presented in the sections of this book covering the individual infectious agents. Here, a general overview is presented.

Few studies on the pathophysiology of respiratory infections have been done in children; therefore, the material presented in this section has been derived mainly from studies in adults.†

*See references 14, 16, 27, 30, 31, 33, 52, 54, 57, 64, 72, 75, 85, 102, 118, 124.

†See references 6, 23, 37, 77, 92, 94, 100, 106, 118, 119, 124, 130, 131.

The clinical syndrome of the common cold can occur in association with more than 100 different viral types and in many instances can occur with either a primary infection or a reinfection with a particular viral type.

Although the primary site of virus inoculation in some colds may be on the conjunctival surface, the vast majority result from inhalation or self-inoculation of virus onto the nasal mucosa. After virus acquisition, infection of the cells of the local respiratory epithelium occurs. This infection varies in the degree of cytopathology on the basis of the viral agent. The infection spreads locally, resulting in an increase in nasal secretions with an increased protein content. Symptoms (nasal stuffiness and throat irritation followed by sneezing) begin on the second or third day and are caused by both cellular damage and irritation. Virus shedding is at its maximum in 2 to 7 days, although some shedding may continue for another 2 weeks. Hilding[65] examined biopsy specimens, scrapings, and smears of nasal secretions and noted that submucosal edema occurred initially, followed by shedding of the ciliated epithelial cells. By the fifth day, the epithelial damage had reached its maximum, with regeneration occurring during the next 10 days. Winther and associates[128] performed similar studies and noted the sloughing of epithelial cells, but they found that the epithelial lining remained continuous with normal cell borders. On the second day of disease, an increase in the number of neutrophils in the epithelium and in the lamina propria occurred. Epithelial mast cells were not involved in the inflammation. The nasal discharge during the second to the seventh day is mucopurulent, owing to its content of desquamated epithelial cells and also polymorphonuclear leukocytes.

In experimental rhinovirus colds in adults, little or no discernible damage to the nasal epithelium has been demonstrated.[55, 118, 129, 130] Arruda and associates[6] noted in adults infected with rhinovirus types 14 and 39 that virus replicates in both ciliated and nonciliated cells in the nasopharynx and that only a very small proportion of the cells were infected.

Because damage to the nasal epithelium is not noted in rhinovirus colds, apparently cell death is not the cause of symptoms. Naclerio and colleagues[89] and Proud and associates[99] have found that kinins are generated locally and that their concentrations correlate with the severity of symptoms. However, the cause-and-effect relationship between kinins and symptoms is questionable because treatment with a bradykinin antagonist failed to lessen symptoms.[117] In addition, steroid therapy was found to reduce the concentration of kinins in nasal wash fluid, but it did not affect clinical symptoms. More recently, researchers have noted that interleukin-1 (IL-1) may contribute to the pathogenesis of rhinovirus infections.[100]

In studies in children with acute URIs, IL-1B, IL-8, IL-6, and tumor necrosis factor-α were found to be elevated markedly in nasal lavage fluid.[92] In a recent study, Pacifico and associates[94] found that IL-8 concentrations and white blood cell and neutrophil counts were significantly greater in children with rhinovirus colds than in well children. In an adult volunteer study, Turner and colleagues[119] noted a significant rank correlation between nasal obstruction severity, rhinorrhea severity, and nasal-wash albumin concentrations and the increase in IL-8 concentration from baseline on days 2 to 4 after virus challenge.

Pedersen and colleagues[95] studied nasal mucociliary transport in naturally acquired colds and noted that transport was reduced markedly during the acute illness and that slight impairment remained for approximately 1 month. They point out that because some children have four to six colds during a winter season, these children may have constantly impaired mucociliary transport.

Although viremia has been noted during infections with some of the viruses that cause colds, viremia is not a known occurrence during the typical common cold. The infection is restricted to the epithelial surfaces of the upper respiratory air passages, including the sinuses and the eustachian tubes. With infection, local interferon is produced and presumably has a major role in controlling the infection.[21] Serum antibody and secretory antibody regularly result from infection. The roles of cell-mediated factors in both immunity and disease pathogenesis of colds are unknown. Levandowski and associates[80] noted in rhinovirus-challenged volunteers that total T cells, and particularly helper T cells, were depressed. The magnitude of this finding correlated with progression of infection and symptoms. In a study in which volunteers received rhinovirus type 39, Skoner and associates[106] found a slight increase in both helper ($CD4^+$) and suppressor ($CD8^+$) T cells during illness.

The role of antibody (both serum and secretory) in the protection against reinfection and clinical colds is complicated. High levels of both secretory and serum antibodies appear to be protective against reinfections.[19, 20, 42, 68–71, 79, 107, 115] Clinically abortive colds probably are reinfection colds with early antibody recall. Fleet and colleagues[42] have demonstrated a short-lived heterologous resistance to rhinovirus colds, which probably is not caused by interferon or antibody.

Unexplained constitutional factors also appear to control the clinical manifestations of colds.[104] Although studies have demonstrated genetic disease susceptibility patterns related to tissue types, no studies relating to common respiratory infections have been done.[24] In experimental coronavirus infections in adults, clinical severity correlated with detectable immunoglobulin E in nasal secretions.[17] This finding suggests that atopy may be related to symptoms in colds caused by coronaviruses.

Although clinical symptoms and virologic data suggest that colds are upper respiratory diseases, some studies of pulmonary function also have indicated occult lower respiratory tract involvement.[5, 22, 97]

Clinical Presentation

Because the common cold is caused by more than 100 different viral types, considerable variation in the clinical manifestations occurs. As indicated in the beginning of this chapter, the limits of illness to be considered under the diagnosis of the common cold have been set arbitrarily but rigidly. A disappointing note is that although many comprehensive studies of respiratory viral illnesses of children have been done, little attention has been given to the details of URI.

Illness in children must be considered under two categories: that of infants and that of older children. The latter is similar to illness in adults. In studies involving 100 young adults, Jackson and colleagues[71] noted that virtually all patients complained of nasal discharge, nasal obstruction, and sore throat; approximately 80 percent had malaise, postnasal discharge, headache, and cough; slightly fewer than 50 percent reported a feverish feeling and chilliness; and approximately 25 percent noted burning eyes and nasal membranes and muscle aching. In older children, the onset of illness is heralded by dryness and irritation in the nose and a scratchy feeling in the throat.[91] The initial symptoms are followed within a few hours by sneezing and watery nasal discharge; chilly feelings and occasionally muscular aches also are noted. Other complaints include headache, general malaise, anorexia, and low-grade fever.

After a variable period of from 1 to 3 days, the illness changes; the nasal secretions become thicker and frequently develop a purulent appearance. Persistent nasal discharge, associated with the trauma of repeated blowing of the nose, leads to excoriation around the nose. Nasal obstruction leads to mouth breathing, which causes drying of the throat, increasing the discomfort in the throat. The usual duration of illness is approximately 7 days, but lingering cough and nasal discharge may persist for 2 weeks or more.

In infants, the manifestations of illness may be more varied. The onset of illness in infants is associated more often with fever (38° C to 39° C [100.4° F to 102.2° F]) than it is in older children. Nasal manifestations in infants are similar to those in older children, but the only other manifestations are irritability and restlessness. Occasionally, coryza is the only symptom. Nasal obstruction may interfere significantly with both feeding and sleeping. Vomiting and diarrhea also may occur.

Differential Diagnosis

Because the clinical entity of the common cold is a somewhat arbitrary grouping of signs and symptoms limited to anatomic boundaries and is caused by many different viral types, the approach to the differential diagnosis must consider both clinical and etiologic criteria. Many upper respiratory illnesses are caused by a large number of infectious agents that should not be confused with colds. For example, a common cold diagnosis should not be considered if objective pharyngitis, other enanthema, or evidence of obstructive airway disease is present.

Because the common cold is an acute, self-limited disease, the diagnosis should not be considered in a child who has persistent nasal signs or symptoms. Subacute or chronic illness should suggest the possibility of adenoiditis or sinusitis.

The most important differential diagnostic considerations are those clinical entities of noninfectious etiology. Allergic rhinitis is a particularly important prospect in the child with "recurrent colds." Careful attention to family history, a search for allergies, the presence or absence of nasal eosinophilia, and the serum immunoglobulin E value will help confirm or exclude this consideration.

Although not reported particularly in pediatric patients, mental stress can lead to vasomotor responses and rhinitis in some susceptible patients. Chemical irritants can cause coldlike symptoms, and the clinical response varies greatly among different individuals. Early symptoms of many illnesses, such as pertussis, epiglottitis, measles, and diphtheria, are those of a cold, but in a short period of time, the more serious nature of the actual illness will be apparent.

Specific Diagnosis

The epidemiologic history is the single most important aspect of specific diagnosis. In children, if exposure history is requested, a contact usually is uncovered. If strict attention to clinical criteria of the common cold have been adopted, routine laboratory study is unnecessary. Frequently, the physician has an urge to take a throat culture to rule out the possibility of group A streptococcal infection. Usually, one is unnecessary because nasal symptoms are not characteristic of acute streptococcal illness except in infancy and pharyngitis is not within the limits of the diagnosis of the common cold. The white blood cell count also is of little use.

Specific diagnosis can be made by the isolation of virus from the nasal secretions. It is performed best by using either a nasal-wash technique[56] or a nasopharyngeal swab. With laboratory techniques of diagnostic virologic facilities such as those in many university hospitals, parainfluenza viruses, respiratory syncytial virus, and most rhinoviruses and influenza viruses will be recovered. Direct antigen detection techniques can be used to identify infections caused by respiratory syncytial virus, parainfluenza viruses, adenoviruses, and influenza viruses. Coronaviruses and some rhinoviruses and influenza strains can be recovered only by special laboratory techniques.

Treatment

Although literally hundreds of cold remedies are available, few offer any benefit to the pediatric patient, and many may be harmful.[47, 48, 67, 108] No clinically available antiviral agents have been shown to be effective in the treatment of colds.

In the approach to the child with a cold, the best assumption is that no therapy whatsoever is indicated in most cases. Then, specific symptomatic care can be added in the individual case when it is needed. Many children and adults feel miserable when they have a cold, and, therefore, therapy with an analgesic often is used. Because aspirin is a risk factor for Reye syndrome in children, the use of acetaminophen rather than aspirin is prudent. The dose per single administration of acetaminophen by year of age is the following: younger than 1 year, 60 mg; 1 to 3 years, 60 to 120 mg; 3 to 6 years, 120 mg; 6 to 12 years, 150 to 300 mg; older than 12 years, 325 to 650 mg. Administration may be repeated three to four times daily in young children and every 4 hours in older children. Acetaminophen rarely should be given to infants younger than 6 months of age.

In adult volunteers with rhinovirus infections, acetaminophen was found to be associated with suppression of the serum neutralizing antibody response, and an increase in nasal symptoms was noted when compared with subjects who received a placebo.[50] In another adult volunteer study, administration of naproxen resulted in a reduction in headache, malaise, myalgia, and cough when compared with placebo.[112]

Relief of nasal obstruction is the most important therapeutic consideration in young children. Locally applied or orally administered, systemically active decongestants are used frequently, but neither their true efficacy nor their adverse effects have been evaluated carefully. Excessive use of sprays and drops with vasoconstrictive drugs clearly can lead to rebound obstruction, which actually prolongs the illness. The associated drying effect of vasoconstrictive drugs administered orally can be expected to be deleterious to normal mechanisms of clearance. In young infants, sympathomimetic-antihistamine mixtures in oral drop dosage form particularly are dangerous because respiratory depression may occur.[48] In addition, in a controlled trial, brompheniramine maleate–phenylpropanolamine hydrochloride was found to be no better than a placebo in relieving cold symptoms in children 6 months to 5 years of age.[25] If vasoactive drugs are used, their use should be restricted to times when maximum benefit will occur (i.e., bedtime) and they should be discontinued within 3 days.

The use of isotonic saline drops and gentle aspiration can be very effective in the temporary relief of nasal obstruction in the infant. Also useful is the general humidification of room air because this moisture tends to dilute tenacious nasal mucus so that its elimination is facilitated.

Antibiotics have no place in the routine therapy of common colds.[49, 74, 81, 93, 103, 110] Occasionally in children, persistent cough is a problem of such magnitude that it disturbs sleep. For cough, codeine and dextromethorphan often are used.[2] However, no well-controlled studies support either the efficacy or safety of either drug as an antitussive in children.

In the past, antihistamines often have been given to children with colds, but efficacy had not been demonstrated.[127] In more recent years, first-generation antihistamines, but not second-generation products, have been shown to lessen rhinorrhea in adults with colds.[87, 88, 117, 118, 123] Doxylamine succinate, clemastine fumarate, chlorpheniramine maleate, and brompheniramine all have been shown to offer benefit in controlled trials. The effect of these antihistamines is due to their anticholinergenic properties. To date, no studies in children have been reported.

In more recent years, a major controversy related to the common cold has ensued over the efficacy of vitamin C, both prophylactically and therapeutically. In two carefully controlled volunteer studies, the administration of 3 g of ascorbic acid per day did not prevent or alter the symptoms of experimental colds.[105, 126] In addition, several large controlled trials in which vitamin C and placebo preparations have been used to prevent and to treat colds have been conducted.[3, 18, 28, 29, 38, 76, 98] In some of these studies, a degree of benefit was reported, whereas in others, no efficacy was noted. Most probably, the reported benefits are a result of statistical artifacts and placebo effect resulting from poor study design rather than specific pharmacologic drug effects. However, the antihistaminic action of vitamin C[125, 132] probably afforded relief to some patients with allergic rhinitis who thought that their illnesses were colds. Because of the many toxic effects of ascorbic acid[11] and because its use in treating respiratory illnesses is questionable at best, giving children vitamin C in excess of normal daily requirements would seem unwarranted.

α_2-Interferon administered intranasally has been shown to be effective in the prevention of rhinovirus colds in controlled clinical trials.[111] However, the effect is variable, and adverse effects of the medication are common occurrences.[114] Intranasal α_2-interferon was not effective in the treatment of naturally occurring colds but demonstrated some benefit in experimental coronavirus colds.[61, 116]

Zinc lozenges have been used to treat the common cold, and the Internet and lay literature are full of claims of efficacy. However, in well-done controlled studies, efficacy has not been demonstrated.[40, 73, 83, 122] In a double-blind placebo-controlled trial, the use of intranasal corticosteroid (fluticasone propionate) offered no clinical benefit in young adults with colds and induced prolonged shedding of rhinovirus.[101]

In a controlled trial in adults, a soluble intercellular adhesion molecule 1 product (tremacamra) reduced the severity of rhinovirus colds.[120] In a recent trial, the antiviral pleconaril induced an early reduction in symptom severity in adults with colds caused by rhinovirus.[62] Pleconaril is an antipicornavirus drug that interacts directly with viral capsid proteins. It blocks virus attachment to cells through intracellular adhesion molecule 1 and subsequent uncoating and release of viral RNA. In another controlled trial, clarithromycin, which may have anti-inflammatory activity, had no effect on the severity of cold symptoms. The intranasal administration of nedocromil sodium has been observed to have a beneficial effect on rhinoviral infections in adult volunteers.[12]

In one study, adults who took sauna baths once or twice a week were found to have fewer colds than had a non-sauna-bathing control group.[39] In another study, volunteers with colds did not benefit from inhaling heated vapor.[43]

Prognosis

The prognosis of common colds in children is excellent. However, secondary complications do occur, and frequently they need careful and prolonged therapy. The most common complications are otitis media, sinusitis, bacterial adenoiditis, bacterial pharyngitis, and lower respiratory bacterial infections.

Prevention

Studies in isolated populations have shown clearly that once a particular respiratory viral infection has run through the entire group, no further respiratory viral illnesses can occur until a new infected person enters the population. This type of evidence indicates that quarantine or isolation-type practices could prevent colds. However, the average urban society of today is so complex that prevention through isolation procedures is impractical. Therefore, efforts to control the spread of respiratory virus should be minimal and practical. However, for children with undue susceptibility to complications, contact with crowds or with infected children and adults should be avoided.

The use of virucidal nasal tissues has been shown to reduce the spread of rhinovirus colds in human volunteers markedly and also to reduce modestly colds in the family setting, but as yet no commercial products are available.[32, 41] Heikkinen and associates[63] found that the intranasal administration of an immunoglobin preparation by nasal sprays twice a day significantly reduced the occurrence of rhinitis in children attending daycare centers. If confirmed, this form of prophylaxis might be useful for selected children.

Fluid extracts of *Echinacea* spp. are popular for both the prevention and treatment of colds.[51, 118, 121] However, no controlled efficacy data are available for children.

REFERENCES

1. Abisheganaden, J. A., Avila, P. C., Kishiyama, J. L., et al.: Effect of clarithromycin on experimental rhinovirus-16 colds: A randomized, double-blind, controlled trial. Am. J. Med. *108*:453–459, 2000.
2. American Academy of Pediatrics Committee on Drugs: Use of codeine- and dextromethorphan-containing cough remedies in children. Pediatrics *99*:918–920, 1997.
3. Anderson, T. W., Beaton, G. H., Corey, P. N., et al.: Winter illness and vitamin C: The effect of relatively low doses. Can. Med. Assoc. J. *112*:823–826, 1975.
4. Andrewes, C. H.: The natural history of the common cold. Lancet *1*:71–75, 1949.
5. Aquilina, A. T., Hall, W. J., Douglas, R. G., Jr., et al.: Airway reactivity in subjects with viral upper respiratory tract infections: The effects of exercise and cold air. Am. Rev. Resp. Dis. *122*:3–10, 1980.
6. Arruda, E., Boyle T. R., Winther, B., et al: Localization of human rhinovirus replication in the upper respiratory tract by in situ hybridization. J. Infect. Dis. *171*:1329–1333, 1995.
7. Badger, G. F., Dingle, J. H., Feller, A. E., et al.: A study of illness in a group of Cleveland families. II. Incidence of the common respiratory diseases. Am. J. Hyg. *58*:31–40, 1953.
8. Badger, G. F., Dingle, J. H., Feller, A. E., et al.: A study of illness in a group of Cleveland families. III. Introduction of respiratory infections into families. Am. J. Hyg. *58*:41–46, 1953.
9. Badger, G. F., Dingle, J. H., Feller, A. E., et al.: A study of illness in a group of Cleveland families. IV. The spread of respiratory infections within the home. Am. J. Hyg. *58*:174–178, 1953.
10. Badger, G. F., Dingle, J. H., Feller, A. E., et al.: A study of illness in a group of Cleveland families. V. Introductions and secondary attack rates as indices of exposure to common respiratory diseases in the community. Am. J. Hyg. *58*:179–182, 1953.
11. Barness, L. A.: Safety considerations with high ascorbic acid dosage. Ann. N. Y. Acad. Sci. *258*:523–528, 1975.
12. Barrow, G. I., Higgins, P. G., Al-Nakib, W., et al.: The effect of intranasal nedocromil sodium on viral upper respiratory tract infections in human volunteers. Clin. Exper. Allergy *20*:45–51, 1989.
13. Brimblecombe, F. S. W., Cruickshank, R., Masters, P. L., et al.: Family studies of respiratory infections. Br. Med. J. *1*:119–128, 1958.
14. Buckland, F. E., and Tyrrell, D. A. J.: Experiments on the spread of colds. I. Laboratory studies on the dispersal of nasal secretion. J. Hyg. Camb. *62*:365–377, 1964.

15. Bush, R. K., Busse, W., Flaherty, D., et al.: Effects of experimental rhinovirus 16 infection on airways and leukocyte function in normal subjects. J. Allergy Clin. Immunol. *61*:80–87, 1978.
16. Bynoe, M. L.: The common cold. Practitioner *197*:739–746, 1966.
17. Callow, K. A., Tyrrell, D. A. J., Shaw, R. J., et al.: Influence of atopy on the clinical manifestations of coronavirus infection in adult volunteers. Clin. Allergy *18*:119–129, 1988.
18. Carr, A. B., Einstein, R., Lai, L. Y. C., et al.: Vitamin C and the common cold: Using identical twins as controls. Med. J. Aust. *2*:411–412, 1981.
19. Cate, T. R., Couch, R. B., and Johnson, K. M.: Studies with rhinoviruses in volunteers: Production of illness, effect of naturally acquired antibody, and demonstration of a protective effect not associated with serum antibody. J. Clin. Invest. *43*:56–67, 1964.
20. Cate, T. R., Rossen, R. D., Douglas, R. G., Jr., et al.: The role of nasal secretion and serum antibody in the rhinovirus common cold. Am. J. Epidemiol. *84*:352–363, 1966.
21. Cate, T. R., Douglas, R. G., Jr., and Couch, R. B.: Interferon and resistance to upper respiratory virus illness. Proc. Soc. Exp. Biol. Med. *131*:631–636, 1969.
22. Cate, T. R., Roberts, J. S., Russ, M. A., et al.: Effects of common colds on pulmonary function. Am. Rev. Resp. Dis. *108*:858–865, 1973.
23. Cherry, J. D.: Newer respiratory viruses: Their role in respiratory illnesses of children. Adv. Pediatr. *20*:225–289, 1973.
24. Cherry, J. D.: Comments. Pediatr. Res. *11*:250–251, 1977.
25. Clemens, C. J., Taylor, J. A., Almquist, J. R., et al.: Is an antihistamine-decongestant combination effective in temporarily relieving symptoms of the common cold in preschool children? J. Pediatr. *130*:463–466, 1997.
26. Cohen, S., Doyle, W. J., Skoner, D. P., et al.: Social ties and susceptibility to the common cold. J. A. M. A. *277*:1940–1944, 1997.
27. Couch, R. B., Cate, T. R., Douglas, R. G., Jr., et al.: Effect of route of inoculation on experimental respiratory viral disease in volunteers and evidence for airborne transmission. Bacteriol. Rev. *30*:517–529, 1966.
28. Coulehan, J. L., Eberhard, S., Kapner, L., et al.: Vitamin C and acute illness in Navajo schoolchildren. N. Engl. J. Med. *18*:973–977, 1976.
29. Coulehan, J. L.: Ascorbic acid and the common cold: Reviewing the evidence. Postgrad. Med. *66*:153–160, 1979.
30. D'Alessio, D. J., Peterson, J. A., Dick, C. R., et al.: Transmission of experimental rhinovirus colds in volunteer married couples. J. Infect. Dis. *133*:28–36, 1976.
31. D'Allessio, D. J., Meschievitz, C. K., Peterson, J. A., et al.: Short-duration exposure and the transmission of rhinoviral colds. J. Infect. Dis. *150*:189–194, 1984.
32. Dick, E. C., Hossain, S. U., Mink, K. A., et al.: Interruption of transmission of rhinovirus colds among human volunteers using virucidal paper handkerchiefs. J. Infect. Dis. *153*:352–356, 1986.
33. Dick, E. C., Jennings, L. C., Mink, K. A., et al.: Aerosol transmission of rhinovirus colds. J. Infect. Dis. *156*:442–448, 1987.
34. Dingle, J. H., Badger, G. F., Feller, A. E., et al.: A study of illness in a group of Cleveland families. I. Plan of study and certain general observations. Am. J. Hyg. *58*:16–30, 1953.
35. Dochez, A. R., Shibley, G. S., and Mills, K. C.: Studies in the common cold. IV. Experimental transmission of the common cold to anthropoid apes and human beings by means of a filtrable agent. J. Exp. Med. *52*:701–716, 1930.
36. Douglas, R. G., Jr., Lindgren, K. M., and Couch, R. B.: Exposure to cold environment and rhinovirus common cold: Failure to demonstrate effect. N. Engl. J. Med. *279*:742–747, 1968.
37. Douglas, R. G., Jr.: Pathogenesis of rhinovirus common colds in human volunteers. Ann. Otol. Rhinol. Laryngol. *79*:563–571, 1970.
38. Elwood, P. C., Hughes, S. J., and St. Leger, A. S.: A randomized controlled trial of the therapeutic effect of vitamin C in the common cold. Practitioner *218*:133–137, 1977.
39. Ernst, E., Pecho, E., Wirz, P., and Saradeth, T.: Regular sauna bathing and the incidence of common colds. Ann. Med. *22*:225–227, 1990.
40. Farr, B. M., Conner, E. M., Betts, R. F., et al.: Two randomized controlled trials of zinc gluconate lozenge therapy of experimentally induced rhinovirus colds. Antimicrob. Agents Chemother. *31*:1183–1187, 1987.
41. Farr, B. M., Hendley, J. O., Kaiser, D. L., et al.: Two randomized controlled trials of virucidal nasal tissues in the prevention of natural upper respiratory infections. Am. J. Epidemiol. *128*:1162–1172, 1988.
42. Fleet, W. F., Couch, R. B., Cate, T. R., et al.: Homologous and heterologous resistance to rhinovirus common cold. Am. J. Epidemiol. *82*:185–196, 1965.
43. Forstall, G. J., Macknin, M. L., Yen-Lieberman, B. R., and Medendorp, S. V.: Effect of inhaling heated vapor on symptoms of the common cold. J. A. M. A. *271*:1109–1111, 1994.
44. Fox, J. P., Hall, C. E., Cooney, M. K., et al.: The Seattle virus watch. II. Objectives, study population and its observation, data processing and summary of illnesses. Am. J. Epidemiol. *96*:270–285, 1972.
45. Foy, H. M., Cooney, M. K., Hall, C., et al.: Case-to-case intervals of rhinovirus and influenza virus infections in households. J. Infect. Dis. *157*:180–182, 1988.
46. Frost, W. H., and Gover, M.: The incidence and time distribution of common colds in several groups kept under continuous observation. *In* Maxcy, K. F. (ed.): Papers of Wade Hampton Frost. New York, Commonwealth Fund, 1941, pp. 359–392.
47. Gadomski, A., and Horton, L.: The need for rational therapeutics in the use of cough and cold medicine in infants. Pediatrics *89*:774–776, 1992.
48. Goldbloom, R. B.: Nasopharyngitis (the common cold). *In* Gellis, S. S., and Kagan, B. M. (eds.): Current Pediatric Therapy. 11th ed. Philadelphia, W. B. Saunders Co., 1984, p. 93.
49. Gordon, M., Lovell, S., and Dugdale, A. E.: The value of antibiotics in minor respiratory illness in children: A controlled trial. Med. J. Aust. *1*:304–306, 1974.
50. Graham, N. M. H., Burrell, C. J., Douglas, R. M., et al.: Adverse effects of aspirin, acetaminophen, and ibuprofen on immune function, viral shedding, and clinical status in rhinovirus-infected volunteers. J. Infect. Dis. *162*:1277–1282, 1990.
51. Grimm, W., and Müller, H.: A randomized controlled trial of the effect of fluid extract of *Echinacea purpurea* on the incidence and severity of colds and respiratory infections. Am. J. Med. *106*:138–143, 1999.
52. Gwaltney, J. M., Jr., Moskalski, P. B., and Hendley, J. O.: Hand-to-hand transmission of rhinovirus colds. Ann. Intern. Med. *88*:463–467, 1978.
53. Gwaltney, J. M., Jr., Moskalski, P. B., and Hendley, J. O.: Interruption of experimental rhinovirus transmission. J. Infect. Dis. *142*:811–815, 1980.
54. Gwaltney, J. M., Jr., and Hendley, J. O.: Transmission of experimental rhinovirus infection by contaminated surfaces. Am. J. Epidemiol. *116*:828–833, 1982.
55. Gwaltney, J. M., Jr., Hendley, J. O., Simon, G., et al.: Rhinovirus infections in an industrial population. I. The occurrence of illness. N. Engl. J. Med. *275*:1261–1268, 1966.
56. Hall, C. B., and Douglas, R. G., Jr.: Clinically useful method for the isolation of respiratory syncytial virus. J. Infect. Dis. *131*:1–5, 1975.
57. Hall, C. B., Douglas, R. G., Jr., Schnabel, K. C., et al.: Infectivity of respiratory syncytial virus by various routes of inoculation. Infect. Immunol. *33*:779–783, 1981.
58. Harris II, J. M., and Gwaltney, J. M., Jr.: Incubation periods of experimental rhinovirus infection and illness. Clin. Infect. Dis. *23*:1287–1290, 1996.
59. Hayden, F. G., and Gwaltney, J. M., Jr.: Intranasal interferon α2 for prevention of rhinovirus infection and illness. J. Infect. Dis. *148*:543–550, 1983.
60. Hayden, F. G., and Gwaltney, J. M., Jr.: Intranasal interferon α2 treatment of experimental rhinoviral colds. J. Infect. Dis. *150*:174–180, 1984.
61. Hayden, F. G., Kaiser, D. L., and Albrecht, J. K.: Intranasal recombinant alfa-2b interferon treatment of naturally occurring common colds. Antimicrob. Agents Chemother. *32*:224–230, 1988.
62. Hayden, F. G., Kim, K., Hudson, S. A., et al.: Pleconaril treatment provides early reduction of symptom severity in viral respiratory infection due to picornaviruses. (Abstract 414) *In* Program and Abstracts 39th Annual Meeting of the Infectious Diseases Society of America. October 25–28, 2001, San Francisco.
63. Heikkinen, T., Ruohola, A., Ruuskanen, O., et al.: Intranasally administered immunoglobulin for the prevention of rhinitis in children. Pedriatr. Infect. Dis. *17*:367–372, 1998.
64. Hendley, J. O., Wenzel, R. P., and Gwaltney, J. M., Jr.: Transmission of rhinovirus colds by self-inoculation. N. Engl. J. Med. *288*:1361–1364, 1973.
65. Hilding, A.: The common cold. Arch. Otolaryngol. *12*:133–150, 1930.
66. Holmes, M. J., and Allen, T. R.: Viral respiratory diseases in isolated communities: A review. Br. Antarct. Surv. Bull. *35*:23–31, 1973.
67. Hutton, N., Wilson, M. H., Mellits, E. D., et al.: Effectiveness of an antihistamine-decongestant combination for young children with the common cold: A randomized, controlled clinical trial. J. Pediatr. *118*: 125–130, 1991.
68. Jackson, G. G., Dowling, H. F., and Anderson, T. O.: Neutralization of common cold agents in volunteers by pooled human globulin. Science *128*:27–28, 1958.
69. Jackson, G. G., Dowling, H. F., Anderson, T. O., et al.: Susceptibility and immunity to common upper respiratory viral infections: The common cold. Ann. Intern. Med. *53*:719–738, 1960.
70. Jackson, G. G., Dowling, H. F., Akers, L. W., et al.: Immunity to the common cold from protective serum antibody: Time of appearance, persistence and relation to reinfection. N. Engl. J. Med. *266*:791–796, 1962.
71. Jackson, G. G., Dowling, H. F., and Muldoon, R. L.: Present concepts of the common cold. Am. J. Public Health *52*:940–945, 1962.
72. Jackson, G. G.: Understanding of viral respiratory illnesses provided by experiments in volunteers. Bacteriol. Rev. *28*:423–430, 1964.
73. Jackson, J. L., Peterson, C., and Lesho, E.: A meta-analysis of zinc salts lozenges and the common cold. Arch. Intern. Med. *157*:2373–2376, 1997.
74. Jacobs, R. F.: Judicious use of antibiotics for common pediatric respiratory infections. Pediatr. Infect. Dis. J. *19*:938–943, 2000.
75. Jennings, L. C., Dick, E. C., Mink, K. A., et al.: Near disappearance of rhinovirus along a fomite transmission chain. J. Infect. Dis. *158*:888–892, 1988.
76. Karlowski, T. R., Chalmers, T. C., Frenkel, L. D., et al.: Ascorbic acid for the common cold: A prophylactic and therapeutic trial. J. A. M. A. *231*: 1038–1042, 1975.
77. Kaul, P., Singh, I., and Turner, R. B.: Effect of nitric oxide on rhinovirus replication and virus-induced interlukin-8 elaboration. Am. J. Respir. Crit. Care Med. *159*:1193–1198, 1999.
78. Kruse, W.: Die erreger von husten und schnupfen. München Med. Wochenschr. *61*:1547, 1914.

79. Lefkowitz, L. B., Jr., Jackson, G. G., and Dowling, H. F.: The role of immunity in the common cold and related viral respiratory infections. Med. Clin. North Am. *47*:1171–1184, 1963.
80. Levandowski, R. A., Ou, D. W., and Jackson, G. G.: Acute-phase decrease of T lymphocyte subsets in rhinovirus infection. J. Infect. Dis. *153*:743–748, 1986.
81. Lexomboon, U., Duangmani, C., Kusalasai, V., et al.: Evaluation of orally administered antibiotics for treatment of upper respiratory infections in Thai children. J. Pediatr. *78*:771–778, 1971.
82. Lobovitz, A. M., Freeman, J., Goldmann, D. A., et al.: Risk of illness after exposure to a pediatric office. N. Engl. J. Med. *313*:425–428, 1985.
83. Mackin, M.L., Piedmonte, M., Calendine, C., et al.: Zinc gluconate lozenges for treating the common cold in children: A randomized controlled trial. J. A. M. A. *279*:1962–1967, 1998.
84. Mäkelä, M. J., Puhakka, T., Ruuskanen, O., et al.: Viruses and bacteria in the etiology of the common cold. J. Clin. Microbiol. *36*(2):539–542, 1998.
85. Meschievitz, C. K., Schultz, S. B., and Dick, E. C.: A model for obtaining predictable natural transmission of rhinoviruses in human volunteers. J. Infect. Dis. *150*:195–201, 1984.
86. Monto, A. S., Cavallaro, J. J., and Keller, J. B.: Seasonal patterns of acute infection in Tecumseh, Mich. Arch. Environ. Health *21*:408–417, 1970.
87. Mossad, S. B.: Treatment of the common cold. B. M. J. *317*:33–36, 1998.
88. Muether, P. S., and Gwaltney, J. M., Jr.: Variant effect of first- and second-generation antihistamines as clues to their mechanism of action on the sneeze reflex in the common cold. Clin. Infect. Dis. *33*:1483–1488, 2001.
89. Naclerio, R. M., Proud, D., Lichtenstein, L. M., et al.: Kinins are generated during experimental rhinovirus colds. J. Infect. Dis. *157*:133–142, 1988.
90. Nafstad, P., Hagen, J. A., Øie, L., et al.: Day care centers and respiratory health. Pediatrics *103*:753–758, 1999.
91. Nelson, W. E.: Infections of the upper respiratory tract. *In* Nelson, W. E. (ed.): Textbook of Pediatrics. 6th ed. Philadelphia, W. B. Saunders, 1954, pp. 770–786.
92. Noah, T. L., Henderson, F. W., Wortman, I. A., et al.: Nasal cytokine production in viral acute upper respiratory infection of childhood. J. Infect. Dis. *171*:584–592, 1995.
93. Nyquist, A., Gonzales, R., Steiner, J., et al.: Antibiotic prescribing for children with colds, upper respiratory tract infections, and bronchitis. J. A. M. A. *279*:875–877, 1998.
94. Pacifico, L., Iacobini, M., Viola, F., et al.: Chemokine concentrations in nasal washings of infants with rhinovirus illness. Clin. Infect. Dis. *31*:834–838, 2000.
95. Pedersen, M., Sakakura, Y., Winther, B., et al.: Nasal mucociliary transport, number of ciliated cells, and beating pattern in naturally acquired common colds. Eur. J. Respir. Dis. *64*(Suppl. 128):355–364, 1983.
96. Pepper, W.: The Medical Side of Benjamin Franklin. Philadelphia, W. J. Campbell, 1911, pp. 50–51, 60–65, 72–73.
97. Picken, J. J., Niewoehner, D. E., and Chester, E. H.: Prolonged effects of viral infections of the upper respiratory tract upon small airways. Am. J. Med. *52*:738–746, 1972.
98. Pitt, H. A., and Costrini, A. M.: Vitamin C prophylaxis in marine recruits. J. A. M. A. *241*:908–911, 1979.
99. Proud, D., Naclerio, R. M., Gwaltney, J. M., et al.: Kinins are generated in nasal secretions during natural rhinovirus colds. J. Infect. Dis. *161*:120–123, 1990.
100. Proud, D., Gwaltney, J. M., Hendley, J. O., et al.: Increased levels of interleukin-1 are detected in nasal secretions of volunteers during experimental rhinovirus colds. J. Infect. Dis. *169*:1007–1013, 1994.
101. Puhakka, T., Mäkelä, M. J., Malmström, K., et al.: The common cold: effects of intranasal fluticasone proportionate treatment. J. Allergy Clin. Immunol. *101*:726–731, 1998.
102. Reed, S. E.: An investigation of the possible transmission of rhinovirus colds through indirect contact. J. Hyg. Camb. *75*:249–258, 1975.
103. Rosenstein, N., Phillips, W. R., Gerber, M., et al.: The common cold—principles of judicious use of antimicrobial agents. Pediatrics *101*: 181–184, 1998.
104. Sargent, F., Lombard, O. M., and Sargent, V. W.: Further studies on stability of resistance to the common cold: The importance of constitution. Am. J. Hyg. *45*:29–32, 1947.
105. Schwartz, A. R., Togo, Y., Hornick, R. B., et al.: Evaluation of the efficacy of ascorbic acid in prophylaxis of induced rhinovirus 44 infection in man. J. Infect. Dis. *128*:500–505, 1973.
106. Skoner, D. P., Whiteside, T. L., Wilson, J. W., et al.: Effect of rhinovirus 39 infection on cellular immune parameters in allergic and nonallergic subjects. J. Allergy Clin. Immunol. *92*:732–743, 1993.
107. Smith, C. B., Purcell, R. H., Bellanti, J. A., et al.: Protective effect of antibody to parainfluenza type I virus. N. Engl. J. Med. *275*:1145–1152, 1966.
108. Smith, M. B. H., and Feldman, W.: Over-the-counter cold medications: A critical review of clinical trials between 1950 and 1991. J. A. M. A. *269*:2258–2263, 1993.
109. Smith, W., Andrewes, C. H., and Laidlaw, P. P.: A virus obtained from influenza patients. Lancet *2*:66–68, 1933.
110. Soyka, L. F., Robinson, D. S., Lachant, N., et al.: The misuse of antibiotics for treatment of upper respiratory tract infections in children. Pediatrics *55*:552–556, 1975.
111. Sperber, S. J., and Hayden, F. G.: Chemotherapy of rhinovirus colds. Antimicrob. Agents Chemother. *32*:409–419, 1988.
112. Sperber, S. J., Hendley, J. O., Hayden, F. G., et al.: Effects of naproxen on experimental rhinovirus colds: A randomized, double-blind, controlled trial. Ann. Intern. Med. *117*:37–41, 1992.
113. Takkouche, B., Regueira, C., and Gestal-Otero, J.: A cohort study of stress and the common cold. Epidemiology *11*:345–349, 2001.
114. Tannock, G. A., Gillett, S. M., Gillett, R. S., et al.: A study of intranasally administered interferon A (rIFN-alpha 2A) for the seasonal prophylaxis of natural viral infections of the upper respiratory tract in healthy volunteers. Epidemiol. Infect. *101*:611–621, 1988.
115. Tremonti, L. P., Lin, J. S. L., and Jackson, G. G.: Neutralizing activity in nasal secretions and serum in resistance of volunteers to parainfluenza virus type 2. J. Immunol. *101*:572–577, 1968.
116. Turner, R. B., Felton, A., Kosak, K., et al.: Prevention of experimental coronavirus colds with intranasal alpha-2b interferon. J. Infect. Dis. *154*:443–447, 1986.
117. Turner, R. B., Sperber, S. J., Sorrentino, J. V., et al.: Effectiveness of clemastine fumarate for treatment of rhinorrhea and sneezing associated with the common cold. Clin. Infect. Dis. *25*:824–830, 1997.
118. Turner, R. B.: The common cold. Pediatr. Ann. *27*:790–795, 1998.
119. Turner, R. B., Weingand, K. W., Yeh, C., et al.: Association between interleukin-8 concentration in nasal secretions and severity of symptoms of experimental rhinovirus colds. Clin. Infect. Dis. *26*:840–846, 1998.
120. Turner, R. B., Wecker, M. T., Pohl, G., et al.: Efficacy of tremacamra, a soluble intercellular adhesion molecule 1, for experimental rhinovirus infection: A randomized clinical trial. J. A. M. A. *281*:1797–1804, 1999.
121. Turner, R. B., Riker, D. K., and Gangemi, J. D.: Ineffectiveness of echinacea for prevention of experimental rhinovirus colds. Antimicrob. Agents Chemother. *44*:1708–1709, 2000.
122. Turner, R. B., and Cetnarowski, W. E.: Effect of treatment with zinc gluconate or zinc acetate on experimental and natural colds. Clin. Infect. Dis. *31*:1202–1208, 2000.
123. Turner, R. B.: The treatment of rhinovirus infections: Progress and potential. Antiviral Res. *49*:1–14, 2001.
124. Tyrrell, D. A. J.: Common Colds and Related Diseases. Baltimore, Williams & Wilkins, 1965.
125. Valic, F., and Zuskin, E.: Pharmacological prevention of acute ventilatory capacity reduction in flax dust exposure. Br. J. Indian Med. *30*:381–384, 1973.
126. Walker, G. H., Bynoe, M. L., and Tyrrell, D. A. J.: Trial of ascorbic acid in prevention of colds. B. M. J. *1*:603–606, 1967.
127. West, S., Brandon, B., Stolley, P., et al.: A review of antihistamines and the common cold. Pediatrics *56*:100–107, 1975.
128. Winther, B., Brofeldt, S., Christensen, B., et al.: Light and scanning electron microscopy of nasal biopsy material from patients with naturally acquired common colds. Acta. Otolaryngol. (Stockh.) *97*:309–318, 1984.
129. Winther, B., Farr, B., Turner, R. B., et al.: Histopathologic examination and enumeration of polymorphonuclear leukocytes in the nasal mucosa during experimental rhinovirus colds. Acta Otolaryngol. (Suppl.) (Stockh.) *413*:19–24, 1984.
130. Winther, B.: Effects on the nasal mucosa of upper respiratory viruses (common cold). Danish Med. *41*:193–204, 1994.
131. Zhu, Z., Tang, W., Gwaltney, J. M., Jr., et al.: Rhinovirus stimulation of interleukin-8 in vivo and in vitro: Role of NF-κB. Am. J. Physiol. *273*:L814–L824, 1997.
132. Zuskin, E., Lewis, A. J., and Bouhuys, A.: Inhibition of histamine-induced airway constriction by ascorbic acid. J. Allergy Clin. Immunol. *51*:218–226, 1973.

Infections of the Oral Cavity

CONSTANTINE SIMOS ■ THOMAS R. FLYNN ■ JOSEPH F. PIECUCH ■ RICHARD G. TOPAZIAN

Although most infections of the oral cavity in children are odontogenic and may be treated simply with local measures, their occasional spread to adjacent or distant fascial spaces or to the maxilla and mandible may result in life-threatening complications. Consequently, careful attention, including liberal use of the dental consultation, should be given to such infections.[14, 50]

Microbiologic Considerations in Dental Infections

NORMAL FLORA

That the oral cavity provides an environment favorable to the growth of microorganisms is substantiated by reports of bacterial counts in the range of 10^8 to 10^{11} organisms/mL of saliva.[3, 6] More than 30 species of bacteria normally can be identified in saliva in varying proportions, depending on a dynamic interaction of different microbial ecosystems, including the tongue, the gingival crevice, and the presence of plaque.[47, 53] Age, anatomic relationships, eruption of teeth, presence of decayed teeth, diet, oral hygiene, antibiotic therapy, systemic disease, cancer chemotherapy,[48] and hospitalization can modify the microbial population. In the older literature, emphasis was placed on the role of *Streptococcus* and *Staphylococcus* spp. in producing odontogenic infections, to the exclusion of most anaerobic bacteria. This emphasis probably was the result of failure to culture satisfactorily for anaerobic organisms, and it is now well known that the ratio of anaerobic to aerobic organisms ranges from 3:1 to 10:1.[3, 7]

The nomenclature of the oral flora is changing rapidly owing to the improved understanding of the genetic make-up of these bacteria provided by molecular biology techniques. Table 9–1 summarizes nomenclatural changes among selected members of the oral flora.[8, 56, 57]

The flora of children is similar to that of adults, with several exceptions. At birth, the oral cavity is sterile, but colonization with *Streptococcus salivarius* is rapid. This organism has been found in 80 percent of cultures taken from 1-day-old infants.[58] The percentage of *Streptococcus* spp. decreases from 98 percent at day 1 to 70 percent at 4 months[45] as other organisms become established. *Staphylococcus* spp., *Neisseria, Veillonella, Actinomyces, Nocardia, Fusobacterium, Bacteroides, Corynebacterium, Candida,* and a variety of coliforms gradually become established by the time the child reaches 1 year of age. As the deciduous dentition erupts, anaerobic organisms become well established in the gingival crevice, yet the spirochetes, *Bacteroides* and *Prevotella* spp., and related oral anaerobes, which commonly are associated with the gingival crevice in adults, appear to be present in fewer numbers in patients younger than 13 to 16 years.[6, 58] Eruption of deciduous teeth also is associated with the establishment of *Streptococcus mutans* and *Streptococcus sanguis,* which adhere to the enamel surface.

TABLE 9–1 ■ TERMINOLOGY CHANGES FOR SELECTED ORAL PATHOGENS

Older Terminology	Current Terminology
Streptococcus viridans	*Streptococcus anginosus*
	Streptococcus intermedius
	Streptococcus constellatus
	Streptococcus mutans
	Streptococcus sanguis
	Streptococcus mitis
	Streptococcus salivarius
	Streptococcus vestibularis
Streptococcus milleri	*Streptococcus anginosus*
	Streptococcus intermedius
	Streptococcus constellatus
Bacteroides melaninogenicus	*Prevotella melaninogenica*
	Prevotella intermedia
	Prevotella oralis
	Prevotella buccae
	Prevotella denticola
	Prevotella nigrescens
	Porphyromonas asaccharolytica
	Porphyromonas gingivalis
	Porphyromonas endodontalis
	Porphyromonas salivosa
	Porphyromonas circumdentaria
Streptococcus faecalis	*Enterococcus faecalis*
Streptococcus faecium	*Enterococcus faecium*
Peptococcus species	*Peptostreptococcus* species (main oral pathogen is *P. micros*)

PATHOGENIC ORGANISMS

Not all residents of the oral flora are pathogens. In the odontogenic infections caries and periodontal disease, a progression from initiating infections caused by oral streptococci toward a predominance of oral anaerobes in the more severe and long-standing infections apparently occurs. For example, caries is initiated primarily by *S. mutans,* a member of the alpha-hemolytic *Streptococcus* viridans group. As tooth decay progresses toward the dental pulp, *Lactobacillus* and *Actinomyces* spp. join the carious milieu. Severe pulpal infections are caused generally by a combination of these same oral facultative streptococci plus obligate anaerobes, such as *Porphyromonas endodontalis,* formerly classified as *B. melaninogenicus.*[61]

Periodontal infections also are polymicrobial; gram-positive aerobes, primarily streptococci, predominate in gingivitis, and the gram-negative anaerobic rods predominate in bone-destroying periodontitis. Juvenile periodontitis (formerly called periodontosis), a particularly aggressive periodontal infection in children and adolescents, shows a predominance of *Actinobacillus actinomycetemcomitans* in its cultivable flora.

Orofacial odontogenic infections that spread beyond the teeth and alveolar processes are polymicrobial, yielding on average four to six isolates per case.[5, 34, 46] Severe orofacial infections have been associated statistically with *Fusobacterium nucleatum.*[24] The concept of the progression from aerobic streptococci to anaerobic gram-negative rods in orofacial infections is supported further by studies that have

TABLE 9–2 ■ MOST FREQUENT PATHOGENS ISOLATED FROM OROFACIAL INFECTIONS IN TWO STUDIES

Microorganism	Percentage of Cases	
	Lewis et al.*	Heimdahl et al.†
Streptococcus milleri	50	31
Peptostreptococcus species	64	31
Other anaerobic streptococci	8	38
Bacteroides (Prevotella) oralis	40	9
Bacteroides (Prevotella) gingivalis	28	‡
Bacteroides (Porphyromonas) melaninogenicus	24	26
Fusobacterium species	14	45

*Data from Lewis, M. A. O., MacFarlane, T. W., and McGowan, D. A.: Quantitative bacteriology of acute dentoalveolar abscesses. J. Med. Microbiol. *21*:101–104, 1986.
†Data from Heimdahl, A., Von Konow, L., Satoh, T., et al.: Clinical appearance of orofacial infections of odontogenic origin in relation to microbiological findings. J. Clin. Microbiol. *22*:299–302, 1985.
‡This organism was not reported in this study.

found a predominance of streptococci in early infections (in the first 3 days of symptoms) and a predominance of anaerobes in late infections.[34] Table 9–2 lists the frequency with which the major pathogens in orofacial infections were isolated in two studies.[24, 34]

Infections originating from nonodontogenic causes (facial trauma, surgical manipulation, tonsillitis) are included in most studies of soft tissue and fascial space infections, and contamination from the skin or oropharynx might allow aerobic organisms, such as *Staphylococcus aureus* and aerobic *Streptococcus* spp., to become established.[6] In contradistinction, infections originating solely from the dental periapical tissues are much more likely to be predominantly anaerobic.

A pitfall in the identification of organisms as described in the older literature was the failure to culture satisfactorily for anaerobic organisms. The more current literature recognizes this fact.[35, 46] The preponderance of anaerobic organisms in odontogenic infections mandates the use of both anaerobic and aerobic culturing techniques in those situations in which cultures are indicated.

Anatomic Considerations

Most severe orofacial infections develop consequent to dental infection—periapical, periodontal, or pericoronal. Spread occurs along anatomic pathways of least resistance.[3, 7, 25, 33, 60] Periodontal and pericoronal infections rarely have major sequelae because they generally drain from the gingival sulcus along the surface of the tooth into the oral cavity. On the other hand, infections associated with the root apices generally are confined within the bony alveolar process (Fig. 9–1). Should spontaneous intraoral drainage occur through either the periodontium or the pulp chamber, further spread through the marrow spaces is unlikely to occur. If such drainage does not occur, spread through bone (osteomyelitis) or perforation of the cortical plate of the affected jaw may take place. Infections associated with root apices close to the buccal cortical plate generally spread buccally, whereas those close to the lingual or palatal cortical plate or to the maxillary sinus spread in those directions (Fig. 9–2). Once penetration of the cortical plate occurs, infection involves the adjacent soft tissues and may manifest as either cellulitis or a soft tissue abscess, which eventually may perforate mucous membrane or skin as a sinus track (Fig. 9–3).

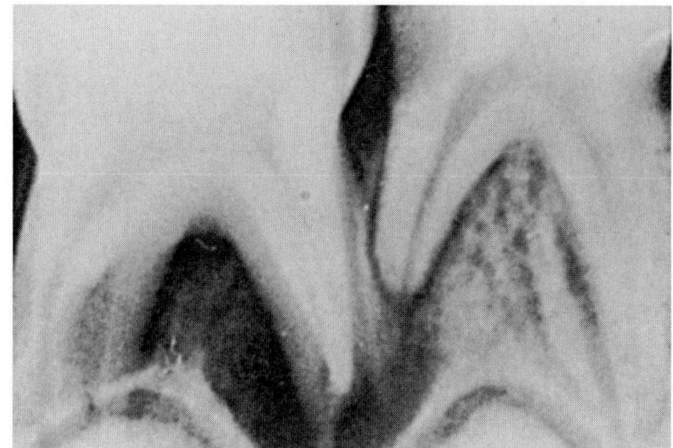

FIGURE 9–1 ■ Radiolucency representing a chronic periapical abscess involving the mesial root of the deciduous second molar and the distal root of the deciduous first molar. The developing mandibular bicuspids are seen inferior to the deciduous roots. The cause of the abscess is the deep carious lesions in both teeth, which appear to have penetrated the pulp chambers.

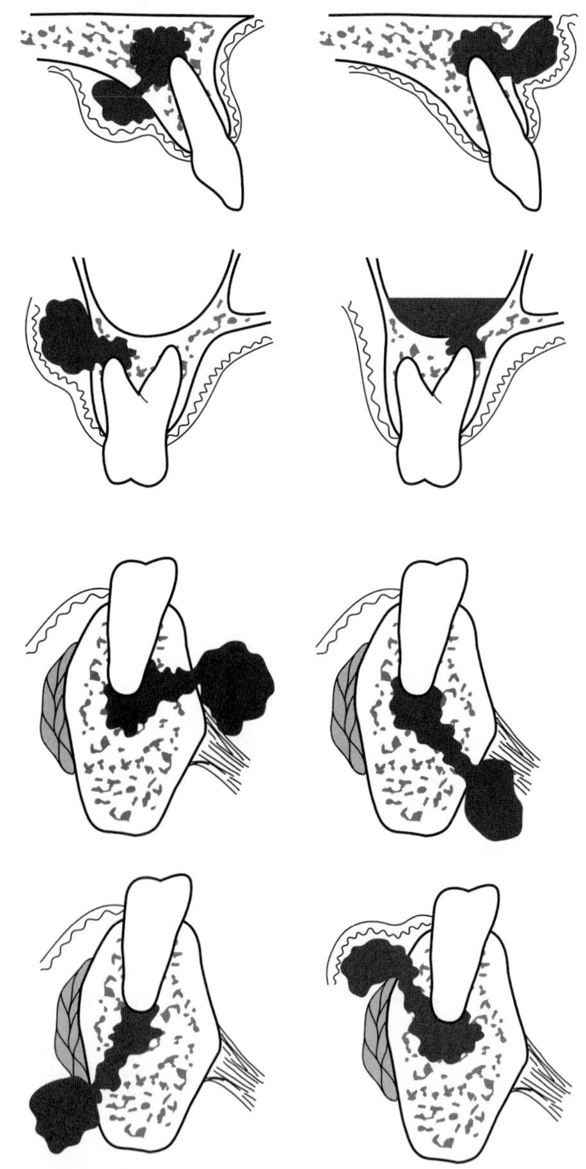

FIGURE 9–2 ■ Possible pathways of spread of periapical infection. (From Shafer, W. G., Hine, M. K., and Levy, B. M.: Textbook of Oral Pathology. 2nd ed. Philadelphia, W. B. Saunders, 1963.)

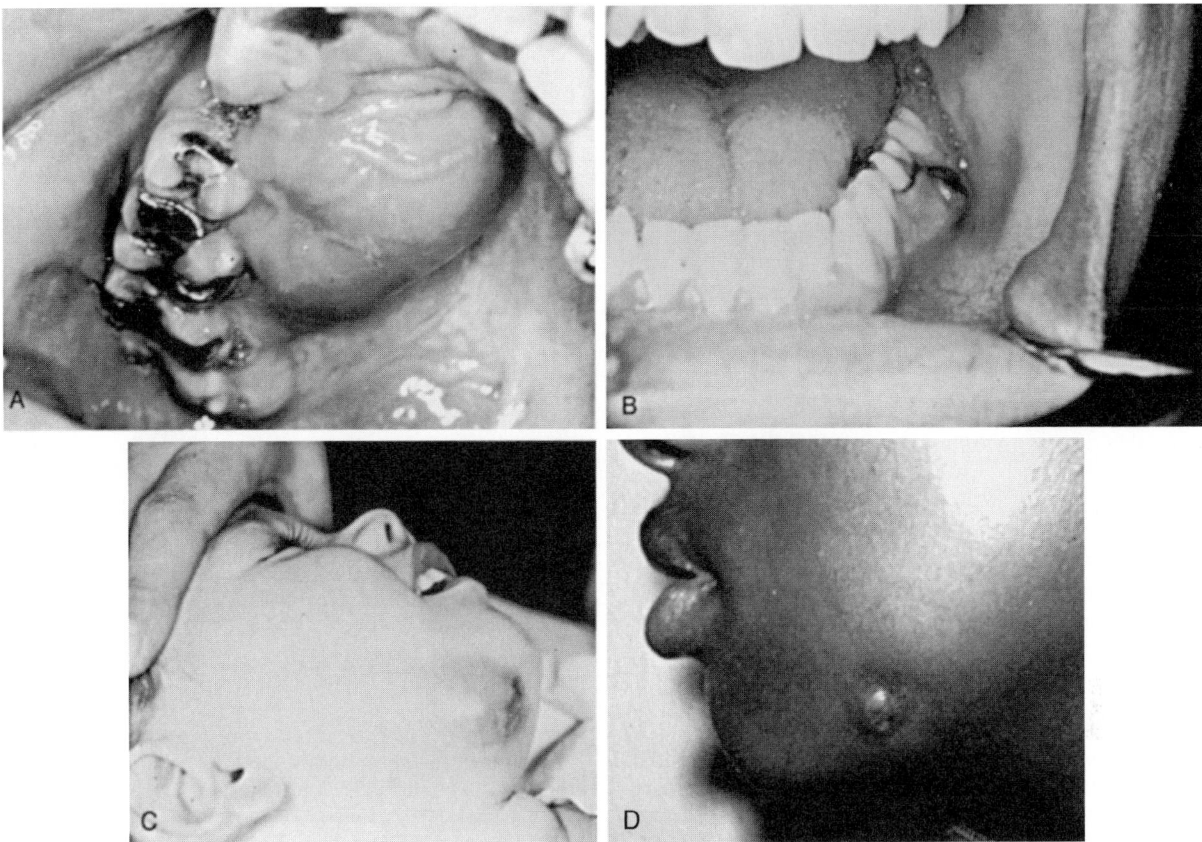

FIGURE 9–3 ■ Spread of odontogenic infection. *A,* Palatal abscess resulting from infected first premolar. *B,* Intraoral mucosal fistula from periapical abscess of mandibular left first molar. *C,* Soft tissue infection secondary to periapical abscess. *D,* Draining cutaneous sinus track from a chronically infected lower molar in an adolescent girl. (*A* from Piecuch, J.: Odontogenic infections. Dent. Clin. North Am. *26*:129–145, 1982. *D* from Flynn, T. R., and Topazian, R. G.: Infections of the oral cavity. *In* Waite, D. E. [ed.]: Textbook of Practical Oral and Maxillofacial Surgery. Philadelphia, Lea & Febiger, 1987.)

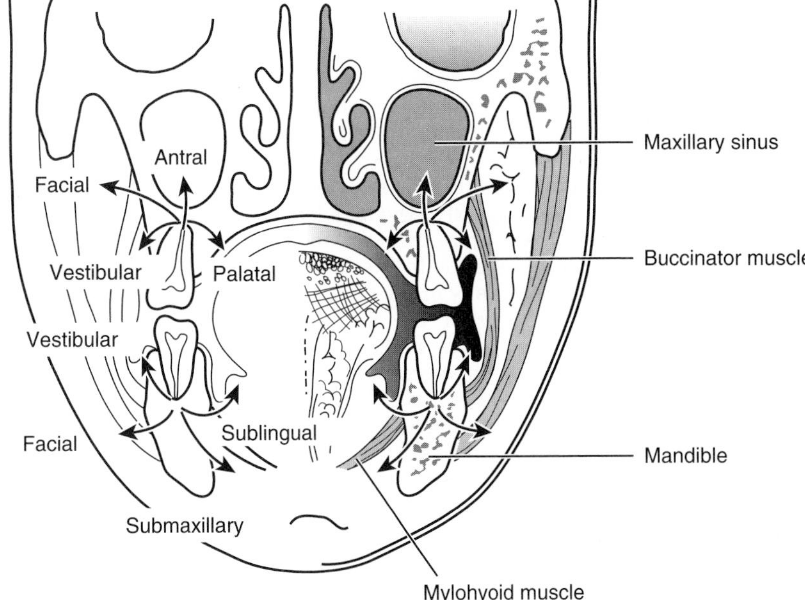

FIGURE 9–4 ■ Common pathways of spread of periapical infection. (From Kruger, G.: Textbook of Oral Surgery. 4th ed. St. Louis, C. V. Mosby, 1980.)

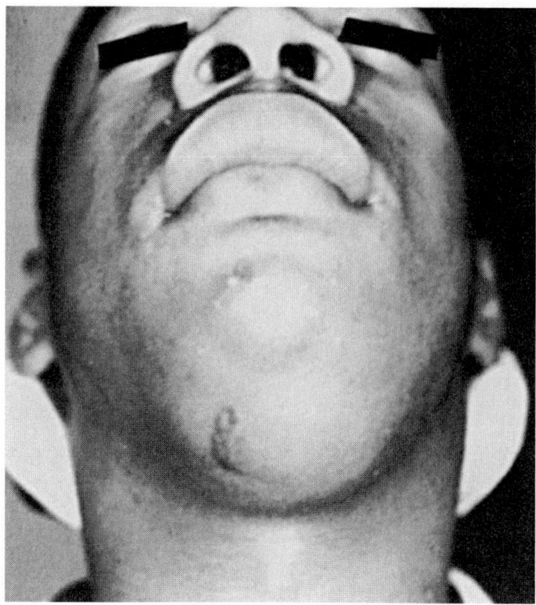

FIGURE 9–5 ■ Submental space abscess.

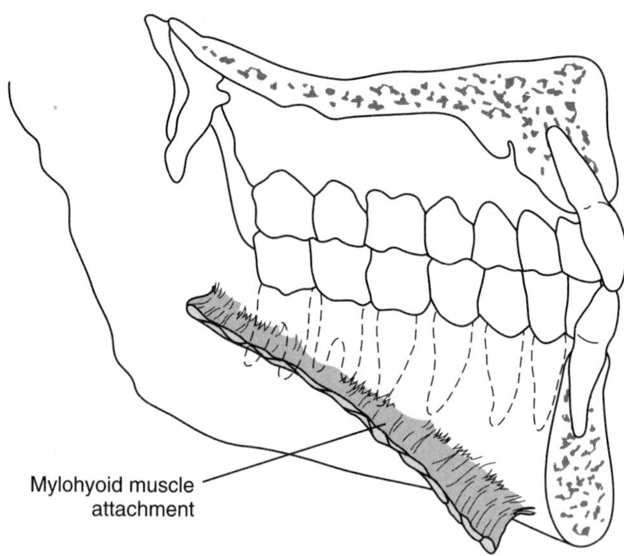

FIGURE 9–6 ■ Relation of tooth apices to the origin of mylohyoid muscle. (From Waite, D.: Textbook of Practical Oral Surgery. Philadelphia, Lea & Febiger, 1978.)

Perforation of periapical infections through bone follows a typical pattern that results from the position of the root apices in relation to the bony cortex and to muscle attachments (Fig. 9–4). Infections involving maxillary anterior teeth and buccal roots of maxillary posterior teeth generally perforate labially or buccally, whereas those involving palatal roots of posterior teeth perforate palatally or rarely into the maxillary sinus. The presence of the buccinator muscle attachment superior to the root apices usually confines these infections and fistulas to the oral cavity. In children, however, maxillary root apices often are superior to the buccinator, and infections may spread to the buccal or infraorbital space or to the periorbital tissues. They eventually may drain through the skin.

Infections of the mandibular incisor or canine tooth may spread either labially or lingually because the alveolar process is thin in this area. Labial perforation, which occurs more commonly, may be confined intraorally if the root apices are superior to the origin of the mentalis muscle but may spread extraorally if the apices are inferior to the mentalis attachment (Fig. 9–5). Mandibular premolar and first molar infections often perforate buccally, whereas the second and third molars perforate lingually.

When spread of mandibular infections occurs lingually, the relationship of the tooth apices to the mylohyoid muscle origin is significant (Fig. 9–6). From the first molar forward, the dental root apices are superior to the mylohyoid, and these infections localize intraorally in the floor of the mouth (sublingual space). The apices of the second and third molars generally are inferior to the mylohyoid, and so the submandibular space will be involved, with an extraoral presentation. As in maxillary infections, the relationship of the buccinator muscle to the root apices determines whether the infection spreads intraorally or extraorally.

Two fascial spaces commonly associated with odontogenic infections are the submandibular and masticator spaces.[17,18,33] The submandibular space is formed within the superficial layer of deep cervical fascia inferior to the mylohyoid muscle and inferomedial to the mandible. Anteriorly and posteriorly, it is limited by the bellies of the digastric muscle. Within this space lies the submandibular gland and portions of the facial artery and anterior facial vein. This space is closely approximated to the sublingual and masticator spaces. Infections of the submandibular space may originate in these adjacent spaces as well as in mandibular posterior teeth.

The masticator space also is formed within the superficial layer of deep cervical fascia. Its name is appropriate because its contents include the masseter, internal and external pterygoid, and temporalis muscles, as well as the mandibular ramus and the inferior alveolar neurovascular bundle. Adjacent are the submandibular, lateral pharyngeal, and retropharyngeal spaces. Infections of the masticator space may originate in adjacent spaces or spread to it from periapical or pericoronal infections of the mandibular second and third molars and maxillary third molar.

Treatment of Odontogenic Infections

Patients with odontogenic infections may present with symptoms ranging from minor to life-threatening. Too often, a patient may be given a thorough systemic and extraoral head and neck evaluation while the intraoral search for the etiologic agent is overlooked.

Thorough oral examination begins with an evaluation of the degree of mandibular opening. Interincisal distance on wide opening extends up to 40 mm or more, even in young children. Painful limitation of oral opening, or trismus, is associated with inflammation of the muscles of mastication and indicates spread of the infection to the masticator space. In association with a high fever, it can represent a serious turn of events. Teeth are inspected visually for caries by percussion for tenderness and by electrical sensitivity or hot and cold stimulation for the pulpal pain response. Gingival tissues are probed for periodontal defects, and salivary glands are palpated for tenderness and milked to observe for purulent discharge from the duct orifices.

GENERAL THERAPEUTIC PRINCIPLES

As with infections elsewhere in the body, the principles of treatment of oral infections involve surgical drainage and antibiotics. Surgical drainage may comprise standard incision and drainage of an orofacial swelling or, in the case of localized periapical infection, endodontic drainage through the pulp or extraction of the offending tooth.

Surgical treatment of odontogenic infections is primary. Dodson and colleagues,[10] in a review of head and neck infections requiring hospitalization of children, found that facial infections of the regions at or above the level of the upper lip and teeth most frequently were upper respiratory or sinus related and that lower face infections primarily were odontogenic. Infections of the upper face resolved without surgery in 65 percent of cases, whereas infections of the lower face resolved without surgery in only 25 percent of cases. Odontogenic infections almost always required some sort of surgical intervention. This finding may be due to the fact that the portal of entry in respiratory infections is through the surface mucosa, whereas the tooth roots carry the invading bacterial pathogens deep into the bone of the jaw, through which the surrounding deep fascial spaces become infected. Respiratory pathogens frequently are viral, and odontogenic infections almost uniformly are bacterial, which may explain the propensity of odontogenic infections to form abscesses that need to be drained. Odontogenic infections treated with only antibiotics almost always recur in worse form than their previous manifestation. On the other hand, the indications for treating with antibiotics in addition to appropriate dental surgical therapy are fever, trismus, lymphadenopathy, osteomyelitis, and immune system compromise. Minor infections localized to the alveolar processes can be treated by tooth extraction, gingival curettage, or root canal therapy, with or without intraoral incision and drainage, without the use of antibiotics in the nonimmunocompromised individual.

Antibiotic selection for odontogenic infections, although ultimately based on Gram stain and aerobic and anaerobic cultures, generally is begun empirically before culture results are available. Penicillin G or V is the logical first choice for outpatient infections on the basis of its lack of toxicity, bactericidal nature, and the sensitivity of most streptococci and oral anaerobes to this drug. Antibiotic sensitivity studies indicate that the oral anaerobes now are largely resistant to erythromycin, however.[49] A study of severe odontogenic infections found penicillin-resistant organisms in 60 percent of cases and therapeutic failure of empirical penicillin in 26 percent of cases.[13] The duration of previous therapy with β-lactam antibiotics also has been correlated with increased numbers of β-lactamase–producing bacteria in persisting infections. Patients with persisting infection after 3 days of treatment with a β-lactam antibiotic had a 50 percent incidence of β-lactamase–producing bacteria in the infection.[29, 21] Clindamycin remains highly effective against the likely oral pathogens, including streptococci and the oral anaerobes; its association with *Clostridium difficile* colitis and its effectiveness in severe orofacial infections indicate that it should be reserved, in this era of increasing microbial resistance to antibiotics, for the most severe cases.

The aforementioned considerations suggest that the empirical antibiotics of choice are penicillin in early and mild odontogenic infections and clindamycin for severe or chronic cases or in a patient with penicillin allergy. Table 9–3 lists our recommendations for empirical antibiotic therapy in odontogenic infections.

Second-line antibiotics in odontogenic infections are the cephalosporins, whose effectiveness against the oral anaerobes has been waning, and metronidazole, which is effective against obligate anaerobes only. The safety and effectiveness of metronidazole in children have been established for treatment of only amebiasis, however.

TABLE 9–3 ■ EMPIRICAL ANTIBIOTICS OF CHOICE FOR ODONTOGENIC INFECTIONS*

Type of Infection		Antibiotic of Choice
Outpatient or early (1st–3rd day of symptoms) infections		Penicillin Clindamycin Cephalexin (or other first-generation cephalosporin)
	Penicillin allergy	Clindamycin Cephalexin (if the penicillin allergy was not the anaphylactoid type—use caution)
Inpatient or chronic infections		Clindamycin Ampicillin + metronidazole Ampicillin + sulbactam
	Penicillin allergy	Clindamycin Cephalosporin IV (if the penicillin allergy was not the anaphylactoid type—use caution) Metronidazole alone (if neither clindamycin nor cephalosporins can be tolerated)

*Empirical antibiotic therapy is used before culture and sensitivity reports are available. Cultures should be taken in severe infections that threaten vital structures.

From Flynn, T. R.: The swollen face—severe odontogenic infections. Emerg. Med. Clin. North Am. *18*:481–519, 2000.

Other considerations that may be of importance in the selection of antibiotics for individual cases are as follows. (1) *Eikenella corrodens,* an occasional pathogen in odontogenic infections, is uniformly resistant to clindamycin, which may explain the lack of effectiveness of clindamycin in some cases. (2) Some cephalosporins do not cross the blood-brain barrier in high concentrations, which may be a factor in antibiotic selection for odontogenic infections that are approaching the cranial cavity. Penicillin is able to cross the blood-brain barrier when the meninges are inflamed. Metronidazole crosses the blood-brain barrier, and, therefore, its use may be justified in severe odontogenic infections approaching the brain in children. Ceftazidime is one cephalosporin that crosses the blood-brain barrier well. (3) Tetracycline is incorporated permanently into newly formed dentin, thereby causing permanent disfiguring discoloration of the dentition. Therefore, it should not be used in children until they are at least 9 years of age, when all but the third molar teeth will have full crown formation. (4) β-Lactamase inhibitors used in combination with β-lactam antibiotics may improve their effectiveness against resistant anaerobes, although the effectiveness of these drugs in odontogenic infections has not been studied. (5) Staphylococci are uncommon pathogens in odontogenic infections, and coverage for staphylococci is not indicated in empirical therapy for these infections, although their role in upper respiratory and sinus infections is well known.

NURSING BOTTLE CARIES

Nursing bottle caries is a pattern of tooth decay affecting mainly the primary upper incisors and frequently the upper and lower primary molars in children of bottle-feeding age. It is caused by a practice of putting the child to bed with a nursing bottle filled with a sugar-containing drink, such as milk, fruit juice, or a soft drink. The child sucks on the bottle intermittently during sleep, when salivary secretion is low, and the sugar-containing liquid stays in the mouth for extended periods. This situation provides an excellent environment for the growth of caries-producing organisms, such as *S. mutans*. Nursing bottle caries can destroy virtually the entire primary dentition of a child as it erupts. Therefore, pediatric physicians and dentists should instruct parents to avoid putting their children to bed with nursing bottles or, if they must do so, to use only water in the bedtime drink.

PERIAPICAL ABSCESS

Extension of microorganisms through the root apex leads to the formation of an abscess. Early in this process, the acute abscess is indistinguishable clinically and radiographically from an acute pulpitis, particularly because radiographic evidence of bone destruction may take 7 to 14 days or more to develop. Sensitivity to heat stimulus (relieved by cold), exquisite sensitivity to percussion, and tenderness to finger pressure on the alveolar process are indications that the tooth has become abscessed. Electric pulp testing may be diagnostic if the tooth shows no response to the electrical stimulus, but a positive pain response may be equivocal in multirooted teeth. Chronic abscesses are diagnosed more easily by looseness of the tooth, suppuration from draining sinus tracks or from the gingival crevice (see Fig. 9–3), and radiolucency on the radiographs (see Fig. 9–1). Depending on the path of least resistance, fluctuant areas may be noted in the buccal or lingual mucosa. Spread through the tissues, or cellulitis, may lead to the classic presentation of swollen face, pain, elevated temperature, and malaise.

In 1951, Krogh[30] demonstrated a 3 percent complication rate when 2626 infected teeth were removed at the time of initial presentation. In 1975, Martis and Karakasis[41] published a similar study in which they treated 1376 acute dentoalveolar abscesses by immediate extraction. A 3 percent complication rate was found in this study as well. A complication was defined as further extension of the infection, requiring additional treatment. Hall and associates[20] published a report in 1968 in which 350 patients with odontogenic cellulitis were divided randomly into two groups. The first group had extractions performed on the day of initial presentation, whereas the second group waited (with antibiotics) until the fourth day for surgical treatment to be performed after "localization" had occurred. The investigators' observations showed that in neither group did extraction spread the cellulitis. In addition, those with earlier extractions recovered more rapidly, whereas those with delayed treatment had a greater need for incision and drainage, which was twice as likely to be extraoral than intraoral. In 1978, Martis and colleagues[42] showed in a series of more than 2000 patients that extraction without antibiotics in the presence of periapical infection led to the same complication rate as did extraction of noninfected teeth.

Considering the prospect of early relief of symptoms as well as a 97 percent chance that extraction (or occasionally root canal treatment) will cure the infection, early surgical intervention clearly is mandatory. The use of antibiotics must be determined on an individual basis according to principles outlined previously.

PERIODONTAL INFECTIONS

Surrounding the teeth is a distinctive, pink keratinized mucosa, the gingiva (Fig. 9–7*A*). Normal gingiva is attached firmly to the alveolar bone and extends between the teeth as the interdental papilla. A thin cuff of free (nonattached) gingiva surrounds each tooth, and the resulting crevice between the free gingiva and the tooth normally is 1 to 3 mm in depth. It is represented by a thin roll of tissue along each tooth in the illustration.

Accumulation of food deposits and bacteria in the gingival crevice may result in gingivitis, a localized inflammation of the free gingiva that presents as an erythematous, nonpainful swelling of the interdental papillae. In severe cases (see Fig. 9–7*B*), the gingival architecture may become distorted, and accumulations of plaque are evident. Although gingivitis is prevalent at all ages, affecting more than 50 percent of children[44] and almost all adults to some degree, it often is most severe in compromised hosts, including patients with diabetes and immunosuppressed patients. Poor oral hygiene is the usual precipitating factor for development of gingivitis, and this condition generally responds to dental scaling and improved oral hygiene.

In adolescents as well as in adults, gingivitis may progress to periodontitis, a progressively severe infection that is characterized by hypertrophied gingivae, tooth mobility caused by irreversible resorption of alveolar bone, and a purulent exudate. Unfortunately, this insidious condition usually is painless and may progress for years before being recognized. Localized periodontal treatment and meticulous oral hygiene may arrest the condition.

A rare variant, juvenile periodontitis,[32] usually is localized to the molar and incisor regions of younger, otherwise healthy children. Deep gingival pocketing and severe bone resorption are characteristic of this process and may result in loss of the dentition in these areas. The etiology is thought to involve a gram-negative anaerobe, *A. actinomycetemcomitans*, and localized bacterial inhibition of leukocyte function. Tetracycline in older patients has been useful in combination with periodontal surgery and meticulous home care.

Acute necrotizing ulcerative gingivitis (see Fig. 9–7*C*) is a specific infection caused by fusiform bacilli and spirochetes. Synonyms include trench mouth and Vincent infection. Erythema at the tips of the interdental papillae soon is supplanted by frank ulceration and foci of spontaneous bleeding. A pseudomembranous necrotic exudate forms along the marginal gingivae and the interdental papillae. The papillae later become blunted. Acute necrotizing ulcerative gingivitis is characterized by pain, foul breath and taste, thick ropy saliva, malaise, and occasionally fever. Theories suggest a concomitant viral etiology. Treatment consists initially of penicillin therapy followed within a few days by localized gingival curettage and oral rinses with 0.5 percent hydrogen peroxide or 0.12 percent chlorhexidine.[37] The safety and effectiveness of chlorhexidine in children have not been established, however.

PERICORONITIS

Impaction of microorganisms and debris under the soft tissue overlying the crown of a tooth, often a mandibular third molar, or any erupting permanent tooth leads to the

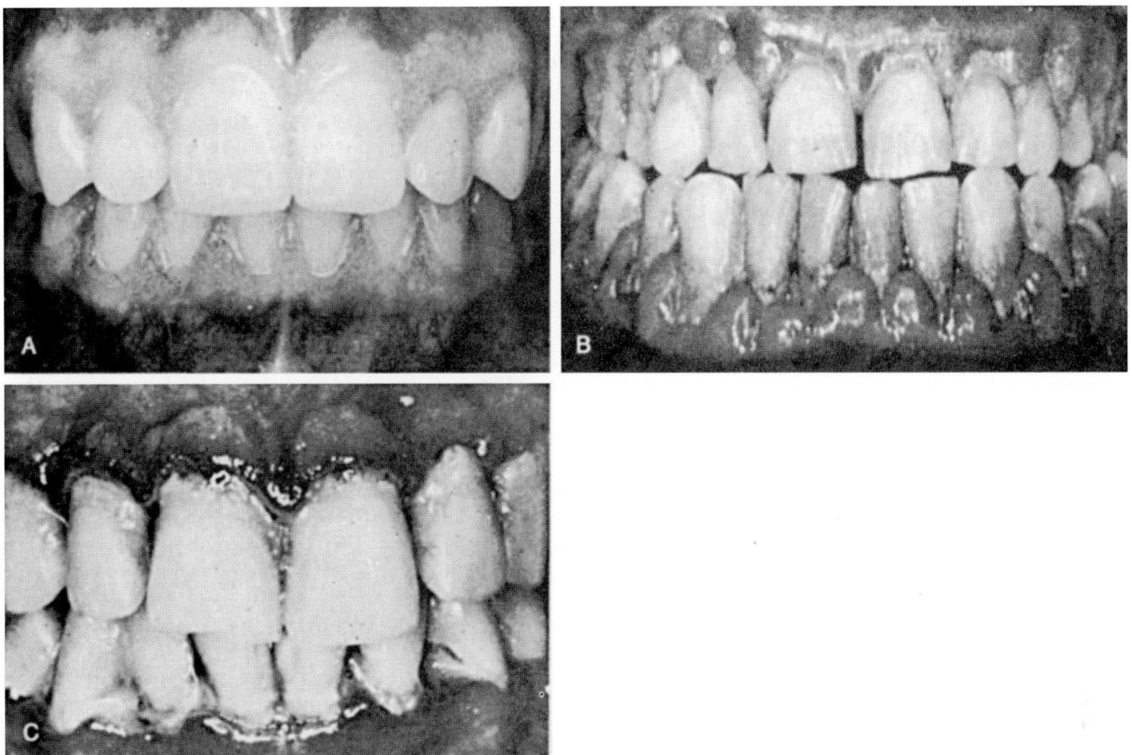

FIGURE 9–7 ■ *A,* Normal gingivae. *B,* Severe gingivitis. The maxillary gingivae exhibit mild inflammation; the mandibular interdental papillae are distorted grossly in form. Accumulations of plaque are prominent adjacent to the mandibular incisors. *C,* Acute necrotizing ulcerative gingivitis.

development of inflammation. Drainage usually occurs spontaneously from under the flap, thus localizing the problem. Blockage of natural drainage may lead to spread of infection to adjacent soft tissues and fascial spaces (Fig. 9–8).

Pericoronitis is a polymicrobial infection; the periodontal pathogens *Prevotella* and *Porphyromonas* spp. and oral spirochetes, such as *Treponema denticola,* usually are the causative organisms. Recently, the *Streptococcus milleri* group bacteria also have been found to have a significant role in acute pericoronitis.[24] These organisms usually are sensitive to penicillin or penicillin in combination with metronidazole. Pericoronitis most frequently occurs about the posterior portion of the crown of the lower third molar because it erupts during adolescence. In most cases, partial eruption of the third molar is caused by insufficient length of the horizontal ramus of the mandible to house all of the teeth. Therefore, part of the third molar is trapped under the oral mucosa covering the buccinator muscle and the superior pharyngeal constrictor because they form the most anterior portion of the oropharynx. In cases in which room is insufficient for the eruption of the third molar, the pericoronitis becomes recurrent or chronic, and the impacted third molar should be removed.

Lower third molars lie in proximity to the pterygomandibular space, a portion of the masticator space. When these infections spread to involve this space, trismus results, which obscures the infection to clinical examination. Therefore, the presence of trismus with a history of pain in the third molar region is an ominous sign of infection involving the masticator space, which, although not manifested by external facial swelling, may begin to involve the deeper parapharyngeal spaces. These infections may become life-threatening. The lower third molar is the most frequent offending tooth in severe odontogenic infections requiring

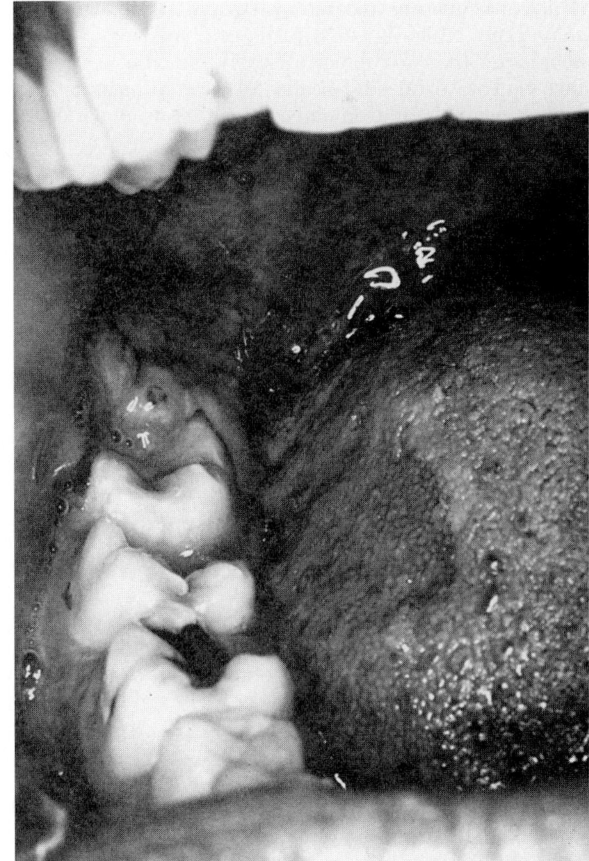

FIGURE 9–8 ■ Pericoronitis.

hospitalization, and these infections occur most frequently in adolescence and young adulthood.[22]

A variety of treatment modalities, including local incision and drainage as well as extraction of the tooth, are applicable to pericoronitis.[42, 54] Penicillin is used if fever or trismus is present. Resolution of symptoms should occur in less than 1 week.

ORAL MANIFESTATIONS OF HUMAN IMMUNODEFICIENCY VIRUS INFECTION IN CHILDREN

The most common oral lesions found in children with human immunodeficiency virus (HIV) disease are oral candidiasis, herpes simplex virus infections, linear gingival erythema, parotid salivary gland enlargement, and recurrent aphthous ulcerations. In contradistinction to adult HIV infection, HIV-associated periodontitis and gingivitis are much less common. Neoplastic oral manifestations of HIV infection, such as Kaposi sarcoma, non-Hodgkin lymphoma, and hairy leukoplakia, continue to be rare. In contrast to adults, children infected with HIV have a greater susceptibility to bacterial infections, especially with encapsulated organisms, such as *Streptococcus pneumoniae* and *Haemophilus influenzae*. Septicemia from an oral focus of infection can become a life-threatening problem in the HIV-infected child, and, therefore, optimal oral health must be established and vigorously maintained in these children.[31] Routine use of chlorhexidine gluconate 0.12 percent mouthrinse may be helpful in minimizing gingivitis, candidiasis, and bacterial superinfections of the oral cavity, although its safety and effectiveness have not been demonstrated in children.

Oral candidiasis is most frequently of the pseudomembranous type, which is seen in the oral cavity as a creamy white plaque that is rubbed off easily, leaving a reddened surface mucosa exposed. Because oral candidiasis is a rare finding in normal children older than 6 months, persistence of oral candidiasis for 2 months or more in a child older than 6 months who has not received antibiotic therapy in the past 2 weeks is suggestive of HIV infection. Persistent oral candidiasis indicates acquired immunodeficiency category P-2D3 (symptomatic infection with secondary infectious diseases) in the Centers for Disease Control and Prevention classification of HIV infection in children younger than 12 years.[28]

Oral candidiasis was associated with a decreased survival time in a study of 99 children with perinatally acquired HIV infection. The median time from birth to the manifestation of the first lesion of oral candidiasis was 2.4 years, and the median time from the appearance of lesions to death was 3.4 years, with a relative hazard rate of 14.2.[27]

Treatment of oral candidiasis lesions is difficult because of frequent recurrence of oral fungal infection with resistant biotypes of *Candida albicans* or colonization by related but more resistant species, such as *Candida krusei, Candida parapsilosis,* and *Candida guilliermondii*. Treatment regimens may progress from nystatin to clotrimazole, fluconazole, and amphotericin B, depending on the extent of disease, clinical response, and culture and sensitivity results.[40] Sudden onset of rampant dental caries has been associated with prolonged oral use of sucrose-containing antifungal antibiotic preparations.[64]

Linear gingival erythema, formerly referred to as HIV gingivitis, is the most common form of periodontal disease seen in children with HIV infection. It is described as a fiery-red, 2- to 3-mm-wide linear band of inflammation of the gingiva. Pain is not associated with the lesion, but the gingivae are likely to bleed during tooth brushing or even spontaneously. The microbiology of this lesion is not clear, but *Candida* spp. may be a possible cause.

Parotid salivary gland enlargement, which may be painful and become secondarily infected, has been reported in 14 to 30 percent of HIV-infected children. The enlargement appears to be caused by infiltration of the glands by T8 lymphocytes and has been associated with increased survival time. The median time was 4.6 years from birth to development of parotid enlargement and 5.4 years from development of lesions to death, with a relative hazard rate of 0.38.[27]

Herpes simplex virus infections, although common occurrences in normal children, appear to be particularly severe and recur more often in HIV-infected children. The lesions appear first as multiple clustered vesicles on the lips or keratinized oral mucosa, which soon rupture to leave painful irregular oral ulcers or crusted labial ulcers. Fever and dysphagia may warrant hospital admission for hydration, nutrition, and therapy with parenteral acyclovir. Less severe cases may be treated with oral acyclovir.

Dental caries is increased in pediatric HIV cohorts. The cause of this finding is not clear. It may be due to xerostomia secondary to parotid enlargement in some cases, prolonged use of sucrose-containing antifungal agents in others, and nursing bottle caries in still others. The association of nursing bottle caries with pediatric HIV infection may be due to their common increased prevalence in urban dwellers with limited economic resources, although nursing bottle caries also is found frequently in children with other chronic diseases.[64]

Complications of Odontogenic Infections

FASCIAL SPACE INFECTIONS

Spread of infection to the fascial spaces may result in dramatic facial swelling and high fever and, if untreated, respiratory embarrassment. The characteristics of the more common fascial space infections related to odontogenic infection are described here.

Infraorbital space infections generally are related to maxillary anterior teeth and are well localized to the infraorbital fossa by the levator labii superioris and levator anguli oris muscles. Facial swelling lateral to the nose is prominent, as is decreased mobility of the upper lip caused by inflammation of these muscles. If the area is fluctuant, intraoral incision and drainage with placement of a small Penrose drain for 1 to 2 days generally provide sufficient treatment. Antibiotics are indicated for all infections of the fascial space.

Trismus is the hallmark of infection of the masticator space. It is caused by spasm in the muscles of mastication, which define this large potential space. The resulting inability to open the mouth hinders access to the airway for endotracheal intubation. In addition, abscesses of the masticator space may rupture into the oropharynx, causing aspiration of pus, or they may pass easily around the medial pterygoid muscle to involve the lateral pharyngeal and retropharyngeal spaces. Figure 9–9 shows a 6-year-old boy whose lower primary molar abscesses spread to involve the buccal, pterygomandibular, and lateral pharyngeal spaces. Extraoral and intraoral drainage, prolonged intubation, and extraction of the offending teeth were required.

Infections of the submandibular space (Fig. 9–10) may be localized unilaterally or may involve bilateral structures.

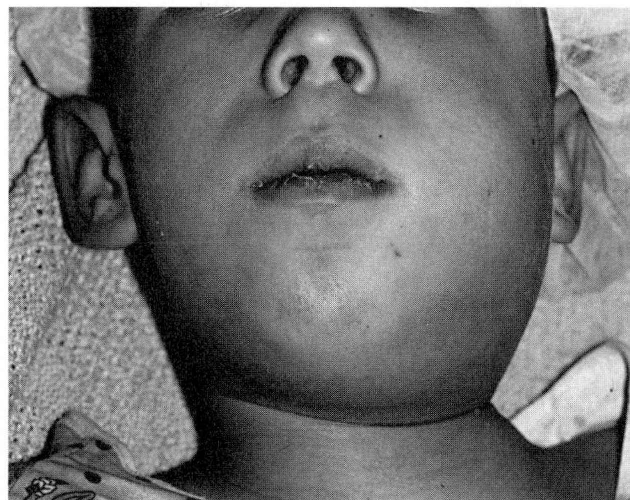

FIGURE 9–9 ■ Lateral pharyngeal space abscess in a 6-year-old boy. Note the swelling above the hyoid bone and anterior to the sternocleidomastoid muscle. Swelling also occurs in the buccal and submandibular spaces.

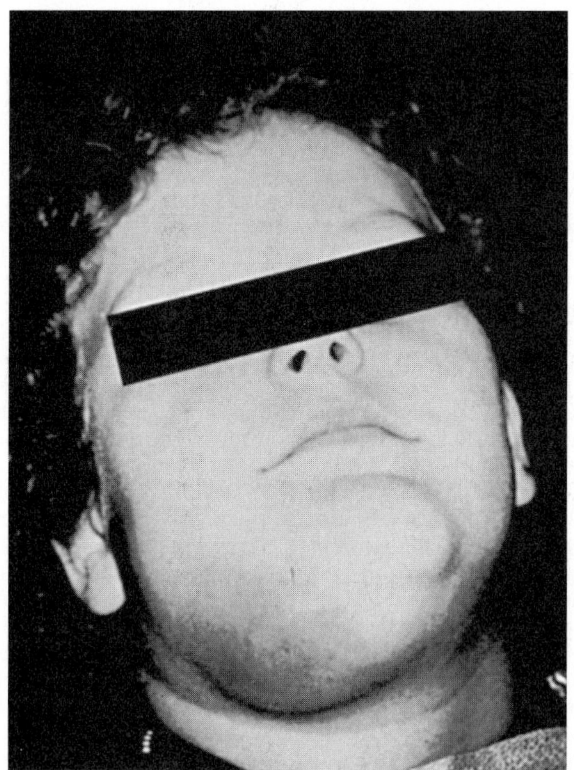

FIGURE 9–10 ■ Submandibular space abscess.

Treatment of submandibular space infection is by means of extraoral incision and drainage.

First described in 1836, Ludwig angina consists of infection of the sublingual and submandibular spaces bilaterally and is characterized by hard, brawny swelling and a minimum of suppuration. The tongue often is edematous and raised to the roof of the mouth, with little mobility (Fig. 9–11). Airway obstruction should be considered imminent, and indeed, the greatest cause of death in Ludwig angina is blockage of the airway by soft tissue swelling, pus, or blood, which occurred in more than 50 percent of its victims in the pre-antibiotic era.[19] Today, death rarely occurs, although the need for tracheostomy or prolonged endotracheal intubation is common. The cause of this infection often is odontogenic infection but also may include laceration of the floor of the mouth and mandibular fracture. Usually a disease of middle-aged people, it is a rare occurrence in children but may occur in greater frequency in the immunologically compromised.[16] Surgical drainage of all four spaces, accompanied by vigorous antibiotic therapy, is indicated.

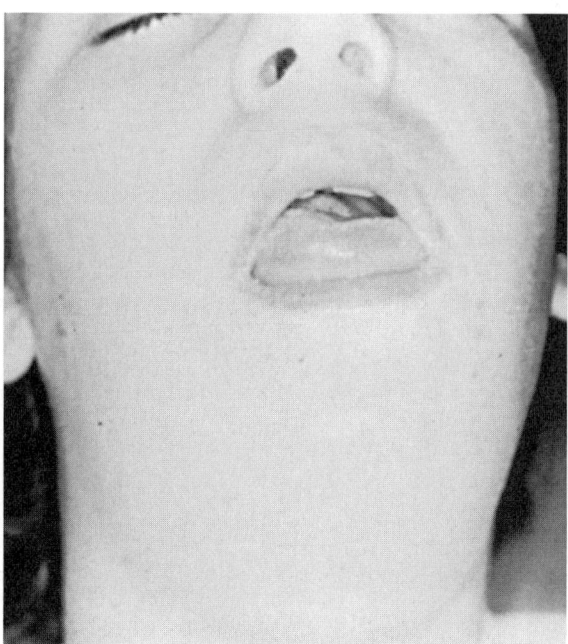

FIGURE 9–11 ■ Ludwig angina.

NECROTIZING FASCIITIS

Necrotizing fasciitis, which causes a frightening loss of skin and underlying tissues, has received considerable notoriety in the press. Cervicofacial necrotizing fasciitis often is odontogenic and typically causes a superficial spreading of cellulitis that follows the platysma muscle from the cheek down the entire neck to the anterior chest wall (Fig. 9–12*A*). Figure 9–12*B* illustrates such a swelling in an 8-year-old boy. The presumptive cause was odontogenic infection of the primary molars, which caused a high fever and a rapidly progressive cellulitis extending from the cheek to the chest. The cause of these infections often is group A streptococci, but a wide variety of microorganisms may be involved. Therefore, wide-spectrum antibiotic therapy is indicated empirically, along with hydration, transfusions if necessary, and support of electrolyte balance, especially with calcium, which may be sequestered by necrotic fat molecules.[1]

ODONTOGENIC SINUSITIS

A significant percentage of cases of sinusitis are odontogenic, especially in adults, because the maxillary sinus follows the erupting permanent tooth roots into the alveolar

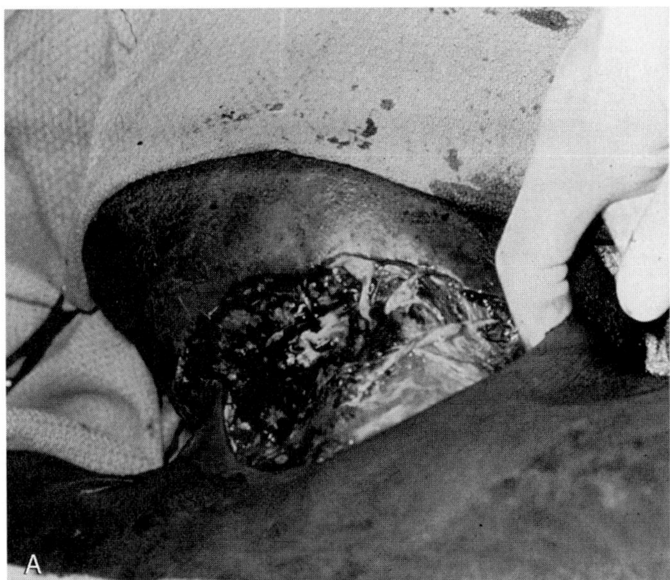

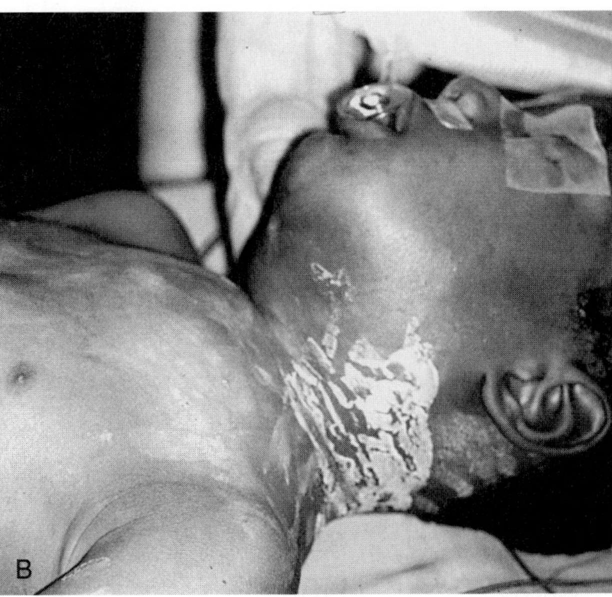

FIGURE 9–12 ■ *A,* Surgical débridement of necrotic skin and platysma muscle of the left neck of a diabetic female patient with necrotizing fasciitis. Note how easily blunt finger dissection can undermine the skin in the plane of the necrotic platysma muscle. *B,* Necrotizing fasciitis in an 8-year-old boy. Note the swelling extending from the buccal space down the neck and onto the anterior chest wall, following the extent of the platysma muscle. The chalky material on the posterior neck is calamine lotion placed by the patient's mother for vesicles that resembled poison ivy.

process. This pneumatization of the alveolar process progresses throughout life and is accelerated by loss of the upper posterior teeth. Dental infections of the periapical upper posterior teeth occasionally rupture through the maxillary sinus floor to involve the paranasal sinuses. Therefore, dental infection should be eliminated in the complete treatment of severe recurrent sinusitis in children.

Figure 9–13 illustrates a case in a 9-year-old boy of left pansinusitis, including ethmoiditis and a subperiosteal orbital abscess associated with infected upper primary molars. His treatment involved a team approach of the dental and otolaryngology services for tooth extraction, incision and drainage of the buccal and infraorbital spaces, endoscopic sinus surgery, and external drainage of the orbital abscess.

BUCCAL AND PERIORBITAL CELLULITIS

A child occasionally presents with an acute buccal or periorbital space swelling and cellulitis with no clinically apparent odontogenic cause. These infections tend to occur in young children, usually those younger than 36 months. A history of recent upper respiratory infection or sinusitis usually exists. Both *H. influenzae* type b and *S. pneumoniae* have been implicated as pathogens in these conditions, although the widespread use of conjugated vaccines has reduced drastically the incidence of invasive disease from *H. influenzae.*[15] A possible mechanism for the inoculation of the soft tissues is migration of organisms through emissary veins piercing the thin cortical bone overlying the lateral surface of the maxillary sinus, in cases with existing sinusitis. Unless the infection is severe, incision and drainage usually are not necessary, and treatment with antibiotics is successful. Blood cultures frequently are positive in more severe cases, and the role of lumbar puncture remains controversial in the overall management of infants and young children.

ORBITAL AND INTRACRANIAL COMPLICATIONS

Odontogenic infections that spread to involve the orbit and the brain are rare occurrences. Orbital and intracranial abscesses may have an odontogenic origin, however, and, therefore, the dental condition of patients with these conditions should be evaluated by a dentist. Probably no more than 5 to 10 percent of orbital cellulitis is odontogenic in origin.[26, 65] This infection generally is unilateral and is characterized by proptosis, chemosis, lid edema, and restriction of extraocular motion secondary to edema.[51] No nerve palsies or visual changes are present. Treatment includes surgical drainage, antibiotics, and elimination of the dental infection.

Cavernous sinus thrombosis, which may be difficult to differentiate clinically from orbital cellulitis, is considerably more serious because microorganisms proliferate intracranially. The risk of death is high. Characteristics include bilateral involvement with rapid progression from one eye to the other, proptosis, chemosis, and lid edema. Extraocular movements are limited because of inflammation of the third, fourth, and sixth cranial nerves. Systemic signs of meningeal irritation and ophthalmoscopic evidence of obstruction of the retinal veins are also present.[7, 51, 60] Treatment includes high doses of parenteral antibiotics, elimination of the causative dental pathosis, and incision and drainage of infected fascial spaces.

Brain abscess and subdural empyema are rare occurrences today compared with several decades ago. Of the large series of brain abscess cases reported, 0 to 4 percent of cases have been attributed to dental causes.[38, 63] However, all of the studies in which the individual case histories are described disclose a pansinusitis intervening between the dental infection and the brain.[39, 55] Therefore, odontogenic brain abscesses appear to occur by direct extension through the paranasal sinuses, usually to the frontal lobe through the frontal sinuses. On the other hand, odontogenic cavernous sinus thrombosis appears to be propagated by an ascending thrombophlebitis.

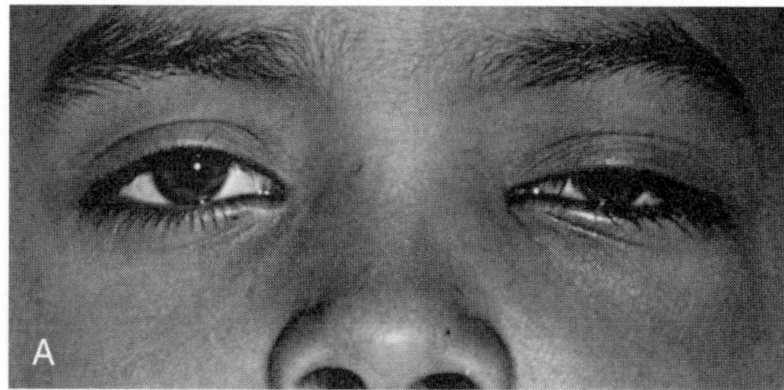

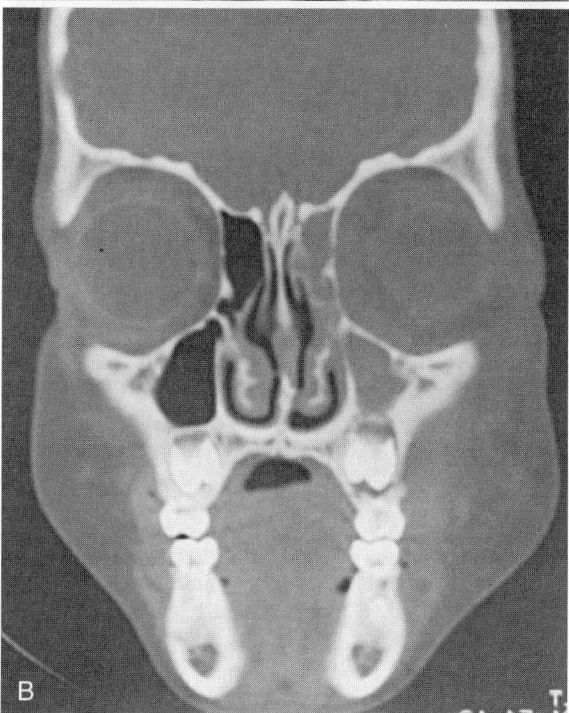

FIGURE 9–13 ■ *A,* A 9-year-old boy with a left pansinusitis and an abscess of the upper left first primary molar. Note the left periorbital discoloration and swelling, with partial ptosis and displacement of the globe laterally. *B,* Computed tomographic scan of the same patient. Note the left maxillary sinus opacification close to the infected tooth, opacification of the ethmoid sinuses, elevation of the periosteum away from the medial orbital wall, and displacement of the globe laterally within the orbit.

Osteomyelitis of the Jaws in Children

Osteomyelitis of the jaws in children usually results from periodontal or, more commonly, periapical infection. Open fracture of the jaws with delayed treatment also is a significant cause of osteomyelitis. Extension from contiguous infections, such as otitis, parotitis, and mastoiditis, occurs much less often.

Osteomyelitis of the jaws occurring in children must be viewed with great concern because it may result in the following problems: (1) loss of primary and permanent teeth; (2) sequestration of segments of the jaws; (3) growth defects, such as mandibular hypoplasia, asymmetry, and ankylosis[12]; (4) disfiguring facial scars and cutaneous fistulas; and (5) lesions suggestive of malignancy, which require open biopsy. For these reasons, osteomyelitis of the jaws in children should be diagnosed rapidly and treated aggressively. A useful classification of this disease is shown in Table 9–4.[62]

TABLE 9–4 ■ OSTEOMYELITIS OF THE JAWS

Suppurative	Nonsuppurative
Acute suppurative	Chronic sclerosing
Chronic suppurative	Facial sclerosing
Primary	Diffuse sclerosing
Secondary	Garré sclerosing
Infantile	Actinomycotic
	Radiation osteomyelitis and necrosis

PREDISPOSING FACTORS

Preexisting systemic disease with accompanying alteration of host resistance plays a major role in the initiation of osteomyelitis of the jaws. It includes such conditions as uncontrolled diabetes, agranulocytosis, leukemia, sickle-cell disease, and febrile illnesses. Conditions that alter the vascularity of bone and thus the ability to combat infections, including bone tumors, fibrous dysplasia, Paget disease, and radiation to the jaws, also are important predisposing conditions. Major maxillofacial injuries resulting in open fractures of the jaws, especially those that are not treated immediately, are an important cause of osteomyelitis.

MICROBIOLOGY

Because the etiology of osteomyelitis of the jaws includes causes other than purely odontogenic infections, the bacterial spectrum is broad. Most instances of osteomyelitis of the jaws are caused by aerobic streptococci (alpha-hemolytic streptococci, *Streptococcus* viridans group), anaerobic streptococci, and other anaerobes, particularly peptostreptococci, fusobacteria, and *Bacteroides* and related genera.[49] Only occasional cases are caused by *S. aureus,* with entry through the skin as the probable route. Other bacteria involved include oral anaerobes, aerobic and microaerophilic cocci, and gram-negative organisms. Specific forms of osteomyelitis are caused by *Actinomyces israelii, Treponema pallidum,* and *Mycobacterium tuberculosis. Salmonella* organisms have been associated with osteomyelitis of the jaws in patients with sickle-cell anemia.[9]

CLINICAL FINDINGS

Osteomyelitis involves the mandible far more frequently than the maxilla because the relatively poor blood supply to the mandible comes primarily from one major vessel and the periosteal blood supply. Four major forms of the disease, which may be distinguished clinically, are (1) acute suppurative; (2) secondary chronic, the form that begins as an acute osteomyelitis and becomes chronic; (3) primary chronic, the form that has no acute phase and always has appeared to be a low-grade infection; and (4) nonsuppurative osteomyelitis. Those most often seen in children are the acute suppurative, the secondary chronic, and one nonsuppurative form, Garré sclerosing osteomyelitis. These conditions are described in some detail.

SUPPURATIVE OSTEOMYELITIS

Suppurative osteomyelitis usually begins with deep and intense pain in the jaws, high intermittent fever, and an obvious cause, most often a deeply carious or discolored tooth. In the early stages, mental nerve paresthesia is occasionally present. During the course of several days, facial swelling develops, and in 10 to 14 days, teeth begin to loosen, pus exudes around the gingival sulcus, and multiple mucosal or cutaneous sinus tracks form. In addition to the draining sinuses, a firm cellulitis is present in the soft tissues accompanied by trismus and cervical lymphadenopathy. A leukocytosis, ranging typically from 8000 to 15,000 cells/mm^3, is present, although it does not ordinarily reach the levels that are seen in acute osteomyelitis of the long bones. After 10 days to 2 weeks, radiographs may show scattered areas of bone destruction suggestive of a moth-eaten appearance (Fig. 9–14), and periosteal reaction characterized by the laying down of new bone commonly is seen. Smears of specimens and cultures, including cultures of bone sequestra, should be taken whenever possible. Interpretation of cultures must be made with caution because of the possibility of skin and oral contaminants in the specimen.

Initially, antibiotics doses adjusted for age are given empirically with a regimen described in Table 9–5. As results from smears and culture are obtained, antibiotics may be changed, unless the infection is responding favorably, in which case no change is made. The involved tooth is removed as early as possible to allow drainage and to provide material for culture.

Antibiotic therapy is continued for at least 2 to 4 weeks after all symptoms subside. If the infection persists, repeated cultures are obtained and the antibiotic is changed if necessary. The greater vascularity of the jaws may explain their more rapid response to antibiotic therapy and surgery compared with long bones. Therefore, the duration of intravenous antibiotic therapy in osteomyelitis of the jaws may not need to be as prolonged as in that of the long bones. Consideration should be given to sequestrectomy, saucerization, or the placement of closed-wound irrigation and suction. Saucerization involves the removal of teeth in the immediate area and removal of the overlying buccal plate of bone, allowing access to the medullary portion and sequestra that may be present. Placement of catheters through an extraoral approach occasionally is necessary for closed irrigation and suction. It permits instillation of antibiotics, allowing direct contact with the bone. Hyperbaric oxygen treatment may be considered in chronic cases refractory to antibiotic treatment.[43]

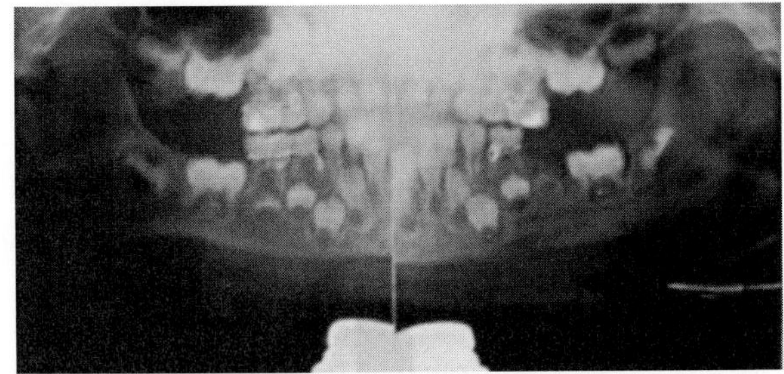

FIGURE 9–14 ■ Radiograph of the jaws of a 4-year-old girl with suppurative osteomyelitis of the left mandible. The film shows marked destruction of the body and ramus of the mandible.

INFANTILE OSTEOMYELITIS

Osteomyelitis of the jaws in the newborn is an uncommon finding but worthy of special mention because of its serious sequelae. It occurs most often a few weeks after birth and usually involves the maxilla. It is not odontogenic in origin but is thought to arise from neonatal trauma to oral tissues, hematogenous spread (from skin, middle ear, mastoid, or tonsils), or an infected nipple.[52] The patient presents with a facial cellulitis centered about the orbit (Fig. 9–15). Irritability and malaise precede cellulitis and are followed by marked elevation in temperature, anorexia, and dehydration. Extraorally, inner canthal swelling, palpebral edema

TABLE 9–5 ■ RECOMMENDED ANTIBIOTIC REGIMEN FOR OSTEOMYELITIS OF THE JAWS

Empirical Therapy	
Regimen I	1. Aqueous penicillin, 250,000 units/kg/24 hr in 6 divided doses IV, *with* 2. Oxacillin, 200 mg/kg/24 hr in 4 divided doses IV. When patient has been asymptomatic for 48 to 72 hours, switch to regimen II.
Regimen II	1. Penicillin V, 50 mg/kg/24 hr in 6 divided doses PO, *with* 2. Dicloxacillin, 75 mg/kg/24 hr in 4 divided doses PO for an additional 2 to 4 weeks
Regimen III	1. Clindamycin, 30 mg/kg/24 hr in 3 divided doses IV, *then* 2. Clindamycin, 30 mg/kg/24 hr in 3 divided doses PO
Initial Therapy with Gram Stain Results	
Smear suggestive of staphylococcal infection	
Regimen IV	Oxacillin, 200 mg/kg/24 hr in 4 divided doses IV. When patient has been asymptomatic for 48 to 72 hours, switch to regimen IV.
Regimen V	Dicloxacillin, 75 mg/kg/24 hr in 4 divided doses PO for an additional 2 to 4 weeks
Smear suggestive of anaerobic infection	
Regimen VI	Aqueous penicillin, 250,000 units/kg/24 hr in 6 divided doses IV. When patient has been asymptomatic for 48 to 72 hours, change to penicillin V, 50 mg/kg/24 hr in 6 divided doses PO for 2 to 4 weeks
Smear suggestive of both staphylococcal and anaerobic organisms	
Regimen I initially	
Therapy in Cases of Allergy to Penicillin (in order of preference)	
1. Clindamycin, 30 mg/kg/24 hr in 3 divided doses IV, *then* Clindamycin, 30 mg/kg/24 hr in 3 divided doses PO	
2. Cephalosporin: Cefazolin, 80 mg/kg/24 hr in 4 divided doses IV Cephalexin, 50 mg/kg/24 hr in 4 divided doses PO	

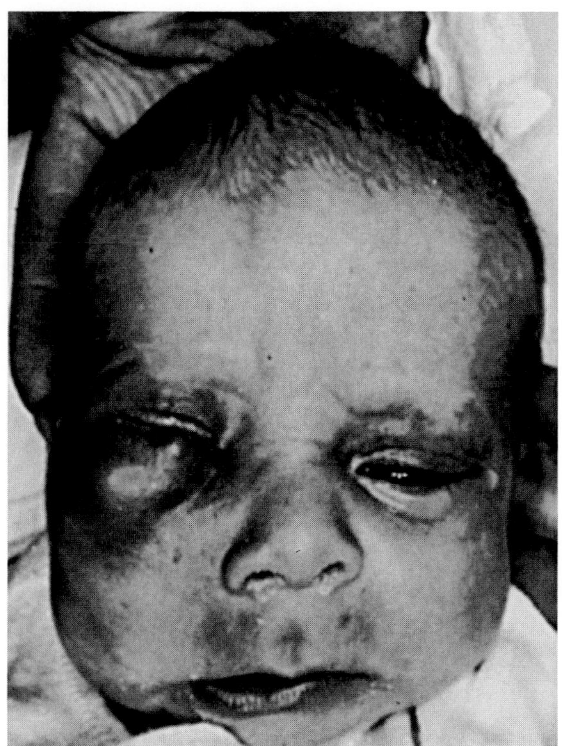

FIGURE 9–15 ■ Characteristic clinical picture of a 3-week-old child with infantile osteomyelitis. (Courtesy of Dr. M. Michael Cohen, Sr.)

with closure of the eye, conjunctivitis, and proptosis may be seen together with a purulent discharge from the nose or from the inner canthus. Oral examination shows swelling of the maxilla on the affected side extending to both the buccal and the palatal regions, with fluctuation often present with multiple sinus tracks. *S. aureus* is the organism usually found.

Aggressive, prompt treatment must be undertaken to prevent permanent optic damage, neurologic complications, loss of tooth buds and bone, and extension to the dural sinuses. Intravenous penicillin and a penicillinase-resistant penicillin are given simultaneously with surgical drainage of all fluctuant areas, repeated Gram smears, and culture and sensitivity testing. Antibiotics are continued orally for 2 to 4 weeks after all signs of the infection have disappeared. If sequestra form, they should be removed conservatively. Of note is that tooth buds may be lost, and surviving teeth may be deformed or discolored after eruption.

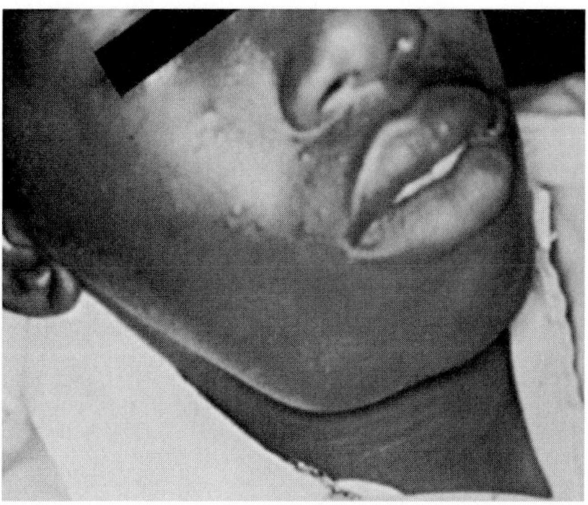

FIGURE 9–16 ■ Enlargement of the right side of the mandible in a 12-year-old patient with Garré sclerosing osteomyelitis. The swelling is hard and nontender.

GARRÉ SCLEROSING OSTEOMYELITIS

This condition, also known as chronic nonsuppurative sclerosing osteomyelitis and proliferative osteomyelitis of Garré,[4] is notable because of the similarity of some of its characteristics to those of other neoperiostoses. It is characterized by a localized, hard, nontender swelling of the mandible (Fig. 9–16). Lymphadenopathy, hyperpyrexia, and leukocytosis are not present. It is associated commonly with a carious tooth, usually the lower first molar (Fig. 9–17),

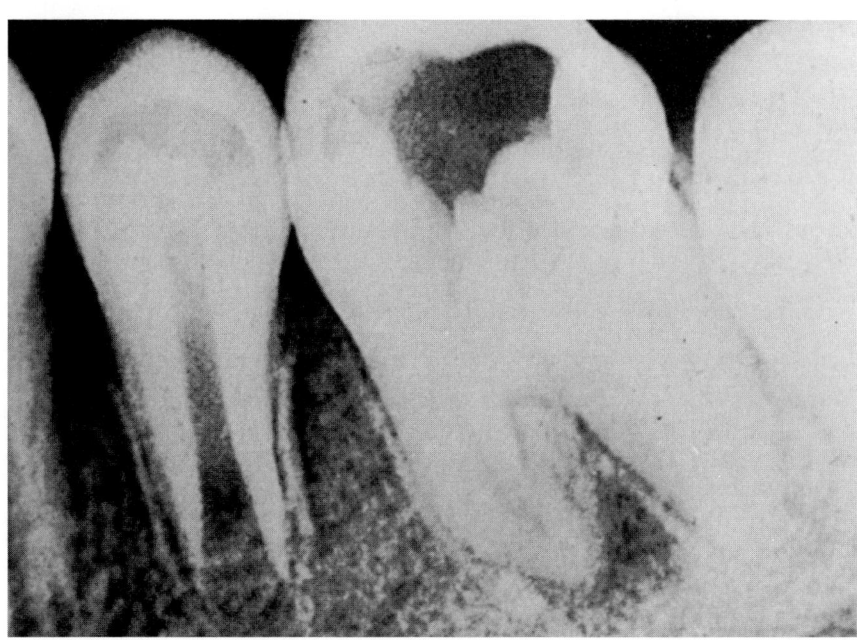

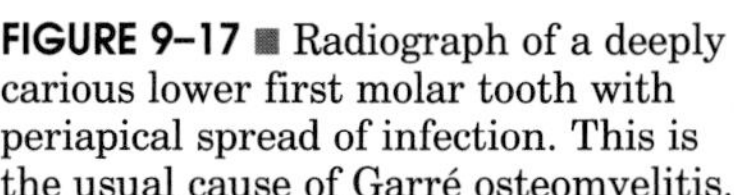

FIGURE 9–17 ■ Radiograph of a deeply carious lower first molar tooth with periapical spread of infection. This is the usual cause of Garré osteomyelitis.

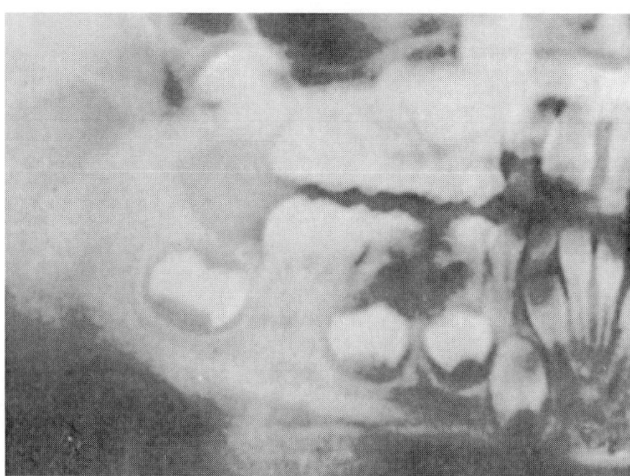

FIGURE 9–18 ■ Characteristic radiograph of Garré osteomyelitis showing the laminated or onion-peel appearance of the mass. (Courtesy of Dr. Larry J. Peterson.)

and a history of a past toothache. It also may be associated with a recent dental extraction or an infected flap of tissue over an erupting tooth.[36] Radiographs are impressive, showing a focal area of well-calcified bone proliferation that is smooth and that often has a laminated or onion-peel appearance (Fig. 9–18).

Garré osteomyelitis is thought to be a response to a low-grade stimulus, such as a dental infection, that influences the potentially active periosteum of young individuals. Its appearance resembles that of infantile cortical hyperostosis (Caffey disease), osteosarcoma, and Ewing sarcoma and must be distinguished from them.[11] Treatment consists of extraction or endodontic treatment of the involved tooth, with continued clinical and radiographic follow-up of the patient to ensure that the new bone formation does not progress. Ordinarily, remodeling occurs over time, but biopsy should be performed to rule out neoplasm if the lesion does not regress. No antibiotic therapy is necessary.

Herpes Simplex Virus Infections

Herpes simplex virus type 1 infections[59] commonly are manifested as herpetic gingivostomatitis. Five stages of infection have been identified: (1) primary mucocutaneous infection, (2) acute infection of ganglia, (3) establishment of latency, (4) reactivation, and (5) recurrent infection.

Primary infection is established by direct contact either with people who have draining lesions or with an asymptomatic carrier who may continue to shed the virus despite the lack of symptoms. The highest incidence of primary infection appears to be between the ages of 2 and 4 years. Infants are protected by maternal antibodies. A series of 19,000 children with gingivostomatitis recorded by Jauretic in 1966 contained no cases in infants younger than 6 months. There appears to be no seasonal variation or male and female difference in incidence.

The incubation period is thought to be approximately 6 days, followed by the development of small vesicles that may coalesce to form larger lesions or ulcers. In severe cases, the lips, gingivae, oral mucosa, and pharynx may be involved. Many patients with primary herpes labialis may be asymptomatic, however, and symptoms may not develop. Healing occurs in 1 to 2 weeks, with gradual crusting of the lesions followed by re-epithelialization.

Latency is thought to continue throughout life, with reactivation occurring at various times, possibly triggered by actinic radiation and emotional or physical stress. Recurrent disease is manifested by vesicles at the mucocutaneous border, which are painful for about 2 days, followed by crusting and complete healing in 7 to 8 days.

Up to 50 percent of the adult population in industrialized countries and a higher percentage in less developed nations may suffer from recurrent herpes labialis. Surprisingly, many if not most adults who suffer from recurrent "cold sores" are not aware that they can transmit the disease and should be counseled in this regard. Likewise, medical, dental, and nursing personnel also should be advised that occurrence of cutaneous lesions (the herpetic whitlow) is not unknown after direct contact of the practitioner's fingers with lesions during the physical examination.

REFERENCES

1. Balcerak, R. J., Sisto, J. M., and Bosack, R. C.: Cervicofacial necrotizing fasciitis: Report of three cases and literature review. J. Oral Maxillofac. Surg. *46*:450–459, 1988.
2. Barkin, R., Bonis, S., Elzhammer, R., et al.: Ludwig's angina in children. J. Pediatr. *87*:563–565, 1975.
3. Bartlett, J. G., and Gorbach, S. L.: Anaerobic infections of the head and neck. Otolaryngol. Clin. North Am. *9*:655–678, 1976.
4. Benca, P. G., Mostofi, R., and Kuo P.: Proliferative periostitis (Garré's osteomyelitis). Oral Surg. *63*:258–260, 1987.
5. Brook, I., Frazier, E. H., and Gher, M. E.: Aerobic and anaerobic microbiology of periapical abscess. Oral Microbiol. Immunol. *6*:123–125, 1991.
6. Busch, D. E.: Anaerobes in infections of the head and neck and ear, nose, and throat. Rev. Infect. Dis. *6*:S115–S122, 1984.
7. Chow, A. W., Roser, S. M., and Brady, F. A.: Orofacial odontogenic infections. Ann. Intern. Med. *88*:392–402, 1978.
8. Coykendall, A. L.: Classification and identification of the viridans streptococci. Clin. Microbiol. Rev. *2*:315–328, 1989.
9. Daramola, J. O.: Massive osteomyelitis of the mandible complicating sickle cell disease: Report of case. J. Oral Surg. *39*:144–146, 1981.
10. Dodson, T. B., Perrott, D. H., and Kaban, L. B.: Pediatric maxillofacial infections: A retrospective study of 113 patients. J. Oral Maxillofac. Surg. *47*:327–330, 1989.
11. Eversole, L. R., Lieder, A. S., Gorwin, J. O., et al.: Proliferative periostitis of Garré: Its differentiation from other neoperiostoses. J. Oral Surg. *37*:725–731, 1979.
12. Fisher, A. D.: Osteomyelitis of the mandible in a child. J. Oral Surg. *353*:60–63, 1977.
13. Flynn, T. R., Wiltz, M., Adamo A. K., et al.: Predicting length of hospital stay and penicillin failure in severe odontogenic infections. Int. J. Oral Maxillofac. Surg. *28*(Suppl. 1):48, 1999.
14. Gilmore, W. C., Jacobus, N. V., Gorbach, S. L., et al.: A prospective double-blind evaluation of penicillin versus clindamycin in the treatment of odontogenic infections. J. Oral Maxillofac. Surg. *46*:1065–1070, 1988.
15. Givner, L. B., Mason, E. O., Barson, W. J., et al.: Pneumococcal facial cellulitis in children. Pediatrics *106*:E61, 2000.
16. Goldberg, M. H., and Topazian, R. G.: Odontogenic infection and deep fascial space infection of dental origin. *In* Topazian, R. G., and Goldberg, M. H. (eds.): Oral and Maxillofacial Infections. 3rd ed. Philadelphia, W. B. Saunders, 1994, pp. 198–250.
17. Granite, E. L.: Anatomic considerations in infections of the face and neck. J. Oral Surg. *34*:34–44, 1976.
18. Grodinsky, M., and Holyoke, E.: The fascia and fascial spaces of the head and neck and adjacent regions. Am. J. Anat. *63*:367–407, 1938.
19. Gross, S., and Nieburg, P.: Ludwig's angina in childhood. Am. J. Dis. Child. *131*:291–292, 1977.
20. Hall, H. D., Gunter, J. W., Jr., Jamison, H. C., et al.: Effect of time of extraction on resolution of odontogenic cellulitis. J. Am. Dent. Assoc. *77*:626–631, 1968.
21. Handal, T., and Olsen, I.: Antimicrobial resistance with focus on oral beta-lactamases. Eur. J. Oral Sci. *108*:163–174, 2000.
22. Haug, R. H., Hoffman, M. J., and Indresano, A. T.: An epidemiologic and anatomic survey of odontogenic infections. J. Oral Maxillofac. Surg. *49*:976–980, 1991.

23. Heidrun, P. L., Reichart, E., Schmitt, W., et al.: Investigation of infectious organisms causing pericoronitis of the mandibular third molar. J. Oral Maxillofac. Surg. *58*:611–616, 2000.
24. Heimdahl, A., Von Konow, L., Satoh, T., et al.: Clinical appearance of orofacial infections of odontogenic origin in relation to microbiological findings. J. Clin. Microbiol. *22*:299–302, 1985.
25. Howe, G.: Orofacial infections and their management. *In* Howe, G. (ed.): Minor Oral Surgery. Bristol, John Wright & Sons, 1966.
26. Kaban, L., and McGill, T.: Orbital cellulitis of dental origin: Differential diagnosis and the use of computed tomography as a diagnostic aid. J. Oral Surg. *38*:682–685, 1980.
27. Katz, M. H., Mastrucci, M. T., Leggott, P. J., et al.: Prognostic significance of oral lesions in children with perinatally acquired human immunodeficiency virus infection. Am. J. Dis. Child. *147*:45–48, 1993.
28. Ketchem, L., Berkowitz, R. J., McIlveen, L., et al.: Oral findings in HIV-seropositive children. Pediatr. Dent. *12*:143–146, 1990.
29. Kuriyama, T., Nakagawa, K., Karasawa, T., et al.: Past administration of beta-lactam antibiotics and increase in the emergence of beta-lactamase–producing bacteria in patients with orofacial odontogenic infections. Oral Surg. Oral Med. Oral Pathol. Oral Radiol. Endod. *89*:186–192, 2000.
30. Krogh, H. W.: Extraction of teeth in the presence of acute infections. J. Oral Surg. *9*:136–151, 1951.
31. Leggott, P. J.: Oral manifestations of HIV infection in children. Oral Surg. *73*:187–192, 1992.
32. Lesco, B., and Brownstein, M. P.: Recognition of periodontal disease in children. Pediatr. Clin. North Am. *29*:457–474, 1982.
33. Levitt, G. W.: Cervical fascia and deep neck infections. Otolaryngol. Clin. North Am. *9*:703–716, 1976.
34. Lewis, M. A. O., MacFarlane, T. W., and McGowan, D. A.: Quantitative bacteriology of acute dentoalveolar abscesses. J. Med. Microbiol. *21*:101–104, 1986.
35. Lewis, M. A. O., MacFarlane, T. W., McGowan, D. A., et al.: Assessment of the pathogenicity of bacterial species plated from acute dentoalveolar abscesses. J. Med. Microbiol. *27*:109–116, 1988.
36. Lichty, G., Langlais, R. P., and Aufdemorte, T.: Garrè's osteomyelitis: Literature review and case report. Oral Surg. *50*:309–313, 1980.
37. Magnusson, B. O., Matsson, L., and Modeen, T.: Gingivitis and periodontal disease in children. *In* Magnusson, B. O., Koch, B., and Poulsen, S. (eds.): Pedodontics: A Systematic Approach. Copenhagen, Munksgaard, 1981.
38. Mampalam, T. J., and Rosenblum, M. L.: Trends in the management of bacterial brain abscesses: A review of 102 cases over 17 years. Neurosurgery *23*:451–458, 1988.
39. Maniglia, A. J., Goodwin, W. J., Arnold, J. E., et al.: Intracranial abscesses secondary to nasal, sinus, and orbital infections in adults and children. Arch. Otolaryngol. Head Neck Surg. *115*:1424–1429, 1989.
40. Marchisio, P., and Principi, N.: Treatment of oropharyngeal candidiasis in HIV-infected children with oral fluconazole. Eur. J. Clin. Microbiol. Infect. Dis. *13*:338, 1994.
41. Martis, C. S., and Karakasis, D. T.: Extractions in the presence of acute infections. J. Dent. Res. *54*:59–61, 1975.
42. Martis, C. S., Karabouta, I., and Lazaridis, N.: Extraction of impacted mandibular wisdom teeth in the presence of acute infection. Int. J. Oral Surg. *7*:541–548, 1978.
43. Marx, R., Johnson, R., and Kline, S.: Prevention of osteoradionecrosis: A randomized prospective clinical trial of hyperbaric oxygen vs. penicillin. J. Am. Dent. Assoc. *111*:49–54, 1985.
44. Massler, M.: Epidemiology of gingivitis in children. J. Am. Dent. Assoc. *45*:319, 1952.
45. McCarthy, C., Snyder, M. G., and Parker, R. B.: The indigenous oral flora of man. I. The newborn to one-year-old infant. Arch. Oral Biol. *10*:61–70, 1975.
46. Moenning, J., Nelson, C., and Kohler, R.: The microbiology and chemotherapy of odontogenic infections. J. Oral Maxillofac. Surg. *43*:976–985, 1989.
47. Morhert, R. E., and Fitzgerald, R. J.: Nutritional determinants of the ecology of the oral flora. Dent. Clin. North Am. *42*:473–489, 1976.
48. O'Sullivan, E. A., Duggal, M. S., Bailey, C. C., et al.: Changes in the oral microflora during cytotoxic chemotherapy in children being treated for acute leukemia. Oral Surg. *76*:161–168, 1993.
49. Peterson, L. J.: Microbiology of head and neck infections. Oral Maxillofac. Clin. North Am. *3*:247, 1991.
50. Piecuch, J. F.: Odontogenic infections. Dent. Clin. North Am. *26*:129–145, 1982.
51. Price, C. D., Hameroff, S. B., and Richards, R. D.: Cavernous sinus thrombosis and orbital cellulitis. South. Med. J. *64*:1243–1247, 1971.
52. Raymon, Y., Oberman, M., Horowitz, I., et al.: Osteomyelitis of the maxilla in the newborn. Int. J. Oral Surg. *6*:90–94, 1977.
53. Rogers, A. H.: The oral cavity as a source of potential pathogens in focal infection. Dent. Clin. North Am. *42*:245–248, 1976.
54. Rud, J.: Removal of impacted lower third molars with acute pericoronitis and necrotizing gingivitis. Br. J. Oral Surg. *7*:153–160, 1970.
55. Schwaber, M. K., Pensak, M. L., and Bartels, L. J.: The early signs and symptoms of neurotologic complications of chronic suppurative otitis media. Laryngoscope *99*:373–375, 1989.
56. Shah, H. N., and Collins, D. M.: *Prevotella,* a new genus to include *Bacteroides melaninogenicus* and related species formerly classified in the genus *Bacteroides*. Int. J. Systemat. Bacteriol. *40*:205–208, 1990.
57. Shah, H. N., and Collins, D. M.: Proposal for reclassification of *Bacteroides asaccharolyticus, Bacteroides gingivalis,* and *Bacteroides endodontalis* in a new genus, *Porphyromonas*. Int. J. Systemat. Bacteriol. *38*:128, 1988.
58. Socransky, S., and Manganiello, S.: The oral microbiota of man from birth to senility. J. Periodontol. *42*:485–496, 1971.
59. Straus, S. E. (moderator): Herpes simplex virus infection: Biology, treatment, prevention. NIH Conference. Ann. Intern. Med. *103*:404, 1985.
60. Summers, G. W.: The diagnosis and management of dental infections. Otolaryngol. Clin. North Am. *9*:717–728, 1976.
61. Sundqvist, G.: Taxonomy, ecology, and pathogenicity of the root canal flora. Oral Surg. *78*:522–530, 1994.
62. Topazian, R. G.: Uncommon infections of the oral and maxillofacial regions. *In* Topazian, R. G., and Goldberg, M. H. (eds.): Oral and Maxillofacial Infections. 3rd ed. Philadelphia, W. B. Saunders, 1994, pp. 407–429.
63. Traub, W. H.: Brain abscess and acute purulent meningitis: Recent developments in clinical microbiology. *In* Schiefer, W., Klinger, M., and Brock, M. (eds.): Brain Abscess and Meningitis: Subarachnoid Hemorrhage: Timing Problems. New York, Springer-Verlag, 1981.
64. Valdez, I. H., Pizzo, P. A., and Atkinson, J. C.: Oral health of pediatric AIDS patients: A hospital-based study. J. Dent. Child. *61*:114–148, 1994.
65. Woods, R.: Pyogenic dental infections: A ten-year review. Aust. Dent. J. *23*:107–111, 1978.

Pharyngitis (Pharyngitis, Tonsillitis, Tonsillopharyngitis, and Nasopharyngitis)

JAMES D. CHERRY

Pharyngitis is an inflammatory illness of the mucous membranes and underlying structures of the throat. The clinical diagnostic category includes tonsillitis, tonsillopharyngitis, and nasopharyngitis; inflammation also frequently involves the nasopharynx, uvula, and soft palate. Illness usually is acute but may also be subacute or chronic. Diagnosis of pharyngitis requires objective evidence of inflammation (erythema, exudate, or ulceration). The symptom of sore throat invariably accompanies pharyngitis, but it should not be used as the sole criterion; sore throat is a common

TABLE 10–1 ■ ETIOLOGIC AGENTS OF NASOPHARYNGITIS

Etiologic Agent	Type of Pharyngeal Lesion*			Relative Importance of Nasal and Pharyngeal Symptoms†		Frequency of Pharyngitis†	Main Season	Duration of Pharyngitis
	Erythematous	Follicular	Exudative	Nasal	Pharyngeal			
Bacteria								
Corynebacterium diphtheriae[159]	+++		++++	+	+++	+	Fall, winter, spring	Acute, subacute
Haemophilus influenzae[152]	++			++	++	+	Fall, winter, spring	Acute, subacute
Neisseria meningitidis[133]	++			+	+++	+	Fall, winter, spring	Acute, subacute
Viruses								
Adenoviruses[10, 29, 77, 101, 113, 132, 136, 148]	++++	++++	++	+	+++	++++	All seasons	Acute
Enteroviruses (polio, coxsackieviruses A and B, echovirus)[19, 28, 77, 78, 101, 129, 130, 153]	+++		+	+	+++	+++	Summer, fall	Acute
Influenza A and B[77, 111, 119, 127, 139]	+++			+	+++	++	Fall, winter	Acute
Parainfluenza 1–4[6, 61, 68, 69, 75, 107, 110, 112, 120, 126, 139]	++		+	+++	+	++	Fall, winter, spring	Acute
Respiratory syncytial[18, 66, 69, 96, 112]	++			+++	+	+	Fall, winter, spring	Acute
Rhinoviruses[63, 77]	+			+++	+	+	Fall, winter, spring	Acute
Rotaviruses[60, 87, 96, 122]	++			++	++	++	Fall, winter, spring	Acute
Rickettsia								
Coxiella burnetii[73]	++			++	++	+	All seasons	Acute

*Pluses indicate the relative degree and severity of the lesion (++++, most marked; +, minimal).
† Each +, 25%.
‡ ++++, 76 to 100 percent; +++, 51 to 75 percent; ++, 26 to 50 percent; +, 1 to 25 percent.

complaint of children with colds in whom no objective evidence of pharyngeal inflammation is present.

Although the clinical finding of pharyngitis suggests an almost exclusive group A streptococcal etiology to many physicians, etiologic considerations should include a multitude of viruses, bacteria, and other infectious and noninfectious agents. Etiologically, pharyngitis is subdivided conveniently into two categories: illness with nasal symptoms (nasopharyngitis) and illness without nasal involvement (pharyngitis or tonsillopharyngitis). In acute illness, nasopharyngitis nearly always is of viral etiology, whereas pharyngitis without nasal signs has diverse etiologic possibilities, including bacteria, viruses, fungi, and other infectious agents. Here, nasopharyngitis and pharyngitis without nasal involvement are considered separately.

History

Although throat inflammation undoubtedly has been a physical finding of disease throughout human existence, only in relatively recent years has attention been given to pharyngitis as a primary complaint. The throat findings of diphtheria were mentioned in the third century AD,[142] and Vincent angina was noted in the military before the Christian era,[40] but group A streptococcal infection and pharyngitis were not clearly associated until World War II.[26, 121] Although Glover and Griffith[53] mentioned streptococcal tonsillitis in 1931, the major reference to streptococci in the pre-antibiotic era was in association with scarlet fever, erysipelas, and suppurative processes.[20]

Nasopharyngitis

ETIOLOGIC AGENTS

Etiologic agents of nasopharyngitis, categorized by type of lesion, frequency and season of occurrence, and duration of illness, are listed in Table 10–1. The relative importance of nasal and pharyngeal manifestations also is presented.

Although Table 10–1 shows three bacterial agents and one rickettsia, the overwhelming majority of nasopharyngitis occurrence is caused by viral infections. The specific infectious agents are discussed fully in their respective sections of this book; therefore, only an overview is presented here.

Adenoviruses are the most common cause of nasopharyngitis; types 1, 2, 3, 4, 5, 6, 7, 7a, 9, 14, and 15 account for most illnesses.[10, 29, 74, 101, 113, 132, 136, 148] Nasopharyngitis also commonly occurs with influenza and parainfluenza viral infections.* Although rhinoviral and respiratory syncytial viral infections are common occurrences in children and both always have nasal manifestations (coryza), the occurrence of objective pharyngeal manifestations is uncommon.[18, 63, 66–69, 74, 96, 112] Respiratory symptoms with cough, nasal discharge, and pharyngitis frequently occur in children with rotaviral gastroenteritis.[60, 87, 122]

*See references 6, 61, 68, 69, 74, 75, 107, 110–112, 119, 120, 127, 139.

EPIDEMIOLOGY

Nasopharyngitis is a common illness of childhood. It tends to be most prevalent in young children, in association with primary infections with respiratory viruses. Nasal symptoms with enteroviruses occur less frequently in school-age children than in preschool-age children. In contrast, older children rarely have pharyngitis with respiratory syncytial viral, parainfluenza viral, and rhinoviral infections. Nasopharyngitis caused by adenoviral infection is a particularly frequent occurrence in the adolescent and young adult in military training.[29, 132, 148]

Nasopharyngitis occurs more commonly during the cold weather months (see Table 10–1). No apparent sex predilection has been found. The method of transmission is similar to that of other respiratory viral infections (see Chapter 8).

PATHOPHYSIOLOGY

The pathophysiology of nasopharyngitis is presented in Chapter 8 and in the pharyngitis section of this chapter, as well as in the chapters discussing the individual viral agents. In nasopharyngitis associated with *Haemophilus influenzae* and *Neisseria meningitidis*, the nasal symptoms probably result from a concomitant respiratory viral infection.[20]

CLINICAL PRESENTATION

Because nasopharyngitis is caused by many different etiologic agents, a reasonable expectation is varied clinical manifestations. These differences are highlighted in Table 10–1. Fever occurs in nearly all cases of nasopharyngitis. With adenoviral and influenza viral disease, the pharyngeal findings are most prominent; with the other respiratory viruses, coryza is more notable than are pharyngeal complaints. In adenoviral infections, follicular pharyngitis is the rule, and exudate is common. In contrast, patients with the other respiratory viral infections usually present with only pharyngeal erythema. Nasopharyngitis of a viral etiology most often is an acute, self-limited disease lasting 4 to 10 days. In general, adenoviral illnesses tend to be more prolonged than are those resulting from the other respiratory viruses. Other symptoms in nasopharyngitis are related to the causative virus. For example, parainfluenza and respiratory syncytial viral infections might also have lower respiratory tract findings (laryngotracheitis, pneumonia, or bronchiolitis), and influenza might be associated with more severe, generalized complaints.

Although respiratory symptoms in association with rotaviral gastroenteritis have been noted frequently, little careful clinical study of the respiratory manifestations has been performed. Lewis and associates,[87] in a careful study, observed a statistically significant occurrence of nasal discharge, cough, and red throat in children with rotaviral diarrhea compared with children with diarrhea caused by other agents.

Nasopharyngitis with *H. influenzae* or *N. meningitidis* infections has been noted mainly in people with septicemia and meningitis. The nasal symptoms (coryza) usually preceded the pharyngitis and the severe systemic disease by a few to several days. In Q fever, the predominant finding is pneumonia. With diphtheria, the exudative pharyngitis and constitutional symptoms are most prominent.

DIFFERENTIAL DIAGNOSIS AND TREATMENT

See the following sections.

Pharyngitis, Tonsillitis, and Tonsillopharyngitis

ETIOLOGIC AGENTS

Etiologic agents of pharyngitis categorized by type of lesion, frequency of occurrence, and duration of illness are presented in Table 10–2. A great number of diverse possibilities exist for the differential diagnosis of pharyngitis. The specific agents or factors are presented in their respective sections of this book, and, therefore, only an overview is given here.

As with all infectious diseases, etiologic prevalence depends on multiple factors (status of the host, age, season, environment, exposure, and type of lesion) that must be considered in each individual case. In otherwise healthy children, the following infectious agents account for more than 90 percent of acute infections with pharyngeal involvement: *Streptococcus pyogenes*; adenoviruses; influenza viruses A and B; parainfluenza viruses 1, 2, and 3; Epstein-Barr virus; enteroviruses; and *Mycoplasma pneumoniae*.*

Although the group A streptococcus is suggested frequently[20] as the only worthy bacterial consideration in the etiology of pharyngitis, the data in Table 10–2 indicate broader possibilities. For example, when streptococci with beta-hemolysis recovered from children and adolescents with pharyngitis are typed, group B, C, and G strains occasionally are found.[5, 23, 25, 48, 64, 144, 145] Turner and associates[145] found that of the group C streptococci, only *Streptococcus equisimilis* caused pharyngitis; *Streptococcus anginosus (Streptococcus milleri)* was part of the normal oropharyngeal flora.

Laboratory accidents have provided evidence that *H. influenzae* can cause pharyngitis,[109, 151] and children with systemic illnesses caused by *H. influenzae* and *N. meningitidis* frequently have an associated marked pharyngitis.[131, 152, 156] *Arcanobacterium haemolyticum* and *Corynebacterium ulcerans* occasionally cause an illness mimicking diphtheria.[13, 59, 76, 80, 92, 114] *A. haemolyticum* also causes an illness that has been confused with streptococcal scarlet fever.[39, 76, 89, 92]

Because anaerobic microorganisms are universal constituents of the normal throat flora, assigning etiologic significance to these agents in throat infections frequently is difficult. However, Vincent stomatitis and angina appear to be the results of mixed infections with anaerobes.[41, 54, 91, 147] Brook and Gober[12] noted a significant association between encapsulated organisms of the *Bacteroides melaninogenicus* group (*Prevotella melaninogenica*) and acute tonsillitis in children. My impression is that acute and subacute infections with anaerobes account for numerous pharyngeal infections in adolescents in which cultures do not reveal group A streptococci and infectious mononucleosis test results are negative. Gonococcal and treponemal infections should be considered in sexually active or known exposed teenagers and other children.[15, 27, 42, 72, 155]

Adenoviral types 1, 2, 3, 4, 5, 6, 7, 7a, 9, 11, 14, 15, and 16 are the most common causes of pharyngitis in young children, and they also are prominent etiologic agents in older

*See references 1, 6, 10, 11, 19, 22, 28, 29, 32, 36, 52, 56, 61, 65, 68, 69, 75, 77, 78, 100–102, 107, 110–113, 119, 120, 126–130, 132, 134, 136, 137, 148, 149, 153.

TABLE 10–2 ■ ETIOLOGIC AGENTS OF PHARYNGITIS

Etiologic Agent or Factor	Type of Lesion*					Frequency of Occurrence†	Duration of Pharyngitis
	Erythematous	Follicular	Exudative	Ulcerative	Petechial		
Bacteria							
Streptococcus pyogenes[11,32,36,52,100,102,128,137]	++++	++	+++		+++	++++	Acute
Other streptococci (groups B, C, and G)[2,23–25,48,64,144,145]	+++	+	++			++	Acute
Corynebacterium diphtheriae[97,128,159]	+++		++++			+	Acute
Corynebacterium pyogenes[150]	++++		++++			+	Acute
Corynebacterium ulcerans[89,114,141]	++++		+++			+	Acute
Arcanobacterium haemolyticum[4,13,39,59,76,80,92]	++++	++	+++			+	Acute
Mixed anaerobes (*Bacteroides* species, *Peptostreptococcus, Fusobacterium* species)[12,14,41,54,91,147]	++++		+	++++		++	Subacute
Actinomyces species[41]	+			+		+	Chronic
Francisella tularensis[71,146,157]	++++		+++			+	Acute,
Haemophilus influenzae[109,138,151,152,156]	++					++	Acute, subacute
Legionella pneumophila[105]	++++					+	Acute
Neisseria meningitidis[131]	++		+			++	Acute
Neisseria gonorrhoeae[72,155]	++		+			+	Acute, subacute, chronic
Leptospira species[70,115]	++++					+	Acute
Treponema pallidum[15,27,42]	+	+		+		+	Subacute
Borrelia species[84]	++++					+	Acute
Streptobacillus moniliformis[118]	+					+	Acute
Yersinia enterocolitica[123,140]	++++		++			+	Acute
Yersinia pseudotuberculosis[125]							
Streptococcus pneumoniae[94]	+			+		+	Acute
Salmonella typhi[3,106]	+					+	Acute
Chlamydia							
Chlamydia pneumoniae[57]	++++					++	Acute
Chlamydia trachomatis[108]	++	+	+			+	Acute, recurrent
Viruses							
Adenoviruses[10,29,101,104,113,132,148]	++++	++++	++			++++	Acute
Influenza A and B[111,119,127,139]	+++					+++	Acute
Parainfluenza 1–4[6,61,68,69,75,107,110,112,120,126,139]	++					+++	Acute
Respiratory syncytial[18,66–69,96,112]	++					+	Acute
Enteroviruses (polio, coxsackieviruses A and B, echovirus)[1,19,28,78,101,129,130,134,153]	+++		+	++		+++	Acute
Epstein-Barr[65,149]	+++	+	++++		++	+++	Acute, subacute
Reoviruses[86,158]	++					+	Acute
Cytomegalovirus[9,82]	+					+	Acute
Herpes simplex[17,20,36,101,154]	++		++	++++		++	Acute
Measles[21]	+++				+	++	Acute
Rubella[21,43]					++	+	Acute
Rhinoviruses[63]	+					+	Acute
Human immunodeficiency virus (HIV)[8]	++						Acute
Mycoplasma							
Mycoplasma pneumoniae[22,52,56,69]	++	+	+			++	Acute
Mycoplasma hominis[103]	+		+			+	Acute
Rickettsia							
Coxiella burnetii[35,73]	++					+	Acute
Fungi							
Candida species[85,133]	+		++++			+++	Acute, subacute, chronic

Continued

TABLE 10–2 ■ ETIOLOGIC AGENTS OF PHARYNGITIS—cont'd

Etiologic Agent or Factor	Type of Lesion*					Frequency of Occurrence†	Duration of Pharyngitis
	Erythematous	Follicular	Exudative	Ulcerative	Petechial		
Parasites							
Toxoplasma gondii[83]	+					+	Acute
Recognized illnesses of uncertain etiology							
Aphthous stomatitis[55, 124]	+			++++		++	Acute, recurrent
PFAPA[38, 90, 95]	++		++			+	Acute, recurrent
Behçet syndrome[93]	+			++++		+	Chronic, recurrent
Kawasaki disease[99]	++					+	Acute
Stevens-Johnson syndrome[21]	+		+	++++		+	Acute
Illness in which host factors or therapeutic agents are primary causes							
Neutropenia, other immunodeficiencies, cancer, chemotherapeutic agents, generalized neoplastic disease[21]	+			++++		++	Chronic

*Pluses indicate the relative degree and severity of the lesion (++++, most marked; +, minimal).

†++++, 76 to 100 percent; +++, 51 to 75 percent; ++, 26 to 50 percent; +, 1 to 25 percent.

children and adolescents.* Pharyngeal involvement frequently is overshadowed by other respiratory symptoms (e.g., cough, coryza) in parainfluenza viral infections and by systemic complaints (e.g., fever, exanthem, meningitis) in enteroviral infections.† An enteroviral etiology should be suspected when small ulcerative lesions are noted that involve the soft palate and uvula as well as the posterior pharyngeal wall (see Chapter 11). Infection with Epstein-Barr virus causes infectious mononucleosis with pharyngeal involvement similar to that resulting from group A streptococcal infection.[65, 149] The clinical manifestations of Epstein-Barr virus are age related; young children rarely have marked pharyngeal involvement.

Acquired cytomegalovirus infection causes an infectious mononucleosis–like syndrome, but pharyngitis occurs less commonly than it does in Epstein-Barr virus mononucleosis.[82] Primary as well as recurrent herpes simplex virus infections occasionally have pharyngeal manifestations.[17, 20, 36, 101] However, many illnesses that are ascribed clinically to herpes simplex virus actually are misidentified instances of aphthous stomatitis. Virtually all instances of herpes simplex virus infections with pharyngitis also will reveal lesions in the anterior mouth and externally around the mouth. Although Koplik spots are known universally as the enanthem of measles, many physicians are unaware of the diffuse nature of the associated measles pharyngitis.[21] Primary infection with human immunodeficiency virus may cause the acute retroviral syndrome with fever, nonexudative pharyngitis, lymphadenopathy, exanthem, arthralgia, myalgia, and lethargy.[8]

*See references 10, 16, 29, 31, 101, 104, 113, 132, 136, 148.

†See references 1, 6, 19, 28, 61, 68, 69, 75, 78, 101, 107, 110, 112, 120, 126, 129, 130, 134, 139, 153.

The role of *Chlamydia* spp. in the cause of pharyngitis is not clear. Grayston and associates[57, 58] noted the occurrence of pharyngitis in adolescents and young adults infected with *Chlamydia pneumoniae*.[57, 58] In a study in children, IgM antibody to *Chlamydia trachomatis* was found in children with pharyngitis.[62] Because cross-reactivity between *C. trachomatis* and *C. pneumoniae* exists, the illnesses studied were likely to be caused by *C. pneumoniae* rather than by *C. trachomatis*. Ogawa and colleagues[108] noted prolonged and recurrent tonsillitis in association with sexually transmitted *C. trachomatis*.

Relatively mild pharyngitis occurs in young children with *M. pneumoniae* infections; in older children, pharyngeal involvement is more pronounced.[22, 52, 56, 69] In young adult volunteers, *Mycoplasma hominis* was noted to cause pharyngitis.[103] Although lower respiratory tract findings and systemic complaints are most marked in Q fever, moderate subjective and mild objective evidence of pharyngitis is also noted.[35, 73] Exudative pharyngeal involvement with *Candida* spp. commonly occurs.[85, 133] *Candida* infection most commonly occurs in children whose normal throat flora has been disrupted and in children who have a compromised immunologic response.

Recurrent aphthous stomatitis usually involves the anterior oral cavity but is occasionally noted with extensive pharyngeal and soft palate lesions.[55, 124] Although L-forms of *Streptococcus sanguis* can be recovered consistently from the lesions of this disease,[55] their role in the etiology is unclear. In 1987, Marshall and colleagues[95] described a new syndrome, periodic fever, aphthous stomatitis, pharyngitis, and adenitis (PFAPA), and it subsequently has been observed by others.[38, 90] In Behçet syndrome, the ulcerative lesions are subacute or chronic and usually not associated with surrounding pharyngeal inflammation.[93] In Kawasaki disease, the pharyngeal mucosa is deeply erythematous.[99]

Pharyngeal involvement is a common occurrence in noninfectious illnesses in which host resistance has been altered. The lesions usually are ulcerative, but secondary bacterial or fungal overgrowth can lead to marked erythematous and exudative findings.

EPIDEMIOLOGY

Pharyngitis is a common occurrence in children, and as noted in Table 10–2, it is the result of many different infectious agents. In general, bacterial pharyngitis occurs more commonly in the cold weather seasons; an enteroviral etiology is most common in the summer and fall. In younger children, viral pharyngitis tends to occur relatively more frequently than does bacterial disease.[31] It has no apparent sex predilection.

Most diseases associated with pharyngitis require close person-to-person contact for spread. Pathogens are transmitted directly by close-range airborne dissemination or indirectly by the hands of the future host. Several foodborne outbreaks of streptococcal pharyngitis have been reported.[37, 44] Prechewing of food by adults also may be a cause of streptococcal pharyngitis in infants.[135]

PATHOPHYSIOLOGY

The pathology and pathophysiology of diseases in which pharyngitis is prominent are presented in the chapters of this book on specific infectious agents (in particular, Chapters 87, 161, and 170).

CLINICAL PRESENTATION

The clinical findings in pharyngitis are highlighted in Table 10–2. Manifestations related to individual pathogens are detailed in the chapters of this book dealing with the specific agents. The onset of pharyngitis usually is sudden and accompanied by fever and the complaint of sore throat. Frequently, parents observe that the child's breath is not normal and that the throat and particularly the tonsils are red. Other initial complaints include headache, nausea, vomiting, and, sometimes, abdominal pain. Anorexia is the rule, as is some degree of lessened activity. Parents also report frequently that the child's cervical lymph nodes are enlarged and tender.

Physical examination usually substantiates the parents' observations—the child is febrile with moderate to severe pharyngeal erythema and some degree of cervical adenitis. As noted in Table 10–2, the pharyngeal response is varied. With acute common infections, the basic lesion is erythema. Associated with erythema can be follicular, ulcerative, and petechial lesions and generalized or circumscribed exudative areas. Follicular lesions are most characteristic of adenoviral infections, whereas exudative lesions occur most commonly in group A streptococcal infections and in infectious mononucleosis. Meland and associates[98] noted that the absence of cough and the presence of swollen lymph nodes had the highest specificity in predicting a streptococcal cause of pharyngitis. Ulcerative lesions are observed most frequently in enteroviral infections (see Chapter 170). Petechiae on the soft palate frequently are seen in group A streptococcal infections but also commonly occur in infectious mononucleosis, measles, and rubella.

Occurrences of pharyngitis in children almost entirely are acute, self-limited diseases; those of viral etiology last 4 to 10 days, and those caused by group A streptococci, if untreated, last slightly longer. Subacute and chronic pharyngeal disease is not a common occurrence in children, but the etiologic possibilities are numerous (see Table 10–2).

Differential Diagnosis

As noted in Table 10–2, the differential considerations in pharyngitis are numerous, as in nasopharyngitis (see Table 10–1). Although considerable overlap exists in the spectrum of illness in pharyngeal infections, many clues help in ruling in or out certain diagnostic possibilities. The diagnosis of pharyngitis requires carefully eliciting epidemiologic and other historical data (i.e., exposure, season, incubation period, age of patient, associated clinical findings), in addition to the observation of pharyngeal physical findings.

The overwhelming majority of acute instances of nasopharyngitis are of viral etiology (see Table 10–1), with adenoviruses accounting for the greatest number of cases. Nasopharyngitis also occurs during epidemic influenza A and B and parainfluenza 1 and 2 and with sporadic parainfluenza 3 infections. In all cases, proper epidemiologic and historical data should be elicited so that early diphtheria and other unusual but treatable illnesses are not diagnosed incorrectly. Retrospective study has indicated that nasopharyngitis occasionally occurs in severe infections from *H. influenzae* and meningococci, so the possibility of these infections should be considered when the epidemiology suggests it.

Although most cases of pharyngitis without nasal symptoms are caused by viral infections, the number of other etiologic possibilities is great. Unfortunately, the approach taken all too frequently by many physicians is to consider all pharyngitis as being of bacterial origin and to treat it with antibiotics. Initial consideration in the child with pharyngitis should be the duration of illness. Subacute, chronic, and recurrent illnesses (see Table 10–2) generally suggest more unusual problems and require a more deliberate approach.

In all instances of acute pharyngitis, ruling out streptococcal disease is mandatory.

Specific Diagnosis

The epidemiologic history and careful clinical categorization are the most important aspects of specific diagnosis. The most pressing diagnostic need in upper respiratory infections in everyday pediatric practice is the distinction of bacterial from viral disease—who and who not to treat with antibiotics. An approach to the problem is presented in Table 10–3.

TABLE 10–3 ■ TREATMENT CONSIDERATIONS IN UPPER RESPIRATORY TRACT INFECTIONS

Clinical Entity	Etiology
Common cold, herpangina, pharyngoconjunctival fever	Viral, 100%
Never-Never Land	
Marked pharyngitis with exudate and fever and cervical lymphadenitis	Bacterial, 70%

Modified from Cherry, J. D.: Newer respiratory viruses: Their role in respiratory illness of children. *In* Schulman, I., et al. (eds.): Advances in Pediatrics, Vol. 20. © 1973, Year Book Medical Publishers, Inc., Chicago. Used by permission.

The child with the common cold, herpangina, or pharyngoconjunctival fever has a viral disease and does not need therapy with antibiotics. In most instances, when these clinical diagnoses are apparent, performing throat cultures for bacterial pathogens is not necessary. The child with severe acute pharyngitis with exudate and fever and cervical lymphadenitis also is treated easily because most of these children have disease resulting from group A streptococci.

Only a relatively small number of children have illnesses at the extremes of those in Table 10–3. Indeed, most of the illnesses seen routinely by the physician dealing with children fall into the large middle area, "never-never land." On clinical grounds, no certain way to make an etiologic diagnosis and specifically to rule out infection caused by *S. pyogenes* exists. Therefore, until relatively recently, the usually recommended approach to management of pharyngitis and nasopharyngitis was to obtain a throat culture to determine whether group A streptococci were present. Several rapid tests for the detection of group A streptococci are available that make the immediate diagnosis and treatment of streptococcal pharyngitis possible in the practice setting.* In general, these rapid tests have high specificity, but sensitivity is less than optimal. Therefore, if early treatment is desirable today, a reasonable approach to the diagnosis of streptococcal pharyngitis is to carry out a rapid test. If the test result is positive, specific therapy is instituted. In the case of a negative rapid test result, a routine throat culture is performed, and therapy is withheld pending the culture results.[117]

A question exists regarding whether early treatment of streptococcal pharyngitis is desirable.[34, 49, 50, 116, 117] Certainly in the public clinic, where following up children with positive throat cultures often is difficult, immediate diagnosis and treatment are important. However, as Pichichero and associates[116] and El-Daher and colleagues[34] have shown, early treatment may result in a decreased desirable antibody response, thus allowing reinfection with type-specific organisms to occur. Therefore, in settings in which the communication between physicians and parents is satisfactory, an advisable approach in many instances is to withhold the institution of treatment for a day or two. Gerber and associates[49, 50] argue against this approach because immediate therapy can reduce the risk of transmission of infection, and they challenge the interpretation of the findings of Pichichero and colleagues and El-Daher and coworkers.[34, 49, 50]

Cultures for other pathogens should be reserved for unusual situations, such as persistent symptoms, indicative epidemiology, or other pertinent historical data. Because *H. influenzae* and *Streptococcus pneumoniae* frequently are part of the normal flora, their isolation is not always etiologically significant. However, if cultures reveal predominant growths of either, quite likely they are contributing to the disease process, and antibiotic therapy directed at them will benefit the patient.[20, 94, 156] When the possibility of disease because of anaerobic agents exists, a Gram-stained smear from an exudative area may be rewarding. When the pharyngeal findings are unique or when many cases of a similar illness are observed, a viral culture from the throat is indicated.

Treatment

The specific treatments of diseases with nasopharyngitis and pharyngitis are presented in chapters of this book that deal with the individual pathogens. Although a multitude of proprietary remedies are available for respiratory infections, and sore throat specifically, none has a place in the care of the pediatric patient. Particularly to be condemned are throat lozenges that contain a large number of useless ingredients, many potentially harmful. Antibiotic-containing lozenges particularly are to be condemned because they may allow streptococcal disease to go unrecognized. Antiseptic mouthwashes have no value, and decongestants and antihistamines have no proven efficacy and frequently lead to troublesome side effects.

Because children with pharyngitis frequently feel ill, therapy with an analgesic is reasonable. Formerly, aspirin was the analgesic usually recommended. However, because aspirin is an etiologic factor in influenza-associated Reye syndrome and because differentiating influenza viral infections from other respiratory viral infections is difficult clinically, using acetaminophen rather than aspirin is prudent. The dose per single administration of acetaminophen by year of age is as follows: younger than 1 year, 60 mg; 1 to 3 years, 60 to 120 mg; 3 to 6 years, 120 mg; 6 to 12 years, 150 to 300 mg; older than 12 years, 325 to 650 mg. Administration may be repeated three or four times daily in young children and every 4 hours in older children. Acetaminophen rarely should be given to infants younger than 6 months. In young children, careful attention to adequate hydration is particularly necessary.

*See references 7, 8, 30, 33, 45–47, 51, 67, 81, 88, 116, 143.

Prognosis

Almost all occurrences of nasopharyngitis and pharyngitis are self-limited, and the overall prognosis is excellent. However, keeping a constant vigil for streptococcal and other more serious diseases is necessary. Failure to diagnose and to treat group A streptococcal infections, syphilis, and other more unusual infections can lead to serious short-term and long-term difficulties.

Prevention

Because pharyngitis and nasopharyngitis are caused by infections with a large number of different respiratory pathogens, no practical specific approach to prevention exists. On occasion, streptococcal disease can be prevented by the judicious use of prophylactic penicillin. For young children or others with undue susceptibility to serious disease with common respiratory pathogens, reducing contact situations (e.g., daycare centers) is prudent.

REFERENCES

1. Ager, E. A., Felsenstein, W. C., Alexander, E. R., et al.: An epidemic of illness due to coxsackievirus group B, type 2. J. A. M. A. *187*:251–256, 1964.
2. Arditi, M., Shulman, S. T., Davis, A. T., et al.: Group C β-hemolytic streptococcal infections in children: Nine pediatric cases and review. Rev. Infect. Dis. *2*:34–45, 1989.
3. Ash, I., McKendrick, G. D. W., Robertson, M. H., et al.: Outbreak of typhoid fever connected with corned beef. Br. Med. J. *1*:1474–1478, 1964.
4. Banck, G., and Nyman, M.: Tonsillitis and rash associated with *Corynebacterium haemolyticum*. J. Infect. Dis. *154*:1037–1039, 1986.
5. Benjamin, J. T., and Perriello, V. A., Jr.: Pharyngitis due to group C hemolytic streptococci in children. J. Pediatr. *89*:254–256, 1976.
6. Bisno, A. L., Barratt, N. P., Swanston, W. H., et al.: An outbreak of acute respiratory disease in Trinidad associated with para-influenza viruses. Am. J. Epidemiol. *91*:68–77, 1970.
7. Bisno, A. L., Gerber, M. A., Gwaltney, J. M., et al.: Diagnosis and management of group A streptococci pharyngitis: A practice guideline. Clin. Infect. Dis. *25*:574–583, 1997.
8. Bisno, A. L.: Acute pharyngitis. N. Engl. J. Med. *344*:205–211, 2001.
9. Bonkowsky, H. L., Lee, R. V., and Klatskin, G.: Acute granulomatous hepatitis: Occurrence in cytomegalovirus mononucleosis. J. A. M. A. *233*:1284–1288, 1975.
10. Brandt, C. D., Kim, H. W., Vargosko, A. J., et al.: Infections in 18,000 infants and children in a controlled study of respiratory tract disease: I. Adenovirus pathogenicity in relation to serologic type and illness syndrome. Am. J. Epidemiol. *90*:484–500, 1969.

11. Breese, B. B.: Streptococcal pharyngitis and scarlet fever. Am. J. Dis. Child. *132*:612–616, 1978.
12. Brook, I., and Gober, A. E.: *Bacteroides melaninogenicus*: Its recovery from tonsils of children with acute tonsillitis. Arch. Otolaryngol. *109*:818–819, 1983.
13. Carlson, P., Kontianinen, S., Renkonen, O. V., et al.: *Arcanobacterium haemolyticum* and streptococcal pharyngitis in Army conscripts. Scand. J. Infect. Dis. *27*:17–18, 1995.
14. Carrie, S., and Fenton, P. A.: Necrobacillosis: An unusual case of pharyngotonsillitis. J. Laryngol. Otol. *108*:1097–1098, 1994.
15. Catalano, P. M., and Schragger, A. H.: Early and latent syphilis. Arch. Dermatol. *92*:433–435, 1965.
16. Centers for Disease Control: Adenovirus type 16—Long Island, New York. M. M. W. R. *28*:530–532, 1979.
17. Cesario, T. C., Poland, J. D., Wulff, H., et al.: Six years' experience with herpes simplex virus in a children's home. Am. J. Epidemiol. *90*:416–422, 1969.
18. Chanock, R. M., Parrott, R. H., Vargosko, A. J., et al.: Respiratory syncytial virus. Am. J. Public Health *52*:918–925, 1962.
19. Cherry, J. D., and Jahn, C. L.: Herpangina: The etiologic spectrum. Pediatrics *36*:632–634, 1965.
20. Cherry, J. D.: Newer respiratory viruses: Their role in respiratory illness of children. Adv. Pediatr. *20*:225–290, 1973.
21. Cherry, J. D.: Personal observations.
22. Cherry, J. D., and Welliver, R. C.: *Mycoplasma pneumoniae* infections of adults and children. West. J. Med. *125*:47–55, 1976.
23. Chretien, J. H., McGinniss, C. G., Thompson, J., et al.: Group B beta-hemolytic streptococci causing pharyngitis. J. Clin. Microbiol. *10*:263–266, 1979.
24. Cimolai, N., Elford, R. W., Bryan, L., et al.: Do the β-hemolytic non-group A streptococci cause pharyngitis? Rev. Infect. Dis. *10*:587–601, 1988.
25. Cimolai, N., Morrison, B. J., MacCulloch, L., et al.: Beta-haemolytic non-group A streptococci and pharyngitis: A case-control study. Eur. J. Paediatr. *150*:776–779, 1991.
26. Commission on Acute Respiratory Diseases: Endemic exudative pharyngitis and tonsillitis: Etiology and clinical characteristics. J. A. M. A. *125*:1163–1169, 1944.
27. Conant, M. A., and Lane, B.: Secondary syphilis misdiagnosed as infectious mononucleosis. Calif. Med. *109*:462–464, 1968.
28. Cramblett, H. G., Moffet, H. L., Black, J. P., et al.: Coxsackievirus infections: Clinical and laboratory studies. J. Pediatr. *64*:406–414, 1964.
29. Dascomb, H. E., and Hilleman, M. R.: Clinical and laboratory studies in patients with respiratory disease caused by adenoviruses (RI-APC-ARD agents). Am. J. Med. *Aug.*:161–174, 1956.
30. Denny, F. W.: Current problems in managing streptococcal pharyngitis. J. Pediatr. *111*:797–806, 1987.
31. Douglas, R. M., Miles, H., Hansman, D., et al.: Acute tonsillitis in children: Microbial pathogens in relation to age. Pathology *16*:79–82, 1984.
32. Dyment, P. G., Klink, L. B., and Jackson, D. W.: Hoarseness and palatal petechiae as clues in identifying streptococcal throat infections. Pediatrics *41*:822–823, 1968.
33. Ebell, M. H., Smith, M. A., Barry, H. C., et al.: Does this patient have strep throat? J. A. M. A. *284*:2912–2918, 2000.
34. El-Daher, N. T., Hijazi, S. S., Rawashedeh, N. M., et al.: Immediate vs. delayed treatment of group A beta-hemolytic streptococcal pharyngitis with penicillin V. Pediatr. Infect. Dis. J. *10*:126–130, 1991.
35. Eshchar, J., Waron, M., and Alkan, W. J.: Syndromes of Q fever. J. A. M. A. *195*:146–149, 1966.
36. Evans, A. S., and Dick, E. C.: Acute pharyngitis and tonsillitis in University of Wisconsin students. J. A. M. A. *190*:699–708, 1964.
37. Farley, T. A., Wilson, S. A., Mahoney, F., et al.: Direct inoculation of food as the cause of an outbreak of group A streptococcal pharyngitis. J. Infect. Dis. *167*:1232–1235, 1993.
38. Feder, H. M., Jr.: Periodic fever, aphthous stomatitis, pharyngitis, adenitis: A clinical review of a new syndrome. Curr. Opin. Pediatr. *12*:253–256, 2000.
39. Fell, H. W. K., Nagington, J., Naylor, G. R. E., et al.: *Corynebacterium haemolyticum* infections in Cambridgeshire. J. Hyg. Camb. *79*:269–275, 1977.
40. Finegold, S. M., Bartlett, J. G., Chow, A. W., et al.: Management of anaerobic infections. Ann. Intern. Med. *83*:375–389, 1975.
41. Finegold, S. M., and Rosenblatt, J. E.: Practical aspects of anaerobic sepsis. Medicine (Baltimore) *52*:311–322, 1973.
42. Fiumara, N. J., and Berg, M.: Primary syphilis in the oral cavity. Br. J. Vener. Dis. *50*:463–464, 1974.
43. Forchheimer, F.: The enanthem of German measles. Phila. Med. J. *II*:15–17, 1898.
44. Fries, S. M.: Diagnosis of group A streptococcal pharyngitis in a private clinic: Comparative evaluation of an optical immunoassay method and culture. J. Pediatr. *126*:933–936, 1995.
45. Gallo, G., Berzero, R., Cattai, N., et al.: An outbreak of group A food-borne streptococcal pharyngitis. Eur. J. Epidemiol. *8*:292–297, 1992.
46. Gerber, M. A.: Comparison of throat cultures and rapid strep tests for diagnosis of streptococcal pharyngitis. Pediatr. Infect. Dis. *8*:820–824, 1989.
47. Gerber, M. A., Spadaccini, L. J., Wright, L. L., et al.: Latex agglutination tests for rapid identification of group A streptococci directly from throat swabs. J. Pediatr. *105*:702–705, 1984.
48. Gerber, M. A., Randolph, M. F., Martin, N. J., et al.: Community-wide outbreak of group G streptococcal pharyngitis. Pediatrics *87*:598–603, 1991.
49. Gerber, M. A.: Effect of early antibiotic therapy on recurrence rates of streptococcal pharyngitis. Pediatr. Infect. Dis. J. *10*:S56–S60, 1991.
50. Gerber, M. A., Randolph, M. F., DeMeo, K. K., et al.: Lack of impact of early antibiotic therapy for streptococcal pharyngitis on recurrence rates. J. Pediatr. *117*:853–858, 1990.
51. Gerber, M. A., Tanz, R. R., Kabat, W., et al.: Optical immunoassay test for group A ß-hemolytic streptococcal pharyngitis: An office-based, multicenter investigation. J. A. M. A. *277*:899–903, 1997.
52. Glezen, W. P., Clyde, W. A., Jr., Senior, R. J., et al.: Group A streptococci, mycoplasmas, and viruses associated with acute pharyngitis. J. A. M. A. *202*:455–460, 1967.
53. Glover, J. A., and Griffith, F.: Acute tonsillitis and some of its sequels: Epidemiological and bacteriological observations. Br. Med. J. *Sept. 19*:521–527, 1931.
54. Gorbach, S. L., and Bartlett, J. G.: Anaerobic infections (three parts). N. Engl. J. Med. *290*:1177–1184, 1237–1245, 1289–1294, 1974.
55. Graykowski, E. A., Barile, M. F., Lee, W. B., et al.: Recurrent aphthous stomatitis: Clinical, therapeutic, histopathologic, and hypersensitivity aspects. J. A. M. A. *196*:637–644, 1966.
56. Grayston, J. T., Alexander, E. R., Kenny, G. E., et al.: *Mycoplasma pneumoniae* infections: Clinical and epidemiologic studies. J. A. M. A. *191*: 369–374, 1965.
57. Grayston, J. T., Campbell, L. A., Kuo, C. C., et al.: A new respiratory tract pathogen: *Chlamydia pneumoniae* strain TWAR. J. Infect. Dis. *161*: 618–625, 1990.
58. Grayston, J. T.: *Chlamydia pneumoniae* (TWAR) infections in children. Pediatr. Infect. Dis. J. *13*:675–685, 1994.
59. Green, S. L., and LaPeter, K. S.: Pseudodiphtheritic membranous pharyngitis caused by *Corynebacterium hemolyticum*. J. A. M. A. *245*: 2330–2331, 1981.
60. Gurwith, M., Wenman, W., Hinde, D., et al.: A prospective study of rotavirus infection in infants and young children. J. Infect. Dis. *144*:218–224, 1981.
61. Harris, D. J., Wulff, H., Ray, C. G., et al.: Viruses and disease: II. An outbreak of parainfluenza type 2 in a children's home. Am. J. Epidemiol. *87*:419–425, 1968.
62. Harrison, H. R., Magder, L. S., Boyce, W. T., et al.: Acute *Chlamydia trachomatis* respiratory infection in childhood: Serologic evidence. Am. J. Dis. Child. *140*:1068–1071, 1986.
63. Higgins, P. G., Ellis, E. M., Woolley, D. A., et al.: Viruses associated with acute respiratory infections in Royal Air Force personnel. J. Hyg. Camb. *68*:647–654, 1970.
64. Hill, H. R., Caldwell, G. G., Wilson, E., et al.: Epidemic of pharyngitis due to streptococci of Lancefield group G. Lancet *2*:371–374, 1969.
65. Hoagland, R. J.: Clinical manifestations of infectious mononucleosis: A report of two hundred cases. Am. J. Med. Sci. *240*:21–28, 1960.
66. Hoekstra, R. E., Herrmann, E. C., Jr., and O'Connell, E. J.: Virus infections in children: Clinical comparison of overlapping outbreaks of influenza A2/Hong Kong/68 and respiratory syncytial virus infections. Am. J. Dis. Child. *120*:14–16, 1970.
67. Hofer, C., Binns, H. J., and Tanz, R. R.: Strategies for managing group A streptococcal pharyngitis. Arch. Pediatr. Adolesc. Med. *151*:824–829, 1997.
68. Holzel, A., Parker, L., Patterson, W. H., et al.: Virus isolations from throats of children admitted to hospital with respiratory and other diseases, Manchester 1962–4. Br. Med. J. *1*:614–619, 1965.
69. Horn, M. E. C., Brain, E., Gregg, I., et al.: Respiratory viral infection in childhood: A survey in general practice, Roehampton 1967–1972. J. Hyg. Camb. *74*:157–168, 1975.
70. Humphrey, T., Sanders, S., and Stadius, M.: Leptospirosis mimicking MLNS. J. Pediatr. *91*:853–854, 1977.
71. Jacobs, R. F., Condrey, Y. M., and Yamauchi, T.: Tularemia in adults and children: A changing presentation. Pediatrics *76*:818–822, 1985.
72. Jamsky, R. J.: Gonococcal tonsillitis: Report of a case. Oral Surg. *44*:197–200, 1977.
73. Johnson, J. E., III, and Kadull, P. J.: Laboratory-acquired Q fever: A report of fifty cases. Am. J. Med. *41*:391–403, 1966.
74. Jordan, W. S., Jr.: Acute respiratory diseases of viral etiology: I. Ecology of respiratory viruses—1961. Am. J. Public Health *52*:897–945, 1962.
75. Kapikian, A. Z., Chanock, R. M., Reichelderfer, T. E., et al.: Inoculation of human volunteers with parainfluenza virus type 3. J. A. M. A. *178*: 537–546, 1961.
76. Karpathios, T., Drakonaki, S., Zervoudaki, A., et al.: *Arcanobacterium haemolyticum* in children with presumed streptococcal pharyngotonsillitis or scarlet fever. J. Pediatr. *121*:735–737, 1992.
77. Kellner, G., Popow-Kraupp, T., Kundi, M., et al.: Contribution of rhinoviruses to respiratory viral infections in childhood: A prospective study in a mainly hospitalized infant population. J. Med. Virol. *25*:455–469, 1988.
78. Kibrick, S.: Current status of Coxsackie and ECHO viruses in human disease. Prog. Med. Virol. *6*:27–70, 1964.

79. Komaroff, A. L., Aronson, M. D., Pass, T. M., et al.: Serologic evidence of chlamydial and mycoplasmal pharyngitis in adults. Science *222*:927–928, 1983.
80. Kovatch, A. L., Schuit, K. E., and Michaels, R. H.: *Corynebacterium hemolyticum* peritonsillar abscess mimicking diphtheria. J. A. M. A. *249*: 1757–1758, 1983.
81. Kurtz, B., Kurtz, M., Roe, M., et al.: Importance of inoculum size and sampling effect in rapid antigen detection for diagnosis of *Streptococcus pyogenes* pharyngitis. J. Clin. Microbiol. *38*:279–281, 2000.
82. Lajo, A., Borque, C., Del Castillo, F., et al.: Mononucleosis caused by Epstein-Barr virus and cytomegalovirus in children: A comparative study of 124 cases. Pediatr. Infect. Dis. J. *13*:56–60, 1994.
83. Lascari, A. D., and Bapat, V. R.: Syndromes of infectious mononucleosis. Clin. Pediatr. *9*:300–305, 1970.
84. Le, C. T.: Tick-borne relapsing fever in children. Pediatrics *66*:963–966, 1980.
85. Lehner, T.: Oral thrush, or acute pseudomembranous candidiasis: A clinicopathologic study of forty-four cases. Oral Surg. *18*:27–37, 1964.
86. Lerner, A. M., Cherry, J. D., Klein, J. O., et al.: Infections with reoviruses. N. Engl. J. Med. *267*:947–952, 1962.
87. Lewis, H. M., Parry, J. V., Davies, H. A., et al.: A year's experience of the rotavirus syndrome and its association with respiratory illness. Arch. Dis. Child. *54*:339–346, 1979.
88. Lieu, T. A., Fleisher, G. R., and Schwartz, J. S.: Cost-effectiveness of rapid latex agglutination testing and throat culture for streptococcal pharyngitis. Pediatrics *85*:246–256, 1990.
89. Lipsky, B. A., Goldberger, A. C., Tompkins, L. S., et al.: Infections caused by nondiphtheria corynebacteria. Rev. Infect. Dis. *4*:1220–1235, 1982.
90. Long, S.: Syndrome of periodic fever, aphthous stomatitis, pharyngitis, and adenitis (PFAPA)—what it isn't. What is it? J. Pediatr. *135*:1–5, 1999.
91. Macdonald, J. B., Socransky, S. S., and Gibbons, R. J.: Aspects of the pathogenesis of mixed anaerobic infections of mucous membranes. J. Dent. Res. *42*(Suppl. 1):529–544, 1963.
92. Mackenzie, A., Fuite, L. A., Chan, F. T. H., et al.: Incidence and pathogenicity of *Arcanobacterium haemolyticum* during a 2-year study in Ottawa. Clin. Infect. Dis. *21*:177–181, 1995.
93. Mamo, J. G., and Baghdassarian, A.: Behçet's disease: A report of 28 cases. Arch. Ophthalmol. *71*:4–14, 1964.
94. Markowitz, M.: Cultures of the respiratory tract in pediatric practice. Am. J. Dis. Child. *105*:12–18, 1963.
95. Marshall, G. S., Edwards, K. M., Butler, J., et al.: Syndrome of periodic fever, pharyngitis, and aphthous stomatitis. J. Pediatr. *110*:43–46, 1987.
96. Maynard, J. E., Fletz, E. T., Wulff, H., et al.: Surveillance of respiratory virus infections among Alaskan Eskimo children. J. A. M. A. *200*: 927–931, 1967.
97. McCloskey, R. V., Eller, J. J., Green, M., et al.: The 1970 epidemic of diphtheria in San Antonio. Ann. Intern. Med. *75*:495–503, 1971.
98. Meland, E., Digranes, A., and Skjaerven, R.: Assessment of clinical features predicting streptococcal pharyngitis. Scand. J. Infect. Dis. *25*:177–183, 1993.
99. Melish, M. E., Hicks, R. M., and Larson, E. J.: Mucocutaneous lymph node syndrome in the United States. Am. J. Dis. Child. *130*:599–607, 1976.
100. Moffet, H. L., Cramblett, H. G., and Smith, A.: Group A streptococcal infections in a children's home: II. Clinical and epidemiologic patterns of illness. Pediatrics *33*:11–17, 1964.
101. Moffet, H. L., Siegel, A. C., and Doyle, H. K.: Nonstreptococcal pharyngitis. J. Pediatr. *73*:51–60, 1968.
102. Mortimer, E. A., Jr., and Boxerbaum, B.: Diagnosis and treatment: Group A streptococcal infections. Pediatrics *36*:930–932, 1965.
103. Mufson, M. A.: *Mycoplasma hominis 1* in respiratory tract infections. Ann. N. Y. Acad. Sci. *174*:798–808, 1970.
104. Nakayama, M., Miyazaki, C., Ueda, K., et al.: Pharyngoconjunctival fever caused by adenovirus type 11. Pediatr. Infect. Dis. J. *11*:6–9, 1992.
105. Nigro, G., Pastoris, M. D., Fantasia, M. M., et al.: Acute cerebellar ataxia in pediatric legionellosis. Pediatrics *72*:847–849, 1983.
106. Nourmand, A., and Ziai, M.: Typhoid and paratyphoid fever in children. Review of symptoms and therapy in 165 cases. Clin. Pediatr. *8*:235–238, 1969.
107. Numazaki, Y., Yano, N., Shigeta, S., et al.: Studies on parainfluenza virus infections among infants and children in Sendai: II. Serologic and epidemiologic investigation. Jpn. J. Microbiol. *12*:343–351, 1968.
108. Ogawa, H., Hashiguchi, K., and Kazuyama, Y.: Prolonged and recurrent tonsillitis associated with sexually transmitted *Chlamydia trachomatis*. J. Laryngol. Otol. *107*:27–29, 1993.
109. Park, W. H., and Cooper, G. V.: Accidental inoculation of influenza bacilli on the mucous membranes of healthy persons with development of infection in at least one: Persistence of type characteristics of the bacilli. J. Immunol. *6*:81–85, 1921.
110. Parrott, R. H., Vargosko, A., Luckey, A., et al.: Clinical features of infection with hemadsorption viruses. N. Engl. J. Med. *260*:731–738, 1959.
111. Parrott, R. H., Kim, H. W., Vargosko, A. J., et al.: Serious respiratory tract illness as a result of Asian influenza and influenza B infections in children. J. Pediatr. *61*:205–213, 1962.
112. Parrott, R. H.: Viral respiratory tract illnesses in children. Bull. N. Y. Acad. Med. *39*:629–648, 1963.
113. Pereira, M. S.: Adenovirus infections. Postgrad. Med. J. *49*:798–801, 1973.
114. Pers, C.: Infection due to *Corynebacterium ulcerans* producing diphtheria toxin: A case report from Denmark. Acta Pathol. Microbiol. Immunol. Scand. *95*:361–362, 1987.
115. Peter, G.: Leptospirosis: A zoonosis of protean manifestations. Pediatr. Infect. Dis. *1*:282–288, 1982.
116. Pichichero, M. E., Disney, F. A., Talpey, W. B., et al.: Adverse and beneficial effects of immediate treatment of group A beta-hemolytic streptococcal pharyngitis with penicillin. Pediatr. Infect. Dis. *6*:635–643, 1987.
117. Pichichero, M. E., Disney, F. A., Green, J. L., et al.: Comparative reliability of clinical, culture, and antigen detection methods for the diagnosis of group A beta-hemolytic streptococcal tonsillopharyngitis. Pediatr. Ann. *21*:798–805, 1992.
118. Place, E. H., and Sutton, L. E.: Erythema arthriticum epidemicum (Haverhill fever). Arch. Intern. Med. *54*:659–684, 1934.
119. Podosin, R. L., and Felton, W. L., II: The clinical picture of Far East influenza occurring at the Fourth National Boy Scout Jamboree: Report of 616 cases. N. Engl. J. Med. *258*:778–782, 1958.
120. Poland, J. D., Wulff, H., Welton, E. R., et al.: Viruses and disease: Studies in a children's home. Am. J. Epidemiol. *84*:92–102, 1966.
121. Rantz, L. A., Boisvert, P. J., and Spink, W. W.: Hemolytic streptococcic and nonstreptococcic diseases of the respiratory tract: A comparative clinical study. Arch. Intern. Med. *78*:369–386, 1946.
122. Rodriguez, W. J., Kim, H. W., Arrobio, J. O., et al.: Clinical features of acute gastroenteritis associated with human reovirus–like agent in infants and young children. J. Pediatr. *91*:188–193, 1977.
123. Rodriguez, W. J., Controni, G., Cohen, G. J., et al.: *Yersinia enterocolitica* enteritis in children. J. A. M. A. *242*:1978–1980, 1979.
124. Rogers, R. S., III: Recurrent aphthous stomatitis: Clinical characteristics and evidence for an immunopathogenesis. J. Invest. Dermatol. *69*:499–509, 1977.
125. Saari, T. N., and Triplett, D. A.: *Yersinia pseudotuberculosis* mesenteric adenitis. J. Pediatr. *85*:656–659, 1974.
126. Saliba, G. S., Glezen, W. P., and Chin, T. D. Y.: Etiologic studies of acute respiratory illness among children attending public schools. Am. Rev. Respir. Dis. *95*:592–602, 1967.
127. Schmidt, J. P., Metcalf, T. G., and Miltenberger, F. W.: An epidemic of Asian influenza in children at Ladd Air Force Base, Alaska, 1960. J. Pediatr. *61*:214–220, 1962.
128. Schmidt, W. C., and Rammelkamp, C. H., Jr.: Bacterial infections of the nasopharynx, with particular reference to the prevention of rheumatic fever and glomerulonephritis. Pediatr. Clin. *Feb.*:139–154, 1957.
129. Scott, T. F. McNair: Clinical syndromes associated with enterovirus and reovirus infections. Adv. Virus Res. *8*:165–197, 1962.
130. Siegel, W., Spencer, F. J., Smith, D. J., et al.: Two new variants of infection with Coxsackievirus group B, type 5, in young children: A syndrome of lymphadenopathy, pharyngitis and hepatomegaly or splenomegaly, or both, and one of pneumonia. N. Engl. J. Med. *268*:1210–1216, 1963.
131. Smith, H. W., Thomas, L., Dingle, J. H., et al.: Meningococcic infections: Report of 43 cases of meningococcic meningitis and 8 cases of meningococcemia. Ann. Intern. Med. *20*:12–32, 1944.
132. Sohier, R., Chardonnet, Y., and Prunieras, M.: Adenoviruses: Status of current knowledge. Prog. Med. Virol. *7*:253–325, 1965.
133. Solomon, P.: Oral moniliasis complicating combined broad-spectrum-antibiotic and antifungal therapy. N. Engl. J. Med. *265*:847–848, 1961.
134. Steigman, A. J., Lipton, M. M., and Braspennickx, H.: Acute lymphonodular pharyngitis: A newly described condition due to Coxsackie A virus. J. Pediatr. *61*:331–336, 1962.
135. Steinkuller, J. S., Chan, K., and Rinehouse, S. E.: Prechewing of food by adults and streptococcal pharyngitis in infants. J. Pediatr. *120*:563–564, 1992.
136. Sterner, G.: Adenovirus infection in childhood: An epidemiological and clinical survey among Swedish children. Acta Paediatr. *142*:5–30, 1962.
137. Stillerman, M., and Bernstein, S. H.: Streptococcal pharyngitis: Evaluation of clinical syndromes in diagnosis. Am. J. Dis. Child. *101*:476–489, 1961.
138. Stollerman, G. H.: Sore throat: A diagnostic and therapeutic dilemma. J. A. M. A. *189*:145–146, 1964.
139. Sutton, R. N. P.: Respiratory viruses in a residential nursery. J. Hyg. Camb. *60*:51–67, 1962.
140. Tacket, C. O., Davis, B. R., Carter, G. P., et al.: *Yersinia enterocolitica* pharyngitis. Ann. Intern. Med. *99*:40–42, 1983.
141. Tomlinson, A. J. H.: Human pathogenic coryneform bacteria: Their differentiation and significance in public health today. J. Appl. Bacteriol. *29*:131–137, 1966.
142. Top, F. H., Sr.: Diphtheria. *In* Top, F. H., Sr., and Wehrle, P. F. (eds.): Communicable and Infectious Diseases. St. Louis, C. V. Mosby, 1972, pp. 190–207.
143. Tsevat, J., and Kotagal, U. R.: Management of sore throats in children. Arch. Pediatr. Adolesc. Med. *153*:681–688, 1999.
144. Turner, J. C., Hayden, G. F., Kiselica, D., et al.: Association of group C beta-hemolytic streptococci with endemic pharyngitis among college students. J. A. M. A. *264*:2644–2647, 1990.

145. Turner, J. C., Fox, A., Fox, K., et al.: Role of group C beta-hemolytic streptococci in pharyngitis: Epidemiologic study of clinical features associated with isolation of group C streptococci. J. Clin. Microbiol. *31*:808–811, 1993.
146. Tyson, H. K.: Tularemia: An unappreciated cause of exudative pharyngitis. Pediatrics *58*:864–866, 1976.
147. Uohara, G. I., and Knapp, M. J.: Oral fusospirochetosis and associated lesions. Oral Surg. *24*:113–123, 1967.
148. Van Der Veen, J.: The role of adenoviruses in respiratory disease. Am. Rev. Respir. Dis. *88*:167–180, 1963.
149. Veltri, R. W., Sprinkle, P. M., and McClung, J. E.: Epstein-Barr virus associated with episodes of recurrent tonsillitis. Arch. Otolaryngol. *101*:552–556, 1975.
150. Von Graevenitz, A.: Which bacterial species should be isolated from throat cultures? Eur. J. Clin. Microbiol. *2*:1–3, 1983.
151. Walker, J. E.: Infection of laboratory worker with bacillus influenzae. J. Infect. Dis. *43*:300–305, 1928.
152. Walker, S. H.: The respiratory manifestations of systemic *Hemophilus influenzae* infection. J. Pediatr. *62*:386–392, 1963.
153. Ward, R.: Poliomyelitis. Pediatr. Clin. North Am. *7*:947–963, 1960.
154. Wat, P. J., Strickler, J. G., Myers, J. L., et al.: Herpes simplex infection causing acute necrotizing tonsillitis. Mayo Clin. Proc. *69*:269–271, 1994.
155. Wiesner, P. J., Tronca, E., Bonin, P., et al.: Clinical spectrum of pharyngeal gonococcal infection. N. Engl. J. Med. *288*:181–185, 1973.
156. Willard, C. Y., and Hansen, A. E.: Bacterial flora of the nasopharynx in children: Influence of respiratory infections and previous antimicrobial therapy. Am. J. Dis. Child. *97*:318–325, 1959.
157. Wills, P. I., Gedosh, E. A., and Nichols, D. R.: Head and neck manifestations of tularemia. Laryngoscope *92*:770–773, 1982.
158. Zalan, E., Leers, W. D., and Labzoffsky, N. A.: Occurrence of reovirus infection in Ontario. Can. Med. Assoc. J. *87*:714–715, 1962.
159. Zalma, V. M., Older, J. J., and Brooks, G. F.: The Austin, Texas, diphtheria outbreak: Clinical and epidemiological aspects. J. A. M. A. *211*:2125–2129, 1970.

Herpangina

JAMES D. CHERRY ■ KARIN A. NIELSEN

Herpangina, a fairly frequent, acute febrile illness that occurs in the summer and fall in temperate climates, is characterized by papular, vesicular, and ulcerative lesions on the anterior tonsillar pillars, soft palate, tonsils, pharynx, and posterior buccal mucosa. It is caused by many different enteroviruses.

History

Zahorsky[45, 46] generally is credited with the identification and characterization of the disease spectrum of herpangina. In his first paper in 1920 entitled "Herpetic Sore Throat," he presented the findings in 82 cases. In 1924, he introduced the name "herpangina" so that the clinical entity would not be confused with other diseases of the mouth and throat. In both papers, Zahorsky noted that Moro previously had referred to a similar illness in 1906. Johnsson and Lindahl[17] also reported that similar syndromes had been observed by Trousseau in 1906 and Marfan in 1924 as well as by Moro in 1906. In 1939, Levine and associates[24] described epidemic herpangina in three summer camps, and in 1941, Breese[4] reported 28 cases that he observed during the summers of 1938 and 1940. In 1951, Huebner and associates[15] and Parrott and colleagues[33] clearly established the etiologic relationship of coxsackieviruses A to herpangina. In 1965, Cherry and Jahn[8] noted from the literature as well as from their own observations that herpangina resulted from infection with many echoviruses and coxsackieviruses B as well as coxsackieviruses A.

Etiologic Agents

Virologic studies in the early 1950s that used suckling mice inoculation clearly indicated that several coxsackieviruses A were the cause of epidemic herpangina.[16, 18, 20, 33, 38, 43] In subsequent years, tissue culture techniques became widely used in diagnostic virology, and many studies revealed additional enteroviral types in association with herpangina.[8] Of interest is that, except for the initial interest in herpangina in 1950, careful study of the etiology of epidemic disease has not been performed. Most herpangina virus–illness associations that have been made during the last 40 years have resulted from secondary findings in other investigations.[1–3, 5, 6, 9–15, 19, 21–23, 25–30, 32, 34–37] A listing of viral agents associated with herpangina is presented in Table 11–1. In recent years, coxsackieviruses B and enterovirus 71 have been implicated most frequently. Of note, however, is that diagnostic studies using suckling mice inoculation have been performed only rarely during the last 30 years. As noted in Table 11–1, herpes simplex virus also can cause a clinical picture suggestive of herpangina.[10, 28] Indeed, Zahorsky[46] suggested that the cause of poliomyelitis also could be etiologic in herpangina because a similar enanthem had been observed in both sporadic and epidemic poliomyelitis.

Epidemiology

See sections on coxsackieviruses and echoviruses in Chapter 170.

Pathophysiology

The pathophysiology of coxsackievirus and that of echovirus infections are presented in their respective sections in Chapter 170. However, specific experimental data related to herpangina are presented by Simkova and Petrovicova.[40] In rhesus monkeys, they found that oropharyngeal lesions typical of herpangina developed in 2 to 7 days after oral, intravenous, or subcutaneous administration of coxsackievirus A4. These studies indicate that the oropharyngeal lesions are the result of multiplication of virus at the secondary infection site after viremia rather than a primary manifestation of initial cellular involvement.

Clinical Manifestations

Although Zahorsky[45, 46] and others[16, 33] have considered herpangina a specific febrile disease, perhaps a more appropriate approach is to restrict the term herpangina to the

TABLE 11–1 ■ ETIOLOGIC AGENTS FOUND IN ASSOCIATION WITH SPORADIC OR EPIDEMIC HERPANGINA

Virus	Occurrence		Reference
	Epidemic	Sporadic	
Coxsackievirus A			
1	+		18, 42, 43
2	+		18, 38, 42, 43
3	+		18, 38, 42, 43
4	+		18, 38, 42, 43
5	+		7, 18, 42, 43
6	+		18, 38, 42, 43
7		+	18, 35
8	+		18, 38, 42, 43
9		+	8, 18, 22, 35
10	+		18, 38, 42, 43
16		+	5, 8, 18
22	+		18, 42, 43
Coxsackievirus B			
1	+	+	8, 12, 26, 35, 42, 43
2		+	1, 12, 18, 27, 35, 42, 43
3		+	11–13, 18, 23, 31, 35, 42–44
4		+	2, 3, 8, 9, 12, 18, 34, 35, 42, 43
5		+	2, 12, 18, 35, 37, 42, 43
Echovirus			
6		+	18
9		+	8, 18, 21, 35, 37
11		+	29, 41
16	+	+	18, 32
17		+	8
22		+	29
25	+		30
Enterovirus 71	+		5, 6, 14, 15, 19, 25, 39
Herpes simplex		+	10, 28

characteristic oropharyngeal lesions. Herpangina is one of the protean manifestations of enteroviral infections, and it can occur in association with exanthem, aseptic meningitis, encephalitis, acute flaccid paralysis, and other clinical constellations.

The onset of herpangina is typical of most enteroviral infections and is characterized by the sudden awareness of fever.[4, 33, 45, 46] No characteristic prodrome usually exists, but young children may be irritable and occasionally listless and anorexic for a few hours before the febrile state is recognized. The initial temperature can be variable, with a range from normal to 41° C (106° F). In general, the temperature tends to be higher in younger patients. Breese[4] noted that the most common temperature in young children was between 39.5° C and 40° C (103° F and 104° F). Older children frequently complain of headache and backache. Vomiting occurs in approximately 25 percent of children younger than 5 years. In one outbreak of illness caused by coxsackievirus A4,[10] initial symptoms were anorexia and drooling (100%); sore throat (50%); coryza (45%); headache (18%); and vomiting, diarrhea, or both (36%).

In most instances of herpangina, the oropharyngeal lesions are present on the first examination at the time of fever or shortly after fever is noted. In the coxsackievirus A4 outbreak described by Forman and Cherry,[10] the enanthem was not observed until 24 to 48 hours after the onset of initial nonspecific symptoms. The characteristic lesions in herpangina are small (1 to 2 mm) vesicles and ulcers. These lesions apparently start as papules, become vesicular, and then ulcerate in a short but variable period. In the experience of one us (J. D. C.), the lesions most commonly observed are ulcers. Breese[4] noted in a number of children seen early in the course of the illness that a petechial appearance preceded the appearance of typical vesicular-ulcerative enanthem.

The lesions usually are discrete, with an average of 5 per patient; some patients will have only 1 or 2 lesions, whereas others may have 14 or more. When seen early, the vesicular lesions are observed to enlarge from 1 to 2 mm to 3 to 4 mm during a 2- to 3-day period.[33] Each vesicular and ulcerative lesion is surrounded by an erythematous ring that varies in size up to 10 mm in diameter. The most common site of the lesions is the anterior tonsillar pillars. Lesions also occur on the soft palate, uvula, tonsils, and pharyngeal wall and occasionally on the posterior buccal surfaces. In some cases, additional lesions have been noted on the dorsum or tip of the tongue. However, by definition, cases in which the primary involvement is on the tongue or anterior mouth and in which the lesions are of a general size greater than 5 mm are not considered to be herpangina.

Aside from the specific lesions, the remainder of the throat appears normal, minimally injected, or erythematous. The usual duration of signs and symptoms is 3 to 6 days. Most cases of herpangina are mild and without complications, but aseptic meningitis and other more severe enteroviral manifestations also occur occasionally. Recently, severe neurologic manifestations have been observed in children with herpangina caused by enterovirus 71.[6, 14, 15, 19, 25, 39] During epidemic disease in Taiwan in 1998, children with herpangina and aseptic meningitis, acute flaccid paralysis, and rhombencephalitis were described.[14, 15, 39] In one study, a biphasic course was described, with herpangina occurring first and neurologic manifestations 2 to 5 days later.[15]

Routine laboratory study is of little value in herpangina. The total white blood cell count may be normal or slightly elevated; the differential count most often is normal.

Differential Diagnosis

The classic appearance of the oropharynx in herpangina makes diagnosis easy. It can be differentiated clearly from bacterial pharyngitis on clinical grounds, so obtaining bacterial cultures seldom is necessary. The follicular lesions of adenoviral infections can be confused with it, but they frequently are exudative, not ulcerative, and associated with a more marked, generalized, erythematous pharyngitis than is herpangina. Additional differential considerations are presented elsewhere (see Chapters 10 and 170).

Specific Diagnosis

In most instances, a clinical diagnosis is all that is necessary. However, because herpangina is a good indicator of enteroviral disease in a community, submission of throat or rectal specimens to a viral diagnostic center can be rewarding.

Treatment, Prognosis, and Prevention

No treatment is necessary other than attention to hydration and observation for signs of more severe enteroviral illness. Except in rare instances (associated myocarditis, encephalitis), the prognosis is excellent. No general preventive measures are necessary, but a wise policy is not to expose young children unnecessarily to persons known to be afflicted.

REFERENCES

1. Ager, E. A., Felsenstein, W. C., Alexander, E. R., et al.: An epidemic of illness due to Coxsackie virus group B, type 2. J. A. M. A. *187:*251–256, 1964.
2. Artenstein, M. S., Cadigan, F. C., Jr., and Buescher, E. L.: Epidemic Coxsackie virus infection with mixed clinical manifestations. Ann. Intern. Med. *60:*196–203, 1964.
3. Artenstein, M. S., Cadigan, F. C., Jr., and Buescher, E. L.: Clinical and epidemiological features of Coxsackie group B virus infections. Ann. Intern. Med. *63:*597–603, 1965.
4. Breese, B. B., Jr.: Aphthous pharyngitis. Am. J. Dis. Child. *61:*669–674, 1941.
5. Chang, L. Y., Lin, T. Y., Huang, Y. C., et al.: Comparison of enterovirus 71 and coxsackie-virus A16 clinical illnesses during the Taiwan enterovirus epidemic, 1998. Pediatr. Infect. Dis. J. *12*:1092–1096, 1999.
6. Chang, L. Y., Lin, T. Y., Hsu, K. H., et al.: Clinical features and risk factors of pulmonary oedema after enterovirus-71-related hand, foot, and mouth disease. Lancet *354*:1682–1686, 1999.
7. Chawareewong, S., Kiangsiri, S., Lokaphadhana, K., et al.: Neonatal herpangina caused by Coxsackie A-5 virus. J. Pediatr. *93:*492–494, 1978.
8. Cherry, J. D., and Jahn, C. L.: Herpangina: The etiologic spectrum. Pediatrics *36:*632–634, 1965.
9. Felici, A., and Gregorig, B.: Contribution to the study of diseases in Italy caused by the Coxsackie B group of viruses. II. Epidemiological, clinical and virological data obtained in the course of a summer outbreak caused by Coxsackie B4 virus. Arch. Ges. Virusforsch. *9:*317–328, 1959.
10. Forman, M. L., and Cherry, J. D.: Enanthems associated with uncommon viral syndromes. Pediatrics *41:*873–882, 1968.
11. Glick, S. M., and Stroud, R.: An unusual case of Coxsackie B infection. Arch. Intern. Med. *109:*97–101, 1962.
12. Hable, K. A., O'Connell, E. J., and Herrmann, E. C., Jr.: Group B coxsackieviruses as respiratory viruses. Mayo Clin. Proc. *45:*170–176, 1970.
13. Hierholzer, J. C., Mostow, S. R., and Dowdle, W. R.: Prospective study of a mixed coxsackie virus B3 and B4 outbreak of upper respiratory illness in a children's home. Pediatrics *49:*744–752, 1972.
14. Ho, M., Chen, E. R., Hsu, K. H., et al.: An epidemic of enterovirus 71 infection in Taiwan. N. Engl. J. Med. *341*:929–935, 1999.
15. Huang, C. C., Liu, C. C., Chang, Y. C., et al.: Neurologic complications in children with enterovirus 71 infection. N. Engl. J. Med. *341*:936–942, 1999.
16. Huebner, R. J., Cole, R. M., Beeman, E. A., et al.: Herpangina: Etiological studies of a specific infectious disease. J. A. M. A. *145:*628–633, 1951.
17. Johnsson, T., and Lindahl, J.: Herpangina: A clinical and virological study. Arch. Ges. Virusforsch. *2:*96–109, 1953.
18. Kibrick, S.: Current status of Coxsackie and ECHO viruses in human disease. Prog. Med. Virol. *6:*27–70, 1964.
19. Komatsu, H., Shimizu, Y., Takeuchi, Y., et al.: Outbreak of severe neurologic involvement associated with Enterovirus 71 infection. Pediatr. Neurol. *20*:17–23, 1999.
20. Kravis, L. P., Hummeler, K., Sigel, M. M., et al.: Herpangina: Clinical and laboratory aspects of an outbreak caused by Group A Coxsackie viruses. Pediatrics *11:*113–119, 1953.
21. Lepow, M. L., Carver, D. H., and Robbins, F. C.: Clinical and epidemiologic observations on enterovirus infection in a circumscribed community during an epidemic of ECHO 9 infection. Pediatrics *26:*12–26, 1960.
22. Lerner, A. M., Klein, J. O., Levin, H. S., et al.: Infections due to Coxsackie virus group A, type 9, in Boston, 1959, with special reference to exanthems and pneumonia. N. Engl. J. Med. *263:*1265–1272, 1960.
23. Lerner, A. M., Klein, J. O., and Finland, M.: Infection with Coxsackie virus group B, type 3, with vesicular eruption: Report of two cases. N. Engl. J. Med. *263:*1305, 1960.
24. Levine, H. B., Hoerr, S. O., and Allanson, J. C.: Vesicular pharyngitis and stomatitis: An unusual epidemic of possible herpetic origin. J. A. M. A. *112:*2020–2022, 1939.
25. Liu, C. C., Tseng, H. W., Wang, S. M., et al.: An outbreak of enterovirus 71 infection in Taiwan, 1998: Epidemiologic and clinical manifestations. J. Clin. Virol. *17*:23–30, 2000.
26. McLean, D. M., Coleman, M. A., Larke, R. P. B., et al.: Viral infections of Toronto children during 1965. I. Enteroviral disease. Can. Med. Assoc. J. *94:*839–843, 1966.
27. Marchessault, V., Pavilanis, V., Podoski, M. O., et al.: An epidemic of aseptic meningitis caused by Coxsackie B type 2 virus. Can. Med. Assoc. J. *85:*123–126, 1961.
28. Marks, M. I.: Herpangina and pleurodynia associated with herpes simplex virus. Pediatrics *48:*305–307, 1971.
29. Moore, M.: Enteroviral disease in the United States, 1970–1979. J. Infect. Dis. *146:*103–108, 1982.
30. Moritsugu, Y., Sawada, K., Hinohara, M., et al.: An outbreak of type 25 Echovirus infections with exanthem in an infant home near Tokyo. Am. J. Epidemiol. *87:*599–608, 1968.
31. Nakayama, T., Urano, T., Osano, M., et al.: Outbreak of herpangina associated with Coxsackievirus B3 infection. Pediatr. Infect. Dis. *8*:495–498, 1989.
32. Neva, F. A., Feemster, R. F., and Gorbach, I. J.: Clinical and epidemiological features of an unusual epidemic exanthem. J. A. M. A. *155:*544–548, 1954.
33. Parrott, R. H., Ross, S., Burke, F. G., et al.: Herpangina: Clinical studies of a specific infectious disease. N. Engl. J. Med. *245:*275–280, 1951.
34. Ray, C. G., Plexico, K. L., Wenner, H. A., et al.: Acute respiratory illness associated with Coxsackie B4 virus in children. Pediatrics *39:*220–226, 1967.
35. Reinhard, K. R.: Ecology of enteroviruses in the western Arctic. J. A. M. A. *183:*410–418, 1963.
36. Sabin, A. B.: Role of ECHO viruses in human disease. *In* Rose, H. M. (ed.): Viral Infections of Infancy and Childhood. Symposium No. 19, Section on Microbiology, New York Academy of Medicine. New York, Hoeber-Harper, 1960, pp. 78–100.
37. St. Geme, J. W., Jr., and Prince, J. T.: Vesicular pharyngitis associated with Coxsackie virus group B, type 5. N. Engl. J. Med. *265:*1255–1256, 1961.
38. Scott, T. F. M.: Clinical syndromes associated with enterovirus and reovirus infection. Adv. Virus Res. *8:*165–197, 1962.
39. Shen, W. C., Tsai, C., Chiu, H., et al.: MRI of Enterovirus 71 myelitis with monoplegia. Neuroradiology *42*:124–127, 2000.
40. Simkova, A., and Petrovicova, A.: Experimental infection of rhesus monkeys with Coxsackie A 4 virus. Acta Virol. *16:*250–257, 1972.
41. Suzuki, N., Ishikawa, K., Horiuchi, T., et al.: Age-related symptomatology of ECHO 11 virus infection in children. Pediatrics *65:*284–286, 1980.
42. Wenner, H. A.: The enteroviruses. Am. J. Clin. Pathol. *57:*751–761, 1972.
43. Wenner, H. A.: Virus diseases associated with cutaneous eruptions. Prog. Med. Virol. *16:*269–336, 1973.
44. Winsser, J., and Altieri, R. H.: A three-year study of Coxsackie virus, group B, infection in Nassau County. Part I. Fecal studies of patients. Am. J. Med. Sci. *247:*269–273, 1964.
45. Zahorsky, J.: Herpetic sore throat. South. Med. J. *13:*871–872, 1920.
46. Zahorsky, J.: Herpangina: A specific infectious disease. Arch. Pediatr. *41:*181–184, 1924.

CHAPTER 12 Pharyngoconjunctival Fever

JAMES D. CHERRY

Pharyngoconjunctival fever is an acute, communicable disease syndrome characterized by fever, pharyngitis, and conjunctivitis. It is caused by several serologic types of adenovirus; illness is both epidemic and sporadic.

History

Shortly after the first isolation of adenoviruses in tissue culture by Rowe and associates[53] in 1953, the clear association of infection with certain adenoviral types and the syndrome of fever, pharyngitis, and conjunctivitis was established.[51] For an approximate 5-year period after the discovery of the adenoviral etiology of pharyngoconjunctival fever, the literature contained numerous confirmatory reports from throughout the world.* In almost all reports, the association

*See references 1, 3, 6–8, 11, 16, 18, 20, 21, 24–27, 31–36, 38–41, 46–49, 56, 58–60, 62, 64–66, 68, 69.

between swimming and the contraction of the syndrome was noted. A quick perusal of the reports would suggest that both the syndrome and the etiologic agents were new discoveries. However, epidemics of pharyngoconjunctival fever–like illness have been noted throughout this century. Béal[4] in 1907 in France was perhaps the first to note the syndrome. In the 1920s, epidemics of febrile disease with conjunctivitis associated with swimming in public pools and lakes were noted in Germany[50] and the United States.[2] Quite probably, "swimming bath conjunctivitis," as described by Derrick[15] in 1943, was caused by adenoviral infection; an epidemic of conjunctivitis studied by Cockburn and associates[11] in Greeley, Colorado, in 1951 was later proved to have been caused by adenovirus type 3.

During the last 33 years, reports of pharyngoconjunctival fever have been relatively few.* My experience suggests that this paucity is not because of a decrease in prevalence of the syndrome but because of a general disinterest in the differential diagnosis of viral respiratory disease.

Etiologic Agents

In epidemic pharyngoconjunctival fever, the most likely etiologic agent is adenovirus 3.† The next most prevalent adenovirus associated with epidemic disease is type 7.[9, 16, 20, 72] One or more epidemics also have been noted with adenoviruses 2, 4, 7a, 11, and 14.[1, 6, 14, 17, 18, 47, 64, 66, 75] Sporadic occurrences of pharyngoconjunctival fever have been observed in association with infections with adenoviruses 1, 2, 3, 4, 5, 6, 7, 7a, 8, 14, 19, and 13/30 (an intermediate type).‡

Epidemiology

Pharyngoconjunctival fever occurs in large community-wide epidemics, in focal outbreaks, and as sporadic cases. Most major community epidemics have occurred in the summertime and have been centered around public swimming facilities. Two community outbreaks involving primarily swimmers have occurred in the wintertime.[9, 22] In swimming-associated outbreaks, infection probably occurs by conjunctival inoculation of adenoviruses from contaminated water. To date, however, the virus has been recovered from the incriminated water in only two outbreaks.[14, 45] In one outbreak, adenovirus type 4 was recovered from water samples on two occasions 14 days apart.[14] More recently, an adenovirus type 3 was recovered from a pool in which 681 campers had symptoms.[45] In this outbreak, both the frequency of swimming and the history of towel sharing increased the risk of acquiring illness. An adenovirus type 3 also was recovered from a sewage outlet area in a lake that was close to a swimming beach.[41]

The incubation period of swimming-associated infections is approximately 5 to 7 days.[5, 22, 36, 66] Secondary cases regularly occur in contacts (most often family members) of swimming-acquired cases. In these instances, the incubation period frequently is slightly longer (9 days).[3, 22] However, this longer period of incubation may be due to a delay in the time of spread of the virus to the contact rather than an actual prolongation of incubation. Secondary cases probably result from large-droplet respiratory spread to the conjunctiva, the upper respiratory tract, or both. An alternative method would be the contamination of the recipient's hands with eye discharge and then autoinoculation of the conjunctiva.

In non–swimming-associated outbreaks of adenoviral respiratory illness with appropriate serotypes, conjunctivitis occurs only rarely.[8, 21, 29, 34, 40, 62] This fact, in conjunction with the finding that pharyngoconjunctival fever occurred after conjunctival administration of virus but not after nasopharyngeal application in volunteers,[6, 57, 69] suggests that the conjunctiva must be inoculated directly for the syndrome to occur. After conjunctival inoculation, pharyngeal spread and systemic illness occur. However, after direct respiratory inoculation, the conjunctiva does not become involved unless respiratory secretions containing virus are applied to the conjunctiva, presumably by autoinoculation. Hospital outbreaks of pharyngoconjunctival fever–like illnesses have been reported.[19, 42] Most instances have occurred in intensive care units. An outbreak of pharyngoconjunctival fever also has been noted in a daycare center.[10]

Although some early epidemic investigations suggested that boys were more susceptible to disease than were girls,[20, 64] the incidence of pharyngoconjunctival fever in children in fact does not differ by sex.[5, 60] In some cultures, boys had more exposure to swimming and, therefore, accounted for more cases of illness. In an outbreak that occurred in children hospitalized in Japan for long-term treatment of bronchial asthma, the attack rate was 68.2 percent in boys and only 6.3 percent in girls. This sex difference was attributed to the fact that the boys and girls took separate daily communal baths. Secondary cases in adult family members occur more commonly in mothers than in fathers, presumably because of greater contact with the children.[5, 22]

Pathophysiology

The route of infection with adenoviruses that are capable of causing pharyngoconjunctival fever determines the pathologic manifestations.

Conjunctival biopsy specimens in volunteer studies revealed an inflammatory response with lymphocytic infiltration of the submucosal layer.[6, 7] Biopsy material from palatine tonsils of infected volunteers revealed both hypertrophy and hyperplasia of the lymphoid tissue with congestion and edema of the surrounding connective tissue.

Clinical Presentation

By definition, pharyngoconjunctival fever is a syndrome characterized by fever, pharyngitis, and conjunctivitis. During epidemics, not all children and adults who have the same infection have the complete syndrome triad. Some patients have only pharyngitis, and some have only conjunctivitis. For purposes of this discussion, all descriptions of frequency of signs and symptoms are calculated from the starting point of 100 percent fever, pharyngitis, and conjunctivitis.

The frequencies of specific signs and symptoms are presented in Tables 12–1 and 12–2.* Although some patients have noted mild prodromal symptoms of headache and malaise, the usual onset of illness is abrupt, with sore

*See references 9, 13, 14, 17, 22, 23, 27, 30, 31, 44, 45, 47, 52, 53, 55, 57, 63, 67, 70, 71, 72, 75.

†See references 3, 5, 6, 8, 11, 22, 24, 26, 32, 35–37, 41, 44, 45, 48, 51, 58, 64, 71, 75.

‡See references 6, 7, 23, 24, 29–31, 34, 38–40, 46, 54, 55, 59–63, 65, 67, 70.

*See references 7, 9, 20, 26, 36, 38, 39, 44, 51, 56, 57, 64.

TABLE 12–1 ■ RELATIVE FREQUENCY OF SYMPTOMS IN EPIDEMIC PHARYNGOCONJUNCTIVAL FEVER

Symptoms	Frequency*
Throat complaints	++++
Soreness	++++
Cough	++
Foreign body sensation	++
Dry feeling	+
Eye complaints	+++
Aching or soreness	+++
Burning sensation	++
Lacrimation	+
Photophobia	+
Nasal complaints	+++
Coryza	++
Stuffiness and/or blockage	++
Sneezing	+
Epistaxis	+
Other complaints	++++
Headache	++++
Anorexia	+++
Malaise	++
Generalized aches and pains	++
Nausea	++
Vomiting	+
Diarrhea	+
Abdominal pain	+

Data from references 7, 9, 20, 26, 36, 38, 39, 44, 51, 56, 57, 64.

*++++, 76 to 100 percent; +++, 51 to 75 percent; ++, 26 to 50 percent; +, 1 to 25 percent.

throat, generalized aches and pains, eye irritation or pain, and fever. Throat complaints vary from mild to severe. In some patients, only a dry, scratchy feeling is reported; others have noted the feeling of a foreign body. On examination, the tonsils and pharyngeal lymphoid tissue are hypertrophied. The degree of pharyngeal redness and infection varies considerably from patient to patient. Approximately one third of those affected will have follicular exudative lesions that cannot be differentiated from streptococcal disease on clinical grounds. Follicular lesions also have been noted on the soft palate, and the papillae of the tongue may be hypertrophied.

Hypertrophy of the adenoids occurs, which results in nasal blockage. Coryza is a common occurrence. Posterior nasal discharge is a common occurrence and leads to cough in many instances. In some investigations, epistaxis has occurred in as many as 20 percent of the cases.[56, 64]

In general, complaints related to the conjunctivitis are fewer than might be suggested by the usual physical appearance. Most patients note some aching or soreness; photophobia and lacrimation are unusual occurrences. The appearance of the palpebral conjunctiva usually is granular. The lesions may be almost microscopic or as large as 2 to 3 mm in diameter. Hemorrhages occasionally are noted on the bulbar surface. Frequently, involvement starts in one eye and does not involve the other eye until 2 or 3 days later. On occasion, the involvement is restricted to one eye.

Some degree of anterior and posterior cervical lymphadenopathy occurs in most patients. Preauricular involvement occurs surprisingly infrequently when the degree of eye involvement is taken into consideration. Generalized lymphadenopathy is observed in 10 to 20 percent of affected patients, and liver and spleen enlargement occurs frequently.

TABLE 12–2 ■ RELATIVE FREQUENCY OF SIGNS IN EPIDEMIC PHARYNGOCONJUNCTIVAL FEVER

Signs	Frequency*
Throat findings	++++
Erythema and infection	++++
Hypertrophied lymphatic tissue	++++
Particular exudate	++
Eye findings	++++
Erythema and infection of palpebral and bulbar conjunctiva	++++
Edema	+++
Granular and follicular involvement	++
Eyes unequally affected	++
Superficial punctate keratitis	+
Lymph node enlargement	++++
Cervical	++++
Preauricular	+
Generalized	+
Fever	++++
≥39° C (≥102.2° F)	+++
Other	
Flushed face	+++
Enlarged liver and/or spleen	+

Data from references 7, 9, 20, 26, 36, 38, 39, 51, 56, 57, 64.

*++++, 76 to 100 percent; +++, 51 to 75 percent; ++, 26 to 50 percent; +, 1 to 25 percent.

Most patients complain of generalized symptoms, but the degree varies considerably among those affected. Temperature higher than 39° C (102.2° F) occurs in more than 50 percent of the patients, and headache is the rule. General malaise and anorexia are common occurrences; gastrointestinal symptoms occur in approximately 25 percent of cases. Vomiting and diarrhea occur most commonly in the younger age groups.

Compared with other respiratory viral infections, the duration of illness with pharyngoconjunctival fever is relatively long. In most patients, the fever is sustained or remittent for 3 to 4 days, and then temperature gradually returns to normal during 24 to 48 hours. Approximately 10 percent of patients will have fever that lasts longer than 7 days. Throat and eye findings usually are improved considerably by the seventh day of illness, but these findings, as well as nasal complaints, fatigue, and headache, may persist for 14 days.

Early in the illness, the total white blood cell count is within normal limits or slightly elevated, with a normal differential count or one with a slight increase in polymorphonuclear leukocytes. During convalescence, many patients have a moderate leukopenia with an equal number of lymphocytes and polymorphonuclear cells. Smears from affected conjunctivae usually do not reveal abnormalities on cytologic examination.

Differential Diagnosis

Because the symptom triad of fever, pharyngitis, and conjunctivitis is virtually unique to pharyngoconjunctival fever, making the diagnosis should be easy. The only difficulty on clinical grounds is in trying to assign a specific type of adenovirus. In general, major epidemic disease is most likely to be caused by type 3 or 7; sporadic cases can occur with types 1 to 8, 14, 19, and 13/30. Manifestations by different adenoviral types have no known differences.

Of some concern in the differential diagnosis is picornavirus epidemic conjunctivitis (acute hemorrhagic conjunctivitis).[43, 73, 74] Two enteroviruses (coxsackievirus A24 and enterovirus 70) have been implicated etiologically in several extensive outbreaks of disease. Affected patients have had severe conjunctivitis with preauricular lymphadenitis, but fever and pharyngitis have not been prominent associated signs. However, in one outbreak, 23 percent of those studied had upper respiratory tract symptoms.[43]

Generalized diseases that on occasion might be confused with pharyngoconjunctival fever include leptospirosis, psittacosis, *Mycoplasma pneumoniae* infection, Q fever, Newcastle disease virus infection, and prodromal measles. Of these illnesses, all but Newcastle disease virus infection have generalized symptoms that are disproportionately more important than those of either conjunctivitis or pharyngitis. Human infection with Newcastle disease virus could be confused easily on clinical grounds with pharyngoconjunctival fever. However, a history of exposure to chickens or other fowl should aid in diagnosis.

Of more difficulty in making a differential diagnosis are illnesses usually characterized by either pharyngitis or conjunctivitis. On occasion, infections with influenza viruses, parainfluenza viruses, enteroviruses (other than coxsackievirus A24 and enterovirus 70), and Epstein-Barr virus are confusing. Although eye complaints do occur in these illnesses, severe conjunctivitis usually does not occur.

The differential diagnosis of conjunctivitis includes bacterial infections caused by *Haemophilus influenzae, Streptococcus pneumoniae, Streptococcus pyogenes,* and *Neisseria gonorrhoeae.* In all of these infections, purulent discharge is greater than that usually observed in pharyngoconjunctival fever. *Chlamydia trachomatis* infections are perhaps the most troublesome in the differential diagnosis. In the past, many cases of swimming pool conjunctivitis were attributed to chlamydial infections. Many such reported cases in reality probably were adenoviral infections. *C. trachomatis* infections can be diagnosed by the demonstration of characteristic inclusions in Giemsa-stained scrapings from the palpebral conjunctivae, by direct immunofluorescence, by enzyme immunoassay, or by culture. Epidemic adenoviral keratoconjunctivitis is another differential diagnostic consideration. Other differential diagnostic possibilities that should cause no difficulty include cat-scratch fever, tularemia, *Acanthamoeba* keratitis, and allergic conjunctivitis.

Specific Diagnosis

In most instances, a clinical diagnosis is all that is necessary. Specific viral diagnosis can be accomplished with ease in any routinely equipped diagnostic virology laboratory. Diagnosis can be made by isolation of virus in tissue culture or by direct antigen detection by indirect immunofluorescence, enzyme-linked immunosorbent assay, or polymerase chain reaction analysis.[10, 12, 52, 67] Cultures from the conjunctivae generally are more diagnostically specific than are those from the throat. The recovery of an adenovirus (particularly type 2) from the throat in an isolated case does not necessarily indicate an etiologic role for the recovered virus. An adenoviral etiology also can be verified by studying paired serum samples for a titer rise to the adenoviral group antigen.

Treatment

In general, no treatment is necessary or effective in pharyngoconjunctival fever. If conjunctivitis persists and becomes purulent, an investigation for bacterial pathogens and appropriate topical antimicrobial therapy are indicated. Use of steroid-containing ophthalmic ointments should be avoided.

Prognosis

The prognosis generally is excellent. Although superficial keratitis occasionally occurs, permanent scarring is not a problem. Sinusitis, otitis media, and bacterial conjunctivitis are rare secondary complications that, if untreated, can result in long-term difficulties.

Prevention

Volunteer studies have clearly indicated that infection and presumable resultant antibody are protective against future disease. Therefore, protection theoretically could be achieved through immunization, but priority to study and to implement an immunization program is low. Because the major cause of pharyngoconjunctival fever caused by adenoviruses is swimming in contaminated water, discretion in bathing locations is advised. Swimming pool water should be chlorinated adequately, and pool filtration systems should be inspected daily. Ill persons should be excluded from swimming pools during their illness and for a period of up to at least 2 weeks after recovery.

REFERENCES

1. Albano, A., Salvaggio, L., and Morrone, G.: Episodio epidemico de febbre faringocongiuntivale da adenovirus di tipo 2. Boll. Ist. Sieroter. Milan. *40:*580–584, 1961.
2. Bahn, C. A.: Swimming bath conjunctivitis. New Orleans Med. Surg. J. *79:*586–590, 1927.
3. Barr, J., Kjellén L., and Svedmyr, A.: Hospital outbreak of adenovirus type 3 infections: A clinical and virologic study on 38 patients partly involved in a nosocomial outbreak. Acta Pediatr. *47:*365–382, 1958.
4. Béal, R.: Sur une forme particuliére de conjonctivité aigue avec follicules. Ann. D'Oculistique *Jan.:*1–33, 1907.
5. Bell, J. A., Rowe, W. P., Engler, J. I., et al.: Pharyngoconjunctival fever: Epidemiological studies of a recently recognized disease entity. J. A. M. A. *157:*1083–1092, 1955.
6. Bell, J. A., Ward, T. G., Huebner, R. J., et al.: Studies of adenoviruses (APC) in volunteers. Am. J. Public Health *46:*1130–1146, 1956.
7. Bell, J. A.: Clinical manifestations of pharyngoconjunctival fever. Am. J. Ophthalmol. *43:*11–14, 1957.
8. Bell, T. M., Turner, G., MacDonald, A., et al.: Type-3 adenovirus infection. Lancet *2:*1327–1329, 1960.
9. Caldwell, G. G., Lindsey, N. J., Wulff, H., et al.: Epidemic of adenovirus type 7 acute conjunctivitis in swimmers. Am. J. Epidemiol. *99:*230–234, 1974.
10. Chomel, J. J., Szymczyszyn, P., Honneger, D., et al.: An epidemic of adenovirus type 1 conjunctivitis. Pediatr. Infect. Dis. J. *8:*885–886, 1989.
11. Cockburn, T. A., Rowe, W. P., and Huebner, R. J.: Relationship of the 1951 Greeley, Colorado, outbreak of conjunctivitis and pharyngitis to type 3 APC virus infection. Am. J. Hyg. *63:*250–253, 1956.
12. Cooper, R. J., Yeo, A. C., Bailey, A. S., and Tullo, A. B.: Adenovirus polymerase chain reaction assay for rapid diagnosis of conjunctivitis. Invest. Ophthalmol. Vis. Sci. *40:*90–95, 1999.
13. Cooper, R. J., Hallett, R., Tullo, A. B., and Klapper, P. E.: The epidemiology of adenovirus infections in Greater Manchester, UK, 1982–96. Epidemiol. Infect. *125:*333–345, 2000.
14. D'Angelo, L. J., Hierholzer, J. C., Keenlyside, R. A., et al.: Pharyngoconjunctival fever caused by adenovirus type 4: Report of a swimming pool-related outbreak with recovery of virus from pool water. J. Infect. Dis. *140:*42–47, 1979.
15. Derrick, E. H.: Swimming-bath conjunctivitis, with a report of 3 probable cases and a note on its epidemiology. Med. J. Aust. *2:*334–336, 1943.

16. Duxbury, A. E., McCutchan, R., White, J., et al.: Epidemic adenovirus infection in a Victorian migrant centre presenting as pharyngoconjunctival fever. Med. J. Aust. *2:*413–417, 1960.
17. Ellis, A. W., McKinnon, G. T., Lewis, F. A., et al.: Adenovirus type 4 in Melbourne, 1969–1971. Med. J. Aust. *1:*209–211, 1974.
18. Epshtein, F. G., Agarkova, L. G., Dreizin, E. Y., et al.: Acute respiratory diseases in children caused by adenovirus of 7a type. Sov. Med. *2:*81–85, 1962.
19. Faden, H., Gallagher, M., Ogra, P., et al.: Nosocomial outbreak of pharyngoconjunctival fever due to adenovirus type 4: New York. M. M. W. R. *27:*49, 1978.
20. Forssell, P., Lapinleimu, K., Strandström, H., et al.: Febrile pharyngitis and conjunctivitis: An epidemic associated with APC virus infection. Ann. Med. Exp. Biol. Fenn. *34:*287–292, 1956.
21. Forssell, P., Halonen, H., Stenstrom, R., et al.: An adenovirus epidemic due to types 1 and 2. Ann. Pediatr. Fenn. *8:*35–44, 1962.
22. Foy, H. M., Cooney, M. K., and Hatlen, J. B.: Adenovirus type 3 epidemic associated with intermittent chlorination of a swimming pool. Arch. Environ. Health *17:*795–802, 1968.
23. Foy, H. M., and Grayston, J. T.: Adenoviruses. *In* Evans, A. S. (ed.): Viral Infections of Humans: Epidemiology and Control. New York, Plenum, 1976.
24. Fukumi, H., Nishikawa, F., Nakamura, K., et al.: Studies on the adenovirus as an etiological agent of pharyngoconjunctival fever. Jpn. J. Med. Sci. Biol. *10:*79–85, 1957.
25. Fukumi, H., Nishikawa, F., Nakamura, K., et al.: Further studies of the cases associated with adenoviruses. Jpn. J. Med. Sci. Biol. *10:*407–418, 1957.
26. Fukumi, H., Nishikawa, F., Mizutani, H., et al.: An epidemic of adenovirus type 3 infections among school children in an elementary school in Tokyo. Jpn. J. Med. Sci. Biol. *11:*129–140, 1958.
27. Fukumi, H., Nishikawa, F., Takemura, M., et al.: Isolation of adenovirus possessing both the antigens of types 3 and 7. Jpn. J. Med. Sci. Biol. *14:*173–181, 1961.
28. Harley, D., Harrower, B., Lyon, M., and Dick, A.: A primary school outbreak of pharyngoconjunctival fever caused by adenovirus type 3. Commun. Dis. Intell. *25:*9–12, 2001.
29. Harris, D. J., Wulff, H., Ray, C. G., et al.: Viruses and disease. III. An outbreak of adenovirus type 7a in a children's home. Am. J. Epidemiol. *93:*399–402, 1971.
30. Herrmann, E. C., Jr.: Experiences in laboratory diagnosis of adenovirus infections in routine medical practice. Mayo Clin. Proc. *43:*635–644, 1968.
31. Huebner, R. J., Rowe, W. P., and Chanock, R. M.: Newly recognized respiratory tract viruses. Annu. Rev. Microbiol. *12:*49–76, 1958.
32. Jansson, E., Wager, O., Forssel, P., et al.: Epidemic occurrence of adenovirus type 7 infection in Helsinki. Ann. Paediatr. Fenn. *8:*24–34, 1962.
33. Jones, B. R.: Sporadic ocular disease associated with adenovirus infection in London. Proc. R. Soc. Med. *50:*758–760, 1957.
34. Jordan, W. S., Jr., Badger, G. F., Curtiss, C., et al.: A study of illness in a group of Cleveland families. X. The occurrence of adenovirus infections. Am. J. Hyg. *64:*336–348, 1956.
35. Kaji, M., Kimura, M., Kamiya, S., et al.: An epidemic of pharyngoconjunctival fever among school children in an elementary school in Fukuoka prefecture. Kyushu J. Med. Sci. *12:*1–8, 1960.
36. Kaji, M., Kamiya, S., Tatewaki, E., et al.: An epidemic of pharyngoconjunctival fever in Moji, Kyushu. Kyushu J. Med. Sci. *12:*241–249, 1961.
37. Kawana, R., Kaneko, M., Matsumoto, I., et al.: An outbreak of pharyngoconjunctival fever due to adenovirus type 3. Jpn. J. Microbiol. *10:*149–157, 1966.
38. Kendall, E. J. C., Riddle, R. W., Tuck, H. A., et al.: Pharyngoconjunctival fever: School outbreaks in England during the summer of 1955 associated with adenovirus types 3, 7, and 14. Br. Med. J. *2:*131–136, 1957.
39. Kimura, S. J., Hanna, L., Nicholas, A., et al.: Sporadic cases of pharyngoconjunctival fever in Northern California, 1955–1956. Am. J. Ophthalmol. *43:*14–16, 1957.
40. Kjellén, L., Sterner, G., and Svedmyr, A.: On the occurrence of adenoviruses in Sweden. Acta Paediatr. *46:*164–176, 1957.
41. Kjellén, L., Zetterberg, B., and Svedmyr, A.: An epidemic among Swedish children caused by adenovirus type 3. Acta Paediatr. *46:*561–568, 1957.
42. Larsen, R. A., Jacobson, J. T., Jacobson, J. A., et al.: Hospital-associated epidemic of pharyngitis and conjunctivitis caused by adenovirus (21/H21 + 35). J. Infect. Dis. *154:*706–709, 1986.
43. Lim, K. H., and Yin-Murphy, M.: An epidemic of conjunctivitis in Singapore in 1970. Singapore Med. J. *12:*247–249, 1971.
44. Martone, W. J., Hierholzer, J. C., Keenlyside, R. A., et al.: An outbreak of adenovirus type 3 disease at a private recreation center swimming pool. Am. J. Epidemiol. *111:*229–237, 1980.
45. McMillan, N. S., Martin, S. A., Sobsey, M. D., et al.: Outbreak of pharyngoconjunctival fever at a summer camp: North Carolina, 1991. M. M. W. R. *41:*342–343, 1992.
46. Merchant, R. K., Rowe, W. P., Kasel, J. A., et al.: Pharyngoconjunctival fever due to type 1 adenovirus: Report of three cases. N. Engl. J. Med. *258:*131–133, 1958.
47. Nakayama, M., Miyazaki, C., Ueda, K., et al.: Pharyngoconjunctival fever caused by adenovirus type 11. Pediatr. Infect. Dis. J. *11:*6–9, 1992.
48. Oker-Blom, N., Wager, W., Strandström, H., et al.: Adenoviruses associated with pharyngoconjunctival fever: Isolation of adenovirus type 7 and serological studies suggesting its etiological role in an epidemic in Helsinki. Ann. Med. Exp. Biol. Fenn. *35:*342–351, 1957.
49. Ormsby, H. L., and Aitchison, W. S.: The role of the swimming pool in the transmission of pharyngeal-conjunctival fever. Can. Med. Assoc. J. *73:*864–866, 1975.
50. Paderstein, R.: Was ist Schwimmbad-Konjunktivitis? Klin. Monat. Augenh. *74:*634–642, 1925.
51. Parrott, T. H., Rowe, W. P., Huebner, R. J., et al.: Outbreak of febrile pharyngitis and conjunctivitis associated with type 3 adenoidal-pharyngeal-conjunctival virus infections. N. Engl. J. Med. *251:*1087–1090, 1954.
52. Player, V., and Westmoreland, D.: Rapid diagnosis of adenovirus pharyngoconjunctival fever: Use of a monoclonal antibody-based ELISA test during an outbreak. J. Virol. Methods *24:*307–312, 1989.
53. Rowe, W. P., Huebner, R. J., Gilmore, L. K., et al.: Isolation of a cytopathogenic agent from human adenoids undergoing spontaneous degeneration in tissue culture. Proc. Soc. Exp. Biol. Med. *84:*570–573, 1953.
54. Schaap, G. J. P., DeJong, J. C., Van Bijsterveld, O. P., et al.: A new intermediate adenovirus type causing conjunctivitis. Arch. Ophthalmol. *97:*2336–2338, 1979.
55. Schwartz, H. S., Vastine, D. W., Yamashiroya, H., et al.: Immunofluorescent detection of adenovirus antigen in epidemic keratoconjunctivitis. Invest. Ophthalmol. *15:*199–207, 1976.
56. Sobel, G., Aronson, B., Aronson, S., et al.: Pharyngoconjunctival fever. Am. J. Dis. Child. *92:*596–612, 1956.
57. Sohier, R., Chardonnet, Y., and Prunieras, M.: Adenoviruses: Status of current knowledge. Prog. Med. Virol. *7:*253–325, 1965.
58. Sterner, G.: Infections with adenovirus type 7 in children and their relationship to acute respiratory disease. Acta Paediatr. *48:*287–298, 1959.
59. Sterner, G., Gerzen, P., Ohlson, M., et al.: Acute respiratory illness and gastroenteritis in association with adenovirus type 7 infections. Acta Paediatr. *50:*457–468, 1961.
60. Sterner, G.: Adenovirus infection in childhood: An epidemiological and clinical survey among Swedish children. Acta Paediatr. *51:*1–30, 1962.
61. Sutton, R. N. P., Pullen, H. J. M., Blackledge, P., et al.: Adenovirus type 7; 1971–74. Lancet *2:*987–991, 1976.
62. Tyrrell, D. A. J., Balducci, D., and Zaiman, T. E.: Acute infections of the respiratory tract and the adenoviruses. Lancet *2:*1326–1330, 1956.
63. Van Bijsterveld, O. P., DeJong, J. C., Muzerie, C. J., et al.: Pharyngoconjunctival fever caused by adenovirus type 19. Ophthalmologica *177:*134–139, 1978.
64. Van Der Veen, J., and Van Der Ploeg, G.: An outbreak of pharyngoconjunctival fever caused by types 3 and 4 adenovirus at Waalwijk, the Netherlands. Am. J. Hyg. *68:*95–105, 1958.
65. Van Der Veen, J.: The role of adenoviruses in respiratory disease. Am. Rev. Respir. Dis. *88:*167–180, 1963.
66. Van Horne, R. G., Saslaw, S., Anderson, G. R., et al.: An intrafamilial epidemic of pharyngoconjunctival fever. Arch. Intern. Med. *99:*70–73, 1957.
67. Vastine, D. W., Schwartz, H. S., Yamashiroya, H. M., et al.: Cytologic diagnosis of adenoviral epidemic keratoconjunctivitis by direct immunofluorescence. Invest. Ophthalmol. *16:*195–200, 1977.
68. Wallis, A. L.: An unusual epidemic. Lancet *2:*290–291, 1955.
69. Ward, T. G., Huebner, R. J., Rowe, W. P., et al.: Production of pharyngoconjunctival fever in human volunteers inoculated with APC viruses. Science *122:*1086–1087, 1955.
70. Ward, T. G.: Viruses of the respiratory tract. Prog. Med. Virol. *15:*126–158, 1973.
71. Yamadera, S., Yamashita, K., Akatsuka, M., et al.: Adenovirus surveillance, 1982–1993, Japan. A report of the National Epidemiological Surveillance of Infectious Agents in Japan. Jpn. J. Med. Sci. Biol. *48:*199–210, 1995.
72. Yamadera, S., Yamashita, K., Akatsuka, M., et al.: Trend of adenovirus type 7 infection, an emerging disease in Japan. A report of the National Epidemiological Surveillance of Infectious Agents in Japan. Jpn. J. Med. Sci. Biol. *51:*43–51, 1998.
73. Yin-Murphy, M., and Lim, K. H.: Picornavirus epidemic conjunctivitis in Singapore. Lancet *1:*857–858, 1972.
74. Yin-Murphy, M.: Simple tests for the diagnosis of picornavirus epidemic conjunctivitis (acute haemorrhagic conjunctivitis). Bull. World Health Organ. *54:*675–679, 1976.
75. Yodfat, Y., and Nishmi, M.: Successive overlapping outbreaks of febrile pharyngitis and pharyngoconjunctival fever associated with adenovirus types 2 and 7, in a kibbutz. Isr. J. Med. Sci. *10:*1505–1509, 1974.

CHAPTER 13

Uvulitis

ELLEN R. WALD

Infections of the uvula have been reported infrequently in the medical literature. When the uvula is the most inflamed structure in the posterior pharynx of a febrile child, acute infection should be suspected. Other causes of uvulitis include trauma (from instrumentation), inhalant irritation (from cannabis use), vasculitis, and allergy.[2, 3, 5]

Etiology

The main bacterial agents that cause uvulitis in children include *Haemophilus influenzae* type b and *Streptococcus pyogenes*.[6] Uvulitis caused by *H. influenzae* may occur concurrently with epiglottitis or as an isolated infection.[8, 13] Uvulitis caused by *S. pyogenes* appears always to occur in concert with pharyngitis. Brook[1] reported two cases of uvulitis caused by anaerobic bacteria, *Fusobacterium nucleatum* and *Prevotella intermedia*. No search for viral agents has been conducted. Several cases of uvulitis caused by *Candida albicans* have been described in immunocompetent toddlers.[7]

In adults, both *Streptococcus pneumoniae* and *H. influenzae* have been reported to cause uvulitis.[4, 12] In many patients, an associated epiglottitis has been present.[9, 12]

Epidemiology

The epidemiology of uvulitis is the epidemiology of its two etiologic agents, *S. pyogenes* and *H. influenzae* type b. As such, it occurs in the school-age child between 5 and 15 years of age (the so-called streptococcal age group) in association with pharyngitis. Similarly, it can be seen in the *H. influenzae* age group (3 months to 5 years) if a child has not received the now routine and universally recommended conjugate vaccine to prevent infections caused by *H. influenzae* type b. Cases of uvulitis in association with epiglottitis have been reported in the United States and in England.[1, 6, 11] Infections caused by *S. pyogenes* and *H. influenzae* primarily occur in the winter and spring, but both types can occur throughout the year.

Pathogenesis

Uvulitis is an acute cellulitis characterized by dramatic swelling and erythema. Infection of the uvula probably arises from direct invasion by *S. pyogenes* or *H. influenzae* type b, both being recognized as normal nasopharyngeal flora. In the latter case, epiglottitis also may arise by direct extension, and the bacteremia may result secondarily from either the uvula or the epiglottis as a primary site of infection.

Uvulitis that is noninfectious may result from injury, chemical irritation, or allergic inflammation. A child ultimately diagnosed to have Kawasaki disease presented with uvulitis.[5]

Clinical Manifestations

In a review of five patients with streptococcal uvulitis, all had associated pharyngitis.[6] The patients presented with low-grade fever and sore throat. Three of the five patients experienced a choking or gagging sensation in the pharynx that induced coughing and spitting; one of these patients also presented with drooling. Although pharyngitis was noted on physical examination, the swelling and erythema of the uvula were most dramatic (Fig. 13–1). None of the patients had evidence of respiratory distress.

In most children with uvulitis and epiglottitis, the presentation usually is typical for epiglottitis, with sudden onset of high fever, dysphagia, and increasing respiratory distress. However, Rapkin[11] reported a case of uvulitis and epiglottitis in which the epiglottitis initially was unsuspected. The same observation has been made in some adults with uvulitis and epiglottitis.[4, 9] Lateral neck radiography (performed in one case to evaluate the possibility of a retropharyngeal abscess) belatedly alerted the clinicians to the correct diagnosis.

In patients with uvulitis and no epiglottitis, the presentation may be similar to that of epiglottitis (acute onset of fever, odynophagia, and drooling) or less specific, with fever and irritability or decreased appetite.[8, 13] The diagnosis in these cases is provided by physical examination of the oropharynx, which shows a swollen and erythematous uvula (see Fig. 13–1).

Diagnosis

The diagnosis of streptococcal uvulitis is suspected when a school-age child presents with low-grade fever, pharyngitis, and uvulitis. The diagnosis is confirmed by the recovery of *S. pyogenes* from a surface culture of the throat or uvula or both.

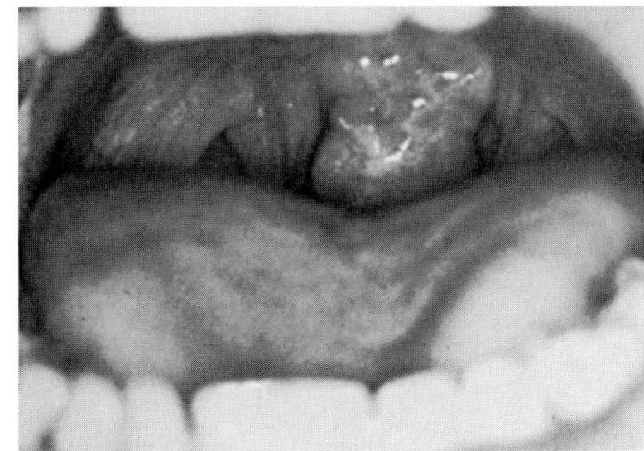

FIGURE 13–1 ■ Swollen (two to three times normal size) and erythematous uvula in a patient without epiglottitis or pharyngitis.

The diagnosis of uvulitis caused by *H. influenzae* is suspected in a highly febrile infant or preschool-age child who has uvular inflammation on physical examination. Lateral neck radiography must be performed to evaluate the possibility of epiglottitis, unless obvious signs of upper respiratory obstruction are present, in which case immediate endoscopy is warranted. If epiglottitis is discovered, the airway must be secured and appropriate parenteral antimicrobials initiated after blood and surface culture specimens are obtained. Any surface culture specimen obtained to search for *H. influenzae* must be plated onto chocolate agar. After appropriate culture specimens are obtained, parenteral antimicrobials should be initiated, as in other infections associated with bacteremia caused by *H. influenzae*.

Differential Diagnosis

The differential diagnosis of the patient with acute onset of fever, dysphagia, and drooling includes herpes simplex gingivostomatitis, uvulitis, epiglottitis, severe pharyngitis, and peritonsillar or retropharyngeal abscess. Although being extremely cautious in examining the pharynx of any patient with suspected epiglottitis is appropriate, some children will tolerate attempted visualization of the oral cavity without becoming unduly upset. Instrumentation with a tongue blade should be avoided. If the examination does not show gingivostomatitis or peritonsillar abscess, lateral neck radiography should be performed. If epiglottitis or retropharyngeal abscess is confirmed, management of the airway and administration of antimicrobials are indicated for epiglottitis, incision and drainage and antimicrobials for retropharyngeal abscess. If the lateral neck is normal and the uvula is inflamed, uvulitis with or without pharyngitis is confirmed.

Treatment

Management of uvulitis is guided primarily by the associated pharyngitis or epiglottitis, if either is present. In the case of streptococcal pharyngitis, penicillin therapy for 10 days is most appropriate. These patients can usually be treated orally with penicillin V, 25 to 50 mg/kg/day, administered in two divided doses.

In the case of uvulitis and epiglottitis, management of the airway is most important and can be accomplished by nasotracheal intubation or tracheotomy. Appropriate parenteral antibiotic therapy is usually initiated.

In the case of uvulitis without epiglottitis in an infant or preschool-age child, antimicrobial therapy should be planned for possible *H. influenzae* type b bacteremia. In general, approximately 50 percent of respiratory isolates of *H. influenzae* are β-lactamase producing. Accordingly, an advanced-generation cephalosporin, such as cefotaxime at 200 mg/kg/day in four divided doses or ceftriaxone at 100 mg/kg/day in one dose or two divided doses, is appropriate. In a patient with serious penicillin hypersensitivity, aztreonam at 100 mg/kg/day in three divided doses is also a satisfactory regimen. After the patient has defervesced and has improved clinically, an oral antimicrobial agent can be substituted. The results of blood and surface cultures now can guide therapy. For an ampicillin-sensitive *H. influenzae* infection, amoxicillin at 45 mg/kg/day in two divided doses should be prescribed to complete a 7- to 10-day course of treatment. For β-lactamase–producing *H. influenzae,* a variety of oral agents, including cefixime at 10 mg/kg in a single daily dose, cefuroxime at 30 mg/kg/day in two divided doses, or amoxicillin–potassium clavulanate at 45 mg/kg/day of amoxicillin in two divided doses, can be prescribed.

Resolution was prompt in the two cases of uvulitis allegedly caused by *C. albicans*; one child was treated with topical nystatin, and the other improved spontaneously.[7]

REFERENCES

1. Brook, I.: Uvulitis caused by anaerobic bacteria. Pediatr. Emerg. Care *13*:221, 1997.
2. Butterton, J. R., and Clawson-Simons, J.: Hymenoptera uvulitis. N. Engl. J. Med. *317*:1291, 1987.
3. Guarisco, J. L., Cheney, M. L., LeJeune, F. E., Jr., et al.: Isolated uvulitis secondary to marijuana use. Laryngoscope *98*:1309–1312, 1988.
4. Jerrard, D. A., and Olshaker, J.: Simultaneous uvulitis and epiglottitis without fever or leukocytosis. Am. J. Emerg. Med. *14*:551–552, 1996.
5. Kazi, A., Gauthier, M., Lebel, M. H., et al.: Uvulitis and supraglottitis: Early manifestations of Kawasaki disease. J. Pediatr. *120*:564–567, 1992.
6. Kotloff, K. L., and Wald, E. R.: Uvulitis in children. Pediatr. Infect. Dis. *2*:392–393, 1983.
7. Krober, M. S., and Weir, M. R.: Acute uvulitis apparently caused by *Candida albicans*. Pediatr. Infect. Dis. J. *10*:73, 1991.
8. Li, K. I., Kiernan, S., and Wald, E. R.: Isolated uvulitis due to *Hemophilus influenzae* type b. Pediatrics *74*:1054–1057, 1984.
9. McNamara, R., and Koobatian, T.: Simultaneous uvulitis and epiglottitis in adults. Am. J. Emerg. Med. *15*:161–163, 1997.
10. McNamara, R.: Clinical characteristics of acute uvulitis. Am. J. Emerg. Med. *12*:51–52, 1994.
11. Rapkin, R. H.: Simultaneous uvulitis and epiglottitis. J. A. M. A. *43*:1843, 1980.
12. Westerman, E. L., and Hutton, J. P.: Acute uvulitis associated with epiglottitis. Arch. Otolaryngol. Head Neck Surg. *112*:448–449, 1986.
13. Wynder, S. G., Lampe, R. M., and Shoemaker, M. E.: Uvulitis and *Hemophilus influenzae* bacteremia. Pediatr. Emerg. Care *2*:23–25, 1986.

Peritonsillar, Retropharyngeal, and Parapharyngeal Abscesses

NIRA A. GOLDSTEIN ■ MARGARET R. HAMMERSCHLAG

A deep neck abscess is a collection of pus in a potential space bounded by fascia.[5] These potential spaces are areas of least resistance to the spread of infection. An infection may begin with a minimal area of cellulitis and progress to a deep neck abscess, which may then extend to invade adjacent potential spaces; these spaces frequently encompass vital structures in the neck. Destruction and dysfunction of these structures represent the major complications of deep neck infections.[32]

Epidemiology of Head and Neck Space Infections in Children

Data concerning the frequency of head and neck space infections in children are limited. A survey conducted by the American Academy of Otolaryngology found the incidence of peritonsillar abscesses to be approximately 30 per 100,000 person-years, or approximately 45,000 cases annually in the United States and Puerto Rico.[24] A retrospective study from the Children's Hospital of Pittsburgh identified 117 children with head and neck space infections seen between 1986 and 1992.[54] The patients ranged in age from 1 month to 18 years, with a mean age of 7.8 years.[54] Peritonsillar space infections (cellulitis and abscesses) occurred most frequently, accounting for 61 (49%) of the cases, followed by retropharyngeal space infections with 27 (22%) of the cases. Only three (2%) parapharyngeal space infections were seen during the period of the study. Broughton[13] reported seeing 14 pediatric patients, 15 months to 17 years of age, with retropharyngeal and parapharyngeal space infections during a 9-year period at the University of Kentucky Medical Center.

Peritonsillar abscesses rarely occur in young children. They occur most commonly in patients in their late adolescence and the early part of the second decade. The mean age of the children with peritonsillar infection in Pittsburgh was 11 years, whereas the mean age of the patients with retropharyngeal space infections was 4 years, similar to the mean age of 4.5 years reported by Thompson and associates[53] in their 36-year review of 65 children with retropharyngeal abscesses treated at the Children's Hospital of Los Angeles. Retropharyngeal abscesses have been reported to occur more frequently in young children.

All of the peritonsillar infections were associated with tonsillitis, and 15 percent had antecedent infectious mononucleosis shown by positive monospot test results.[54] Results of a meta-analysis of 15 previously reported series of patients with peritonsillar abscess reported by Herzon[24] found prior tonsillar infection rates ranging from 11 to 56 percent, with an overall rate of 36 percent. The relatively high incidence of peritonsillar abscess reported in the American Academy of Otolaryngology study raised the possibility that the decreasing rate of tonsillectomy might increase the risk for development of peritonsillar abscess.[24]

Peritonsillar Abscess (Quinsy)

A peritonsillar abscess (quinsy) is circumscribed medially by the fibrous wall of the tonsil capsule and laterally by the superior constrictor muscle. Pus may be localized in the superior pole, midpoint, or inferior pole or rarely may be dispersed, with multiple loculations in the peritonsillar space. The superior pole is the most common location, with a frequency range of 41.2 to 70 percent; the remaining inferior locations account for the balance.[6, 9, 34]

The etiology of peritonsillar abscesses is not constant. They may occur after any "virulent" tonsillitis, with extension through the fibrous tonsil capsule.

CLINICAL MANIFESTATIONS

The recent history may include a sore throat with occasional unilateral pain, malaise, low-grade pyrexia, chills, diaphoresis, dysphagia, reduced oral intake, trismus, and a muffled "hot potato voice." Trismus results from irritation and reflex spasm of the internal pterygoid muscle. Sixty-three percent of the children with peritonsillar infection from the Pittsburgh series had trismus.[54] Impaired palatal motion from edema contributes to the muffled voice.

Physical examination reveals minimal to moderate toxicity, dehydration, and drooling. Inspection of the oropharynx may be compromised by trismus. The soft palate is displaced toward the unaffected side, swollen and red, and frequently palpably fluctuant. The edematous uvula is pushed across the midline. The displaced tonsil and its crypts rarely are coated with exudate. The breath is fetid, and ipsilateral, tender, cervical adenopathy is present. The white blood cell count is elevated, with a predominance of polymorphonuclear leukocytes.

Brodsky and associates[10] attempted to identify the clinical signs that might distinguish peritonsillar abscess from peritonsillar cellulitis in a group of 21 children admitted to the Children's Hospital of Buffalo from 1985 through 1987. No significant difference in age, duration of sore throat, fever, or white blood cell count was noted, although a greater degree of pharyngotonsillar bulge and muffled voice was found in the patients with abscess. However, patients with peritonsillar cellulitis improved after receiving 24 hours of intravenous antibiotics, whereas patients with peritonsillar abscess had no change or worsening of symptoms. Blotter and colleagues[7] confirmed these findings in a group of 102 patients admitted to Children's Hospital of Columbus, Ohio, between 1995 and 1998.

In uncomplicated cases, computed tomographic (CT) scan has not been as useful as have clinical assessment and follow-up evaluation in the management of peritonsillar abscess. CT scans are useful in young children with suspected peritonsillar abscess who are not cooperative with examination or children with other suspected deep neck infections.[20]

TREATMENT

Traditionally, management of peritonsillar abscess in children involved hospital admission for intravenous hydration, antibiotic therapy and analgesia, and either intraoral incision and drainage of the abscess or "acute quinsy tonsillectomy" with removal of the medial wall of the abscess. Although older children may tolerate incision and drainage under local anesthetic, the procedure is not well tolerated in young children and risks potential injury to adjacent vascular structures. The administration of a general anesthetic is required for tonsillectomy in all age groups and often is required for incision and drainage in young children. Acute tonsillectomy often was performed to prevent future recurrence of the peritonsillar abscess. Although it is a commonly accepted clinical observation, a high recurrence rate of peritonsillar abscess has not been well documented. A meta-analysis reported by Herzon[24] of 19 studies from the United States, Europe, and Israel involving 1399 patients found recurrence rates of peritonsillar abscess of 10 to 15 percent. The rates of recurrence appear to be lower in the United States (0% to 17%) than in the series reported from Europe and Israel (3% to 22%). A retrospective analysis of 290 patients treated for peritonsillar abscess found that patients who had a history of recurrent tonsillitis before development of the abscess had a fourfold greater rate of recurrence than did those with no history (40% versus 9.6%).[29] The authors recommended that patients with a history of recurrent tonsillitis before admission be treated with tonsillectomy.[29] The risks of acute tonsillectomy are not greater than those associated with delayed tonsillectomy.[33, 38] In addition, the morbidity of patients caused by two hospitalizations involving two procedures is reduced by acute tonsillectomy.[3, 8, 9] An additional benefit of the acute tonsillectomy is the ability to evacuate inferior pole abscesses that technically are difficult to drain by needle aspiration or incision and drainage.[34]

Studies have suggested that many peritonsillar abscesses can be managed by simple needle aspiration combined with antibiotic therapy on an outpatient basis.[10, 24, 44, 46, 48, 54, 55] An extensive meta-analysis of 10 studies conducted from 1961 through 1994 involving 496 patients with peritonsillar abscesses found that needle aspiration had an overall success rate of 94 percent (range, 85% to 100%).[24] This success rate compares favorably with that reported for incision and drainage. Weinberg and associates[55] successfully performed needle aspiration in 41 of 43 children, aged 7 to 18 years, with a mean age of 13.9 years. All were admitted for intravenous antibiotic therapy, two (5%) required repeated aspiration for resolution, and five (12%) did not respond and required acute tonsillectomy. Other studies, which have included both adults and children with peritonsillar abscesses, have reported that 0 to 14 percent of patients require hospitalization, although the ages of the patients requiring hospitalization have not been reported.[24, 44, 48] Younger children often require admission to correct dehydration.[20] Younger children also are more likely than are older children to respond to intravenous antibiotics alone and to have negative findings at surgical drainage.[7] The use of conscious sedation has been reported to be a safe and effective approach for the drainage of peritonsillar abscesses in children.[49]

A suggested approach to the management of children with peritonsillar abscess is as follows.[25] Cooperative children should undergo needle aspiration of the abscess and treatment with antibiotics. Children who can tolerate liquids orally may be managed as outpatients, and the remainder should be admitted for hydration and administration of intravenous antibiotics. Approximately 4 percent of children will require a repeated aspiration for resolution.[25] Children who remain symptomatic after undergoing needle aspiration require incision and drainage or acute quinsy tonsillectomy, depending on the prior history of recurrent tonsillitis. Children who cannot tolerate needle aspiration on initial presentation are admitted for administration of intravenous antibiotics. If no response occurs within 24 hours, incision and drainage or acute tonsillectomy is performed, depending on the prior history of recurrent tonsillitis. Delayed tonsillectomy is reserved for children who recover from the peritonsillar abscess without general anesthesia but have a history of recurrent tonsillitis or prior peritonsillar abscess.

Untreated peritonsillar abscess may point, with spontaneous rupture, or extend to the pterygomaxillary space, with potentially fatal complications. Upper airway obstruction, septicemia, and vascular catastrophe may occur. Necrotizing fasciitis also has been reported in adults with peritonsillar abscess.[21, 56]

Retropharyngeal Abscess (Posterior Visceral Space, Retrovisceral Space, and Retroesophageal Space Abscesses)

The anterior wall of the retropharyngeal space is the middle layer of the deep cervical fascia, which abuts the posterior esophageal wall (the superior pharyngeal constrictor muscle). The deep layer of the deep cervical fascia circumscribes the posterior wall of this potential space. Inferiorly, these two fasciae fuse to limit the depth of this pocket at a level between the first and second thoracic vertebrae. A retropharyngeal abscess can erode inferiorly through the junction of these fasciae to extend posteriorly into the prevertebral space (Fig. 14–1*A*). Subsequently, pus in the prevertebral space can descend inferiorly below the diaphragm to the psoas muscles.

The retropharyngeal space contains two paramedial chains of lymph nodes that receive drainage from the nasopharynx, adenoids, posterior paranasal sinuses, middle ear, and eustachian tube. These structures are prominent in early childhood and atrophy at puberty.[22] Retropharyngeal abscesses are common occurrences in young children and are thought to be secondary to suppurative adenitis of these retropharyngeal nodes.[2] Other sources of infection are penetrating foreign bodies, endoscopy, trauma, pharyngitis, vertebral body osteomyelitis, petrositis, dental procedures,[54] and branchial cleft anomalies.[26] In one series of 17 cases of retropharyngeal abscesses presenting to the Children's Hospital, Denver, Colorado, 7 children (41%), including 2 neonates (most likely associated with attempts at intubation), had perforations of the hypopharynx or esophagus.[39] In the Pittsburgh series, 63 percent of the children with retropharyngeal abscess had antecedent tonsillitis, pharyngitis, or viral upper respiratory tract infection.[54] Two children had previous trauma; however, no details on the type of trauma were given. In adults, tuberculosis and syphilis were common causes of retropharyngeal abscesses in the pre-antibiotic era.[42] Four of seven patients treated for retropharyngeal abscess at Columbia-Presbyterian Medical Center in New York during a 6-year period had serologic evidence of acute primary Epstein-Barr viral infection.[51]

CLINICAL MANIFESTATIONS

The symptoms of retropharyngeal abscess frequently begin insidiously after mild antecedent infection. Airway stridor from edema, cellulitis, or an obstructing mass is a common occurrence. Laryngeal edema may cause dyspnea and tachypnea. Dysphagia, drooling, and odynophagia may occur. No trismus occurs, but a stiff neck secondary to muscle tenderness may be present, along with an ipsilateral tender cervical adenopathy. Thirty-three percent of the 27 children with retropharyngeal abscess in the Pittsburgh series had torticollis or limitation of neck motion.[54] In the adult, the symptoms may be milder. Complaints of chest pain by an adult may reflect mediastinal extension.

Early in the course, midline or unilateral swelling of the posterior pharynx occurs. Later, gentle palpation may demonstrate a large fluctuant mass in the posterior pharynx. Vigorous palpation is to be avoided because it may cause the abscess to rupture into the upper airway. As with other abscesses, the white blood cell count is increased, with a predominance of granulocytes.

Plain films of the neck often are the initial radiologic study performed, but they must be taken with the patient in a true lateral position, with the neck in extension, and on inspiration, or the child's retropharyngeal soft tissues may appear abnormally thickened. Widening of the prevertebral soft tissues exceeding the anteroposterior diameter of the contiguous vertebral bodies or thickening of the retropharyngeal space greater than 7 mm at C2 in both children and adults, or 14 mm at C6 in children or 22 mm at C6 in adults, suggests retropharyngeal inflammation. Rarely, a prevertebral soft tissue mass, air-fluid level, or gas may be seen. The normal cervical lordosis may be lost or reversed secondary to muscle spasm or local inflammation (Fig. 14–2).

CT scan has rendered the diagnosis and management of deep neck space infections more precise.[17, 31, 52] In contrast

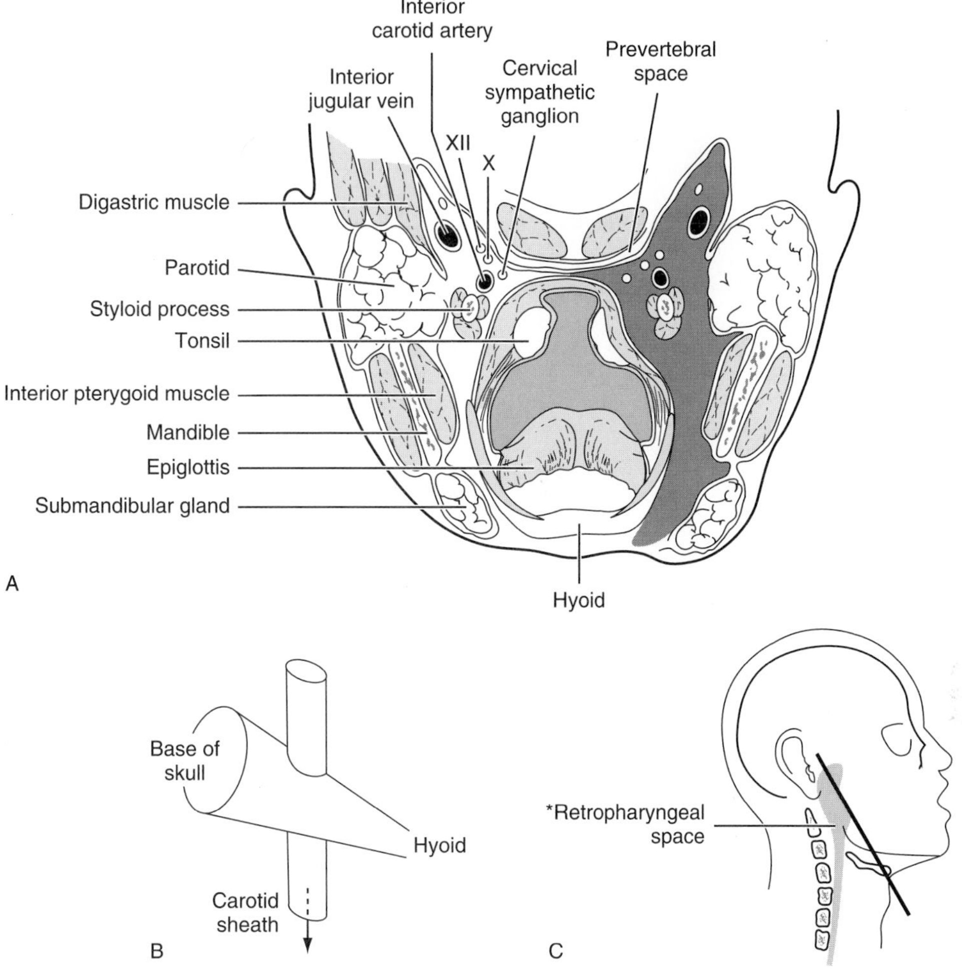

FIGURE 14–1 ■ *A,* Oblique transverse section of the oropharynx posterosuperiorly and the hypopharynx anteroinferiorly. Depicted are a peritonsillar abscess on the right and a pterygomaxillary space abscess on the left. The asterisk indicates the retropharyngeal space. *B,* The "cone" of the potential pterygomaxillary space with its carotid sheath. *C,* The vertical dimensions of the retropharyngeal space. The black oblique line repesents the level of the drawing in *A.*

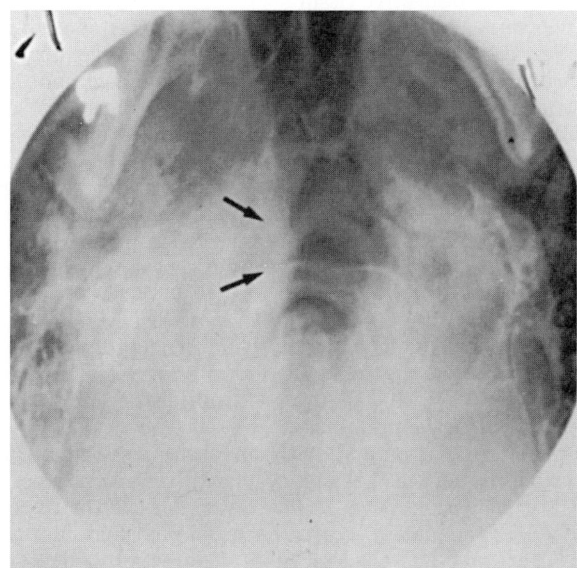

FIGURE 14–2 ■ Lateral neck radiograph demonstrating a retropharyngeal abscess containing gas and causing convexity of the cervical vertebrae.

to conventional radiologic studies, the CT scan distinguishes cellulitis of the neck, which usually does not require surgical treatment, from a deep neck abscess, which requires surgical drainage. With its ability to define differences in tissue density, CT scanning permits accurate determination of the extent of the abscess and its extension and involvement of adjacent spaces.[17, 31, 52] An abscess is distinguished from cellulitis by a low-attenuation homogeneous area surrounded by a ring enhancement of contrast material. When more than one space is involved, accurate assessment of these spaces may ensure sufficient surgical drainage. Vascular structures can be identified, as can potential complications such as venous thrombosis. Gas may also be detected by CT (Fig. 14–3).

A 10-year retrospective study from the Massachusetts Eye and Ear Infirmary compared preoperative CT scans with intraoperative findings in 38 patients who underwent surgical exploration of the parapharyngeal or retropharyngeal space within 48 hours after the scans were performed. Overall, the intraoperative findings confirmed the CT scan interpretation in 76.3 percent of the patients.[31] Of the 38 patients, 5 (13.2%) had CT scans indicative of abscesses that were not confirmed at surgery. Exploration of the parapharyngeal or retropharyngeal space revealed cellulitis. The

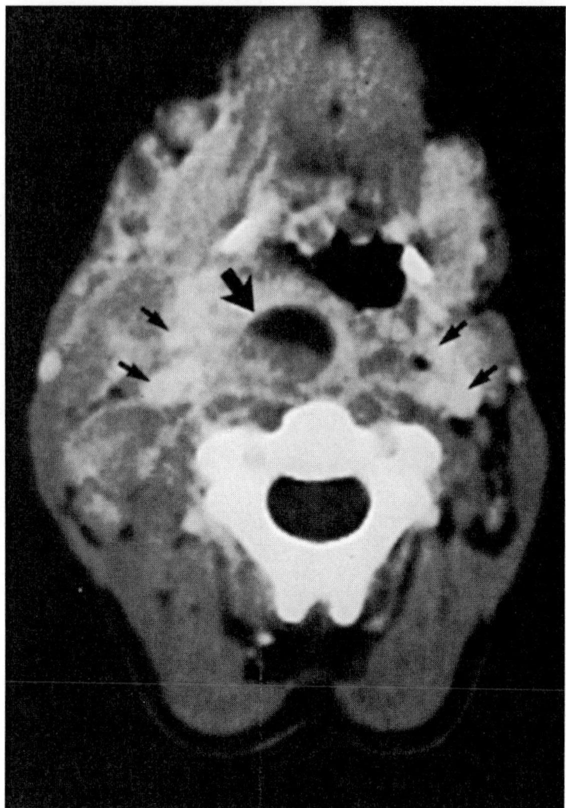

FIGURE 14–3 ■ Axial computed tomographic scan from a patient with a retropharyngeal abscess at the level of the base of the tongue demonstrating the abscess with its rim containing gas *(large arrow)*. The patient is supine, with the gas displaced superiorly. The great vessels are lateral to the abscess *(small arrows)*.

false-negative rate was 10.5 percent. The sensitivity of CT scanning for detection of parapharyngeal or retropharyngeal space abscess was 87.9 percent. Similar findings were reported in the Pittsburgh series; the sensitivity of CT scanning for differentiating an abscess from cellulitis was 91 percent.[54] In three cases, the radiologist's blinded CT scan interpretation did not correlate with the operative findings. Two patients with false-positive interpretations had retropharyngeal infections and underwent needle aspiration. The positive predictive value of CT scans in detection of abscess versus cellulitis was 83 percent.

TREATMENT

The treatment of choice is administration of intravenous antibiotics and incision and drainage. If the mass is small, a peroral incision with the patient in the Rose position (supine with the neck hyperextended) may provide some drainage, but a slight risk of aspiration exists. If the mass is large or if fever persists after peroral drainage, an external incision is preferred. A tracheotomy may be required if risk of compromising the airway exists.

Posterior mediastinitis can result from the spread of infection from the retropharyngeal area into the prevertebral space. Other complications may be seen when the abscess extends to the parapharyngeal space and involves the great vessels and cranial nerves.

Reports have documented that patients with small retropharyngeal abscesses may respond to treatment with intravenous antibiotics alone. Broughton[13] described the experience at the University of Kentucky Medical Center, where 8 of 14 patients with deep neck infections seen during a 9-year period were treated successfully by antibiotics alone. All were reported to have small abscesses on CT scan. However, possibly some had only cellulitis. In the Pittsburgh study, 15 of the children with parapharyngeal or retropharyngeal space infections underwent surgical intervention; 11 (73%) underwent incision and drainage, and 4 (27%) underwent needle aspiration.[54] All had successful outcomes. Twelve (44%) of the children with retropharyngeal infections were treated with intravenous antibiotics alone, and all did well. Close clinical follow-up is mandatory for children treated with intravenous antibiotics alone. Children who do not improve within 24 to 48 hours require surgical drainage.

Parapharyngeal Abscess (Pterygomaxillary, Pharyngomaxillary, Lateral, and Pharyngeal Space Abscesses)

The potential parapharyngeal or pterygomaxillary space is an inverted conical cavity (see Fig. 14–1*B*) lying along an oblique axis roughly parallel to the ramus of the mandible (see Fig. 14–1*C*). The base of the skull at the jugular foramen forms the base of the "cone," and its apex is at the hyoid bone (see Fig. 14–1*B*). The buccopharyngeal fascia, lateral to the superior pharyngeal constrictor, delineates the medial boundary, and the parotid gland and its partially dehiscent deep layer of the superficial cervical fascia form the lateral wall of this cone. The internal pterygoid muscle and mandible demarcate the cone on its anterolateral aspect. The pterygomaxillary space is contiguous with the peritonsillar, submandibular, and retropharyngeal spaces, all of which are potential avenues of egress for an extending pterygomaxillary space abscess (see Fig. 14–1*A*).

The posterior portion of the cone contains the contents of the carotid sheath (carotid artery and internal jugular vein), the cranial nerves IX through XII, and the cervical sympathetic chain. Anterior are the internal pterygoid muscle and fatty connective tissue.

Involvement of these structures determines the clinical manifestations and complications of the pterygomaxillary space abscess. An abscess in the posterior compartment may show medial displacement of the lateral pharyngeal wall and parotid space induration and swelling, with variable overlying facial nerve weakness, carotid artery erosion and hemorrhage,[30] internal jugular vein thrombosis, decreased gag reflex and dysphagia, ipsilateral vocal cord paralysis, weakness of the ipsilateral trapezius muscle, ipsilateral lingual deviation, and Horner syndrome from cervical sympathetic chain involvement.[14]

Extension of the abscess into the anterior compartment causes trismus from irritation of the internal pterygoid muscle. Induration at the angle of the jaw and medial displacement of the tonsil and pharyngeal wall also occur with an anterior compartment abscess.

By the time a patient with an abscess seeks medical attention, the source of the pterygomaxillary space infection may be unclear. Reports indicate variable causes: incompletely or inadequately treated bacterial pharyngitis, tonsillitis,[2] peritonsillar abscess, dental infections, bacterial parotitis, otitis, mastoiditis (Bezold abscess from a mastoid tip infection traveling along the digastric muscles), petrositis, cervical adenitis with suppuration, cervical vertebral tubercular adenitis in the adult,[4, 40] foreign bodies,[14, 15] trauma, intravenous drug abuse,[23] branchial cleft anomalies,[50] and cat-scratch disease.[57] A few cases of pterygomaxillary abscesses in children have been reported, and they tended to occur in later childhood and adolescence. Only three cases of parapharyngeal abscess and cellulitis were reported in the Pittsburgh series,[54] and only three cases were reported in a 15-year review of pediatric neck abscesses from Rainbow Babies and Children's Hospital in Cleveland, Ohio.[16]

CLINICAL MANIFESTATIONS

In addition to the symptoms noted in the preceding description, tender cervical swelling, induration and erythema of the side of the neck, torticollis, sore throat, dysphagia, trismus, hoarseness, malaise, chills, and diaphoresis may occur. Variable low-grade pyrexia with occasional temperature spikes occurs. Examination discloses variable toxicity, respiratory tract distress, laryngeal edema, medial displacement of the lateral pharyngeal wall and inferior tonsil pole, trismus, and, infrequently, drooling. Palpation of the neck reveals a tender, high cervical mass, initially diffuse and later fluctuant. Pharyngeal blood clots may presage carotid artery erosion. Bleeding from or blood clots in the external auditory canal have been noted in patients with carotid artery erosion and dissection of the abscess through the junction of the bony and cartilaginous external auditory canal.

The complications of pterygomaxillary abscesses are related to the structures involved: involvement of the carotid artery can produce hemiplegia from emboli; internal jugular vein thrombosis with cephalad extension may lead to a cavernous sinus thrombosis, whereas inferior extension leads to internal jugular vein thrombosis. Internal jugular vein thrombosis is characterized by spiking temperature, toxicity with intense diaphoresis, headaches, and increased intracranial pressure. Septic pulmonary emboli occasionally are present.

Extension into the retropharyngeal region by a pterygomaxillary abscess may lead to a posterior mediastinitis. Airway obstruction occurring secondary to laryngeal edema and aspiration pneumonia from suppuration of the abscess into the pharynx have been reported. Initially, the pterygomaxillary abscess may be difficult to differentiate from a peritonsillar abscess, but the peritonsillar abscess usually is less toxic and has a distinct, soft palatal fluctuation.

As described for the diagnosis of retropharyngeal abscess, CT is an extremely useful tool for distinguishing parapharyngeal abscess from cellulitis and for localizing the abscess for surgical planning. In a review of 47 children who presented with deep neck infections to the Children's Hospital of Buffalo during a 5½-year period, CT scan demonstrated that 34 (77%) of 44 patients who underwent CT scan had involvement of both the parapharyngeal and retropharyngeal spaces.[41] The involvement of both spaces had implications for the approach to surgical drainage.

TREATMENT

Intravenous antibiotic therapy with incision and drainage is the primary treatment. An otolaryngologic consultation should be obtained for this potentially complex surgery of the neck. The incision should be external, with sufficient exposure to provide immediate access to the common carotid artery for ligation, should there be carotid artery erosion.[35] An intraoral drainage and incision procedure traditionally has been condemned because rapid access to the vital structures of the neck is not possible with this approach. However, Nagy and associates[41] successfully treated 21 of 22 children with either parapharyngeal or combined parapharyngeal and retropharyngeal abscesses through an intraoral approach. The authors emphasized that CT with intravenous contrast enhancement demonstrated that all of the abscesses were located medial to the great vessels and were adjacent to the pharyngeal wall.

The use of CT has made it possible for some patients with parapharyngeal abscesses to be managed with intravenous antibiotics. However, the number of reported cases is small and usually analyzed with cases of retropharyngeal abscess.[13, 41] Nagy and associates[41] treated 3 (13%) of 24 children with small parapharyngeal abscesses by intravenous antibiotics alone. Close clinical follow-up is necessary for children with parapharyngeal cellulitis or small parapharyngeal abscesses that are treated conservatively with intravenous antibiotics. Surgical drainage should be performed in children who do not improve within 24 to 48 hours.

Microbiology of Deep Neck Abscesses

Group A streptococci *(Streptococcus pyogenes)* and *Staphylococcus aureus* have been considered to be the organisms most frequently associated with pharyngeal space infections. However, studies have demonstrated the presence of oral anaerobes in these infections; these organisms may be responsible for the gas seen on lateral neck radiographs (see Fig. 14–2). This finding is not surprising because the main portals of entry for pharyngeal space infections are the nasopharynx, oropharynx, paranasal sinuses, mastoid, and lower molars, all areas that are colonized with anaerobes.

The most complete microbiologic data available are from studies of peritonsillar abscesses. Flödstrom and Hallander[19] in 1976 reported the results of bacterial cultures on aspirates of pus from 37 patients with peritonsillar abscesses. The ages of the patients were not given. Group A streptococci were isolated from 17 of these patients, whereas 15 had an increase in their antistreptolysin O or anti-DNAase titers. Anaerobes were found in 28 of the cultures, including those of 8 patients that also disclosed the presence of streptococci. The most common anaerobic species isolated were fusobacteria (13), peptostreptococci (16), and *Bacteroides* spp. (18). Among the aerobic organisms, *S. aureus* was isolated four times and *Haemophilus influenzae* twice. No isolates of aerobic gram-negative enteric organisms were present. Jokipii and colleagues[27] performed semiquantitative cultures of aspirated pus from 42 peritonsillar abscesses and found similar results. Group A streptococci, the aerobic bacteria most frequently isolated, were isolated in pure culture 4 of 10 times. Anaerobes were more abundant than aerobes; the most important species, both in frequency and quantitatively, were *Bacteroides, Peptostreptococcus,* and *Fusobacterium*. Most of the infections were polymicrobial, with two to seven bacteria in 83 percent of the specimens. Subsequent studies from the United States and Finland have reported similar findings.[12, 28, 46, 47] Kieff and associates[28a] found that streptococci were the most frequent isolates; group A streptococci and other non-group A beta-hemolytic streptococci were present in more than 30 percent of patients, and alpha-hemolytic streptococci accounted for another 27.2 percent. The pathogenic role of anaerobic bacteria in peritonsillar abscesses has been reinforced by reports of complications caused by fusobacterial infection in children.[43, 45] *Fusobacterium* and *Bacteroides* spp. have been associated with septic thrombophlebitis and pulmonary emboli from the jugular veins.

Data on the microbiology of retropharyngeal and parapharyngeal abscesses in children are more limited. However, and not surprisingly, the organisms isolated are similar to those found in peritonsillar abscesses, but with a higher number of anaerobic species. Brook[11] examined aspirated pus from 14 children 1 to 6 years of age (median age, 3 years, 2 months) with retropharyngeal abscesses. Anaerobes were isolated from all patients; they were the only organisms isolated in two patients (14%) and were mixed with aerobes in the remainder (86%). The predominant anaerobic species were *Bacteroides, Peptostreptococcus,* and *Fusobacterium.* The predominant aerobic species were alpha- and gamma-hemolytic streptococci, *S. aureus, Haemophilus* spp., and group A beta-hemolytic streptococci. Seventy-one percent of the isolates were β-lactamase positive and included all isolates of the *S. aureus* group, 6 of 18 of the *Bacteroides melaninogenicus* group (33%), and 2 of 3 of the *Bacteroides oralis* group. Dodds and Maniglia[16] reported the results of cultures from nine retropharyngeal and three parapharyngeal abscesses from children and adolescents. The organisms isolated were similar to those reported by Brook,[11] but the microbiology was not as complete because the study was retrospective and not all specimens may have been processed for anaerobic culture. Streptococcal species were the isolates that occurred most frequently, followed by *S. aureus* and *H. influenzae.* One isolate each of *Fusobacterium necrophorum, Escherichia coli,* and *Klebsiella pneumoniae* was found. Asmar[1] performed cultures on material from 17 children with retropharyngeal abscesses; viridans streptococci were isolated from 11 of the abscesses, *S. aureus* from 8, and group A streptococci from 6. The most frequently identified anaerobes were *Peptostreptococcus* species. Overall, 45 aerobic and 18 anaerobic species were identified.

Rarely, retropharyngeal abscess may result from anterior extension from cervical osteomyelitis. This condition has been described with tuberculosis[42] and atypical mycobacteria causing a retropharyngeal abscess in a similar clinical setting. Barratt and colleagues[2] reported one case of retropharyngeal abscess caused by *Coccidioides immitis* in a 24-year-old woman with Hodgkin disease. The infection also was secondary to cervical vertebral osteomyelitis. Other rare and unusual causes of deep neck abscesses include cat-scratch disease *(Bartonella),*[57] *Streptococcus pneumoniae,*[38a] and Kawasaki disease.[25a]

Because a large variety of organisms can be found in pharyngeal space infections, obtaining adequate culture specimens is of the greatest importance. The optimal material for culture is an aspirate of the pus obtained at operation. Throat swabs or swabs of the abscess obtained after drainage usually are inadequate because of contamination with normal oropharyngeal flora. The pus, when obtained, can be transported in a capped syringe if anaerobic transport media are not available. Most pathogenic obligate anaerobes can survive in a purulent exudate, despite extended periods of exposure to air.[18] A Gram stain of the exudate will provide important clues to the bacterial etiology. A Gram stain showing a mixture of organisms suggests a mixed aerobic-anaerobic infection.

Although use of a β-lactamase–resistant antibiotic may be necessary in the treatment of deep neck abscesses because of the presence of β-lactamase–producing bacteria, including *S. aureus* and *Bacteroides* spp.,[11, 12, 54] results of two studies suggest that penicillin alone was equivalent to broad-spectrum antibiotics for treatment of peritonsillar abscesses.[28a, 58] Yilmaz and colleagues[58] compared procaine penicillin with intramuscular administration of ampicillin-sulbactam in outpatient treatment of 40 patients with peritonsillar abscesses that were drained perorally. No statistical difference in duration of symptoms and clinical recovery was found between the two groups. Kieff and associates[28a] retrospectively evaluated 103 patients with peritonsillar abscesses who were treated with incision and drainage. Fifty-eight patients were treated with broad-spectrum antibiotics, alone and in combination, including ampicillin-sulbactam, clindamycin, cephalosporins, and metronidazole; 45 patients were treated with penicillin alone. All patients were hospitalized after drainage, and the clinical outcomes, including duration of hospitalization and fever, did not differ significantly between the two groups. No significant difference in the organisms isolated was found, and failure and complication rates also did not differ.

No comparative treatment studies for retropharyngeal or parapharyngeal abscesses have been reported. Treatment in these cases should be based on the results of cultures, as stated before. Drugs that may be effective include ampicillin-sulbactam, expanded-spectrum cephalosporins such as ceftriaxone, oxacillin or nafcillin, ticarcillin–clavulanic acid, and piperacillin-tazobactam. The cephalosporins may need to be used in combination with clindamycin or metronidazole for adequate anaerobic coverage. Erythromycin is less satisfactory because it has less activity against *Bacteroides fragilis* and *Fusobacterium.* The routine use of aminoglycoside antibiotics is not indicated because aerobic gram-negative enteric rods are rarely found in these infections. Antibiotic therapy is effective only in conjunction with adequate surgical drainage, however.

REFERENCES

1. Asmar, B. I.: Bacteriology of retropharyngeal abscess in children. Pediatr. Infect. Dis. J. *9*:595–596, 1990.
2. Barratt, G. E., Koopmann, C. F., and Coulthard, S. W.: Retropharyngeal abscess: A ten year experience. Laryngoscope *94*:455–463, 1984.
3. Bateman, G. H., and Kodicek, J.: Primary quinsy tonsillectomy. Ann. Otol. Rhinol. Laryngol. *68*:315–321, 1959.
4. Beck, A. L.: Deep neck infection. Ann. Otol. Rhinol. Laryngol. *56*:722–765, 1947.
5. Beck, A. L.: Deep neck infection. Ann. Otol. Rhinol. Laryngol. *56*:439–481, 1947.
6. Beeden, A. G., and Evans, J. N. G.: Quinsy tonsillectomy: A further report. J. Laryngol. Otol. *84*:443–448, 1970.
7. Blotter, J. W., Yin, L., Glynn, M., and Wiet, G. J.: Otolaryngology consultation for peritonsillar abscess in the pediatric population. Laryngoscope. *110*:1698–1701, 2000.
8. Bonding, P.: Tonsillectomy à chaud. J. Laryngol. Otol. *81*:1171–1182, 1973.
9. Brandon, E. C., Jr.: Immediate tonsillectomy for peritonsillar abscess. Trans. Am. Acad. Ophthalmol. Otolaryngol. *77*:412–416, 1973.
10. Brodsky, L., Sobie, S. R., Korwin, D., et al.: A clinical prospective study of peritonsillar abscess in children. Laryngology *98*:780–783, 1988.
11. Brook, I.: Microbiology of retropharyngeal abscesses in children. Am. J. Dis. Child. *141*:202–204, 1987.
12. Brook, I., Frazier, E. H., and Thompson, D. H.: Aerobic and anaerobic microbiology of peritonsillar abscess. Laryngoscope *101*:289–292, 1991.
13. Broughton, R. A.: Nonsurgical management of deep neck infections in children. Pediatr. Infect. Dis. J. *11*:14–18, 1992.
14. Chassaignae, E.: Traite Pratique de la Suppuration et du Drainage Chirurgal. Vol. II. Paris, Masson, 1859.
15. Danforth, H. B., and Brown, A. K., Jr.: A foreign body etiology of pterygomaxillary space abscess. Laryngoscope *73*:1485, 1963.
16. Dodds, B., and Maniglia, A. J.: Peritonsillar and neck abscesses in the pediatric age group. Laryngoscope *98*:956–959, 1988.
17. Endicott, J. N., Nelson, R. J., and Saraceno, C. A.: Diagnosis and management decisions in infections of the deep fascial spaces of the head and neck utilizing computerized tomography. Laryngoscope *92*:630–633, 1982.
18. Finegold, S. M.: Anaerobic Bacteria in Human Disease. New York, Academic Press, 1977, pp. 129–141.
19. Flödstrom, A., and Hallander, H. O.: Microbiological aspects of peritonsillar abscesses. Scand. J. Infect. Dis. *8*:157–160, 1976.
20. Friedman, N. R., Mitchell, R. B., Pereira, K. D., et al.: Peritonsillar abscess in early childhood: Presentation and management. Arch. Otolaryngol. Head Neck Surg. *123*:630–632, 1997.

21. Greinwald, J. H., Wilson, J. F., and Haggerty, P. G.: Peritonsillar abscess: An unlikely cause of necrotizing fasciitis. Ann. Otol. Rhinol. Laryngol. *104*:133–137, 1995.
22. Grodinsky, M.: Retropharyngeal and lateral pharyngeal abscesses: An anatomic and clinical study. Ann. Surg. *110*:177–199, 1939.
23. Har-El, G., Aroesty, J. H., Shaha, A., and Lucente, F. E.: Changing trends in deep neck abscess: A retrospective study of 110 patients. Oral Surg. Oral Med. Oral Pathol. *77*:446–450, 1994.
24. Herzon, F. S.: Peritonsillar abscess: Incidence, current management practices, and a proposal for treatment guidelines. Laryngoscope *105*:1–17, 1995.
25. Herzon, F. S., and Nicklaus, P.: Pediatric peritonsillar abscess: Management guidelines. Curr. Probl. Pediatr. *26*:270–278, 1996.
25a. Homicz, M. R., Carvalho, D., Kearns, D. B., et al.: An atypical presentation of Kawasaki disease resembling a retropharyngeal abscess. Int. J. Pediatr. Otolaryngol. *54*:45–49, 2000.
26. Huang, R. Y., Damrose, E. J., Alavi, S., et al.: Third branchial cleft anomaly presenting as a retropharyngeal abscess. Int. J. Pediatr. Otorhinolaryngol. *54*:167–172, 2000.
27. Jokipii, A. M. M., Jokipii, L., Sipila, P., et al.: Semiquantitative culture results and pathogenic significance of obligate anaerobes in peritonsillar abscesses. J. Clin. Microbiol. *26*:957–961, 1988.
28. Jousimies-Somer, H., Savolainen, S., Makitie, A., et al.: Bacteriologic findings in peritonsillar abscesses in young adults. Clin. Infect. Dis. *16*:S292–S298, 1993.
28a. Kieff, D. A., Bhattacharyya, N., Siegel, N. S., and Salman, S. D.: Selection of antibiotics after incision and drainage of peritonsillar abscesses. Otolaryngol. Head Neck Surg. *120*:57–61, 1999.
29. Kronenberg, J., Wolf, M., and Leventon, G.: Peritonsillar abscess: Recurrence rate and the indication for tonsillectomy. Am. J. Otolaryngol. *8*:82–84, 1987.
30. Langenbrunner, D. J., and Dajani, S.: Pharyngomaxillary space abscess with carotid artery erosion. Arch. Otolaryngol. *94*:447–457, 1971.
31. Lazor, J. B., Cunningham, J., Eavey, R. D., et al.: Comparison of computed tomography and surgical findings in deep neck infections. Otolaryngol. Head Neck Surg. *111*:746–750, 1994.
32. Leavitt, G. W.: Cervical fascia and deep neck infections. Otolaryngol. Clin. North Am. *9*:703–716, 1976.
33. Lee, K. J., Traxler, J. H., Smith, A. W., et al.: Tonsillectomy: Treatment of peritonsillar abscess. Trans. Am. Acad. Ophthalmol. Otolaryngol. *77*:417–421, 1973.
34. Licameli, G. R., and Grillone, G. A.: Inferior pole peritonsillar abscess. Otolaryngol. Head Neck Surg. *118*:95–99, 1998.
35. Liston, R. L.: On a variety of false aneurysm. Br. Foreign Med. Rev. *15*:155–161, 1843.
36. de Marie, S., Tham, R., van der Mey, A. G. L., et al.: Clinical infections and nonsurgical treatment of parapharyngeal space infections complicating throat infection. Rev. Infect. Dis. *11*:975–982, 1989.
37. Mattucci, K., and Samet, C.: Pterygomaxillary space abscess. N. Y. State J. Med. *74*:1409–1412, 1974.
38. McCurdy, J. A., Jr.: Peritonsillar abscess. Arch. Otol. *103*:414–415, 1977.
38a. Medina, M., Goldfarb, J., Traquina, D., et al.: Cervical adenitis and deep neck infection caused by *Streptococcus pneumoniae*. Pediatr. Infect. Dis. J. *16*:823–824, 1997.
39. Morrison, J. E., Jr., and Pashley, N. R.: Retropharyngeal abscess in children: A 10-year review. Pediatr. Emerg. Care *4*:9–11, 1988.
40. Mosher, H. P.: The submaxillary fossa approach to deep pus in the neck. Trans. Am. Acad. Ophthalmol. Otolaryngol. *34*:19–36, 1926.
41. Nagy, M., Pizzuto, M., Backstrom, J., and Brodsky, L.: Deep neck infections in children: A new approach to diagnosis and treatment. Laryngoscope *107*:1627–1634, 1997.
42. Neumann, J. L., and Schlueter, D. P.: Retropharyngeal abscess as the presenting feature of tuberculosis of the cervical spine. Am. Rev. Respir. Dis. *110*:508–511, 1974.
43. Oleske, J. M., Starr, S. E., and Nahmias, A. J.: Complications of peritonsillar abscess due to *Fusobacterium necrophorum*. Pediatrics *57*:570–571, 1976.
44. Ophir, D., Bawnik, J., Porat, M., et al.: Peritonsillar abscess: A prospective evaluation of outpatient management by needle aspiration. Arch. Otolaryngol. *114*:661–663, 1988.
45. Rubinstein, E., Onderdonk, A. B., and Rahal, J. J.: Peritonsillar infection and bacteremia caused by *Fusobacterium gonidiaformans*. J. Pediatr. *85*:673, 1974.
46. Savolainen, S., Jousimies-Somer, H. R., Makitie, A. A., et al.: Peritonsillar abscess. Arch. Otolaryngol. Head Neck Surg. *119*:521–524, 1993.
47. Sprinkle, P. M., Veltri, R. W., and Kantor, C. M.: Abscesses of the head and neck. Laryngoscope *84*:1142–1148, 1974.
48. Stringer, S. P., Schaefer, S. D., and Close, L. G.: A randomized trial for outpatient management of peritonsillar abscess. Arch. Otolaryngol. *114*:278–298, 1988.
49. Suskind, D. L., Park, J., Piccirillo, J. F., et al.: Conscious sedation: A new approach for peritonsillar abscess drainage in the pediatric population. Arch. Otolaryngol. Head Neck Surg. *125*:1197–1200, 1999.
50. Takimoto, T., and Itoh, M.: Parapharyngeal abscess associated with the second pharyngeal pouch. J. Laryngol. Otol. *107*:456–457, 1993.
51. Takoudes, T. G., and Haddad, J.: Retropharyngeal abscess and Epstein-Barr virus infection in children. Ann. Otol. Rhinol. Laryngol. *107*:1072–1075, 1998.
52. Thawley, S. E., Godo, M., and Fuller, T. R.: Computerized tomography in the evaluation of head and neck lesions. Laryngoscope *88*:451–459, 1978.
53. Thompson, J. W., Cohen, S. R., and Reddix, P.: Retropharyngeal abscess in children: A retrospective and historical analysis. Laryngoscope *98*:589–592, 1988.
54. Ungkanont, K., Yellon, R. F., Weissman, J. L., et al.: Head and neck space infections in infants and children. Otolaryngol. Head Neck Surg. *112*:375–382, 1995.
55. Weinberg, E., Brodsky, L., Stanievich, J., et al.: Needle aspiration of peritonsillar abscess in children. Arch. Otolaryngol. Head Neck Surg. *119*:169–172, 1993.
56. Wenig, B. L., Shikowitz, M. J., and Abramson, A. L.: Necrotizing fasciitis as a lethal complication of peritonsillar abscess. Laryngoscope *94*:1576–1579, 1984.
57. Yeh, S. H., Zangwill, K. M., Hall, B., et al.: Parapharyngeal abscess due to cat-scratch disease. Clin. Infect. Dis. *30*:599–601, 2000.
58. Yilmaz, T., Ünal, Ö. F., Figen, G., et al.: A comparison of procaine penicillin with sulbactam-ampicillin in the treatment of peritonsillar abscesses. Eur. Arch. Otolaryngol. *255*:163–165, 1998.

Cervical Lymphadenitis

C. MARY HEALY ■ CAROL J. BAKER

Cervical lymphadenopathy is enlargement of the lymph nodes in the neck. Cervical lymphadenitis implies that inflammation of a node or nodes is present. The inflammatory response by the host is triggered by some form of injury or invasion proximal to the involved lymph node or nodes. The nodes become affected secondarily by drainage through connecting afferent lymphatic channels. The injury may be acute or chronic, infectious or noninfectious. Proper anatomic definition of the inflamed node or nodes,[65] combined with a knowledge of the structures of the head and neck drained by them, may allow identification of a portal of entry for infectious agents, the most common cause of cervical lymphadenitis in infants and children.

Figure 15–1 illustrates the regional lymph nodes commonly affected in infants and children with cervical adenitis. The superficial cervical lymph nodes lie on top of the sternocleidomastoid muscle along the course of the external jugular vein. They receive afferents from the superficial tissues of the neck, mastoid, superficial parotid (preauricular) nodes, and submaxillary glands. Their efferents terminate in the upper deep cervical lymph nodes. The mastoid lymph nodes overlie the mastoid process of the

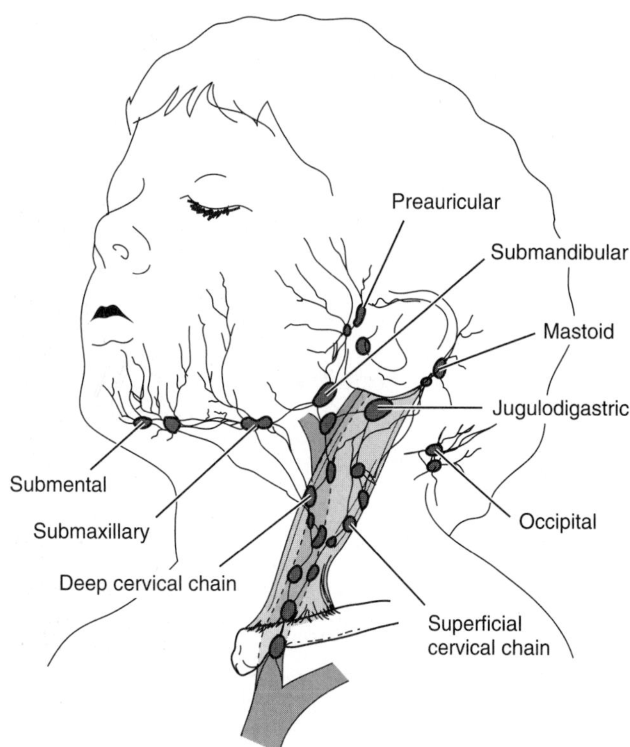

FIGURE 15–1 ■ The lymphatic drainage and lymph nodes involved in infants and children with cervical lymphadenitis.

temporal bone and receive drainage from the parietal scalp and inner surface of the pinna. The occipital lymph nodes lie on the upper part of the trapezius and receive afferents from the occipital scalp and superficial portions of the upper posterior neck. Their efferents terminate in the deep cervical glands, as do those from the mastoid nodes. The deep cervical lymph nodes lie deep to the sternomastoid muscle along the entire length of the internal jugular vein and are divided into upper and lower groups. The jugulodigastric gland, a member of the upper group, lies at the angle of the jaw below the posterior belly of the digastric muscle. The lymphoid tissue of the palatine tonsil is drained into this gland; thus, it frequently becomes enlarged in patients with "tonsillitis" or with tuberculous infection originating from the tonsils. The larynx, trachea, thyroid gland, and esophagus drain into the lower deep cervical glands. The submental lymph nodes, which lie between the digastric muscles below the myohyoid, receive superficial and deep drainage from the anterior tongue, lower lip, and chin, from both sides of the midline. They send efferents to the submandibular and upper deep cervical glands. The submandibular lymph nodes lie adjacent to the submandibular salivary gland and receive wide, superficial drainage from the lateral aspect of the lower lip, the vestibule of the nose, the cheeks, the medial parts of the eyelids, and the forehead. Deep drainage to these nodes arises from the posterior part of the mouth, gums, teeth, and tongue, as well as from superficial and submental lymph nodes.

Because most of the lymphatic drainage of the head and neck goes to the submaxillary and deep cervical nodes, these glands are involved in more than 80 percent of cases of cervical adenitis in young children. Submental and superficial cervical lymphadenitis is observed less frequently.

Epidemiology

The epidemiology of infectious cervical adenitis is that of its infectious agents. Although cervical lymphadenitis can be a manifestation of focal viral infections of the oropharynx or respiratory tract, often it is part of a more generalized reticuloendothelial response to systemic infection. Viruses commonly associated with prominent cervical adenitis include Epstein-Barr virus, cytomegalovirus, and human immunodeficiency virus (HIV). In HIV-infected children, cervical adenitis may either herald or be a part of the more generalized lymphadenopathy associated with this infection. Although human herpesvirus 6 (HHV-6), the cause of roseola in infants (exanthem subitum), is associated with the development of a mononucleosis syndrome and cervical adenopathy in adults,[3] lymphadenitis is not a prominent feature in children with primary infection.[49] Adenoviral and enteroviral infections are causes of generalized lymphadenopathy, rather than of cervical adenitis alone. The epidemiology of cervical adenitis varies with age, geographic location, and socioeconomic status. In general, lower socioeconomic status is associated with a higher incidence of infection in younger children.

When bacterial in origin, with the exception of group A streptococci and *Mycobacterium tuberculosis*, the agents isolated from these glands are those normal inhabitants of the nose, mouth, pharynx, and skin—*Staphylococcus aureus*, anaerobes, atypical mycobacteria, *Actinomyces israelii*—and person-to-person transmission does not occur. In contrast, infection of cervical lymph nodes with group A streptococci and *M. tuberculosis* results from contact with human infection by way of airborne droplets. Except in neonates, in whom male dominance has been reported in cases caused by group B streptococci,[11] infectious lymphadenitis has no sexual or seasonal predilection.[13, 34] Any age group may be affected. In neonates, *S. aureus* and group B streptococci are the most common pathogens. Suppurative cervical lymphadenitis caused by *Staphylococcus epidermidis* in an otherwise healthy infant has been reported.[103] Nonetheless, despite the high frequency of nasal colonization by this organism, it remains a rare etiologic agent. Rarely, *Streptococcus pneumoniae* has been reported as causing suppurative adenitis[78] in the older child. Some studies[34, 118, 133] indicate that *S. aureus* has the leading role in infancy, whereas group A streptococci and *S. aureus* are equally likely to be pathogenic in childhood. Other reports of the relationship between age and probable etiologic agent have varied.[13, 24] Together, *S. aureus* and *Staphylococcus pyogenes* accounted for 65 to 89 percent of consecutive cases in prospectively evaluated series.[13, 34, 133] An increasing incidence of nosocomial and community-acquired methicillin-resistant *S. aureus* (MRSA) infections in the United States and elsewhere,[21, 39, 44, 52, 83] coupled with the recognition that the highest rates of community-acquired MRSA colonization and invasive disease are found in children,[39, 83] requires that MRSA be considered a possible etiology. Some studies have found no difference in clinical syndromes caused by either methicillin-susceptible or methicillin-resistant strains,[52] whereas other studies have documented that more skin and soft tissue infections are caused by community-acquired MRSA strains.[39, 44] Although prospective studies of the impact of MRSA on pediatric adenitis are lacking, one retrospective case series from 1996 to 1998 identified 354 cases of community-acquired MRSA infections in Minnesota, and 8 (2%) presented as adenitis.[83]

The epidemiology of bacterial lymphadenitis varies by geographic location. Resurgence of infection with *Yersinia pestis* (bubonic plague) in the southwestern United States

TABLE 15–1 ■ DIFFERENTIATION OF *MYCOBACTERIUM TUBERCULOSIS* AND ATYPICAL MYCOBACTERIAL CERVICAL ADENITIS

	Atypical MCA	*M. tuberculosis*
Age	1–6 years	All ages
Race	White	Black, Asian
Exposure to tuberculosis	Absent	Present
Abnormal chest radiographs	Rare	Often
Residence	Suburban	Urban
PPD-S >15 mm	Uncommon	Often
Bilateral involvement	Rare	Not uncommon

MCA, mycobacterial cervical adenitis; PPD-S, purified protein derivative-S.

means that in areas where it is endemic, it must also be considered in the differential diagnosis. Furthermore, epidemic diphtheria, reported in the Russian Federation in 1990, has spread to several countries of the former Soviet Union and must be added to the list of possible causes of cervical lymphadenitis in that area.[31]

The distinctive epidemiological features of mycobacterial infection are summarized in Table 15–1. Scrofula caused by *M. tuberculosis* is a relatively rare disease. When it does occur, it usually affects adults and older children. In contrast, children with atypical mycobacterial infection almost always are 1 to 6 years of age, live in suburban or rural communities, and have no history of contact with *M. tuberculosis*.[19, 33, 35, 43, 61, 113, 125, 130] Whereas *M. tuberculosis* is an infection acquired primarily by inhalation, both the gastrointestinal tract and the respiratory tract may serve as the primary portal of entry for atypical mycobacteria.[43, 87, 94, 98] Atypical infection appears to have an ethnic predilection for whites and tuberculous infections for blacks, Asians, and the Australian Aboriginal population.[86]

The advent of the HIV pandemic has had a major impact on the nature and frequency of mycobacterial infections. A marked increase in the incidence of tuberculous infection in HIV-infected adults has occurred, as has a similar trend in HIV-infected children. Annualized case rates for tuberculosis in HIV-infected children have increased from 58 per 100,000 during the years 1981 to 1985 to 478 per 100,000 during the years 1990 to 1992.[46] The increase in the number of cases is not confined to HIV-infected children. The increased prevalence of tuberculous infection in the community means that all children are at increased risk of being exposed to an infectious adult.[20] Of additional concern in the early 1990s was the frequency with which drug-resistant tuberculosis was detected in children, with as many as 15 percent of isolates resistant to isoniazid and rifampin.[46] Four percent or more of *M. tuberculosis* isolates from patients in 46 states and the District of Columbia during 1993 to 1998 were resistant to isoniazid.[32]

The incidence of nontuberculous mycobacterial infections appears to be rising, although some of this apparent increase most likely results from improvements in diagnostic methods. An association between cold weather and the incidence of cervical adenitis caused by atypical mycobacteria has been suggested by some studies describing a winter predominance[68, 130] or a steady incidence throughout the year in a cold climate.[43] Until the 1970s, *Mycobacterium scrofulaceum* was the usual etiologic agent isolated from children, followed by *Mycobacterium avium-intracellulare*.[130] This trend has reversed, with *M. avium-intracellulare* now accounting for 50 to 98 percent of culture-proven cases.[40, 51, 67, 68, 85, 86, 119, 130] Previously uncommon species, such as *Mycobacterium kansasii, Mycobacterium malmoense, Mycobacterium fortuitum,* and *Mycobacterium haemophilum,* also are detected more frequently.[10, 40, 67, 68, 85, 86] Some of them probably are responsible for many cases of culture-negative mycobacterial lymphadenitis because of their fastidious growth requirements. New diagnostic methods have led to case reports of cervical adenitis secondary to slow-growing species such as *Mycobacterium lentiflavum* and *Mycobacterium interjectum*.[48, 115] Cervical lymphadenitis caused by *Mycobacterium chelonae* occurs rarely, usually involves the submandibular glands, and typically occurs in patients with antecedent histories of dental disease.[5]

Cervical lymphadenopathy often is the direct result of infection with HIV. However, the development of acute tender adenitis in an HIV-infected child should provoke a search for another etiology. Although the typical childhood pathogens remain the most common invaders in this setting, as in other immunocompromised children, more unusual opportunists also should be sought.[46] Patients with HIV infection and newly commenced on potent antiretroviral agents may develop a new onset of mycobacterial lymphadenitis (both tuberculous and nontuberculous mycobacteria). When it occurs, it is more localized, is associated with more sinus formation, and more often is caused by nontuberculous *(M. avium-intracellulare)* than tuberculous mycobacteria.[95]

Cat-scratch disease is a common cause of lymphadenitis in children and young adults.[22] In 1988, English and associates[38] first isolated a pleomorphic gram-negative bacillus, later identified as *Afipia felis*, from lymph nodes of patients with cat-scratch disease. *Bartonella henselae* (formerly called *Rochalimaea henselae*), a morphologically similar but genetically distinct pleomorphic gram-negative bacillus, now is recognized to cause most cat-scratch disease.[1]

The cervical nodes are the second most common site of cat-scratch disease involvement. Although unusual and severe manifestations of this infection have been described in adult patients with acquired immunodeficiency syndrome (AIDS),[57, 105] for the most part it remains a mild, self-limited infection in children and adolescents, showing no ethnic group predilection. Seasonal variation with an increased incidence in fall, winter, and early spring does occur in temperate zones. A history of animal contact with cats usually can be elicited.[26] The importance of bites and scratches by kittens in transmitting this disease has been well defined.[75] However, the absence of a history of traumatic contact with cats in a substantial number of cases has raised the possibility that other modes of transmission exist. Zangwill and associates[134] have suggested that fleas might serve as vectors of transmission. Their hypothesis is strengthened by the detection of *Bartonella* DNA by polymerase chain reaction analysis in collections of fleas from cats owned by two infected patients.[134]

Pathophysiology

Although cervical lymphadenitis is a common entity in pediatric clinical practice, little information exists about its pathogenesis. Viral cervical adenitis may be part of either a local response to viruses invading the oropharynx or respiratory tract (e.g., adenoviruses, coxsackieviruses) or a more generalized reticuloendothelial response to systemic viral infection (e.g., Epstein-Barr virus, cytomegalovirus, HHV-6, HIV). Infection attributed to group A streptococci and *S. aureus* is presumed to enter the cervical lymphatics from the oropharynx and anterior nares, respectively. In the patient with group A streptococcal pharyngitis or tonsillitis, whether infection remains localized at the pharyngotonsillar tissues or spreads to cervical lymph nodes and results in suppuration primarily is a function of the host defense. For example, although peak attack rates for group A streptococcal pharyngitis are observed among school-age children, suppurative cervical adenitis rarely occurs. In contrast, infants and children younger than 3 years rarely have group A streptococci isolated from throat cultures, but this age group is the one more commonly afflicted with suppurative cervical lymphadenitis.[97]

In infections attributed to *S. aureus,* colonization of the anterior nares is thought to be a prerequisite for cervical lymphadenitis. Brook and Winter[22, 23] came to this conclusion because organisms of identical phage types were isolated from the anterior nares and the cervical abscesses of their patients. An investigation of children in St. Louis found no such correlation between isolates from nasal and cervical node cultures.[13] The role of *S. aureus* as a primary pathogen has been the subject of some debate. Thirty percent of aspirates in most series yield mixed cultures of *S. aureus* and group A streptococci, and antistreptolysin O titers frequently are elevated significantly in the sera of patients whose lymph nodes yielded a pure culture of *S. aureus*. In a California study, 65 percent of patients had node aspirates yielding a pure culture of *S. aureus,* and 41 percent of these exhibited an immune response to one or more of the extracellular antigens of group A streptococci.[133] Similarly, despite the high prevalence of penicillin resistance among *S. aureus,* many children improve with penicillin or ampicillin treatment, suggesting that although streptococci and staphylococci may coexist in these nodes, staphylococci may play a subsidiary role as secondary invaders. Most children with isolates of *S. aureus* from suppurative lymph nodes show no evidence of coexistent streptococcal infection or viral upper respiratory infection. In this more common circumstance, *S. aureus* apparently has the capacity to be a primary invader.

Recovery of anaerobic bacteria from cervical nodes suggests invasion of the lymphatics by normal mouth flora, often as a result of local tissue destruction by periodontal disease.[24] The delineation of the pathophysiology of cervical lymphadenitis of diverse bacterial etiology will require an understanding of the interaction between a given microorganism (inoculum size, elaboration of extracellular enzymes, ability to adhere to epithelium) and the host (humoral and surface immune capacity, degree of trauma, and so on).

Tuberculous cervical lymphadenopathy occurs within months of the initial exposure, through pulmonary infection and involvement of the regional and then more distant lymph nodes. Because the process is relatively rapid, chest radiographic evidence of active pulmonary disease often is present. Nontuberculous mycobacteria are ubiquitous in the environment. Oropharyngeal acquisition and local infection lead to involvement of the lymph nodes. Most children with nontuberculous mycobacterial cervical lymphadenitis are immunocompetent, although a study suggests that those who develop necrotic nodes may have deficient production of interferon-γ.[85] Although *Mycobacterium avium* skin test positivity has been linked with pet birds, no clear relationship with lymphadenitis has been shown.[64] The observation that discontinuation of childhood bacille Calmette-Guérin (BCG) vaccination has been associated with an increase in atypical mycobacterial infection in many countries suggests that this vaccine may have a protective effect.[126] However, progressive cervical adenitis after BCG vaccination has also been reported.[88]

Clinical Presentation

The clinical manifestations of cervical lymphadenitis vary considerably but are consistent with the diverse causes associated with enlargement of cervical nodes in infants and children. Categorizing the mode of presentation as either acute or subacute and chronic is useful, for although the boundaries are ill-defined and much overlap exists, common causes tend to fall fairly consistently within one or another category. Cervical lymphadenitis of acute onset may be categorized further as either bilateral or unilateral. In most situations, acute, bilateral cervical adenitis is either part of a generalized reticuloendothelial response to a systemic infection or a localized reaction to acute pharyngitis. Presence or absence of associated features (pharyngitis, enanthems or exanthems, generalized adenopathy, hepatosplenomegaly) aids in the differentiation.

Acute unilateral cervical lymphadenitis is caused by streptococcal or staphylococcal infection in 53 to 89 percent of cases.[13, 34, 54, 133] In newborns, *S. aureus* is the most common cause, and clinical features are similar to those seen in older children. Group B streptococci have been described as causative in a "cellulitis-adenitis" syndrome in infancy.[11] These infants differ from those with staphylococcal adenitis in that they are younger and more often are male; they have a greater frequency of systemic symptoms, irritability, and anorexia, and 94 percent have associated bacteremia. The typical patient presents with fever, facial or submandibular cellulitis, and ipsilateral otitis media.[11]

The patient with disease attributed to *S. aureus* or group A streptococci typically is 1 to 4 years of age (70% to 80%), and the male-to-female ratio is equal. Few criteria help to differentiate streptococcal from staphylococcal infections clinically. Cervical adenitis can occur as part of the "streptococcosis" syndrome of infancy, with an onset heralded by coryza, an irregular low-grade fever, nasal discharge with excoriation and crusting around the nares, vomiting, and loss of appetite. Enlargement of lymph nodes occurs within a few days of onset and resolves, as do other symptoms, without treatment within 6 to 8 weeks.[97] Suppuration of cervical glands may occur at any time during this interval, but it seldom occurs if antimicrobial therapy is given early in the illness. Group A streptococci should also be suspected as a cause of cervical adenitis in the patient with typical vesiculopustular or crusted lesions of impetigo involving the face or scalp.

Systemic symptoms in children with staphylococcal or streptococcal cervical adenitis usually are minimal or absent unless associated with cellulitis, metastatic foci of infection, or bacteremia. The primary site of lymph node involvement by frequency is submandibular (50%–60%), upper cervical (25%–30%), submental (5%–8%), occipital (3%–5%), and lower cervical (2%–5%).[13, 34, 131] Involved nodes generally vary in size from 2.0 to 6.0 cm in diameter, and one fourth to one third become fluctuant. Patients with lymphadenitis caused by *S. aureus* are more likely to have suppuration and a longer duration of symptoms before diagnosis than are those with disease caused by other bacterial agents.[13, 118] Among patients who develop suppurative adenitis, 86 percent do so within 2 weeks of onset[131] (Fig. 15–2). Approximately one third of patients in one study had concomitant lymphadenopathy at other anatomic sites.[13] Patients frequently have a history of recent upper respiratory tract symptoms, including sore throat (40%), earache or coryza (16%), and impetigo (32%), as well as signs of pharyngitis, tonsillitis, or otitis media.[13, 34] However, these symptoms do not help to delineate etiology. Hepatomegaly or splenomegaly occurs rarely and, if present,

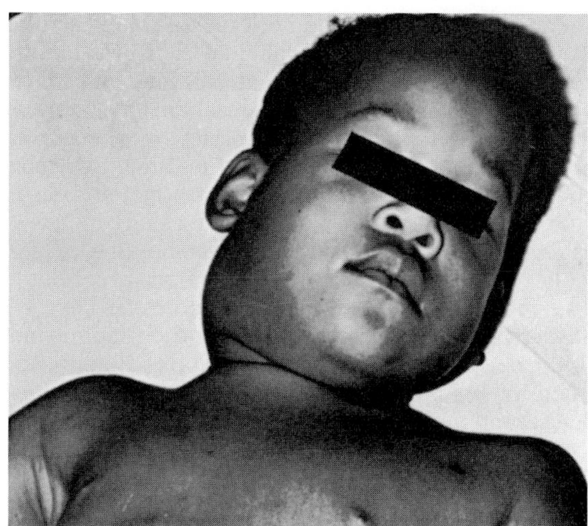

FIGURE 15–2 ■ A 2-year-old boy with fever and unilateral inflammation of the cervical lymph nodes of 2 days' duration. Needle aspirate culture of this nonfluctuant node grew *Staphylococcus aureus*. Antistaphylococcal therapy resulted in complete resolution of adenitis without surgical drainage.

should suggest bacteremia or generalized disease processes (e.g., infectious mononucleosis, reticuloendotheliosis, tuberculosis, HIV infection).

Kawasaki disease may present as a febrile illness associated with bilateral or unilateral cervical lymphadenopathy and may be confused with the more common acute pyogenic infections.[128] Other features (conjunctivitis, oral manifestations, changes in the peripheral extremities, polymorphic erythematous rash) are required criteria for the diagnosis.[79] Although originally called mucocutaneous lymph node syndrome, unilateral lymph node enlargement of at least 1.5 cm is an inconsistent feature.[15, 79] Lymphadenopathy usually subsides when the fever subsides, although it may follow a more chronic course in some cases.

The rapid development of painful lymphadenitis, quickly succeeding the sudden onset of fever, chills, weakness, and headache, is one of the classic presentations of infection caused by *Y. pestis*. The groin is the site most often involved. However, other locations, including the cervical area, may be affected. Rapidly diagnosing and providing treatment are critical because infection can be fulminant.

In cases of diphtheria, cervical adenopathy develops secondary to infection of the posterior structures of the mouth and proximal pharynx. A whitish-gray membrane covers the mucosal surfaces. In severe cases, the cervical adenopathy, which typically is bilateral, can result in a "bull neck" appearance.

Careful physical examination of the head and neck, particularly areas drained by affected lymph nodes, may yield important clues about etiology. The presence of periodontal disease is associated with a higher incidence of anaerobic organisms causing adenitis[24]; the history or presence of tick bites suggests the possibility of tularemia[114]; and the presence of papular or pustular lesions, suggesting an inoculation site, raises the possibility of rarer causes of infection, including *Nocardia*, actinomycosis, sporotrichosis, plague, and cutaneous diphtheria as well as cat-scratch disease.

Mycobacterial infections, cat-scratch disease, and toxoplasmosis are among the more common entities presenting as subacute or chronic lymphadenitis. The epidemiologic and clinical features that aid in the differentiation of typical and atypical mycobacterial infections are summarized in

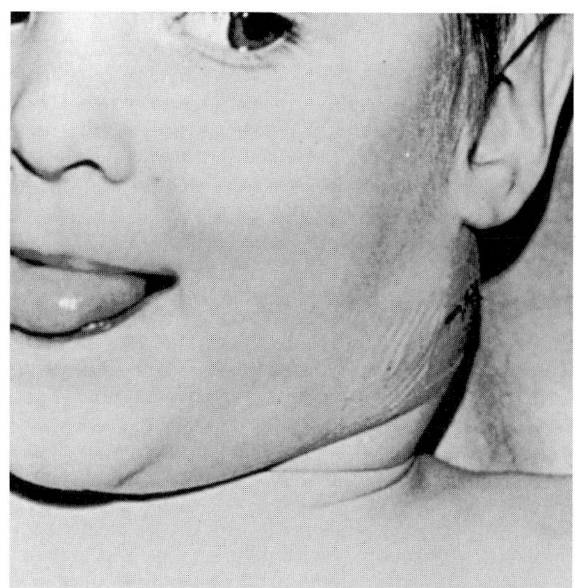

FIGURE 15–3 ■ A 4-year-old boy who had bilateral nontender enlargement of lymph nodes of 6 weeks' duration without other symptoms. Purified protein derivative-S resulted in 18-mm induration, excisional biopsy acid-fast stain was positive, and cultures grew *Mycobacterium tuberculosis*.

Table 15–1. The clinical manifestations are virtually identical[19, 30, 81] (Fig. 15–3). Typically, the child presents with a history of painless (so-called cold) cervical node swelling. The submandibular cervical nodes usually are involved in atypical mycobacterial infection,* whereas other cervical nodes are involved more frequently with *M. tuberculosis*.[4, 19, 56, 74, 106] As the infection progresses, the skin overlying the node may develop a pinkish or violaceous discoloration caused by increased vascularity, although no increase in skin temperature occurs. This finding may be followed by adherence of the skin to the underlying mass. If left untreated, fluctuation and spontaneously draining sinus tracks may develop.

The patient with *M. tuberculosis* infection is more likely than one with atypical mycobacterial disease to be older than 4 years of age and to have generalized lymphadenopathy (10% to 20% of cases), bilateral node enlargement (10% of cases), a history of exposure to tuberculosis (93% of cases), and an urban residence.[19, 74, 91] However, duration of adenopathy, fever, and presence or absence of constitutional symptoms exhibit no differences. An abnormal chest radiograph has been noted in 28 to 71 percent of cases caused by *M. tuberculosis*,[106, 107, 116, 125] in contrast to the 98 to 100 percent of normal chest radiographs of patients with atypical mycobacterial disease.[43, 104, 106, 119, 124] In a summary of 447 reported childhood cases of atypical mycobacterial infections from 15 countries, Lincoln and Gilbert[63] detected only six cases of bilateral cervical node involvement, four with abnormal chest radiographs, and none with nodal enlargement other than cervical. Similar findings have been reported by other researchers.[104, 124] Intradermal testing with purified protein derivative–S uncommonly produces more than 15 mm of induration at 48 hours in the child with atypical mycobacterial infection, but reactions between 5 and 15 mm are relatively common.[70] Reactions of 10 to 20 mm can occur with *Mycobacterium marinum* and *M. fortuitum* infection.[94] Skin

*See references 4, 19, 40, 51, 67, 68, 74, 104, 106, 119, 124, 130.

reaction to intradermal purified protein derivative may persist, even when children are retested many years after having an infection.[130]

Cat-scratch disease may appear days to weeks after the initial inoculation occurs. A history of contact with a cat or kitten or a scratch characteristically is present. Later, when the primary lesion may have healed, tender regional adenopathy appears. Although axillary nodes most frequently are affected, 25 percent of children have isolated cervical node involvement. Middle cervical and parotid nodes are involved more often than are submandibular ones.[100] Constitutional symptoms, present early in the course of the illness, usually are mild and may have resolved by the time the adenitis appears. Fever is observed in one fourth of patients and has a mean duration of 5 to 7 days.[69] Nodes suppurate in one tenth to one third of patients.[26, 29] Rare manifestations include Parinaud syndrome,[27] encephalopathy,[66] exanthems[26] (usually of the erythema nodosum type), and osteolytic lesions.[28]

Acquired toxoplasmosis may present as regional lymphadenopathy, frequently with involvement of posterior cervical nodes.[77, 99, 122] Most children exhibit few if any constitutional symptoms. If present, fatigue and generalized myalgia are prominent. The characteristic location combined with a history of exposure to cats or of eating undercooked meats should raise this diagnostic possibility, and the diagnosis then may be confirmed by appropriate serologic testing. This etiology for cervical adenopathy in children living in the United States is uncommon.

Chronic, recurrent cervical adenitis forms part of the PFAPA syndrome, a chronic syndrome first described in 1987.[76] It is characterized by periodic episodes of high fever ($<39°$ C) lasting 3 to 6 days and recurring every 3 to 8 weeks in association with aphthous ulcers, pharyngitis, and cervical adenitis. In most children, onset of disease occurs before they reach 5 years of age, the syndrome is self-limited, and recovery without long-term sequelae is the rule. Oral steroids are effective in aborting an attack.[92, 123]

A rare disorder of unknown etiology that also may present as painless cervical adenopathy, with or without fever, is subacute necrotizing lymphadenitis (Kikuchi lymphadenitis). A disorder recognized most frequently in young women, it invariably runs a benign course with spontaneous resolution occuring over the course of 3 to 4 months.[42, 127] Pediatric cases have been reported.[84, 111] Whether it is infectious in nature, perhaps the result of infection with a single novel agent or a nonspecific host response to any of a variety of agents, remains to be determined. Finally, with a history of subacute or chronic lymphadenitis, careful physical examination should be undertaken to exclude obvious local causes (i.e., seborrhea, head lice, *Tinea capitis*, and chronic otitis media) before an extensive diagnostic work-up is initiated.

Differential Diagnosis

Cervical swellings are encountered frequently in pediatric practice, and most of them represent lymph nodes. When considering the diagnostic possibilities in patients with cervical lymphadenitis, one must first ascertain whether the pathologic process actually involves a lymph node, then whether its cause is infectious, and if it is infectious, the likely etiologic agent. The duration of the cervical swelling aids in the differential diagnosis because most tumors or developmental anomalies have been noted for weeks. Rapid enlargement may occur in developmental anomalies, but it usually results from secondary infection. Location is a most helpful clue because midline masses rarely represent lymph nodes, and the most common neck masses of congenital origin (thyroglossal duct cyst, branchial cleft cyst, and cystic hygromas) have characteristic anatomic locations.

Of the midline masses, thyroglossal duct cysts are by far the most common.[58, 96] They may occur anywhere from the foramen caecum to the thyroid, are midline, and move on tongue protrusion. They may have an associated sinus track, midline or just lateral to it, from which cloudy mucus sometimes can be expressed. They may become infected secondarily, but in the noninfected state, they are nontender, smooth, and round with well-defined margins. Thyroglossal duct cysts must be differentiated from other midline masses, including epidermoid cysts, lipomas, thyroid tumors, and the rare midline lymph node.

The second most common benign congenital neck mass is the branchial cleft cyst. It usually arises from the second branchial cleft and lies at the anterior border of the sternocleidomastoid muscle. Although such cysts usually manifest themselves as skin dimples, they may become infected secondarily and present as inflammatory swellings or draining sinus tracks. A careful examination should detect a sinus track. Branchial cleft cysts can present at any age but usually do so during early school age.

Cystic hygromas, considerably less common than thyroglossal duct or branchial cleft cysts, are the third most frequent cause of congenital neck masses. They arise from lymphatics derived from either the jugular vein or mesenchymal tissue. They may occur elsewhere but most commonly are found posterior to the sternocleidomastoid muscle in the supraclavicular fossa. Most such hygromas present in the first 2 years of life, many being noted at birth or soon thereafter. They are soft, compressible tumors that transilluminate well, and, although benign in themselves, they may cause symptoms through pressure exerted on surrounding structures. Confusion may arise when cystic hygromas increase in size in association with an upper respiratory tract infection; this event causes increased lymph flow, so that the hygroma persists while other lymph nodes decrease in size after resolution of the infection. In most circumstances, palpation and transillumination readily distinguish these congenital malformations.

These four cervical masses—thyroglossal duct cysts, thyroid tumors, branchial cleft cysts, and cystic hygromas—accounted for 63.7 percent of lesions in children with persistent cervical masses reported by Moussatos and Baffes.[81] Other lesions included neurogenic tumors, parotid tumors, and miscellaneous benign tumors (12.3%). The remainder of masses represented lymph nodes. As a rule, masses located completely anterior to the sternocleidomastoid muscle are benign. The exception is the thyroid tumor.[81] Malignant neoplasms that mimic cervical lymph nodes usually are located in the posterior triangle or are multiple masses extending across both the anterior and posterior triangles. In contrast, approximately 50 percent of masses in the posterior triangle represent malignant neoplasms, and most of them are of lymphoid origin. Whereas most cysts and tumors present as solitary, unilateral, nontender masses, lymph nodes of noninfectious etiology frequently are multiple and bilateral, although they may be mildly tender.

Noninfectious chronic inflammatory involvement of cervical lymph nodes may represent a variety of uncommon, usually benign, but sometimes malignant entities (Table 15–2). Fifty percent of malignant neck masses in children are caused by lymphomas, Hodgkin and non-Hodgkin. Neuroblastoma is the second most common malignant neoplasm, accounting for 15 percent. The likelihood of a given diagnosis is age-dependent, with neuroblastoma

TABLE 15–2 ■ ETIOLOGY OF CERVICAL ADENITIS: NONINFECTIOUS

	Isolated Cervical	Cervical Associated with Generalized Adenopathy
Malignancy		
Hodgkin disease	+	+
Non-Hodgkin lymphomas	+	+
Rhabdomyosarcoma	+	–
Neuroblastoma	+	+
Leukemia	+	+
Metastatic carcinoma	+	–
Thyroid tumors	+	–
Drugs		
Isoniazid	–	+
Phenytoin (Dilantin)	–	+
Serum sickness	–	+
Collagen Vascular Disease		
Juvenile rheumatoid arthritis	–	+
Systemic lupus erythematosus	–	+
Miscellaneous		
Sarcoidosis	–	+
Reticuloendotheliosis	–	+
Sinus histiocytosis with massive lymphadenopathy	+	+
Histiocytosis X	–	+
Postvaccinial	+	–
Storage disorders	–	+
Kawasaki disease	+	+
Masses Simulating Adenopathy		
Cystic hygroma	+	–
Branchial cleft cyst	+	–
Thyroglossal duct cyst	+	–
Epidermoid cyst	+	–
Sternocleidomastoid tumor	+	–

TABLE 15–3 ■ ETIOLOGY OF CERVICAL ADENITIS: INFECTIOUS

	Isolated Cervical	Cervical Associated with Generalized Adenopathy
Bacterial		
Staphylococcus aureus	+	–
Group A streptococci	+	+
Mycobacterium tuberculosis	+	+
Atypical mycobacteria	+	–
Bartonella henselae	+	–
Gram-negative enterics	+	–
Anaerobes	+	–
Haemophilus influenzae	+	–
Yersinia pestis	–	+
Actinomyces israelii	+	–
Diphtheria	+	–
Tularemia	+	–
Brucellosis	–	+
Syphilis	+	+
Viral		
Measles	+	+
Rubella	+	+
Epstein-Barr virus	+	+
Herpes simplex	+	–
Human herpesvirus 6	+	+
Cytomegalovirus	+	+
Mumps	+	–
Varicella	+	+
HIV	+	+
Fungal		
Histoplasmosis	+	+
Cryptococcus	+	–
Aspergillosis	+	–
Candida	+	–
Sporotrichosis	+	–
Parasitic		
Toxoplasma gondii	+	+

being more common than is Hodgkin disease in the younger age groups.[54] Thyroid tumors are the third most frequent neck malignant mass. Other entities to be included in the differential diagnosis are leukemia,[25] metastatic carcinoma,[81] phenytoin (Dilantin)-induced pseudolymphoma,[25] serum sickness,[25] storage disorders (Gaucher disease, Niemann-Pick disease), collagen vascular disease,[25] sarcoidosis,[55] sinus histiocytosis with massive lymphadenopathy,[12, 102] reticuloendotheliosis or histiocytosis X,[25] and postvaccinal lymphadenitis.[90] Except for malignant neoplasms, these disease entities almost always are associated with lymphadenopathy that is not limited to the cervical region and have a variety of clinical and laboratory findings that allow the correct diagnosis to be made.

A large number of infectious agents have been reported in association with cervical adenitis in infants and children (Table 15–3). Among patients evaluated prospectively with needle aspirate cultures of affected lymph nodes, *S. aureus* or group A streptococci are the organisms isolated most commonly.[13, 24, 34, 118, 133] No significant difference has been reported that will distinguish between patients with adenitis attributed to streptococci or staphylococci with respect to sex, ethnicity, dental problems, symptoms, presence of fever, or site or size of lymph nodes. However, in those patients from whom *S. aureus* is isolated, a longer duration of disease before diagnosis, a larger percentage of fluctuant lymph nodes,[13, 118] and a tendency toward slower resolution are found.[34] Most patients with bacterial cervical lymphadenitis, including those with mycobacterial infection, are 1 to 6 years of age. Older children are more likely to have negative lymph node aspirate cultures.[13, 113, 118]

Anaerobes rarely were associated with cervical adenitis in early studies.[13, 34] Proper bacteriologic techniques for the isolation of these fastidious organisms allowed Brook[24] to report anaerobes alone in 18 percent and mixed anaerobic and aerobic bacteria in 20 percent of patients, suggesting that anaerobic organisms may play a more significant role in the etiology of cervical lymphadenitis than recognized previously. Therefore, the older child with "negative" cultures, especially the one with poor dental hygiene or periodontal disease, may have anaerobic infection, as did the 9-year-old boy in Figure 15–4. Needle aspiration of this cervical mass yielded *Peptococcus, Peptostreptococcus, Bacteroides fragilis,* and viridans streptococci. Resolution of the lymphadenitis occurred promptly after incision and drainage and penicillin therapy. Dental disease or manipulation also should suggest the possibility of cervicofacial actinomycosis (lumpy jaw). These patients have a submandibular mass and frequently a fistula from the skin to the oral cavity.[16]

Less commonly occurring bacteria,[62] as well as viruses, fungi, and parasites, can cause cervical lymphadenitis in children. These patients usually have less evidence of acute inflammation, with or without adenopathy at additional sites, as well as historical and physical findings that suggest unusual causes of cervical lymph gland enlargement.

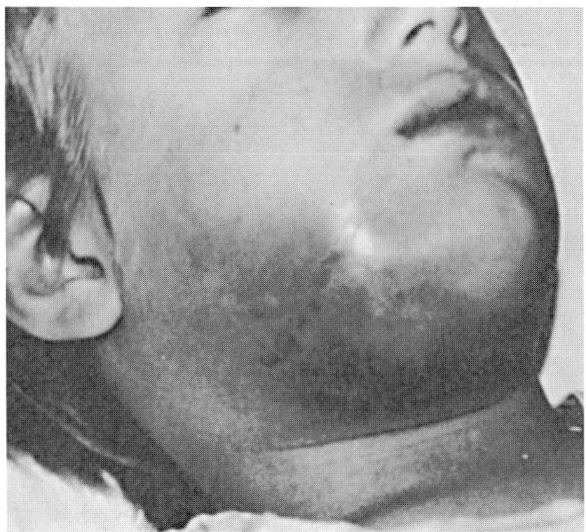

FIGURE 15–4 ■ A 9-year-old boy who developed high fever and markedly tender submental lymph node inflammation after a tooth extraction. Cultures from this fluctuant mass grew three anaerobes and viridans streptococci.

Specific Diagnosis

A detailed history to ascertain preceding dental problems, presence of skin lesions, animal exposure (including exposure to fleas and ticks), duration of illness, presence of associated symptoms, contact with tuberculosis, presence of risk factors for HIV infection, drug use (especially phenytoin) or other unusual ingestions (undercooked meat, unpasteurized dairy products), recent travel outside the geographic region of residence, and sites of occult infection drained by the affected node may yield important diagnostic clues in the patient with cervical lymphadenitis. Physical examination should include careful inspection for dental disease, noncervical lymphadenopathy, hepatosplenomegaly, and oropharyngeal or skin lesions.

Radiologic evaluation of adenitis is not necessary in most mild to moderate cases. Ultrasonography often is performed when the presenting neck mass is very large, is increasing in size, or has not responded to initial antibiotic therapy. It is useful in diagnosing suppuration and expediting incision and drainage. High-resolution and color Doppler ultrasonography (with or without contrast enhancement) defining longitudinal/transverse nodal ratio and vascularity patterns has had some success in differentiating benign and malignant lymph nodes in adults.[2, 80, 82, 132] In children, in whom most adenopathy is infectious or reactive in etiology, ultrasonography is less discriminating. In one study of 146 children, unilateral lymph nodes and cystic necrosis were found only in lymphadenitis caused by cat-scratch disease, bacterial infection, or tuberculous infection.[93] However, individual sonographic findings were not specific for diagnosis, although these findings combined with clinical signs were helpful. No patients with nontuberculous mycobacterial adenitis were evaluated in this study. Some studies report characteristic low-density, ring-enhancing lesions with minimal or absent inflammatory stranding of subcutaneous fat on computed tomography and magnetic resonance imaging of nontuberculous mycobacterial adenitis in children.[51, 101] These findings may be helpful in differentiating this etiology from other bacterial causes when the diagnosis is not suspected clinically or early in the course. Differences in clinical presentation between the two entities, however, should obviate the need for such imaging in all but the most complicated cases.

In the acute stage of cervical lymphadenitis, needle aspiration of the affected node is a valuable diagnostic tool. Sixty to 88 percent of patients with acute cervical lymphadenitis subjected to needle aspiration of the affected node for bacterial and mycobacterial culture have an etiologic agent recovered.[13, 24, 56, 133] Only inflamed nodes should be aspirated, but they need not be fluctuant. No serious complications of this procedure have been recorded. The largest or most fluctuant node should be selected, and the skin should be cleansed and anesthetized. Skin anesthesia can be induced effectively by use of a topical anesthetic cream (e.g., lidocaine-prilocaine [EMLA]) placed on the selected aspiration site under an occlusive dressing 30 to 45 minutes before the procedure is performed. An 18- or 20-gauge needle attached to a 20-mL syringe is used. If no material is aspirated, 1 to 2 mL of sterile *nonbacteriostatic* saline is injected into the node and reaspirated. The aspirate should be inoculated directly from the syringe onto aerobic (including chocolate agar) and anaerobic media as well as onto Sabouraud agar (fungi) and into a broth media suitable for the early detection of mycobacteria, such as the BACTEC radiometric assay. In this last system, the release of labeled carbon dioxide in an automated ion chamber system can detect mycobacteria as early as 12 to 17 days after inoculation of the broth.[112] Performing Gram and acid-fast stains is mandatory, and their readings will serve as a guide in selecting initial antimicrobial therapy. Polymerase chain reaction assays to identify tuberculous and nontuberculous mycobacteria have confirmed their presence in gastric aspirates and in specimens obtained from lymph nodes by aspiration or biopsy.[37, 41, 47, 48, 110, 115] This technique shows great promise in providing a rapid and specific diagnosis but is not as yet routinely available. Thioglycolate broth and anaerobically incubated blood agar plates are incapable of providing optimal conditions for the isolation of many anaerobic bacteria.[13] Therefore, optimal methods for cultivation of fastidious anaerobes should be employed because anaerobic organisms may be recovered in as many as 20 percent of cases.[24] Cultures of infected skin lesions and exudates on tonsils also should be performed but not to the exclusion of needle aspiration.

Isolation of group A streptococci from the throat or skin cultures of a patient with lymphadenitis does *not* confirm the etiology of the lymph node inflammation. Patients have been noted to have isolation of group A streptococci from throat and of *S. aureus* from lymph node aspirate cultures.[13, 97] Intradermal skin testing for tuberculosis with purified protein derivative (5 TU) tuberculin should be performed. Induration of 15 mm or greater is suggestive of infection with *M. tuberculosis,* whereas reactions of 5 to 14 mm may be caused by either a tuberculous or nontuberculous mycobacterial infection.[70] In an attempt to develop a rational approach to the use and interpretation of differential skin testing, Huebner and associates,[53] using standardized tuberculous (purified protein derivative–T) and nontuberculous mycobacterial antigens, studied 144 children with chronic cervical adenopathy, of whom 123 had mycobacterial culture results available. The low incidence of tuberculosis within the study population (four cases) prevented making an interpretation about the utility of these antigens for distinguishing disease caused by *M. tuberculosis* from that caused by other mycobacteria. Children with culture-confirmed mycobacterial lymphadenopathy had significantly larger reactions to nontuberculous mycobacterial antigens than did those with microscopy-negative and culture-negative results. The study was terminated prematurely because of an unacceptably high incidence of a blistering skin reaction to nontuberculous mycobacterial antigens.

Intradermal skin testing, with use of a crude extract from affected nodes, historically has been used to establish the diagnosis of cat-scratch disease.[26] However, a diagnosis usually is based on the presence of regional adenopathy, a history of cat exposure (particularly if the patient has a history of a scratch or a primary skin lesion), and negative results of laboratory studies for other causes of lymphadenopathy. *B. henselae*, the more common etiologic agent of this disease, can be isolated from blood if lysis-centrifugation blood culture or the BACTEC blood culture system is used. Isolates then may be identified by use of a commercially available system (MicroScan Rapid Anaerobe Panel, Baxter, Sacramento, CA).[1] Serologic methods for the detection of IgG antibodies to *B. henselae* are available[1, 134] and should be considered the "gold standard" diagnostic method. Abdominal ultrasonography is supportive if typical microabscesses are seen in the liver or spleen, but a normal study does not exclude the diagnosis. In few cases would a lymph node biopsy be undertaken to exclude other, more serious, pathologic processes.

If, after the aforementioned evaluation has been performed, the etiology of the adenitis remains uncertain or the lymphadenopathy has persisted with no detectable response to antimicrobial therapy, a more intense diagnostic evaluation is indicated. Studies may include a complete blood count; a venereal disease research laboratory test; serology for Epstein-Barr virus, cytomegalovirus, HHV-6, HIV, histoplasmosis, coccidioidomycosis, toxoplasmosis, tularemia, *B. henselae,* and *Brucella;* and a radiograph of the chest. If the diagnosis remains in doubt and the node persists, enlarges, is hard, or is fixed to the adjacent structures, biopsy *should* be performed. Biopsy material should be submitted for the studies outlined earlier for lymph node aspirate cultures as well as for routine histology; Giemsa, periodic acid–Schiff, and methenamine silver stains; and, in select cases only, viral cultures. If the histology reveals noncaseating granulomas and the child has a history of cat exposure, the most likely diagnosis is cat-scratch disease,[69, 72] and serologic testing is indicated. Sarcoidosis involving lymph nodes would have a similar histologic appearance but is a rare finding in children and a condition in which isolated cervical node involvement has not been observed.[55, 109]

Older children are more likely to have negative cultures of lymph node aspirates[13, 118] and to be more frequent candidates for excisional lymph node biopsy. They also are more likely to have lymphomas. Thus, excising appropriate tissue, especially from adolescents, is important so that precise diagnostic interpretation can be made. It can be facilitated by the proper selection of a lymph node for biopsy; intact removal of the node chosen; and proper fixation, cutting, and staining of the specimen. If only one node or one anatomic group of nodes is enlarged, the largest node should be excised. If several groups of lymph nodes are involved, the site for biopsy should be selected according to the likelihood of diagnostic yield. Biopsy specimens from the lower neck and supraclavicular area have the highest yield.[59] Other areas, including the upper cervical, submandibular, axillary, and parotid lymph nodes, are much more likely to be affected by reactive hyperplasia, which may or may not be related to the underlying disease process. If lymphoma is suspected, needle biopsies or frozen sections are contraindicated.[18, 25]

Even under optimal conditions, many reactive processes, including rheumatoid arthritis, toxoplasmosis, phenytoin-induced adenopathy, dermatopathic adenitis, and infectious mononucleosis, have been noted to simulate lymphoma.[25] Obtaining a thorough history and appropriate serologic studies is useful for excluding reactive processes known to simulate lymphoma.

Treatment

Optimal management of the child with cervical lymphadenitis depends on making an accurate assessment of the underlying etiology. Because almost all cases are associated with infectious agents, every effort should be made to ascertain the etiologic agent so that specific therapy can be initiated. Aspiration of the affected lymph node for Gram and acid-fast stains will serve as a guide for initial therapy, and culture and antimicrobial susceptibility will form the basis for prescribing specific treatment in patients with bacterial lymphadenitis.[13, 34] However, when the patient presents with typical findings of acute bacterial lymphadenitis, empirical therapy may be undertaken without prior needle aspiration. In this situation, close follow-up is essential because failure to show some clinical response after 48 hours of therapy is an indication for this diagnostic procedure to be performed.

Acute suppurative cervical lymphadenitis most frequently is caused by infection with *S. aureus* or group A streptococci.[13, 23, 34, 108, 118, 133] In nodes that progress to abscess formation, *S. aureus* is the single most frequently isolated agent,[13, 34, 108] and drainage is mandatory. Because of the frequency of infection caused by *S. aureus* or group A streptococcus, empirical antimicrobial therapy should be directed against these two agents. Penicillinase-resistant penicillins should be used. If the patient requires parenteral therapy, oxacillin, nafcillin (150 mg/kg/day) or cefazolin (100 mg/kg/day) may be used. When oral therapy is deemed to be adequate, dicloxacillin (50 mg/kg/day) or cephalexin (25–50 mg/kg/day) is recommended. Augmentin, the fixed combination of amoxicillin and clavulanic acid, provides good activity against methicillin-susceptible staphylococci and streptococci and has an expanded spectrum of activity against the oral anaerobic organisms. These features, combined with its palatability, render it an attractive alternative to the traditional penicillinase-resistant penicillins. However, clavulanate-associated diarrhea can be a problem in some children. In penicillin-allergic patients, cephalosporins may be used. Once-daily ceftriaxone (50–100 mg/kg/day) is an attractive and effective alternative to the parenteral antibiotics that require more frequent administration. Cefixime is not active against *S. aureus* and is not a suitable agent for the empirical treatment of bacterial adenitis. In areas where community-acquired MRSA is high, clindamycin (30 mg/kg/day) for parenteral or oral use is appropriate for empirical or alternative therapy. Clindamycin has good activity against anaerobes and methicillin-susceptible *S. aureus;* in addition, community-acquired MRSA isolates usually are clindamycin-susceptible.[39, 52, 83] In the severely ill child needing hospitalization or with signs of airway compromise, vancomycin (45 mg/kg/day) in combination with another agent is appropriate treatment until culture results are obtained. Trimethoprim-sulfamethoxazole (10 mg/kg/day of the trimethoprim component) is an alternative choice for oral therapy of community-acquired MRSA infections[39, 52, 83] but should not be used initially because it is not active against group A streptococcus. Antibiotic therapy may need to be modified if an obvious primary focus of infection suggests a different etiologic agent. For example, in the patient with periodontal or dental disease, adequate anaerobic activity is mandatory; therapy with penicillin V (50 mg/kg/day), Augmentin (40 mg/kg/day), or clindamycin (30 mg/kg/day) should be initiated pending results of cultures.

Patients with marked lymph node enlargement, moderate to severe systemic symptoms, or concomitant cellulitis frequently require parenteral therapy for the first few days. This therapy allows a high concentration of the drug within the inflamed tissue and may promote more rapid localization, especially in patients with staphylococcal adenitis. Although the use of parenteral drugs must be individualized, most infants and children with staphylococcal or streptococcal lymphadenitis respond to orally administered antimicrobials.

Adenitis caused by group A streptococci should be treated with penicillin G (100,000 IU/kg/day) or penicillin V (50 mg/kg/day) for a total of 10 days. In the child with penicillin allergy, erythromycin ethyl succinate (40 mg/kg/day) or cephalexin (25–50 mg/kg/day) may be used. Both drugs have been demonstrated to be effective in the treatment of cervical lymphadenitis.[13, 22] Treatment should be continued for at least 10 days or approximately 5 days after signs of local inflammation and systemic toxicity have disappeared, whichever is longer. If required, analgesics should be given and not overlooked in infants and children too young to verbalize their discomfort. The average duration of antibiotic therapy is 10 days, unless abscess formation occurs late in the first or early in the second week of treatment.[22] In this situation, incision and drainage are indicated,[13, 23, 34] and therapy should be continued until resolution of the acute process occurs, usually within another 5 to 7 days.

Some clinical improvement is to be expected within 48 hours after initiation of therapy, and it will be manifested by a decrease in inflammation and tenderness of the lymph node as well as a fall in the maximum daily temperature. The size of the lymph node may not show evidence of regression at this stage, and total resolution of fever should not be expected. Recording accurate measurements of the node at the time of presentation is important because a subjective evaluation is an unreliable indicator of lymph node evolution during therapy. If no clinical improvement is noted by 48 hours, needle aspiration is recommended. Furthermore, the history and physical examination should be reassessed and a more detailed laboratory evaluation initiated. Regression of lymph node size is slow, usually requiring 4 to 6 weeks or more. Persistence of significant enlargement beyond 6 to 8 weeks, even in the face of good initial response to antimicrobial therapy, demands that an underlying disorder be excluded. Once signs of acute inflammation have resolved, prolonged antimicrobial therapy is of little value because penetration of antimicrobials through the fibrous capsule of the node is poor.[22] Spontaneous regression occurs in most patients, although it may require several weeks. Uncommonly, reactivation of inflammation may occur, and a meticulous search for an untreated primary source of bacterial infection, such as a secondarily infected dermatitis, infestation, foreign body, or dental abscess, should be undertaken. Re-treatment should include specific measures to eliminate the predisposing condition.

If Gram stain of the lymph node aspirate suggests a microorganism other than *S. aureus* or group A streptococci, initial antimicrobial therapy should be directed at the most likely agent until culture results are known. Because attempts to perform careful Gram stains and careful anaerobic cultures of lymph node aspirates in most reported series have been limited, the large number of infants and children with sterile aspirates may be attributed, in part, to a failure to isolate fastidious anaerobes indigenous to the mouth. These microorganisms should respond to penicillin G therapy. For penicillin-resistant organisms, clindamycin is a useful alternative drug. In the first 2 months of life, group B streptococci and *S. aureus* are important pathogens to consider in selecting initial therapy. Penicillinase-resistant penicillins are active against both agents. If group B streptococci are isolated, penicillin G can be substituted. Final bacteriologic identification and antimicrobial susceptibility tests should be the ultimate guide to specific antimicrobial therapy in all patients. Treatment of cervical lymph node infections associated with rarely encountered bacteria, fungi, and parasites listed in Table 15–3 is discussed under those specific disease entities.

Although controversy exists as to whether cervical adenitis associated with *M. tuberculosis* in a child is truly a localized process, only rarely do patients have disseminated infection.[35, 46, 89] When infection is not localized, pulmonary or hilar lymph node involvement occurs commonly.[35, 56, 91, 133] A 6-month regimen of isoniazid (10 mg/kg/day), rifampin (15–20 mg/kg/day), and pyrazinamide (30 mg/kg/day) currently is recommended for the treatment of uncomplicated intrathoracic pulmonary tuberculosis or isolated cervical lymphadenitis in children.[6] Triple therapy is given daily for the first 2 months of therapy, after which isoniazid and rifampin are administered, either daily or on a twice-weekly basis, for the following 4 months. Directly observed therapy is an option when noncompliance is suspected. In areas where multiple-drug resistance in *M. tuberculosis* is prevalent, ethambutol (25 mg/kg/day) or streptomycin (20–40 mg/kg/day) is added for initial treatment until drug susceptibilities are known. The addition of a fourth drug should occur after consultation with an expert in the field; both drugs may have toxic effects, and careful assessment of the risks and benefits is warranted. Detailed discussion of the treatment of tuberculosis in children is provided in Chapter 101. Response to antituberculous therapy is usual, with rapid resolution of symptoms and marked regression of lymph nodes occurring within 3 months. However, nodes remain palpable for months because scarring and fibrosis are regular accompaniments to resolution of disease. Draining sinuses, a common complication of lymph node aspiration or incision and drainage before the advent of effective antituberculous chemotherapy, no longer develop.[91]

Cervical lymphadenitis attributed to atypical mycobacteria occurs much more commonly in the young child than that caused by *M. tuberculosis.* These microorganisms demonstrate in vitro resistance to commonly employed antituberculous drugs. Resistance is particularly common among Runyon groups II and III mycobacteria (*M. scrofulaceum* and *M. intracellulare,* respectively). Surgical excision remains the treatment of choice for nontuberculous mycobacterial lymphadenitis,[8, 36, 40, 68, 71, 94, 119] and total removal of all the visibly affected nodes is recommended.[4, 8, 30, 50, 94, 104, 130] Early (within 1 month of onset) removal of affected nodes was associated significantly with better aesthetic results in one series.[68] Thorough curettage has been found to be effective,[89] but it results in higher rates of relapse.[40] Antituberculous therapy generally has been ineffective.[74] The new macrolides clarithromycin and azithromycin, rifampin and its analogue rifabutin, ethambutol, amikacin, and cefoxitin show activity against nontuberculous mycobacteria.[36, 120] Clarithromycin monotherapy and combination therapy with clarithromycin and ethambutol or rifampin has been successful in the treatment of nontuberculous lymphadenitis.[17, 45, 51, 67, 121] In the largest series, 10 children (7 of whom had initial incision and drainage or aspiration) were treated for 1 to 14 months with a regimen of clarithromycin (20–30 mg/kg/day) in combination with ethambutol

(12.5–19 mg/kg/day) or rifampin (6–20 mg/kg/day). Five were cured; the remainder needed further surgical procedures.[51] Six of seven patients treated for 6 months in another series had not relapsed after a mean follow-up of 3 years.[67] Rifabutin was used in all children in this study, resulting in side effects in four (neutropenia, yellow skin pigmentation) that disappeared after dose reduction. In HIV-infected children receiving protease inhibitors, rifabutin generally is contraindicated (indinavir and nelfinavir are the preferred protease inhibitors) but can be given at a much reduced dosage if deemed necessary.[8] Despite the lack of prospective studies, macrolide-containing regimens are promising options for the treatment of nontuberculous mycobacterial adenitis when complete excision of the affected node would endanger the facial nerve or its branches or when a reduction in size of the swelling would facilitate a complete and aesthetic excision at a later stage. The optimal duration of therapy is not known, but regimens of 4 to 6 months or longer are usual. Currently, macrolide monotherapy or combination therapy should be viewed as a valuable adjunct when surgery is not feasible or is refused.

Cat-scratch disease usually is a benign, self-limited disorder requiring no specific therapy. The use of antimicrobials is controversial, but rifampin, trimethoprim-sulfamethoxazole, azithromycin, ciprofloxacin, and parenteral gentamicin may be useful in promoting defervescence and in clinical resolution of systemic cat-scratch disease.[7, 9, 14, 73] If the lymph node progresses to fluctuation, needle aspiration may hasten resolution and also relieve discomfort. Surgical excision may be required in a minority of patients who have persistence despite needle aspiration or who develop draining sinuses.

Prognosis

With effective antimicrobial therapy, complete resolution of cervical lymphadenitis caused by *S. aureus,* group A streptococci, and *M. tuberculosis* is the rule. Delay in diagnosis or initiation of therapy may prolong the clinical course and even may result in complications or sequelae, such as sinus tracks (mycobacteria),[19, 91] abscess formation,[22, 33] cellulitis or bacteremia *(S. aureus* and *S. pyogenes),*[13] acute glomerulonephritis (group A streptococci),[34] disseminated disease *(M. tuberculosis),*[56] or even mycotic carotid artery aneurysm.[129] Except for abscess formation, these complications are rare occurrences. Although lymph node infection caused by *S. aureus* is more likely to result in abscess formation, at least one study has noted a significantly greater duration of infection before initiation of treatment for patients in whom *S. aureus* was isolated from the abscess cavity cultures.[13] The extracellular products of this organism (coagulase, fibrinolysin, hyaluronidase) in part explain its propensity for abscess formation, which may occur in 50 to 70 percent of patients.[23, 34, 131] Even in patients whose course is complicated by suppuration, appropriate drainage in conjunction with specific antimicrobial therapy results in prompt resolution of signs and symptoms, and only rarely will relapse occur. Today, physicians seldom recommend surgical excision of affected nodes, with the exception of disease caused by atypical mycobacteria, for which surgical excision remains the treatment of choice. Antimicrobial therapy has been responsible for the disappearance of those events commonly associated with cervical adenitis historically: thrombosis of the internal jugular vein, rupture of the carotid artery, generalized septic embolic phenomena, mediastinal abscess, purulent pericarditis, and even death.[60, 117, 131]

With the advent of effective antituberculous agents, the prognosis for tuberculous cervical adenitis also is excellent. With surgical excision early in the course of lymphadenitis caused by atypical mycobacterial infection, resolution can be anticipated.[40, 68, 104] Persistent and recurrent disease is the most frequent complication encountered.[130] Macrolide monotherapy or combination therapy is useful in ameliorating these complications or in cases for which surgery is not feasible.[94] Cat-scratch disease usually is a benign, self-limited disorder only rarely requiring therapeutic intervention, such as needle aspiration, to relieve pain.

Prevention

Initiating appropriate medical and, occasionally, surgical therapy for predisposing conditions (e.g., dental caries, abscess, group A streptococcal pharyngitis or nasopharyngitis, purulent otitis media, impetigo, other infections involving the face and scalp) and minimizing the exposure of infants and children to adults with active tuberculosis should reduce the incidence of cervical lymphadenitis. Some authors suggest that decreased exposure to animals may result in fewer infections,[13] especially for adenitis attributed to toxoplasmosis or cat scratches.[29, 99]

REFERENCES

1. Adal, K. A., Cockerell, C. J., and Petri, W. A., Jr.: Cat scratch disease, bacillary angiomatosis, and other infections due to *Rochalimaea.* N. Engl. J. Med. *330*:1509–1515, 1994.
2. Ahuja, A. T., Ying, M., Ho, S. S., et al.: Distribution of intranodal vessels in differentiating benign from metastatic neck nodes. Clin. Radiol. *56*:197–201, 2001.
3. Akashi, K., Eizuru, Y., Sumiyoshi, Y., et al.: Brief report: Severe infectious mononucleosis-like syndrome and primary human herpes 6 infection in an adult. N. Engl. J. Med. *329*:168–171, 1993.
4. Altman, R. P., and Margileth, A. M.: Cervical lymphadenopathy from atypical mycobacteria: Diagnosis and surgical treatment. J. Pediatr. Surg. *10*:419–422, 1975.
5. Alvi, A., and Myssiorek, D.: *Mycobacterium chelonae* causing recurrent neck abscess. Pediatr. Infect. Dis. J. *12*:617–618, 1993.
6. American Academy of Pediatrics: Tuberculosis. *In* Pickering, L. K. (ed.): 2000 Red Book: Report of the Committee on Infectious Diseases. 25th ed. Elk Grove Village, IL, American Academy of Pediatrics, 2000, pp. 600–601.
7. American Academy of Pediatrics: Cat-scratch disease. *In* Pickering, L. K. (ed.): 2000 Red Book: Report of the Committee on Infectious Diseases. 25th ed. Elk Grove Village, IL, American Academy of Pediatrics, 2000, pp. 201–203.
8. American Academy of Pediatrics: Diseases caused by nontuberculous mycobacteria. *In* Pickering, L. K. (ed.): 2000 Red Book: Report of the Committee on Infectious Diseases. 25th ed. Elk Grove Village, IL, American Academy of Pediatrics, 2000, pp. 613–618.
9. Arisoy, E. S., Correa, A. G., Wagner, M. L., et al.: Hepatosplenic cat-scratch disease in children: Selected clinical features and treatment. Clin. Infect. Dis. *28*:778–784, 1999.
10. Armstrong, K. L., James, R. W., Dawson, D. J., et al.: *Mycobacterium haemophilum* causing perihilar or cervical lymphadenitis in healthy children. J. Pediatr. *121*:202–205, 1992.
11. Baker, C. J.: Group B streptococcal cellulitis-adenitis in infants. Am. J. Dis. Child. *136*:631–633, 1982.
12. Bankaci, M., Morris, R. F., Stool, S. E., et al.: Sinus histiocytosis with massive lymphadenopathy: Report of its occurrence in two siblings with retropharyngeal involvement in both. Ann. Otol. Rhinol. Laryngol. *87*:327–331, 1978.
13. Barton, L. L., and Feigin, R. D.: Childhood cervical lymphadenitis: A reappraisal. J. Pediatr. *84*:846–852, 1974.
14. Bass, J. W., Freitas, B. C., Freitas, A. D., et al: Prospective randomized double blind placebo-controlled evaluation of azithromycin for treatment of cat-scratch disease. Pediatr. Infect. Dis. J. *17*:447–452, 1998.
15. Bell, D. M., Morens, D. M., Holman, R. C., et al.: Kawasaki syndrome in the United States. Am. J. Dis. Child. *137*:211–214, 1983.
16. Bennhoff, D. F.: Actinomycosis: Diagnostic and therapeutic considerations and a review of 32 cases. Laryngoscope *94*:1198–1217, 1984.
17. Berger, C., Pfyffer, G. E., and Nadal, D.: Treatment of nontuberculous mycobacterial lymphadenitis with clarithromycin plus rifabutin. J. Pediatr. *128*:383–386, 1996.
18. Betsill, W. L., Jr., and Hajdu, S. I.: Percutaneous aspiration biopsy of lymph nodes. Am. J. Clin. Pathol. *73*:471–479, 1980.

19. Black, B. G., and Chapman, J. S.: Cervical adenitis in children due to human and unclassified mycobacteria. Pediatrics *33*:887–893, 1984.
20. Braun, M. M., and Cauthen, G.: Relationship of the human immunodeficiency virus epidemic to pediatric tuberculosis and bacillus Calmette-Guérin immunization. Pediatr. Infect. Dis. J. *11*:220–220, 1992.
21. Bronzwaer, S. L., Buchholz, U., Kool, J. L., et al.: EARSS activities and results: Update. Eur. Surveill. *6*:2–5, 2001.
22. Brook, A. H., and Winter, G. B.: Cervicofacial suppurative lymphadenitis due to staphylococcal infection in childhood. Br. J. Oral Surg. *8*:257–263, 1971.
23. Brook, A. H., and Winter, G. B.: Staphylococcal cervicofacial lymphadenitis in children. Lancet *2*:660–661, 1972.
24. Brook, I.: Aerobic and anaerobic bacteriology of cervical adenitis in children. Clin. Pediatr. *19*:693–696, 1980.
25. Butler, J. J.: Non-neoplastic lesions of lymph nodes of man to be differentiated from lymphomas. Natl. Cancer Inst. Monogr. *32*:233–249, 1969.
26. Carithers, H. A.: Cat-scratch disease: An overview based on a study of 1200 patients. Am. J. Dis. Child. *139*:1124–1133, 1985.
27. Carithers, H. A.: Oculoglandular disease of Parinaud: A manifestation of cat-scratch disease. Am. J. Dis. Child. *132*:1195–1200, 1978.
28. Carithers, H. A.: Cat-scratch disease associated with an osteolytic lesion. Am. J. Dis. Child. *137*:968–970, 1983.
29. Carithers, H. A., Carithers, C. M., and Edwards, R. O., Jr.: Cat-scratch disease: Its natural history. J. A. M. A. *207*:312–316, 1969.
30. Castro, D. J., Hoover, L., Castro, D. J., et al.: Cervical mycobacterial lymphadenitis. Arch. Otolaryngol. *111*:816–819, 1985.
31. Centers for Disease Control and Prevention: Diphtheria epidemic: New independent states of the former Soviet Union. M. M. W. R. *44*:177–181, 1995.
32. Centers for Disease Control and Prevention: Progress toward the elimination of tuberculosis—United States, 1998. M. M. W. R. *48*:732–736, 1999.
33. Chapman, J. S., and Guy, L. R.: Scrofula caused by atypical mycobacteria. Pediatrics *23*:323–331, 1959.
34. Dajani, A. S., Garcia, R. E., and Wolinsky, E.: Etiology of cervical lymphadenitis in children. N. Engl. J. Med. *268*:1329–1333, 1963.
35. Davis, S. D, and Comstock, G. W.: Mycobacterial cervical adenitis in children. J. Pediatr. *58*:771–778, 1961.
36. Diagnosis and treatment of disease caused by nontuberculous mycobacteria. This official statement of the American Thoracic Society was approved by the Board of Directors, March 1997. Medical Section of the American Lung Association. Am. J. Respir. Crit. Care Med. *156*:S1–S25, 1997.
37. El Amin, N. M., Hanson, H. S., Petterson, B., et al.: Identification of nontuberculous mycobacteria: 16S rRNA gene sequence analysis vs. conventional methods. Scand. J. Infect. Dis. *32*:47–50, 2000.
38. English, C. K., Wear, D. J., Margileth, A. M., et al.: Cat-scratch disease: Isolation and culture of the bacterial agent. J. A. M. A. *259*:1347–1352, 1988.
39. Fergie, J. E., and Purcell, K.: Community-acquired methicillin-resistant *Staphylococcus aureus* infections in South Texas children. Pediatr. Infect. Dis. J. *20*:860–863, 2001.
40. Flint, D., Mahadevan, M., Barber, C., et al.: Cervical lymphadenitis due to non-tuberculous mycobacteria: Surgical treatment and review. Int. J. Pediatr. Otorhinolaryngol. *53*:187–194, 2000.
41. Frevel, T., Schafer, K. L., Totsch, M., et al.: PCR based detection of mycobacteria in paraffin wax embedded material routinely processed for morphologic examination. J. Clin. Pathol. *52*:283–288, 1999.
42. Fujimori, T., Shioda, K., and Sussman, E. B.: Subacute necrotising lymphadenitis: A clinicopathologic study. Acta Pathol. Jpn. *31*:791–797, 1981.
43. Gill, M. J., Fanning, E. A., and Chomyc, S.: Childhood lymphadenitis in a harsh northern climate due to atypical mycobacteria. Scand. J. Infect. Dis. *19*:77–83, 1987.
44. Gorak, E. J., Yamada, S. M., and Brown, J. D.: Community-acquired methicillin-resistant *Staphylococcus aureus* in hospitalized adults and children without known risk factors. Clin. Infect. Dis. *29*:797–800, 1999.
45. Green, P. A., von Reyn, C. F., and Smith, R. P., Jr.: *Mycobacterium avium* complex parotid lymphadenitis: Successful therapy with clarithromycin and ethambutol. Pediatr. Infect. Dis. J. *12*:615–617, 1993.
46. Gutman, L. T., Moye, J., Zimmer, B., et al: Tuberculosis in human immunodeficiency virus-exposed or -infected United States children. Pediatr. Infect. Dis. J. *13*:963–968, 1994.
47. Haas, W. H., Amthor, B., Engelmann, G., et al.: Preoperative diagnosis of *Mycobacterium avium* lymphadenitis in two immunocompetent children by polymerase chain reaction of gastric aspirates. Pediatr. Infect. Dis. J. *17*:1016–1020, 1998.
48. Haase, G., Kentrup, H., Skopnik, H., et al.: *Mycobacterium lentiflavum:* An etiologic agent of cervical lymphadenitis. Clin. Infect. Dis. *25*:1245–1246, 1997.
49. Hall, C. B., Long, C. E., Schnabel, K. C., et al.: Human herpesvirus-6 infection in children. N. Engl. J. Med. *331*:432–438, 1994.
50. Harris, B. H., Webb, W., Wilkinson, A. H., et al.: Mycobacterial lymphadenitis. J. Pediatr. Surg. *17*:589–590, 1982.
51. Hazra, R., Robson, C. D., Perez-Atayde, A. R., et al.: Lymphadenitis due to nontuberculous mycobacteria in children: Presentation and response to therapy. Clin. Infect. Dis. *28*:123–129, 1999.
52. Herold, B. C., Immergluck, L. C., Maranan, M. C., et al.: Community-acquired methicillin-resistant *Staphylococcus aureus* in children with no identified predisposing risk. J. A. M. A. *279*:593–598, 1998.
53. Huebner, R. E., Schein, M. F., Cauthen, G. M., et al: Usefulness of skin testing with mycobacterial antigens in children with cervical lymphadenopathy. Pediatr. Infect. Dis. J. *11*:450–456, 1992.
54. Jaffe, B. F.: Pediatric head and neck tumors: A study of 178 cases. Laryngoscope *83*:1644–1651, 1973.
55. Kendig, E. L., Jr.: The clinical picture of sarcoidosis in children. Pediatrics *54*:289–292, 1974.
56. Kent, D. C.: Tuberculous lymphadenitis: Not a localized disease process. Am. J. Med. Sci. *254*:866–873, 1967.
57. Koehler, J. E., LeBoit, P. E., Egbert, B. M., et al.: Cutaneous vascular lesions and disseminated cat-scratch disease in patients with the acquired immunodeficiency syndrome (AIDS) and AIDS-related complex. Ann. Intern. Med. *109*:449–455, 1988.
58. Knight, P. J., Hamoudi, A. B., and Vassy, L. E.: The diagnosis and treatment of midline neck masses in children. Surgery 93:603–611, 1983.
59. Knight, P. J., Mulne, A. F., and Vassy, L. E.: When is lymph node biopsy indicated in children with enlarged peripheral nodes? Pediatrics *69*:391–396, 1982.
60. Kratz, R. C., Stine, F. A., Grover, J. W., et al.: Suppurations of the neck. Arch. Otolaryngol. *70*:692–695, 1959.
61. Lai, K. K., Stottmeier, K. D., Sherman, I. H., et al: Mycobacterial cervical lymphadenopathy: Relation of etiologic agents to age. J. A. M. A. *251*: 1286–1288, 1984.
62. Lampe, R. M., Baker, C. J., Septimus, E. J., et al.: Cervicofacial nocardiosis in children. J. Pediatr. *99*:593–595, 1981.
63. Lincoln, E. M., and Gilbert, L. A.: Disease in children due to mycobacteria other than *Mycobacterium tuberculosis.* Am. Rev. Respir. Dis. *105*:683–714, 1972.
64. Lind, A., Larsson, L. O., Bentzon, M. W., et al.: Sensitivity to sensitins and tuberculin in Swedish children. I. A study of school-children in an urban area. Tubercle *72*:29–36, 1991.
65. Lockhart, R. D., Hamilton, G. F., and Fyfe, F. W.: Anatomy of the Human Body. Philadelphia, J. B. Lippincott, 1959, pp. 662–664.
66. Lyon, L. W.: Neurologic manifestations of cat-scratch disease: Report of a case and review of the literature. Arch. Neurol. *25*:23–27, 1971.
67. Losurdo, G., Castagnola, E., Cristino, E., et al.: Cervical lymphadenitis caused by nontuberculous mycobacteria in immunocompetent children: Clinical and therapeutic experience. Head Neck *20*:245–249, 1998.
68. Maltezou, H. C., Spyridis, P., and Kafetzis, D.: Nontuberculous mycobacterial lymphadenitis in children. Pediatr. Infect. Dis. J *18*:968–970, 1999.
69. Margileth, A. M.: Cat scratch disease: Nonbacterial regional lymphadenitis: The study of 145 patients and a review of the literature. Pediatrics *42*:803–818, 1968.
70. Margileth, A. M.: The use of purified protein derivative mycobacterial skin test antigens in children and adolescents: Purified protein derivative skin test results correlated with mycobacterial isolates. Pediatr. Infect. Dis. *2*:225–231, 1983.
71. Margileth, A. M.: Management of nontuberculous (atypical) mycobacterial infections in children and adolescents. Pediatr. Infect. Dis. *4*:119–121, 1985.
72. Margileth, A. M.: Cat-scratch disease update. Am. J. Dis. Child. *138*:711–713, 1984.
73. Margileth, A. M.: Antibiotic therapy for cat-scratch disease: Clinical study of therapeutic outcome in 268 patients and a review of the literature. Pediatr. Infect. Dis. J. *11*:474–478, 1992.
74. Margileth, A. M., Chandra, R., and Altman, R. P.: Chronic lymphadenopathy due to mycobacterial infection: Clinical features, diagnosis, histopathology, and management. Am. J. Dis. Child. *138*:917–921, 1984.
75. Margileth, A. M., Wear, D. J., Hadfield, T. L., et al.: Cat-scratch disease: Bacteria in skin at the primary inoculation site. J. A. M. A. *252*:928–931, 1984.
76. Marshall, G. S., Edwards, K. M., Butler, J., et al.: Syndrome of periodic fever, pharyngitis, and aphthous stomatitis. J. Pediatr. *110*:43–46, 1987.
77. McCabe, R. E., Brooks, R. G., Dorfman, R. F., et al.: Clinical spectrum in 107 cases of toxoplasmic lymphadenopathy. Rev. Infect. Dis. *9*:754–774, 1987.
78. Medina, M., Goldfarb, J., Traquinna, D., et al.: Cervical adenitis and deep neck infection caused by *Streptococcus pneumoniae.* Pediatr. Infect. Dis. J. *16*:823–824, 1997.
79. Melish, M. E., Hicks, R. V., and Reddy, R.: Kawasaki syndrome: An update. Hosp. Pract. *17*:99–105, 1982.
80. Moritz, J. D., Ludwig, A., and Oestmann, J. W.: Contrast-enhanced color Doppler sonography for evaluation of enlarged cervical lymph nodes in head and neck tumors. Am. J. Roentgenol. *174*:1279–1284, 2000.
81. Moussatos, G. H., and Baffes, T. G.: Cervical masses in infants and children. Pediatrics *32*:251–256, 1963.
82. Na, D. G., Lim, H. K., Byun, H. S., et al.: Differential diagnosis of cervical lymphadenopathy: Usefulness of color Doppler sonography. Am. J. Roentgenol. *168*:1311–1316, 1997.
83. Naimi, T. S., LeDell, K. H., and Boxrud, D. J.: Epidemiology and clonality of community-acquired methicillin-resistant *Staphylococcus aureus* in Minnesota, 1996–1998. Clin. Infect. Dis. *33*:990–996, 2001.
84. Nambiar, S., Chandra, R. S., Schwartz, R. H., et al.: Seven-year-old Indian girl with fever and cervical lymphadenitis. Kikuchi-Fujimoto disease. Pediatr. Infect. Dis. J. *20*:464–465, 469, 2001.

85. Nylen, O., Berg-Kelly, K., and Andersson, B.: Cervical lymph node infections with non-tuberculous mycobacteria in preschool children: Interferon gamma deficiency as a possible cause of clinical infection. Acta Paediatr. *89*:1322–1325, 2000.
86. O'Brien, D. P., Currie, B. J., and Krause, V. L.: Nontuberculous mycobacterial disease in northern Australia: A case series and review of the literature. Clin. Infect. Dis. *31*:958–968, 2000.
87. O'Brien, R. J., Geiter, L. J., and Snider, D. E., Jr.: The epidemiology of nontuberculous mycobacterial diseases in the United States. Am. Rev. Respir. Dis. *135*:1007–1014, 1987.
88. Oguz, F., Mujgan, S., Alper, G., et al.: Treatment of bacillus Calmette-Guérin associated lymphadenitis. Pediatr. Infect. Dis. J *11*:87, 1992.
89. Olson, N. R.: Nontuberculous mycobacterial infections of the face and neck: Practical considerations. Laryngoscope *91*:1714–1726, 1981.
90. Omokoku, R., and Castells, S.: Post-DPT inoculation cervical lymphadenitis in children. N. Y. State J. Med. *81*:1667–1668, 1981.
91. Ord, R. J., and Matz, G. J.: Tuberculous cervical lymphadenitis. Arch. Otolaryngol. *99*:327–329, 1974.
92. Padeh, S., Brezniak, N., Zemer, D., et al.: Periodic fever, aphthous stomatitis, pharyngitis, and adenopathy syndrome: Clinical characteristics and outcome. J. Pediatr. *135*:98–101, 1999.
93. Papakonstantinou, O., Bakantaki, A., Paspalaki, P., et al.: High-resolution and color Doppler ultrasonography of cervical lymphadenopathy in children. Acta Radiol. *42*:470–476, 2001.
94. Perlman, D. C., D'Amico, R., and Salomon, N.: Mycobacterial infections of the head and neck. Curr. Infect. Dis. Rep. *3*:233–241, 2001.
95. Phillips, P., Kwiatkowski, M. B., and Copland, M.: Mycobacterial lymphadenitis associated with the initiation of combination antiretroviral therapy. J. AIDS *20*:122–128, 1999.
96. Pounds, L. A.: Neck masses of congenital origin. Pediatr. Clin. North Am. *28*:841–844, 1981.
97. Powers, G. F., and Boisvert, P. L.: Age as a factor in streptococcosis. J. Pediatr. *25*:481–504, 1944.
98. Prince, D. S., Peterson, D. D., Steiner, R. M., et al.: Infection with *Mycobacterium avium* complex in patients without predisposing conditions. N. Engl. J. Med. *321*:863–868, 1989.
99. Rafaty, F. M.: Cervical adenopathy secondary to toxoplasmosis. Arch Otolaryngol. *103*:547–549, 1977.
100. Ridder, G. J., Richter, B., Disko, U., et al.: Gray-scale sonographic evaluation of cervical lymphadenopathy in cat-scratch disease. J. Clin. Ultrasound *29*:140–145, 2001.
101. Robson, C. D., Hazra, R., Barnes, P. D., et al.: Nontuberculous mycobacterial infection of the head and neck in immunocompetent children. CT and MR findings. Am. J. Neuroradiol. *20*:1829–1835, 1999.
102. Rosai, J., and Dorfman, R. F.: Sinus histiocytosis with massive lymphadenopathy: A newly recognized benign clinicopathological entity. Arch. Pathol. *87*:63–70, 1969.
103. Ryan-Poirier, K., and Patrick, C. C.: Cervical adenitis caused by *Staphylococcus epidermidis*. J. Clin. Microbiol. *31*:426–427, 1993.
104. Schaad, U. B., Votteler, T. P., McCracken, G. H., et al.: Management of atypical mycobacterial lymphadenitis in childhood: A review based on 380 cases. J. Pediatr. *95*:356–360, 1979.
105. Schlossberg, D., Morad, Y., Krouse, T. B., et al: Culture-proved disseminated cat-scratch disease in acquired immunodeficiency syndrome. Arch. Intern. Med. *149*:1437–1439, 1989.
106. Schroder, K. E., Elverland, H. H., Mair, I. W. S., et al: Granulomatous cervical lymphadenitis. J. Otolaryngol. *8*:127–131, 1979.
107. Schuit, K. E., and Powell, D. A.: Mycobacterial lymphadenitis in childhood. Am. J. Dis. Child. *132*:675–677, 1978.
108. Scobie, W. G.: Acute suppurative adenitis in children: Review of 964 cases. Scott. Med. J. *14*:352–354, 1969.
109. Siltzbach, L. E., and Greenberg, G. M.: Childhood sarcoidosis: A study of 18 patients. N. Engl. J. Med. *279*:1239–1244, 1968.
110. Singh, K., Muralidar, M., Kumar, A., et al: Comparison of in house polymerase chain reaction techniques for the detection of *Mycobacterium tuberculosis* DNA in granulomatous lymphadenopathy. J. Clin. Pathol. *53*:355–361, 2000.
111. Smith, H. L., II: Necrotizing lymphadenitis (Kikuchi's disease). Pediatrics *91*:152, 1993.
112. Sommers, H. M., and Good, R. C.: Mycobacterium. *In* Lennette, E. H., Balows, A., Hausler, W. J., Jr., et al. (eds.): Manual of Clinical Microbiology. 4th ed. American Society for Microbiology, 1985, pp. 216–240.
113. Spark, R. P., Fried, M. L., Bean, C. K., et al: Nontuberculous mycobacterial adenitis of childhood. Am. J. Dis. Child. *142*:106–108, 1988.
114. Speert, D. P., Britt, W. J., and Kaplan, E. L.: Tick-borne tularemia presenting as ulcerative lymphadenitis. Clin. Pediatr. *18*:239–241, 1979.
115. Springer, B., Kirschner, P., Rost-Meyer, G., et al.: *Mycobacterium interjectum,* a new species isolated from a patient with chronic lymphadenitis. J. Clin. Microbiol. *31*:3083–3089, 1993.
116. Starke, J. R., and Taylor-Watt, K. T.: Tuberculosis in the pediatric population of Houston, Texas. Pediatrics *84*:28–35, 1989.
117. Stuteville, O. H.: Otorhinolaryngologic surgery: The spread of infections in the head and neck. J. Int. Coll. Surg. *29*:750–754, 1958.
118. Sundaresh, H. P., Kumar, A., Hokanson, J. T., et al.: Etiology of cervical lymphadenitis in children. Am. Fam. Physician *24*:147–151, 1981.
119. Suskind, D. L., Handler, S., Tom, L. W. C., et al.: Nontuberculous mycobacterial cervical adenitis. Clin. Pediatr. (Phila.) *36*:403–409, 1997.
120. Tartaglione, T.: Treatment of nontuberculous mycobacterial infections: Role of clarithromycin and azithromycin. Clin. Ther. *19*:626–638, 1997.
121. Tessier, M.-H., Amoric, J. C., Mechinaud, F., et al.: Clarithromycin for atypical mycobacterial lymphadenitis in nonimmunocompromised children. Lancet *344*:1778, 1994.
122. Thomaidis, T., Anastassea-Vlachou, K., Mandalenaki-Lambrou, C., et al.: Chronic lymphoglandular enlargement and toxoplasmosis in children. Arch. Dis. Child. *52*:403–407, 1977.
123. Thomas, K. T., Feder, H. M., Jr., Lawton, A. R., et al.: Periodic fever syndrome in children. J. Pediatr. *135*:15–21, 1999.
124. Thompson, J. N., Watanabe, M. J., Greene, G. R., et al.: Atypical mycobacterial cervical adenitis: Clinical presentation. Laryngoscope *90*:287–294, 1980.
125. Tomblin, J. L., and Roberts, F. J.: Tuberculous cervical lymphadenitis. Can. Med. Assoc. J. *121*:324–330, 1979.
126. Trinka, L., Dankova, D., and Svandova, E.: Six years experience with the discontinuation of the BCG vaccination. IV. Protective effect of BCG vaccination against *Mycobacterium avium intracellulare* complex. Tuber. Lung Dis. *75*:348–352, 1994.
127. Turner, R. R., Martin, J., and Dorfman, R. F.: Necrotizing lymphadenitis: A study of 30 cases. Am. J. Surg. Pathol. *7*:115–123, 1983.
128. Waggoner-Fountain, L. A., Hayden, G. F., and Hendley, J. O.: Kawasaki syndrome masquerading as bacterial lymphadenitis. Clin. Pediatr. *34*:185–189, 1995.
129. Wells, R. G., and Sty, J. R.: Cervical lymphadenitis complicated by mycotic carotid artery aneurysm. Pediatr. Radiol. *21*:402–403, 1991.
130. Wolinsky, E.: Mycobacterial lymphadenitis in children: A prospective study of 105 nontuberculous cases with long-term follow-up. Clin. Infect. Dis. *20*:954–963, 1995.
131. Wright, N. L.: Cervical infections. Am. J. Surg. *113*:379–386, 1967.
132. Wu, C. H., Lee, M. M., Huang, K. C., et al.: A probability prediction rule for malignant cervical lymphadenopathy using sonography. Head Neck *22*:223–228, 2000.
133. Yamauchi, T., Ferrieri, P., and Anthony, B. F.: The aetiology of acute cervical adenitis in children: Serological and bacteriological studies. J. Med. Microbiol. *13*:37–43, 1980.
134. Zangwill, K. M., Hamilton, D. H., Perkins, B. A., et al.: Cat scratch disease in Connecticut: Epidemiology, risk factors, and evaluation of a new diagnostic test. N. Engl. J. Med. *329*:8–13, 1993.

Parotitis

JOHN R. CLARK, JR. ■ JUDITH R. CAMPBELL

Parotitis, inflammation of the parotid gland, is caused by a variety of infectious agents and noninfectious systemic illnesses. Several definitions are used to describe the clinical presentations and etiologic processes that lead to parotid gland swelling and inflammation. *Suppurative parotitis*, first described in the 1800s, is a serious bacterial infection in neonates and postsurgical patients.[42] *Epidemic parotitis*, particularly prevalent in the prevaccine era, primarily was caused by mumps virus infection.[49] In the postvaccine era, this form of parotitis also is caused by other viral pathogens and, therefore, is referred to as *viral parotitis*. Rarely, a more indolent, slowly progressive, granulomatous infection may occur that is referred to as *granulomatous parotitis*. *Recurrent parotitis of childhood* is a unique illness that is characterized by multiple episodes of acute and subacute parotid gland swelling. The histologic findings in this disease include architectural changes in the ducts and chronic inflammation. Many noninfectious systemic illnesses cause persistent or recurrent parotid gland swelling and inflammation, which is referred to as *chronic parotitis*. Bilateral parotid enlargement is a frequent presentation of human immunodeficiency virus (HIV) infection as part of *diffuse infiltrative lymphocytosis syndrome*.

Pathophysiology

Despite the various agents that cause parotitis, involvement of the gland occurs mainly by three mechanisms. The most common one is a localized infection limited to the gland and surrounding structures. Parotitis may be a manifestation of a systemic infection, as in mumps, or rarely may develop secondary to hematogenous seeding during periods of transient bacteremia. Several common contributing factors and pathophysiologic mechanisms lead to swelling of the gland. The parotid is well encapsulated and consists of a superficial and a deep lobe that are separated by the facial nerve. The parotid duct (Stensen duct) traverses the buccal soft tissue anteriorly and exits opposite the second upper molar. Thin, watery secretions from the parotid gland cleanse the ductal system and have some bacteriostatic properties, thereby preventing accumulation of bacteria and debris.[32] Factors that predispose individuals to the development of parotitis include side effects of certain drugs and diseases that lead to dehydration, xerostomia, or ductal obstruction[32, 42] (Table 16–1). Decreased salivary flow allows retrograde migration of bacteria. Stasis in the ductal system, caused by ductal ectasia, inflammation, calculi, or strictures, allows proliferation of bacteria and inflammation within the gland.

TABLE 16–1 ■ PREDISPOSING FACTORS FOR PAROTITIS

Drug-Induced Xerostomia
Anticholinergics
Antihistamines
Antidepressants
Phenothiazines
Beta blockers
Diuretics
General anesthesia
Disease-Related Xerostomia
Sjögren syndrome
Diabetes mellitus
Chronic liver disease
Cystic fibrosis
Obstruction
Dental appliances
Oral tumors
Radiation therapy
Trauma

Etiology

Infectious parotitis may be caused by aerobes, anaerobes, mycobacteria, and viruses (Table 16–2). In all age groups, *Staphylococcus aureus* is the organism most commonly associated with suppurative parotitis.[40, 42] Gram-negative pathogens (e.g., *Escherichia coli* and *Klebsiella* and *Pseudomonas* species) also may cause suppurative parotitis, particularly in neonates and debilitated or hospitalized patients.[10, 28, 41, 42] The role of anaerobic organisms in this infection has become apparent, especially when poor oral hygiene and oral pathology are associated features.[4, 5, 35] In cases of recurrent parotitis of childhood, *Streptococcus* spp. are the bacteria most commonly isolated.[18, 37, 40] Granulomatous parotitis most often is caused by *Mycobacterium tuberculosis* and may occur in the absence of systemic or disseminated tuberculous disease.[32, 38, 45] Other causes of granulomatous parotitis include *Mycobacterium avium–intracellulare*, *Actinomyces* spp., and gram-negative intracellular organisms (*Francisella tularensis* and *Brucella* spp.).[22, 32, 52] In the postvaccine era, the most common viral cause of parotitis still is the paramyxovirus mumps virus. However, coxsackieviruses, Epstein-Barr virus, influenza A virus, parainfluenza viruses, herpes simplex virus, cytomegalovirus, and lymphocytic-choriomeningitis virus all have been implicated in cases of parotitis.[1, 2, 25, 27, 29, 31, 32]

TABLE 16–2 ■ PAROTITIS: REPORTED INFECTIOUS ETIOLOGIES

Aerobic Bacteria
Staphylococcus aureus
Alpha-hemolytic streptococci
Streptococcus pneumoniae
Streptococcus pyogenes
Viridans streptococci
Haemophilus species
Moraxella catarrhalis
Pseudomonas aeruginosa
Escherichia coli
Proteus species
Salmonella species
Klebsiella species
Anaerobic Bacteria
Peptostreptococcus species
Prevotella species
Fusobacterium species
Actinomyces species
Mycobacteria
Mycobacterium tuberculosis
Mycobacterium avium–intracellulare
Other mycobacteria
Viruses
Mumps
Coxsackieviruses A and B
Echoviruses
Epstein-Barr virus
Influenza A
Parainfluenza viruses 1 and 3
Cytomegalovirus
Herpes simplex virus type 1
Lymphocytic-choriomeningitis virus
Human immunodeficiency virus

Clinical Presentation and Diagnosis

A detailed history and physical examination are critical in assisting the clinician in determining the most likely etiology of parotid gland swelling. One should determine the onset and duration of symptoms, their periodicity, and the character of salivary secretions. In addition, the presence of a systemic disease must be excluded. Examination of the parotid gland is achieved best by simultaneous palpation of the intraoral and extraoral salivary structures. Gentle external pressure should be applied to the gland, and the parotid duct should be examined for evidence of purulent secretions or surrounding erythema.

Suppurative parotitis occurs most commonly in neonates or patients with dehydration, poor oral hygiene, malnutrition, immunosuppression, oral trauma, sepsis, or any medication or disease that decreases salivary secretions.[16] Most often, the disease is unilateral; however, bilateral suppurative parotitis may occur in as many as 17 percent of cases.[42] The disease is characterized by acute onset of pain, swelling, warmth, and induration of the involved gland and purulent discharge from the Stensen duct. Associated physical findings may include fever, trismus, malaise, and cervical adenitis. In suppurative parotitis, the Gram stain and culture (aerobic and anaerobic) of purulent material from the duct can provide a specific microbiologic diagnosis. In addition, elevation of the white blood cell count with a neutrophil predominance may help differentiate this form of parotitis from viral parotitis and parotid disease of a noninfectious etiology.

Mumps is the most common form of viral parotitis and is characterized by a prodrome of fever, malaise, anorexia, and headache. Usually, the following day, unilateral or bilateral earache and parotid tenderness develop. The gland or glands enlarge during the subsequent 2 to 3 days, and the orifice of the Stensen duct is erythematous and swollen, yet secretions from the duct are clear. At the point of maximal swelling, the angle of the jaw is obliterated and the earlobe lifted upward and out. The other salivary glands are involved in as many as 10 percent of cases.[37] Rare systemic manifestations of mumps infection include epididymo-orchitis, meningitis, meningoencephalitis, and oophoritis. Other viral agents may produce similar clinical manifestations and can be differentiated from mumps only by culture and hemagglutination inhibition, complement fixation, or enzyme-linked immunosorbent assay serology. In viral parotitis, the white blood cell count may be normal, slightly elevated, or depressed, with a lymphocytic predominance.

Granulomatous parotitis typically presents as a painless, slowly enlarging mass without surrounding inflammation. It may be misdiagnosed as a slow-growing tumor until the correct diagnosis often is made by biopsy and culture. Both *M. tuberculosis* and *M. avium–intracellulare* may cause infection in the parenchyma of the gland or in intraglandular or periglandular lymph nodes.[38, 52] Clinical evidence of systemic tuberculous disease usually is absent. Parotitis has been observed as an extension of nontuberculous cervical adenitis.[52] Actinomycosis of the parotid gland causes a slowly enlarging, nodular, nontender gland; however, associated oral or cervicofacial infection usually is present. Fistulas draining yellow or white material with sulfur granules are common.[22]

Recurrent parotitis of childhood is a rare disease, with onset that typically occurs before the child reaches 10 years of age and a peak incidence at approximately 6 years of age.[15, 37] Some authors hypothesize that an underlying congenital abnormality, such as sialectasis, is a common predisposing feature. Clinically, these children experience repeated episodes of fever, pain, and unilateral swelling of the parotid gland. Purulent material often can be expressed from the Stensen duct and, when cultured, often yields streptococcal organisms. Sialography and ultrasound reveal multiple areas of sialectasis throughout the parotid glands bilaterally even if only one side is symptomatic. The frequency of attacks is highly variable, and each episode of parotitis may last as long as 2 weeks, when it resolves spontaneously.[9] Several authors have noted that recurrences become less frequent with increasing age and that the disease tends to cease at the onset of puberty or early adulthood.[15, 37]

Human Immunodeficiency Virus and Parotid Enlargement

Bilateral parotid enlargement is a common finding in children infected with HIV. This entity in HIV-positive children is associated with the HLA-DR11 phenotype, but the significance of this finding is unclear.[24, 48] Bilateral parotid enlargement frequently is seen as part of diffuse infiltrative lymphocytosis syndrome, which is characterized by proliferation of CD8-positive lymphocytes within the circulation and is of unclear etiology. Growth of the parotid is secondary to infiltration of CD8 lymphocytes into the gland, follicular hyperplasia of intraparotid lymphoid tissue (as occurs in lymph nodes throughout the body in HIV infection), and development of diffuse intraparotid, lymphoepithelial cysts.[7, 33] Epstein-Barr virus has been proposed as an impetus for CD8 lymphoproliferation because the virus has been isolated from parotid tissue of some affected patients.[8] However, the absence of positive serology for the virus renders it an unlikely causative agent. HIV, which may be the inciting agent, has been detected in dendritic cells, macrophages, and lymphocytes isolated from the parotid glands of affected patients.[8]

Parotid enlargement may be present in as many as 20 to 50 percent of children with HIV infection and acquired immunodeficiency syndrome (AIDS).[26, 30, 47, 50] The median time from birth to development of parotid enlargement is 4.6 years, and often it is the first manifestation of HIV infection acquired during the perinatal period in an otherwise healthy older child.[24, 26] HIV-positive children with enlarged parotid glands tend to have a slower progression to death than do those afflicted with oral herpes or candidiasis.[26] Usually, both parotid glands are involved, and an affected patient presents with enlarged, tender parotid glands, xerostomia, and increased serum amylase level.[6] Severity of pain and size of the gland tend to fluctuate without apparent cause.

Among the differential diagnoses for parotid enlargement in an HIV-positive patient is viral and bacterial parotitis. Some patients have preexisting xerostomia that may increase their susceptibility to parotitis. In addition, the immunocompromised state of patients with AIDS may predispose them to infection of the parotid gland with other agents, such as cytomegalovirus, Epstein-Barr virus, and bacteria.[20, 44, 51]

Differential Diagnosis

Parotitis most often is diagnosed based on clinical presentation, microbiology, serology, and response to empirical therapy. Ultrasound may be useful as a screening tool to prompt the necessity for more sensitive modalities if the sonograph is abnormal.[36] Computed tomography is most useful in evaluating for anatomic defects, radiolucent calculi, or abscess formation in the parotid gland.[43] X-ray sialography is the gold standard in examining the parotid gland ducts; however, sialograms are contraindicated in the setting of acute infection. Magnetic resonance sialography is a promising alternative and has several advantages. Unlike x-ray sialography, magnetic resonance sialography is not contraindicated during acute parotitis and does not require injection of contrast material or involve manipulation of the Stensen duct.[17] Nonetheless, experience with magnetic resonance sialography is limited, and this mode alone may not be sufficiently sensitive to detect tertiary salivary ductules or calculus disease.[17, 54]

Noninfectious causes of parotid swelling and inflammation include collagen vascular diseases (Sjögren syndrome and systemic lupus erythematosus), metabolic disorders (hepatic disease, hyperlipoproteinemia, hyperuricemia), endocrine disorders (diabetes mellitus, hypothyroidism), tumors, leukemic infiltration, drugs (antineoplastic chemotherapy), and poisons (iodine).[32, 37, 40] Sjögren syndrome, the most common cause of noninfectious parotitis, is caused by lymphocyte-mediated destruction of the exocrine glands.[21,40] Patients with this disease have diminished or absent glandular secretions and mucosal dryness; therefore, xerostomia and keratoconjunctivitis sicca are prominent clinical features. In addition, the parotid glands are enlarged bilaterally, are firm, and have an irregular contour. Sialography reveals sialectasia, and saliva from these patients has unique biochemical characteristics. Antibodies to nuclear antigens SS-A and SS-B can be detected in the sera of patients with Sjögren syndrome.[40] One should remember that patients with chronic noninfectious parotitis have changes in the ductular architecture or strictures that can predispose them to episodes of infectious parotitis.

Treatment

Treatment of parotitis includes rehydration, parotid massage, discontinuation of any medications that diminish salivary flow, and sialalogues (e.g., lemon drops, hard candy, chewing gum), which increase salivary flow.[3, 32, 40, 42] In cases of suspected suppurative parotitis, a broad-spectrum antibiotic regimen that is effective against *S. aureus*, *Streptococcus* spp., gram-negative organisms, and anaerobes should be administered empirically, pending specific culture results. Antibiotic regimens frequently employed include penicillinase-resistant penicillins, first-generation cephalosporins, and clindamycin in combination with an aminoglycoside.[3] If the patient has been hospitalized for a prolonged period or if the predominant organisms on Gram stain of the purulent discharge are gram-negative, ceftazidime should be considered as initial empiric therapy.[40, 42] Surgical incision and drainage of purulent fluid are indicated if there is slow or no response to medical therapy or fluctuance increases.[46] The treatment of viral parotitis consists of antipyretics, analgesia, and hydration. In cases of mycobacterial infection, excision of the gland may be required, in addition to specific antimycobacterial therapy.[38, 45] Reports have described successful treatment with clarithromycin and azithromycin of parotitis caused by atypical mycobacteria.[19] In contrast, actinomycosis of the parotid gland is managed medically with penicillin G.[22] Children with recurrent parotitis should be treated with antibiotics during acute episodes, but chronic suppressive antimicrobial therapy is not recommended. Tympanic neurectomy involves severing the parasympathetic secretomotor fibers of the tympanic plexus to the parotid. This procedure attenuates secretion from the gland and, therefore, relieves sialectasis and further episodes of parotitis in more than 70 percent of patients.[14, 39] Only 10 to 20 percent of these patients will require parotidectomy for persistence of symptoms beyond puberty.[12] Although it is the optimal treatment for complete resolution of recurrent parotitis, it carries a risk for facial nerve injury.

Complications

With improved fluid management of postsurgical patients and the use of broad-spectrum antimicrobial agents, complications secondary to infectious parotitis now are rare events. In neonates or immunocompromised patients, sepsis may be a severe complication of this infection. Abscess formation may result from delayed or ineffective therapy. Compromise of the facial nerve may occur and can resolve with successful treatment of the infected gland.[34] The most serious and rare complication is extension to other structures of the head and neck and along fascial planes to the face, external auditory canal, jugular vein, mandible, and even the mediastinum.

Prevention

Suppurative parotitis can be prevented in postsurgical patients by maintaining adequate hydration and good oral hygiene. The most common form of viral parotitis, mumps, can be prevented by appropriate vaccination. Between 1968 and 1993, a 99 percent reduction in the incidence of new cases of mumps occurred.[53] However, in the mid-1980s, a relative resurgence of mumps in previously vaccinated populations was noted.[11, 23] The current recommendation to revaccinate children with measles-mumps-rubella vaccine when they are 11 or 12 years of age is expected to reduce the occurrence of mumps in previously vaccinated children.[13]

REFERENCES

1. Arditi, M., Langman, C. B., Christensen, M., et al.: Probable herpes simplex virus type 1–related acute parotitis, nephritis and erythema multiforme. Pediatr. Infect. Dis. J. 7:427–429, 1988.
2. Brill, S. J., and Gilfillan, R. Acute parotitis associated with influenza type A: A report of twelve cases. N. Engl. J. Med. *296*:1391–1392, 1977.
3. Brook, I. Diagnosis and management of parotitis. Arch. Otolaryngol. Head Neck Surg. *118*:469–471, 1992.
4. Brook, I., and Finegold, S. M. Acute suppurative parotitis caused by anaerobic bacteria: Report of two cases. Pediatrics *62*:1019–1020, 1978.
5. Brook, I., Frazier, E. H., and Thompson, D. H. Aerobic and anaerobic microbiology of acute suppurative parotitis. Laryngoscope *101*:170–172, 1991.
6. Chanock, S. J., and McIntosh, K. Pediatric infection with the human immunodeficiency virus: Issues for the otorhinolaryngologist. Otolaryngol. Clin. North Am. *22*:637–660, 1989.
7. Chapnik, J. S., Noyek, A. M., Berris, B., et al.: Parotid gland enlargement in HIV infection: Clinical/imaging findings. J. Otolaryngol. *19*:189–194, 1990.
8. Chetty, R., Vaithilingum, M., and Thejpal, R. Epstein-Barr virus status and the histopathological changes of parotid gland lymphoid infiltrates in HIV-positive children. Pathology *31*:413–417, 1999.
9. Chitre, V. V., and Premchandra, D. J. Recurrent parotitis. Arch. Dis. Child. *77*:359–363, 1997.
10. Chiu, C., and Lin, T. Clinical and microbiological analysis of six children with acute suppurative parotitis. Acta. Paediatr. *85*:106–108, 1996.
11. Cochi, S. L., Preblud, S. R., and Orenstein, W. A. Perspectives on the relative resurgence of mumps in the United States. Am. J. Dis. Child. *142*:499–507, 1988.
12. Cohen, H. A., Gross, S., Nussinovitch, M., et al.: Recurrent parotitis. Arch. Dis. Child. *67*:1036–1037, 1992.
13. Committee on the Control of Infectious Diseases, American Academy of Pediatrics 1994 Red Book: Report of the Committee on the Control of Infectious Diseases. 23rd ed. Evanston, IL, American Academy of Pediatrics, 1994.
14. Daud, A. S., and Pahor, A. L. Tympanic neurectomy in the management of parotid sialectasis. J. Laryngol. Otol. *109*:1155–1158, 1995.

15. Ericson, S., Zetterlund, B., and Ohman, J. Recurrent parotitis and sialectasis in childhood: Clinical, radiologic, immunologic, bacteriologic, and histologic study. Ann. Otol. Rhinol. Laryngol. *100*:527–535, 1991.
16. Fathalla, B., Collins, D., and Ezhuthachan, S. Acute suppurative parotitis: Uncommon presentation in a premature infant. J. Perinatol. *1*:57–59, 2000.
17. Fischbach, R., Kugel, H., Ernst, S., et al.: MR sialography: Initial experience using a T2-weighted fast SE sequence. J. Comput. Assist. Tomogr. *21*:826–830, 1997.
18. Giglio, M. S., Landaeta, M., and Pinto, M. E. Microbiology of recurrent parotitis. Pediatr. Infect. Dis. J. *16*:386–390, 1997.
19. Green, P. A., Fordham von Reyn, C., and Smith, Jr. *Mycobacterium avium* complex parotid lymphadenitits: Successful therapy with clarithromycin and ethambutol. Pediatr. Infect. Dis. J. *12*:615–617, 1993.
20. Hanekom, W. A., Chadwick, E. G., and Yogev, R. Pneumococcal parotitis in a human immunodeficiency virus-infected child. Pediatr. Infect. Dis. J. *14*:1113–1114, 1995.
21. Hearth-Holmes, M., Baethge, B. A., Abreo, F., et al.: Autoimmune exocrinopathy presenting as recurrent parotitis of childhood. Arch. Otolaryngol. Head Neck Surg. *119*:347–349, 1993.
22. Hensher, R., and Bowerman, J. Actinomycosis of the parotid gland. Br. J. Oral Maxillofac. Surg. *23*:128–134, 1995.
23. Hersh, B. S., Fine, P. E. M., Kent, W. K., et al.: Mumps outbreak in a highly vaccinated population. J. Pediatr. *119*:187–193, 1991.
24. Itescu, S. Diffuse infiltrative lymphocytosis syndrome in children and adults infected with HIV-1: A model of rheumatic illness caused by acquired viral infection. Am. J. Reprod. Immunol. *28*:247–250, 1992.
25. Jantausch, B. A., Wiedermann, B. L., and Jeffries, B. Parainfluenza virus type 2 meningitis and parotitis in an 11-year-old child. South. Med. J. *88*:230–231, 1995.
26. Katz, M. H., Mastrucci, M. T., Leggot, P. J., et al.: Prognostic significance of oral lesions in children with perinatally acquired human immunodeficiency virus infection. Am. J. Dis. Child. *147*:45–48, 1993.
27. Krilov, L. R., and Swenson, P. Acute parotitis associated with influenza A infection. J. Infect. Dis. *152*:853, 1985.
28. Leake, D., and Leake, R. Neonatal suppurative parotitis. Pediatrics *46*:203–207, 1970.
29. Lee, A. C. W., Lim, W. L., and So, K. T. Epstein-Barr virus associated parotitis. J. Paediatr. Child Health *33*:177–178, 1997.
30. Lepage, P., Van de Perre, P., Van Vliet, G., et al.: Clinical and endocrinologic manifestations in perinatally human immunodeficiency virus type 1-infected children aged 5 years or older. Am. J. Dis. Child. *145*:1248–1251, 1991.
31. Lewis, J. M., and Utz, J. P. Orchitis, parotitis and meningoencephalitis due to lymphocytic-choriomeningitis virus. N. Engl. J. Med. *265*:776–780, 1961.
32. Loughran, D. H., and Smith, L. G. Review: Infectious disorders of the parotid gland. N. J. Med. *85*:311–314, 1988.
33. Mandel, L., Kim, D., and Uy, C. Parotid gland swelling in HIV diffuse infiltrative CD8 lymphocytosis syndrome. Oral Surg. Oral Med. Oral Pathol. Oral Radiol. Endod. *85*:565–568, 1998.
34. Mathur, N. B., Goyal, R. K., and Khalil, A. Neonatal suppurative parotitis with facial palsy. Indian Pediatr. *25*:806–807, 1988.
35. Matlow, A., Korentager, R., Keystone, E., et al.: Parotitis due to anaerobic bacteria. Rev. Infect. Dis. *10*:420–423, 1988.
36. Murray, M. E., Buckenham, T. M., and Joseph, A. E. A. The role of ultrasound in screening patients referred for sialography: A possible protocol. Clin. Otolaryngol. *21*:21–23, 1996.
37. Myer, C., and Cotton, R. T. Salivary gland disease in children: A review. Part 1: Acquired non-neoplastic disease. Clin. Pediatr. *25*:314–322, 1986.
38. O'Connell, J. E., George, M. K., Speculand, B., et al.: Mycobacterial infection of the parotid gland: An unusual case of parotid swelling. J. Laryngol. Otol. *107*:561–564, 1993.
39. Perera, A. M., Kumar, B. N., and Pahor, A. L. Long-term results of tympanic neurectomy for chronic parotid sialectasis. Rev. Laryngol. Otol. Rhinol. *121*:95–98, 2000.
40. Pou, A. M., Johnson, J. T., and Weissman, J. Management decisions in parotitis. Compr. Ther. *21*:85–92, 1995.
41. Pruett, T. L., and Simmons, R. L. Nosocomial gram-negative bacillary parotitis. J. A. M. A. *251*:252–253, 1984.
42. Raad, I. I., Sabbagh, M. F., and Caranasos, G. J. Acute bacterial sialadenitis: A study of 29 cases and review. Rev. Infect. Dis. *12*:591–601, 1990.
43. Rabinov, J. D. Imaging of salivary gland pathology. Radiol. Clin. North Am. *38*:1047–1057, 2000.
44. Redleaf, M. I., Bauer, C. A., and Robinson, R. A. Fine-needle detection of cytomegalovirus parotitis in a patient with acquired immunodeficiency syndrome. Arch. Otolaryngol. Head Neck Surg. *120*:414–416, 1994.
45. Rowe-Jones, J. M., Vowles, R., Leighton, S. E. J., et al.: Diffuse tuberculous parotitis. J. Laryngol. Otol. *106*:1094–1095, 1992.
46. Sabatino, G., Verrotti, A., de Martino, M., et al.: Neonatal suppurative parotitis: A study of five cases. Eur. J. Pediatr. *158*:312–314, 1999.
47. Schuval, S. J., Bonagura, V. R., and Ilowite, N. T. Rheumatologic manifestations of pediatric human immunodeficiency virus infection. J. Rheumatol. *20*:1578–1582, 1993.
48. Schuval, S. J., O'Reilly, M. E., and Bonagura, V. R. Increased frequency of HLA-DR11 in pediatric human immunodeficiency virus-associated parotid gland enlargement. Clin. Diagn. Lab. Immunol. *4*:258–260, 1997.
49. Simpson, R. E. H. Infectiousness of communicable diseases in the household (measles, chickenpox, and mumps). Lancet *2*:549–554, 1952.
50. Sperling, N. M., and Lin, P. Parotid disease associated with human immunodeficiency virus infection. Ear Nose Throat J. *69*:475–477, 1990.
51. Stellbrink, H., Albrecht, H., and Greten, H. Pneumococcal parotitis and cervical lymph node abscesses in an HIV-infected patient. Clin. Invest. *72*:1037–1040, 1994.
52. Tunkel, D. E. Atypical mycobacterial adenitis presenting as a parotid abscess. Am. J. Otolaryngol. *16*:428–432, 1995.
53. van Loon, F. P., Holmes, S. J., Sirotkin, B. I., et al.: Mumps surveillance—United States, 1988–1993. M. M. W. R. Morb. Mortal. Wkly. Rep. *44*:1–14, 1995.
54. Varghese, J. C., Thornton, F., Lucey, B. C., et al.: A prospective comparative study of MR sialography and conventional sialography of salivary disease. A. J. R. Am. J. Roentgenol. *173*:1497–1503, 1999.

Sinusitis

JAMES D. CHERRY ■ NINA L. SHAPIRO ■ JAIME G. DEVILLE

Sinusitis is an inflammation of the mucosal lining of one or more of the paranasal sinuses. Although this inflammation of sinus mucosa most probably occurs to some degree with every upper respiratory tract infection that produces rhinitis, the vast majority of these episodes apparently have a spontaneous resolution. Recent reports estimate that between 5 and 10 percent of upper respiratory infections are complicated by acute sinusitis.[1, 142, 151] This rate represents a significant increase from earlier reports,[31] possibly because of a greater awareness of the illness and improved imaging techniques. However, the growing number of children in daycare has led to an actual increase in the incidence of upper respiratory tract infections.[151, 155] In addition, recognition that sinus infection can have a negative effect on the health of the growing numbers of children with chronic pulmonary disease has increased the interest in this disease.[90]

When considering a diagnosis of sinusitis in a child, the major problem is to distinguish simple upper respiratory tract infection or allergic inflammation from secondary bacterial infection of the sinuses. Unless complications such as periorbital cellulitis or cavernous sinus thrombosis render the diagnosis obvious, the clinician has no reliable way to establish a diagnosis of acute sinusitis in the office setting. Sometimes, symptoms and signs of sinusitis occur simultaneously with rhinitis, but most often, they occur after an episode of rhinitis. Infection in the sinuses usually persists after the preceding rhinitis has resolved. Sinusitis is classified by the duration of clinical symptoms: acute (up to 3 weeks), subacute (3 to 10 weeks), and chronic (more than 10 weeks). Available data comparing acute and subacute sinusitis are sparse; both entities may prove to have similar etiology, diagnosis, and prognosis; therefore, the distinction appears to be arbitrary and to have no clinical significance.

History

Purulent sinusitis and its relationship to orbital inflammation have been known for more than 2000 years.[62] Nathaniel Highmore, a 17th-century English physician and anatomist, is given credit for the separation of dental and antral disease.[109] John Hunter indicated the importance of surgical drainage in purulent sinusitis and suggested perforating the partition between the maxillary antrum and the nose.[109] During the first half of the 20th century, sinusitis was responsible for considerable morbidity and mortality, and surgical care of sinusitis frequently was lifesaving. Since the advent of antibiotics, sinusitis has had a lower medical profile. However, interest in this topic has increased. The advent of the newer surgical techniques of functional endoscopic sinus surgery that yield comparable results to sinus puncture and aspiration,[139] which now have been applied to children; improved diagnostic imaging studies; and the greater social importance of upper respiratory tract infections for parents who must be absent from work to seek treatment for their children[90] are just some of the factors involved.

Anatomy

All the paranasal sinuses develop as outpouchings of the nasal cavity. Three shelflike structures, the inferior, middle, and superior turbinates, are on the lateral nasal wall. The superior turbinate is not well developed in the first year of life.[167] Beneath each turbinate is the corresponding meatus into which the sinuses open; that is, the frontal, maxillary, and anterior ethmoid sinuses open into the middle meatus. The sphenoid and posterior ethmoid cells open high in the nasal vault into the superior meatus.[152]

The maxillary sinuses develop early in the second trimester of fetal life as lateral outpouchings in the posterior aspect of the middle meatuses. They are present at birth,[5, 95, 123, 167] with floors barely below the attachment of the inferior turbinates.[152] They expand rapidly by the time the child is 4 years of age.[167] Ultimately, at full size, the lateral borders of the maxillary sinuses reach the lateral orbital rims. The position of the floors of the sinuses is determined by the eruption of the dentition.[152] The ostia of the maxillary sinuses are located high on the medial walls of the sinuses, which impedes gravitational drainage of secretions; ciliary activity is required to move secretions from the body of the maxillary sinuses through the ostia into the nose.[152]

The ethmoid sinuses develop in the fourth month of gestation[152] and are present at birth.[95, 123, 167] They are not a single large cavity but a grouping of cells, 3 to 15 in number, each with its own opening or ostium. They have a honeycombed radiographic appearance and are small anteriorly and large posteriorly. The walls of the ethmoid labyrinth, especially the lateral walls bordering on the orbits, are thin; they are referred to as the *lamina papyracea*.[152]

Development of the frontal sinuses is variable. In adults, 80 percent have bilateral frontal sinuses, 1 to 4 percent have agenesis of the frontal sinuses, and the remainder have unilateral hypoplasia. The position of the frontal sinuses is supraorbital after 4 years of age, but they are not distinguished radiographically from the ethmoid sinuses until the child is 6 to 8 years of age. The frontal sinuses do not reach adult size for another 8 to 10 years.[152]

The onset of development of the sphenoid sinuses occurs during the child's first 2 years of life, but they remain rudimentary until about 6 years of age. They have reached their permanent size, although not their permanent shape, by the time the child is 12 years of age.[167]

Although the full development of the sinuses may take 20 years, by the time the child is 12 years of age, the nasal cavity and the paranasal sinuses nearly have completed their development and have reached adult proportions.[167] Sinus disease in postpubertal adolescents is thus similar to that in adults.

The mucosal lining of all the paranasal sinuses is composed of ciliated columnar epithelium and goblet cells.[126] It is continuous and similar to that lining the nasal cavity, except that the mucosa in the nose is thicker and contains more glands. The epithelium of all the paranasal sinuses and nasal cavity is covered in part by a mucus blanket.

Pathophysiology

The pathogenesis of sinus infection undoubtedly is similar to that of otitis media. The middle ear, with its extension, the eustachian tube, and the paranasal sinuses normally are sterile, but their contiguous areas (nasopharynx and nose) have a dynamic microbial flora. Under normal conditions, ciliary function with mucus flow can be expected to keep the sinuses clear of pathogens. The cilia within the sinuses propel the mucus toward their respective ostia, and from there, nasal ciliary action moves the mucus blanket posteriorly toward the pharynx. However, insults that damage the ciliary epithelium and affect the morphology, number, and function of cilia and those that alter the production or viscosity of the mucus blanket lead to obstruction of the flow of mucus, which allows the inoculation of large numbers of microorganisms into the sinuses, which can lead to infection. In a study in adults in whom sneezing, coughing, and nose blowing were stimulated or initiated voluntarily, intranasal pressures were measured, and the deposition of contrast medium (that before the initiation of the event had been inoculated into the nasopharynx) was determined by computed tomography (CT) scan.[58] Results of this study showed that nose blowing introduced viscous fluid into the maxillary sinuses, whereas coughing or sneezing did not generate enough pressure to propel fluid into the sinuses. Once instituted, sinus infection is complicated further by inflammatory obstruction of the ostium leading to the nose.

Recurrent chronic sinusitis implies a problem with local mucociliary defense, a defect in systemic immunity, or a fixed anatomic sinus obstruction. Often, the predisposing factors work in tandem, as in a child with a septal deformity and a viral illness.[90] In chronic sinusitis, the mucosa is thickened, and marked edema, vessel dilation, and infiltration of inflammatory cells are present.[141] Goblet cells are decreased in density, and seromucous glands are increased in density compared with their presence in normal sinuses. The single most important factor leading to purulent sinus infection in children as well as in adults is upper respiratory viral infection.[25, 39, 90, 151]

Wald and colleagues[151] in a prospective study involving a large number of children younger than 3 years of age demonstrated a doubling of the rate of sinusitis (defined as upper respiratory symptoms persisting longer than 15 days) among children in a daycare setting compared with children not in daycare. The differences presumably were due to increased exposure to viral respiratory illnesses. Radiographic studies in children with acute colds regularly indicate abnormalities of the maxillary sinuses, suggesting that the infection involves these areas.[93] These asymptomatic sinus opacifications may persist for 2 weeks after the symptoms of the upper respiratory illness have resolved.[36, 79, 152] Viral infection that involves the sinuses rarely is differentiated from its primary manifestations, such as the common cold, nasopharyngitis, and influenza, and recovery is the rule. However, if the effect of the viral infection on the mucosal surface is severe and is associated with the inoculation of one or more pathogenic bacterial agents and obstruction of an ostium, then disease will occur.

The mechanisms by which upper respiratory viral infections set the stage for secondary bacterial infection in the sinuses are complex. Using in situ hybridization, rhinovirus RNA was demonstrated inside epithelial cells of maxillary sinus in 50 percent of a small number of adults with acute sinusitis.[107] This finding is remarkable because in experimental rhinovirus infections, only a small percentage of nasal epithelial cells were noted to contain rhinovirus RNA.[6] These differences may only reflect differences in inoculum between experimental and natural infection, but they may indicate heavier infection in the sinuses than in the nose. Symptoms in upper respiratory viral infections are not caused by extensive damage to ciliated nasal epithelium but rather to aspects of the host response[6, 57, 100, 102, 105, 110, 111, 166] (see Chapter 8).

Other irritants can set the stage for sinus infection. For example, swimming in ocean, lake, or chlorinated pool water can lead to sinus involvement. Drying of the nasal mucosa, which occurs commonly during the winter in cold climates, may be a precipitating factor. Children with respiratory allergies are prone to sinusitis,[46, 113–115] and allergy probably is the second most prevalent predisposing factor in childhood sinusitis, acting through mucosa congestion and perhaps depressing local and systemic immune responses.[90, 128] The treatment of respiratory allergies may contribute to sinusitis because ciliary damage occurring after the administration of nasal decongestants has been demonstrated in organ culture and animal studies.[36, 37, 96] Richards and colleagues[118] reported a diagnosis of atopy in 62 percent of a selected cohort of pediatric patients who had documented recurrent sinusitis and were referred to allergy clinics in Los Angeles. Dental infections or extractions also can lead to maxillary sinusitis if the tooth root is adjacent to the maxillary sinus floor.[27]

Sudden change in pressure, as with diving or during descent in an airplane, physically can overcome local mucociliary defense mechanisms and lead to the sudden onset of acute sinusitis.[90] Defects of ciliary function, such as those occurring in the immotile cilia syndrome and Kartagener syndrome, predispose the child to chronic sinusitis.[40, 68, 77, 115, 123, 132] Refractory sinusitis also occurs commonly in children with primary and acquired immunodeficiency diseases.[24, 90, 97, 124, 129, 143, 148] A growing population of immunocompromised children undergoing treatment for malignancies and organ transplantations, as well as young patients with maternally transmitted and blood-transmitted acquired immunodeficiency syndrome, constitute another growing population with a potential for developing sinusitis that is difficult to manage. Finally, anatomic obstruction caused by septal deformities, craniofacial anomalies, foreign bodies, adenoidal hypertrophy, or nasal masses or polyps predisposes children to sinusitis. Nasal polyps in young children usually are not caused by allergies and, therefore, should constitute an indication for evaluation for cystic fibrosis.[90]

Immunologic mechanisms clearly are important in the pathogenesis of sinus infections, as indicated by the high prevalence of chronic sinus infections in children with immunodeficiencies.[24, 90, 97, 124, 129, 143] Sinus and nasal mucus contains immunoglobulin A (IgA), IgG, and IgM and lysozymes.[20, 122] Secretory IgA, which is produced locally, is the predominant immunoglobulin in nasal mucus.[60] IgG antibodies in nasal mucus result from passive leakage from plasma cells in the epithelium and submucosa and from the serum.[14] In general, with increasing age and resulting from previous exposures, these immunoglobulins develop species- and type-specific antibodies that block epithelial colonization by specific microorganisms.

Shapiro and associates[129] studied 61 children with refractory sinusitis and found that 34 had abnormal immunologic studies. Abnormal findings included poor response to pneumococcal type 7 antigen after immunization, IgG3 subclass deficiency, low serum IgA or IgG values, and elevated serum IgE values.

Etiology

Although most studies on the etiology of sinusitis have involved adults, adequate pediatric data are available. The findings in studies of adults can be applied appropriately to adolescents as well.

Examining the results of anterior nasal cultures from normal subjects and from those with respiratory illnesses is important here to clear up confusion regarding the make-up of normal flora. During early investigations of the common cold, Shibley and associates[130] noted that in a group of 13 people followed for 4 to 9 months, neither *Haemophilus influenzae* nor hemolytic streptococci were obtained from nasal culture when the subjects were well. However, when their study subjects were ill with colds, *H. influenzae* was recovered from 9 percent of the cultures and hemolytic streptococci from 6 percent. In a study of 500 consecutive medical patients, Jacobson and Dick[71] noted in all but two instances that the recovery of pneumococci and hemolytic streptococci from the nose correlated with nasal or sinus disease. Studies in children have disclosed more varied results. Dunlap and Harvey[39, 61] were able to recover *H. influenzae*, pneumococci, and hemolytic streptococci from the noses of normal children with some consistency. However, they were interested in carriage and spread of organisms, and, therefore, the state of well-being of their subjects was not delineated clearly.

Orobello and colleagues[103] found that cultures of ipsilateral middle meatus correlated well with maxillary (83%) and ethmoid (80%) sinus cultures. However, nasopharyngeal cultures correlated less well, with only 45 and 40 percent of maxillary and ethmoid sinus cultures, respectively, being similar.

Yang[168] studied children in a day nursery and noted that neither pneumococci nor *H. influenzae* could be recovered from the noses of well children. Hays and Mullard[64] only rarely could find *Streptococcus pneumoniae*, beta-hemolytic streptococci, or *H. influenzae* in nose cultures from normal children. In an extensive study, Box and associates[13] noted pneumococci in nasal specimens of 38 percent of children without respiratory illness, but in only 3 percent was the growth of great magnitude (more than 100 colonies per plate). In the same study, *Haemophilus* spp. and beta-hemolytic streptococci were recovered from 14 and 1 percent, respectively, of the cultured specimens from noses. In comparison,

TABLE 17–1 ■ ETIOLOGIC AGENTS IN SINUSITIS ANALYZED BY PATIENT AGE AND TYPE OF ILLNESS

	Frequency				Age Group (years)		
	Overall	Acute	Subacute	Chronic	≤5	6–12	>12
Aerobic Bacteria							
Haemophilus influenzae	++++	++++	++++	++++	++++	++++	++++
Streptococcus pneumoniae	++++	++++	++++	++++	++++	++++	++++
Moraxella catarrhalis	+++	+++	++	+	+++	+	++
Staphylococcus aureus	++	+	+	++	++	++	++
Streptococcus pyogenes	++	++	++	++	+	++	++
Alpha- and nonhemolytic streptococci	+		+	+			++
Staphylococcus epidermidis	+		+	+		+	++
Alcaligenes species	+			+			++
Escherichia coli	+			+			++
Klebsiella pneumoniae	+			+			++
Pseudomonas aeruginosa	+			+			++
Other*	+			+			++
Anaerobic Bacteria							
Peptococcus species	++	+	+	++		+	++
Peptostreptococcus species	++	+	+	++			++
Bacteroides species	++	+	+	++			++
Veillonella	++	+	+	++			++
Other†	+		+	+			+
Mycoplasma							
Mycoplasma pneumoniae	+	+					+
Other							
L-forms	+			+			+
Mixed: aerobes and anaerobes	++	+	+	++			++
Mixed *Haemophilus influenzae* with other organisms	++	+	+	++		+	++
Other‡	+	+		+		+	+

*Serratia, diphtheroids, *Enterococcus* species, *Neisseria* species, *Haemophilus* species, *Proteus* species, *Acinetobacter, Citrobacter* species, *Eikenella corrodens.*

†*Fusobacterium* species, *Bifidobacterium, Propionibacterium.*

‡Rhinovirus, adenovirus, *Aspergillus* species, other fungi.

Data from references 7, 12, 16, 18, 24, 38, 43, 44, 51, 74, 75, 80, 89, 104, 115, 116, 135, 136, 140, 145, 146, 153, 154, 157–159.

in the same study, pneumococci and *Haemophilus* spp. were recovered from 57 and 25 percent, respectively, of the cultures of patients with respiratory illness.

In a study performed in the Finnish military, nasal cultures from 183 healthy recruits revealed the following frequencies of specific organisms: *H. influenzae,* 4 percent; *S. pneumoniae,* 1 percent; *Moraxella catarrhalis,* 3 percent; and *Streptococcus pyogenes,* 0 percent.[75] In contrast, in 185 recruits with acute maxillary sinusitis, the percentages of nasal isolates for the same organisms were 61, 25, 7, and 6 percent, respectively. In 91 percent of cases in which a sinus aspirate culture yielded an isolate, the same organism was found in a nasal sample. Similar results have been obtained in other studies performed in adults with acute sinusitis, in which nontypable *H. influenzae* and *S. pneumoniae* account for approximately 74 percent of all bacterial strains recovered in sinus aspirates.[59] In all studies, *Staphylococcus aureus* clearly is part of the normal nasal flora. It is present in well or sick children approximately 50 percent of the time.

To summarize, pneumococci, *H. influenzae, M. catarrhalis,* or *S. pyogenes* seldom is found in the nose of a normal child and should suggest a nasal or paranasal infectious illness. However, the recovery of *S. aureus* cannot be correlated with disease.

A review of many reports of children indicates that *S. pneumoniae, H. influenzae,* and *M. catarrhalis* are the etiologic agents that occur most commonly in acute and subacute ethmoid and maxillary sinusitis.* In one of the studies[158] of sinus aspirates from 50 children, *S. aureus* was not isolated from the maxillary sinus. Several studies of pediatric patients with chronic sinusitis suggest an increased importance of anaerobes and staphylococcal species.[17, 18, 34, 148] In other studies in children with chronic sinusitis who have undergone surgery, a predominance of coagulase-negative staphylococci, viridans streptococci, and *S. aureus* was noted.[98, 103] Several studies[48, 62, 163] documenting that *S. pneumoniae, H. influenzae,* and *M. catarrhalis* were the most common etiologic agents were concerned primarily with orbital involvement; between 50 and 85 percent of cases of orbital cellulitis had radiographic evidence of sinusitis. Orbital complications of ethmoiditis primarily affect children. *Staphylococcus* spp., *S. pneumoniae,* and other streptococci have been found in children with orbital involvement from ethmoiditis[3] or frontal sinusitis.[47]

In Table 17–1, etiologic agents of sinusitis are listed by age of patient and type of illness. Clearly, in all age groups and in acute, subacute, and chronic disease, *H. influenzae* and *S. pneumoniae* are the principal pathogens in the vast majority of cases. Also clear is that a large number of different bacterial species have been recovered from the sinuses of affected patients. In young children, more than 90 percent of all cases of sinusitis are caused by five organisms: *H. influenzae, S. pneumoniae, M. catarrhalis, S. aureus,* and *S. pyogenes*. In the adolescent, the same organisms, plus largely penicillin-sensitive anaerobes, account for most cases. As noted in Table 17–1, a vast array of gram-negative enteric and other bacilli have been recovered from patients with sinusitis, in most instances from those who have had various forms of antibiotic therapy before culture. Also

*See references 48, 62, 64, 67, 68, 89, 95, 146, 153, 154, 157, 158, 163.

important is to note that organisms previously considered to be nonpathogens, such as *Staphylococcus epidermidis*, have been implicated etiologically.

Although clinically recognized sinusitis has occurred rarely in patients with *Mycoplasma pneumoniae* infection, Griffin and Klein[52] noted radiographic evidence of sinusitis in approximately two thirds of a group of Navy recruits with *M. pneumoniae* pneumonia. In adults with chronic suppurative maxillary sinusitis, mycoplasmas have been sought but not recovered.[12, 51, 137] Bhattacharyya and colleagues[12] noted L-forms in 21 percent of all sinuses in patients with chronic disease.

Fungal diseases of the sinuses have been well described in adults.[161] Acute fulminate fungal sinusitis is seen in immunosuppressed individuals and is associated with high morbidity and mortality rates.[28, 134] *Aspergillus* spp. are the most common fungal causes of sinusitis. Many cases of chronic sinusitis from which a microorganism is not recovered have been thought to be caused by *Aspergillus* spp. infections.[76] The presence of eosinophils, Charcot-Leyden crystals, and hyphae found retrospectively, and not noted on the original examination, in mucus recovered from sinuses suggests that some cases of chronic sinusitis may represent *Aspergillus* hypersensitivity. This allergic aspergillosis in the sinuses is similar to allergic bronchopulmonary aspergillosis. In a series of six patients who were 8 to 16 years of age and had allergic aspergillosis sinusitis, all presented with nasal polyposis and facial deformity, indicating advanced disease.[91] Mucormycosis, an infection caused by Zygomycetes (formerly Phycomycetes), is seen in immunocompromised children and adults.[85] *Drechslera* spp., *Bipolaris* spp., and *Curvalaria lunata* have been added to the list of fungi that can cause sinusitis in children.[11, 44, 133]

Although sinusitis has been reported as a complication of Epstein-Barr virus infection, the sinus infections appear to be a complication of steroid treatment and not specifically the viral infection.[49] *Nocardia* spp. have been reported as a cause of acute sinusitis in an adult transplant recipient[119] and of chronic sinusitis in both immunocompetent and immunocompromised individuals.[144]

Epidemiology

Although sinus involvement occurs commonly with respiratory viral infection, sinusitis seldom is identified as a specific illness in previously healthy children. In a survey of all office visits, totaling 2613, Breese and colleagues[15] noted only six children (0.23%) in whom the initial diagnosis was sinusitis. The true incidence of sinusitis in childhood is unknown. In 1989, Wald and colleagues[153] estimated that between 0.5 and 5 percent of upper respiratory tract infections are complicated by acute sinusitis. More recent estimates by the same authors have been as high as 10 percent.[151] The most recent estimates of greater incidence could be related to a heightened awareness and concern for lost work days by working parents, a possible correlation between pulmonary problems in an increasing number of children with chronic lung disease, better imaging techniques, increased interest in endoscopic sinus surgery,[139] more disease because of more exposure due to more children in daycare,[90] and an increased recognition or perhaps incidence of allergy-related illness.[117, 118] Seasonal prevalence has not been studied, but a reasonable assumption is that disease would increase during the cold-weather months because it is the time of greatest respiratory viral activity. Cases in older children also can be expected to occur more frequently in association with swimming.

Although it is not well documented, sinusitis appears to be more of a problem in geographic areas where marked temperature changes occur. In children, sinusitis appears to occur more commonly in boys than in girls.[63, 95] Ueda and Yoto[142] found abnormal findings in the maxillary sinuses in 135 (6.7%) of 2013 children who presented to an outpatient department with upper respiratory symptoms; of this group, 65 percent were boys and 35 percent were girls. Manning and associates[92] found similar distribution in a group of 60 children diagnosed by CT or magnetic resonance imaging (MRI) scans. Host factors are important in sinusitis because the illness occurs more commonly in allergic children; in children with chronic ear infections; and in patients with cystic fibrosis, primary humoral immunodeficiencies, and Kartagener syndrome.[19, 68, 101, 123] Although an association between sinus disease and asthma appears to exist, controversy continues regarding whether sinusitis and other upper airway stimuli can induce asthma.[45, 118, 127, 169] However, a review of hospital admissions of patients with status asthmaticus at the Children's Hospital of Los Angeles showed a marked increase in admissions, and sinusitis was diagnosed in 23 percent.[117] Children with various immunologic defects frequently have sinusitis.

Sinusitis is noncontagious from person to person, but point-source outbreaks are possible from swimming in heavily contaminated water. A cluster of seven cases of invasive nosocomial fungal sinusitis in severely neutropenic patients has been described. It was caused by the release of airborne fungal spores from soil reservoirs that were distributed during hospital construction during a 2-year period.[86]

Clinical Presentation

The clinical symptoms of sinusitis vary by age. Older children and adolescents have localized complaints similar to those of adults, whereas in young children, the findings are related less clearly to the sinuses.[150] Table 17–2 presents the overall frequencies of symptoms, signs, and laboratory findings for acute, subacute, and chronic disease.

In young children, disease involves only the ethmoid and maxillary sinuses. In these children, illness frequently has its onset after an upper respiratory viral infection. However, a period of general improvement may occur between the acute respiratory illness and the onset of symptoms related to sinus infection. The most prominent symptom in all children, and particularly in those younger than 10 years of age, is persistent rhinorrhea. The discharge frequently is purulent, but it can be serous or even watery on occasion. Associated with rhinorrhea is cough, which becomes more prominent with increasing duration of disease. The cough particularly is troublesome at night because it is caused by the stimulation of the sinus drainage as it traverses the pharyngeal wall. The posterior drainage also occasionally causes vomiting. Fever is of variable occurrence in sinusitis and, in a general way, is related inversely to both age and duration of illness. Malodorous breath often is reported by parents. The first evidence of illness in some children is fever and periorbital swelling. In most instances, periorbital cellulitis is a manifestation of ethmoid sinusitis.

Although facial pain and headache are frequent complaints of sinus disease in adults, they have been noted only in approximately one third of the cases in children and are unusual occurrences in the young child. The main symptom in the older child and adolescent is rhinorrhea. However, in the older patient with more chronic disease, the nasal symptoms may be minimal or absent. Troublesome postnasal drip is a frequent complaint.

TABLE 17–2 ■ CLINICAL FINDINGS IN ACUTE, SUBACUTE, AND CHRONIC SINUSITIS OF CHILDREN

	Occurrence (%)	
	Acute and Subacute Sinusitis	Chronic Sinusitis
Symptoms		
Fever	50	20
Rhinorrhea	80	80
Cough (persistent and evening)	50	90
Pain/headache	30	30
Sore throat	20	20
Periorbital swelling	30	0
Vomiting	20	10
Allergic history	20	40
Malodorous breath	20	20
Signs		
Rhinorrhea	80	80
Temperature ≥38.3° C (≥101° F)	20	0
Sinus tenderness	20	10
Otlis media	40	60
Posterior pharyngeal pus	0	10
Transillumination positive	30	10
Periorbital swelling	30	0
Malodorous breath	20	20
Laboratory		
Abnormal radiographs	100	100
Maxillary	90	90
Ethmoid	40	40
Frontal and sphenoid	10	10
Unilateral	70	10
Bilateral	30	90
Erythrocyte sedimentation rate elevation	50	10
White blood cell count elevation with an increased percentage of band form neutrophlls	40	10

Data from references 2, 9, 63, 66, 72, 77, 78, 95, 101, 115, 118, 123, 135, 154.

Physical signs in sinusitis also differ by age. Nasal discharge is the most frequent finding in all age groups. However, young children are more likely to have a serous or watery discharge than are adolescents. Temperature elevation occurs more commonly in acute disease and in association with orbital cellulitis. Sinus tenderness, a common finding in older patients, is noted only rarely in children. Particularly significant is tenderness with percussion of the upper molars. Examination of the throat frequently reveals free exudate. Occasionally, the breath is malodorous.

The ears are abnormal in almost one half of all patients with sinusitis. In acute disease in young children, this can be acute otitis media, but usually the findings are more suggestive of serous disease. Acute sinusitis frequently is unilateral, whereas chronic disease more often is bilateral.

Children with chronic sinusitis frequently have only minimal complaints. The parent will note that the child does not feel well and frequently will report that the child has had a persistent respiratory infection for months. In a series of children with chronic (longer than 3 months) upper respiratory complaints who were referred to allergy clinics, 60 percent had sinusitis.[101] In this study, the combination of moderate to severe rhinorrhea and cough with minimal sneezing was reported to have a specificity of 95 percent and a sensitivity of 38 percent in predicting the presence of chronic sinusitis. In the referred children in this study, sinusitis was found in 63 percent of atopic children and in 75 percent of nonatopic children.

Laboratory studies other than cultures and radiography are not very useful in the evaluation of the child with sinusitis. Herz and Gfeller[66] noted that in their study, erythrocyte sedimentation rates were elevated in only approximately one half of the patients, and leukocytosis occurred in only one third. In general, younger children with orbital cellulitis and ethmoid sinusitis are more likely to have both elevated sedimentation rates and white blood cell counts. The American Academy of Pediatrics (AAP) Subcommittee of Sinusitis and Committee on Quality Improvement recently recommended that the diagnosis of acute bacterial sinusitis be based on clinical criteria in children who present with upper respiratory symptoms that are either persistent (nasal or postnasal discharge of any quality with or without daytime cough for longer than 10 to 14 days) or severe (temperature higher than 39° C and purulent nasal discharge present concurrently for at least 3 or 4 consecutive days in a child who appears ill).[3]

Differential Diagnosis

Differential considerations in sinusitis are not many and are more concerned with whether sinus involvement in a particular child is the primary event or a secondary problem related to a more general host defect. Children with recurrent and chronic sinusitis should be evaluated for respiratory allergy, cystic fibrosis, immunologic deficiency, and Kartagener and other immotile-cilia syndromes.

Foreign bodies in the nose can be mistaken for sinusitis, as can cysts in the maxillary antra. Nasal structural defects (congenital and acquired), such as palatal clefts, unilateral choanal atresia, nasal polyps, and septal deviation, can be confused with sinusitis, but more commonly these problems are predisposing factors in sinus infections.

Dental infections frequently are mistaken for maxillary sinus disease. However, dental infections can lead by direct extension to sinus involvement. Primary infections in the region of the eye also occur without sinus disease. In young children, a chronic infection of the adenoids can be confused clinically with sinusitis. Infections with *Bordetella pertussis* can be confused with subacute sinusitis.

Specific Diagnosis

Although persistent nasal symptoms and the presence of other clinical findings as listed in Table 17–2 indicate a diagnosis of sinusitis, the only certain way to make the diagnosis is by obtaining roentgenograms and cultures reflecting sinus flora. Although some physicians have suggested that maxillary sinus roentgenograms frequently are abnormal for normal children,[93, 131] other data indicate that abnormal roentgenograms are infrequent for normal children older than 1 year of age.[79] During infancy, the maxillary sinuses are so small that minimal mucosal edema may "opacify" a sinus on a radiograph. In young children, roentgenographic examination should consist of two views: lateral and Waters. In older children, Caldwell and basal projections also should be performed. One should point out that roentgenograms in acute upper respiratory viral infections as a rule will be abnormal; these roentgenograms are not false-positive ones but are the result of viral infections. However, from a therapeutic point of view, sinus roentgenograms usually should not be obtained unless nasal symptoms in an upper respiratory illness have not shown signs of improvement after 5 to 7 days.

Plain-film radiographic examination has been supplanted mainly by CT and MRI for the diagnosis of sinusitis. Many endoscopic sinus surgeons consider CT to be a mandatory part of the preoperative evaluation. MRI is useful in cases that may be complicated by orbital or intracranial extension. The high prevalence of incidental sinus opacification in asymptomatic infants and children noted radiographically has been confirmed by CT studies.[30, 50] Since the advent of MRI, researchers have realized that a significant number of incidental sinus abnormalities also occur in adults. These findings in both children and adults may be from subclinical or resolving respiratory infections or due to unrecognized allergies.[29]

CT has been recognized widely as the standard for the diagnosis of paranasal sinus disease. In particular, coronal thin-section images offer excellent delineation of lesions in the osteomeatal complex.[170] Obtaining axial images is useful for evaluating periorbital and intraorbital complications.[42] In some institutions, a so-called screening CT of the sinuses is performed with a limited number of slices.[55] It can be offered at a cost and radiation exposure that are similar to those associated with plain-film studies but with much greater accuracy. Unfortunately, all young children and infants require sedation for CT, which limits its suitability.

The AAP Subcommittee of Sinusitis and Committee on Quality Improvement recently recommended that imaging studies are not necessary to confirm a diagnosis of clinical sinusitis in children 6 years of age or younger.[3] The need for radiographic evidence as a confirmatory test in children older than 6 years of age with severe symptoms remains controversial. The American College of Radiology considers that the diagnosis of acute uncomplicated sinusitis should be made only on clinical grounds.[94] CT scans of the sinuses should be reserved for those patients in whom surgery is being considered as a management strategy.[3] In a recent meta-analysis of acute uncomplicated sinusitis in children,[70] poor concordance was observed among clinical criteria, plain radiographs, CT scans, ultrasonography, and fluid aspiration. Therefore, more studies will be necessary to determine the optimal set of clinical criteria and other laboratory or radiologic studies for diagnosis of this condition.

Which radiographic technique (plain radiography, CT, or MRI) is selected for evaluation of the child with presumed sinusitis should be determined by availability of techniques and the expertise of the radiologist as well as by clinical symptoms. Roentgenograms, in most instances, should not be obtained early in the illness of children with uncomplicated upper respiratory complaints because of the high incidence of transient abnormalities.[4] Radiography is indicated for children with continuing symptoms of sinusitis after extensive medical therapy or for children with possible complications of sinusitis. CT is optimal.[4] A limited CT scan with axial cuts may be obtained. It will allow for excellent visualization of sinus anatomy and pathology while limiting the radiation exposure to the child. A limited sinus CT scan has radiation similar to that of a sinus plain-film series. In the absence of low-cost screening CT, plain radiography should be the initial imaging study in most children who have symptoms of sinus disease.[29] Children who have periorbital swelling or proptosis should undergo immediate contrast-enhanced CT studies in both axial and coronal planes. If symptoms or CT findings suggest intracranial extension, MRI should be performed.[4, 29]

Although ultrasonography would appear to offer an alternative to sinus roentgenography, some question remains about its dependability unless one normal air-filled maxillary sinus or one opacified maxillary sinus is present for comparison.[154, 159] The hallmark of specific diagnosis in sinusitis is similar to that of other infectious diseases: the culture of infected material. Many physicians erroneously considered it an impossible task because of the inability of obtaining material directly from the sinuses of children. However, as discussed in the section on etiology, nasal cultures that are properly performed will reveal the causative organism in most instances. Nasal culture should be taken from the region of the maxillary ostium in the middle meatus. An important point is that cultures should be obtained from this area and not from the nasopharynx. Wald and associates[159] found no correlation between bacteria isolated directly from the maxillary sinuses and nasopharyngeal and throat culture isolates. Best results are obtained when a vasoconstrictor, such as 0.25 percent phenylephrine hydrochloride, is administered first and the culture is obtained with a wire-cotton swab under direct vision. With this technique, material frequently can be obtained as it comes from the sinus ostium. Bilateral cultures always should be obtained. In serious cases, such as in children with neurologic complications, or in treatment failures, performing antral puncture for culture can be lifesaving. Anaerobic and aerobic cultures should be performed on any material recovered by antral puncture.

Treatment

ACUTE AND SUBACUTE SINUSITIS

The successful treatment of acute and subacute sinusitis in children primarily depends on the administration of an appropriate antibiotic, in adequate dosage, for a sufficient period. In most instances, therapy should be instituted before obtaining the results of cultures. Antibiotic selection in this situation is not a great problem in children because the etiologic agent is *H. influenzae*, *S. pneumoniae*, *M. catarrhalis*, *S. aureus*, or *S. pyogenes* in more than 90 percent of acute cases.

Initial selection of an antibiotic should be based on the severity of the clinical illness and must take into consideration the antibiotic resistance patterns of the common causative organisms as well as the cost and ease of administration of the treatment regimen. Today, approximately 50 percent of nontypable *H. influenzae* and 100 percent of *M. catarrhalis* strains produce β-lactamases and are resistant to amoxicillin.[32, 33] In addition, between 15 and 38 percent of *S. pneumoniae* strains have either intermediate (7%–19%) or complete (7%–19%) penicillin resistance.[10, 22, 35]

The AAP Subcommittee of Sinusitis and Committee on Quality Improvement, in their Clinical Practice Guideline: Management of Sinusitis, recommended amoxicillin as first-line therapy for children younger than 2 years of age suspected of having acute bacterial sinusitis of mild to moderate severity and who do not attend daycare and who have not recently been treated with an antimicrobial agent. They recommend an amoxicillin dose of either 45 mg/kg/day in two divided doses or 90 mg/kg/day in two divided doses. They recommend cefdinir (14 mg/kg/day in one or two doses), cefuroxime (30 mg/kg/day in two divided doses), or cefpodoxime (10 mg/kg/day once daily) for the child who is "allergic" to amoxicillin if the past allergic reaction was not a type 1 hypersensitivity reaction. If the past allergic reaction was of a type 1 nature, they recommend clarithromycin (15 mg/kg/day in two divided doses) or azithromycin (10 mg/kg/day on day 1 followed by 5 mg/kg/day as a single dose for 4 days). Furthermore, they suggest clindamycin (30 to 40 mg/kg/day in three divided doses) as an alternative therapy for the penicillin-allergic patient who is known to be infected with a penicillin-resistant pneumococcal strain. Their recommendation is based on the safety, tolerability, low cost, and narrow spectrum of amoxicillin and a calculated success rate based on data regarding treatment of acute otitis media.

The committees further recommended that children who did not improve while receiving the lower amoxicillin dose, those with more severe illness, and those who attend daycare should be treated with high-dose amoxicillin-clavulanate (80 to 90 mg/kg/day of amoxicillin component in two divided doses). For children with vomiting, a single dose of ceftriaxone (50 mg/kg/day) given either intravenously or intramuscularly is suggested. After this regimen, the child's therapy is switched to an oral regimen.

The committees' suggestions presented above applied only to children younger than 2 years of age; however, because the spectrum of etiologic agents is similar to that for older children, it should also apply for those older than 2 years of age.

In contrast to the committees' recommendations presented above, we consider that a more appropriate approach is to use only high-dose amoxicillin or amoxicillin-clavulanate (90 mg/kg/day in two divided doses). The duration of treatment in the outpatient setting has not been studied adequately. Wald[147] suggests that therapy should be continued for 7 days after the child becomes free of symptoms.

The seriously ill child should be hospitalized, and therapy for β-lactamase–producing staphylococci and highly resistant pneumococci should be implemented, in addition to coverage for amoxicillin-resistant *H. influenzae* and *M. catarrhalis*. This coverage is achieved best with nafcillin (150 to 200 mg/kg per 24 hours every 6 hours) or vancomycin (40 mg/kg per 24 hours every 6 hours) and cefotaxime (100 to 200 mg/kg per 24 hours every 6 hours) or ceftriaxone (100 mg/kg per 24 hours every 12 hours). Therapy should be adjusted on the basis of clinical response and culture results. The dosage and duration of antimicrobial therapy in sinusitis are critical. Penicillins penetrate the sinuses relatively poorly.[8, 41, 56, 73, 87] The duration of therapy should be a minimum of 10 days.

The relief of obstruction at the sinus ostia and the establishment of drainage are time-honored principles of therapy. To achieve these goals, locally applied and systemically active vasoconstrictive drugs are used. However, to date, no evidence supports their therapeutic effectiveness. The beneficial effects of oral, systemically active, vasoconstrictive drugs are hampered by the fact that their drying effect may be deleterious to the mucus blanket. Topical vasoconstrictor drugs (e.g., phenylephrine hydrochloride and oxymetazoline) are plagued by rebound vasodilation. We consider that these drugs should be used rarely in acute disease; their main use is to relieve pain caused by obstruction, and they should be used only for 2 to 3 days.

CHRONIC AND RECURRENT SINUSITIS

Allergic disorders are common occurrences in chronic and recurrent sinusitis.[90, 149] Children should be evaluated for allergy, and when identified, specific treatment should be employed. Specific allergens and irritants should be avoided (e.g., through air filtering, removal of pets, avoidance of tobacco smoke), and pharmacologic management should be implemented.

Nasal saline washes (twice daily in each nostril) are useful because they liquefy secretions and enhance mucociliary transport, which improves sinus drainage and ventilation. Antihistamines may be useful if allergic rhinitis is a contributing factor to the chronic sinus infection. Anti-inflammatory agents also may be useful. In selected cases, use of either topically applied corticosteroids or cromolyn sodium may be beneficial. Corticosteroids should be used carefully because their use on occasion can lead to superinfection in the sinuses with *Pseudomonas* spp., other highly resistant gram-negative bacilli, or fungi. For effective corticosteroid use, Wald[149] suggests using a topical decongestant first so that the steroid preparation can reach the affected areas better.

In chronic or recurrent disease, antimicrobial treatment should be based on culture and sensitivity data. Specific antimicrobial agents are the same as those employed in acute and subacute disease, but treatment should be prolonged for 3 weeks or more and for 7 days after the resolution of symptoms. *Aspergillus* and *Bipolaris* spp. and other fungal infections require prolonged therapy with an antifungal agent to which the specific agent is susceptible. Itraconazole, ketoconazole, and fluconazole all have been effective in selected cases. Allergic fungal sinusitis can be treated with endoscopic sinus débridement of all fungal and polypoid disease, followed by topical and systemic corticosteroids and close follow-up including frequent endoscopic cleaning.[26, 81, 82, 112] Allergic aspergillosis of the sinuses can be managed with topical steroids without specific antifungal therapy (see Chapter 28).

In the past, surgical therapy for sinusitis in children was of questionable benefit. Surgical therapy included diagnostic and therapeutic irrigation; permanent drainage procedures in children with complications of sinusitis and in those who had immune defects; and such procedures as adenoidectomy,[84] septoplasty, and turbinectomy to relieve anatomic obstructions in order to improve nasal and sinus ventilation. In one uncontrolled study of children with otitis media with effusion and sinusitis, the sinusitis was improved 6 months after adenoidectomy in 56 percent of children, whereas only 24 percent of similar children who did not undergo surgery had similar improvement.[138]

Historically, creating nasoantral windows was the most common major surgical procedure for treating chronic sinusitis in children.[53, 99] However, long-term success with this procedure was poor because of the high rate of closure of the windows. A new interest in sinus surgery has resulted from the introduction of endoscopic techniques. Several studies have found endoscopic surgery to be safe and effective.[54, 83, 88, 108, 120] Pediatric endoscopic sinus surgery now is recognized as a viable option for children with chronic recurrent sinusitis refractory to medical therapy.[23] A meta-analysis of 832 children who underwent endoscopic sinus surgery from 1986 to 1996 revealed an overall 88.4 percent positive outcome after surgery.[65]

The goal of functional endoscopic sinus surgery is to remove obstruction at the osteomeatal complex where the mucociliary flow from the frontal, maxillary, and ethmoid sinuses converges.[83, 120] This removal results in improved drainage and restoration of normal physiologic function of the frontal, maxillary, and ethmoid sinuses. Surgery involves an anterior ethmoidectomy and enlargement of the natural ostium of the maxillary sinus. Follow-up surgery performed 2 to 3 weeks after the initial surgery sometimes is necessary to remove crusts, blood clots, any stenting material, granulative tissue, and adhesions.[160]

In a study of 210 children with a history of chronic sinusitis for 3 months or longer, functional endoscopic sinus surgery resulted in successful outcomes in 165 (79%).[83] The follow-up period was from 3 to 36 months (mean, 18 months), and all of the infections in these children had failed to respond to prior extensive medical management. In this series, no major complications occurred.

Functional endoscopic sinus surgery should be considered for children with chronic or recurrent sinusitis that has failed extensive, prolonged, and adequate medical management. This management includes specific antimicrobial therapy for specific organisms identified by culture; the diagnosis and treatment of allergic and other contributing conditions, such as cystic fibrosis, asthma, or immunologic disorders; and a trial of prophylactic antimicrobial agents.

Orbital and intracranial abscesses and cavernous sinus thrombosis secondary to sinus infection require emergency surgery, which often is lifesaving.[121, 125, 162, 164] Cellulitis, osteomyelitis, and meningitis also frequently require surgery if they do not respond to antimicrobial therapy.[121] Surgery in these cases involves drainage of the sinuses and abscesses. Endoscopic techniques may allow for intranasal drainage and avoidance of development of facial scars.[5] Surgical procedures also may be indicated for the child with acute or chronic disease resulting from an identified underlying problem, such as an immunologic deficiency.[165]

Prognosis

The prognosis of identified and adequately treated sinusitis in otherwise normal children is excellent. However, all too frequently, children suffer with subnormal health because sinusitis goes unrecognized; it may be treated only partially because of other clinical impressions, which contributes to the chronicity of the problem. Sinusitis is likely to be recurrent in children with a history of previous chronic disease and in children with repeated adverse exposure, such as swimming in contaminated or irritating water. Children with allergic respiratory disease also are likely to have frequent recurrences. Sinusitis in the immunocompromised child frequently is resistant to cure; long-term continuous therapy can be of benefit in such patients, however.

Serious complications occur in untreated sinusitis. They include meningitis; osteomyelitis; cavernous sinus thrombosis; and epidural, subdural, brain, and orbital abscesses.[125, 162, 164] Signs and symptoms of neurologic involvement in sinusitis frequently call for aggressive surgical management of the sinusitis as well as the intracranial and paracranial lesions.

Paranasal sinusitis also has been noted on occasion to be associated with bronchial asthma.[106, 114] Its successful treatment has resulted in clearing of the asthma.[69, 127]

Prevention

Sinusitis, as such, is not preventable in most instances. However, in some individuals, change of lifestyle can do much to improve the situation. For example, sinusitis in some children clearly is related to their swimming habits and, therefore, can be controlled by elimination of swimming or perhaps by the use of nose plugs. Good allergic management, including intranasal corticosteroid or cromolyn therapy, will prevent sinus disease in certain atopic children. Relief of nasal airway obstruction caused by allergic rhinitis, enlarged adenoids, or other anatomic problems also should help to prevent sinusitis. Early attention to persistent nasal discharge also can be expected to lessen the damage associated with sinus infection.

REFERENCES

1. Aitken, M., and Taylor, J. A.: Prevalence of clinical sinusitis in young children followed by primary care pediatricians. Arch. Pediatr. Adolesc. Med. *152*:244–248, 1998.
2. Alfaro, V. R.: Nasal sinus disease in children. Pediatr. Clin. North Am. *9*:1061–1072, 1962.
3. American Academy of Pediatrics. Subcommittee on Management of Sinusitis and Committee on Quality Improvement: Clinical practice guideline: Management of sinusitis. Pediatrics *108*:798–808, 2001.
4. April, M. M., Zinreich, J., Baroody, F. M., et al.: Coronal CT scan abnormalities in children with chronic sinusitis. Laryngoscope *103*:985–990, 1993.
5. Arjmand, E. M., Lusk, R. P., and Muntz, H. R.: Pediatric sinusitis and subperiosteal orbital abscess formation: Diagnosis and treatment. Otolaryngol. Head Neck Surg. *109*:886–894, 1993.
6. Arruda, E., Boyle, T. R., Winther, B., et al.: Localization of human rhinovirus replication in the upper respiratory tract by in situ hybridization. J. Infect. Dis. *171*:1329–1333, 1995.
7. Axelsson, A., and Brorson, J. E.: The correlation between bacteriological findings in the nose and maxillary sinus in acute maxillary sinusitis. Laryngoscope *88*:2003–2011, 1973.
8. Axelsson, A., Grebelius, N., Jensen, C., et al.: Treatment of acute maxillary sinusitis. IV. Ampicillin, cephradine and erythromycin estolate with and without irrigation. Acta Otol. *79*:466–472, 1975.
9. Axelsson, A., and Runze, U.: Symptoms and signs of acute maxillary sinusitis. Otol. Rhinol. Laryngol. *38*:298–308, 1976.
10. Baquero, F., and Loza, E.: Antibiotic resistance of microorganisms involved in ear, nose and throat infections. Pediatr. Infect. Dis. J. *13*:S9–S14, 1994.
11. Berry, A. J., Kerkering, T. M., Giordano, A. M., et al.: Phaeohyphomycotic sinusitis. Pediatr. Infect. Dis. *3*:150–152, 1984.
12. Bhattacharyya, T. K., Mehra, Y. N., and Agarwal, S. C.: Incidence of bacterial, L-form and mycoplasma in chronic sinusitis. Acta Otol. *74*:293–296, 1972.
13. Box, Q. T., Cleveland, R. T., and Willard, C. Y.: Bacterial flora of the upper respiratory tract. I. Comparative evaluation by anterior nasal, oropharyngeal, and nasopharyngeal swabs. Am. J. Dis. Child. *102*:293–301, 1961.
14. Brandtzaeg, P.: Mucosal immunology: With special reference to specific immune defense of the upper respiratory tract. Otorhinolaryngology *50*:225–235, 1988.
15. Breese, B. B., Disney, F. A., and Talpey, W.: The nature of a small pediatric group practice: Part I. Pediatrics *38*:264–277, 1966.
16. Brook, I.: Beta-lactamase-producing bacteria in head and neck infection. Laryngoscope *98*:428–431, 1988.
17. Brook, I., Yocum, P., Shah, K.: Aerobic and anaerobic bacteriology of concurrent chronic otitis media with effusion and chronic sinusitis in children. Arch. Otolarynol. Head Neck Surg. *126*:174–176, 2000.
18. Brook, I.: Bacteriologic features of chronic sinusitis in children. J. A. M. A. *246*:967–969, 1981.
19. Buering, I., Friedrich, B., Schaaf, J., et al.: Chronic sinusitis refractory to standard management in patients with humoral deficiencies. Clin. Exp. Immunol. *109*:468–472, 1997.
20. Carenfelt, C., Lundberg, C., and Karlen, K.: Immunoglobulins in maxillary sinus secretion. Acta Otol. *82*:123–130, 1976.
21. Carenfelt, C., and Lundberg, C.: Purulent and nonpurulent maxillary sinus secretions with respect to pO_2, pCO_2, and pH. Acta Otol. *84*:138–144, 1977.
22. Centers for Disease Control and Prevention. Geographic variation in penicillin resistance in *Streptococcus pneumoniae*-selected sites, United States, 1997. M. M. W. R. Morb. Mortal. Wkly Rep. *48*:656–661, 1999.
23. Chan, K. H., Winslow, C. P., Levin, M. J., et al.: Clinical practice guidelines for the management of chronic sinusitis in children. Otolaryngol. Head Neck Surg. *120*:328–334, 1999.
24. Cherry, J. D.: Infection in the compromised host. *In* Stiehm, E. R. (ed.): Immunologic Disorders in Infants and Children. 4th ed. Philadelphia, W. B. Saunders, 1996, pp. 975–1013.
25. Colman, B. H.: Sinusitis. Practitioner *215*:725–731,1975.
26. Corey, J. P., Delsupene, K. G., Ferguson, B. J.: Allergic fungal sinusitis: Allergic, infectious, or both? Otolaryngol. Head Neck Surg. *113*:110–119, 1995.
27. Dawes, J. D. K.: Diagnosis and treatment of sinusitis. Br. Med. J. *1*:843–845, 1966.
28. de Shazo, R. D., O'Brien, M., Chapin, K., et al.: A new classification and diagnostic criteria for invasive fungal sinusitis. Arch. Otolaryngol Head Neck Surg. *127*:1181–1188, 1997.
29. Diament, M. J.: The diagnosis of sinusitis in infants and children: X-ray, computed tomography, and magnetic resonance imaging: Diagnostic imaging of pediatric sinusitis. J. Allergy Clin. Immunol. *90*:442–444, 1990.
30. Diament, M. J., Senac, M. O., Jr., Gilsanz, V., et al.: Prevalence of incidental paranasal sinuses opacification in pediatric patients: A CT study. J. Comput. Assisted Tomogr. *11*:426–431, 1987.
31. Dingle, J. H., Badjer, D. F., and Jordan, W. S., Jr.: Patterns of Illness: Illness in the Home. Cleveland, Western Reserve University, 1964, p. 347.

32. Doern, G. V., Brueggemann, A. B., Pierce, G., et al.: Antibiotic resistance among clinical isolates of *Haemophilus influenzae* in the United States in 1994 and 1995 and detection of beta-lactamase-positive strains resistant to amoxicillin-clavulanate: Results of a national multicenter surveillance study. Antimicrob. Agents Chemother. *41*:292–297, 1997.
33. Doern, G. V., Jones, R. N., Pfaller, M. A., et al.: *Haemophilus influenzae* and *Moraxella catarrhalis* from patients with community-acquired respiratory tract infections: Antimicrobial susceptibility patterns from the SENTRY Antimicrobial Surveillance Program (United States and Canada, 1997). Antimicrob. Agents Chemother. *43*:385–389, 1999.
34. Don, D. M., Yellon, R. F., Casselbrant, M. L., et al.: Efficacy of a stepwise protocol that includes intravenous antibiotic therapy for the management of chronic sinusitis in children and adolescents. Arch. Otolaryngol. Head Neck Surg. *127*:1093–1098, 2001.
35. Dowell, S. F., Butler, J. C., Giebink, G. S., et al.: Acute otitis media: Management and surveillance in an era of pneumococcal resistance—a report from the Drug-resistant *Streptococcus pneumoniae* Therapeutic Working Group. Pediatr. Infect. Dis. J. *18*:1–9, 1999.
36. Dudley, J. P., and Cherry, J. D.: The effect of mucolytic agents and topical decongestants on the ciliary activity of chicken tracheal organ cultures. Pediatr. Res. *11*:904–906, 1977.
37. Dudley, J. P., and Cherry, J. D.: Effects of topical nasal decongestants on the cilia of a chicken embryo tracheal organ culture system. Laryngoscope *88*:110–116, 1978.
38. Dudley, J. P., Goldstein, E. J. C., George, W. L., et al.: Sinus infection due to *Eikenella corrodens*. Arch. Otol. *104*:462–463, 1978.
39. Dunlap, M. B., and Harvey, H. S.: Host influence on upper respiratory flora. N. Engl. J. Med. *255*:640–646, 1956.
40. Eliasson, R., Mossberg, B., Camner, P., et al.: The immotile cilia syndrome: A congenital ciliary abnormality as an etiologic factor in chronic airway infections and male sterility. N. Engl. J. Med. *297*:1–6, 1977.
41. Eneroth, C. M., Lundberg, C., and Wretlind, B.: Antibiotic concentrations in maxillary sinus secretions and in the sinus mucosa. Chemotherapy *21*(Suppl. 1):1–7, 1975.
42. Fernbach, S. K., and Naidich, T. P.: CT diagnosis of orbital inflammation in children. Neuroradiology *22*:7–13, 1981.
43. Frederick, J., and Braude, A. I.: Anaerobic infection of the paranasal sinuses. N. Engl. J. Med. *290*:135–137, 1974.
44. Frenkel, L. M., Kuhls, T. L., Nitta, K., et al.: Recurrent bipolaris sinusitis following surgical and antifungal therapy. Pediatr. Infect. Dis. *6*:1130–1132, 1987.
45. Friday, G. A., and Fireman, P.: Sinusitis and asthma: Clinical pathogenic relationships. Clin. Chest Med. *9*:557–565, 1988.
46. Friedman, R., Ackerman, M., Wald, E., et al.: Asthma and bacterial sinusitis in children. J. Allergy Clin. Immunol. *74*:185–189, 1984.
47. Garcia, C. E., Cunningham, M. J., Randall, A. C., et al.: The etiologic role of frontal sinusitis in pediatric orbital abscesses. Am. J. Otolaryngol. *14*:449–452, 1993.
48. Gellady, A. M., Shulman, S. T., and Ayoub, E. M.: Periorbital and orbital cellulitis in children. Pediatrics *61*:272–277, 1978.
49. Givner, L. B., McGehee, D., Taber, L. H., et al.: Sinusitis, orbital cellulitis and polymicrobial bacteremia in a patient with primary Epstein-Barr virus infection. Pediatr. Infect. Dis. *3*:254–156, 1984.
50. Glasier, C. M., Archer, D. P., and Williams, K. D.: Incidental paranasal sinus abnormalities on CT of children: Clinical correlation. Am. J. Neuroradiol. 7:861–864, 1986.
51. Gnarpe, H., and Lundberg, C.: L-phase organisms in maxillary sinus secretions. Scand. J. Infect. Dis. *3*:257–259, 1971.
52. Griffin, J. P., and Klein, E. W.: Role of sinusitis in primary atypical pneumonia. Clin. Med. *78*:23–27, 1971.
53. Gross, C. W.: Surgical management: An otolaryngologist's perspective. Pediatr. Infect. Dis. *4*:567, 1985.
54. Gross, C. W., Gurucharri, M. J., Lazar, R. H., et al.: Functional endonasal sinus surgery (FESS) in the pediatric age group. Laryngoscope *99*:272–275, 1989.
55. Gross, C. W., McGeady, S. J., Kerut, T., et al.: Limited-slide CT in the evaluation of paranasal sinus disease in children. Am. J. Roentgenol. *156*:367–369, 1991.
56. Gullers, K., Lundberg, C., and Malmborg, A. S.: Penicillin in paranasal sinus secretions. Chemotherapy *14*:303–307, 1969.
57. Gwaltney, M. J., Jr., Hendley, J. O., Simon, G., et al.: Rhinovirus infections in an industrial population. I. The occurrence of illness. N. Engl. J. Med. *275*:1261–1268, 1966.
58. Gwaltney, M. J., Jr., Hendley, J. O., Phillips, C. D., et al.: Nose blowing propels nasal fluid into the paranasal sinuses. Clin. Infect. Dis. *30*:387–391, 2000.
59. Hamory, B. H., Sande, M. A., Sydnor, A., Jr., et al.: Etiology and antimicrobial therapy of acute maxillary sinusitis. J. Infect. Dis. *139*:197–202, 1979.
60. Hansson, L. A., Ahlstedt, S., Andersson, B., et al.: Mucosal immunity. Ann. N. Y. Acad. Sci. *409*:1–21, 1983.
61. Harvey, H. S., and Dunlap, M. B.: Seasonal prevalence of upper respiratory pathogens. N. Engl. J. Med. *264*:684–686, 1961.
62. Hawkins, D. B., and Clark, R. W.: Orbital involvement in acute sinusitis: Lessons from 24 childhood patients. Clin. Pediatr. *16*:464–471, 1977.
63. Haynes, R. E., and Cramblett, H. G.: Acute ethmoiditis: Its relationship to orbital cellulitis. Am. J. Dis. Child. *114*:261–267, 1967.
64. Hays, G. C., and Mullard, J. E.: Can nasal bacterial flora be predicted from clinical findings? Pediatrics *49*:596–599, 1972.
65. Hebert, R. L., Bent, J. P.: Meta-analysis of pediatric functional endoscopic sinus surgery. Laryngoscope. *108*:796–799, 1998.
66. Herz, G., and Gfeller, J.: Sinusitis in paediatrics. Chemotherapy *23*:50–57, 1977.
67. Holdaway, M. D., and Turk, D. C.: Capsulated *Haemophilus influenzae* and respiratory tract disease. Lancet *1*:358–360, 1967.
68. Hoshaw, T. C., and Nickman, N. J.: Sinusitis and otitis in children. Arch. Otol. *100*:194–195, 1974.
69. Ikeda, K., Tanno, N., Tamura, G., et al.: Endoscopic sinus surgery improves pulmonary function in patients with asthma associated with chronic sinusitis. Ann. Otol. Rhinol. Laryngol. *108*:355–359, 1999.
70. Ioannidis, J. P., and Lau, J.: Technical report: Evidence for the diagnosis and treatment of acute uncomplicated sinusitis in children: a systematic overview. Pediatrics. *108*:E57, 2001.
71. Jacobson, L. O., and Dick, G. F.: Normal and abnormal bacterial flora of the nose. J. A. M. A. *117*:2222–2225, 1941.
72. Jaffe, B. F.: Chronic sinusitis in children: Comments on pathogenesis and management. Clin. Pediatr. *13*:944–948, 1974.
73. Jeppesen, F., and Illum, P.: Concentration of ampicillin in antral mucosa following administration of ampicillin sodium and privampicillin. Acta. Otol. *73*:428–432, 1972.
74. Jousimies-Somer, H. R., Savolainen, S., and Ylikoski, J. S.: Bacteriological findings of acute maxillary sinusitis in young adults. J. Clin. Microbiol. *26*:1919–1925, 1988.
75. Jousimies-Somer, H. R., Savolainen, S., and Ylikoski, J. S.: Comparison of the nasal bacterial floras in two groups of healthy subjects and in patients with acute maxillary sinusitis. J. Clin. Microbiol. *27*:2736–2743, 1989.
76. Katzenstein, A. L., Sale, S. R., and Greenberger, P. A.: Pathologic findings in allergic aspergillus sinusitis. Am. J. Surg. Pathol. *7*:439–443, 1983.
77. Kern, E. B.: Sinusitis. J. Allergy Clin. Immunol. *73*:25–31, 1984.
78. Kogutt, M. S., and Swischuk, L. E.: Diagnosis of sinusitis in infants and children. Pediatrics *52*:152–156, 1973.
79. Kovatch, A. L., Wald, E. R., Ledesma-Medina, J., et al.: Maxillary sinus radiographs in children with nonrespiratory complaints. Pediatrics *73*:306–308, 1984.
80. Krajina, Z., Koskovic, F., and Babic, I.: The bacteriology of the respiratory tract in various pathological conditions. Acta Otol. *67*:453–459, 1969.
81. Kupferberg, S. B., and Bent, J. P.: Allergic fungal sinusitis in the pediatric population. Arch. Otolaryngol. Head Neck Surg. *122*:1381–1384, 1996.
82. Kupferberg, S. B., Bent J. P., Kuhn, F. A.: Prognosis for allergic fungal sinusitis. Otolaryngol. Head Neck Surg. *117*:35–41, 1997.
83. Lazar, R. H., Ramzi, R. Y., and Gross, C. W.: Pediatric functional endonasal sinus surgery: A review of 210 cases. Head Neck *14*:92–98, 1992.
84. Lee, D., Rosenfeld, R. M.: Adenoid bacteriology and sinonasal symptoms in children. Otolaryngol. Head Neck Surg. *116*:301–307, 1997.
85. Lehrer, R. I., Howard, D. H., Sypherd, P. S., et al.: Mucormycosis. Ann. Intern. Med. *93*:93–108, 1980.
86. Lueg, E. A., Ballagh, R. H., and Forte, V.: Analysis of the recent cluster of invasive fungal sinusitis as the Toronto Hospital for Sick Children. J. Otolaryngol. *25*:366–370, 1996.
87. Lundberg, C., and Malmburg, A. S.: Studies of antibiotics in sinus secretions. Rhinology *9*:166–168, 1971.
88. Lusk, R. P., and Muntz, H. R.: Endoscopic sinus surgery in children with chronic sinusitis: A pilot study. Laryngoscope *100*:654–658, 1990.
89. Lystad, A., Berdal, P., and Lund-Iversen, L.: The bacterial flora of sinusitis with an in vitro study of the bacterial resistance to antibiotics. Acta Otol. *188*(Suppl.):390–399, 1963.
90. Manning, S. C.: Pediatric sinusitis. Otolaryngol. Clin. North Am. *26*:623–638, 1993.
91. Manning, S. C., Vuitch, F., Weinberg, A. G., et al.: Allergic aspergillosis: A newly recognized form of sinusitis in the pediatric population. Laryngoscope *99*:681–685, 1989.
92. Manning, S. C., Biavati, M. J., and Phillips, D. L.: Correlation of clinical sinusitis signs and symptoms to imaging findings in pediatric patients. Int. J. Pediatr. Otorhinolaryngol. *37*:65–74, 1996.
93. Maresh, M. M., and Washburn, A. H.: Paranasal sinuses from birth to late adolescence. II. Clinical and roentgenographic evidence of infection. Am. J. Dis. Child. *60*:841–861, 1940.
94. McAllister, W. H., Parker, B. R., Kushner, D. C., et al.: Sinusitis in the pediatric population. *In* ACR Appropriateness Criteria. Reston, VA.: American College of Radiology, 2000. *http://www.acr.org/cgi-bin/fr?tmpl:appcrit,pdf:0811-818* sinusitis-ac.pdf.
95. McLean, D. C.: Sinusitis in children: Lessons from 25 patients. Clin. Pediatr. *9*:342–345, 1970.
96. Min, Y. G., Kim, H. S., Suh, S. H., et al.: Paranasal sinusitis after long-term use of topical nasal decongestants. Acta Otolaryngol. *116*:465–471, 1996.

97. Mofenson, L. M., Korelitz, J., Pelton, S., et al.: Sinusitis in children infected with human immunodeficiency virus: Clinical characteristics, risk factors, and prophylaxis. Clin. Infect. Dis. *21*:1175–1181, 1995.
98. Muntz, H. R., and Lusk, R. P.: Bacteriology of the ethmoid bullae in children with chronic sinusitis. Arch. Otolaryngol. Head Neck Surg. *117*:179–181, 1991.
99. Muntz, H. R., and Lusk, R. P.: Nasal antral windows in children: A retrospective study. Laryngoscope *100*:643–646, 1990.
100. Naclerio, R. M., Proud, D., Lichtenstein, L. M., et al.: Kinins are generated during experimental rhinovirus colds. J. Infect. Dis. *157*:133–142, 1988.
101. Nguyen, K. L., Corbett, M. L., Garcia, D. P., et al.: Chronic sinusitis among pediatric patients with chronic respiratory complaints. J. Allergy Clin. Immunol. *92*:824–830, 1993.
102. Noah, T. L., Henderson, F. W., Wortman, I. A., et al.: Nasal cytokine production in viral acute upper respiratory infection of childhood. J. Infect. Dis. *171*:584–592, 1995.
103. Orobello, P. W., Park, R. I., Belcher, L. J., et al.: Microbiology of chronic sinusitis in children. Arch. Otolaryngol. Head Neck Surg. *117*:980–983, 1991.
104. Palva, T., Grumlaut-Onroos, J. A., and Palva, A.: Bacteriology and pathology of chronic maxillary sinusitis. Acta Orol. *54*:159–175, 1962.
105. Pedersen, M., Sakakura, Y., Winther, B., et al.: Nasal mucociliary transport, number of ciliated cells, and beating pattern in naturally acquired common colds. Eur. J. Respir. Dis. *128*(Suppl.):355–364, 1983.
106. Phipatanakul, C. S., and Slavin, R. G.: Bronchial asthma produced by paranasal sinusitis. Arch. Otol. *100*:109–112, 1974.
107. Pitkaranta, A., Starck, M., Savolainen, S., et al.: Rhinovirus RNA in the maxillary sinus epithelium of adult patients with acute sinusitis. Clin. Infect. Dis. *33*:909–911, 2001.
108. Poole, M. D.: Pediatric sinusitis is not a surgical disease. Ear Nose Throat J. *71*:622–623, 1992.
109. Proctor, D. F.: The historical background of modern otolaryngology. *In* Ravitch, M. M. (ed.): The Nose, Paranasal Sinuses and Ears in Childhood. Springfield, IL, Charles C Thomas, 1963, pp. 3–19.
110. Proud, D., Naclerio, R. M., Gwaltney, J. M., et al.: Kinins are generated in nasal secretions during natural rhinovirus colds. J. Infect. Dis. *161*:120–123, 1990.
111. Proud, D., Gwaltney, J. M., Hendley, J. O., et al.: Increased levels of interleukin-1 are detected in nasal secretions of volunteers during experimental rhinovirus colds. J. Infect. Dis. *169*:1007–1013, 1994.
112. Quraishi, H. A., Ramadan, H. H.: Endoscopic treatment of allergic fungal sinusitis. Otolaryngol. Head Neck Surg. *117*:29–34, 1997.
113. Rachelefsky, G. S., Katz, R. M., and Siegel, S. C.: Chronic sinusitis in children with respiratory allergy: The role of antimicrobials. J. Allergy Clin. Immunol. *69*:382–387, 1982.
114. Rachelefsky, G. S., Katz, R. M., and Siegel, S. C.: Chronic sinus disease with associated reactive airway disease in children. Pediatrics *73*:526–529, 1984.
115. Rachelefsky, G. S., Katz, R. M., and Siegel, S. C.: Chronic sinusitis in the allergic child. Pediatr. Clin. North Am. *35*:1091–1101, 1988.
116. Rantanen, T., and Arvilommi, H.: Double-blind trial of doxycycline in acute maxillary sinusitis: A clinical and bacteriological study. Acta Otol. *76*:58–62, 1973.
117. Richards, W.: Hospitalization of children with status asthmaticus: A review. Pediatrics *84*:111–118, 1989.
118. Richards, W., Roth, R., and Church, F.: Underdiagnosis and undertreatment of chronic sinusitis in children. Clin. Pediatr. *30*:88–92, 1991.
119. Roberts, S. A., Bartley, J., Braatvedt, G., et al.: *Nocardia asteroids* as a cause of sphenoidal sinusitis: Case report. Clin. Infect. Dis. *21*:1041–1042, 2001.
120. Rosenfeld, R. M.: Pilot study of outcomes in pediatric rhinosinusitis. Arch. Otol. Head Neck Surg. *121*:729–736, 1995.
121. Rosenfeld, R. A., and Rowley, A. H.: Infectious intracranial complications of sinusitis, other than meningitis, in children: 12-year review. Clin. Infect. Dis. *18*:750–754, 1994.
122. Rossen, R. D., Butler, W. T., Cate, T. R., et al.: Protein composition of nasal secretion during respiratory virus infection. Proc. Soc. Exp. Biol. Med. *119*:1169–1176, 1965.
123. Rulon, J. T.: Sinusitis in children. Postgrad. Med. *48*:107–112, 1970.
124. Rynnel-Dagoo, B., Forsgren, J., Freijd, A., et al.: Rationale for antibiotic therapy in pediatric ear, nose and throat infections: Immunologic issues. Pediatr. Infect. Dis. J. *13*:15–20, 1994.
125. Sable, N. S., Hengerer, A., and Powell, K. R.: Acute frontal sinusitis with intracranial complications. Pediatr. Infect. Dis. *3*:58–61, 1984.
126. Schenck, N. L., and Rauchbach, E.: Frontal sinus disease. IV. Cellular response to experimentally induced infection. Laryngoscope *86*:1726–1733, 1976.
127. Senior, B. A., Kennedy, D. W., Tanabodee, J., et al.: Long-term impact of functional endoscopic sinus surgery on asthma. Otolaryngol. Head Neck Surg. *121*:66–68, 1999.
128. Shapiro, G. G.: The role of nasal airway obstruction in sinus disease and facial development. J. Allergy Clin. Immunol. *82*:935–940, 1988.
129. Shapiro, G. G., Virant, F. S., Furukawa, C. T., et al.: Immunologic defects in patients with refractory sinusitis. Pediatrics *87*:311–316, 1991.
130. Shibley, G. S., Hanger, F. M., and Dochez, A. R.: Studies in the common cold. I. Observations of the normal bacterial flora of nose and throat with variations occurring during colds. J. Exp. Med. *43*:415–431, 1926.
131. Shopfner, C. E., and Rossi, J. O.: Roentgenogram evaluation of the paranasal sinuses in children. A. J. R. Am. J. Roentgenol. *118*:176–186, 1973.
132. Shurin, P. A.: Etiology and antimicrobial therapy of paranasal sinusitis in children. Ann. Otol. Rhinol. Laryngol. *90*(Suppl.):72–74, 1981.
133. Sobol, S. M., Love, R. G., Stutman, H. R., et al.: Phaeohyphomycosis of the maxilloethmoid sinus caused by *Drechslera spicifera*: A new fungal pathogen. Laryngoscope *94*:620–627, 1984.
134. Sohail, M. A., Al Khabori, M., Hyder, J., et al.: Acute fulminant fungal sinusitis: Clinical presentation, radiological findings and treatment. Acta Trop. *80*:177–185, 2001.
135. Sparrevohn, U. R., and Buch, A.: The bacteriology of maxillary sinusitis. I. Technique. Acta. Otol. *34*:425–436, 1946.
136. Spector, S. L., English, G. M., McIntosh, K., et al.: Adenovirus in the sinuses of an asthmatic patient with apparent selective antibody deficiencies. Am. J. Med. *55*:227–231, 1973.
137. Sprinkle, P.: Current status of mycoplasmatales and bacterial variants in chronic otolaryngic disease. Laryngoscope *82*:737–747, 1972.
138. Takahashi, H., Fujita, A., and Hanjo, I.: Effect of adenoidectomy on otitis media with effusion, tubal function, and sinusitis. Am. J. Otol. *10*:208–213, 1989.
139. Talbot, G. H., Kennedy, D. W., Scheld, W. M., et al.: Rigid nasal endoscopy versus sinus puncture and aspiration for microbiologic documentation of acute bacterial maxillary sinusitis. Clin. Infect. Dis. *33*:1668–1675, 2001.
140. Tinkelman, D. G., and Silk, H. J.: Clinical and bacteriologic features of chronic sinusitis in children. Am. J. Dis. Child. *143*:938–941, 1989.
141. Tos, M., and Mogensen, C.: Mucus production in chronic maxillary sinusitis. Acta Otol. *97*:151–159, 1984.
142. Ueda, D., Yoto, Y.: The ten-day mark as a practical diagnostic approach for acute paranasal sinusitis in children. Pediatr. Infect. Dis. *15*:576–579, 1996.
143. Umetsu, D. J., Ambrosino, D. M., Quinti, I., et al.: Recurrent sinopulmonary infection and impaired antibody response to bacterial capsular polysaccharide antigen in children with selective IgG subclass deficiency. N. Engl. J. Med. *313*:1247–1251, 1985.
144. Unzaga, M. J., Crovetto, M. A., Santamaria, J. M., et al.: Maxillary sinusitis caused by *Nocardia nova*. Clin. Infect. Dis. *23*:184–185, 1996.
145. Urdal, K., and Berdal, P.: The microbial flora in 81 cases of maxillary sinusitis. Acta Otol. *37*:20–25, 1949.
146. Van Cauwenberge, P., Verschraegen, G., and Van Renterghem, L.: Bacteriological findings in sinusitis (1963–1975). Scand. J. Infect. Dis. *9*:72–77, 1976.
147. Wald, E. R.: Sinusitis. Pediatr. Ann. *27*:811–818, 1998.
148. Wald, E. R.: Microbiology of acute and chronic sinusitis in children and adults. Am. J. Med. Sci. *316*:13–20, 1998.
149. Wald, E. R.: Chronic sinusitis in children. J. Pediatr. *127*:339–347, 1995.
150. Wald, E. R.: Sinusitis in infants and children. Ann. Otol. Rhinol. Laryngol. Suppl. *155*:37–41, 1992.
151. Wald, E. R., Guerra, N., and Byers, C.: Upper respiratory tract infection in young children: Duration of and frequency of complications. Pediatrics *87*:129—133, 1991.
152. Wald, E. R.: Rhinitis and acute and chronic sinusitis. *In* Bluestone, C. D., Stool, S. E., and Scheetz, M. D. (eds.): Pediatric Otorhinolaryngology. 2nd ed. Philadelphia, W. B. Saunders, 1990, pp. 729–944.
153. Wald, E. R., Byers, C., Guerra, N., et al.: Subacute sinusitis in children. J. Pediatr. *115*:28–32, 1989.
154. Wald, E. R.: Sinusitis in children. Pediatr. Infect. Dis. *7*:S150–S153, 1988.
155. Wald, E. R., Dashefky, B., Byers, C., et al.: Frequency and severity of infections in day care. J. Pediatr. *112*:540–546, 1988.
156. Wald, E. R., Chiponis, D., and Ledesma-Medina, J.: Comparative effectiveness of amoxicillin and amoxicillin-clavulanate potassium in acute paranasal sinus infections in children: A double-blind, placebo-controlled trial. Pediatrics *77*:795–800, 1986.
157. Wald, E. R.: Epidemiology, pathophysiology and etiology of sinusitis. Pediatr. Infect. Dis. *4*:S51–S81, 1985.
158. Wald, E. R., Reilly, J. S., Casselbrant, M., et al.: Treatment of acute maxillary sinusitis in childhood: A comparative study of amoxicillin and cefaclor. J. Pediatr. *104*:297–302, 1984.
159. Wald, E. R., Milmoe, G. J., Bowen, A. D., et al.: Acute maxillary sinusitis in children. N. Engl. J. Med. *304*:749–754, 1981.
160. Walner, D. L., Falaglia, M., Willging, J. P., et al.: The role of second-look nasal endoscopy after pediatric functional endoscopic sinus surgery. Arch. Otolaryngol. Head Neck Surg. *124*:425–428, 1998.
161. Washburn, R. G., Kennedy, D. W., Begley, M. G., et al.: Chronic fungal sinusitis in apparently normal hosts. Medicine *67*:231–247, 1988.
162. Wassermann, D.: Acute paranasal sinusitis and cavernous sinus thrombosis. Arch. Otol. *86*:99–103, 1967.

163. Watters, E. C., Wallar, P. H., Hiles, D. A., et al.: Acute orbital cellulitis. Arch. Ophthalmol. *94*:785–788, 1976.
164. Whitaker, C. W.: Intracranial complications of ear, nose, and throat infections. Laryngoscope *81*:1375–1380, 1971.
165. Whiatick, B. J., Willging, P., Myer, C. M., et al.: Functional endoscopic sinus surgery in the immunocompromised child. Otolaryngol Head Neck Surg. *105*:818–825, 1991.
166. Winther, B.: Effects on the nasal mucosa of upper respiratory viruses (common cold). Danish Med. Bull. *41*:193–204, 1994.
167. Wold, G., Anderhuber, W., and Kuhn, F.: Development of the paranasal sinuses in children: Implications for paranasal sinus surgery. Ann. Otol. Rhinol. Laryngol. *102*:705–711, 1993.
168. Yang, H. S.: Nasal flora of the children in a day nursery. Am. J. Dis. Child. *61*:262–272, 1941.
169. Zimmerman, B., Stringer, D., Feanning, S., et al.: Prevalence of abnormalities found by sinus x-ray in childhood asthma: Lack of relation to severity of asthma. J. Allergy Clin. Immunol. *80*:268–273, 1987.
170. Zinreich, S. J., Kennedy, D. W., Rosenbaum, A. E., et al.: Paranasal sinuses: CT imaging requirements for endoscopic surgery. Radiology *163*:769–775, 1987.

Otitis Externa

RALPH D. FEIGIN ■ JOSHUA J. ALEXANDER

Otitis externa is a common finding in children, especially during the summer. Approximately 5 to 20 percent of patients visiting their physician during the summer months in tropical and subtropical areas have infections of the external ear.[35] The precise cause of otitis externa is unknown. The disease seems to be multifactorial in etiology and involves an interaction of host and environmental factors.[3]

Etiology

The external auditory canal has many features designed to protect the surface epithelium from invading pathogens. Hairs located on the outer one third of the canal actively push debris toward the opening of the external auditory meatus. The continuous flow of epithelium from the tympanic membrane to the external meatus, coupled with the rolling motion of the lateral external auditory canal, also serves to facilitate the movement of debris toward the external auditory meatus. Apocrine and sebaceous glands produce cerumen, which provides an acid pH medium that acts as a chemical barrier against infection. Factors that disrupt these natural protective mechanisms produce conditions that are favorable for the development of otitis externa. They include high temperature and humidity, increased sweating,[17] allergy, stress, trauma, removal of cerumen, alkaline pH, environmental bacterial contamination, and maceration.[35]

Swimming has been associated with the development of otitis externa. Prolonged immersion, frequent showering and hair washing,[32] repeated ear cleansing, and use of cotton swabs and cerumen scoops can lead to the complete removal of the acid medium required to protect the epithelium. Maceration of the skin follows, permitting bacteria to enter. Divers have a higher degree of skin trauma and maceration and a higher rate of otitis externa than do other individuals.[34, 38, 44] The use of occlusive head gear, such as divers' hoods and earplugs, is associated with increased bacterial colonization of the external ear.[5] At this time, no direct relationship exists between bacterial colonization of the external auditory canal and otitis externa. However, the combination of prolonged immersion and occlusion may predispose the diver to an increased risk for developing otitis externa.

Several studies have shown that the incidence of otitis externa increases as the bacterial counts in the water increase. Among nondiving children on an Israeli kibbutz using a highly contaminated swimming pool (more than 3000 bacteria per 100 mL of water), the rate of otitis externa was as high as 36 percent.[38] Investigators found an association between the degree of *Pseudomonas* spp. colonization in five Ontario lakes and the incidence of otitis externa.[36] Other investigators, however, have reported no correlation between bacterial counts of the water in which an individual is immersed and extent of infection.[7] Many physicians consider that the hot, humid summer weather is the cause of "swimmer's ear."

Children with chronic serous otitis media may have an increased incidence of otitis externa. Continuous negative pressure causes abnormal desquamation of epithelium and accumulation of wax in the canal, often leading to maceration of the skin as a result of water trapped in the debris. Restoration of normal ear pressure in 15 patients who suffered from chronic otitis externa resulted in marked improvement of the symptoms and clinical findings.[19]

Several additional factors may predispose children to the development of otitis externa. Impacted cerumen can trap water in the proximal part of the canal, leading to maceration of the underlying skin. Cleansing the ear with soapy water often replaces the acid medium with an alkaline film. Contact dermatitis related to hairsprays, shampoo, hearing aids, or earrings; antibiotics prescribed for the treatment of otitis externa; and bacteria present in the canal secondary to chronic-draining otitis media may cause otitis externa. Otitis externa in an infant has been associated with a bath sponge contaminated by *Pseudomonas aeruginosa*.[37] Other factors that predispose children to the development of otitis externa include (1) a congenitally narrow external auditory meatus, (2) acquired narrowing of the external auditory canal or meatus secondary to inflammation, (3) small external auditory canals in certain disorders caused by chromosomal defects (e.g., Down syndrome), (4) bathing with immersion of the ears in bath water, and (5) infection transmitted by or from the hands to the ears. Many systemic illnesses also have been associated with infection. They include anemia, vitamin deficiencies, seborrhea, psoriasis,

Langerhans cell histiocytosis, and anxiety (neurodermatitis). Even relapsing acute myelogenous leukemia may present as otitis externa.[29]

Bacteriology

In approximately 30 percent of normal individuals, the external canal is sterile. *Staphylococcus epidermidis* can be recovered from the external auditory canal in 50 percent of individuals; in 3 percent, *Staphylococcus aureus* may be recovered.[42] As many as 31 percent of normal patients have fungi, *Aspergillus niger,* or *Candida albicans* as part of the normal flora of the external ear.[40]

The pathogens cultured most frequently from patients with otitis externa are *S. aureus* and *P. aeruginosa*, the latter being more prominent in tropical climates. *Proteus vulgaris*, *Proteus mirabilis*, *Acinetobacter calcoaceticus*, *Enterococcus faecalis*, diphtheroids, *Escherichia coli*, *Klebsiella* spp., *Peptostreptococcus* spp., and *Bacteroides* spp. are other agents that have been implicated in the etiology of this disease process.[6, 9, 11, 17, 27, 35, 45]

Infection with *Vibrio alginolyticus* several months after exposure to saltwater has been reported.[28]

Otomycosis, or fungal otitis externa, is responsible for approximately 10 percent of otitis externa in the United States. *Aspergillus* causes 80 to 90 percent of the cases of otomycosis. The next most common fungal pathogen involved is *Candida* spp. such as *Candida albicans* or *Candida parapsilosis.* Other fungi that may cause otitis externa include Phycomycetes and *Rhizopus* and *Penicillium* spp.[13, 25]

Clinical Manifestations

According to Senturia and colleagues,[35] otitis externa can be divided into three stages: preinflammatory, acute, and chronic. During the preinflammatory stage, the lipid cover is removed, leading to maceration and pruritus. As the patient scratches in an attempt to relieve the discomfort, he or she often traumatizes the skin, predisposing it to bacterial invasion. On examination, the canal may appear to be normal.

The acute stage also may be divided into three stages. In mild disease, the canal is erythematous and edematous. Often, a clear, odorless discharge and exfoliative debris in the canal are present. In moderate otitis externa, itching and pain are prominent. The lumen is occluded partially with seropurulent debris. Mild periauricular edema also may be present. Severe disease with marked periauricular edema and complete obliteration of the canal causes intense pain upon chewing and movement of the tragus. Examination of the external auditory canal of patients with chronic otitis reveals thickened edematous skin with eczematous gray, brown, or greenish secretion.

Diagnosis and Differential Diagnosis

Most patients present for evaluation of ear pain, which may vary in intensity from mild to severe. Often, marked tenderness is associated with movement of the tragus. The skin of the ear canal is attached directly to the periosteum and perichondrium. Edema in the canal compresses the nerves directly against bone. Because the skin of the auricle is connected directly to the canal epithelium, any movement of the auricle is transmitted to the canal, causing pain secondary to nerve compression. In chronic cases, itching, tinnitus,[1] hearing loss (conductive), or a feeling of fullness may bring the patient to the physician. A caseous discharge may or may not be present. Hearing usually is normal if the canal is clear and can be evaluated by tuning fork, tympanography, or audiography.

The differential diagnosis of otitis externa includes both benign and malignant conditions. The list includes furunculosis, foreign bodies, suppurative and nonsuppurative otitis media, bullous myringitis, herpes zoster oticus,[17] mastoiditis, benign necrotizing otitis externa,[43] malignant otitis externa, and various malignancies.[22]

Furunculosis usually is found in the outer one half of the canal, where sebaceous glands or hair follicles become obstructed and infected, most commonly by *S. aureus*.[17] Physical examination reveals a "localized" area of infection. Pain usually is relieved after incision and drainage of the abscess with a No. 11 blade, 18-gauge needle, or both.[30]

Children commonly place small objects in the external canal. Foreign bodies may incite a localized inflammatory reaction secondary to trauma. These objects usually can be removed with careful use of a cerumen scoop under otoscopic or microscopic guidance or by saline lavage. Local or general anesthesia may be required to remove an object trapped at the isthmus.[4]

Acute otitis media generally causes ear pain that is not exacerbated by movement of the tragus. Discharge is not present unless the tympanic membrane has erupted. When the tympanic membrane perforates, bloody discharge often is present, and the intensity of the pain diminishes substantially. Once the discharge is removed from the canal, the tympanic membrane can be examined. It often is erythematous and inflamed. These patients generally have temperatures of 40° C to 40.5° C (104° F to 105° F) and have an elevated white blood cell count. Commonly, tympanometry demonstrates a type B tracing.[45] Appropriate oral antibiotic therapy is indicated.

Bullous myringitis may involve both the tympanic membrane and the external canal. Serous or hemorrhagic blebs cause severe pain. Fever generally is absent, and hearing is not affected unless the child also has otitis media. The blebs may need to be incised if pain is severe.

Herpes zoster oticus (Ramsay Hunt syndrome) is a cranial neuritis caused by varicella-zoster virus. It is manifested by a vesicular eruption on the pinna and external auditory meatus, severe otalgia, and ipsilateral facial paralysis. Diagnosis is made by viral culture of an open vesicle, and treatment consists of administration of topical and intravenous acyclovir.[17]

Acute mastoiditis causes sagging of the posterior canal wall that may look like simple edema. These patients have extreme tenderness over the mastoid process and usually have minimal tragal and auricular tenderness. Swelling may blunt the postauricular crease and cause anterior deviation of the auricle. Mastoid radiography should distinguish a case of severe otitis externa from mastoiditis, whereas computed tomography and magnetic resonance imaging help define deep tissue inflammation or abscess.[18]

Benign necrotizing otitis externa is a relatively rare condition that can present with otorrhea, pruritus of the ear, and mild otalgia. It is characterized by the development of an avascular bony sequestration in the tympanic plate and can be treated by long-term conservative management or surgery.[43]

Malignant external otitis is not seen commonly in the pediatric age group, except in children with chronic illness or malnourishment[12] or those who are immunosuppressed.[31] It occurs most frequently in the elderly diabetic population and is caused most commonly[17] by *P. aeruginosa*. The infection begins in the canal, often after minor trauma, and spreads rapidly to involve the soft tissue, cartilage, bone, nerves, and parotid gland. Pain is severe, and discharge is copious. In contrast to simple otitis externa, edema and active granulation tissue are found in the canal. Movement of the temporomandibular joint and palpation below the external canal cause extreme pain. Patients who develop facial paralysis, which occurs more commonly in children than in adults with this condition, have an ominous prognosis. An erythrocyte sedimentation rate appears to be a sensitive index for malignant otitis externa,[17] and a technetium 99m bone scan may be helpful in early[17] detection of the osteomyelitis that is associated with this condition.[10] Complications of malignant external otitis noted in children are stenosis of the external auditory canal, auricular cartilage deformity, tympanic membrane necrosis,[12] and sensorineural hearing loss.[41] A positive bone scan itself, however, should not be considered to be diagnostic of malignant external otitis because positive scans have been noted in children with severe otitis externa.[23] A biopsy specimen also should be sent for histopathology to rule out a primary or metastatic malignancy.[17] Malignancy also may masquerade as otitis externa. Squamous cell carcinoma is the most common presentation; however, basal cell carcinoma and adenocarcinoma, as well as metastatic lymphoma, can be found in the external canal. Ear canal malignancy may manifest with a bloody discharge, deafness, or a nonhealing ulcer or otalgia. Malignancy should be considered if the pain is out of proportion to the degree of skin involvement.

Treatment

The goals of treatment are to relieve pain, cleanse the canal, restore the protective epithelial barrier, and prevent reinfection. In the preinflammatory stage, the canal can be flushed with 3 percent hypertonic saline or Burow solution (two tablets in 1 pint of water) three times daily. The canal should be dried with a cotton swab after each irrigation. If no infection is present, topical corticosteroid creams, such as Benisone, Kenalog, or Tridesilon, may be used three times each day. If the canal is infected, Neosporin-G cream, administered three times per day, may be provided. Acetic acid (VSōl) should be used to restore the acid pH 1 or 2 weeks after this treatment. Ofloxacin otic solution 0.3 percent has been reported to be efficacious in the treatment of otitis externa. Bacterial eradication rates ranged from 81 to 100 percent in clinical trials.[39]

In contrast to the preinfected stage, irrigation should be avoided when the canal is infected mildly. Cortisporin solution or suspension (a mixture of polymyxin, neomycin, and hydrocortisone in an acid pH medium that is active against both staphylococci and gram-negative rods) should be used four times daily. An important point to remember is that hypersensitivity to neomycin may occur, complicating the existing otitis externa. This hypersensitivity may be masked by the steroid application when moderate or severe infection is found.

If the external ear canal is very swollen and painful, Burow solution, acetic acid, or Cortisporin may be placed in the canal on a cotton wick in an attempt to reduce swelling. Anodynes also may be used as needed. Taking a culture of the canal before the initiation of therapy is important. After the swelling has decreased, colistin sulfate or clindamycin drops should be used until the patient has been symptom-free for 1 to 2 weeks. In children who have indwelling tympanostomy tubes, local therapy should be used with care because direct contact with the otic nerves can cause permanent damage.

Analgesics, as well as antibiotic coverage with tetracycline (in children older than 8 years of age), ampicillin, or cephalosporins, may be indicated, especially if the child is febrile. Cellulitis that accompanies otitis externa is secondary to infection with gram-positive organisms that usually respond to these antibiotics. Systemic therapy with oxacillin or nafcillin may be required in patients with severe chondritis associated with otitis media when chondritis is caused by *S. aureus*. Therapy with an appropriate aminoglycoside or ciprofloxacin if the patient is 18 years of age or older[14] should be considered when otitis is caused by *P. aeruginosa*. For the duration of therapy, the patient should be advised to avoid showers and excessive exercise. Severely infected external auditory canals may require drainage of abscesses that may be present. Drainage should be performed only after 24 hours of antibiotic coverage. In cases in which anaerobic bacteria are isolated or their presence is suspected, the use of imipenem, cefoxitin, or the combination of amoxicillin or ticarcillin and clavulanic acid may be warranted.[6]

Fungal disease is managed best by careful cleansing with hydrogen peroxide[2] and thorough drying followed by[26] treatment of the canal by the physician once a day for 3 days with *m*-cresyl acetate.[35] Other treatment regimens include sulfanilamide powder insufflated into the canal to form a thin layer. Usually, one treatment is sufficient.[21] Gentian violet, Burow solution, 5-fluorocytosine,[20] 3 percent iodochlorhydroxyquin (Vioform), 2 percent ketoconazole cream,[15] nystatin-triamcinolone (Mycolog-II) ointment,[26] clotrimazole (Lotrimin) drops, thimerosal (Merthiolate),[33] and tolnaftate also may be effective.[8, 24] Itraconazole (Sporanox) has been effective for the treatment of *Aspergillus* spp.–associated otitis externa.

Finally, the rare case of otitis externa caused by Langerhans cell histiocytosis may be treated successfully with topical 20 percent nitrogen mustard otic drops.[16]

Prevention

Patients with a history of otitis externa related to water activities should minimize exposure to water by using earplugs while bathing or swimming. After prolonged swimming, acetic acid (2%) drops may decrease recurrence of otitis externa by neutralizing the alkaline effects of pool water.[2, 17]

REFERENCES

1. Agius, A. M., Pickles, J. M., and Burch, K. L.: A prospective study of otitis externa. Clin. Otol. *17*:150–154, 1992.
2. Biedlingmaier, J. F.: Two ear problems you may not need to refer. Postgrad. Med. *96*:141–148, 1994.
3. Bierel, J. F. (ed.): Logan Turner's Disease of Nose and Throat. Boston, Wright, 1982, pp. 338–344.
4. Bressler, K.: Ear foreign-body removal: A review of 98 consecutive cases. Laryngoscope *103*:367–370, 1993.
5. Brook, I., and Coolbaugh, J. C.: Changes in the bacterial flora of the external ear canal from the wearing of occlusive equipment. Laryngoscope *94*:963–964, 1984.
6. Brook, I., Frazier, E. H., and Thompson, D. H.: Aerobic and anaerobic microbiology of external otitis. Clin. Infect. Dis. *15*:955–958, 1992.
7. Calderon, R. L., and Ad Mood, E. W.: Epidemiological assessment of water quality and "swimmer's ear." Arch. Environ. Health *37*:300–305, 1982.
8. Caruso, V. G., and Meyerhopt, W. L.: Trauma and infection of the external ear. In Paparella, M. M., and Shumrick, D. A. (eds.): Otolaryngology II. Philadelphia, W. B. Saunders, 1980, pp. 1345–1349.
9. Clark, W. B., Brook, I., Bianki, D., et al.: Microbiology of otitis externa. Otolaryngol. Head Neck Surg. *116*:23–25, 1997.

10. Cohen, D., Friedman, P., and Eilon, A.: Malignant external otitis versus acute external otitis. J. Laryngol. Otol. *101*:211–215, 1987.
11. Dibb, W. L.: Microbial aetiology of otitis externa. J. Infect. 22:233–239, 1991.
12. Evans, P., and Hofmann, L.: Malignant external otitis: A case report and review. Am. Fam. Physician *49*:427–431.
13. Fairbanks, D. N.: Otic topical agents. Ear Nose Throat J. *60*:239–242, 1981.
14. Gehanno, P.: Ciprofloxacin in the treatment of malignant external otitis. Chemotherapy 40(Suppl. 1):*35*–40, 1994.
15. Gintautiene, K., Lamarca, C., Duvalsaint, F., et al.: Effect of ketoconazole on external otitis. Proc. West. Pharmacol. Soc. *34*:351–352, 1991.
16. Hadfield, P. J., Birchall, M. A., and Albert, D. M.: Otitis externa in Langerhans' cell histiocytosis: The successful use of topical nitrogen mustard. Int. J. Pediatr. Otorhinolaryngol. *30*:143–149, 1994.
17. Hirsch, B.: Infections of the external ear. Am. J. Otolaryngol. *13*:145–155, 1992.
18. Hopkin, R. J., Bergeson, P. S., Pinckard, R. C., et al.: Otitis externa posing as mastoiditis. Arch. Pediatr. Adolesc. Med. *148*:1346–1349, 1994.
19. Khalifa, M. S., Abdel Nabi, E. A., and Labib, K. L.: Middle ear pressure changes in relation to recurrent otitis externa. J. Laryngol. Otol. *98*:241–242, 1984.
20. Kintzel, P., Trausch, D. E., and Copfer, A. L.: Otic administration of amphotericin B 0.25% in sterile water. Ann. Pharmacother. *28*:333–335, 1994.
21. Kopstein, E.: Otitis externa: Unorthodox but effective treatments. Laryngoscope *94*:1248, 1984.
22. Lee, K. J.: Differential Diagnosis Otolaryngology. New York, Arco, 1978, pp. 110–114.
23. Levin, W. J., Shary, J. H., III, Nichols, L. T., et al.: Bone scanning in severe external otitis. Laryngoscope *96*:1193–1195, 1986.
24. Liston, S. L., and Siegel, L. G.: Tinactin in the treatment of fungal otitis externa. Laryngoscope *96*:699, 1986.
25. Lopez, L., and Evens, R. P.: Drug therapy of aspergillus otitis externa. Otolaryngol. Head Neck Surg. *88*:649–651, 1980.
26. Lucente, F. E.: Fungal infections of the external ear. Otolaryngol. Clin. North Am. *26*:995–1006, 1993.
27. Mugliston, T., and O'Donoghue, G.: Otomycosis: A continuing problem. J. Laryngol. Otol. *99*:327–333, 1985.
28. Mukherji, A., Schroeder, S., Deyling, C., et al.: An unusual source of *Vibrio alginolyticus*-associated otitis: Prolonged colonization or freshwater exposure? Arch. Otolaryngol. Head Neck Surg. *126*:790–791, 2000.
29. Padmore, R. F., Bedard, Y., and Chapnick, J.: Relapse of acute myelogenous leukemia presenting as acute otitis externa. Cancer *53*:569–572, 1984.
30. Potsic, W. P.: Office pediatric otology. Otolaryngol. Clin. North Am. *25*:781–789, 1992.
31. Rubin, J., Yu, V. L., and Stool, S. E.: Malignant external otitis in children. J. Pediatr. *113*:965–970, 1988.
32. Russell, J. D., Donnelly, M., McShane, D. P., et al.: What causes acute otitis externa? J. Laryngol. Otol. *107*:898–901, 1993.
33. Schneider, M. L.: Merthiolate in treatment of otomycosis. Laryngoscope 91:1194–1195, 1981.
34. Senturia, B. H., and Carr, C. D.: Studies of the factors considered responsible for diseases of the external ear. Laryngoscope *68*:2052–2077, 1958.
35. Senturia, B. H., Morris, D. M., and Lucente, F.: Disease of the External Ear: An Otologic-Dermatologic Manual. New York, Grune & Stratton, 1980, pp. 31–59.
36. Seyfried, P., and Cook, R. J.: Otitis externa infections related to *Pseudomonas aeruginosa* levels in 5 Ontario lakes. Can. J. Public Health *75*:83–91, 1984.
37. Sheth, K. J., Miller, R. J., Sheth, N. K., et al.: *Pseudomonas aeruginosa* otitis externa in an infant associated with a contaminated infant bath sponge. Pediatrics *77*:920–921, 1986.
38. Simchen, E., Franklin, D. D., and Hillel, S.: "Swimmer's ear" among children of kindergarten age and water quality of swimming pools in 11 kibbutzim. Israel J. Med. Sci. *20*:584–588, 1984.
39. Simpson, K. L., and Markham, A.: Ofloxacin otic solution: A review of its use in the management of ear infections. Drugs *58*:509–531, 1999.
40. Singer, D. E., Freenan, E., Hoffert, W. R., et al.: Otitis externa: Bacteriological and mycological studies. Ann. Otol. Rhinol. Laryngol. *24*:317–330, 1952.
41. Sobie, S., Brodsky, L., and Stanievich, J. F.: Necrotizing external otitis in children: Report of two cases and review of the literature. Laryngoscope *97*:598–601, 1987.
42. Stewart, J. D.: Chronic exudative otitis. J. Laryngol. Otol. 65:24–32, 1951.
43. Wormold, P. J.: Surgical management of benign necrotizing otitis externa. J. Laryngol. Otol. *108*:101–105, 1994.
44. Wright, D. N., and Alexander, J. M.: Effect of water on the bacterial flora of swimmers' ears. Arch. Otolaryngol. *99*:15–18, 1974.
45. Yelland, M.: Otitis externa in general practice. Med. J. Aust. *156*:325–330, 1992.

Otitis Media

JEROME O. KLEIN ■ CHARLES D. BLUESTONE

The term *otitis media* denotes inflammation of the mucoperiosteal lining of the middle ear. *Acute otitis media* is the rapid onset of signs and symptoms of acute infection within the middle ear. *Otitis media with effusion* is an inflammation of the middle ear in which a collection of liquid is present in the middle ear space and no signs or symptoms of acute infection are present. *Middle ear effusion* denotes liquid in the middle ear. The effusion may be serous, a thin, watery liquid; mucoid, a thick, viscid, mucus-like liquid; purulent; or a combination of these forms. Fluctuating or persisting loss of hearing is present in most patients who have middle ear effusion; hearing impairment is the most frequent complication of acute otitis media or otitis media with effusion. Suppurative complications of otitis media occur when inflammation and infection extend beyond the mucoperiosteal lining of the middle ear (e.g., mastoiditis, epidural abscess).

Incidence and Epidemiology of Acute Otitis Media

Acute otitis media is one of the most common infectious diseases of childhood. A survey of diagnoses made in office practices in the United States in 1990 identified 24.5 million visits at which the principal diagnosis was otitis media; diagnoses of otitis media had increased from 9.91 million visits recorded in 1975.[151] In Boston, Teele and associates[168] found that about 33 percent of pediatric office visits for illness of any kind were attributable to acute otitis media or otitis media with effusion. The same group of investigators reported that, by 1 year of age, 62 percent of children had at least one episode of acute otitis media and 17 percent had three or more episodes.[169] By 3 years of age, more than 80 percent of children had at least one episode of acute otitis media and 46 percent had three or more episodes.

A similar preponderance of cases of acute otitis media during the first or second year of life with a decline in incidence rate thereafter has been reported by investigators from locations as diverse geographically as Finland;[135, 155] Sweden;[77] Cleveland, Ohio;[104] Huntsville, Alabama;[75] and Galveston, Texas.[15] The results of these studies suggest that by the time they reach 3 years of age, children may be categorized into three groups of about equal size relative to acute infections of the middle ear: one group is free of ear infections; a second group may have occasional episodes of otitis media, usually associated with infections of the respiratory tract; and a third group is otitis-prone, subject to repeated (three or more) episodes of acute infection.

A prospective study beginning in 1991 of more than 2000 Pittsburgh children surveyed during their first 2 years of life provided insight into the prevalence of otitis media, the amount of antibiotic used, and the proportion of children who required surgery for severe and recurrent disease:[124] middle ear effusion was present 20.4 and 16.6 percent of time during their first and second years of life, respectively; mean number days of antimicrobial therapy for otitis media was 41.9 and 48.6 days in the first and second years of life (more than 90% of all antibiotic treatment in the first 2 years of life was for otitis media), respectively; and 1.8 and 4.2 percent of the children had myringotomy and insertion of tympanostomy tubes in the first and second years of life, respectively.

HOST RISK FEATURES

The peak age-specific attack rate occurs between 6 and 18 months of age (Table 19–1). The frequent occurrence of otitis media in otherwise healthy infants is in part a reflection of the fact that the eustachian tube of the young child is shorter, floppier, straighter, and more horizontal than is that of the older child. Thus, organisms from the nasopharynx reach the middle ear more readily than they do in older individuals. By 3 years of age, the incidence of acute otitis media decreases because of changes in the child's anatomy and physiology and maturing immune mechanisms. Children who have had little or no experience with otitis media by the time they reach age 3 years are unlikely to develop problems with middle ear infections unless some predisposing factor, such as tumor or fracture of the base of the skull or a facial bone or acquired immune deficiency, occurs.

Acute otitis media, like most bacterial infections in children, appears to occur more commonly in boys than in girls.[169] A genetic predisposition to acute otitis media has been demonstrated by a study in twins[30]; histories of severe and recurrent ear infections in siblings and parents are found frequently in families with an otitis-prone child.[53, 169] Although prematurity has not been associated previously with predisposition to middle ear infection, a study from the Netherlands suggests that a gestational age of younger than 33 weeks and very low birth weight (less than 1500 g) are risk factors for developing recurrent otitis media.[44] Age at first episode of acute otitis media is associated significantly with recurrent episodes.[169]

TABLE 19–1 ■ RISK FACTORS FOR SEVERE AND RECURRENT ACUTE OTITIS MEDIA

Male gender
Familial aggregation: disease in siblings and parents
Very low birth weight (<1500 g) and gestational age younger than 33 wk
Early onset of disease
Race: Native American, Alaskan Eskimo, Australian Aborigine
Poverty: Crowded living conditions, poor sanitation, lack of access to medical care
Prone sleeping position
Use of pacifier
Not breast-fed
Group daycare
Exposure to smoke and environmental antigens
Congenital or acquired immunodeficiency

Predisposing factors for race and ethnicity may be difficult to separate from poor social and economic conditions. Particularly high rates of the disease have been observed among Eskimos,[81, 136, 144] Native Americans,[160] and Australian aboriginal children.[112] Factors of poverty predisposing children to development of respiratory infections and otitis media include crowded living conditions, poor sanitation, and limited access to medical care.[107]

Although most children with recurrent and severe otitis media have no obvious predisposing factor, a small number have altered host defenses, including anatomic changes (e.g., cleft palate or uvula, submucous cleft), alterations of normal physiologic defenses (e.g., patulous eustachian tube, barotrauma), and congenital or acquired immunologic deficiencies (e.g., immunoglobulin deficiency, chronic granulomatous disease, malignancy). Active middle ear disease is a constant event in children with cleft palate.[119, 120] Children with acquired immunodeficiency syndrome have a higher age-specific incidence of otitis media beginning at 6 months of age, compared with uninfected children.[6] Nasotracheal intubation has been identified as a factor in the development of acute otitis media and otitis media with effusion in neonates and older children.[13, 41, 129]

ENVIRONMENTAL RISK FACTORS

An increased incidence of respiratory infections, including otitis media among children in group daycare compared with those receiving home care, has been documented in the United States,[67, 114, 146] Sweden,[69] and Finland.[3, 154] A survey of children in Memphis, Tennessee, found that children in daycare experienced more episodes of otitis media and also were more likely to have placement of ventilation tubes[7] (see Table 19–1). By the second year of life, 21 percent of Pittsburgh, Pennsylvania, children observed from birth who were in group daycare (seven children or more) had surgical procedures for middle ear disease (almost all were myringotomy and placement of tubes), compared with only 3 percent of children in home care.[179] The increase in incidence of otitis media from 9.91 million office visits in 1975 to 24.5 million office visits in 1990 is associated with increased usage of group daycare for young infants.[151]

Placing infants in daycare usually is necessitated by the professional needs of one or both parents. Paid maternal leave, as is fostered in some European countries, results in an increased proportion of mothers who are breast-feeding and delayed entry of infants into out-of-home daycare. As an example, in the Czech Republic, paid maternal leave is available to all women for 9 months after giving birth and is optional to the child's third birthday. Paid parental leave now is reaching a stage of discussion and experimental programs in the United States. The Federal Family and Leave Act guarantees only 6 weeks of unpaid leave, but more generous programs are available in Massachusetts, Vermont, Maryland, and Washington.

Children who are breast-fed have fewer incidents of ear disease than do infants who are bottle-fed. In a Boston,

Massachusetts, study,[169] breast-feeding for 3 months or more was associated with decreased risk of developing acute otitis media in the first year of life. Although bottle-fed infants are placed in a reclining or horizontal position and the breast-fed infant is held in a vertical position, the data suggest that a constituent of breast milk is the important factor and not position during feeding. Of children with cleft palate who were provided breast milk or formula in a similar container, those who received breast milk had fewer cases of middle ear effusion.[121]

Sleep position and use of a pacifier have been identified as risk features in two recent studies. More episodes of acute otitis media were identified in children who slept prone (compared with those who slept supine) in an investigation of 14,000 infants in Bristol, England.[54] Use of a pacifier increased the risk for development of recurrent acute otitis media in Finnish children attending daycare centers.[115] More than three episodes of acute otitis media occurred in 29.5 percent of children younger than 2 years of age using pacifiers and in 20.6 percent of those not doing so; in children 2 to 3 years of age, the incidences of recurrent acute otitis media were 30.6 percent and 13.2 percent, respectively. Although data from these studies need to be corroborated, suggesting to parents that infants sleep in the supine position and limiting use of a pacifier may be opportunities to decrease the incidence of acute otitis media.

Allergy to environmental antigens plays a role in congestion of the mucosa of the eustachian tube. Exposure to smoke can result in goblet cell hyperplasia, mucus hypersecretion, ciliostasis, and decreased mucociliary transport.[173] The availability of a biochemical marker, cotinine, in saliva, serum, or urine has rendered documentation of passive exposure to tobacco smoke more reliable than that provided by history alone. High concentrations of serum cotinine were associated by Etzel and colleagues[46] with increased incidence of acute otitis media and increased duration of middle ear effusion. Kim and colleagues[85] in Houston, Texas, documented the association of invasive pneumococcal infections in children and adults with increased environmental exposures to sulfur dioxide (a marker for air pollution) and higher counts of ragweed pollen.

Studies in both the United Kingdom and the United States demonstrate seasonal variation in the occurrence of acute otitis media. The pattern within a period of a year is sinusoidal, with the peak incidence in December through March and lowest incidence in July through September.[76, 109] These findings do not correlate with general climatic conditions because the U.S. studies were performed in Texas and Washington, D.C., and the United Kingdom study in northern England. The incidence, however, coincides with the peak incidence of respiratory infections in both countries.

Etiologic Agents

The microbiologic causes of otitis media have been documented by appropriate cultures of middle ear effusions obtained by needle aspiration. Many bacteriologic studies of acute otitis media have been performed, and the results are consistent in demonstrating the importance of *Streptococcus pneumoniae* and *Haemophilus influenzae* and a minor role for *Moraxella catarrhalis* and group A streptococci. These bacterial pathogens also may be present in fluids obtained from children with otitis media with effusion. The extensive use of the conjugate pneumococcal vaccine may result in a decrease in acute otitis media caused by *S. pneumoniae* and a proportional increase in disease caused by *H. influenzae* and *M. catarrhalis*. Respiratory viruses alone or in combination with bacteria have been identified in 17 percent of middle ear fluids of children with acute otitis media.[140] *Chlamydia trachomatis* is responsible for some episodes of otitis media in infants 6 months of age or younger.

Bacteria may be isolated from middle ear fluid in approximately two thirds of patients with acute otitis media (Table 19–2). The isolates obtained by needle tympanocentesis in studies of acute otitis media in children during the period 1985 to 1992 are shown in Table 19–2. The bacterial pathogen recovered most commonly from the middle ear of patients in each study was *S. pneumoniae*, which was found in 27 to 52 percent of cases. Nontypable strains of *H. influenzae* were isolated in 16 to 52 percent of cases. *M. catarrhalis* (previously *Branhamella catarrhalis*) accounted for 2 to 15 percent of cases of acute otitis media.[176] Concomitant isolation of two or more organisms in the same effusion occurs in as many as 7 percent of cases. Disparate results of cultures in children with bilateral acute otitis media occur in approximately 20 percent of cases.[128]

Relatively few pneumococcal serotypes are responsible for most cases of otitis media caused by *S. pneumoniae*. The most common types, in order of decreasing frequency, are 19, 23, 6, 14, 3, and 18.[62, 80] All of these serotypes except serotype 3 are included in the conjugate and polysaccharide pneumococcal vaccines that are currently available.

Most *H. influenzae* organisms isolated from middle ear fluid are nontypable.[72, 73, 158] In unimmunized children, type b strains may be responsible for approximately 10 percent of children with *Haemophilus* spp. otitis, and approximately one fourth of these children have or develop bacteremia or meningitis.[64] Previously thought to be limited to preschool-aged children, *H. influenzae* now is known to cause otitis media in older children and adolescents.[147, 149] Thirty to sixty percent or more of *H. influenzae*[19] B and 75 percent of *M. catarrhalis*[92, 153, 176] organisms isolated from middle ear fluids produce β-lactamase.

Several clinical situations warrant special consideration: (1) the occurrence of purulent conjunctivitis in association with acute otitis media (conjunctivitis-otitis syndrome) usually is attributable to nontypable *H. influenzae*[23, 24]; (2) acute otitis media occurs commonly among children hospitalized in intensive care units, and the bacteriology may be reflective of the hospital environment[41]; (3) renewed signs of acute otitis media within 14 days usually represent relapse, whereas signs occurring 21 or more days after a prior infection are likely to indicate a new infection or recurrence[28];

TABLE 19–2 ■ BACTERIAL PATHOGENS ISOLATED FROM MIDDLE EAR ASPIRATES IN INFANTS AND CHILDREN WITH ACUTE OTITIS MEDIA (PERCENTAGE OF CHILDREN WITH PATHOGEN, 1985–1992)*

Pathogen	Mean	Range
Streptococcus pneumoniae	38	27–52
Haemophilus influenzae	27	16–52
Moraxella catarrhalis	10	2–15
Group A *Streptococcus*	3	0–11
Staphylococcus aureus	2	0–16
Miscellaneous bacteria	8	0–24
None or nonpathogens	28	12–35

*Percentage greater than 100 because of more than 1 pathogen per middle ear effusion.

From Bluestone, C. D., and Klein, J. O.: Otitis Media in Infants and Children. 3rd ed. Philadelphia, W. B. Saunders, 2001.

and (4) children with tympanostomy tubes may develop acute otitis media caused by organisms associated with otitis externa as well as acute otitis media (e.g., *Staphylococcus aureus, Pseudomonas aeruginosa, Staphylococcus epidermidis, S. pneumoniae, and H. influenzae*).[145]

The bacteriology of otitis media with effusion mimics that of acute otitis media.[56, 57, 110, 138, 150, 161] In contrast, the etiologic agents of chronic suppurative otitis media with persistent perforation include *P. aeruginosa, S. aureus,* anaerobic bacteria, and enteric gram-negative bacilli.[25, 83, 118] *Mycobacterium tuberculosis* is a rare but important cause of chronic suppurative otitis media with persistent perforation.[181]

Bacteria found in middle ear aspirates usually are present in the nasopharynx of children with acute otitis media, but multiple pathogens may be present in the nasopharynx that are not present in the middle ear.[47] Although not useful for specific microbiologic diagnosis of acute otitis media, nasopharyngeal cultures are of value for monitoring antibiotic susceptibility patterns of bacterial pathogens associated with acute otitis media. Several investigators have noted quantitative differences in the nasopharyngeal flora of patients with and without otitis media, and these differences may play a role in the pathogenesis of middle ear disease. Long and colleagues[97] described a significant association between the recovery of abundant *H. influenzae* (at least 50% total colony count) from the nasopharynx and bacteriologically confirmed otitis media. An additional finding was that a semiquantitative nasopharyngeal culture was sensitive and specific in predicting the middle ear pathogen. Similar nasopharyngeal colonization rates for *S. pneumoniae* occur in ill and healthy children.[68, 96, 97] Gray and coworkers[62] have correlated the occurrence of acute otitis media with nasopharyngeal acquisition of new serotypes of *S. pneumoniae*.

Sterile cultures are noted after needle tympanocentesis in approximately one third of patients with acute otitis media. This finding in part may reflect limitations of bacterial culture methods because antigen detection tests often indicate the presence of pneumococcal capsular polysaccharide in sterile middle ear fluid.[93, 99]

Use of polymerase chain reaction for bacterial and viral genome sequences adds an additional technique for identifying the role of microorganisms in acute otitis media and otitis media with effusion. Post and colleagues[133] identified DNA of *S. pneumoniae, H. influenzae,* and *M. catarrhalis* in patients with otitis media with effusion whose cultures were negative for these bacterial species.

The clinical history suggests that viral infection serves as a frequent initiating event of acute otitis media by producing congestion of the mucosa of the upper respiratory tract. In addition, epidemiologic data support an association between viral respiratory infection and the occurrence of acute otitis media.[66] Infection with respiratory syncytial virus, influenza viruses, and adenoviruses was associated with a greater risk for developing otitis media than was infection with other viruses. In contrast to this epidemiologic association is the low viral isolation rate from middle ear fluid in patients with otitis media. A virus was isolated from only 29 of 663 (4.4%) specimens obtained by tympanocentesis and reviewed by Klein and Teele in 1976.[91] A higher virus identification rate in middle ear fluid using culture and antigen detection has been reported.[34, 86, 143] Ruuskanen and colleagues[140] summarized eight studies published between 1982 and 1990 using immunoassay or isolation; virus was identified in middle ear fluids in 17 percent of the samples: as a single agent in 6 percent and in combination with a bacterial pathogen in 11 percent. Viruses identified in middle ear fluids have included respiratory syncytial virus, influenza viruses, adenoviruses, parainfluenza viruses, enteroviruses, and rhinoviruses. Concomitant isolation of viral and bacterial pathogens from middle ear fluid appears to be a common finding.[34, 143] Reverse transcriptase polymerase chain reaction was used by Pitkaranta and colleagues[132] to identify viruses in middle ear fluids of children with acute otitis media and otitis media with effusion; evidence of rhinovirus was found in 22 and 19 percent, respectively, and respiratory syncytial virus in 18 and 8 percent, respectively.

A role for *Mycoplasma pneumoniae* in the etiology of otitis media was suggested by the observation of myringitis in nonimmune adults inoculated with the organism.[139] A subsequent study attempted to isolate the organism from middle ear fluid in patients with otitis media but was successful in only 1 of 771 patients.[91] This study suggests that mycoplasmas are an infrequent cause of acute otitis media.

C. trachomatis has been implicated as a cause of acute otitis media. Tipple and colleagues[171] recovered *C. trachomatis* from 3 of 11 middle ear specimens in infants with chlamydial pneumonia. Each of the patients had clinical findings consistent with acute otitis media. Chang and associates[32] isolated *C. trachomatis* from 3 of 26 unselected patients with otitis media. In contrast, Hammerschlag and coworkers[63] failed to recover the organism from any of 68 patients with otitis media. Thus, *C. trachomatis* may play a limited role in the development of acute otitis media during the first months of life. In contrast, *Chlamydia pneumoniae* rarely is a cause of respiratory disease in children younger than 5 years of age.[117] The organism was isolated from the middle ear fluid of a patient with otitis media with effusion, but a prospective study of 75 children 6 months to 12 years of age referred for myringotomy or placement of tympanostomy tubes failed to identify *C. pneumoniae* in the middle ear fluids.[60]

Although *S. pneumoniae* and *H. influenzae* are responsible for most cases of bacterial otitis media, *M. catarrhalis* and group A streptococci are responsible for some cases and should be considered in choosing appropriate antimicrobial agents. The incidence of acute otitis media caused by *M. catarrhalis* in most studies is less than 10 percent but was noted to be as high as 22 and 27 percent in 1983 reports from Pittsburgh[92] and Cleveland,[153] respectively, and 18.4 percent in a study of Finnish children observed between 1995 and 1997.[84] Most strains of *M. catarrhalis* isolated from middle ear fluids produce β-lactamase, and some patients fail to improve if they are treated with a β-lactamase–susceptible drug.

During the preantibiotic era, otitis caused by group A streptococci frequently was associated with scarlet fever and often was of a severe and destructive form. In recent years, group A streptococci have been isolated frequently in some studies from Scandinavia but have been found infrequently in most studies from the United States.

Tuberculous otitis was an occasional cause of severe middle ear disease at the turn of the century in the United States and Western Europe and still occurs in developing countries. Otitis caused by *M. tuberculosis* is characterized by a painless, watery otorrhea through single or multiple perforations of the tympanic membrane.[156]

Other bacteria, including *S. aureus* (which occurs infrequently in the United States but appears to be the etiologic agent in as many as 10% of cases in Japan[4]), gram-negative enteric bacilli (responsible for approximately 20% of otitis media cases in neonates but a rare finding in older infants), anaerobic bacteria, *Clostridium tetani*, and *Corynebacterium diphtheriae*, are responsible for occasional cases of acute otitis media.

ETIOLOGY IN THE NEONATE

Clinical investigators have performed needle tympanocentesis to isolate bacterial pathogens causing otitis media in the first 6 weeks of life. A total of 169 infants were included in four of these studies.[12, 18, 152, 170] Bacteria were isolated from middle ear fluid in 68 percent of cases. As in older children, *S. pneumoniae* and *H. influenzae* were the organisms isolated most frequently. Other than the more frequent occurrence of disease caused by gram-negative enteric organisms (approximately 20% of cases) and the occasional isolation of other neonatal pathogens (e.g., group B streptococci), the bacteriology of otitis media in this age group was similar to that in older children.

Pathogenesis

The pathogenesis of otitis media is likely to follow the following sequence of events in most children. The patient has an antecedent event (usually caused by an upper respiratory viral infection) that results in congestion of the respiratory mucosa throughout the respiratory tract, including the nose, nasopharynx, eustachian tube, and middle ear; congestion of the mucosa in the eustachian tube results in obstruction of the narrowest portion of the tube, the isthmus. The obstruction results in negative pressure in the middle ear and then development of middle ear effusion. The secretions of the mucosa of the middle ear, which usually drain through the eustachian tube, now have no egress and accumulate in the middle ear. The effusion may be asymptomatic (i.e., lacking the signs and symptoms of acute infection) and is termed *otitis media with effusion*. If pathogenic bacteria or viruses that colonize the nasopharynx are present in the middle ear after obstruction of the eustachian tube has taken place, the organisms multiply, resulting in an acute suppurative infection, an abscess, characterized by signs and symptoms of acute infection such as fever and otalgia.[20, 21, 58, 142] For children with recurrent episodes of acute otitis media or otitis media with effusion, anatomic or physiologic abnormalities of the eustachian tube appear to be predisposing factors. Also possible is that subtle changes in immune response occur that predispose to frequent episodes of otitis media. Experimental studies provide evidence that virus-induced impairments in neutrophil migration and bacterial killing also may be important in the pathogenesis of acute otitis media.[2]

With growth of the skull and change in the position, length, and width of the eustachian tube over time, the predilection to otitis media in accompanying acute infections of the upper respiratory tract in the first 3 years of life diminishes and the patient has fewer episodes of acute otitis media. Children younger than 3 years of age with similar respiratory infections are predisposed to the complication of acute infection of the middle ear, whereas older children challenged by the same microorganism have the signs of the upper respiratory infection but need not have the complicating ear infection.

The pathogenesis of persistent middle ear effusion or otitis media with effusion remains uncertain. An effective antimicrobial agent sterilizes the acute bacterial infection of acute otitis media. The middle ear effusion, now sterile, may persist for weeks to months. The median duration of middle ear effusion after acute otitis media is approximately 23 days (Fig. 19–1). The type of antibacterial drug used does not appear to alter the duration of fluid in the middle ear after acute infection.

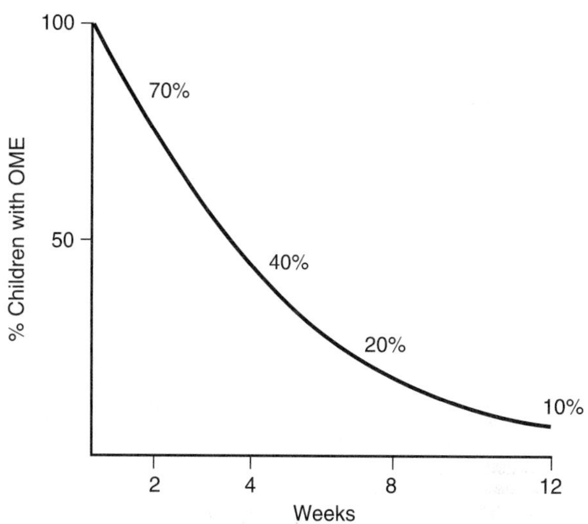

FIGURE 19–1 ■ Persistence of middle ear effusion after onset of acute otitis media. (Modified from Teele, D. W., Klein, J. O., and Rosner, B. A.: Epidemiology of otitis media in children. Ann. Otol. Rhinol. Laryngol. *89*:5–6, 1980; *In* Bluestone, C. D., and Klein, J. O.: Otitis Media in Infants and Children. 3rd ed. Philadelphia, W. B. Saunders, 2001.)

Pathophysiology

TYMPANIC MEMBRANE

In the presence of otitis media, changes in the tympanic membrane occur rapidly. The presence of congested blood vessels, edema (which obscures normal landmarks), and bulging or sagging of Shrapnell membrane indicate not only a myringitis (inflammation of the tympanic membrane) but also the presence of fluid in the middle ear space. Blebs that appear on the surface epithelium are a consequence of acute otitis media or edema or hydropic degeneration of the membrane.

Inflammation may occur on outer epithelial or inner mucosal sides of the fibrous layer (middle layer) of the drum. In severe cases, infection may involve the fibrous layer itself. The membrane thickens as a result of edema and infiltration of polymorphonuclear leukocytes. All three layers of the drum may undergo dissolution, owing to pressure necrosis resulting from the expanding middle ear abscess or thrombophlebitis of tympanic veins, with resulting perforation. With evacuation of the contents of the middle ear abscess, healing may be rapid, and the perforation usually seals within a few days. In the process of healing, metaplasia of the epithelium, hyaline degeneration, calcium deposition, and scar formation may occur. Occasionally, when a perforation is close to the margin of the annulus or occurs in Shrapnell membrane, the skin of the external auditory canal and the surface squamous epithelium of the tympanic membrane may grow through the aperture and invade the middle ear. This event may lead to formation of a cholesteatoma (epidermal inclusion cyst). Even if the perforation heals, a differential in gas pressure across the tympanic membrane caused by malfunction of the eustachian tube may result in resorption of gas in the middle ear cavity and negative pressure in the middle ear, which causes retraction of Shrapnell membrane or an atrophic scar into the middle ear or mastoid attic.

EUSTACHIAN TUBE

The eustachian tube is approximately 3.8 cm long in the adult. It opens in the fossa of Rosenmüller and then extends upward, backward, and laterally to open in the upper anterior wall of the tympanic cavity (protympanum). In the child, the tube is shorter and floppier. The eustachian tube is composed of two portions: the cartilaginous portion extending into the nasopharynx and the bony portion originating in the middle ear. The upper third of the tube is bony; the middle ear opening is the widest; and the medial end (the part joining the cartilaginous eustachian tube), or isthmus, is the narrowest. Pneumatic peritubal air cells arising from the middle ear cavity surround it and can extend to the petrous apex. The internal carotid artery lies anteromedial to this region (Fig. 19–2).

The lower two thirds of the eustachian tube is a narrow, slitlike, fibrocartilaginous passage. It makes a 160-degree angle with the bony portion at its junction. The cross-section of the tube looks like a shepherd's crook, with a cartilaginous superior and medial surface and a fibrous lateral surface.

Three muscles are associated with the eustachian tube. The tensor tympani muscle lies on top of it; the levator palatini muscle lies under it; and the tensor palatini muscle arises on the tube, scaphoid fossa, and spine of sphenoid and then courses around the hook of the hamulus and forms an aponeurosis with its mate (from the opposite side) in the soft palate. This muscle is the only one that acts directly on the eustachian tube.

The eustachian tube area, protympanum, and hypotympanum are lined by ciliated columnar epithelium with goblet cells or secretory cells (respiratory epithelium, schneiderian epithelium). The epithelium is continuous with the upper airway system and paranasal sinuses. This area also contains a well-defined subepithelial connective tissue layer, which thins out and may be absent nearing the antrum and mastoid air cell system. The movement of the cilia and mucus blanket always is toward the eustachian tube and nasopharynx. The tube is surrounded by a plexus of lymphoid channels. It has an arterial supply from a branch of the middle meningeal or accessory meningeal artery and from branches of the artery of the pterygoid canal. The nerve supply is from the tympanic plexus (IX) (sensory) and sphenopalatine ganglion (sympathetics and parasympathetic palatine fiber).

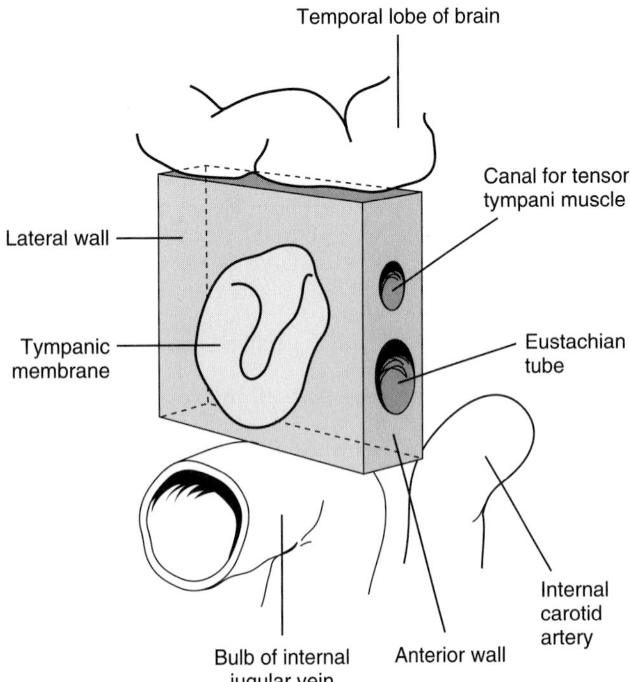

FIGURE 19–2 ■ The middle ear. (From Klein, J. O., and Daum, R. S.: The Diagnosis and Management of the Patient with Otitis Media. Copyright Biomedical Information Corporation, New York, 1985.)

Whereas the bony portion is rigid and patulous, the medial two thirds normally is held closed by elastic recoil of the fibrocartilaginous tissue. Thus, contraction of the tensor palatini muscle that inserts in the anterolateral wall opens the tube on swallowing. On the average, the adult swallows once per minute while awake and once every 5 minutes while asleep. Suckling children usually swallow five times per minute.

Mucus and ciliary action flow from the middle ear to the eustachian tube. The eustachian tube acts as a unidirectional valve that favors outflow from the middle ear to the pharynx. Reverse flow can be induced by an increase in pressure in the nasopharynx (Valsalva, barotrauma). Thus, during occlusion of the eustachian tube, the oxygen and carbon dioxide (and other gases) are absorbed from the middle ear by diffusion into the rich vasculature, and a negative pressure is created. A patent eustachian tube is a critical prerequisite for subsidence of middle ear disease.

Clinical Presentation

Children with acute otitis media may have nonspecific signs and symptoms, including fever, irritability, headache, apathy, anorexia, vomiting, and diarrhea. Signs of respiratory viral infection, including cough and coryza, usually are present before the specific signs of ear infection occur. Fever occurs in approximately one third[148] to two thirds[113] of children with otitis media.

Specific signs and symptoms associated with otitis media and its complications and sequelae include the following.

Otalgia, or ear pain, is the most common complaint of infants and children with acute otitis media. The symptom is suggested in young infants who are pulling at the ear or excessively irritable. Some infants will not have earache; Hayden and Schwartz[66] identified absence of ear pain in approximately one fifth of 335 consecutively diagnosed episodes of otitis media, usually among children older than 2 years of age.

Otorrhea is discharge from the middle ear through a perforation in the tympanic membrane or from the external auditory canal when inflamed. The acute perforation usually is central in the membrane. Relief of the pressure on the tympanic membrane results in immediate relief of pain and usually a decrease in temperature. Because the tympanic membrane has a dense network of blood vessels, rapid repair of the membrane occurs, and the perforation usually is unapparent within 24 to 72 hours. If the tympanic membrane seals and mucous membrane infection still is present, fluid may reaccumulate with renewed acute signs of otitis media.

Hearing loss occurs whenever fluid fills the middle ear space, whether the fluid is associated with acute infection or with otitis media with effusion. When fluid fills the middle ear space, the median hearing loss is 25 dB (the equivalent of having plugs in the ear canals).[51]

Vertigo occurs but is not a common complaint of children with otitis media. Vertigo occurs more commonly in unilateral than bilateral disease and also may be caused by labyrinthitis. Older children describe a feeling of spinning, whereas younger children may not be able to verbalize these symptoms but manifest disequilibrium by falling or stumbling.

Tinnitus is an uncommon complaint in children, but when it does occur, the symptom often is caused by otitis media and eustachian tube dysfunction.

Swelling about the ear, especially in the postauricular area, may be a sign of mastoiditis.

Facial paralysis in children occurs as a complication of acute otitis media or chronic otitis media with perforation of the tympanic membrane or as a result of an enlarging cholesteatoma.

Conjunctivitis has been associated with acute otitis media caused by nontypable strains of *H. influenzae*. The conjunctivae are injected, with tearing or purulent discharge.[24]

Craniofacial anomalies, such as cleft palate, mandibulofacial dysostosis, and Down syndrome, may predispose to frequent ear disease. Hypernasal speech suggests velopharyngeal insufficiency.

Otoscopy

Examination of the ear should begin with observation of the auricle and the external auditory meatus. Palpation of the periauricular areas should be performed to indicate presence of periostitis or diffuse external otitis. The ear canal should be examined for inflammation or cerumen that obstructs vision of the tympanic membrane.

For proper assessment of the tympanic membrane and its mobility, a pneumatic otoscope in which the diagnostic head has a secure seal should be used. The speculum should have the largest lumen that can fit comfortably into the child's cartilaginous external auditory meatus. The important landmarks of the tympanic membrane that can be visualized with the otoscope are indicated in Figure 19–3. The otoscopic examination should include observation of these conditions of the tympanic membrane:

1. *Position*: normal is slightly convex; bulging indicates increased pressure from positive air pressure or fluid; a retracted drum indicates negative pressure with or without effusion; fullness of the tympanic membrane is apparent initially in the posterosuperior portion of the pars tensa and the pars flaccida because these two areas are the most highly compliant parts of the membrane.
2. *Appearance and color*: the normal color is pearly gray and translucent; any congestion of the mucous membrane of the middle ear will be reflected in congestion of the vessels of the tympanic membrane and appear pink or with congested vessels; a blue discoloration suggests blood in the middle ear associated sometimes with basal skull fracture; the inflamed middle ear mucosa usually is reflected in a bright red tympanic membrane.
3. *Integrity of the membrane*: all four quadrants of the tympanic membrane should be inspected for presence or absence of perforation, retraction pockets, or cholesteatoma.
4. *Mobility*: application of positive and negative pressures by the pneumatic otoscope enables the viewer to determine the presence of an air-filled space (rapid excursion of the membrane on positive and negative pressures) or fluid-filled space (limited or no excursion of the membrane); a middle ear with negative pressure will not respond to otoscopic negative pressure, and a middle ear with high positive pressure will not respond to otoscopic positive pressure (Fig. 19–4).

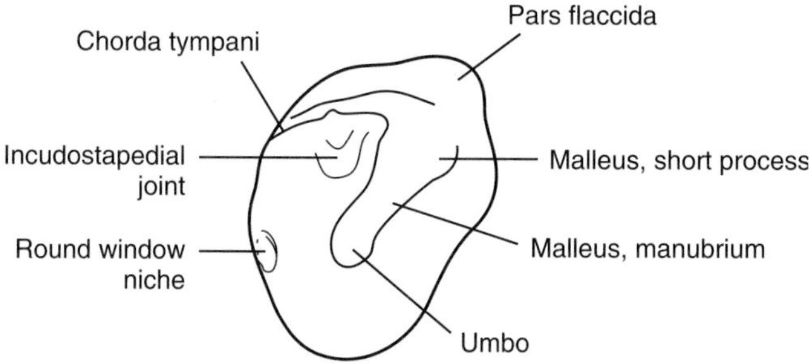

FIGURE 19–3 ■ Important landmarks of the tympanic membrane that usually can be visualized with the otoscope. (From Bluestone, C. D., and Klein, J. O.: Otitis Media in Infants and Children. 3rd ed. Philadelphia, W. B. Saunders, 2001.)

TYMPANOMETRY

Tympanometry measures the compliance of the tympanic membrane[26, 38, 48, 106, 109, 134, 137, 172] (Fig. 19–5). Under normal circumstances, the pressure in the middle ear virtually is the same as the external ambient pressure; the eustachian tube functions to equate middle ear pressure to atmospheric pressure. If for any reason a pressure differential occurs across the tympanic membrane, stress will be applied to the drum. Middle ear compliance, therefore, varies as a function of the pressure differential across the tympanic membrane. Where blockage of the eustachian tube with no fluid in the middle ear occurs, the tympanometry curve will have a shape similar to that observed on a normal tympanogram, but the point of maximal compliance will be shifted to the negative pressure side because maximal compliance is reached when the tympanic membrane reaches a peak of compliance (i.e., when external canal pressure is reduced to the same level as in the middle ear).

If ossicular discontinuity or a flaccid or atrophic tympanic membrane is present, the drum is highly compliant, and a highly peaked tympanogram is obtained. Abnormal tympanograms obtained in the presence of fluid in the middle ear are characterized by the following:

1. Reduced height of the curve (i.e., the middle ear has reduced compliance)
2. Shift to negative pressure sides of the curve and point of maximal compliance (i.e., eustachian tube blockage)
3. A flat curve without definite peak, the most characteristic feature

Although tympanometry with the electroacoustic impedance bridge has proved to be a satisfactory method for detecting the presence of fluid in the middle ear cavity, technical difficulties exist in obtaining accurate readings in infants and children, including requirement for a secure seal of the probe in the ear canal, the need for a period of quiet to obtain an accurate reading, and decreased accuracy in infants younger than 7 months of age (because of the highly compliant external auditory canals).[125] In addition, only a few of many instruments currently on the market in the United States have data about sensitivity and specificity based on tympanometric patterns of otoscopic results before myringotomy.[50, 116] Less persuasive data are available from studies correlating tympanometry and otoscopy findings.[26, 36, 48, 106, 134]

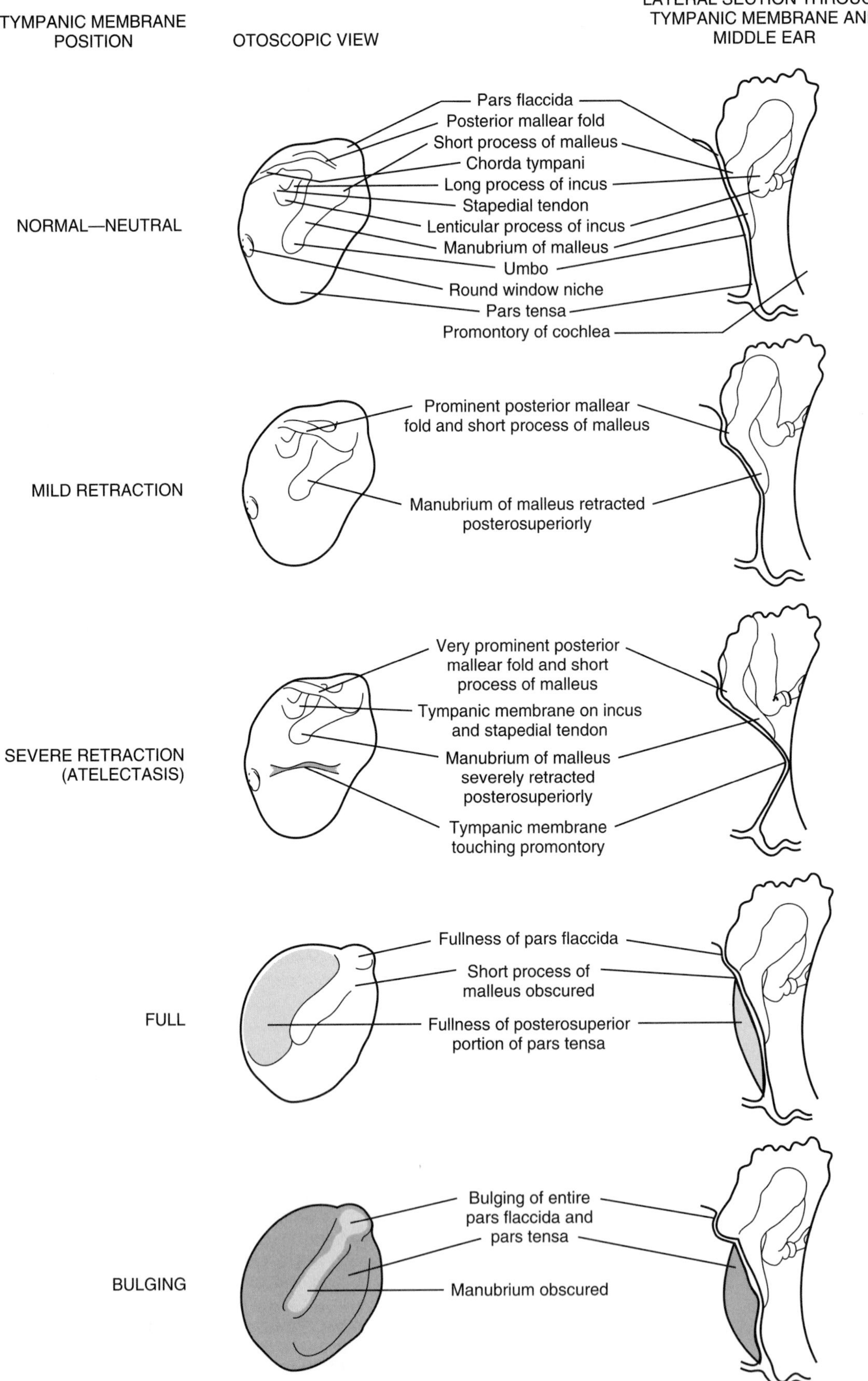

FIGURE 19–4 ■ Otoscopic views and corresponding lateral sections through the tympanic membranes and middle ear demonstrate the various positions of the drum with their respective anatomic landmarks. (From Bluestone, C. D., and Klein, J. O.: Otitis Media in Infants and Children. 3rd ed. Philadelphia, W. B. Saunders, 2001.)

	TYMPANOGRAM TYPES	COMMON VARIANTS	PRESUMPTIVE DIAGNOSIS OF TYPANIC MEMBRANE MIDDLE EAR CONDITION
1.	Normal	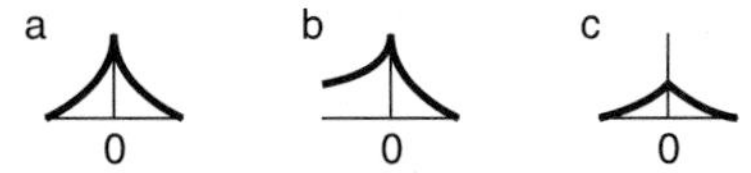 a b c 0 0 0	Normal
2.	High compliance (normal pressure)	 0	Flaccid tympanic membrane or ossicular discontinuity
3.	Negative pressure (normal compliance)	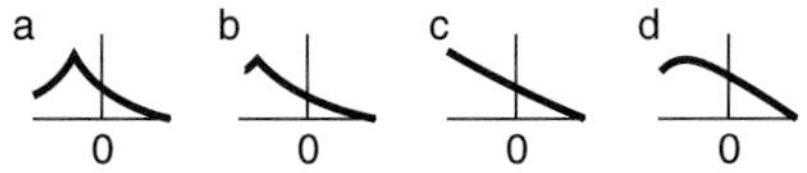 a b c d 0 0 0 0	High negative pressure with or without middle ear effusion
4.	High negative pressure and high compliance	 0	Flaccid tympanic membrane and high negative pressure (or ossicular discontinuity and high negative pressure)
5.	High positive pressure	a b 0 0	High positive pressure with or without middle ear effusion
6.	Low compliance	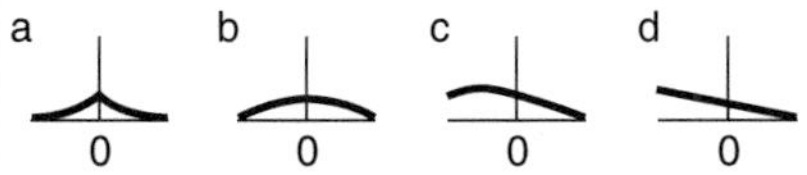 a b c d 0 0 0 0	Middle ear effusion, and/or thickened tympanic membrane, and/or ossicular fixation and/or adhesive otitis media

FIGURE 19–5 ■ Tympanogram types related to presumptive conditions of the middle ear. (From Bluestone, C. D., and Klein, J. O.: Otitis Media in Infants and Children. 3rd ed. Philadelphia, W. B. Saunders, 2001.)

ACOUSTIC REFLECTOMETRY

The acoustic otoscope, or reflectometer (MDI Instruments, Chester, NJ), is a handheld instrument that utilizes a microphone in the probe tip placed in the opening of the child's external ear canal. Both a professional and consumer model were developed. The tip measures the level of transmitted and reflected sound from a less than 90-dB sound source that varies from 1800 to 4400 Hz in a 750-msec period. Acoustic energy is reflected back toward the probe tip from the ear canal and eardrum. The operating principle is based on the fact that a sound wave in a closed tube will be reflected when it strikes the end of the tube. Sound reflectivity is measured in units that indicate the status of a fluid-filled or air-filled middle ear.[37] Babonis and associates[5] found that tympanometry and reflectometry had comparable accuracy in predicting middle ear effusion documented by myringotomy. Acoustic reflectometry has some technical advantages when compared with tympanometry; accurate readings can be obtained in crying children, and a secure seal of the probe tip in the ear canal is not required.

AUDIOMETRIC TESTS

Audiometric testing may be employed to measure auditory acuity and evaluate conductive hearing losses, but assessment of hearing is not an accurate method for identifying middle ear effusion. Hearing loss is the most prevalent complication of otitis media and is present uniformly whenever fluid fills the middle ear. The audiogram usually reveals a mild to moderate conductive hearing loss (median is 27 dB).[51] Obstruction of the eustachian tube early in the clinical course of otitis media results in absorption of gases from the middle ear and drum retraction. The reduced compliance of the drum results in increased stiffness in the ossicular chain system. The audiogram reveals a low-frequency conductive hearing loss. As serous effusion appears and the middle ear fills with serum and pus, the ossicular system has an increased mass applied to it and the audiogram flattens out, resulting in a high-frequency conductive hearing loss.

TYMPANOCENTESIS AND MYRINGOTOMY

Tympanocentesis, a needle aspiration of the middle ear effusion, is used primarily for diagnosis of presence or absence of an effusion and for microbiologic study. Because cultures of the upper respiratory tract are of limited value in providing specific microbiologic diagnosis of otitis media, only materials obtained by aspiration of the middle ear abscess can be considered a true reflection of the etiology of acute otitis media. Myringotomy is an incision in the anterior lower quadrant of the tympanic membrane for therapeutic drainage.

Tympanocentesis or myringotomy should be considered in patients who at onset appear toxic or are seriously ill, in patients who are toxic after initiation of antimicrobial therapy, in the presence of suppurative complications (including mastoiditis and meningitis), and in the immunologically deficient patient in whom an unusual organism may be present.

RADIOGRAPHY

Roentgenographic evaluation of the temporal bone is indicated when complications or sequelae of otitis media are suspected or present. Plain radiographs are of limited value in the diagnosis of osteitis of the mastoid or cholesteatoma; computed tomography and magnetic resonance imaging are more precise and should be obtained if a suppurative intratemporal or intracranial complication is suspected.

Differential Diagnosis

Inflammation or foreign body in the external ear canal may produce ear pain simulating that of acute otitis media. When external otitis or furunculosis of the external canal is present, the patient often has severe itching in the ear canal and pain elicited by manipulation of the pinna. The canal may be narrowed and so tender that performing an otoscopic examination is not possible.

An erythematous tympanic membrane may be caused by an upper respiratory tract infection with congestion of the mucosa lining the entire respiratory tract, including the middle ear. A "red drum" also may be produced by trauma or aggressive examination of the external canal and may appear suddenly in the crying child.

Otalgia may be associated with infections of the tonsils, adenoids, teeth, nasopharynx, hypopharynx, or larynx. Tumors in those regions can refer pain to the ipsilateral ear along the 10th cranial nerve. Lymphomas, leukemias, and rhabdomyosarcomas involving the palate, nasopharynx, or base of the skull eventually occlude one or both eustachian tubes, producing serous effusions and otalgia.

Acute otitis media must be differentiated from an acute exacerbation of an unrelated disease in a patient with persistent middle ear effusion. Because fluid persists for weeks to months after each episode of acute otitis media, an intercurrent infection, not associated with middle ear disease, may be misdiagnosed as acute otitis media because of the presence of acute systemic signs of an infectious illness plus a middle ear effusion. This event may be one of the frequent reasons for overdiagnosis of acute otitis media. At present, no technique, other than tympanocentesis, is readily available to distinguish a relapse of acute otitis media from a new and recurrent episode of acute otitis media or from an intercurrent and unrelated infection associated with persistent middle ear effusion.

Otitis Media with Effusion

The presence of a relatively asymptomatic middle ear effusion has many synonyms, such as secretory, nonsuppurative, and serous otitis media, but the most acceptable term is *otitis media with effusion*. After every episode of acute otitis media, fluid persists in the middle ear for weeks to months[167] (see Fig. 19–1). In a study of Boston children, 70 percent of the patients still had effusion at 2 weeks; 40 percent had it at 1 month; 20 percent at 2 months; and 10 percent at 3 months. Similar results of persistent middle ear effusion after an episode of acute otitis media have been noted in all other clinical studies of acute otitis media. The incidence or prevalence of otitis media with effusion that is unrecognized by parents and, therefore, not brought to medical attention has been studied extensively.[29, 49, 131] The prevalence of effusion varied with age and the time of year. Incidence of otitis media with effusion peaked during the second year of life and was more prevalent in winter than in summer months.[49, 131, 164] In some children, the duration of otitis media with effusion may be as short as 1 or several days.[16] Because hearing loss is present whenever fluid fills the middle ear space, physicians are concerned about the many children with prolonged time spent with effusion; the accompanying hearing loss; and possible adverse effects on speech, language, and cognitive development.

The pathogenesis of otitis media with effusion remains uncertain. Although appropriate antibacterial agents are effective in sterilizing the middle ear effusion in acute otitis media, the drugs do not rid the ear of the fluid. At some later point, bacteria may re-enter the fluid-filled middle ear space. Bacteria can be recovered from one third to one half of specimens obtained at the time of myringotomy or tympanostomy tube insertion.[56, 57, 110, 138, 150] The bacteriology in such cases has mimicked closely the bacteriology of acute otitis media, with *S. pneumoniae* and *H. influenzae* being the predominant organisms isolated. The significance of this finding at present is unknown. The bacteria merely may colonize middle ear fluid without producing inflammation, or they may play a role in the production or persistence of middle ear fluid. In addition to live bacteria, nonviable bacteria, pneumococcal capsular polysaccharide, and endotoxin have been found in chronic middle ear effusions.[40, 56, 93]

Much attention has been given to the nature and composition of the middle ear effusion. The presence of biologic mediators of inflammation in the middle ear fluid has been demonstrated[14, 94, 157]; they include chemotactic factors, macrophage-inhibiting factors, activated complement, histamine, prostaglandins, leukotrienes,[78, 79, 111] and immune complexes.[178] Elevated levels of immunoglobulin A (IgA), IgE, IgM, and IgG also have been noted in serous effusions.

Clinical evaluation depends on otologic examination and audiologic and tympanometric testing. Symptoms of this disease include conductive deafness that usually is fluctuant and may be position dependent. The patient may have a dull earache or a sensation of fullness in the ear. The eardrum usually is dull with a poor light reflex and may be retracted. Color may be pale pink or have a ground-glass appearance.

Complications and Sequelae: Intratemporal

Intracranial suppurative complications of otitis media, including meningitis, brain abscess, and lateral sinus thrombosis, are relatively uncommon occurrences today in developed countries (Fig. 19–6). Intratemporal complications that occur within the aural cavity and adjacent structures of the temporal bone occur more commonly. They include acute and chronic perforation of the tympanic membrane, chronic suppurative otitis media, mastoiditis, cholesteatoma and retraction pocket, adhesive otitis media, tympanosclerosis, and ossicular discontinuity and fixation. The most frequent complication is hearing loss that occurs whenever the middle ear cavity is filled with fluid.

HEARING LOSS

Fluctuating or persisting loss of hearing is present in most children who have middle ear effusion; impairment of hearing is the most prevalent complication of otitis media with effusion. Audiograms of children with middle ear effusion usually reveal a mild to moderate conductive loss in the range of 15 to 40 dB.[51] With such deficits, the softer speech sounds and voiceless consonants may be missed. The hearing loss is not influenced by the quality of fluid in the middle ear; ears with thin fluids are impaired to the same degree as those with fluids of gluelike consistency.[27, 180] The hearing impairment usually is reversed with resolution of the effusion. Uncommonly, permanent conductive hearing loss occurs because of irreversible changes from the inflammatory reaction, resulting in adhesive otitis media or ossicular

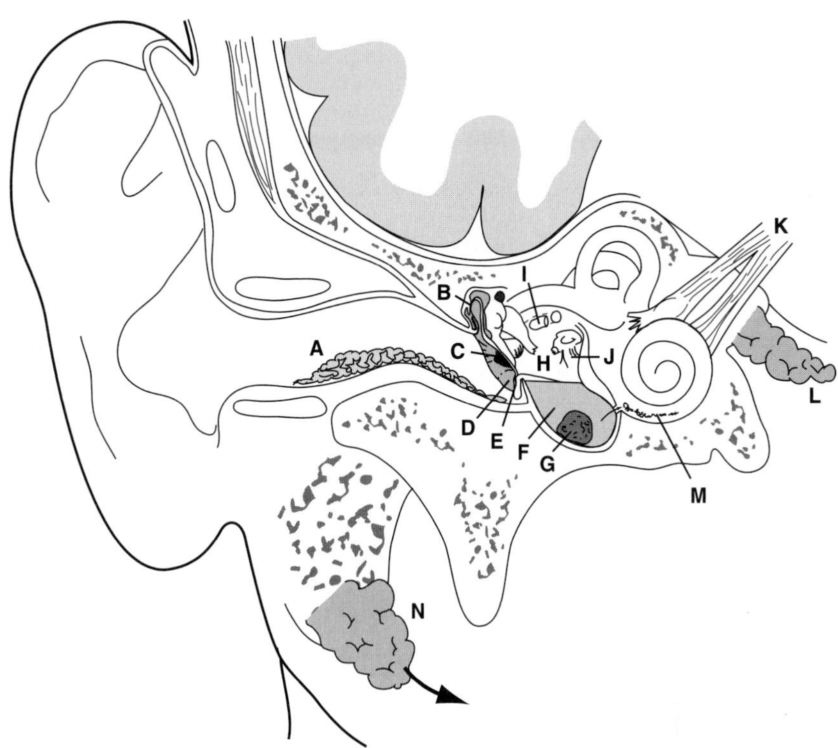

FIGURE 19–6 ■ Intratemporal complications and sequelae of otitis media include the following: *A,* Infectious eczematoid dermatitis. *B,* Cholesteatoma. *C,* Retraction pocket of tympanic membrane. *D,* Tympanosclerosis. *E,* Perforation of tympanic membrane. *F,* Chronic suppurative otitis media. *G,* Cholesterol granuloma. *H,* Ossicular discontinuity. *I,* Facial paralysis. *J,* Adhesive otitis media with fixation of the ossicles. *K,* Hearing loss. *L,* Petrositis. *M,* Labyrinthitis. *N,* Mastoiditis with extension into the neck (Bezold abscess). (From Bluestone, C. D., and Klein, J. O.: Otitis Media in Infants and Children. 3rd ed. Philadelphia, W. B. Saunders, 2001.)

discontinuity. High negative pressure in the middle ear or atelectasis in the absence of effusion also may cause conductive loss.

Sensorineural hearing loss after a case of acute otitis media may occur as a result of increased tension and stiffness of the round-window membrane and is reversible. A permanent sensorineural loss may occur as a result of spread of infection or products of inflammation through the round-window membrane.[98]

EFFECTS OF OTITIS MEDIA ON DEVELOPMENT OF THE CHILD

Children with severe or recurrent otitis media have prolonged time spent with middle ear effusion. Hearing impairment accompanies the effusion in most children. If the hearing impairment occurs at a time of rapid intellectual growth, the result may be impaired development of speech, language, and cognitive abilities (Fig. 19–7). Because language acquisition is dynamic during infancy, any problems in receiving or interpreting sound signals might have a significant effect on development of speech and language. Softer speech sounds and voiceless consonants, in particular, may be missed or confused when effusion is present in the middle ear. Although many studies have been performed and are reviewed in a recent clinical practice guideline (*Otitis Media with Effusion in Young Children*) published by the Agency for Health Care Policy and Research of the U.S. Department of Health and Human Services,[162] the limitations of design of many of the studies and inconsistencies of the results limit conclusions about the effect of otitis media on development. The interested reader should consult the guideline for a valuable review and extensive bibliography. A recent study by Paradise and colleagues[123] indicates that early placement of ventilating tubes in children with prolonged time spent with middle ear fluid did not measurably improve developmental outcomes at age 3 years. Nonetheless, some infants and young children with recurrent otitis media and prolonged time spent with middle ear effusion possibly have substantive loss in potential for development of speech, language, and cognitive abilities. Selected references about long-term outcomes of otitis media include studies by Gravel and Wallace,[61] Teele and colleagues,[166] and Friel-Patti and associates[52] and recently published reviews by Berman[11] and Klein.[90]

CHILD BEHAVIOR AND QUALITY-OF-LIFE OUTCOMES

Disturbances in the child's behavior associated with otitis media have been reported to include restlessness, frequent disobedience, impaired task orientation in the classroom,

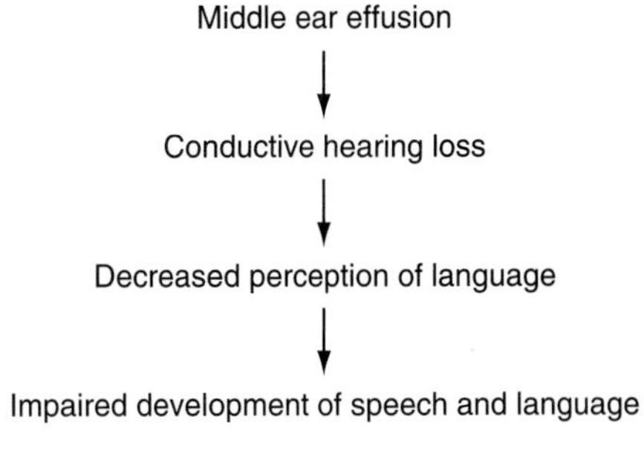

FIGURE 19–7 ■ Long-term sequelae of middle ear effusion. (From Bluestone, C. D., and Klein, J. O.: Otitis Media in Infants and Children. 3rd ed. Philadelphia, W. B. Saunders, 2001.)

short attention span and distractibility, attention deficits, and restricted social interaction. Only selected children may be most affected. Paradise and colleagues[122] found that stress in the parent–child relationship and behavior problems were highest among children from the most socioeconomically disadvantaged homes.

The working parent who has spent a sleepless night attending to a child who is fretful because of ear pain may have work-related and home-related stress. Chase[33] described the response of parents of 1-year-old children to structured interaction tasks; parents of a child who had one or more episodes of otitis media were less effective in gaining the child's attention, less able to respond effectively when the child was distracted from the task, and less able to help the child understand and perform the task.

PERFORATION OF THE TYMPANIC MEMBRANE

Acute perforation (not caused by trauma) usually is secondary to acute otitis media but also may occur during the course of otitis media with effusion. The perforation occurs because of pressure of the expanding middle ear contents on the membrane, resulting in local ischemia and tissue damage, usually in the central portion of the membrane. With rupture, the middle ear contents are discharged into the external ear canal, with instant relief of pain and defervescence in acute infection. Because the membrane is highly vascular, the perforation may seal quickly and not be evident within hours to days. If the mucous membrane of the middle ear remains inflamed, fluid may reaccumulate behind the resealed tympanic membrane.

Chronic perforation may occur after an acute episode, spontaneous extrusion, or removal of a tympanostomy tube. If squamous epithelium grows at the edges of the perforation, healing may be prevented, and the perforation will persist. The term *chronic suppurative otitis media* is limited to a stage of ear disease in which chronic inflammation of the middle ear and mastoid occurs and in which a nonintact tympanic membrane (caused by perforation or tympanostomy tube) and otorrhea are present. Mastoiditis usually is present, and a cholesteatoma may have formed.

CHOLESTEATOMA

The cholesteatoma usually is a cystic structure lined by squamous epithelium resting on a fibrous strand. The contents of the cyst are the products of desquamation, keratinization, and pus formulation. Cholesteatoma may invade, causing local bone erosion and destruction of the ossicular chain. Aural cholesteatomas can be classified as congenital or acquired.

A congenital cholesteatoma is a congenital rest of epithelial tissue and appears as a white cystlike structure within the middle ear or temporal bone.

Acquired cholesteatoma may be secondary to implantation of epithelial tissue or may be a sequela of otitis media or a retraction pocket, or both. Implantation cholesteatoma may develop either from epithelium that has migrated through a perforation of the tympanic membrane or from intra-aural epithelium remaining after middle ear or mastoid surgery. Infection caused by such organisms as *S. aureus, P. aeruginosa, Proteus* spp., nonhemolytic streptococci, and *Aspergillus* spp. may be present. The process of alternating infection and healing will cause the advancement of squamous epithelium into the middle ear and antrum.[48, 95, 141] The persistent infection also stimulates proliferation of the mucoperiosteum of the attic region, thus creating an accelerated tissue growth (increased production of collagenase) and a destructive and expansive process. It is characterized by a foul smell, pus, squames, and bone destruction.

Management of cholesteatoma is surgical removal of the entire cyst. Antimicrobial therapy may be necessary if secondary infection is present.

ADHESIVE OTITIS MEDIA

Adhesive otitis media is a result of healing after chronic inflammation of the middle ear and mastoid. Fibrous tissue proliferates in the muscosal lining and may impair movement of the ossicles and result in conductive hearing loss. Adhesive changes may bind the eardrum to the ossicles and surrounding middle ear structures and cause resorption of the ossicles.

TYMPANOSCLEROSIS

Tympanosclerosis, or scarring of the tympanic membrane, may be a sequela of chronic middle ear inflammation or trauma. White plaques are present in the tympanic membrane, with nodular deposits in the submucosal layers. The histopathology is marked by hyaline degeneration resulting from a healing reaction characterized by fibroblastic invasion of the submucosa followed by thickening and fusion of the fibers.

OSSICULAR DISCONTINUITY AND FIXATION

Ossicular chain abnormalities, including osteitis, may be secondary to chronic inflammation in the middle ear or the presence of a retraction pocket or cholesteatoma. The long process of the incus most commonly is involved. Erosion of the blood supply, cholesteatoma, or adhesive otitis media may be the cause of the bone erosion and disarticulation. Conductive hearing loss is present to a varying degree. Diagnosis may be assisted by computed tomography or magnetic resonance imaging.

MASTOIDITIS

Reports from Denmark,[130] Italy,[100] and the United States[82] indicate that mastoiditis continues to be an important complication of acute otitis media in developed countries, although at a low rate. In developing countries, untreated otitis media may lead to persistent perforation of the tympanic membrane, dysarticulation of ossicles, and mastoiditis. Berman[10] estimated that mastoiditis occurred as a complication of otitis media in developing countries in as many as 0.74 percent of cases of otitis based on community and school surveys and in 1.7 to 18 percent, respectively, based on hospital clinical record reviews. In a survey of eight children's hospitals in the United States between 1993 and 1998 for pneumococcal diseases, Kaplan and colleagues[82] identified 34 children with pneumococcal mastoiditis; serogroup 19 accounted for 57 percent of the isolates. The cases occurred primarily in children younger than 2 years of age.

At birth, the mastoid consists of a single cell, the antrum, connected to the middle ear by a small channel, the aditus ad antrum. Pneumatization of the mastoid bone takes place soon after birth and usually is extensive by the time one reaches 2 years of age. Likely, whenever acute otitis media occurs, some degree of mastoiditis is present. With healing of the middle ear infection, healing of the mastoid also takes place. In a small number of cases, mastoid disease progresses with hyperemia and edema of the mucosal lining of the pneumatized cells; accumulation of serous and then purulent exudates in the cells; demineralization of the cellular walls and necrosis of bone; and, finally, formation of abscess cavities caused by coalescence of adjacent cells after destruction of the cell walls. Pus may escape into contiguous areas, including the posterior cranial fossa, the middle cranial fossa, the sigmoid and lateral sinuses, the canal of the facial nerve, the semicircular canals, and the petrous tip of the temporal bone.

Signs of acute mastoiditis with periostitis include fever, otalgia, postauricular erythema, tenderness, and slight swelling. The pinna may be displaced inferiorly and anteriorly.

Initial management of acute mastoiditis includes administration of parenteral antibiotics and myringotomy to provide drainage of the middle ear and mastoid contents. Surgical drainage of the mastoid should be performed if the symptoms of the acute infection, including fever and otalgia, persist. If the infection progresses, causing destruction of the bony trabeculae, a mastoid empyema, mastoidectomy should be performed to prevent spread of the infection to adjacent structures.

PETROSITIS

Petrositis occurs when suppurative infection extends from the middle ear and mastoid into the petrous portion of the temporal bone. Signs of petrositis include pain behind the eye, deep ear pain, persistent ear discharge, and sixth nerve palsy. The triad of pain behind the eye, aural discharge, and sixth nerve palsy is known as Gradenigo syndrome. Management is similar to that described earlier for mastoiditis.

LABYRINTHITIS

Spread of acute otitis media into the cochlear and vestibular apparatus through the round (less commonly, the oval) window results in inflammation of the labyrinth. The signs of labyrinthitis include sudden, progressive, or fluctuating sensorineural hearing loss or vertigo in association with otitis media or mastoiditis. Signs of suppurative labyrinthitis (in the absence of meningitis) warrant performing aggressive otologic surgery and administering parenteral antimicrobial therapy.

FACIAL PARALYSIS

Facial paralysis may occur as a sequela of acute otitis media because of exposure of the facial nerve in the middle ear cleft caused by a bony dehiscence. The palsy usually is unilateral. The paralysis usually resolves with medical therapy for acute otitis media, but if paralysis of the facial nerve persists, decompression may be necessary.

Complications and Sequelae: Intracranial

The middle ear and mastoid air cells are adjacent to the dura of the posterior and middle cranial fossa, the sigmoid venous sinus of the brain, and the inner ear (Fig. 19–8). Suppuration in the middle ear or mastoid may spread to these structures, producing suppurative complications, such as meningitis, extradural abscess, subdural empyema, focal encephalitis, brain abscess, and lateral sinus thrombosis. Intracranial

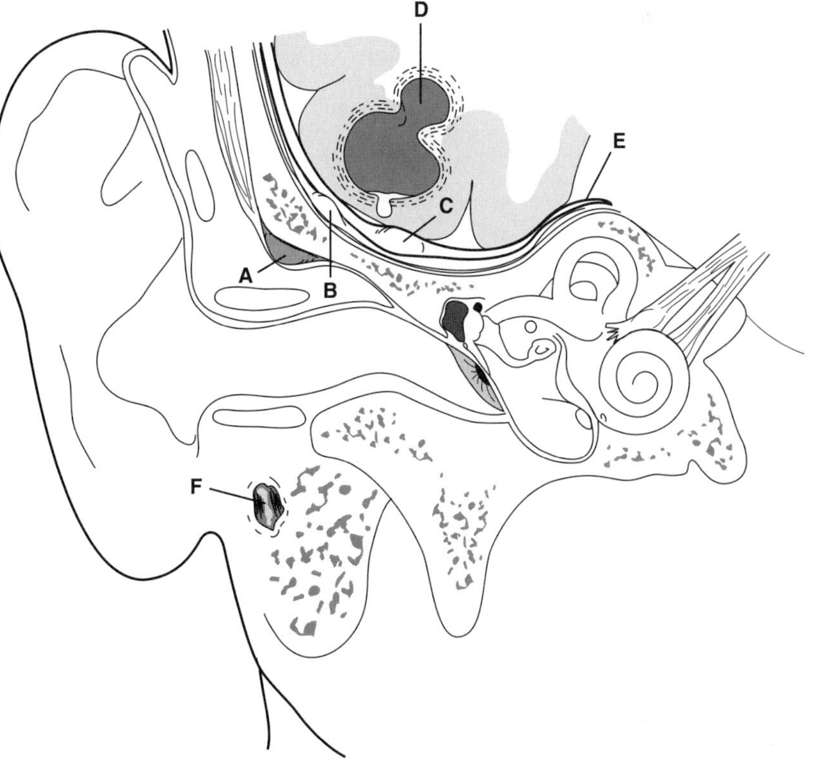

FIGURE 19–8 ■ Suppurative complications of otitis media and mastoiditis. *A,* Subperiosteal abscess. *B,* Extradural abscess. *C,* Subdural empyema. *D,* Brain abscess. *E,* Meningitis. *F,* Lateral sinus thrombosis. (From Bluestone, C. D., and Klein, J. O.: Otitis Media in Infants and Children. 3rd ed. Philadelphia, W. B. Saunders, 2001.)

complications should be suspected when the child with acute or chronic otitis media develops persistent and severe headache, severe otalgia, and change in affect or level of responsiveness. Conversely, children with diagnosed intracranial infection, such as meningitis, should have middle ear or mastoid disease assessed as the origin of the central nervous system disease.

Intracranial extension of infection from the middle ear into the intracranial area may occur because of any of the following:

1. Progressive thrombophlebitis, permitting infection to spread through the intact bone
2. Erosion of the bony walls of the middle ear or mastoid
3. Extension along preformed pathways such as the round window, dehiscent sutures, skull fractures, and congenital or surgically acquired bony dehiscences

The microbiology, pathogenesis, diagnosis, and management of intracranial complications of otitis media and mastoiditis are discussed extensively elsewhere (see Chapters 20, 38, 39, and 43).

Management of Acute Otitis Media

Management of acute otitis media focuses on the choice of an appropriate antimicrobial agent. Decongestants and antihistamines may provide some comfort for the patient who has congestion of the upper respiratory tract but provide no benefit in terms of earlier resolution of the middle ear infection. The antimicrobial agent should have a spectrum of activity that includes *S. pneumoniae* and *H. influenzae* and has documented clinical and microbiologic efficacy, limited side effects, availability in a convenient dosage schedule, palatability when provided in suspension, and reasonable cost.

The patient treated with appropriate antimicrobial therapy should have substantial resolution of signs and symptoms within 72 hours and absence of signs of relapse, recurrence, or suppurative sequelae.

The daily dosage schedules of 15 antimicrobial agents useful in acute otitis media are listed in Table 19–3. In addition, ofloxacin otic has been approved by the U.S. Food and Drug Administration (FDA) for treatment of acute otitis media in children with tympanostomy tubes in place.

CLINICAL IMPLICATIONS OF ANTIBIOTIC RESISTANCE

Increased resistance of bacterial pathogens to available antimicrobial agents has been a constant concern since the introduction of antimicrobial agents. Multidrug-resistant pneumococci add complexity to the choice of optimal antimicrobial agents for acute otitis media. At present, the incidence of strains of pneumococci that are nonsusceptible to penicillin averages approximately 25 percent in the United States but is more than twice that in southeastern and southwestern states. Reasons for the regional differences are not known. The major risk factors for presence of multidrug-resistant pneumococci are recent (within 30 days) administration of an antimicrobial agent and attendance in daycare. In addition, the increasing proportion of β-lactamase–producing strains of *H. influenzae* and *M. catarrhalis,* now between 30 and 75 percent in the United States, warrants consideration in choice of optimal agents.

TABLE 19–3 ■ DAILY DOSAGE SCHEDULE FOR ANTIMICROBIAL AGENTS USEFUL IN ACUTE OTITIS MEDIA*

Agent	24-Hour Dosage
Amoxicillin	40–80 mg/kg in 2–3 doses
Amoxicillin-clavulanate	40–80 mg/kg in 2 doses (90 mg/kg in 2 doses for Augmentin ES600)
Cefprozil	30 mg/kg in 2 doses
Cefpodoxime	10 mg/kg in 2 doses
Cefaclor	40 mg/kg in 2–3 doses
Cefixime	8 mg/kg in 1 dose
Cefuroxime axetil	30 mg/kg in 2 doses
Loracarbef	30 mg/kg in 2 doses
Ceftriaxone	50 mg/kg in 1 dose† (1–3 days)
Ceftibuten	9 mg/kg in 1 dose†
Cefdinir	14 mg/kg in 1–2 doses
Erythromycin-sulfisoxazole	50 mg/kg erythromycin, 150 mg/kg sulfisoxazole in 4 doses
Clarithromycin	15 mg in 2 doses
Azithromycin	30 mg/kg in 1 dose (1 day) 10 mg/kg in 1 dose (3 days) 10 mg/kg in 1 dose day 1; 5 mg/kg in 1 dose (days 2–5)
Trimethoprim-sulfamethoxazole (TMP-SMZ)	8 mg TMP, 40 mg SMZ in 2 doses

*Approved for use in the United States for treatment of acute otitis media (August 2003).
†Intramuscular route.

DIFFUSION OF ANTIMICROBIAL AGENTS INTO MIDDLE EAR FLUIDS

Most antimicrobial agents of value for treatment of acute otitis media achieve significant concentrations in middle ear fluid. The concentrations are, in general, parallel to, although lower than, concentrations of drug in serum. Purulent fluids have higher concentrations of drug than do mucoid or serous fluids. Penicillins and cephalosporins achieve concentrations in middle ear fluids that are approximately one fifth to one third the levels present in serum. Sulfonamides and erythromycin achieved middle ear concentrations that were approximately 50 percent of serum concentrations. An extensive review of concentrations achieved in middle ear fluids is provided in the textbook *Pediatric Otolaryngology,* edited by Bluestone, Stool, and Kenna.[22]

STERILIZATION OF MIDDLE EAR FLUIDS BY ANTIMICROBIAL AGENTS

To define the ability of antimicrobial agents to eradicate bacterial pathogens from middle ear fluids of children with acute otitis media, investigators have used serial aspirates of the infected fluids.[39, 71, 74, 105, 108] The initial aspirate identifies the bacterial pathogen of the acute middle ear infection; the second aspirate, obtained days after initiation of therapy, defines the ability of the drug to eradicate the infection. The results of these tests generally are consistent with data available from in vitro assays of the drugs against the major bacterial pathogens and the concentrations of drug achieved in the middle ear fluids.[87] Penicillin-susceptible pneumococcal infections were sterilized by most penicillins, cephalosporins, and macrolides; failure rates of 10 percent or more were identified only in infections treated with cefaclor, cefixime, and cefpodoxime; sulfonamides alone were ineffective, but trimethoprim-sulfamethoxazole was effective.

Dagan[39] reviewed sterilization of middle ear fluids by antimicrobial agents for pneumococci that were penicillin-susceptible and -nonsusceptible. The sterilization of middle ear fluids infected with susceptible strains was consistent with prior data. Nonsusceptible strains were less readily eradicated from the middle ear fluid, and the failure rates were twofold or more than those for penicillin-susceptible strains. As examples, the failure rates for penicillin-nonsusceptible versus penicillin-susceptible strains were 20 versus 10 percent, respectively, for amoxicillin; 53 versus 0 percent, respectively, for ceftriaxone administered as one dose; 9 versus 0 percent, respectively, for ceftriaxone administered as three consecutive daily doses; 62 versus 10 percent, respectively, for cefaclor; 92 versus 5 percent, respectively, for azithromycin; and 79 versus 0 percent, respectively, for trimethoprim-sulfamethoxazole.

Sterilization of middle ear fluids infected with *H. influenzae* was influenced by the strain differences—β-lactamase–positive or –negative for β-lactam drugs. Failure rates for amoxicillin were 21 percent when the strain was β-lactamase negative but were similar to placebo, 60 percent, when the strain produced β-lactamase. Ceftriaxone eradicated all isolates of *H. influenzae* whether or not they produced β-lactamase. Cefuroxime axetil was more effective (15% failures) when compared with cefaclor (40% failures). Failures for azithromycin were comparable to placebo, 57 versus 52 percent, respectively. Although similar data based on dual ear aspirates are not available for middle ear infections caused by *M. catarrhalis*, the high proportion of β-lactamase–producing strains suggests microbiologic results similar to those of *H. influenzae*.

STERILIZATION OF MIDDLE EAR FLUIDS WITHOUT ANTIBACTERIAL AGENTS

Using the same technique of dual aspirates to identify the microbiologic efficacy of antibacterial drugs, Howie[70] identified sterilization of infected middle ear fluids without drugs. A placebo replaced active therapy in the dual aspirate study: 2 to 7 days after the initial aspirate identified the presence of pneumococci or *H. influenzae*, 19 percent of the pneumococci and 48 percent of the *Haemophilus* strains no longer were present. The differential clearing of the bacteria with persistence of most pneumococci but resolution of one half of the infections caused by nontypable *H. influenzae* likely will be associated with some immune or bacteriostatic factor in the middle ear inflammatory exudate that acts to inhibit growth of these organisms. These data of spontaneous resolution need to be considered in evaluating the efficacy of new and old antibacterial drugs.

ARE ANTIMICROBIAL AGENTS INDICATED FOR ALL CHILDREN WITH ACUTE OTITIS MEDIA?

Before the introduction of sulfonamides in 1936, management of acute otitis media included watchful waiting or, when the suppurative process produced severe clinical signs, use of myringotomy to drain the middle ear abscess. Spread of infection to the mastoid, meninges, or other intracranial foci was a feared complication of otitis media. Early therapeutic trials identified the value of using antimicrobial agents for resolution of clinical signs and decreased incidence of suppurative complications. However, most children with acute otitis media respond clinically without use of antimicrobial agents. Those children who improve without antimicrobial drugs include the one third with acute otitis media who have a bacteriologically sterile effusion and are presumed to have a viral infection and those who have bacterial infections that clear without antimicrobial agents (20% of pneumococcal infections, 50% of infections caused by nontypable strains of *H. influenzae,* and approximately 75% of acute otitis media caused by *M. catarrhalis*).[87] Because of the increased incidence of bacterial pathogens resistant to available antimicrobial agents and the data associating extensive use of the drugs with development of resistant strains, limiting the use of antimicrobial agents for children with acute otitis media has been suggested.

On the basis of studies performed by van Buchem and colleagues[174, 175] and other investigators, many physicians in Western Europe manage acute otitis media by symptomatic treatment and observation and use antimicrobial agents only if the illness persists for 3 or more days. Of concern is the paucity of information about withholding antimicrobial agents for children younger than 2 years of age with acute otitis media. In the United States, interest in this management plan has increased, but the recommendations of the Centers for Disease Control and Prevention (CDC) and the American Academy of Pediatrics focus on increasing the accuracy of diagnosis, avoiding use of antimicrobial agents for otitis media with effusion, and continuing use of these drugs for treatment of acute otitis media.[43]

CHOICE OF ANTIMICROBIAL AGENTS

Oral amoxicillin remains the first-line antimicrobial agent for treating acute otitis media because of the expected low failure rates. The drug-resistant *S. pneumoniae* Therapeutic Working Group of the CDC[42] suggested that an increase in dosage used of amoxicillin for empiric treatment from 40 to 45 mg/kg/day to 80 to 90 mg/kg/day would be effective for more nonsusceptible strains. The CDC group chose three agents for therapy of children who had failed amoxicillin treatment: high-dose amoxicillin-clavulanate, cefuroxime axetil, or intramuscular ceftriaxone. The use of high-dose amoxicillin-clavulanate responds to concern about failure of amoxicillin in cases of acute otitis media caused by β-lactamase–producing *H. influenzae*. However, if failure occurred because of a high-level resistant strain of *S. pneumoniae*, the same dosage of amoxicillin in the combination would not be advantageous. Cefuroxime axetil, cefpodoxime, and cefdinir have equivalent profiles in vitro against *S. pneumoniae* and *H. influenzae*. Because of bitter taste, cefuroxime and cefpodoxime are not well accepted by young patients, and the better taste of cefdinir increased acceptability and compliance. Intramuscular ceftriaxone was most effective in eradicating nonsusceptible pneumococci when provided in three daily doses, but an alternative regimen is to provide a single dose and, if signs do not resolve at 48 hours, to proceed to a second or third dose.[89]

DOSAGE SCHEDULES

Dosage schedules of the antimicrobial agents of value for therapy of acute otitis media have been determined on the basis of studies of the pharmacokinetics and results of clinical trials (see Table 19–3).

DURATION OF THERAPY

Duration of therapy is based on clinical trials and tradition. Most clinical trials and standard pediatric practice include a 10-day course of an antimicrobial agent. The FDA recently approved a 5-day schedule of once-a-day azithromycin administered orally based on studies comparing the clinical efficacy of 5-day azithromycin with 10-day amoxicillin-clavulanate courses. These data suggest that short courses of therapy may be appropriate for many children with acute otitis media, although some children (likely those with severe and recurrent disease) will require more prolonged schedules.

CLINICAL COURSE AFTER INITIATION OF THERAPY

The clinical course of a child who receives appropriate antimicrobial therapy includes significant resolution of acute signs within 48 to 72 hours. Instructions to the parent should indicate the need to contact the physician if the signs or symptoms worsen at any time or are unimproved at 72 hours. Persistent ear pain or systemic signs, such as fever, signal the need for reevaluation to examine for other foci of infections, to determine the need for another antimicrobial agent, or to perform tympanocentesis or myringotomy to incise and drain the middle ear abscess and culture the fluid to identify the pathogen. If a new antibiotic is needed, one with β-lactamase stability and activity against penicillin-resistant pneumococci (if such information is available from local surveillance studies) should be chosen.

Follow-up visits should be made to determine that the child has recovered from the acute infection and to diagnose persistent middle ear effusion if it is present. The utility of the traditional 10- to 14-day visit was reassessed by Hathaway and coworkers[65] and Mandel and colleagues[102]; these investigators concluded that the follow-up visit can be extended to 4 to 6 weeks after onset of treatment in those children whose parents thought the disease had resolved at 10 to 14 days. For those who still had signs or symptoms of disease (other than persistent middle ear effusion), the 10- to 14-day visit was recommended.

Visits at 4 to 6 weeks and repeated at 1-month intervals if effusion is present are of value in determining the duration of middle ear effusion after the acute episode and identifying children who may be candidates for placement of tympanostomy tubes.

SYMPTOMATIC THERAPY

Administration of antipyretics and analgesics and application of local heat usually are helpful in treating the child with an acute painful and febrile episode. Topical agents such as Auralgan Otic and narcotic analgesia with codeine or analogs are effective for the patient with moderate or severe pain. An oral decongestant, such as pseudoephedrine hydrochloride, may relieve nasal congestion, and antihistamines may help patients with known or suspected nasal allergy. The efficacy of antihistamines and decongestants for resolution of middle ear effusion is unproven.

MANAGEMENT OF ACUTE OTITIS MEDIA IN THE CHILD WITH TYMPANOSTOMY TUBES

Children with tympanostomy tubes also suffer from acute otitis media. Because the tube permits drainage of the middle ear fluid and an abscess does not develop, the major pathology is inflammation of the mucous lining of the middle ear and the dominant clinical sign is otorrhea. The bacterial pathogens include those responsible for acute otitis media *(S. pneumoniae, H. influenzae,* and *M. catarrhalis)* and bacteria that may invade the middle ear from the external canal *(S. aureus* and *P. aeruginosa).* Although amoxicillin or amoxicillin-clavulanate was the usual choice for treatment of acute otitis media in the child with tympanostomy tubes, ofloxacin otic solution administered topically twice a day for 10 days was equivalent clinically and superior microbiologically (because of activity against *P. aeruginosa*) to amoxicillin-clavulanate administered orally three times a day for 10 days.[59]

Management of Otitis Media with Effusion

The following options have been investigated for management of the child with prolonged middle ear fluid or with otitis media with effusion:

1. Another 10-day course of a broad-spectrum antimicrobial agent that has activity against β-lactamase–producing organisms because bacterial pathogens are found in approximately one fourth of patients with otitis media with effusion; a meta-analysis of blinded studies identified resolution of effusion in 14 percent of cases.[163]
2. Myringotomy or myingotomy and tympanostomy tubes to drain the middle ear fluid, aerate the middle ear space, and permit the middle ear mucosa to return to normal.[103]
3. Adenoidectomy with or without tonsillectomy for children who have recurrences after an initial placement of tympanostomy tubes.[55]
4. Steroid therapy alone or with an antibiotic. This therapy has been demonstrated to be effective in some children with otitis media with effusion. Berman[9] recommended a regimen of prednisone, 1 mg/kg/day (given orally in two doses) for 7 days with an antibiotic for 14 to 21 days. Children without a history of varicella infection who have been exposed to the virus in the month before treatment should not receive prednisone because of the risk for developing disseminated disease. The guidelines published by the Agency for Health Care Policy and Research concluded that the data were insufficient in sample size or duration of observation to recommend use of steroids for otitis media with effusion.[164]

Topical or systemic nasal decongestants, antihistamines, and anti-inflammatory agents,[1, 177] alone or in combination, have been found to be of limited or no value in the management of otitis media with effusion.

We favor an initial course of a broad-spectrum antibiotic for children with otitis media with effusion for 3 or more months. If the effusion does not resolve, use of tympanostomy tubes is the most efficient method for managing prolonged middle ear effusion. The use of tympanostomy tubes first was suggested more than 100 years ago by Politzer, but the procedure did not become readily available until it was reintroduced by Armstrong in 1954. Myringotomy and placement of ventilating tubes result in the following immediate benefits to the patient with otitis media with effusion: the effusion is drained, and the fluid-filled space is aerated; the middle ear secretions, which constantly are being formed by the secretory cells of the mucosa, are drained; the chronically diseased mucosa (characterized by hypertrophic secretory cells) returns to normal; the hearing impairment caused by the middle ear fluid disappears; concern for effects of hearing loss on development of speech and cognitive abilities is diminished; and the child who was not responsive or attentive (a condition often unrecognized as hearing impairment by the parent) becomes more social and more involved with siblings, parents, and playmates. The procedure may be disadvantageous for the following reasons: general anesthesia is required; the cost is significant; and, although uncommon, sequelae, such as persistent otorrhea, permanent perforation, scarring of the membrane, and cholesteatoma, may occur.

Current recommendations for pediatric otitis media with effusion include follow-up visits for 1 to 2 months after the acute episode. When the effusion persists for 3 or more months, the child should receive medical treatment with a course of antibiotics (2 to 3 weeks) or in conjunction with a 7-day regimen of prednisone. If the effusion fails to resolve with medical management, the child should be referred to an otolaryngologist for consideration of placement of tympanostomy tubes with or without adenoidectomy.[103, 126]

Prevention

ADVISING PARENTS

Parents of children who have severe and recurrent otitis media or risk factors for developing middle ear infections should be advised of measures that may reduce the incidence of infection, such as breast-feeding; enrolling children in small, rather than large, group daycare centers; and reducing exposure to tobacco smoke. In addition, data about the risks for developing recurrent otitis media associated with the prone sleeping position and use of a pacifier, although requiring corroboration, may be added to the discussion with the parent. Physicians also may advise parents that the seasonal incidence of otitis media suggests that their child's condition is expected to improve in late spring and summer and that aggressive measures of management, including chemoprophylaxis and surgery, may be postponed until the course of disease has been determined in the next respiratory season.

PNEUMOCOCCAL VACCINES

The approval by the FDA in February 2000 of a safe and effective seven-valent conjugate pneumococcal vaccine (PCV7) that was immunogenic in infants as young as 2 months of age promises to decrease substantially the incidence of pneumococcal diseases, including acute otitis media. The results of two large PCV7 clinical trials have been published: an evaluation of the efficacy of the vaccine for prevention of invasive bacterial disease, pneumoniae, and otitis media in approximately 38,000 Northern California infants[17] and a clinical and microbiologic study of the efficacy of PCV7 for prevention of acute otitis media in 1662 Finnish infants.[45]

In the Northern California study, the efficacy of PCV7 for prevention of episodes of acute otitis media was based solely on clinical criteria. The vaccine was 7.8 percent effective in preventing otitis media, and children who received the vaccine were 24.9 percent less likely to have surgical procedures for placement of ventilating tubes than were children who received the control vaccine (conjugate polysaccharide meningococcal group C).

The Finnish trial provided specific microbiologic data based on aspirates of middle ear fluids in children who had acute otitis media. Children who received PCV7 had 6 percent fewer episodes of acute otitis media, and culture-confirmed pneumococcal episodes were reduced by 34 percent. Children who received PCV7 experienced a 57 percent reduction in episodes caused by pneumococcal serotypes included in the vaccine and a 51 percent reduction in episodes caused by cross-reactive pneumococcal serotypes. A 33 percent increase in episodes of acute otitis media caused by nonvaccine pneumococcal serotypes and an 11 percent increase in episodes caused by *H. influenzae* occurred.

With the widespread use of PCV7 (14 million doses had been distributed by the spring of 2001), we will learn more about the efficacy of the vaccine for treating acute otitis media. Surveillance of the effects of PCV7 will include number of episodes of acute otitis media, number of office visits and prescriptions for this diagnosis, incidence of multidrug-resistant strains of *S. pneumoniae,* and incidence of carriage of vaccine and nonvaccine serotypes.

The 23-type polysaccharide vaccine currently available produces an independent antibody response in children 2 years of age or older and adults. Studies of polysaccharide vaccines in Finland and the United States have indicated that the vaccines were effective in preventing type-specific pneumococcal otitis media if an adequate immune response occurred, but the number of types producing an adequate response in children younger than 2 years of age was limited.[101, 159, 165] Administration of the polysaccharide vaccine in older children may provide protection against types not included in PCV7 and has been recommended by the American Academy of Pediatrics and the Advisory Committee on Immunization Practices of the Surgeon General for high-risk children 2 years of age and older who have received PCV7. For children 2 years of age and older who continue to have severe and recurrent acute otitis media, use of the polysaccharide vaccine after administration of PCV7 may be of value for protection against additional serotypes.

INFLUENZA VIRUS VACCINES

Influenza virus vaccine resulted in a reduction in cases of influenza A as well as a 36 percent decline in otitis media in children attending a daycare center.[35] A similar reduction (30%) in episodes of febrile otitis media also was reported in children after administration of a live, attenuated cold-adapted intranasal vaccine.[8] As of September 2002, the cold-adapted live vaccine had not yet been approved by the FDA. Use of influenzavirus vaccines currently available should be part of the strategy for reducing the incidence of acute otitis media for children with recurrent and severe disease.

CHEMOPROPHYLAXIS

Use of chemoprophylaxis has succeeded in reducing the number of new symptomatic episodes of acute otitis media in children who have a history of recurrent infections. Children at risk for developing severe and recurrent disease should be considered for chemoprophylaxis despite the concern for development of resistant strains of bacterial pathogens after use of the regimen of a modified dosage of an antimicrobial agent. The results of reports of controlled clinical trials of modified courses of antimicrobial agents compared with those in which placebo or historical controls were used have been reviewed.[88] Most of these studies used a sulfonamide or a broad-spectrum penicillin. Most reports indicated benefit to the enrollees in reduction of new episodes when they were compared with controls: amoxicillin efficacy varied from 44 to 67 percent, and sulfonamide efficacy ranged from 40 to 88 percent (although the efficacy of sulfonamides was reported as only 8% in one study).

We recommend the following protocol based on the results of these studies. Criteria for enrollment include three documented episodes of acute otitis media in 6 months or four episodes in 12 months. Because children who have episodes of acute infection early in life or have siblings with severe and recurrent ear infections are prone to develop otitis media, prophylaxis also should be considered for children who have one episode in the first 6 months of life plus a family history of ear infections or who have two episodes in the first year of life.

A sulfonamide or amoxicillin is the agent used most often and provides the advantages of demonstrated efficacy, safety, and low cost. The drug is administered at one half the therapeutic dose (administered once a day); amoxicillin is given at a dose of 20 mg/kg, and sulfisoxazole is given at a dose of 50 mg/kg.

Chemoprophylaxis should be provided during the fall, winter, and early spring months (when respiratory tract infections are most frequent) for a period of up to 6 months.

Children, when free of signs of acute infection, should be examined at approximately 2-month intervals to determine whether middle ear effusion is present. Management of prolonged middle ear effusion should be considered separately from prevention of recurrences of acute infection.

Acute infections are expected to occur, although at a lower rate, during the course of prophylaxis. The infection should be treated with the alternative regimen; a cephalosporin or amoxicillin-clavulanate would be suitable alternatives, irrespective of the prophylactic agent used.

SURGICAL OPTIONS

When nonsurgical methods of prevention fail to prevent recurrent otitis media, surgery is a reasonable option. Among the options that have been demonstrated to be effective is insertion of tympanostomy tubes, with or without adenoidectomy. Casselbrant and colleagues[31] randomized children into treatment groups receiving amoxicillin, tympanostomy tube placement, or placebo and found that both amoxicillin and insertion of the tympanostomy tube were effective. But, with the current concern about the association of low-dose, long-term antimicrobial prophylaxis and emergence of resistant otitis pathogens,[42] myringotomy and placement of tympanostomy tubes is more desirable than is antimicrobial prophylaxis. When tympanostomy tubes extrude and the child continues to have recurrent episodes of otitis media, replacement of the tympanostomy tubes in conjunction with adenoidectomy has been demonstrated to be effective.[126] However, as recently shown by Paradise and coworkers,[127] neither the addition of adenoidectomy nor adenotonsillectomy is effective in children not treated previously with tympanostomy tubes, when prevention of otitis media is the only indication.

REFERENCES

1. Abramovich, S., O'Grady, J., Fuller, A., et al.: Naproxen in otitis media with effusion. J. Laryngol. Otol. *100*:263–266, 1986.
2. Abramson, J. S., Giebink, G. S., Mills, E. L., et al.: Polymorphonuclear leukocyte dysfunction during influenza virus infection in chinchillas. J. Infect. Dis. *143*:836–845, 1981.
3. Alho, O. P., Koivu, M., Sorri, M., et al.: Risk factors for recurrent acute otitis media and respiratory infection in infancy. Int. J. Pediatr. Otorhinolaryngol. *19*:151–161, 1990.
4. Baba, S.: Recent aspects of clinical bacteriology in otitis media. Presented at Presymposium on Management of Otitis Media, Kyoto, January 12, 1985.
5. Babonis, T. R., Weir, M. R., and Kelly, P. C.: Impedance tympanometry and acoustic reflectometry at myringotomy. Pediatrics *87*:475–480, 1991.
6. Barnett, E. D., Klein, J. O., Pelton, S. I., et al.: Otitis media in children born to human immunodeficiency virus-infected mothers. Pediatr. Infect. Dis. J. *11*:360–364, 1992.
7. Bell, D. W., Gleiber, D. W., Mercer, A. A., et al.: Illness associated with child day care: A study of incidence and cost. Am. J. Public Health *79*:479–484, 1989.
8. Belshe, R. B., Mendelman, P. M., Treanor, J., et al.: The efficacy of live attenuated, cold-adapted trivalent, intranasal influenza virus vaccine in children. N. Engl. J. Med. *338*:1459–1461, 1998.
9. Berman, S.: Otitis media in children. N. Engl. J. Med. *332*:1560–1565, 1995.
10. Berman, S.: Otitis media in developing countries. Pediatrics *96*:126–131, 1995.
11. Berman, S.: Management of otitis media and functional outcomes related to language, behavior, and attention: Is it time to change our approach? Pediatrics *107*:1175–1177, 2001.
12. Berman, S. A., Balkany, T. J., and Simmons, M. A.: Otitis media in infants less than 12 weeks of age: Differing bacteriology among in-patients and out-patients. J. Pediatr. *93*:453–454, 1978.
13. Berman, S. A., Balkany, T. J., and Simmons, M. A.: Otitis media in the neonatal intensive care unit. Pediatrics *62*:168, 1978.
14. Bernstein, J. M.: Biologic mediators of inflammation in middle ear effusion. Ann. Otol. Rhinol. Laryngol. *85*(Suppl. 25):90–96, 1976.
15. Biles, R. E., Bufler, P. A., and O'Donnell, A. A.: Epidemiology of otitis media: A community study. Am. J. Public Health *70*:593–598, 1980.
16. Birch, L., and Elbrond, O.: Daily impedance audiometric screening of children in a day-care institution: Changes through one month. Scand. Audiol. *14*:5–8, 1985.
17. Black, S., Shinefield, H., Fireman, B., et al.: Efficacy, safety and immunogenicity of heptavalent pneumococcal conjugate vaccine in children. Northern California Kaiser Permanente Vaccine Study Center Group. Pediatr. Infect. Dis. J. *19*:187–195, 2000.
18. Bland, R. D.: Otitis media in the first six weeks of life: Diagnosis, bacteriology and management. Pediatrics *49*:187–197, 1972.
19. Bluestone, C. D.: Management of otitis media in infants and children: Current role of old and new antimicrobial agents. Pediatr. Infect. Dis. *7*:S129–S136, 1988.
20. Bluestone, C. D., and Beery, Q. C.: Concepts on the pathogenesis of middle-ear effusions. Ann. Otol. Rhinol. Laryngol. *85*:182–186, 1976.
21. Bluestone, C. D., Cantekin, E. I., and Beery, Q. C.: Effect of inflammation on the ventilatory function of the eustachian tube. Laryngoscope *87*:493–507, 1977.
22. Bluestone, C. D., Stool, S. E., Kenna, M. A. (eds.): *Pediatric Otolaryngology*. Vol. 1, 3rd ed. Philadelphia, W. B. Saunders, 1996, pp. 515–517.
23. Bodor, F. F.: Systemic antibiotics for treatment of the conjunctivitis-otitis media syndrome. Pediatr. Infect. Dis. *8*:287–290, 1989.
24. Bodor, F. F., Marchant, C. D., Shurin, P. A., et al.: Bacterial etiology of conjunctivitis-otitis media syndrome. Pediatrics *76*:26–28, 1985.
25. Brook, I.: Prevalence of beta-lactamase-producing bacteria in chronic suppurative otitis media. Am. J. Dis. Child. *139*:280–283, 1985.
26. Brooks, D. N.: Hearing screening: A comparative study of an impedance method and pure tone testing. Scand. Audiol. *2*:67–72, 1973.
27. Brown, D. T., Marsh, R. R., and Potsic, W. P.: Hearing loss induced by viscous fluids in the middle ear. Int. J. Pediatr. Otorhinolaryngol. *5*:39– 46, 1983.
28. Carlin, S. A., Marchant, C. D., Shurin, P. A., et al.: Early recurrences of otitis media: Reinfection or relapse? J. Pediatr. *110*:20–25, 1987.
29. Casselbrant, M. D., Brostoff, L. M., Cantekin, E. I., et al: Otitis media with effusion in preschool children. Laryngoscope *95*:428–436, 1985.
30. Casselbrant, M. L., Mandel, E. M., Fall, P. A., et al.: The heritability of otitis media: A twin and triplet study. J. A. M. A. *202*:2125–2130, 1999.
31. Casselbrant, M. L., Kaleida, P. H., Rockette, H. E., et al.: Efficacy of antimicrobial prophylaxis and tympanostomy tube insertion for prevention of recurrent acute otitis media: Results of randomized clinical trial. Pediatr. Infect. Dis. J. *11*:278–286, 1992.
32. Chang, M. J., Rodriguez, W. J., and Mohla, C.: *Chlamydia trachomatis* in otitis media in children. Pediatr. Infect. Dis. *1*:95–97, 1982.
33. Chase, C.: Hearing loss and development: A neuropsychologic perspective. *In* Eavey, R. D., and Klein, J. O. (eds.): Hearing Loss in Childhood: A Primer. Report of the 102nd Ross Conference on Pediatric Research. Columbus, OH, Ross Laboratories, 1992, pp. 88–94.
34. Chonmaitree, T., Howie, V. M., and Truant, A. L.: Presence of respiratory viruses in middle ear fluids and nasal wash specimens from children with acute otitis media. Pediatrics *77*:698–702, 1986.
35. Clements, D. A., Langdon, L., Bland, C., and Walter, E.: Influenza A vaccine decreased the incidence of otitis media in 6- to 30-month old children in day care. Arch. Pediatr. Adolesc. Med. *149*:1113–1117, 1997.

36. Coffey, J. D., Jr., Martin, A. D., and Booth, H. N.: *Neisseria catarrhalis* in exudative otitis media. Arch. Otolaryngol. *86*:403–406, 1967.
37. Combs, J. T.: Two useful tools for exploring the middle ear. Contemp. Pediatr. *10*:60–75, 1993.
38. Cooper, J. E., Jr., Gates, G. A., Owen, J. H., et al.: An abbreviated impedance bridge technique for school screening. J. Speech Hear. Disord. *40*:260–269, 1975.
39. Dagan, R.: Treatment of acute otitis media: Challenges in the era of antibiotic resistance. Vaccine *19*:S9–S16, 2001.
40. DeMaria, T. F., Prior, R. B., Briggs, B. R., et al.: Endotoxin in middle ear effusions from patients with chronic otitis media with effusion. *In* Lim, D. J., Bluestone, C. D., Klein, J. O., et al. (eds.): Recent Advances in Otitis Media with Effusion. Philadelphia, Decker, 1984, pp. 123–125.
41. Derkay, C. S., Bluestone, C. D., Thompson, A. E., et al.: Otitis media in the pediatric intensive care unit: A prospective study. Otolaryngol. Head Neck Surg. *100*:292–299, 1989.
42. Dowell, S. F., Butler, J. C., Giebink, G. S., et al.: Acute otitis media management and surveillance in an era of pneumococcal resistance: A report from the Drug-Resistant *Streptococcus pneumoniae* Therapeutic Working Group. Pediatr. Infect. Dis. J. *18*:1–9, 1999.
43. Dowell, S. F., Marcy, S. M., Phillips, W. R., et al.: Principles of judicious use of antimicrobial agents for pediatric upper respiratory tract infections. Pediatrics *101*(Suppl.): 163–165, 1998.
44. Engel, J. A. M., Anteunis, L. J. C., Hendriks, J. J. T., et al: Epidemiological aspects of otitis media with effusion in infancy. *In* Abstracts of the Sixth International Symposium on Recent Advances in Otitis Media, Fort Lauderdale, June 4–8, 1995, p. 15.
45. Eskola, J., Kilpi, T., Palmu, A., et al.: Efficacy of a pneumococcal conjugate vaccine against acute otitis media. N. Engl. J. Med. *344*:403–409, 2001.
46. Etzel, R. A., Pattishall, E. N., Haley, N. J., et al.: Passive smoking and middle ear effusion among children in day care. Pediatrics *90*:228–232, 1992.
47. Faden, H., Stanievich, J., Brodsky, L., et al.: Changes in nasopharyngeal flora during otitis media of childhood. Pediatr. Infect. Dis. J. *9*:623, 1990.
48. Fernandez, C., Lindsay, J. R., Moskowitz, M.: Some observations on the pathogenesis of middle ear cholesteatoma. Arch. Otolaryngol. *69*:537–546, 1959.
49. Fiellau-Nikolajsen, M.: Tympanometry in three-year-old children. II. Seasonal influence on tympanometric results in nonselected groups of three-year-old children. Scand. Audiol. *8*:181–185, 1979.
50. Finitzo, T., Friel-Patti, S., Chinn, K., et al.: Tympanometry and otoscopy prior to myringotomy: Issues in diagnosis of otitis media. Int. J. Pediatr. Otorhinolaryngol. *24*:101–110, 1992.
51. Fria, T. J., Cantekin, E. I., and Eichler, J. A.: Hearing acuity of children with otitis media with effusion. Arch. Otolaryngol. Head Neck Surg. *111*:10–16, 1985.
52. Friel-Patti, S., Finitzo-Hieber, T., Conti, G., et al.: Language delay in infants associated with middle ear disease and mild fluctuating hearing impairment. Pediatr. Infect. Dis. *1*:104–109, 1982.
53. Fry, J., Dillane, J. B., Jones, R. F. M., et al.: The outcome of acute otitis media. Br. J. Prev. Soc. Med. *23*:205–209, 1969.
54. Gannon, M. M., Haggard, M. P., Golding, J., et al.: Sleeping position: A new environmental risk factor for otitis media? *In* Abstracts of the Sixth International Symposium on Recent Advances in Otitis Media. Fort Lauderdale, June 4–8, 1995, p. 24.
55. Gates, G. A., Avery, C. A., Prihoda, T. A., et al.: Effectiveness of adenoidectomy and tympanostomy tubes in the treatment of chronic otitis media with effusion. N. Engl. J. Med. *317*:1444–1451, 1987.
56. Giebink, G. S., Juhn, S. K., Weber, M. L., et al.: The bacteriology and cytology of chronic otitis media with effusion. Pediatr. Infect. Dis. *1*:98–103, 1982.
57. Giebink, G. S., Mills, E. L., Huff, J. S., et al.: The microbiology of serous and mucoid otitis media. Pediatrics *63*:915–919, 1979.
58. Giebink, G. S., and Quie, P. G.: Otitis media: The spectrum of middle ear inflammation. Annu. Rev. Med. *29*:285–306, 1978.
59. Goldblatt, E. L., Dohar, J., Nozza, R. J., et al.: Topical ofloxacin versus systemic amoxicillin/clavulanate in purulent otorrhea in children with tympanostomy tubes. Int. J. Pediatr. Otorhinolaryngol. *46*:91–101, 1998.
60. Goo, Y. A., Hori, M. K., Voorhres, J. H., Jr, et al.: Failure to detect *Chlamydia pneumoniae* in ear fluids from children with otitis media. Pediatr. Infect. Dis. J. *14*:1000–1001, 1995.
61. Gravel, J. S., and Wallace, I. F.: Listening and language at 4 years of age: Effects of early otitis media. J. Speech Hear. Res. *35*:588–595, 1992.
62. Gray, B. M., Converse, G. M., III, and Dillon, H. C., Jr.: Serotypes of *Streptococcus pneumoniae* causing disease. J. Infect. Dis. *140*:979–983, 1979.
63. Hammerschlag, M. R., Hammerschlag, P. E., and Alexander, E. R.: The role of *Chlamydia trachomatis* in middle ear effusions in children. Pediatrics *66*:615–617, 1980.
64. Harding, A. L., Anderson, P., Howie. V. M., et al.: *Hemophilus influenzae* isolated from children with otitis media. *In* Sell, S. H., and Karzon, D. T. (eds.): *Hemophilus influenzae*. Nashville, Vanderbilt University Press, 1973.
65. Hathaway, T. J., Katz, H. P., Dershewitz, R. A., et al.: Acute otitis media: Who needs post-treatment follow-up? Pediatrics *94*:143, 1994.
66. Hayden, G. F., and Schwartz, R. H.: Characteristics of earache among children with acute otitis media. Am. J. Dis. Child. *139*:721–723, 1985.
67. Henderson, F. W., Collier, A. M., Sanyal, M. A., et al.: A longitudinal study of respiratory viruses and bacteria in the etiology of acute otitis media with effusion. N. Engl. J. Med. *306*:1377–1383, 1982.
68. Hendley, J. O., Sande, M. A., Stewart, P. M., et al.: Spread of *Streptococcus pneumoniae* in families: Carriage rates and distribution of types. J. Infect. Dis. *132*:55–68, 1975.
69. Hesselvik, L.: Respiratory infections among children in day nurseries. Acta. Paediatr. Scand. *74*(Suppl.):33–103, 1949.
70. Howie, V. M.: Eradication of bacterial pathogens from middle ear infections. Clin. Infect. Dis. *14*(Suppl. 2):209–210, 1992.
71. Howie, V. M.: Otitis media. Pediatr. Rev. *18*:320–323, 1993.
72. Howie, V. M., and Ploussard, J. H.: Bacterial etiology and antimicrobial treatment of exudative otitis media: Relation of antibiotic therapy to relapses. South. Med. J. *64*:233–239, 1971.
73. Howie, V. M., Ploussard, J. H., and Lester, R. L., Jr.: Otitis media: A clinical and bacteriological correlation. Pediatrics *45*:29–35, 1970.
74. Howie, V. M., and Ploussard, J. H.: The "in vivo" sensitivity test: Bacteriology of middle ear exudate during antimicrobial therapy in otitis media. Pediatrics *44*:940–944, 1969.
75. Howie, V. M., Ploussard, J. H., and Sloyer, J. The "otitis-prone" condition. Am. J. Dis. Child. *129*:676–678, 1975.
76. Howie, V. M., and Schwartz, R. H.: Acute otitis media: One year in general pediatric practice. Am. J. Dis. Child. *137*:155–158, 1983.
77. Ingvarsson, L., Lundgren, A., and Oloffson, B.: Epidemiology of acute otitis media in children: A cohort study in an urban population. *In* Lim, D. J., Bluestone, C. D., Klein, J. O., et al. (eds.): Recent Advances in Otitis Media with Effusion. Philadelphia, Decker, 1984, pp. 19–22.
78. Jung, T. T. K., Smith, D. M., Juhn, S. K., et al.: Prostaglandins and otitis media: Studies in the chinchilla. Otolaryngol. Head Neck Surg. *88*:316–323, 1980.
79. Jung, T. T. K., Juhn, S. K., and Michael, A. F.: Localization of prostaglandin-forming cyclooxygenase in middle ear and external canal tissue. Otolaryngol. Head Neck Surg. *91*:187–192, 1983.
80. Kamme, C., Ageberg, M., and Lundgren, K.: Distribution of *Diplococcus pneumoniae* types in acute otitis media in children and influence of the types on the clinical course in penicillin V therapy. Scand. J. Infect. Dis. *2*:183–190, 1970.
81. Kaplan, G. J., Fleshman, J. K., Bender, T. R., et al.: Long-term effects of otitis media: A 10-year cohort study of Alaskan Eskimo children. Pediatrics *52*:577–585, 1973.
82. Kaplan, S. L., Mason, E. O., Wald, E. R., et al.: Pneumococcal mastoiditis in children. Pediatrics *106*:695–699, 2000.
83. Kenna, M. A., and Bluestone, C. D.: Microbiology of chronic suppurative otitis media in children. Pediatr. Infect. Dis. *5*:223–225, 1986.
84. Kilpi, T., Herva, E., Kaijalainen, T., et al.: Bacteriology of acute otitis media in a cohort of Finnish children followed for the first two years of life. Pediatr. Infect. Dis. J. *20*:654–662, 2001.
85. Kim, P. E., Musher, D. M., Glezen, W. P. et al.: Association of invasive pneumococcal disease with season, atmosphere conditions, air pollution and the isolation of respiratory viruses. Clin. Infect. Dis. *22*:100–106, 1996.
86. Klein, B. S., Dollete, F. R., and Yolken, R. H.: The role of respiratory syncytial virus and other viral pathogens in acute otitis media. J. Pediatr. *101*:16–20, 1982.
87. Klein, J. O.: Microbiologic efficacy of antibacterial drugs for acute otitis media. Pediatr. Infect. Dis. *12*:973–975, 1993.
88. Klein, J. O.: Preventing recurrent otitis: What role for antibiotics? Contemp. Pediatr. *11*:44–60, 1994.
89. Klein, J. O.: Review of consensus reports on management of acute otitis media. Pediatr. Infect. Dis. J. *18*:1150–1153, 1999.
90. Klein, J. O.: The burden of otitis media. Vaccine *19*:S2–S8, 2001.
91. Klein, J. O., and Teele, D. W.: Isolation of viruses and mycoplasmas from middle ear effusions: A review. Ann. Otol. Rhinol. Laryngol. *85*(Suppl. 25):140–144, 1976.
92. Kovatch, A. L., Wald, E. R., and Michaels, R. H.: β-Lactamase-producing *Branhamella catarrhalis* causing otitis media in children. J. Pediatr. *102*:261–263, 1983.
93. Leinonen, M. K.: Detection of pneumococcal capsular polysaccharide antigens by latex agglutination, counterimmunoelectrophoresis, and radioimmunoassay in middle ear exudates in acute otitis media. J. Clin. Microbiol. *11*:135–140, 1980.
94. Lim, D. J., Bluestone, C. D., Saunders, W. H., et al.: Report of research committee on middle ear effusions. Ann. Otol. Rhinol. Laryngol. *85*(Suppl. 25):1–295, 1976.
95. Lim, D. J., and Saunders, W. H.: Acquired cholesteatoma: Light and electron microscopic observations. Ann. Otol. Rhinol. Laryngol. *81*:1–11, 1972.
96. Loda, F. A., Collier, A. M., Glezen, W. P., et al.: Occurrence of *Diplococcus pneumoniae* in the upper respiratory tract of children. J. Pediatr. *87*:1087–1093, 1975.
97. Long, S. S., Heuretig, F. M., Teter, M. J., et al.: Nasopharyngeal flora and acute otitis media. Infect. Immunol. *41*:987–991, 1983.

98. Lundman, L., Juhn, S. K., Bagger-Sjoback, D., et al.: Permeability of the normal round window membrane to *Haemophilus influenzae* type b endotoxin. Acta. Otolaryngol. 112:524–529, 1992.
99. Luotonen, J., Herva, E., Karma, P., et al.: The bacteriology of acute otitis media in children with special reference to *Streptococcus pneumoniae* as studied by bacteriological and antigen detection methods. Scand. J. Infect. Dis. 113:177–183, 1981.
100. Magliulo, G., Vingola, G. M., Petti, R., et al.: Acute mastoiditis in pediatric age group. Int. J. Otorhinoloaryngol. *31*:147–151, 1995.
101. Makela, P. H., Leinonen, M., Pukander, J., et al.: A study of the pneumococcal vaccine in prevention of clinically acute attacks of recurrent otitis media. Rev. Infect. Dis. *3*(Suppl.):124–133, 1981.
102. Mandel, E. M., Casselbrant, M. L., Rockette, H. E., et al.: Efficacy of 20- vs. 10-day antimicrobial treatment for acute otitis media. Pediatrics *96*:5–13, 1995.
103. Mandel, E. M., Rockette, H. E., Bluestone, C. D., et al.: Myringotomy with and without tympanostomy tubes for chronic otitis media with effusion. Arch. Otolaryngol. Head Neck Surg. *115*:1217–1224, 1989.
104. Marchant, C. D., Shurin, P. A., Turczyk, V. A., et al.: Course and outcome of otitis media in early infancy: A prospective study. J. Pediatr. *104*:826–831, 1984.
105. Marchant, C. D., Shurin, P. A., Turcyzk, V. A., et al.: A randomized controlled trial of cefaclor compared with trimethoprim-sulfamethoxazole for treatment of acute otitis media. J. Pediatr. *105*:633–638, 1984.
106. McCandless, G. A., and Thomas, G. K.: Impedance audiometry as a screening procedure for middle ear disease. Trans. Am. Acad. Ophthalmol. Otolaryngol. *78*:98–102, 1974.
107. McEldowney, D., and Kessner, D. M.: Review of the literature: Epidemiology of otitis media. *In* Gloric, A., and Gerwin, K. S. (eds.): Otitis Media. Springfield, IL, Charles C Thomas, 1972.
108. McLinn, S. E.: Cefaclor in treatment of otitis media and pharyngitis in children. Am. J. Dis. Child. *134*:560–563, 1980.
109. Medical Research Council Working Party Report: Acute otitis media in general practice. Lancet *2*:510–514, 1957.
110. Meyerhoff, W. L., and Giebink, G. S.: Pathology and microbiology of otitis media. Laryngoscope *92*:273–277, 1982.
111. Mogi, G.: Secretory IgA and antibody activities in middle ear effusions. Ann Otol Rhinol Laryngol *85*(Suppl. 25):97–102, 1976.
112. Morris, P. S.: A systematic review of otitis media in Australian Aboriginal children. *In* Abstracts of the Sixth International Symposium on Recent Advances in Otitis Media, Fort Lauderdale, June 4–8, 1995, p. 11.
113. Mortimer, E. A., Jr., and Watterson, R. L., Jr.: A bacteriologic investigation of otitis media in infancy. Pediatrics *17*:359–366, 1956.
114. Murwitz, E. S., Gunn, W. J., Pinsky, P. F., et al.: Risk of respiratory illness associated with day-care attendance: A nationwide study. Pediatrics *87*:62–69, 1991.
115. Niemela, M., Uhari, M., and Mottonen, M.: A pacifier increases the risk of recurrent acute otitis media in children in day care centers. Pediatrics *96*:884–888, 1995.
116. Nozza, R. J., Bluestone, C. D., Kardatzke, D., et al.: Towards the validation of aural acoustic immittance measures for the diagnosis of middle ear effusion in children. Ear Hearing *13*:442–453, 1992.
117. Ogawa, H., Fujisawa, T., and Kazuyama, Y.: Isolation of *Chlamydia pneumoniae* from middle ear aspirates of otitis media with effusion: A case report. J. Infect. Dis. *162*:1000–1001, 1990.
118. Papastavros, T., Giamarellou, H., and Varlejides, S.: Role of aerobic and anaerobic microorganisms in chronic suppurative otitis media. Laryngoscope *96*:438–442, 1986.
119. Paradise, J. L., and Bluestone, C. D.: Early treatment of the universal otitis media of infants with cleft palate. Pediatrics *53*:48–54, 1974.
120. Paradise, J. L., Bluestone, C. D., and Felder, H.: The universality of otitis media in 50 infants with cleft palate. Pediatrics *44*:35–42, 1969.
121. Paradise, J. L., Elster, B. A., and Tan, L. Evidence in infants with cleft palate that breast milk protects against otitis media. Pediatrics *94*:853, 1994.
122. Paradise, J. L., Feldman, H. M., Colborn, D. K., et al.: Parental stress and parent-rated child behavior in relation to otitis media in the first three years of life. Pediatrics *104*:1264–1273, 1999.
123. Paradise, J. L., Feldman, H. M., Campbell, T. F., et al.: Effect of early or delayed insertion of tympanostomy tubes for persistent otitis media on developmental outcomes at the age of three years. N. Engl. J. Med. *334*:1179–1187, 2001.
124. Paradise, J. L., Rockette, H. E., Colburn, D. K., et al.: Otitis media in 2253 Pittsburgh-area infants: Prevalence and risk factors during the first two years of life. Pediatrics *99*:318–333, 1997.
125. Paradise, J. L., Smith, C. G., and Bluestone, C. D.: Tympanometric detection of middle ear effusion in infants and young children. Pediatrics *56*:198–210, 1976.
126. Paradise, J. L., Bluestone, C. D., Rogers, K. D., et al.: Efficacy of adenoidectomy for recurrent otitis media in children previously treated with tympanostomy tube placement: Results of parallel randomized and nonrandomized trials. J. A. M. A. *263*:2066–2073, 1990.
127. Paradise, J. L., Bluestone, C. D., Colburn, D. K., et al.: Adenoidectomy and tonsillectomy for recurrent acute otitis media: Parallel randomized and nonrandomized trials. J. A. M. A. *263*:2066–2073, 1990.
128. Pelton, S. I., Teele, D. W., Shurin, P. A., et al.: Disparate cultures of middle ear fluids in bacterial otitis media. Am. J. Dis. Child. *134*:951–953, 1980.
129. Persico, M., Barker, G. A., and Mitchell, D. P.: Purulent otitis media: A "silent" source of sepsis in the pediatric intensive care unit. Otolaryngol. Head Neck Surg. *93*:330, 1985.
130. Petersen, C. G., Oveson, T., and Petersen, C. B.: Acute mastoidectomy in a Danish county from 1977 to 1996 with focus on the bacteriology. Int. J. Pediatr. Otorhinolaryngol. *45*:21–29, 1998.
131. Pitkaranta, A., Jero, J., Aruda, E., et al.: Polymerase chain reaction–based detection of rhinovirus, respiratory syncytial virus and coronavirus in otitis media with effusion. J. Pediatr. *133*:390–394, 1998.
132. Pitkaranta, A., Virolainen, A., Jero, J., et al.: Detection of rhinovirus, respiratory syncytial virus and coronavirus infections in acute otitis media by reverse transcriptase polymerase chain reaction. Pediatrics *102*:291–299, 1998.
133. Post, J. C., Preston, R. A., Aul, J. J., et al.: Molecular analysis of bacterial pathogens in otitis media with effusion. J. A. M. A. *273*:1598–1604, 1995.
134. Poulsen, G., and Tos, M.: Screening tympanometry in newborn infants and during the first six months of life. Scand. Audiol. *7*:159–166, 1978.
135. Pukander, J., Luotonen, J., Sipila, M., et al.: Incidence of acute otitis media. Acta. Otolaryngol. *93*:447–453, 1982.
136. Reed, D., and Brody, J.: Otitis media in urban Alaska. Alaska Med. *8*:64–67, 1966.
137. Renvall, U., and Holmquist, J.: Tympanometry revealing middle ear pathology. Ann. Otol. Rhinol. Laryngol. *85*(Suppl. 25):209–215, 1976.
138. Riding, K. H., Bluestone, C. D., Michaels, R. H., et al.: Microbiology of recurrent and chronic otitis media with effusion. J. Pediatr. *93*:739–743, 1978.
139. Rifkind, D. R., Chanock, R., Kranetz, H., et al.: Ear involvement (myringitis) and primary atypical pneumonia following inoculation of volunteers with Eaton agent. Am. Rev. Respir. Dis. *85*:479–489, 1962.
140. Ruuskanen, O., Arola, M., Heikkinen, T., et al.: Viruses in acute otitis media: Increasing evidence for clinical significance. Pediatr. Infect. Dis. J. *10*:425, 1991.
141. Ruedi, L.: Cholesteatoma formation in the middle ear in animal experiments. Acta. Otolaryngol. *50*:233–242, 1959.
142. Sanyal, M. A., Henderson, F. W., Stempel, E. C., et al.: Effect of upper respiratory tract infection on eustachian tube ventilatory function in the preschool child. J. Pediatr. *97*:11–15, 1980.
143. Sarkkinen, H., Ruuskanen, I., Meurman, O., et al.: Identification of respiratory virus antigens in middle ear fluids of children with acute otitis media. J. Infect. Dis. *151*:444–448, 1985.
144. Schaefer, O.: Otitis media and bottle feeding. An epidemiological study of infant feeding habits and incidence of recurrent and chronic middle ear disease in Canadian Eskimos. Can. J. Public Health *62*:478–489, 1971.
145. Schneider ML. Bacteriology of otorrhea from tympanostomy tubes. Arch. Otolaryngol. Head Neck Surg. *115*:1225–1226, 1989.
146. Schwartz, B., Giebink, G. S., Henderson, F. W., et al.: Respiratory infections in day care. Pediatrics *84*:1018–1020, 1994.
147. Schwartz, R. H., and Rodriguez, W. J.: Acute otitis media in children eight years old and older: A reappraisal of the role of *Hemophilus influenzae*. Am. J. Otolaryngol. *2*:19–21, 1981.
148. Schwartz, R. H., Rodriguez, W. J., Brook, I., et al.: The febrile response in acute otitis media. J. A. M. A. *245*:2057–2058, 1981.
149. Schwartz, R. H., Rodriguez, W. J., Khan, W. N., et al.: Acute purulent otitis media in children older than 5 years: Incidence of *Hemophilus* as a causative organism. J. A. M. A. *238*:1032–1033, 1977.
150. Senturia, B. H.: Classification of middle ear effusion. Ann. Otol. Rhinol. Laryngol. *79*:358–370, 1970.
151. Schappert, S. M.: Office visits for otitis media: United States, 1975–90. From Vital and Health Statistics of the Centers for Disease Control/National Center for Health Statistics *214*:1–18, 1992.
152. Shurin, P. A., Howie, V. M., Pelton, S. I., et al.: Bacterial etiology of otitis media during the first 6 weeks of life. J. Pediatr. *92*:893–896, 1978.
153. Shurin, P. A., Marchant, C. D., Kim, C. H., et al.: Emergence of beta-lactamase-producing strains of *Branhamella catarrhalis* as important agents of acute otitis media. Pediatr. Infect. Dis. *2*:34–38, 1983.
154. Sipila, M., Karma, P., Pukander, J., et al.: The Bayesian approach to the evaluation of risk factors in acute and recurrent acute otitis media. Acta. Otolaryngol. *106*:94–101, 1988.
155. Sipila, M., Pukander, J., and Karma, P.: Incidence of acute otitis media up to the age of 1½ years in urban infants. Acta. Otolaryngol. *104*:138–145, 1987.
156. Skolnik, P. R., Nadol, J. B., Jr., and Baker, A. S.: Tuberculosis of the middle ear: Review of the literature with an instructive case report. Rev. Infect. Dis. *8*:403, 1986.
157. Skoner, D. P., Stillwagon, P. K., Casselbrandt, M. L., et al.: Inflammatory mediators in chronic otitis media with effusion. Arch. Otolaryngol. Head Neck Surg. *114*:1131–1133, 1988.
158. Sloyer, J. L., Jr., Cate, C. C., Howie, V. M., et al.: Immune response to acute otitis media in children. II. Serum and middle ear fluid antibody in otitis media due to *H. influenzae*. J. Infect. Dis. *132*:685–688, 1975.

159. Sloyer, J. L., Jr., Ploussard, J. H., and Howie, V. M.: Efficacy of pneumococcal polysaccharide vaccine in preventing acute otitis media in infants in Huntsville, Alabama. Rev. Infect. Dis. *3*(Suppl.):119–123, 1981.
160. Spivey, G. H., and Hirschhorn, N.: A migrant study of adopted Apache children. Johns Hopkins Med. J. *140*:43–46, 1977.
161. Sriwardhana, K. B., Howard, A. J., and Dunkin, K. T.: Bacteriology of otitis media with effusion. J. Laryngol. Otol. *103*:253–256, 1989.
162. Stool, S. E., Berg, A. O., Berman, S., et al.: Otitis Media with Effusion in Young Children: Clinical Practice Guideline. Number 12. AHCPR Publication No. 94-0622. Rockville, MD, Agency for Health Care Policy and Research, Public Health Service, U.S. Department of Health and Human Services, July 1994.
163. Stool, S. E., Berg, A. O., Berman, S., et al.: Otitis Media with Effusion in Young Children: Clinical Practice Guideline. Number 12. AHCPR Publication No. 94-0622. Rockville, MD, Agency for Health Care Policy and Research, Public Health Service, U.S. Department of Health and Human Services, July 1994, p. 48.
164. Stool, S. E., Berg, A. O., Berman, S., et al.: Otitis Media with Effusion in Young Children: Clinical Practice Guideline Number 12. AHCPR Publication No. 94-0622. Rockville, MD, Agency for Health Care Policy and Research, Public Health Service, U.S. Department of Health and Human Services, July 1994, p. 52.
165. Teele, D. W., Klein, J. O., et al., for the Greater Boston Collaborative Otitis Media Study Group: Use of pneumococcal vaccine for prevention of recurrent acute otitis media in infants in Boston. Rev. Infect. Dis. *3*(Suppl.):113–118, 1981.
166. Teele, D. W., Klein, J. O., Chase, C., et al.: Otitis media in infancy and intellectual ability, school achievement, speech, and language at age 7 years. J. Infect. Dis. *162*:685–694, 1990.
167. Teele, D. W., Klein, J. O., and Rosner, B. A.: Epidemiology of otitis media in children. Ann. Otol. Rhinol. Laryngol. *89*(Suppl. 68):5–6, 1980.
168. Teele, D. W., Klein, J. O., Rosner, B., et al.: Middle ear disease and the practice of pediatrics. J. A. M. A. *249*:1026–1029, 1983.
169. Teele, D. W., Klein, J. O., Rosner, B., et al.: Epidemiology of otitis media during the first seven years of life in children in greater Boston: A prospective cohort study. J. Infect. Dis. *160*:83–94, 1989.
170. Tetzlaff, T. R., Ashworth, C., and Nelson, J.D.: Otitis media in children less than 12 weeks of age. Pediatrics *59*:827–832, 1977.
171. Tipple, M. A., Beem, M. O., and Saxon, E. M.: Clinical characteristics of the afebrile pneumonia associated with *Chlamydia trachomatis* infection in infants less than 6 months of age. Pediatrics *63*:192–197, 1979.
172. Tos, M., Poulson, G., and Hancke, A. B.: Screening tympanometry during the first year of life. Acta. Otolaryngol. *88*:388–394, 1979.
173. U.S. Department of Health and Human Services: The health consequences of smoking: A report from the Surgeon General. Department of Health. Human Services Publication (DHS)84-50205. Rockville, MD, Office on Smoking and Health, 1984, p. 292.
174. van Buchem, F. L., Dunk, J. H. M., and van't Hof, M. A.: Therapy of acute otitis media: Myringotomy, antibiotics or neither? A double-blind study in children. Lancet *2*:883–887, 1981.
175. van Buchem, F. L., Peeters, M. F., and van't Hof, M. A.: Acute otitis media: A new treatment strategy. Br. Med. J. *290*:1033–1037, 1985.
176. Van Hare, G. F., Shurin, P. A., Marchant, C. D., et al.: Acute otitis media caused by *Branhamella catarrhalis*: Biology and therapy. Rev. Infect. Dis. *9*:16–27, 1987.
177. Varsano, I. B., Volovitz, B. M., and Grossman, J. E.: Effect of naproxen, a prostaglandin inhibitor, on acute otitis media and persistence of middle ear effusion in children. Ann. Otol. Rhinol. Laryngol. *98*:389–392, 1989.
178. Veltri, R. W., and Sprinkle, P. M.: Secretory otitis media: An immune complex disease. Ann. Otol. Rhinol. Laryngol. *85*(Suppl. 25):135–319, 1976.
179. Wald, E. R., Dashefsky, B., Byers, C., et al.: Frequency and severity of infections in day care. J. Pediatr. *112*:540–564, 1988.
180. Weiderhold, M. L., Zajtchuk, J. T., Vap, J. G., et al.: Hearing loss in relation to physical properties of middle ear effusions. Ann. Otol. Rhinol. Laryngol. *85*:185–189, 1980.
181. Yaniv, E.: Tuberculous otitis: An underdiagnosed disease. Am. J. Otolaryngol. *8*:356–360, 1987.

Mastoiditis

KAREN LEWIS ■ NINA L. SHAPIRO ■ JAMES D. CHERRY

Mastoiditis, a suppurative infection of the mastoid air cells, is a potential complication of all cases of otitis media caused by the continuity of the mucoperiosteal lining of the mastoid with that of the middle ear.[17] The spectrum of disease in mastoiditis ranges from asymptomatic cases with apparent spontaneous resolution to progressive disease with life-threatening complications.[6] Since the advent of antibiotic therapy, mastoiditis is seen much less frequently, but the frequency of complications remains the same.[16, 18, 63] With mastoiditis occurring less commonly, physicians are less apt to consider the diagnosis, especially when the clinical picture has been masked by antibiotic therapy or when the process is chronic and of low grade. Proper antibiotic therapy, often accompanied by surgical drainage, can halt and prevent serious complications if mastoiditis is diagnosed early.

History

Before the advent of antibiotics, mastoiditis was a frequent complication of otitis media that could be treated only by expectant waiting or surgery.[29, 31] When surgery was used, many patients with mastoiditis were cured by simple mastoid drainage alone, with a mortality rate quoted at 2 percent.[31] However, intracranial complications of mastoiditis carried a very grave prognosis. In the preantibiotic era, between 1928 and 1933, 25 of every 1000 deaths at Los Angeles County Hospital in California were caused by intracranial complications of otitis media, such as meningitis, venous sinus thrombosis, and brain abscess. In contrast, between 1949 and 1954, only 2.5 per 1000 deaths at the same hospital were caused by complications of otitis or mastoiditis. The use of antibiotics in treating mastoiditis initially led to a marked decrease in the surgical approach to treatment of this illness.[6, 63] However, the realization that infection can persist and complications of mastoiditis can occur even while the patient is receiving antibiotic therapy has resulted in the present-day combined approach of antibiotics and surgery.[18, 22, 40, 44]

Bacteriology

The bacteriology of acute mastoiditis differs somewhat from that of acute otitis media (Table 20–1). In acute otitis media, *Streptococcus pneumoniae* is the most frequent pathogen isolated (30%), with *Haemophilus influenzae* being the second most common (22%), *Moraxella catarrhalis* being the third most common (7%), and group A beta-hemolytic streptococci being a distant fourth (2%) (see Chapter 19). However, studies on acute mastoiditis (defined as symptoms of less than 1 month's duration) show that whereas *S. pneumoniae* still is the first most common isolate, *Streptococcus pyogenes* and *Staphylococcus aureus* are the second and third most common isolates, respectively.[16, 22, 25, 40, 44] *H. influenzae* has been isolated from the middle ear of

TABLE 20–1 ■ SUMMARY OF BACTERIAL ISOLATES FROM THE MIDDLE EAR, SUBPERIOSTEAL ABSCESS, OR MASTOID OF CHILDREN WITH MASTOIDITIS IN FIVE STUDIES

	Acute Mastoiditis				Chronic Mastoiditis
Isolates	**Ginsburg et al.[16]**	**Hoppe et al.[25]**	**Ogle and Lauer[44]**	**Nadal et al.[40]**	**Brook[4]**
Streptococcus pneumoniae	14	13	7	9	1
Streptococcus pyogenes	8	4	3	4	2
Staphylococcus aureus	8	2	2	4	8
Haemophilus influenzae	1	—	3	1	—
Pseudomonas species	2	—	1	3	7
Other gram-negative bacilli	1	1	—	1	7
Anaerobes	2	—	3	2	61
Mycobacterium tuberculosis	1	—	—	—	—
Staphylococcus epidermidis	1	2	5	—	—
Streptococcus viridans	1	—	1	—	—
Candida albicans	—	—	1	—	—
Other	4*	—	2†	—	4‡
Total no. of patients	57	28	30	54	24

**Eikenella corrodens,* microaerophilic streptococci, nonenterococcal group D streptococci, group D streptococci.
†*Morganella morganii,* nonhemolytic streptococci.
‡Alpha-hemolytic streptococci.

patients with mastoiditis but less often than one would expect, given its frequent recovery in acute otitis media without mastoiditis. Gram-negative bacteria, enterococci, anaerobes, and *Mycobacterium tuberculosis* also have been isolated occasionally in patients with acute mastoiditis.

Chronic mastoiditis has a bacteriologic spectrum different from that of acute mastoiditis. Aerobic cultures of chronic mastoiditis and chronic otitis media both show predominantly *S. aureus* and gram-negative bacilli, especially *Pseudomonas aeruginosa.*[4, 12, 49] In addition, a wide variety of anaerobic organisms can be isolated from an infected mastoid and middle ear.[4, 12] Brook[4] studied the aerobic and anaerobic bacteriology of chronic otitis media (of at least 3 months' duration) in 24 children. Anaerobic isolates alone were found in 17 percent, aerobic organisms alone in 4 percent, and mixed aerobic and anaerobic infections in 79 percent. All cases had from two to seven different bacterial isolates. *Peptococcus* spp., *Actinomyces* spp., and *Bacteroides melaninogenicus* (*Prevotella melaninogenica*) were the anaerobic organisms isolated most commonly. Of note is that 17 patients were infected with β-lactamase–producing organisms (i.e., *S. aureus* or *P. melaninogenica, Bacteroides fragilis,* or other *Bacteroides* spp. that were resistant to ampicillin).

M. tuberculosis currently is an uncommon cause of mastoiditis in the United States but still is a cause of chronically draining ears in lower socioeconomic groups and immigrants from endemic areas.[38] Case reports of mastoiditis implicate such organisms as nontuberculous mycobacteria,[43] *Aspergillus fumigatus,*[20] *Paragonimus*-like trematodes,[45] *Nocardia asteroides,*[36] *Actinomyces* spp.,[54] *Blastomyces dermatitidis,*[27] and *Histoplasma capsulatum.*[36] *Pneumocystis carinii* otitis media and mastoiditis have occurred as the first manifestation of acquired immunodeficiency syndrome.[15]

Anatomy and Pathophysiology

The mastoid process comprises the posterior part of the temporal bone and, as such, is adjacent to many important structures. Within the mastoid is an interconnecting system of air cells divided by bony septa that drain superiorly into the middle ear by way of a narrow aditus.[6, 17] Only the superior portion of the mastoid air space, the antrum, is present at birth; pneumatization of the mastoid starts soon after birth and usually is completed well by the time the child reaches 2 years of age.[3, 31] Structures lying anteromedial to the mastoid process include the middle ear and ossicles, the facial nerve, the posterior bony wall of the external auditory canal, the jugular vein, and the internal carotid artery. Posteromedially, the mastoid borders the posterior cranial fossa and the sigmoid sinus. Superiorly, the mastoid borders the middle cranial fossa. Medially, the mastoid cortex encases the cochlea and semicircular canals. The soft tissues and muscles of the lateral neck are located inferiorly. Any or all of these adjacent structures can be affected by extension of a suppurative process in the mastoid.

A certain amount of mastoid inflammation accompanies all cases of otitis media because the mastoid air spaces are continuous with the middle ear cavity and both are lined by a continuous mucoperiosteum.[3, 17] The first stage of an ear and mastoid infection is associated with hyperemia of the middle ear and the mastoid air cell mucosa. If the infection persists, an exudative stage develops, with serum, fibrin, polymorphonuclear cells, and red blood cells accumulating in the middle ear and mastoid. The accumulation of purulent exudate increases the middle ear pressure, eventually resulting in perforation of the tympanic membrane, followed by mucopurulent drainage from the middle ear and mastoid air cells. Some children also have such marked mucoperiosteal swelling that the drainage of pus from the mastoid is blocked. The pus under pressure creates an environment of local acidosis, hypoxia, and ischemia, causing decalcification and resorption of the bony septa. The term *coalescent mastoiditis* is applied to this process because with the destruction of the bony septa, the mastoid air cells coalesce into large cavities. Osteomyelitis of the adjacent bone may develop, with subsequent bony erosion and eventual extension of the infection into surrounding structures.[3, 17]

Congenital cholesteatomas usually present as a "squamous pearl" in the anterosuperior quadrant of the middle ear, abutting the tympanic membrane. They may be associated with recurrent otitis media.[35] Acquired cholesteatomas, on the other hand, often are a result of chronic infections and tympanic membrane perforation. The perforation allows for squamous material from the external auditory canal to enter the middle ear space.[46] This tissue contains osteolytic enzymes, leading to bony erosion or mastoid air cell obstruction.[41] Cholesteatomas also may cause slow, insidious erosion of underlying bone, predisposing to extramastoid spread of infection months or years later.[17, 49]

Clinical Presentation

The classic presentation of acute mastoiditis is a febrile child with ear pain, postauricular swelling, and postauricular tenderness developing days to weeks after the beginning of acute otitis media (Fig. 20–1).[16, 40, 44] If antibiotics were used to treat the otitis media, the child may have appeared to improve, only to become ill again while still receiving therapy or once the antibiotics were stopped; conversely, the child may not have responded to the antibiotics at all. Examination of the tympanic membrane in acute mastoiditis usually shows that it is abnormal.[16, 22, 40] Early in the course of illness, periosteal inflammation will produce swelling and tenderness and sometimes redness over the mastoid process.[3, 16] Palpable postauricular fluctuance occurs later, when pus from the mastoid air cells breaks through the underlying bony cortex and forms a subperiosteal abscess.[21] In children older than 1 year of age, the most common area where fluctuance is felt lies behind the ear, where it pushes the earlobe up and out; however, in children younger than 1 year of age, the fluctuance often may present above the ear, pushing the pinna down and out.[16]

Chronic mastoiditis is a much more indolent disease process than is acute mastoiditis. It develops when longstanding middle ear disease, usually over months to years, has been present.[49] Fever and postauricular swelling may or may not be present. Persistent or intermittent mucopurulent drainage from a previously perforated eardrum is very suggestive of chronic mastoiditis. Hearing loss and ear pain also may accompany chronic mastoiditis.[49] All these symptoms can be mild enough to be ignored until serious intracranial suppuration occurs. Persistent ear drainage, persistent ear pain, or an otitis media nonresponsive to antibiotics should prompt a search for mastoiditis.

Complications

Complications of mastoiditis include subperiosteal abscess,[21] Bezold abscess,[13] facial nerve paralysis,[57] meningitis,[6, 16] brain abscess,[6, 16] cerebellar abscess,[3] epidural abscess,[3] subdural empyema, labyrinthitis,[17] venous sinus thrombophlebitis,[11] bacteremia,[6, 37] benign intracranial hypertension, osteomyelitis of the temporal bone with occasional extension to adjacent bones,[3, 17] hearing loss,[47] septic pulmonary emboli,[26] and cerebrospinal fluid otorrhea.[17]

Subperiosteal abscesses appear as a postauricular fluctuant mass that obscures the postauricular sulcus. They occur when pus in the mastoid breaks through the bony cortex or extends along vascular channels and dissects under the overlying periosteum.[21]

A Bezold abscess develops when a mastoid infection erodes through the bony cortex of the inferior aspect of the mastoid tip and dissects down the tissue planes to form a deep neck abscess. Fluctuance over the mastoid is not felt. Rather, swelling and tenderness are present below the mastoid process and under the sternocleidomastoid muscle.[13]

The facial nerve runs close to the mastoid and the middle ear, rendering it vulnerable to injury when extension of mastoid or middle ear infection occurs.[17] Pressure on and inflammation of the facial nerve from symptomatic or asymptomatic mastoiditis can lead to transient or permanent facial nerve paralysis that usually is unilateral, although bilateral facial palsy from mastoiditis can occur.[3, 57]

Because the temporal bone that houses the mastoid air cells constitutes the floor of the middle and posterior cranial fossa, bony erosion from osteomyelitis, preexisting bony defects, or spread of infection along vascular channels can allow for intracranial spread of mastoid infections into the middle and posterior cranial fossae. The infection may remain confined to the extradural space as an extradural abscess or may penetrate the dura and produce a subdural empyema, a brain abscess, a cerebellar abscess, or meningitis.[3, 5, 17]

Invasion of infection into the bony labyrinth through the oval or round window will trigger a labyrinthitis, with initial tinnitus, hearing loss, nausea, and dizziness progressing to severe vertigo, ear pain, vomiting, nystagmus, and balance difficulties.[17]

Intracranial venous sinus thrombophlebitis is a rare but potentially fatal complication of mastoiditis.[3, 17, 55] The lateral aspect of the sigmoid sinus is formed by the temporal bone. Therefore, venous sinus thrombophlebitis results when an underlying mastoiditis extends through the temporal bone in close proximity to the lateral or sigmoid venous

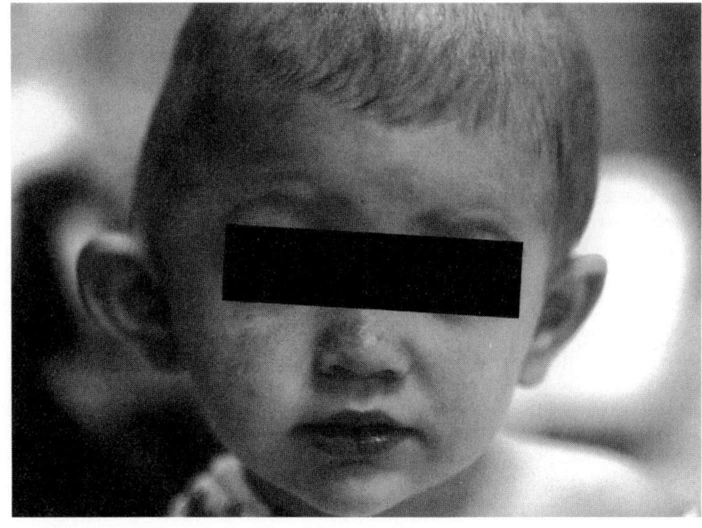

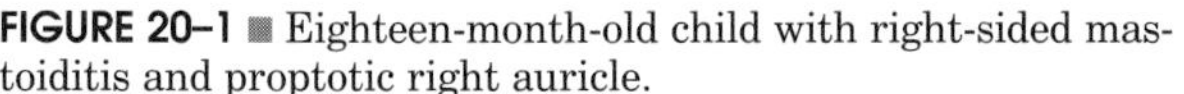

FIGURE 20–1 ■ Eighteen-month-old child with right-sided mastoiditis and proptotic right auricle.

sinus. A perisinus abscess initially is formed, followed by formation of a mural thrombus in the sinus wall. The thrombus eventually may occlude the entire sinus, or it may suppurate and spread along the sinus, resulting in septicemia, increased intracranial pressure, septic emboli, and extension of infection to other intracranial structures.[11, 14] The classic findings of a septic thrombosis of the lateral sinus are spiking fevers, shaking chills, and tenderness along the jugular vein associated with acute or chronic otitis. A palpable "cord" at the jugular vein (indicating a jugular vein thrombus) also may be present. However, when only a perisinus abscess is present or if the patient is being treated partially with antibiotics, the only symptoms may be a low-grade fever and headache.[19, 55]

Benign intracranial hypertension can be seen in association with lateral sinus obstruction secondary to mastoiditis and is termed *otitic hydrocephalus*. On rare occasions, otitic hydrocephalus can be seen with mastoiditis in the absence of lateral sinus thrombosis. The decreased venous drainage caused by the venous sinus obstruction results in increased intracranial pressure, headache, papilledema, and sixth nerve palsy without enlarged ventricles or a space-occupying lesion.[17, 19]

Permanent conductive hearing loss occurs when the middle ear mastoid infection is severe enough to damage or destroy the ossicles. Tuberculous mastoiditis classically presents with marked conductive hearing loss that often is not reversible.

Osteomyelitis secondary to mastoiditis can spread to adjacent bones. Involvement of the petrous portion of the temporal bone produces a syndrome that was described by Gradenigo in 1907 with a triad of abducens paralysis or paresis, severe pain in the distribution of the trigeminal nerve, and suppurative otitis media; additional cranial nerve deficits also may occur. Antibiotics may mask the classic signs of petrositis and allow progression to severe intracranial complications such as meningitis and epidural abscess. Petrositis may be suspected only when antibiotic and surgical management for mastoiditis fails to control chronic ear drainage.[17]

M. tuberculosis mastoiditis is uncommon but should be considered in children who have chronic ear discharge despite antibiotic therapy. Children can go for months or years with chronic draining ears before the diagnosis of tuberculous mastoiditis is considered.[5, 38] Children from lower socioeconomic homes, immigrants from endemic areas, and children with tuberculosis contacts in the family are at risk. The classic presentation in the preantibiotic era was an afebrile young child with painless persistent watery ear drainage, an enlarged preauricular lymph node, a history of tuberculosis contact, and often facial nerve paralysis.[51, 58]

However, tuberculous mastoiditis not always is painless.[60] Sometimes, the diagnosis initially is suspected only when a mastoidectomy wound does not heal.[33, 49] Early in the disease, physical examination may reveal small yellow spots (caseating granulomas) on a thickened and hyperemic tympanic membrane. These spots coalesce early and produce tympanic membrane perforations.[33] The discharge through these perforations initially is watery, but later it becomes purulent.[32] Pale, avascular granulation tissue is abundant throughout the middle ear and mastoid and often is seen in the external auditory canal and around the tympanic membrane perforation.[51, 60] Both preauricular and postauricular nontender, enlarged lymph nodes may be present,[32, 36] and early and severe hearing loss is a characteristic problem.[60] Often, evidence of tuberculosis elsewhere in the body will be present.[60] A 5-tuberculin unit purified protein derivative skin test usually, but not always, is positive.[38]

Differential Diagnosis

Postauricular swelling, a chronically draining ear, or radiographic evidence of mastoid abnormalities also can appear in other disease entities. Postauricular lymphadenopathy can occur secondary to a scalp infection, causing postauricular swelling. However, the swelling would be discrete, would not displace the pinna, and would not obliterate the postauricular sulcus.[16] Severe otitis externa may lead to periauricular cellulitis, with postauricular swelling, erythema, and tenderness.[24] Mumps can cause parotid swelling, pushing the earlobe up and out, but the swelling is over the parotid gland rather than located postauricularly. Histiocytosis,[34] acute lymphocytic leukemia,[39] acute myelogenous leukemia,[56] Burkitt lymphoma,[59] aneurysmal bone cysts,[9] and other benign and malignant tumors of the mastoid bone[8] also can present with symptoms clinically suggestive of mastoiditis. Kawasaki disease may mimic acute mastoiditis with postauricular lymph node swelling and ear pain.[50] Children with severe and recurrent ear infections may have an underlying congenital or acquired immunodeficiency.

Specific Diagnosis

The diagnosis of mastoiditis can be made on clinical grounds alone when a child has an acute episode of fever, otitis media, and posterior auricular tenderness and fluctuance. Mastoiditis is much less suspect when swelling and tenderness over the mastoid process are absent, such as when an infection has been masked by antibiotic treatment or when it has extended to an area other than over the mastoid process. Mastoiditis needs to be considered in all cases of otitis media not responding to antibiotics and in all intracranial suppurative diseases that do not have an apparent focus.

Obtaining an aspirate from the middle ear is an important part of properly diagnosing and managing mastoiditis. Gram stains of aspirates from the middle ear are quite accurate and, as such, can help in the initial selection of antibiotic therapy for chronic mastoiditis. Brook[4] found that in 24 children with tympanocentesis, one half of the Gram stains showed a complete correlation with subsequent culture results and the other half showed a partial correlation (one bacterial species was not seen). Leukocytes were seen on all the Gram stains. In addition, cultures from the middle ear accurately reflect mastoid disease.[16, 37]

Ginsburg and associates[16] compared the results of cultures of middle ear aspirates and mastoid cultures in 16 of their patients with acute mastoiditis and found that the same bacterial species was isolated from both sites. A sterile aspiration through an intact tympanic membrane gives the most accurate culture information. If the tympanic membrane is perforated, the purulent drainage may be contaminated by colonizing ear canal flora. However, an aspirate for culture generally should be obtained from the ear drainage, preferably from as close to the perforation as possible. Aspiration of postauricular fluctuance also is useful in identifying the responsible organisms.[21, 44] In addition, specimens should be obtained directly from the mastoid at surgery. All of them should be sent for both aerobic and anaerobic cultures with proper anaerobic transport technique. If the child has had a chronic ear infection or if the child is in a high-risk population for acquiring tuberculosis, mycobacterial stains and cultures also should be obtained, and a purified protein derivative should be placed.

A lumbar puncture should be performed if the clinical presentation is suggestive of meningeal irritation; a computed tomographic (CT) scan should be taken before performing the lumbar puncture if papilledema or a suggestion of focal intracranial extension is present. Lymphocytosis of the cerebrospinal fluid suggests a parameningeal focus of infection. An immunologic evaluation should be considered if a child has had recurrent episodes of otitis media leading to mastoiditis.

Peripheral white blood cell counts in mastoiditis may be normal or elevated, often with an increase in band-form neutrophils.[22, 40] The erythrocyte sedimentation rate often is elevated in acute mastoiditis, but in chronic mastoiditis, it usually is within normal limits.[47]

Mastoiditis often can be diagnosed on clinical findings alone. However, when a patient is not improving on medical therapy, radiologic imaging of the temporal bone is needed.

Changes in the temporal bone are seen best by CT scan.[52] Early in the course of mastoiditis, nonspecific clouding of the middle ear and mastoid is seen. With time, necrosis and coalescence of the bony septa occur. Other CT findings in mastoiditis include hypoaeration of the mastoid and adjacent bony destruction. Figure 20–2 shows a CT scan of a child with unilateral mastoiditis complicated by lateral sinus thrombosis and elevated intracranial pressure.

Magnetic resonance imaging is valuable to search for suppurative intracranial complications of mastoiditis.[52, 53] In addition, sometimes magnetic resonance angiography is needed to diagnose sigmoid sinus thrombosis.[7]

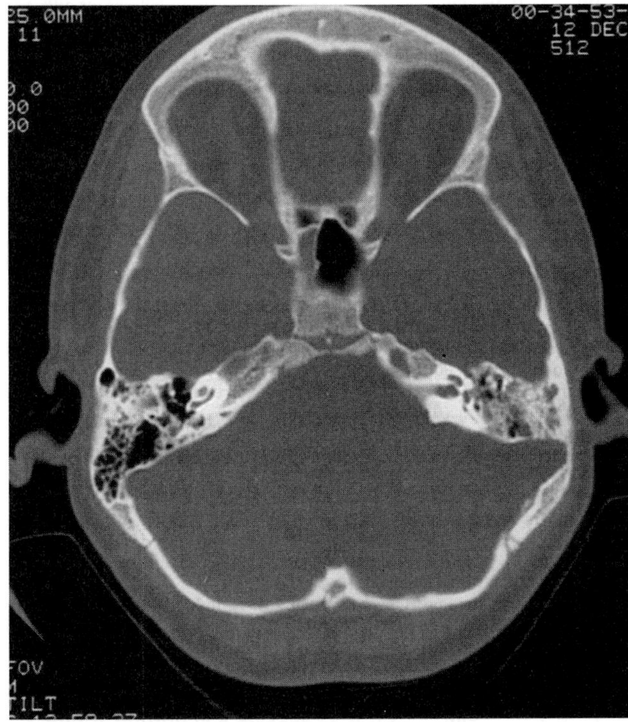

FIGURE 20–2 ■ Computed tomographic scan of the head of a 12-year-old boy with left lateral sinus thrombosis and increased intracranial pressure complicating left mastoiditis. The left mastoid air cells are opacified with marked loss of the fine bony septa, in contrast to the right mastoid air cells.

Treatment

The pediatrician and the otolaryngologist should work together on the management of a child with suspected or proven mastoiditis because all children with mastoid infections are potential surgical candidates. Some kind of drainage for the middle ear should be provided early in the course of therapy, for both therapeutic and diagnostic purposes. It could consist of tympanocentesis with subsequent tympanostomy tubes[16, 40, 44] or a myringotomy.[22] A specific etiologic diagnosis is more important today than in the past because of the increasing incidence of infections caused by penicillin-resistant pneumococci and methicillin-resistant coagulase-positive staphylococci.[1, 23, 28, 42, 48]

If the patient has an acute onset of posterior auricular swelling and tenderness with minimal or no posterior auricular fluctuance and no signs of intracranial complications, he or she is likely to respond to antibiotic therapy alone.[22, 40, 44]

Indications for surgical intervention include postauricular fluctuance; a history of chronic ear drainage with postauricular swelling or bony changes on radiographs; facial nerve palsy; nausea, vomiting, and vertigo suggestive of labyrinthitis; meningitis; brain abscess; venous sinus thrombosis with or without intracranial hypertension; epidural or subdural empyema; and petrositis. In addition, if the patient initially is treated medically, a mastoidectomy is indicated if progression of postauricular swelling or fluctuance or persistence of fever, ear pain, or purulent ear drainage occurs while the child is receiving parenteral antibiotics.[17, 22, 40, 44]

All surgical treatment should include culture of the middle ear or mastoid, either by tympanocentesis or during surgery. If a notable middle ear effusion is present, middle ear drainage and pressure equalization should be done by tympanostomy tube placement or a wide circumferential myringotomy.

If postauricular subperiosteal abscess or a Bezold abscess is present, then incision and drainage need to be performed. They should be combined with myringotomy and tube placement. In addition, consideration should be given to performing a simple mastoidectomy to remove any diseased mastoid cells or inflammatory mucosa. When a mastoidectomy is performed, a biopsy of the inflammatory tissue should be sent to exclude lesions such as eosinophilic granuloma or rhabdomyosarcoma.

For intracranial complications (such as subdural or cerebral abscess), a mastoidectomy needs to be performed. Draining the mastoid at the same time as draining the intracranial abscess has been done safely in the same operative setting.[30]

If a patient is found to have a cholesteatoma, a modified radical mastoidectomy should be performed, with complete removal of the cholesteatoma. The child with a cholesteatoma will likely need a second-look operation at a later date to monitor for recurrent disease.

Ototopical drops should be included in the postoperative care. Ciprofloxacin ear drops appear to be less toxic than are aminoglycoside drops.[10, 61, 62]

All children with mastoiditis should have audiograms. They will help to distinguish a purely conductive loss (indicative of middle ear involvement) from a sensorineural loss (a sign of inner ear involvement).

The initial choice of antibiotics for mastoiditis must be made empirically, based on the knowledge of the most likely organisms. Because acute mastoiditis most often is caused by *S. pneumoniae* or *S. pyogenes* and less often by *S. aureus* and *H. influenzae,* oxacillin (150 mg/kg/day divided every 6 hours) and cefotaxime (200 mg/kg/day divided every 6 hours) can be recommended. However, in cases of severe

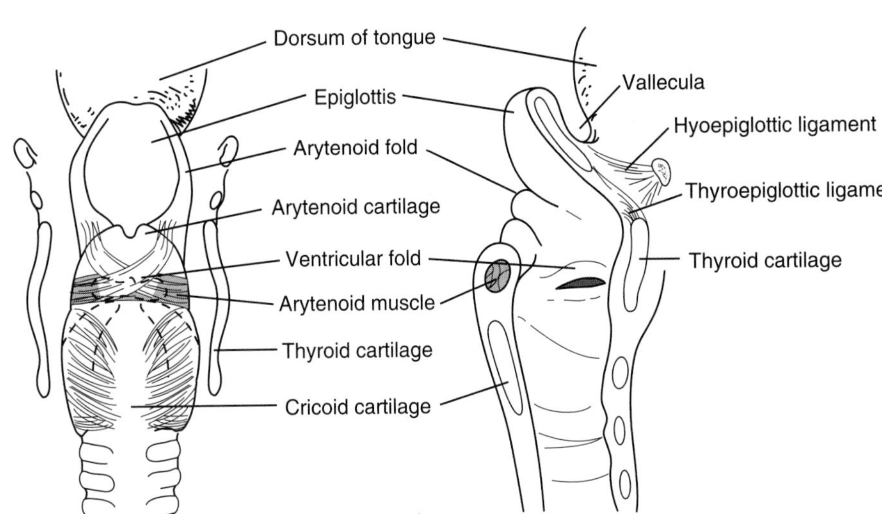

FIGURE 21–1 ■ Anatomic relationships of the supraglottic larynx, posterior view (*left*) and sagittal view (*right*).

Epiglottitis also can result from noninfectious causes. Hot foods and water can cause thermal epiglottitis, as can poisoning with corrosive agents including cocaine alkaloid.[16, 98, 102, 107]

Anatomy

The thin, elastic, leaflike epiglottic cartilage is attached to the anterior surface of the thyroid cartilage by the thyroepiglottic ligament (Fig. 21–1). The hypoepiglottic ligament also provides support, anchoring the epiglottis to the hyoid bone. The superior aspect of the epiglottis arches slightly posteriorly. Stratified squamous epithelium covers the anterior surface of the epiglottis and the superior third of the posterior portion; respiratory epithelium covers the remaining posterior surface. The stratified squamous epithelium is loosely adherent, creating a large potential space for the accumulation of inflammatory cells and edema fluid.

The arytenoepiglottic folds arise from the epiglottis and terminate posteriorly near the paired arytenoid cartilages. These structures commonly are involved in the supraglottic infection and occasionally are the site of serious disease without epiglottitis per se.[16] Immediately anterior to the epiglottis are the valleculae epiglotticae, where saliva pools before deglutition.

Pathophysiology

Supraglottic cellulitis with marked edema involving the epiglottis, arytenoepiglottic folds, ventricular bands, and arytenoids is the hallmark of this illness. As the edema increases, the epiglottis curls posteriorly and inferiorly. Inspiration tends to draw the inflamed supraglottic ring into the laryngeal inlet, whereas expiration is unopposed.[166] This "ball-valve" mechanism is thought to produce slight hypoxia without hypercapnia.[156] Diffuse infiltration with polymorphonuclear leukocytes, hemorrhage, edema, and fibrin deposition can be seen microscopically; this can progress to microabscesses, with *H. influenzae* type b occasionally seen in the tissue.[92, 151] Frank abscess formation has been documented in adults.[116, 121, 149, 154, 180, 207, 213] Infection of the supraglottic larynx may spread inferiorly to involve the paraglottic space,[81] but as a rule, neither upward extension into the laryngeal lymphatics nor downward extension into the subglottic region occurs.[18, 92]

Infection of the supraglottic structures probably arises from direct invasion by *H. influenzae* type b with subsequent development of bacteremia. The bacteremia appears to be relatively short in duration and of low concentration, as suggested by several observations: (1) the serum concentration of the capsular polysaccharide is directly proportional to the concentration and duration of bacteremia,[157] (2) children with epiglottitis have less *H. influenzae* type b capsular polysaccharide in their sera than do patients with meningitis,[203] and (3) the density of *H. influenzae* type b in blood is significantly lower in patients with epiglottitis than in patients with meningitis.[109, 155, 182] In 23 patients with epiglottitis, the geometric mean number of organisms was 123 colony-forming units (CFU)/mL, whereas the geometric mean number in 43 patients with meningitis was 2203 CFU/mL ($p < .001$).[109]

What predisposes the epiglottitis to infection is unknown. Possibly, mild trauma to the epiglottis occurs during food intake, which could result in damage to the mucosal surface, which in turn could allow the invasion of organisms that already were present in the upper respiratory tract. Also possible is that a viral infection damages the mucosal surface so that secondary bacterial infection could occur.

Acute-phase sera in most children with epiglottitis lack specific bactericidal and hemagglutinating antibody. Seroconversion regularly occurs after infection.[29, 122]

Conflicting evidence exists relating to a possible genetic difference between patients with *H. influenzae* type b epiglottitis and other individuals.[5, 77, 186, 213] Whisnant and associates[213] surveyed human leukocyte antigens (HLA) and erythrocytic antigens among 30 children with epiglottitis and 20 patients with meningitis. HLA-A11 was found in 17 and 3 percent of the patients with meningitis and epiglottitis, respectively ($p < .01$). HLA-B5 occurred in 13 and 3 percent of patients with epiglottitis and meningitis, respectively ($p < .05$), whereas B40 occurred more often (23% versus 10%) in patients with meningitis than in those with epiglottitis ($p < .05$). Moreover, the frequency of A28 and B17 antigens was higher among the patients with epiglottitis than in uninfected control subjects.[213] However, the results of another study did not confirm these observations.[77]

The distribution and frequency of MNS erythrocyte antigens in patients with epiglottitis may differ from those observed in others. For example, the NNSS genotype occurred in 6.4 percent of patients with epiglottitis and 0.5 percent of healthy control subjects ($p < .0002$),[213] but this difference was not confirmed.[77] However, the results of two studies suggest that the MNS genotype occurs less often in patients with *H. influenzae* type b meningitis than in patients with epiglottitis.[77, 213] In one study, white children with *H. influenzae* type b meningitis lacked G2m(n), an allotype antigen of IgG2 subclass heavy chains, more frequently than did control subjects.[5] In another study in a white population in Finland, however, this difference was not noted.[185] The frequency of the Km(1) immunoglobulin allotype in children with epiglottitis did not differ significantly from the prevalence of that marker in blacks or whites. However, in blacks with *H. influenzae* type b meningitis, the Km(1) marker occurred less frequently in patients than in control subjects.[77]

The identification of one outer-membrane protein subtype of *H. influenzae* type b that was associated relatively infrequently with epiglottitis suggests that isotype-specific differences in the propensity of *H. influenzae* type b to cause epiglottitis may exist.[183]

Clinical Manifestations

The classic onset of epiglottitis in children is abrupt, and progression of disease is rapid; careful history on occasion reveals the occurrence of a trivial antecedent upper respiratory tract infection.* The total duration of illness before hospitalization usually is less than 24 hours and occasionally as short as 2 hours. In one study in which 142 medical records of children with epiglottitis were reviewed, the duration of illness before tracheotomy was found to be 12 hours or less in 73 percent and more than 24 hours in only four patients.[44]

The most common presentation of acute epiglottitis in children includes the sudden onset of fever, severe sore throat, dysphagia, and drooling. Airway obstruction always occurs and is rapidly progressive. It is manifested by distress on inspiration, a choking sensation, irritability, restlessness, and anxiety. The speech is muffled or thick sounding, but hoarseness usually does not occur. The child usually insists on sitting up with a characteristic posture with the arms back, the trunk leaning forward, the neck hyperextended, and the chin pushed forward. This posture increases the diameter of the obstructed airway.

In contrast with acute laryngotracheitis, in which marked inspiratory stridor occurs, the degree of observed stridor in epiglottitis often is not severe. This apparent lack of respiratory distress often leads the unwary physician to underestimate the severity of the child's illness. With progression, the air exchange becomes progressively worse, and hypoxia, hypercapnia, and acidosis develop. These findings cause increased irritability, restlessness, and disorientation, and if an artificial airway is not established, the child will experience a sudden cardiorespiratory arrest.

Fever occurs in virtually all children; most temperatures are between 38.8° C and 40.0° C (101.8° F and 104° F). Blood leukocyte counts almost always are elevated; the mean total count was about 20,000 cells/mm^3 in five studies.[4, 19, 44, 89, 209] The differential cell count reveals an increased percentage of neutrophils and band forms; most patients have absolute band counts that are more than 500 cells/mm^3.

The clinical picture of epiglottitis in adults is more indolent than that in children.[80, 179, 217] In two studies, an average of 1 to 3 days elapsed before medical aid was sought. The mean temperature was 38.2° C (100.7° F), and some patients were afebrile; the temperature range was 36.6° C to 40.0° C (97.8° F to 104° F). Blood leukocyte counts averaged 17,000/mm^3 (range, 8000 to 32,000/mm^3). Sore throat and dysphagia were universal occurrences. Zwahlen and Regamy[217] reviewed the clinical features of 100 reported adult cases of epiglottitis. Of these, 78 percent had dyspnea; 49 percent, dysphonia; 41 percent, cyanosis; and 38 percent, stridor. Forty-six percent had edema of the neck. A precordial purring or fluttering sensation was described by one adult patient.[158]

Differential Diagnosis

The hallmark of the successful management of acute epiglottitis is an awareness of the condition and an understanding of the rapidity of its progression. A correct early diagnosis frequently is lifesaving. Acute epiglottitis must be differentiated from seven other conditions with symptoms of acute upper airway obstruction. Aspects of the differential diagnosis are presented in the text in Chapter 22 and in Table 22–5.

In epiglottitis, the important differential points are a lack of a croupy cough; the presence of a swollen, cherry-red epiglottis; the sitting posture of the child with the chin pushed forward and, also, a reluctance or refusal to lie down; and the relatively greater apprehension and anxiety of the child than the degree of chest retraction suggests. In contrast, the child with acute laryngotracheitis has a normal epiglottis on examination, always has a typical barking cough, is comfortable in a supine position, and frequently appears to have only minimal apprehension in spite of retractions in which the sternum appears to be indenting 2 inches or more.

Acute angioneurotic edema that involves the epiglottis can mimic acute epiglottitis. However, in this condition, the temperature usually is normal and the patient appears less toxic. This condition usually is brought on by a specific allergic reaction after the ingestion of a food or medicine.

Supraglottitis should be considered in children with uvulitis because their clinical features may overlap and both infections may be present. Concomitant uvulitis and epiglottitis were described with *H. influenzae* type b bacteremia in children[99, 147] and *S. pneumoniae* bacteremia in an adult.[211] Isolated uvulitis has been associated with *H. influenzae* type b bacteremia and group A beta-hemolytic streptococcal pharyngitis.[99, 115] Uvulitis in the absence of epiglottitis was described in a child with odynophagia, drooling, and *H. influenzae* type b bacteremia.[115]

A foreign body lodged in a vallecula or the larynx or penetrating posterior pharyngeal tissues may mimic the signs and symptoms of acute supraglottitis.[208] A paravertebral collection of pus, from cervical osteomyelitis or parapharyngeal abscess, rarely can spread anteriorly and produce acute "croup." Congenital anomalies and laryngeal papillomas can be excluded by their chronic course. *Candida albicans* has caused neonatal laryngeal obstruction without radiologic epiglottitis.[142]

Infection of supraglottic structures by *Mycobacterium tuberculosis* occurs less commonly than does glottic involvement; tuberculous laryngitis is an exceedingly rare occurrence in children and always is associated with pulmonary lesions.[59] The onset is considerably more insidious than is that of *H. influenzae* type b supraglottitis. Nasopharyngeal diphtheria may mimic acute epiglottitis and may be associated with a serosanguineous nasal discharge.

Chronic epiglottic enlargement with edema was observed in two children with cancer who had received radiotherapy to the neck. Their clinical features were not confused with those of acute supraglottitis, although one patient had dysphagia and snored.[216] Severe, chronic inflammatory

*See references 13, 14, 18, 19, 29, 32, 44, 60, 80, 89, 91, 114, 119, 122, 123, 131, 139, 144, 172, 201, 212.

epiglottitis with associated granulomatous lymphangitis was found on histologic examination of tissue obtained from a 19-month-old black child who had epiglottic enlargement without erythema for 3 months.[208] "Tuberculoid" granulomatous lesions were seen at histologic examination of an epiglottic biopsy specimen obtained from a 22-year-old man, HIV status unknown, who presented with weight loss, sore throat, and dysphonia of 1 month's duration.[130] The epiglottitis and arytenoepiglottic folds of this patient were erythematous and edematous.

Lymphangiectasis of the epiglottis produced airway obstruction with stridor and intermittent cyanosis in a 4-month-old white boy. On histologic examination, the epiglottis consisted of multiple dilated lymphatic vessels lined by a single layer of epithelial cells with no discernible wall. The stroma contained scattered lymphocytes and a few neutrophils. This lesion spontaneously regressed, and the child was normal at 1 year of age.[196]

Specific Diagnosis

The clinical picture of sore throat, dysphagia, drooling, anxiety, and inspiratory distress without significant stridor and the characteristic sitting position should suggest the presumptive diagnosis in most cases. The definitive anatomic diagnosis is made by the visualization of the epiglottis and the etiologic diagnosis by culture of an organism from the blood or the surface of the epiglottis. An *H. influenzae* type b etiology also can be established by the demonstration of antigenemia or antigenuria.[177, 203]

In the typical case, the epiglottis is fiery-red and greatly swollen. In children, the epiglottis can be seen by simple depression of the tongue with a tongue blade. In older children and adults, indirect or direct laryngoscopy usually is necessary to confirm the diagnosis. On occasion, the obstruction is caused by swelling of the ventricular bands and the arytenoepiglottic folds so that the epiglottis may appear relatively normal.

Major controversy exists relating to the safety of using a tongue depressor in examination of a child with suspected epiglottitis because sudden cardiorespiratory arrest has been noted to occur. However, most instances of cardiorespiratory arrest that I am aware of occurred after the child was forced into a supine position rather than because of the examination itself. In many instances, patients with presumptive epiglottitis can be examined in an upright position with a tongue blade or by the use of indirect laryngoscopy.

Case management should be individualized. In the child with moderate or advanced disease, the clinical diagnosis should be apparent without an intraoral examination. In this situation, intraoral examination should not be performed, but the child should be prepared for the establishment of an airway. This preparation should be rapid but controlled so that intubation can be performed in an operating room.

The diagnosis of epiglottitis can be established by the classic appearance on a lateral neck radiograph (Fig. 21–2).[145, 209] However, my opinion is that this radiographic procedure rarely is necessary; all too often it leads to a delay in the necessary definitive therapy.[44, 92, 129] The use of the lateral neck radiograph should be reserved for subacute cases in which the specific diagnosis after clinical examination is not clear.

The lateral film of the neck, delineating the soft tissues, taken with the patient upright, gives the best view of the upper airway anatomy (see Fig. 21–2). The hypopharynx is dilated; normal cervical lordosis may be replaced by a straight or kyphotic contour. The valleculae are narrowed and may be obliterated. A thickened mass of tissue stretching from the valleculae to the arytenoids emphasizes the appropriateness of the term *supraglottitis*. In adults with epiglottitis, the widths of the epiglottis and arytenoepiglottic folds uniformly exceed 8 and 7 mm, respectively.[163]

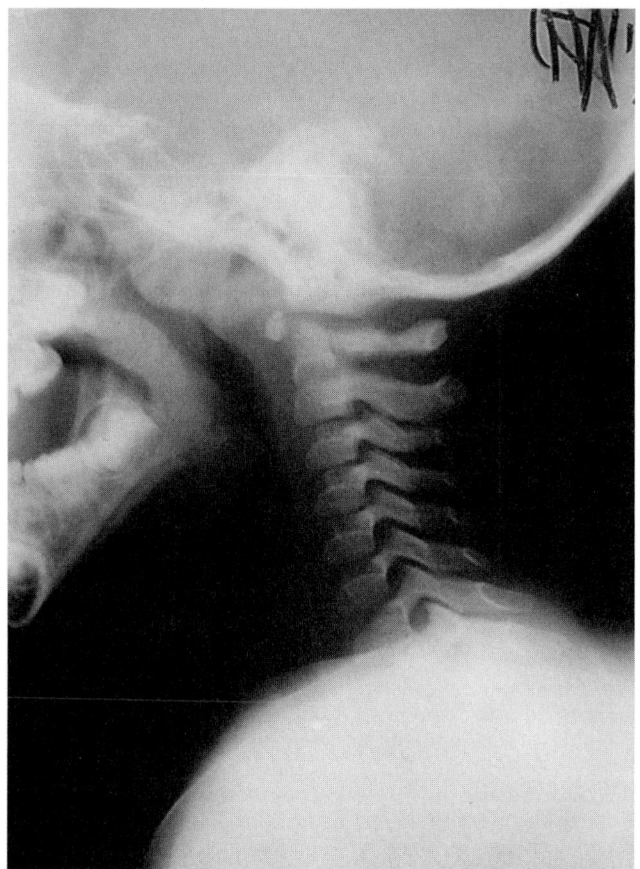

FIGURE 21–2 ■ A lateral neck radiograph from a child with acute epiglottitis showing the swollen epiglottis (thumb sign) encroaching on the airway. (Courtesy of Dr. Ines Bouchat.)

When performed, radiography of the neck in the anteroposterior projection usually reveals that tracheal narrowing is absent. However, some children with acute supraglottitis have localized subglottic narrowing indistinguishable from that found in acute laryngotracheitis.[167, 175]

All patients with suspected epiglottitis should have a blood culture, and a culture specimen should be obtained from the surface of the epiglottis when an artificial airway is established. Today, cultures are of increasing importance because of the change in epidemiology of *H. influenzae* type b infection and the resulting increased likelihood of an organism other than *H. influenzae* type b causing the illness. A white blood cell count with a differential also may provide useful information. In children who have received antimicrobial treatment before cultures, performing a direct antigen test for *H. influenzae* type b on the blood and urine is worthwhile.

Treatment

The treatment of acute epiglottitis should be relatively simple in that it involves only two main aspects of therapy: an airway must be established, and an appropriate antimicrobial agent needs to be administered. However, in the past, the mortality rate due to epiglottitis has varied from

0 to 32 percent,[44, 80] suggesting major differences in the implementation of treatment.

Most deaths occur in transit to the hospital or within the first few hours after arrival. Once the diagnosis is suspected, the patient should be attended constantly by individuals skilled in resuscitation with appropriate equipment for airway stabilization and ventilatory support. Delays of 2 or 3 hours have proved fatal; every effort should be made to reduce the time needed to secure a patient's airway and to initiate antibiotic therapy, before which unnecessary stress should be avoided. In most cases, radiographic confirmation should be omitted. Blood tests, extensive history taking, and delay in transport should be eliminated.

Medical centers and pediatric services that have planned protocols for the diagnostic investigation and treatment of patients with suspected acute epiglottitis generally have better morbidity and mortality statistics than do services that do not. Pediatricians, radiologists, otolaryngologists, and anesthetists may contribute to the assessment and management of a case; having roles and responsibilities of each service defined in advance minimizes confusion and renders the institution of care easier.

SECURING THE AIRWAY

In general, the cornerstone of all management plans is the establishment of an airway in all children in whom the diagnosis of epiglottitis is made.[39] In 1938, Sinclair[171] recognized that tracheostomy was lifesaving. Berenberg and Kevy[19] advocated hospitalization for all patients with epiglottitis but tracheostomy only "if necessary." However, Bass and associates[13] have a compelling argument for performing routine tracheostomy. Among 83 patients with documented epiglottitis, 11 of whom were adults, these authors noted that 16 of 83 (19%) had life-threatening obstruction when first seen. An additional 14 (17%) progressed to this point within 6 hours of admission; 9 of 83 (11%) required emergency tracheostomy while hospitalized. Of these nine, two died and one suffered anoxic brain damage. All nine were being monitored carefully, with bedside tracheostomy equipment available and trained personnel nearby. Six of the adults required tracheostomy for survival.[13] Margolis and colleagues[123] noted that elective tracheostomy, performed at the time of diagnosis, eliminated fatalities in 15 consecutive patients. This observation was in contrast to 4 deaths in 20 patients observed until tracheostomy "was required."

A large body of literature attests to the safety and efficacy of nasotracheal intubation as a replacement for tracheostomy,* which has a complication rate of 50 percent.[187, 212] Biologically inert tubes, with their decreased risk of complicating subglottic stenosis,[169] and the recollection that endotracheal tube insertion was universal before tracheostomy[129] was an accepted procedure led to the routine use of nasotracheal intubation in this disease. Nasotracheal intubation requires a shorter duration of airway maintenance: 32 patients with epiglottitis managed with tracheostomy had a mean duration of intubation of 7.5 days and a mean hospitalization of 8.8 days. In contrast, a nasotracheal tube was used for a mean of 38 hours with a 6.5-day hospitalization in five patients.[129] Diaz and Lockhart[54] managed 104 patients with nasotracheal intubation. The mean intubation time was 53 ± 14.9 hours; 7 patients (6.8%) extubated themselves, and 2 required reintubation. Laryngeal edema occurred in three patients (2.9%) who had been intubated. In two, subglottic granulations required excision.

My belief, as well as that of Daum and Smith,[51] is that the argument for performing elective tracheostomy or, preferably, intubation in all children with supraglottitis is compelling, and the procedure should be performed immediately after diagnosis. Whether this "stimulus-response" approach is necessary for adults with epiglottitis is controversial.[12, 65, 80, 140, 166, 170, 179] Mayo Smith and associates[124] compared selected clinical features in adults with epiglottitis at the time of diagnosis who died or received an artificial airway with those of adults who recovered without airway intervention. Few differences emerged. Patients who died or who were managed with airway intervention had respiratory distress and bacteremia more often than did those who recovered without airway intervention. Obviously, the presence of bacteremia was not known on presentation. Moreover, the mortality among all adults managed expectantly was 4.6 percent, a figure comparable to the mortality rate (6.1%) of children in a series reported before recommendations for routine securing of the airway at diagnosis.[37, 124] The preponderance of evidence until very recently has suggested that securing the airway in all adults with supraglottitis by nasotracheal intubation should reduce mortality rates.[7, 10, 12, 13, 20, 21, 48, 98, 124] However, Frantz and associates[66] reported an analysis of 129 cases of acute epiglottitis in adults in which no deaths occurred in the cohort, and 85 percent were managed without airway intervention.

To aid in intubation and to reduce long-term sequelae, most investigators have advocated use of a nasotracheal tube 0.5 to 1.0 mm smaller than that predicted by the patient's age.[83, 129, 160] Recommendations for tube size are shown in Table 21–2.[113, 169]

Published criteria for extubation (summarized in reference 14) include those based on duration of therapy and those based on daily examination of the epiglottis and supraglottic structures by direct laryngoscopy[52] or fiberoptic bronchoscopy.[138, 198]

Long-term complications appear rarely with nasotracheal intubation. Thirty-three children with epiglottitis managed with nasotracheal intubation (mean duration of intubation, 55 hours) were evaluated 1 to 8 years later. By history and measurement of peak expiratory flow rates, no complications were found.[160] Although additional long-term data are necessary to ensure absence of residua, elective nasotracheal intubation appears to be the procedure of choice.

Several reports documented the recognition of idiopathic pulmonary edema before[111] or, more commonly, after[24, 52, 56, 68, 94, 178, 190] insertion of an endotracheal tube to relieve laryngeal obstruction caused by epiglottitis. One hypothesis to explain this phenomenon is that airway obstruction

TABLE 21–2 ■ SIZE OF NASOTRACHEAL TUBES RECOMMENDED FOR CHILDREN WITH ACUTE SUPRAGLOTTITIS[144, 170]

Age	Size (mm)
Birth–6 mo	3.0
6 mo–3 yrs	3.5
3 yrs–5 yrs	4.0
Older than 5 yrs	4.5

*See references 14, 45, 83, 106, 123, 139, 146, 160, 169, 187, 189.

produces markedly negative intrapleural pressure with increased venous return to the right side of the heart with decreased left ventricular output and increased pulmonary blood volume.[108] These changes increase the pulmonary microvascular pressure and produce pulmonary hyperemia and edema. Endotoxemia may play a role in altering vascular permeability but is not necessary for recognition of this complication of airway obstruction because abrupt onset of pulmonary edema was described when airway obstruction caused by croup, foreign body, and malignant neoplasm was relieved acutely.[35] The frequency of pulmonary edema complicating intubation in supraglottitis was approximately 9 percent,[175] and it has occurred in an adult.[150] Continuous positive airway pressure in all intubated patients with epiglottitis probably will provide prophylaxis against this complication,[54, 68] but controlled data are lacking.

ANTIBIOTICS

The mainstay of antibiotic therapy for acute epiglottitis in the recent past has been ceftriaxone (50 to 100 mg/kg/day given every 12 hours intravenously) or cefotaxime (100 to 200 mg/kg/day given every 6 hours intravenously) because virtually all cases in both children and adults were caused by *H. influenzae* type b. However, in the present conjugate vaccine era, the incidence of all invasive *H. influenzae* type b disease has decreased dramatically. Therefore, in children previously vaccinated, the etiology is likely to be attributable to another organism. Culture results today have added significance because one possible etiology that would require a change in therapy is *S. aureus*.

No controlled data exist about the duration of antimicrobial administration, but a course of 7 days seems appropriate. In the event that group A streptococci are isolated from the airway, penicillin is the drug of choice. A semisynthetic penicillinase-resistant penicillin or vancomycin should be used for *S. aureus,* whereas erythromycin is indicated for *Corynebacterium diphtheriae.*

OTHER SUPPORTIVE MEASURES

Some authors have advocated steroid therapy on the basis of anecdotal experience in patients with epiglottitis, but no controlled data exist to support its use, and such therapy may be hazardous: among 91 patients with epiglottitis who received steroid therapy, 4 (4%) had evidence of bleeding from the gastrointestinal tract that was sufficient in 2 to require transfusion,[55] a phenomenon observed by others.[103] Therapy with racemic epinephrine is without benefit.

Expert respiratory nursing care is essential. Inadvertent extubation must be avoided, particularly in the first 24 hours. Judicious use of sedatives that do not appreciably depress respiration may be appropriate.

Complications

Extraepiglottic complications are not common occurrences in children with acute epiglottitis. In one study involving 72 children with epiglottitis, investigators noted that 25 percent had pneumonia, 25 percent had cervical adenitis, 8 percent had tonsillitis, and 5 percent had otitis media.[131] The other common invasive manifestations of *H. influenzae* type b infections (meningitis, arthritis, and cellulitis) are rarely found in conjunction with epiglottitis.[131, 159]

Prevention

PROPHYLAXIS OF HOUSEHOLD CONTACTS

In the pre–conjugate vaccine era, household contacts of patients with *H. influenzae* type b infection were at increased risk for acquiring *H. influenzae* type b infection.[76] Whether an increased risk occurred in daycare contacts was unresolved.[50] Although contacts of patients with *H. influenzae* type b epiglottitis younger than 5 years are colonized less frequently than are contacts of patients with other *H. influenzae* type b invasive infections,[49] secondary disease was described in household contacts when an index patient had epiglottitis.[1, 73, 74, 193] Secondary *H. influenzae* type b epiglottitis was described in a child[1] and two adults who were household contacts of a patient with *H. influenzae* type b meningitis.[73, 74] *H. influenzae* type b epiglottitis occurred in two siblings[79] who presented within 1 day.

Rifampin prophylaxis, 20 mg/kg/day (600 mg/dose maximum) for 4 days, is recommended for all unvaccinated members of a patient's contact group when the index patient has *H. influenzae* type b epiglottitis and at least one contact in the group is 4 years of age or younger.[6, 38]

The recognition that adults occasionally may acquire secondary infection, particularly epiglottitis, on exposure to children with invasive *H. influenzae* type b infection has prompted some experts to extend prophylaxis to all of a patient's contact groups, regardless of the presence of one or more contacts who are 4 years of age or younger. All experts, however, recommended that adults and older children be made aware of the signs and symptoms of *H. influenzae* type b disease, particularly when the patient's contact group would not receive prophylaxis under current guidelines.

REFERENCES

1. Addy, M. G., Ellis, P. D. M., and Turk, D. C.: *Haemophilus* epiglottitis: Nine recent cases in Oxford. Br. Med. J. *1*:40–41, 1972.
2. Alba, D., Perna, C., Torres, E., et al.: Isolated candidal epiglottitis: Report of a fatal case. Clin. Infect. Dis. *22*:732–733, 1996.
3. Alexander, H. E., Ellis, C., and Leidy, C.: Treatment of type-specific *H. influenzae* infections in infancy and childhood. J. Pediatr. *20*:673–698, 1942.
4. Alho, O.-P., Jokinen, K., Pirila, T., et al.: Acute epiglottitis and infant conjugate *Haemophilus influenzae* type b vaccination in northern Finland. Arch. Otolaryngol. Head Neck Surg. *121*:898–902, 1995.
5. Ambrosino, D. M., Schiffman, G., Gottschlich, E. C., et al.: Correlation between G2m(n) immunoglobulin allotype and human antibody response and susceptibility to polysaccharide encapsulated bacteria. J. Clin. Invest. *75*:1935–1942, 1985.
6. American Academy of Pediatrics: *Haemophilus influenzae* infections. *In* Pickering, L. K. (ed.): 2000 Red Book: Report of the Committee on Infectious Diseases. 25th ed. Elk Grove Village, IL, American Academy of Pediatrics, 2000, pp. 203–217.
7. Andreassen, U. K., Husum, B., Tos, M., et al.: Acute epiglottitis in adults: A management based on a 17-year material. Acta Anaesthesiol. Scand. *28*:155–157, 1984.
8. Barnham, M., Kerby, J., Chandler, R. S., et al.: Group C streptococci in human infection: A study of 308 isolates with clinical correlations. Epidemiol. Infect. *102*:379–390, 1989.
9. Baron, B. J.: Comments on a case of extremely acute edematous laryngitis. Br. Med. J. *2*:1328, 1887.
10. Bass, J. W.: Routine tracheotomy for epiglottitis: What are the odds? J. Pediatr. *83*:510–511, 1973.
11. Bass, J. W.: Personal communication, 1977.
12. Bass, J. W.: Response to CPC. N. Engl. J. Med. *298*:342–343, 1978.
13. Bass, J. W., Steele, R. W., and Wiebe, R. A.: Acute epiglottitis: A surgical emergency. J. A. M. A. *229*:671–675, 1974.
14. Battaglia, J. D., and Lockhart, C. H.: Management of acute epiglottitis by nasotracheal intubation. Am. J. Dis. Child. *129*:334–336, 1975.
15. Baugh, R., and Baker, S. R.: Epiglottitis in children: Review of 24 cases. Otolaryngol. Head Neck Surg. *90*:157–162, 1982.
16. Baxter, J. D.: Acute epiglottitis in children. Laryngoscope *77*:1358–1367, 1967.

17. Belfer, R. A.: Group A beta-hemolytic streptococcal epiglottitis as a complication of varicella infection. Pediatr. Emerg. Care *12:*203–204, 1996.
18. Benjamin, B., and O'Reilly, B.: Acute epiglottitis in infants and children. Ann. Otol. *85:*565–572, 1976.
19. Berenberg, W., and Kevy, S.: Acute epiglottitis in childhood: A serious emergency, readily recognized at the bedside. N. Engl. J. Med. *258:*870–874, 1958.
20. Bishop, M. L.: Epiglottitis in the adult. Anesthesiology *55:*701–702, 1981.
21. Bishop, M. J., and Weymuller, E. A.: Adult epiglottitis revisited. Anesthesiology *57:*545–546, 1982.
22. Black, M. J., Harbour, J., Remsen, K. A., et al.: Acute epiglottitis in adults. J. Otolaryngol. *10:*23–27, 1981.
23. Blackstock, D., Adderley, R. J., and Steward, D. J.: Epiglottitis in young infants. Anesthesiology *69:*97–100, 1987.
24. Blankson, V. N.: Pulmonary edema complicating epiglottitis. J. Med. Soc. N. J. *80:*939–941, 1983.
25. Bogger-Goren, S.: Acute epiglottitis caused by herpes simplex virus. Pediatr. Infect. Dis. *6:*1133, 1987.
26. Bolivar, R., Gomez, L. G., Luna, M., et al.: *Aspergillus* epiglottitis. Cancer *51:*367–370, 1983.
27. Bottenfield, G. W., Arcinue, E. L., Sarnaik, A., et al.: Diagnosis and management of acute epiglottitis: Report of 90 consecutive cases. Laryngoscope *90:*822–825, 1980.
28. Bower, C. M., and Suen, J. Y.: Adult acute epiglottitis caused by *Serratia marcescens*. Otolaryngol. Head Neck Surg. *115:*156–159, 1996.
29. Branefors-Helander, P., and Jeppsson, P. H.: Acute epiglottitis: A clinical, bacteriological and serological study. Scand. J. Infect. Dis. *7:*103–111, 1975.
30. Breivik, H., and Klaastad, O.: Acute epiglottitis in children. Br. J. Anaesth. *50:*505–509, 1978.
31. Briggs, W. H., and Altenau, M. M.: Acute epiglottitis in children. Otolaryngol. Head Neck Surg. *88:*665–669, 1980.
32. Brilli, R. J., Benzing, G., and Cotcamp, D. H.: Epiglottitis in infants less than two years of age. Pediatr. Emerg. Care *5:*16–21, 1989.
33. Broadhurst, L. E., Erickson, R. L., and Kelley, P. W.: Decreases in invasive *Haemophilus influenzae* diseases in US Army children, 1984 through 1991. J. A. M. A. *269:*227–231, 1993.
34. Broughton, S. J., and Warren, R. E.: A review of *Haemophilus influenzae* infections in Cambridge 1975–1981. J. Infect. *9:*30–42, 1984.
35. Burtner, D. D., and Goodman, M.: Anesthetic and operative management of potential upper airway obstruction. Arch. Otolaryngol. *104:*657–661, 1978.
36. Butt, W., Shann, F., Walker, C., et al.: Acute epiglottitis: A different approach to management. Crit. Care Med. *16:*43–47, 1988.
37. Cantrell, R. W., Bell, R. A., and Morioka, W. T.: Acute epiglottitis: Intubation versus tracheostomy. Laryngoscope *88:*994–1005, 1978.
38. Centers for Disease Control: Immunization Practices Advisory Committee: *Haemophilus* b conjugate vaccine for prevention of *Haemophilus influenzae* type b disease among infants and children 2 months of age and older. M. M. W. R. *40*(RR-1):1–7, 1991.
39. Cherry, J. D.: Acute epiglottitis, laryngitis, and croup. *In* Remington, J. S., and Swartz, M. N. (eds.): Current Clinical Topics in Infectious Diseases. New York, McGraw-Hill, 1981, pp. 1–30.
40. Cherry, J. D.: Croup. *In* Kiple, K. F. (ed.): The Cambridge World History of Human Disease. Cambridge, Cambridge University Press, 1993, pp. 654–657.
41. Cherry, J. D.: Unpublished data, 1973.
42. Chow, A. W., Bushkell, L. L., Yoshikawa, T. T., et al.: *Haemophilus parainfluenzae* epiglottitis with meningitis and bacteremia in an adult. Am. J. Med. Sci. *267:*365–368, 1974.
43. Claesson, B., Trollfors, B., Ekström-Jodal, B., et al.: Incidence and prognosis of acute epiglottitis in children in a Swedish region. Pediatr. Infect. Dis. *3:*534–538, 1984.
44. Cohen, S. R., and Chai, J.: Epiglottitis: Twenty-year study with tracheotomy. Ann. Otol. *87:*461–467, 1978.
45. Coker, S. B., and Scherz, R. G.: Safe alternative to tracheostomy in acute epiglottitis. Am. J. Dis. Child. *129:*136, 1975.
46. Coulehan, J. L., Michaels, R. H., Hallowell C., et al.: Epidemiology of *Haemophilus influenzae* type b disease among Navajo Indians. Public Health Rep. *99:*404–409, 1984.
47. Dagan, R., and the Israeli Pediatric Bacteremia and Meningitis Group: A two-year prospective, nationwide study to determine the epidemiology and impact of invasive childhood *Haemophilus influenzae* type b infection in Israel. Clin. Infect. Dis. *15:*720–725, 1992.
48. Darnell, J. C.: Acute epiglottitis in adults: Report of a case and review of the literature. J. Indiana State Med. Assoc. *69:*21–23, 1976.
49. Daum, R. S., Glode, M. P., Goldmann, D. A., et al.: Rifampin chemoprophylaxis for household contacts of patients with invasive infections due to *Haemophilus influenzae* type b. J. Pediatr. *98:*485–491, 1981.
50. Daum, R. S., Granoff, D. M., Gilsdorf, J., et al.: *H. influenzae* type b infections in day care attendees: Implications for management. Rev. Infect. Dis. *8:*46–55, 1986.
51. Daum, R. S., and Smith, A. L.: Epiglottitis (supraglottitis). *In* Feigin, R. D., and Cherry, J. D. (eds.): Textbook of Pediatric Infectious Diseases. 3rd ed. Philadelphia, W. B. Saunders, 1992, pp. 197–209.
52. Davis, H. W., Gartiner, J. C., Galvis, A. G., et al.: Acute upper airway obstruction: Croup and epiglottitis. Pediatr. Clin. North Am. *28:*859–880, 1981.
53. Devita, M. A., and Wagner, I. J.: Acute epiglottitis in the adult. Crit. Care Med. *14:*1082–1083, 1986.
54. Diaz, J. H., and Lockhart, C. H.: Early diagnosis and airway management of acute epiglottitis in children. South. Med. J. *75:*399–403, 1982.
55. DiTirro, F. R., Silver, M. H., and Hengerer, A. S.: Acute epiglottitis: Evolution of management in the community hospital. Int. J. Pediatr. Otorhinolaryngol. *7:*145–152, 1984.
56. Donnelly, J., Overtun, J. H., and Mellis, C. M.: Pulmonary oedema following relief of epiglottitis. Anaesth. Intensive Care *9:*290–291, 1981.
57. Drake-Lee, A. B., Broughton, S. J., and Grace, A.: Children with epiglottitis. Br. J. Clin. Pract. *38:*218–220, 1984.
58. Dudley, J. P.: Supraglottitis and *Hemophilus parainfluenzae*: Pathogenic potential of the organism. Ann. Otol. Rhinol. Laryngol. *96:*400–402, 1987.
59. Dworetzky, J. P., and Risch, O. C.: Laryngeal tuberculosis: A study of 500 cases of pulmonary tuberculosis with a resume based on twenty-eight years of experience. Ann. Otol. Rhinol. Laryngol. *50:*745–761, 1941.
60. Faden, H. S.: Treatment of *Haemophilus influenzae* type b epiglottitis. Pediatrics *63:*402–407, 1979.
61. Farley, M. M., Stephens, D. S., Brachman, P. S., Jr., et al.: Invasive *Haemophilus influenzae* disease in adults: A prospective, population-based surveillance. Ann. Intern. Med. *116:*806–812, 1992.
62. Fearon, B. W., and Bell, R. D.: Acute epiglottitis: A potential killer. Can. Med. Assoc. J. *112:*760–766, 1975.
63. Fogarty, J., Moloney, A. C., and Newell, J. B.: The epidemiology of *Haemophilus influenzae* type b disease in the Republic of Ireland. Epidemiol. Infect. *114:*451–463, 1995.
64. Fontanarosa, P. B., Polsky, S. S., and Goldman, G. E.: Adult epiglottitis. J. Emerg. Med. *7:*223–231, 1989.
65. Frantz, T. D., and Rasgon, B. M.: Acute epiglottitis: Changing epidemiologic patterns. Otolaryngol. Head Neck Surg. *109:*457–460, 1993.
66. Frantz, T. D., Rasgon, B. M., and Quesenberry, C. P., Jr.: Acute epiglottitis in adults: Analysis of 129 cases. J. A. M. A. *272:*1358–1360, 1994.
67. Freeman, L., and Wolford, R.: Acute epiglottitis caused by methicillin-resistant *Staphylococcus aureus* in adults. Clin. Infect. Dis. *26:* 1240–1241, 1998.
68. Galvis, A. G., Stool, S. E., and Bluestone, C. D.: Pulmonary edema following relief of acute upper airway obstruction. Ann. Otol. *89:*124–128, 1980.
69. Garpenholt, O., Hugosson, S., Fredlund, H., et al.: Epiglottitis in Sweden before and after introduction of vaccination against *Haemophilus influenzae* type b. Pediatr. Infect. Dis. J. *18:*490–493, 1998.
70. Gerber, A. C., and Pfenninger, J.: Acute epiglottitis: Management by short duration of intubation and hospitalisation. Intensive Care Med. *12:*407–411, 1986.
71. Giani, G., Quirino, F., Sacrini, A., et al.: Supraglottitis due to herpes simplex virus type 1 in an adult. Clin. Infect. Dis. *22:*382–383, 1996.
72. Glickman, M., and Klein, R. S.: Acute epiglottitis due to *Pasteurella multocida* in an adult without animal exposure. Emerg. Infect. Dis. *3:*408–409, 1997.
73. Glode, M. P., Halsey, N. A., Murray, M., et al.: Epiglottitis in adults: Association with *Haemophilus influenzae* type b colonization and disease in children. Pediatr. Infect. Dis. *3:*548–551, 1984.
74. Glode, M. P.: Post exposure prophylaxis for bacterial meningitis. *In* Sande, M. A., Smith, A. L., and Root, R. K. (eds.): Bacterial Meningitis. New York, Churchill Livingstone, 1985.
75. Gorelick, M. H., and Baker, M. D.: Epiglottitis in children, 1979 through 1992: Effects of *Haemophilus influenzae* type b immunization. Arch. Pediatr. Adolesc. Med. *148:*47–50, 1994.
76. Granoff, D. M., and Daum, R. S.: Spread of *Haemophilus influenzae* type b: Recent epidemiologic and therapeutic considerations. J. Pediatr. *97:*854–860, 1980.
77. Granoff, D. M., Pandey, J. P., Boies, E., et al.: Response to immunization with *Haemophilus influenzae* type b polysaccharide-pertussis vaccine and risk of *Haemophilus* meningitis in children with the Km(1) immunoglobulin allotype. J. Clin. Invest. *74:*1708–1714, 1984.
78. Grattan-Smith, T., Forer, M., Kilham, H., et al.: Viral supraglottitis. J. Pediatr. *110:*434–435, 1987.
79. Handler, S. D., Plotkin, S. A., Potsic, W. P., et al.: *Haemophilus influenzae* epiglottitis occurring concurrently in two siblings. Clin. Pediatr. *21:*634–635, 1982.
80. Hawkins, D. B., Miller, A. H., Sachs, G. B., et al.: Acute epiglottitis in adults. Laryngoscope *83:*1211–1220, 1973.
81. Healy, G. B., Hyams, V. J., and Tucker, G. F.: Paraglottic laryngitis in association with epiglottitis. Ann. Otol. Rhinol. Laryngol. *94:*618–621, 1985.
82. Hébert, P. C., Ducic, Y., Boisvert, D., et al.: Adult epiglottitis in a Canadian setting. Laryngoscope *108:*64–69, 1998.
83. Heldtander, P., and Lee, P.: Treatment of acute epiglottitis in children by long-term intubation. Acta Otolaryngol. *75:*379–381, 1973.
84. Hodge, K. M., and Ganzel, T. M.: Diagnostic and therapeutic efficiency in croup and epiglottitis. Laryngoscope *97:*621–625, 1987.

85. Howard, A. J., Dunkin, K. T., Musser, J. M., et al.: Epidemiology of *Haemophilus influenzae* type b invasive disease in Wales. Br. Med. J. *303*:441–445, 1991.
86. Isenberg, D. A., Lipkin, D. P., Mowbray, J. F., et al.: Fatal pneumococcal epiglottitis in lupus overlap syndrome. Clin. Rheumatol. *3*:529–532, 1984.
87. Jenkins, W. A.: *Pasteurella multocida* as a cause of acute adult epiglottitis. Am. J. Emerg. Med. *15*:323, 1997.
88. Jerrard, D. A., and Olshaker, J.: Simultaneous uvulitis and epiglottitis without fever or leukocytosis. Am. J. Emerg. Med. *14*:551–552, 1996.
89. Johnson, G. K., Sullivan, J. L., and Bishop, L. A.: Acute epiglottitis: Review of 55 cases and suggested protocol. Arch. Otolaryngol. *100*:333–337, 1974.
90. Johnson, R. H., and Rumans, L. W.: Unusual infections caused by *Pasteurella multocida*. J. A. M. A. *237*:146–147, 1977.
91. Johnstone, J. M., and Lawy, H. S.: Acute epiglottitis in adults due to infection with *Haemophilus influenzae* type b. Lancet *2*:134–136, 1967.
92. Jones, H. M.: Acute epiglottitis: A personal study over twenty years. Proc. R. Soc. Med. *63*:706–712, 1970.
93. Jones, R. N., Slepack, J., and Bigelow, J.: Ampicillin-resistant *Haemophilus paraphrophilus* laryngoepiglottitis. J. Clin. Microbiol. *4*: 405–407, 1976.
94. Kanter, R. K., and Watchko, J. F.: Pulmonary edema associated with upper airway obstruction. Am. J. Dis. Child. *138*:356–358, 1984.
95. Kennedy, C. A., and Rosen, H.: *Kingella kingae* bacteremia and adult epiglottitis in a granulocytopenic host. Am. J. Med. *85*:701–702, 1988.
96. Kessler, H. A., Schade, R., and Trenhome, G. M.: Acute pneumococcal epiglottitis in immunocompromised adults. Scand. J. Infect. Dis. *12*: 207–210, 1980.
97. Kharasch, S., Vinci, R., and Reece, R.: Esophagitis, epiglottitis, and cocaine alkaloid ("crack"): "Accidental" poisoning or child abuse? Pediatrics *86*:117–119, 1990.
98. Khilanani, U., and Khatib, R.: Acute epiglottitis in adults. Am. J. Med. Sci. *287*:65–70, 1984.
99. Kotloff, K. L., and Wald, E. R.: Uvulitis in children. Pediatr. Infect. Dis. *2*:392–393, 1983.
100. Kristensen, K., Kaaber, K., Ronne, T., et al.: Epidemiology of *Haemophilus influenzae* type b infections among children in Denmark in 1985 and 1986. Acta Paediatr. Scand. *79*:587–592, 1990.
101. Kristensen, K.: *Haemophilus influenzae* type b infections in adults. Scand. J. Infect. Dis. *21*:651–653, 1989.
102. Kulick, R. M., Selbst, S. M., Baker, M.D., et al.: Thermal epiglottitis after swallowing hot beverages. Pediatrics *81*:441–444, 1988.
103. Kyrcz, R. W., and Indyk, D.: Atypical acute epiglottitis with gastrointestinal bleeding. J. Fam. Pract. *27*:102–103, 1988.
104. Lacroix, J., Ahronheim, G., Arcand, P., et al.: Group A streptococcal supraglottitis. J. Pediatr. *109*:20–24, 1986.
105. Lacroix, J., Ahronheim, G., and Girouard, G.: *Pseudomonas aeruginosa* supraglottitis in a six-month-old child with severe combined immunodeficiency syndrome. Pediatr. Infect. Dis. *7*:739–741, 1988.
106. Lacroix, J., Blanc, V. F., Weber, M., et al.: Étude de 100 cas consécutifs d'epiglottite aiguë. L'Union Médicale du Canada *111*:774–779, 1982.
107. Lai, S. H., Wong, K. S., Liao, S. L., et al.: Noninfectious epiglottitis in children: Two case reports. Int. J. Pediatr. Otorhinolaryngol. *55*:57–60, 2000.
108. Lang, S. A., Duncan, P. G., Shephard, D. A. E., et al.: Pulmonary edema associated with airway obstruction. Can. J. Anaesth. *37*:210–218, 1990.
109. La Scolea, L. J., Rosales, S. V., Welliver, R. C., et al.: Mechanisms underlying the development of meningitis or epiglottitis in children after *Haemophilus influenzae* type b bacteremia. J. Infect. Dis. *151*:1162–1165, 1985.
110. Lederman, M. M., Lowder, J., and Lerner, P. I.: Bacteremic pneumococcal epiglottitis in adults with malignancy. Am. Rev. Respir. Dis. *125*: 117–118, 1982.
111. Lee, S. C., Meislin, H., and Iserson, K. V.: Epiglottitis presenting as acute pulmonary edema. Ann. Emerg. Med. *14*:60–63, 1985.
112. Lemierre, A., Meyer, A., and Laplane, R.: Maladies infectieuses: Les septicemies à bacille de Pfeiffer. Ann. Med. *39*:97–119, 1936.
113. Levison, H., Tabachnik, E., and Newth, C. J. L.: Wheezing in infancy, croup and epiglottitis. Curr. Probl. Pediatr. *12*:1–65, 1982.
114. Lewis, J. K., Gartner, J. C., and Galvis, A. G.: A protocol for management of acute epiglottitis. Clin. Pediatr. *17*:494–496, 1978.
115. Li, K. I., Kiernan, S., Wald, E. R., et al.: Isolated uvulitis due to *Haemophilus influenzae* type b. Pediatrics *74*:1054–1057, 1984.
116. Lindquist, J. R., Franzen, R. E., and Ossoff, R. H.: Acute infectious supraglottitis in adults. Ann. Emerg. Med. *9*:256–259, 1980.
117. Lipson, A., Kronick, J. B., Tewfik, L., et al.: Group B streptococcal supraglottitis in a 3-month-old infant. Am. J. Dis. Child. *140*:411–412, 1986.
118. Liptak, G. S., McConnochie, K. M., Roghmann, K. J., et al.: Decline of pediatric admissions with *Haemophilus influenzae* type b in New York State, 1982 through 1993: Relation to immunizations. J. Pediatr. *130*: 923–930, 1997.
119. Losek, J. D., Dewitz-Zink, B. A., Melzer-Lange, M., et al.: Epiglottitis: Comparison of signs and symptoms in children less than 2 years old and older. Ann. Emerg. Med. *19*:55–58, 1990.
120. Mace, S. E.: Acute epiglottitis in adults. Am. J. Emerg. Med. *3*:543–550, 1985.
121. Macneil, A., Campbell, A. M., and Clark, L. J.: Adult acute epiglottitis in association with infection of an epiglottic cyst. Anaesth. Intensive Care *17*:211–212, 1989.
122. Margolis, C. Z., Colletti, R. B., and Grundy, G.: *Haemophilus influenzae* type b: The etiologic agent in epiglottitis. J. Pediatr. *87*:322–323, 1975.
123. Margolis, C. Z., Ingram, D. L., and Meyer, J. H.: Routine tracheotomy in *Hemophilus influenzae* type b epiglottitis. J. Pediatr. *81*:1150–1153, 1972.
124. Mayo Smith, M. F., Hirsch, P. J., Wodzinski, S. F., et al.: Acute epiglottitis in adults. N. Engl. J. Med. *314*:1133–1139, 1986.
125. McGregor, A. R., Dawson, K. P., and Abbott, G. D.: Acute epiglottitis in childhood, Christchurch 1970–84. N. Z. Med. J. *98*:1011–1013, 1985.
126. McIntyre, P. B., Leeder, S. R., and Irwig, L. M.: Invasive *Haemophilus influenzae* type b disease in Sydney children 1985–1987: A population-based study. Med. J. Aust. *154*:832–837, 1991.
127. Mehtar, S., Bangham, L., Kalmanovitch, D., et al.: Adult epiglottitis due to *Vibrio vulnificus*. Br. Med. J. *296*:827–828, 1988.
128. Midwinter, K. I., Hodgson, D., and Yardley, M.: Paediatric epiglottitis: The influence of the *Haemophilus influenzae* b vaccine, a ten-year review in the Sheffield region. Clin. Otolaryngol. *24*:447–448, 1999.
129. Milko, D. A., Marshak, G., and Striker, T. W.: Nasotracheal intubation in the treatment of acute epiglottitis. Pediatrics *53*:674–677, 1974.
130. Mitchell, D. B., and Drake-Lee, A. B.: Chronic nonspecific granulomatous epiglottitis. J. Laryngol. Otolaryngol. *99*:1305–1308, 1985.
131. Molteni, R. A.: Epiglottitis: Incidence of extraepiglottis infection: Report of 72 cases and review of the literature. Pediatrics *58*:526–531, 1976.
132. Murphy, T. V., Osterholm, M. T., Pierson, L. M., et al.: Prospective surveillance of *Haemophilus influenzae* disease in Dallas County, Texas, and in Minnesota. Pediatrics *79*:173–180, 1987.
133. Murphy, T. V., Granoff, D. M., Pierson, L. M., et al.: Invasive *Haemophilus influenzae* type b disease in children <5 years of age in Minnesota and in Dallas County, Texas, 1983–1984. J. Infect. Dis. *165*(Suppl. 1):S7–S10, 1992.
134. Musharrafieh, U. M., Araj, G. F., and Fuleihan, N. S.: Viral supraglottitis in an adult: A case presentation and literature update. J. Infect. *39*:157–160, 1999.
135. Myer, C. M., 3rd.: *Candida* epiglottitis: Clinical implications. Am. J. Otolaryngol. *18*:428–430, 1997.
136. Nelson, K., Watanakunakorn, C., and Watkins, D. A.: Acute epiglottitis due to serogroup Y *Neisseria meningitidis* in an adult. Clin. Infect. Dis. *23*:1192–1193, 1996.
137. Nguyen, R., and Leclerc, J.: Cervical necrotizing fasciitis as a complication of acute epiglottitis. J. Otolaryngol. *26*:129–131, 1997.
138. Nussbaum, E.: Fiberoptic laryngoscopy as a guide to tracheal extubation in acute epiglottitis. J. Pediatr. *102*:269–270, 1983.
139. Oh, T. H., and Motoyama, E. K.: Comparison of nasotracheal intubation and tracheostomy in management of acute epiglottitis. Anaesthesiology *46*:214–216, 1977.
140. Park, K. W., Darvish, A., and Lowenstein, E.: Airway management for adult patients with acute epiglottitis: A 12-year experience at an academic medical center (1984–1995). Anesthesiology *88*:254–261, 1998.
141. Peltola, H.: *Haemophilus influenzae* type b disease and vaccination in Europe: Lessons learned. Pediatr. Infect. Dis. J. *17*:S126–S132, 1998.
142. Perrone, J. A.: Laryngeal obstruction due to *Monilia albicans* in a newborn. Laryngoscope *80*:288–291, 1970.
143. Quigley, C., Kaczmarski, E. B., Jones, D. M., et al.: *Haemophilus influenzae* type b disease in north-west England. J. Infect. *26*:215–220, 1993.
144. Rabe, E. F.: Infectious croup: III. *Hemophilus influenzae* type b croup. Pediatrics *2*:559–566, 1948.
145. Rapkin, R. H.: The diagnosis of epiglottitis: Simplicity and reliability of radiographs of the neck in the differential diagnosis of the croup syndrome. J. Pediatr. *80*:96–98, 1972.
146. Rapkin, R. H.: Nasotracheal intubation in epiglottitis. Pediatrics *56*:110–112, 1975.
147. Rapkin, R. H.: Simultaneous uvulitis and epiglottitis. J. A. M. A. *243*:1843, 1980.
148. Richens, J., and Montgomery, J.: Acute epiglottitis (supraglottitis) in the puerperium caused by infection with group A *Streptococcus*. Papua New Guinea Med. J. *31*:293–294, 1988.
149. Ridgeway, N. A., Verghese, A., Perlman, P. E., et al.: Epiglottic abscess due to group B *Streptococcus* communication. Ann. Otol. Rhinol. Laryngol. *93*:277–278, 1984.
150. Rivera, M., Hadlock, F. P., and O'Meara, M. I.: Pulmonary edema secondary to acute epiglottitis. A. J. R. Am. J. Roentgenol. *132*:991–992, 1979.
151. Robbins, J. P., and Fitz-Hugh, G. S.: Epiglottitis in the adult. Laryngoscope *81*:700–706, 1971.
152. Rose, F. B., Garman, R. F., Falkenberg, K. J., et al.: Adult epiglottitis, cellulitis and *Streptococcus pneumoniae* bacteremia. Scand. J. Infect. Dis. *14*:301–302, 1982.
153. Rothstein, S. G., Persky, M. S., Edelman, B. A., et al.: Epiglottitis in AIDS patients. Laryngoscope *99*:389–392, 1989.

154. Russell, G. A., Gresham, G. A., and Wight, D. G. D.: Acute epiglottitis in adults not due to *Haemophilus*. J. Laryngol. Otol. *99:*1035–1038, 1985.
155. Santosham, M., and Moxon, E. R.: Detection and quantitation of bacteremia in childhood. J. Pediatr. *91:*719–721, 1977.
156. Scheidemandel, H. H. E., and Page, R. S.: Special considerations in epiglottitis in children. Laryngoscope *85:*1738–1745, 1975.
157. Scheifele, D. W., Daum, R. S., Syriopoulou, V., et al.: Comparison of two antigen detection techniques in a primate model of *H. influenzae* type b infection. Infect. Immun. *26:*827–831, 1979.
158. Schiffman, F. J., and Lichtman, H. C.: Paroxysmal precordial purring sign in epiglottitis. Lancet *335:*609, 1990.
159. Schuh, S., Huang, A., and Fallis, J. C.: Atypical epiglottitis. Ann. Emerg. Med. *17:*168–170, 1988.
160. Schuller, D. E., and Birch, H. G.: The safety of intubation in croup and epiglottitis: An eight-year follow-up. Laryngoscope *85:*33–46, 1975.
161. Schultes, A., and Agia, G. A.: Acute *Haemophilus parainfluenzae* epiglottitis in an adult. Postgrad. Med. *75:*207–211, 1984.
162. Schultz, R. L., and Morrison, W. V.: Short term intubation in children with acute epiglottitis. South. Med. J. *75:*158–160, 1982.
163. Schumaker, H. M., Doris, P. E., and Birnbaum, G.: Radiographic parameters in adult epiglottitis. Ann. Emerg. Med. *13:*588–590, 1984.
164. Schwam, E., and Cox, J.: Fulminant meningococcal supraglottitis: An emerging infectious syndrome? Emerg. Infect. Dis. *5:*464–467, 1999.
165. Schwartz, R. H., Knerr, R. J., Hermansen, K., et al.: Acute epiglottitis caused by β-hemolytic group C streptococci. Am. J. Dis. Child. *136:*558–559, 1982.
166. Scully, R. E., Galdabini, J. J., and McNeely, B. U.: Presentation of case. N. Engl. J. Med. *297:*878–883, 1977.
167. Shackelford, G. D., Siegel, M. J., and McAlister, W. H.: Subglottic edema in acute epiglottitis in children. Am. J. Roentgenol. *131:*603–605, 1978.
168. Shalit, M., Gross, D. J., and Levo, Y.: Pneumococcal epiglottitis in systemic lupus erythematosus on high-dosage corticosteroids. Ann. Rheum. Dis. *41:*615–616, 1982.
169. Shann, F. A., Phelan, P. D., Stocks, J. G., et al.: Prolonged nasotracheal intubation of tracheostomy in acute laryngotracheobronchitis and epiglottitis? Aust. Paediatr. J. *11:*212–217, 1975.
170. Shih, L., Hawkins, D. B., and Stanley, R. B., Jr.: Acute epiglottitis in adults: A review of 48 cases. Ann. Otol. Rhinol. Laryngol. *97:*527–529, 1988.
171. Sinclair, S. E.: *Haemophilus influenzae* type b in acute laryngitis with bacteremia. J. A. M. A. *117:*170–173, 1941.
172. Singer, J. I., and McCabe, J. B.: Epiglottitis at the extremes of age. Am. J. Emerg. Med. *6:*228–231, 1988.
173. Sivalingam, P., and Tully, A. M.: Acute meningococcal epiglottitis and septicaemia in a 65-y-old man. Scand. J. Infect. Dis. *30:*196–198, 1998.
174. Slack, C. L., Allen, G. C., Morrison, J. E., et al.: Post-varicella epiglottitis and necrotizing fasciitis. Pediatrics *105:*e13, 2000.
175. Slovis, T. L., and Arcinue, E.: Subglottic edema in acute epiglottitis in children. Letter. Am. J. Roentgenol. *132:*500, 1979.
176. Sly, P. D., Landau, L. I., and Wagener, J. S.: Acute epiglottitis in childhood: Report of an increased incidence in Victoria. Aust. N. Z. J. Med. *14:*131–134, 1984.
177. Smith, E. W. P., and Ingram, D. L.: Counterimmunoelectrophoresis in *Haemophilus influenzae* type b epiglottitis and pericarditis. J. Pediatr. *85:*571–573, 1975.
178. Soliman, M. G., and Richer, P.: Epiglottitis and pulmonary edema in children. Can. Anaesth. Soc. J. *25:*270–276, 1978.
179. Solomon, P., Weisbrod, M., Irish, J. C., et al.: Adult epiglottitis: the Toronto Hospital experience. J. Otolaryngol. *27:*332–336, 1998.
180. Stanley, R. E., and Liange, T. S.: Acute epiglottitis in adults (the Singapore experience). J. Otolaryngol. *102:*1017–1021, 1988.
181. Stuart, M. J., and Hodgetts, T. J.: Adult epiglottitis: Prompt diagnosis saves lives. Br. Med. J. *308:*329–330, 1994.
182. Sullivan, T. D., La Scotea, L. J., and Neter, E.: Relationship between the magnitude of bacteremia and the clinical disease. Pediatrics *69:*669–702, 1982.
183. Takala, A., Eskola, J., Bol, P., et al.: *Haemophilus influenzae* type b strains of outer membrane subtypes 1 and 1c cause different types of invasive disease. Lancet *2:*647–649, 1987.
184. Takala, A., Eskola, J., and Alphen, L.: Spectrum of invasive *Haemophilus influenzae* type b disease in adults. Arch. Intern. Med. *150:*2573–2576, 1990.
185. Takala, A. K., Sarvas, H., Kela, E., et al.: Susceptibility to invasive *Haemophilus influenzae* type b disease and the immunoglobulin G2m(n) allotype. J. Infect. Dis. *163:*637–639, 1991.
186. Tejani, A., Mahadevan, R., Dobias, B., et al.: Occurrence of HLA types in *H. influenzae* type b disease. Tissue Antigens *17:*205–211, 1981.
187. Templer, J. W.: Trauma to the larynx and cervical trachea. *In* English, G. M. (ed.): Otolaryngology. Hagerstown, MD, Harper & Row, 1976.
188. Theisen, D. F.: Angina epiglottidea anterior: Report of three cases. Albany Med. Ann. *21:*395–405, 1900.
189. Tos, M.: Nasotracheal intubation instead of tracheotomy in acute epiglottitis in children. Acta Otolaryngol. *75:*382–383, 1973.
190. Travis, K. W., Todres, I. D., and Shannon, D. C.: Pulmonary edema associated with croup and epiglottitis. Pediatrics *59:*695–698, 1977.
191. Trollfors, B., Brorson, J. E., Clarsson, B., et al.: Invasive infections caused by *Haemophilus* species other than *Haemophilus influenzae* infection. Infection *13:*12–14, 1985.
192. Trollfors, B., Nylen, O., and Strangert, K.: Acute epiglottitis in children and adults in Sweden 1981–1983. Arch. Dis. Child. *65:*491–494, 1990.
193. Trollfors, B.: Invasive *Haemophilus influenzae* infections in household contacts of patients with *Haemophilus influenzae* meningitis and epiglottitis. Acta Paediatr. Scand. *80:*795–797, 1991.
194. Trollfors, B., Nylen, O., Carenfelt, C., et al.: Aetiology of acute epiglottitis in adults. Scand. J. Infect. Dis. *30:*49–51, 1998.
195. Tveteras, K., and Kristensen, S.: Acute epiglottitis in adults: Bacteriology and therapeutic principles. Clin. Otolaryngol. *12:*337–343, 1987.
196. Tyler, D. C., and Haas, J. E.: Airway obstruction due to epiglottic lymphangiectasis: A case report. Int. J. Pediatr. Otorhinol. *6:*285–289, 1983.
197. Valdepena, H. G., Wald, E. R., Rose, E., et al.: Epiglottitis and *Haemophilus influenzae* immunization: The Pittsburgh experience: A five-year review. Pediatrics *96:*424–427, 1995.
198. Vauthy, P. A., and Reddy, R.: Acute upper airway obstruction in infants and children: Evaluation by the fiberoptic bronchoscope. Ann. Otol. Rhinol. Laryngol. *89:*417–418, 1980.
199. Vernham, G. A., and Crowther, J. A.: Acute myeloid leukaemia presenting with acute *Branhamella catarrhalis* epiglottitis. J. Infect. *26:*93–95, 1993.
200. Vernon, D. D., and Sarnaik, A. P.: Acute epiglottitis in children: A conservative approach to diagnosis and management. Crit. Care Med. *14:*23–25, 1986.
201. Vetto, R. R.: Epiglottitis: A report of thirty-seven cases. J. A. M. A. *173:*990–994, 1960.
202. Walsh, T. J., and Gray, W. C.: *Candida* epiglottitis in immunocompromised patients. Chest *91:*482–485, 1987.
203. Ward, J. I., Siber, G. R., Scheifele, D. W., et al.: Rapid diagnosis of *Haemophilus influenzae* type b infections by latex particle agglutination and counterimmunoelectrophoresis. J. Pediatr. *93:*37–42, 1978.
204. Ward, J. I., Lum, M. K. W., Margolis, H. S., et al.: *Haemophilus influenzae* disease in Alaskan Eskimos: Characteristics of a population with an unusual incidence of invasive disease. Lancet *1:*1281–1285, 1981.
205. Ward, J.: *Haemophilus influenzae*. *In* Feigin, R. D., and Cherry, J. D. (eds.): Textbook of Pediatric Infectious Diseases. 4th ed. Philadelphia, W. B. Saunders, 1998.
206. Warner, J. A., and Finlay, W. E. I.: Fulminating epiglottitis in adults: Report of three cases and review of the literature. Anaesthesia *40:*348–352, 1985.
207. Warshawski, J., Havas, T. E., McShane, D. P., et al.: Adult epiglottitis. J. Otolaryngol. *15:*362–364, 1986.
208. Watts, F. B., Jr., and Slovis, T. L.: The enlarged epiglottis. Pediatr. Radiol. *5:*133–136, 1977.
209. Weber, M. L., Desjardins, R., Perreault, G., et al.: Acute epiglottitis in children: Treatment with nasotracheal intubation: Report of 14 consecutive cases. Pediatrics *57:*152–155, 1976.
210. Wenger, J. K.: Supraglottitis and group A *Streptococcus*. Pediatr. Infect. Dis. J. *16:*1005–1007, 1997.
211. Westerman, E. L., and Hutton, J. P.: Acute uvulitis associated with epiglottitis. Arch. Otolaryngol. Head Neck Surg. *112:*448–449, 1986.
212. Wetmore, R. F., and Handler, S. D.: Epiglottitis: Evolution in management during the last decade. Ann. Otol. *88:*822–826, 1979.
213. Whisnant, J. K., Rogentine, G. N., Gralnick, M. A., et al.: Host factors and antibody response in *Haemophilus influenzae* type b meningitis and epiglottitis. J. Infect. Dis. *133:*448–455, 1976.
214. Wolf, M., Strauss, B., Kronenberg, J., et al.: Conservative management of adult epiglottitis. Laryngoscope *100:*183–185, 1990.
215. Young, N., Finn, A., and Powell, C.: Group B streptococcal epiglottitis. Pediatr. Infect. Dis. J. *15:*95–96, 1996.
216. Yousefzadeh, D. K., Tewfik, H. H., and Franken, E. A.: Epiglottic enlargement following radiation treatment and head and neck tumors. Pediatr. Radiol. *10:*165–168, 1981.
217. Zwahlen, A., and Regamy, C.: Les épiglottites aiguës de l'adulte. Schweiz. Med. Wochenschr. *108:*447–482, 1978.

Croup (Laryngitis, Laryngotracheitis, Spasmodic Croup, Laryngotracheobronchitis, Bacterial Tracheitis, and Laryngotracheobronchopneumonitis)

JAMES D. CHERRY

The term *croup* is used to identify several different respiratory illnesses characterized by varying degrees of inspiratory stridor, cough, and hoarseness resulting from obstruction in the region of the larynx. The etiology of croup syndromes is diverse, and the consideration of noninfectious possibilities in the differential diagnosis is of major importance. A classification of etiologic considerations in supraglottic, laryngeal, and infraglottic acute obstructions is presented in Table 22–1.

Epiglottitis (discussed in Chapter 21) and diphtheria (presented in Chapter 95) are mentioned here only for historical perspective and as a consideration in differential diagnosis. Croup is presented under the subheadings of laryngitis, laryngotracheitis, spasmodic croup, laryngotracheobronchitis, bacterial tracheitis, and laryngotracheobronchopneumonitis.

Historical Aspects

The word *croup* is derived from the Anglo-Saxon word *kropan,* "to cry aloud."[26] Until the 20th century, most crouplike illnesses were thought to be diphtheria. Diphtheritic croup is an ancient disease that has been traced to the time of Homer. The historical trail of diphtheria disappeared in the 5th century and did not reappear until 1100 years later. In the 16th century, epidemics were noted in Europe. Top[193] credits Bretonneau for differentiating diphtheritic croup from spasmodic croup in 1826. In the 20th century, the history of croup is marked by three important events: (1) the rapid decline in incidence of diphtheria associated with the use of toxoid, (2) the introduction and widespread use of antibiotics, and (3) the advent of tissue culture techniques, resulting in the establishment of viruses as etiologic agents. After these three events occurred, a prevalent academic view was that all croup was of viral etiology, and bacteria generally were dismissed as causative agents.[34, 55, 161] However, a careful review of many publications from the first half of the 20th century clearly indicates a causative role for several bacteria, in addition to *Corynebacterium diphtheriae,* in croup.* Bacterial croup (bacterial tracheitis) was rediscovered in 1979.†

In the 1940s, Davison separated spasmodic croup from other, more severe forms of croup.[41] The clinical and pathologic aspects of this entity were poorly defined, and today it often is not separated clinically from more severe forms of croup.

TABLE 22–1 ■ CLINICAL CONSIDERATIONS IN ACUTE SUPRAGLOTTIC, LARYNGEAL, AND INFRAGLOTTIC OBSTRUCTIONS

Infectious
Acute epiglottitis
Laryngitis
Laryngeal diphtheria
Laryngotracheitis
Laryngotracheobronchitis
Laryngotracheobronchopneumonitis
Bacterial tracheitis
Spasmodic croup
Mechanical
Foreign body
Secondary to trauma resulting from intubation
Allergic
Acute angioneurotic edema

Data from references 27, 28, 34, 60, 62, 144, 159.

Terminology

The terminology and classification of infectious illnesses involving the larynx and infraglottic region have evolved over time. Unfortunately, classifications often have mixed etiologic systems with anatomic systems and thereby have led to confusion. For example, croup often has been presented in articles under the heading of laryngotracheobronchitis when the authors actually were discussing laryngotracheitis.[98, 123, 133, 156, 168, 173, 191] The term *membranous croup* has been used as the title for papers dealing with bacterial croup.[45, 76] This use is confusing because membranous croup historically was diphtheria. Many papers dealing with bacterial croup also have been titled bacterial tracheitis.‡ This term seems inappropriate because most cases of bacterial croup seen today have lower respiratory tract involvement as well as tracheal findings. Table 22–2 lists the classifications and definitions used in this chapter.

In the present era, the physician's knowledge of the clinical symptoms of croup and of the relationship of history and physical findings to the needs of therapy and general prognosis has generally declined.

Etiology

The etiologic agents in laryngitis, spasmodic croup, laryngotracheitis, laryngotracheobronchitis, and laryngotracheobronchopneumonitis are presented by frequency and

*See references 8, 16, 17, 40, 41, 59, 68, 88, 96, 134, 143, 148, 164, 165.

†See references 27, 28, 31, 45, 49, 50, 54, 56, 58, 72, 76, 78, 97, 102, 121, 122, 132, 137, 142, 144, 178, 185, 186, 190, 201, 209.

‡See references 31, 49, 50, 54, 56, 58, 97, 102, 121, 122, 142, 178, 201, 209.

TABLE 22–2 ■ CLASSIFICATION AND DEFINITION OF INFECTIOUS ILLNESSES INVOLVING THE LARYNX AND INFRAGLOTTIC REGION[28, 39, 60, 143]

Category	Other Terms	Definitions
Laryngitis		Inflammation of the larynx resulting in hoarseness; usually occurs in older children and adults in association with common upper respiratory viral infection
Laryngeal diphtheria	Membranous croup, true croup, diphtheritic croup	Infection involving the larynx and other areas of the upper and lower airway due to *Corynebacterium diphtheriae*, resulting in a gradually progressive obstruction of the airway and associated inspiratory stridor
Laryngotracheitis	False croup, virus croup, acute obstructive subglottic laryngitis	Inflammation of the larynx and trachea usually caused by infection with parainfluenza and influenza viruses; occasionally secondary bacterial infection
Laryngotracheobronchitis and laryngotracheobronchopneumonitis	Membranous laryngotracheobronchitis, pseudomembranous croup	Inflammation of the larynx, trachea, and bronchi and/or lung; usually similar in onset to laryngotracheitis but more severe illness; bacterial infection frequently has causative role
Bacterial croup	Bacterial tracheitis, membranous croup, membranous tracheitis, membranous laryngotracheobronchitis, pseudomembranous croup	A severe form of laryngotracheitis, laryngotracheobronchitis, or laryngotracheobronchopneumonitis due to bacterial infection
Spasmodic croup	Spasmodic laryngitis, catarrhal spasm of the larynx, subglottic allergic edema	An illness characterized by the sudden onset at night of inspiratory stridor; associated with mild upper respiratory infection without inflammation or fever but with edema in the subglottic region

Modified from Cherry, J. D.: Acute epiglottitis, laryngitis, and croup. *In* Remington, J. S., and Swartz, M. N. (eds.): Current Clinical Topics in Infectious Diseases. Vol. 2. New York, McGraw-Hill, 1981. Reproduced with permission of The McGraw-Hill Companies.

severity of illness in Table 22–3. Laryngitis is a common manifestation of infection with many respiratory viruses in older children, adolescents, and adults. Outbreaks of laryngitis in closed population groups (such as boarding schools and military training camps) most frequently are caused by adenovirus types 4 and 7, and community outbreaks most often are noted in association with epidemic influenza. Sporadic instances of laryngitis most often are caused by adenoviral infections. Laryngitis also has been reported in association with group A streptococcal infections; interestingly, the incidence of this association has varied from 2 to 40 percent.[14, 139, 198]

Generally accepted today is that both acute laryngotracheitis and spasmodic croup, which are rarely differentiated clinically, are caused by infection with many different viruses. Although a large number of studies of respiratory viral infection exist, almost no attempt has been made to delineate the differences in etiologic spectrum by severity of illness.

Parainfluenza virus type 1 is the most common cause of acute laryngotracheitis and is responsible for frequent and clearly delineated fall and winter epidemics. Croup with parainfluenza type 2 virus is seldom severe but on occasion is related to small outbreaks. Parainfluenza virus type 3 is a frequent cause of sporadic but severe illness.

The most severe laryngotracheitis has been noted in association with influenza A viral infections. Both respiratory syncytial virus and several different adenoviruses frequently are isolated in croup. In general, these illnesses are not severe, but lower respiratory involvement occasionally is a problem. Laryngeal, tracheal, and bronchial involvement commonly occurs in measles.[30] Although rhinoviruses, *Mycoplasma pneumoniae*, enteroviruses, herpes simplex virus, and reoviruses have been associated with croup, they generally cause only minimal distress.

Bacteria, other than *Haemophilus influenzae* in epiglottitis and *C. diphtheriae* in membranous croup, generally were dismissed as causative agents in croup until relatively recently.[34, 55, 161] However, a careful review of many publications on laryngotracheobronchitis from the first half of the 20th century indicates a role for several common bacterial pathogens.* In 1979, bacterial croup was rediscovered,[97] and many reports of this illness have been published since then.† In the reports from the pre-antibiotic era, *Streptococcus pyogenes* was the pathogen implicated most commonly. Since 1979, *Staphylococcus aureus* has been the agent implicated most commonly. Other important bacteria are *Streptococcus pneumoniae* and *H. influenzae*. More recently, *Moraxella catarrhalis* has been found to be the causative agent in several cases.[10, 58, 102, 209] In most instances, bacterial croup is likely to be the result of bacterial superinfection in viral disease.‡ *Cryptosporidium* also has been recovered from the trachea of an infant with a subacute illness.[77]

Epidemiology

Croup accounts for approximately 15 percent of lower respiratory tract disease seen in pediatric practice. In a large 11-year study in a pediatric practice in Chapel Hill, North Carolina, Denny and associates[48] noted the incidence of croup by age and sex. Their data are presented in Table 22–4. The highest attack rate occurred in children 7 to 36 months of age. Few cases occurred after the sixth birthday. Hoekelman[81] studied the occurrence of illness prospectively in 246 full-term, first-born, well babies during their first

*See references 8, 16, 17, 31, 41, 42, 49, 56, 59, 68, 72, 88, 96, 134, 143, 148, 164, 165, 185, 190, 201.

†See references 10, 45, 50, 54, 58, 76, 78, 102, 121, 122, 132, 137, 142, 144, 178, 186, 209.

‡See references 20, 31, 54, 76, 96, 122, 132, 142, 144, 147.

TABLE 22–3 ■ ETIOLOGIC AGENTS IN LARYNGITIS, SPASMODIC CROUP, LARYNGOTRACHEITIS, LARYNGOTRACHEOBRONCHITIS, AND LARYNGOTRACHEOBRONCHOPNEUMONITIS PRESENTED BY FREQUENCY AND SEVERITY OF ILLNESS

Category	Etiologic Agents	Frequency*	Associated with Outbreaks	Severity†	References
Laryngitis	Adenoviruses				
	Types 4 and 7	++++	Yes	+ to +++	38, 84, 183, 198
	Types 2, 3, 5, 8, 11, 14, and 21	+++	No	+ to +++	
	Influenza viruses Types A and B	++++	Yes	+ to ++++	6, 84, 149, 198
	Parainfluenza viruses				84, 198
	Type 1	++	Yes	+ to +++	
	Types 2 and 3	+	Yes	+ to ++	
	Rhinoviruses and respiratory syncytial virus	++	No	+ to ++	84, 155, 163, 198
	Enteroviruses	+	No	+	84, 198
	Streptococcus pyogenes	+ to +++	Yes	+ to ++	14, 139
Laryngotracheitis and spasmodic croup	Parainfluenza viruses	++++		+ to +++	11, 22–24, 29, 46, 48, 65, 66, 69, 79, 83, 85, 113, 118, 124, 125, 127, 141, 149, 153, 154, 157, 199
	Type 1	++++	Yes		
	Type 2	++	Yes		
	Type 3	++	No		
	Influenza viruses	++			19, 22, 23, 29, 46, 48, 57, 61, 65, 69, 85, 86, 124, 127, 141, 149, 153, 154, 157, 199
	Type A	+++	Yes	+ to ++++	
	Type B	+	Yes	+ to ++	
	Respiratory syncytial virus	++	No	+ to ++	21–24, 29, 46, 48, 65, 66, 69, 85, 113, 125, 138, 153, 154, 156, 194, 200, 206, 210
	Measles virus	++	Yes	+ to +++	30
	Adenoviruses Unspecified types and types 1, 2, 3, 5, 6, and 7	++	No	+ to ++	13, 22–24, 29, 46, 69, 83, 85, 113, 118, 124, 125, 141, 153, 154, 156, 181, 194, 199, 200
	Rhinoviruses	+	No	+	29, 65, 69, 124, 141
	Mycoplasma pneumoniae	+	No	+	22, 24, 29, 46–48, 69, 85, 125
	Enteroviruses	+	No	+	23, 29, 35, 65, 66, 69, 85, 93, 124, 138, 182, 194, 206
	Coxsackievirus type A9	+	No	+	
	Coxsackievirus types B4 and B5	+	No	+	
	Echoviruses types 4, 11, and 21	+	No	+	
	Herpes simplex viruses	+	No	+	85, 90, 114, 141, 182
	Reoviruses	+	No	+	210
Laryngotracheobronchitis and laryngotracheo-bronchopneumonitis	Parainfluenza viruses types 1, 2, and 3	+	No	+++	16, 66, 70, 83, 125, 134, 151, 153
	Influenza viruses types A and B	+	No	+++	57, 61, 86, 154
	Staphylococcus aureus, *S. pyogenes*, *Streptococcus pneumoniae*, *Haemophilus influenzae*, and *Moraxella catarrhalis*	++	No	++++	8, 10, 16, 17, 41, 42, 45, 50, 54, 58, 59, 68, 76, 78, 88, 96, 97, 102, 121, 122. 132, 133, 143 144, 148, 164, 165, 178, 209
	Other bacteria	±	No	++++	58, 76, 78, 102, 121, 137, 209
	Cryptosporidium	–	No	++	77

*++++, most frequent; +++, frequent; ++, occasional; +, rare; –, questionable. †++++, most severe; +++, severe; ++, not severe; +, minimal distress.

TABLE 22–4 ■ INCIDENCE OF CROUP BY PATIENT'S AGE AND SEX, CHAPEL HILL, NC, 1964 TO 1975

Age (years)	Incidence/100 Children/ Year (M/F)	Incidence by Sex (M/F)
0–½	2.76/2.01	1.37
½–1	4.95/2.86	1.73
1–2	5.60/3.66	1.53
2–3	3.55/2.63	1.35
3–4	2.55/1.60	1.59
4–5	1.69/1.16	1.46
5–6	1.15/0.92	1.25
6	0.47/0.44	1.07
All ages	1.82/1.27	1.43

From Denny, F. W., Murphy, T. F., Clyde, W. A., Jr., et al.: Croup: An 11-year study in a pediatric practice. Pediatrics *71*:871–876, 1983. Used by permission.

year of life. Three infants (1.2%) had croup during the study year. The analysis of a pediatric practice with approximately 3000 active records and approximately 10,000 yearly visits of children younger than 5 years disclosed 5 cases of croup in a group of 50 consecutive hospitalized patients.[15]

Although croup occurs occasionally in older children, most cases occur within the first 3 years of life. A review of 211 children hospitalized for croup during a 2-year period at Cardinal Glennon Memorial Hospital for Children in St. Louis showed that 26 percent of those cases were in children younger than 1 year and 73 percent were in those younger than 3 years.[64] Similar data on age have been observed by others.[48, 55, 60, 168, 172]

Croup occurs decidedly more commonly in boys than in girls (see Table 22–4). In our studies, two of every three hospitalized children were boys.[64] Berg,[9] Kravitz,[115] and Rosales and Davenport[168] noted similar sex-related illness ratios. The 3-year seasonal pattern of croup as manifested by emergency department visits at Cardinal Glennon Memorial Hospital for Children is presented in Figure 22–1. In each of the years, late fall–early winter peaks occurred. In the Chapel Hill studies, an increase was noted in the number of croup cases beginning in September, with a peak in October and November and then a decrease during the next 7-month period.[48] In a 2-year emergency department study in Toronto involving 1700 cases, the peak month of visits and hospital admissions was found to be October.[172] Marx and associates[128] reviewed the National Hospital Discharge Survey data for hospitalizations for croup between 1979 and 1993. They also examined Centers for Disease Control and

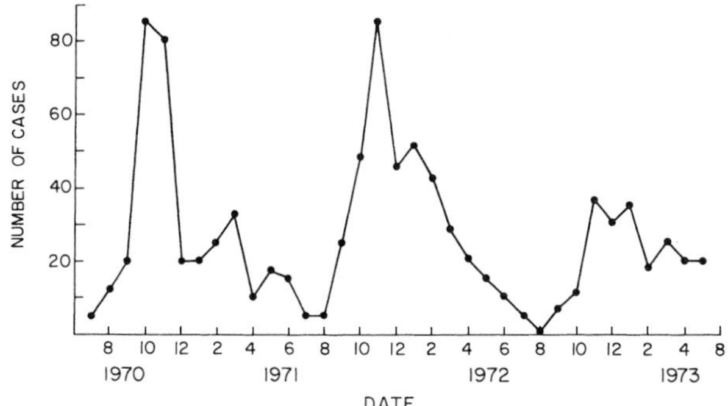

FIGURE 22–1 ■ Seasonal occurrence of croup, Cardinal Glennon Memorial Hospital for Children emergency department, July 1970 to June 1973.

Prevention laboratory-based surveillance data and published reports with virus isolation studies. Major peaks in hospitalizations for croup occurred in October of odd-number years at the time of peak parainfluenza virus type 1 activity. Minor peaks in hospitalizations for croup occurred each year in February when influenza A and B and respiratory syncytial viral infections were common occurrences. Epidemic peaks of acute laryngotracheitis reflect community-wide activity with parainfluenza 1 and 2 viruses or influenza A or B outbreaks.[48, 70, 128]

In the Toronto study, the time of the visit to the emergency department was analyzed.[172] The peak number of visits occurred between 10:00 PM and 4:00 AM. During this period, approximately 17 percent of those children seen were admitted to the hospital. In contrast, of children seen between noon and 6:00 PM, approximately 50 percent were admitted to the hospital.

Because croup is caused by the same viruses that cause other respiratory illnesses, the method of spread probably is similar for all (see discussion of the common cold in Chapter 8). In children, most spread involves close person-to-person contact, with large droplets of virus-containing nasal secretions being applied to the nose from the hands of the future host or by close-range airborne acquisition. Parainfluenza viruses are common causes of colds in adults, so older persons with relatively trivial illnesses may be the source of the more severe childhood croup.

Pathophysiology

ACUTE LARYNGITIS, LARYNGOTRACHEITIS, LARYNGOTRACHEOBRONCHITIS, AND LARYNGOTRACHEOBRONCHOPNEUMONITIS

Although the eventual site of clinically important pathologic change in laryngotracheitis is within the larynx and trachea, the initial acquisition of infection is similar to that of other respiratory viral infections and occurs within the upper air passages, including the nasal and pharyngeal epithelial surfaces. After acquisition of virus, infection of the cells of the local respiratory epithelium occurs, spreading locally to involve the larynx and trachea. The initial symptoms of nasal stuffiness and throat irritation reflect the primary sites of involvement. Studies in organ culture systems have shown that several respiratory viruses inhibit tracheal ciliary function and eventually lead to marked destruction of the epithelium as well as evidence of viral infection in the lamina propria.[111, 162]

Laryngoscopic studies in acute laryngotracheitis reveal redness and swelling of the lateral walls of the trachea, just below the vocal cords.[40, 41, 188] Because the subglottic trachea is surrounded by a firm cartilaginous ring, the inflammatory swelling can occur only by encroaching on the patency of the airway; the subglottic space often is reduced to a slit 1 to 2 mm wide. As the disease progresses, the tracheal lumen becomes further obstructed by a fibrinous exudate, and its surface is covered by pseudomembranes composed of the exudative material. The vocal cords frequently are swollen, and their mobility is impaired.

Histologic study of postmortem material from the larynx and trachea reveals marked edema and cellular infiltration in the lamina propria, submucosa, and adventitia. The cellular infiltrate includes histiocytes, lymphocytes, plasma cells, and polymorphonuclear leukocytes.[16, 17, 140, 148, 165]

The older literature indicates that the classic laryngotracheobronchitis and the same disease with pneumonia represent the extension of disease from the trachea to the bronchi and alveoli. The progressive obstructive disease with exudate and pseudomembrane obstruction at the bronchial and bronchiolar levels usually is the result of secondary bacterial involvement. In bacterial croup, the tracheal wall is infiltrated with inflammatory cells, and ulceration and microabscess formation occur.[122] In uncomplicated croup, failure of gas exchange within the lung, in addition to hypoxia resulting from subglottic tracheal obstruction, may occur.[145, 191]

Because parainfluenza viral infections are common occurrences in young children and because only a small number get croup, host factors probably are important factors in the pathogenesis. Welliver and associates[204] found that children with croup caused by parainfluenza viruses were much more likely to have virus-specific IgE antibody in their secretions than were children with parainfluenza infections who did not have croup. In the same study, researchers found that the severity of illness correlated directly with the specific IgE antibody titer. In another study, Welliver and colleagues[203] found that lymphocytes from children with croup showed greater stimulation on exposure to parainfluenza virus antigen than did those from children with noncroup upper respiratory parainfluenza viral infections. In the same patients with croup, the investigators also found a diminished histamine-induced suppression of lymphocyte reactivity to parainfluenza viral antigens. These findings suggest a defect in suppressor function in patients with croup.

BACTERIAL TRACHEITIS

As noted earlier, the bronchi and lungs also usually are involved in bacterial tracheitis, and this illness is caused by secondary bacterial infection in viral laryngotracheitis, laryngotracheobronchitis, or laryngotracheobronchopneumonitis.* In addition to the findings in laryngotracheitis of viral origin, thick pus is present within the lumen of the trachea and lower air passages as well.[78, 102, 121, 132] Ulcerations, pseudomembranes, and microabscesses also are present.

SPASMODIC CROUP

Spasmodic croup is somewhat of an enigma because it occurs in association with respiratory viral infections similar to those that cause more severe laryngotracheitis. Using direct laryngoscopy, Davison[40] noted that the subglottic tissues in spasmodic croup showed noninflammatory edema. Although definitive proof is lacking, a reasonable assumption is that in spasmodic croup, no direct viral involvement of the tracheal epithelium occurs, and the obstruction is the result of the relatively sudden occurrence of a noninflammatory edema within the submucosa of the subglottic trachea. The reason for this sudden edematous swelling is unknown, but it is readily reversible; the tendency for its occurrence appears to run in families. Hide and Guyer[80] noted that children who had recurrent croup were more likely to have a family history of allergy compared with children who did not have recurrent croup. Studies by Zach[211] suggest that children with recurrent croup have a hyperreactivity airway disorder and a tendency toward having low serum IgA levels.

*See references 2, 25–28, 31, 45, 49, 50, 54, 58, 72, 78, 97, 102, 121, 122, 144, 147, 178, 186.

Clinical Presentation

ACUTE LARYNGITIS

Clinical characteristics of laryngitis are presented in Table 22–5. Laryngitis is mainly a disease of older children, adolescents, and adults that is disturbing but self-limited. The specific clinical manifestation is hoarseness. Other symptoms depend on the causative infectious agent. Adenoviruses and influenza viruses cause the most severe instances of laryngitis. With these viruses, fever usually occurs, and sore throat, headache, muscle aches and pains, and prostration are common symptoms. In contrast, patients with laryngitis resulting from rhinoviral, parainfluenza viral, or respiratory syncytial viral infections have minimal or no fever and few systemic complaints. They usually have pronounced nasal symptoms (coryza and stuffiness), however.

On occasion, hoarseness may persist, which may be a result of secondary bacterial infection of the upper respiratory tract.

ACUTE LARYNGOTRACHEITIS

Although the clinical spectrum of acute laryngotracheitis varies considerably, its manifestations usually are significantly different from those of the other acute diseases with obstruction in the region of the larynx (see Table 22–5). Onset of illness usually is not alarming and suggests the onset of a cold. Initial symptoms are nasal complaints and include dryness, irritation, and coryza. Ordinary cough and the complaint of sore throat occur frequently. Fever is a usual occurrence within the first 24 hours, which is not true of the common cold. After a period as short as a few hours but usually after 12 to 48 hours, upper airway obstructive signs and symptoms are seen. The cough first becomes "croupy" (sounding like a barking seal), then evidence of respiratory stridor (difficulty associated with inspiration) gradually increases. Examination at this time reveals a child with a hoarse voice, coryza, a normal or minimally inflamed pharynx, and a slightly increased respiratory rate with a prolonged inspiratory phase. Temperature nearly always ranges between 37.8° C and 40.5° C (100° F and 105° F).

The speed of progression and final degree of upper airway obstruction are variable. Some children will have hoarseness and barking cough but no other evidence of obstruction; in these cases, the symptoms last for approximately 3 to 7 days, with a gradual return to normal. In other cases, the obstruction is progressive and leads to severe respiratory distress with supraclavicular and infraclavicular and sternal retractions, cyanosis of varying degrees, and apprehension. With hypoxia, the cardiac rate increases, and the child becomes restless. Without intervention, asphyxial death will occur rapidly in some children. In others, the problem of hypoxia is more prolonged, and respiratory fatigue may lead to the patient's demise. The duration of illness in the severely affected child, regardless of therapy, is rarely less than 7 days and is frequently as long as 14 days.

Laboratory study in acute laryngotracheitis is of only minimal value. The white blood cell count frequently is elevated above 10,000 cells/mm^3, and the number of polymorphonuclear cells predominates.[29, 146] Very high white blood cell counts (>20,000) with a large number of band-form neutrophils should suggest bacterial superinfection or the possibility of acute epiglottitis. The posteroanterior chest radiograph reveals the subglottic narrowing, and a lateral neck radiograph indicates the size of the epiglottis.

ACUTE LARYNGOTRACHEOBRONCHITIS AND LARYNGOTRACHEOBRONCHOPNEUMONITIS (BACTERIAL TRACHEITIS)

Laryngotracheobronchitis and laryngotracheobronchopneumonitis are far less common occurrences than are laryngotracheitis and spasmodic croup; however, these illnesses occur more commonly than generally realized.* These entities may be considered an extension of acute laryngotracheitis, as numerous descriptions in the literature suggest.† The severity of the illness is due to secondary bacterial infection. Initial symptoms and signs are similar to those of laryngotracheitis (see Table 22–5). The afflicted child usually has mild to moderately severe illness for 2 to 7 days and then suddenly becomes markedly worse. On occasion, both upper and lower airway obstructions appear to occur simultaneously. In many children, the distress from tracheal obstruction is of such magnitude that the symptoms and signs of lower respiratory involvement go unnoticed. Symptoms and signs associated with extension of disease to the bronchi, bronchioles, and lung substance include rales, air trapping, wheezing, and a further increase in the respiratory rate. Obstruction in these illnesses usually is of such a degree that either intubation or tracheostomy is necessary.

Several instances of laryngotracheobronchopneumonitis with toxic shock syndrome have been observed.[18, 25, 147, 179, 186] In general, the children with these staphylococcal infections initially have the onset of croup, then the more severe manifestations of bacterial tracheitis develop, and finally the exanthem and other manifestations of toxic shock syndrome develop. An infant with both tracheitis and supraglottitis caused by *M. catarrhalis* has been described.[2] Other findings in laryngotracheobronchitis and laryngotracheobronchopneumonitis are presented in Table 22–5.

SPASMODIC CROUP

In recent years, the clinical entity of spasmodic croup has been incorporated by many physicians into the overall diagnosis of croup. Although distinguishing mild cases of laryngotracheitis from spasmodic croup is difficult at the onset in some instances, the delineation of the two entities clearly is important from the prognostic and therapeutic perspectives (see Table 22–5).

Spasmodic croup occurs in children 3 months to 3 years of age. The onset always occurs at night, and the characteristic presentation occurs in a child who previously was thought to be well or to have had a mild cold with coryza as the only symptom. The child awakens at night with sudden dyspnea, croupy cough, and inspiratory stridor. There is no fever. The symptoms are apparently the result of sudden subglottic edema; relief is achieved easily by general reassurance and administration of moist air. The occurrence of spasmodic croup tends to run in families, with repeated attacks occurring in some children. After one attack, the child is likely to have another attack the same evening and on three or four successive evenings. These attacks can be prevented by employing mild sedation at bedtime and ensuring that the bedroom air is adequately humidified.

*See references 10, 27, 31, 45, 49, 50, 54, 58, 72, 76, 78, 97, 102, 121, 122, 132, 137, 142, 186, 209.

†See references 8, 16, 17, 41, 42, 59, 68, 88, 102, 134, 148, 160, 161, 164, 165.

Differential Diagnosis

The therapeutic approaches to the various acute obstructions in the region of the larynx vary markedly. Therefore, making a correct diagnosis is essential and frequently lifesaving. Table 22–5 lists the differential points of eight conditions with symptoms and signs of acute upper airway obstruction.

The most frequent serious differential diagnostic problem is the recognition of acute epiglottitis and its separation from the less fulminant laryngotracheitis. In epiglottitis, the important differential points are lack of a croupy cough; the presence of a swollen, cherry-red epiglottis; the sitting posture of the child with the chin pushed forward and a reluctance or refusal to lie down; and the relatively greater apprehension and anxiety of the patient than the degree of chest retraction suggests. In contrast, the child with acute laryngotracheitis has a normal epiglottis on examination, always has a typical barking cough, is comfortable in a supine position, and frequently appears to have only minimal apprehension in spite of retractions in which the sternum appears to be indenting 2 inches or more.

Early in the course of epiglottitis, the diagnosis can be confirmed only by the observation of the epiglottis, which can be performed without difficulty.[112] Later in the disease, the posture of the child and the history of rapidly progressing disease render the differential from laryngotracheitis readily apparent, so that examination of the epiglottis directly (a dangerous procedure if the child is forced to lie down) or indirectly by a lateral neck radiograph rarely is indicated and usually is contraindicated.

Laryngotracheobronchitis and laryngotracheobronchopneumonitis can be recognized by signs of lower respiratory involvement (rales, air trapping, wheezing, and pulmonary infiltrates on the radiograph). Bacterial disease should be suspected in laryngotracheobronchitis and laryngotracheobronchopneumonitis and when symptoms and signs become worse in laryngotracheitis. A lateral radiograph can be useful in the evaluation because it may reveal soft tissue densities within the trachea.

Lateral neck and chest radiographs are regarded by many physicians as definitive tests to determine whether to rule out epiglottitis and laryngotracheitis. However, in a careful study by Stankiewicz and Bowes,[161] the sensitivity and specificity of both radiographs were low.

Although a rare occurrence today, laryngeal diphtheria always should be considered and ruled out in croup. Important in this regard are the history of immunization, the pharyngeal evidence of diphtheria, the relative slowness of the disease to progress, and a greater degree of hoarseness caused by direct laryngeal membrane formation.

Spasmodic croup rarely should be confused with acute laryngotracheitis, but a perusal of the literature indicates that the two entities most commonly are considered laryngotracheitis, which is unfortunate because prognostic and therapeutic considerations for the two entities are different. Spasmodic croup always is of sudden onset at night, occurs without fever, and is relieved by simple therapeutic modalities.

The possibility of foreign body and angioneurotic edema always must be considered in upper airway obstructive disease. Differential points are presented in Table 22–5. Rarely, acute upper airway obstruction occurs in adolescents as a result of psychogenic and emotional factors.[67, 106, 171]

Specific Diagnosis

The epidemiologic history frequently is an important factor in making a specific diagnosis. Obtaining bacterial culture

TABLE 22–5 ■ DIFFERENTIAL DIAGNOSIS OF ACUTE OBSTRUCTION IN THE REGION OF THE LARYNX

Category	Acute Epiglottitis	Laryngeal Diphtheria	Laryngitis	Acute Laryngotracheitis	Laryngotracheobronchitis and Laryngotracheobronchopneumonitis (Including Bacterial Tracheitis)	Spasmodic Croup	Foreign Body	Acute Angioneurotic Edema
Common age of occurrence	1 to 8 years	All ages	Older children and adults	3 months to 3 years	3 months to 3 years	3 months to 3 years	All ages	All ages
Past and family history	Not contributory	No or inadequate immunization	Not contributory	Family history of croup	May be family history of croup	Family history of croup; perhaps previous attack	Occasional history of ingestion	Allergic history; perhaps previous attack
Prodrome	Occasionally coryza	Usually pharyngitis	Usually stuffy nose or coryza	Usually coryza	Usually coryza	Minimal coryza	None	Occasionally cutaneous allergic manifestations
Onset (time to full-blown disease)	Rapid; 4 to 12 hours	Slowly for 2- to 3-day period	Variable; 12 hours to 4 days	Moderate but variable; 12 to 48 hours	Usually gradually progressive; 12 hours to 7 days	Sudden; always at night	Usually sudden	Rapid
Symptoms on presentation								
Fever	Yes; usually 39.5° C (103° F)	Yes; usually 37.8° C to 38.5° C (100° F to 101° F)	Yes; 37.8° C to 39.4° C (100° F to 103° F) with adenoviral and influenza viral infections; usually minimal with other viruses	Yes; variable, 37.8° C to 40.5° C (100° F to 105° F)	Yes; variable, 37.8° C to 40.5° C (100° F to 105° F)	No	No, unless secondary infection	No
Hoarseness and barking cough	No	Yes	Yes	Yes	Yes	Yes	Usually no	No
Dysphagia	Yes; usually severe	Usually yes	No	No	No	No	Frequently yes	Yes
Inspiratory stridor	Yes; moderate to severe	Yes; minimal to severe	No	Yes; minimal to severe	Yes; usually severe	Yes; moderate	Variable	Yes
Toxic appearance	Severe	Usually no	No	Usually minimal	Usually moderate; may be severe	No	No	No

Signs on presentation								
Oral cavity	Pharyngitis and excessive salivation	Membranous pharyngitis	Normal or mild to moderate pharyngitis	Usually minimal pharyngitis	Usually minimal pharyngitis	Normal	Normal	Pale appearance
Epiglottis	Cherry-red and swollen	Usually normal; may contain membrane	Normal	Normal	Normal	Normal	Normal	Swollen and pale
Radiographs	Swollen epiglottis on lateral film	Not useful	Not useful	Subglottic narrowing on PA film	Subglottic narrowing on PA film; irregular soft tissue densities within trachea on lateral film	Not useful	May reveal foreign body	Swollen epiglottis on lateral film
Laboratory								
Leukocyte count	Usually markedly elevated with increased percentage of band forms	Usually elevated with increased percentage of band forms	Usually normal	Mildly elevated with > 70% polymorphonuclear cells	Variable; usually mildly elevated with 70% polymorphonuclear cells; may be increased band count	Normal	Normal, unless secondary infection	Normal; sometimes eosinophilia
Bacteriology	Throat and blood cultures yield *Haemophilus influenzae* type b	Smear and culture from membrane reveal organism	Usually normal flora in throat; occasionally *Streptococcus pyogenes* in throat	Only important if secondary infection suspected	Normal throat flora; tracheal culture often yields *S. pyogenes, Staphylococcus aureus, Streptococcus pneumoniae*, or *H. influenzae*	Normal flora	Only important if secondary infection suspected	Normal flora
Clinical course	Rapidly progressive; cardiorespiratory arrest will occur within hours if not treated	Slowly progressive obstruction of the airway	Hoarseness persists at a constant degree about 4 to 7 days; occasionally persists 2 to 3 weeks	Variable speed of progression of obstruction; usually does not require surgical intervention	Degree of obstruction usually severe; persists 7 to 14 days; frequently requires surgical intervention	Symptoms of short duration with treatment; repeated attacks common	Variable depending on size and substance of foreign body	Variable; sometimes leads to rapid asphyxia without therapy

Data from references 40, 41, 45, 54, 63, 76, 78, 97, 121, 122, 136, 192.

specimens from the throat, laryngeal region, and blood is helpful in diagnosing epiglottitis and also important in identifying laryngotracheitis, laryngotracheobronchitis, and laryngotracheobronchopneumonitis when secondary infection is suspected. The white blood cell count should be obtained because it can be helpful when secondary bacterial infection is considered.

A specific etiologic diagnosis can be made by the isolation of virus or its identification by a direct antigen test from a nasopharyngeal specimen. The diagnostic virologic facilities of many medical centers enable identification of parainfluenza viruses, respiratory syncytial viruses, adenoviruses, most rhinoviruses, and influenza viruses.

Treatment

During the last 60 years, the treatment of croup has created considerable controversy: tracheostomy versus no tracheostomy, intubation versus tracheostomy, warm versus cold humidification, antibiotics versus no antibiotics, steroids versus no steroids, sedation versus no sedation, and racemic epinephrine therapy versus mist therapy alone. Few of these controversies have been resolved scientifically, but the passage of time has lessened the importance of some of the discrepant opinions.

Of most importance in the evaluation of therapeutic modalities and the specific approach to therapy in croup is making an accurate differential diagnosis. Unfortunately, a look at the most important controversy (the use of steroids) indicates that in most instances, cases of spasmodic croup, in which a favorable outcome invariably can be expected, were not separated clinically from cases of laryngotracheitis, in which the outcome is less predictable.

ACUTE LARYNGOTRACHEITIS

In managing acute laryngotracheitis, each case must be treated individually: one child will need minimal simple therapy (i.e., mist therapy), whereas another will require consideration of all modalities. In all children with acute laryngotracheitis, attention should be given to the anxiety and apprehension of the patient and parents and to the immediate institution of mist therapy. The parents should be reassured immediately, and of importance is that the child not be separated from them. Physical examination should be performed rapidly by one physician, and all but absolutely necessary procedures should be deferred. The early institution of mist therapy will do much to relieve anxiety, but a parent should be at the bedside because mist tents can be frightening to a child.

The judicious use of sedatives also aids in relieving apprehension and anxiety. Sedatives should not be used continuously or in dosages that will suppress respirations, however.

In the past, mist therapy was the cornerstone of management of croup. However, in recent years, the value of this therapy has been questioned because two small studies performed in 1978 and 1984 failed to indicate efficacy.[12, 120] In my opinion, properly employed mist therapy in croup is still useful today. Nebulization in laryngotracheitis will prevent desiccation of the inflamed epithelial surfaces and help prevent inspissation of secretions and exudate.[150] The viscosity of the exudate will be reduced, thus allowing its easier removal by coughing.[51] Mist therapy also may stimulate nasal and laryngeal receptors that cause slowing of the respiratory rate, which will benefit the child with croup.[170]

Contrary to popular belief, the temperature of the nebulized air need not be cold but should be comfortable to the child. Before the availability of the current generation of humidification devices, steam was the usual method used to supply moisture. In the enclosed environment, it often led to excessive temperatures, which caused distress to the child. Excessively cold moist air is equally distressing.

Oxygen should be administered to the child who is hypoxemic from respiratory distress. The studies of Newth and associates[145] and Taussig and colleagues[191] indicate that mild hypoxemia occurs more commonly than is realized clinically. The drying effect of oxygen is counterproductive to the removal of tracheal exudate, so it should not be used routinely.

Since 1952, numerous communications in the English medical literature have described the use of corticosteroids in croup. Most of these reports contain testimonial information about the efficacy of one steroid preparation or another. Nine double-blind, controlled studies also were conducted before 1989.[52, 53, 93, 112, 117, 119, 176, 184, 187] Eden and Larkin,[53] in 1964, noted no difference between control and methylprednisolone therapy in a study of 50 children with acute croup. In 1967, Eden and colleagues[52] studied another 50 patients and could find no benefit from dexamethasone compared with a control preparation. Sussman and colleagues[187] also could not demonstrate any benefit from dexamethasone therapy. In contrast to these three studies, Skowron and coworkers[176] noted a slight benefit regarding duration of stridor, retractions, fever, and days in the hospital in a group receiving dexamethasone. However, they suggested that steroids not be used routinely for laryngotracheitis because the overall benefits were minimal and a potential risk exists in administration of steroids. In 1969, James[93] noted that dexamethasone-treated patients recovered from their obstructive symptoms more quickly than did the control group. In another study involving 30 children, Leipzig and associates[119] concluded that dexamethasone in an adequate dose (0.3 mg/kg initially and repeated in 2 hours) given intramuscularly hastens the recovery from uncomplicated croup. Unfortunately, this study and its predecessors have major inadequacies in design.[28, 196] In a study with 72 children, Koren and colleagues[112] noted that dexamethasone did not offer any benefit to patients with laryngotracheitis but did decrease significantly the respiratory rate in children with spasmodic croup compared with placebo-treated control subjects. Although these findings were statistically significant, the benefits were not clinically significant.

Two additional modest studies of the use of dexamethasone in croup were published, as were a meta-analysis of the evidence from the various randomized trials and a set of related editorials and a review.[4, 101, 117, 174, 177, 184] Kuusela and Vesikari[117] concluded that dexamethasone was beneficial in acute spasmodic croup, and Super and associates[184] concluded that dexamethasone is beneficial in reducing the overall severity of moderate to severe acute laryngotracheitis during the first day of treatment.

The 1989 meta-analysis suggested that the use of steroids in children hospitalized with croup resulted in a significantly increased number with clinical improvement 12 hours and 24 hours after treatment and a reduced incidence of endotracheal intubation than occurred in the control subjects.[101] In this analysis, improvement at 12 hours was noted to be greater in those children who received higher initial doses of steroid (≥125 mg of cortisone) than in those who received lower doses.

In the early 1990s, nebulized steroids were evaluated in the treatment of croup, which led to another round of testimonials, controlled studies, and treatment articles supporting the efficacy of steroids.* Since the 1989 meta-analysis, more than 15 additional, controlled, steroid treatment trials have been performed, and another meta-analysis was published in 1999.[5, 10] On the basis of the two meta-analyses and the specific studies analyzed, most reviews on the management of croup recommend the routine use of steroids (administered orally, intramuscularly, or by nebulization) in the treatment of croup.†

In the past, when I reviewed the data on the use of steroids in croup, what concerned me was that the specific clinical entity that was being treated was poorly defined and that no evidence indicated that steroids worked in any illness other than spasmodic croup.[28] Today, my analysis of the available data still results in concern and some skepticism. In their meta-analysis, Ausejo and colleagues[5] noted that publication bias played a part in the results. They therefore stated that this problem rendered their findings of positive efficacy somewhat less certain. Of most concern to me today is that the risks of steroid use have not been evaluated and that because of small sample sizes in all available studies they cannot be evaluated by meta-analysis.

I have seen lower respiratory tract complications develop in three children receiving steroid treatment for croup. In one case, an adenoviral pneumonia worsened, and in the other cases, bacterial tracheitis with pneumonia occurred. In the study of Super and colleagues,[184] two steroid-treated patients developed pneumonia during therapy; none of the control subjects developed pneumonia. In a more recent trial in which 28 children received nebulized dexamethasone, two children with neutropenia developed bacterial tracheitis.[94] Burton and associates[20] reported the occurrence of *Candida* laryngotracheitis as a complication of steroid and antibiotic treatment in a child with croup.

In summary, a single dose of a systemic steroid, such as dexamethasone administered intramuscularly or orally (0.6 mg/kg), or the limited use of nebulized budesonide probably is safe and may be useful in the child with more severe spasmodic croup. Steroids should not be used in laryngotracheobronchitis, laryngotracheobronchopneumonitis, or epiglottitis.

Because laryngotracheitis is a disease of viral etiology, what seems apparent is that antibiotic therapy would not be indicated and consequently not employed. However, in our analysis of more than 200 hospitalized children with laryngotracheitis, we noted that antibiotics had been administered to 85 percent.[64] A review of the records in many instances revealed that the physician had given antibiotic therapy because the possibility of epiglottitis had not been ruled out adequately. In several instances, the epiglottis had been observed and thought to be somewhat reddened or questionably enlarged.

A second consideration with regard to antibiotic therapy in croup is that the most dramatic reduction in mortality rates coincides with the introduction and widespread use of antibiotics. In my opinion, many of the deaths attributed to croup in the pre-antibiotic era were caused by secondary bacterial infections. Although use of antibiotics contributed to the reduction in the number of deaths caused by croup, other factors may be important. At about the same time that antibiotics were introduced, disease caused by *S. pyogenes* decreased in incidence and severity. Reasons for the decreased frequency of streptococcal disease were not clear.

Most patients with laryngotracheitis today do not need antibiotic therapy. However, in severe cases in which bacterial sepsis cannot be ruled out, antibiotic therapy should be employed. The pathogens to consider include pneumococci, group A streptococci, *S. aureus,* and *H. influenzae.* In patients with laryngotracheitis in whom fever persists or signs change, secondary infection should be considered. In these instances, appropriate culture specimens should be obtained before initiation of therapy (see the section on laryngotracheobronchitis for specific antibiotic therapy).

The use of nebulized racemic epinephrine, which was introduced by Jordan[98] in 1966 and popularized by Jordan and other members of the Utah group,[1, 99] has been adopted widely throughout the United States and elsewhere.[104, 116, 123, 136, 169, 173] The usual method of nebulization of racemic epinephrine is by intermittent positive-pressure breathing, and this form of therapy was associated with a marked reduction in tracheostomies in several series.

In 1973, Gardner and associates[63] performed the first double-blind, controlled study in which racemic epinephrine was nebulized by a compressor without intermittent positive-pressure breathing. They found that saline-treated patients responded as well to therapy as did the racemic epinephrine recipients. In retrospect, this study can be criticized because the investigators failed to differentiate spasmodic croup from laryngotracheitis. In 1975, Taussig and associates[191] reported a small but carefully conducted study with intermittent positive-pressure breathing and racemic epinephrine in which they noted acute improvement in all cases, recurrence of symptoms in 2 hours, and no change in partial pressure of oxygen with clinical improvement; 24 to 36 hours after therapy, treated and untreated children were clinically similar. In another significant study that involved children hospitalized with severe croup without improvement after admission to a high-humidity mist room, Westley and colleagues[207] showed that racemic epinephrine therapy caused definite short-term improvement in children compared with saline treatment. This study is particularly important because a parainfluenza viral etiology was documented in more than 65 percent of the study's subjects, and all cases were clearly laryngotracheitis and not spasmodic croup.

In summary, the following points can be made about the use of racemic epinephrine in the treatment of croup: (1) many children with croup will respond to moist air alone; (2) significant rebound occurs after racemic epinephrine therapy, so it frequently needs to be repeated many times; (3) in the hospitalized child with severe acute laryngotracheitis, it should be used. Tracheotomy or endotracheal intubation can be prevented in some cases. The most important issue today regarding the use of racemic epinephrine is whether it can be used safely for outpatient therapy.[32, 103, 158] In the past, most experts advised against the use of racemic epinephrine in the outpatient setting because of the known rebound that occurs. Some data suggest that with careful observation for a sufficient period (at least 2 hours) after administration, patients can be managed safely and hospitalizations decreased.[32, 103, 158] In a small study, investigators found that the administration of a helium-oxygen mixture (Heliox) resulted in improvement in children with croup similar to that with racemic epinephrine treatment.[202]

The establishment of a mechanical airway seldom is necessary in patients with laryngotracheitis today. The planned procedure has a better outcome than does the procedure performed under emergency conditions. Traditionally, tracheostomy was the preferred method when a mechanical airway was needed.[7, 62, 212] However, when careful attention

*See references 5, 37, 71, 73, 87, 92, 94, 95, 100, 107–110, 131, 166, 167, 205.

†See references 3, 36, 43, 44, 71, 73, 89, 92, 95, 108–110, 166, 167.

is given to tube size and other aspects of placement and maintenance, nasotracheal intubation compares favorably with tracheostomy.[7, 212] The management of the child with a mechanical airway requires trained pediatric intensive care physicians and the facilities of an adequately staffed intensive care unit.

Two antiviral drugs have activity against viruses that cause laryngotracheitis.[75, 91, 130, 189, 208] Amantadine is approved for use in treating influenza A viral infections, and ribavirin is active against parainfluenza viruses, influenza A and B viruses, and respiratory syncytial virus (see Chapter 238, Antiviral Agents, and Chapter 181, Influenza Viruses). At present, consideration of amantadine in therapy for severe croup that occurs during documented epidemics caused by influenza A virus would seem reasonable. However, few trials of this mode of therapy have been conducted in children, and it has not been demonstrated to be beneficial to adults with pulmonary complications of influenza. Both influenza A and B can be treated with neuraminidase inhibitors (zanamivir and oseltamivir), but these agents are not approved for use in young children.[33]

LARYNGOTRACHEOBRONCHITIS AND LARYNGOTRACHEOBRONCHOPNEUMONITIS (BACTERIAL TRACHEITIS)

In general, all the treatment considerations discussed for laryngotracheitis, except steroids and racemic epinephrine by aerosol, apply to laryngotracheobronchitis and laryngotracheobronchopneumonitis. Most important, however, because most patients have bacterial disease, antibiotics should be administered to all patients after appropriate culture specimens are obtained. Empirical therapy should be directed against *S. aureus, S. pyogenes, S. pneumoniae,* and *H. influenzae*. At present, initial treatment with oxacillin (150 mg/kg/day every 6 hours intravenously) and a third-generation cephalosporin, such as cefotaxime (150 mg/kg/day every 6 hours intravenously), is reasonable. The physician should be aware of the possibility of the presence of a methicillin-resistant staphylococcus. In severe cases, vancomycin (40 mg/kg/day intravenously every 6 hours) may be used instead of oxacillin.

Most children with advanced laryngotracheobronchitis or laryngotracheobronchopneumonitis will need the placement of a mechanical airway. Whenever possible, this procedure should be done electively rather than as an emergency.

SPASMODIC CROUP

The major problem in therapy for spasmodic croup is overtreatment. Many physicians are unfamiliar with the benign nature of this disease and will institute intermittent positive-pressure breathing, steroids, and other unnecessary therapies. Spasmodic croup responds to the administration of moist air in all instances.

Further attacks of spasmodic croup the same evening or during the next few nights can be prevented by the use of mild sedation at bedtime.

LARYNGITIS

Patients with laryngitis should rest their voices as much as possible. Increased fluid intake and the use of a vaporizer will help liquefy secretions and should provide symptomatic relief. Because group A streptococcal infection is a cause of laryngitis, culture should be performed. If it is positive, penicillin or a suitable alternative antimicrobial agent should be administered. In children and adolescents with prolonged hoarseness, sinusitis should be considered. Radiographs of the sinuses and a quantitative culture from the nose should be performed in search of a predominant abnormal bacterial flora. If either is positive, therapy with appropriate antibiotics is indicated. If laryngeal symptoms are persistent, the child should undergo laryngoscopic examination and other appropriate studies to exclude tumor, foreign body, and other chronic diseases.

Prognosis

The prognosis of acute laryngotracheitis has improved markedly during the last 50 years. Today, a child with croup only rarely requires a mechanical airway, and virtually all deaths should be preventable. The child should be observed for the following complications: hypoxemia and cardiorespiratory failure, pulmonary edema,[195] pneumothorax and pneumomediastinum, mechanical problems caused by tracheotomies and nasotracheal tubes, and secondary bacterial infections.

Children with a history of croup have a higher prevalence of increased bronchial reactivity than do children without such history.[74, 126, 205]

Prevention

At present, acute laryngotracheitis is not preventable. Trials with attenuated parainfluenza viral vaccines were not effective.[197] The widespread use of influenza vaccines could reduce the incidence of croup caused by influenza A and B viruses.

REFERENCES

1. Adair, J. C., Ring, W. H., Jordan, W. S., et al.: Ten-year experience with IPPB in the treatment of acute laryngotracheobronchitis. Anesth. Analg. *50*:649–655, 1971.
2. Alligood, G. A., and Kenny, J. F.: Tracheitis and supraglottitis associated with *Branhamella catarrhalis* and respiratory syncytial virus. Pediatr. Infect. Dis. *8*:190, 1989.
3. American Academy of Pediatrics: Parainfluenza. *In* Pickering, L. K. (ed.): 2000 Red Book: Report of the Committee on Infectious Diseases. 25th ed. Elk Grove Village, IL, American Academy of Pediatrics, 2000, pp. 419–420.
4. Anonymous: Steroids and croup. Lancet *2*:1134–1136, 1989.
5. Ausejo, M., Saenz, A., Pham, B., et al.: The effectiveness of glucocorticoids in treating croup: Meta-analysis. BMJ *319*:595–600, 1999.
6. Banatvala, J. E., Reiss, B. B., Anderson, T. B., et al.: Asian influenza in 1963 in two general practices in Cambridge, England. Can. Med. Assoc. J. *93*:593–597, 1965.
7. Barker, G. A.: Current management of croup and epiglottitis. Pediatr. Clin. North Am. *26*:565–579, 1979.
8. Baum, H. L.: Acute laryngotracheobronchitis. J. A. M. A. *91*:1097–1102, 1928.
9. Berg, R. B.: Weight and sex of children hospitalized with infectious croup: An analysis of 850 cases. Pediatrics *31*:18–21, 1963.
10. Bernstein, T., Brilli, R., and Jacobs, B.: Is bacterial tracheitis changing? A 14-month experience in a pediatric intensive care unit. Clin. Infect. Dis. *27*:458–462, 1998.
11. Bisno, A. L., Barratt, N. P., Swanston, W. H., et al.: An outbreak of acute respiratory disease in Trinidad associated with para-influenza viruses. Am. J. Epidemiol. *91*:68–77, 1970.
12. Bourchier, D., Dawson, K. P., and Ferguson, D. M.: Humidification in viral croup: A controlled trial. Aust. Paediatr. J. *20*:289–291, 1984.
13. Brandt, C. D., Kim, H. W., Vargosko, A. J., et al.: Infections in 18,000 infants and children in a controlled study of respiratory tract disease. I. Adenovirus pathogenicity in relation to serologic type and illness syndrome. Am. J. Epidemiol. *90*:484–500, 1969.
14. Breese, B. B.: Diagnosis of streptococcal pharyngitis. *In* Breese, B. B., and Hall, C. B. (eds.): Beta Hemolytic Streptococcal Diseases. Boston, Houghton Mifflin, 1978, pp. 79–96.

15. Breese, B. B., Disney, F. A., and Talpey, W.: The nature of a small pediatric group practice. Part I. Pediatrics *38*:264–277, 1966.
16. Brennemann, J., Clifton, W. M., Frank, A., et al.: Acute laryngotracheobronchitis. Am. J. Dis. Child. *55*:667–695, 1938.
17. Brighton, G. R.: Laryngotracheobronchitis. Ann. Otol. Rhinol. Laryngol. *49*:1070–1082, 1940.
18. Britto, J., Habibi, P., Walters, S., et al.: Systematic complications associated with bacterial tracheitis. Arch. Dis. Child. *74*:249–250, 1996.
19. Brocklebank, J. T., Court, S. D. M., McQuillin, J., et al.: Influenza-A infection in children. Lancet *2*:497–500, 1972.
20. Burton, D. M., Seid, A. B., Kearns, D. B., et al.: *Candida* laryngotracheitis: A complication of combined steroid and antibiotic usage in croup. Int. J. Pediatr. Otorhinol. *23*:171–175, 1992.
21. Chanock, R. M., Parrott, R. H., Johnson, K. M., et al.: Myxoviruses: Parainfluenza. Am. Rev. Respir. Dis. *88*(pt 2):152–166, 1962.
22. Chanock, R., Chambon, L., Chang, W., et al.: WHO respiratory disease survey in children: A serological study. Bull. World Health Organ. *37*:363–369, 1967.
23. Chanock, R. M., and Parrott, R. H.: Acute respiratory disease in infancy and childhood: Present understanding and prospects for prevention: E. Mead Johnson Address, October 1964. Pediatrics *36*:21–39, 1965.
24. Chapman, R. S., Henderson, F. W., Clyde, W. A., Jr., et al.: The epidemiology of tracheobronchitis in pediatric practice. Am. J. Epidemiol. *114*:786–797, 1981.
25. Chenaud, M., Leclerc, F., and Martinot, A.: Bacterial croup and toxic shock syndrome. Eur. J. Pediatr. *145*:306–307, 1986.
26. Cherry, J. D.: Croup. *In* Kiple, K. F. (ed.): The Cambridge World History of Human Disease. Cambridge, Cambridge University Press, 1993, pp. 654–657.
27. Cherry, J. D.: Acute epiglottitis, laryngitis and croup. *In* Remington, J. S., and Swartz, M. N. (eds.): Current Clinical Topics in Infectious Diseases. New York, McGraw-Hill, 1981, pp. 1–30.
28. Cherry, J. D.: The treatment of croup: Continued controversy due to failure of recognition of historic, ecologic, etiologic and clinical perspectives. J. Pediatr. *94*:352–354, 1979.
29. Cherry, J. D.: Newer respiratory viruses: Their role in respiratory illnesses of children. *In* Schulman, I. (ed.): Advances in Pediatrics. Vol. 20. Chicago, Year Book, 1973, pp. 225–289.
30. Cherry, J. D.: Measles. *In* Feigin, R. D., and Cherry, J. D. (eds.): Textbook of Pediatric Infectious Diseases. 4th ed. Philadelphia, W. B. Saunders, 1998.
31. Conley, S. F., Beste, D. J., and Hoffmann, R. G.: Measles-associated bacterial tracheitis. Pediatr. Infect. Dis. J. *12*:414–415, 1993.
32. Cornell, H. M., and Bolte, R. G.: Outpatient use of racemic epinephrine in croup. Am. Fam. Phys. *46*:683–684, 1992.
33. Couch, R.B.: Prevention and treatment of influenza. N. Engl. J. Med. *343*:1778–1787, 2000.
34. Cramblett, H. G.: Croup: Present day concept. Pediatrics *25*:1071–1076, 1960.
35. Cramblett, H. G., Moffett, H. L., Black, J. P., et al.: Coxsackie virus infections: Clinical and laboratory studies. J. Pediatr. *64*:406–414, 1964.
36. Cressman, W. R., and Myer, C. M., III: Diagnosis and management of croup and epiglottitis. Pediatr. Clin. North Am. *41*:265–276, 1994.
37. Cruz, M. N., Stewart, G., and Rosenberg, N.: Use of dexamethasone in the outpatient management of acute laryngotracheitis. Pediatrics *96*:220–223, 1995.
38. Dascomb, H. E., and Hilleman, M. R.: Clinical and laboratory studies in patients with respiratory disease caused by adenoviruses (R1-APC-ARD agents). Am. J. Med. *21*:161, 1956.
39. Davison, F. W.: Inflammatory diseases of the larynx of infants and small children. Ann. Otol. Rhinol. Laryngol. *76*:753, 1967.
40. Davison, F. W.: Acute laryngeal obstruction in children. J. A. M. A. *171*:1301–1305, 1959.
41. Davison, F. W.: Acute obstructive laryngitis in children. Penn. Med. J. *53*:250–254, 1950.
42. Davison, F. W.: Acute laryngotracheobronchitis: Further studies on treatment. Arch. Otolaryngol. *47*:455–464, 1948.
43. Dawson, K., Cooper, D., Cooper, P., et al.: The management of acute laryngo-tracheo-bronchitis (croup): A consensus view. J. Paediatr. Child Health *28*:223–224, 1992.
44. DeBoeck, K.: Croup: A review. Eur. J. Pediatr. *154*:432–436, 1995.
45. Denneny, J. C., and Handler, S. D.: Membranous laryngotracheobronchitis. Pediatrics *70*:705–707, 1982.
46. Denny, F. W., and Clyde, W. A., Jr.: Acute lower respiratory tract infections in nonhospitalized children. J. Pediatr. *108*:635–646, 1986.
47. Denny, F. W., Clyde, W. A., Jr., and Glezen, W. P.: *Mycoplasma pneumoniae* disease: Clinical spectrum, pathophysiology, epidemiology, and control. J. Infect. Dis. *123*:74–92, 1971.
48. Denny, F. W., Murphy, T. F., Clyde, W. A., Jr., et al.: Croup: An 11-year study in a pediatric practice. Pediatrics *71*:871–876, 1983.
49. Donnelly, B. W., McMillan, J. A., and Weiner, L. B.: Bacterial tracheitis: Report of eight new cases and review. Rev. Infect. Dis. *12*:729–735, 1990.
50. Dudin, A. A., Thalji, A., and Rambaud-Cousson, A.: Bacterial tracheitis among children hospitalized for severe obstructive dyspnea. Pediatr. Infect. Dis. *9*:293–295, 1990.
51. Dulfano, M. J., Adler, K., and Wooten, O.: Physical properties of sputum. IV. Effects of 100 percent humidity and water mist. Am. Rev. Respir. Dis. *107*:130–132, 1972.
52. Eden, A. N., Kaufman, A., and Yu, R.: Corticosteroids and croup: Controlled double-blind study. J. A. M. A. *200*:403–404, 1967.
53. Eden, A. N., and Larkin, V. D. P.: Corticosteroid treatment of croup. Pediatrics *33*:768–769, 1964.
54. Edwards, K. M., Dundon, M. C., and Altemeier, W. A.: Bacterial tracheitis as a complication of viral croup. Pediatr. Infect. Dis. *2*:390–391, 1983.
55. Eichenwald, H. F.: Respiratory infections in children. Hosp. Pract. *11*:81–90, 1976.
56. Eid, N. S., and Jones, V. F.: Bacterial tracheitis as a complication of tonsillectomy and adenoidectomy. J. Pediatr. *125*:401–402, 1994.
57. Eller, J. J., Fulginiti, V. A., Plunket, D. C., et al.: Attack rates for hospitalized croup in children in a military population: Importance of A2 influenza infection. Pediatr. Res. *6*:386, 1972.
58. Ernst, T. N., and Philp, M.: Bacterial tracheitis caused by *Branhamella catarrhalis*. Pediatr. Infect. Dis. *6*:574, 1987.
59. Everett, A. R.: Acute laryngotracheobronchitis: An analysis of 1,175 cases with 98 tracheotomies. Laryngoscope *61*:113–123, 1951.
60. Fearon, B.: Acute obstructive laryngitis in infants and children. Hosp. Med. *4*:51–67, 1968.
61. Forbes, J. A.: Severe effects of influenza viral infection. Med. J. Aust. *44*:75–79, 1958.
62. Fried, M. P.: Controversies in the management of supraglottitis and croup. Pediatr. Clin. North Am. *26*:931–942, 1979.
63. Gardner, H. G., Powell, K. R., Roden, V. J., et al.: The evaluation of racemic epinephrine in the treatment of infectious croup. Pediatrics *52*:68–71, 1973.
64. Gardner, H. G., Powell, K. R., and Cherry, J. D.: Unpublished data, 1973.
65. Gardner, P. S., McQuillin, J., McGuckin, R., et al.: Observations on clinical and immunofluorescent diagnosis of parainfluenza virus infections. Br. Med. J. *2*:7–12, 1971.
66. Gardner, P. S.: Virus infections and respiratory disease of childhood. Arch. Dis. Child. *43*:629–645, 1968.
67. Geist, R., and Tallett, S. E.: Diagnosis and management of psychogenic stridor caused by a conversion disorder. Pediatrics *86*:315–317, 1990.
68. Gittens, T. R.: XXXIII. Laryngitis and tracheobronchitis in children: Special reference to nondiphtheritic infections. Ann. Otol. Rhinol. Laryngol. *41*:422–438, 1932.
69. Glezen, W. P., Loda, F. A., Clyde, W. A., Jr., et al.: Epidemiologic patterns of acute lower respiratory disease of children in a pediatric group practice. J. Pediatr. *78*:397–406, 1971.
70. Glezen, W. P., Loda, F. A., and Denny, F. W.: The parainfluenza viruses. *In* Evans, A. S. (ed.): Viral Infections of Humans: Epidemiology and Control. New York, Plenum, 1976, pp. 337–349.
71. Godden, C. W., Campbell, M. J., Hussey, M., et al.: Double blind placebo controlled trial of nebulised budesonide for croup. Arch. Dis. Child. *76*:155–158, 1997.
72. Gold, S. M., Shott, S. R., and Myer, C. M., III: Radiological case of the month. Arch. Pediatr. Adolesc. Med. *150*:97–98, 1996.
73. Griffin, S., Ellis, S., Fitzgerald-Barron, A., et al.: Nebulised steroid in the treatment of croup: A systematic review of randomized controlled trials. Br. J. Gen. Pract. *50*:135–141, 2000.
74. Gurwitz, D., Corey, M., and Levison, H.: Pulmonary function and bronchial reactivity in children after croup. Am. Rev. Respir. Dis. *122*: 95–99, 1980.
75. Hall, C. B., McBride, J. T., Walsh, E. E., et al.: Aerosolized ribavirin treatment of infants with respiratory syncytial viral infection: A randomized double-blind study. N. Engl. J. Med. *308*:1443–1447, 1983.
76. Han, B. K., Dunbar, J. S., and Striker, T. W.: Membranous laryngotracheobronchitis (membranous croup). A. J. R. Am. J. Roentgenol. *133*:53–58, 1979.
77. Harari, M. D., West, B., and Dwyer, B.: *Cryptosporidium* as cause of laryngotracheitis in an infant. Lancet *1*:1207, 1986.
78. Henry, R. L., Mellis, C. M., and Benjamin, B.: Pseudomembranous croup. Arch. Dis. Child. *58*:180–183, 1983.
79. Herrmann, E. C., Jr., and Hable, K. A.: Experiences in laboratory diagnosis of parainfluenza viruses in routine medical practice. Mayo Clin. Proc. *45*:177–188, 1970.
80. Hide, D. W., and Guyer, B. M.: Recurrent croup. Arch. Dis. Child. *60*:585–586, 1985.
81. Hoekelman, R. A.: Infectious illness during the first year of life. Pediatrics *59*:119–121, 1977.
82. Holdaway, M. D.: Croup and epiglottitis: Diagnosis and action. Drugs *13*:452–457, 1977.
83. Holzel, A., Parker, L., Patterson, W. H., et al.: Virus isolations from throats of children admitted to hospital with respiratory and other diseases, Manchester 1962–4. Br. Med. J. *1*:614–619, 1965.
84. Hope-Simpson, R. E., and Higgins, P. G.: A respiratory virus study in Great Britain: Review and evaluation. Prog. Med. Virol. *11*:354–407, 1969.
85. Horn, M. E. C., Brain, E., Gregg, I., et al.: Respiratory viral infection in childhood: A survey in general practice, Roehampton 1967–1972. J. Hyg. Camb. *74*:157–168, 1975.

86. Howard, J. B., McCracken, G. H., Jr., and Luby, J. P.: Influenza A_2 virus as a cause of croup requiring tracheotomy. J. Pediatr. *81*:1148–1150, 1972.
87. Husby, S., Agertoft, L., Mortensen, S., et al.: Treatment of croup with nebulised steroid (budesonide): A double-blind, placebo-controlled study. Arch. Dis. Child. *68*:352–355, 1993.
88. Hyde, C. I., and Ruchman, J.: Acute infectious edematous laryngitis in which recovery followed tracheotomy. Arch. Pediatr. *48*:124–129, 1931.
89. Infectious Diseases and Immunization Committee, Canadian Paediatric Society: Steroid therapy for croup in children admitted to hospital. Can. Med. Assoc. J. *147*:429–430, 1992.
90. Inglis, A. F., Jr.: Herpes simplex virus infection: A rare cause of prolonged croup. Arch. Otolaryngol. Head Neck Surg. *119*:551–552, 1993.
91. Jackson, G. G., and Stanley, E. D.: Prevention and control of influenza by chemoprophylaxis and chemotherapy: Prospects from examination of recent experience. J. A. M. A. *235*:2739–2742, 1976.
92. Jaffe, D.M.: The treatment of croup with glucocorticoids. N. Engl. J. Med. *339*:553–555, 1998.
93. James, J. A.: Dexamethasone in croup: A controlled study. Am. J. Dis. Child. *117*:511–516, 1969.
94. Johnson, D. W., Schuh, S., Koren, G., et al.: Outpatient treatment of croup with nebulized dexamethasone. Arch. Pediatr. Adolesc. Med. *150*:349–355, 1996.
95. Johnson, D. W., Jacobson, S., Edney, P. C., et al.: A comparison of nebulized budesonide, intramuscular dexamethasone, and placebo for moderately severe croup. N. Engl. J. Med. *339*:498–503, 1998.
96. Johnson, M. C.: Acute laryngotracheobronchitis in infants: Report of three cases. Arch. Otolaryngol. *17*:230–234, 1933.
97. Jones, R., Santos, J. I., and Overall, J. C., Jr.: Bacterial tracheitis. J. A. M. A. *242*:721–726, 1979.
98. Jordan, W. S.: Laryngotracheobronchitis: Evaluation of new therapeutic approaches. Rocky Mt. Med. J. *63*:69, 1966.
99. Jordan, W. S., Graves, C. L., and Elwyn, R. A.: New therapy for postintubation laryngeal edema and tracheitis in children. J. A. M. A. *212*:585–588, 1970.
100. Kaditis, A. G., and Wald, E. R.: Viral croup: A current diagnosis and treatment. Pediatr. Infect. Dis. J. *17*:827–834, 1998.
101. Kairys, S. W., Olmstead, E. N., and O'Connor, G. T.: Steroid treatment of laryngotracheitis: A meta-analysis of the evidence from randomized trials. Pediatrics *83*:683–693, 1989.
102. Kasian, G. F., Bingham, W. T., Steinberg, J., et al.: Bacterial tracheitis in children. Can. Med. Assoc. J. *140*:46–50, 1989.
103. Kelley, P. B., and Simon, J. E.: Racemic epinephrine use in croup and disposition. Am. J. Emerg. Med. *10*:181–183, 1992.
104. Kepes, E. R., Martinez, L. R., Andrews, I. C., et al.: Racemic epinephrine in postintubation laryngeal edema. N. Y. State J. Med. *72*:583–584, 1972.
105. Kibrick, S.: Current status of coxsackie and ECHO viruses in human disease. Prog. Med. Virol. *6*:27–70, 1964.
106. Kissoon, N., Kronick, J. B., and Frewen, T. C.: Psychogenic upper airway obstruction. Pediatrics *81*:714–717, 1988.
107. Klassen, T. P., Feldman, M. E., Watters, L. K., et al.: Nebulized budesonide for children with mild to moderate croup. N. Engl. J. Med. *331*:285–289, 1994.
108. Klassen, T. P., Watters, L. K., Feldman, M. E., et al.: The efficacy of nebulized budesonide in dexamethasone-treated outpatients with croup. Pediatrics *97*:463–466, 1996.
109. Klassen, T. P., Craig, W. R., Moher, D., et al.: Nebulized budesonide and oral dexamethasone for treatment of croup: A randomized controlled trial. J.A.M.A. *279*:1629–1632, 1998.
110. Klassen T.P.: Croup: A current perspective. Emerg. Med. *46*:1167–1178, 1999.
111. Klein, J. D., and Collier, A. M.: Pathogenesis of human parainfluenza type 3 virus infection in hamster tracheal organ culture. Infect. Immunol. *10*:883–888, 1974.
112. Koren, G., Frand, M., Barzilay, Z., et al.: Corticosteroid treatment of laryngotracheitis vs spasmodic croup in children. Am. J. Dis. Child. *137*:941–944, 1983.
113. Korppi, M., Halonen, P., Kleemola, M., et al.: The role of parainfluenza viruses in inspiratory difficulties in children. Acta Paediatr. Scand. *77*:105–111, 1988.
114. Krause, I., Schonfeld, T., Ben Ari, J., et al.: Prolonged croup due to herpes simplex virus infection. Eur. J. Pediatr. *157*:567–569, 1998.
115. Kravitz, H.: Sex distribution of hospitalized children with acute respiratory diseases, gastroenteritis and meningitis. Clin. Pediatr. *4*:484–491, 1965.
116. Kristjansson, S., Berg-Kelly, K., and Winso, E.: Inhalation of racemic adrenaline in the treatment of mild and moderately severe croup: Clinical symptom score and oxygen saturation measurements for evaluation of treatment effects. Acta Paediatr. *83*:1156–1160, 1994.
117. Kuusela, A. L., and Vesikari, T.: A randomized double-blind, placebo-controlled trial of dexamethasone and racemic epinephrine in the treatment of croup. Acta Paediatr. Scand. *77*:99–104, 1988.
118. Laxdal, O. E., Robertson, H. E., Braaten, V., et al.: Acute respiratory infections in children. I. An intensive study of etiology in an open community. Can. Med. Assoc. J. *88*:1049–1054, 1963.
119. Leipzig, B., Oski, F. A., Cummings, C. W., et al.: A prospective randomized study to determine the efficacy of steroids in treatment of croup. J. Pediatr. *94*:194–196, 1979.
120. Lenney, W., and Milner, A. D.: Treatment of acute viral croup. Arch. Dis. Child. *53*:704–706, 1978.
121. Liston, S. L., Gehrz, R. C., and Jarvis, C. W.: Bacterial tracheitis. Arch. Otolaryngol. *107*:561–564, 1981.
122. Liston, S. L., Gehrz, R. C., Siegel, L. G., et al.: Bacterial tracheitis. Am. J. Dis. Child. *137*:764–767, 1983.
123. Lockhart, C. H., and Battaglia, J. D.: Croup (laryngotracheal bronchitis) and epiglottitis. Pediatr. Ann. *6*:262–269, 1977.
124. Loda, F. A., Clyde, W. A., Jr., Glezen, W. P., et al.: Studies on the role of viruses, bacteria, and *M. pneumoniae* as causes of lower respiratory tract infections in children. J. Pediatr. *72*:161–176, 1968.
125. Loda, F. A., Glezen, W. P., and Clyde, W. A., Jr.: Respiratory disease in group day care. Pediatrics *49*:428–437, 1972.
126. Loughlin, G. M., and Taussig, L. M.: Pulmonary function in children with a history of laryngotracheobronchitis. J. Pediatr. *94*:365–369, 1979.
127. Macasaet, F. F., Kidd, P. A., Bolano, C. R., et al.: The etiology of acute respiratory infections. III. The role of viruses and bacteria. J. Pediatr. *72*:829–839, 1968.
128. Marx, A., Török, T. J., Holman, R. C., et al.: Pediatric hospitalizations for croup (laryngotracheobronchitis): Biennial increases associated with human parainfluenza virus 1 epidemics. J. Infect. Dis. *176*:1423–1427, 1997.
129. Mauro, R. D., Poole, S. R., and Lockhart, C. H.: Differentiation of epiglottitis from laryngotracheitis in the child with stridor. Am. J. Dis. Child. *142*:679–682, 1988.
130. McClung, H. W., Knight, V., Gilbert, B. E., et al.: Ribavirin aerosol treatment of influenza B virus infection. J. A. M. A. *249*:2671–2674, 1983.
131. McDonogh, A. J.: The use of steroids and nebulised adrenaline in the treatment of viral croup over a seven-year period at a district hospital. Anaesth. Intensive Care *22*:175–178, 1994.
132. McKenzie, M., Norman, M. G., Anderson, J. D., et al.: Upper respiratory tract infection in a 3-year-old girl. J. Pediatr. *105*:129–133, 1984.
133. McLean, D. M., Roy, T. E., O'Brien, M. J., et al.: Parainfluenza viruses in association with acute laryngotracheobronchitis, Toronto, 1960–61.Can. Med. Assoc. J. *85*:290–294, 1961.
134. McNab, J. C. G.: Acute streptococcal infection of the trachea in an infant, aged fifteen months. J. Laryngol. *30*:337–338, 1915.
135. Meade, R. H., III: Laryngeal obstruction in children. Pediatr. Clin. North Am. *9*:233–262, 1962.
136. Melnick, A., Berger, R., and Green, G.: Spasmodic croup in children: Personal experiences with intermittent positive pressure breathing in therapy. Clin. Pediatr. *11*:615–617, 1972.
137. Miller, B. R., Arthur, J. D., Parry, W. H., et al.: Atypical croup and *Chlamydia trachomatis*. Lancet *1*:1022, 1982.
138. Miller, D. G., Gabrielson, M. O., and Horstmann, D. M.: Clinical virology and viral surveillance in a pediatric group practice: The use of double-seeded tissue culture tubes for primary virus isolation. Am. J. Epidemiol. *88*:245–256, 1968.
139. Mogabgab, W. J.: Beta-hemolytic streptococcal and concurrent infections in adults and children with respiratory disease, 1958 to 1969. Am. Rev. Respir. Dis. *102*:23–34, 1970.
140. Morgan, E. A., and Wishart, D. E. S.: Laryngo-tracheobronchitis: A statistical review of 549 cases. Can. Med. Assoc. J. *56*:8–15, 1947.
141. Mufson, M. A., Krause, H. E., Mocega, H. E., et al.: Viruses, *Mycoplasma pneumoniae* and bacteria associated with lower respiratory tract disease among infants. Am. J. Epidemiol. *91*:192–202, 1970.
142. Naqvi, S. H., and Dunkle, L. M.: Bacterial tracheitis and viral croup. Pediatr. Infect. Dis. *3*:282–283, 1984.
143. Neffson, A. H.: Acute laryngotracheobronchitis: A 25-year review. Am. J. Med. Sci. *208*:524–547, 1944.
144. Nelson, W. E.: Bacterial croup: A historical perspective. J. Pediatr. *105*:52–55, 1984.
145. Newth, C. J. L., Levison, H., and Bryan, A. C.: The respiratory status of children with croup. J. Pediatr. *81*:1068–1073, 1972.
146. Nichol, K. P., and Cherry, J. D.: Bacterial-viral interrelations in respiratory infections of children. N. Engl. J. Med. *277*:667–672, 1967.
147. Nijssen-Jordan, C., Donaldson, J. D., and Halperin, S. A.: Bacterial tracheitis associated with respiratory syncytial virus infection and toxic shock syndrome. Can. Med. Assoc. J. *142*:233–234, 1990.
148. Orton, H. B., Smith, E. L., Bell, H. O., et al.: Acute laryngotracheobronchitis: Analysis of sixty-two cases with report of autopsies in eight cases. Arch. Otolaryngol. *33*:926–960, 1941.
149. Paisley, J. W., Bruhn, F. W., Lauer, B. A., et al.: Type A2 influenza viral infections in children. Am. J. Dis. Child. *132*:34–36, 1978.
150. Parks, C. R.: Mist therapy: Rationale and practice. J. Pediatr. *76*:305–313, 1970.
151. Parrott, R. H.: Viral respiratory tract illnesses in children. Bull. N. Y. Acad. Med. *39*:629–648, 1963.

152. Parrott, R. H., Kim, H. W., Vargosko, A. J., et al.: Serious respiratory tract illness as a result of Asian influenza and influenza B infections in children. J. Pediatr. *61*:205–213, 1962.
153. Parrott, R. H., Vargosko, A. J., Kim, H. W., et al.: Acute respiratory diseases of viral etiology. III. Myxoviruses: Para influenza. Am. J. Public Health *52*:907–917, 1962.
154. Parrott, R. H., Vargosko, A. J., Kim, H. W., et al.: Clinical syndromes among children. Am. Rev. Respir. Dis. *88*:73–76, 1962.
155. Person, D. A., and Herrmann, E. C., Jr.: Experiences in laboratory diagnosis of rhinovirus infections in routine medical practice. Mayo Clin. Proc. *45*:517, 1970.
156. Plachtova-Pecenkova, I., Brockova, M., Fecova, D., et al.: Note on the aetiology of acute laryngotracheobronchitis in children: Findings in the autumn of 1965 and the spring of 1966. J. Hyg. Epidemiol. Microbiol. Immunol. *12*:227–237, 1968.
157. Poland, J. D., Welton, E. R., and Chin, T. D. Y.: Influenza virus B as a cause of acute croup syndrome. Am. J. Dis. Child. *107*:54, 1964.
158. Prendergast, M., Jones, J. S., and Hartman, D.: Racemic epinephrine in the treatment of laryngotracheitis: Can we identify children for outpatient therapy? Am. J. Emerg. Med. *12*:613–616, 1994.
159. Rabe, E. F.: Infectious croup. I. Etiology. Pediatrics *2*:255–265, 1948.
160. Rabe, E. F.: Acute inflammatory disorders of the larynx and laryngotracheal area. Pediatr. Clin. North Am. *4*:169–182, 1957.
161. Rabe, E. F.: Infectious croup. II. "Virus" croup. Pediatrics *2*:415–427, 1948.
162. Reed, S. E., and Boyde, A.: Organ cultures of respiratory epithelium infected with rhinovirus or parainfluenza virus studied in a scanning electron microscope. Infect. Immunol. *6*:68–76, 1972.
163. Reilly, C. M., Hoch, S. M., Stokes, J., Jr., et al.: Clinical and laboratory findings in cases of respiratory illness caused by coryzaviruses. Ann. Intern. Med. *57*:515–525, 1962.
164. Richards, L.: Fulminating laryngo-tracheo-bronchitis. Ann. Otol. Rhinol. Laryngol. *42*:1014–1040, 1933.
165. Richards, L.: A further study of the pathology of acute laryngo-tracheobronchitis in children. Ann. Otol. Rhinol. Laryngol. *47*:326–341, 1938.
166. Rittichier, K. K., and Ledwith, C. A.: Outpatient treatment of moderate croup with dexamethasone: Intramuscular versus oral dosing. Pediatrics *106*:1344–1348, 2000.
167. Roberts, G. W., Master, V. V., Staugas, R. E., et al.: Repeated dose inhaled budesonide versus placebo in the treatment of croup. J. Paediatr. Child Health *35*:170–174, 1999.
168. Rosales, J. K., and Davenport, H. T.: Acute laryngotracheobronchitis and epiglottitis. Can. Anaesth. Soc. J. *9*:467–478, 1962.
169. Rull, J., and Hargitai, R.: Laryngitis subglottica kezelese mikronephrin tulnyomasos belelegeztetesevel. Orvosi Hetilap *115*:2727–2731, 1974.
170. Sasaki, C. T., and Suzuki, M.: The respiratory mechanism of aerosol inhalation in the treatment of partial airway obstruction. Pediatrics *59*:689–694, 1977.
171. Schalen, L., and Andersson, K.: Differential diagnosis and treatment of psychogenic voice disorder. Clin. Otolaryngol. *17*:225–230, 1992.
172. Sendi, K., Crysdale, S., and Yoo, J.: Tracheitis: Outcome of 1,700 cases presenting to the emergency department during two years. J. Otolaryngol. *21*:20–24, 1992.
173. Singer, O. P., and Wilson, W. J.: Laryngotracheobronchitis: 2 years' experience with racemic epinephrine. Can. Med. Assoc. J. *115*:132–134, 1976.
174. Skolnik, N. S.: Treatment of croup: A critical review. Am. J. Dis. Child. *143*:1045–1049, 1989.
175. Skolnik, N.: Croup. J. Fam. Pract. *37*:165–170, 1993.
176. Skowron, P. N., Turner, J. A. P., and McNaughton, G. A.: The use of corticosteroid (dexamethasone) in the treatment of acute laryngotracheitis. Can. Med. Assoc. J. *94*:528–531, 1966.
177. Smith, D. S.: Corticosteroids in croup: A chink in the ivory tower? J. Pediatr. *115*:256–257, 1989.
178. Sofer, S., and Chernick, V.: Increased need for tracheal intubation for croup in relation to bacterial tracheitis. Can. Med. Assoc. J. *128*:160–161, 1983.
179. Solomon, R., Truman, T., and Murray, D. L.: Toxic shock syndrome as a complication of bacterial tracheitis. Pediatrics *4*:298–299, 1985.
180. Stankiewicz, J. A., and Bowes, A. K.: Croup and epiglottitis: A radiologic study. Laryngoscope *95*:1159–1160, 1985.
181. Sterner, G., Gerzen, P., Ohlson, M., et al.: Acute respiratory illness and gastroenteritis in association with adenovirus type 7 infections. Acta Paediatr. *50*:457–468, 1961.
182. Stott, E. J., Bell, E. J., Eadie, M. B., et al.: A comparative virological study of children in hospital with respiratory and diarrhoeal illnesses. J. Hyg. Camb. *65*:9–23, 1967.
183. Stuart-Harris, C. H.: The adenoviruses and respiratory disease in man. Lectures on the Scientific Basis of Medicine *8*:148–164, 1958–59.
184. Super, D. M., Cartelli, N. A., Brooks, L. J., et al.: A prospective randomized double-blind study to evaluate the effect of dexamethasone in acute laryngotracheitis. J. Pediatr. *115*:323–329, 1989.
185. Suresh, G. K., Dhawan, A., and Kohli, V.: Tracheal diphtheria mimicking bacterial tracheitis. Pediatr. Infect. Dis. J. *11*:502, 1992.
186. Surh, L., and Read, S. E.: Staphylococcal tracheitis and toxic shock syndrome in a young child. J. Pediatr. *105*:585–587, 1984.
187. Sussman, S., Grossman, M., Magoffin, R., et al.: Dexamethasone (16 alpha-methyl, 9 alpha-fluoroprednisolone) in obstructive respiratory tract infections in children: A controlled study. Pediatrics *34*:851–855, 1964.
188. Szpunar, J., Glowacki, J., Laskowski, A., et al.: Fibrinous laryngotracheobronchitis in children. Arch. Otolaryngol. *93*:173–178, 1971.
189. Taber, L. H., Knight, V., Gilbert, B. E., et al.: Ribavirin aerosol treatment of bronchiolitis associated with respiratory syncytial virus infection in infants. Pediatrics *72*:613–618, 1983.
190. Tan, A. K. W., and Manoukian, J. J.: Hospitalized croup (bacterial and viral): The role of rigid endoscopy. J. Otolaryngol. *21*:48–53, 1992.
191. Taussig, L. M., Castro, O., Beaudry, P. H., et al.: Treatment of laryngotracheobronchitis (croup): Use of intermittent positive-pressure breathing and racemic epinephrine. Am. J. Dis. Child. *129*:790–793, 1975.
192. Temple, A. R.: Recent advances in diagnosis and management of croup. J. Fam. Pract. *2*:85–89, 1975.
193. Top, F. H., Sr.: Diphtheria. *In* Top, F. H., Sr., and Wehrle, P. F. (eds.): Communicable and Infectious Diseases. St. Louis, C. V. Mosby, 1972, pp. 190–207.
194. Toth, M., and Major, V.: Virological investigation of hospitalized cases of pseudocroup and acute laryngotracheobronchitis. Acta Microbiol. *12*:189–200, 1965.
195. Travis, K. W., Todres, I. D., and Shannon, D. C.: Pulmonary edema associated with croup and epiglottitis. Pediatrics *59*:695–698, 1977.
196. Tunnessen, W. W., Jr., and Feinstein, A. R.: The steroid-croup controversy: An analytic review of methodologic problems. J. Pediatr. *96*:751–756, 1980.
197. Tyeryar, F. J., Jr., Richardson, L. S., and Belshe, R. B.: Report of a workshop on respiratory syncytial virus and parainfluenza viruses. J. Infect. Dis. *137*:835–846, 1978.
198. Tyrrell, D. A. J.: Common Colds and Related Diseases. Baltimore, Williams & Wilkins, 1965.
199. Vargosko, A. J., Chanock, R. M., Huebner, R. J., et al.: Association of type 2 hemadsorption (parainfluenza 1) virus and Asian influenza A virus with infectious croup. N. Engl. J. Med. *261*:1–9, 1959.
200. Vihma, L.: Surveillance of acute viral respiratory diseases in children. Acta Paediatr. Scand. *192*(Suppl.):8–53, 1969.
201. Walker, P., and Crysdale, W. S.: Croup, epiglottitis, retropharyngeal abscess, and bacterial tracheitis: Evolving patterns of occurrence and care. Int. Anesth. Clin. *30*:57–70, 1992.
202. Weber, J. E., Chudnofsky, C. R., Younger, J. G., et al.: A randomized comparison of helium-oxygen mixture (Heliox) and racemic epinephrine for the treatment of moderate to severe croup. Pediatrics *107*:E96, 2001. Available at: http://www.pediatrics.org/cgi/content/full/107/6/e96
203. Welliver, R. C., Sun, M., and Rinaldo, D.: Defective regulation of immune response in croup due to parainfluenza virus. Pediatr. Res. *19*: 716–720, 1985.
204. Welliver, R. C., Wong, D. T., Middleton, E., Jr., et al.: Role of parainfluenza virus-specific IgE in pathogenesis of croup and wheezing subsequent to infection. J. Pediatr. *101*:889–896, 1982.
205. Welliver, R.C.: Croup: Continuing controversy. Semin. Pediatr. Infect. Dis. *6*:90–95, 1995.
206. Wenner, H. A., Christodoulopoulou, G., Weston, J., et al.: The etiology of respiratory illnesses occurring in infancy and childhood. Pediatrics *31*:4–17, 1963.
207. Westley, C. R., Cotton, E. K., and Brooks, J. G.: Nebulized racemic epinephrine by IPPB for the treatment of croup: A double-blind study. Am. J. Dis. Child. *132*:484–487, 1978.
208. Wilson, S. Z., Gilbert, B. E., Quarles, J. M., et al.: Treatment of influenza A (H1N1) virus infection with ribavirin aerosol. Antimicrob. Agents Chemother. *26*:200–203, 1984.
209. Wong, V. K., and Mason, W. H.: *Branhamella catarrhalis* as a cause of bacterial tracheitis. Pediatr. Infect. Dis. *6*:945–946, 1987.
210. Wulff, H., Kidd, P., and Wenner, H. A.: Etiology of respiratory infections: Further studies during infancy and childhood. Pediatrics *33*:30–44, 1964.
211. Zach, M. S.: Airway reactivity in recurrent croup. Eur. J. Respir. Dis. *128*(Suppl.):81–88, 1983.
212. Zulliger, J. J., Schuller, D. W., Beach, T. P., et al.: Assessment of intubation in croup and epiglottitis. Ann. Otol. Rhinol. Laryngol. *91*:403–406, 1982.

Lower Respiratory Tract Infections

CHAPTER 23 Acute Bronchitis

JAMES D. CHERRY

Bronchitis is a common diagnosis in pediatric practice, although little unanimity exists among physicians regarding its exact clinical constellation, and in the true pathologic sense, it probably never occurs as an isolated entity. Acute bronchitis is a febrile illness with cough, rhonchi, and referred breath sounds.[13] Asthmatic bronchitis (infectious asthma), similar to acute bronchitis but with associated wheezing and expiratory distress, is discussed in Chapter 25. On pathologic examination, the clinical illness of acute bronchitis reflects acute inflammatory disease of the larger air passages, including the trachea and the large and medium-sized bronchi.[22]

Etiology

The various infectious agents incriminated in acute bronchitis are presented in Table 23–1. Infections with adenoviruses, influenza viruses, parainfluenza viruses, respiratory syncytial virus, and *Mycoplasma pneumoniae* account for the overwhelming majority of cases of acute bronchitis in children. These agents, plus many rhinoviruses and a few enteroviruses, account for virtually all cases in the United States today.

Of the adenoviruses, type 7 has been associated most commonly with acute bronchitis in children. However, in military recruits, including adolescents, adenovirus types 4 and 7 cause epidemic acute respiratory disease, in which bronchitis is a usual occurrence.[19, 58]

Influenza A virus infection is a common cause of severe acute bronchitis, particularly at the time of antigenic shift of influenza A virus subtype and pandemic disease. Acute bronchitis caused by influenza A virus also is a regular occurrence between pandemics in new susceptible individuals (young children) in the population. Influenza B virus also is an important cause of bronchitis, and it was a more common causative agent than was influenza A virus in one large longitudinal study.[11]

All cases of measles involve the bronchi; but fortunately, measles has been an uncommon disease since the widespread use of vaccines. Of the parainfluenza viruses, type 3 is associated most commonly with acute bronchitis. Respiratory syncytial virus is a common cause of acute bronchitis, particularly in the very young child. The recently identified human metapneumovirus (HMPV) is another cause of acute bronchitis.[51]

Of the bacterial agents listed in Table 23–1, only *Haemophilus influenzae* clearly can be incriminated. *Bordetella pertussis* infection involves the trachea and bronchi, but fever is uncommon, and therefore the illness is outside the definition of acute bronchitis. When sought, *M. pneumoniae* is a surprisingly common cause of bronchitis. *Chlamydia pneumoniae* has been found to be the cause of bronchitis in adolescents and young adults.[28]

Epidemiology

The epidemiology of the common viruses that are associated with bronchitis is presented in Section XVII. Chapman and associates[11] published the results of a study of acute bronchitis in a single private group pediatric practice in Chapel Hill, North Carolina. The study occurred during a 104-month period, during which 5489 episodes of lower respiratory illness occurred. Of these illnesses, 40.1 percent were acute bronchitis. The bronchitis attack rate was highest during the second year of life (6.71%), and then it decreased gradually to approximately 2.0 percent in teenagers. In contrast to the age-specific attack rates, the ratio of bronchitis cases to all lower respiratory illness cases increased with age. In the first year of life, the ratio was 0.29; in children 12 years of age or older, it was 0.69.

During the first 6 years of life, respiratory syncytial virus and parainfluenza virus type 3 were the most common etiologic agents noted in the Chapel Hill study. During the first 2 years of life, adenoviruses also commonly were associated with bronchitis. After age 6 years, *M. pneumoniae* and influenza A and B viruses were the most common etiologic agents. In a study of cough illnesses of 6 days' duration or longer in university students, investigators found that 15 of 31 students with laboratory evidence of *Bordetella* spp. infection were considered by their primary care providers to have bronchitis.[40]

The incidence of acute bronchitis peaks in the winter months, declines to midsummer, and rises again through the fall. Attack rates generally are higher in boys than in girls.[11, 34, 59] A sex difference is most pronounced during the first 6 years of life.

Pathophysiology and Pathology

Because acute bronchitis is an illness characterized by clinical features and one not usually associated with death, knowledge of its pathophysiology and pathology is meager. The general pathophysiology of human infections with viruses and *M. pneumoniae* that cause acute bronchitis is presented more completely in the sections of this book related to the individual infectious agents.

In virtually all cases of acute bronchitis, evidence of upper respiratory viral infection (pharyngitis, rhinitis) also is present. Tracheal and bronchial infection apparently is the result of distal spread. In bronchitis, the clinical features

TABLE 23–1 ■ INFECTIOUS AGENTS ASSOCIATED WITH ACUTE BRONCHITIS

Agent	Importance in Causation*	References
Viruses		
Adenovirus types 1–7, 12	+++	1, 2, 4, 8–10, 14, 20, 23, 24, 31, 32, 36, 48, 53, 56, 59, 60, 63
Enterovirus	+	26, 31, 32, 53
Coxsackieviruses B	+	8
Echoviruses 8, 12, 14	+	57
Polioviruses	+	23, 57
Herpes simplex	+	23, 53, 57
Influenza	+++	1, 5, 7–11, 14, 20, 24, 26, 55, 57
A	++	5, 8, 10, 11, 26, 31, 32, 55, 57
B	++	8, 10, 11, 26, 31
C	+	1
Measles	+	14, 22, 46
Mumps	+	57
Parainfluenza	+++	1, 5, 8–11, 14, 23–26, 29, 31, 36, 53, 55, 57, 60
1	++	8–11, 20, 26, 29
2	++	5, 8–10, 26, 29
3	+++	1, 2, 5, 8–11, 20, 26, 29, 32, 55
4	+	25
Respiratory syncytial	+++	1–3, 7–11, 14, 20, 23, 24, 26, 30–33, 39, 49, 53, 54, 56, 57, 60
Human metapneumovirus	+	51
Rhinoviruses	++	8, 14, 23, 24, 26, 31, 32, 45, 52, 53
Bacteria		
Bordetella pertussis	+	22
Bordetella parapertussis	–	
Haemophilus influenzae	–	36, 61
Moraxella catarrhalis	–	18, 27
Streptococcus pneumoniae	–	36
Streptococcus pyogenes	–	36, 44, 53
Other		
Chlamydia psittaci	+	10
Chlamydia pneumoniae	+	28
Mycoplasma pneumoniae	+++	8–11, 14, 20, 26, 31, 47

*+++, very common; ++, common; +, rare; –, of questionable etiologic significance.

result from damage to the ciliated epithelium of the lower trachea and the large and medium-sized bronchi.[22] Although the cytopathology of the different infectious agents is different,[64] the resulting obstruction of the air passages leads to similar symptoms. The duration of symptoms depends to some extent on the specific initial infectious agent and, in cases of prolonged illness, on secondary bacterial infection.

An intriguing note is that in acute bronchitis, the larynx and subglottic trachea are not involved prominently. Conversely, today, bronchial involvement is seen only occasionally in croup.

Clinical Presentation

Initial manifestations of acute bronchitis are upper respiratory in nature and, depending on the etiologic agent, either predominantly nasal, as in the common cold, or show additional objective evidence of pharyngitis, as in nasopharyngitis. Fever usually is present, and temperature varies from 37.8° C to 39° C (100° F to 103° F) on most occasions. Cough always is present, and its onset can be insidious or abrupt. Initially, the cough is dry and harsh and often brassy in younger children. As the illness progresses, the cough becomes looser. In older children, purulent sputum is raised and expectorated. In younger children, the swallowing of often tenacious sputum frequently leads to gagging and vomiting. Older children may complain of chest pain resulting from coughing.

On initial physical examination, a variable degree of rhinitis usually is present; many patients will have diffuse pharyngeal erythema. As the disease progresses, these upper respiratory signs generally decrease. Examination of the chest reveals rhonchi and referred breath sounds. Coarse, changing rales are noted frequently.

In the usual case of acute bronchitis, the illness can be separated into three phases: a 1- to 2-day prodromal period when fever and upper respiratory symptoms predominate, a 4- to 6-day period of marked tracheobronchial symptoms with some fever and general discomfort, and a recovery period that may last 1 or 2 weeks and is characterized by cough and expectoration. On occasion, the recovery period is particularly distressing and is associated with a low-grade fever, suggesting secondary bacterial infection. Bronchitis caused by *C. pneumoniae* often is insidious in onset and frequently associated with or preceded by pharyngitis.[28, 35] Illness persists for several weeks but responds to appropriate antibiotic therapy.

Laboratory study in acute bronchitis is of limited use. Children in whom throat cultures reveal pathogenic bacteria in predominant growth tend to have more severe illness than do children with only viral infections.[12, 41] The white blood cell count is usually greater than 10,000 cells/mm^3, and approximately one third of the cases have a predominance of neutrophils.[41] The chest radiograph is normal unless associated pulmonary involvement is present.

Differential Diagnosis and Specific Diagnosis

Because acute bronchitis is a clinical entity caused by multiple etiologic agents, the most difficult differential aspect of diagnosis is the selection of the specific infectious cause. Also of importance is the separation of acute, self-limited bronchitis from chronic, more serious problems such as cystic fibrosis, allergic respiratory disease, and sinusitis.

An epidemiologic history frequently can help in assigning a particular virus, *M. pneumoniae, C. pneumoniae,* or *B. pertussis,* as the presumptive etiologic agent. For example, if epidemic bronchiolitis is occurring in the community, respiratory syncytial virus would be a likely cause. Similarly, predictions of causation by influenza virus, parainfluenza virus, adenoviruses, *M. pneumoniae, C. pneumoniae,* or *B. pertussis* can be made through clinical epidemiologic observations. Specific etiologic diagnosis can be made through the isolation of an organism or its identification by a direct antigen test from the nasopharyngeal secretions. Serologic study on paired sera may be useful for the diagnosis of *M. pneumoniae, C. pneumoniae,* and *B. pertussis*.

Children with protracted illnesses or febrile exacerbations should be examined by culture and radiograph for secondary bacterial infection of the tracheobronchial tree or the lungs, or both. Children with chronic recurrent illnesses should be tested for cystic fibrosis, allergic conditions, and anatomic problems, such as gastroesophageal reflux and tracheoesophageal fistula.

Treatment

Treatment of acute bronchitis is distinguished more by what *not* to do than by specific modalities. In most mild cases, no specific therapy is indicated.

For the many children who feel miserable during the initial phases of acute bronchitis, analgesic therapy may be useful. Formerly, aspirin was the recommended analgesic. However, because aspirin is an etiologic factor in influenza-associated Reye syndrome and because differentiating influenza viral infections from other respiratory viral infections is difficult, it is prudent to use acetaminophen rather than aspirin. The dose per single administration of acetaminophen by year of age is as follows: younger than 1 year, 60 mg; 1 to 3 years, 60 to 120 mg; 3 to 6 years, 120 mg; 6 to 12 years, 150 to 300 mg; older than 12 years, 325 to 650 mg. Administration may be repeated three or four times daily in young children and every 4 hours in older children. Acetaminophen rarely should be given to infants younger than 6 months of age.

As a result of widespread advertising, a common practice of individuals with acute bronchitis is to use an array of cold remedies, which contain various combinations of antihistamines, decongestants, and antitussives. None has been demonstrated to be useful in acute bronchitis, and in certain stages of illness, they may aggravate the recovery process. Repeated bouts of coughing occasionally result in emesis, exhaustion, or insomnia, and the careful use of antitussive agents (codeine or dextromethorphan) can be useful.[16] Cough suppressants should be used with caution when a cough is productive, however.

Intake of fluids should be encouraged to prevent overall dehydration and to decrease the viscosity of new secretions. Use of mist therapy also will help in thinning the exudate-containing respiratory secretions.[21, 43]

In severe cases of acute bronchitis, treatment with specific antiviral agents should be considered. When influenza A virus is the likely etiologic agent, amantadine, rimantadine, zanamivir, or oseltamivir therapy may be of benefit (only amantadine is approved for use in young children).[17]

As noted in Table 23–1, most cases of acute bronchitis are caused by viruses, so antibiotic therapy would appear not to be indicated.[42, 62] However, in cases in which fever returns or no trend toward recovery is seen by the seventh day of illness, the possibility of secondary bacterial infection should be considered. The association of sinusitis or a throat culture with a predominant growth of a respiratory pathogen (*Streptococcus pneumoniae, Streptococcus pyogenes, Moraxella catarrhalis, H. influenzae*) is an indication for therapy. Infection with *M. pneumoniae* also should be treated, but unlike treatment of pneumonia, the therapy usually will not show an impressive response. Bronchitis caused by *C. pneumoniae* should be treated with erythromycin (50 mg/kg/day divided every 6 hours) for 10 to 14 days.[28]

Prognosis

The prognosis in acute bronchitis usually is excellent. Although the duration of cough can be disturbing to both parent and child, full recovery is the rule. Several studies suggest that lower respiratory illness in the first few years of life may be associated with persistent respiratory symptoms and with abnormalities in lung function in later life.[6, 15, 37, 38] Although none of these studies has followed children with acute bronchitis specifically, the findings in other illnesses (bronchiolitis and croup) indicate a need to observe children with episodes of acute bronchitis carefully as well.

Prevention

At present, no practical method of prevention of acute bronchitis in children exists. However, because most cases result from infections with common respiratory viruses, the development of vaccines could be expected to be helpful.

REFERENCES

1. Aitken, C. J. D., Moffat, M. A. J., and Sutherland, J. A. W.: Respiratory illness and viral infection in an Edinburgh nursery. J. Hyg. Camb. *65*:25–36, 1967.
2. Avila, M. M., Carballal, G., Rovaletti, H., et al.: Viral etiology in acute lower respiratory infections in children from a closed community. Am. Rev. Respir. Dis. *140*:634–637, 1989.
3. Berglund, B., and Strahlmann, C. H.: Respiratory syncytial virus infections in hospitalized children: Evaluation of the virus isolation and complement-fixation techniques in the virological diagnosis: Clinical and epidemiological characteristics. Acta Paediatr. Scand. *56*:1–10, 1967.
4. Brandt, C. D., Kim, H. W., Vargosko, A. J., et al.: Infections in 18,000 infants and children in a controlled study of respiratory tract disease. I. Adenovirus pathogenicity in relation to serologic type and illness syndrome. Am. J. Epidemiol. *90*:484–500, 1969.
5. Brocklebank, J. T., Court, S. D. M., McQuillin, J., et al.: Influenza A infection in children. Lancet *1*:497–500, 1972.
6. Burrows, B., Knudson, R. J., and Lebowitz, M. D.: The relationship of childhood respiratory illness to adult obstructive airway disease. Am. Rev. Respir. Dis. *115*:751–760, 1977.
7. Caul, E. O., Waller, D. K., Clarke, S. K. R., et al.: A comparison of influenza and respiratory syncytial virus infections among infants admitted to hospital with acute respiratory infections. J. Hyg. Camb. *77*:383–392, 1976.
8. Chanock, R. M., and Parrott, R. H.: Acute respiratory disease in infancy and childhood: Present understanding and prospects for prevention: E. Mead Johnson Address, October 1964. Pediatrics *36*:21–39, 1965.
9. Chanock, R. M., Mufson, M. A., and Johnson, K. M.: Comparative biology and ecology of human virus and mycoplasma respiratory pathogens. Prog. Med. Virol. *7*:208–252, 1965.
10. Chanock, R., Chambon, L., Chang, W., et al.: WHO respiratory disease survey in children: A serological study. Bull. World Health Organ. *37*:363–369, 1967.
11. Chapman, R. S., Henderson, F. W., Clyde, W. A., Jr., et al.: The epidemiology of tracheobronchitis in pediatric practice. Am. J. Epidemiol. *114*:786–797, 1981.
12. Cherry, J. D., Diddams, J. A., and Dick, E. C.: Rhinovirus infections in hospitalized children: Provocative bacterial interrelationships. Arch. Environ. Health *14*:390–396, 1967.

13. Cherry, J. D.: Newer respiratory viruses: Their role in respiratory illnesses of children. *In* Schulman, I. (ed.): Advances in Pediatrics. Vol. 20. Chicago, Year Book, 1973, pp. 225–290.
14. Cherry, J. D.: Personal observations.
15. Colley, J. R. T., Douglas, J. W. B., and Reid, D. D.: Respiratory disease in young adults: Influence of early childhood lower respiratory tract illness, social class, air pollution, and smoking. Br. Med. J. *8*:195–198, 1973.
16. Committee on Drugs: Use of codeine- and dextromethorphan-containing cough syrups in pediatrics. Pediatrics *62*:118–122, 1978.
17. Couch, R. B.: Prevention and treatment of influenza. N. Engl. J. Med. *343*:1778–1787, 2000.
18. Darelid, J., Lofgren, S., and Malmvall, B. E.: Erythromycin treatment is beneficial for longstanding *Moraxella catarrhalis* associated cough in children. Scand. J. Infect. Dis. *25*:323–329, 1993.
19. Dascomb, H. E., and Hilleman, M. R.: Clinical and laboratory studies in patients with respiratory disease caused by adenoviruses (RI-APC-ARD agents). Am. J. Med. *21*:161–174, 1956.
20. Denny, F. W., and Clyde, W. A., Jr.: Acute lower respiratory tract infections in nonhospitalized children. J. Pediatr. *108*:635–646, 1986.
21. Dulfano, M. J., Adler, K., and Wooten, O.: Physical properties of sputum. IV. Effects of 100 percent humidity and water mist. Am. Rev. Respir. Dis. *107*:130–132, 1973.
22. Edwards, G.: Acute bronchitis: Aetiology, diagnosis, and management. Br. Med. J. *1*:963–966, 1966.
23. Gardner, P. S.: Virus infections and respiratory disease of childhood. Arch. Dis. Child. *43*:629–645, 1968.
24. Gardner, P. S.: How etiologic, pathologic, and clinical diagnoses can be made in a correlated fashion. Pediatr. Res. *11*:254–261, 1977.
25. Gardner, S. D.: The isolation of parainfluenza 4 subtypes A and B in England and serological studies of their prevalence. J. Hyg. Camb. *67*:545–550, 1969.
26. Glezen, W. P., Loda, F. A., Clyde, W. A., Jr., et al.: Epidemiologic patterns of acute lower respiratory disease of children in a pediatric group practice. J. Pediatr. *78*:397–406, 1971.
27. Gottfard, P., and Brauner, A.: Children with persistent cough: Outcome with treatment and role of *Moraxella catarrhalis*? Scand. J. Infect. Dis. *26*:545–551, 1994.
28. Grayston, J. T., Campbell, L. A., Kuo, C. C., et al.: A new respiratory tract pathogen: *Chlamydia pneumoniae* strain TWAR. J. Infect. Dis. *161*:618–625, 1990.
29. Herrmann, E. C., Jr., and Hable, K. A.: Experiences in laboratory diagnosis of parainfluenza viruses in routine medical practice. Mayo Clin. Proc. *45*:177–188, 1970.
30. Hilleman, M. R.: Respiratory syncytial virus. Am. Rev. Respir. Dis. *88*(Suppl.):181–189, 1963.
31. Horn, M. E. C., Brain, E., Gregg, I., et al.: Respiratory viral infection in childhood: A survey in general practice, Roehampton 1967–1972. J. Hyg. Camb. *74*:157–168, 1975.
32. Kellner, G., Popow-Kraupp, T., Kundi, M., et al.: Contribution of rhinoviruses to respiratory viral infections in childhood: A prospective study in a mainly hospitalized infant population. J. Med. Virol. *25*:455–469, 1988.
33. Kim, H. W., Arrobio, J. O., Brandt, C. D., et al.: Epidemiology of respiratory syncytial virus infection in Washington, D.C. I. Importance of the virus in different respiratory tract disease syndromes and temporal distribution of infection. Am. J. Epidemiol. *98*:216–225, 1973.
34. Kravitz, H.: Sex distribution of hospitalized children with acute respiratory diseases, gastroenteritis and meningitis. Clin. Pediatr. *4*:484–491, 1965.
35. Kuo, C. C., Jackson, L. A., Campbell, L. A., et al.: *Chlamydia pneumoniae* (TWAR). Clin. Microbiol. Rev. *8*:451–461, 1995.
36. Laxdal, O. E., Robertson, H. E., Braaten, V., et al.: Acute respiratory infections in children. I. An intensive study of etiology in an open community. Can. Med. Assoc. J. *88*:1049–1054, 1963.
37. Lebowitz, M. D., and Burrows, B.: The relationship of acute respiratory illness history to the prevalence and incidence of obstructive lung disorders. Am. J. Epidemiol. *105*:544–554, 1977.
38. Leeder, S. R., Woolcock, A. J., and Blackburn, C. R. B.: Prevalence and natural history of lung disease in New South Wales schoolchildren. Int. J. Epidemiol. *3*:15–23, 1974.
39. McClelland, L., Hilleman, M. R., Hamparian, V. V., et al.: Studies of acute respiratory illnesses caused by respiratory syncytial virus. 2. Epidemiology and assessment of importance. N. Engl. J. Med. *264*:1169–1175, 1961.
40. Mink, C. A. M., Cherry, J. D., Christenson, P., et al.: A search for *Bordetella pertussis* infection in university students. Clin. Infect. Dis. *14*:464–471, 1992.
41. Nichol, K. P., and Cherry, J. D.: Bacterial-viral interrelations in respiratory infections of children. N. Engl. J. Med. *277*:667–672, 1967.
42. O'Brien, K. L., Dowell, S. F., Schwartz, B., et al.: Cough illness/bronchitis—principles of judicious use of antimicrobial agents. Pediatrics *101*:178–181, 1998.
43. Parks, C. R.: Mist therapy: Rationale and practice. J. Pediatr. *76*:305–313, 1970.
44. Pereira, M. S.: Adenovirus infections. Postgrad. Med. J. *49*:798–801, 1973.
45. Person, D. A., and Herrmann, E. C., Jr.: Experiences in laboratory diagnosis of rhinovirus infections in routine medical practice. Mayo Clin. Proc. *45*:517–526, 1970.
46. Robbins, F. C.: Measles: Clinical features. Am. J. Dis. Child. *103*:266–273, 1962.
47. Saliba, G. S., Glezen, W. P., and Chin, T. D. Y.: *Mycoplasma pneumoniae* infection in a resident boys' home. Am. J. Epidemiol. *86*:408–418, 1967.
48. Similä, S., Jouppila, R., Salmi, A., et al.: Encephalomeningitis in children associated with an adenovirus type 7 epidemic. Acta Paediatr. Scand. *59*:310–316, 1970.
49. Spence, L., and Barratt, N.: Respiratory syncytial virus associated with acute respiratory infections in Trinidadian patients. Am. J. Epidemiol. *88*:257–266, 1968.
50. Sterner, G., Gerzen, P., Ohlson, M., et al.: Acute respiratory illness and gastroenteritis in association with adenovirus type 7 infections. Acta Paediatr. *50*:457–468, 1961.
51. Stockton, J., Stephenson, I., Fleming, D., and Zambon, M.: Human *Metapneumovirus* as a cause of community-acquired respiratory illness. Emerg. Infect. Dis. *8*:897–901, 2002.
52. Stott, E. J., Eadie, M. B., and Grist, N. R.: Rhinovirus infections of children in hospital: Isolation of three possibly new rhinovirus serotypes. Am. J. Epidemiol. *90*:45–52, 1969.
53. Stuart-Harris, C. H.: The present status of the respiratory viruses and acute respiratory disease in man. Israel J. Med. Sci. *2*:255–268, 1966.
54. Suto, T., Yano, N., Ikeda, M., et al.: Respiratory syncytial virus infection and its serologic epidemiology. Am. J. Epidemiol. *82*:211–224, 1965.
55. Sutton, R. N. P.: Respiratory viruses in a residential nursery. J. Hyg. Camb. *60*:51–67, 1962.
56. Toth, M., Barna, M., and Voltay, B.: Aetiology of acute respiratory diseases in infants and children. Acta Paediatr. Hung. *6*:367–374, 1965.
57. Urquhart, G. E. D., Moffat, M. A. J., Calder, M. A., et al.: An aetiological study of respiratory infection in children, Edinburgh City Hospital, 1961–1963. J. Hyg. Camb. *63*:187–199, 1965.
58. van der Veen, J.: The role of adenoviruses in respiratory disease. Am. Rev. Respir. Dis. *88*:167–180, 1963.
59. van Lierde, S., Corbeel, L., and Eggermont, E.: Clinical and laboratory findings in children with adenovirus infections. Eur. J. Pediatr. *148*:423–525, 1989.
60. Vihma, L.: Surveillance of acute viral respiratory diseases in children. Acta Paediatr. Scand. *192*(Suppl.):7–53, 1969.
61. Walker, S. H.: The respiratory manifestations of systemic *Haemophilus influenzae* infection. J. Pediatr. *62*:386–392, 1963.
62. Watson, R. L., Dowell, S. F., Jayaraman, M., et al.: Antimicrobial use for pediatric upper respiratory infections: Reported practice, actual practice, and parent beliefs. Pediatrics *104*:1251–1257, 1999.
63. Yodfat, Y., and Nishmi, M.: Successive overlapping outbreaks of febrile pharyngitis and pharyngoconjunctival fever associated with adenovirus types 2 and 7, in a Kibbutz. Israel J. Med. Sci. *10*:1505–1509, 1974.
64. Zinserling, A.: Peculiarities of lesions in viral and mycoplasmal infections of the respiratory tract. Virchows Arch. A *356*:259–273, 1972.

CHAPTER

24 Chronic Bronchitis

I. CELINE HANSON ■ WILLIAM T. SHEARER

Chronic bronchitis is a serious and costly health problem in adults.[24] Of the estimated 16 million adults with chronic obstructive pulmonary disease (COPD), most have chronic bronchitis.[13] In the adult literature, chronic bronchitis is described classically as "a clinical disorder characterized by excessive mucus production in the bronchial tree with manifestation, i.e., cough, present on most days for a maximum of 3 months in the year and not less than 2 successive years."[1] For most pediatricians and in the pediatric literature, the clinical entity of chronic bronchitis is ill defined and most commonly synonymous with asthmatic bronchitis.[38] Lack of uniform or standardized definitions of chronic bronchitis leads to wide discrepancies in reported childhood prevalence (Table 24–1), and the listed etiologic agents often overlap with those agents presumed to be responsible for acute or asthmatic bronchitis. The pathology of the disease entity also is unclear. Bronchoscopy of pediatric patients with chronic bronchitis has revealed findings not dissimilar to those noted in children with asthma, which reflects the inclusion of asthma in the spectrum of the chronic bronchitis complex.[26] Pediatric bronchoscopic evaluation yields heterogeneous histomorphic findings (granulocyte and mononuclear cell predominance at lavage and biopsy) that are distinct from findings in adults with chronic bronchitis.[35]

Differential Diagnosis

Because chronic bronchitis is accepted by most physicians as being a complex of symptoms characterized by persistent cough with or without wheezing,[5, 18, 26] it is imperative that the physician address those diseases that include chronic bronchitis with consideration of the spectrum of signs and symptoms with which they may present. Table 24–2 includes a list of illnesses that are associated with recurrent lower respiratory tract illnesses or chronic cough for longer than 3 months. Heading the list is asthma,[11, 40] defined as reversible obstructive airways disease with a significant inflammatory component leading to increased edema and production of mucus, as discussed in Chapter 25. Recurrent episodes of acute bronchitis often are interpreted as chronic bronchitis, although the intermittent nature of these episodes and absence of a persistent cough usually distinguish this group of patients clinically.[4, 14] Specific viral infections (rhinovirus, parainfluenza virus) in children with or without allergic rhinitis may provoke airway hyperreactivity and late asthmatic reactions, which may be confused symptomatically with chronic bronchitis.[7, 20] Persistent lower tract infections (i.e., *Chlamydia* spp., pertussis, and *Mycobacterium* spp.) frequently present with the complex of symptoms described and are evaluated best with chest radiographs in a search of enlarged hilar nodes or interstitial lung infiltrates. Respiratory tract secretions for appropriate bacterial and viral culture and serum for determinations of antibacterial antibodies should be obtained. In the case of tuberculosis, a delayed hypersensitivity skin test for *Mycobacterium tuberculosis* antigen should be applied.

Cystic fibrosis, the most common inherited lethal condition in whites, with an incidence of approximately 1 in 2000 births, is manifested by failure to thrive, steatorrhea, nasal polyps, and recurrent lower respiratory tract symptoms and is identified easily by abnormally elevated chloride levels (>60 mEq/L) as measured by the sweat iontophoresis test.[16]

Primary ciliary dyskinesia encompasses the immotile cilia disorders and Kartagener syndrome (rhinosinusitis, bronchitis or bronchiectasis, and situs inversus). Patients with these illnesses suffer from defects in mucociliary transport, as evidenced by a decrease in ciliary beat frequency. Electron microscopy of bronchial cilia shows structural defects classically with absent dynein arms.[32] Diagnosis is made by bronchial or, in some cases, nasal turbinate biopsy.

The primary immune disorders associated most frequently with recurrent sinopulmonary infections include selective immunoglobulin A (IgA) deficiency,[9] hypogammaglobulinemia (both primary and secondary), IgG subclass deficiencies, and ataxia telangiectasia. Selective IgA deficiency, the form of the immunodeficiency most commonly encountered, with an incidence of 1 in 500, is accompanied by a propensity for atopy and an increase in associated autoimmune disease (most often rheumatoid arthritis and systemic lupus erythematosus). The diagnosis is made readily by evaluation of quantitative serum immunoglobulins defining IgA levels of less than 10 mg/dL. IgG subclass deficiencies have been detected most recently in patients with depressed IgA levels (i.e., <60 mg/dL)[28] and, in addition, are linked to recurrent infections, particularly otitis, sinusitis, and recurrent lower respiratory tract infections.[34] The patient with ataxia telangiectasia has both depressed serum IgA concentrations and marked dysfunction of the swallowing mechanism, leading to recurrent lower respiratory tract infections probably secondary to recurrent aspiration. These patients are identified by the classic telangiectases of the skin and conjunctiva in association with aberrant and progressively deteriorating neurologic symptoms and immunodeficiency (depressed IgA and IgE and aberrant T-cell–mediated immunity). Some of these patients have depressed IgG subclasses (IgG2, IgG4) as well.[28] Graft-versus-host disease affecting the lungs has been described in immunocompromised patients after

TABLE 24–1 ■ PREVALENCE OF CHILDHOOD BRONCHITIS

Reference	Study	Prevalence of Bronchitis
Bland et al.[3]	1974—Kent schoolchildren (acute and chronic)	5.5%
Burrows and Lebowitz[6]	1975—Arizona children (chronic)	7.1%
Burrows et al.[5]	1977—Arizona retrospective questionnaire (chronic)	46.4%
Kubo et al.[18]	1978—Japanese children (chronic and recurrent)	1.4%
Peat et al.[29]	1980—Sydney schoolchildren (acute and chronic)	20.0%

Modified from Morgan, W. T., and Taussig, L. M.: The chronic bronchitis complex in childhood. Pediatr. Clin. North Am. *31*:851–864, 1984.

TABLE 24–2 ■ CONDITIONS ASSOCIATED WITH CHRONIC COUGH (3 MONTHS OR LONGER) OR LOWER RESPIRATORY TRACT ILLNESS

I. Asthma
II. Recurrent episodes of bronchitis (*Chlamydia* species, pertussis, mycobacteria)
III. Cystic fibrosis
IV. Primary ciliary dyskinesia
  A. Kartagener syndrome
  B. Immotile cilia syndrome
V. Immunodeficiency
  A. Selective IgA deficiency
  B. Subclass of IgG deficiency
  C. Hypogammaglobulinemia (primary and secondary)
  D. Ataxia telangiectasia
  E. Graft-versus-host disease status after bone marrow transplantation
  F. Prematurity
  G. HIV infection
VI. Anatomic lesions
  A. Foreign body
  B. Status after esophageal atresia repair
  C. Mediastinal tumors
  D. Congenital heart disease
VII. Irritants
  A. Milk aspiration (gastroesophageal reflux, tracheoesophageal fistula)
  B. Tobacco smoke
  C. Pollution
  D. Occupational exposure

Modified from Morgan, W. T., and Taussig, L. M.: The chronic bronchitis complex in childhood. Pediatr. Clin. North Am. *31*:851–864, 1984.

undergoing bone marrow transplantation.[3] The lesion is caused by chronic pulmonary lymphocytic infiltrates and pulmonary fibrosis mimicking the symptom complex of chronic bronchitis and often is indistinguishable radiographically or clinically from those infections that characteristically are pathogenic (i.e., *Pneumocystis carinii, Candida albicans, Aspergillus* species).

Secondary immune disorders (prematurity and pediatric human immunodeficiency virus [HIV] infection) also may be associated with significant sinopulmonary infections. Premature infants with attendant severe respiratory distress syndrome requiring positive-pressure ventilation may develop bronchopulmonary dysplasia (BPD). Diagnostic criteria include hypoxia requiring oxygen supplementation, characteristic diffuse interstitial markings on chest radiograph, and clinical signs of pulmonary disease (tachypnea, intercostal retractions).[31] In one series, more than 60 percent of surviving children with BPD were documented to have significant pulmonary disease and associated morbidity (i.e., increased hospitalizations).[33] Continued improved care for premature infants and resultant decreased incidence of mortality may increase the population of infants afflicted with BPD. Pediatric HIV infection is estimated to affect 1200 to 1800 infants in the United States annually and is associated with serious lower respiratory tract illness.[23] In particular, lymphoid interstitial pneumonitis or pulmonary lymphoid hyperplasia, reported in 25 percent of all children with acquired immunodeficiency syndrome, may produce chronic cough, sputum production, and hypoxia. Definitive diagnosis is by biopsy. Characteristic radiographic findings of diffuse bilateral interstitial or nodular infiltrates in an HIV-infected infant without known infectious etiologies may lead to a presumptive diagnosis. Despite more efficacious primary antiretroviral therapy that restores immunocompetence, lower respiratory tract infections (viral, bacterial, fungal) are still common occurrences in children infected with HIV.[23] In the face of improved survival for HIV-infected children, the incidence of chronic radiographic lung changes (parenchymal consolidations and nodular disease for longer than 3 months) has been described in 33 percent of children by the time they are 4 years of age.[27] The diagnosis of HIV infection is by viral diagnostic assays (HIV culture, polymerase chain reaction, p24 antigen, immune complex–dissociated p24 antigen) for perinatally exposed infants younger than 18 months of age and by serology (enzyme-linked immunosorbent assay and confirmational assays [Western blot analysis, indirect fluorescent antibody assay]) for perinatally exposed infants 18 months of age or older.[8]

Anatomic lesions that lead to pulmonary obstructive airway disease can simulate the complex of chronic bronchitis. The infant with chronic cough, poor feeding habits, and failure to thrive should undergo evaluation for gastroesophageal reflux and tracheoesophageal fistula, which most easily are identified by barium swallow or pH probe monitoring. Mediastinal tumors can produce extrinsic obstruction, leading to recurrent cough and wheezing. Congenital heart disease should be considered in this patient group and can be evaluated with chest radiography, electrocardiography, and echocardiography.

Respiratory tract irritants have been implicated as a cause of chronic cough, as documented in adult populations of industrial European nations.[15, 25, 39] An assessment of the public health impact of pollution in Austria, France, and Switzerland concluded that air pollution caused 6 percent of all mortality, or 40,000 attributable cases per year.[19] Of note is that nonindustrial, rural communities, such as the forest zone of Nigeria, report virtually no chronic bronchitis, whereas metropolitan New York reports an increased risk for development of both upper and lower respiratory tract infections in both adults and children who reside in those parts of the city with the highest ambient air levels of sulfur dioxide and particulate air pollution.[22] After exposure to urban air particulate matter, animal models with induced chronic bronchitis (exposure to 200 ppm of sulfur dioxide for 6 weeks) have shown pathologic changes consistent with exacerbation of their chronic bronchitis, namely, changes in ventilatory capacity and marked pulmonary inflammation.[10] A correlation between tobacco smoking and reduced ventilatory capacity in adults has been reported by many investigators. Peat and associates[29] described teenagers in Sydney, Australia, with recurrent episodes of bronchitis with worsened lung function when coupled with tobacco smoking. A meta-analysis of 21 relevant publications on relations between exposure to environmental tobacco smoke and lower respiratory tract infection in infancy and early childhood concluded that exposure to environmental smoke resulted in adverse childhood respiratory outcomes.[21] They included an increased number of lower respiratory tract infections and an increased number of hospitalizations for these infections. These data suggest that for physicians to obtain a smoking history not only for the patient but also for other household members is imperative. Occupational exposures long have been cited for exacerbating pulmonary diseases and possibly causing persistent lower respiratory tract irritation presenting as chronic cough. Classic examples of exposure to dust leading to increased risk are described in coal miners in Great Britain, foundry workers in the Rhine-Ruhr area of Germany, potters in West Virginia, and farmers in Croatia; also well documented is that tobacco smoking accentuates the irritant effect of occupational exposure for these adult patients.[42]

Epidemiology and Etiology

Differentiating the impact of clinical, social, and environmental factors on lower respiratory tract disease, including chronic bronchitis, has been problematic and has led to conflicting outcomes in epidemiologic assessments.[6, 12, 17, 37] In addition, the lack of a standardized definition of chronic bronchitis in the pediatric literature leads to confusing data when attempting to appreciate the prevalence or etiology of the disease complex.[26, 38] In Table 24–1, the information from Kubo and associates[18] separates acute recurrent bronchitis, asthmatic bronchitis, and chronic bronchitis, leading to a drop in the prevalence from a proposed 46.4 percent (in the Arizona questionnaire) to 1.4 percent.[26] Considerable overlap also exists in evaluating etiologic agents for chronic bronchitis. The same viral agents proposed as the exacerbating factors of asthmatic bronchitis (see Chapter 25) are implicated in exacerbations of chronic bronchitis.[14, 18] They include rhinoviruses, parainfluenza viruses, respiratory syncytial virus, influenza A and B viruses, adenoviruses, and enteroviruses. Persistent adenovirus infection has been implicated as a cause of childhood chronic bronchitis. In a study of 11 children with chronic bronchitis, transbronchial biopsy revealed no evidence of persistent adenovirus infection (culture or polymerase chain reaction),[30] suggesting that viral infections may precipitate cough, but their roles in the pathologic findings associated with chronic bronchitis should be questioned. For a group of 40 pediatric patients with chronic bronchitis and exacerbations of cough and fever, predominant bacterial pathogens isolated from washed sputum are listed in Table 24–3 and include *Haemophilus influenzae, Streptococcus pneumoniae,* and *Staphylococcus aureus*.[18] These bacteria also are implicated as etiologic agents in the triggering of asthmatic bronchitis. Treatment of exacerbations of chronic bronchitis with antibiotic therapy usually is effective in reducing volume of sputum and purulence but shows no parallel elimination of the cultured micro-organisms.

Treatment

When a specific diagnosis is found in association with chronic cough or wheezing, therapy is directed toward the primary disease entity as well as the clinical presentation of cough. Hence, bronchodilators (theophylline preparations, β-adrenergic agents, cromolyn sodium, corticosteroids) and anticholinergic agents are used, when appropriate, for the treatment of chronic cough associated with asthma or acute exacerbations of COPD.[36] Appropriate positioning techniques (prone 30 degrees), feeding schedules, and medications (e.g., bethanecol) are indicated in the approach to infants with gastroesophageal reflux. The patient with hypogammaglobulinemia or an IgG subclass deficiency can be aided with supplemental intravenous immunoglobulin preparations currently available commercially (100 to 400 mg/kg/dose every 2 to 4 weeks) in an attempt to decrease the incidence of infections.

That those patients with such chronic pulmonary diseases as cystic fibrosis, asthma, or ciliary dyskinesias understand the pulmonary irritant effect of tobacco smoking, dust exposure, and air pollution is imperative. A change of occupation may be essential for their well-being. Also imperative is to stress the irritant effect of parental smoking on the already compromised pulmonary function of the child. Antibiotic therapy for chronic bronchitis usually is reserved for only those patients with severe illness in whom the likelihood of secondary bacterial infection is great. In these instances, therapy usually consists of amoxicillin (45 to 90 mg/kg per 24 hours), erythromycin (40 mg/kg per 24 hours), or, in adolescents, tetracycline (25 to 50 mg/kg per 24 hours) for 5 to 10 days. Although concerns about resistant flora might suggest expansion to newer antibiotics, such use has not been proven efficacious in chronic pulmonary diseases, especially COPD.[2, 36, 41] For the patient receiving methylxanthine therapy, of importance is to remember that certain antibiotics, such as erythromycin, lead to elevated serum concentrations of theophylline, which renders toxicity more likely to occur. As with patients who have obstructive lung disease, attention must be aimed at careful and sequential monitoring of pulmonary function. The prognosis for chronic bronchitis is varied and is dependent on the specific etiology of this syndrome.

TABLE 24–3 ■ DOMINANT PATHOGENS IN WASHED SPUTUM OF CHRONIC BRONCHITIS (40 CASES)

	No. of Cases
Haemophilus influenzae and *Streptococcus pneumoniae*	21 (52.5%)
Haemophilus influenzae	17 (42.5%)
Staphylococcus aureus	2 (5.0%)
Superinfection with gram-negative rods	
Pseudomonas aeruginosa	4
Klebsiella pneumoniae	2
Escherichia coli	1
Enterobacter cloacae	1

From Kubo, S., Funabashi, S., Uehara, S., et al.: Clinical aspects of "asthmatic bronchitis" and chronic bronchitis in infants and children. J. Asthma Res. *15*:99–132, 1978.

REFERENCES

1. American Thoracic Society: Chronic bronchitis, asthma, and pulmonary emphysema. Thorax *15*:762–768, 1980.
2. Ball, P., Baquero, F., Cars, O., et al.: Antibiotic therapy of community respiratory tract infections: Strategies for optimal outcomes and minimized resistance emergence. Antimicrob. Chemother. *49*:31–40, 2002.
3. Beschorner, W. E., Saral, R., Hutchins, G. M., et al.: Lymphocytic bronchitis associated with graft-versus-host disease in recipients of bone marrow transplants. N. Engl. J. Med. *299*:1030–1036, 1978.
4. Boule, M., Gaultier, C., Tournier, G., et al.: Lung function in children with recurrent bronchitis. Respiration *38*:127–134, 1979.
5. Burrows, B., Knudsen, R. J., and Lebowitz, M. D.: The relationship of childhood respiratory illness to adult obstructive airway disease. Am. Rev. Respir. Dis. *115*:751–759, 1977.
6. Burrows, B., and Lebowitz, M. D.: Characteristics of chronic bronchitis in a warm dry region. Am. Rev. Respir. Dis. *112*:365–370, 1975.
7. Busse, W. W.: Respiratory infections: Their role in airway responsiveness and the pathogenesis of asthma. J. Allerg. Clin. Immun. *85*:671–684, 1990.
8. Centers for Disease Control and Prevention: 1994 Revised classification system for human immunodeficiency virus infection in children less than 13 years of age. M. M. W. R. Morb. Mortal. Wkly. Rep. *43*:1–17, 1994.
9. Chipps, B. E., Talama, R. C., and Winklestein, J. A.: IgA deficiency, recurrent pneumonia, and bronchiectasis. Chest *73*:519–526, 1978.
10. Clarke, R. W., Catalano, P. J., Koutrakis, P., et al.: Urban air particulate inhalation alters pulmonary function and induces pulmonary inflammation in a rodent model of chronic bronchitis. Inhal. Toxicol. *11*:637–656, 1999.
11. Cloutier, M. M., and Laughlin, G. M.: Chronic cough in children: A manifestation of airway hyperreactivity. Pediatrics *67*:6–12, 1981.
12. Dodge, R., Burrows, B., Lebowitz, M. D., et al.: Antecedent features of children in whom asthma develops during the second decade of life. J. Allerg. Clin. Immun. *92*:744–749, 1993.
13. Faulkner, M. A., and Hilleman, D. E.: The economic impact of chronic obstructive pulmonary disease. Expert Opin. Pharmacother. *3*:219–228, 2002.

14. Horn, M. E. C., and Gregg, I.: Role of viral infection and host factors in acute episodes of asthma and chronic bronchitis. Chest *63*:44–85, 1973.
15. Irwin, R. S., Corrao, W. M., and Pratter, M. R.: Chronic persistent cough in the adult. Am. Rev. Respir. Dis. *123*:413–417, 1981.
16. Klein, R. B., and Huggins, B. W.: Chronic bronchitis in children. Semin. Respir. Med. *9*:13–22, 1994.
17. Kolnaar, B. G. M., Van den Bosch, W. J. H. M., Van den Hoogen, H. J. M., et al.: The clustering of respiratory diseases in early childhood. Fam. Med. *26*:106–110, 1994.
18. Kubo, S., Funabashi, S., Uehara, S., et al.: Clinical aspects of "asthmatic bronchitis" and chronic bronchitis in infants and children. J. Asthma Res. *15*:99–132, 1978.
19. Kunzli, N., Kaiser, R., Medina, S., et al.: Public-health impact of outdoor and traffic-related air pollution: A European assessment. Lancet *356*:795–801, 2000.
20. Lemanske, R. F., Dick, E. C., Swenson, C. A., et al.: Rhinovirus upper respiratory tract infection increases airway hyperreactivity and late asthmatic reactions. J. Clin. Invest. *83*:1–10, 1989.
21. Li, J. S., Peat, J. K., Zuan, W., et al.: Meta-analysis on the association between environmental tobacco smoke (ETS) exposure and the prevalence of lower respiratory tract infection in early childhood. Pediatr. Pulmonol. *27*:5–13, 1999.
22. Love, G. T., Lan, S. P., Shy, C. M., et al.: The incidence and severity of acute respiratory illness in families exposed to different levels of air pollution, New York metropolitan area 1971–1972. Arch. Environ. Health *36*:66–74, 1981.
23. Mato, S. P., and Van Dyke, R. B.: Pulmonary infections in children with HIV infection. Semin. Respir. Infect. *17*:33–46, 2002.
24. McGuire, A., Irwin, D. E., Fenn, P., et al.: The excess cost of acute exacerbations of chronic bronchitis in patients aged 45 and older in England and Wales. Value Health *4*:370–375, 2001.
25. Monto, A. S., and Ross, H.: Acute respiratory illness in the community: Effect of family composition, smoking, and chronic symptoms. Br. J. Prev. Soc. Med. *31*:101–108, 1977.
26. Morgan, W. T., and Taussig, L. M.: The chronic bronchitis complex in childhood. Pediatr. Clin. North Am. *31*:851–864, 1984.
27. Norton, K. I., Kattan, M., Rao, J. S., et al: Chronic radiographic lung changes in children with vertically transmitted HIV-1 infection. A. J. R. Am. J. Roentgenol. *176*:1553–1558, 2001.
28. Oxelius, V. A.: Quantitative and qualitative investigations of serum IgG subclasses in immunodeficiency diseases. Clin. Exp. Immunol. *36*: 112–116, 1979.
29. Peat, J. K., Woolcock, A. J., Leider, S. R., et al.: Asthma and bronchitis in Sydney school children. I. Prevalence during a six-year study. Am. J. Epidemiol. *111*:721–727, 1980.
30. Pichler, M., Herrmann, G., Schmidt, H., et al.: Persistent adenoviral infection and chronic obstructive bronchitis in children: is there a link? Pediatr. Pulmonol. *32*:367–371, 2001.
31. Redding, G. J., Brown, G. F., Jacobs, M., et al.: Bronchopulmonary dysplasia (BPD). Pediatr. Pulmonol. *3*(Suppl.):3–13, 1989.
32. Rossman, C. M., Forrest, J. B., Ruffin, R. E., et al.: Immotile cilia syndrome in persons with and without Kartagener's syndrome. Am. Rev. Respir. Dis. *121*:1011–1016, 1980.
33. Rozycki, H. J., and Kirkpatrick, B. V.: New developments in bronchopulmonary dysplasia. Pediatr. Ann. *22*:532–538, 1993.
34. Schur, P. H., Borel, H., Gelfand, E. W., et al.: Selective gamma-G globulin deficiencies in patients with recurrent pyogenic infections. N. Engl. J. Med. *283*:631–634, 1970.
35. Smith, T. F., Ireland, T. A., Zaatari, G. S., et al.: Characteristics of children with endoscopically proved "chronic bronchitis." Am. J. Dis. Child. *139*:1039–1044, 1985.
36. Stoller, J. K.: Acute exacerbations of chronic obstructive pulmonary disease. N. Engl. J. Med. *346*:988–994, 2002.
37. Strachan, D. P., Seagrott, V., and Cook, D. G.: Chest illness in infancy and chronic respiratory disease in later life: An analysis by month of birth. Int. J. Epidemiol. *23*:1060–1068, 1994.
38. Taussig, L. M., Smith, S. M., and Blumenfeld, R.: Chronic bronchitis in childhood: What is it? Pediatrics *67*:1–5, 1981.
39. Wanner, H. U.: Effects of atmospheric pollution on human health. Experientia *49*:754–758, 1993.
40. Williams, H., and McNicol, K.: Prevalence and natural history of wheezing bronchitis and asthma in children: An epidemiological study. B. M. J. *4*:321–325, 1969.
41. Zhanel, G. G., Ennis, K., Vercaigne, L., et al.: A critical review of the fluoroquinolones: Focus on respiratory infections. Drugs *62*:13–59, 2002.
42. Zock, J. P., Sunyer, J., Kogevinas, M., et al.: Occupation, chronic bronchitis, and lung function in young adults: An international study. Am. J. Respir. Crit. Care Med. *163*:1572–1577, 2001.

Bronchiolitis and Infectious Asthma

ROBERT C. WELLIVER

Bronchiolitis and infectious asthma, which also is called asthmatic bronchitis or wheezy bronchitis, are common illnesses of children, characterized by symptoms of upper respiratory tract infection and signs of obstructive airway disease. Bronchiolitis and infectious asthma often are considered to be distinct entities, and not all infants who develop bronchiolitis have infectious asthma in later life. Nonetheless, studies indicate that the two illnesses are quite similar in terms of clinical presentation, pathologic findings, and mechanisms of pathogenesis. Differences in terms of etiologic agents that precipitate episodes of illness or in terms of response to therapy are more a function of the patient's age (particularly older or younger than 3 years) than of any underlying disease process. *Infectious asthma*, therefore, is considered as a term defining the occurrence of repeated episodes of bronchiolitis, and the two conditions are discussed together.

Definitions

Bronchiolitis is an acute communicable disease predominantly manifesting in infancy and characterized by cough, coryza, fever, grunting, tachypnea, retractions, inspiratory crackles, expiratory wheezing, and air trapping. The age at which the first (and the most severe) episodes most commonly occur is 2 to 6 months. *Infectious asthma* is a term that generally refers to infection-induced wheezing occurring beyond infancy. Nonetheless, a given patient may experience bronchiolitis during the first months of life and a recurrent episode caused by the same virus in the second year, suggesting an identical underlying nature of the two illnesses.

History

Although all practicing pediatricians today are familiar with the term *bronchiolitis* and associate it with an acute clinical illness with the signs and symptoms of obstructive emphysema, it has been recognized in the medical literature for only a relatively brief period.

In the early years of the 20th century, the term *capillary bronchitis* was used to describe an inflammatory illness of the smallest alveoli.[59] However, the condition could not be distinguished clinically from pneumonia, and whether the pathologic entity (i.e., bronchiolitis) ever occurred separately from pneumonia was doubted. In the 11th edition of

Holt's Diseases of Infancy and Childhood,[76] published in 1940, capillary bronchitis is discussed only briefly and is considered under pneumococcal pneumonia. Not until the sixth edition of the *Textbook of Pediatrics,*[124] published in 1954, was acute bronchiolitis listed as a heading; even at that time, it was associated with interstitial pneumonitis.

In contrast to the delayed textbook recognition of bronchiolitis, good clinical descriptions were presented in journals. In 1941, Hubble and Osborn[80] published "Acute Bronchiolitis in Children," in which an epidemic of bronchiolitis involving 50 hospitalized children was described. Pratt[138] in 1944 and Nelson and Smith[125] in 1945 presented excellent clinical papers. Studies in the late 1950s and early 1960s established the etiologic association of respiratory syncytial virus (RSV) and other viruses with acute bronchiolitis.[7, 24–27, 150]

Etiologic Agents

RSV is the major cause of bronchiolitis in infancy and virtually the only important etiologic consideration when the disease is epidemic.* In sporadic instances of bronchiolitis, other infectious agents have been found to have etiologic associations. The relative frequency of infectious agents in the overall cause of bronchiolitis is presented in Table 25–1. These data were compiled from 12 reports in which respiratory illness in children was observed over an extended period of time, and in most instances, a large number of clinical illness categories were being studied. In the nonepidemic situation, more than 50 percent of the isolates or instances of serologic evidence of infection are infectious agents other than RSV. During epidemics in the colder months, virologic and serologic studies indicate RSV as the cause in 80 percent or more of the cases, especially in severe ones. In contrast, sporadic disease rarely is associated with a more than 50 percent association of infectious agent and illness, despite the fact that infections undoubtedly are the cause of sporadic and epidemic bronchiolitis.[112]

Children surviving infantile bronchiolitis often have recurrent episodes of wheezing that, on clinical grounds, seem to be precipitated by upper respiratory infections. Studies designed to determine the infectious agents responsible for these repeated wheezing episodes have yielded variable results, presumably because they involve patients of different ages followed during different seasons of the year.[9, 58, 104, 113–116] A comprehensive study based on more than a decade of observation of children from birth through 15 years of age[71] revealed that viruses and *Mycoplasma pneumoniae* are the most common etiologic agents (Table 25–2). RSV is the most common cause of recurrent, wheezing-associated respiratory illness occurring in young children, including those who previously experienced bronchiolitis, which strongly suggests the identical nature of infection-related wheezing episodes occurring in children of different ages. With increasing patient age, rhinoviruses and *M. pneumoniae* account for most infection-induced wheezing episodes. The parainfluenza and influenza viruses are important causes of such wheezing episodes throughout childhood, whereas coronaviruses and adenoviruses are less common causes in infancy. RSV remains an important cause of wheezing in adolescents[71] and can cause airway obstruction in middle-aged and elderly individuals.[181]

The role of bacteria as primary agents, synergistically active participants, or secondary invaders in bronchiolitis has interested investigators for many years. No evidence has been found of a primary role for bacteria in bronchiolitis of infants.[7, 100] The data on synergistic viral-bacterial infections also are not convincing. Wood and colleagues[195] in 1954 and Sell[155] in 1960 reported results of studies in which bacteriologic and serologic evidence tended to associate *Haemophilus influenzae* infections with bronchiolitis. Some of the children from these studies later were shown serologically to have had RSV infection.[29] Later studies showed evidence of mixed viral-bacterial infections in bronchiolitis[105, 127] and other lower respiratory illnesses.[127] However, these serologically defined mixed infections were found no more commonly among patients with bronchiolitis than among patients with mild upper respiratory tract disease, whereas RSV was recovered 10 times as often from patients with lower respiratory tract disease as from patients with upper respiratory tract disease alone.[105] A role of any significance for mixed viral-bacterial infection in bronchiolitis of infancy is unlikely to exist. Bacterial superinfection is an uncommon occurrence in bronchiolitis (at least in developed countries), as is discussed later in this chapter (see Complications and Prognosis).

The association of asthma and infectious illnesses was appreciated throughout the 20th century. Initial reports tended to relate bacterial agents to wheezing; as early as 1909, Carmalt-Jones[21] reported improvement of patients with asthma in association with injections of a bacterial vaccine. Throughout the first half of the 20th century, "bacterial allergy" was the main consideration in infection-related wheezing, and controversy raged about the therapeutic merits of bacterial vaccines. Despite widespread use of bacterial vaccines in the treatment of infectious asthma, no evidence that bacterial organisms of the normal flora precipitate asthmatic attacks exists.[67, 77, 118, 119, 179] However, in children with sinus infections with *Streptococcus pneumoniae* or *H. influenzae*, eradication of the infection may result in marked improvement of the asthma. Administration of antibiotic therapy for bacterial sinusitis is justified, but therapeutic trials of antibiotics for infantile bronchiolitis or recurrent episodes of wheezing[79] have not yielded beneficial results. The routine use of antibiotics prophylactically or therapeutically in acute wheezing episodes in children cannot be defended. In particular, after a diagnosis of RSV or parainfluenza virus infection has been established, antibiotic courses started empirically can be stopped with safety.

TABLE 25–1 ■ INFECTIOUS AGENTS ASSOCIATED WITH ACUTE BRONCHIOLITIS

Infectious Agent	Relative	Frequency (%)
Respiratory syncytial virus		50
Parainfluenza viruses		25
Type 1	(8)	
Type 2	(2)	
Type 3	(15)	
Adenoviruses		5
Mycoplasma pneumoniae		5
Rhinoviruses		5
Influenza viruses		5
Type A	(3)	
Type B	(2)	
Enteroviruses		2
Herpes simplex virus		2
Mumps virus		<1

Data from references 21, 23, 25, 47, 54, 89, 100, 105, 120, 170.

*See references 7, 8, 11, 21, 23–28, 47, 54, 89, 100, 101, 105, 120, 132, 142, 150, 170.

TABLE 25–2 ■ PRINCIPAL AGENTS RECOVERED FROM CHILDREN OF DIFFERENT AGES WITH WHEEZING PRECIPITATED BY INFECTION

Agent*	Frequency of Isolation of Each Age Group†			
	0–2 years	2–5 years	5–9 years	9–15 years
Respiratory syncytial virus	++++	+++	++	++
Adenoviruses	++	++	+	0
Parainfluenza viruses	++	++	++	++
Rhinoviruses	+	+ to ++	++ to +++	++ to +++
Mycoplasma pneumoniae	+	++	+++	++++

*Other agents that more rarely precipitate wheezing include enteroviruses, herpes simplex virus, cytomegalovirus, coronaviruses, influenza viruses, mumps virus, varicella-zoster virus, *Bordetella pertussis*, and *Coxiella burnetii*.
†++++, very common; +++, common; ++, occasional; +, uncommon.
Data from references 9, 48, 58, 71, 77, 104, 113, 114, 116, 155.

Epidemiology

Bronchiolitis predominantly is a disease of infancy, although a similar disease occurring in older children arbitrarily may be referred to as another diagnostic entity. In a study involving 1148 children, the peak age of incidence was between 2 and 6 months, with more than 80 percent of the cases occurring during the first year of life.[132] In a study of families in or near Houston, Texas, rates of RSV infection were 68.8 per 100 children in the first year of life and 82.6 per 100 children in the second year, including many reinfections. Lower respiratory illness was caused by RSV in 22.4 of 100 children in the first year of life. Of all RSV infections occurring in children younger than 12 months of age, one third were accompanied by lower respiratory illness. Although the attack rate of RSV decreased with age, the frequency with which lower respiratory disease occurred among those infected remained relatively constant (Table 25–3), at least until they reached 4 years of age.[56] In the area of Tucson, Arizona, a study of 1179 children enrolled in a health maintenance organization found that the rate of lower respiratory illness in the first year of life was 32.9 episodes per 100 children; 60 percent of these episodes were diagnosed as bronchiolitis.[197]

Studies in the Washington, D.C., area[89] estimated the risk of hospitalization for bronchiolitis among infants between 0 and 12 months old to be 10 per 1000. A combined study involving 10 centers in Great Britain[31] concluded that the frequency of hospitalization for lower respiratory tract disease (predominantly wheezing) caused by RSV was 1 per 114 infants younger than 1 year of age and 1 per 476 children younger than 5 years of age. Peak rates of hospitalization were observed for children from 1 to 3 months of age (1 in 56).

TABLE 25–3 ■ ATTACK RATES OF RESPIRATORY SYNCYTIAL VIRUS

Age (mo)	Child Years	Infections per 100 Child Years	LRI per 100 Child Years	LRI per 100 Infections
0–12	125	68.8	22.4	32.6
13–24	92	82.6	13.0	15.8
25–36	65	46.2	10.8	23.3
37–48	39	33.3	7.7	23.1

LRI, lower respiratory tract infections.
From Glezen, W. P., Taber, L.H., Frank, A. L., et al.: Risk of primary infection and reinfection with respiratory syncytial virus. Am. J. Dis. Child. *140*:543–546, 1986.

Studies completed in North Carolina[71] in which the incidence of all wheezing-associated respiratory infection (those requiring hospitalization and those mild enough to permit outpatient management) was determined in a group practice showed that the incidence of such illness was 11.4 cases per 100 children in the first year of life, 6.0 per 100 children in the second year, and 1.3 per 100 children in elementary school.

Epidemic bronchiolitis caused by RSV is markedly seasonal in temperate climates, with peak activity in the period from January to May and virtually no activity from August to October.[89] In contrast to the number of bronchiolitis cases caused by RSV, a few sporadic cases caused by other agents are seen throughout the entire year. In their study of 1179 cases, Kim and associates[89] found that 77 percent of the cases of RSV infection occurred between December and June. The lowest incidence occurred in August (2%). In equatorial climates, RSV activity is spread throughout the year.

Bronchiolitis occurs more frequently in boys; the male-to-female ratio is approximately 1.5:1.[47] In older children, wheezing attributable to viral and mycoplasma infections also occurs more frequently in males (male-to-female ratio of 1.35:1) until they reach 9 years of age, when the incidence becomes equal for the sexes.[71]

Environmental factors are a major determinant of risk for hospitalization for lower respiratory illness caused by RSV, with the incidence of hospitalization for infants 1 to 3 months of age residing in rural, urban, or heavily industrialized areas of Great Britain being 1 in 80, 1 in 60, and 1 in 40, respectively. The figures for all children younger than 5 years of age were 1 in 714, 1 in 588, and 1 in 227, respectively.[31] Studies from Tucson, Arizona, indicate that many socioeconomic factors are associated with an increased risk of developing lower respiratory infection at the time of infection with RSV. These factors include absence of breast feeding, low level of maternal education, and exposure to cigarette smoke. The greatest risk was conferred by sharing sleeping quarters with two or more individuals.[197]

Annual rates of hospitalization and death for RSV infection in the United States have been reported.[156, 157] Approximately 123,000 infants younger than 1 year of age are hospitalized annually with bronchiolitis, with RSV infection accounting for 51,000 to 82,000 of these hospitalizations. Including cases diagnosed as pneumonia, RSV infection results in 70,000 to 120,000 hospitalizations annually. The annual incidence of hospitalization for bronchiolitis increased from 12.9 per 1,000 infants in 1980 to 31.2 per 1,000 in 1996, suggesting an increased severity of illness developing during this interval. Between 1979 and 1997, an average of 95 bronchiolitis-associated deaths occurred annually, with 77 percent occurring during the RSV epidemic season. Of all bronchiolitis-associated deaths, approximately 20 percent occurred in infants with underlying heart disease, lung disease, or premature birth. RSV infection might have resulted in 171 to 510 deaths annually, which included cases of bronchiolitis and pneumonia.

Clinical Presentation

Acute bronchiolitis occurs most commonly in infants 2 to 12 months of age. In most instances, the patient's history reveals exposure to an adult or older child with a common cold or other relatively trivial respiratory infection. Occasionally, as in the daycare setting, the child is exposed to other children with more marked respiratory illness. After exposure, the incubation period is approximately 5 to 7 days. The initial signs include copious nasal discharge (often serous in the early stage), cough, irritability, poor feeding, and vomiting in some cases. The child usually has fever, with rectal temperatures ranging from normal to 40.6° C (105.4° F) (mean, 39° C [102° F]).[142] Nasal congestion with tenacious secretions and progressive cough and dyspnea dominate the clinical picture. Symptoms of upper respiratory infection persist for several days, and the onset of lower respiratory infection usually is precipitous, with the time of the onset of wheezing often recognizable from the caretaker's description of the illness. The maximum severity of illness generally is attained within 24 hours of the first signs of lower respiratory illness. Apnea may occur and may be severe enough to require mechanically assisted ventilation.[12]

At the time of hospital admission, all patients have cough and evidence of respiratory distress. Examination reveals fever in 50 to 80 percent of cases. The pulse is rapid, and the respiratory rate usually is between 40 and 80 breaths per minute. The breathing is labored, with flaring of the alae nasae; grunting; abdominal breathing; and supraclavicular, subcostal, and intercostal retractions. The degree of retraction of the lower chest wall may be a particularly accurate indicator of the severity of the illness. Wheezing often is audible without the use of a stethoscope, and the chest is full. Hyperresonance may be detected on percussion, and auscultation generally reveals harsh rhonchi, high- or low-pitched expiratory wheezes, or fine inspiratory rales. Occasionally, wheezing is not audible despite other evidence of airway obstruction. A prolonged expiratory phase of breathing may occur, suggesting the presence of a more severe degree of illness. Cyanosis also occurs in severe cases.

Other findings include a mild conjunctivitis in one third of the cases, pharyngitis of varied severity in approximately one half of the affected infants, and otitis media in 5 to 15 percent of the cases. The abdomen frequently appears distended, and the liver and spleen usually are palpable; the organs are not enlarged but are pushed down because of emphysema and the flattened diaphragm.

The hospital course of bronchiolitis is variable. Significant improvement occurred in one half of the cases within 2 days in one large study.[1] In the same study, approximately one third of the cases had a gradual course without evidence of clear-cut improvement at any one time; 71 percent of the patients were afebrile by the third hospital day. In another study performed more than 25 years later,[57] the average duration of hospitalization was 3.4 days. Longer stays were required for infants with initial oxygen saturations of less than 90 percent and those younger than 6 weeks of age at the onset of illness. Reasonable criteria for admission in otherwise healthy infants, therefore, seem to include hypoxia (i.e., oxygen saturation of less than 90 to 92 percent), age younger than 6 weeks, and a degree of respiratory distress sufficient to reduce fluid intake to inadequate levels. Other criteria include apnea, immunodeficiency, and the presence of significant underlying heart or lung disease. Most patients can be discharged from the hospital within 2 to 3 days after admission, although mild wheezing still may be present.

In 121 hospitalized patients, the total white blood cell count was less than 12,500/mm^3 in 74 percent, and in 15 determinations had more than 60 percent neutrophils.[1] In another study, a mean leukocyte count of 16,000/mm^3 was determined for children with lower respiratory tract disease, including bronchiolitis, as was an increased percentage of band form neutrophils compared with that of a control group. As in most infections, eosinophil counts in peripheral blood are reduced at the time of acute RSV infection. Nevertheless, eosinophil counts still are greater in infants with RSV bronchiolitis (particularly in male patients) than in infants with upper respiratory illness alone caused by RSV.[52]

Abnormalities of blood gas tensions and pH occur and are related to the severity of disease. Hypoxemia is a common occurrence; clinical cyanosis is not a reliable index of arterial oxygen tension (Pao_2).[34, 158] The respiratory rate is related inversely to the Pao_2, except when respiratory failure is imminent. In mild to moderate cases, carbon dioxide retention does not occur because the alveoli that are functioning can compensate for alveoli that are not ventilated. In severe disease, the blood pH is low and the $Paco_2$ is elevated.[37, 158] The technique of pulse oximetry has obviated the need for arterial blood gas sampling, except in severe cases for which hypercarbia is a concern.

In certain patients, clinical findings (e.g., degree of chest wall retractions, wheezing) often are out of proportion to the degree of hypoxia as measured by pulse oximetry.[121, 184] Infants with marked dyspnea must be evaluated carefully because respiratory failure may occur precipitously, despite their relatively reassuring oximetry readings. A more meaningful scoring system to assess severity of illness has been developed.[60]

The roentgenographic appearance of the chest in bronchiolitis varies considerably.[93] Anteroposterior x-ray films may be normal in mild cases. In moderate to severe illness, radiographs often appear exceptionally clear because of hyperinflation. The diaphragms often are flattened or depressed. The costophrenic angle is less acute, and the hilar vascular shadows are stretched. Frequently, areas of atelectasis give the appearance of pneumonitis, although true consolidation is quite uncommon. The heart usually appears small.

On the lateral radiograph, the diaphragm is depressed markedly, and reversal of the normal convexity frequently is seen. The anteroposterior diameter of the chest is increased.

With recurrent wheezing episodes, the prodrome may be considerably shorter in duration with little or no fever. Coryza may become progressively less noticeable or may even be absent in older children. In these afebrile children with brief prodromes, differentiation of infection-induced wheezing from more conventional asthma becomes essentially impossible clinically.[189]

Pathophysiology

The pathophysiology of bronchiolitis deservedly has been the focus of numerous investigations. Several original theories can be discounted reliably, whereas others deserve further study. Pathologic examinations of the lung in bronchiolitis or human airways in organ culture[72] reveal necrosis of the respiratory epithelium with destruction of the ciliated layer; mononuclear cell invasion of the peribronchial tissues; edema of the submucosa and adventitia; and obstruction of small airways with dense plugs of mucus, fibrin, and alveolar debris. An associated interstitial pneumonitis may occur, and patchy areas of atelectasis are common occurrences.[2, 193] Recovery apparently is complete histologically,[193] although mucus plugging the airway still was prominent in an infant 5 weeks after an acute episode of bronchiolitis. This infant had experienced a full clinical recovery (despite the persistent mucus plugging some areas of the lung) before eventually dying of acute pneumococcal pneumonia.[123]

Infants particularly are prone to the development of severe illness as a result of infection of the small airways for many reasons, including the small diameters of their airways. The infant lung is deficient in collateral alveolar ventilation through the pores of Kohn, which develop only in later life.[106] Atelectatic areas cannot be re-expanded readily. Other studies have demonstrated that the small airways in children younger than the age of 5 years contribute fivefold to sevenfold more to total airway resistance than do small airways of adults.[75] Viral infections involving small airways in young children are, therefore, more likely to manifest as serious clinical illnesses than are similar infections in adults. Nonetheless, these abnormalities exist in all infants. In contrast, most infants infected with RSV do not develop lower respiratory illness, which suggests that host or environmental factors may be involved in determining the pathogenesis of RSV infection. A list of environmental factors is presented in Table 25–4, and potentially important host factors are described later.

One factor that appears to predispose to the development of lower respiratory illness with RSV infection is the infecting dose of virus. Infants with greater quantities of RSV in their nasopharyngeal secretions are more likely to exhibit severe illness.[15] The fact that crowding is associated with greater risk of developing lower respiratory infection also suggests the importance of the initial inoculum.[193]

Another risk factor for the development of lower respiratory infection may be the relative diameter of the airway. When pulmonary function testing is completed on healthy infants before lower respiratory infection occurs, certain infants have relatively lower air flows (and presumably narrower airways) than do other infants. When followed prospectively, these infants are somewhat more likely to develop wheezing early in life than are infants with larger

TABLE 25–4 ■ FACTORS ASSOCIATED WITH AN INCREASED RISK AND SEVERITY OF BRONCHIOLITIS AND OF POSTBRONCHIOLITIC MORBIDITY

Factor	Increase in Frequency	Increase in Severity	Increase in Later Morbidity
Crowding	+++	+++	?
Passive smoking	+++	+++	++
Male gender	+	++	++
Absence of breast-feeding	+	+	?
Family history of asthma	±	±	±
Personal atopy	–	–	+++
Congenitally small airways	++	?	–
Airway reactivity	–	+	++
RSV-specific IgE response	++	++	++

+++, implies strong relationship; ++, implies moderate relationship; +, implies weak relationship; ±, implies controversial relationship; –, implies no relationship; ?, implies unknown relationship;
RSV, respiratory syncytial virus.
Data from references 16, 31, 55, 62, 71, 94, 103, 108, 109, 160, 175, 186, 188, 190, 191, 197–200.

airways.[108] The presence of congenitally smaller airways may place infants at greater risk for developing bronchiolitis. These abnormalities of lung function no longer are associated with an increased risk of wheezing after the child reaches 3 years of age. Instead, evidence of atopy then becomes the principal risk factor for recurrent wheezing.[109]

Several studies have demonstrated that the airways of infants are intrinsically more reactive to bronchospastic stimuli than are airways of older children,[97, 175] particularly in children from families with asthma.[199] How long this increased reactivity persists is unknown, and no study has demonstrated that infants with greater degrees of hereditary airway hyperreactivity are more likely to develop bronchiolitis or recurrent virus-induced wheezing. In later childhood, repeated occurrences of viral infections are necessary to sustain this increased reactivity.[183] In addition to the hereditary airway hyperreactivity, viruses themselves may induce increases in reactivity. Viral infections that clinically appear to be restricted to the upper respiratory tract in adults and children nonetheless result in transient, increased constrictive responses of the airway to a variety of stimuli, including histamine, irritants, and other agents, as well as small airway dysfunction.[3, 4, 10, 33, 42, 99] These constrictive responses after infection may occur as a result of denudation of airway epithelium with exposure and subsequent activation of airway irritant receptors, thereby effecting bronchoconstriction through stimulation of the parasympathetic nervous system.[42] Whether these changes could account for the severe degree of airway obstruction observed in bronchiolitis is in doubt, in that the abnormalities are relatively mild compared with the markedly increased reactivity that is observed in asthmatic individuals after exposure to allergens. These virus-induced changes were observed in all infected individuals, including those who did not experience wheezing at the time of the virus infection. However, if airways already are hyperreactive in infants, on a hereditary basis or as a result of a preceding viral infection, the subsequent stimulus of RSV infection may be sufficient to cause airway obstruction.

Immunologic deficits may be expected to lead to more severe forms of virus-induced respiratory illness. However, studies of the antibody response to RSV infection in serum and in respiratory secretions show that the response is similar among patients with bronchiolitis or simple upper respiratory illness alone due to this agent.[86, 187, 193] Antibody-directed cellular cytotoxicity expressed against tissue culture cells infected with RSV also is similar in patients with all forms of illness caused by this agent.[84, 152] Although investigators have shown that cells infected with RSV can activate complement through classic and alternate pathways,[165] studies suggest that in vivo activation of the complement cascade occurs with equal frequency among patients with all forms of illness caused by the virus.[85] When studied during the acute illness, cell-mediated immune responses (measured by lymphoproliferation) to RSV and parainfluenza virus[153, 185] are greater among patients with bronchiolitis than among those with upper respiratory illness alone caused by these agents. Cytotoxic T-lymphocyte activity is not detected easily in infants with bronchiolitis,[5] but no evidence exists of a deficiency of cytotoxic activity among these patients. In infants with the acquired immunodeficiency syndrome (AIDS), RSV infection may be unusually persistent, but bronchiolitis apparently is no more severe than in immunologically normal infants.[22, 91] Immunologic deficiency apparently can be excluded as a potential contributing factor in bronchiolitis.

Immunologic hypersensitivity has been suggested as playing a role in the development of severe bronchiolitis.

Original field trials demonstrated that a formalin-inactivated RSV vaccine induced humoral and cell-mediated immune responses to the virus. Nonetheless, vaccinated subjects manifested more severe forms of illness than did unvaccinated controls when subjects in each group subsequently were infected naturally.[88] The resulting disease in vaccine recipients was quite similar in form to bronchiolitis occurring after natural RSV infection, but an increased rate of hospitalization and two deaths occurred in vaccinated individuals. Some form of hypersensitivity apparently was induced by vaccination.

Other studies of unvaccinated, naturally infected infants also suggest that immunologic sensitization to RSV plays a role in the pathogenesis of the disease. In one study, infants with fatal RSV pneumonia had abundant virus but little immunoglobulin in lung tissues, whereas infants with bronchiolitis had demonstrable immunoglobulin but no detectable virus.[50] This study included an extremely small number of patients. The concept that serum IgG antibody to RSV, acquired by vaccination or transplacentally, might sensitize the host has been dispelled by results of studies demonstrating that severe bronchiolitis may occur in the absence of circulating antibody[133] and that titers of maternal antibody actually correlate with protection against infection caused by the virus.[55, 129]

Support for the concept that cell-mediated immune sensitization to RSV may play a role in the pathogenesis of bronchiolitis comes from the results of several studies. Cell-mediated immune responses to viral antigen were greater among recipients of an inactivated RSV vaccine than among control subjects who previously had experienced natural infection.[90] Exaggerated cell-mediated immune responses also were observed among infants younger than 6 months of age at the time of infection with RSV (the group at the highest risk for bronchiolitis) compared with infants infected at a later age.[153] Studies of infants acutely infected with RSV[185] and parainfluenza virus have demonstrated enhanced cell-mediated immune responses among patients with bronchiolitis compared with upper respiratory illness alone caused by either agent.

The exact mechanism by which cell-mediated hypersensitivity may contribute to bronchiolitis requires further investigation. Mice infused with cytotoxic T lymphocytes previously sensitized to RSV (by restimulation of cells with RSV in vitro) develop much more severe lung pathology and exhibit higher death rates after having RSV infection than did mice infected without previous infusion of sensitized cells.[98] These results have not been confirmed in humans, partly because of the difficulty in demonstrating cytotoxic T lymphocytes in the peripheral blood of acutely infected subjects. An effect related to an exaggerated release of lymphokines also is possible. Lymphokines released by activated T lymphocytes (e.g., interleukin-3, interleukin-5) are capable of activating eosinophils and mast cells to release proinflammatory factors.[43]

Immediate hypersensitivity to viral antigens has received much consideration as a potential contributing factor in bronchiolitis. The relation of a family history of asthma to the development of bronchiolitis in infancy remains controversial.[94, 160, 167, 200] However, production of virus-specific IgE and subsequent release of mediators of bronchoconstriction have been documented in infants hospitalized with bronchiolitis caused by RSV and the parainfluenza viruses.[16, 186, 188, 189] In bronchiolitis caused by RSV, the quantities of virus-specific IgE produced and histamine present in respiratory secretions correlate with the severity of illness, as measured by degree of arterial oxygen tension.[188] Leukotriene C_4 is a product of mast cells and eosinophils and is a potent stimulant of airway smooth muscle constriction and mucus secretion. This mediator is released into the airway in acute bronchiolitis,[182] as is histamine,[188] and histamine and prostaglandins are found in increased concentrations in serum.[161]

A possible role for eosinophils in the pathogenesis of bronchiolitis is supported by the finding of increased concentrations of eosinophil cationic protein in secretions of infants with bronchiolitis and an overall correlation of concentrations of this protein with the degree of hypoxia.[51, 52] Peripheral blood eosinophil counts are depressed during the acute phase of most infectious diseases, including RSV infection. Nevertheless, eosinophil counts in peripheral blood are higher in infants with bronchiolitis than in those with upper respiratory illness only, particularly in boys.[52] This finding is of interest because boys generally have more severe forms of bronchiolitis. Evidence suggests that the development of more severe forms of RSV bronchiolitis may be a result of immunologic hypersensitivity, possibly IgE-mediated hypersensitivity responses, occurring in the lung. Eosinophils were observed in the lung tissues at autopsy in the two infants who developed fatal RSV bronchiolitis after receiving the formalin-inactivated vaccine mentioned earlier.[88] This finding suggests that IgE-mediated hypersensitivity may have played a role in the adverse responses to that vaccine and in the pathogenesis of bronchiolitis itself.

An interesting, although contrasting, viewpoint is that eosinophils contribute to the clearance of viruses after infection. This view is supported by the fact that eosinophils contain enzymes with ribonuclease activity, which inactivates RSV.[37, 38] IgE and eosinophil-dependent mechanisms may be important in recovery from viral infections, much as they are in parasitic infections.

The airways of asthmatic individuals are infiltrated by T-lymphocytes (predominantly helper T lymphocytes) and eosinophils. Helper T (T_H) cells can be classified as type 1 (T_H1), which produce primarily interferon-γ and interleukin 2 (IL-2), or as type 2 (T_H2), which produce IL-4, IL-5, IL-13, and others. This finding is important because IL-4, IL-5, and IL-13 are important factors in promoting IgE synthesis and eosinophil migration. Asthma is thought by some researchers to be a result of a T_H2 bias in the airway. An attractive hypothesis is that RSV infection induces airway obstruction and wheezing by inciting the same type of T_H2 responses as observed in asthma. Interferon-γ and IL-4 are found in respiratory secretions of infants with RSV bronchiolitis, but IL-5 and IL-13 rarely are detectable in serum or secretions,[53, 180] suggesting that bronchiolitis is not characterized by a T_H2 lymphocyte bias.

Chemokines are proteins released by airway epithelial cells, inflammatory cells, fibroblasts, and other cell types that are chemotactic for leukocytes. Certain chemokines (e.g., IL-8) are active on a broad variety of leukocytes. Others, such as macrophage inflammatory protein 1-alpha (MIP-1α), the monocyte chemotactic proteins (MCP) types 1 through 4, eotaxin, and regulated on activation, normal T-cell expressed and secreted (RANTES), are more selective for eosinophils, basophils, mast cells, and T lymphocytes. These chemokines represent an alternative to T_H2 lymphocytes in terms of initiating the inflammatory response in asthma and bronchiolitis. Studies suggest that MIP-1α, eotaxin, and MCP may be particularly important in the pathogenesis of bronchiolitis because they correlate with the degree of hypoxia observed during acute illness.[53] Abnormalities of chemokine responses, rather than helper T-cell responses, may underlie the pathogenesis of bronchiolitis.

Other studies have identified potential mechanisms by which viral infections may precipitate airway obstruction in subjects with airways prone to constriction, although their actual role in expression of clinical illness remains to be defined. Immune complexes of RSV and its antibody stimulate metabolism of granulocyte arachidonic acid to bronchoactive metabolites such as thromboxanes.[44] Viral infections induce beta-adrenergic blockade in granulocytes of asthmatic individuals,[18] although whether such changes also occur in cells in the respiratory tract that regulate airway diameter is not known. Exposure of leukocytes to viral antigens in vitro enhances basophil histamine release on appropriate stimulation.[19, 82] Damage to the respiratory epithelium may have an enhancing effect on the magnitude of the IgE response to inhaled antigens[135]; viral infections could contribute in this way to the development of wheezing. Various studies of other potential mechanisms by which the immune response may exacerbate illness are under way in animal models.

Diagnosis

DIFFERENTIAL DIAGNOSIS

A tendency exists to attribute all infantile respiratory distress occurring after the immediate newborn period to bronchiolitis. However, the list of causes of infantile dyspnea consists of conditions that are associated with upper and lower airway obstruction. Recognition of upper airway obstructive disease should cause little difficulty because the problem is one of distress with inspiration rather than air trapping. Illnesses that cause lower airway obstructive disease and diseases that suggest this problem are listed in Table 25–5.

The differential diagnosis of allergic disease causes the most difficulty. Generally, the first episode of allergic respiratory disease, when associated with infection, cannot be separated from bronchiolitis by any objective measures. Anatomic defects such as vascular rings can cause obstruction of the airway at many locations; inspiratory or expiratory distress, or a combination, can occur. Frequently, a child with an anatomic defect does not have any detectable difficulty until the occurrence of a trivial respiratory infection, which complicates the diagnostic picture.

TABLE 25–5 ■ DIFFERENTIAL DIAGNOSTIC CONSIDERATIONS IN ACUTE BRONCHIOLITIS AND INFECTIOUS ASTHMA

- Allergy
  - Asthma
  - Allergic pneumonias (e.g., allergic aspergillosis)
- Anatomic cause
  - Vascular ring, lung cysts, lobar emphysema
  - Pneumothorax, hydrothorax, chylothorax
  - Foreign body
- Circulatory failure
  - Congenital and acquired heart disease
  - Anemia
  - Nephritis
- Infections
  - Viral, chlamydial, rickettsial, mycoplasmal, bacterial, and fungal pneumonias
  - Migrating parasites
- Irritants
  - Inhalation of toxic substances (e.g., chlorine gas)
  - Aspiration pneumonia
  - Gastroesophageal reflux
- Metabolic cause
  - Poisons (e.g., salicylate)
  - Acidosis

Foreign bodies should be considered even in very young infants. Gastroesophageal reflux disease has become recognized as a frequent cause of wheezing in young infants. Because of its obvious therapeutic implications, bacterial pneumonia is the most important differential consideration, although wheezing occurs very infrequently in association with bacterial pneumonia.[104, 105]

SPECIFIC DIAGNOSIS

Because bronchiolitis and infectious asthma are clinical diseases with arbitrary boundaries and multiple etiologic agents, outlining a method for specific diagnosis is difficult. When illness is epidemic, RSV usually is the cause. In nonepidemic situations, a careful history and appropriate laboratory studies and radiographs should be considered to exclude the other differential diagnostic possibilities that are listed in Table 25–5.

A specific etiologic diagnosis can be made by the isolation of virus from the nasopharynx. The diagnostic virologic facilities of many medical centers enable the isolation in tissue culture of RSV, parainfluenza and influenza viruses, adenoviruses, rhinoviruses, enteroviruses, and herpesviruses. The use of the shell vial technique has been applied to RSV infection with success.[164] The polymerase chain reaction (PCR) technique also shows promise in amplification of small quantities of RSV RNA from clinical specimens, although its having superiority to other methods does not appear likely.[134] Rapid detection of viral antigen of RSV directly in nasopharyngeal secretions by commercially available (e.g., enzyme-linked immunosorbent assay [ELISA]) or fluorescent antibody techniques is the method of choice in most laboratories for several reasons. The accuracy of these techniques is superior to that of standard cell culture (at least in infants) because antigens remain stable under transport conditions that inactivate live virus, and results are available several days earlier than by cell culture. Infections with influenza and parainfluenza viruses and adenoviruses also can be identified by rapid detection techniques, and reliable commercial kits permitting simultaneous testing for each of these agents are the standard in most laboratories.

Treatment

The cornerstone of therapy for bronchiolitis is the administration of oxygen because sicker patients usually are hypoxemic.[40, 158] Oxygen saturation should be maintained at 92 percent or higher. Usually, an oxygen concentration of 30 or 40 percent can achieve this goal, and the patient's respiratory status can be monitored by pulse oximetry; however, blood gas determinations should be obtained when indicated by clinical findings (e.g., cyanosis, agitation). A common practice is to place children with bronchiolitis in tents and administer mist vigorously. Although oxygen should be humidified, the use of mists and aerosols except to deliver specific antiviral therapy is discouraged; mist can act as an irritant, causing reflex bronchoconstriction, and the water usually does not reach the lower airways.[6]

Although dehydration is a potential problem in children with bronchiolitis because of vomiting and lack of intake, care must be taken not to overhydrate such patients. Because edema is an important part of the pathology of bronchiolitis, excess water may contribute to airway obstruction.

Beta-adrenergic bronchodilators have been employed frequently in bronchiolitis. Slight improvements in air flow, in oxygenation, and in clinical illness scores have been reported,[66, 92, 96, 149] but these effects are not likely to be meaningful clinically; hospitalization is not prevented, and hospital stays are not shortened.[36, 45] Improvements observed after the administration of the first dose of these compounds usually are not observed after subsequent doses. In one study, oral and aerosolized beta-adrenergic agents were compared with inactive substances given by the corresponding route. The degree of improvement was the same in all four groups.[49] Combinations of salbutamol and dexamethasone also have no objective effect.[173]

In the past, epinephrine often was administered subcutaneously to older infants in an attempt to differentiate allergic disease from true bronchiolitis. This approach rarely was successful in differentiating one illness from the other or in improving the condition of the patient. However, studies have suggested that aerosolized, racemic epinephrine produced greater improvement than did the use of beta-adrenergic aerosols alone.[149] Other studies of alpha-adrenergic agents have resulted in the same conclusion. In general, the minor improvements in pulmonary function obtained using alpha-adrenergics or racemic epinephrine are not clinically meaningful; mortality is not improved, nor is the duration of stay in the intensive care unit or in the hospital reduced.

Aerosolized sympathomimetic drugs are used frequently in older children with wheezing presumed to be caused by viral infections, with somewhat better results than those in infants.[78, 96, 136, 148] Nonetheless, no evidence exists that this form of therapy reduces the need for hospitalization of these patients. Aerosols of ipratropium also have been administered in bronchiolitis without observable benefit.[154]

Possible explanations for poor responses to bronchodilators include a paucity of beta-adrenergic receptors in infancy[144]; decreased amounts of smooth muscle capable of responding to bronchodilators surrounding the terminal airways[141]; the nature of the airway obstruction itself (intense mucous plugging)[193]; and, presumably, persistence of virus in the airway, stimulating continued inflammation and/or release of bronchoconstrictive mediators.

In summary, trials of alpha- or beta-adrenergic aerosols may be attempted in all seriously ill patients,[13, 40] although persistence with either of these approaches in the absence of an initial response may prove harmful.[81, 128] A child treated for croup with multiple doses of racemic epinephrine developed ventricular tachycardia and a small myocardial infarction,[20] emphasizing the need to avoid the careless use of these compounds in viral respiratory infections.

Corticosteroids have been employed repeatedly in treating bronchiolitis. Controlled studies have failed to reveal any benefit in terms of prevention of hospitalization, reduced duration of hospitalization, reduced need for intubation, or reduced frequency of recurrent wheezing episodes after bronchiolitis.[14, 34, 35, 46, 95, 143] In the child with nonrespiratory indications for the administration of corticosteroids, these drugs need not be withheld because of fear of complications, although the duration of viral shedding may be extended in individuals treated with steroids.

Early experience with the antiviral substance ribavirin in bronchiolitis suggested that mild subjective benefits and improvement in oxygenation occurred after near-continuous aerosol administration of this compound.[63, 64, 84, 146, 171] The degree of improvement in patients treated with ribavirin was not marked. No study has demonstrated whether the administration of ribavirin could prevent deaths, avoid the need for mechanical ventilation, or shorten the duration of hospital stays. Perhaps the most convincing study suggesting a beneficial effect of ribavirin involved the use of the drug in patients already receiving mechanically assisted ventilation. In this study, recipients of ribavirin had a shorter duration of assisted ventilation, oxygen therapy, and hospitalization.[163] Controls in this study received water by aerosol, although inhalation of hypotonic solutions can provoke bronchospasm in certain individuals.[117] A study conducted subsequently in a similar patient population but using saline as a control substance found only trends in favor of ribavirin that were not statistically significant.[111]

Ribavirin is quite expensive and is difficult to use because of the need for prolonged aerosol administration. Although the drug is hygroscopic and may precipitate in ventilatory circuits of mechanical ventilators, it can be administered safely to infants on mechanically assisted ventilation if filters are used to prevent plugging of the circuits.[131] Because ribavirin is teratogenic in rodents, concern has arisen regarding the safety of health care workers exposed to aerosols of the drug.[68, 145] Ribavirin has not been detected in plasma or urine samples of health care providers caring for patients receiving ribavirin by aerosol. Although absorption probably occurs in these workers, the amount absorbed is negligible. Women who already are pregnant may be excused from caring for patients receiving ribavirin, but implementing further measures does not seem justifiable at this time.

A meta-analysis of studies using ribavirin demonstrated slight benefits in morbidity and mortality rates that were not statistically significant.[140] A beneficial effect of ribavirin in patients with life-threatening bronchiolitis cannot be excluded completely, but the drug does not appear to be of benefit from a cost-effectiveness standpoint in those with any less severe degree of illness.

Other approaches to therapy of RSV infection include the use of interferon-α,[30] vitamin A,[126] and nitric oxide.[133] The results of these studies were negative. Surfactant[87, 177] and leukotriene receptor antagonists[162] have been used in very small studies of bronchiolitis or virus-induced wheezing, with positive effects that require confirmation. Preparations containing a very high titer of neutralizing antibody against RSV have been tested in the prevention and treatment of RSV infection in high-risk populations.[60, 69, 176] The results of the prophylaxis studies were positive, as discussed later. However, a significant therapeutic effect of these compounds could not be identified after RSV infection was established.[107]

Because bronchiolitis is a viral disease, antibiotics are not useful or necessary. Unfortunately, in many instances, the radiographic picture suggests pneumonia and the blood leukocyte count is elevated; the physician, therefore, feels compelled to administer antibiotics. Most authorities do not use antibiotics in bronchiolitis or discontinue their use after RSV infection is confirmed because bacterial infection of the lung is rare in bronchiolitis even when infiltrates are identified on chest radiographs. In one large study, secondary bacterial infection occurred in no more than 7 (1.2%) of 565 children with RSV infection.[65] Institution of antibiotics should be considered during the course of therapy when a change in illness suggests the possibility of secondary bacterial infection. When antibiotic therapy is to be administered because of the possibility of pneumonia, the usual etiologic agents should be considered (*S. pneumoniae* or possibly *Staphylococcus aureus*) and ampicillin, oxacillin, or ceftriaxone may be employed. When secondary infection is a possibility, *S. aureus* and other hospital-associated organisms must be considered.

The child with bronchiolitis generally is more comfortable in the supine position with the head end of the crib slightly elevated. Infant seats are used frequently but are not optimal because the child's head tends to fall to the side or forward, which constricts the upper airway. The sitting position also causes a possibly deleterious upward pressure on the diaphragm.

If respiratory failure occurs (virtually absent inspiratory breath sounds, severe inspiratory retractions, inability to maintain an oxygen saturation of more than 90% in 40% ambient oxygen, cyanosis in 40% oxygen, decreased or absent response to painful stimuli, and a $Pa{CO_2}$ of 65 mm Hg or higher), ventilatory assistance, such as nasotracheal intubation, neuromuscular blockade, and positive-pressure ventilation,[39, 130] is indicated.

Prevention

The development of a method to prevent RSV infection remains a high priority. Initially, a formalin-inactivated RSV vaccine was prepared in a fashion similar to that of the early poliovirus vaccine. This vaccine was ineffective and even enhanced the severity of subsequent RSV-related illness in vaccinees.[88] Later, a live, temperature-sensitive vaccine was developed by adapting RSV to grow at low temperatures in cell culture. This attenuated vaccine was designed to grow at the lower temperatures of the upper respiratory tract but be inactive at the higher temperatures in the lung. In initial field trials, the vaccine strain caused febrile respiratory illnesses in seronegative vaccinees but did not replicate adequately in seropositive subjects.[28] Further trials of temperature-sensitive mutant RSV strains as vaccines currently are in progress.

Another vaccine candidate consists of a purified preparation of the RSV fusion protein, the protein responsible for fusion of the viral and host epithelial cell lipid membranes. This vaccine apparently is effective in previously infected children older than 18 months[178] but is ineffective in its current formulation in younger children. Numerous other vaccine candidates, including other protein subunits, RSV nucleic acid vaccines, bovine RSV strains, and human strains with gene deletions or given with immunologically active adjuvants, have been developed. Many of them are in early clinical trials, but development of a successful vaccine is not imminent.

In contrast to the largely negative experience with vaccine development, protection against serious illness caused by RSV infection has been achieved using a pooled preparation of human serum obtained from donors with very high titers of neutralizing antibody against RSV.[60] This compound, when administered during the RSV season on a monthly basis to infants and young children with a history of birth at less than 32 weeks' gestation or to those with bronchopulmonary dysplasia, caused a marked reduction in the severity of illness and rate of hospitalization after RSV infection. A similar benefit could not be demonstrated in patients with underlying congenital heart disease, and some potentially harmful effects were observed in infants with cyanotic heart disease.

These trials have been repeated successfully using a mouse monoclonal antibody against the RSV fusion protein.[176] The antibody is reconstructed so that it has more than 95 percent of the protein structure of a human antibody. This compound is approximately 50 percent effective in preventing RSV-related hospitalization when administered to high-risk infants, and it has received approval for use in infants born prematurely with or without lung disease of premature birth. Separate trials in infants with congenital heart disease are under way; early results suggest that the monoclonal antibody is safe and moderately effective in this population as well.

Complications and Prognosis

Virtually all cases of bronchiolitis in healthy children resolve without acute complications. Secondary bacterial infection in bronchiolitis now is an extremely uncommon occurrence. Scott and colleagues[151] identified minor electrocardiographic abnormalities in 2 percent of 188 children with bronchiolitis.

The overall mortality in bronchiolitis is determined largely by the presence of underlying illness. Henderson and Rosenzweig[70] in 1951 and Dennis and associates[36] in 1960 determined a 2 percent mortality rate during extensive studies of hospitalized cases in Detroit, Michigan, and Oakland, California. Heycock and Noble[74] found a 5.5 percent death rate during an 8-year period in which 1230 cases were reviewed. During a 5-year study period, Ackerman[1] observed no deaths in 207 cases, but two deaths occurred after the study. A multicenter study in Great Britain[31] estimated the mortality rate due to RSV infection in infancy at 0.5 percent. Deaths should occur rarely, except among infants with severe underlying cardiac or pulmonary disease; even in these cases, mortality should not exceed 3 percent of cases.[122]

The relation of bronchiolitis to the subsequent development of asthma long has been controversial. As many as 50 percent of patients with bronchiolitis have recurrent episodes of wheezing, although this figure falls to approximately 10 percent by adolescence and may not be above that of the general population by this time.[103, 166] Whether this recurrent wheezing is caused by RSV infection or, alternatively, suggests that RSV infection in early life is an indicator of a tendency toward airway obstruction is still being investigated. Recurrent wheezing after a case of bronchiolitis could be a reflection of an inherited asthmatic trait. Some studies find a strong correlation between atopic family history and recurrent wheezing,[41, 48, 147, 192, 200] whereas others, particularly those from Great Britain,[139, 159, 160] do not. Titers of total serum IgE[137] and peripheral blood eosinophil counts[200] have some predictive value for the development of recurrent wheezing after bronchiolitis. Two studies demonstrated that peripheral blood eosinophilia during viral infections, particularly RSV bronchiolitis, predicts the development of recurrent wheezing during school ages.[40, 110] Atopy appears to explain at least some of the recurrent wheezing after bronchiolitis.

RSV infection in early infancy could damage the developing airway, rendering the airway more prone to obstruction in later life. Pulmonary function tests performed in former bronchiolitis patients up to 12 years after an episode of bronchiolitis reveal an increased frequency of airway hyperreactivity in response to challenge with exercise or chemical agents, increased ratios of residual volume to total lung capacity, and reduced expiratory air flow at low lung volumes.[61, 83, 139, 159, 168, 174, 194] Although these abnormalities are observed commonly in individuals with asthma, they could not be explained in several of the previous studies simply by the presence of a personal or family history of atopy.[62, 139, 159] However, some of these retrospective studies demonstrated that a single episode of RSV bronchiolitis was not associated with long-term lung dysfunction; abnormal lung function was observed only if at least two episodes of lower respiratory illness had occurred before the age of 2 years.

Prospective studies demonstrate that recurrent wheezing through age 3 years after bronchiolitis (but not beyond) is related to abnormalities of lung function that existed before RSV infection occurred. Wheezing persisting beyond the age of 3 years was related, at least partially, to the atopic status of the host.[109] No study has demonstrated a relationship between the severity of the initial bronchiolitis episode and the degree of abnormality of long-term lung function.[61, 62, 139, 159]

In summary, some factor other than atopy may determine in part the apparent lung abnormalities seen after a case of bronchiolitis,[102, 190, 197, 198] but no direct evidence supports that this other factor is the initial episode of RSV infection itself.

RSV infection may induce persistent airway hyperreactivity. Retrospective studies have demonstrated that airway reactivity is greater in individuals 1 decade after an episode of infantile bronchiolitis than in control populations without a history of bronchiolitis.[61, 139] However, airway reactivity in all children is greater than that in adults, and it is greatest in children of atopic families and in those exposed to cigarette smoke.[199] Airway hyperreactivity after bronchiolitis is not necessarily a reflection of the RSV infection itself. One prospective study found no relationship between RSV bronchiolitis and the degree of airway reactivity at age 2 years.[3]

RSV infection possibly can promote sensitization to allergens. In animal models, critically timed RSV infection can enhance temporarily the degree of airway reactivity induced after sensitization to an allergen.[135] Whether this phenomenon occurs in humans is unknown. However, the absence of T_H2-like cytokine responses at the time of RSV bronchiolitis[53] suggests that RSV infection in infancy likely does not promote a persistent atopic state in the host.

RSV infection more likely results in the release of mediators of airway obstruction such as histamine and leukotrienes through a mechanism other than T_H2 cytokine responses. Chemokines such as MIP-1α, which cause mast cell and basophil degranulation, are possible candidates. Release of these mediators at the time of RSV infection may result in wheezing in susceptible individuals. These same individuals may again develop wheezing at the time of allergen exposure in childhood (particularly if they are atopic), but the relationship of bronchiolitis in infancy and such subsequent childhood wheezing would not be causal but rather would be based on the underlying susceptibility of the airway to obstruction.

The overall outlook for infantile bronchiolitis generally is excellent. In a follow-up study conducted at my institution,[190] severe lung disease was not observed in former bronchiolitis patients. All oxygen saturation levels were greater than 95 percent, and at least some of the air flow obstruction present at age 7 to 9 years was reversible with a single bronchodilator treatment, as was confirmed later.[166] Single episodes of infantile bronchiolitis (in the absence of passive smoke exposure and without recurrent wheezing episodes) have not been associated with abnormalities of lung function or airway hyperreactivity in later childhood.[83, 169, 183] The natural history of postbronchiolitic wheezing in childhood is for episodes of wheezing to become progressively milder,[61, 102, 139, 159] and the frequency of postbronchiolitic wheezing eventually falls to essentially the same rate as that of children who did not experience bronchiolitis in infancy.[73, 102] Nonetheless, the overall prognosis is not entirely benign, and exposure to noxious environmental elements may result in an accelerated deterioration of lung function in later life.[32, 192, 196] The combination of respiratory tract illness in early life and subsequent cigarette smoking especially may be harmful.[172] Individuals who develop bronchiolitis in infancy should avoid smoking in later life, as well as occupations that are associated with exposure to irritants in the air.

REFERENCES

1. Ackerman, B. D.: Acute bronchiolitis: A study of 207 cases. Clin. Pediatr. *1*:75–81, 1962.
2. Adams, J. M., Imagawa, D. T., and Zike, K.: Epidemic bronchiolitis and pneumonitis related to respiratory syncytial virus. JAMA. *176*:1037–1039, 1961.
3. Adler, A., Ngo, L., and Tager, I. B.: Association of tobacco smoke exposure and respiratory syncytial virus infection with airways reactivity in early childhood. Pediatr. Pulmonol. *32*:418–427, 2001.
4. Aquilina, A. T., Hall, W. J., Douglas, G., et al.: Airway reactivity in subjects with viral upper respiratory tract infections: The effects of exercise and cold air. Am. Rev. Respir. Dis. *122*:3–10, 1980.
5. Bangham, R. M., Cannon, M. J., Karzon, D. T., et al.: Cytotoxic T-cell response to respiratory syncytial virus in mice. J. Virol. *56*:55–59, 1985.
6. Bau, S. K., Aspin, N., Wood, D. E., et al.: The measurement of fluid deposition in humans following mist tent therapy. Pediatrics. *48*:605–612, 1971.
7. Beem, M., Wright, F. H., Fasan, D. M., et al.: Observations on the etiology of acute bronchiolitis in infants. J. Pediatr. *61*:864–869, 1962.
8. Beem, M., Wright, F. H., Hamre, D., et al.: Association of the chimpanzee coryza agent with acute respiratory disease in children. N. Engl. J. Med. *263*:523–530, 1960.
9. Berger, I., Argaman, Z., Schwartz, S. B., et al.: Efficacy of corticosteroids in acute bronchiolitis: Short-term and long-term follow-up. Pediatr. Pulmonol. *26*:162–166,1998.
10. Boushey, H. A., Holtzman, M. J., Sheller, J. R., et al.: Bronchial hyperreactivity. Am. Rev. Respir. Dis. *121*:389–413, 1980.
11. Brandt, C. D., Kim, H. W., Arrobio, J. O., et al.: Epidemiology of respiratory syncytial virus infection in Washington, D.C. III. Composite analysis of eleven consecutive yearly epidemics. Am. J. Epidemiol. *98*:355–364, 1973.
12. Bruhn, F. W., Mokrohisky, S. T., and McIntosh, K.: Apnea associated with respiratory syncytial virus infection in young infants. J. Pediatr. *90*:382–386, 1977.
13. Brooks, L. J., and Cropp, G. J. A.: Theophylline therapy in bronchiolitis: A retrospective study. Am. J. Dis. Child. *135*:934–936, 1981.
14. Brunette, M. G., Lands, L., and Thibodeau, L. P.: Childhood asthma: Prevention of attacks with short-term corticosteroid treatment of upper respiratory tract infection. Pediatrics. *81*:624–629, 1988.
15. Buckingham, S. C., Bush, A. J., and Devincenzo, J. P.: Nasal quantity of respiratory syncytial virus correlates with disease severity in hospitalized infants. Pediatr. Infect. Dis. J. *19*:113–117, 2000.
16. Bui, R. H. D., Molinaro, G. A., Kettering, J. D., et al.: Virus-specific IgE and IgG4 antibodies in serum of children infected with respiratory syncytial virus. J. Pediatr. *110*:87–90, 1987.
17. Burrows, B., Knudson, R. J., and Lebowitz, M. D.: The relationship of childhood respiratory illness to adult obstructive airway disease. Am. Rev. Respir. Dis. *115*:751–760, 1977.
18. Busse, W. W.: Decreased granulocyte response to isoproterenol in asthma during upper respiratory infections. Am. Rev. Respir. Dis. *115*:783–791, 1977.
19. Busse, W. W., Swenson, C. A., Borden, E. C., et al.: Effect of influenza A virus on leukocyte histamine release. J. Allergy Clin. Immunol. *71*: 382–388, 1983.
20. Butte, M. J., Nguyen, B. X., Hutchison, T. J., et al.: Pediatric myocardial infarction after racemic epinephrine administration. Pediatrics. *104*: 103–104, 1999.
21. Carmalt-Jones, D. W.: The treatment of bronchial asthma by a vaccine. Br. Med. J. *2*:1049–1050, 1909.
22. Chandwani, S., Borkowsky, W., Krasinski, K., et al.: Respiratory syncytial virus infection in human immunodeficiency virus-infected children. J. Pediatr. *117*:251–254, 1990.
23. Chanock, R., Chambon, L., Chang, W., et al.: WHO Respiratory Disease Survey in Children: A serologic study. Bull. World health Organ. *37*: 363–369, 1967.
24. Chanock, R. M., Parrott, R. H., Vargosko, A. J., et al.: IV. Respiratory syncytial virus. Am. J. Public Health. *52*:918–925, 1962.
25. Chanock, R. M., Mufson, M. A., and Johnson, K. M.: Comparative biology and ecology of human virus and mycoplasma respiratory pathogens. Prog. Med. Virol. *7*:208–252, 1965.
26. Chanock, R. M., and Parrott, R. H.: Acute respiratory disease in infancy and childhood: Present understanding and prospects for prevention. Pediatrics. *36*:21–39, 1965.
27. Chanock, R. M., Kim, H. W., Vargosko, A. J., et al.: Respiratory syncytial virus. I. Virus recovery and other observations during a 1960 outbreak of bronchiolitis, pneumonia, and minor respiratory diseases in children. JAMA. *176*:647–653, 1961.
28. Chanock, R. M., and Murphy, B. R.: Use of temperature-sensitive and cold-adapted mutant viruses in immunoprophylaxis of acute respiratory tract disease. Rev. Infect. Dis. *2*:421–431, 1980.
29. Cherry, J. D.: Newer respiratory viruses: Their role in respiratory illness of children. Adv. Pediatr. *20*:225–290, 1973.
30. Chipps, B. E., Sullivan, W. F., and Portnoy, J. M.: Alpha-2a-interferon for treatment of bronchiolitis caused by respiratory syncytial virus. Pediatr. Infect. Dis. J. *12*:653–658, 1993.
31. Clarke, S. K. R., Gardner, P. S., Poole, P. M., et al.: Respiratory syncytial virus infection: Admissions to hospital in industrial, urban, and rural areas. Br. Med. J. *2*:796–798, 1978.
32. Colley, J. R. T., Douglas, J. W. B., and Reid, D. D.: Respiratory disease in young adults: Influence of early childhood lower respiratory tract illness, social class, air pollution, and smoking. Br. Med. J. *3*:195–198, 1973.

33. Collier, A. M., Pimmel, R. L., Hasselblad, V., et al.: Spirometric changes in normal children with upper respiratory infections. Am. Rev. Respir. Dis. *117*:47–53, 1978.
34. Connolly, J. H., Field, C. M. B., Glasgow, J. F. T., et al.: A double blind trial of prednisolone in epidemic bronchiolitis due to respiratory syncytial virus. Acta Paediatr. Scand. *58*:116–120, 1969.
35. Dabbous, I. A., Tkachyk, J. S., and Stamm, S. J.: A double blind study on the effects of corticosteroids in the treatment of bronchiolitis. Pediatrics. *37*:477–484, 1966.
36. Dobson, J. V., Stephens-Grof, S. M., McMahon, S. R., et al. The use of albuterol in hospitalized infants with bronchiolitis. Pediatrics. *101*:361–368, 1998.
37. Domachowske, J. B., Dyer, K. D., Bonville, C. A., and Rosenberg, H. F.: Recombinant human eosinophil-derived neurotoxin/RNase 2 functions as an effective antiviral agent against respiratory syncytial virus. J. Infect. Dis. *177*:1458–1464, 1998.
38. Domachowske, J. B., Bonville, C. A., Dyer, K. D., and Rosenberg, H. F.: Evolution of antiviral activity in the ribonuclease A gene superfamily: Evidence for a specific interaction between eosinophil-derived neurotoxin (EDN/RNase 2) and respiratory syncytial virus. Nucleic Acids Res. *26*:5327–5332, 1998.
39. Downes, J. J., Wood, D. W., Striker, T. W., et al.: Acute respiratory failure in infants with bronchiolitis. Anesthesiology. *29*:426–434, 1968.
40. Ehlenfield, D. R., Cameron, K., and Welliver, R. C.: Eosinophilia at the time of bronchiolitis predicts childhood reactive airway disease. Pediatrics. *105*:79–83, 2000.
41. Eisen, A. H., and Bacal, H. L.: The relationship of acute bronchiolitis to bronchial asthma: A 4 to 14 year follow-up. Pediatrics *31*:859–861, 1963.
42. Empey, D. W., Laitinen, L. A., Jacobs, L., et al.: Mechanisms of bronchial hyperreactivity in normal subjects after upper respiratory tract infection. Am. Rev. Respir. Dis. *113*:131–139, 1976.
43. Fabian, I., Kletter, Y., Mor, S., et al.: Activation of human eosinophil and neutrophil functions by haematopoietic growth factors: Comparisons of IL-1, IL-3, IL-5 and GM-CSF. Br. J. Haematol. *80*:137–143, 1992.
44. Faden, H., Kaul, T. N., and Ogra, P. L.: Activation of oxidative and arachidonic acid metabolism in neutrophils by respiratory syncytial virus antibody complexes: Possible role in disease. J. Infect. Dis. *148*:110–116, 1983.
45. Flores, G., and Horwitz, R.: Efficacy of β_2-agonists in bronchiolitis: A reappraisal and meta-analysis. Pediatrics. *100*:233–239, 1997.
46. Fox, G. F., Everard, M. E., Marsh, M. J., and Milner, A. D.: Randomized controlled trial of budesonide for the prevention of post-bronchiolitis wheezing. Arch. Dis. Child. *80*:343–347, 1999.
47. Foy, H. M., Cooney, M. K., Maletzky, A. J., et al.: Incidence and etiology of pneumonia, croup and bronchiolitis in preschool children belonging to a prepaid medical care group over a four-year period. Am. J. Epidemiol. *97*:80–92, 1973.
48. Freeman, G. L., and Todd, R. H.: The role of allergy in viral respiratory tract infections. Am. J. Dis. Child. *104*:330–334, 1962.
49. Gadomski, A. M., Aref, G. H., Badr El Din, O., et al.: Oral versus nebulized albuterol in the management of bronchiolitis in Egypt. J. Pediatr. *124*:131–138, 1994.
50. Gardner, P. S., McQuillin, J., and Court, S. D. M.: Speculation on pathogenesis in death from respiratory syncytial virus infection. Br. Med. J. *1*:327–332, 1970.
51. Garofalo, R., Kimpen, J. L. L., Welliver, R. C., et al.: Eosinophil degranulation in naturally acquired respiratory syncytial virus infection. J. Pediatr. *120*:28–32, 1992.
52. Garofalo, R., Dorris, A., Ahlstedt, S., et al.: Peripheral blood eosinophil counts and eosinophil cationic protein content of respiratory secretions in bronchiolitis: Relationship to severity of disease. Pediatr. Allergy Immunol. *5*:111–117, 1994.
53. Garofalo, R. P., Patti, J., Hintz, K. E., et al.: Macrophage inflammatory protein-1_α (not T-helper type 2 cytokines) is associated with severe forms of respiratory syncytial virus bronchiolitis. J. Infect. Dis. *184*:383–389, 2001.
54. Glezen, W. P., Loda, F. A., Clyde, W. A., Jr., et al.: Epidemiologic patterns of acute lower respiratory disease of children in a pediatric group practice. J. Pediatr. *78*:397–406, 1971.
55. Glezen, W. P., Paredes, A., Allison, J. E., et al.: Risk of respiratory syncytial virus infection for infants from low-income families in relationship to age, sex, ethnic group, and maternal antibody level. J. Pediatr. *98*:708–715, 1981.
56. Glezen, W. P., Taber, L. H., Frank, A. L., et al.: Risk of primary infection and reinfection with respiratory syncytial virus. Am. J. Dis. Child. *140*: 543–546, 1986.
57. Green, M., Brayer, A. F., Schenkman, K. A., et al.: Duration of hospitalization in previously well infants with respiratory syncytial virus infection. Pediatr. Inf. Dis. J. *8*:601–605, 1989.
58. Gregg, I.: The role of viral infection in asthma and bronchitis. *In* Proudfoot, A. T. (ed.): Symposium on Viral Diseases. Edinburgh, T. A. Constable, 1975, pp. 82–98.
59. Griffith, J. P. C., and Mitchell, A. G.: The Diseases of Infants and Children. Vol. II. Philadelphia, W. B. Saunders, 1927, pp. 274–355.
60. Groothuis, J. R., Simoes, E. A. F., Levin, M. J., et al.: Prophylactic administration of a respiratory syncytial virus immune globulin to high-risk infants and young children. N. Engl. J. Med. *329*:1524–1530, 1993.
61. Gurwitz, D., Mindorff, C., and Levison, H.: Increased incidence of bronchial reactivity in children with a history of bronchiolitis. J. Pediatr. *98*:551–555, 1981.
62. Hall, C. B., Hall, W. J., Gala, C. L., et al.: Long-term prospective study in children after respiratory syncytial virus infection. J. Pediatr. *105*: 358–364, 1984.
63. Hall, C. B., McBride, J. T., Walsh, E. E., et al.: Aerosolized ribavirin treatment of infants with respiratory syncytial viral infection. N. Engl. J. Med. *308*:1443–1447, 1983.
64. Hall, C. B., McBride, J. T., Gala, C. L., et al.: Ribavirin treatment of respiratory syncytial virus infection in infants with underlying cardiopulmonary disease. JAMA. *254*:3047–3051, 1985.
65. Hall, C. B., Powell, K. R., Schnabel, K. C., et al.: Risk of secondary bacterial infection in infants hospitalized with respiratory syncytial viral infection. J. Pediatr. *113*:266–271, 1988.
66. Hammer, J., Numa, A., and Newth, C. J. L.: Albuterol responsiveness in infants with respiratory failure caused by respiratory syncytial virus infection. J. Pediatr. *127*:485–490, 1995.
67. Hampton, S. F., Johnson, M. C., and Galakatos, E.: Studies of bacterial hypersensitivity in asthma. I. The preparation of antigen of *Neisseria catarrhalis*, the induction of asthma by aerosols, the performance of skin and passive transfer tests. J. Allergy. *34*:63–95, 1963.
68. Harrison, R., Bellows, J., Rempel, D., et al.: Assessing exposures of health-care personnel to aerosols of ribavirin: California. MMWR. Morb. Mortal. Wkly. Rep. *37*:560–563, 1988.
69. Hemming, V. G., and Prince, G. A.: Immunoprophylaxis of infections with respiratory syncytial virus: Observations and hypothesis. Rev. Infect. Dis. *12*:S470–S475, 1990.
70. Henderson, A. T., and Rosenzweig, S.: Bronchiolitis in infancy: Clinical study with special emphasis on the cardiac complications. U. S. Armed Forces Med. J. *2*:943–952, 1951.
71. Henderson, F. W., Clyde, W. A., Jr., Collier, A. M., et al.: The etiologic and epidemiological spectrum of bronchiolitis in pediatric practice. J. Pediatr. *95*:183–190, 1979.
72. Henderson, F. W., Hu, S. C., and Collier, A. M.: Pathogenesis of respiratory syncytial virus infection in ferret and fetal human tracheas in organ culture. Am. Rev. Respir. Dis. *118*:29–37, 1978.
73. Henderson, F. W., Stewart, P. W., Burchinal, M. R., et al.: Respiratory allergy and the relationship between early childhood lower respiratory illness and subsequent lung function. Am. Rev. Respir. Dis. *145*:283–290, 1992.
74. Heycock, J. B., and Noble, T. C.: 1,230 Cases of acute bronchiolitis in infancy. Br. Med. J. *5309*:879–881, 1962.
75. Hogg, J. C., Williams, J., Richardson, J. B., et al.: Age as a factor in the distribution of lower-airway conductance and in the pathologic anatomy of obstructive lung disease. N. Engl. J. Med. *282*:1283–1287, 1970.
76. Holt, L. E., and Howland, J.: Diseases of the lungs: Peculiarities of the thorax in children. *In* Holt, L. E., and McIntosh, R. (eds.): Holt's Diseases of Infancy and Childhood. 11th ed. New York, D. Appleton-Century, 1940, pp. 498, 513.
77. Horn, M. E. C., Brain, E., Gregg, I., et al.: Respiratory viral infection in childhood: A survey in general practice, Roehampton 1967–1972. J. Hyg. (Camb.) *74*:157–168, 1975.
78. Horn, M. E. C., Brain, E. A., Gregg, I., et al.: Respiratory viral infection and wheezy bronchitis in childhood. Thorax. *34*:23–28, 1979.
79. Horn, M. E. C., Reed, S. E., and Taylor, P.: Role of viruses and bacteria in acute wheezy bronchitis in childhood: A study of sputum. Arch. Dis. Child. *54*:587–592, 1979.
80. Hubble, D., and Osborn, G. R.: Acute bronchiolitis in children. Br. Med. J. *1*:107–110, 1941.
81. Hughes, D. M., Lesouef, P. N., and Landau, L. I.: Effect of salbutamol on respiratory mechanics in bronchiolitis. Pediatr. Res. *22*:83–86, 1987.
82. Ida, S., Hooks, J. J., Siraganian, R. P., et al.: Enhancement of IgE-mediated histamine release from human basophils by viruses: Role of interferon. J. Exp. Med. *145*:892–906, 1977.
83. Kattan, M., Keens, T. G., Lapierre, J. G., et al.: Pulmonary function abnormalities in symptom-free children after bronchiolitis. Pediatrics. *59*:683–688, 1977.
84. Kaul, T. N., Welliver, R. C., and Ogra, P. L.: Development of antibody dependent cell-mediated cytotoxicity in the respiratory tract after natural infection with respiratory syncytial virus. Infect. Immun. *37*:492–498, 1982.
85. Kaul, T. N., Welliver, R. C., and Ogra, P. L.: Appearance of complement components and immunoglobulins on nasopharyngeal epithelial cells following naturally acquired infection with respiratory syncytial virus. J. Med. Virol. *9*:149–158, 1982.
86. Kaul, T. N., Welliver, R. C., Wong, D. T., et al.: Secretory antibody response to respiratory syncytial virus infection. Am. J. Dis. Child. *135*:1013–1016, 1981.
87. Kerr, M. H., and Paton, J. Y.: Surfactant protein levels in severe respiratory syncytial virus infection. Am. J. Resp. Crit. Care Med. *159*:1115–1118, 1999.

88. Kim, H. W., Canchola, J. G., Brandt, C. D., et al.: Respiratory syncytial virus disease in infants despite prior administration of antigenic inactivated vaccine. Am. J. Epidemiol. *89*:422–434, 1969.
89. Kim, H. W., Arrobio, J. O., Brandt, C. D., et al.: Epidemiology of respiratory syncytial virus infection in Washington, D.C. I. Importance of the virus in different respiratory tract disease syndromes and temporal distribution of infection. Am. J. Epidemiol. *98*:216–225, 1973.
90. Kim, H. W., Leikin, S. L., Arrobio, J., et al.: Cell-mediated immunity to respiratory syncytial virus induced by inactivated vaccine or by infection. Pediatr. Res. *10*:75–78, 1976.
91. King, J. C., Jr., Burke, A. R., Clemens, J. D., et al.: Respiratory syncytial virus illnesses in human immunodeficiency virus and noninfected children. Pediatr. Infect. Dis. J. *12*:733–739, 1993.
92. Klassen, T. P., Rowe, P. C., Sutcliffe, T., et al.: Randomized trial of salbutamol in acute bronchiolitis. J. Pediatr. *118*:807–811, 1991.
93. Koch, D. A.: Roentgenologic considerations of capillary bronchiolitis. Am. J. Roentgenol. Radiat. Ther. Nucl. Med. *82*:433–436, 1959.
94. Laing, I., Riedel, F., Yap, P. L., et al.: Atopy predisposing to acute bronchiolitis during an epidemic of respiratory syncytial virus. BMJ *284*:1070–1072, 1982.
95. Leer, J. A., Jr., Green, J. L., Heimlich, E. M., et al.: Corticosteroid treatment in bronchiolitis: A controlled, collaborative study in 297 infants and children. Am. J. Dis. Child. *117*:495–502, 1969.
96. Lenney, W., and Milner, A. D.: Alpha and beta adrenergic stimulants in bronchiolitis and wheezy bronchitis in children under 18 months of age. Arch. Dis. Child. *53*:707–709, 1978.
97. Lesouef, P. N., Geelhoed, G. C., Turner, D. J., et al.: Response of normal infants to inhaled histamine. Am. Rev. Respir. Dis. *139*:62–66, 1989.
98. Liew, F. Y., and Russell, S. M.: Inhibition of pathogenic effect of effector T cells by specific suppressor T cells during influenza virus infection in mice. Nature. *304*:541–543, 1983.
99. Little, J. W., Hall, W. J., Douglas, R. G., et al.: Airway hyperreactivity and peripheral airway dysfunction in influenza A infection. Am. Rev. Respir. Dis. *118*:295–303, 1978.
100. Loda, F. A., Clyde, W. A., Jr., Glezen, W. P., et al.: Studies on the role of viruses, bacteria, and *M. pneumoniae* as causes of lower respiratory tract infections in children. J. Pediatr. *72*:161–176, 1968.
101. Loda, F. A., Glezen, W. P., and Clyde, W. A., Jr.: Respiratory disease in group day care. Pediatrics. *49*:428–437, 1972.
102. McConnochie, K. M., and Roghmann, K. J.: Bronchiolitis as a possible cause of wheezing in childhood: New evidence. Pediatrics. *74*:1–10, 1984.
103. McConnochie, K. M., and Roghmann, K. J.: Wheezing at age 8 and 13 years: Changing importance of bronchiolitis and passive smoking. Pediatr. Pulmonol. *6*:138–146, 1989.
104. McGeorge, M.: Severe obstructive bronchiolitis in infancy: Treatment with hydrocortisone. Clin. Pediatr. *3*:11–18, 1964.
105. Macasaet, F. F., Kidd, P. A., Bolano, C. R., et al.: The etiology of acute respiratory infections. III. The role of viruses and bacteria. J. Pediatr. *72*:829–839, 1968.
106. Macklin, C. C.: Alveolar pores and their significance in the human lung. Arch. Pathol. *21*:202, 1936.
107. Malley, R., DeVincenzo, J., Ramilo, O., et al.: Reduction of respiratory syncytial virus in tracheal aspirates in intubated infants by use of humanized monoclonal antibody to RSV F protein. J. Infect. Dis. *178*:1555–1561, 1998.
108. Martinez, F. D., Morgan, W. J., Wright, A. L., et al.: Diminished lung function as a predisposing factor for wheezing respiratory illness in infants. N. Engl. J. Med. *319*:1112–1117, 1988.
109. Martinez, F. D., Wright, A. L., Taussig, L. M., et al.: Asthma and wheezing in the first six years of life. N. Engl. J. Med. *332*:133–138, 1995.
110. Martinez, F. D., Stern, D. A., Wright, A. L., and Taussig, L. M.: Differential immune responses to acute lower respiratory illnesses in early life and subsequent development of persistent wheezing and asthma. J Allergy Clin. Immunol. *102*:915–920, 1998.
111. Meert, K. L., Sarnaik, A. P., Gelmini, M. J., et al.: Aerosolized ribavirin in mechanically ventilated children with respiratory syncytial virus lower respiratory tract disease: A prospective, double-blind, randomized trial. Crit. Care Med. *22*:566–572, 1994.
112. Miller, D. G., Gabrielson, M. O., and Horstmann, D. M.: Clinical virology and viral surveillance in a pediatric group practice: The use of double-seeded tissue culture tubes for primary virus isolation. Am. J. Epidemiol. *88*:245–256, 1968.
113. Minor, T. E., Baker, J. W., Dick, E. C., et al.: Greater frequency of viral respiratory infections in asthmatic children as compared with their nonasthmatic siblings. J. Pediatr. *85*:472–477, 1974.
114. Minor, T. E., Dick, E. C., De Meo, A. N., et al.: Viruses as precipitants of asthmatic attacks in children. JAMA. *227*:292–298, 1974.
115. Minor, T. E., Dick, E. C., Baker, J. W., et al.: Rhinovirus and influenza type A infections as precipitants of asthma. Am. Rev. Respir. Dis. *113*: 149–153, 1976.
116. Mitchell, I., Inglis, J. M., and Simpson, H.: Viral infection as a precipitant of wheeze in children: Combined home and hospital study. Arch. Dis. Child. *53*:106–111, 1978.
117. Moler, F. W., Bandy, K. P., and Custer, J. R.: Ribavirin therapy for acute bronchiolitis: Need for appropriate controls. J. Pediatr. *119*:509, 1991.
118. Mueller, H. L.: The dual role of infection in asthma of childhood. Postgrad. Med. *50*:225–229, 1971.
119. Mueller, H. L., and Lanz, M.: Hyposensitization with bacterial vaccine in infectious asthma: A double-blind study and a longitudinal study. JAMA. *208*:1379–1383, 1969.
120. Mufson, M. A., Krause, H. E., Mocega, H. E., et al.: Viruses, *Mycoplasma pneumoniae* and bacteria associated with lower respiratory tract disease among infants. J. Epidemiol. *91*:192–202, 1970.
121. Mulholland, E. K., Olinsky, A., and Shann, F.: Clinical findings and severity of acute bronchiolitis. Lancet. *335*:1259–1261, 1990.
122. Navas, L., Wang, E., de Carvalho, V., et al.: Improved outcome of respiratory syncytial virus infection in a high-risk hospitalized population of Canadian children. J. Pediatr. *121*:348–354, 1992.
123. Neilson, K. A., and Yunis, E. J.: Demonstration of respiratory syncytial virus in an autopsy series. Pediatr. Pathol. *10*:491–502, 1990.
124. Nelson, W. E.: Viral or probable viral infections. *In* Nelson, W. E. (ed.): Pediatrics. 6th ed. Philadelphia, W. B. Saunders, 1954, pp. 823–828, 1438–1446.
125. Nelson, W. E., and Smith, L. W.: Generalized obstructive emphysema in infants. J. Pediatr. *26*:36–55, 1945.
126. Neuzil, K. M., Gruber, W. C., Chytil, F., et al.: Safety and pharmacokinetics of vitamin A therapy for infants with respiratory syncytial virus infections. Antimicrob. Agents Chemother. *39*:1191–1193, 1995.
127. Nichol, K. P., and Cherry, J. D.: Bacterial-viral interrelations in respiratory infections of children. N. Engl. J. Med. *277*:667–672, 1967.
128. O'Callaghan, C., Milner, A. D., and Swarbrick, A.: Paradoxical deterioration in lung function after nebulised salbutamol in wheezy infants. Lancet. *2*:1424–1425, 1986.
129. Ogilvie, M. M., Vathenen, S., Radford, M., et al.: Maternal antibody and respiratory syncytial virus infection in infancy. J. Med. Virol. *7*:263–271, 1981.
130. Outwater, K. M., and Crone, R. K.: Management of respiratory failure in infants with acute viral bronchiolitis. Am. J. Dis. Child. *138*:1071–1075, 1984.
131. Outwater, K. M., Meissner, C., and Peterson, M. B.: Ribavirin administration to infants receiving mechanical ventilation. Am. J. Dis. Child. *142*:512–515, 1988.
132. Parrott, R. H., Kim, H. W., Arrobio, J. O., et al.: Epidemiology of respiratory syncytial virus infection in Washington, D.C. II. Infection and disease with respect to age, immunologic status, race and sex. Am. J. Epidemiol. *98*:289–300, 1973.
133. Patel, N. R., Hammer, J., Nichani, S., et al.: Effect of nitric oxide on respiratory mechanics in ventilated infants with RSV bronchiolitis. Intensive Care Med. *25*:81–87, 1999.
134. Paton, A. W., Paton, J. C., Lawrence, A. J., et al.: Rapid detection of respiratory syncytial virus in nasopharyngeal aspirates by reverse transcription and polymerase chain reaction amplification. J. Clin. Microbiol. *30*:901–904, 1992.
135. Peebles, R. S., Sheller, J. R., Johnson, J. E., et al. Respiratory syncytial virus infection prolongs methacholine-induced airway hyperresponsiveness in ovalbumin-sensitized mice. J. Med. Virol. *57*:186–192, 1999.
136. Phelan, P. D., and Williams, H. E.: Sympathomimetic drugs in acute viral bronchiolitis: Their effect on pulmonary resistance. Pediatrics. *44*:493–497, 1969.
137. Polmar, S. H., Robinson, L. D., Jr., and Minnefor, A. B.: Immunoglobulin E in bronchiolitis. Pediatrics. *50*:279–284, 1972.
138. Pratt, E. L.: Acute bronchiolitis in infants. Med. Clin. North Am. *28*:1098–1107, 1944.
139. Pullan, C. R., and Hey, E. N.: Wheezing, asthma, and pulmonary dysfunction 10 years after infection with respiratory syncytial virus in infancy. Br. Med. J. *284*:1665–1669, 1982.
140. Randolph, A. G., and Wang, E. E. L.: Ribavirin for respiratory syncytial virus infection: A systematic overview. Arch. Pediatr. Adolesc. Med. *150*:942–947, 1996.
141. Reid, L.: Influence of the pattern of structural growth of lung on susceptibility to specific infectious diseases in infants and children. Pediatr. Res. *11*:210–215, 1977.
142. Reilly, C. M., Stokes, J., Jr., McClelland, L., et al.: Studies of acute respiratory illnesses caused by respiratory syncytial virus. 3. Clinical and laboratory findings. N. Engl. J. Med. *264*:1176–1182, 1961.
143. Richter, H., and Seddon, P.: Early nebulized budesonide in the treatment of bronchiolitis and the prevention of postbronchiolitis wheezing. J. Pediatr. *132*:849–853, 1998.
144. Roan, Y., and Galant, S. P.: Decreased neutrophil beta adrenergic receptors in the neonate. Pediatr. Res. *16*:591–593, 1982.
145. Rodriguez, W. J., Bui, R. H. D., Connor, J. D., et al.: Environmental exposure of primary care personnel to ribavirin aerosol when supervising treatment of infants with respiratory syncytial virus infections. Antimicrob. Agents Chemother. *31*:1143–1146, 1987.
146. Rodriguez, W. J., Kim, H. W., Brandt, C. D., et al.: Aerosolized ribavirin in the treatment of patients with respiratory syncytial virus disease. Pediatr. Infect. Dis. J. *6*:159–163, 1987.

147. Rooney, J. C., and Williams, H. E.: The relationship between proved viral bronchiolitis and subsequent wheezing. J. Pediatr. *79*:744–747, 1971.
148. Rutter, N., Milner, A. D., and Hiller, E. J.: Effect of bronchodilators on respiratory resistance in infants and young children with bronchiolitis and wheezy bronchitis. Arch. Dis. Child. *50*:719–722, 1975.
149. Sanchez, I., De Koster, J., Powell, R., et al.: Effect of racemic epinephrine and salbutamol on clinical score and pulmonary mechanics in infants with bronchiolitis. J. Pediatr. *122*:145–151, 1993.
150. Sandiford, B. R., and Spencer, B.: Respiratory syncytial virus in epidemic bronchiolitis of infants. Br. Med. J. *5309*:881–882, 1962.
151. Scott, L. P., III, Gutelius, M. F., and Parrott, R. H.: Children with acute respiratory tract infections: An electrocardiographic survey. Am. J. Dis. Child. *119*:111–113, 1970.
152. Scott, R., DeLandazuri, M. O., Gardner, P. S., et al.: Human antibody-dependent cell-mediated cytotoxicity against target cells infected with respiratory syncytial virus. Clin. Exp. Immunol. *28*:19–26, 1977.
153. Scott, R., Kaul, A., Scott, M., Chiba, Y., et al.: Development of in vitro correlates of cell-mediated immunity to respiratory syncytial virus infection in humans. J. Infect. Dis. *137*:810–817, 1978.
154. Seidenberg, J., Masters, I. B., Hudson, I., et al.: Effect of ipratropium bromide on respiratory mechanics in infants with acute bronchiolitis. Aust. Paediatr. J. *23*:169–172, 1987.
155. Sell, S. H. W.: Some observations on acute bronchiolitis in infants. Am. J. Dis. Child. *100*:31–39, 1960.
156. Shay, D. K., Holman, R. C., Roosevelt, G. E., et al.: Bronchiolitis-associated mortality and estimates of respiratory syncytial virus-associated deaths among US children, 1979–1997. J. Infect. Dis. *183*:16–22, 2001.
157. Shay, D. K., Holman, R. C., Newman, R. D., et al.: Bronchiolitis-associated hospitalizations among US children, 1980–1996. JAMA. *282*:1440–1446, 2001.
158. Simpson, H., Matthew, D. J., Inglis, J. M., et al.: Virological findings and blood gas tensions in acute lower respiratory tract infections in children. Br. Med. J. *2*:629–632, 1974.
159. Sims, D. G., Downham, M. A. P. S., Gardner, P. S., et al.: Study of 8-year-old children with a history of respiratory syncytial virus bronchiolitis in infancy. Br. Med. J. *1*:11–14, 1978.
160. Sims, D. G., Gardner, P. S., Weightman, D., et al.: Atopy does not predispose to RSV bronchiolitis or postbronchiolitic wheezing. Br. Med. J. *282*:2086–2088, 1981.
161. Skoner, D. P., Fireman, P., Caligiuri, L., et al.: Plasma elevations of histamine and a prostaglandin metabolite in acute bronchiolitis. Am. Rev. Respir. Dis. *142*:359–364, 1990.
162. Skoner, D.: Montelukast in 2- to 5-year-old children with asthma. Pediatr. Pulmonol. *21*:46–48, 2001.
163. Smith, D. W., Frankel, L. R., Mathers, L. H., et al.: A controlled trial of aerosolized ribavirin in infants receiving mechanical ventilation for severe respiratory syncytial virus infection. N. Engl. J. Med. *325*:24–29, 1991.
164. Smith, M. C., Creutz, C., and Huang, Y. T.: Detection of respiratory syncytial virus in nasopharyngeal secretions by shell vial technique. J. Clin. Microbiol. *29*:463–465, 1991.
165. Smith, T. F., McIntosh, K., Fishaut, M., et al.: Activation of complement by cells infected with respiratory syncytial virus. Infect. Immun. *33*: 43–48, 1981.
166. Stein, R. T., Sherrill, D., Morgan, W. J., et al.: Respiratory syncytial virus in early life and risk of wheeze and allergy by age 13 years. Lancet. *354*:541–545, 1999.
167. Stempel, D. A., Clyde, W. A., Jr., Henderson, F. W., et al.: Serum IgE levels and the clinical expression of respiratory illnesses. J. Pediatr. *97*:185–190, 1980.
168. Stokes, G. M., Milner, A. D., Hodges, I. G. C., et al.: Lung function abnormalities after acute bronchiolitis. J. Pediatr. *98*:871–874, 1981.
169. Strope, G. L., Stewart, P. W., Henderson, F. W., et al.: Lung function in school-age children who had mild lower respiratory illnesses in early childhood. Am. Rev. Respir. Dis. *144*:655–662, 1991.
170. Sturdy, P. M., McQuillin, J., and Gardner, P. S.: A comparative study of methods for the diagnosis of respiratory virus infections in childhood. J. Hyg. (Camb.) *67*:659–670, 1969.
171. Taber, L. H., Knight, V., Gilbert, B. E., et al.: Ribavirin aerosol treatment of bronchiolitis associated with respiratory syncytial virus infection in infants. Pediatrics. *72*:613–618, 1983.
172. Tager, I. B., Weiss, S. T., Munoz, A., et al.: Longitudinal study of the effects of maternal smoking on pulmonary function in children. N. Engl. J. Med. *309*:699–703, 1983.
173. Tal, A., Bavilski, C., Yohai, D., et al.: Dexamethasone and salbutamol in the treatment of acute wheezing in infants. Pediatrics. *71*:13–18, 1983.
174. Taussig, L. M.: Clinical and physiologic evidence of the persistence of pulmonary abnormalities after respiratory illnesses in infancy and childhood. Pediatr. Res. *11*:216–218, 1977.
175. Tepper, R. S., Rosenberg, D., and Eigen, H.: Airway responsiveness in infants following bronchiolitis. Pediatr. Pulmonol. *13*:6–10, 1992.
176. The Impact RSV study group: Palivizumab, a humanized respiratory syncytial virus monoclonal antibody, reduces hospitalization from respiratory syncytial virus infection in high-risk infants. Pediatrics. *102*:531–537, 1998.
177. Tibby, S. M., Hatherill, M., Wright, S., et al.: Exogenous surfactant supplementation in infants with respiratory syncytial virus bronchiolitis. Am. J. Resp. Crit. Care Med. *162*:1251–1256, 2000.
178. Tristram, D. A., Welliver, R. C., Mohar, C. K., et al.: Immunogenicity and safety of respiratory syncytial virus subunit vaccine in seropositive children 18–36 months old. J. Infect. Dis. *167*:191–195, 1993.
179. Twarog, F. J., and Colten, H. R.: Rational management of allergic disease: The role of immunotherapy. Pediatrics. *60*:320–323, 1977.
180. van Schaik, S. M., Tristram, D. A., Nagpal, I. S., et al.: Increased production of interferon-γ and cysteinyl leukotrienes in virus-induced wheezing. J. Allergy Clin. Immunol. *103*:630–636, 1999.
181. Vikerfors, T., Grandien, M., and Olcen, P.: Respiratory syncytial virus infections in adults. Am. Rev. Respir. Dis. *136*:561–564, 1987.
182. Volovitz, B., Welliver, R. C., DeCastro, G., et al.: The release of leukotrienes in the respiratory tract during infection with respiratory syncytial virus: Role in obstructive airway disease. Pediatr. Res. *24*:504–507, 1988.
183. Voter, K. Z., Henry, M. M., Stewart, P. W., et al.: Lower respiratory illness in early childhood and lung function and bronchial reactivity in adolescent males. Am. Rev. Respir. Dis. *137*:302–307, 1988.
184. Wang, E. E. L., Milner, R. A., Navas, L., et al.: Observer agreement for respiratory signs and oximetry in infants hospitalized with lower respiratory infections. Am. Rev. Respir. Dis. *145*:106–109, 1992.
185. Welliver, R. C., Kaul, A., and Ogra, P. L.: Cell-mediated immune response to respiratory syncytial virus infection: Relationship to the development of reactive airway disease. J. Pediatr. *94*:370–375, 1979.
186. Welliver, R. C., Kaul, T. N., and Ogra, P. L.: The appearance of cell-bound IgE in respiratory-tract epithelium after respiratory-syncytial-virus infection. N. Engl. J. Med. *303*:1198–1202, 1980.
187. Welliver, R. C., Kaul, T. N., Putnam, T. I., et al.: The antibody response to primary and secondary infection with respiratory syncytial virus: Kinetics of class-specific responses. J. Pediatr. *96*:808–813, 1980.
188. Welliver, R. C., Wong, D. T., Sun, M., et al.: The development of respiratory syncytial virus-specific IgE and the release of histamine in nasopharyngeal secretions after infection. N. Engl. J. Med. *305*:841–846, 1981.
189. Welliver, R. C., Wong, D. T., Middleton, E., Jr., et al.: Role of parainfluenza virus-specific IgE in pathogenesis of croup and wheezing subsequent to infection. J. Pediatr. *101*:889–896, 1982.
190. Welliver, R. C., and Duffy, L.: The relationship of RSV-specific immunoglobulin E antibody responses in infancy, recurrent wheezing, and pulmonary function at age 7–8 years. Pediatr. Pulmonol. *15*:19–27, 1993.
191. Williams, H., and McNicol, K. N.: Prevalence, natural history, and relationship of wheezy bronchitis and asthma in children: An epidemiological study. Br. Med. J. *4*:321–325, 1969.
192. Wittig, H. J., Cranford, N. J., and Glasner, J.: The relationship between bronchiolitis and childhood asthma: A follow-up study of 100 cases of bronchiolitis in infancy. J. Allergy. *30*:19–23, 1959.
193. Wohl, M. E. B., and Chernick, V.: Bronchiolitis. Am. Rev. Respir. Dis. *118*:759–781, 1978.
194. Wohl, M. E. B., Stigol, L. C., and Mead, J.: Resistance of the total respiratory system in healthy infants and infants with bronchiolitis. Pediatrics. *43*:495–509, 1969.
195. Wood, S. H., Buddingh, G. J., and Abberger, B. F., Jr.: An inquiry into the etiology of acute bronchiolitis of infants. Pediatrics. *13*:363–372, 1954.
196. Woolcock, A. J., Leeder, S. R., Peat, J. K., et al.: The influence of lower respiratory illness in infancy and childhood and subsequent cigarette smoking on lung function in Sydney schoolchildren. Am. Rev. Respir. Dis. *120*:5–14, 1979.
197. Wright, A. L., Taussig, L. M., Ray, C. G., et al.: The Tucson children's respiratory study. II. Lower respiratory illness in the first year of life. Am. J. Epidemiol. *129*:1232–1246, 1989.
198. Wright, A. L., Holberg, C., Martinez, F. D., et al.: Relationship of parental smoking to wheezing and nonwheezing lower respiratory tract illnesses in infancy. J. Pediatr. *118*:207–214, 1991.
199. Young, S., Le Souf, P., Geelhoed, G., et al.: The influence of a family history of asthma and parental smoking on airway responsiveness in early infancy. N. Engl. J. Med. *324*:1168–1174, 1991.
200. Zweiman, B., Schoenwetter, W. F., Pappano, J. E., Jr., et al.: Patterns of allergic respiratory disease in children with a past history of bronchiolitis. J. Allergy Clin. Immunol. *48*:283–289, 1971.

CHAPTER 26

Nonbacterial Pneumonia

KENNETH M. BOYER

Nonbacterial pneumonias are the most frequent pulmonary infections encountered in pediatrics.* Numerous terms based on their causes, clinical manifestations, or histologic features are used for these conditions. Although their connotations differ, viral pneumonia, atypical pneumonia, infant pneumonitis, and interstitial pneumonia are encountered frequently. The varied causes, excluding bacteria and fungi, cover a broad taxonomic spectrum. With improvements in microbiologic techniques, the number of known causative agents continues to increase. Defining etiology once was the province of the epidemiologist and virologist, but a sufficient body of knowledge has accumulated to permit informed diagnostic judgment to be made by practicing physicians and rapid specific diagnosis by clinical microbiology laboratories. Although most nonbacterial pneumonias have a good prognosis, occasionally they are life-threatening. Therapy directed against the causative agent may shorten the course or avert serious complications. At times, it is lifesaving.

This chapter provides an overview of pneumonia syndromes caused by viruses, mycoplasmas, and chlamydiae, as well as by *Coxiella burnetii* (a rickettsia) and *Pneumocystis carinii* (an apicomplexan parasite).

Historical Aspects

The development of systematic bacteriology in the late 19th century led to the widespread thought that pneumonias were bacterial infections with differences in manifestations (bronchial, lobular, lobar) that primarily were the result of differences in anatomic localization. During the 1918 influenza pandemic, most postmortem examinations of patients with pneumonia revealed numerous bacteria in the lungs. A variety of different species were identified, not exclusively *Haemophilus influenzae,* the organism at that time regarded as the cause of influenza. In a few cases in which no bacteria were found, Goodpasture[82] and Winternitz and colleagues[237] found distinctive histopathologic lesions in the lung that prompted researchers to conclude that they were induced by a nonbacterial agent. Isolation of influenza A virus by Smith and associates[220] in 1933 altered the prevailing bacteriologic and anatomic concepts of pneumonia and ushered in a new era of etiologic diagnosis of respiratory syndromes.

The first isolation of influenza virus and subsequent isolation of *Chlamydia psittaci* (psittacosis) and *C. burnetii* (Q fever) involved transmission of infection to experimental animals such as ferrets and chick embryos. The development of tissue culture techniques in the 1950s enabled researchers to identify numerous other common respiratory viruses—adenoviruses, parainfluenza viruses, respiratory syncytial virus (RSV), enteroviruses, and rhinoviruses. The major etiologic agent of primary atypical pneumonia had been passed to experimental animals in the 1940s, but it was not identified as a mycoplasma definitely until 1962.[38]

In the 1960s and 1970s, the most valuable studies of nonbacterial respiratory infection in pediatrics were comprehensive longitudinal investigations in which epidemiologic and clinical patterns of illness were defined. These studies established that most lower respiratory tract infections in infants and young children are caused by nonbacterial agents, principally respiratory viruses and *Mycoplasma pneumoniae.* The attention of current investigators is being directed increasingly at developing methods for rapid diagnosis, chemotherapy, and prevention, although new agents (e.g., Sin Nombre hantavirus,[104, 230] and human metapneumovirus,[231] and the coronavirus related to the severe acute respiratory syndrome [SARS][51a, 129a]) continue to be associated with distinctive pneumonia syndromes.

Etiology

Three *Mycoplasma* spp., 1 *Rickettsia* sp., 3 *Chlamydia* spp., 1 protozoan parasite, and at least 16 different virus groups have been associated with pneumonia syndromes in children. The overall importance of these agents is not measured simply by their incidence. Some agents, though quite common, generally give rise to relatively mild illness; others, less frequently encountered, characteristically may cause serious disease. In Table 26–1, the major agents in various age groups are presented by their overall frequency, their typical degree of severity, and their mode of access to the lung. Although the incidence data are representative of numerous major epidemiologic studies,* one should recall that the proportion of pneumonias of unproven cause in most such studies has been approximately 50 percent. Possible explanations for the high percentage of such cases include a bacterial etiology[164]; partial treatment with antimicrobial agents[120]; late collection of viral cultures and sera[66]; suboptimal storage, transport, or cultivation of specimens[76, 204]; and as yet unidentified agents. The use of antibody tests for bacterial pathogens and immunoassays and polymerase chain reaction assays for viruses account for the higher rates of diagnosis in some recent studies.[103, 120, 241]

RSV generally is accepted as the agent found most frequently in pediatric pneumonias, particularly those associated with bronchiolitis.† Although infection with this virus is quite common in all age groups, lower respiratory tract involvement is especially prominent in infancy.

The three parainfluenza viruses (types 1, 2, and 3) are second only to RSV as causes of lower respiratory tract disease in infants and younger children. Parainfluenza 3 is the agent most frequently found in pneumonia[78, 80, 111, 187]; infection by parainfluenza 1 and 2 generally produces laryngotracheitis.

*See references 33, 34, 38, 43, 48, 65, 66, 76, 79, 81, 111, 115, 134, 138, 141, 144, 169, 172, 176, 183, 185, 229.

*See references 33, 34, 38, 43, 49, 57, 64–66, 76, 79, 81, 111, 134, 138, 144, 147, 169, 172, 176, 183, 185, 229.

†See references 16, 18, 22, 25, 105, 116, 124, 154, 168, 221, 228.

TABLE 26–1 ■ ETIOLOGIC AGENTS IN NONBACTERIAL PNEUMONIA

Etiologic Agents	Frequency*			Usual Degree of Severity†			Mode of Access to Lung
	0–3 mo	4 mo–5 yr	6–16 yr	0–3 mo	4 mo–5 yr	6–16 yr	
Virus							
Respiratory syncytial virus	+++	++++	+	++	++	+	Respiratory
Human metapneumovirus	+	++	?	++	++	?	Respiratory
Parainfluenza viruses							
Type 1	+	++	+	++	++	+	Respiratory
Type 2	+	+	+	++	++	+	Respiratory
Type 3	++	+++	++	++	++	+	Respiratory
Influenza viruses							
Type A	++	+++	+++	++	++	+	Respiratory
Type B	++	++	+	++	++	+	Respiratory
Adenoviruses‡	+	++	++	+++	++	+	Respiratory
Rhinoviruses§	+	+	+	–	++	+	Respiratory
Enteroviruses‖	+	+	+	++	++	+	Respiratory (hematogenous)
Coronaviruses	–	+	+	–	++	+++	Respiratory
Measles virus	+	++	++	+++	++	++	Respiratory (hematogenous)
Rubella virus	+	–	–	++	–	–	Hematogenous
HIV	+	++	+	++	++	++	Hematogenous
Varicella-zoster virus	+	+	+	+++	+++	+++	Hematogenous (respiratory)
Cytomegalovirus	+++	+	+	++	+++	+++	Hematogenous (respiratory)
Epstein-Barr virus	–	+	++	–	++	+	Hematogenous (respiratory)
Herpes simplex virus	++	+	+	++++	+++	+++	Hematogenous (respiratory)
Mycoplasmas							
Mycoplasma pneumoniae	–	+	++++	–	++	+	Respiratory
Mycoplasma hominis	?	–	–	?	–	–	Respiratory
Ureaplasma urealyticum	?	–	–	?	–	–	Respiratory
Chlamydiae							
Chlamydia pneumoniae	–	+	+++	–	+	+	Respiratory
Chlamydia psittaci	+	+	+	–	++	++	Respiratory
Chlamydia trachomatis	++++	–	–	++	–	–	Respiratory
Rickettsiae							
Coxiella burnetii	–	+	+	–	++	++	Respiratory (hematogenous)
Protozoa							
Pneumocystis carinii	+	++	+	+++	+++	+++	Respiratory

*++++, most frequent; +++, frequent; ++, infrequent; +, rare; –, no reported cases; ?, uncertain.
†++++, often fatal; +++, severe; ++, usually hospitalized; +, home management; –, no reported cases; ?, uncertain.
‡Types 1, 2, 3, 4, 5, 7, 14, and 21.
§Ninety or more types known.
‖Coxsackieviruses A9, A16, B1, B4, and B5; echoviruses 9, 11, 19, 20, and 22.

Influenza A and B viruses are not as prevalent overall as are RSV and parainfluenza viruses, but during periods of epidemic spread, they may become predominant isolates in hospitalized children with lower respiratory tract disease.[13, 24, 81, 125, 182, 186, 212]

Adenoviruses commonly are isolated in children with pneumonia* and pertussis syndrome.[23, 44, 175, 179] Their overall impact in the causation of nonbacterial pneumonia in children probably is somewhat less than that of the aforementioned agents; however, many fatal illnesses have been reported. Their common asymptomatic carriage and potential for endogenous activation by unrelated illnesses can render causation difficult to prove.[63, 175] Of the 51 known adenoviruses, types 1, 2, 3, 4, 5, 7, 14, 21, and 35 clearly have been associated with pneumonia.[23, 126] In certain aboriginal populations such as the Maori, Native Americans, and Inuit, adenoviruses commonly produce severe infection.[107, 130] In military recruits, adenoviruses are second to *M. pneumoniae* as a cause of atypical pneumonia.[50]

Rhinoviruses[13, 73, 188, 201, 226] have been associated less frequently with pneumonia, although upper respiratory infection with the multiple serotypes of these organisms occurs frequently. Some degree of lower respiratory involvement by rhinoviruses also is indicated by their documented role in exacerbations of asthma[165] and bronchitis.[160] Among the enteroviruses, primary viral pneumonia has been documented best with coxsackieviruses A9[135] and B1,[53] although coxsackieviruses A16, B4, and B5 and echoviruses 9, 11, 19, 20, and 22 also have been reported.[38, 91, 216] Human metapneumonovirus, recently described in children with upper and lower respiratory tract infection in the Netherlands,[231] accounted for 10 percent of otherwise unexplained respiratory infections. The clinical symptoms in infected children resembled those caused by RSV.[177, 231] Coronaviruses have been implicated as causes of pneumonia in a few seroepidemiologic studies, but until recently tissue culture recovery of these agents has been rare.[123, 157] However, the current global epidemic of SARS appears to be caused by a novel coronavirus, the Urbani strain.[51a, 129a]

Pneumonia is the most frequent serious complication of measles. Kohn and Koiransky[128] demonstrated by careful radiographic study that 55 percent of routine measles cases had pulmonary infiltrates early in the illness, thus suggesting viral rather than bacterial causation. Secondary bacterial pneumonia in measles is caused by common respiratory pathogens: *Streptococcus pneumoniae, H. influenzae, Streptococcus pyogenes,* and *Staphylococcus aureus.* Progressive, fatal, primary measles pneumonia (Hecht giant-cell pneumonia) occurs in immunocompromised patients, particularly those with hematologic malignancy or infection with

*See references 5, 7, 17, 23, 26, 35, 76, 106, 108, 119, 174, 191, 225, 240.

human immunodeficiency virus type 1 (HIV-1).[129, 148, 214, 215] The typical measles rash often is absent. In some persons immunized with killed measles virus vaccine during the 1960s, an unusual nodular pneumonia, along with vasculitis of the distal extremities, developed after infection with wild measles virus. Although no longer seen, atypical measles remains important because its pathogenetic mechanism has implications for the development of new vaccines.[68]

Viruses that may attack the lungs by hematogenous spread include varicella-zoster virus (VZV), Epstein-Barr virus (EBV), rubella virus, cytomegalovirus (CMV), herpes simplex virus (HSV), and HIV. Rubella virus, CMV, and HSV may cause interstitial pneumonia in congenitally or perinatally infected infants.[8, 100, 239, 244] CMV and VZV are causes of life-threatening pneumonia in immunocompromised hosts.[113, 192, 236] Pneumonia has been noted in association with primary EBV infections.[6, 56] Pulmonary infiltration also is a component of the fatal X-linked lymphoproliferative syndrome caused by EBV.[197] One of the characteristic features of HIV infection in children is lymphocytic interstitial pneumonitis, an indolent but progressive process that occurs in approximately a quarter of children in whom acquired immunodeficiency syndrome (AIDS) develops.[207] Both HIV RNA and EBV DNA have been demonstrated in the lung tissue of affected children.[4] The relative contributions of the two agents to the pathogenesis of lymphocytic interstitial pneumonitis are not understood clearly, although EBV is suspected to be the trigger.[122]

Of the 15 known *Mycoplasma* spp. that infect humans, only *M. pneumoniae* is a well-established cause of pneumonia. In children younger than 2 years of age, infection is a common occurrence, but pneumonia is unusual. In children older than 5 years of age, *M. pneumoniae* is the most common etiology of nonbacterial pneumonia.[40, 66] Studies have associated genital mycoplasmas, in particular *Ureaplasma urealyticum* and *Mycoplasma hominis,* with congenital and perinatally acquired pneumonia. However, proof of causation is not secure.[30, 31]

Three *Chlamydia* spp. have been associated with pneumonia. *C. psittaci* is the well-recognized cause of psittacosis (ornithosis). *Chlamydia trachomatis,* the established agent of inclusion blennorrhea in neonates, causes a characteristic afebrile pneumonitis syndrome in infants 4 to 14 weeks of age.[15] In urban areas in the United States where the condition first was studied carefully—Chicago, Seattle, San Francisco, and Birmingham—it was the most frequent cause of pneumonia in that age group.[52, 102] With widespread screening and treatment of pregnant women for *Chlamydia,* the incidence of this condition appears to be decreasing. *C. pneumoniae* was isolated first in 1965 and recognized as a cause of pneumonia in 1986.[84] It now is emerging as one of the more frequent causes of pneumonia in older children and young adults.[85, 209]

Of the rickettsiae, only *C. burnetii* is associated with pneumonia, in the form of Q fever. This infection may be severe but, because of its restricted ecologic niche, is a rare occurrence in children.

P. carinii, a protozoan parasite, is an important cause of pneumonia in compromised hosts,[113, 192, 236] although its incidence in children receiving chemotherapeutic regimens for malignancy has been reduced dramatically with the use of trimethoprim-sulfamethoxazole (TMP-SMX) prophylaxis.[112] *P. carinii* is an established cause of pneumonia in premature and debilitated infants[71] and, with *C. trachomatis,* CMV, and genital mycoplasmas, has been associated with the afebrile pneumonitis syndrome of infancy.[52, 190, 223, 224] It is the most frequent cause of death in infants with HIV infection, although the incidence now is reduced markedly in U.S. populations as a result of early diagnosis and treatment of perinatal HIV infection and by the institution of chemoprophylaxis with TMP-SMX.[202, 217]

Epidemiology

The major contributors to the overall epidemiology of nonbacterial pneumonia in children are RSV, parainfluenza viruses,

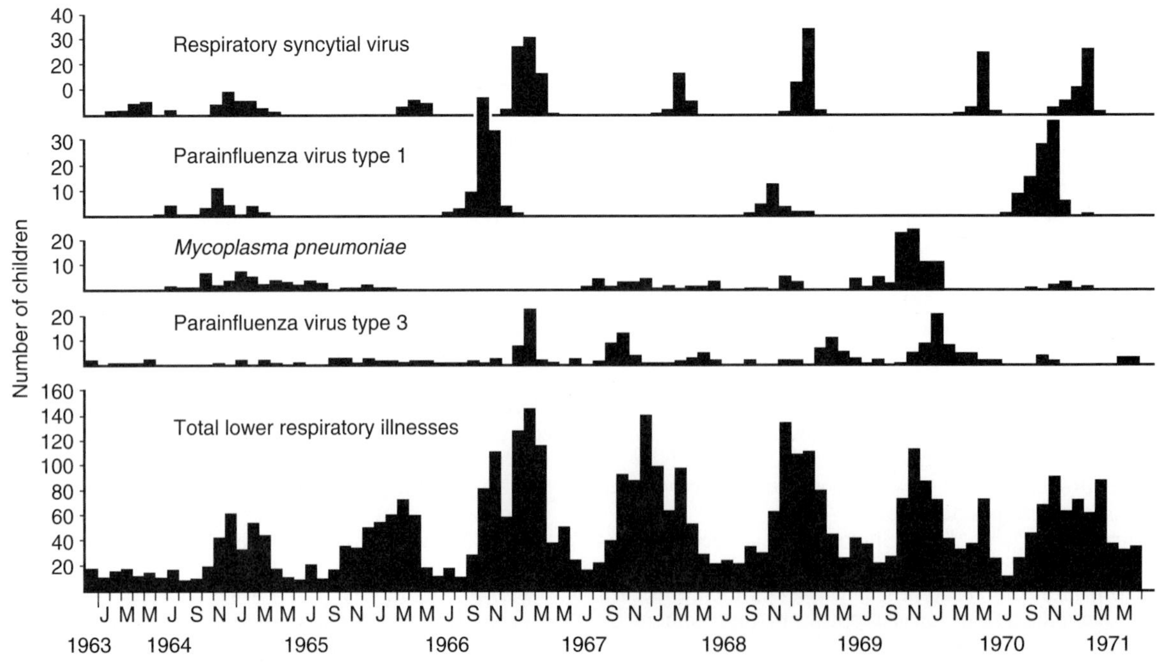

FIGURE 26–1 ■ Number of isolations, according to month, of four major respiratory pathogens from children with lower respiratory illnesses in Chapel Hill, North Carolina. (From Glezen, W. P., and Denny, F. W.: Epidemiology of acute lower respiratory disease in children. N. Engl. J. Med. *288*:500, 1973. Reprinted with permission from the New England Journal of Medicine.)

M. pneumoniae, and, to a lesser extent, influenza viruses A and B.[49] Because of their brief incubation periods and high degree of communicability, these agents often spread through communities in well-defined waves[76, 78] (Fig. 26–1). During intervals between epidemics, RSV, parainfluenza 1 and 2, and influenza viruses A and B rarely are isolated. Between peaks, *M. pneumoniae* and parainfluenza 3 tend to persist endemically. During respiratory disease seasons in the colder months, an interference phenomenon has been noted whereby peaks of infection by particular agents seldom occur simultaneously[76] (Fig. 26–2).

Annual incidence rates of childhood pneumonia show a rough inverse correlation with age and range from 40 per 1000 in children younger than 5 years of age to 7 per 1000 in adolescents 12 to 15 years of age.[66, 172] RSV is the most common etiologic agent in children younger than 5 years of age; in those older than 5 years, *M. pneumoniae* is most common.[66] Most studies have shown a male preponderance in pediatric lower respiratory infections on the order of 1.25:1. The increased rates of lower respiratory infection in lower socioeconomic groups correlate best with family size, a reflection of environmental crowding.[76]

Pregnancy, chronic lung disease, valvular heart disease, and neuromuscular conditions in adults predispose to greater severity of viral, particularly influenzal, pneumonia.[143] In children, congenital heart disease and bronchopulmonary dysplasia are associated with greater severity of viral pneumonia, especially with RSV.[145] Pulmonary deterioration in patients with cystic fibrosis has been shown to be accelerated by respiratory viral infection.[233] In treated hematologic malignancy, marrow transplantation, and immunosuppressed states, common respiratory viruses have been recognized increasingly as causes of severe pneumonia and respiratory failure.[98, 101] Children with these underlying conditions also are prone to the development of serious pulmonary infection with such agents as measles virus, VZV, and CMV, which have the capacity for hematogenous dissemination and viral latency. Pediatric HIV infection has added a new category of immunocompromised children susceptible to these pathogens, as well as to the common bacterial agents of pneumonia. Profoundly immunocompromised patients, such as those with severe combined immunodeficiency disease, are prone to the acquisition of progressive as well as prolonged pulmonary disease caused by common respiratory viruses.[118]

Transmission of the more common agents of lower respiratory tract disease most often occurs by means of droplet spread from relatively close contact with a source case. Direct inoculation at the alveolar level probably does not occur in most cases because of the extremely small size of aerosolized particles necessary for such transmission to be accomplished. Studies of nosocomially transmitted RSV infection have shown the importance of adults with relatively trivial upper respiratory tract infection as intermediates in transmission to susceptible young infants.[94] School-age children often introduce respiratory viral agents into households and, thus, are the source of secondary infections in parents and younger siblings.[76] The increasing use of group daycare by working parents has been associated with enhanced transmission of numerous respiratory pathogens[140, 197] and certainly has extended the definition of "school age" to a younger group of children.

Pathogenesis and Pathology

After inoculation of the upper respiratory tract, viral agents that cause pneumonia proliferate and spread by contiguity to involve the lower and more distal portions of the respiratory tract. Infected epithelium loses its ciliary appendages, rounds up, and sloughs into the air passages, with subsequent stasis of mucus and accumulation of cellular

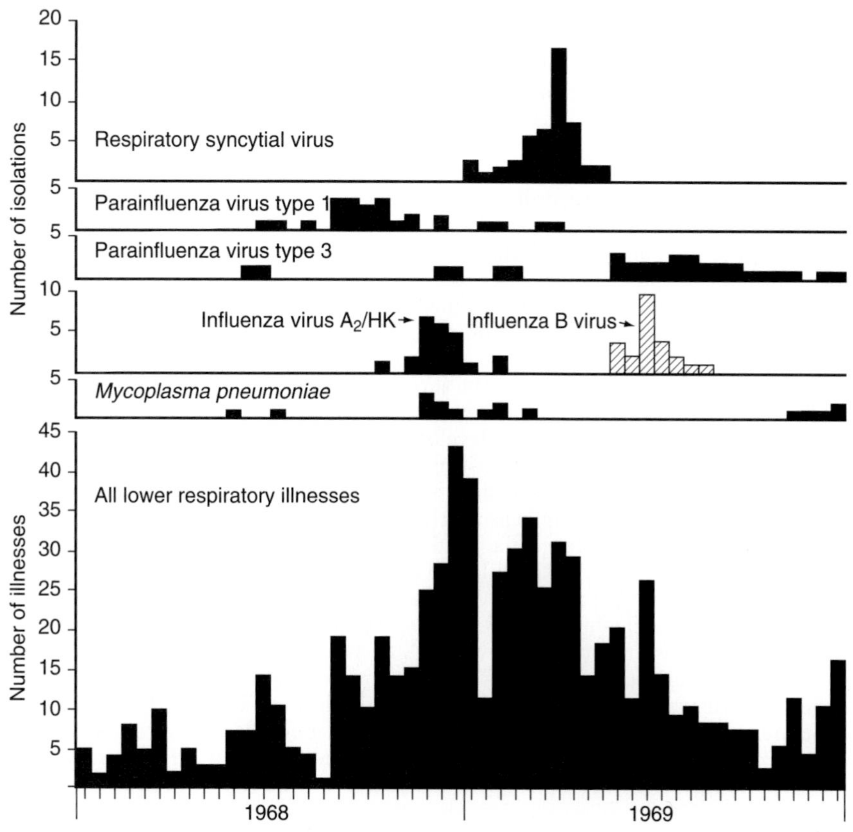

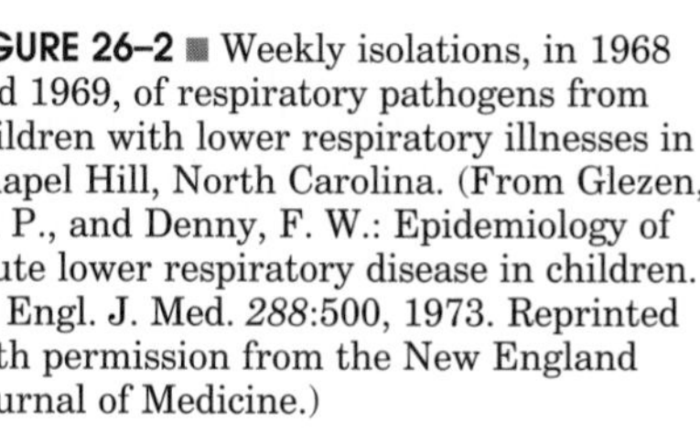

FIGURE 26–2 ■ Weekly isolations, in 1968 and 1969, of respiratory pathogens from children with lower respiratory illnesses in Chapel Hill, North Carolina. (From Glezen, W. P., and Denny, F. W.: Epidemiology of acute lower respiratory disease in children. N. Engl. J. Med. *288*:500, 1973. Reprinted with permission from the New England Journal of Medicine.)

debris.[1, 29, 245] When infection extends to the terminal airways, the alveolar lining cells lose their structural integrity, and, as a result, surfactant production is lost, hyaline membranes form, and pulmonary edema develops. The inflammatory response at the site of tissue damage results in mononuclear infiltration of submucosal and interstitial structures, which further contributes to narrowing of air passages and alveolocapillary block of gas exchange. Relative expiratory obstruction gives rise to hyperinflation and "air trapping." Complete obstruction or stop-valve mechanisms result in atelectasis. Ventilation-perfusion mismatch further exacerbates the hypoxia.

The relative rarity of fatal outcomes in patients with the common etiologies of nonbacterial pneumonia has resulted in a relatively narrow view of the characteristic pathology, limited largely to autopsy studies of overwhelming illness in infants and military recruits. The pathology associated with infection by RSV, adenoviruses, and influenza virus A has been studied most extensively in humans. Studies of the pathology of RSV, parainfluenza virus, and *Mycoplasma* infection have been aided by animal model systems such as mice,[83] the Syrian hamster,[77] and the cotton rat.[88]

Five major pathologic findings have been described in fatal human infections, any or all of which may be present in a given case: acute bronchiolitis, necrotizing bronchiolitis, interstitial pneumonia, alveolar pneumonia, and diffuse alveolar damage. Acute bronchiolitis is characterized by relatively superficial and reversible destruction of ciliated respiratory epithelium, along with accompanying mononuclear infiltration. Necrotizing bronchiolitis extends to the deeper submucosal layers lining the respiratory tract and may not be as readily reversible. It is associated particularly with adenoviral pneumonia.[14] Interstitial pneumonia is a diffuse process in which the inflammatory mononuclear response predominantly involves the peribronchial alveolar septa. In alveolar pneumonia, the alveoli are filled with degenerating lining cells and mononuclear or polymorphonuclear inflammatory cells with or without hyaline membranes. Hyaline membranes consist of fibrin deposits triggered by local release of tissue factor–factor VII complexes, as well as inhibitors of fibrinolysis.[19] When hyaline membranes are present, the process is described as diffuse alveolar damage. It is the histopathologic hallmark of the acute phase of adult respiratory distress syndrome.[205, 206] Acute bronchiolitis and interstitial pneumonia are observed in most cases of fatal nonbacterial pneumonia, regardless of cause.[1] Alveolar pneumonia may reflect bacterial superinfection, adult respiratory distress syndrome, or agonal changes associated with intensive ventilator support and oxygen toxicity.

Three important factors that influence the pathologic expression of nonbacterial pneumonia in children are anatomy, preexisting pulmonary disease, and immunity. In young infants, the small caliber of the terminal airways and the absence of interconnections between alveolar spaces (pores of Kohn) contribute to the development of wheezing and lobular atelectasis.[171, 238] Preexisting pulmonary disease (e.g., bronchopulmonary dysplasia) is characterized by emphysema, squamous metaplasia of the tracheobronchial tree, hypertrophied goblet cells, and enhanced airway smooth muscle reactivity. An inability to clear the excessive secretions triggered by infection in patients with bronchopulmonary dysplasia often leads to bronchospasm, atelectasis, and respiratory failure.

Immunopathologic mechanisms have been invoked to explain the disparity between infants and older children in the clinical expression of infection by RSV and *M. pneumoniae*.[32, 158] Interaction between RSV-infected epithelial cells and specific IgE, with the subsequent release of histamine, has been postulated as an immune mechanism for bronchospasm in RSV disease.[234] Cumulative immunity after repeated natural infections by *M. pneumoniae* may account for the more impressive clinical expression of illness in older children and adults.[61] Specific cell-mediated immunity, detectable at low levels in young children but increased in adults, probably contributes to the pathogenesis.

Opportunistic nonbacterial pathogens generally take advantage of the defects in cell-mediated immunity induced by immunosuppressive therapy or HIV infection. A variety of unique pathologic manifestations of viral pneumonia, including giant-cell pneumonia (leukemia or HIV infection with superimposed measles),[148, 214, 215] lymphoid interstitial pneumonitis or pulmonary lymphoid hyperplasia (HIV with associated EBV infection),[4, 207] and graft-versus-host disease (bone marrow allograft with associated CMV infection), may ensue in these circumstances.[55, 227, 236]

Clinical Manifestations

Acute nonbacterial pneumonia in infants and young children generally occurs after 1 or 2 days of coryza, decreased appetite, and low-grade fever. The onset usually is gradual, with increasing fretfulness, respiratory congestion, vomiting, cough, and fever. In very young infants, fever may be minimal and apneic spells may be the most prominent (and frightening) initial complaint.[27] The most reliable physical findings are those of respiratory distress: tachypnea (respiratory rate ≥50/min[37]), tachycardia, nasal flaring, and retractions, but without the stridor characteristic of upper airway obstruction. In patients with atelectasis or air trapping, grunting may be present. Cyanosis generally accompanies the apneic spells or coughing attacks but may be present at rest in advanced disease or in those with underlying chronic cardiopulmonary conditions.

Other physical findings are quite variable and in fact may be normal. Wheezing occurs in infants with associated bronchiolitis or bronchospasm. Hyperresonance may be noted if air trapping is present. Diminished local percussion or breath sounds may indicate lobar consolidation or atelectasis. In interstitial pneumonia, fine crackling rales may be present diffusely or locally. Also important in initial assessment is an evaluation of the young child's state of hydration because increased insensible loss from fever and hyperventilation, coupled with anorexia, can result in significant deficits in fluid.

The afebrile pneumonitis syndrome of young infants, in contrast to the usual acute viral pneumonias affecting this age group, is subacute to chronic in its development and is nonseasonal. Characteristic features include the absence of fever, a "staccato" cough pattern (individual coughs separated by inspirations), and diffuse rales on auscultation.[15] Radiographic findings usually consist of interstitial infiltrates with subsegmental atelectasis. Hypergammaglobulinemia and mild eosinophilia are abnormalities frequently detected in the laboratory.

Most infants with HIV/AIDS and *P. carinii* pneumonia have a progressive febrile course leading to respiratory failure over the course of 1 to 3 weeks. Typical upper respiratory symptoms may be absent, and these infants may fail to respond to conventional antibiotic therapy. When pneumonia actually is detected by chest radiography, the severity of involvement may not be appreciated because abnormalities often are subtle early in the course. However, even with mild radiographic abnormalities, hypoxia may be obvious and severe. Frequently, the discovery of HIV seropositivity first raises this diagnostic possibility. An important observation is that

P. carinii pneumonia may develop in infants with HIV/ AIDS who have CD4 lymphocyte counts in the "normal" range.[217]

Nonbacterial pneumonia in older children and adolescents clinically is more nearly like that in adults. Premonitory complaints generally include such systemic symptoms as malaise, myalgia, and anorexia, in addition to upper respiratory symptoms. "Chilliness" may occur, but rigors generally are absent. Cough usually is irritative and nonproductive. A temperature higher than 39° C (102.2° F) is an unusual event. Although tachypnea, flaring, and retractions typically are present, they may be less apparent than in an infant or young child. Findings on examination of the chest are more reliable than in infancy and may include local percussion dullness or diminished breath sounds and local or diffuse fine rales. Because apnea rarely occurs in older patients, cyanosis is an ominous sign of advanced disease and respiratory failure. Progression to acute respiratory failure occurs in a disturbingly high proportion of patients with the recently described SARS.[132a, 194a] Although mild dehydration often is present, generally it is not evident on examination. Nonspecific rash suggests a viral or mycoplasmal cause.[39]

Radiologic findings in nonbacterial pneumonia are variable and depend on the child's age and the infecting agent.[45, 46, 149, 152, 181, 203, 218] In infants and young children, bilateral air trapping and perihilar infiltrates are the most frequent findings. Patchy areas of consolidation may represent lobular atelectasis or alveolar pneumonia. In older children and adolescents, lobar involvement more frequently is definable, but typically the affected areas are not consolidated completely. Although lobar consolidation may occur in nonbacterial pneumonias, this finding should be distinguished from atelectasis and is more consistent with a bacterial etiology. Similarly, although small pleural effusions may be detected on decubitus films in patients with nonbacterial pneumonia,[62] effusions are much more suggestive of a bacterial etiology.

Peripheral leukocyte counts are quite variable in nonbacterial pneumonia.[66, 176, 194] Leukocytosis occurs most frequently in children with influenza and parainfluenza pneumonia,[66] but high counts are more consistent with a bacterial etiology.[66, 153] Gram staining of sputum or tracheal secretions from patients with nonbacterial pneumonia tends to show epithelial cells as the predominant cell type, with a mixed bacterial population representing the patient's pharyngeal flora. A predominance of neutrophils may be seen, but this finding generally reflects bacterial superinfection or preexisting chronic pulmonary disease.

Differential Diagnosis

In the differential diagnosis of nonbacterial pneumonia, the following factors need to be considered: status of the host—normal or compromised; the environment—animate (human and other animal exposure) or inanimate; the age of the patient; and, finally, the season. In certain epidemiologic settings, the diagnosis of nonbacterial pneumonia may be made with relative certainty. Often, however, this category of pulmonary infection is a diagnosis of exclusion. The major conditions to be differentiated include noninfectious pulmonary disease; bacterial pneumonia amenable to conventional antibiotics; and the more unusual bacterial, fungal, or parasitic infections that may require specialized forms of therapy.

Noninfectious conditions that may simulate nonbacterial pneumonia are summarized in Table 26–2. These conditions are particularly relevant to consider in a child with persistent or recurrent pulmonary disease. The line of demarcation between infectious and noninfectious conditions not always is sharp. In a child with sickle-cell anemia, for example, pulmonary vascular occlusive crisis is manifested as fever, leukocytosis, and patchy pulmonary infiltrates (the acute chest syndrome).[11, 193] Differentiation from pneumococcal, *Haemophilus,* or mycoplasmal pneumonia, to which a child with sickle-cell anemia has increased susceptibility, may be difficult or impossible. Early recognition of noninfectious conditions either mimicking or underlying pneumonia may prevent recurrence or improve the prognosis. Aspiration resulting from gastroesophageal reflux, for example, is a relatively common correctable cause of recurrent diffuse pneumonia.[41] Early recognition and treatment of cystic fibrosis as an underlying condition have clear beneficial effects in reducing irreversible pulmonary damage.[180]

Pneumonias caused by pyogenic bacteria are classically lobar in distribution and exhibit consolidation on radiographs. Atelectasis, on the other hand, is a common event in viral pneumonia and must be distinguished from true consolidation. Pleural effusions, circular infiltrates, consolidations with convex margins, and pneumatoceles all favor a bacterial etiology. In a young child, high fever with significant leukocytosis also favors a bacterial etiology.[155] In contrast to patients with lower counts, children with pneumonia who had leukocyte counts greater than 15,000/mm^3 were found to have a high probability of rapid defervescence with antimicrobial therapy in one emergency department study, presumably on the basis of a bacterial etiology.[153]

TABLE 26–2 ■ NONINFECTIOUS CONDITIONS THAT MAY SIMULATE NONBACTERIAL PNEUMONIA IN CHILDREN

Technical	Damage by physical agents	Collagen disease (SLE, JRA)
Poor inspiratory film	Lipoid pneumonia	Sarcoidosis
Underpenetrated film	Kerosene pneumonia	Neoplasm
Physiologic	Near-drowning	Histiocytosis X
Prominent thymus	Smoke inhalation	Bronchogenic cyst
Breast shadows	Iatrogenic pulmonary damage	Vascular ring
Chronic pulmonary disease	Drugs (bleomycin, nitrofurantoin)	Pulmonary sequestration
Asthma	Radiation pneumonitis	Cystic adenomatoid malformation
Bronchiectasis	Graft-versus-host disease	Congenital lobar emphysema
Bronchopulmonary dysplasia	Atelectasis	Alpha$_1$-antitrypsin deficiency
Pulmonary fibrosis	Mucus plug	Allergic alveolitis
Cystic fibrosis	Foreign body	Dust (farmer's lung)
Recurrent aspiration	Congestive heart failure	Mold (allergic aspergillosis)
Gastroesophageal reflux	Pulmonary infarction	Excreta (pigeon breeder's lung)
Tracheoesophageal fistula	Sickle vaso-occlusive crisis	Pulmonary hemosiderosis
Cleft palate	Fat embolism	Desquamative interstitial pneumonitis
Neuromuscular disorders	Pleural effusion	Adult respiratory distress syndrome
Familial dysautonomia	Pleural reaction	

JRA, juvenile rheumatoid arthritis; SLE, systemic lupus erythematosus.

Other laboratory investigations, such as the erythrocyte sedimentation rate, C-reactive protein, and reduction of nitroblue tetrazolium by leukocytes, frequently are positive in children with bacterial respiratory infection.[58, 151, 178] In my opinion, however, these tests add little to careful initial clinical examination, roentgenographic findings, a differential white count, and if accessible, a Gram stain of tracheal secretions in excluding a bacterial cause.[153] Specific detection techniques for bacterial antigens, used with urine or respiratory secretions, occasionally are helpful. However, false-negative results occur frequently. Because a bacterial etiology cannot be excluded with certainty, these tests seldom are used in clinical laboratories.[115, 208]

Positive cultures of blood, pleural fluid, or lung aspirates provide definite evidence of the etiology of bacterial pneumonia. Because of the common asymptomatic carriage of potential pulmonary pathogens in children, however, the diagnostic value of upper respiratory tract bacterial cultures is debated.[12, 79, 139] In a child with a suspected nonbacterial pneumonia, the finding of "normal flora" in nasopharyngeal or endotracheal secretions is reassuring. In a child who is not doing well, a predominant pathogen in such cultures can be helpful in selecting or altering antimicrobial therapy.[20, 38]

Among the less common causes of pneumonia, tuberculosis should never be forgotten. Tuberculin testing should be considered in the initial evaluation and is especially important in children residing in urban areas, in recent immigrants, and in Native Americans. Fungal pneumonia, particularly coccidioidomycosis, histoplasmosis, and blastomycosis, should be considered in children residing in or visiting endemic areas. Often, a suggestive history, such as exposure to excavations (backyard swimming pools, geologic or archeologic "digs"), clean-up chores in old sheds and barns, and exposure to dust storms, may be elicited. Erythema nodosum and eosinophilia are common clinical clues to these entities. Immunodiffusion serologic testing often yields the diagnosis. Other fungal pneumonias, such as aspergillosis and cryptococcosis, occur in the setting of immunosuppression. These conditions, coupled with the possibility of *Pneumocystis,* fungal, resistant bacterial, and CMV pneumonia, warrant the use of bronchoalveolar lavage or open lung biopsy as a definitive approach to diagnosis in compromised hosts.[67, 239] In an appropriate epidemiologic setting, progressive or recurrent pneumonia should prompt obtaining serologic testing for HIV. At present, pulmonary disease is the most common defining condition in pediatric AIDS.[207] Pulmonary paragonimiasis caused by the lung fluke *Paragonimus westermani* has been recognized as a cause of chronic pneumonia in Indochinese immigrants in the United States.[28]

Specific Diagnosis

Isolation of virus can be performed in most major medical centers and public health laboratories. With the possible exception of HSV and adenoviruses, respiratory viruses rarely are carried asymptomatically. Thus, identification of an agent in upper respiratory secretions is strong evidence for its causative role in pneumonia. Conventional virologic techniques provide the most sensitive and specific means of identification (see Chapter 249). However, most of the common respiratory viral pathogens, as well as chlamydiae and mycoplasmas, now are identified readily by "rapid" techniques. The available methods and reagents are expanding rapidly and include fluorescent antibody techniques, enzyme-linked immunosorbent assay, direct DNA probes, and polymerase chain reaction.[36, 54, 72, 137, 166] Clinical specimens may be tested directly or after pre-incubation in tissue culture systems. In an individual case, serologic diagnosis of acute respiratory viral infection is, in general, less satisfactory than virologic diagnosis. The difficulty with serology relates to timing of specimens, choice of antigens to test, and variation in the quality and specificity of available reagents.

On the other hand, laboratory facilities for the actual isolation of chlamydiae, mycoplasmas, and rickettsiae are less readily available to the clinician. Thus, serologic techniques are important means for making a specific diagnosis. Acute-phase reactants (e.g., cold agglutinins in *M. pneumoniae* infection) are of greatest diagnostic help during acute illness but are not invariably present. Serologic tests also can be helpful in diagnosing chlamydial pneumonitis in infants—high levels of IgG-specific antibodies are found uniformly at initial evaluation.[15] *Pneumocystis* infection usually is diagnosed by visualizing organisms in specimens obtained by bronchoalveolar lavage during bronchoscopy or by open lung biopsy. Silver impregnation and direct immunofluorescence staining techniques have the greatest sensitivity. Noninvasive diagnosis by serologic and molecular biologic techniques is being investigated.[136, 189, 224]

Because of the epidemiologic behavior of nonbacterial respiratory infections, a reasonable guess regarding the specific cause often can be based on such factors as age, season, and associated clinical features. If the presence of a particular nonbacterial agent in a community can be established by isolation or serologic means, however, the probability of other patients with similar manifestations having illness caused by that agent is increased greatly. Regional viral surveillance programs, such as those performed in Rochester[93] and Houston,[75] can be particularly helpful to practicing pediatricians in this regard.

Treatment

Therapy for nonbacterial pneumonia primarily is expectant and supportive. However, specific therapies are available for some of these conditions. Rapid etiologic diagnosis permits appropriate use of these therapies, particularly for hospitalized patients and compromised hosts. Although they shorten the course of illness, they frequently have a less dramatic therapeutic effect than do specific antibiotic therapies for bacterial infections.

The course of uncomplicated viral pneumonia is not influenced by the administration of antibiotics. However, in the vast majority of cases in which pulmonary involvement is uncovered, antibiotic therapy is administered because bacterial disease cannot be ruled out with certainty and combined viral-bacterial infection is a common occurrence.[120] In all but the most mild cases, this approach is both reasonable and practical. Of importance, however, is that antibiotic therapy in routine cases be appropriate for the most common bacterial pathogens *(S. pneumoniae* and *H. influenzae).* The increasing prevalence of penicillin-resistant pneumococci now renders treatment with ceftriaxone or cefotaxime a reasonable choice. Concomitant treatment with a macrolide drug should be considered in the age groups younger than 3 months and older than 6 years because of the high prevalence of chlamydial and mycoplasmal etiologies.[117, 156] In immunocompromised hosts or when secondary infection is a possibility, *S. aureus* (including methicillin-resistant strains) and other hospital-associated and opportunistic pathogens must be considered.[143]

In fulminant viral pneumonia caused by varicella in a compromised host, specific antiviral chemotherapy with acyclovir may be lifesaving, but one should recall that as many as 50 percent of patients with this condition have complicating bacterial sepsis that requires antibiotic therapy as well.[59] Treatment with amantadine, rimantadine, or oseltamivir should be considered in children with viral pneumonia in the context of a community epidemic of influenza A. Treatment of lymphocytic interstitial pneumonia in pediatric AIDS patients includes antiretroviral therapy with prednisone pulses for increasing hypoxia.[159] Progressive CMV interstitial pneumonia in bone marrow or solid organ transplant recipients is treated best with ganciclovir and intravenous immunoglobulin, ideally with high-titer antibody activity.[55]

TMP-SMX and pentamidine are equally effective for the treatment of *P. carinii* pneumonitis, but the former is the drug of choice because of its lower toxicity. TMP-SMX may be given orally (20 mg/kg/day of the TMP component divided every 6 hours) or intravenously (15 mg/kg/day divided every 8 hours). Pentamidine should be reserved for patients who are intolerant of TMP-SMX. Atovaquone is a future therapeutic option, pending more complete information on its pharmacokinetic profile in pediatrics. Completion of a course of therapy with any agent should be followed by direct transition to long-term chemoprophylaxis.

Inhalational administration of the antiviral compound ribavirin has been used successfully to treat viral pneumonia caused by RSV and influenza.[74, 97, 127] Anecdotal experience and in vitro activity suggest that it also may be beneficial in parainfluenza and measles virus infection.[9] Early studies indicated that ribavirin was of particular value for the treatment of RSV infection in nonventilated infants with underlying cardiopulmonary disease[96] and in previously normal infants with RSV pneumonia and respiratory failure.[219] However, several multicenter re-evaluations of the use of ribavirin therapy for RSV-infected infants with and without respiratory failure have yielded equivocal results.[132, 161, 167, 235] These observations, coupled with the high cost of the drug,[60] concerns about its possible teratogenicity in medical personnel,[3] and the complexity of its administration during mechanical ventilation,[47] have led to reassessment of its use and a change in American Academy of Pediatrics recommendations from "should be used"[3] to "may be considered."[199]

Bronchospasm is present in a substantial proportion of nonbacterial pneumonias. Airway reactivity may be preexisting or arise as part of the pathogenesis of the pneumonia itself. In most hospitals, intervention, particularly with inhaled bronchodilators, has become part of the routine management of any patient with wheezing, regardless of age or mechanism. Rigorous pulmonary function studies have shown that only approximately 50 percent of previously normal infants with RSV-associated respiratory failure respond to inhaled albuterol.[99] However, in several double-blind controlled trials, inhaled albuterol and racemic epinephrine both have shown statistically significant overall benefit.[162, 200, 210, 213] Other studies of the use of albuterol and ipratropium in mildly ill infants have been less convincing.[69, 232] Interestingly, none of the available studies of ribavirin therapy for RSV bronchiolitis and pneumonia has controlled for the effects of concomitant inhaled bronchodilator therapy.

The use of systemic corticosteroids in nonbacterial pneumonia should be approached with caution. In patients with preexisting asthma or bronchopulmonary dysplasia and acute deterioration triggered by pneumonia, steroids are a noncontroversial element of treatment. In adult patients with AIDS and rapidly progressive *P. carinii* pneumonia, short-course steroid therapy clearly is beneficial.[21, 70] Comparable data do not exist for pediatric patients with HIV/AIDS. In infants and children without preexisting lung disease, steroid therapy for viral bronchiolitis with or without concomitant pneumonia has shown neither consistent benefit nor harm.[133, 222] The value of steroids probably strikes a balance between their anti-inflammatory effects in short-term use and their immunosuppressive effects with more prolonged administration.

Other key elements of supportive therapy include maintenance of adequate hydration, high humidity, and oxygenation and ventilation; mobilization of lower respiratory secretions; and particularly in young infants, continuous monitoring of respiration. Because of increased insensible loss caused by fever, hyperventilation, and anorexia, mild dehydration frequently is observed initially, and continuing loss is to be expected during the acute phase of illness. Thus, restoration of deficits and adequate maintenance of fluid intake are desirable. Maintaining nutrition often is difficult when respiratory distress is present; oral feeding is limited or contraindicated. Parenteral nutrition through peripheral veins is adequate during acute self-limited pneumonia. Situations involving more prolonged hospitalization or mechanical ventilation should lead to early consideration of central alimentation.

The therapeutic benefit of mist tents is debated because negligible amounts of nebulized water actually reach the bronchiolar level.[184] However, high humidity is required to prevent the drying effects of supplemental oxygen therapy; slowing evaporation probably also serves to reduce the viscosity of mucus secretions and the magnitude of insensible fluid loss. Mobilization of respiratory secretions by means of vibration and postural drainage is indicated in nonbacterial pneumonias complicated by atelectasis,[142] but it is not helpful in the absence of excessive secretions or mucus plugging.[173] Progression of infiltrates and hypoxia occasionally occurs secondary to pulmonary edema and may require diuretic therapy.

Because of the presence of ventilation-perfusion abnormalities and alveolocapillary block, most children with nonbacterial pneumonia have some degree of hypoxemia. In a child with respiratory distress, provision of supplemental oxygen reduces anxiety and ventilation rates. Increases in inspired oxygen to approximately 30 percent are provided easily by nasal cannulas, which are the most convenient means of administration. More severe respiratory distress or cyanosis requires documentation of respiratory status by means of arterial blood gas determination and more exact regulation of inspired oxygen administered by mask or hood. Noninvasive monitoring by means of oximetry can reduce the need for frequent blood gas sampling and arterial lines.[95] Consistent oxygen saturation of 95 percent or more should be the target. In respiratory failure, mechanical ventilation may be required to maintain oxygenation and prevent retention of carbon dioxide.[51, 90, 150] In this instance, management in an intensive care unit setting is mandated, with invasive monitoring of gas exchange.

Apnea and bradycardia occur commonly in young infants with RSV, parainfluenza, and influenza viral pneumonia.[27, 42] This complication occurs particularly frequently in infants with a history of premature birth. Although the mechanism for these episodes is uncertain, continuous cardiorespiratory monitoring of any young infant with viral pneumonia is prudent.

Acetaminophen should be used to control high fever and will benefit the patient in terms of comfort as well as a reduction in oxygen and nutritional requirements. Expectorants, antihistamines, and cough suppressants, though widely prescribed for upper respiratory tract infections in children and adults, probably have no place in the management of acute nonbacterial pneumonia. In convalescence, persistent irritative coughing that interferes with sleep may be alleviated by the judicious use of codeine or dextromethorphan.[2]

Prognosis

In the pre-antibiotic era, pneumonia (of which most cases were "bronchopneumonia") was the most frequent cause of death in children. At present, a fatal outcome rarely occurs but always is a possibility. It is most likely to occur in young infants or compromised hosts.

The incidence of long-term complications of nonbacterial pneumonia is unknown. However, these conditions probably play a role in the development of some cases of bronchiectasis, chronic pulmonary fibrosis, desquamative interstitial pneumonitis, bronchiolitis obliterans, and unilateral hyperlucent lung (Swyer-James syndrome). These complications are well-documented sequelae of measles and adenoviral and influenza viral pneumonia.[121, 130, 131, 146] They occur most frequently today in children who have survived complex and prolonged hospitalization involving aggressive ventilator management of respiratory failure.[205, 206]

At a minimum, children with pneumonia should be re-evaluated clinically 2 to 3 weeks after diagnosis. Provided that the child is asymptomatic, has returned to normal activities, and has a benign physical examination, a follow-up radiograph is not required.[87] Repeated chest radiographs are necessary for children with complicated clinical courses, underlying pulmonary disease, or previous episodes of pneumonia or if signs or symptoms of respiratory difficulty persist at the time of follow-up. One should recognize that approximately 20 percent of even uncomplicated pneumonias will show persistent radiographic abnormalities 3 to 4 weeks after diagnosis, but a selective approach to follow-up films permits early recognition of atelectasis, unresolved infiltrates, or progressive disease.

Prevention

Nosocomial spread of respiratory viruses occurs readily in pediatric wards and involves intermediate carriage by medical personnel who have acquired mild upper respiratory tract infections.[92] A reasonable approach to interdicting nosocomial transmission is to group patients with pneumonia and exclude personnel with symptomatic respiratory illness from ward duties.

Of the common viral causes of pneumonia, vaccines at present are available for only influenza A and B. Annual influenza vaccination with "split-product" vaccines is recommended for children with chronic respiratory disease, HIV/AIDS, and other conditions predisposing them to the development of pneumonia.[195] Adenoviral vaccines have been used widely in the military, but their manufacture has been discontinued recently. Attenuated, inactivated, and subunit vaccines against RSV, parainfluenza 3, and *M. pneumoniae* have received considerable investigative effort but have not yet proved to be effective.[114, 170]

In compromised hosts, intramuscular passive immunization with pooled immunoglobulin and varicella-zoster immunoglobulin is an established postexposure measure to prevent the acquisition of measles and varicella pneumonia, respectively. Palivizumab is a "humanized" mouse monoclonal antibody specific for the fusion protein of RSV and is administered intramuscularly.[242] It mostly has replaced RSV-specific intravenous immunoglobulin as a means of preventing RSV lower respiratory tract infection in infants with prematurity or other high-risk conditions.[86, 196] Other products, such as specific Fab immunoglobulin fragments produced by recombinant DNA technology, are being studied.[10]

P. carinii pneumonia can be prevented in pediatric patients with hematologic malignancy or HIV/AIDS by prophylactic administration of TMP-SMX. This medication has become a part of the routine management of these conditions and has reduced the incidence of *P. carinii* infection dramatically.[89, 112, 202] Unless HIV infection reasonably can be excluded by multiple HIV cultures or polymerase chain reaction, seropositive HIV-exposed infants should receive chemoprophylaxis from 4 to 6 weeks of age up to 12 months of age, regardless of their immune status. Seropositive children 1 to 5 years of age should receive prophylaxis if their CD4 counts are less than 500 cells/μL or the CD4 percentage is less than 15. The criterion for prophylaxis in older children and adults is a CD4 count less than 200 cells/μL or a percentage less than 15. The recommended dosage of TMP-SMX is 150 mg/m^2/day of TMP divided into two doses given on 3 successive days each week.[202]

Opportunistic CMV pneumonia, a major hazard in seronegative high-risk premature infants and recipients of allogeneic bone marrow transplants, can be prevented effectively by the exclusive use of CMV-seronegative blood products.[244] In marrow transplant recipients who are seropositive and thus at risk for reactivation disease, prophylactic acyclovir, ganciclovir, and intravenous immunoglobulin have been shown to reduce rates of infection and interstitial pneumonia.[163, 211, 227]

REFERENCES

1. Aherne, W., Bird, T., Court, S. D. M., et al.: Pathological changes in virus infection of the lower respiratory tract in children. J. Clin. Pathol. *23*:7–18, 1970.
2. American Academy of Pediatrics Committee on Drugs. Use of codeine- and dextromethorphan-containing cough syrups in pediatrics. Pediatrics *62*:118–122, 1978.
3. American Academy of Pediatrics Committee on Infectious Diseases. Use of ribavirin in the treatment of respiratory syncytial virus infection. Pediatrics *92*:501–504, 1993.
4. Andiman, W. A., Eastman, R., Martin, K., et al.: Opportunistic lymphoproliferations associated with Epstein-Barr viral DNA in infants and children with AIDS. Lancet *2*:1390–1393, 1985.
5. Andiman, W. A., Jacobson, R. I., and Tucker, G.: Leukocyte-associated viremia with adenovirus type 2 in an infant with lower-respiratory-tract disease. N. Engl. J. Med. *297*:100–101, 1977.
6. Andiman, W. A., McCarthy, P., Markowitz, R. I., et al.: Clinical, virologic, and serologic evidence of Epstein-Barr virus infection in association with childhood pneumonia. J. Pediatr. *99*:880–886, 1981.
7. Angella, J. J., and Connor, J. D.: Neonatal infection caused by adenovirus type 7. J. Pediatr. *72*:474–478, 1968.
8. Ballard, R. A., Drew, W. L., Hufnagle, K. G., et al.: Acquired cytomegalovirus infection in preterm infants. Am. J. Dis. Child. *133*:482–485, 1979.
9. Banks, G., and Fernandez, H.: Clinical use of ribavirin in measles: A summarized review. *In* Smith, R. A., Knight, V., and Smith, J. A. D. (eds.): Clinical Applications of Ribavirin. New York, Academic Press, 1984, pp. 203–209.
10. Barbas, C. F., Crowe, J. E., Cababa, D., et al.: Human monoclonal Fab fragments derived from a combinatorial library bind to respiratory syncytial virus F glycoprotein and neutralize infectivity. Proc. Natl. Acad. Sci. U. S. A. *89*:10164–10168, 1992.
11. Barrett-Connor, E.: Acute pulmonary disease and sickle cell anemia. Am. Rev. Respir. Dis. *104*:159, 1971.
12. Barrett-Connor, E.: The nonvalue of sputum culture in the diagnosis of pneumococcal pneumonia. Am. Rev. Respir. Dis. *103*:845–848, 1971.
13. Bauer, C. R., Elie, K., Spene, L., et al.: Hong Kong influenza in a neonatal unit. J. A. M. A. *223*:1233–1235, 1973.
14. Becroft, D. M. O.: Histopathology of fatal adenovirus infection of the respiratory tract in young children. J. Clin. Pathol. *20*:561–569, 1967.
15. Beem, M., and Saxon, E.: Respiratory-tract colonization and a distinctive pneumonia syndrome in infants infected with *Chlamydia trachomatis*. N. Engl. J. Med. *296*:306–310, 1977.
16. Beem, M., Wright, F. H., Hamre, D., et al.: Association of the chimpanzee coryza agent with acute respiratory disease in children. N. Engl. J. Med. *263*:523–530, 1960.
17. Benyesh-Melnick, M., and Rosenberg, H. S.: The isolation of adenovirus type 7 from a fetal case of pneumonia and disseminated disease. J. Pediatr. *64*:83–87, 1964.
18. Berkovich, S., and Taranko, L.: Acute respiratory illness in the premature nursery associated with respiratory syncytial virus infections. Pediatrics *34*:735–760, 1964.

19. Bertozzi, P., Astedt, B., Zenzius, L., et al.: Depressed bronchoalveolar urokinase activity in patients with adult respiratory distress syndrome. N. Engl. J. Med. *322*:890–897, 1990.
20. Boyer, K. M., and Cherry, J. D.: Pneumonias in children. Curr. Top. Pediatr. *1*:169–182, 1979.
21. Bozzette, S. A., Sattler, F. R., Chin, J., et al.: A controlled trial of early adjunctive treatment with corticosteroids for *Pneumocystis carinii* pneumonia in the acquired immunodeficiency syndrome. N. Engl. J. Med. 323:1451–1457, 1990.
22. Brandt, C. D., Kim, H. W., Arrobio, J. O., et al.: Epidemiology of respiratory syncytial virus infection in Washington, DC. III. Composite analysis of eleven consecutive yearly epidemics. Am. J. Epidemiol. *98*:355–364, 1973.
23. Brandt, C. D., Kim, H. W., Vargosko, A. J., et al.: Infections in 18,000 infants and children in a controlled study of respiratory tract disease. I. Adenovirus pathogenicity in relation to serologic type and illness syndrome. Am. J. Epidemiol. *90*:484–500, 1969.
24. Brocklebank, J. T., Court, S. D. M., McQuillin, J., et al.: Influenza-A infection in children. Lancet *2*:497–500, 1972.
25. Brodie, H. R., and Spencer, L. P.: Respiratory syncytial virus infections in children in Montreal: A retrospective study. Can. Med. Assoc. J. *109*:1199–1201, 1973.
26. Brown, R. S., Nogrady, M. B., Spence, L., et al.: An outbreak of adenovirus type 7 infection in children in Montreal. Can. Med. Assoc. J. *108*:434–439, 1973.
27. Bruhn, F. W., Mokrohisky, S. T., and McIntosh, K.: Apnea associated with respiratory syncytial virus infection in young infants. J. Pediatr. *40*:382–386, 1977.
28. Burton, K., Yogev, R., London, N., et al.: Pulmonary paragonimiasis in Laotian refugee children. Pediatrics *70*:246–248, 1982.
29. Carson, J. L., Collier, A. M., and Hu, S. S.: Acquired ciliary defects in nasal epithelium of children with acute viral upper respiratory infections. N. Engl. J. Med. *312*:463–468, 1985.
30. Cassell, G. H., Waites, K. B., and Crouse, D. T.: Mycoplasmal infections. *In* Remington, J. S., and Klein, J. O. (eds.): Infectious Diseases of the Fetus and Newborn Infant. 4th ed. Philadelphia, W. B. Saunders, 1995, pp. 619–655.
31. Cassell, G. H., Waites, K. B., Crouse, D. T., et al.: Association of *Ureaplasma urealyticum* infection of the lower respiratory tract with chronic lung disease and death in very-low-birthweight infants. Lancet *2*:240–245, 1988.
32. Chanock, R. M., Kapikian, A. Z., Mills, J., et al.: Influence of immunological factors in respiratory syncytial virus disease. Arch. Environ. Health *21*:347–356, 1970.
33. Chanock, R. M., Mufson, M. A., and Johnson, K. M.: Comparative biology and ecology of human virus and mycoplasma respiratory pathogens. Prog. Med. Virol. *7*:208–252, 1965.
34. Chanock, R. M., and Parrott, R. H.: Acute respiratory disease in infancy and childhood: Present understanding and prospects for prevention. Pediatrics *36*:21–39, 1965.
35. Chany, C., Lepine, P., Lelong, M., et al.: Severe and fatal pneumonia in infants and young children associated with adenovirus infections. Am. J. Hyg. *67*:367–378, 1958.
36. Chao, R. K., Fishaut, M., Schwartzman, J. D., et al.: Detection of respiratory syncytial virus in nasal secretions from infants by enzyme-linked immunosorbent assay. J. Infect. Dis. *139*:483–486, 1979.
37. Cherian, T., John, T. J., Simoes, E., et al.: Evaluation of simple clinical signs for the diagnosis of acute lower respiratory tract infection. Lancet *2*:125–128, 1988.
38. Cherry, J. D.: Newer respiratory viruses: Their role in respiratory illnesses of children. Adv. Pediatr. *20*:225–290, 1973.
39. Cherry, J. D., Hurwitz, E. S., and Welliver, R. C.: *Mycoplasma pneumoniae* infections and exanthems. J. Pediatr. *87*:369–373, 1975.
40. Cherry, J. D., and Welliver, R. C.: *Mycoplasma pneumoniae* infections of adults and children. West. J. Med. *125*:47–55, 1976.
41. Christie, D. L., O'Grady, L. R., and Mack, D. V.: Incompetent lower esophageal sphincter and gastroesophageal reflux in recurrent acute pulmonary disease of infancy and childhood. J. Pediatr. *93*:23–27, 1978.
42. Church, N. R., Anas, N. G., Hall, C. B., et al.: Respiratory syncytial virus–related apnea in infants: Demographics and outcome. Am. J. Dis. Child. *138*:247–250, 1984.
43. Claesson, B. A., Trollfors, B., Brolin, I., et al.: Etiology of community-acquired pneumonia in children based on antibody responses to bacterial and viral antigens. Pediatr. Infect. Dis. J. *8*:856–862, 1989.
44. Connor, J. D.: Evidence for an etiologic role of adenoviral infection in pertussis syndrome. N. Engl. J. Med. *283*:390–394, 1970.
45. Conte, P., Heitzman, E. R., and Marakarian, B.: Viral pneumonia: Roentgen pathological correlations. Radiology *95*:267–272, 1970.
46. Courtnoy, I., Lande, A. E., and Turner, R. B.: Accuracy of radiographic differentiation of bacterial from nonbacterial pneumonia. Clin. Pediatr. (Phila) *28*:261–264, 1989.
47. Demers, R. R., Parker, J., Frankel, L. R., et al.: Administration of ribavirin to neonatal and pediatric patients during mechanical ventilation. Respir. Care *31*:1188–1196, 1986.
48. Dennehy, P. H., and McIntosh, K.: Viral pneumonia in childhood. *In* Weinstein, L., and Fields, B. N. (eds.): Seminars in Infectious Disease. Vol 5. Pneumonias. New York, Thieme-Stratton, 1983.
49. Denny, F. W.: The replete pediatrician and the etiology of lower respiratory tract infections. Pediatr. Res. *3*:463–470, 1969.
50. Dingle, J., and Langmuir, A. D.: Epidemiology of acute respiratory disease in military recruits. Am. Rev. Respir. Dis. *97*:1–65, 1968.
51. Downes, J. J., Wood, D. W., Striker, T. W., et al.: Acute respiratory failure in infants with bronchiolitis. Anesthesiology *29*:426–434, 1968.
51a. Drosten, C., Günther, S., Preiser, W., et al.: Identification of a novel coronavirus in patients with severe acute respiratory syndrome. N. Engl. J. Med. *348*:1967–1976, 2003.
52. Dworsky, M., and Stagno, S.: Newer agents causing pneumonitis in early infancy. Pediatr. Infect. Dis. J. *1*:188–195, 1982.
53. Eckert, H. L., Portnoy, B., Salvatore, M. A., et al.: Group B Coxsackie virus infection in infants with acute lower respiratory disease. Pediatrics *39*:526–531, 1967.
54. Eisenstein, B. J.: The polymerase chain reaction: A new method of using molecular genetics for medical diagnosis. N. Engl. J. Med. *322*:178–183, 1990.
55. Emanuel, D., Cunningham, I., Jules-Elysee, K., et al.: Cytomegalovirus pneumonia after bone marrow transplantation successfully treated with the combination of ganciclovir and high-dose intravenous immune globulin. Ann. Intern. Med. *109*:777–782, 1988.
56. Evans, A. S.: Infectious mononucleosis in University of Wisconsin students: Report of a five-year investigation. Am. J. Hyg. *71*:342–362, 1960.
57. Evans, A. S.: Epidemiological concepts and methods. *In* Evans, A. S. (ed.): Viral Infections of Humans: Epidemiology and Control. New York, Plenum Publishing, 1976, pp. 1–32.
58. Feigin, R. D., Shackelford, P. G., Choi, S. C., et al.: Nitroblue tetrazolium dye test as an aid in the differential diagnosis of febrile disorders. J. Pediatr. *78*:230–237, 1971.
59. Feldman, S., Hughes, W. T., and Daniel, C. B.: Varicella in children with cancer: Seventy-seven cases. Pediatrics *56*:388–397, 1975.
60. Feldstein, T. J., Swegarden, J. L., Atwood, G. F., et al.: Ribavirin therapy: Implementation of hospital guidelines and effect on usage and cost of therapy. Pediatrics *46*:14–17, 1995.
61. Fernald, G. W., and Clyde, W. A.: Pulmonary immune mechanisms in *Mycoplasma pneumoniae* disease. *In* Kirkpatrick, C. H., and Reynolds, H. Y. (eds.): Immunologic and Infectious Reactions in the Lung. New York, Marcel Dekker, 1976, pp. 101–130.
62. Fine, N. L., Smith, L. R., and Sheedy, P. F.: Frequency of pleural effusions in mycoplasmal and viral pneumonias. N. Engl. J. Med. *283*:790–793, 1970.
63. Fox, J. P., Brandt, C. D., Wasserman, F. E., et al.: The Virus Watch Program: A continuing surveillance of viral infections in metropolitan New York families. VI. Observations of adenovirus infections, virus excretion patterns, antibody response, efficiency of surveillance, patterns of infection, and relation to illness. Am. J. Epidemiol. *89*:25–50, 1969.
64. Fox, J. P., and Hall, C. E.: Viruses in Families. Surveillance of Families as a Key to Epidemiology of Virus Infections. Littleton, MA, PSG Publishing, 1980.
65. Foy, H. M., Cooney, M. K., Maletzky, A. J., et al.: Incidence and etiology of pneumonia, croup and bronchiolitis in preschool children belonging to a prepaid medical care group over a four-year period. Am. J. Epidemiol. *97*:80–92, 1973.
66. Foy, H. M., Cooney, M. K., McMahon, R., et al.: Viral and mycoplasmal pneumonia in a prepaid medical care group during an eight-year period. Am. J. Epidemiol. *97*:93–102, 1973.
67. Frankel, L. R., Smith, D. W., and Lewiston, N. J.: Bronchoalveolar lavage for diagnosis of pneumonia in the immunocompromised child. Pediatrics *81*:785–788, 1988.
68. Fulginiti, V. A., Eller, J. J., Downie, A. W., et al.: Altered reactivity to measles virus: Atypical measles in children previously immunized with inactivated measles virus vaccines. J. A. M. A. *202*:1075–1080, 1967.
69. Gadomski, A. M., Lichtenstein, R., Horton, L., et al.: Efficacy of albuterol in the management of bronchiolitis. Pediatrics *43*:907–912, 1994.
70. Gagnon, S., Boota, A. M., Fischl, M. A., et al.: Corticosteroids as adjunctive therapy for severe *Pneumocystis carinii* pneumonia in the acquired immunodeficiency syndrome: A double-blind, placebo-controlled trial. N. Engl. J. Med. *323*:1444–1450, 1990.
71. Gajdusek, D. C.: *Pneumocystis carinii:* Etiologic agent of interstitial plasma cell pneumonia of premature and young infants. Pediatrics *19*:543–565, 1957.
72. Gardner, P. S.: How etiologic, pathologic, and clinical diagnoses can be made in a correlated fashion. Pediatr. Res. *11*:254–261, 1977.
73. George, R. B., and Mogabgab, W. J.: Atypical pneumonia in young men with rhinovirus infections. Ann. Intern. Med. *71*:1073–1078, 1969.
74. Gilbert, B. E., Wilson, S. Z., Knight, V., et al.: Ribavirin small-particle aerosol treatment of infections caused by influenza virus strains A/Victoria/7/83 (H1N1) and B/Texas/1/84. Antimicrob. Agents Chemother. *27*:309–313, 1985.
75. Glezen, W. P.: Acute Respiratory Disease Update. Houston, Baylor College of Medicine, 1985.

76. Glezen, W. P., and Denny, F. W.: Epidemiology of acute lower respiratory disease in children. N. Engl. J. Med. *288*:498–505, 1973.
77. Glezen, W. P., and Denny, F. W.: Effect of passive antibody on parainfluenza virus type 3 pneumonia in hamsters. Infect. Immun. *14*:212–216, 1976.
78. Glezen, W. P., Frank, A. L., Taber, L. H., et al.: Parainfluenza virus type 3: Seasonality and risk of infection and reinfection in young children. J. Infect. Dis. *150*:851–857, 1984.
79. Glezen, W. P., Loda, F. A., Clyde, W. A., et al.: Epidemiologic patterns of acute lower respiratory disease of children in a pediatric group practice. J. Pediatr. *78*:397–406, 1971.
80. Glezen, W. P., Loda, F. A., and Denny, F. W.: The parainfluenza viruses. *In* Evans, A. S. (ed.): Viral Infections of Humans: Epidemiology and Control. New York, Plenum Publishing, 1976, pp. 337–349.
81. Glezen, W. P., Paredes, A., and Taber, L. H.: Influenza in children: Relationship to other respiratory agents. J. A. M. A. *243*:1345–1349, 1980.
82. Goodpasture, E. W.: The significance of certain pulmonary lesions in relation to the etiology of influenza. Am. J. Med. Sci. *158*:863–870, 1919.
83. Graham, B., Davis, T., Tang, Y., et al.: Immunoprophylaxis and immunotherapy of respiratory syncytial virus–infected mice with respiratory syncytial virus–specific immune serum. Pediatr. Res. *34*:167–172, 1993.
84. Grayston, J. T., Campbell, L. A., Kuo, C.-C., et al.: A new respiratory tract pathogen: *Chlamydia pneumoniae* strain TWAR. J. Infect. Dis. *161*:618–625, 1990.
85. Grayston, J. T., Kuo, C.-C., Wang, S. P., et al.: A new *Chlamydia psittaci* strain, TWAR, isolated in acute respiratory tract infection. N. Engl. J. Med. *315*:161–168, 1986.
86. Groothius, J. R., Simoes, E. A., Levin, M. J., et al.: Prophylactic administration of respiratory syncytial virus immune globulin to high-risk infants and young children. N. Engl. J. Med. *329*:1524–1530, 1993.
87. Grossman, L. K., Wald, E. R., Nair, P., et al.: Roentgenographic follow-up of acute pneumonia in children. Pediatrics *63*:30–31, 1979.
88. Gruber, W., Wilson, S., Throop, P., et al.: Immunoglobulin administration and ribovirus infection of the cotton rat. Pediatr. Res. *21*:270–274, 1987.
89. Guidelines for prophylaxis against *Pneumocystis carinii* pneumonia for children infected with human immunodeficiency virus. M. M. W. R. Recomm. Rep. *40*(RR-2):1–13, 1991.
90. Habib, D. M., and Perkin, R. M.: Continuous distending pressure and assisted ventilation. *In* Levin, D. L., and Morriss, F. C. (eds.): Essentials of Pediatric Intensive Care. St. Louis, Quality Medical Publishing, 1990, pp. 897–910.
91. Hable, K. A., O'Connell, E. J., and Herrmann, E. C., Jr.: Group B Coxsackieviruses as respiratory viruses. Mayo Clin. Proc. *45*:170–176, 1970.
92. Hall, C. B.: The shedding and spreading of respiratory syncytial virus. Pediatr. Res. *11*:236–239, 1977.
93. Hall, C. B.: Infectious Disease Newsletter. Rochester, NY, University of Rochester School of Medicine, 1985.
94. Hall, C. B., Douglas, R. G., Geiman, J. M., et al.: Nosocomial respiratory syncytial virus infections. N. Engl. J. Med. *293*:1343–1346, 1975.
95. Hall, C. B., Hall, W. J., and Speers, D. M.: Clinical and physiological manifestations of bronchiolitis and pneumonia: Outcome of respiratory syncytial virus. Am. J. Dis. Child. *133*:798–802, 1979.
96. Hall, C. B., McBride, J. T., Gala, L. L., et al.: Ribavirin treatment of respiratory syncytial viral infection in infants with underlying cardiopulmonary disease. J. A. M. A. *254*:3047–3051, 1985.
97. Hall, C. B., McBride, J. T., Walsh, E. E., et al.: Aerosolized ribavirin treatment of infants with respiratory syncytial virus infection: A randomized double-blind study. N. Engl. J. Med. *308*:1443–1447, 1983.
98. Hall, C. B., Powell, K. R., MacDonald, N. E., et al.: Respiratory syncytial viral infection in children with compromised immune function. N. Engl. J. Med. *315*:77–81, 1986.
99. Hammer, J., Numa, A., and Neroth, C. J.: Albuterol responsiveness in infants with respiratory failure caused by respiratory syncytial virus infection. J. Pediatr. 127:485–490, 1995.
100. Hanshaw, J. B., and Dudgeon, J. A.: Viral Diseases of the Fetus and Newborn. Philadelphia, W. B. Saunders, 1978.
101. Harrington, R. D., Hooton, T. M., Hackman, R. C., et al.: An outbreak of respiratory syncytial virus in a bone marrow transplant center. J. Infect. Dis. *165*:987–993, 1992.
102. Harrison, H. R., English, M. G., Lee, C. K., et al.: *Chlamydia trachomatis* infant pneumonitis: Comparison with matched controls and other infant pneumonitis. N. Engl. J. Med. *298*:702–708, 1978.
103. Heiskanen-Kosma, T., Korppi, M., Jokimen, C., et al.: Etiology of childhood pneumonia: Serologic results of a prospective, population-based study. Pediatr. Infect. Dis. J. *17*:986–991, 1998.
104. Heiskanen-Kosma, T., Korppi, M., Laurila, A., et al.: *Chlamydia pneumoniae* is an important cause of community-acquired pneumonia in school-aged children: Serologic results of a prospective, population-based study. Scand. J. Infect. Dis. *31*:255–259, 1999.
105. Henderson, F. W., Clyde, W. A., Collier, A. M., et al.: The etiologic and epidemiologic spectrum of bronchiolitis in pediatric practice. J. Pediatr. *95*:183–190, 1979.
106. Henson, D., and Mufson, M. A.: Myocarditis and pneumonitis with type 21 adenovirus infection: Association with fatal myocarditis and pneumonitis. Am. J. Dis. Child. *121*:334–336, 1971.
107. Herbert, F. A., Mahon, W. A., Wilkinson, D., et al.: Pneumonia in Indian and Eskimo infants and children. Part I. A clinical study. Can. Med. Assoc. J. *96*:257–265, 1967.
108. Herbert, F. A., Wilkinson, D., Burchak, E., et al.: Adenovirus type 3 pneumonia causing lung damage in childhood. Can. Med. Assoc. J. *116*:274–276, 1977.
109. Herrmann, E. C., Jr.: Experiences in laboratory diagnosis of adenovirus infections in routine medical practice. Mayo Clin. Proc. *43*:635–644, 1968.
110. Herrmann, E. C., Jr., and Hable, K. A.: Experiences in laboratory diagnosis of parainfluenza viruses in routine medical practice. Mayo Clin. Proc. *45*:177–188, 1970.
111. Horn, M. E. C., Brain, E., Gregg, I., et al.: Respiratory viral infection in childhood: A survey in general practice, Roehamptom, 1967–1972. J. Hyg. (Camb.) *74*:157–168, 1975.
112. Hughes, W. T.: Five-year absence of *Pneumocystis carinii* pneumonitis in a pediatric oncology unit. J. Infect. Dis. *150*:305–306, 1984.
113. Hughes, W. T., Feldman, S., and Cox, F.: Infectious diseases in children with cancer. Pediatr. Clin. North Am. *21*:583–615, 1974.
114. Institute of Medicine, National Academy of Sciences: New Vaccine Development. Establishing Priorities. Diseases of Importance in the United States. Washington, DC, National Academy Press, 1985.
115. Isaacs, D.: Problems in determining the etiology of community-acquired childhood pneumonia. Pediatr. Infect. Dis. J. *8*:143–148, 1989.
116. Jacobs, J. W., Peacock, D. B., Corner, B. D., et al.: Respiratory syncytial and other viruses associated with respiratory disease in infants. Lancet *1*:871–876, 1971.
117. Jadavji, T., Law, B., Lebel, M. H., et al.: A practical guide for the diagnosis and treatment of pediatric pneumonia. C. M. A. J. *156*(Suppl.):703–711, 1997.
118. Jarvis, W. R., Middleton, P. J.: and Gelfand, E. W.: Significance of viral infections in severe combined immunodeficiency disease. Pediatr. Infect. Dis. J. *2*:187–192, 1983.
119. Jasson, E., Wager, O., Forssell, P., et al.: Epidemic occurrence of adenovirus type 7 infection in Helsinki. Ann. Paediatr. Fenn. *8*:24–34, 1962.
120. Juven, T., Mertsola, J., Waris, M., et al.: Etiology of community-acquired pneumonia in 254 hospitalized children. Pediatr. Infect. Dis. J. *19*:293–298, 2000.
121. Kattan, M., Keens, T. G., LaPierre, J. G., et al.: Pulmonary function abnormalities in symptom-free children after bronchiolitis. Pediatrics *59*:683–688, 1977.
122. Katz, B. Z., Berkman, A. B., and Shapiro, E. D.: Serologic evidence of active Epstein-Barr virus infection in Epstein-Barr virus–associated lymphoproliferative disorders of children with acquired immunodeficiency syndrome. J. Pediatr. *120*:228–232, 1992.
123. Kaye, H. S., Marsh, H. B., and Dowdle, W. R.: Seroepidemiologic survey of coronavirus (strain OC 43) related infections in a children's population. Am. J. Epidemiol. *94*:43–49, 1971.
124. Kim, H. W., Arrobio, J. O., Brandt, C. D., et al.: Epidemiology of respiratory syncytial virus infection in Washington, D.C. I. Importance of the virus in different respiratory tract disease syndromes and temporal distribution of infection. Am. J. Epidemiol. *98*:216–225, 1973.
125. Kim, H. W., Brandt, C. D., Arrobio, J. O., et al.: Influenza A and B virus infection in infants and young children during the years 1957–1976. Am. J. Epidemiol. *109*:464–479, 1979.
126. Kim, K. S., and Gohd, R. S.: Fatal pneumonia caused by adenovirus type 35. Am. J. Dis. Child. *135*:473–475, 1981.
127. Knight, V., Wilson, S. Z., Quarles, J. M., et al.: Ribavirin small-particle aerosol treatment of influenza. Lancet *2*:945–950, 1981.
128. Kohn, J. L., and Koiransky, H.: Successive roentgenograms of the chest of children during measles. Am. J. Dis. Child. *38*:258–270, 1929.
129. Krasinski, K., and Borkowsky, W.: Measles and measles immunity in children infected with human immunodeficiency virus. J. A. M. A. *261*:2512–2516, 1989.
129a. Ksiazek, T. G., Erdman, D., Goldsmith, C.S., et al.: A novel coronavirus associated with severe acute respiratory syndrome. N. Engl. J. Med. *348*:1953–1966, 2003.
130. Lang, W. R., Howden, C. W., Laws, J., et al.: Bronchopneumonia with serious sequelae in children with evidence of adenovirus type 21 infection. B. M. J. *1*:73–79, 1969.
131. Laraya-Cuasay, L. R., Deforest, A., Huff, D., et al.: Chronic pulmonary complications of early influenza virus infection in children. Am. Rev. Respir. Dis. *116*:617–625, 1977.
132. Law, B. J., Wang, E. E., and Stephens, D.: Ribavirin does not reduce hospital stay in patients with respiratory syncytial virus lower respiratory tract infection. Abstract. Pediatr. Res. *37*:110, 1995.
132a. Lee, N., Hui, D. H., Wu, A., et al.: A major outbreak of severe acute respiratory syndrome in Hong Kong. N. Engl. J. Med. *348*:1986–1994, 2003.
133. Leer, J. A., Bloomfield, N. J., Green, J. L., et al.: Corticosteroid treatment in bronchiolitis: A controlled collaborative study in 297 infants and children. Am. J. Dis. Child. *117*:495–503, 1969.

134. Lepow, M. L., Balassanian, N., Emmerich, J., et al.: Interrelationships of viral, mycoplasmal, and bacterial agents in uncomplicated pneumonia. Am. Rev. Respir. Dis. *97*:533–545, 1968.
135. Lerner, A. M., Klein, J. O., Levin, H. S., et al.: Infections due to Coxsackie virus group A, type 9, in Boston, 1959, with special reference to exanthems and pneumonia. N. Engl. J. Med. *263*:1265–1272, 1960.
136. Liebovitz, E., Pollack, H., Moore, T., et al.: Comparison of PCR and standard cytological staining for detection of *Pneumocystis carinii* from respiratory specimens from patients with or at high risk for infection by human immunodeficiency virus. J. Clin. Microbiol. *33*:3004–3007, 1995.
137. Liu, C.: Diagnosis of influenzal infection by means of fluorescent antibody. Am. Rev. Respir. Dis. *83*(Suppl.):130–138, 1960.
138. Loda, F. A., Clyde, W. A., Jr., Glezen, W. P., et al.: Studies on the role of viruses, bacteria, and *M. pneumoniae* as causes of lower respiratory tract infections in children. J. Pediatr. *72*:161–176, 1968.
139. Loda, F. A., Collier, A. M., Glezen, W. P., et al.: Occurrence of *Diplococcus pneumoniae* in the upper respiratory tract of children. J. Pediatr. *87*:1087–1093, 1975.
140. Loda, F. A., Glezen, W. P., and Clyde, W. A., Jr.: Respiratory disease in group daycare. Pediatrics *49*:428–437, 1972.
141. Long, S. S.: Treatment of acute pneumonia in infants and children. Pediatr. Clin. North Am. *30*:297–321, 1983.
142. Lough, M. D., Doershuk, C. F., and Stern, R. C.: Pediatric Respiratory Therapy. 3rd ed. Chicago, Year Book Medical Publishers, 1985.
143. Louria, D. B., Blumenfield, H. L., Ellis, J. T., et al.: Studies on influenza in the pandemic of 1958–59. II. Pulmonary complications of influenza. J. Clin. Invest. *38*:213–265, 1959.
144. Macasaet, F. F., Kidd, P. A., Bolanco, C. R., et al.: The etiology of acute respiratory infections. III. The role of viruses and bacteria. J. Pediatr. *72*:829–839, 1968.
145. MacDonald, N. E., Hall, C. B., Suffin, S. D., et al.: Respiratory syncytial viral infection in infants with congenital heart disease. N. Engl. J. Med. *307*:397–400, 1982.
146. MacPherson, R. I., Cumming, G., and Chernick, V.: Unilateral hyperlucent lung in childhood: A complication of viral pneumonia. J. Can. Assoc. Radiol. *20*:225–231, 1969.
147. Maletzky, A. J., Cooney, M. K., Luce, R., et al.: Epidemiology of viral and mycoplasmal agents associated with childhood lower respiratory illness in a civilian population. J. Pediatr. *78*:407–414, 1971.
148. Markowitz, L. E., Chandler, F. W., Boldan, E. O., et al.: Fatal measles pneumonia without rash in a child with AIDS. J. Infect. Dis. *158*:480–483, 1988.
149. Markowitz, R. I., and Ruchelli, E.: Pneumonia in infants and children: Radiological-pathological correlation. Semin. Roentgenol. *33*:151–162, 1998.
150. Martin, L. D., Rafferty, J. F., Walker, L. K., et al.: Principles of respiratory support and mechanical ventilation. *In* Rogers, M. C. (ed.): Textbook of Pediatric Intensive Care. Baltimore, Williams & Wilkins, 1992, pp. 134–203.
151. McCarthy, P. L., Frank, A. L., Ablow, R. C., et al.: Value of the C-reactive protein test in the differentiation of bacterial and viral pneumonia. J. Pediatr. *92*:454–456, 1978.
152. McCarthy, P. L., Spiesel, S. Z., Stashwick, C. A., et al.: Radiographic findings and etiologic diagnosis in ambulatory childhood pneumonias. Clin. Pediatr. (Phila.) *20*:686–691, 1981.
153. McCarthy, P. L., Tomasso, L., and Dolan, T. F.: Predicting fever responses of children with pneumonia treated with antibiotics. Clin. Pediatr. (Phila.) *19*:753–760, 1980.
154. McClelland, L., Hilleman, M. R., Hamparian, V. V., et al.: Studies of acute respiratory illnesses caused by respiratory syncytial virus. 2. Epidemiology and assessment of importance. N. Engl. J. Med. *264*:1169–1175, 1961.
155. McGowan, J. E., Bratton, L., Klein, J. D., et al.: Bacteremia in febrile children seen in a "walk-in" pediatric clinic. N. Engl. J. Med. *288*:1309–1312, 1973.
156. McIntosh, K.: Community-acquired pneumonia in children. N. Engl. J. Med. *346*:429–437, 2002.
157. McIntosh, K., Chao, R. K., Krause, H. E., et al.: Coronavirus infection in acute lower respiratory tract disease of infants. J. Infect. Dis. *130*:502–507, 1974.
158. McIntosh, K., and Fishaut, J. M.: Immunopathologic mechanisms in lower respiratory tract disease in infants due to respiratory syncytial virus. Prog. Med. Virol. *26*:94–118, 1980.
159. McKinney, R. E., Maha, M. A., Connor, E. M., et al.: A multicenter trial of oral zidovudine in children with advanced human immunodeficiency virus disease. N. Engl. J. Med. *324*:1018–1025, 1991.
160. McNamara, M. J., Phillips, I. A., and Williams, O. B.: Viral and *Mycoplasma pneumoniae* infections in exacerbations of chronic lung disease. Am. Rev. Respir. Dis. *100*:19–24, 1969.
161. Meert, K. L., Sarnaik, A. P., Gelmino, M. J., et al.: Aerosolized ribavirin in mechanically ventilated children with respiratory syncytial virus lower respiratory tract disease: A prospective, double-blind, randomized trial. Crit. Care Med. *22*:566–572, 1994.
162. Menon, K., Sutcliffe, T., and Klassen, T. P.: A randomized trial comparing the efficacy of epinephrine with salbutamol in the treatment of acute bronchiolitis. J. Pediatr. *126*:1004–1007, 1995.
163. Meyers, J. D., Reed, E. C., Shepp, D. H., et al.: Acyclovir for prevention of cytomegalovirus infection and disease after allogeneic marrow transplantation. N. Engl. J. Med. *318*:70–75, 1988.
164. Mimica, L., Donoso, E., Howard, J. E., et al.: Lung puncture in the etiological diagnosis of pneumonia. Am. J. Dis. Child. *122*:278–282, 1971.
165. Minor, T. E., Dick, E. C., DeMeo, A. N., et al.: Viruses as precipitants of asthmatic attacks in children. J. A. M. A. *227*:292–298, 1974.
166. Mintz, L., Ballard, R. A., Sniderman, S. H., et al.: Nosocomial respiratory syncytial virus infections in an intensive care nursery: Rapid diagnosis by direct immunofluorescence. Pediatrics *64*:149–153, 1979.
167. Moler, F. W., Steinhart, C. M., Ohmit, S. E., et al.: Effectiveness of ribavirin in otherwise well infants with respiratory syncytial virus–associated respiratory failure. J. Pediatr. *128*:422–428, 1996.
168. Morrell, R. E., Marks, M. I., Champlin, R., et al.: An outbreak of severe pneumonia due to respiratory syncytial virus in isolated Arctic populations. Am. J. Epidemiol. *101*:231–237, 1975.
169. Mufson, M. A., Krause, H. E., Mocega, H. E., et al.: Viruses, *Mycoplasma pneumoniae,* and bacteria associated with lower respiratory tract disease among infants. Am. J. Epidemiol. *91*:912–202, 1970.
170. Murphy, B. R., Hall, S. L., Kulkarni, A. B., et al.: An update on approaches to the development of respiratory syncytial virus and parainfluenza virus type 3 vaccines. Virus Res. *32*:13–36, 1994.
171. Murphy, S., and Florman, A. L.: Lung diseases against infection: A clinical correlation. Pediatrics *72*:1–15, 1983.
172. Murphy, T. F., Henderson, F. W., Clyde, W. A., Jr., et al.: Pneumonia: An eleven-year study in a pediatric practice. Am. J. Epidemiol. *113*:12–21, 1981.
173. Murray, J. F.: The ketchup-bottle method. N. Engl. J. Med. *300*:1155–1157, 1979.
174. Nahmias, A. J., Griffith, D., and Snitzer, J.: Fatal pneumonia associated with adenovirus type 7. Am. J. Dis. Child. *114*:36–41, 1967.
175. Nelson, K. E., Gavitt, F., Batt, M. D., et al.: The role of adenoviruses in the pertussis syndrome. J. Pediatr. *86*:335–341, 1975.
176. Nichol, K. P., and Cherry, J. D.: Bacterial-viral interrelationships in respiratory infections of children. N. Engl. J. Med. *277*:667–672, 1967.
177. Nissen, M. D., Siebert, D. J., Mackay, I. M., et al.: Evidence of human metapneumovirus in Australian children. Med. J. Aust. *176*:188, 2002.
178. Nohynek, H., Valkeila, E., Leinonen, M., et al.: Erythrocyte sedimentation rate, white blood cell count and serum C-reactive protein in assessing etiologic diagnosis of acute lower respiratory infection in children. Pediatr. Infect. Dis. J. *14*:484–490, 1995.
179. Olson, L. C., Miller, G., and Hanshaw, J. B.: Acute infectious lymphocytosis presenting as a pertussis-like illness: Its association with adenovirus type 12. Lancet *1*:200–201, 1964.
180. Orenstein, D. M., Boat, T. F., Stern, R. C., et al.: The effect of early diagnosis and treatment in cystic fibrosis. Am. J. Dis. Child. *131*:973–975, 1977.
181. Osborne, D.: Radiologic appearance of viral disease of the lower respiratory tract in infants and children. A. J. R. Am. J. Roentgenol. *130*:29–33, 1978.
182. Paisley, J. W., Bruhn, F. W., Lauer, B. A., et al.: Type A_2 influenza viral infections in children. Am. J. Dis. Child. *132*:34–36, 1978.
183. Paisley, J. W., Lauer, B. A., McIntosh, K., et al.: Pathogens associated with acute lower respiratory tract infection in young children. Pediatr. Infect. Dis. J. *3*:14–19, 1984.
184. Parks, C. R.: Mist therapy: Rationale and practice. J. Pediatr. *76*:305–313, 1970.
185. Parrott, R. H.: Viral respiratory tract illness in children. Bull. N. Y. Acad. Med. *39*:629–648, 1963.
186. Parrott, R. H., Kim, H. W., Vargosko, A. J., et al.: Serious respiratory tract illness as a result of Asian influenza and influenza B infections in children. J. Pediatr. *61*:205–213, 1962.
187. Parrott, R. H., Vargosko, A., Luckey, A., et al.: Clinical features of infection with hemadsorption viruses. N. Engl. J. Med. *260*:731–738, 1959.
188. Person, D. A., and Herrmann, E. C., Jr.: Experiences in laboratory diagnosis of rhinovirus infections in routine medical practice. Mayo Clin. Proc. *45*:517–526, 1970.
189. Pifer, L. L: *Pneumocystis carinii:* A diagnostic dilemma. Pediatr. Infect. Dis. J. *2*:177–183, 1983.
190. Pifer, L. L., Hughes, W. J., Stagno, S., et al.: *Pneumocystis carinii* infection: Evidence for high prevalence in normal and immunosuppressed children. Pediatrics *61*:35–41, 1978.
191. Pinkerton, H., and Carroll, S.: Fatal adenovirus pneumonia in infants: Correlation of histologic and electron microscopic observations. Am. J. Pathol. *65*:543–548, 1971.
192. Pizzo, P.: Infectious complications in the child with cancer. J. Pediatr. *98*:341–354, 513–523, 1981.
193. Poncz, M., Kane, E., and Gill, F. M.: Acute chest syndrome in sickle cell disease: Etiology and clinical correlates. J. Pediatr. *107*:861–866, 1985.
194. Portnoy, B., Hanes, B., Salvatore, M. A., et al.: The peripheral white blood count in respirovirus infection. J. Pediatr. *68*:181–188, 1966.

194a. Poutanen, S. M., Low, D. E., Henry, B., et al.: Identification of severe acute respiratory syndrome in Canada. N. Engl. J. Med. *348*:1995–2005, 2003.
195. Prevention and control of influenza: Recommendations of the Immunization Practices Advisory Committee (ACIP). M. M. W. R. Recomm. Rep. *39*(RR-7):1–15, 1990.
196. Prevention of respiratory syncytial virus infections: Indications for the use of palivizumab and update on the use of RSV-IGIV. American Academy of Pediatrics Committee on Infectious Diseases and Committee on Fetus and Newborn. Pediatrics *102*:1211–1216, 1998.
197. Public health considerations of infectious diseases in child day care centers. The Child Day Care Infectious Disease Study Group. J. Pediatr. *105*:683–701, 1984.
198. Purtilo, D. T., Sakamoto, F., Barnabei, V., et al.: Epstein-Barr virus induced diseases in boys with X-linked lymphoproliferative syndrome. Am. J. Med. *73*:49–56, 1982.
199. Reassessment of the indications for ribavirin therapy in respiratory syncytial virus infection. American Academy of Pediatrics Committee on Infectious Diseases. Pediatrics *97*:137–140, 1996.
200. Reijowen, T., Korppi, M., Pitkakangas, S., et al.: The clinical efficacy of nebulized racemic epinephrine and albuterol in acute bronchiolitis. Arch. Pediatr. Adolesc. Med. *149*:686–692, 1995.
201. Reilly, C. M., Hoch, S. M., Stokes, J., Jr., et al.: Clinical and laboratory findings in cases of respiratory illness caused by coryzaviruses. Ann. Intern. Med. *57*:515–525, 1962.
202. 1995 Revised guidelines for prophylaxis against *Pneumocystis carinii* pneumonia for children infected with or perinatally exposed to human immunodeficiency virus. National Pediatric and Family HIV Resource Center and National Center for Infectious Diseases, Centers for Disease Control and Prevention. M. M. W. R. Recomm. Rep. *44*(RR-4):1–11, 1995.
203. Rice, R. P., and Loda, F. A.: A roentgenographic analysis of respiratory syncytial virus pneumonia in infants. Radiology *87*:1021–1027, 1966.
204. Ross, C. A., Stott, E. J., McMichael, S., et al.: Problems of laboratory diagnosis of respiratory syncytial virus infection in childhood. Arch. Virusforsch. *14*:553–562, 1964.
205. Royall, J. A., and Levin, D. L.: Adult respiratory distress syndrome in pediatric patients. I. Clinical aspects, pathophysiology, pathology, and mechanisms of lung injury. J. Pediatr. *112*:169–180, 1988.
206. Royall, J., and Levin, D. L.: Adult respiratory distress syndrome in pediatric patients. II. Management. J. Pediatr. *112*:335–347, 1988.
207. Rubinstein, A., Morecki, R., Silverman, B., et al.: Pulmonary disease in children with acquired immune deficiency syndrome and AIDS-related complex. J. Pediatr. *108*:498–503, 1986.
208. Rusconi, F., Rancilio, L., Assael, B. M., et al.: Counter immunoelectrophoresis and latex particle agglutination in the etiologic diagnosis of presumed bacterial pneumonia in pediatric patients. Pediatr. Infect. Dis. J. *7*:781–785, 1988.
209. Saikku, P., Ruutu, P., Leinonen, M., et al.: Acute lower-respiratory-tract infection associated with chlamydial TWAR antibody in Filipino children. J. Infect. Dis. *158*:1095–1097, 1988.
210. Sanchez, I., DeKoster, J., Powell, R. E., et al.: Effect of racemic epinephrine and salbutamol on clinical score and pulmonary mechanics in infants with bronchiolitis. J. Pediatr. *122*:145–151, 1993.
211. Schmidt, G. M., Horak, D. A., Niland, J. C., et al.: A randomized, controlled trial of prophylactic ganciclovir for cytomegalovirus pulmonary infections in recipients of allogeneic bone marrow transplants. N. Engl. J. Med. *324*:1005–1011, 1991.
212. Schmidt, J. P., Metcalf, T. G., and Miltenberger, F. W.: An epidemic of Asian influenza in children at Ladd Air Force Base, Alaska, 1960. J. Pediatr. *61*:214–220, 1962.
213. Schuh, S., Canny, G., Reisman, J. J., et al.: Nebulized albuterol in acute bronchiolitis. J. Pediatr. *117*:633–637, 1990.
214. Siegel, M. M., Walter, T. K., and Ablin, A. R.: Measles pneumonia in childhood leukemia. Pediatrics *60*:38–40, 1977.
215. Siegel, S., Johnston, S., and Adair, S.: Isolation of measles virus in primary rhesus monkey cells from a child with acute interstitial pneumonia who cytologically had giant-cell pneumonia without a rash. Am. J. Clin. Pathol. *94*:464–469, 1990.
216. Siegel, W., Spencer, F. J., Smith, D. J., et al.: Two new variants of infection with Coxsackie virus group B, type 5, in young children: A syndrome of lymphadenopathy, pharyngitis and hepatomegaly or splenomegaly, or both, and one of pneumonia. N. Engl. J. Med. *268*: 1210–1216, 1963.
217. Simonds, R. J., Lindegren, M. L., Thomas, P., et al.: Prophylaxis against *Pneumocystis carinii* pneumonia among children with perinatally acquired human immunodeficiency virus infection in the United States. N. Engl. J. Med. *332*:786–790, 1995.
218. Simpson, W., Hacking, P. M., Court, S. D. M., et al.: The radiological findings in respiratory syncytial virus infection in children. II. The correlation of radiological categories with clinical and virological findings. Pediatr. Radiol. *2*:155–160, 1974.
219. Smith, D. W., Frankel, L. R., Mathers, L. H., et al.: A controlled trial of aerosolized ribavirin in infants receiving mechanical ventilation for severe respiratory syncytial virus infection. N. Engl. J. Med. *325*:24–29, 1991.
220. Smith, W., Andrewes, C. H., and Laidlaw, P. P.: A virus isolated from influenza patients. Lancet *2*:66–68, 1933.
221. Spence, L., and Barratt, N.: Respiratory syncytial virus associated with acute respiratory infections in Trinidadian patients. Am. J. Epidemiol. *88*:257–266, 1968.
222. Springer, C., Bar-Yishay, E., Uwayyad, K., et al.: Corticosteroids do not affect the clinical or physiological status of infants with bronchiolitis. Pediatr. Pulmonol. *9*:181–185, 1990.
223. Stagno, S., Brasfield, D. M., Brown, M. B., et al.: Infant pneumonitis associated with cytomegalovirus, *Chlamydia, Pneumocystis* and *Ureaplasma*: A prospective study. Pediatrics *68*:322–329, 1981.
224. Stagno, S., Pifer, L. L., Hughes, W. T., et al.: *Pneumocystis carinii* pneumonitis in young immunocompetent infants. Pediatrics *66*:56–62, 1980.
225. Steen-Johnsen, J., Orstavik, I., and Attramadal, A.: Severe illnesses due to adenovirus type 7 in children. Acta Paediatr. Scand. *58*:157–163, 1969.
226. Stott, E. J., Eadie, M. B., and Grist, N. R.: Rhinovirus infections of children in hospital: Isolation of three, possibly new rhinovirus serotypes. Am. J. Epidemiol. *90*:45–52, 1969.
227. Sullivan, K. M., Kopecky, K. J., and Jocom, J.: Immunomodulatory and antimicrobial efficacy of intravenous immunoglobulin in bone marrow transplantation. N. Engl. J. Med. *323*:705–712, 1990.
228. Suto, T., Yano, N., Ikeda, M., et al.: Respiratory syncytial virus infection and its serologic epidemiology. Am. J. Epidemiol. *82*:211–224, 1965.
229. Turner, R. B., Lande, A. E., Chase, P., et al.: Pneumonia in pediatric outpatients: Cause and clinical manifestations. J. Pediatr. *111*:194–200, 1987.
230. Update: Hantavirus pulmonary syndrome—United States, 1999. M. M. W. R. Morb. Mortal. Wkly. Rep. *48*(24):521–525, 1999.
231. van den Hoogen, B. G., de Jong, J. C., Groen, J., et al.: A newly discovered human pneumovirus isolated from young children with respiratory disease. Nat. Med. *7*:719–724, 2001.
232. Wang, E. E., Milner, R., Allen, U., et al.: Bronchodilators for treatment of mild bronchiolitis: A factorial randomized trial. Arch. Dis. Child. *67*:289–293, 1992.
233. Wang, E. E. L., Prober, C. G., Manson, B., et al.: Association of respiratory viral infections with pulmonary deterioration in patients with cystic fibrosis. N. Engl. J. Med. *311*:1653–1658, 1984.
234. Welliver, R. C., Wong, D. T., Sun, M., et al.: The development of respiratory syncytial virus–specific IgE and the release of histamine in nasopharyngeal secretions after infection. N. Engl. J. Med. *305*:841–846, 1981.
235. Wheeler, J. G., Wofford, J., and Turner, R. B.: Historical cohort evaluation of ribavirin efficacy in respiratory syncytial virus infection. Pediatr. Infect. Dis. J. *12*:209–213, 1993.
236. Winston, D. J., Gale, R. P., Meyer, D. V., et al.: Infectious complications of human bone marrow transplantation. Medicine (Baltimore) *58*:1–31, 1979.
237. Winternitz, M. C., Wason, I. M., and McNamara, F. P.: The Pathology of Influenza. New Haven, CT, Yale University Press, 1920.
238. Wohl, M. E. B., and Mead, J.: Age as a factor in respiratory disease. *In* Chernick, V., and Kendig, E. L. (eds.): Disorders of the Respiratory Tract in Children. Philadelphia, W. B. Saunders, 1990, pp. 175–182.
239. Wolff, L. J., Bartlett, M. S., Baehner, R. L., et al.: The causes of interstitial pneumonitis in immunocompromised children: An aggressive systematic approach to diagnosis. Pediatrics *60*:41–45, 1977.
240. Wright, H. T., Jr., Beckwith, J. B., and Gwinn, J. L.: A fatal case of inclusion body pneumonia in an infant infected with adenovirus type 3. J. Pediatr. *64*:528–533, 1964.
241. Wubbel, L., Muniz, L., Ahmed, A., et al.: Etiology and treatment of community-acquired pneumonia in ambulatory children. Pediatr. Infect. Dis. J. *18*:98–104, 1999.
242. Wyde, P. R., Moore, D. K., Hepburn, T., et al.: Evaluation of the protective efficacy of reshaped human monoclonal antibody RSHZ19 against respiratory syncytial virus in cotton rats. Pediatr. Res. *38*: 543–550, 1995.
243. Yeager, A. S.: Transfusion-acquired cytomegalovirus infection in newborn infants. Am. J. Dis. Child. *128*:478–483, 1974.
244. Yeager, A. S., Grumet, F. C., Hafleigh, E. G., et al.: Prevention of transfusion-acquired cytomegalovirus infections in newborn infants. J. Pediatr. *98*:281–287, 1981.
245. Zinserling, A.: Peculiarities of lesions in viral and *Mycoplasma* infections of the respiratory tract. Virchows Arch. Pathol. Anat. *356*:259–273, 1972.

CHAPTER 27

Bacterial Pneumonias

JEROME O. KLEIN

Bacterial pneumonia is an inflammation of the lung caused by a bacterial pathogen. The pneumonias may be classified in anatomic terms, such as lobar pneumonia, bronchopneumonia, and interstitial pneumonia; however, this disease usually is categorized by the etiologic agent, as in pneumococcal or staphylococcal pneumonia.

History

Pneumonia has been a frequent and serious human illness throughout recorded history. Histologic examination of Egyptian mummies (1250 to 1000 BC) revealed hepatization of the lungs compatible with acute pneumococcal pneumonia. The disease was well known to the Greeks and Romans, and the symptoms and management (including a drainage procedure for empyema) were described by Hippocrates. Laennec described the pathologic changes and physical signs of pneumonia and pleurisy in 1819, and Rokitansky distinguished lobar pneumonia from bronchopneumonia in 1842.

In 1881, Pasteur in France and Sternberg in the United States independently isolated, cultured, and described the pneumococcus. Each used inoculation of rabbits with human saliva. Pasteur used saliva from a child who had died of clinical rabies, whereas Sternberg used material from a normal subject. A fatal septicemia resulted in the rabbits, and the organisms were isolated from their blood. In 1882, Friedländer described the pneumococcus in pathologic sections of lung and pleura and in fluid obtained by lung puncture from living patients with pneumonia. In the same laboratory, Christian Gram exposed the sections to a sequence of dyes: aniline–gentian violet, a weak solution of iodine, ethanol, and Bismarck brown. Pairs of elongated cocci retained the dark aniline–gentian violet dye. The organism was referred to as *pneumococcus* by Fraenkel in 1886 because of its role as a cause of pulmonary infection.

Early methods of treating pneumonia included bloodletting; leeching; inhalation of chloroform; subcutaneous injection of gold, silver, and platinum solutions; and oral administration of mercury, quinine, and digitalis. The investigations of the pneumococcus in the late 19th century led to the use in 1891 of small subcutaneous doses of rabbit serum for treatment of patients with pneumonia. These treatments usually failed, but after the many antigenically separable types of the pneumococcus were recognized, specific antisera were prepared. These materials provided prompt and striking symptomatic improvement and a marked reduction in the fatality rate for pneumococcal pneumonia. Problems arose because of hypersensitivity reactions to the animal serums and the difficulty of making type-specific diagnoses. Responses to these problems included partial elimination of some of the animal protein and adaptation of the Neufeld technique for typing of pneumococci in sputum and body fluids. Use of rabbit antisera resulted in a significant increase in survival of patients with pneumonia caused by *Haemophilus influenzae*, and antistreptococcal horse serum or human serum obtained from patients convalescing from scarlet fever was used with success in patients with streptococcal pneumonia. Serotherapy was discarded after the introduction of the sulfonamides and penicillin.

Soon after the introduction of the sulfonamides for clinical use in 1935, sulfapyridine was identified as the most potent of the compounds for treatment of pneumococcal disease. By 1943, however, sulfonamide-resistant strains were reported.[75] In 1941, Abraham and colleagues[3] and, in 1943, Keefer and colleagues[42] reported the efficacy of penicillin in treatment of life-threatening infections caused by gram-positive cocci, including *Streptococcus pneumoniae*. Penicillin-resistant pneumococci were identified in epidemic form in South Africa in the 1970s and since have been identified throughout the world.

The approval of a heptavalent conjugate polysaccharide vaccine (Prevnar, Wyeth-Lederle Vaccines) by the U.S. Food and Drug Administration (FDA) in February 2000 was the culmination of more than a century of efforts to provide protection for infants, the age group with the highest attack rates for pneumococcal diseases. Whole-cell vaccines had been investigated at the turn of the century and were administered to more than 1 million individuals without serious adverse events but with uncertain benefit. The importance of capsular polysaccharides to provide serotype-specific antigens was described in the 1930s, and a quadrivalent capsular polysaccharide pneumococcal vaccine was successful in reducing serotype-specific pneumonia in military recruits.[47] The results of the military trial led to licensure of a hexavalent capsular polysaccharide vaccine for general use after World War II. However, the introduction of penicillin and other potent antimicrobials focused physicians' attention on treatment rather than prevention, and use of the vaccine lagged. As a result of limited use, the first polysaccharide vaccines were withdrawn in the 1950s.

A 14-valent pneumococcal polysaccharide vaccine was introduced in the United States in 1977, and a 23-valent vaccine was introduced in 1983. Most of the polysaccharides were poor immunogens for children younger than 2 years of age, and the vaccines were used only in children who were 2 years of age or older and at risk for contracting invasive pneumococcal infections (e.g., children with sickle-cell disease, functional asplenia, or nephrosis). In October 1990, a conjugate polysaccharide vaccine for *H. influenzae* type b was approved by the FDA. Use of the vaccine has led to a significant decrease in the incidence of invasive disease, including pneumonia caused by *H. influenzae* type b. Similar technology was used to produce a pneumococcal conjugate vaccine. Approval by the FDA in 2000 resulted in recommendations for universal immunization in infants and selected children 2 to 5 years of age. By the spring of 2001, more than 14 million doses of the pneumococcal conjugate vaccine had been distributed.

Further information about early studies of the pneumococcus and bacterial pneumonias is provided in two reference works of great value that were reprinted in 1979 by the Harvard University Press: *The Biology of the Pneumococcus* by Benjamin White and *Pneumonia* by Roderick Heffron.

These works first were published in 1938 and 1939, respectively, by the Commonwealth Fund, New York. Watson and colleagues[82] wrote a brief history of the pneumococcus, highlighting landmarks in infectious disease discovery, including the development of Gram stain, the role of the capsule in resistance to phagocytosis, use of polysaccharides as vaccines, and evidence that DNA encodes genetic information. Symposia proceedings have focused on the pneumococcus,[64] polysaccharide pneumococcal vaccines,[41] *H. influenzae*,[23] and lower respiratory tract infections in children in developing countries.[9, 27]

Microbiology

Because of the difficulty of documenting the microbiology of pneumonia in infants and young children, accurate data concerning the incidence and specific agents of bacterial pneumonia in children are lacking. Austrian[7] estimates that bacteria are responsible for one tenth to one third of all cases of acute pneumonias. A presumptive diagnosis of bacterial or mixed bacterial and viral infection based on antigen detection and antibody assays was made in 45 percent of Finnish children who were hospitalized for lower respiratory tract infections.[55] Bacteriologic findings based on results of lung punctures from 1069 children in developing countries identified *S. pneumoniae*, *H. influenzae*, and *Staphylococcus aureus* as the leading pathogens.[68]

Now, as in the past, *S. pneumoniae* is the leading bacterial cause of pneumonia in all age groups except the newborn infant. *H. influenzae* type b was an important cause of pneumonia in young infants until the introduction of the conjugate polysaccharide vaccine in October 1990. In areas with high rates of immunization, pneumonia and invasive disease caused by *H. influenzae* now are uncommon. Other species of bacteria are of importance in special groups: group B *Streptococcus, S. aureus*, and some gram-negative enteric bacilli are responsible for pneumonia in the newborn infant; group A *Streptococcus* may cause pneumonia in children with viral infections, particularly measles, chickenpox, and influenza; pneumonia caused by *S. aureus* and gram-negative enteric bacilli is a concern in children with malignancy or those who have altered host defense mechanisms. Anaerobic bacteria play significant roles in aspiration pneumonia and lung abscess. Only a few cases of pneumonia caused by *Legionella pneumophila* have been reported in children. Other species of bacteria responsible for occasional cases of pneumonia include *Neisseria meningitidis*, *Bordetella pertussis*, *Bartonella henselae*,[1] *Bacillus anthracis*, *Salmonella typhosa*, *Francisella tularensis,* and leptospirosis (associated with pulmonary hemorrhage).[85]

STREPTOCOCCUS PNEUMONIAE

Although approximately 90 immunologically distinct types of *S. pneumoniae* have been identified on the basis of capsular polysaccharide antigens, relatively few types are responsible for most disease in children. Types 1, 3, 6, 7, 14, 18, 19, and 23 are the types most frequently implicated in pneumonia in children; all but 1 and 3 are included in the heptavalent pneumococcal conjugate polysaccharide vaccine.

The spectrum of lower respiratory tract illness caused by *S. pneumoniae* ranges from a mild to moderate disease that can be managed without hospitalization to a severe and life-threatening disease that may be complicated by empyema or extrapulmonary manifestations, including meningitis. The usual case has a sudden onset, lobar involvement, abrupt termination after appropriate chemotherapy is instituted, and rapid restoration of the involved area of the lung to normal. Although the classic pattern of pneumococcal pneumonia has a lobar distribution, bronchopneumonia and interstitial pneumonia are frequent occurrences.

Multidrug-resistant strains of pneumococci were reported from South Africa[5] in 1977. Some of the strains were highly resistant to penicillin G, requiring more than 4 μg/mL for inhibition, and were resistant to other drugs. As of September 2001, multidrug-resistance included β-lactam drugs, tetracyclines, chloramphenicol, macrolides, clindamycin, trimethoprim-sulfamethoxazole, and other sulfonamides. Resistance of pneumococci to quinolones rarely occurs, and no vancomycin-resistant strains of pneumococci have been reported. The rate of resistant pneumococci varies in different countries. Incidence is highest in the Far East, with Korea, Taiwan, and Thailand reporting resistance rates in excess of 80 percent. Spain and France have the highest rates of pneumococcal resistance in Europe (30%–40%), whereas The Netherlands and Germany have resistance rates below 5 percent.

Resistance of *S. pneumoniae* to penicillin is caused by alterations of penicillin-binding proteins. Penicillin resistance is defined by the minimal inhibitory concentrations (MIC) of pneumococci: less than 0.1 μg/mL = susceptibility; 0.1 μg/mL or higher = nonsusceptibility; among nonsusceptible strains, 0.1 to 1.0 μg/mL = intermediate status; and 2 μg/mL or greater = high-level resistance. No clinical features distinguish infection caused by a resistant pneumococcal strain, nor does virulence of infection appear to be increased.

Surveys of susceptibilities of *S. pneumoniae* in the United States show steadily increasing rates of resistance throughout the country.[31] Prevalence varies by region, with rates highest in the Southeast and lowest in the Northeast and Pacific regions. These regional differences are unexplained. Results of surveys of antimicrobial resistance of pneumococcal strains are published frequently; a source of current information is available on the Centers for Disease Control and Prevention (CDC) web site (www.cdc.gov). A report[25] of antimicrobial resistance among clinical isolates of *S. pneumoniae* in the United States during 1999 to 2000 revealed 34 percent were nonsusceptible to penicillin, including 21.5 percent with high-level resistance; MICs to all β-lactam antimicrobials increased as penicillin MICs increased. Resistance rates among non–β-lactam agents were 25 percent for macrolides, 9 percent for clindamycin, and 30 percent for trimethoprim-sulfamethoxazole. Resistance to vancomycin was not detected. The management issues raised by the appearance of resistant pneumococci are discussed in the section on chemotherapy for specific pathogens.

HAEMOPHILUS INFLUENZAE

H. influenzae type b accounts for most cases of pneumonia caused by this species. Pneumonia caused by *H. influenzae* types a, c, or d is reported rarely, but in a study of serotypes isolated from children with pneumonia in developing countries, types a, c, d, e, or f were responsible for 10 percent of cases.[69] Nontypeable strains are responsible for an uncertain number of cases of pneumonia and are isolated from patients with chronic bronchitis, bronchiectasis, and cystic fibrosis who have acute exacerbations of disease.

In developing countries, nontypeable strains of *H. influenzae* are important causes of pneumonia. The nontypeable strains gain access to the lung through spread from the upper respiratory tract but are less likely than are type b strains to invade the bloodstream. The diagnosis of nontypeable *H. influenzae* pneumonia in the living child is made only by lung aspiration or blood culture.[69] Of 32 isolates of *H. influenzae* obtained from blood or lung puncture of children with pneumonia in Papua New Guinea, 18 were nontypeable, 8 were types other than b, and 6 were b; all 6 patients with type b obtained from culture of the lung aspirate also were bacteremic. Only 4 of 18 patients with nontypeable *H. influenzae* in the lung puncture were bacteremic.[70] Of 105 isolates of *Haemophilus* spp. from cultures of blood from children with lower respiratory tract infection in Pakistan, 10 were *Haemophilus parainfluenzae*, 61 were *H. influenzae* type b, and 34 were nontypeable.[83] Similar data were reported in patients with lobar pneumonia in the Gambia.[80] Nontypeable *H. influenzae* is unlikely to be diagnosed as the cause of pneumonia if microbiologic diagnosis relies on cultures of blood alone. These data also suggest that pneumonia caused by nontypeable *H. influenzae* probably is underdiagnosed in developed and developing countries.

The clinical presentation of pneumonia caused by *H. influenzae* is indistinguishable from that caused by *S. pneumoniae* and includes mild, moderate, and severe disease. In a series of cases in children seen at the Boston City Hospital, 17 children with pneumonia and bacteremia caused by *H. influenzae* type b were identified in a 5-year period; only 4 of the children were judged to be sufficiently ill for admission to a hospital.[49] All of 13 children with mild to moderate pneumonia and bacteremia were treated successfully as outpatients. The relatively mild course of pneumonia in these patients contrasts with findings of other investigators who based their reports on the records of children admitted to the hospital.[6, 18, 39, 62] A report of 65 children with *H. influenzae* pneumonia hospitalized at Parkland Memorial Hospital in Dallas during the 14-year period beginning July 1964 included 24 children with pleural effusion, 7 with pneumothorax, and 1 who developed pneumatoceles; 10 children had associated meningitis, and 3 had purulent pericarditis.[32] Type b was the pathogen cultured most frequently from empyema fluids in children receiving care in Bethesda during the period 1974 to 1987.[18]

Beginning in the 1970s, β-lactamase–producing strains of nontypeable and type b *H. influenzae* were reported throughout the United States.[81] The enzyme cleaves the β-lactam ring of susceptible penicillins, rendering the antibiotic inactive against the enzyme-producing strain. In the United States, 33.5 percent and 41.6 percent of strains of *H. influenzae* in two 1997 surveys were β-lactamase–positive.[38, 74] Strains of *H. influenzae* that were β-lactamase–negative but resistant to amoxicillin and amoxicillin-clavulanate also have been identified. A survey in the United States in 1994 and 1995[24] identified 38.9 percent of *H. influenzae* resistant to amoxicillin, including 4.5 percent of strains resistant to amoxicillin-clavulanate (presumably resistant on the basis of a mechanism other than production of β-lactamase).

STAPHYLOCOCCUS AUREUS

Pneumonia and other serious infections caused by *S. aureus* are of particular concern in newborn infants, patients with altered host defenses, and patients with prior viral respiratory infection (e.g., influenza). In the United States and western Europe, the most severe problem with staphylococcal disease in newborn infants occurred in the 1950s and ended around 1965. The cyclic appearance and disappearance of virulent strains of *S. aureus* has no satisfactory explanation. The phage type 80/81, which was so devastating in the 1950s, no longer is a major problem in the United States or Europe. Nevertheless, rare cases of fatal and rapidly progressive staphylococcal pneumonia still occur.[58]

In older children, staphylococcal pneumonia may not be differentiated clinically or radiologically from other bacterial pneumonias. In young infants, the course usually is severe; the onset is abrupt, with tachypnea, significant dyspnea, and restlessness. Progression of disease is rapid, and empyema, abscesses, and pneumatoceles are common findings. Although pneumatoceles are associated with staphylococcal pneumonia, they also may be seen in children with pneumonia caused by *S. pneumoniae*, group A *Streptococcus*, and *H. influenzae*. Pneumatoceles may persist for many months but are not a significant cause of morbidity, and they usually require no specific therapy.

GROUP B *STREPTOCOCCUS*

Early-onset disease in the newborn infant caused by group B *Streptococcus* presents as a multisystem illness during the first week of life and frequently is characterized by pneumonia, the clinical and radiologic pattern of which simulates respiratory distress syndrome.[2] The pattern of group B *Streptococcus* on chest radiograph includes diffuse pulmonary granularity and air bronchograms, similar to the pattern seen in infants with respiratory distress syndrome. Apnea and shock are more likely to occur in cases of pneumonia caused by group B *Streptococcus*. Infants with infections caused by group B *Streptococcus* require lower respiratory pressures on mechanical ventilation than do infants with respiratory distress syndrome. At autopsy, hyaline membranes similar to those seen in infants with respiratory distress syndrome have been observed in the lungs of infants who died of pneumonia caused by group B *Streptococcus*, and gram-positive cocci were identified within the hyaline membranes.

ANAEROBIC BACTERIA

Improvements in techniques for isolation and identification of the various genera and species of anaerobic bacteria have provided a better understanding of the anaerobic flora of humans and the roles of these organisms in disease. Anaerobes are present on the skin, in the mouth, in the intestines, and in the genital tract. Anaerobic bacteria may be responsible for pneumonia and lung abscesses in a host who is subject to aspiration. The anaerobic bacteria most commonly responsible for pulmonary infection include *Fusobacterium* spp., *Bacteroides melaninogenicus, Bacteroides fragilis, Peptococcus,* and *Peptostreptococcus*. The initial lesion of anaerobic infection of the lower respiratory tract is a pneumonitis with a slowly progressive clinical course. Lung abscess and necrotizing pneumonia may be a late consequence of the anaerobic pneumonitis.[11, 19]

LEGIONELLA PNEUMOPHILA

In August 1976, 221 cases of respiratory illness caused by an unknown agent occurred among 4500 participants at an American Legion convention in Philadelphia. The disease was marked by high fever, recurrent chills, prominent myalgia, abnormal liver function, and a toxic encephalopathy in addition to respiratory signs. Patients had nonproductive coughs, and their radiologic patterns showed patchy bronchopneumonia that in some cases progressed to lobar consolidation. Some patients responded promptly to therapy with erythromycin.

Investigators at the CDC of the Public Health Service isolated small pleomorphic rods from lung tissues taken at autopsy. The rods were stained with silver-impregnation methods and were visualized by direct immunofluorescence; however, they were seen poorly or not at all with Gram stain. The organism was designated *Legionella pneumophila.*

The genus *Legionella* includes aerobic, fastidious, gram-negative rods that require cysteine and some form of iron for growth. Eighteen separable species have been identified. The natural habitat of *L. pneumophila* is aquatic reservoirs, including rivers, lakes, air-conditioning cooling towers, and water distribution systems. Almost all cases of respiratory infection in children have been associated with *L. pneumophila*, except for one case caused by *Legionella micdadei* (the Pittsburgh pneumonia agent).[46] Diagnosis is made by culture on buffered yeast extract agar, direct fluorescent antibody staining of respiratory tract secretions, and demonstration of antibody by indirect immunofluorescence.

Seroepidemiologic studies suggest that subclinical or minor infections occur in some children.[54, 65] Prospective studies of children with lower respiratory disease, however, identified few cases caused by *L. pneumophila*.[4, 59] Legionellosis in children with leukemia in relapse[46] and chronic granulomatous disease[61] indicates that the organism should be added to the list of agents that cause pneumonia in the immunocompromised child.

GROUP A *STREPTOCOCCUS*

Pneumonia caused by group A *Streptococcus* is uncommon. Surveys of children hospitalized with pneumonia in Dallas[76] during a 9-year period and in Denver[53] and Chicago[39] during a 5-year period identified only five, three, and two cases, respectively, caused by group A *Streptococcus*. Pneumonia caused by group A *Streptococcus* may develop after viral infection, such as influenza, measles, and chickenpox, but it also occurs in children without previous illness. The disease is characterized by necrosis of respiratory tract mucosa and lung tissue with edema and localized hemorrhage. Clinical signs include chills, high and prolonged fever, dyspnea, and pleuritic chest pain. Patients remain febrile for a mean of 10 days,[76] long after the initiation of therapy with appropriate antibacterial drugs. Bacteremia and pleural effusion are frequent occurrences, and pneumatoceles may occur. The typical pleural effusion begins as a serous fluid, progresses to be serosanguineous, and may become fibrinopurulent.

NEISSERIA MENINGITIDIS

N. meningitidis usually is associated with asymptomatic carriage in the upper respiratory tract, and pneumonia occurs relatively uncommonly. When pneumonia caused by *N. meningitidis* does occur, it usually is caused by group Y and is accompanied in some cases by bacteremia.[37, 84] No distinctive clinical pattern occurs in children, and the diagnosis usually is made by culture of blood.[10, 33]

GRAM-NEGATIVE ENTERIC BACILLI

Pneumonia caused by gram-negative enteric bacilli occurs in newborn infants and children with altered host defense mechanisms but is seen rarely in normal infants and children. Pneumonia caused by *Pseudomonas aeruginosa* and, to a lesser extent, by *Burkholderia cepacia* is a particular problem in children with cystic fibrosis and may occur as a severe, progressive disease leading to a fatal, necrotizing bronchopneumonia. Pneumonia caused by *Klebsiella pneumoniae* is severe, with fever, chills, and a pattern of necrosis and destruction of lung tissue.

Epidemiology

The respiratory pathogens *S. pneumoniae, H. influenzae*, group A *Streptococcus*, and *S. aureus* are common inhabitants of the upper respiratory tract. These organisms may be isolated from many healthy children, and differentiating the many children who are colonized (i.e., multiplication of microorganisms without signs or symptoms of disease and without immune response), children who have asymptomatic or inapparent infection (i.e., multiplication of organisms without signs or symptoms of disease but with immune response), and children with disease (i.e., clinical signs or symptoms that result from multiplication of microorganisms) is important. Colonization may persist for several months. The reason for colonization in some individuals and inapparent infection or disease in others is unknown. Current theories are considered in the section on pathogenesis.

Humans are the only known source for the common bacterial pathogens responsible for respiratory disease. Transmission occurs in most cases by droplet spread, the brief passage of the infectious agent through the air when the source and the patient are near each other (usually within several feet); spread occurs also during talking or sneezing. Airborne spread occurs in some cases of staphylococcal infection; organisms within droplet nuclei, dust particles, or skin squames are carried through the air for distances of more than several feet.

The incubation period of bacterial pneumonia is difficult to determine, probably because of factors such as viral infection that play a role in the development of disease. Similarly, the period of communicability is not known accurately but probably is approximately 24 hours after administration of effective antimicrobial therapy for *S. pneumoniae* and *H. influenzae*.

Bacterial pneumonia may occur during all seasons but is most prevalent during the winter and spring months. Presumably, crowding in indoor spaces during these seasons favors direct transmission of infected droplets.

The highest incidence of pneumonia is in the very young and the very old. Passively acquired antibody to *S. pneumoniae* and *H. influenzae* type b is protective during the first few months of life. After the first months, if infected, the infant is susceptible to the disease until active immunity is induced as a response to inapparent infection or overt disease.

An overall male predominance is found in almost all series of bacterial pneumonia in children. Series of cases of *H. influenzae* pneumonia showed the male predominance to be 2:1 or greater.[6, 39, 62] More cases of pneumococcal pneumonia occur in boys than girls in all pediatric age groups.[36]

Nosocomial pneumonia occurs in children at risk for aspiration, ventilated patients, and children with underlying pulmonary and cardiac disease and immunodeficiencies. Gram-negative bacillary organisms are responsible for most of the bacterial pneumonias acquired in the hospital, followed in importance by gram-positive organisms. Compliance with infection control measures in intensive care units is critical to prevention of nosocomial pneumonias.[40]

Although Heffron[36] cites several studies suggesting that blacks are peculiarly susceptible to pneumonia and to pneumococcus infections in general, no studies of the incidence of disease in different racial groups that are controlled adequately for socioeconomic factors, access to medical care, and other features important in the transmission of disease have been reported.

Bacterial pneumonia occurs uncommonly in epidemic form in the community, although the incidence of disease increases during periods of epidemic viral infection, as occurs with influenza outbreaks. Legionnaires' disease usually occurs in clusters of cases; most outbreaks have been related to airborne spread from contaminated air-conditioning cooling towers. Hospital-acquired infection may be epidemic (e.g., infections in newborn nurseries during the period of prevalence of virulent strains of *S. aureus*). Common-source outbreaks of pneumonia caused by gram-negative enteric bacilli may result from contaminated aqueous solutions used in humidification equipment.

Pathogenesis

Most bacterial pneumonias are a result of colonization of the nasopharynx followed by aspiration or inhalation of organisms. The lung is protected from bacterial infection by a variety of mechanisms, including filtration of particles in the nares, prevention of aspiration of infected secretions by the epiglottal reflex, expulsion of aspirated materials by the cough reflex, entrapment and expulsion of organisms by mucus-secreting and ciliated cells, ingestion and killing of bacteria by alveolar macrophages, neutralization of bacteria by local and systemic nonspecific and specific immune substances (i.e., complement, opsonins, and antibodies), and transport of particles from the lung by lymphatic drainage. Pulmonary infection may occur when one or more of these barriers are altered, inhibited, or destroyed. Hematogenous spread to the lung by means of infected emboli arising from a suppurative focus, such as an abscess of the skin or soft tissue caused by *S. aureus*, is an infrequent occurrence.

Animal models suggest that the inflammatory responses in the lung are caused by cell wall components of gram-positive organisms or endotoxins of gram-negative bacteria.[21, 77] An increase in cell wall components and endotoxin may occur after antibiotic-caused cell death, with resulting increase in inflammation. The first stage in the healing produced by appropriate antimicrobial drugs may be accompanied by clinical deterioration caused by an early increase in inflammation in the lung.

Pneumonia caused by *S. pneumoniae* begins with acute inflammation and hyperemia of the lower respiratory mucosa, exudation of edema fluid, deposition of fibrin, and infiltration of alveoli by polymorphonuclear leukocytes (i.e., "red hepatization"), followed by predominance of fibrin deposition and macrophage activity (i.e., "white hepatization"). Exudate in the alveoli is digested enzymatically and absorbed or removed by coughing. Resolution then occurs, with return of lung morphology and physiology to normal. In contrast, when the pneumonia is caused by *S. aureus* or *K. pneumoniae*, destruction of tissue and formation of multiple small abscesses frequently occur.

Although clinicians have observed that symptoms and signs of minor respiratory infection caused by viruses frequently precede development of bacterial pneumonia, precise documentation of antecedent viral infection is scant. Studies in animal models of infection with influenza and reoviruses[43] demonstrate a limited period of vulnerability of the lung to bacterial challenge after viral infection. The effects of the viral infection appear to be mediated by alterations in the activity of the alveolar macrophage. A brief period of impaired function of these phagocytic cells results from the viral infection. Staphylococcal[28, 50] or pneumococcal pneumonias[29, 30] may occur during or shortly after infection caused by influenza virus. Severe pneumococcal pneumonia has been associated with outbreaks of influenza,[57] and increased mortality rates from pneumonia in children occur during epidemics of influenza.[26] No evidence indicates that infections with other respiratory viruses precede development of bacterial pneumonias.[50] As an example, Hall and colleagues[34] found that the risk of secondary bacterial infection developing in infants hospitalized with respiratory syncytial viral infection was low (1.2% of 565 children studied over the course of 9 years).

Anatomic, physiologic, or immune defects predispose patients to lower respiratory tract infection. They include congenital anomalies (i.e., cleft palate, tracheoesophageal fistula, or sequestration of lung); congenital or acquired defects in immune function; aspiration (e.g., in children with familial dysautonomia, in the comatose patient, in the child who has a nasogastric feeding tube in place, after seizure, during anesthesia)[48]; and alterations in the quality of mucus secretions (e.g., in patients with cystic fibrosis). Various types of pulmonary infections may develop in children who are being treated with cytotoxic and immunosuppressive drugs for malignancy or for collagen vascular disease or who are recipients of organ transplants. Patients with immune deficits may develop pneumonia caused by aerobic and anaerobic gram-negative bacilli, staphylococci, *Legionella* spp., *Nocardia*, various fungi (including *Aspergillus* and *Candida* spp. and *Pneumocystis carinii)*, and such viruses as cytomegalovirus. Some of the infections in patients with depressed immune response represent reactivation of a latent infection.

The newborn infant can acquire pneumonia by several routes, including transplacental infection, aspiration of organisms present in the birth canal during delivery, and postnatal infection in the nursery or at home from human sources or contaminated equipment or materials.

Clinical Manifestations

The signs and symptoms of bacterial pneumonia vary with the bacterial pathogen, the age of the patient, and the severity of the disease. Some organisms are associated with a specific pattern of disease, such as the lobar pneumonia of *S. pneumoniae* and the empyema, abscess, and pneumatocele formation caused by *S. aureus*; however, any of these manifestations may result from infection caused by any of the bacterial pathogens. In young infants, signs may be nonspecific and findings sparse on physical examination. Radiologic evidence of pneumonia may be found in infants who appear to have minimal disease or whose signs are more likely to be associated with upper respiratory tract infection. In older children, most cases are mild, and undoubtedly many cases occur and remain unrecognized because signs of disease do not warrant radiography of the chest. The child with pneumonia who requires hospitalization represents a small but unknown fraction of all children with pneumonia.

Symptoms and signs of pneumonia in children may be classified for convenience into five categories: nonspecific manifestations of infection and toxicity; general signs of lower respiratory tract disease; signs of pneumonia; signs of pleural fluid; and signs of extrapulmonary disease.

Nonspecific manifestations of infection and toxicity include fever, headache, malaise, gastrointestinal complaints, restlessness, and apprehension. Rigors may occur and vary from symptoms of chilliness to a sign of teeth-chattering chills.

General signs of lower respiratory tract disease include tachypnea; dyspnea, including shallow or grunting respirations; cough; expectoration of sputum; and flaring of the alae nasae. Because of the importance of tachypnea as a sign of lower respiratory tract disease, reference values for normal patients should be known.[66] Respiratory rates are correlated inversely with age during the first 3 years of life and vary between a median of 47 breaths per minute in the first months of life to 38 at the end of the first year to 28 by 3 years of age. In older children, rates vary between 15 and 25 breaths per minute. Asleep subjects have lower respiratory rates than awake subjects. On the basis of these data, definitions of tachypnea for the purpose of diagnosing lower respiratory tract infection are 50 breaths per minute in infants 1 to 11 months of age, 40 per minute in children 1 to 4 years of age, and 30 per minute in children 5 years of age or older.[45]

Other general signs of pneumonia include a protective position and abdominal findings. The patient may lie on the affected side of the lung with legs drawn up because of chest pain. Abdominal distention may result from gastric dilatation because of swallowed air or paralytic ileus. The liver may be displaced downward by the right diaphragm or may be enlarged if congestive heart failure complicates the pneumonia.

Signs of pneumonia may be subtle in the young infant. Percussion usually is not of value in the infant or in the older child if distribution of the pneumonia is patchy. Dullness to percussion is associated more often in the young child with the presence of pleural fluid than with the involvement of the parenchyma of the lung. Auscultatory findings may include rales but are less consistent than are those in the older child. Abnormal findings in the older child include dullness to percussion, decreased tactile and vocal fremitus on palpation, and decreased breath sounds and rales over involved areas on auscultation. Intercostal retraction indicates recruitment of accessory muscles that becomes necessary to assist respiration when significant involvement of the lung is present.

Irritation of the pleura is accompanied by chest pain that may be severe and may limit chest movement. A friction rub may be detected over the involved area of pleura. As the effusion enlarges, dyspnea may increase, but pleuritic pain may diminish and become a dull ache. The pain of pleural irritation may be present at the site of inflammation. If the involved area includes the diaphragm, the pain may be referred to the posterior and lateral neck. Abdominal pain may be so severe as to suggest acute appendicitis. Pleural irritation over the right upper lobe may elicit meningismus, a sign of meningeal irritation without evidence of inflammation. Empyema may extend to involve the mediastinum or pericardium or may penetrate the chest wall to present as a soft tissue abscess (i.e., empyema necessitans). Signs of extension of empyema should be sought in the patient who does not respond appropriately to chemotherapy and surgical drainage.

Extrapulmonary infection, including abscesses of the skin and soft tissues, otitis media, sinusitis, and meningitis, may occur concomitantly with bacterial pneumonia. Pericarditis and epiglottitis are particularly likely to be associated with pneumonia caused by *H. influenzae* type b.

Diagnosis

MICROBIOLOGIC DIAGNOSIS

Effective chemotherapy is available for treatment of all forms of bacterial pneumonia in children. Optimal treatment, however, requires definition of the etiologic agent. The physician must differentiate viral or mycoplasmal from bacterial pneumonia; if the agent is bacterial, the probable species must be considered. An effort should be made to obtain adequate materials for bacteriologic diagnosis; they include sputum, secretions from the posterior nasopharynx, and blood. The physician also should consider tracheal aspiration in young children unable to produce sputum, thoracentesis when pleural fluid is present, percutaneous lung aspiration in children who are critically ill, and lung biopsy when tissue diagnosis is important.

Methods for Obtaining Material for Examination and Culture

Sputum usually is not available from children until they are 5 years of age; younger children usually swallow their secretions. A Gram-stained smear of sputum is of value in providing immediate information about the bacterial pathogen; the presence of a significant number of organisms associated with or ingested by polymorphonuclear leukocytes suggests the likely pathogen, whereas the presence of epithelial cells indicates that the material is from the mouth and that further attempts should be made to obtain sputum. The adequacy of the specimen for microbiologic evaluation may be defined by the presence of 10 or more polymorphonuclear cells per low-power field and fewer than 25 squamous epithelial cells per low-power field.

Secretions from the nasopharynx include organisms that may be responsible for pneumonia, but results of culture of the nasopharynx may be unrevealing or misleading because of the high rate of carriage of bacterial pathogens. Tracheal aspiration through a catheter may be of diagnostic assistance when it is performed with direct laryngoscopy but is less valuable when the catheter is passed through the nose or mouth because of contamination with organisms present in the upper respiratory tract. Use of a double-lumen catheter ensures that the specimen remains free of contaminants.

Culture of blood provides specific bacteriologic diagnosis. Bennett and Beeson[13] suggested that most patients with pneumococcal pneumonia have bacteremia at some time during their illness. Reports of pneumococcal pneumonia in adults indicate an incidence of bacteremia of approximately 25 percent.[8, 36] Data on the occurrence of bacteremia in children are less well documented. In a study of Boston children,[73] bacteremia occurred in 8 of 100 consecutive febrile children younger than 2 years of age with radiologic evidence of pneumonia who were seen in a "walk-in" clinic. This and other studies of febrile children seen in clinics for ambulatory children reveal many cases of unsuspected bacteremia in children with pneumonia caused by *S. pneumoniae*,[16] *H. influenzae*,[49] and *N. meningitidis*.[10] The proportion of children with pneumonia who are bacteremic is uncertain, but some data are available from studies of concurrent cultures of blood and lung aspirate. Of 43 Gambian children younger than 10 years of age with pneumonia who had concurrent cultures of blood and lung aspirate, bacterial pathogens were cultured from lung aspirates only in 19 children, from blood in 4, and from blood and lung in 10 patients.[80]

The availability of flexible bronchoscopy and bronchoalveolar lavage has added another approach to obtain optimal specimens for microbiologic diagnosis of pneumonia.[12] The technique provides a direct view of bronchial and lung pathology, may provide evidence of endobronchial obstructions, and may identify and remove mucus or mucopurulent plugs. These techniques have been of particular value in the diagnosis of pulmonary disease in children with acquired immunodeficiency syndrome.[14]

Thoracentesis should be considered whenever fluid is present in the pleural space and microbiologic diagnosis is unrevealed by cultures of sputum, blood, or tracheal aspirate. Pleural biopsy should be performed at the time of thoracentesis if tuberculosis or tumor is included in the differential diagnosis. The area to be aspirated is defined by physical examination (i.e., the point of maximal dullness), chest radiography, and ultrasonography. Gram or acid-fast stain of the fluid may provide immediate information about the pathogen. Fluid should be sent for culture; cytology; and determination of glucose, protein, and pH.

Aspiration of pulmonary exudate (i.e., lung puncture) can provide direct, specific, and immediate information about the causative agent of pneumonia. The procedure is performed as would be a thoracentesis. Lung puncture should be considered for the child who is critically ill and for whom a specific diagnosis is of immediate importance in guiding antimicrobial therapy; the child whose condition deteriorates after initial therapy and for whom an etiologic agent has not been identified; and the child who has an underlying disease complicating the pneumonia or who is receiving drugs limiting normal host defense mechanisms.[44] A reappraisal of lung tap in children indicated that a bacteriologic cause was identified in approximately 50 percent of cases and that adverse events were few.[79] Performing open or closed lung biopsy is necessary if tissue diagnosis is important.

Transtracheal percutaneous aspiration is a safe and useful method of obtaining secretions from the lower respiratory tract of adults with pneumonia who are unable to produce adequate sputum. This method bypasses the mouth flora and permits the investigator to obtain direct culture of tracheal secretions. Transtracheal aspiration has not been used in young children with pneumonia because pediatricians lack experience with the technique and are concerned about the safety of the procedure. Only one report is available; Brook and Finegold[19] used transtracheal aspiration without apparent morbidity to determine the bacteriology of lung abscesses in 10 institutionalized children 23 months to 14 years of age.

Special Methods of Isolation and Identification

Clinical microbiology laboratories have facilities for isolation and identification of aerobic bacterial pathogens associated with pneumonia, but anaerobic bacteria require special techniques. Because many anaerobic bacteria are exquisitely sensitive to oxygen, anaerobic transport media must be provided, and special methods must be used to handle materials on arrival in the laboratory.

Identification of bacterial antigens from secretions and body fluids is possible with the use of precipitin reaction, counterimmunoelectrophoresis, latex agglutination, and enzyme-linked immunosorbent assay. Identification of antigen is of particular help when prior administration of antimicrobial agents prevents successful isolation of bacteria.

Counterimmunoelectrophoresis of nasopharyngeal secretions may distinguish patients with pneumococcal pneumonia from those who are carriers of this organism.[20] Detection in urine of polysaccharide antigens of *S. pneumoniae* and *H. influenzae* type b has been used for rapid diagnosis of pneumonia.[17, 78] Questions about sensitivity and specificity of the technique remain to be answered. Preliminary studies suggest value for polymerase chain reaction (PCR) for detection of *S. pneumoniae* in whole blood and serum in patients with pneumonia.[67, 86] Michelow and colleagues[52] reviewed the diagnosis of lower respiratory infections caused by *S. pneumoniae* by culture, PCR (i.e., whole blood, buffy coat, or plasma), serology, and urinary antigen.

Laboratory Tests

Elevated white blood cell counts (>15,000 cells/mm^3) frequently but not invariably occur in patients with bacterial pneumonia. A white blood cell count below 5000 cells/mm^3 usually is associated with severe and overwhelming disease. Determinations of erythrocyte sedimentation rate and measurement of C-reactive protein did not distinguish virus from bacterial pneumonia in Finnish children.[58]

The presence of an immune response to infection may be used to document bacterial pneumonia in retrospect. Serologic tests for bacterial pathogens of importance in pneumonia are available only from investigative laboratories.

Chest Radiography

Although the diagnosis of pneumonia may be suggested by clinical signs, pneumonia is defined by chest radiography. In addition to plain radiography, tomography and computed tomography may be used to provide special detail about cavitation, calcification, and patency of central airways.

Radiographic findings may not correlate with clinical signs in young infants. Significant pneumonia may be found by radiography in the absence of clinical signs. Pleural effusion may be identified only with the use of a radiograph taken in the lateral decubitus position. The radiologic pattern may lag behind clinical improvement for weeks to months.

A chest radiograph should be obtained at the conclusion of the illness to determine that the pneumonia has cleared and that no underlying process, such as foreign body, congenital malformation, or residual atelectasis, is present. The precise timing for performing such a study is uncertain, but it should be when resolution is expected, approximately 4 to 6 weeks after initial signs appear.

Of particular interest in the clinical trial of the heptavalent conjugate pneumococcal vaccine conducted in Northern California (see Prevention section) was the insight obtained in the proportion of radiologically identifiable pneumonias that were caused by the pneumococcus.[15] Children immunized with the conjugate pneumococcal vaccine had approximately one-third fewer episodes of radiographically confirmed pneumonia than did children who received the control vaccine. Because approximately 80 percent of the pneumococcal types thought to be responsible for pneumonia in infants were in the vaccine, these data suggest that the pneumococcus was responsible for roughly 40 percent of pneumonias identified by abnormal radiographs. Because lobar pneumonia frequently is caused by the pneumococcus, the 63 percent decrease in radiographically confirmed lobar consolidation in infants who had received the pneumococcal conjugate vaccine was less surprising.

DIFFERENTIAL DIAGNOSIS

The differential diagnosis of bacterial pneumonia includes nonbacterial pneumonias and noninfectious causes of pulmonary disease. During each period of life, certain nonbacterial agents are prominent causes of pneumonia. Pneumonia in the neonate may result from congenital infection or infection acquired at the time of delivery because of rubella, toxoplasmosis, herpes simplex infection, cytomegalovirus infection, or syphilis. In children between 2 weeks and 6 months of age, *Chlamydia trachomatis* is an important cause of a syndrome of afebrile pneumonia. Throughout childhood, most pneumonias are caused by the respiratory viruses, including adenoviruses, influenza viruses, parainfluenza viruses, respiratory syncytial virus, echoviruses, and coxsackieviruses A and B. *Mycoplasma pneumoniae* is an uncommon cause of pneumonia in preschool-age children but is an important cause of pneumonia in school-age children, adolescents, and young adults.

Nonbacterial pneumonias that are susceptible to available antimicrobial agents include disease caused by fungi (e.g., histoplasmosis, blastomycosis), *Rickettsia* (i.e., Q fever), and *Chlamydia* (i.e., TWAR agent and psittacosis).

A most important consideration is tuberculosis in children with persistent pulmonary disease who do not respond to penicillin or alternatives to penicillin. All children living in areas that have a high risk for tuberculosis should have a tuberculin skin test if admitted to the hospital with a lower respiratory tract infection.

Noninfectious causes of pulmonary lesions include aspiration of gastric contents, aspiration of foreign body, drug reactions, sequestration of lobe, congestive heart failure, atelectasis, sarcoidosis, malignancy or tumor, alveolar proteinosis, pulmonary hemosiderosis, and desquamating interstitial pneumonia.

The bacterial causes of acute empyema include *S. aureus, S. pneumoniae, H. influenzae*, gram-negative bacilli, and anaerobic bacteria.[18] Bloody exudates (when thoracentesis occurs without trauma) suggest malignancy, infarct of the lung, connective tissue disorder, pancreaticopleural fistula, or tuberculosis.

CLINICAL GUIDELINES IN DEVELOPING COUNTRIES

Acute infections of the lower respiratory tract are the single most important cause of death in children younger than 5 years of age in developing countries.[72] The authors of the Programme for the Control of Respiratory Infections of the World Health Organization (WHO) developed clinical guidelines for case diagnosis of pneumonia for use in developing countries. In these areas, diagnosis and management are provided for children by health care personnel who work in facilities where laboratory and radiologic tests are limited or do not exist.[63] The goals of the program are to simplify diagnosis to the smallest number of readily identifiable signs, to provide a system for classification of the illness, and to define the basis for use of antibacterial agents. The guidelines include assessment of fever, nutrition, lethargy, and color (i.e., presence or absence of cyanosis); measurement of the respiratory rate; observations of chest wall movement to detect retractions; and auscultation for stridor and wheezes.

The guidelines distinguish levels of disease for purposes of management. *Very severe pneumonia* includes central cyanosis and an inability to drink. *Severe pneumonia* includes chest indrawing, without cyanosis, and the ability to drink. *Pneumonia* includes no chest indrawing but sustained tachypnea (>60 breaths/min for infants younger than 2 months of age, >50 breaths/min for children 2 to 12 months of age, >40 breaths/min for children 12 months to 5 years of age). *No pneumonia* includes cough in the absence of chest indrawing and tachypnea. The suggested management includes hospitalization and administration of parenteral antibiotics for children with very severe and severe pneumonia; home care and administration of oral antibiotics for children with pneumonia; and for children with cough but without signs of severe respiratory illness, no antibiotics but assessment and treatment of other problems.

The ability of nurses and nursing assistants in Swaziland to recognize pneumonia using the WHO's protocols was evaluated by Simoes and McGrath.[71] Signs of severe disease, including stridor and abnormal sleepiness, often were overlooked, as was audible wheeze, but tachypnea and chest wall retractions were well recognized. In a study of Chinese children, tachypnea (50 cycles/min for infants 2 to 11 months of age and 40 cycles/min for children 1 to 5 years of age) was a good predictor of radiologically defined pneumonia and was recommended for use by village health workers in diagnosing pneumonia. Nasal flaring, retractions, stridor, and cyanosis of the tongue had high predictive values but were observed infrequently.[22] A respiratory rate of more than 50 cycles per minute or retractions were predictive of pneumonia in children with cough evaluated in Papua New Guinea.[35]

Management of Bacterial Pneumonia

Therapy should be initiated promptly after bacterial pneumonia is diagnosed or strongly suspected. Initial therapy is guided by knowledge of the likely bacterial pathogens in the child's age group because examination of the sputum or tracheal aspirate usually is unavailable in patients younger than school age. The physician must decide whether hospitalization is required for optimal management of the child. Most children with mild to moderate disease can be treated at home. Children who require hospitalization include those with severe disease who require hydration, oxygen, or observation; those who are toxic and have a significant degree of pulmonary dysfunction; and those whose families lack the ability to provide therapy and supportive care. Special concern is warranted for infants in the first year of life, when signs of respiratory disease are subtle and disease may progress rapidly.

INITIAL CHOICE OF ANTIMICROBIAL AGENTS BY AGE GROUP

Neonatal Pneumonia

The treatment of neonatal pneumonia is similar to that of other severe neonatal infections. Initial therapy must include coverage for gram-positive cocci, particularly group B *Streptococcus*, and gram-negative bacilli.

A penicillin is the drug of choice for the gram-positive organisms. If the physician has reason to suspect staphylococcal infection, a penicillinase-resistant penicillin is chosen. If the risk of staphylococcal infection is not significant, penicillin G or ampicillin is used. The latter drug may provide a theoretical advantage because of greater in vitro activity against some enterococci and some gram-negative bacilli, particularly *Escherichia coli* and *Proteus mirabilis*, when used alone or in combination with an aminoglycoside.

Choice of therapy for suspected gram-negative bacillary infection depends on the antibiotic susceptibility pattern for recent isolates obtained from newborn infants. An aminoglycoside such as gentamicin has an effective range of in vitro activity. Amikacin and tobramycin have similar activity but may be effective for strains of gram-negative enteric bacilli that are resistant to gentamicin.

Initial therapy is reevaluated when the results of cultures are available. Duration of therapy depends on the causative agent. Pneumonia caused by group B *Streptococcus* or gram-negative enteric bacilli is treated for 7 to 10 days; disease caused by *S. aureus* requires 3 to 6 weeks of antimicrobial therapy, according to the severity of the disease.

Pneumonias in Children 1 Month to 10 Years of Age

Most cases of bronchopneumonias at this age are caused by respiratory viruses. If the initial clinical and radiologic findings are consistent with viral infection and the child can be observed closely, antimicrobial agents may be withheld pending the results of cultures. *S. pneumoniae* and *H. influenzae* (nontypeable and type b) are the major bacterial agents responsible for bacterial pneumonia in this age group. The rate of disease caused by *H. influenzae* type b is low in children who were immunized previously with the conjugate vaccine. Although a varying proportion of pneumococci are multidrug-resistant organisms, the concentrations of parenteral ampicillin are sufficient to achieve concentrations in the blood and lung that can inhibit and kill all but the most resistant strains. If the child is critically ill, vancomycin should be substituted for ampicillin because pneumococci are not resistant to it. Strains of β-lactamase–producing *H. influenzae* resistant to amoxicillin and other susceptible penicillins have been isolated throughout the United States. Nonetheless, amoxicillin still is appropriate initial therapy for the young child with mild disease. If the child is moderately or seriously ill, drugs with efficacy against *S. pneumoniae* and β-lactamase–producing *H. influenzae*, including ampicillin–sulbactam or cephalosporins (i.e., cefuroxime, ceftriaxone, cefotaxime, or ceftazidime), should be administered by parenteral routes.

S. aureus now is an uncommon cause of pneumonia in this age group. However, if clinical signs compatible with staphylococcal disease are present, initial therapy should include a parenteral penicillinase-resistant penicillin.

Because *M. pneumoniae* and *Chlamydia pneumoniae* are common causes of pneumonia in school-age children and adolescents, presumptive therapy should include coverage for *S. pneumoniae, M. pneumoniae,* and *C. pneumoniae* in children older than 5 years of age. Erythromycin, azithromycin, and clarithromycin are appropriate drugs for coverage of both pathogens.

Pneumonia in the Child 10 Years of Age or Older

S. pneumoniae, M. pneumoniae, and *C. pneumoniae* are the major treatable causes of pneumonia in this age group. *H. influenzae* occurs relatively infrequently, and initial therapy need not include coverage for this organism. Therapy outlined earlier for the school-age child continues to be appropriate for the child 10 years of age or older.

CHEMOTHERAPY FOR SPECIFIC PATHOGENS

Pneumococcal Pneumonia

Penicillin G is the drug of choice for children with pneumonia caused by *S. pneumoniae*. For most children with mild to moderately severe disease, an oral penicillin is suitable. Phenoxymethyl penicillin (penicillin V) administered orally provides significant antibacterial activity, as well as approximately twice the peak serum level provided by an equivalent dose of buffered oral penicillin G. Children who appear to be toxic, who have underlying disease, or who have complications (e.g., abscesses, empyema) require the higher serum and tissue antibacterial activity that is provided by aqueous penicillin G administered by the intravenous or intramuscular route.

Strains of nonsusceptible *S. pneumoniae* have become prevalent in most communities in the United States. Clinical failures have occurred in some patients with meningitis caused by penicillin-resistant pneumococci, but few failures have been identified in cases of sepsis or pneumonia treated with a penicillin or cephalosporin in an adequate dosage schedule. Results of a study of adults with bacteremic pneumonia caused by penicillin-resistant pneumococci suggested that patients with highly resistant strains (MICs were 4.0 and 8.0 μg/mL) failed to respond to a penicillin, whereas patients with strains having lower MICs did respond.[60] Susceptibility tests should be performed on all isolates of *S. pneumoniae* from sputum and body fluids (i.e., blood, cerebrospinal fluid, and pleural fluid). Presumptive therapy for mild to moderate pneumonias need not be altered because of concern for resistant pneumococci, but severe pneumonias should be treated with high-dosage parenteral therapy providing high serum and tissue concentrations and stability to β-lactamases, such as intravenous ceftriaxone and cefotaxime. The most appropriate regimen is chosen when results of culture and susceptibility tests are available. Vancomycin is effective uniformly against all pneumococci, including highly resistant strains, and should be considered if the susceptibility tests indicate the strain is multidrug-resistant and uniquely susceptible to vancomycin.

The dosage schedule for mild to moderate disease and severe disease is provided in Chapter 235. The duration of therapy depends on the clinical response, but therapy should be continued for at least 3 days after defervescence and significant resolution of radiologic and clinical signs; usually, a period of 5 to 7 days is sufficient.

Pneumonia Caused by *Haemophilus influenzae*

Nontypeable and type b strains of *H. influenzae* are susceptible to various antimicrobial agents, including ampicillin or amoxicillin (non–β-lactamase producers), oral or parenteral cephalosporins, the sulfonamides, and aminoglycosides. All have been used with success in systemic infections (including pneumonia) caused by this agent. Amoxicillin is considered the drug of choice for treating young children with mild to moderate pulmonary disease. Because of the concern for β-lactamase–producing strains of *H. influenzae*, a parenteral second-generation (cefuroxime) or third-generation cephalosporin (ceftriaxone, cefotaxime, or ceftazidime) should be used as initial therapy in patients with severe disease when this microorganism is known or strongly suspected to be the pathogen.

The child with mild to moderate disease should be treated for a minimum of 7 days, including a period without fever of at least 3 days. The child with severe disease should be treated for 2 to 3 weeks.

Staphylococcal Pneumonia

The high incidence of staphylococci resistant to penicillin G, in the hospital and in the community, requires the use of a penicillinase-resistant penicillin whenever staphylococcal pneumonia is diagnosed or suspected. Subsequently, if the culture and sensitivity data indicate that the organism is susceptible to penicillin G, the drug should be used because of its greater efficacy and lower cost. Clinical trials indicate that all penicillinase-resistant penicillins are equally effective in treating staphylococcal pneumonia. Although the incidence of staphylococci in the community that are resistant to penicillinase-resistant penicillins is low (approximately 1% in reports from U.S. centers), resistance should be suspected if appropriate clinical response does not occur after the use of one of these penicillins. Vancomycin has been used successfully for patients with pneumonia caused by one of these resistant strains of *S. aureus*.

The rapid development of empyema, pneumatoceles, and abscesses demands close observation and meticulous nursing care. The antibiotic should be administered parenterally using a high dosage schedule for 2 to 3 weeks; an oral preparation then may be given for 1 to 3 weeks. The total duration of antibiotic therapy depends on the initial response, the presence of pulmonary and extrapulmonary complications, and the rapidity of resolution of the pneumonia.

Pneumonia Caused by Anaerobic Bacteria

Most anaerobic bacteria that cause pneumonia, including strains of *B. fragilis*, are highly susceptible to penicillin G. Some strains of *B. fragilis* may be resistant to penicillin G and susceptible to chloramphenicol, clindamycin, or cefoxitin. The duration of therapy depends on the extent of the disease; pneumonia without complications clears rapidly with appropriate therapy; 7 days of therapy usually is sufficient.

Pneumonia Caused by Gram-Negative Bacilli

The initial choice of therapy is guided by the following factors: the source of the infection, the disease process present (e.g., burn, cystic fibrosis), host susceptibility to infection (e.g., deficient immune mechanisms), and the antimicrobial susceptibility pattern for these organisms in the community or hospital. The basis for choice of antibiotic is similar to that outlined for neonatal pneumonia suspected to be caused by gram-negative bacilli. The duration of therapy must be tailored to the clinical course and the response to therapy. Cases of pneumonia with minimal pulmonary lesions and limited symptoms should be treated for at least 3 days after defervescence. Severe cases of pneumonia should be treated for 2 to 3 weeks.

Therapy for the Child Who Is Allergic to Penicillin

A child who has a significant history of allergic reaction to any of the penicillins must be considered sensitive to all of them, and alternative antimicrobial agents must be considered for therapy. Cephalothin and cefazolin have been used with success in the treatment of staphylococcal and pneumococcal pneumonia and may be used as alternatives to penicillin. Erythromycin; the new macrolides, clarithromycin and azithromycin; and clindamycin are active in vitro against gram-positive cocci and are effective in the treatment of pneumococcal, staphylococcal, and anaerobic pneumonias. Because some staphylococci may be resistant to these antibiotics, testing the organism for susceptibility is important. Vancomycin may be considered for use in the patient who is allergic to penicillin and who has severe staphylococcal disease.

Adjuncts to Chemotherapy

Administration of antimicrobial agents is only part of the management of the child with pneumonia. Close observation, nursing care (including suction of excess secretions), and the following supportive measures are of the utmost importance:

1. Maintenance of fluid and electrolyte balance
2. Humidification provided by cool mist
3. Oxygen for severe dyspnea
4. Cleansing of the mouth
5. Sparing use of antipyretics because the temperature course provides a guideline for the therapeutic response

More extensive procedures may be required in special circumstances:

1. Bronchoscopy is important in documenting the presence of a foreign body, tumor, or congenital anomaly.
2. Intubation of the trachea or tracheotomy may be considered when the patient has difficulty clearing secretions and more efficient suction of the lower respiratory tree is required.
3. Drainage of pleural effusions may be necessary when an accumulation of fluid compromises respiration. Thick, tenacious empyema may require intercostal tube drainage or closed-tube thoracostomy. Empyema caused by *S. aureus* may require placement of a tube, whereas the less viscid effusion associated with *S. pneumoniae* and *Streptococcus pyogenes* rarely requires more than frequent thoracentesis. Empyema caused by *H. influenzae* may be thick and viscid, requiring placement of a chest tube, or less viscid, requiring only thoracentesis. Single or multiple thoracenteses are adequate when the volume of fluid is small and the quality of the fluid allows ready drainage, as usually is true with empyema caused by *S. pneumoniae* or group A *Streptococcus*. When large amounts of fluid are present or the fluid is thick and viscid, a closed drainage system with intercostal chest tube under negative pressure is placed; this placement frequently is necessary for empyema caused by *S. aureus*. The tube should be removed as soon as its drainage function is completed because delay might result in local tissue injury, secondary infection, or sinus formation.
4. Intrapleural instillation of antibiotic should be considered in cases of empyema when the fluid is loculated because of fibrous adhesions. If a chest tube is in place, antibiotics are instilled after irrigation through the tube. In susceptible infections, aqueous penicillin G (10,000 to 50,000 units), ampicillin (10 to 50 mg), or a penicillinase-resistant penicillin or cephalosporin (10 to 50 mg) may be inoculated in 10 mL of diluent (i.e., sterile water or normal saline) after the tube is clamped. The clamp is maintained for 1 hour and then released for drainage. The instillations should be repeated three to four times each day that the tube remains in place. If thoracenteses are done, antibiotic is introduced after the pleural fluid is aspirated.

Prognosis

In uncomplicated cases of pneumococcal pneumonia in children in the United States, the mortality rate is very low (<1%). A review of mortality from pneumonia in children in the United States, 1939 through 1996, identified reductions in mortality that were thought to reflect expanded access to medical care for poor children.[26] In developing countries, pneumonia is a major cause of mortality, accounting for more than one fourth of deaths in children younger than 5 years of age. One half of the pneumonia-related mortality occurs in children younger than 1 year of age. The WHO estimates that approximately 4 million childhood deaths are caused each year by pneumonia.

Lung morphology and physiology usually return to normal after completion of appropriate antimicrobial therapy. Fibrothorax is a rare occurrence; almost all children resolve thickened pleurae with no effect on lung growth and function. Even after having extensive disease associated with empyema caused by *S. aureus* or *H. influenzae*, children have normal growth and development and normal pulmonary function after recovery.[51] Deaths still result from bacterial pneumonias; however, most deaths of children result from abrupt, overwhelming disease. Asmar and colleagues[6] reported 2 deaths in 43 children with pneumonia caused by *H. influenzae*; both deaths occurred before antibiotics could be administered.

Prevention

The approval of a conjugate polysaccharide pneumococcal vaccine by the FDA in February 2000, followed by the recommendations of the various authoritative groups (e.g., American Academy of Pediatrics, American Academy of

Family Physicians and Advisory Committee on Immunization Practices of the Surgeon General) for universal immunization of infants and selective immunization of children at risk who are 2 to 5 years of age, added the most effective mode of prevention of pneumococcal diseases yet available. The available vaccine (Prevnar, Wyeth Lederle Vaccines, Pearl River, NY) is a heptavalent vaccine in which the individual polysaccharides have been purified and directly conjugated to the protein carrier CRM 197, a nontoxic variant of diphtheria toxin. The conjugate vaccine induces type-specific antibodies in infants as young as 2 months of age.

The safety and efficacy of the vaccine for prevention of pneumonia was studied in a trial of approximately 38,000 children in Northern California by Black and Shinefield and their colleagues at the Kaiser Permanente Vaccine Study Center.[15] Children were randomly assigned to receive the conjugate pneumococcal vaccine or a conjugate polysaccharide meningococcal group C vaccine. Pneumonia was defined clinically and radiologically. Infants and children who had received the pneumococcal vaccine demonstrated an 11 percent reduction in clinical episodes of pneumonia, a 35 percent decrease in radiographically confirmed pneumonia, and a 63 percent decrease in radiographically confirmed lobar consolidation.

The 23-type pneumococcal polysaccharide vaccine produces a satisfactory independent antibody response but only in children older than 2 years of age. The polysaccharide vaccine is recommended for children 2 years of age and older who are at risk for developing invasive disease (e.g., sickle cell disease, human immunodeficiency virus infection or other immunodeficiencies, malignancy, nephrosis) after they have received the appropriate number of doses of the conjugate vaccine.

Children who have sickle-cell anemia or who have functional or anatomic asplenia are at risk for developing overwhelming disease caused by *S. pneumoniae*. Daily antimicrobial prophylaxis is recommended for these children irrespective of their immunization status. The chemoprophylactic regimen used most commonly is daily administration of oral penicillin V (125 mg twice daily for children <5 years; 250 mg twice daily for children ≥5 years).

A polysaccharide vaccine for prevention of *H. influenzae* type b disease was introduced in the United States in April 1985. As was true of other polysaccharide vaccines, infants younger than 18 months of age had an inadequate immune response to the capsular polysaccharide. The development of a conjugate vaccine by coupling the capsular saccharide of *H. influenzae* type b and a protein resulted in protective antibodies in infants as young as 2 months of age. The conjugate *H. influenzae* type b vaccine was approved by the FDA in the fall of 1990 and has resulted in virtual elimination of disease caused by *H. influenzae* type b in infants and children.

REFERENCES

1. Abbasi, S., and Chesney, P. J.: Pulmonary manifestations of cat-scratch disease: A case report and review of the literature. Pediatr. Infect. Dis. J. *14*:547–548, 1995.
2. Ablow, R. C., Driscoll., S. G., Effmann, E. L., et al.: A comparison of early-onset group B streptococcal neonatal infection and the respiratory distress syndrome of the newborn. N. Engl. J. Med. *294*:65–70, 1976.
3. Abraham, E. P., Gardner, A. D., Chain, E., et al.: Further observations on penicillin. Lancet. *2*:177–189, 1941.
4. Anderson, R. D., Lauer, B. A., Fraser, D. W., et al.: Infections with *Legionella pneumophila* in children. J. Infect. Dis. *13*:386–390, 1981.
5. Applebaum, P. C., Bhamjee, A., Scragg, J. N., et al.: *Streptococcus pneumoniae* resistant to penicillin and chloramphenicol. Lancet. *2*:995, 1977.
6. Asmar, B. I., Slovis, T. L., Reed, J. O., et al: *Haemophilus influenzae* type b pneumonia in 43 children. J. Pediatr. *93*:389–393, 1978.
7. Austrian, R.: Treatment of pneumonia. Mod. Treat. *1*:909–923, 1964.
8. Austrian, R., and Gold, J.: Pneumococcal bacteremia with especial reference to bacteremic pneumococcal pneumonia. Ann. Intern. Med. *60*:759–776, 1964.
9. Bale, J. R.: Creation of a research program to determine the etiology and epidemiology of acute respiratory tract infection in children in developing countries. Rev. Infect. Dis. *12*(Suppl. 8):S861–S866, 1990.
10. Baltimore, R. S., and Hammerschlag, M.: Meningococcal bacteremia: Clinical and serologic studies of infants with mild illness. Am. J. Dis. Child. *131*:1001–1004, 1977.
11. Bartlett, J. G.: Anaerobic bacterial pneumonitis. Am. Rev. Respir. Dis. *119*:19–23, 1979.
12. Baselski, V. S., and Wunderink, R. G.: Bronchoscopic diagnosis of pneumonia. Clin. Microbiol. Rev. *7*:533–558, 1994.
13. Bennett, I. L., Jr., and Beeson, P. B.: Bacteremia: A consideration of some experimental and clinical aspects. Yale J. Biol. Med. *26*:241–262, 1954.
14. Birriel, J. A., Jr., Adams, J. A., Saldana, M. A., et al.: Role of flexible bronchoscopy and bronchoalveolar lavage in the diagnosis of pediatric acquired immunodeficiency syndrome–related pulmonary disease. Pediatrics. *87*:897–899, 1991.
15. Black, S., Shinefield, H., Ray, P., et al.: Efficacy of heptavalent conjugate pneumococcal vaccine (Wyeth Lederle) in 37,000 infants and children: Impact on pneumonia, otitis media and an update on invasive disease—Results of the Northern California Kaiser Permanente Efficacy Trial. Proceedings of the 39th Interscience Conference on Antimicrobial Agents and Chemotherapy, 1999, p. 379, #1398.
16. Bratton, L., Teele, D. W., and Klein, J. O.: Outcome of unsuspected pneumococcemia in children not initially admitted to the hospital. J. Pediatr. *90*:703–706, 1977.
17. Bromberg, K., Tannis, G., and Rodgers, A.: Pneumococcal C and type polysaccharide detection in the concentrated urine of patients with bacteremia. Med. Microbiol. Immunol. *179*:335–338, 1990.
18. Brook, I.: Microbiology of empyema in children and adolescents. Pediatrics *85*:722–726, 1990.
19. Brook, I., and Finegold, S. M.: Bacteriology and therapy of lung abscess in children. J. Pediatr. *94*:10–12, 1979.
20. Congeni, B. L., and Nankervis, G. A.: Diagnosis of pneumonia by counterimmunoelectrophoresis of respiratory secretions. Am. J. Dis. Child. *1132*:684–688, 1978.
21. Cundell, D., Masure, H. R., and Tuomanen, E. I.: The molecular basis of pneumococcal infection: A hypothesis. Clin. Infect. Dis. *21*(Suppl. 3):S204–S212, 1995.
22. Dai, Y., Foy, H. M., Zonghan, Z., et al.: Respiratory rate and signs in roentgenographically confirmed pneumonia among children in China. Pediatr. Infect. Dis. J. *14*:48–50, 1995.
23. Daum, R. S., Granoff, D. M., Mäkelä, P. H., et al. (guest eds.): Epidemiology, pathogenesis, and prevention of *Haemophilus influenzae* disease. J. Infect. Dis. *165*(Suppl. 1):S1–S206, 1992.
24. Doern, G. V., Brueggemann, A. B., Pierce, G., et al.: Antibiotic resistance among clinical isolates of *Haemophilus influenzae* in the United States in 1994–1995 and detection of β-lactamase-positive strains resistant to amoxicillin-clavulanate: Results of a national multicenter surveillance study. Antimicrob. Agents Chemother. *41*:292–297, 1997.
25. Doern, G. V., Heilman, K. P., Huynh, H. K., et al.: Antimicrobial resistance among clinical isolates of *Streptococcus pneumoniae* in the United States during 1999–2000 including a comparison of resistance rates since 1994–1995. Antimicrob. Agents Chemother. *45*:1721–1729, 2001.
26. Dowell, S. F., Kupronis, B. A., Zell, E. R., and Shay, D. K.: Mortality from pneumonia in children in the United States, 1939 through 1996. N. Engl. J. Med. *342*:1399–1407, 2000.
27. Edelstein, P. H.: Antimicrobial chemotherapy for legionnaires' disease: A review. Clin. Infect. Dis. *21*(Suppl. 3):S265–S276, 1995.
28. Finland, M., Peterson, O. L., and Strauss, E.: Staphylococcic pneumonia occurring during an epidemic of influenza. Arch. Intern. Med. *70*:183–205, 1942.
29. Finland, M., Ory, E. M., Meads, M., et al.: Influenza and pneumonia: Serological studies during and after an outbreak of influenza. Br. J. Lab. Clin. Med. *33*:32–46, 1948.
30. Finland, M., Barnes, M. W., and Samper, B. A.: Influenza virus isolations and serological studies made in Boston during the winter of 1943–1944. J. Clin. Invest. *24*:192–208, 1945.
31. Friedland, E. R., and McCracken, G. H., Jr.: Management of infections caused by antibiotic-resistant *Streptococcus pneumoniae*. N. Engl. J. Med. *331*:377–382, 1994.
32. Ginsburg, C. M., Howard, J. B., and Nelson, J. D.: Report of 65 cases of *Haemophilus influenzae* b pneumonia. Pediatrics *64*:283–286, 1979.
33. Goldwater, P. N., and Rice, M. S.: Primary meningococcal pneumonia in a nineteen-month-old child. Pediatr. Infect. Dis. J. *14*:155–156, 1995.
34. Hall, C. B., Powell, K. R., Schnabel, K. C., et al.: Risk of secondary bacterial infection in infants hospitalized with respiratory syncytial viral infection. J. Pediatr. *113*:266–271, 1988.
35. Harari, M., Shann, F., Spooner, V., et al.: Clinical signs of pneumonia in children. Lancet *338*:928–930, 1991.
36. Heffron, R.: Pneumonia with Special Reference to Pneumococcus Lobar Pneumonia. New York, Commonwealth Fund, 1939, pp. 308, 312, 549; reissued by Harvard University Press, Boston, 1979.

37. Hersh, J. H., Gold, R., and Lepow, M. L.: Meningococcal group Y pneumonia in an adolescent female. J. Pediatr. *64*:222–224, 1979.
38. Jacobs, M. R., Bajaksouzian, S., Zilles, A., et al.: Susceptibilities of *Streptococcus pneumoniae* and *Haemophilus influenzae* to 10 oral antimicrobial agents based on pharmacodynamic parameters: 1997 US surveillance study. Antimicrob. Agents Chemother. *43*:1901–1908, 1999.
39. Jacobs, N. M., and Harris, V. J.: Acute *Haemophilus* pneumonia in childhood. Am. J. Dis. Child. *133*:603–605, 1979.
40. Jacobs, R. F.: Nosocomial pneumonia in children. Infection *19*:64–72, 1991.
41. Kass, E. H. (ed.): Assessment of the pneumococcal polysaccharide vaccine. Rev. Infect. Dis. *3*(Suppl.):S1–S197, 1981.
42. Keefer, C. S., Blake, F. G., Marshall, E. K., Jr., et al.: Penicillin in the treatment of infections: A report of 500 cases. J. A. M. A. *122*:1217–1224, 1943.
43. Klein, J. O., Green, G. M., Tilles, J. G., et al.: Effect of intranasal reovirus infection on antibacterial activity of mouse lung. J. Infect. Dis. *119*:43–50, 1969.
44. Klein, J. O., and Gellis, S. S.: Diagnostic needle aspiration in pediatric practice. Pediatr. Clin. North Am. *18*:219–231, 1971.
45. Korppi, M.: Physical signs in childhood pneumonia. Pediatr. Infect. Dis. J. *14*:405–406, 1995.
46. Kovatch, A. L., Jardine, D. S., Dowling, J. N., et al.: Legionellosis in children with leukemia in relapse. Pediatrics *73*:811–815, 1984.
47. MacLeod, C. M., Hodges, R., Heidelberger, M., et al.: Prevention of pneumococcal pneumonia by immunization. J. Exp. Med. *82*:445–465, 1945.
48. Marik, P. E.: Aspiration pneumonitis and aspiration pneumonia. N. Engl. J. Med. *344*:665–671, 2001.
49. Marshall, R., Teele, D. W., and Klein, J. O.: Unsuspected bacteremia due to *Haemophilus influenzae*: Outcome in children not initially admitted to hospital. J. Pediatr. *95*:690–695, 1979.
50. Martin, C. M., Kunin, C. M., Gottlieb, L. S., et al.: Asian influenza A in Boston, 1957–1958. II. Severe staphylococcal pneumonia complicating influenza. Arch. Intern. Med. *103*:532–542, 1959.
51. McLaughlin, F. J., Goldmann, D. A., Rosenbaum, D. M., et al.: Empyema in children: Clinical course and long-term follow-up. Pediatrics *73*:587–593, 1984.
52. Michelow, I. C., Lozano, J., Olsen, K., et al.: Diagnosis of *Streptococcus pneumoniae* lower respiratory infection in hospitalized children by culture, polymerase chain reaction, serology and urinary antigen. Clin. Infect. Dis. In press.
53. Molteni, R. A.: Group a beta-hemolytic streptococcal pneumonia: Clinical course and complications of management. Am. J. Dis. Child. *131*:1366–1371, 1977.
54. Muldoon, R. L., Jaecker, D. L., and Kiefer, H. K.: Legionnaires' disease in children. Pediatrics *67*:329–332, 1981.
55. Nohynek, H., Eskola, J., Laine, E., et al.: The causes of hospital-treated acute lower respiratory tract infection in children. Am. J. Dis. Child. *145*:618–622, 1991.
56. Nohynek, H., Valkeila, E., Leinonen, M., et al.: Erythrocyte sedimentation rate, white blood cell count and serum C-reactive protein in assessing etiologic diagnosis of acute lower respiratory infections in children. Pediatr. Infect. Dis. J. *14*:484–490, 1995.
57. O'Brien, K. L., Walters, M. I., Sellman, J., et al.: Severe pneumococcal pneumonia in previously healthy children: The role of preceding influenza infection. Clin. Infect. Dis. *30*:784–789, 2000.
58. Olcay, L., Secmeer, G., Gogus, S., and Akcoren, Z.: Pathological case of the month: Fatal hemorrhagic staphylococcal pneumonia. Arch. Pediatr. Adolesc. Med. *149*:925–926, 1995.
59. Orenstein, W. A., Overturf, G. D., Leedom, J. M., et al.: The frequency of *Legionella* infection prospectively determined in children hospitalized with pneumonia. J. Pediatr. *99*:403–406, 1981.
60. Pallares, R., Linares, J., Vadillo, M., et al.: Resistance to penicillin and cephalosporin and mortality from severe pneumococcal pneumonia in Barcelona, Spain. N. Engl. J. Med. *333*:474–480, 1995.
61. Peerless, A. G., Liebhaber, M., Anderson, S., et al.: *Legionella* pneumonia in chronic granulomatous disease. J. Pediatr. *106*:783–785, 1985.
62. Potter, A. R., and Fischer, G. W.: *Haemophilus influenzae*, the predominant cause of bacterial pneumonia in Hawaii. Pediatr. Res. *11*:504, 1977.
63. Programme for the Control of Acute Respiratory Infections: Acute Respiratory Infections in Children: Case Management in Small Hospitals in Developing Countries. Geneva, World Health Organization, 1990.
64. Quie, P. G., Giebink, G. S., and Winkelstein, J. A. (guest eds.): The pneumococcus. Rev. Infect. Dis. *3*:183–396, 1981.
65. Renner, E. D., Helms, C. M., Hierholzer, W. J., Jr., et al.: Legionnaires' disease in pneumonia patients in Iowa: A retrospective seroepidemiologic study, 1972–1977. Ann. Intern. Med. *90*:603–606, 1979.
66. Rusconi, R., Castagneto, M., Gagliardi, L., et al.: Reference values for respiratory rate in the first 3 years of life. Pediatrics *94*:350–355, 1994.
67. Salo, P., Ortqvist, A., and Leinonen, M.: Diagnosis of bacteremic pneumococcal pneumonia by amplification of pneumolysin gene fragment in serum. J. Infect. Dis. *171*:479–482, 1995.
68. Shann, F.: The management of pneumonia in children in developing countries. Clin. Infect. Dis. *21*(Suppl. 3):S218–S225, 1995.
69. Shann, F.: *Haemophilus influenzae* pneumonia: Type b or non-type b? Lancet *354*:1488–1490, 1999.
70. Shann, F., Germer, S., Hazlett, D., et al.: Aetiology of pneumonia in children in Goroka Hospital, Papua New Guinea. Lancet *2*:537–541, 1984.
71. Simoes, E. A. F., and McGrath, E. J.: Recognition of pneumonia by primary health care workers in Swaziland with a simple clinical algorithm. Lancet *340*:1502–1503, 1992.
72. Steinhoff, M. C. (ed.): Belagio conference on the pathogenesis and prevention of pneumonia in children in developing regions. Rev. Infect. Dis. *13*(Suppl. 6), 1991.
73. Teele, D. W., Pelton, S. E., Grant, J. A., et al.: Bacteremia in febrile children under 2 years of age: Results of cultures of blood of 600 consecutive febrile children seen in a "walk-in" clinic. J. Pediatr. *87*:227–231, 1975.
74. Thornsberry, C., Ogilvie, P. T., Holley, H. P., Jr., and Sahm, D. F.: Survey of susceptibilities of *Streptococcus pneumoniae, Haemophilus influenzae* and *Moraxella catarrhalis* isolates to 26 antimicrobial agents: A prospective US study. Antimicrob. Agents Chemother. *43*:2612–2623, 1999.
75. Tillett, W. S., Cambier, M. J., and Harris, W. H., Jr.: Sulfonamide-fast pneumococci: A clinical report of two cases of pneumonia together with experimental studies on the effectiveness of penicillin and tyrothricin against sulfonamide-resistant strains. J. Clin. Invest. *22*:249–255, 1943.
76. Trujillo, M., and McCracken, G. H., Jr.: Prolonged morbidity in children with group A beta-hemolytic streptococcal pneumonia. Pediatr. Infect. Dis. J. *13*:411–412, 1994.
77. Tuomanen, E. I., Austrian, R., and Masure, H. R.: Pathogenesis of pneumococcal infection. N. Engl. J. Med. *332*:1280–1284, 1995.
78. Turner, R. B., Hayden, F. G., and Hendley, J. O.: Counterimmunoelectrophoresis of urine for diagnosis of bacterial pneumonia in pediatric outpatients. Pediatrics *71*:780–783, 1983.
79. Vuori-Holopainen, E., and Peltola, H.: Reappraisal of lung tap: Review of an old method for better etiologic diagnosis of childhood pneumonia. Clin. Infect. Dis. *32*:715–726, 2001.
80. Wall, R. A., Corrah, P. T., Mabey, D. C. W., et al.: The etiology of lobar pneumonia in the Gambia. Bull. World Health Organ. *64*:553–558, 1986.
81. Ward, J. I., Tsai, T. F., Filice, G. A., et al.: Prevalence of ampicillin- and chloramphenicol-resistant strains of *Haemophilus influenzae* causing meningitis and bacteremia: National survey of hospital laboratories. J. Infect. Dis. *138*:421–424, 1978.
82. Watson, D. A., Musher, D. M., Jacobson, J. W., et al.: A brief history of the pneumococcus in biomedical research: A panoply of scientific discovery. Clin. Infect. Dis. *17*:913–924, 1993.
83. Weinberg, G. A., Ghafoor, A., Ishaq, Z., et al.: Clonal analysis of *Hemophilus influenzae* isolated from children from Pakistan with lower respiratory tract infections. J. Infect. Dis. *160*:634–643, 1989.
84. Winstead, J. M., McKinsey, D. S., Tasker, S., et al.: Meningococcal pneumonia: Characterization and review of cases seen over the past 25 years. Clin. Infect. Dis. *30*:87–94, 2000.
85. Zaki, S. R., Shieh, W-J, and the Epidemic Working Group at Ministry of Health in Nicaragua, Pan American Health Organization, US Department of Agriculture, and Centers for Disease Control and Prevention: Leptospirosis associated with outbreak of acute febrile illness and pulmonary hemorrhage, Nicaragua, 1995. Lancet *347*: 535–536, 1996.
86. Zhang, Y., Isaacman, D. J., Wadowsky, R. M., et al.: Detection of *Streptococcus pneumoniae* in whole blood by PCR. J. Clin. Microbiol. *33*:596–601, 1995.

Chronic Interstitial Pneumonitis and Hypersensitivity Pneumonitis

LELAND L. FAN

CHRONIC INTERSTITIAL PNEUMONITIS IN CHILDREN

The interstitial lung diseases (ILDs) in children include a large, heterogeneous group of mostly rare conditions characterized by restrictive lung disease and disordered gas exchange.[7, 30, 33] In many of these disorders, injury to the alveolar wall gives rise to an inflammatory response with subsequent repair that potentially can lead to pulmonary fibrosis. Although specific entities, such as desquamative interstitial pneumonitis (DIP), are described in adults and children, the frequency and distribution of these diseases are different in adults and children, and some unique forms of ILD in children have not been described in adults.

Classification

A general classification of pediatric ILDs is given in Table 28–1. Although certain factors, such as aspiration, infection, hypersensitivity reactions to organic dusts, and drug toxicity, are known to cause ILD in children, most pediatric cases are of unknown origin. Pediatric ILD can exist as an isolated, primary pulmonary disorder or as part of a more systemic process, such as sarcoidosis or collagen vascular disease.

INFECTION IN CHRONIC LUNG DISEASE

The roles of infectious agents, such as adenovirus,[99] influenza virus,[50] *Mycoplasma*,[91] and *Chlamydia*,[39] in the development of chronic lung disease in children have been well documented. Virtually any organism that infects the lower respiratory tract is capable of producing chronic diffuse lung disease if the injury is severe enough, although most infected children have acute, self-limited disease that resolves completely.

Probably the best example of postinfectious chronic lung disease is found in children who develop bronchiolitis obliterans after having severe adenovirus pneumonia.[99] Bronchiolitis obliterans is characterized by a fibrosing process of the small airways resulting in severe, nonreversible obstruction of the airways. Occasionally, severe involvement of one lung leads to the development of a unilateral, small, hyperlucent lung, known as Swyer-James syndrome.[99] Patients with severe adenovirus pneumonia have immune complexes containing adenovirus antigen in the lung and increased serum levels of interleukin-6, interleukin-8, and tumor necrosis factor–α.[59, 60] These studies suggest that abnormal or excessive host immunologic and inflammatory responses may be important in the development of chronic lung disease from adenovirus in infants and young children. Other infectious agents known to cause bronchiolitis obliterans include *Mycoplasma*, measles, parainfluenza, pertussis, and respiratory syncytial virus.[13]

Other organisms have been associated with pediatric chronic lung disease. Perinatal infection or colonization with *Ureaplasma urealyticum* has been implicated in inducing pulmonary inflammation and subsequent development of bronchopulmonary dysplasia in premature neonates.[42] Parvovirus has been linked to autoimmune disease associated with ILD and other organ involvement.[9]

In a prospective study of immunocompetent children with chronic diffuse infiltrates, I found an infectious agent as the underlying cause of chronic ILDs in 10 (20%) of 51 pediatric ILD cases.[27] Identified agents included adenovirus alone in four patients, adenovirus and cytomegalovirus in two, varicella in one, Epstein-Barr virus in one, *Chlamydia* in one,

TABLE 28–1 ■ CLASSIFICATION OF PEDIATRIC INTERSTITIAL LUNG DISEASES

Pediatric Interstitial Lung Diseases of Known Etiology
- Aspiration syndromes
- Chronic infection (viral, bacterial, fungal, parasitic)
  - Immunocompetent host
  - Immunocompromised host
- Bronchopulmonary dysplasia
- Hypersensitivity pneumonitis (and other environmental exposures)
- Lipid storage diseases

Pediatric Interstitial Lung Diseases of Unknown Etiology
- **Primary Pulmonary Disorders**
  - Usual interstitial pneumonitis (UIP)
  - Desquamative interstitial pneumonitis (DIP)
  - Lymphocytic interstitial pneumonitis (LIP) and related disorders
  - Nonspecific interstitial pneumonitis (NSIP)
  - Pulmonary hemosiderosis
  - Pulmonary infiltrates with eosinophilia
  - Bronchiolitis obliterans
  - Bronchiolitis obliterans with organizing pneumonia (BOOP)
  - Alveolar proteinosis
  - Pulmonary vascular disorders (proliferative and congenital)
  - Pulmonary lymphatic disorders
  - Pulmonary microlithiasis
- **Systemic Disorders with Pulmonary Involvement**
  - Connective tissue disease
  - Malignancies
  - Histiocytosis
  - Sarcoidosis
  - Neurocutaneous syndromes

Unique Forms of Interstitial Lung Disease in Infancy
- Neuroendocrine cell hyperplasia of infancy (NEHI)[70]
- Follicular bronchitis/bronchiolitis[41]
- Cellular interstitial pneumonitis of infancy[80]
- Acute pulmonary hemorrhage of infancy (APHI)[25]
- Chronic pneumonitis of infancy[44]
- Surfactant protein deficiencies[62,63]
- Familial desquamative interstitial pneumonitis (FDIP)[93]
- Idiopathic pulmonary fibrosis of infancy[66]

Adapted from Fan, L. L.: Pediatric interstitial lung disease. *In* Schwarz, M. I., and King, T. E. (eds.): Interstitial Lung Disease. 3rd ed. Hamilton, Ontario, B.C. Decker, 1998, pp. 103–118.

and *Toxocara* in one. Chronic or acute infections with long-term sequelae account for many cases of ILD of known origin in children.

CLASSIC FORMS OF IDIOPATHIC INTERSTITIAL PNEUMONIAS

The classic forms, which Liebow and Carrington originally described largely in adults, included usual interstitial pneumonitis (UIP), DIP, lymphocytic interstitial pneumonitis (LIP), and bronchiolitis obliterans organizing pneumonia (BOOP).[52] Katzenstein and Myers redefined four pathologic categories of idiopathic pulmonary fibrosis to include UIP, DIP/respiratory bronchiolitis interstitial lung disease (DIP/RBILD), acute interstitial pneumonia (AIP, formerly known as Hamman-Rich syndrome), and nonspecific interstitial pneumonia (NSIP).[45]

With the possible exception of UIP and RBILD, these forms of ILD also occur in childhood, but they are rare. A more common pattern of chronic ILD in children is a cellular interstitial pneumonia without the specific histologic features of the classic forms.[80]

Usual Interstitial Pneumonitis

The term UIP, mainly described in adults, refers to a specific pathologic process characterized by ongoing and progressive lung disease, which is patchy in distribution and variable in histology. This pattern is caused by the recruitment of initially normal lung units by an inflammatory and later fibrotic process. The most important histologic features of UIP are fibroblastic foci, which are thought to be the sites from which this process originates.[45] As the recruitment progresses, all stages of reaction—from early acute lesions with hyaline membrane formation, through chronic inflammatory lesions with a mixed mononuclear infiltrate, to late fibrotic lesions—coexist. True examples of this process are exceedingly rare events in children, if they exist at all, although many children with less specific or less well-defined histologic processes have been given this diagnosis. The tendency to use this term in children with a wide variety of nonspecific processes may account for the better prognosis of children with UIP compared with adults, who generally have a very poor prognosis. Although more than 100 children with UIP, cryptogenic fibrosing alveolitis, or idiopathic pulmonary fibrosis have been reported in the literature, many did not have biopsy confirmation of the diagnosis.* The inclusion of heterogeneous conditions into a single diagnostic category may impair significantly evaluation of potential etiologies and therapeutic regimens.

Desquamative Interstitial Pneumonitis

As in adults, DIP in children is a uniform and monotonous histologic process, characterized by hyperplasia of alveolar epithelial cells and an abundance of macrophages within airspaces. These cells within airspaces, initially misidentified as desquamated epithelial cells, give the condition its name.[30] Inflammatory cells, including histiocytes, lymphocytes, plasma cells, and eosinophils, are present but usually only in small numbers. There may be minimal and generally uniform widening of alveolar septa by increased connective tissue, but fibrosis is not a notable feature. In some cases, DIP-like reactions occur in association with more specific lesions and may obscure the more specific picture. Although DIP and UIP have been suggested to represent different stages of the same disease process, this association has not been demonstrated convincingly in children.

DIP in childhood appears to be a different process from DIP in adults, in that it is not decreasing in incidence, the mortality rate is higher, and it is not linked to smoking.[32, 86, 87, 90, 94] DIP occasionally has been associated with infection, particularly congenital rubella[8] and cytomegalovirus infection.[81] A familial version of DIP, which carries a high mortality rate, also exists.[5, 10, 32, 93] One study linked familial DIP with surfactant protein C deficiency.[62] In another case, a congenital defect of the pulmonary surfactant system, not associated with known mutations of the surfactant protein synthesis, has been reported.[20]

Lymphocytic Interstitial Pneumonitis

LIP is the most common of the classically described interstitial pneumonias in children, but rather than being an actual interstitial pneumonitis, it is a form of pulmonary lymphoproliferative disease. It is characterized histologically by a diffuse infiltrate of mature lymphocytes, with smaller numbers of plasma cells and histiocytes in the pulmonary interstitium, including the alveolar wall.[47, 48] The infiltrate also may be found along lymphatic pathways and, therefore, is evident in bronchovascular and interlobular septa, but usually it spares the pleura. The lymphocytes are small noncleaved cells that may accumulate as small nodules, sometimes with germinal centers. Generally, the lymphocytes are polyclonal, with B cells and a variety of T cells identified.[68] Neither fibrosis nor airspace disease is prominent in this disease.

LIP is distinguished histologically from the other benign lymphoid disorders of the lung, which include intraparenchymal lymph nodes, hyperplasia of the bronchial associated lymphoid tissue, nodular lymphoid hyperplasia, and angioimmunoblastic lymphadenopathy.[47, 48] Although many clinicians or pathologists assume that hyperplasia of the bronchial associated lymphoid tissue and nodular lymphoid hyperplasia are stages in the evolution of LIP, this association has not been proved. LIP may exist as an isolated and sometimes familial disorder,[64] but it usually is associated with abnormalities of immune status, including autoimmune disorders[53, 96] and immunodeficiency states.[16] This disease is a well-described complication of pediatric acquired immunodeficiency syndrome (AIDS) and occurs in as many as 30 percent of children affected perinatally with human immunodeficiency virus type 1.[43, 68, 76–78, 83] Children with AIDS and LIP tend not to develop opportunistic infections, such as those caused by *Pneumocystis carinii*. The better prognosis of this group probably is related to less immune compromise. Although Epstein-Barr virus has been isolated from the lungs of some AIDS[2, 26] and non-AIDS patients with LIP,[57] its role in the development of LIP remains unclear.

Clinical Presentation

Most children with ILD have insidious symptoms that may go unrecognized for years. Some of these children have been misdiagnosed as having asthma and treated with bronchodilators.[32] Although a history of wheezing can be elicited in one half of the patients, it can be documented by physical examination in only approximately 20 percent of them. More

*See references 14, 21, 32, 38, 40, 66, 74, 86, 88, 102.

typical symptoms include cough, dyspnea, chronic tachypnea and retractions, exercise limitation, and frequent respiratory infections. One distinguishing feature is that symptoms tend to be more continuous with ILD and more episodic with asthma.

A careful history should be taken to assess the severity of disease and to obtain information that may contribute to making a diagnosis. A search for precipitating factors should include a careful feeding history to rule out potential causes of aspiration; any prior acute or severe respiratory infections; and environmental exposures, especially to birds or molds. Hemoptysis may indicate a pulmonary vascular disorder or hemosiderosis. Joint disease or rash may indicate a systemic process such as connective tissue disease. A family history of relatives or siblings with similar lung conditions may be clues to genetic or familial lung diseases, such as a defect in surfactant proteins.

On physical examination, tachypnea and retractions often are observed, and crackles commonly are heard, particularly at the bases. In severe cases, cyanosis, clubbing, an increased P2 (elevated pulmonic component of the second heart sound), and evidence of growth failure are seen.

Diagnostic Evaluation

A systematic approach to the pediatric patient with ILD is essential for the physician confronted with such a large differential of rare conditions. Diagnostic studies can be divided into those used to assess extent and severity of disease, to identify disorders that predispose to ILD, and to identify the primary ILD (Table 28–2). For adults with ILD, Raghu suggested a diagnostic process that uses a thorough history and physical examination first, noninvasive tests next, and then invasive studies, including bronchoalveolar lavage and transbronchial biopsy followed by open lung biopsy if the previous less invasive studies do not provide a specific diagnosis.[71] Based on experience from a retrospective chart review of 48 children with ILDs,[32] my colleagues and I independently developed an algorithm remarkably similar to that of Raghu and used it prospectively in the evaluation of 51 children presenting with ILDs.[27] In this study, a specific diagnosis was established by history and physical alone in 1 patient, noninvasive studies alone in 8 others, and invasive studies, including lung biopsy, in another 26. Of the remaining patients, eight had a suggestive diagnosis and eight had no specific diagnosis. This study suggests that a systematic approach to the diagnosis of pediatric ILD is useful and that some patients can be diagnosed with noninvasive studies, but most require invasive studies, including lung biopsy.

TABLE 28–2 ■ DIAGNOSTIC STUDIES FOR PEDIATRIC INTERSTITIAL LUNG DISEASE

To Assess Extent and Severity of Disease
- Chest radiographs, high-resolution computed tomography
- Pulmonary function studies: spirometry; pulse oximetry and arterial blood gases (resting, sleeping, and with exercise); diffusion, pressure-volume curve, infant studies
- Electrocardiogram, echocardiogram

To Identify Primary Disorders that Predispose to ILD
- Human immunodeficiency virus (HIV) infection
- Immune studies: immunoglobulins including IgE, skin tests for delayed hypersensitivity, response to immunizations, T and B subsets, complement, others as indicated
- Barium swallow, pH probe

To Identify Primary ILD
- Antinuclear antibody
- Angiotensin-converting enzyme
- Antineutrophil cytoplasmic antibody
- Antiglomerular basement membrane antibody
- Hypersensitivity screen
- Infectious disease evaluation: cultures, titers, skin tests
- Cardiac catheterization (in selected cases)
- Bronchoalveolar lavage and transbronchial biopsy
- Transthoracic biopsy

ILD, interstitial lung disease.
From Fan, L. L.: Pediatric interstitial lung disease. *In* Schwarz, M. I., and King, T. E. (eds.): Interstitial Lung Disease. 3rd ed. Hamilton, Ontario, B. C. Decker, 1998, pp. 103–118.

PULMONARY FUNCTION TESTS

Pulmonary functions studies typically show a pattern of restrictive lung disease with a reduced forced vital capacity (FVC) and forced expiratory volume in 1 second (FEV_1), and normal FEV_1/FVC ratio.[32] Severity of illness can be graded by oxygen saturation and the development of pulmonary hypertension.[29] Patients with mild disease most often are normoxic under all conditions, but with progression of disease and ventilation-perfusion mismatch, they may experience desaturation with exercise or during sleep. Patients with more advanced disease are hypoxemic at rest. The development of pulmonary hypertension often indicates a poor prognosis.

HIGH-RESOLUTION COMPUTED TOMOGRAPHY

High-resolution computed tomography (HRCT) has become an important diagnostic modality in the evaluation of children with ILD. This technique combines thin-section CT with a high-frequency resolution algorithm and reduces the field of view to image one lung or a portion of one lung. Compared with plain chest radiographs, HRCT provides more precise detail about the extent and distribution of parenchymal disease, and this information can be used to select favorable biopsy sites. In a study of 20 children with biopsy-confirmed ILDs, 56 percent of the confident first-choice diagnoses on HRCT were correct.[54] Diseases were classified into five distinct groups based on dominant HRCT features: geographic hyperlucency (i.e., bronchiolitis obliterans or bronchocentric granulomatosis), septal thickening (i.e., lymphangiomatosis, hemangiomatosis, or microlithiasis), ground glass opacification (i.e., DIP, LIP, or HSP), lung cysts and nodules (i.e., histiocytosis), and consolidation (i.e., aspiration, BOOP). In this study, HRCT increased the level of diagnostic confidence for the diagnosis of pediatric ILD, improved diagnostic accuracy, and provided a useful classification system.

BRONCHOALVEOLAR LAVAGE

The recovery of pulmonary cells and alveolar lining fluid by bronchoalveolar lavage (BAL) has been used to diagnose certain pulmonary disorders and to study mechanisms of disease in children. The technique can be performed under direct vision with a pediatric flexible fiberoptic bronchoscope or as a blind technique with a catheter placed through an endotracheal tube.

The most common indication for performing pediatric BAL has been the detection of infection in the immunocompromised host, with a diagnostic yield of approximately

50 percent in patients who did not have AIDS and 75 percent in patients with AIDS.[34] BAL also can identify aspiration or pulmonary hemorrhage by the detection of lipid-laden or hemosiderin-laden macrophages, respectively. However, the presence of lipid- or hemosiderin-laden macrophages in BAL may be sensitive but not specific for aspiration or alveolar hemorrhage syndromes.[31] BAL also has been used to diagnose alveolar proteinosis, lysosomal storage disorders, and histiocytosis in children.[31]

I found that BAL was diagnostic of a primary disorder in only 5 of 29 immunocompetent children with diffuse infiltrates.[31] Aspiration was detected in three and infection in two. The differential diagnosis was narrowed in 15 patients by the presence of lymphocytosis, neutrophilia, or eosinophilia. A secondary disorder was uncovered in eight patients. This study suggests that BAL provides some useful information in children with ILDs but that its ability to determine the primary cause is limited.

LUNG BIOPSY

As in adult ILD, lung biopsy remains the gold standard for the diagnosis of pediatric ILD because most diseases are classified in terms of previously defined histopathologic patterns. An amount of lung tissue adequate for diagnosis has been obtained by using transbronchial biopsy (TBB), percutaneous needle biopsy, conventional open lung biopsy (OLB), and video-assisted thoracoscopy (VAT).

Transthoracic lung biopsy (i.e., OLB or VAT) remains the most reliable way to obtain adequate tissue for diagnosis. No matter what technique is used, lung biopsy material must be processed in a consistent manner to ensure optimal interpretation. This process includes the preparation of imprints from biopsy tissue and the preservation of tissue using several modalities for optimal diagnostic yield. Tissue for light microscopy should be fixed in expansion by methods previously reported.[30] Interpretation of the biopsy by a pathologist with considerable expertise in pediatric lung disease is critical because the normal lung of an infant is much different from that of an older child or adolescent, and any pathologic findings must be interpreted in light of the normal age-dependent variations of lung architecture.

As in adults, the use of VAT is rapidly becoming the method of choice for lung biopsy in children. Technical modifications have allowed its use even in infants.[75] In a prospective study of a small group of immunocompetent children with ILDs, I found that the diagnostic yield for OLB (57%) and VAT (54%) was comparable, but the morbidity from VAT clearly was lower in terms of duration of surgery, chest tube, and hospitalization.[28] Although multiple-lobe biopsies directed by HRCT have been advocated for the diagnosis of adult and pediatric ILDs, this study did not show a difference in diagnostic yield for single versus multiple lobe biopsies. Overall, the diagnostic yield from transthoracic lung biopsy (OLB and VAT) was disappointing, in large part because of an extremely low diagnostic yield in children younger than 2 years of age. However, this study was performed before many of the newly reported diffuse lung diseases in infants were described (see Table 28–1).

Treatment

Supportive care includes adequate nutrition, annual influenza vaccination, aggressive treatment of intercurrent infections, a carefully supervised fitness and exercise program, avoidance of inhalant hazards such as tobacco smoke, selective use of bronchodilators, and oxygen for chronic hypoxemia. Patients with underlying systemic disorders need primary treatment for that disorder, such as gamma-globulin for hypogammaglobulinemia. Specific therapy for primary ILD, such as anti-infective therapy for chronic infections, interferon-α for pulmonary hemangiomatosis,[98] and lung lavage for alveolar proteinosis,[56] should be used when possible. When environmental agents such as bird antigens are causative, avoidance is critical (see the Hypersensitivity Pneumonitis section).

In general, corticosteroids remain the treatment of choice for most patients with ILD on the presumption that suppression of inflammation may reduce the risk of fibrosis.[30] Although controlled clinical studies are lacking, corticosteroids have been used to treat such diverse types of diffuse lung diseases as UIP, DIP, LIP, and hypersensitivity pneumonitis.[34] In my retrospective study of pediatric ILDs, corticosteroids were judged to be effective in 40 percent (12 of 30) of treated children with ILD in terms of improved clinical status, decreased oxygen requirements, and improved pulmonary function.[32] A trial of prednisone or equivalent corticosteroid (1 to 2 mg/kg/day) for at least 6 to 8 weeks probably is warranted.

Alternative, but unproved, therapy includes pulse steroid therapy, hydroxychloroquine, azathioprine, cyclophosphamide, methotrexate, cyclosporin, and intravenous gamma-globulin. Of these, hydroxychloroquine probably has been used the most.[3, 32, 86, 87] The precise mechanism of action is unknown, but chloroquine and hydroxychloroquine have demonstrated immunosuppressive effects with the ability to inhibit the functional capabilities of monocytes and the generation of antibody-forming cells. Hydroxychloroquine is preferred over chloroquine because the former has less retinal toxicity. The recommended dose in children for the treatment of ILD is 10 mg/kg/day.

The fact that many alternative pharmacologic approaches are considered for children and adults with ILDs implies that conventional therapy often is ineffective. New strategies are being developed based on animal models of pulmonary fibrosis and advances in the cellular and molecular biology of inflammatory reactions. Such therapies will be directed against the action of certain cytokines, oxidants, and growth factors that may be involved in the fibrotic process. The potential to deliver specific inflammatory inhibitors or inhibitors of collagen biosynthesis directly to the lung through aerosolization suggests that disease processes in the lung may be more amenable to novel therapies than those in other internal organs would be.

More children are receiving lung transplantation for end-stage ILD. For example, 48 children with ILD have received lung transplantation at St. Louis Children's Hospital. The indications for transplantation included infant ILD (10), childhood ILD (5), secondary pulmonary fibrosis (5), infant pulmonary alveolar proteinosis (12), pulmonary hemosiderosis (2), bronchopulmonary dysplasia (5), and bronchiolitis obliterans (9) (George Mallory, personal communication, 2001). The 5-year survival of children with ILD is approximately 60 percent, which is slightly higher than that of children receiving transplants for cystic fibrosis or pulmonary hypertension. No evidence of recurrence of underlying lung disease in the allografts has been found.

Outcome

The prognosis of children with ILDs varies. Infants with neuroendocrine cell hyperplasia of infancy generally do well, although they may be symptomatic and require oxygen for years.[70] At the other end of the spectrum are children with growth failure, pulmonary hypertension, and severe fibrosis who do poorly.

The overall mortality rates for pediatric ILDs remain high. In a series of 25 children with fibrosing alveolitis or DIP, Sharief and coworkers[86] reported a poor response to treatment in nine patients with four deaths. In a review of 28 patients with DIP, Stillwell and colleagues[90] reported that only 17 patients survived. In a series of children with a variety of ILDs that have been described more recently, Nicholson and associates,[61] using available follow-up data, reported 4 deaths among 17 patients.

I reviewed the outcomes of 99 children with chronic ILDs seen in Denver, Colorado, over a 15-year period (1980 through 1994).[29] As expected, a wide variety of disorders were encountered, and 15 deaths were recorded, with a probability that a patient would survive to 24, 48, and 60 months after onset of symptoms of 83, 72, and 64 percent, respectively. Of the clinical features present at the time of initial evaluation, weight greater than the 5th percentile, crackles, clubbing, family history of ILD, and duration of symptoms were not associated with decreased survival. However, a severity of illness score, based on increasing levels of hypoxemia and the presence or absence of pulmonary hypertension, was related significantly to survival, with an increasing score associated with a higher probability of decreased survival. A simple scoring system appears to be a useful measure of outcome in children with ILD.

HYPERSENSITIVITY PNEUMONITIS

Hypersensitivity pneumonitis (HP), also known as extrinsic allergic alveolitis, is a form of immune-mediated ILD that develops in response to repeated inhalation of finely dispersed organic antigens.[17] A wide variety of organic particles, including mammalian and avian proteins, fungi, thermophilic bacteria, and certain small-molecular-weight, volatile and nonvolatile chemical compounds, are known to induce HP in susceptible individuals.[36]

Acute and chronic forms have been described, and repeated exposure can lead to irreversible lung damage. Although exposure to antigens capable of provoking HP occurs commonly in the home and work environment, the overall incidence of HP in the general population is low. An estimated 5 to 15 percent of persons exposed to high levels of a specific organic antigen will develop clinical disease.

Pathology and Pathogenesis

Pathologically, the disease is characterized by a diffuse and predominantly mononuclear cell inflammation of the small airways and pulmonary parenchyma, often associated with poorly formed, non-necrotizing granulomata.[84] Foamy macrophages commonly are seen in the airspaces. With advanced disease, interstitial and intra-alveolar fibrosis develops and is indistinguishable from other causes of pulmonary fibrosis.

The mechanisms by which organic dusts induce these characteristic pathologic features of the disease are understood poorly. Evidence supports a type III and a type IV hypersensitivity reaction, as defined by Coombs and Gell.[51] A type III reaction is suggested by the presence of precipitating antibody to the offending antigen, immune complex deposition, and activation of complement. A type IV reaction is suggested by an increased percentage of T lymphocytes in BAL fluid, with a strong predominance of $CD8^+$ subsets and a low CD4/CD8 ratio, and the presence of granulomata on lung biopsy. Considering the small proportion of exposed individuals who develop clinical symptoms, complex interactions among the nature of the antigen, the intensity and duration of the exposure, and the host response in susceptible individuals most likely are involved.

Etiology

As shown in Table 28–3, HP in adults is caused by a wide variety of occupational and environmental exposures. [84] In contrast, HP in children is caused mainly by exposure to an array of domestic birds (83%) and fungi (17%), based on a review of 83 reported pediatric cases.* HP also has been reported in a child receiving methotrexate.[18] Familial cases have been identified,[1] with a report describing a mother (who died of the disease) and all of her five children who developed HP from exposure to wild city pigeons.[22]

Clinical Presentation

In the reported pediatric cases previously referenced, the mean age (±SD) was 10 (±3.9) years. The youngest reported patient with HP developed symptoms at 8 months of age.[23]

In the acute form, symptoms mimic a flulike illness, with high fever, chills, dry cough, dyspnea, and malaise. These symptoms begin several hours after exposure and diminish during the next 12 to 24 hours if no additional exposure occurs. Physical examination reveals a dyspneic, ill-appearing child, often with bibasilar crackles. Transient hypoxemia and nodular pulmonary infiltrates often are present.

In the chronic form, children have insidious and progressive symptoms. In the reported pediatric cases for which the following specific symptoms were recorded, exercise intolerance was experienced in 98 percent (61 of 62), cough in 97 percent (66 of 68), weight loss in 92 percent (34 of 37), and fever in 75 percent (38 of 51). On physical examination, crackles were detected in 69 percent (41 of 61) and clubbing in 32 percent (10 of 31) of cases.

Diagnosis

A careful and thorough environmental history is critical to detect potential antigens. The following criteria are considered essential for the diagnosis of HP in adults:

- Symptoms compatible with HP
- Evidence of exposure to appropriate antigen by history or detection in serum or BAL antibody
- Findings compatible with HP on chest radiograph or HRCT
- BAL lymphocytosis (if BAL performed)
- Pulmonary histologic changes compatible with HP (if lung biopsy performed)
- Positive "natural challenge" (i.e., reproduction of symptoms and laboratory abnormalities after exposure to the suspected environment)[82]

*See references 4, 6, 11, 12, 14, 15, 19, 22–24, 35, 37, 46, 49, 58, 65, 67, 69, 73, 79, 85, 89, 92, 95, 97, 100, 101.

TABLE 28–3 ■ ETIOLOGIC AGENTS OF HYPERSENSITIVITY PNEUMONITIS

Disease	Antigen	Source
Fungi and Bacteria		
Farmer's lung	*Faeni rectivirgula*	Moldy hay, grain, silage
Ventilation pneumonitis; humidifier lung; air conditioner lung	*Thermoactinomyces vulgaris, Thermoactinomyces sacchari, Thermoactinomyces candidus, Klebsiella oxytoca*	Contaminated forced air systems, water reservoirs
Bagassosis	*T. vulgaris*	Moldy sugarcane (i.e., bagasse)
Mushroom worker's lung	*Thermoactinomyces sacchari*	Moldy mushroom compost
Suberosis	*Thermoactinomyces viridis, Penicillium glabrum*	Moldy cork
Detergent lung; washing powder lung	*Bacillus subtilis* enzymes	Detergents (during processing or use)
Malt worker's lung	*Aspergillus fumigatus, Aspergillus clavatus*	Moldy barley
Sequoiosis	*Graphium, Pullularia,* and *Trichoderma* spp., *Aureobasidium pullulans*	Moldy wood dust
Maple bark stripper's lung	*Cryptostroma corticale*	Moldy maple bark
Cheese washer's lung	*Penicillium casei, A. clavatus*	Moldy cheese
Woodworker's lung	*Alternaria* spp., wood dust	Oak, cedar, and mahogany dust; pine and spruce pulp
Paprika slicer's lung	*Mucor stolonifer*	Moldy paprika pods
Sauna taker's lung	*Aureobasidium* spp., other sources	Contaminated sauna water
Familial HP	*B. subtilis*	Contaminated wood dust in walls
Wood trimmer's lung	*Rhizopus* spp., *Mucor* spp.	Contaminated wood trimmings
Composter's lung	*T. vulgaris, Aspergillus*	Compost
Basement shower HP	*Epicoccum nigrum*	Mold on unventilated shower
Hot-tub lung	*Cladosporium* spp.	Hot-tub mists, mold on ceiling
Wine maker's lung	*Botrytis cincrea*	Mold on grapes
Woodsman's disease	*Penicillium* spp.	Oak and maple trees
Thatched-roof lung	*Saccharomonospora viridis*	Dead grasses and leaves
Tobacco grower's lung	*Aspergillus* spp.	Tobacco plants
Potato riddler's lung	Thermophilic actinomycetes, *Faeni rectivirgula, T. vulgaris, Aspergillus* spp.	Moldy hay around potatoes
Summer-type pneumonia	*Trichosporon cutaneum*	Contaminated old houses
Dry rot lung	*Merulius lacrymans*	Rotten wood
"Stipatosis"	*A. fumigatus,* thermophilic actinomycetes	Esparto dust
Machine operator's lung	*Pseudomonas fluorescens*	Aerosolized metal-working fluid
Amoebae		
Humidifier lung	*Naegleria gruberi, Acanthamoeba polyphaga, Acanthamoeba castellani*	Contaminated water
Animal proteins		
Pigeon breeder's or pigeon fancier's disease	Avian droppings, feathers, serum	Parakeets, budgerigars, pigeons, chickens, turkeys
Pituitary snuff taker's lung	Pituitary snuff	Bovine and porcine pituitary proteins
Fish meal worker's lung	Fish meal	Fish meal dust
Bat lung	Bat serum protein	Bat droppings
Furrier's lung	Animal-fur dust	Animal pelts
Animal handler's lung; laboratory worker's lung	Rats, gerbils	Urine, serum, pelts, proteins
Insect proteins		
Miller's lung	*Sitophilus granarius* (i.e., wheat weevil)	Dust-contaminated grain
Lycoperdonosis	Puffball spores	Lycoperdon puffballs
Chemical		
Pauli's reagent alveolitis	Sodium diazobenzene sulfate	Laboratory reagent
Chemical worker's lung	Isocyanates, trimellitic anhydride	Polyurethane foams, spray paints, elastomers, special glues
Vineyard sprayer's lung	Copper sulfate	Bordeaux mixture
Pyrethrum HP	Pyrethrum	Pesticide
Epoxy resin lung	Phthalic anhydride	Heated epoxy resin
Unknown		
Bible printer's lung		Moldy typesetting water
Coptic lung (mummy handler's lung)		Cloth wrappings of mummies
Grain measurer's lung		Cereal grain
Coffee worker's lung		Coffee-bean dust
Tap water lung		Contaminated tap water
Tea grower's lung		Tea plants
Mollusk-shell HP		Sea-snail shell
Swimming pool worker's lung		Aerosolized endotoxin from pool-water, sprays, and fountains

HP, hypersensitivity pneumonia.
From Selman, M.: Hypersensitivity pneumonitis. *In* Schwarz, M. I., and King, T. E. (eds.): Interstitial Lung Disease. 3rd ed. Hamilton, Ontario, B. C. Decker, 1998, pp. 393–422.

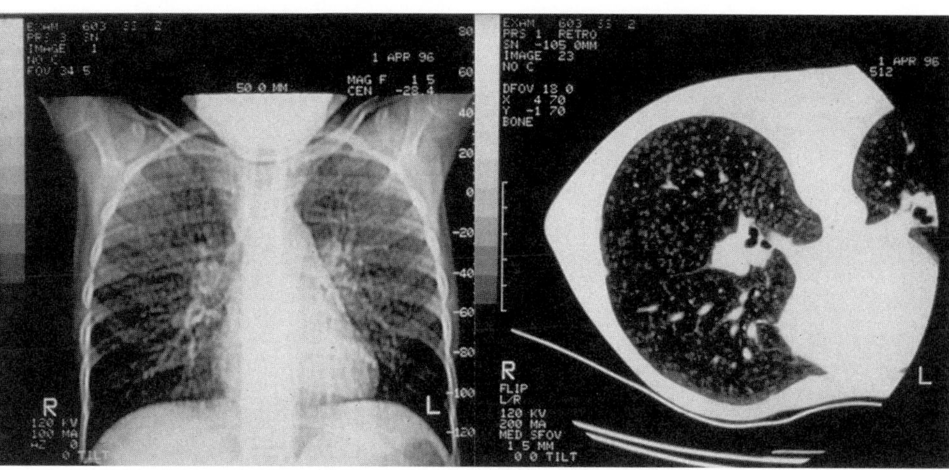

FIGURE 28–1 ■ Hypersensitivity pneumonitis from cockatiel antigens in an adolescent. The chest radiograph shows bilateral reticulonodular infiltrates. High-resolution computed tomography shows diffuse, multiple, fine nodules. (Courtesy of Robin Deterding, M.D., University of Colorado, Denver, CO.; From Fan, L. L.: Pediatric interstitial lung disease. *In* Schwarz, M. I., and King, T. E. [eds.]: Interstitial Lung Disease. 3rd ed. Hamilton, Ontario, B. C. Decker, 1998, pp. 103–118.)

Minor criteria that are nonspecific but almost always present in HP include bibasilar crackles, decreased diffusing capacity, and arterial hypoxemia at rest or with exercise. Children with HP also meet most of these criteria, although BAL has not been performed often in pediatric cases, and diffusing capacity cannot be performed easily in children younger than 6 to 7 years of age.

In the acute form, classic features on chest radiograph and HRCT include poorly defined micronodules with predominance in the upper and middle lung zones (Fig. 28–1). On HRCT, an additional characteristic feature is widespread ground-glass attenuation. In the more chronic phase, diffuse interstitial infiltrates may predominate, with progression to fibrosis and honeycombing that are indistinguishable from UIP.[55] In the reported pediatric cases of HP, chest radiographs were abnormal in 83 percent (69 of 83).

Pulmonary function tests typically show a restrictive defect sometimes with an obstructive component. In reported pediatric cases, the mean (±SD) FEV_1 and FVC, in the children tested, were 55.3 percent (±20.2%) and 53.1 percent (±21.1%) of predicted, respectively. The pressure-volume curve is shifted down and to the right, consistent with decreased compliance. Although resting room air oxygen saturation may be normal, desaturation with exercise or sleep may occur. In patients with long-standing disease, resting oxygen desaturation can be demonstrated. In the pediatric cases for which oxygenation was documented, 84 percent (31 of 37) had hypoxemia at rest. Pulmonary hypertension may be present with advanced disease, but unlike other forms of pediatric ILDs, it may reverse completely with successful treatment.

Detection of precipitating IgG antibodies to the offending antigen can be useful in confirming the diagnosis in a patient with documented exposure and typical clinical features (Fig. 28–2). However, as many as 50 percent of individuals who are exposed to a particular antigen will develop precipitating antibodies, and only a small percentage of these will develop HP.[17] Conversely, not all individuals with symptomatic HP have positive precipitins. In reported pediatric cases, positive precipitins were found in 71 (89%) of 80 children tested. Because the quality of antigen material may vary in commercial laboratories, obtaining a sample of the suspected antigen directly from the original source and testing it against the patient's serum in a reputable laboratory is preferable.

Although provocation challenge (i.e., inhalation of the putative antigen in controlled laboratory conditions) has been useful in adults,[72] it has not been employed in children as often. Provocation challenge was used in only 20 of the 83 children reported in the literature, and 11 (55%) were positive.

BAL obtained from flexible fiberoptic bronchoscopy typically shows a lymphocytosis with a low CD4/CD8 ratio. Lung tissue obtained from transbronchial biopsy in older children and adults (Fig. 28–3) or transthoracic (open or thoracoscopic) biopsy shows the characteristic histologic features described previously. Of the 83 reported pediatric cases of HP, nine biopsies were obtained, and all showed typical histologic changes.

Treatment and Outcome

The mainstay of treatment is eliminating exposure to the offending antigen. In the literature, exposure was eliminated in 97 percent (63 of the 65) of the pediatric cases, with improvement occurring in all but one fatal case.

Corticosteroids often result in rapid improvement in symptoms and reversal of radiographic and lung function

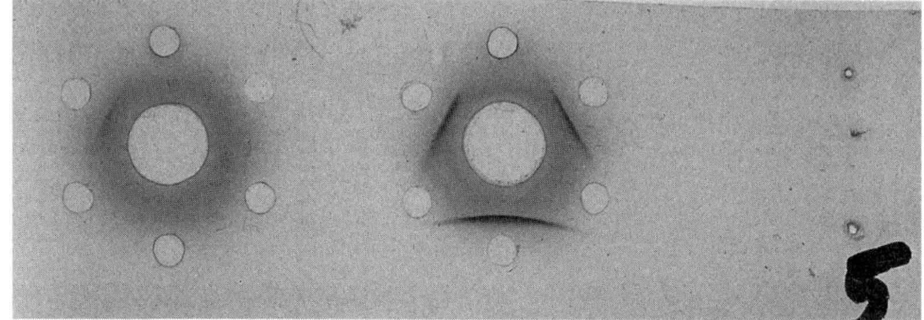

FIGURE 28–2 ■ Serum-precipitating antibodies against cockatiel antigens in the patient shown in Figure 28–1. (Courtesy of Robin Deterding, M.D., University of Colorado, Denver, CO.)

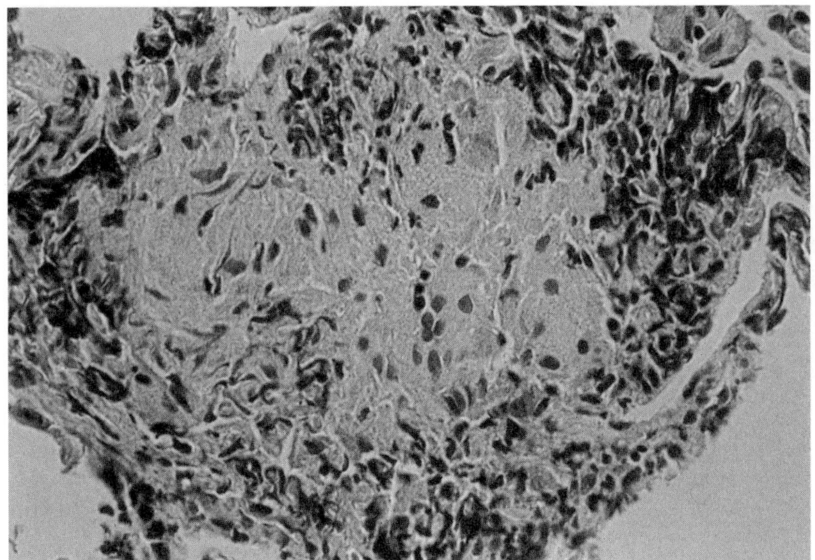

FIGURE 28–3 ■ Transbronchial biopsy in the patient shown in Figure 28–1 demonstrates a poorly formed granuloma consistent with hypersensitivity pneumonitis. (Courtesy of Robin Deterding, M.D., University of Colorado, Denver, CO.)

abnormalities unless irreversible changes in the lung have occurred. Corticosteroids were used in 60 percent (39 of 65) of the reported pediatric cases, with a positive response in all but the one fatal case.

The outcome of children with HP, properly diagnosed and treated, is excellent. In the 65 pediatric cases of HP with reported outcomes, 63 improved or became asymptomatic, 1 patient remained unchanged, and 1 patient died. In the fatal case, an 11-year-old girl developed classic features of HSP after several years of exposure to budgerigars and other birds.[97] Despite removal of the offending antigens and treatment with corticosteroids and D-penicillamine, she died of respiratory failure 13 months later. The overall prognosis for children with HSP is excellent, provided a prompt diagnosis is made and appropriate treatment consisting of antigen removal and the judicious use of corticosteroids is instituted.

REFERENCES

1. Allen, D. H., Basten, A., Williams, G. V., and Woolcock, A. J.: Familial hypersensitivity pneumonitis. Am. J. Med. *59*:505–514, 1975.
2. Andiman, W. A., Eastman, R., Martin, K., et al.: Opportunistic lymphoproliferations associated with Epstein-Barr viral DNA in infants and children with AIDS. Lancet *2*:1390–1393, 1985.
3. Avital, A., Godfrey, S., Maayan, C., et al.: Chloroquine treatment of interstitial lung disease in children. Pediatr. Pulmonol. *18*:356–360, 1994.
4. Balasubramaniam, S. K., O'Connell, E. J., Yunginger, J. W., et al.: Hypersensitivity pneumonitis due to dove antigens in an adolescent. Clin. Pediatr. *26*:174–176, 1987.
5. Balasubramanyan, N., Murphy, A., O'Sullivan, J., and O'Connell, E. J.: Familial interstitial lung disease in children: Response to chloroquine treatment in one sibling with desquamative interstitial pneumonitis. Pediatr. Pulmonol. *23*:55–61, 1997.
6. Barker, P. M., and Warner, J. O.: "Atypical pneumonia" due to parakeet sensitivity: Bird fancier's lung in a 10-year-old girl. Br. J. Dis. Chest *78*:404–407, 1984.
7. Bokulic, R. E., and Hilman, B. C.: Interstitial lung disease in children. Pediatr. Clin. North Am. *41*:543–567, 1994.
8. Boner, A., Wilmott, R. W., Dinwiddie, R., et al.: Desquamative interstitial pneumonia and antigen-antibody complexes in two infants with congenital rubella. Pediatrics *72*:835–839, 1983.
9. Bousvaros, A., Sundel, R., Thorne, G. M., et al.: Parvovirus B19–associated interstitial lung disease, hepatitis, and myositis. Pediatr. Pulmonol. *26*:265–269, 1998.
10. Buchino, J. J., Keenan, W. J., Algren, J. T., and Bove, K. E.: Familial desquamative interstitial pneumonitis occurring in infants. Am. J. Med. Genet. Suppl. *3*:285–291, 1987.
11. Bureau, M. A., Fecteau, C., Patriquin, H., et al.: Farmer's lung in early childhood. Am. Rev. Respir. Dis. *119*:671–675, 1979.
12. Chandra, S., and Jones, H. E.: Pigeon fancier's lung in children. Arch. Dis. Child. *47*:716–718, 1972.
13. Chang, A. B., Masel, J. P., and Masters, B.: Post-infectious bronchiolitis obliterans: Clinical, radiological and pulmonary function sequelae. Pediatr. Radiol. *28*:23–29, 1998.
14. Chetty, A., Bhuyan, U. N., Mitra, D. K., et al.: Cryptogenic fibrosing alveolitis in children. Ann. Allergy *58*:336–340, 1987.
15. Chiron, C., Gaultier, C., Boule, M., et al.: Lung function in children with hypersensitivity pneumonitis. Eur. J. Respir. Dis. *65*:79–91, 1984.
16. Church, J. A., Isaacs, H., Saxon, A., et al.: Lymphoid interstitial pneumonitis and hypogammaglobulinemia in children. Am. Rev. Respir. Dis. *124*:491–496, 1981.
17. Craig, T. J., and Richerson, H. B.: Update on hypersensitivity pneumonitis. Compr. Ther. *22*:559–564, 1996.
18. Cron, R. Q., Sherry, D. D., and Wallace, C. A.: Methotrexate-induced hypersensitivity pneumonitis in a child with juvenile rheumatoid arthritis. J. Pediatr. *132*:901–902, 1998.
19. Cunningham, A. S., Fink, J. N., and Schlueter, D. P.: Childhood hypersensitivity pneumonitis due to dove antigens. Pediatrics *58*:436–442, 1976.
20. Cutz, E., Wert, S., Nogee, L. M., and Moore, A. M.: Deficiency of lamellar bodies in alveolar type II cells associated with fatal respiratory disease in a full-term infant. Am. J. Respir. Crit. Care Med. *161*:608–614, 2000.
21. Desmarquest, P., Tamalet, A., Fauroux, B., et al.: Chronic interstitial lung disease in children: Response to high-dose intravenous methylprednisolone pulses. Pediatr. Pulmonol. *26*:332–338, 1998.
22. du Marchie Sarvaas, G., Merkus, P. J., and de Jongste, J. C.: A family with extrinsic allergic alveolitis caused by wild city pigeons: A case report. Pediatrics *105*:E62, 2000.
23. Eisenberg, J. D., Montanero, A., and Lee, R. G.: Hypersensitivity pneumonitis in an infant. Pediatr. Pulmonol. *12*:186–190, 1992.
24. El-Hefny, A., Ekladious, E. M., El-Sharkawy, S., et al.: Extrinsic allergic bronchiolo-alveolitis in children. Clin. Allergy *10*:651–658, 1980.
25. Epstein, C. E., and Fan, L. L.: Alveolar hemorrhage syndromes: Update on pulmonary hemosiderosis. J. Respir. Dis. Pediatrician *3*:49–56, 2001.
26. Fackler, J. C., Nagel, J. E., Adler, W. H., et al.: Epstein-Barr virus infection in a child with acquired immunodeficiency syndrome. Am. J. Dis. Child. *139*:1000–1004, 1985.
27. Fan, L. L., Kozinetz, C. A., Deterding, R. R., and Brugman, S. M.: Evaluation of a diagnostic approach to pediatric interstitial lung disease. Pediatrics *101*:82–85, 1998.
28. Fan, L. L., Kozinetz, C. A., Wojtczak, H. A., et al.: Diagnostic value of transbronchial, thoracoscopic, and open lung biopsy in immunocompetent children with chronic interstitial lung disease. J. Pediatr. *131*:565–569, 1997.
29. Fan, L. L., and Kozinetz, C. A.: Factors influencing survival in children with chronic interstitial lung disease. Am. J. Respir. Crit. Care Med. *156*:939–942, 1997.
30. Fan, L. L., and Langston, C.: Chronic interstitial lung disease in children. Pediatr. Pulmonol. *16*:184–196, 1993.
31. Fan, L. L., Lung, M. C., and Wagener, J. S.: The diagnostic value of bronchoalveolar lavage in immunocompetent children with chronic diffuse pulmonary infiltrates. Pediatr. Pulmonol. *23*:8–13, 1997.

32. Fan, L. L., Mullen, A. L., Brugman, S. M., et al.: Clinical spectrum of chronic interstitial lung disease in children. J. Pediatr. *121*:867–872, 1992.
33. Fan, L. L.: Evaluation and therapy of chronic interstitial pneumonitis in children. Curr. Opin. Pediatr. *6*:248–254, 1994.
34. Fan, L. L.: Pediatric interstitial lung disease. *In* Schwarz, M. I., and King, T. E. (eds.): Interstitial Lung Disease. 3rd ed. Hamilton, Ontario, B. C. Decker, 1998, pp. 103–118.
35. Grammer, L. C., Roberts, M., Lerner, C., and Patterson, R.: Clinical and serologic follow-up of four children and five adults with bird-fancier's lung. J. Allergy Clin. Immunol. *85*:655–660, 1990.
36. Grammer, L.C.: Occupational allergic alveolitis. Ann. Allergy Asthma Immunol. *83*:602–606, 1999.
37. Grech, V., Vella, C., and Lenicker, H.: Pigeon breeder's lung in childhood: Varied clinical picture at presentation. Pediatr. Pulmonol. *30*:145–148, 2000.
38. Hacking, D., Smyth, R., Shaw, N., et al.: Idiopathic pulmonary fibrosis in infants: Good prognosis with conservative management. Arch. Dis. Child. *83*:152–157, 2000.
39. Harrison, H. R., Taussig, L. M., and Fulginiti, V. A.: *Chlamydia trachomatis* and chronic lung disease in childhood. Pediatr. Infect. Dis. J. *1*:29–33, 1982.
40. Hewitt, C. J., Hull, D., and Keeling, J. W.: Fibrosing alveolitis in infancy and childhood. Arch. Dis. Child. *52*:22–37, 1977.
41. Hull, J., Chow, C. W., and Robertson, C. F.: Chronic idiopathic bronchiolitis of infancy. Arch. Dis. Child. *77*:512–515, 1997.
42. Jobe, A. H., and Bancalari, E.: Bronchopulmonary dysplasia. Am. J. Respir. Crit. Care Med. *163*:1723–1729, 2001.
43. Joshi, V. V., Oleske, J. M., Minnefor, A. B., et al.: Pathologic pulmonary findings in children with the acquired immunodeficiency syndrome: A study of ten cases. Hum. Pathol. *16*:241–246, 1985.
44. Katzenstein, A. L., Gordon, L. P., Oliphant, M., and Swender, P. T.: Chronic pneumonitis of infancy. A unique form of interstitial lung disease occurring in early childhood. Am. J. Surg. Pathol. *19*:439–447, 1995.
45. Katzenstein, A. L., and Myers, J. L.: Idiopathic pulmonary fibrosis: Clinical relevance of pathologic classification. Am. J. Respir. Crit. Care Med. *157*:1301–1315, 1998.
46. Keith, H. H., Holsclaw, D. S., and Dunsky, E. H.: Pigeon breeder's disease in children. A family study. Chest *79*:107–110, 1981.
47. Koss, M. N.: Pulmonary lymphoid disorders. Semin. Diagn. Pathol. *12*:158–171, 1995.
48. Kradin, R. L., and Mark, E. J.: Benign lymphoid disorders of the lung, with a theory regarding their development. Hum. Pathol. *14*:857–867, 1983.
49. Krasnick, J., Patterson, R., Stillwell, P. C., et al.: Potentially fatal hypersensitivity pneumonitis in a child. Clin. Pediatr. *34*:388–391, 1995.
50. Laray-Cuasay, L. R., DeForest, A., Huff, D., et al.: Chronic pulmonary complications of early influenza virus infection in children. Am. Rev. Respir. Dis. *116*:617–625, 1977.
51. Larsen, G. L.: Hypersensitivity lung disease. Annu. Rev. Immunol. *3*:59–85, 1985.
52. Liebow, A. A., and Carrington, C. B.: The interstitial pneumonias. *In* Simon, M., Potchen, E. J., and Le May, M. (eds.): Frontiers of Pulmonary Radiology. New York, Grune & Stratton, 1968, pp. 102–141.
53. Lovell, D., Lindsley, C., and Langston, C.: Lymphoid interstitial pneumonia in juvenile rheumatoid arthritis. J. Pediatr. *105*:947–950, 1984.
54. Lynch, D. A., Hay, T., Newell, J. D., et al.: Pediatric diffuse lung disease: Diagnosis and classification using high-resolution CT. A.J.R. Am. J. Roentgenol. *173*:713–718, 1999.
55. Lynch, D. A., Newell, J. D., Logan, P. M., et al.: Can CT distinguish hypersensitivity pneumonitis from idiopathic pulmonary fibrosis? A.J.R. Am. J. Roentgenol. *165*:807–811, 1995.
56. Mahut, B., Delacourt, C., Scheinmann, P., et al.: Pulmonary alveolar proteinosis: Experience with eight pediatric cases and a review. Pediatrics *97*:117–122, 1996.
57. Malamou-Mitsi, V., Tsai, M. M., Gal, A. A., et al.: Lymphoid interstitial pneumonia not associated with HIV infection: Role of Epstein-Barr virus. Mod. Pathol. *5*:487–491, 1992.
58. Miller, M. M., Patterson, R., Fink, J. N., and Roberts, M.: Chronic hypersensitivity lung disease with recurrent episodes of hypersensitivity pneumonitis due to a contaminated central humidifer. Clin. Allergy *6*:451–462, 1976.
59. Mistchenko, A. S., Diez, R. A., Mariani, A. L., et al.: Cytokines in adenoviral disease in children: Association of interleukin-6, interleukin-8, and tumor necrosis factor alpha levels with clinical outcome. J. Pediatr. *124*:714–720, 1994.
60. Mistchenko, A. S., Lenzi, H. L., Thompson, F. M., et al.: Participation of immune complexes in adenovirus infection. Acta. Paediatr *81*:983–988, 1992.
61. Nicholson, A. G., Kim, H., Corrin, B., et al.: The value of classifying interstitial pneumonitis in childhood according to defined histological patterns. Histopathology *33*:203–211, 1998.
62. Nogee, L. M., Dunbar, A. E., Wert, S. E., et al.: A mutation in the surfactant protein C gene associated with familial interstitial lung disease. N. Engl. J. Med. *344*:573–579, 2001.
63. Nogee, L. M.: Surfactant protein-B deficiency. Chest *111*:129S–135S, 1997.
64. O'Brodovich, H. M., Moser, M. M., and Lu, L.: Familial lymphoid interstitial pneumonia: a long-term follow-up. Pediatrics *65*:523–528, 1980.
65. O'Connell, E. J., Zora, J. A., Gillespie, D. N., and Rosenow, E. C.: Childhood hypersensitivity pneumonitis (farmer's lung): Four cases in siblings with long-term follow-up. J. Pediatr. *114*:995–997, 1989.
66. Osika, E., Muller, M. H., Boccon-Gibod, L., et al.: Idiopathic pulmonary fibrosis in infants. Pediatr. Pulmonol. *23*:49–54, 1997.
67. Park, S. M., and Tremper, L.: Hypersensitivity pneumonitis in pediatric patients. Immunol. Allergy Pract. *9*:420–423, 1987.
68. Pitt, J.: Lymphocytic interstitial pneumonia. Pediatr. Clin. North Am. *38*:89–95, 1991.
69. Purtilo, D. T., Brem, J., Ceccaci, L., et al.: A family study of pigeon breeders' disease. J. Pediatr. *86*:569–571, 1975.
70. Pye, C., Fan, L. L., and Langston, C.: Pulmonary neuroendocrine cell hyperplasia in persistent tachypnea of infancy. Mod. Pathol. *11*:4P, 1998.
71. Raghu, G.: Interstitial lung disease: A diagnostic approach. Are CT scan and lung biopsy indicated in every patient? Am. J. Respir. Crit. Care Med. *151*:909–914, 1995.
72. Ramirez-Venegas, A., Sansores, R. H., Perez-Padilla, R., et al.: Utility of a provocation test for diagnosis of chronic pigeon breeder's disease. Am. J. Respir. Crit. Care Med. *158*:862–869, 1998.
73. Reiss, J. S., Weiss, N. S., Payette, K. M., and Strimas, J.: Childhood pigeon breeder's disease. Ann. Allergy *32*:208–212, 1974.
74. Riedler, J., Golser, A., and Huttegger, I.: Fibrosing alveolitis in an infant. Eur. Respir. J. *5*:359–361, 1992.
75. Rothenberg, S. S., Wagner, J. S., Chang, J. H., and Fan, L. L.: The safety and efficacy of thoracoscopic lung biopsy for diagnosis and treatment in infants and children. J. Pediatr. Surg. *31*:100–103, 1996.
76. Rubinstein, A., Bernstein, L. J., Charytan, M., et al.: Corticosteroid treatment for pulmonary lymphoid hyperplasia in children with the acquired immune deficiency syndrome. Pediatr. Pulmonol. *4*:13–17, 1988.
77. Rubinstein, A., Morecki, R., and Goldman, H.: Pulmonary disease in infants and children. Clin. Chest Med. *9*:507–517, 1988.
78. Rubinstein, A., Morecki, R., Silverman, B., et al.: Pulmonary disease in children with acquired immune deficiency syndrome and AIDS-related complex. J. Pediatr. *108*:498–503, 1986.
79. Saltos, N., Saunders, N. A., Bhagwandeen, S. B., and Jarvie, B.: Hypersensitivity pneumonitis in a mouldy house. Med. J. Aust. *2*:244–246, 1982.
80. Schroeder, S. A., Shannon, D. C., and Mark, E. J.: Cellular interstitial pneumonitis in infants. A clinicopathologic study. Chest *101*:1065–1069, 1992.
81. Schroten, H., Manz, S., Kohler, H., et al.: Fatal desquamative interstitial pneumonia associated with proven CMV infection in an 8-month-old boy. Pediatr. Pulmonol. *25*:345–347, 1998.
82. Schuyler, M., and Cormier, Y.: The diagnosis of hypersensitivity pneumonitis. Chest *111*:534–536, 1997.
83. Scott, G. B., Hutto, C., Makuch, R. W., et al.: Survival in children with perinatally acquired human immunodeficiency virus type 1 infection. N. Engl. J. Med. *321*:1791–1796, 1989.
84. Selman, M.: Hypersensitivity pneumonitis. *In* Schwarz, M. I., and King, T. E. (eds.): Interstitial Lung Disease. 3rd ed. Hamilton, Ontario, B. C. Decker, 1998, pp. 393–422.
85. Shannon, D. C., Andrews, J. L., Recavarren, S., and Kazemi, H.: Pigeon breeder's lung disease and interstitial pulmonary fibrosis. Am. J. Dis. Child. *117*:504–510, 1969.
86. Sharief, N., Crawford, O. F., and Dinwiddie, R.: Fibrosing alveolitis and desquamative interstitial pneumonitis. Pediatr. Pulmonol. *17*:359–365, 1994.
87. Springer, C., Maayan, C., Katzir, Z., et al.: Chloroquine treatment in desquamative interstitial pneumonia. Arch. Dis. Child. *62*:76–77, 1987.
88. Steinkamp, G., Muller, K. M., Schirg, E., et al.: Fibrosing alveolitis in childhood. A long-term follow-up. Acta Paediatr. Scand. *79*:823–831, 1990.
89. Stiehm, E. R., Reed, C. E., and Tooley, W. H.: Pigeon breeder's lung in children. Pediatrics *39*:904–915, 1967.
90. Stillwell, P. C., Norris, D. G., O'Connell, E. J., et al.: Desquamative interstitial pneumonitis in children. Chest *77*:165–171, 1980.
91. Stokes, D., Sigler, A., Khouri, N. F., and Talamo, R. C.: Unilateral hyperlucent lung (Swyer-James syndrome) after severe *Mycoplasma pneumoniae* infection. Am. Rev. Respir. Dis. *117*:145–152, 1978.
92. Swingler, G. H.: Summer-type hypersensitivity pneumonitis in southern Africa. A report of 5 cases in one family. S. Afr. Med. J. *77*:104–107, 1990.
93. Tal, A., Maor, E., Bar-Ziv, J., and Gorodischer, R.: Fatal desquamative interstitial pneumonia in three infant siblings. J. Pediatr. *104*:873–876, 1984.
94. Teague, W. G., Sutphen, J. L., and Fechner, R. E.: Desquamative interstitial pneumonitis complicating inflammatory bowel disease of childhood. J. Pediatr. Gastroenterol. Nutr. *4*:663–667, 1985.
95. Tsai, E., Couture, D., and Hughes, D. M.: A pediatric case of pigeon breeder's disease in Nova Scotia. Can. Respir. J. *5*:507–510, 1998.

96. Uziel, Y., Hen, B., Cordoba, M., and Wolach, B.: Lymphocytic interstitial pneumonitis preceding polyarticular juvenile rheumatoid arthritis. Clin. Exp. Rheumatol. *16*:617–619, 1998.
97. Vergesslich, K. A., Gotz, M., and Kraft, D.: [Bird breeder's lung with conversion to fatal fibrosing alveolitis]. Dtsch. Med. Wochenschr. *108*:1238–1242, 1983.
98. White, C. W., Sondheimer, H. M., Crouch, E. C., et al.: Treatment of pulmonary hemangiomatosis with recombinant interferon alfa-2a. N. Engl. J. Med. *320*:1197–1200, 1989.
99. Wohl, M. E. B., and Chernic, V.: Bronchiolitis. Am. Rev. Respir. Dis. *118*:759–781, 1978.
100. Wolf, S. J., Stillerman, A., Weinberger, M., and Smith, W.: Chronic interstitial pneumonitis in a 3-year-old child with hypersensitivity to dove antigens. Pediatrics *79*:1027–1029, 1987.
101. Yee, W. F., Castile, R. G., Cooper, A., et al.: Diagnosing bird fancier's disease in children. Pediatrics *85*:848–852, 1990.
102. Zapletal, A., Houstek, J., Samanek, M., et al.: Lung function in children and adolescents with idiopathic interstitial pulmonary fibrosis. Pediatr. Pulmonol. *1*:154–166, 1985.

CHAPTER 29

Pleural Effusions and Empyema

J. GARY WHEELER ■ RICHARD F. JACOBS

Collections of fluid in the pleural space have been described in the literature as transudates, pleural effusions, exudates, purulent pleurisy, parapneumonic effusions, empyema, and complicated empyema. Unfortunately, a great deal of inexactitude exists in the use of these terms, and, therefore, comparing methods of diagnosis and management from one study to another is difficult. Standardized definitions are used in this chapter to describe pleural fluid collections.

The term *transudative pleural effusion* refers to fluid in the pleural space that is a nonpurulent effusion and typically nonpneumonic in origin. The term *purulent effusions* refers to effusions that are more cellular (exudative) and typically pneumonic in origin. The term *empyema* is used to describe purulent effusions with chemical or microbial evidence of a more severe process requiring drainage. *Complicated empyema* describes the processes associated with loculations or a fibropurulent rind requiring more aggressive manipulations for cure. *Parapneumonic effusion* is a general term referring to any pleural exudative process resulting from an inflammatory process in the lung. Although these definitions are arbitrary and the literature is inconsistent in the use of these terms, a relatively standard approach to the classification of these four types of effusions and their management has evolved.

The first description of parapneumonic infection is attributed to Hippocrates, who in the fourth century BC advocated incision and drainage of empyema 2 weeks after the onset of symptoms. Since then, the physiology and microbiology of effusions have been described, and parapneumonic diseases and the management of fluid collections of the pleural space have been defined. In most cases, the directions of Hippocrates still are relevant: "...set him upon a stool, which is not wobbly; someone should hold his hands, then shake him by the shoulders and listen to see on which side a noise is heard. And right at this place—preferably on the left—make an incision, then it produces death more rarely."[50] This description of open drainage to normal atmospheric pressures was recognized to be associated with significant mortality rates from hemodynamic instability in 1918, when the Empyema Commission of the United States Army recommended that the practice be abandoned.[49] Thereafter, closed-tube drainage was introduced, and mortality rates fell. Developments in radiology, antimicrobials, and surgery resulted in further improvements in care. Today, the major cause of mortality is related to the underlying disease because the management of parapneumonic effusions in children is largely successful and without residual morbidity. The physician must understand the risks for development of pleural effusion and empyema, as well as indications for thoracentesis, implications of the results of pleural fluid studies, and the optimal medical and surgical management of the effusions and empyema.

Epidemiology

Parapneumonic effusions are known and expected complications in children with respiratory tract infections. The frequency of effusions can be as high as 20 percent of patients with viral or mycoplasmal pneumonia[20, 25, 72] and 75 percent of patients with proven *Staphylococcus aureus* pneumonia.[5] Empyema has been reported to occur in 6.3 of 1000 admissions of Israeli children[55] and as a complication of pneumonia in 1 percent of children in the United States.[15] One of the most extensive studies of empyema in children was from Dallas; 12 episodes per year during a 19-year period were described.[22] In adults, empyema follows a primary pulmonary process in 55 to 60 percent of cases, surgery in 20 percent, trauma in 6 percent, spontaneous pneumothorax in 35 percent, and other causes in 2 percent.[49, 70] Hoff and associates[33] found that 11 percent of cases in children had an underlying illness, including hyperimmunoglobulin E syndrome, hypogammaglobulinemia, acute lymphocytic leukemia, cerebral palsy, Down syndrome, and postsurgical and congenital thrombocytopenia. The remainder were related to a primary pulmonic process. Freij and associates[22] found a rate of 8.3 percent with similar risk factors. The mortality rate is highest in the first 2 years of life. After 2 years of age, children have better outcomes than do adults; generally, they have less intrinsic lung disease, have greater elasticity of their chest wall, and heal more quickly than do older individuals.[13, 27]

Pathophysiology

The pleurae are mesodermally derived tissues that are approximately 30 to 40 µm thick and permeable to liquid and gas.[7, 43] The parietal pleurae, which adhere to the chest wall, are fed from the intrathoracic and superior phrenic arteries and have sensory enervation. The visceral pleurae are splanchnic in origin, with blood flow from the pulmonic and pericardiophrenic arteries and no sensory enervation.

The lymphatic structures of the visceral pleurae are microscopic vessels called *lacunae*. They are denser in the lower lobes to accommodate greater venous pressure. Parietal structures called *stomas* are 4- to 10-µm-diameter pores that connect the pleurae to lymphatics. These stomas have valvular function during expiration and inspiration and can filter large structures, such as red blood cells and macrophages.[43] The venous drainage of visceral pleura is into the pulmonic veins and from the parietal pleura into intercostal and bronchial veins. Lymphatic structures are woven below and around the mesothelial cells and ultimately drain into mediastinal, intercostal, and mammary nodes. The structure of the pleura is a surface of mesothelial cells and layers of lymphatic sinuses and pores, elastic fibers, and loose vascular connective tissue and a fibroelastic layer covering the lungs and chest wall.[43]

The precise flow and distribution of pleural fluid have been debated for some time. Because of the differences in venous pressure in the intercostal and pulmonary veins, fluid is thought to flow from the parietal venous system to the visceral system by drifting from the high pressure in parietal tissues into the negative-pressure pleural space, with reabsorption on the visceral side. The latter is caused by a relatively low venous pressure system on the parietal side and the relatively high oncotic pressure of the pulmonic venous system compared with the pleural space.

The dynamics of this process are described in Starling's equation:

$$\text{Fluid movement} = k \bullet [\{HP_c - HP_{ip}\} - \{COP_c - COP_{ip}\}]$$

in which k is the filtration coefficient (a measure of the permeability of capillaries to fluid), HP is the hydrostatic pressure, and COP is the colloid osmotic pressure of capillaries (c) and the intrapleural compartment (ip).[12]

The consensus is that, although the impact of Starling forces on venous flow may play a role in the normal situation, parietal lymphatics absorb most of the excess fluids in pathologic situations and play an important role in normal physiology as well, removing up to 250 to 500 mL/day in adults.[75] They are the only mechanism for absorbing cells and other debris from the pleura.

A few studies in the past have shown that as much as 20 mL of pleural fluid is found normally in 30 percent of resting adults, 70 percent of exercising adults,[5] and 46 to 67 percent of postpartum women.[33] Some fluid may be transported from the peritoneum to the pleura through small communications.[5] This hypothesis is supported by reports of patients with infected abdominal fluid and pleural effusions in whom the same organisms are recovered in both sites.[11]

The raison d'être of the pleural space is unknown. Some mammals, such as elephants, do not have a pleural space.[85] This fact has served as the rationale for using some methods of management of pleural disease that have included chemical obliteration of the pleural space. In the normal situation, pleural fluid in small amounts is a necessary requirement for optimal lubrication of the pleural space and for mechanical coupling of the lung and chest wall.[43] The accumulation of excess fluid (i.e., effusion) occurs in a limited set of circumstances, through excess production or deficient absorption. Increased production occurs when vessels are leaky (e.g., in septic shock) or active secretion of fluid with mesothelial inflammation (e.g., pleural infection) is present. Decreased absorption occurs with lowered oncotic pressure (e.g., nephrosis), increased pulmonary hydrostatic pressure (e.g., congestive heart failure), or lymphatic obstruction (e.g., malignancy).[84]

The mechanisms behind pleural effusions may vary among different infectious diseases. Effusion can be a "sympathetic" pleural response to a bacterial infection in the lung associated with inflammatory cytokines and altered venous or lymphatic drainage because of local edema. Direct or hematogenous extension of a bacterial process can occur in the pleura. *Mycoplasma* particularly is pathogenic in patients with sickle-cell disease, presumably because of pulmonary sludging, which raises pulmonic venous drainage pressures and results in accumulation of effusions. In pneumococcal disease, effusions often develop several days after the acute infection, when bacteria no longer can be recovered. These effusions may be related to immune complex disease.[12] In patients with tuberculosis, the most common cause of pleural effusions is thought to be the rupture of an old granuloma into the pleural space, with a hypersensitivity response not unlike the skin test response,[13] which in part explains the low yield in cultures.

After an inflammatory process is initiated, it tends to progress through three classic stages.[3] The first, defined as a *purulent effusion*, is the acute exudative stage, with a thin pleural exudate characterized by normal glucose, lactate dehydrogenase, and pH. The transitional fibropurulent stage, categorized as *empyema*, is characterized by turbid fluid, decreased glucose concentration (<60 mg/dL) and pH (7.2 to 7.35), and elevated lactate dehydrogenase level (>200 U/L). The chronic organizing stage is notable for a very low pH (<7.2) and glucose level (<40 mg/dL), lactate dehydrogenase concentration greater than 1000 U/L, and development of loculations and peel. This fluid is found in patients with *complicated empyema*.

Often, the pleural fluid quality can be predicted based on the clinical course of the patient without sampling the fluid. A patient with anasarca caused by heart failure or nephrosis with bilateral effusions may not need to have an effusion analyzed if otherwise stable. However, if the same patient has fever, examination of the fluid is necessary to exclude a secondary bacterial infection. Pleural fluid analysis is most helpful when the underlying disease is unknown or when a primary pulmonic process is suspected. When patients have effusions caused by hydrostatic imbalance, the effusion is a transudate. Its protein and cell count do not exceed the range of normal pleural fluid (5000 cells/mm and <2 g of protein).[5, 75] Patients who have an active inflammatory process may have an exudate (defined by excess protein and cells). In children, the most common cause of exudative pleural processes is pneumonia. In adults, most pleural effusions are related to congestive heart failure or malignancy,[48] but pneumonia is the most common cause of empyema.[60] Table 29–1 summarizes the general differences among pleural effusions.

A list of causes of effusions is found in Table 29–2. Some of these causes, particularly iatrogenic causes, such as invasive procedures and drugs, are important to consider in the differential diagnosis of a difficult patient. Others are associated with specific syndromes, such as adult respiratory distress syndrome[77] and yellow nail–lymphedema syndrome.[79] Motor vehicle accidents have been identified as a common cause of serosanguineous effusions when disruption of normal mechanical lung function and hematoma occur.[69]

Microbiology

Among children with parapneumonic effusions, no prospective study has established firmly the frequency with which effusions occur and how many are associated with particular microbes. Although respiratory viruses infrequently cause symptomatic effusions, the sheer number of cases and the presence of asymptomatic cases likely would render viral

TABLE 29–1 ■ CHARACTERISTICS OF PLEURAL EFFUSIONS

	Transudative	Purulent Effusion	Empyema	Complicated Empyema
Appearance	Serous	Thin exudate	Turbid	Thick pus
Mean WBC	1000	5300	25,500	55,000
PMN%	50%	>90%	>95%	>95%
Protein (fluid/serum ratio)	<0.5	>0.5	>0.5	>0.5
LDH (fluid/serum ratio)	<0.6	>0.6	>0.6	>0.6
LDH (IU/L)		>200	>200	>1000
Glucose mg/dL	>60	<60	<60	<40
pH*	7.4–7.5	7.35–7.45	7.2–7.35	<7.2
Imaging	Fluid	Fluid	Fluid	Loculations, thick peel, scoliosis

*Should be examined immediately or stored at 0° C.
LDH, lactate dehydrogenase; PMN, polymorphonuclear neutrophils; WBC, white blood cell count.

infection the most common cause. Definite viral disease has been associated with cytomegalovirus, Epstein-Barr virus, measles, and adenovirus.[22, 24, 37, 54] Other pathogens, such as *Mycoplasma* and *Chlamydia*, are difficult to diagnose but may account for a significant number of pneumonic infections in older children and adolescents that may be associated with effusions in as many as 20 percent of cases.[20, 24, 72] Viral, chlamydial, and mycoplasmal organisms rarely are isolated in patients with effusions requiring intervention.

Several papers have established the role of different bacterial pathogens in childhood effusions. A study of 227 children by Freij and colleagues[22] found *S. aureus* (29%), *Streptococcus pneumoniae* (22%), and *Haemophilus influenzae* (18%) as the three most frequent causes of parapneumonic effusions (Table 29–3). Other studies have verified the relative frequency of these pathogens and are listed in Table 29–4. However, the incidence of *H. influenzae* has fallen dramatically with the universal vaccination of infants using conjugate *H. influenzae* type b vaccines.[1] The hope is that the conjugated pneumococcal vaccine will lead to a similar drop in the incidence of pneumococcal disease. Certain groups of children (e.g., neonates,[22] immunocompromised hosts, patients with preexisting chest tubes that become infected with nosocomial pathogens, patients with a ruptured viscus, and patients with foreign body aspiration) are at higher risk for acquiring gram-negative infections.

TABLE 29–2 ■ CAUSES OF PLEURAL EFFUSION

- Capillary leak
  - Sepsis syndrome
  - Vasculitis associated with immune complex disease
    - Connective tissue diseases
    - Inflammatory bowel disease
  - Malignancy (lymphoreticular, sarcoma, neuroblastoma)
  - Toxins (e.g., TSST-1*)
  - Drugs (phenytoin, isoniazid, nitrofurantoin, amiodarone, methotrexate, bleomycin)
  - Myxedema
  - Trauma
- Increased hydrostatic pressure
  - Congestive heart failure
  - Sickle-cell disease
  - Pulmonary venous hypertension
  - Superior vena cava syndrome
  - Pregnancy
- Decreased oncotic pressure
  - Nephrosis
  - Cirrhosis
  - Protein malnutrition
- Obstructed lymphatics
  - Congenital lymphangiectasia
  - Yellow nail syndrome
  - Radiation injury
  - Neoplasia (metastatic disease)
  - Pneumonia
- Pleural inflammation
  - Pneumonia
  - Lung abscess with pleural fistula
  - Pleural infection (e.g., tuberculosis)
  - Esophageal rupture
  - Pancreatitis
- Iatrogenic
  - Drugs
  - Central-line misplacement

*Toxic shock syndrome toxin-1.

Administration of antibiotics before the diagnosis of empyema is made influences the recovery of organisms. In one report, the incidence of prethoracentesis antibiotics was 71 percent in culture-negative effusions and only 41 percent in culture-positive effusions.[33] Pretreatment with antibiotics may be associated with a decrease in the number of positive blood cultures and in the number of patients from whom *S. pneumoniae* are recovered.[60] Freij and associates[22] have reported the frequency of parapneumonic effusions occurring in children with pneumonia caused by specific pathogens. The rates of effusion by organism were as follows: group A *Streptococcus*, 86 to 91 percent; *S. aureus*, 72 to 76 percent; *S. pneumoniae*, 57 percent; *H. influenzae*, 49 to 75 percent; *Mycoplasma*, 21 percent; and adenoviruses, 11 to 33 percent. Anaerobes were sought carefully by Brook and Frazier,[11] who found them infrequently in patients younger than 6 years of age. They rarely were found in patients with primary pneumonia, occurring most often in patients with lung abscess and aspiration pneumonia.[11] In older patients (7 to 17 years), anaerobes were recovered as isolated pathogens in 44 percent of cases.[11] Virtually every bacterial organism has been associated with pleural effusion at one time or another. *Brucella*[39] and *Yersinia*[36] may be associated with the development of pleural effusions. The diagnosis in such cases often is suggested by a unique history in the patient.

Mycobacterial and fungal effusions are rare findings in children but are well described. In four published reviews, only two patients (from Nigeria) were reported to have *Mycobacterium tuberculosis*.[22, 33, 51, 54] In a series of 303 children younger than 2 years of age with tuberculosis, 3.3 percent had an effusion.[32] In adolescents with tuberculosis, the incidence of effusion with tuberculosis likely approximates that of adult disease. In one series of adult patients with primary tuberculous disease, pleural effusion occurred in 29 percent of cases.[16] In another adult series, primarily of

TABLE 29–3 ■ DISTRIBUTION OF PATHOGENS BY AGES

Pathogen	No. of Cases					
	0–6 Months	7–12 Months	13–24 Months	25 Months–5 Years	6–15 Years	Total
Staphylococcus aureus	27 (41)*	11 (17)	10 (15)	6 (9)	12 (18)	66 (100)
Streptococcus pneumoniae	7 (14)	13 (27)	16 (33)	8 (16)	5 (10)	49 (100)
Haemophilus	4 (10)	15 (38)	18 (45)	3 (7)	0	40 (100)
Sterile	3 (6)	9 (17)	17 (31)	11 (20)	14 (26)	54 (100)
Mixed bacteria	6 (60)	1 (10)	0	1 (10)	2 (20)	10 (100)
Streptococci	1 (20)	0	1 (20)	2 (40)	1 (20)	5 (100)
Gram-negative rods	2 (67)	0	1 (33)	0	0	3 (100)
All cases	50 (22)	49 (21)	63 (28)	31 (14)	34 (15)	227 (100)

*Numbers in parentheses, percentage of cases.
From Freij, B. J., Kusmiesz, H., Nelson, J. D., et al.: Parapneumonic effusions and empyema in hospitalized children: A retrospective review of 227 cases. Pediatr. Infect. Dis. J. 3:578–591, 1984.

reactivation disease, pleural effusion occurred in only 1 percent of the patients.[27] Histoplasmosis has been associated with pleural effusion in 0 to 6 percent of childhood histoplasmosis cases.[62] Blastomycosis has been associated with pleural effusions in 0 to 40 percent of cases.[61, 73] Effusions resulting from other fungi (e.g., *Coccidioides, Aspergillus*) have been described.[49] Parasitic diseases manifesting with effusions are uncommon but found in patients with *Entamoeba histolytica* disease, most often from rupture of a hepatic abscess into the pleural space.[49] Echinococcal disease also has been reported.[21]

Pleural effusion associated with adult human immunodeficiency virus (HIV) infection has been reported in 14.6 percent of hospital admissions in one series in which 67 of 160 cases were infectious. Fifty of those cases were associated with bacterial pneumonia, 10 with tuberculosis, and 5 with *Pneumocystis carinii* pneumonia.[2] Another report on patients infected with HIV suggested that empyema was seen primarily in patients with intravenous drug abuse.[8] For whatever reason, we have not seen empyema frequently in our HIV-infected population, perhaps because of the recent use of more effective antiretroviral therapy.

Drug resistance in community-acquired pneumonia is an issue that complicates the management of parapneumonic effusions. Intermediate or fully resistant *S. pneumoniae* have been found in 12.8 percent and 10.1 percent of isolates, respectively, in a 1993–2000 study from multiple pediatric centers. Seven and one-half percent were cephalosporin-resistant.[78]

Methicillin-resistant *S. aureus* (MRSA) is another concern in empyema. A report showed that 22.3 percent of isolates of *S. aureus* were methicillin resistant; 43 percent of them were community acquired.[35]

DIAGNOSIS

CLINICAL PRESENTATION

The clinical presentation of transudative effusions compared with purulent effusions ordinarily is distinctive, but a continuum of symptoms is shared by both. Many of the symptoms associated with pleural processes are caused by the underlying disease that precipitated the effusion, rendering a distinct syndrome difficult to recognize in patients. Disease caused by some pathogens (e.g., anaerobes, fungi, mycobacteria) also may follow a more insidious course, obscuring the symptoms of effusion. A history always should be obtained to identify systemic diseases, such as immunodeficiency diseases, cancer, and rheumatic diseases, or medications that may be associated with effusions.

Symptoms most specific for parapneumonic processes are dyspnea and pleuritic pain. Dyspnea occurs when the volume of the effusion mechanically interferes with breathing or when pain prevents adequate gas exchange. Pain occurs with irritation of the parietal pleura and on inspiration (i.e., pleurisy). Fever is generated by the inflammatory response and pathogen-specific components (e.g., lipopolysaccharide, toxins). With an acute bacterial process, the fever can be high and hectic, mimicking that with an abscess. Patients in the chronic organizational phase generally have less fever. Cough and malaise are secondary symptoms. Hemoptysis and purulent sputum also may occur. The onset of symptoms of a purulent effusion may be delayed in time and distinct from the symptoms found at the onset of the pneumonia in older children; infants, however, usually have no symptom-free period.[13] In the early phases of effusions, the patient may have no symptoms.

TABLE 29–4 ■ PERCENTAGE OF PATHOGENS RECOVERED IN PURULENT EFFUSIONS FROM CHILDREN

Site/Years (No. of Patients)	*Staphylococcus aureus*	*Streptococcus pneumoniae*	*Haemophilus influenzae*	Other Pathogens	Sterile	Reference
Dallas/1964–82 (227)	29	22	18	8	24	22
Nashville/1977–89 (61)	11	34	3	11	39	32
Washington, D.C./1973–85 (33)	15	12	21	52	NR	11
Nigeria/1989–91 (57)	63	NR	NR	37	NR	50
Israel/1972–81 (37)	14	41	NR	35	11	54
Dallas/1992–98 (135)	8	32	1	13	46	18

NR, not reported.

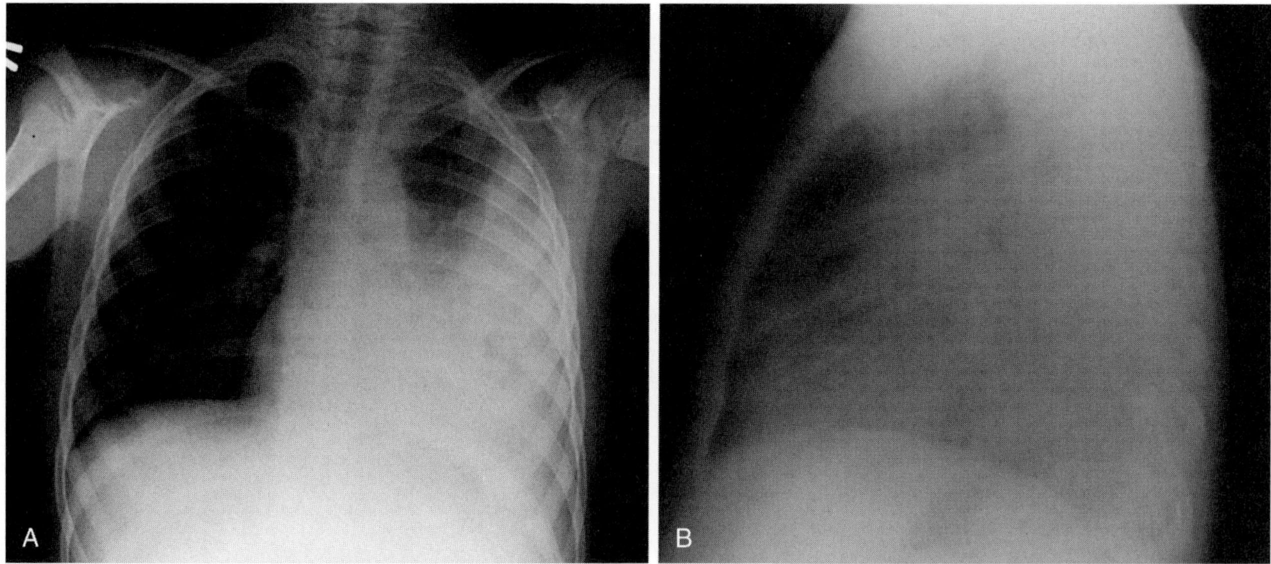

FIGURE 29–1 ■ Posterior *(A)* and lateral *(B)* chest radiographs demonstrate a left pleural effusion in a 9-year-old girl who had symptoms of chest wall pain, fever, and vomiting. After 1 week, her chest wall pain and shortness of breath continued, and she was admitted to the hospital and treated with cefuroxime and erythromycin for pneumonia. An ultrasound examination performed 2 days later showed a large pleural effusion that was drained, with a glucose level less than 20 mg/dL, lactate dehydrogenase level greater than 99,000 U/L, protein level of 4.5 g/dL, and white blood cell count of 51,000 mm^3. Gram stain of the fluid showed gram-positive cocci, but the culture was negative. After failure to respond to intravenous antibiotics alone, the patient was taken to the operating room, where an empyema and several small abscesses were drained, along with decortication and repair of multiple bronchopleural fistulas. She was discharged 9 days later and received an additional 10 days of intravenous imipenem-cilastatin. She was well 1 month after hospital discharge.

The physical examination usually is revealing. The child is tachypneic in more than 70 percent of cases, but breathing is shallow as a result of the child's attempt to minimize pain. Fever and cough usually occur in more than 90 percent of patients with purulent effusions.[51] The patient may appear toxic, with acute infection. Patients often posture toward the affected side. Classically, auscultation reveals a decrease in breath sounds and occasionally detects a pleural rub, but they often are absent in the very young child. Rales from an associated pneumonia may be heard. Depending on the stage of the process, percussion may reveal a level of dullness associated with free-flowing effusion. As the process organizes, it may be less evident. Empyemas can erode through the chest wall into the subcutaneous tissue (i.e., empyema necessitatis) or into a bronchus (i.e., bronchopleural fistula).

IMAGING

The diagnosis most often is made by radiographic examination of the chest. Consolidation of a lobe of the lung is present, with an effusion obscuring the diaphragm (Fig. 29–1). A standard posteroanterior standing view reveals blunting of the costal diaphragmatic gutter. As fluid tracks along the lateral and posterior chest wall, a meniscus configuration is seen. Distinguishing it from pleural thickening may be difficult, and in such cases, a decubitus or cross-table view of the chest allows free-flowing fluid to layer out on the dependent chest wall. In older children and adults, a decubitus layer of fluid of more than 10 mm is considered a sufficient volume of fluid to attempt to extract by thoracentesis.[46] With large volumes of fluid (>1000 mL),[71] compression of the lung and shift of the trachea away from the effusion (Fig. 29–2) may occur. As an empyema develops and organizes, discrete pockets of fluid (i.e., loculations) may form within the pleural cavity (see Fig. 29–2). Occasionally, they are confused with lung abscess. Scoliosis also is well defined by the chest radiograph and occasionally is used as an indication for surgery.[33] The observation of an air-fluid level in the pleural space signifies that air has been generated in the pleural space (by gas-forming organisms) or has entered through a pneumothorax, perforated viscus, or bronchopleural fistula.

Ultrasonography has demonstrated great utility in providing better guidance for thoracentesis of pleural fluid. It is noninvasive and allows definition of empyema by showing internal echoes and septations (see Fig. 29–2).[73, 87] Transudates uniformly are anechoic, although approximately one third of exudates also are anechoic.[87] Ultrasonography is not as precise as is computed tomography (CT) in differentiating a lung abscess from an empyema. CT and magnetic resonance imaging occasionally are required to distinguish parenchymal from pleural disease or to locate a fistula.[75] CT particularly is useful in the patient whose chest radiograph shows total opacification of the lung, and such tomographic scanning is considered by some physicians to be the study of choice in this situation.[33] Ultrasound can have false-negative results, and CT can have false-positive findings on examination of pleural effusions. One study of adults showed that neither effectively predicted the stage of the effusion or predicted the surgical outcome.[38]

THORACENTESIS

Thoracentesis plays an important role in the management of parapneumonic effusions and in 90 percent of adult cases yields useful information.[17] Some investigators would argue that primary video-assisted thoracoscopic surgery (VATS) should be performed without thoracentesis.[18] The decision to obtain fluid from the pleural cavity should be made if fluid is adequate in volume and anatomically accessible and if a microbial diagnosis has not been made or presumed and

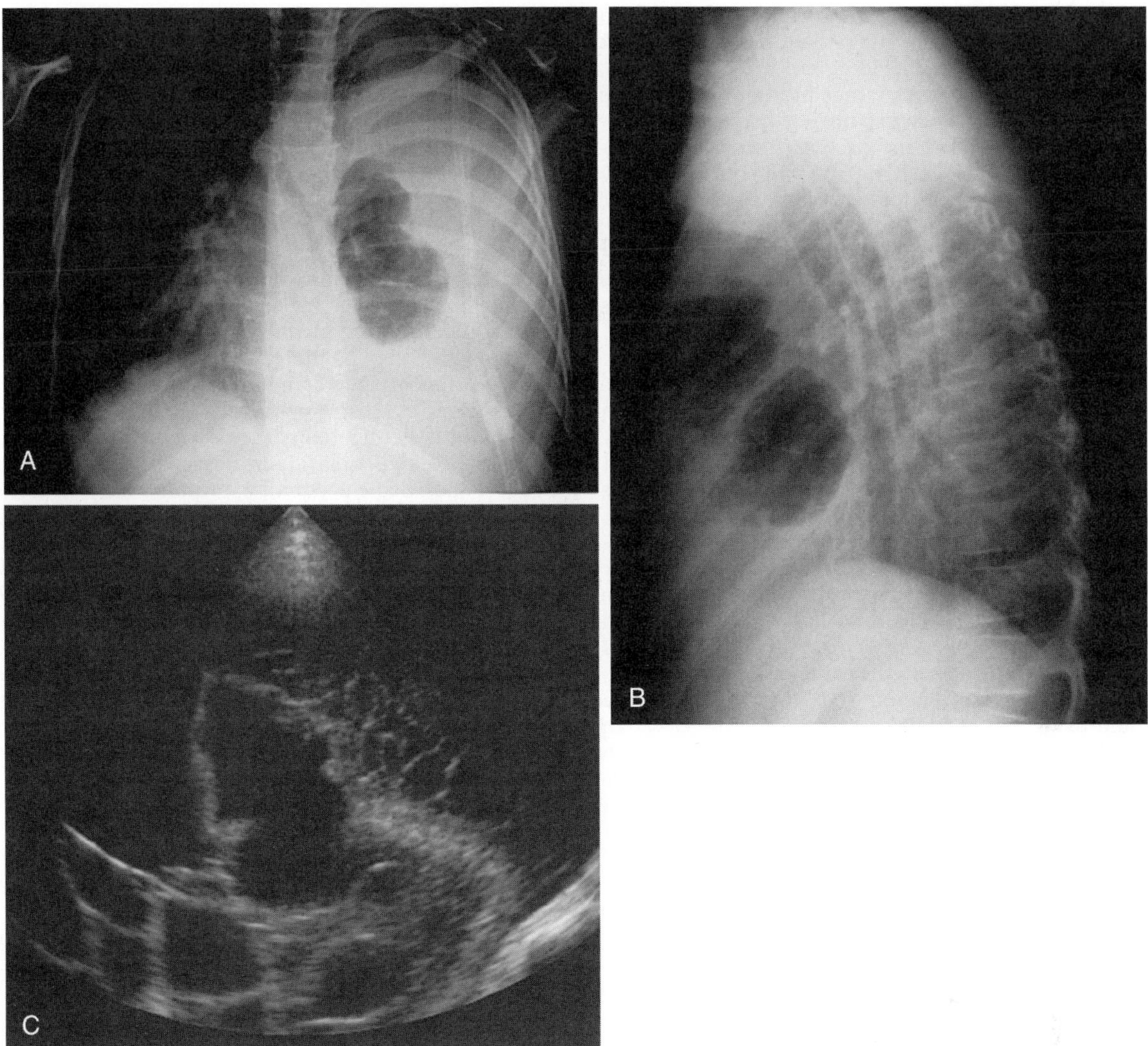

FIGURE 29–2 ■ *A–C,* Chest radiograph and ultrasound examination images from a 7-year-old boy with a 5-day history of vomiting, diarrhea, and low-grade fever. He had varicella 2 weeks earlier. The patient was hospitalized for dehydration and developed left-sided chest pain and a mild cough. Intravenous nafcillin was begun, but his condition deteriorated over the next 4 days, with an enlarging effusion and tracheal shift. Loculations were found on ultrasound examination images shown. He had a thoracotomy performed on day 6 with decortication and removal of a fibrinous rind. He was afebrile within 24 hours and received 1 week of intravenous antibiotics and 1 week of oral antibiotics. The patient was well on follow-up examination after discharge.

antibiotic therapy is intended or if pulmonary function is compromised by the effusion and imaging does not reveal evidence of organization to determine whether further intervention is necessary.

The volume and location of the fluid can be determined precisely by ultrasound examination if the physical examination does not allow localization of the fluid. When a healthy child with apparent or culture-confirmed pneumococcal pneumonia that is community acquired has a small pleural effusion, thoracentesis usually is not required. Small effusions generally can resorb, and a 50 percent chance of recovering the etiologic organism from blood cultures exists.[22] We suggest, however, that when the clinical presentation is atypical or a moderately sized effusion exists, thoracentesis almost always is indicated to define the microbial process. Atypical situations include a history of trauma, foreign body aspiration, prolonged or chronic disease, and underlying systemic diseases (e.g., congestive heart failure, malignancy).

In a classic paper published in 1972, Light and associates[48] established the methodology by which transudates could be differentiated from exudates. Such criteria are valuable in determining if antibiotic treatment is indicated, particularly in patients with underlying diseases that predispose them to sterile effusions but who may have a comorbid infectious condition. An exudate was defined by any of the following criteria: a fluid-to–serum protein ratio of greater than 0.5, a lactate dehydrogenase fluid-to-serum ratio of greater than 0.6, a glucose concentration less than 50 mg/dL, and a pH level less than 7.2. This study was based on the results from 150 adult patients, 103 of whom had exudates.[48]

The criteria of Light and associates have been embraced and are used as guidelines in the management of parapneumonic effusions in adults and children. In 1984, Peterman and Speicher,[59] using adult data, recommended a two-step process to separate transudates from exudates using only the protein and lactate dehydrogenase serum-to–pleural fluid ratios in the initial evaluation. If a patient had an apparent exudate, additional studies, including cultures, stains, pH, and glucose, were indicated. Another study of 297 adults compared several criteria for separating transudates and exudates and concluded that the criteria of Light and associates still yielded a high sensitivity (98%) and a specificity of 77 percent. A pleural fluid cholesterol concentration greater than 60 mg/dL also was used and had a sensitivity of 88 percent and specificity of 91 percent for exudates.[67] Although the cholesterol was not recommended for routine use, it was suggested as an extra screening test for patients with congestive heart failure in whom diuretic therapy might lead to increased concentration of pleural fluid protein.[15, 30, 67]

After an exudate is verified, determination must be made about whether chest-tube drainage or other procedures such as VATS are needed. This determination is accomplished by examining several aspects of the pleural fluid. In 1980, Light and associates[47] described pleural fluid findings in adults with exudates in an attempt to determine which patients needed early chest-tube drainage of their effusions. Thirty-seven adults with acute pneumonia and parapneumonic effusions were studied. Ten patients were considered to have complicated cases if they required chest tubes or had positive cultures at the time of thoracentesis. No clinical differences were found between the complicated and uncomplicated cases. Patients who required chest tubes had a pleural fluid pH of less than 7 and a glucose level less than 40 mg/dL. All patients with uncomplicated effusions had a pH greater than 7.2 and lactate dehydrogenase level less than 1000 mL. Patients with a pH between 7.0 and 7.2 fell into both categories. Anaerobes were recovered from 6 of 10 complicated cases, and *S. pneumoniae* was recovered from 15 of 27 uncomplicated cases. Cell count and protein analysis were not helpful in separating complicated from uncomplicated cases.

The application of these criteria to children has received limited study. In one series of 61 children, patients who required chest tubes or decortication had a mean pleural fluid pH of 7.24 and 7.10, respectively, compared with those who were treated with antibiotics only (pH=7.35). The mean pleural fluid glucose concentration was 74 g/L in the group treated with antibiotics, 10 g/L in the group treated with chest tubes, and 24 g/L in the group treated by decortication.[33] These data suggest that the criteria of Light and associates for glucose are appropriate in children but that the pH at which chest tubes are indicated may be higher for children than for adults. Additional studies are needed to confirm these observations.

Standard Gram stain and bacterial culture (aerobic and anaerobic) are indicated when thoracentesis is performed in patients in whom diagnosis of infection is entertained. The Gram stain usually is positive in patients with bacterial infections; when such infections exist, Gram stain may be used to direct empiric therapy until culture results are known. In one study of children, 12 of 54 sterile effusions from patients with negative blood cultures had a positive Gram stain.[22] Some experts consider that a positive Gram stain is indicative of a more severe process and that such patients are more likely to require more invasive surgical procedures.[13]

When the total white blood cell count and differential are performed, supportive information may be gained. Rarely do the results of a peripheral white blood cell count change the clinical management of the patient. The total white blood cell count in empyema fluid can vary from 5000 to 625,000 cells/mm^3, with median values ranging from 5000 to 55,000.[22, 33] Virtually all cells are neutrophils in bacterial infections. Marked eosinophilia may be seen in parasitic, fungal, tuberculous, or hypersensitivity disease and when blood is found in the pleural space.[13] A large number of small lymphocytes suggests malignancy or tuberculosis.[19, 29, 86] Other studies are required when the history suggests another underlying process. When tuberculosis is suspected by history, specific mycobacterial stains and cultures should be obtained. Identification of mycobacteria by stain and culture may be equivalent to the rate of identification of the disease process by pleural biopsy (~25%).[57] Specific mycobacterial and fungal stains also should be obtained using a Ziehl-Neelsen/auramine stain and potassium hydroxide. Application of newer methods for diagnosis, such as polymerase chain reaction and tuberculostearic acid by mass spectroscopy, may be indicated.

When malignancy or metastases are suspected, cytology is necessary.[29] Most effusions in children that prove to be malignant are of lymphoreticular origin. Amylase sometimes is measured and is elevated in cases of esophageal rupture, acute hemorrhagic peritonitis, or pulmonary infarction.[45, 71] Countercurrent immunoelectrophoresis and other antigen detection systems occasionally are used for diagnosis and are useful in pretreated individuals. They are widely available only for disease caused by *S. pneumoniae* and *H. influenzae* type b and not for disease caused by *S. aureus* or anaerobes. Samples for antigen detection require special preparation before analysis because of increased levels of pleural fluid protein, which can create false-positive test results. The tests add expense and rarely influence management decisions.

ADDITIONAL DIAGNOSTIC STUDIES

An intradermal skin test should be applied to any child with a parapneumonic effusion to evaluate tuberculosis as a possible cause. One third of patients with tuberculous effusions have a negative purified protein derivative skin test result.[6] Early morning gastric aspirates are recommended if tuberculosis is suspected.[80] Blood cultures also are indicated, because as many as one third of patients can have positive blood cultures and negative pleural fluid Gram stain and culture results.[22] Sputum is a less reliable source from which to determine the microbial cause of an effusion but may be helpful in a patient with purulent sputum and a single predominant organism. It can be diagnostic in older children with reactivation or cavitary tuberculosis and in cases of blastomycosis and histoplasmosis. Cold agglutinins or *Mycoplasma* serology may confirm the cause of a pleural effusion, although the nonspecificity of cold agglutinins and the delay in the rise in antibody titers render these data of marginal use in the acute management of the patient. Viral cultures are useful in only the more unusual cases and generally provide information that is not helpful in the initial management of the patient. Rapid diagnostic antigen assays, such as the rapid tests for influenza A and B, may be of use in defining the primary cause of respiratory disease but do not help exclude secondary bacterial pathogens causative of pneumonia and a parapneumonic effusion. When other diseases, such as Wegener granulomatosis[4] and lupus erythematosus, are suspected, disease-specific tests, such as antineutrophil cytoplasmic antibody and anti–nucleic acid antibody, are indicated.

Management

If a patient has an underlying disease process associated with pleural effusion and thoracentesis has excluded bacterial infection (e.g., normal protein and lactate dehydrogenase fluid-to-serum ratio, normal glucose level, negative cultures and Gram stain results), no further treatment is indicated other than treatment of the underlying disease. These patients continue to be at risk for developing infection of the effusion and may require repeat examination of pleural fluid at a later period if infection is suggested clinically.

If empyema is suggested by thoracentesis or surgical findings, empiric antibiotic therapy is indicated. Therapy always should include antimicrobials that are effective against *S. aureus* and *S. pneumoniae*. Acceptable regimens include nafcillin, clindamycin, first-generation cephalosporins, and cefuroxime. In patients who are vaccinated fully against *H. influenzae* (primary series and booster) and for whom the Gram stain is negative, empiric coverage against *H. influenzae* is not required. If *H. influenzae* is suspected, addition of a third-generation cephalosporin (i.e., ceftriaxone or cefotaxime) or single-drug use of cefuroxime or ampicillin-sulbactam would be effective. Ticarcillin-clavulanate, imipenem-cilastatin, meropenem, and piperacillin-tazobactam and cefepime are more costly alternatives.

In patients at risk for acquiring gram-negative disease (e.g., neonates, postsurgical patients), addition of an aminoglycoside or an advanced generation cephalosporin (i.e., cefepime, ceftriaxone, or cefotaxime) is required. Extended-spectrum semisynthetic penicillins (e.g., ticarcillin-clavulanate, piperacillin-tazobactam) also are effective, as are carbapenems. In patients with renal failure or cephalosporin hypersensitivity, aztreonam is effective therapy for gram-negative infections. Ceftazidime or cefepime, broad-spectrum β-lactams with or without a β-lactamase inhibitor (i.e., ticarcillin-clavulanic acid, imipenem cilastatin, meropenem, or piperacillin-tazobactam), or aminoglycosides are indicated for *Pseudomonas* infection.

Surgical drainage is considered to be a critical factor in resolving anaerobic infection. Clindamycin and metronidazole are effective, particularly when postsurgical infection or a ruptured gastrointestinal viscus is present. Upper respiratory tract anaerobes may be resistant to penicillins because of β-lactamase–producing oral flora (particularly the *Prevotella* and *Porphyromonas* spp.).[11] In these situations, penicillin sensitivity should be documented before a penicillin is used as primary therapy.

For patients who have drug-resistant *S. pneumoniae*, most lung infections without associated central nervous system disease respond to high-dose penicillin (minimal inhibitory concentration [MIC] >2 μg/mL) or cephalosporins (MIC >2 μg/mL).[44, 58] When the pneumococcus is highly resistant to penicillin and cephalosporins and the patient's disease fails to improve, therapy with vancomycin, clindamycin, or both drugs may be required. Recovery of MRSA requires vancomycin therapy. Clindamycin sensitivity should be determined because many MRSA isolates are susceptible to clindamycin in vitro. Intravenous clindamycin can be switched to oral clindamycin, offering a management advantage over vancomycin.

With appropriate antibiotic therapy, the duration of fever in uncomplicated cases of purulent effusions usually is less than 48 to 72 hours.[56] When fever persists beyond 72 hours, surgical drainage may be required. The duration of antibiotic therapy is based on the response of the patient to the medical and surgical therapy provided. In one series of pediatric patients, the duration of antibiotic therapy for patients who did not have surgical drainage was 10.4 days, and for those with chest-tube drainage or decortication, the duration of intravenous therapy was 15.7 and 13.4 days, respectively.[33] The duration of combined intravenous and oral therapy was 12 to 24 days in the study reported by Freij and associates,[22] with patients with *S. pneumoniae* infection receiving the shortest courses of antibiotic therapy and those infected with *S. aureus* being treated for longer periods[22] (Table 29–5). A prudent standard is to continue treatment for a minimum of 1 week beyond the last febrile day.

Closed-chest-tube drainage has been the standard treatment of parapneumonic effusions in four classes of patients: those in whom thick, purulent material is found at thoracentesis; those with a pleural fluid pH level less than 7.35 and glucose level less than 60 mg/dL; those for whom antibiotic therapy has not been associated with a timely clinical response (72 hours); and those in whom pulmonary function is compromised, as demonstrated by severe hypoxemia or hypercapnia.

When closed-chest-tube drainage is not associated with clinical improvement and defervescence of disease or if the lung parenchyma is trapped by the fibrinopurulent peel or fever persists, decortication often is required. If the pleural involvement is limited, a small incision (mini-thoracotomy) can be employed.[63] Ultrasonography and CT are required to define these conditions.

Decortication has been advocated as a more expedient way to manage patients. One study reported that patients who had decortication had shorter hospital stays (11.6 days) compared with patients who had thoracentesis or tube thoracostomy (28.3 days).[23] Total hospital days also were reduced in another study when patients treated with decortication (16.6 days) were compared with those treated by chest-tube drainage (21.4 days).[33] In both cases, morbidity from the operative procedure was minimal. Decortication appears to have some advantages in advanced disease in which fibrosis in the pleural cavity has resulted in a large peel. Hoff and associates[33] used an empyema scoring system to assess the need for decortication. Any two of the following are considered indicative of severe disease and need for decortication: anaerobic infection, a pH less than 7.2, glucose level less than 40 mg/dL, scoliosis, and lung entrapment.[33]

Other surgical techniques to reduce operative mortality and promote earlier hospital discharge have been proposed.[40, 41] VATS is the most popular technique and is gaining support in many centers. Although general anesthesia is required for thoracoscopy, only two small incisions are needed: one through the existing chest-tube tract for a telescope and the second through which operating instruments are passed. This procedure allows adhesiolysis and débridement and should be performed before a thick peel develops.

Proponents of VATS argue that a brief operative procedure and the attendant risks of anesthesia outweigh the child's suffering during thoracentesis (and chest tube placement). More importantly, a definitive procedure is performed rather than running the risk of having to perform subsequent chest tube placements and thoracotomy. The hospital stay is shortened. Doski and colleagues reported a series of 139 children that were studied from 1992 through 1998.[18] By comparing historical cohorts, they showed a shorter length of stay (7 vs. 11 and 12 days) for children who underwent VATS than for groups of children who had thoracentesis, chest-tube drainage, or fibrinolytic therapy and rescue VATS for failure. (Twelve of 98 patients who received traditional therapy required thoracotomy, whereas none in the primary VATS group did.) A small, randomized study of 20 patients was conducted from 1994 through 1996 and showed that VATS was superior to chest-tube drainage with fibrinolytic therapy (CT-F). Compared with CT-F, VATS resulted in a higher primary success rate (91% vs. 44%), fewer hospital days (8.7 vs. 12.8), and lower costs (about $16,000 vs. $24,000).[83] Other studies have shown similar results.[26, 38, 53, 64]

TABLE 29–5 ■ SUMMARY OF SURGICAL MANAGEMENT

	No. of Cases						
Procedures	*Staphylococcus aureus*	*Streptococcus pneumoniae*	*Haemophilus*	*Sterile*	*Mixed*	*Streptococcus*	GNR
DT only	5 (7.5)*	15 (31)	16 (40)	25 (46)	0	1 (20)	0
MT	5 (7.5)	5 (10)	5 (12)	2 (4)	0	0	0
D ± T	56 (85)	29 (59)	19 (48)	27 (50)	10 (100)	4 (80)	3 (100)
Thoracotomy	1 (2)	0	1 (3)	1 (2)	0	1 (20)	0
Open drainage	1 (2)	2 (4)	0	0	1 (10)	1 (20)	0
Decortication	2 (3)	0	0	3 (6)	0	0	0
	Duration of Drainage (Days)						
	n = 39	n = 24	n = 15	n = 22	n = 7	n = 4	n = 2
Range	1–43	2–12	3–41	1–20	4–54	3–6	3
Median	7	4.5	6	4.5	7	5.5	3
Mean	11.8	5.5	9.4	6.4	15.4	5	3
SD	11.1	3.0	9.6	4.7	18.5	1.4	0

*Numbers in parentheses, percentage of cases.
†Includes only surviving children who required closed-chest-tube drainage only and in whom the exact duration of drainage was known.
GNR, gram-negative rods; DT, diagnostic thoracentesis; MT, multiple thoracenteses; D ± T, closed drainage with or without initial thoracentesis.
From Freij, B. J., Kusmiesz, H., Nelson, J. D., et al.: Parapneumonic effusions and empyema in hospitalized children: A retrospective review of 227 cases. Pediatr. Infect. Dis. J. 3:578–591, 1984.

The use of radiologist-directed thoracentesis with pigtail catheters for drainage with fibrinolytic therapy has been promoted as a way to reduce the number of operative procedures and achieve shorter hospital stays. Our early experience with these procedures has shown no improvement over standard chest-tube thoracostomy, and complications have shown them to be inferior to primary VATS. A report confirmed this observation in patients with empyema.[65]

In cases of chronic empyema, other approaches are used. A closed tube can be converted into an open-drainage tube. This conversion is accomplished safely a minimum of 10 to 14 days into the course of an empyema when the visceral and parietal pleurae fuse and a pneumothorax can be avoided safely.[49] Other options include open drainage by rib resection and creation of a pleural window. The window ultimately closes with lung expansion and granulation, with disappearance of the pleural space.

The use of streptokinase in children with pleural effusion was reported in 1993.[68] The investigators used 12,000 to 91,000 U/kg of streptokinase over the course of 5 days in five children with persistent empyema that had been unresponsive to chest-tube drainage and antibiotics; they reported that the treatment had immediate beneficial effects. The occasional side effects caused by streptokinase reported in adults have generated concern about its safety.[9, 66] In addition, the cost of urokinase is less than that of streptokinase. Urokinase has been used in children with minimal adverse effects.[31, 42, 66, 76] In adults, these different agents appear to be equivalent,[10] although commercial shortages of the products have occurred. This therapy may have value in patients with organizing pleural inflammation and inadequate drainage caused by loculations of pleural fluid without a peel.

Rarely are full thoracotomy and pneumonectomy required for severe pneumonic and parapneumonic disease. An occasional complication of empyema is persistent organized fluid or air collections in the pleural space, particularly in adults. A high rate of success has been reported using talc pleurodesis in these situations, as well as in patients with noninfectious persistent effusions.[81, 85] Long-term complications of this therapy include development of bronchogenic carcinoma and mesothelioma (asbestos-free preparations presumably are not associated with the development of these neoplastic conditions).

One frequent cause of bloody pleural effusions is motor vehicle accidents.[49, 69] In one series of 100 children, 56 percent had pleural effusions associated with pulmonary contusions. They were treated with closed-chest-tube drainage; no antibiotics were used, and no infectious complications occurred.[69] Management of pleural hematoma secondary to trauma occasionally is complicated by infection because the bloody pleural fluid is an excellent growth medium. One study suggested that empyema is less common in post-traumatic effusion with closed-chest-tube drainage than repeated thoracentesis.[82]

Different biases continue to exist in the management of parapneumonic effusions in children. In suspected empyema based on the clinical history and chest radiograph, we consider that a practical and effective approach is to perform an ultrasound study. If the study suggests empyema, primary VATS should be performed. If the study result is negative, thoracentesis should be done, and if consistent with empyema, VATS should be done. An algorithm incorporating alternatives for the management of pleural collections is shown in Figure 29–3.

Complications from closed-chest-tube drainage include bleeding, infection of the exit wound, bronchopleural fistula, and laceration of the lung. Because of these rare complications, chest-tube placement, performed in the past by the pediatrician, now is delegated more frequently to the surgeon.

Prognosis and Long-Term Outcome

The long-term outcome of patients with effusions depends on the underlying cause of the effusion. Patients with empyema who previously were well recover satisfactorily in most cases. Occasional rare complications, such as temporary paralysis of the diaphragm, have been reported.[52] In three retrospective reviews, the percentage of patients who required

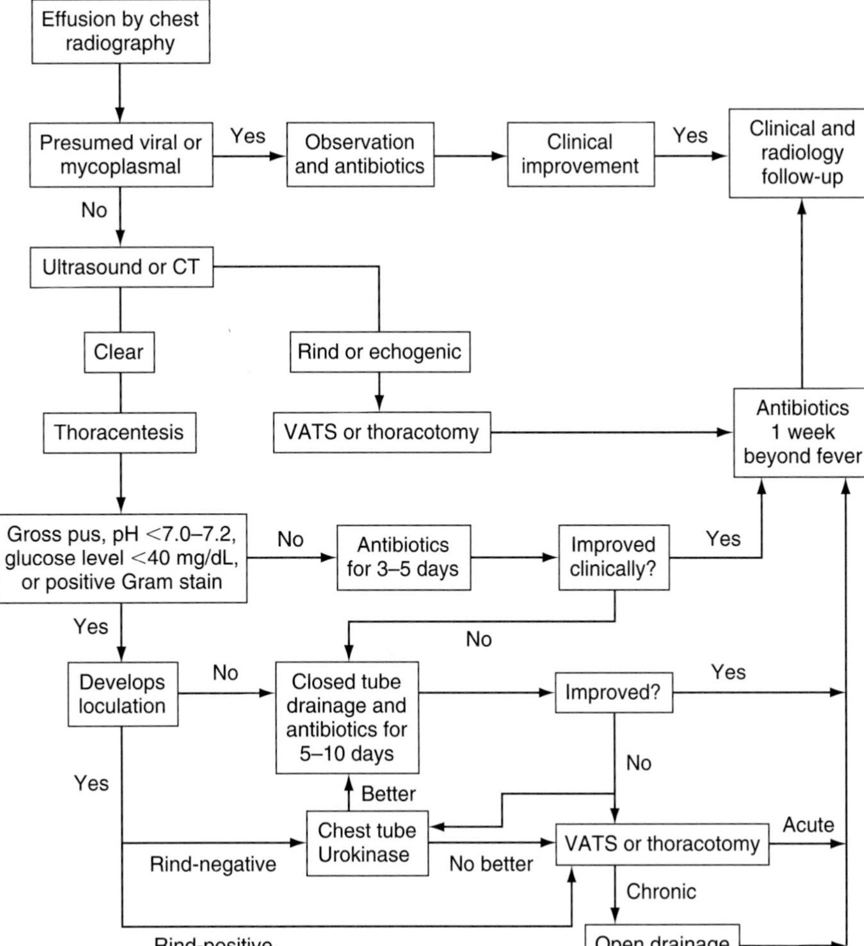

FIGURE 29–3 ■ Algorithm for the management of pleural fluid collections. CT, computed tomography; VATS, Video-assisted thoracic surgery.

closed-chest-tube drainage or other surgical procedures ranged from 62 to 80 percent.[22, 33, 55] The rate of decortication ranged from 4 percent[22] to 43 percent.[33] The relationship of surgical management to the pathogen causing the infection is shown in Table 29–5. The immediate mortality rate for children in recent years has been 0 to 10.8 percent.[22, 33, 51, 55] In one of these studies, the mortality rate was highest for children younger than 1 year of age.[22] Studies conducted to evaluate long-term, specific pulmonary disability using pulmonary function tests and lung volumes have shown normalization of these study results over time.[56]

REFERENCES

1. Adams, W. G., Deaver, K. A., Cochi, S. L., et al.: Decline of childhood *Haemophilus influenzae* type b (Hib) disease in the HIB vaccine era. JAMA *269*:221–226, 1993.
2. Afessa B.: Pleural effusion and pneumothorax in hospitalized patients with HIV infection—The pulmonary complications, ICU support, and prognostic factors of hospitalized patients with HIV (PIP) study. Chest *117*(4):1031–1037, 2000.
3. Andrews, N. C., Parker, E. F., Shaw, R. R., et al.: Management of non-tuberculous empyema. Am. Rev. Respir. Dis. *85*:935, 1962.
4. Bambery, P., Sakhuja, V., Behera, D., et al.: Pleural effusions in Wegener's granulomatosis: Report of five patients and a brief review of the literature. Scand. J. Rheumatol. *20*:445–447, 1991.
5. Baum, G. L.: Diseases of the pleura. Hosp. Med. *5*:6–25, 1969.
6. Berger, H. W., and Mejia, E.: Tuberculous pleurisy. Chest *63*:43–50, 1973.
7. Black, L. F.: The pleural space and pleural fluid. Mayo Clin. Proc. *47*:494–506, 1972.
8. Borge, J. H., Michavila, I. A., Mendez J. M., et al.: Thoracic empyema in HIV-infected patients—Microbiology, management, and outcome. Chest *113*:732–738, 1998.
9. Bouros, D., Schiza, S., Panagou, P., et al.: Role of streptokinase in the treatment of acute loculated parapneumonic pleural effusions and empyema. Thorax *49*:852–855, 1994.
10. Bouros, D., Schiza, S., Patsourakis, G., et al.: Intrapleural streptokinase versus urokinase in the treatment of complicated parapneumonic effusions—a prospective, double-blind study. Am. J. Respir. Crit. Care Med. *115*:291–295, 1997.
11. Brook, I., and Frazier, E. H.: Aerobic and anaerobic microbiology of empyema. Chest *103*:1502–1507, 1993.
12. Brown, R. B., and Weinstein, L.: Pleural effusions. *In* Feigin, R. D., and Cherry, J. D. (eds.): Textbook of Pediatric Infectious Diseases. 3rd ed. Philadelphia, W. B. Saunders, 1992, pp. 309–315.
13. Brusch, J. L., and Weinstein, L.: Pleural empyema. *In* Feigin, R. D., and Cherry, J. D. (eds.): Textbook of Pediatric Infectious Diseases. 3rd ed. Philadelphia, W. B. Saunders, 1992, pp. 315–320.
14. Chartrand, S. A., and McCracken, G. H., Jr.: Staphylococcal pneumonia in infants and children. Pediatr. Infect. Dis. J. *1*:19–23, 1982.
15. Chonmaitree, T., and Powell, K. R.: Parapneumonic pleural effusion and empyema in children. Clin. Pediatr. *22*:414–419, 1983.
16. Choyke, P. L., Sostman, H. D., Curtis, A. M., et al.: Adult onset of pulmonary tuberculosis. Radiology *148*:357, 1983.
17. Collins, T. R., and Dahn, S. A.: Thoracentesis: Clinical value, complications, technical problems and patient experience. Chest. *91*:817–822, 1987.
18. Doski, J. J., Lou, D., Hicks, B. A., et al.: Management of parapneumonic collections in infants and children. J. Pediatr. Surg. *35*:265–270, 2000.
19. Epstein, D. M., Kline, L. R., Albeida, S. M., et al.: Tuberculous pleural effusions. Chest *91*:106–109, 1987.
20. Fine, N. L., Smith, L. R., and Sheedy, P. E.: Frequency of pleural effusions in mycoplasma and viral pneumonias. N. Engl. J. Med. *283*:790–793, 1970.
21. Fitzgerald, D., Harvey, J., Isaacs, D., et al.: The case of the persistent pleural effusions. Pediatr. Infect. Dis. J. *10*:475, 479–480, 1991.

22. Freij, B. J., Kusmiesz, H., Nelson, J. D., et al.: Parapneumonic effusions and empyema in hospitalized children: A retrospective review of 227 cases. Pediatr. Infect. Dis. J. *3*:578–591, 1984.
23. Golladay, E. S., and Wagner, C. W.: Management of empyema in children. Am. J. Surg. *158*:618–621, 1989.
24. Gothof, B. S., Kamilli, I., Keller, C., et al.: Pleural effusions in acute mononucleosis. Bildgebung. *58*:218–220, 1991.
25. Grix, A., and Giammona, J. T.: Pneumonitis with pleural effusion in children due to *Mycoplasma pneumoniae*. Am. Rev. Respir. Dis. *109*:665–671, 1974.
26. Grewal, H., Jackson, R. J., Wagner, C. W., et al.: Early video-assisted thoracic surgery in the management of empyema. Pediatrics *103*:1–5, 1999.
27. Groff, D. B., Randolph, J. G., and Blader, B.: Empyema in childhood. JAMA *195*:572–574, 1966.
28. Hadlock, F. P., Park, S. K., Awe, R. J., et al.: Unusual findings in adult pulmonary tuberculosis. A. J. R. Am. J. Roentgenol. *134*:1015, 1980.
29. Hallman, J. R., and Geisinger, K. R.: Cytology of fluids from pleural, peritoneal and pericardial cavities in children. Cytol. Fluids *38*:209–217, 1994.
30. Hamm, H., Brohan, U., Bohmer, R., et al.: Cholesterol in pleural effusions: A diagnostic aid. Chest *92*:296–302, 1987.
31. Handman, H. P., and Reuman, P. D.: The use of urokinase for loculated thoracic empyema in children: A case report and review of the literature. Pediatr. Infect. Dis. J. *12*:958–959, 1993.
32. Hardy, J. B., and Kendy, E. L., Jr.: Tuberculous pleurisy with effusion in infancy. J. Pediatr. *26*:138, 1945.
33. Hoff, S. J., Neblett, W. W., Edwards, K. M., et al.: Parapneumonic empyema in children: Decortication hastens recovery in patients with severe pleural infections. Pediatr. Infect. Dis. J. *10*:194–199, 1990.
34. Hughson, W. G., Friedman, P., Feigin, D. S., et al.: Postpartum pleural effusion: A common radiographic finding. Ann. Intern. Med. *97*:856–858, 1982.
35. Hussain, F. M., Boyle-Vavra, S., Bethel, C. D., et al.: Current trends in community acquired methicillin resistant *Staphylococcus aureus* at a tertiary care pediatric facility. Pediatr. Infect. Dis. J. *19*:1163–1166, 2000.
36. Kane, D. R., and Reuman, P. D.: *Yersinia enterocolitica* causing pneumonia and empyema in a child and a review of the literature. Pediatr. Infect. Dis. J. *11*:591–593, 1992.
37. Kato, Y., Miyata, I., Sakuma, S., et al.: A case of cytomegalovirus mononucleosis associated with pleural effusion. Acta Paediatr. Jpn. *36*:280–283, 1994.
38. Kearney, S. E., Davies, C. W. H., Davies, R. J. O., et al.: Computed tomography and ultrasound in parapneumonic effusions and empyema. Clin. Radiol. *55*:542–547, 2000.
39. Kerem, E., Diav, O., Navon, P., et al.: Pleural fluid characteristics in pulmonary brucellosis. Thorax *49*:89–90, 1994.
40. Kercher, K. W., Attorri, R. J., Hoover, J. D., et al.: Thoracoscopic decortication as first-line therapy for pediatric parapneumonic empyema—A case series. Chest *118*:24–27, 2000.
41. Kern, J. A., and Rodgers, B. M.: Thoracoscopy in the management of empyema in children. J. Pediatr. Surg. *28*:1128–1132, 1993.
42. Kornecki, A., and Sivan, Y.: Treatment of loculated pleural effusion with intrapleural urokinase in children. J. Ped. Surg. *32*:1473–1475, 1997.
43. Lee, K. F., and Olak, J.: Anatomy and physiology of the pleural space. Chest Surg. Clin. North Am. *4*:391–403, 1994.
44. Leggiadro, R. J., Davis, Y., and Tenover, F. C.: Outpatient drug-resistant pneumococcal bacteremia. Pediatr. Infect. Dis. J. *13*:1144–1145, 1995.
45. Light, R. W.: Pleural effusions. Med. Clin. North Am. *61*:1339–1351, 1977.
46. Light, R. W.: Pleural Diseases. Philadelphia, Lea & Febiger, 1983.
47. Light, R. W., Girard, W. M., Jenkinson, S. G., et al.: Parapneumonic effusions. Am. J. Med. *69*:507–512, 1980.
48. Light, R. W., Macgregor, M. I., Luchsinger, P. C., et al.: Pleural effusions: The diagnostic separation of transudates and exudates. Ann. Intern. Med. *77*:507–513, 1972.
49. Magovern, C. J., and Rusch, V. W.: Parapneumonic and post-traumatic pleural space infections. Chest Surg. Clin. North Am. *4*:561–582, 1994.
50. Major, R. H.: Classic Descriptions of Disease. 2nd ed. Springfield, IL, Charles C Thomas, 1939, p. 620.
51. Mangete, E. D. O., Kombo, B. B., and Legg-Jack, T. E.: Thoracic empyema: A study of 56 patients. Arch. Dis. Child. *69*:587–588, 1993.
52. Mazzare, M. A., and Park, M. K.: Empyema causing paralysis of hemidiaphragm. Arch. Pediatr. Adolesc. *149*:342–343, 1995.
53. Meier, A. H., Smith, B., Raghavan, A., et al.: Rational treatment of empyema in children. Arch. Surg. *135*:907–912, 2000.
54. Meyer, K., Girgis, N., and McGravey, V.: Adenovirus associated with congenital pleural effusion. Clin. Lab. Observ. *107*:433, 1985.
55. Meyerovitch, J., Shohet, I., and Rubinstein, E.: Analysis of thirty-seven cases of pleural empyema. Eur. J. Clin. Microbiol. *4*:337–339, 1985.
56. Murphy, D., Lockhart, C. H., and Todd, J. K.: Pneumococcal empyema. Am. J. Dis. Child. *134*:659–662, 1980.
57. Nance, K. V., Shermer, R. W., and Askin, F. B.: Diagnostic efficacy of pleural biopsy as compared with that of pleural fluid examination. Mod. Pathol. *4*:320–324, 1991.
58. Pallares, R., Linares, J., Vadillo, M., et al.: Resistance to penicillin and cephalosporin and mortality from severe pneumococcal pneumonia in Barcelona, Spain. N. Engl. J. Med. *333*:474–480, 1995.
59. Peterman, T. A., and Speicher, C. E.: Evaluating pleural effusions: A two-stage laboratory approach. JAMA *252*:1051–1053, 1984.
60. Pothula, V., and Krellenstein, D. J.: Early aggressive surgical management of parapneumonic empyemas. Chest *105*:832–836, 1994.
61. Powell, D. A., and Schult, K. E.: Acute pulmonary blastomycosis in children: Clinical course and follow-up. Pediatrics *63*:736–740, 1979.
62. Quasney, M. W., and Leggiadro, R. J.: Pleural effusion associated with histoplasmosis. Pediatr. Infect. Dis. J. *12*:415–418, 1993.
63. Raffensperger, J. G., Luck, S. R., Shkolnik, A., et al.: Mini-thoracotomy and chest tube insertion for children with empyema. J. Thorac. Cardiovasc. Surg. *84*:497–504, 1982.
64. Rescorla, F. J., West, K. W., Gingalewski, C. A., et al.: Efficacy of primary and secondary video-assisted thoracic surgery in children. J. Pediatr. Surg. *35*:134–138, 2000.
65. Roberts, J. S., Bratton, S. L., Brogan, T. V.: Efficacy and complications of percutaneous pigtail catheters for thoracostomy in pediatric patients. Chest *114*:1116–1121, 1998.
66. Robinson, L. A., Moulton, A. L., Fleming, W. H., et al.: Intrapleural fibrinolytic treatment of multiloculated thoracic empyemas. Ann. Thorac. Surg. *57*:803–814, 1994.
67. Romero, S., Candela, A., Martin, C., et al.: Evaluation of different criteria for the separation of pleural transudate from exudates. Chest *104*:399–404, 1993.
68. Rosen, H., Nadkarni, V., Therous, M., et al.: Intrapleural streptokinase as adjunctive treatment for persistent empyema in pediatric patients. Chest *103*:1190–1192, 1993.
69. Roux, P., and Fisher, R. M.: Chest injuries in children: An analysis of 100 cases of blunt chest trauma from motor vehicle accidents. J. Pediatr. Surg. *27*:551–555, 1992.
70. Sahn, S. A.: Pleural manifestations of pulmonary disease. Hosp. Pract. *16*:73–89, 1981.
71. Sahn, S. A.: The differential diagnosis of pleural effusions. West. J. Med. *137*:99–108, 1982.
72. Sahn, S. A.: Pleural effusions in the atypical pneumonias. Semin. Respir. Infect. *3*:322–334, 1988.
73. Schutze, G. S.: Blastomycosis. Clin. Infect. Dis. *22*:496–502, 1996.
74. Sherman, M. M., Subramanian, V., and Berger, R. L.: Management of thoracic empyema. Am. J. Surg. *133*:474–479, 1977.
75. Stewart, P. B.: The rate of formation and lymphatic removal of fluid in pleural effusions. J. Clin. Invest. *42*:258–262, 1963.
76. Stringel, G., and Hartman A. R.: Intrapleural instillation of urokinase in the treatment of loculated pleural effusions in children. J. Pediatr. Surg. *29*:1539–1540, 1994.
77. Tagliabue, M., Casella, T. C., Zincone, G. E., et al.: CT and chest radiography in the evaluation of adult respiratory distress syndrome. Acta Radiol. *35*:230–234, 1994.
78. Tan, T. Q., Mason, E. O., Wald, E. R., et al.: Clinical characteristics of children with complicated pneumococcal pneumonia caused by *Streptococcus pneumoniae*. Pediatrics *110*:1–6, 2002.
79. Tita, J. A., Wiedemann, H. P., and Weinstein, C. E.: Pleural effusions and abnormal nails. Hosp. Pract. *21*:65–68, 1986.
80. Vallejo, J. T., Ong, L. T., and Starke, J. R.: Clinical features, diagnosis and treatment of tuberculosis in infants. Pediatrics *94*:1–7, 1994.
81. Vargas, F. S., Milanez, J. R., Filomeno, L. T., et al.: Intrapleural talc for the prevention of recurrence in benign or undiagnosed pleural effusions. Chest *106*:1771–1775, 1994.
82. Varkey, B., Rose, H. D., Kutty, C. P. K., et al.: Empyema thoracis during a ten-year period: Analysis of 72 cases and comparison to a previous study (1952–1967). Arch. Intern. Med. *141*:1771–1776, 1981.
83. Wait, M. A., Sharma, S., Hohn, J., et al.: A randomized trial of empyema therapy. Chest *111*:1548–1551, 1997.
84. Weiner-Kronish, J. P., and Broaddus, V. C.: Interrelationship of pleural and pulmonary interstitial liquid. Annu. Rev. Physiol. *55*:209–226, 1993.
85. Weissberg, D., and Ben-Zeev, I.: Talc pleurodesis. J. Thorac. Cardiovasc. Surg. *106*:689–695, 1993.
86. Yam, L. T.: Diagnostic significance of lymphocytes in pleural effusions. Ann. Intern. Med. *66*:972–982, 1967.
87. Yang, P. C., Luh, K. T., Chang, D. B., et al.: Value of sonography in determining the nature of pleural effusion: Analysis of 320 cases. Am. J. Radiol. *159*:29–33, 1992.

CHAPTER 30

Lung Abscess

J. GARY WHEELER ■ RICHARD F. JACOBS

A lung abscess is an area of necrotic material in the parenchyma of the lung initiated or complicated by infectious organisms. Although possibly originating from a pneumonia, it is distinguished by liquefaction and destruction of parenchymal tissue, organization, and cavitation. A lung abscess may erupt and form an adjacent empyema. Strictly, however, empyema is defined by involvement of the pleural tissues.

Lung abscess has been stereotyped in the past as a disease of male alcoholics that was managed with surgery.[48] Descriptions of pediatric patients have helped characterize this process and distinguish it from the presentation found in older reviews of adult patients. The incidence of lung abscess has dropped precipitously in the modern era. Smith[43] reported lung abscesses in 0.33 percent of pediatric admissions in 1934, and Emanuel and Shulman[13] reported a rate of 0.012 percent from 1985 to 1990. In major pediatric referral centers in Chicago, Houston, Dallas, and Montreal, the incidence of lung abscesses has ranged in the last 2 decades from 1.5 to 4.7 cases per year.[4, 13, 26, 44] Many of these cases developed in compromised hosts, whereas normal hosts were affected more frequently in the preantibiotic era. This downward trend also has been observed for adults.[36]

Improvements in pediatric diagnosis and care have resulted in a decrease in the relative numbers of cases related to underlying diseases. The morbidity and mortality rates also have fallen with employment of antibiotic therapy and modern critical care. In 1920, Wessler and Schwarz[48] reported a 33 percent mortality rate, with "invalidism" and hemiplegia occurring in another 27 percent.[48] The mortality rates in the two latest reports of lung abscess were 11 and 4 percent.[13, 44]

Although lung abscesses occur in all ages of children, two studies have suggested that the trend is away from children younger than 5 years of age to an older population.[13, 32] In four studies, the median age ranged from 7 to 9.3 years.[4, 7, 13, 17, 44] No consistent racial or sexual predisposition to this condition in children has been identified. In the 1950s, one series found boys to be more at risk than were girls.[24] In adults, a twofold greater risk exists for men.[30, 36] Specific risk factors for development of lung abscess are found in Table 30–1. Most are related to some predisposition to aspiration, hematogenous spread, or compromised immunity.

Pathophysiology

Two main mechanisms explain formation of a lung abscess. The first mechanism is the introduction of pathogens directly into the air spaces, which typically results in solitary abscesses. It most commonly follows aspiration, with a resultant neutrophilic reaction and necrosis. Aspiration is thought to be the prevalent precipitating factor in adults, particularly in individuals with significant dental disease.[6] Most lung abscesses related to aspiration are polymicrobial and include anaerobes. The prevalence of fluoride and the relatively low incidence of dental disease in children may be additional factors for the reduced incidence of lung abscess in children, although aspiration pneumonia does occur in the absence of dental disease.

The second mechanism in the formation of lung abscess is hematogenous spread. Hematogenous seeding of the lung can lead to an initial pneumonia that develops into an abscess with further organization and cavitation. Primary pneumonia rarely progresses to necrosis and abscess in modern times; this phenomenon is explained in large part by the ready accessibility of antibiotics. Emboli from the venous circulation (i.e., septic thrombophlebitis) and right side of the heart (i.e., endocarditis) can cause single or multiple lung abscesses, which often are subpleural. Infection in the head and neck area also is a risk factor for vascular spread to the lung with resultant lung abscess.[40] This complication occurred very commonly in past eras. Lung abscesses complicated tonsillectomies in as many as one third of cases in a 1920 report.[48] They were theorized to result from aspiration during the operative procedure[43] and characteristically developed 13 to 14 days after the procedure.[48] Great improvements in modern pediatric anesthesia with careful efforts to prevent aspiration have rendered this complication an uncommon event today.

A lung abscess tends to have irregular margins, with occasional bullae, and it can dissect into adjacent tissues, such as the mediastinum, bronchi, and pleural space. If the abscess ruptures into a bronchus, air enters and an air-fluid level can be seen radiographically. Dissection into the pleural space creates a purulent effusion, with air noted only if an anaerobic process is present. Dissection into the mediastinum causes a widening of the mediastinum. Air is detected if communication occurs with a bronchus or in the presence of anaerobes. Multiple lung abscesses occur more frequently in hematogenous or embolic disease and are found more often with more sensitive tools, such as computed tomography (CT). Modern reviews of children have suggested that single abscesses are found more frequently than are multiple abscesses.[7, 13, 44]

Microscopically, a lung abscess is definable by a collection of necrotic material; highly neutrophilic inflammation; a surrounding irregular, fibrotic wall; and microvascular

TABLE 30–1 ■ UNDERLYING RISKS FOR 46 SECONDARY LUNG ABSCESSES IN PEDIATRIC PATIENTS

Risk	No.
Neuropsychiatric causes	16
Hematologic/oncologic disorders	11
Primary pulmonary disease	8
Immunodeficiency	4
Congenital heart disease	2
Solvent aspiration	1
Foreign body aspiration	1
Prematurity	1
Chromosomal disorder	1
Endocrinopathy	1

Data from references 13 and 44, and unpublished data from Little Rock, Arkansas, 1989 to 1994.

infarcts. Lymphocytes often are present and seem to play a regulatory role in the formation of the abscess.[41] The infrequency of lung abscesses in patients with human immunodeficiency virus (HIV) infection may be explained by this observation.

The role of preceding viral infection in undermining phagocytic host defenses is supported by the observations of preceding respiratory symptoms in patients with lung abscesses.[1] They manifest primarily in cold weather[4, 13] and typically after well-defined viral illnesses, such as varicella, measles, and influenza.[22, 24, 47] The impact of chemotherapy on phagocytes also may explain the increased numbers of lung abscesses in patients with leukemia and other cancers.

On a macroscopic scale, lung abscesses do have a tendency to develop in all parts of the lung. If associated with aspiration, the anatomic site depends on whether the subject was supine or erect at the time of aspiration. Supine patients develop abscesses in the posterior upper and lower lobes, and erect patients develop infection in the middle and basilar lower lobes. In general, the tendency is for aspiration-related abscesses to develop more on the right than the left, presumably because of the more vertical anatomy of the right stem bronchus.[13, 21]

Physicians have grouped lung abscesses into primary and secondary categories, presuming that primary and secondary abscesses have different microbiologic factors, management approaches, and outcomes. The arbitrary nature of this distinction is apparent when appreciating how much the microbiology, clinical course, management, and outcome of both conditions overlap.[30] Primary abscesses occur in previously normal hosts without a history of trauma or aspiration of a foreign body. Secondary abscesses occur in the setting of underlying medical illnesses predisposing to infection, airway obstruction, embolization, or aspiration. In an earlier series, secondary abscesses were found more often in children younger than 1 year of age,[24] but this difference was not corroborated in a later study.[13] Primary abscesses were found in 64 percent of patients in Chicago,[13] 33 percent in Houston,[44] and 45 percent in Little Rock (unpublished data, 1989 to 1994). A large study in Toronto from 1956 to 1965 described only 30 percent of abscesses as primary.[24]

In the modern era, lung abscess should trigger a search to exclude underlying factors that may have prognostic value and lead to treatment of the underlying disease. The classic lung abscess syndrome in adults is represented by the alcoholic who aspirates during an alcoholic binge. In children, a classic presentation would be any child with altered mental status, associated swallowing dysfunction, or both conditions. Foreign bodies can obstruct normal clearance of pathogens and precipitate the development of a lung abscess. However, they are a surprisingly rare cause in some reports.[13, 25] Obstruction also predisposes to lung abscess in adults who have carcinoma of the lung and rarely in children with metastatic disorders. Ineffective cough in patients with neurodegenerative or myopathic disorders is another risk factor for developing lung abscess, similar to that in the adult alcoholic. Patients with leukemia or who are receiving chemotherapy also are at increased risk. Occasionally, a bronchogenic cyst can become infected and mimic a lung abscess. Tricuspid or pulmonary valve endocarditis in children with complicated congenital heart disease places them at risk for developing lung abscesses.

Immunodeficiency is another risk factor for development of a lung abscess. Patients with chronic granulomatous disease and hyper-IgE syndrome typically are found to have lung abscesses. Patients with hypogammaglobulinemia may develop abscesses, although bronchiectasis is the more characteristic finding. The same is true for patients with immotile cilia syndromes and cystic fibrosis, although in the latter group, disease abscesses are surprisingly uncommon.[9] Among pediatric patients, HIV-1 infection has not been reported as a risk factor in series from Chicago and Houston.[13, 44] Additional causes are listed in Table 30–1.

Microbiology

The microbiology of lung abscesses appears to be evolving as patients and antibiotics change.[36] In the preantibiotic era, streptococci and *Mycobacterium tuberculosis* were the causes of lung abscesses most commonly reported. After penicillin use began and tuberculosis skin testing, treatment, and control programs became widespread, staphylococci most frequently were recovered from lung abscesses.[37] Development of better culture techniques also increased the identification of anaerobes in lung abscess material; in past eras, these organisms probably were present but not recovered. Anaerobes were suspected by the fetid odor of abscesses, the time course of postoperative aspiration infections, and Gram stains of tissue and pus, which showed fusobacteria and spirochetes.[43, 48] Table 30–2 summarizes the microbiology of pediatric lung abscesses reported from 1976 to 1995.

The primary role of anaerobes in lung abscesses has been assumed in aspiration pneumonias. Anaerobes are prominent in the oral cavity and have been recovered from the abscesses of patients with dental disease.[6] However, in many past studies, lung abscess materials were not transported and cultured for optimal anaerobic growth. Successful growth was described when specimens were transported in a closed syringe, with culture inoculation beginning in less than 10 minutes.[7] Later studies, in which optimal culture methods were employed, corroborated the role of anaerobes in lung abscesses in children.[7, 44] In one study of mentally retarded

TABLE 30–2 ■ MICROBIOLOGY OF PEDIATRIC LUNG ABSCESS

Organism	No.
Staphylococcus aureus	15
Coagulase-negative *Staphylococcus*	2
Streptococcus pyogenes	5
Streptococcus pneumoniae	8
Alpha-hemolytic *Streptococcus*	13
Other aerobic *Streptococcus*	7
Enterococci	2
Branhamella catarrhalis	3
Escherichia coli	9
Klebsiella	8
Pseudomonas spp.	10
Serratia	1
Haemophilus spp.	7
Other gram-negative organisms	2
Bacteroides spp.	19
Peptostreptococcus	12
Other anaerobes	26
Candida spp.	3
Aspergillus	2
Mucor	1
Mycobacterium tuberculosis	1
Total	156

This information was reported in the literature from 1976 to 1995. The isolates were recovered by direct aspiration of abscess contents, bronchoscopic aspiration, transtracheal aspiration, blood culture, or culture of surgical specimens. Data from case reports focused on procedures are included, whereas data from those focused on the organism recovered are not.[4, 7, 11, 13, 19, 20, 22, 23, 25, 26, 32, 34, 42, 44, 46] children with seizure disorders, poor dental care, and suspected aspiration, transtracheal polymicrobial infections with aerobes were found in 9 of 10 samples.[7] An average of 6.2 isolates were recovered per patient. *Peptostreptococcus* and *Bacteroides* spp. were the anaerobes recovered most frequently.[7] In a larger group of 45 children, 15 of whom had primary abscesses, 14 had polymicrobial infections.[44] Older children with neurologic disorders were the primary patients with anaerobes in both studies. Anaerobes, along with *Streptococcus pneumoniae*, nontypeable *Haemophilus influenzae*, and *Staphylococcus aureus*, have been recovered from normal patients.[44]

The role of tissue lysins and toxins depends on the pathogen and is thought to be critical for the development of lung abscesses. In mixed infections, synergy probably occurs among the pathogens, which leads to maximally destructive qualities, as proposed by Smith in 1934.[43]

Nosocomial pathogens are becoming more frequent causes of lung abscesses as a result of the increased numbers of patients with extended hospitalizations and advanced-generation antibiotics. The widespread use of third-generation cephalosporin antibiotics has resulted in resistant *Enterobacter* spp. and other gram-negative organisms being recovered in secondary lung abscesses. In the report by Tan and associates,[44] fungal abscesses always were associated with debilitated, chronically hospitalized patients. Immunosuppression no doubt contributes to the recovery of other unsuspected organisms (e.g., *Legionella*, *Neisseria mucosa*, *S. pneumoniae*, *Citrobacter*)[12, 18, 38, 39] and underscores the value of obtaining specimens in chronically hospitalized patients, atypical cases, and patients not responding to empiric treatment.

Among otherwise normal hosts, tuberculosis can be a cause of single and multiple abscesses. The number of tuberculosis cases presenting as lung abscess has increased dramatically in the past decade, and tuberculosis probably will be associated more frequently with lung abscesses in the future. In patients with an international travel history, unusual pathogens such as parasites (e.g., hydatid cysts)[14] and regional bacteria (e.g., *Pseudomonas pseudomallei*) should be considered.

An important lesson for the physician is the relevance of various respiratory cultures to the microbiology of lung abscesses. Rarely is sputum of use in defining the pathogens in a lung abscess because of three factors. First, sputum typically is contaminated with abundant mouth flora. Second, if the lung abscess is not ruptured, no direct communication of the pathogens in the abscess occurs with the airway. Third, sputum is difficult to obtain in preadolescent children. Obtaining cough cultures, performed by gagging a young child and culturing the coughed sputum collected on a swab before it can be swallowed, frequently is unsuccessful. However, useful information occasionally is acquired by the skilled clinician.

Bronchoscopy is effective in recovering relevant organisms if the abscess has ruptured and has therapeutic value because it may assist in clearing secretions from the airway. It has been performed infrequently in pediatric practice in the past because of a lack of skilled personnel and pediatric equipment. Bronchoscopy is used rarely to drain the abscess, but when performed, highly informative microbiologic information may be obtained. Transtracheal aspirates, also performed in few pediatric patients, have similar value. The upper airway frequently is colonized in debilitated patients, and microbiologic information so obtained must be interpreted with care. Direct aspiration of the abscess, typically under CT or ultrasound guidance,[45] is an ideal way to provide microbiologic data and plan antimicrobial therapy. Aspiration may have therapeutic value in decompressing the abscess.

Clinical Features

Most patients with lung abscesses have had symptoms 1 to 3 weeks before hospitalization.[13] Fever is reported to be associated with 100 percent of primary abscesses[13, 24] and 84 percent of a mixed group of primary and secondary abscesses.[44] All patients with secondary abscesses in a small series had fever.[7] Cough occurs in 53 to 67 percent of cases.[24, 44] Initially, it may be nonproductive, becoming purulent when rupture into a bronchus occurs. With necrosis, hemoptysis can occur. Ipsilateral chest or shoulder pain also has been described in some patients, particularly older children.[13, 25] Weight loss may be present if the abscess is of more than a few days' duration. Other symptoms are listed in Table 30–3.[44]

Some differences in presentation by age exist. Neonates and young infants typically are febrile, without localizing symptoms. Older children also are febrile but may have more cough or tachypnea and focal pain.

The clinical features of a lung abscess vary with the causative organisms and patient risk factors. Patients with bacterial pneumonia can present with dramatic onset of fever and overwhelming respiratory failure, such as in staphylococcal pneumonia. In these cases, the patient often has a recent history of influenza or varicella infection. Staphylococcal abscesses may not be noticed on chest radiographs until the patient already is on ventilatory support because of the time required for an abscess to organize. Similar presentations are typical of group A beta-hemolytic *Streptococcus* and *S. pneumoniae* infections. Often, a patient has received antibiotics, and a temporary defervescence in symptoms occurs before the hectic fevers of an abscess reemerge. In the latter situation, the respiratory symptoms may be less notable but virtually always are present.[13] This biphasic presentation was described more than 60 years ago in postoperative aspiration[43] and continues to be typical of many lung abscesses.

Subacute presentations are typical in patients with tuberculosis or fungal abscesses and usually are associated with other chronic systemic symptoms, such as anorexia,

TABLE 30–3 ■ SYMPTOMS AND SIGNS IN PATIENTS WITH LUNG ABSCESS

Symptom	No. of Cases	%
Fever	38	84
Cough	24	53
Dyspnea	17	38
Chest pain	11	24
Anorexia	9	20
Purulent sputum	8	18
Rhinorrhea	7	16
Malaise/lethargy	5	11
Hemoptysis	4	9
Diarrhea	4	9
Nausea/vomiting	3	7
Irritability	3	7
Otitis media	2	4
Convulsions	2	4
Weight loss	1	2
Sore throat	1	2
Lymphadenopathy	1	2

From Tan, T. Q., Seilheimer, D. K., and Kaplan, S. L.: Pediatric lung abscess: Clinical management and outcome. Pediatr. Infect. Dis. J. *14*:51–55, 1995.

weight loss, and malaise. The symptoms of cough may be prominent. Aspiration pneumonia may take an indolent or acute course, depending primarily on the organisms in the abscess, the volume of aspirated material, and the status of the host.

The physical findings in lung abscess are limited. Children almost always have fever,[24,44] whereas adults present with fever less frequently (19%).[36] Tachypnea is a variable finding. Typically, auscultation is unrevealing, except in cases of very large abscesses, in which loss of normal breath sounds is perceived. Adults and older children seem to have more discrete physical findings, with rales and decreased breath sounds in approximately one third of adult cases,[36] but they are uncommon findings in young children.[3]

An abscess can rupture into the bronchus, the mediastinum, or the pleura. In all cases, these complications are significant. In children, all organisms seem capable of causing these complications, but polymicrobial and anaerobic infections are suspected most often. Rupture into the bronchus may not be harmful if the volume of the abscess cavity does not overwhelm the host's ability to cough and clear the material. In the immunocompromised host, it may lead to disseminated pneumonia and further abscesses or death. Among adult patients who died of lung abscess, 22 percent were found to have died of aspiration of the abscess contents.[16] In the otherwise healthy individual, rupture into the bronchus can be beneficial because it decompresses the abscess and allows more rapid healing of the affected tissues. It is associated with the sudden production of foul-smelling, abundant, and sometimes blood-stained sputum. Frank hemoptysis is an uncommon occurrence. Rupture into the mediastinum can be life-threatening, can be associated with chest pain and cardiac compromise, and requires surgery to drain the resulting mediastinitis. Rupture into the pleural space results in pleuritic pain, enhancement of symptoms on inspiration, and often a more toxic presentation. It also may require drainage.

Routine laboratory information is of limited help. The white blood cell count and erythrocyte sedimentation rate are elevated nonspecifically, and a left shift of the white blood cell differential count typically occurs.[13] Certain laboratory tests, such as the purified protein derivative tuberculosis skin test, HIV serology, or sweat chloride test, may be helpful in revealing an underlying cause. Except for the tuberculosis skin test, such studies should not be performed routinely and should be directed by a family history or other findings, such as chronic diarrhea or lymphadenopathy. Blood cultures are helpful but are positive in less than 10 percent of cases.[13,44]

Differential Diagnosis

The major differential diagnoses in the management of a lung abscess are anatomic. A lung abscess must be differentiated from pneumonia, necrotizing pneumonia, pneumatocele, loculated empyema, and a purulent pleural effusion with a bronchopleural fistula. CT or ultrasound may confirm an abscess by documenting central cavitation and differentiating pleural from parenchymal tissues. An abscess may be confused with a congenital cyst, pseudocyst, hydatid cyst, saccular bronchiectasis, pneumatocele, or sequestration. Chest CT allows definition of these entities in many cases by identifying the associated structures, such as the vascular supply and pleural borders.

Apart from the anatomic and infectious causes of lung abscess, the other very rare cause is cancer. Unrecognized metastatic disease from Ewing sarcoma or osteosarcomas with associated central necrosis can mimic an abscess or, by obstructing a bronchus, can promote abscess formation.

Diagnosis

The diagnosis of lung abscess almost always is made by imaging the lung. In most cases, the plain radiograph is adequate to define a lung abscess (Fig. 30–1), showing a thickened cavity with an air-fluid level that can be accentuated by placing the patient in the lateral decubitus or erect position. Atelectasis often occurs as an expanding abscess compressing adjacent tissues. Pleural thickening may occur if the abscess is subpleural. Hilar adenopathy occurs in subacute situations. Visualization can be performed with bronchoscopy if the abscess ruptures into the bronchus. It is limited by the

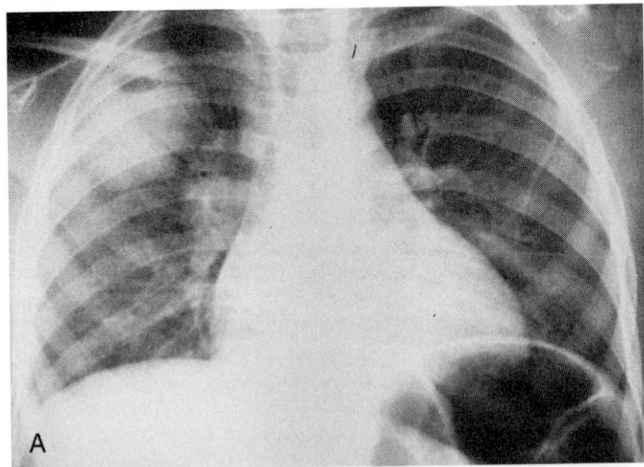

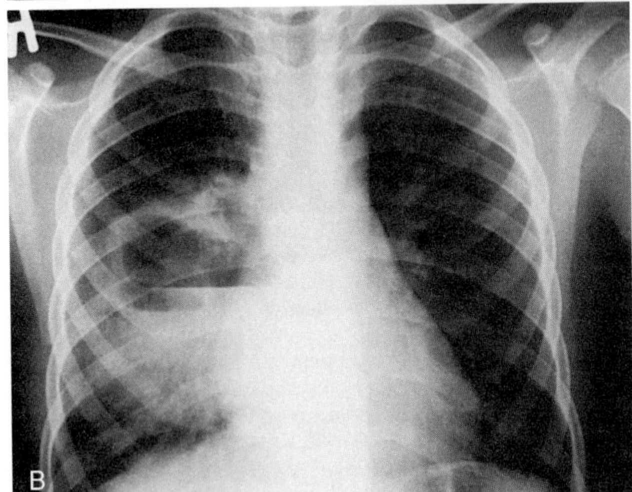

FIGURE 30–1 ■ *A,* Plain chest film of a 4-year-old black boy with symptoms, including cough and fever of 104° F, for 4 days. He was treated initially with oral cefaclor and re-presented with this radiograph demonstrating an air-fluid level in the right upper lobe. On intravenous cefuroxime, he was afebrile in 48 hours and went home on oral cefuroxime axetil after 4 days. *B,* Plain chest film of a 6-year-old black boy who presented after 5 days of symptoms with high fever, productive cough, dyspnea, and abdominal pain. The plain chest film reveals multiple air-fluid levels. Nafcillin and cefotaxime were begun. On day 4, an ultrasound-guided diagnostic aspiration recovered thick purulent material, but Gram stain and all cultures, including anaerobic and fungal, were negative. He was afebrile in 7 days and went home on amoxicillin-clavulanic acid at 10 days.

location of the abscess and skill of the bronchoscopist. The procedure usually is not performed for anatomic diagnosis but rather to obtain microbiologic specimens or exclude a foreign body.

CT is optimal in its ability to identify smaller or multiple abscesses, document the impact of the abscess on adjacent tissues, identify cystic processes mimicking an abscess, and define an abscess for which an organized pneumonia obscures an air-fluid level on plain film.[19] The CT image of a lung abscess reveals an air-fluid level with an active rim, and the abscess is distinguished from necrotizing pneumonia, which lacks enhancement on contrast studies and lacks a distinct air-fluid level.[17] Nuclear imaging is described[10] but used rarely and adds little to the information obtained by CT.

After a presumed abscess is defined by imaging, needle aspiration of the abscess or bronchoscopic recovery of abscess fluid should allow confirmation and identification of the infectious cause of the process. Based on available pediatric studies, whether either procedure hastens recovery or reveals the microbiologic cause in pretreated individuals cannot be predicted. In an interesting case report in which an infant had abscesses in both lungs, the time to recovery was equal in the abscess that was drained and the other abscesses that were treated medically.[27] An adult study using thin-needle aspiration showed positive cultures in 92 percent of patients not pretreated with antibiotics and in 70 percent of those pretreated.[35]

Directly aspirating a lung abscess may be difficult or unsuccessful if the abscess is not large or peripheral, and complications such as lung laceration and sterile pleural effusions are real risks. However, two groups[17, 44] have had satisfactory pediatric experience using direct aspiration under CT guidance (Fig. 30–2). Bronchoscopy particularly is valuable if foreign bodies are suspected or pus can be recovered. When material is obtained, a putrid quality is a clue that anaerobic organisms are present. Typically, the abscess contains pure neutrophils. Occasionally, counterimmune electrophoresis or other antigen detection systems may assist in the microbiologic diagnosis when cultures are negative.[15] Because of the special handling required, these technologies usually are employed only after standard cultures have failed.

Treatment

Although surgery has a role in specific situations, the treatment of lung abscess in children often is successful when antibiotics alone are used.[37] In most cases, the need for surgery is limited to instances of failed antibiotic therapy or to an abscess complicated by rupture into adjacent tissues. Newer techniques such as hyperbaric oxygen[8] have been proposed as adjuvant therapy.

The initial choice of antibiotics almost always is presumptive because abscess material may not be available. For primary lung abscesses in which no risk factors are identified and in the absence of positive blood cultures, the recommended approach is to begin therapy with a regimen that covers *S. aureus, S. pneumoniae*, and the anaerobic microorganisms that normally are found in the upper respiratory tract. Clindamycin, ampicillin plus sulbactam, or ticarcillin plus clavulanate frequently are used in this setting.

For patients at risk for aspiration or who are immunocompromised, gram-negative pathogens also must be considered. This spectrum of pathogens can be addressed with one of several drug regimens: clindamycin and cefotaxime (or an aminoglycoside); ticarcillin plus clavulanate or piperacillin plus tazobactam; or nafcillin (or cefazolin), gentamicin, and metronidazole. Patients with cystic fibrosis are particularly vulnerable to *Pseudomonas* spp. and should receive an aminoglycoside plus an additional antipseudomonal penicillin or cephalosporin. Carbapenem therapy would be an alternative, but data on its use in children are limited. When endocarditis is present, coverage (e.g., vancomycin plus gentamicin with or without anaerobic coverage) should be provided for staphylococci, streptococci, and enterococci while awaiting results of blood cultures.

Physicians hope that the special problem of drug-resistant *S. pneumoniae* will remain limited because this pathogen rarely is isolated in lung abscesses. However, without effective outpatient therapy, more cases of pneumonia may progress to necrosis or abscess, and as a result, a resurgence of this disease may occur. Reports from Spain suggest that most patients with resistant organisms (penicillin G, minimum inhibitory concentrations of 0.12 to 2.0) still are sensitive clinically to achievable doses of penicillins.[33]

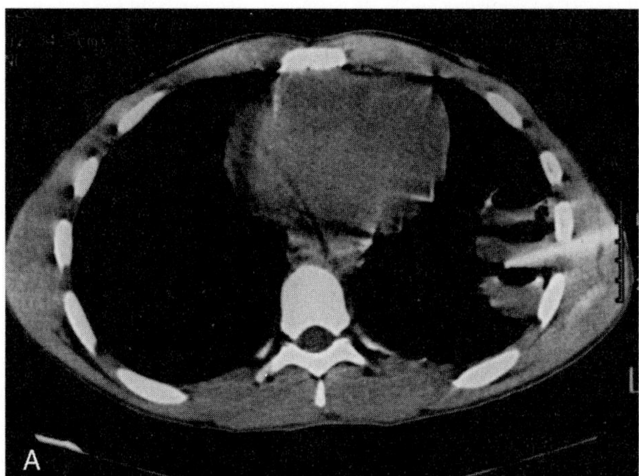

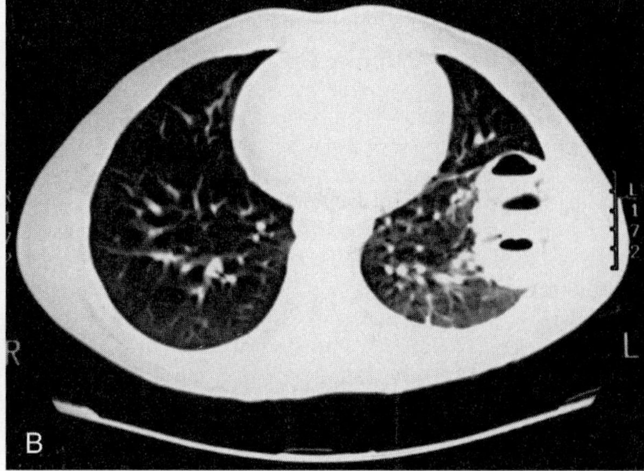

FIGURE 30–2 ■ This scan is that of a 15-year-old white boy who, 4 days before admission, reported a mild aspiration during fresh-water swimming. He awoke the next day with chest and back pain. He then developed low-grade fever. His plain chest film showed a large, thick-walled abscess in the left lower lobe. The computed tomographs show insertion of a 20-gauge needle into the abscess on the first day of admission *(A)* and detail of the wall thickness and cavitation *(B)*. *Haemophilus influenzae* grew from the aspirate. Ampicillin-sulbactam was initiated and continued for 14 days.

With culture information available, therapy is directed specifically at the pathogens isolated. However, in most patients, oral or intravenous antibiotic therapy has been administered before aspiration of a lung abscess and may affect which organisms are recovered.[13] For this reason, coverage should be extended to include organisms that are likely to be present but are not recovered, such as anaerobes in a setting of aspiration.

All bacterial lung abscesses should be treated with intravenous therapy until the patient is stabile and no longer toxic. In approximately two thirds to four fifths of patients, this condition occurs within 3 to 7 days of instituting intravenous therapy.[13, 26] After the patient has been afebrile 48 to 72 hours, initiation of oral therapy may be considered. Certain oral drugs, such as amoxicillin plus clavulanate and clindamycin, achieve therapeutic serum levels and are effective against the spectrum of organisms in lung abscesses.

The length of total therapy for a lung abscess should be 2 to 3 weeks. Complicated infections should be treated intravenously until fever has disappeared and no evidence of continuing inflammation exists. An additional 2 to 3 weeks of oral treatment should follow. Radiographic resolution of a lung abscess that is not drained occurs over the course of weeks. Even with drainage, resolution may not occur more rapidly. Chest radiography should be repeated every 1 to 2 weeks until complete resolution is documented.

Tuberculous lung abscesses may rupture spontaneously into the pleura. Treatment is not directed so much at the immediate abscess or pleuritis but at preventing spread if it erupts into a bronchus. Preventing reactivation several years later is another goal of therapy.

Clinical failure is defined by persistent fever and toxicity. Not clearly defined is the length of time treatment with intravenous antibiotics should continue before declaring therapy a failure. Suggestions in the literature range from 1 to 3 weeks.[2, 4, 37] When clinical failure occurs, several options are available, including drainage of the abscess, which permits identification of the organisms causing the disease process.

Performing bronchoscopy may allow direct perforation of the abscess and evacuation of its contents. However, a risk of fatality occurring from aspiration of abscess contents exists.[18]

Catheter drainage or needle aspiration (once or more) also is possible under fluoroscopy, ultrasonography, or CT guidance.[11, 17, 22, 23, 25, 34, 46] It can be performed by simple CT-guided needle aspiration, which leads to relief of symptoms in approximately two thirds of cases within 48 hours.[17] Pleural fistulas are a consequence in as many as one fifth of cases.[17] The risk is lowest if the abscess is peripheral and adhesion of the opposing pleural surfaces is a consequence of the inflammatory process. When this adhesion occurs, the needle or catheter does not traverse the pleural space. Catheter drainage may be attempted in abscesses larger than 20 cc or 4 cm in diameter[2, 17] using 8- to 10-French pigtail catheters. Smaller abscesses are technically difficult to manage. Chest tube thoracostomy once was the standard therapy of lung abscesses,[29, 31] and it now is recommended when conservative therapy fails. It may play a role in patients with large abscesses if the abscess abuts the parietal pleura and provides a direct path from the exterior surface to the abscess.[28] Significant complications, such as hemothorax, bronchopleural fistula, and empyema, which occur in a few cases, are associated with tube thoracostomy.[28]

Another possible surgical indication is proximity of a lung abscess to the mediastinum. In the face of antibiotic failure, an open lung procedure and wedge resection may be required, depending on the location of the abscess.[5] The procedure typically is successful and often obviates lobectomy.[20, 48] In the complicated case, such as with a gangrenous lung, lobar resection may be necessary. Although the management of the infant with a lung abscess has been addressed with similar approaches, it has required surgery somewhat more commonly than in older children.[42, 47]

Prognosis

The outcome for pediatric patients usually is very good when lung abscesses are uncomplicated, and recovery is more rapid than in adults.[30] Most patients have complete symptomatic and radiographic resolution in 3 to 6 weeks, with normal pulmonary function tests at follow-up.[4, 13] Complicated disease associated with thoracostomy tubes and empyema more likely leads to residual symptoms (e.g., pleurisy) and persistent effusions or pleural thickening on radiographs. In reports published since 1982, one half of the patients with lung abscess have required surgical intervention, such as thoracentesis to drain an empyema, lobectomy, or decortication, and 20 percent have required lobectomy or decortication.[4, 7, 13, 44] If patients require lung resection, they may experience immediate surgical complications; long-term exercise tolerance may be limited; and other problems, such as scoliosis, may develop. One study, however, found normal pulmonary functions in patients studied after undergoing lobectomy.[32] Rarely, a residual cavity may develop and become superinfected. The mortality rate is 4 to 11 percent[13, 44] for patients with primary and secondary lung abscesses.[13, 44] Higher risk of morbidity and mortality occurs in patients with secondary abscesses who have complications caused by either a decrease in host resistance or underlying disease.[13, 36, 44]

REFERENCES

1. Abramson, J. S., and Mills, E. L.: Depression of neutrophil function induced by viruses and its role in secondary microbial infections. Rev. Infect. Dis. *10*:326–341, 1988.
2. Al-Salem, A. H., and Ali, E. A.: Computed tomography-guided percutaneous needle aspiration of lung abscesses in neonates and children. Pediatr. Surg. Int. *12*:417–419, 1997.
3. Asher, M. I., and Beaudry, P. H.: Lung abscess. *In* Chernick, V., and Kendig, E. L. (eds.): Disorders of the Respiratory Tract in Children. 5th ed. Philadelphia, W. B. Saunders, 1990, pp. 429–435.
4. Asher, M. I., Spier, S., Beland, M., et al.: Primary lung abscess in childhood: The long-term outcome of conservative management. Am. J. Dis. Child. *136*:491–494, 1982.
5. Ball, W. S., Jr., Bisset, G. S., III, and Towbin, R. B.: Percutaneous drainage of chest abscesses in children. Radiology *171*:431–434, 1989.
6. Bartlett, J. G., Gorbach, S. L., Tally, F. P., et al.: Bacteriology and treatment of primary lung abscess. Am. Rev. Respir. Dis. *109*:510–516, 1974.
7. Brook, I., and Finegold, S. M.: Bacteriology and therapy of lung abscess in children. J. Pediatr. *94*:10–12, 1979.
8. Bulynin, V. I., Koshelev, P. I., and Barsukov, V. A.: Treatment of acute lung abscess using hyperbaric oxygenation. Grudnaia Serdechno-Sosudistaia Khir. *5*:37–41, 1990.
9. Canny, G. J., Marcotte, J. E., and Levison, H.: Lung abscess in cystic fibrosis. Thorax *41*:221–222, 1985.
10. Cook, P. S., Datz, F. L., Disbro, M. A., et al.: Pulmonary uptake in indium-111 leukocyte imaging: Clinical significance in patients with suspected occult infections. Radiology *150*:557–561, 1984.
11. Cuestas, R. A., Kienzle, G. D., and Armstrong, J. D., II: Percutaneous drainage of lung abscesses in infants. Pediatr. Infect. Dis. J. *8*:390–392, 1989.
12. Dobranowski, J., and Stringer, D. A.: Diagnosis of *Legionella* lung abscess by percutaneous needle aspiration. J. Can. Assoc. Radiol. *40*:43–44, 1989.
13. Emanuel, B., and Shulman S. T.: Lung abscess in infants and children. Clin. Pediatr. *34*:2–6, 1995.
14. Fitzgerald, D., Harvey, J., Issacs, D., et al.: The case of the persistent pleural effusion. Pediatr. Infect. Dis. J. *10*:475–477, 1991.

15. Hanukoglu, A., Gutman, R., Fried, D., et al.: Lung abscess caused by *Streptococcus pneumoniae* type 3: The importance of counterimmunoelectrophoresis in laboratory diagnosis. Infection *12*:39–40, 1984.
16. Harper, P., and Terry, P. B.: Fatal lung abscesses: Review of 11 years experience. South. Med. J. *74*:281–283, 1981.
17. Hoffer, F. A., Bloom, D. A., Colin, A. A., and Fishman, S. J.: Lung abscess versus necrotizing pneumonia: Implications for interventional therapy. Pediatr. Radiol. *29*:87–91, 1999.
18. Hussain, Z., Lannigan, R., and Austin, T. W.: Pulmonary cavitation due to *Neisseria mucosa* in a child with chronic neutropenia. Eur. J. Clin. Microbiol. Infect. Dis. *7*:175–176, 1988.
19. Johnson, J. F., Shiels, W. E., White, C. B., et al.: Concealed pulmonary abscess: Diagnosis by computed tomography. Pediatrics. *78*:283–286, 1986.
20. Kosloske, A. M., Ball, W. S., Jr., Butler, C., et al.: Drainage of pediatric lung abscess by cough, catheter, or complete resection. J. Pediatr. Surg. *21*:596–600, 1986.
21. Kuhn, C.: Bacterial infections. *In* Thurlbeck, W. M., and Churg, A. M. (eds.): Pathology of the Lung. 2nd ed. New York, Thieme Medical Publishers, 1995, p. 285.
22. Levine, M. M., Ashman, R., and Heald, F.: Anaerobic (putrid) lung abscess in adolescence. Am. J. Dis. Child. *130*:77–81, 1976.
23. Lorenzo, R. L., Bradford, G. F., Black, J., et al.: Lung abscesses in children: Diagnostic and therapeutic needle aspiration. Radiology. *157*:79–80, 1985.
24. Mark, P. H., and Turner, J. A.: Lung abscess in childhood. Thorax *23*:216, 1968.
25. Mayer, T., Matlak, M. E., Condon, V., et al.: Computed tomographic findings of neonatal lung abscess. Am. J. Dis. Child. *136*:39, 1982.
26. McCracken, G. H.: Lung abscess in childhood. Hosp. Pract. *13*:35–36, 1978.
27. Melhem, R. E.: Percutaneous drainage of chest abscesses in children. Radiology *173*:575–576.
28. Mengoli, L.: Giant lung abscess treated by tube thoracostomy. J. Thorac. Cardiovasc. Surg. *90*:186–194, 1985.
29. Monaldi, V.: Endocavitary aspiration in the treatment of lung abscess. Chest *29*:193–201, 1956.
30. Neild, J. E., Eykyn, S. J., and Phillips, I.: Lung abscess and empyema. J. Med. *57*:875–882, 1985.
31. Neuhof, H., and Touroff, A. S. W.: Acute putrid abscess of the lung: Hyperacute variety. J. Thorac. Surg. *12*:98–106, 1936.
32. Nonoyama, A., Tanaka, K., Osako, T., et al.: Surgical treatment of pulmonary abscess in children under ten years of age. Chest *85*:358–362, 1984.
33. Pallares, R., Linares, J., Vadillo, M., et al.: Resistance to penicillin and cephalosporin and mortality from severe pneumococcal pneumonia in Barcelona, Spain. N. Engl. J. Med. *333*:474–480, 1995.
34. Parker, L. A., Melton, J. W., Delany, D. J., et al.: Percutaneous small bore catheter drainage in the management of lung abscesses. Chest *92*:213–218, 1987.
35. Pena Grinan, N., Munoz Lucena, F., Vargas Romero, J., et al.: Yield of percutaneous needle lung aspiration in lung abscess. Chest *97*:69–74, 1990.
36. Pohlson, E. C., McNamara, J. J., Char, C., et al.: Lung abscess: A changing pattern of the disease. Am. J. Surg. *150*:97–101, 1985.
37. Powell, K.: Primary pulmonary abscess. Am. J. Dis. Child. *136*:489–490, 1982.
38. Purdy, G. D., Cullen, M., Yedlin, S., et al.: An unusual neonatal case presentation: *Streptococcus pneumoniae* pneumonia with abscess and pneumatocoele formation. J. Perinatol. *8*:378–381, 1987.
39. Shamir, R., Horev, G., Merlob, P., et al.: *Citrobacter diversus* lung abscess in a preterm infant. Pediatr. Infect. Dis. J. *9*:221–222, 1990.
40. Shanks, G. D., and Berman, J. D.: Anaerobic pulmonary abscesses: Hematogenous spread from head and neck infections. Clin. Pediatr. *25*:520–522, 1986.
41. Shapiro, M. E., Kasper, D. L., Zaleznik, D. F., et al.: Cellular control of abscess formation: Role of T cells in the regulation of abscesses formed in response to *Bacteroides fragilis*. J. Immunol. *137*:341–345, 1986.
42. Siegel, D., and McCracken, G. H., Jr.: Neonatal lung abscess. Am. J. Dis. Child. *133*:947–949, 1979.
43. Smith, D. T.: The diagnosis and treatment of pulmonary abscess in children. J. A. M. A. *103*:971–974, 1934.
44. Tan, T. Q., Seilheimer, D. K., and Kaplan, S. L.: Pediatric lung abscess: Clinical management and outcome. Pediatr. Infect. Dis. J. *14*:51–55, 1995.
45. van Sonnenberg, E., D'Agostino, H. B., Casola, G., et al.: Lung abscess: CT-guided drainage. Radiology *178*:347–351, 1991.
46. Weber, T. R., Vane, D. W., Krishna, G., et al.: Neonatal lung abscess: Resection using one-lung anesthesia. Ann. Thorac. Surg. *36*:464–467, 1983.
47. Weissberg, D.: Percutaneous drainage of lung abscess. J. Thorac. Cardiovasc. Surg. *87*:308–312, 1984.
48. Wessler, H., and Schwarz, H.: Abscess of the lung in infants and children. Am. J. Dis. Child. *19*:137–140, 1920.

CHAPTER 31 Cystic Fibrosis

LISA SAIMAN ■ PETER W. HIATT

Cystic fibrosis (CF) is the most common inherited lethal disease of the white population. It occurs primarily in individuals of central and western European origin and affects more than 30,000 Americans. The estimated incidence in the United States is 1 in 2000 to 2600 live white births,[209] 1 in 19,000 live African American births, 1 in 11,500 live Hispanic births, and 1 in 25,000 live Asian American births.[119] CF has an autosomal recessive mode of inheritance. Affected individuals are phenotypic homozygotes, and both parents usually are heterozygotes or carriers. The carrier frequency in white individuals in the United States is approximately 1 in 25, with full siblings of children with CF having a 1 in 4 chance of being affected.

A range of different mutations in a single gene located on the long arm of chromosome 7 are responsible for the defective protein product in CF.[118] The most common mutation (ΔF508) is the absence of three sequential nucleotides, which leads to the deletion (Δ) of phenylalanine (F) at position 508 on the CF transmembrane conductance regulator protein (CFTR). Approximately 70 percent of individuals with CF have this mutation. To date, more than 700 mutations in the CFTR gene have been identified. Certain populations, including Ashkenazi Jews, have a relatively low incidence of the ΔF508 mutation.[119]

Five classes of mutations have been proposed to account for reduced CFTR chloride channel function.[201] Class 1 mutations are those in which stop codons or frame shift mutations cause early termination of mRNA translation and minimal to no protein production. In class 2 mutations (ΔF508), protein fails to mature, again resulting in little CFTR expression at the cell membrane. Class 3 and 4 mutations are associated with defective regulation and decreased conductance of chloride at the cell membrane. Thus, production of protein and transit to the cell surface occur, but chloride conductance is altered or nonexistent. Class 5 consists of splice site mutations, and such mutations affect the amount of CFTR produced. The presence of more than 700 mutations for CFTR has prompted investigators to evaluate the association of genotype with clinical disease. The CF phenotype-genotype consortium has demonstrated that certain mutations from classes 3 to 5 are associated with pancreatic sufficiency; however, a poor correlation of CF genotype with the severity of pulmonary disease has been noted. The wide variation in pulmonary disease observed in CF may reflect the effects of environment, patient compliance, polymorphisms in CFTR, and modifier genes that affect CFTR function.

CFTR is a glycoprotein expressed at relatively low levels by surface epithelial cells in the lungs, sweat glands, pancreas, liver, large intestine, and testes.[153] Higher-level expression has been reported in submucosal glands. CFTR appears to be very similar to a group of membrane transport proteins known as the ABC transporter superfamily.[83] Researchers have confirmed that CFTR functions as an apical chloride channel mediated by cyclic adenosine monophosphate. CFTR appears to regulate the activities of separate chloride and sodium channels by balancing the rates of secretion of chloride and absorption of sodium.[60] CFTR, therefore, appears to be responsible for the proper hydration of secretions in the airways, pancreas, and other tissues. Thus, an inability to secrete chloride and excessive absorption of sodium and water contribute to altered luminal secretions in patients with CF. In the lungs, this condition leads to decreased airway surface liquid, decreased mucociliary clearance, and a predisposition for chronic bacterial infections.

Clinical Manifestations

Individuals with CF have exocrine gland dysfunction that results in progressive suppurative obstructive lung disease, pancreatic insufficiency (85–90%), elevated sweat electrolytes, male infertility (>95%), and female infertility (70–80%). Less common manifestations include hepatobiliary disease, osteoarthropathy, diabetes mellitus, nasal polyposis, and meconium ileus[32] (Table 31–1).

The potential relationship between genotype (the genetic constitution of an individual) and phenotype (the physical expression of that genotype) in CF is an active area of clinical investigation. To date, correlation of genotype with phenotype has not led to many clear associations between the severity or course of pulmonary disease and the type of genetic mutations.[27, 93] The influence of factors such as infection with respiratory viruses, colonization with bacterial pathogens, nutrition, passive smoke exposure, and changing medical therapy has complicated the analysis. Multiple mutations and lack of complete understanding of the physiologic function of CFTR have delayed our gaining an understanding of the genotypic influence on phenotype in CF.

A strong association between pancreatic function and genotype has been reported for individuals homozygous for ΔF508.[16] Most subjects homozygous for ΔF508 are pancreatic insufficient.[38] Obstruction of the pancreatic duct begins in utero and results in fibrosis and loss of exocrine pancreatic function. Because pancreatic fluid from patients with CF is low in enzyme and bicarbonate concentrations, such patients have maldigestion of both fat and protein. Clinically, children commonly have steatorrhea, protein-calorie malnutrition, muscle wasting, and progressive failure to thrive. A voracious appetite is characteristic, and stools are described as bulky, greasy, and foul smelling. Approximately 10 to 15 percent of patients have sufficient preservation of pancreatic function to allow normal digestion of food (pancreatic sufficient).[48] At least five mutations from classes 3 to 5 described earlier are associated with pancreatic sufficiency, whereas almost all patients homozygous for ΔF508 are pancreatic insufficient.[38]

TABLE 31–1 ■ CLINICAL FEATURES OF CYSTIC FIBROSIS AT DIAGNOSIS

Age and Clinical Feature	Approximate Incidence (%)
0–2 Years	
Meconium ileus	10–15
Obstructive jaundice	
Hypoproteinemia/anemia	
Bleeding diathesis	
Heat prostration/hyponatremia	
Failure to thrive	
Steatorrhea	85
Rectal prolapse	20
Bronchitis/bronchiolitis	
Staphylococcal pneumonia	
2–12 Years	
Malabsorption	85
Recurrent pneumonia/bronchitis	60
Nasal polyps	6–36
Intussusception	1–5
13 Years+	
Chronic pulmonary disease	70
Clubbing	
Abnormal glucose tolerance	20–30
Diabetes mellitus	7
Chronic intestinal obstruction	10–20
Recurrent pancreatitis	
Focal biliary cirrhosis	15–25
Portal hypertension	2–5
Gallstones	4–14
Aspermia	98

From Maclusky, I., and Levison, H.: Kendig's Disorders of the Respiratory Tract in Children. 5th ed. Philadelphia, W. B. Saunders, 1990, p. 701.

Liver disease in CF is associated with pancreatic insufficiency.[133] Focal biliary cirrhosis develops in roughly 25 percent of CF patients, but less than 5 percent progress to multilobar biliary cirrhosis and portal hypertension. Meconium ileus, the thick inspissated meconium that mechanically obstructs the distal ileum, occurs in 8 to 15 percent of newborns with CF. It also is associated with pancreatic insufficiency.[92] A similar syndrome (distal intestinal obstructive syndrome) mimicking meconium ileus can occur in older children and young adults with CF. Adult males with congenital absence of the vas deferens can have abnormal CF alleles with little clinical expression of disease other than in the reproductive system.

Pulmonary disease is the primary cause of morbidity and mortality in patients with CF.[208] The lungs are morphologically normal at birth; however, within weeks they begin showing evidence of small airway abnormalities and inflammation. Progressive bronchiectasis develops with time and leads to advanced destruction of the airways and parenchyma (Figs. 31–1 and 31–2). Bronchiectatic cysts are prominent, especially in the upper lobes. Death eventually results from respiratory failure. Progressive deterioration in pulmonary function occurs despite the routine use of antimicrobial agents. A pathogenic role for bacteria is suggested by the presence of immune complexes in the lungs, clinical improvement after treatment with antibiotics, and the improved survival observed since the introduction of therapy with antipseudomonal agents.

Many children with CF are evaluated initially during infancy for recurrent wheezing or persistent bronchiolitis. These findings often resolve with therapy. As mucopurulent secretions increase, chronic cough develops.[32] Digital clubbing occurs gradually and correlates with the severity of

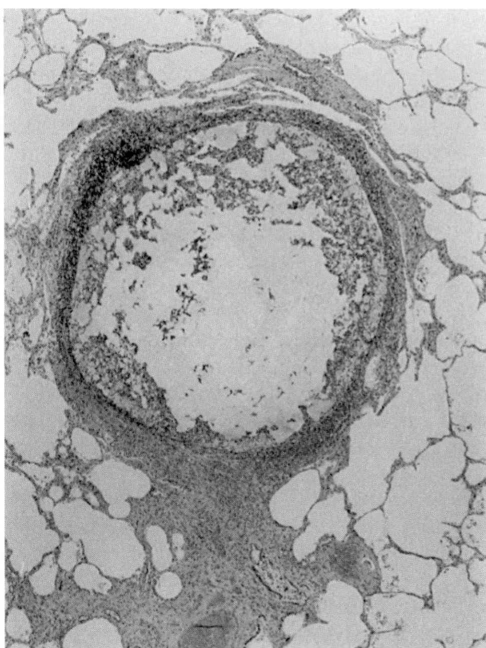

FIGURE 31–1 ■ Early stages of lung disease in cystic fibrosis are demonstrated in this lung specimen. Airway inflammation and bronchiectasis are present. The surrounding lung parenchyma is normal.

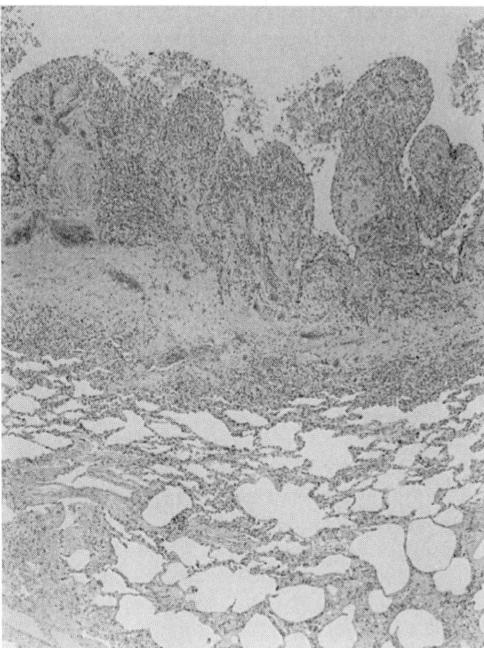

FIGURE 31–2 ■ Late stages of pulmonary disease are illustrated. Epithelial ulceration of the airway, loss of smooth muscle from the airway wall, inflammation, and bronchiectasis are present in the large airway at the top of the photomicrograph. Compression of the surrounding lung parenchyma occurs as bronchiectasis increases.

lung disease. On examination, the patient has evidence of crackles and decreased breath sounds secondary to mucopurulent secretions. Acute exacerbations may develop and require administration of intravenous antibiotic therapy and frequent hospitalization. As lung disease progresses, exercise tolerance decreases, dyspnea increases, and respiratory failure develops. Marked heterogeneity in the rate of progression of pulmonary disease has been noted. Some patients live to the fifth decade of life, whereas others succumb to respiratory failure before their 10th birthday.

In the year 2000, the mean survival age for individuals with CF was 32 years. Survival for children born during and after 2001 is expected to increase, with the median age approaching the fifth decade of life. In the United States, more than one third of people with CF are 18 years or older, and within 10 years, one half will be older than 18 years. Thus, as life expectancy has increased, CF has become a disease of both children and adults.

Diagnosis

In the absence of newborn screening, in utero diagnosis, or a family history of CF, strong clinical suspicion is required for early recognition of CF. Most children have a history of recurrent lower respiratory tract disease and symptoms secondary to malabsorption. Approximately 10 percent of children will have meconium ileus at birth or a family history of CF, or both. The quantitative pilocarpine iontophoresis sweat test is one acceptable test to establish a diagnosis of CF.[39] A sweat chloride concentration greater than 60 mmol/L is consistent with a diagnosis of CF. Values between 40 and 60 mmol/L are considered borderline, and values less than 40 mmol/L are normal. Some data suggest that a sweat chloride concentration greater than 40 mmol/L in infants younger than 3 months is highly consistent with a diagnosis of CF. The sweat test should be repeated on two separate occasions. Identification of two CF mutations by genotype is highly specific, but less sensitive. At most, only 80 to 85 percent of CF alleles are identified with the current commercially available screening panels. The ΔF508 mutation is found in 70 percent of CF chromosomes in people from the United States. However, because each patient has two chromosomes, only 50 percent of patients are homozygous for ΔF508. Current commercially available screening detects 32 to 70 mutations, including 2 mutations in 80 percent of descendants from northern Europe and roughly 60 percent of mutations in African Americans.

Nasal potential difference measurements assess the transepithelial electrical potential difference across the nasal epithelium. Different patterns of potential difference are found in patients with CF and those with normal epithelia. Although nasal potential difference measurements can be very helpful in patients with nondiagnostic sweat tests and only one identified CF mutation, the test is available at less than 10 percent of accredited CF centers in the United States.

Newborn screening programs have been implemented in some states in America as well as the United Kingdom, Australia, and Europe. Using low values of trypsinogen in dried blood specimens obtained in routine screening programs for metabolic disorders, these programs identify newborns with CF. Improved nutritional status as a result of newborn screening has been reported in a controlled, randomized trial in Wisconsin.[55] Ninety percent of screened infants in whom CF was diagnosed at birth maintained their weight at greater than the 10th percentile versus only 60 percent of unscreened controls. These differences diminished with time as clinical symptoms led to a diagnosis of CF in the unscreened controls, and the two groups' nutritional status was comparable at 5 to 6 years of age. Without screening, the diagnosis is made in approximately 60 percent of patients by 1 year of age and in close to 90 percent by 5 years of age. Thus, early diagnosis through neonatal screening appears to improve nutritional outcome in the first 5 years

TABLE 31–2 ■ DIAGNOSIS OF CYSTIC FIBROSIS

One or More Phenotypic Features
Chronic sinopulmonary disease
Gastrointestinal and nutritional abnormalities
Salt loss syndromes—acute salt depletion
Chronic metabolic alkalosis
Male urogenital abnormalities resulting in obstructive azoospermia

Plus Laboratory Evidence of CFTR Abnormality (One or More)
Elevated sweat chloride concentrations
Identification of two CFTR mutations
In vivo demonstration of abnormal ion transport across nasal epithelium

CFTR, cystic fibrosis transmembrane conductance regulator.

of life, yet whether these programs are associated with improved pulmonary outcomes and improved long-term survival remains unclear.

In summary, the diagnosis of CF should be based on the presence of one or more clinical features (Table 31–2), a positive newborn screening test, and laboratory evidence of abnormal CFTR function. Laboratory evidence includes elevated sweat chloride concentrations, two identifiable CF mutations, or abnormal in vivo nasal potential difference measurements made across the nasal epithelium.

Pathogenesis

Current knowledge of the cell biology, biochemistry, and physiology of CF is incomplete. As suggested previously, the pathogenesis is initiated by a defect in the gene responsible for production of the transporter protein CFTR.[117] Altered salt and water transport leads to abnormal secretions in the respiratory tract, pancreas, gastrointestinal tract, sweat glands, and other exocrine glands. In the lungs, abnormal respiratory tract secretions leading to decreased airway surface liquid appear to decrease mucociliary clearance and impair defenses to inhaled particulate matter and various microbial pathogens. These features lead to bacterial colonization and infection, inflammation, airway obstruction, and progressive lung destruction. Although the clinical features of CF are well described, the exact process by which alterations in CFTR lead to disease is unknown.

Altered chloride channel function helps explain disease in the sweat glands, intestine, pancreas, and male genital tract. Loss of chloride from sweat can alter secretion of intestinal fluids and potentially yield dehydrated pancreatic fluid. Plugging of pancreatic ducts leads to pancreatic atrophy and loss of digestive enzymes and islet cells. The same ductular plugging and atrophy may occur in the male and female genital tracts. Multiple hypotheses have been proposed to define the mechanism of airway colonization with *Pseudomonas aeruginosa*. Although several studies have assessed this problem, the exact mechanism of infection and colonization remains unknown. The primary hypothesis for airway infection in CF is altered mucociliary clearance secondary to abnormal salt and water transport. As the normal function of CFTR is being defined, additional hypotheses are being put forward to explain the mechanism of early airway infection and inflammation. These hypotheses involve altered epithelial cell receptors for bacteria, abnormal mucins that enhance bacterial binding or impair airway clearance, and inactivation of epithelial-derived bactericidal activity.

Chronic bacterial infection of the airway is responsible for progressive respiratory impairment and death in most patients with CF. Bacterial colonization and infection of the lower respiratory tract occur early in human infants with CF (Fig. 31–3), and airway inflammation often is established at the time that the disease becomes clinically apparent.[9]

Adherence of bacteria to respiratory epithelial cells is a necessary antecedent to the development of infection and inflammation-induced airway damage in CF.[56, 164, 214] Nonmucoid *P. aeruginosa* isolates appear to adhere via pili,[164] whereas the exopolysaccharide alginate mediates adherence of mucoid strains of the organism. Local production of cytokines and other proteins in response to bacterial infection may play an important role in modulating the chronic airway inflammation.[171] Airway inflammation in CF is characterized by marked neutrophilic infiltration with release of

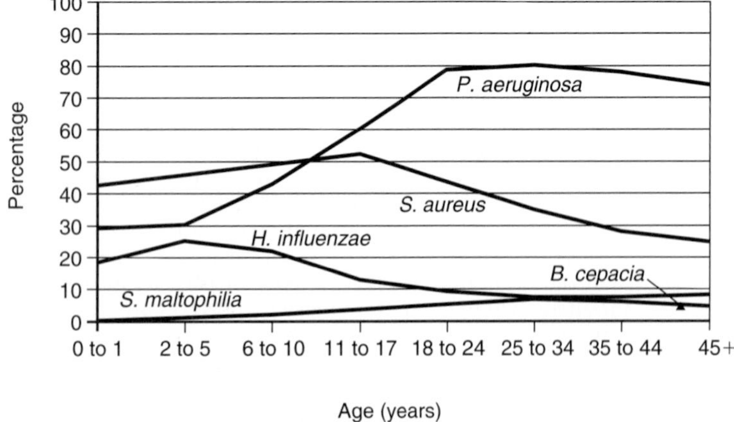

FIGURE 31–3 ■ Age-specific prevalence of pathogens in CF patients. (Courtesy of the Cystic Fibrosis National Patient Registry, 2000.)

bioactive lipids, oxygen metabolites, myeloperoxidase, and lysozyme.[56] Proteases (e.g., elastase) derived from both neutrophils and bacteria directly damage respiratory epithelium and cleave proteins that are important in host defense.[183, 193] Chronic infection with retention of the byproducts of inflammation ultimately leads to the severe bronchiectatic changes and derangements in gas exchange characteristic of end-stage CF.

Several in vivo studies have assessed the location of bacterial adherence within the lungs of CF subjects and the attachment of bacteria to CF and non-CF cells in vitro.[12, 194] *P. aeruginosa* is found within the lumen of airways of CF patients obtained at autopsy.[12] These organisms are observed within the inflammatory exudates of the airways and not within epithelial cells lining the lung or in alveolar spaces. In vitro studies have demonstrated adherence of *P. aeruginosa* in areas of epithelial cell destruction.[139, 142, 194] However, no adherence to the apical membrane of intact epithelial cells has been noted. In contrast, cell culture models show evidence that defects in CFTR enhance bacterial binding to immortalized airway epithelial cells.[160] A tetrasaccharide (asialo-G_{M1}) is expressed more on CF than non-CF cells and promotes binding of *P. aeruginosa* to the epithelial membrane. Pseudomonal exoproducts such as neuraminidase increase the amount of asialo-G_{M1} available for bacterial binding and thereby facilitate bacterial adherence to airway epithelial cells.[26, 164]

Mucins also may play an important role in binding bacteria within the airway. Sialylated and neutral forms of mucins bind *P. aeruginosa.*[145] Removal of sialylic acid from mucin by neuraminidase reduces the adherence of *P. aeruginosa.* Although mucins are important in lung defense, the means by which abnormal CFTR function affects mucin-bacterial binding remains unclear. Deletion of CFTR could result in a biochemically altered mucin, a change in the clearance of mucin, or altered bacterial binding.

Airway epithelial cells are vital in maintaining a pathogen-free environment within the airway. Smith and colleagues[175] demonstrated that a monolayer of airway epithelial cells were able to kill bacteria when placed on their apical surface. In contrast, CF epithelia were unable to clear the bacterial load. Surface fluid washed from the normal cells demonstrated bactericidal activity; however, fluid from the CF monolayer lacked bacterial killing properties. Goldman and associates[67] duplicated the results of this study with a different model. They implicated a human defensin, hBD-1, as the primary agent responsible for bacterial killing. Defensins are low-molecular-weight proteins produced by epithelial cells that are cytotoxic to bacteria and thought to be salt sensitive. How deletion of CFTR affects the function of these molecules and other antimicrobial substances produced by the respiratory epithelium, such as lysozyme, is unclear.

Excessive oxidant production by CF neutrophils has been proposed as a mechanism of airway injury. Activation of reduced nicotinamide adenine dinucleotide phosphate (NADPH) within neutrophils results in the production of precursors used by myeloperoxidase to generate chloramines. Chloramines are oxidants with long half-lives and, if produced in excess, have the potential to damage airway epithelium.[20] One study has examined the activity of NADPH and myeloperoxidase in producing chloramines in CF and non-CF subjects.[205] Significant differences were observed between groups in myeloperoxidase activity and chloramine release, both of which were increased in CF subjects. Treatment of CF neutrophils with amiloride reduced the generation of oxidants, which suggests that altered intracellular ion concentrations or pH may regulate myeloperoxidase activity. Thus, CFTR may alter oxidant production in neutrophils. Alternatively, other investigators have suggested that circulating neutrophils may be primed to respond to a phagocytic stimulus and that these differences in oxidant generation represent increased neutrophil activity.[72, 151]

CFTR, in addition to affecting oxidant production, also may regulate glutathione production in cells transfected with CFTR.[102] Glutathione is an antioxidant found in large amounts in airway lung fluid from normal subjects[29]; however, it is reduced in CF patients.[157] Mutant CFTR, therefore, may alter glutathione transport and consequently impair defense against oxidant injury. Thus, both increased oxidant production from neutrophils and impaired antioxidant transport in airway epithelial cells can be altered by mutant CFTR, thereby increasing the potential for oxidant injury in the CF airway.

Production of cell adherence molecules and inflammatory cytokines is intact in patients with CF.[49, 94] However, defects in bacterial opsonization, a reduction in anti-inflammatory cytokines, and proinflammatory effects of bacterial DNA have been reported. Although humoral antibody responses and neutrophil phagocytosis from peripheral blood are normal, increased elastase in the CF airway can alter opsonic receptors and thereby impair phagocytosis. The large amounts of elastase present in bronchoalveolar lavage (BAL) fluid from the airways of CF patients overwhelm normal antiprotease activity. This condition can lead to local impairment in phagocytosis of bacteria within the airway lumen and thus contribute to bacterial persistence.

Proinflammatory mediators are elevated in BAL fluid from patients with CF, as are macrophages expressing intracellular cytokines.[15] In contrast, some anti-inflammatory cytokines (interleukin-10 [IL-10]) are found in reduced amounts in BAL fluid from CF subjects. These observations have prompted some investigators to assess IL-10 production by bronchial epithelial cells in normal and CF subjects.[15] Bronchial epithelial cells from normal individuals produce significantly greater amounts of IL-10 than do cells from CF subjects. Enhanced macrophage production of proinflammatory cytokines and decreased production of IL-10 have fostered a hypothesis that the CF gene defect may contribute to airway inflammation to such an extent that the inflammation exceeds the normal expected response to bacterial infection. Alternatively, CFTR could have no effect on the production of this anti-inflammatory cytokine, and IL-10 could be down-regulated. Although understanding of the pathogenesis of CF is far from complete, better elucidation of the biology of CFTR should result in the development and institution of new therapeutic modalities.

Microbiology of Cystic Fibrosis

EPIDEMIOLOGY OF PATHOGENS IN CYSTIC FIBROSIS

Ever since investigators provided the initial descriptions of CF, researchers have appreciated that patients are infected with a unique, though predictable, cascade of pathogens, including *Staphylococcus aureus,* nontypeable *Haemophilus influenzae,* and *P. aeruginosa.*[6, 25, 63, 112] The mucoid phenotype of *P. aeruginosa* is a pathognomonic feature of CF and a marker of chronic lung infection.[71] The CF lung can harbor very high concentrations of *P. aeruginosa;* as many as 10^8 to 10^9 organisms per gram of sputum may be present.[207] *Burkholderia cepacia* complex can be particularly virulent and associated with increased morbidity and mortality.[36, 69, 154]

AGE-SPECIFIC PREVALENCE OF PATHOGENS

The CF Foundation in the United States has maintained an annual CF National Patient Registry since 1962.[57] The age-specific prevalence of pathogens in CF patients in the United States, as reported to this registry in 2000, is shown in Figure 31–3.[42] During the first decade of life, *S. aureus* is the most common pathogen and is harbored by 40 percent of children and adolescents. Nontypeable *H. influenzae* also is a prevalent pathogen early in life and is cultured from the respiratory tracts of 15 percent of children.[42] These organisms are replaced during adolescence and adulthood largely by *P. aeruginosa.* However, *P. aeruginosa* may be the first pathogen isolated and is recovered from 30 percent of infants during the first year of life; by the time they are 18 years of age, approximately 80 percent of American patients with CF are infected with *P. aeruginosa.* Overall, *B. cepacia* complex is found in 3 to 4 percent of patients and 10 percent of adults. Similar patterns of infection are noted in CF patients from around the world.

EMERGING PATHOGENS

During the past decade, researchers increasingly have appreciated that several other microorganisms also may colonize or infect the respiratory tract of patients with CF. These microorganisms include intrinsically multidrug-resistant, nonfermenting, gram-negative bacilli such as several newly defined genomovars (species) of *Burkholderia* (including genomovar III, *Burkholderia vietnamiensis,* and *Burkholderia multivorans*)[104] (Table 31–3), *Stenotrophomonas maltophilia,* and *Achromobacter xylosoxidans.*[73] In addition, patients may be colonized with *Aspergillus* spp. and be susceptible to allergic bronchopulmonary aspergillosis[62] or be colonized or infected with nontuberculous mycobacteria (NTM).[126] Furthermore, many more common pathogens found in CF patients, including *P. aeruginosa*[163, 187] and methicillin-resistant *S. aureus* (MRSA), may become multidrug-resistant.[64]

The etiologies behind these emerging pathogens are multifactorial. The life expectancy of CF patients has increased during the past 4 decades and is now 32 years of age.[42] CF patients are treated with frequent and prolonged courses of antimicrobial agents, including oral, intravenous, and aerosolized agents. On average, CF patients receive 0.6 courses of intravenous antibiotics per year for the management of pulmonary exacerbations,[42] and approximately 90 percent of patients will receive oral agents at least once during a 6-month period.[21] Evidence of nosocomial acquisition of some pathogens, including *B. cepacia* complex, *P. aeruginosa,* and MRSA, has been noted and is described in further detail later. Finally, during the past 15 years, detection of many potential pathogens has improved. Clinical microbiology laboratories processing CF specimens are using several selective media, particularly for *B. cepacia* complex, and are speciating non–lactose-fermenting gram-negative bacilli.[63, 74, 185] This procedure may have led to recent increases in the prevalence of some microorganisms because of ascertainment bias.

TABLE 31–3 ■ MEMBERS OF THE *BURKHOLDERIA CEPACIA* COMPLEX, 2001

Species (Genomovar)	Binomial Designation	Reference
I	*B. cepacia*	Vandamme 1997
II	*B. multivorans*	Vandamme 1997
III	Pending	Vandamme 1997
IV	*B. stabilis*	Vandamme 1997, 2000
V	*B. vietnamiensis*	Vandamme 1997
VI	Pending	Coenye, LiPuma 2001
VII	*B. ambifaria*	Coenye, Mahenthiralingam 2001
(VIII)	Pending	*
IX	*B. pyrrocinia*	*

*Manuscripts in preparation.

NONBACTERIAL PATHOGENS

Numerous studies have evaluated the role of nonbacterial infections in causing pulmonary exacerbations in CF. A clear correlation between respiratory viral infection and exacerbation of lung disease has been demonstrated in most of these reports.* Most studies have focused on school-age and adult patients with CF. Few studies were controlled, and many failed to use active viral surveillance. Most infections were identified by a fourfold rise in antibody titer. Abman and colleagues,[2] in assessing the effects of respiratory viral infections in infants with CF, found that hospitalization with respiratory syncytial virus (RSV) correlated with a poor early clinical course.

Chronic cough, pneumonia, and wheezing are early pulmonary findings in infants with CF. Two studies have reported prolonged bronchiolitis-like syndromes in infants younger than 6 months.[61, 107] These infants required intensive respiratory therapy, including bronchodilators, chest physiotherapy, and mechanical ventilation in selected infants. In a prospective study, Abman and associates[2] identified viral pathogens in 12 hospitalized infants with CF. Seven of the 12 isolates were RSV. Infants infected with RSV experienced prolonged hospitalizations, one half needed mechanical ventilation, and 75 percent required supplemental oxygen at hospital discharge. When evaluated at a mean of 28 months after hospitalization, infants hospitalized with RSV were noted to have chronic respiratory symptoms and worse radiograph scores. Hiatt and coworkers assessed the effects of respiratory viral infection in infants with CF and found that one half of the CF infants infected with RSV required hospitalization.[76] Although severe sequelae were not observed, pulmonary function was markedly worse after hospitalization. These studies suggest that viral respiratory infection, especially RSV, has a significant detrimental impact on the early respiratory course of infants with CF.

The interrelationship between the acquisition of *P. aeruginosa* and the development of viral respiratory infection remains clouded. Petersen and Ong and their colleagues[127, 138] reported more severe pulmonary disease when viral infection was accompanied by *Pseudomonas* colonization, yet Przyklenk and associates[143] found no correlation. Synergism between bacterial and respiratory viral infection was suggested by Przyklenk and coworkers after an increase in bacterial colony-forming units was found in the sputum of CF subjects. Hordvik and colleagues[79] and Efthimiou and coworkers[51] noted that patients with CF and severe pulmonary disease recovered slowly from viral infection. The underlying severity of lung disease was critical in predicting response to viral respiratory infection.

*See references 3, 51, 79, 127, 138, 143, 147, 180, 198, 210.

Role of the Clinical Microbiology Laboratory

Ongoing communication between the clinical microbiology laboratory and the CF care team is critical to provide appropriate care and infection control and to further our understanding of the epidemiology of pathogens in patients with CF. Every 5 years, the executive committee of the U.S. CF Foundation conducts site visits of accredited CF care centers in the United States ($n = 117$) and meets with the director of the clinical microbiology laboratory in an effort to ensure standardized practices.[165]

SPECIMEN PROCESSING

Respiratory tract specimens from patients with CF, including those obtained after lung transplantation, should be labeled "CF specimens" to ensure proper processing. Timely transport will optimize recovery of pathogens; ideally, specimens should be received by the laboratory within 3 to 4 hours of collection or stored at 4° C and processed within 24 hours. Sputum is the ideal specimen, and at least 1.0 mL should be collected to ensure adequate volume for plating on selective media. Sputum should be Gram-stained to assess whether a specimen contains bacteria and neutrophils rather than epithelial cells. Throat cultures often are obtained in children too young to expectorate, but they do not always predict the presence of pathogens in the lower airway.[155] BAL specimens generally are reserved for research protocols, lung transplant recipients, or patients with atypical courses who are not producing sputum.

SELECTIVE MEDIA

Selective media are needed to identify specific pathogens, although using them may be costly and time consuming. Current recommendations for selective media are shown in Table 31–4. *S. aureus* from patients with CF may be thymidine deficient and require mannitol salt agar for growth.[165] Detection of *B. cepacia* complex is enhanced markedly by the use of oxidative-fermentative bacitracin–polymyxin B lactose (OFBPL) agar or *B. cepacia* selective media (BCSM).[63, 74] Multicenter studies conducted by the Centers for Disease Control and Prevention in the 1980s demonstrated that the use of selective media for *B. cepacia* improved the yield of *Burkholderia* spp. from patients with CF.[185] In addition, specimens can be plated on Mycosel agar to identify *Aspergillus* spp., although this mold also will grow on blood agar. Throat swabs from nonexpectorating patients also should be plated on selective media.[172] If NTM is suspected, sputum must be processed with an additional decontamination step to avoid overgrowth by *P. aeruginosa.*[202] However, performing quantitative cultures is not recommended except for a research study.

ANTIMICROBIAL SUSCEPTIBILITY TESTING

The optimal methodology for antimicrobial susceptibility testing for both mucoid and non-mucoid strains of *P. aeruginosa* has been elucidated recently. In studies of 500 multidrug-resistant strains of *P. aeruginosa* from patients with CF, five different antimicrobial susceptibility testing methods were compared: a reference microbroth dilution assay, Kirby Bauer disks, E-tests, and the automated, commercial systems Vitek and Microscan. The agar-based diffusion methods (Kirby Bauer disks and the E-test) proved most accurate when compared with the reference methodologies.[23, 24, 159] The commercial systems Vitek and Microscan had unacceptably high rates of very major (i.e., false-susceptible) and major (i.e., false-resistant) errors. Thus, the National Committee for Clinical Laboratory Standards endorses the use of antibiotic-impregnated disks.[120]

In summary, clinical microbiology laboratories that process respiratory tract specimens from patients with CF should use standardized, validated methods. This procedure is particularly important in the era of managed care because specimens may be processed by commercial laboratories, and many laboratories affiliated with academic institutions are experiencing fiscal challenges.

TABLE 31–4 ■ RECOMMENDED MEDIA AND PROCESSING FOR RECOVERY OF CYSTIC FIBROSIS PATHOGENS

Organism	Recommended Media or Processing*†
Staphylococcus aureus	Mannitol salt agar Columbia/colistin-nalidixic acid agar
Haemophilus influenzae	Horse blood or chocolate agar (supplemented or not with 300 mg/L bacitracin) incubated anaerobically
Pseudomonas aeruginosa	MacConkey agar
Burkholderia cepacia complex	OFPBL agar, PC agar, BCSA
Stenotrophomonas maltophilia	MacConkey agar, VIA agar DNase agar confirmatory media or biochemical or molecular identification
Achromobacter xylosoxidans	MacConkey agar Biochemical identification assay
Mycobacterial spp.	NALC-NaOH and oxalic acid decontamination step
Yeast	Mycosel agar‡
Other gram-positive organisms	Sheep blood agar supplemented with neomycin and gentamicin (streptococcal selective agar)
Other gram-negatives organisms	MacConkey agar

*Detection of some pathogens may be enhanced by prolonging incubation for as long as 4 days to allow slow-growing colonies to become apparent.
†All media are commercially available.
‡*Aspergillus* species and other molds do not grow well on Mycosel agar but do grow well (though not selectively) on many of the media used for cystic fibrosis specimens, especially OFPBL. Confirmation of the identification of molds should be done with standard biochemical and phenotypic methods.
BCSA, *Burkholderia cepacia* selective agar; NALC, *N*-acetyl-L-cysteine; OFPBL, oxidative-fermentative bacitracin-polymyxin B lactose; PC, *Pseudomonas cepacia*; VIA, vancomycin-imipenem agar.

Specific Cystic Fibrosis Pathogens

NONTYPEABLE *HAEMOPHILUS INFLUENZAE*

H. influenzae frequently is the earliest pathogen isolated from patients with CF. Advent of the *H. influenzae* vaccine has not had an impact on the prevalence of this organism because patients with CF harbor nontypeable strains. In general, this pathogen is susceptible to a wide variety of agents and amenable to treatment.

STAPHYLOCOCCUS AUREUS

S. aureus is the most common pathogen isolated from patients with CF during the first decade of life. Patients generally retain the same clone of methicillin-susceptible *S. aureus* for their lifetime.[19, 169] Notably, MRSA is found in 6.7 percent (range, 0–19%) of patients and generally appears in older patients. MRSA can be associated with deterioration in both pediatric and adult patients.[113, 191] Recent hospitalization is a risk factor for development of MRSA, and such infection suggests nosocomial acquisition.[64]

PSEUDOMONAS AERUGINOSA

P. aeruginosa is the most common and important pathogen in patients with CF. Initial colonization occurs with non-mucoid, antibiotic-susceptible strains that express pili, flagella, and the lipopolysaccharide O side chain.[70] Initial attachment to a solid surface (e.g., mucin or respiratory epithelial cells) occurs via flagella and type IV pili.[37] Attachment then activates genes that synthesize extracellular polysaccharide (alginate),[47] and *P. aeruginosa* strains become mucoid, grow as microcolonies, and are thought to create biofilms.[37] The LasR-LasI system (quorum-sensing genes) promotes the initial formation of microcolonies, which later differentiate into alginate-encased mature biofilms. Thus, biofilms are the proposed mechanism by which *P. aeruginosa* permanently infects the CF respiratory tract and eludes host defenses and antimicrobial agents, and accordingly, biofilms are a potential target for therapeutic interventions.

Bacteria in biofilms avoid ciliary clearance, evade phagocytosis, and are antibiotic-resistant.[173] Unlike bacteria that are planktonically grown, biofilm bacteria are not killed by antibiotics because the targets of conventional antibiotics, such as penicillin-binding proteins, are not expressed by bacteria growing in biofilms.[37] Thus, antibiotics given during acute pulmonary exacerbations may kill planktonic bacteria shed by biofilms, but they cannot eliminate the antibiotic-resistant sessile biofilm communities. This finding has enormous clinical implications because current antibiotic susceptibility testing methodologies use planktonically growing organisms.

P. aeruginosa also produces numerous virulence factors that have been studied in animal models of sepsis, acute lung infection, and bacteremia. Such factors are chemotactic stimuli to neutrophils and include pili, exotoxin A and exoenzyme S, leukocidin, phospholipase C, elastase, and alkaline protease.[30, 177, 189] Exotoxins may increase the viscosity of secretions and impair ciliary clearance, as well as cause small airway obstruction and, ultimately, lung destruction.

Infection with *P. aeruginosa* is associated with increased morbidity and mortality. Children infected with *P. aeruginosa* are more likely to have cough and lower chest radiograph scores than are uninfected children.[81] Investigators have shown that infants younger than 2 years of age who are infected with both *S. aureus* and *P. aeruginosa* have lower pulmonary function, chest radiograph scores, and 10-year survival rates than do uninfected children.[4] *P. aeruginosa* infection is associated with a gradual deterioration in the mean percent predicted forced expiratory volume in 1 second (FEV_1).[93, 130] However, researchers increasingly are appreciating that the mucoid phenotype of *P. aeruginosa* is associated with a more rapid decline in lung function.[75, 131]

BURKHOLDERIA CEPACIA

Infection with *B. cepacia* complex and the associated "cepacia syndrome" was reported first in 1979 in adolescent Canadian patients with CF.[86, 186] The cepacia syndrome is characterized by a virulent course, high fever, bacteremia, rapid deterioration in lung function, and early death. In general, patients with CF do not have bacteremia caused by any other pathogens. Perhaps more frightening to the CF community than the cepacia syndrome itself was the realization that patient-to-patient transmission of *B. cepacia* was occurring, as described later. However, researchers also have realized that *B. cepacia* complex apparently is associated with different clinical courses: the cepacia syndrome versus a more gradual deterioration in lung function versus transient colonization without any apparent adverse effect on pulmonary function.

Through a series of genetic and phenotypic studies, researchers have discovered that *B. cepacia* actually is a complex of several different species called genomovars that are distinguishable by their physiologic and genetic characteristics.[35] The genomovars of the *B. cepacia* complex are shown in Table 31–3, but in all likelihood, more genomovars will be defined in the future. Recent work by several international investigators has described the epidemiology and clinical courses associated with different genomovars.[104, 108, 178] Most CF isolates are genomovar II or III, which can be associated with a more rapidly progressive course.[106] Patient-to-patient transmission may occur via the cable pilus[182] or the *B. cepacia* epidemiologic strain marker (BCESM),[109] but most transmissible strains do not express these markers. In general, *B. multivorans* strains are associated with transient colonization and not with clinical deterioration,[109] but dissemination and clinical deterioration can be caused by this genomovar.[104] Thus, an expanded knowledge of different genomovars may lead to different clinical management, including different strategies for infection control.

STENOTROPHOMONAS MALTOPHILIA

S. maltophilia is an intrinsically multiple antibiotic-resistant, gram-negative bacillus that is well known as a hospital-acquired pathogen in non-CF patients and is being isolated with increasing frequency from the respiratory tract of patients with CF. The overall prevalence of this organism in patients with CF is 6.7 percent (range, 0–27%),[42] and in single-center studies the prevalence has ranged from 10 to 25 percent.[45, 46] In a recent randomized, placebo-controlled study of aerosolized tobramycin in 520 patients with CF who were 6 years or older, the prevalence of *S. maltophilia* was 10.7 percent at baseline,[25] whereas the national rate reported to the CF Registry was 2.9 to 3.9 percent in comparably aged patients. Thus, a suggestion is that the national rate may be an underestimate because clinical laboratories may not identify this potential pathogen. Transient colonization also may be common; Demko and colleagues reported that 50 percent of patients had only a single positive culture for this microorganism.[45] Long-term use of antibiotics has been shown to be a potential risk factor for acquisition of *S. maltophilia*.[188]

The role of this organism as a pathogen in CF is still under investigation. A recent case-control study did not show a significant difference in lung function or mortality when patients with and without *S. maltophilia* were compared.[68] However, anecdotal reports support the observation that this organism is a pathogen in some patients with CF, and in a cross-sectional analysis of the CF National Patient Registry from 1990 to 1997, the rate of intravenous antibiotic use in patients infected with *S. maltophilia* was comparable to the rate in patients infected with *P. aeruginosa* or *B. cepacia*.[161] Demko and coworkers found that the 5-year survival rate of patients with *S. maltophilia* ($n = 211$) who had severe lung function at initial isolation of this organism was 40 percent; patients without *S. maltophilia* (n = 471) had a 5-year survival rate of 72 percent.[45]

ACHROMOBACTER XYLOSOXIDANS

A. xylosoxidans may be isolated from the respiratory tracts of patients with CF, but the clinical significance of this organism remains unclear. In 1997, the last year that this organism was reported to the CF patient registry, 2.7 percent of patients harbored this multidrug-resistant, gram-negative bacillus.[40] However, 8.7 percent of patients in the aerosolized tobramycin trial had positive cultures for *A. xylosoxidans* at enrollment, again suggesting that the reported prevalence is low.[22] *A. xylosoxidans* may be misidentified as another nonfermenting gram-negative bacillus, and conversely, *P. aeruginosa, B. cepacia* complex, and *S. maltophilia* may be misidentified as *A. xylosoxidans.*[158] The impact of this organism may be difficult to assess because *A. xylosoxidans* generally is cultured from patients concomitantly infected with *P. aeruginosa,* but an association has been found between *A. xylosoxidans* and pulmonary exacerbations.[50, 54]

ASPERGILLUS AND *SCEDOSPORIUM* SPECIES

Patients with CF are colonized frequently with *Aspergillus* spp., with allergic bronchopulmonary aspergillosis developing in a minority. Invasive infections with *Aspergillus* spp. may develop only in lung transplant recipients, as described later. Approximately 10 percent of patients with CF harbor *Aspergillus* spp., most often *Aspergillus fumigatus,*[41] although baseline data from the aerosolized tobramycin trial indicated that 24.5 percent of patients had positive cultures.[21] Antibiotics, including oral and aerosolized agents, are risk factors for colonization with *Aspergillus* spp.[13, 148]

Overall, allergic bronchopulmonary aspergillosis will develop in 2 to 10 percent of CF patients and can be associated with a dramatic loss of lung function.[53, 62, 110, 118] The wide range in prevalence may be due to a lack of standardized diagnostic criteria, variability in laboratory procedures, and limited recognition by physicians. This immunologically mediated syndrome is marked by a brisk IgE response, specific antibody to *A. fumigatus*, peripheral eosinophilia, and symptoms of reactive airway disease. Short-lived pulmonary infiltrates may be noted on chest radiographs. Although *Aspergillus* spp. normally do not invade the parenchyma, the airways become impacted with mucus containing fibrin, eosinophils, and mononuclear cells, which can result in permanent damage, including airway obstruction and proximal bronchiectasis.[53]

Scedosporium spp. can be isolated from the lungs of patients with CF, but at present, the clinical significance of these fungi remains unknown. In the aerosolized tobramycin trial, 2.4 percent of patients harbored saprophytic fungi,[22] and Cimon and coauthors reported that 8.6 percent of 128 patients monitored for 5 years were colonized or infected with *Scedosporium apiospermum.*[34]

NONTUBERCULOUS MYCOBACTERIA

Since the early 1990s, researchers increasingly have appreciated that NTM may be pathogens in patients with CF.[125] This prevalence may be due in part to the increased length of survival of patients with CF, as well as improved culture techniques; special culture techniques have been developed to prevent overgrowth by *P. aeruginosa.*[202] Olivier and colleagues conducted a natural history study of NTM in patients with CF in 21 American CF centers from 1993 to 1997.[125] Using standardized mycobacteriologic methods,[203] these investigators found that the overall prevalence of colonization or infection with NTM was 13 percent. *Mycobacterium avium* complex and *Mycobacterium abscessus* were the species most commonly identified and represented 72 and 16 percent of isolates, respectively. Patients with NTM were older and had a better mean percent predicted FEV_1, a lower prevalence of *P. aeruginosa*, and a higher prevalence of *S. aureus* than did patients without NTM. This finding suggests a "healthy survivor" effect in that older, relatively stable patients were more likely to harbor NTM.

In an individual patient, determining whether NTM are colonizing the lung or causing disease can be difficult. Signs and symptoms of mycobacterial disease are nonspecific and may be consistent with CF pulmonary exacerbations. Though less common, night sweats and recurrent fever can provide clues to this diagnosis. Radiographic signs generally are nonspecific, but small nodules in the lung periphery may be noted on high-resolution computed tomography.[126] Patients with acid-fast bacilli demonstrated on several sputum specimens are thought to be more likely infected than colonized with NTM.[5] However, clinicians often resort to a diagnostic/therapeutic trial of antimycobacterial agents to assess the impact of NTM on clinical status. Oral agents may not be absorbed well by patients with CF, so determining serum levels for antimycobacterial agents may be useful.[137] Thus, further studies are needed to determine whether NTM cause a progressive deterioration in lung function and, if so, what the optimal therapy is.

Treatment of Pathogens in Patients with Cystic Fibrosis

One of the cornerstones of care for patients with CF remains the aggressive use of oral, intravenous, and aerosolized antibiotics. The increasing longevity of patients with CF has paralleled the development of effective anti-*Pseudomonas* antibiotics. Antibiotics are used during several stages of CF lung disease. They have been used as prophylaxis to prevent the acquisition of pathogens and to delay chronic infection with *P. aeruginosa,* as treatment for pulmonary exacerbations, and as suppressive therapy in patients chronically infected with *P. aeruginosa.* At present, the primary goal of antibiotic therapy in patients with CF is to reduce rather than eradicate the number of organisms in the lung and thereby decrease inflammation.[146]

PROPHYLAXIS TO PREVENT ACQUISITION OF *STAPHYLOCOCCUS AUREUS*

Relatively few studies of antibiotic prophylaxis in patients with CF have been performed. Thus far, studies have focused on prevention of *S. aureus* infection in an attempt to delay acquisition of *P. aeruginosa.* From 1985 to 1992, British investigators conducted a study in which 42 infants with newly diagnosed CF were randomized to 12 months of treatment with flucloxacillin and compared with a control group in which antimicrobial treatment was provided when "clinically indicated."[14, 199] Infants treated with flucloxacillin had fewer infections with *S. aureus* and fewer hospitalizations, but both groups had similar pulmonary function. In a placebo-controlled trial conducted in the

United States, 119 patients with newly [illegible]nosed CF (mean age, 16 months) were randomized to [illegible] cephalexin or placebo for 5 to 7 years. At the end [illegible] study, the two groups did not have different pulm[illegible]nction, nutritional status, or chest radiograph sc[illegible] did they have a difference in the number of pul[illegible]xacerbations. Children treated with cephalexin [illegible]sed infection with *S. aureus,* but *increased* infect[illegible] *P. aeruginosa* (H. C. Stutman, personal comm[illegible]). Similarly, Ratjen and colleagues demonstrat[illegible] patients who received antistaphylococcal agents [illegible] a significantly higher rate of acquisition of *P. aeruginosa* and no improvement in lung function.[149] Thus, antistaphylococcal prophylaxis, though practiced in the United Kingdom, has not been endorsed widely in the United States because of concern about the emergence of resistance, the increased risk of acquiring *P. aeruginosa,* and the lack of impact on lung function. Future studies no doubt will be performed on the prevention of acquisition of *P. aeruginosa,* but to date, no randomized, placebo-controlled studies have addressed the efficacy of this approach.

STRATEGIES TO DELAY CHRONIC COLONIZATION WITH *PSEUDOMONAS AERUGINOSA*

Another "prophylactic" strategy is the use of antibiotics to prevent or delay chronic colonization with *P. aeruginosa,* defined as 6 months' or longer duration of infection.[89] This strategy has been used mainly in Europe and was described initially in the Danish CF center.[69, 89, 184, 195, 197] The rationale for this approach is that during initial infection or colonization with *P. aeruginosa,* the organism burden is low, a biofilm has not been established, and antimicrobial therapy may eradicate or reduce the number of bacteria. In general, colistin and ciprofloxacin have been administered every 3 months after the initial isolation of *P. aeruginosa.*[59] These studies have been somewhat flawed in that the outcomes of the treated patients have been compared with historic controls rather than controls treated with placebo.[184] Resistance to the therapeutic regimen has been observed as well.

Elborn and associates conducted a prospective, randomized, multicenter study in the United Kingdom to compare routine treatment every 3 months with antimicrobial treatment as needed for pulmonary exacerbations.[52] In this study, no significant differences between the two groups were noted in lung function, radiographic scores, or height and weight, but the patients were older and had established infection with *P. aeruginosa.*

The CF community in Australia also has used intravenous antibiotics followed by the administration of ciprofloxacin or aerosolized agents on initial recovery of *P. aeruginosa* and found that 6 of 24 children no longer had *P. aeruginosa* isolated for more than 12 months.[8]

Despite concern about the emergence of antimicrobial resistance, a growing consensus in the United States is that a strategy to prevent or delay chronic colonization with *P. aeruginosa* merits further study, particularly in young children before they experience a significant decline in lung function. In a small study, Wiesemann and coworkers demonstrated that treatment of young patients with aerosolized tobramycin within 7 to 12 weeks of initial infection or colonization with *P. aeruginosa* led to a shorter time to conversion from a positive to a negative culture when compared with placebo.[204] At present, pharmacokinetic studies and phase II studies of aerosolized tobramycin inhalation are being performed in young children in anticipation of this approach.[156]

TREATMENT OF PULMONARY EXACERBATIONS

Pseudomonas aeruginosa

Currently, treatment of pulmonary exacerbations is the most accepted indication for the use of antimicrobial agents. Numerous treatment trials on the antibiotic management of pulmonary exacerbations caused by *P. aeruginosa* have been performed, but several pivotal trials have led to the principles that guide the management strategies used by most physicians treating patients with CF today. Several placebo-controlled trials demonstrated that placebo-treated patients had increased morbidity and mortality rates.[65, 82, 200] Regelmann and colleagues showed that the combination of a β-lactam agent and an aminoglycoside reduced sputum bacterial density and improved pulmonary function when compared with placebo in hospitalized patients treated with bronchodilators and chest physiotherapy.[150] Smith and associates conducted a trial comparing the use of a β-lactam agent (azlocillin) with or without an aminoglycoside (tobramycin).[174] Patients treated with the combination of agents had a significant reduction in bacterial density and a longer time to re-admission for a new exacerbation than did patients treated with azlocillin alone.

Studies also have compared various agents, singly or in combination, although no regimen has proved superior. Most studies have enrolled small numbers of patients and concluded that the comparative treatment regimens were equivalent in efficacy, but they were insufficiently powered to detect differences in treatment groups.[17, 66, 87, 99, 111, 136, 168, 170] Furthermore, many studies demonstrated the emergence of resistance to the study drug at the completion of therapy, which did not correlate with clinical response to treatment.[90, 129] At present, a larger multicenter trial of ceftazidime and tobramycin versus meropenem and tobramycin is being performed; preliminary results indicate that outcomes are comparable with the two regimens (J. Blumer, personal communication). Finally, two studies examining the safety and efficacy of single daily dosing of tobramycin versus multiple daily dosing are being performed in the United Kingdom and the United States (J. Tureen, personal communication). These studies are critical for determining whether an increased risk of ototoxicity and nephrotoxicity occurs in patients with CF who receive repeated aminoglycoside courses.

Antibiotic dosages must be higher because the volume of distribution and clearance are increased in patients with CF.[44] In general, the choice of parenteral antibiotic agents is based on identification and susceptibility of the microorganisms isolated from respiratory tract cultures. Many agents have activity against *P. aeruginosa.* Accepted treatment of a pulmonary exacerbation consists of two parenteral agents from different antibiotic classes to provide "synergy" and delay the emergence of resistance.[117, 146, 163] Most commonly, a β-lactam agent with activity against *P. aeruginosa,* such as ticarcillin-clavulanate (Timentin), piperacillin, or ceftazidime, is combined with an aminoglycoside agent, generally tobramycin.

Agents are administered for 10 to 21 days, and responses to therapy are multifaceted. The agents rarely eradicate *P. aeruginosa,* emergence of resistance to the study drug or drugs is noted frequently, and the impact on bacterial density is inconsistent. Molecular studies have confirmed that resistance develops in the infecting strains rather than the acquisition of more resistant strains.[124] With treatment, patients experience an improved sense of well-being, as well as improved pulmonary function.[128] The Epidemiologic Study of Cystic Fibrosis analyzed the relationship between pulmonary function and treatment of pulmonary exacerbations; centers with patients in the upper quartile of pulmonary function treated pulmonary exacerbations more frequently than did centers with patients in the lower quartile.[116]

In vitro synergy studies have been performed by the CF Referral Center for Susceptibility and Synergy Testing to guide clinical care for multidrug-resistant strains of *P. aeruginosa.*[163, 165] The activity of clinically achievable concentrations of pairs of antimicrobial agents with different mechanisms of action (e.g., a β-lactam agent is paired with an aminoglycoside) is tested. To determine whether a combination of agents is synergistic, a fractional inhibitory concentration is calculated; synergy is defined as a fourfold reduction in the minimal inhibitory concentration (MIC) of agents alone in comparison to agents in combination. Most multidrug-resistant strains, defined as resistance to all the agents in two or more classes of antibiotics,[163, 165] can be inhibited by one or more combinations of agents. A randomized trial to study the clinical efficacy of synergy studies currently is under way in Canada.[1]

Mild exacerbations often are treated with oral ciprofloxacin[33, 77] with or without aerosolized agents such as tobramycin or colistin. Treatment trials supporting the use of aerosolized antibiotics for the management of mild exacerbations are lacking.

The CF community has not arrived at a consensus regarding the equivalence of inpatient versus outpatient management of pulmonary exacerbations. Outpatient management has advantages; it is less costly, is less disruptive to patients and their families, and has less risk of the patient acquiring nosocomial pathogens. However, patients may improve more with hospitalization because of better compliance with bed rest, chest physiotherapy, and bronchodilator treatments.[18]

Staphylococcus aureus and *Haemophilus influenzae*

Antibiotics with activity against *S. aureus* and *H. influenzae* also are included in the treatment of a pulmonary exacerbation if these pathogens are present. The clinical utility of antistaphylococcal agents is demonstrated best by early studies of infants with CF who were treated with penicillin before the nearly universal acquisition of β-lactamases by *S. aureus*.[6, 112] Infants treated during the antibiotic era had markedly improved survival. Vancomycin is used for the treatment of MRSA when this organism is considered a pathogen. No trials of treatment with linezolid in patients with CF had been performed at the time of this writing.

Burkholderia cepacia Complex

Management of *B. cepacia* complex is more problematic because of higher levels of intrinsic antibiotic resistance and a paucity of clinical trials. Initial isolates may be susceptible to ciprofloxacin, β-lactam antibiotics, chloramphenicol, trimethoprim-sulfamethoxazole, meropenem, and minocycline, but with the exception of *Burkholderia gladioli*, all *Burkholderia* spp. are resistant to aminoglycosides. As described for the management of *P. aeruginosa,* combinations of agents are used to treat a pulmonary exacerbation. Meropenem and minocycline had the most in vitro activity against 652 multidrug-resistant *Burkholderia* strains isolated from patients with CF and tested at the CF Referral Center; this combination inhibited 28 and 33 percent of strains, respectively.[22] Temocillin has been used in Europe to treat pulmonary exacerbation caused by *B. cepacia.*[190] However, resistance can develop and severely limits therapeutic options. Several investigators have performed synergy studies, including studies with two or more drug combinations, and demonstrated an improvement in pulmonary function.[1, 152, 167] Currently, an open-label trial of meropenem for the treatment of pulmonary exacerbations in patients with CF is being performed (J. Blumer, personal communication).

Stenotrophomonas maltophilia and *Achromobacter xylosoxidans*

At the time of this writing, no treatment trials for patients with CF and infected with either *S. maltophilia* or *A. xylosoxidans* have been performed. Appropriate treatment is hampered further by a lack of standardized methods for susceptibility testing and lack of consensus regarding which antimicrobial agents should be tested. However, similar strategies are used for the treatment of these organisms as described earlier for *P. aeruginosa* and *B. cepacia* complex; two or more parenteral agents are used for prolonged periods.

The CF Referral Center has been studying the susceptibility patterns of *S. maltophilia* and *A. xylosoxidans.* In a survey of 263 isolates of *S. maltophilia* taken from 218 patients with CF from 1995 to 1998, doxycycline, ticarcillin plus clavulanate, piperacillin plus tazobactam, and trimethoprim-sulfamethoxazole were most active and inhibited 78, 39, 18, and 13 percent of isolates, respectively.[167] A recent study of 94 isolates of *A. xylosoxidans* from 77 patients demonstrated that meropenem plus imipenem, or piperacillin with or without tazobactam, was most active.[158]

Allergic Bronchopulmonary Aspergillosis

Treating allergic bronchopulmonary aspergillosis can be very difficult. Although steroids are the treatment of choice because this disorder is immunologically mediated, the response to steroids is variable. Some investigators have attempted to use antifungal therapy such as oral itraconazole or aerosolized amphotericin with reported response, but no controlled trials have been performed.[117] Monitoring serum levels of itraconazole is desirable because this agent may be malabsorbed. No reports of the use of newer agents such as voriconazole or the echinocandins exist in the population of patients with CF.

Chronic Suppressive Therapy

Antibiotics are used frequently in patients with CF to prolong the time between pulmonary exacerbations and to slow the progression in lung deterioration. This strategy is termed *chronic suppressive therapy* or *maintenance therapy*. Numerous oral agents that may not be bactericidal for *P. aeruginosa* (e.g., amoxicillin-clavulanate, trimethoprim-sulfamethoxazole, or macrolide agents) are used empirically, sometimes in rotation, with anecdotal support coming from patients and physicians. The use of oral antibiotics is widespread; during a 6-month period, 90 percent of patients received at least one course of oral antibiotics.[25] However, no clinical trials support this practice, which may, in fact, contribute to antibiotic resistance.

For decades, aerosolized agents, such as tobramycin, colistin, gentamicin, and amikacin, and various β-lactam antibiotics, including carbenicillin and cephaloridine, also have been used for the management of chronic infections.[28] Most recently, a multicenter phase III, double-blind, placebo-controlled, randomized treatment trial of aerosolized tobramycin (TOBI, Pathogenesis, Seattle) was performed in patients with CF who were chronically infected with *P. aeruginosa*.[148] Patients received 300 mg of tobramycin delivered by jet nebulizer twice daily every other month for 6 months. The rationale for giving therapy every other month was to delay the emergence of resistance, reduce cost, and increase compliance. Treated patients had a 10 percent improvement in FEV_1 when compared with patients who received placebo; the latter patients experienced a 2 percent decline in FEV_1. This decline is comparable to the 2 to 4 percent annual decline noted in natural history studies of children with CF and the 1 to 2 percent annual decline seen in adults.[43] Treated patients also had a reduction in bacterial density, fewer days of hospitalization, and fewer days of administration of intravenous antibiotics. In subset analyses, adolescents had the greatest improvement in pulmonary function. During treatment, patients receiving tobramycin had increased tinnitus that was unassociated with hearing loss. Minimal systemic absorption of tobramycin occurred because serum levels of tobramycin generally were less than 1 µg/mL.

Although this study confirmed the efficacy of aerosolized tobramycin in patients with CF and chronically infected with *P. aeruginosa*, several questions remain. In routine antimicrobial susceptibility testing, the breakpoint for resistance to tobramycin is an MIC of 16 µg/mL or greater. However, 100-fold higher concentrations of tobramycin are delivered by the aerosol route without toxicity; the median concentration of tobramycin in the trial was 1200 µg/g of sputum. Thus, the conventional breakpoint for resistance to tobramycin is irrelevant for drug delivered by aerosolization, but at present, the breakpoint for aerosolized tobramycin is unknown. Furthermore, commercially available susceptibility tests do not measure MICs above 16 µg/mL. During the 6-month trial, resistance to tobramycin did develop; a trend toward higher MICs (median MIC, 2 µg/mL) occurred in the treatment group when compared with the placebo group (median MIC, 1 µg/mL). However, only a minority of patients had isolates with tobramycin MICs of 128 µg/mL or greater, and the impact of these higher MICs on clinical efficacy could not be determined because of the small number of such patients. Although patients receiving aerosolized tobramycin required significantly less intravenous antibiotics during the trial, concern remains that resistance will limit the effectiveness of intravenous tobramycin.

Investigators also examined the emergence of intrinsically tobramycin-resistant pathogens. Although the prevalence of *B. cepacia*, *S. maltophilia*, and *A. xylosoxidans* did not increase during the study period, the prevalence of *Aspergillus* but not allergic bronchopulmonary aspergillosis did. Whether this observation reflects the natural history of CF or the use of aerosolized tobramycin remains unclear. Ongoing studies are needed to address these concerns.

Macrolide Antibiotics

Much recent interest has been generated in the potential use of macrolide agents in CF[80]; this interest stems from the successful treatment of diffuse pan-bronchiolitis (DPB) with erythromycin, azithromycin, and clarithromycin.[95, 101] DPB, a chronic lung disease diagnosed primarily in Japanese adults, has several clinical features similar to those found in CF, including progressive lung disease caused by both mucoid and non-mucoid strains of *P. aeruginosa*.[181] DPB may be mild CF; patients with DPB do not have the common CFTR mutations found in white patients, but they do have mutations in CFTR.[213] Though not bactericidal for *P. aeruginosa,* low-dose macrolide agents chronically administered to patients with DPB has reduced both morbidity and mortality rates.

In vitro studies have provided the scientific rationale for this clinical efficacy: subinhibitory concentrations of macrolide agents reduce the production of several virulence factors by *P. aeruginosa*,[114, 115] including the formation of biofilm.[85, 96] Macrolide antibiotics also may have an anti-inflammatory effect and decrease cytokine production by neutrophils, monocytes, and bronchial epithelial cells.[84, 211]

Preliminary open-label clinical studies have suggested that macrolides also may be beneficial for patients with CF in that long-term therapy improved pulmonary function and body weight.[88] A double-blind, placebo-controlled, cross-over study using azithromycin was conducted in Australia and demonstrated an improvement in pulmonary function in the treatment group.[206] Currently, a double-blind, randomized, placebo-controlled trial is under way in the United States to test the safety and efficacy of prolonged therapy with azithromycin in children and adults with CF who are chronically infected with *P. aeruginosa*.[162] These studies are critical to defining the efficacy of this oral agent in CF.

Lung Transplantation

Lung transplantation currently is considered a last resort for the end-stage pulmonary disease of CF.[212] Bilateral lung and, less commonly, heart-lung and single-lung transplantation from living related donors has been performed in CF patients. By 1997, 847 American patients with CF and approximately 300 patients with CF from Canada, the United Kingdom, and France had undergone lung transplantation. Overall, the 1-, 3-, and 5-year survival rates for patients with CF who received transplants since 1992 are 70, 53, and 48 percent, respectively.[7]

Patients with CF present unique challenges for successful lung transplantation. Advantages include the relative youth of these patients, who have many years of productive life ahead. The life-threatening manifestations of CF generally are limited to the lungs, except for patients with diabetes and advanced liver disease. In addition, patients with CF have experience with complex medical regimens. However, the optimal time to list a patient for lung transplantation is difficult to determine because the natural history of CF cannot be predicted precisely and the usual wait for available lungs is 18 to 24 months.[98]

Although CF does not develop in the transplanted lungs, they can become infected with the pretransplant pathogens or newly acquired pathogens, including *B. cepacia*.[91, 106, 176, 179] Thus, controversy has ensued about whether microbiologic criteria, including pretransplant infection with multidrug-resistant pathogens, should be considered contraindications to lung transplantation for patients with CF. Several centers have published their experience with infections after lung transplantation in patients with CF. Patients at Duke University experienced infections with pretransplant pathogens, including invasive aspergillosis; sepsis with *S. maltophilia, B. cepacia,* and *B. gladioli;* and sternal wound infections.[91] Other investigators have reported that the morbidity and mortality caused by *P. aeruginosa* infection post-transplant are not higher in patients with CF than in those who do not have CF.[58, 123] However, patients with CF who are infected with *B. cepacia* generally have increased morbidity and mortality rates. In Toronto, 7 of 15 patients died, including those who acquired *B. cepacia* after transplantation, and evidence of patient-to-patient transmission was documented.[176] Although Steinbach and colleagues[179] did not detect patient-to-patient transmission, an increased mortality rate was noted with *B. cepacia* but not with multidrug-resistant *P. aeruginosa*.[7] Patients infected with genomovar III had increased mortality rates after undergoing lung transplantation when compared with patients infected with other genomovars pretransplant.[7] Finally, patients with CF are at risk of acquiring invasive aspergillosis after undergoing transplantation, but at lower rates than in non-CF patients.[123, 132] Many of these patients with CF were colonized with *Aspergillus* spp. before undergoing transplantation.

The U.S. CF Foundation held a consensus conference on lung transplantation in 1996.[212] The committee concluded that microbiologic contraindications to transplantation were limited to active hepatitis B and human immunodeficiency virus. The decision to perform transplantation in patients infected with *B. cepacia* complex or multidrug-resistant *P. aeruginosa* or in those colonized with *Aspergillus* spp. should be made on a case-by-case basis. Potentially, an understanding of the genomovar infecting a patient may be a useful predictor of mortality.

Anti-inflammatory Therapy

Chronic inflammation associated with chronic bacterial colonization has been implicated as playing a critical role in CF lung disease. Nonsteroidal agents and glucocorticoids have been used as potential medications for anti-inflammatory therapy. A randomized trial using oral prednisone (1 or 2 mg/kg every other day) demonstrated a reduction in the rate of decline in pulmonary function in patients with CF, but such treatment was associated with significant steroid-related side effects.[10] Three short-term trials using inhaled steroids have led to mixed results and, therefore, no clear direction for chronic use.[11, 121, 196] High-dose ibuprofen (20 to 30 mg/kg twice per day) used for a 4-year period led to a decreased rate of decline in pulmonary function with few reported side effects.[97] Several anti-inflammatory agents, including antiproteases and antioxidants, have been proposed as potential therapies, but they remain under investigation and are not a part of routine clinical practice.

Prevention

IMMUNIZATIONS

Unfortunately, no effective vaccine against *P. aeruginosa* has been developed. However, appropriate use of currently available vaccines is advocated strongly. Annual influenza vaccination is recommended for patients with CF. Although these patients do not have an increased risk of acquiring *Streptococcus pneumoniae* infection, they should receive the pneumococcal vaccine Prevnar during routine childhood immunization. The RSV subunit vaccine PFP-2 (purified fusion protein vaccine is a fusion glycoprotein that induces serum neutralizing antibodies) has been studied in children with CF over the course of two RSV seasons.[141] Initial results showed that the RSV subunit vaccine was safe and immunogenic and reduced the number of lower respiratory tract infections.[140] Children with CF who received the vaccine had significantly fewer lower respiratory tract infections. A placebo-controlled trial of RSV monoclonal antibody (palivizumab) to prevent RSV disease in young infants with CF has been performed, but analysis is ongoing.

INFECTION CONTROL PRECAUTIONS

Infection control in CF poses unique issues. Patients with CF can acquire pathogens from each other rather than from non-CF patients or healthy individuals. Recommendations for infection control have implications for treatment, transplantation, and the psychosocial well-being of patients, families, and staff. Infection control strategies should address both inpatient and outpatient settings (e.g., the CF clinics and pulmonary function test laboratories), as well as non–health care settings, including family education day, CF summer camps, and multiple patient families.[162]

Although the source of most pathogens in patients with CF is unknown, recognition that patient-to-patient spread can occur has been increasing. Such spread is best described for *B. cepacia* complex, and risk factors associated with transmission are shown in Table 31–5.[69, 105, 135, 136, 144, 192] The consensus is that patients harboring this pathogen should be segregated from other patients with CF and not cohorted together because of concern that some strains of *B. cepacia* complex may be more virulent and replace other strains.[109] Thus, a patient with CF and *B. cepacia* complex is hospitalized in a single room and kept apart from other patients with CF. Furthermore, patients infected with

TABLE 31–5 ■ RISK FACTORS ASSOCIATED WITH ACQUISITION OF *BURKHOLDERIA CEPACIA* COMPLEX

Risk Factor(s)	Comment
Attendance at a cystic fibrosis summer camp (Pegues)	Risk of acquisition (6% incidence) increased with time spent at camp and prevalence of *B. cepacia* at the camp
Sleeping in the same cabin	
Sharing a personal item	
Dancing with a *B. cepacia*-infected camper	
Attendance at a summer educational program (LiPuma 1994)	3 of 15 patients (20%) acquired the same ribotype
Participation in an adult cystic fibrosis group (Smith)	Disband meetings thought to represent extensive social contact
Social contact (Govan, Smith)	
Kissing	
Intimate contact	
Prolonged car rides	
Sibling with *B. cepacia* complex	
Handshaking	2 of 68 cultures positive: 1 from a patient and 1 from an investigator (Pegues)
	3 patients' hands became contaminated after coughing (Govan 1993)
Inpatient exposure	
Recent hospitalization (Pegues 1994)	Risk of acquisition increased if hospitalized within 3 mo and if hospitalized longer
Use of a specific shower	Interviews with health care workers indicated poor adherence to contact precautions
Sharing a hospital room with another patient infected with *B. cepacia*	
Cared for by a medical student	
Respiratory therapy equipment	Reservoirs of large-volume nebulizers grew *B. cepacia*
Sharing equipment	
Hospital nebulizers (Burdge)	
Spirometer (Isles)	
Mouthpiece filters (Govan)	

B. cepacia are seen on different clinic days in many CF centers. To date, only one case of transmission of *B. cepacia* complex between CF and non-CF patients has been reported.[78]

Similarly, patients with CF and MRSA in the respiratory tract should be placed in private rooms without access to common areas. Interpatient spread of MRSA among patients with CF and non-CF patients has been reported.[64]

Perhaps of most concern have been several recent reports of clonal spread of *P. aeruginosa* among patients with CF. These examples have involved obvious phenotypes that triggered an investigation of possible patient-to-patient spread, including an increase in ceftazidime-resistant *P. aeruginosa*[31] or initial colonization of young children with mucoid strains of *P. aeruginosa.*[8, 122] These reports have lead CF centers in Europe to favor cohorting and segregating patients with *P. aeruginosa,* particularly those with antibiotic-resistant strains, in both hospital and clinic settings.[59]

Examples of patient-to-patient spread of other potential pathogens in patients with CF have been scant. They have included rare instances of shared clones of *S. maltophilia, A. xylosoxidans*,[100] and NTM[125] among siblings or patients who were hospitalized together.

A recent CF Consensus for Infection Control was held and emphasized the importance of standard precautions, hand hygiene, and microbiologic surveillance that included the use of selective media and quarterly culturing of the respiratory tract.[166] Additional areas that were stressed were appropriate sterilization, disinfection, and environmental cleaning.

Conclusions

In conclusion, the microbiology of patients with CF is complex and changing. Although the pathogenesis of lung infections is being investigated actively, current hypotheses suggest multiple etiologies. Appropriate microbiologic processing of respiratory tract specimens is critical to ensure an accurate understanding of the epidemiology of CF lung disease and to provide appropriate treatment and infection control. Current treatment strategies are directed largely at management of deteriorations in pulmonary function, but increasingly, strategies are being directed at prevention and preservation of lung function.

REFERENCES

1. Aaron, S. D.: Multiple combination bactericidal antibiotic testing for patients with cystic fibrosis infected with *Burkholderia cepacia.* Am. J. Respir. Crit. Care Med. *161*:1206–1212, 2000.
2. Abman, S. H., Accurso, F. J., and Sokol, R. J.: Hypoalbuminemia in young infants with cystic fibrosis. Letter. J. Pediatr. *116*:841, 1990.
3. Abman, S. H., Ogle, J. W., Butler, S. N., et al.: Role of respiratory syncytial virus in early hospitalizations for respiratory distress of young infants with cystic fibrosis. J. Pediatr. *113*:826, 1988.
4. Abman, S. H., Ogle, J. W., Harbeck, R. J., et al.: Early bacteriologic, immunologic, and clinical courses of young infants with cystic fibrosis identified by neonatal screening. J. Pediatr. *119*:211–217, 1991.
5. American Thoracic Society: Diagnosis and treatment of disease caused by nontuberculous mycobacteria. Am. J. Respir. Crit. Care Med. *156*(Suppl.):1–25, 1997.
6. Anderson, D. H.: Therapy and prognosis of fibrocystic disease of the pancreas. Pediatrics *3*:406–417, 1949.
7. Aris, R. M., Gilligan, P. H., Neuringer, I. P., et al.: The effects of panresistant bacteria in cystic fibrosis patients on lung transplant outcome. Am. J. Respir. Crit. Care Med. *155*:1699–1704, 1997.
8. Armstrong, D. S., Grimwood, K., Carlin, J. B., et al.: Lower airway inflammation in infants and young children with cystic fibrosis. Am. J. Respir. Crit. Care Med. *156*:1197–1204, 1997.
9. Armstrong, D. S., Grimwood, K., Carzino, R., et al.: Lower respiratory infection and inflammation in infants with newly diagnosed cystic fibrosis. B. M. J. *310*:1571, 1995.
10. Auberbach, H. S., Williams, M., Kirkpatrick, J. A., and Colten, H. R.: Alternate day prednisone reduced morbidity and improves pulmonary function in cystic fibrosis. Lancet *2*:686–688, 1985.
11. Balfour-Lynn, I. M., Klein, N. J., and Dinwiddie, R.: Randomized controlled trial of inhaled corticosteroids (fluticasone propionate) in cystic fibrosis. Arch. Dis. Child. *77*:124–130, 1997.
12. Baltimore, R. S., Christie, C. D., and Smith, G. J.: Immunohistopathologic localization of *Pseudomonas aeruginosa* in lungs from patients with cystic fibrosis. Implications for the pathogenesis of progressive lung deterioration. Am. Rev. Respir. Dis. *140*:1650–1661, 1989.
13. Bargon, J., Dauletbaev, N., Kohler, B., et al.: Prophylactic antibiotic therapy is associated with an increased prevalence of *Aspergillus* colonization in adult cystic fibrosis patients. Respir. Med. *93*:835–838, 1999.
14. Beardsmore, C. S., Thompson, J. R., Williams, A., et al.: Pulmonary function in infants with cystic fibrosis: The effect of antibiotic treatment. Arch. Dis. Child. *71*:133–137, 1994.
15. Bonfield, T. L., Konstan, M. W., Burfeind, P., et al.: Normal bronchial epithelial cells constitutively produce the anti-inflammatory cytokine interleukin-10, which is downregulated in cystic fibrosis. Am. J. Respir. Cell Mol. Biol. *13*:257–261, 1995.
16. Borgo, G., Mastella, G., Gasparini, P., et al.: Pancreatic function and gene deletion F508 in cystic fibrosis. J. Med. Genet. *27*:665, 1990.
17. Bosso, J. A., and Black, P. C.: Controlled trial of aztreonam vs. tobramycin and azlocillin for acute pulmonary exacerbations of cystic fibrosis. Pediatr. Infect. Dis. J. *7*:171–176, 1988.
18. Bosworth, D. G., and Nielson, D. W.: Effectiveness of home versus hospital care in the routine treatment of cystic fibrosis. Pediatr. Pulmonol. *24*:42–47, 1997.
19. Branger, C., Gardye, C., and Lambert-Zechovsky, N.: Persistence of *Staphylococcus aureus* strains among cystic fibrosis patients over extended periods of time. J. Med. Microbiol. *45*:294–301, 1996.
20. Brown, R. K., and Kelly, F. J.: Role of free radicals in the pathogenesis of cystic fibrosis. Thorax *49*:738–742, 1994.
21. Burns, J. L., Emerson, J., Stapp, J. R., et al.: Microbiology of sputum from patients at cystic fibrosis centers in the United States. Clin. Infect. Dis. *27*:158–163, 1998.
22. Burns, J., and Saiman, L.: *Burkholderia cepacia* infections in cystic fibrosis. Pediatr. Infect. Dis. J. *18*:155–156, 1999.
23. Burns, J. L., Saiman, L., Whittier, S., et al.: Comparison of agar diffusion methodologies for antimicrobial susceptibility testing of *Pseudomonas aeruginosa* isolated from cystic fibrosis patients. J. Clin. Microbiol. *38*:1818–1822, 2000.
24. Burns, J. L., Saiman, L., Whittier, S., et al.: Comparison of two commercial systems (Vitek and MicroScan-WalkAway) for antimicrobial susceptibility testing of *Pseudomonas aeruginosa* isolates from cystic fibrosis patients. Diagn. Microbiol. Infect. Dis. *39*:257–260, 2001.
25. Burns, J. L., Van Dalfsen, J. M., Shawar, R. M., et al.: Effect of chronic intermittent administration of inhaled tobramycin on respiratory microbial flora in patients with cystic fibrosis. J. Infect. Dis. *179*:1190–1196, 1999.
26. Caclano, G., Kazys, M., Saiman, L., and Prince, A.: Production of the *Pseudomonas aeruginosa* neuraminidase is increased under hyperosmolar conditions and is regulated by genes involved in alginate expression. J. Clin. Invest. *89*:1866–1874, 1992.
27. Campbell, P. W., Phillips, J. A., Krishnamani, M. R. S., et al.: Cystic fibrosis: Relationship between clinical status and F508 deletion. J. Pediatr. *118*:239, 1991.
28. Campbell, P. W., 3rd, and Saiman, L.: Use of aerosolized antibiotics in patients with cystic fibrosis. Chest *116*:775–788, 1999.
29. Cantin, A. M., North, S. L., Hubbard, R. C., and Cystal, R. G.: Normal alveolar epithelial lining fluid contains high levels of glutathione. J. Appl. Physiol. *63*:152–158, 1987.
30. Cash, H. A., Woods, D. E., McCullough, B., et al.: A rat model of chronic respiratory infection with *Pseudomonas aeruginosa.* Am. Rev. Respir. Dis. *119*:453–459, 1979.
31. Cheng, K., Smyth, R. L., Govan, J. R., et al.: Spread of beta-lactam–resistant *Pseudomonas aeruginosa* in a cystic fibrosis clinic. Lancet *348*:639–642, 1996.
32. Chernick, V. C., and Kendig, E. L.: Disorders of the Respiratory Tract in Children. 5th ed. Philadelphia, W. B. Saunders, 1990, pp. 692–730.
33. Church, D. A., Kanga, J. F., Kuhn, R. J., et al.: Sequential ciprofloxacin therapy in pediatric cystic fibrosis: Comparative study vs. ceftazidime/tobramycin in the treatment of acute pulmonary exacerbations. The Cystic Fibrosis Study Group. Pediatr. Infect. Dis. J. *16*:97–105, 123–126, 1997.
34. Cimon, B., Carrere, J., Vinatier, J. F., et al.: Clinical significance of *Scedosporium apiospermum* in patients with cystic fibrosis. Eur. J. Clin. Microbiol. Infect. Dis. *19*:53–56, 2000.
35. Coenye, T., Vandamme, P., Govan, J. R., and LiPuma, J. J.: Taxonomy and identification of the *Burkholderia cepacia* complex. J. Clin. Microbiol. *39*:3427–3436, 2001.
36. Corey, M., and Farewell, V.: Determinants of mortality from cystic fibrosis in Canada, 1970–1989. Am. J. Epidemiol. *143*:1007–1017, 1996.
37. Costerson, J. W., Steward, P. S., and Greenberg, E. P.: Bacterial biofilms: A common cause of persistent infections. Science *284*:1318–1322, 1999.
38. Cutting, G. R.: Genotype defect: Its effect on cellular function and phenotypic expression. Semin. Respir. Crit. Care Med. *15*:356, 1994.

39. Cystic Fibrosis Consensus Conference: Microbiology and Infectious Disease in Cystic Fibrosis. Vol. V, Section l. Cystic Fibrosis Foundation, Bethesda, MD, May 17–18, 1994, pp. 1–26.
40. Cystic Fibrosis Foundation Patient Registry: Annual Report. Bethesda, MD, 1997.
41. Cystic Fibrosis Foundation Patient Registry: Annual Report. Bethesda, MD, 1999.
42. Cystic Fibrosis Foundation Patient Registry: Annual Report. Bethesda, MD, 2000.
43. Davis, P. B., Byard, P. J., and Konstan, M. W.: Identifying treatments that halt progression of pulmonary disease in cystic fibrosis. Pediatr. Res. *41*:161–165, 1997.
44. de Groot, R., and Smith, A. L.: Antibiotic pharmacokinetics in cystic fibrosis: Differences and clinical significance. Clin. Pharmacol. *13*:228–253, 1987.
45. Demko, C. A., Stem, R. C., and Doershuk, C. F.: *Stenotrophomonas maltophilia* in cystic fibrosis: Incidence and prevalence. Pediatr. Pulmonol. *25*:304–308, 1998.
46. Denton, M., and Kerr, K. G.: Microbiological and clinical aspects of infection associated with *Stenotrophomonas maltophilia.* Clin. Microbiol. Rev. *11*:57–80, 1998.
47. Deretic, V., Schurr, M. J., Yu, H.: *Pseudomonas aeruginosa,* mucoidy and the chronic infection phenotype in cystic fibrosis. Trends Microbiol. *3*:351–356, 1995.
48. Di Sant'Agnese, P. A.: Fibrocystic disease of the pancreas with normal or partial pancreatic function. Pediatrics *15*:683, 1955.
49. Doring, G.: Mechanisms of airway inflammation in cystic fibrosis. Pediatr. Allergy Immunol. *7*:63–66, 1996.
50. Dunne, W. M., Jr., and Maisch, S.: Epidemiological investigation of infections due to *Alcaligenes* species in children and patients with cystic fibrosis: Use of repetitive-element-sequence polymerase chain reaction. Clin. Infect. Dis. *20*:836–841, 1995.
51. Efthimiou, J., Hodson, M. E., Taylor, P., et al.: Importance of viruses and *Legionella pneumophila* in respiratory exacerbations of young adults with cystic fibrosis. Thorax *39*:150, 1984.
52. Elborn, J. S., Prescott, R. J., Stack, B. H. R., et al.: Elective versus symptomatic antibiotic treatment in cystic fibrosis patients with chronic *Pseudomonas* infection of the lungs. Thorax *55*:355–358, 2000.
53. Elliot, M. W., and Newman Taylor, A. J.: Allergic bronchopulmonary aspergillosis. Clin. Exp. Allergy *27*:55–59, 1997.
54. Fabbri, A., Tacchella, A., Manno, G., et al.: Emerging microorganisms in cystic fibrosis. Chemioterapia *6*:32–37, 1987.
55. Farrell, P. M., Kosorok, M. R., Laxova, A., et al.: Nutritional benefits of neonatal screening for cystic fibrosis. Wisconsin Cystic Fibrosis Neonatal Screening Study Group. N. Engl. J. Med. *337*:963–969, 1997.
56. Fick, R. B., Jr., Sonoda, F., and Hornick, D. B.: Emergence and persistence of *Pseudomonas aeruginosa* in the cystic fibrosis airway. Semin. Respir. Infect. 7:168, 1992.
57. FitzSimmons, S. O.: The changing epidemiology of cystic fibrosis. J. Pediatr. *122*:1–9, 1993.
58. Flume, P. A., Egan, T. M., Paradowski, L. J., et al.: Infectious complications of lung transplantation: The impact of cystic fibrosis. Am. J. Respir. Crit. Care Med. *149*:1601–1607, 1994.
59. Frederiksen, B., Koch, C., and Hoiby, N.: Antibiotic treatment of initial colonization with *Pseudomonas aeruginosa* postpones chronic infection and prevents deterioration of pulmonary function in cystic fibrosis. Pediatr. Pulmonol. *23*:330–335, 1997.
60. Gabriel, S. E., Clarke, L. L., Boucher, R. C., et al.: CFTR and outward rectifying chloride channels are distinct proteins with a regulatory relationship. Nature *363*:263, 1993.
61. Garland, J. S., Chan, Y. M., Kelly, K. J., et al.: Outcome of infants with cystic fibrosis requiring mechanical ventilation for respiratory failure. Chest *96*:136, 1989.
62. Geller, D. E., Kaplowitz, H., Light, M. J., and Colin, A. A.: Allergic bronchopulmonary aspergillosis in cystic fibrosis: Reported prevalence, regional distribution, and patient characteristics. Scientific Advisory Group, Investigators, and Coordinators of the Epidemiologic Study of Cystic Fibrosis. Chest *116*:639–646, 1999.
63. Gilligan, P. H.: Microbiology of airway disease in patients with cystic fibrosis. Clin. Microbiol. Rev. *4*:35–51, 1991.
64. Givney, R., Vickery, A., Halliday, A., et al.: Methicillin-resistant *Staphylococcus aureus* in a cystic fibrosis unit. J. Hosp. Infect. *35*:27–36, 1997.
65. Gold, R., Carpenter, S., Heurter, H., et al.: Randomized trial of ceftazidime versus placebo in the management of acute respiratory exacerbations in patients with cystic fibrosis. J. Pediatr. *111*:907–913, 1987.
66. Gold, R., Overmeyer, A., Knie, B., et al.: Controlled trial of ceftazidime vs. ticarcillin and tobramycin in the treatment of acute respiratory exacerbations of cystic fibrosis. Pediatr. Infect. Dis. J. *4*:172–177, 1985.
67. Goldman, M. N., Anderson, G. M., Stolzenbert, E. D., et al.: Human beta-defensin-1 is a salt-sensitive antibiotic in lung that is inactivated in cystic fibrosis. Cell *88*:553–560, 1997.
68. Goss, C. H., Otto, K., Aitken, M. L., and Rubenfeld, G. D.: Detecting *Stenotrophomonas maltophilia* does not reduce survival of patients with cystic fibrosis. Am. J. Respir. Crit. Care Med. *166*:356–361, 2002.
69. Govan, J. R., Brown, P. H., Maddison, J., et al.: Evidence for transmission of *Pseudomonas cepacia* by social contact in cystic fibrosis. Lancet *342*:15–19, 1993.
70. Govan, J. R., and Nelson, J. W.: Microbiology of lung infection in cystic fibrosis. Br. Med. Bull. *48*:912–930, 1992.
71. Govan, J. R. W., and Deretic, V.: Microbial pathogenesis in cystic fibrosis: Mucoid *Pseudomonas aeruginosa* and *Burkholderia cepacia.* Microb. Rev. *60*:539–574, 1993.
72. Graft, D. R., Mischler, E., Farrell, P. M., and Busse, W.: Granulocyte chemiluminescence in patients with cystic fibrosis. Am. Rev. Respir. Dis. *125*:540–543, 1982.
73. Hancock, R. E. W.: Resistance mechanisms in *Pseudomonas aeruginosa* and other nonfermentative gram negative bacteria. Clin. Infect. Dis. *27*(Suppl.):93–99, 1998.
74. Henry, D., Campbell, M., McGimpsey, C., et al.: Comparison of isolation media for recovery of *Burkholderia cepacia* complex from respiratory secretions of patients with cystic fibrosis. J. Clin. Microbiol. *37*:1004–1007, 1999.
75. Henry, R. L., Mellis, C. M., and Petrovic, L.: Mucoid *Pseudomonas aeruginosa* is a marker of poor survival in cystic fibrosis. Pediatr. Pulmonol. *12*:158–161, 1992.
76. Hiatt, P. W., Grace, S. C., Kozinetz, C. A., et al.: Effects of viral lower respiratory tract infection on lung function in infants with cystic fibrosis. Pediatrics *103*:619–626, 1999.
77. Hodson, M. E., Roberts, C. M., Butland, R. J. A., et al.: Oral ciprofloxacin compared with conventional intravenous treatment for *Pseudomonas aeruginosa* infections in adults with cystic fibrosis. Lancet *1*:235–237, 1987.
78. Holmes, A., Nolan, R., Taylor, R., et al.: An epidemic of *Burkholderia cepacia* transmitted between patients with and without cystic fibrosis. J. Infect. Dis. *179*:1197–1205, 1999.
79. Hordvik, N. L., Konig, P., Hamory, B., et al.: Effects of acute viral respiratory tract infections in patients with cystic fibrosis. Pediatr. Pulmonol. 7:217, 1989.
80. Howe, R. A., and Spencer, R. C.: Macrolides for the treatment of *Pseudomonas aeruginosa* infections? J. Antimicrob. Chemother. *40*:153–155, 1997.
81. Hudson, V. L., Wielinski, C. L., and Regelmann, W. E.: Prognostic implications of initial oropharyngeal bacterial flora in patients with cystic fibrosis diagnosed before the age of two years. J. Pediatr. *122*:854–860, 1993.
82. Hyatt, A. C., Chipps, B. E., Kumor, K. M., et al.: A double-blind controlled trial of anti-*Pseudomonas* chemotherapy of acute respiratory exacerbations in cystic fibrosis. J. Pediatr. *99*:307–311, 1981.
83. Hyde, S. C., Emsley, P., Hartshorn, M. J., et al.: Structural model of ATP-binding proteins associated with cystic fibrosis, multi-drug resistance and bacterial support. Nature *346*:362, 1990.
84. Ichikawa, Y., Ninomiya, H., Koga, H., et al.: Erythromycin reduces neutrophils and neutrophil-derived elastolytic-like activity in the lower respiratory tract of bronchiolitis patients. Am. Rev. Respir. Dis. *146*:196–203, 1992.
85. Ichimiya, T., Takeoka, K., Hiramatsu, K., et al.: The influence of azithromycin on the biofilm formation of *Pseudomonas aeruginosa* in vitro. Chemotherapy *42*:186–191, 1996.
86. Isles, A., Maclusky, I., Corey, M., et al.: *Pseudomonas cepacia* infection in cystic fibrosis: An emerging problem. J. Pediatr. *104*:206–210, 1984.
87. Jackson, M. A., Kusmiesz, H., Shelton, S., et al.: Comparison of piperacillin vs. ticarcillin plus tobramycin in the treatment of acute pulmonary exacerbations of cystic fibrosis. Pediatr. Infect. Dis. J. *5*:440–443, 1986.
88. Jaffe, A., Francis, J., Rosenthal, M., et al.: Long-term azithromycin may improve lung function in children with cystic fibrosis. Lancet *351*:420, 1998.
89. Jensen, T., Pedersen, S. S., Hoiby, N., et al.: Use of antibiotics in cystic fibrosis: The Danish approach. Antibiot. Chemother. *42*:237–246, 1989.
90. Jewett, C. V., Ledbetter, J., Lyrene, R. K., et al.: Comparison of cefoperazone sodium vs. methicillin, ticarcillin, and tobramycin in treatment of pulmonary exacerbations in patients with cystic fibrosis. J. Pediatr. *106*:669–672, 1985.
91. Kanj, S. S., Tapson, V., Davis, D., et al.: Infections in patients with cystic fibrosis following lung transplantation. Chest *112*:924–930, 1997.
92. Kerem, E., Corey, M., Kerem, B., et al.: Clinical and genetic comparisons of patients with cystic fibrosis with and without meconium ileus. J. Pediatr. *114*:767, 1989.
93. Kerem, E., Corey, M., Kerem, B., et al.: The relationship between genotype and phenotype in cystic fibrosis—analysis of the most common mutation (ΔF508). N. Engl. J. Med. *323*:1517, 1990.
94. Khair, O. A., Davies, R. J., and Devalia, J. L.: Bacterial-induced release of inflammatory mediators by bronchial epithelial cells. Eur. Respir. J. *9*:1913–1922, 1996.
95. Kobayashi, H., Takeda, H., Sakayori, S., et al.: Study on azithromycin in treatment of diffuse panbronchiolitis. [Japanese, abstract in English.] J. Jpn. Assoc. Infect. Dis. *69*:711–722, 1995.
96. Kondoh, K., Hashiba, M., and Baba, S.: Inhibitory activity of clarithromycin on biofilm synthesis with *Pseudomonas aeruginosa.* Acta Otolaryngol. Suppl. *525*:56–60, 1996.

97. Konstan, M. W., Byard, P. J., Hoppel, C. L., and Davis, P. B.: Effect of high-dose ibuprofen in patients with cystic fibrosis. N. Engl. J. Med. *332*:848–854, 1995.
98. Kotloff, R. M., and Zuckerman, J. B.: Lung transplantation for cystic fibrosis: Special considerations. Chest *109*:787–798, 1996.
99. Krilov, L. R., Blumer, J. L., Stern, R. C., et al.: Imipenem/cilastatin in acute pulmonary exacerbations of cystic fibrosis. Rev. Infect. Dis. 7(Suppl.):482–489, 1985.
100. Krzewinski, J. W., Nguyen, C. D., Foster, J. M., and Burns, J. L.: Use of random amplified polymorphic DNA polymerase chain reaction to determine the epidemiology of *Stenotrophomonas maltophilia* and *Achromobacter (Alcaligenes) xylosoxidans* from patients with cystic fibrosis. J. Clin. Microbiol. *39*:3597–3602, 2001.
101. Kudoh, S., Azuma, A., Yamamoto, M., et al.: Improvement of survival in patients with diffuse panbronchiolitis treated with low-dose erythromycin. Am. J. Respir. Crit. Care Med. *157*:1829–1832, 1998.
102. Linsdell, R., and Hanrahan, J. W.: Glutathione permeability of CFTR. Am. J. Physiol. *175*:C323–C326, 1998.
103. LiPuma, J. J.: *Burkholderia cepacia* epidemiology and pathogenesis: Implications for infection control. Curr. Opin. Pulm. Med. *4*:337–341, 1998.
104. LiPuma, J. J.: *Burkholderia cepacia* complex: A contraindication to lung transplantation in cystic fibrosis? Transpl. Infect. Dis. *3*:149–160, 2001.
105. LiPuma, J. J., Dasen, S. E., Nielson, D. W., et al.: Person-to-person transmission of *Pseudomonas cepacia* between patients with cystic fibrosis. Lancet *336*:1094–1096, 1990.
106. LiPuma, J. J., Spilker, T., Gill, L. H., et al.: Disproportionate distribution of *Burkholderia cepacia* complex species and transmissibility markers in cystic fibrosis. Am. J. Respir. Crit. Care Med. *164*:92–96, 2001.
107. Lloyd-Still, J. D., Kahw, K. T., and Shwachman, H.: Severe respiratory disease in infants with cystic fibrosis. Pediatrics *53*:678, 1974.
108. Mahenthiralingam, E., Bischof, J., Byrne, S. K., et al.: DNA-based diagnostic approaches for identification of *Burkholderia cepacia* complex, *Burkholderia vietnamiensis, Burkholderia multivorans, Burkholderia stabilis*, and *Burkholderia cepacia* genomovars I and III. J. Clin. Microbiol. *38*:3165–3173, 2000.
109. Mahenthiralingam, E., Vandamme, P., Campbell, M. E., et al.: Infection with *Burkholderia cepacia* complex genomovars in patients with cystic fibrosis: Virulent transmissible strains of genomovar III can replace *B. multivorans*. Clin. Infect. Dis. *33*:1469–1475, 2001.
110. Mastella, G., Rainisio, M., Harms, H. K., et al.: Allergic bronchopulmonary aspergillosis in cystic fibrosis. A European epidemiological study. Epidemiologic Registry of Cystic Fibrosis. Eur. Respir. J. *16*:464–471, 2000.
111. McLaughlin, F. J., Matthews, W. J., Strieder, D. J., et al.: Clinical and bacteriological responses to three antibiotic regimens for acute exacerbations of cystic fibrosis: Ticarcillin-tobramycin, azlocillin-tobramycin, and azlocillin-placebo. J. Infect. Dis. *147*:559–567, 1983.
112. Mearns, M. B.: Treatment and prevention of pulmonary complications of cystic fibrosis in infancy and early childhood. Arch. Dis. Child. *47*:5–11, 1972.
113. Miall, L. S., McGinley, N. T., Brownlee, K. G., and Conway, S. P.: Methicillin-resistant *Staphylococcus aureus* (MRSA) infection in cystic fibrosis. Arch. Dis. Child. *84*:160–162, 2001.
114. Mizukane, R., Hirakata, Y., Kaku, M., et al.: Comparative in vitro exoenzyme-suppressing activities of azithromycin and other macrolide antibiotics against *Pseudomonas aeruginosa*. Antimicrob. Agents Chemother. *38*:528–533, 1994.
115. Molinari, C., Guzman, C. A., Pesce, A., et al.: Inhibition of *Pseudomonas aeruginosa* virulence factors by subinhibitory concentrations of azithromycin and other macrolide antibiotics. J. Antimicrob. Chemother. *31*:681–688, 1993.
116. Morgan, W. J., Butler, S. M., Johnson, C. A., et al.: Epidemiologic study of cystic fibrosis: Design and implementation of a prospective, multicenter, observational study of patients with cystic fibrosis in the U.S. and Canada. Pediatr. Pulmonol. *28*:231–241, 1999.
117. Moss, R. B.: Cystic fibrosis: Pathogenesis, pulmonary infection, and treatment. Clin. Infect. Dis. *21*:839–851, 1995.
118. Moss, R. B., and King, V. V.: Management of sinusitis in cystic fibrosis by endoscopic surgery and serial antimicrobial lavage. Reduction in recurrence requiring surgery. Arch. Otolaryngol. *121*:566, 1995.
119. Murphy, T. M., and Rosenstein, B. J.: Cystic Fibrosis Lung Disease: Approaching the 21st Century. University of Chicago, Pritzker School of Medicine. Chicago, Gardiner Caldwell SynerMed., 1995.
120. National Committee for Clinical Laboratory Standards: Performance Standards for Antimicrobial Susceptibility Testing; 11th Informational Supplement. Vol. 21, NCCLS Document M100-S11. Wayne, PA, NCCLS, 2001.
121. Nikolaizik, W. H., and Schöni, M. H.: Pilot study to assess the effect of inhaled corticosteroids on lung function in patients with cystic fibrosis. J. Pediatr. *128*:271–274, 1996.
122. Nixon, G. M., Armstrong, D. S., Carzino, R., et al.: Clinical outcome after early *Pseudomonas aeruginosa* infection in cystic fibrosis. J. Pediatr. *138*:699–704, 2001.
123. Nunley, D. R., Grgurich, W., Iacono, A. T., et al.: Allograft colonization and infections with *Pseudomonas* in cystic fibrosis lung transplant recipients. Chest *113*:1235–1243, 1998.
124. Ogle, J. W., Reller, B., and Vasil, M. L.: Development of resistance in *Pseudomonas aeruginosa* to imipenem, norfloxacin, and ciprofloxacin during therapy: Proof provided by typing with a DNA probe. J. Infect. Dis. *157*:743–748, 1988.
125. Olivier, K. N., Weber, D. J., et al.: Prevalence of nontuberculous mycobacteria in persons with cystic fibrosis. Multicenter study of a potential pathogen in a susceptible population. Int. J. Tuberc. Lung Dis. *5*:1122–1128, 2001.
126. Olivier, K. N., Yankaskas, J. R., and Knowles, M. R.: Nontuberculous mycobacterial pulmonary disease in cystic fibrosis. Semin. Respir. Infect. *11*:272–284, 1996.
127. Ong, E. L., Ellis, M. E., Webb, A. K., et al.: Infective respiratory exacerbations in young adults with cystic fibrosis: Role of viruses and atypical microorganisms. Thorax *44*:739, 1989.
128. Orenstein, D. M., Pattishall, E. N., Nixon, R. A., et al.: Quality of well-being before and after antibiotic treatment of pulmonary exacerbation in patients with cystic fibrosis. Chest *98*:1081–1084, 1990.
129. Padoan, R., Cambisano, W., Costantini, D., et al.: Ceftazidime monotherapy vs. combined therapy in *Pseudomonas* pulmonary infections in cystic fibrosis. Pediatr. Infect. Dis. J. *6*:648–653, 1987.
130. Pamukcu, A., Bush, A., and Buchdahl, R.: Effects of *Pseudomonas aeruginosa* colonization on lung function and anthropometric variables in children with cystic fibrosis. Pediatr. Pulmonol. *19*:10–15, 1995.
131. Parad, R. B., Gerard, C. J., Zurakowski, D., et al.: Pulmonary outcome in cystic fibrosis is influenced primarily by mucoid *Pseudomonas aeruginosa* infection and immune status and only modestly by genotype. Infect. Immun. *67*:4744–4750, 1999.
132. Paradowski, L. J.: Saprophytic fungal infections and lung transplantation—revisited. J. Heart Lung Transplant. *16*:524–531, 1997.
133. Parks, R. W., and Grand, R. J.: Gastrointestinal manifestations of cystic fibrosis: A review. Gastroenterology *81*:1143, 1981.
134. Parry, M. F., and Neu, H. C.: Tobramycin and ticarcillin therapy for exacerbations of pulmonary disease in patients with cystic fibrosis. J. Infect. Dis. *134*(Suppl.):194–197, 1976.
135. Pegues, D. A., Carson, L. A., Tablan, O. C., et al.: Acquisition of *Pseudomonas cepacia* at summer camps for patients with cystic fibrosis. Summer Camp Study Group. J. Pediatr. *124*:694–702, 1994.
136. Pegues, D. A., Schidlow, D. V., Tablan, O. C., et al.: Possible nosocomial transmission of *Pseudomonas cepacia* in patients with cystic fibrosis. Arch. Pediatr. Adolesc. Med. *148*:805–812, 1994.
137. Peloquin, C. A.: Using therapeutic drug monitoring to dose the antimycobacterial drugs. Clin. Chest Med. *18*:79–87, 1997.
138. Petersen, N. T., Hoiby, N., Mordhorst, C. H., et al.: Respiratory infections in cystic fibrosis patients caused by virus, chlamydia and mycoplasma: Possible synergism with *Pseudomonas aeruginosa*. Acta Paediatr. Scand. *70*:623, 1981.
139. Philippon, S., Streckert, H. J., and Morgenroth, K.: In vitro study of the bronchial mucosa during *Pseudomonas aeruginosa* infection. Virchows Arch. A Pathol. Anat. *423*:39–43, 1993.
140. Piedra, P. A., Grace, S., Jewell, A., et al.: Purified fusion protein vaccine protects against lower respiratory tract illness during respiratory syncytial virus season in children with cystic fibrosis. Pediatr. Infect. Dis. J. *15*:23–31, 1996.
141. Piedra, P. A., Grace, S., Jewell, A., et al.: Sequential annual administration of purified fusion protein vaccine against respiratory syncytial virus in children with cystic fibrosis. Pediatr. Infect. Dis. J. *17*: 217–224, 1998.
142. Plotkowski, M. C., Chevillard, M., Pierrot, D., et al.: Differential adhesion of *Pseudomonas aeruginosa* to human respiratory epithelial cells in primary culture. J. Clin. Invest. *87*:2018–2028, 1991.
143. Przyklenk, B., Bauernfeind, A., Bertele, R. M., et al.: Viral infections of the respiratory tract in patients with cystic fibrosis. Serodiagn. Immunother. Infect. Dis. *2*:217, 1988.
144. *Pseudomonas cepacia* at summer camps for persons with cystic fibrosis. M. M. W. R. Morb. Mortal. Wkly. Rep. *42*:456–459, 1993.
145. Ramphal, R., Houdret, N., Koo, L., et al.: Differences in adhesion of *Pseudomonas aeruginosa* to mucin glycopeptides from sputa of patients with cystic fibrosis and chronic bronchitis. Infect. Immun. *57*: 3066–3071, 1989.
146. Ramsey, B. W.: Management of pulmonary disease in patients with cystic fibrosis. N. Engl. J. Med. *333*:179–188, 1996.
147. Ramsey, B. W., Gore, E. J., Smith, A. L., et al.: The effect of respiratory viral infections on patients with cystic fibrosis. Am. J. Dis. Child. *143*:662, 1989.
148. Ramsey, B. W., Pepe, M. S., Quan, J. M., et al.: Intermittent administration of inhaled tobramycin in patients with cystic fibrosis. N. Engl. J. Med. *340*:23–30, 1999.
149. Ratjen, F., Comes, G., Paul, K., et al.: Effect of continuous antistaphylococcal therapy on the rate of *P. aeruginosa* acquisition in patients with cystic fibrosis. Pediatr. Pulmonol. *31*:13–16, 2001.
150. Regelmann, W. E., Elliott, G. R., Warwich, W. J., and Clawson, C. C.: Reduction of sputum *Pseudomonas aeruginosa* density by antibiotics improves lung function in cystic fibrosis more than do bronchodilators and chest physiotherapy alone. Am. Rev. Respir. Dis. *141*: 914–921, 1990.

151. Regelman, W. E., Lunde, N. M., Porter, P. T., and Quie, T. G.: Increased monocyte chemiluminescence in cystic fibrosis patients and in their parents. Pediatr. Res. *20*:619–622, 1986.
152. Richards, R. M. E., Hamilton, V. E. S., and Thomas, M. R.: In-vitro investigation of the antibacterial activity of agents which may be used for the oral treatment of lung infections in CF patients. J. Antimicrob. Chemother. *42*:171–178, 1998.
153. Riordan, J. R., Rommens, J. M., Kerem, B. S., et al.: Identification of the cystic fibrosis gene: Cloning and characterization of the complementary DNA. Science *245*:1066, 1989.
154. Rosenfeld, M., Davis, R., FitzSimmons, S., et al.: Gender gap in cystic fibrosis mortality. Am. J. Epidemiol. *145*:794–803, 1997.
155. Rosenfeld, M., Emerson, J., Accurso, F., et al.: Diagnostic accuracy of oropharyngeal cultures in infants and young children with cystic fibrosis. Pediatr. Pulmonol. *28*:321–328, 1999.
156. Rosenfeld, M., Gibson, R., McNamara, S., et al.: Serum and lower respiratory tract drug concentrations after tobramycin inhalation in young children with cystic fibrosis. J. Pediatr. *139*:527–572, 2001.
157. Roum, J. H., Buhl, R., McElvaney, N. G., et al.: Systemic deficiency of glutathione in cystic fibrosis. J. Appl. Physiol. *75*:2419–2424, 1993.
158. Saiman, L.: Misidentification and antimicrobial susceptibility testing of *Alcaligenes xylosoxidans* isolated from patients with cystic fibrosis. J. Clin. Microbiol. *39*:3942–3945, 2001.
159. Saiman, L., Burns, J. A., Whittier, S., et al.: Evaluation of reference dilution test methods for antimicrobial susceptibility testing of *Pseudomonas aeruginosa* isolates from patients with cystic fibrosis. J. Clin. Microbiol. *37*:2987–2991, 1999.
160. Saiman, L., Caclano, G., Gruenert, D., and Prince, A.: Comparison of adherence of *Pseudomonas aeruginosa* to respiratory epithelial cells from cystic fibrosis patients and healthy subjects. Infect. Immun. *60*:2808–2814, 1992.
161. Saiman, L., and Edwards, L.: What is the association between CF pathogens and morbidity and mortality? Pediatr. Pulmonol. Suppl. *20*:147–148, 2000.
162. Saiman, L., MacDonald, N., Burns, J., et al.: Infection control in cystic fibrosis: Practical recommendations for the hospital, clinic, and social settings. Am. J. Infect. Control *28*:381–385, 2000.
163. Saiman, L., Mehar, F., Niu, W. W., et al.: Antibiotic susceptibility of multiply resistant *Pseudomonas aeruginosa* isolates from CF patients, including transplant candidates. Clin. Infect. Dis. *23*:532–537, 1996.
164. Saiman, L., and Prince, A.: *Pseudomonas aeruginosa* pili bind to asialoGM1 which is increased to the surface of cystic fibrosis epithelial cells. J. Clin. Invest. *92*:1875–1880, 1993.
165. Saiman, L., Schidlow, D., and Smith, A. L.: Cystic Fibrosis Foundation: The Diagnosis of Cystic Fibrosis: Consensus Statement. Vol. VII, Section I. Consensus Conferences Concept in Care, Bethesday, MD, 1996.
166. Saiman, L., Siegel, J., and the Consensus Committee: Infection control recommendations for patients with cystic fibrosis: Microbiology, important pathogens, and infection control practices to prevent patient-to-patient transmission. In press.
167. San Gabriel, P., Liu, Z., et al.: Antibiotic susceptibility and synergy testing of *Burkholderia cepacia* and *Stenotrophomonas maltophilia*. Paper presented at the Cystic Fibrosis North American Meeting, October 1998, Montreal.
168. Schaad, U. B., Wedgwood-Krucko, J., Guenin, K., et al.: Antipseudomonal therapy in cystic fibrosis: Aztreonam and amikacin versus ceftazidime and amikacin administered intravenously followed by oral ciprofloxacin. Eur. J. Clin. Microbiol. Infect. Dis. *8*:858–865, 1989.
169. Schlichting, C., Branger, C., Fournier, J. M., et al.: Typing of *Staphylococcus aureus* by pulsed-field gel electrophoresis, zymotyping, capsular typing, and phage typing: Resolution of clonal relationships. J. Clin. Microbiol. *31*:227–232, 1993.
170. Scully, B. E., Ores, C. N., Prince, A. S., and Neu, H. C.: Treatment of lower respiratory tract infections due to *Pseudomonas aeruginosa* in patients with cystic fibrosis. Rev. Infect. Dis. 7(Suppl):669–674, 1985.
171. Shelhamer, J. H., Levine, S. J., Wu, T., et al.: NIH conference. Airway inflammation. Ann. Intern. Med. *123*:288, 1995.
172. Shreve, M. R., Butler, S., Kaplowitz, H. J., et al.: Impact of microbiology practice on cumulative prevalence of respiratory tract bacteria in patients with cystic fibrosis. J. Clin. Microbiol. *37*:753–757, 1999.
173. Singh, P. K., Schaefer, A. L., Parsek, M. R., et al.: Quorum-sensing signals indicate that cystic fibrosis lungs are infected with bacterial biofilms. Nature *407*:762–764, 2000.
174. Smith, A. L., Doreshuk, C., Goldmann, D., et al.: Comparison of a β-lactam alone versus β-lactam and an aminoglycoside for pulmonary exacerbation in cystic fibrosis. J. Pediatr. *134*:413–421, 1999.
175. Smith, J. J., Travis, S. M., Greenberg, E. P., and Welsh, M. J.: Cystic fibrosis airway epithelia fail to kill bacteria because of abnormal airway surface fluid. Cell *85*:229–236, 1996.
176. Snell, G. I., de Hoyos, A., Krajden, M., et al.: *Pseudomonas cepacia* in lung transplantation recipients with cystic fibrosis. Chest *103*:466–471, 1993.
177. Sorenson, R., Walter, R. L., and Klinger, J. D.: Infection and immunity to *Pseudomonas.* Clin. Rev. Allergy *9*:47–74, 1991.
178. Speert, D. P., Henry, D., Vandamme, P., et al.: Epidemiology of *Burkholderia cepacia* complex in patients with cystic fibrosis, Canada. Emerg. Infect. Dis. *8*:181–187, 2002.
179. Steinbach, S., Sun, L., Jiang, R. Z., et al.: Transmissibility of *Pseudomonas cepacia* infection in clinic patients and lung-transplant recipients with cystic fibrosis. N. Engl. J. Med. *331*:981–987, 1994.
180. Stroobant, J.: Viral infection in cystic fibrosis. J. R. Soc. Med. *79*:19, 1986.
181. Sugiyama, Y.: Diffuse panbronchiolitis. Clin. Chest Med. *14:*765–772, 1993.
182. Sun, L., Jiang, R. Z., Steinbach, S., et al.: The emergence of a highly transmissible lineage of cbl+ *Pseudomonas (Burkholderia) cepacia* causing CF center epidemics in North America and Britain. Nat. Med. *1*:661–666, 1995.
183. Suter, S.: The role of bacterial proteases in the pathogenesis of cystic fibrosis. Am. J. Respir. Crit. Care Med. *150*(Suppl.):118, 1994.
184. Szaff, M., Hoiby, N., and Flensborg, E. W.: Frequent antibiotic therapy improves survival of cystic fibrosis patients with chronic *Pseudomonas aeruginosa* infection. Acta Paediatr. Scand. *72*:651–657, 1983.
185. Tablan, O. C., Carson, L. A., Cusick, L. B., et al.: Laboratory proficiency test results on use of selective media for isolating *Pseudomonas cepacia* from simulated sputum specimens of patients with cystic fibrosis. J. Clin. Microbiol. *25*:485–487, 1987.
186. Tablan, O. C., Chorba, T. L., Schidlow, D. V., et al.: *Pseudomonas cepacia* colonization in patients with cystic fibrosis: Risk factors and clinical outcome. J. Pediatr. *107*:382–387, 1985.
187. Taccetti, G., Campana, S., and Marianelli, L.: Multiresistant non-fermentative gram-negative bacteria in cystic fibrosis patients: The results of an Italian multicenter study. Eur. J. Epidemiol. *15*:85–88, 1999.
188. Talmaciu, I., Varlotta, L., Mortensen, J., and Schidlow, D. V.: Risk factors for emergence of *Stenotrophomonas maltophilia* in cystic fibrosis. Pediatr. Pulmonol. *30*:10–15, 2000.
189. Tang, H., Kays, M., and Prince, A.: Role of *Pseudomonas aeruginosa* pili in acute pulmonary infection. Infect. Immun. *63*:1278–1285, 1995.
190. Taylor, R. F., Gaya, H., and Hodson, M. E.: Temocillin and cystic fibrosis: Outcome of intravenous administration in patients infected with *Pseudomonas cepacia.* J. Antimicrob. Chemother. *29*:341–344, 1992.
191. Thomas, S. R., Gyi, K. M., Gaya, H., and Hodson, M. E.: Methicillin-resistant *Staphylococcus aureus:* Impact at a national cystic fibrosis centre. J. Hosp. Infect. *40*:203–209, 1998.
192. Thomassen, M., Demko, C., Doershuk, C. F., et al.: *Pseudomonas cepacia:* Decrease in colonization in patients with cystic fibrosis. Am. Rev. Respir. Dis. *134*:669–671, 1986.
193. Tosi, M. F., Zakem, H., and Berger, M.: Neutrophil elastase cleaves C3bi on opsonized *Pseudomonas* as well as CR1 on neutrophils to create a functionally important opsonin receptor mismatch. J. Clin. Invest. *86*:300, 1990.
194. Ulrich, M., Herbert, S., Berger, J., et al.: Localization of *Staphylococcus aureus* in infected airways of patients with cystic fibrosis and in a cell culture model of *S. aureus* adherence. Am. J. Respir. Cell Mol. Biol. *19*:83–91, 1998.
195. Valerius, N. H., Koch, C., and Hoiby, N.: Prevention of chronic *Pseudomonas aeruginosa* colonisation in cystic fibrosis by early treatment. Lancet *338*:725–726, 1991.
195a. Vandamme P., Holmes B., Vancanneyt M., et al.: Occurrence of multiple genomovars of *Burkholderia cepacia* in cystic fibrosis patients and proposal of *Burkholderia multivorans* sp. nov. Int. J. Syst. Bacteriol. *47*:1188–1200, 1997.
196. Van Haren, E. H. J., Lammers, J.-W. J., Festen, J., et al.: The effects of inhaled corticosteroid budesonide on lung function and bronchial hyperresponsiveness in adult patients with cystic fibrosis. Respir. Med. *89:*209–214, 1995.
197. Vazquez, C., Municio, M., Corera, M., et al.: Early treatment of *Pseudomonas aeruginosa* colonization in cystic fibrosis. Acta Paediatr. *82*:308–309, 1993.
198. Wang, E. E., Prober, C. G., Manson, B., et al.: Association of respiratory viral infections with pulmonary deterioration in patients with cystic fibrosis. N. Engl. J. Med. *311*:1653, 1984.
199. Weaver, L. T., Green, M. R., Nicholson, K., et al.: Prognosis in cystic fibrosis treated with continuous flucloxacillin from the neonatal period. Arch. Dis. Child. *70*:84–89, 1994.
200. Weintzen, R., Prestidge, C. R., Kramer, R. I., et al.: Acute pulmonary exacerbations in cystic fibrosis: A double-blind trial of tobramycin and placebo therapy. Am. J. Dis. Child. *134*:1134–1138, 1980.
201. Welsh, M. J., and Smith, A. E.: Molecular mechanisms of CFTR chloride channel dysfunction in cystic fibrosis. Cell *73*:1251–1254, 1993.
202. Whittier, S., Hopfer, R. L., Knowles, M. M., and Gilligan, P. H.: Improved recovery of mycobacteria from respiratory secretions of patients with cystic fibrosis. J. Clin. Microbiol. *31*:861–864, 1993.
203. Whittier, S., Olivier, K., Gilligan, P. H., et al.: Proficiency testing of clinical microbiology laboratories using modified decontamination procedures for detection of nontuberculous mycobacteria in sputum samples from cystic fibrosis patients. The Nontuberculous Mycobacteria in Cystic Fibrosis Study Group. J. Clin. Microbiol. *35*:2706–2708, 1997.
204. Wiesemann, H. G., Steinkamp, G., Ratjen, F., et al.: Placebo-controlled, double-blind randomized study of aerosolized tobramycin for early treatment of *Pseudomonas aeruginosa* colonization in cystic fibrosis. Pediatr. Pulmonol. *25*:88–92, 1998.

205. Witko-Sarsat, V., Callen, R. C., Paulais, M., et al.: Disturbed myeloperoxidase-dependent activity of neutrophils in cystic fibrosis homozygotes and heterozygotes, and its correction by amiloride. J. Immunol. *157*:2728–2735, 1996.
206. Wolter, J., Seeney, S., Bell, S., et al.: Effect of long term treatment with azithromycin on disease parameters in cystic fibrosis: A randomized trial. Thorax 57:212–216, 2002.
207. Wong, K., Roberts, M. C., Owens, L., et al.: Selective media for the quantitation of bacteria in cystic fibrosis sputum. J. Med. Microbiol. *17*:113–119, 1984.
208. Wood, R. E., Board, T. F., and Doershuk, C. F.: State of the art: Cystic fibrosis. Am. Rev. Respir. Dis. *113*:833, 1976.
209. Wood, R. E., Board, T. F., and Doershuk, C. F.: Cystic fibrosis. Am. Rev. Respir. Dis. *113*:841, 1976.
210. Wright, P. F., Khaw, K. T., Oxman, M. N., et al.: Evaluation of the safety of amantadine-HCl and the role of respiratory viral infections in children with cystic fibrosis. J. Infect. Dis. *134*:144, 1976.
211. Yanagihara, K., Tomono, K., Sawai, T., et al.: Effect of clarithromycin on lymphocytes in chronic respiratory *Pseudomonas aeruginosa* infection. Am. J. Respir. Crit. Care Med. *155*:337–342, 1997.
212. Yankaskas, J. R., and Mallory, G. B.: Lung transplantation in cystic fibrosis: Consensus conference statement. Chest *113*:217–226, 1998.
213. Yoshimura, K., Iizuka, S., Anzai, C., et al.: Diffuse panbronchiolitis is closely associated with mutations of the CFTR gene. Abstract. Paper presented at the American Thoracic Society Meeting, May 2000, p. 77.
214. Zar, H., Saiman, L., Quittell, L., et al.: Binding of *Pseudomonas aeruginosa* to respiratory epithelial cells from patients with various mutations in the cystic fibrosis transmembrane regulator. J. Pediatr. *126*:230–233, 1995.

SECTION III

Infections of the Heart

CHAPTER 32

Infective Endocarditis

JEFFREY R. STARKE

Infective endocarditis results when microorganisms adhere to the endocardial surface of the heart. This process usually occurs on heart valves, although septal defects and mural surfaces can be affected. Most episodes of endocarditis begin on endocardium that has been altered by congenital defects, previous disease, surgery, or trauma. The clinical manifestations depend on the degree of compromise of cardiac function and the occurrence of embolic phenomena. Even though bacteria are responsible for most cases, instances of infective endocarditis caused by fungi, chlamydiae, rickettsiae, and perhaps viruses have been described. Advances in the practice of general pediatrics and cardiology during the past 3 decades have contributed to changes in the predisposing conditions and etiologic agents of "modern" infective endocarditis. Before the 1950s, rheumatic fever was the major underlying condition, but its incidence has declined greatly since then.[264] Concurrently, improvements in the medical and surgical management of children with congenital heart disease have increased survival rates. At present, approximately 80 to 90 percent of children with infective endocarditis have congenital heart disease.[20, 65, 228, 301, 364, 395, 443] Many cases occur after cardiac surgery, especially for replacement of valves and creation of shunts with prosthetic materials.[289] The reported incidence of infective endocarditis in neonates is increasing, probably because of the use of sophisticated and highly invasive techniques in neonatal intensive care nurseries.[79, 282, 342]

Historically, infective endocarditis has been classified as acute or subacute based on the progression of untreated disease.[375] The acute form has a fulminant course with high fever, systemic toxicity, and death from sepsis in several days to 6 weeks. The most common etiologic agents are *Staphylococcus aureus, Streptococcus pyogenes,* and *Streptococcus pneumoniae.* Children with the acute form often have no underlying cardiac lesion. Subacute disease usually occurs in patients with previous valvular disease or after cardiac surgical intervention. It is characterized by a more indolent course (6 weeks to several months), with low-grade fever, vague systemic complaints, and various embolic phenomena. Viridans streptococci are the most common etiologic agents. This classification ignores the frequent overlap in clinical manifestations caused by various organisms,[375] especially the staphylococci and fungi, which are causes of an increasing number of subacute cases in the postcardiac surgical setting. Classification based on specific etiologic agents is preferable because it has implications for the usual clinical course, predisposing factors, and appropriate medical and surgical management.

Epidemiology

The incidence of infective endocarditis in adults has been difficult to determine because the methods of study and criteria for diagnosis vary among series.[25, 106, 445] Accurate figures on the incidence of infective endocarditis in children are difficult to obtain. The most common method of reporting incidence in pediatric series expresses the number of cases of infective endocarditis as the numerator and the total number of hospital admissions during the analyzed period as the denominator. Zakrzewski and Keith[472] reported an incidence of endocarditis of 1 in 4500 pediatric admissions at the Hospital for Sick Children in Toronto from 1952 to 1962, whereas Van Hare and colleagues[443] at Case Western Reserve found an incidence of 1 in 1280 in the period from 1972 to 1982. In a large series from Boston Children's Hospital spanning the period between 1933 and 1972, the incidence before 1963 was 1 in 4500 pediatric admissions, whereas that for 1963 to 1972 was 1 in 1800 admissions.[199] A study from a children's hospital in Australia reported an incidence of 1 in 4500 hospital admissions between 1971 and 1983.[388] More recently, one Japanese center reported an annual incidence of 0.9 cases per 1000 children seen at the cardiology clinic.[137] Although differences in referral patterns at these centers may have introduced bias into these figures, the incidence of infective endocarditis in children appears to be rising. This rise might be explained by the increased survival of children with all forms of cardiovascular disease and an increase in the percentage of cases that occur after cardiac surgery and are related to intravascular catheters.[126, 206, 289, 364] Early surgical correction of many types of congenital heart disease along with effective perioperative antibiotic prophylaxis regimens ultimately may lower the incidence of postoperative infective endocarditis. However, the increasing use of invasive therapeutic modalities, especially intravenous catheters and pacemakers, may lead to an increased incidence of so-called nosocomial endocarditis.[126, 270]

The average age of children with infective endocarditis is increasing, a phenomenon that may reflect the longer life expectancy created by improved therapy for children at risk. From 1930 to 1950, the mean age for children with infective endocarditis was close to 5 years.[199] Between 1960 and the present, it increased to 8.5 and then to 13 years.[137, 147, 199, 228, 269, 364, 395] The number of reports of infective endocarditis in children younger than 2 years had been small but has increased significantly during the past 15 years.[33, 147, 282] The clinical course of infective endocarditis in these young children often is atypical, and some cases are diagnosed at autopsy.[198] Before the 1950s, this disease was a rare event in neonates, with only eight autopsy cases reported.[256] Several reports suggest a rapidly increasing rate associated with the development of intensive supportive care in neonates.[40, 79, 275, 282, 286, 312, 313, 342] Symchych and colleagues[416] found a 3 percent incidence of bacterial endocarditis among all neonatal autopsies. Endocarditis in neonates frequently occurs on the tricuspid valve when associated with an indwelling central venous catheter.[430] Congenital heart defects also predispose neonates to the development of infectious endocarditis.[79]

Any form of structural cardiac disease may predispose to infective endocarditis, especially when associated with turbulence of blood flow.[398] In autopsy and clinical series, children with ventricular septal defect, tetralogy of Fallot, left-sided valvular disease, and systemic-pulmonary arterial communication were at highest risk, whereas those with pulmonary stenosis, coarctation of the aorta, and secundum atrial septal defect were at low risk.[356, 364] Hypertrophic obstructive cardiomyopathy rarely is associated with infective endocarditis.[67] Isolated pulmonic or tricuspid valve endocarditis can occur in "otherwise normal" children and adolescents with sepsis or focal bacterial infection,[302] but usually it is associated with congenital heart disease, intravenous catheters, or intravenous drug abuse.[60, 299] A bicuspid aortic valve is recognized as an important risk factor for the development of infective endocarditis, especially in elderly men.[276] The underlying heart diseases in 266 pediatric cases of infective endocarditis are listed in Table 32–1.[206]

A cooperative study on the natural history of aortic stenosis, pulmonary stenosis, and ventricular septal defect has reported data from a controlled pediatric population collected over a period of 4 to 15 years.[145] In patients not undergoing surgical correction, the risk of acquiring endocarditis by 30 years of age in those with ventricular septal defects was 9.7 percent versus 1.4 percent for aortic stenosis and 0.9 percent for pulmonic stenosis. Aortic valvotomy in children with aortic stenosis actually increases the relative risk, whereas successful repair of ventricular septal defect significantly decreases long-term susceptibility to infective endocarditis.[146] Similarly, endocarditis is an extremely rare occurrence after ligation of patent ductus arteriosus. At present, palliative systemic-to-pulmonary shunting is the surgical procedure most often complicated by infective endocarditis.[364] In a review of 115 patients with tetralogy of Fallot, Kaplan and colleagues[208] reported an 8 percent incidence of infective endocarditis after placement of a Pott shunt.

The increasing use of prosthetic valves and valved conduit repairs in children with complex heart disease may lead to a larger number of cases of infective endocarditis in the future.[207, 213, 395] Most medical centers report an incidence of prosthetic-valve endocarditis of 2 to 4 percent after surgery,[50, 148, 359, 398] with the aortic and mitral valves being affected most frequently.[187, 258]

TABLE 32–1 ■ UNDERLYING HEART DISEASE IN 266 CHILDREN WITH INFECTIVE ENDOCARDITIS

Congenital heart disease		78%
Tetralogy of Fallot	24%	
Ventricular septal defect	16%	
Congenital aortic stenosis	8%	
Patent ductus arteriosus	7%	
Transposition of great vessels	4%	
Others	19%	
Rheumatic heart disease		14%
No heart disease		8%

From Kaplan, E. L.: Infective endocarditis in the pediatric age group: An overview. *In* Kaplan, E. L., and Taranta, A. V. (eds.): Infective Endocarditis: An American Heart Association Symposium. Dallas, American Heart Association, 1977, pp. 51–54.

Older studies arbitrarily divided prosthetic-valve endocarditis into two categories—early and late—based on whether the infection occurred within 60 days of valve placement or later.[28] The rationale for categorization by time was based on apparent differences in bacteriologic, pathogenetic, and prognostic associations. So-called early cases most often were caused by coagulase-negative staphylococci, gram-negative bacilli, and fungi, whereas oral and enterococcal streptococci, along with staphylococci, predominated in late cases.[211] These older reports suggested that early cases were acquired via intraoperative valve contamination or were secondary to postoperative extracardiac infections, whereas late cases were acquired by the same mechanisms as native-valve endocarditis. Nosocomial bacteremia at any time after valve placement is a significant risk factor for endocarditis.[115] Finally, the mortality rate was thought to be higher in early versus late infection.

However, more recent studies have blurred this arbitrary time distinction between early and late prosthetic-valve endocarditis.[50, 187, 359] The risk probably is highest in the first 6 to 12 months and decreases to its lowest beyond 1 year after valve replacement. Coagulase-negative staphylococci are the dominant organisms both before and after the 60th postoperative day.[50, 210] Clinical and epidemiologic data also suggest that prosthetic-valve infection caused by staphylococci within the first year after placement probably is acquired at the time of surgery.[28] Identified risk factors for the development of prosthetic-valve endocarditis in adults include native-valve endocarditis, black race, male sex, a mechanical (versus biologic) prosthesis, and prolonged cardiopulmonary bypass time[187]; no comparable information is available for children.

Mitral valve endocarditis occurs frequently on an anatomically normal valve in patients with other predisposing factors.[127] An association between mitral valve prolapse and infective endocarditis has been recognized in adults and children. This heart lesion is being detected with increasing frequency in adolescent girls and may be only one component of a developmental syndrome.[380] In adults, 40 to 50 percent of cases of infective endocarditis associated with isolated insufficient mitral valves occur in patients with mitral prolapse.[75] In some series of native-valve endocarditis, mitral valve prolapse has been the most common underlying lesion.[276] The reported incidence of infective endocarditis in patients with mitral valve prolapse has varied markedly among studies, from low rates of 14 per 100,000 per year to 5 of 58 patients monitored prospectively for 9 to 22 years.[175] A retrospective epidemiologic analysis involving matched cases and controls yielded an odds ratio of 8.2, indicative of a substantially higher risk for development of endocarditis in patients with mitral valve prolapse than in normal controls.[72]

That the risk of developing infective endocarditis is not uniform for all patients with mitral valve prolapse has become apparent. The risk is increased in patients with a preexisting systolic murmur (but not for those with an isolated click and no murmur), echocardiographically demonstrated regurgitation, and valvular redundancy.[81, 175, 257, 266] The signs and symptoms of endocarditis associated with mitral valve prolapse may be more subtle than those of other types of left-sided endocarditis.[127, 310] However, significant complications are relatively common occurrences and sometimes require valve replacement during the acute illness or during convalescence.[15, 402]

Fungal endocarditis is a rare disorder in children but should be suspected in certain clinical and epidemiologic settings. It is more likely to occur after cardiac surgery and rarely occurs on native heart valves. It occurs more commonly in neonates being treated in intensive care settings than in older children.[79] Other predisposing factors include (1) the presence of an indwelling vascular catheter, (2) prolonged use of antibiotics, (3) intrinsic (immunodeficiency diseases, malignancy, malnutrition) or extrinsic (corticosteroids, cytotoxic drugs) immunosuppression, (4) bowel surgery resulting in transient fungemia, (5) intravenous drug abuse, and (6) preexisting or concomitant bacterial endocarditis.

Many conditions other than structural heart disease predispose children to infective endocarditis. The most important is the presence of an indwelling central venous catheter, especially in patients who are seriously ill or immunocompromised.[147, 245, 433, 457] The catheter acts as a foreign body and presumably causes microscopic damage by abrading endocardial and valve surfaces; such damage results in nonbacterial thrombotic vegetation.[20] Infection of intracardiac pacemaker wires also can lead to endocarditis.[10] The most common sources of organisms are infection acquired during the placement procedure and infection of the pacemaker pouch. Infective endocarditis, usually of the tricuspid valve, has developed in children with ventriculoatrial shunts placed for the treatment of hydrocephalus.[206] In patients with arteriovenous fistulas created for hemodialysis, bacterial vegetations may develop in the fistula and on heart valves.[239, 345] Rarely, penetrating wounds or foreign bodies can initiate endocarditis.[178, 265] One important group of patients with an increased risk for development of infective endocarditis is intravenous drug abusers.[272, 460] In this group of patients, two thirds have no evidence of underlying heart disease. A predilection for involvement of the tricuspid valve, followed by the mitral and aortic valves, has been noted.[136] Roentgenographic evidence of septic pulmonary emboli and signs of tricuspid insufficiency dominate the clinical findings.[375] Within this group of patients, increased rates of infective endocarditis and mortality are associated with infection by human immunodeficiency virus (HIV), particularly as CD4 cell counts fall below 200/mm^3.[313, 336]

Although the incidence of infective endocarditis in children may be rising, the prognosis has improved dramatically during the past several decades. Current mortality rates usually are close to 10 percent.[292, 364, 379, 388] Most survivors remain hemodynamically stable at long-term follow-up.[130, 379] However, patients who experience infective endocarditis appear to be at higher risk for developing recurrent endocarditis than are those with similar cardiac abnormalities who have not had previous endocarditis.[398] The patient's functional class before treatment appears to be most predictive of long-term functional status. In one study, 22 percent of children surviving infective endocarditis required surgery related to the infection, including vegetectomy, evacuation of a hematoma, atrioventricular valve replacement, and placement or replacement of a graft or intracardiac shunt.[364]

Pathophysiology

Clinical observations, autopsy studies, and work with experimental animal models have demonstrated that the occurrence of several independent events is required for the development of subacute infectious endocarditis. The endocardial surface usually is disrupted by stress or injury commonly caused by the turbulence of blood. This surface damage results in the deposition of fibrin and platelets, which form nonbacterial thrombotic vegetations. If bacteria adhere to these deposits, infective endocarditis results. The surface of the infected vegetation becomes protected by a cover of fibrin and platelets. A tremendous proliferation of organisms may ensue (as many as 10^9 colony-forming units per gram).[102] The protective sheath isolates the organisms from the action of host neutrophils and antibiotics. The clinical manifestations and complications of infective endocarditis are related to both the hemodynamic changes caused by local infection and the occurrence of embolization and metastatic infection.

In experimental animals, the valvular surface must be damaged, usually by an intravenous catheter, to produce infective endocarditis.[16] The first step in the pathogenesis of subacute infective endocarditis in humans is the development of hemodynamic factors that favor endocardial damage. In an autopsy study of 1024 patients with infective endocarditis, Lepeschkin[240] showed that the location of the endocardial lesions correlates with the impact of pressure, thus making a strong argument for the role of mechanical stress as a critical factor in evolution of the lesions. When associated with valvular insufficiency, infective endocarditis usually occurs on the atrial surface of the mitral valve and the ventricular surface of the aortic valve. Injection of a bacterial aerosol into the air stream passing through a Venturi tube demonstrates how high pressure drives an infected fluid into a low-pressure sink.[351] This process establishes maximal deposition of bacteria in the low-pressure sink immediately beyond the orifice. Mitral insufficiency creates a Venturi effect when blood is driven from the high-pressure left ventricle into a low-pressure atrium; maximal deposition occurs around the mitral annulus on the atrial side. Similarly, with aortic valve insufficiency, the high-pressure source is the aorta and the low-pressure sink is the left ventricle, which leads to deposition on the ventricular surface of the valve.

Lesions also are created more directly by a jet stream causing endocardial damage. For example, in a small, restrictive ventricular septal defect with a left-to-right shunt, a Venturi effect leads to the development of lesions on the right ventricular septal side of the defect, whereas secondary lesions created by the jet effect are located on the right ventricular wall opposite the defect.[452] Heart defects with a surface area large enough to prevent a significant pressure gradient and those in which smaller volumes minimize the gradient do not create the jet and Venturi effects. This difference helps explain the rarity of endocarditis in patients with atrial septal defects and the increased risk of infection complicating small, but not large, ventricular septal defects.

Once endocardial damage has occurred, collagen is exposed, and platelet and fibrin deposition ensues in a manner analogous to formation of the primary plug of normal hemostasis after vascular injury.[196, 453] The sterile platelet-fibrin thrombus that is formed subsequently is referred to as a nonbacterial thrombotic vegetation. In experimental animals, many exogenous stresses, including exposure to cold, high altitude, high cardiac output states, hormonal manipulations, and passage of a sterile catheter across a heart valve, lead to formation of this lesion. Formation of the vegetation reflects two pathogenic mechanisms: hypercoagulability and endothelial damage.[375] To establish experimental infective endocarditis without initial formation of the vegetation is nearly impossible. Microscopic examination demonstrates that this lesion is the one to which microorganisms attach during the early stages of experimental endocarditis. Nonbacterial thrombotic vegetations have been found in both adults and children with malignancy, chronic wasting diseases, uremia, connective tissue diseases, and congenital heart disease and after the

TABLE 32–2 ■ BACTEREMIA AFTER VARIOUS PROCEDURES IN ADULTS AND CHILDREN

Initiating Event	Percentage of Positive Blood Cultures	Predominant Organisms
Dental extraction (children)	30–65	*Streptococcus*, diphtheroids
Chewing gum, candy, paraffin	0–51	*Streptococcus, Staphylococcus epidermidis*
Tooth brushing	0–26	*Streptococcus*
Tonsillectomy	28–38	*Streptococcus, Haemophilus*, diphtheroids
Bronchoscopy (rigid scope)	15	*Streptococcus, S. epidermidis*
Bronchoscopy (fiberoptic)	0	
Orotracheal intubation	0	
Nasotracheal intubation/suctioning	16	*Streptococcus*, aerobic gram-negative rods
Sigmoidoscopy/colonoscopy	0–9.5	*Enterococcus*, aerobic gram-negative rods
Upper gastrointestinal endoscopy	8–12	*Streptococcus, Neisseria, S. epidermidis*, diphtheroids, other
Percutaneous liver biopsy	3–14	Pneumococcus, aerobic gram-negative rods, *Staphylococcus aureus*, other
Urethral catheterization	8	Not stated
Manipulation of *S. aureus* suppurative foci	54	

From Everett, E. D., and Hirschmann, J. U.: Transient bacteremia and endocarditis prophylaxis: A review. Medicine (Baltimore) *56*:61–77, 1977, © 1977, The Williams & Wilkins Company, Baltimore.

placement of intracardiac catheters,[250, 317] and they have been associated with embolism and infarction in distant organs.[36]

Once a nonbacterial thrombotic vegetation has been established, transient bacteremia or fungemia may result in colonization of the lesion. Transient bacteremias are common occurrences, especially with traumatization of a mucosal surface. Table 32–2 lists the incidence of bacteremia in adults and children after various procedures.[114, 349] The bacteremia usually is of low grade and is proportional to the amount of trauma produced by the procedure and the number of organisms inhabiting the surface. In addition, "silent" bacteremia probably occurs frequently. Many persons have circulating antibodies to their own oral flora, as well as an increase in peripheral T cells sensitized to the flora of their dental plaque.[375] Some children with congenital heart disease may be at increased risk for gingival colonization and subsequent development of bacteremia with organisms associated with infectious endocarditis, such as the HACEK microbes *(Haemophilus spp., Actinobacillus actinomycetemcomitans, Cardiobacterium hominis, Eikenella corrodens, Kingella kingae)*.[399]

The ability of microorganisms to adhere to the platelet-fibrin thrombus is a critical factor in the development of infective endocarditis.[86, 164, 196] In a canine model, *S. aureus* and the viridans streptococci, which frequently cause infective endocarditis, adhere more readily to normal aortic leaflets than do organisms uncommon in endocarditis.[156] Within isolates of *S. aureus,* strains devoid of microencapsulation are less capable of inducing endocarditis in an experimental model than are encapsulated strains.[17] Specific products released by these organisms, including dextran, mannan, teichoic acid, and slime, may enhance their ability to colonize the vegetation.[196, 221] The amount of dextran produced by various viridans streptococci in broth correlates with both their adherence and their ability to produce endocarditis in the rabbit model.[287, 377] *Candida albicans* is readily adherent and produces infective endocarditis in rabbits more easily than does *Candida krusei*, a nonadherent yeast rarely implicated in human infective endocarditis.[373] In addition, endocarditis-producing strains of streptococci and staphylococci are more potent stimulators of platelet aggregation than are other bacteria that do not produce infective endocarditis.[71, 173, 287] This action may accelerate the formation of an infected vegetation or increase the removal of organisms from the circulation. The importance of adherence by organisms has been studied by pre-incubating organisms with many classes of antibiotics. After incubation at subinhibitory concentrations, adhesion of streptococcal species to fibrin-platelet matrices and damaged canine valves is decreased.[378] Antibiotics may prevent development of infective endocarditis by both bacterial killing and inhibition of adherence to the vegetation.[151]

Host tissue factors undoubtedly play an important role in adherence of bacteria to the developing thrombus. Once bacteria become adherent to a nonbacterial thrombus, activation of the coagulation system ensues. Some organisms that produce endocarditis may be able to initiate procoagulant activity via microbial enzymes. Activation of the intrinsic coagulation pathway is triggered by exposed connective tissue components and platelet aggregation.[221] However, activation of the extrinsic coagulation pathway probably is the major stimulus for growth of vegetations. Elements of the extracellular matrix, including fibronectin, laminin, and collagen, have been shown to facilitate the adherence of bacteria on fibrin-platelet matrices.[413, 432] Fibronectin may be the host receptor for organisms within the nonbacterial thrombotic vegetation.[229, 252] Laminin-binding proteins have been found on the cell walls of organisms recovered from patients with endocarditis.[393]

The platelet-organism interaction is complex and not understood completely. *Streptococcus sanguis* produces two cell surface antigens that promote platelet aggregation: a class I antigen promotes adhesion of *S. sanguis* to platelets, whereas coexpression of a class II antigen promotes platelet adhesion or aggregation.[174] The induced platelet aggregation appears to be an important determinant of further development of vegetation and progression of disease in experimental endocarditis. In addition, production of streptococcal exopolysaccharide inversely correlates with platelet adhesion while inhibiting aggregation, thus indicating that surface molecules may enhance endocarditis at only certain pathogenic steps.[410] Platelets also may be involved in host defense within the vegetation. After exposure to thrombin, platelets may release microbicidal proteins with bactericidal activity against some gram-positive cocci; resistance to these proteins may be a virulence factor for *S. aureus* in the development of endocarditis.[308, 469]

As bacterial colonization of a nonbacterial thrombotic vegetation progresses, it enlarges by further bacterial

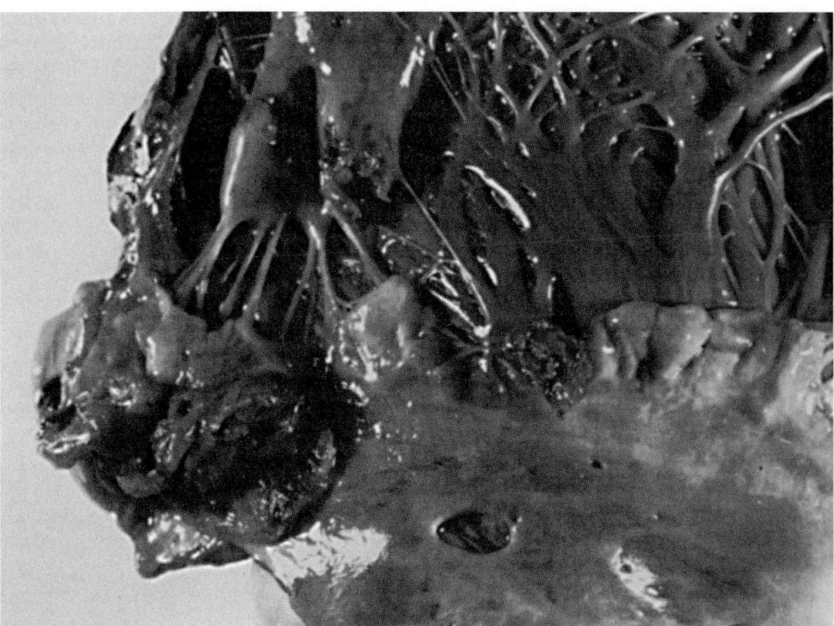

FIGURE 32–1 ■ Subacute endocarditis of the mitral valve with vegetation and rupture of the papillary muscle caused by *Staphylococcus aureus*. (Courtesy of Dr. Edith P. Hawkins, Texas Children's Hospital, Houston.)

proliferation and platelet-fibrin deposition (Fig. 32–1). Kissane[226] describes three histologic zones: (1) necrotic endocardium; (2) a broad zone of bacterial colonies, pyknotic nuclear debris, and fibrin; and (3) a thin coating on the surface of fibrin and leukocytes. The location of bacterial colonies below the surface and the minimal infiltration by phagocytic cells create an environment of impaired host resistance that results in extreme bacterial proliferation. The structure of the vegetation diminishes the penetration of antibiotics into the bacterial layer. In addition, the metabolic activity of bacteria within this lesion is slowed, thus rendering antibiotics less effective. The formation of vegetations and erosion of heart valves may cause valvular incompetence and thereby result in cardiac failure.

Immunopathologic factors may have important roles in both the development and sequelae of infective endocarditis.[29] The susceptibility of a gram-negative bacillus to complement-mediated bactericidal activity is critical to its potential to create endocarditis; only "serum-resistant" organisms produce infective endocarditis in humans and experimental animals.[101] Gram-positive cocci are a more frequent cause of infective endocarditis than are gram-negative bacilli. Gram-positive organisms are resistant to this bactericidal activity; phagocytosis is required for killing.

The frequent presence of hypergammaglobulinemia, splenomegaly, and monocytes in the blood of patients with infective endocarditis indicates stimulation of the humoral and cellular immune systems. Macroglobulins, cryoglobulins, and agglutinating, opsonic, and complement-fixing antibodies have been associated with infective endocarditis.[179, 236] Studies in animals pre-immunized with heat-killed streptococci before inducing aortic valve trauma and infection suggest that circulating antibody has a protective role.[376, 439] However, antibody to *S. aureus* or *Staphylococcus epidermidis* does not prevent the development of endocarditis in immunized animals, perhaps because this antibody does not enhance opsonophagocytosis.[375] The continuous antigenic challenge created by intravascular organisms leads to increased production of specific antibody (including opsonic, agglutinating, and complement-fixing antibodies), cryoglobulins, macroglobulins, and antibodies to bacterial heat shock protein,[338] as well as to the subsequent formation of circulating immune complexes. These complexes are found with increased frequency in patients with a long duration of illness, hypocomplementemia, extravalvular manifestations, and right-sided disease.[31] Quantitative levels of circulating immune complexes may be helpful in distinguishing endocarditic from nonendocarditic sepsis and in monitoring anti-infective therapy. Effective treatment usually leads to a prompt decrease in these levels,[30] whereas relapses may be characterized by rising titers.[214] The diffuse glomerulonephritis occasionally noted with infective endocarditis is caused by subepithelial deposition of immune complexes and complement.[161] Immune complexes can be demonstrated in some diffuse purpuric lesions seen with endocarditis.[251] Bacterial antigens have been found within these complexes.[186]

Further evidence of stimulation of the immune system in infective endocarditis is the development of rheumatoid factor in approximately 50 percent of adults with disease of longer than 6 weeks' duration.[459] Titers of rheumatoid factor correlate with hypergammaglobulinemia and, as with immune complex levels, decrease with therapy and increase during relapse. The role of rheumatoid factor in the disease process is unknown, but it may be involved by blocking IgG opsonic activity, stimulating phagocytosis, or accelerating microvascular damage.[375] Antinuclear, antiendocardial, antisarcolemmal, and antimyolemmal antibodies also have been identified in patients with infective endocarditis; their role in pathogenesis is unclear.[259]

The pathologic changes that occur in the heart in association with infective endocarditis are secondary to local extension of the infection. The vegetations vary in size from a millimeter to several centimeters; frequently they are singular, but they may be multiple. Valvular stenosis may result from large lesions. Vegetations secondary to certain organisms, especially *Candida, Haemophilus,* and *S. aureus* in acute cases, often are large and friable, with a propensity for embolization.[470] Ulcerative lesions may occur and lead to perforation of the valve and subsequent congestive heart failure. Other local complications include rupture of the chordae tendineae or papillary muscle (see Fig. 32–1), valve ring abscess with subsequent fistula formation and pericardial empyema,[41, 55] aneurysms of the sinus of Valsalva or ventricle,[140, 372] myocarditis, and myocardial infarction.[119] Persistent fever occurring during appropriate medical therapy for infective endocarditis may reflect a persistent vegetation, especially with right-sided disease, or extension of infection into a valve ring and adjacent structures.[97] In such cases, surgery frequently is required.

The pathologic changes in distant organs usually are secondary to embolization with subsequent infarction or metastatic infection. In many cases of infective endocarditis, the causative organism is of low pathogenicity; infections caused by septic emboli often are low grade because of the reduced propensity of these organisms to invade tissue. However, the emboli in acute *S. aureus* endocarditis frequently cause severe metastatic infections and overwhelming sepsis. Emboli from right-sided heart lesions lodge in the lungs and cause pulmonary infarcts and abscesses, which usually are small and multiple. Left-sided lesions may embolize to any organ but most commonly affect the brain, kidney, spleen, and skin.[303] Cerebral emboli have been detected in 30 percent of cases in adults and children and have caused infarction, abscess, mycotic aneurysm, subarachnoid hemorrhage, meningitis, and acute hemiplegia of childhood.[52, 158, 167, 202, 271, 365] Kidney abscess is a rare occurrence, but infarcts are noted in most patients at autopsy.[284] Amyloidosis involving primarily the kidneys is a rare complication of chronic infective endocarditis.[172] Splenic abscess also is a rare event but can be a fatal complication if undetected.[200] The most common manifestation of embolization to the skin is petechiae. Janeway lesions are septic emboli consisting of bacteria, neutrophils, necrosis, and subcutaneous hemorrhage. Osler nodes are areas of thrombosis and necrosis. They may be related to both immune complex deposition and septic emboli.[3]

Clinical Manifestations

The signs and symptoms of infective endocarditis are determined by the extent of local cardiac disease, the continuous bacteremia, and the degree of involvement of distant organs as a result of embolization, metastatic infection, and circulating immune complexes. Consequently, the clinical findings are highly variable and mimic those of many other diseases.[362] Unexplained embolic phenomena in any organ should suggest the diagnosis of endocarditis, especially in children with known heart disease. Patients with acute bacterial endocarditis initially may be seen with florid sepsis; the endocarditis is diagnosed at autopsy. The indolent manifestations of subacute endocarditis may evolve for weeks or months before medical care is sought. Endocarditis frequently occurs in children with preexisting heart disease, so subtle changes in cardiac function may be difficult to detect early in the course. Table 32–3 lists the frequency of the major clinical manifestations of bacterial endocarditis in infants and children.

Fever is the most common symptom of infective endocarditis, but it is absent in 10 percent of cases. It usually is of low grade and has no specific pattern. Chills may accompany the fever, but they rarely are seen in children. Persistent fever during antimicrobial therapy is an uncommon occurrence. Prolonged (>2 weeks) fever is associated with certain etiologic agents (*S. aureus,* gram-negative bacilli, fungi), with culture-negative endocarditis, and with complications such as embolization of major vessels, intracardiac or peripheral abscess, tissue infarction, a need for cardiac surgery, and a higher mortality rate.[42, 237] Nonspecific symptoms such as malaise, anorexia, weight loss, and fatigue are common findings. Arthralgia occurs in 24 percent of patients. The arthralgia frequently is multiple and most commonly affects the large joints. Although adults initially may have synovitis,[69] it is a rare finding in children. Osteoarticular infection in association with infective endocarditis in adults occurs almost exclusively in intravenous drug users[371]; it is seen very rarely in children. Gastrointestinal complaints are noted in 16 percent of cases and include nausea, vomiting, and abdominal pain. Chest pain occurs in approximately 10 percent of older children and generally is mild and nonspecific. Although chest pain usually is related to diffuse myalgias, it may be secondary to pulmonary complications or cardiac lesions, especially if the tricuspid valve is involved.

Heart murmurs occur in more than 90 percent of children with infective endocarditis, but the vast majority of patients have underlying heart disease with preexisting murmurs. The appearance of a new murmur or significant change in a previous one occurs in only 25 percent of cases. Significant blood flow turbulence caused by compromised valvular function must have occurred for a murmur to be detected or to change. The frequent absence of changes in the cardiac examination early in the disease contributes to the long average delay in diagnosis, especially in children with preexisting heart disease. Congestive heart failure occurs in 30 percent of children with infective endocarditis and is especially common in those in whom a new murmur of valvular insufficiency develops. Endocarditis should be suspected in any child who has rheumatic or congenital heart disease and unexplained deterioration in cardiac function. Although valvular regurgitation is the most common hemodynamic complication of endocarditis, significant obstruction of a valve or shunt requiring rapid surgery rarely occurs.[66]

Neurologic signs and symptoms are reported in approximately 20 percent of children with endocarditis. They may dominate the clinical findings, especially in endocarditis

TABLE 32–3 ■ CLINICAL MANIFESTATIONS OF BACTERIAL ENDOCARDITIS IN CHILDREN

Symptom	Average (%)	Range (%)	Physical Finding	Average (%)	Range (%)
Fever	90	56–100	Splenomegaly	55	36–67
Malaise	55	40–79	Petechiae	33	10–50
Anorexia/weight loss	31	8–83	Embolic phenomenon	28	14–50
Heart failure	30	9–47	New or change in heart murmur	24	9–44
Arthralgia	24	16–38	Clubbing	14	2–42
Neurologic	18	12–21	Osler nodes	7	7–8
Gastrointestinal	16	9–36	Roth spots	5	0–6
Chest pain	9	5–20	Janeway lesion	5	0–10
			Splinter hemorrhages	5	0–10

Data from references 43, 77, 137, 199, 228, 269, 362, 388, 395, 424, 443.

caused by *S. aureus*.[167, 365] The sudden development of cerebral lesions in an infant or child should suggest this diagnosis. The manifestations are those that commonly accompany a cerebral infarct or abscess—namely, acute hemiplegia of childhood, seizures, ataxia, aphasia, sensory loss, focal neurologic deficits, and alterations in mental status. They may be the initial feature of endocarditis or may occur years after the infection has been eradicated.[473] Mycotic aneurysms of the cerebral vessels occur rarely in cases of pediatric endocarditis.[56] They usually are single, small, and peripheral but may lead to subarachnoid hemorrhage. Whereas computed tomographic scanning of the brain is useful for delineating central nervous system involvement in patients with infective endocarditis, magnetic resonance imaging may be more sensitive for detecting small infarctions and changes secondary to cerebral edema.[34] Other neurologic manifestations associated with endocarditis include cranial nerve palsies, neuropathy, visual changes, choreoathetosis, seizures, and toxic encephalopathy.

Splenomegaly is a common manifestation of endocarditis in children and occurs in 55 percent of cases. It is found frequently in patients with long-standing disease and other evidence of immune system activation. The spleen generally is nontender and may be associated with mild hepatomegaly. Splenic infarction and abscess are rare events but should be suspected in patients with left upper quadrant abdominal pain that radiates to the left shoulder, a pleural friction rub, or left pleural effusion.

Skin manifestations occur less commonly in children than in adults.[251] Clubbing is found in 10 to 20 percent of children with endocarditis but frequently is related to underlying heart disease. Petechiae are noted in approximately one third of patients, especially those with long-standing disease. They are found most commonly on the extremities, oral mucosa, and conjunctivae. Splinter hemorrhages are linear red or brown streaks seen in the nail beds. They are present in only 5 percent of children with endocarditis and are associated with other conditions.[223] Three other types of lesions are more specific for infective endocarditis but occur in only 5 to 7 percent of patients: Osler nodes, small (2 to 10 mm), painful nodular lesions found in the pads of the fingers or toes; Janeway lesions, usually painless hemorrhagic macular plaques that frequently occur on the palms and soles[117]; and Roth spots, small pale retinal lesions associated with areas of hemorrhage located near the optic disk.

Other than fever and, perhaps, splenomegaly, no single sign or symptom occurs in more than 50 percent of children with endocarditis. That no classic clinical manifestation exists for this disease is obvious because the chance that even three or more signs will be present is extremely low. The appearance of any one of these clinical features in a child with predisposing heart disease should raise suspicion of infective endocarditis and lead to an appropriate diagnostic evaluation.

The clinical findings of infective endocarditis in infants and neonates are less specific than are those in older children. The onset more often is acute and related to overwhelming infection.[198, 278] In the pre-antibiotic era, these children often had other foci of infection, such as osteomyelitis, meningitis, and pneumonia, that dominated the clinical picture. The widespread use of antibiotics since 1941 has caused a decrease in the number of cases of infective endocarditis occurring secondary to other suppurative infections.[278] Although early studies concluded that congenital heart disease was not an important predisposing factor to endocarditis in infants,[143, 458] more recent reports suggest that it is.[79, 198] At present, infants with heart defects undergo corrective and palliative surgery at a younger age than in the past. Infants in whom postoperative endocarditis does develop probably will have clinical findings more similar to those in older children.

Infective endocarditis is a rare occurrence in neonates and frequently is associated with indwelling vascular catheters.[267] It may affect the tricuspid valve and have a fairly "silent" clinical manifestation. Persistent bacteremia or fungemia should lead to a search for a cardiac focus of infection. Deterioration in pulmonary function, coagulopathies, thrombocytopenia, and low-grade murmurs often develop in neonates. Skin abscesses and hepatomegaly also are common findings. The prognosis of infective endocarditis associated with neonatal intensive care usually is favorable, perhaps because the diagnosis often is established relatively early and antibiotics are given rapidly.[364]

Reported series of infective endocarditis in children with prosthetic valves are scarce. In early disease, fever may be the only finding because the other signs of endocarditis are masked by the medical and surgical complications occurring in the immediate postoperative period. Late infections generally produce clinical findings similar to those in native-valve endocarditis. Clinical evidence of systemic embolization occurs in as many as 40 percent of patients. Neurologic complications carry a particularly poor prognosis for survival.[219] A new or changing murmur often indicates valvular insufficiency caused by a paravalvular leak. Florid cardiac failure is the major manifestation if local infection or an abscess creates valve instability and acute, severe regurgitation.

The signs and symptoms of infective endocarditis in intravenous drug abusers may be similar, but they have several more distinctive features of their illness. Two thirds of these patients have no predisposing heart disease. The valve most commonly affected is the tricuspid, which leads to a predominance of pulmonary signs and symptoms resulting from pleural effusion, pulmonary infarction, and lung abscesses. Signs of tricuspid insufficiency (gallop rhythm, pulsatile liver, regurgitant murmur) are found in one third of cases.[375] A large number of patients have extracardiac sites of infection that are helpful in diagnosis.[422]

Laboratory Findings

The most important diagnostic procedure is the blood culture. Because many bacteria that usually are not pathogenic cause infective endocarditis, scrupulous aseptic technique must be used to distinguish causative agents from contaminants. The yield of organisms is not increased by obtaining blood from arterial puncture or cardiac catheterization.[32] The bacteremia usually is of low grade and continuous. The first two cultures will yield the organism 90 percent of the time; in two thirds of cases, all blood cultures will be positive.[456] Therefore, isolated positive cultures generally are not significant. Previous outpatient antibiotic therapy may change the yield significantly. In one study, culture positivity in cases of proven endocarditis was 64 percent in patients who received antibiotics before blood was drawn for culture versus 100 percent in patients without exposure to antibiotics.[320] Blood should be injected into hypertonic media if the patient has been exposed to antibiotics.

When *Candida* endocarditis is suspected, several additional points should be considered. Isolation of *Candida* spp. may require incubation for 1 week or longer. All blood cultures from a patient with *Candida* endocarditis may not be positive, in contrast to the usual situation with bacterial endocarditis; several positive cultures may be interspersed among negative cultures. In patients with fungal endocarditis, *Candida* is isolated commonly from other infected sites, such as urine, sputum, synovial fluid, cerebrospinal fluid, lymph nodes, and bone marrow.[366]

Three to five samples of blood for culture should be obtained from different sites within the first 24 hours in children with suspected endocarditis. Though difficult in smaller children, obtaining 3 to 5 mL of blood per culture is desirable for optimal yield. The samples should be injected into thioglycolate and trypticase soy (or brain-heart infusion) broth and held for at least 3 weeks to detect slow-growing organisms. If gram-positive cocci grow in the broth but fail to grow on subculture, nutritionally variant streptococci should be suspected and subculture performed on media with either L-cysteine or pyridoxal phosphate.[53, 401] Poured plates may be used to estimate the degree of bacteremia.

Negative blood cultures are noted in 10 to 15 percent of patients with clinically diagnosed endocarditis.[435] However, if the patients had not received antibiotic therapy previously and blood for culture was obtained properly, these cases have been less than 5 percent of the total. Potential reasons for negative cultures include (1) right-sided endocarditis; (2) previous administration of antibiotics; (3) fungal (especially *Aspergillus*) endocarditis; (4) endocarditis caused by *Bartonella* spp., rickettsiae, chlamydiae, or viruses; (5) mural endocarditis; (6) slow growth of organisms (*Candida, Haemophilus, Brucella,* nutritionally variant streptococci); (7) anaerobic infection; and (8) nonbacterial thrombotic endocarditis or an incorrect diagnosis.[162, 166, 326, 435] In some instances, intraleukocytic organisms may be seen in layered peripheral blood, even when cultures are negative.[333] If surgical resection of vegetations or valve replacement is performed, an etiology may be demonstrated by appropriate histologic examination and stains for bacteria and fungi. Organisms also may be isolated from extracardiac sites (bone marrow, urine).

Many nonspecific laboratory findings are abnormal in patients with infective endocarditis (Table 32–4). The erythrocyte sedimentation rate is elevated in 80 to 90 percent of cases. However, frequently it is normal or low when congestive heart failure or renal failure is present. Serum C-reactive protein levels usually are elevated initially and return to normal during successful therapy.[274] An increase during therapy may be due to treatment failure but also can be caused by drug allergy or intercurrent infection. Rheumatoid factor rarely has been measured in a series of pediatric patients, but when measurements have been made, they have been positive in 25 to 50 percent of children with endocarditis. A positive test may be a diagnostic aid in cases of culture-negative endocarditis when other causes are excluded. Serial measurements may provide evidence of efficacy of therapy, although a fall in the titer of rheumatoid factor may lag behind the clinical and bacteriologic response.[448] Hypocomplementemia is seen in association with glomerulonephritis. Anemia is present in approximately 40 percent of patients, especially in those with long-standing disease. Although hemolysis may occur in the areas of turbulence in the heart, more often it is an anemia of chronic disease. Because many patients with cyanotic heart disease normally have a compensatory polycythemia, a serial drop in hematocrit is of more significance than is a single measurement. Leukocytosis occurs in a few patients, but leukopenia is a rare finding in the absence of acute endocarditis with overwhelming sepsis. Hematuria and proteinuria, present in 25 to 50 percent of cases, usually are secondary to microemboli in the kidneys and may be accompanied by "pyuria," casts, and bacteriuria.

TABLE 32–4 ■ SELECTED LABORATORY FINDINGS OF BACTERIAL ENDOCARDITIS IN CHILDREN

Laboratory Finding	Average (%)	Range (%)
Positive blood culture	87	68–98
Elevated erythrocyte sedimentation rate	80	71–96
Low hemoglobin (anemia)	44	19–79
Positive rheumatoid factor	38	25–55
Hematuria	35	28–47

Data from references 43, 77, 137, 199, 228, 269, 388, 395, 424, 443.

Circulating immune complexes are present in most adult cases of subacute endocarditis, as measured by Raji cell radioimmunoassay[425] or the ^{125}I-Clq binding assay.[474] They frequently are absent in acute endocarditis.[214] Low levels of immune complexes have been found in 32 percent of adults with septicemia but not endocarditis, in 10 percent of normal controls, and in 40 percent of noninfected intravenous drug abusers.[31] However, levels higher than 100 µg/mL are correlated highly with the presence of endocarditis. Serial measurement of immune complex levels may aid in monitoring therapeutic efficacy.[30] Systematic investigation of immune complexes has been reported infrequently in children with endocarditis. When immune complexes have been sought, most patients,[443] including two of three children with culture-negative endocarditis, have had significant levels.[448]

In cases in which infective endocarditis is suspected but blood cultures remain negative, serologic testing for specific organisms may prove helpful. Several techniques measure antibody to teichoic acids, which are major components of the cell wall of *S. aureus.* These antibodies are present in more than 85 percent of adults with staphylococcal endocarditis, but the false-positive rate is as high as 10 percent.[300] False-negative results correlate with a short (<2 weeks) duration of illness. Specific information about the accuracy of this test in children is lacking, and the tests are not readily available. Serologic testing is available or under investigation for many other organisms that cause infective endocarditis, including *Bartonella, Brucella, Candida, Aspergillus, Histoplasma, Cryptococcus, Chlamydia,* and *Coxiella.*[203, 224] In general, the usefulness of these tests in children with endocarditis is unproven. Some patients with nonspirochetal bacterial endocarditis who reside in locales endemic for Lyme disease will have significantly elevated levels of antibodies reactive to *Borrelia burgdorferi.*[205] Diagnostic confusion may occur because the signs and symptoms of infective endocarditis and Lyme disease can be quite similar.

Radiographic techniques have not been a great aid in the diagnosis of infective endocarditis. The findings on plain chest roentgenograms are nonspecific, but evidence of complications, such as septic pulmonary emboli or congestive heart failure, may be helpful. Computed tomography may help in the diagnosis of an infected shunt.[436] Immunoscintigraphy using technetium-labeled antigranulocyte antibodies may yield useful information when the echocardiographic findings are equivocal.[288] Cineangiography is the definitive method to determine the anatomic alterations in the heart resulting from infective endocarditis, but it rarely is necessary in children.

The electrocardiogram also is useful in the evaluation of patients with endocarditis because it will detect arrhythmias and conduction disturbances that complicate the disease. Ventricular ectopy may be related to myocardial ischemia, myocarditis, or myocardial abscess. New conduction defects imply extension of infection beyond the valve ring into the myocardium. Any degree of atrioventricular block, a new left bundle branch block, or a new right bundle branch block with a left anterior hemiblock may represent extension of infection from the aortic valve into the ventricular septum. Junctional tachycardia, Wenckebach atrioventricular block, or complete heart block may be produced by extension of the infection from the mitral valve annulus into the atrioventricular node or proximal His bundle. In general, an unstable conduction block is more likely to develop in patients with aortic valve endocarditis than in those with mitral infection.[96]

Echocardiography has become a valuable adjunct to the diagnosis and treatment of endocarditis in children.[94, 152, 230, 347, 360, 361, 381] Color Doppler is a sensitive modality for detection of valvular insufficiency, and the results may influence surgical and medical treatment decisions.[128] Echocardiography can be performed via the traditional transthoracic or the transesophageal approach.[330] The sensitivity and specificity of transthoracic echocardiography still are being defined, with positive results in 36 to 100 percent of children in various series of pediatric patients.[45, 94, 215, 364]

In general, two-dimensional echocardiography is more sensitive than is the M-mode technique, especially in cases of right-sided endocarditis,[316] and it is superior in diagnosing complications of the destructive process.[283] The smallest size vegetation detectable is approximately 2 mm, but the acoustic impedance of the mass relative to the surrounding structures is a more important factor than is size in identifying the vegetation. Echocardiography has identified vegetations in culture-negative cases.[215] Its accuracy in prosthetic-valve endocarditis is diminished by the difficulty in resolution around the prosthetic device.[296, 404] Serial evaluation of valvular vegetations generally does not assist in assessing the efficacy of antibiotic therapy because diminution or disappearance of vegetations may take place long after the completion of successful medical treatment.[225, 354, 446]

The use of transthoracic echocardiography to predict the clinical course and need for operative intervention in patients with endocarditis is controversial.[5] A synopsis of many reports that have assessed the role of transthoracic echocardiography in the diagnosis and management of infective endocarditis suggests the following: (1) because of variable sensitivity among studies for detection of vegetations, a negative study does not rule out endocarditis, especially when foreign material is present within the heart; (2) false-positive studies are quite rare (the specificity is high); (3) the reliability of transthoracic echocardiography depends on the experience of the examiner and the technical adequacy of the study; (4) transthoracic echocardiography is valuable in assessing local complications of endocarditis on native valves; and (5) in most but not all studies, patients with a vegetation identified by transthoracic echocardiography have an increased risk for the development of systemic emboli and congestive heart failure.[191, 215, 254, 348, 369, 403]

Although some investigators think that the presence of a vegetation should hasten early surgery, most suggest that a positive echocardiogram is adjunctive evidence that should be considered along with other clinical parameters when considering surgical intervention. One study suggested that the relative risk for embolic events associated with echocardiographically visualized lesions is microorganism-dependent, with a significant attributable risk seen only in patients with viridans streptococcal infection.[396] Absence of a vegetation on transthoracic echocardiography may define a subset of patients at low risk for the development of embolic complications.

Transesophageal echocardiography is a newer technique that has been studied extensively in adults with infective endocarditis.[85] It uses a 5-MHz phased-array transducer with Doppler and color flow encoding capabilities mounted on the tip of a flexible endoscope.[375] Biplane transesophageal echocardiography is considered the standard technique and is superior to transthoracic echocardiography because of improved spatial resolution, lack of acoustic interference from the lungs and chest wall, and closer proximity to posterior structures, such as the mitral valve and left atrium.[84] Multiplane transesophageal echocardiography facilitates and abbreviates the examination procedure and may be more accurate in providing the dimensions of a vegetation associated with infective endocarditis.[84, 194]

Transesophageal echocardiography generally is well tolerated by children, even with the use of an adult probe (when the child's weight is more than 7 kg),[381] and rarely is associated with bacteremia.[83, 233, 329] Transesophageal echocardiography usually is more sensitive than is transthoracic echocardiography in the detection of intracardiac vegetations and is positive in 70 to 95 percent of adults with strongly suspected endocarditis.[293, 387] It is significantly more sensitive in the detection of vegetations and complications in infected prosthetic valves.[220, 321, 353, 404, 417] Transesophageal echocardiography is particularly useful for detecting an aortic root abscess or involvement of the sinus of Valsalva in adults, and it should be considered in children with aortic valve endocarditis and changing aortic root dimensions on a standard transthoracic echocardiograph.[128] It appears to be less helpful for detection of vegetations in right-sided endocarditis.[370] Although a negative transesophageal echocardiographic study does not exclude endocarditis,[392] the procedure should be considered for patients with suspected endocarditis and a negative transthoracic echocardiograph and when perivalvular extension of infection is suspected.

To aid in the diagnosis of infective endocarditis, various sets of clinical criteria have been suggested. The von Reyn criteria were described in 1982, but echocardiographic findings were not included in the case definitions.[445] In addition, isolation of a typical infective endocarditis pathogen from blood cultures was not considered. A new set of case definitions and diagnostic criteria were proposed by investigators from Duke[104] (Tables 32–5 and 32–6). The inclusion of echocardiographic and blood culture findings in these new criteria has resulted in more flexibility, a higher proportion of "definite" cases, and a more accurate reflection of current clinical practice. These criteria have been validated in large series of infective endocarditis in adults and children.[92, 104, 176, 368] In two pediatric series of clinically defined endocarditis, no cases were rejected by the Duke criteria, whereas 25 and 19 percent were rejected by the von Reyn criteria.[92, 405] In one study, three of six pathologically confirmed cases were rated as only probable or rejected by the von Reyn criteria, whereas all were definite by the Duke criteria.[92] Several recent studies have proposed minor modifications of the Duke criteria, especially for prosthetic-valve endocarditis.[232, 244]

Microbiology

A wide variety of microorganisms are capable of causing infective endocarditis in humans. Table 32–7 lists the organisms isolated from patients in major pediatric series. Gram-positive cocci are the etiologic agents in 90 percent of cases in which an organism is isolated. Streptococci remain the bacteria isolated most frequently, although the percentage of cases caused by staphylococci and fungi has been increasing during the past 2 decades.[199, 278, 364, 395, 424, 443, 470] Polymicrobial infective endocarditis, especially in nosocomial settings, also appears to be increasing in incidence.[18] The characteristics of selected organisms and the type of disease that they produce are considered in the following subsections.

TABLE 32–5 ■ DEFINITION OF TERMS USED IN THE DUKE CRITERIA FOR INFECTIVE ENDOCARDITIS

Major Criteria

1. Positive blood culture
   a. Typical microorganisms for IE from ≥2 blood cultures
      (1) Viridans streptococci,* *Streptococcus bovis,* or HACEK group *or*
      (2) Community-acquired *Staphylococcus aureus* or enterococci, in the absence of another primary focus, *or*
   b. Persistently positive blood cultures, with recovery of a microorganism consistent with IE from
      (1) Blood cultures drawn ≥12 hr apart *or*
      (2) All of 3 or a majority of 4 or more separate blood cultures, with first and last drawn ≥1 hr apart
2. Evidence of endocardial involvement
   a. Positive echocardiogram for IE
      (1) Oscillating intracardiac mass on valve or supporting structures, in the path of regurgitant jets, or on implanted material, in the absence of an alternative anatomic explanation, *or*
      (2) Abscess *or*
      (3) New partial dehiscence of a prosthetic valve *or*
   b. New valvular regurgitation (increase or change in preexisting murmur is not sufficient)

Minor Criteria

1. Predisposing heart condition or intravenous drug use
2. Fever ≥38° C
3. Vascular phenomena: major arterial emboli, septic pulmonary infarcts, mycotic aneurysm, intracranial hemorrhage, conjunctival hemorrhages, Janeway lesions
4. Immunologic phenomena: glomerulonephritis, Osler nodes, Roth spots, rheumatoid factor
5. Microbiologic evidence: positive blood culture but not meeting major criteria as noted previously† or serologic evidence of active infection with organism consistent with IE
6. Echocardiogram: consistent with IE but not meeting major criteria as noted previously

*Including nutritionally variant strains (*Abiotrophia* species).
†Excluding single positive cultures for coagulase-negative staphylococci and organisms that do not cause IE.
HACEK, *Haemophilus* species, *Actinobacillus actinomycetemcomitans, Cardiobacterium hominis, Eikenella corrodens, Kingella kingae;* IE, infective endocarditis.
From Durack, D. T., Lukes, A. S., Bright, D. K., et al.: New criteria for diagnosis of infective endocarditis: Utilization of specific echocardiographic findings. Am. J. Med. *96*:200–209, 1994.

TABLE 32–6 ■ DUKE CRITERIA FOR THE DIAGNOSIS OF INFECTIVE ENDOCARDITIS

Definite

1. Pathologic criteria
   a. Microorganisms: demonstrated by culture or histology in a vegetation, in a vegetation that has embolized, or in an intracardiac abscess *or*
   b. Pathologic lesions: vegetation or intracardiac abscess present and confirmed by histology showing endocarditis
2. Clinical criteria (see Table 32–5)
   a. 2 major criteria *or*
   b. 1 major and 3 minor criteria *or*
   c. 5 minor criteria

Possible

1. Findings consistent with IE that fall short of "definite" but not "rejected"

Rejected

1. Firm alternative diagnosis explaining evidence of IE *or*
2. Resolution of IE syndrome with antimicrobial therapy for ≤4 days *or*
3. No pathologic evidence of IE at surgery or autopsy with antibiotic therapy for ≤4 days

IE, infective endocarditis. From Durack, D. T., Lukes, A. S., Bright, D. K., et al.: New criteria for diagnosis of infective endocarditis: Utilization of specific echocardiographic findings. Am. J. Med. *96*:200–209, 1994.

STREPTOCOCCI

Several terminologies have been used to classify streptococci. The Lancefield system defines groups (A, B, C, D, E, F, G, H) by serologic reactions. The viridans streptococci are alpha-hemolytic or nonhemolytic, may be Lancefield nontypeable *(Streptococcus milleri, Streptococcus mitior, Streptococcus salivarius,* most *Streptococcus mutans,* and *S. sanguis)* or typeable *(Streptococcus bovis* group D, some *S. sanguis* group H, some *S. milleri* group F), and display similar characteristics in vivo. They are the most frequent etiologic agents in subacute infective endocarditis and cause 40 percent of cases in children. They may cause rapidly progressive invasive disease.[180, 412]

Viridans streptococci are common pathogens in patients with underlying heart disease but less common in postoperative patients. They are part of the indigenous flora of the human mouth and gastrointestinal tract, and procedures that disrupt mucosal integrity in these areas predispose to development of viridans streptococcal bacteremia. In the pediatric population, most blood and cerebrospinal fluid isolates of viridans and nonhemolytic streptococci are not from patients with infective endocarditis.[165] Most strains are exquisitely susceptible to penicillin, although previous administration of antibiotics may promote infection with resistant strains.[241] Nutritionally variant viridans streptococci, recently reclassified as *Abiotrophia defectiva,* are recognized as one cause of culture-negative endocarditis in children.[64, 120, 304, 350] These organisms grow in broth but will not grow on subculture agar-based plates. Bacteriologic failure has occurred in 40 percent of reported cases of endocarditis caused by these organisms despite susceptibility to the antibiotics used.[401] Most viridans streptococci have low pathogenicity; however, *S. milleri* has a predilection for suppurative complications.[298] The prognosis of endocarditis caused by nonenterococcal streptococci is excellent with good medical and surgical management; the cure rate is more than 90 percent, although complications (emboli, congestive heart failure) occur in as many as 30 percent of cases.

Enterococcal endocarditis occurs much less commonly in children than in adults[279, 421] and accounts for only 4 percent of pediatric cases. The organism normally inhabits the gastrointestinal and genitourinary tracts; instrumentation of these areas may cause enterococcal bacteremia. More than 40 percent of adult patients have no underlying heart disease.[346] Endocarditis should be considered in all infants and children with unexplained enterococcal bacteremia.

TABLE 32–7 ■ ETIOLOGIC AGENTS OF BACTERIAL ENDOCARDITIS IN CHILDREN

Organism	Average (%)	Range (%)
Streptococci		
Viridans	40.3	17–72
Enterococci	4.0	0–12
Pneumococci	3.3	0–21
Beta-hemolytic	2.7	0–8
Other	1.1	0–16
Staphylococci		
Staphylococcus aureus	23.8	5–40
Coagulase-negative staphylococci	4.7	0–15
Gram-negative aerobic bacilli	4.0	0–15
Fungi	1.1	0–12
Miscellaneous bacteria	2.4	0–10
Culture-negative	12.6	2–32

Data from references 43, 51, 77, 197–199, 228, 278, 364, 395, 424, 443.

Although the incidence of enterococcal bacteremia appears to be increasing in some neonatal intensive care units, the incidence of associated endocarditis seems to be very low. Factors that may suggest endocarditis in patients with enterococcal bacteremia include (1) preexisting heart disease, (2) community acquisition, (3) a cryptogenic source, and (4) the absence of polymicrobial bacteremia.[260] Differentiation of enterococci from other group D streptococci *(S. bovis)* is important because their respective therapeutic approaches are different.

Endocarditis caused by beta-hemolytic streptococci occurred more commonly in the pre-antibiotic era than today. Most cases are caused by Lancefield group B or G organisms,[1, 12, 139, 451] whereas group C and A streptococci rarely cause endocarditis.[39, 98, 153, 249, 340] Group A, B, or C streptococcal infection may lead to large, bulky vegetations, easily seen by echocardiography, and to embolic complications.[13, 285] Even though group B streptococcal bacteremia is a common finding in newborn infants, endocarditis caused by this organism occurs rarely in this age group. Similarly, *S. pneumoniae* accounted for 10 to 15 percent of endocarditis cases in the pre-antibiotic era but currently causes less than 1 percent.[142, 190, 314] Pneumococcal endocarditis may involve either the aortic or the mitral valve,[110, 428] and less than 50 percent of affected children have underlying heart disease. The clinical course often is fulminant.[107, 238, 331] Concurrent meningitis or pneumonia (or both) occurs frequently. Valvular dysfunction and cardiac decompensation are common findings.[42, 49] Early surgical intervention may be required because the mortality rate is 75 percent when medical management alone is used.[190]

STAPHYLOCOCCI

Staphylococci cause 20 to 30 percent of cases of infective endocarditis in children. *S. aureus* is the etiologic agent in most cases of acute endocarditis and frequently infects normal heart valves.[133, 291] The course often is fulminant when the mitral or aortic valve is involved, with frequent suppurative complications occurring both in the heart (myocardial abscess, pericarditis, valve ring abscess) and in other organs.[113, 204] *S. aureus* is responsible for more than 50 percent of cases of endocarditis in intravenous drug abusers, but their disease tends to be less severe.[62, 63] The origin of the infecting organism is the addict's own nose or skin, not the injection paraphernalia.[434] Endocarditis associated with indwelling vascular catheters or prosthetic valves frequently is caused by *S. aureus.*[195] Endocarditis must be suspected in any patient with *S. aureus* bacteremia, even when a peripheral focus of infection is present. However, most patients with *S. aureus* bacteremia do not have endocarditis.

The incidence of *S. epidermidis* endocarditis is rising rapidly.[9] Though a rare cause of endocarditis that occurs in patients without underlying heart disease, it is a common etiologic agent of endocarditis occurring after cardiac surgery.[218] This organism is the leading agent in prosthetic-valve endocarditis, for which it causes 25 to 67 percent of early cases and 25 to 33 percent of late cases.[148, 187, 210] Coagulase-negative staphylococcal endocarditis also has been associated with mitral valve prolapse and the use of intravascular catheters in premature neonates.[19, 309] Although metastatic infection rarely occurs, *S. epidermidis* can be locally invasive; the mortality rate of *S. epidermidis* prosthetic-valve endocarditis approaches 75 percent when valve replacement is not performed. Cases of infective endocarditis caused by other species of coagulase-negative staphylococci, such as *Staphylococcus capitis,* appear to be rare.[246]

GRAM-NEGATIVE ORGANISMS

Whereas gram-negative bacteria cause 4 to 5 percent of cases of infective endocarditis in children, the percentage of children with gram-negative enteric bacteremia in whom endocarditis develops is extremely low. Endocarditis should be suspected in patients with gram-negative infection when bacteremia persists despite usually appropriate antibiotic therapy.[58] Burn patients,[184] immunosuppressed hosts, narcotic addicts, and prosthetic-valve recipients are at an increased risk for development of gram-negative endocarditis. However, in the early postoperative period after cardiac surgery, sustained gram-negative bacillary bacteremia commonly is caused by other foci of infection and does not imply the presence of endocarditis. Many species of gram-negative enteric organisms have caused infective endocarditis in children, but no clear pattern has emerged. Among the gram-negative organisms more commonly reported are *Brucella, Escherichia coli, Serratia, Klebsiella-Enterobacter, Salmonella,* and *Pseudomonas.*[93, 227, 253, 414] Endocarditis caused by *Salmonella* has been reported in patients with HIV infection.[125] It most often affects previously abnormal heart valves. Endocarditis is a rare complication of tularemia.[418] Cure of left-sided endocarditis caused by the Enterobacteriaceae seldom is achieved with medical therapy alone.[375] Most information about gram-negative enteric endocarditis is limited to case reports and general medicine reviews; discussion of individual organisms is beyond the scope of this review.

Other gram-negative organisms associated with infective endocarditis are the so-called HACEK coccobacilli (*Haemophilus, Actinobacillus, Cardiobacterium, Eikenella,* and *Kingella*).[87] These organisms caused 57 percent of cases of gram-negative endocarditis seen at the Mayo Clinic from 1958 to 1979.[144] Endocarditis caused by *Haemophilus influenzae* has been reported in only four children.[82, 263] Cases caused by *Haemophilus parainfluenzae* and *Haemophilus aphrophilus* occur slightly more commonly.[35, 68, 88, 193, 255] They generally are seen in the setting of preexisting valvular disease and run a subacute course. However, central nervous system complications and emboli to major peripheral arteries are frequent occurrences.[68] Infective endocarditis in children caused by other organisms of the HACEK group is an extremely rare event.[8, 121, 290, 318, 339, 455] All the bacteria in this group are fastidious, may require 2 to 3 weeks for primary isolation, and need subculturing onto chocolate agar in an atmosphere of 5 to 10 percent carbon dioxide for optimal growth. These procedures should be performed in all cases of culture-negative endocarditis.

Neisseria gonorrhoeae was responsible for 10 percent of cases in the pre-antibiotic era, but fewer than 40 episodes have been reported since 1942.[124, 188] It frequently attacks previously normal heart valves and is manifested as an acute illness.[419] Valvular destruction with a need for valve replacement occurs commonly. At present, nonpathogenic *Neisseria* spp. are isolated more frequently in endocarditis than are gonococci, but they usually attack abnormal or prosthetic valves.[46, 170, 185, 328, 382]

Although 1 percent of cases of infective endocarditis in adults are caused by anaerobic bacteria,[122] reports of anaerobic endocarditis in children are exceedingly rare.[73, 305, 390, 395, 408]

GRAM-POSITIVE BACILLI

Infective endocarditis caused by *Corynebacterium* spp. is an unusual finding but may occur on normal or previously abnormal valves.[280] Both toxigenic[91] and nontoxigenic[160, 391, 426] strains of *Corynebacterium diphtheriae* cause endocarditis in children, thus demonstrating that the toxigenic and invasive properties of the organism are independent. Infection occurs most often on native valves and may be quite aggressive and lead to major vascular complications. *Listeria monocytogenes* endocarditis rarely occurs, has a high mortality rate, and, unlike other forms of listeriosis, usually is not associated with immunocompromised hosts.[27, 59] It has not been associated with listeriosis in neonates. Fewer than 40 cases of *Lactobacillus* endocarditis have been reported.[159, 183, 411] Endocarditis caused by *Erysipelothrix rhusiopathiae* is found predominately in adults who are farmers or exposed to farm animals or products.[155, 168] Most cases of *Bacillus* endocarditis involve the tricuspid valve in intravenous drug users, but other patients have been affected, including those with prosthetic valves.[400] *Gemella morbillorum,* formerly known as *Streptococcus morbillorum,* is a gram-positive coccus that normally resides in the gastrointestinal tract and is a rare cause of endocarditis.[116, 234]

OTHER ORGANISMS

Many different bacteria, including *Acinetobacter,*[157] *Stenotrophomonas,*[352] *Nocardia,*[450] *Actinomyces,*[231] *Streptobacillus,*[358] and *Rothia,*[409] have been associated rarely with endocarditis.[48] Mycobacterial endocarditis is an exceedingly infrequent event.[138]

Infective endocarditis caused by *Coxiella burnetii,* the causative agent of Q fever, is well documented in northern Africa, Europe, and Australia.[2, 47, 235, 243] Most cases are chronic (occurring over a 6- to 12-month period) and involve the aortic valve. Clues to diagnosis include exposure to parturient cats or rabbits, massive splenomegaly, hypergammaglobulinemia, and thrombocytopenia.[327] The diagnosis usually is confirmed by measurement of antibodies against phase I and phase II antigens, but the organism has been isolated from leukocytes in a shell vial assay and has been demonstrated by immunohistologic techniques.[47, 150] At least 20 well-documented cases of infective endocarditis caused by *Chlamydia psittaci* and *Chlamydia pneumoniae* have been reported.[177, 203, 268, 380, 386] Most patients have had preexisting heart disease and a subacute course.[262] *Legionella* has been implicated in several cases of prosthetic-valve endocarditis.[429] *Bartonella quintana* and *Bartonella henselae* have been identified as the cause of endocarditis in "culture-negative" cases.[99, 192, 394] Most described cases have been in immunocompetent individuals. The diagnosis was established by serology, polymerase chain reaction, or special culture techniques.[21, 123, 131, 341]

Although culture of bacteria remains the primary method to establish the microbial cause of infective endocarditis, the number of organisms causing endocarditis that cannot be cultivated by standard culture methods is growing.[132, 181] More recently, universal and species-specific primers have been designed to amplify bacterial DNA directly from resected valves. Among the organisms causing endocarditis identified by these methods are *Bartonella, Tropheryma whippelii, Coxiella, Mycoplasma, Haemophilus, Abiotrophia, Gemella, Cardiobacterium,* and *Streptococcus.*[141, 154, 181, 248, 337]

FUNGI

Most cases of fungal endocarditis in children have been described as occurring after cardiovascular surgery and prolonged intravenous and antibiotic therapy.[109] More recently, cases have been reported in neonates[273] and after prosthetic-valve placement.[307] The most common causative organism is *C. albicans,* although disease has been attributed to other *Candida* spp., including *C. krusei, Candida parapsilosis, Candida stellatoidea, Candida tropicalis,* and *Candida guilliermondii.*[335, 366, 383] Among intravenous drug abusers, *Candida* spp. other than *C. albicans* are more common causes of endocarditis.[357] The clinical manifestation usually is indolent and not specific, with symptoms occurring from weeks to months before diagnosis. Signs and symptoms caused by emboli to large vessels, especially those supplying the brain, kidney, spleen, and extremities, should alert the physician to the possibility of fungal endocarditis. Large, friable vegetations occur frequently and can be detected by echocardiography.[406] Cutaneous and ocular manifestations of systemic *Candida* infection may be present.[44] The prognosis of *Candida* endocarditis is poor and related to the propensity for septic emboli, the tendency for invasion into the myocardium, and the poor penetration of antifungal agents into the bulky vegetation. The diagnosis frequently is delayed by the tendency for negative or intermittently positive blood cultures to occur in this disease.[201] Surgical intervention usually is required.

Aspergillus spp., including *Aspergillus flavus, Aspergillus fumigatus, Aspergillus terreus,* and *Aspergillus niger,* are the second most frequent causes of fungal endocarditis, and such infections have been reported in 16 children.[23, 24] Two thirds of these patients had underlying heart disease. *Aspergillus* endocarditis has been found in immunocompromised hosts with no previous cardiac problems.[467] The most common initial manifestations are fever and embolic phenomena, especially to the central nervous system.[447] Fewer than 15 cases have been diagnosed antemortem, three by culture of peripheral emboli. In none of the patients were antemortem blood cultures positive. Most cases occur after open heart surgery; the most likely source of the organism is airborne inoculation of the heart during the operation.[23] Surgical removal of all infected material is recommended, although only one child has been treated successfully.

Other fungi that rarely cause endocarditis include *Histoplasma capsulatum, Coccidioides immitis, Cryptococcus neoformans, Torulopsis glabrata, Trichosporon beigelii,*[217] and *Fusarium* spp.[182]

Treatment

In the pre-antibiotic era, infective endocarditis was a uniformly fatal disease. With the current improved methods of diagnosis and therapy, 80 to 90 percent of children with this disease can be expected to survive. Mortality rates are higher for acute staphylococcal infection, fungal endocarditis, and prosthetic-valve endocarditis, although the tendency toward earlier surgical intervention for these entities may improve survival rates. The cornerstone of successful therapy is selection of antibiotics with specific activity against the causative organism. Better analysis of pharmacodynamic variables, such as bactericidal activity and the post-antibiotic effects of various drugs, may assist in the selection of optimal therapeutic regimens.[76, 222, 462] Although persistent infection occasionally complicates treated endocarditis,[344] deterioration in cardiac function is the major cause of morbidity and mortality.

Several general principles provide the basis for the current recommendations for treatment of endocarditis. Parenteral administration of antibiotics is preferred because erratic absorption of oral antibiotics, especially in infants, can lead to therapeutic failure. Although patient selection criteria for the use of outpatient parenteral antibiotic therapy for endocarditis in adults have been suggested, no data have been published about this practice for children.[7] Prolonged treatment, usually 4 to 6 weeks or longer, is necessary to sterilize the vegetations and prevent relapse. Bacteriostatic antibiotics are not effective and lead to frequent relapses or failure to eradicate the infection, or both. Antibiotic combinations may produce a rapid bactericidal effect through synergistic mechanisms of action. When synergy exists, smaller doses of each drug may be used, thereby reducing toxic side effects. However, certain drug combinations (penicillin and chloramphenicol, for example) can be antagonistic and their use should be avoided.

Blood should be drawn for culture for several days to evaluate the effect of the antibiotics. Negative follow-up cultures do not guarantee the success of therapy, but persistent positive cultures usually require that a change or addition to the antibiotic regimen be made. Observation of the patient's clinical course is extremely important. When fever is present initially, the temperature often returns to normal within a few days after therapy is started. However, fever can persist for weeks in patients whose eventual outcome is good. Such patients must be monitored closely for cardiac arrhythmias and congestive heart failure, which may require intensive care observation and electrocardiographic monitoring. Evidence of major embolic phenomena must be sought diligently by physical examination.

Several laboratory tests may aid in monitoring therapy. In all cases of bacterial endocarditis, the minimal inhibitory concentration (MIC) and minimal bactericidal concentration (MBC) must be determined for the antibiotics being used because disk susceptibility testing is unreliable and not quantitative. When combinations of antibiotics are used, tests for bactericidal synergy, such as broth dilution, "checkerboards," or time-kill curves, may give additional information. The role of monitoring the inhibitory and bactericidal activity of the patient's serum is highly controversial. The Schlichter test determines the maximal dilutions of a patient's serum that in vitro inhibit and kill an inoculum of the organism causing the endocarditis.[318, 343] Standardization of this test is poor, with laboratories using variations in inoculum size, composition of the broth, timing of samples (at expected peak or trough antibiotic concentrations in serum), methods of dilution, and determination of the bactericidal end-point. In the rabbit endocarditis model, peak serum bactericidal titers greater than 1:8 correlate with therapeutic success.[57] A retrospective review of 17 reports of serum bactericidal activity in patients with endocarditis failed to show any correlation between titers greater than 1:8 and therapeutic success.[74] A prospective study suggested adjusting antibiotic doses to achieve peak titers of 1:64 or greater and trough titers of 1:32 or greater.[454] At present, no generally accepted recommendation can be made. In general, to attempt to achieve a peak serum bactericidal titer of at least 1:8 or greater seems reasonable if serious drug toxicity is not encountered. However, this level may not be attainable with certain organisms such as the enterococcus and gram-negative bacilli. Serum bactericidal testing may be particularly useful when synergistic combinations or less well established antibiotic regimens are used or when response to therapy is suboptimal.[466]

Little information is available concerning optimal antibiotic therapy for infective endocarditis in children; most treatment regimens are adapted from studies of adults with endocarditis.[463] In general, these regimens have been equally successful (and generally less toxic) in children. Table 32–8 lists recommended doses of the commonly used antibiotics.

After initial evaluation of a patient with suspected infective endocarditis, the physician must make a clinical judgment about when to initiate therapy. If the findings are strongly indicative of the diagnosis or the child is very ill, treatment should be started as soon as blood has been drawn for culture. Initial empiric therapy depends on the clinical setting in which the tentative diagnosis is made. If the infection is subacute, a combination of penicillin G and an aminoglycoside usually is recommended for its activity against viridans streptococci, enterococci, and most gram-negative organisms. If *S. aureus* endocarditis is a strong consideration (acute manifestation, narcotic addicts), a penicillinase-resistant penicillin should be added to this regimen. Patients who recently have undergone cardiac surgery, especially prosthetic-valve placement, are treated best with an aminoglycoside and vancomycin to "cover" for nosocomial infection caused by resistant *S. epidermidis;* some physicians add penicillin G to this regimen to improve activity against streptococci. When culture and susceptibility data are known, antibiotic therapy can be changed as needed. In areas where community-acquired methicillin-resistant *S. aureus* isolates are a concern, vancomycin should be added to the nafcillin.

TABLE 32–8 ■ SUGGESTED INTRAVENOUS ANTIBIOTIC DOSES AND SCHEDULES FOR INFECTIVE ENDOCARDITIS IN CHILDREN

Antibiotic	Daily Dose/kg	Divided Doses Every
Aqueous crystalline penicillin G sodium	200,000–300,000 U	4 hr
Ampicillin sodium	200–300 mg	4–6 hr
Cefazolin	100 mg	6–8 hr
Ceftriaxone	75–100 mg	12–24 hr
Gentamicin sulfate	3.0–7.5 mg	8 hr
Nafcillin sodium	100–200 mg (max., 12 g)	4–6 hr
Oxacillin sodium	100–200 mg (max., 12 g)	4–6 hr
Rifampin	20 mg	8–12 hr
Vancomycin hydrochloride	30–60 mg	6–12 hr

Most strains of viridans streptococci, *S. pyogenes,* and nonenterococcal group D streptococci are exquisitely susceptible to penicillin, with an MIC of less than 0.2 μg/mL. However, 15 to 20 percent of viridans streptococci have an MIC of 0.2 μg/mL or greater and are defined arbitrarily as relatively resistant. In addition, some strains (particularly *S. mutans* and *S. mitior*) demonstrate tolerance, that is, an MIC to penicillin of less than 0.1 μg/mL but an MBC that is more than 10-fold higher (1.25 to 50 μg/mL). Most strains of nutritionally dependent streptococci are tolerant to penicillin.[375] Clinical failure may occur in endocarditis caused by these tolerant organisms when penicillin alone is used for treatment,[6] but except for nutritionally dependent streptococci, therapy for tolerant viridans streptococci generally should be the same as for susceptible strains.

Although most experts recommend that endocarditis caused by relatively resistant streptococci be treated with high doses of penicillin combined with 2 to 4 weeks of an aminoglycoside, some authorities consider that penicillin alone usually is adequate therapy.[38, 95] Synergy in vitro between penicillin or vancomycin and streptomycin, gentamicin, or kanamycin can be demonstrated against virtually all penicillin-susceptible streptococci.[449] This observation correlates with a more rapid rate of eradication of bacteria from cardiac vegetations in the rabbit endocarditis model when synergistic combinations of antibiotics are used.[102, 105] However, streptomycin is not synergistic for strains with high-level streptomycin resistance; gentamicin

TABLE 32–9 ■ SUGGESTED REGIMENS FOR TREATMENT OF NATIVE-VALVE ENDOCARDITIS CAUSED BY PENICILLIN-SUSCEPTIBLE VIRIDANS STREPTOCOCCI AND *STREPTOCOCCUS BOVIS* (MIC ≤0.1 μg/mL) IN ADULTS

Antibiotic(s)	Duration (wk)	Comments
Aqueous crystalline penicillin G sodium	4	Preferred for patients with impairment of the eighth cranial nerve or renal function
or		
Ceftriaxone sodium	4	
Aqueous crystalline penicillin G sodium or ceftriaxone	2	Gentamicin peak serum concentration of approximately 3 μg/mL is desirable
plus		
Gentamicin sulfate	2	
Vancomycin hydrochloride	4-6	Recommended for patients allergic to β-lactam antibiotics

From Wilson, W. R., Karchmer, A. W., Dajani, A. S., et al.: Antibiotic treatment of adults with infective endocarditis due to streptococci, enterococci, staphylococci, and HACEK microorganisms. J.A.M.A. *274*:1706–1713, 1995. Copyright 1995, American Medical Association.

is the preferred second drug for these rare isolates.[111] In pediatric patients, gentamicin usually is substituted for streptomycin because of its lower toxicity.

Several regimens have been examined in adults with penicillin-susceptible viridans streptococcal endocarditis (Table 32–9). A 2-week course of penicillin alone leads to an unacceptable relapse rate. However, a 2-week course of intramuscular procaine penicillin and streptomycin cured 99 percent of adults with penicillin-susceptible streptococcal endocarditis.[464] These results are similar to those obtained with β-lactams alone for 4 weeks[212] or penicillin for 4 weeks combined with streptomycin for the first 2 weeks. The 2-week penicillin-gentamicin regimen is the least expensive and is the preferred therapy in uncomplicated cases of penicillin-susceptible streptococcal endocarditis in young adults.[375] In general, the regimen of 4 weeks of penicillin alone is preferred for patients in renal failure or at high risk for aminoglycoside-induced ototoxicity. Vancomycin or ceftriaxone administered for 4 weeks can be used in patients with penicillin-susceptible viridans streptococcal endocarditis who have a penicillin allergy.[134, 135, 384, 407] The regimen of 4 weeks of penicillin plus an initial 2 weeks of gentamicin is recommended in adults with a complicated course (symptoms for >3 months)[261] or with infection caused by relatively penicillin-resistant organisms (Table 32–10). Most nutritionally deficient streptococci are tolerant to penicillin. For patients with endocarditis caused by these organisms, 4 to 6 weeks of penicillin with the addition of an aminoglycoside is recommended[38, 463] (Table 32–11). In patients with streptococcal infection of prosthetic valves or other prosthetic materials, a 6-week regimen of penicillin supplemented with an aminoglycoside is recommended. Of emphasis is that none of the regimens discussed has been evaluated specifically in children with endocarditis.

TABLE 32–10 ■ SUGGESTED THERAPY FOR NATIVE-VALVE ENDOCARDITIS CAUSED BY STRAINS OF VIRIDANS STREPTOCOCCI AND *STREPTOCOCCUS BOVIS* RELATIVELY RESISTANT TO PENICILLIN G (MIC, 0.1 AND 0.5 μg/ml) IN ADULTS

Antibiotic(s)	Duration (wk)	Comments
Aqueous crystalline penicillin G sodium	4	Cefazolin or other first-generation cephalosporins may be substituted for penicillin in patients whose penicillin hypersensitivity is not of the immediate type
or		
Ceftriaxone sodium		
plus		
Gentamicin sulfate	2	
Vancomycin hydrochloride	4–6	Recommended for patients allergic to β-lactam antibiotics

From Wilson, W. R., Karchmer, A. W., Dajani, A. S., et al.: Antibiotic treatment of adults with infective endocarditis due to streptococci, enterococci, staphylococci, and HACEK microorganisms. J.A.M.A. *274*:1706–1713, 1995. Copyright 1995, American Medical Association.

TABLE 32–11 ■ SUGGESTED THERAPY FOR ENDOCARDITIS CAUSED BY ENTEROCOCCI AND OTHER SELECTED STREPTOCOCCI* IN ADULTS

Antibiotic(s)	Duration (wk)	Comments
Aqueous crystalline penicillin G sodium	4–6	Four-week therapy recommended for patients with symptoms <3 mo in duration. Six-week therapy recommended for patients with symptoms >3 mo in duration
plus		
Gentamicin sulfate	4–6	
Ampicillin sodium	4–6	
plus		
Gentamicin sulfate	4–6	
Vancomycin hydrochloride	6	Recommended for patients allergic to β-lactam antibiotics
plus		
Gentamicin sulfate	6	

*This table is for endocarditis caused by gentamicin- or vancomycin-susceptible enterococci, viridans streptococci with an MIC greater than 0.5 μg/mL, *Abiotrophia* species, or prosthetic-valve endocarditis secondary to viridans streptococci or *Streptococcus bovis*.
MIC, minimal inhibitory concentration.
From Wilson, W. R., Karchmer, A. W., Dajani, A. S., et al.: Antibiotic treatment of adults with infective endocarditis due to streptococci, enterococci, staphylococci, and HACEK microorganisms. J.A.M.A. *274*:1706–1713, 1995. Copyright 1995, American Medical Association.

TABLE 32–12 ■ SUGGESTED THERAPY FOR ENDOCARDITIS CAUSED BY STAPHYLOCOCCI IN THE ABSENCE OF PROSTHETIC MATERIAL IN ADULTS

Antibiotic(s)	Duration	Comments
	Methicillin-Susceptible Staphylococci*	
Nafcillin sodium or oxacillin sodium	6 wk	Benefit of additional aminoglycoside has not been established
optional addition of		
Gentamicin sulfate	3–5 days	
Cefazolin or other first-generation cephalosporin	6 wk	For patients with non-immediate-type hypersensitivity to penicillin
optional addition of		
Gentamicin sulfate	3–5 days	
Vancomycin hydrochloride	6 wk	Recommended for patients allergic to penicillin
	Methicillin-Resistant Staphylococci	
Vancomycin hydrochloride	≥6 wk	
plus		
Rifampin	≥6 wk	
Gentamicin	2 wk	

*If *Staphylococcus* is penicillin-susceptible (minimal inhibitory concentration ≤0.1 μg/mL), aqueous crystalline penicillin G sodium can be used for 6 weeks instead of nafcillin or oxacillin.

Data from Wilson, W. R., Karchmer, A. W., Dajani, A. S., et al.: Antibiotic treatment of adults with infective endocarditis due to streptococci, enterococci, staphylococci, and HACEK microorganisms. J.A.M.A. *274*:1706–1713, 1995; and Ferrieri, P., Gewitz, M. H., Gerber, M. A., et al.: Unique features of endocarditis in children. Pediatrics *109*:931–943, 2002.

Most strains of enterococci have an MIC to penicillin of 0.4 μg/mL or greater and an MBC of 6.25 μg/mL or greater.[297] All β-lactam antibiotics are bacteriostatic against enterococci and cannot be used alone. However, plasmid-mediated β-lactamase production has been found in rare strains of *Enterococcus faecalis*. Ampicillin-sulbactam overcomes the enzyme production and is effective as therapy.[423] Although therapy with penicillin alone is ineffective, the combination of penicillin and an aminoglycoside is synergistic and produces a bactericidal effect on most enterococcal strains.[279] Unfortunately, 20 to 50 percent of enterococcal strains demonstrate very high resistance (MIC >2000 μg/mL) to streptomycin, and synergy between penicillin and streptomycin does not occur.[171, 374] High-level resistance to gentamicin has been found in some isolates, and the incidence is increasing in certain locales.[108, 247, 319] When these isolates are encountered, all aminoglycosides should be tested because the organism may be susceptible to one while resistant to others.[452] Fortunately, these strains rarely cause endocarditis.[297] Although vancomycin-resistant enterococci have emerged as important nosocomial pathogens, they rarely cause endocarditis. Optimal therapy for these strains has not been established, but a combination of high-dose penicillin plus vancomycin and gentamicin may be effective in some cases.[54] Vancomycin-resistant enterococcal endocarditis has been treated successfully with oral linezolid.[11] The usual regimens for enterococcal endocarditis are listed in Table 32–11.

Most isolates of *S. aureus* are resistant to penicillin, but endocarditis caused by penicillin-susceptible (MIC <0.1 μg/mL) isolates can be treated with this agent. In general, a semisynthetic penicillinase-resistant penicillin given for 4 to 6 weeks is the drug of choice[323, 397] (Table 32–12). The addition of gentamicin to nafcillin produces an enhanced bactericidal effect in vitro and in experimental staphylococcal endocarditis in rabbits.[339, 367] However, the value of this combination in patients has not been proved, and generally it is reserved for children with overwhelming infection. In penicillin-allergic patients or in those with methicillin-resistant *S. aureus,* vancomycin alone has been recommended, although treatment failures in children with endocarditis have been reported.[118, 189, 242] The addition of rifampin or the use of β-lactam drugs after desensitization is necessary in some cases.[26, 291] Ciprofloxacin has been used, but treatment failures have occurred because of the emergence of resistance.[295, 420] The combination of vancomycin and rifampin for at least 6 weeks, plus the addition of gentamicin for the first 2 weeks, is recommended for the treatment of endocarditis caused by methicillin-resistant *S. aureus,* although clinical trial data are not available.[128] Nosocomial infections with *S. epidermidis* usually are treated with vancomycin because of the high incidence of methicillin resistance among these isolates. The addition of rifampin and gentamicin to either nafcillin or vancomycin may increase bactericidal activity and is recommended in cases of prosthetic-valve endocarditis secondary to any staphylococci[38, 463] (Table 32–13).

Therapy for endocarditis caused by gram-negative organisms must be individualized in accordance with in vitro susceptibility and synergy studies. Six to 8 weeks of combination therapy with two or more drugs may be required, especially with endocarditis caused by *Klebsiella* or *Pseudomonas*.[129, 322] Surgical intervention frequently is necessary, especially for infection of the mitral or aortic valves. Endocarditis caused by *Haemophilus* and other fastidious gram-negative organisms usually is responsive to ampicillin alone, but the addition of an aminoglycoside may improve the outcome[68, 463] (Table 32–14). Anaerobic bacilli are generally susceptible to penicillin, but infection caused by resistant *Bacteroides fragilis* is treated best by combinations including metronidazole, ticarcillin-clavulanate, or imipenem.

Survival rates of only 10 to 20 percent in patients with fungal endocarditis are related to the poor ability of presently available antifungal agents to sterilize the vegetations. Only rare cures with medical therapy alone have been reported.[366] Most investigators think that early surgical intervention is mandatory in every patient who has conclusive evidence of intracardiac fungal infection.[437, 438] Only 33 cases of successful treatment of fungal prosthetic-valve endocarditis have been reported, even when surgery was performed.[149]

Although a prolonged course of antifungal therapy before surgery does not improve the outcome, chemotherapy should be given in conjunction with operative treatment. The drug of choice is amphotericin B at a dose of 0.5 to 1.0 mg/kg/day. This antibiotic may be either fungistatic or fungicidal, depending on the infecting organism. Even

TABLE 32–13 ■ SUGGESTED THERAPY FOR ENDOCARDITIS CAUSED BY STAPHYLOCOCCI IN THE PRESENCE OF A PROSTHETIC VALVE OR OTHER PROSTHETIC MATERIAL IN ADULTS

Antibiotic(s)	Duration (wk)	Comments
	Methicillin-Susceptible Staphylococci	
Nafcillin sodium or oxacillin sodium	≥6	First-generation cephalosporins or vancomycin should be used in patients allergic to β-lactam antibiotics
plus		
Rifampin	≥6	Rifampin plays a unique role in eradication of staphylococci from prosthetic material
plus		
Gentamicin sulfate	2	
	Methicillin-Resistant Staphylococci	
Vancomycin hydrochloride	≥6	
plus		
Rifampin	≥6	
plus		
Gentamicin sulfate	2	

From Wilson, W. R., Karchmer, A. W., Dajani, A. S., et al.: Antibiotic treatment of adults with infective endocarditis due to streptococci, enterococci, staphylococci, and HACEK microorganisms. J.A.M.A. *274*:1706–1713, 1995. Copyright 1995, American Medical Association.

though the toxicity of amphotericin B appears to be less severe in children than in adults, side effects that may necessitate alterations in the usual regimen may occur and include fever, chills, phlebitis, anemia, hypocalcemia, renal tubular acidosis, nephrotoxicity, and thrombocytopenia. The optimal dosage of amphotericin B is unknown; total doses of 20 to 50 mg/kg commonly are used. 5-Fluorocytosine[277] and rifampin may act synergistically with amphotericin B against many strains of fungi, but their roles in fungal endocarditis are unproven. Fluconazole is less effective than is amphotericin B for the prophylaxis or treatment of experimental *Candida* endocarditis,[465] but it has been used successfully in a few patients.[78, 444]

Treatment of culture-negative endocarditis is problematic.[22] In general, the same criteria used to choose empiric therapy for infective endocarditis can be followed. Antibiotics usually are continued for 6 weeks, and ongoing surveillance for an etiologic agent must be performed. In 52 adults with culture-negative endocarditis, survival correlated with the initial clinical response to antibiotics; most deaths were caused by systemic emboli or congestive heart failure.[326]

Surgery has become a valuable adjunct to medical therapy in the management of infective endocarditis.[25, 315, 325, 332] Several echocardiographic findings are suggestive of a possible need for surgical intervention[25, 128] (Table 32–15). Among the generally accepted indications for surgical intervention during active endocarditis are (1) refractory congestive heart failure,[281, 427, 461] (2) uncontrolled infection,[262] (3) more than one serious embolic episode, (4) fungal endocarditis, (5) most cases of prosthetic-valve endocarditis,[4, 90, 112, 363, 471] and (6) local suppurative complications, including perivalvular or myocardial abscess with conduction system abnormalities.[37, 355, 385, 415, 468] The usual indication for surgical intervention is congestive heart failure in left-sided lesions and persistent infection in right-sided disease. Among children with endocarditis after undergoing previous cardiac surgery, repair or takedown of infected graft material commonly is the reason for surgery.[70, 311] In general, operative mortality is low even if surgery is performed during the active infection.[275, 294, 306] The hemodynamic status of the patient rather than the activity of the infection is the critical factor in determining the timing of cardiac surgery or valve replacement.[209] The aortic valve is the site most often requiring surgical intervention.[334, 431]

TABLE 32–14 ■ SUGGESTED THERAPY FOR ENDOCARDITIS CAUSED BY HACEK ORGANISMS IN ADULTS

Antibiotic(s)	Duration (wk)	Comments
Ceftriaxone sodium	4	Cefotaxime sodium or other third-generation cephalosporins may be substituted
Ampicillin sodium	4	
plus		
Gentamicin sulfate	4	

HACEK, *Haemophilus* species, *Actinobacillus actinomycetemcomitans, Cardiobacterium hominis, Eikenella corrodens, Kingella kingae.*
From Wilson, W. R., Karchmer, A. W., Dajani, A. S., et al.: Antibiotic treatment of adults with infective endocarditis due to streptococci, enterococci, staphylococci, and HACEK microorganisms. J.A.M.A. *274*:1706–1713, 1995. Copyright 1995, American Medical Association.

Prevention

Accepted medical practice is to give prophylactic antibiotics to susceptible patients in an attempt to prevent infective endocarditis.[100, 216, 389] The rationale for such treatment is

TABLE 32–15 ■ ECHOCARDIOGRAPHIC FEATURES SUGGESTING A POSSIBLE NEED FOR SURGICAL INTERVENTION IN ENDOCARDITIS

Vegetation
Persistent vegetation after systemic embolization
  Anterior mitral valve leaflet, particularly >10 mm
  Embolic event during first 2 wk of therapy
  ≥2 embolic events
Increase in vegetation size after 4 wk of therapy

Valvular Dysfunction
Acute aortic or mitral insufficiency with signs of ventricular failure
Heart failure unresponsive to medical therapy
Valve perforation or rupture

Perivalvular Extension
Valvular dehiscence, rupture, or fistula
New heart block
Large abscess or extension of abscess

Data from Bayer, A., Bolger, A., Taubert, K., et al.: Diagnosis and management of infective endocarditis and its complications. Circulation *98*:2936–2948, 1998; and Ferrieri, P., Gewitz, M. H., Gerber, M. A., et al.: Unique features of infective endocarditis in children. Pediatrics *109*:931–943, 2002.

TABLE 32–16 ■ CARDIAC CONDITIONS FOR WHICH ENDOCARDITIS PROPHYLAXIS IS RECOMMENDED

High Risk
Prosthetic cardiac valves, including bioprosthetic and homograft valves
Previous bacterial endocarditis
Complex cyanotic congenital heart disease
Surgically constructed systemic-pulmonary shunts or conduits

Moderate Risk
Most other congenital cardiac malformations (except isolated secundum atrial septal defect or mitral valve prolapse without regurgitation)
Acquired valvular dysfunction
Hypertrophic cardiomyopathy
Mitral valve prolapse with valvular regurgitation and/or thickened leaflets

From Dajani, A. S., Taubert, K. A., Wilson, W., et al.: Prevention of bacterial endocarditis: Recommendations by the American Heart Association. Clin. Infect. Dis. *75*:1448–1458, 1997.

TABLE 32–17 ■ PROCEDURES FOR WHICH ENDOCARDITIS PROPHYLAXIS IS RECOMMENDED

Dental
Extractions and periodontal procedures (surgery, scaling, planing, probing)
Implant placement and reimplantations
Endodontal (root canal) instrumentation
Subgingival placement of antibiotic fibers or strips
Initial placement of orthodontic bands (not brackets)
Intraligamentary local anesthetic injections
Prophylactic cleaning with probable bleeding

Respiratory
Tonsillectomy and/or adenoidectomy
Surgery involving respiratory mucosa
Rigid-scope bronchoscopy

Gastrointestinal Tract
Sclerotherapy for esophageal varices
Esophageal stricture dilation
Endoscopic retrograde cholangiography (biliary obstruction)
Biliary tract surgery
Surgical procedures that involve intestinal mucosa

Genitourinary Tract
Cystoscopy
Urethral dilation
Prostate surgery

From Dajani, A. S., Taubert, K. A., Wilson, W., et al.: Prevention of bacterial endocarditis: Recommendations by the American Heart Association. Clin. Infect. Dis. *75*:1448–1458, 1997.

based on studies indicating that antibiotics can reduce the incidence of bacteremia after various procedures in humans[114] and can prevent experimental endocarditis in animals.[324] However, no controlled trials have documented the efficacy of endocarditis prophylaxis in humans.[441] Prevention of bacterial infection is most likely to be successful and cost-effective when a single antibiotic is directed against a single pathogen and when the disease occurs with high frequency in the absence of prophylaxis. Prevention of endocarditis does not meet these ideals because a variety of drugs are used against a variety of organisms and the disease rarely occurs even if prophylaxis is not given.[100] Less than 10 percent of all endocarditis cases can be attributed to bacteremia caused by previous medical, surgical, or dental procedures.[440] Many cases of prophylaxis failure have been reported,[103] but only 12 percent of such patients received antibiotic regimens recommended by the American Heart Association. For reasons that are not clear, mitral valve prolapse was the condition associated most frequently with prophylaxis failure.

The most common errors in attempted prevention of endocarditis include inadequate medical histories taken by dentists and other health professionals to identify high-risk patients, initiation of prophylactic antibiotics too early, continuation of preventive therapy too long, the use of low-dose antibiotics, lack of prophylaxis for minor dental procedures, and confusion between prevention of rheumatic fever and prevention of infective endocarditis.[163, 169] Several studies have shown that adult patients at risk for development of infective endocarditis often have inadequate knowledge of their cardiac lesion, endocarditis, and the recommended prophylaxis.[61, 442] One recent study demonstrated that the parents of children with heart defects have a low level of knowledge about the importance of good oral health in preventing endocarditis.[89]

The Committee on Rheumatic Fever, Endocarditis and Kawasaki Disease of the Council on Cardiovascular Diseases in the Young of the American Heart Association has published recommendations for bacterial endocarditis prophylaxis.[80] The cardiac conditions and procedures for which endocarditis prophylaxis is indicated are listed in Tables 32–16 and 32–17. The recommended antibiotic regimens are shown in Tables 32–18 and 32–19. The major change in the

TABLE 32–18 ■ PROPHYLACTIC REGIMENS FOR DENTAL, ORAL, RESPIRATORY TRACT, OR ESOPHAGEAL PROCEDURES

Situation	Agent	Regimen
Standard general prophylaxis	Amoxicillin	Adults: 2.0 g; children: 50 mg/kg PO 1 hr before procedure
Unable to take oral medications	Ampicillin	Adults: 2.0 g IM or IV; children: 50 mg/kg IM or IV within 30 min before procedure
Allergic to penicillin	Clindamycin	Adults: 600 mg; children: 20 mg/kg PO 1 hr before procedure
	or	
	Cephalexin or cefadroxil	Adults: 2.0 mg; children: 50 mg/kg PO 1 hr before procedure
	or	
	Azithromycin or clarithromycin	Adults: 500 mg; children: 15 mg/kg PO 1 hr before procedure
Allergic to penicillin and unable to take oral medications	Clindamycin	Adults: 600 mg; children: 20 mg/kg IV within 30 min before procedure
	or	
	Cefazolin	Adults: 1.0 g; children: 25 mg/kg IM or IV within 30 min before procedure

From Dajani, A. S., Taubert, K. A., Wilson, W., et al.: Prevention of bacterial endocarditis: Recommendations by the American Heart Association. Clin. Infect. Dis. *75*:1448–1458, 1997.

TABLE 32–19 ■ PROPHYLACTIC REGIMENS FOR GENITOURINARY OR GASTROINTESTINAL (EXCLUDING ESOPHAGEAL) PROCEDURES

Situation	Agents	Regimen
High-risk patients	Ampicillin plus gentamicin	Adults: ampicillin, 2.0 g IM or IV, plus gentamicin, 1.5 mg/kg (not to exceed 120 mg) within 30 min of starting the procedure; 6 hr later, ampicillin, 1 g IM/IV, or amoxicillin, 1 g PO Children: ampicillin, 50 mg/kg IM or IV (not to exceed 2.0 g), plus gentamicin, 1.5 mg/kg within 30 min of starting the procedure; 6 hr later, ampicillin, 25 mg/kg IM/IV or amoxicillin, 25 mg/kg PO
High-risk patients allergic to ampicillin/amoxicillin	Vancomycin plus gentamicin	Adults: vancomycin, 1.0 g IV over 1–2 hr, plus gentamicin, 1.5 mg/kg IV/IM (not to exceed 120 mg); complete injection/infusion within 30 min of starting the procedure Children: vancomycin, 20 mg/kg IV over 1–2 hr, plus gentamicin, 1.5 mg/kg IV/IM; complete injection/infusion within 30 min of starting the procedure
Moderate-risk patients	Amoxicillin or ampicillin	Adults: amoxicillin, 2.0 g PO 1 hr before procedure, or ampicillin, 2.0 g IM/IV within 30 min of starting the procedure Children: amoxicillin, 50 mg/kg PO 1 hr before procedure, or ampicillin, 50 mg/kg IM/IV within 30 min of starting the procedure
Moderate-risk patients allergic to ampicillin/amoxicillin	Vancomycin	Adults: vancomycin, 1.0 g IV over 1–2 hr: complete infusion within 30 min of starting the procedure Children: vancomycin, 20 mg/kg IV over 1–2 hr; complete infusion within 30 min of starting the procedure

From Dajani, A. S., Taubert, K. A., Wilson, W., et al.: Prevention of bacterial endocarditis: Recommendations by the American Heart Association. Clin. Infect. Dis. *75*:1448–1458, 1997.

most recent recommendations is the suggested use of amoxicillin—instead of penicillin V—for standard oral prophylaxis. Amoxicillin is recommended because it is absorbed better from the gastrointestinal tract and provides higher and more sustained serum levels. Endocarditis prophylaxis also is recommended for patients with indwelling transvenous cardiac pacemakers, ventriculoatrial shunts for hydrocephalus, and arteriovenous shunts for renal dialysis.

Although immunization against bacteria that commonly cause endocarditis (such as viridans streptococci) has been proposed, this approach remains a theoretic possibility.[14]

REFERENCES

1. Agarwala, B. N.: Group B streptococcal endocarditis in a neonate. Pediatr. Cardiol. *9*:51–53, 1988.
2. Al-Hajjar, S., Qadri, S. M. H., Al-Sabban, E., and Jager, C.: *Coxiella burnetii* endocarditis in a child. Pediatr. Infect. Dis. J. *16*:911–912, 1997.
3. Alpert, J. S., Krous, H. F., Dalen, J. E., et al.: Pathogenesis of Osler's nodes. Ann. Intern. Med. *85*:471–476, 1976.
4. Alsip, S. G., Blackstone, E. H., Kirklin, J. W., et al.: Indications for cardiac surgery in patients with infective endocarditis. Am. J. Med. *78*:138–142, 1985.
5. Aly, A. M., Simpson, P. M., and Humes, R. A.: The role of transthoracic echocardiography in the diagnosis of infective endocarditis in children. Arch. Pediatr. Adolesc. Med. *153*:950–954, 1999.
6. Anderson, A. W., and Cruickshank, J. G.: Endocarditis due to viridans-type streptococci tolerant to beta-lactam antibiotics: Therapeutic problems. B. M. J. *285*:85, 1982.
7. Andrews, M. M., and von Reyn, C. F.: Patient selection criteria and management guidelines for outpatient parenteral antibiotic therapy for native valve infective endocarditis. Clin. Infect. Dis. *33*:203–209, 2001.
8. Anolik, R., Berkowitz, R. J., Campos, J. M., et al.: *Actinobacillus* endocarditis associated with periodontal disease. Clin. Pediatr. (Phila.) *20*:633–655, 1981.
9. Arber, N., Militano, A., Ben-Yehuda, A., et al.: Native valve *Staphylococcus epidermidis* endocarditis: Report of seven cases and review of the literature. Am. J. Med. *90*:758, 1991.
10. Arber, N., Pras, E., Copperman, Y., et al.: Pacemaker endocarditis: Report of 44 cases and review of the literature. Medicine (Baltimore) *73*:299–305, 1994.
11. Babcock, H. M., Ritchie, D. J., Christiansen, E., et al.: Successful treatment of vancomycin-resistant *Enterococcus* endocarditis with oral linezolid. Clin. Infect. Dis. *32*:1373–1375, 2001.
12. Backes, R. J., Wilson, W. R., and Geraci, J. E.: Group B streptococcal infective endocarditis. Arch. Intern. Med. *145*:693–696, 1985.
13. Baddour, L. M.: Infective endocarditis caused by β-hemolytic streptococci. The Infectious Diseases Society of America's Emerging Infections Network. Clin. Infect. Dis. *26*:66–71, 1998.
14. Baddour, L. M.: Immunization for prevention of infective endocarditis. Curr. Infect. Dis. Rep. *1*:126–128, 1999.
15. Baddour, L. M., and Bisno, A. L.: Infective endocarditis complicating mitral valve prolapse: Epidemiologic, clinical and microbiological aspects. Rev. Infect. Dis. *8*:117–137, 1986.
16. Baddour, L. M., Christensen, G. D., Lowrance, J. H., et al.: Pathogenesis of experimental endocarditis. Rev. Infect. Dis. *11*:452–463, 1989.
17. Baddour, L. M., Lowrance, C., Albus, A., et al.: *Staphylococcus aureus* microcapsule expression attenuates bacterial virulence in a rat model of experimental endocarditis. J. Infect. Dis. *165*:749–753, 1992.
18. Baddour, L. M., Meyer, J., and Henry, B.: Polymicrobial infective endocarditis in the 1980's. Rev. Infect. Dis. *13*:963–970, 1991.
19. Baddour, L. M., Phillips, T. N., and Bisno, A. L.: Coagulase-negative staphylococcal endocarditis: Occurrence in patients with mitral valve prolapse. Arch. Intern. Med. *146*:119–121, 1986.
20. Baltimore, R. S.: Infective endocarditis in children. Pediatr. Infect. Dis. J. *11*:907–912, 1992.
21. Baorto, E., Payne, M., Slater, L., et al.: Culture-negative endocarditis caused by *Bartonella henselae*. J. Pediatr. *132*:1051–1054, 1998.
22. Barnes, P. D., and Crook, D. W. M.: Culture negative endocarditis. J. Infect. *35*:209–213, 1997.
23. Barst, R. J., Prince, A. S., and Neu, H. C.: *Aspergillus* endocarditis: Case report and review of the literature. Pediatrics *68*:73–78, 1981.
24. Barst, R. J., Prince, A. S., and Neu, H. C.: Echocardiography in *Aspergillus* endocarditis. Pediatrics *69*:252–253, 1982.
25. Bayer, A., Bolger, A., Taubert, K., et al.: Diagnosis and management of infective endocarditis and its complications. Circulation *98*:2936–2948, 1998.
26. Bayer, A. S.: Infective endocarditis. Clin. Infect. Dis. *17*:313–332, 1993.
27. Bayer, A. S., Chow, A. W., and Guze, L. B.: *Listeria monocytogenes* endocarditis: Report of a case and review of the literature. Am. J. Med. Sci. *273*:319–323, 1977.
28. Bayer, A. S., Nelson, R. J., and Slama, T. G.: Current concepts in prevention of prosthetic valve endocarditis. Chest *97*:1203–1207, 1990.
29. Bayer, A. S., and Theofilopoulos, A. N.: Immunopathogenetic aspects of infective endocarditis. Chest *97*:204–212, 1990.
30. Bayer, A. S., Theofilopoulos, A. N., Dixon, F. J., et al.: Circulating immune complexes in experimental streptococcal endocarditis: A monitor of therapeutic efficacy. J. Infect. Dis. *139*:1–8, 1979.
31. Bayer, A. S., Theofilopoulos, A. N., Eisenberg, R., et al.: Circulating immune complexes in infective endocarditis. N. Engl. J. Med. *295*:1500–1505, 1976.
32. Beeson, P. B., Brannon, E. S., and Warren, J. V.: Observations on the sites of removal of bacteria from the blood in patients with bacterial endocarditis. J. Exp. Med. *81*:9–23, 1945.
33. Berkowitz, F. E., and Dansky, R.: Infective endocarditis in black South African children: Report of 10 cases with some unusual features. Pediatr. Infect. Dis. J. *8*:787–791, 1989.

34. Bertorini, T. E., Laster, R. E., Thompson, B. F., et al.: Magnetic resonance imaging of the brain in bacterial endocarditis. Arch. Intern. Med. *149*:815–817, 1989.
35. Bieger, R. C., Brewer, N. S., and Washington, J. A.: *Haemophilus aphrophilus*: A microbiological and clinical review and report of 42 cases. Medicine (Baltimore) *57*:345–355, 1978.
36. Biller, J., Challa, V. R., Toole, J. F., et al.: Nonbacterial thrombotic endocarditis: A neurologic perspective of clinicopathologic correlations of 99 patients. Arch. Neurol. *39*:95–98, 1982.
37. Bishara, J., Leibovici, L., Gartman-Israel, D., et al.: Long-term outcome of infective endocarditis: The impact of early surgical intervention. Clin. Infect. Dis. *33*:1636–1643, 2001.
38. Bisno, A. L., Dismukes, W. E., Durack, D. T., et al.: Antimicrobial treatment of infective endocarditis due to viridans streptococci, enterococci and staphylococci. J. A. M. A. *261*:1471–1477, 1989.
39. Blair, D. C., and Martin, D. B.: Beta hemolytic streptococcal endocarditis: Predominance of non–group A organisms. Am. J. Med. Sci. *276*:269–277, 1978.
40. Blieden, L. C., Morehead, R. R., Burke, B., et al.: Bacterial endocarditis in the neonate. Am. J. Dis. Child. *124*:747–749, 1972.
41. Blumberg, E. A., Karlis, D. A., Chandrasekaran, K., et al.: Endocarditis-associated paravalvular abscesses. Chest *107*:898–903, 1995.
42. Blumberg, E. A., Robbins, N., Adimora, A., et al.: Persistent fever in association with infective endocarditis. Clin. Infect. Dis. *15*:983–990, 1992.
43. Blumenthal, S., Griffiths, S. P., and Morgan, B. C.: Bacterial endocarditis in children with heart disease: A review based on the literature and experience with 58 cases. Pediatrics *26*:993–1017, 1960.
44. Bodey, G. P., and Luna, M.: Skin lesions associated with disseminated candidiasis. J. A. M. A. *229*:1466–1468, 1974.
45. Bricker, J., Latson, L., Huhta, J., et al.: Echocardiographic evaluation of infective endocarditis in children. Clin. Pediatr. (Phila.) *24*:312–319, 1985.
46. Brodie, E., Adler, J. L., and Daly, A. K.: Bacterial endocarditis due to an unusual species of encapsulated *Neisseria*. Am. J. Dis. Child. *122*:433–437, 1972.
47. Brouqui, P., Dumler, J. S., and Raoult, D.: Immunohistologic demonstration of *Coxiella burnetii* in the valves of patients with Q fever endocarditis. Am. J. Med. *97*:451–458, 1994.
48. Brouqui, P., and Raoult, D.: Endocarditis due to rare and fastidious bacteria. Clin. Microbiol. Rev. *14*:177–207, 2001.
49. Bruyn, G. A. W., Thompson, J., and Van Der Meer, J. W. M.: Pneumococcal endocarditis in adult patients: A report of five cases and review of the literature. Q. J. Med. *74*:33–40, 1990.
50. Calderwood, S., Swinski, L., Waternaux, C., et al.: Risk factors for the development of prosthetic valve endocarditis. Circulation *72*:31–37, 1985.
51. Caldwell, R. L., Hurwitz, R. A., and Girod, D. A.: Subacute bacterial endocarditis in children. Am. J. Dis. Child. *122*:312–315, 1971.
52. Canter, M. C., and Hart, R. G.: Neurologic complications of infective endocarditis. Neurology *41*:1015, 1991.
53. Carey, R. B., Gross, K. C., and Roberts, R. B.: Vitamin B_6–dependent *Streptococcus mitior (mitis)* isolated from patients with systemic infections. J. Infect. Dis. *131*:722–725, 1975.
54. Caron, F., Carbon, C., and Gutmann, L.: Triple-combination penicillin-vancomycin-gentamicin for experimental endocarditis caused by a moderately penicillin- and highly glycopeptide-resistant isolate of *Enterococcus faecium*. J. Infect. Dis. *164*:888–893, 1991.
55. Carpenter, J. L.: Perivalvular extension of infection in patients with infectious endocarditis. Rev. Infect. Dis. *13*:127–138, 1991.
56. Carr, P., Wright, M., and Handler, L. C.: Endocarditis-related cerebral aneurysms: Radiologic changes with treatment. A. J. N. R. Am. J. Neuroradiol. *16*:745, 1995.
57. Carrizosa, J., and Kaye, D.: Antibiotic concentrations in serum, serum bactericidal activity, and results of therapy of streptococcal endocarditis in rabbits. Antimicrob. Agents Chemother. *12*:479–483, 1977.
58. Carruthers, M.: Endocarditis due to enteric bacilli other than salmonellae: Case reports and literature review. Am. J. Med. Sci. *273*:203, 1977.
59. Carvajal, A., and Frederiksen, W.: Fatal endocarditis due to *Listeria monocytogenes*. Rev. Infect. Dis. *10*:616–623, 1988.
60. Cassling, R. S., Rogler, W. C., and McManus, B. M.: Isolated pulmonic valve infective endocarditis: A diagnostically elusive entity. Am. Heart J. *109*:558–567, 1985.
61. Cetta, F., and Warnes, C. A.: Adults with congenital heart disease: Patient knowledge of endocarditis prophylaxis. Mayo Clin. Proc. *70*:50–54, 1995.
62. Chambers, H. F., Korzeniowski, O. M., Sande, M. A., et al.: *Staphylococcus aureus* endocarditis: Clinical manifestation in addicts and nonaddicts. Medicine (Baltimore) *62*:170–174, 1983.
63. Chambers, H. F., Miller, R. T., and Newman, M. D.: Right-sided *Staphylococcus aureus* endocarditis in intravenous drug abusers: Two-week combination therapy. Ann. Intern. Med. *109*:619–624, 1988.
64. Chang, H.-H., Lu, C.-Y., Hsueh, P.-R., et al.: Endocarditis caused by *Abiotrophia defectiva* in children. Pediatr. Infect. Dis. J. *21*:697–700, 2002.
65. Channer, K. S., Joffe, H. S., and Jordan, S. C.: Presentation of infective endocarditis in childhood and adolescence. J. R. Coll. Physicians Lond. *23*:152–155, 1989.
66. Charney, R., Keltz, T. N., Attai, L., et al.: Acute valvular obstruction from streptococcal endocarditis. Am. Heart J. *125*:544, 1993.
67. Chen, M.-R.: Infective endocarditis in hypertrophic obstructive cardiomyopathy. J. Clin. Ultrasound *20*:612–614, 1992.
68. Chunn, C. J., Jones, S. R., McCutchan, J. A., et al.: *Haemophilus parainfluenzae* infective endocarditis. Medicine (Baltimore) *56*:99–113, 1977.
69. Churchill, M. A., Geraci, J. E., and Hunder, G. G.: Musculoskeletal manifestations of bacterial endocarditis. Ann. Intern. Med. *87*:754–759, 1977.
70. Citak, M., Rees, A., and Mavroudis, C.: Surgical management of infective endocarditis in children. Ann. Thorac. Surg. *54*:755–758, 1992.
71. Clawson, C. C., Rao Gunda, H. R., and White, J. G.: Platelet interaction with bacteria. IV. Stimulation of the release reaction. Am. J. Pathol. *81*:411–417, 1975.
72. Clemens, J. O., Horwitz, R. I., Jaffee, C. C., et al.: A controlled evaluation of the risk of bacterial endocarditis in persons with mitral-valve prolapse. N. Engl. J. Med. *307*:776–781, 1982.
73. Cofsky, R. D., and Seligman, S. J.: *Peptococcus magnus* endocarditis. South. Med. J. *78*:361–362, 1985.
74. Coleman, D. L., Horwitz, R. I., and Andriole, V. T.: Association between serum inhibitory and bactericidal concentrations and therapeutic outcome in bacterial endocarditis. Am. J. Med. *73*:260–267, 1982.
75. Corrigan, D., Bolen, J., Hancock, E. W., et al.: Mitral valve prolapse and endocarditis. Am. J. Med. *63*:315–318, 1977.
76. Cremieux, A.-C., and Carbon, C.: Pharmacokinetics and pharmacodynamic requirements for antibiotic therapy of experimental endocarditis. Antimicrob. Agents Chemother. *36*:2069–2074, 1992.
77. Cutler, J. G., Ongley, P. A., Schwachman, H., et al.: Bacterial endocarditis in children with heart disease. Pediatrics *22*:706–714, 1958.
78. Czwerwiec, F. S., Bilsker, M. S., Kamerman, M. L., et al.: Long-term survival after fluconazole therapy of candidal prosthetic valve endocarditis. Am. J. Med. *94*:545–546, 1993.
79. Daher, A. H., and Berkowitz, F. E.: Infective endocarditis in neonates. Clin. Pediatr. (Phila.) *20*:198–206, 1995.
80. Dajani, A. S., Taubert, K. A., Wilson, W., et al.: Prevention of bacterial endocarditis: Recommendations by the American Heart Association. Clin. Infect. Dis. *75*:1448–1458, 1997.
81. Danchin, N., Voiriot, P., Briancon, S., et al.: Mitral valve prolapse as a risk factor for infective endocarditis. Lancet *1*:743–745, 1989.
82. Danford, D. A., Kugler, J. D., Cheatham, J. P., et al.: *Hemophilus influenzae* endocarditis: Successful treatment with ampicillin and early valve replacement. Neb. Med. J. *38*:88–91, 1984.
83. Daniel, W. G., Erbel, R., Kasper, W., et al.: Safety of transesophageal echocardiography: A multicenter survey of 10,419 examinations. Circulation *83*:817–821, 1991.
84. Daniel, W. G., Mugge, A., Grote, J., et al.: Evaluation of endocarditis and its complications by biplane and multiplane transesophageal echocardiography. Am. J. Card. Imaging *9*:100–105, 1995.
85. Daniel, W. G., Mugge, A., Martin, R. P., et al.: Improvement in the diagnosis of abscesses associated with endocarditis by transesophageal echocardiography. N. Engl. J. Med. *324*:795–800, 1991.
86. Dankert, J., Krijgsveld, J., van der Werff, J., et al.: Platelet microbicidal activity is an important defense factor against viridans streptococcal endocarditis. J. Infect. Dis. *184*:597–605, 2001.
87. Das, M., Badley, A. D., Cockerill, F. R., et al.: Infective endocarditis caused by HACEK microorganisms. Annu. Rev. Med. *48*:25–33, 1997.
88. Das, I., De Giovanni, J. V., and Gray, J.: Endocarditis caused by *Haemophilus parainfluenzae* identified by 16 S ribosomal RNA sequencing. J. Clin. Pathol. *50*:72–74, 1997.
89. da Silva, D. B., Sovza, I. P., and Cunha, M. C.: Knowledge, attitudes and status of oral health in children at risk for infective endocarditis. Int. J. Pediatr. Dent. *12*:124–131, 2002.
90. David, T. E.: The surgical treatment of patients with prosthetic valve endocarditis. Semin. Thorac. Cardiovasc. Surg. *7*:47–53, 1995.
91. Davidson, S., Rotem, Y., Bogkowski, B., et al.: *Corynebacterium diphtheriae* endocarditis. Am. J. Med. Sci. *271*:351–353, 1976.
92. Del Pont, J. M., DeCicco, L. T., Vartalitis, C., et al.: Infective endocarditis in children: Clinical analyses and evaluation of two diagnostic criteria. Pediatr. Infect. Dis. J. *14*:1079–1086, 1995.
93. Delvecchio, G., Fracasetti, O., and Lorenzi, N.: *Brucella* endocarditis. Int. J. Cardiol. *33*:328–329, 1991.
94. Dillon, T., Meyer, R. A., Korfhagen, J. C., et al.: Management of infective endocarditis using echocardiography. J. Pediatr. *96*:552–558, 1980.
95. DiNubile, M. J.: Treatment of endocarditis caused by relatively resistant nonenterococcal streptococci: Is penicillin enough? Rev. Infect. Dis. *12*:112–117, 1990.
96. DiNubile, M. J., Calderwood, S. B., Steinhaus, D. M., et al.: Cardiac conduction abnormalities complicating native valve active infective endocarditis. Am. J. Cardiol. *58*:1213–1217, 1986.
97. Douglas, A., Moore-Gillon, J., and Eykyn, S.: Fever during treatment of infective endocarditis. Lancet *1*:1341–1343, 1986.

98. Downing, G. J., and Spirazza, C.: Group C beta-hemolytic streptococcal endocarditis. Pediatr. Infect. Dis. J. *5*:703–704, 1986.
99. Drancourt, M., Mainardi, J. L., Brouqui, P., et al.: *Bartonella (Rochalimaea) quintana* endocarditis in three homeless men. N. Engl. J. Med. *332*:419–423, 1995.
100. Durack, D. T.: Prevention of infective endocarditis. N. Engl. J. Med. *332*:38–44, 1995.
101. Durack, D. T., and Beeson, P. B.: Protective role of complement in experimental *Escherichia coli* endocarditis. Infect. Immun. *16*:213–214, 1977.
102. Durack, D. T., Beeson, P. B., and Petersdorf, R. G.: Experimental bacterial endocarditis. III. Production and progress of the disease in rabbits. Br. J. Exp. Pathol. *54*:142–151, 1973.
103. Durack, D. T., Kaplan, E. L., and Bisno, A. L.: Apparent failure of endocarditis prophylaxis: Analysis of 52 cases submitted to a national registry. J. A. M. A. *250*:2318–2322, 1983.
104. Durack, D. T., Lukes, A. S., Bright, D. K., et al.: New criteria for diagnosis of infective endocarditis: Utilization of specific echocardiographic findings. Am. J. Med. *96*:200–209, 1994.
105. Durack, D. T., Pelletier, L. L., and Petersdorf, R. G.: Chemotherapy of experimental streptococcal endocarditis. II. Synergism between penicillin and streptomycin against penicillin-sensitive streptococci. J. Clin. Invest. *53*:829–836, 1974.
106. Durack, D. T., and Petersdorf, R. G.: Changes in the epidemiology of endocarditis. *In* Kaplan, E. L., and Taranta, A. V. (eds.): Infective Endocarditis: An American Heart Association Symposium. Dallas, American Heart Association, 1977, p. 3.
107. Edwards, K., Hruby, N., and Christy, C.: Pneumococcal endocarditis in infants and children: Report of a case and review of the literature. Pediatr. Infect. Dis. J. *9*:652–657, 1990.
108. Eliopoulos, G. M., Thauvin-Eliopoulos, C., and Moellering, R. C., Jr.: Contribution of animal models in the search for effective therapy for endocarditis due to enterococci with high-level resistance to gentamicin. Clin. Infect. Dis. *15*:58–62, 1992.
109. Ellis, M. E., Al-Abdely, H., Sandridge, A., et al.: Fungal endocarditis: Evidence in the world literature, 1965–1995. Clin. Infect. Dis. *32*:50–62, 2001.
110. Elward, K., Hruby, N., and Christy, C.: Pneumococcal endocarditis in infants and children: Report of a case and review of the literature. Pediatr. Infect. Dis. J. *9*:652–657, 1990.
111. Enzler, M. J., Rouse, M. S., Henry, N. K., et al.: In vitro and in vivo studies of streptomycin-resistant, penicillin-susceptible streptococci from patients with infective endocarditis. J. Infect. Dis. *155*:954–958, 1987.
112. Ergin, M. A.: Surgical techniques in prosthetic valve endocarditis. Semin. Thorac. Cardiovasc. Surg. 7:54–56, 1995.
113. Esperson, F., and Frimodt-Moller, N.: *Staphylococcus aureus* endocarditis: A review of 119 cases. Arch. Intern. Med. *146*:1118–1121, 1986.
114. Everett, E. D., and Hirschmann, J. U.: Transient bacteremia and endocarditis prophylaxis: A review. Medicine (Baltimore) *56*:61–77, 1977.
115. Fang, G., Keys, T. F., Gentry, L. O., et al: Prosthetic valve endocarditis resulting from nosocomial bacteremia. Ann. Intern. Med. *119*:560, 1993.
116. Farmaki, E., Roilides, E., Darilis, E., et al.: *Gemella morbillorum* endocarditis in a child. Pediatr. Infect. Dis. J. *19*:751–753, 2000.
117. Farrior, J. B., and Silverman, M. E.: A consideration of the differences between a Janeway lesion and an Osler's node in infectious endocarditis. Chest *70*:239–243, 1976.
118. Faville, R. J., Zaska, D. E., Kaplan, E. L., et al.: *Staphylococcus aureus* endocarditis: Combined therapy with vancomycin and rifampin. J. A. M. A. *240*:1963–1965, 1978.
119. Feder, H. M., Chameides, L., and Diana, D. J.: Bacterial endocarditis complicated by myocardial infarction in a pediatric patient. J. A. M. A. *247*:1315–1316, 1982.
120. Feder, H. M., Olsen, N., McLaughlin, J. C., et al.: Bacterial endocarditis caused by vitamin B_6-dependent viridans group *Streptococcus*. Pediatrics *66*:309–312, 1980.
121. Felius, A., Fleer, A., and Mouloert, A.: *Actinobacillus actinomycetemcomitans* endocarditis in a child with a prosthetic heart valve. Infection *12*:260–261, 1984.
122. Felmer, J. M., and Dowell, V. R.: Anaerobic bacterial endocarditis. N. Engl. J. Med. *283*:1188–1192, 1970.
123. Fenollar, F., Lepidi, H., and Raoult, D.: Whipple's endocarditis: Review of the literature and comparisons with Q fever, *Bartonella* infection and blood culture–positive endocarditis. Clin. Infect. Dis. *33*:1309–1316, 2001.
124. Fernandez, G. C., Chapman, A. J., Bolli, R., et al.: Gonococcal endocarditis: A case series demonstrating modern presentation of an old disease. Am. Heart J. *108*:1326–1334, 1984.
125. Fernandez-Guerrero, M. L., Torres-Perea, R., Gomez-Rodrigo, J., et al.: Infectious endocarditis due to non-*typhi Salmonella* in patients infected with human immunodeficiency virus: Report of two cases and review. Clin. Infect. Dis. *22*:853–855, 1996.
126. Fernandez-Guerrero, M. L., Verdejo, C., Azofra, J., et al.: Hospital-acquired infectious endocarditis not associated with cardiac surgery: An emerging problem. Clin. Infect. Dis. *20*:16–23, 1995.
127. Fernicola, D. J., and Roberts, W. C.: Clinicopathologic features of active infective endocarditis isolated to the native mitral valve. Am. J. Cardiol. *71*:1186–1197, 1993.
128. Ferrieri, P., Gewitz, M. H., Gerber, M. A., et al.: Unique features of infective endocarditis in children. Pediatrics *109*:931–943, 2002.
129. Fichtenbaum, C. H., and Smith, M. J.: Treatment of endocarditis due to *Pseudomonas aeruginosa* with imipenem. Clin. Infect. Dis. *14*:353–354, 1992.
130. Fisher, R. G., Moodie, D. S., and Rice, R.: Pediatric bacterial endocarditis: Long-term follow-up. Cleve. Clin. Q. *52*:41–45, 1985.
131. Fournier, P. E., Lelievre, H., Eykyn, S. J., et al.: Epidemiologic and clinical characteristics of *Bartonella henselae* endocarditis: A study of 48 patients. Medicine (Baltimore) *80*:245–251, 2001.
132. Fournier, P. E., and Raoult, D.: Non-culture laboratory methods for the diagnosis of infectious endocarditis. Curr. Infect. Dis. Rep. *1*:136–141, 1999.
133. Fowler, V. G., Jr., Sanders, L. C., Kong, L. K., et al.: Infective endocarditis due to *Staphylococcus aureus*: 59 prospectively identified cases with follow-up. Clin. Infect. Dis. *28*:106–114, 1999.
134. Francioli, P., Etienne, J., Hoigue, R., et al.: Treatment of streptococcal endocarditis with a single daily dose of ceftriaxone sodium for 4 weeks: Efficacy and outpatient treatment feasibility. J. A. M. A. *267*:264–267, 1992.
135. Francioli, P., Ruch, W., Stamboulian, D., et al.: Treatment of streptococcal endocarditis with a single daily dose of ceftriaxone and netilmicin for 14 days: A prospective multicenter study. Clin. Infect. Dis. *21*:1406–1410, 1995.
136. Frontera, J. A., and Graclon, J. D.: Right-side endocarditis in injection drug users: Review of proposed mechanisms of pathogenesis. Clin. Infect. Dis. *30*:374–379, 2000.
137. Fukushige, J., Igarashi, H., and Veda, K.: Spectrum of infective endocarditis during infancy and childhood: 20-year review. Pediatr. Cardiol. *15*:127–131, 1994.
138. Galil, K., Thurer, R., Glatter, K., et al.: Disseminated *Mycobacterium chelonae* infection resulting in endocarditis. Clin. Infect. Dis. *23*:1322–1323, 1996.
139. Gallagher, P. G., and Watanakunakorn, C.: Group B streptococcal endocarditis: Report of seven cases and review of the literature. Rev. Infect. Dis. *8*:175–188, 1986.
140. Garty, B., Berant, M., Weinhouse, E., et al.: False aneurysm of the right ventricle due to endocarditis in a child. Pediatr. Cardiol. *8*:275–277, 1987.
141. Gauduchon, V., Benito, Y., Celard, M., et al.: Molecular diagnosis of recurrent *Streptococcus mutans* endocarditis by PCR amplification and sequencing. Clin. Microbiol. Infect. 7:36–37, 2001.
142. Gelfand, M. S., and Threlkeld, M. G.: Subacute bacterial endocarditis secondary to *Streptococcus pneumoniae*. Am. J. Med. *93*:91, 1992.
143. Gelfman, R., and Levine, S. A.: The incidence of acute and subacute bacterial endocarditis in congenital heart disease. Am. J. Med. Sci. *204*:324–333, 1942.
144. Geraci, J. E., and Wilson, W. R.: Endocarditis due to gram-negative bacteria. Mayo Clin. Proc. *57*:145–148, 1982.
145. Gersony, W. M., and Hayes, C. J.: Bacterial endocarditis in patients with pulmonary stenosis, aortic stenosis or ventricular septal defect. Circulation *56*:84–89, 1977.
146. Gersony, W. M., Hayes, C. J., Driscoll, D. J., et al.: Bacterial endocarditis in patients with aortic stenosis, pulmonary stenosis, or ventricular septal defect. Circulation *87*(Suppl. 1):121–126, 1993.
147. Geva, T., and Frand, M.: Infective endocarditis in children with congenital heart disease: The changing spectrum, 1965–85. Eur. Heart J. *9*:1244–1249, 1988.
148. Ghann, J. W., and Dismukes, W. E.: Prosthetic valve endocarditis: An overview. Kardiovaskulare Erkrankungan *8*:320–331, 1983.
149. Gilbert, H. M., Peters, E. D., Lang, S. J., et al.: Successful treatment of fungal prosthetic valve endocarditis: Case report and review. Clin. Infect. Dis. *22*:348–354, 1996.
150. Gil-Grande, R., Aguado, J. M., Pastor, C., et al.: Conventional viral cultures and shell vial assay for diagnosis of apparently culture-negative *Coxiella burnetii* endocarditis. Eur. J. Clin. Microbiol. Infect. Dis. *14*:64–67, 1995.
151. Glauser, M. P., Bernard, J. P., Moreillon, P., et al.: Successful single-dose amoxicillin prophylaxis against experimental streptococcal endocarditis: Evidence for two mechanisms of protection. J. Infect. Dis. *147*:568–575, 1983.
152. Goessler, M. C., Riggs, T. W., DeLeon, S., et al.: Echocardiographic diagnosis of tricuspid valve endocarditis in a child with a normal heart. Pediatr. Cardiol. *2*:141–143, 1982.
153. Goldberg, P., Shulman, S. T., and Yogev, R.: Group C streptococcal endocarditis. Pediatrics *75*:114–116, 1985.
154. Goldenberg, D., Kunzli, A., Vogt, P., et al.: Molecular diagnosis of bacterial endocarditis by broad-range PCR amplification and direct sequencing. J. Clin. Microbiol. *35*:2733–2739, 1997.
155. Gorby, G. L., and Peacock, J. E.: *Erysipelothrix rhusiopathiae* endocarditis: Microbiologic, epidemiologic and clinical features of an occupational disease. Rev. Infect. Dis. *10*:317–325, 1988.

156. Gould, K., Ramirez-Ronda, C. H., Holmes, R. K., et al.: Adherence of bacteria to heart valves in vitro. J. Clin. Invest. *56*:1364–1370, 1975.
157. Gradon, J. D., Chapnick, E. K., and Lutwick, L. I.: Infective endocarditis of a native valve due to *Acinetobacter*: Case report and review. Clin. Infect. Dis. *14*:1145–1148, 1992.
158. Gransden, W. R., Eykyn, S. J., and Leach, R. M.: Neurologic presentations of native valve endocarditis. Q. J. Med. *73*:1135–1142, 1989.
159. Griffiths, J. K., Daly, J. S., and Dodge, R. A.: Two cases of endocarditis due to *Lactobacillus* species: Antimicrobial susceptibility, review and discussion of therapy. Clin. Infect. Dis. *15*:250–255, 1992.
160. Guard, R. W.: Non-toxigenic *Corynebacterium diphtheriae* causing subacute bacterial endocarditis: Case report. Pathology *11*:533–535, 1979.
161. Gutman, R. A., Striker, G. E., Gilliland, B. C., et al.: The immune complex glomerulonephritis of bacterial endocarditis. Medicine (Baltimore) *51*:1–5, 1972.
162. Hall, B., and Dowling, H. F.: Negative blood cultures in bacterial endocarditis: A decade's experience. Med. Clin. North Am. *50*:159–170, 1966.
163. Hall, G., Heimdahl, A., and Nord, C. E.: Bacteremia after oral surgery and antibiotic prophylaxis for endocarditis. Clin. Infect. Dis. *29*:1–10, 1999.
164. Hall, L. H., and Herndon, B. L.: Association of cell adherent glycocalyx and endocarditis production by viridans group streptococci. J. Clin. Microbiol. *28*:1698–1700, 1990.
165. Hamoudi, A. C., Hriban, M. M., Marcon, M. J., et al.: Clinical relevance of viridans and nonhemolytic streptococci isolated from blood and cerebrospinal fluid in a pediatric population. Am. J. Clin. Pathol. *93*:270, 1990.
166. Hampton, J. R., and Harrison, M. J.: Sterile blood cultures in bacterial endocarditis. Q. J. Med. *36*:167–174, 1967.
167. Hart, R. G., Foster, J. W., Luther, M. F., et al.: Stroke in infective endocarditis. Stroke *21*:695–700, 1990.
168. Hayek, L. J. H. E.: *Erysipelothrix* endocarditis affecting a porcine xenograft heart valve. J. Infect. *27*:203, 1993.
169. Hayes, P. A., and Fasules, J.: Dental screening of pediatric cardiac surgical patients. A. S. D. C. J. Dent. Child. *68*:255–258, 2001.
170. Heiddal, S., Sverrisson, J. T., Ynguason, E. E., et al.: Native-valve endocarditis due to *Neisseria sicca*: Case report and review. Clin. Infect. Dis. *16*:667–670, 1993.
171. Hellinger, W. C., Rouse, M. S., Robadan, P. M., et al.: Continuous intravenous versus intermittent ampicillin therapy of experimental endocarditis caused by aminoglycoside-resistant enterococci. Antimicrob. Agents Chemother. *36*:1272–1275, 1992.
172. Herbert, M. A., Milford, D. V., Silove, E. D., et al.: Secondary amyloidosis from long-standing bacterial endocarditis. Pediatr. Nephrol. *9*:33–35, 1995.
173. Herzberg, M. C., Brintzenhote, K. C., and Clawson, C. C.: Aggregation of human platelets and adhesion of *Streptococcus sanguis*. Infect. Immun. *39*:1457–1469, 1983.
174. Herzberg, M. C., MacFarlane, G. D., Gong, K., et al.: The platelet interactivity phenotype of *Streptococcus sanguis* influences the course of experimental endocarditis. Infect. Immun. *60*:4809–4818, 1992.
175. Hickey, A. J., MacMahon, S. W., and Wilcken, D. E. L.: Mitral valve prolapse and bacterial endocarditis: When is antibiotic prophylaxis necessary? Am. Heart J. *109*:431–435, 1985.
176. Hoen, B., Selton-Suty, C., Danchin, N., et al.: Evaluation of the Duke criteria versus the Beth Israel criteria for the diagnosis of infective endocarditis. Clin. Infect. Dis. *21*:905, 1995.
177. Hoen, B., Selton-Suty, C., Lacassin, F., et al.: Infective endocarditis in patients with negative blood cultures: Analysis of 88 cases from a one-year nationwide survey in France. Clin. Infect. Dis. *20*:501–506, 1995.
178. Holland, F., II, Fernandez, L., Jacobs, J., and Bolooki, H.: Clostridial endocarditis following penetrating cardiac trauma. Clin. Infect. Dis. *24*:87–88, 1997.
179. Horwitz, D., Quismorio, F. P., and Friou, G. J.: Cryoglobulinemia in patients with infective endocarditis. Clin. Exp. Immunol. *19*:131–137, 1975.
180. Hosea, S. W.: Virulent *Streptococcus viridans* bacterial endocarditis. Am. Heart J. *101*:174–176, 1981.
181. Houpikian, P., and Raoult, D.: Diagnostic methods: Current best practices and guidelines for identification of difficult-to-culture pathogens in infective endocarditis. Infect. Dis. Clin. North Am. *16*:377–392, 2002.
182. Hsu, C.-M., Lee, P.-I., Chen, J.-M., et al.: Fatal *Fusarium* endocarditis complicated by hemolytic anemia and thrombocytopenia in an infant. Pediatr. Infect. Dis. J. *13*:1146–1148, 1994.
183. Husni, R. N., Gordon, S. M., Washington, J. A., and Longworth, D. L.: *Lactobacillus* bacteremia and endocarditis: Review of 45 cases. Clin. Infect. Dis. *25*:1048–1055, 1997.
184. Hyams, K. C., Mader, J. T., Pollard, R. B., et al.: *Serratia* endocarditis in a pediatric burn patient. J. A. M. A. *246*:983–984, 1981.
185. Ingram, R. J. H., Cornere, B., and Ellis-Pegler, R. B.: Endocarditis due to *Neisseria mucosa*: Two case reports and review. Clin. Infect. Dis. *15*:321–324, 1992.
186. Inman, R. D., Redecha, P. B., Knechtle, S. J., et al.: Identification of bacterial antigens in circulating immune complexes of infective endocarditis. J. Clin. Invest. *70*:271–280, 1982.
187. Ivert, T. S., Dismukes, W. E., Cobbs, C. G., et al.: Prosthetic valve endocarditis. Circulation *69*:223–232, 1984.
188. Jackman, J. D., Jr., and Glamann, D. B.: Gonococcal endocarditis: Twenty-five year experience. Am. J. Med. Sci. *301*:221, 1991.
189. Jackson, M. A., and Hicks, R. A.: Vancomycin failure in staphylococcal endocarditis. Pediatr. Infect. Dis. J. *6*:750–752, 1987.
190. Jackson, M. J., and Rutledge, J.: Pneumococcal endocarditis in children. Pediatr. Infect. Dis. J. *1*:120–122, 1982.
191. Jaffe, W. M., Morgan, D. E., Pearlman, A. S., et al.: Infective endocarditis, 1983–1988: Echocardiographic findings and factors influencing morbidity and mortality. J. Am. Coll. Cardiol. *15*:1227–1233, 1990.
192. Jalava, J., Kotilainen, P., Nikkari, S., et al.: Use of the polymerase chain reaction and DNA sequencing for detection of *Bartonella quintana* in the aortic valve of a patient with culture-negative infective endocarditis. Clin. Infect. Dis. *21*:891–896, 1995.
193. Jemsek, J. G., Greenberg, S. B., Gentry, L. O., et al.: *Haemophilus parainfluenzae* endocarditis: Two cases and review of the literature in the past decade. Am. J. Med. *66*:51–57, 1979.
194. Job, F. P., Franke, S., Lethen, H., et al.: Incremental valve of biplane and multiplane transesophageal echocardiography for the assessment of active infective endocarditis. Am. J. Cardiol. *75*:1033–1037, 1995.
195. John, M. D. V., Hibberd, P. L., Karchmer, A. W., et al.: *Staphylococcus aureus* prosthetic valve endocarditis: Optimal management and risk factors for death. Clin. Infect. Dis. *26*:1307–1309, 1998.
196. Johnson, C. M.: Adherence events in the pathogenesis of infective endocarditis. Infect. Dis. Clin. North Am. *7*:21–36, 1993.
197. Johnson, C. M., and Rhodes, K. H.: Pediatric endocarditis. Mayo Clin. Proc. *57*:86–94, 1982.
198. Johnson, D. H., Rosenthal, A., and Nadas, A.: Bacterial endocarditis in children under 2 years of age. Am. J. Dis. Child. *129*:183–186, 1975.
199. Johnson, D. H., Rosenthal, A., and Nadas, A.: A forty-year review of bacterial endocarditis in infancy and childhood. Circulation *51*:581–588, 1975.
200. Johnson, J. D., Raff, M. J., Barnwell, P. A., et al.: Splenic abscess complicating infectious endocarditis. Arch. Intern. Med. *143*:906–912, 1983.
201. Johnson, P. G., Lee, J., Domanski, M., et al.: Late recurrent *Candida* endocarditis. Chest *99*:1531–1533, 1991.
202. Jones, H. K., and Siekert, R. G.: Neurologic manifestations of infective endocarditis. Brain *112*:1295–1315, 1989.
203. Jones, R. B., Priest, J. B., and Kuo, C.: Subacute chlamydial endocarditis. J. A. M. A. *247*:655–658, 1982.
204. Julander, I.: Unfavourable prognostic factors in *Staphylococcus aureus* septicemia and endocarditis. Scand. J. Infect. Dis. *17*:179–187, 1985.
205. Kaell, A. T., Volkman, D. J., Gorevic, P. D., et al.: Positive Lyme serology in subacute bacterial endocarditis: A study of four patients. J. A. M. A. *264*:2916–2918, 1990.
206. Kaplan, E. L.: Infective endocarditis in the pediatric age group: An overview. *In* Kaplan, E. L., and Taranta, A. V. (eds.): Infective Endocarditis: An American Heart Association Symposium. Dallas, American Heart Association, 1977, pp. 51–54.
207. Kaplan, E. L., Rich, H., Gersony, W., et al.: A collaborative study of infective endocarditis in the 1970's: Emphasis on infections in patients who have undergone cardiovascular surgery. Circulation *59*:327–335, 1979.
208. Kaplan, S., Helmworth, J. A., Ahern, E. N., et al.: Results of palliative procedures for tetralogy of Fallot in infants and young children. Ann. Thorac. Surg. *5*:489–495, 1968.
209. Karalis, D. G., Blumberg, A. E., Vilaro, J. F., et al.: Prognostic significance of valvular regurgitation in patients with infective endocarditis. Am. J. Med. *90*:193–197, 1991.
210. Karchmer, A. W., Archer, G. L., and Dismukes, W. E.: *Staphylococcus epidermidis* causing prosthetic valve endocarditis: Microbiologic and clinical observations as guides to therapy. Ann. Intern. Med. *98*:447–455, 1983.
211. Karchmer, A. W., Dismukes, W. E., Buckley, M. J., et al.: Late prosthetic valve endocarditis: Clinical features influencing therapy. Am. J. Med. *64*:199–206, 1978.
212. Karchmer, A. W., Moellering, R. C., Maki, D. G., et al.: Single-antibiotic therapy for streptococcal endocarditis. J. A. M. A. *241*:1801–1806, 1979.
213. Karl, T., Wensley, D., Stark, J., et al.: Infective endocarditis in children with congenital heart disease: Comparison of selected features in patients with surgical correction or palliation and those without. Br. Heart J. *58*:57–65, 1987.
214. Kauffman, R. H., Thompson, J., Valentijn, R. M., et al.: The clinical implications and the pathogenetic significance of circulating immune complexes in infective endocarditis. Am. J. Med. *71*:17–25, 1981.
215. Kavey, R. W., Frank, D. M., Byrum, C. J., et al.: Two-dimensional echocardiographic assessment of infective endocarditis in children. Am. J. Dis. Child. *137*:851–856, 1983.
216. Kaye, D.: Prevention of bacterial endocarditis: 1991. Ann. Intern. Med. *114*:803–804, 1991.

217. Keay, S., Denning, D. W., and Stevens, D. A.: Endocarditis due to *Trichosporon beigelii*: In vitro susceptibility of isolates and review. Rev. Infect. Dis. *13*:383–386, 1991.
218. Keys, T. F., and Hewitt, W. L.: Endocarditis due to micrococci and *Staphylococcus epidermidis*. Arch. Intern. Med. *132*:216–220, 1973.
219. Keyser, D. L., Biller, J., Coffman, T. T., et al.: Neurologic complications of late prosthetic valve endocarditis. Stroke *21*:472, 1990.
220. Khandheria, B. K.: Transesophageal echocardiography in the evaluation of prosthetic valves. Am. J. Card. Imaging *9*:106–114, 1995.
221. Kielhofner, M. A., and Hamill, R. J.: Role of adherence in infective endocarditis. Tex. Heart J. *16*:239–249, 1989.
222. Kihuchi, K., Enari, T., Minami, S., et al.: Postantibiotic effects and postantibiotic sub-MIC effects of benzyl penicillin on viridans streptococci isolated from patients with infective endocarditis. J. Antimicrob. Chemother. *34*:687–696, 1994.
223. Kilpatrick, Z. M., Greenberg, P. A., and Sanford, J. P.: Splinter hemorrhages: Their clinical significance. Arch. Intern. Med. *115*:730–735, 1965.
224. Kimbrough, R. C., Ormsbee, R. A., Peacock, M., et al.: Q fever endocarditis in the United States. Ann. Intern. Med. *91*:400–402, 1979.
225. King, M. E., and Weyman, A. E.: Echocardiographic findings in infective endocarditis. Cardiovasc. Clin. *13*:147–165, 1983.
226. Kissane, J. M.: Pathology of Infancy and Childhood. 2nd ed. St. Louis, C. V. Mosby, 1975, pp. 417–418.
227. Komshian, S. V., Tablan, O. C., Palutke, W., et al.: Characteristics of left-sided endocarditis due to *Pseudomonas aeruginosa* in the Detroit Medical Center. Rev. Infect. Dis. *12*:693–702, 1990.
228. Kramer, H., Bourgeois, M., Liersch, R., et al.: Current clinical aspects of bacterial endocarditis in infancy, childhood and adolescence. Eur. J. Pediatr. *140*:253–259, 1983.
229. Kuypers, J. M., and Proctor, R. A.: Reduced adherence to traumatized rat heart valves by a low–fibronectin-binding mutant of *Staphylococcus aureus*. Infect. Immun. *57*:2306–2312, 1989.
230. Laird, W. P., Nelson, J. D., Weinberg, A. G., et al.: Fatal *Hemophilus influenzae* endocarditis diagnosed by echocardiography in an infant. Pediatrics *64*:292–295, 1979.
231. Lam, S., Samraj, J., Rahman, S., et al.: Primary actinomycotic endocarditis: Case report and review. Clin. Infect. Dis. *16*:481–485, 1993.
232. Lamas, C. C., and Eykyn, S. J.: Suggested modifications to the Duke criteria for the clinical diagnosis of native valve and prosthetic valve endocarditis: Analysis of 118 pathologically proven cases. Clin. Infect. Dis. *25*:713–719, 1997.
233. Lamich, R., Alonso, C., Guma, J. R., et al.: Prospective study of bacteremia during transesophageal echocardiography. Am. Heart J. *125*:1454, 1993.
234. La Scola, B., and Raoult, D.: Molecular identification of *Gemella* species from three patients with endocarditis. J. Clin. Microbiol. *36*:866–871, 1998.
235. Laufer, D., Lew, P. D., Obertiansli, I., et al.: Chronic Q fever endocarditis with massive splenomegaly in childhood. J. Pediatr. *108*:535–539, 1986.
236. Laxdal, T., Messner, R. P., and Williams, R. S.: Opsonic, agglutinating and complement-fixing antibodies in patients with subacute bacterial endocarditis. J. Lab. Clin. Med. *71*:638–675, 1968.
237. Lederman, M. M., Sprague, L., Wallis, R. S., et al.: Duration of fever during treatment of infective endocarditis. Medicine (Baltimore) *71*:52, 1992.
238. Lefort, A., Mainordi, J.-L., Selton-Suty, C., et al.: *Streptococcus pneumoniae* endocarditis in adults: A multi center study in France in the era of penicillin resistance (1991–1998). The Pneumococcal Endocarditis Study Group. Medicine (Baltimore) *79*:327–337, 2000.
239. Leonard, A., Raij, L., and Shapiro, F. C.: Bacterial endocarditis in regularly dialyzed patients. Kidney Int. *4*:407–422, 1973.
240. Lepeschkin, E.: On the relation between the side of valvular involvement in endocarditis and the blood pressure resting on the valve. Am. J. Med. Sci. *224*:318–319, 1952.
241. Levin, R. M., Pulliam, L., Mondry, C., et al.: Penicillin-resistant *Streptococcus constellatus* as a cause of endocarditis. Am. J. Dis. Child. *136*:42–45, 1982.
242. Levine, D. P., Fromm, B. S., and Reddy, B. R.: Slow response to vancomycin or vancomycin plus rifampin in methicillin-resistant *Staphylococcus aureus* endocarditis. Ann. Intern. Med. *115*:674–680, 1991.
243. Levy, P. Y., Drancourt, M., Etienne, J., et al.: Comparison of different antibiotic regimens for therapy of 32 cases of Q fever endocarditis. Antimicrob. Agents Chemother. *35*:533–537, 1991.
244. Li, J. S., Sexton, D. J., Mick, N., et al.: Proposed modifications to the Duke criteria for the diagnosis of infective endocarditis. Clin. Infect. Dis. *30*:633–638, 2000.
245. Liepman, M. K., Jones, P. G., and Kauffman, C. A.: Endocarditis as a complication of indwelling right atrial catheters in leukemic patients. Cancer *54*:804–807, 1984.
246. Lina, B., Celard, M., Vandenesch, F., et al.: Infective endocarditis due to *Staphylococcus capitis*. Clin. Infect. Dis. *15*:173–174, 1992.
247. Lipman, M. L., and Silva, J.: Endocarditis due to *Streptococcus faecalis* with high-level resistance to gentamicin. Rev. Infect. Dis. *11*:325–328, 1989.
248. Lisby, G., Gutschik, E., and Durack, D. T.: Molecular methods for diagnosis of infective endocarditis. Infect. Dis. Clin. North Am. *16*:393–412, 2002.
249. Liu, V. C., Stevenson, J. G., and Smith, A. L.: Group A *Streptococcus* mural endocarditis. Pediatr. Infect. Dis. J. *11*:1060–1062, 1992.
250. Liwnicz, B. H., and Lepow, H.: Nonbacterial thrombotic endocarditis in a premature child: Clinical significance and possible relationships to subvalvular hematoma. N. Y. State J. Med. *76*:912–916, 1976.
251. Lowenstein, M. B., Urman, J. D., Abeles, M., et al.: Skin immunofluorescence in infective endocarditis. J. A. M. A. *238*:1163–1165, 1977.
252. Lowrance, J. H., Baddour, L. M., and Simpson, W. A.: The role of fibronectin binding in a rat model of experimental endocarditis caused by *Streptococcus sanguis*. J. Clin. Invest. *86*:7, 1990.
253. Lubani, M., Sharda, D., and Helin, I.: Cardiac manifestations in brucellosis. Arch. Dis. Child. *61*:569–572, 1986.
254. Lutas, E. M., Roberts, R. B., Devereux, R. B., et al.: Relation between the presence of echocardiographic vegetations and the complication rate in infective endocarditis. Am. Heart J. *112*:107–113, 1986.
255. Lynn, D. C., Kane, J. G., and Parker, R. H.: *Haemophilus parainfluenzae* endocarditis: A review of forty cases. Medicine (Baltimore) *56*:115–128, 1977.
256. Macauley, D.: Acute endocarditis in infancy and early childhood. Am. J. Dis. Child. *88*:715–721, 1954.
257. MacMahon, S. W., Hickey, A. J., Wilcken, D. E. L., et al.: Risk of infective endocarditis in mitral valve prolapse with and without precordial systolic murmurs. Am. J. Cardiol. *58*:105–108, 1986.
258. Madison, J., Wang, K., Gobel, F. L., et al.: Prosthetic aortic valve endocarditis. Circulation *51*:940–949, 1975.
259. Maisch, B., Eichstadt, H., and Kochsiek, K.: Immune reactions in infective endocarditis. I. Clinical data and diagnostic relevance of antimyocardial antibodies. Am. Heart J. *106*:329–344, 1983.
260. Maki, D. G., and Agger, W. A.: Enterococcal bacteremia: Clinical features, the risk of endocarditis and management. Medicine (Baltimore) *67*:248–269, 1988.
261. Malacoff, R. F., Frank, E., and Andriole, V. T.: Streptococcal endocarditis (non-enterococcal, non–group A): Single vs. combination therapy. J. A. M. A. *241*:1807–1810, 1979.
262. Mansur, A. J., Grinberg, M., Lemosdaluz, P., et al.: The complications of infective endocarditis. Arch. Intern. Med. *152*:2428, 1992.
263. Marinell, P. V., Diana, D. J., and Todd, W. A.: Survival of a child after *Hemophilus influenzae* b endocarditis. Pediatr. Infect. Dis. J. *2*:46–47, 1983.
264. Markowitz, M.: The decline of rheumatic fever: Role of medical intervention. Lewis W. Wannamaker Memorial Lecture. J. Pediatr. *106*:545–550, 1985.
265. Markowitz, S. M., Szentpetery, S., Lower, R. R., et al.: Endocarditis due to accidental penetrating foreign bodies. Am. J. Med. *60*:571–576, 1976.
266. Marks, A. R., Choong, C. Y., Sanfilippo, A. J., et al.: Identification of high-risk and low-risk subgroups of patients with mitral-valve prolapse. N. Engl. J. Med. *370*:1031–1036, 1989.
267. Marks, K. A., Zucker, N., Kopelushnik, J., et al.: Infective endocarditis successfully treated in extremely low birth weight infants with recombinant tissue plasminogen activator. Pediatrics *109*:153–158, 2002.
268. Marrie, T. J., Harczy, M., Mann, O. E., et al.: Culture-negative endocarditis probably due to *Chlamydia pneumoniae*. J. Infect. Dis. *161*:127–129, 1990.
269. Martin, J. M., Neches, W. H., and Wald, E. R.: Infective endocarditis: 35 years of experience at a children's hospital. Clin. Infect. Dis. *24*:669–675, 1997.
270. Martino, P., Micozzi, A., Venditti, M., et al.: Catheter-related right-sided endocarditis in bone marrow transplant recipients. Rev. Infect. Dis. *12*:250–257, 1990.
271. Masuda, J., Yutani, C., Waki, R., et al.: Histopathologic analysis of the mechanisms of intracranial hemorrhage complicating infective endocarditis. Stroke *23*:843, 1992.
272. Mathew, J., Addai, T., Anand, A., et al.: Clinical features, site of involvement, bacteriologic findings and outcome of infective endocarditis in intravenous drug users. Arch. Intern. Med. *155*:1641–1648, 1995.
273. Mayayo, E., Moralejo, J., Camps, J., et al.: Fungal endocarditis in premature infants: Case report and review. Clin. Infect. Dis. *22*:366–368, 1996.
274. McCartney, A. C., Orange, G. U., Pringle, S. D., et al.: Serum C reactive protein in infective endocarditis. J. Clin. Pathol. *41*:44–48, 1988.
275. McGuinness, G. A., Schieken, R. M., and Maguire, G. F.: Endocarditis in the newborn. Am. J. Dis. Child. *134*:577–580, 1980.
276. McKinsey, D. S., Ratts, T. E., and Bisno, A. L.: Underlying cardiac lesions in adults with infective endocarditis: The changing spectrum. Am. J. Med. *82*:681–688, 1987.
277. Medoff, G., Comfort, M., and Kabayashi, G.: Synergistic action of amphotericin B and 5-fluorocytosine against yeast-like organisms. Proc. Soc. Exp. Biol. Med. *138*:571–574, 1971.

278. Mendelsohn, G., and Hutchins, G. M.: Infective endocarditis during the first decade of life. Am. J. Dis. Child. *133*:619–622, 1979.
279. Megran, D. W.: Enterococcal endocarditis. Clin. Infect. Dis. *15*:63–71, 1992.
280. Merzbach, D., Freundlich, E., Metzker, A., et al.: Endocarditis due to *Corynebacterium*. J. Pediatr. *67*:792–796, 1965.
281. Middlemost, S., Wisenbaugh, T., Meyerowitz, C., et al.: A case for early surgery in native left-sided endocarditis complicated by heart failure: Results in 203 patients. J. Am. Coll. Cardiol. *18*:663–667, 1991.
282. Millard, D. D., and Shulman, S. T.: The changing spectrum of neonatal endocarditis. Clin. Perinatol. *15*:587–608, 1988.
283. Mintz, G. S., Kotler, M. N., Segal, B. L., et al.: Comparison of two-dimensional and M-mode echocardiography in the evaluation of patients with infective endocarditis. Am. J. Cardiol. *43*:738–745, 1979.
284. Mittal, B. V.: Renal lesions in infective endocarditis. J. Postgrad. Med. *33*:193–197, 1987.
285. Mohan, U. R., Walters, S., and Kroll, J. S.: Endocarditis due to group A β-hemolytic *Streptococcus* in children with potentially lethal sequelae: 2 cases and review. Clin. Infect. Dis. *30*:624–625, 2000.
286. Moodie, D. S., and Gallen, W. J.: Pneumococcal endocarditis in a 7 week old infant. Am. J. Dis. Child. *129*:980–983, 1975.
287. Moreillon, P., Que, Y. A., Bayer, A. S.: Pathogenesis of streptococcal and staphylococcal endocarditis. Infect. Dis. Clin. North Am. *16*:297–318, 2002.
288. Morguet, A. J., Munz, D. L., Ivancevic, V., et al.: Immunoscintigraphy using technetium-99m–labeled anti–NCA-95 antigranulocyte antibodies as an adjunct to echocardiography in subacute infective endocarditis. J. Am. Coll. Cardiol. *23*:1171–1188, 1994.
289. Morris, C. D., Reller, M. D., and Menosch, V. D.: Thirty year incidence of infective endocarditis after surgery for congenital heart defect. J. A. M. A. *279*:599–603, 1998.
290. Morrison, V. A., and Wagner, K. F.: Clinical manifestations of *Kingella kingae* infections: Case report and review. Rev. Infect. Dis. *11*:776–782, 1989.
291. Mortara, L. A., and Bayer, A. S.: *Staphylococcus* bacteremia and endocarditis: New diagnostic and therapeutic concepts. Infect. Dis. Clin. North Am. *7*:53–67, 1993.
292. Moy, R. J. D., George, R. H., DeGiovanni, J. V., et al.: Improving survival in bacterial endocarditis. Arch. Dis. Child. *61*:394–399, 1986.
293. Mugge, A., Daniel, W. G., Frank, G., et al.: Echocardiography in infective endocarditis: Reassessment of prognostic implications of vegetation size determined by the transthoracic and transesophageal approach. J. Am. Coll. Cardiol. *14*:631–638, 1989.
294. Mullany, C. J., Chau, Y. L., Schaff, H. V., et al.: Early and late survival after surgical treatment of culture-positive active endocarditis. Mayo Clin. Proc. *70*:517–525, 1995.
295. Munoz, P., Berenguer, J., Rodriguez-Greixems, M., et al.: Ciprofloxacin and infective endocarditis. Infect. Dis. Clin. Pract. *2*:119, 1993.
296. Murphy, J. G., and Foster-Smith, K.: Management of complications of infective endocarditis with emphasis on echocardiographic findings. Infect. Dis. Clin. North Am. *7*:153–165, 1993.
297. Murray, B. E.: The life and times of the *Enterococcus*. Clin. Microbiol. Rev. *3*:46–65, 1990.
298. Murray, H. W., Gross, K. C., Masur, H., et al.: Serious infections caused by *Streptococcus milleri*. Am. J. Med. *64*:759–765, 1978.
299. Musewe, N. N., Hecht, B. M., Hesslein, P. S., et al.: Tricuspid valve endocarditis in two children with normal hearts: Diagnosis and therapy of an unusual clinical entity. J. Pediatr. *110*:735–738, 1987.
300. Nagel, J. G., Tuazon, C. V., Cardella, T. A., et al.: Teichoic acid serologic diagnosis of staphylococcal endocarditis. Ann. Intern. Med. *82*:13–18, 1975.
301. Nagunuma, M.: Infective endocarditis in children. Jpn. Circ. J. *49*:545–552, 1985.
302. Naidoo, D. P.: Right-sided endocarditis in the non-drug addict. Postgrad. Med. J. *69*:615–620, 1993.
303. Nakayama, D. K., O'Neill, J. A., Wagner, H., et al.: Management of vascular complications of bacterial endocarditis. J. Pediatr. Surg. *21*:636–639, 1986.
304. Narasimhan, S. L., and Weinstein, A. J.: Infective endocarditis due to a nutritionally deficient *Streptococcus*. J. Pediatr. *96*:61–62, 1980.
305. Nastro, L. J., and Finegold, S. M.: Endocarditis due to anaerobic gram-negative bacilli. Am. J. Med. *54*:482–496, 1973.
306. Nelson, R. J., Harley, D. P., French, W. J., et al.: Favorable ten-year experience with valve procedures for active infective endocarditis. J. Thorac. Cardiovasc. Surg. *87*:493–502, 1984.
307. Nguyen, M. H., Nguyen, M. L., Yu, V. L., et al.: *Candida* prosthetic valve endocarditis: Prospective study of six cases and review of the literature. Clin. Infect. Dis. *22*:262–267, 1996.
308. Nicolau, D. P., Freeman, C. D., Nightingale, C. H., et al.: Reduction of bacterial titers by low-dose aspirin in experimental aortic valve endocarditis. Infect. Immun. *61*:1593–1595, 1993.
309. Noel, G. J., O'Loughlin, J. E., and Edelson, P. J.: Neonatal *Staphylococcus epidermidis* right-sided endocarditis: Description of five catheterized infants. Pediatrics *82*:234–239, 1988.
310. Nolan, C. M., Kane, J. J., and Grunow, W. A.: Infective endocarditis and mitral prolapse: A comparison with other types of endocarditis. Arch. Intern. Med. *141*:447–450, 1981.
311. Nomura, F., Penny, D. J., Menahem, S., et al.: Surgical intervention for infective endocarditis in infancy and childhood. Ann. Thorac. Surg. *60*:90–95, 1995.
312. O'Callaghan, C., and McDougall, P.: Infective endocarditis in neonates. Arch. Dis. Child. *63*:53–57, 1988.
313. Oelberg, D. G., Fisher, D. J., Gross, D. M., et al.: Endocarditis in high-risk neonates. Pediatrics *71*:392–397, 1983.
314. Okumura, A., Ito, K., Kondo, M., et al.: Infective endocarditis caused by highly penicillin-resistant *Streptococcus pneumoniae:* Successful treatment with cefuzonam, ampicillin and imipenem. Pediatr. Infect. Dis. J. *14*:327–329, 1995.
315. Olaison, L., and Pettersson, G.: Current best practices and guidelines: Indications for surgical intervention in infective endocarditis. Infect. Dis. Clin. North Am. *16*:453–476, 2002.
316. Panidis, I. P., Kotler, M. N., Mintz, G. S., et al.: Right heart endocarditis: Clinical and echocardiographic features. Am. Heart J. *107*:759–764, 1984.
317. Patchell, R. A., White, C. L., Clark, A. W., et al.: Nonbacterial thrombotic endocarditis in bone marrow transplant patients. Cancer *55*:631–635, 1985.
318. Patrick, W. D., Brown, W. D., Bowmer, M. I., et al.: Infective endocarditis due to *Eikenella corrodens:* Case report and review of the literature. Can. J. Infect. Dis. *1*:139, 1990.
319. Patterson, J. E., and Zervos, M. J.: High-level gentamicin resistance in *Enterococcus:* Microbiology, genetic basis and epidemiology. Rev. Infect. Dis. *12*:644–652, 1990.
320. Pazin, G. J., Saul, S., and Thompson, M. E.: Blood culture positivity: Suppression by out-patient antibiotic therapy in patients with bacterial endocarditis. Arch. Intern. Med. *142*:263–269, 1982.
321. Pedersen, W. R., Walker, M., Olson, J. D., et al.: Value of transesophageal echocardiography as an adjunct to transthoracic echocardiography in evaluation of native and prosthetic valve endocarditis. Chest *100*:351–356, 1991.
322. Pefanis, A., Giamarellou, H., Karayiannakos, P., et al.: Efficacy of ceftazidime and aztreonam alone or in combination with amikacin in experimental left-sided *Pseudomonas aeruginosa* endocarditis. Antimicrob. Agents Chemother. *37*:308–313, 1993.
323. Pefanis, A., Thauvin-Eliopoulos, C., Eliopoulos, G. M., et al.: Activity of ampicillin-sulbactam and oxacillin in experimental endocarditis caused by beta-lactamase hyperproducing *Staphylococcus aureus*. Antimicrob. Agents Chemother. *37*:507–511, 1993.
324. Pelletier, L. L., Durack, D. T., and Petersdorf, R. G.: Chemotherapy of experimental streptococcal endocarditis. IV. Further observations on prophylaxis. J. Clin. Invest. *56*:319–330, 1975.
325. Perry, K. S., Tresch, D. D., Brooks, H. L., et al.: Operative approach to endocarditis. Am. Heart J. *108*:561–566, 1984.
326. Pesanti, E. L., and Smith, I. M.: Infective endocarditis with negative blood cultures: An analysis of 52 cases. Am. J. Med. *66*:43–50, 1979.
327. Peter, O., Flepp, M., Bestetti, G., et al.: Q fever endocarditis: Diagnostic approaches and monitoring of therapeutic effects. Clin. Invest. *70*:932, 1992.
328. Pollack, S., Mogtader, A., and Lange, M.: *Neisseria subflava* endocarditis: Case report and review of the literature. Am. J. Med. *76*:752–758, 1984.
329. Pongratz, G., Henneke, K. H., von der Grun, M., et al.: Risk of endocarditis in transesophageal echocardiography. Am. Heart J. *125*:190–193, 1993.
330. Popp, R. L.: Echocardiography. N. Engl. J. Med. *323*:165, 1990.
331. Powderly, W. G., Stanley, S. L., and Medoff, G.: Pneumococcal endocarditis: Report of a series and review of the literature. Rev. Infect. Dis. *8*:786–791, 1986.
332. Powell, D. C., Bivens, B. A., Bell, R. M., et al.: Endocarditis: Increasingly a surgical disease. Am. Surg. *48*:5–10, 1982.
333. Powers, D. L., and Mandell, G. L.: Intraleucocytic bacteria in endocarditis patients. J. A. M. A. *227*:313–315, 1974.
334. Prager, R. L., Maples, M. D., Hammon, J. W., et al.: Early operative intervention in aortic bacterial endocarditis. Ann. Thorac. Surg. *32*:347–350, 1981.
335. Prinsloo, J. G., and Pretorius, P. J.: *Candida albicans* endocarditis. Am. J. Dis. Child. *111*:446–447, 1966.
336. Pulvirenti, J. J., Kerns, E., Benson, C., et al.: Infective endocarditis in injection drug users: Importance of human immunodeficiency virus serostatus and degree of immunosuppression. Clin. Infect. Dis. *22*:40–45, 1996.
337. Qin, X., and Urdahl, K. B.: PCR and sequencing of independent genetic targets for the diagnosis of culture negative bacterial endocarditis. Diagn. Microbiol. Infect. Dis. *40*:145–149, 2001.
338. Qoronfleh, M. W., Weraarchakul, W., and Wilkinson, B. S.: Antibodies to a range of *Staphylococcus aureus* and *Escherichia coli* heat shock proteins in sera from patients with *S. aureus* endocarditis. Infect. Immun. *61*:1567–1570, 1993.

339. Rabin, R. L., Wong, P., Noonan, J. A., et al.: *Kingella kingae* endocarditis in a child with a prosthetic aortic valve and bifurcation graft. Am. J. Dis. Child. *137*:403–404, 1983.
340. Ramirez, C. A., Naragi, S., and McCulley, D. J.: Group A beta-hemolytic streptococcus endocarditis. Am. Heart J. *108*:1383–1386, 1984.
341. Raoult, D., Fournier, P. E., Dramcourt, M., et al.: Diagnosis of 22 new cases of *Bartonella* endocarditis. Ann. Intern. Med. *125*:646–652, 1996.
342. Rastogi, A., Luken, J. A., Pildes, R. S., et al.: Endocarditis in the neonatal intensive care unit. Pediatr. Cardiol. *14*:183–186, 1993.
343. Reller, L. B.: The serum bactericidal test. Rev. Infect. Dis. *8*:803–807, 1986.
344. Reymann, M. T., Holley, H. P., and Cobbs, C. G.: Persistent bacteremia in staphylococcal endocarditis. Am. J. Med. *65*:729–739, 1978.
345. Ribot, S., Rothfeld, D., and Frankel, H. J.: Infectious endocarditis in maintenance hemodialysis patients. Am. J. Med. Sci. *264*:183–188, 1972.
346. Rice, L. B., Calderwood, S. B., Eliopoulos, G. M., et al.: Enterococcal endocarditis: A comparison of prosthetic and native valve disease. Rev. Infect. Dis. *13*:1–7, 1991.
347. Rice, M. J., McDonald, R. W., Reller, M. D., et al.: Pediatric echocardiography: Current role and a review of technical advances. J. Pediatr. *128*:1–14, 1996.
348. Robbins, M. J., Frater, R. W. M., Soeiro, R., et al.: Influence of vegetation size on clinical outcome of right-sided infective endocarditis. Am. J. Med. *80*:165–171, 1986.
349. Roberts, G. J., Gardner, P., and Simmons, N. A.: Optimum sampling time for detection of dental bacteremia in children. Int. J. Cardiol. *35*:311–315, 1992.
350. Roberts, K. B., and Sidlak, M. J.: Satellite streptococci: A major cause of "negative" blood cultures in bacterial endocarditis? J. A. M. A. *241*:2293–2294, 1979.
351. Rodbard, S.: Blood velocity and endocarditis. Circulation *27*:18–28, 1963.
352. Rodero, F. G., del Mar Masia, M., Cortes, J., et al.: Endocarditis caused by *Stenotrophomonas maltophilia:* Case report and review. Clin. Infect. Dis. *23*:1261–1265, 1996.
353. Rogers, J., Walker, M., Olson, J. D., et al.: Value of transesophageal echocardiography as an adjunct to transthoracic echocardiography in evaluation of native and prosthetic valve endocarditis. Chest *100*:351–355, 1991.
354. Rohmann, S., Erbel, R., Darius, H., et al.: Prediction of rapid versus prolonged healing of infective endocarditis by monitoring vegetation size. J. Am. Soc. Echocardiogr. *4*:465–474, 1991.
355. Rohmann, S., Seifert, T., Erbel, R., et al.: Identification of abscess formation in native-valve infective endocarditis using transesophageal echocardiography: Implications for surgical treatment. Thorac. Cardiovasc. Surg. *39*:273–280, 1991.
356. Rose, A. G.: Infective endocarditis complicating congenital heart disease. S. Afr. Med. J. *53*:739–743, 1978.
357. Rubinstein, E., Noreiga, E. R., Simberkoff, M. S., et al.: Fungal endocarditis: Analysis of 24 cases and review of the literature. Medicine (Baltimore) *54*:331–344, 1975.
358. Rupp, M. E.: *Streptobacillus moniliformis* endocarditis: Case report and review. Clin. Infect. Dis. *14*:769–772, 1992.
359. Rutledge, R., Kim, B. J., and Applebaum, R. E.: Actuarial analysis of the risk of prosthetic valve endocarditis in 1,598 patients with mechanical and bioprosthetic valves. Arch. Surg. *120*:469–472, 1985.
360. Sable, C. A., Rome, J. J., Martin, G. R., et al.: Indications for echocardiography in the diagnosis of infective endocarditis in children. Am. J. Cardiol. *75*:801–804, 1995.
361. Sachdev, M., Peterson, G. E., and Jollis, J. G.: Imaging techniques for diagnosis of infective endocarditis. Infect. Dis. Clin. North Am. *16*:319–338, 2002.
362. Sadiq, M., Nazir, M., and Sheikh, S. A.: Infective endocarditis in children—incidence, pattern, diagnosis and management in a developing country. Int. J. Cardiol. *78*:175–182, 2001.
363. Saffle, J. R., Gardner, P., Schoenbaum, S. C., et al.: Prosthetic valve endocarditis: The case for prompt valve replacement. J. Thorac. Cardiovasc. Surg. *73*:416–420, 1977.
364. Saiman, L., Prince, A., and Gersony, W. M.: Pediatric infective endocarditis in the modern era. J. Pediatr. *122*:847–853, 1993.
365. Salgado, A. V., Furlan, A. J., Keys, T. F., et al.: Neurologic complications of endocarditis: A 12-year experience. Neurology *39*:173–178, 1989.
366. Sanchez, P. J., Siegel, J. D., and Fishbein, J.: *Candida* endocarditis: Successful medical management in three preterm infants and review of the literature. Pediatr. Infect. Dis. *10*:239–243, 1991.
367. Sande, M. A., and Courtney, K. B.: Nafcillin-gentamicin synergism in experimental *Staphylococcus* endocarditis. J. Lab. Clin. Med. *88*: 118–124, 1976.
368. Sandre, R. M., and Shatran, S. D.: Infective endocarditis: Review of 135 cases over 9 years. Clin. Infect. Dis. *22*:276–286, 1996.
369. Sanfilippo, A. J., Picard, M. H., Newell, J. B., et al.: Echocardiographic assessment of patients with infectious endocarditis: Prediction or risk for complications. J. Am. Coll. Cardiol. *18*:1191–1199, 1991.
370. San Roman, J. A., Vilacosta, I., Zamorano, J. L., et al.: Transesophageal echocardiography in right-sided endocarditis. J. Am. Coll. Cardiol. *21*:1226–1230, 1993.
371. Sapico, F. L., Liquete, J. A., and Sarma, R. J.: Bone and joint infections in patients with infective endocarditis: Review of a 4-year experience. Clin. Infect. Dis. *22*:783–787, 1996.
372. Sapsford, R. N., Fitchett, D. H., Tarin, D., et al.: Aneurysm of left ventricle secondary to bacterial endocarditis. J. Thorac. Cardiovasc. Surg. *78*:79–86, 1979.
373. Scheld, W. M., Calderone, R. A., Alliegro, G. M., et al.: Yeast adherence in the pathogenesis of *Candida* endocarditis. Proc. Soc. Exp. Biol. Med. *168*:208–217, 1981.
374. Scheld, W. M., and Mandell, G. L.: Enigmatic enterococcal endocarditis. Ann. Intern. Med. *100*:904–905, 1984.
375. Scheld, W. M., and Sande, M. A.: Endocarditis and intravascular infections. *In* Mandell, G., Bennett, J. E., and Dolin, R. (eds.): Principles and Practices of Infectious Diseases. 4th ed. New York, Churchill Livingstone, 1995, pp. 740–782.
376. Scheld, W. M., Thomas, J. H., and Sande, M. A.: Influence of preformed antibody on experimental *Streptococcus sanguis* endocarditis. Infect. Immun. *25*:781–785, 1979.
377. Scheld, W. M., Valone, J. A., and Sande, M. A.: Bacterial adherence in the pathogenesis of endocarditis: Interaction of bacterial dextran, platelets and fibrin. J. Clin. Invest. *61*:1394–1398, 1978.
378. Scheld, W. M., Zak, O., Vosbeck, K., et al.: Bacterial adhesion in the pathogenesis of endocarditis: Effect of subinhibitory antibiotic concentrations on streptococcal adhesion in vitro and the development of endocarditis in rabbits. J. Clin. Invest. *68*:1381, 1981.
379. Schollin, J., Bjarke, B., and Wesstrom, G.: Follow-up study on children with infective endocarditis. Acta Paediatr. *78*:615–619, 1989.
380. Schulte, J. E., Gaffney, F. A., Bland, L., et al.: Distinctive anthropometric characteristics of women with mitral valve prolapse. Am. J. Med. *71*:553–558, 1981.
381. Scott, P. J., Blackburn, M. E., Wharton, G. A., et al.: Transesophageal echocardiography in neonates, infants and children: Applicability and diagnostic value in everyday practice of a cardiothoracic unit. Br. Heart J. *68*:488–492, 1992.
382. Scott, R. M.: Bacterial endocarditis due to *Neisseria flava.* J. Pediatr. *78*:673–675, 1971.
383. Seeling, M. S., Speth, C. P., Kozinn, P. J., et al.: Patterns of *Candida* endocarditis following cardiac surgery: Importance of early diagnosis and therapy (an analysis of 91 cases). Prog. Cardiovasc. Dis. *17*:125–160, 1974.
384. Sexton, D. J., Tenenbaum, M. J., Wilson, W. R., et al.: Ceftriaxone once daily for four weeks compared with ceftriaxone plus gentamicin once daily for two weeks for treatment of endocarditis due to penicillin-susceptible streptococci. Clin. Infect. Dis. *27*:1470–1474, 1998.
385. Shah, F. S., Fennelly, G., Weingarten-Arams, J., et al.: Endocardial abscesses in children: Case report and review of the literature. Clin. Infect. Dis. *29*:1478–1482, 1999.
386. Shapiro, D. S., Kenney, S. C., Johnson, M., et al.: *Chlamydia psittaci* endocarditis diagnosed by blood culture. N. Engl. J. Med. *326*:1192–1195, 1992.
387. Shively, B. K., Gurule, F. T., Roldan, C. A., et al.: Diagnostic value of transesophageal compared with transthoracic echocardiography in infective endocarditis. J. Am. Coll. Cardiol. *18*:391–397, 1991.
388. Sholler, G. F., Hawker, R. E., and Celermajer, J. M.: Infective endocarditis in childhood. Pediatr. Cardiol. *6*:183–186, 1986.
389. Simmons, N. A.: Recommendations for endocarditis prophylaxis. J. Antimicrob. Chemother. *31*:437–438, 1993.
390. Singhi, S. C., Singh, S., and Bidwai, P. S.: *Peptococcus* endocarditis. Indian J. Pediatr. *25*:876–878, 1988.
391. Sirisanthana, V., and Sirisanthana, T.: *Corynebacterium diphtheriae* endocarditis. Pediatr. Infect. Dis. J. *2*:470–471, 1983.
392. Sochowski, R. A., and Chan, K.-L.: Implication of negative results on a monoplane transesophageal echocardiographic study in patients with suspected infective endocarditis. J. Am. Coll. Cardiol. *21*:216, 1993.
393. Sommer, P., Gleyzal, C., Guerret, S., et al.: Induction of a putative laminin-binding protein of *Streptococcus gordonii* in human infective endocarditis. Infect. Immun. *60*:360–365, 1992.
394. Spach, D. H., Kanter, A. S., Daniels, N. A., et al.: *Bartonella (Rochalimaea)* species as a cause of apparent "culture-negative" endocarditis. Clin. Infect. Dis. *20*:1044–1047, 1995.
395. Stanton, B. F., Baltimore, R. S., and Clemens, J. D.: Changing spectrum of infective endocarditis in children. Am. J. Dis. Child. *138*:720–725, 1984.
396. Steckelberg, J. M., Murphy, J. G., Ballard, D., et al.: Emboli in infective endocarditis: The prognostic value of echocardiography. Ann. Intern. Med. *114*:635–640, 1991.
397. Steckelberg, J. M., Rouse, M. S., Tallan, B. M., et al.: Relative efficacies of broad-spectrum cephalosporins for treatment of methicillin-susceptible *Staphylococcus aureus* experimental infective endocarditis. Antimicrob. Agents Chemother. *37*:554–558, 1993.
398. Steckelberg, J. M., and Wilson, W. R.: Risk factors for infective endocarditis. Infect. Dis. Clin. North Am. *7*:9–19, 1993.

399. Steelman, R., Einzig, S., Balian, A., et al.: Increased susceptibility to gingival colonization by specific HACEK microbes in children with congenital heart disease. J. Clin. Pediatr. Dent. *25*:91–94, 2000.
400. Steen, M. K., Bruno-Murtha, L. A., Chaux, G., et al.: *Bacillus cereus* endocarditis: Report of a case and review. Clin. Infect. Dis. *14*:945–946, 1992.
401. Stein, D. S., and Nelson, K. E.: Endocarditis due to nutritionally deficient streptococci: Therapeutic dilemma. Rev. Infect. Dis. *9*:908–916, 1987.
402. Sternik, L., Zehr, K. J., Orszulak, T. A., et al.: The advantage of repair of mitral valve in acute endocarditis. J. Heart Valve Dis. *11*:91–97, 2002.
403. Stewart, J. A., Silamperi, D., Harris, P., et al.: Echocardiographic documentation of vegetative lesions in infective endocarditis: Clinical implications. Circulation *61*:374–380, 1980.
404. Stewart, W. J., and Shan, K.: The diagnosis of prosthetic valve endocarditis by echocardiography. Semin. Thorac. Cardiovasc. Surg. *7*:7–12, 1995.
405. Stockheim, J. A., Chadwick, E. G., Kessler, S., et al.: Are the Duke criteria superior to Beth Israel criteria for diagnosis of infective endocarditis in children? Clin. Infect. Dis. *27*:1451–1456, 1998.
406. Stopfuchen, H., Benzing, F., Jungst, B., et al.: Echocardiographic diagnosis of *Candida* endocarditis of the tricuspid valve and of the right atrium in a young infant. Pediatr. Cardiol. *4*:49–51, 1983.
407. Stramboulian, D., Bonvehi, P., Arevalo, C., et al.: Antibiotic management of outpatients with endocarditis due to penicillin-susceptible streptococci. Rev. Infect. Dis. *13*(Suppl. 2):160–163, 1991.
408. Stuart, G., and Wren, C.: Endocarditis with acute mitral regurgitation caused by *Fusobacterium necrophorum*. Pediatr. Cardiol. *13*:230–232, 1992.
409. Sudduth, E. J., Rozich, J. D., and Farrar, W. E.: *Rothia dentocariosa* endocarditis complicated by perivalvular abscess. Clin. Infect. Dis. *17*:772–775, 1993.
410. Sullam, P. M., Costerton, J. W., Yamasaki, R., et al.: Inhibition of platelet binding and aggregation by streptococcal exopolysaccharide. J. Infect. Dis. *167*:1123–1130, 1993.
411. Sussman, J. I., Baron, E. J., Goldberg, S. M., et al.: Clinical manifestations and therapy of *Lactobacillus* endocarditis: Report of a case and review of the literature. Rev. Infect. Dis. *8*:771–776, 1986.
412. Sussman, J. I., Baron, E. J., Tenenbaum, M. J., et al.: Viridans streptococcal endocarditis: Clinical, microbiological and echocardiographic correlations. J. Infect. Dis. *154*:597–603, 1986.
413. Switalski, L. M., Murchison, H., Timpl, R., et al.: Binding of laminin to oral and endocarditis strains of viridans streptococci. J. Bacteriol. *169*:1095–1101, 1987.
414. Sykes, R. M.: *Salmonella* endocarditis in a Nigerian child. East Afr. Med. J. *61*:326–327, 1984.
415. Symbas, P. N., Vlasis, S. E., Zacharupoulos, L., et al.: Immediate and long-term outlook for valve replacement in acute bacterial endocarditis. Ann. Surg. *195*:721–724, 1982.
416. Symchych, P. S., Krauss, A. W., and Winchester, P.: Endocarditis following intracardiac placement of umbilical venous catheters in neonates. J. Pediatr. *90*:287–289, 1977.
417. Taams, M. A., Gussenhoven, E. J., Bos, E., et al.: Enhanced morphological diagnosis in infective endocarditis by transesophageal echocardiography. Br. Heart J. *63*:109–113, 1990.
418. Tancik, C. A., and Dillaha, J. A: *Francisella tularensis* endocarditis. Clin. Infect. Dis. *30*:399–400, 2000.
419. Tanowitz, H. B., Alder, J. J., and Chirito, E.: Gonococcal endocarditis. N. Y. State J. Med. *42*:2782–2783, 1972.
420. Tebas, P., Martinez, R., Roman, F., et al.: Early resistance to rifampin and ciprofloxacin in the treatment of right-sided *Staphylococcus aureus* endocarditis. J. Infect. Dis. *163*:204–205, 1991.
421. Teixeira, O. H., Carpenter, B., and Vlad, P.: Enterococcal endocarditis in early infancy. Can. Med. Assoc. J. *127*:612–613, 1982.
422. Thadelpall, H., and Francis, C. K.: Diagnostic clues in metastatic lesions of endocarditis in addicts. West. J. Med. *128*:1–7, 1978.
423. Thal, L. A., Vazquez, J., Perri, M. B., et al.: Activity of ampicillin plus sulbactam against β-lactamase producing enterococci in experimental endocarditis. J. Antimicrob. Chemother. *31*:182, 1993.
424. Thapar, M. K., Rao, P. S., Feldman, D., et al.: Infective endocarditis: A review. Paediatrician 7:65–84, 1978.
425. Theofilopoulos, A. N., Wilson, C. B., and Dixon, F. J.: The Raji cell radioimmune assay for detecting immune complexes in human sera. J. Clin. Invest. *57*:169–182, 1976.
426. Tiley, S. M., Kociuba, K. R., Heron, L. G., et al.: Infective endocarditis due to nontoxigenic *Corynebacterium diphtheriae:* Report of seven cases and review. Clin. Infect. Dis. *16*:271–275, 1993.
427. Tolan, R. W., Jr., Kleiman, M. B., Frank, M., et al.: Operative intervention in active endocarditis in children: Report of a series of cases and review. Clin. Infect. Dis. *14*:852–862, 1992.
428. Tolaymat, A., Rhatigan, R. M., and Levin, S.: Pneumococcal endocarditis in infants. South. Med. J. *72*:448–451, 1979.
429. Tompkins, L. S., Roessler, B. J., Redd, S. C., et al.: *Legionella* prosthetic-valve endocarditis. N. Engl. J. Med. *318*:530–535, 1988.
430. Tornos, M. P., Castro, A., Toran, N., et al.: Tricuspid valve endocarditis in children with normal valves. Am. Heart J. *118*:624–625, 1989.
431. Tornos, M. P., Permanyer-Miralda, G., Olona, M., et al.: Long-term complications of native valve infective endocarditis in non-addicts: A 15-year follow-up study. Ann. Intern. Med. *117*:567–572, 1992.
432. Toy, P. T. C. Y., Lai, W., Drake, T. A., et al.: Effect of fibronectin on adherence of *Staphylococcus aureus* to fibrin thrombi in vitro. Infect. Immun. *48*:83–86, 1985.
433. Tsao, M. M., and Katz, D.: Central venous catheter–induced endocarditis: Human correlate of the animal experimental model of endocarditis. Rev. Infect. Dis. *6*:783–790, 1984.
434. Tuazon, C. V., and Sheagren, J. W.: Staphylococcal endocarditis in parenteral drug abusers: Source of the organism. Ann. Intern. Med. *82*:788–790, 1975.
435. Tunkel, A. R., and Kaye, D.: Endocarditis with negative blood cultures. N. Engl. J. Med. *326*:1215–1217, 1992.
436. Turner, S. W., Wyllie, J. P., Hamilton, J. R. L., et al.: Diagnosis of infected modified Blalock-Taussig shunt by computed tomography. Ann. Thorac. Surg. *59*:1216–1217, 1995.
437. Turnier, E., Kay, J. H., Bernstein, S., et al.: Surgical treatment of *Candida* endocarditis. Chest *67*:262–268, 1975.
438. Utley, J. R., Mills, J., and Roe, B. B.: The role of valve replacement in the treatment of fungal endocarditis. J. Thorac. Cardiovasc. Surg. *69*:255–258, 1975.
439. van de Rijn, I.: Analysis of cross-protection between serotypes and passively transferred immune globulin in experimental nutritionally variant streptococcal endocarditis. Infect. Immun. *56*:117–121, 1988.
440. van der Meer, J. T. M., Thompson, J., Valkenburg, H. A., et al.: Epidemiology of bacterial endocarditis in the Netherlands. II. Antecedent procedures and use of prophylaxis. Arch. Intern. Med. *152*:1869–1873, 1992.
441. van der Meer, J. T. M., van Wijk, W., Thompson, J., et al.: Efficacy of antibiotic prophylaxis for prevention of native valve endocarditis. Lancet *339*:135, 1992.
442. van der Meer, J. T. M., van Wijk, W., Thompson, J., et al.: Awareness of need and actual use of prophylaxis: Lack of patient compliance in the prevention of bacterial endocarditis. J. Antimicrob. Chemother. *29*:187–194, 1992.
443. Van Hare, G. F., Ben-Shacher, G., Liebman, J., et al.: Infective endocarditis in infants and children during the past 10 years: A decade of change. Am. Heart J. *107*:1235–1240, 1984.
444. Venditti, M., De Bernardis, F., Micozzi, A., et al.: Fluconazole treatment of catheter-related right-sided endocarditis caused by *Candida albicans* and associated with endophthalmitis and folliculitis. Clin. Infect. Dis. *14*:422–426, 1992.
445. Von Reyn, C. F., Levy, B. S., Arbert, R. D., et al.: Infective endocarditis: An analysis based on strict case definitions. Ann. Intern. Med. *94*:505–517, 1982.
446. Vuille, C., Nidor, F. M., Weyman, A., and Picard, M. H.: Natural history of vegetations during successful medical treatment of endocarditis. Am. Heart J. *128*:1200–1209, 1994.
447. Walsh, T. J., and Hutchins, G. M.: *Aspergillus* mural endocarditis. Am. J. Clin. Pathol. *71*:640–644, 1979.
448. Walterspiel, J. N., and Kaplan, S. L.: Incidence and clinical characteristics of "culture negative" infective endocarditis in a pediatric population. Pediatr. Infect. Dis. J. *5*:328–332, 1986.
449. Watanakunakorn, C., and Glotzbecker, C.: Synergism with aminoglycosides of penicillin, ampicillin and vancomycin against nonenterococcal group D streptococci and viridans streptococci. J. Med. Microbiol. *10*:133–137, 1977.
450. Watson, A., French, P., and Wilson, M.: *Nocardia asteroides* native valve endocarditis. Clin. Infect. Dis. *32*:660–661, 2001.
451. Weinberg, A. G.: Group B streptococcal endocarditis detected by echocardiography. J. Pediatr. *92*:335–336, 1978.
452. Weinstein, A. J., and Moellering, R. C.: Penicillin and gentamicin therapy for enterococcal infections. J. A. M. A. *223*:1030–1032, 1973.
453. Weinstein, L., and Schlesinger, J. J.: Pathoanatomic, pathophysiologic and clinical correlations in endocarditis. N. Engl. J. Med. *291*:832–837, 1122–1126, 1974.
454. Weinstein, M. P., Stratton, C. W., Ackley, A., et al.: Multicenter collaborative evaluation of a standardized bactericidal test as a prognostic indicator in infective endocarditis. Am. J. Med. 78:262–269, 1985.
455. Wells, L., Ritter, N., and Donald, F.: *Kingella kingae* endocarditis in a sixteen-month-old child. Pediatr. Infect. Dis. J. *20*:454–455, 2001.
456. Werner, A. S., Cobbs, C. G., Kaye, D., et al.: Studies on the bacteremia of bacterial endocarditis. J. A. M. A. *202*:199–203, 1967.
457. Wheeler, J. G., and Weesner, K. M.: *Staphylococcus aureus* endocarditis and pericarditis in an infant with a central venous catheter. Clin. Pediatr. (Phila.) *23*:46–47, 1984.
458. White, P. D.: The incidence of endocarditis in earliest childhood. Am. J. Dis. Child. *32*:536–549, 1926.
459. Williams, R. C., and Kunkel, H. G.: Rheumatoid factor, complement and conglutinin aberrations in patients with subacute bacterial endocarditis. J. Clin. Invest. *41*:666–675, 1962.

460. Wilson, L. E., Thomas, D. L., Astemborski, J., et al.: Prospective study of infective endocarditis among injection drug users. J. Infect. Dis. *185*:1761–1766, 2002.
461. Wilson, W. R., Davidson, G. K., Guiliani, E., et al.: Cardiac valve replacement in congestive heart failure due to infective endocarditis. Mayo Clin. Proc. *54*:223–226, 1979.
462. Wilson, W. R., Gilbert, D. N., Bisno, A. L., et al.: Evaluation of new anti-infective drugs for the treatment of infective endocarditis. Clin. Infect. Dis. *15*(Suppl. 1):89–95, 1992.
463. Wilson, W. R., Karchmer, A. W., Dajani, A. S., et al.: Antibiotic treatment of adults with infective endocarditis due to streptococci, enterococci, staphylococci, and HACEK microorganisms. J. A. M. A. *274*:1706–1713, 1995.
464. Wilson, W. R., Thompson, R. L., Wilkowske, C. J., et al.: Short-term therapy for streptococcal infective endocarditis. J. A. M. A. *245*:360–363, 1981.
465. Witt, M. D., and Bayer, A. S.: Comparison of fluconazole and amphotericin B for prevention and treatment of experimental *Candida* endocarditis. Antimicrob. Agents Chemother. *35*:2481–2485, 1991.
466. Wolfson, J. S., and Swartz, M. N.: Serum bactericidal activity as a monitor of antibiotic therapy. N. Engl. J. Med. *312*:968–975, 1985.
467. Woods, G. L., Wood, R. P., and Shaw, B. W.: *Aspergillus* endocarditis in patients without prior cardiovascular surgery: Report of a case in a liver transplant recipient and review. Rev. Infect. Dis. *11*:263–272, 1989.
468. Yankah, A. C., Klose, H., Petzina, R., et al.: Surgical management of acute aortic root endocarditis with viable homograft: 13 years experience. Eur. J. Cardiothorac. Surg. *21*:260–267, 2002.
469. Yeaman, M. R., Norman, D. C., and Bayer, A. S.: *Staphylococcus aureus* susceptibility to thrombin-induced platelet microbicidal protein is independent of platelet adherence and aggregation in vitro. Infect. Immun. *60*:2368–2374, 1992.
470. Yokochi, K., Sakamato, H., Mikajima, T., et al.: Infective endocarditis in children: A current diagnostic trend and the embolic complications. Jpn. Circ. J. *50*:1294–1297, 1986.
471. Yu, V. L., Fang, G. D., Keys, T. F., et al.: Prosthetic valve endocarditis: Superiority of surgical valve replacement versus medical therapy alone. Ann. Thorac. Surg. *58*:1073–1077, 1994.
472. Zakrzewski, T., and Keith, J. D.: Bacterial endocarditis in infants and children. J. Pediatr. *67*:1179–1193, 1965.
473. Ziment, I.: Nervous system complications in bacterial endocarditis. Am. J. Med. *47*:593–607, 1969.
474. Zubler, R. H., Lange, G., Lambert, P. H., et al.: Detection of immune complexes in unheated sera by a modified ^{125}I-Clq binding test. J. Immunol. *116*:232–239, 1976.

Infectious Pericarditis

SHELDON L. KAPLAN ■ RICHARD A. FRIEDMAN

Purulent pericarditis generally refers to bacterial infection of the pericardium. Inflammation of the pericardium, however, may result from numerous nonbacterial microorganisms or may occur with a variety of noninfectious illnesses (Table 33–1). Regardless of the cause of pericarditis, the responses of the pericardium are limited to acute inflammation, effusion with or without tamponade, and fibrosis with or without constriction.[16] Because untreated purulent pericarditis is rapidly fatal, suspecting the disease early and approaching the diagnosis aggressively are important.

Anatomy and Function

The pericardium is composed of two loosely approximated layers: visceral and parietal. The visceral pericardium is composed of mesothelial tissue, which closely follows the contour of the heart and extends for a short distance beyond the atria and ventricles to the great vessels. The outer parietal pericardium is a more fibrous structure, composed of layers of collagen interlaced with elastic fibers. The pericardial sac is attached to the diaphragm below, to the sternum in front, and to the thoracic vertebrae, esophagus, and aorta posteriorly. It is surrounded by the lungs on either side and is related closely to the main bronchi and the mediastinal lymph nodes. The phrenic and vagus nerves supply a network of pain fibers to the parietal pericardium.

The dynamics of the pericardial fluid are understood poorly. The pericardial membrane is active in the transfer of water, electrolytes, and relatively small molecules. Molecules of large molecular weight, however, are absorbed poorly from the pericardial space because lymphatic channels are sparse and drainage must occur primarily through the epicardial capillaries.[59]

The function of the pericardium was summarized by Ainger[1]: prevention of overdistention of the heart, protection of the heart from infection and adhesions, maintenance of the heart within a fixed geometric position within the chest, and regulation of the interaction between the stroke volumes of the two ventricles.

Bacterial Pericarditis

POPULATION AND INCIDENCE

Although purulent pericarditis is not a common infection in the pediatric age group, it remains an important one to recognize because of its life-threatening nature. In an extensive early literature review of purulent pericarditis, one half of 425 cases occurred in children younger than 13 years of age.[6] In a review of 162 reported children with pericarditis from 1950 to 1977, 67 percent of the children were 48 months old or younger.[25] From 1962 to 1974, 67 cases were recognized at St. Louis Children's Hospital (Table 33–2).[77] During this 12-year period, pericardial disease of all causes occurred in approximately 1 of every 850 hospital admissions.[77] Twelve (18%) of these children had purulent pericarditis. Most cases in younger children are infectious. Acute pericarditis was found in 20 children between 1987 and 1997 in a hospital in Iran.[67] The causes of pericarditis were bacterial in eight (40%), collagen vascular disease in six (30%), viral in four (20%), and secondary to mediastinal mass invasion in two

TABLE 33–1 ■ CAUSES OF PERICARDITIS

Idiopathic

Benign
Recurrent

Infectious

Purulent
1. Bacterial: *Staphylococcus aureus, Haemophilus influenzae,* streptococci, *Neisseria meningitidis, Streptococcus pneumoniae,* anaerobes, *Francisella tularensis, Salmonella,* enteric bacilli, *Pseudomonas, Listeria, Neisseria gonorrhoeae, Actinomyces,* nocardiosis
2. Tuberculosis
3. Fungal: histoplasmosis, coccidioidomycosis, aspergillosis, candidiasis, blastomycosis, cryptococcosis

Viral
1. Coxsackieviruses B
2. Other: influenza A and B, mumps, echoviruses, adenoviruses, infectious mononucleosis, hepatitis, measles, cytomegalovirus

Other
1. Rickettsial: typhus, Q fever
2. Mycoplasmal: *Mycoplasma pneumoniae*
3. Parasitic: *Entamoeba histolytica, Echinococcus*
4. Spirochetal: syphilis, leptospirosis
5. Chlamydial: psitticosis
6. Protozoal: toxoplasmosis

Noninfectious

Postpericardiotomy syndrome
Rheumatic fever
Connective tissue disorders: JRA, SLE, dermatomyositis, periarteritis nodosa
Trauma: blunt or penetrating
Metabolic: uremia, myxedema
Hypersensitivity: serum sickness, pulmonary infiltrates with eosinophilia, Stevens-Johnson syndrome, drugs (hydralazine, procainamide, chemotherapy)
Neoplasm: leukemia, metastatic
Postirradiation

JRA, juvenile rheumatoid arthritis; SLE, systemic lupus erythematosus.

(10%). Although rare, purulent pericarditis also can occur in neonates.[48] In most series, a marked male predominance has been noted.

ETIOLOGY

Primary purulent pericarditis is a rare disease and accounted for only 7 of 50 cases of pericarditis reported by Gersony and McCracken.[30] The disease is associated most often with infection from another site, with hematogenous or direct spread to the pericardium. Feldman[25] reviewed all cases of bacterial pericarditis reported in the English language literature from 1950 to 1977. Bacteria were isolated in 146 (90%) of 162 cases. No other infection was found in 10 patients. The most common concomitant site involved was the lung, especially for *Staphylococcus aureus, Haemophilus influenzae,* and *Streptococcus pneumoniae.* When septic arthritis, osteomyelitis, or skin infections were found, *S. aureus* most often was the cause of pericarditis. *Neisseria meningitidis* and *H. influenzae* most often were responsible for concomitant meningitis and pericarditis.

Before the introduction of antibiotics, pneumococcal and streptococcal organisms were the most frequent causes of purulent pericarditis in children. Most cases were associated with pulmonary infections. Nearly one half the patients with streptococcal pericarditis had associated postinfluenzal pneumonia. Hemolytic streptococci were isolated most often; 10 percent were nonhemolytic streptococci, and 5 percent were viridans streptococci. Kauffman and colleagues[50] reviewed 113 cases of pneumococcal pericarditis reported since 1900. Preceding pneumonia was present in 93 percent and empyema in 66 percent. Pericarditis was thought to be a late event resulting from delay in administering appropriate therapy for pneumonia.

TABLE 33–2 ■ PERICARDITIS IN CHILDREN, 1962–1974 (ST. LOUIS CHILDREN'S HOSPITAL)*

Etiology	Number of Patients
Unknown	28
Purulent	12
Juvenile rheumatoid arthritis	9
Acute rheumatic fever	8
Uremia	5
Viral	2
Blunt chest trauma	2
Dermatomyositis	1

*Patients with postpericardiotomy pericarditis and those with small effusions at autopsy were excluded from consideration.
From Strauss, A. W., Santa Maria, M., and Goldring, D.: Constrictive pericarditis in children. Am. J. Dis. Child. *129*:822–826, 1975. Copyright 1975, American Medical Association.

S. aureus is the organism most commonly responsible for purulent pericarditis in children.[5, 25, 30, 42, 67] Most cases are the result of hematogenous seeding of the pericardium from staphylococcal pneumonia with empyema, acute osteomyelitis, or soft tissue abscesses. Occasionally, the pericardium is infected during the course of staphylococcal endocarditis. *S. aureus* is the organism recovered most frequently when purulent pericarditis develops within 3 months of open heart surgery. The clinical course of acute staphylococcal pericarditis is dominated by severe toxemia. In addition to the necrotizing infection produced by *S. aureus,* the organism often releases a potent exotoxin, which produces shock and contributes to the high mortality. *S. aureus* was isolated from 73 percent of infants who died of purulent pericarditis in the series reported by Gersony and McCracken.[30] It was responsible for 50 percent of cases in children between 1 and 4 years of age in the review by Feldman.[25] In seven patients younger than 1 month of age, *S. aureus* was isolated from four. This finding is corroborated in literature from other countries.[17, 45, 67] In one of the latest series, Thebaud and colleagues[80] reported 19 children with purulent pericarditis in a children's hospital in Paris between 1979 and 1994. The mean age of the children was 3 years (range, 3 months to 10 years). The organisms isolated were *S. aureus* (3 cases), *H. influenzae* (4), group A *Streptococcus* (3), *S. pneumoniae* (3), and *N. meningitidis* (1). Concomitant infections included pneumonia (6), osteomyelitis (3), cellulitis (1), and sinusitis (1). *S. aureus* pericarditis as a complication of varicella has been reported in several children.[8]

In the prevaccine era, the second most frequently encountered organism was *H. influenzae* type b.[14] It was responsible for 22 percent (35 of 163) of the cases in Feldman's review.[25] A single site of coexisting infection, the lung, was identified in 16 of the 35 cases. Meningitis as a single other site of infection was found in 5 of 35 patients, and multiple involvement was found in 7 of 35.[25] Echeverria and colleagues[22] summarized 33 cases from the literature. Pulmonary infiltrates and empyema were seen in 64 percent of patients. Nearly 85 percent had symptoms of an upper respiratory tract infection in the preceding 5 to 12 days. Because the *H. influenzae* type b conjugate vaccine has been given routinely to young infants in developed countries, this organism has been eliminated as a cause of invasive infections, including pericarditis.

Pneumococcal, streptococcal, and meningococcal pericarditis have diminished in frequency since the introduction of penicillin.[6] Go and coworkers[32] summarized the 15 reported cases of pneumococcal pericarditis from 1980 to 1998. One was a child. Only four cases did not have an underlying risk factor. In a surveillance study of invasive pneumococcal infections in eight pediatric hospitals, only three cases of pericarditis have been observed in more than 2500 cases of systemic pneumococcal infection during the 6-year period of 1993 through 1999.[49] Pericardial involvement occurs in approximately 5 percent of young adults with meningococcemia.[19, 39] The clinical course generally is milder than that observed with other types of purulent pericarditis. Pericardial involvement rarely is detected at the time of hospital admission. Pericarditis became apparent by the third day in 13 of 17 patients reported by Dixon and Sanford.[19] In some, it did not occur until late in the course of therapy. Whether this late-onset pericardial effusion is a part of the meningococcal infection or is related to immune complexes is unclear.[19, 62, 72] Primary meningococcal pericarditis that occurs without clinical evidence of meningococcemia, meningitis, or any other focal infection has been reported in 16 patients, including 6 children 18 years old or younger (range, 2 to 18 years).[3] Meningococcal serotype C was identified in 11 (79%) of 14 cases for which the serotype was known. Cardiac tamponade developed in 88 percent of the patients.

Occasionally, other microorganisms cause acute purulent pericarditis. Feldman[25] reported that 11 (8%) of 146 cases of pericarditis in children were caused by *Pseudomonas aeruginosa*. *P. aeruginosa* has caused pericarditis in an immunocompetent adult with cystic fibrosis.[2] Pericarditis can occur with pneumonic tularemia, salmonellosis, sepsis from enteric bacilli, listeriosis, and disseminated gonococcal disease.[6] Anaerobic bacteria should be suspected when pericarditis develops in association with lung abscess, intra-abdominal infection, or a penetrating wound. Callanan and colleagues[10] reported the rapid development of constrictive pericarditis after purulent pericarditis caused by anaerobic streptococcal infection. The child had a history of blunt trauma to the chest with no evidence of a penetrating wound 3 weeks before cardiac tamponade developed. The incidence of anaerobic infection may be underestimated because of improper handling of specimens for culture.[25] Prolonged symptoms related to pericarditis can be associated with *Mycoplasma pneumoniae* infection.[23]

Mycobacterium tuberculosis, once a common cause of acute pericarditis in the United States,[5] now is responsible more often for chronic pericardial disease. This infection is a complication of miliary tuberculosis and rarely a primary infection. In the series of 2500 children with tuberculosis reported by Lincoln and Savell,[55] pericarditis was diagnosed in 0.4 percent and found at necropsy in 5 percent of patients. Review of 100 cases of tuberculous pericarditis in South African blacks by Desai[18] revealed a marked male predominance (72%). The duration of symptoms, consisting of cough and peripheral edema, in most patients was 0 to 120 days. Most patients were febrile and had congestive heart failure. Generalized lymphadenopathy occurred in nearly 30 percent of patients, pulsus paradoxus occurred in one half, and a friction rub was audible in 25 percent. Of the 52 patients who had pericardiocentesis, 40 percent yielded fluid, but none was positive for acid-fast bacilli. Pericardial effusion was demonstrated in 82 patients, 16 of whom died of tamponade and another 16 of whom developed constricting pericarditis.

The four stages of tuberculous pericarditis have been described as dry, effusive, absorptive, and constrictive.[64] Granulomata usually are found in the dry stage and heal with no sequelae. The effusive stage occurs commonly with tuberculous lymphadenitis, and 15 to 200 mL of fluid usually accumulates in the pericardial space. The absorptive stage is characterized by thickening of the pericardium with fibrin deposition. Further fibrin deposition plus calcification occurs during the constrictive phase. The disease may progress through all stages or remain in one stage.

Latent infection in the mediastinal lymph nodes with spread directly into the pericardium is thought to be the mode of involvement with *M. tuberculosis.*[64] The lymph nodes at the tracheal bifurcation often are the source.

Histoplasma pericarditis generally occurs with pulmonary, rather than disseminated, disease.[66] Coccidioidomycosis[13] and, rarely, blastomycosis[38] also may cause pericardial disease. Other pathogenic fungi include *Aspergillus* and *Candida.* These fungi are more serious considerations in patients who are immunosuppressed, have serious burns, or are receiving long-term broad-spectrum antibiotics after undergoing cardiac surgery.[69]

PATHOLOGY AND PATHOGENESIS

Pericarditis begins with fine deposits of fibrin adjacent to the great vessels; it causes the pericardial membrane to lose its smoothness and translucency. Numerous granulocytes may extend into the myocardium.[34]

Bacterial pericarditis most commonly results from direct extension of infection from involved lung and pleura. Pulmonary infections may spread to the pericardium through the bronchial circulation.[37] Pericarditis also can develop through hematogenous dissemination from infection elsewhere. Pericarditis also may be the result of an immunologically induced response to a primary infection.

As pericardial fluid accumulates, intrapericardial pressure rises. The rate of rise is a function of the speed of accumulation and the compliance of the pericardium. With slow accumulation of fluid, large volumes can be accommodated because of the gradual expansion of the parietal pericardium. As the compliance of the pericardium reaches its maximum, however, further accumulation of even small volumes of fluid results in an abrupt increase in intrapericardial pressure. If pericardial fluid accumulates at a rapid rate, marked elevation in intrapericardial pressure may occur with much smaller volumes of fluid. As little as 100 mL can cause severe tamponade in a small child, whereas up to 3 L may accumulate slowly in an older child and not result in tamponade.[1]

The most significant hemodynamic effect of pericardial effusion is restriction of ventricular filling. Ventricular end-diastolic, atrial, and venous pressures rise on the right and left sides of the heart equally. When restriction of ventricular filling becomes more pronounced, the ventricular stroke volume and cardiac output fall. In an attempt to maintain cardiac output, tachycardia and peripheral vasoconstriction occur. Systemic arterial blood pressure and pulse pressure are reduced markedly. Tamponade occurs when these compensatory mechanisms fail to maintain adequate cardiac output.

CLINICAL MANIFESTATIONS

A diagnosis of purulent pericarditis should be suspected in any patient with septicemia who develops cardiomegaly.

The classic signs and symptoms of pericarditis are precordial pain, pericardial friction rub, evidence of cardiac fluid, and muffled heart sounds.[12] Chest pain is not a common symptom, especially in small children; the reported rates vary from 15 to 80 percent.[4, 6, 30, 42, 59, 63, 83] Acute abdominal symptoms may manifest as the presenting complaints of some children.[20]

The most common symptoms and signs of pericarditis are fever, tachypnea, and tachycardia. They also are presenting features of associated systemic infection. However, if the cardiac shadow is radiographically enlarged, with or without a friction rub, and the tachypnea and tachycardia are out of proportion to the fever, myocardial dysfunction or pericarditis should be suspected. An evanescent or ubiquitous rub may be detected. The typical sound of a rub is that of a high-frequency murmur,[65] which may have a to-and-fro or triphasic pattern but may not have any correlation with the cardiac cycle.[26] Frequently, the rub is heard better with the patient leaning forward or kneeling.[26] A rub may be differentiated from a murmur by pressing the diaphragm of the stethoscope firmly against the chest wall; this pressure amplifies the rub, and the typical scratchy quality becomes more apparent as the examiner opposes the visceral and parietal pericardium by compression of the chest. Rubs have been known to increase with inspiration.[74] Although a rub is less likely to be heard in the presence of a large effusion, it still may exist.[26] The heart sounds usually are muffled, and the palpable ventricular impulse generally is diminished. Both findings, however, may be present in congestive heart failure, but they may be absent with tamponade.

Cardiac tamponade may be an early complication of pericarditis associated with a systemic infection. Cardiac tamponade means that there is compression of the heart by a tense pericardial sac, usually full of fluid, resulting in a decrease in venous return to the cardiac chambers and a decrease in cardiac output. During inspiration, the intrathoracic pressure falls, and venous return to the cavae increases. The tense pericardial sac limits the amount of blood that can enter the right atrium because of diastolic compression; a paradoxical rise in jugular venous pressure occurs during inspiration (i.e., Kussmaul sign)[51] (Fig. 33–1).

During inspiration, a small drop in systolic blood pressure and cardiac output normally occurs and is caused by an increase in pulmonary venous capacitance. It is exaggerated with pericardial tamponade (>10 mm Hg drop in blood pressure) because of the restricted inflow into the cardiac chambers. This clinical sign has been called *paradoxical pulse,* but it actually is an exaggeration of the normal respiratory cycle[33] (Fig. 33–2).

DIAGNOSIS

Radiographic appearance of a rapidly increasing cardiothoracic ratio without increasing pulmonary vascular markings is more suggestive of pericardial effusion than of congestive heart failure caused by myocardial dysfunction (Fig. 33–3). Fluoroscopy alone generally is of little value; myocardial dysfunction and pericarditis can impair cardiac contractility.

The size of the pericardial shadow does not necessarily indicate the severity of hemodynamic effects. It is a function of the rapidity of accumulation and the volume of pericardial fluid. When acute infection results in sudden cardiac tamponade, the heart size may be normal. A large, globular heart shadow with no evidence of increased pulmonary vasculature, particularly in a patient who has signs of right-sided heart failure, is strong evidence for pericardial disease. The lack of pulmonary overcirculation helps to distinguish this condition from myocarditis; however, determining whether pulmonary infiltrates also exist may be difficult.

A plain lateral chest radiograph may demonstrate findings consistent with a pericardial effusion.[53] Separation of more than 2 mm between the anterior mediastinal and subepithelial "fat stripes" suggests an effusion. Obliteration of the retrosternal space without evidence of thymic or right ventricular enlargement also indicates pericarditis.

The extent of electrocardiographic abnormalities may be explained by the amount of pericardial effusion and the presence of superficial myocardial injury or myocarditis. Pericardial effusion gives rise to low-voltage QRS complexes as the result of the damping effect of pericardial fluid between the chest wall and the myocardium. Accumulation of fluid and fibrin under pressure also may produce an injury pattern manifested by ST-segment deviation. More than 90 percent of patients have elevation of the ST segment, which occurs most frequently in leads I, II, V_5, and V_6. Widespread T-wave inversion indicative of epicarditis may be seen in the same leads in which ST-segment elevation occurs.

Spodick[75] described four stages of electrocardiographic changes in acute pericarditis. In stage I, ST-segment elevation is pronounced and the PR segment may be depressed. In stage II, the ST segment begins to return to the isoelectric line, the amplitude of the T wave diminishes, and the PR

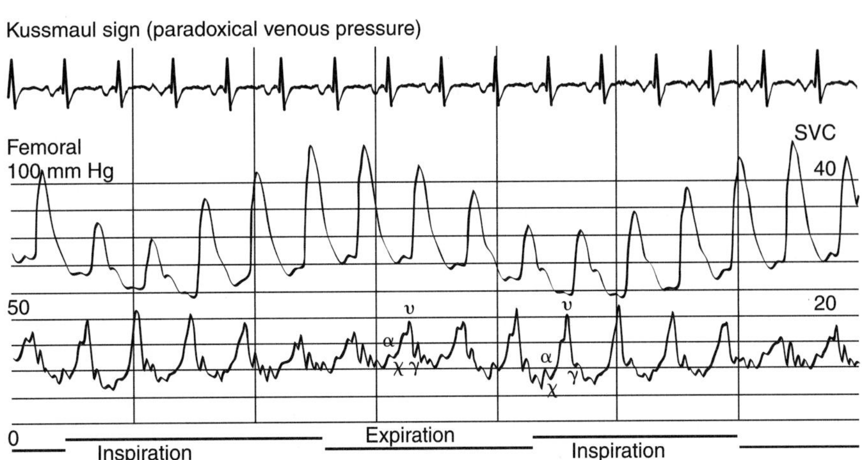

FIGURE 33–1 ■ Simultaneous recording of right atrial and femoral artery pressures. Notice the increased V wave and exaggerated decrease in the femoral artery pulse with inspiration.

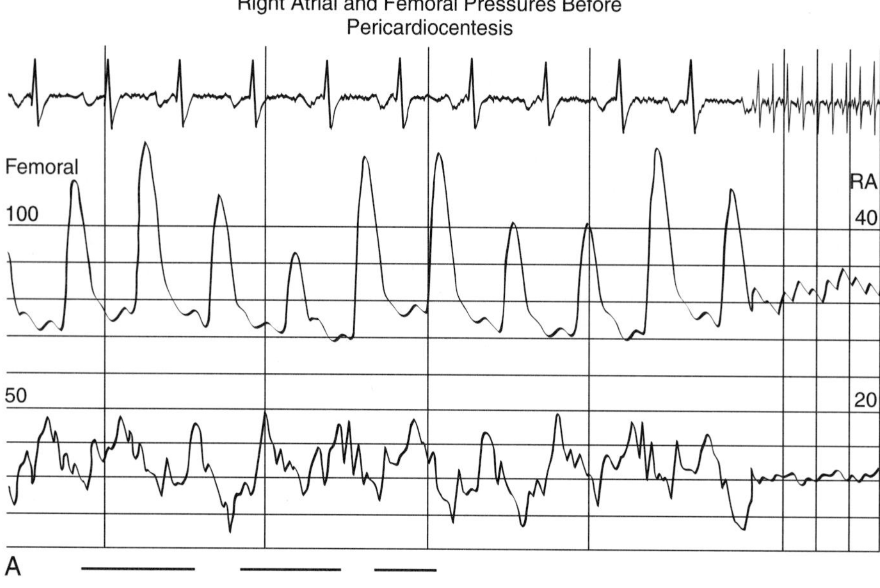

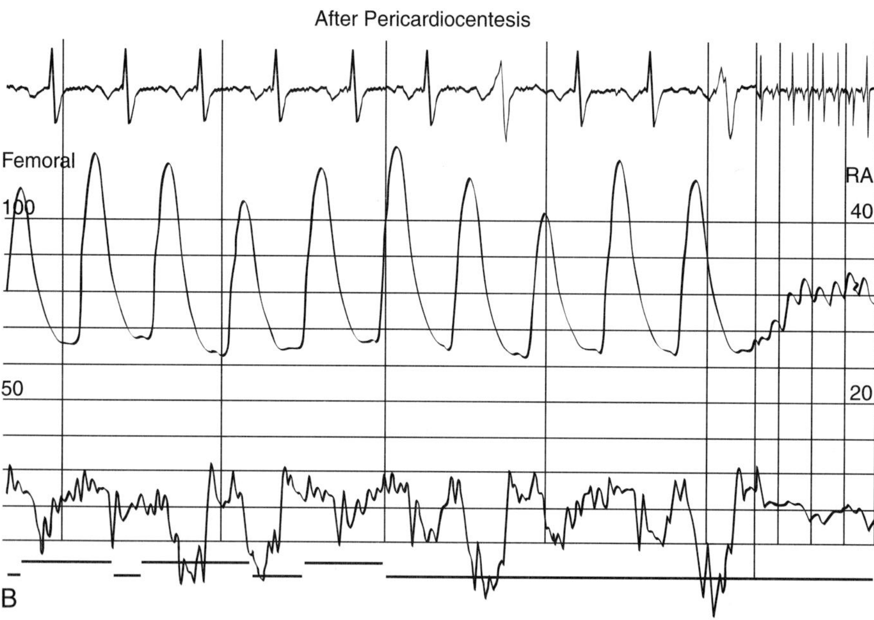

FIGURE 33–2 ■ Recordings of femoral artery and right atrial pressures before *(A)* and after *(B)* pericardiocentesis. *A,* There is an exaggerated decrease in the fall of femoral artery pressure with inspiration and a sustained increase in right atrial pressure. *B,* The recording demonstrates a more normal variation of femoral pressure and a lower right atrial pressure.

segment is depressed. By stage III, the ST segment has returned to the isoelectric line and the T-wave inversion occurs. An incompletely inverted T wave (i.e., a diphasic wave or an upright T wave with a notched summit) sometimes is observed. In stage IV, these changes may resolve completely. T-wave abnormalities, however, may persist for life and do not necessarily indicate active disease.

Ginzton and Laks[31] compared the electrocardiograms of 19 patients with acute pericarditis with those of 20 healthy patients. By forming a ratio of the amplitude of the ST-segment and T-wave height in all patients, a value of 0.25 or greater in lead V_6 had a positive and negative predictive value of 1.0 for determining the presence of pericarditis. This finding also was true in leads I, V_4, and V_5, although the predictive values were not as high as in lead V_6. Using Spodick's criteria for their patients, Ginzton and Laks[31] were unable to distinguish healthy, normal individuals from patients with acute pericarditis. Their method may prove to be more reliable, although a large study enrolling children has not been performed.

The presence of electrical alternans is seen in a large pericardial effusion. It refers to the alternation in electrical amplitude of the T wave and the QRS complex with each cardiac cycle. Electrical alternans is thought to result from the rotational and pendular motion of the heart suspended in pericardial fluid.

Deviations from classic patterns occasionally occur, and single electrocardiographic changes are not uncommon findings. For example, all 12 children reported by Okoroma and colleagues[63] had ST-segment elevation, whereas only three had concomitant low voltage.

Although many textbooks cite the frequent occurrence of dysrhythmias with pericarditis, they are an unusual occurrence in the absence of coexisting heart disease. In one study, 20 of 49 patients with acute pericarditis had no underlying heart disease.[76] Seven patients had no

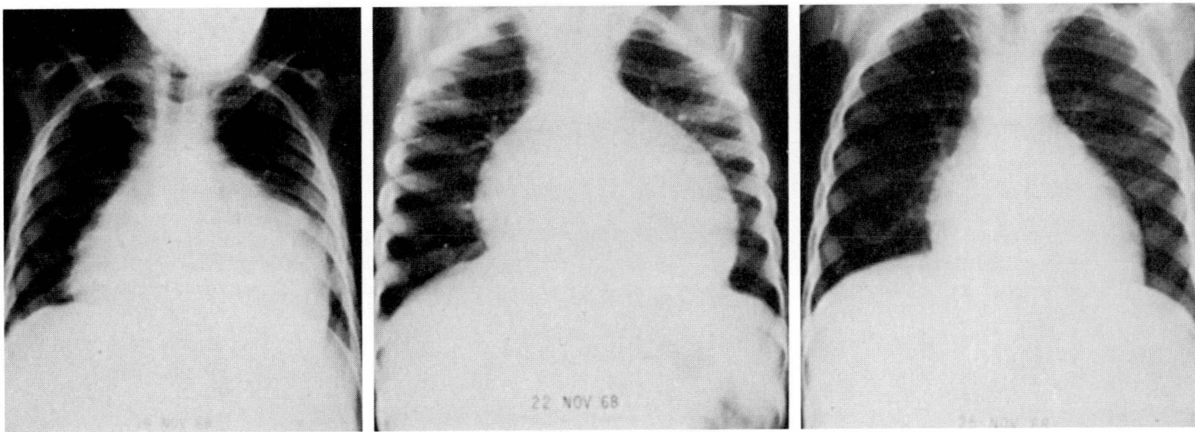

FIGURE 33–3 ■ In a patient with pericarditis, the first two radiographs demonstrate an enlarged cardiac shadow without an increase in pulmonary vascular markings. The third shows a marked decrease in apparent heart size after pericardiocentesis.

dysrhythmias documented on 24-hour Holter monitoring, and 10 of 20 had infrequent single ectopic beats. Only three patients had supraventricular tachycardia.

M-mode echocardiography is the most sensitive method for diagnosis of significant pericardial effusion.[36, 43] With a small to moderate effusion, only a "fluid space" is seen posteriorly (Fig. 33–4*B*). With a larger effusion, fluid is seen anteriorly and posteriorly, and the septal motion becomes grossly abnormal. The heart may give the appearance of freely swinging (see Fig. 33–4*A*). Newer echocardiographic techniques, such as two-dimensional sector scanning, are no more useful than is the conventional M-mode.

Friedland and colleagues[28] prospectively performed transthoracic two-dimensional echocardiography in 36 children with staphylococcal bacteremia; 89 percent had at least one suspected focus of infection, and 19 had community-acquired infections. Vegetations were detected in four children without clinical manifestations of endocarditis. Two other children, including one without suggestive clinical features, had significant pericarditis detected. The researchers concluded that echocardiography should be considered for children with bacteremia caused by *S. aureus,* even when an obvious noncardiac source of infection exists.

Computed tomography and magnetic resonance imaging of the chest are other modalities used to examine the pericardium.[7] They may help to differentiate a bacterial pericarditis from other conditions involving the pericardium. Occult or unsuspected pericarditis has been discerned with radionuclide techniques in immunocompromised patients and in trauma patients.[35, 71]

A pericardial effusion may be diagnosed by noticing a discrepancy between the position of a catheter placed adjacent to the lateral wall of the right atrium and the right cardiac border. An injection of radiopaque contrast material into the right atrium may delineate these findings further. Pressure measurements at the time of cardiac catheterization reveal the elevated right atrial pressure and further emphasize the exaggeration of venous, systemic, and left ventricular pressures imposed by inspiration (see Fig. 33–2). Injection of carbon dioxide or air into the pericardium percutaneously may delineate further the pericardial effusion fluoroscopically and differentiate freely moving fluid from loculated areas (Fig. 33–5).

The diagnosis of purulent pericarditis is established definitively only by direct examination of pericardial fluid. Purulent fluid is characterized by a predominance of

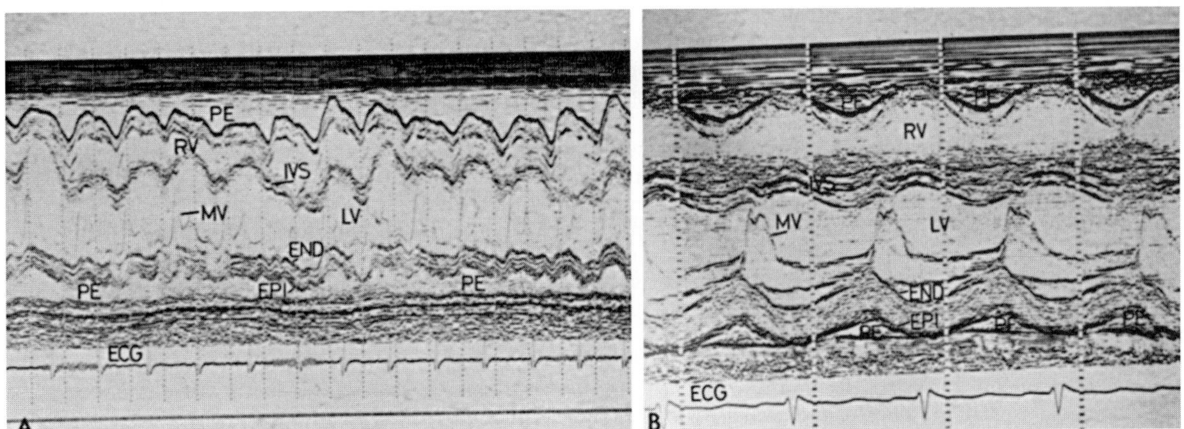

FIGURE 33–4 ■ Serial echocardiograms of a child before pericardiocentesis *(A)* and after pericardiocentesis *(B)*. *A,* Notice the large effusion anteriorly and posteriorly with the "swinging" movement of the septum and anterior and posterior walls. *B,* The heart movement is normal, and there remains only a small effusion anteriorly and posteriorly. END, endocardium; EPI, epicardium; IVS, interventricular septum; LV, left ventricle; MV, mitral valve; PE, pericardial effusion; RV, right ventricle.

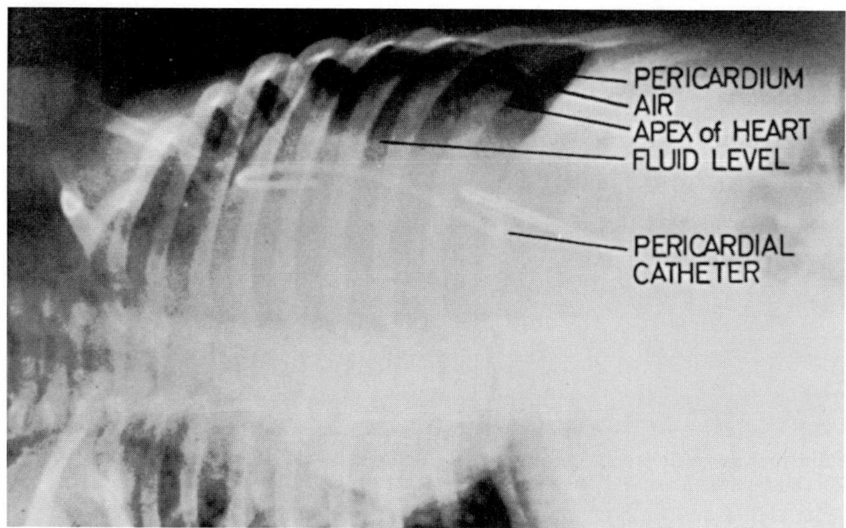

FIGURE 33–5 ■ Chest radiograph of a patient lying on the right side with a catheter in the pericardium. Air has been injected through the catheter, outlining the pericardium and fluid within the sac.

polymorphonuclear leukocytes; however, it also may occur early in the course of viral and tuberculous pericarditis. Proper handling of pericardial fluid is crucial to recovery and identification of the etiologic agent:

1. Fluid should be placed directly into broth capable of supporting aerobic and anaerobic microorganisms. The fluid should be plated directly onto agar media, such as blood agar, chocolate agar, or MacConkey agar.
2. Cultures also should be submitted for identification of *M. tuberculosis*, fungi, and viruses.
3. Several slides should be prepared for immediate examination by Gram stain and stain for acid-fast bacilli. Unstained slides should be stored in case of controversy or the need for special histochemical stains.
4. Antigen detection for *S. pneumoniae* or perhaps polymerase chain reaction for other microorganisms may be useful in selected cases, particularly when the patient has received prior antimicrobial therapy.

The causative microorganism is isolated from blood cultures in many patients. When indicated, cerebrospinal fluid also should be cultured. Because purulent pericarditis often occurs after infections of the lung or pleural space, thoracentesis can reveal the etiologic agent in many cases. Documentation of empyema together with evidence of pericardial disease correlates highly with purulent pericarditis. Van Reken and associates,[81] however, reported a child with *H. influenzae* type b pneumonia and empyema from whom only coxsackievirus A9 was isolated from nonpurulent pericardial fluid.

Acid-fast bacilli are seen on stained smears of pericardial fluid from 15 to 42 percent of patients with tuberculous pericarditis.[5] Examination of pericardial biopsy by routine methods and with special stains such as the auramine O stain can increase the frequency of identification of *M. tuberculosis*.[61] A negative purified protein derivative (PPD) skin test does not exclude the diagnosis of tuberculous pericarditis.

Grossly bloody pericardial fluid is observed frequently in patients with *Histoplasma* pericarditis, and an aspirate of the effusion reveals a predominance of mononuclear leukocytes. Growth of *Histoplasma capsulatum* from pericardial fluid rarely is successful. Demonstrating the typical intracellular yeast forms on special stain of pericardial tissue also is helpful. Elevation of the yeast phase of the complement-fixation titer in pericardial fluid allows making a more rapid diagnosis.[66] Serum precipitin antibodies to *H. capsulatum* also indicate acute histoplasmosis and are helpful when present. Detecting the polysaccharide of *H. capsulatum* in urine or other body fluids is a rapid and sensitive means by which to establish the diagnosis of histoplasmosis.

DIFFERENTIAL DIAGNOSIS

Any patient with a rapidly increasing heart size in the absence of increasing pulmonary vascular markings should be suspected of having a pericardial effusion. Purulent pericarditis must be differentiated from pericardial effusion caused by collagen diseases, other infectious agents (e.g., viral, tuberculous, rickettsial, protozoan), neoplastic disorders, metabolic disorders, and congestive heart failure.[12] Glycogen storage disease, congenital heart disease, primary myocardial disease, cardiac tumors, and coronary artery aberrations (i.e., anomalous origin from the pulmonary artery, medial wall necrosis, and Kawasaki disease) may be confused with pericardial effusion.[12] Appropriate analysis of pericardial fluid usually permits differentiation of purulent pericarditis from pericarditis caused by other disorders.

TREATMENT

Purulent pericarditis is a potentially life-threatening illness that requires pericardial decompression and open drainage, appropriate antimicrobial therapy, and intense supportive therapy.

Ainger[1] stated that more than one half of the children with purulent pericarditis require early or emergency drainage of the pericardium for relief of critical tamponade. Although bedside needle pericardiocentesis may be lifesaving or necessary for rapid diagnosis, Fowler and Manitasas[26] reported three deaths related to pericardiocentesis performed by inexperienced physicians. Complications include arrhythmias resulting from myocardial injury, laceration of the coronary arteries leading to hemopericardium and tamponade, and pneumothorax. Ledbetter[54] described a 10-year-old girl with staphylococcal pericarditis who developed an aortic aneurysm after undergoing multiple pericardiocentesis procedures for recurrent tamponade. The subxiphoid approach is recommended, and Hoffman and Stanger[41] have described the proper technique.

Decompression and drainage of the pericardium are safest in a controlled environment, such as in an operating room or under fluoroscopy in the catheterization laboratory. If the patient is awake and agitated, premedication with intravenous diazepam (1 mg per year of age) or ketamine (0.5 to 1 mg/kg) may be given.

If pericardiocentesis does not relieve symptoms successfully and evidence of tamponade continues, immediate surgical drainage is necessary. Multiple attempts may prove unsuccessful and can lead to serious complications. The pus surrounding the heart may be too thick to be aspirated, as has been seen especially with *H. influenzae* infection.[57] Surgical creation of a pericardial window with a drain occasionally is necessary for complete removal of fluid, which accumulates rapidly. In preparation for evacuation of the pericardial fluid during tamponade, adequate cardiac output can be maintained by stimulating the heart with pharmacologic agents that cause a chronotropic and an inotropic effect. Isoproterenol administered intravenously at a rate of 0.05 to 0.10 μg/kg/min is our drug of choice. It does not replace evacuating the fluid, but it gains time until the aspiration or drainage can be performed.

Medications that tend to decrease heart rate and intravascular volume are contraindicated because they further compromise the patient. Wyler and colleagues[82] warn against the use of halothane anesthesia because of its known depressant effect on myocardial function. They described two patients who had reversible cardiac arrest when this agent was used during surgery to relieve tamponade.

Controversy exists regarding the approach and extent of surgery.[24, 26, 27, 52, 58, 70] A left anterolateral thoracotomy through the fifth intercostal space or a subxiphoid approach with removal of the xiphoid process appears best. Most surgeons favor the creation of a pericardial "window"; however, some favor more extensive removal of pericardial tissue. This decision may be influenced by the severity of pericardial inflammation or the presence of bloody pericardial fluid because these conditions have greater potential for producing acute or chronic constriction. Care must be taken during the procedure not to injure the phrenic nerves. Morgan and colleagues[57] reviewed 15 children with purulent pericarditis between 1971 and 1981. *H. influenzae* occurred in 7 of 15 patients. Most patients had pericardiocentesis followed by an anterior interphrenic pericardiectomy and recovered completely. In a series of nine children with *H. influenzae* pericarditis, all received a limited left thoracotomy with subxiphoid approach for pericardiostomy, and no deaths occurred.[14] Video-assisted thoracoscopic approaches to managing pericarditis have been described, but further experience is necessary for pediatric patients.[56] For selected patients for whom surgery cannot be performed in a timely manner, the instillation of intrapericardial streptokinase or urokinase or other thrombolytic agents has been successful in draining purulent pericarditis and preventing the need for a more extensive surgical procedure.[47]

Antimicrobial therapy alone is insufficient for the successful treatment of purulent pericarditis. The survival of patients with purulent pericarditis is improved significantly when early pericardial drainage is performed (Table 33–3). In the preantibiotic era, draining the pericardium decreased the mortality rate from nearly 100 to 45 percent.[6] Occasionally, patients with meningococcal pericarditis have been managed successfully without pericardial drainage.[16] Fyfe and colleagues[29] described 73 of 79 patients with *H. influenzae* pericarditis seen between 1928 and 1984. The mortality rate before 1960 was 64 percent (7 of 11 patients), although 5 of 7 deaths were reported before the antibiotic era. From 1960 to 1969, the mortality rate was 36 percent, and from 1970 to 1979, it dropped to 11.5 percent. From 1980 to 1984, 25 cases with no mortality were reported.

TABLE 33–3 ■ INFLUENCE OF PERICARDIAL DRAINAGE ON SURVIVAL IN PURULENT PERICARDITIS IN CHILDREN

Treatment	Survived	Died
Antibiotics alone	5	28
Antibiotics and pericardial drainage	45	10

Data from references 4, 27, 50, 60.

When the etiologic agent cannot be detected rapidly, the initial antibiotic regimen should consist of two or more drugs. Because *S. aureus* is a major pathogen, a penicillinase-resistant penicillin, such as nafcillin or oxacillin, must be included in a dose of 200 mg/kg/24 hours (maximum, 12 g). In regions where infections caused by methicillin-resistant *S. aureus* have occurred in the community, when strains of *S. pneumoniae* resistant to the extended-spectrum cephalosporins are present, or when the infection is nosocomially acquired, vancomycin should be used in a dose of 40 to 60 mg/kg/day in four divided doses (maximum, 4 g). Cefotaxime (200 to 300 mg/kg/day in three or four divided doses) or ceftriaxone (100 mg/kg/day in one or two doses) should be administered to provide protection against *S. pneumoniae* (including penicillin-resistant strains), *N. meningitidis*, and *H. influenzae* type b for children who may be inadequately immunized. An aminoglycoside antibiotic should be added to this combined drug therapy when purulent pericarditis occurs after cardiac surgery, in association with genitourinary infections, or in the immunocompromised host.

For the patient who is allergic to penicillin, vancomycin, clindamycin, or cefazolin is substituted for the treatment of susceptible *S. aureus;* some patients who are allergic to penicillin are sensitive to cephalosporins.

The duration of therapy is empiric and is determined in part by the nature of concomitant infection. Generally, after a pathogen is isolated and the antimicrobial susceptibilities are known, the most specific antimicrobial agent is continued intravenously for 3 to 4 weeks.

Using chemotherapy to treat tuberculous pericarditis has had a major impact on mortality. Before its use, the mortality rate in the acute phase was 80 to 90 percent. The other 10 to 20 percent of patients died of constrictive pericarditis or miliary tuberculosis.[64] The use of three or four drugs, including isoniazid, pyrazinamide, rifampin, and possibly streptomycin, for a period of 9 to 12 months is recommended. Corticosteroids seem to be helpful in reducing the inflammatory response to infection and enhancing the resorption of pericardial fluid.[64] Mortality rates also are decreased with steroid therapy, although the development of constrictive pericarditis does not seem to be affected.[21] Prednisone (1 mg/kg/24 hours) or an equivalent dose of other preparations for 6 to 8 weeks is recommended. In selected cases, pericardiectomy may be indicated to prevent constrictive pericarditis.

Amphotericin B, alone or with other systemic agents, is indicated for treatment of fungal pericarditis. However, it rarely is required for successful therapy of *Histoplasma* pericarditis, for which nonsteroidal anti-inflammatory agents are recommended for 2 to 12 weeks, depending on the clinical resolution of symptoms and physical findings of pericarditis.[84] Steroids may be tried for 1 to 2 weeks. As with bacterial pericarditis, open pericardiectomy is critical for the successful treatment of *Candida* pericarditis.[69]

General supportive therapy in the acute stage of infection may include the administration of oxygen, volume expansion to increase ventricular filling pressure, and isoproterenol to facilitate systolic emptying. Digitalis and diuretics should be used cautiously and only when indicated by decreased myocardial function. Serial electrocardiograms may indicate the presence of occult arrhythmias and alert the physician to the degree of myocardial involvement. The patient must be monitored carefully for signs of reaccumulation of pericardial fluid and for the development of acute constrictive pericarditis. Strauss and colleagues[77] reported this complication in 2 of 12 children with purulent pericarditis. Acute constriction may develop within weeks of the initial pericardial infection[4, 9] and has been reported as early as the eighth day.[68] Constrictive pericarditis may be suspected by increasing jugular and central venous pressure, weight gain, enlarging liver, worsening dyspnea, and decreased urinary output. The persistence of heart failure when the cardiac silhouette is becoming smaller also suggests the development of constrictive pericarditis. Complete pericardiectomy should be performed promptly when constriction is suspected.

PROGNOSIS

The current mortality rate for acute purulent pericarditis ranges from 25 to 75 percent. Accurate statistics are difficult to compute from the literature because the nature and severity of underlying disease have not been considered. Factors that contribute to mortality are the delay in recognition, absence of early surgical drainage, presence of cardiac tamponade, degree of myocardial involvement, etiologic agent (particularly *S. aureus*), and age of the patient. Long-term follow-up of children with purulent pericarditis is recommended. They should be followed carefully for the presence of a constrictive component as a sequela to the acute infection. Most children, however, recover fully and return to normal activity.

Viral Pericarditis

In 1951, Christian[15] suggested that viral infections were responsible for cases of idiopathic or benign pericarditis. A viral cause, however, has not been substantiated in many patients.

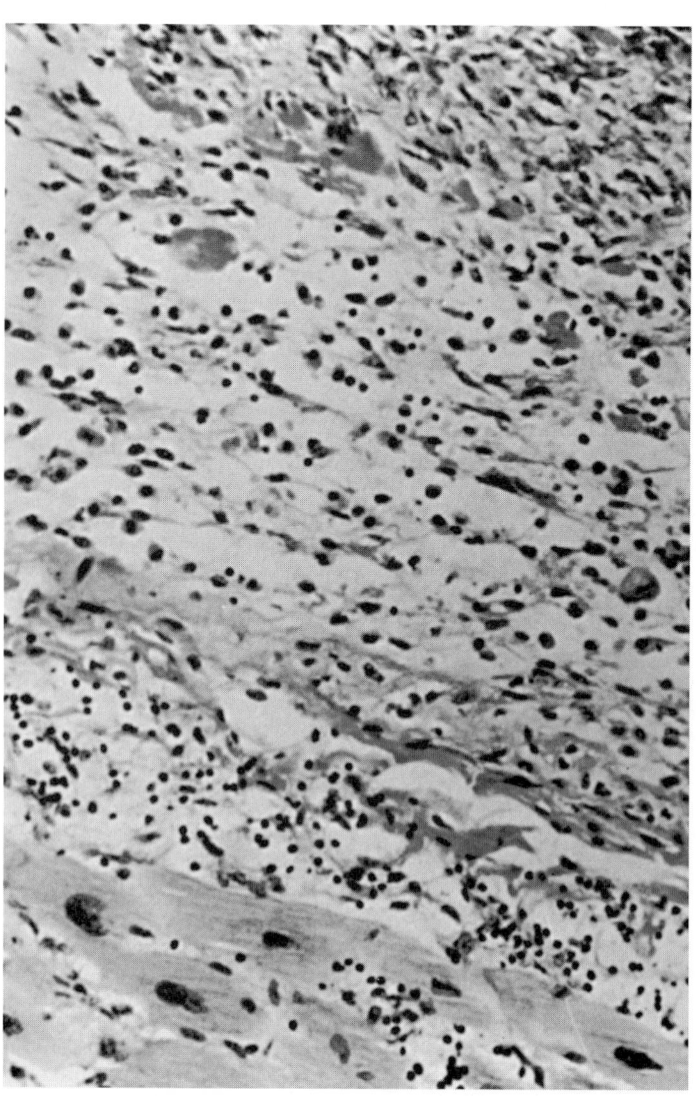

FIGURE 33–6 ■ In this case of viral pericarditis, there is a layer of fibrin and fibroblasts along the pericardial surface. The mononuclear cell infiltrate in the epicardium extends into the outer myocardium (hematoxylin and eosin staining, ×400). (Courtesy of Edith P. Hawkins, M.D., Texas Children's Hospital, Houston.)

ETIOLOGY

The principal viruses implicated in pericarditis are the coxsackieviruses.[60] Adenoviruses have been recovered less frequently.[46] Associations with varicella,[79] cytomegalovirus,[11] smallpox vaccinations, influenza,[40] influenza vaccinations,[78] and infectious mononucleosis[44, 73] have been reported.

CLINICAL MANIFESTATIONS

In approximately 40 to 75 percent of cases, the patient has a history of upper respiratory tract infection for 10 days to 2 weeks preceding the onset of symptoms. Fever and chest and abdominal pain are the most common symptoms.[15] A friction rub may be heard in 50 to 80 percent of cases.[83] Children with viral pericarditis generally are less toxic and experience smaller elevations in body temperature than do those with purulent pericarditis. Some, however, appear acutely ill. Large amounts of pericardial fluid accumulation and tamponade are rare findings.

INVESTIGATIVE TECHNIQUES

The electrocardiographic, radiographic, echocardiographic, and nuclear scanning findings described for patients with purulent pericarditis also are observed in patients with viral pericarditis. The peripheral leukocyte count, however, may reveal fewer polymorphonuclear leukocytes than in patients with bacterial pericarditis. Mononuclear cell infiltrates in the pericardium with extension into the myocardium may be seen (Fig. 33–6).

If obtained, pericardial fluid should be sent for cell count and viral culture. Nasopharyngeal and rectal samples also should be obtained and cultured for viruses. Acute and convalescent sera should be obtained so that appropriate titers can be measured if a virus is isolated.

COURSE AND PROGNOSIS

Viral pericarditis generally resolves spontaneously over the course of 3 to 4 weeks.[60] Large pericardial effusions and tamponade are rare.[12] Generally, bed rest for approximately 1 week and analgesics for pain are the only therapy that is required. Constrictive pericarditis is a rare occurrence, but pericarditis may recur.[60]

REFERENCES

1. Ainger, L. E.: Diseases of the pericardium. In Kelley, V. C. (ed.): Practice of Pediatrics. Vol. III. New York, Harper Medical, Looseleaf Reference Services, 1969.
2. Altemeier, W. A., Tonelli, M. R., and Aitken, M. L.: Pseudomonal pericarditis complicating cystic fibrosis. Pediatr. Pulmonol. *27*:62–65, 1999.
3. Baevsky, R. H.: Primary meningococcal pericarditis. Clin. Infect. Dis. *20*:213–215, 1999.
4. Benzing, G., III, and Kaplan, S.: Purulent pericarditis. Am. J. Dis. Child. *106:*287–294, 1963.
5. Boyd, G. L.: Tuberculous pericarditis in children. Am. J. Dis. Child. *86:*293–300, 1953.
6. Boyle, J. D., Pearce, M. L., and Guze, L. B.: Purulent pericarditis: Review of literature and report of eleven cases. Medicine (Baltimore) *40:*119–144, 1961.
7. Breen, J. F.: Imaging of the pericardium. J. Thorac. Imaging *16*:47–54, 2001.
8. Brumund, M. R., Truemper, E. J., and Pearson-Shaver, A. L.: Disseminated varicella and staphylococcal pericarditis after topical steroids. J. Pediatr. *131*:162–163, 1997.
9. Caird, R., Conway, N., and McMillan, I. K. R.: Purulent pericarditis followed by early constriction in young children. Br. Heart J. *35:*201–203, 1973.
10. Callanan, D. L., Morriss, M. J., Kaplan, S. L., et al.: Constrictive pericarditis due to *Streptococcus sanguis*. South. Med. J. *74:*377–378, 1981.
11. Campbell, P. T., Li, J. S., Wall, T. C., et al.: Cytomegalovirus pericarditis: Case series and review of the literature. Am. J. Med. Sci. *309:*229–234, 1995.
12. Cayler, G. G., and Riley, H. D.: Non-rheumatic inflammatory cardiovascular diseases. *In* Moss, A. J., and Adams, F. H. (eds.): Heart Disease in Infants, Children and Adolescents. Baltimore, Williams & Wilkins, 1968, p. 851.
13. Chapman, M. G., and Kaplan, L.: Cardiac involvement in coccidioidomycosis. Am. J. Med. *23:*87–98, 1957.
14. Cheatham, J. E., Grantham, R. N., Peyton, M. D., et al.: *Haemophilus influenzae* purulent pericarditis in children. J. Thorac. Cardiovasc. Surg. *79:*933–936, 1980.
15. Christian, H. A.: Nearly ten decades of interest in idiopathic pericarditis. Am. Heart J. *42*:654, 1951.
16. Connolly, D. C., and Burchell, H. B.: Pericarditis: A ten-year survey. Am. J. Cardiol. *7:*7–13, 1961.
17. Corachan, M., Poore, P., Hadley, G. P., et al.: Purulent pericarditis in Papua, New Guinea: Report of 12 cases and review of the literature in a tropical environment. Trans. R. Soc. Trop. Med. Hyg. *77:*341–343, 1983.
18. Desai, H. N.: Tuberculous pericarditis. A review of 100 cases. S. Afr. Med. J. *55:*877–880, 1979.
19. Dixon, L. M., and Sanford, H. S.: Meningococcal pericarditis in the antibiotic era. Milit. Med. *136:*433–438, 1971.
20. Donnelly, L. F., Kimball, T. R., and Barr, L. L.: Purulent pericarditis presenting as acute abdomen in children: Abdominal imaging findings. Clin. Radiol. *54*:691–693, 1999.
21. Dooley, D. P., Carpenter, J. L., and Rademacher, S.: Adjunctive corticosteroid therapy for tuberculosis: A critical reappraisal of the literature. Clin. Infect. Dis. *25*:872–877, 1997.
22. Echeverria, P., Smith, E. W. P., Ingram, D., et al.: *Haemophilus influenzae* b pericarditis in children. Pediatrics *56:*808–818, 1975.
23. Farraj, R. S., McCully, R. B., Oh, J. K., and Smith, T. F.: *Mycoplasma*-associated pericarditis. Mayo Clin. Proc. *72*:33–36, 1997.
24. Farrow, C. D., Jr., Brom, A. G., and Nauta, J.: The surgical treatment of pericarditis: A follow-up study. Dis. Chest *48:*478–483, 1965.
25. Feldman, W. E.: Bacterial etiology and mortality of purulent pericarditis in pediatric patients: Review of 162 cases. Am. J. Dis. Child. *133:*641–644, 1979.
26. Fowler, N. O., and Manitasas, G. T.: Infectious pericarditis. Prog. Cardiovasc. Dis. *16:*323–336, 1973.
27. Fredriksen, R. T., Cohen, L., and Mullins, C. B.: Pericardial window or pericardiocentesis for pericardial effusions. Am. Heart J. *82:*158–162, 1971.
28. Friedland, I. R., du Plessis, J., and Cilliers, A.: Cardiac complications in children with *Staphylococcus aureus* bacteremias. J. Pediatr. *127*:746–748, 1995.
29. Fyfe, D. A., Hagler, D. J., Puga, F. J., et al.: Clinical and therapeutic aspects of *Haemophilus influenzae* pericarditis in pediatric patients. Mayo Clin. Proc. *59:*415–422, 1984.
30. Gersony, W. M., and McCracken, G. H.: Purulent pericarditis in infancy. Pediatrics. *40:*224–232, 1967.
31. Ginzton, L. E., and Laks, M. M.: The differential diagnosis of acute pericarditis from the normal variant: New electrocardiographic criteria. Circulation *65:*1004–1009, 1982.
32. Go, C., Asnis, D. S., and Saltzman, H.: Pneumococcal pericarditis since 1980. Clin. Infect. Dis. *27*:1338–1340, 1998.
33. Golinko, R. V., Kaplan, N., and Rudolph, A. M.: The mechanism of pulsus paradoxus during acute pericardial tamponade. J. Clin. Invest. *42:*229, 1963.
34. Gore, I., and Kline, I. K.: Pericarditis and myocarditis. A. Pericarditis. *In* Gould, S. E. (ed.): Pathology of the Heart and Great Vessels. 3rd ed. Springfield, IL, Charles C Thomas, 1968, p. 724.
35. Greenberg, M. L., Niebulski, H. I. J., Uretsky, B. F., et al.: Occult purulent pericarditis detected by iridium-111 leukocyte imaging. Chest *85:*701–703, 1984.
36. Gutgesell, H. P., and Paquet, M.: Atlas of Pediatric Echocardiography. Hagerstown, MD, Harper & Row, 1978, p. 161.
37. Hahn, R. S., Holman, E., and Fuerichs, J. B.: The role of the bronchial artery circulation in the etiology of pulmonary and pericardial suppuration. J. Thorac. Surg. *27:*121, 1954.
38. Herman, G. R., Marchand, E. J., and Grur, G. H.: Pericarditis: Clinical and laboratory data of 130 cases. Am. Heart J. *43:*641–652, 1952.
39. Herrick, W. W.: Meningococcal pericarditis. Med. Clin. North Am. *2:*411, 1918.
40. Hildebrandt, H. M., Maassab, H. F., and Willis, P. W.: Influenza virus pericarditis. Am. J. Dis. Child. *104:*579, 1962.
41. Hoffman, J. I. E., and Stanger, P.: Diseases of the pericardium. *In* Rudolph, A. (ed.): Pediatrics. New York, Appleton-Century-Crofts, 1977, pp. 1474–1477.

42. Horan, J. M.: Acute staphylococcal pericarditis. Pediatrics *19:*36–43, 1957.
43. Horowitz, M. S., Schultz, C. S., Stinson, E. B., et al.: Sensitivity and specificity of echocardiography diagnosis of pericardial effusion. Circulation *50:*239, 1974.
44. Hudgins, J. M.: Infectious mononucleosis complicated by myocarditis and pericarditis. J. A. M. A. *235:*262, 1976.
45. Jaiyesimi, F., Abioye, A. A., and Antia, A. U.: Infective pericarditis in Nigerian children. Arch. Dis. Child. *54:*384–390, 1979.
46. Johnson, R. T., Portnoy, B., Rodgers, N. G., et al.: Acute benign pericarditis: Virologic study of 34 patients. Arch. Intern. Med. *108:*823, 1961.
47. Juneja, R., Kothari, S. S., Saxena, A., et al.: Intrapericardial streptokinase in purulent pericarditis. Arch. Dis. Child. *80:*275–277, 1999.
48. Kanarek, K. S., and Coleman, J.: Purulent pericarditis in a neonate. Pediatr. Infect. Dis. J. *10:*549–550, 1991.
49. Kaplan, S. L., Mason, E. O., Jr., Wald, E. R., et al.: Six-year multicenter surveillance of invasive pneumococcal infections in children. Pediatr. Infect. Dis. J. *21:*141–147, 2002.
50. Kauffman, C. A., Watanakunakorn, C., and Phair, J. P.: Purulent pneumococcal pericarditis: A continuing problem in the antibiotic era. Am. J. Med. *54:*743–750, 1973.
51. Kussmaul, A.: Ueber schwieglige mediastino-perikarditis und der paradoxen puls. Klin. Wochenschr. *10:*443, 1873.
52. Lajos, T. Z., Black, H. E., Cooper, R. G., et al.: Pericardial compression. Ann. Thorac. Surg. *19:*47–53, 1975.
53. Lane, E. J., and Carsky, E. W.: Epicardial fat: Lateral plain film analysis in normals and in pericardial effusion. Radiology *91:*1–5, 1968.
54. Ledbetter, M. K.: Aortic aneurysm complicating staphylococcal pericarditis. Okla. State Med. Assoc. *74:*222–225, 1981.
55. Lincoln, E. M., and Savell, E. M.: Tuberculosis in Children. New York, McGraw-Hill, 1963.
56. Mack, M. M., Acuff, T., Hazelrigg, S., and Landreneau, R.: Thoracoscopic approach for the pericardium. Endosc. Surg. Allied Technol. *1:*271–274, 1993.
57. Morgan, R. J., Stephenson, L. W., Woolf, P. K., et al.: Surgical treatment of purulent pericarditis in children. J. Thorac. Cardiovasc. Surg. *85:*527–531, 1983.
58. Mullen, D. C., Dillon, M. L., Young, W. G., Jr., et al.: Pericardiectomy in non-tuberculous pericarditis. J. Thorac. Cardiovasc. Surg. *58:*517–529, 1969.
59. Nadas, A. S., and Levy, J. M.: Pericarditis in children. Am. J. Cardiol. *7:*109–117, 1961.
60. Neill, C. A., and Harouturuan, L. M.: Diseases of the pericardium. *In* Watson, H. (ed.): Paediatric Cardiology. London, Lloyd-Luke, 1968, p. 703.
61. Nelson, C. T., and Taber, L. H.: Diagnosis of tuberculous pericarditis with a fluorochrome stain. Pediatr. Infect. Dis. J. *14:*1004–1006, 1995.
62. O'Connell, B.: Pericarditis following meningococcal meningitis. Am. J. Dis. Child. *126:*265–267, 1973.
63. Okoroma, E., Perry, L. W., and Scott, L. P.: Acute bacterial pericarditis in children: Report of 25 cases. Am. Heart J. *90:*709–713, 1975.
64. Orbtals, D. W., and Avioli, L. V.: Tuberculous pericarditis. Arch. Intern. Med. *139:*231–234, 1979.
65. Phillips, J. H., and Burch, G. E.: Selected clues in cardiac auscultation. Am. Heart J. *63:*1, 1962.
66. Picardi, J. L., Kaufmann, C. A., Schwarz, J., et al.: Pericarditis caused by *Histoplasma capsulatum*. Am. J. Cardiol. *37:*82–88, 1976.
67. Roodmeyma, S., and Sadeghian, N.: Acute pericarditis in childhood: A 10-year experience. Pediatr. Cardiol. *21:*363–367, 2000.
68. Rubenstein, J. J., Goldblatt, A., and Daggett, W. M.: Acute constriction complicating purulent pericarditis in infancy. Am. J. Dis. Child. *124:*591–594, 1972.
69. Schrank, J. H., Jr., and Dooley, D. P.: Purulent pericarditis caused by *Candida* species: Case report and review. Clin. Infect. Dis. *21:*182–187, 1995.
70. Sethi, G. K., Nelson, R. M., and Jenson, C. B.: Surgical management of acute septic pericarditis. Chest *63:*732–735, 1973.
71. Shreiner, D. P., Krishnaswami, V., and Murphy, J. H.: Unsuspected purulent pericarditis detected by gallium-67 scanning. Clin. Nucl. Med. *6:*411–412, 1981.
72. Simon, H. B., Tarr, P. I., Hutter, A. M., et al.: Primary meningococcal pericarditis: Diagnosis by countercurrent immunoelectrophoresis. J. A. M. A. *235:*278–280, 1976.
73. Smith, J. N., Jr.: Complications of infectious mononucleosis. Ann. Intern. Med. *44:*861, 1956.
74. Spodick, D. H.: Pericardial rub: Prospective multiple observer investigation of pericardial friction in 100 patients. Am. J. Cardiol. *35:*357, 1975.
75. Spodick, D. H.: Acute Pericarditis. New York, Grune & Stratton, 1959, p. 17.
76. Spodick, D. H.: Frequency of arrhythmias in acute pericarditis determined by Holter monitoring. Am. J. Cardiol. *53:*842–845, 1984.
77. Strauss, A. W., Santa-Maria, M., and Goldring, D.: Constrictive pericarditis in children. Am. J. Dis. Child. *129:*822–826, 1975.
78. Streifler, J. J., Dux, S., Garty, M., et al.: Recurrent pericarditis: A rare complication of influenza vaccination. Br. Med. J. *283:*526–527, 1981.
79. Tatter, D., Gerard, P. W., and Silverman, A. H.: Fatal varicella pericarditis in a child. Am. J. Dis. Child. *108:*88, 1964.
80. Thebaud, B., Sisi, D., and Kachaner, J.: Purulent pericarditis in children: A 15-year experience. Arch. Pediatr. *3:*1084–1090, 1996.
81. Van Reken, D., Strauss, A., Hernandez, A., et al.: Infectious pericarditis in children. J. Pediatr. *85:*165–169, 1974.
82. Wyler, F., Knulsi, D., Rutishauser, M., et al.: Pericarditis purulenta in children. Helv. Paediatr. Acta *32:*135–140, 1977.
83. Weir, E. K., and Joffe, H. S.: Purulent pericarditis in children: An analysis of 28 cases. Thorax *32:*438, 1977.
84. Wheat, J., Sarosi, G., McKinsey, D., et al.: Practice guidelines for the management of patients with histoplasmosis. Clin. Infect. Dis. *30:*688–695, 2000.

Myocarditis

RICHARD A. FRIEDMAN ■ DESMOND F. DUFF ■ KENNETH O. SCHOWENGERDT JR. ■ JESUS G. VALLEJO ■ JEFFREY A. TOWBIN

Myocarditis refers to inflammation of muscular walls of the heart.[221] The clinical presentation and cause may be quite varied. In this chapter, we concentrate on proven or presumed infectious causes for myocarditis. This entity may go unrecognized in a large number of patients whose illness may resolve spontaneously, or it may lead to significant morbidity and mortality.

Myocarditis may occur with many, if not all, of the common infectious illnesses that afflict infants and children (Table 34–1). Myocarditis also may occur as a manifestation of hypersensitivity or toxic reaction to certain drugs (see Table 34–1).

In the early part of the 20th century, most cases were classified as idiopathic, and a diffuse or focal interstitial inflammation was identified on histologic examination. Fiedler[57] was the first to document the pathologic changes in an adult, and the entity of diffuse or focal, idiopathic or isolated interstitial myocarditis often carries the eponym of *Fiedler myocarditis*. Rheumatic fever, diphtheria, and other bacterial infections were the only diseases recognized as associated with myocarditis, although some experts suspected that viruses might play a significant etiologic role in many cases.[206]

After the discovery by Dalldorf and Sickles[38] in 1947 of the coxsackievirus group and the subsequent isolation and

TABLE 34–1 ■ CAUSES OF MYOCARDITIS

Agent	Reference
Viruses	
Coxsackieviruses A	72, 93
Coxsackieviruses B	12, 19, 45, 72, 93, 102, 113, 120, 125, 134, 155, 190, 194, 202, 241
Echoviruses	19, 34, 47, 87, 242
Polio viruses	60, 62, 207
Rubella virus	5, 72, 141
Measles virus	198
Adenoviruses	22, 92
Vaccinia virus	70, 160
Mumps virus	70, 131, 196, 207
Herpes simplex virus	256
Epstein-Barr virus (infectious mononucleosis)	70, 95, 104, 105
Cytomegalovirus	59, 226, 238
Rhinoviruses	218
Hepatitis viruses	105, 165
Arboviruses	169
Influenza viruses	47, 135, 244
Varicella virus	59, 63, 156
Rickettsia	
Rickettsia rickettsii	105
Rickettsia tsutsugamushi	171
Bacteria	
Meningococcus	78, 197
Klebsiella	197
Leptospira	105
Staphylococcus	70, 197
Syphilis	105
Haemophilus influenzae	70
Hemolytic streptococci	70, 105
Tuberculosis	105
Typhoid	105
Mycoplasma	
Mycoplasma pneumoniae	61, 70, 204
Chlamydia psittaci	105
Protozoa	
Trypanosoma cruzi	62, 105
African trypanosomiasis	160
Toxoplasmosis	105
Amebiasis	142
Other Parasites	
Toxocara canis	243
Trichinosis	36, 76, 98, 219
Fungi and Yeasts	
Actinomycosis	105
Coccidioidomycosis	105
Histoplasmosis	37
Candida	197
Toxin	
Diphtheria	17, 132, 231, 260
Scorpion	127
Drugs	
Sulfonamides	60, 253
Phenylbutazone	97
Cyclophosphamide	9
Neomercazole	105
Hypersensitivity/Autoimmunity	
Rheumatoid arthritis	153
Rheumatic fever	197, 207
Ulcerative colitis	162
Systemic lupus erythematosus	88
Other	
Sarcoidosis	105
Scleroderma	259
Idiopathic	48, 57, 136, 173, 186, 227, 250, 251
Cornstarch	26

identification of many viruses, the number of cases of myocarditis classified as idiopathic diminished rapidly.

As a clinical entity, myocarditis is uncommon in children, representing 0.3 percent of the 14,322 patients seen by the Cardiology Service at Texas Children's Hospital between 1954 and 1977. This experience is similar to that reported by Toronto Children's Hospital for the years 1951 to 1964.[117] Apparently, however, not all cases of myocarditis are recognized clinically, and a much higher incidence is recorded in autopsy series. At Texas Children's Hospital, an autopsy incidence of 1.15 percent was found from 4343 studies performed between 1954 and 1977. This rate is considerably lower than the incidence of 6.83 percent reported by Saphir and colleagues[206] in 1944 for 1420 autopsies performed on children. In Saphir's series, 32 of the 97 cases had or probably had rheumatic carditis, whereas only 2 cases occurred in the Texas Children's Hospital series. The discrepancy is even more alarming when these observations are compared with the observations of Burch and colleagues,[27] who demonstrated evidence of interstitial myocarditis in the hearts of 29 of 50 infants and young children undergoing routine postmortem studies. Zee-Cheng and associates[260] and Parrillo and coworkers[181] found that a substantial number of patients undergoing endomyocardial biopsy for unexplained myocardial dysfunction had histologic findings suggestive of myocarditis. Other investigators[225, 226] discovered evidence of myocarditis in patients presenting with ventricular dysrhythmias. Pomerance[185] cautioned pathologists against the overdiagnosis of myocarditis, indicating that minor foci of inflammatory cells exist in approximately 5 percent of "normal" hearts. He suggests that the term *myocarditis* should be used only when the pathologist is convinced that the lesion is of a magnitude of clinical significance. However, as noted by Gore and Saphir[74] and Saphir and associates,[206] unless a thorough study of the myocardium is made, focal inflammation may be missed, and if strategically placed, a small inflammatory lesion may lead to significant disease (e.g., life-threatening arrhythmia such as complete heart block).

Some of the discrepancies between the clinical and autopsy series may be explained by the fact that, in a significant number of cases, the manifestations of myocarditis are subclinical and may be recognized only by electrocardiographic changes or perhaps not at all. In many instances, myocarditis is but one component of a generalized illness, and the cardiac dysfunction, if mild, may be overlooked.

Epidemiology

Although myocarditis generally is a sporadic disease, epidemics have been reported. Most of the epidemics have been caused by coxsackievirus group B and have affected infants in the newborn period.[49, 55] Gear and Measroch[69] were the first to identify coxsackievirus B in association with myocarditis after a nursery epidemic in a maternity home in what was southern Rhodesia. Subsequent reports of nursery epidemics appeared from Rhodesia,[156] South Africa,[111] the Netherlands,[238] the United States,[120] and Singapore.[107]

Infections with coxsackieviruses and echoviruses are common occurrences in the general population.[79] Illnesses caused by these viruses include upper respiratory tract infections, gastroenteritis, orchitis, infectious mononucleosis-like syndromes, pleurodynia, meningoencephalitis, hepatitis, pneumonia, hemolytic-uremic syndrome, and carditis.[45, 100, 133] Lerner and colleagues[133] state that by adult life most people in the United States have significant titers of type-specific protective antibodies.

As the risk of infection in childhood is reduced because of generally improved socioeconomic conditions, a susceptible adult population will be created.[81] This concept has important ramifications for pregnant women. Infection in the mother late in pregnancy may lead to intrauterine fetal infection or early postnatal infection of the newborn infant.

Spread after birth predominantly occurs by the fecal-oral route or by the airborne route. Coxsackievirus B attaches to target cells by receptors that are not shared with other members of the enterovirus group. These receptors are thought to be an essential element in viral replication and may determine tissue tropism.[254]

Approximately 50 percent of infections with both groups of viruses are subclinical.[133] In the 1965 outbreak of coxsackievirus B infection in Europe, 5 percent of the infected patients had cardiac manifestations.[58, 65] That same year, outbreaks in Scotland, Finland, and Austria occurred, and a higher incidence of myocarditis was documented. Approximately 12 percent of those affected presented with some cardiac dysfunction.[80, 254] Myocarditis has been associated with coxsackievirus B serotypes 1 through 6, and the most severe disease has occurred with types 3 and 4.[100, 119, 120] Some appreciation of the frequency also may be gained from the observations of Burch and colleagues,[27] who used an immunofluorescent technique to demonstrate coxsackievirus B antigens in 41 percent of 29 infants and children who had evidence of interstitial myocarditis at routine autopsy. Wentworth and colleagues[250] reviewed the autopsies of 2427 patients in southern Ontario, Canada. Of the 1299 cases of unexpected deaths, 20 were thought to be caused by viral myocarditis. Nine of the 20 had positive serologic evidence for coxsackievirus B infection. Less frequently, coxsackievirus A virus and echoviruses have been implicated as causes of myocarditis (see Table 34–1). Cases of idiopathic myocarditis peak during the summer months, a period corresponding to the peak fecal excretion of the enteroviruses.

Karjalainen and colleagues[115] prospectively examined 104 conscripts during a 1978 influenza A virus (H1N1) epidemic in Sweden. The incidence of myocarditis was 9 percent of the 67 verified cases of influenza virus infection.

In 1965, 260,222 cases of measles were reported in the United States; this number declined to 24,031 in 1975. Cardiac involvement in measles usually occurs after the onset of the illness, although at least one case has been described during the prodromal phase.[35]

The teratogenicity of the rubella virus in the first 4 months of pregnancy is well known. Ainger and colleagues,[5] however, demonstrated that, because of the persistence of the virus in the fetus, extensive involvement of the myocardium may lead to severe myocarditis. Of 47 infants with congenital rubella, 10 had myocarditis: 7 of the 10 had active disease, and 4 died. Morbidity in the survivors was severe. Rubella immunization programs have succeeded in reducing the number of congenital cases, and only 28 cases of congenital rubella were recorded in the mortality and morbidity statistics of the United States in 1975.[158]

Infection of the newborn with herpes simplex virus occurs in approximately 1 of 7500 deliveries.[18] Most infections are caused by type 2 virus, which is acquired from the genital tract of the mother in 95 percent of cases. Approximately 1 percent of pregnant women in the lowest socioeconomic groups have evidence of herpes. The spectrum of disease ranges from inapparent infection to a fatal encephalopathy. Myocardial involvement has been described, and herpesvirus has been isolated from the myocardium at autopsy.[255] Recognition of genital herpes and delivery of the infant by cesarean section reduce the incidence of myocarditis caused by this agent.

Osama and colleagues[177] prospectively investigated 312 cases of varicella over the course of a 1-year period. Eighteen (5.8%) of the 312 cases showed evidence of myocarditis. A statistically significant increase in myocarditis was found in patients who complained of skeletal myalgia.

Although diphtheria now is rare, 285 cases were reported in the United States in 1975,[158] compared with 160 cases in 1965.[157] The median for the years 1960 through 1964 was 463 cases, and the median for the years 1970 through 1974 was 224 cases. Approximately one third of the cases have electrocardiographic findings suggesting myocardial involvement,[62] although the rate of myocardial involvement may be as high as 84 percent with severe infections.[17] The heart is involved only when the fauces are infected, but cardiac complications are the most common cause of death.

Pathology

IMMUNOLOGIC ASPECTS

The histologic and gross anatomic changes seen in patients with viral myocarditis have been examined extensively with the use of animal models. An understanding of the immunologic response to viral infection in these models is essential in trying to explain the spectrum of injuries seen in the hearts of patients with myocarditis.

The group B coxsackieviruses have been studied the most extensively for their ability to induce myocarditis.[1] Rabin and associates[187] showed that, after parenteral injection of coxsackievirus B in mice, viremia was detected at 24 to 72 hours and maximal growth in tissue occurred at 72 to 96 hours. After that time, virus titers declined and could not be found 7 to 10 days after inoculation.[254] An inverse relationship exists between virus and antibody concentrations, implying that the latter is responsible at least partially for viral clearance.[9] Evidence shows that macrophages also are active in viral clearance.[174] The appearance of macrophages in coxsackievirus B myocarditis is typical for this disease 5 to 10 days after infection.[132, 254]

Two mechanisms, probably in combination, account for the injuries from coxsackievirus B seen in myocarditis. Direct myofiber destruction by the viral particle has been demonstrated.[13, 73, 102] A second mechanism cited is cell-mediated destruction of myofibers, and it is responsible for the greatest damage to the myocardium. Mice pretreated with antithymocyte serum lack a normal immunologic response to infection and develop a significantly less extensive necrosis of myocardial tissue than do similarly infected animals that are treated with normal rabbit serum.[254] T-cell–deficient animals clear viremia normally and do not develop significant myocarditis. This finding suggests that the T cells are not required for elimination of virus but do play a key role in the major inflammatory response to infection.[102, 254] However, mice treated within 24 hours of or before infection with neutralizing antibody failed to develop myocarditis.[148, 149, 188, 255] The combination of macrophages and antibody suppresses viral infection, and T lymphocytes participate in the injury of myocytes.

Woodruff[254] points out that T cells can cause injury through several mechanisms: accumulation of activated macrophages, production of antibody and antibody-dependent cell-mediated cytotoxicity or lysis by antibody and complement, and direct action of cytotoxic T cells. Huber and associates,[102] using BALB/c mice infected with coxsackievirus B3, showed that cytolytic T cells were the agents responsible for the major part of myocardial cell injury. These cells damaged virus-infected and noninfected myocytes in T-cell–deficient animals.

Generation of cytotoxic T cells is thought to be stimulated by infected host cells and not by the virus. The effector cells then recognize virus-specific and major histocompatibility antigens (modified H2 antigens) on the cell surface and act to destroy them through that recognition. The ongoing injury then may be considered an autoimmune process.[102, 254] Support for this concept is provided by Pacque and colleagues.[178] Using CD-1 mice infected with coxsackievirus B3, they found a potassium chloride–extractable antigen in the hearts of mice previously infected with a group B coxsackievirus that was specifically immunoreactive with immune mouse peritoneal exudate cells (i.e., stimulated production of a migration inhibitory factor). No viral activity was detected in the animals that had this extractable antigen. Similar experiments in a primate model confirmed earlier findings in mice and lent further support to similar circumstances in humans.[179] Experimental evidence also has shown that the antigen responsible for cytotoxic T-cell activity is not detectable by antiserum that contains antibodies directed at structural components of the viral capsid. Antiviral serum also has been ineffective in preventing injury.[253] Natural killer cells have been implicated in the destruction of noninfected myocardial cells.[254] The exact mechanism of their activity is unknown.

Other viral agents have been used to produce myocarditis in animals. Sakamoto and colleagues,[203] using influenza A virus (H2N2), produced myocarditis in mice. However, mice pretreated with irradiation or athymic mice did not develop myocarditis. Using encephalomyocarditis virus, which is a picornavirus similar to the coxsackieviruses, Matsumori and Kawai[148, 150] produced a model of acute and chronic myocarditis in mice. Their model showed that acute myocarditis could progress and produce a picture of dilated cardiomyopathy similar to that seen in humans after recovery from an acute episode of myocarditis.

Studies in humans with myocarditis have been performed. Maisch and colleagues[141] demonstrated antibody-mediated cytolysis in 30 percent of 144 patients with myocarditis of unknown origin and in 18 of 19 patients with confirmed viral infection (i.e., coxsackievirus B, influenza A, or mumps). The titer of a muscle-specific antimyolemmal antibody found in these patients correlated closely with the degree of cytolysis induced in vitro with rat cardiocytes. Examining the number of positive and negative responses of neutralizing antibody to coxsackieviruses B1 to B6, Hori and colleagues[97] found that adult patients with myocarditis had been exposed to a greater number of groups than had the normal control subjects. These investigators suggest that an essential step in the development of myocarditis is the infection of one group by coxsackievirus B and immunization against that type plus other types of coxsackievirus B from previous exposure. However, a few cases of myocarditis in that group showed evidence of exposure to only one type of coxsackievirus B, creating some doubt about this hypothesis.

A defect in cell-mediated immunity also has been found in patients with myocarditis. Eckstein and colleagues[53] showed a significant reduction in suppressor cell (concanavalin A–induced) activity in patients with myocarditis and congestive cardiomyopathy compared with healthy controls.

Studies have pointed to the effect of humoral effectors in promoting autoimmune myocarditis after viral clearance has occurred. Autoantibodies to various cellular components (e.g., antimyosin, adenine nucleotide translocator protein) have been described.[16] Inflammatory cytokines, including tumor necrosis factor and interleukin-1, have been demonstrated in a rat model; they possibly amplify injury by reducing catecholamine-induced ventricular contractility.[82] Anti–tumor necrosis factor antibodies administered to mice before inoculation with encephalomyocarditis virus improved survival and produced less necrosis and inflammatory cellular infiltrate by day 14 after introduction of the virus.[257]

Specific molecules known as cell adhesion molecules may be involved with the progression of the inflammatory response in myocarditis. One such molecule is intercellular adhesion molecule-1 (ICAM-1). ICAM-1 appears after inflammatory injury, and the expression of this molecule is up-regulated by cytokines such as interleukin-1 and tumor necrosis factor–α.[51, 96, 183] ICAM-1 expression is increased in mice infected with coxsackievirus B3.[214] Treatment with anti–ICAM-1 monoclonal antibody reduced the myocardial inflammation seen with the same virus.[213]

Although unequivocal proof of direct viral and humoral damage to myocytes in humans is lacking, animal models strongly suggest that it is a contributing factor. The immune response to viral infection certainly plays a major role in the damage seen long after viral clearance and may be the key element in terms of therapy for preventing further injury (Fig. 34–1).

GROSS AND MICROSCOPIC FEATURES

Isolated or idiopathic myocarditis probably is a rare pathologic entity. The pathologic cardiac findings usually are nonspecific; similar gross and microscopic changes occur regardless of the causative agent.[57, 74, 104, 173, 185, 197, 206] However, the histology sometimes suggests a specific cause.

Grossly, all four chambers of the heart are enlarged, and the cardiac weight is increased. The heart usually is flabby and pale. In some instances, especially with coxsackievirus B infections, petechial hemorrhages may be seen on the epicardial surfaces; pericardial fluid may be tinged with blood. On cut section, the ventricular muscle walls may be thinned. Occasionally, the ventricles are hypertrophied or increased in thickness because of edema. The valves are spared. The endocardial surface usually is unaffected but occasionally may be thickened and appear glistening white. This important observation suggests to some investigators that endocardial fibroelastosis, which manifests as congestive cardiomyopathy, represents a progression from acute viral myocarditis.[85, 106] In an elegant study of 64 hearts of children who had myocarditis or endocardial fibroelastosis, Hutchins and Vie[106] found 18 with endocardial fibroelastosis only, 5 with myocarditis only, and 41 with features of both diseases. When the history disclosed that the time from onset of illness to death was 2 weeks or less, only myocarditis was evident. When the time interval was between 2 weeks and 4 months, a combined picture was seen, whereas only endocardial fibroelastosis with occasional trivial myocarditis was evident when the time from onset of disease to death was more than 4 months. These findings are

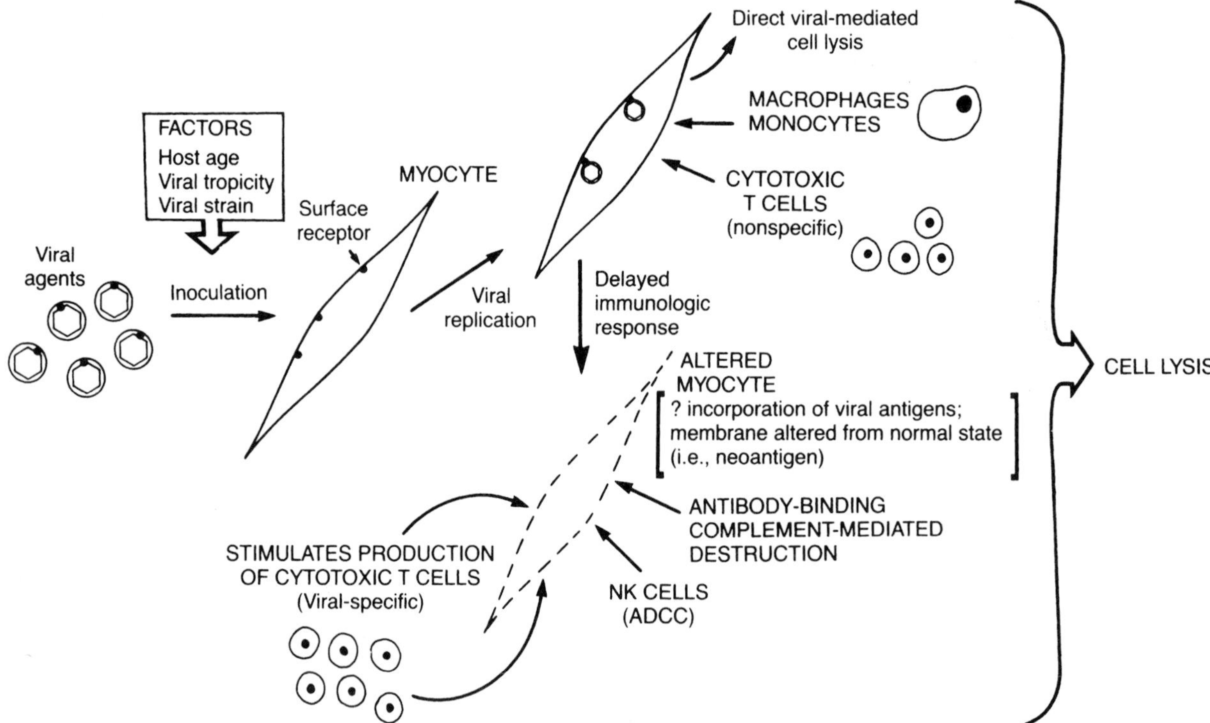

FIGURE 34–1 ■ Schema for the pathogenesis of myocarditis. Viral agents attach to cells by means of surface receptors. After a cell is infected, the cell cycle is changed. Direct virus-mediated cytolysis occurs. Cellular effectors of injury (i.e., macrophages, monocytes, and nonspecific cytotoxic T cells) are involved in the primary reaction. Myocytes that survive are altered in their structure. Cytotoxic T cells specifically targeted against the altered myocyte, natural killer (NK) cells, and complement-activated antibody-mediated cardiocytolysis or antibody-dependent cellular cytotoxicity (ADCC) take part in the secondary reaction. (Partially adapted from Maisch, B., Trostel-Soeder, R., Stechemesser, E., et al.: Diagnostic relevance of humoral and cell-mediated immune reactions in patients with acute viral myocarditis. Clin. Exp. Immunol. *48*:533, 1982.)

supported by Hastreiter and Miller,[85] who found microscopic evidence of myocarditis after transthoracic needle biopsy of the myocardium in a child who had the classic clinical picture of endocardial fibroelastosis, including left ventricular hypertrophy on electrocardiography.

Fruhling and associates[66] were able to extend these observations by demonstrating coxsackievirus B3 in the myocardium of 13 of 28 infants with endocardial fibroelastosis. Van Reken and associates[239] described a 5-month-old infant who died after the sudden onset of congestive cardiac failure and who had endocardial fibroelastosis and an echovirus 9 myocarditis documented at autopsy. The virus was isolated from the heart and from the lungs, liver, and lymph nodes.

Saphir and Field[207] observed mural thrombi in the left ventricular cavity in some patients with myocarditis and minute emboli in coronary and cerebral vessels. Coronary emboli, although rare, may play a role in the causation of cardiac dysrhythmias, which sometimes accompany myocarditis.

The microscopic picture of acute myocarditis typically shows a focal or diffuse interstitial collection predominantly composed of mononuclear cells, lymphocytes, plasma cells, and eosinophils. Polymorphonuclear leukocytes rarely are seen unless the cause of the carditis is bacterial. Virus particles and inclusion bodies are recognized only rarely.[189, 197]

In severe infections with any agent, but especially with coxsackieviruses and diphtheria exotoxin, a loss of cross-striation in the muscle fibers, edema, and, sometimes, extensive necrosis of the myocardium occur. The diphtheria exotoxin has a particular affinity for conductive tissue; dysrhythmias, including complete heart block, are relatively common occurrences in this form of myocarditis. The exotoxin interferes with protein synthesis by inhibiting a translocating enzyme in the delivery of amino acids. Carnitine metabolism also is affected, which results in triglyceride accumulation and a typical picture of fatty changes seen in myofibers.[194]

Although the perivascular accumulation of lymphocytes and plasma cells is described in coxsackievirus B myocarditis, it is a minor finding. When myocarditis is caused by rickettsiae,[106] varicella,[59, 156] trypanosomes,[62, 184] or other parasites[60, 241] or when it occurs as a reaction to sulfonamide,[60, 249] this pattern dominates.

Myocarditis seen with bacterial infections usually differs from that of presumed viral origin (Figs. 34–2 to 34–5). The myocardial changes are similar to the extracardiac findings. Microabscesses and patchy focal suppurative changes may be observed.[194] Frequently, a perimyocarditis may be seen with concomitant bacterial infection of pericardium and myocardium.

Trichinella spp. usually cause a focal infiltrate consisting of lymphocytes and eosinophils. Larvae usually cannot be identified.

Chagas disease (discussed more extensively later) may affect 50 percent of a population in an endemic area and is the most common causative agent of myocarditis in South America. Survivors of acute infection may suffer significant long-term morbidity, and the clinical course may result in protracted heart failure and death. Trypanosomes usually are visible, with neutrophils, lymphocytes, macrophages, and eosinophils all present in the same lesion.[194]

Some cases of myocarditis manifest only as disturbances in electrical conduction within the heart. Fortunately, in most instances, arrhythmias are transitory. Cases of sudden

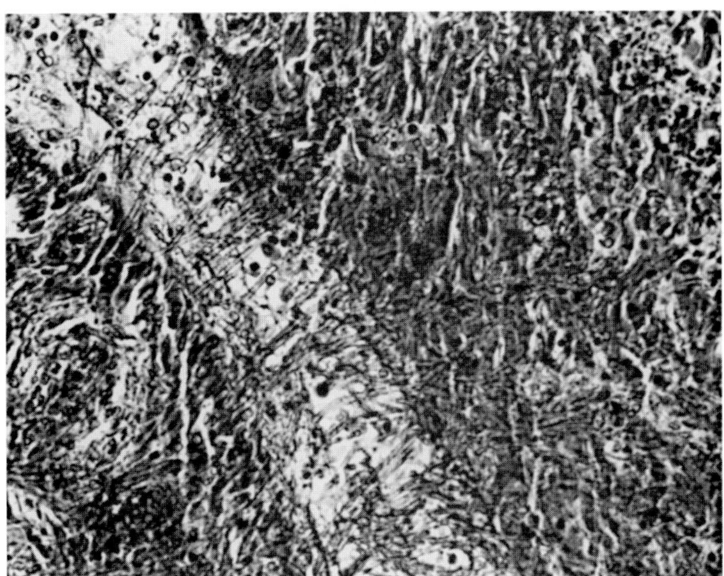

FIGURE 34–2 ■ *Candida albicans* myocarditis. Notice the focal necrosis of the myocardium with central masses of hyphae and necrotic debris surrounded by mononuclear cell infiltrate (hematoxylin and eosin staining, ×160). (Courtesy of Edith Hawkins, M.D., Houston, TX.)

death associated with myocarditis are well documented, but the mode of death often is obscure.

Sudden infant death syndrome, a distressingly common entity that affects 1 of every 500 infants, may be caused by cardiac arrhythmias in some cases.[65] James[109] found a resorptive, degenerative process in the bundle of His and the left margin of the atrioventricular node but no inflammatory cells in the cases he studied of infants who died in Northern Ireland. He concluded, however, that lethal arrhythmias of conduction disturbances may be caused by a developmental histologic change in these critical regions of the heart. Jankus[110] demonstrated lymphocytic infiltrates in the region of the main bundle and left fascicle in a 3-month-old patient who died suddenly. However, no degenerative changes were found, and the significance of these findings remains speculative.

Giant cells with or without granulomata are markers for the diagnosis of giant-cell myocarditis.[104] Granulomata have been observed in the myocardium in patients with tuberculosis, syphilis, rheumatoid arthritis, rheumatic heart disease, sarcoidosis, and certain fungal and parasitic infestations. Occasionally, giant cells have been seen in interstitial myocarditis (idiopathic or Fiedler). In a significant number of cases, giant-cell myocarditis occurs, but no cause is found. Two types of giant cells are recognized, one of which appears to be myogenic in origin and is thought to represent transitional forms of myocardial fibers. This type of cell has been found without granulomata. The second and more characteristic giant cell probably is derived from interstitial histiocytes. The latter type typically is seen in patients with myocarditis of nonviral cause, whereas the former represents a response to viral infection. Hudson[104] described similar cells in an adult who had received neo-mercazole (carbimazole) therapy, and Hodge and Lawrence[95] reported two cases of granulomatous myocarditis associated with phenylbutazone therapy.

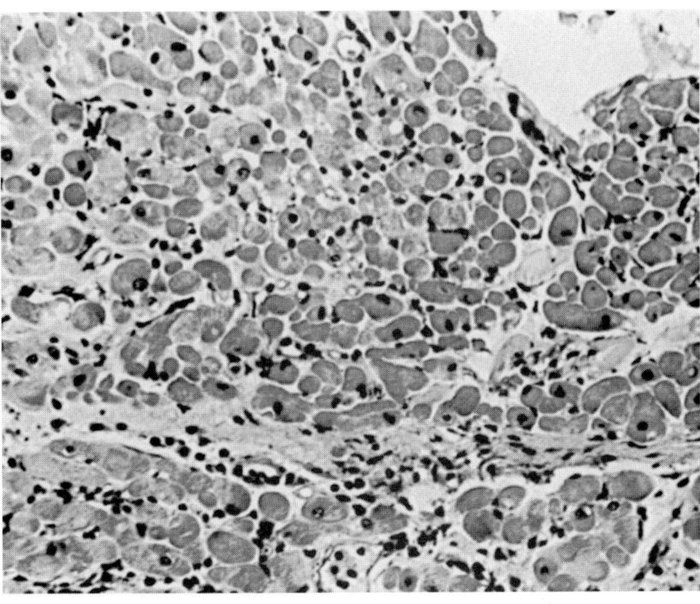

FIGURE 34–3 ■ Right ventricular biopsy. The presumed viral myocarditis is characterized by focal mononuclear cell infiltrates (hematoxylin and eosin staining, ×160). (Courtesy of Edith Hawkins, M.D., Houston, TX.)

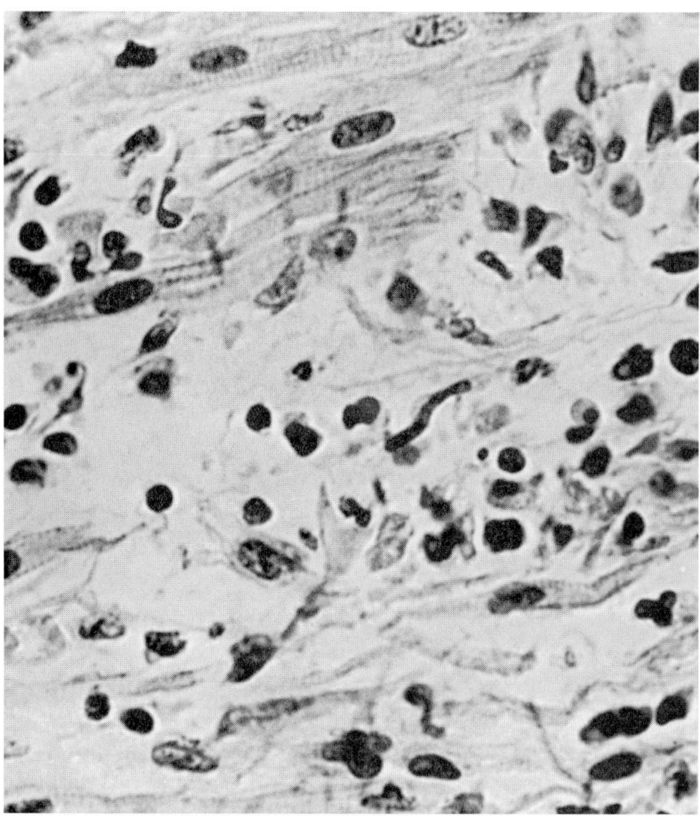

FIGURE 34–4 ■ Section of myocardium. Picornavirus myocarditis characterized by interstitial edema, mononuclear cell infiltrates, and focal myofiber disruption (hematoxylin and eosin staining, ×400). (Courtesy of Edith Hawkins, M.D., Houston, TX.)

Pathophysiology

With extensive interstitial inflammation, muscle-cell injury, or both, myocardial contractility is reduced. As a consequence, the heart enlarges and the end-diastolic volume of the ventricle increases. In the normal heart, an increase in filling volume leads, by the Starling mechanism, to an increased force of contraction, ejection fraction, and cardiac output. In patients with myocarditis, the myocardium is unable to respond in this manner, and cardiac output is reduced. Systemic blood flow may, however, be maintained by use of the cardiac reserve, mediated by the sympathetic nervous system and leading to vasoconstriction of the skin vessels and an increase in heart rate. With progressive disease or any stress (e.g., infection, anemia, fever), the heart may be unable to meet the oxygen demands of the tissues, and the clinical picture of congestive cardiac failure may become evident. Increased end-diastolic volume leads to progressive increase in ventricular end-diastolic pressure, which leads to increased filling pressure, and left atrial and pulmonary venous hydrostatic pressure may be elevated above the colloid osmotic pressure, which normally prevents transudation of fluid across the capillary membranes. Pulmonary congestion and edema, as well as systemic

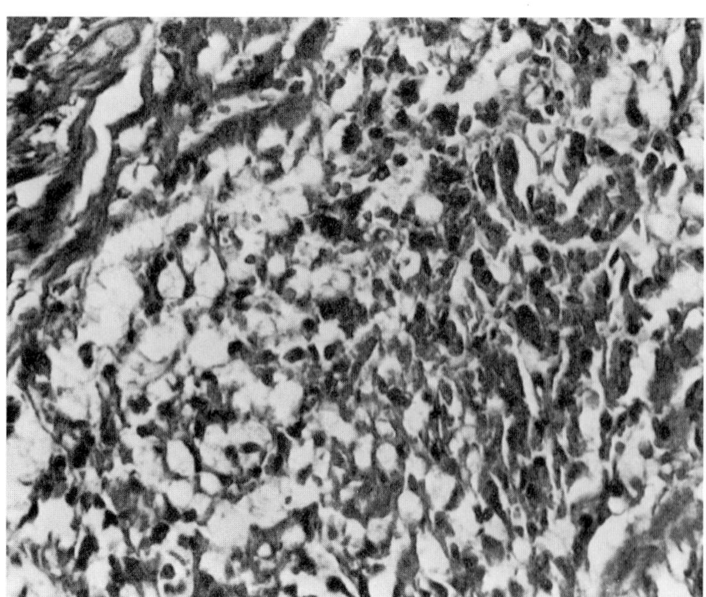

FIGURE 34–5 ■ Section of myocardium. Vaccinia (smallpox vaccine) myocarditis. Note mononuclear cell infiltrates and fatty degenerative changes (hematoxylin and eosin staining, ×400). (Courtesy of Edith Hawkins, M.D., Houston, TX.)

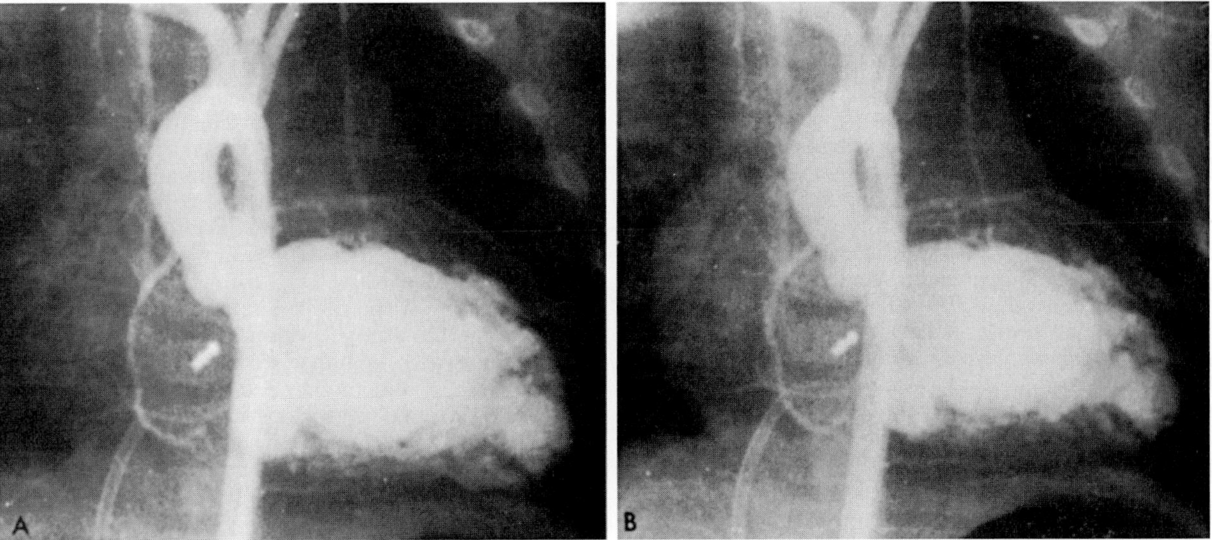

FIGURE 34–6 ■ The end-diastolic *(A)* and end-systolic *(B)* frames from a left ventriculogram of a patient with idiopathic myocarditis show irregularity of the wall and poor contractility.

venous engorgement (manifested in infants primarily as hepatic enlargement), are common findings in the more acute forms of myocarditis. In some infants and young children, the presentation predominantly is that of right-sided heart failure.[195]

An appreciation of the disturbance of myocardial function may be gained from the angiographic frames in Figure 34–6. The left ventricle is dilated considerably, and the outline is irregular in diastole and systole. The ejection fraction is reduced significantly at 35 percent instead of the normal 60 to 75 percent.

Another means of evaluating left ventricular function is the noninvasive technique of cardiac ultrasound. Normal standards have been established for children by Gutgesell and colleagues[83]; an example is shown in Figure 34–7*A*. The normal shortening fraction (i.e., percentage change in ventricular dimensions between end-diastole and end-systole) is 35 ± 4 percent, irrespective of age (range, 28–44%). Figure 34–7*B* illustrates the case of a 4-year-old child with idiopathic myocarditis and demonstrates ventricular dilatation with markedly reduced motion of the left ventricular posterior wall and septum, leading to a shortening fraction of only 12 percent. Further assessment of ventricular function also can be achieved by measuring systolic time intervals obtained from simultaneous recording of the electrocardiogram and the semilunar valve opening and closing points on the echocardiogram.[83]

Clinical Presentation

The clinical presentation of myocarditis varies considerably with the age of the patient and the virulence of the organism. At one end of the spectrum is a fulminant and rapidly fatal illness, and at the other, no apparent clinical disturbance at all. The newborn infant especially is susceptible to the severe form of myocarditis usually caused by the coxsackieviruses B,[120, 238] but it also is recognized with rubella[5] and herpes simplex[256] viral infections and with toxoplasmosis.[62, 104]

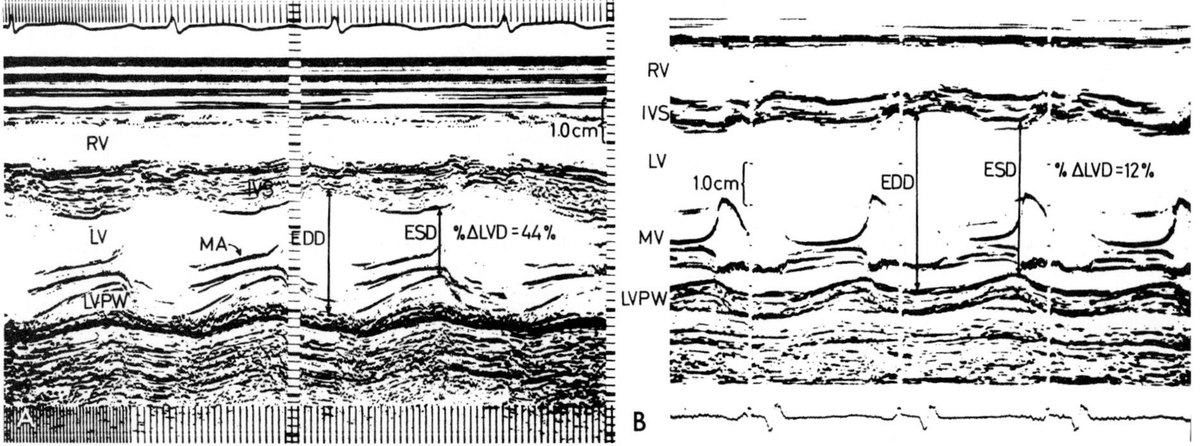

FIGURE 34–7 ■ *A*, Normal echocardiogram of a 4-year-old child. *B*, Echocardiogram of a 4-year-old child with idiopathic myocarditis shows left ventricular dilatation and severely reduced shortening fraction. EDD, end-diastolic dimension; ESD, end-systolic dimension; IVS, interventricular septum; LVPW, left ventricular posterior wall; MA, mitral apparatus; MV, mitral valve, %ΔLVD, percent change in left ventricular dimension (shortening fraction).

In many of these infections, myocarditis is but one component of a generalized illness, often with severe hepatitis and encephalitis.[119, 120] In some instances, however, infections with these organisms may produce only a mild clinical disturbance.[25, 108] In the report by Brightman and colleagues,[25] a nursery epidemic of coxsackievirus B5 infection in preterm infants was recognized only by chance because a virologic survey was in progress at the time in their institution. Sporadic cases also occurred among term infants. No instances of myocarditis occurred, and all the infants recovered. Findings were lethargy, failure to gain weight, and, in some infants, evidence of aseptic meningitis. As described in the review by Kibrick and Benirschke[120] of 25 infants with coxsackievirus B myocarditis, vague symptoms such as lethargy and anorexia may herald the onset of the severe disease, emphasizing that close attention should be paid to all symptoms, especially in the newborn, no matter how nonspecific. Four infants had episodes of vomiting, and fever was documented for more than one half of the cases; occasionally, the temperature was subnormal. Cyanosis; respiratory distress; and tachycardia, cardiomegaly, or electrocardiographic changes occurred in 19 of 23 infants. Tachypnea, a respiratory rate higher than 60 per minute in the newborn, is an early sign of heart failure in the young infant and should alert the clinician to this diagnosis.

In older infants and children, the manifestations of myocarditis generally are less fulminant than those in newborns.[117, 195, 201, 245, 252] However, an acute and fatal illness has been associated with idiopathic myocarditis[136] and the myocarditis associated with enteroviruses,[120] adenoviruses,[89] mumps,[127] chickenpox,[59] diphtheria,[17] cytomegalovirus,[232] and many of the other causes listed in Table 34–1. Some older children have been reported with acute, substernal chest pain consistent with angina and have electrocardiographic changes of acute myocardial infarction.[101, 152] The usual clinical picture is that of an acute or a subacute illness, which often begins with a mild upper respiratory infection and a low-grade fever.[10] Some infants have only vague, nonspecific suggestions of disease (e.g., irritability, periodic episodes of pallor) before the onset of cardiorespiratory symptoms, which begin a few days to 2 weeks after the onset of the initial symptoms. Abdominal pain may be a prominent complaint in some children.[245]

On examination, these infants and children often are anxious and apprehensive, but some appear apathetic and listless. Pallor may be striking, and mild cyanosis may be present. The skin may be cold and mottled. Respirations are rapid and labored, and grunting may be prominent. The pulse is thready, and blood pressure usually is normal or slightly reduced unless the infant is in profound shock. The precordium is quiet, without a prominent cardiac impulse. Tachycardia, sometimes marked, is discernible. The heart sounds are muffled, and a prominent gallop rhythm usually is heard. Fine and colleagues[58] found the most sensitive clinical sign of myocarditis to be a soft first sound at the apex. However, a prolonged PR interval, which may be a nonspecific finding in many febrile illnesses,[212] also can cause a soft first sound without any other evidence of myocarditis. A high-pitched systolic murmur of mitral insufficiency is heard in some cases. The breath sounds are harsh. Scattered rhonchi and, occasionally, fine crepitations in the lung bases may be detected. Almost uniformly, the liver is enlarged; edema is a rare finding. Some infants are less distressed and have signs of only mild congestive cardiac failure, without the signs of peripheral circulatory failure. Others have no signs of cardiac compromise, and myocarditis is recognized only as part of a generalized illness by a disturbance in the electrocardiographic pattern.

MYOCARDITIS IN CASES OF HUMAN IMMUNODEFICIENCY VIRUS INFECTION

Infection with human immunodeficiency virus (HIV) may affect the heart adversely. Cardiac dysfunction, including congestive heart failure, may occur; many patients who have died and undergone autopsy demonstrate myocarditis. Anderson and associates[7] retrospectively analyzed 71 consecutive necropsy patients who died of acquired immunodeficiency syndrome (AIDS) and found that 52 percent had evidence of myocarditis. Opportunistic agents could account for only a few of the cases, and most were considered idiopathic. Another study[15] examined autopsy specimens of 26 consecutive cases. Lymphocytic myocarditis was seen in nine patients (35%), and another seven patients had lymphocytic infiltrates without myocytolysis. Acierno[3] correctly points out that a distinction must be made between AIDS-associated myocarditis and secondary myocarditis due to known pathogens or idiopathic myocarditis. Hypersensitivity or allergic-type vasculitis may occur in this disease state, with an uncontrolled hypergammaglobulinemia inducing a type I hypersensitivity reaction. Reilly and colleagues[192] found a 45 percent incidence of myocarditis in 58 consecutive autopsy cases. Congestive heart failure, ventricular tachycardia, and other electrocardiographic abnormalities were seen in nearly 60 percent of those patients. Two patients died suddenly, both with myocarditis. One study of eight children who died of noncardiac causes demonstrated myocarditis in two of four patients who underwent autopsy examination. One of the patients had disseminated cytomegalovirus infection, including numerous inclusions on microscopic examination of the heart.[224]

Myocardial inflammation, with or without cell destruction, is a frequent finding in patients infected with HIV. The exact mechanism of this response, whether to the virus itself or to opportunistic agents or other toxic reactions, is not clear. Specific therapy for myocarditis in these patients has not been elucidated, and no recommendations, other than inotropic support with anticongestive and afterload-reducing agents, can be made.

Diagnosis

CLINICAL CHARACTERISTICS AND RADIOGRAPHIC EVIDENCE

Myocarditis often is difficult to diagnose, but it should be suspected in any infant or child who presents with congestive heart failure and who has or recently has had a febrile illness. The history should include information regarding travel, exposure to tuberculosis, recent drug ingestion, and illnesses in other family members or schoolmates.

A quiet precordium in the presence of a gallop rhythm and decreased intensity or muffling of the heart sounds are findings that strongly suggest the diagnosis. A tachycardia out of proportion to the level of fever also should be viewed with suspicion. A physiologic third heart sound is a common finding in normal healthy children and in those with anemia and fever. Sometimes, as with fever and associated tachycardia, the cardiac rhythm may have a gallop cadence. In association with it, however, the precordium is hyperactive, and the heart sounds are crisp and have increased intensity. An unusually prominent third heart sound suggests a disturbance of ventricular compliance without other evidence of compromised cardiac function and should be investigated further with an echocardiogram, a chest radiograph, and an electrocardiogram.

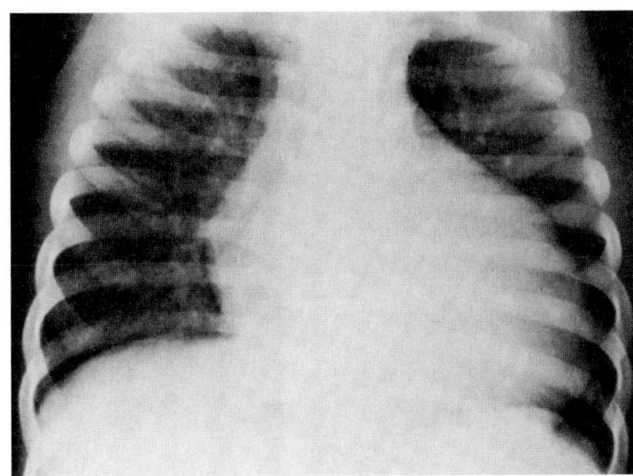

FIGURE 34–8 ■ Marked cardiomegaly with a mild increase in the pulmonary venous pattern in the upper lobes.

Chest radiographs of infants and children who have signs of congestive cardiac failure invariably show cardiomegaly, usually of a severe degree (Fig. 34–8). All four chambers may be enlarged, and evidence of pulmonary venous congestion often is found.

Sometimes, especially in newborn infants, the first sign of illness is acute circulatory collapse, and in this circumstance, the cardiac size may be normal. The same is true of children who have an arrhythmia rather than congestive heart failure. Other patients may present Stokes-Adams attacks caused by complete heart block.[135]

The occurrence of an arrhythmia, especially after a febrile illness, should alert the clinician to look for other signs of myocarditis.[34, 218] Lind and Hulquist[136] detected significant dysrhythmias in five infants with isolated myocarditis. Four of the five infants died, and three of these children had paroxysmal atrial tachycardia. Paroxysmal atrial tachycardia has been reported in patients with viral myocarditis[34, 218] and has been described in patients with diphtheritic myocarditis.[17] Atrial ectopic tachycardia may mimic sinus tachycardia and, if not carefully evaluated, may be the primary cause for significant myocardial dysfunction. Complete heart block has been described in children in association with acute idiopathic myocarditis[113, 135] and with rubella,[73, 137] coxsackievirus,[208] and respiratory syncytial virus[14, 71] infections. In some instances, it is permanent,[14, 72, 209] and in others, temporary.[72, 113] The electrocardiogram is an essential diagnostic tool for all patients with suspected myocarditis.

The classic electrocardiographic pattern in myocarditis is one of diffuse low-voltage QRS complexes (<5 mm total amplitude) with low-amplitude or slightly inverted T waves and a small or absent Q wave in leads V_5 and V_6 (Fig. 34–9). The low-voltage signal may be present in the standard leads and the precordial leads. Figure 34–10 depicts the electrocardiogram of an infant with acute myocarditis and shows a pattern of acute myocardial ischemia. Figure 34–11*A* shows multifocal extrasystoles and severe intraventricular conduction delay in a patient with diphtheritic myocarditis; the electrocardiogram of this child returned to normal over a period of 3 months (see Fig. 34–11*B*). The electrocardiogram from a 5-month-old infant who had mild fever, diarrhea, and vomiting for 3 to 4 days before admission is shown in Figure 34–12. The 2:1 atrioventricular block was associated with normal QRS complexes. This abnormality persisted in the absence of clinical symptoms for 1 year. Figure 34–13 shows a left bundle branch block that was identified in a 10-month-old infant with acute idiopathic myocarditis. Anomalous origin of the left coronary artery from the pulmonary artery was suspected but was excluded by catheterization. This electrocardiographic pattern persisted for at least 6 months.

Karjalainen[116] studied the electrocardiograms of 87 conscripts between 18 and 30 years of age, 28 of whom had myocarditis. The most frequent findings were T-wave changes of reduced amplitude or inversion in the left chest leads. Sinus tachycardia followed by premature ventricular depolarizations was the most common dysrhythmia. Take and colleagues[228] examined serial electrocardiograms of

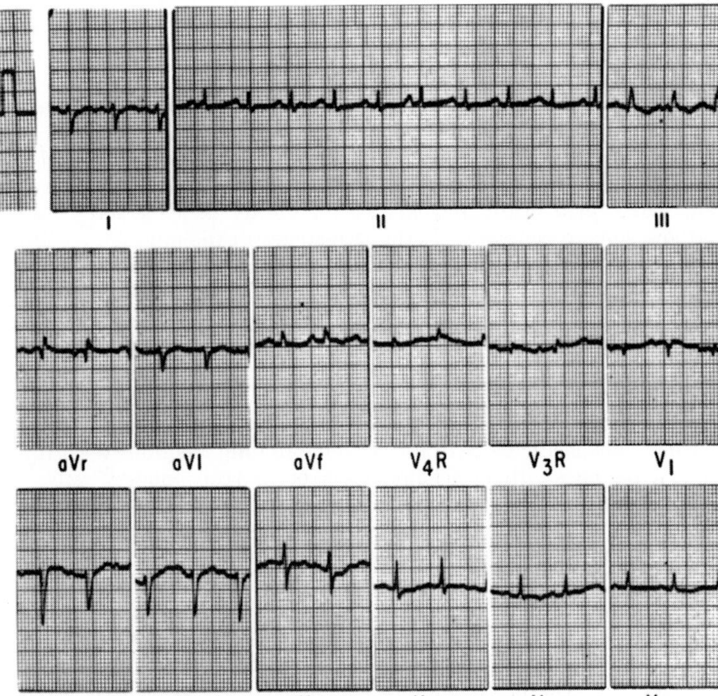

FIGURE 34–9 ■ Diffuse low-voltage or QRS complexes with T-wave flattening and 1-mm Q waves in the lateral precordial leads represents the classic pattern in myocarditis.

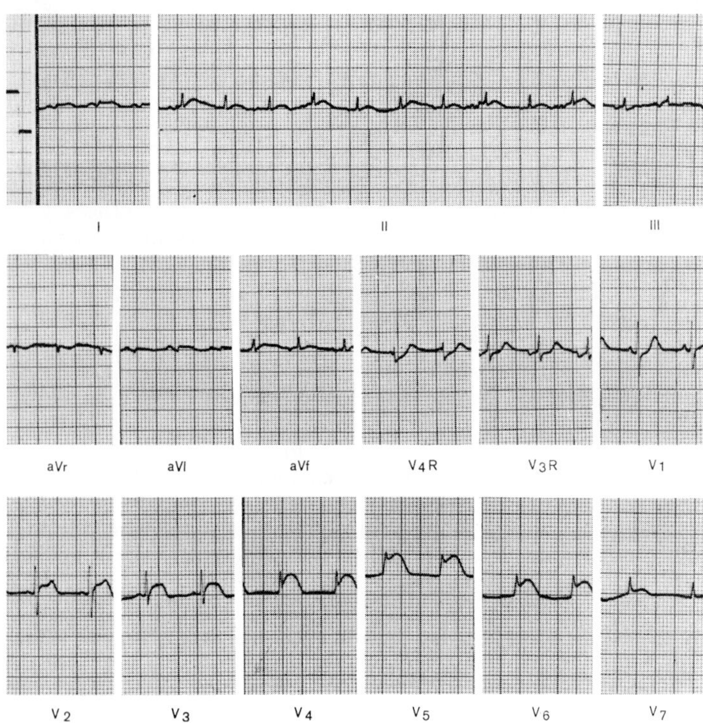

FIGURE 34–10 ■ In addition to low voltage, there is evidence of acute myocardial ischemia with 4- to 5-mm ST-segment elevation dominantly in the middle and lateral precordial leads.

16 patients with confirmed viral myocarditis. They found four patterns: complete normalization even in the presence of severe myocardial damage in the acute stage; "pseudo-infarction" patterns with Q waves and poor R-wave progression; permanent conduction disturbances that might require pacemaker support; and chronic dysrhythmias, predominantly ventricular tachycardia and supraventricular tachycardia. Hoshino and colleagues[99] induced coxsackievirus B3 myocarditis in Syrian golden hamsters and found that 80 percent of them had ST-segment or T-wave (or both) changes in the surface electrocardiogram. Most of the changes were seen between days 2 and 4, when mortality rates were highest. The endocardial third of the myocardium was most involved histologically, which suggested that the subendocardial myocardial injury corresponded to the observed ST-segment and T-wave changes. Kishimoto and coworkers,[125] using DBA/2 mice, induced myocarditis with encephalomyocarditis virus. Acute changes were correlated with advanced atrioventricular block and with atrial and ventricular premature depolarizations. Sinus tachycardia and low voltage were seen in the late stages in the animals that survived. Over the long term, the QRS voltages recovered toward normal, possibly reflecting loss of myocardial edema or development of ventricular hypertrophy, or both, as a compensatory mechanism for poor ventricular function.

Although T-wave and ST-segment changes are the most sensitive indices of myocardial ischemia, they also appear to be rather nonspecific. Prolongation of the PR interval is another nonspecific electrocardiographic finding frequently noted in patients with febrile illnesses. Scott and colleagues[212] demonstrated a 1.49 percent prevalence of these findings in a group of 737 infants and children with respiratory tract infections, but they also found a similar incidence among 108 control children without respiratory infection or other febrile illness. Abt and Vinnecour[2] recorded PR prolongation and T-wave changes in infants and children who were suffering from pneumonia without other signs of myocarditis. The QT interval has been prolonged in cases of acute myocarditis, but it also appears to be a rather nonspecific finding associated with certain infectious diseases, such as measles[198] and poliomyelitis.[114] Thus, a diagnosis of myocarditis cannot be established with certainty on the basis of these nonspecific changes.

The echocardiogram is useful in assessing ventricular function and helps to exclude pericardial effusion as the cause of the cardiomegaly. This ultrasound technique is an invaluable aid in the assessment of patients with suspected myocarditis.[200]

Nuclear imaging has been advocated as a potentially helpful laboratory screening test. Some evidence suggests that using gallium 67 to screen patients with idiopathic dilated cardiomyopathy may select a subgroup of patients who could benefit from endomyocardial biopsy. The biopsy specimen then could be used to confirm the presence of active inflammation. O'Connell and colleagues[170] studied 68 patients with dilated cardiomyopathy who underwent 71 parallel studies with endomyocardial biopsy and gallium scanning. For five of six patients, biopsy samples that showed myocarditis also showed dense gallium uptake, and only 9 of 65 negative biopsies had "equivocally positive" gallium scans. A 36 percent incidence of myocarditis on biopsy was found for positive scans, and only a 1.8 percent incidence of myocarditis on biopsy was found for negative scans. No large studies enrolling children have been performed, but this technique may prove to be a safe and relatively effective method for selecting children for biopsy and for following the effects of immunosuppressive therapy on the inflammatory response to the viral infection.

Techniques for examining heart muscle biopsy specimens promise to help us diagnose and plan therapy more accurately. These techniques include nucleic acid hybridization and enzymatic amplification,[235] which can be used to clone viral RNA or DNA. The offending virus, whose "fingerprint" is present, can be identified, yielding important epidemiologic information and possibly therapeutic guidance.

Indium 111 antimyosin imaging[44] and the presence of major histocompatibility complex class I and II antigens measured by radioimmunoassay using monoclonal antibodies[90]

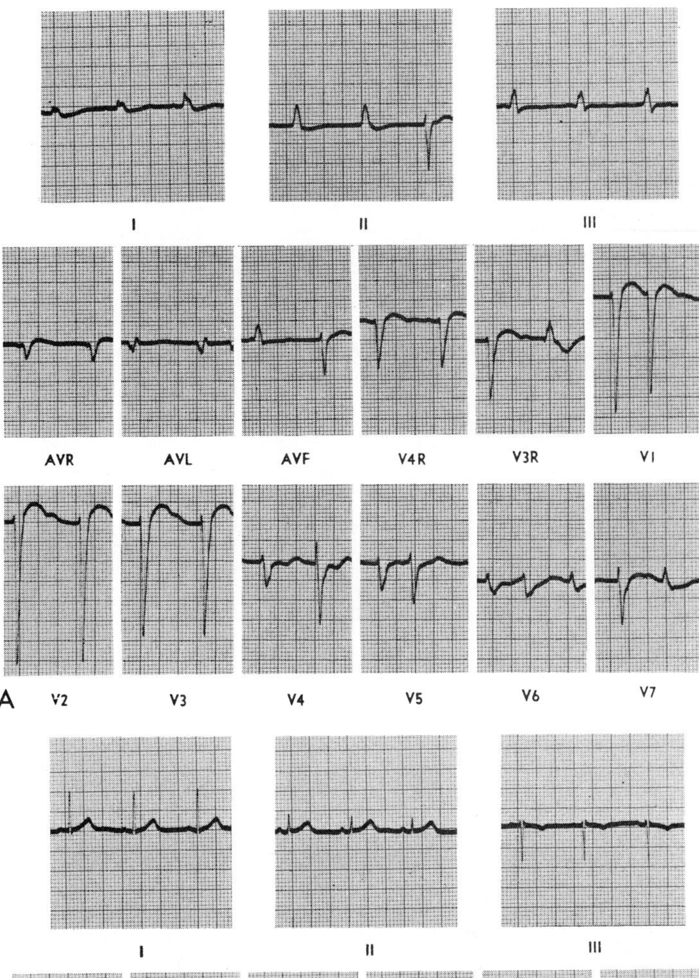

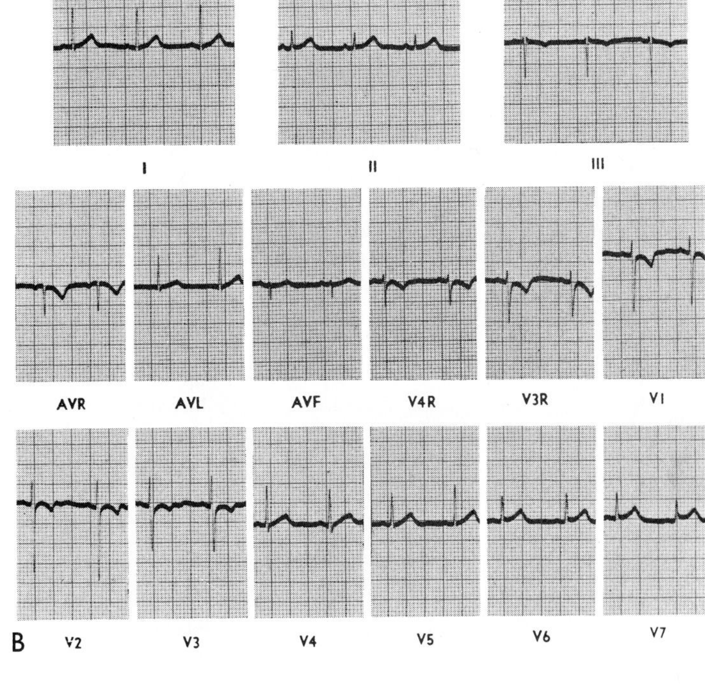

FIGURE 34–11 ■ *A,* Multifocal premature beats are caused by atrioventricular dissociation and left bundle branch block resulting from diphtheritic myocarditis. *B,* A normal electrocardiogram is shown for the same patient 3 months after an episode of myocarditis.

can detect patients with active myocarditis. High titers (≥1:20) of an IgG antibody (i.e., heart-reactive antibodies) measured by indirect immunofluorescence have been reported in patients with biopsy-confirmed myocarditis.[167] Although none of the methods is yet clinically applicable to all patients, these noninvasive tests offer some hope that the diagnosis of inflammatory heart disease will become safer.

To undertake a hemodynamic study in patients with a classic picture of acute myocarditis, including an electrocardiogram that reveals low voltage, is unnecessary and potentially dangerous. If the clinical or electrocardiographic presentation is atypical (i.e., left ventricular hypertrophy with left axis deviation, infarction pattern, or left bundle branch block), the infant should be studied for exclusion of anomalous origin of the left coronary artery or another unsuspected anomaly.

Endomyocardial biopsy has become a relatively safe and effective means for sampling heart muscle.[6] The technique originally was introduced in 1962 in Japan by Sakakibara and Konno[202] but did not gain wide acceptance in the United States for another 10 or more years. Its widest application has been in monitoring the effectiveness of immunosuppressive therapy in heart transplant patients who may undergo the procedure multiple times.

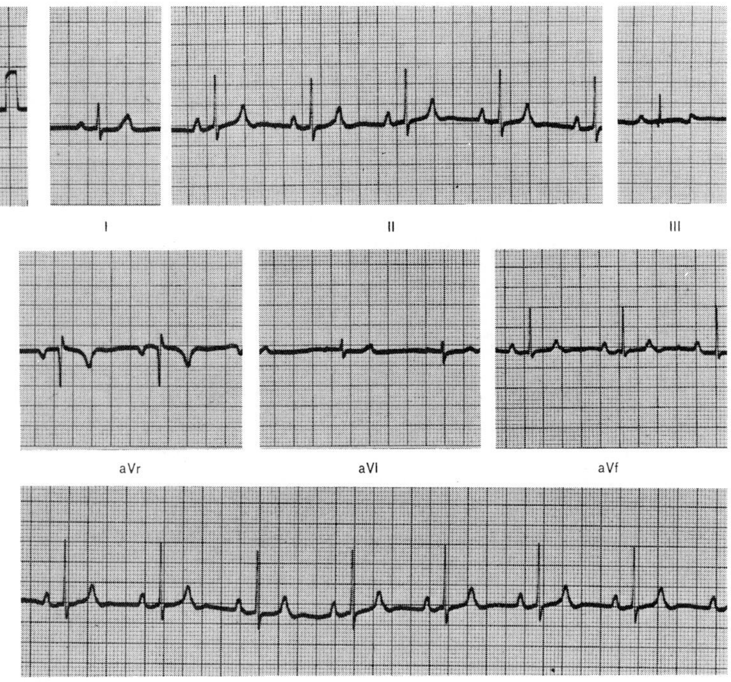

FIGURE 34–12 ■ Second-degree atrioventricular block with an effective ventricular rate of 60 beats per minute. The blocked P wave is placed on top of the T wave in each cycle.

Endomyocardial biopsy used for establishing the diagnosis of myocarditis and possibly classifying the phase (i.e., active, healing, or healed) of viral infection may have a direct impact on the type of therapy employed. Classification of myocarditis based on histologic evidence found on biopsy specimens has proved to be a difficult and sometimes controversial task. No widespread agreement exists on the criteria for establishing the diagnosis of myocarditis from biopsy samples. Sampling error due to the small amounts of tissue obtained and the focal nature of sampling and the disease process may lead to misdiagnosis. Samples usually are obtained from the right ventricular septum or apex and should contain at least three and optimally five pieces of tissue. Some investigators[236] have found sampling from other areas of the heart (e.g., left ventricle) to be more sensitive, but these techniques have not been applied widely.

Cases of "borderline myocarditis" (i.e., specimens containing increased numbers of inflammatory cells but without evidence of myocyte necrosis) may require a repeat biopsy to confirm the diagnosis. Dec and colleagues[41] confirmed the diagnosis of myocarditis in four of six patients with an initial diagnosis of borderline myocarditis. They did not demonstrate any significant advantage to sampling the left ventricle during the repeat study. Overinterpretation or

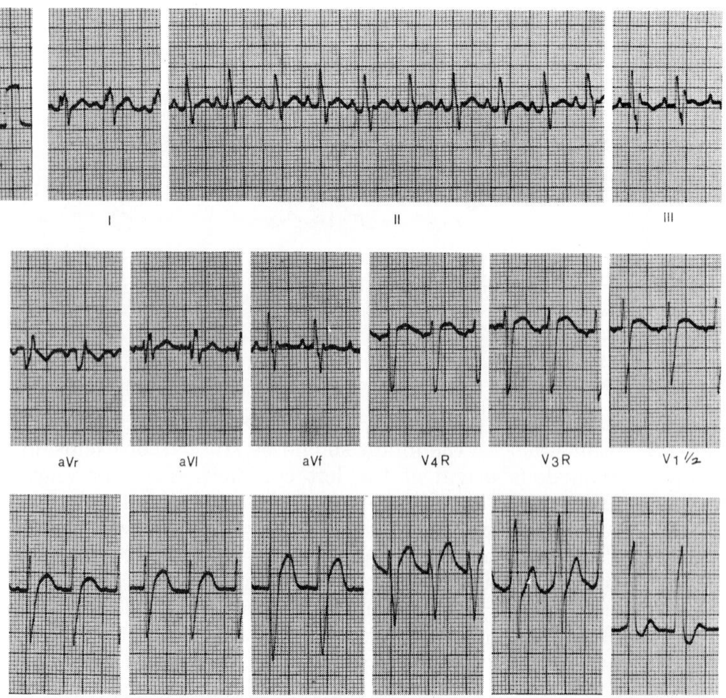

FIGURE 34–13 ■ Sinus tachycardia (rate, 150 beats per minute) and left bundle branch block.

misinterpretation has been cited as a major problem in the reading of biopsy specimens. Some studies[225, 226, 244] used this technique to establish a diagnosis of myocarditis in patients presenting with idiopathic congestive cardiomyopathy and in patients with serious ventricular dysrhythmias with otherwise structurally normal hearts. Edwards and associates[54] looked at endomyocardial biopsy samples from 170 biopsies and found that more than five lymphocytes per high-power field was consistent with a diagnosis of active lymphocytic myocarditis.

Using endomyocardial biopsy, Fenoglio and coworkers[56] diagnosed myocarditis in 34 patients presenting with congestive heart failure of unknown origin. They classified these patients on the basis of clinical and histologic findings in an attempt to establish subgroups of patients who might benefit from immunosuppressive therapy. Three groups were established: acute, rapidly progressive, and chronic. Immunosuppressive therapy was thought to be significantly beneficial only for the latter group in terms of clinical improvement. Dec and colleagues[43] studied 27 patients referred for endomyocardial biopsy because of congestive heart failure of unknown origin. Two thirds of the patients had biopsy samples read as positive for myocarditis, but unlike the study of Fenoglio and colleagues,[56] in which the histologic grouping was slightly different, no correlation was found between histologic classification and outcome. Moreover, outcome did not differ between the group receiving immunosuppressives and the group not receiving immunosuppressives. Biopsy results were negative for 30 percent of the patients who already demonstrated all the clinical criteria of myocarditis and were positive for two of five patients without any clinical evidence of myocarditis (i.e., viral-like illness, pericarditis, or laboratory evidence of viral infection).

Olsen[176] reviewed 1200 biopsy specimens from patients with a clinical diagnosis of idiopathic dilated congestive cardiomyopathy and found that slightly more than 25 percent had a diagnosis of myocarditis established on the basis of critical evaluation of their tissue specimens. No large study of pediatric patients has been conducted to confirm this finding in the young.

Most physicians would agree that many cases of idiopathic dilated cardiomyopathy probably are the sequelae of unrecognized acute viral myocarditis. The role of endomyocardial biopsy in attempting to salvage patients by selecting them for specific therapy has some validity. The hope is that early intervention in some patients guided by this technique will prevent them from progressing to needing transplantation or to death from intractable heart failure.

MOLECULAR DIAGNOSTIC STUDIES

In Situ Hybridization

In 1986, Bowles and colleagues[23] demonstrated the utility of molecular biologic analysis of tissue samples in the diagnosis of myocarditis. Using in situ hybridization, they were able to demonstrate enteroviral RNA in the myocardium of patients suspected of having myocarditis. The investigators also showed that enteroviral RNA could be identified in the myocardial tissue samples obtained from patients with end-stage dilated cardiomyopathy, and the suggestion that some cases of dilated cardiomyopathy were caused by a previous episode of subclinical myocarditis gained scientific support. The ability to diagnose enteroviral myocarditis and the finding of enteroviral RNA in patients with dilated cardiomyopathy later were confirmed by other investigators.[10, 11, 24] Unfortunately, because of questions of excessive false-positive results, variations among laboratories, and the difficulty in performing the test routinely in hospital laboratories, this method never gained practical popularity.

Polymerase Chain Reaction

Initially described and perfected by Mullis and Faldona,[164] the polymerase chain reaction (PCR) has been used extensively in molecular biology. Jin and associates[112] first described the usefulness of PCR in identifying the viral genome in myocardial samples obtained from patients with suspected myocarditis. Using reverse-transcriptase PCR, which uses RNA to amplify the corresponding complementary DNA before final DNA amplification, the researchers were able to identify an enteroviral genome from cardiac tissue samples. Patients with dilated cardiomyopathy were shown to harbor an enteroviral genome within myocardial specimens. Confirmation of the utility of PCR in the etiologic diagnosis of a viral genome in patients with clinical myocarditis and idiopathic dilated cardiomyopathy quickly followed.[33, 52, 75, 91, 163, 182, 191, 246, 247] However, controversy existed because reports of high levels of false-positive results,[52] contamination,[33] and low sensitivity[246] were published. The strength of this rapid (<5 hours) and powerful method of amplification of a specific viral genome is also its weakness. The method depends on the quality and quantity of nucleic acid extraction, but contamination may be commonplace in some laboratories. If any requirements are altered, amplification may not occur, leading to false-negative or false-positive (i.e., contamination) results.

Numerous publications have demonstrated that PCR is a rapid and sensitive method for the diagnosis of enteroviral myocarditis and that it is probably the test of choice in the diagnosis of all virus-induced cardiac disease. For instance, Towbin and colleagues[233] used PCR to successfully diagnose adenoviral myocarditis in a fetus with nonimmune hydrops fetalis. In this case, the adenoviral genome was amplified from fetal blood and maternal blood at 29 weeks' gestation and again at delivery at 34 weeks' gestation using blood from baby and mother, as well as placental specimens. Treatment with digoxin in utero helped the fetus improve clinically, and the newborn infant had normal cardiac function at delivery. Using viral primers designed to amplify enterovirus, adenovirus, cytomegalovirus, and herpes simplex virus nucleic acid, Martin and associates[143] reported 34 patients with suspected acute myocarditis for whom 68 percent of samples analyzed were PCR-positive. In this report, samples from 17 control patients were PCR-negative. Adenovirus was the most common viral genome identified (58%), and enteroviruses were the second most common (29%). A few reported cases were PCR-positive for herpes simplex virus and cytomegalovirus.

Griffin and colleagues[77] studied 58 patients with myocarditis and 28 patients with dilated cardiomyopathy caused by endocardial fibroelastosis. All tissue samples were obtained at autopsy; 79 percent of samples were fixed with formalin, and 21 percent were fresh-frozen with liquid nitrogen. The investigators demonstrated that 59 percent of the autopsy-confirmed cases of myocarditis were PCR-positive; 53 percent of the positive samples had adenovirus, 32 percent had enterovirus, and the remainder of PCR-positive cases had amplified herpes simplex virus and cytomegalovirus. The researchers convincingly demonstrated that fixed tissue samples were useful for PCR analysis, with essentially no differences in the percentage of samples amplified using either method. Particularly important was the finding that the enterovirus, an RNA virus, could be identified effectively using fixed specimens.

This finding suggests that previous or current cases of myocarditis in which no cause could be identified by culture, serology, or microscopy can be studied by PCR of autopsy samples, with the cause identified retrospectively or prospectively. The investigators also identified adenoviral genome in 21 percent of the cases of endocardial fibroelastosis, with no other viral genome identified.[211] This study, coupled with the report by Martin and associates,[143] suggested that adenovirus is a major cause of myocarditis. Although previous reports of adenoviral myocarditis had been published,[22, 32, 67, 77, 89, 215, 222, 240] the virus was considered a minor and unimportant cause of disease by most experts. Closer evaluation of these reports, however, demonstrates that a relatively high percentage of cases identified by culture and serology were caused by adenovirus, superseded only by the enteroviruses, coxsackieviruses, and echoviruses. Lozinski and coworkers[138] confirmed the importance of adenovirus in their study of cases of myocarditis for which no cause had been found previously; in this case, 66 percent of the previously unidentified cases were identified as adenovirus.

Schowengerdt and colleagues[210] showed that a variety of viruses might be the inciting cause of rejection in patients after undergoing heart transplantation. Using PCR of endomyocardial biopsy specimens, the investigators demonstrated a direct correlation between histologic rejection and PCR-positive viral study results. Studying patients undergoing serial endomyocardial biopsies, they found that the viral genome could be amplified in transplant-rejecting patients who previously had negative PCR analyses. In these cases, as the rejection grade improved, the PCR results again became negative. The most common viruses correlated with rejection were adenoviruses, cytomegalovirus, and parvovirus. The researchers postulated that this form of rejection probably is another form of myocarditis, and this hypothesis has been supported by other clinical studies.[248]

Future Directions of Diagnostic Methods

The current diagnostic methods are an improvement over past methods, but they lack the sensitivity to identify all cases of myocarditis and are unable to pinpoint the areas of myocardium hardest hit by the viral infection. Moreover, the role of inflammatory mediators is not well studied by these methods. Several new approaches, including in situ PCR and inflammatory mediators, are likely to help rectify these inadequacies.

The in situ PCR method combines PCR and in situ hybridization to identify where in the affected tissue the viral genome resides. A sample of myocardium can be shown to have the viral genome within certain myocytes but not in others. This knowledge may help explain the patchy nature of the infiltrate and the selective areas of dysfunction.

Using PCR and other methods, a variety of inflammatory mediators, such as cytokines and adhesion molecules, can be analyzed. In certain cases of clinical myocarditis, for instance, the histologic pattern appears "negative for myocarditis." Martin and colleagues[143] showed that the viral genome, particularly adenovirus, may be amplified in some of these cases. In these and other cases in which the causative agent is not identified, the cascade of inflammatory mediators probably is up-regulated,[128, 168, 234] and identification of this response could help to diagnose inflammatory heart disease.

These methods and others will continue to improve the diagnostic armamentarium for myocarditis and expand our understanding of this heterogeneous disease. Once understood, specific therapy is more likely to become available.

VIROLOGIC AND BACTERIOLOGIC STUDIES

For each infant or child with a diagnosis of acute myocarditis, an attempt should be made to identify the offending organism. If the patient is seen early in the illness, isolation of the virus from throat washings, stool, blood, or the myocardium may be possible. Support for an active infection is obtained by demonstrating a fourfold rise in antibody titer to the virus that has been isolated.[22, 86, 92, 209, 243]

Lerner and Wilson[132] suggested criteria that would help define an etiologic association between a coxsackievirus infection and myocarditis. High-order associations included isolation of the virus from the myocardium, the endocardium, or pericardial fluid and localization of type-specific virus in myocardium, endocardium, or pericardium at sites of pathologic change. Moderate-order associations are determined when virus is isolated from pharynx or feces and a fourfold increase in type-specific, neutralizing, hemagglutination-inhibiting, or complement-fixing antibodies is demonstrated or when virus is isolated from pharynx or feces with a concurrent serum titer of 1:32 or greater of type-specific IgM-neutralizing or hemagglutination-inhibiting antibodies.

Schmidt and colleagues[209] stress the usefulness of the IgM-specific antibody titer. Coxsackieviruses B1, B3, B4, B5, and B6 are identifiable with this method. Immunofluorescent methods may be used during histologic analysis to identify specific antigens in the myocardium.[27] In chronic illness, attempts at virologic identification are less fruitful.[80]

Blood for aerobic and anaerobic cultures should be obtained from any infant with fever and signs of compromised cardiovascular function. The erythrocyte sedimentation rate and white blood cell count usually are elevated in acute myocarditis; occasionally, a leukemoid reaction may be identified.[4] A normal value for these tests does not exclude myocarditis. Elevations of serum glutamic oxaloacetic and glutamic pyruvic transaminase levels have been detected, especially in diphtheritic myocarditis,[227] but they may be elevated in any patient with acute myocardial damage. Although a high level of serum transaminase activity usually is an ominous prognostic sign, Tahernia[227] found the electrocardiogram to be a more sensitive indicator of the ultimate outcome in children with diphtheritic myocarditis. Creatine phosphokinase and lactate dehydrogenase enzymes also should be measured. Okuni and coworkers[172] noticed that elevation of isoenzyme 1 of lactate dehydrogenase appeared to be very specific in their patients with idiopathic myocarditis.

Differential Diagnosis

Any cause of circulatory failure, especially when onset is acute, may mimic myocarditis. In newborn infants, heart failure associated with hypoxia, hypoglycemia, and hypocalcemia is well recognized, whereas circulatory collapse may occur with any infection and without direct involvement of the myocardium. A careful history may help to elucidate possible precipitating factors. Biochemical investigations to exclude hypoglycemia and hypocalcemia always should be conducted in any newborn infant who has signs of heart failure. Blood cultures should be obtained when infection is suspected.

Many infants with structural cardiac defects (e.g., hypoplastic left heart syndrome, aortic valve stenosis) may not have audible murmurs when severely ill. Murmurs, however, usually appear with treatment and improvement in cardiac function. The precordium usually is hyperactive, rather than quiet, and the heart sounds are clear and increased in intensity, rather than muffled. The electrocardiogram usually shows severe right ventricular hypertrophy in the former condition and shows right ventricular or left ventricular hypertrophy in the latter; the electrocardiogram is useful in the differential diagnosis. The findings on an echocardiogram often are diagnostic.

Beyond the immediate neonatal period, endocardial fibroelastosis, anomalous left coronary artery arising from the pulmonary artery, Cori type II glycogen storage disease (i.e., Pompe disease), medial necrosis of the coronary arteries, left atrial myxoma,[166] and other congestive cardiomyopathies of undetermined cause are the major disease entities that require differentiation from myocarditis.[62, 117] Common to all of these disorders is moderate to severe cardiomegaly, usually associated with congestive cardiac failure, gallop rhythm, and the infrequent occurrence or absence of murmurs. The murmurs are associated primarily with anomalous left coronary artery and endocardial fibroelastosis. They are not more than grade 3/6 in intensity, are high pitched, are apically located, and represent some degree of mitral insufficiency. Idiopathic myocarditis occurs primarily after the patient reaches 6 months of age,[195] whereas most of the conditions described earlier manifest before the child is 6 months of age.

Endocardial fibroelastosis, a relatively common cause of congestive cardiac failure in infants, is impossible to differentiate from acute myocarditis on the basis of clinical examination alone.

Anomalous origin of the left coronary artery should be identified. The electrocardiogram usually shows left axis deviation of the QRS complex in the frontal plane, left ventricular hypertrophy, and a pattern of anterolateral myocardial infarction. It is recognized as a QR pattern with inverted T waves in standard leads I and AVL, as well as a broad Q wave with inverted T waves in precordial leads V_5 and V_6 and loss of anterior forces in the mid-precordial leads. For definitive diagnosis, cardiac catheterization is essential.

Pericarditis, frequently caused by viruses, usually occurs in children rather than in infants. The clinical history may be identical to that of patients with myocarditis; however, considering the degree of cardiomegaly, cardiovascular function is compromised less than in patients with myocarditis, although cardiac tamponade may occur in some cases. Differentiation from myocarditis may be made clinically if the patient has a friction rub, no gallop rhythm, and a typical pattern of chest pain. However, further studies may be required for making a conclusive diagnosis. The echocardiogram is invaluable in establishing this diagnosis. It is the most sensitive and least traumatic technique available and easily identifies an effusion. Myocarditis and pericarditis may occur together. This combination is seen most frequently in the pancarditis of rheumatic fever but may occur also in coxsackievirus B infections and in many of the collagen vascular and autoimmune diseases. Myocarditis has been associated with rheumatoid arthritis,[153] systemic lupus erythematosus,[87] and ulcerative colitis.[162]

Treatment

STANDARD APPROACHES

Intensive medical care is required during the acute stage of the illness. Heart rate, respiratory rate, and blood pressure should be monitored frequently, and a careful assessment of urine output and fluid intake is mandatory. All patients require bed rest. Experimental studies in mice have shown that exercise increases virus replication in the myocardium and increases the mortality from myocarditis by 100 percent.[68, 133] Although extrapolating directly from experimental studies in animals to the human situation always is dangerous, suggesting strict bed rest during the early stages of acute myocarditis appears to be a prudent measure. For infants or children with signs of congestive cardiac failure or shock, oxygen should be administered to maintain a normal arterial blood oxygen tension.

No specific therapeutic modality is known that can reverse the myocardial injury directly, but much can be done to maintain adequate tissue perfusion, prevent metabolic disturbances, and support myocardial function. When congestive cardiac failure is identified, digitalis should be administered. Because of the apparent increased sensitivity of the inflamed myocardium to digitalis, rapid digitalization in less than 24 hours should be avoided. The oral route is preferred over the intravenous route, although the latter may be required when the patient is in shock. A dose of 0.03 mg/kg, rather than 0.04 mg/kg, should be used as a total digitalizing dose. One half of the total dose is given initially, and the remainder is divided equally and administered at 8-hour intervals. Digitalization may effect dramatic improvement.[194]

Diuretics also are used frequently to treat cardiac failure. Diuretics have no direct beneficial effect on the myocardium; they should be used cautiously because rapid reduction in extracellular fluid volume may lead to shock, and the loss of potassium associated with vigorous diuresis may precipitate digitalis toxicity. When it is used, we prefer furosemide (Lasix) in a dosage of 1 mg/kg. The frequency of administration depends on the clinical state of the patient.

In some instances, especially in the newborn infant, the primary presentation may be that of shock. The blood pressure usually is maintained close to normal levels until late in the course of disease; therefore, it cannot be a reliable index of the severity of the patient's condition. Cold extremities, increasing heart rate, and low urine output are much more sensitive indicators of a reduction in effective circulating blood volume. Although the hearts of these infants and children respond poorly to volume loading, a colloid transfusion may help in selected patients. Albumin, as a 5 percent solution in Ringer's lactate, or whole blood may be given in an initial dose of 5 mL/kg. The total amount administered should be guided by the response of the patient in terms of perfusion, urine output, heart rate, and central venous pressure. These patients may require a high filling pressure (e.g., 12 to 18 mm Hg) to achieve any cardiac output, compared with 5 mm Hg, which would achieve sufficient filling in the normal heart. If the patient remains in shock despite these high filling pressures, a positive inotropic agent is required. We prefer dopamine because it exerts an inotropic effect on the heart and concomitantly dilates the renal vessels, thereby improving urine output. The usual dosage is 2 to 10 μg/kg/min. As the dose increases to 20 μg/kg/min, dopamine has a more dominant alpha-adrenergic effect and may increase systemic peripheral resistance; we usually avoid doses above 15 μg/kg/min. Dobutamine, which is a sympathomimetic amine that stimulates $beta_1$ and $beta_2$ as well as alpha-adrenergic receptors, may be quite useful when used in combination with dopamine. It has significant inotropic activity while decreasing left ventricular filling pressure. Dobutamine does not induce the positive chronotropic effect and increased ventricular irritability that is seen with dopamine. Used in combination with low doses of dopamine (<10 μg/kg/min), dobutamine, in doses up to 10 μg/kg/min, may result in significant positive inotropism while preventing a sinus tachycardia that may compromise cardiac output further. Isoproterenol, a commonly used inotropic agent, should be avoided because it causes a significant increase in heart rate and may affect cardiac function adversely. When these drugs are used, ensuring normal acid-base balance is important because action of the agents is decreased significantly by acidosis.

Agents such as sodium nitroprusside, phentolamine, and the nitrates have been used in adults. They have been used less extensively in children, primarily in the early postoperative period after open heart surgery, to improve cardiac function. They improve cardiac output by indirectly reducing systemic arterial resistance or venous filling pressure, or both. One study[191] demonstrated a marked improvement in the reduction of inflammation, necrosis, and dystrophic calcification in mice infected with coxsackievirus B3 when they were treated early after infection with captopril, an angiotensin-converting enzyme inhibitor.[193] Besides its known afterload-reducing effects, this agent, which contains sulfhydryl groups in its chemical structure, is capable of scavenging oxygen-free radicals in vitro. This ability may enable the drug to reduce myocyte damage by free radicals during the acute phase of the infection.

Another study failed to demonstrate any significant correlation between improved ventricular function and histologic improvement in patients with myocarditis treated with immunosuppressive therapy. Rather, a rise in the ejection fraction during the first 3 months of therapy seemed predictive of a good outcome.[42] Intravenously administered afterload-reducing agents should not be used unless facilities are available for constantly monitoring the left ventricular filling pressure (i.e., mean wedge pressure) and unless that pressure is elevated.

Arrhythmias should be recognized and treated vigorously. Digitalis should be used with caution, and intravenous administration of this drug should be performed only if the oral route is not possible. Rather than used as inotropic support, digitalis can be used to help control supraventricular arrhythmias. Levels must be monitored, especially when renal function is suspect. Lidocaine should be administered intravenously in a dose of 1 mg/kg for the acute treatment of complex ventricular arrhythmias, such as couplets and ventricular tachycardia. In cases of intractable ventricular arrhythmias, intravenously administered procainamide, 10 to 15 mg/kg as a loading dose followed by a drip of 40 to 70 μg/kg/min, can be used. Monitoring the serum level on a daily basis beginning several hours after the drip is started is essential to prevent toxic side effects. Alternatively, amiodarone given intravenously can be used for life-threatening ventricular arrythmias. Beginning with a loading dose between 10 and 15 mg/kg and following with a drip of 10 to 15 mg/kg/day may be very successful in suppressing ventricular tachycardia. Measures of contractility using echocardiographic techniques also are vital because procainamide is a negative inotrope. The use of intravenously administered amiodarone has been approved by the U.S. Food and Drug Administration and should be considered if the more standard therapy outlined earlier fails. However, despite aggressive management of ventricular tachycardia in the acute setting, it may prove to be a terminal event in many cases.

A temporary pacing catheter should be inserted when complete heart block occurs; in many instances, it allows time for spontaneous recovery of atrioventricular conduction. A permanent pacemaker may be required; if so, it should be inserted as an elective, rather than emergency, procedure. A demand pacemaker only should be used because in most instances a return to normal rhythm is expected; use of this type of pacemaker avoids the risk of competition between the patient's inherent rhythm and the pacemaker, as would occur with a fixed-rate device. If infants or children experience Stokes-Adams attacks, a transthoracic pacing wire may have to be inserted as an emergency procedure.

Antibiotics should not be given routinely unless a bacterial infection is suspected and appropriate cultures have been obtained before their use.

IMMUNOSUPPRESSIVE AGENTS

The use of immunosuppressive agents in the treatment of viral or suspected viral myocarditis remains controversial. Early animal studies suggested an exacerbation of virus-induced cytotoxicity when such agents were given in the acute setting and possible interference with the production of interferon.[121, 122, 199] A report[31] of 13 children with biopsy-confirmed myocarditis treated with prednisone approximately 3 weeks after symptoms occurred demonstrated a marked reduction in inflammation at the follow-up biopsy. However, this study was uncontrolled and may not truly represent an accurate account of the role of immunosuppressive therapy. Mason and colleagues[145] used endomyocardial biopsy as a means of diagnosing and following the effects of immunosuppressive therapy in 10 patients. Eight patients received a combination of prednisone and azathioprine, and two patients received prednisone alone. Four patients improved clinically and histologically while on therapy. Two patients who had their medications discontinued suffered relapses, which were reversed with reinstitution of therapy. Only one patient worsened while on therapy, and that patient died. Although the study by Mason and associates was uncontrolled, the reversal of congestive heart failure seen in the two patients who were restarted on therapy suggests the beneficial effect of these agents.

Daly and colleagues[39] treated nine patients using combined immunosuppressive therapy with prednisolone and azathioprine. Seven of the nine patients showed definite hemodynamic and histologic improvement after receiving 2 months of therapy. However, after 4 months off therapy, only four of the seven patients still showed significant improvement. One patient improved with reinstitution of therapy, and two patients deteriorated. Dec and colleagues[43] treated nine patients in their study with single or combined immunosuppressive therapy. They saw improvement in 4 of 9; however, 6 of 18 patients not receiving immunosuppressive agents also improved, nullifying any statistically significant difference between the two groups. Lymphocytic myocarditis was found in 6 of 12 patients with no obvious cardiac disease but with high-grade ventricular dysrhythmias and who had undergone right ventricular endomyocardial biopsy.[244] All six patients received combined immunosuppressive therapy with prednisone and azathioprine. At follow-up, five of six patients had been cured of the dysrhythmia, and active myocardial inflammation had disappeared, as confirmed by repeat biopsy. Although this study was uncontrolled, the fact that none of the patients progressed to a cardiomyopathic state or died of their illness strongly suggests a beneficial effect.

Kereiakes and Parmley[118] tabulated most of the studies showing the effects of immunosuppressive therapy in patients with myocarditis. Sixty percent of 82 biopsy-confirmed cases of myocarditis showed improvement with steroids alone or in combination with azathioprine. Patients with lower-grade inflammatory changes appear to do better than patients with higher-grade changes. Complications of immunosuppressive therapy, including opportunistic infections[145, 225] and a cushingoid state,[199] have been reported and may limit the amount and type of therapy. Hobbs and associates[94] treated 34 adults with biopsy-confirmed myocarditis with combined prednisone and azathioprine. Survival was no better for patients with histologic improvement than for those with persistent infiltrates. Most patients experienced side effects, some of them lethal, from the corticosteroids. Hence, the potential benefits of this type of therapy must be weighed against the risks of immunosuppression in each patient. Steroids also have been used in diphtheritic myocarditis[231] but apparently do not prevent the observed electrocardiographic changes seen in untreated patients or the associated neuritis.

The long-awaited results of the Myocarditis Treatment Trial Investigators have been published.[146] The study was performed with adult patients, but the results probably are applicable to most children with this disease. Random assignment was made of 111 patients with a histopathologic diagnosis of myocarditis to one of three treatment groups. The first group received azathioprine and prednisone; the second group received cyclosporine and prednisone; and the third group received no immunosuppressive therapy (i.e., they received conventional supportive therapy). Patients were treated for 24 weeks. Although three different indices of left ventricular function were studied, no difference was found between the groups treated with immunosuppressive agents and the control (conventional therapy) group. More importantly, survival was no different among the groups. The investigators concluded that immunosuppressive therapy was not beneficial in most patients with histologically confirmed myocarditis.

A multicenter study of the use of intravenous gammaglobulin in children with myocarditis is ongoing. This study is based on the early results of Drucker and associates,[50] who investigated the use of this agent in 21 of 46 children with myocarditis. Patients who received this drug had better left ventricular function at follow-up. Survival *tended* to be higher at 1 year, although the data did not reach statistical significance because of the small number of patients in the study. Whether this drug proves to be beneficial or these early results mirror the early published experience with corticosteroids remains to be seen.

Prognosis

The prognosis of acute myocarditis caused by coxsackievirus B infection in the newborn infant is poor. Kibrick and Benirschke[120] reported a 75 percent mortality rate among 25 infants with coxsackievirus B myocarditis. The greatest number of deaths occurred in the first week of the illness. No apparent sequelae occurred in the six infants who survived, although no long-term follow-up data were available. The outlook in other infants and children with clinically recognized myocarditis is somewhat better, but mortality rates remain significant (10% to 25%). Hastreiter and Miller[85] observed complete recovery in 50 percent of patients. Another 25 percent became asymptomatic, but abnormal electrocardiograms or chest radiographs persisted. An abnormality may not be evident on the electrocardiogram unless the patients are exercised.[20] Despite lack of symptoms, many adult patients have a reduced working capacity associated with exercise stress testing.[21]

The outcome of myocarditis is related in part to the cause. Patients with diphtheritic myocarditis who have arrhythmias or conduction abnormalities have a very poor prognosis. Tahernia[227] found in his study that all patients with disturbances of conduction died. Begg[17] also reported a 100 percent mortality rate for patients with diphtheritic myocarditis who developed supraventricular tachycardia.

Chronic arrhythmias may persist long after the acute disease has passed. Friedman and colleagues[63] performed a retrospective analysis of 12 patients with biopsy-confirmed myocarditis and complex ventricular arrhythmias at the time of presentation (11 with ventricular tachycardia). Five of the 12 patients still were receiving antiarrhythmic therapy at a median follow-up of 50 months. Complex ventricular arrhythmias still were present in these patients (three with ventricular tachycardia and two with couplets or multiforms), requiring ongoing therapy. The investigators concluded that although the arrhythmias were controlled more easily than at presentation of the patients, ongoing surveillance was essential in ensuring the suppression of these potentially life-threatening arrhythmias. Children who recover from myocarditis, regardless of cause, should be followed indefinitely.

Prevention

COMMON CAUSES OF MYOCARDITIS

Because enteroviruses may be spread by the airborne route, any newborn infant with myocarditis should be isolated with his or her mother. Individuals employed in newborn nurseries who develop signs or symptoms of enteroviral infection should be excluded from the nursery until they have recovered.

Immunization programs help to reduce the incidence of myocarditis associated with diphtheria and many of the other common infectious agents.[258]

Matsumori and colleagues[147] induced myocarditis with encephalomyocarditis virus in mice. Using ribavirin early after inoculation, they were able to show a significant reduction in myocardial injury and inflammation, presumably caused by inhibition of viral replication. No studies have been conducted in humans, but this model is a promising first step in possible prevention and therapy of virus-induced myocarditis.

The use of myocardial biopsy techniques may help to define further the cause of idiopathic cardiomyopathies, and with the probable availability of specific antiviral agents in the future, prevention of viral myocarditis may become a reality.

PARASITIC MYOCARDITIS

Parasitic myocarditis is an uncommon form of heart disease in the United States. In contrast, in Central and South America, infection with the protozoan *Trypanosoma cruzi* (i.e., American trypanosomiasis or Chagas disease) is a prominent cause of myocarditis.[129] Myocardial disease caused by infection with other parasites, including *Trichinella, Toxoplasma,* and *Toxocara,* has been reported in the literature.

The major cardiovascular manifestation of Chagas disease is an extensive myocarditis that typically becomes evident years or even decades after the initial infection. The disease is transmitted to humans by various species of blood-sucking reduviid insects. After inoculation, the protozoa multiply and then migrate widely throughout the body. The mechanism by which *T. cruzi* invades mammalian cells is largely unknown, but experimental studies suggest that an essential step is triggering of activation of the transforming growth factor–β (TGF-β) signaling pathway by *T. cruzi.*

Cells deficient in TGF-β receptors are protected against penetration and replication by adherent parasites. In contrast, administration of exogenous TGF-β enhances *T. cruzi* invasion.[154] Acute Chagas disease usually is an illness of children but can occur at any age.[123] Histologic examination of the heart during the acute phase reveals intracellular parasites with a marked cellular infiltrate, particularly around myocytes that have ruptured and released the parasites.[180] A well-established fact is that intracellular parasites are found in cardiac myocytes only during the acute phase of illness. Severe myocarditis develops in only a small proportion of acute cases, and most deaths are caused by the resultant congestive heart failure and pericardial effusion. Nonspecific electrocardiographic changes are seen, but the life-threatening arrhythmias that are frequent occurrences in chronic Chagas disease generally do not occur. In most patients with more acute disease (90% of cases), symptoms resolve gradually over a period of weeks to months.

Chronic progressive Chagas develops in 10 to 20 percent of previously asymptomatically infected individuals.[139] It is manifested by a chronic, diffuse, progressive fibrosing myocarditis that involves the myocytes and the atrioventricular conduction system.[159, 161] On gross examination, the heart usually is enlarged and flaccid. Thrombus formation is a frequent occurrence, and in some cases, thrombus may fill much of the apex of the left ventricle. Immune-mediated cardiac injury, caused primarily by infiltrating mononuclear cells, probably is the main mechanism responsible for the development of chronic Chagas heart disease. This hypothesis is supported by several observations. Animal models of *T. cruzi* infection have demonstrated lysis of nonparasitized cardiac myocytes by immune effector cells[8]; depletion of $CD4^+$ T-lymphocyte subpopulations abrogates myocardial injury in a murine model of chronic Chagas disease; and myocardial damage can be induced in healthy animals by passive transfer of $CD4^+$ T cells from *T. cruzi*–infected mice.[205] Although $CD4^+$ T cells appear to be critical in myocardial injury, $CD8^+$ T cells may have a protective role. Mice depleted of $CD8^+$ T cells have a robust parasitemia, but almost no inflammatory infiltrates are seen in the parasite-infected tissues.[229]

Histologic examination reveals focal but widespread areas of cellular infiltrates composed of plasma cells, eosinophils, mast cells, and macrophages.[159] Extensive fibrosis occurs, replacing previously damaged myocardial tissue. In contrast to the situation observed in acute disease, the presence of parasites (a rare finding) in tissue has little correlation with myocardial pathology. Inflammatory changes in the right bundle branch and the anterior fascicle of the left bundle branch explain the frequent occurrence of right bundle branch and left anterior fascicular block.[161]

The clinical manifestations of chronic Chagas disease range from isolated rhythm disturbances to advanced disease characterized by cardiomegaly, chronic congestive heart failure, and arrhythmias. Syncope also is a frequent problem of the disease. In one series of 53 patients with chronic Chagas disease, the most frequent causes of recurrent syncope were ventricular tachycardia (43%) with a poor prognosis and paroxysmal atrioventricular block (21%) with a favorable prognosis.[144] Sudden death caused by ventricular fibrillation is a constant threat and may develop before cardiomegaly or heart failure is diagnosed.[29, 144]

The diagnosis of chronic Chagas disease cannot be made only on the basis of histologic examination of the heart. Serologic testing is the method of choice for establishing the diagnosis of chronic Chagas disease. Several highly sensitive serologic tests for the detection of anti–*T. cruzi* antibodies, such as indirect hemagglutination, complement fixation, indirect immunofluorescence, and enzyme-linked immunosorbent assay, are available.[124, 217] Unfortunately, these assays lack specificity, and false-positive results have been reported in patients with other infectious diseases, such as malaria, leishmaniasis, and syphilis.[123] The current emphasis on the management of Chagas disease is on prevention because a chemotherapeutic agent that eradicates the parasite in the chronic stage of the disease is not available.

Myocarditis is one of the most serious complications of trichinosis. The disease develops when undercooked meat contaminated with infective larvae of *Trichinella* is eaten. Myocardial invasion by *Trichinella spiralis* has been well described,[219] but encystment within the myocardium has been reported only rarely.[98] At autopsy, the heart may be dilated and a pericardial effusion may be identified. Histologically, a prominent focal infiltrate composed of lymphocytes and eosinophils with interstitial edema and scattered hemorrhages commonly is found.[219] Myocarditis usually is mild, with few clinical signs and symptoms. However, this myocarditis may range from chest pain to fatal congestive heart failure and may mimic acute myocardial infarction.[36, 76] In one series of 114 patients with trichinosis, 21 percent had abnormal electrocardiograms.[213] Abnormalities included prolongation of the PR interval, low voltage or prolongation of the QRS complex, and flattened T waves. Despite electrocardiographic evidence of myocardial involvement, fewer than 0.1 percent of patients with trichinosis die of this complication.[76] The definitive diagnosis of trichinosis is based on demonstration of the larval forms in tissue biopsy samples, usually from a large tender area such as the gastrocnemius muscle. Serologic testing is available through state laboratories and the Centers for Disease Control and Prevention (CDC). Typically, serum antibody titers become positive during or after the third week of illness. The efficacy of mebendazole or albendazole in the treatment of myocarditis caused by *Trichinella* infection has not been evaluated adequately.

Toxocara canis, the principal cause of visceral larva migrans, is a rare cause of myocarditis. Most reported cases have occurred in children younger than 3 years of age.[40, 64, 241] Children especially are susceptible to infection with *Toxocara* because of their habit of crawling on the ground and putting various objects into their mouths. The myocardial lesions noted on histologic examination have included granulomata and extensive eosinophilic infiltrates with foci of muscle necrosis.[40, 241] The clinical presentation may be that of acute respiratory distress caused by congestive heart failure, requiring administration of oxygen and diuretic therapy. However, asymptomatic infection involving the heart also has been reported.[40] The definitive diagnosis requires microscopic identification of the larvae in biopsy specimens of the liver or heart, but this finding is infrequent. An enzyme immunoassay for *Toxocara* serum antibodies, which is available at the CDC, can provide presumptive evidence of toxocariasis.

Toxoplasma gondii may cause myocarditis as part of disseminated infection or, less frequently, as an isolated cardiac infection. In infants with congenital toxoplasmosis, the clinical manifestations usually are those of meningoencephalitis, but at autopsy, extensive myocardial involvement has been documented.[261] Outside the newborn period, infection with this intracellular parasite most commonly occurs in immunosuppressed individuals with malignant diseases, patients with AIDS,[28] and patients who have undergone cardiac or bone marrow transplantation.[139] Histologic examination of the heart reveals focal interstitial infiltrates consisting of histiocytes, lymphocytes, plasma cells, eosinophils, and very few polymorphonuclear cells.[230] Toxoplasma is seen as basophilic masses within a pseudocyst in normal or damaged myocardial fibers. Clinical manifestations may include arrhythmias (atrial and ventricular), atrioventricular block, atypical chest pain, pericarditis, and heart failure.[129, 230] The diagnosis of toxoplasmic myocarditis requires the exclusion of other specific forms of heart disease and the establishment of evidence of toxoplasmosis with serologic testing. The diagnosis may be aided by endomyocardial biopsy.[139] Treatment with pyrimethamine and sulfonamides (especially sulfadiazine) has been reported in patients with isolated toxoplasmic myocarditis, but the response to therapy has varied. In one series of toxoplasmic myocarditis, relapses occurred in 17 percent of cases after therapy.[130]

Myocardial disease also has been reported after infection with *Echinococcus granulosus* and *Plasmodium falciparum*.[151] Cardiac involvement is estimated to occur in less than 2 percent of cases of echinococcosis.[46] When it does occur, the cysts usually are located in the intramyocardial region and protrude into the adjacent cardiac chambers. The clinical manifestations primarily depend on the location and size of the cyst. Rupture of the cyst is the most dreaded complication because it may lead to pericarditis, anaphylactic shock, or pulmonary emboli. Two-dimensional echocardiography is the preferred imaging study to detect and localize cysts.[175] Myocardial changes also have been documented in fatal malaria, particularly when caused by *P. falciparum*. Histologically, blocking of the coronary arteries and capillaries with parasites, local hemorrhage, and deposit of pigment occurs.[144, 220] However, clinical findings suggestive of cardiac involvement are rare. In a series of 49 patients with falciparum malaria, no electrocardiographic evidence of cardiac involvement was found.[220]

Myocarditis also has occurred in association with primary amebic meningoencephalitis caused by *Naegleria*. In a retrospective study, focal or diffuse myocarditis was documented in more than 40 percent of cases.[142] However, myocardial involvement is not a clinically significant manifestation of this uniformly fatal central nervous system infection.

REFERENCES

1. Abelmann, W. H.: Virus and the heart. Circulation *44*:950–956, 1971.
2. Abt, A. F., and Vinnecour, M. I.: Electrocardiographic studies during pneumonia in infants and children. Am. J. Dis. Child. *47*:737, 1934.
3. Acierno, L. J.: Cardiac complications in acquired immunodeficiency syndrome (AIDS): A review. J. Am. Coll. Cardiol. *13*:1144, 1989.
4. Ainger, L. E.: Acute aseptic myocarditis: Corticosteroid therapy. J. Pediatr. *64*:716–723, 1964.
5. Ainger, L. E., Lawyer, N. G., and Fitch, C. W.: Neonatal rubella myocarditis. Br. Heart J. *28*:691, 1966.
6. Ali, N., Ferrans, V. J., Roberts, W. C., et al.: Clinical evaluation of transvenous catheter technique for endomyocardial biopsy. Chest *63*:399–402, 1973.
7. Anderson, D. W., Virmani, R., Reilly, J. M., et al.: Prevalent myocarditis at necropsy in acquired immunodeficiency syndrome. J. Am. Coll. Cardiol. *11*:792, 1988.
8. Andrade, Z. A., Andrade, S. G., Correa, R., et al.: Myocardial changes in acute *Trypanosoma cruzi* infection. Ultrastructural evidence of immune damage and the role of microangiopathy. Am. J. Pathol. *144*:1403–1411, 1994.
9. Appelbaum, F., Stranchen, J. A., Graw, R. G., Jr., et al.: Acute lethal carditis caused by high-dose combination chemotherapy: A unique clinical and pathological entity. Lancet *1*:58–62, 1976.
10. Archard, L. C., Bowles, N. E., Olsen, E. G. J., et al.: Detection of persistent coxsackievirus in dilated cardiomyopathy and myocarditis. Eur. Heart J. *8*:437–440, 1987.
11. Archard, L. C., Greeke, C. A., Richardson, P. J., et al.: Persistence of enteroviral RNA in dilated cardiomyopathy: A progression from myocarditis. *In* Schultheiss, H. E. (ed.): New Concepts in Viral Heart Disease. New York, Springer-Verlag, 1988, pp. 349–362.
12. Babb, J. M., Stoneman, M. E. R., and Stern, H.: Myocarditis and croup caused by coxsackie virus type B5. Arch. Dis. Child. *36*:551–556, 1961.
13. Bablanian, R.: Structure and functional alterations in cultured cells infected with cytocidal viruses. Prog. Med. Virol. *19*:40–83, 1975.
14. Bairan, A. C., Cherry, J. D., Fagan, L. F., et al.: Complete heart block and respiratory syncytial virus. Am. J. Dis. Child. *127*:264–265, 1974.
15. Baroldi, G., Corallo, S., Moroni, M., et al.: Focal lymphocytic myocarditis in acquired immunodeficiency syndrome (AIDS): A correlative morphologic and clinical study in 26 consecutive fatal cases. J. Am. Coll. Cardiol. *12*:463, 1988.
16. Barry, W. H.: Mechanisms of immune-mediated myocyte injury. Circulation *5*:2421–2432, 1994.
17. Begg, M. D.: Diphtheritic myocarditis: EKG study. Lancet *1*:857, 1937.
18. Behrman, R. E.: Neonatology: Diseases of the Fetus and Infant. St. Louis, C. V. Mosby, 1973.
19. Bell, E. J., and Grist, N. R.: Echo viruses, carditis and acute pleurodynia. Am. Heart J. *82*:133, 1971.
20. Bengtssen, E., and Lamberger, B.: Five-year follow-up study of cases suggestive of acute myocarditis. Am. Heart J. *72*:751, 1966.
21. Bergstrom, K., Erikson, U., Nordbring, F., et al.: Acute non-rheumatic myopericarditis: A follow-up study. Scand. J. Infect. Dis. *2*:7–16, 1970.
22. Berkovich, S., Rodriguez-Torres, R., and Lin, J. S.: Virologic studies in children with acute myocarditis. Am. J. Dis. Child. *115*:207, 1968.
23. Bowles, N. E., Richardson, P. J., Olsen, E. G. J., et al.: Detection of coxsackie-B-virus specific RNA sequences in myocardial biopsy samples from patients with myocarditis and dilated cardiomyopathy. Lancet *1*:1120–1123, 1986.
24. Bowles, N. E., Rose, M. L., Taylor, P., et al.: End-stage dilated cardiomyopathy: Persistence of enterovirus RNA in myocardium at cardiac transplantation and lack of immune response. Circulation *80*:1128–1136, 1989.
25. Brightman, V. J., McNair Scott, T. F., Westphal, M., et al.: An outbreak of coxsackie B5 virus infection in a newborn nursery. J. Pediatr. *69*:179, 1966.
26. Brynjolfsson, G., Eshaghy, B., Talano, J. V., et al.: Granulomatous myocarditis secondary to cornstarch. Am. Heart J. *94*:353–358, 1977.
27. Burch, G. E., Sun, S. C., Chu, K. C., et al.: Interstitial and coxsackie virus–myocarditis in infants and children: A comparative histologic and immunofluorescent study of 50 autopsied hearts. J. A. M. A. *203*:1–8, 1968.
28. Cappel, M. S., Mikhail, N., Ortega, A., et al.: Toxoplasma myocarditis in AIDS. Am. Heart J. *123*:1728–1729, 1992.
29. Carrasco, H. A., Guerrero, L., Parada, H., et al.: Ventricular arrhythmias and left ventricular myocardial function in chronic chagasic patients. Int. J. Cardiol. *28*:35–41, 1980.
30. Carrasco, H. A., Parada, H., Guerrero, L., et al.: Prognostic implications of clinical, electrocardiographic and hemodynamic findings in chronic Chagas disease. Int. J. Cardiol. *43*:27–38, 1994.
31. Chan, K. Y., Iwahara, M., Benson, L. N., et al.: Immunosuppressive therapy in the management of acute myocarditis in children: A clinical trial. J. Am. Coll. Cardiol. *17*:458, 1991.
32. Chany, C., Lepine, P., Lelong, M., et al.: Severe and fatal pneumonia in infants and young children associated with adenovirus infections. Am. J. Hyg. *67*:367–378, 1958.
33. Chapman, N. M., Tracy, S., Gauntt, C. J., et al.: Molecular detection and identification of enteroviruses using enzymatic amplification and nucleic acid hybridization. J. Clin. Microbiol. *28*:843–850, 1990.
34. Cherry, J. D., Jahn, C. L., and Meyer, T. C.: Paroxysmal atrial tachycardia associated with echo 9 virus infection. Am. Heart J. *73*:681, 1967.
35. Cohen, N. A.: Myocarditis in prodromal measles. Am. J. Clin. Pathol. *40*:50–53, 1963.
36. Compton, S. J., Celeum, C. L., Lee, C., et al.: Trichinosis with ventilatory failure and persistent myocarditis. Clin. Infect. Dis. *16*:500–504, 1993.
37. Crawford, S. E., Crook, W. G., Harrison, W. W., et al.: Histoplasmosis as a cause of acute myocarditis and pericarditis: Report of occurrence in siblings and review of the literature. Pediatrics *29*:92, 1961.
38. Dalldorf, G., and Sickles, G. M.: An unidentified filterable agent isolated from the faeces of children with paralysis. Science *108*:61–62, 1984.
39. Daly, K., Richardson, P. J., Olsen, E. G. J., et al.: Acute myocarditis: Role of histological and virological examination in the diagnosis and assessment of immunosuppressive treatment. Br. Heart J. *51*:30–35, 1984.
40. Dao, A. H., and Viromani, R.: Visceral larva migrans involving the myocardium: Report of 2 cases and review of the literature. Pediatr. Pathol. *6*:449–456, 1986.
41. Dec, G. W., Fallon, J. T., Southern, J. F., et al.: "Borderline myocarditis": An indication for repeat endomyocardial biopsy. J. Am. Coll. Cardiol. *15*:283, 1990.
42. Dec, G. W., Fallon, J. T., Southern, J. F., et al.: Relation between histological findings on early repeat right ventricular biopsy and ventricular function in patients with myocarditis. Br. Heart J. *60*:332, 1988.
43. Dec, G. W., Palacios, I. F., Fallon, J. T., et al.: Acute myocarditis in the spectrum of acute dilated cardiomyopathy. N. Engl. J. Med. *312*:885–890, 1985.
44. Dec, G. W., Palacios, I., Yasuda, T., et al.: Antimyosin antibody cardiac imaging: Its role in the diagnosis of myocarditis. J. Am. Coll. Cardiol. *16*:97, 1990.
45. Dery, P., Marks, M. I., and Shapera, R.: Clinical manifestations of coxsackievirus infections in children. Am. J. Dis. Child. *128*:464–468, 1974.

46. Dighiero, J., Canabal, E. J., Aguiree, C. V., et al.: *Echinococcus* disease of the heart. Circulation *17*:127–132, 1958.
47. Downham, M. A. P. S., Gardner, P. S., McQuillin, J., et al.: Role of respiratory viruses in childhood mortality. B. M. J. *1*:235–239, 1975.
48. Drennan, J. M.: Acute isolated myocarditis in newborn infants. Arch. Dis. Child. *28*:288–291, 1953.
49. Drew, J. H.: Echo 11 outbreak in a nursery associated with myocarditis. Aust. Paediatr. J. *9*:90–95, 1973.
50. Drucker, N. A., Colan, S. D., Lewis, A. B., et al.: Gamma globulin treatment of acute myocarditis in the pediatric population. Circulation *89*:252–257, 1994.
51. Dustin, M. L., Staunton, D. E., and Springer, T. A.: Supergene families in the immune system. Immunol. Today *9*:213–215, 1988.
52. Easton, A., and Eglin, R. P.: The detection of coxsackievirus RNA in cardiac tissue by in situ hybridization. J. Gen. Virol. *69*:285–291, 1988.
53. Eckstein, R., Mempel, W., and Bolte, H. D.: Reduced suppressor cell activity in congestive cardiomyopathy and in myocarditis. Circulation *65*:1224–1229, 1982.
54. Edwards, W. D., Holmes, D. R., and Reeder, G. S.: Diagnosis of active lymphocytic myocarditis by endomyocardial biopsy: Quantitative criteria for light microscopy. Mayo Clin. Proc. *57*:419–425, 1982.
55. Eichenwald, H. F., and Shinefield, H. R.: Viral infections of the fetus and of the premature and newborn infant. Adv. Pediatr. *12*:249, 1962.
56. Fenoglio, J. J., Ursell, P. C., Kellogg, C. F., et al.: Diagnosis and classification of myocarditis by endomyocardial biopsy. N. Engl. J. Med. *308*:12–18, 1983.
57. Fiedler, A.: Ueber akute interstitielle myokarditis. *In* Festschrift zur Feier des funfzigjahrigen Besteheen des Strastkrankenhauses zu Dresden-Friedrichstadt. Dresden, Baensch, 1899, p. 3.
58. Fine, I., Brainerd, H., and Sokolow, M.: Myocarditis in acute infectious diseases: A clinical and electrocardiographic study. Circulation *2*:859, 1950.
59. Fowler, O. N.: Myocardial Diseases. New York, Grune & Stratton, 1973, pp. 253–279.
60. French, A. J., and Weller, C. J.: Interstitial myocarditis following the clinical and experimental use of sulfonamide drugs. Am. J. Pathol. *18*:109, 1942.
61. Friedli, B., Renevey, F., and Rouge, J. C.: Complete heart block in a young child presumably due to mycoplasma pneumonial myocarditis. Acta Paediatr. Scand. *66*:385–388, 1977.
62. Friedman, F. W., Lesch, M., and Sonnenblick, H. E.: Neonatal Heart Disease. New York, Grune & Stratton, 1973, p. 210.
63. Friedman, R. A., Kearney, D. L., Moak, J. P., et al.: Persistence of ventricular arrhythmia after resolution of occult myocarditis in children and young adults. J. Am. Coll. Cardiol. *24*:780–783, 1994.
64. Friedman, S., and Hervada, A.: Severe myocarditis with recovery in a child with visceral larva migrans. J. Pediatr. *90*:322–323, 1977.
65. Froggatt, P., Lynas, M. A., and Marshall, T. K.: Sudden death in babies: Epidemiology. Am. J. Cardiol. *22*:457–468, 1968.
66. Fruhling, L., Koru, R., Lavillaureix, J., et al.: Chronic fibroelastic myoendocarditis of the newborn and the infant (fibroelastosis). New morphological, etiological and pathogenic data. Relation to certain cardiac abnormalities. Ann. Anat. Pathol. *7*:227, 1962.
67. Gardiner, A. J. S., and Short, D.: Four faces of acute myopericarditis. Br. Heart J. *35*:433–442, 1973.
68. Gatmaitan, B. G., Chason, J. L., and Lerner, A. M.: Augmentation of the virulence of murine coxsackie B3 myocardiopathy by exercise. J. Exp. Med. *131*:1132–1136, 1970.
69. Gear, J. H., and Measroch, V.: South African Institute for Medical Research Annual Report for 1952. South African Institute for Medical Research, 1953, pp. 38–39.
70. Gerzen, P., Granath, A., Holmgren, B., et al.: Acute myocarditis: A follow-up study. Br. Heart J. *34*:575–583, 1972.
71. Giles, T. D., and Gohd, R. S.: Respiratory syncytial virus and heart disease: A report of two cases. J. A. M. A. *236*:1128–1130, 1976.
72. Goldfinger, D., Schreiber, W., and Wosika, P. H.: Permanent heart block following German measles. Am. J. Med. *2*:320, 1947.
73. Goodman, G. C.: The cytopathology of enteroviral infection. Int. Rev. Exp. Pathol. *5*:67–110, 1966.
74. Gore, I., and Saphir, O.: Myocarditis: A classification of 1402 cases. Am. Heart J. *34*:827, 1947.
75. Grasso, M., Arbustini, E., Silini, E., et al.: Search for coxsackievirus B_3 RNA in idiopathic dilated cardiomyopathy using gene amplification by polymerase chain reaction. Am. J. Cardiol. *69*:658–664, 1992.
76. Gray, D. F., Morse, B. S., and Phillips, W. F.: Trichinosis with neurologic and cardiac involvement. Ann. Intern. Med. *57*:230–244, 1962.
77. Griffin, L. D., Kearney, D., Ni., J., et al.: Analysis of formalin-fixed and frozen myocardial autopsy samples for viral genome in childhood myocarditis and dilated cardiomyopathy with endocardial fibroelastosis using polymerase chain reaction (PCR). Cardiovasc. Pathol. *4*:3–11, 1995.
78. Grist, N. R., and Bell, E. J.: Enteroviruses and cardiac disease. Lancet *2*:1188, 1970.
79. Grist, N. R., and Bell, E. J.: Coxsackie viruses and the heart. Am. Heart J. *77*:295–300, 1969.
80. Grist, N. R.: Viruses and myocarditis. Postgrad. Med. J. *48*:746–749, 1972.
81. Grist, N. R., and Bell, E. J.: A six-year study of coxsackievirus B infections in heart disease. J. Hyg. (Camb.) *73*:165–172, 1974.
82. Gulick, T., Chung, M. L., Pieper, S. J., et al.: Interleukin-1 and tumor necrosis factor inhibit cardiac myocyte beta-adrenergic responsiveness. Proc. Natl. Acad. Sci. U. S. A. *86*:6753–6757, 1989.
83. Gutgesell, H. P., Paquet, M., Duff, D. F., et al.: Evaluation of left ventricular size and function by echocardiography: Results in normal children. Circulation. *56*:457–462, 1977.
84. Harris, M. J.: Sudden infant death syndrome. Med. J. Aust. Letter *2*:190, 1975.
85. Hastreiter, A. R., and Miller, R. A.: Management of primary endomyocardial disease: The myocarditis-endocardial fibroelastosis syndrome. Pediatr. Clin. North Am. *11*:401–430, 1964.
86. Haynes, R. E., Cramblett, H. G., Hilty, M. D., et al.: Echo virus type 3 infections in children: Clinical and laboratory studies. J. Pediatr. *80*:589–595, 1972.
87. Hejtmanick, R. M., Wright, C. J., Quint, R., et al.: The cardiovascular manifestations of systemic lupus erythematosus. Am. Heart J. *68*:119–130, 1964.
88. Helin, M., Sarola, J., and Lapinleimu, K.: Cardiac manifestations during a coxsackie B5 epidemic. Br. Med. J. *3*:97, 1968.
89. Henson, D., and Mufson, M. A.: Myocarditis and pneumonitis with type 21 adenovirus infection: Association with fatal myocarditis and pneumonitis. Am. J. Dis. Child. *121*:334–336, 1971.
90. Herskowitz, A., Ahmed-Ansari, A., Neumann, D. A., et al.: Induction of major histocompatibility complex antigens within the myocardium of patients with active myocarditis: A non-histologic marker of myocarditis. J. Am. Coll. Cardiol. *15*:624, 1990.
91. Hilton, D. A., Variend, S. and Pringle, J. H.: Demonstration of coxsackievirus RNA in formalin-fixed tissue sections from childhood myocarditis by in situ hybridization and the polymerase chain reaction. J. Pathol. *170*:45–51, 1993.
92. Hirschman, Z. S., and Hammer, S. G.: Coxsackie virus myopericarditis: A microbiological and clinical review. Am. J. Cardiol. *34*:224–232, 1974.
93. Hoagland, R. J.: Cardiac involvement in infectious mononucleosis. Am. J. Med. Sci. *232*:252, 1956.
94. Hobbs, R. E., Pelegrin, D., Ratliff, N. B., et al.: Lymphocytic myocarditis and dilated cardiomyopathy: Treatment with immunosuppressive agents. Cleve. Clin. J. Med. *56*:628, 1989.
95. Hodge, P. R., and Lawrence, J. R.: Two cases of myocarditis associated with phenylbutazone therapy. Med. J. Aust. *1*:640, 1957.
96. Hogg, N., Bates, P. A., and Harvey, J.: Structure and function of intercellular adhesion molecule 1. Chem. Immunol. *50*:98–115, 1991.
97. Hori, H., Matoba, T., Shingu, M., et al.: The role of cell mediated immunity in coxsackie B viral myocarditis. Jpn. Circ. J. *45*:1409, 1981.
98. Horlich, S. S., and Bichnell, R. E.: Trichiniasis with widespread infestation of many tissues. N. Engl. J. Med. *201*:816–819, 1929.
99. Hoshino, T., Matsumori, A., Kawai, C., et al.: Electrocardiographic abnormalities in Syrian golden hamsters with coxsackievirus B1 myocarditis. Jpn. Circ. J. *46*:1305–1312, 1982.
100. Hosier, D. M., and Newton, W. A., Jr.: Serious coxsackie infection in infants and children. Am. J. Dis. Child. *96*:251–267, 1958.
101. Hoyer, M. H., and Fischer, D. R.: Acute myocarditis simulating myocardial infarction in a child. Pediatrics *87*:250, 1991.
102. Huber, S. A., Job, L. P., and Woodruff, J. F.: Lysis of infected myofibers by coxsackie virus B-3 immune T-lymphocytes. Am. J. Pathol. *98*:681, 1980.
103. Hudgins, J. M.: Infectious mononucleosis complicated by myo- and pericarditis. J. A. M. A. *235*:2626–2627, 1976.
104. Hudson, R. E. B.: Myocardial involvement (myocarditis) in infections, infestation and drug therapy. Cardiovasc. Pathol. *1*:782–854, 1965.
105. Hughes, W. T., and Rathauser, V.: Rocky Mountain spotted fever in children. Pediatr. Dig., 1970, pp. 29–34.
106. Hutchins, G. H., and Vie, S. A.: The progression of interstitial myocarditis to idiopathic endocardial fibro-elastosis. Am. J. Pathol. *66*:483–496, 1972.
107. Hwang, W. S., Chan, M. C., Wong, H. B., et al.: Fatal coxsackie virus infections of the newborn. Singapore Med. J. *16*:244–248, 1975.
108. Jahn, C. L., and Cherry, J. D.: Mild neonatal illness associated with heavy enterovirus infection. N. Engl. J. Med. *274*:394, 1966.
109. James, T. N.: Sudden death in babies: New observations on the heart. Am. J. Cardiol. *22*:479, 1968.
110. Jankus, A.: Inflammatory changes in the cardiac conducting system in sudden infant death syndrome. Med. J. Aust. *1*:594–595, 1975.
111. Javett, S. N., Heymann, S., Mundel, B., et al.: Myocarditis in the newborn infant: A study of an outbreak associated with coxsackie group B virus infection in a maternity home in Johannesburg. J. Pediatr. *48*:1–22, 1956.
112. Jin, O., Sole, M. J., and Butany, J. W.: Detection of enterovirus RNA in myocardial biopsies from patients with myocarditis and cardiomyopathy using gene amplification by polymerase chain reaction. Circulation *82*:8–16, 1990.

113. Johnson, J. L., and Lee, L. P.: Complete atrioventricular heart block secondary to acute myocarditis requiring intracardiac pacing. J. Pediatr. *78*:312–316, 1971.
114. Joos, H. A., and Yu, P. N. G.: Electrocardiographic observations in poliomyelitis: Changes of the Q-T interval in twenty-three cases. Am. J. Dis. Child. *80*:22, 1950.
115. Karjalainen, J., Nieminen, M. S., and Heikkila, J.: Influenza A1 myocarditis in conscripts. Acta Med. Scand. *20*:27–30, 1980.
116. Karjalainen, J.: Functional and myocarditis induced T wave abnormalities. Chest *83*:6, 1983.
117. Keith, J. D., Rowe, R. D., and Vlad, P.: Heart Disease in Infancy and Childhood. 2nd ed. New York, Macmillan, 1967, pp. 996–1019.
118. Kereiakes, D. J., and Parmley, W. W.: Myocarditis and cardiomyopathy. Am. Heart J. *108*:1318–1325, 1984.
119. Kibrick, S., and Benirschke, K.: Acute aseptic myocarditis and meningoencephalitis in the newborn child infected with coxsackie virus group B3. N. Engl. J. Med. *255*:883, 1956.
120. Kibrick, S., and Benirschke, K.: Severe generalized disease (encephalohepatomyocarditis) occurring in the newborn period and due to infection with coxsackievirus group B: Evidence of intrauterine infection with this agent. Pediatrics *22*:857–874, 1958.
121. Kilbourne, E. D., Smart, K. M., and Pokorny, B. A.: Inhibition by cortisone of the synthesis and action of interferon. Nature *190*:650–651, 1961.
122. Kilbourne, E. D., Wilson, C. B., and Perrier, D.: The induction of gross myocardial lesions by a coxsackie (pleurodynic) virus and cortisone. J. Clin. Invest. *35*:362, 1956.
123. Kirchhoff, L. V.: *Trypanosoma* species (American trypanosomiasis, Chagas disease): Biology of trypanosomes. *In* Mandell, G. L., Bennett, J. E., and Dolin, R. (eds.): Mandell, Douglas and Bennett's Principles and Practices of Infectious Diseases. 4th ed. New York, Churchill Livingstone, 1995, pp. 2442–2450.
124. Kirchhoff, L. V., Gam, A. A., Gusmao, R., et al.: Increased specificity of serodiagnosis of Chagas disease by detection of antibody to the 72- and 90-kDa glycoproteins of *Trypanosoma cruzi*. J. Infect. Dis. *155*:561–564, 1987.
125. Kishimoto, C., Matsumori, A., Ohmae, M., et al.: Electrocardiographic findings in experimental myocarditis in DBA/2 mice. J. Am. Coll. Cardiol. *3*:1461–1468, 1984.
126. Kothari, U. R., Shah, S. S., Doshi, H. V., et al.: Myocarditis from scorpion sting: A clinical and electrocardiographic study of 50 cases. Indian Heart J. *28*:88–92, 1976.
127. Kussy, J. C.: Fatal mumps myocarditis. Minn. Med. *57*:285–286, 1974.
128. Lane, J. R., Neuman, D. A., Lafond-Walker, A., et al.: Role of IL-1 and tumor necrosis factor in coxsackie virus-induced autoimmune myocarditis. J. Immunol. *151*:1682–1690, 1993.
129. Laranja, F. S., Dias, E., Nobrega, G., et al.: Chagas disease: A clinical, epidemiologic and pathologic study. Circulation *14*:1035–1060, 1956.
130. Leak, D., and Meghji, M.: Toxoplasmic infection in cardiac disease. Am. J. Cardiol. *43*:841–849, 1979.
131. Ledbetter, M. K., Cannon, A. B., and Costa, A. F.: The electrocardiogram in diphtheritic myocarditis. Am. Heart J. *68*:599, 1964.
132. Lerner, A. M., and Wilson, M. F.: Virus myocardiopathy. Progr. Med. Virol. *15*:63–91, 1973.
133. Lerner, A. M., Wilson, F. M., and Reyes, M. P.: Enteroviruses and the heart (with special emphasis on the probable role of coxsackieviruses, group B, types 1–5). Mod. Concepts Cardiovasc. Dis. *64*:7–10, 1975.
134. Lewes, D., Rainford, D. J., and Lane, W. F.: Symptomless myocarditis and myalgia in viral and *Mycoplasma pneumoniae* infections. Br. Heart J. *36*:924–932, 1974.
135. Lim, C. H., Toh, C. C., Chia, B. L., et al.: Stokes-Adams attacks due to acute nonspecific myocarditis. Am. Heart J. *38*:123, 1949.
136. Lind, J., and Hulquist, G. T.: Isolated myocarditis in newborn and young infants. Am. Heart J. *38*:123, 1949.
137. Logue, B. L., and Hanson, J. L.: Complete heart block in German measles. Am. Heart J. *30*:205, 1945.
138. Lozinski, G. M., Davis G. G., Krous, H. F., et al.: Adenovirus myocarditis: Retrospective diagnosis by gene amplification from formalin-fixed, paraffin-embedded tissues. Hum. Pathol. *25*:831–834, 1994.
139. Luft, B. J., Billingham, M., and Remington, J. S.: Endomyocardial biopsy in the diagnosis of toxoplasmic myocarditis. Transplant. Proc. *6*:1871–1873, 1986.
140. Magure, J. H., Hoff, R., Sherlock, I., et al.: Cardiac morbidity and mortality due to Chagas disease: Prospective electrocardiographic study of a Brazilian community. Circulation *75*:1140–1145, 1987.
141. Maisch, B., Trostel-Soeder, R., Stechemesser, E., et al.: Diagnostic relevance of humoral and cell-mediated immune reactions in patients with acute viral myocarditis. Clin. Exp. Immunol. *48*:533, 1982.
142. Markowitz, S. M., Martinez, A. J., Duna, R. J., et al.: Myocarditis associated with primary amebic *(Naegleria)* meningoencephalitis. Am. J. Clin. Pathol. *62*:619–628, 1974.
143. Martin, A. B., Webber, S., Fricker, F. J., et al.: Acute myocarditis: Rapid diagnosis by PCR in children. Circulation *90*:330–339, 1994.
144. Martinez, M. F., Sosa, E., Nishioka, S., et al.: Clinical and electrophysiologic features of syncope in chronic chagasic heart disease. J. Cardiovasc. Electrophysiol. *5*:563–570, 1994.
145. Mason, J. W., Billingham, M. E., and Ricci, D. R.: Treatment of acute inflammatory myocarditis assisted by endomyocardial biopsy. Am. J. Cardiol. *45*:1037–1044, 1980.
146. Mason, J. W., O'Connell, J. B., Herskowitz, A., et al.: A clinical trial of immunosuppressive therapy for myocarditis: The Myocarditis Treatment Trial Investigators. N. Engl. J. Med. *333*:269–275, 1995.
147. Matsumori, A., Wang, H., Abelman, W. H., et al.: Treatment of viral myocarditis with ribavirin in an animal preparation. Circulation *71*:834–839, 1985.
148. Matsumori, A., and Kawai, C.: An experimental model for congestive heart failure after encephalomyocarditis virus myocarditis in mice. Circulation *65*:1230–1235, 1982.
149. Matsumori, A., Crumpacker, C., Abelmann, W. H., et al.: Virus vaccine and passive immunization for the prevention of viral myocarditis in mice. Circulation *68*(Suppl. III):338, 1983.
150. Matsumori, A., and Kawai, C.: An experimental model of congestive (dilated) cardiomyopathy: Dilation and hypertrophy of the heart in the chronic stage in DBA/2 mice with myocarditis caused by encephalomyocarditis virus. Circulation *66*:355–360, 1982.
151. Merkel, W. C.: *Plasmodium falciparum* malaria: The coronary and myocardial lesion observed at autopsy in two cases of acute fulminating *Plasmodium falciparum* infection. Arch. Pathol. *41*:290–298, 1946.
152. Miklozek, C. L., Crumpacker, C. S., Royal, H. D., et al.: Myocarditis presenting as acute myocardial infarction. Am. Heart J. *115*:768, 1988.
153. Miller, J. J., and French, J. W.: Myocarditis in juvenile rheumatoid arthritis. Am. J. Dis. Child. *131*:205–209, 1977.
154. Ming, M., Ewen, M. E., Pereira, M. E.: Trypanosome invasion of mammalian cells requires activation of the TGF beta signaling pathway. Cell *82*:287–296, 1995.
155. Montgomery, J., Gear, J., Prinsloo, F. R., et al.: Myocarditis of the newborn: Outbreak in maternity home in southern Rhodesia associated with coxsackie group B virus infection. S. Afr. Med. J. *29*:608–612, 1955.
156. Moore, C. M., Henry, J., Benzing, G., III, et al.: Varicella myocarditis. Am. J. Dis. Child. *118*:899–902, 1969.
157. Morbidity and Mortality Weekly Report. U.S. Department of Health, Education and Welfare. *14(1)*, 1965.
158. Morbidity and Mortality Weekly Report. U.S. Department of Health, Education and Welfare. *24(19)*, 1975.
159. Morris, S. A., Tanowitz, H. B., Wittner, M., et al.: Pathophysiological insights into the cardiomyopathy of Chagas disease. Circulation *82*:1900–1909, 1990.
160. Moschos, A., Papaioannou, A. C., Nicolopoulos, D., et al.: Cardiac complications after vaccination for smallpox. Helv. Paediatr. Acta *31*:257–260, 1976.
161. Mott, K. E., and Hagstrom, J. W. C.: The pathologic lesions of the cardiac autonomic system in chronic Chagas myocarditis. Circulation *31*:273–286, 1965.
162. Mowat, N. A., Bennett, P. N., Finlayson, J. K., et al.: Myopericarditis complicating ulcerative colitis. Br. Heart J. *36*:724–727, 1974.
163. Muir, P., Nicholson, F., Jhetan, M., et al.: Rapid diagnosis of enterovirus infection by magnetic bead extraction and polymerase chain reaction detection of enterovirus RNA in clinical specimens. J. Clin. Microbiol. *31*:31–38, 1993.
164. Mullis, K. B., and Faldona, F. A.: Specific synthesis of DNA in vitro via a polymerase catalyzed chain reaction. Methods Enzymol. *155*:335–350, 1988.
165. Nagaratnam, N., Gunawardene, K. R., and DeSilva, D. P.: Myocardial involvement in infectious hepatitis. Postgrad. Med. J. *47*:785–788, 1971.
166. Neches, W. H., Park, S. C., Lenox, C. C., et al.: Left atrial myxoma: Clinical presentation suggesting acute myocarditis. J. A. M. A. *229*: 1906–1907, 1974.
167. Neumann, D. A., Burek, C. L., Baughman, K. L., et al.: Circulating heart-reactive antibodies in patients with myocarditis or cardiomyopathy. J. Am. Coll. Cardiol. *16*:839, 1990.
168. Neuman, D. A., Lane, J. R., Allen, G. S., et al.: Viral myocarditis leading to cardiomyopathy: Do cytokines contribute to pathogenesis? Clin. Immunol. Pathol. *68*:181–190, 1993.
169. Obeyesekere, I., and Hermon, Y.: Myocarditis and cardiomyopathy after arbovirus infections (dengue and chikungunya fever). Br. Heart J. *34*:821–827, 1972.
170. O'Connell, J. B., Henken, R., Robinson, J., et al.: Gallium-67 imaging in patients with dilated cardiomyopathy and biopsy proven myocarditis. Circulation *70*:58–62, 1984.
171. Ognibene, A. J., O'Leary, D. S., Czarnecki, S. W., et al.: Myocarditis and disseminated intravascular coagulation in scrub types. Am. J. Med. Sci. *262*:233–239, 1971.
172. Okuni, M., Yamada, T., Mochizuki, S., et al.: Studies on myocarditis in childhood with special reference to the possible role of immunological process and the thymus in the chronicity of the disease. Jpn. Circ. J. *39*:463–470, 1975.

173. Okuni, M., and Takamiya, Y.: Primary myocardial disease in children, with special references to idiopathic myocarditis. Jpn. Circ. J. *35*:771–776, 1971.
174. Oldstone, M. B. A.: Virus neutralization and virus induced immune complex disease. Prog. Med. Virol. *19*:84–119, 1975.
175. Oliver, J. M., Sotillo, J. F., Dominguez, F. J., et al.: Two-dimensional echocardiographic features of *Echinococcus* of the heart and blood vessels. Circulation *78*:327–337, 1988.
176. Olsen, E. G. J.: The role of biopsy in the diagnosis of myocarditis. Herz. *10*:21–25, 1985.
177. Osama, S. M., Krishnamurti, S., and Gupta, D. N.: Incidence of myocarditis in varicella. Indian Heart J. *31*:315–320, 1979.
178. Pacque, R. E., Strauss, D. C., Nealon, T. J., et al.: Fractionation and immunologic assessment of KC1-extractable cardiac antigens in coxsackievirus B3 virus induced myocarditis. J. Immunol. *123*:358–364, 1979.
179. Pacque, R. E., Gauntt, C. J., and Nealon, T. J.: Assessment of cell mediated immunity against coxsackie B3 induced myocarditis in a primate model (*Papio papio*). Infect. Immunol. *31*:470–479, 1981.
180. Palacios-Pru, E., Carrasco, H., Scoraza, C., et al.: Ultrastructural characteristics of different stages of human Chagas myocarditis. Am. J. Trop. Med. Hyg. *41*:29–40, 1989.
181. Parrillo, J. E., Aretz, H. T., Palacios, I., et al.: The results of transvenous endomyocardial biopsy can frequently be used to diagnose myocardial disease in patients with idiopathic heart failure. Circulation *69*:93–101, 1984.
182. Petitjean, J., Kopecka, H., Freymuth, F., et al.: Detection of enteroviruses in endomyocardial biopsy by molecular approach. J. Med. Virol. *37*:76–82, 1992.
183. Pober, J. S., Gimbrone, M. A., Lapierre, L. A., et al.: Overlapping patterns of activation of human endothelial cells by interleukin 1, tumor necrosis factor, and immune interferon. J. Immunol. *137*:1893–1896, 1986.
184. Poltera, A. A., Cox, J. N., and Owor, R.: Pancarditis affecting the conducting system and all valves in human African trypanosomiasis. Br. Heart J. *38*:827–837, 1976.
185. Pomerance, A.: Classification of the secondary cardiomyopathies: The pathologist's view. Postgrad. Med. J. *48*:714–721, 1972.
186. Pomerance, A., and Davies, M. J. (eds.): The Pathology of the Heart. Philadelphia, J. B. Lippincott, 1975.
187. Rabin, E. R., Hassan, S. A., Jenson, A. B., et al.: Coxsackie virus B3 myocarditis in mice. Am. J. Pathol. *44*:775–797, 1964.
188. Rager-Zisman, B., and Allison, A. C.: Effects of immunosuppression on coxsackie B3 virus infection in mice and passive protection by circulating antibody. J. Gen. Virol. *19*:339, 1973.
189. Rantakallio, P., Saukronen, A. L., Krause, U., et al.: Follow-up study of 17 cases of neonatal coxsackie B5 meningitis and one with suspected myocarditis. Scand. J. Infect. Dis. *2*:25–28, 1970.
190. Ray, C. G., Portman, J. N., Stamm, S. J., et al.: Hemolytic-uremic syndrome and myocarditis: Association with coxsackievirus B infection. Am. J. Dis. Child. *122*:418–420, 1971.
191. Redline, R. W., Genest, D. R., and Tycko, B.: Detection of enteroviral infection in paraffin-embedded tissue by the RNA polymerase chain reaction technique. Am. J. Clin. Pathol. *96*:568–571, 1991.
192. Reilly, J. M., Cunnion, R. E., Anderson, D. W., et al.: Frequency of myocarditis, left ventricular dysfunction and ventricular tachycardia in the acquired immune deficiency syndrome. Am. J. Cardiol. *62*:789, 1988.
193. Rezkalla, S., Kloner, R. A., Khatib, G., et al.: Beneficial effects of captopril in acute coxsackievirus B3 murine myocarditis. Circulation *81*:1039, 1990.
194. Robbins, S. L., and Cotran, R. S.: Pathologic Basis of Disease. 2nd ed. Philadelphia, W. B. Saunders, 1979, p. 694.
195. Rosenbaum, H. D., Nadas, A. S., and Neuhauser, E. B. D.: Primary myocardial disease in infancy and childhood. Am. J. Dis. Child. *86*:28–44, 1953.
196. Rosenberg, E. H.: Acute myocarditis in mumps (epidemic parotitis). Arch. Intern. Med. *76*:257, 1945.
197. Rosenberg, H. S., and McNamara, D. G.: Acute myocarditis in infancy and childhood. Prog. Cardiovasc. Dis. *7*:179–197, 1964.
198. Ross, L. J.: Electrocardiographic findings in measles. Am. J. Dis. Child. *83*:282–291, 1952.
199. Rytel, M. W., and Kilbourne, E. D.: Differing susceptibility of adolescent and adult mice to non-lethal infection with coxsackie virus B3 (S5596). Proc. Soc. Exp. Biol. Med. *137*:443–448, 1971.
200. Sahn, D. J., Vaucher, Y., Williams, D. E., et al.: Echocardiographic detection of large left-to-right shunts and cardiomyopathies in infants and children. Am. J. Cardiol. *38*:73–79, 1976.
201. Sainani, G. S., Dekate, M. P., and Rao, C. P.: Heart disease caused by coxsackie virus B infection. Br. Heart J. *37*:819–823, 1975.
202. Sakakibara, S., and Konno, S.: Endomyocardial biopsy. Jpn. Heart J. *3*:537, 1962.
203. Sakamoto, M., Suzuki, F., Arai, S., et al.: Experimental myocarditis induced in mice by infection with influenza A2 virus. Microbiol. Immunol. *25*:173–181, 1981.
204. Sands, M. J., Jr., Satz, J. E., Turner, W. E., Jr., et al.: Pericarditis and perimyocarditis associated with active *Mycoplasma pneumoniae* infection. Ann. Intern. Med. *86*:544–548, 1977.
205. dos Santos, R. R., Rossi, M. A., Laus, J. L., et al.: Anti-CD4 abrogates rejection and reestablishes long-term tolerance to syngeneic newborn hearts grafted in mice chronically infected with *Trypanosoma cruzi*. J. Exp. Med. *175*:29–39, 1992.
206. Saphir, O., Simon, W. A., and Reingold, M. I.: Myocarditis in children. Am. J. Dis. Child. *67*:294–312, 1944.
207. Saphir, O., and Field, M.: Complications of myocarditis in children. J. Pediatr. *45*:457–463, 1954.
208. Schieken, R. M., and Myers, M. G.: Complete heart block in viral myocarditis. J. Pediatr. *87*:831–832, 1975.
209. Schmidt, N. J., Magoffin, R. L., and Lennette, E. H.: Association of group B coxsackieviruses with cases of pericarditis, myocarditis or pleurodynia by demonstration of immunoglobulin M antibody. Infect. Immunol. *8*:341–348, 1973.
210. Schowengerdt, K. O., Ni, J., Denfield, S. W., et al.: Diagnosis, surveillance, and epidemiologic evaluation of viral infection in pediatric cardiac transplant recipients using the polymerase chain reaction (PCR). J. Heart Lung Transplant. 2002. In press.
211. Schryer, M. J., and Karnauchow, P. N.: Endocardial fibroelastosis: Etiologic and pathogenetic considerations in children. Am. Heart J. *88*:557–565, 1974.
212. Scott, L. P., III, Gutelius, M. F., and Parrott, R. H.: Children with acute respiratory tract infections: An electrocardiographic survey. Am. J. Dis. Child. *119*:111–113, 1970.
213. Seko, Y., Matsuda, H., Kato, K., et al.: Expression of intercellular adhesion molecule-1 in murine hearts with acute myocarditis caused by coxsackievirus B3. J. Clin. Invest. *91*:1327–1336, 1993.
214. Seko, Y., Yamazaki, T., Shinkai, Y., et al.: Cellular and molecular bases for the immunopathology of the myocardial cell damage involved in acute viral myocarditis with special reference to dilated cardiomyopathy. Jpn. Circ. J. *56*:1062–1072, 1992.
215. Shingu, M.: Laboratory diagnosis of viral myocarditis: A review. Jpn. Circ. J. *53*:87–93, 1989.
216. Solarz, S.: An electrocardiographic study on one-hundred fourteen consecutive cases of trichinosis. Am. Heart J. *34*:230–240, 1947.
217. Spencer, H. C., Allain, D. S., Sulzer, A. J., et al.: Evaluation of the micro-enzyme-labeled immunosorbent assay for antibodies to *Trypanosoma cruzi*. Am. J. Trop. Med. Hyg. *29*:179–182, 1980.
218. Spencer, M. J., Cherry, J. D., Adams, F. H., et al.: Supraventricular tachycardia in an infant associated with a rhinoviral infection [letter]. J. Pediatr. *86*:811–812, 1975.
219. Spink, W. W.: Cardiovascular complications of trichinosis. Arch. Intern. Med. *56*:238–245, 1935.
220. Sprague, H. B.: The effects of malaria on the heart. Am. Heart J. *31*:426–430, 1946.
221. Stedman's Medical Dictionary. 2nd ed. Baltimore, Williams & Wilkins, 1966.
222. Sterner, G.: Adenovirus infections in childhood: An epidemiological and clinical survey among Swedish children. Acta Paediatr. *142*:1–30, 1962.
223. Sterner, G., Agell, B. O., Wahren, B., et al.: Acquired cytomegalovirus infection in older children and adults: A clinical study of hospitalized patients. Scand. J. Infect. Dis. *2*:95–103, 1970.
224. Stewart, J. M., Kaul, A., Gromisch, D. S., et al.: Symptomatic cardiac dysfunction in children with human immunodeficiency virus infection. Am. Heart J. *117*:140, 1989.
225. Strain, J. E., Grose, R. M., Factor, S. M., et al.: Results of endomyocardial biopsy in patients with spontaneous ventricular tachycardia but without apparent structural heart disease. Circulation *68*:1171–1181, 1983.
226. Sugrue, D. D., Holmes, D. R., Gersh, B. J., et al.: Cardiac histologic findings in patients with life threatening ventricular arrhythmias of unknown origin. J. Am. Coll. Cardiol. *4*:952–957, 1984.
227. Tahernia, A. C.: Electrocardiographic abnormalities and transaminase levels in diphtheritic myocarditis. J. Pediatr. *75*:1008–1014, 1969.
228. Take, M., Sekiguchi, M., Hiroe, M., et al.: Long-term follow-up of electrocardiographic findings in patients with acute myocarditis proven by endomyocardial biopsy. Jpn. Circ. J. *46*:1227–1234, 1982.
229. Tarleton, R. L., Zhang, L., and Downs, M. O.: "Autoimmune rejection" of neonatal heart transplants in experimental Chagas disease is a parasite-specific response to infected host tissue. Proc. Natl. Acad. Sci. U. S. A. *94*:3932–3937, 1997.
230. Theologides, A., and Kennedy, B. J.: Toxoplasmic myocarditis and pericarditis. Am. J. Med. *47*:169–173, 1969.
231. Thisyakorn, U. S. A., Wongvanich, J., and Kumpeng, V.: Failure of corticosteroid therapy to prevent diphtheritic myocarditis or neuritis. Pediatr. Infect. Dis. *3*:126–128, 1984.
232. Tiula, E., and Leinikki, P.: Fatal cytomegalovirus infection in a previously healthy boy, with myocarditis and consumption coagulopathy as presenting signs. Scand. J. Infect. Dis. *4*:57–60, 1972.
233. Towbin, J. A., Griffin, L. D., Martin, A. B., et al.: Intrauterine adenoviral myocarditis presenting as non-immune hydrops fetalis: Diagnosis by polymerase chain reaction. Pediatr. Infect. Dis. J. *13*:144–150, 1994.

234. Toyozaki, T., Saito, T., Takano, H., et al.: Expression of intercellular adhesion molecule-1 on cardiac myocytes for myocarditis before and during immunosuppressive therapy. Am. J. Cardiol. *72*:441–444, 1993.
235. Tracy, S., Wiegand, V., McManus, B., et al.: Molecular approaches to enteroviral diagnosis in idiopathic cardiomyopathy and myocarditis. J. Am. Coll. Cardiol. *15*:1688, 1990.
236. Unverferth, D. V., Fetters, J. K., Uretsky, B., et al.: Right versus left heart biopsies: Different information. Circulation. *70*(Suppl. II):402, 1984.
237. Van Creveld, S., de Groot, J. W., Hartog, H. A. P., et al.: Diagnosis and treatment of acute interstitial myocarditis in infancy. Ann. Paediatr. *183*:193–202, 1954.
238. Van Creveld, S., and de Jager, H.: Myocarditis in newborns caused by coxsackie virus: Clinical and pathological data. Ann. Paediatr. *187*:100, 1956.
239. Van Reken, D. E., Geffen, W. A., and Cramer, S. F.: Clinical conference: Sudden congestive heart failure in a 5-month-old infant. J. Pediatr. *85*:724–729, 1974.
240. Van Zaane, K. D., and Van der Veen, J.: Quelques symtomes cliniques particuliers chez les enfants attenints d'ure infection a' adenovirus. Presse Med. *70*:1021–1022, 1962.
241. Vargo, T. A., Singer, D. B., Gillette, P. C., et al.: Myocarditis due to visceral larva migrans. J. Pediatr. *90*:322–323, 1977.
242. Verel, D., Warrack, A. J., Potter, C. W., et al.: Observations on the A2 England influenza epidemic: A clinicopathological study. Am. Heart J. *92*:290–296, 1976.
243. Verlinde, J. D., Van Tongeren, H. A. E., and Kret, A.: Myocarditis in newborns due to coxsackie B virus: Virus studies. Ann. Paediatr. *187*:113, 1956.
244. Vignola, P. A., Aonuma, K., Swage, P., et al.: Lymphocytic myocarditis presenting as unexplained ventricular arrhythmias: Diagnosis with endomyocardial biopsy and response to immunosuppression. J. Am. Coll. Cardiol. *4*:812–819, 1984.
245. Weber, M. W., Baldwin, J. S., and Hall, J. W.: Acute isolated myocarditis: Review of the literature and a report of a case in a 10-year-old child. Pediatrics *3*:829–835, 1949.
246. Weiss, L. M., Movahed, L. A., Billingham, M. E., et al.: Detection of coxsackievirus, B_3 RNA in myocardial tissue by the polymerase chain reaction. Am. J. Pathol. *138*:497–503, 1991.
247. Weiss, L. M., Liu, X.-F., Chang, K. L., et al.: Detection of enteroviral RNA idiopathic dilated cardiomyopathy and other human cardiac tissues. J. Clin. Invest. *90*:156–159, 1992.
248. Weiss, L. M., Movahed, L. A., Berry, G. J., et al.: In situ hybridization studies for viral nucleic acids in heart and lung allograft biopsies. Am. J. Clin. Pathol. *93*:675–679, 1990.
249. Wells, A. H., and Sax, S. G.: Isolated myocarditis, probably of sulfonamide origin. Am. Heart J. *30*:522, 1945.
250. Wentworth, P., Jentz, L. A., and Croal, A. E.: Analysis of sudden unexpected death in southern Ontario, with emphasis on myocarditis. Can. Med. Assoc. J. *120*:676–706, 1979.
251. Whitehead, J. E.: Silent infections and the epidemiology of viral carditis. Am. Heart J. *85*:711–713, 1973.
252. Williams, H., O'Reilly, R. N., and Williams, A.: Fourteen cases of idiopathic myocarditis in infants and children. Arch. Dis. Child. *28*:271–283, 1953.
253. Wong, C. Y., Woodruff, J. J., and Woodruff, J. F.: Generation of cytotoxic T lymphocytes during coxsackie B-3 infection. II. Characterization of effector cells and demonstration of cytotoxicity against viral infected fibers. J. Immunol. *118*:1165–1169, 1977.
254. Woodruff, J. F.: Viral myocarditis: A review. Am. J. Pathol. *101*:427–484, 1980.
255. Woodruff, J. F.: The influence of quantitated post-weaning undernutrition on coxsackie virus B3 infection of adult mice. II. Alteration of host defense mechanisms. J. Infect. Dis. *121*:164, 1970.
256. Wright, H. T., Jr.: Fatal infection in a newborn infant due to herpes simplex virus. J. Pediatr. *67*:130–132, 1965.
257. Yamada, T., Matsumori, A., and Sasayama, S.: Therapeutic effect of anti-tumor necrosis factor-alpha antibody on the murine model of viral myocarditis induced by encephalomyocarditis virus. Circulation *89*:846–851, 1994.
258. Yogman, M., and Echeverria, P.: Scleredema and carditis: Report of a case and review of the literature. Pediatrics *54*:108–110, 1974.
259. Zalma, V. M., Older, J. J., and Brooks, G. F.: The Austin, Texas, diphtheria outbreak: Clinical and epidemiological aspects. J. A. M. A. *211*:2125, 1970.
260. Zee-Cheng, C. S., Tsai, C. C., Palmer, D. C., et al.: High incidence of myocarditis by endomyocardial biopsy in patients with idiopathic congestive cardiomyopathy. J. Am. Coll. Cardiol. *3*:63–70, 1984.
261. Zwelzer, W. M.: Infantile toxoplasmosis. Arch. Pathol. *38*:1–19, 1944.

CHAPTER 35 Acute Rheumatic Fever

DIANA LENNON

Acute rheumatic fever is an inflammatory disease of the heart, joints, central nervous system, and subcutaneous tissues that develops after a nasopharyngeal infection by one of the group A beta-hemolytic streptococci. The pathogenesis of this disease, a clinical syndrome without a specific diagnostic test, remains an enigma, and specific treatment is not available. However, prevention of initial and recurrent attacks is possible with penicillin prophylaxis. Rheumatic fever is especially important because of the heart disease that often ensues, and such disease may lead to chronic progressive damage and premature death. As succinctly stated by Lasegue many years ago, "Rheumatic fever licks the joints and bites the heart,"[131] a statement that holds true today. The unexpected upsurge in this disease in the United States in the late 1980s and into the 1990s and reports of increasing numbers of invasive group A streptococcal infections have renewed interest in group A streptococci and their abilities. In addition, recognition that rheumatic fever is the leading cause of acquired heart disease in children and young adults worldwide has led to action.[105]

Epidemiology

The overall incidence and severity of acute rheumatic fever have decreased in recent years in developed areas of Western countries and in prosperous countries of Asia.[3] Reliable morbidity data on the occurrence of acute rheumatic fever in total populations are lacking because studies often consider only a segment of a population. However, the trend seems clear. Some of the best long-term data come from Denmark, where rheumatic fever has been a reportable disease for many years[147]; a steady decline has been occurring since 1900, except for a peak during World War II (Fig. 35–1). In the United States, rheumatic fever is not a reportable disease, but mortality rates (Fig. 35–2) and hospital discharge rates (Fig. 35–3 and Table 35–1) have shown a steady decline. Although this decline was already under way, it appears to have been accelerated by the introduction of penicillin.[88]

The really dramatic decline in the incidence of rheumatic fever began in the United States in the late 1940s

FIGURE 35–1 ■ Reported annual incidence of acute rheumatic fever in Denmark, 1862 to 1962. (Adapted from Public Health Board of Denmark: Reported rheumatic fever incidence in Denmark, 1862–1962. *In* Vendsborg, P., Fauerholdt, L., and Olsen, K. H.: Decreasing incidence of a history of acute rheumatic fever in chronic rheumatic heart disease. Cardiologica *53*:332–340, 1968. Used with permission of S. Karger A. G., Basel.)

(see Fig. 35–2). During the late 1950s, the 1960s, and the early 1970s, studies in the United States showed annual rates of between 13.5 and 62.5 first attacks per 100,000 children 5 to 14 years of age; however, these studies are not strictly comparable in design.[27, 36, 59, 123] Some of them were conducted in low-income urban areas, locations in which the incidence of rheumatic fever was thought to be higher. Secondary prevention of rheumatic fever with penicillin prophylaxis to protect against recurrent attacks probably became widespread in the 1960s. Denny and colleagues[47] showed the possibility of preventing initial attacks with injectable penicillin in 1950 in military camps. Similar controlled studies were not repeated in the general population or with oral penicillin.

The most compelling evidence that appropriate medical intervention helps reduce the number of initial attacks of rheumatic fever comes from a study by Gordis of health care availability in an inner-city Baltimore population at risk.[59] The rate of acute rheumatic fever was reduced by 60 percent over a decade in only the census tracts receiving a comprehensive care program, with that reduction occurring only in patients with an identifiable preceding clinical respiratory infection. A similar trend with small numbers of patients was seen for the Navajo and Papago Native American populations in school-based intervention programs[9, 36] and in an Alaskan program.[25] Other school-based interventions[110] have reduced streptococcal prevalence rates but have not gone the necessary further step to show a reduction in rheumatic fever morbidity in a controlled, carefully demarcated population.

An unexplained high incidence of acute rheumatic fever persists in Hawaii, especially in Polynesian and part-Polynesian children.[33] Similarly, rates are inexplicably higher in larger populations of Polynesian children in New Zealand.[80] Furthermore, in some areas of the continental United States, the rate of endemic rheumatic fever continues to exceed that of the general population in some children traditionally considered to be at risk (urban blacks), though not in others (recent Hispanic immigrants).[51] In contrast, in a hospital-based study in another urban area, Hispanic children, reflecting the pediatric population being served, were the most affected.[62]

However, since the beginning of 1985, the number of patients with acute rheumatic fever in several centers on the U.S. mainland has increased.[21, 35, 48, 66, 79, 145, 146, 150, 151, 163] Even though these numbers are not large, they represent a definite increase, but focal outbreaks may be reflected rather than increased activity nationwide (Table 35–2).[138] In fact, nationally, the number of diagnoses of acute rheumatic fever may have continued to decline gradually from 1984 through 1990.[138] The populations (aside from clusters in military populations[2, 150]) generally do not seem to be those considered to have been at risk in the past: most patients are white and middle class and live in suburban or rural communities with ready access to medical care. In the Utah and Tennessee outbreaks,[146, 156] the families were larger than the state average. The military outbreaks[2, 151] were the first in 2 decades in U.S. military personnel. Factors other than the widespread use of antibiotics and improved availability

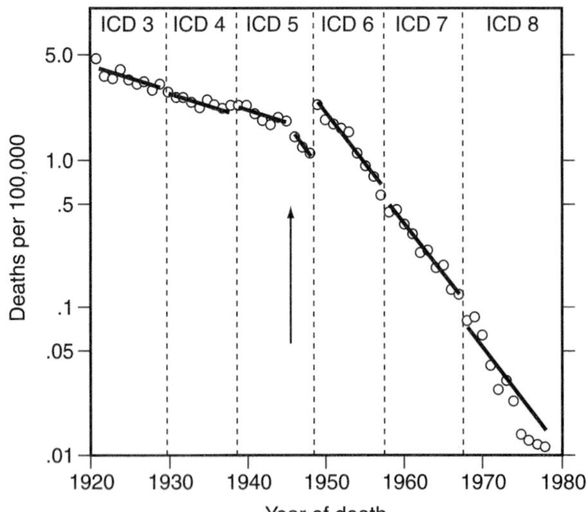

FIGURE 35–2 ■ U.S. national mortality from rheumatic fever in persons 5 to 19 years old, 1921 through 1978. Values are age adjusted to the 1950 U.S. population. Trend lines are fitted for each era (1921 through 1945 and 1946 through 1978) separately and take International Classification of Diseases (ICD) revisions into account. The *arrow* separates the two eras. (Reprinted, by permission, from Massell, B. F., Chute, C. G., Walker, A. M., et al.: Penicillin and the marked decrease in morbidity and mortality from rheumatic fever in the United States. N. Engl. J. Med. *318*:280–286, 1988.)

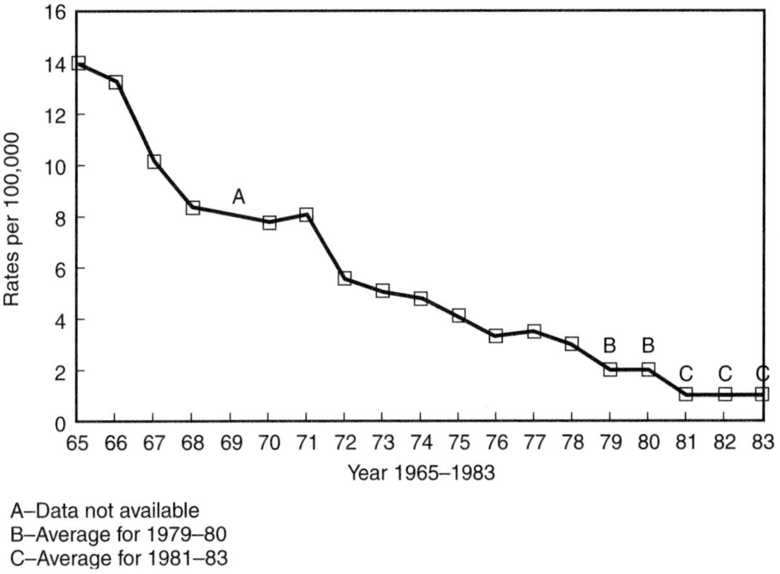

FIGURE 35–3 ■ Annual rates (per 100,000) of discharge of patients with rheumatic fever from short-stay nonfederal hospitals in the United States, 1965 to 1983. (From National Hospital Discharge Survey, NCHS. Adapted from Gordis, L.: The virtual disappearance of rheumatic fever in the United States: Lessons in the rise and fall of disease. Circulation *72*:1155–1162, 1985.)

A–Data not available
B–Average for 1979–80
C–Average for 1981–83

of health care may be important. Overcrowded living circumstances long have been considered to be a risk factor,[109] although this hypothesis has failed to be substantiated as an important risk factor by conditional logistic regression in a modern-day study.[148]

The disquieting feature in these recent outbreaks was the severity of the illness, especially in the Salt Lake City, Utah, outbreak: 68 percent of patients had carditis (Table 35–3), 19 percent had severe carditis with or without congestive heart failure, and 3 patients required mitral valve replacement. Earlier U.S. reports documented clinical carditis in initial attacks of rheumatic fever in 40 to 51 percent of patients (1951 through 1965).[87] Longitudinal observations at the same institution suggest a decreasing frequency of clinical carditis (73% from 1921 to 1930, 51% from 1951 to 1960).[23, 93] Rheumatic fever in its milder form with arthritis as the sole major manifestation may cause difficulty in making a diagnosis,[64] and the patient may not be admitted to the hospital, which could affect estimates of rates of carditis in studies that are not population based. With the use of Doppler echocardiography, carditis rates in the Utah patients rose to 85 percent (see Table 35–3). A reappraisal of diagnostic and descriptive data on rheumatic fever and its outcomes may be needed. The duration of secondary penicillin prophylaxis and endocarditis prophylaxis is an important consideration for patients with nonclinical carditis. However, the place of this new technology should be assessed carefully by longitudinal studies (see "Laboratory Findings").

TABLE 35–1 ■ REPORTED INCIDENCE OF ACUTE RHEUMATIC FEVER IN STUDIES IN THE UNITED STATES, 1970–1981

Location	Years of Study	Rate/100,000	Age Range (yr)
Fairfax, VA	1970–1980	1.14	0–18
Rhode Island	1976–1980	0.23	5–17
Memphis, TN	1977–1981	1.88	5–17
Baltimore, MD	1977–1981	0.50	5–19
San Fernando, CA	1971–1980	0.63	5–17

Adapted from Veasy, L. G., Wiedmeier, S. E., Orsmond, G. S., et al.: Resurgence of acute rheumatic fever in the intermountain area of the U.S. N. Engl. J. Med. *316*:421–427, 1987; and Markowitz M., and Kaplan, E. L.: Reappearance of rheumatic fever. Adv. Pediatr. *36*:44, 1989.

The prevalence of rheumatic heart disease, which represents the result of many years of exposure to the risks of acquiring acute rheumatic fever, appears to have declined in the United States over the course of many years.[102]

Many different racial and ethnic groups have been deemed unusually susceptible to rheumatic fever. They usually have been minority groups within a given area who are of lower socioeconomic status than the general population (e.g., Malays in Singapore, Arabs in Israel, Bantus in South Africa, Maori in New Zealand, African Americans in the United States, aborigines in Australia).[3, 29, 86] In the United States, when differences in socioeconomic status or degree of crowding were taken into account,[58] the greater differences in the incidence of rheumatic fever,[57] prevalence of rheumatic heart disease,[102] and mortality from acute rheumatic fever and rheumatic heart disease disappeared,[115] at least in the population studied. Rates in African Americans were slower to decline. They became very low in the 1970s, at least in some areas.[78] However, Gordis and associates[60] caution that some other socioeconomically determined factor closely paralleling crowding could be the actual determinant of rheumatic fever. Most authorities agree that the reduction in both the incidence and severity of rheumatic fever that has been noted in the United States and Western Europe might be due in part to a higher standard of living and less crowding. In a case-control study in the former Yugoslavia, home dampness, change of place of residence during the last 5 years, low maternal education, body weight below normal, frequent incidents of sore throat, and positive family history of rheumatic fever were found to be significant risk factors.[148]

The recognition of a relationship between group A streptococcal throat infection and rheumatic fever grew out of observations of the latter occurring after outbreaks of scarlet fever.[108] The attack rate noted after group A streptococcal throat infection varied widely (from 3% at Warren Air Force Base[117] to 0.39% in Chicago children[128]). Further observations in the latter study revealed that exudative pharyngitis, a positive throat culture with persistence of group A streptococci beyond 21 days, and the development of significant antibody (antistreptolysin O [ASO]) responses were associated with a higher attack rate that approached 3 percent in the children studied.

Rheumatic fever, like streptococcal infection, occurs most commonly in children 5 to 15 years of age. First attacks of

TABLE 35–2 ■ REPORTED OUTBREAKS OF ACUTE RHEUMATIC FEVER IN THE UNITED STATES: SELECTED EPIDEMIOLOGIC FEATURES

	Salt Lake City, Utah[129, 130]	Columbus, Ohio[58]	Akron, Ohio[30]	Pittsburgh, Pennsylvania[131, 145]	San Diego, California[124]	Tennesee[138*]
Time	1985–1992	6/84–9/86	1986	1987–6/90	12/86–7/87	1/87–7/88
Number of cases	274	40	23	60	50	26
White (%)	93	80	96	97	50	80
Family income	80% middle	73% middle	\$20,000–\$40,000	3 of 17 on assistance[131]	NA	\$18,000
Suburban-rural residents	Majority[129]	85%	Many	75%[136]	NA	20%
History of sore throat ($n^{\dagger}$)	77 (46)	22 (NA)	18 (NA)	4/17 (3/17)[131] 28/43 (11/43)[145‡]	6 (3)	15 (7)
Family history of rheumatic fever (%)	NA	5	16	64[131]	NA	NA
Recurrences	27	1	0	2	1	0
M types of group A streptococci isolated from						
Patients	1 × M-1; 1 × M-5	NA	M-1, -5, -18	NA	§	Mucoid M-18/T-1 Mucoid nontypeable
Families	3 × M-3; 1 × M-1 1 × M-18; 1 × M-78	NA	M-6	NA	NA	NA
Community	9 × M-18 (8/9 mucoid) 1 × M-4, M-5, M-6, M-9, M-11, M-12 6 nontypeable	Mucoid M-18	NA	NA	NA	Mucoid M-18

*Family size greater than the state average.
†Number who sought treatment.
‡Respiratory illness.
§San Diego: five of seven available sera positive for antibodies to M-18, three of seven positive for M-1 antibodies, two of seven positive for M-5 and M-6 antibodies, and one of seven positive for M-24 antibodies.
Adapted from Veasy, L. G., Wiedmeier, S. E., Orsmond, G. S., et al.: Resurgence of acute rheumatic fever in the intermountain area of the U.S. N. Engl. J. Med. *316*:421–427, 1987. Adapted from Markowitz, M., and Kaplan, E. L.: Reappearance of rheumatic fever. Adv. Pediatr. *36*:39–68, 1989 (see Table 35–1).

rheumatic fever rarely occurs in children younger than 3 years of age or in adults older than 40 years of age because of the relative infrequency of streptococcal infection at these ages.

The incidence of acute rheumatic fever is highest in the spring and winter months in temperate zones and coincides with the seasonal variation in streptococcal pharyngitis. This incidence may be related to the greater tendency for spread of streptococcal infection by closer contact during the colder and damper months,[131, 148] at least in some climates.

Pathogenesis

Evidence points toward every episode of acute rheumatic fever being preceded by a group A streptococcal upper respiratory tract infection. The events that occur after such infection and that culminate in rheumatic fever remain poorly defined, thus suggesting a complex interaction of numerous factors. With a resurgence of interest in this disease after recent outbreaks, laboratory data collected with the use of modern technologies must be evaluated carefully and correlated with the epidemiology of the disease.[68] Pathogenesis involves the host, the environment (see "Epidemiology"), and group A streptococci, individually and collectively.

So-called rheumatogenic strains of group A streptococci have been discussed much, most recently in relation to the latest focal upsurges in rheumatic fever.[71] However, because no factor has been described or isolated, such strains remain a hypothesis.[19] To date, rheumatic fever has been shown to occur only after nasopharyngeal infection.[152] Why the site of infection appears to predispose to the development of

TABLE 35–3 ■ CLINICAL MANIFESTATIONS IN FOUR OUTBREAKS OF ACUTE RHEUMATIC FEVER

Manifestation	Salt Lake City, Utah, 1985–1992 (274 Patients) (%)	Columbus, Ohio, 1984–1986 (40 Patients) (%)	Northeastern Ohio, 1986 (23 Patients) (%)	Pittsburgh, Pennsylvania, 1985–6/1990 (60 Patients) (%)	San Diego, California, Naval Base, 1986–1987 (10 Patients) (%)	Tennessee, 1987–1988 (26 Patients) (%)
Arthritis	36	62	78	43	100	58
Carditis	68*	50	30	52	30	73
Chorea	37	17	9	37	0	31
Erythema marginatum	4	12	1	0	0	4
Subcutaneous nodules	3	0	0	0	10	0

*Eighty-five percent with Doppler ultrasound examination.
Adapted from Markowitz, M., and Kaplan, E. L.: Reappearance of rheumatic fever. Adv. Pediatr. *36*:39–68, 1989.

rheumatic fever remains an enigma, perhaps related to skin lipids.[75] Acute glomerulonephritis develops after skin or throat infections with a nephritogenic type of group A *Streptococcus* (e.g., M-49, M-12).[152] Certain streptococcal M protein serotypes are implicated strongly and repetitively in epidemics of acute rheumatic fever. Serotypes M-3, M-5, M-14, M-18, and M-24 have been reported more than once in outbreaks, and M-1, M-6, M-19, M-27, and M-29 have been reported once only.[19] Distinct nucleotide sequences that determine different gene subfamilies encoding the M or M-like protein antigenic domain ("emm gene") may be the cause of these variations in streptococcal rheumatogenic potential, depending on the site of infection.[18] Other equally prevalent M types rarely, if ever, have been associated with epidemics of the disease[19] or have failed to cause recurrences in susceptible patients.[22] The current resurgence lends limited support for this concept: no predominance of a single serotype within a specific geographic zone was identified in any of the published outbreaks (see Tables 35–2 and 35–4). Specific M types and their production of mucoidal colonies (see Table 35–4), considered to be related to the amount of M protein and virulence,[153] may be more relevant to epidemic than to endemic rheumatic fever. In Auckland, New Zealand, an average of 45 new cases of acute rheumatic fever occur annually in children (annual age-specific rate of 20/100,000/yr). Nine years (1984–1992) of surveillance of group A streptococcal isolates from hospitalized pediatric patients (one centralized children's facility for 8 of the 9 years in question) yielded 2410 isolates. Only 3 of 38 throat isolates (32 from well-documented cases of rheumatic fever, 6 from siblings) were strains described as possibly rheumatogenic (one each of M-1, M-3, and M-6).[92] None was described as mucoidal.[92] In that series, M types 6, 53, 55, and 66 (and NZ 1437 when sibling isolates were included as cases) were statistically more likely to be associated with a case of acute rheumatic fever. Both streptococcal collections[90] (see Table 35–4) are limited samples and may not be

TABLE 35–4 ■ GROUP A STREPTOCOCCI ISOLATED FROM PATIENTS WITH RHEUMATIC FEVER AND FROM THEIR SIBLINGS (1986 TO MAY 1988)

	No. of			No. (%)
Serotype	*Cases*	*Siblings*	*Total*	**Mucoidal**
OF-Negative				
M-1, T-1	6	2	8	7 (88)
M-3, T-3	3	6	9	1 (11)
M-18, T-18	6	2	8	7 (88)
M-5, T-5/27/44	1	3	4	1 (25)
M-6, T-6	3	0	3	2 (67)
M-41, T-13	1	0	1	0 (0)
Subtotal	20	13	33	18 (55)
OF-Positive				
OF-75, T-25	2	0	2	0 (0)
OF-77, T-13	2	0	2	0 (0)
OF-78, T-11	0	2	2	0 (0)
OF-48, T-28	1	0	1	1 (100)
M-2, T-2	1	0	1	0 (0)
M-4, T-4	1	0	1	0 (0)
Subtotal	7	2	9	1 (11)
Total	27	15	42	19 (45)

OF, opacity factor.
From Kaplan, E. L., Johnson, D. R., and Cleary, P. P.: Group A streptococcal serotypes isolated from patients and sibling contacts during the resurgence of rheumatic fever in the U.S. in the mid-1980s. J. Infect. Dis. *159*:101–103, 1989.

representative. In addition, as in most series, group A streptococcal isolates are isolated from a minority of cases and are not supported by streptococcal or type-specific antibody data. Strain selectivity is a further consideration. No documented evidence has shown that all members of an M type may be equally able to elicit acute rheumatic fever. Some streptococci from a particular serotype may be associated with both acute rheumatic fever and acute post-streptococcal glomerulonephritis, although the two sequelae rarely occur simultaneously.[84, 91] M types have been shown to be composed of genetically diverse streptococci, not all of which may be established within a community.[92] The M type denotes possibly nothing more than a shared type-specific marker, with the property of rheumatogenicity as yet remaining elusive. Streptococcal strains that are opacity factor–negative (a lipoprotein lipase) are unlikely to be rheumatogenic according to earlier data[156] (see Table 35–4). Such may be the case in areas where M types reflecting endemic streptococcal skin disease occur more commonly and are associated with rheumatic fever.[72, 91, 129] Surveillance of group A streptococci in different geographic zones must be encouraged to guide vaccine development.

Although current evidence strongly implicates an immunologic mechanism in the pathophysiology of rheumatic fever, the details of how the disease develops are by no means clear.[28, 132] Evidence to date strongly suggests an abnormal cell-mediated and humoral immune response to cell membrane streptococcal antigens, which because of molecular mimicry of human tissues, may result in continued damage to the cardiovascular and nervous systems.[28, 132] The findings of circulating immune complexes in most patients[37] and the deposition of C3 and immunoglobulin in the myocardium of patients dying of acute rheumatic fever support an abnormal immune response in rheumatic fever.[70]

M proteins from highly rheumatogenic group A streptococcal types share antigenic determinants with myosin, with the sarcolemma of cardiac muscle,[41, 42] and with antigens of articular cartilage and synovium.[12] Thus, the immune response to streptococci may mistake the host antigens as foreign and result in tissue damage. Other streptococcal antigens, such as the group A carbohydrate component, are candidates for mistaken cross-reaction with a glycoprotein in human heart valves.[56] Group A streptococci have components that can amplify or down-regulate the immune response.[28]

The site of the initial streptococcal infection may be important: lymphatic channels have been demonstrated between the tonsils and the heart.[28] Unusual compartmentalization of rheumatic antigen–positive non-T cells has been demonstrated in patients with acute rheumatic fever, with no positive cells detected in rheumatic tonsils but increased numbers in peripheral blood.[61]

Cell-mediated immunity to streptococcal antigens also is enhanced in patients with rheumatic fever.[132] The lymphocytic infiltrate of heart valves was found to be composed predominantly of $CD4^+$ helper cells.[116] Increased expression of HLA-DR on fibroblasts, which can present antigens to $CD4^+$ lymphocytes (cytotoxic/suppressor T cells), has been observed on the heart valves of patients with acute carditis.[7] The cytotoxicity induced in normal human helper and suppressor cells in vitro by purified protein from a type M-5 group A streptococcal organism has been shown to destroy several human cell types, including cultured myocardial cells.[43] T-cell subset study results are conflicting,[101, 132] but production of interleukins is reported to be enhanced.[100, 164] The role of M protein and streptococcal pyrogenic exotoxins as superantigens is being explored and perhaps might explain the exaggeration of the streptococcal immune response.[89, 140]

The genetic background of the human host appears to influence susceptibility to rheumatic fever. Aggregation of rheumatic fever cases in families has been recognized for quite some time.[111] However, low concordance for inheritance has been reported in monozygotic twins,[137] although affected siblings have significant concordance for arthritis, residual rheumatic heart disease, and chorea.[130] Pataroyo and associates[107] found that the B lymphocytes of patients with rheumatic fever have a specific marker (883 alloantigen) associated with host rheumatic susceptibility.[161, 162] It appears to transcend ethnicity[107] and may be similar to an immune response gene.[132] This work has been extended to family members of rheumatic fever patients with the use of monoclonal antibodies.[50, 122] The approach has the potential to identify those individuals with an altered risk for development of rheumatic fever or heart disease and thus could allow targeted primary prevention. Class I HLA molecules have not been associated with acute rheumatic fever. Many studies in different populations have shown an association with HLA-DR but without a single HLA marker for susceptibility.[132] Genetic factors alone seem highly unlikely to be responsible for susceptibility to rheumatic fever.[88]

Immunity to group A streptococci, and thus to rheumatic fever, depends on antibodies to the M protein; such antibodies can opsonize the bacteria in the presence of neutrophils.[16] Until lately, immunity was thought to be strain-specific and dependent on antibodies to the variable serotype-specific regions of the protein, and vaccine development has followed this pathway.[15] Antibodies against the variable amino-terminal end of the M protein opsonize streptococci in a type-specific manner, but the results of experiments in animals suggest that the conserved carboxyl-terminal end also may be an immune target. Some human evidence suggests that this conserved epitope acts as a subunit vaccine.[114] Complexities in this area include the risk of inducing cross-reacting antibodies that could injure rather than protect.[95] Separation of the peptide fragments of M proteins (epitopes) that evoke type-specific and not cross-reacting antibodies is an important step.[26, 37] With more than 80 different defined serotypes of group A streptococci, research programs are in progress to define strategies of vaccination other than induction of the N-terminal serotypic M protein–specific opsonic antibodies or to investigate ways to combine multiple M protein N-terminal epitopes into a vaccine that is highly immunogenic for each individual determinant.[24]

Rheumatic Fever in Developing Countries

Rheumatic heart disease is considered by some physicians to be one of the few preventable chronic diseases.[113] In spite of impressive declines in incidence in developed countries (see Figs. 35–1 to 35–3), globally, rheumatic heart disease remains the most common form of acquired heart disease.[76] Four fifths of the world's population live in developing countries, where the prevalence of rheumatic heart disease suggests that the incidence of acute rheumatic fever remains at high levels in areas characterized by crowded living quarters and lower socioeconomic conditions. In Soweto, South Africa, the prevalence of rheumatic heart disease has been estimated at 7.1 per 1000 schoolchildren.[97] Given the difference in medical care delivery, estimates of the incidence of acute rheumatic fever must be viewed with caution. However, estimates suggest an annual incidence of 200 to 400 cases per 100,000 population in Soweto.[76] In India, the prevalence of rheumatic heart disease in schoolchildren has been estimated to be between 1.0 and 5.4 cases per 1000.[106] The incidence of rheumatic fever (as judged by hospital admissions for rheumatic heart disease between 1966 and 1980) has remained stable in India during this period of rapid decline in the United States and the West.[3] Community-based secondary penicillin prophylaxis programs in developing countries are considered cost-effective and more achievable than primary prevention.[76]

Pathology[124]

The unique pathologic lesion of rheumatic fever is the Aschoff body, generally considered to be a granuloma that results from injury to collagen fibers. Classically, these lesions are found in the heart, usually in the left atrial appendage, but similar foci can be found in the synovia of the joints and in and about joint capsules, tendons, and fascia.

The early pathologic response to rheumatic fever may be an exudative reaction with Aschoff-like bodies as an inflammatory focus. They are cardiac or extracardiac, with a central area of fibrinoid necrosis surrounded mostly by polymorphonuclear leukocytes. Clinically, this condition may be manifested as arthritis and spontaneously subside in 2 to 4 weeks. No residual joint damage results. The proliferative phase of classic Aschoff nodules, which consists of central necrosis surrounded by a rosette of large mononuclear cells, giant multinuclear cells, and other cell types, is confined to the heart and usually causes pancarditis with simultaneous involvement of all three layers (the pericardium, the myocardium, and the endocardium). This event may result in permanent valvular damage in the following order of frequency: the mitral valve, the aortic valve, the tricuspid valve, and, rarely, the pulmonary valve. Therefore, the heart disease encountered clinically usually is mitral regurgitation, aortic regurgitation, or both. The scarring that leads to valvular stenosis (mitral or aortic) typically takes decades to develop but may occur much faster in hyperendemic areas. However, this process is not the full story because although rheumatic mitral valve stenosis occurs is somewhat more commonly in India[126] and occasionally occurs in other less advantaged populations, it was never a common occurrence in the United States or the United Kingdom at the height of rheumatic fever incidence.[136]

The presence of Aschoff bodies is not evidence of rheumatic activity because these lesions are found in biopsy specimens of the left atrial appendage many years after an acute attack of rheumatic fever. Little is known about the pathology of Sydenham chorea, and the pathologic changes cannot be related to the clinical manifestations. Patients rarely die of this form of rheumatic fever.

Clinical Course

The stage is set for the development of rheumatic fever in a susceptible host after a pharyngeal infection by one of the types of group A beta-hemolytic streptococci. If the infection is not treated, most persons recover from the acute effects of the disease. Acute rheumatic fever develops in approximately 1 to 3 percent of children with known epidemic untreated exudative pharyngitis and a culture positive for group A streptococci. The frequency drops to less than 1 percent, as shown in the one controlled study involving children,[128] when patients with less severe or less precisely diagnosed streptococcal infections are included. The preceding pharyngitis is not recognized as an illness by the patient or parents in approximately 10 to 33 percent of cases of acute rheumatic fever, although 50 to 60 percent of patients remember having a sore throat.[59] In some series, this figure was lower (see Table 35–2). The infection is followed by a latent period that averages 19 days in duration,[118] during which time the patient seems well. The range appears to be between 1 and 5 weeks but has been difficult to establish.[30] The average latent period is the same for recurrent attacks as for initial episodes.[30]

Acute rheumatic fever then begins. Table 35–3 suggests a clinical profile in the United States, although recurrent cases with their increased risk for carditis are included. In a prospective study in India, 67 percent of initial episodes were associated with migrating arthritis involving one or more of the large joints[125] accompanied by a fever of 38 to 39°C, malaise, and anorexia. Just as the redness, swelling, and pain in a knee subside, the whole process may start again in the ankle. The elbows and wrists are also likely to be involved. Typically, multiple joints are involved, in tandem with overlap over time, when symptoms are not suppressed by anti-inflammatory therapy. The whole polyarthritic episode usually subsides over the course of 4 weeks, with no residua remaining. Carditis generally appears early in the illness (first 2 weeks) if it is going to occur.[1] The joint inflammation may be low grade in some persons, without limitation of motion or outward manifestations of redness and swelling (arthralgia).

At examination, the striking findings are the patient's pallor and discomfort, especially on movement of the affected joints. The pulse is rapid. Examination of the heart may reveal, in at least half of patients, a grade II/IV apical pansystolic murmur that is transmitted to the axilla (mitral insufficiency) with or without an apical mid-diastolic flow murmur (Carey-Coombs murmur); half of these patients also may experience an early diastolic grade II/IV murmur at the left sternal edge (aortic insufficiency). In addition, less commonly the child can have congestive heart failure or cardiac enlargement, indicative of active carditis. Carditis is more likely to occur in younger children. Pericarditis may be suspected with muffled heart sounds, a frictional rub, or chest pain. It becomes less common as acute rheumatic fever in a population becomes less severe. Death is a rare, but well-described, sequela of the acute phase of the disease. Murmurs of mitral and aortic stenosis are associated with chronic, but not with acute, rheumatic valve disease. The distinctive rash, erythema marginatum, is observed in approximately 10 percent of patients (Fig. 35–4). It is not pruritic or painful. The pink, slightly raised macules usually seen initially on the trunk and proximal ends of the extremities and never on the face fuse centrally and coalesce to form a serpiginous pattern. The lesions may disappear after a few hours or may reappear intermittently over a period of weeks, especially after a warm shower or bath. Subcutaneous nodules, usually associated with severe carditis, also occur uncommonly (less than 10% of patients). They are firm and painless and are found over bony surfaces or prominences and over tendons. Acute rheumatic fever is not likely to be diagnosed on the basis of the latter two major criteria without another major criterion.

Sydenham chorea, or St. Vitus dance, may be the only manifestation of rheumatic fever, or it may be associated with other disease manifestations. It becomes less common as acute rheumatic fever becomes less severe in a population. Chorea is characterized by purposeless (most often bilateral, uncoordinated, involuntary) movements, mostly of the hands, feet, and face, that develop over a period of weeks and are accentuated by excitement and emotional stress. They disappear during sleep. Sensation remains intact. The speech can be explosive and indistinct and the handwriting clumsy. Handwriting is a useful objective means of monitoring the course of the disease. The child has difficulty counting rapidly and holding the protruded tongue still. The fingers and wrists are hyperextended when the fingers are outstretched, and the palms usually are turned outward when the arms are held above the head. Handgrip generally is weak and may consist of spasmodic contractions followed by rapid relaxation. The patient may be easily irritated and quarrelsome. Chorea typically is a delayed manifestation of rheumatic fever and may develop after other signs of the disease have subsided. Chorea not uncommonly appears 2 to 6 months after the streptococcal infection. Most observers think that residual heart disease occurs less commonly when chorea is the only manifestation of rheumatic fever, but the importance of prophylaxis to prevent recurrent attacks and possible subsequent carditis was reaffirmed in Kuwait.[83] Permanent serious residual neurologic deficits have not been observed. A 25-year review found the duration of chorea to be 1 to 22 weeks, with a median of 12 weeks.[103] Recurrent attacks are not uncommon events. The neuropsychiatric sequelae of chorea were reviewed recently.[98]

The average duration of an attack of acute rheumatic fever is approximately 3 months when unaltered by anti-inflammatory therapy.[87] Less than 5 percent of cases persist longer than 6 months with active symptoms, so-called chronic rheumatic fever.[136]

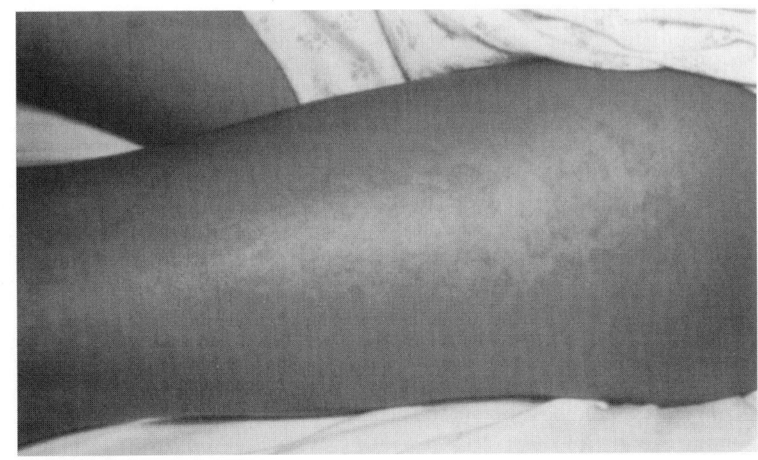

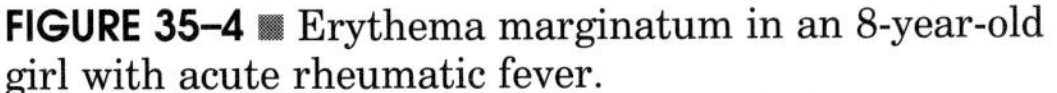

FIGURE 35–4 ■ Erythema marginatum in an 8-year-old girl with acute rheumatic fever.

Laboratory Findings[63, 87]

The degree of inflammation in patients with acute rheumatic fever is measured by nonspecific indicators, such as the erythrocyte sedimentation rate (ESR) and C-reactive protein (CRP). Unless the patient has taken corticosteroids or salicylates, these test results almost always are positive in patients with polyarthritis or acute carditis, whereas they often are normal in patients with chorea. The magnitude of the ESR is proportional to the intensity of the inflammatory reaction but is not site-specific (i.e., it can be high with polyarthritis or carditis). The ESR may be decreased in congestive heart failure, whereas CRP may be elevated in congestive heart failure attributable to any cause. The ESR may remain elevated for 6 weeks to 3 months in an untreated attack of acute rheumatic fever. Anti-inflammatory agents may damp down the ESR, but it will rebound if they are stopped before the rheumatic process has run its course. Chronic elevation of the ESR (more than 6 months) is not understood but is not sufficient reason on its own to limit a patient's activities.[136] The CRP may reflect the patient's rheumatic activity more precisely than may the ESR.[87]

Chest radiographs are useful for detecting cardiomegaly, which may be caused by dilatation, preexisting heart disease, or pericardial effusion. The degree of enlargement is helpful in judging severity. The electrocardiogram may show a prolonged atrioventricular conduction time, usually evidenced by a prolonged PR interval or even greater degrees of heart block.[121] In general, an increase in the PR interval in tracings with comparable rates is considered significant.[87] Atrioventricular conduction abnormalities per se bear no relation to the ultimate prognosis of patients. Changes of myocarditis and pericarditis also are seen. The roles of two-dimensional and Doppler echocardiography in the diagnosis and determination of the prognosis of acute rheumatic fever are becoming clearer.[1, 52, 63, 144–146, 159] In a prospective blinded study using febrile controls and strict color and pulsed Doppler criteria, pathologic left-sided heart regurgitation could be differentiated from physiologic regurgitation.[1] Several centers using similar strict criteria have observed subclinical carditis in acute rheumatic fever.[53, 54, 145, 146] The status of echocardiographic evidence as a major or minor criterion remains to be settled. It has important implications for patients with polyarthritis as a sole major criterion[63] or patients without major criteria and only echocardiographic evidence of mitral or aortic regurgitation.

A positive throat culture for group A beta-hemolytic streptococci as evidence of a recent streptococcal infection seldom is found, and as many as 50 percent of such patients could be carriers of the organism.[74] A positive culture may be helpful if it can be related to the time of the acute infection.

Corroboration of a previous streptococcal infection may be documented by numerous streptococcal antibody tests.[158] Antibody titers may be elevated in the absence of clinical or bacteriologic evidence of streptococcal pharyngitis. The ASO titer is the most popular antibody test, and it measures the inhibition of rabbit red blood cells by specific antibody to streptolysin O, an extracellular product of beta-hemolytic streptococci that in its reduced form hemolyzes red blood cells. The "normal" level for an ASO titer usually is defined as the highest titer exceeded by only 20 percent of a population, but it is influenced importantly by age, geography, season, and other factors.[73] ASO titers of 500 Todd units or greater are rare findings in normal schoolchildren and are good evidence of a recent streptococcal infection. ASO titers below 250 Todd units could be considered normal; titers of 250 to 320 should be considered borderline elevated. Approximately 50 percent of patients with acute rheumatic fever have ASO titers in this range, and approximately 60 percent have titers of 500 or greater.[63] Conversely, ASO titers can be normal in as many as 20 percent of acute rheumatic patients.[133] A recent streptococcal infection is more likely to be demonstrated if more than one antibody titer is measured (e.g., antistreptokinase and antihyaluronidase).[133] Anti–deoxyribonuclease B is the most favored because of better reproducibility. The Jones criteria[63] (Table 35–5) call for an elevated or rising titer of an antistreptococcal antibody. The onset of clinical acute rheumatic fever usually coincides with the peak of the streptococcal antibody response. It may stay elevated for many weeks. However, the absence of an elevated antistreptococcal titer, if three different antibodies are measured, means that the clinician can be 95 percent certain that the patient has not had a streptococcal infection within the recent past. In patients with pure chorea, however, antibody levels may have declined to normal because of the length of the latent period between the development of streptococcal infection and the manifeastation of this symptom. A slide agglutination test is available (Streptozyme antibody test, Wampole Laboratories, Stamford, CT). This test cannot be recommended at this time because of inconsistencies in results caused by variations in different lots of test material.[157]

TABLE 35–5 ■ GUIDELINES FOR THE DIAGNOSIS OF AN INITIAL ATTACK OF RHEUMATIC FEVER (JONES CRITERIA, 1992 UPDATE)*

Major Manifestations†
Carditis
Polyarthritis
Chorea
Erythema marginatum
Subcutaneous nodules
Minor Manifestations†
Clinical findings
Arthralgia
Fever
Laboratory findings
Elevated acute-phase reactants
Elevated erythrocyte sedimentation rate
Elevated C-reactive protein
Prolonged PR interval
Supporting Evidence of Antecedent Group A Streptococcal Infection
Positive throat culture or rapid streptococcal antigen test
Elevated or rising streptococcal antibody titer

*If supported by evidence of preceding group A streptococcal infection, the presence of two major manifestations or of one major and two minor manifestations indicates a high probability of acute rheumatic fever.

†See text for details.

Guidelines for the diagnosis of rheumatic fever. Jones criteria, 1992 update. Special Writing Group of the Committee on Rheumatic Fever, Endocarditis, and Kawasaki Disease in the Young of the American Heart Association. J. A. M. A. *268*:2069–2073, 1992. Copyright 1992, American Medical Association.

The synovial fluid in joints affected by acute rheumatic fever contains 10,000 to 100,000 white blood cells/mm^3, which are mostly neutrophils. The protein concentration is approximately 4 g/dL, glucose levels are normal, and a good mucin clot is present.[65]

Diagnosis

The signs and symptoms of rheumatic fever vary greatly, depending on the stage of the disease, the epidemiology of the rheumatic fever in that place at that time, the severity of the disease, and the sites of involvement. In the absence of a diagnostic test or pathognomonic sign, Jones suggested a series of criteria (major and minor) (see Table 35–5) that have stood the test of time, with ongoing modifications.[85]

The keystone on which the Jones criteria (1992 update[63]) rest is the demonstration of a recent streptococcal infection. Because relatively few acute rheumatics have positive throat cultures, demonstration of a previous streptococcal infection by a rising titer of one or more of the extracellular streptococcal antibodies is critical confirmatory evidence for the establishment of a recent streptococcal infection. Of emphasis is that the mere presence of an elevated titer to one or more of the streptococcal antibodies (see "Laboratory Findings") means only that the subject has had a recent group A beta-hemolytic streptococcal infection.

Clinical manifestations in recent outbreaks are summarized in Table 35–3. Before this time, during the period of declining incidence in the United States, carditis was found in less than half of rheumatic patients and generally was less severe.[93] Joint involvement alone was, therefore, the most common manifestation and rendered arriving at a diagnostic certainty difficult.[64] A common avoidable error is the premature administration of salicylates or corticosteroids before the signs and symptoms become distinct; such therapy leaves in doubt the necessity of administering secondary prophylaxis without a firm diagnosis.

In contrast to the revised Jones criteria (1965), more updated criteria[63] (1992) are designed to establish a diagnosis of the initial attack of acute rheumatic fever; therefore, a previous attack of rheumatic fever or rheumatic heart disease no longer is a minor manifestation. Echocardiography currently is not a stand-alone criterion for the diagnosis of acute rheumatic fever (see "Laboratory Findings"); however, chorea and indolent carditis are considered stand-alone criteria for the diagnosis of rheumatic fever. Recurrences of rheumatic fever in patients with a reliable past history of rheumatic fever or clear-cut rheumatic heart disease can be diagnosed by the demonstration of a single major or several minor criteria if supporting evidence of a recent group A streptococcal infection is present.

So-called post-streptococcal arthritis has been discussed as a possible entity when the initial symptoms and signs are atypical for acute rheumatic fever, fail to respond to salicylate therapy, or both. In some cases, rheumatic heart disease has ensued.[45] In all such patients who fulfill the Jones criteria, a diagnosis of rheumatic fever should be considered, particularly for the purpose of administering secondary penicillin prophylaxis.[11] The role of echocardiography in this diagnostic situation has not been clarified.

Differential Diagnosis

Many other diseases might be confused with acute rheumatic fever: rheumatoid arthritis, suppurative bacterial arthritis (especially gonococcal arthritis in adolescents), reactive arthritis (e.g., after *Yersinia*[77] or *Mycoplasma*[99] infection), infective endocarditis, sickle-cell anemia, leukemia, and Lyme disease.[112]

With the help of the Jones criteria and time, these diseases usually can be excluded. For example, heart involvement with rheumatoid arthritis is a rare event. In suppurative arthritis, demonstration of the infecting bacteria by smear and recovery by culture provide the answer. With sickle-cell disease, the bone is affected and not the joint, and a sickle-cell preparation helps establish the diagnosis. A blood smear usually establishes the diagnosis of leukemia.

Common errors include diagnosing acute rheumatic fever when a single joint is involved, when an innocent murmur is present, when a nonspecific rash (especially an urticarial or an erythema multiforme rash) erroneously is called erythema marginatum, and when other symptoms similar to chorea (e.g., tics, phenothiazine-induced extrapyramidal syndrome) are misinterpreted.[67] Committing a child to many years of penicillin prophylaxis requires careful decision making at the time of diagnosis.

Treatment[39, 135]

Therapy for acute rheumatic fever is symptomatic: control the inflammation, decrease the fever, and keep cardiac failure in check. Neither salicylates nor corticosteroids are thought to affect severity or outcome.[139] If the physician thinks that a patient has acute rheumatic fever, a trial of salicylates is indicated as symptomatic therapy. Characteristically, the joint inflammation and fever subside in 24 to 48 hours with salicylate treatment if the serum level is 10 to 20 mg/dL, which usually is achieved by a dose of 60 to 100 mg/kg/24 hr (not exceeding 6 g/day in divided doses). This dose may be increased, but one is advised to measure serum salicylate levels and thereby adjust the dosage regimen. A higher dosage may result in the undesirable development of salicylism (tinnitus and hyperpnea). Except for occasional patients with rheumatoid arthritis, no other forms of arthritis respond in this dramatic way to aspirin. Salicylate therapy is recommended for 1 to 2 weeks and then can be reduced gradually. Newer nonsteroidal anti-inflammatory drugs (NSAIDs) for the treatment of acute rheumatic fever have been studied in limited fashion.[143] Naproxen (10 to 20 mg/kg/day) had a dramatic effect similar to that of aspirin and was well tolerated. Advantages are twice-daily administration, the availability of elixir, less hepatotoxicity, and no need to determine serum levels.

No evidence has substantiated that steroid therapy is superior or that treatment with steroid or aspirin decreases the severity or prevents the development of residual heart disease.[4, 139] Both are palliative and not curative. They are, however, effective anti-inflammatory agents for controlling the acute exudative manifestations of rheumatic fever. Steroids are more likely to reduce acute symptoms promptly and, therefore, may be indicated for severely ill patients in whom inflammatory edema of the myocardium may be life-threatening during the acute stage of the illness.[142] The effect of NSAIDs has not been evaluated adequately. Acetaminophen, also not critically evaluated, is used by some clinicians to provide some symptomatic relief as the signs and symptoms evolve into a diagnosable picture of acute rheumatic fever.

A recent randomized controlled trial of intravenous immunoglobulin, a proven immunomodulator, in acute rheumatic fever failed to alter the natural history, with no detectable difference noted in the clinical, laboratory, or echocardiographic parameters found during the subsequent 12 months.[149]

Bed rest has not been studied critically.[87] Restriction of physical activity until the rheumatic process has become quiescent is a time-honored method of treatment. It has been based on the assumption that the workload of the inflamed heart is related to the degree of residual scarring. Suggested guidelines include as much as 6 weeks of bed rest, depending on whether carditis is present, followed by gradual ambulation indoors over an equally long period before outside activity, in modified fashion, takes place. Patients with severe carditis who have congestive heart failure are managed more conservatively.

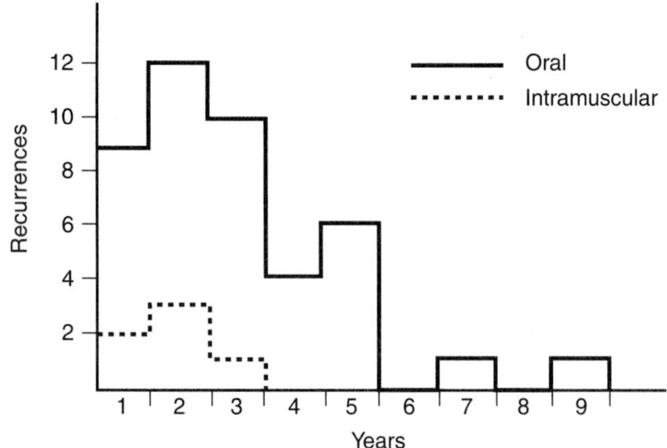

FIGURE 35–5 ■ Influence of oral and intramuscular penicillin prophylaxis on the recurrence of rheumatic fever. Time is between the last attack and recurrence (years). (From Newman, J. E., Lennon, D. R., and Wong-Toi, W.: Patients with rheumatic fever recurrences. N. Z. Med. J. *97*:678–680, 1984.)

All patients should receive intramuscular benzathine penicillin, even if the throat culture does not reveal group A beta-hemolytic streptococci. Patients then can be placed on the secondary preventive treatment regimen, which may be either oral penicillin V, 250 mg twice a day, or injections of benzathine penicillin, 1.2 million U every 4 weeks. The parenteral route has been shown to be more effective by the author's group[104] (Fig. 35–5) and others.[160] In high-risk situations, administration of benzathine penicillin every 3 weeks has been advised.[82]

Rarely, a patient has profound myocarditis and congestive heart failure. In these circumstances, the patient should have the benefit of the usual measures for the treatment of congestive heart failure: bed rest, diuretics, and if needed, oxygen and digoxin. Feinstein and Areralo[49] did not find a higher incidence of digoxin toxicity in patients with active carditis than in those with inactive rheumatic heart disease.

CARDIAC SURGERY IN ACTIVE RHEUMATIC HEART DISEASE

Aggressive surgical therapy, with increasing acceptance that mitral repair rather than replacement is the treatment of choice for mitral regurgitation,[8] also may be indicated in patients with severe active rheumatic heart disease. Strauss and associates[134] proposed that a child with rheumatic heart disease be catheterized and considered a candidate for surgery in the presence of any one of the following criteria:

1. Congestive heart failure and true chronic rheumatic fever
2. Congestive heart failure and a cardiothoracic ratio greater than 0.6
3. Functional class IV
4. Atrial fibrillation

They suggested that the decision to operate be based on the severity of the disability and the hemodynamic disturbance rather than the activity or inactivity of the rheumatic process. From the 1990s onward, two-dimensional or Doppler echocardiography has spared the patient from having cardiac catheterization. Extensive published experience in South Africa[13] and France[32] with excellent results has challenged the concept that congestive heart failure and death during active carditis are caused by myocarditis rather than incompetence of the valve. Careful postoperative management, including at least 4 months of physical rest, diuretics, and vasodilatation with angiotensin-converting enzyme inhibitors, is thought to improve the long-term outcome by avoiding increased blood pressure and myocardial contractility before the repair has consolidated. The acute rheumatic activity usually subsides within 2 to 3 weeks of obtaining valve competence.[13]

Prognosis

The prognosis for patients with acute rheumatic fever depends on the initial manifestations, as shown clearly in the 20-year follow-up study from the prepenicillin era by Bland and Jones.[23] A patient with marked cardiomegaly, congestive heart failure, or pericarditis had about a 70 to 80 percent chance of dying in the 10 years before the advent of secondary prevention programs, open heart surgery, and use of prosthetic valves. The prognosis today is not as ominous, although the recurrence rates (with the attendant increased risk of carditis in individual patients) reported after some outbreaks[145, 163] suggest a careful look at secondary prevention and its delivery. The risk of having rheumatic heart disease at 1-[139] and 10-year[34] follow-up is as high as 70 percent for patients with cardiomegaly or heart failure indicative of the severity of their myocarditis and who survive. Most of these patients have mitral insufficiency, and approximately 50 percent of them also have aortic insufficiency. Approximately 50 percent of patients initially are left with residual heart disease after an attack of rheumatic fever. This rate is about the same as that 25 to 30 years ago. However, approximately 25 percent of these patients return to normal cardiac status, with a higher chance if the cardiac involvement is mild. Of patients with no or questionable carditis[139] during their attack of rheumatic fever, only 6 percent were found to have heart murmurs when re-examined 10 years later. Heart disease was present at follow-up in 30 percent of the patients initially found to have only apical systolic murmurs and in 40 percent of those with basal diastolic murmurs during the acute phase. Patients with chorea may have a slightly lower incidence of residual heart disease.[83]

Prevention[39]

Denny and associates[47, 155] made one of the most important research contributions in the last 50 years when they showed that rheumatic fever can be prevented in most susceptible subjects if the preceding pharyngeal infection by one of the group A beta-hemolytic streptococci is treated adequately. These studies used depot penicillin G. The effectiveness of other antimicrobial agents (benzathine penicillin, chlortetracycline [Aureomycin], sulfadiazine, oxytetracycline) in the prevention of rheumatic fever also was studied.[46] Eradication of the streptococcus was shown to be essential,[30] and a 10-day course of penicillin treatment was found to be more effective than a 5-day course.[154] From these studies, penicillin, a bactericidal agent with activity against streptococci, became the drug of choice. Efficacy studies against rheumatic fever per se were performed only in military populations with injectable penicillin. The ability of oral penicillin to eradicate streptococci in throats is not equal to the ability of injectable penicillin to do so.[14] A complete explanation for the decline in rheumatic fever remains unclear.

Streptococcal pharyngeal infection should be identified before treatment is started. Such an infection can be diagnosed by throat culture or by using a rapid diagnostic antigen-detection kit.[39, 44, 81, 120] The true place of these kits in the clinical setting is evolving. Most tests have high specificity, so a patient with acute pharyngitis and a positive test result should be treated. Many of the tests have less than desirable sensitivity and should be confirmed by a throat culture. One study found that in a third of persons with false-negative rapid antigen-detection test results, streptococcal antibody titers rose subsequently, thus suggesting infection.[55] Military studies have shown that primary preventive treatment with penicillin is effective even if started as late as 9 days after the infection develops,[31] so physicians can wait 24 to 48 hours for verification of infection by recovery of group A beta-hemolytic streptococci. A dose of 1.2 million U of benzathine penicillin intramuscularly (0.6 million U if ≤27 kg) is usually adequate treatment. Because of the discomfort and a possible, but small risk associated with intramuscular penicillin,[5] oral penicillin V (250 mg two or three times a day for children; 500 mg two or three times a day for adolescents and adults) may be preferred in areas in which the incidence of rheumatic fever is low. Erythromycin estolate (20 to 40 mg/kg/day in two to four divided doses; maximum, 1 g/day) may be used in patients who are allergic to penicillin. Erythromycin ethylsuccinate (40 mg/kg/day two to four times daily; maximum, 1 g/day) is an alternative therapy. All oral treatments should be given for 10 days. Although certain new wider-spectrum agents have been administered in shorter courses with the desired streptococcal eradication, on the basis of penicillin's narrow spectrum of antimicrobial activity, the infrequency with which it produces adverse reactions, and its modest cost, it is the drug of choice for nonallergic patients.[20]

Reappearance of acute rheumatic fever in a specific geographic region should draw attention to therapeutic, preventive, and epidemiologic measures for control of the disease. A targeted approach to particularly high-risk population groups in schools may be cost-effective and efficacious.[25, 36, 110, 113, 123, 141] Because treatment of pharyngitis seems likely to have contributed to the declining incidence of rheumatic fever, obtaining throat cultures (or a rapid antigen test) and administering penicillin treatment, if positive for group A streptococci, still are recommended in low-risk populations, although this recommendation is being challenged by some physicians.[96] In addition, a negative culture avoids unnecessarily prescribing antibiotics in the 70 to 80 percent of children with a sore throat attributable to viral pharyngitis.[127] Prompt administration of antibiotic therapy may shorten the duration of symptoms in patients with group A beta-hemolytic streptococcal pharyngitis.[119] Cultures should be used selectively in age groups in which rheumatic fever rarely occurs (e.g., younger than 4 years of age or older than 20 years). Signs and symptoms usually not associated with streptococcal infection, such as simple coryza, hoarseness, cough, conjunctivitis, anterior stomatitis, and diarrhea,[39] may help target the approach in a low-risk population.

A follow-up throat culture taken after a course of treatment for streptococcal pharyngitis is not recommended routinely unless the patient remains symptomatic or is from a family with a rheumatic member. Such follow-up cultures probably identify long-term carriers for whom repeated courses of antibiotics generally are not indicated.[127] Streptococcal carriers appear to pose little threat to themselves regarding the development of sequelae from streptococcal infection or dissemination of the organism to those around them. However, when a symptomatic viral upper respiratory tract infection develops in such a carrier, distinguishing whether the group A streptococci isolated indicate current streptococcal infection or identify that individual as a chronic carrier frequently is not possible. In one study, only 43 percent of children with paired sera from whom group A streptococci were recovered showed a significant antibody response to one of two different streptococcal antibodies.[74] Often, a reasonable approach is to administer a single course of therapy. Indications for obtaining cultures from household contacts vary according to circumstances.[39] Family contacts of high-risk patients should have a culture performed and receive treatment if the culture is positive.

Recurrent attacks of rheumatic fever can be prevented by continuous penicillin prophylaxis, either orally or parenterally.[38] The parenteral route has been shown to be more effective (1.2 million U of benzathine penicillin intramuscularly at 28-day intervals).[160] In this comprehensive study, children experienced a recurrence rate of only 0.4 per 100 patient-years of observation (Table 35–6). An international study of allergic reactions to long-term benzathine penicillin prophylaxis found that the benefits of preventing recurrence far outweighed the risk of development of a serious allergic reaction.[5] In areas of particularly high risk, administration of benzathine penicillin every 21 days may be more efficacious[82] because serum levels of penicillin toward the end of the time can be unreliable,[69] although this decision should be offset against practicability, cost, and probable compliance. A recent publication supports the use of 1 percent lidocaine hydrochloride as a diluent for benzathine penicillin G to increase tolerability.[6]

Patients allergic to penicillin may be given erythromycin (250 mg twice a day). Oral regimens that have been studied for efficacy are penicillin and sulfadiazine (see Table 35–6). Sulfadiazine is not readily available in the United States.[10] The lesser efficacy of oral regimens is related at least in part to compliance difficulties.

The risk of rheumatic fever occurring after a group A streptococcal infection rises from an attack rate of 1 to 3 percent with the first attack of streptococcal pharyngitis to 25 to 75 percent with subsequent attacks.[47] Those who have had carditis are at increased risk for development of further carditis. Those who have not had clinical carditis have a considerably less risk of cardiac involvement after a recurrence.[83]

The risk of recurrence depends on several other factors, such as the length of time since the most recent attack and the risk of acquiring streptococcal throat infections according to occupation or living circumstances. If possible, the length of prophylaxis should be individualized. The suggested length is a minimum of 5 years' prophylaxis and a

TABLE 35–6 ■ PROPHYLAXIS AND ATTACK RATES OF STREPTOCOCCAL INFECTION AND RHEUMATIC FEVER RECURRENCE

	Parenteral Benzathine Penicillin	Oral Penicillin	Oral Sulfadiazine
Number of years	560	545	576
Number and rate of all streptococcal infections, exclusive of the carrier state	24/4.3	101/18.5	102/17.7
Number and rate of rheumatic recurrences	2/0.4	30/5.5	16/2.8

Adapted from Wood, H. F., Feinstein, A. R., Taranta, A., et al.: Rheumatic fever in children and adolescents: A long-term epidemiologic study of subsequent prophylaxis, streptococcal infections, and clinical sequelae. III. Comparative effectiveness of three prophylaxis regimens in preventing streptococcal infections and rheumatic recurrences. Ann. Intern. Med. *60* (Suppl. 5):31–45, 1964, with permission.

maximum of lifelong prophylaxis.[38] This approach has been validated in a study from Chile.[17]

Of equal importance is the prevention of infective endocarditis in patients with rheumatic heart disease or in those who have had rheumatic fever by the administration of antimicrobial drugs before and after surgical procedures on the eyes, ears, mouth (dental extractions), nose, throat, and gastrointestinal and genitourinary tracts.[38, 40]

Conclusion

Although having effective prophylaxis against a disease[94] for which the pathophysiology is understood incompletely and for which no pharmacologic cure exists is gratifying, rheumatic fever and its sequelae still occur in an appreciable number of young people. This rate is, in large part, a reflection of complacency about rheumatic fever and rheumatic heart disease by doctors and patients, although at least in some parts of the world it reflects living conditions. Renewed educational effort regarding prevention of this disorder is needed by both physicians and the public. The available preventive methods should be applied vigorously.

REFERENCES

1. Abernathy, M., Bass, N., Sharpe, N., et al.: Doppler echocardiography and the early diagnosis of carditis in acute rheumatic fever. Aust. N. Z. J. Med. *24*:530–535, 1994.
2. Acute rheumatic fever among army trainees—Fort Leonard Wood, Missouri, 1987–1988. M. M. W. R. Morb. Mortal. Wkly. Rep. *37*(34):519–522, 1988.
3. Agarwal, B. L.: Rheumatic Fever and Rheumatic Heart Disease in Developing Countries. India, Arnold Publishers, 1988, pp. 24–25.
4. Albert, D. A., Hafel, L., and Karrison, T.: The treatment of rheumatic carditis: A review and meta-analysis. Medicine (Baltimore) *74*:1–12, 1995.
5. Allergic reactions to long-term benzathine penicillin prophylaxis for rheumatic fever. International Rheumatic Fever Study Group. Lancet *337*:1308–1310, 1990.
6. Amir, J., Ginat, S., Cohen, Y. H., et al.: Lidocaine as a diluent for administration of benzathine penicillin G. Pediatr. Infect. Dis. J. *17*:890–893, 1998.
7. Amoils, B., Morrison, R. C., Wadee, A. A., et al.: Aberrant expression of HLA-DR antigen on valvular fibroblasts from patients with active rheumatic carditis. Clin. Exp. Immunol. *66*:88–94, 1986.
8. Antunes, M. J.: Mitral valvuloplasty, a better alternative: Comparative study between valve reconstruction and replacement for rheumatic mitral valve disease. Eur. J. Cardiothorac. Surg. *4*:257–264, 1990.
9. Atha, M., Enos, E., Frank, C., et al.: How an American Indian tribe controlled the streptococcus. World Health Forum *3*:423–428, 1982.
10. Availability of sulfadiazine—United States. M. M. W. R. Morb. Mortal. Wkly. Rep. *41*(50):950–951, 1992.
11. Ayoub, E. M., and Majeed, H. A.: Poststreptococcal reactive arthritis. Curr. Opin. Rheumatol. *12*:306–310, 2000.
12. Baird, R. W., Bronze, M. S., Kraus, W., et al.: Epitopes of group A streptococcal M protein shared with antigens of articular cartilage and synovium. J. Immunol. *146*:3132–3137, 1991.
13. Barlow, J. B.: Aspects of active rheumatic carditis. Aust. N. Z. J. Med. *22*:592–600, 1992.
14. Bass, J. W.: Streptococcal pharyngitis in children: A comparison of four treatment schedules with intramuscular benzathine penicillin. J. A. M. A. *235*:1112, 1976.
15. Beachey, E. H., Bronze, M., Dale, K. B., et al.: Protective and autoimmune epitopes of streptococcal M proteins. Vaccine *6*:192–196, 1988.
16. Beachey, E. H., Seyer, J. M., Dale, J. B., et al.: Type-specific protective immunity evoked by synthetic peptide of *Streptococcus pyogenes* M protein. Nature *292*:457–459, 1981.
17. Berrios, X., del Campo, E., Guzman, B., et al.: Discontinuing rheumatic fever prophylaxis in selected adolescents and young adults: A prospective study. Ann. Intern. Med. *118*:401–406, 1993.
18. Bessen, D. E., Sotiv, C. M., Readdy, T. L., et al.: Genetic correlates of throat and skin isolates of group A streptococci. J. Infect. Dis. *173*:896–900, 1996.
19. Bisno, A. L.: The concept of rheumatogenic and nephritogenic group A streptococci. *In* Read, S. E., and Zabriskie, J. B. (eds.): Streptococcal Diseases and the Immune Response. New York, Academic Press, 1980, pp. 789–804.
20. Bisno, A. L., Gerber, M. A., Gwaltney, J. M., et al.: Diagnosis and management of group A streptococcal pharyngitis: A practice guideline. Clin. Infect. Dis. *25*:574–583, 1997.
21. Bisno, A. L., and Land, M. A.: Incidence of acute rheumatic fever in Memphis and Shelby County, Tennessee, 1977–1981. *In* Shulman, A. (ed.): Management of Pharyngitis in an Era of Declining Rheumatic Fever. Columbus, OH, Ross Laboratories, 1984, pp. 13–24.
22. Bisno, A. L., Pearce, I. A., and Stollerman, G. H.: Streptococcal infections that fail to cause recurrences of rheumatic fever. J. Infect. Dis. *136*:278–285, 1977.
23. Bland, E. F., and Jones, T. D: Rheumatic fever and rheumatic heart disease: A twenty-year report on 1,000 patients followed since childhood. Circulation *4*:836–843, 1951.
24. Brandt, E. R., and Good, M. F.: Vaccine strategies to prevent rheumatic fever. Immunol. Res. *19*:89–103, 1999.
25. Brant, L. J., Bender, T. R., and Bross, D. S.: Evaluation of an Alaskan streptococcal control program: Importance of the program's intensity and duration. Prev. Med. *15*:632–642, 1986.
26. Bronze, M. S., Beachey, E. H., and Dale, J. B.: Protective and heart-cross-reactive epitopes located within the NH_2 terminus of type 19 streptococcal M protein. J. Exp. Med. *167*:1849–1859, 1988.
27. Brownell, K. D., and Baileu-Rose, F.: Acute rheumatic fever in children. J. A. M. A. *224*:1593–1597, 1973.
28. Cairns, L. M.: Immunological studies in rheumatic fever: The immunology of rheumatic fever. N. Z. Med. J. *101*:388–391, 1988.
29. Carapetis, J. R., Wolft, D. R., and Currie, B. J.: Acute rheumatic fever and rheumatic heart disease in the Top End of Australia's Northern Territory. Med. J. Aust. *164*:146–149, 1996.
30. Catanzaro, F. J., Rammelkamp, C. H., Jr., and Chamovitz, R.: Prevention of rheumatic fever by treatment of streptococcal infections. II. Factors responsible for failures. N. Engl. J. Med. *259*:51–57, 1958.
31. Catanzaro, F. J., Stetson, C. A., Morris, A. J., et al.: The role of the streptococcus in the pathogenesis of rheumatic fever. Am. J. Med. *17*:749–756, 1954.
32. Chauvaud, S., Perier, P., Touati, G., et al.: Long-term results of valve repair in children with acquired mitral valve incompetence. Circulation *74*(Suppl. 1):104–109, 1986.
33. Chun, L. T., Reddy, D. V., and Yamamoto, L. G.: Rheumatic fever in children and adolescents in Hawaii. Pediatrics *79*:549–552, 1987.
34. Combined Rheumatic Fever Study Group, 1965: A comparison of short-term, intensive prednisone and acetylsalicylic acid therapy in the treatment of acute rheumatic fever. N. Engl. J. Med. *272*:63–70, 1965.
35. Congeni, B., Rizzo, C., Congeni, J., et al.: Outbreak of acute rheumatic fever in northeast Ohio. J. Pediatr. *111*:176–179, 1987.
36. Coulehan, J., Grant, S., Reisinger, K., et al.: Acute rheumatic fever and rheumatic heart disease on the Navajo Reservation, 1962–77. Public Health Rep. *95*:62–68, 1980.
37. Cunningham, M., and Russell, M.: Study of heart-reactive antibody in antisera and hybridoma culture fluids against group A streptococci. Infect. Immun. *42*:531–538, 1983.
38. Dajani, A. S., Bisno, A. L., Chung, K., et al.: Prevention of bacterial endocarditis. Recommendations by the American Heart Association. J. A. M. A. *264*:2919–2922, 1990.
39. Dajani, A., Taubert, K., Ferrieri, P., et al.: Treatment of acute streptococcal pharyngitis and prevention of rheumatic fever: A statement for health professionals. Pediatrics *96*:758–764, 1995.
40. Dajani, A. S., Taubert, K. A., Wilson, W., et al.: Prevention of bacterial endocarditis: Recommendations by the American Heart Association. J. A. M. A. *277*:1794–1801, 1997.
41. Dale, J. B., and Beachey, E. H.: Protective antigenic determinant of streptococcal M protein shared with sarcolemmal membrane protein of human heart. J. Exp. Med. *156*:1165–1176, 1982.
42. Dale, J. B., and Beachey, E. H.: Epitopes of streptococcal M proteins shared with cardiac myosin. J. Exp. Med. *162*:583–591, 1985.
43. Dale, J. B., and Beachey, E. H.: Human cytotoxic T lymphocytes evoked by group A streptococcal M proteins. J. Exp. Med. *166*:1825–1837, 1987.
44. Daly, J. A., Korgenski, E. K., Munson, A. C., et al.: Optical immunoassay for streptococcal pharyngitis: Evaluation of accuracy with routine and mucoid strains associated with acute rheumatic fever outbreak in the intermountain area of the U.S. J. Clin. Microbiol. *32*:531–532, 1994.
45. de Cunto, C. L., Giannini, E. H., Fink, C. W., et al.: Prognosis of children with post-streptococcal reactive arthritis. Pediatr. Infect. Dis. J. *7*:683–686, 1988.
46. Denny, F. W.: A 45-year perspective on the streptococcus and rheumatic fever: The Edward H. Kass lecture in infectious disease history. Clin. Infect. Dis. *19*:1110–1122, 1994.
47. Denny, F. W., Wannamaker, L. W., Brink, W. R., et al.: Prevention of rheumatic fever: Treatment of the preceding streptococcal infection. J. A. M. A. *143*:151–153, 1950.
48. Eckerd, J. M., and McJunkin, J. E.: Recent increase in incidence of acute rheumatic fever in southern West Virginia. Scientific Newsfront *85*:279–281, 1989.
49. Feinstein, A. R., and Areralo, A. C.: Manifestations and treatment of congestive heart failure in young patients with rheumatic heart disease. Pediatrics *33*:661, 1964.

50. Feldman, B. M., Zabriskie, J. B., Silverman, E. D., et al.: Diagnostic use of B-cell alloantigen D8/17 in rheumatic chorea. J. Pediatr. *123*:84–86, 1993.
51. Ferguson, G. W., Shultz, J. M., and Bisno, A. L.: Epidemiology of acute rheumatic fever in a multiethnic multiracial urban community: The Miami–Dade County experience. J. Infect. Dis. *164*:720–725, 1991.
52. Figueroa, F. E., Fernandez, M. S., Valdes, P., et al.: Prospective comparison of clinical and echocardiographic diagnosis of rheumatic carditis: Long term follow up of patients with subclinical disease. Heart *85*:407–410, 2001.
53. Folger, G. M., Jr., and Hajar, R.: Doppler echocardiographic findings of mitral and aortic valve regurgitation in children manifesting only rheumatic arthritis. Am. J. Cardiol. *63*:1278–1280, 1989.
54. Folger, G. M., Jr., Hajar, R., Robida, A., et al.: Occurrence of valvular heart disease in acute rheumatic fever without evident carditis: Colour flow Doppler identification. Br. Heart J. *67*:434–438, 1992.
55. Gerber, M. A., Randolph, M. A., Chanatry, J., et al.: Antigen detection test for streptococcal pharyngitis: Evaluation of sensitivity with respect to true infections. J. Pediatr. *108*:654–658, 1986.
56. Goldstein, I., Halpern, B., and Robert, L.: Immunologic relationship between streptococcal A polysaccharide and structural glycoproteins of heart valve. Nature *213*:44–47, 1967.
57. Gordis, L.: Studies in the epidemiology and preventability of rheumatic fever. I. Demographic factors and the incidence of acute attacks. J. Chronic Dis. *21*:645–654, 1969.
58. Gordis, L.: Studies in the epidemiology and preventability of rheumatic fever. II. Socio-economic factors and the incidence of acute attacks. J. Chronic Dis. *21*:655–666, 1969.
59. Gordis, L.: Effectiveness of comprehensive-care programs in preventing rheumatic fever. N. Engl. J. Med. *289*:331–335, 1973.
60. Gordis, L., Lilienfeld, A., and Rodriguez, R.: A community-wide study of acute rheumatic fever in adults: Epidemiologic and preventive factors. J. A. M. A. *210*:862–865, 1969.
61. Gray, E. D., Regelmann, W. E., Abdin, Z., et al.: Compartmentalization of cells bearing "rheumatic" cell surface antigens in peripheral blood and tonsils in rheumatic heart disease. J. Infect. Dis. *155*:247–252, 1987.
62. Griffiths, S. P., and Gersony, W. M.: Acute rheumatic fever in New York City (1969–1988): A comparative study of two decades. J. Pediatr. *116*:882–887, 1990.
63. Guidelines for the diagnosis of rheumatic fever. Jones criteria, 1992 update. Special Writing Group of the Committee on Rheumatic Fever, Endocarditis, and Kawasaki Disease of the Council on Cardiovascular Disease in the Young of the American Heart Association. J. A. M. A. *268*:2069–2073, 1992.
64. Herold, B. C., and Shulman, S. T.: Poststreptococcal arthritis. Pediatr. Infect. Dis. J. *7*:681–682, 1988.
65. Homer, C., and Shulman, S. T.: Clinical aspects of acute rheumatic fever. J. Rheumatol. *18*(Suppl. 29):2–13, 1991.
66. Hosier, D. M., Graenen, J., Teske, D. W., et al.: Resurgence of rheumatic fever. Am. J. Dis. Child. *141*:730–733, 1987.
67. Kaplan, E. L.: Acute rheumatic fever. Pediatr. Clin. North Am. *25*:817–829, 1978.
68. Kaplan, E. L.: Epidemiological approaches to understanding the pathogenesis of rheumatic fever. Int. J. Epidemiol. *14*:499–501, 1985.
69. Kaplan, E. L., Berrios, X., Speth, J., et al.: Pharmacokinetics of benzathine penicillin G: Serum levels during the 28 days after intramuscular injection of 1,200,000 units. J. Pediatr. *115*:146–150, 1989.
70. Kaplan, M. H., Bolande, R., Rakaita, L., et al.: Presence of bound immunoglobulins and complement in the myocardium in acute rheumatic fever. N. Engl. J. Med. *271*:637–645, 1964.
71. Kaplan, E. L., Johnson, D. R., and Cleary, P. P.: Group A streptococcal serotypes isolated from patients and sibling contacts during the resurgence of rheumatic fever in the U.S. in the mid-1980s. J. Infect. Dis. *159*:101–103, 1989.
72. Kaplan, E. L., Johnson, D. R., Nanthapisud, P., et al.: A comparison of group A streptococcal serotypes isolated from the upper respiratory tract in the USA and Thailand: Implications. Bull. World Health Organ. *70*:433–437, 1992.
73. Kaplan, E. L., Rothermel, C. D., and Johnson, D. R.: Antistreptolysin O and anti–deoxyribonuclease B titers: Normal values for children ages 2 to 12 in the U.S. Pediatrics *101*:86–88, 1998.
74. Kaplan, E. L., Top, F. H., Dudding, B. A., et al.: Diagnosis of streptococcal pharyngitis: Differentiation of acute infection from the carrier state in the symptomatic child. J. Infect. Dis. *123*:490–501, 1971.
75. Kaplan, E. L., and Wannamaker, L. W.: Streptolysin O: Suppression of its antigenicity by lipids extracted from skin. Proc. Soc. Exp. Biol. Med. *146*:205–208, 1974.
76. Kumar, R.: Controlling rheumatic heart disease in developing countries. World Health Forum *16*:47–51, 1995.
77. Laitinen, O., Leirisalo, M., and Allander, E.: Rheumatic fever and *Yersinia* arthritis: Criteria and diagnostic problems in a changing disease pattern. Scand. J. Rheumatol. *4*:145–157, 1975.
78. Land, M. A., and Bisno, A. L.: Acute rheumatic fever: A vanishing disease in suburbia. J. A. M. A. *249*:895–898, 1983.
79. Leggiardro, R. J., Birnbaum, S. E., Chase, N. A., et al.: A resurgence of acute rheumatic fever in a mid-south children's hospital. South. Med. J. *83*:1418–1420, 1990.
80. Lennon, D., Martin, D., Wong, E., et al.: Longitudinal study of poststreptococcal disease in Auckland: Rheumatic fever, glomerulonephritis, epidemiology and M typing 1981–86. N. Z. Med. J. *101*:396–398, 1988.
81. Lieu, T. A., Fleisher, G. R., and Schwartz, J. S.: Cost-effectiveness of rapid latex agglutination and throat culture for streptococcal pharyngitis. Pediatrics *85*:246–256, 1990.
82. Lue, H. C., Wu, M. H., Wang, J. K., et al.: Long-term outcome of patients with rheumatic fever receiving benzathine penicillin G prophylaxis every three weeks versus every four weeks. J. Pediatr. *125*:812–816, 1994.
83. Majeed, H. A., Yousof, A. M., Khuffash, F. A., et al.: The natural history of acute rheumatic fever in Kuwait: A prospective 6-year follow-up report. J. Chronic Dis. *39*:361–369, 1986.
84. Majeed, H. A., Yousof, A. M., Rotta, J., et al.: Group A streptococcal strains in Kuwait: A nine-year prospective study of prevalence and associations. Pediatr. Infect. Dis. J. *11*:295–300, 1992.
85. Markowitz, M.: Evolution and critique of changes in the Jones criteria for diagnosis of rheumatic fever. N. Z. Med. J. *101*:392–394, 1988.
86. Markowitz, M.: Streptococcal disease in developing countries. Pediatr. Infect. Dis. J. *10*(Suppl.):11–38, 1991.
87. Markowitz, M., and Gordis, L.: Rheumatic Fever. Philadelphia, W. B. Saunders, 1972, pp. 62–63, 80–102, 133–136.
88. Markowitz, M., and Kaplan, E. L.: Reappearance of rheumatic fever. Adv. Pediatr. *36*:39–68, 1989.
89. Marrack, P., and Kappler, J.: The staphylococcal exotoxins and their relatives. Science *248*:705–711, 1990.
90. Martin, D. R.: Rheumatogenic streptococci reconsidered. N. Z. Med. J. *101*:394–396, 1988.
91. Martin, D. R., and Single, L. A.: Molecular epidemiology of group A *Streptococcus* M type 1 infections. J. Infect. Dis. *167*:1112–1117, 1993.
92. Martin, D. R., Voss, L. M., Walker, S. J., et al.: Acute rheumatic fever in Auckland, New Zealand: Spectrum of associated group A streptococci different from expected. Pediatr. Infect. Dis. J. *13*:264–269, 1994.
93. Massell, B., Amezcua, F., and Pelargonio, S.: Evolving picture of rheumatic fever: Data from 40 years at the House of the Good Samaritan. J. A. M. A. *188*:287–294, 1964.
94. Massell, B. F., Chute, C. G., Walker, A. M., et al.: Penicillin and the marked decrease in morbidity and mortality from rheumatic fever in the United States. N. Engl. J. Med. *318*:280–286, 1988.
95. Massell, B. F., Honikman, L. H., and Amezcua, J.: Rheumatic fever following streptococcal vaccine: Report of 3 cases. J. A. M. A. *207*: 1115–1119, 1969.
96. McIsaac, W. J., Goel, V., Slaughter, P. M., et al.: Reconsidering sore throats II: Alternative approach and practical office tool. Can. Fam. Physician *43*:495–500, 1997.
97. McLaren, M. J., Hawkins, D. M., Koornhof, H. J., et al.: Epidemiology of rheumatic heart disease in black school children of Soweto, Johannesburg. B. M. J. *3*:474–477, 1975.
98. Moore, D. P.: Neuropsychiatric aspects of Sydenham's chorea: A comprehensive review. J. Clin. Psychiatry *57*:407–414, 1996.
99. Moore, P., and Mortland, T.: *Mycoplasma pneumoniae* infection mimicking acute rheumatic fever. Pediatr. Infect. Dis. J. *13*:81–82, 1994.
100. Morris, K., Mohan, C., Wahi, P., et al.: Enhancement of IL-1, IL-2 production and IL-2 receptor generation in patients with acute rheumatic fever and active rheumatic heart disease: A prospective study. Clin. Exp. Immunol. *91*:429–436, 1993.
101. Morris, K., Mohan, C., Wahi, P. L., et al.: Increased inactivated T cells and reduction in suppressor/cytotoxic T cells in acute rheumatic fever and active heart disease: A longitudinal study. J. Infect. Dis. *167*:3979–3983, 1993.
102. Morton, W. E., Huhn, L. A., and Litchy, J. A.: Rheumatic heart disease epidemiology: Observations on 17,366 Denver schoolchildren. J. A. M. A. *199*:879–884, 1967.
103. Nausieda, P. A., Grossman, B. J., Koller, W. C., et al.: Sydenham chorea: An update. Neurology *30*:331–334, 1980.
104. Newman, J. E., Lennon, D. R., and Wong-Toi, W.: Patients with rheumatic fever recurrences. N. Z. Med. J. *97*:678–680, 1984.
105. Nordet, P.: WHO/ISFC Global programme for the prevention & control of RH/RHD. J. Inf. Fed. Cardiol. *3*:4–5, 1993.
106. Padmavati, S.: Rheumatic heart disease: Prevalence and preventive measures in the Indian subcontinent. Heart *86*:127, 2001.
107. Pataroyo, M. E., Winchester, R. J., Vejerano, A., et al.: Association of a B cell alloantigen with susceptibility to rheumatic fever. Nature *278*:173–174, 1979.
108. Paul, J. R.: Epidemiology of Rheumatic Fever. 3rd ed. New York, American Heart Association, 1957, pp. 46–56.
109. Perry, C. B., and Roberts, J. A. F.: A study on the variability in the incidence of rheumatic heart disease within the city of Bristol. B. M. J. *193*(Suppl.):154–158, 1937.
110. Phibbs, B., Lundin, S. R., Watson, W. B., et al.: Experience of a Wyoming county streptococcal control project. West. J. Med. *148*:546–550, 1988.
111. Pickles, W. N.: A rheumatic family. Lancet *2*:241, 1943.

112. Pinals, R.: Polyarthritis and fever. N. Engl. J. Med. *330*:769–774, 1994.
113. Prevention of rheumatic heart disease. Lancet *1*:143–144, 1982.
114. Pruksakorn, S., Currie, B., Brandt, E., et al.: Towards a vaccine for rheumatic fever: Identification of a conserved target epitope on M protein of group A streptococci. Lancet *334*:639–642, 1994.
115. Quinn, R. W., and Federspiel, C. F.: The incidence of rheumatic fever in metropolitan Nashville, 1963–1969. Am. J. Epidemiol. *99*:273–280, 1974.
116. Raizada, V., Williams, R. C., Chopra, P., et al.: Tissue distribution of lymphocytes in rheumatic heart valves as defined by monoclonal anti-T cell antibodies. Am. J. Med. *74*:90–96, 1983.
117. Rammelkamp, C. H., Denny, F. W., and Wannamaker, L. W.: Studies on the epidemiology of rheumatic fever in the armed services. *In* Thomas, L. (ed.): Rheumatic Fever. Minneapolis, University of Minnesota Press, 1972, p. 72.
118. Rammelkamp, C. H., Jr., and Stolzer, B. L.: The latent period before the onset of acute rheumatic fever. Yale J. Biol. Med. *34*:386–398, 1961.
119. Randolph, M. F., Gerber, M. A., De Meo, K. K., et al.: Effect of antibiotic therapy on the clinical course of streptococcal pharyngitis. J. Pediatr. *106*:870–875, 1985.
120. Redd, S. C., Facklam, R. R., Collin, S., et al.: Rapid group A streptococcal antigen detection kit: Effect on antimicrobial therapy for acute pharyngitis. Pediatrics *82*:576–581, 1988.
121. Reddy, D. V., Chun, L. T., and Yamamoto, L. G.: Acute rheumatic fever with advanced degree AV block. Clin. Pediatr. (Phila.) *28*:326–328, 1989.
122. Regelmann, W. E., Talbot, R., Cairns, L., et al.: Distribution of cells bearing "rheumatic" antigens in peripheral blood of patients with rheumatic fever/rheumatic heart disease. J. Rheumatol. *16*:931–935, 1989.
123. Rhodes, P., and Jackson, H.: Rheumatic fever in Colorado: A conquered disease? J. A. M. A. *234*:157–158, 1975.
124. Robbins, S. L.: The heart: Rheumatic fever and rheumatic heart disease. *In* Cotran, R. S., Kumar, V., and Robbins, S. L. (eds.): Robbins Pathologic Basis of Disease. 4th ed. Philadelphia, W. B. Saunders, 1994, pp. 547–550.
125. Sanyal, S. K., Berry, A. M., Duggal, S., et al.: Sequelae of the initial attack of acute rheumatic fever in children from north India. Circulation *65*:375–379, 1982.
126. Sanyal, S. K., Thapar, M. K., Ahmed, S. H., et al.: The initial attack of acute rheumatic fever during childhood in north India: A prospective study of the clinical profile. Circulation *49*:7–12, 1974.
127. Shulman, S. T.: The decline of rheumatic fever: What impact on our management of pharyngitis? Am. J. Dis. Child. *128*:426–427, 1984.
128. Siegal, A. C., Johnson, E. E., and Stollerman, G. H.: Controlled studies of streptococcal pharyngitis in a pediatric population. N. Engl. J. Med. *265*:559–566, 1961.
129. Single, L. A., and Martin, D. R.: Clonal differences within M-types of the group A streptococci revealed by pulsed field gel electrophoresis. FEMS Microbiol. Lett. *91*:85–90, 1992.
130. Spagnuolo, M., and Taranta, M.: Rheumatic fever in siblings: Similarity of its clinical manifestations. N. Engl. J. Med. *278*:183–188, 1968.
131. Stollerman, G. H.: Rheumatic Fever and Streptococcal Infection. New York, Grune & Stratton, 1975, pp. 79–86.
132. Stollerman, G. H.: Rheumatogenic streptococci and autoimmunity. Clin. Immunol. Immunopathol. *61*:131–142, 1991.
133. Stollerman, G. H., Lewis, A. J., Schultz, I., et al.: Relationship of immune response to group A streptococci to the course of acute, chronic and recurrent rheumatic fever. Am. J. Med. *20*:163–169, 1956.
134. Strauss, A. W., Goldring, D., Kissane, J., et al.: Valve replacement in acute rheumatic heart disease. J. Thorac. Cardiovasc. Surg. *67*:659–670, 1974.
135. Taranta, A., and Markowitz, M.: Rheumatic Fever. 2nd ed. Dordrecht, Germany, Kluwer, 1989, pp. 61–65.
136. Taranta, A., Spagnuolo, M., and Feinstein, A. R.: "Chronic" rheumatic fever. Ann. Intern. Med. *56*:367–388, 1962.
137. Taranta, A., Torosdag, S., Metrakos, J. D., et al.: Rheumatic fever in monozygotic and dizygotic twins. Circulation *20*:778, 1959.
138. Taubert, K. A., Rowley, A. H., and Shulman, S. T.: Seven-year national survey of Kawasaki disease and acute rheumatic fever. Pediatr. Infect. Dis. J. *13*:704–708, 1994.
139. The natural history of rheumatic fever and rheumatic heart disease. Ten year report of a cooperative clinical trial of ACTH, cortisone and aspirin. Circulation *32*:457–476, 1965.
140. Tomai, M., Kotb, M., Majumdar, G., et al.: Superantigenicity of streptococcal M protein. J. Exp. Med. *172*:359–362, 1990.
141. Tompkins, R. K., Burnes, D. C., and Cable, W. E.: An analysis of the cost-effectiveness of pharyngitis management and acute rheumatic fever prevention. Ann. Intern. Med. *86*:481–492, 1977.
142. Treatment of rheumatic fever. Editorial. N. Engl. J. Med. *272*:101–102, 1965.
143. Uziel, Y., Hashkes, P. J., Kassem, E., et al.: The use of naproxen in the treatment of children with rheumatic fever. J. Pediatr. *137*:269–271, 2000.
144. Veasy, L. G.: Time to take soundings in acute rheumatic fever. Lancet *357*:1994–1995, 2001.
145. Veasy, L. G., Tani, L. Y., and Hill, H. R.: Persistence of acute rheumatic fever in the intermountain area of the U.S. J. Pediatr. *124*:9–11, 1994.
146. Veasy, L. G., Wiedmeier, S. E., Orsmond, G. S., et al.: Resurgence of acute rheumatic fever in the intermountain area of the U.S. N. Engl. J. Med. *316*:421–427, 1987.
147. Vendsborg, P., Fauerholdt, L., and Olsen, K. H.: Decreasing incidence of a history of acute rheumatic fever in chronic rheumatic heart disease. Cardiologica *53*:332–340, 1968.
148. Vlajinac, H., Adanja, B., Markinkovic, J., et al.: Influence of socio-economic and other factors on rheumatic fever occurrence. Eur. J. Epidemiol. *7*:702–704, 1991.
149. Voss, L. M., Wilson, N. J., Neutze, J. M., et al.: Intravenous immunoglobulin in acute rheumatic fever: A randomized controlled trial. Circulation *103*:401–406, 2001.
150. Wald, E. R., Dashefsky, B., Feidt, C., et al.: Acute rheumatic fever in western Pennsylvania and the Tri-State Area. Pediatrics *80*:371–374, 1987.
151. Wallace, M. R., Garst, P. D., Papadimos, T. J., et al.: The return of acute rheumatic fever in young adults. J. A. M. A. *262*:2557–2561, 1989.
152. Wannamaker, L. W.: Differences between streptococcal infections of the skin and of the throat. N. Engl. J. Med. *282*:23–30, 78–85, 1970.
153. Wannamaker, L. W.: Virulence factors in streptococci. Scand. J. Infect. Dis. *31*(Suppl.):22–27, 1982.
154. Wannamaker, L. W., Denny, F. W., Perry, W. D., et al.: The effect of penicillin prophylaxis on streptococcal disease rates and the carrier state. N. Engl. J. Med. *249*:1–7, 1953.
155. Wannamaker, L. W., Rammelkamp, C. H., Jr., Denny, F. W., et al.: Prophylaxis of acute rheumatic fever by treatment of the preceding streptococcal infection with various amounts of depot penicillin. Am. J. Med. *10*:673–695, 1951.
156. Westlake, R. M., Graham, T. A., and Edwards, K. M.: An outbreak of acute rheumatic fever in Tennessee. Pediatr. Infect. Dis. J. *9*:97–100, 1990.
157. WHO evaluation of the Streptozyme test for streptococcal antibodies. Bull. World Health Organ. *64*:504, 1986.
158. Widdowson, J. P., Maxted, W. R., Notley, C. M., et al.: The antibody responses in man to infection with different serotypes of group A streptococci. J. Med. Microbiol. *7*:483, 1974.
159. Wilson, N. J., and Neutze, J. M.: Echocardiographic diagnosis of subclinical carditis in acute rheumatic fever. Int. J. Cardiol. *50*:1–6, 1995.
160. Wood, H. F., Feinstein, A. R., Taranta, A., et al.: Rheumatic fever in adolescents: A long-term epidemiologic study of subsequent prophylaxis, streptococcal infections, and clinical sequelae. III. Comparative effectiveness of three prophylaxis regimens in preventing streptococcal infections and rheumatic recurrences. Ann. Intern. Med. *60*(Suppl.):31–45, 1964.
161. Zabriskie, J. B.: Rheumatic fever: A model for the pathological consequences of microbial-host mimicry. Clin. Exp. Rheum. *4*:65–73, 1986.
162. Zabriskie, J. B., Lavench, D., Williams, R. C., et al.: Rheumatic fever–associated B cell alloantigens as identified by monoclonal antibodies. Arthritis Rheum. *28*:1047–1051, 1985.
163. Zangwill, K. M., Wald, E. M., and Londino, A. V.: Acute rheumatic fever in western Pennsylvania: A persistent problem into the 1990's. J. Pediatr. *118*:561–563, 1991.
164. Zedan, M. M., El-Shennawy, F. A., Abou-Bakr, H. M., et al.: Interleukin-2 in relation to T cell subpopulations in rheumatic heart disease. Arch. Dis. Child. *67*:1373–1375, 1992.

CHAPTER 36

Noninfectious Carditis

DAVID R. FULTON ■ JANE G. SCHALLER

Many diseases, primarily of the rheumatic disease category, are associated with carditis that presumably is noninfectious in nature. Rheumatic fever, the principal rheumatic disease affecting the heart, is presented in Chapter 35. Cardiac manifestations of other rheumatic diseases, including juvenile rheumatoid arthritis (JRA), ankylosing spondylitis, Reiter disease, systemic lupus erythematosus (SLE), the various vasculitis syndromes, scleroderma, dermatomyositis, and miscellaneous other diseases, are discussed here. All at times may mimic infectious diseases.

The etiologies and pathogenetic mechanisms of the rheumatic diseases are poorly understood. All are associated with chronic inflammation of various connective tissues throughout the body. Heart disease results when cardiac connective tissue is affected by such inflammation. Various regions of the heart, including the pericardium, myocardium, endocardium, coronary blood vessels, and conduction system, can be involved. In some diseases, notably SLE, immune complex disease appears to be responsible for much of the inflammation and tissue damage; however, the primary causes of lupus itself and those of the associated immune complex formation remain obscure. Immune complex mechanisms also have been demonstrated in seropositive rheumatoid arthritis and certain forms of vasculitis. The finding of hepatitis antigen as the causal agent in some instances of polyarteritis, presumably by an immune complex mechanism, suggests that infectious agents in fact may play roles in some rheumatic disease syndromes. However, the mechanisms of inflammation observed in most rheumatic diseases remain unknown; for example, although beta-hemolytic streptococcal infections long have been a known antecedent event for rheumatic fever, the ways in which such infections cause disease have yet to be elucidated.

Diagnosis of the various rheumatic diseases rests largely on the clinical appearance of patients; certain laboratory tests and radiographs also may be helpful. Each rheumatic disease presents a reasonably characteristic type and pattern of tissue involvement; for example, rheumatoid arthritis is characterized by chronic synovitis, dermatomyositis by inflammation of muscle and skin, and scleroderma by hardening of the skin and subcutaneous tissues. Researchers have no explanation for the varying and distinctive patterns of tissue involvement in these diseases. Although no laboratory tests are diagnostic, investigations such as antinuclear antibodies, rheumatoid factors, histocompatibility antigens, radiographs, and tissue histology may be useful in classifying patients (Table 36–1).

Types of cardiac involvement that have been observed in the various rheumatic diseases are summarized in Table 36–2. Cardiac involvement, particularly pericarditis and myocarditis, can occur as isolated events without a proven infectious or rheumatic etiology. The rheumatic and allied conditions (other than rheumatic fever) most frequently associated with cardiac involvement include Kawasaki disease (coronary vasculitis or myocarditis, or both, affect approximately 50% of patients), systemic-onset JRA (pericarditis affects 25 to 50% of patients), and SLE (various heart lesions affect 20 to 40% of patients).

TABLE 36–1 ■ CLINICAL AND LABORATORY FEATURES OF RHEUMATIC DISEASES

Disease	Characteristic Clinical Features	Laboratory Characteristics
Juvenile rheumatoid arthritis	Chronic synovitis Several subgroups Systemic onset RF-negative polyarthritis RF-positive polyarthritis Pauciarthritis—chronic iridocyclitis Pauciarthritis—sacroiliitis	Radiographic evidence of destructive arthritis—10–30% RF—10% (RF-positive polyarthritis subgroup) ANA—25% (associated with chronic iridocyclitis)
Ankylosing spondylitis	Sacroiliitis Spinal arthritis	HLA-B27—95% Radiographic sacroiliitis—100% Radiographic spinal arthritis—late
Systemic lupus erythematosus	Multisystem disease Facial rash—50%	ANA—100% Other "autoantibodies" and lowered levels of serum hemolytic complement DNA antibodies—50%
Dermatomyositis	Myositis, rash	Elevated serum levels of "muscle" enzymes Abnormal electromyogram and MRI Histologic myositis
Scleroderma	Cutaneous involvement	ANA, common (Sc 170 positive)
Vasculitis	Multisystem disease Several distinct syndromes Henoch-Schönlein vasculitis Kawasaki disease Polyarteritis nodosa and variance	Histologic vasculitis Abnormal cardiac echo Arteriography

ANA, antinuclear antibodies; MRI, magnetic resonance imaging; RF, rheumatoid factors.

TABLE 36–2 ■ CARDIAC MANIFESTATIONS OF RHEUMATIC DISEASES

	Pericarditis	Myocarditis	Endocarditis	Coronary Vasculitis
Juvenile rheumatoid arthritis	Systemic onset + RF*-positive +	Systemic onset ± RF-positive ±	RF-positive ±	–
Ankylosing spondylitis	±	±	+ (Aortitis)	–
Systemic lupus erythematosus	+	+	+	+
Dermatomyositis	±	±	–	–
Scleroderma	+	+	±	–
Vasculitis	+	±	+	+

*RF, rheumatoid factors; ±, <5% of patients; +, ≥5% of patients; –, not associated.

Pericarditis

In pericarditis, the pericardium, or outer layer of the heart, is the site of inflammation. The pericardium may become thickened as a result of inflammation or fibrosis. Excessive production of pericardial fluid may give rise to pericardial effusions. If the pericardium merely is inflamed, no cardiac enlargement may be apparent, but friction rubs may be heard; they often are transient and changeable. If the pericardium becomes chronically fibrotic, signs of constrictive pericarditis may ensue. If enough excess pericardial fluid is produced, signs of pericardial effusion will result. If cardiac output is compromised by pericardial constriction from either pericardial thickening or pressure from pericardial effusion, physical signs of cardiac tamponade or cardiac failure may occur.

The pericarditis associated with rheumatic diseases may be entirely asymptomatic. The most common symptom is pain, which generally is in a substernal or anterior precordial location, often is exacerbated by lying flat, and sometimes is referred to the left shoulder or arm. Dyspnea or tachypnea also may be present. With large pericardial effusions or with constrictive pericarditis, signs of heart failure may be noted. Physical findings of pericarditis include pericardial friction rubs, tachypnea, cardiac enlargement, and congestive heart failure. With constrictive pericarditis, hepatomegaly is a cardinal sign.

The diagnosis of pericarditis rests first on suspicion of its presence. The possibility of pericarditis should be considered in any patient with rheumatic disease and chest pain or dyspnea. The diagnosis depends on demonstration of a pericardial friction rub or pericardial fluid or thickening. The latter may be suspected on the basis of physical findings or chest radiography and confirmed by echocardiography. Echocardiography can detect small effusions not sufficient to suggest cardiac enlargement on radiography.[134] Electrocardiographic changes of pericarditis are not specific and may be lacking. In many instances, the pericarditis of rheumatic diseases is entirely subclinical and may be found only on incidental echocardiography[10] or at autopsy.[91] On the other hand, some individuals with symptoms suggestive of pericarditis may have entirely normal findings, including echocardiography.

In the rheumatic diseases, pericarditis generally is serofibrinous in nature. Similar pleuritis, with or without pleural effusion, also often is present. This type of pericarditis resembles viral rather than bacterial pericarditis. The course generally is benign, although congestive heart failure sometimes occurs. Attacks often are self-limited but may recur. In a few rheumatic diseases, notably seropositive rheumatoid arthritis, the subsequent development of chronic constrictive pericarditis has been reported. Pericardiocentesis performed to determine a rheumatic etiology usually is not diagnostic.[110]

JUVENILE RHEUMATOID ARTHRITIS

Significant pericarditis[10, 51, 91] is associated with two subgroups of JRA: systemic-onset and seropositive disease; it occurs rarely in other patients.

In systemic-onset JRA, from 25 to 50 percent of patients have clinical signs of pericarditis,[122] and higher percentages can be found by echocardiography to have pericardial effusions.[10] This pericarditis is serofibrinous in nature and often associated with a similar pleuritis. Pericarditis generally occurs during febrile periods of active systemic JRA and diminishes with remission of the other systemic manifestations, usually within a period of approximately 6 months. Symptoms include chest pain, dyspnea, tachypnea, and pain on lying flat in the supine position. Friction rubs, often transient, may be heard, and heart sounds may be muffled. Radiographic evidence of cardiac enlargement and electrocardiographic changes suggestive of pericarditis may be present. Rarely, congestive heart failure ensues. The diagnosis of pericarditis is made on the basis of the history and physical and laboratory findings. Infectious pericarditis must be considered in the differential diagnosis, particularly if patients are receiving corticosteroids. Pain also must be differentiated from inflammation of the costosternal junctions and other small joints of the anterior chest wall.

Therapy is geared to the underlying systemic JRA. Nonsteroidal agents or salicylates may be effective in treating children with only mild pericarditis. Maximal therapeutic effect may require several weeks. Congestive heart failure from the pericarditis of systemic-onset JRA seldom occurs; most pericarditis is relatively benign. Chest pain and dyspnea may be troublesome and require analgesics or codeine for relief; the use of narcotics for long periods should be avoided, however. If pericardial effusions are very large or occur in the presence of congestive heart failure, corticosteroid therapy in doses of 1 to 2 mg/kg body weight of prednisone per 24 hours (40 to 60 mg/24 hr for a teenager) should result in rapid resolution of the pericarditis. Pericardiocentesis rarely is necessary, although tamponade has been reported.[154]

The prognosis for the pericarditis of systemic-onset JRA is excellent,[91, 135] although rare deaths have been reported.[51] Subsequent development of chronic constrictive pericarditis is not associated with systemic-onset JRA. Bouts of pericarditis generally subside within weeks to months, but some patients have recurrent pericarditis associated with subsequent attacks of systemic manifestations in future years.

Pericarditis also occurs in seropositive JRA, a subgroup similar to classic adult-onset rheumatoid arthritis.[122] This pericarditis generally is serofibrinous, although granulomatous lesions resembling rheumatoid nodules sometimes are found in affected pericardium, and occasionally chronic fibrosis with subsequent constriction occurs.[6, 43, 79, 109, 138] Pericarditis has been diagnosed by physical or electrocardiographic changes in 10 percent of adult rheumatoid patients,[79] by echocardiographic changes in 50 percent of adult rheumatoid patients with nodules,[6] and in 40 percent of adult rheumatoid patients at autopsy.[138] Such pericarditis often occurs years after the onset of disease and, thus, rarely is recognized during the childhood years. Few other extra-articular manifestations are associated, although affected patients often have severe joint disease. The course of the pericarditis generally is benign, except for patients with chronic fibrosis and pericardial constriction. Pericardiectomy in patients with seropositive disease has been successful in relieving symptoms.[30] Therapy is that for the underlying disease; occasionally, corticosteroids are needed. Distinction must be made from infectious pericarditis occurring as an independent event and from inflammation of chest wall joints.

SYSTEMIC LUPUS ERYTHEMATOSUS

Serofibrinous pericarditis occurs in 20 to 50 percent of patients with SLE.[7, 34, 56, 78, 126] Histologic examination of affected pericardium may show hematoxylin bodies, fairly characteristic of SLE, and pericardial fluid may contain typical lupus erythematosus cells, which are formed in vitro.[56] Deposits of immunoglobulins and complement have been identified in the pericardium.[65]

The clinical manifestations and diagnostic tests for pericarditis are similar to those described for systemic-onset JRA: chest pain, dyspnea, friction rub, tachycardia, distant heart sounds, congestive heart failure, cardiac enlargement, nonspecific electrocardiographic changes, and evidence of pericardial effusion on echocardiography.[2, 54] Pericarditis may occur as an isolated event in SLE and even may be the initial manifestation of disease; it also may occur as a part of multisystemic disease at any time during the course of SLE. The use of procainamide has led to a drug-induced SLE that has been associated with constrictive pericarditis.[17, 134] Infectious pericarditis must be differentiated from SLE, particularly in patients receiving corticosteroids. Other cardiac manifestations of lupus (coronary vasculitis, myocardial infarction, and endocarditis) also must be differentiated, as must the pleural or pulmonary disease of lupus or inflammation of the anterior chest wall joints.

The pericarditis of lupus generally is benign and responds well to treatment of the underlying disease. Occasionally, large pericardial effusions or congestive heart failure may demand immediate initiation of therapy with corticosteroids. Pericardial thickening can be assessed by echocardiography.[29] Pericardiocentesis rarely is required in younger patients.[1, 31, 71] Pain may respond to aspirin, nonsteroidal anti-inflammatory drugs, or codeine. The prognosis for the pericarditis of SLE is excellent; although bouts may be chronic or recurrent, they very infrequently interfere with cardiac function and rarely, if ever, result in chronic constriction.[65]

MIXED CONNECTIVE TISSUE DISEASE

Mixed connective tissue disease is a rheumatic disease syndrome that combines the clinical and laboratory features of SLE, rheumatoid arthritis, dermatomyositis, and scleroderma; it is characterized by the presence of high titers of a specific antinuclear antibody reactive with ribonucleoprotein.[127, 129] Pericarditis similar to that of SLE occurs in some patients.

OTHER RHEUMATIC DISEASES OCCASIONALLY ASSOCIATED WITH PERICARDITIS

Polyarteritis and other vasculitis syndromes,[115] scleroderma,[15, 18, 97, 131, 144] and dermatomyositis occasionally are associated with pericarditis.[137] Findings are similar to those described earlier. Chronic fibrosis and constriction occur rarely, if ever.

ISOLATED IDIOPATHIC PERICARDITIS

Pericarditis occurs in numerous individuals with no stigmata of either infectious or rheumatic disease.[69, 151] This pericarditis may occur as a single event or may recur; pleuritis may be associated with it. High fever and elevated sedimentation rates may occur, but no clinical or laboratory findings are diagnostic of any rheumatic or infectious disease. Although the etiology of this type of pericarditis is unknown, undiagnosed viral pericarditis may be the cause in some cases; the predilection for viral pericarditis to recur is well known. Chest trauma also may be followed by pericarditis. Also possible is that some "isolated pericarditis" represents undiagnosed rheumatic disease with pericarditis as the sole manifestation. Long-term observations are required to sort out the natural history and ultimate outcome. Patients generally respond to salicylates; sometimes, administration of corticosteroids is required.

Myocarditis

Myocardial inflammation may be entirely subclinical or may cause significant cardiac dysfunction. Myocardial dysfunction results in loss of normal myocardial contractility with subsequent cardiac dilatation, decreased cardiac output, congestive heart failure, and cardiac arrhythmias. Pathologic changes include collections of inflammatory cells or deposition of fibrinoid in the myocardium, with varying degrees of damage and loss of myocardial fibers. The symptoms of myocarditis are those referable to compromised cardiac function or arrhythmias; generally, pain is not present. Physical findings may include hypotension, tachycardia, tachypnea, diminished intensity of heart sounds, narrow pulse pressure, hepatomegaly, and rhythm disturbances. Chest radiographs may show increased cardiac size that is not attributable to pericardial fluid. However, early in the course of acute myocarditis, the heart may appear small despite significant cardiac decompensation. Electrocardiographic changes may include low voltage, left ventricular hypertrophy, nonspecific ST and T wave changes, and various abnormalities in cardiac rhythm.[85] Echocardiography may be helpful in excluding pericardial effusion as a component of cardiac enlargement and in identifying an enlarged, poorly contractile left ventricle. Serum levels of the enzymes found in cardiac muscle may be elevated. The diagnosis of myocarditis is made on the basis of clinical and laboratory findings. Occasionally, endomyocardial biopsy may be helpful, particularly in establishing a viral etiology. Pericarditis often is associated with myocarditis.

Subclinical myocarditis, defined by only electrocardiographic changes or as an incidental autopsy finding, may be found in many rheumatic diseases but apparently is of little clinical consequence. Clinically significant myocarditis quite rarely occurs in rheumatic diseases other than rheumatic fever but has been noted in SLE, various vasculitis syndromes, systemic-onset JRA, dermatomyositis, and scleroderma. The differential diagnosis of myocarditis associated with rheumatic diseases includes viral and other infectious myocarditis, various other known familial or metabolic cardiomyopathies, and cardiac amyloidosis.

Treatment of myocarditis is multifaceted. Digitalis should be used cautiously because many of these patients are sensitive to dosages in the therapeutic range. Diuretic therapy to decrease preload to the myocardium should be considered; however, many individuals require elevated central venous pressure to maintain adequate cardiac output. Afterload reduction therapy with milrinone or nitrates has been a major contribution to management but is dependent on accurate determination of the underlying hemodynamics. For patients with hemodynamic embarrassment, central venous management, preferably with a pulmonary artery wedge catheter, is mandatory. Patients with high-degree atrioventricular block and congestive heart failure may require temporary cardiac pacing. Intravenous gamma-globulin is effective in Kawasaki disease and some instances of viral myocarditis but seldom has been used for the myocarditis of rheumatic diseases.

JUVENILE RHEUMATOID ARTHRITIS

Myocarditis is a rare event but occurs occasionally[10, 95, 100] in patients with systemic-onset JRA who also have pericarditis. Congestive heart failure may be severe, but it generally responds to corticosteroids and diuresis. Patients may be extremely sensitive to digitalis preparations. Episodes of myocarditis may be self-limited or may become chronic.

Myocarditis also has been reported in seropositive rheumatoid arthritis, although it rarely is of clinical significance[85, 132] and often is an incidental postmortem finding. Granulomatous lesions resembling rheumatoid nodules may be found in the myocardium and rarely may cause heart block.[59] Diffuse myocarditis also may be present.

SYSTEMIC LUPUS ERYTHEMATOSUS

Myocarditis occurs in some patients with lupus, as witnessed by electrocardiographic changes and autopsy findings.[34] However, this type of heart involvement occurs less commonly in patients with SLE than does either pericarditis or endocarditis. Patients with active myositis appear more likely to manifest myocarditis. High titers of anti-ribonucleoprotein antibody also are found in this subset of patients.[14] Pathologic changes include fibrinoid deposition in the myocardium, myocardial inflammation, and inflammation of coronary blood vessels. The myocarditis generally is mild; the subsequent development of congestive heart failure and cardiac arrhythmias is unusual, but the development of complete heart block with death has been reported more frequently and has been associated with early onset of atherosclerotic vascular disease and myocardial infarction.[11, 45, 150] Therapy is directed toward the underlying disease.

DERMATOMYOSITIS AND POLYMYOSITIS

Although skeletal muscle involvement is, by definition, present in all patients, recognized involvement of heart muscle occurs only rarely in dermatomyositis and polymyositis. Myocardial involvement may, however, be a rare cause of cardiac arrhythmia, heart block, or congestive heart failure.[93, 123, 130] Reviews of autopsy material suggest that subclinical myocardial inflammation may not be a rare event.[130]

SCLERODERMA

Myocardial involvement, a potentially fatal event in scleroderma, occurs in a significant number of patients with systemic scleroderma (progressive systemic sclerosis)[66, 117] but rarely, if ever, in association with morphea or linear scleroderma.[82] A strong association has been found between the presence of myositis and myocarditis.[41, 149] The myocardial involvement of scleroderma is characterized histologically by collections of inflammatory cells in the myocardium, myocardial fibrosis, degeneration of myocardial fibers, and thickening of coronary blood vessels, although in one series of patients the coronary blood vessels were reported to be normal.[18] Symptoms include cardiac arrhythmias, cardiac enlargement, or congestive heart failure; some patients have precordial pain suggestive of angina. Laboratory findings include electrocardiographic changes[40] and cardiac enlargement on chest radiographs. Abnormalities in cardiac function as indicated by exercise testing and thallium scanning may predate the clinical evidence of myocarditis.[39] Cardiac conditions to be differentiated include hypertensive cardiac disease secondary to associated renal hypertension and cor pulmonale resulting from the pulmonary hypertension of scleroderma lung disease. No specific therapy exists for the heart disease of scleroderma; administration of drugs such as corticosteroids, cytotoxic agents, and penicillamine may be warranted in patients with life-threatening disease.[103] Conventional therapy for heart failure is indicated if present. Regular follow-up with electrocardiography and Holter monitoring is indicated because of the likelihood of the development of serious rhythm disturbances.[149] Scleroderma heart disease generally is slowly and relentlessly progressive and may be fatal.

POLYARTERITIS AND VASCULITIS

Myocardial involvement occurs at times in polyarteritis nodosa, sometimes as a result of multiple small cardiac infarcts secondary to vasculitis of the coronary blood vessels.[61] Inflammatory myocarditis of clinical significance is an unusual event, but electrocardiographic changes suggestive of myocarditis at times are seen in Henoch-Schönlein vasculitis, and subclinical myocarditis may not be a rare event.[3, 64]

Endocarditis

In endocarditis, inflammation of the inner layer of the heart causes either diffuse thickening of the endocardium (as in endocardial fibroelastosis) or valvular disease. Valvulitis is the identifying sign of acute rheumatic fever but occurs relatively rarely in other rheumatic disease syndromes. In endocarditis, the endocardium, particularly the part forming the valve leaflets, becomes inflamed, thickened, and fibrotic, with possible resultant compromise of cardiac contractility (as in endocardial fibroelastosis) or valve function. Pathologic changes in valve leaflets similar to those in mild rheumatic fever have been described in numerous rheumatic diseases but usually are of little clinical significance. SLE, ankylosing spondylitis, some of the vasculitis syndromes, and seropositive rheumatoid arthritis at times are associated with clinically significant endocarditis. Heart valves damaged by endocarditis may function poorly, compromise cardiac function, or act as foci for bacterial endocarditis.

The clinical manifestations of endocarditis are limited unless cardiac compromise or symptoms of coexisting pericarditis or coronary vascular disease are present. Signs include valvular heart murmurs, thickened valve leaflets seen on echocardiography, selective cardiac enlargement on chest radiography, certain electrocardiographic changes, and abnormal findings on cardiac catheterization. The diagnosis rests on one or more of such findings. Distinction must be made from bacterial endocarditis, not always an easy task in a febrile rheumatic disease patient with a heart murmur. In rheumatic diseases other than rheumatic fever, distinction also must be made between coexisting rheumatic fever and valvular heart disease caused by the particular rheumatic disease present in the patient. In addition, congenital heart disease must be differentiated from endocarditis.

JUVENILE RHEUMATOID ARTHRITIS

Significant valvular heart disease rarely, if ever, occurs in the seronegative JRA subgroups.[122] Patients with JRA and pathologic heart murmurs should be suspected of having coexisting congenital heart disease or bacterial endocarditis. Mitral regurgitation may be present in severe myocarditis resulting from ventricular dilatation or papillary muscle dysfunction.

Valvular heart disease occurs occasionally in patients with seropositive rheumatoid arthritis. In one instance, in a child with seropositive JRA, severe aortic regurgitation necessitated replacement of the aortic root with a pulmonary autograft, but the patient later died of congestive heart and allograft failure.[124] At autopsy, the pulmonary allograft showed a thickened annulus with retracted valve cusps and histologic evidence of a rheumatic process.[145] Rheumatoid granulomatous lesions have been found in affected valve leaflets. Autopsy series have reported a high incidence of valvular lesions resembling those of chronic rheumatic fever in adult rheumatoid patients; however, few of these patients have had clinically significant heart disease,[135] and similar lesions also have been described in "normal" nonrheumatoid adults.[9, 12, 132]

ANKYLOSING SPONDYLITIS

Ankylosing spondylitis and the spondyloarthropathies may be associated with aortitis and aortic valvular disease with resulting aortic insufficiency.[16, 52, 63, 136] This type of endocarditis occurs in approximately 5 percent of patients with spondylitis, generally some years after the onset of disease; hence, it rarely is seen in children. A similar type of heart disease has been noted occasionally in Reiter disease.[106] Pathologic changes include an inflammatory process of the proximal aorta and aortic valve; the histology is reminiscent of luetic aortitis. Myocarditis, heart block, and cardiac arrhythmias also may be present. The only associated symptoms are those of cardiac decompensation or arrhythmia. Signs include the murmur of aortic insufficiency and characteristic findings of aortic insufficiency on echocardiography and cardiac catheterization.[140] Advances in the use of Doppler echocardiography permit sensitive identification of aortic regurgitation before auscultatory findings become apparent. This type of heart disease has no known form of prevention or specific therapy. Aortic valve replacement may be required. Bacterial endocarditis must be differentiated from ankylosing spondylitis.

SYSTEMIC LUPUS ERYTHEMATOSUS

Verrucous endocarditis, or Libman-Sacks endocarditis, is a frequent autopsy finding in SLE.[34] One or more heart valves may be affected. Vegetations are present on one or both surfaces of the valve leaflets; they also may spread to the chordae, papillary muscles, and mural endocardium. Histologic changes include fibrinoid deposition with an accompanying inflammatory response but with minimal fibrosis and scarring. In distinction to the endocarditis of rheumatic fever, valve leaflets rarely are destroyed or seriously deformed in SLE; hence, cardiac function rarely is affected. Affected valve leaflets may be predisposed to the subsequent development of bacterial endocarditis, however. No clinical symptoms are associated with Libman-Sacks endocarditis. Signs include cardiac murmurs, which may be quite changeable, but attempts to correlate murmurs in patients with lupus and the valve changes found at autopsy have not been uniformly successful, and whether the murmurs found so commonly in SLE patients always are related to the observed endocarditis is not certain. A diagnosis of Libman-Sacks endocarditis is difficult to make in a living patient, although valvular murmurs certainly suggest its presence. Echocardiography occasionally may be helpful in demonstrating thickened valve leaflets.[29, 37, 49]

The differential diagnosis must include bacterial endocarditis; making this distinction may be difficult in a febrile patient with SLE and a heart murmur. A thorough search for possible infectious agents should be made in such patients. The frequent treatment of lupus patients with medications that interfere with host inflammatory and immune responses, such as corticosteroids and cytotoxic agents, compounds the problem. Myocarditis, pericarditis, and the pulmonary disease of lupus also must be differentiated from endocarditis in SLE.

No therapy is indicated for Libman-Sacks endocarditis per se; it rarely interferes significantly with cardiac function, nor does it cause significant chronic valvular damage. If the possibility exists that the patient has bacterial endocarditis, appropriate evaluation and antibiotic therapy should be instituted.

A few patients with SLE incur significant damage to either the mitral or aortic valve, particularly the aortic valve, with resulting clinical heart disease.[9, 36] In such patients, initiation of vigorous anti-inflammatory therapy might be indicated in an attempt to stop the valve destruction, but the possibility of bacterial endocarditis always must be considered.

Cardiac Disease in Infants of Mothers with Systemic Lupus Erythematosus

Infants of mothers with SLE may show transient manifestations of the disease, presumably transplacentally passed[70, 121, 146]; findings include discoid lupus, thrombocytopenia, hemolytic anemia, leukopenia, and positive tests for antinuclear antibodies. Such infants also may be affected by cardiac diseases that not always are transient. Fatal endocardial fibroelastosis has been reported in three infants of mothers with connective tissue disease.[60, 62, 92] Congenital complete heart block is a sequela, usually permanent, of maternal SLE[4, 23, 96] with an approximate frequency of 50 percent in infants with neonatal lupus.[5, 20, 50, 87, 148] Antibodies to the soluble tissue ribonucleoprotein antigens

SSA/Ro or SSB/La (or both) are found in the serum of infants with neonatal lupus, as well as in maternal serum.[125] Many of these mothers do not have clinical manifestations of lupus, although some eventually progress to overt expression of the disease; others have clinical manifestations of Sjögren syndrome. The development of congenital complete heart block correlates with the presence of anti-SSA/Ro or anti-SSB/La antibodies, or both,[114] but the exact relationship of these antibodies to damage to the conduction system still is uncertain. Serum from infants younger than 3 months of age has been found to contain antibody; however, none has been identified in infants older than 6 months old, thus suggesting transplacental transfer of this antibody. The presence of fetal bradycardia resulting from complete heart block should suggest fetal SLE and prompt investigation of the antibody status of the mother. When hemodynamically significant, the bradycardia may cause fetal hydrops with ascites and pleural and pericardial effusions necessitating close serial assessment. Maternal treatment with steroids or plasmapheresis is of unclear benefit.[21, 22, 139, 153] Postmortem immunofluorescent studies have demonstrated antibody throughout the heart of an infant with congenital complete heart block and positive serology for anti-Ro (SSA).[92] The mother was clinically well and had a high serum antinuclear antibody titer. The cardiac examination was marked by elements of fibroelastosis, dystrophic calcification, and sparse inflammation, findings suggesting that intrauterine cardiac damage may result from maternally transferred autoantibody.

Reports in adults have demonstrated aortic and mitral regurgitation in individuals with antiphospholipid antibodies.[105] Fetal death followed by maternal death 28 hours later has been reported in a woman with elevated titers of anticardiolipin antibody. The fetal postmortem examination showed placental infarction and multiorgan infarction from intravascular thrombosis of small vessels.[8] Further investigation is necessary to determine whether the presence of these antiphospholipid antibodies can be used as a marker in children at risk for development of valvulitis.[24, 42]

Vasculitis

Endocarditis and valvulitis have been reported rarely in polyarteritis, Henoch-Schönlein vasculitis, and other vasculitis syndromes. The symptoms, signs, and diagnostic measures are similar to those described earlier. Aschoff bodies, thought by some researchers to be pathognomonic of rheumatic fever, have been described in vasculitis.[38]

Aortic valvular disease, with resultant aortic insufficiency, is one of the cardinal findings in Cogan syndrome,[25, 28] an unusual vasculitis variant characterized also by interstitial keratitis and nerve deafness. Histologic examination of affected valve leaflets has shown nonspecific acute and chronic inflammation with areas of fibrinoid necrosis but no demonstrable immunoglobulin or complement deposits. Therapy with corticosteroids has been considered helpful in some patients.

Takayasu aortitis, another vasculitis variant characterized by inflammation of the aorta and its major branches, also has been associated at times with endocarditis and valvular disease.[26]

Coronary Vasculitis

Coronary vasculitis, characterized by inflammation of the coronary blood vessels, occurs in several rheumatic disease syndromes, including SLE, polyarteritis nodosa and its variants, and Kawasaki disease. Inflamed vessels may become weakened, with the subsequent formation of an aneurysm, or become narrowed and produce coronary insufficiency or myocardial infarction. Coronary vasculitis may be entirely silent or may be associated with the subacute anginal symptoms of chest pain or with the sudden catastrophic symptoms of massive myocardial infarction or ruptured coronary aneurysm (severe chest pain, tachycardia, vascular collapse, sudden heart failure). The diagnosis of coronary vasculitis is difficult to make antemortem. Electrocardiographic changes suggestive of myocardial ischemia or myocardial infarction, echocardiograms showing coronary aneurysms, and increased serum levels of enzymes found in myocardial muscle may be helpful. Coronary arteriography, if necessary, may be diagnostic.

SYSTEMIC LUPUS ERYTHEMATOSUS

Coronary vasculitis probably occurs in a significant number of patients with SLE as part of a systemic vasculitis.[13, 34, 67, 126] Such coronary vasculitis is largely subclinical; any symptoms of chest pain may be difficult to differentiate from those of the pericarditis that occurs so commonly in patients with SLE.

Myocardial infarction is emerging as a cause of death in relatively young patients with SLE,[45, 68, 99, 112, 142] including children. Histologic changes postmortem may show accelerated atherosclerosis of coronary vessels, indistinguishable from the atherosclerotic heart disease of older patients. The role of SLE coronary vasculitis in initiating or accelerating this process is not known; other possible risk factors include the nephrotic syndrome, prolonged corticosteroid therapy, hypertension, familial atherosclerosis, and diabetes.

POLYARTERITIS NODOSA

Coronary vasculitis is a known concomitant of polyarteritis nodosa.[61, 111, 114] Massive myocardial infarction or ruptured aneurysms have been reported; smaller foci of myocardial damage may contribute to the "myocarditis" damage occasionally seen in polyarteritis nodosa. The symptoms, signs, and diagnostic measures are similar to those described earlier. Coronary arteriography might be diagnostic in some patients. Therapy with corticosteroids and perhaps with some of the cytotoxic agents is warranted, although not uniformly successful in severe polyarteritis nodosa.

Infantile Polyarteritis Nodosa

Infantile polyarteritis nodosa has been considered a rare variant of polyarteritis nodosa that is seen almost exclusively in infants and young children. Coronary vasculitis is the cardinal manifestation, and indeed, sometimes the coronary vessels are the sole site of vasculitis.[75, 104, 116] The distribution of vascular involvement is peculiar; relatively large coronary vessels and other visceral vessels (such as the mesenteric arteries) are affected, but smaller vessels (such as those of muscle and skin) usually are spared. This condition now is generally considered to be very similar, if not identical to, Kawasaki disease.

KAWASAKI DISEASE

A fascinating constellation of signs designated as Kawasaki disease (see also Chapter 82) was noted initially in Japan and later in many other countries[44, 73, 76]; hundreds of

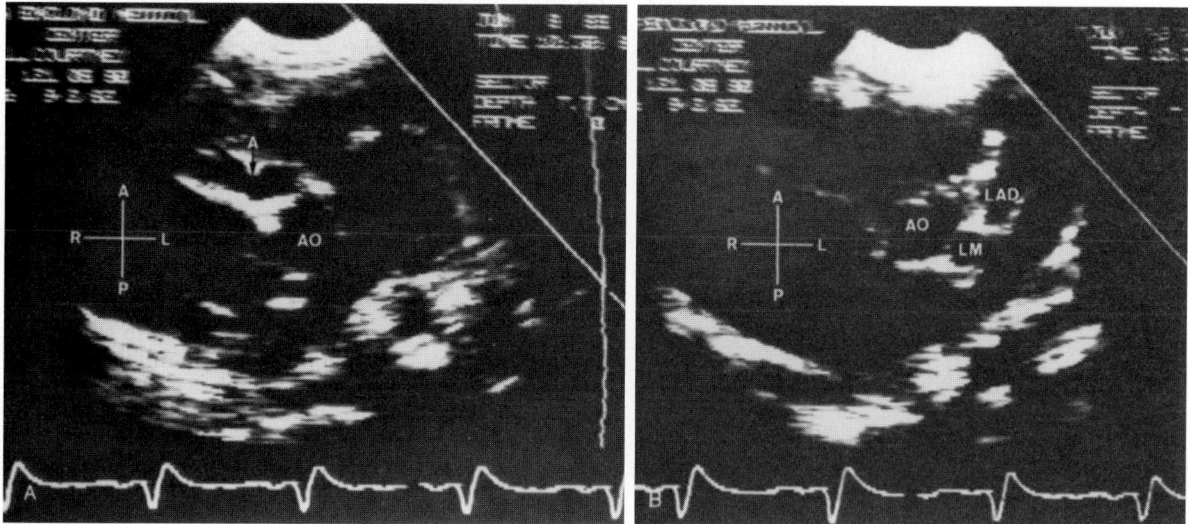

FIGURE 36–1 ■ *A,* Two-dimensional echocardiogram showing a cross-sectional short-axis view of the heart. The proximal right coronary artery (A) is dilated markedly after takeoff from the aortic root (AO). *B,* Two-dimensional echocardiogram of the aorta (AO) and left coronary artery in the same patient depicting aneurysm formation of the left main coronary artery (LM) and the left anterior descending coronary artery (LAD).

thousands of cases have been recognized in Japanese children. The disease has been noted with increasing frequency in the United States for the past 40 years.[84, 98] This disease affects children primarily in the first 5 years of life, although cases also occur in older children.[102]

The diagnosis rests entirely on clinical grounds: a characteristic combination of prolonged high fever, multiform rash, mucositis, conjunctivitis, erythema of the hands and feet with characteristic late peeling of the digits, and lymphadenopathy. An estimated 0.1 to 0.3 percent of children with Kawasaki disease die of coronary vasculitis and are found at autopsy to have changes indistinguishable from those of infantile polyarteritis nodosa.

No specific laboratory tests are diagnostic of the disease, but supportive evidence includes marked thrombocytosis. In addition, two-dimensional echocardiography has demonstrated accurately dilatation and aneurysms of the proximal coronary arteries (Fig. 36–1), as well as less specific signs of cardiac inflammation, including abnormal ventricular wall motion, pericardial effusion, mitral regurgitation, and diminished cardiac function.[27, 55, 94, 120, 155] Arteriography has confirmed coronary abnormalities in 15 to 20 percent of untreated children with Kawasaki disease (Figs. 36–2 and 36–3), and of those affected, approximately 50 percent will be noted to undergo regression of lesions by echocardiography, arteriography, or both modalities[72, 119] (Fig. 36–4).

After a clinical diagnosis in the acute stage of the illness has been made, the treatment of choice is high-dose intravenous gamma-globulin. Efficacy has been demonstrated in several studies using total doses between 1 and 2 g/kg given

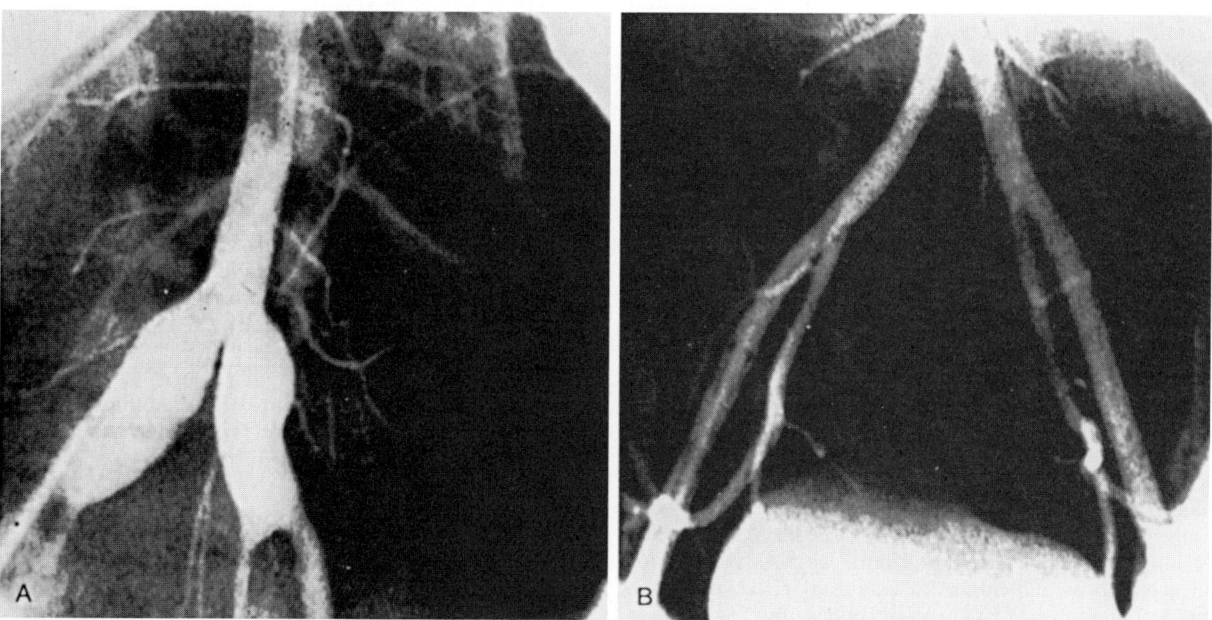

FIGURE 36–2 ■ *A,* Angiogram made in the abdominal aorta of a 3-year-old girl showing bilateral aneurysms of the iliac arteries 2 months after the onset of Kawasaki disease. *B,* A repeat study 1 year later shows dramatic improvement in both vessels.

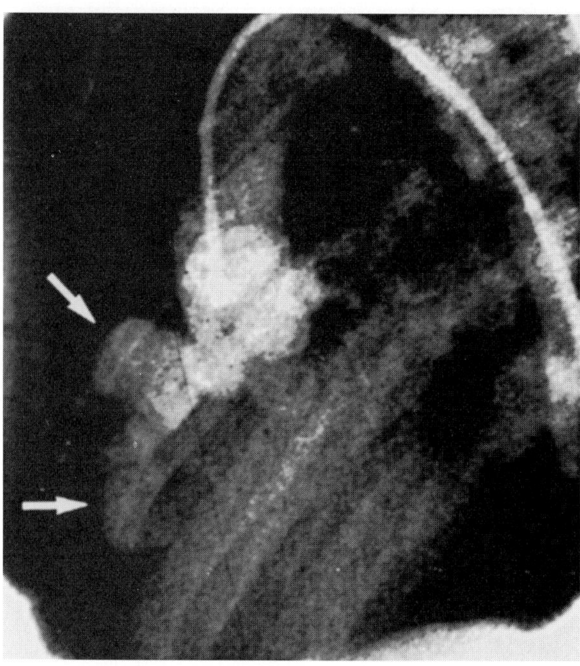

FIGURE 36–3 ■ Multiple aneurysms of the right coronary artery *(arrows)* delineated by an aortic root angiogram in a 3-year-old girl 2 months after the onset of Kawasaki disease.

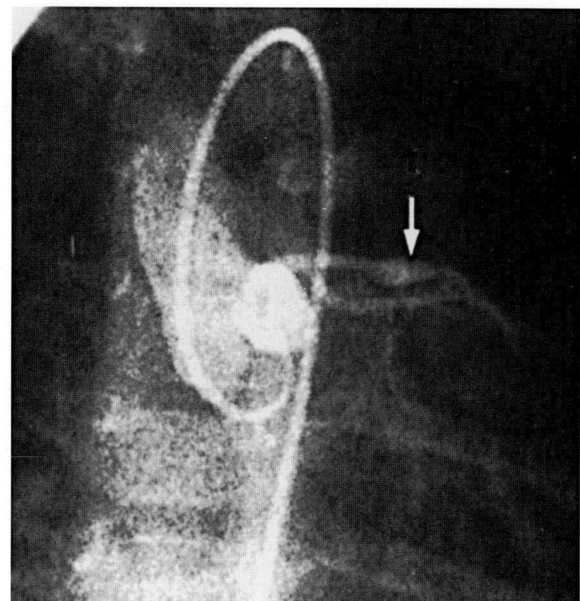

FIGURE 36–4 ■ Aortic root cineangiogram of an isolated aneurysm of the left coronary artery system in a 2-year-old boy.

as a course either in a single dose or divided over as many as 4 days.[107, 108, 143] The widely accepted regimen is to treat with 2 g/kg as a single dose administered over the course of 8 to 12 hours. Complications associated with intravenous immunoglobulin treatment seldom occur and usually are minor (rash, fever, edema), although in some children congestive heart failure may be precipitated or exacerbated. Preparations currently in use have not resulted in documented transmission of human immunodeficiency virus infection.

Salicylates are used as adjunctive therapy at 100 mg/kg/day in four divided doses until the patient is afebrile and then continued on a 5-mg/kg dose schedule during the early acute phase because activation of coagulation has been shown to occur in the first 3 weeks of the illness.[19] Elevations in beta-thromboglobulin, thromboxane A_2, and thromboxane B_2 support the theory of platelet activation in this illness and suggest a need for antiplatelet therapy.[19, 58] Simultaneously, the low plasma prostacyclin levels present in the first week of the illness suggest endothelial cell dysfunction related to the vasculitis. These levels remain low through the first 2 months of illness. The relationship of high thromboxane and low prostacyclin levels in this disease may predispose to the development of coronary vasoconstriction and platelet aggregation potentiating ischemia. Corticosteroid therapy, once considered detrimental, now is considered useful in selected cases that do not respond to immunoglobulin therapy.[113, 128, 152]

In the presence of persistent coronary abnormalities, low-dose aspirin is continued indefinitely. Giant aneurysms, defined as lesions exceeding 8 mm in diameter, are associated more frequently with myocardial ischemia, myocardial infarction, or death. Although more aggressive therapy would seem to be indicated, no single approach has been accepted universally. Most clinicians choose to add warfarin therapy to low-dose aspirin until the aneurysms decrease to less than 8 mm in diameter. The surgical experience involving aortocoronary bypass grafting for symptomatic patients or for critically narrowed vessels in the absence of symptoms has improved greatly.[80, 118, 133, 147] Balloon angioplasty has not been widely successful and may predispose to rupture of calcified vessels. The early Japanese experience with Rotablator therapy is promising. The prevalence of this disease and the uncertain impact on the expected acquired atherosclerotic lesions of the population necessitate continued follow-up by cardiologists. Long-term evaluation is important, particularly for patients with known vascular involvement.[32, 47]

The etiology of Kawasaki disease remains elusive,[44] as does its greater frequency in Japan than in other countries.[35] Most investigators continue to suspect an infectious etiology, but debate continues regarding whether a conventional antigen or a superantigen is instrumental. Why primary Kawasaki disease is so rare in adults also has not been explained,[141] although some children who have had Kawasaki disease clearly may have cardiovascular manifestations in early adulthood.[57]

REFERENCES

1. Aiuto, L. T., Stambouly, J. J., and Boxer, P. A.: Cardiac tamponade in an adolescent female: An unusual manifestation of systemic lupus erythematosus. Clin. Pediatr. (Phila.) *32*:500–567, 1993.
2. Al-Abbad, A. J., Cabral, D. A., Sanatani, S., et al.: Echocardiography and pulmonary function testing in childhood onset systemic lupus erythematosus. Lupus *10*:32–27, 2001.
3. Allen, D. M., Diamond, L. K., and Howell, D. A.: Anaphylactoid purpura in children (Henoch-Schönlein syndrome). Am. J. Dis. Child. *99*:833–854, 1960.
4. Alterburger, K. M., Jedziniak, M., Roper, W. L., et al.: Congenital complete heart block associated with hydrops fetalis. J. Pediatr. *91*:618–620, 1977.
5. Askanase, A. D., Friedman, D. M., Copel, J., et al.: Spectrum and progression of conduction abnormalities in infants born to mothers with anti-SSA/Ro-SSB/La antibodies. Lupus *11*:145–151, 2002.
6. Bacon, P. A., and Gibson, D. G.: Cardiac involvement in rheumatoid arthritis. Ann. Rheum. Dis. *33*:20–24, 1974.

7. Bastos, C. J., Queiroz, A. C., and Martinelli, R.: Cardiac involvement in systemic lupus erythematosus: Anatomopathological study. Rev. Assoc. Med. Bras. *39*:161–164, 1993.
8. Bendon, R. W., Wilson, J., Getahun, B., et al.: A maternal death due to thrombotic disease associated with anticardiolipin antibody. Arch. Pathol. Lab. Med. *111*:370–372, 1987.
9. Bernhard, G. C., Lange, R. L., and Hensly, G. T.: Aortic disease with valvular insufficiency as the principal manifestation of systemic lupus erythematosus. Ann. Intern. Med. *71*:81–87, 1969.
10. Bernstein, B., Takahashi, M., and Hanson, V.: Cardiac involvement in juvenile rheumatoid arthritis. J. Pediatr. *85*:313–317, 1974.
11. Bilazarian, S. D., Taylor, A. J., Brezinski, D., et al.: High-grade atrioventricular heart block in an adult with systemic lupus erythematosus: The association of nuclear RNP (U1 RNP) antibodies, a case report, and review of the literature. Arthritis Rheum. *32*:1170–1174, 1989.
12. Bonfiglio, T., and Atwater, E. C.: Heart disease in patients with seropositive rheumatoid arthritis: A controlled autopsy study and review. Arch. Intern. Med. *124*:714–719, 1969.
13. Bonfiglio, T., Botti, R., and Hagstrom, J.: Coronary arthritis, occlusion, and myocardial infarction due to lupus erythematosus. Am. Heart J. *83*:153–158, 1972.
14. Borenstein, D. G., Fye, W. B., Arnett, F. C., et al.: The myocarditis of systemic lupus erythematosus: Association with myocarditis. Ann. Intern. Med. *89*:619–624, 1978.
15. Botstein, G. R., and LeRoy, E. C.: Primary heart disease in systemic sclerosis (scleroderma): Advances in clinical and pathologic features, pathogenesis, and new therapeutic approaches. Am. Heart J. *102*:913–919, 1981.
16. Bottiger, L. E., and Edhag, O.: Heart block in ankylosing spondylitis and uropolyarthritis. Br. Heart J. *34*:487–492, 1972.
17. Browning, C. A., Bishop, R. L., Heilpern, R. J., et al.: Accelerated constrictive pericarditis in procainamide-induced systemic lupus erythematosus. Am. J. Cardiol. *53*:376–377, 1984.
18. Bulkley, B. H., Ridolfi, R., Salyer, W. R., et al.: Myocardial lesions of progressive systemic sclerosis: A cause of cardiac dysfunction. Circulation *53*:483–490, 1976.
19. Burns, J. C., Glode, M. P., Clarke, S. H., et al.: Coagulopathy and platelet activation in Kawasaki syndrome: Identification of patients with high risk for development of coronary artery aneurysms. J. Pediatr. *105*:206–211, 1984.
20. Buyon, J. P.: Neonatal lupus: Bedside to bench and back. Scand. J. Rheumatol. *25*:271–276, 1996.
21. Buyon, J., Roubey, R., Swersky, S., et al.: Complete congenital heart block: Risk of occurrence and therapeutic approach to prevention. J. Rheumatol. *15*:1104–1108, 1988.
22. Carreira, P. E., Guiterrez-Larraya, F., and Gomez-Reino, J. J.: Successful intrauterine therapy with dexamethasone for fetal myocarditis and heart block in a woman with systemic lupus erythematosus. J. Rheumatol. *20*:1204–1207, 1993.
23. Chameides, L., Truex, R. C., Vetter, V., et al.: Association of maternal systemic lupus erythematosus with congenital complete heart block. N. Engl. J. Med. *297*:1204–1207, 1977.
24. Chartash, E., Lang, D. M., Paget, S. A., et al.: Aortic insufficiency and mitral regurgitation in patients with systemic lupus erythematosus and the antiphospholipid syndrome. Am. J. Med. *86*:407–412, 1989.
25. Cheson, B. D., Bluming, A. Z., and Alroy, J.: Cogan's syndrome: A systemic vasculitis. Am. J. Med. *60*:549–555, 1976.
26. Chhetri, M. K., Pal, N. C., Neelakantan, C., et al.: Endocardial lesion in a case of Takayasu's arteriopathy. Br. Heart J. *32*:859–862, 1970.
27. Chung, K. J., Brandt, L., Fulton, D. R., et al.: Cardiac and coronary arterial involvement in infants and children from New England with mucocutaneous lymph node syndrome (Kawasaki disease): Angiocardiographic-echocardiographic correlations. Am. J. Cardiol. *50*:136–142, 1982.
28. Cogan, D. G., and Dickersin, G. R.: Nonsyphilitic interstitial keratitis with vestibuloauditory symptoms. Arch. Ophthalmol. *71*:172–175, 1964.
29. Collins, R. L., Turner, R. A., Nomeir, A. M., et al.: Cardiopulmonary manifestations of systemic lupus erythematosus. J. Rheumatol. *5*:299–306, 1978.
30. Cooper, D. K. C., Cleland, W. P., and Bentall, H. H.: Collagen diseases as a cause of constrictive pericarditis. Thorax *33*:368–371, 1978.
31. Costallat, L. T., and Coimbra, A. M.: Systemic lupus erythematosus: Clinical and laboratory aspects related to age at disease onset. Clin. Exp. Rheum. *12*:603–607, 1994.
32. Dajani, A. S., Taubert, K. A., Takahashi, M., et al.: Guidelines for long-term management of patients with Kawasaki disease. Report from the Committee on Rheumatic Fever, Endocarditis, and Kawasaki Disease, Council on Cardiovascular Disease in the Young, American Heart Association. Circulation *89*:916–922, 1994.
33. Denbow, C. E., Lie, J. T., Tancredi, R. G., et al.: Cardiac involvement in polymyositis: A clinicopathologic study of 20 autopsied patients. Arthritis Rheum. *22*:1088–1092, 1979.
34. Doherty, N. E., and Siegel, R. J.: Cardiovascular manifestations of systemic lupus erythematosus. Am. Heart J. *110*:1257–1265, 1985.
35. Du, Z. D., Zhang, T., Liang, L., et al.: Epidemiologic picture of Kawasaki disease in Beijing from 1995 through 1999. Pediatr. Infect. Dis. J. *21*:103–107, 2002.
36. Durand, I., Blaysat, G., Chauvaud, S., et al.: Extensive fibrous endocarditis as first manifestation of systemic lupus erythematosus. Arch. Pediatr. *50*:685–688, 1993.
37. Elkayam, V., Weiss, S., and Laniado, S.: Pericardial effusion and mitral valve involvement in systemic lupus erythematosus. Ann. Rheum. Dis. *36*:349–353, 1977.
38. Fogel, B. J., Weinberg, T., and Markowitz, M.: A fatal connective tissue disease following a wasp sting. Am. J. Dis. Child. *114*:325–329, 1967.
39. Follansbee, W. P., Curtiss, E. I., Medoger, T. A., et al.: Physiologic abnormalities of cardiac function in progressive systemic sclerosis with diffuse scleroderma. N. Engl. J. Med. *310*:142–148, 1984.
40. Follansbee, W. P., Curtiss, E. I., and Ranko, P. S.: The electrocardiogram in systemic sclerosis (scleroderma): Study of 102 consecutive cases with functional correlations and review of the literature. Am. J. Med. *79*:183–192, 1985.
41. Follansbee, W. P., Zerbe, T. R., and Medsger, T. A.: Cardiac and skeletal muscle disease in systemic sclerosis (scleroderma): A high-risk association. Am. Heart J. *125*:194–203, 1993.
42. Ford, P. M., Ford, S. E., and Lillicrap, D. P.: Association of lupus anticoagulant with severe valvar heart disease in systemic lupus erythematosus. J. Rheumatol. *15*:597–600, 1988.
43. Franco, A. E., Levine, H. D., and Hall, A. P.: Rheumatoid pericarditis: Report of 17 cases diagnosed clinically. Ann. Intern. Med. *77*:837–844, 1972.
44. Freeman, A. F., and Shulman, S. T.: Recent developments in Kawasaki disease. Curr. Opin. Infect. Dis. *14*:357–361, 2001.
45. Friedman, D. M., Lazanas, H. M., and Fierman, A. H.: Acute myocardial infarction in pediatric systemic lupus erythematosus. J. Pediatr. *117*:263–266, 1990.
46. Fulton, D. R., Meissner, H. C., and Peterson, M. B.: Effects of current therapy of Kawasaki disease on eicosanoid metabolism. Am. J. Cardiol. *61*:1323–1327, 1988.
47. Fulton, D. R., and Newburger, J. W.: Long-term cardiac sequelae of Kawasaki disease. Curr. Rheumatol. Rep. *2*:324–329, 2000.
48. Furusho, K., Sato, K., Soeda, T., et al.: High-dose intravenous gammaglobulin for Kawasaki disease. Lancet *2*:1359, 1983.
49. Galve, E., Candell-Riera, J., Pierau, C., et al.: Prevalence, morphologic types, and evolution of cardiac valvular disease in systemic lupus erythematosus. N. Engl. J. Med. *319*:817–823, 1988.
50. Gladman, G., Silverman, E. D., Yuk-Law, et al.: Fetal echocardiographic screening of pregnancies of mothers with anti-Ro and/or anti-La antibodies. Am. J. Perinatol. *19*:73–80, 2002.
51. Goldenberg, J., Ferraz, M. B., Pessoa, A. P., et al.: Symptomatic cardiac involvement in juvenile rheumatoid arthritis. Int. J. Cardiol. *34*:57–62, 1992.
52. Graham, D. C., and Smythe, H. A.: The carditis and aortitis of ankylosing spondylitis. Bull. Rheum. Dis. *9*:171–174, 1958.
53. Grenadier, E., Allen, H. D., Goldberg, S. J., et al.: Left ventricular wall motion abnormalities in Kawasaki's disease. Am. Heart J. *107*:966–973, 1984.
54. Guevara, J. P., Clark, B. J., and Athreya, B. H.: Point prevalence of cardiac abnormalities in children with systemic lupus erythematosus. J. Rheumatol. *28*:854–859, 2001.
55. Hamashima, Y., Kishi, K., and Tasaka, K.: Rickettsia-like bodies in infantile acute febrile mucocutaneous lymph node syndrome. Lancet *2*:42, 1973.
56. Harvey, A., Shulman, L., Tumulty, P., et al.: Systemic lupus erythematosus: A review of the literature and clinical analysis of 138 cases. Medicine (Baltimore) *33*:291–437, 1954.
57. Hayashida, N., Tayama, E., Teshima, H., et al.: Coronary artery bypass grafting in an adult case with Kawasaki disease. Ann. Thorac. Cardiovasc. Surg. *8*:47–50, 2002.
58. Hidaka, T., Nakano, M., Ueta, T., et al.: Increased synthesis of thromboxane A_2 by platelets from patients with Kawasaki disease. J. Pediatr. *102*:94–96, 1983.
59. Hoffman, F. G., and Leight, L.: Complete atrioventricular block associated with rheumatoid disease. Am. J. Cardiol. *16*:585–592, 1965.
60. Hogg, G. R.: Congenital acute lupus erythematosus associated with subendocardial fibroelastosis. Am. J. Clin. Pathol. *28*:648–654, 1957.
61. Holsinger, D. R., Osmundson, P. J., and Edwards, J. E.: The heart in periarteritis nodosa. Circulation *25*:610–618, 1962.
62. Hull, D., Binns, B. A. O., and Joyce, D.: Congenital heart block and widespread fibrosis due to maternal lupus erythematosus. Arch. Dis. Child. *41*:688–690, 1966.
63. Huppertz, H., Voigt, I., Muller-Scholden, J., et al.: Cardiac manifestations in patients with HLA B27–associated juvenile arthritis. Pediatr. Cardiol. *21*:141–147, 2000.
64. Imai, T., and Matsumoto, S.: Anaphylactoid purpura with cardiac involvement. Arch. Dis. Child. *45*:727–729, 1970.
65. Jacobson, E. J., and Reza, M. L.: Constrictive pericarditis in systemic lupus erythematosus: Demonstration of immunoglobulins in the pericardium. Arthritis Rheum. *21*:972–974, 1978.

66. James, T. N.: De subitaneis mortibus. VIII. Coronary arteries and conduction system in scleroderma heart disease. Circulation *50*:844–856, 1974.
67. James, T., Rupe, C., and Monto, R.: Pathology of the cardiac conduction system in systemic lupus erythematosus. Ann. Intern. Med. *63*:402–410, 1965.
68. Jensen, G., and Sigurd, B.: Systemic lupus erythematosus and acute myocardial infarction. Chest *64*:653–654, 1973.
69. Johnson, R. T., Portnoy, B., Rogers, N. G., et al.: Acute benign pericarditis: Virologic study of 34 patients. Arch. Intern. Med. *108*:823–832, 1961.
70. Jordan, J. M., Valenstein, P., and Kredich, D. W.: Systemic lupus erythematosus with Libman-Sachs endocarditis in a 9-month-old infant with neonatal lupus erythematosus and congenital heart block. Pediatrics *84*:574–578, 1989.
71. Kahl, L. E.: The spectrum of pericardial tamponade in systemic lupus erythematosus. Arthritis Rheum. *35*:1343–1349, 1992.
72. Kato, H., Ichinose, E., Yoshioaka, F., et al.: Fate of coronary aneurysms in Kawasaki disease: Serial coronary angiography and long-term follow-up study. Am. J. Cardiol. *49*:1758–1766, 1982.
73. Kato, H., Koike, S., Yamamoto, M., et al.: Coronary aneurysms in infants and young children with acute febrile mucocutaneous lymph node syndrome. J. Pediatr. *86*:892–898, 1975.
74. Kato, H., Koike, S., and Yokoyama, T.: Kawasaki disease: Effect of treatment on coronary artery involvement. Pediatrics *63*:175–179, 1979.
75. Kawai, S., Okada, R., Sigimoto, H., et al.: An autopsied case of a 2-month-old infant with granulomatous pancarditis having severe vasculitis and valvulitis. Jpn. Circ. J. *47*:1325–1330, 1983.
76. Kawasaki, T., Kasaki, T., Kosaki, F., et al.: A new infantile acute febrile mucocutaneous lymph node syndrome (MLNS) prevailing in Japan. Pediatrics *54*:271–276, 1974.
77. Kijima, Y., Kamiya, T., Suzuki, A., et al.: A trial procedure to prevent aneurysm formation of the coronary arteries by steroid pulse therapy in Kawasaki disease. Jpn. Circ. J. *46*:1239–1242, 1982.
78. King, K. K., Kornreich, H. K., Bernstein, B. H., et al.: The clinical spectrum of systemic lupus erythematosus in childhood. Arthritis Rheum. *20*:287–294, 1977.
79. Kirk, J., and Cosh, J.: The pericarditis of rheumatoid arthritis. Q. J. Med. *38*:397–423, 1969.
80. Kitamura, S., Kawachi, K., Harima, R., et al.: Surgery for coronary heart disease due to mucocutaneous lymph node syndrome (Kawasaki disease): Report of six patients. Am. J. Cardiol. *51*:444–448, 1983.
81. Kitamura, S., Kawashima, Y., Fujita, T., et al.: Aortocoronary bypass grafting in a child with coronary artery obstruction due to mucocutaneous lymph node syndrome: Report of a case. Circulation *53*:1035–1040, 1975.
82. Kornreich, H. K., King, K. K., Bernstein, B. H., et al.: Scleroderma in childhood. Arthritis Rheum. *20*:343–350, 1977.
83. Kusakawa, S., and Heiner, D. C.: Elevated level of immunoglobulin E in the acute febrile mucocutaneous lymph node syndrome. Pediatr. Res. *10*:108–111, 1976.
84. Landing, B. H., and Larson, E. J.: Are infantile periarteritis nodosa with coronary artery involvement and fatal mucocutaneous lymph node syndrome the same? Comparison of 20 patients from North America with patients from Hawaii and Japan. Pediatrics *59*:651–662, 1977.
85. Latinen, O., Kentala, E., and Leirisalo, M.: Electrocardiographic findings in patients with connective heart disease. Scand. J. Rheumatol. *7*:193–198, 1978.
86. Lebowitz, W. B.: The heart in rheumatoid arthritis (rheumatoid disease): A clinical and pathological study of 62 cases. Ann. Intern. Med. *58*:102–123, 1963.
87. Lee, L. A.: Neonatal lupus: Clinical features, therapy, and pathogenesis. Curr. Rheumatol. Rep. *3*:391–395, 2001.
88. Leung, D. Y. M., Chu, E. T., Wood, N., et al.: Immunoregulatory T cell abnormalities in mucocutaneous lymph node syndrome. J. Immunol. *130*:2002–2004, 1983.
89. Leung, D. Y. M., Meissner, H. C., Fulton, D. R., et al.: Toxic shock syndrome toxin–secreting *Staphylococcus aureus* in Kawasaki syndrome. Lancet *342*:1385–1388, 1993.
90. Leung, D. Y. M., Seigel, L., Grady, S., et al.: Immunoregulatory abnormalities in mucocutaneous lymph node syndrome. Clin. Immunol. Immunopathol. *23*:100–112, 1982.
91. Lietman, P. S., and Bywaters, E. G. L.: Pericarditis in juvenile rheumatoid arthritis. Pediatrics *32*:855–860, 1963.
92. Litsey, S. E., Noonan, J. A., O'Connor, W. N., et al.: Maternal connective tissue disease and congenital heart block: Demonstration of immunoglobulin in cardiac tissue. N. Engl. J. Med. *312*:98–100, 1985.
93. Lynch, P. G.: Cardiac involvement in chronic polymyositis. Br. Heart J. *33*:416–419, 1971.
94. Maeda, T., Yoshida, H., Funabashki, T., et al.: Subcostal 2-dimensional echocardiographic imaging of peripheral left coronary artery aneurysms in Kawasaki disease. Am. J. Cardiol. *52*:48–52, 1983.
95. Marin-Garcia, J., Sheridan, R., and Hanissian, A. S.: Echocardiographic detection of early cardiac involvement in juvenile rheumatoid arthritis. Pediatrics *73*:394–397, 1984.
96. McCue, C. M., Mantakas, M. E., Tingelstad, J. B., et al.: Congenital heart block in newborns of mothers with connective tissue disease. Circulation *56*:82–90, 1977.
97. McWhorter, J. E., IV, and LeRoy, E. C.: Pericardial disease in scleroderma (systemic sclerosis). Am. J. Med. *56*:566–575, 1974.
98. Melish, M. E., Hicks, R. M., and Larson, E. J.: Mucocutaneous lymph node syndrome in the United States. Am. J. Dis. Child. *130*:599–607, 1976.
99. Meller, J., Conde, C. A., Deppisch, L. M., et al.: Myocardial infarction due to coronary atherosclerosis in three young adults with systemic lupus erythematosus. Am. J. Cardiol. *35*:309–314, 1975.
100. Miller, J. J., III: Carditis in juvenile rheumatoid arthritis. Arthritis Rheum. *20*:243, 1977.
101. Miller, J. J., and French, J. W.: Myocarditis in juvenile rheumatoid arthritis. Am. J. Dis. Child. *131*:205–209, 1977.
102. Momenah, T., Sanatani, S., Potts, J., et al.: Kawasaki disease in the older child. Pediatrics *102*:e7, 1998.
103. Muers, M., and Stokes, W.: Treatment of scleroderma heart by D-penicillamine. Br. Heart J. *38*:864–867, 1976.
104. Munro-Faure, H.: Necrotizing arteritis of the coronary vessels in infancy: Case report and review of the literature. Pediatrics *23*:914–926, 1959.
105. Nayak, A. K., and Komatireddy, G.: Cardiac manifestations of the antiphospholipid antibody syndrome: A review. Mo. Med. *99*:171–178, 2002.
106. Neu, L. T., Jr., Reider, R. A., and Mack, R. E.: Cardiac involvement in Reiter's disease: Report of a case with review of the literature. Ann. Intern. Med. *53*:215–220, 1960.
107. Newburger, J. W., Takahashi, M., Beiser, A. S., et al.: A single intravenous infusion of gammaglobulin as compared with four infusions in the treatment of acute Kawasaki syndrome. N. Engl. J. Med. *324*:1633–1639, 1991.
108. Newburger, J. W., Takahashi, M., Burns, J. C., et al.: The treatment of Kawasaki syndrome with intravenous gamma globulin. N. Engl. J. Med. *315*:341–347, 1986.
109. Nomeir, A. M., Turner, R., and Watts, E.: Cardiac involvement in rheumatoid arthritis. Ann. Intern. Med. *79*:800–806, 1973.
110. Permanyer-Miralda, G., Sagristà-Sauleda, J., and Soler-Soler, J.: Primary acute pericardial disease: A prospective series of 231 consecutive patients. Am. J. Cardiol. *56*:623–630, 1985.
111. Przybojewski, J. K.: Polyarteritis nodosa in the adult. S. Afr. Med. J. *60*:512–518, 1984.
112. Rahman, P., Urowitz, M. B., Gladman, D. D., et al.: Contribution of traditional risk factors to coronary artery disease in patients with systemic lupus erythematosus. J. Rheumatol. *26*:2363–2368, 1999.
113. Raman, V., Kim, J., Sharkey, A., et al.: Response of refractory Kawasaki disease to pulse steroid and cyclosporin A therapy. Pediatr. Infect. Dis. J. *20*:635–637, 2001.
114. Ramsey-Goldman, R., Hom, D., Deng, J. S., et al.: Anti SS-A antibodies and fetal outcome in maternal systemic lupus erythematosus. Arthritis Rheum. *29*:1269–1273, 1986.
115. Reidbord, H. E., McCormack, L. J., and O'Duffy, J. D.: Necrotizing angiitis. II. Findings at autopsy in twenty-seven cases. Cleve. Clin. Q. *32*:191–204, 1965.
116. Roberts, F. B., and Fetterman, G. H.: Polyarteritis nodosa in infancy. J. Pediatr. *63*:519–529, 1963.
117. Sackner, M., Heinz, E., and Steinberg, A.: The heart in scleroderma. Am. J. Cardiol. *17*:542–559, 1966.
118. Sandiford, F. M., Vargo, T. A., Shih, J., et al.: Successful triple coronary artery bypass in a child with multiple coronary aneurysms due to Kawasaki's disease. J. Thorac. Cardiovasc. Surg. *79*:283–287, 1980.
119. Sasaguri, Y., and Kato, H.: Regression of aneurysms in Kawasaki disease: A pathological study. J. Pediatr. *100*:225–231, 1982.
120. Satomi, G., Nakamura, K., Narai, S., et al.: Systemic visualization of coronary arteries by two-dimensional echocardiography in children and infants: Evaluation in Kawasaki's disease and coronary arteriovenous fistulas. Am. Heart J. *107*:497–505, 1984.
121. Schaller, J. G.: Lupus phenomena in the newborn. Arthritis Rheum. *20*:312–314, 1977.
122. Schaller, J., and Wedgwood, R. J.: Is juvenile rheumatoid arthritis a single disease? A review. Pediatrics *50*:940–953, 1972.
123. Schaumberg, H. H., Nielsen, S. L., and Yurchak, P. M.: Heart block in polymyositis. N. Engl. J. Med. *284*:480–481, 1971.
124. Schoof, P. H., Cromme-Digkhuis, A. H., Bogers, A. J. J. C., et al.: Aortic root replacement with pulmonary autograft in children. J. Thorac. Cardiovasc. Surg. *107*:367–373, 1994.
125. Scott, J. S., Maddison, P. J., Taylor, P. V., et al.: Connective tissue disease, antibodies to ribonucleoprotein, and congenital heart block. N. Engl. J. Med. *309*:209–212, 1983.
126. Seaman, A. J., and Christerson, J. W.: Demonstration of L. E. cells in pericardial fluid: Report of a case. J. A. M. A. *149*:145–147, 1952.
127. Sharp, G. C., Irvin, W. S., Tan, E. M., et al.: Mixed connective tissue disease: An apparently distinct rheumatic disease syndrome associated with a specific antibody to an extractable nuclear antigen (ENA). Am. J. Med. *52*:148–159, 1972.

128. Shinohara, M., Sone, K., Tomomasa, T., et al.: Corticosteroids in the treatment of the acute phase of Kawasaki disease. J. Pediatr. *135*:411–413, 1999.
129. Singsen, B. H., Bernstein, B. H., Kornreich, H. K., et al.: Mixed connective tissue disease in childhood: A clinical and serologic survey. J. Pediatr. *90*:893–900, 1977.
130. Singsen, B. H., Goldreyer, B., Stanton, R., et al.: Childhood polymyositis with cardiac conduction defects. Am. J. Dis. Child. *130*:72–74, 1976.
131. Smith, J. W., Clements, P. J., Levismen, J., et al.: Echocardiographic features of progressive systemic sclerosis (PSS): Correlation with hemodynamic and post mortem studies. Am. J. Med. *66*:28–33, 1979.
132. Sokoloff, L.: Cardiac involvement in rheumatoid arthritis and allied disorders: Current concepts. Mod. Concepts Cardiovasc. Dis. *33*: 847–850, 1964.
133. Suma, K., Takeuchi, Y., Shiroma, K., et al.: Early and late postoperative studies in coronary arterial lesions resulting from Kawasaki's disease in children. J. Thorac. Cardiovasc. Surg. *84*:224–229, 1983.
134. Sunder, S. K., and Shah, A.: Constrictive pericarditis in procainamide-induced lupus erythematosus syndrome. Am. J. Cardiol. *36*:960–962, 1975.
135. Svantesson, H., Bjorkhem, G., and Elborough, R.: Cardiac involvement in juvenile rheumatoid arthritis: A follow-up study. Acta Paediatr. Scand. *72*:345–350, 1983.
136. Takkunen, J., Vuopala, V., and Isomaki, H.: Cardiomyopathy in ankylosing spondylitis. I. Medical history and results of clinical examination in a series of 55 patients. Ann. Clin. Res. *2*:106–112, 1970.
137. Tami, L. F., and Bhasin, S.: Polymorphism of the cardiac manifestations in dermatomyositis. Clin. Cardiol. *16*:260–264, 1993.
138. Thadani, U., Iveson, J. M. I., and Wright, V.: Cardiac tamponade, constrictive pericarditis and pericardial resection in rheumatoid arthritis. Medicine (Baltimore) *54*:261–270, 1975.
139. Theander, E., Brucato, A., Gudmundsson, S., et al.: Primary Sjögren's syndrome—treatment of fetal incomplete atrioventricular block with dexamethasone. J. Rheumatol. *28*:373–376, 2001.
140. Thomas, D., Hill, W., Geddes, R., et al.: Early detection of aortic dilatation in ankylosing spondylitis using echocardiography. Aust. N. Z. J. Med. *12*:10–13, 1982.
141. Tomiyama, J., Hasegawa, Y., Kumagai, Y., et al.: Acute febrile mucocutaneous lymph node syndrome (Kawasaki disease) in adults: Case report and review of the literature. Jpn. J. Med. *30*:285–289, 1991.
142. Tsakraklides, V. G., Bleiden, L. C., and Edwards, J. E.: Coronary atherosclerosis and myocardial infarction associated with systemic lupus erythematosus. Am. Heart J. *87*:637–641, 1974.
143. Tse, S. M., Silverman, E. D., McCrindle, B. W., et al.: Early treatment with intravenous immunoglobulin in patients with Kawasaki disease. J. Pediatr. *140*:450–455, 2002.
144. Uhl, G. S., and Koppes, G. M.: Pericardial tamponade in systemic sclerosis (scleroderma). Br. Heart J. *42*:345–348, 1979.
145. van Suylen, R. J., Schoof, P. H., Bos, E., et al.: Pulmonary autograft failure after aortic root replacement in a patient with juvenile rheumatoid arthritis. Eur. J. Cardiothorac. Surg. *6*:571–572, 1992.
146. Vonderheid, E. C., Koblenzer, P. J., Ming, P. M. L., et al.: Neonatal lupus erythematosus. Arch. Dermatol. *112*:698–705, 1976.
147. Wada, J., Endo, M., Takao, A., et al.: Mucocutaneous lymph node syndrome: Successful aortocoronary bypass homograft in a four-year-old boy. Chest *77*:443–446, 1980.
148. Watson, R. M., Lane, A. T., Barnett, N. K., et al.: Neonatal lupus erythematosus: A clinical, serological and immunogenetic study with review of literature. Medicine (Baltimore) *63*:362–378, 1984.
149. West, S. G., Killian, P. J., and Lawless, O. J.: Association of myositis and myocarditis in progressive systemic sclerosis. Arthritis Rheum. *22*:1088–1092, 1979.
150. White, P. H.: Pediatric systemic lupus erythematosus and neonatal lupus. Rheum. Dis. Clin. North Am. *20*:119–127, 1994.
151. Wolff, L., and Grunfeld, O.: Pericarditis. N. Engl. J. Med. *268*:419–426, 1963.
152. Wright, D. A., Newburger, J. W., Baker, A., et al.: Treatment of immune globulin-resistant Kawasaki disease with pulsed doses of corticosteroids. J. Pediatr. *128*:146–149, 1996.
153. Yamada, H., Kata, E. H., Ebina, Y., et al.: Fetal treatment of congenital heart block ascribed to anti-SSA antibody: Case reports with observation of cardiohemodynamics and review of the literature. Am. J. Reprod. Immunol. *42*:226–232, 1999.
154. Yancy, C. L., Doughty, R. A., Cohlan, B. A., et al.: Pericarditis and cardiac tamponade in juvenile rheumatoid arthritis. Pediatrics *68*:369–373, 1981.
155. Yoshikawa, J., Yanagihara, K., Owaki, T., et al.: Cross-sectional echocardiographic diagnosis of coronary artery aneurysms in patients with the mucocutaneous lymph node syndrome. Circulation *59*:133–139, 1979.

Mediastinitis

MORVEN S. EDWARDS

The mediastinum includes the extrapleural portion of the thoracic cavity situated between the two pleural sacs. The superior and inferior portions are separated arbitrarily by a line extending from the lower manubrium to the fourth thoracic vertebra. The superior mediastinum contains the thymus gland, trachea, esophagus, and aortic arch. The inferior mediastinum is divided into the anterior compartment, containing lymphatic tissue and fat; the middle compartment, containing the heart, pericardium, aorta, bifurcation of the trachea, main bronchi, and numerous lymph nodes; and the posterior compartment, containing the esophagus, thoracic duct, descending aorta, and vagus nerve. Infections of the mediastinum are relatively uncommon, but they often pose a serious threat to the vital structures in the vicinity and may prove extremely difficult to diagnose. Two forms are recognized: acute mediastinitis, which is a fulminant, septic process, and chronic mediastinitis, which is an indolent infection that produces late symptoms caused by compression of adjacent structures.

Acute Mediastinitis

The major causes of acute mediastinitis are classified etiologically as traumatic perforation of the esophagus, nontraumatic extension from extramediastinal infections, and postoperative median sternotomy wound infections (Table 37–1).

PERFORATION OF THE ESOPHAGUS

The most common cause of acute mediastinitis is perforation of the esophagus.[41, 48] The stomach and duodenum represent more frequent sites of the perforations of the alimentary tract, usually caused by intrinsic diseases of these organs. In contrast, the esophagus has a thin, vulnerable wall and is perforated more easily.

Perforations of the esophagus usually occur at a site of normal or pathologic narrowing, and a high correlation

TABLE 37–1 ■ ACUTE MEDIASTINITIS

Perforated esophagus
- Spontaneous or postemetic
- Foreign body
- Instrumentation (e.g., esophagoscopy, instrumental dilatation)
- Postoperative (e.g., esophageal, proximal stomach, or thoracic surgery)
- Blunt or penetrating trauma

Extension of infections from adjacent structures
- "Space infections" of the head and neck
- Lungs, pleura, lymph nodes, pericardium, tracheostomy
- Subphrenic infection
- Osteomyelitis of vertebrae
- Hematogenous dissemination of infection from a remote site

Postoperative median sternotomy wound infection

exists between the location of the lesion and the cause of rupture. The normal esophagus has three narrow sites: the proximal end, located at the level of the cricopharyngeal muscle; the midthoracic segment, where the aortic arch and left main stem bronchus indent the esophagus; and the transdiaphragmatic segment. Most perforations caused by instrumentation and foreign bodies involve the proximal end, which is the narrowest segment. Perforations at this level usually are located in the posterior wall, giving egress to the prevertebral or retrovisceral space. Perforations at the level of the aortic arch usually are caused by ingested foreign bodies. The usual location of spontaneous perforations is the transdiaphragmatic area. In most such cases, a longitudinal tear occurs on the left posterolateral wall just above the cardia, where the esophagus has little connective tissue support and its intrinsic musculature is relatively weak.

Perforation of the esophagus may be spontaneous, as a consequence of retching or vomiting or air blast injuries, or traumatic.[1, 12] Traumatic perforation may occur after ingestion of a foreign body or as a complication of endoscopic or open surgical procedures. In one large series of acute purulent mediastinitis, ingestion of a foreign body or extraction caused one third of cases of esophageal origin.[7]

Perforations from instrumentation may produce precipitous symptoms during the procedure from transmural laceration.[48] Alternatively, a superficial tear occurs and becomes the site of suppurative infection that subsequently extends through remaining layers; several hours or days may elapse between instrumentation and the onset of symptoms. Repair of esophageal atresia is a common condition associated with a tear of the esophagus during childhood. In one review, 7 of 41 infants had a clinically significant esophageal disruption requiring reoperation 1 to 18 days after repair of esophageal atresia.[6] Mediastinitis complicated repair of esophageal atresia in 3.6 percent of 223 cases in another large series.[46] Postoperative perforations of the esophagus usually represent infectious complications of anastomotic leaks occurring after esophageal resection or of esophageal-pleural fistulas occurring after thoracic surgery. Most of these infections do not become apparent until weeks or months after surgery.

Children with mediastinitis from erosion of the esophagus caused by a foreign body tend to have small and well-contained perforations. Sharp objects such as pins and bone fragments may cause immediate transmural penetration. More commonly and especially with blunt objects such as coins, teeth, and food particles (e.g., corn chips), the foreign body becomes impacted in the esophagus.[45] Eventually, suppurative necrosis of the wall occurs, with the onset of symptoms days, weeks, or even months after the ingestion.[29]

The predominant symptoms of acute mediastinitis developing after perforation of the esophagus are neck and chest pain, respiratory distress, and dysphagia. Chills, fever of 37.8° C to 39° C (100° F to 102° F), and leukocytosis also are common. Infants present with tachycardia; respiratory difficulty, including increased respiratory rate; retractions; stridor; or a supplemental oxygen requirement.[29] Some patients may have a staccato breathing pattern characterized by an inspiratory halt with resumption of inspiration after a brief rest.[14] The onset of symptoms usually is abrupt, and the disease tends to follow a fulminant course. Approximately 20 to 30 percent of patients are comatose or hypotensive when first seen.[1] Mortality rates are 15 to 40 percent and are especially high for patients who are not seen and properly treated in the early stages of the disease.[1, 7, 12, 46, 48] Mortality rates for children are lower than those for adults. An exception is postoperative perforation of the esophagus, which tends to follow a somewhat more indolent course.

Physical examination often reveals cervical tenderness and subcutaneous emphysema in patients with proximal perforations, whereas patients with lower perforations of the esophagus are more likely to have signs suggesting an acute abdominal catastrophe. Examination of the lung fields often shows them to be abnormal, but the findings are nonspecific. The Hamman sign consists of "crunching" sounds heard in synchrony with the heartbeat along the left sternal border or cardiac apex. This finding is observed in approximately 50 percent of cases of mediastinal emphysema, but it also is found with left pneumothorax, dilated esophagus, gastric dilatation, bullous emphysema, and pneumoperitoneum.

Routine laboratory tests other than the chest radiograph generally are of little value. Analysis of pleural fluid usually shows a sterile exudate early in the disease course. Pleural fluid amylase levels often are normal within the first 24 hours after perforation. After 24 hours, the pleural fluid amylase level is elevated disproportionately compared with serum levels.

The principal findings on chest radiographs are a widened mediastinum, subcutaneous and mediastinal emphysema, and pleural effusions. Pleural effusions are more common occurrences with lower perforations of the esophagus and usually involve the left side. Basilar or retrocardiac infiltrates ascribed to chemical pneumonitis may be detected in the pulmonary segment adjacent to the site of perforation. Additional changes often include basilar atelectasis, a pneumothorax, or a hydropneumothorax. Radiopaque foreign bodies may be detected with plain radiographs, but they often are demonstrated better with mediastinal tomography or fluoroscopy.

Radiographic demonstration of gas in the soft tissue is highly suggestive of perforation of the esophagus if interpreted in the context of a compatible clinical presentation. Gas in the prevertebral tissue or superior mediastinum is most common with perforation of the upper esophagus. However, other conditions such as chest wall trauma or perforation of the trachea also may cause mediastinal emphysema.

The diagnosis of acute mediastinitis caused by perforation of the esophagus often can be made on the basis of the clinical setting coupled with the previously noted abnormalities of routine chest radiographs, mediastinal tomography, fluoroscopy (during ingestion of nonirritating water-soluble contrast media), computed tomography (CT) with contrast, or spiral CT.[53] Esophagoscopy is unnecessary and is contraindicated except for removing a foreign body.

The treatment of perforations of the esophagus in all patients includes supportive measures and antimicrobials. Supportive measures include intravenous fluid support, maintenance of an adequate airway, esophageal rest (i.e., no food), and careful monitoring of vital functions. Many patients are critically ill when seen and require stabilization before performance of diagnostic tests or surgery is feasible. Some children, especially those with perforation of the esophagus by a foreign body and mediastinitis, can be treated without surgical intervention. Conservative management can be considered for children in whom the perforation is a small, well-contained lesion in the upper esophagus in the absence of underlying esophageal pathology.[29] Surgical drainage and repair have been the standard treatment historically and should be undertaken for large perforations, when there is communication with the pleural space or abdomen, when vascular erosion is a concern, and in the setting of underlying esophageal pathology.

Selection of antimicrobial treatment optimally is determined by bacteriologic studies. Unfortunately, valid specimens for meaningful culture seldom are obtained, and a paucity of data are reported concerning documented pathogens. Blood and pleural fluid cultures should be obtained, but they usually are negative, except late in the course. As a consequence, decisions with regard to antimicrobials necessarily are empiric and should be directed against oral anaerobic bacteria and streptococci.[2, 4, 8, 23]

EXTENSION FROM INFECTIONS OF ADJACENT STRUCTURE

The mediastinum would appear to be a prime location for the spread of infections from contiguous structures. Anatomically, it is a central focus of lymph drainage, fascial planes from the abdomen and supraclavicular region transgress the mediastinum, and the adjacent pulmonary system is one of the most frequent sites of serious infection. Nonetheless, the mediastinum rarely is involved secondarily in suppurative infections.

In the preantimicrobial era, peritonsillar abscess, Ludwig angina, and other infections of the head and neck were relatively common causes of acute mediastinitis.[8, 17, 41, 57] Since penicillin has become available, these infections occur less frequently. When they do occur, the usual initial focus is pharyngitis, retropharyngeal abscess,[51] or a dental infection. These infections spread beyond the usual anatomic barriers to involve spaces of the neck or perimandibular area. The term *space infection* refers to suppurative involvement of potential spaces formed by fascial planes that extend from the head to the thorax.[4] The principal spaces that serve as conduits to the mediastinum are the visceral division of the deep cervical fascia that envelops the esophagus, trachea, larynx, and thyroid gland and the carotid sheath, which extends from the base of the skull, passes through the posterior pharyngomaxillary space along the prevertebral fascia, and enters the chest. Conditions other than pharyngitis and dental infections that may lead to suppurative involvement of these spaces include mastoiditis, laryngectomy, mediastinotomy, tracheostomy, and surgery or trauma of the oral airways. Placement of airway stents for management of tracheal or bronchial stenoses in children can be complicated by mediastinitis.[27]

In children, penetrating injury from an oral or oropharyngeal wound may serve as the entry site for infection extending to the mediastinum. Children have developed mediastinitis after receiving intraoral injuries caused by falling with a toothbrush in the mouth.[32] Infection spreads to the mediastinum through the retropharyngeal space. Other sharp objects, such as fish bones, may perforate the esophagus, with resultant infection.[43] Often, a penetrating wound to the oropharynx is caused by falling on a sharp or pointed object (i.e., the pencil injury). Occasionally, foreign bodies retained in the esophagus for months to years can have life-threatening complications, such as bronchoesophageal fistula or mediastinitis. The reported items causing such morbidity include coins, a heart pendant, a clothespin spring, and a toy soldier.[20] Suppurative pleuropulmonary infections rarely are complicated by mediastinal involvement. Extension of infection from vertebrae, ribs, or sternum also is unusual.

The major bacteria responsible for suppurative infections that originate in the oral cavity and extend to the mediastinum are group A beta-hemolytic streptococci and the anaerobic bacteria that are considered normal oral flora.[4, 8, 26, 40, 41] The former is the most frequent pathogen when the pharynx is the original portal of entry. Anaerobic bacteria, principally *Prevotella* species, *Bacteroides* spp., fusobacteria, and peptostreptococci, are the major pathogens in spreading infections of dental origin. Clindamycin often is regarded as the agent of choice for streptococci and anaerobes, although some authorities prefer other regimens likely to be effective, including penicillin plus metronidazole, cefoxitin, cefotetan, imipenem, or a β-lactam–β-lactamase inhibitor.[2, 8, 16, 23]

Surgical drainage is the cornerstone of treatment in "space infections." Transcervical incisions usually are employed when spread to the superior mediastinum has occurred. Extension of the infection below the level of the fourth thoracic vertebra requires a parasternal or paravertebral approach, depending on whether the anterior or posterior mediastinum is involved.

Mediastinitis Due to Median Sternotomy Wound Infections

Sternal wound infections complicate 0.1 to 7.1 percent of median sternotomy incisions for cardiac surgery in children.[11, 37, 44, 52] Sternal wound infections have been classified as superficial when infection is limited to the skin and soft tissue overlying the sternum and deep when infection extends to the sternum or mediastinal contents.[11, 44] Alternatively, Mehta et al[37] used the Centers for Disease Control and Prevention definition of surgical-site infection (SSI), which distinguishes superficial (i.e., skin and subcutaneous tissue) or deep (i.e., fascia and muscle) incisional SSIs from organ-space SSIs.[25] The rate is somewhat higher after cardiac transplantation.[28, 55] Mediastinitis is considered a major complication, with potential involvement of contiguous structures, including prosthetic valves, grafts, pericardium, lung, and chest wall. Contemporary data indicate that the incidence of mediastinitis after median sternotomy in children is 2 to 3.9 percent.[37, 52] According to Pollock and colleagues,[44] postoperative wound infection more frequently is a complication of double-outlet right ventricle repair, truncus repair, switch, valvulatory or conduit procedures than of repair of an atrial septal defect, a ventricular septal defect, or tetralogy of Fallot. Mediastinal infection has developed from an infection of a retained epicardial pacemaker lead.[24]

Risk factors for development of sternal wound infections in children are listed in Table 37–2. They may be classified as preoperative, intraoperative, or postoperative risk factors. In general, the sicker the child, the greater the risk for development of sternal wound infection. Factors not associated with risk for infection have included emergency surgery or prior infections.[37] Outbreaks of mediastinitis and endocarditis have been reported with *Mycobacterium chelonei* or *Mycobacterium fortuitum,* presumably reflecting contact with nonsterile water.[30] Epidemics also have been

TABLE 37–2 ■ RISK FACTORS FOR STERNAL WOUND INFECTIONS IN CHILDHOOD

Preoperative Factors
Young infant with underlying disorders
Severe illness (assessed by high American Society of Anesthesiologists score) and long preoperative hospital stay
Inadequate antimicrobial prophylaxis
High leukocyte band count
Intraoperative Factors
Perfusion time exceeding 1 hour
Delayed sternal closure
Postoperative Factors
High pediatric risk of mortality (PRISM) score (≥10) on admission to pediatric intensive care unit
Perfusion time in excess of 1 hour
Excessive bleeding
Reexploration for bleeding
Increased leukocyte band count (day 1)
Long duration of ventilatory support
Prolonged inotropic support
Low cardiac output state
Longer hospital stay

Data from references 11, 37, 44, 52.

traced to operating room personnel, who may serve as the source of *Staphylococcus aureus* or other bacteria.[18]

The mean time from surgery to onset of wound infection is 10 to 15 days postoperatively, but it may be delayed for a month when the onset is indolent. The clinical features of sternal wound infections include local pain and tenderness, erythema, purulent drainage, wound dehiscence, persistent or recurrent postoperative fever, and leukocytosis. Less frequently, sternal instability with a rocking motion is identified, although it may indicate nonunion without necessarily implicating infection. The most common sequence is fever and systemic toxicity followed by signs of a sternal wound infection with cellulitis or purulent drainage. CT, often with aspiration, is an important adjunct in the diagnosis.[28] The findings may include mediastinal soft tissue swelling, pleural effusions, and sternal dehiscence or erosion, but CT of the chest does not always reveal abnormalities.[39, 56] Consideration should be given to use of alternate testing modalities, such as magnetic resonance imaging, when infection is suspected. Lack of compelling radiographic evidence of infection should not delay drainage when clinical signs are evident.

The treatment of median sternotomy infections includes prolonged courses of antibiotics and surgical débridement. Selection of an antimicrobial optimally is based on culture results of blood, needle aspirates, or tissue specimens obtained from the infected site. Empiric therapy given while awaiting results of culture should be based on the likely pathogens. The most frequent pathogens in an era of almost universal use of antimicrobial prophylaxis are *S. aureus* (including methicillin-resistant *S. aureus* [MRSA]). In adults, MRSA mediastinitis is associated with higher rates of overall mortality, mediastinitis-related mortality, and treatment failure than is infection caused by methicillin-sensitive *S. aureus* (MSSA), but this association has not been reported for children.[38] Gram-negative enteric bacteria and *Pseudomonas* are less common causes of mediastinitis. Polymicrobial infection may occur in as many as one fourth of patients.[5] *Candida* spp. should be considered in any patient with infection of the mediastinum, particularly when broad-spectrum antimicrobials have been used.[9] Almost any microorganism gaining entry to the mediastinum can, in theory, serve as the nidus for infection, and *Mycoplasma hominis*, *Ureaplasma urealyticum*, *Nocardia*, and *Aspergillus* have been reported.[19, 33, 34, 54] *M. fortuitum* also can be a cause of apparently culture-negative mediastinitis and has been reported in a child after undergoing a Fontan operation.[50] MRSA and coagulase-negative staphylococci usually are treated with vancomycin because of resistance to β-lactams; rifampin or gentamicin sometimes is added to enhance antimicrobial activity. Empiric antibiotics should be modified based on results from wound or blood cultures. Systemic antibiotics should be given for at least 3 to 6 weeks.

Adequate surgical débridement is the most important facet of treatment. It usually reveals gross pus and often shows sternal osteomyelitis. The wound should be reopened and débrided for removal of all infected tissue. A distinction needs to be made between superficial and deep infections. Superficial infections can be treated simply with incision, packing, and a short course of antibiotics, usually for 10 to 14 days. With deep involvement, débriding devitalized bone and irrigating the mediastinum are necessary. The wound may be managed with closed irrigation, open-wound packing, a muscle flap procedure, or an omental flap procedure.[3, 22, 42, 55] Reconstruction of the pectoralis muscle flap has been an effective treatment for deep sternal wound infections, even in the neonatal age group.[13]

Chronic Mediastinitis

Chronic mediastinitis is an indolent infection involving the paratracheal region, carina, and hilum. Two histologic forms are recognized: granulomatous and fibrotic. The clinical presentation and location of lesions for these two forms are identical, and considerable overlap in histologic findings may be present. Consequently, many authorities consider that common etiologic mechanisms are responsible and that the fibrotic form represents the end stage of granulomatous mediastinitis.[49] Nonetheless, one type of fibrotic mediastinitis stands apart in being associated with a fibrotic process at another anatomic site such as the retroperitoneum. Additional distinctive features of fibrotic mediastinitis are that symptomatic disease is more common and that an etiologic organism rarely is demonstrated.

Chronic mediastinitis occurs in virtually any age group. Many patients are asymptomatic, and the lesion initially is detected by routine chest radiographs showing a widened superior mediastinum near the tracheal bifurcation or the hilum with a lobulated configuration.[15] Mediastinal calcifications also may be present. Concomitant changes in the pulmonary parenchyma demonstrable by chest radiograph are variable. Symptoms, when manifested, usually reflect compression of adjacent structures such as the superior vena cava, esophagus, and tracheobronchial tree. Low-grade fever, anemia, and weight loss also may be present. A review of 180 reported cases showed that 26 percent of 103 patients with granulomatous mediastinitis were symptomatic, compared with 83 percent of 77 individuals with fibrotic mediastinitis.[49] The most common signs and symptoms are those ascribed to obstruction of the superior vena cava.

Histoplasmosis is the most common identifiable cause of chronic mediastinitis; less common causes are tuberculosis, blastomycosis, sarcoidosis, nocardiosis, actinomycosis, and lymphomas.[10, 15, 21, 31, 35] A review of 180 cases of histoplasmosis and tuberculosis accounted for 27 percent of cases of granulomatous mediastinitis and 4 percent with fibrotic mediastinitis. Most (31%) were enigmatic, but many investigators believe that histoplasmosis accounts for most of the idiopathic cases.

Two types of mediastinal fibrosis caused by histoplasmosis are recognized. The most common type, mediastinal granuloma, is caused by a cluster of nodes that coalesce and form an encapsulated mass that may be large and compress adjacent structures, especially the superior vena cava or esophagus. Surgical resection often is feasible but advocated only when the obstruction is significant. The second type is healed histoplasmosis with sclerosis. The thick, fibrotic capsule may invade contiguous structures, causing stenosis of pulmonary arteries, pulmonary veins, superior vena cava, or bronchi. These lesions may require resection.

The diagnostic evaluation of patients with possible chronic mediastinitis should include a chest radiograph, CT or magnetic resonance imaging,[47] tuberculin skin test, and histoplasmosis serology. Cultures of sputum for *Mycobacterium tuberculosis* and pathogenic fungi rarely are positive. The antigen assay for *Histoplasma capsulatum* using blood and urine usually is negative, and skin tests for this fungus are not helpful. Complement-fixation titers usually exceed 1:8 in patients with chronic histoplasmosis. A vascular imaging study is indicated if there is evidence of venous or vena caval obstruction or of arterial involvement.

Calcifications or radiographic stability over a prolonged period suggests a benign condition, and if obstructive symptoms are lacking, surgery often can be deferred.[36] Caution in this approach is necessary because thymomas and teratomas may cause calcified masses in the superior mediastinum, and both require surgical resection. Resected tissue should be cultured and studied extensively on histologic sections for evidence of *M. tuberculosis* and fungi. When *H. capsulatum* is responsible, it usually is detected histologically; fungal cultures rarely are positive.[35, 36] The role of amphotericin B when surgically excised tissue shows *H. capsulatum* is controversial, but most authorities concur that drug treatment is unnecessary if cultures are negative.[36] Newer agents used for histoplasmosis, such as ketoconazole, fluconazole, and itraconazole, also play an uncertain role in therapy.

Acknowledgments

The author acknowledges the contribution of Dr. John G. Bartlett in the previous edition of this chapter. Many sections required minimal changes apart from the addition of recently published information.

REFERENCES

1. Abbott, O. A., Mansour, K. A., Logan, W. D., Jr., et al.: A traumatic so-called "spontaneous" rupture of the esophagus. J. Thorac. Cardiovasc. Surg. *59:*67–83, 1970.
2. Applebaum, P. C., Spangler, S. K., Jacobs, M. R.: Beta-lactamase production and susceptibilities to amoxicillin, amoxicillin-clavulanate, ticarcillin, ticarcillin-clavulanate, cefoxitin, imipenem, and metronidazole of 320 non–*Bacteroides fragilis Bacteroides* isolates and 129 fusobacteria from 28 U.S. centers. Antimicrob. Agents Chemother. *34*:1546–1550, 1990.
3. Backer, C. L., Pensler, J. M., Tobin, G. R., et al.: Vascularized muscle flaps for life-threatening mediastinal wounds in children. Ann. Thorac. Surg. *57:*797–801, 1994.
4. Bartlett, J. G., and Gorbach, S. L.: Anaerobic infections of the head and neck. Otolaryngol. Clin. North Am. *9:*655–678, 1976.
5. Brook, I.: Microbiology of postthoracotomy sternal wound infection. J. Clin. Microbiol. *27*:806–807, 1989.
6. Chavin, K., Field, G., Chandler, J., et al.: Save the child's esophagus: Management of major disruption after repair of esophageal atresia. J. Pediatr. Surg. *31*:48–52, 1996.
7. Cherveniakov, A., and Cherveniakov, P.: Surgical treatment of acute purulent mediastinitis. Eur. J. Cardiovasc. Thorac. Surg. *6*:407–410, 1992.
8. Civen, R., Vaisanen, M. L., and Finegold, S. M.: Peritonsillar abscess, retropharyngeal abscess, mediastinitis and nonclostridial anaerobic myonecrosis: A case report. Clin. Infect. Dis. *16*(Suppl. 4):S299–S303, 1992.
9. Clancy, C. J., Nguyen, M. H., and Morris, A. J.: Candidal mediastinitis: An emerging clinical entity. Clin. Infect. Dis. *25*:608–613, 1997.
10. Dukes, R. J., Strimlan, C. V., Dines, D. E., et al.: Esophageal involvement of mediastinal granuloma. J. A. M. A. *236:*2313–2315, 1976.
11. Edwards, M. S., and Baker, C. J.: Median sternotomy wound infections in children. Pediatr. Infect. Dis. J. *2*:105–109, 1983.
12. Enquist, R. W., Blanck, R. R., and Butler, R. H.: Nontraumatic mediastinitis. J. A. M. A. *236:*1048–1049, 1976.
13. Erez, E., Katz, M., Sharoni, E., et al.: Pectoralis major muscle flap for deep sternal wound infection in neonates. Ann. Thorac. Surg. *69*:572–577, 2000.
14. Feldman, R., and Gromischm, D. S.: Acute suppurative mediastinitis. Am. J. Dis. Child. *121:*79–81, 1971.
15. Ferguson, T. B., and Burford, T. H.: Mediastinal granuloma. Ann. Thorac. Surg. *1:*125–141, 1965.
16. Finegold, S. M., and Wexler, H. M.: Therapeutic implications of bacteriologic findings in mixed aerobic-anaerobic infections. Antimicrob. Agents Chemother. *32*:611–616, 1988.
17. Garatea-Crelgo, J., and Gay-Escoda, C.: Mediastinitis from odontogenic infection: Report of three cases and review of the literature. Int. J. Oral Maxillofac. Surg. *20*:65–68, 1991.
18. Gaynes, R., Marosok, R., Mowry-Hanley, J., et al.: Mediastinitis following coronary artery bypass surgery: A 3-year review. J. Infect. Dis. *163*:117–121, 1991.
19. Geers, T. A., Taege, A. J., Longworth, D. L., et al.: *Ureaplasma urealyticum*: Unusual cause of culture-negative mediastinitis. Clin. Infect. Dis. *29*:949–950, 1999.
20. Gilchrist, B. F., Valerie, E. P., Nguyen, M., et al.: Pearls and perils in the management of prolonged, peculiar, penetrating esophageal foreign bodies in children. J. Pediatr. Surg. *32*:1429–1431, 1997.
21. Goodwin, R. A., Nickell, J. A., and Des Prez, R. M.: Mediastinal fibrosis complicating healed primary histoplasmosis and tuberculosis. Medicine (Baltimore) *51:*227–246, 1972.
22. Gottlieb, L. J., Pielet, R. W., Karp, R. B., et al.: Rigid internal fixation of the sternum in postoperative mediastinitis. Arch. Surg. *129*:489–493, 1994.
23. Gudiol, F., Manresa, F., Pallares, R., et al.: Clindamycin vs. penicillin for anaerobic lung infections. Arch. Intern. Med. *150*:2525–2531, 1990.
24. Hachiro, Y., Kikuchi, S., Ito, M., et al.: Infection of a retained permanent epicardial pacemaker lead. Ann. Thorac. Surg. *71*:2038–2039, 2001.
25. Horan, T. C., Gaynes, R. P., Martone, W. J., et al.: CDC definitions of nosocomial surgical site infections, 1992: A modification of CDC definitions of surgical wound infections. Am. J. Infect. Control *20*:271–274, 1992.
26. Howell, H. S., Prinz, R. A., and Pickleman, J. R.: Anaerobic mediastinitis. Surg. Gynecol. Obstet. *143:*353–359, 1976.
27. Jacobs, J. P., Quintessenza, J. A., Botero, L. M., et al.: The role of airway stents in the management of pediatric tracheal, carinal, and bronchial disease. Eur. J. Cardiothorac. Surg. *18*:505–512, 2000.
28. Karwande, S. V., Renlund, D. G., Olsen, S. L., et al.: Mediastinitis in heart transplantation. Ann. Thorac. Surg. *54*:1039–1045, 1992.
29. Kerschner, J. E., Beste, D. J., Conley, S. F., et al.: Mediastinitis associated with foreign body erosion of the esophagus in children. Int. J. Pediatr. Otorhinolaryngol. *59*:89–97, 2001.
30. Kuritsky, J. N., Bullen, M. G., Broome, C. V., et al.: Sternal wound infections and endocarditis due to organisms of the *Mycobacterium fortuitum* complex. Ann. Intern. Med. *98:*938–939, 1983.
31. Langerstrom, C. F., Mitchell, H. G., Graham, B. S., et al.: Chronic fibrosing mediastinitis and superior vena caval obstruction from blastomycosis. Ann. Thorac. Surg. *54*:764–765, 1992.
32. Law, R. C., Fouque, C. A., Waddell, A., et al.: Penetrating intra-oral trauma in children. BMJ *314*:50–51, 1997.
33. Lequier, L., Robinson, J., and Vaudry, W.: Sternotomy infection with *Mycoplasma hominis* in a neonate. Pediatr. Infect. Dis. J. *14*:1010–1011, 1995.
34. Mattila, P. S., Carlson, P., Sivonen, A., et al.: Life-threatening *Mycoplasma hominis* mediastinitis. Clin. Infect. Dis. *29*:1529–1537, 1999.
35. Mathisen, D. J., and Grillo, H. C.: Clinical manifestations of mediastinal fibrosis and histoplasmosis. Ann. Thorac. Surg. *54*:1053–1057, 1992.
36. Medeiros, A. A.: Case records of the Massachusetts General Hospital (chronic mediastinitis due to histoplasmosis). N. Engl. J. Med. *295:*381–388, 1976.
37. Mehta, P. A., Cunningham, C. K., Colella, C. B., et al.: Risk factors for sternal wound and other infections in pediatric cardiac surgery patients. Pediatr. Infect. Dis. J. *19*:1000–1004, 2000.
38. Mekontso-Dessap, A., Kirsch, M., Brun-Buisson, C., et al.: Poststernotomy mediastinitis due to *Staphylococcus aureus*: Comparison of methicillin-resistant and methicillin-susceptible cases. Clin. Infect. Dis. *32*:877–883, 2001.
39. Misawa, Y., Fuse, K., and Hasegawa, T.: Infectious mediastinitis after cardiac operations: Computed tomographic findings. Ann. Thorac. Surg. *65*:622–624, 1998.
40. Murray, P. M., and Finegold, S. M.: Anaerobic mediastinitis. Rev. Infect. Dis. *6:*5123–5127, 1984.

41. Neuhof, H.: Acute infections of the mediastinum with special reference to mediastinal suppuration. J. Thorac. Surg. *6*:194–195, 1936.
42. Newman, L. S., Szczukowski, L. C., Bain, R. P., et al.: Suppurative mediastinitis after open heart surgery. Chest *94*:546–553, 1988.
43. Nozoe, T., Kitamura, M., Adachi, Y., et al.: Successful conservative treatment for esophageal perforation by a fish bone associated with mediastinitis. Hepatogastroenterology *45*:2190–2192, 1998.
44. Pollock, E. M. M., Ford-Jones, E. L., Rebeyka, I., et al.: Early nosocomial infections in pediatric cardiovascular surgery patients. Crit. Care Med. *18*:378–384, 1990.
45. Reino, A. J., Jahn, A. F., Parsons, J., et al.: Traumatic pneumomediastinum in a child secondary to corn chip perforation of the esophagus. Pediatr. Emerg. Care *9*:211–215, 1993.
46. Rokitansky, A. M., Kolankaya, V. A., Seidl, S., et al.: Recent evaluation of prognostic risk factors in esophageal atresia—a multicenter review of 223 cases. Eur. J. Pediatr. Surg. *3*:196–201, 1993.
47. Rossi, S. E., McAdams, H. P., Rosado-de-Christenson, M. L., et al.: Fibrosing mediastinitis. Radiographics *21*:737–757, 2001.
48. Salo, J. A., Isolauri, J. O., Heikkila, L. J., et al.: Management of delayed esophageal perforation with mediastinal sepsis. J. Thorac. Cardiovasc. Surg. *106*:1088–1091, 1993.
49. Schowengerdt, C. G., Suyemoto, R., and Main, F. B.: Granulomatous and fibrous mediastinitis. J. Thorac. Cardiovasc. Surg. *57*:365–379, 1969.
50. Syed, A. U., Hussain, R., Bhat, A. N., et al.: Mediastinitis due to *Mycobacterium fortuitum* infection following Fontan operation in a child. Scand. Cardiovasc. J. *31*:311–313, 1997.
51. Sztajnbok, J., Grassi, M. S., Katayama, D. M., et al.: Descending suppurative mediastinitis: Nonsurgical approach to this unusual complication of retropharyngeal abscesses in childhood. Pediatr. Emerg. Care *15*:341–343, 1999.
52. Tabbutt, S., Duncan, B. W., McLaughlin, D., et al.: Delayed sternal closure after cardiac operations in a pediatric population. J. Thorac. Cardiovasc. Surg. *113*:886–893, 1997.
53. Tecce, P. M., Fishman, E. K., and Kuhlman, J. E.: CT evaluation of the anterior mediastinum: Spectrum of disease. Radiographics *14*:973–990, 1994.
54. Wenger, P. N., Brown, J. M., McNeil, M. M., et al.: *Nocardia farcinica* sternotomy site infections in patients following open heart surgery. J. Infect. Dis. *178*:1539–1543, 1998.
55. Whitehead, B., Helms, P., Goodwin, M., et al.: Heart-lung transplantation for cystic fibrosis. Arch. Dis. Child. *66*:1022–1026, 1991.
56. Yamaguchi, H., Yamauchi, H., Yamada, T., et al.: Diagnostic validity of computed tomography for mediastinitis after cardiac surgery. Ann. Thorac. Cardiovasc. Surg. *7*:94–98, 2001.
57. Zeitoun, I. M., and Dhanarajani, P. J.: Cervical cellulitis and mediastinitis caused by odontogenic infections: Report of two cases and review of the literature. J. Oral Maxillofac. Surg. *53*:203–208, 1995.

Central Nervous System Infections

CHAPTER 38

Bacterial Meningitis beyond the Neonatal Period

RALPH D. FEIGIN ■ ERIC PEARLMAN

Bacterial meningitis is an inflammation of the meninges caused by bacterial infection. The term *leptomeningitis* denotes inflammation of the arachnoid and pia mater, the usual distribution of meningitis. Infections of the neonate, including bacterial meningitis, are presented in Chapter 74, and infections of the central nervous system (CNS) caused by mycobacteria are discussed in Chapter 101.

Incidence and Epidemiology

Before the discovery and use of antibiotics, bacterial meningitis generally was fatal. Although antibiotic therapy has improved dramatically the prognosis in patients afflicted with bacterial meningitis, bacterial meningitis continues to be a significant cause of morbidity and mortality in children. Whereas the number of deaths attributed to many different infectious diseases in the United States decreased by 10- to 200-fold between 1935 and 1968, the number of reported deaths caused by bacterial meningitis decreased by only half during the same period.[324, 325] In 1972, the Centers for Disease Control and Prevention (CDC) estimated that in the United States, 29,000 cases of meningitis were caused by *Haemophilus influenzae* type b, 4800 cases were caused by *Streptococcus pneumoniae,* and 4600 cases were caused by *Neisseria meningitidis*.

Population-based studies in South Carolina, Minnesota, Vermont, and New Mexico in the 1970s suggested that the actual incidence of bacterial meningitis ranged between 5.4 and 7.3 cases per 100,000 population.[48, 110–113] Studies reported in 1995 suggested that the incidence in individuals between 1 and 23 months of age ranged between 0.7 (for *H. influenzae* type b) and 6.6 (for *S. pneumoniae*) cases per 100,000 population.

Before the widespread use of conjugate *H. influenzae* type b vaccine, *H. influenzae* type b was the most common cause of bacterial meningitis in children in the United States, Canada, and Scandinavia, but this pattern was not universal.[138] Davey and associates[65] reported that between 1968 and 1977, *N. meningitidis* was the most common cause and *H. influenzae* type b the second most common cause of bacterial meningitis for children and young adults in Great Britain. Mortality rates in this group of patients were 3.5 percent for those with meningococcal meningitis, 7.7 percent for children with *H. influenzae* meningitis, and 30 percent for patients with pneumococcal meningitis.

By 1995 in the United States, the most frequent cause of bacterial meningitis in children older than 1 month to 24 months of age was *S. pneumoniae,* followed by *N. meningitidis,* group B streptococcus, and *H. influenzae* (Table 38–1). In children younger than 1 month, the most common cause of bacterial meningitis was group B streptococcus, followed by *S. pneumoniae*.[284] *Escherichia coli* and *Listeria monocytogenes* are the other common causes of meningitis in neonates 2 to 6 weeks of age.[6, 29] *N. meningitidis* was the most common cause for the age group 2 to 29 years, followed by *S. pneumoniae*.

The child between 6 and 12 months of age appears to be at greatest risk for acquiring bacterial meningitis; 90 percent of reported cases occur between 1 month and 5 years of age.[110] The age distribution of patients with bacterial meningitis has not changed appreciably during the past 40 years.[240, 297]

EPIDEMIOLOGY OF *HAEMOPHILUS INFLUENZAE* MENINGITIS

The most dramatic change in the epidemiology of bacterial meningitis since the advent of antibiotics has occurred in the past 10 to 15 years because of licensure of conjugate vaccines against *H. influenzae* type b.[281] The first vaccine available was *H. influenzae* type b capsular polysaccharide (polyribosylribitol phosphate [PRP]), which was licensed in April 1985 for use in children 18 to 59 months of age. Newer vaccines with improved immunogenicity for children of younger ages were developed by covalently linking the capsular polysaccharide with protein antigens. In October 1990, the first conjugate, PRP diphtheria CRM_{197} protein conjugate (HbOC), was approved for infant use, and in 1991, the Advisory Committee on Immunization Practices and the American Academy of Pediatrics recommended universal infant immunization at 2, 4, and 6 months of age with either HbOC or PRP–meningococcal protein conjugate (PRP-OMP) vaccines.[8, 50]

The *Haemophilus influenzae* Study Group[5] noted that the number of cases of *H. influenzae* meningitis in children younger than 5 years reported through the National Bacterial Meningitis Reporting System began declining rapidly in 1988 (Fig. 38–1). In another CDC surveillance project conducted from 1989 to 1997, the race-adjusted incidence of invasive *H. influenzae* type b disease among children younger than 5 years declined from 34 to 0.4 per 100,000, a 99 percent reduction.[53]

Schoendorf and colleagues[283] evaluated national trends in mortality from meningitis from 1980 to 1991. From 1980 through 1987, mortality rates from *H. influenzae* meningitis decreased an average of 8.5 percent a year, from 1.72 per

TABLE 38–1 ■ AGE-SPECIFIC INCIDENCE IN 1995 OF BACTERIAL MENINGITIS PER 100,000 POPULATION

Age	*Haemophilus influenzae*	*Streptococcus pneumoniae*	*Neisseria meningitidis*	Group B Streptococcus
<1 mo	0	15.7	0	125.00
1–23 mo	0.7	6.6	4.5	2.8
2–29 yr	0.1	0.5	1.1	0.1
30–59 yr	0.2	1.0	0.3	0.05
>60 yr	0.07	1.9	0.1	0.1

From Schuchat, A., Robinson, K., Wenger, J. D., et al.: Bacterial meningitis in the United States in 1995. N. Engl. J. Med. *337*:970–976, 1997.

100,000 children in 1980 to 0.94 per 100,000 children in 1987. From 1988 to 1991, however, mortality rates decreased an average of 48 percent a year, with a death rate of 0.11 per 100,000 children in 1991. The estimated case-fatality rate for *H. influenzae* meningitis was 3.3 percent from 1980 to 1987 and 2.3 percent from 1988 to 1991. In comparison, mortality rates from *S. pneumoniae* decreased 10 percent annually from 1980 to 1987 and 3 percent annually from 1988 to 1991. Similarly, mortality rates from meningococcal meningitis decreased by 13 percent annually from 1980 to 1987 and 12 percent annually from 1988 to 1991.

The dramatic decrease in the incidence of *H. influenzae* meningitis probably has been affected by several factors. The precipitous drop that occurred shortly after universal immunization of infants strongly suggests that this practice has affected the epidemiology of this disease. Conjugate vaccination protects against nasopharyngeal colonization,[224] thus decreasing the carriage rate of *H. influenzae* type b and diminishing the reservoir for transmission, as well as providing immunity from infection. These factors would lessen the likelihood of development of infection in underimmunized children as well. Other changes in medical practice, such as the widespread use of outpatient antibiotics and improvements in supportive care, may have some effect, as demonstrated by the decrease in case-fatality rates for *H. influenzae* meningitis, the steady decrease in mortality rates before vaccination, and the decrease in instances of meningococcal and pneumococcal disease.

Before universal vaccination, the incidence of *H. influenzae* meningitis varied worldwide. The incidence of *H. influenzae* meningitis in Scandinavian children younger than 5 years averaged 16 to 28 cases per 100,000 children from 1975 to 1984.[243] The incidence of *H. influenzae* meningitis in the Netherlands was 22 cases per 100,000 children younger than 5 years.[326] A universal vaccination program in that country appears to have led to a marked decrease in the incidence, with 6 reported cases of meningitis caused by *H. influenzae* in a 1-year period after implementation of universal vaccination of infants compared with 34 cases per 100,000 children in a 1-year period before vaccination.

The incidence of *H. influenzae* meningitis is markedly higher in nonindustrialized populations. Before the vaccination era, Alaskan Eskimos had an annual incidence of 282 cases per 100,000 children younger than 5 years.[338] The Navajo and White Mountain Apache Native Americans had a much higher incidence compared with that of Native Americans in other regions of the United States,[61, 203] and the incidence among Australian aboriginals and among certain African populations, such as those in Gambia and Senegal, was 3 to 10 times higher than that of populations in the United States and Europe.[34, 130, 151]

In one study, the incidence of *H. influenzae* meningitis was 3.5-fold higher in blacks than in whites, but this distribution of cases appeared to be related more closely to poverty than to race.[110] In whites, no increase in incidence occurred in overcrowded households, but the incidence was higher in rural than in urban areas. Fraser and associates[110] postulated that the increased incidence in rural whites and in blacks was related to lack of access to early medical care.

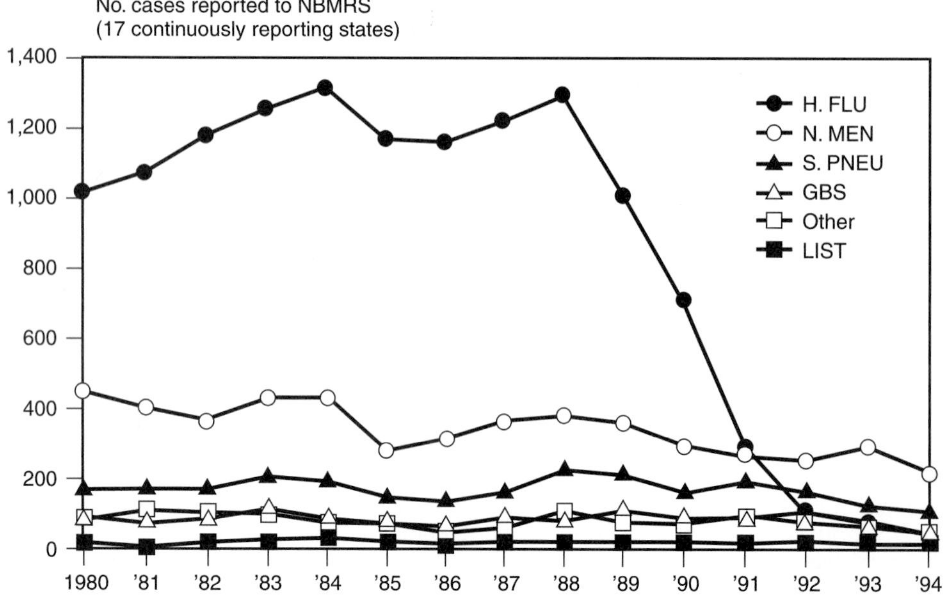

FIGURE 38–1 ■ Incidence of bacterial meningitis in individuals from birth to 19 years of age. A marked decline in the incidence of *Haemophilus influenzae* type b meningitis is noted during the period between 1988 and 1994. GBS, group B streptococcus; H. FLU, *Haemophilus influenzae* type b; LIST, *Listeria monocytogenes;* NBMRS, National Bacterial Meningitis Reporting System; N. MEN, *Neisseria meningitidis;* S. PNEU, *Streptococcus pneumoniae.*

Ward and colleagues[336] studied prospective data obtained in 19 states to determine the risk of spread of severe *H. influenzae* illness among household contacts of patients with *H. influenzae* meningitis. The risk in children younger than 1 year of age was 6 percent; in children younger than 4 years, 2.1 percent; and in children younger than 6 years, 0.5 percent. The risk of *H. influenzae* disease occurring in household contacts younger than 6 years is similar to the risk of secondary meningococcal disease occurring in all household contacts, indicating a need for effective antimicrobial prophylaxis.

Spread of *H. influenzae* disease in daycare centers also is well documented.[27, 132, 212] The precise risk of acquiring secondary *H. influenzae* type b infection in daycare centers remains unclear.

Recurrent invasive *H. influenzae* type b disease has been reported. Detailed studies suggest that age and high incidence of disease alone are not the only factors contributing to the recurrence of the disease.[43] Patients who have recurrent disease caused by *H. influenzae* type b may represent a subset of a population with unusual disease susceptibility. In addition, children who develop invasive infection caused by *H. influenzae* type b after receiving appropriate conjugate vaccine frequently have subnormal immunoglobulin concentrations and should undergo immune evaluation.[156]

EPIDEMIOLOGY OF MENINGITIS CAUSED BY *STREPTOCOCCUS PNEUMONIAE*

The highest rate of invasive pneumococcal infection occurs in children younger than 2 years. In a population-based surveillance study of invasive pneumococcal infection in southern California, the age-specific incidence of invasive pneumococcal disease for children 2 years old or younger was 145 cases per 100,000. For children 2 to 4 years old and 5 to 14 years old, the age-specific incidence dropped to 25 per 100,000 and 5 per 100,000, respectively.[350] The age-specific incidence for pneumococcal meningitis was 21, 12, 6, 2, and 0.5 cases per 100,000 for the age groups 0 to 6 months, 7 to 12 months, 13 to 24 months, 25 to 60 months, and older than 60 months, respectively.

The risk for development of sepsis or meningitis caused by *S. pneumoniae* depends to some extent on the serotype with which the child is colonized. Although 90 pneumococcal serotypes have been identified, invasive disease, including sepsis and meningitis, in children younger than 6 years old is associated most commonly with serotypes 14, 6B, 19F, 18C, 23F, 4, and 9V.[46] The risk of contracting pneumococcal meningitis is 5- to 36-fold greater among blacks than among whites and is independent of income or population density.[110] In one study, 11 percent of the black population with pneumococcal pneumonia had sickle-cell disease, a factor known to predispose the individual to pneumococcal disease.[110] On the basis of these data, Fraser and associates[110] suggested that 1 of every 24 children with sickle-cell disease may develop pneumococcal meningitis by 4 years of age. This incidence is 36-fold greater than the incidence of pneumococcal meningitis in a normal black population and 314-fold greater than that in white children. Daycare attendance, underlying disease, and lack of breast feeding were risk factors for acquiring invasive pneumococcal infections in a large case-control study that included children from the United States and Canada.[198] Although cigarette smoking is a major risk factor for the development of invasive pneumococcal disease in adults, whether exposure to cigarette smoke increases the risk of developing systemic pneumococcal infection in children remains unclear.[138, 236] The greatest mortality occurs in very old and very young patients and has been estimated to be 20 to 60 percent.[103, 112, 113, 126]

Pneumococcal infections generally occur sporadically. Household contacts of a patient with pneumococcal disease are not considered to be at increased risk of acquiring secondary infection. However, the occurrence of concurrent pneumococcal disease (meningitis and bacteremia) in the household setting has been reported.[20, 293]

The incidence of systemic infection with penicillin-resistant *S. pneumoniae* has been increasing steadily worldwide since it first was reported in Australia in the 1960s.[150] It has become an increasing problem in the United States since the mid-1980s.[306, 311, 312] In 1995, a CDC multistate surveillance study showed that 35 percent of *S. pneumoniae* cerebrospinal fluid (CSF) isolates were resistant to penicillin.[284]

The first report of meningitis caused by resistant pneumococci was published in 1974,[230] and numerous case reports have appeared subsequently. Tan and colleagues[311] found that patients with systemic infections caused by penicillin-resistant pneumococci were more likely to have received a course of antibiotics within a month before their infection than were matched control subjects who had infections caused by pneumococci but whose isolates were susceptible to penicillin.

More recently, an increase has occurred in the number of cases of systemic infection and meningitis caused by *S. pneumoniae* organisms resistant to penicillin and third-generation cephalosporins. In 1998, CDC surveillance of multiple areas around the United States found that 24 percent of pneumococcal isolates associated with invasive infections were nonsusceptible to penicillin; 14 percent of isolates were nonsusceptible to cefotaxime.[342] As with many studies, rates of resistance were higher among children younger than 5 years. In a prospective study involving eight children's hospitals nationwide during a 6-year period starting September 1993, a significant increase in the proportion of isolates nonsusceptible to penicillin or ceftriaxone was found. In the sixth year of the study ending August 1998, 37 percent and 11 percent of invasive isolates were nonsusceptible to penicillin and ceftriaxone, respectively.[174] Isolates of penicillin-resistant and third-generation cephalosporin–resistant *S. pneumoniae* have been recovered in other regions of the world as well.[116, 119, 258] Treatment failures in patients with *S. pneumoniae* meningitis resistant to penicillin and third-generation cephalosporins have led to changes in the empirical therapy of suspected bacterial meningitis, as discussed in the treatment section.[18, 39, 119, 180, 295]

EPIDEMIOLOGY OF MENINGOCOCCAL MENINGITIS

The carriage rate for *N. meningitidis* in the civilian population has been estimated at various times to be between 1 and 15 percent. Carriage rates in military personnel during epidemic periods have been considerably greater. Meningococcal carriers generally are adults (older than 21 years) who harbor the organism for months.

No correlation has been noted between meningococcal meningitis and crowding within households, but disease appears to be more prevalent in urban than in rural areas. In a civilian population, meningococcal meningitis generally is a disease of children and young adults who have been exposed to an adult carrier, usually in the same family, or to individuals with disease or who are carrying the organism in a daycare center setting. The estimated likelihood of severe meningococcal disease in family contacts occurring simultaneously with the first case is 1 percent.[194] The rate is 1000-fold greater than the risk in the community. The risk of meningitis in daycare center contacts of children with meningococcal disease is 1 per 1000.

In a CDC surveillance study of invasive meningococcal disease in the United States, the average annual incidence of disease was 1.1 per 100,000 population for the years 1992 to 1996.[263] The highest age-specific incidence occurred in infants younger than 1 year of age, with the peak incidence in infants 4 to 5 months old (15.9 cases per 100,000). The age-specific incidence declined sharply until the 10- to 14-year age range, at which point it began to increase again during the adolescent and early adult years. During the teenage range, the incidence peaked between 15 and 19 years of age (1.5 to 2.2 cases per 100,000). Overall, serogroup C caused 35 percent of cases; serogroup B, 32 percent; and serogroup Y, 26 percent. In the decade of the 1990s, serogroup Y became more common among older patients and caused more pneumonia than did the other serogroups. Thirty percent of serogroup B disease occurred in children younger than 1 year. An increased risk of contracting meningococcal infection also exists in college students, especially freshmen who reside on campus in the dormitories.[152]

Another change in the epidemiology of meningococcal disease in the United States relates to the increasing number of outbreaks (more than 10 cases per 100,000 population during 3 months), generally caused by serogroup C. Although these outbreaks account for only 2 to 3 percent of the total number of cases, they cause tremendous public concern and anxiety, which frequently result in misunderstanding of the nature of an outbreak by the media and the public.[159]

One otherwise unprecedented outbreak occurred in a sixth-grade elementary school classroom.[86] Five children from a class of 24 developed meningococcal meningitis. In addition, two siblings of one of the index cases also developed meningococcal infection. Detailed epidemiologic investigation suggested that close contact in the classroom (nose-to-nose distances of 34 inches or less) correlated with an increased rate of carriage of *N. meningitidis* and with an increased risk for development of invasive meningococcal disease.

Major outbreaks of meningococcal meningitis have occurred worldwide. In the late 1980s and early 1990s, major epidemics of meningococcal meningitis caused by a specific clone (III-1) of serogroup A *N. meningitidis* occurred throughout sub-Saharan Africa.[2, 143, 147, 246, 270] The origins of a pandemic spread of clone III-1 were traced to epidemics in Asia in the early 1980s, with spread through the Near East.[1] An outbreak occurred during the annual pilgrimage to Mecca in 1987,[218, 219] with pilgrims carrying clones back to their countries of origin, including the United States and the United Kingdom. Epidemics of closely related strains of clone III-1 serogroup A meningococcal meningitis occurred in the Sudan,[270] Ethiopia,[147] and Chad in 1988[219] and in Kenya[246] in 1989. A report in 1992 described an epidemic of clone III-1 in the Central African Republic in an area traditionally outside the "meningitis belt."[143] These epidemics generally begin during the dry season and decline at onset of the rainy season. Major outbreaks have occurred in Brazil, in Finland, and at multiple sites in Africa.[70, 243, 343] Shifts within a given community or within a country as a whole from one serogroup to another also are associated with an increased incidence of disease for several years after the new serogroup is introduced into the community.[263] The mechanisms underlying the changing patterns of meningococcal serogroups that cause disease are unknown.

Meningococcal infections also occur more frequently in patients with a deficiency of the terminal components (C5–C8) of the complement system.[81] More recently, an increased risk for contracting meningococcal meningitis has been reported in individuals with an inherited deficiency of C9[229] and with properdin deficiency.[301] Individuals with a complement-depleting underlying illness also are at particular risk for invasive disease.[245] Screening for complement deficiency in pediatric patients with meningococcal disease is recommended.[195]

Pathophysiology

ORGANISMS ENCOUNTERED

Any organism may produce meningitis in a susceptible individual. *S. pneumoniae* and *N. meningitidis* are the responsible agents in approximately 95 percent of healthy children older than 2 months. In compromised hosts, infection with other organisms may occur more frequently. The specific organism sometimes may be predicted on the basis of the type of deficit that is present in the host.

ROUTES OF INFECTION

Bacterial infection of the normally sterile leptomeningeal spaces can occur from a distant focus through the bloodstream or by direct invasion from a contiguous focus. Meningitis usually is the result of hematogenous dissemination of organisms from a distant site of infection,[297] often from the respiratory tract. The meninges thus are seeded with microorganisms during a bacteremic period. Bacterial meningitis in children with otitis media generally follows bacteremia, although direct invasion of the meninges may occur as a complication of otitis media.

The route of infection in bacterial meningitis has been studied by use of a variety of animal models, but the experimental infection was initiated in most cases in a manner that did not mimic human disease. Bacterial meningitis has been induced in rats[220] and monkeys[277] after intranasal inoculation of *H. influenzae* type b. Bacteremia developed hours before meningitis could be detected histologically, a finding that supports the concept that meningitis follows hematogenous dissemination from nasopharyngeal colonization or infection. Marginating bacteria could be detected by fluorescent staining initially in the lateral and dorsal longitudinal (sagittal) sinuses and subsequently spread to the leptomeninges. In the rat model, otitis media appeared to develop by spread of infection from the subarachnoid space to the inner ear and then to the middle ear.

Meningitis may develop after bacterial invasion from a contiguous focus of infection, as in infection of the mastoid or paranasal sinuses, or as a complication of otitis media. Fracture through the paranasal sinuses as a result of head trauma may precede development of meningitis caused by *S. pneumoniae* and *H. influenzae*, which may be recurrent. Direct invasion also may occur in individuals with dermoid sinus tracks or meningomyeloceles, where a direct communication between the skin and the meninges is present. In this setting, infection usually is produced by organisms found on the skin. Recurrent meningitis has been reported in patients with basiethmoidal encephaloceles[309] as well as a congenital defect in the stapedial footplate.[154] Surgical obliteration of the fistula with temporal muscle and fascia prevented the recurrence of meningitis. Meningitis also may develop subsequent to osteomyelitis of the skull or vertebral column. Rarely, meningitis may develop in the normal host with commensurate microorganisms after tooth extraction or dental fillings.[58, 289]

Neurosurgical procedures, particularly those designed for diversion of CSF in children who have hydrocephalus, may lead to subsequent development of meningitis. A chemical meningitis also may occur after neurosurgical procedures, especially those involving the posterior fossa.[107] In these patients, evidence of inflammation develops rapidly, with elevation of temperature on the first postoperative day.

Infection of the CNS may result from environmental contamination or manipulation. Meningeal infection may be acquired in utero transplacentally or during delivery through contact with the cervix or vaginal canal, which may be colonized with a variety of organisms, particularly group B streptococci and *L. monocytogenes*.[6, 21] The newborn infant, the patient with cystic fibrosis, or the burned child may develop septicemia and meningitis as a result of persistent heavy colonization with *Staphylococcus aureus*. A humidified atmosphere promotes the colonization and growth of such organisms as *Serratia marcescens* and *Pseudomonas aeruginosa*. Placing a patient in this setting leads to an increased frequency of infection with these organisms. Indwelling catheters can predispose a person to infection by bacterial (and fungal) organisms that generally are of low virulence in the normal host.

Factors Predisposing the Host to Bacterial Meningitis

Those factors that predispose the host to the development of infection in other sites also predispose the host to the development of bacterial infection of the CNS. A strong interrelationship exists among factors relating to the host, the organism, and the environment with regard to the pathogenesis and outcome of meningitis. Although presented separately, they must be considered a complex interplay of factors that leads to infection.

An increased incidence of bacterial meningitis is observed in the very young; males are affected more frequently than are females, and the severity of disease also is increased in these groups. Fraser and associates[113] reported that the greatest morbidity after bacterial meningitis occurred in individuals affected between birth and 4 years of age. The newborn infant is predisposed to septicemia and meningitis by factors that reflect physiologic deficiencies or immaturity of host defense mechanisms. They include (1) decreased phagocytic and bactericidal activity of polymorphonuclear leukocytes, (2) defects in the response of neonatal leukocytes to chemotactic factors, (3) a deficiency in the capacity of leukocytes to support opsonization, and (4) defects in microtubular length and number that decrease the motility of the neonatal leukocytes compared with those from older children. Deficiencies in serum complement components (C1q, C3, and C5), low levels of serum properdin, and low concentrations of serum IgM and IgA have been documented repeatedly. Despite transplacental acquisition of IgG, antibodies against specific infective agents may be lacking. The precise age at which each of these factors reaches the concentration and functional activity noted in older children and adults is unclear and undoubtedly varies somewhat from individual to individual. In part, meningitis in children between 1 month and 1 year of age may reflect qualitative or quantitative differences of the inflammatory and immunologic responses in older children compared with infants.

The increased risk for development of meningitis in the normal host with less than completely mature immunologic and inflammatory responses to infection may be attributable to age alone. This factor is exemplified in the report of Cole and associates,[56] who studied the risk of recurrent bacteremia in young children. Within 18 months of having bacteremic illness, none of 42 children older than 24 months had a documented additional episode of bacteremia or systemic infection. However, 15 of 135 children (11%) younger than 24 months at the time of the initial bacteremic disease had at least one additional documented bacteremic illness. Of these 15 children, 14 contracted both infections while they were younger than 2 years. Seven of these 15 children had meningitis. Only two patients had documented congenital or hereditary disorders of immunoglobulin or complement concentration or function.

A genetic determination for the predilection of some normal children for the development of bacteremia and meningitis has been suggested.[319] The ability of the host to produce, within the CSF, interleukin (IL)–12 and tumor necrosis factor-α (TNF-α)–induced interferon-γ is important in the natural immunity to various microorganisms that may cause meningitis.[187]

Congenital or acquired abnormalities of the immune system may predispose the host to the acquisition of bacterial infections. Congenital deficiency of the three major immunoglobulin classes may predispose the host to the acquisition of severe bacterial infection. Congenital defects of thymic-dependent, small lymphocyte function or combined T and B defects are detrimental to host defense. A deficiency of $CD4^+$ helper-inducer T cells in patients with bacterial meningitis has been reported and may contribute to the impaired antibody synthesis to bacterial capsular polysaccharides in this disease.[257] Multiple studies have demonstrated that deficiencies of various components of the complement system and increased consumption or loss of complement have been associated with increased risk for development of bacterial meningitis caused by encapsulated organisms.*

An increased incidence of overwhelming infection, including meningitis, occurs after splenectomy, but the likelihood of development of such infection depends on the age of the child at the time of splenectomy, the time since splenectomy, and the original indication for splenectomy.[82] Congenital asplenia or polysplenia also has been associated with an increased incidence of septicemia and meningitis caused by *S. pneumoniae,*[82] *H. influenzae* type b, and gram-negative enteric microorganisms.

Children with sickle-cell disease and other hemoglobinopathies experience meningitis caused by *S. pneumoniae, H. influenzae,* and *Salmonella* spp. more frequently than do normal children.

Children with malignant neoplasms with or without neutropenia appear to be susceptible to development of meningitis caused by organisms of low virulence that pose a minimal threat to normal children, presumably because of abnormalities in immunologic function.[302] A decreased production of normal immunoglobulins, delayed and defective antibody responses to antigenic stimuli, production of abnormal immunoglobulins, depression in the clearance mechanisms of the reticuloendothelial system, and depression of cellular immunity have been documented in children with malignant neoplasms involving the reticuloendothelial system. In addition, the use of irradiation or immunosuppressive agents and antimetabolites predisposes the host to the development of infection in the CNS. Attributing the occurrence of bacterial meningitis in this population directly

*See references 79, 81, 123, 155, 195, 200, 229, 245, 257, 266, 271, 329.

to these agents rather than to the disease for which this therapy has been provided may be difficult. Meningitis occurring after neurosurgical manipulation for tumors of the CNS in non-neutropenic children usually develops within a month of the neurosurgery.[302]

Malnutrition also predisposes children and adults to infectious disease. Impaired cellular immune responses, low levels of serum complement, impaired phagocytic activity of neutrophils, and decreased serum concentrations of transferrin have been documented in malnourished children.[94]

Patients with systemic diseases, such as diabetes mellitus, renal insufficiency, adrenal insufficiency, cystic fibrosis, hypoparathyroidism, and exudative enteropathy, have an increased frequency and severity of CNS infections.[37] Children with diabetes mellitus, coma caused by drug overdose, and Cushing syndrome have been shown to be at increased risk for development of bacteremia or meningitis caused by *H. influenzae* type b.[197] Some type of underlying condition was noted for 21 percent (37 of 181) of the children with pneumococcal meningitis in a multicenter surveillance study.[16] The most common of these conditions was some disorder of the CNS, which occurred in 16 children (9%). Defective chemotaxis, phagocytosis, and bactericidal function accompany these disorders and may explain, in part, the increased susceptibility of these individuals to infection.[94, 95]

In the normal host, bacterial infections at sites other than the leptomeninges are associated with an increased incidence of CNS infection. Infection may spread hematogenously to the meninges in children with endocarditis, pneumonia, or thrombophlebitis or by direct extension from sinusitis, mastoiditis, or osteomyelitis of the skull. Development of meningitis subsequent to performance of lumbar puncture in children younger than 1 year has been described.[106, 317]

Pathology

The most detailed account in English of the pathologic changes occurring with meningitis was written in 1948 by Adams, Kubik, and Bonner.[4] They described the meningeal, cerebral, and vascular changes found post mortem in 14 patients who succumbed to *H. influenzae* 14 hours to 76 days after the onset of disease. Although most patients in their series received inadequate treatment (effective antibiotic therapy was not available), the pathologic findings they describe differ little from those of subsequent reports by Smith and Landing,[298] Rorke and Pitts,[262] and Dodge and Swartz,[77] whose patients died despite administration of antibiotics. These descriptions are summarized later.

A meningeal exudate varying in thickness may be found (Fig. 38–2). Purulent material is distributed widely but may accumulate about the veins and venous sinuses, over the convexity of the brain, in the depths of the sulci, in the sylvian fissures, within the basal cisterns, and around the cerebellum. The spinal cord may be encased in pus. Ventriculitis (purulent material within the ventricles) has been noted repeatedly in children who died of their diseases. Subsequent experience suggests that ventriculitis may be a relatively common finding in children with bacterial meningitis who survive, particularly neonates. Invasion of the ventricular wall with perivascular collections of purulent material has been noted. Loss of ependymal lining and subependymal gliosis may be seen. In some studies, purulent exudate tended to be thicker over the convexity of the brains in patients with pneumococcal meningitis than in those patients with other forms of meningitis.[77, 262]

Vascular and parenchymatous changes have been demonstrated at necropsy. Polymorphonuclear infiltrates extending to the subintimal region of small arteries and veins have been associated with the exudative meningeal process. Thrombosis of small cortical veins associated with necrosis of the cerebral cortex may be noted. Occlusion of one of the major venous sinuses, subarachnoid hemorrhage secondary to a necrotizing arteritis, and necrosis of the cerebral cortex in the absence of identifiable thrombosis of small vessels rarely may be observed. Reactive microglia and astrocytes may be identified in the cerebral cortex, particularly subadjacent to regions of heavy subarachnoid exudate. Because no bacteria are found in the cerebral cortex, these pathologic changes should be viewed as a noninfectious encephalopathy. "Toxic or circulatory factors" were suggested as possible causes by Adams and associates.[5] Dodge and Swartz[77] suggested systemic hypoxia and fever as additional possible causes. They also noted that an increase in intracranial pressure might interfere with cerebral circulation.

Damage to the cerebral cortex, reflecting the effects of vascular occlusion, hypoxia, bacterial invasion, toxic encephalopathy, bacterial factors, inflammatory mediators, small molecule effectors, or some combination of these factors, provides an adequate explanation for impaired consciousness, deficits in motor and sensory functions, seizures, and retardation that may be observed.

Hydrocephalus that develops in patients beyond the newborn period is an uncommon complication of meningitis. Most often, hydrocephalus is communicating and is the result of adhesive thickening of the arachnoid about the cisterns at the base of the brain. Less frequently, the aqueduct of Sylvius or the foramina of Magendie and Luschka are obstructed by fibrosis and reactive gliosis. The ensuing ventricular dilatation may be coupled with coexistent necrosis of nervous tissue because of the meningitis itself or because of occlusion of cerebral veins and, rarely, arteries. Cerebral necrosis plus increased intraventricular pressure may result in total dissolution of the cerebrum.

Subdural effusions occur frequently during the course of meningitis. The exact pathogenesis is not known. However, the high incidence of effusion and the fact that subdural fluid collections may be found early in the course of bacterial

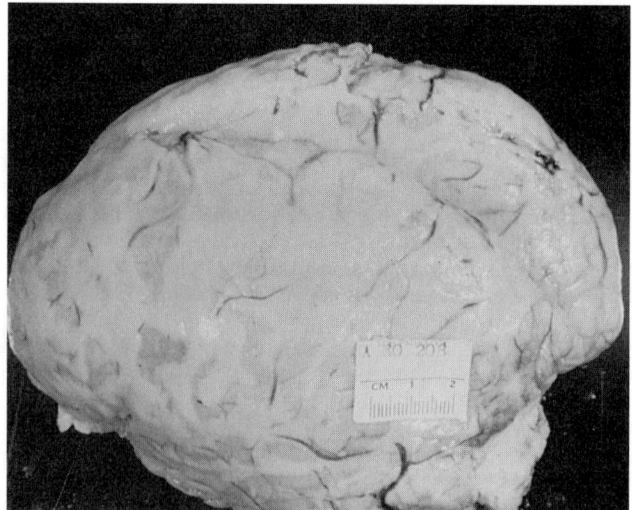

FIGURE 38–2 ■ Note extensive purulent exudate over entire cerebral cortex in a patient who died as a result of bacterial meningitis.

meningitis in children suggest that subdural effusions should be considered a concomitant occurrence with meningeal inflammation rather than a complication of the disease. Numerous veins traverse the subdural space, and inflammation of these veins and of the dural capillaries could produce an increase in vascular permeability and loss of albumin-rich fluid into the subdural space.[70] The ratio of albumin to gamma globulin is higher in the subdural fluid of children with meningitis than it is in serum.[135] When the inflammatory process subsides, formation of fluid generally ceases, but its presence may persist because of a continued transudation through newly formed vessels in the subdural membrane.

Subdural empyema, as opposed to subdural effusion, occurs rarely. It was observed in only two of the cases reported by Adams and associates,[5] in 1 of 34 patients examined by Smith and Landing,[298] and in none of the patients studied by Dodge and Swartz.[77]

Many factors contribute to the increase in intracranial pressure in patients with meningitis. Endotoxin and fragments of the cell wall of gram-positive organisms are capable of inducing the release of IL-1 and TNF from macrophages and other sources.[74, 215] These substances, in addition to other interleukins and arachidonic acid metabolites, affect many systems, including endothelial cells, and profoundly affect the function of the vasculature and its interaction with neutrophils and other inflammatory cells. These substances play an important role in the pathogenesis of increased intracranial pressure and cerebral edema in patients with meningitis by altering cerebral blood flow, intracranial blood volume, and permeability of the cerebral vasculature.[233] Intercellular junctions, which normally are tight, are open in experimental meningitis, which is associated with an increased permeability to circulating albumin.[252] Pinocytotic vesicles also are noted within the cytoplasm of endothelial cells. Swelling of cellular elements (cytotoxic edema) also has been noted.

Alterations in CSF resorption further exacerbate cerebral edema and increased intracranial pressure. In experimental meningitis, resorption of CSF is diminished as an accumulation of proteins, leukocytes, and other materials interferes with the function of the arachnoid villus.[280]

During the course of meningitis, excess secretion of antidiuretic hormone (ADH) occurs, which induces water retention and exacerbates electrolyte abnormalities already created secondary to the inflammatory processes occurring in the CNS. Cellular electrolyte disturbances may depolarize neuronal membranes, predisposing the host to seizure activity. Increased oxidation of glucose and increased lactate production, as well as depletion of high-energy compounds such as adenosine 5′-triphosphate and phosphocreatine, are observed. Hypoglycorrhachia results primarily from decreased transport of glucose across the inflamed choroid plexus and from increased use of glucose by host tissues. Use of glucose by bacteria and polymorphonuclear leukocytes is of less relative importance.[77, 279]

PATHOGENESIS

Most cases of bacterial meningitis progress through four steps: (1) infection or colonization of the upper respiratory tract, (2) invasion of the blood from a respiratory focus, (3) seeding of the meninges by a blood-borne organism, and (4) inflammation of the meninges and brain. Less commonly, infection of the leptomeninges can occur by contiguous spread or hematogenous dissemination from another remote site. The nasopharyngeal mucosa is colonized with *S. pneumoniae, N. meningitidis,* or other microorganisms, resulting most commonly in an asymptomatic carrier state or minor upper respiratory tract illness. This attachment is mediated by specific microbial cell surface components. *N. meningitidis* strains possess fimbriae that bind to cell surface receptors on nasopharyngeal mucosal cells[71] and appear to be transported across specialized cells within phagocytic vacuoles.[310] Once in the bloodstream, the common pathogenic organisms (*S. pneumoniae, H. influenzae, N. meningitidis, E. coli* K1, and group B streptococcus) are capable of evading host defense mechanisms through capsular polysaccharides, which inhibit neutrophil phagocytosis and classic complement-mediated bactericidal activity. These bacteria then traverse the blood-brain barrier, most likely at the cerebral capillaries and choroid plexus. Fimbriae of *E. coli* have been shown to facilitate attachment in these regions.[241] Once in the CSF, and because of insufficient opsonic and phagocytic activity in the CSF, organisms multiply rapidly, liberating cell wall or membrane components (lipopolysaccharide, lipoteichoic acid, peptidoglycan, bacterial toxins).

Host defenses within the CSF before and after bacterial invasion seem to rely on two important mechanisms available to the host to clear bacteria.[292] One clearance system requires a type-specific antibody, a functional classic complement system for opsonization, and the presence of competent polymorphonuclear leukocytes for phagocytosis. The second system is dependent on the interaction of nonspecific or low-affinity antibody and the alternative complement pathway for opsonization of the organism. Clearance by this system occurs in the absence of polymorphonuclear leukocytes.

Complement and opsonic proteins either are found at very low concentrations or are absent entirely within normal CSF.[108, 292] Thus, the CSF is devoid of those factors required for bacterial clearance. When bacteria first invade the meninges, the lack of complement and opsonic proteins within the sanctuary of the CNS may permit the bacteria to multiply unrestrained for some time. The slow response of polymorphonuclear leukocytes and the lack of serum-specific antibody available during the initial inflammatory response enhance the probability that bacterial infection will be established.[33, 84, 128, 334, 352]

The specific pathophysiologic changes in bacterial meningitis are the result of the bacterial products and the inflammatory response of the host to those products. Initial bactericidal antibiotic therapy results in a rapid release of bacterial products such as endotoxins, teichoic acid, and peptidoglycans. Augmented permeability of the blood-brain barrier can be induced by bacterial products alone, which cause disruption of the tight junctions between capillary endothelial cells and marked increase in pinocytotic activity within endothelial cells. An influx of serum albumin into the CSF is accompanied by other low-molecular-weight proteins, including components of the complement cascade.[162]

TNF-α and IL-1 appear to be key mediators in initiation of meningeal inflammation. Both proteins stimulate vascular endothelial cells to induce adhesion and passage of neutrophils into the CNS and trigger inflammatory processes. Astrocytes and microglia are capable of producing TNF-α.[320] TNF-α concentrations are elevated (1) in CSF but not in serum; (2) in animal models of bacterial meningitis; and (3) in patients with bacterial meningitis caused by *H. influenzae, N. meningitidis, S. pneumoniae,* and *Streptococcus agalactiae*[225] but not in patients with culture-proven viral meningitis.[255] IL-1 activity can be detected in infants and children with bacterial meningitis, and its presence is correlated significantly with CSF inflammatory abnormalities,

TNF-α concentrations, and adverse outcome.[225] TNF-α and IL-1 are capable of inducing phospholipase A_2 activity, which in turn triggers the production of platelet-activating factor and activates the arachidonic acid pathway. This process leads to the generation of prostaglandins, thromboxanes, and leukotrienes from membrane phospholipids of endothelial and polymorphonuclear cells, which modulate multiple aspects of the inflammatory process.

These cytokines activate adhesion-promoting receptors on cerebral vascular endothelial cells, resulting in attraction and attachment of leukocytes to sites of stimuli. These leukocytes release proteolytic compounds that allow intercellular junctions to be traversed. These enzymes in conjunction with platelet-activating factor and the arachidonic acid metabolites injure the vascular endothelium, resulting in increased permeability of the blood-brain barrier and activation of the coagulation cascade.

Superoxide and hydrogen peroxide are secreted by TNF-α–stimulated macrophages, including brain microglia, and leukocytes[250, 257]; hydrogen peroxide induces extensive neuronal damage.[237] In addition, macrophages secrete excitatory amino acids, such as glutamate, that potentially kill *N*-methyl-D-aspartate receptor–positive cells.[190]

For gram-positive bacterial meningitis, lipoteichoic acid peptidoglycans are the bacterial surface elements that induce inflammation.[322] The threshold concentration that triggers inflammation is approximately 10^5 bacterial cell equivalents of cell wall pieces.[322] For gram-negative meningitis, endotoxin is the major inflammatory component, with peptidoglycan serving as an important cofactor.[45] The inflammatory threshold is approximately 2 pg of endotoxin or approximately 10^5 bacterial cell equivalents.[345]

Cytokines now appear to be the primary drivers of the inflammatory response. The following cytokines are involved in the inflammatory response noted in bacterial meningitis: IL-1, IL-3, IL-4, IL-6, IL-8, IL-10, IL-12, interferon-γ, macrophage inflammatory protein, transforming growth factor-β, and TNF-α.[72, 114, 327]

The chemokines are a superfamily of small chemoattractant cytokines that play an important role in the initiation and modulation of inflammation in bacterial meningitis.[304] Complement factors are up-regulated in bacterial meningitis. The activated complement cascade in CSF, acting on up-regulated complement receptors on brain cells, potentially mediates direct brain damage.[41] Complement factors also are chemoattractants that enhance CSF leukocytosis and thereby indirectly produce brain damage in patients with bacterial meningitis.[83]

The most potent final effectors of brain damage in bacterial meningitis appear to be host-derived, low-molecular-weight mediators, such as hydrogen peroxide, hydroxyl radicals, and hypochlorous acid.[253] Nitric oxide also can be induced in brain cells in response to bacterial products.[178] Nitric oxide and superoxide radicals react to form peroxynitrite anion, which decomposes and forms nitrogen dioxide, hydroxyl radicals, and strong oxidant compounds.[30] Peroxynitrite appears to be an important neuronal toxin.[185]

The various pathways to neuronal cell death are shown in Figure 38–3. A detailed review of the molecular mechanisms of brain damage in bacterial meningitis has been provided by Braun and Tuomanen.[41] The role of inflammatory mediators and oxygen radicals in the pathogenesis of bacterial meningitis also is detailed in a review by Leib and Tauber.[196]

The increasing concentrations of chemotactic factors in the subarachnoid space lead to accumulation of large numbers of neutrophils in the CSF. The growth of bacteria is not slowed significantly by this response,[83] and the large number of neutrophils actually may have a deleterious effect, causing tissue damage and poor disease outcome.[88, 96] Impaired phagocytosis by neutrophils in the meningeal spaces may be related to weak activity in fluid medium, lack of complement activity and opsonization, and poor penetration of IgM and IgG through the blood-brain barrier, even during acute *H. influenzae* and *S. pneumoniae* meningitis.[129]

Bacterial cell wall fragments, endotoxin, or both also contribute to vascular permeability. In experimental *E. coli* meningitis, the CSF endotoxin concentration increased markedly after treatment with β-lactam antibiotics. This increase was associated with an increase in brain water content. This effect could be blocked by polymyxin or a monoclonal antibody, both of which inactivate endotoxin.[314]

The inflammatory and vascular events described earlier act synergistically to produce the clinical symptoms and long-term sequelae that are noted in patients with bacterial meningitis. Vascular permeability leads to vasogenic edema. Inflammatory and electrolyte changes lead to cytotoxic edema. Alterations in production and absorption of CSF lead to interstitial edema. The cytokines also trigger increased

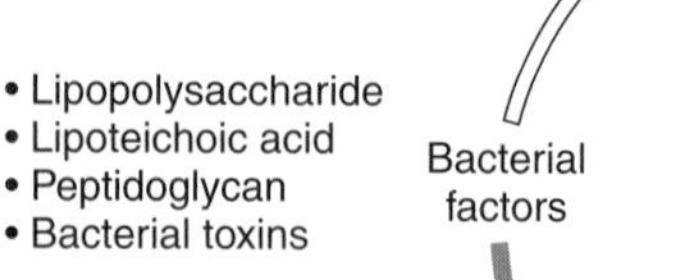

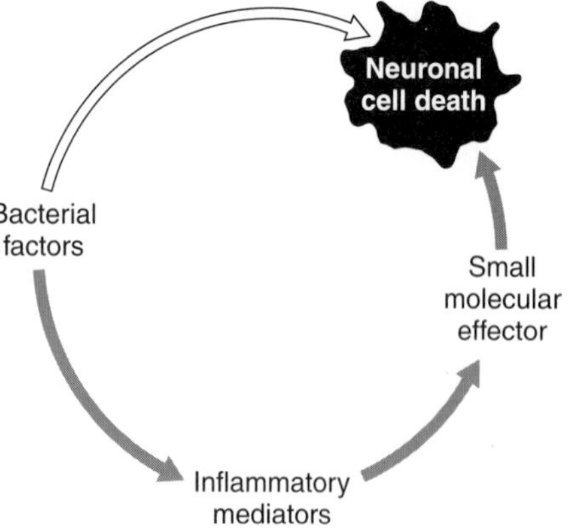

- Reactive oxygen species (superoxide, peroxynitrite)
- Reactive nitrogen species (nitric oxide)
- Excitatory amino acids (glutamate, aspartate, glycine, taurine, alanine)

- Cytokines (TNF, IL-1, IL-6, IL-8, IL-10, PAF, TGFβ)
- Arachidonic acid metabolites (prostaglandins, leukotrienes)
- Complement

FIGURE 38–3 ■ Pathways to neuronal cell death. Although bacterial products can induce directly some neuronal toxicity, host-derived inflammatory agents are the primary source of final mediators of injury. IL, interleukin; PAF, platelet-activating factor; TGF, transforming growth factor; TNF, tumor necrosis factor. (From Braun, J. S., and Tuomanen, E. I.: Molecular mechanisms of brain damage in bacterial meningitis. Adv. Pediatr. Infect. Dis. *14*:49–71, 1999.)

cerebral blood flow and further formation of edema, resulting in increased intracranial pressure.[19] The increased intracranial pressure and vasculitis lead to a subsequent decrease in cerebral blood flow, which does not appear to be caused by loss of autoregulation.[19] Activation of the coagulation cascade predisposes the patient to venous, microvascular, and, rarely, arterial thrombosis. Direct neurotoxic damage by inflammatory cells also may contribute to the neuropathologic changes seen in bacterial meningitis.

Clinical Manifestations and Pathophysiologic Relationships

Inflammation of the meninges generally is associated with nausea, vomiting, irritability, anorexia, headache, confusion, back pain, and nuchal rigidity. In many cases, Kernig and Brudzinski signs will be noted. Kernig sign is present when the leg is flexed 90 degrees at the hips and cannot be extended more than 135 degrees. Brudzinski sign is present if the thighs and legs are flexed involuntarily when the neck is flexed. All of these findings suggest irritation of inflamed sensory nerves, which in turn produces a reflex contraction of certain muscles in an attempt to minimize pain. These findings also can be the result of increased intracranial pressure and an associated distortion of nerve roots. These signs can be accompanied by hyperesthesia and photophobia. Currently, no satisfactory pathophysiologic explanation for photophobia exists. Signs of meningeal inflammation may be minimal in the infant, but irritability, restlessness, and poor feeding may be noted. Nuchal rigidity and Kernig and Brudzinski signs may occur late in the young child. Nuchal rigidity may not be elicited in comatose patients or when signs of focal or diffuse neurologic impairment are present. At the time of initial evaluation, 60 to 80 percent of children have a stiff neck.[165] A review of 1064 cases of bacterial meningitis in children beyond the neonatal period revealed that 16 (1.5%) had no meningeal signs during their entire period of hospitalization, despite the presence of CSF pleocytosis.[125] Fever, a hallmark of infection, generally is present; its absence in a patient with signs of meningeal inflammation, although infrequent, is far from unusual.

Increased intracranial pressure is the rule; it may be reflected by complaints of headache in older children and by a bulging fontanelle and diastasis of sutures in the infant. Papilledema is an uncommon finding in acute meningitis, presumably because of the relatively brief duration of increased pressure at the time of diagnosis. When papilledema is observed, venous sinus occlusion, subdural empyema, or brain abscess should be sought.

Signs of cerebral edema may be present. Vasogenic edema occurs as a consequence of increased permeability of the blood-brain barrier. Interstitial edema may occur secondary to decreased clearance of CSF at the arachnoid villi and subsequent obstructive hydrocephalus. Cytotoxic cerebral edema mediated by the release of toxic factors from neutrophils and bacteria leads to increased concentration of intracellular water and sodium and loss of intracellular potassium. In many cases (88% in one prospective study[87]), meningitis is associated with the release of ADH, causing water retention and a relative dumping of sodium by the kidney. If the patient then is given excessive free water during therapy, a further increase in intracranial pressure may be noted.

Transient or permanent paralysis of cranial nerves may be noted. Deafness or disturbances in vestibular function are relatively common findings; optic nerve involvement with blindness rarely occurs. Involvement of the eighth cranial nerve may reflect disease at the level of the cochlear and vestibular end-organs, which may be related to concomitant infection of the inner ear. Paralysis of extraocular and facial nerves may be noted. Torticollis has been reported in two children with partially treated meningitis.[210] Obtundation, stupor, coma, and focal neurologic signs may be seen in children with bacterial meningitis. The relative frequency with which these findings are noted may be seen in Table 38–2, in which data for 235 children with bacterial meningitis who were enrolled prospectively have been analyzed according to the type of organism responsible for their meningitis. Overall, 14.9 percent of children were semicomatose or comatose at the time of admission; rates for children with pneumococcal or meningococcal meningitis were higher than those for children with *H. influenzae* disease. Focal neurologic signs were present at the time of admission in 16.5 percent of the total group (34.3% of children with pneumococcal meningitis). The presence of focal neurologic signs at the time of admission indicated poor prognosis and could be correlated with persistent abnormal neurologic examinations at 1, 3, and 6 months ($p < .01$) and at 1 year after discharge ($p < .03$). The presence of focal signs at the time of admission also correlated with the presence of retardation ($p < .001$), as determined by detailed psychometric testing after discharge.

In general, when focal signs are noted in the absence of seizures, cortical necrosis, occlusive vasculitis, or thrombosis of cortical veins has occurred. Thrombosis of meningeal vessels or cortical necrosis may be associated with hemiparesis or quadriparesis as well as with focal seizures. These signs may appear during the first 3 or 4 days of illness or, less commonly, may be noted after the first or second week of infection. A highly significant association ($p < .001$) between neurologic signs indicative of cerebral injury and late (1 to 15 years after the acute infection) afebrile seizures has been noted.[247] Ataxia has been a presenting sign of

TABLE 38–2 ■ FREQUENCY OF SELECTED FINDINGS IN CHILDREN WITH BACTERIAL MENINGITIS

	Total Group	*Haemophilus influenzae*	*Streptococcus pneumoniae*	*Neisseria meningitidis*	Others
Number of patients	235	151	35	26	23
Level of consciousness (%)					
Irritable or lethargic	184 (78.3)	117 (77.5)	24 (68.6)	21 (80.8)	22 (95.7)
Somnolent	16 (6.8)	13 (8.6)	1 (2.8)	1 (3.8)	1 (4.3)
Obtunded-semicomatose	27 (11.5)	15 (9.9)	8 (22.9)	4 (15.4)	0 (0)
Comatose	8 (3.4)	6 (4.0)	2 (5.7)	0 (0)	0 (0)
Focal neurologic signs on admission (%)	37 (16.5)	22 (14.6)	12 (34.3)	2 (7.7)	1 (4.3)
Seizures before admission (%)	48 (20.4)	35 (23.2)	8 (23)	3 (11.5)	2 (8.7)
Seizures in hospital (%)	61 (26)	43 (28)	12 (34)	5 (19)	1 (4.5)

meningitis in numerous children and adults. Schwartz[286] described four children who presented with ataxia as an initial symptom. Adolescents with meningitis may present with behavioral abnormalities that may be confused with drug abuse or psychiatric disorders.[24]

Approximately 20 percent of children with bacterial meningitis experience seizures before admissions, and approximately 26 percent have them during the first or second day in the hospital. Green and colleagues[139] retrospectively examined the frequency of seizures before or at the time of presentation in children with meningitis. They found that 111 of 410 (27%) children with bacterial meningitis had seizures at or before the time of diagnosis; 88 of these children had complex seizures (focal, prolonged, or more than one in a 24-hour period). They found that all children with bacterial meningitis who presented with seizures had other signs or symptoms of meningitis, such as altered level of consciousness, nuchal rigidity, or complex seizures and petechial rash. The frequency of seizure activity is similar for children with *H. influenzae* type b or pneumococcal meningitis; seizures occur in children with meningitis caused by these organisms approximately twice as frequently as in children with meningococcal meningitis. In one study of 181 children with pneumococcal meningitis, 41 (23%) developed seizures before admission; 75 percent of preadmission seizures were generalized.[16]

Overall, seizures are noted in approximately 30 percent of children with bacterial meningitis. Seizures noted before or during the first several days of hospitalization are of no particular prognostic significance. In particular, their occurrence does not herald the development of a permanent seizure disorder. Seizures that are difficult to control or that persist beyond the fourth hospital day, as well as seizures that occur for the first time late in the hospital course, may be of greater significance and have been associated with permanent sequelae of meningitis. Children with focal seizures have a greater likelihood for development of sequelae of meningitis than do those with generalized seizure activity. Focal or prolonged seizures probably are indicative of serious cerebral vascular disturbances or cerebral infarction. Seizures that occur before admission have correlated positively with abnormal audiometric studies and permanent hearing handicaps. Seven percent of patients with bacterial meningitis have focal or generalized seizures 3 months to 15 years after recovery from bacterial meningitis.[247]

Collections of fluid in the subdural space can be demonstrated in as many as 50 percent of infants and children during acute illness.[77] In a prospective study of infants 1 to 18 months of age with bacterial meningitis, subdural effusions were noted in 43 percent of those with *H. influenzae* meningitis, 30 percent of those with pneumococcal meningitis, and 22 percent of those with meningococcal meningitis. Subdural effusions were found in 24 percent (25 of 103) of the children undergoing neuroimaging in the multicenter pediatric surveillance study of pneumococcal meningitis.[16] No greater incidence of neurologic sequelae or developmental delay was found on long-term follow-up in patients with effusion compared with those with bacterial meningitis who did not have effusion.[296, 299]

Subdural effusions may cause enlargement in head circumference or may be responsible for abnormal transillumination of the skull. Vomiting, seizures, a full fontanelle, focal neurologic signs, or persistent fever may be noted at times, but these signs occur with such frequency in children with bacterial meningitis who do not have subdural effusions that it is difficult to attribute their occurrence to the subdural effusion.[89]

Blindness and optic atrophy may be related to optic arachnoiditis or infarction of the occipital lobe. Spastic paraparesis with sensory loss in the lower extremities may be secondary to meningomyelitis, spinal cord infarction, or both.

Arthralgia and myalgia are noted in many patients with bacterial meningitis, reflecting the systemic nature of the disease. Arthritis also may occur and does so most commonly during the course of meningococcal disease; generally, it is transient. Early findings of arthritis may be related to direct invasion of the joint by the meningococcus. Arthritis that develops late in the course of meningococcal or *H. influenzae* meningitis may be an immune complex–mediated event. Petechial or purpuric lesions may be seen in 50 percent of patients with meningococcal meningitis[77] but also may accompany any infectious or noninfectious disease process in which vasculitis occurs. Purpura, shock, and hypothermia indicate a poor prognosis.

Pericardial effusions may be present; they generally resolve during the course of antibiotic therapy. In some cases, they are the cause of persistent fever, and pericardiocentesis or an open drainage procedure may be required.

Shock may be associated with any form of overwhelming bacteremia but occurs most often in patients with fulminant meningococcemia. In a prospective study, 3.8 percent of children with meningococcal meningitis developed profound hypotension. In the same study, shock occurred in 5.5 percent of children with *H. influenzae* meningitis. Endotoxin has been detected by *Limulus* lysate assay in the blood and CSF of children with meningococcal and *H. influenzae* meningitis.[264] Sixteen percent of the children in the multicenter pneumococcal meningitis study were in shock on admission.[16] Signs of disseminated intravascular coagulation may accompany hypotension in these patients.

Facial cellulitis (including buccal and periorbital cellulitis), pneumonia, epiglottitis, endophthalmitis, and other suppurative manifestations can present at the time of admission in any patient with bacterial meningitis. In one study of children with buccal cellulitis, less than 10 percent (7 of 73) had concomitant bacterial meningitis documented by lumbar puncture as part of their initial evaluation.[22] Five of the seven children had no clinical evidence of meningeal irritation. *H. influenzae* and *S. pneumoniae* were cultured from two patients with periorbital cellulitis and no clinical evidence of meningeal irritation or abnormal CSF cell counts or chemistries.[272] In the largest review of facial cellulitis caused by *S. pneumoniae*, 15 of 52 children had a lumbar puncture performed; 2 (13.3%) had a pleocytosis (18 white blood cells—52% polymorphonuclear leukocytes, and 9 white blood cells—91% polymorphonuclear leukocytes).[136] The Gram stain and cultures of the CSF specimens were negative. Lumbar puncture should be considered for children with facial cellulitis who are younger than 18 months and possibly bacteremic with *S. pneumoniae*.

Differential Diagnosis

The signs and symptoms described earlier suggest meningeal or intracranial pathologic processes but are not pathognomonic of acute bacterial infection. Tuberculous meningitis, fungal meningitis, aseptic meningitis, brain abscess, intracranial or spinal epidural abscesses, bacterial endocarditis with embolism, subdural empyema with or without thrombophlebitis, ruptured dermoid cysts, ruptured spinal ependymomas, and brain tumors may show similar signs and symptoms. Differentiation of these disorders depends on careful examination of CSF obtained by lumbar puncture and additional immunologic, radiographic, and isotopic studies as delineated later.

Diagnosis

Early diagnosis and treatment of bacterial meningitis are imperative in reducing mortality rates and morbidity. Physicians must perform a lumbar puncture on any child in whom they suspect the diagnosis after a careful history and physical examination have been performed, unless specific contraindications to this procedure (e.g., clinical signs of increased intracranial pressure in a patient with a closed fontanelle and closed sutures) are present.

An association between performance of a lumbar puncture during bacteremia and the later development of meningitis has been reported.[106] This association was evident only in children younger than 1 year. The perceptive physician selects children for lumbar puncture in whom clinical signs suggest developing meningitis before the CSF findings are diagnostic. These data suggest a need for careful observation and, if appropriate, hospitalization and antimicrobial therapy for infants younger than 1 year who undergo lumbar puncture and who concomitantly have risk factors (e.g., concurrent high temperature and white blood cell counts) for the development of bacteremia.

CSF findings characteristic of various inflammatory diseases of the CNS are shown in Table 38–3.

Measurement of pressure, often neglected in infants and young children, is an important component of each CSF examination. When the pressure is very high, only enough fluid to permit a careful examination should be removed. Compression of the jugular vein should be avoided unless compression of the spinal cord is suspected. Xanthochromic CSF derives its color primarily from bilirubin pigment. Hemorrhage, bilirubin staining in icteric patients who have meningitis (i.e., neonates, leptospirosis), or an elevated protein concentration of CSF may be associated with xanthochromia.

CSF should be examined immediately. The total number of white blood cells (WBCs) should be counted in a counting chamber, and after cytocentrifugation, a differential cell count should be performed on a Wright-stained smear of the sediment. The normal CSF of children 3 months of age or older contains fewer than 6 WBCs/mm^3. Ninety-five percent of children older than 3 months have no polymorphonuclear leukocytes in the CSF; thus, the presence of a polymorphonuclear leukocyte in the CSF may be regarded as abnormal. When a lumbar puncture has been performed in a febrile child and a single polymorphonuclear leukocyte has been noted, careful clinical observation is imperative, and treatment should be considered until the results of the culture of the CSF are known.

If the lumbar puncture has been traumatic, a total cell count can be performed in a counting chamber. The red blood cells (RBCs) then can be lysed by acetic acid and a cell count repeated. If the total number of WBCs compared with the number of RBCs is in excess of that in whole blood, one can assume the presence of CSF pleocytosis. One simple way to estimate the WBC count in the presence of RBCs is to allow 1 WBC per 1000 RBCs/mm^3. CSF protein should be measured (usually elevated in bacterial meningitis), and the CSF glucose concentration should be compared with the blood glucose concentration that has been obtained concomitantly. In patients with bacterial meningitis, depression of CSF glucose and of the ratio of CSF to blood glucose (normally approximately 66%) is the rule.

Separate smears should be made, and one should be Gram stained for bacteria. A Kinyoun stain for mycobacteria is performed if tuberculous meningitis is suspected. The probability of visualizing bacteria on a Gram stain of CSF depends on the number of organisms present. The percentage of positive smears is 25 percent with less than 10^3 colony-forming units (CFU)/mL, 60 percent in the range of 10^3 to 10^5 CFU/mL, and 97 percent with more than 10^5 CFU/mL.[189] Quellung and agglutination reactions can provide immediate identification of various organisms if the appropriate type of specific antisera is available. Treating the child with bacterial meningitis with an antibiotic before performing initial lumbar puncture usually does not alter markedly the morphologic or chemical results obtained (Table 38–4). In patients with *H. influenzae* meningitis (Table 38–5) who were pretreated, CSF cultures frequently grew *H. influenzae*; a tendency exists for pretreatment of children with pneumococcal or meningococcal disease to render the CSF sterile (see Table 38–4). Even when children received appropriate antibiotics for their meningitis intravenously for 44 to 68 hours, the bacterial character of the chemical and morphologic findings could be discerned in most cases.[36]

The CSF should be cultured on a blood agar plate and a chocolate agar plate. The CSF specimens always should be cultured, even when the fluid appears to be crystal-clear and acellular or nearly so.

In the 1970s, countercurrent immunoelectrophoresis was shown to be a useful technique for rapid diagnosis (within 1 hour) and management of bacterial meningitis caused by *H. influenzae* type b, *S. pneumoniae, N. meningitidis* (groups A, C, W135, and D), and group B streptococcus. It may be used to detect antigens from K1 strains of *E. coli* or *L. monocytogenes*.[97, 209] The methodology is sensitive and can detect nonviable bacteria, thus permitting the detection of bacterial antigen, even in patients who have been pretreated with appropriate antibiotics. If this technique is employed, it is imperative to use antisera that have the greatest possible sensitivity and specificity.[157, 288] Group B meningococcal antiserum, which is available commercially, is unreliable. When pneumococcal antisera are used, material obtained from the State Serum Institute in Copenhagen, Denmark, has proved to be highly efficacious; sensitivity is enhanced by using the various pools of pneumococcal antisera in addition to the omniserum. A negative result of countercurrent immunoelectrophoresis does not exclude the diagnosis of bacterial meningitis.

Latex particle agglutination commercial kits are available for detecting the polysaccharide antigens of *H. influenzae* type b, *S. pneumoniae, N. meningitidis,* and group B streptococcus. Latex particle agglutination is superior to countercurrent immunoelectrophoresis in detecting PRP antigen of *H. influenzae* type b in CSF and serum. However, nonspecific agglutination of latex particles in serum, urine, and other body fluids may result in an indeterminate test result.[64, 158, 278, 339] A commercial latex particle agglutination kit containing antibody-coated latex particles for *H. influenzae* type b, *S. pneumoniae,* and *N. meningitidis* serogroups is available. The Food and Drug Administration does not recommend latex agglutination testing of urine of infants for group B streptococcus as a method for inferring invasive disease with this organism. Latex agglutination of urine for group B streptococcus or *N. meningitidis* should be avoided because of the high frequency of false-positive results.

The clinical utility of rapid antigen detection in CSF has been questioned in recent years since the decline in frequency of invasive infections caused by *H. influenzae* type b. A positive test response rarely alters the approach to

TABLE 38–3 ■ CEREBROSPINAL FLUID FINDINGS IN SUPPURATIVE DISEASES OF THE CENTRAL NERVOUS SYSTEM AND MENINGES

Condition	Pressure (mm H_2O)	Leukocytes/mm^3	Protein (mg/dL)	Sugar (mg/dL)	Specific Findings
Acute bacterial meningitis	Usually elevated; average, 300	Several hundred to more than 60,000; usually a few thousand; occasionally fewer than 100 (especially meningococcal or early in disease); polymorphonuclears predominate	Usually 100 to 500, occasionally more than 1000	Fewer than 40 in more than half the cases	Organism usually seen on smear or recovered on culture in more than 90% of cases
Subdural empyema	Usually elevated; average, 300	Fewer than 100 to a few thousand; polymorphonuclears predominate	Usually 100 to 500	Normal	No organisms on smear or by culture unless concurrent meningitis
Brain abscess	Usually elevated	Usually 10 to 200; fluid rarely is acellular; lymphocytes predominate	Usually 75 to 400	Normal	No organisms on smear or by culture
Ventricular empyema (rupture of brain abscess)	Considerably elevated	Several thousand to 100,000; usually more than 90% polymorphonuclears	Usually several hundred	Usually fewer than 40	Organisms may be cultured or seen on smear
Cerebral epidural abscess	Slight to modest elevation	Few to several hundred or more cells; lymphocytes predominate	Usually 50 to 200	Normal	No organisms on smear or by culture
Spinal epidural abscess	Usually reduced with spinal block	Usually 10 to 100; lymphocytes predominate	Usually several hundred	Normal	No organisms on smear or by culture
Thrombophlebitis (often associated with subdural empyema)	Often elevated	Few to several hundred; polymorphonuclears and lymphocytes	Slightly to moderately elevated	Normal	No organisms on smear or by culture
Bacterial endocarditis (with embolism)	Normal or slightly elevated	Few to fewer than 100; lymphocytes and polymorphonuclears	Slightly elevated	Normal	No organisms on smear or by culture
Acute hemorrhagic encephalitis	Usually elevated	Few to more than 1000; polymorphonuclears predominate	Moderately elevated	Normal	No organisms on smear or by culture
Tuberculous infection	Usually elevated; may be low with dynamic block in advanced stages	Usually 25 to 100, rarely more than 500; lymphocytes predominate, except in early stages when polymorphonuclears may account for 80% of cells	Nearly always elevated; usually 100 to 200; may be much higher if dynamic block	Usually reduced; less than 50 in 75% of cases	Acid-fast organisms may be seen on smear of protein coagulum (pellicle) or recovered from inoculated guinea pig or by culture
Cryptococcal infection	Usually elevated; average, 225	Average, 50 (0 to 800); lymphocytes predominate	Average, 100; usually 20 to 500	Reduced in more than half of cases; average, 30; often higher in patients with concomitant diabetes mellitus	Organisms may be seen in India ink preparation and on culture (Sabouraud medium); usually will grow on blood agar; may produce alcohol in cerebrospinal fluid from fermentation of glucose
Syphilis (acute)	Usually elevated	Average, 500; usually lymphocytes; rarely polymorphonuclears	Average, 100; gamma globulin often high, with abnormal colloidal gold curve	Normal (rarely reduced)	Positive reagin test result for syphilis; spirochete not demonstrable by usual techniques of smear or by culture
Sarcoidosis	Normal to considerably elevated	0 to fewer than 100 mononuclear cells	Slight to moderate elevation	Normal	No specific findings

TABLE 38–4 ■ COMPARISON OF CEREBROSPINAL FLUID (CSF) FINDINGS IN PATIENTS WITH UNTREATED AND PRETREATED MENINGITIS

	Untreated	Pretreated
Number of patients	143	91
Total white blood cell count × 10^3		
Mean ± 1 SD	4.9 ± 6.5	4.1 ± 5.0
Range	0–55	0.006–25.5
Percentage polys		
Mean ± 1 SD	84 ± 21	81 ± 25
Range	0–100	0–100
Glucose (mg/dL)		
Mean ± 1 SD	35 ± 28	32 ± 25
Range	0–109	0–100
CSF/blood glucose (%)		
Mean ± 1 SD	29 ± 21	29 ± 21
Range	0–78	0–94
Protein (mg/dL)		
Mean ± 1 SD	226 ± 228	174 ± 193
Range	13–2290	10–1640
Culture-positive	135	71
Gram stain-positive	114	62

therapy. Maxson and associates[207] examined this issue and suggested that bacterial antigen tests be reserved for those patients with suspected bacterial meningitis whose initial CSF Gram stain was negative and whose culture was negative after 48 hours of incubation. Perkins and associates[244] reviewed all latex particle agglutination tests performed during a 10-month period at two hospitals and reached the same conclusion. Finlay and colleagues[104] suggested that latex agglutination testing of CSF be used only when the Gram stain is negative or when the Gram stain is consistent with meningococci. In the latter case, clarifying the meningococcal serotype quickly may have implications, in large outbreaks, for recommending meningococcal vaccine for type A, C, Y, or W135 disease.

TABLE 38–5 ■ CEREBROSPINAL FLUID (CSF) FINDINGS IN UNTREATED AND PRETREATED PATIENTS WITH *HAEMOPHILUS INFLUENZAE* MENINGITIS

	Untreated	Pretreated
Number of patients	92	57
Total white blood cell count × 10^3		
Mean ± 1 SD	5.6 ± 7.6	4.0 ± 4.8
Range	0.001–55	0.094–25.0
Percentage polys		
Mean ± 1 SD	91 ± 15	83 ± 22
Range	0–108	0–99
Glucose (mg/dL)		
Mean ± 1 SD	34 ± 27.5	29 ± 26
Range	0–109	0–99
CSF/blood glucose (%)		
Mean ± 1 SD	29 ± 21	24 ± 20
Range	0–78	0–82
Protein (mg/dL)		
Mean ± 1 SD	214 ± 129	187 ± 227
Range	25–752	29–1640
CIE (μg/mL)		
Mean ± 1 SD	1.83 ± 2.63	2.36 ± 4.73
Range	0–10.24	0–20.48
Culture-positive	91	51
Gram stain-positive	81	45
CIE-positive	77/88	50/55

CIE, counterimmunoelectrophoresis.

The rapidity with which results of bacterial antigen tests are obtained renders them tempting as a means to establish an early diagnosis. The degree to which they affect clinical decisions is not clear.[207] Performing these tests is not necessary for every patient suspected of having bacterial meningitis, but they could play a role in certain circumstances, such as when patients have a clinical presentation suggestive of bacterial meningitis and pretreatment with antibiotics or with a traumatic lumbar puncture. Antigen detection is useful in developing countries, where CSF culture yields are lower.[67]

Polymerase chain reaction (PCR) analysis of CSF has been used to detect microbial DNA in patients with bacterial meningitis. Primers are available for the detection of *S. pneumoniae, N. meningitidis,* and *H. influenzae* type b simultaneously. Species-specific amplicons have been detected in 89 percent of patients with proven streptococcal, meningococcal, or *H. influenzae* type b meningitis.[254] No false-positive results were noted.

Kotilainen and associates[188] used PCR and DNA sequencing techniques in a prospective study of CSF from patients with suspected bacterial meningitis. The bacterial 23S rRNA gene was amplified from the CSF of 5 of 46 adults with possible infection of the CNS. After sequencing of the 16S or 23S rRNA gene PCR products, 98.3 percent to 100 percent homology with *N. meningitidis* was observed in all five patients. This PCR method was not timely enough for routine laboratory use because it required 2 to 5 days to obtain results that could be reported to the physicians.

Dagan and associates[62] have described the use of PCR for detection of *S. pneumoniae* within CSF. du Plessis and associates[78] have developed a seminested PCR strategy based on the amplification of the pneumococcal penicillin-binding protein 2B gene to detect penicillin-susceptible or penicillin-nonsusceptible *S. pneumoniae* within CSF. PCR detected pneumococci in all of the 18 culture-positive CSF specimens (of 285 total specimens tested). No false-positives were noted. This test required only a few hours to perform and used only 15 μL of CSF.

PCR is most useful in documenting rapidly viral antigens within CSF, thereby reducing the use of antibiotics in selected patients who are treated for presumptive bacterial disease but who may have viral meningitis.[265, 282, 328] Dicuonzo and associates[73] also documented the great sensitivity of oligoprobes on amplified DNA for the diagnosis of *H. influenzae,* streptococcal, and *Mycobacterium tuberculosis* meningitis. No false-negative results occurred in culture-positive CSF specimens.

C-reactive protein (CRP) measurement has been proposed as a test that may be of value in distinguishing bacterial from viral meningitis. In some studies, overlap in CRP determinations between these groups of patients has been observed. For this reason, we do not consider that one can rely on the CRP result to distinguish bacterial from viral meningitis with sufficient certainty.[92, 127, 161] Nonetheless, in the best study to date, serum CRP was superior to CSF parameters in distinguishing Gram stain–negative bacterial from viral meningitis.[303] Among 92 patients with viral meningitis, 93 percent had serum CRP levels within the normal range (<20 mg/L). Only one child with Gram stain–negative bacterial meningitis had a serum CRP value within the normal range.

Numerous metabolic changes have been reported to occur in the CSF and blood of patients with meningitis (Table 38–6). CSF lactate has been noted to be elevated significantly in patients with bacterial meningitis. The increase in CSF lactate apparently is related to decreased cerebral blood flow, cerebral hypoxia, and a change to anaerobic metabolism by the brain. Concentration of CSF lactate tends to parallel the

TABLE 38–6 ■ METABOLIC CHANGES REPORTED IN PATIENTS WITH BACTERIAL MENINGITIS

CSF lactate increased
CSF pH decreased
CSF lactate dehydrogenase increased
Creatine phosphokinase increased
Aspartate transaminase increased
CSF and blood elastase-α-proteinase inhibitor increased
CSF vasopressin increased

CSF, cerebrospinal fluid.

CSF cellular response.[267] Although the concentration of CSF lactate in patients with bacterial meningitis generally is greater than that in patients with aseptic meningitis, such is not always the case. In some patients with aseptic meningitis, CSF lactate has been in the range generally observed in patients with bacterial infections. Conversely, in patients who proved to have bacterial meningitis but who had equivocal clinical and CSF findings, measurement of CSF lactate failed to differentiate bacterial from nonbacterial infection.[267] Thus, the determination of the concentration of CSF lactate cannot be used reliably to differentiate viral from bacterial meningitis in the individual patient.[186]

Depression of the pH of CSF also has been described in patients with bacterial meningitis. The depression of pH in CSF is more transient than is the elevation of CSF lactic acid, and, therefore, its measurement is of even less value in differential diagnosis.[341]

Lactate dehydrogenase, creatine phosphokinase, and aspartate transaminase may be elevated in patients with bacterial meningitis. In some cases, total lactate dehydrogenase activity within CSF may be similar in patients with bacterial and aseptic meningitis, but lactate dehydrogenase isoenzymic analysis may permit differentiation of bacterial from nonbacterial infection. This procedure is time-consuming and cumbersome and does not permit a specific etiologic diagnosis in any patient.[167, 232]

Despite the application of impeccable clinical judgment, examination of CSF, and use of one or more of the rapid diagnostic techniques, situations arise in which differentiation of bacterial from aseptic meningitis remains problematic. In these cases, a predominance of polymorphonuclear leukocytes generally is found in the CSF, the CSF cell count is less than 100 cells/mm^3, the CSF glucose concentration is normal or nearly so, and the Gram stain result is negative. In fact, most children with aseptic meningitis have a predominance of polymorphonuclear leukocytes on their initial CSF examination.[234] In addition, although the patients exhibit signs and symptoms suggestive of meningitis, they do not appear acutely ill. Some investigators have advocated withholding antibiotic therapy in these individuals and repeating the lumbar puncture after 6 to 12 hours of close observation.[3, 93] Usually, the repeated examination of CSF either substantiates the impression of aseptic meningitis (a shift to a lymphocytic differential is noted) or points more conclusively to a bacterial process. This course of action is not recommended if the patient has been pretreated with antibiotics or is younger than 1 year. On occasion, children will have a mild CSF pleocytosis, which may have a predominance of polymorphonuclear leukocytes, after they experience seizures.[347, 349] In general, CSF abnormalities should not be attributed to seizures unless other causes of CNS inflammation have been excluded.

Additional laboratory data are helpful and should be obtained. Blood cultures should be obtained in every patient suspected of having bacterial meningitis. In one prospective study in which blood was obtained for culture from every patient, the cultures were positive in 80 percent of children with *H. influenzae* meningitis, in 52 percent of children with pneumococcal meningitis, and in 33 percent of children with meningococcal meningitis.[90] Forty-four percent of the entire group had received some form of antibiotic therapy before admission to the hospital and before these blood cultures were performed. If these individuals were excluded, positive blood cultures were obtained from 90 percent, 80 percent, and 91 percent of children with meningitis caused by *H. influenzae, S. pneumoniae,* and *N. meningitidis*, respectively.

A thorough search for foci of infection adjacent to or remote from the meninges should be performed. Repetitive neurologic evaluation also should be performed and appropriate laboratory studies undertaken to define the extent of neurologic dysfunction.

When the concentration of bacteria within the blood is high, a Gram-stained smear of a buffy coat obtained from the blood may reveal the presence of microorganisms. If petechial lesions are present, a smear of the lesions after puncture with a small lancet may reveal microorganisms on Gram stain. A chest radiograph may be helpful in disclosing a focus of infection.

Radioisotope scanning may be helpful in selected patients, such as those with a leak of CSF. The pattern of distribution of radioactivity recorded by gamma camera coincides with the accumulation of purulent material. Increased concentration of isotope may relate to the inflammatory response within the meninges or in the periventricular region or to alteration in the blood-brain barrier.[131] Localized concentrations of radionuclide may be seen in children with meningitis, most likely as a result of cerebral vasculitis or infarction.[77] Confirmation of impaired cerebral circulation, including occlusion and narrowing of arteries, sluggish circulation, and retrograde flow, has been provided by the studies of Gado and associates.[120] In these studies, resolution of the arterial lesions was demonstrated in subsequent angiograms in two patients, despite the persistence of neurologic deficits; these findings prompted the authors to suspect vascular spasm at the earlier stage of disease. Hydrocephalus contributed to sluggish circulation through intracerebral vessels in two patients. Tyson and colleagues[323] demonstrated at least transient disturbance in the circulation of CSF in 45 percent of patients with meningitis, but persistent hydrocephalus is a rare complication of purulent meningitis.

Computed tomography (CT) and magnetic resonance imaging (MRI) are noninvasive techniques that permit the prospective and repetitive assessment of children with meningitis. These techniques permit detection of ventricular dilatation, subdural effusion, decrease in brain mass, and presence of vascular lesions or of brain infarcts (Fig. 38–4). With these procedures, ventricular dilatation may be noted acutely in many children who never develop hydrocephalus after recovery from their disease.[90] Neuroimaging may be indicated in the following situations: (1) focal neurological signs; (2) persistently positive CSF cultures despite appropriate antibiotic therapy; (3) persistent elevation of CSF polymorphonuclear leukocytes (more than 30% to 40%) after more than 10 days of therapy; and (4) recurrent meningitis.[182]

Recurrent bacterial meningitis may be the result of a communication between the nasal passage or ear and the meninges. If rhinorrhea or otorrhea is present, a leak may be suspected, but documenting that CSF is present and locating the site of leakage are difficult when the sample is small or contaminated. Sectional (2 mm) coronal cranial CT has been reported to be a relatively easy, noninvasive method for delineating anatomic abnormalities in children with recurrent meningitis.[309]

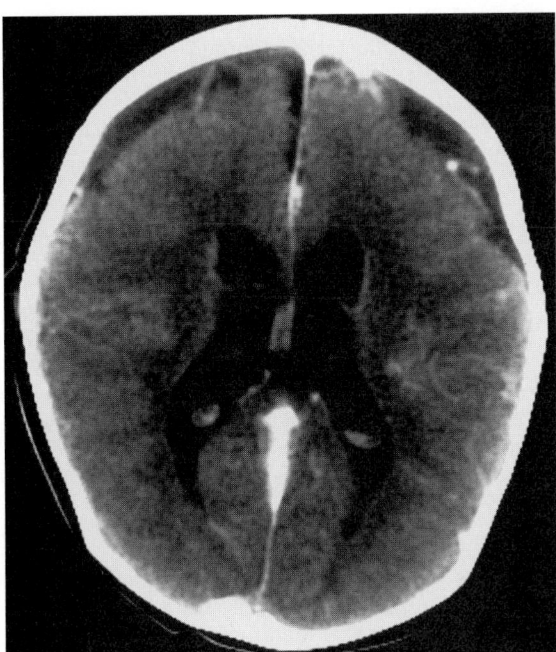

FIGURE 38–4 ■ Computed tomographic scan of a 2-year-old child with bacterial meningitis. Moderately severe ventricular dilatation and the presence of bilateral extracerebral fluid collections overlying the convexities of the brain (subdural effusions) are noted. Note the several prominent vessels that run through the subdural space.

Meurman and associates[214] demonstrated that an extra band of transferrin is located in the β_2-fraction after protein electrophoresis of CSF. This extra β_2-transferrin band could not be demonstrated in serum, nasal secretions, saliva, tears, or perilymph and endolymph. The amount of sample required is small (<50 μL). We have applied this immunochemical method successfully in documenting that fluid found draining from the nose or ear was CSF. Differential suction may permit demonstration of the site of the anatomic communication between the nose, the ear, and the meninges. Moderate contamination with other body fluids does not invalidate the method. The method also is noninvasive and safe for the patient.

Treatment

ANTIMICROBIAL THERAPY

Prompt treatment of bacterial meningitis with an appropriate antibiotic is essential. The initial selection always should be made before definitive cultures are available and ideally should be based on incidence and susceptibility patterns in the local community.[181]

For many years, ampicillin and chloramphenicol were preferred as the initial empirical therapy for children older than 3 months thought to have bacterial meningitis. The development of newer cephalosporins and other antibiotics that have excellent bactericidal activity against *H. influenzae* type b, *N. meningitidis,* and *S. pneumoniae* within the CSF led to the current approaches to initial therapy of childhood meningitis. Cefotaxime and ceftriaxone are included in the empirical treatment regimen of choice in most centers.[179]

Cefotaxime sodium is a third-generation cephalosporin that has a broad spectrum of activity against both gram-positive and gram-negative organisms. It possesses a high level of resistance to hydrolysis by β-lactamase. It penetrates the blood-brain barrier and provides bactericidal activity in the CSF equivalent to or greater than that of antibiotics that have been used conventionally for treatment of bacterial meningitis in children.[221] It is an excellent choice for inclusion in empirical therapy in children 1 month of age or older but must be used with ampicillin for initial therapy in children younger than 1 month because *L. monocytogenes* and enterococci cannot be treated with cefotaxime but will be sensitive to ampicillin. Vancomycin in a dose of 60 mg/kg/day in four divided doses is recommended in addition to cefotaxime for empirical therapy of children with meningitis because of the frequency with which penicillin- and cephalosporin-resistant pneumococci have been isolated in recent years worldwide. Cefotaxime is given as a daily dose of 225 to 300 mg/kg/day in three or four divided doses intravenously. The higher dosage is preferred by some experts because the higher CSF concentrations achieved by high-dose therapy may be beneficial for patients whose disease may be caused by *S. pneumoniae* when the organisms are of intermediate susceptibility to third-generation cephalosporins.[59]

Ceftriaxone is another third-generation cephalosporin that possesses broad antimicrobial activity against the organisms that cause bacterial meningitis. Ceftriaxone readily penetrates the CSF of patients with inflamed meninges. In patients who receive adjunctive therapy with dexamethasone, meningeal inflammation may be reduced, possibly decreasing the penetration of antibiotics into the CSF. Gaillard and colleagues[121] found that concentration of ceftriaxone in the CSF of children with bacterial meningitis treated with dexamethasone was similar to that found in those not treated with steroids. The half-life of ceftriaxone in serum is approximately 4 hours; a twice-daily dose regimen provides both serum and CSF concentrations far in excess of the minimal bactericidal concentrations of most organisms that cause bacterial meningitis. Several prospective randomized studies have demonstrated that ceftriaxone is comparable to ampicillin plus chloramphenicol for the treatment of bacterial meningitis in children.[17, 28, 44, 60, 68, 133, 308]

Ceftriaxone therapy has been associated with an increased incidence of diarrhea, which is mild and self-limited. An increased incidence of "gallbladder sludge," or precipitation of ceftriaxone salts in the gallbladder, diagnosed ultrasonographically, also occurs and generally is asymptomatic but occasionally is associated with clinical symptoms of cholecystitis.[17, 276] Ceftriaxone also has a high protein-binding capacity and can displace bilirubin from albumin in vitro[144] and, therefore, needs to be used cautiously in neonates.

When ceftriaxone is used for the treatment of bacterial meningitis, it can be administered in a dose of 100 mg/kg/24 hours in two divided doses or one daily dose intravenously. Although a once-daily dose has proved to be effective,[38, 115, 142] is convenient, and lends itself particularly to home therapy for selected patients (after an initial period of hospitalization), we do not advocate single daily dosing; dosing errors, delayed doses, or missed doses undoubtedly will occur, and inadequate treatment could result. Moreover, although ceftriaxone can be given intramuscularly, a single dose by this route may be impractical.[38] The solution used for intramuscular administration should contain no more than 250 mg/mL. A 15-kg child receiving a daily dose of 80 mg/kg would require 4.8 mL of fluid, a volume too large for injection in a single site in an infant. In addition, for non–penicillin-susceptible but ceftriaxone-susceptible organisms, administration twice a day may be preferred.[59]

Ampicillin and chloramphenicol have been and continue to be effective as initial treatment of bacterial meningitis when organisms are susceptible to these agents, but they are used infrequently. Ampicillin may be provided intravenously in a dose of 300 mg/kg/24 hours in six divided doses. An initial bolus of 100 mg/kg is given. Chloramphenicol is administered intravenously in a dose of 100 mg/kg/24 hours in four divided doses. No loading dose of chloramphenicol is required.

An increasing number of strains of *S. pneumoniae* that are relatively or completely resistant to penicillin and third-generation cephalosporins have been identified.[42] Tan and coworkers[313] reported a retrospective analysis of five children who had pneumococcal meningitis caused by strains that were penicillin resistant and that had minimal inhibitory concentrations (MICs) to cefotaxime or ceftriaxone of 0.5 to 2 μg/mL compared with strains that were penicillin resistant but susceptible to cefotaxime or ceftriaxone (MIC ≥ 0.25 μg/mL) and found no difference in clinical outcome at the time of discharge. After publication of this report and others with similar findings, the National Committee for Clinical Laboratory Standards established the current guidelines for interpreting the MIC for cefotaxime or ceftriaxone for pneumococci isolated from patients with bacterial meningitis. The guidelines indicate that strains with an MIC of 2 μg/mL or greater are considered resistant, those with an MIC of 1 μg/mL are intermediate, and those with an MIC of 0.5 μg/mL or less are considered fully susceptible.[231]

Vancomycin has been used successfully to treat penicillin-resistant pneumococcal meningitis[39, 119] and experimental models of cephalosporin-resistant pneumococcal meningitis.[117] In eight reports of treatment failures with third-generation cephalosporins, a variety of treatment regimens were used, all with success. Vancomycin, alone or in combination with rifampin, chloramphenicol, or both, was used most frequently. The recommendation for empirical therapy of bacterial meningitis advocated by the Committee of Infectious Diseases of the American Academy of Pediatrics is to include vancomycin in addition to a third-generation cephalosporin in patients 1 month of age or older.[10] If nonsusceptibility to penicillin (MIC ≥ 0.1 μg/mL) and cephalosporins (MIC ≥ 0.1 μg/mL) is documented, treatment is continued with vancomycin plus cefotaxime or ceftriaxone (a synergistic effect is achieved when they are used together) with or without rifampin to complete an appropriate course. Vancomycin should be given at a dose of 60 mg/kg/24 hours in four divided doses. Peak serum concentrations of vancomycin in children whose renal function is normal should be between 30 and 40 μg/mL.

Antibiotic tolerance is the ability of an organism to grow in the presence of antibiotics and frequently is a precursor phenotype to resistance. Clinical isolates of *S. pneumoniae* that are tolerant to vancomycin have been reported in the United States.[235] Meningitis caused by a vancomycin-tolerant organism in a patient was treated successfully with cefotaxime (300 mg/kg/day in four divided doses) plus vancomycin (60 mg/kg/day in four divided doses) and rifampin (20 mg/kg/day in two divided doses). Chloramphenicol also may be a suitable alternative for the treatment of these organisms if the pneumococcus proves to be sensitive to this antibiotic. However, pneumococcal isolates resistant to penicillin or extended-spectrum cephalosporins frequently are not susceptible to chloramphenicol.

Cefuroxime is a second-generation cephalosporin that has been shown to be effective in vitro against *H. influenzae* type b, *S. pneumoniae,* and *N. meningitidis*. Initial clinical studies found that cefuroxime had equivalent effectiveness compared with ampicillin plus chloramphenicol. However, subsequent studies demonstrated delayed sterilization of the CSF; relapse during or after treatment was higher, and more frequent sensorineural hearing loss occurred than with use of ampicillin, chloramphenicol, cefotaxime, and ceftriaxone.[15, 69, 190, 191, 193, 275] Therefore, cefuroxime *should not be used* to treat bacterial meningitis in children.

Ceftazidime has been efficacious in the treatment of meningitis caused by *P. aeruginosa*.[153, 216, 259, 260] Cefoperazone and cefoxitin within CSF may fail to reach concentrations required to kill all susceptible strains of *H. influenzae* and *S. pneumoniae* and cannot be recommended for the treatment of bacterial meningitis in children.[47, 101] Cefpirome concentrations in CSF of patients with bacterial meningitis were found to be significantly higher than the minimum bactericidal concentrations for *N. meningitidis, H. influenzae,* and *S. pneumoniae,*[346] but studies documenting its effectiveness in large numbers of children have not been performed.

Cefepime is a fourth-generation cephalosporin that has been studied for the treatment of bacterial meningitis. In vitro, cefepime offers no advantage over cefotaxime or ceftriaxone for penicillin-resistant *S. pneumoniae*.[176] In addition, no in vitro data exist for the efficacy of cefepime against cefotaxime-resistant pneumococci. In two clinical trials, the effect of cefepime was found to be equivalent to that of either cefotaxime or ceftriaxone.[268, 269] However, no penicillin- or ceftriaxone-resistant pneumococci were encountered in either study. Thus, the role of cefepime for the treatment of bacterial meningitis is unclear.

Aztreonam is an antimicrobial agent that belongs to the monobactam family of antibiotics. It is effective against most gram-negative organisms, including *P. aeruginosa*. Limited data suggest its efficacy in the treatment of *Pseudomonas* and *H. influenzae* meningitis, suggesting a potential role for this agent in the treatment of patients who are allergic to penicillin and who are infected with these or other gram-negative organisms.[177, 192, 321]

If a history of *significant* allergy to penicillin or cephalosporin (anaphylaxis, urticaria, exfoliative dermatitis) is documented, vancomycin plus rifampin or chloramphenicol may be used. A cross-reactivity of approximately 10 to 15 percent has been noted for cephalosporins in penicillin-allergic patients.

When meningitis is caused by *Streptococcus pyogenes,* ampicillin or penicillin provides effective therapy. If meningitis is caused by a penicillin-resistant strain of *S. aureus*, oxacillin or nafcillin should be employed, using 200 mg/kg/24 hours intravenously in six divided doses. Vancomycin is effective against *S. aureus* strains resistant to penicillin and to semisynthetic penicillin derivatives[145] or in patients with *S. aureus* meningitis who are penicillin allergic. Vancomycin also may be useful in treatment of meningitis caused by *Flavobacterium meningosepticum*.[75] Metronidazole is effective in treatment of anaerobic infection of the CNS when response to conventional therapy has been suboptimal. A dose of 40 mg/kg/24 hours in three or four divided doses results in CSF concentrations of greater than 10 μg/mL.[32]

Imipenem and meropenem have been evaluated for the treatment of meningitis. These carbapenems are active against the bacteria that cause meningitis, but the use of imipenem-cilastatin has been associated with drug-induced seizures.[348]

The safety and efficacy of meropenem and cefotaxime were compared in a prospective randomized trial of 190 children with bacterial meningitis.[183] Seizures occurred within 24 hours before administration of antibiotic therapy in 16 percent of patients randomized to receive meropenem and in 7 percent of patients randomized to receive cefotaxime. Seizures occurred in patients after administration of therapy in 6 percent of children receiving meropenem and in 1 percent of those receiving cefotaxime. None of these seizures could be attributed to drug therapy. All patients responded to therapy with clinical improvement, and bacterial eradication was proved by repeated lumbar puncture in 100 percent of patients in both groups. No significant difference in short-term outcomes occurred between the two groups. Odio and associates[238] compared the efficacy and safety of meropenem with cefotaxime for the treatment of bacterial meningitis in 258 children who were randomly assigned to the meropenem or cefotaxime group. Clinical cure with or without sequelae was achieved in 97 and 96 percent of the meropenem- and cefotaxime-treated patients, respectively. At 7 weeks after treatment was concluded, 54 percent of patients treated with meropenem and 58 percent of patients treated with cefotaxime had no sequelae. Seizures were noted in 12 percent of the patients treated with meropenem and in 17 percent of those treated with cefotaxime; none of the seizures was considered to be drug related. These data suggest that meropenem is effective in the treatment of bacterial meningitis in children. Few children with pneumococcal meningitis in either study had isolates that were nonsusceptible to cefotaxime. Thus, no conclusions can be drawn regarding the usefulness of meropenem in treating pneumococcal meningitis caused by isolates with a cefotaxime or ceftriaxone MIC equal to or greater than 2 μg/mL. Meropenem should be studied further in children who may have meningitis that is caused by organisms resistant to extended-spectrum cephalosporins. For meropenem-susceptible isolates, meropenem alone or in combination with other drugs may provide a satisfactory alternative for patients who do not tolerate vancomycin.[59]

Current recommendations for antibiotic treatment of various microorganisms are provided in Table 38–7. An appropriate antibiotic should be continued until the patient is afebrile for 5 days but at least for 7 to 10 days in every patient. Although some data support a shorter course of therapy, we continue to recommend 10 days of treatment for pneumococcal and *H. influenzae* type b meningitis and 7 days for *N. meningitidis* meningitis.[160, 201, 206] If clinical improvement is noted within 24 hours, a repeated lumbar puncture is not necessary, in most cases, during the course of treatment or after treatment has been completed. If infection is caused by *S. pneumoniae* that is resistant to penicillin and to third-generation cephalosporins, we recommend a repeated lumbar puncture at 48 to 72 hours to document bacterial sterilization of the CSF. If clinical improvement is slower than anticipated or is not noted, a repeated examination of the CSF is indicated at any time.

In the 1970s, lumbar puncture frequently was performed at the conclusion of therapy. Data from studies performed at that time (Table 38–8) reveal that WBC counts and protein concentrations within the CSF generally had not returned completely to normal and that the CSF-to-blood glucose ratio may have remained depressed. In every case, Gram stain of the CSF should reveal no organisms and cultures should be sterile. If a lumbar puncture is performed at the conclusion of therapy, we consider re-treatment to be mandatory if organisms are seen or grown. It also may be considered if more than 30 percent of the cells are polymorphonuclear leukocytes or if the CSF glucose concentration and the CSF-to-blood glucose ratio are less than 20 mg/dL and 20 percent, respectively.

Bacteriologic relapse after treatment of meningitis (particularly that caused by *H. influenzae* and treated with ampicillin) was highlighted in numerous reports.[23, 55, 57, 148, 149] Precise assessment of the frequency of relapse in children who have received an appropriate antibiotic to which the organism is sensitive or an appropriate dose intravenously and for an extended period has been difficult. The relapse rate is currently less than 1 percent.

Some physicians have discharged children with meningitis from the hospital before the conclusion of a course of therapy and prescribed home management. Benefits of home therapy include a decreased risk of acquiring nosocomial infection, a return of the child to his or her normal environment sooner, and a decrease in the total cost of therapy. Financial savings of outpatient, once-daily ceftriaxone for pediatric meningitis have been estimated to be $200 per day.[249]

Bradley and colleagues[38] reported the results of 54 children with bacterial meningitis treated as outpatients from 1 to 8 days (mean, 4.6 days) with intramuscular ceftriaxone given once daily. Each dose was given in conjunction with a physician's examination. Each child had to be afebrile for 24 to 48 hours before initiation of home therapy, free of neurologic dysfunction except for auditory or vestibular dysfunction, and without evidence of inappropriate secretion of ADH before being considered for outpatient therapy. No child required readmission or developed neurologic sequelae or relapse.

Powell and Mawhorter[249] reported a retrospective review of 26 patients with meningitis or other serious bacterial infections who received some portion of their therapy as an outpatient with ceftriaxone; none of the patients experienced relapse or recurrence.

Waler and Rathore[335] suggest 10 criteria for considering outpatient therapy for children with bacterial meningitis: (1) the child has received inpatient therapy for at least 6 days, (2) the child is afebrile for at least 24 to 48 hours before initiation of outpatient therapy, (3) the child has no significant neurologic dysfunction or focal findings, (4) the child has no seizure activity, (5) the child is clinically stable, (6) the child is taking all fluids by mouth, (7) the first dose of outpatient antibiotic is received in the hospital, (8) the antibiotic is administered in the office or emergency department setting or by qualified home health nursing, (9) daily examination is performed by a physician, and (10) parents are reliable and have transportation and a telephone. The dose of ceftriaxone of 80 to 100 mg/kg/24 hours intramuscularly may need to be aliquoted to account for the volume of diluent needed to achieve a concentration of no greater than 250 mg/mL. If oral chloramphenicol is used, therapeutic serum concentrations of 15 to 25 μg/mL must be documented before discharge and maintained.

H. influenzae type b organisms have been recovered from the throats of patients after completion of a course of treatment for *H. influenzae* type b meningitis. Therefore, when members of a household to which the patient will return include children 4 years of age or younger, the patient should be given rifampin, 20 mg/kg once daily for 4 days, to prevent the occurrence of secondary cases. Children with meningococcal meningitis also should receive chemoprophylaxis to eradicate nasopharyngeal carriage before discharge unless they were treated with cefotaxime or ceftriaxone.

ADJUNCTIVE THERAPY

As described earlier, the pathogenesis and subsequent sequelae of bacterial meningitis are as much a consequence of the host response to infection as of the bacterial organisms themselves. Anti-inflammatory agents used as adjuncts to antimicrobial therapy may decrease the degree of tissue injury during the course of the disease.

Corticosteroids have been suggested as an adjunct to therapy of bacterial meningitis because they may (1) decrease intracranial pressure by decreasing meningeal inflammation and brain water content; (2) modulate the production of cytokines, which in turn lessens the meningeal inflammatory

TABLE 38–7 ■ RECOMMENDATIONS FOR ANTIBIOTIC THERAPY

Organism	Antibiotic(s)	Recommended Dosages IV
Bacteroides fragilis	Chloramphenicol Metronidazole	100 mg/kg/d in 4 dd 30 mg/kg/d in 4 dd
Bacteroides other than *B. fragilis*	Penicillin G	300,000 units/kg/d in 6 dd
Clostridium	Penicillin G	300,000 units/kg/d in 6 dd
Corynebacterium	Penicillin G Erythromycin	300,000 units/kg/d in 6 dd 50 mg/kg/d in 4 dd
*Enterobacter, Klebsiella, Escherichia coli**	Ampicillin Gentamicin Amikacin Cefotaxime Ceftriaxone Ticarcillin	300 mg/kg/d in 6 dd 7.5 mg/kg/d in 3 dd 15 mg/kg/d in 3 dd 200 mg/kg/d in 4 dd 100 mg/kg/d in 2 dd 300 mg/kg/d in 4 dd
Haemophilus influenzae	Ampicillin Cefotaxime Ceftriaxone Chloramphenicol	300 mg/kg/d in 6 dd 200 mg/kg/d in 4 dd 100 mg/kg/d in 1 or 2 dd 100 mg/kg/d in 4 dd
Listeria monocytogenes	Ampicillin Gentamicin Trimethoprim-sulfamethoxazole	300 mg/kg/d in 6 dd 7.5 mg/kg/d in 3 dd 20 mg/kg/d in 4 dd (TMP component)
Neisseria meningitidis	Penicillin G	300,000 units/kg/d in 6 dd
Neisseria gonorrhoeae	Penicillin G (if sensitive to penicillin) Ceftriaxone	300,000 units/kg/d in 6 dd 100 mg/kg/d in 1 or 2 dd
Proteus mirabilis (indole-negative)	Ampicillin	300 mg/kg/d in 6 dd
Proteus mirabilis (indole-positive)	Cefotaxime Gentamicin Amikacin Ticarcillin	200 mg/kg/d in 4 dd 7.5 mg/kg/d in 3 dd 22.5 mg/kg/d in 3 dd 300 mg/kg/d in 4-6 dd
Pseudomonas	Gentamicin Ticarcillin Piperacillin Amikacin Ceftazidime Meropenem	7.5 mg/kg/d in 3 dd 450 mg/kg/d in 4 or 6 dd 300 mg/kg/d in 4 or 6 dd 15-20 mg/kg/d in 3 dd 150-200 mg/kg/d in 3 dd 120 mg/kg/d in 3 dd
Salmonella	Ampicillin Cefotaxime Gentamicin Chloramphenicol	300 mg/kg/d in 6 dd 200 mg/kg/d in 4 dd 7.5 mg/kg/d in 3 dd 100 mg/kg/d in 4 dd
Staphylococcus aureus (penicillinase-negative)†	Penicillin G	300,000 units/kg/d in 6 dd
Staphylococcus aureus (penicillinase-positive)†	Oxacillin or nafcillin	200 mg/kg/d in 6 dd
Staphylococcus aureus (resistant to semisynthetic penicillins)	Vancomycin plus rifampin	60 mg/kg/d in 4 dd 20 mg/kg/d in 2 dd
Staphylococcus (coagulase-negative)	Vancomycin plus rifampin	60 mg/kg/d in 4 dd 20 mg/kg/d in 2 dd
Streptococcus pneumoniae†	Penicillin G Chloramphenicol Vancomycin Cefotaxime/ceftriaxone Rifampin‡	300,000 units/kg/d in 6 dd 100 mg/kg/d in 4 dd 60 mg/kg/d in 4 dd 225–300 mg/kg/d in 3 or 4 dd/100 mg/kg/d in 1 or 2 dd 20 mg/kg/d in 2 dd
Unknown (<1 mo of age)	Ampicillin plus cefotaxime plus vancomycin	300 mg/kg/d in 6 dd 200 mg/kg/d in 4 dd 60 mg/kg/d in 4 dd
Unknown (>1 mo of age)	Cefotaxime or ceftriaxone plus vancomycin Nafcillin (if question of staphylococcal infection) Gentamicin (if question of *Pseudomonas*)	225–300 mg/kg/d in 4 dd 100 mg/kg/d in 1 or 2 dd 60 mg/kg/d in 4 dd 200 mg/kg/d in 6 dd 7.5 mg/kg/d in 3 dd

*Trimethoprim-sulfamethoxazole in a dose or 20 mg (trimethoprim) and 100 mg (sulfamethoxazole) kg/day IV in 4 divided doses (dd) has been used successfully in selected patients with gram-negative enteric meningitis.

†Vancomycin may be provided in a dose of 60 mg/kg/day in 4 dd IV if patients are allergic to penicillin or penicillin derivatives or in the case of *Streptococcus pneumoniae* for multidrug-resistant pneumococci or pneumococci that are highly resistant to penicillin. In these cases, addition of rifampin also may be considered.

‡Should never be used alone.

TABLE 38–8 ■ CEREBROSPINAL FLUID FINDINGS AT CONCLUSION OF ANTIBIOTIC TREATMENT

	Total White Blood Cell Count		Polymorphonuclear Leukocytes (%)		Protein (mg/dL)		Glucose (mg/dL)		CSF-to-Blood Glucose Ratio	
	Mean ± 1 SD	Range	Mean ± 1 SD	Range	Mean ± 1 SD	Range	Mean ± 1 SD	Range	Mean ± 1 SD	Range
Total group	41 ± 80	0–850	5.5 ± 12	0–90	46 ± 72	7–970	47 ± 12.7	21–91	55.7 ± 17	23–156
Haemophilus influenzae	53 ± 98	0–850	5.5 ± 11	0–90	43 ± 37	10–334	47 ± 13	31–100	55 ± 17	31–100
Ampicillin	56 ± 107	0–850	5.9 ± 12	0–90	44 ± 43	13–334	46 ± 14	21–91	53 ± 17	33–89
Chloramphenicol	49 ± 83	0–325	5.1 ± 10.7	0–50	41 ± 26	7–127	48 ± 11	27–90	57 ± 13	30–100
Streptococcus pneumoniae	29 ± 30	0–110	5.5 ± 11.5	0–45	42 ± 39	7–211	48 ± 9	22–68	57 ± 13	22–91
Neisseria meningitidis	16 ± 27	0–132	3.4 ± 7.9	0–27	39 ± 46	7–188	47 ± 11	29–77	47 ± 19	23–100
Others	11 ± 18	0–77	7.3 ± 19	0–75	70 ± 197	10–970	48 ± 18	37–73	70 ± 28	44–156

response; and (3) decrease the incidence of sensorineural hearing loss or other neurologic complications of meningitis.[190, 237]

Corticosteroids may play a role in acute management of increased intracranial pressure and cerebral herniation, although no data specifically indicate that corticosteroids decrease cerebral edema caused by bacterial meningitis. Odio and colleagues[237] found that dexamethasone therapy in children with bacterial meningitis decreased opening lumbar CSF pressure 12 hours after administration of the first dose, but this effect was lost by 24 hours of treatment. The significance of these findings is unclear because the steroids were not given as specific therapy for increased intracranial pressure, and most of the subjects were not demonstrating signs of impending herniation.

In experimental *H. influenzae* meningitis, administration of dexamethasone 1 hour before but not 1 hour after administration of ceftriaxone was associated with significantly reduced TNF-α concentration and indices of inflammation in the CSF.[226] Administration of dexamethasone has been associated with decreased concentration in CSF of prostaglandin E_2 and decreased leakage of some proteins from serum into CSF in rabbits with experimental pneumococcal meningitis.[163] In patients with bacterial meningitis, steroid-treated patients had significantly lower concentrations of IL-1β, TNF-α, platelet-activating factor, and prostaglandin E_2 in their CSF than did those who received antibiotics alone.[213, 227, 237] Patients tend to become afebrile sooner when they receive dexamethasone but have an increased incidence of secondary fevers.[333]

Although our understanding of the pathophysiologic events associated with initiation of the acute inflammatory response has been enhanced by recent data, the ability of dexamethasone to reduce long-term complications of bacterial meningitis remains controversial. None of the pediatric studies of the use of dexamethasone for treatment of bacterial meningitis has demonstrated an overall change in mortality.

In randomized, placebo-controlled trials of dexamethasone as adjunctive therapy in bacterial meningitis[190, 237, 274, 333] and in retrospective studies[134, 175] published since 1988, 68 percent (227 of 333) of steroid recipients in the six randomized trials had meningitis caused by *H. influenzae* type b; the remaining 32 percent had meningitis caused by *S. pneumoniae* (38) or *N. meningitidis* (41).[251] A meta-analysis of nine controlled trials published before 1991 failed to document a reduced risk of neurologic abnormality at hospital discharge or follow-up examination.[153a] A more recent meta-analysis of randomized clinical trials of dexamethasone as adjunctive therapy for bacterial meningitis suggests a beneficial effect for *H. influenzae* meningitis and a possible beneficial effect in preventing severe hearing loss in *S. pneumoniae* meningitis, but only if it is given early.[211] Most patients with *S. pneumoniae* meningitis in the studies that were reviewed were not treated with vancomycin. The effects of dexamethasone use with vancomycin for bacterial meningitis caused by *S. pneumoniae,* which are resistant to third-generation cephalosporins, is not clear. This issue is important because the penetrance of vancomycin across the blood-brain barrier is not optimal, and selected studies show that it is reduced further when dexamethasone is used concomitantly.[16, 40, 118, 217]

Odio and associates[237] found that the administration of dexamethasone immediately before the initiation of cefotaxime therapy was associated with a lower incidence of neurologic sequelae (14% compared with 38% in patients receiving cefotaxime alone). They found no significant difference in auditory sequelae compared with those of control subjects. The frequency of neurologic sequelae in placebo-treated patients was significantly higher than that noted in other studies.[274, 316, 333]

Studies by Lebel and associates[190] and Schaad and colleagues[274] failed to demonstrate a significant reduction in the incidence of neurologic sequelae in comparisons of steroid- with placebo-treated patients. A prospective, multicentered, placebo-controlled study evaluated 143 children with bacterial meningitis caused by *H. influenzae* type b (58%), *S. pneumoniae* (23%), and *N. meningitidis* (17%).[333] Patients were treated with ceftriaxone and placebo or ceftriaxone and dexamethasone administered within 4 hours of the first dose of antibiotics. No significant difference in neurologic or developmental outcome was found between patients who received steroids or placebo.

Sensorineural hearing loss is a significant sequela of bacterial meningitis. In the two randomized studies performed by Lebel and associates,[190] patients treated with dexamethasone were significantly less likely to have moderate or severe bilateral sensorineural hearing loss; however, in one study, patients were treated with cefuroxime, which has been shown to result in delayed sterilization of the CSF and a higher rate of hearing loss compared with treatment with ceftriaxone.[275] An additional 100 infants and children with bacterial meningitis were treated with ceftriaxone for 10 days and either dexamethasone or placebo for 4 days. A significant reduction in moderate to severe hearing loss in children with *H. influenzae* type b meningitis ($p < .001$) was reported. No significant differences in other neurologic sequelae were found between the two groups. In addition, two patients receiving dexamethasone developed gastrointestinal bleeding severe enough to require transfusion, and two others developed heme-positive stools. Odio and associates[237] found no significant difference in the incidence of moderate or severe hearing impairment between placebo and steroid groups (16% and 6%, respectively).

The Swiss Meningitis Group[274] found that treatment of children with dexamethasone 10 minutes before administration of ceftriaxone and then for 2 days subsequently resulted in persistent hearing loss in 5 percent (3) of children who had received dexamethasone and in 15 percent (8) of those who received placebo, a difference that was not significant. One child treated with steroid and five children treated with placebo had unilateral hearing loss only. The group also documented a transient mild to moderate hearing impairment in five children treated with dexamethasone and four children treated with placebo; in six of the nine, the impairment was caused by a conductive disturbance. Dexamethasone did not alter the incidence or natural history of the transient hearing impairment.

In a multicenter study,[333] audiologic measurements were made early in the course of the disease (within 24 hours of admission) as well as 6 weeks to 12 months after recovery from disease. The authors found no significant difference in the incidence of persistent moderate or severe hearing loss between children who received dexamethasone within 4 hours of antibiotics and those who received placebo, with the exception of bilateral deafness in children with *H. influenzae* type b meningitis (5 of 72 in the placebo-treated group versus 0 of 67 in the dexamethasone-treated group; $p = .02$). The overall incidence of moderate to severe hearing loss was 14.7 percent (10.3% unilateral and 4.4% bilateral) in the dexamethasone-treated group and 22.9 percent (13.5% unilateral and 9.4% bilateral; $p = .33$ for bilateral loss) in the placebo-treated group. Of note, these authors found that 22 children (8 in the dexamethasone-treated group and 14 in the placebo-treated group) had bilateral moderate or severe hearing loss at the initial evaluation. Only one child with *H. influenzae* meningitis and unilateral deafness at initial examination progressed to bilateral deafness. At follow-up, the resolution of hearing loss was nearly identical for each group, with 8 of the 22 children having normal hearing at follow-up, 5 having unilateral deafness, and 9 having bilateral deafness. These results suggest that hearing loss occurs early in the course of meningitis and that early auditory brain stem response results need to be interpreted cautiously with regard to long-term audiologic sequelae. A strong relationship was noted between hearing loss early in the disease and a low concentration of CSF glucose at presentation of meningitis, a finding that has been reported previously.[76]

The Infectious Diseases Committee of the American Academy of Pediatrics states that dexamethasone therapy should be considered for pneumococcal meningitis in infants and children 6 weeks of age and older.[10] Dexamethasone is also recommended for treatment of infants and children with *H. influenzae* type b meningitis by the Red Book Committee.[12] The reluctance on the part of some experts to recommend dexamethasone for pneumococcal meningitis is predicated on data that fail to show any diminution in morbidity or mortality rates from meningitis when meningitis is caused by *S. pneumoniae* and dexamethasone is used. The CSF concentrations of vancomycin, ceftriaxone, cefotaxime, and rifampin when they are given in dosages recommended for meningitis in children treated with dexamethasone *generally* are adequate to treat meningitis caused by most nonsusceptible strains of *S. pneumoniae*. Dexamethasone can lead to decreased fever and a misleading impression of clinical improvement, even though sterilization of the CSF has not been achieved. Dexamethasone should not be used if aseptic or nonbacterial meningitis is suspected; if it is started before the diagnosis of nonbacterial meningitis is made, it should be discontinued immediately. It should not be used in "partially treated" meningitis. No data exist on which to base a recommendation for use of dexamethasone in the treatment of bacterial meningitis in infants younger than 6 weeks or in those with congenital or acquired abnormalities of the CNS, with or without a prosthetic device. In fact, one prospective study in infants concluded that adjunctive dexamethasone therapy does not improve the outcome of neonatal bacterial meningitis.[63] Dexamethasone plus vancomycin may decrease the transport of vancomycin into the CSF of experimental animals with pneumococcal meningitis, but this finding was not observed in nine children who were treated with vancomycin as well as dexamethasone (0.6 mg/kg/day).[184] Dexamethasone should be used cautiously when vancomycin is used to treat meningitis caused by *S. pneumoniae* that may be resistant to penicillin, third-generation cephalosporins, or both.[40, 171]

If dexamethasone is used, it should be used in all patients, regardless of disease severity, and it should be administered as early as possible in the course of treatment in a dose of 0.15 mg/kg/dose intravenously every 6 hours for no more than 4 days. One study[274] found no difference in children treated for 2 days instead of 4 days with 0.4 mg/kg/dose every 12 hours.

Except for hearing loss after *H. influenzae* type b meningitis, no clear evidence establishes that dexamethasone dramatically alters the long-term sequelae of meningitis, and its use is not without risk of causing adverse events. The markedly decreased frequency of meningitis caused by *H. influenzae* type b and the increased frequency of meningitis caused by *S. pneumoniae* not susceptible to penicillin (for which therapy with vancomycin may be necessary) suggest that initiation of dexamethasone should be considered carefully and that the clinician caring for the patient should evaluate the risk-to-benefit ratio of such therapy.

Other inhibitors of inflammatory mediators or of mediator effector molecules such as nitric oxide are being studied in experimental animal models of bacterial meningitis. Although their use is attractive theoretically because of the damage produced by the inflammatory cascade, none has emerged as a realistic potential candidate for general clinical use at this time (i.e., 2003).

Supportive Care

In addition to antibiotic therapy, management of bacterial meningitis includes measures that apply generally to the critically ill child.[182] Careful monitoring and attention to detail are essential. Pulse rate, blood pressure, and respiratory rate should be measured carefully every 15 minutes until stable and then every hour while the patient is in the intensive care unit. Temperature should be measured every 4 hours. A thorough neurologic examination should be performed at the time of admission and at least daily thereafter. A rapid assessment of neurologic function should be performed several times a day for the first several days of treatment. Body weight should be measured daily for at least the first 3 or 4 days. Head circumference should be measured in children younger than 18 months of age at the time of admission and repeated daily if concerns about increased intracranial pressure persist.

The following laboratory data are suggested if results of lumbar puncture indicate bacterial meningitis: (1) total peripheral WBC count and differential, (2) hemoglobin concentration, (3) hematocrit, (4) platelet count, and (5) serum electrolytes (serum and urine osmolalities may be useful in selected patients). Urine volume and specific gravity should be monitored. A low WBC count may suggest a poor prognosis. Anemia associated with *H. influenzae* type b septicemia has been reported[290, 291] and has been attributed to immune hemolysis of RBCs that are coated with soluble bacterial antigens.[290]

Every child with meningitis should be evaluated carefully in a manner that will permit identification of inappropriate secretion of ADH, recognition of seizure activity, and detection of the development of subdural effusions. Body weight, serum electrolytes (serum and urine osmolalities in selected patients), urine volume, and specific gravity determinations should be made at the time of admission and observed closely (every 6 to 12 hours) for the first 24 to 36 hours in the hospital and daily for several days thereafter. Initially, the child should receive nothing by mouth because of the risk of vomiting and aspiration. In addition, delivery of all fluid intravenously ensures greater accuracy in measurement of intake and output during the critical early days of therapy. Inappropriate secretion of ADH has been documented in 88 percent of children enrolled in a prospective study of bacterial meningitis.[87] Elevated serum concentrations of ADH in the presence of hyponatremia have been documented by direct measurement of ADH concentration in serum obtained from the same children.[91]

An electrolyte solution containing approximately 40 mEq/L of sodium and chloride, 35 mEq/L of potassium, and 20 mEq/L of acetate or lactate should be administered at a rate of 1000 to 1200 mL/m^2/24 hours in the patient without evidence of dehydration or shock. Fluid restriction is continued until it can be documented (frequently within 2 hours), on the basis of objective measures, that ADH secretion is not a factor or has resolved. The best indicators of retention of fluid in excess of solute are the body weight and serum sodium concentration. As serum sodium concentration approaches normal (140 mEq/L), fluid administration may be liberalized progressively to normal maintenance levels of 1500 to 1700 mL/m^2/24 hours.

Powell and associates[250] found that elevated concentrations of arginine vasopressin in patients with bacterial meningitis who were clinically dehydrated responded to maintenance fluids plus deficit replacement with 0.9 percent saline. This study confirms that the syndrome of inappropriate secretion of ADH should not be diagnosed in the presence of dehydration. Decreased intravascular volume is a physiologic stimulus for the release of ADH, and, therefore, its release is not inappropriate. Fluid restriction is not advocated for patients who are dehydrated; rehydration should be performed with careful and frequent assessment of fluid and electrolyte status.

Singhi and colleagues[294] examined the effect of fluid restriction on body water and outcome of 50 consecutive children who had been hospitalized with acute meningitis. These children were divided into two groups, those with hyponatremia and those without hyponatremia. Patients in both groups then were randomly assigned to receive either normal maintenance or restricted fluids (65% to 70% of the volume of that received by the maintenance subgroup). Thus, as few as 11 and no more than 15 patients were randomized to any of the four subgroups in the study. No significant difference in overall outcome or intact survival was found when comparisons were made between fluid-restricted and non–fluid-restricted groups or within each group between the subgroups that received restricted fluids or maintenance fluids. However, after combination of the subgroups that received restricted fluids with those that received maintenance fluids, a trend toward higher intact survival and lower mortality was noted in the non–fluid-restricted groups. Nonetheless, children who had an extracellular water reduction of 10 mL/kg or greater in 48 hours had a significantly lower intact survival (10 of 28, 36%) than did those with less than 10 mL/kg or no reduction of extracellular water (15 of 22, 64%). The mortality rate was also higher in the former group (7 of 28, 25%) than in the latter group (2 of 22, 9%). The authors concluded that fluid restriction did not improve the outcome of acute meningitis and that a decrease in extracellular water volume at 48 hours may increase the likelihood of having an adverse outcome.

This study is particularly difficult to interpret within the context of previous information in the literature. In studies of large numbers of children with bacterial meningitis, evidence of inappropriate secretion of ADH correlated significantly ($p < .01$) with abnormal neurologic findings, even 3 months after discharge, and with low IQ scores.[96] The original studies were performed in patients who were *not* fluid restricted.[89] As a result of these findings, coupled with documentation of inappropriate secretion of ADH, a recommendation was made to restrict fluids in patients who are hyponatremic at admission. Fluids are restricted only until evidence for inappropriate secretion of ADH can be excluded (usually within 2 hours). The average patient in subsequent studies reported by Kaplan and Feigin[168] was fluid restricted for only 0.75 days. The mortality rate in the largest single study reported by Feigin[85] of individuals who were fluid restricted was 0.5 percent compared with 9 and 25 percent in the groups reported in the studies by Singhi and associates.[294] Moreover, Singhi and associates[294] did not assess other important outcome variables, such as the number of patients with hearing loss or those whose psychometric performance might or might not have been impaired. The total number of patients in any of their study groups was relatively small. Although their data are intriguing, other differences either in the population studied or in the management of the patients may have accounted for these differences. In addition to the increased mortality rates of the patients studied by Singhi and associates[294] noted earlier, an extraordinarily high frequency of hydrocephalus and a very high frequency of seizures and status epilepticus also were noted, compared with groups of patients who have been studied in the United States. Because cerebral edema and increased intracranial pressure have been noted as major disturbances in seriously ill patients with meningitis and because many of the deaths and some of the sequelae have been related to the effects of cerebral edema and intracranial hypertension, we continue to recommend fluid restriction in patients with hyponatremia who are not dehydrated and liberalization of fluids as soon as the effects of excess ADH secretion have been dissipated (usually less than 1 day).

Meningitis complicated by shock creates a complex fluid management problem. Shock associated with meningitis is secondary to septicemia and generally is treated with intravenous infusion of large quantities of fluid to maintain blood pressure and adequate tissue perfusion (see Chapter 69). Patients with meningitis without shock or dehydration benefit from initial fluid restriction to avoid worsening of cerebral edema and severe hyponatremia with subsequent seizures. Children with meningitis and shock should receive sufficient quantities of isotonic fluid to maintain a systolic blood pressure of 80 to 90 mm Hg, a urine output equal to or greater than 500 mL/m^2/24 hours, and adequate cerebral perfusion as indicated by mental status. Central venous pressure monitoring is useful to guide fluid resuscitation and to prevent fluid overload. The addition of albumin (1 g/kg) to intravenously administered fluids may decrease the total volume of fluid needed to maintain adequate perfusion. Vasopressors, such as dopamine, dobutamine, and isoproterenol, also may provide support of blood pressure and perfusion and reduce requirements for intravenously administered fluids.

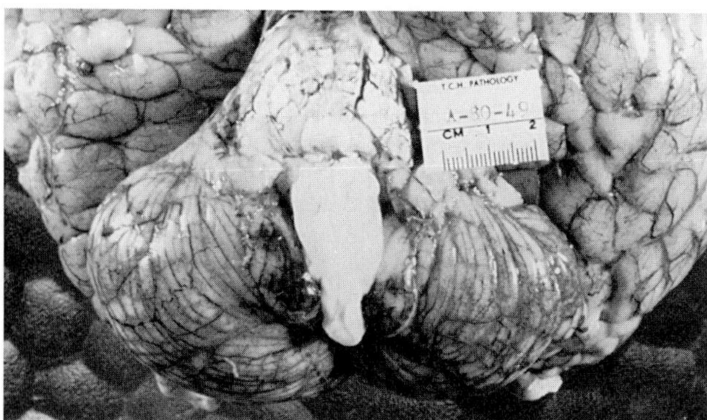

FIGURE 38–5 ■ Inflammation and hemorrhage of cerebellar tonsils from child with cerebellar herniation through the foramen magnum due to bacterial meningitis. (From Kaplan, S.: Current management of common bacterial meningitides. Reproduced with permission of Pediatrics in Review 7:77, copyright 1985.)

When increased intracranial pressure is suggested by such signs as progressive lethargy, increased muscle tone, or bulging anterior fontanelle, elevating the head approximately 30 degrees may be helpful. Increased intracranial pressure associated with deterioration in mental status or signs of cerebral herniation (Fig. 38–5) may be treated more vigorously with mannitol administered intravenously (0.5 g/kg) infused during 30 minutes and repeated as necessary. If steroids are used for this purpose, the recommended steroid is dexamethasone in a dose of 10 to 12 mg/m^2/day in four divided doses for no more than 4 or 5 days.[169]

Head circumference measurement and transillumination permit assessment of the development of subdural effusions or may suggest other causes for an enlarging head. CT may be helpful in detecting large subdural effusions or hydrocephalus. Because effusions can be considered part of the pathophysiologic changes that occur with bacterial meningitis, obtaining CT scans to evaluate effusions does not need to be part of the routine evaluation of a child with meningitis. Neuroimaging (CT or MRI) should be performed in children with focal neurologic signs. In children with hemiparesis or quadriparesis, CT or MRI may document cerebrovascular abnormalities. CT also should be performed in children with papilledema on an emergency basis before proceeding with the initial lumbar puncture. *Administration of antibiotics should not be delayed for diagnostic imaging in patients in whom bacterial meningitis is suspected.*

Treatment of subdural effusions, consisting of subdural paracentesis, should take place only when one suspects that the effusions are responsible for seizures or for prolonged fever as a result of subdural empyema. Paracentesis also may be useful if the effusion is responsible for symptoms of increased intracranial pressure or is the cause of focal neurologic signs.[87, 96] In most cases, subdural taps are not required.

Seizures, when noted, are treated expeditiously. A patent airway must be maintained and appropriate anticonvulsants administered. Sodium phenobarbital (7 mg/kg loading dose) may be administered parenterally followed by a maintenance dose of 5 mg/kg/day in two divided doses. If necessary, diazepam (up to 0.2 mg/kg) or lorazepam (0.05 mg/kg/dose up to 4 mg maximum) infused intravenously for 1 to 2 minutes may be used. If prolonged seizure control is needed, phenytoin (5 mg/kg/day) in two divided doses may be used. Phenytoin generally does not depress the respiratory center to the same extent as phenobarbital does, and it also may benefit the patient by inhibiting the secretion of ADH. If the seizure activity no longer is apparent after the second hospital day and the patient has no focal neurologic signs at the time of discharge from the hospital, anticonvulsants may be discontinued. Phenytoin and phenobarbital can induce hepatic microsomal enzymes; their use may increase the rate of metabolism of chloramphenicol and possibly cause a significant decrease in the serum concentration of this antibiotic if it has been used for treatment of meningitis.[248]

An electroencephalogram is indicated in patients with meningitis and seizures when focal seizures are noted, seizures persist more than 72 hours after presentation, seizures occur after the third day of hospitalization, a subdural effusion is noted, or prolonged alteration in sensorium is present. An electroencephalogram may be of value in distinguishing abnormal intermittent posturing from movements associated with seizure activity.

Persistent fever (lasting longer than 8 or 9 days) has been noted.[23] In the multicenter pneumococcal study, the mean duration of fever was 4.4 ± 3.9 days.[15] Suppurative complications, including subdural or pleural empyema, septic arthritis, and pericarditis, should be sought carefully. The rare occurrence of brain abscess in association with bacterial meningitis may lead to persistent fever as well. Furthermore, nosocomial intercurrent infection, usually viral, may cause prolonged fever in a child with meningitis. Complications of therapy, such as suppurative thrombophlebitis or a urinary tract infection after prolonged catheterization, are additional considerations. Persistent fever may be related to the severity of the infection. Poor therapeutic response (especially in multidrug-resistant organisms) occurs, and repeated lumbar puncture must be considered on an individual basis. Drug fever often is cited but rarely is the cause of persistent fever and remains a diagnosis of exclusion.

Prognosis and Sequelae

The prognosis in individual patients with bacterial meningitis depends on many factors, including the following: (1) the age of the patient, (2) the time course or progression of illness before antibiotic therapy is effective, (3) the specific microorganism causing the disease, (4) the number of organisms[99] or the quantity of capsular polysaccharide material present in the meninges and CSF at the time of diagnosis, (5) the rapidity with which CSF is sterilized after initiation of antibiotic therapy, and (6) the presence of disorders that may compromise host response to infection.[193]

The younger the patient and the greater the antigenic load at the time of admission, the worse the prognosis. Bacterial colony counts appear to be a more reliable indication of sequelae than is antigen concentration. Seizures, subdural effusions, bacteremia, and a more prolonged period of fever occur more frequently in children who have more than 10^7 CFU/mL of a particular organism in their CSF at the time of admission.[100] Children with colony counts equal to or greater than 10^7 CFU/mL also are significantly more likely to experience hearing loss and speech disturbance than are children with meningitis but lower concentrations of bacteria within CSF specimens.[100] The presence of TNF in serum has been associated with a fatal outcome in patients with meningococcal meningitis.[331] Elevated concentrations of IL-1β and TNF within the CSF of patients with bacterial meningitis also have been correlated significantly ($p < .002$) with a higher incidence of neurologic sequelae of disease.[225]

The mortality rate for bacterial meningitis in children who are beyond the neonatal period has been reduced to between 1 and 5 percent. Although antibiotic therapy has reduced the mortality rate, as many as 50 percent of the survivors of meningitis have some sequelae of their disease.[77, 96, 124, 307] Most studies from which estimates of sequelae have been derived have been retrospective, and the patients were enrolled for a period of many years (1951–1968). Although antibiotic treatment of these individuals may have been relatively standardized during this period, ancillary methods employed in their care were not controlled.

The frequency of complications of meningitis can be assessed most appropriately by prospective evaluation. In 1975, Sell[287] began a prospective study of 50 infants and children who recovered from *H. influenzae* meningitis. Fifty percent of this group were entirely normal, 9 percent were normal except for behavioral problems, and 28 percent had significant handicaps. The major handicaps noted included hearing loss (10% to 11%), language disorders or delayed language development (15%), impaired vision (2% to 4%), mental retardation (10% to 11%), motor abnormalities (3% to 7%), and seizures (2% to 8%). Twenty-one postmeningitic children were paired with a sibling and tested by the Wechsler Intelligence Scale for Children. The mean IQ of the postmeningitic children was 86, and that of control children was 97 ($p < .05$). Comparison of results for individual pairs revealed that 29 percent of postmeningitic children scored one full standard deviation below their siblings; no survivor had a score one standard deviation higher than his or her sibling. Feldman and Michaels[98] reported that children who recovered from meningitis caused by *H. influenzae* and who were evaluated 10 to 12 years later maintained grades and scores comparable with those of their siblings as they progressed to middle school. Their academic success may require more school and family support to compensate for the minor differences in IQs that had been noted.

A study by Taylor and associates[316] attempted to gain additional insight into the sequelae of *H. influenzae* meningitis, with particular emphasis on neuropsychologic function. Although the study was retrospective, it permitted a more detailed neuropsychologic assessment made at an earlier age than that reported by investigators in previous studies. In addition, the index patients were compared with their siblings who were closest in age and the same sex, and the study was controlled for occupational and educational status. Only 14 percent of children who had been afflicted with *H. influenzae* meningitis had any residual neurologic sequelae. Mean full-scale IQ was 102 for the index children and 109 for the control children.

The more recent results of our large prospective study of bacterial meningitis in children revealed that 32.8 percent of children had abnormalities detectable on neurologic examination at the time of discharge, but by 5 years after discharge, specific deficits were noted in only 11.1 percent of the total group.[88] As a result of the onset of late seizures in some of these patients, the frequency of neurologic sequelae 15 years after discharge was 14 percent.[247] Specific complications or sequelae of meningitis in these patients are shown in Table 38–9. Shortly after discharge, hemiparesis or quadriparesis was noted in 30 patients (12.4% of the total group), but at 1 year after discharge, paralysis was noted in only 5. These data reflect the tendency for even major neurologic defects to clear unpredictably with time. This important observation suggests the need to maintain cautious optimism in discussing long-term complications of meningitis with parents.

In 1995, Grimwood and colleagues[141] reported the results of a prospective cohort study of 158 meningitis survivors, ages 3 months to 14 years, who were treated in a single center between 1983 and 1986. Between 1991 and 1993, 130 children (82% of the original cohort) were evaluated at a mean age of 8.4 years and a mean of 6.7 years after their meningitis. Blended, audiologic, behavioral, neurologic, neuropsychologic, and sociodemographic assessments were compared with those of sex- and grade-matched control children. A systematic increase in the risk of abnormality or for poorer functioning was noted across all categories tested in children with meningitis versus control children. The differences reached statistical significance for tests of fine motor function, intelligence, neuropsychologic function, school behavior, and auditory figure-ground differentiation. Eleven children who had experienced meningitis (8.5% of the cohort studied) had major deficits (hydrocephalus, persistent seizures, spasticity, blindness, IQ below 70, or profound hearing loss). Twenty-four (18.5%) of the survivors of meningitis, and 14 (10.8%) of the control children had minor deficits (IQ of 70 to 80, inability to read, abnormalities in speech discrimination possibly referable to mild to moderate hearing loss, and school behavior problems). Overall, one in four of the children in this study had either a serious disabling sequela or a functionally important behavior disorder or neuropsychologic or auditory dysfunction that adversely affected academic performance.

Meta-analysis of 19 reports of prospectively enrolled and evaluated cohorts from developed countries published between 1980 and 1990[26] determined the mean probability of mortality to be 3.8 percent for *H. influenzae* type b, 7.5 percent for *N. meningitidis,* and 15.3 percent for *S. pneumoniae,*

TABLE 38–9 ■ COMPLICATIONS OF SEQUELAE OF MENINGITIS

	Total	*Haemophilus influenzae*	*H. influenzae* (ampicillin)	*H. influenzae* (chloramphenicol)	*Streptococcus pneumoniae*	*Neisseria meningitidis*	Others
Number	235	151	90	61	35	26	23
Deaths <12 hr in hospital	4	4	3	1	0	0	0
Deaths >12 hr in hospital	1	0	0	0	0	1	0
Shock	8	6	5	1	1	1	0
Paralysis							
Early	30	18	7	11	7	3	2
Persistent	5	4	1	3	4	0	0
Persistent tone	5	4	1	3	1	2	0
Ataxia							
Early	7	5	2	3	2	0	0
Persistent	1	1	0	1	0	0	0
Visual problems	7	4	2	2	3	0	0
Clinically significant hearing deficit	25	17	6	11	5	2	1
Hydrocephalus	1	1	1	0	0	0	0

with an overall probability of 4.8 percent. The mean probabilities of sequelae in the survivors were deafness, 10.5 percent; mental retardation, 4.2 percent; spasticity, paresis, or both, 3.5 percent; and seizure disorder, 4.2 percent. The mean probability of no detectable sequelae was 83.6 percent.

Other specific sequelae or complications of bacterial meningitis that have been observed include cranial nerve involvement, hemiparesis or quadriparesis, muscle hypertonia, ataxia, permanent seizure disorders, and the development of obstructive hydrocephalus. Subdural effusions (as noted earlier) are so frequent in young children that they can be considered a part of the general disease process rather than a persistent or troublesome complication of the meningeal infection. Development of brain abscess after bacterial meningitis is exceedingly rare[102]; when it is found, the possibility that it preceded the development of meningeal infection must be entertained, and a careful search for other sites of such infections as endocarditis should be initiated.

Arditi and associates[16] reviewed the outcomes of 180 children with 181 cases of pneumococcal meningitis who were enrolled in a prospective multicenter study between 1993 and 1996. Fourteen (7.7%) of 180 children died. No deaths were related to treatment failure caused by an antibiotic-resistant strain. Of the 166 surviving children, 41 (25%) developed motor defects, and 48 (32%) of 151 children had moderate to severe unilateral or bilateral hearing loss. By CT or MRI, brain infarcts were noted in 39 of 103 (38%), subdural effusions in 25 of 103 (24%), hydrocephalus in 22 of 103 (21%), cerebritis in 12 of 103 (12%), and brain edema in 6 of 103 (6%).

So far, the outcome of patients with pneumococcal meningitis caused by penicillin- or cefotaxime-nonsusceptible isolates has not been different from that caused by susceptible strains.[16, 105] This finding is explained, in part, because vancomycin has been administered empirically to most children with suspected bacterial meningitis since the mid-1990s in the United States as well as in other parts of the world where treatment failures have been reported as a result of antibiotic-resistant *S. pneumoniae*.[239]

Evoked response audiometry was used to detect hearing deficits in the patients described by Feigin and Dodge.[88] Some deficit in auditory nerve function was documented by this sensitive technique in 6 percent of children with *H. influenzae* meningitis, in 31 percent of children with pneumococcal meningitis, and in 10.5 percent of children with meningococcal disease.

Significant hearing loss after bacterial meningitis has been reported frequently. The mechanisms responsible for hearing deficits include spread of infection along the auditory canal and cochlear aqueduct, serous or purulent labyrinthitis, and, with time, replacement of the membranous labyrinth with fibrous tissue and new bone.[31, 164, 199, 202, 261] Deafness generally is noted early in the course of bacterial meningitis and is independent of the therapy provided.[76, 166, 172, 223, 287, 330] Ataxia has been reported as a presenting sign of bacterial meningitis in children with hearing loss noted in the same individuals at a later date.[170, 286] Presumably, the insult to the vestibular and auditory systems occurred concomitantly in these children. The early loss of hearing noted by several investigators suggests that hearing loss is *not* associated specifically with the use of a particular antimicrobial agent. Early diagnosis and treatment apparently will not prevent the development of deafness in many children who develop loss of hearing as a consequence of bacterial meningitis.

Estimates of the frequency of hearing loss in retrospective studies vary from 2.4 to 29 percent.[165, 228] In our prospective studies, 7 percent of children have experienced marked to extensive (75-dB loss or greater) hearing losses.[166, 172] Overall, 48 of 151 (32%) of the children with pneumococcal meningitis in the multicenter study had unilateral or bilateral moderate to severe hearing loss.[16] On occasion, hearing loss noted early may improve during a period of weeks to months.[261]

In our studies, no correlation has been found between loss of hearing and either the age of the patient at the onset of meningitis or the duration of illness before admission.[76, 172] A significant correlation was noted between hearing loss and the presence of seizures before admission, the duration of fever in the hospital after therapy had been initiated (which presumably reflects more severe disease), treatment with antibiotics administered orally before a definitive diagnosis of bacterial meningitis, and a depressed CSF-to-blood glucose ratio at the time of admission.[76, 172, 173]

Because hearing deficits occur so commonly in patients with bacterial meningitis, hearing evaluation by evoked response audiometry in young, uncooperative children is recommended routinely at the time of or shortly after discharge from the hospital. Repeated audiometric evaluation is recommended after discharge if the results of the initial examination are abnormal. Pure tone audiometry can be used for older, cooperative children. Differentiation of hearing deficits due to conductive disturbances from those related to damage to the eighth cranial nerve is important. Some children who have repetitive episodes of otitis media may experience conductive loss that is unrelated to the meningitis.

In our studies, the mean IQ (±1 SD) of the entire group of patients (235) after recovery was 94 (±23), with a range of 33 to 150. Twenty-nine children (17.3%) had IQs less than 80, and 22 (11.6%) had IQs less than 70. A comparison of these patients with their siblings and other control children revealed no significant difference in mean IQ. A significantly greater proportion ($p < .01$) of children who recovered from meningitis had IQs less than 80 than did children from control groups. These results differ from those of Sell,[287] which were noted previously. Tejani and associates[318] also prospectively evaluated children who had recovered from bacterial meningitis using siblings as controls. They reported no significant differences in the verbal performances or full-scale IQs between patients with meningitis and the sibling control population.

The prospective nature of these studies has permitted an assessment of factors that herald a poor prognosis and that may be discernible at or near the time of admission. Evidence of inappropriate secretion of ADH was correlated significantly ($p < .01$) with abnormal neurologic examinations at 3 months after discharge and with low IQs. The age of the child correlated inversely with the development of subdural effusion ($p < .01$), the occurrence of hearing deficits ($p < .02$), and low IQ ($p < .05$). Thus, the significantly increased impact of the disease on young children could be documented conclusively. The presence of focal neurologic findings in patients who were not postictal at the time of admission correlated significantly ($p < .001$) with abnormal neurologic examination, which was noted previously. Focal deficits indicative of cerebral injury noted at admission or during the course of hospitalization were associated significantly ($p < .001$) with the development of late (1 to 15 years after discharge) afebrile seizures.[247] Thus, focal neurologic findings at the time of admission proved to be a most reliable predictor of permanent sequelae of bacterial meningitis. Focal deficits at admission also correlated significantly with low IQs ($p < .001$), even at 2 and 3 years after discharge from the hospital. The quantity of antigen in the initial CSF specimen and the number of organisms present also correlated significantly ($p < .01$) with sequelae of meningitis.[96]

Only one study assessed the value of the Pediatric Risk of Mortality (PRISM) score in predicting outcomes of bacterial meningitis.[205] This study was performed in a subgroup of children requiring mechanical ventilation. The single best predictor of death and functional states on follow-up evaluation was the PRISM score. When the score was less than 20 within the first 24 hours of admission to the pediatric intensive care unit, a favorable outcome was noted in 82 percent. When the score was 20 or higher, a favorable outcome was noted in only 30 percent ($p < .009$).

CT has revealed evidence of cerebral infarction in children who had a diagnosis of bacterial meningitis established within 1 or 2 days of the onset of symptoms of a febrile illness.[300] In most of these cases, evidence of abnormalities in cerebrovascular dynamics (arteritis, thrombosis, thrombophlebitis), ventricular dilatation, or both have been observed. In some of these cases, infarction has been associated with profound hypotension related to endotoxemia (personal experience). Brain infarction apparently is *not* related causally to a delay in diagnosis and therapy in many cases.

Prevention

HAEMOPHILUS INFLUENZAE MENINGITIS

In the past 10 years, methods of preventing meningitis caused by *H. influenzae* type b have improved. The dramatic decrease in the incidence of *H. influenzae* type b invasive disease and meningitis has been attributed to the introduction of vaccines that initially were found to be effective at 15 months of age[8] and then later found to be effective as early as 2 months of age.[283] Currently, three conjugate vaccines are approved for infants beginning at 2 months of age: HbOC, PRP-OMP, and PRP conjugated to tetanus toxoid (PRP-T). The Advisory Committee on Immunization Practices and the American Academy of Pediatrics recommend universal infant immunization with HbOC or PRP-T at 2, 4, and 6 months of age or PRP-OMP at 2 and 4 months of age.[12, 50]

Passive immunization of infants has also been studied with use of bacterial polysaccharide immunoglobulin.[7, 273] This preparation given in a single intramuscular dose of 0.5 mL/kg provides significant protection for infants from *H. influenzae* type b disease for 3 or 4 months.

The single most comprehensive study concerning the spread of *H. influenzae* type b infection among household contacts was coordinated by the CDC.[336] Data collected from 19 states were analyzed prospectively. *H. influenzae* meningitis was reported in 1403 patients. Eighty-two percent of exposed families were investigated for the occurrence of *H. influenzae* disease within 30 days of its onset in the index patient. Systemic disease caused by *H. influenzae* type b developed in 9 of 1687 contacts (0.5%) who were younger than 6 years. The risk of infection in patients younger than 4 years was 2.1 percent; the risk in children younger than 1 year was 6 percent. The risk of secondary infection of household contacts in the 30 days after onset of meningitis in the index case was 585 times greater than the age-adjusted risk in the general population and was similar to the risk of secondary meningococcal disease in household contacts. This nationwide study provided an important impetus for finding a chemoprophylactic regimen that could prevent secondary infection in household contacts.

A nationwide, collaborative, placebo-controlled trial was conducted subsequently among household (children younger than 6 years) and daycare center contacts of people with invasive *H. influenzae* type b disease.[25] Four of 765 placebo-treated contacts experienced secondary disease versus none of 1112 rifampin-treated contacts ($p = .027$).

The Infectious Diseases Committee of the American Academy of Pediatrics recommends that rifampin be provided orally once each day for 4 days in a dose of 20 mg/kg (maximum dose, 600 mg/day) to all household contacts (children and adults), irrespective of age in those households with at least one unvaccinated contact younger than 4 years.[12] The dose for infants younger than 1 month is not established, but it may be lowered to 10 mg/kg. However, rifampin prophylaxis is not required when all of the household contacts younger than 4 years have been fully immunized. All members of households with a fully immunized but immunocompromised child, regardless of age, should receive rifampin because of concern that the immunization may not have been effective.

When two or more cases of invasive disease have occurred within 60 days and unimmunized or incompletely immunized children attend a daycare facility, rifampin should be administered to all personnel and attendees. When a single case has been reported, the use of rifampin is controversial, and many experts recommend *no* prophylaxis.[12]

Unimmunized or incompletely immunized children should receive a dose of vaccine and should be scheduled for completion of the recommended age-specific immunization schedule.

No data document the safety of rifampin administered during pregnancy. Therefore, prophylaxis with rifampin is not recommended for pregnant women who are contacts of infected infants.

Patients receiving rifampin should be advised routinely that their urine, sweat, and tears will be stained orange. Individuals should be advised to refrain from using contact lenses while receiving rifampin therapy because the lenses may be stained permanently.

PNEUMOCOCCAL INFECTION

In a large randomized trial conducted by Black and colleagues,[35] more than 37,000 infants received either the 7-valent pneumococcal vaccine containing polysaccharides of serotypes 4, 6B, 9V, 14, 18C, 19F, and 23F conjugated to CRM_{197} or meningococcal serogroup C oligosaccharide conjugated to the same protein. Vaccines were administered at 2, 4, 6, and 12 to 15 months of age. The pneumococcal conjugate vaccine was found to be 97.4 percent efficacious in preventing acquisition of invasive pneumococcal infections caused by vaccine serotype isolates. As a result of this study, the 7-valent pneumococcal protein conjugate vaccine is recommended by the Advisory Committee on Immunizations Practices and the Infectious Diseases Committee of the American Academy of Pediatrics for all children younger than 24 months to prevent invasive pneumococcal infections.[11, 54] Vaccine also is recommended for children 25 to 60 months of age with high risk of acquiring invasive disease and should be considered for otherwise normal children in this age range with other risk features that may increase their risk for development of systemic pneumococcal infection. The reader is referred to the CDC and American Academy of Pediatrics statements and the chapter on pneumococcal infections for the details of these recommendations.

MENINGOCOCCAL INFECTION

We advocate the use of chemoprophylaxis in all household members of a patient with meningococcal meningitis and in daycare and nursery school contacts, preferably within 24 hours of the diagnosis of the primary case.[13] Prophylaxis may be provided for persons who had contact with the patient's oral secretions through kissing or sharing toothbrushes or eating utensils during the 7 days before onset of disease in the index case. Prophylaxis is not recommended routinely for health care personnel unless they have had close exposure through mouth-to-mouth resuscitation, intubation, or suctioning before antibiotic therapy was initiated. Schoolroom classmates and hospital contacts of patients usually are not given prophylactic treatment.

Minocycline and rifampin have proved to be 80 to 90 percent effective in eradicating carriage of meningococci.[146] Both drugs are secreted in the saliva in concentrations greater than the MICs for meningococci. The use of minocycline has been accompanied by frequent and significant vestibular reactions, even after a single dose of 100 mg, and, in our opinion, generally should not be used.[48, 51, 52, 344]

Rifampin is the drug of choice in most instances and can be used in a dose of 600 mg twice daily for four doses in adults and in doses of 10 mg/kg/dose for four doses in children between 1 and 12 years of age. A dose of 5 mg/kg every 12 hours for four doses can be used in children between 3 months and 1 year of age.[222] The emergence of rifampin-resistant strains in treated meningococcal carriers has been reported to occur with a frequency of 0 to 27 percent.[66, 80, 340]

A single intramuscular dose of ceftriaxone has proved to be an effective alternative to rifampin for prophylaxis in meningococcal contacts.[285] This approach to prophylaxis may be particularly useful in circumstances in which compliance with the use of oral rifampin is considered questionable. The efficacy of ceftriaxone has been confirmed for only group A strains, but its effect is likely to be similar for other serogroups. Ceftriaxone has the advantage of easier dosage and administration and safety in pregnancy.[13] Ceftriaxone may be given intramuscularly in a dose of 125 mg for individuals younger than 12 years and in a dose of 250 mg for individuals 12 years of age and older.

Ciprofloxacin given to adults in a single oral dose of 500 mg has been effective in eradicating meningococcal carriage.[13] At present, ciprofloxacin is not recommended for individuals younger than 18 years or for pregnant women.

Because secondary cases may occur several weeks or more after onset of disease in the index case, meningococcal vaccine may be used as an adjunct to chemoprophylaxis when an outbreak is caused by a serogroup contained in the vaccine. Recommendations for the administration of the meningococcal serogroup C vaccine to control outbreaks have been outlined by the CDC.[49]

A serogroup-specific quadrivalent meningococcal vaccine against group A, C, 4, and W135 *N. meningitidis* has been approved for use in the United States in children 2 years of age and older. The vaccine consists of 50 μg each of the respective purified bacterial polysaccharides. It may be given subcutaneously as a single 0.5-mL dose and can be given concurrently with other vaccines.

A single dose of serogroup C vaccine seems to be approximately 70 percent effective, for a period of 6 to 9 months, in preventing meningococcal disease in children who are older than 2 years.[315] Single 50-μg injections in children younger than 2 years do not produce adequate antibody responses.[315] A serogroup A polysaccharide vaccine has been field tested by the World Health Organization and is effective in children 3 months of age or older.[242, 332] Serogroup-specific monovalent vaccines may be used to control outbreaks of disease caused by either type A or type C meningococci and may be of value for travelers to countries with epidemic disease.[13, 85] The vaccine is administered as a single dose parenterally in the volume specified by the package insert. Reactions noted after immunizations previously have been mild and infrequent; localized erythema of 1 or 2 days' duration is not unusual. The safety of the vaccine in pregnant women has not been established.

An effective serogroup B meningococcal vaccine has not been produced to date. In an effort to enhance the immunologic activity of meningococcal serogroup B polysaccharide, it has been complexed noncovalently with serotype 2 outer-membrane proteins. The product has been shown to be safe and immunogenic in humans.[351] This preparation offers the hope that an appropriately immunogenic serogroup B meningococcal vaccine may be available in the near future.[109]

Immunization with the meningococcal quadrivalent vaccine is recommended for children 2 years of age or older in high-risk groups, including those with anatomic or functional asplenia and those with terminal deficiencies of the complement system or with properdin deficiency. The American College Health Association recommends immunization of college students. The American Academy of Pediatrics recommends that health care workers inform college students and their parents of the risk of contracting meningococcal disease during college and the potential benefits of immunization. The meningococcal vaccine should be made available to those students requesting immunization.[9]

Like other protein conjugate vaccines, meningococcal C conjugate vaccines are more immunogenic than is the pure polysaccharide vaccine in infants younger than 2 years of age.[204] Because of a high incidence of meningococcal disease in the United Kingdom, a meningococcal serogroup C CRM_{197} was administered in a phased program beginning November 1999 to all children younger than 18 years.[256] Surveillance studies to assess short-term efficacy have shown a 97 percent efficacy for teenagers and a 92 percent efficacy for toddlers in the prevention of meningococcal serogroup C infection.

REFERENCES

1. Achtman, M.: Molecular epidemiology of epidemic bacterial meningitis. Rev. Med. Microbiol. *1*:29–38, 1990.
2. Achtman, M.: Clonal properties of meningococci from epidemic meningitis. Trans. R. Soc. Trop. Med. Hyg. *85*(Suppl.):24–31, 1991.
3. Adair, C. V., Gould, R. L., and Smadel, J. E.: Aseptic meningitis, a disease of diverse etiology: Clinical and etiologic studies on 854 cases. Ann. Intern. Med. *39*:675–704, 1953.
4. Adams, R. D., Kubik, C. S., and Bonner, F. J.: The clinical and pathological aspects of influenzal meningitis. Arch. Pediatr. *65*:354–376, 1948.
5. Adams, W. G., Deaver, K. A., Cochi, S. L., et al.: Decline of childhood *Haemophilus influenzae* type b (Hib) disease in the Hib vaccine era. J. A. M. A. *269*:221–226, 1993.
6. Allbritton, W. L., Wiggins, G. L., and Feeley, J. C.: Neonatal listerioses: Distribution of serotypes in relation to age at onset of disease. J. Pediatr. *88*:481–483, 1976.
7. Ambrosino, D. M., Landesman, S. H., Gorham, C. C., et al.: Passive immunization against disease due to *Haemophilus influenzae* type b: Concentrations of antibody to capsular polysaccharide in high-risk children. J. Infect. Dis. *153*:1–7, 1986.
8. American Academy of Pediatrics, Committee on Infectious Diseases: *Haemophilus influenzae* type b conjugate vaccines: Recommendations for immunization of infants and children 2 months of age and older: Update. Pediatrics *88*:169–172, 1991.
9. American Academy of Pediatrics, Committee on Infectious Diseases: Meningococcal disease prevention and control strategies for practice-based physicians (Addendum: Recommendations for college students). Pediatrics *106*:1500–1504, 2000.
10. American Academy of Pediatrics: Pneumococcal infections. *In* Pickering, L. K. (ed.): 2000 Red Book: Report of the Committee on Infectious Diseases. 25th ed. Elk Grove Village, IL, American Academy of Pediatrics, 2000, pp. 454–456.
11. American Academy of Pediatrics, Committee on Infectious Diseases: Policy Statement: Recommendations for the prevention of pneumococcal infections, including the use of pneumococcal conjugate vaccine (Prevnar), pneumococcal polysaccharide vaccine, and antibiotic prophylaxis. Pediatrics *106*:362–366, 2000.
12. American Academy of Pediatrics: *Haemophilus influenzae* infections. *In* Pickering, L. K. (ed.): 2000 Red Book: Report of the Committee on Infectious Diseases. 25th ed. Elk Grove Village, IL, American Academy of Pediatrics, 2000, pp. 262–272.

13. American Academy of Pediatrics: Meningococcal infections. *In* Pickering, L. K. (ed.): 2000 Red Book: Report of the Committee on Infectious Diseases. 25th ed. Elk Grove Village, IL, American Academy of Pediatrics, 2000, pp. 396–401.
14. Anderson, G., Smithee, L., Rados, M., et al.: Progress toward elimination of *Haemophilus influenzae* type b disease among infants and children—United States, 1987–1993. M. M. W. R. Morb. Mortal. Wkly. Rep. *43*:144–148, 1994.
15. Arditi, M., Herold, B. C., and Yogev, R.: Cefuroxime treatment failure and *Haemophilus influenzae* meningitis: Case report and review of the literature. Pediatrics *84*:132–135, 1989.
16. Arditi, M., Mason, E., Jr., Bradley, J., et al.: Three-year multicenter surveillance of pneumococcal meningitis in children: Clinical characteristics, and outcome related to penicillin susceptibility and dexamethasone use. Pediatrics *102*:1087–1097, 1998.
17. Aronoff, S. C., Reed, M. O., O'Brien, C. A., et al.: Comparison of the efficacy and safety of ceftriaxone to ampicillin/chloramphenicol in the treatment of childhood meningitis. Antimicrob. Agents Chemother. *13*:143–151, 1984.
18. Asensi, F., Otero, M. C., Perez-Tamarit, D., et al.: Risk/benefit in the treatment of children with imipenem-cilastatin for meningitis caused by penicillin-resistant pneumococcus. J. Chemother. *5*:133–134, 1993.
19. Ashwal, S., Tomasi, L., Schneider, S., et al.: Bacterial meningitis in children: Pathophysiology and treatment. Neurology *42*:739–748, 1992.
20. Asmar, B. I., and Dajani, A. S.: Concurrent pneumococcal disease in two siblings. Am. J. Dis. Child. *136*:946–947, 1982.
21. Baker, C. J., and Barrett, F. F.: Transmission of group B streptococci among parturient women and their neonates. J. Pediatr. *83*:919–925, 1972.
22. Baker, R. C., and Bausher, J. C.: Meningitis complicating acute bacteremic facial cellulitis. Pediatr. Infect. Dis. *5*:421–423, 1986.
23. Balagtas, R. C., Levin, S., Nelson, K. E., et al.: Secondary and prolonged fevers in bacterial meningitis. J. Pediatr. *77*:957–964, 1970.
24. Baldwin, L. N., Henderson, A., Thomas, P., et al.: Acute bacterial meningitis in young adults mistaken for substance abuse. B. M. J. *306*:775–776, 1993.
25. Band, J., Fraser, D. W., and Ajello, G.: Prevention of *Hemophilus influenzae* type b disease. J. A. M. A. *25*:2381–2386, 1984.
26. Baraff, L. J., Lee, S., and Schriger, D. L.: Outcomes of bacterial meningitis in children: A meta-analysis. Pediatr. Infect. Dis. J. *12*:389–394, 1993.
27. Barenkamp, S. J., Granoff, D. M., and Munson, R. S., Jr.: Outer-membrane protein subtypes of *Haemophilus influenzae* type b and spread of disease in day-care centers. J. Infect. Dis. *144*:210–217, 1981.
28. Barson, W. J., Miller, M. A., Brady, M. T., et al.: Prospective comparative trial of ceftriaxone versus conventional therapy for treatment of bacterial meningitis in children. Pediatr. Infect. Dis. *4*:362–368, 1985.
29. Baumgartner, E. T., Augustine, A., and Steele, R. W.: Bacterial meningitis in older neonates. Am. J. Dis. Child. *137*:1052–1054, 1983.
30. Beckman, J. S., Beckman, T. W., Chen, J., et al.: Apparent hydroxyl radical production by peroxynitrite: Implications for endothelial injury from nitric oxide and superoxide. Proc. Natl. Acad. Sci. U. S. A. *87*:1620–1624, 1990.
31. Berlow, S. J., Caldarelli, D. D., Matz, G. J., et al.: Bacterial meningitis: A prospective investigation. Laryngoscope *90*:1445–1452, 1980.
32. Berman, B. W., King, F. H., Jr., Rubenstein, D. S., et al.: *Bacteroides fragilis* meningitis in a neonate successfully treated with metronidazole. J. Pediatr. *93*:793–795, 1978.
33. Bernhardt, L. L., Semberkoff, M. S., and Rahal, J. J., Jr.: Deficient cerebrospinal fluid opsonization in experimental *Escherichia coli* meningitis. Infect. Immun. *32*:411–413, 1981.
34. Bijlmer, H. A.: World-wide epidemiology of *Haemophilus influenzae* meningitis: Industrialized versus non-industrialized countries. Vaccine *9*(Suppl.):S5–S9, 1991.
35. Black, S., Shinfield, H., Fireman, B., et al.: Efficacy, safety and immunogenicity of heptavalent pneumococcal vaccine in children. Pediatr. Infect. Dis. J. *19*:187–195, 2000.
36. Blazer, S., Berant, M., and Alon, U.: Bacterial meningitis: Effect of antibiotic treatment on cerebrospinal fluid. Am. J. Clin. Pathol. *80*:386–387, 1983.
37. Bohr, V., Hansen, B., Jessen, O., et al.: Eight hundred and seventy-five cases of bacterial meningitis. Part I of a three-part series: Clinical data, prognosis, and the role of specialized hospital departments. J. Infect. *7*:21–30, 1983.
38. Bradley, J. S., Ching, D. K., and Phillips, S. E.: Outpatient therapy of serious pediatric infections with ceftriaxone. Pediatr. Infect. Dis. J. *7*:160–164, 1988.
39. Bradley, J. S., and Conner, J. D.: Ceftriaxone failure in meningitis caused by *Streptococcus pneumoniae* with reduced susceptibility to beta-lactam antibiotics. Pediatr. Infect. Dis. J. *10*:871–873, 1991.
40. Brady, M. T., Kaplan, S. L., and Taber, L. H.: Association between persistence of pneumococcal meningitis and dexamethasone administration. J. Pediatr. *99*:924–926, 1981.
41. Braun, J. S., and Tuomanen, E. I.: Molecular mechanisms of brain damage in bacterial meningitis. Adv. Pediatr. Infect. Dis. *14*:49–71, 1999.
42. Breiman, R. F., Butler, J. C., Tenover, F. C., et al.: Emergence of drug-resistant pneumococcal infections in the United States. J. A. M. A. *271*:1831–1835, 1994.
43. Brenneman, G., Silimperi, D., and Ward, J.: Recurrent invasive *Haemophilus influenzae* type b disease in Alaskan natives. Pediatr. Infect. Dis. J. *6*:388–392, 1987.
44. Bryan, J. P., Rocha, H., da Silva, H. R., et al.: Comparison of ceftriaxone and ampicillin plus chloramphenicol for the therapy of acute bacterial meningitis. Antimicrob. Agents Chemother. *28*:361–368, 1985.
45. Burroughs, M., Cabellos, C., Prasad, S., et al.: Bacterial components and the pathophysiology of injury to the blood-brain barrier: Does cell wall add to the effects of endotoxin in gram-negative meningitis? J. Infect. Dis. *165*:S82–S85, 1992.
46. Butler, J. C., Breiman, R. F., and Lipman, H. B.: Serotype distribution of *Streptococcus pneumoniae* infections among preschool children in the United States, 1978–1994: Implications for development of conjugate vaccine. J. Infect. Dis. *171*:885–889, 1995.
47. Cable, D., Overturf, G., and Edralin, G.: Concentrations of cefoperazone in cerebrospinal fluid during bacterial meningitis. Antimicrob. Agents Chemother. *23*:688–691, 1983.
48. Centers for Disease Control: Bacterial meningitis and meningococcemia: United States—1978. M. M. W. R. Morb. Mortal. Wkly. Rep. *28*:277–278, 1979.
49. Centers for Disease Control and Prevention: Control and prevention of meningococcal disease and control and prevention of serogroup C meningococcal disease: Evaluation and management of suspected outbreaks. M. M. W. R. Morb. Mortal. Wkly. Rep. *46*(RR-5):1–21, 1997.
50. Centers for Disease Control: *Haemophilus* b conjugate vaccines for prevention of *Haemophilus influenzae* type b disease among infants and children two months of age and older: Recommendations of the Immunization Practices Advisory Committee (ACIP). M. M. W. R. Morb. Mortal. Wkly. Rep. *40*:1–7, 1991.
51. Centers for Disease Control: Vestibular reactions to minocycline after meningococcal prophylaxis—New Jersey. M. M. W. R. Morb. Mortal. Wkly. Rep. *24*:9–11, 1975.
52. Centers for Disease Control: Vestibular reactions to minocycline followup—Georgia, New York, Vermont. M. M. W. R. Morb. Mortal. Wkly. Rep. *24*:55–56, 1975.
53. Centers for Disease Control and Prevention: Progress toward eliminating *Haemophilus influenzae* type b disease among infants and children—United States, 1987–1997. M. M. W. R. Morb. Mortal. Wkly. Rep. *47*:993–998, 1998.
54. Centers for Disease Control and Prevention: Recommendations of the Advisory Committee on Immunization Practices. Preventing pneumococcal disease among infants and young children. M. M. W. R. Morb. Mortal. Wkly. Rep. *49*(RR-9):1–35, 2000.
55. Cherry, J. D., and Sheenan, C. P.: Bacteriologic relapse in *Haemophilus influenzae* meningitis: Inadequate ampicillin therapy. N. Engl. J. Med. *278*:1001–1003, 1968.
56. Cole, F. S., Saryan, J. A., and Smith, A. L.: The risk of additional systemic bacterial illness in infants with systemic *Streptococcus pneumoniae* disease. J. Pediatr. *99*:91–94, 1981.
57. Coleman, S. J., Auld, E. B., Connor, J. D., et al.: Relapse of *Hemophilus influenzae* type b meningitis during intravenous therapy with ampicillin. J. Pediatr. *74*:781–784, 1969.
58. Colville, A., Davies, W., Heneghan, M., et al.: A rare complication of dental treatment: *Streptococcus oralis* meningitis. Br. Dent. J. *175*: 133–134, 1993.
59. Committee on Infectious Diseases of the American Academy of Pediatrics: Therapy for children with invasive pneumococcal infections. Pediatrics *99*:289–299, 1997.
60. Congeni, B. L.: Comparison of ceftriaxone and traditional therapy of bacterial meningitis. Antimicrob. Agents Chemother. *25*:40–44, 1984.
61. Coulehan, J. L., Michaels, R. H., Hallowell, C., et al.: Epidemiology of *Haemophilus influenzae* type b disease among Navajo Indians. Public Health Rep. *99*:404–409, 1984.
62. Dagan, R., Shriker, O., Hazan, I., et al.: Prospective study to determine clinical relevance of detection of pneumococcal DNA in sera of children by PCR. J. Clin. Microbiol. *36*:669–673, 1998.
63. Daoud, A. S., Batieha, A., Al-Sheyyab, M., et al.: Lack of effectiveness of dexamethasone in neonatal bacterial meningitis. Eur. J. Pediatr. *158*:230–233, 1999.
64. Daum, R. S., Silber, G. R., Kamon, J. S., et al.: Evaluation of a commercial latex particle agglutination test for rapid diagnosis of *Haemophilus influenzae* type b infection. Pediatrics *69*:466–471, 1982.
65. Davey, P. G., Cruikshank, J. K., McManus, I. C., et al.: Bacterial meningitis—ten years' experience. J. Hyg. *88*:383–401, 1982.
66. Deal, W. B., and Sanders, E.: Efficacy of rifampin in treatment of meningococcal carriers. N. Engl. J. Med. *281*:641–645, 1969.
67. Deivanayagam, N., Ashaok, T. P., Nedunchelian, K., et al.: Evaluation of CSF variables as a diagnostic test for bacterial meningitis. J. Trop. Pediatr. *39*:284–287, 1993.
68. Del Rio, M., Chrane, D., Shelton, S., et al.: Ceftriaxone versus ampicillin and chloramphenicol for treatment of bacterial meningitis in children. Lancet *1*:1241–1244, 1983.
69. Del Rio, M. D. A., Chrane, D. F., Shelton, S., et al.: Pharmacokinetics of cefuroxime in infants and children with bacterial meningitis. Antimicrob. Agents Chemother. *22*:990–994, 1982.

70. de Morais, J. S., Munford, R. S., Rise, J. N., et al.: Epidemic disease due to serogroup L *Neisseria meningitidis* in São Paulo, Brazil. J. Infect. Dis. *129*:568–571, 1974.
71. Devoe, I. W., and Gilchrist, J. E.: Pili on meningococci from primary cultures of nasopharyngeal carriers and cerebrospinal fluid of infants with acute disease. J. Exp. Med. *141*:297–305, 1975.
72. Diab, A., Zhu, J., Lindquist, L., et al.: *Haemophilus influenzae* and *Streptococcus pneumoniae* induce different intracerebral mRNA cytokine patterns during the course of experimental bacterial meningitis. Clin. Exp. Immunol. *109*:233–241, 1997.
73. Dicuonzo, G., Lorino, G., Lilli, D., et al.: Use of oligoprobes on amplified DNA in the diagnosis of bacterial meningitis. Eur. J. Clin. Microbiol. Infect. Dis. *18*:352–357, 1999.
74. Dinarello, C. A., and Mier, J. W.: Lymphokines. N. Engl. J. Med. *317*:940–945, 1987.
75. Di Pentima, M. C., Mason, E. O., Jr., and Kaplan, S. L.: In vitro antibiotic synergy against *Flavobacterium meningosepticum*: Implications for therapeutic options. Clin. Infect. Dis. *26*:1169–1176, 1998.
76. Dodge, P. R., Davis, H., Feigin, R. D., et al.: Prospective evaluation of hearing impairment as a sequela of acute bacterial meningitis. N. Engl. J. Med. *311*:869–874, 1984.
77. Dodge, P. R., and Swartz, M. N.: Bacterial meningitis: A review of selected aspects. II. Special neurologic problems, postmeningitic complications and clinicopathological correlations. N. Engl. J. Med. *272*:1003–1010, 1965.
78. du Plessis, M., Smith, A. M., and Klugman, K. P.: Rapid detection of penicillin-resistant *Streptococcus pneumoniae* in cerebrospinal fluid by a seminested-PCR strategy. J. Clin. Microbiol. *36*:453–457, 1998.
79. Edwards, K. M., Alford, R., Gewurz, H., et al.: Recurrent bacterial infections associated with C^3 nephritic factor and hypocomplementemia. N. Engl. J. Med. *308*:1138–1141, 1983.
80. Eickhoff, T. C.: In-vitro and in-vivo studies of resistance to rifampin in meningococci. J. Infect. Dis. *123*:414–420, 1971.
81. Ellison, R. T., III, Kohler, P. F., Curd, J. G., et al.: Prevalence of congenital or acquired complement deficiency in patients with sporadic meningococcal disease. N. Engl. J. Med. *308*:913–916, 1983.
82. Eraklis, A. J., Kevy, S. V., Diamond, L. K., et al.: Hazard of overwhelming infection after splenectomy in childhood. N. Engl. J. Med. *276*:1225–1229, 1967.
83. Ernst, J. D., Decazes, J. M., and Sande, M. A.: Experimental pneumococcal meningitis: The role of leukocytes in pathogenesis. Infect. Immun. *41*:275–279, 1983.
84. Ernst, J. D., Hartiala, K. T., Goldstein, I. M., et al.: Complement (C5)-derived chemotactic activity accounts for accumulation of polymorphonuclear leukocytes in cerebrospinal fluid of rabbits with pneumococcal meningitis. Infect. Immun. *46*:81–86, 1984.
85. Feigin, R. D.: Bacterial meningitis beyond the newborn period. *In* Feigin, R. D., and Cherry, J. D. (eds.): Textbook of Pediatric Infectious Diseases. 2nd ed. Philadelphia, W. B. Saunders, 1987, pp. 439–465.
86. Feigin, R. D., Baker, C. J., Herwaldt, L. A., et al.: Epidemic meningococcal disease in an elementary-school classroom. N. Engl. J. Med. *307*:1255–1257, 1982.
87. Feigin, R. D., and Dodge, P. R.: Bacterial meningitis: Newer concepts of pathophysiology and neurologic sequelae. Pediatr. Clin. North Am. *23*:541–556, 1976.
88. Feigin, R. D., and Dodge, P. R.: Personal communications, 1974–1991.
89. Feigin, R. D., and Dodge, P. R.: Personal data.
90. Feigin, R. D., and Dodge, P. R.: Personal experience: Unpublished data for prospective studies of bacterial meningitis, 1974–1979.
91. Feigin, R. D., and Kaplan, S.: Inappropriate secretion of antidiuretic hormone (ADH) in children with bacterial meningitis. Am. J. Clin. Nutr. *30*:1482–1484, 1977.
92. Feigin, R. D., McCracken, G. H., and Klein, J. O.: Diagnosis and management of meningitis. Pediatr. Infect. Dis. J. *11*:785–814, 1992.
93. Feigin, R. D., and Shackelford, P. G.: Sequential lumbar puncture as a diagnostic aid in aseptic meningitis. N. Engl. J. Med. *289*:571–574, 1973.
94. Feigin, R. D., and Shearer, W. T.: Opportunistic infection in children. Part I. In the compromised host. J. Pediatr. *87*:507–514, 1975.
95. Feigin, R. D., and Shearer, W. T.: Opportunistic infection in children. Part II. In the compromised host. J. Pediatr. *87*:677–694, 1975.
96. Feigin, R. D., Stechenberg, B. W., Chang, M. J., et al.: Prospective evaluation of treatment of *Hemophilus influenzae* meningitis. J. Pediatr. *88*:773–775, 1976.
97. Feigin, R. D., Wong, M., Shackelford, P. G., et al.: Countercurrent immunoelectrophoresis of urine as well as CSF and blood for the diagnosis of bacterial meningitis. J. Pediatr. *89*:773–774, 1976.
98. Feldman, H. M., and Michaels, R. H.: Academic achievement in children 10 to 12 years after *Haemophilus influenzae* meningitis. Pediatrics *81*:339–344, 1988.
99. Feldman, W. E.: Concentrations of bacteria in cerebrospinal fluid of patients with bacterial meningitis. J. Pediatr. *88*:549–552, 1976.
100. Feldman, W. E., Ginsburg, C. B., McCracken, G. H., et al.: Relation of concentrations of *Haemophilus influenzae* type b in cerebrospinal fluid to late sequelae of patients with meningitis. J. Pediatr. *100*:209–218, 1982.
101. Feldman, W. E., Moffitt, S., and Manning, N. S.: Penetration of cefoxitin into cerebrospinal fluid of infants and children with bacterial meningitis. Antimicrob. Agents Chemother. *21*:468–471, 1982.
102. Feldman, W. E., and Schwartz, J.: *Haemophilus influenzae* type b brain abscess complicating meningitis: Case report. Pediatrics *72*:473–475, 1983.
103. Finland, M., and Barnes, M. W.: Acute bacterial meningitis at Boston City Hospital during 12 selected years, 1935–1972. J. Infect. Dis. *136*:400–415, 1977.
104. Finlay, F. O., Witherow, H., and Rudd, P. T.: Latex agglutination testing in bacterial meningitis. Arch. Dis. Child. *73*:160–161, 1995.
105. Fiore, A. E., Moroney, J. F., Farley, M. M., et al.: Clinical outcomes of meningitis caused by *Streptococcus pneumoniae* in the era of antibiotic resistance. Clin. Infect. Dis. *30*:71–77, 2000.
106. Fischer, G. W., Brenz, R. W., Alden, E. R., et al.: Lumbar puncture and meningitis. Am. J. Dis. Child. *129*:590–592, 1975.
107. Forgacs, P., Geyer, C. A., and Freidberg, S. R.: Characterization of chemical meningitis after neurological surgery. Clin. Infect. Dis. *32*:179–185, 2001.
108. Franciosi, R. A., Knostman, J. D., and Zimmerman, R. A.: Group B streptococcal neonatal and infant infections. J. Pediatr. *82*:707–718, 1973.
109. Frasch, C. E., Pepple, B. S., Cate, T. R., et al.: Immunogenicity and clinical evaluation of group B *Neisseria meningitidis* outer membrane protein vaccines. *In* Weinstein, L., and Fields, B. N. (eds.): Seminar in Infectious Diseases. Vol. 4. Bacterial Vaccines. New York, Thieme-Stratton, 1982, pp. 263–267.
110. Fraser, D. W., Darby, C. P., Koehler, R. E., et al.: Risk factors in bacterial meningitis: Charleston County, South Carolina. J. Infect. Dis. *127*:271–277, 1973.
111. Fraser, D. W., Geil, C. C., and Feldman, R. A.: Bacterial meningitis in Bernalilla County, New Mexico: A comparison with three other American populations. Am. J. Epidemiol. *100*:29–34, 1974.
112. Fraser, D. W., Henke, C. E., and Feldman, R. A.: Changing patterns of bacterial meningitis in Olmstead County, Minnesota, 1935–1970. J. Infect. Dis. *128*:300–307, 1973.
113. Fraser, D. W., Mitchell, J. E., Silverman, L. P., et al.: Undiagnosed bacterial meningitis in Vermont children. Ann. J. Epidemiol. *102*:394–399, 1975.
114. Frei, K., Piani, D., Pfister, H. W., et al.: Immune-mediated injury in bacterial meningitis. Int. Rev. Exp. Pathol. *34*:183–192, 1993.
115. Frenkel, L. D., and the Multicenter Ceftriaxone Pediatric Study Group: Once-daily administration of ceftriaxone for the treatment of selected serious bacterial infections in children. Pediatrics *82*:486–491, 1988.
116. Friedland, I. R., and Klugman, K. P.: Antibiotic-resistant pneumococcal disease in South African children. Am. J. Dis. Child. *146*:920–923, 1992.
117. Friedland, I. R., Paris, M., Ehrett, S., et al.: Evaluation of antimicrobial regimens for treatment of experimental penicillin- and cephalosporin-resistant pneumococcal meningitis. Antimicrob. Agents Chemother. *37*:1630–1636, 1993.
118. Friedland, I. R., Paris, M., Shelton, S., et al.: Time-kill studies of antibiotic combinations against penicillin-resistant and -susceptible *Streptococcus pneumoniae*. J. Antimicrob. Chemother. *34*:231–237, 1994.
119. Friedland, I. R., Shelton, S., Paris, M., et al.: Dilemmas in diagnosis and management of cephalosporin-resistant *Streptococcus pneumoniae* meningitis. Pediatr. Infect. Dis. J. *12*:196–200, 1993.
120. Gado, M., Axley, J., Appleton, D. B., et al.: Angiography in the acute and post-treatment phases of *Haemophilus influenzae* meningitis. Radiology *110*:439–444, 1974.
121. Gaillard, J. L., Abadie, G., Cheron, J., et al.: Concentrations of ceftriaxone in cerebrospinal fluid of children with meningitis receiving dexamethasone therapy. Antimicrob. Agents Chemother. *38*:1209–1210, 1994.
122. Garcia, H., Kaplan, S. L., and Feigin, R. D.: Cerebrospinal fluid concentration of arginine vasopressin in children with bacterial meningitis. J. Pediatr. *98*:67–70, 1981.
123. Garred, P., Michaelsen, T. E., Bjune, G., et al.: A low serum concentration of mannan-binding protein is not associated with serogroup B or C meningococcal disease. Scand. J. Immunol. *37*:468–470, 1993.
124. Gary, N., Powers, N., and Todd, J. K.: Clinical identification and comparative prognosis of high-risk patients with *Haemophilus influenzae* meningitis. Am. J. Dis. Child. *143*:307–311, 1989.
125. Geiseler, P. J., and Nelson, K. E.: Bacterial meningitis without clinical signs of meningeal irritation. South. Med. J. *75*:448–450, 1982.
126. Geiseler, P. J., Nelson, K. E., and Levin, S.: Community-acquired purulent meningitis: A review of 1,316 cases during the antibiotic era, 1954–1976. Rev. Infect. Dis. *2*:725–744, 1980.
127. Gerdes, L. U., Jorgensen, P. E., Nexo, E., et al.: C-reactive protein and bacterial meningitis: A meta-analysis. Scand. J. Clin. Lab. Invest. *58*:383–393, 1998.
128. Giampaolo, C., Scheld, W. M., Boyd, J., et al.: Leukocyte and bacterial interrelationships in experimental meningitis. Ann. Neurol. *9*:328–333, 1982.
129. Gigliotti, F., Lee, D., Insel, R. A., et al.: IgG penetration into the cerebrospinal fluid in a rabbit model of meningitis. J. Infect. Dis. *156*:394–398, 1987.
130. Gilbert, G.: Epidemiology of *Haemophilus influenzae* type b disease in Australia and New Zealand. Vaccine *9*(Suppl.):S10–S13, 1991.

131. Gilday, D. L.: Various radionuclide patterns of cerebral inflammation in infants and children. A. J. R. Am. J. Roentgenol. *120*:247–253, 1974.
132. Ginsburg, C. M., McCracken, G. H., Jr., and Parke, J. J.: *Haemophilus influenzae* type b disease in a day-care center. Pediatr. Res. *11*:435, 1977.
133. Girgis, N. I., Abu El Ella, A. H., Farid, Z., et al.: Intramuscular ceftriaxone versus ampicillin-chloramphenicol in childhood bacterial meningitis. Scand. J. Infect. Dis. *20*:613–617, 1988.
134. Girgis, N. I., Farid, Z., Mikhail, I. A., et al.: Dexamethasone treatment for bacterial meningitis in children and adults. Pediatr. Infect. Dis. J. *5*:210–215, 1989.
135. Gitlin, D.: Pathogenesis of subdural collections of fluid. Pediatrics *16*:345–351, 1955.
136. Givner, L. B., Mason, E. O., Jr., Barson, W. J., et al.: Pneumococcal facial cellulitis in children. Pediatrics *106*:e61, 2000.
137. Gold, R.: Bacterial meningitis—1982. Am. J. Med. *75*:98–101, 1983.
138. Gold, R.: Epidemiology of bacterial meningitis. Infect. Dis. Clin. North Am. *13*:515–525, 1999.
139. Green, S. M., Rothrock, S. G., Clem, K. J., et al.: Can seizures be the sole manifestation of meningitis in febrile children? Pediatrics *92*:527–534, 1993.
140. Greenfield, S., and Feldman, H. A.: Familial carriers and meningococcal meningitis. N. Engl. J. Med. *277*:487–502, 1967.
141. Grimwood, K., Anderson, V. A., Bond, L., et al.: Adverse outcomes of bacterial meningitis in school-age survivors. Pediatrics *95*:646–656, 1995.
142. Grubbauer, H. M., Dornbusch, H. J., Dittrich, P., et al.: Ceftriaxone monotherapy for bacterial meningitis in children. Chemotherapy *36*:441–447, 1990.
143. Guibourdenche, M., Caugant, D. A., Hervé, V., et al.: Characteristics of serogroup A *Neisseria meningitidis* strains isolated in the Central African Republic in February 1992. Eur. J. Clin. Microbiol. Infect. Dis. *13*:174–177, 1994.
144. Gulian, J.-M., Gonard, V., Dalmasso, C., et al.: Bilirubin displacement by ceftriaxone in neonates: Evaluation by determination of "free" bilirubin and erythrocyte-bound bilirubin. J. Antimicrob. Chemother. *19*:823–829, 1987.
145. Gump, D. W.: Vancomycin for treatment of bacterial meningitis. Rev. Infect. Dis. *3*:S289–S292, 1981.
146. Guttler, R. B., Counts, G. W., Avent, C. K., et al.: Effect of rifampin and minocycline on meningococcal carrier rates. J. Infect. Dis. *124*:199–205, 1971.
147. Haimanot, R. T., Caugant, D. A., Fekadu, D., et al.: Characteristics of serogroup A *Neisseria meningitidis* responsible for an epidemic in Ethiopia, 1988–89. Scand. J. Infect. Dis. *22*:171–174, 1990.
148. Hall, B. D.: Failure of ampicillin in meningitis. Lancet *1*:1033, 1968.
149. Haltalin, K. C., and Smith, J. B.: Reevaluation of ampicillin therapy for *Haemophilus influenzae* meningitis: An appraisal based on a review of cases of persistent or recurrent infection. Am. J. Dis. Child. *122*:328–336, 1971.
150. Hansman, D., and Andrews, G. A.: A resistant pneumococcus. Lancet *2*:264–265, 1967.
151. Hansman, D., Hanna, J., and Morey, F.: High prevalence of invasive *Haemophilus influenzae* disease in central Australia, 1986. Lancet *2*:927, 1986.
152. Harrison, L. H., Dwyer, D. M., Maples, C. T., et al.: Risk of meningococcal infection in college students. J. A. M. A. *281*:1906–1910, 1999.
153. Hatch, D., Overturf, G. D., Kovacs, A., et al.: Treatment of bacterial meningitis with ceftazidime. Pediatr. Infect. Dis. *5*:416–420, 1986.
153a. Haven, P. L., Wendelgerger, K. J., Hoffman, G. M., et al.: Corticosteroids as adjunctive therapy in bacterial meningitis. Am. J. Dis. Child. *143*:1051–1055, 1989.
154. Hirakawa, K., Kurokawa, M., Yajin, K., et al.: Recurrent meningitis due to a congenital fistula in the stapedial footplate. Arch. Otolaryngol. *109*:697–700, 1983.
155. Hogasen, K., Michaelsen, T., Mellbye, O. J., et al.: Low prevalence of complement deficiencies among patients with meningococcal disease in Norway. Scand. J. Immunol. *37*:487–489, 1993.
156. Holmes, S. J., Lucas, A. H., Osterholm, M. T., et al.: Immunoglobulin deficiency and idiotype expression in children developing *Haemophilus influenzae* type b disease after vaccination with conjugate vaccine. The Collaborative Study Group. J. A. M. A. *266*:1960–1965, 1991.
157. Ingram, D. L., Anderson, P., and Smith, D. H.: Counter-current immunoelectrophoresis in the diagnosis of systemic disease caused by *Hemophilus influenzae*, type b. J. Pediatr. *81*:1156–1159, 1972.
158. Ingram, D. L., Pearson, A. W., and Occhiuti, A. R.: Detection of bacterial antigens in body fluids with the Wellcogen *Haemophilus influenzae* b, *Streptococcus pneumoniae*, and *Neisseria meningitidis* (ACYW135) latex agglutination tests. J. Clin. Microbiol. *18*:1119–1121, 1983.
159. Jackson, L. A., Schuchat, A., Reeves, M. W., et al.: Serogroup C meningococcal outbreaks in the United States: An emerging threat. J. A. M. A. *273*:383–389, 1995.
160. Jadavji, T., Biggar, W. D., Gold, R., et al.: Sequelae of acute bacterial meningitis in children treated for seven days. Pediatrics *78*:21–25, 1985.
161. Jaye, D. L., and Waites, K. B.: Clinical applications of C-reactive protein in pediatrics. Pediatr. Infect. Dis. J. *16*:735–746, 1997.
162. Kadurugamuwa, J. L., Hengstler, B., and Zak, O.: Cerebrospinal fluid protein profile in experimental pneumococcal meningitis and its alteration by ampicillin and anti-inflammatory agents. J. Infect. Dis. *159*:26–34, 1989.
163. Kadurugamuwa, J. L., Hengstler, B., and Zak, O.: Effects of antiinflammatory drugs on arachidonic-acid metabolites and cerebrospinal fluid (CSF) proteins during infectious pneumococcal meningitis in rabbits. Pediatr. Infect. Dis. *6*(Suppl.):1153–1154, 1987.
164. Kaene, W. M., Postic, W. P., Rowe, L. D., et al.: Meningitis and hearing loss in children. Otolaryngology *105*:39–44, 1979.
165. Kaplan, S. L.: Clinical presentations, diagnosis, and prognostic factors of bacterial meningitis. Infect. Dis. Clin. North Am. *13*:579–594, 1999.
166. Kaplan, S. L., Catlin, F. I., Weaver, T., et al.: Onset of hearing loss in children with bacterial meningitis. Pediatrics *73*:575–578, 1984.
167. Kaplan, S. L., and Feigin, R. D.: Rapid identification of the invading microorganism. Pediatr. Clin. North Am. *27*:783–803, 1980.
168. Kaplan, S. L., and Feigin, R. D.: The syndrome of inappropriate secretion of antidiuretic hormone in children with bacterial meningitis. J. Pediatr. *92*:758–761, 1978.
169. Kaplan, S. L., and Fishman, M. A.: Supportive therapy for bacterial meningitis. Pediatr. Infect. Dis. J. *6*:670–677, 1987.
170. Kaplan, S. L., Goddard, J., VanKleeck, M., et al.: Ataxia and deafness in children due to bacterial meningitis. Pediatrics *68*:8–13, 1981.
171. Kaplan, S. L., and Mason, E. O., Jr.: Management of infections due to antibiotic-resistant *Streptococcus pneumoniae*. Clin. Microbiol. Rev. *11*:628–644, 1998.
172. Kaplan, S. L., Mason, E. O., Jr., Mason, S. K., et al.: Prospective comparative trial of moxalactam versus ampicillin or chloramphenicol for treatment of *Haemophilus influenzae* type b meningitis. J. Pediatr. *104*:447–453, 1984.
173. Kaplan, S. L., Smith, E. O., Wills, C., et al.: Association between preadmission oral antibiotic therapy and cerebrospinal fluid findings and sequelae caused by *Haemophilus influenzae* type b meningitis. Pediatr. Infect. Dis. *5*:626–632, 1986.
174. Kaplan, S. L., Mason, E. O., Jr., Wald, E. R., et al.: Six-year multicenter surveillance of invasive pneumococcal infections in children. Pediatr. Infect. Dis. J. *21*:141–147, 2002.
175. Kennedy, W. A., Hoyt, M. J., and McCracken, G. H.: The role of corticosteroids in children with pneumococcal meningitis. Am. J. Dis. Child. *145*:1374–1478, 1991.
176. Kessler, R. E.: Cefepime microbiologic profile and update. Pediatr. Infect. Dis. J. *20*:331–336, 2001.
177. Kilpatrick, M., Girgis, N., Farid, Z., et al.: Aztreonam for treating meningitis caused by gram-negative rods. Scand. J. Infect. Dis. *23*:125–126, 1991.
178. Kim, Y. S., and Tauber, M. G.: Neurotoxicity of glia activated by gram-positive bacterial products depends on nitric oxide production. Infect. Immun. *64*:3148–3153, 1996.
179. Klass, P. E., Klein, J. O.: Therapy of bacterial sepsis, meningitis and otitis media in infants and children: 1992 poll of directors of programs in pediatric infectious diseases. Pediatr. Infect. Dis. J. *11*:702–705, 1992.
180. Kleiman, M. D., Weinberg, G. A., Reynolds, J. K., et al.: Meningitis with beta-lactam–resistant *Streptococcus pneumoniae*: The need for early repeat lumbar puncture. Pediatr. Infect. Dis. J. *12*:782–784, 1993.
181. Klein, J. O., Feigin, R. D., and McCracken, G. H., Jr.: Report of the Task Force on Diagnosis and Management of Meningitis. Pediatrics *78*:S959–S982, 1986.
182. Kline, M. W., and Kaplan, S. L.: Computed tomography in bacterial meningitis of childhood. Pediatr. Infect. Dis. J. *7*:855–857, 1988.
183. Klugman, K. P., Dagan, R., and The Meropenem Meningitis Study Group: Randomized comparison of meropenem with cefotaxime for treatment of bacterial meningitis. Antimicrob. Agents Chemother. *39*:1140–1146, 1995.
184. Klugman, K. P., Friedland, I. R., and Bradley, J. S.: Bactericidal activity against cephalosporin-resistant *Streptococcus pneumoniae* in cerebrospinal fluid of children with acute bacterial meningitis. Antimicrob. Agents Chemother. *39*:1988–1992, 1995.
185. Koedel, U., Bernatowicz, A., Paul, R., et al.: Experimental pneumococcal meningitis: Cerebrovascular alterations, brain edema, and meningeal inflammation are linked to the production of nitric oxide. Ann. Neurol. *37*:313–323, 1995.
186. Komorowski, R. N., Farmer, S. G., and Hause, L. L.: Cerebrospinal fluid lactic acid in diagnosis of meningitis. J. Clin. Microbiol. *8*:89–92, 1978.
187. Kornelisse, R. F., Hack, C. E., Savelkoul, H. F., et al.: Intrathecal production of interleukin-12 and gamma interferon in patients with bacterial meningitis. Infect. Immun. *65*:877–881, 1997.
188. Kotilainen, P., Jalava, J., Meurman, O., et al.: Diagnosis of meningococcal meningitis by broad-range bacterial PCR with cerebrospinal fluid. J. Clin. Microbiol. *36*:2205–2209, 1998.
189. LaScolea, L. J., Jr., and Dryja, D.: Quantitation of bacteria in cerebrospinal fluid and blood of children with meningitis and its diagnostic significance. J. Clin. Microbiol. *19*:187–190, 1984.

190. Lebel, M. H., Freij, B. J., Syrogiannopoulos, G. A., et al.: Dexamethasone therapy for bacterial meningitis: Results of two double-blind, placebo-controlled trials. N. Engl. J. Med. *319*:964–971, 1988.
191. Lebel, M. H., Hoyt, M. J., and McCracken, G. H.: Comparative efficacy of ceftriaxone and cefuroxime for treatment of bacterial meningitis. J. Pediatr. *114*:1049–1054, 1989.
192. Lebel, M. H., and McCracken, G. H., Jr.: Aztreonam: Review of the clinical experience and potential uses in pediatrics. Pediatr. Infect. Dis. J. *7*:331–339, 1988.
193. Lebel, M. H., and McCracken, G. H., Jr.: Delayed cerebrospinal fluid sterilization and adverse outcome of bacterial meningitis in infants and children. Pediatrics *83*:161–167, 1989.
194. Leedom, J. M., Ivler, D., Mathies, A. W., et al.: The problem of sulfadiazine-resistant meningococci. Antimicrob. Agents Chemother. *6*:281–292, 1966.
195. Leggiadro, R. J., and Winkelstein, J. A.: Prevalence of complement deficiencies in children with systemic meningococcal disease. Pediatr. Infect. Dis. J. *6*:75–76, 1987.
196. Leib, S. L., and Tauber, M. D.: Pathogenesis of bacterial meningitis. Infect. Dis. Clin. North Am. *13*:527–548, 1999.
197. Lerman, S. J.: Systemic *Hemophilus influenzae* infection: A study of risk factors. Clin. Pediatr. *21*:360–364, 1982.
198. Levine, O. S., Farley, M., Harrison, L. E., et al.: Risk factors for invasive pneumococcal disease in children: A population-based case-control study in North America. Pediatrics *103*:e28, 1999.
199. Liebman, E. P., Ronis, M. L., Loyrinic, J. H., et al.: Hearing improvement following meningitis deafness. Arch. Otolaryngol. *90*:470–473, 1969.
200. Lim, D., Gerurz, A., Lint, T. F., et al.: Absence of the sixth component of complement in a patient with repeated episodes of meningococcal meningitis. J. Pediatr. *89*:42–47, 1976.
201. Lin, T. Y., Chrane, D. F., Nelson, J. D., et al.: Seven days of ceftriaxone therapy is as effective as ten days' treatment for bacterial meningitis. J. A. M. A. *253*:3559–3563, 1985.
202. Lindsay, J.: Profound childhood deafness: Inner ear pathology. Ann. Otol. Rhinol. Laryngol. *82*(Suppl. 5):88–102, 1973.
203. Losonsky, G. A., Santosham, M., Sehgal, V. M., et al.: *Haemophilus influenzae* disease in the White Mountain Apaches: Molecular epidemiology of a high risk population. Pediatr. Infect. Dis. *3*:539–547, 1984.
204. MacLennan, J. M., Shackley, F., Heath, P. T., et al.: Safety, immunogenicity, and induction of immunologic memory by a serogroup C meningococcal conjugate vaccine in infants. A randomized controlled trial. J. A. M. A. *283*:2795–2801, 2000.
205. Madagame, E. T., Havens, P. L., Bresnahan, J. M., et al.: Survival and functional outcome of children requiring mechanical ventilation during therapy for acute bacterial meningitis. Crit. Care Med. *23*:1279–1283, 1995.
206. Marks, W. A., Stutman, H. R., Marks, M. I., et al.: Cefuroxime versus ampicillin plus chloramphenicol in childhood bacterial meningitis: A multicenter randomized controlled trial. J. Pediatr. *109*:123–130, 1986.
207. Maxson, S., Lewno, M. J., and Schutze, G. E.: Clinical usefulness of cerebrospinal fluid bacterial antigen studies. J. Pediatr. *125*:235–238, 1994.
208. McCracken, G. J., Jr., and Lebel, M. H.: Dexamethasone therapy for bacterial meningitis in infants and children. Am. J. Dis. Child. *143*:287–289, 1989.
209. McCracken, G. H., Sarff, L. D., Glode, M. P., et al.: Relation between *Escherichia coli* K1 capsular polysaccharide antigen and clinical outcome in neonatal meningitis. Lancet *2*:246–250, 1974.
210. McIntosh, D., Brown, J., Hanson, R., et al.: Torticollis and bacterial meningitis. Pediatr. Infect. Dis. J. *12*:160–161, 1993.
211. McIntyre, P. B., Berkey, C. S., King, S. M., et al.: Dexamethasone as adjunctive therapy in bacterial meningitis. J. A. M. A. *278*:925–931, 1997.
212. Melish, M. E., Nelson, A. J., Martin, T. E., et al.: Epidemic spread of *Hemophilus influenzae* type b disease in a day care center. Pediatr. Res. *10*:348, 1976.
213. Mertsola, J., Kennedy, W. A., Waagner, D., et al.: Endotoxin concentrations in cerebrospinal fluid correlate with clinical severity and neurologic outcome of *Haemophilus influenzae* type b meningitis. Am. J. Dis. Child. *145*:1099–1103, 1991.
214. Meurman, O. H., Irjala, K., Suonpaa, J., et al.: A new method for the identification of cerebrospinal fluid leakage. Acta Otolaryngol. *87*:366–369, 1979.
215. Michie, H. R., Manogue, K. R., Spriggs, D. R., et al.: Detection of circulation tumor necrosis factor after endotoxin administration. N. Engl. J. Med. *318*:1481–1486, 1988.
216. Modai, J., Vittecoq, D., Decazes, J. M., et al.: Penetration of ceftazidime into cerebrospinal fluid of patients with bacterial meningitis. Antimicrob. Agents Chemother. *24*:126–128, 1983.
217. Moellering, R. C.: Pharmacokinetics of vancomycin. J. Antimicrob. Chemother. *14*:43–52, 1984.
218. Moore, P. S., Harrison, L. H., Telzak, E. E., et al.: Group A meningococcal carriage in travelers returning from Saudi Arabia. J. A. M. A. *260*:2686–2689, 1988.
219. Moore, P. S., Reeves, M. W., Schwartz, B., et al.: Intercontinental spread of an epidemic group A *Neisseria meningitidis* strain. Lancet *2*:260–263, 1989.
220. Moxon, E. R., Smith, A. L., Averill, D. R., et al.: *Hemophilus influenzae* meningitis in infant rats after intranasal inoculation. J. Infect. Dis. *129*:154–162, 1974.
221. Mullaney, D. T., and John, J. F.: Cefotaxime therapy: Evaluation of its effect on bacterial meningitis, CSF drug levels, and bactericidal activity. Arch. Intern. Med. *143*:1705–1708, 1983.
222. Mumford, R. J., deVasconelas, Z. J. S., Phillips, C. J., et al.: Eradication of carriage of *Neisseria meningitidis* in families: A study in Brazil. J. Infect. Dis. *129*:644–649, 1974.
223. Munoz, O., Benitez-Diaz, L., Martinez, M. C., et al.: Hearing loss after *Hemophilus influenzae* meningitis: Follow-up study with auditory brainstem potentials. Ann. Otol. Rhinol. Laryngol. *92*:272–275, 1983.
224. Murphy, T. V., Pastor, P., Medley, F., et al.: Decreased *Haemophilus* colonization in children vaccinated with *Haemophilus influenzae* type b conjugate vaccine. J. Pediatr. *122*:517–523, 1993.
225. Mustafa, M. M., Lebel, M. H., Ramilo, O., et al.: Correlation of interleukin 1β and cachectin concentrations in cerebrospinal fluid and outcome from bacterial meningitis. J. Pediatr. *115*:208–213, 1989.
226. Mustafa, M. M., Ramilo, O., Mertsola, J., et al.: Modulation of inflammation and cachectin activity in relation to treatment of experimental *Haemophilus influenzae* type b meningitis. J. Infect. Dis. *160*:818–825, 1989.
227. Mustafa, M. M., Ramilo, O., Saez-Llorens, X., et al.: Cerebrospinal fluid prostaglandins, interleukin 1β, and tumor necrosis factor in bacterial meningitis: Clinical and laboratory correlations in placebo and dexamethasone-treated patients. Am. J. Dis. Child. *144*:883–887, 1990.
228. Nadol, J. B., Jr.: Hearing loss as a sequela of meningitis. Laryngoscope *88*:739–755, 1978.
229. Nagata, M., Hara, T., Aoki, T., et al.: Inherited deficiency of ninth component of complement: An increased risk of meningococcal meningitis. J. Pediatr. *114*:260–264, 1989.
230. Naraqui, S., Kirkpatrick, G. P., and Kabins, S.: Relapsing pneumococcal meningitis: Isolation of an organism with decreased susceptibility to penicillin G. J. Pediatr. *85*:671–673, 1974.
231. National Committee for Clinical Laboratory Standards: Performance Standards for Antimicrobial Testing. Tenth informational supplement (aerobic dilution). M100-S10(M7)Table 2G. MIC Interpretive Standards (μg/mL) for *Streptococcus pneumoniae*. NCCLS, Wayne, PA, January 2000.
232. Neches, W., and Platt, M.: Cerebrospinal fluid LDH in 287 children including 53 cases of meningitis of bacterial and non-bacterial etiology. Pediatrics *41*:1097–1103, 1968.
233. Niemoller, U. M., and Tauber, M. G.: Brain edema and increased intracranial pressure in the pathophysiology of bacterial meningitis. Eur. J. Clin. Microbiol. Infect. Dis. *8*:109–117, 1989.
234. Negrini, B., Kelleher, K. J., and Wald, E. R.: Cerebrospinal fluid findings in aseptic versus bacterial meningitis. Pediatrics *105*:316–319, 2000.
235. Novak, R., Henriques, B., Charpentier, E., et al.: Emergency of vancomycin tolerance in *Streptococcus pneumoniae*. Nature *399*:590–593, 1999.
236. Nuorti, J. P., Butler, J. C., Farley, M. M., et al.: Cigarette smoking and invasive pneumococcal disease. N. Engl. J. Med. *342*:681–689, 2000.
237. Odio, C. M., Faingezicht, I., and Paris, M.: The beneficial effects of early dexamethasone administration in infants and children with bacterial meningitis. N. Engl. J. Med. *324*:1515–1531, 1991.
238. Odio, C. M., Puig, J. R., Feris, J. M., et al.: Prospective, randomized investigator-blinded study of the efficacy and safety of meropenem vs. cefotaxime therapy in bacterial meningitis in children. Pediatr. Infect. Dis. J. *18*:581–590, 1999.
239. Olivier, C., Cohen, R., Begue, P., et al.: Bacteriologic outcome of children with cefotaxime- or ceftriaxone-susceptible and -nonsusceptible S*treptococcus pneumoniae* meningitis. Pediatr. Infect. Dis. J. *19*: 1015–1017, 2000.
240. Parke, J. C., Jr., Schneerson, R., and Robbins, J. B.: The attack rate, age, incidence, racial distribution and case fatality rate of *Hemophilus influenzae*, type b meningitis in Mecklenburg County, North Carolina. J. Pediatr. *81*:765–769, 1972.
241. Parkkinen, J., Korhonen, T. K., Pere, A., et al.: Binding sites in the rat brain for *Escherichia coli* S fimbriae associated with neonatal meningitis. J. Clin. Invest. *81*:860–865, 1988.
242. Peltola, H., Makela, P. H., Kayhty, H., et al.: Clinical efficacy of meningococcus group A capsular polysaccharide vaccine in children three months to five years of age. N. Engl. J. Med. *297*:686–691, 1977.
243. Peltola, H., Rod, T. O., Jonsdottir, K., et al.: Life-threatening *Haemophilus influenzae* infections in Scandinavia: A five-country analysis of the incidence and the main clinical and bacteriologic characteristics. Rev. Infect. Dis. *12*:708–715, 1990.
244. Perkins, M. D., Mirrett, S., and Reller, R. B.: Rapid bacterial antigen detection is not clinically useful. J. Clin. Microbiol. *33*:1486–1491, 1995.
245. Peter, G., Weigart, M. B., Bissel, A. R., et al.: Meningococcal meningitis in familial deficiency of the fifth component of complement. Pediatrics *67*:882–886, 1981.

246. Pinner, R. W., Onyango, F., Perkins, B. A., et al.: Epidemic meningococcal disease in Nairobi, Kenya, 1989. J. Infect. Dis. *166*:359–364, 1992.
247. Pomeroy, S. L., Holmes, S. J., Dodge, P. R., et al.: A prospective evaluation of the neurologic sequelae of bacterial meningitis in children with special emphasis on late seizures. N. Engl. J. Med. *323*:1651–1657, 1990.
248. Powell, D. A., Nahata, M. C., Durrell, D. C., et al.: Interactions among chloramphenicol, phenytoin and phenobarbital in a pediatric patient. J. Pediatr. *98*:1001–1003, 1981.
249. Powell, K. R., and Mawhorter, S.: Outpatient treatment of serious infections in infants and children with ceftriaxone. J. Pediatr. *110*:889–901, 1987.
250. Powell, K. R., Sugarman, L. I., Eskenazi, A. I., et al.: Normalization of plasma arginine vasopressin concentrations when children with meningitis are given maintenance plus replacement fluid therapy. J. Pediatr. *117*:515–522, 1990.
251. Prober, C. G.: The role of steroids in the management of children with bacterial meningitis. Pediatrics *95*:29–31, 1995.
252. Quagliarello, V. J., Long, W. J., and Scheld, W. M.: Morphologic alterations of the blood brain barrier with experimental meningitis in the rat: Temporal sequence and role of encapsulation. J. Clin. Invest. *77*:1084–1095, 1986.
253. Quagliarello, V. J., and Scheld, W. M.: Bacterial meningitis: Pathogenesis, pathophysiology, and progress. N. Engl. J. Med. *327*:864–872, 1992.
254. Radstrom, P., Backman, A., Qian, N., et al.: Detection of bacterial DNA in cerebrospinal fluid by an assay for simultaneous detection of *Neisseria meningitidis, Haemophilus influenzae,* and streptococci using a semi-nested PCR strategy. J. Clin. Microbiol. *32*:1738–1744, 1994.
255. Ramilo, O., Mustafa, M. M., Porter J., et al.: Detection of interleukin-1β but not tumor necrosis factor-alpha in cerebrospinal fluid of children with aseptic meningitis. Am. J. Dis. Child. *144*:349–352, 1990.
256. Ramsay, M. E., Andrews, N., Kaczmarski, E. B., et al.: Efficacy of meningococcal serogroup C conjugate vaccine in teenagers and toddlers in England. Lancet *357*:195–196, 2001.
257. Raziuddin, S., El-Awad, M. E., and Mir, N. A.: Bacterial meningitis: T cell activation and immunoregulatory $CD4^+$ T cell subset alteration. J. Allergy Clin. Immunol. *87*:1115–1120, 1991.
258. Ridgway, E. J., Allen, K. D., Neal, T. J., et al.: Penicillin-resistant pneumococcal meningitis. Lancet *339*:931, 1992.
259. Rodriguez, W. J., Khan, W. N., Gold, B., et al.: Ceftazidime in the treatment of meningitis in infants and children over one month of age. Am. J. Med. *79*(Suppl. 2A):52–55, 1985.
260. Rodriguez, W. J., Puig, J. R., Khan, W. N., et al.: Ceftazidime vs. standard therapy for pediatric meningitis: Therapeutic, pharmacologic and epidemiologic observations. Pediatr. Infect. Dis. *5*:408–415, 1986.
261. Roeses, R. J., and Campbell, J. C.: Recovery of auditory function following meningitis deafness. J. Speech Hear. Dis. *40*:405–411, 1975.
262. Rorke, L. B., and Pitts, F. W.: Purulent meningitis: The pathological basis of clinical manifestations. Clin. Pediatr. *2*:64–71, 1963.
263. Rosenstein, N. E., Perkins, B. A., Stephens, D. S., et al.: The changing epidemiology of meningococcal disease in the United States, 1992–1996. J. Infect. Dis. *180*:1894–1901, 1999.
264. Ross, S., Rodriguez, W., Controni, G., et al.: Limulus lysate test for gram-negative bacterial meningitis: Bedside application. J. A. M. A. *233*:1366–1369, 1975.
265. Rotbart, H. A.: Diagnosis of enteroviral meningitis with the polymerase chain reaction. J. Pediatr. *117*:85–89, 1990.
266. Rowe, P. C., McLean, R. H., Wood, R. A., et al.: Association of homozygous C4B deficiency with bacterial meningitis. J. Infect. Dis. *160*:448–451, 1989.
267. Rutledge, J., Benjamin, D., Hood, L., et al.: Is the CSF lactate measurement useful in the management of children with suspected bacterial meningitis? J. Pediatr. *98*:20–24, 1981.
268. Saez-Llorens, X., Castano, E., Garcia, R., et al.: Prospective randomized comparison of cefepime and cefotaxime for treatment of bacterial meningitis in infants and children. Antimicrob. Agents Chemother. *39*:937–940, 1995.
269. Saez-Llorens, X., and O'Ryan, M.: Cefepime in the empiric treatment of meningitis in children. Pediatr. Infect. Dis. *20*:356–361, 2001.
270. Salih, M. A., Ahmed, H. S., Karrar, Z. A., et al.: Features of a large epidemic of group A meningococcal meningitis in Khartoum, Sudan, in 1988. Scand. J. Infect. Dis. *22*:161–170, 1990.
271. Sanal, O., Loos, M., Ersoy, F., et al.: Complement component deficiencies and infection: C5, C8, C3. Eur. J. Pediatr. *151*:676–679, 1992.
272. Sankrithi, U. M., and Lipuma, J. J.: Clinically inapparent meningitis complicating periorbital cellulitis. Pediatr. Emerg. Care 7:28–29, 1991.
273. Santhosham, M., Reid, R., and Ambrosino, D. M.: Prevention of *Haemophilus influenzae* type b infections in high-risk infants treated with bacterial polysaccharide immune globulin. N. Engl. J. Med. *317*:923–929, 1987.
274. Schaad, U. B., Lips, U., Gnehm, H. E., et al.: Dexamethasone therapy for bacterial meningitis in children. Lancet *342*:457–461, 1993.
275. Schaad, U. B., Suter, S., Gianella-Borradori, A., et al.: A comparison of ceftriaxone and cefuroxime for the treatment of bacterial meningitis in children. N. Engl. J. Med. *322*:141–147, 1990.
276. Schaad, U. B., Wedgwood-Krucko, J., and Tschaeppeler, H.: Reversible ceftriaxone-associated biliary pseudolithiasis in children. Lancet *2*:1411–1413, 1988.
277. Scheifele, D., Daum, R., Syriopoulou, V., et al.: A primate model of *Hemophilus influenzae*, type b meningitis. 16th Interscience Conference on Antimicrobial Agents and Chemotherapy, Chicago, October 27–29, 1976. Abstract 238.
278. Scheifele, D. W., Ward, J. I., and Siber, G. R.: Advantage of latex agglutination over countercurrent immunoelectrophoresis in the detection of *Haemophilus influenzae* type b antigen in serum. Pediatrics *68*:888–891, 1981.
279. Scheld, W. M.: Pathophysiological correlates in bacterial meningitis. J. Infect. *3*(Suppl. 1):5–18, 1981.
280. Scheld, W. M.: Pathogenesis and pathophysiology of pneumococcal meningitis. *In* Sande, M. A., Smith, A. L., and Root, R. K. (eds.): Bacterial Meningitis. New York, Churchill Livingstone, 1985, pp. 37–69.
281. Schlech, W. F., Ward, J. L., Band, J. D., et al.: Bacterial meningitis in the United States, 1978–1981: The National Bacterial Meningitis Surveillance Study. J. A. M. A. *253*:1749–1954, 1985.
282. Schlesinger, Y., Sawyer, M. H., and Storch, G.A.: Enteroviral meningitis in infancy: Potential role for polymerase chain reaction in patient management. Pediatrics *94*:157–162, 1994.
283. Schoendorf, K. C., Adams, W. G., Kiely, J. L., et al.: National trends in *Haemophilus influenzae* meningitis mortality and hospitalization among children, 1980 through 1991. Pediatrics *93*:663–668, 1994.
284. Schuchat, A., Robinson, K., Wenger, J. D., et al.: Bacterial meningitis in the United States in 1995. N. Engl. J. Med. *337*:970–976, 1997.
285. Schwartz, B., Al-Tobaiqi, A., Al-Ruwais, A., et al.: Comparative efficacy of ceftriaxone and rifampin in eradicating pharyngeal carriage of group A *Neisseria meningitidis*. Lancet *1*:1239–1242, 1988.
286. Schwartz, J. F.: Ataxia in bacterial meningitis. Neurology *22*:1071–1074, 1972.
287. Sell, S. H.: Long-term sequelae of bacterial meningitis in children. Pediatr. Infect. Dis. *2*:90–93, 1983.
288. Shackelford, P. G., Campbell, J., and Feigin, R. D.: Countercurrent immunoelectrophoresis in the evaluation of childhood infection. J. Pediatr. *85*:478–481, 1974.
289. Shetty, N., de Keyser, P., and Ridgway, G. L.: Acute bacterial meningitis after dental fillings. J. Infect. *37*:89–90, 1998.
290. Shurin, S. B., and Anderson, P.: Anemia associated with *H. influenzae* b (Hib) septicemia is due to immune hemolysis of RBC coated with soluble bacterial antigens. Pediatr. Res. *17*:932, 1983.
291. Sills, R. H., Caserta, M. T., and Landaw, S. A.: Decreased erythrocyte deformability in the anemia of bacterial meningitis. J. Pediatr. *101*:395–398, 1982.
292. Simberkoff, M. D., Moldovec, N. H., and Rahal, J. J., Jr.: Absence of detectable bactericidal and opsonic activities in normal and infected human cerebrospinal fluids: A regional host defense deficiency. J. Lab. Clin. Med. *95*:362–372, 1980.
293. Singer, J. I., and Berger, O. G.: Simultaneous occult pneumococcal bacteremia in identical twins. J. Pediatr. *98*:250–251, 1981.
294. Singhi, S. C., Singhi, P. D., Srinivas, B., et al.: Fluid restriction does not improve the outcome of acute meningitis. Pediatr. Infect. Dis. J. *14*:495–503, 1995.
295. Sloas, M. M., Barrett, F. F., Chesney, P. J., et al.: Cephalosporin treatment failure in penicillin- and cephalosporin-resistant *Streptococcus pneumoniae* meningitis. Pediatr. Infect. Dis. J. *11*:662–666, 1992.
296. Smith, A. L.: Neurologic sequelae of meningitis. N. Engl. J. Med. *319*:1012–1014, 1988.
297. Smith, D. H., Ingram, D. L., Smith, A. L., et al.: Bacterial meningitis. Pediatrics *52*:586–600, 1973.
298. Smith, J. F., and Landing, B. H.: Mechanisms of brain damage in *H. influenzae* meningitis. J. Neuropathol. Exp. Neurol. *19*:248–265, 1960.
299. Snedeker, J. D., Kaplan, S. L., Dodge, P. R., et al.: Subdural effusion and its relationship with neurologic sequelae of bacterial meningitis in infancy: A prospective study. Pediatrics *86*:163–170, 1990.
300. Snyder, R. D., Stovring, J., Cushing, A. H., et al.: Cerebral infarction in childhood bacterial meningitis. J. Neurol. Neurosurg. Psychiatry *44*:581–585, 1981.
301. Soderstrom, C., Sjoholm, A. G., Svensson, R., et al.: Another Swedish family with complete properdin deficiency: Association with fulminant meningococcal disease in one male family member. Scand. J. Infect. Dis. *21*:259–265, 1989.
302. Sommers, L. M., and Hawkins, D. S.: Meningitis in pediatric cancer patients: A review of forty cases from a single institution. Pediatr. Infect. Dis. J. *18*:902–907, 1999.
303. Sormunen, P., Kallio, M. J. T., Kilpi, T., et al.: C-reactive protein is useful in distinguishing Gram stain–negative bacterial meningitis from viral meningitis. J. Pediatr. *134*:725–729, 1999.
304. Spanaus, K. S., Nadal, D., Pfister, H. W., et al.: C-X-C and C-C chemokines are expressed in the cerebrospinal fluid in bacterial meningitis and mediate chemotactic activity on peripheral blood–derived polymorphonuclear and mononuclear cells in vitro. J. Immunol. *158*:1956–1964, 1997.

305. Speer, C. P., Rethwilm, M., and Gahr, M.: Elastase-alpha 1-proteinase inhibitor: An early indicator of septicemia and bacterial meningitis in children. J. Pediatr. *111*:667–671, 1987.
306. Spika, J. S., Facklam, R. R., Plikaytis, B. D., et al. (The Pneumococcal Surveillance Working Group): Antimicrobial resistance of *Streptococcus pneumoniae* in the United States, 1979–1987. J. Infect. Dis. *163*:1273–1278, 1991.
307. Sproles, E. T., III, Azerrad, J., Williamson, C., et al.: Meningitis due to *Hemophilus influenzae*: Long-term sequelae. J. Pediatr. *75*:782–788, 1969.
308. Steele, R. W., and Bradsher, R. W.: Comparison of ceftriaxone with standard therapy for bacterial meningitis. J. Pediatr. *103*:138–141, 1983.
309. Steele, R. W., McConnell, J. R., Jacobs, R. F., et al.: Recurrent bacterial meningitis: Coronal thin-section cranial computed tomography to delineate anatomic defects. Pediatrics *76*:950–953, 1985.
310. Stephen, D. S., and McGee, Z. A.: Attachment of *Neisseria meningitidis* to human mucosal surfaces: Influence of pili and type of receptor cell. J. Infect. Dis. *143*:525–532, 1981.
311. Tan, T. Q., Mason, E. O., Jr., and Kaplan, S. L.: Penicillin-resistant systemic pneumococcal infections in children: A retrospective case-control study. Pediatrics *92*:761–767, 1993.
312. Tan, T. Q., Mason, E. O., Jr., and Kaplan, S. L.: Systemic infections due to *Streptococcus pneumoniae* relatively resistant to penicillin in a children's hospital: Clinical management and outcome. Pediatrics *90*:928–933, 1992.
313. Tan, T. Q., Schutze, G. E., Mason, E. O., Jr., et al.: Antibiotic therapy and acute outcome of meningitis due to *Streptococcus pneumoniae* considered intermediately susceptible to broad-spectrum cephalosporins. Antimicrob. Agents Chemother. *38*:918–923, 1994.
314. Tauber, M. G., Shibl, A. M., Hackbarth, C. J., et al.: Antibiotic therapy endotoxin concentration in cerebrospinal fluid and brain edema in experimental *Escherichia coli* meningitis in rabbits. J. Infect. Dis. *156*:456–462, 1987.
315. Tauney, A. E., Galvao, P. A., DeMorais, J. S., et al.: Disease prevention by meningococcal serogroup C polysaccharide vaccine in pre-school children—São Paulo, Brazil. Unpublished.
316. Taylor, H. G., Mills, E. L., Ciampi, A., et al.: The sequelae of *Haemophilus influenzae* meningitis in school-age children. N. Engl. J. Med. *323*:1657–1663, 1990.
317. Teele, D. W., Dashefsky, B., Rakusan, T., et al.: Meningitis after lumbar puncture in children with bacteremia. N. Engl. J. Med. *305*:1079–1081, 1981.
318. Tejani, A., Dobias, B., and Sambursky, J.: Long-term prognosis after *H. influenzae* meningitis: Prospective evaluation. Dev. Med. Child. Neurol. *24*:338–343, 1982.
319. Tejani, A., Mahadevan, R., and Dobias, B.: Occurrence of HLA types in *H. influenzae* type b disease. Tissue Antigens *17*:205–211, 1981.
320. Tracey, K. J., Vlassara, J., and Cerami, A.: Cachectin/tumor necrosis factor. Lancet *1*:1122–1125, 1989.
321. Trujillo, H., Harry, N., Arango, A., et al.: Aztreonam in the treatment of aerobic, gram-negative bacillary infections in pediatric patients. Chemotherapy *35*(Suppl.):25–30, 1989.
322. Tuomanen, E., Liu, H., Hengstler, B., et al.: The induction of meningeal inflammation by components of the pneumococcal cell wall. J. Infect. Dis. *151*:859–868, 1985.
323. Tyson, J. E., Gilmartin, R. C., Jr., Friedman, B. I., et al.: ^{131}I-HSA cisternography in children with meningitis. *In* Harbert, J. C. (ed.): Cisternography and Hydrocephalus. Springfield, IL, Charles C Thomas, 1972, pp. 413–432.
324. U.S. Department of Commerce, Bureau of the Census: Mortality Statistics, 1935. Washington, D.C., Government Printing Office, 1937.
325. U.S. Department of Health, Education and Welfare, Public Health Service: Vital Statistics of the United States, 1968. Vol. II. Mortality. Washington, D.C., Government Printing Office, 1970.
326. van Alphen, L., Spanjaard, L., van der Ende, A., et al.: Predicted disappearance of *Haemophilus influenzae* type b meningitis in Netherlands. Lancet *344*:195, 1994.
327. van Furth, A. M., Roord, J. J., and van Furth, R.: Roles of proinflammatory and anti-inflammatory cytokines in pathophysiology of bacterial meningitis and effect of adjunctive therapy. Infect. Immun. *64*:4883–4890, 1996.
328. van Vliet, K. E., Glimaker, M., Lebon, P., et al.: Multicenter evaluation of the Amplicor Enterovirus PCR test with cerebrospinal fluid from patients with aseptic meningitis. J. Clin. Microbiol. *36*:2652–2657, 1998.
329. Veeder, M. H., Folds, J. D., Yount, W. J., et al.: Recurrent bacterial meningitis associated with C8 and IgA deficiency. J. Infect. Dis. *144*:399–402, 1981.
330. Vienny, H., Despland, P. A., Lutschg, J., et al.: Early diagnosis and evolution of deafness in childhood bacterial meningitis: A study using brainstem auditory evoked potentials. Pediatrics *73*:579–586, 1984.
331. Waage, A., Halstensen, A., and Espevik, T.: Association between tumour necrosis factor in serum and fatal outcome in patients with meningococcal disease. Lancet *1*:355–357, 1987.
332. Wahden, M. H., Rizk, F., and El-Akkad, A. M.: A controlled field trial of a serogroup A meningococcal polysaccharide vaccine. Bull. World Health Organ. *48*:667–673, 1973.
333. Wald, E. R., Kaplan, S. L., Mason, E. O., Jr., et al.: Dexamethasone therapy for children with bacterial meningitis. Pediatrics *95*:21–28, 1995.
334. Waldvogel, F. A.: Pathophysiological mechanisms in pneumococcal infection: Two examples—pleural empyema and acute bacterial meningitis. *In* Majno, G., Cotran, R. S., and Kaufman, N. (eds.): Current Topics in Inflammation and Infection. Baltimore, Williams & Wilkins, 1982, pp. 115–122.
335. Waler, J. A., and Rathore, M. H.: Outpatient management of pediatric bacterial meningitis. Pediatr. Infect. Dis. J. *14*:89–92, 1995.
336. Ward, J. I., Fraser, D. W., Baraff, L. J., et al.: *Hemophilus influenzae* meningitis: A national study of secondary spread in household contacts. N. Engl. J. Med. *19*:122–126, 1979.
337. Ward, J. I., Gorman, C., Philips, C., et al.: *Haemophilus influenzae* type b disease in a day care center. J. Pediatr. *92*:713–717, 1978.
338. Ward, J. I., Lum, M. K. W., Hall, D. B., et al.: Invasive *Haemophilus influenzae* type b disease in Alaska: Background epidemiology for a vaccine efficacy trial. J. Infect. Dis. *153*:17–26, 1986.
339. Ward, J. I., Siber, G. I., Scheifele, D. W., et al.: Rapid diagnosis of *Hemophilus influenzae* type b infections by latex particle agglutination and counterimmunoelectrophoresis. J. Pediatr. *93*:37–42, 1978.
340. Weidmer, C. E., Dunkel, T. B., Pettyjohn, F. S., et al.: Effectiveness of rifampin in eradicating the meningococcal carrier state in a relatively closed population: Emergence of resistant strains. J. Infect. Dis. *24*:172–178, 1971.
341. Weil, M. L.: Infections of the nervous system. *In* Menkes, J. H. (ed.): Textbook of Child Neurology. Philadelphia, Lea & Febiger, 1980, pp. 276–304.
342. Whitney, C. G., Farley, M. M., Hadler, J., et al.: Increasing prevalence of multi-drug resistant *Streptococcus pneumoniae* in the United States. N. Engl. J. Med. *343*:1917–1924, 2000.
343. Whittle, H. C., and Greenwood, B. M.: Meningococcal meningitis in the northern savanna of Africa. Trop. Doct. *6*:99–104, 1976.
344. Williams, D. N., Laughlin, L. W., and Lee, Y. H.: Minocycline: Possible vestibular side-effects. Lancet *2*:744–746, 1974.
345. Wispelwey, B., Lesse, A. J., Hansen, E. J., et al.: *Haemophilus* lipopolysaccharide-induced blood brain barrier permeability during experimental meningitis in the rat. J Clin. Invest. *82*:1339–1346, 1988.
346. Wolff, M., Chavanet, P., Kazmierczak, A., et al.: Diffusion of cefpirome into the cerebrospinal fluid of patients with purulent meningitis. J. Antimicrob. Chemother. *29A*:59–62, 1992.
347. Wong, M., Schlaggar, B. L., and Landt, M.: Postictal cerebrospinal fluid abnormalities in children. J. Pediatr. *138*:373–377, 2001.
348. Wong, V. K., Wright, H. T., Jr., Ross, L. A., et al.: Imipenem/cilastatin treatment of bacterial meningitis in children. Pediatr. Infect. Dis. J. *10*:122–125, 1991.
349. Woody, R. C., and Yamauchi, T.: Cerebrospinal fluid cell counts in childhood idiopathic status epilepticus. Pediatr. Infect. Dis. J. *7*:298–299, 1988.
350. Zangwell, K. M., Vadheim, C. M., Vannier, A. M., et al.: Epidemiology of invasive pneumococcal disease in Southern California: Implications for the design and conduct of a pneumococcal conjugate vaccine efficacy trial. J. Infect. Dis. *174*:752–759, 1996.
351. Zollinger, W. D., Mandrell, R. E., Guffiss, J. M., et al.: Complex of meningococcal group B polysaccharide and type 2 outer membrane protein immunogenic in man. J. Clin. Invest. *63*:836–848, 1979.
352. Zwahlen, A., Nydegger, U. E., Vaudaux, P., et al.: Complement-mediated opsonic activity in normal and infected human cerebrospinal fluid: Early response during bacterial meningitis. J. Infect. Dis. *145*:635–646, 1982.

CHAPTER 39

Paramenigeal Infections

HOWARD P. GOODKIN ■ SCOTT L. POMEROY

Abscess formation may occur in the parenchyma of the central nervous system, in the subdural space, or in the epidural space. Although brain abscess, subdural empyema, cranial epidural abscess, and spinal epidural infections are discussed as separate entities, two or more conditions may coexist in a patient. All can alter neurologic function by direct destruction of nervous tissue, by infarction after inflammatory occlusion of veins and arteries, or by compression caused by mass effect.

Brain Abscess

Brain abscess is an uncommon occurrence in children. Jadavji and colleagues[26] identified 74 children between the ages of 3 weeks and 18 years who were diagnosed with a brain abscess at the Hospital for Sick Children (Toronto, Canada) between January 1960 and June 1984, for a mean of three identified cases annually. As expected, the incidence of brain abscess is likely to vary by geographic location.[20, 39]

The mortality rate associated with brain abscesses appears to be decreasing. This reduction probably is the result of the advent of head imaging and its use to guide the management of brain abscesses, improvements in surgical techniques, and advances in antibiotics. Fischer and associates[17] found a reduction in mortality rate from 36 percent before 1970 to 14 percent after 1970. Tekkök and colleagues[44] described a similar decline, from 30 percent in the era before the use of computed tomography (CT) to 6 percent in the last 5 years of their study and zero in the last 3 years of their study. Other case series also have reported a mortality rate of zero.[27]

Although mortality appears to be decreasing, a significant percentage of children continue to have residual neurologic deficits, including epilepsy, permanent motor or sensory dysfunction, visual field defects, and personality change.[17, 20, 24] Some children also require placement of a ventriculoperitoneal shunt.[11]

SOURCES OF INFECTION, PATHOGENESIS, AND PATHOLOGY

Organisms invade the parenchyma of the brain usually as a consequence of contiguous infection of nonneural tissues or as the result of hematogenous spread from a remote site. In children, as in adults, brain abscess rarely results from bacterial meningitis, although an abscess may give rise to meningitis as a consequence of rupture into the ventricle or rarely into the subarachnoid space. In infants, especially in neonates, which came first often is uncertain, and it probably could occur either way. In this very young group, the abscess may be enormous before the lesion is recognized.[37]

Initially, a rather diffuse inflammatory response in the brain occurs, with polymorphonuclear leukocytes predominating (i.e., cerebritis). Over a period of many days to weeks, necrosis and liquefaction occur in the center of the lesion. Reactive astroglia, fibroblasts, and macrophages surround the nidus of tissue destruction. Mononuclear and polymorphonuclear leukocytes may be seen scattered throughout this zone. The resulting capsule may, in chronic abscesses, be several millimeters to centimeters in thickness. Especially in the early stages of the process, widespread edema may be present within the white matter around the abscess cavity.

Figure 39–1 shows the gross appearance of a well-defined abscess of hematogenous origin. In Figures 39–2 through 39–4, various microscopic features are illustrated.

Britt and Enzmann[6] reported a correlation between the histopathologic stages of abscess formation and clinical and CT findings in experimental animals and in humans. As outlined by Barkovich,[4] the histopathologic stage of abscess formation also corresponds to specific findings on magnetic resonance imagery (MRI) of the head.

When symptoms and signs of intracranial disease develop in a patient with infection of the middle ear, mastoids, paranasal sinuses, or soft tissues of the face, orbit, or scalp, brain abscess should be considered in the differential diagnosis. The infection most often is subacute or chronic and spreads intracranially by infected veins or, less commonly, by osteomyelitis. An abscess also may complicate comminuted fractures of the skull and develop after intracranial surgery, including the insertion of shunts to divert cerebrospinal fluid (CSF) from a lateral ventricle to another compartment of the body (e.g., right atrium, peritoneal cavity). In infants and young children, a sharp object may penetrate the skull, leaving minimal external evidence of trauma, especially in case of orbital trauma because the posterior wall of the orbit is so thin that a pencil point or sharp stick has been incriminated as the mode for introducing the infective agent in frontal lobe abscess[2, 23] and rarely in cerebellar abscess.[1] Congenital lesions, including dermal sinuses, usually occur over the posterior fossa, and various forms of ruptured anterior (nasal) and posterior encephaloceles may provide direct access for microorganisms to reach brain tissue.

Patients with congenital cyanotic heart disease in whom venous blood is shunted into the systemic circulation, bypassing the lungs, are prone to develop brain abscesses. Curiously, this development rarely occurs in patients younger than the age of 2 years, and the abscess or abscesses usually are in areas of brain perfused by the middle cerebral arteries. Evidence of associated endocarditis is rare in these cases, although acute bacterial endocarditis may be complicated by septic infarction of brain and abscess formation.[36] Peripheral arteriovenous shunts, lung abscess, pulmonary thrombophlebitis, and collections of purulent material elsewhere in the body may provide an infective source for a cerebral abscess. Patients with congenital or acquired immune suppression also are at increased risk for developing brain abscesses. Esophageal dilation has been associated with brain abscess, but it appears to be a rare entity for which the pathogenesis is unknown.[32] In some cases, no source can be found.

A wide range of microorganisms, including most bacteria and certain fungi and parasites, can be recovered from brain abscesses. A single abscess may contain anaerobic and aerobic bacteria.[7, 8] These facts must be considered when the pus

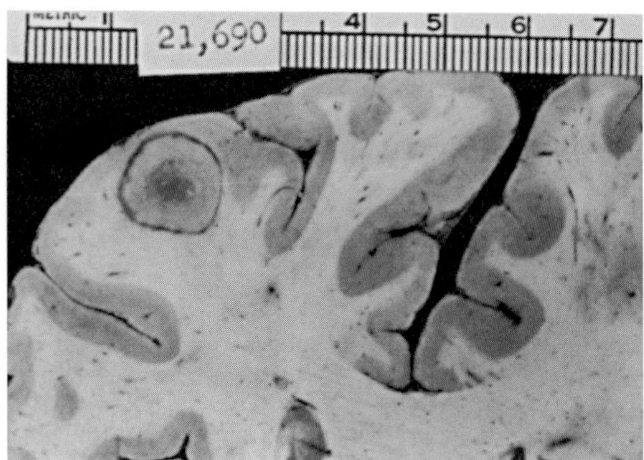

FIGURE 39–1 ■ Circumscribed cerebral abscess of hematogenous origin.

is subjected to laboratory investigation. Smears of the sample should be examined microscopically after Gram staining and after staining for acid-fast bacilli and fungi. Cultures should be incubated under appropriate conditions for aerobic and anaerobic bacteria, mycobacteria, and fungi. Unless this matter is appreciated, the examiner may conclude inappropriately that the pus is sterile. Sterile pus has been reported in approximately 25 percent of abscesses, but the techniques used in attempting recovery of an agent rarely were described sufficiently to afford reasonable assurance that no viable microorganisms were present.

Among the aerobic species frequently seen are strains of streptococci, staphylococci, *Escherichia coli*, *Proteus*, *Nocardia*, and *Haemophilus influenzae*. Anaerobic bacteria, including various species of peptostreptococci, streptococci, fusobacteria, and *Bacteroides*, have been cultured most commonly. *Haemophilus aphrophilus*, which thrives in an environment rich in carbon dioxide, has been recovered rarely from brain abscesses in children. Pneumococci have been cultured infrequently in recent years, which contrasts with earlier findings. *Salmonella* organisms may be recovered.[29, 30] Gram-negative organisms such as *Proteus* and

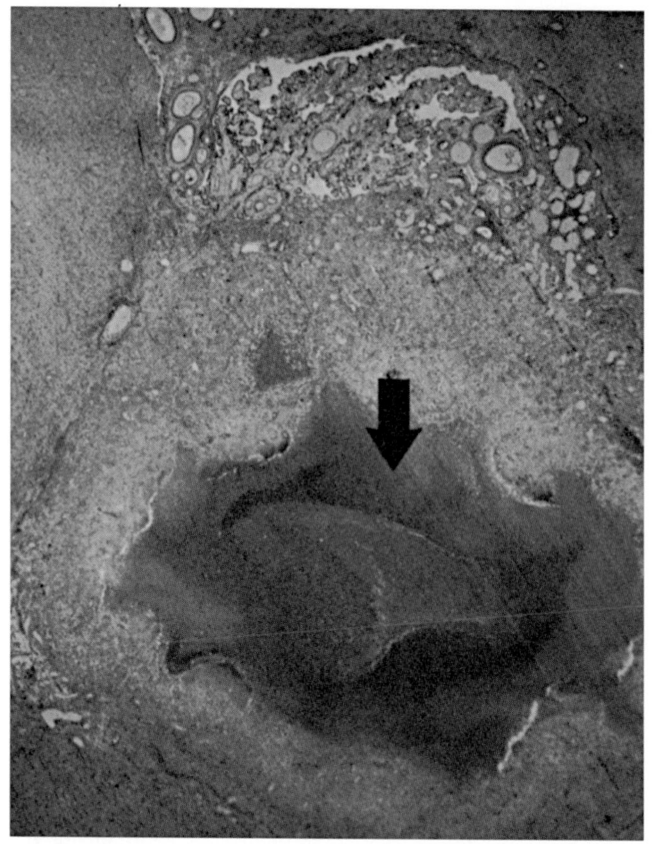

FIGURE 39–2 ■ Area of necrosis and liquefaction in a cerebral abscess *(arrow)*.

Citrobacter,[37] but not *E. coli*, are recovered commonly from abscesses in neonates. Offending fungi include *Cladosporium trichoides* and species of *Candida* and *Aspergillus*; but they, as well as amebic abscesses, are uncommon occurrences, at least in the United States. However, opportunistic infections have become increasingly important with induced

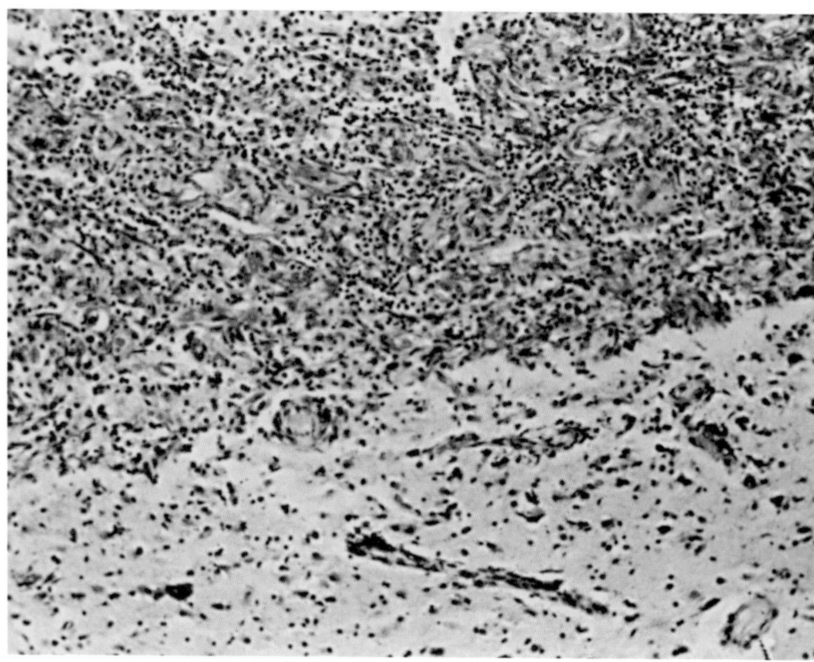

FIGURE 39–3 ■ Astroglia and fibroblasts forming the capsule of a cerebral abscess.

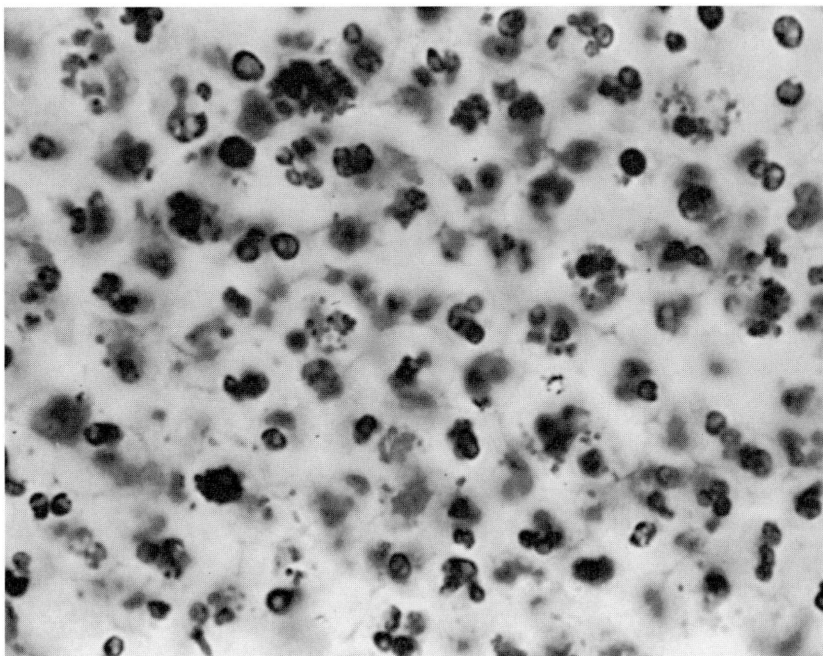

FIGURE 39–4 ■ Mononuclear and polymorphonuclear leukocytes are in the center of a cerebral abscess.

immunosuppression and with the advent of acquired immunodeficiency syndrome (AIDS). In particular, fungal abscesses may occur in immunosuppressed patients, although abscesses caused by many other organisms, including *Toxoplasma gondii,* also are occurring more frequently.[19, 35]

CLINICAL MANIFESTATIONS

The clinical courses of patients with brain abscesses are protean. During the initial stages of disease, fever, generalized malaise, vomiting, and headache may occur and often are localized to the region of the infection. In infants and young children, the presence of headache is difficult to document, although in infants, the anterior fontanelle may bulge, reflecting increased intracranial pressure. Focal neurologic signs depend on the site of the lesion or lesions and may be prominent or inconspicuous and develop suddenly or slowly. For example, a patient with a frontal abscess may exhibit few symptoms and signs except for raised intracranial pressure for weeks or months, whereas abscesses involving regions of the central nervous system concerned with motor, sensory, language, or visual functions usually cause deficits relatively early in the course of the disease.

Leukocytosis and an elevated sedimentation rate may or may not occur, and recovery of a microorganism from the blood would be exceptional except for septicemia related to an acute endocarditis. The CSF characteristically is sterile, although inflammatory cells (a few to 400 polymorphonuclear cells and lymphocytes) and a modest elevation in protein with a normal concentration of glucose often can be found. The CSF pressure usually is elevated. Because of this pressure, caution must be exercised to prevent a disturbance in intracranial dynamics precipitating herniation of cerebral tissue at the tentorium or foramen magnum, a complication occurring all too frequently, even in the absence of lumbar puncture. When brain abscess is a serious diagnostic consideration, especially in the presence of signs of increased intracranial pressure, a CT or other scan should be obtained before performing a lumbar puncture. If evidence of a probable abscess is demonstrated by imaging, lumbar puncture should be avoided.

Chronic abscesses are accompanied less frequently by systemic symptoms and laboratory evidence of infection. Rather, they produce symptoms and signs of an intracranial mass lesion and may be confused with neoplastic disease. An exception exists when rupture of the abscess into the ventricular system evokes a catastrophic complication, which is discussed later.

Frontal Lobe Abscess

In infants and children, infection of facial tissues or ethmoidal sinuses, often with orbital cellulitis, leads most frequently to intracranial infection by way of veins that drain into the cavernous sinus, which may itself become infected and thrombosed.[42] Amputation of a nasal meningoencephalocele leading to a cerebrospinal rhinorrhea predisposes to intracranial spread of infection, including abscess. Apical dental abscesses in older children are a potential source.[31] In neonates, abscesses frequently are multiple and involve the frontal lobes most commonly, although the source of the infection leading to formation of an abscess frequently is obscure.[37]

In older children, papilledema is a common finding, and disturbed behavior of the child may lead to the incorrect diagnosis of a primary psychiatric disorder. Forced grasping and sucking may be prominent, and hemiparesis later evolves. Because frontal lobe lesions remain relatively silent, rather massive abscess cavities can develop before focal neurologic signs appear. Frequently, depressed consciousness and signs of temporal lobe herniation, often with rupture into the lateral ventricle, preclude receiving effective treatment before death.

Temporal Lobe Abscess

Most temporal lobe abscesses are of otogenic origin. Developing as they do because of mastoiditis and phlebitis, associated infection within the epidural and subdural space occurs commonly, and lateral sinus and cortical vein thromboses also occur. Although reports indicate that the abscess may develop on the side opposite to the ear disease, we have not observed it. Nonfluent or fluent dysphasia can be witnessed when the dominant hemisphere is involved, and a contralateral upper quadrant field defect or complete homonymous hemianopsia may be demonstrated. Extension anteriorly can interfere with motor function, affecting the face and arm most conspicuously. Herniation of the mesial temporal lobe through the incisura of the tentorium usually produces an ipsilateral third nerve palsy and upper brain stem dysfunction. Prognosis is poor when the diagnosis is delayed until this stage.

Parietal Lobe Abscess

Usually of hematogenous origin, a parietal lobe abscess often is relatively asymptomatic with regard to focal neurologic features until it encroaches on the sensorimotor cortex. Extension posteriorly and inferiorly may cause an inferior quadrant field defect and homonymous hemianopsia or dysphasia when the dominant hemisphere is involved. Dyspraxia and spatial neglect contralaterally suggest dysfunction of the nondominant hemisphere.

Cerebellar Abscess

As with temporal lobe abscesses, cerebellar abscesses usually are of otogenic origin. The same pathogenic factors prevail as in temporal lobe abscesses, but the infection extends below the tentorium. Occasionally, an infection of the soft tissues of the neck, such as a carbuncle, leads to development of a cerebellar abscess.

Most cerebellar abscesses develop in the hemispheres so that the neurologic syndrome is lateralized, with ataxia and tremor occurring ipsilateral to the lesion. Dizziness and nystagmus (most prominent on gaze to the side of the lesion) may be discerned if the lesion extends close to the midline, in which case, ataxia of gait is to be expected. Skew deviation of the eyes and abducens nerve palsy may be seen. Vomiting is prominent, and papilledema occurs in approximately one half of the cases; these findings are related primarily to increased intracranial pressure from the mass itself or from swelling of surrounding uninfected tissue, either of which may impair circulation of the CSF. Sudden death results from apnea associated with herniation of cerebellar tissue through the foramen magnum. Upward herniation through the incisura of the tentorium can produce symptoms and signs similar to those observed in downward herniation from supratentorial lesions.

Brain Stem Abscess

Brain stem abscesses are rare occurrences and infrequently are diagnosed during life. Otogenic or hematogenous sources have been reported. Most often, the lesion is confused clinically with a primary glioma because of multiple cranial nerve palsies and signs of involvement of ascending and descending tracts.

RUPTURE OF BRAIN ABSCESS INTO THE VENTRICULAR SYSTEM

Rupture of an abscess into the ventricle with consequent ventricular empyema is a dreaded complication because the mortality rate exceeds 50 percent, and residual neurologic deficits, including hydrocephalus, are the rule in those who survive. Frequently, rupture occurs before the diagnosis of abscess has been established and surgical removal can be accomplished. A sudden worsening in the patient's clinical state heralds this event. High fever, shock, meningismus, and altered consciousness are prominent among the clinical signs. Rupture of the abscess into the ventricle is seen more frequently in patients with deep-seated abscesses or in immunocompromised patients.[43] Whereas a modest pleocytosis and elevated protein concentration in CSF may have been identified earlier, the findings of 50,000 to 100,000 polymorphonuclear leukocytes and markedly reduced sugar concentration in the CSF are usual findings. Organisms may be demonstrated on smear of the CSF and cultured from the fluid. In other words, the patient has developed purulent meningitis, and treatment must include high doses of antibiotics and surgery (see the Treatment section). The concurrence of abscess and meningitis in the past has led to the assumption that brain abscess can be a complication of meningitis, but this rarely, if ever, is the case, although meningitis may develop during the incipient stages of abscess formation after intracranial invasion of organisms from a contiguous extracranial source. In such circumstances, the abscess may appear to be consequent on the leptomeningitis. Given a potential source of infection in the ear or paranasal sinuses, the clinician must be wary and appreciate the possibility of this sequence of events. Abscess has been reported to complicate *Citrobacter* meningitis in infants, but careful pathologic study has demonstrated vasculitis and liquefaction necrosis of the white matter without capsule formation.[18]

DIAGNOSIS

MRI is the modality of choice for the diagnosis and localization of cerebral abscesses. Similar MRI findings can be observed in infarction, demyelinating disorders, and neoplastic processes. Diffusion-weighted MRI and magnetic resonance spectroscopy have been shown to be effective methods in differentiating cerebral abscesses from tumors.[10, 14] Figure 39–5 illustrates the appearance on MRI scan of a right frontal cerebral abscess in a 10-year-old girl. However, CT scanning remains an excellent alternative if MRI is not available (Fig. 39–6). Intravenous administration of contrast material is advised because the abscess may be missed otherwise.[28, 40]

The presence of gas within the abscess cavity on head imaging suggests communication of the abscess with air outside the skull, although gas-forming bacteria in the abscess cavity may be responsible on rare occasions.[46]

Abnormalities on electroencephalography may be localized and can help in excluding a more generalized, bilateral intracranial disease, such as encephalitis. Unilateral slow waves (delta, 1 to 3/sec) characterize the usual electroencephalographic findings in cases of cerebral abscess.

After the diagnosis of brain abscess has been established, a careful search should be made for a source of infection serving as a site of origin for hematogenous spread or direct inoculation of organisms into the central nervous system. In addition to data obtained from the history and physical examination, the MRI or CT evaluation should be extended to include the mastoids and paranasal sinuses. An echocardiogram should be obtained to assess for concurrent endocarditis. Other testing should be guided by the history and findings of physical examination.

TREATMENT

No prospective clinical trials have compared various surgical and medical treatment strategies available to guide the management of cerebral abscesses in children. Most surgical and medical treatment guidelines are based on populations consisting primarily of adult patients. However, appropriate

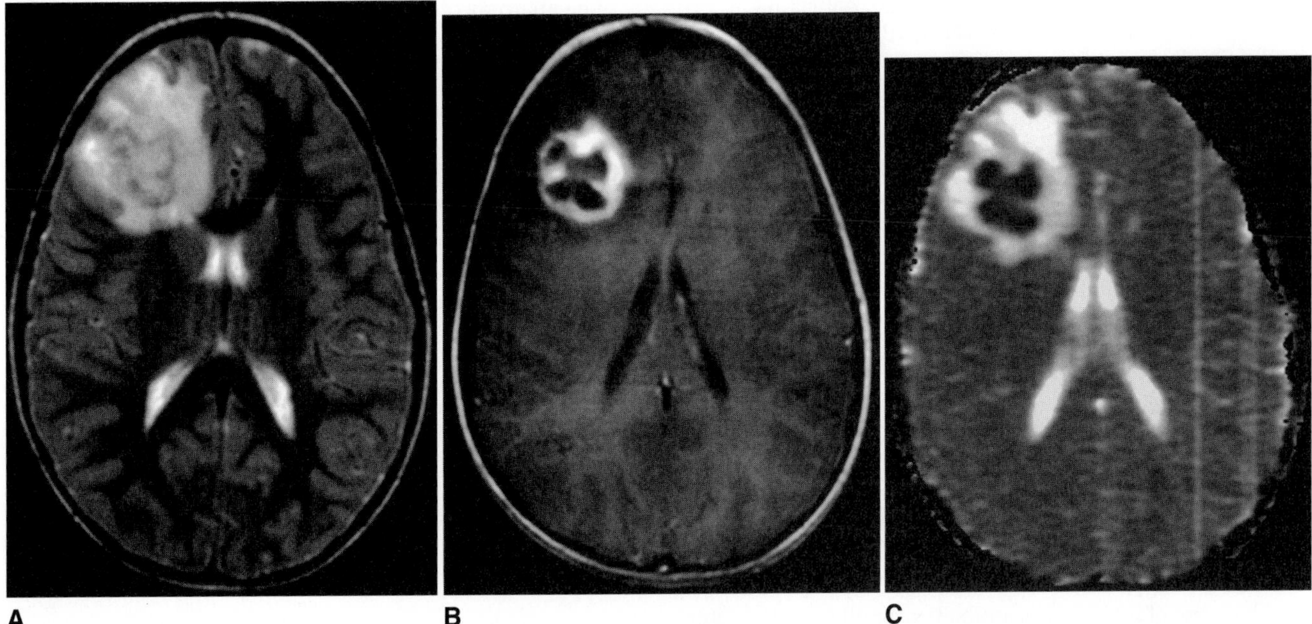

FIGURE 39–5 ■ Bacterial abscess in a 10-year-old girl. *A,* The axial T2-weighted image shows an irregular mass in the right frontal lobe with a hypointense wall *(arrows)* and surrounding vasogenic edema. *B,* Gadolinium-enhanced, T1-weighted image shows intense, smooth enhancement of the capsule. *C,* Apparent diffusion coefficient map from a line-scan, diffusion-weighted study shows decreased signal within the cavity, compatible with restricted diffusion and suggesting an abscess cavity rather than tumor necrosis. (Courtesy of F. Kim, M.D., Northwestern University School of Medicine, Chicago.)

management of brain abscesses apparently requires a combined surgical and medical approach (but see Leys and colleagues[33]), with isolated medical management limited to patients who are neurologically intact and in whom the abscess is in the cerebritis stage [21] or the abscess or abscesses are small [38] or to patients who are too unstable to undergo a surgical procedure.

The initial treatment of solitary and multiple brain abscesses is the aspiration of the cavity contents followed by the initiation of empiric antibiotic coverage while the cultures are maturing. Although not universally accepted,[13] serial CT scans or, in young infants, real-time ultrasonography probably is the best means for monitoring the response to treatment. Mamelak and colleagues[34] have suggested performing head imaging biweekly or on any sign of clinical deterioration, with further aspiration if the cavity enlarges or fails to diminish in size after 3 to 4 weeks. Because excisions may be associated with increased risk of neurologic sequelae, surgery should be reserved for patients who do not respond to the strategy of repeated aspiration and medical management and when an abscess results in a significant mass effect.

While results of cultures are pending, the selection of antibiotics should be guided by the primary source of infection, pertinent patient history, and the results of microscopic examination of the pus (Table 39–1). The duration of therapy is empirical and, in children, has ranged from 10 days (in a child after surgical excision[39]) to 8 weeks. Generally, the duration of treatment should be 4 to 8 weeks, with a shorter duration of therapy reserved only for patients with complete surgical excision of the abscess. Based on a single abstract,[9] the Infection in Neurosurgery Working Party of the British Society for Antimicrobial Chemotherapy[13] recommended that the duration of antibiotic therapy, as well as a switch from parenteral to oral therapy, should be guided by the serum C-reactive protein level. However, in the absence of a randomized, controlled, multicenter study, we recommend at least a

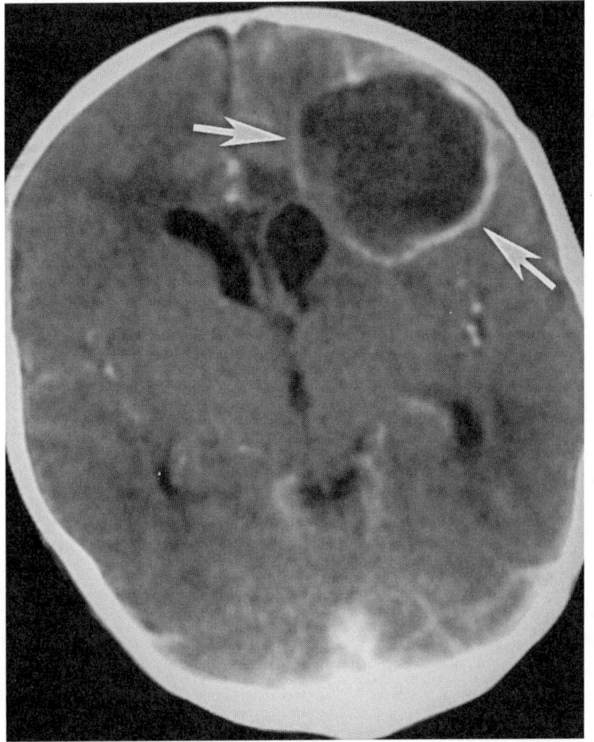

FIGURE 39–6 ■ Contrast-enhanced computed tomography shows a ring-enhancing left frontal cerebral abscess *(arrows)* in a 3-week-old boy with concurrent *Enterobacter* meningitis. (Courtesy of C. D. Robson, M.D., Harvard Medical School, Boston, and P. D. Barnes, M.D., Stanford University School of Medicine, Stanford, CA.)

TABLE 39–1 ■ SUGGESTED INITIAL EMPIRIC ANTIBIOTIC THERAPY FOR BRAIN ABSCESS IN CHILDREN

Primary Source	Antibiotic Regimen*
Paranasal sinuses	Nafcillin or vancomycin, cefotaxime or ceftriaxone, and metronidazole
Teeth	Penicillin, cefotaxime or ceftriaxone, and metronidazole
Middle ear	Nafcillin or vancomycin, cefotaxime or ceftriaxone, and metronidazole
Penetrating trauma	Vancomycin and cefotaxime or ceftriaxone
Metastatic/cryptogenic	Vancomycin, cefotaxime or ceftriaxone, and metronidazole
Congenital heart disease	Vancomycin, cefotaxime or ceftriaxone, and metronidazole
Ventriculoperitoneal shunt	Vancomycin and ceftazidime

*Immunosuppressed children should be treated with broad coverage and with consideration of amphotericin B therapy. Antituberculous therapy should be considered for children with exposure to tuberculosis. Antibiotic regimens are likely to vary by geographic location based on resistant organisms.

4-week course of intravenous antibiotics for all patients. After completion of the antibiotic regimen, head imaging should be continued at regular intervals (every 2 to 4 months) for at least 1 year or until all abscesses have resolved.

With the advent of head imaging and the current methods of treatment employing head imaging, an overall reduction in mortality has occurred; however, a high proportion of children with cerebral abscesses develop neurologic deficits. Eradication of potential sources of infection before the abscess has developed is logical preventive medicine. Early diagnosis and treatment are imperative and can be facilitated by the liberal use of MRI or CT scanning when this diagnosis is even a remote consideration.

Subdural Empyema

Pyogenic infection in the subdural space is designated as subdural empyema or sometimes, but less correctly, as subdural abscess. The sources of infection and microorganisms responsible are the same as those encountered in brain abscess. It is a relatively rare disease; only one case was seen at St. Louis Children's Hospital during a period when 122 patients with bacterial meningitis and 3 patients with cerebral abscess were treated. The primary source of subdural empyema in this single case was not found, which increasingly is true for the pediatric experience. Farmer, Wise, and Jacobson[16, 25] found associated meningitis in six of eight infants with subdural empyema (seen over a 16-year period), suggesting that the latter was a complication of the former. We also have encountered this situation, albeit rarely, and the subdural fluid usually is turbid rather than frankly purulent.

In older children, the infection appears not to follow leptomeningitis. Although leptomeningitis may complicate subdural empyema, infections of the paranasal sinuses and mastoid region, usually chronic, spread to the subdural space directly because of osteomyelitis or by way of infected veins that penetrate the skull. Extension to cortical veins and to major venous sinuses frequently is associated with subdural empyema, as discussed elsewhere in this section. Why in some cases the infection is restricted to one or another anatomic site or sites (e.g., epidural space, subdural space, parenchyma of the brain or blood vessels) is unknown. Subdural empyema may be hematogenous in origin. It is an infrequent but recognized complication of intracranial surgery.

The anatomy of the subdural space is such that the infection often extends widely over one or both cerebral hemispheres, and accumulation of pus in the parafalcine region is well known.

CLINICAL MANIFESTATIONS

The symptoms and signs of the primary source of infection may be prominent, subtle, or absent. Increasingly severe headache, high fever, signs of meningeal irritation, and progressive neurologic deficits referable to the site of the lesion are reported in the typical untreated case. Focal or generalized seizures are prominent, especially in cases of cortical injury from associated vasculitis. Signs of increased intracranial pressure become prominent as the mass of pus enlarges. In infants, a fullness of fontanelle, vomiting, and depressed responsiveness are seen. Transillumination of the skull can be positive. Older children also may develop papilledema. As the intracranial pressure rises, symptoms and signs progress, ultimately leading to temporal lobe or cerebellar herniation and the characteristic syndromes of these complications.

DIAGNOSIS

The laboratory findings reflect the active infectious process. Peripheral leukocytosis and a predominance of polymorphonuclear leukocytes with immature cells are seen.

The CSF in infants reflects the common association with leptomeningitis, and the findings depend on when the fluid is examined. Before the meningitis has been treated adequately, organisms may be cultured; the glucose concentration may be low and the protein concentration high in the CSF. Later, the CSF findings are those of treated meningitis, but viable organisms can be recovered from the subdural collections when the CSF is sterile. Specific antigens may be demonstrated in subdural collections by tests such as countercurrent immunoelectrophoresis in the absence of viable organisms. In older children, the characteristic CSF findings include elevated pressure with a few to a few hundred or more leukocytes, with polymorphonuclear leukocytes predominating. The protein concentration frequently is elevated, the glucose concentration normal, and the fluid sterile.

In the past 2 or more decades, subdural empyema in children has become more difficult to diagnose clinically because of antimicrobial therapy. When initiated early, it may attenuate the dramatic nature of the disease, especially the symptoms and signs of acute infection. Because the diagnosis of subdural empyema often is confused with that of brain abscess, radiographic studies are necessary to establish the correct diagnosis. CT scanning (Fig. 39–7) and MRI are effective noninvasive techniques, as previously discussed in relation to brain abscess. Cerebral angiography can demonstrate a failure of the cerebral vessels to approximate the inner surface of the skull. These studies reveal the extent of subdural disease and may define an epidural abscess or other infectious exudate collection concurrent with subdural empyema (Fig. 39–8).

TREATMENT

Until a causative organism is identified, the patient should receive broad-spectrum antibiotics intravenously in dosages appropriate for bacterial meningitis. After the offending organism is identified, the sensitivities of that organism to specific medications dictate selection of more precise antibiotic therapy.

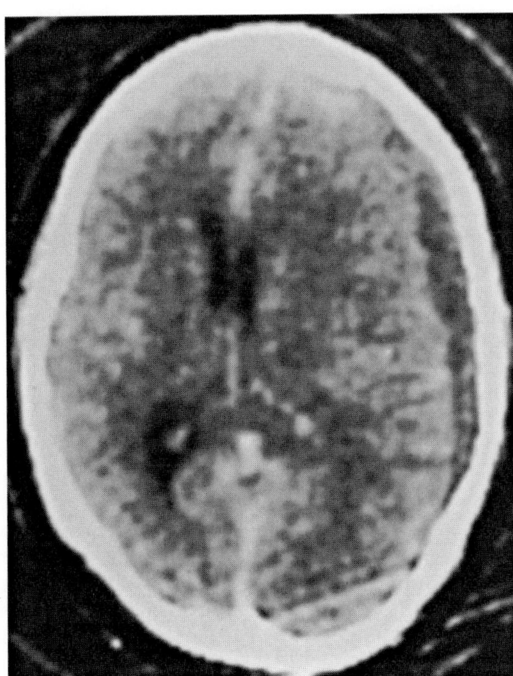

FIGURE 39–7 ■ Computed tomography shows a subdural empyema with marked displacement of the ventricular system.

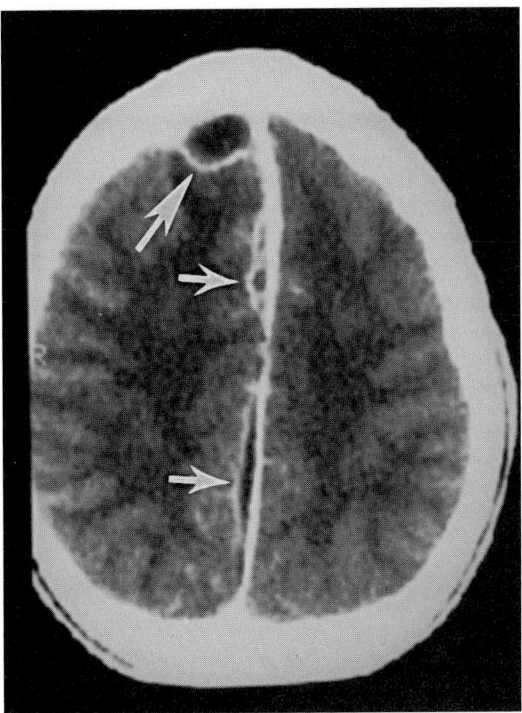

FIGURE 39–8 ■ Contrast-enhanced computed tomography demonstrates a right frontal epidural abscess *(large arrow)* concurrent with an interhemispheric subdural abscess *(small arrows)* in a 13-year-old boy who developed headache, fever, and vomiting after fracture of the right frontal sinus. (Courtesy of C. D. Robson, M.D., Harvard Medical School, Boston, and P. D. Barnes, M.D., Stanford University School of Medicine, Stanford, CA.)

In infants, antibiotic therapy may be sufficient when the fluid is cloudy only, but if thick, purulent material is obtained by subdural paracentesis or, in older children, if the clinical and radiographic evidence indicates a subdural empyema, surgery is requisite. Depending on individual circumstances, craniotomy or multiple burr holes with irrigation of the subdural space should be accomplished.

Unfortunately, the mortality and morbidity rates are high (20% to 40%) in most series but lower in some.[15, 41, 47] Early diagnosis and treatment are imperative, and the early use of CT scanning appears to be responsible for improved therapeutic results.[47]

Cranial Epidural Abscess

Because the dura mater is adherent to the inner aspect of the cranium, epidural abscesses rarely attain a large size, and they consequently do not exert significant pressure on the brain. They are important because they can serve as a focus for spread of infection into the subdural space, leptomeninges, or brain. The infection may involve local penetrating vessels and lead to their occlusion, with extension to venous sinuses and other vessels. Infection of the middle ear, mastoid bone, or ancillary air sinuses may lead to epidural abscess, as in the case of subdural empyema and brain abscess. Often, epidural abscess coexists with the other lesions and presumably develops first. Osteomyelitis may be evident, which usually is the case with mastoiditis and often is evident after head injury with comminuted fracture of the skull or after intracranial surgery. An adolescent boy with osteomyelitis and epidural abscess complicating a wrestling injury was reported.[45]

Local pain, tenderness, and fever may be the only signs. Treatment usually includes antibiotic drugs and surgery in the presence of osteomyelitis. Exclusion of associated intracranial infections is mandatory; the epidural infection serves to raise these diagnostic possibilities.

Spinal Epidural Infections

Spinal epidural infections may be acute or chronic, and they may be restricted in their extent or extend longitudinally over many segments of the spinal cord because the epidural space offers no resisting structures. Most often, the process affects the posterior region of the spine, with maximal pus or granulomatous tissue found over the dorsal aspect of the cord or spinal roots. However, in Danner and Hartman's [12] series from the New York Hospital, in approximately one half of the patients, the pus primarily was anterior to the cord. In the case of spinal osteomyelitis, the pus may be more viscous ventrally. Occasionally, the purulent material may encircle the neural elements. In infants and children, this condition is rare; no case was encountered at the St. Louis Children's Hospital during the 39 months in which 122 cases of bacterial meningitis were seen. In an extensive report by Baker and colleagues[3] covering a 27-year period at the Massachusetts General Hospital, only 6 of 39 patients were younger than 20 years of age, and the youngest was 11. The incidence ranged from 0.2 to 1.2 hospital admissions each year. In approximately one half of the patients in this series, acute purulent material was discovered at operation or autopsy, with *Staphylococcus aureus* incriminated in more than one half of the cases. In the remainder, a granulomatous process was found, associated with a wide variety of bacteria. No instance of tuberculous infection occurred, although in many regions of the world, this organism remains an important consideration. Nonbacterial infective agents may include fungi or parasites.

The neural dysfunction probably results from direct compression of the spinal cord, roots, and nerves, but impaired circulation from associated inflammation and occlusion of vessels is at least a contributory factor in some cases. Determining with certainty the extent to which each of the previous mechanisms contributes to neural dysfunction often is difficult. Extensive necrosis of the cord may result in advanced cases in which a prompt diagnosis has not been made.

SOURCES OF INFECTION

In tuberculous and other chronic infections, osteomyelitis and intervertebral disk infection are common occurrences, but those afflicted primarily are adults.[29] Acute spinal epidural infections usually occur after hematogenous spread from furuncles, pharyngitis, dental abscesses, decubitus ulcers, and urinary tract and wound infections. They may complicate spinal surgery, and lumbar puncture rarely has been implicated as a source.[5] Osteomyelitis occurs uncommonly. The patient may have a history of minor trauma to the back. Presumably, trauma results in local tissue injury or hemorrhage, forming a nidus for the developing infection.

CLINICAL MANIFESTATIONS

Fever is the rule, and the temperature is higher in patients with acute infections. Such patients appear septic, and toxic delirium occurs frequently. Heusner,[22] in his classic paper dealing primarily with acute epidural abscesses, divided the clinical phases as follows: (1) spinal ache, (2) root pain, (3) weakness, and (4) paralysis. Although certain therapeutic implications render this separation a useful way to consider the disorder, phases 3 and 4 are combined in the following discussion. That the various stages often overlap is axiomatic.

Phase 1: Spinal Ache

Spinal ache was a universal finding in Heusner's experience.[22] In a report from Baker and associates,[3] all 39 patients had backache of various degrees of severity. Local tenderness was absent in only two of their patients and should be searched for by carefully tapping over the spine.

Phase 2: Root Pain

Root pain is characteristic and is an early symptom that may assist in localization of the pathologic process. Root pain especially is prominent with lumbosacral disease in which roots are implicated without involvement of the spinal cord. The diagnosis is suspected infrequently until functional motor and sensory losses occur, which is unfortunate because therapy is most effective during the early stages. Progression to symptoms and signs of spinal cord involvement usually occurs within a few days, except when the process is granulomatous, in which case the course tends to be prolonged, extending over several or more weeks.

Phases 3 and 4: Weakness and Paralysis

After weakness and impaired sensation referable to disease of the spinal cord appear, the progression to paralysis can be rapid, and performing immediate surgical treatment is imperative to maximize the likelihood of reasonable functional recovery. However, even appropriate therapy at this stage often is ineffective in restoring normal neurologic functions. Death occurs in at least 20 percent of cases; this rate has not changed significantly since 1948, despite the availability of a wide range of antibiotic agents.

DIAGNOSIS

The diagnosis of spinal epidural infection is established by MRI of the spine (Fig. 39–9). Imaging also may reveal evidence of concurrent osteomyelitis of the spine, which is found in approximately 20 percent of chronic lesions. After epidural abscess is discovered, immediate neurosurgical intervention is necessary to prevent long-term neurologic sequelae. At the time of surgery, stains and cultures for aerobic and anaerobic bacteria, mycobacteria, and fungi should be obtained. If lumbar puncture is attempted when epidural abscess is suspected, the spinal needle (with stylet) is advanced slowly into the lumbar region, with periodic removal of the stylet and with suction applied gently *before* the thecal sac is entered. If purulent material is obtained, the diagnosis is established, and the pus must be examined by a Gram-stained smear and cultured on various media under aerobic and anaerobic conditions. The leptomeninges should not be penetrated if purulent material is encountered; otherwise, CSF should be obtained. Characteristically, the CSF is clear or slightly opalescent and yellow if there is a block. Pleocytosis with a few too many hundred cells (with lymphocytes predominating) reflects a contiguous infectious process, but in the absence of meningitis, no organisms can

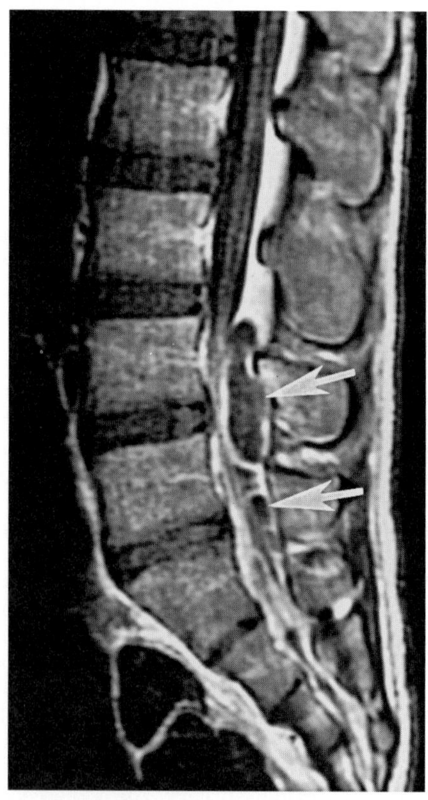

FIGURE 39–9 ■ The gadolinium-enhanced, sagittal, T1-weighted magnetic resonance image shows a rim-enhancing lumbar spinal epidural abscess *(arrows)* in a 15-year-old boy with a 3-week history of lower back pain, followed by rapidly progressing left leg numbness and decreased bowel and bladder function. *Staphylococcus aureus* was cultured from purulent fluid removed after L4-L5 laminectomy was performed. (Courtesy of C. D. Robson, M.D., Harvard Medical School, Boston, and P. D. Barnes, M.D., Stanford University School of Medicine, Stanford, CA.)

be identified, and the CSF glucose concentration should be normal. The protein concentration always is elevated, and the level may be very high (several hundred to 2000 mg/dL) in the case of a partial or total manometric block.

The differential diagnosis includes myelitis caused by bacterial meningitis, syphilis, viruses, and a parainfectious process, as well as by the syndrome of acute transverse myelopathy of unknown cause. Spinal ache is most prominent in acute transverse myelopathy, but as a general rule, the entire illness is compressed in time, with paresis or paralysis evolving over the course of hours or a few days from the onset of disease. Impaired circulation of CSF does not occur in this or the aforementioned disorders. Rarely, a lymphoma may mimic a spinal epidural abscess. Spinal cord tumors, vascular malformations, and arachnoiditis are considerations when the course of disease is prolonged and evidence of sepsis is minimal or absent, as occurs with chronic epidural infections.

TREATMENT

Prompt surgical removal of purulent or granulomatous material is essential. It should be combined with intravenous administration of an appropriate antibiotic. Initial empiric antibiotic coverage is similar to that for brain abscess, although antifungal therapy need not be included unless cultures or stains are positive for fungi. Treatment typically should be continued for 3 to 4 weeks but prolonged for twice this period if the patient has osteomyelitis. Despite advances, the morbidity and mortality rates for spinal epidural abscess remain distressingly high. As many as one third of children with the disease die, and another one third are left with permanent neurologic sequelae, including weakness, incontinence, and sensory abnormalities. Rapid diagnosis and treatment are essential to ensure a successful outcome.

REFERENCES

1. Amano, K., and Kamano, S.: Cerebellar abscess due to penetrating orbital wound. J. Comput. Assist. Tomogr. *6*:1163–1166, 1982.
2. Anonymous: Case records of the Massachusetts General Hospital. Weekly clinicopathological exercises. Case 13-1973. N. Engl. J. Med. *288*:674–679, 1973.
3. Baker, A. S., et al.: Spinal epidural abscess. N. Engl. J. Med. *293*:463–468, 1975.
4. Barkovich, A. J.: Pediatric Neuroimaging. Philadelphia, Lippincott Williams & Wilkins, 2000.
5. Bergman, I., et al.: Epidural abscess and vertebral osteomyelitis following serial lumbar punctures. Pediatrics. *72*:476–480, 1983.
6. Britt, R. H., and Enzmann, D. R.: Clinical stages of human brain abscesses on serial CT scans after contrast infusion. Computerized tomographic, neuropathological, and clinical correlations. J. Neurosurg. *59*:972–989, 1983.
7. Brook, I.: Aerobic and anaerobic bacteriology of intracranial abscesses. Pediatr. Neurol. *8*:210–214, 1992.
8. Brook, I.: Brain abscess in children: Microbiology and management. J. Child. Neurol. *10*:283–288, 1995.
9. Brown, E. M., et al.: Short-course antimicrobial therapy for brain abscess and subdural empyema. Proceedings of the 123rd Meeting of the Society of British Neurological Surgeons. J. Neurol. Neurosurg. Psychiatry. *57*:390–395, 1994.
10. Castillo, M.: Imaging brain abscesses with diffusion-weighted and other sequences. AJNR. Am. J. Neuroradiol. *20*:1193–1194, 1999.
11. Ciurea, A. V., et al.: Neurosurgical management of brain abscesses in children. Childs Nerv. Syst. *15*:309–317, 1999.
12. Danner, R. L., and Hartman, B. J.: Update on spinal epidural abscess: 35 cases and review of the literature. Rev. Infect. Dis. *9*:265–274, 1987.
13. De Louvois, J., et al.: The rational use of antibiotics in the treatment of brain abscess. Report by the "Infection in Neurosurgery" Working Party of the British Society for Antimicrobial Chemotherapy. Br. J. Neurosurg. *14*:525–530, 2000.
14. Desprechins, B., et al.: Use of diffusion-weighted MR imaging in differential diagnosis between intracerebral necrotic tumors and cerebral abscesses. AJNR. Am. J. Neuroradiol. *20*:1252–1257, 1999.
15. Dill, S. R., et al.: Subdural empyema: Analysis of 32 cases and review. Clin. Infect. Dis. *20*:372–386, 1995.
16. Farmer, T. W., and Wise, G. R.: Subdural empyema in infants, children and adults. Neurology. *23*:254–261, 1973.
17. Fischer, E. G., et al.: Cerebral abscess in children. Am. J. Dis. Child. *135*:746–749, 1981.
18. Foreman, S. D., et al.: Neonatal *Citrobacter* meningitis: Pathogenesis of cerebral abscess formation. Ann. Neurol. *16*:655–659, 1984.
19. Hagensee, M. E., et al.: Brain abscess following marrow transplantation: Experience at the Fred Hutchinson Cancer Research Center, 1984–1992. Clin. Infect. Dis. 19:402–408, 1994.
20. Hegde, A. S., et al.: Brain abscess in children. Childs Nerv. Syst. *2*:90–92, 1986.
21. Heineman, H. S., et al.: Intracranial suppurative disease. Early presumptive diagnosis and successful treatment without surgery. J. A. M. A. *218*:1542–1547, 1971.
22. Heusner, A. P.: Nontuberculous spinal epidural infections. N. Engl. J. Med. *239*:845–854, 1948.
23. Horner, F. A., et al.: Broken pencil points as a cause of brain abscess. N. Engl. J. Med. *271*:342–345, 1964.
24. Idriss, Z. H., et al.: Brain abscesses in infants and children: Current status of clinical findings, management and prognosis. Clin. Pediatr. (Phila.) *17*:738–740, 745–746, 1978.
25. Jacobson, P. L., and Farmer, T. W.: Subdural empyema complicating meningitis in infants: Improved prognosis. Neurology. *31*:190–193, 1981.
26. Jadavji, T., et al.: Brain abscesses in infants and children. Pediatr. Infect. Dis. *4*:394–398, 1985.
27. Jamjoom, A.: Childhood brain abscess in Saudi Arabia. Ann. Trop. Paediatr. *17*:95–99, 1997.
28. Joubert, M. J., and Stephanov, S.: Computerized tomography and surgical treatment in intracranial suppuration. Report of 30 consecutive unselected cases of brain abscess and subdural empyema. J. Neurosurg. *47*:73–78, 1977.
29. Kaufman, D. M., et al.: Infectious agents in spinal epidural abscesses. Neurology *30*:844–850, 1980.
30. Kondziolka, D., et al.: Factors that enhance the likelihood of successful stereotactic treatment of brain abscesses. Acta Neurochir. *127*:85–90, 1994.
31. Lampe, R. M., et al.: Brain abscess following dental extraction in a child with cyanotic congenital heart disease. Pediatrics *61*:659–660, 1978.
32. Leahy, W. R., et al.: Cerebral abscess in children secondary to esophageal dilatation. Pediatrics *59*:300–301, 1977.
33. Leys, D., et al.: Management of focal intracranial infections: Is medical treatment better than surgery? J. Neurol. Neurosurg. Psychiatry *53*: 472–475, 1990.
34. Mamelak, A. N., et al.: Improved management of multiple brain abscesses: A combined surgical and medical approach. Neurosurgery *36*:76–85, 1995.
35. Piazza, E., et al.: Intracerebral mass lesions in patients affected by AIDS. Acta Neurochir. *83*:116–120, 1986.
36. Pruitt, A. A., et al.: Neurologic complications of bacterial endocarditis. Medicine (Baltimore). *57*:329–343, 1978.
37. Renier, D., et al.: Brain abscesses in neonates. A study of 30 cases. J. Neurosurg. *69*:877–882, 1988.
38. Rosenblum, M. L., et al.: Nonoperative treatment of brain abscesses in selected high-risk patients. J. Neurosurg. *52*:217–225, 1980.
39. Saez-Llorens, X. J., et al.: Brain abscess in infants and children. Pediatr. Infect. Dis. J. *8*:449–458, 1989.
40. Shaw, M. D., and Russell, J. A.: Value of computed tomography in the diagnosis of intracranial abscess. J. Neurol. Neurosurg. Psychiatry *40*:214–220, 1977.
41. Smith, H. P., and Hendrick, E. B.: Subdural empyema and epidural abscess in children. J. Neurosurg. *58*:392–397, 1983.
42. Sutton, D. L., and Ouvrier, R. A.: Cerebral abscess in the under 6 month age group. Arch. Dis. Child. *58*:901–905, 1983.
43. Takeshita, M., et al.: Current treatment strategies and factors influencing outcome in patients with bacterial brain abscess. Acta Neurochir. *140*:1263–1270, 1998.
44. Tekkok, I. H., and Erbengi, A.: Management of brain abscess in children: Review of 130 cases over a period of 21 years. Childs Nerv. Syst. *8*:411–416, 1992.
45. Tudor, R. B., et al.: Pott's puffy tumor, frontal sinusitis, frontal bone osteomyelitis, and epidural abscess secondary to a wrestling injury. Am. J. Sports. Med. *9*:390–391, 1981.
46. Young, R. F., and Frazee, J.: Gas within intracranial abscess cavities: An indication for surgical excision. Ann. Neurol. *16*:35–39, 1984.
47. Zimmerman, R. D., et al.: Subdural empyema: CT findings. Radiology. *150*:417–422, 1984.

Additional Reading

Calfee, D. P., and Wispelwey, B.: Brain abscess. Semin. Neurol. *20*:353–360, 2000.

Cochrane, D. D.: Consultation with the specialist. Brain abscess. Pediatr. Rev. *20*:209–215, 1999.

Mathisen, G. E., and Johnson, J. P.: Brain abscess. Clin. Infect. Dis. *25*:763–779, 1997.

CHAPTER 40

Fungal Meningitis

J. THOMAS CROSS, JR. ■ RICHARD F. JACOBS

Fungi are rare causes of meningitis in children. *Candida albicans*, *Cryptococcus neoformans*, and *Coccidioides immitis* are the isolates found most commonly in the pediatric age group. Making a diagnosis can be difficult. Fungal meningitis frequently is chronic, and patients may have few symptoms. The lack of obvious meningeal signs and symptoms and the relatively uncommon incidence of a fungal cause often delay the diagnosis. Inherent problems with the diagnosis of fungal infections of the central nervous system (CNS) begin with the basic microbiology of the organisms. Their fastidious growth, the prolonged time needed for culture, and the requirement of special media can render making a diagnosis in meningitis difficult.

Because cultivating many fungi from the cerebrospinal fluid (CSF) frequently is difficult, the use of serologic tests for antibodies and antigens help define the infection quicker and with more sensitivity. These tests can be performed on CSF, serum, and, in some instances, urine.[170] For most infections, amphotericin B is the drug of choice, although its supremacy is being tested by some of the newer azoles and the introduction of lipid formulations of amphotericin B. Namdar and colleagues[108] compared Abelcet, Amphotec, and AmBisome in the neonatal and pediatric populations. CNS disease caused by fungi generally has a high morbidity and mortality rate.

Epidemiology

The epidemiology of fungal meningitis depends on many factors. The geographic location of the patient or travel to an endemic area can be an important clue to defining the cause of the infection. The geographic distribution of fungal meningitis varies in the United States and worldwide. Histoplasmosis generally occurs in endemic areas of the Mississippi River valley.[169] Coccidioidomycosis occurs in the San Joaquin Valley and the desert Southwest of the United States and in Mexico.[3, 113] Cryptococcosis distribution is worldwide rather than in discrete endemic areas, but it seems to be associated with pigeon droppings and nesting areas of other birds.[93] Blastomycosis has a sporadic pattern of infectivity but generally occurs in states bordering the Mississippi and Ohio River basins, with occasional outbreaks occurring in the Great Lakes region and Canada.[47, 78, 136] *Candida* spp., *Aspergillus* spp., *Sporothrix schenckii*, and other fungal pathogens generally are not defined by geographic boundaries but depend more on environmental exposures and the immunocompetence of the individual patient. Uncommon species of yeasts and fungi, including *Rhodotorula rubra*, *Aureobasidium mansoni*, *Clavispora lusitaniae*, and *Bipolaris spicifera*, have been reported in nosocomial cases of meningitis.[65, 84]

Many fungal infections (particularly those caused by *Candida* spp. and *Histoplasma*) usually are not responsible for causing meningitis, unless the host is immunocompromised. Cases of cryptococcal meningitis have increased dramatically in association with the acquired immunodeficiency syndrome (AIDS) epidemic. A review from the mid-1980s by the Centers for Disease Control and Prevention showed an incidence rate of 6.8 percent for cryptococcal meningitis in patients with AIDS; however, the rate in pediatric AIDS patients was 10 times lower (0.6 percent).[137] In the pre-AIDS era, patients known to be at risk for acquiring disseminated cryptococcosis included patients with lymphoma, patients on high-dose corticosteroid therapy, and patients with underlying cellular immune dysfunction.[22] Risk factors for developing *Candida* spp. meningitis are similar to those for candidemia: prolonged antimicrobial therapy, indwelling venous catheters, hyperalimentation, corticosteroid use, recent intra-abdominal surgery, and intravenous drug abuse.[130, 150] Pediatric cases occur most commonly in the neonate, particularly in the very-low-birth-weight infant.[9, 53, 67, 70, 142] In the early 1980s, 3.8 percent of infants weighing less than 1500 g in a large pediatric teaching hospital developed systemic fungal infections, most of which were caused by *Candida* spp. The mean birth weight was 809 g, with 86 percent of the infants weighing less than 1000 g.

Inhalation is the most common means by which many fungi infect the host. Other fungi can be inoculated directly into the skin; this inoculation can occur in the outdoor environment or in the hospital setting (e.g., intravenous catheters), especially in very-low-birth-weight infants.[9]

Clinical Manifestations

Infections caused by *Candida* spp. in very-low-birth-weight newborns can be particularly difficult to diagnose because of the broad range of symptoms. Most infants with disseminated candidiasis with meningitis present with respiratory distress and a supplemental oxygen requirement, and most progress to require mechanical ventilation.[9] *Candida* usually is identified in endotracheal washings, urine, and blood in patients with *Candida* meningitis, but the infants have symptoms on average 11 days before the diagnosis is made. Ophthalmologic examinations may be very important in identifying disseminated *Candida* infections.[27] A careful funduscopic examination also can help determine if increased intracranial pressure is present with the presence of papilledema. Marked abdominal distention also occurs commonly in disseminated *Candida* infections in low-birth-weight infants and frequently is associated with guaiac-positive stools. Most patients also have temperature instability, elevated white blood cell counts, and feeding intolerance. Hepatomegaly may indicate the presence of systemic infection.

Physical manifestations that are diagnostic for other causes of fungal meningitis (e.g., *Cryptococcus, Blastomyces, Histoplasma*) rarely are found because the infections usually are chronic. However, looking carefully for other manifestations of fungal infections, especially the presence of skin lesions, is very important. All superficial lesions, nodules, and draining abscesses should be investigated because they may give a clue to the cause of subacute and chronic infections (e.g., *Coccidioides, Blastomyces, Cryptococcus*).[59] Fungal stains, including India ink, should be performed on all biopsy specimens and drainage material, and all specimens should be processed for culture. Bone involvement is a common occurrence with certain fungal infections (e.g., *Cryptococcus, Blastomyces*).

The significance of isolating a fungus from CSF cannot be overemphasized. The finding of fungal organisms should be considered a true infection and appropriate antifungal therapy initiated. However, the significance of a single CSF culture for *Candida* or an unlikely meningeal pathogen *(Paecilomyces)* with an otherwise normal CSF should lead the physician to consider the possibility of contamination.[5] Repeat CSF cultures should be sought in such patients.

INFECTION WITH SPECIFIC ORGANISMS

Candidal Meningitis

Candidal meningitis remains a relatively rare disease in children. Arisoy and associates[5] reported that 2 percent of all positive CSF cultures were fungal organisms. *Candida* spp. accounted for 94.5 percent of the fungal isolates. Nine of 23 patients were newborns, eight of whom were very-low-birth-weight infants. Risk factors for positive CSF fungal cultures from neonates included antimicrobial therapy, umbilical catheterization, total parenteral nutrition, intubation, and prematurity.[40, 41] Risk factors in children beyond the neonatal period included concurrent bacterial infection, chronic systemic or CNS disease, and the presence of central venous catheters. Histopathology models in animals have revealed hyphal invasion, vasculitis, abscesses, and acute and chronic inflammatory infiltration of meninges and brain parenchyma.[69]

Children with human immunodeficiency virus (HIV) infection are at risk for acquiring disseminated *Candida* infections, including meningitis. In one study, 27 percent of HIV-infected patients with disseminated *Candida* infections had CNS involvement.[90] Nearly all HIV-infected patients who develop *Candida* infection do so as a result of hospital-acquired infection. Predisposing factors include oral candidiasis, central venous catheters, prolonged antibiotic therapy, and total parenteral nutrition. In HIV-infected patients, neutropenia surprisingly is not a major risk factor. However, simultaneous pulmonary disease, particularly viral, bacterial, or *Pneumocystis carinii* pneumonias, exists in most of HIV-infected patients with disseminated *Candida* infection. Most patients are febrile for more than 14 days, with peak temperatures of more than 39°C before the diagnosis is made.

The incidence of infection with *Candida* species other than *C. albicans* has increased dramatically in immunocompromised children, particularly those with malignancies. In a case series of children with leukemia, *Candida tropicalis* meningitis was uniformly fatal.[44] In addition to patients with malignancies and HIV infections, other children at risk for developing infection have been reported, including a child with myeloperoxidase deficiency.[95]

Candida spp. have become another concern because of the development of resistance. Intensive efforts to develop standardized, reproducible, and clinically relevant susceptibility testing methods for the fungi have resulted in the development of the NCCLS M27-A methodology for susceptibility testing of yeasts for the azole agents.[124] Reliable breakpoints are not available for amphotericin B. Unfortunately, isolates of *Candida glabrata* and *Candida krusei* with increasing resistance to amphotericin B have been described.[168] *Candida lusitaniae* has shown resistance to amphotericin B, and meningitis in an adult patient with a resistant strain has been reported.[131] *C. krusei* has been noted to have azole resistance, particularly in immunocompromised patients receiving suppressive azole therapy. These fungal infections already are difficult to treat, without the added burden of drug resistance. If patients with *Candida* spp. (including *C. albicans*) meningitis are slow to clear infection or unexpected relapse occurs, susceptibility testing is recommended.

Candida meningitis usually responds to therapy with intravenous amphotericin B alone or in combination with oral flucytosine. The use of flucytosine is controversial; however, most reports support its use in meningitis. Flucytosine has been difficult to use in low-birth-weight infants because of the immaturity of their gastrointestinal tracts and the risks of their developing necrotizing enterocolitis. The use of amphotericin alone for systemic candidiasis, including meningitis, in neonates has been used successfully in patients who could not tolerate oral medication.[21] The *most* important factor in successful treatment was the initiation of therapy quickly, once systemic *Candida* infection was suspected and frequently before the organism was isolated. Prolonged delays in initiating therapy result in high mortality rates. Amphotericin B initiated at a dose of 0.25 mg/kg of body weight diluted in 5 or 10 percent dextrose-water can be infused over the course of 2 to 4 hours. In most neonates, the drug dosage can be increased in 0.25 mg/kg increments at 6- to 12-hour intervals until the desired 1 mg/kg daily dose is attained. In older children and adolescents, a test dose may be given, with an initial dose of 0.1 mg/kg (1 mg, maximum). If this dose is tolerated, the initial dose of therapy (0.25 mg/kg) is given. Many authorities now feel that a test dose is unnecessary and that cautious infusion of the first dose is adequate.[36] In severely ill patients, the dose can be increased rapidly in 6- to 12-hour intervals to 1 mg/kg/dose. Flucytosine generally is recommended in a dose of 150 mg/kg/day, divided every 6 hours. The use of flucytosine often requires monitoring and adjustment of dosage based on serum determinations.

Large, controlled trials using the azoles and newer agents for *Candida* meningitis are lacking. Huttova reported eight neonates with candidal meningitis treated with intravenous fluconazole with and without amphotericin B.[64] Numbers from the study were too small to make conclusive recommendations. Liposomal amphotericin B was used successfully in five of six cases of *Candida* meningitis in newborn infants.[132] Marr and associates[99] reported on the use of fluconazole plus flucytosine for the treatment of *Candida* meningitis in a very-low-birth-weight infant.

Cryptococcosis

Cryptococcal meningitis was a relatively rare occurrence in the United States in the pre-HIV era. However, with the growth of the AIDS epidemic, this infection has become a common cause of meningitis in adults in certain areas of the United States and infects 2 to 9 percent of adult patients with AIDS.[28, 35, 80, 175] It remains a relatively uncommon occurrence in pediatric patients.[109, 125] Cryptococcosis is a systemic fungal infection, and meningitis is its most serious manifestation. Patients with initial pulmonary involvement may have very few symptoms but can present with fever, cough, weight loss, and dyspnea on exertion.[100] In adult studies, progressively severe headaches without the presence of fever were common findings.[152] Patients with cryptococcal meningitis frequently have few symptoms but can present with nausea, dizziness, and irritability. Nuchal rigidity usually is absent. Careful examination for cranial nerve palsies, which are found in approximately one fifth of adult patients, should be performed. Diplopia, in particular, is one of the most common manifestations of cryptococcal meningitis. Papilledema is seen in nearly one third of patients with cryptococcal meningitis.[34] Patients with coexistent AIDS frequently have very few symptoms.[35]

Pediatric patients with cryptococcal meningitis usually present with signs and symptoms not referable to the CNS.[141] Leggiadro and associates[89] reported on 13 children with AIDS compiled from 11 institutions who were diagnosed with extrapulmonary cryptococcosis. Meningitis was diagnosed in 62 percent of these patients and was the most common clinical manifestation of extrapulmonary disease. Patients who initially responded to antifungal therapy did not die of the fungal infection but succumbed to other illnesses related to their immunodeficiency. Death, however, can occur even in an immunocompetent child on effective therapy.[128]

Leggiadro and associates[88] reported on eight children with acute lymphoblastic leukemia who developed extrapulmonary cryptococcosis. Of these immunocompromised children, 63 percent had meningitis. Fever was the most common symptom, occurring in 60 percent of the children with meningitis. Headache was present in only 40 percent. A significant number of the children (40%) were completely asymptomatic and had lumbar punctures performed as routine management of their acute lymphoblastic leukemia, with the subsequent unexpected growth of *C. neoformans* on culture. One child had cutaneous lesions, and another had ptosis and an unsteady gait. Treatment in this series of patients included amphotericin B (intravenous, intrathecal, or both), alone or combined with oral flucytosine. In these patients with acute lymphoblastic leukemia, relapse was a major complication, occurring in 60 percent of patients thought to have been treated successfully. The relapses occurred within 2 to 6 months of completing therapy. Treatment of the relapses generally included combination therapy of amphotericin B and flucytosine, with the occasional use of intrathecal amphotericin B.

Other illnesses that may lead to cryptococcal meningitis include systemic lupus erythematosus being treated with corticosteroids alone or in combination with azathioprine,[2, 88, 92, 122] chronic mucocutaneous candidiasis,[66, 163] and hyper-IgE syndrome.[147] Zoonotic transmission from a pet cockatoo was described in an immunocompromised adult.[110]

Direct examination of the CSF using the India ink test can provide an immediate presumptive diagnosis of cryptococcal meningitis. The sensitivity of this test is variable, but in studies of adult patients with AIDS, positive results with the stain approached 75 percent.[28] Other useful stains include silver, periodic acid–Schiff, and mucicarmine. Gram stain of CSF is insensitive and unreliable.

Diagnosis of cryptococcal meningitis is aided by the use of serologic tests. The most common test is the cryptococcal capsular polysaccharide antigen test, which can be performed on serum, CSF, or other sterile body fluids. The sensitivity of this test is nearly 100 percent for the serum of patients who are HIV-positive.[29, 80, 175] The CSF antigen test appears in some studies to be less sensitive, with a 91 percent sensitivity.[28] False-positive results caused by cross-reactions of antigens in disseminated infections with *Trichosporon beigelii* have been reported.[102] Culture still is the gold standard for diagnosing and monitoring the success of therapy.

Treatment of cryptococcal meningitis is prolonged and, in immunocompromised patients, frequently requires lifelong maintenance therapy. In adults with HIV infection, multiple regimens have been suggested. Practice guidelines have been published for patients with cryptococcal meningitis who are HIV-negative or -positive.[129] For those who are HIV negative, amphotericin B (0.7 to 1 mg/kg/day) plus flucytosine (100 mg/kg/day in four divided doses) for 2 weeks and then fluconazole (400 mg) for a minimum of 10 weeks or alternatively amphotericin B (0.7 to 1 mg/kg day) plus flucytosine (100 mg/kg/day) for 6 to 10 weeks is recommended. A repeat lumbar puncture is recommended at 2 weeks. If cultures still are positive, prolonged induction therapy should be continued and fluconazole once started for therapy should be continued for 6 to 12 months. The investigators who proposed the guidelines do not recommend initiating therapy with fluconazole alone. The use of AmBisome (4 mg/kg) for 6 to 10 weeks is a possible alternative if the patient cannot tolerate amphotericin B or azole therapy.

For HIV-infected patients, the practice guideline study group recommends induction therapy of amphotericin B (0.7 to 1 mg/kg/day) plus flucytosine (100 mg/kg/day in four divided doses) for 2 weeks and then fluconazole (400 mg/day) for a minimum of 10 weeks.[129] When flucytosine cannot be administered, amphotericin B is an acceptable alternative. The use of lipid formulations of amphotericin B may be helpful in patients who cannot tolerate amphotericin B because of renal toxicity.[31] AmBisome has been effective at doses of 4 mg/kg/day.[87]

In patients with renal compromise associated with amphotericin B, flucytosine levels must be monitored carefully. The recommendation is that the dose of flucytosine be reduced to 75 to 100 mg/kg/day and continuing doses be adjusted to maintain serum flucytosine levels between 25 and 60 μg/mL.[6, 45] Serum cryptococcal antigens are not useful in monitoring response to therapy, and the use of CSF cryptococcal antigens to monitor response to therapy also is controversial. The best method to judge successful therapy is by the demonstration of sterility of CSF fungal cultures.

In pediatrics, a combination of amphotericin B and flucytosine has been used most frequently. In children with AIDS, amphotericin B in a dose of 0.5 to 1.0 mg/kg/day with or without flucytosine (150 mg/kg/day in four divided doses) is recommended for 4 to 8 weeks, followed by maintenance therapy with fluconazole (3 to 6 mg/kg/day) indefinitely.[167]

Histoplasmosis

Infection with *Histoplasma capsulatum,* usually a benign and self-limited disease, is endemic in many parts of the United States. Disseminated disease, including meningitis, is a rare occurrence in children.[75] Case reports of adults generally describe immunocompromised individuals.[51, 157] Clinical presentations reported in the literature show a wide variability in the manifestation of meningitis. In these cases, 39 percent of patients presented with meningitis associated with acute dissemination, 25 percent with single histoplasmoma that presented as symptomatic mass lesions alone or with dissemination, 25 percent with chronic meningitis without evidence of dissemination, and the remainder with meningitis as a manifestation of recurrent disease. Rarely, embolization to the brain caused by *Histoplasma* endocarditis has been associated with meningitis.[169]

Meningitis occurring in patients with AIDS has become relatively common in endemic areas. In one report, disseminated histoplasmosis caused 8 percent of the AIDS-defining illnesses in children.[134] The duration of symptoms is quite variable. In patients who do not have AIDS, the symptoms generally last longer than 6 months and can last as long as 7 years.[38, 51, 117, 164] In the patient with AIDS, symptoms usually manifest more acutely and in a much shorter time-frame.[169] In this series, neurologic findings occurred in all but 6 percent of the patients.[169] The most common signs and symptoms include depressed consciousness (29%), headaches (24%), confusion (22%), cranial nerve deficits (19%), other focal deficits (16%), seizures (14%), personality changes (12%), and ataxia (11%). Findings more commonly observed with acute bacterial meningitis, such as meningismus, a Babinski sign, or papilledema, were seen in less than 8 percent of the cases. In adult patients who do not have AIDS, the death rate is approximately 12 percent, with a relapse rate of 44 percent. In adult patients with AIDS, the death rate is as high as 100 percent in some series.[4, 169]

Diagnosis can be aided by serologic testing. High levels of anti–*H. capsulatum* antibodies were detected in the serum of 70 percent of patients tested. CSF serology was helpful in 75 percent of patients who were tested. Culture of the CSF was positive for less than half of the cases in one review.[75] However, in a second series in patients with AIDS, blood cultures were positive for 49 percent, bone marrow for 53 percent, respiratory secretions for 58 percent, and brain or meninges cultures for 75 percent of those tested. Serologic testing can be negative because 10 to 25 percent of patients with disseminated disease lack a positive antibody response. The serology also can be falsely positive in patients with other fungal diseases or tuberculosis. The antibody response to acute *Histoplasma* infection may remain elevated for years, without evidence of dissemination or meningeal disease. The use of *Histoplasma* antigen has become widely held as a useful test in the immunocompromised patient with disseminated *Histoplasma*. Data from Wheat and associates[169] showed that antigen was found in the urine of six of seven patients with AIDS and meningitis.

Treatment with amphotericin B is considered standard therapy. A total dose of at least 30 mg/kg is considered by many physicians to be necessary to ensure a cure. Children with meningitis caused by *H. capsulatum* should have the dose of amphotericin B increased rapidly to 1 mg/kg/day. The use of intrathecal amphotericin B is not recommended for *H. capsulatum* meningitis. According to a practice guideline for adults, liposomal amphotericin B (3 to 5 mg/kg/day or every other day, given 3 to 4 months) may be considered for patients who have failed therapy with amphotericin B followed by fluconazole.[171] Johnson and colleagues[71] reported on a trial comparing amphotericin B with liposomal amphotericin B (AmBisome, LAmB) as induction therapy and showed the agents had similar efficacy for treating disseminated histoplasmosis. LeMonte and associates[91] found that amphotericin B combined with fluconazole might have antagonistic effects for treatment of histoplasmosis, but data are needed to access combination therapy for meningitis. AIDS patients whose induction therapy was successful must remain on an anti-*Histoplasma* agent indefinitely. A few cases of children with disseminated histoplasmosis and AIDS have been reported but none with meningitis, and in these children, antifungal therapy must be continued indefinitely.[24, 134] The case report by Schutze and associates[134] demonstrated that ketoconazole was ineffective for preventing recurrence of nonmeningeal disseminated disease, and with ketoconazole's poor CNS penetration, it is likely to be ineffective for prophylaxis of meningitis. In patients with AIDS, some success has occurred with the use of itraconazole for suppressive therapy in disseminated disease. However, few data exist on the use of itraconazole for suppressive therapy for meningitis or other CNS lesions caused by *Histoplasma*. Based on the available data, intravenous amphotericin B in a weekly dose of 1 mg/kg is the best agent for maintenance therapy in patients with meningitis. In one case report, fluconazole was effective in an adult with *Histoplasma* meningitis refractory to amphotericin B therapy.[151]

Coccidioidomycosis

C. immitis meningitis is a more common cause of chronic meningitis than is *Histoplasma*. Approximately 1 percent of children with symptomatic pulmonary disease develop disseminated disease.[72] From 15 to 20 percent of patients with disseminated coccidioidomycosis develop meningitis.[72, 77] History of exposure is a very important factor in diagnosing this disease and relies on careful questioning of the patient about travel to or residence in an endemic area.[148, 149] Exposure of wounds by colonized soil has been implicated in at least one pediatric case.[107] An association between facial cutaneous coccidioidomycosis and meningitis has been described.[7]

CSF shows a mononuclear pleocytosis with an elevated protein and decreased glucose concentration. Diagnosing coccidioidal meningitis is made easier by the availability of reliable serologic tests. Smith and associates[143] showed that complement-fixing antibodies appeared in the CSF only in patients with meningitis and provided a sensitivity of 76 percent. Ninety-six percent sensitivity was seen when the complement-fixation test was incubated at 4°C.[114] McGinnis,[101] in his review of the literature based on pooling five studies, showed that *Coccidioides* could be cultured from the CSF in 76 percent of patients with meningitis and was seen on direct examination of the CSF in only 8 percent of the cases. He concluded that these values were too high and were likely skewed because of reporting bias. Other experts in the field also consider that the rate of positive CSF cultures is much lower (approximately 33%) and that finding the organism in the CSF by direct examination rarely occurs.[146]

Coccidioidomycosis in infancy was described more than 40 years ago and continues to be a problem today.[153] Infants usually have severe disease with high mortality rates and morbidity. In the 1980s, two studies described children with *Coccidioides* spp. meningitis who were treated with oral, intravenous, or intrathecal imidazoles.[61, 138] The authors reported promising results with the use of ketoconazole and imidazole therapy when compared with standard intravenous or intrathecal amphotericin B.

If untreated, *Coccidioides* meningitis uniformly is fatal. Therapy with intravenous and intrathecal amphotericin B reduced the mortality rate to 30 percent.[114] The use of fluconazole has been found in adult studies to have a success rate as high as 79 percent.[49] It appears safe in clinical use, despite a case report of a pregnant woman with *Coccidioides* meningitis treated with fluconazole who delivered a child with congenital malformations. However, the child was thought to have an autosomal recessive disorder (Antley-Bixler syndrome) and not teratogenic malformations caused by fluconazole.[86] Fluconazole may be the superior agent for sustaining remission of meningitis caused by *Coccidioides* because of its oral bioavailability, the toxicity associated with amphotericin B, and the elimination of the need for intrathecal administration.[120]

Galgiani and coworkers[48] have written practice guidelines for the treatment of coccidioidomycosis in adults. Therapy with oral fluconazole is preferred, with most authorities recommending 400 mg/day orally, although some physicians begin with higher doses of 800 to 1000 mg/day. Fluconazole in a dose of 400 to 600 mg/day for 9 to 12 months has been shown to be effective in adults.[49, 155] A corresponding dose of 6 mg/kg/day in pediatric patients also has been used, but no controlled studies using this agent in pediatric patients have been published. If treatment is begun with azole therapy, it should be continued for life.[33]

Itraconazole has proven efficacy in nonmeningeal coccidioidomycosis, with 63 percent of adult patients treated showing a complete response.[156] Dosages of itraconazole of 400 to 600 mg/day have been reported to be effective in adults. Because itraconazole has variable oral bioavailability, many authorities recommend monitoring for adequate serum drug levels.[162] The use of itraconazole for meningeal involvement led to great hope for the use of an oral agent in this disease.[154] Unfortunately, adult patients with *Coccidioides* meningitis had high relapse rates (40% to 50%), which rendered them dependent on lifelong therapy with itraconazole.[57] However, the alternative of continued intrathecal amphotericin B renders this treatment much more appealing.

In children, well-developed, controlled clinical trials with large patient numbers do not exist for the azoles; therefore, some authorities consider intravenous and intrathecal amphotericin B the standard therapy for coccidioidal meningitis. It also is recommended for patients who do not respond to fluconazole or itraconazole treatment. Some experts initially use a combination of oral azole with intrathecal amphotericin B with the thought that responses are more prompt with this approach. Amphotericin B can be administered intrathecally into the lumbar area or into the cisterna magna, or by using an Ommaya reservoir.[32, 50, 82, 174] In younger children, intraventricular or intracisternal therapy using the Ommaya reservoir allows ease of administration but has the disadvantage of increasing susceptibility to secondary bacterial infection. The initial dose of amphotericin B administered into the CSF is 0.025 mg. The dose then is increased by doubling until a maintenance dose of 0.1 to 0.5 mg is attained. After this dose has been achieved, therapy can be given every other day, alternating with the intravenous administration of amphotericin B. Therapy is continued until the child's condition has stabilized, at which point intrathecal therapy gradually can be stretched out to every 3 weeks. This program is continued until the CSF indices are normal and culture results have been negative for at least 1 year. Miconazole, an imidazole compound that no longer is commercially available, was used in the treatment of *Coccidioides* meningitis and, in combination with oral ketoconazole, had good results in nine children.[138]

Blastomycosis

Blastomyces dermatitidis is an uncommon cause of chronic meningitis and is difficult to diagnose premortem unless the patient has other signs of systemic blastomycosis. However, when systemic blastomycosis occurs, it involves the CNS in as many as 5 percent of cases.[18] Common sites for this organism include bone, genitourinary tract, and skin.[10, 19] Although examination of CSF obtained by lumbar puncture usually is negative (9% sensitivity), ventricular fluid (four of four patients tested) appears to have a higher yield.[81] Typically, fungal meningitis is associated with a lymphocytic pleocytosis; however, meningitis caused by *B. dermatitidis* frequently has a neutrophilic predominance.[60] Previously, blastomycosis most often affected patients who were immunocompetent. Patients with AIDS are at a high risk for developing chronic infection.[60] Because of the difficulty in diagnosing meningitis caused by *B. dermatitidis* and its similarities to tuberculous meningitis, patients usually are treated for presumptive tuberculous meningitis.[54, 106] Although meningitis is the most common form of CNS blastomycosis, solitary mass lesions also can occur.[126]

Diagnosis relies on the characteristic histopathologic appearance in tissues and occasionally on culture of CSF obtained from the ventricles. However, if the difficulty in performing these procedures is prohibitive, looking for other sources of blastomycosis, including sputum and urine, is indicated. A study in patients with AIDS showed that sputum examination was useful for the diagnosis of disseminated blastomycosis.[115]

Treatment of systemic blastomycosis, including meningitis, relies on amphotericin B in a dose of 1 mg/kg/day.[145] The duration of therapy is unknown, but adults with systemic disease usually require a minimum of 2 g to prevent relapse of nonmeningeal disease.[116] In adult patients who have been "cured" of their meningitis, doses between 2400 and 3150 mg were required, which would correspond to a total dose of 35 to 45 mg/kg in a child. The use of lipid formulations of amphotericin B has not been reported for CNS blastomycosis, but this treatment according to current practice guidelines of the Mycoses Study Group may be an alternative for patients unable to tolerate amphotericin B because of toxicity.[26] Azoles should not be considered for primary treatment of CNS blastomycosis. Schutze and colleagues[133] report that children respond less satisfactorily to oral azole therapy than do adults.

Aspergillosis

CNS infections with *Aspergillus fumigatus* and other *Aspergillus* spp. in immunocompromised patients usually are fatal. Conditions that place the patient at risk include organ transplantation, malignancies, and neutropenia. In most reported cases, patients were receiving high-dose corticosteroid therapy in addition to broad-spectrum antibiotics.[11, 83] Many patients had fever, and pulmonary findings preceded neurologic manifestations. *Aspergillus* infection of the CNS usually is acquired by hematogenous spread from the lungs. Other modes of acquisition include extension from a contiguous focus (sinuses) and intravenous drug abuse.[105]

Brain abscesses are the most typical manifestation of *Aspergillus* spp. infection in the CNS, but meningoencephalitis, isolated spinal cord lesions, aqueductal stenosis, and mycotic aneurysms also have been described.[25, 42, 161, 165, 173] The use of magnetic resonance imaging has been suggested to be superior to computed tomography for the delineation of CNS lesions in patients with bone marrow transplantation.[103] The lesions are consistent with acute infarcts.

Some of the early reports of CNS aspergillosis were for infants who appeared to be normal.[1, 96] The diagnosis of meningitis relies on CSF cultures, but the results of a bronchoscopy or biopsy frequently are more helpful and provide a more expedient diagnosis. Use of *Aspergillus* antigen in the CSF has been helpful, and it may be used for serial observations during the course of therapy.[166] Because the disease is uniformly fatal, the importance of treating pulmonary aspergillosis before the development of meningeal involvement cannot be overemphasized. Amphotericin B in doses of 1 to 1.5 mg/kg/day is recommended, with or without the addition of flucytosine, rifampin, or both agents.[55, 160] Itraconazole has been used successfully in one case report, as has voriconazole.[104, 166]

Sporotrichosis

Sporothrix schenckii, although primarily a lymphocutaneous disease, has been reported to cause meningitis.[39, 46, 79, 118, 140] Many of the cases recently described have occurred in adults with AIDS as an underlying risk factor.[37, 127] Meningeal seeding may occur through hematogenous spread from the lungs, as is seen in most other fungal infections.[39] Meningeal involvement with sporotrichosis produces CSF indices and abnormalities similar to those seen with the other fungal meningitides.[38] CSF fungal culture is insensitive for the diagnosis of meningitis caused by sporotrichosis. The use of *S. schenckii* antibody in the CSF has been effective in diagnosing meningitis in patients without other overt signs of this infection.[135]

Treating this infection is very difficult. Amphotericin B alone has been successful on occasion.[76] Some experts recommend the addition of flucytosine, but no studies have evaluated the efficacy of this combination. The azoles, particularly itraconazole, had excellent results in nonmeningeal disease, but successful treatment of meningitis with this agent has not been proved.

Mucormycosis

Meningitis caused by *Mucor* spp. or other zygomycetes usually occurs as a result of direct extension from paranasal sinus disease. Infection with these organisms most commonly is seen in the immunocompromised host and particularly in patients with diabetes mellitus or those receiving high doses of corticosteroids. Patients (particularly dialysis patients) undergoing chelation therapy with deferoxamine are at risk for developing infection.[16, 17, 74, 172] The association with deferoxamine therapy is seen with *Cunninghamella*.[123] *Mucor* spp. causing CNS disease has been reported in children but is a very rare occurrence.[58, 68] Treatment employs amphotericin B in doses of 1 to 1.5 mg/kg/day but usually is unsuccessful. Surgical excision of rhinocerebral infection is recommended along with antifungal therapy.

Other Fungal Infections

Acremonium spp. are common soil fungi that may cause chronic meningitis in humans.[112] *Xylohypha bantiana*, an uncommon dematiaceous fungus, caused a fungal brain abscess in an adolescent girl; this report increases the number of cases reported in the literature to nearly 40.[111] Cerebral chromoblastomycosis also has been reported.[139] Other fungal organisms causing CNS infection include *Paracoccidioides brasiliensis* (i.e., South American blastomycosis),[119] *Prototheca wickerhamii*,[73] *B. capitatus*,[52] *Rhodotorula* spp.,[98, 121] *Pseudallescheria boydii*,[13] *Aureobasidium mansoni*,[65] *Clavispora lusitaniae*,[65] and *Bipolaris spicifera*.[84]

Diagnosis

Specific information about each organism's diagnosis is discussed in previous sections. Table 40–1 provides specific data for some of the fungal meningitides. Overall, the problem with diagnosing many of these infections is that most patients have nonspecific signs and symptoms without reference to the CNS. Standard culture media may not be useful for these organisms, and cultures can take weeks before an organism is identified. The use of antigen and antibody testing has proved quite useful for the diagnosis of *Cryptococcus*, *Coccidioides*, and *Histoplasma* infections. The hope is that polymerase chain reaction technology may be helpful in the future, as it has been for bacterial and mycobacterial diagnoses. Neonates may have only a mild CSF pleocytosis. In one series of 16 neonates with definite *Candida* meningitis, the median CSF white blood cell count was 53 cells/mm^3 (range, 0 to 1120 cells/mm^3).[43]

CSF examination may be helpful in some instances. As much CSF as can be removed safely should be obtained, especially at the time of ventriculography or pneumoencephalography.[38] A minimum of 5 mL of spinal fluid has been suggested, based on experimental work.[94] Repeated cultures of large volumes of CSF may be helpful.[38] The fluid obtained should be centrifuged and the sediment saved for culture and India ink preparation. The supernatant is sent for serologic tests. The India ink test should be interpreted with caution and must be followed with cultures because artifacts frequently can cause misinterpretation.[38] The cumulative efficacy of repeated lumbar punctures for cryptococcal meningitis improved the sensitivity of the India ink smear from 26 percent in one lumbar puncture to 52.6 percent with the second.[101] If large volumes are available, membrane filtration may be used to concentrate the fungal elements. The membrane containing the fungi is placed aseptically on isolation media and incubated at 30°C for as long as 4 weeks. The CSF that passes through the membrane then can be used for serology or chemistry determinations.[101] The remaining CSF can be inoculated onto Sabouraud glucose agar, blood agar, and brain-heart infusion agar or into broth media or into both types of media. CSF cultures generally are unhelpful for *Histoplasma*, *Blastomyces*, and other dimorphic fungi.

TABLE 40–1 ■ FUNGAL CEREBROSPINAL FLUID CHARACTERISTICS[54, 61, 101, 168]

Organism	WBCs	Protein	Glucose	Smears	Serology	Cultures
Blastomyces	Variable up to 15,000 cells/mm^3 with PMNs or lymphocytes	Elevated up to 300 mg/dL	Normal or low	Rare on smear	No good serology	CSF cultures rarely +; increased yield with ventricular taps
Candida	Mean = 600 cells/mm^3 up to 1900 cells/mm^3 with lymphocytes or PMNs	Elevated	Low or normal	40% + on smears	Serology not helpful	CSF cultures useful
Coccidioides	100–750 WBCs, mostly lymphocytes	150–2000 mg/dL	21–62% serum	Rare on smear	CSF CF Ab + in 75–95%	CSF cultures + in 33–60%
Cryptococcus	40–400 WBCs, mostly lymphocytes	High	Low	India ink + in 25–50%	CSF and serum cryptococcal Ag + in 85–90%	CSF cultures + in 75%
Histoplasma	0–300 WBCs, lymphocytes, or PMNs; most 11–101/mm^3	Usually elevated but can be normal	Usually low (<40 mg/dL) to normal	Rare on smear	Polysaccharide Ag in urine, blood, CSF + in 61%	CSF cultures + in 27–65%

+, positive; Ab, antibody; Ag, antigen; CF, complement fixation; CSF, cerebrospinal fluid; PMNs, polymorphonuclear leukocytes; WBCs, white blood cells.

Serologic techniques are extremely useful for *Cryptococcus* and *Coccidioides*. Approximately 100 percent sensitivity is seen with serum cryptococcal antigen tests in HIV-positive patients.[29, 80, 175] The CSF antigen test in HIV-positive patients appears in some studies to be less sensitive (91%).[28] In patients not infected with HIV, the sensitivity of the serologic test in the CSF approaches 90 percent.[62] For coccidioidal meningitis, the sensitivity rate is more than 76 percent.[114, 143]

Candida can be cultured but may require a prolonged incubation period, necessitating institution of empiric therapy while awaiting cultures. For other organisms, such as *Histoplasma*, *Blastomyces*, and *Coccidioides*, culturing other body fluids, such as blood, urine, sputum, or draining wounds, can be helpful.

Antifungal Agents and Treatment Guidelines

Amphotericin B remains the treatment of choice for most CNS fungal infections. Amphotericin B has less than 5 percent oral bioavailability and is more than 90 percent protein bound.[14] It has a very prolonged terminal elimination half-life of 15 days, with only approximately 3 percent of the parent compound found unchanged in the urine.[8] CSF concentrations are approximately 2 to 4 percent of those found in serum.[50, 159] The dose recommended varies, depending on the organism and the severity of the illness. However, in most children and infants, a dose of 1 mg/kg/day appears to be satisfactory, particularly in view of the increased clearance of the drug compared with that in adults.[12, 144]

Toxicity and adverse effects are universal with the use of amphotericin B. Acetaminophen and diphenhydramine may be helpful in reducing the incidence of fever, nausea, and chills. The effective use of hydrocortisone to reduce febrile reactions has been documented.[158] However, great variability of patient responses to this treatment occurs. The use of corticosteroids can potentiate water retention and amphotericin B–induced hypokalemia; the dosage of corticosteroids should be kept to a minimum.[50] If chills occur, they can be terminated with the use of meperidine.[20]

Amphotericin B induces reversible impairment of renal function in 80 percent of patients during the first 2 weeks of therapy.[23] In most cases, renal function returns to normal after cessation of administration of the drug. The manifestations of its toxicity include renal tubular acidosis, azotemia, oliguria, and potassium-magnesium wasting. Other nephrotoxic drugs worsen the azotemia. Renal failure in adult studies has been shown to be ameliorated by the use of salt loading.[63] The adult studies used 500 mL of a 0.9 percent sodium chloride solution as prehydration and posthydration therapy; in children, 10 mL/kg appears to work as well. Hypokalemia along with hypomagnesemia occurs frequently and may require supplementation. A normocytic, normochromic anemia occurs in many patients who receive amphotericin B, with an 18 to 35 percent decrease in hemoglobin seen after 10 weeks of therapy; this anemia appears partly related to changes in erythropoietin levels.[97]

One approach to minimize amphotericin B toxicity while maintaining the drug's pharmacologic spectrum and clinical utility is the use of liposomal and lipid-complexed formulations. The three formulations approved for clinical use include amphotericin B lipid complex (Abelcet, Liposome Company, Princeton, NJ), amphotericin B colloidal dispersion (Amphotec, Amphocil, Sequus Pharmaceuticals, Menlo Park, CA), and liposomal amphotericin B (AmBisome, NeXstar Pharmaceuticals, Boulder, CO; Fujisawa USA, Deerfield, IL). Although each of these lipid delivery systems is unique and has different pharmacokinetic and pharmacodynamic profiles, no clinical comparisons of lipid formulations have been conducted in children. Their use is discussed briefly in the case reports that exist for the individual infections listed previously. Most of the published literature in pediatrics is of cases for which AmBisome has been used.

Ketoconazole has not been an effective agent for treating most fungal CNS disease processes. It has been supplanted by the newer azoles, fluconazole and itraconazole, because of their better bioavailability and more favorable results in clinical trials.

Fluconazole is a very effective agent for the suppression of cryptococcal meningitis in patients with AIDS and immunocompetent patients and appears to be superior to amphotericin B for prolonged maintenance therapy in patients with AIDS. Fluconazole absorption by the gastrointestinal tract is not affected by the presence of food or gastric acidity.[15] Fluconazole is highly water soluble and minimally bound to plasma proteins.[85] The terminal elimination half-life of fluconazole is 22 to 31 hours, with 80 percent of the drug excreted unchanged in the urine.[30] Fluconazole readily penetrates into CSF in inflamed or noninflamed meninges, achieving levels that are 60 to 80 percent of serum levels. Rifampin, cyclosporin A, and phenytoin have significant interactions with fluconazole. Adverse effects are relatively uncommon occurrences, especially compared with those associated with amphotericin B. Less than 5 percent of patients have nausea and vomiting. Asymptomatic elevations of plasma aminotransferases occur in less than 1 to 7 percent of patients.[30]

Data for itraconazole use in pediatrics are very limited, and itraconazole is not recommended at this time for CNS fungal infections in children. Itraconazole has increased absorption when taken with food.[161] Itraconazole is highly protein bound (>99%); less than 1 percent is excreted unchanged in urine.[56] CSF concentrations are relatively low compared with those of fluconazole; however, itraconazole is much more lipophilic, allowing it to show efficacy in treatment of some fungal meningitides. Additional data on it and the other azoles should be forthcoming in the next several years, particularly for treatment of coccidioidal meningitis in children. Promising results from an adult study have been published.[154]

Conclusion

With the large increase in the number of immunocompromised children caused by the epidemic of HIV, the advent of new antineoplastic agents, the growth of organ transplantation, and the increased use of corticosteroids, the relative rarity of fungal meningitides has been replaced by a burgeoning upswing in the incidence and prevalence of these infections. New modalities for diagnosis are needed because many of these fungal infections still require weeks for identification. We expect that trials in progress will help determine the role of azoles, amphotericin B, lipid formulations of amphotericin B, or combinations of these drugs as the optimal treatment of many fungal meningitides.

REFERENCES

1. Allan, G. W., and Anderson, D. H.: Generalized aspergillosis in an infant 18 days of age. Pediatrics. *26*:432–440, 1960.
2. al-Rasheed, S. A., and al-Fawaz, I. M.: Cryptococcal meningitis in a child with systemic lupus erythematosus. Ann. Trop. Paediatr. *10*:323–326, 1990.

3. Ampel, N. M., Wieden, M. A., and Galgiani, J. N.: Coccidioidomycosis: Clinical update. Rev. Infect. Dis. *11*:897, 1989.
4. Anaissie, E., Fainstein, V., Samo, T., et al.: Central nervous system histoplasmosis: An unappreciated complication of the acquired immunodeficiency syndrome. Am. J. Med. *84*:215–217, 1988.
5. Arisoy, E. S., Arisoy, A. E., and Dunne, W. M., Jr.: Clinical significance of fungi isolated from cerebrospinal fluid in children. Pediatr. Infect. Dis. J. *13*:128–133, 1994.
6. Armstrong, D.: Treatment of opportunistic fungal infections. Clin. Infect. Dis. *16*:1–9, 1993.
7. Arsura, E. L., Kilgore, W. B., Caldwell, J. W., et al.: Association between facial cutaneous coccidioidomycosis and meningitis. West. J. Med. *169*:13–16, 1998.
8. Atkinson, A. J., and Bennett, J. E.: Amphotericin B pharmacokinetics in humans. Antimicrob. Agents Chemother. *13*:271, 1978.
9. Baley, J. E., Kliegman, R. M., and Fanaroff, A. A.: Disseminated fungal infections in very low-birth-weight infants: Clinical manifestations and epidemiology. Pediatrics. *73*:144–152, 1984.
10. Baumgardner, D. J., Buggy, B. P., Mattson, B. J., et al.: Epidemiology of blastomycosis in a region of high endemicity in north central Wisconsin. Clin. Infect. Dis. *15*:629–635, 1992.
11. Beal, M. F., O'Carroll, C. P., Kleinman, G. M., et al.: Aspergillosis of the central nervous system. Neurology *32*:473–479, 1982.
12. Benson, J. M., and Nahata, M. C.: Pharmacokinetics of amphotericin B in children. Antimicrob. Agents Chemother. *33*:1989–1993, 1989.
13. Berenguer, J., Diaz-Mediavilla, J., Urra, D., et al.: Central nervous system infection caused by *Pseudallescheria boydii*: Case report and review. Rev. Infect. Dis. *11*:890--896, 1989.
14. Block, E. R., Bennett, J. E., Livoti, L. G., et al.: Flucytosine and amphotericin B: Hemodialysis effects on the plasma concentration and clearance. Ann. Intern. Med. *80*:613–617, 1974.
15. Blum, R., A., D'Andrea, D. T., Florentino, B. M., et al.: Increased gastric pH and the bioavailability of fluconazole and ketoconazole. Ann. Intern. Med. *114*:755–757, 1991.
16. Boelaert, J. R., de Locht, M., Van Cutsem, J., et al.: Mucormycosis during deferoxamine therapy is a siderophore-mediated infection: In vitro and in vivo animal studies. J. Clin. Invest. *91*:1979–1986, 1993.
17. Boelaert, J. R., Vergauwe, P. L., and Vandepitte, J. M.: Mucormycosis infection in dialysis patients. Ann. Intern. Med. *107*:782–783, 1987.
18. Bradsher, R. W.: Blastomycosis. Clin. Infect. Dis. *14* (Suppl. 1): S582–S590, 1992.
19. Bradsher, R. W., Rice, D. C., and Abernathy, R. S.: Ketoconazole therapy for endemic blastomycosis. Ann. Intern. Med. *103*:872–879, 1985.
20. Burks, L. C., Aisner, J., Fortner, C. L., et al.: Meperidine for the treatment of shaking chills and fever. Arch. Intern. Med. *140*:483–484, 1980.
21. Butler, K. M., Rench, M. A., and Baker, C. J.: Amphotericin B as a single agent in the treatment of systemic candidiasis in neonates. Pediatr. Infect. Dis. J. *9*:51–56, 1990.
22. Butler, W. T., Alling, D. W., Spickard, A., et al.: Diagnostic and prognostic value of clinical and laboratory findings in cryptococcal meningitis: A follow-up study of forty patients. N. Engl. J. Med. *270*:59–66, 1964.
23. Butler, W. T., Bennett, J. E., Alling, D. W., et al.: Nephrotoxicity of amphotericin B: Early and late effects in 81 patients. Ann. Intern. Med. *61*:175–187, 1964.
24. Byers, M., Feldman, S., and Edwards, J.: Disseminated histoplasmosis as the acquired immunodeficiency syndrome-defining illness in an infant. Pediatr. Infect. Dis. J. *11*:127–128, 1992.
25. Casey, A. T., Wilkins, P., and Uttley, D.: Aspergillosis infection in neurosurgical practice. Br. J. Neurosurg. *8*:31–39, 1994.
26. Chapman, S. W., Bradsher, R. W., Campbell, G. D., et al.: Practice guidelines for the management of patients with blastomycosis. Clin. Infect. Dis. *30*:679–683, 2000.
27. Chen, J. Y.: Neonatal candidiasis associated with meningitis and endophthalmitis. Acta Pediatr. Jpn. *36*:261–265, 1994.
28. Chuck, S. L., and Sande, M. A.: Infections with *Cryptococcus neoformans* in the acquired immunodeficiency syndrome. N. Engl. J. Med. *321*:794–799, 1989.
29. Clark, R. A., Greer, D., Atkinson, W., et al.: Spectrum of *Cryptococcus neoformans* infection in 68 patients infected with human immunodeficiency virus. Rev. Infect. Dis. *12*:768–777, 1990.
30. Como, J. A., and Dismukes, W. E.: Oral azole drugs as systemic antifungal therapy. N. Engl. J. Med. *330*:263–272, 1994.
31. Coukell, A. J., and Brogden, R. N.: Liposomal amphotericin B. Therapeutic use in the management of fungal infections and visceral leishmaniasis. Drugs *55*:585–612, 1998.
32. Dennis, M., and Rasch, J. R.: The Ommaya Reservoir in fungal meningitis: A case report. *In* Ajello, L. (ed.): Coccidioidomycosis. Tucson, AZ, University of Arizona Press, 1967, pp. 119–122.
33. Dewsnup, D. H., Galgiani, J. N., Graybill, J. R., et al.: Is it ever safe to stop azole therapy for *Coccidioides immitis* meningitis? Ann. Intern. Med. *124*:305–310, 1996.
34. Diamond, R. D.: *Cryptococcus neoformans. In* Mandell, G. L., Bennett, J. E., and Dolin, R. (eds.): Principles and Practice of Infectious Diseases. 4th ed. New York, Churchill Livingstone, 1995, pp. 2331–2340.
35. Dismukes, W. E.: Cryptococcal meningitis in patients with AIDS. J. Infect. Dis. *157*:624–628, 1988.
36. Dismukes, W. E.: Introduction to antifungal drugs. Clin. Infect. Dis. *30*:653–657, 2000.
37. Donabedian, H., O'Donnell, E., Olszewski, C., et al.: Disseminated cutaneous and meningeal sporotrichosis in an AIDS patient. Diagn. Microbiol. Infect. Dis. *18*:111–115, 1994.
38. Ellner, J. J., and Bennett, J. E.: Chronic meningitis. Medicine (Baltimore). *55*:341–396, 1976.
39. Ewing, G. E., Bosl, G. J., and Peterson, P. K.: *Sporothrix schenckii* meningitis in a farmer with Hodgkin's disease. Am. J. Med. *68*:455–457, 1980.
40. Faix, R. G.: Systemic *Candida* infections in infants in intensive care nurseries: High incidence of central nervous system involvement. J. Pediatr. *105*:616–622, 1984.
41. Faix, R. G., Kovarik, S. M., Shaw, T. R., et al.: Mucocutaneous and invasive candidiasis among very low birth weight (<1500 grams) infants in intensive care nurseries: A prospective study. Pediatrics *83*:101–107, 1989.
42. Feely, M., and Steinberg, M.: *Aspergillus* infection complicating transsphenoidal yttrium-90 pituitary implant. J. Neurosurg. *46*:530–532, 1977.
43. Fernandez, M., Moylett, E. H., Noyala, D. E., et al.: Candida meningitis in neonates. Clin. Infect. Dis. *31*:458–463, 2000.
44. Flynn, P. M., Marina, N. M., Rivera, G. K., et al.: *Candida tropicalis* infections in children with leukemia. Leuk. Lymphoma *10*:369–376, 1993.
45. Francis, P., and Walsh, T. J.: Evolving role of flucytosine in immunocompromised patients: New insights into safety, pharmacokinetics, and antifungal therapy. Clin. Infect. Dis. *15*:1003–1008, 1992.
46. Freeman, J. W., and Ziegler, D. K.: Chronic meningitis caused by *Sporotrichum schenckii*. Neurology *27*:989–992, 1977.
47. Furcolow, M. L., Chick, E. W., Busey, J. F., et al.: Prevalence and incidence studies of human and canine blastomycosis. I. Cases in the United States, 1885–1968. Am. Rev. Respir. Dis. *102*:60–67, 1970.
48. Galgiani, J. N., Ampel, N. M., Catanzaro, A., et al.: Practice guidelines for treatment of coccidioidomycosis. Clin. Infect. Dis. *30*:658–661, 2000.
49. Galgiani, J. N., Catanzaro, A., Cloud, G. A., et al.: Fluconazole therapy for coccidioidal meningitis: The NIAID-Mycoses Study Group. Ann. Intern. Med. *119*:28–35, 1993.
50. Gallis, H. A., Drew, R. H., and Pickard, W. W.: Amphotericin B: 30 years of clinical experience. Rev. Infect. Dis. *12*:308–329, 1990.
51. Gelfand, J. A., and Bennett, J. E.: Active *Histoplasma* meningitis of 22 years duration. J. A. M. A. *233*:1294–1295, 1975.
52. Girmenia, C., Micozzi, A., Venditti, M., et al.: Fluconazole treatment of *Blastoschizomyces capitatus* meningitis in an allogeneic bone marrow recipient. Eur. J. Clin. Microbiol. Infect. Dis. *10*:752–756, 1991.
53. Glick, C., Graves, C. R., and Feldman, S.: Neonatal fungemia and amphotericin B. South. Med. J. *86*:1368–1371, 1993.
54. Gonyea, E. F.: The spectrum of primary blastomycotic meningitis: A review of central nervous system blastomycosis. Ann. Neurol. *3*:26–39, 1978.
55. Gordon, M. A., Holzman, R. S., Senter, H., et al.: *Aspergillus oryzae* meningitis. J. A. M. A. *235*:2122–2123, 1976.
56. Grant, S. M., and Clissold, S. P.: Itraconazole: A review of its pharmacodynamic and pharmacokinetic properties and therapeutic use in superficial and systemic mycoses. Drugs *37*:310–344, 1989.
57. Graybill, J. R.: Future directions of antifungal chemotherapy. Clin. Infect. Dis. *14* (Suppl. 1):S170–S181, 1992.
58. Hale, L. M.: Orbital-cerebral phycomycosis: Report of a case and a review of the disease in infants. Arch. Ophthalmol. *86*:39–43, 1971.
59. Hamner, R. W., Baum, E. W., and Pritchett, P. S.: Coccidioidal meningitis diagnosed by skin biopsy. Cutis. *29*:603–610, 1982.
60. Harley, W. B., Lomis, M., and Haas, D. W.: Marked polymorphonuclear pleocytosis due to blastomycotic meningitis: Case report and review. Clin. Infect. Dis. *18*:816–818, 1994.
61. Harrison, H. R., Galgiani, J. N., Reynolds, A. F., Jr., et al.: Amphotericin B and imidazole therapy for coccidioidal meningitis in children. Pediatr. Infect. Dis. *2*:216–221, 1983.
62. Hay, R. J., Mackenzie, D. W. R., Campbell, C. K., et al.: Cryptococcosis in the United Kingdom and the Irish Republic: An analysis of 69 cases. J. Infect. *2*:13–22, 1980.
63. Heidemann, H. T., Gerkens, J. F., Spickard, W. A., et al.: Amphotericin B nephrotoxicity in humans decreased by salt repletion. Am. J. Med. *75*:476–481, 1983.
64. Huttova, M., Hartmanova, I., Kralinsky, K., et al.: *Candida* fungemia in neonates treated with fluconazole: Report of forty cases, including eight with meningitis. Pediatr. Infect. Dis. J. *17*:1012–1015, 1998.
65. Huttova, M., Kralinsky, K., Horn, J., et al.: Prospective study of nosocomial fungal meningitis in children—Report of 10 cases. Scand. J. Infect. Dis. *30*:485–487, 1998.
66. Imperato, P. J., Buckley, C. E., and Callaway, J. L.: *Candida* granuloma. Arch. Dermatol. *97*:139–146, 1968.
67. Isaacs, D., Barfield, C. P., Grimwood, K., et al.: Systemic bacterial and fungal infections in infants in Australian neonatal units: Australian Study Group for Neonatal Infections. Med. J. Aust. *162*:198–201, 1995.
68. Isaacson, C., and Levin, S. E.: Gastrointestinal mucormycosis in infancy. S. Afr. Med. J. *35*:581–584, 1961.

69. Jafari, H. S., Saez-Llorens, X., Grimprel, E., et al.: Characteristics of experimental *Candida albicans* infection of the central nervous system in rabbits. J. Infect. Dis. *164*:389–395, 1991.
70. Johnson, D. E., Thompson, T. R., Green, T. P., et al.: Systemic candidiasis in very low-birth-weight infants (<1500 grams). Pediatrics *73*:138–143, 1984.
71. Johnson P., Wheat, L. J., Cloud, G., et al.: A multicenter randomized trial comparing amphotericin B (AmB) and liposomal amphotericin B (AmBisome, LAmB) as induction therapy of disseminated histoplasmosis (DH) in AIDS patients. Abstract L40e. Proceedings of the 7th Conference on Retroviruses and Opportunistic Infections, San Francisco, 30 January–2 February 2000. San Francisco, Foundation for Retrovirology and Human Health, 2000.
72. Kafka, J. A., and Catanzaro, A.: Disseminated coccidioidomycosis in children. J. Pediatr. *98*:355–361, 1981.
73. Kaminski, Z. C., Kapila, R., Sharer, L. R., et al.: Meningitis due to *Prototheca wickerhamii* in a patient with AIDS. Clin. Infect. Dis. *15*:704–706, 1992.
74. Kaneko, T., Abe, F., Ito, M., et al.: Intestinal mucormycosis in a hemodialysis patient treated with desferrioxamine. Acta. Pathol. Jpn. *41*:561–566, 1991.
75. Karalakulasingam, R., Arora, K. K., and Adams, G.: Meningoencephalitis caused by *Histoplasma capsulatum*: Occurrence in a renal transplant and review of the literature. Arch. Intern. Med. *136*:217–220, 1976.
76. Kauffman, C. A.: Old and new therapies for sporotrichosis. Clin. Infect. Dis. *21*:981–985, 1995.
77. Kelly, P. C.: Coccidioidal meningitis. *In* Stevens, D. A. (ed.): Coccidioidomycosis: A Text. New York, Plenum Medical Book Co., 1980, pp. 163–194.
78. Klein, B. S., Vergeront, J. M., Weeks, R. J., et al.: Isolation of *Blastomyces dermatitidis* in soil associated with a large outbreak of blastomycosis in Wisconsin. N. Engl. J. Med. *314*:529–534, 1986.
79. Klein, R. C., Ivens, M. S., Seabury, J. H., et al.: Meningitis due to *Sporotrichum schenckii*. Arch. Intern. Med. *118*:145–149, 1966.
80. Kovacs, J. A., Kovacs, A. A., Polis, M., et al.: Cryptococcosis in the acquired immunodeficiency syndrome. Ann. Intern. Med. *103*:533–538, 1985.
81. Kravitz, G. R., Davies, S. F., Eckman, M. R., et al.: Chronic blastomycotic meningitis. Am. J. Med. *71*:501–505, 1981.
82. Kucers, A., and Bennett, N. McK.: Amphotericin B. *In* Kucers, A., and Bennett, N. McK. (eds.): The Use of Antibiotics. 4th ed. Philadelphia, J. B. Lippincott, 1987, pp. 1441–1477.
83. Lammens, M., Robberecht, W., Waer, M., et al.: Purulent meningitis due to aspergillosis in a patient with systemic lupus erythematosus. Clin. Neurol. Neurosurg. *94*:39–43, 1992.
84. Latham, R. H.: *Bipolaris spicifera* meningitis complicating a neurosurgical procedure. Scand. J. Infect. Dis. *32*:102–103, 2000.
85. Lazar, J. D., and Hilligoss, D. M.: The clinical pharmacology of fluconazole. Semin. Oncol. *17*(Suppl. 6):14–18, 1990.
86. Lee, B. E., Feinberg, M., Abraham, J. J., et al.: Congenital malformations in an infant born to a woman treated with fluconazole. Pediatr. Infect. Dis. J. *11*:1062–1064, 1992.
87. Leenders, A. C., Riss, P., Portegies, P., et al: Liposomal amphotericin B (AmBisome) compared with amphotericin B followed by oral fluconazole in the treatment of AIDS-associated cryptococcal meningitis. AIDS. *11*:1463–1471, 1997.
88. Leggiadro, R. J., Barrett, F. F., and Hughes, W. T.: Extrapulmonary cryptococcosis in immunocompromised infants and children. Pediatr. Infect. Dis. J. *11*:43–47, 1992.
89. Leggiadro, R. J., Kline, M. W., and Hughes, W. T.: Extrapulmonary cryptococcosis in children with acquired immunodeficiency syndrome. Pediatr. Infect. Dis. J. *10*:658–662, 1991.
90. Leibovitz, E., Rigaud, M., Chandwani, S., et al.: Disseminated fungal infections in children infected with human immunodeficiency virus. Pediatr. Infect. Dis. J. *10*:888–894, 1991.
91. LeMonte, A. M., Washum, K. E., Smedema, M. L., et al.: Amphotericin B combined with itraconazole or fluconazole for treatment of histoplasmosis. J. Infect. Dis. *182*:545–550, 2000.
92. Lesser, R. L., Simon, R. M., Leon, H., et al.: Cryptococcal meningitis and internal ophthalmoplegia. Am. J. Ophthalmol. *87*:682–687, 1979.
93. Littman, M. L., and Walter, J. E.: Cryptococcosis: Current status. Am. J. Med. *45*:922–932, 1968.
94. Louria, D. B., Feder, N., Mitchell, W., et al.: Influence of fungus strain and lapse on time in experimental histoplasmosis and of volume of inoculum in cryptococcosis upon recovery of the fungi. J. Lab. Clin. Med. *53*:311–317, 1959.
95. Ludviksson, B. R., Thorarensen, O., Gudnason, T., et al.: *Candida albicans* meningitis in a child with myeloperoxidase deficiency. Pediatr. Infect. Dis. J. *12*:162–164, 1993.
96. Luke, J. L., Bolande, R. P., and Gross, S.: Generalized aspergillosis and *Aspergillus endocarditis* in infancy. Pediatrics. *31*:115–122, 1963.
97. MacGregor, R. R., Bennett, J. E., and Erslev, A. J.: Erythropoietin concentration in amphotericin B–induced anemia. Antimicrob. Agents Chemother. *14*:270–273, 1978.
98. Marinova, I., Szabadosova, V., Brandeburova, O., et al.: *Rhodotorula* spp. fungemia in an immunocompromised boy after neurosurgery successfully treated with miconazole and 5-flucytosine: Case report and review of the literature. Chemotherapy *40*:287–289, 1994.
99. Marr, B., Gross, S., Cunningham, C., Weiner, L. Candidal sepsis and meningitis in a very-low-birth-weight infant successfully treated with fluconazole and flucytosine. Clin. Infect. Dis. *19*:795–796, 1994.
100. McDonald, R., Greenberg, E. N., and Kramer, R.: Cryptococcal meningitis. Arch. Dis. Child. *45*:417–420, 1970.
101. McGinnis, M. R.: Detection of fungi in cerebrospinal fluid. Am. J. Med. *75*:129–138, 1983.
102. McManus, E. J., and Jones, J. M.: Detection of a *Trichosporon beigelii* antigen cross-reactive with *Cryptococcus neoformans* capsular polysaccharide in serum from a patient with disseminated *Trichosporon* infection. J. Clin. Microbiol. *21*:681–685, 1985.
103. Miaux, Y., Ribaud, P., Williams, M, et al.: MR of cerebral aspergillosis in patients who have had bone marrow transplantation. AJNR Am. J. Neuroradiol. *16*:555–562, 1995.
104. Mikolich, D. J., Kinsella, L. J., Skowron, G., et al.: *Aspergillus* meningitis in an immunocompetent adult successfully treated with itraconazole. Clin. Infect. Dis. *23*:1318–1319, 1996.
105. Morrow, R., Wong, B., Finkelstein, W. E., et al.: Aspergillosis of the cerebral ventricles in a heroin abuser: Case report and review of the literature. Arch. Intern. Med. *143*:161–164, 1983.
106. Morse, H. G., Nichol, W. P., Cook, D. M., et al.: Central nervous system and genitourinary blastomycosis: Confusion with tuberculosis. West. J. Med. *139*:99–103, 1983.
107. Morwood, D. T., Nichter, L. S., and Wong, V.: An unusual complication of an open-head injury: Coccidioidal meningitis. Ann. Plast. Surg. *23*:437–441, 1989.
108. Namdar, R., Anderson, J. D., and Kline, S. S.: Abelcet, Amphotec, and AmBisome in the neonatal and pediatric populations: A literature review. J. Pediatr. Pharm. Pract. *3*:13–28, 1998.
109. Nicholas, S. W., Dondheimer, D. L., Willoughby, A. D., et al.: Human immunodeficiency virus infection in childhood, adolescence, and pregnancy: A status report and national research agenda. Pediatrics *83*:293–308, 1989.
110. Nosanchuk, J. D., Shoham, S., Fries, B. C., et al.: Evidence of zoonotic transmission of *Cryptococcus neoformans* from a pet cockatoo to an immunocompromised adult. Ann. Intern. Med. *132*:205–208, 2000.
111. Palaoglu, S., Sav, A., Basak, T., et al.: Cerebral phaeohyphomycosis. Neurosurgery *33*:894–897, 1993.
112. Papadatos, C., Pavatou, M., and Alexiou, D.: *Cephalosporium* meningitis. Pediatrics *44*:749–751, 1969.
113. Pappagianis, D: Epidemiology of coccidioidomycosis. *In* Stevens D. A. (ed.): Coccidioidomycosis: A Text. New York, Plenum Medical, 1980, p. 63.
114. Pappagianis, D., and Crane, R.: Survival in coccidioidal meningitis since introduction of amphotericin B. *In* Ajello, L. (ed.): Coccidioidomycosis: Current Clinical and Diagnostic Status. Miami, Symposia Specialists Medical Books, 1977, pp. 223–237.
115. Pappas, P. G., Pottage, J. C., Powderly, W. G., et al.: Blastomycosis in patients with the acquired immunodeficiency syndrome. Ann. Intern. Med. *116*:847–853, 1992.
116. Parker, J. D., Doto, I. L., and Tosh, F. E.: A decade of experience with blastomycosis and its treatment with amphotericin B. Am. Rev. Respir. Dis. *99*:895–902, 1969.
117. Parsons, R. J., and Zarafonetis, C. J. D.: Histoplasmosis in man: Report of seven cases and a review of seventy-one cases. Arch. Intern. Med. *75*:1–23, 1945.
118. Penn, C. C., Goldstein, E., and Bartholomew, M. R.: *Sporothrix schenckii* meningitis in a patient with AIDS. Clin. Infect. Dis. *15*:741–743, 1992.
119. Pereira, W. C., Tenuto, R. A., Raphael, A., et al.: Localizacaco encefalica da blastomicose Sul-Americana. Arq. Neuro-Psiquiat. (Sao Paulo). *23*:113–126, 1965.
120. Perez, J. A., Jr., Johnson, R. A., Caldwell, J. W., et al.: Fluconazole therapy in coccidioidal meningitis maintained with intrathecal amphotericin B. Arch. Intern. Med. *155*:1665–1668, 1995.
121. Pore, R. S., and Chen, J.: Meningitis caused by *Rhodotorula*. Sabouraudia. *14*:331–335, 1976.
122. Rapaport, S. I., Ames, S. B., and Duvall, B. J.: A plasma coagulation defect in systemic lupus erythematosus arising from hypoprothrombinemia combined with antiprothrombinase activity. Blood. *15*:212–227, 1960.
123. Rex, J. H., Ginsberg, A. M., Fries, L. F., et al.: *Cunninghamella bertholetiae* infection associated with deferoxamine therapy. Rev. Infect. Dis. *10*:1187–1194, 1988.
124. Rex, J. H., Pfaller, M. A., Galgiani, J. N., et al.: Development of interpretative breakpoints for antifungal susceptibility testing: Conceptual framework and analysis of in vitro–in vivo correlation data for fluconazole, itraconazole, and *Candida* infections. Clin. Infect. Dis. *24*:235–247, 1997.
125. Rogers, M. F., Thomas, P. A., Starcher, E. T., et al.: Acquired immunodeficiency syndrome in children: Report of the Centers for Disease Control national surveillance, 1982–1985. Pediatrics *79*:1008–1014, 1987.
126. Ross, K. L., Bryan, J. P., Maggio, W. W., et al.: Intracranial blastomycoma. Medicine (Baltimore). *66*:224–235, 1987.

127. Rotz, L. D., Slater, L. N., Wack, M. F., et al.: Disseminated sporotrichosis with meningitis in a patient with AIDS. Infect. Dis. Clin. Pract. *5*:566–568, 1996.
128. Ruggierei, M., Polizzi, A., Vitaliti, M. C., et al.: Fatal biphasic brainstem and spinal leptomeningitis with Cryptococcus neoformans in a non-immunocompromised child. Acta Paediatr. *88*:671–674, 1999.
129. Saag, M. S., Graybill, R. J., Larsen, R. A., et al.: Practice guidelines for the management of cryptococcal disease. Clin. Infect. Dis. *30*:710–718, 2000.
130. Salaki, J. S., Louria, D. B., and Chmel, H.: Fungal and yeast infections of the central nervous system: A clinical review. Medicine (Baltimore), *63*:108–132, 1984.
131. Sarma, P. S., Durairaj, P., and Padhye, A. A.: *Candida lusitaniae* causing fatal meningitis. Postgrad. Med. J. *69*:878–880, 1993.
132. Scarcella, A., Pasquariello, M. B., Guigliano, B., et al: Liposomal amphotericin B treatment for neonatal fungal infections. Pediatr. Infect. Dis. J. *17*:146–148, 1998.
133. Schutze, G. E., Hickerson, S. L., Fortin, E. M., et al.: Blastomycosis in children. Clin. Infect. Dis. *22*:496–502, 1996.
134. Schutze, G. E., Tucker, N. C., and Jacobs, R. F.: Histoplasmosis and perinatal human immunodeficiency virus. Pediatr. Infect. Dis. J. *11*:501–502, 1992.
135. Scott, E. N., Kaufman, L., Brown, A. C., et al.: Serologic studies in the diagnosis and management of meningitis due to *Sporothrix schenckii*. N. Engl. J. Med. *317*:935–940, 1987.
136. Sekshon, A. S., Borgorus, M. S., and Sims, H. V.: Blastomycosis: Report of three cases from Alberta with a review of Canadian cases. Mycopathologia *1*:53–63, 1979.
137. Selik, R., Starcher, E., and Curran J.: Opportunistic diseases reported in AIDS patients: Frequencies, associations, and trends. AIDS. *1*:175–182, 1987.
138. Shehab, Z. M., Britton, H., and Dunn, J. H.: Imidazole therapy of coccidioidal meningitis in children. Pediatr. Infect. Dis. J. 7:40–44, 1988.
139. Shimosaka, S., and Waga, S.: Cerebral chromoblastomycosis complicated by meningitis and multiple fungal aneurysms after resection of a granuloma: Case report. J. Neurosurg. *59*:158–161, 1983.
140. Shoemaker, E. H., Bennett, H. D., Fields, W. S., et al.: Leptomeningitis due to *Sporotrichum schenckii*. Arch. Pathol. *64*:222, 1957.
141. Siewers, C. M. F., and Cramblett, H. G.: Cryptococcosis (torulosis) in children: A report of four cases. Pediatrics *34*:393–400, 1964.
142. Smego, R. A., Perfect, J. R., and Durack, D. T.: Combined therapy with amphotericin B and 5-fluorocytosine for *Candida* meningitis. Rev. Infect. Dis. *6*:791–801, 1984.
143. Smith, C. E., Saito, M. T., and Simons, S. A.: Pattern of 39,500 serologic tests in coccidioidomycosis. J. A. M. A. *160*:546–552, 1956.
144. Starke, J. R., Mason, E. O., Jr., Kramer, W. G., et al.: Pharmacokinetics of amphotericin B in infants and children. J. Infect. Dis. *155*:766–774, 1987.
145. Steele, R. W., and Abernathy, R. S.: Systemic blastomycosis in children. Pediatr. Infect. Dis. J. *2*:304–307, 1983.
146. Stevens, D.: *Coccidioides immitis. In* Mandell, G. L., Bennett, J. E., and Dolin, R. (eds.): Principles and Practice of Infectious Diseases. 4th ed. New York, Churchill Livingstone, 1995, pp. 2365–2375.
147. Stone, B. D., and Wheeler, J. G.: Disseminated cryptococcal infection in a patient with hyperimmunoglobulinemia E syndrome. J. Pediatr. *117*:92–95, 1990.
148. Takeda, K., Oritsu, M., and Sakuta, M.: A case of coccidioidomycosis with central nervous system involvement. Rinsho Shinkeigaku. *33*:1184–1187, 1993.
149. Taylor, G. D., Boettger, D. W., Miedzinski, L. J., et al.: Coccidioidal meningitis acquired during holidays in Arizona. Can. Med. Assoc. J. *142*:1388–1390, 1990.
150. Taylor, G. D., Buchanan-Chell, M., Kirkland, T., et al.: Trends and sources of nosocomial fungaemia. Mycoses *37*:187–190, 1994.
151. Tiraboschi, I., Parera, I. C., Pikielny, R., et al.: Chronic *Histoplasma capsulatum* infection of the central nervous system successfully treated with fluconazole. Eur. Neurol. *32*:70–73, 1992.
152. Tjia, T. L., Yeow, Y. K., and Tan, C. B.: Cryptococcal meningitis. J. Neurol. Neurosurg. Psychiatry *48*:853–858, 1985.
153. Townsend, T. E., and McKay, R. W.: Coccidioidomycosis in infants. Am. J. Dis. Child. *86*:51–53, 1953.
154. Tucker, R. M., Denning, D. W., Dupont, B., et al.: Itraconazole therapy for chronic coccidioidal meningitis. Ann. Intern. Med. *112*:108–112, 1990.
155. Tucker, R. M., Galgiani, J. N., Denning, D. W., et al.: Treatment of coccidioidal meningitis with fluconazole. Rev. Infect. Dis. *12*(Suppl. 3):S390–S399, 1990.
156. Tucker, R. M., Williams, P. L., Arathoon, E. G., et al.: Treatment of mycoses with itraconazole. Ann. N. Y. Acad. Sci. *544*:451–470, 1988.
157. Tynes, B. S., Crutcher, J. C., and Utz, J. P.: Histoplasma meningitis. Ann. Intern. Med. *59*:615–621, 1963.
158. Tynes, B. S., Utz, J. P, Bennett, J. E., et al.: Reducing amphotericin B reactions: A double-blind study. Am. Rev. Respir. Dis. *87*:264–268, 1963.
159. Utz, J. P., Garriques, I. L., Sande, M. A., et al: Therapy of cryptococcosis with a combination of flucytosine and amphotericin B. J. Infect. Dis. *132*:368–373, 1975.
160. Van de Wyngaert, F. A., Sindic, C. J., Rousseau, J. J., et al.: Spinal arachnoiditis due to *Aspergillus meningitis* in a previously healthy patient. J. Neurol. *233*:41–43, 1986.
161. van Landeghem, F. K., Stiller, B., Lehmann, T. N., et al.: Aqueductal stenosis and hydrocephalus in an infant due to aspergillus infection. Clin. Neuropathol. *19*:26–29, 2000.
162. Van Peer, A., Woestenborghs, R., Heykants, J., et al.: The effects of food and dose on the oral systemic availability of itraconazole in healthy subjects. Eur J. Clin. Pharmacol. *36*:423–426, 1989.
163. Van't Wout, J. W., DeGraeff-Meeder, E. R., Paul, L. C., et al.: Treatment of two cases of cryptococcal meningitis with fluconazole. Scand. J. Infect. Dis. *20*:193–198, 1988.
164. Venger, B. H., Landon, G., and Rose, J. E.: Solitary histoplasmoma of the thalamus: Case report and literature review. Neurosurgery *20*:784–787, 1987.
165. Venugopal, P. V., Venugopal, T. V., Thiruneelakantan, D., et al.: Cerebral aspergillosis: Report of two cases. Sabouraudia. *15*:225–230, 1977.
166. Verweij, P. E., Brinkman, K., Kremer, H. P. H., et al.: *Aspergillus* meningitis: Diagnosis by nonculture-based microbiological methods and management. J. Clin. Microbiol. *37*:1186–1189, 1999.
167. Walsh, T. J.: Fungal infections complicating pediatric HIV infection. *In* Pizzo, P. A., and Wilfert, C. M. (eds.): Pediatric AIDS: The Challenge of HIV Infection in Infants, Children, and Adolescents. 2nd ed. Baltimore, Williams & Wilkins, 1994, pp. 321–343.
168. Wanger, A., Mills, K., Nelson, P. W., and Rex, J. H.: Comparison of Etest and National Committee for Clinical Laboratory Standards broth microdilution method for antifungal susceptibility testing: Enhanced ability to detect amphotericin B–resistant isolates. Antimicrob. Agents. Chemother. *39*:2520–2522, 1995.
169. Wheat, L. J., Batteiger, B. E., and Sathapatayavongs, B.: *Histoplasma capsulatum* infections of the central nervous system: A clinical review. Medicine (Baltimore). *69*:244–260, 1990.
170. Wheat, L. J., Connolly-Stringfield, P. A., Baker, R. L., et al.: Disseminated histoplasmosis in the acquired immune deficiency syndrome: Clinical findings, diagnosis and treatment and review of the literature. Medicine (Baltimore). *69*:361–374, 1990.
171. Wheat, J., Sarosi, G., McKinsey, D., et al.: Practice guidelines for the management of patients with histoplasmosis. Clin. Infect. Dis. *30*:688–695, 2000.
172. Windus, D. W., Stokes, J. J., Julian, B. A., et al.: Fatal *Rhizopus* infections in hemodialysis patients receiving deferoxamine. Ann. Intern. Med. *107*:678–680, 1987.
173. Young, R. C., Bennett, J. E., Vogel C. L., et al. Aspergillosis: The spectrum of the disease in 98 patients. Medicine (Baltimore). *49*: 147–173, 1970.
174. Zealear, D. S., and Winn, W. A.: The neurosurgical approach in the treatment of coccidioidal meningitis: Report of ten cases. *In* Ajello, L. (ed.): Coccidioidomycosis. Tucson, AZ, University of Arizona Press, 1967, pp. 43–53.
175. Zuger, A., Louie, E., Holzman, R. S., et al.: Cryptococcal disease in patients with the acquired immunodeficiency syndrome: Diagnostic features and outcome of treatment. Ann. Intern. Med. *104*:234–240, 1986.

CHAPTER 41

Eosinophilic Meningitis

BARBARA W. STECHENBERG

Eosinophilic meningitis may include any meningitis, infectious or noninfectious, in which one finds a cerebrospinal fluid pleocytosis with a significant percentage of eosinophils. Such a finding strongly suggests invasion of the central nervous system (CNS) by a helminthic parasite. In the last 20 years, the term *eosinophilic meningitis* has been applied more specifically to a typical form of meningitis caused by *Angiostrongylus cantonensis* (Chen), a rat lungworm found primarily in the Pacific Islands and Southeast Asia.

The first documented case of eosinophilic meningitis was reported from Taiwan in 1945.[1] The patient was a 15-year-old boy who developed severe headache and vomiting. Examination of the cerebrospinal fluid (CSF) revealed 528 leukocytes, of which 50 percent were eosinophils. Ten actively moving nematodes also were recovered from the specimen. Since the early 1960s, many new cases have been reported, with particularly large numbers from Thailand,[19, 20] Tahiti,[24] Taiwan,[35] and Hawaii.[10]

Etiologic Agents

The organism that presumably is involved in most cases is the rodent lungworm. *A. cantonensis,* which as an adult is 17 to 25 mm long and 0.25 to 0.36 mm at its maximum width, has a smooth cuticle and three minute lips at the cephalic end. The male has a copulatory bursa supported by bursal rays.

In its life cycle, rodents such as *Rattus rattus* are the principal hosts. These rodents ingest mollusks containing third-stage larvae, which travel from the liver and lung into the general circulation. The larvae selectively leave the circulation to enter the CNS within the first 48 hours. There they develop into young adults in approximately 2 weeks.[32] From the brain, they travel to the pulmonary arteries, where their eggs are laid. The eggs hatch in the pulmonary capillaries; the first-stage forms then travel from the alveolar spaces up the rat trachea to the gastrointestinal tract, from which they are eliminated in the feces. The larvae can survive for approximately 2 weeks under humid conditions. The third-stage larvae develop in the intermediate hosts in about 2 weeks.

Another form of eosinophilic meningitis has been attributed to the nematode *Gnathostoma spinigerum.* The adult *G. spinigerum* is stout and reddish and has a globose cephalic bulb that is separated from the body by a slight constriction. The head and anterior part of the body have spines. Males and females may be 11 to 25 mm and 25 to 54 mm in length, respectively. The adults lie coiled in lesions along the alimentary canal, from which they release eggs into the feces, where they become embryonated. The eggs hatch on reaching water, releasing a larva that is ingested by a copepod *(Cyclops)* and continues to develop. When the infected copepod is eaten by a fish, frog, snake, or bird, a third-stage larva develops and becomes encapsulated in the intermediate host. When it is ingested by the definitive host (cats, dogs, hogs, mink, humans), the parasite localizes in the stomach wall.[25]

Epidemiology

The geographic distribution of eosinophilic meningitis depends on the distribution of *A. cantonensis.* A large number of cases have been reported from Taiwan and Thailand. Other areas include Vietnam, the Society Islands (especially Tahiti), Hawaii, the Marshall Islands, and Ponape. Rodents infected with the worm have been documented in other areas of the Pacific Islands and Asia. Disease has been reported from Cuba, Egypt, and many other countries. As infected rodents are carried to other countries on cargo ships, spread of these organisms will continue to increase. Two cases have been diagnosed in the continental United States in travelers from endemic regions.[6, 15] An outbreak was described in 12 of 23 young adults who had traveled together to Jamaica.[28]

The seasonal incidence of the disease varies in different areas, but the months of highest prevalence usually correspond with the more humid periods in each country.

Patients with eosinophilic meningitis have eaten terrestrial snails, slugs, fish, or freshwater shrimp, all of which can serve as intermediate hosts for the parasites.[29–31] In Thailand, the most common source is the *Pila* snails, which are eaten raw or pickled.[17] They may be served as an appetizer with alcoholic beverages, which may explain, in part, the increased incidence of the disease in males.[19] The giant African snail *Achatina fulica* is found commonly in Taiwan and may carry thousands of roundworm larvae, thus explaining the higher incidence of recovery of organisms from the patients on Taiwan.[31] The larvae also may remain infective in water for about 60 hours. Cases have been associated with the ingestion of leafy vegetables, presumed to be contaminated by slugs or snails.[10]

The distribution of disease among age groups is variable. In Thailand, most of the cases occur in the third to fourth decade of life, but in Taiwan and Hawaii, most cases occur in children younger than 15 years.[19, 35] Although eosinophilic meningitis rarely occurs in very young children, one report documented disease in five children younger than 2 years.[27]

Pathogenesis

The pathogenesis of this disease in humans has not been studied rigorously but is presumed to parallel that in the rodent host. The larvae are ingested, make their way into the general circulation, and selectively enter the CNS. The number of nematodes found on autopsy specimens has been varied. In a Taiwanese 5-year-old girl, 150 nematodes were found on the surface of the cerebrum and cerebellum and in the subarachnoid spaces, and more than 500 were recovered from the normal saline in which the spinal cord and meninges were placed. *A. cantonensis* also were found in the pulmonary arteries.[35]

Pathologic specimens have demonstrated a leptomeningitis in which plasma cells and eosinophils predominate. Tortuous tracks of variable size in the brain and spinal cord parenchyma surrounded by variable reaction and degenerating neurons may be present. Granuloma may form around dead *A. cantonensis*.[16, 23]

Hemorrhagic, necrotic tracks caused by the organisms have been associated more commonly with *G. spinigerum* infection,[4] but even *Angiostrongylus* is capable of causing a vascular reaction, including thrombosis and rupture of vessels and arteritis, leading to formation of an aneurysm.[16] The tracks caused by *G. spinigerum* may be larger and more necrotic.

Clinical Manifestations

On the basis of information obtained from patients with a history of ingestion of the intermediate hosts, the incubation period is between 7 and 30 days. Most patients with typical eosinophilic meningitis have an abrupt onset of their disease; a more insidious onset may be noted in 20 percent of cases. Headache is the most common and distressing symptom. It usually is intermittent but is frequent and severe. Other common symptoms are nausea, vomiting (often projectile), intermittent somnolence, malaise, anorexia, constipation, and fever with temperatures usually reaching a maximum of 38° C to 39° C in the early phase of the disease, although many patients have no documented fever. Nuchal rigidity is seen more commonly in the older patients, often in association with severe headache. Paresthesias occur in a large variety of locations and are expressed as pain, numbness, itching, or a sense of worms crawling on the skin. Some patients also note diplopia with or without strabismus. Convulsions are unusual occurrences.

The findings on physical examination are normal in half the patients. Physical findings may include mild hepatomegaly, mild changes in deep tendon reflexes (usually decreased), nuchal rigidity, absent abdominal wall reflexes, and, less commonly, ophthalmoplegia or facial paralysis. Twelve percent of Thai patients had abnormal ophthalmoscopic examinations.[9]

Examination of the CSF reveals grossly turbid or opalescent fluid in most patients, with leukocyte counts usually between 100 and 5000/mm^3. All counts usually reach their maximum in the first 3 weeks of disease, dropping sharply thereafter. In general, the percentage of eosinophils in the CSF is high, often greater than 50 percent. Fluids with higher cell counts tend to have a higher percentage of eosinophils.[20, 35] The proportion of eosinophils may decrease after the first 4 weeks. CSF protein concentration is moderately high (often 50 to 200 mg/dL), but the glucose concentration usually is normal.

Peripheral white blood cell count is variable, but the differential cell count often shows striking eosinophilia. Examination of the feces may reveal concurrent infestation with other parasites, such as *Ascaris* or *Trichuris*.

The clinical manifestations of the eosinophilic radiculomyeloencephalitis thought to be associated with *G. spinigerum* overlap to some degree with those of typical eosinophilic meningitis. Headache is less prominent, however. Many of the patients report sharp, shooting pains of the trunk or limbs, flaccid paralyses, and impairment of superficial sensation.[18] Impairment of the sensorium may be sudden in association with cerebral hemorrhage. Grossly bloody spinal fluid is a common finding when myeloencephalitis is present, but it is extremely rare in typical eosinophilic meningitis.

Differential Diagnosis

The diagnosis of eosinophilic meningitis caused by *A. cantonensis* can be made definitively only by isolation of the parasite from the CSF. In regions where the nematodes are endemic, many cases are diagnosed only on the basis of the typical clinical manifestations and the markedly reduced probability of other causes. Serology and intradermal skin testing have been unreliable in the past, although the enzyme-linked immunosorbent assay appears to show more promise for diagnosis.[2]

Other helminths may invade the CNS of humans and may be associated with an eosinophilic pleocytosis.[33] They include *Taenia solium,* the pork tapeworm causing cerebrospinal cysticercosis; *Schistosoma* spp.; *Paragonimus westermani;* and *Echinococcus*. The diseases produced generally have a chronic and intermittent course. Signs of a space-occupying lesion and convulsions are found frequently. Visceral myiasis with invasion of the CNS by botfly larvae may cause CSF eosinophilia.[3] Several cases of eosinophilic meningitis associated with the raccoon ascarid *Baylisascaris procyonis* have been reported in children.[7, 8] The larvae of *Trichinella spiralis* and *Toxocara canis* can invade the CNS, but pleocytosis appears to be an unusual occurrence[3, 35]; the evidence for an association of eosinophilic meningitis with these parasites often is circumstantial.[11]

Neurosyphilis and tuberculous meningitis rarely have been associated with eosinophils in the CSF, as have several malignant neoplasms, particularly lymphomas, involving the CNS.[11, 14] Other known causes of significant eosinophilic pleocytosis include intrathecal injection of various foreign proteins, rabies vaccination, the insertion of rubber tubing into the CNS during neurosurgery, lymphocytic choriomeningitis,[11] coccidioidomycosis,[22, 26] and Rocky Mountain spotted fever.[5] Eosinophilic pleocytosis has been documented in infants with congenital toxoplasmosis and late-onset group B streptococcal meningitis.[13, 34] Eosinophilia in the CSF indicating hypersensitivity has been difficult to document, although one case report described the association of eosinophilic meningitis and ibuprofen therapy.[21] A study documented more than 5 percent eosinophils in the ventricular fluid of patients with shunt pathology, particularly malfunction.[12]

Treatment

In a study in Thailand in which the disappearance of headache was used as the criterion for improvement, no significant differences were noted among groups when 284 patients were treated with analgesics alone, 96 patients were treated with analgesics and steroids (30 to 60 mg of prednisone daily for 5 days), and 56 patients were treated with analgesics and antibiotics (penicillin or tetracycline).[15] A recent study that compared adult patients given a 2-week course of prednisolone (60 mg/day) with persons treated with a placebo showed a significant decrease in the number of patients with headache and in the duration of headache in the prednisolone-treated group.[4a] Treatment with thiabendazole also has been tried without significant benefit.

Course and Prognosis

In most patients, eosinophilic meningitis is a self-limited disease characterized by repeated attacks of severe headache, vomiting, intermittent fever, and somnolence. Many patients experience a dramatic improvement soon after undergoing a lumbar puncture, so repeated lumbar punctures may be performed at weekly intervals to relieve the headache. In the majority of patients, most symptoms disappear within 4 weeks of onset, often within a few days after the first lumbar puncture is performed, leaving no sequelae. The mortality rate in large series from Thailand and Taiwan has been less than 5 percent; the incidence of permanent sequelae also has been less than 5 percent for *Angiostrongylus* infection.[20, 34] The mortality in gnathostomiasis is higher, ranging from 7.7 to 25 percent.[25] No evidence that immunity develops after recovery from infection exists; many recurrences have been reported.[20, 24, 35]

Prevention

Prevention of the disease can be effected only by rodent control and proper cooking of mollusks, shrimp, fish, and other intermediate hosts. Careful washing of fruits and vegetables that may be contaminated by rodent feces also is important. The larvae may remain infective in water for as long as 60 hours, so protection of the water supply should be attempted.

REFERENCES

1. Beaver, P. C., and Rosen, L.: Memorandum on the first report of *Angiostrongylus* in man by Nomura and Lin, 1945. Am. J. Trop. Med. Hyg. *13:*589–590, 1964.
2. Bhopale, M. K., Limaye, L. S., Pradhan, V. R., et al.: Studies on suspected clinical and experimental angiostrongyliasis: Serological responses. J. Hyg. Epidemiol. Microbiol. Immunol. *29*:283–288, 1985.
3. Char, D. F. B., and Rosen, L.: Eosinophilic meningitis among children in Hawaii. J. Pediatr. *70:*28–35, 1967.
4. Chitanondh, H., and Rosen, L.: Fatal eosinophilic encephalomyelitis caused by the nematode *Gnathostoma spinigerum.* Am. J. Trop. Med. Hyg. *16:*638–645, 1967.

4a. Chotmongkol, V., Sawanyawisuth, K., and Thavornpirak, Y.: Corticosteroid treatment of eosinophilic meningitis. Clin. Infect. Dis. *31*:660–662, 2000.

5. Crennan, J. M., and VanScoy, R. E.: Eosinophilic meningitis caused by Rocky Mountain spotted fever. Am. J. Med. *80*:288–289, 1986.
6. Fischer, P. R.: Eosinophilic meningitis. West. J. Med. *139*:372–373, 1983.
7. Fox, A. S., Kazacos, K. R., Gould, N. S., et al.: Fatal eosinophilic meningoencephalitis and visceral larva migrans caused by the raccoon ascarid *Baylisascaris procyonis.* N. Engl. J. Med. *312*:1619–1623, 1985.
8. Huff, D. S., Neatie, R. C., Binder, M. J., et al.: Case 4: The first fatal *Baylisascaris* infection in humans: An infant with eosinophilic meningoencephalitis. Pediatr. Pathol. *2*:345–352, 1984.
9. Kanchanaranya, C., and Punyagupta, S.: Case of ocular angiostrongyliasis associated with eosinophilic meningitis. Am. J. Ophthalmol. *71*:931–934, 1971.
10. Koo, J., Pien, F., and Kliks, M. M.: *Angiostrongylus* (parastrongylus) eosinophilic meningitis. Rev. Infect. Dis. *10*:1155–1162, 1988.
11. Kuberski, T.: Eosinophils in the cerebrospinal fluid. Ann. Intern. Med. *91:*70–75, 1979.
12. McClinton, D., Caraccio, C., and Englander, R.: Predictors of ventriculoperitoneal shunt pathology. Pediatr. Infect. Dis. J. *20*:593–597, 2001.
13. Miron, D., Snelling, L. K., Josephson, S. L., et al.: Eosinophilic meningitis in a newborn with group B streptococcal infection. Pediatr. Infect. Dis. J. *12*:966–967, 1993.
14. Mulligan, M. J., Vasu, R., Grossi, C. E., et al.: Case report: Neoplastic meningitis with eosinophilic pleocytosis in Hodgkin's disease: A case with cerebellar dysfunction and a review of the literature. Am. J. Med. Sci. *296*:322–326, 1988.
15. Noskin, G. A., McMenamin, M. B., and Grohmann, S. M.: Eosinophilic meningitis due to *Angiostrongylus cantonensis.* Neurology *42*:1423–1424, 1992.
16. Nye, S. W., Tangchai, P., and Sundarakiti, S.: Lesion of the brain in eosinophilic meningitis. Arch. Pathol. *89:*9–19, 1970.
17. Punyagupta, S.: Eosinophilic meningoencephalitis in Thailand: Summary of nine cases and observations on *Angiostrongylus cantonensis* as a causative agent and *Pila ampullacea* as a new intermediate host. Am. J. Trop. Med. Hyg. *14:*370–374, 1965.
18. Punyagupta, S., Limtrakul, C., Vichipanthu, P., et al.: Radiculomyeloencephalitis associated with eosinophilic pleocytosis: Report of nine cases. Am. J. Trop. Med. Hyg. *17:*551–560, 1968.
19. Punyagupta, S., Bunnag, T., Juttijudata, P., et al.: Eosinophilic meningitis in Thailand: Epidemiologic studies of 484 typical cases and the etiologic role of *Angiostrongylus cantonensis.* Am. J. Trop. Med. Hyg. *19:*950–958, 1970.
20. Punyagupta, S., Juttijudata, P., and Bunnag, T.: Eosinophilic meningitis in Thailand: Clinical studies of 484 typical cases probably caused by *Angiostrongylus cantonensis.* Am. J. Trop. Med. Hyg. *24:*921–931, 1975.
21. Quinn, J. P., Weinstein, R. A., and Caplan, L. R.: Eosinophilic meningitis and ibuprofen therapy. Neurology *34:*108–109, 1984.
22. Ragland, A. S., Arsura, E., Ismail, Y., et al.: Eosinophilic pleocytosis in coccidioidal meningitis: Frequency and significance. Am. J. Med. *95*:254–256, 1993.
23. Rosen, L., Chappel, R., Laqueur, G. L., et al.: Eosinophilic meningoencephalitis caused by a metastrongylid lungworm of rats. J. A. M. A. *179:*620–624, 1962.
24. Rosen, L., Loison, G., Laigret, J., et al.: Studies on eosinophilic meningitis. 3. Epidemiologic and clinical observations on Pacific Islands and the possible etiologic role of *Angiostrongylus cantonensis.* Am. J. Epidemiol. *85:*17–44, 1967.
25. Rusnak, J. M., and Lucey, D. R.: Clinical gnathostomiasis: Case report and review of the English language literature. Clin. Infect. Dis. *16*:33–50, 1993.
26. Schermoly, M. J., and Hinthorn, D. R.: Eosinophilia in coccidioidomycosis. Arch. Intern. Med. *148*:895–896, 1988.
27. Shih, S.-L., Hsu, C.-H., Huanig, F.-Y., et al.: *Angiostrongylus cantonensis* infection in infants and young children. Pediatr. Infect. Dis. J. *11*:1064–1065, 1992.
28. Slom, T. J., Cortese, M. M., Gerber, S. I., et al.: An outbreak of eosinophilic meningitis caused by *Angiostrongylus cantonensis* in travelers returning from the Caribbean. N. Engl. J. Med. *346*:668–675, 2002.
29. Wallace, G. D., and Rosen, L.: Studies on eosinophilic meningitis. 2. Experimental infection of shrimp and crabs with *Angiostrongylus cantonensis.* Am. J. Epidemiol. *84:*120–131, 1966.
30. Wallace, G. D., and Rosen, L.: Studies on eosinophilic meningitis. 4. Experimental infection of freshwater and marine fish with *Angiostrongylus cantonensis.* Am. J. Epidemiol. *85:*395–402, 1967.
31. Wallace, G. D., and Rosen, L.: Studies on eosinophilic meningitis. V. Molluscan hosts of *Angiostrongylus cantonensis* on Pacific Islands. Am. J. Trop. Med. Hyg. *18:*206–216, 1969.
32. Wallace, G. D., and Rosen, L.: Studies on eosinophilic meningitis. VI. Experimental infection of rats and other homoiothermic vertebrates with *Angiostrongylus cantonensis.* Am. J. Epidemiol. *89:*331–344, 1969.
33. Weller, P. F., Eosinophilic meningitis. Am. J. Med. *95*:250–253, 1993.
34. Woods, C. R., and Englund, J.: Congenital toxoplasmosis presenting with eosinophilic meningitis. Pediatr. Infect. Dis. J. *12*:347–348, 1993.
35. Yii, C.: Clinical observations on eosinophilic meningitis and meningoencephalitis caused by *Angiostrongylus cantonensis* on Taiwan. Am. J. Trop. Med. Hyg. *25:*233–249, 1976.

CHAPTER 42

Aseptic Meningitis and Viral Meningitis

JAMES D. CHERRY ■ KARIN A. NIELSEN

Aseptic meningitis is an inflammatory process of the meninges. It is a relatively common occurrence and is caused by many different etiologic factors. The cerebrospinal fluid (CSF) is characterized by pleocytosis, increased protein, and the absence of microorganisms on Gram stain and on routine culture. Usually, the illnesses are self-limited; with some etiologies, however, the resulting diseases may be severe, protracted, recurrent, or progressive and lead to disability and death.

Serous meningitis, lymphocytic meningitis, and *nonparalytic poliomyelitis* are terms that were used in the past to denote aseptic meningitis. Viral meningitis is an inflammation of the leptomeninges caused by infections with many different viruses. Viruses are the cause of most cases of aseptic meningitis.

History

Aseptic meningitis is a syndrome that first was described by Wallgren in 1925.[194] Wallgren's criteria for this diagnosis included (1) an acute onset with obvious signs and symptoms of meningeal involvement; (2) alteration of CSF typical of meningitis, which may show a small or large number of cells; (3) absence of bacteria in the CSF, as demonstrated by appropriate culture; (4) a relatively short, benign course of illness; (5) absence of local parameningeal infection (e.g., otitis, sinusitis, trauma) or a general disease that might have meningitis as a secondary manifestation; and (6) absence from the community of epidemic disease, of which meningitis is a feature. In 1951, Wallgren[193] redefined aseptic meningitis as a syndrome likely to be encountered in a large number of different infectious diseases.

The clinical occurrence of aseptic meningitis first was recognized in epidemic poliomyelitis and in mumps at the beginning of the 20th century.[65, 198] Rivers and Scott[150] reported the recovery of lymphocytic choriomeningitis (LCM) virus from the CSF of several patients with aseptic meningitis in 1935, and in 1934, Johnson and Goodpasture[98] proved that mumps was caused by a virus.

The discovery of coxsackieviruses in 1948 by Dalldorf and Sickles[51] and the introduction of tissue culture in 1949 by Enders, Weller, and Robbins,[66] which resulted in the discovery of echoviruses, paved the way for the widespread investigation into the etiology of aseptic meningitis.

Rasmussen[145] reported on 374 cases evaluated at the Walter Reed Army Institute of Research laboratory between 1941 and 1946 and found the probable or definite etiology in 26 percent of "viral" disease of the central nervous system (CNS). Mumps and LCM viruses were the two etiologic agents identified in his study.

In 1953, Adair and associates[4] reviewed 480 additional cases of aseptic meningitis occurring in military personnel and their dependents from 1947 through 1952 and were able to confirm the etiology in 25 percent of those patients. Herpes simplex virus (HSV) and *Leptospira* spp. were added to the previously identified mumps and LCM viruses as causes of aseptic meningitis. Meyer and associates[124] extended these studies to include 713 more children and adults with acute CNS syndromes of "viral" etiology admitted to military and Veterans Administration hospitals between 1953 and 1958. Of these 713 patients, 430 had the clinical syndrome of aseptic meningitis. Approximately 80 percent of these patients were hospitalized in the United States. An etiologic diagnosis was determined in 71 percent of patients with aseptic meningitis. In addition to the agents identified earlier, poliovirus, coxsackieviruses of groups A and B, and echoviruses and arthropod-borne viruses were identified as causes of aseptic meningitis. Lepow and colleagues[113, 114] reported the probable viral etiology in 54 percent of the 407 patients they studied in Cleveland between 1955 and 1958. Lennette and associates[112] in 1958 determined a viral etiology in 65 percent of 511 children and adults with presumed viral CNS disease in Los Angeles; 368 of these patients were diagnosed as having aseptic meningitis. Sköldenberg[169] analyzed 3117 patients admitted to the Hospital for Infectious Diseases in Stockholm between 1955 and 1964 with the diagnosis of aseptic meningitis, with or without encephalitis or myelitis, and a virologic or clinical diagnosis (or both) of an associated virus infection was established in 72.6 percent. Berlin and associates[18] performed a surveillance study of aseptic meningitis in pediatric ambulatory clinics and emergency departments of three Baltimore hospitals between July 1986 and December 1990. They identified a single viral agent in 169 (62 percent) of the 274 cases with laboratory study; 168 enteroviruses and 1 adenovirus were identified.

Today, with the use of polymerase chain reaction (PCR), as well as culture and appropriate serologic study, the etiology of most cases of aseptic meningitis can be determined.

Etiology

Etiologic agents and factors in aseptic meningitis are listed in Table 42–1. At present, the diagnostic work-up of aseptic meningitis usually is not undertaken vigorously, and, therefore, the etiologic agent is identified in only approximately 10 percent of all cases. However, epidemiologic study and intensive investigations at some centers indicate that most cases result from viral infections. Enteroviruses account for approximately 85 percent of all cases of aseptic meningitis.[38, 54–56, 130] The following enteroviruses have been associated with aseptic meningitis: polioviruses 1 to 3; coxsackieviruses A 1 to 14, 16 to 18, 21, 22, and 24; coxsackieviruses B 1 to 6; echoviruses 1 to 9, 11 to 27, and 29 to 33; and enterovirus 71. In recent years, multiple outbreaks of aseptic meningitis caused by enteroviruses were described. They included outbreaks caused by echovirus 30 in Romania, Belarus, Australia, Japan, Switzerland, Germany, Turkey, and the Arabian Gulf.[7, 42, 81, 100, 105, 148, 164, 188, 189] Echovirus 13 was responsible for reported outbreaks of aseptic meningitis in the United States and Germany.[30, 59] Enterovirus 71 caused a major epidemic in Taiwan from 1998 to 1999, with multiple cases of hand, foot, and mouth disease associated with aseptic meningitis and other neurologic manifestations.[96, 115, 117] Similar

TABLE 42–1 ■ ETIOLOGIC AGENTS, FACTORS, AND DISEASES ASSOCIATED WITH ASEPTIC MENINGITIS

Viruses
Enteroviruses (echoviruses, coxsackieviruses A and B, polioviruses, and enteroviruses)
Arboviruses (in the United States: Eastern equine, Western equine, Venezuelan equine, West Nile, St. Louis, Powassan, California, Colorado tick fever. In other areas of the world, many other arboviruses are important.)
Mumps
Herpes simplex type 2
Human herpesvirus type 6
HIV-1
Adenoviruses
Varicella-zoster
Epstein-Barr
Lymphocytic choriomeningitis
Encephalomyocarditis
Cytomegalovirus
Rhinoviruses
Measles
Rubella
Influenza A and B
Parainfluenza
Hendra; Nipah
Parvovirus B19
Rotaviruses
Coronaviruses
Variola

Postvaccine
Measles
Vaccinia
Polio
Rabies

Bacteria
Mycobacterium tuberculosis
Atypical mycobacterias
Pyogenic—partially treated
Leptospira species (leptospirosis)
Treponema pallidum (syphilis)
Borrelia species (relapsing fever)
Borrelia burgdorferi (Lyme disease)
Nocardia species (noncardiosis)
Bartonella henselae
Brucella species

Fungi
Blastomyces dermatitidis
Coccidioides immitis
Cryptococcus neoformans
Histoplasma capsulatum
Candida species
Other: *Alternaria* species, *Aspergillus* species, *Cephalosporium* species, *Cladosporium trichoides, Dreschslera hawaiiensis, Paracoccidioides brasiliensis, Petriellidium boydii, Sporotrichum schenckii, Ustilago* species, *Zygomycete* species

Chlamydia
Chlamydia psittaci
Chlamydia pneumoniae

Rickettsia
Rickettsia rickettsii (Rocky Mountain spotted fever)
Rickettsia prowazekii (typhus)
Coxiella burnetii
Ehrlichia canis

Mycoplasma
Mycoplasma pneumoniae
Mycoplasma hominis

Parasites (eosinophilic meningitis)
Roundworms: *Angiostrongylus cantonensis, Gnathostoma spinigerum, Baylisascaris procyonis, Strongyloides stercoralis, Trichinella spiralis, Toxocara canis*
Tapeworms: Cysticercosis
Flukes: *Paragonimus westermani*, schistosomiasis, fascioliasis

Parasites (noneosinophilic meningitis)
Toxoplasma gondii (toxoplasmosis)
Naegleria fowleri
Acanthamoeba

Parameningeal Infections

Malignancy
Leukemia
Central nervous system tumor

Immune Diseases
Behçet syndrome
Lupus erythematosus
Sarcoidosis

Miscellaneous
Kawasaki disease
Heavy metal poisoning
Intrathecal injections (contrast media, antibiotics, etc.)
Foreign bodies (shunt, reservoir)
Antimicrobial agents
Other drugs
Epidermoid, dermoid, other cysts

outbreaks of aseptic meningitis caused by enterovirus 71 were reported in Australia and Japan.[123, 166] Echoviruses 4 and 7 also were involved in the Romanian outbreak of aseptic meningitis caused primarily by echovirus 30 in 1999.[32] Outbreaks of aseptic meningitis caused by echovirus 4 were reported in Italy and Israel/Palestine.[88, 142] Echovirus 11 was responsible for an outbreak of aseptic meningitis among institutionalized children in Israel,[173] whereas echovirus 9 was identified as the primary enterovirus serotype in an outbreak in Japan.[6]

A case of aseptic meningitis caused by vaccine-derived poliovirus was reported in the Philippines in 2001.[29] It was in association with two pediatric cases of acute flaccid paralysis during the same time period. Viral isolates from all three patients revealed type 1 polioviruses derived from the Sabin vaccine strain. The most common specific enteroviral types in the vaccine era in the United States are coxsackievirus B5 and echoviruses 4, 6, 9, and 11. In recent years, echovirus 30 has been associated increasingly with cases of aseptic meningitis. Arboviruses account for approximately 5 percent of cases of aseptic meningitis in North America, St. Louis encephalitis virus being the most common.[25, 34, 36, 41] Infection with La Crosse encephalitis virus (a California encephalitis virus subtype) often resembles herpes encephalitis, but it may present as aseptic meningitis in children. In a study of 127 patients, mainly children, hospitalized in the southern United States with La Crosse virus infection, headache, fever, vomiting, and seizures were predominant findings. Thirteen percent of these patients had aseptic meningitis.[122] Tick-borne encephalitis can present as aseptic meningitis in endemic areas. Tick-borne encephalitis virus cases were reported recently in studies conducted in Slovenia and Sweden, and in mild cases, the clinical presentation was that of aseptic meningitis.[84, 118] In the prevaccine era, mumps virus was the agent responsible for the greatest number of cases of aseptic meningitis; today in the United States, use of vaccine has rendered mumps meningitis a rare event.[35]

Aseptic meningitis is an occasional manifestation of acute and recurrent genital infections with HSV-2.[11, 17, 49, 61, 170, 185] In contrast with HSV-1 CNS infections, which without treatment usually are fatal, HSV-2 aseptic meningitis in otherwise immunocompetent patients is a benign, self-limited illness. Adenoviral types 1, 2, 3, 5, 6, 7, 12, 14, and 32 have been associated with meningitis and meningoencephalitis.[18, 47, 54–56, 68, 104, 137, 167, 172] Although they rarely occur, adenoviral CNS infections tend to be more severe than are enteroviral infections. Pleocytosis is noted occasionally in herpes zoster, but neurologic involvement in primary varicella-zoster viral infections usually is an encephalitis rather than a benign meningitis.[54, 143, 147, 197] Echevarria and colleagues[64] detected DNA sequences specific for varicella-zoster virus in the CSF of six patients with acute aseptic meningitis who had no cutaneous lesions. Meningoencephalitis with sequelae in an infant with human herpesvirus type 6 (HHV-6) has been reported.[205] A variety of neurologic disorders, including aseptic meningitis, are rare complications of Epstein-Barr virus infection.[67, 82, 177, 187] A recent report identified HHV-7 in the CSF by PCR in six children with neurologic diseases, including aseptic meningitis, meningoencephalitis, facial palsy, vestibular neuritis, and febrile seizures.[140] The role of HHV-7 as a causative agent in aseptic meningitis remains to be determined.

On occasion, meningitis or meningoencephalitis occurs as a manifestation of acute illness with HIV-1 infection.[12, 87] Neurologic manifestations develop 3 to 6 weeks after primary infection at the same time as an infectious mononucleosis-like illness.

Although LCM virus was an important historical cause of aseptic meningitis, it rarely is recognized today as a cause of meningitis, except in animal-exposure outbreak situations.[13, 14, 19, 57, 124] In 1974, 8 cases of aseptic meningitis caused by LCM virus were found in New York State.[57] Many sporadic instances of LCM virus infection probably go unrecognized. Physicians should be alert to the possibility in all situations of rodent (pet or wild) exposure. Encephalomyocarditis virus is another rodent virus that rarely is recognized in humans.[195] It is associated with a variety of neurologic manifestations, including aseptic meningitis.[72]

Most noncongenital infections with cytomegalovirus (CMV) in nonimmunocompromised patients are unrecognized. However, occasional instances of aseptic meningitis have been noted.[54–56] Rarely, aseptic meningitis has been noted during illnesses caused by rhinoviruses, influenza A and B viruses, parainfluenza viruses, parvovirus B19 virus, rotaviruses, and coronaviruses.* Most infections with measles, rubella, and variola viruses that involve the CNS are encephalitic.[37, 39, 40, 127]

Neurologic illness is a rare complication of measles, smallpox, polio, and rabies viral vaccines. In most instances, the illnesses are complex and severe, but on occasion, aseptic meningitis is the only manifestation.[18, 29, 37, 41, 128, 175] Aseptic meningitis and encephalitis resulting from administration of mumps vaccine have been noted in Canada, Brazil, and Europe.[8, 10, 44, 45, 62, 121, 126] The Leningrad 3 and Urabe Am 9 strains of vaccine viruses have been implicated. In the United States, where the Jeryl Lynn vaccine strain has been used exclusively, the rate of encephalitis in vaccinees has been no higher than that of the observed background incidence of similar illness in the population.[35] More recently, a preliminary analysis of the Vaccine Safety Datalink (VSD) project demonstrated a possible increased risk of developing aseptic meningitis after immunization with Jeryl Lynn mumps strain 8 to 14 days following receipt of the vaccine. However, a follow-up case-control evaluation of hospitalized cases failed to demonstrate an increased risk.[21]

Certain bacteria are important to recognize as etiologic agents in aseptic meningitis because the illnesses are treatable and early initiation of therapy is crucial. Of most importance is tuberculous meningitis. Early treatment of this illness nearly always results in complete cure, whereas diagnostic delay or inadequate treatment frequently results in permanent neurologic sequelae. Lyme disease, relapsing fever, brucellosis, and leptospirosis, as well as rickettsial infections, are illnesses, acquired either directly or indirectly from animals, in which aseptic meningitis may be a part of the disease process.* Partially treated common bacterial meningitides are a relatively common cause of meningitis in which cultures of CSF fail to grow organisms. Fortunately, antigen detection systems, such as latex agglutination, can be useful in identifying the causative agents in some of these cases.

A large number of fungi and yeasts cause meningitis.[159] Many fungal meningitides occur only in immunocompromised patients. The following agents are the most common causes of meningitis in children and adults with normal immunologic status: *Blastomyces dermatitidis, Coccidioides immitis, Cryptococcus neoformans, Cladosporium* species, *Histoplasma capsulatum,* and *Paracoccidioides brasiliensis.*

Mycoplasma pneumoniae is an important cause of neurologic illness.[27, 141] Pönkä[141] noted that 8 of 560 hospitalized patients with *M. pneumoniae* infections had aseptic meningitis and 18 had encephalitis or meningoencephalitis. *Mycoplasma hominis* and *Ureaplasma urealyticum* are rare causes of neonatal meningitis.[73, 119, 191, 192] Meningitis and meningoencephalitis have been associated with *Chlamydia pneumoniae* infections.[171, 179]

Parasites are an occasional cause of aseptic meningitis. Of much interest is eosinophilic meningitis, which is caused by *Angiostrongylus cantonensis*, a rat lungworm.[43, 87, 151, 196] Aseptic meningitis caused by *A. cantonensis* has been observed on several islands in the Pacific, and the infection may be acquired by the consumption of freshwater shrimp.

Recently, Syrogiannopoulos and associates[181] noted aseptic meningitis in 15 of 117 (12.8 %) infants younger than 90 days old with urinary tract infections. Numerous drugs and biologicals have been implicated in aseptic meningitis.† Of most importance in pediatrics are trimethoprim-sulfamethoxazole and intravenous immunoglobulin. Other causes of aseptic meningitis are listed in Table 42–1.‡ Aseptic meningitis is a common manifestation in Kawasaki disease.[79]

Epidemiology

Because many different types of organisms cause aseptic meningitis, no unified epidemiologic pattern exists. The epidemiology of the specific individual infectious agents or diseases is presented in detail in the various respective chapters of this book, and only a brief overview is presented here.

Because approximately 85 percent of all cases of aseptic meningitis are caused by enteroviral infections, the basic epidemiologic pattern of aseptic meningitis reflects these agents. In temperate climates, most cases occur in the summer and fall; infection with enteroviruses is spread directly from person to person, and the incubation period usually is 4 to 6 days. Epidemiologic considerations in aseptic meningitis caused by agents other than enteroviruses depend markedly on season, geography, climatic conditions, animal exposures, and many other factors related to the specific pathogens.

*See references 9, 28, 50, 54–56, 95, 132, 133, 136, 149, 190, 202.

*See references 20, 23, 78, 97, 99, 107, 110, 138, 174, 201, 204, 207.
†See references 13, 26, 58, 69, 80, 86, 120, 125, 131, 144, 203.
‡See references 33, 60, 71, 77, 90, 94, 106–108, 111, 120, 165, 180.

Clinical Manifestations

Aseptic meningitis has many different causes (see Table 42–1), and clinical manifestations vary somewhat with the different diseases. In some instances, the signs and symptoms resulting from meningeal inflammation dominate the clinical illness, whereas in other instances, the main signs and symptoms reflect other organ system involvement. Clinical manifestations in aseptic meningitis, regardless of etiology, also vary markedly by patient age.

ENTEROVIRUSES

Enteroviruses are the most common cause of aseptic meningitis, and they can be considered the prototype for a description of general clinical manifestations of aseptic meningitis.*

However, even among the enteroviruses, significant differences in clinical manifestations exist among the different viral types. Some general aspects of epidemic enteroviral aseptic meningitis are presented by viral type in Chapter 170.

The onset of illness generally is acute, although it may be insidious over the course of a week or so or may be preceded by a nonspecific acute febrile illness of a few days' duration. Almost all children have fever, and most older children have headache, which most often is retroorbital or frontal in location. Photophobia is a common occurrence. Temperature elevation is variable, ranging from 38° to 40.5° C (100.4° to 105° F), and usually lasts approximately 5 days. Occasionally, fever is biphasic, with the initial elevation occurring before the onset of neurologic signs and symptoms. Anorexia, nausea, and vomiting are common complaints, and abdominal pain and diarrhea also are reported frequently.

Meningeal signs (stiff neck and back, tightness of the hamstring muscles, Brudzinski and Kernig signs) usually are present, but deep tendon reflexes usually are normal or hyperactive. Seizures occur occasionally, usually when concomitant high fever is present. Muscle weakness rarely is reported, but myalgia occasionally is noted. In young children, fever, irritability, and lethargy are the most common findings. Infants may be irritable and show resentment to handling, and the fontanelle may be tense.

Other manifestations of enteroviral infections also occur in children with aseptic meningitis. Most common is pharyngitis, which occurs during infection with all of the neurotropic enteroviral types. Rash occurs commonly but varies by viral type. With echovirus 9 meningitis, 30 to 50 percent of children have rashes, whereas with echovirus 6, exanthem is rare. Cases of meningitis caused by enterovirus 71 frequently are accompanied by hand, foot, and mouth syndrome. Enanthem, pleurodynia, pericarditis, myocarditis, and conjunctivitis are other findings noted in children with enteroviral aseptic meningitis. Illness often is biphasic with fever, an interlude, then return of fever and neurologic manifestations.

CSF leukocyte counts vary from a few cells to a few thousand/mm^3; the median is in the range of 100 to 500 cells/mm^3. The percentage of neutrophils also varies greatly. Initially, a predominance of neutrophils commonly occurs, but later, CSF examinations show a decline in the percentage of neutrophils. The CSF protein usually is elevated mildly, and the glucose concentration most often is normal; rarely, hypoglycorrhachia is noted.

The duration of illness is variable. Usually, disability because of neurologic involvement lasts 1 to 2 weeks.

*See references 2, 6, 7, 22, 29–32, 42, 52, 59, 70, 74, 83, 85, 88, 89, 91, 92, 96, 100, 102, 103, 109, 115, 146, 153, 155–158, 160, 168, 178, 182, 199.

ASEPTIC MENINGITIS CAUSED BY OTHER AGENTS

In meningitis caused by arboviruses, brain involvement usually occurs as well (meningoencephalitis). However, with both St. Louis and California viral infections in children, the illness commonly is benign without changes in sensorium or other findings indicative of brain involvement. Seizures occur more commonly in arboviral meningitides than in enteroviral illnesses of otherwise comparable severity. When neurologic disease caused by mumps is recognized, usually evidence of brain involvement is present. However, CSF examination in mild cases of mumps often reveals pleocytosis.

Tuberculous meningitis usually has a gradual onset over a period of 2 to 3 weeks. Initially, personality changes, irritability, anorexia, listlessness, and low-grade fever may be present, followed by signs of increased intracranial pressure, such as drowsiness, stiff neck, cranial nerve palsies, inequality of the pupils, vomiting, and convulsions. Finally, coma, irregular pulse and respirations, and high fever occur. In fungal diseases, the course of meningitis is similar to that in tuberculosis. In both tuberculosis and several fungal meningitides, such as those caused by *C. immitis, H. capsulatum,* and *C. neoformans*, historical and radiographic evidence of pulmonary disease may be present.

Aseptic meningitis caused by *M. pneumoniae* is unique in that it frequently occurs a few days to 3 weeks after a respiratory illness (pharyngitis, bronchitis, or pneumonia). In nonenteroviral aseptic meningitides, the CSF findings generally are similar to those in enteroviral disease. In general, the likelihood of a predominance of neutrophils is less in other aseptic meningitides, and low glucose levels are likely in parameningeal bacterial infections, partially treated bacterial meningitides, brain tumors, leukemic infiltration, *M. pneumoniae* infections, fungal infections, and tuberculosis.

RECURRENT ASEPTIC MENINGITIS (MOLLARET MENINGITIS)

In 1944, Mollaret[129] described three patients with recurrent aseptic meningitis whom he had observed over a period of 15 years. Subsequently, many other cases have been reported, and some cases have been noted in children.[24, 45, 46, 93, 139, 176, 184] The illness is characterized by recurrent attacks of fever with meningeal signs and symptoms. The attacks last several days and are separated by symptom-free periods of weeks or months. During attacks, CSF pleocytosis, which in addition to neutrophils and lymphocytes contains endothelial cells (Mollaret cells), occurs. The disease remits spontaneously. The disease has been considered of unknown etiology, but Steel and colleagues[176] recovered HSV-1 from the CSF of a patient during a recurrence. Epstein-Barr virus infection has been associated with recurrent meningitis, and recurrent meningitis has been found to be an early manifestation of systemic lupus erythematosus.[82, 161] Studies using the PCR or DNA probes suggest that HSV-2 is the major cause of recurrent aseptic meningitis.[15, 45, 139, 183, 184] A 30-year-old man had Mollaret meningitis (seven episodes) attributed to exposure to wood preservatives.[157] Recurrent aseptic meningitis in an 8-year-old girl secondary to an intracranial cyst has been reported.[106]

Differential Diagnosis

Careful analysis of the history and epidemiologic circumstances may point toward one of the specific causes listed in

Table 42–1. During the summer and autumn, the presence of pleurodynia, herpangina, or unexplained febrile eruptions in the community suggests the possibility of enteroviral infections; the coexistence of acute paralytic disorders in other patients suggests poliomyelitis; encephalitis in horses points to the possibility of an arbovirus infection; a history of swimming in waters contaminated by urine from infected animals suggests leptospiral infection. Exposure to ticks might suggest Lyme disease, relapsing fever, or rickettsial disease, depending on the geographic location and other symptoms of the illness. Knowledge of clear-cut exposure to or concurrent evidence of mumps or of one of the common exanthems is helpful in making the differential diagnosis.

The association of pneumonia or other respiratory illness preceding aseptic meningitis strongly suggests the possibility of *M. pneumoniae* as the etiologic agent.

Most difficult from the diagnostic, therapeutic, and prognostic points of view are instances of incipient or partially treated bacterial (especially when caused by *Haemophilus influenzae*) or mycobacterial meningitis. The clinical findings; the dosage of antibiotic previously used; the spinal fluid smear, latex agglutination, or other rapid antigen identification test; the culture; and the glucose level may be helpful in diagnosing bacterial meningitis. The quantitative determination of C-reactive protein in the CSF also may be useful in differentiating bacterial from viral meningitis.[1, 48, 53, 134, 135] Lindquist and associates[116] found that the determination of CSF concentrations of lactate was the most useful test in differentiating bacterial from nonbacterial causes of meningitis. Studies suggest that the presence of tumor necrosis factor-α in the CSF is a rare finding in viral infections but a common one in bacterial disease.[5, 63, 75] When tuberculous meningitis is suspected, a careful evaluation of contacts, a careful examination of an appropriately stained smear from the pellicle of the CSF that was allowed to settle, and a positive tuberculin reaction may confirm the diagnosis. Because combined bacterial and viral infection has occurred, examinations of CSF should be repeated if the slightest doubt exists. The possibility that the observed meningeal reaction is of neither viral nor bacterial origin must be considered. Finally, CNS tumor must be considered in the differential diagnosis, particularly if hypoglycorrhachia and prominent signs of increased intracranial pressure are present.[108]

Specific Diagnosis

Obtaining a meticulous history is essential and must evaluate exposure in the past 2 to 3 weeks to illness in contacts; exposure to mosquitoes, ticks, and animals during recent vacations, picnics, and so on; awareness of illness in animals, especially horses and other Equidae, in the patient's environment; recent travel from the home area; recent injections or medications of any kind; and the possibility of accidental exposure to heavy metals.

The CSF must be examined carefully to exclude disorders that respond to specific therapy. Smears for bacteria, appropriate rapid antigen identification tests, and cultures of the CSF are mandatory; the history and clinical findings may indicate the need for performing acid-fast stain and culture of the sediment for mycobacteria. Other circumstances may indicate the need for excluding fungal or protozoal infection; atypical cells may require cytopathologic study to exclude neural neoplasms, which may present acutely.

In any patient suspected of having viral meningitis, spinal fluid, blood, feces, and throat swabs should be collected and sent to a laboratory offering viral diagnostic services. An additional serum specimen should be collected 10 to 21 days later so that paired serum specimens can be examined for antibody titer increases. This pairing particularly is useful in arboviral, LCM viral, encephalomyocarditis viral, leptospiral, borrelial, rickettsial, mycoplasmal, and toxoplasmal infections. Although these studies may not provide an immediate diagnosis, they may give early warning of a specific epidemic, and they are useful for prognostication, particularly in very young infants.

Several studies indicate that an enteroviral etiology of aseptic meningitis can be diagnosed by the demonstration of enteroviral RNA by PCR assay.*

Treatment

Hospitalization usually is necessary because of the possibility of treatable bacterial disease and the frequent need for fluid therapy for dehydration. Treatment is symptomatic. Headache and hyperesthesia are treated with rest, analgesics, and a reduction in room light, noise, and visitors. Antipyretics are recommended for fever. Using acetaminophen rather than aspirin is prudent because of the associated risk for Reye syndrome with the latter antipyretic. Codeine, morphine, and the phenothiazine derivatives often are used for pain and vomiting, but they rarely are necessary in children, and they should be avoided because they may induce misleading signs and symptoms. The investigational antiviral drug pleconaril has been shown to be effective in the treatment of enteroviral meningitis.[152]

Several weeks after apparent recovery, careful neuromuscular assessment should be conducted to ensure that muscular weakness is not a sequel. Bilateral audiometry is recommended, especially when mumps virus was involved.

Treatment for such illnesses as tuberculous meningitis, fungal meningitides, and other illnesses for which specific therapies are available is covered in specific chapters of this book.

Prognosis

The prognosis in aseptic meningitis depends on the etiology. Some illnesses have an ominous prognosis (tuberculous meningitis, parameningeal infections, rickettsial infections), but the patients usually do well if appropriate specific therapy is instituted early in the course of the illness. In *C. immitis* meningitis, the prognosis for cure is guarded even with early optimal therapy.

In enteroviral and other viral meningitides, children usually recover completely. Some patients complain of fatigue, irritability, decreased ability to concentrate, muscle pain, muscle weakness and spasm, and incoordination for several weeks after an acute illness. Although the outcome of enteroviral meningitis most often is without residual, some infants who have enteroviral meningitis in the first few months of life have an increased risk for having altered language development.[16, 200] Therefore, formally evaluating such children from ages 3 to 6 years is important.

Prevention

The universal use of polio and mumps vaccines in children clearly is effective in controlling these two diseases. Control

*See references 3, 6, 76, 88, 101, 105, 154, 162, 163, 186, 206.

of insect vectors by suitable spraying methods and eradication of insect breeding sites is important in the control of many arboviruses. The control of animal vectors such as mice and rats alters the incidence of infections with LCM and encephalomyocarditis viruses.

REFERENCES

1. Abramson, J. S., Hampton, K. D., Babu, S., et al.: The use of C-reactive protein from cerebrospinal fluid for differentiating meningitis from other central nervous system diseases. J. Infect. Dis. *151*:854–858, 1985.
2. Abzug, M. J., Levin, M. J., and Rotbart, H. A.: Profile of enterovirus disease in the first two weeks of life. Pediatr. Infect. Dis. J. *12*:820–824, 1993.
3. Abzug, M. J., Loeffelholz, M., and Rotbart, H. A.: Clinical and laboratory observations: Diagnosis of neonatal enterovirus infection by polymerase chain reaction. J. Pediatr. *126*:447–450, 1995.
4. Adair, C. V., Gauld, R. L., and Smadel, J. E.: Aseptic meningitis, a disease of diverse etiology: Clinical and etiologic studies on 854 cases. Ann. Intern. Med. *39*:675–704, 1953.
5. Akalin, H., Akdis, A. C., Mistik, R., et al.: Cerebrospinal fluid interleukin-1 beta/interleukin-1 receptor antagonist balance and tumor necrosis factor concentrations in tuberculous, viral and acute bacterial meningitis. Scand. J. Infect. Dis. *26*:667–674, 1994.
6. Akasu, Y.: Outbreak of aseptic meningitis due to ECHO-9 in northern Kyushu island in the summer of 1997. Kurume Med. J. *46*:97–104, 1999.
7. Amvrosiena, T. V., Titov, L. P., Mulders, M., et al.: Viral water contamination as the cause of aseptic meningitis outbreak in Belarus. Cent. Eur. J. Public Health. *9*:154–157, 2001.
8. Anonymous: Mumps meningitis and MMR vaccination. Lancet *2*:1015–1016, 1989.
9. Arisoy, E. S., Demmler, G. J., Thakar, S., et al.: Meningitis due to parainfluenza virus type 3: Report of two cases and review. Clin. Infect. Dis. *17*:995–997, 1993.
10. Arruda, W. O., Kondageski, C.: Aceptic meningitis in a large MMR vaccine campaign (590,609 people) in Curitiba, Parana, Brazil, 1998. Rev. Inst. Med. Trop. Sao Paulo *43*:301–302, 2001.
11. Atia, W. A., Ratnatunga, C. S., Greenfield, C., et al.: Aseptic meningitis and herpes simplex proctitis: A case report. Br. J. Vener. Dis. *58*:53–58, 1982.
12. Atwood, W. J., Berger, J. R., Kaderman, R., et al.: Human immunodeficiency virus type 1 infection of the brain. Clin. Microbiol. Rev. *6*:339–366, 1993.
13. Auxier, G. G.: Aseptic meningitis associated with administration of trimethoprim and sulfamethoxazole. Am. J. Dis. Child. *144*:144–145, 1990.
14. Barton, L. L., Hyndman, N. J.: Lymphocytic choriomeningitis virus: reemerging central nervous system pathogen. Pediatrics *105*:835, 2000.
15. Bachmeyer, C., de la Blanchardière, A., Lepercq, J., et al.: Recurring episodes of meningitis (Mollaret's meningitis) with one showing an association with herpes simplex virus type 2. J. Infect. *32*:247–248, 1996.
16. Bergman, I., Painter, M. J., Wald, E. R., et al.: Outcome in children with enteroviral meningitis during the first year of life. J. Pediatr. *110*:705–709, 1987.
17. Bergstrom, T., Vahlne, A., Alestig, K., et al.: Primary and recurrent herpes simplex virus type 2-induced meningitis. J. Infect. Dis. *162*:322–330, 1990.
18. Berlin, L. E., Rorabaugh, M. L., Heldrich, F., et al.: Aseptic meningitis in infants <2 years of age: Diagnosis and etiology. J. Infect. Dis. *168*:888–892, 1993.
19. Biggar, R. J., Woodall, J. P., Walter, P. D., et al.: Lymphocytic choriomeningitis outbreak associated with pet hamsters: Fifty-seven cases from New York State. J. A. M. A. *232*:494–500, 1975.
20. Bingham, P. M., Galetta, S. L., Athreya, B., et al.: Neurologic manifestations in children with Lyme disease. Pediatrics *96*:1053–1056, 1995.
21. Black, S., Shinefield, H., Ray, P., et al.: Risk of hospitalization because of aseptic meningitis after measles-mumps-rubella vaccination in one- to two-year-old children: An analysis of the Vaccine Safety Datalink (VSD) Project. Pediatr. Infect. Dis. *16*:500–503, 1997.
22. Bowen, G. S., Fisher, M. C., DeForest, A., et al.: Epidemic of meningitis and febrile illness in neonates caused by echo type 11 virus in Philadelphia. Pediatr. Infect. Dis. *2*:359–363, 1983.
23. Bruhn, F. W.: Lyme disease. Am. J. Dis. Child. *138*:467–470, 1984.
24. Bruyn, G. W., Straathof, L. J. A., and Raymakers, G. M. J.: Mollaret's meningitis: Differential diagnosis and diagnostic pitfalls. Neurology *12*:745–753, 1962.
25. Calisher, C. H.: Medically important arboviruses of the United States and Canada. Clin. Microbiol. Rev. *7*:89–116, 1994.
26. Carlson, J., and Wiholm, B. E.: Trimethoprim-associated aseptic meningitis. Scand. J. Infect. Dis. *19*:687–691, 1987.
27. Cassell, G. H., and Cole, B. C.: Mycoplasmas as agents of human disease. N. Engl. J. Med. *304*:80–89, 1981.
28. Cassinotti, P., Schultze, D., Schlageter, P., et al.: Persistent human parvovirus B19 infection following an acute infection with meningitis in an immunocompetent patient. Eur. J. Clin. Microbiol. Infect. Dis. *12*:701–704, 1993.
29. Centers for Disease Control: Acute flaccid paralysis associated with circulating vaccine-derived poliovirus—Philippines, 2001. M. M. W. R. Morb. Mortal. Wkly. Rep. *50*:874–875, 2001.
30. Centers for Disease Control: Echovirus type 13—United States, 2001. M. M. W. R. Morb. Mortal. Wkly. Rep. *50*:777–780, 2001.
31. Centers for Disease Control: Enterovirus surveillance—United States, 1997–1999. M. M. W. R. Morb. Mortal. Wkly. Rep. *49*:913–916, 2000.
32. Centers for Disease Control: Outbreak of aseptic meningitis associated with multiple enterovirus serotypes—Romania, 1999. M. M. W. R. Morb. Mortal. Wkly. Rep. *49*:669–671, 2000.
33. Centers for Disease Control: Outbreak of Hendra-like virus—Malaysia and Singapore, 1998–1999. M. M. W. R. Morb. Mortal. Wkly. Rep. *48*:265–269, 1999.
34. Centers for Disease Control: Arboviral surveillance: United States, 1990. M. M. W. R. Morb. Mortal. Wkly. Rep. *39*:593–598, 1990.
35. Centers for Disease Control: ACIP: Mumps prevention. M. M. W. R. Morb. Mortal. Wkly. Rep. *38*:388–400, 1989.
36. Centers for Disease Control: Arboviral infections of the central nervous system: United States, 1985. M. M. W. R. Morb. Mortal. Wkly. Rep. *35*:341–350, 1986.
37. Centers for Disease Control: Measles surveillance, 1977–1981. Issued September 1982.
38. Centers for Disease Control: Enterovirus surveillance, summary 1970–1979. Issued November 1981.
39. Centers for Disease Control: Encephalitis surveillance, annual summary 1978. Issued May 1981.
40. Centers for Disease Control: Neurotropic diseases surveillance, summary 1974–1976. Issued October 1977.
41. Centers for Disease Control: Neurotropic viral diseases surveillance: Aseptic meningitis, annual summary 1975. Issued July 1977.
42. Cernescu, C., Tardei, G., Ruta, S., et al.: An outbreak of aseptic meningitis due to Echo 30 virus in Romania during the 1999 summer. Rom. J. Virol. *50*:99–106, 1999.
43. Char, D. F. B., and Rosen, L.: Eosinophilic meningitis among children in Hawaii. J. Pediatr. *70*:28–35, 1967.
44. Cizman, M., Mozetic, M., Radescek-Rakar, R., et al.: Aseptic meningitis after vaccination against measles and mumps. Pediatr. Infect. Dis. *8*:302–308, 1989.
45. Cohen, B. A., Rowley, A. H., and Long, C. M.: Herpes simplex type 2 in a patient with Mollaret's meningitis: Demonstration by polymerase chain reaction. Ann. Neurol. *35*:112–116, 1994.
46. Coleman, W. S., Lischner, H. W., and Grover, W. D.: Recurrent aseptic meningitis without sequelae. J. Pediatr. *87*:89–91, 1975.
47. Connor, J. D., Buchta, R. M., DeGenaro, F., Jr., et al.: Potpourri of adenoviral infections. West. J. Med. *120*:55–61, 1974.
48. Corrall, C. J., Pepple, J. M., Moxon, E. R., et al.: C-reactive protein in spinal fluid of children with meningitis. J. Pediatr. *99*:365–369, 1981.
49. Craig, C. P., and Nahmias, A. J.: Different patterns of neurologic involvement with herpes simplex virus types 1 and 2: Isolation of herpes simplex virus type 2 from the buffy coat of two adults with meningitis. J. Infect. Dis. *127*:365–372, 1973.
50. Craver, R. D., Gohd, R. S., Sundin, D. R., et al.: Isolation of parainfluenza virus type 3 from cerebrospinal fluid associated with aseptic meningitis. Clin. Microbiol. Infect. Dis. *99*:705–707, 1993.
51. Dalldorf, G., and Sickles, G. M.: An unidentified, filtrable agent isolated from the feces of children with paralysis. Science *108*:61–62, 1948.
52. Davies, J. W., McDermott, A., and Severs, D.: Epidemic virus meningitis due to echo 9 virus in Newfoundland. Can. Med. Assoc. J. *79*:162–167, 1958.
53. DeBeer, F. C., Kirsten, G. F., Gie, R. P., et al.: Value of C reactive protein measurement in tuberculous, bacterial, and viral meningitis. Arch. Dis. Child. *59*:653–656, 1984.
54. Deibel, R., and Flanagan, T. D.: Central nervous system infections: Etiologic and epidemiologic observations in New York State, 1976–1977. N. Y. State J. Med. *79*:689–695, 1979.
55. Deibel, R., Flanagan, T. D., and Smith, V.: Central nervous system infections: Etiologic and epidemiologic observations in New York State, 1975. N. Y. State J. Med. *77*:1398–1404, 1977.
56. Deibel, R., Flanagan, T. D., and Smith, V.: Central nervous system infections in New York State: Etiologic and epidemiologic observations, 1974. N. Y. State J. Med. *75*:2337–2342, 1975.
57. Deibel, R., Woodall, J. P., Decher, W. J., et al.: Lymphocytic choriomeningitis virus in man: Serologic evidence of association with pet hamsters. J. A. M. A. *232*:501–504, 1975.
58. Derbes, S. J.: Trimethoprim-induced aseptic meningitis. J. A. M. A. *252*:2865–2866, 1984.
59. Diedrich, S., and Schreier, E.: Aseptic meningitis in Germany associated with enterovirus type 13. B. M. C. Infect. Dis. *1*:14, 2001.
60. Dimmitt, D. C., Fishbein, D. B., and Dawson, J. E.: Human ehrlichiosis associated with cerebrospinal fluid pleocytosis: A case report. Am. J. Med. *87*:677–678, 1989.
61. Do, A. N., Green, P. A., and Demmler, G. J.: Herpes simplex virus type 2 meningitis and associated genital lesions in a three-year-old child. Pediatr. Infect. Dis. J. *13*:1014–1016, 1994.

62. Dourado, I., Cunha, S., Teixeira, M. G., et al.: Outbreak of aseptic meningitis associated with mass vaccination with a urabe-containing measles-mumps-rubella vaccine: Implications for immunization program. Am. J. Epidemiol. *151*:524–530, 2000.
63. Dulkerian, S. J., Kilpatrick, L., Costarino, A. T., Jr., et al.: Cytokine elevations in infants with bacterial and aseptic meningitis. J. Pediatr. *126*:872–876, 1995.
64. Echevarria, J. M., Casas, I., Tenorio, A., et al.: Detection of varicella-zoster virus-specific DNA sequences in cerebrospinal fluid from patients with acute aseptic meningitis and no cutaneous lesions. J. Med. Virol. *43*:331–335, 1994.
65. Enders, J. F.: Mumps. *In* Rivers, T. M., and Horsfall, F. L. (eds.): Viral and Rickettsial Infections of Man. Philadelphia, J. B. Lippincott, 1959, pp. 780–789.
66. Enders, J. R., Weller, T. H., and Robbins, F. C.: Cultivation of the Lansing strain of poliomyelitis virus in cultures of various human embryonic tissues. Science *109*:85–87, 1949.
67. Evans, A. S., and Niederman, J. C.: Epstein-Barr virus. *In* Evans, A. S. (ed.): Viral Infections of Humans. Epidemiology and Control. 2nd ed. New York, Plenum Medical, 1982, pp. 253–281.
68. Faulkner, R., and Van Rooyen, C. E.: Adenoviruses types 3 and 5 isolated from the cerebrospinal fluid of children. Can. Med. Assoc. J. *87*:1123–1125, 1962.
69. Fobelo, M. J., Corzo Delgado, J. E., Romero Alonso, A., et al.: Aseptic meningitis related to valacyclovir. Ann. Pharmacother. *35*:128–129, 2001.
70. Forbes, J. A.: Meningitis in Melbourne due to ECHO virus. Part I. Clinical aspects. Med. J. Aust. *1*:246–248, 1958.
71. Fryden, A., Kihlstrom, E., Maller, R., et al.: A clinical and epidemiological study of "ornithosis" caused by *Chlamydia psittaci* and *Chlamydia pneumoniae* (strain TWAR). Scand. J. Infect. Dis. *21*:681–691, 1989.
72. Gajdusek, D. C.: Review article: Encephalomyocarditis virus infection in childhood. Pediatrics *16*:902–906, 1955.
73. Garland, S. M., and Murton, L. J.: Neonatal meningitis caused by *Ureaplasma urealyticum*. Pediatr. Infect. Dis. *6*:868–870, 1987.
74. Gilbert, G. L., Dickson, K. E., Waters, M. J., et al.: Outbreak of enterovirus 71 infection in Victoria, Australia, with a high incidence of neurologic involvement. Pediatr. Infect. Dis. *7*:484–488, 1988.
75. Glimaker, M., Kragsbjerg, P., Forsgren, M., et al.: Tumor necrosis factor–alpha in cerebrospinal fluid from patients with meningitis of different etiologies: High levels of TNF-alpha indicate bacterial meningitis. J. Infect. Dis. *167*:882–889, 1993.
76. Glimaker, M., Johansson, B., Olcen, P., et al.: Detection of enteroviral RNA by polymerase chain reaction in cerebrospinal fluid from patients with aseptic meningitis. Scand. J. Infect. Dis. *25*:547–557, 1993.
77. Golden, S. E.: Aseptic meningitis associated with *Ehrlichia canis* infection. Pediatr. Infect. Dis. *8*:335–337, 1989.
78. Gonzalez Garcia, H., Ernandez Alonso, J. F., de Paz Garcia, M., et al.: Meningitis as the first and only manifestation of brucellosis. An. Esp. Pediatr. *53*:280–282, 2000.
79. Gonzalez Pascual, E., Villanueva Lamas, J., Ros Viladoms, J., et al.: Kawasaki disease: A report of 50 cases. An. Esp. Pediatr. *50*:39–43, 1999.
80. Gordon, M. F., Allon, M., and Coyle, P. K.: Drug-induced meningitis. Neurology *40*:163–164, 1990.
81. Gosbell, I., Robinson, D., Chant, K., et al.: Outbreak of echovirus 30 meningitis in Wingecaribee Shire, New South Wales. Commun. Dis. Intell. *24*:121–124, 2000.
82. Graman, P. S.: Mollaret's meningitis associated with acute Epstein-Barr virus mononucleosis. Arch. Neurol. *44*:1204–1205, 1987.
83. Grist, N. R., Bell, E. J., and Assaad, F.: Enteroviruses in human disease. Prog. Med. Virol. *24*:114–157, 1978.
84. Gunther, G., Haglund, M., Lindquist, L., et al.: Tick-borne encephalitis in Sweden in relation to aseptic meningo-encephalitis of other etiology: A prospective study of clinical course and outcome. J. Neurol. *244*: 230–238, 1997.
85. Guthrie, N.: Coxsackie B5 meningitis: Report of an outbreak in a high school football squad. J. Tenn. State Med. Assoc. *55*:355–356, 1962.
86. Haase, K. K., Lapointe, M., Haines, S. J.: Aseptic meningitis after intraventicular administration of gentamicin. Pharmacotherapy *21*: 103–107, 2001.
87. Hammer, S. M., and Connolly, K. J.: Viral aseptic meningitis in the United States: Clinical features, viral etiologies, and differential diagnosis. Curr. Clin. Top. Infect. Dis. *12*:1–25, 1992.
88. Handsher, R., Shulman, L. M., Abramovitz, B., et al.: A new variant of echovirus 4 associated with a large outbreak of aseptic meningitis. J. Clin. Virol. *13*:29–36, 1999.
89. Hanninen, P., and Pohjonen, R.: Echovirus type 6 meningitis: Clinical and virological observations during an epidemic in Turku in 1968. Scand. J. Infect. Dis. *3*:121–125, 1971.
90. Haynes, R. E., Sanders, D. Y., and Cramblett, H. G.: Rocky Mountain spotted fever in children. J. Pediatr. *76*:685–693, 1970.
91. Haynes, R. E., Cramblett, H. G., and Kronfol, H. J.: Echovirus 9 meningoencephalitis in infants and children. J. A. M. A. *208*:1657–1660, 1969.
92. Helin, I., Widell, A., Borulf, S., et al.: Outbreak of coxsackievirus A-14 meningitis among newborns in a maternity hospital ward. Acta Paediatr. Scand. *76*:234–238, 1987.
93. Hermans, P. E., Goldstein, N. P., and Wellman, W. E.: Mollaret's meningitis and differential diagnosis of recurrent meningitis. Am. J. Med. *52*:128–140, 1972.
94. Heusner, A. P.: Nontuberculous spinal epidural infections. N. Engl. J. Med. *239*:845–854, 1948.
95. Holzel, A., Smith, P. A., and Tobin, J. O. H.: A new type of meningoencephalitis associated with a rhinovirus. Acta Paediatr. Scand. *54*: 168–174, 1965.
96. Huang, C. C., Liu, C. C., Chang, Y. C., et al.: Neurologic complications in children with enterovirus 71 infection. N. Engl. J. Med. *341*:936–942, 1999.
97. Jhaveri, R., Cherry, J. D., Phillips, S., et al.: Erythema migrans after ceftriaxone treatment of aseptic meningitis caused by *Borrelia burgdorferi*. Pediatr. Infect. Dis. J. *20*:1010–1012, 2001.
98. Johnson, C. D., and Goodpasture, E. W.: An investigation of the etiology of mumps. J. Exp. Med. *59*:1–20, 1934.
99. Jorbeck, H. J. A., Guftafsson, P. M., Lind, H. C. F., et al.: Tick-borne *Borrelia* meningitis in children. Acta Paediatr. Scand. *76*:228–233, 1987.
100. Kajiwara, I., Kusaba, T., Hayashida, I., et al.: Clinical study of an outbreak of aseptic meningitis due to echovirus type 30 in Munakata City in 1997–1998. Kansenshogaku Zasshi *74*:231–236, 2000.
101. Kammerer, U., Kunkel, B., and Korn, K.: Nested PCR for specific detection and rapid identification of human picornaviruses. J. Clin. Microbiol. *32*:285–291, 1994.
102. Karzon, D. T., and Barron, A. L.: An epidemic of aseptic meningitis syndrome due to echo virus type 6. I. Correlation of enterovirus isolation with illness. II. Clinical study. III. Sequelae. Pediatrics *29*:409–417, 418–431, 432–437, 1962.
103. Karzon, D. T., Eckert, G. L., Barron, A. L., et al.: Aseptic meningitis epidemic due to echo 4 virus. Am. J. Dis. Child. *101*:610–622, 1961.
104. Kelsey, D. S.: Adenovirus meningoencephalitis. Pediatrics *61*:291–293, 1978.
105. Khalfan, S., Aymaard, M., Lina, B., et al.: Epidemics of aseptic meningitis due to enteroviruses following national immunization days in Bahrain. Ann. Trop. Paediatr. *18*:101–109, 1998.
106. Kitai, I., Navas, L., Rohlicke, C., et al.: Recurrent aseptic meningitis secondary to an intracranial cyst: A case report and review of clinical features and imaging modalities. Pediatr. Infect. Dis. J. *11*:671–675, 1992.
107. Kochar, D. K., Agarwal, N., Jain, N., et al.: Clinical profile of neurobrucellosis: A report on 12 cases from Bikar (north-west India). Assoc. Physicians India *48*:376–380, 2000.
108. Kriss, T. C., Kriss, V. M., and Warf, B. C.: Recurrent meningitis: The search for the dermoid or epidermoid tumor. Pediatr. Infect. Dis. J. *14*:697–700, 1995.
109. LaForest, R. A., McNaughton, G. A., Beale, A. J., et al.: Outbreak of aseptic meningitis (meningoencephalitis) with rubelliform rash: Toronto, 1956. Can. Med. Assoc. J. *77*:1–4, 1957.
110. Lecour, H., Miranda, M., Magro, C., et al.: Human leptospirosis: A review of 50 cases. Infection *16*:8–12, 1989.
111. Lee, K. E., Umapathi, T., Tan, C. B., et al.: The neurological manifestations of Nipah virus encephalitis, a novel paramyxovirus. Ann. Neurol. *46*:428–432, 1999.
112. Lennette, E. H., Magoffin, R. L., and Knouf, E. G.: Viral central nervous system disease: An etiologic study conducted at the Los Angeles County General Hospital. J. A. M. A. *179*:687–695, 1962.
113. Lepow, M. L., Carver, D. H., Wright, H. T., Jr., et al.: A clinical, epidemiologic and laboratory investigation of aseptic meningitis during the four-year period 1955–1958. I. Observations concerning etiology and epidemiology. N. Engl. J. Med. *266*:1181–1187, 1962.
114. Lepow, M. L., Coyne, N., Thompson, L. B., et al.: A clinical, epidemiologic and laboratory investigation of aseptic meningitis during the four-year period 1955–1958. II. The clinical disease and its sequelae. N. Engl. J. Med. *266*:1188–1193, 1962.
115. Liao, H. T., Hung, K. L.: Neurologic involvement in an outbreak of enterovirus 71 infection: A hospital-based study. Acta Paediatr. Taiwan *42*:27–32, 2001.
116. Lindquist, L., Linne, T., Hansson, L. O., et al.: Value of cerebrospinal fluid analysis in the differential diagnosis of meningitis: A study in 710 patients with suspected central nervous system infection. Eur. J. Clin. Microbiol. Infect. Dis. *7*:374–380, 1988.
117. Liu, C. C., Tseng, H. W., Wang, S. M., et al.: An outbreak of enterovirus 71 infection in Taiwan, 1998: Epidemiologic and clinical manifestations. J. Clin. Virol. *177*:23–30, 2000.
118. Logar, M., Arnez, M., Kolbl, J., et al.: Comparison of the epidemiological and clinical features of tick-borne encephalitis in children and adults. Infection *28*:74–77, 2000.
119. Mardh, P. A.: *Mycoplasma hominis* infection of the central nervous system in newborn infants. Sex. Transm. Dis. *10*:331–334, 1983.
120. Martin, M. A., Massanari, R. M., Nghiem, D. D., et al.: Nosocomial aseptic meningitis associated with administration of OKT3. J. A. M. A. *259*:2002–2005, 1988.
121. McDonald, J. C., Moore, D. L., and Quennec, P.: Clinical and epidemiologic features of mumps meningoencephalitis and possible vaccine-related disease. Pediatr. Infect. Dis. *8*:751–755, 1989.

122. McJunkin, J. E., de los Reyes, E. C., Irazuzta, J. E., et al.: La Crosse encephalitis in children. N. Engl. J. Med. *345*:148–149, 2001.
123. McMinn, P., Stratov, I., Nagarajan, L., et al.: Neurological manifestations of enterovirus 71 infection during an outbreak of hand, foot and mouth disease in Western Australia. Clin. Infect. Dis. *32*:236–242, 2001.
124. Meyer, H. M., Jr., Johnson, R. T., Crawford, I. P., et al.: Central nervous system syndromes of "viral" etiology: A study of 713 cases. Am. J. Med. *29*:334–347, 1960.
125. Mifsud, A. J.: Drug-related recurrent meningitis. J. Infect. *17*:151–153, 1988.
126. Miller, E., Goldacre, M., Pugh, S., et al.: Risk of aseptic meningitis after measles, mumps, and rubella vaccine in UK children. Lancet *341*:979–982, 1993.
127. Miller, H. G., Stanton, J. B., and Gibbons, J. L.: Parainfectious encephalomyelitis and related syndromes: A critical review of the neurological complications of certain specific fevers. Q. J. Med. *100*:427–505, 1956.
128. Miller, H. G., and Stanton, J. B.: Neurological sequelae of prophylactic inoculation. Q. J. Med. *89*:1–27, 1954.
129. Mollaret, P.: La meningite endothelio-leukocytaire multirecurrente benigne: Syndrome nouveau ou maladie nouvelle? Rev. Neurol. *72*:57–76, 1944.
130. Moore, M.: Enteroviral disease in the United States, 1970–1979. J. Infect. Dis. *146*:103–108, 1982.
131. Muller, M. P., Richardson, D. C., Walmsley, S. L.: Trimethoprim-sulfamethoxazole induced aseptic meningitis in a renal transplant patient. Clin. Nephrol. *55*:80–84, 2001.
132. Okumura, A., and Ichikawa, T.: Aseptic meningitis caused by human parvovirus B19. Arch. Dis. Child. *68*:784–785, 1993.
133. Paisley, J. W., Bruhn, F. W., Lauer, B. A., et al.: Type A2 influenza viral infections in children. Am. J. Dis. Child. *132*:34–36, 1978.
134. Peltola, H., and Valmari, P.: Serum C-reactive protein as detector of pretreated childhood bacterial meningitis. Neurology *35*:251–253, 1985.
135. Peltola, H. O.: C-reactive protein for rapid monitoring of infections of the central nervous system. Lancet *1*:980–983, 1982.
136. Pereira, A. C., Barros, R. A., do Nascimento, J. P., et al.: Two family members with a syndrome of headache and rash caused by human parvovirus B19. Braz. J. Infect. Dis. *5*:37–39, 2001.
137. Pereira, M. S., and MacCallum, F. O.: Infection with adenovirus type 12. Lancet *1*:198–199, 1964.
138. Peter, G.: Leptospirosis: A zoonosis of protean manifestations. Pediatr. Infect. Dis. *1*:282–288, 1982.
139. Picard, F. J., Dekaban, G. A., Silva, J., et al.: Mollaret's meningitis associated with herpes simplex type 2 infection. Neurology *43*:1722–1727, 1993.
140. Pohl-Koppe, A., Blay, M., Jager, G., et al.: Human herpes virus type 7 in the cerebrospinal fluid of children with central nervous system disease. Eur. J. Pediatr. *160*:351–358, 2001.
141. Pönkä, A.: Central nervous system manifestations associated with serologically verified *Mycoplasma pneumoniae* infection. Scand. J. Infect. Dis. *12*:175–184, 1980.
142. Portolani, M., Pecorari, M., Pietrosemoli, P., et al.: Outbreak of aspetic meningitis by echo 4: Prevalence of clinical cases among adults. New Microbiol. *24*:11–15, 2001.
143. Preblud, S. R.: Age-specific risks of varicella complications. Pediatrics *68*:14–17, 1981.
144. Rao, S. P., Teitlebaum, J., and Miller, S. T.: Intravenous immune globulin and aseptic meningitis. Am. J. Dis. Child. *146*:539–540, 1992.
145. Rasmussen, A. F.: The laboratory diagnosis of lymphocytic choriomeningitis and mumps. *In* Rocky Mountain Conference on Infantile Paralysis. Denver, University of Colorado School of Medicine, 1946, p. 45.
146. Reeves, W. C., Quiroz, E., Brenes, M. M., et al.: Aseptic meningitis due to echovirus 4 in Panama City, Republic of Panama. Am. J. Epidemiol. *125*:562–575, 1987.
147. Reimer, L. G., and Reller, L. B.: CSF in herpes zoster meningoencephalitis. Arch. Neurol. *38*:668, 1981.
148. Reintjes, R., Pohle, M., Vieth, U., et al.: Community-wide outbreak of enteroviral illness caused by echovirus 30: A cross-sectional survey and a case-control study. Pediatr. Infect. Dis. J. *18*:104–108, 1999.
149. Riski, H., and Hovi, T.: Coronavirus infections of man associated with diseases other than the common cold. J. Med. Virol. *6*:259–265, 1980.
150. Rivers, T. M., and Scott, T. F. M.: Meningitis in man caused by a filterable virus. Science *81*:439–440, 1935.
151. Rosen, L., Loison, G., Laigret, J., et al.: Studies on eosinophilic meningitis. 3. Epidemiologic and clinical observations on Pacific islands and the possible etiologic role of *Angiostrongylus cantonensis*. Am. J. Epidemiol. *85*:17–44, 1967.
152. Rotbart, H. A., O'Connell, J. F., McKinlay, M. A.: Treatment of human enterovirus infections. Antiviral Res. *38*:1–14, 1998.
153. Rotbart, H. A.: Enteroviral infections of the central nervous system. Clin. Infect. Dis. *20*:971–981, 1995.
154. Rotbart, H. A., Sawyer, M. H., Fast, S., et al.: Diagnosis of enteroviral meningitis by using PCR with a colorimetric microwell detection assay. J. Clin. Microbiol. *32*:2590–2592, 1994.
155. Rotem, C. E.: Meningitis of virus origin. Lancet *1*:502–504, 1957.
156. Rothenberg, R., Murphy, W., O'Brien, C. L., et al.: Aseptic meningitis associated with ECHO virus type 9: An outbreak in Norfolk, Va. South. Med. J. *63*:280–285, 1970.
157. Rottach, K.: Mollaret's meningitis: A new aetiologic feature. Eur. Neurol. *36*:172–173, 1996.
158. Sabin, A. B., Krumbiegel, E. R., and Wigand, R.: ECHO type 9 virus disease: Virologically controlled clinical and epidemiologic observations during a 1957 epidemic in Milwaukee with notes on concurrent similar diseases associated with coxsackie and other ECHO viruses. Prog. Pediatr. *96*:197–219, 1958.
159. Salaki, J. S., Louria, D. B., and Chmel, H.: Fungal and yeast infections of the central nervous system: A clinical review. Medicine *63*:108–132, 1984.
160. Samuda, G. M., Chang, W. K., Yeung, C. Y., et al.: Monoplegia caused by enterovirus 71: An outbreak in Hong Kong. Pediatr. Infect. Dis. *6*:206–208, 1987.
161. Sands, M. L., Ryczak, M., and Brown, R. B.: Recurrent aseptic meningitis followed by transverse myelitis as a presentation of systemic lupus erythematosus. J. Rheumatol. *15*:862–864, 1988.
162. Sawyer, M. H., Holland, D., Aintablian, N., et al.: Diagnosis of enteroviral central nervous system infection by polymerase chain reaction during a large community outbreak. Pediatr. Infect. Dis. J. *13*:177–182, 1994.
163. Schlesinger, Y., Sawyer, M. H., and Storch, G. A.: Enteroviral meningitis in infancy: Potential role for polymerase chain reaction in patient management. Pediatrics *94*:157–162, 1994.
164. Schumaker, J. D., Chuard, C., Renevey, F., et al.: Outbreak of echovirus type 30 meningitis in Switzerland. Scand. J. Infect. Dis. *31*:539–542, 1999.
165. Shaked, Y., and Samra, Y.: Q fever meningoencephalitis associated with bilateral abducens nerve paralysis, bilateral optic neuritis and abnormal cerebrospinal fluid findings. Infection *17*:394–396, 1989.
166. Shinora, M., Uchida, K., Shimada, S., et al.: Characterization of enterovirus type 71 isolated in Saitama Prefecture in 2000. Kansenshogaku Zasshi *75*:490–494, 2001.
167. Simila, S., Jouppila, R., Salmi, A., et al.: Encephalomeningitis in children associated with an adenovirus type 7 epidemic. Acta Paediatr. Scand. *59*:310–316, 1970.
168. Singer, J. I., Maur, P. R., Riley, J. P., et al.: Management of central nervous system infections during an epidemic of enteroviral aseptic meningitis. J. Pediatr. *96*:559–563, 1980.
169. Sköldenberg, B.: On the role of viruses in acute infectious diseases of the central nervous system: Clinical and laboratory studies on hospitalized patients. Scand. J. Infect. Dis. *3*(Suppl.):5–95, 1975.
170. Sköldenberg, B., Jeansson, S., and Wolontis, S.: Herpes simplex virus type 2 and acute aseptic meningitis. Scand. J. Infect. Dis. *7*:227–232, 1975.
171. Socan, M., Beovic, B., and Kese, D.: *Chlamydia* pneumonia and meningoencephalitis. N. Engl. J. Med. *331*:406, 1994.
172. Sohier, R., Chardonnet, Y., and Prunieras, M.: Adenoviruses: Status of current knowledge. Prog. Med. Virol. *7*:253–325, 1965.
173. Somekh, E., Shobat, T., Hansher, R., et al.: An outbreak of echovirus 11 in a children's home. Epidemiol. Infect. *126*:441–444, 2001.
174. Southern, P. M., Jr.: Relapsing fever. *In* Tice, F. (ed.): Practice of Medicine. Vol. 3. Scranton, PA, Hoeber Medical Div., Harper & Row, 1969, pp. 1–19.
175. Spillane, J. D., and Wells, C. E. C.: The neurology of Jennerian vaccination: A clinical account of the neurological complications which occurred during the smallpox epidemic in South Wales in 1962. Brain *87*:1–44, 1964.
176. Steel, J. G., Dix, R. D., and Baringer, J. R.: Isolation of herpes simplex virus type 1 in recurrent (Mollaret) meningitis. Ann. Neurol. *11*:17–21, 1982.
177. Sumaya, C. V., and Ench, Y.: Epstein-Barr virus infectious mononucleosis in children. I. Clinical and general laboratory findings. Pediatrics *75*:1003–1010, 1985.
178. Sumaya, C. V., and Corman, L. I.: Enteroviral meningitis in early infancy: Significance in community outbreaks. Pediatr. Infect. Dis. *1*:151–154, 1982.
179. Sundelof, B., Gnarpe, H., and Gnarpe, J.: An unusual manifestation of *Chlamydia pneumoniae* infection: Meningitis, hepatitis, iritis and atypical erythema nodosum. Scand. J. Infect. Dis. *25*:259–261, 1993.
180. Suzuki, N., Terada, S., and Inoue, M.: Neonatal meningitis with human parvovirus B19 infection. Arch. Dis. Child. Fetal Neonatal Ed. *73*:F196–F197, 1995.
181. Syrogiannopoulos, G. A., Grivea, I. A., Anastassiou, E. D., et al.: Sterile cerebrospinal fluid pleocytosis in young infants with urinary tract infection. Pediatr. Infect. Dis. J. *20*:927–930, 2001.
182. Syverton, J. T., McLean, D. M., daSilva, M. M., et al.: Outbreak of aseptic meningitis caused by coxsackie B5 virus: Laboratory, clinical and epidemiologic study. J. A. M. A. *164*:2015–2019, 1957.
183. Tang, Y., Cleavinger, P. J., Li, H., et al.: Analysis of candidate-host immunogenetic determinants in herpes simplex virus-associated Mollaret's meningitis. Clin. Infect. Dis. *30*:176–178, 2000.
184. Tedder, D. G., Ashley, R., Tyler, K. L., et al.: Herpes simplex virus infection as a cause of benign recurrent lymphocytic meningitis. Ann. Intern. Med. *121*:334–338, 1994.
185. Terni, M., Caccialanza, P., Cassai, E., et al.: Aseptic meningitis in association with herpes progenitalis. N. Engl. J. Med. *285*:503–504, 1971.
186. Thoren, A., and Widell, A.: PCR for the diagnosis of enteroviral meningitis. Scand. J. Infect. Dis. *26*:249–254, 1994.

187. Tsutsumi, H., Kamazaki, H., and Nakata, S.: Sequential development of acute meningoencephalitis and transverse myelitis caused by Epstein-Barr virus during infectious mononucleosis. Pediatr. Infect. Dis. J. *13*:665–667, 1994.
188. Uysal, G., Ozkaya, E., Guven, A.: Echovirus 30 outbreak of aseptic meningitis in Turkey. Pediatr. Infect. Dis. J. *19*:490, 2000.
189. Vieth, U. C., Kunzelmann, M., Diedrich, S., et al.: An echovirus 30 outbreak with high meningitis attack rate among children and household members at four day-care centers. Eur. J. Epidemiol. *15*:655–658, 1999.
190. Vreede, R. W., Schellekens, H., and Zuijderwijk, M.: Isolation of parainfluenza virus type 3 from cerebrospinal fluid. J. Infect. Dis. *165*:1166, 1992.
191. Waites, K. B., Duffy, L. B., Crouse, D. T., et al.: Mycoplasmal infections of cerebrospinal fluid in newborn infants from a community hospital population. Pediatr. Infect. Dis. *9*:241–245, 1990.
192. Waites, K. B., Rudd, P. T., Crouse, D. T., et al.: Chronic *Ureaplasma urealyticum* and *Mycoplasma hominis* infections of central nervous system in preterm infants. Lancet *1*:17–21, 1988.
193. Wallgren, A.: Die ätiologie der enzephalomeningitis bei kindern, besonders des syndromes der akuten abakteriellen (aseptichen) meningitis. Acta Paediatr. Scand. *40*:541–565, 1951.
194. Wallgren, A.: Une nouvelle maladie infectieuse du système nerveux central? Acta Paediatr. Scand. *4*(Suppl.):158–182, 1925.
195. Warren, J.: Encephalomyocarditis viruses. *In* Horsfall, F. L., and Tamm, I. (eds.): Viral and Rickettsial Infections of Man. Philadelphia, J. B. Lippincott, 1965, pp. 562–568.
196. Weller, P. F.: Eosinophilic meningitis. Am. J. Med. *95*:250–253, 1993.
197. Weller, T. H.: Varicella-Herpes zoster virus. *In* Evans, A. S. (ed.): Viral Infections of Humans: Epidemiology and Control. 2nd ed. New York, Plenum Medical, 1982, pp. 569–595.
198. Wickman, I.: Studien über poliomyelitis acuta: Zugleich ein beitrag zur kenntnis der myelitis acuta. Berlin, S. Karger, Engl. Trans. Nev. and Ment. Dis. Monog. Ser. No. 16, 1905. p. 1913,
199. Wilfert, C. M., Lehrman, S. N., and Katz, S. L.: Enteroviruses and meningitis. Pediatr. Infect. Dis. *2*:333–341, 1983.
200. Wilfert, C. M., Thompson, R. J., Jr., Sunder, T. R., et al.: Longitudinal assessment of children with enteroviral meningitis during the first three months of life. Pediatrics *67*:811–815, 1981.
201. Williams, C. L., Strobino, B., Lee, A., et al.: Lyme disease in childhood: Clinical and epidemiologic features of ninety cases. Pediatr. Infect. Dis. *9*: 10–14, 1990.
202. Wong, C. J., Price, Z., and Bruckner, D. A.: Aseptic meningitis in an infant with rotavirus gastroenteritis. Pediatr. Infect. Dis. *3*:244–246, 1984.
203. Wong, J. G., Hathaway, S. C., Paat, J. J., et al.: Drug-induced meningitis: A case involving trimethoprim-sulfamethoxazole. Postgrad. Med. *96*: 117–124, 1994.
204. Wong, M. L., Kaplan, S., Dunkle, L. M., et al.: Leptospirosis: A childhood disease. J. Pediatr. *90*:532–537, 1977.
205. Yanagihara, K., Tanaka-Taya, K., Itagaki, Y., et al.: Human herpesvirus 6 meningoencephalitis with sequelae. Pediatr. Infect. Dis. J. *14*:240–242, 1995.
206. Yerly, S., Gervaix, A., Simonet, V., et al.: Rapid and sensitive detection of enteroviruses in specimens from patients with aseptic meningitis. J. Clin. Microbiol. *34*:199–201, 1996.
207. Young, E. J.: Human brucellosis. Rev. Infect. Dis. *5*:821–842, 1983.

Encephalitis and Meningoencephalitis

JAMES D. CHERRY ■ W. DONALD SHIELDS

Encephalitis is an inflammation of the brain, and meningoencephalitis is a similar inflammatory illness in which both the brain and meninges are involved. The diagnosis of encephalitis can be established with absolute certainty only by the microscopic examination of brain tissue, and similarly the etiology is established only by the recovery from or the demonstration in brain tissue of an infectious agent. In clinical practice, the diagnosis frequently is based on neurologic manifestations, the recovery of infectious agents from other sites in the body, the serologic evidence of a specific infection, and relevant epidemiologic findings.

Encephalitis frequently is classified as primary or as postinfectious or parainfectious.[36] Primary encephalitis is an illness in which encephalitis is the major manifestation. Symptoms are caused by direct invasion and replication of an infectious agent in the central nervous system (CNS), resulting in objective clinical evidence of cerebral or cerebellar dysfunction. Postinfectious or parainfectious encephalitis occurs after or in combination with other illnesses that are not CNS illnesses or after a vaccine or other product has been administered. Manifestations may be mediated immunologically.

When neurologic clinical findings suggest encephalitis, but inflammation of the brain has not occurred (such as in Reye syndrome), the condition is identified by the less specific term *encephalopathy*. Frequently, when encephalitis or meningoencephalitis occurs, other areas of the nervous system, such as the spinal cord (myelitis), nerve roots (radiculitis), and nerves (neuritis), also are involved.

History

Rabies encephalitis was recognized in ancient times in Europe and Asia.[117] In 100 AD, Celsus noted the relationship of animal rabies to human disease. "Sleeping sickness" associated with epidemic influenza was noted early in the 18th century.[235] For the past 100 years, epizootics of encephalitis in equine animals have been observed in the United States, and in 1933, St. Louis encephalitis virus was isolated from the brains of humans dying from epidemic encephalitis.[164, 178] Meningoencephalitis was recognized at the beginning of the 20th century as a complication of mumps.[72] Nonpolio enteroviruses have been known for the past 50 years to be a cause of encephalitis; during the same period, more than 400 zoonotic arthropod-borne viruses have been discovered, and of these, 100 or more cause encephalitis in humans.[17]

Etiology

Etiologic agents in acute encephalitis, meningoencephalitis, and acute illnesses with an encephalitic component are presented in Table 43–1. All of the infectious agents or diseases are presented more fully and are referenced more completely in other areas of this book (see Index).

VIRUSES

Adenoviruses are uncommon but not rare causes of encephalitis and meningoencephalitis.[41, 59, 60, 66, 133, 174, 179] Adenoviral types 1, 2, 3, 5, 6, 7, 11, 12, and 32 have been recovered from either the brain or cerebrospinal fluid (CSF) in afflicted patients. Recently, a syndrome of transient encephalopathy associated with adenovirus type 3 has been described.[220] Herpes simplex virus type 2 (HSV-2) is a leading cause of severe and frequently fatal encephalitis in neonates.[240] In older children, the usual cause is HSV-1.[49, 113, 131, 155, 166, 184, 192, 230] Recurrent genital infection with HSV-2 occasionally is associated with an aseptic meningitis, but this type 2 virus almost never causes encephalitis in other than the newborn period.

Encephalitis can occur in association with primary infection with varicella-zoster virus (VZV) (chickenpox) and with endogenous recurrent disease (herpes zoster).[29, 51, 57, 70, 115, 134, 136, 191, 216] In chickenpox, the rate of encephalitis is

TABLE 43–1 ■ ETIOLOGIC AGENTS IN ACUTE ENCEPHALITIS AND ACUTE MENINGOENCEPHALITIS

Etiologic Agents	Frequency*
Viruses	
Spread person-to-person only	
Adenoviruses	+ +
Herpes simplex types 1 and 2	+ + +
Human herpesvirus type 6	+ +
Human herpesvirus type 7	+
Varicella-zoster	+ +
Epstein-Barr	+
Cytomegalovirus	+ +
Variola	+
Enteroviruses	+ +
Reoviruses	+
Rubella	+ +
Influenza A and B	+ +
Respiratory syncytial	+
Parainfluenza 1-3	+
Mumps	+ + +
Measles	+ +
Hepatitis B	+
Human parvovirus	+
Hepatitis A	+
Rotavirus	+
BK	+
Spread to people by mosquitoes or ticks	
Arboviruses†—those that occur in the United States are the following: St. Louis, West Nile, Eastern equine, Western equine, Venezuelan equine, California, Powassan, and Colorado tick fever	+ + +
Spread by warm-blooded mammals	
Rabies	+ + +
Herpesvirus simiae (herpes B)	+
Lymphocytic choriomeningitis	+ +
Encephalomyocarditis	+
Vesicular stomatitis	+
Equine morbillivirus (Hendra)	+
Nipah	+
Bacteria	
Haemophilus influenzae, Neisseria meningitidis, Streptococcus pneumoniae, Mycobacterium tuberculosis, and other bacterial meningitides often have an encephalitic component.	+ + +
Spirochetal infections: *Treponema pallidum, Leptospira, Borrelia burgdorferi,* and other *Borrelia* species infections	+ + +
Brucella species	+
Actinomyces and *Nocardia*	+
Bartonella henselae	+
Other	
Chlamydia psittaci, Chlamydia pneumoniae	+
Rickettsial infections: Rocky Mountain spotted fever, ehrlichiosis, Q fever, and typhus	+ + +
Mycoplasma infections: *Mycoplasma pneumoniae* and *Mycoplasma hominis*	+ +
Fungal: *Coccidioides immitis, Cryptococcus neoformans,* and other fungal meningitides often have an encephalitic component.	+ +
Protozoal: *Plasmodium* species, *Trypanosoma* species, *Naegleria* species, *Acanthamoeba* species, *Balamuthia mandrillaris,* and *Toxoplasma gondii*	+ + +
Helminths: *Trichinella spiralis, Schistosoma* species, *Strongyloides stercoralis, Baylisascaris procyonis*	+ +
Drug: trimethoprim	+

*Frequency refers to the rate of occurrence of encephalitis or encephalitis component in the particular disease cited and not its relative overall occurrence; + + + = frequent, + + = infrequent; + = rare.

†See Chapters 175, 178, 179, 191, and 192 for viral diseases in other countries transmitted by arthropods.

approximately 0.3 per 1000 cases,[42] and the case-fatality rate is approximately 17 percent.[186] Between 0.5 and 5 percent of patients with herpes zoster have encephalitis.[116] This complication occurs more commonly in immunocompromised patients.

In infectious mononucleosis, encephalitis occurs in less than 1 percent of cases; in addition, encephalitis rarely is the sole manifestation of Epstein-Barr virus infection.[54, 56, 107, 229] Caruso and associates[32] reported five children with subacute and chronic neurologic deficits associated with apparent primary Epstein-Barr viral infections. Severe chronic involvement of the brain is a common occurrence in congenital cytomegalovirus (CMV) infection.[101] Encephalitis due to acquired CMV infection is a relatively uncommon occurrence and usually occurs in immunocompromised children.[107, 215] Several cases have been described in previously healthy patients, however. Human herpesvirus type 6 (HHV-6) is an important cause of acute febrile illness, as well as roseola infantum, in young children.[100] Febrile convulsions occur commonly in HHV-6 infections, and encephalitis is a rare complication of roseola. Studies indicate that HHV-6 is an infrequent cause of encephalitis in children.[113, 114, 157, 243] Human herpesvirus type 7 (HHV-7) also has been implicated as a causative agent in encephalitis.[184, 225] Smallpox (variola virus infection), before its worldwide eradication, was a rare cause of encephalitis.

Enteroviruses now are the leading viral cause of neurologic disease in children in the United States, and they are a major cause of encephalitis.* The following viral types have been associated with encephalitis: coxsackieviruses A2, 4 to 7, 9, 10, 16, and B1–5; echoviruses 1 to 9, 11 to 25, 27, 30, and 33; and enterovirus 71. In 1998, an extensive epidemic of enterovirus 71 disease occurred in Taiwan.[44, 110, 149, 234] Manifestations of illness in this epidemic were varied, and a large number of children had severe neurologic events. They included meningitis, meningoencephalitis, encephalitis, cerebellitis, and polio-like syndrome. In particular, a large number of children had brain stem encephalitis, with numerous fatalities. A variety of neurologic illnesses, including encephalitis, have occurred rarely in reoviral infections.[71, 121, 134, 137, 246]

Neurologic involvement is a common manifestation of congenital rubella virus infection,[102] and encephalitis is a rare complication of noncongenital disease.[165] Some data suggest a rate of encephalitis in rubella between 1 per 5000 and 1 per 10,000 cases.[41] In the prevaccine era, the encephalitis rate in 1 epidemic in 1964 was 1 per 5000 cases, and in another epidemic in 1942, it was 1 per 6000 cases.[153, 212] In addition to Reye syndrome (see Chapter 57), which is an uncommon but important neurologic disease associated with influenza viral infections, encephalitis also occurs with some regularity as a manifestation of influenza viral infection.† During every influenza epidemic, university hospital pediatric services see one or two cases of encephalitis in children with influenza. Sato and colleagues[204] reported two children with reversible frontal lobe syndromes associated with influenza A viral infections. On rare occasions, encephalitis occurs during the course of respiratory infections with respiratory syncytial virus and parainfluenza virus infections.[10, 20, 42, 59, 61, 134, 233]

Before the widespread use of mumps vaccine, this virus was the leading cause of meningoencephalitis in the United States. Today, mumps is a rare event. The rate of encephalitis in mumps is approximately 3 episodes per 1000 cases.[37] The death-to-case rate is 1.4 percent. In the prevaccine era, measles was an important cause of severe encephalitis in children.[40, 42] Measles is a relatively rare event in the United States, and, therefore, encephalitis occurs uncommonly, at a rate of 0.74 per 1000 cases of measles. The death-to-case rate is 14 percent.

Hepatitis B virus is a rare cause of encephalitis, and encephalitis has been reported as a complication of erythema infectiosum on two occasions (human parvovirus infection).[10, 11, 99] Encephalitis and cerebellitis have been noted in association with rotavirus gastroenteritis,[150, 172] and a primary infection with BK virus was noted in a 34-year-old man with monophasic encephalitis.[232] A case of encephalitis in a 3-year-old boy caused by vesicular stomatitis virus has been presented.[190] This virus can be spread by direct contact with infected animals or by insects.

Arboviruses are the most important worldwide cause of severe encephalitis. The occurrence of specific arboviruses is both seasonal and highly geographic. More than 400 different arboviruses exist, and information about illnesses caused by specific types in various areas of the world is detailed in Chapters 175, 178, 179, 191, and 192.[17, 107, 124] In the United States, eight arboviruses (eastern equine, western equine, Venezuelan equine, St. Louis, Powassan, West Nile, California, and Colorado tick fever) that cause encephalitis have been isolated. Illness caused by St. Louis virus has been the most common arboviral disease in the United States. In 1999, an epidemic of West Nile virus encephalitis occurred in New York City and two surrounding counties.[152] The epidemic was related to a simultaneous epizootic among American crows and other bird species. The epizootic has continued and spread throughout the eastern United States.[35]

Each year in the United States, the causative agent is not determined in approximately 75 percent of the cases of encephalitis. However, the seasonal occurrence (summer and fall) of these cases of undetermined etiology suggests that these cases most likely are caused by enteroviruses and arboviruses.

Human rabies is an uncommon occurrence in the United States, but more than 20,000 cases and deaths occur worldwide every year.[242] Since the early 1970s, approximately two cases of rabies have occurred per year in the United States, and approximately 50 percent of the cases have occurred in children and teenagers.[3, 39] Encephalitis caused by herpes B virus is rare; it occurs predominantly in monkey handlers and usually after monkey bites.[112] Except in outbreak situations, lymphocytic choriomeningitis virus rarely is recognized as a cause of encephalitis.[19] However, serologic surveys have indicated that neurologic disease caused by this virus is not rare in the United States.[60–62, 118, 164] Rare cases of encephalitis are caused by encephalomyocarditis virus; infection of humans with this virus is fairly common, but most infections go unrecognized.[222]

A fatal case of encephalitis caused by a novel paramyxovirus (equine morbillivirus; Hendra virus) has been reported in an adult.[180] This virus previously had been noted in association with fatal respiratory infections in horses and humans. Another new paramyxovirus (Nipah virus) was responsible for an extensive outbreak of encephalitis in pig farmers in Malaysia.[85, 145]

BACTERIA

Signs and symptoms of acute encephalitis (drowsiness, coma, convulsions, mental confusion) commonly occur in *Haemophilus influenzae, Neisseria meningitidis,* and *Streptococcus pneumoniae* bacterial meningitides, but the true etiology usually is established easily by the examination of

*See references 16, 41, 49, 59–61, 66, 95, 107, 123, 127, 133, 141, 164, 168, 170, 174.

†See references 16, 41, 51, 59–61, 76, 83, 84, 134, 174, 181, 191, 248.

the CSF. Spirochetal infections are a more common cause of nervous system disease, specifically encephalitis, than generally is appreciated. Encephalitis is a recognized complication of leptospirosis, Lyme disease, and relapsing fever.[20, 26, 183, 217] *Brucella* spp. are an infrequent cause of meningoencephalitis.[244] Encephalitis caused by *Bartonella henselae* is an uncommon complication of cat-scratch disease.[30, 162, 175, 219]

Neurologic disease is a relatively common complication of pertussis. A 10-year study in the United States indicated a rate of neurologic disease in infants of approximately 9 per 1000 cases.[73] An extensive review by Miller and associates[165] suggested that the neurologic disease occurring with pertussis rarely, if ever, is inflammatory, and, therefore, it is better classified as an encephalopathy.

OTHER AGENTS

Encephalitis is an uncommon event in psittacosis, occurring in 1 to 3 percent of cases.[31, 80] It can be caused by both *Chlamydia psittaci* and *Chlamydia pneumoniae.* Neurologic involvement commonly occurs in Rocky Mountain spotted fever.[105, 126] In one study, two thirds of the ill children had evidence of encephalitis. Neurologic sequelae are common events.[87] Neurologic involvement also occurs in nonspotted fever rickettsial infections.[67, 86, 148, 192, 210] *Coxiella burnetii, Ehrlichia canis, Rickettsia typhi,* and *Rickettsia canada* all have been implicated.

Mycoplasma pneumoniae is an important cause of encephalitis.[21, 33, 53, 135, 185, 213] Pönkä[185] noted that 4.8 percent of hospitalized patients with *M. pneumoniae* infections had CNS manifestations, and most of them had encephalitis or meningoencephalitis. *Mycoplasma hominis* is a rare cause of neonatal meningoencephalitis.[151]

A large number of fungi cause neurologic illness.[203] These illnesses occur most commonly in immunocompromised patients, but some infections occur in apparently normal people. Meningitis and brain abscess are the most common pathologic events, but encephalitis is associated commonly with meningitis. The following fungal agents are the most common causes of meningoencephalitis in children and adults with normal immunologic status: *Blastomyces dermatitidis, Coccidioides immitis, Cryptococcus neoformans, Cladosporium* spp., *Histoplasma capsulatum,* and *Paracoccidioides brasiliensis.*

Involvement of the brain in parasitic infections is a common occurrence, and the reader is referred to Section XXII for a complete review. Cerebral malaria is a common complication of *Plasmodium falciparum* infection. Meningoencephalitis and enlarging cerebral mass lesions rarely occur in acute acquired toxoplasmosis.[227] The free-living amoeba *Naegleria fowleri* is a rare cause of encephalitis, but infection with this agent usually is fatal.[207, 223] Most cases occur in children and young adults and are caused by swimming or playing in contaminated water. Fatal encephalitis also has resulted from infection with *Balamuthia mandrillaris*, a soil amoeba formerly thought to be innocuous.[92, 231] *Baylisascaris procyonis*, a raccoon roundworm, has been associated with severe and often fatal encephalitis in children.[34] A recurrent encephalitis caused by administration of trimethoprim has been reported.[106]

POSTIMMUNIZATION

Neurologic disease, including encephalitis and meningoencephalitis, has occurred after immunization with a variety of prophylactic and therapeutic preparations. Depending on the type of immunizing agent, the encephalitis can be the result of an immunologic reaction, a CNS infection with the vaccine virus, or a combination of infection and immunologic reaction. Historically, many of the observed neurologic reactions occurred after the administration of antiserums prepared in animals in the treatment of specific diseases. Antiserums to the following diseases or infectious agents have been noted in association with neurologic illness: tetanus, diphtheria, scarlet fever, tuberculosis, gas gangrene, pneumococcus, gonococcus, meningococcus, and streptococci.[2, 111, 128, 166, 197] Of 100 neurologic syndromes complicating administration of serum reviewed by Miller and Stanton,[166] only 10 percent were of a cerebral or meningeal type.

Neurologic disease was a common complication of rabies vaccine derived from animal nervous tissue.[166] The incidence of complication was between 3 per 1000 and 1 per 6000 cases.[22, 166] Approximately 10 percent of the neurologic disease attributed to this rabies vaccine was meningoencephalitic or encephalomyelitic. Encephalitis has not been observed after the use of the human diploid cell rabies vaccine presently available.[38]

Encephalitis was an important complication of smallpox vaccination.[4, 25, 77, 90, 123, 143, 171, 218] The rate of encephalitis varied markedly from one study to another, from 1 in 4000 primary vaccinations in the Netherlands[171] to approximately 1 in 80,000 primary vaccinations in the United States.[142]

Neurologic disease, including encephalitis, occurs rarely after the administration of typhoid-paratyphoid vaccine.[166] Neurologic disease also rarely has been attributed to administration of tetanus toxoid and diphtheria toxoid, but the manifestations rarely are central.

Encephalitis and encephalopathy have been observed after the administration of influenza immunization.[82, 91, 198, 241] However, in the extensive surveillance that occurred in the United States during the period October 1, 1976 to December 16, 1976, when 45,651,113 people received the A/New Jersey/76 influenza vaccine, no epidemiologic evidence of an association between vaccine and encephalitis was noted.[98] Two children who developed acute disseminated encephalomyelitis after receiving Japanese B encephalitis vaccination have been reported.[176]

Neurologic disease developing after pertussis immunization is a well-known event.[46–48] Pathologic evidence in fatal cases suggests encephalopathy rather than encephalitis.[55] Because neurologic illness similar to that which occurs after the administration of pertussis vaccination is not an infrequent event in infants who have not been vaccinated, establishing a true rate of pertussis vaccine encephalopathy or that such an entity exists at all has been difficult. The analysis of studies suggests that encephalopathy caused by pertussis vaccine does not occur.[47, 48, 94]

Neurologic disease, including encephalitis, is a rare complication of measles immunization.[40, 43, 78, 140] The rate in vaccinees in the United States is less than 1 per million. In contrast, the finding in the National Childhood Encephalopathy Study in England, Scotland, and Wales indicated a rate of 1 per 87,000 immunizations.[1] This high rate of encephalopathy may be an artifact due to the misclassification of complicated febrile convulsions as encephalopathy. Meningoencephalitis is a rare complication of mumps immunization with some vaccine virus strains.[158] It has not been a problem in the United States, however.

A fatal encephalitis occurred in a 3-year-old child after receiving 17D yellow fever vaccine.[188]

POSTINFECTIOUS ENCEPHALITIS

Postinfectious or parainfectious encephalitis is an illness that occurs after a demonstrated or presumed viral infection and is thought to be immune mediated rather than due to a direct effect of the virus in nerve cells.[93, 118–120, 201] This theory has been studied extensively by Johnson and Griffin[93, 119, 120] in encephalitis associated with measles. They have described a periventricular demyelinating disease and have not been able to isolate measles virus or identify measles antigens in nervous tissue. However, other investigators, including one of us (J. D. C.), have recovered measles virus from the CSF and brain of affected patients.[78, 161, 163, 189, 209] We suggest that immune mechanisms play a role in the pathogenesis of measles and perhaps other postinfectious neurologic illnesses, but the process is stimulated by the direct presence of the antigen in the nervous system. The mechanism of disease is important regarding possible treatment: steroids might be useful in immune-mediated disease but could be detrimental in an acute viral infection.

In contrast with measles, other apparent postinfectious encephalitides that usually have a subacute onset are immune mediated and have multifocal white-matter lesions.[5, 9, 24, 97, 129, 160, 171] Specifically, acute disseminated encephalomyelitis usually is subacute in onset and is characterized by optic neuritis, myelitis, ataxia, hemiparesis, cranial nerve palsies, and multifocal white-matter lesions that are indistinguishable on magnetic resonance imaging (MRI) from those seen in multiple sclerosis. Patients with this illness respond dramatically to treatment with steroids and perhaps intravenous immunoglobulin.

CHRONIC ENCEPHALITIC OR ENCEPHALOPATHIC ILLNESSES

"Slow infections" that cause encephalitic and encephalopathic illness in humans have been recognized for many years. Many of these illnesses now are recognized as viral infections or caused by prions. Viral illnesses include progressive multifocal leukoencephalopathy (JC, SV40, and BK viruses), subacute sclerosing panencephalitis (measles virus), and acquired immunodeficiency syndrome (human immunodeficiency virus type 1 [HIV-1] and type 2 [HIV-2]). Prion diseases, called *transmissible spongiform encephalopathies*, include kuru, Jakob-Creutzfeldt disease, and Gerstmann-Sträussler-Scheinker disease.[187] They are related to scrapie of sheep and bovine spongiform encephalopathy (mad cow disease), which are prion diseases of animals. These chronic illnesses are presented in Chapter 160.

Epidemiology

Because encephalitis has many different causes, no unified epidemiologic pattern exists. The specific epidemiology of each infectious agent or disease is presented in detail in the various respective chapters of this book; only a brief overview is presented here. Most cases occur in the summer and fall, reflecting arboviral and enteroviral etiologies. Encephalitis caused by arboviruses occurs in localized outbreaks and epidemics with boundaries determined by the range of particular mosquito vectors and the prevalence of natural reservoir animals.

Arboviruses are zoonoses in which humans are infected accidentally by an arthropod vector, humans not being essential in the life cycle of arboviruses. Most commonly, mosquitoes or other insects acquire arboviruses by biting infected birds, which often have prolonged viremia without illness. The insect vectors, although preferring birds, bite other vertebrates, including humans and horses. Encephalitis in horses and mules may be the first indication of incipient trouble in an area; veterinarians often are the first to detect an impending epidemic. Rural exposure is not a sine qua non; urban and suburban outbreaks are frequent.

Although enteroviral disease, including aseptic meningitis, occurs in epidemics, severe encephalitis caused by these agents usually is a sporadic event.

Sporadic cases of encephalitis occur in any season; epidemiologic considerations that must be reviewed in a search for the causative agent include geographic area; climatic conditions; animal, water, food, soil, and personal exposures; and host factors.

Pathogenesis

Because encephalitis and meningoencephalitis have multiple causes, the lack of a unified pathogenesis is not surprising.* Clinical manifestations of encephalitis can result from either a direct or an indirect effect of an infectious agent on the brain. Rabies, arbovirus infection, herpes simplex, and enteroviral encephalitides are examples in which the viral infections directly involve tissue cells within the brain. In contrast, encephalitic symptoms in bacterial meningitides and in rickettsial infections may be caused by the vasculitis and liberated toxins of the surrounding infection. In addition, in many postinfectious or parainfectious encephalitides, immunologic events clearly are important in the pathogenesis. In this category are measles and *M. pneumoniae* infections.

Postinfectious or parainfectious encephalitis is an acute demyelinating disease of the brain in which the findings suggest an autoimmune process. Usually, little evidence of an active infectious process is present when symptoms occur. However, viral or other agents initially probably invaded the CNS and then were cleared but were a trigger for the subsequent disease. An immune (T-cell) response to myelin basic protein occurs.

In most encephalitides, such as those caused by arboviruses, mumps, and enteroviruses, the CNS infection is secondary to a primary viral infection elsewhere in the body. In general, the infectious agents, whether from ingestion, as in enteroviral infections, or from the bite of a mosquito, as in an arboviral infection, enter the lymphatic system. In the lymphatics, viral multiplication occurs, which results in seeding of the bloodstream and then infection of other organs in the body. Viral multiplication then occurs at these secondary infection sites; extensive secondary viremia occurs; and then the CNS becomes infected. Actual involvement of nervous tissue may result from growth across or passive diffusion through brain capillaries or centripetal axonal transport of virus from the olfactory neuroepithelium to the olfactory bulb.[169]

Infection of the brain also may occur through the peripheral nerves. This retrograde spread of virus is important in rabies and HSV encephalitis.

Pathology

Determining the etiology of encephalitis at autopsy is difficult, although morphologic identification of falciparum malaria, trypanosomiasis, and fungal encephalitis is possible.[55, 118, 165, 166, 218] In viral encephalitides, the histopathologist may recognize rabies (Negri bodies) or an agent of the herpesvirus group (intranuclear inclusion bodies).

*See references 4, 18, 33, 53, 68, 75, 78, 87, 93, 96, 102, 107, 116, 118, 164–166, 169, 238.

Tissue sections of the brain generally reveal meningeal congestion and mononuclear infiltration, perivascular cuffs of lymphocytes and plasma cells, some perivascular tissue necrosis with myelin breakdown, neuronal disruption in various stages (including ultimately neuronophagia), and endothelial proliferation or necrosis. A marked degree of demyelination with preservation of neurons and their axons is considered to be predominantly postinfectious or parainfectious (autoimmune) encephalitis. The severity and the extent of observed lesions vary with the infectious agent as well as with the degree of reaction of the host. The cerebral cortex, especially the temporal lobe, often is affected severely by HSV; the arboviruses tend to affect the entire brain; and rabies has a predilection for the basal structures. Involvement of the spinal cord, nerve roots, and peripheral nerves is variable.

Clinical Manifestations

The clinical findings in encephalitis are determined by the severity of involvement and anatomic localization of the affected portions of the nervous system, the inherent pathogenicity of the offending agent, and the immune and other reactive mechanisms of the patient ("host factors"). Accordingly, a wide range of severity of clinical manifestations exists even with the same etiologic agent. Evidence of brain parenchymal involvement is the hallmark of encephalitis. Children with encephalitis may demonstrate evidence of diffuse disease, such as behavioral or personality changes; decreased consciousness; and generalized seizures or localized changes, such as focal seizures, hemiparesis, movement disorders, cranial nerve defects, and ataxia. Some children may appear to be mildly affected initially only to lapse into coma and sudden death. In others, the illness is ushered in by high fever, violent convulsions interspersed with bizarre movements, and hallucinations alternating with brief periods of clarity, and the children emerge with relatively few sequelae.

Most commonly, the initial manifestations resemble an undifferentiated acute systemic illness with fever, headache, or, in infants, screaming spells, abdominal distress, nausea, and vomiting. Signs of an associated mild nasopharyngitis may suggest a respiratory infection. As the temperature rises, new findings direct attention to the nervous system: mental dullness eventuating in stupor; bizarre movements; convulsions; nuchal rigidity, often not as pronounced as in purely meningitic illness; and focal neurologic signs, which may be stationary, progress, or fluctuate. Loss of bowel and bladder control and unprovoked emotional outbursts may occur.

SPECIFIC FORMS OF ENCEPHALITIS

Specific forms of encephalitis or complicating manifestations of encephalitis include Guillain-Barré syndrome, acute transverse myelitis, acute hemiplegia, brain stem encephalitis, and acute cerebellar ataxia. Acute cerebellar ataxia is characterized by an abrupt onset of truncal ataxia resulting in varying degrees of gait disturbance and balance abnormalities. Children with this illness have tremulousness of the head and trunk when in the upright position and of the extremities when attempting to move them against gravity. The duration of illness varies from 3 to 4 days to several weeks, and as many as 30 percent of those affected have minimal to moderate permanent residual ataxia.

Brain stem encephalitis is a rare disorder but is important because clinical signs appear much like those of a brain stem glioma. The differentiation is made by the time of onset of symptoms. Brain stem glioma usually has slowly progressive symptoms over several weeks or months. Brain stem encephalitis evolves over the course of as few as 1 to 7 days. Both disorders may be associated with radiographic evidence of brain stem enlargement. Brain stem encephalitis resolves after 1 to 4 weeks' duration, whereas a tumor continues to progress until radiation therapy is given.

Most cases of brain stem encephalitis appear to be postinfectious and, thus, are similar to postinfectious cerebellar ataxia, Miller-Fisher syndrome, or Guillain-Barré syndrome. Indeed, the conditions often overlap.[6] In postinfectious cases, the onset of brain stem encephalitis begins 1 to 3 weeks after a nonspecific viral infection. However, brain stem encephalitis has been reported to occur as a result of specific, identifiable, and possibly treatable infectious agents, including HSV,[196, 206] VZV,[199, 221] and CMV,[81, 122] as well as *Listeria monocytogenes*[7, 13] *Propionibacterium acnes*[28] and *Campylobacter jejuni*.[245] Some patients with a typical clinical picture of brain stem encephalitis have had anti-GQ1b antibodies in the serum,[45] which may represent a subgroup of postinfectious brain stem encephalitis. Brain stem encephalitis may arise in HIV-infected patients and may be due to one of the treatable causes, such as herpes simplex encephalitis.[81, 101, 198] Recent reports suggest that intravenous immunoglobulin may be an effective therapy in some patients.[79]

Differential Diagnosis

The evaluation of the patient with an acute CNS illness (encephalopathy) must be considered carefully, and the sequence of tests should be dictated by the specific circumstances of the individual patient. Several disease processes may have a presentation similar to that of encephalitis or meningoencephalitis. The differential diagnosis of acute encephalopathy includes the following:

1. Metabolic diseases, such as hypoglycemia, uremic encephalopathy, hepatic encephalopathy, and rare genetic inborn errors of metabolism, including disorders of glucose or ammonia metabolism
2. Toxic disorders, such as drug ingestion or Reye syndrome
3. Mass lesions, such as tumor or abscess
4. Subarachnoid hemorrhage from arteriovenous malformation or aneurysm
5. Embolic lesions caused by bacterial endocarditis
6. Acute demyelinating disorders, including acute multiple sclerosis and acute hemorrhagic leukoencephalitis
7. Status epilepticus, especially nonconvulsive status epilepticus, such as complex-partial status or absence status
8. Infectious diseases, including viral, bacterial, fungal, chlamydial, mycoplasmal, and parasitic
9. Postinfectious diseases, including Guillain-Barré syndrome, brain stem encephalitis, Miller-Fisher syndrome, and acute cerebellar ataxia
10. Acute confusional migraine

Evaluation of the Patient with Encephalopathy or Possible Encephalitis

Obtaining a careful history and performing a physical and neurologic examination are essential in all patients who present with a history consistent with encephalitis. The differential diagnosis previously presented indicates that encephalitis is only one of many disorders that can present with an acute or subacute picture of encephalopathy. Although the diagnosis of encephalitis may be determined best with a lumbar puncture (LP) and evaluation of the CSF, LP may be contraindicated in some disorders and, if performed inappropriately, may lead to serious complications and even death. For example, a child who has a cerebellar tumor with acute obstruction of the fourth ventricle may present with a decreasing level of consciousness caused by the rapidly rising intracranial pressure (ICP). Nuchal rigidity may be present. The family may not have recognized the more subtle changes in cerebellar functions for the months before the acute obstruction developed and may give a history of acute encephalopathy. In that case, an LP could result in herniation through the foramen magnum. Thus, an essential matter is that the patient be assessed for the possibility of increased ICP and the potential for herniation. The history should be reviewed carefully, questioning specifically for symptoms of neurologic problems that manifested in the days or weeks before the acute disorder occurred. The physical examination must be performed with special attention given to focal neurologic abnormalities, cerebellar signs, and evidence of increased ICP. Conducting a careful funduscopic examination is important but may be impossible in an agitated patient or young child. However, the presence of papilledema would indicate that neuroimaging should be performed before carrying out the LP. If spontaneous venous pulsations are noted on funduscopic examination, ICP is not increased, and the LP can be performed without imaging the patient. In addition to LP, neuroimaging and electroencephalography (EEG) can be of great assistance in determining the cause of the encephalopathy and in determining the most appropriate course of therapy. The history and physical examination will be a guide to the most appropriate first test to perform, but, as a general rule, neuroimaging is the most likely to be helpful. The exception would be a child in nonconvulsive status epilepticus. The history may suggest encephalitis as the most likely diagnosis, but in some patients, nonconvulsive status epilepticus may be clinically indistinguishable from encephalitis.

NEUROIMAGING

Most patients with encephalopathy should undergo neuroimaging to aid diagnosis of treatable conditions, such as HSV encephalitis. Computed tomography (CT) scanning is helpful in the acute setting to identify abnormalities such as tumor or abscess and to decide whether performing an LP is safe. CT, however, is not as helpful as is MRI in detecting the subtle changes associated with encephalitis.[27, 147, 211] MRI should be the imaging technique of choice if it is readily available. In many cases of viral encephalitis, CT and MRI yield normal results or only nonspecific changes such as swelling[237] or edema.[147] An important exception is herpes simplex encephalitis. As previously noted, MRI is more sensitive than is CT. In one study, CT initially was positive in only 42 percent of cases, whereas MRI was positive in all cases.[130] MRI in HSV characteristically shows abnormalities in the medial temporal lobes, inferior frontal cortex, and insula.[146, 239] The likelihood of finding the abnormalities may be increased by using T2-weighted imaging and fluid attenuated inversion-recovery (FLAIR) sequences[8, 125] or diffusion-weighted imaging (DWI).[208, 224] However, the localization of abnormalities may be very different from the classic pattern in young children. In neonatal herpes encephalitis, widespread changes occur in the periventricular white matter, often sparing the medial temporal and inferior frontal lobes. Another pattern recently was described in children between 4 and 13 months of age in whom the cortex and adjacent white matter of the hemispheres were abnormal.[146]

In addition to herpes, other encephalitides may yield abnormal neuroimaging. CT and MRI results often are abnormal with disorders caused by arbovirus or enterovirus infections. When imaging is abnormal, it usually is nonspecific, demonstrating areas of decreased density (with CT) or increased signal intensity (with MRI) in the gray or white matter. Recently, a variety of MRI abnormalities with certain viral encephalitides have been reported. The basal ganglia, brain stem, and thalami have been reported to be abnormal on MRI imaging of patients with eastern equine encephalitis[63] and Japanese encephalitis.[109, 138] These differences help to distinguish HSV from other, nontreatable causes of viral encephalitis. Postinfectious disorders most often are associated with selective oligodendrocyte involvement.[15] Imaging thus shows increased signal in white matter with T2-weighted MRI or low density white matter with CT.[12, 24, 104, 129, 177] Patients with acute hemorrhagic leukoencephalitis, a rare disease that is rapidly progressive and often fatal, may present with a clinical picture similar to that of herpes simplex encephalitis. In contradistinction to HSV infection, however, the CT results often are abnormal within the first 1 or 2 days.[200, 236] Thus, if a patient with suspected herpes simplex encephalitis has abnormal CT results early in the course, acute hemorrhagic leukoencephalitis should be considered.

Another imaging technique that has been reported to be helpful in the diagnosis of encephalitis is single photon emission computed tomography (SPECT). Initial reports suggest that SPECT is more sensitive than is CT. Ackerman and colleagues[1] found that SPECT demonstrated greater sensitivity and more precise localization than did conventional radionuclide scanning and CT. Launes and associates[144] studied 14 encephalitis patients and found that SPECT detected temporal lobe abnormalities in all 6 of the patients with HSV encephalitis and yielded normal results in the remaining 8 who had other etiologies. Recently, a few cases of normal MRI scans but abnormal SPECT in patients with herpes simplex encephalitis have been reported.[103, 154] If SPECT is performed, it appears that ^{99m}Tc-hexamethyl propyleneamine oxime is superior to ^{99m}Tc-ethyl cysteinate dimer.[58, 74] As a general rule, SPECT should be reserved for cases with normal MRI and a nondiagnostic EEG in which herpes simplex encephalitis is still strongly suspected.

Intracranial ultrasonography in the neonate has been shown to be helpful in the diagnosis and follow-up of infants with herpes simplex virus or cytomegalovirus infections.[155]

ELECTROENCEPHALOGRAM

As a general rule, an EEG should be performed in most patients with encephalitis. EEG results of patients with encephalitis generally are normal or nonspecifically abnormal, showing diffuse slowing. However, critical exceptions to the general rule exist. In the setting of acute encephalopathy, comatose patients may be in nonconvulsive status epilepticus,[225] which requires immediate and appropriate intervention. On the other hand, the presence of periodic lateralized epileptiform discharges (PLEDs) in the EEG results strongly suggests the possibility of herpes simplex encephalitis but also may be an indication of seizures.[14] Early in the course of herpes encephalitis, generalized slowing of the background frequencies and focal slowing over the affected temporal lobe may occur. Within a few days, the characteristic PLEDs pattern develops in most cases. Later in the course, the background activity between the bursts of

PLEDs gradually may flatten. Occasionally, other areas of the brain appear to be involved, primarily with HSV. PLEDs, although strongly suggestive of HSV encephalitis, are not diagnostic. PLEDs have been reported with stroke and infectious mononucleosis encephalitis,[89] and periodic complexes are characteristic of the slow virus and prion disorders, including Jakob-Creutzfeldt disease and subacute sclerosing panencephalitis. The EEG abnormalities in neonatal herpes encephalitis are similar. The characteristic EEG results yield periodic or pseudoperiodic complexes, usually triangular or sharp waves, occurring in a multifocal pattern.[167] In one study of 34 infants with herpes encephalitis, 21 underwent EEG; the results of 19 of the 21 were abnormal. The results of 3 showed only focal slowing, but the other 16 showed the characteristic periodic or pseudoperiodic complexes.[202] The authors then reviewed 500 other neonatal EEG records and found 20 with similar complexes. Eleven patients had meningoencephalitis of unknown etiology, 3 had hemorrhage, and 2 suffered asphyxia. Four were placed in a miscellaneous category. Thus, periodic or pseudoperiodic complexes in neonatal EEG results strongly suggest HSV encephalitis, but they are not diagnostic.

Specific Diagnosis

A meticulous history is essential and must evaluate exposure in the past 2 to 3 weeks to illness in contacts; exposure to mosquitoes, ticks, and animals during recent vacations, picnics, and so on; awareness of illness in animals, especially horses and other Equidae, in the patient's environment; recent travel from the home area; recent injections of any kind; and the possibility of accidental exposure to heavy metals, pesticides, or other questionable substances.

The CSF must be examined carefully to exclude other disorders that respond to specific therapy. Smears for bacteria, appropriate rapid antigen identification tests, and cultures of the CSF are mandatory; the history and clinical findings may indicate the need for acid-fast stain and culture of the sediment for mycobacteria. Other circumstances may indicate the need for excluding fungal or protozoal infection; atypical cells may require cytopathologic study to exclude neural neoplasms that may present acutely.

The availability of polymerase chain reaction (PCR) has allowed the definitive and rapid diagnosis of HSV encephalitis, thus eliminating the need for brain biopsy.[65, 139, 205, 230, 240] HSV DNA was detected in the CSF of 53 of 54 patients with biopsy-proven herpes simplex encephalitis.[139] The etiology of encephalitis caused by other herpes group viruses also has been determined by PCR assay of CSF.[57, 157, 229] In addition to its use in herpesvirus infections, PCR is useful in neurologic illnesses caused by enteroviruses and *M. pneumoniae* and in the future likely will be useful in other encephalitides.[21, 132, 194]

In viral encephalitis, the CSF frequently is clear; the leukocyte count ranges from none to several thousand, often with a significant percentage of polymorphonuclear cells initially, moderate or no elevation of protein, and an initially normal level of glucose relative to the simultaneously determined blood glucose level. In any patient suspected of having viral meningoencephalitis, spinal fluid, blood, feces, and throat swabs should be collected and sent to a laboratory offering viral diagnostic services. An additional serum specimen should be collected 10 to 21 days later. Although these studies may not provide an immediate diagnosis, they may give early warning of a specific epidemic, and the use of specific antiviral chemotherapy may be indicated by the preliminary culture results.

Inquiry regarding recent illness, recent injections, and, especially, recent exposures away from the home environment sometimes is helpful. The incubation periods of some arboviruses are such that mosquito bites acquired at least 1 week earlier or insect bites now healed may give a clue. Occasionally, patients who have traveled to Africa or Asia in preceding weeks present with encephalitis caused by viruses, trypanosomiasis, or falciparum malaria with bizarre systemic and CNS signs and symptoms.

Treatment

Acyclovir should be used to treat herpes simplex and varicella-zoster encephalitis and perhaps encephalitis caused by Epstein-Barr virus. CMV encephalitis should be treated with ganciclovir. Pleconaril should be considered for treatment of enteroviral encephalitis and amantadine, or rimantadine for treatment of encephalitis caused by influenza A virus and oseltamivir for influenza B virus. Specific antimicrobial treatment should be used for infections caused by spirochetes, chlamydia, mycoplasma, fungi, and parasites.

General treatment is nonspecific and empiric, aimed at maintaining life and supporting each involved organ system. The effectiveness of various recommended regimens in most instances has not been evaluated objectively.

Until a bacterial etiology and, in particular, a brain abscess are excluded substantially, parenteral antibiotic therapy should be administered.

Anticipating and being prepared for convulsions, cerebral edema, hyperpyrexia, inadequate respiratory exchange, disturbed fluid and electrolyte balance, aspiration and asphyxia, abrupt cardiac and respiratory arrest of central origin, cardiac decompensation, and gastrointestinal bleeding are crucial. The syndrome of disseminated intravascular coagulation may be an additional complication. For these reasons, all patients with severe encephalitis should receive care in intensive care units. Cardiac monitoring should be maintained. Repeat CT and MRI scans are helpful in following comatose patients and often show signs of brain swelling before the patient has the typical clinical indicators of ICP, such as Cushing triad (systolic hypertension, bradycardia, and slowing of respirations), dilated pupils, and decorticate or decerebrate posturing. The Cushing triad is an unreliable indicator of increased ICP, and, when the other signs of increased ICP occur, they often do so late in the course, when the patient's cerebral perfusion already is at risk.[159] If brain swelling becomes a problem, placing an ICP monitor may be necessary. The ICP then should be maintained below 15 mm Hg if at all possible using the standard techniques for reduction of ICP, including hyperventilation, osmotic diuretics, and removal of CSF. As a last resort, inducing a barbiturate coma may be necessary. A related consequence of ICP is the syndrome of inappropriate antidiuretic hormone secretion. Careful monitoring of the fluid and electrolyte balance is essential in all seriously ill encephalitis patients.

All fluids, electrolytes, and medications initially are given parenterally. In patients with prolonged states of coma, parenteral hyperalimentation is indicated. Normal blood levels of glucose, magnesium, and calcium must be maintained to minimize the threat of convulsions.

Status epilepticus caused by encephalitis should be treated vigorously using a structured protocol to ensure optimal control.[214, 228] The current standard initial therapy is intravenous lorazepam, 0.1 to 0.2 mg/kg, up to 4 mg maximum. Seizures associated with encephalitis may be refractory to the usual therapy, and other anticonvulsants may be required to achieve and maintain control of seizures. In patients who fail initial therapy and are in medically refractory status epilepticus, continuous EEG monitoring usually is recommended to monitor the efficacy of the therapy, especially when the patient is in nonconvulsive status epilepticus.[64, 226] If after a second attempt, lorazepam fails to control the seizures, intravenous phenytoin (preferably phosphenytoin in children) is the next drug of choice. The dose is 18 to 20 mg/kg, maximum 1000 mg, given over 20 minutes. Phosphenytoin is preferred because it can be administered faster and does not cause sclerosis of the veins as does phenytoin and is not as likely to cause cardiac arrhythmias. Virtually all patients who require therapy beyond lorazepam will need to be intubated to prevent respiratory embarrassment. If phosphenytoin is unsuccessful, or as an alternative to phosphenytoin, intravenous midazolam has gained favor in recent years.[52, 182] The initial dose is 0.1 to 0.2 mg/kg over 5 minutes with a maintenance infusion starting at 0.05 mg/kg/hr up to a maximum of 0.4 mg/kg/hr. Another alternative therapy is propofol, which generally is administered by an anesthesiologist.

Many methods have been proposed to minimize cerebral edema and to diminish the consequences of cerebral anoxia; these measures are difficult to evaluate and generally are reserved for patients with severe illness whose condition appears to be desperate.

1. Dexamethasone, 0.1 to 0.2 mg/kg intravenously in an initial dose followed by 0.05 to 0.1 mg/kg intravenously every 4 to 6 hours, is given. This large dose should be reduced gradually after a few days if recovery or improvement is evident. Dexamethasone probably should not be used in acute viral diseases because steroids may potentiate the viral infection.

2. Other substances employed in an effort to reduce elevated ICP include (a) mannitol, given intravenously, as a 20 percent solution in a dose of 0.25 to 1 g/kg over a 30- to 60-minute period (this may be repeated every 8 to 12 hours), and (b) glycerol, by nasogastric tube, using 0.5 to 1.0 mL/kg diluted with twice that volume of orange juice. This regimen is nontoxic and may be repeated every 6 hours for an extended period.

For more than 40 years, steroids and adrenocorticotropic hormone frequently have been used as empiric therapy for encephalitis. However, no controlled studies have demonstrated any efficacy. In two comparative studies of measles encephalitis, steroids were found to offer no benefit, and in both studies, the steroid recipients appeared to have had worse outcomes.[23, 247] More recently, in a carefully controlled study, no benefit of high-dose dexamethasone was found in the treatment of acute encephalitis caused by Japanese encephalitis virus.[108]

In contrast with these investigations are more recent clinical experiences in the treatment of acute disseminated encephalomyelitis, in which MRI studies have indicated multifocal white-matter lesions.[24, 97, 129, 160] Patients treated with steroids have responded dramatically, with clinical improvement and resolution of the lesions as demonstrated by MRI. Steroids, along with specific antibiotic therapy, also may offer benefit in the treatment of encephalitis caused by *M. pneumoniae* infection.[135, 213]

Our opinion is that steroids should not be used to treat encephalitis if the patient has an active infection unless the infection can be treated concomitantly with an effective antimicrobial agent. Plasmapheresis and intravenous immunoglobulin have been used empirically to treat brain stem encephalitis as well as other encephalitides, but no studies have been done that indicate such therapies are helpful.[173]

Equipment and personnel for handling such emergencies as cardiac and respiratory arrest must be on hand constantly. Early consultation with an anesthesiologist or intensive care specialist is useful in anticipating the need for artificially assisted respiration.

Supportive and rehabilitative efforts are important after the patient recovers. Motor incoordination, convulsive disorders, squint, total or partial deafness, or behavioral disturbances may appear only after some time. Visual disturbances caused by chorioretinopathy and perceptual amblyopia also may make a delayed appearance. Special facilities and, at times, institutional placement may become necessary.

Prognosis

The prognosis in all encephalitides is guarded with respect to both immediate outcome and sequelae. Sequelae involving the CNS may be intellectual, motor, psychiatric, epileptic, visual, or auditory. Cardiovascular, intraocular, pulmonary, hepatic, and other systems sometimes are affected permanently. The short-term and long-term prognoses depend to some extent on etiology and age. Young infants usually have severe disease and sequelae. In general, HSV carries a worse prognosis for survival and residual disability than do the enteroviruses.

Rautonen and associates[193] examined prognostic factors in childhood acute encephalitis at the Children's Hospital, University of Helsinki, during a 20-year period from 1968 to 1987. In this study were 462 cases with the following etiologies: mumps virus, measles virus, rubella virus, VZV, HSV, enteroviruses, respiratory viruses, *M. pneumoniae*, other agents, and cause undetermined. They found that mortality was fivefold greater in infants compared with older children. Children who were disorientated or unconscious before admission had fourfold and 25-fold greater risks for death and severe damage, respectively, than had children whose level of consciousness had been normal. Patients with HSV or *M. pneumoniae* infection had the greatest risks for death or serious residual damage when compared with children with encephalitis of other etiologies.

California encephalitis has a low mortality rate but occurs most frequently in the pediatric age group. Of those patients who experience seizures in the acute phase of their disease, 25 percent have a permanent seizure disorder.[88] Psychologic sequelae were present in 15 percent in one series but were not found to be significant in several series if the children were evaluated several years after their illnesses.[50, 156, 195]

Prognosis in encephalitis caused by western equine virus is guarded; 56 percent of infants younger than 1 month of age have had recurring seizures with marked motor and behavioral changes. After 1 year of age, the sequelae appear to diminish; only 5 percent of adults have neurologic sequelae. Fifty-seven percent of infants who survived western equine virus infection and who were younger than 1 year of age at the time of infection had major neurologic sequelae requiring either a special school or institutionalization late in life. Severe retardation, paralysis, spasticity, recurrent convulsions, hearing deficits, and speech difficulties all were reported as complications.[69, 75]

Eastern equine encephalitis has a high mortality rate. Infants and children younger than 5 years of age who survive usually have severe sequelae consisting of mental retardation, convulsions, and paralysis. These consequences are in contradistinction to adults older than 40 years of age who survive, who recover completely or have only slight damage.

St. Louis encephalitis has a low mortality rate. Although neurologic sequelae are reported, their incidence is low in the pediatric age group.

Prevention

The widespread use of effective attenuated viral vaccines for measles, mumps, and rubella almost has eliminated CNS complications from these diseases in the United States. The control of encephalitis caused by arboviruses has been less successful because specific vaccines for the arbovirus diseases that occur in North America are not available. Control of insect vectors by suitable spraying methods and eradication of insect breeding sites is useful.

REFERENCES

1. Ackerman, E. S., Tumeh, S. S., Charron, M., et al.: Viral encephalitis: Imaging with SPECT. Clin. Nucl. Med. *13*:640–643, 1988.
2. Allen, I. M.: The neurological complications of serum treatment: With report of a case. Lancet *2*:1128–1131, 1931.
3. Anderson, L. J., Nicholson, K. G., Tauxe, R. V., et al.: Human rabies in the United States, 1960 to 1979: Epidemiology, diagnosis and prevention. Ann. Intern. Med. *100*:728–735, 1984.
4. Angulo, J. J., Pimenta-de-Campos, E., and de Salles-Gomes, L. F.: Postvaccinial meningo-encephalitis: Isolation of the virus from the brain. J. A. M. A. *187*:151–153, 1964.
5. Apak, R. A., Köse, G., Anlar, B., et al.: Acute disseminated encephalomyelitis in childhood: Report of 10 cases. J. Child. Neurol. *14*:198–201, 1999.
6. Arai, M., Odaka, M., Yuki, N., et al.: A patient with overlapping Bickerstaff's brainstem encephalitis, Miller Fisher syndrome and Guillian-Barré syndrome during the clinical course. Eur. J. Neurol. *9*:115–116, 2002.
7. Armstrong, R. W., and Fung, P. C.: Brainstem encephalitis (Rhombencephalitis) due to *Listeria monocytogenes:* Case report and review. Clin. Infect. Dis. *16*:1089–1093, 1993.
8. Ashikaga, R., Araki, Y., Ishida, O.: MR FLAIR imaging of herpes simplex encephalitis. Radiat. Med. *14*:349–352, 1996.
9. Assa, A., Watemberg, N., Bujanover, Y., et al.: Demyelinative brainstem encephalitis responsive to intravenous immunoglobulin therapy. Pediatrics *104*:301–303, 1999.
10. Assaad, F., and Borecka, I.: Nine-year study of WHO virus reports on fatal viral infections. Bull. W. H. O. *55*:445–453, 1977.
11. Balfour, H. H., Jr., Schiff, G. M., and Bloom, J. E.: Encephalitis associated with erythema infectiosum. J. Pediatr. *77*:133–136, 1970.
12. Barnes, P. D., Poussaint, T. Y., and Burrows, P. E.: Imaging of pediatric central nervous system infections. Neuroimaging Clin. North Am. *4*:367–391, 1994.
13. Barontini, F., and Leoncini, F.: Brainstem encephalitis due to *Listeria monocytogenes*: Favourable outcome after early antibiotic therapy. Ital. J. Neurol. Sci. *10*:85–87, 1989.
14. Baykan, B., Kinay, D., Gokyigit, A., et al.: Periodic lateralized epileptiform discharges: Association with seizures. Seizure *9*:402–406, 2000.
15. Becker, L. E.: Infections of the developing brain. Am. J. Neuroradiol. *13*:537–550, 1992.
16. Beghi, E., Nicolosi, A., Kurland, L. T., et al.: Encephalitis and aseptic meningitis, Olmsted County, Minnesota, 1950–1981. I. Epidemiology. Ann. Neurol. *16*:283–294, 1984.
17. Berge, T. O. (ed.): International Catalogue of Arboviruses including Certain Other Viruses of Vertebrates. 2nd ed. Atlanta, U.S. Dept. of Health, Education and Welfare, Public Health Service, No. (CDC) 75-8301, 1975.
18. Bergey, G. K., Coyle, P. K., Kromholz, A., et al.: Herpes simplex encephalitis with occipital localization. Arch. Neurol. *39*:312–313, 1982.
19. Biggar, R. J., Woodall, J. P., Walter, P. D., et al.: Lymphocytic choriomeningitis outbreak associated with pet hamsters: Fifty-seven cases from New York State. J. A. M. A. *232*:494–500, 1975.
20. Bingham, P. M., Galetta, S. L., Athreya, B., et al.: Neurologic manifestations in children with Lyme disease. Pediatrics *96*:1053–1056, 1995.
21. Bitnun, A., Lee Ford-Jones, E., Petric, M., et al.: Acute childhood encephalitis and *Mycoplasma pneumoniae*. Clin. Infect. Dis. *32*:1674–1684, 2001.
22. Blatt, N. H., and Lepper, M. H.: Reactions following antirabies prophylaxis: Report on sixteen patients. Am. J. Dis. Child. *86*:395–402, 1953.
23. Boe, J., Solberg, C. O., and Saeter, T.: Corticosteroid treatment for acute meningoencephalitis: A retrospective study of 346 cases. Br. Med. J. *1*:1094–1095, 1965.
24. Boulloche, J., Parain, D., Mallet, E., et al.: Postinfectious encephalitis with multifocal white matter lesions. Neuropediatrics *20*:173–175, 1989.
25. Brown, E. H.: Complications of smallpox vaccination. Postgrad. Med. J. *41*:634–635, 1965.
26. Bruhn, F. W.: Lyme disease. Am. J. Dis. Child. *138*:467–470, 1984.
27. Cakmakci, H., Kovanlikaya, A., Obuz, F., et al.: Herpes encephalitis in children, MRI assessment. Turkish J. Pediatr. *40*:559–566, 1998.
28. Camarata, P. J., McGeachie, R. E., and Haines, S. J.: Dorsal midbrain encephalitis caused by *Propionibacterium acnes*: Report of two cases. J. Neurosurg. *72*:654–659, 1990.
29. Carithers, H. A., and Margileth, A. M.: Cat-scratch disease: Acute encephalopathy and other neurologic manifestations. Am. J. Dis. Child. *145*:98–101, 1991.
30. Carmack, M. A., Twiss, J., Enzmann, D. R., et al.: Multifocal leukoencephalitis caused by varicella-zoster virus in a child with leukemia: Successful treatment with acyclovir. Pediatr. Infect. Dis. J. *12*:402–406, 1993.
31. Carr-Locke, D. L., and Mair, H. J.: Neurological presentation of psittacosis during a small outbreak in Leicestershire. Br. Med. J. *3*:853–854, 1976.
32. Caruso, J. M., Tung, G. A., Gascon, G. G., et al.: Persistent preceding focal neurologic deficits in children with chronic Epstein-Barr virus encephalitis. J. Child. Neurol. *15*:791–796, 2000.
33. Cassell, G. H., and Cole, B. C.: Mycoplasmas as agents of human disease. N. Engl. J. Med. *304*:80–89, 1981.
34. Centers for Disease Control: Raccoon Roundworm Encephalitis—Chicago, Illinois, and Los Angeles, California, 2000. M. M. W. R. Morb. Mortal. Wkly. Rep. *50*:1153–1155, 2002.
35. Centers for Disease Control: West Nile virus activity—eastern United States, 2001. M. M. W. R. Morb. Mortal. Wkly. Rep. *50*:617–619, 2001.
36. Centers for Disease Control: Case definitions for public health surveillance. M. M. W. R. Morb. Mortal. Wkly. Rep. *39*:1–43, 1990.
37. Centers for Disease Control: Mumps surveillance, January 1977–December 1982. Issued September 1984.
38. Centers for Disease Control: Rabies prevention: United States, 1984. M. M. W. R. Morb. Mortal. Wkly. Rep. *33*:393–408, 1984.
39. Centers for Disease Control: Rabies surveillance: Annual summary 1980–1982. Issued August 1983.
40. Centers for Disease Control: Measles surveillance: Annual report 1977–1981. Issued September 1982.
41. Centers for Disease Control: Encephalitis surveillance: Annual summary 1978. Issued May 1981.
42. Centers for Disease Control: Encephalitis surveillance: Annual summary 1977. Issued December 1979.
43. Centers for Disease Control: Measles surveillance: 1973–1976. Issued July 1977.
44. Chang, L. Y., Lin, T. Y., Huang, Y. C., et al.: Comparison of enterovirus 71 and coxsackie-virus A16 clinical illnesses during the Taiwan enterovirus epidemic, 1998. Pediatr. Infect. Dis. J. *18*:1092–1096, 1999.
45. Chataway, S. J. S., Larner, A. J., Kapoor, R.: Anti-GQ1b antibody status, magnetic imaging, and the nosology of Bickerstaff's brainstem encephalitis. Eur. J. Neurol. *8*:355–357, 2001.
46. Cherry, J. D.: The epidemiology of pertussis and pertussis immunization in the United Kingdom and the United States: A comparative study. Curr. Probl. Pediatr. *14*:1–78, 1984.
47. Cherry, J. D.: "Pertussis vaccine encephalopathy": It is time to recognize it as the myth that it is. J. A. M. A. *263*:1679–1680, 1990.
48. Cherry, J. D., Brunell, P. A., Golden, G. S., et al.: Report of the Task Force on Pertussis and Pertussis Immunization—1988. Pediatrics *81*:939–984, 1988.
49. Chonmaitree, T., Menegus, M. A., Schervish-Swierkosz, E. M., et al.: Enterovirus 71 infection: Report of an outbreak with two cases of paralysis and a review of the literature. Pediatrics *67*:489–493, 1981.
50. Chun, R. W. M., Thompson, W. H., Grabow, J. D., et al.: California arbovirus encephalitis in children. Am. J. Dis. Child. *124*:530–533, 1968.
51. Cizman, M., and Jazbec, J.: Etiology of acute encephalitis in childhood in Slovenia. Pediatr. Infect. Dis. J. *12*:903–908, 1993.
52. Claassen, J., Hirsch, L. J., Emerson, R. G., et al.: Continuous EEG monitoring and midazolam infusion for refractory nonconvulsive status epilepticus. Neurology *57*:1036–1042, 2001.
53. Clyde, W. A., Jr.: Neurological syndromes and mycoplasmal infections. Arch. Neurol. *37*:65–66, 1980.
54. Connelly, K. P., and DeWitt, L. D.: Neurologic complications of infectious mononucleosis. Pediatr. Neurol. *10*:181–184, 1994.
55. Corsellis, J. A. N., Janota, I., and Marshall, A. K.: Immunization against whooping cough: A neuropathological review. Neuropathol. Appl. Neurobiol. *9*:261–270, 1983.
56. Dagan, R., and Shahak, E.: Prolonged meningoencephalitis due to Epstein-Barr virus with favorable outcome in a young infant. Infection *21*:400–402, 1993.
57. Dangond, F., Engle, E., Yesseyan, L., et al.: Pre-eruptive varicella cerebellitis confirmed by PCR. Pediatr. Neurol. *9*:491–493, 1993.
58. DeDeyn, P. P., Van den Broucke, P. W., Pickut, B. A., et al.: Perfusions and thallium single photon emission computed tomography in herpes simplex encephalitis. J. Neurol. Sci. *157*:96–99, 1998.
59. Deibel, R., and Flanagan, T. D.: Central nervous system infections: Etiologic and epidemiologic observations in New York State, 1976–1977. N. Y. State J. Med. *79*:689–695, 1979.

60. Deibel, R., Flanagan, T. D., and Smith, V.: Central nervous system infections: Etiologic and epidemiologic observations in New York State, 1975. N. Y. State J. Med. *77*:1398–1404, 1977.
61. Deibel, R., Woodall, J. P., Decher, W. J., et al.: Lymphocytic choriomeningitis virus in man: Serologic evidence of association with pet hamsters. J. A. M. A. *232*:501–504, 1975.
62. Deibel, R., Flanagan, T. D., and Smith, V.: Central nervous system infections in New York State: Etiologic and epidemiologic observations, 1974. N. Y. State J. Med. *75*:2337–2342, 1975.
63. Deresiewicz, R. L., Thaler, S. J., Hsu, L., et al.: Clinical and neuroradiologic manifestations of eastern equine encephalitis. N. Engl. J. Med. *336*:1867–1874, 1997.
64. DeLorenzo, R. J., Waterhouse, E. J., Towne, A. R., et al.: Persistent nonconvulsive status epilepticus after the control of convulsive status epilepticus. Epilepsia *39*:833–840, 1998.
65. DeVincenzo, J. P., and Thorne, G.: Mild herpes simplex encephalitis diagnosed by polymerase chain reaction: A case report and review. Pediatr. Infect. Dis. J. *13*:662–664, 1994.
66. Donat, J. F., Rhodes, K. H., Groover, R. V., et al.: Etiology and outcome in 42 children with acute nonbacterial meningoencephalitis. Mayo Clin. Proc. *55*:156–160, 1980.
67. Drancourt, M., Raoult, D., Xeridat, B., et al.: Q fever meningoencephalitis in five patients. Eur. J. Epidemiol. *7*:134–138, 1991.
68. Dutt, M. K., and Johnston, I. D. A.: Computed tomography and EEG in herpes simplex encephalitis. Arch. Neurol. *39*:99–102, 1982.
69. Earnest, M. P., Goolishian, H. A., Calverley, J. R., et al.: Neurologic, intellectual, and psychologic sequelae following western equine encephalitis: A study of 35 cases. Neurology *21*:969–974, 1971.
70. Elliott, K. J.: Other neurological complications of herpes zoster and their management. Ann. Neurol. *35*:S57–S61, 1994.
71. El-Rai, F. M., and Evans, A. S.: Reovirus infections in children and young adults. Arch. Environ. Health *7*:700–704, 1963.
72. Enders, J. F.: Mumps. *In* Rivers, T. M., and Horsfall, F. L., Jr. (eds.): Viral and Rickettsial Infections of Man. Philadelphia, J. B. Lippincott, 1959, pp. 780–789.
73. Farizo, K. M., Cochi, S. L., Zell, E. R., et al.: Epidemiological features of pertussis in the United States, 1980–1989. Clin. Infect. Dis. *14*:708–719, 1992.
74. Fazekas, F., Roob, G., Payer, F., et al.: Technetium-99m-ECD SPECT fails to show focal hyperemia of acute herpes encephalitis. J. Nucl. Med. *39*:790–792, 1998.
75. Finlay, K. H., Fitzgerald, L. H., Richter, R. W., et al.: Western encephalitis and cerebral ontogenesis. Arch. Neurol. *16*:140–167, 1967.
76. Flewett, T. H., and Hoult, J. G.: Influenzal encephalopathy and postinfluenzal encephalitis. Lancet *2*:11–15, 1958.
77. Flexner, S.: Postvaccinal encephalitis and allied conditions. J. A. M. A. *94*:305–311, 1930.
78. Forman, M. L., and Cherry, J. D.: Isolation of measles virus from the cerebrospinal fluid of a child with encephalitis following measles vaccination. Evanston, IL, The Program for the American Pediatric Society, 1967.
79. Fox, R. J., Kasner, S. E., Galetta, S. L., et al.: Treatment of Bickerstaff's brainstem encephalitis with immune globulin. J. Neurol. Sci. *15*:88–90, 2000.
80. Fryden, A., Kihlstrom, E., Maller, R., et al.: A clinical and epidemiological study of "ornithosis" caused by *Chlamydia psittaci* and *Chlamydia pneumoniae* (strain TWAR). Scand. J. Infect. Dis. *21*:681–691, 1989.
81. Fuller, G. N., Guiloff, R. J., Scaravilli, F., et al.: Combined HIV-CMV encephalitis presenting with brainstem signs. J. Neurol. Neurosurg. Psychiatry *52*:975–979, 1989.
82. Genz, R. D., and Beecham, H. J.: Meningoencephalitis after influenza inoculation. N. Engl. J. Med. *299*:721–722, 1978.
83. Glezen W. P., Paredes, A., and Taber, L. H.: Influenza in children: Relationship to other respiratory agents. J. A. M. A. *243*:1345–1349, 1980.
84. Glezen, W. P.: Consideration of the risk of influenza in children and indications for prophylaxis. Rev. Infect. Dis. *2*:408–420, 1980.
85. Goh, K. J., Tan, C. T., Chew, N. K., et al.: Clinical features of Nipah virus encephalitis among pig farmers in Malaysia. N. Engl. J. Med. *342*:1229–1235, 2000.
86. Golden, S. E.: Aseptic meningitis associated with *Ehrlichiae canis* infection. Pediatr. Infect. Dis. *8*:335–337, 1989.
87. Gorman, R. J., Saxon, S., and Snead, O. C.: Neurologic sequelae of Rocky Mountain spotted fever. Pediatrics *67*:354–357, 1981.
88. Grabow, J. D., Matthews, G. G., Chun, R. W. M., et al.: The electroencephalogram and clinical sequelae of California arbovirus encephalitis. Neurology *19*:394–404, 1969.
89. Greenberg, D. A., Weinkle, D. J., and Aminoff, M. J.: Periodic EEG complexes in infectious mononucleosis encephalitis. J. Neurol. Neurosurg. Psychiatry *45*:648–651, 1982.
90. Greenberg, M.: Complications of vaccination against smallpox. Am. J. Dis. Child. *76*:492–502, 1948.
91. Greenberg, S. B., Taber, L., Septimus, E., et al.: Computerized tomography in brain biopsy proven herpes simplex encephalitis. Arch. Neurol. *38*:58–59, 1981.
92. Griesemer, D. A., Barton, L. L., Reese, C. M., et al.: Amebic meningoencephalitis caused by *Balamuthia mandrillaris*. Pediatr. Neurol. *10*:249–254, 1994.
93. Griffin, D. E.: Post-infectious and post-vaccinal disorders of the central nervous system. Immunol. Allergy Clin. North Am. *8*:239–249, 1988.
94. Griffith, A. H.: Permanent brain damage and pertussis vaccination: Is the end of the saga in sight? Vaccine *7*:199–210, 1989.
95. Grist, N. R., Bell, E. J., and Assaad, F.: Enteroviruses in human disease. Prog. Med. Virol. *4*:114–157, 1978.
96. Gross, W. L., Ravens, K. G., and Hansen, H. W.: Meningoencephalitic syndrome following influenza vaccination. J. Neurol. *217*:219–222, 1978.
97. Grossman, M., and Azimi, P. H.: An encephalitis syndrome in a seven-year-old. Pediatr. Infect. Dis. J. *14*:550–555, 1995.
98. Guerrero, I. C., Retailliau, H. F., Brandling-Bennett, A. D., et al.: No increased meningoencephalitis after influenza vaccine. N. Engl. J. Med. *300*:565, 1979.
99. Hall, C. B., and Horner, F. A.: Encephalopathy with erythema infectiosum. Am. J. Dis. Child. *131*:65–67, 1977.
100. Hall, C. B., Long, C. E., Schnabel, K. C., et al.: Human herpesvirus-6 infection in children: A prospective study of complications and reactivation. N. Engl. J. Med. *331*:432–438, 1994.
101. Hamilton, R. L., Achim, C., Grafe, M. R., et al.: Herpes simplex virus brainstem encephalitis in an AIDS patient. Clin. Neuropathol. *14*:45–50, 1995.
102. Hanshaw, J. B., Dudgeon, J. A., and Marshall, W. C.: Congenital cytomegalovirus. *In* Hanshaw, J. B., Dudgeon, J. A., and Marshall, W. C. (eds.): Viral Diseases of the Fetus and Newborn. 2nd ed. Philadelphia, W. B. Saunders, 1985, pp. 92–131.
103. Hasegawa, Y., Morishita, M., Ikeda, T., et al.: Early diagnosis of herpes simplex virus encephalitis by single photon emission computed tomography (SPECT) in patients with normal MRI. Rinsho Shinkeigaku Clin. Neurol. *36*:475–480, 1996.
104. Hattori, H., Kawamori, J., Takao, T., et al.: Computed tomography in postinfluenzal encephalitis. Brain Dev. *5*:564–567, 1983.
105. Haynes, R. E., Sanders, D. Y., and Cramblett, H. G.: Rocky Mountain spotted fever in children. J. Pediatr. *76*:685–693, 1970.
106. Hedlund, J., Aurelius, E., and Andersson, J.: Recurrent encephalitis due to trimethoprim intake. Scand. J. Infect. Dis. *22*:109–112, 1990.
107. Ho, D. D., and Hirsch, M. S.: Acute viral encephalitis. Med. Clin. North Am. *69*:415–429, 1985.
108. Hoke, C. H., Jr., Vaughn, D. W., Nisalak, A., et al.: Effect of high-dose dexamethasone on the outcome of acute encephalitis due to Japanese encephalitis virus. J. Infect. Dis. *165*:631–637, 1992.
109. Huang, C. R., Chang, W. N., Lui, C. C., et al.: Neuroimages of Japanese encephalitis: Report of three patients. Ching-Hua I Hseuh Tsa Chih *60*:105–108, 1997.
110. Huang, C. C., Liu, C. C., Chang, Y. C., et al.: Neurologic complications in children with enterovirus 71 infection. N. Engl. J. Med. *341*:936–942, 1999.
111. Hughes, R. R.: Neurological complications of serum and vaccine therapy. Lancet *2*:464–467, 1944.
112. Hummeler, K., Davidson, W. L., Henle, W., et al.: Encephalomyelitis due to infection with *Herpesvirus simiae* (herpes B virus): A report of two fatal, laboratory-acquired cases. N. Engl. J. Med. *261*:64–67, 1959.
113. Irving, W. L., Chang, J., Raymond, D. R., et al.: Roseola infantum and other syndromes associated with acute HHV-6 infection. Arch. Dis. Child. *65*:297–300, 1990.
114. Ishiguro, N., Yamada, S., Takahashi, T., et al.: Meningoencephalitis associated with HHV-6 related exanthem subitum. Acta Paediatr. Scand. *79*:987–989, 1990.
115. Jackson, M. A., Burry, V. F., and Olson, L. C.: Complications of varicella requiring hospitalization in previously healthy children. Pediatr. Infect. Dis. J. *11*:441–445, 1992.
116. Jemsek, H., Greenberg, S. B., Taber, L., et al.: Herpes zoster-associated encephalitis: Clinicopathologic report of 12 cases and review of the literature. Medicine *62*:81–97, 1983.
117. Johnson, H. N.: Rabies. *In* Rivers, T. M., and Horsfall, F. J., Jr. (eds.): Viral and Rickettsial Infections of Man. 3rd ed. Philadelphia, J. B. Lippincott, 1959, pp. 405–431.
118. Johnson, R. T.: Viral Infections of the Nervous System. New York, Raven Press, 1982, pp. 87–128.
119. Johnson, R. T.: The pathogenesis of acute viral encephalitis and postinfectious encephalomyelitis. J. Infect. Dis. *155*:359–364, 1987.
120. Johnson, R. T.: The virology of demyelinating diseases. Ann. Neurol. *36*:S54–S60, 1994.
121. Joske, R. A., Keall, D. D., Leak, P. J., et al.: Hepatitis-encephalitis in humans with reovirus infection. Arch. Intern. Med. *113*:811–816, 1964.
122. Kanzaki, A., Yubuki, S., and Yuki, N.: Bickerstaff's brainstem encephalitis associated with cytomegalovirus infection. J. Neurol. Neurosurg. Psychiatry *58*:260–261, 1993.
123. Kaplan, M. H., Klein, S. W., McPhee, J., et al.: Group B coxsackievirus infections in infants younger than three months of age: A serious childhood illness. Rev. Infect. Dis. *5*:1019–1032, 1983.
124. Kappus, K. D., Sather, G. E., Kaplan, J. E., et al.: Human arboviral infections in the United States in 1980. J. Infect. Dis. *145*:283–286, 1982.

125. Kato, T., Ishii, C., Furusho, J., et al.: Early diagnosis of herpes encephalopathy using fluid-attenuated inversion recovery pulse sequences. Pediatr. Neurol. *19*:58–61, 1998.
126. Katz, D. A., Dworzack, D. L., Horowitz, E. A., et al.: Encephalitis associated with Rocky Mountain spotted fever. Arch. Pathol. Lab. Med. *109*:771–773, 1985.
127. Kennedy, C.: Acute viral encephalitis in childhood. Br. Med. J. *310*:139–140, 1995.
128. Kennedy, F.: Certain nervous complications following the use of therapeutic and prophylactic sera. Am. J. Med. Sci. *177*:555–559, 1929.
129. Kesselring, J., Miller, D. H., Robb, S. A., et al.: Acute disseminated encephalomyelitis: MRI findings and the distinction from multiple sclerosis. Brain *113*:291–302, 1990.
130. Koelfen, W., Freund, M., Guckel, F., et al.: MRI of encephalitis in children: Comparison of CT and MRI in the acute stage with long-term follow-up. Neuroradiology *38*:73–79, 1996.
131. Kohl, S., and James, A. R.: Herpes simplex virus encephalitis during childhood: Importance of brain biopsy diagnosis. J. Pediatr. *107*: 212–215, 1985.
132. Kolski, H., Ford-Jones, E. L., Richardson, S., et al.: Etiology of acute childhood encephalitis at The Hospital for Sick Children, Toronto, 1994–1995. Clin. Infect. Dis. *26*:398–409, 1998.
133. Koskiniemi, M., Manninen, V., Vaheri, A., et al.: Acute encephalitis: A survey of epidemiological, clinical and microbiological features covering a twelve-year period. Acta Med. Scand. *209*:115–120, 1981.
134. Koskiniemi, M., and Vaheri, A.: Effect of measles, mumps, rubella vaccination on pattern of encephalitis in children. Lancet *1*:31–34, 1989.
135. Koskiniemi, M.: CNS manifestations associated with *Mycoplasma pneumoniae* infections: Summary of cases at the University of Helsinki and review. Clin. Infect. Dis. *17*:S52–S57, 1993.
136. Kovacs, S. O., Kuban, K., and Strand, R.: Lateral medullary syndrome following varicella infection. Am. J. Dis. Child. *147*:823–825, 1993.
137. Krainer, L., and Aronson, B. E.: Disseminated encephalomyelitis in humans with recovery of hepato-encephalitis virus (HEV). J. Neuropathol. Exp. Neurol. *18*:339–342, 1969.
138. Kumar, S., Misra, U. K., Kalita, J., et al.: MRI in Japanese encephalitis. Neuroradiology *39*:180–184, 1997.
139. Lakeman, F. D., Whitley, R. J., and the NIAID Collaborative Antiviral Study Group: Diagnosis of herpes simplex encephalitis: Application of polymerase chain reaction to cerebrospinal fluid from brain-biopsied patients and correlation with disease. J. Infect. Dis. *171*:857–863, 1995.
140. Landrigan, P. J., and Witte, J. J.: Neurologic disorders following live measles virus vaccination. J. A. M. A. *223*:1459–1462, 1973.
141. Landry, M. L., Ponseca, S. S., Cohen, S., et al.: Fatal enterovirus type 71 infection: Rapid detection and diagnostic pitfalls. Pediatr. Infect. Dis. J. *14*:1095–1100, 1995.
142. Lane, J. M., Ruben, F. L., Neff, J. M., et al.: Complications of smallpox vaccination, 1968: Results of ten statewide surveys. J. Infect. Dis. *122*:303–309, 1970.
143. Lane, J. M., Ruben, R. L., Neff, J. M., et al.: Complications of smallpox vaccination, 1968: National surveillance in the United States. N. Engl. J. Med. *281*:1201–1208, 1969.
144. Launes, J., Nikkinen, P., Lindroth, L., et al.: Diagnosis of acute herpes simplex encephalitis by brain perfusion single photon emission computed tomography. Lancet *1*:1188–1191, 1988.
145. Lee, K. E., Tan, C. B., Tjia, H. T. L., et al.: The neurological manifestations of Nipah virus encephalitis, a novel paramyxovirus. Ann. Neurol. *46*:428–432, 1999.
146. Leonard, J. R., Moran, C. J., Cross, D. T., et al.: MR imaging of herpes simplex type 1 encephalitis in infants and young children: A separate pattern of findings. A. J. R. Am. J. Roentgenol. *174*:1651–1655, 2000.
147. Lester, J. W., Carter, M. P., and Reynolds, T. L.: Herpes encephalitis: MR monitoring of response to acyclovir therapy. J. Comput. Assist. Tomogr. *12*:941–943, 1988.
148. Linnemann, C. C., Jr., Pretzman, C. I., and Peterson, E. D.: Acute febrile cerebrovasculitis: A non-spotted fever group rickettsial disease. Arch. Intern. Med. *149*:1682–1684, 1989.
149. Liu, C. C., Tseng, H. W., Wang, S. M., et al.: An outbreak of enterovirus 71 infection in Taiwan, 1998: Epidemiologic and clinical manifestations. J. Clin. Virol. *17*:23–30, 2000.
150. Lynch, M., Lee, B., Azimi, P., et al.: Rotavirus and central nervous system symptoms: cause or contaminant? Case reports and review. Clin. Infect. Dis. *33*:932–938, 2001.
151. Mardh, P. A.: *Mycoplasma hominis* infection of the central nervous system in newborn infants. Sex. Transm. Dis. *10*:331–334, 1983.
152. Marfin, A. A., and Gubler, D. J.: West Nile encephalitis: An emerging disease in the United States. Clin. Infect. Dis. *33*:1713–1719, 2001.
153. Margolis, F. J., Wilson, J. L., and Top, F. H.: Postrubella encephalomyelitis: Report of cases in Detroit and review of literature. J. Pediatr. *23*:158–165, 1943.
154. Masdeu, J. C., VanHeertum, R. L., Abdel-Dayem, H.: Viral infections of the brain. J. Neuroimaging Suppl. *1*:S40–S44, 1995.
155. Matsumoto, N., Yano, S., Miyao, M., et al.: Two-dimensional ultrasonography of the brain: Its diagnostic usefulness in herpes simplex encephalitis and cytomegalic inclusion disease. Brain Dev. *5*:327–333, 1983.
156. Matthews, C. G., Chun, R. W. M., Grabow, J. D., et al.: Psychological sequelae in children following California arbovirus encephalitis. Neurology *18*:1023–1030, 1968.
157. McCullers, J. A., Lakeman, F. D., and Whitley, R. J.: Human herpesvirus 6 is associated with focal encephalitis. Clin. Infect. Dis. *21*:571–576, 1995.
158. McDonald, J. C., Moore, D. L., and Quennec, P.: Clinical and epidemiologic features of mumps meningoencephalitis and possible vaccine-related disease. Pediatr. Infect. Dis. *8*:751–755, 1989.
159. McDowall, D. G.: Monitoring the brain. Anesthesiology *45*:117–134, 1976.
160. McHugh, K., and McMenamin, J. B.: Acute disseminated encephalomyelitis in childhood. Irish Med. J. *80*:412–414, 1987.
161. McLean, D. M., Best, J. M., Smith, P. A., et al.: Viral infections of Toronto children during 1965. II. Measles encephalitis and other complications. Can. Med. Assoc. J. *94*:905–910, 1966.
162. Melis, K., Bochner, A., Vandenberghe, P., et al.: Cat-scratch disease with reversible encephalopathy. Eur. J. Pediatr. *149*:2–25, 1989.
163. Meulin, V. T., Kackell, Y., Muller, D., et al.: Isolation of infectious measles virus in measles encephalitis. Lancet *2*:1172–1175, 1972.
164. Meyer, H. M., Jr., Johnson, R. T., Crawford, I. P., et al.: Central nervous system syndromes of "viral" etiology: A study of 713 cases. Am. J. Med. *2*:334–347, 1960.
165. Miller, H. G., Stanton, J. B., and Gibbons, J. L.: Parainfectious encephalomyelitis and related syndromes. Q. J. Med. *100*:427–505, 1956.
166. Miller, H. G., and Stanton, J. B.: Neurological sequelae of prophylactic inoculation. Q. J. Med. *89*:1–27, 1954.
167. Mizrahi, E. M., and Tharp, B. R.: A characteristic EEG pattern in neonatal herpes simplex encephalitis. Neurology *32*:1215–1220, 1982.
168. Modlin, J. F., Dagan, R., Berlin, L. E., et al.: Focal encephalitis with enterovirus infections. Pediatrics *88*:841–845, 1991.
169. Monath, T. P., Cropp, C. B., and Harrison, A. K.: Mode of entry of a neurotropic arbovirus into the central nervous system: Reinvestigation of an old controversy. Lab. Invest. *48*:399–410, 1983.
170. Moore, M.: Enteroviral disease in the United States, 1970–1979. J. Infect. Dis. *146*:103–108, 1982.
171. Nanning, W.: Prophylactic effect of antivaccinia gammaglobulin against post-vaccinal encephalitis. Bull. W. H. O. *27*:317–324, 1962.
172. Nigrovic, L. E., Lumeng, C., Landrigan, C., et al.: Rotavirus cerebellitis? Clin. Infect. Dis. *34*:130, 2002.
173. Nishikawa, M., Ichiyama, T., Hayashi, T., et al.: Intravenous immunoglobulin therapy in acute disseminated encephalomyelitis. Pediatr. Neurol. *21*:583–586, 1999.
174. Noah, N. D., and Urquhart, A. M.: Virus meningitis and encephalitis in 1979. J. Infect. *2*:379–383, 1980.
175. Noah, R. L., Bresee, J. S., Gorensek, M. J., et al.: Cluster of five children with acute encephalopathy associated with cat-scratch disease in South Florida. Pediatr. Infect. Dis. J. *14*:866–869, 1995.
176. Ohtaki, E., Murakami, Y., Komori, H., et al.: Acute disseminated encephalomyelitis after Japanese B encephalitis vaccination. Pediatr. Neurol. *8*:137–139, 1992.
177. Okuno, T., Takao, T., Ito, M., et al.: Contrast-enhanced hypodense areas in a case of acute disseminated encephalitis following influenza A virus. Comput. Radiol. *6*:215–217, 1982.
178. Olitsky, P. K., and Casals, J.: Arthropod-borne group A virus infections of man. *In* Rivers, R. M., and Horsfall, F. L., Jr. (eds.): Viral and Rickettsial Infections of Man. Philadelphia, J. B. Lippincott, 1959, pp. 286–304.
179. Osamura, T., Mizuta, R., Yoshioka, H., et al.: Isolation of adenovirus type 11 from the brain of a neonate with pneumonia and encephalitis. Eur. J. Pediatr. *152*:496–499, 1993.
180. O'Sullivan, J. D., Allworth, A. M., Peterson, D. L., et al.: Fatal encephalitis due to novel paramyxovirus transmitted from horses. Lancet *349*:93–95, 1997.
181. Paisley, J. W., Bruhn, F. W., Lauer, B. A., et al.: Type A2 influenza viral infections in children. Am. J. Dis. Child. *132*:34–36, 1978.
182. Parent, J. M., Lowenstein, D. H.: Treatment of refractory generalized status epilepticus with continuous infusion of midazolam [Abstract]. Neurology *4*:1837–1840, 1994.
183. Peter, G.: Leptospirosis: A zoonosis of protean manifestations. Pediatr. Infect. Dis. *1*:282–288, 1982.
184. Pohl-Koppe, A., Blay, M., Jäger, G., et al.: Human herpes virus type 7 DNA in the cerebrospinal fluid of children with central nervous system diseases. Eur. J. Pediatr. *160*:351–358, 2001.
185. Pönkä, A.: Central nervous system manifestations associated with serologically verified *Mycoplasma pneumoniae* infection. Scand. J. Infect. Dis. *12*:175–184, 1980.
186. Preblud, S. R.: Age-specific risks of varicella complications. Pediatrics *68*:14–17, 1981.
187. Prusiner, S. B., and Hsiao, K. K.: Human prion diseases. Ann. Neurol. *35*:385–395, 1994.

188. Public Health Service, U.S. Dept. Health, Education and Welfare, joint statement: Fatal viral encephalitis following 17D yellow fever vaccine inoculation: Report of a case in a 3-year-old child. J. A. M. A. *198*: 203–204, 1966.
189. Purdham, D. R., and Batty, P. F.: A case of acute measles meningoencephalitis with virus isolation. J. Clin. Pathol. *27*:994–996, 1974.
190. Quiroz, E., Moreno, N., Peralta, P. H., et al.: A human case of encephalitis associated with vesicular stomatitis virus (Indiana serotype) infection. Am. J. Trop. Med. Hyg. *39*:312–314, 1988.
191. Rantala, H., and Uhari, M.: Occurrence of childhood encephalitis: A population-based study. Pediatr. Infect. Dis. J. *8*:426–430, 1989.
192. Raoult, D., and Marrie, T.: Q fever. Clin. Infect. Dis. *20*:489–496, 1995.
193. Rautonen, J., Koskiniemi, M., and Vaheri, A.: Prognostic factors in childhood acute encephalitis. Pediatr. Infect. Dis. J. *10*:441–446, 1991.
194. Read, S. J., Jeffery, K. J., and Bangham, C. R.: Aseptic meningitis and encephalitis: The role of PCR in the diagnostic laboratory. J. Clin. Microbiol. *35*:691–696, 1997.
195. Rie, H. E., Hilty, M. D., and Cramblatt, H. G.: Intelligence and coordination following California encephalitis. Am. J. Dis. Child. *125*:824–827, 1973.
196. Robb, L., and Butt, W.: Brain stem encephalitis due to herpes simplex virus. Aust. Paediatr. J. *25*:246–247, 1989.
197. Robinson, L. J.: Neurologic complications following the administration of vaccines and serums: Report of a case of peripheral paralysis following the injection of typhoid vaccine. N. Engl. J. Med. *216*:831–837, 1937.
198. Rosenberg, G. A.: Meningoencephalitis following an influenza vaccination. N. Engl. J. Med. *283*:1209–1210, 1970.
199. Rosenblum, M. K.: Bulbar encephalitis complicating trigeminal zoster in the acquired immune deficiency syndrome. Hum. Pathol. *20*:292–295, 1989.
200. Rothstein, T., and Shaw, C. M.: Computerized tomography as a diagnostic aid in acute hemorrhagic leukoencephalitis. Ann. Neurol. *13*:331–333, 1983.
201. Rubeiz, H., and Roos, R. P.: Viral meningitis and encephalitis. Semin. Neurol. *12*:165–177, 1992.
202. Sainio, K., Granstrom, M. L., Pettay, O., et al.: EEG in neonatal herpes simplex encephalitis. Electroencephalogr. Clin. Neurophysiol. *56*:556–561, 1983.
203. Salaki, J. S., Louria, D. B., and Chmel, H.: Fungal and yeast infections of the central nervous system: A clinical review. Medicine *63*:108–132, 1984.
204. Sato, S., Kumada, S., Koji, T., et al.: Reversible frontal lobe syndrome associated with influenza virus infection in children. Pediatr. Neurol. *22*:318–321, 2000.
205. Schlesinger, Y., Butler, R. S., and Brunstrom, J. E.: Expanded spectrum of herpes simplex encephalitis in childhood. J. Pediatr. *126*:234–241, 1995.
206. Schmidbauer, M., Budka, H., and Amros, P.: Herpes simplex virus (HSV) DNA in microglial nodular brainstem encephalitis. J. Neuropathol. Exp. Neurol. *48*:645–652, 1989.
207. Seidel, J. S., Harmatz, P., Visvesvara, G. S., et al.: Successful treatment of primary amebic meningoencephalitis. N. Engl. J. Med. *306*:346–348, 1982.
208. Sener, R. N.: Herpes simplex encephalitis: Diffusion MR imaging findings. Comput. Med. Imaging Graph. *25*:391–397, 2001.
209. Shaffer, M. F., Rake, G., and Hodes, H. L.: Isolation of virus from a patient with fatal encephalitis complicating measles. Am. J. Dis. Child. *64*:815–819, 1942.
210. Shaked, Y., and Samra, Y.: Q fever meningoencephalitis associated with bilateral abducens nerve paralysis, bilateral optic neuritis and abnormal cerebrospinal fluid findings. Infection *17*:394–395, 1989.
211. Shaw, D. W. W., and Cohen, W. A.: Viral infections of the CNA in children: Imaging features. A. J. R. Am. J. Roentgenol. *160*:125–133, 1993.
212. Sherman, F. E., Michaels, R. H., and Kenny, F. M.: Acute encephalopathy (encephalitis) complicating rubella. J. A. M. A. *192*:675–681, 1965.
213. Sheth, R. D., Goulden, K. J., and Pryse-Phillips, W. E.: The focal encephalopathies associated with *Mycoplasma pneumoniae*. Can. J. Neurol. Sci. *20*:319–323, 1993.
214. Shields, W. D.: Status epilepticus. Pediatr. Clin. North Am. *36*:383–393, 1989.
215. Siegman-Igra, Y., Michaeli, D., Doron, A., et al.: Cytomegalovirus encephalitis in a noncompromised host. Isr. J. Med. Sci. *20*:163–166, 1984.
216. Sillimsan, C. C., Tedder, D., Ogle, J. W., et al.: Unsuspected varicella-zoster virus encephalitis in a child with acquired immunodeficiency syndrome. J. Pediatr. *123*:418–422, 1993.
217. Southern, P. M., Jr.: Relapsing fever. *In* Tice, F. (ed.): Practice of Medicine. Vol. 3. Scranton, PA, Hoeber Medical Division, Harper & Row, 1969, pp. 1–19.
218. Spillane, J. D., and Wells, C. E. C.: The neurology of Jennerian vaccination: A clinical account of the neurological complications which occurred during the smallpox epidemic in South Wales in 1962. Brain *87*:1–44, 1964.
219. Steiner, M. M., Vuckovitch, D., and Hadawi, S. A.: Cat-scratch disease with encephalopathy: Case report and review of the literature. J. Pediatr. *62*:514–520, 1963.
220. Straussberg, R., Harel, L., Levy, Y., et al.: A syndrome of transient encephalopathy associated with adenovirus infection. Pediatrics *107*:E69, 2001.
221. Tagawa, Y., Nobuhiro, Y.: Bickerstaff's brainstem encephalitis associated with shingles. J. Neurol. *247*:218–219, 2000.
222. Tesh, R. B.: The prevalence of encephalomyocarditis virus neutralizing antibodies among various human populations. Am. J. Trop. Med. Hyg. *27*:144–149, 1978.
223. Thong, T. H.: Primary amoebic meningoencephalitis: Fifteen years later. Med. J. Aust. *1*:352–354, 1980.
224. Tokunaga, K., Kira, R., Takemoto, M., et al.: Diagnostic usefulness of diffusion-weighted magnetic resonance imaging in influenza-associated encephalopathy or encephalitis. Brain Dev. *22*:451–453, 2000.
225. Torigoe, S., Koide, W., Yamada, M., et al.: Human herpesvirus 7 infection associated with central nervous system manifestations. J. Pediatr. *129*:301–305, 1996.
226. Towne, A. R., Waterhouse, E. J., Boggs, J. G., et al.: Prevalence of nonconvulsive status epilepticus in comatose patients. Neurology *54*:340–345, 2000.
227. Townsend, J. J., Wolinsky, J. S., Baringer, J. R., et al.: Acquired toxoplasmosis: A neglected cause of treatable nervous system disease. Arch. Neurol. *32*:335–343, 1975.
228. Treatment of convulsive status epilepticus. Recommendation of the Epilepsy Foundation of America's Working Group on Status Epilepticus. J. A. M. A. *270*:854–859, 1993.
229. Tsutsumi, H., Kamazaki, H., Nakata, S., et al.: Sequential development of acute meningoencephalitis and transverse myelitis caused by Epstein-Barr virus during infectious mononucleosis. Pediatr. Infect. Dis. J. *13*:665–667, 1994.
230. Uren, E. C., Johnson, P. D. R., Montanaro, J., et al.: Herpes simplex virus encephalitis in pediatrics: Diagnosis by detection of antibodies and DNA in cerebrospinal fluid. Pediatr. Infect. Dis. J. *12*:1001–1006, 1993.
231. Visvesvara, G. S., Martinez, A. J., Schuster, F. L., et al.: *Leptomyxid ameba*, a new agent of amebic meningoencephalitis in humans and animals. J. Clin. Microbiol. *28*:2750–2756, 1990.
232. Voltz, R., Gundula, J., Seelos, K., et al.: BK virus encephalitis in an immunocompetent patient. Arch. Neurol. *53*:101–103, 1996.
233. Wallace, S. J., and Zealley, H.: Neurological, electroencephalographic, and virological findings in febrile children. Arch. Dis. Child. *45*:611–623, 1970.
234. Wang, S. M., Liu, C. C., Tseng, H. W., et al.: Clinical spectrum of enterovirus 71 infection in children in southern Taiwan, with an emphasis on neurological complications. Clin. Infect. Dis. *29*:184–190, 1999.
235. Warren, J.: Encephalitis lethargica. *In* Rivers, T. M., and Horsfall, F. L., Jr. (eds.): Viral and Rickettsial Infections of Man. Philadelphia, J. B. Lippincott, 1959, pp. 914–915.
236. Watson, R. T., Ballinger, W. E., and Quisling, R. G.: Acute hemorrhagic leukoencephalitis: Diagnosis by computed tomography. Ann. Neurol. *15*:611–612, 1984.
237. Weisberg, L. A.: The role of CT in the evaluation of patients with intracranial CNS infectious-inflammatory disorders. Comput. Radiol. *8*:29–36, 1984.
238. Whitley, R. J.: Viral encephalitis. N. Engl. J. Med. *323*:242–250, 1990.
239. Whitley, R. J., Cobbs, C. G., Alford, C. A., Jr., et al.: Diseases that mimic herpes simplex encephalitis: Diagnosis, presentation and outcome. J. A. M. A. *262*:234–239, 1989.
240. Whitley, R. J., and Lakeman, F.: Herpes simplex virus infections of the central nervous system: Therapeutic and diagnostic considerations. Clin. Infect Dis. *20*:414–420, 1995.
241. Woods, C. A., and Ellison, G. W.: Encephalopathy following influenza immunization. J. Pediatr. *65*:745–748, 1964.
242. World Health Organization: World Health Statistics Annual. Vol. 11, Infectious Diseases: Cases and Deaths. Geneva, World Health Organization, 1978.
243. Yoshikawa, T., Nakashima, T., Suga, S., et al.: Human herpesvirus-6 DNA in cerebrospinal fluid of a child with exanthem subitum and meningoencephalitis. Pediatrics *89*:888–890, 1992.
244. Young, E. J.: Human brucellosis. Rev. Infect. Dis. *5*:821–842, 1983.
245. Yuki, N., Odaka, M., and Hirata, K.: Bickerstaff's brainstem encephalitis subsequent to *Campylobacter jejuni* enteritis. J. Neurol. Neurosurg. Psychiatry *68*:680–681, 2000.
246. Zalan, E., Leers, W. D., and Labzoffsky, N. A.: Occurrence of reovirus infection in Ontario. Can. Med. Assoc. J. *87*:714–715, 1962.
247. Ziegra, S. R.: Corticosteroid treatment for measles encephalitis. J. Pediatr. *39*:322–323, 1961.
248. Zinserling, A. V., Aksenov, O. A., Melnikova, V. F., et al.: Extrapulmonary lesions in influenza. Tohoku J. Exp. Med. *140*:259–272, 1983.

Transverse Myelitis or Myelopathy

HOWARD P. GOODKIN ■ SCOTT L. POMEROY

Transverse myelitis is a clinical syndrome characterized by the acute or subacute development of complete or partial loss of neurologic function as the result of an intrinsic spinal cord lesion. Most often, the lesion involves a limited number of spinal segments, usually in the cervical or thoracic cord.

This syndrome commonly is thought to be the result of a cell-mediated autoimmune process,[1] probably similar to that resulting in acute disseminated encephalomyelitis or Guillain-Barré syndrome. Typically, the presumed trigger is an infection or vaccine. However, as emphasized by Paine and Byers in 1953,[27] other pathologic processes, including spinal cord ischemia and direct infection of the spinal cord, can mimic the symptoms and signs of transverse myelitis. For this reason, many neurologists prefer the term *transverse myelopathy*.

Etiology and Pathogenesis

The spectrum of probable causes is broad, and the pathophysiologic process often is not well defined. Multiple infectious agents, including a variety of viruses (e.g., varicella-zoster virus,[13, 22] Epstein-Barr virus[34]), parasites (e.g., schistosomiasis[26]), and bacteria (e.g., *Borrelia burgdorferi*[29] and *Mycoplasma pneumoniae*[24]), have been linked to the form of transverse myelitis that has a presumed postinfectious cell-mediated autoimmune etiology. Those cases of transverse myelitis observed after vaccinations[6, 17] also are likely to be the result of a similar autoimmune process. However, in some instances, the transverse myelitis possibly is the result of the organism directly invading the neuropil of the spinal cord and the direct inflammatory response that results.

Transverse myelitis also has been observed in systemic inflammatory diseases, such as systemic lupus erythematosus,[21] and in isolated central nervous system autoimmune disorders, such as multiple sclerosis. In the case of systemic lupus erythematosus and other systemic inflammatory diseases, whether the transverse myelitis is the result of a cell-mediated autoimmune process that directly attacks the neural cells or, instead, a vasculitic-hypercoagulable process that results in thrombosis and spinal cord ischemia and possibly necrosis is uncertain.[3, 10, 19]

Transverse myelitis also has been described after the inadvertent intra-arterial injection of benzathine penicillin, after the intrathecal administration of chemotherapeutic agents, and after radiation therapy.[35] The pathophysiologic process leading to transverse myelitis in these cases probably is not an autoimmune process but, instead, a direct toxic effect or thrombosis.[32] In many other patients for whom no clear etiology has been determined, reason exists to suspect an ischemic etiology, such as anterior spinal artery embolism.[5, 9, 27, 36] However, the cause remains unknown in most patients who have the typical clinical presentation.

Prevalence

During a 20-year period, 62 Jewish patients in Israel were diagnosed with transverse myelitis, for an average incidence rate of 1.3 per million residents.[7] During a 10-year period, Jeffery and colleagues[16] estimated a combined incidence in New Mexico of 4.6 per million per year for idiopathic transverse myelitis and myelitis as a symptom of multiple sclerosis.

Age at onset in these two studies was between approximately 1.5 and 82 years. In general, this syndrome is encountered more commonly in adults than in children. In the Israeli study, the incidence rate was higher in patients older than 40 years, and the lowest incidence rate occurred in those younger than 10 years. A similar decreased incidence in patients younger than 6 years was noted in Australia.[12]

Altrocchi[4] described 67 patients (44 adults and 23 children) who were encountered during a 25-year period (1938–1962) at the Columbia Presbyterian Medical Center in New York. Males and females were affected about equally. Other case series[2, 7, 16] have favored a male predominance.

Pathology

Pathologic findings have not been consistent, confirming that transverse myelitis is not the result of a single pathophysiologic mechanism. The findings have included varying degrees of destruction affecting either the white or gray matter or often both, usually in an asymmetric fashion. This irregular pattern of involvement persists over the longitudinal extent of the lesion, which may involve several segments of the spinal cord. Demyelination, neuronal injury, and incomplete or complete necrosis of neural tissue have been described and may at times be associated with inflammatory cells, macrophages, or proliferation of astroglia (Fig. 44–1). The form of the reaction probably is related to the duration of the disease and its cause. Thickening of small arteries and veins within or adjacent to the parenchyma of the spinal cord has been prominent in only a few of the recorded cases.

Clinical Manifestations

The onset usually is abrupt. The neurologic deficit evolves from the initial symptoms to maximal disability within hours to a few days or, at most, 4 weeks. A premonitory history of an upper respiratory tract infection, gastroenteritis, "flu-like" symptoms, or minor trauma is reported in as many as 50 percent of patients. This premonitory history more typically is obtained in the patients younger than 40 years.

The earliest symptoms are muscle weakness (usually involving the lower limbs), sensory aberrations, back discomfort, and root pain. Dunne and associates[12] have suggested that paresthesia as an initial symptom is rare in

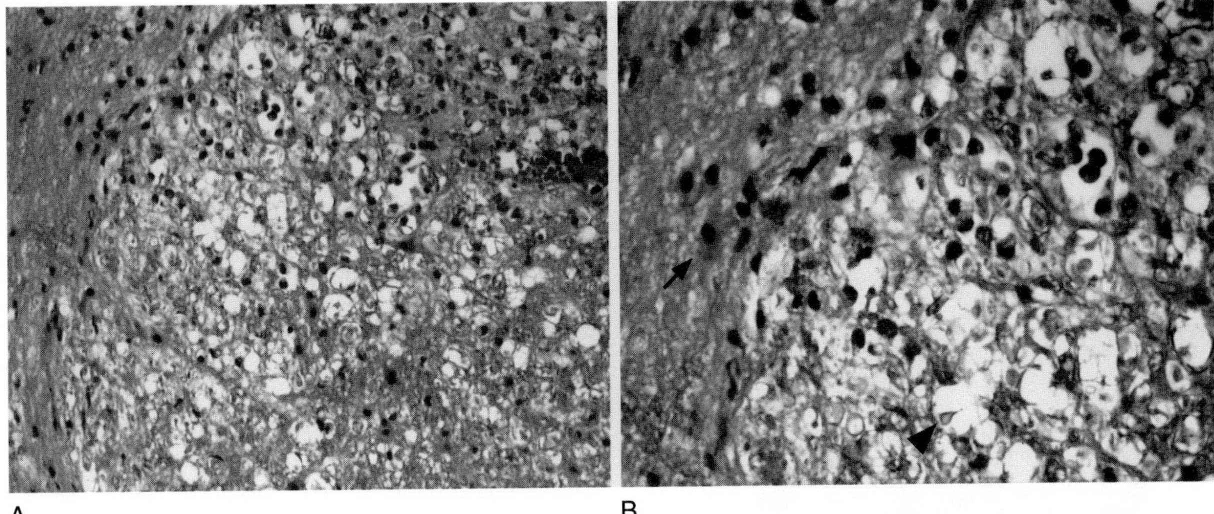

FIGURE 44–1 ■ *A,* Surgical biopsy specimen (hematoxylin and eosin stain) of spinal cord white matter demonstrating marked edema, vacuolation of the neuropil, gliosis, and axonal swelling. There is infiltration of the parenchyma by numerous macrophages, scattered lymphocytes, and occasional neutrophils. *B,* High-power view. The *arrowhead* demonstrates a swollen axon with surrounding vacuolated myelin sheath. The *arrow* points to a hypertrophic reactive astrocyte (gliosis). (Courtesy of Dr. K. Ligon.)

children, although it is common in adults. Signs may be asymmetric, but bilateral involvement of the spinal cord is invariable at some time. In the course of the disorder, bladder and bowel dysfunction are nearly universal as paresis of the limbs and sensory disturbances progress. The bladder dysfunction may be slight (urinary hesitancy) to severe (overflow incontinence). Two patients in the series studied by Dunne and associates[12] presented with urinary retention as the initial symptom.

The degree of paraparesis is variable, but moderate to severe weakness of the legs occurs in approximately two thirds of patients. Weakness may affect the arms in as many as one quarter of the patients. Muscle tone usually is decreased, and stretch reflexes often are absent at the time of presentation. As the syndrome progresses, spasticity prevails and Babinski signs usually are present.

Sensory loss also is seen in approximately two thirds of reported cases. Pain and temperature are affected more often than are position and vibratory sensations. Segmental paresthesias and dysesthesias may occur. A sensory level, most commonly in the thoracic region, is present in most patients.

Meningeal signs are encountered in as many as one third of patients. Fever occurs in approximately half of patients, although it may be referable to complicating infections of the lung or urinary tract.

Diagnosis

Although the diagnosis of transverse myelitis can be suspected on clinical grounds, it is one of exclusion. Therefore, the physician should consider those diseases that demand specific and prompt treatment.

A spinal epidural abscess is a neurosurgical emergency. It can closely mimic transverse myelitis, although the course of transverse myelitis usually is more rapid. Magnetic resonance imaging (MRI) should be performed on an emergent basis to establish this diagnosis. Intraspinal neoplasms and other compressive tumors also will be excluded by imaging of the spinal cord, except in those rare instances in which an acutely inflamed, swollen spinal cord may mimic an intra-axial mass.

Differentiation from Guillain-Barré syndrome can be difficult to make because both syndromes can present with complaints of sensory dysesthesias, flaccid weakness, and lower extremity areflexia shortly after the resolution of an antecedent viral infection. Sensory examination should permit localization of the lesion to either the spinal cord or peripheral nerves (stocking-and-glove distribution). If the clinical diagnosis still is in doubt or if an overlap syndrome (e.g., myeloradiculitis or acute disseminated encephalomyeloradiculitis) is suspected, further evaluation should include imaging of the spinal cord and electromyography or nerve conduction studies.

Syphilis, especially the meningovascular form, can mimic a nonspecific myelitis and deserves immediate attention.

Although currently a rare occurrence in industrialized countries, poliovirus needs to be considered in the differential diagnosis of an acute and subacute presentation of a flaccid paralysis, especially if an asymmetric distribution is present.

Infection with human T-lymphotropic virus 1 (HTLV-1), a retrovirus, can result in a spastic paraparesis, a sensory level, and bladder dysfunction. This HTLV-associated myelopathy, also referred to as tropical spastic paraparesis, usually is a gradual or subacute process; however, acute cases do occur. Differentiation from transverse myelitis may be important because treatment of tropical spastic paraparesis with interferon alfa may be beneficial.[15] Because the MRI findings of this condition may mimic those of transverse myelitis, differentiation will be based on the presence of elevated cerebrospinal fluid (CSF) and serum titers to HTLV-1.

The treatable nutritional myelopathies evolve more slowly and have a pattern of spinal cord involvement that is more diffuse. Other evidence of vitamin B_{12} deficiency or pellagra should render excluding these disorders relatively easy.

A vascular nevus at the segmental level of the spinal cord lesion should signal the possibility of an intraspinal vascular malformation that can be defined by selective spinal cord angiography.

A diagnosis of multiple sclerosis may become obvious only when lesions of the central nervous system are disseminated in time and space.

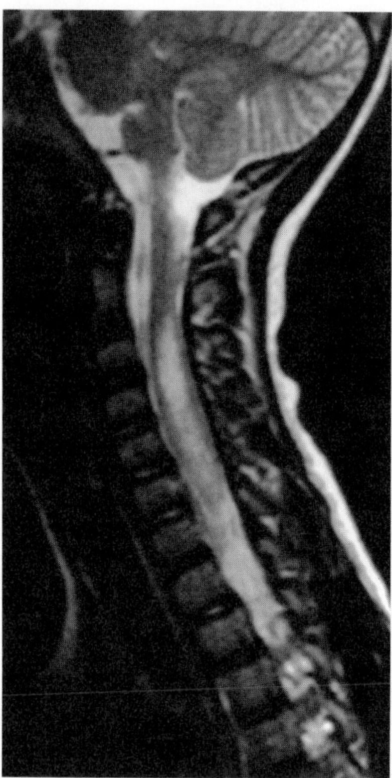

FIGURE 44–2 ■ Sagittal T2-weighted magnetic resonance image reveals increased signal and expansion of the cervicothoracic spinal cord in an 8-year-old boy who presented with subacute onset of paraplegia. The surgical biopsy specimen shown in Figure 44–1 is from the same patient. (Courtesy of Dr. F. Kim.)

Clinical Evaluation

The initial clinical evaluation of all patients presenting with a flaccid paraparesis should include MRI of the spinal cord and a lumbar puncture. MRI findings in transverse myelitis have been variable. In the acute setting, local enlargement of the spinal cord and increased signal intensity on long TR/TE (T2) sequences may be present[30] (Fig. 44–2). However, only a slight increase in signal intensity on long TR sequences[8] and even normal cord intensity have been reported.[23] Choi and associates[11] retrospectively reviewed the initial MRI findings in 17 patients with the diagnosis of transverse myelitis. A centrally located region of high signal intensity occupying more than two thirds of the cross-sectional area of the spinal cord was observed in 88 percent of the patients on axial T2-weighted images. In 53 percent of the patients, this region of hyperintensity was observed to span a length of up to three or four vertebral segments. Cord expansion was observed in only 47 percent of the patients, and contrast enhancement was present in only 53 percent of the patients.

The CSF findings are extremely variable. During the acute stage of the disease, the CSF may be normal or acellular with only a slight rise in the protein concentration, or several hundred or more leukocytes may be present, often with a predominance of polymorphonuclear cells. The concentration of protein may be elevated to several hundred milligrams per deciliter, and the percentage of gammaglobulin can be increased significantly. The glucose concentration is typically normal.

Once the diagnosis of transverse myelitis is established, every effort should be made to determine a specific etiology because specific therapies may be required. This evaluation should be tailored to each patient's history and presentation. If a specific etiology is uncertain, initial laboratory evaluation should be aimed at identifying an infectious cause or a systemic inflammatory disorder and should include (1) viral and bacterial cultures of the CSF, blood, and possibly throat and stool; (2) polymerase chain reaction analysis of the CSF for herpes simplex virus, varicella-zoster virus, Epstein-Barr virus, and cytomegalovirus; (3) serum titers of Epstein-Barr virus and *Mycoplasma pneumoniae;* (4) oligoclonal bands and myelin basic protein in the CSF and oligoclonal bands in the serum; and (5) erythrocyte sedimentation rate, antinuclear antibody titer, and rheumatoid factor titer.[18]

Treatment

Treatment of an idiopathic transverse myelitis or myelopathy is not specific. In those cases in which the high and middle cervical regions are involved, patients are at risk for development of respiratory compromise and need supportive care. Patients with significant bladder and bowel dysfunctions require catheterization and a bowel regimen.

The efficacy of pharmacologic doses of glucocorticoids is unproved; however, two nonrandomized studies[20, 31] have suggested that this therapy reduces the time to full recovery, and in neither study were significant side effects observed.

Prognosis

Proper supportive care, including therapy for complicating infections, prevention of pressure sores, and attention to urinary tract function, renders the prognosis for survival excellent.

The degree of recovery is variable, with little recovery occurring after 6 months. Poor prognostic indicators include an acute presentation[12, 28, 36] and evidence of alpha motor neuron damage.[12, 14, 25] In Paine and Byers' classic paper on the subject, only one patient died and 60 percent of the patients had a complete or nearly complete recovery.[27] In a more recent retrospective study,[12] none of 21 patients died and 61 percent (13) of the patients had a complete or nearly complete recovery. Although cases of relapsing transverse myelitis have been reported,[33] recurrent neurologic problems are rare occurrences among survivors.

REFERENCES

1. Abramsky, O., and Teitelbaum, D.: The autoimmune features of acute transverse myelopathy. Ann. Neurol. *2*:36–40, 1977.
2. al Deeb, S. M., Yaqub, B. A., Bruyn, G. W., and Biary, N. M.: Acute transverse myelitis. A localized form of postinfectious encephalomyelitis. Brain *120*:1115–1122, 1997.
3. Allen, I. V., Millar, J. H. D., Kirk, J., and Shillington, R. K. A.: Systemic lupus erythematosus clinically resembling multiple sclerosis and with unusual pathological and ultrastructural features. J. Neurol. Neurosurg. Psychiatry *42*:392–401, 1979.
4. Altrocchi, P. H.: Acute transverse myelopathy. Arch. Neurol. *9*:111–119, 1963.
5. Arlazoroff, A., Klein, C., Blumen, N., and Ohry, A.: Acute transverse myelitis, a possible vascular etiology. Med. Hypotheses *30*:27–30, 1989.
6. Bakshi, R., and Mazziotta, J. C.: Acute transverse myelitis after influenza vaccination: Magnetic resonance imaging findings. J. Neuroimaging *6*:248–250, 1996.
7. Berman, M., Feldman, S., Alter, M., et al.: Acute transverse myelitis: Incidence and etiologic considerations. Neurology *31*:966–971, 1981.
8. Bitzan, M.: Rubella myelitis and encephalitis in childhood. A report of two cases with magnetic resonance imaging. Neuropediatrics *18*:84–87, 1987.
9. Bots, G. T., Wattendorff, A. R., Buruma, O. J., et al.: Acute myelopathy caused by fibrocartilaginous emboli. Neurology *31*:1250–1256, 1981.

10. Brey, R. L., and Escalante, A.: Neurological manifestations of antiphospholipid antibody syndrome. Lupus 7:S67–S74, 1998.
11. Choi, K. H., Kee, K. S., Chung, S. O., et al.: Idiopathic transverse myelitis: MR characteristics. A. J. N. R. Am. J. Neuroradiol. *17*:1151–1160, 1996.
12. Dunne, K., Hopkins, I. J., and Shield, L. K.: Acute transverse myelopathy in childhood. Dev. Med. Child Neurol. *28*:198–204, 1986.
13. Heller, H. M., Carnevale, N. T., and Steigbigel, R. T.: Varicella zoster virus transverse myelitis without cutaneous rash. Am. J. Med. *88*:550–551, 1990.
14. Irani, D. N., and Kerr, D. A.: 14-3-3 protein in the cerebrospinal fluid of patients with acute transverse myelitis. Lancet *355*:901, 2000.
15. Izumo, S., Goto, I., and Itoyama, Y.: Interferon-alpha is effective in HTLV-1-associated myelopathy: A multicenter, randomized, double-blind, controlled trial. Neurology *46*:1016–1021, 1996.
16. Jeffery, D. R., Mandler, R. N., and Davis, L. E.: Transverse myelitis. Retrospective analysis of 33 cases, with differentiation of cases associated with multiple sclerosis and parainfectious events. Arch. Neurol. *50*:532–535, 1993.
17. Joyce, K. A., and Rees, J. E.: Transverse myelitis after measles, mumps, and rubella vaccine. BMJ *311*:422, 1995.
18. Knebusch, M., Strassburg, H. M., and Reiners, K.: Acute transverse myelitis in childhood: Nine cases and review of the literature. Dev. Med. Child Neurol. *40*:631–639, 1998.
19. Kovacs, B., Lafferty, T. L., Brent, L. H., and DeHoratius, R. J.: Transverse myelopathy in systemic lupus erythematosus: An analysis of 14 cases and review of the literature. Ann. Rheum. Dis. *59*:120–124, 2000.
20. Lahat, E., Pillar, G., Ravid, S., et al.: Rapid recovery from transverse myelopathy in children treated with methylprednisolone. Pediatr. Neurol. *19*:279–282, 1998.
21. Linssen, W. H., Fiselier, T. J. W., Gabreëls, F. J. M., et al.: Acute transverse myelopathy as the initial manifestation of probable systemic lupus erythematosus in a child. Neuropediatrics *19*:212–215, 1988.
22. McCarthy, J. T., and Amer, J.: Postvaricella acute transverse myelitis: A case presentation and review of the literature. Pediatrics *62*:202–204, 1978.
23. Merine, D., Wang, H., Kumar, A. J., et al.: CT myelography and MR imaging of acute transverse myelitis. J. Comput. Assist. Tomogr. *11*: 606–608, 1987.
24. Mills, R. W., and Schoolfield, L.: Acute transverse myelitis associated with *Mycoplasma pneumoniae* infection: A case report and review of the literature. Pediatr. Infect. Dis. J. *11*:228–231, 1992.
25. Misra, U. K., and Kalita, J.: Can electromyography predict the prognosis of transverse myelitis? J. Neurol. *245*:741–744, 1998.
26. Nazer, H., Hugosson, C., and Posas, H.: Transverse myelitis in a child with Down's syndrome and schistosomal colitis. Ann. Trop. Paediatr. *13*:353–357, 1993.
27. Paine, R. S., and Byers, R. K.: Transverse myelopathy in childhood. Am. J. Dis. Child. *85*:151–163, 1953.
28. Ropper, A. H., and Poskanzer, D. C.: The prognosis of acute and subacute transverse myelopathy based on early signs and symptoms. Ann. Neurol. *4*:51–59, 1978.
29. Rousseau, J. J., Lust, C., Zangerlie, P. F., and Bigaigon, G.: Acute transverse myelitis as presenting neurological feature of Lyme disease. Lancet *2*:1222–1223, 1986.
30. Sanders, K. A., Khandji, A. G., and Mohr, J. P.: Gadolinium-MRI in acute transverse myelopathy. Neurology *40*:1614–1616, 1990.
31. Sebire, G., Hollenberg, H., Meyer, L., et al.: High dose methylprednisolone in severe acute transverse myelopathy. Arch. Dis. Child. *76*:167–168, 1997.
32. Stafford, W. W., Mena, H., Piskun, W. S, and Weir, M. R.: Transverse myelitis from intraarterial penicillin. Neurosurgery *15*:552–556, 1984.
33. Tippett, D. S., Fishman, P. S., and Panitch, H. S.: Relapsing transverse myelitis. Neurology *41*:703–706, 1991.
34. Tsutsumi, H., Kamazaki, H., Nakata, S., et al.: Sequential development of acute meningoencephalitis and transverse myelitis caused by Epstein-Barr virus during infectious mononucleosis. Pediatr. Infect. Dis. J. *13*:665–667, 1994.
35. Weir, M. R., and Fearnow, R. G.: Transverse myelitis and penicillin. Pediatrics *71*:988, 1983.
36. Wilmshurst, J. M., Walker, M. C., and Pohl, K. R. E.: Rapid onset transverse myelitis in adolescence: Implications for pathogenesis and prognosis. Arch. Dis. Child. *80*:137–142, 1999.

Additional Reading

Rust, R. S.: Multiple sclerosis, acute disseminated encephalomyelitis, and related conditions. Semin. Pediatr. Neurol. 7:66–90, 2000.

CHAPTER 45 Guillain-Barré Syndrome

DANIEL G. GLAZE

The Guillain-Barré syndrome (GBS) is an acute, demyelinating disease of the peripheral nervous system. With the decline in the incidence of poliomyelitis, GBS has emerged as the most frequent cause of acute, severe generalized human paralytic disease.[199] This disorder typically occurs several weeks after an upper respiratory or gastrointestinal tract illness, but it has been associated with other factors, including immunization and surgery. It is characterized by progressive motor weakness, hyporeflexia, and minor sensory disturbances. An elevated protein concentration contrasts with a relatively normal cell count in the cerebrospinal fluid (CSF). No diagnostic test for GBS exists; the diagnosis is based on the clinical features supported by other data, including CSF protein elevation, electrophysiologic changes, and pathologic changes of the peripheral nerves. The precise diagnostic limits of GBS remain uncertain.[9] The consensus is that GBS is mediated immunologically. However, the specific immunologic alterations necessary to initiate the events that result in demyelinization of human peripheral nerve are unclear. The primary treatment modality is supportive care, but the efficacy of other therapies, such as plasma exchange transfusion and intravenous immune globulin (IVIg) therapy, in shortening the duration of the illness and decreasing the need for mechanical ventilation has been demonstrated.[55, 96, 216, 217] This chapter presents an overview of GBS, including diagnostic inclusion and exclusion criteria, the role of preceding viral infection and immunization, immunologic aspects, and treatment modalities.

History

Although bearing the names of Guillain and Barré, this disorder was recognized first by Landry in 1859.[115] He described 10 patients who usually first had generalized weakness, then paresthesia and transitory muscle cramps, and then rapidly ascending paralysis that involved the respiratory muscles last. He named this disorder acute ascending paralysis, postulated that it occurred after another illness, and considered it to be a severe disease because 2 of the 10 patients died. Other reports of this disorder appeared, but in 1916, Guillain, Barré, and Strohl[79] clearly characterized it and first called attention to the "albuminocytologic dissociation" (increased CSF protein with absence of cells). Barré and Guillain favored an infectious cause; in 1955, Waksman and Adams[223] pointed out the similarity in the clinical and pathologic pictures between GBS and experimental allergic neuritis in rabbits. Melnick,[136] in 1963, found antibodies to nervous tissue in 19 of 38 patients with GBS. In 1960, Osler and Sidell[156] indicated the need for exact diagnostic criteria for GBS and presented 12 diagnostic criteria restricting the definition of the disorder. Most subsequent studies arrived at a broader concept of the disorder.[6, 10, 59] After the reports of significant increase of GBS in association with the 1976 inoculation program for swine influenza and sponsored by the National Institute of Neurological and Communicative Disorders and Stroke (NINCDS), inclusion and exclusion diagnostic criteria were proposed.[9–11]

Diagnostic Criteria

The diagnosis of GBS is based on the clinical history and examination and supported by clinical laboratory (i.e., CSF) and electrodiagnostic (i.e., nerve conduction velocities) evaluations. The "typical" case of GBS often follows a recognizable nonspecific infection, more often viral than bacterial, after a period of a few days or weeks. The paralytic stage usually begins with pain or paresthesia, followed by hypotonic, ascending paralysis without pyramidal tract involvement, and loss of deep tendon reflexes rather than hyperreflexia or pathologic reflexes. Initial weakness usually is noted in the lower extremities and less commonly in the upper extremities or the face. A significant number of patients experience minimal to moderate sensory loss in a glove-stocking distribution. Maximum paralysis is reached in approximately 3 weeks, with more acute than chronic courses occurring. In 46 to 75 percent of persons, cranial nerves, including VII, IX/X, or both, may be affected, giving rise to facial weakness and difficulties in swallowing. Respiratory weakness occurs in 12 to 20 percent of patients, and some may require mechanical ventilation. Pain, usually described as similar to muscle discomfort after exercise, has been reported to occur in 55 percent of patients with GBS, and it may precede weakness in a few patients.[179] On presentation, 79 percent of children with GBS and younger than 6 years may have pain. Pain may be present for more than a week before a correct diagnosis is made and commonly involves the back and lower extremities.[145] Routine laboratory findings are unremarkable, except for characteristic elevation of CSF protein (typical values of 50 to 200 mg/dL) without appearance of cells. CSF protein concentration usually peaks during the second to eighth weeks, with a slow decline thereafter. Although most patients experience "complete" recovery, some (20%) have permanent residual disease (weakness, muscle atrophy) or rarely (1% to 4%) die of respiratory failure.[16, 132]

As Asbury has emphasized,[9] the problem is not with recognition of a typical case but with knowing the delimiting boundaries of the disorder. To define those limits, criteria have been reported and are presented in Table 45–1.[11, 12] These criteria include features required for diagnosis: progressive motor weakness of more than one limb and areflexia.

Clinical features supporting the diagnosis include the following: progression of symptoms with signs of motor weakness ceasing to progress by 4 weeks into the illness; symmetry of symptoms; sensory, cranial nerve, and autonomic dysfunction; recovery; and absence of fever. Laboratory features supporting diagnosis include CSF protein elevation after the first week of symptoms or rise on serial lumbar punctures and fewer than 10 mononuclear leukocytes/mm^3.

TABLE 45–1 ■ CRITERIA FOR DIAGNOSIS OF GUILLAIN-BARRÉ SYNDROME[11,12]

Required
Progressive motor weakness in more than one extremity
Areflexia (at least distal with hyporeflexia of the biceps and knee jerks)

Strongly Supportive
Clinical features (in order of importance)
- Progression: ceases by 4 weeks
- Relative symmetry
- Mild sensory symptoms or signs
- Cranial nerve involvement
- Recovery: usually 2–4 weeks after progression ceases
- Autonomic dysfunction
- Absence of fever at onset of neurologic symptoms

Cerebrospinal Fluid Features
Protein: elevated after first week of symptoms, or rising on serial lumbar punctures
Cells: 10 or fewer mononuclear leukocytes/mm^3

Electrodiagnostic features
Nerve conduction slowing

Casting Doubt
Marked, persistent asymmetry of weakness
Persistent bladder or bowel dysfunction
Bowel or bladder dysfunction at onset
More than 50 mononuclear leukocytes/mm^3 in cerebrospinal fluid
Presence of polymorphonuclear leukocytes in cerebrospinal fluid
Sharp sensory level

Rule Out the Diagnosis
Current history of hexacarbon abuse
Abnormal porphyrin metabolism
Recent diphtheria infection
Evidence of lead neuropathy or intoxication
Purely sensory syndrome
Definite diagnosis of poliomyelitis, botulism, hysterical paralysis, or toxic neuropathy

The major features of physiologic studies of GBS include an early conduction block, an early reduction in distal evoked compound muscle action potential amplitude, and a later reduction in motor conduction velocity.[40] Electrodiagnostic features supporting diagnosis include evidence of nerve conduction slowing in approximately 80 percent of cases characterized by conduction velocity usually less than 60 percent of normal, patchy distribution, and some unaffected nerves; conduction studies yield normal results in the other 20 percent.[9, 10]

Certain features cast doubt on or rule out the diagnosis. They include a purely sensory syndrome; a current history of hexacarbon abuse; abnormal porphyrin metabolism (increased excretion of porphobilinogen and δ-aminolevulinic acid in the urine); evidence of recent diphtheritic infection or lead neuropathy and intoxication; or a definite diagnosis of a condition such as poliomyelitis, botulism, hysterical paralysis, or toxic neuropathy (nitrofurantoin, dapsone, or organophosphorus).[9, 10]

A diagnostic process has been suggested.[9] If the clinical features and temporal evolution are typical and without variant features or features that rule out GBS, the diagnosis may be made on clinical grounds alone. Laboratory findings, such as CSF protein elevation, may not appear until after a week, and electrodiagnostic findings may never appear. However, if clinical features are unusual, laboratory studies may provide important supportive information, and a diagnosis of GBS may have to be delayed to evaluate these test results fully. Asbury and Cornblath[12] reported that certain variant features are seen on occasion in otherwise typical cases of GBS. These variant features include fever at onset of neuritic symptoms, severe sensory loss with pain, progression beyond 4 weeks, cessation of progression without recovery or with major permanent residual deficit, sphincter dysfunction, central nervous system involvement, no rise in CSF protein in the period of 1 to 10 weeks after onset of symptoms, and counts of 11 to 50 mononuclear leukocytes/mm^3 in CSF. These authors suggested that the presence of one of these symptoms, signs, or laboratory results should raise doubt about the validity of the diagnosis and that the presence of two or more suggest that the diagnosis of GBS is incorrect. Manifestations of systemic illness or constitutional symptoms or both preceding or coinciding with signs and symptoms of involvement of the peripheral nervous system also should suggest a diagnosis of a systemic illness or intoxication and not GBS. In human immunodeficiency virus (HIV)–seropositive patients with features consistent with GBS, CSF cell counts frequently are elevated.[12, 42]

Clinical Variants

GBS typically has an acute onset followed by rapidly ascending weakness. In some patients, onset is stuttering with periods of progression and plateaus before reaching the nadir of involvement. Onset is subacute in some patients, with a slow progression that can take place during a few weeks.[134] In addition to weakness and areflexia, other individual features may be observed in patients with GBS. They include total and incomplete external ophthalmoplegia[71, 76]; papilledema[43]; and autonomic dysfunction, including hypertension, postural hypotension, and cardiovascular disturbances.[39, 43, 44, 200] Hypertension may be a consequence of sympathetic nervous system hypersensitivity and increased excretion of catecholamines[43] but has been associated with increased renin-angiotensin activity.[187] Cardiovascular disturbances have been reported to be more prevalent in patients with GBS who are severely paralyzed and require mechanical ventilation.[39] Autonomic dysfunction in GBS, including tachycardia and other arrhythmias, may contribute to morbidity.[44]

A pure motor axonal form of GBS is recognized. This form, acute motor axonal neuropathy (AMAN, in contrast to the "classic" form, acute inflammatory demyelinating polyradiculoneuropathy or AIDP), initially was characterized mainly in north China.[130] There it occurs as a summertime epidemic pattern mostly in children and young adults. AMAN is characterized by selective involvement of motor fibers, less sensory and cranial nerve involvement, and a high incidence of preceding diarrhea. Recovery from the motor form is good and similar to recovery in AIDP.[13] In a study from Argentina, 30 percent of children with GBS had electrodiagnostic findings consistent with AMAN. In comparison to those with AIDP, children with AMAN were younger and more likely to reside in urban or rural areas without running water. GBS in these children with AMAN evolved more acutely, reached a higher maximum disability score, required assisted ventilation more often, had lower mean level of CSF protein, improved more slowly, and had a poorer outcome.[157]

One criticism of the NINCDS Ad Hoc Committee criteria is that they are too restrictive.[9, 11] The criteria initially were designed for use during field studies of GBS. Certain variants are allowed: fever at onset of neuritic symptoms; severe sensory loss with pain; occasional progression beyond 4 weeks; major permanent residual deficits; transient bladder paralysis; and, possibly, central nervous system involvement such as ataxia (cerebellar), dysarthria, extensor plantar responses, and ill-defined sensory levels. These features need not exclude the diagnosis of GBS.[9, 10]

Specific variants in which the clinical features are atypical but may fall in the spectrum of GBS have been described.[9, 10] Findings of ophthalmoplegia, ataxia, and areflexia have been designated Miller Fisher syndrome.[65, 176] The rapid onset of these symptoms usually indicates a benign course with fairly complete recovery within weeks to months.[9, 10] Sensory loss and areflexia without motor weakness or simultaneous onset of symmetric cranial nerve dysfunction may be accepted as variants of GBS if they are characterized by rapid onset and recovery, elevation of CSF protein, and the typical electrodiagnostic pattern of demyelination.[9, 10, 154] The combination of acute motor and sensory axonal neuropathy (AMSAN) and the presentation of acute sensory neuropathy characterized by symmetric glove-and-stocking sensory loss for pain and temperature (acute numbness) with normal muscle strength and tendon reflexes (acute small-fiber sensory neuropathy [ASFSN]) are suggested as variants of GBS.[5a, 191a]

Epidemiology

Trends in the incidence of GBS are difficult to assess because earlier epidemiologic studies[16, 23, 118, 199] were based on small numbers of cases and lacked common and well-defined diagnostic criteria for GBS. The results of these studies may not be comparable because of diagnostic and methodologic differences.[16] Schonberger and associates[191] have reviewed these epidemiologic data for GBS.

CASE REPORTS

Leneman[117] reported an extensive list of 1100 cases. Of these cases, 638 were associated with a variety of infectious diseases, 150 with allergic phenomena or immune responses, 96 with metabolic or endocrine disturbances, 14 with toxic agents, 33 with neoplasms, 1 with an influenza vaccination, and 365 with no known antecedent or underlying disease. However, as has been emphasized,[191] determining whether reported associations are etiologic or merely coincidental is difficult.

CASE-CONTROL STUDIES

Five studies[5, 52, 102, 137, 203] that compared the frequency of suspected etiologic factors in a group of patients with GBS and a selected group without GBS were reviewed. These studies provided evidence that important risk factors for GBS are recent nonspecific antecedent respiratory infection (48%[137]; 43% to 65% of GBS cases in other reports[101, 118]), recent gastrointestinal infection (32%),[102] or recent cytomegalovirus (CMV) infection (32.6%).[52] Three studies[5, 116, 203] found no association of human leukocyte antigen type with GBS.

INCIDENCE RATES IN WELL-DEFINED POPULATIONS

In 10 studies reviewed,* the crude average annual incidence rate of GBS per 100,000 population ranged from 0.6 to 1.9. The similarities of these incidence rates have been suggested

*See references 16, 23, 28, 78, 89, 101, 102, 111, 118, 149.

to be consistent with a hypothesis that the triggering agents responsible for GBS are widespread and multiple and that susceptibility to GBS in geographically scattered populations is similarly low.[191] However, higher incidence rates have been reported, including an increased risk within a 5-week period after A/New Jersey influenza vaccine was administered during 1976.[190] Also, for a large, well-defined Colorado population, an incidence of 4 cases per 100,000 per year for 1981 to 1983 was reported, which contrasted with an incidence of 1.2 cases per 100,000 per year for 1975 to 1980.[101] The increased incidence could not be explained on the basis of characteristics of the patients or predisposing factors. These studies of incidence rates have indicated a higher incidence for males and, in one study, for whites compared with blacks.[191] Peak incidences in the first decade of life,[180] in the fifth and sixth decades,[171, 199] or in both younger and older patients[199] have been observed. These findings may be due to socioeconomic factors, which might influence the age at which viral infections were acquired, or to age-dependent immune system peculiarities.[199] No clear seasonal or geographic clustering of GBS has been observed.

One study[16] has presented an evaluation of GBS using more rigid criteria proposed by the NINCDS Ad Hoc Committee (Table 45–2). The incidence of GBS from 1935 to 1980 in Olmsted County, Minnesota, was 1.8 per 100,000 person-years (age and sex adjusted). The rate increased from 1.2 (1935 to 1956) to 2.4 (1970 to 1980). Males were affected more than were females (2.3 vs. 1.2). The incidence rate increased with age from 0.8 in those younger than 18 years to 3.2 for those 60 years or older. In the 4 weeks preceding the onset of neurologic symptoms, 65 percent of the 48 patients had an antecedent infection, including 21 patients with upper respiratory tract illnesses, 10 with gastrointestinal tract illnesses, and 9 with nonspecific febrile illnesses. A nadir was reached after onset at an average of 8 days. Duration of illness was an average of 12 weeks. Two (4%) of the 48 patients died as a result of GBS; minimal residua were observed in approximately 20 percent, whereas no patient had severe residua.

TABLE 45–2 ■ ANTECEDENT FACTORS

Strongly Suggestive Evidence
Cytomegalovirus
Epstein-Barr virus
Coxsackieviruses A
Campylobacter jejuni
Mycoplasma pneumoniae

Suggestive Evidence
A/New Jersey 1976 influenza immunization

Survey Study or Anecdotal Reports
Viral agents
- Echoviruses
- Coxsackieviruses A and B
- Influenza viruses A and B
- Measles
- Varicella virus
- Rubella
- Mumps
- Hepatitis viruses
- Herpes simplex viruses
- Rabies
- HIV

Nonviral agents
- *Francisella (Pasteurella) tularensis* (tularemia)
- *Chlamydia*
- *Plasmodium* (malaria)
- *Toxoplasma gondii*
- *Mycobacterium tuberculosis*

Noninfectious agents
- Immunizations
  - Trivalent oral poliovirus
  - Diphtheria-tetanus-pertussis
  - Measles-mumps-rubella
  - Rabies
  - Influenza, other than A/New Jersey
  - Polyvalent pneumococcal
  - Hepatitis
  - *Haemophilus influenzae type b*
- Surgery
- Trauma
- Epidural anesthesia
- Neoplasm (Hodgkin)
- Vasculitides (systemic lupus erythematosus)
- Drug hypersensitivities
- Heroin addiction
- Drug (zimeldine)

SENTINEL NEUROLOGISTS' SURVEILLANCE OF GUILLAIN-BARRÉ SYNDROME IN THE UNITED STATES

Between January 1, 1978, and March 31, 1979, neurologists who were members of the American Association of Neuropathologists were surveyed by the Centers for Disease Control and Prevention.[191] This survey indicated that the incidence rate for males was 39 percent higher than that for females and 50 to 60 percent higher for whites than for blacks. The incidence rates were highest for persons 50 to 74 years of age. Sixty-seven percent of the patients for whom information was available indicated that they had had an antecedent illness within 8 weeks before the onset of GBS: 58 percent primarily respiratory, 22 percent gastrointestinal, and 10 percent both respiratory and gastrointestinal. The peak interval between the antecedent respiratory or gastrointestinal tract illness and the onset of GBS was 2 weeks. Five percent of patients with GBS had undergone surgery within 8 weeks before the onset of GBS; the significance of this rate in comparison with the general population has not been confirmed.

INCIDENCE IN PEDIATRIC POPULATIONS

A report based on a retrospective epidemiologic survey conducted in southern California found the mean annual incidence of GBS to be 0.60 (95% confidence intervals, 0.48 to 0.73) per 100,000 children younger than 15 years.[170] This study was based on the review of medical records of all children discharged from 22 hospitals caring for children in Los Angeles and Orange counties with the diagnosis of any kind of neuropathy. The criteria proposed by the GBS study group were used to identify the children with GBS and excluded those with a history or evidence of poliomyelitis, diphtheria, botulism, hexacarbon abuse, porphyria, lead intoxication, toxic neuropathy, exposure to organophosphates, or tic paralysis.[9, 10, 12] From 1980 to 1986, 93 affected children younger than 15 years living in the study area were identified. Eighty-eight had progressive motor weakness of more than one limb; five had Miller Fisher variant with ataxia, areflexia, and ophthalmoplegia. Ninety-two had an initial lumbar puncture, and all of these had CSF cell counts of no more than 50 monocytes or 2 polymorphonuclear leukocytes; 79 had a repeated lumbar puncture, and all of these had elevated CSF protein after 1 week of symptoms. In all patients, disease progressed for days to a few weeks, and recovery ensued 2 to 4 weeks after progression of symptoms was halted. Eighty-eight had relative symmetry of weakness, and 22 had autonomic dysfunction. In 71 patients (76%), the onset of GBS was preceded by an infection. No significant difference in the incidence of GBS was noted between boys and girls, among ethnic groups, or in the annual and monthly occurrence. The incidence was significantly higher in 2-year-old children than in any other group.[170]

Age-related differences in the expression of GBS in children have been observed.[187] In children younger than 5 years, a greater incidence of bulbar nerve (cranial nerves IX, X, XII) dysfunction occurred. In children younger than 5 years, muscle weakness was the most frequent initial symptom, occurring in 72 percent. In children older than 5 years, limb pain was the most frequent initial symptom (53.4%). The interval between previous illness and onset of GBS was shorter for children older than 5 years and typically was 2 to 14 days. No statistically significant differences occurred in respiratory complications or fatal outcome between the groups of older and younger children with GBS.

Pathology and Pathogenesis

GBS has been described as a distinctive neuropathy characterized pathologically by inflammatory lesions scattered throughout the peripheral nervous system.[151, 166] Asbury and associates[10, 11] studied 19 fatal cases and observed that the pathologic hallmark of this disorder is a perivenular mononuclear inflammatory infiltrate, which was observed throughout the peripheral nervous system, even in the cases of shortest clinical course (1 to 4 days). They observed that the lesions were predominantly lymphocytic and that the inflammatory infiltrate tended to cluster about small endoneural and epineural vessels, particularly veins, in a seemingly random, multifocal manner. All levels, including anterior and posterior roots, ganglia, proximal and distal nerve trunks, terminal twigs, cranial nerves, and sympathetic chains and ganglia, appeared vulnerable to attack. The site of maximal involvement correlated with the degree of premorbid clinical findings. Segmented demyelination was the predominant form of nerve fiber damage, and myelin destruction was restricted to these regions of nerve trunks that were infiltrated by inflammatory cells.

Subsequent reports have confirmed the observation that primary demyelination occurs only in tissue infiltrated by inflammatory cells. These studies have shown that the destructive process is affected by macrophages in the presence of lymphocytes and directed only at that part of the Schwann cell plasma membrane forming the myelin sheath.[26, 165, 166, 226, 231] However, Kanda and associates[99] reported the findings of a necropsy of early fulminant GBS in an adult. Using semithin sections, they observed less extensive mononuclear infiltration and found nerve fibers with myelin splitting, even in regions where inflammatory cell reaction was not conspicuous. Small myelinated fibers were preferentially involved, and no abnormalities of unmyelinated fibers occurred. Sensory roots were involved as severely as were motor roots. These authors concluded that the underlying pathologic mechanism of GBS is heterogeneous. They suggested that some cases involve only perivascular infiltration and are cell mediated. Other cases may involve demyelination without lymphocytic infiltration and are mediated primarily humorally.

ROLE OF INFECTION

The onset of GBS frequently follows an acute febrile infectious illness. GBS has been reported to occur after childhood illnesses, such as mumps,[32] varicella,[21, 45, 224] measles,[53, 120, 161] and rubella.[50, 184] However, these childhood illnesses rarely are associated with GBS.[50] Epidemiologic studies have indicated the significant occurrence of upper respiratory or gastrointestinal tract illnesses before the onset of GBS and support the concept that both these categories of illness constitute important risk factors for GBS.[102, 137] One case-control study[137] reported a higher incidence of elevated specific complement-fixation antibody titers in GBS cases compared with control cases for infectious mononucleosis and parainfluenza. Although influenza A and B infections have been observed in patients with GBS,[19, 147, 148, 225] this case-control study found no significantly higher incidence of elevated complement-fixation titers in patients with GBS compared with control subjects for influenza A or B.[137] In addition, during outbreaks of influenza A2 in 1960 to 1961 and influenza B in 1961 to 1962, the incidence of GBS was high; however, the largest number of cases occurred from November 1959 to October 1960, when the prevalence of influenza was comparatively low.[137]

Infectious hepatitis has been reported in association with GBS,[159, 163] and four case reports have observed hepatitis B antigenemia in patients with GBS.[64, 131, 144, 145] Acute viral hepatitis rarely is complicated by GBS. GBS has been associated with serologically documented cases of acute A, B, non-A/non-B, and delta hepatitis.[121, 205, 210] Immune complexes containing hepatitis B surface antigen in the serum and CSF were found in patients with GBS. These complexes were present with acute hepatitis B during the acute phase of GBS and disappeared when the neurologic symptoms resolved.[135, 205, 210] However, a causal association has not been established, and the fact that many of the populations at risk for hepatitis B and A also are at risk for acquiring infections with other viruses, such as Epstein-Barr virus and CMV, has been emphasized.[205]

Echoviruses and various serotypes of coxsackieviruses A and B viral isolates have been described in patients with GBS.[61, 67, 94, 103, 104, 137, 158, 213] Most isolates were obtained from stool, although isolates were obtained from CSF in a few cases.[50] Recovery of virus does not prove causation; some isolates were recovered when enterovirus was prevalent in the community and in one instance equaled the frequency from control subjects.[50, 127] Direct isolation of coxsackievirus A4 from nerve roots and dorsal root ganglia has been reported.[61] GBS also has been reported to occur after herpes simplex type 2 encephalitis,[139, 195] in association with HIV infection,[42] and during the course of rabies infection.[219]

Laboratory research has suggested an important association exists between herpesviruses and GBS. Dowling and Cook[50] reported that 15 percent of patients with GBS tested had IgM antibody in high titer against CMV antigen in tissue culture cells.

Other studies also have observed an association between CMV and GBS.[8, 35, 52, 97, 141, 162, 189] Dowling and Cook[50] reported a wide spectrum of antecedent illness, ranging from asymptomatic infection to typical respiratory tract and gastrointestinal tract symptoms, in CMV-positive patients. A predilection for CMV-positive GBS was found to occur in patients younger than 30 years, corresponding to the age incidence described in heterophil-negative, CMV-induced, mononucleosis-like illness.[50] Time clustering of cases was observed, with CMV antibody–positive cases appearing in 10- to 16-week clusters. Dowling and Cook[50] suggest that in cases associated with preceding surgery, GBS may be consequent to CMV, either acquired during transfusion or caused by activation of latent virus, or occurrence of nontransfusion, non-A/non-B hepatitis. Dowling and Cook[49] also observed the frequent (8%) occurrence of IgM antibodies to Epstein-Barr virus in GBS. In contrast, less than 2 percent (1 of 75) of GBS patients demonstrated IgM herpes simplex virus–specific antibody.[18] These studies indicate that two herpesviruses are common antecedents of the syndrome, but the precise mechanism by which they initiate destruction of myelin is not known. However, Hart and Kennedy[83] emphasized the difficulty of establishing CMV as a cause of GBS. Using serologic tests, they confirmed active CMV infection in three patients with GBS. They reported that CMV can be isolated in as many as 1 percent of asymptomatic persons and in as many as 10 percent of pregnant women. Isolation may be coincidental. These authors suggested that latent CMV may be activated by other viruses, and isolation may reflect such a nonspecific phenomenon. GBS has been observed in association with HIV infection.[42] Elevated levels of circulating antibody to Epstein-Barr virus, CMV, and other infectious agents are common findings in these patients and may be directly responsible for some cases of GBS occurring in association with HIV infection.

Nonviral infectious agents may precede occurrence of GBS. Indeed, a preceding infection with *Campylobacter jejuni* associated with a diarrheal illness commonly occurs.[172, 174, 175] After two case reports,[34, 167] a retrospective study was conducted to determine serologic evidence of recent *C. jejuni* infection in GBS.[98] Thirty-eight percent (20) of 56 GBS patients were found to have serum evidence, CSF serologic evidence (including documentation of rise in titer, two or more elevated antibody titers, or positive CSF titer), or both. Twenty percent of these patients with GBS had preceding diarrheal illnesses. Groups of normal control subjects and those with other neurologic disorders had no evidence of having had a recent *C. jejuni* infection. IgA- and IgM-specific antibody was found only in the CSF of patients with recent *C. jejuni* infection, suggesting production of specific antibodies in the nervous system because their passive diffusion into the CSF is unlikely. GBS patients with serologic evidence of *C. jejuni* appeared to have a significantly more severe illness; 90 percent of these patients required mechanical ventilation. A report noted mild illness in GBS patients with positive serology and stool culture for *C. jejuni*.[167] During a prospective, case-controlled study in a cohort of patients with GBS (96 patients) or Miller Fisher syndrome (7 patients) who were admitted to hospitals throughout England and Wales between November 1992 and April 1994, Rees and associates[174] found evidence of recent *C. jejuni* infection in 26 percent of the patients with GBS or Miller Fisher syndrome, compared with 16 percent of household controls and 1 percent of age-matched hospital controls. No specific serotypes were associated with GBS. Seventy percent of the patients with *C. jejuni* infection reported having had a diarrheal illness within 12 weeks before the onset of the neurologic illness. *C. jejuni* was associated with axonal degeneration, slow recovery, and greater disability after 1 year. The median interval from onset of diarrhea to the onset of symptoms for all *C. jejuni*–positive patients was 9 days, suggesting that GBS is a consequence of an immune response to *C. jejuni* rather than a direct effect of the organism or one of its toxins.[95]

Mycoplasma pneumoniae is the second most prominent nonviral agent reported in association with GBS. One report observed that 5 percent of patients with GBS had serologic evidence of active *Mycoplasma* infection.[72] GBS has been reported rarely after infection with *Haemophilus influenzae, Francisella tularensis* (tularemia), *Chlamydia* (psittacosis), *Plasmodium* (malaria), *Mycobacterium tuberculosis,* and *Toxoplasma gondii*.[22, 75, 137, 140, 142, 155, 188, 222]

In summary, patients with GBS frequently give a history of prodromal symptoms. An association between GBS and an infectious agent long has been considered. McFarlin[129] has suggested that demyelination of peripheral nerve results from direct infection of Schwann cells by the infectious agent, producing prodromal symptoms, or from immunologic mechanisms triggered by the infection. McFarlin[129] favors the second possibility because epidemiologic and virologic surveys of patients with GBS have failed to identify reactivity with a single infectious agent and because the disorder can be triggered by other events, including surgery and immunizations. In addition, the clinical course may be shortened by plasmapheresis.

ROLE OF IMMUNIZATION

GBS occurs infrequently after immunization, including smallpox, diphtheria, tetanus, pertussis, combined mump-srubella, hepatitis B, rabies, *H. influenzae* type b, and polyvalent pneumococcal vaccines.[46, 69, 81, 92, 105] However, a nationwide GBS surveillance conducted from December 16, 1976, until January 31, 1977, suggested an excess risk of developing GBS was related to A/New Jersey influenza vaccine for persons 18 years of age or older.[27] The peak time of onset of GBS was 2 to 3 weeks after the vaccine was received. For the 10 weeks after vaccination with A/New Jersey vaccine, the risk was approximately 13.3 cases per 100,000 for vaccine recipients, which was five to six times higher than that in unvaccinated persons (2.6 per 100,000).[190, 191]

A subsequent survey of persons older than 18 years vaccinated in the 1978 to 1979 influenza campaign revealed that the relative risk of developing vaccine-associated GBS (those vaccinated within 8 weeks before the onset of GBS) was 1.4, which was significantly below the risk, 6.2, associated with A/New Jersey vaccine for the equivalent 8-week period.[27, 92, 191] The survey of 1979 to 1980 also did not reveal an increased incidence of GBS for vaccinated versus nonvaccinated persons.[92, 100, 191] The clustering of GBS onset in the second and third weeks after the influenza vaccinations administered in 1976 was not observed after vaccinations administered in either 1978 to 1979 or 1979 to 1980.[191] These results suggested that A/New Jersey influenza vaccine differed from subsequent influenza vaccines in its ability to trigger GBS.[191] The neurotigenic P2 protein of peripheral nerve myelin has been shown to have been present in the 1976 influenza vaccine and to have been biologically active.[198] P2 may have been a factor in the production of GBS after administration of the A/New Jersey influenza vaccination in susceptible persons.[197] Asbury[9] concluded that an "epidemic" of GBS actually took place, but the precise cause of the illness remains undetermined. Whether a special antigenic site was on the A/New Jersey viral product remains unclear. Patients with GBS who were vaccinated were spread throughout all 141 lots, and the problem could not be traced to individual lots or a single manufacturer. Surveillance for GBS in the subsequent (1979) influenza programs did not show any excess cases of GBS.[9]

GBS has occurred after the administration of rabies vaccine prepared in suckling mouse brain.[25, 87] A severe protracted course with involvement of cranial nerves, increased mortality rate (20%), and increased long-term sequelae were observed. GBS occurs less commonly after immunization with Sample-type vaccine prepared in brain and spinal cord of mature animals.

The number of GBS cases was increased in both children and adults in Finland in 1985 after a mass vaccination program with oral polio vaccine.[104, 212] This one-time campaign involved the entire Finnish population, and further study of the association between oral polio vaccine and GBS in Finland was not possible. This relationship was examined further during a retrospective epidemiologic survey in southern California.[170] No apparent temporal association between GBS and oral polio vaccine was noted. The frequency of GBS was low in the age groups during which children usually are immunized (before 2 years of age and 5 years of age). Researchers concluded that the failure to find a correlation between the usual age of oral polio vaccine immunization and the incidence of GBS by age coupled with the failure to find any children with GBS with onset within 1 month of receiving oral polio vaccine immunization provided strong evidence against a causal relationship between oral polio vaccine administration and GBS. They suggested that the differences noted in the outcomes of these studies may be related to the fact that the entire population in the study in Finland already was vaccinated with inactivated polio vaccine and that different types of oral polio vaccine were used in Finland and California.

IMMUNOLOGIC FACTORS

Current opinion strongly favors the hypothesis that GBS is an autoimmune disease. Much evidence suggests that GBS represents an aberrant immune response to peripheral nerve components.[6] McFarlin[129] suggested that the following factors support an autoimmune mechanism in GBS: plasmapheresis shortens the clinical course of GBS; sera from patients with GBS contain IgM antibodies against a component of peripheral nerve myelin; lipid antigen reacts with these antibodies; and at least one lipid, sulfate-3-glucoronyl paragloboside, can produce an experimental disease similar to GBS. This hypothesis is supported by the similarities of GBS, experimental allergic neuritis, and Marek disease.[207, 223] Serum antibodies or antibody-like factors have been demonstrated in peripheral nervous system tissues in experimental allergic neuritis and in GBS.* P2, a neurotigenic component of peripheral nervous system myelin administered in complete Freund adjuvant, has been shown to induce experimental allergic neuritis[223]; sensitization to P2 has been reported in GBS.[2, 3, 4, 197] Sensitized lymphocytes capable of producing demyelination have been found in experimental allergic neuritis and GBS.[7, 63, 74, 229] Evidence of hypersensitization to peripheral nervous system antigens by use of the technique of macrophage migration inhibition factor assay has been reported in experimental allergic neuritis[196] and GBS.[74, 108, 123, 177] However, the cause of GBS and the nature of the antigen or antigens against which the immune response is directed are not known precisely. Studies have provided evidence that an intense immunologic response is an invariable accompaniment of the disease.[4, 36, 93, 182, 185] Both cell-mediated immunity and humoral immunity have been found to be altered in GBS and may contribute to the pathogenesis and pathology of GBS.

Several lines of investigation have implicated a cell-mediated immunologic reaction to the constituent of myelin as being of primary importance in the pathogenesis of GBS.[3, 4, 6, 74, 93, 108, 185] Activated lymphocytes can be identified in early phases of GBS.[48] Secretion of mediators, such as macrophage migration inhibitory factor (a measure of T-cell sensitization), in the presence of P2 protein has been demonstrated during the acute phase of GBS.[17, 74, 108, 177, 197] By means of in vitro lymphocytic transformation technique, some researchers found lymphocytes sensitized to P2 in GBS[4]; others have not confirmed these results and suggest that P2 may not be the antigen in GBS.[93] Goust and associates[74] have reported circulating immune complexes in GBS and an association between increased immune complex and decreased suppressor cell function. Abnormal T-cell subsets have been reported,[124] but other investigators did not reproduce this finding.[90, 93] Additional evidence of cell-mediated immunity in GBS is suggested by studies observing demyelinization of rat peripheral nerves in tissue culture by circulating immunocytes from patients with GBS or lymph node cells from animals with experimental allergic neuritis.[7, 93, 186]

Activation of T cells has been reported in GBS.[4, 85, 86, 206] Alterations in T-cell subsets, including decreased numbers of $CD3^+$ and $CD4^+$ and increased CD19, have been observed.[232] These changes normalized after plasmapheresis in patients who improved. Taylor and Hughes[206] observed an increase in the levels of T cells bearing activator markers (interleukin-2 receptor and transferrin receptor) in the serum of GBS patients compared with normal control subjects. Hartung and associates[85, 86] have demonstrated T-cell activation in the acute phase of GBS, as evidenced by increased interleukin-2 receptor expression on T cells, increased serum concentrations of interleukin-2 and soluble interleukin-2 receptor, and increased numbers of DR-positive circulating T cells. They reported that increased soluble interleukin-2 receptor concentrations that were found in several samples decreased with clinical improvement. The suggested role of activated T cells in GBS could include cytotoxic effect on Schwann cells, myelinotoxic effects, recruitment of macrophages in a delayed hypersensitivity reaction, or helping B cells to produce antibody against myelin. Activated T cells also may play a role in recovery.[85, 86]

Both protective and destructive roles have been ascribed to antibodies in GBS.[7, 230] One suggestion is that the destructive effects of antibodies are mediated either directly by lysis of peripheral myelin with or without a requirement for complement or indirectly by opsonizing myelin, which then is attacked by macrophages.[93] Serum and CSF immunoglobulins of restricted electrophoretic heterogenicity have been reported to be increased in GBS, and these increased levels return toward normal with clinical improvement.[36, 38, 122] Autoantibodies to erythrocytes and circulating antigen-antibody complexes have been found in GBS.[37, 38, 48, 51, 74] Antineural antibody in GBS sera was demonstrated first by Melnick[136]; antineural antibodies also have been reported in the CSF of patients with GBS.[182] The cytotoxic effect of GBS serum in vitro has been reported.[36, 39, 54] Several studies have suggested the presence of antineuronal antibodies in GBS patients. Indirect immunofluorescence has been used to demonstrate that sera of patients with GBS have IgG antibody to monkey dorsal root ganglia.[49]

Some findings indicate that sera from patients with GBS react with multiple antigens in peripheral nerve myelin.[51, 110, 168, 233] Complement-fixing antibodies to peripheral nerve myelin have been detected in the serum of patients with GBS.[109, 136] Rising titers of complement-fixing antiperipheral nerve myelin antibodies (IgM) were found during the acute phase of GBS, and decreasing titers were observed during convalescence.[109] Koski and associates[109, 110] found that some of the antiperipheral nerve myelin antibody in all serum from patients with GBS that was tested binds a neutral glycolipid of human peripheral nerve myelin and cross-reacts with Forssman antigen, a cross-species antigen found in many infectious diseases. These investigators suggested that IgM antibodies, triggered by multiple infectious agents in patients with GBS, can bind to a glycolipid surface determinant of human peripheral nerve myelin and, after penetration of the damaged blood-nerve barrier, participate in the demyelination of peripheral nerves

*See references 37, 47, 122, 125, 150, 182, 183, 207, 209, 218.

through activation of complement. Yu and associates[233] found that sera from patients with GBS reacted with antigens in peripheral nerve myelin, including one lipid, SGPG; in rabbits, immunization with SGPG produced weakness and physiologic abnormalities consistent with a demyelinating neuropathy.

PATHOGENESIS

GBS is regarded as an autoimmune disorder involving both cellular and humoral immune mechanisms.[216] Immunologic studies have not resulted in a simple concept of the pathogenesis of GBS. The animal model of GBS, experimental allergic neuritis, has allowed analysis of the pathogenetic mechanisms involved in the demyelinating process.[216] In the Lewis rat, the disease can be transferred by $CD4^+$ T cells reactive to neuroautoantigens P2 and P0. In the rabbit, experimental allergic neuritis serum injected intraneurally demyelinates rat nerve largely because of antigalactocerebroside antibody.[164] In humans, no peripheral nerve antigen has been identified as the responsible target.[216] Involvement of the cellular immune system has been implicated. T and B cells become activated at the onset of GBS, as indicated by an increase of activation markers, including interleukin-2, soluble interleukin-2 receptor, and tumor necrosis factor-α in serum and CSF.[15, 84, 193, 216] The serum levels of these markers decrease with recovery.[15, 193] Disruption of myelin has been reported secondary to increased serum concentrations of the cytokine tumor necrosis factor-α.[193] Increased serum concentrations of tumor necrosis factor-α are detected in 50 percent of patients with GBS as well as in 26 percent of patients with unrelated neuropathies and other neurologic disorders. Increased serum concentrations of tumor necrosis factor-α are not specific for GBS. Tumor necrosis factor-α serum concentrations correlate with clinical severity, decrease as patients recover,[193] and are similar in patients with GBS whether or not preceding infections were noted. Thus, these elevations likely are not merely secondary to the antecedent infection. In contrast, soluble concentrations of interleukin-2 receptor are elevated in healthy relatives of GBS patients as well as in GBS patients. These data suggest that these concentrations may be secondary to environmental or infectious factors rather than related to the pathogenic mechanism responsible for GBS.[193] The involvement of complement is suggested by findings that include increased concentrations of the soluble terminal complement in serum and CSF and increases of C3a and C5a in CSF alone.[84, 164, 216] One study demonstrated a breakdown of the blood-nerve barrier by activated T cells, allowing the development of focal conduction block and demyelinization in the presence of circulating antimyelin antibodies.[164] Elevated serum concentrations of endothelial leukocyte adhesion molecule-1 have been demonstrated in GBS during the acute phase, with serum concentrations returning to normal by 14 days. Endothelial leukocyte adhesion molecule-1 may be important by virtue of breakdown of the blood-nerve barrier.[155]

The diversity of preceding infectious factors and the observation that GBS may occur after noninfectious factors, such as surgery, trauma, epidural anesthesia, drug administration, and immunizations[6, 27, 62, 202] (see Table 45–2), have suggested that infection is not a necessary precondition for the development of GBS. A single factor, such as the release of antigen, may be common to the mechanism leading to nerve damage; the peripheral nervous system may possess a limited repertoire of pathologic responses and may react to diverse insults in a restricted fashion; or both may be true.[196] As noted, numerous reports have indicated alterations of both cell-mediated immunity and humoral immunity in GBS and have suggested an immunologic basis for the demyelinization in GBS. However, the exact mechanism and precise interaction of a preceding event and the patient's cell-mediated and humoral immune responses in causing demyelinization are not known. Whether GBS is the result of an autoimmune process or represents neural injury from an immune response to viral antigen that might be present in neural tissue is not clear.[36] Proposed mechanisms for the immunopathogenesis of GBS lesions have included antibody or cell-mediated immunity to an infectious agent with secondary neural injury, autoantibody or cell-mediated immunity to peripheral nervous system tissue, and demyelinization caused by deposition of circulatory antigen-antibody complexes in blood vessels of peripheral nerves.[36] One suggestion is that GBS is a syndrome and not a disease and that it may have several different causes.[201]

Increasingly, researchers have noted that the expression of GBS varies considerably.[56, 216] Although the NINCDS Ad Hoc Committee proposed criteria for the research diagnosis of GBS, this committee recognized the occurrence of heterogeneous clinical presentations with fever, severe sensory loss or pain, and progression beyond 4 weeks as variants. Ataxic (Miller Fisher syndrome) and autonomic variants also have been described. In view of these findings, establishing minimal criteria for the diagnosis of GBS may be difficult. For example, insistence on areflexia is too restrictive; pain may occur in half of patients and should not be an exclusion criterion. GBS could be viewed as a family of closely related diseases that can be categorized by class of axon (motor, sensory, autonomic, or mixtures), pathologic process (inflammatory-demyelinating, antibody attack), preceding infection, associated antibody, underlying disease mechanism, or response to treatment.[216]

The clinical variability of GBS may reflect different pathogenetic mechanisms. Pathology results suggest the heterogeneity of GBS. Studies by Asbury and coworkers[9–12] indicated the early occurrence of inflammatory cells as the primary mechanism resulting in demyelination. The lesions were found along all of the nerve but with variable expression among patients corresponding to their clinical deficits. The role of lymphocytic infiltration has been reappraised. Lymphocytic infiltration varies widely among persons with GBS. Severe demyelination can occur without lymphocytic infiltration. Heterogeneity is suggested further by the experimental allergic neuritis models.[216] The rat experimental allergic neuritis model is a T-cell–dependent response to the antigen P2. In the rabbit model, demyelination results from a B-cell–dependent response to galactocerebroside. These models suggest that the variability of GBS may depend on the relative contribution of T-cell and B-cell responses.

Serum antibodies against such major glycolipids as GM_1, GD_{1b}, and LM_1 have been reported in the acute phase of GBS.[60, 152, 221, 235] In GBS, the specificity of antiganglioside antibodies is variable.[30, 227] The presence of anti-GM_1 ganglioside IgG antibodies may be associated with a more severe and predominantly motor form of GBS. Among 132 patients with GBS participating in the Dutch GBS trial and for whom suitable pretreatment serum was available, 25 (19%) demonstrated high anti-GM_{1b} antibody titers of the IgG (N = 15) or IgM (N = 14) class or both (N = 4). Patients who were antibody positive more frequently experienced preceding diarrhea and had serologic evidence of recent *C. jejuni* infection without antecedent evidence of CMV, Epstein-Barr virus, or *M. pneumoniae* infection than did patients who were antibody negative. In the antibody patients who were antibody positive, the onset was more rapid, limb weakness was more severe, distal weakness was more prominent, and recovery time was more prolonged. These patients less frequently had a sensory deficit or cranial nerve involvement.[234]

Serum anti-GQ_{1b} ganglioside antibodies have been observed in the Miller Fisher variant of GBS.[30, 95, 227] As many as 82 percent of patients with the Miller Fisher variant of GBS may have IgG antibodies to another ganglioside, GQ_{1b}. The circulating anti-GQ_{1b} IgG antibodies induce presynaptic and postsynaptic blockade. After recovery, this blocking activity was lost and sera became negative for anti-GQ_{1b} antibodies. These IgG antibodies may play a pathogenic role in the Miller Fisher variant of GBS.[24]

These findings suggest some association between antigenic specificities of antiglycolipid antibodies and clinical forms of GBS. However, the exact role of these antibodies—neurotoxic, directly responsible for the symptoms, or as incidental byproducts—is not established clearly.[30, 216, 227] A decline in anti-GD_{1b} ganglioside titers in relation to clinical recovery has been reported in patients with GBS following plasma exchange.[174a] Although studies confirm the activation of the immune system in GBS, whether the increase in activation markers is caused by preceding infection, why they are found only in some but not all patients with GBS, and what their role is in destruction of myelin remain unknown.

Evidence for shared antigenic determinants among certain infective agents associated with GBS and various antigens within peripheral nerve includes the following: shared antigenic determinants between herpes simplex ribonucleotide reductase and peripheral nerve P0 glycoprotein have been demonstrated; amino acid sequence homology between CMV and varicella-zoster virus and P0 glycoprotein has been observed; and antibodies to ganglioside have been detected in patients with GBS after *C. jejuni* and *M. pneumoniae* infection.[5b, 164] Some studies indicate that molecular mimicry may contribute to the presence of antiganglioside antibodies after *C. jejuni* infection.[60, 152, 235] Humoral immune mechanisms directed at an infectious agent may cross-react with antigens of the peripheral nervous system and cause an immunopathologic disease. The family of glycoconjugates, including gangliosides, is one candidate of the myelin antigenic groups with which antibodies have been identified in GBS. The frequency of these antibodies may be as high as 35 percent of patients with GBS. Nonetheless, the presence of high titers of antiglycoconjugate antibodies is not necessarily correlated with the more severe course of this disease.[60, 77, 98, 221]

The association of *C. jejuni* infection preceding presentation of GBS and the occurrence of antiganglioside antibodies may contribute to an understanding of pathogenesis of GBS. *C. jejuni* has a lipopolysaccharide capsule that is rich in glycoconjugates containing sialic acid and that resemble human glycoconjugates.[77] A terminal tetrasaccharide immunogenically identical to the ganglioside GM_1 in human peripheral nerve has been demonstrated on the outer membrane of a *Campylobacter* strain cultured from a patient with GBS.[14] Serologic evidence of an antecedent *C. jejuni* infection has been shown to correlate with the presence of anti-GM_1 antibodies.[60, 95, 221, 235] Anti-GM_1 IgG antibodies in GBS sera recognize surface epitopes on whole *Campylobacter* bacteria, and this recognition is strain specific. *Campylobacter* isolated from patients with GBS and with enteritis have been found to have similar ganglioside-like moieties. This finding indicates that patients who develop GBS respond differently to the ganglioside-like epitopes on *Campylobacter* than do non-GBS diarrhea patients.[95] The finding also suggests a role for host susceptibility as a determinant for outcome after *Campylobacter* infection.[194]

C. jejuni but not *Escherichia coli* bacteria can absorb GM_1 antibodies of the IgG class.[152] Studies suggest that molecular mimicry might play a role in the pathogenesis of GBS. Molecular mimicry is suggested further by the observation that the GQ_{1b} epitope is present in the lipopolysaccharide fractions of *C. jejuni* isolated from patients with the Miller Fisher variant.[227, 235] Direct infection of cells of the peripheral nervous system leading to an immune attack seems unlikely in the case of *C. jejuni* because extraintestinal infection and especially peripheral nervous system infection probably are not relevant. *C. jejuni* may generate toxins that directly damage peripheral nerves. Although strain-specific toxins may play a role in post–*C. jejuni* GBS, an immune mechanism remains most likely.[77] Especially appealing is that the association with *C. jejuni* provides indirect support for the "shared epitope" or "molecular mimicry" model of the immunopathogenesis of GBS.[194] One hypothesis is that an infectious agent with a specific antigenetic repertoire induces an immune response involving T-cell activation and antibodies that cross-react with gangliosides in peripheral nerves.[60]

GBS has been considered to be a single disorder referred to as acute inflammatory demyelinating polyneuropathy. However, not all GBS is demyelinating. Axonal GBS now is well recognized. In the motor axonal form of GBS, the nodes of Ranvier of the motor fibers are the primary targets. The earliest changes appear to be antibody and complement mediated, and T lymphocytes are a rare finding in nerve. The axonal form of GBS has been associated with antiganglioside GM_1 antibody and *C. jejuni* infection. Most of the Chinese cases appear to be triggered by recent *C. jejuni* infection in the gut. Surface lipopolysaccharides of *C. jejuni* strains associated with GBS contain epitopes that are similar or identical to GM_1 ganglioside that is concentrated at the nodes of Ranvier. This finding supports the role of molecular mimicry for inducing GBS.[13] Conflicting results have been reported concerning the relation of GM_1 antibody to axonal degeneration.[114] Antibodies to other gangliosides have been reported to be elevated in sera of patients with GBS during the acute phase. Only a 50 percent concordance between serological evidence of *C. jejuni* infection and presence of anti-GM_1 antibody was found during large studies. GBS patients with anti-GM_1 antibodies have had identified infections that included *C. jejuni* (23%), CMV (10%), *M. pneumoniae* (6%), and Epstein-Barr virus (3%).[153] Microorganisms other than *C. jejuni* may trigger antiganglioside response and elicit axonal GBS. Whether the presence of anti-GM_1 antibodies is associated with extensive axonal loss and poor outcome is a matter of controversy. Some GBS patients with anti-GM_1 antibodies recover quickly or have conduction abnormalities suggestive of demyelination.[88, 114, 173, 220]

Outcome

Most patients with GBS recover spontaneously. However, epidemiologic studies have indicated that 10 to 23 percent of patients may require mechanical ventilation, 7 to 22 percent have some disability, 3 to 10 percent relapse, and 2 to 5 percent die.[9, 29, 66, 88, 107, 126, 169, 228] Patients may be left with residual symptoms, such as facial weakness, weakness in the lower extremities with footdrop, weakness and atrophy of hands, and autonomic dysfunction (impotence and urinary retention).[134] In the North American study of the effect of plasmapheresis,[80] the median time to recovery of independent walking was 85 days for control subjects compared with 169 days for patients who received mechanical ventilation.

This same study indicated that children walked at 52 days. Five prognostic factors were identified: age, requirement for respiratory support, rate of progress, abnormal physiologic characteristics of peripheral nerve function, and plasmapheresis.

In children, complete recovery from motor or sensory deficit after an episode of GBS has been reported in 70 percent of cases after 12 months and in 82 percent after 15 years.[181] Kleyweg and associates[107] compared the outcome of GBS in groups of children and adults. They observed that 22 percent of the children compared with 30 percent of adults required mechanical ventilation, with a median duration of 21.5 days in the children and 32 days in the adults. Mean duration of hospitalization was 84 days for the children and 86 days in the adult group. Two of 18 children died. At 1 year, 77 percent of the children had a good outcome, and at 2 years, 83 percent had a good outcome; for the adults, good outcomes at 1 and 2 years were observed in 86 and 92 percent, respectively. Significant slowing of motor and sensory nerve conduction or electromyographic abnormalities may persist for weeks to years after recovery.[169, 181] Reported unfavorable signs for complete recovery in children included a period longer than 18 days of plateau between greatest weakness and beginning weakness, weakness and maximum motor deficit of greater than 3 weeks, or marked paralysis alone (need for assisted ventilation).[58, 181, 228]

Treatment

No specific treatment exists for GBS. Intensive nursing and medical care are essential for proper management. Most deaths are related to respiratory failure, pulmonary embolism, and autonomic dysfunction.[91] Respiratory function must be monitored closely, especially during the acutely progressive phase. The need for endotracheal intubation and mechanical ventilation has been suggested if vital capacity falls below 12 to 15 mL/kg, arterial Po_2 falls below 70 mm Hg, or clinical signs of fatigue develop; tracheostomy may be indicated if paralysis is prolonged.[178] Physiotherapy and preventive measures for pulmonary embolism are indicated. Because of autonomic dysfunction, the electrocardiogram and blood pressure must be monitored. Hyponatremia is a reported complication and probably is caused by inappropriate secretion of antidiuretic hormone[160]; fluid and sodium balance and adequate nourishment must be maintained. Reassurance and attention to anxiety, anger, and depression are important during the progressive phase of GBS, especially for patients being ventilated.[91]

Other treatment modalities have been used in an attempt to hasten recovery, to shorten ventilatory and intensive care unit time, and to decrease the incidence of residual neurologic deficits. Adrenocorticotropic hormone, prednisone, and prednisolone have been used in GBS with varying results. In one controlled study, in eight patients with mild or moderate GBS, adrenocorticotropic hormone shortened the duration of GBS but not the hospital stay.[204] The opposite conclusion was reached from a larger, randomized trial of prednisolone in severely affected patients requiring ventilation.[73] Improvement was less in the prednisolone group than in the control group. A controlled, randomized trial of plasma exchange combined with prednisone was compared with supportive care alone in patients with GBS.[138] Improvement in the treated group over the control subjects was not significant; the investigators suggested that the potential beneficial effect of plasma exchange (discussed later) may have been adversely affected by prednisone. Steroids appear to have little effect on GBS. A beneficial effect of steroids on chronic or subacute demyelinating polyradiculoneuropathy has been reported.[31, 57, 143] Steroids also have hastened improvement in experimental allergic neuritis when they were begun before or at the time of onset of neurologic signs; such an effect would be difficult to demonstrate in GBS, in which making the diagnosis and initiating treatment within 24 hours from the onset of symptoms rarely are possible.[91] McKhann[131] suggested that assessment of steroids in GBS may have been complicated because of relatively late administration of steroids in GBS.

The efficacy of plasmapheresis has been demonstrated in two large clinical trials in adults involving 245 patients in the North American trial and 220 patients in the French trial.[68, 80] Initial clinical trials in adults, randomized and controlled but unmasked in design, demonstrated that plasma exchange begun in the first 2 weeks of the illness had a significant beneficial effect in the rate of recovery.[13] In the North American trial, a total of 200 to 500 mL/kg of plasma was exchanged on three to five occasions.[80] In the French study, two plasma volumes were exchanged on 4 alternative days.[68] In the patients treated by plasmapheresis in both studies, improvement started earlier, the need for artificial respiration was reduced significantly, and the median time until independent locomotion was decreased by 32 and 41 days, respectively, compared with the control group. Plasma exchange was beneficial even in those individuals with the worst prognostic factors. Plasma exchange appeared to halt the progression of GBS and to improve the degree and the rate of recovery. Even mild cases may respond favorably to plasma exchange.[214] A further study suggested that two exchanges are better than none for mild GBS, four exchanges are more beneficial than two for moderate GBS, and six exchanges confer no further benefit than do four on severe GBS.[13] Plasmapheresis may be beneficial in patients treated up to 30 days after the onset of disease, although it is more beneficial when started within 7 days of onset of disease.[170a] Studies in children also have demonstrated the efficacy of plasmapheresis for treatment of GBS. In children, the benefits have included decrease in the number of days of mechanical ventilation and time until motor recovery as well as a decrease in the overall cost of care.[96, 217] Although plasmapheresis can be a cumbersome procedure with many technical difficulties, it has been used safely in critically ill children as young as 8 months. Mild hypotension related to rapid fluid removal has been reported, but no major complications or deaths related to plasmapheresis have been reported in pediatric patients with GBS. Reported complications in adults include hypotension, transfusion reactions, hypocalcemia, arrhythmias, cardiopulmonary arrest, and infection caused by transmitted blood products or sepsis secondary to indwelling catheters.

In children, a short intensive course of plasmapheresis has been recommended for those with significant motor weakness, rapid progress of symptoms, impending respiratory failure, or bulbar insufficiency. Significant motor weakness includes having a limited ability to walk, being bed bound, or needing ventilatory assistance. Plasmapheresis should be initiated within the first 7 days of the onset of disease symptoms.[96, 217]

Contraindication to the use of plasmapheresis in some patients with GBS and complications and lack of universal availability of plasmapheresis led to a study of IVIg as an alternative to plasmapheresis therapy. A multicenter study conducted in the Netherlands compared IVIg with plasmapheresis.[215, 216] A dose of 0.4 g/kg/day of IVIg was administered on 5 consecutive days. Significantly more patients (53%) treated with IVIg improved during the first 4 weeks compared with the group treated by plasmapheresis (34%).

Other outcome variables, including time until functional improvement, the proportion of patients with multiple complications, and the proportion of patients needing artificial ventilation in the second week, favored therapy with IVIg. The researchers concluded that IVIg is at least as effective as treatment by plasmapheresis. Randomized controlled trials in adults show that IVIg and plasma exchange are equally effective in reducing the time to functional recovery. The combination of plasma exchange followed by IVIg is not significantly better than is IVIg or plasma exchange alone. Approximately 10 percent of patients with GBS deteriorate after initial improvement or stabilization with IVIg or plasma exchange treatment and often require repeated treatment. These treatment-related clinical fluctuations are seen more frequently in relatively young patients with severe motor and sensory involvement associated with preceding or ongoing CMV infection. For adult patients with GBS, the suggested candidates for treatment with IVIg or plasma exchange include those unable to walk without assistance and still within the first 2 weeks.[214] Because of ease of administration and a favorable side effect profile, IVIg has been suggested as first-line therapy for GBS.[214]

Of patients with GBS who participated in the Dutch GBS trial, those with high anti-GM_{1b} antibody titers responded to IVIg faster than to plasma exchange. Patients who were positive for anti-GM_{1b} antibody and were treated with plasma exchange had a significantly slower recovery than did patients who were negative for anti-GM_{1b} and were treated with plasma exchange. This association was absent in those treated with IVIg. Patients with GBS and anti-GM_{1b} IgM antibodies did not differ significantly from patients who were anti-GM_{1b} negative. Patients who were positive for antibody frequently had serologic evidence of recent *C. jejuni* infection without evidence of other infectious agents such as CMV or Epstein-Barr virus.[214, 234] Similar results are reported for a group of Japanese patients with GBS who were positive for IgG anti-GM_1 antibody. Those treated with IVIg, in comparison to those treated with plasma exchange, were more likely to regain independent locomotion at 6 months and were more likely to have rapid recovery within 4 weeks and less delayed recovery.[113] These findings suggest that therapy may be optimized by considering subgroups in respect to the pattern of antiganglioside antibodies and antecedent infection. For the subgroup positive for IgG anti-GM_1 antibody, IVIg therapy may be a more efficacious treatment than is plasma exchange.

No large trials of IVIg therapy have been performed exclusively in children. Small studies indicate improvement in children similar to that in adults when plasmapheresis or IVIg therapy is used. A retrospective review of children receiving plasmapheresis compared with children treated with IVIg revealed a shorter time for improvement and fewer days of mechanical ventilation in the group treated by IVIg.[197] Abd-Allah and associates[1] retrospectively reviewed the clinical course of seven children (mean age, 5 to 8 years) treated with IVIg (0.4 g/kg/day for 5 days). Clinical improvement occurred on average within 2.4 ± 1.3 days of beginning IVIg. Except for a brief episode of hypotension in one patient, no complications were associated with IVIg. One child had a relapse 2 weeks after discharge. This child improved but had significant residual effects after a second course of IVIg and treatment with plasma exchange. These results were similar to those of a comparison group of eight children treated with plasma exchange alone. The need for admission to the pediatric intensive care unit and duration of stay were lower in the IVIg-treated group. Similar results were observed in 74 children with GBS identified from the literature and successfully treated with IVIg.[1]

Advantages of IVIg therapy for GBS include its wide availability, ease of administration, safety, and absence of serious complications. Therapy with IVIg generally is less expensive than is plasmapheresis.[217]

In children, reported complications of plasmapheresis or IVIg therapy have included headache (aseptic meningitis), hypotension, dyspnea, diuresis, fever, and transient microscopic hematuria.[96, 217] In adults, high-dose IVIg has been observed to increase blood viscosity, which appears to occur immediately after completion of the IVIg infusion; the effect decreases during the next month. A concern is that such an effect might impair blood flow and trigger a cardiovascular or cerebrovascular embolus and ischemic event.[41] Other reported adverse reactions have included nephrotoxicity,[119] pain at the site of infusion, flushing, chest tightness, chills, fever, dizziness, and nausea. An uncontrolled study reported symptomatic relapse of GBS.[20] Researchers have suggested that antibody specificities of different immunoglobulin preparations vary considerably, which may yield different therapeutic results. Further deterioration during IVIg or plasmapheresis treatment may occur. Approximately 10 percent of patients with GBS treated with either IVIg or plasmapheresis may improve initially and deteriorate subsequently. Re-treatment is not associated with further improvement. More than one third of patients start to improve during the second week of treatment.[215, 216] Thus, researchers have suggested that the chosen therapy be continued at least until the second week after its initiation. Subsequently, a change in therapy may be appropriate. In most cases, a subsequent change in therapy has been of little benefit because most patients are at the end of their third or beginning of their fourth week of disease; any treatment then is unlikely to be beneficial.[215, 216]

In summary, controlled studies in adults and retrospective studies in children suggest that therapy with IVIg is at least as effective as plasmapheresis.[1, 215–217] The mode of action of IVIg therapy is not known. Suggested potential mechanisms have included provision of a source of anti-idiotypic antibodies with selective reduction or suppression of antimyelin antibodies, provision of neutralizing or antitoxin antibodies, and enhancement of competitive macrophage inhibition.[23a, 192]

REFERENCES

1. Abd-Allah, S. A., Jansen, P. W., Ashwal, S., et al.: Intravenous immunoglobulin as therapy for pediatric Guillain-Barré syndrome. J. Child Neurol. *12*:376–380, 1997.
2. Abramsky, O., and Korn-Luhetzky, I.: Association with autoimmune diseases and cellular immune response to the neurotigenic protein in Guillain-Barré syndrome. Trans. Am. Neurol. Assoc. *105*:350–354, 1980.
3. Abramsky, O., Teitelbaum, D., and Arnon, R.: Experimental allergic neuritis induced by a basic neurotigenic protein (P_1L) of human peripheral nerve origin. Eur. J. Immunol. 7:213–217, 1977.
4. Abramsky, O., Webb, C., Teitelbaum, D., et al.: Cell mediated immunity to neural antigens in idiopathic polyneuritis and myeloradiculitis. Neurology *25*:1154–1159, 1975.
5. Adams, D., Gibson, J. D., Thomas, P. K., et al.: HLA antigens in Guillain-Barré syndrome. Lancet *2*:504–505, 1977.

5a. Alaedini, A., Briana, C., Wirguin, I., et al.: Detection of anti-ganglioside antibodies in Guillain-Barré syndrome. Indian J. Med. Res. *113*:234–238, 2001.

5b. Ang, C., Tio-Gillen, A., Groen, J., et al.: Cross-reactive antigalactocerebroside antibodies and *Mycoplasma pneumoniae* infections in Guillain-Barré syndrome. J. Neuroimmunol. *130*:179, 2002.

6. Arnason, B. G. W.: Inflammatory polyradiculoneuropathies. *In* Dyck, P. J., Thomas, P. K., and Lambert E. H. (eds.): Peripheral Neuropathy. Vol. 2. Philadelphia, W. B. Saunders, 1975, pp. 1110–1148.
7. Arnason, B. G. W., Winkler, G. F., and Hadler, N. M.: Cell mediated demyelination of peripheral nerve in tissue culture. Lab. Invest. *21*:1–10, 1969.
8. Arnold, A. G., Lawrence, D. S., and Corbitt, G.: Cytomegalovirus infection and the Guillain-Barré syndrome. Postgrad. Med. J. *54*:112–114, 1978.

9. Asbury, A. K.: Diagnostic considerations in Guillain-Barré syndrome. Ann. Neurol. *9*(Suppl.):1–5, 1981.
10. Asbury, A. K.: Guillain-Barré syndrome: Historical aspects. Ann. Neurol. *27*(Suppl.):S2–S6, 1990.
11. Asbury, A. K., Arnason, B. G., Karp, H. R., et al.: Criteria for diagnosis of Guillain-Barré syndrome. Ann. Neurol. *3*:565–566, 1978.
12. Asbury, A. K., and Cornblath, D. R.: Assessment of current diagnostic criteria for Guillain-Barré syndrome. Ann. Neurol. *27*(Suppl.):S21–S24, 1990.
13. Asbury, A. K., and McKhann, G. M.: Changing views of Guillain-Barré Syndrome. Ann. Neurol. *41*:287–288, 1997.
14. Banerjii, N. K., and Miller, J. H. D.: Guillain-Barré syndrome in children with special reference to serial nerve conduction studies. Dev. Med. Child Neurol. *14*:56–63, 1972.
15. Bansil, S., Mithen, F. A., Cook, S. D., et al.: Clinical correlation with serum-soluble interleukin-2 receptor levels in Guillain-Barré syndrome. Neurology *41*:1302–1305, 1991.
16. Beghi, E., Kurland, L. T., Mulder, D. W., et al.: Guillain-Barré syndrome: Clinicoepidemiologic features and effect of influenza vaccine. Arch. Neurol. *42*:1053–1057, 1985.
17. Behan, P. O., Lamarche, J. B., Feldman, R. G., et al.: Lymphocyte transformation in the Guillain-Barré syndrome. Lancet *1*:421, 1970.
18. Bernsen, H. J., Van-Loon, A. M., Poels, R. F., et al.: Herpes simplex virus specific antibody determined by immunoblotting in cerebrospinal fluid of a patient with the Guillain-Barré syndrome. J. Neurol. Neurosurg. Psychiatry *52*:788–791, 1989.
19. Bertrand, A., Janbon, F., Clot, J., et al.: Guillain-Barré polyradiculoneuritis and influenza virus. Presse Med. *79*:2328, 1971.
20. Bleck, T. P.: IVIg for GBS: Potential problems in the alphabet soup. Neurology *43*:857–858, 1993.
21. Boucharlat, J., Groslambert, R., and Chateau, R.: Polyradiculoneuritis as a symptom of varicella (a case report). J. Med. Lyon *49*:1443–1445, 1968.
22. Bouchez, B., Poirriez, J., Arnott, G. E., et al.: Acute polyradiculoneuritis during toxoplasmosis. J. Neurol. *231*:347, 1985.
23. Brewis, M., Poskanzer, D. C., Rolland, C., et al.: Neurological diseases in an English city. Acta Neurol. Scand. *42*(Suppl. 24):1–89, 1966.
23a. Buchwald, B., Ahangari, R., Weishaupt, A., and Toyka, K. V.: Intravenous immnoglobulins neutralize blocking antibodies in Guillain-Barré syndrome. Ann. Neurol. *51*:673–680, 2002.
24. Buchwald, B., Bufler, J., Carpo, M., et al.: Combined pre- and postsynaptic action of IgG antibodies in Miller Fisher syndrome. Neurology *56*:67–74, 2001.
25. Cabrera, J., Griffin, D. E., and Johnson, R. T.: Unusual features of the Guillain-Barré syndrome after rabies vaccine prepared in suckling mouse brains. J. Neurol. Sci. *81*:239–245, 1987.
26. Carpenter, S.: An ultrastructural study of an acute fatal case of the Guillain-Barré syndrome. J. Neurol. Sci. *15*:125–140, 1972.
27. Centers for Disease Control: National surveillance for Guillain-Barré syndrome January 1978–March 1979. M. M. W. R. *28*:547–548, 1979.
28. Chen, K. M., Brody, J. A., and Kurland, L. T.: Patterns of neurologic disease on Guam. I. Epidemiologic aspects. Arch. Neurol. *19*:573–578, 1968.
29. Cheng, Q., Jian, G. X., Press, R., et al.: Clinical epidemiology of Guillain-Barré syndrome in adults in Sweden 1996–1997: A prospective study. Eur. J. Neurol. *7*:685–692, 2000.
30. Chiba, A., Kusunoki, S., Shimizu, T., et al.: Serum IgG antibody to ganglioside GQ_{1b} is a possible marker of Miller Fisher syndrome. Ann. Neurol. *31*:677–679, 1992.
31. Colan, R. V., Snead, O. C., Oh, S. S., et al.: Steroid-responsive polyneuropathy with subacute onset in childhood. J. Pediatr. *97*:374–377, 1980.
32. Collens, W. S., and Rabinowitz, M. A.: Mumps polyneuritis: Quadriplegia with bilateral facial paralysis. Arch. Intern. Med. *41*:61–65, 1928.
33. Constant, O. C., Bentley, C. C., Denman, A. M., et al.: The Guillain-Barré syndrome following *Campylobacter enteritis* with recovery after plasmapheresis. J. Infect. *6*:89–91, 1983.
34. Constantino, T., and Weintraub, A.: The Guillain-Barré syndrome as a complication of the postperfusion syndrome. Am. Heart J. *84*:678–680, 1972.
35. Cook, S. D., and Dowling, P. C.: The role of autoantibody and immune complexes in the pathogenesis of Guillain-Barré syndrome. Ann. Neurol. *9*(Suppl.):70–79, 1981.
36. Cook, S. D., Dowling, P. C., Murray, M. R., et al.: Circulating demyelinating factors in acute idiopathic polyneuropathy. Arch. Neurol. *24*:136–144, 1971.
37. Cook, S. D., Dowling, P. C., and Whitaker, J. N.: Serum immunoglobulins in the Guillain-Barré syndrome. Neurology *20*:403, 1970.
38. Cook, S., Murray, M. R., Whitaker, J. N., et al.: Myelinotoxic antibody in the Guillain-Barré syndrome. Neurology *19*:284, 1969.
39. Cooper, W. O., Daniels, S. R., and Loggie, J. M.: Prevalence and correlates of blood pressure elevation in children with Guillain-Barré syndrome. Clin. Pediatr. (Phila) *37*:621–624, 1998.
40. Cornblath, D. R.: Electrophysiology in Guillain-Barré syndrome. Ann. Neurol. *27*(Suppl.):S17–S20, 1990.
41. Dalakas, M. C.: High-dose intravenous immunoglobulin and serum viscosity: A risk of precipitating thromboembolic events. Neurology *44*:223–226, 1994.
42. Dalakas, M. C., and Pezeshkpour, G. H.: Neuromuscular disease associated with human immunodeficiency virus infection. Ann. Neurol. *23*(Suppl.):S38–S48, 1988.
43. Davidson, D. L. W., and Jellinek, E. H.: Hypertension and papilloedema in the Guillain-Barré syndrome. J. Neurol. Neurosurg. Psychiatry *40*:144–148, 1977.
44. Davies, A. G., and Dingle, H. R.: Observations on cardiovascular and neuroendocrine disturbance in the Guillain-Barré syndrome. J. Neurol. Neurosurg. Psychiatry *35*:176–179, 1972.
45. Davis, J., and Rowlatt, R. J.: Transient severe hypertension and polyradiculitis after chickenpox. Br. Med. J. *2*:1608, 1978.
46. D'Cruz, O. F., Shapiro, E. D., Spiegelman, K. N., et al.: Acute inflammatory demyelinating polyradiculoneuropathy (Guillain-Barré syndrome) after immunization with *Haemophilus influenzae* type b conjugate vaccine. J. Pediatr. *115*:743–746, 1989.
47. Dowling, P. C., Bosch, V. V., Cook, S. D., et al.: Serum immunoglobulins in Guillain-Barré syndrome. J. Neurol. Sci. *57*:435–440, 1982.
48. Dowling, P. C., and Cook, S. D.: Circulating complexes in neurologic disease. J. Neuropathol. Exp. Neurol. *1*:161, 1972.
49. Dowling, P. C., and Cook, S. D.: Antibodies to dorsal root ganglia in Guillain-Barré syndrome. Neurology *23*:423, 1973.
50. Dowling, P. C., and Cook, S. D.: Role of infection in Guillain-Barré syndrome: Laboratory confirmation of herpesviruses in 41 cases. Ann. Neurol. *9*(Suppl.):44–55, 1981.
51. Dowling, P. C., Cook, S. D., and Whitaker, J. N.: Cold agglutinin in positive Guillain-Barré syndrome. Trans. Am. Neurol. Assoc. *95*:234–235, 1970.
52. Dowling, P., Menonna, J., and Cook, S.: Cytomegalovirus complement fixation antibody in Guillain-Barré syndrome. Neurology *27*:1153–1156, 1977.
53. Drueke, T. B., Pujade-Lauraine, E., Poisson, M., et al.: Measles virus and Guillain-Barré syndrome during long-term hemodialysis. Am. J. Med. *60*:444–446, 1976.
54. Dubois-Dalcq, M., Buyse, M., Buyse, G., et al.: The action of Guillain-Barré syndrome serum on myelin: A tissue culture and electron-microscopic analysis. J. Neurol. Sci. *13*:67–83, 1971.
55. Dutch Guillain-Barré Study Group: Treatment of Guillain-Barré syndrome with high dose immune globulin combined with methylprednisone: A pilot study. Ann. Neurol. *35*:749–752, 1994.
56. Dyck, P. J.: Is there an axonal variety of GBS? Neurology *43*:1277–1280, 1993.
57. Dyck, P. J., O'Brien, P. C., Oviatt, K. F., et al.: Prednisone improves chronic inflammatory demyelinating polyradiculoneuropathy more than no treatment. Ann. Neurol. *11*:136–141, 1982.
58. Eberle, E., Brink, S., Azen, S., et al.: Early predictors of incomplete recovery in children with Guillain-Barré polyneuritis. J. Pediatr. *86*:356–359, 1975.
59. Eiben, R. M., and Gersiny, W. M.: Recognition, prognosis and treatment of the Guillain-Barré syndrome (acute idiopathic polyneuritis). Med. Clin. North Am. *47*:1371–1380, 1963.
60. Enders, U., Karch, H., Toyka, K. V., et al.: The spectrum of immune responses to *Campylobacter jejuni* and glycoconjugates in Guillain-Barré syndrome and in other neuroimmunological disorders. Ann. Neurol. *34*:136–144, 1993.
61. Estrada-Gonzales, R., and Mas, P.: Virological studies in acute polyradiculoneuritis—Landry-Guillain-Barré syndrome: Various findings in relation to coxsackie A4 virus. Neurol. Neurocir. Psiquiatr. *18*(Suppl. 2–3):527–531, 1977.
62. Fagius, J., Osterman, P. O., and Siden, A.: Guillain-Barré syndrome following zimeldine treatment. J. Neurol. Neurosurg. Psychiatry *48*:65–69, 1985.
63. Feasby, T. E., Hahn, A. F., and Gilber, J. J.: Passive transfer of demyelinating activity in Guillain-Barré polyneuropathy. Neurology *30*:363, 1980.
64. Feutren, G., Gerbal, J.-L., Allinquant, B., et al.: Association of Guillain-Barré syndrome and B-virus hepatitis: Simultaneous presence of anti-DS-DNA antibodies and HBs antigen in cerebrospinal fluid. J. Clin. Lab. Immunol. *11*:161–164, 1983.
65. Fisher, M.: An unusual variant of acute idiopathic polyneuritis syndrome of ophthalmoplegia, ataxia and areflexia. N. Engl. J. Med. *255*:57–65, 1956.
66. Fletcher, D. D., Lawn, N. D., Wolter, T. D., et al.: Long-term outcome in patients with Guillain-Barré syndrome requiring mechanical ventilation. Neurology *54*:2311–2315, 2000.
67. Forbes, F. J., Brumlik, J., and Harding, H. B.: Acute ascending polyradiculomyelitis associated with Echo 9 virus. Dis. Nerv. Syst. *28*:537–540, 1967.
68. French Cooperative Group of Plasma Exchange in Guillain-Barré Syndrome: Efficiency of plasma exchange in Guillain-Barré syndrome: Role of replacement fluids. Ann. Neurol. *22*:753–761, 1987.
69. Friedland, M. L., and Wittels, E. G.: An unusual neurologic reaction following polyvalent pneumococcal vaccine in a patient with hairy cell leukemia. Am. J. Hematol. *14*:189, 1983.
70. Gashi, F., and Kenrick, M. M.: Guillain-Barré syndrome: Review of the literature, case presentation, and psychiatric management. South. Med. J. *68*:1524–1528, 1975.

71. Gibberd, F. B.: Ophthalmoplegia in acute polyneuritis. Arch. Neurol. *23*:161–164, 1970.
72. Goldschmidt, B., Menonna, J., Fortunato, T., et al.: Mycoplasma antibody in Guillain-Barré syndrome and other neurological disorders. Ann. Neurol. *7*:108–112, 1980.
73. Goodall, J. A. D., Kosmidis, J. C., and Geddes, A. M.: Effect of corticosteroids on course of Guillain-Barré syndrome. Lancet *1*:524–526, 1974.
74. Goust, J. M., Chenais, F., Carnes, J. E., et al.: Abnormal T cell subpopulations and circulating immune complexes in the Guillain-Barré syndrome and multiple sclerosis. Neurology *28*:421–425, 1978.
75. Grattan, C. E. H., and Berman, P.: Chlamydial infection as a possible aetiological factor in the Guillain-Barré syndrome. Postgrad. Med. J. *58*:776–777, 1982.
76. Green, S. H.: Polyradiculitis (Landry-Guillain-Barré syndrome) with total external ophthalmoplegia: Encephalo-myelo-radiculo-neuropathy. Dev. Med. Clin. Neurol. *13*:369–373, 1976.
77. Griffin, J. W., and Ho, T. W. H.: The Guillain-Barré syndrome at 75: The *Campylobacter* connection. Ann. Neurol. *34*:125–127, 1993.
78. Gudmundsson, K. R.: Prevalence and occurrence of some rare neurological diseases in Iceland. Acta Neurol. Scand. *45*:114–118, 1969.
79. Guillain, G., Barré, J. A., and Strohl, A.: Sur un syndrome de radiculonevrite avec hyperalbuminose du liquide cephalo-rachidien sans regraphiques des reflexes tendineux. Bull. Soc. Med. Hop. Paris *40*:1462–1470, 1916.
80. Guillain-Barré Syndrome Study Group: Plasmapheresis and acute Guillain-Barré syndrome. Neurology *35*:1096–1104, 1985.
81. Gunderman, J. R.: Guillain-Barré syndrome: Occurrence following combined mumps-rubella vaccine. Am. J. Dis. Child. *125*:834–835, 1973.
82. Hall, S. M., Hughes, R. A. C., Alkinson, P. F., et al.: Motor nerve biopsy in severe Guillain-Barré syndrome. Ann. Neurol. *31*:441–444, 1992.
83. Hart, I. K., and Kennedy, P. G.: Guillain-Barré syndrome associated with cytomegalovirus infection. Q. J. Med. *67*:425–430, 1988.
84. Hartung, H. P.: Immune-mediated demyelination. Ann. Neurol. 33:563–567, 1993.
85. Hartung, H. P., Hughes, R. A., Taylor, W. A., et al.: T-cell activation in Guillain-Barré syndrome and in MS: Elevated serum levels of soluble IL-2 receptors. Neurology *40*:215–218, 1990.
86. Hartung, H. P., and Toyka, K. V.: T-cell and macrophage activation in experimental autoimmune neuritis and Guillain-Barré syndrome. Ann. Neurol. *27*(Suppl.):S57–S63, 1990.
87. Hemachudha, T., Griffin, D. E., Chen, W. W., et al.: Immunologic studies of rabies vaccination–induced Guillain-Barré syndrome. Neurology *38*:375–378, 1988.
88. Ho, T. W., Li, C. Y., Cornblath, D. R., et al.: Patterns of recovery in the Guillain-Barré syndromes. Neurology *48*:695–700, 1997.
89. Hogg, J. E., Kobrin, D. E., and Schoenberg, B. S.: The Guillain-Barré syndrome, epidemiologic and clinical features. J. Chronic Dis. *32*: 227–231, 1974.
90. Hughes, R. A. C., Aslan, S., and Gray, I. A.: Lymphocyte subpopulations and suppression cell activity in acute polyradiculoneuritis (Guillain-Barré syndrome). Clin. Exp. Immunol. *51*:448–454, 1983.
91. Hughes, R. A. C., Kadlubowski, M., and Hufschmidt, A.: Treatment of acute inflammatory polyneuropathy. Ann. Neurol. *9*(Suppl.):125–133, 1981.
92. Hurwitz, E. S., Schonberger, L. B., Nelson, D. B., et al.: Guillain-Barré syndrome and the 1978–1979 influenza vaccine. N. Engl. J. Med. *304*:1557–1561, 1981.
93. Iqbal, A., Oger, J. J.-F., and Arnason, B. G.: Cell-mediated immunity in idiopathic polyneuritis. Ann. Neurol. *9*(Suppl.):65–68, 1981.
94. Jackson, A. L.: A clinical study of the Landry-Guillain-Barré syndrome with reference to aetiology, including the role of coxsackie virus infections. S. Afr. J. Lab. Clin. Med. 7:121–137, 1961.
95. Jacobs, B. C., Endtz, H., van der Meche, F. G., et al.: Serum anti-GQ_{1b} IgG antibodies recognize surface epitopes on *Campylobacter jejuni* from patients with Miller Fisher syndrome. Ann. Neurol. *37*:260–264, 1995.
96. Jansen, P. W., Perkin, R. M., and Ashwal, S.: Guillain-Barré syndrome in childhood: Natural course and efficacy of plasmapheresis. Pediatr. Neurol. *9*:16–20, 1993.
97. Kabins, S., Keller, R., Peitchel, R., et al.: Acute idiopathic polyneuritis caused by cytomegalovirus. Arch. Intern. Med. *136*:100–101, 1976.
98. Kaldor, J., and Speed, B. R.: Guillain-Barré syndrome and *Campylobacter jejuni*: A serological study. Br. Med. J. *288*:1867–1870, 1984.
99. Kanda, T., Hayashi, H., Tanabe, H., et al.: A fulminant case of Guillain-Barré syndrome: Topographic and fibre size related analysis of demyelinating changes. J. Neurol. Neurosurg. Psychiatry *52*:857–864, 1989.
100. Kaplan, J. E., Katona, P., Hurwitz, E. S., et al.: Guillain-Barré syndrome in the United States, 1979–1980 and 1980–1981: Lack of an association with influenza vaccination. J. A. M. A. *248*:696–700, 1982.
101. Kaplan, J. E., Poduska, P. J., McIntosh, G. C., et al.: Guillain-Barré syndrome in Larimer County, Colorado: A high incidence area. Neurology *35*:581–584, 1985.
102. Kennedy, R. H., Danielson, M. A., Mulder, D. W., et al.: Guillain-Barré syndrome: A 42 year epidemiologic and clinical study. Mayo Clin. Proc. *53*:93–99, 1978.
103. Kibrich, S.: Current status of coxsackie and Echo viruses in human disease. Prog. Med. Virol. *6*:27–70, 1964.
104. Kinnunen, E., Färkkilä, M., Hovi, T., et al.: Incidence of Guillain-Barré syndrome during a nationwide oral poliovirus vaccine campaign. Neurology *39*:1034–1036, 1989.
105. Kisch, A. L.: Guillain-Barré syndrome following smallpox vaccination: Report of a case. N. Engl. J. Med. *258*:83, 1958.
106. Kleinman, H., Ramras, K. G., Cooney, M. K., et al.: Aseptic meningitis due to Echo virus type 7. N. Engl. J. Med. *267*:1116–1121, 1962.
107. Kleyweg, R. P., van der Meche, F. G., Loonen, M. C., et al.: The natural history of the Guillain-Barré syndrome in 18 children and 50 adults. J. Neurol. Neurosurg. Psychiatry *52*:853–856, 1989.
108. Knowles, M., Saunders, M., Currie, S., et al.: Lymphocyte transformation in the Guillain-Barré syndrome. Lancet *2*:1168–1170, 1969.
109. Koski, C. L.: Characterization of complement-fixing antibodies to peripheral nerve myelin in Guillain-Barré syndrome. Ann. Neurol. *27*(Suppl.): S44–S47, 1990.
110. Koski, C. L., Chou, D. K., and Jungalwala, F. B.: Anti–peripheral nerve myelin antibodies in Guillain-Barré syndrome bind a neutral glycolipid of peripheral myelin and cross-react with Forssman antigen. J. Clin. Invest. *84*:280–287, 1989.
111. Kurland, L. T.: Descriptive epidemiology of selected neurologic and myopathic disorders with particular reference to a survey in Rochester, Minnesota. J. Chronic Dis. *8*:378–418, 1958.
112. Kurland, L. T., Wiederholt, W. C., Kirkpatrick, J. W., et al.: Swine influenza vaccine and Guillain-Barré syndrome: Epidemic or artifact? Arch. Neurol. *42*:1089–1090, 1985.
113. Kuwabara, S., Mori, M., Ogawara, K., et al.: Intravenous immunoglobulin therapy for Guillain-Barré syndrome with IgG anti-GM_1 antibody. Muscle Nerve *24*:54–58, 2001.
114. Kuwabara, S., Yuki, N., Koga, M., et al.: IgG anti-GM_1 antibody is associated with reversible conduction failure and axonal degeneration in Guillain-Barré syndrome. Ann. Neurol. 44:202–208, 1998.
115. Landry, O.: Note sur la paralysis ascendante aique. Gaz. Hebdom. Med. Chir. *6*:472–474, 486–488, 1859.
116. Latovitzki, N., Suciu-Foca, N., Penn, A. S., et al.: HLA typing and Guillain-Barré syndrome. Neurology *29*:743–745, 1979.
117. Leneman, F.: The Guillain-Barré syndrome. Arch. Intern. Med. *118*:139–144, 1966.
118. Lesser, R. P., Hauser, W. A., Kurland, L. T., et al.: Epidemiologic features of the Guillain-Barré syndrome. Neurology *23*:1269–1272, 1973.
119. Levy, J. B., and Pusey, C. D.: Nephrotoxicity of intravenous immunoglobulin. Q. J. Med. *93*:751–755, 2000.
120. Lidin-Janson, G., and Strannegard, O.: Two cases of Guillain-Barré syndrome and encephalitis after measles. Br. Med. J. *2*:572, 1972.
121. Lin, S. M., Ryu, S. T., and Liaw, Y. F.: Guillain-Barré syndrome associated with acute delta-hepatitis virus superinfection. J. Med. Virol. *28*:144–145, 1989.
122. Link, H.: Immunoglobulin abnormalities in Guillain-Barré syndrome. J. Neurol. Sci. *18*:11–23, 1973.
123. Lisak, R. P., Kuchmy, D., Armati-Gulsin, P. J., et al.: Serum-mediated Schwann cell cytotoxicity in the Guillain-Barré syndrome. Neurology *34*:1240–1243, 1984.
124. Lisak, R. P., Zweiman, B., Guerrero, F., et al.: Circulating T-cell subsets in Guillain-Barré syndrome. J. Neuroimmunol. *8*:93–101, 1985.
125. Lisak, R. P., Zweiman, B., and Norman, M.: Antimyelin antibodies in neurologic diseases: Immunofluorescent demonstration. Arch. Neurol. *32*:163–167, 1975.
126. Loffel, N. B., Rossi, L. W., Mumenthaler, M., et al.: The Landry-Guillain-Barré syndrome: Complications, prognosis, and natural history in 123 cases. J. Neurol. Sci. *33*:71–79, 1977.
127. Lopez, F., Lopez, J. H., Holquin, H., et al.: An outbreak of acute polyradiculoneuropathy in Columbia in 1968. Am. J. Epidemiol. *98*:226–230, 1973.
128. McFarland, H. R., and Heller, G. L.: Guillain-Barré disease complex: A statement of diagnostic criteria and analysis of 100 cases. Arch. Neurol. *14*:196–201, 1966.
129. McFarlin, D. E.: Immunological parameters in Guillain-Barré syndrome. Ann. Neurol. *27*(Suppl.):S25–S29, 1990.
130. McKhann, G. M., Cornblath, D. R., Griffin, J. W., et al.: Acute motor axonal neuropathy: A frequent cause of acute placid paralysis in China. Ann. Neurol. *33*:333–342, 1993.
131. McKhann, G. M.: Guillain-Barré syndrome: Clinical and therapeutic observations. Ann. Neurol. *27*(Suppl.):S13–S16, 1990.
132. McLeod, J. G., Walsh, J. C., Prineas, J. W., et al.: Acute idiopathic polyneuritis: A clinical and electrophysiological follow-up study. J. Neurol. Sci. *27*:145–162, 1976.
133. Marks, J. S., and Halpin, T. J.: Guillain-Barré syndrome in recipients of A/New Jersey influenza vaccine. J. A. M. A. *243*:2490–2494, 1980.
134. Marshall, J.: The Landry-Guillain-Barré syndrome. Brain *86*:55–66, 1963.
135. Marti-Masso, J. F., Obeso, J. A., Cosme, A., et al.: Guillain-Barré syndrome associated with a type B acute hepatitis. Med. Clin. (Barc.) *73*:447–450, 1979.
136. Melnick, S. C.: Thirty-eight cases of the Guillain-Barré syndrome: An immunological study. Br. Med. J. *1*:368–373, 1963.
137. Melnick, S. C., and Flewelt, T. H.: Role of infection in the Guillain-Barré syndrome. J. Neurol. Neurosurg. Psychiatry *27*:385–407, 1964.

138. Mendell, J. R., Kissel, J. T., Kennedy, M. S., et al.: Plasma exchange and prednisone in Guillain-Barré syndrome: A controlled randomized trial. Neurology *35*:1551–1555, 1985.
139. Menonna, J., Goldschmidt, B., Haidri, N., et al.: Herpes simplex virus IgM specific antibodies in Guillain-Barré syndrome and encephalitis. Acta Neurol. Scand. *56*:223–231, 1977.
140. Mori, M., Kuwabara, S., Miyake, M., et al.: *Haemophilus influenzae* infection and Guillain-Barré syndrome. Brain *123*:2171–2178, 2000.
141. Mozes, B., Pines, A., Sayar, Y., et al.: Guillain-Barré syndrome associated with acute cytomegalovirus mononucleosis syndrome. Eur. Neurol. *23*:237–239, 1984.
142. Mushinski, J. F., Taniguchi, R. M., and Stiefel, J. W.: Guillain-Barré syndrome associated with ulceroglandular tularemia. Neurology *14*:877–879, 1964.
143. Newman, M. J., and Nelson, N.: Treatment of subacute polyneuritis with corticosteroids. Can. J. Neurol. Sci. *1*:180–184, 1974.
144. Ng, P. L., Powell, I. W., and Campbell, C. P.: Guillain-Barré syndrome during the pre-icteric phase of acute type B viral hepatitis. Aust. N. Z. J. Med. *5*:367–369, 1975.
145. Nguyen, D. K., Agenarioti-Belanger, S., and Vanasse, M.: Pain and the Guillain-Barré syndrome in children under 6 years old. J. Pediatr. *134*:773–776, 1999.
146. Niermeyer, P., and Girs, C. H.: Guillain-Barré syndrome in acute HBS Ag-positive hepatitis. Br. Med. J. *4*:732–733, 1975.
147. Novak, M.: Guillain-Barré syndrome as a sequela of influenza. Cesk. Neurol. Neurochir. *38*:314–316, 1975.
148. Nowicki, J.: Neurological syndromes occurring in the course of influenza. Neurol. Neurochir. Pol. *7*:695–699, 1973.
149. Nyland, H.: Epidemiology of Guillain-Barré syndrome in mid-western Norway. Acta Neurol. Scand. *57*(Suppl. 67):223, 1978.
150. Nyland, H., and Aarli, J. A.: Guillain-Barré syndrome: Demonstration of antibodies to peripheral nerve tissue. Acta Neurol. Scand. *58*:35–43, 1978.
151. Nyland, H., Matre, R., and Mork, S.: Immunological characterization of sural nerve biopsies from patients with Guillain-Barré syndrome. Ann. Neurol. *9*(Suppl.):80–86, 1981.
152. Oames, P. G., Jacobs, B. C., Hazenberg, M. P. H., et al.: Anti-GM_1 IgG antibodies and *Campylobacter* bacteria in Guillain-Barré syndrome: Evidence of molecular mimicry. Ann. Neurol. *38*:170, 1995.
153. Ogawara, K., Kuwabara, S., Mori, M., et al.: Axonal Guillain-Barré syndrome: Relation to anti-ganglioside antibodies and *Campylobacter jejuni* infection in Japan. Ann. Neurol. *48*:624–631, 2000.
154. Oh, S. J., LaGanke, C., and Claussen, G. C.: Sensory Guillain-Barré syndrome. Neurology *56*:82–86, 2001.
155. Oka, N., Akiguchi, I., Kawasaki, T., et al.: Elevated serum levels of endothelial leukocyte adhesion molecules in Guillain-Barré syndrome and chronic inflammatory demyelinating polyneuropathy. Ann. Neurol. *35*:621–624, 1994.
156. Osler, L. D., and Sidell, A. D.: The Guillain-Barré syndrome: The need for exact diagnostic criteria. N. Engl. J. Med. *262*:964–969, 1960.
157. Paradiso, G., Tripoli, J., Galicchio, S., et al.: Epidemiological, clinical and electrodiagnostic findings in childhood Guillain-Barré syndrome: A reappraisal. Ann. Neurol. *46*:701–707, 1999.
158. Parker, W., Witt, J. C., Dawson, J. W., et al.: Landry-Guillain-Barré syndrome: The isolation of an Echovirus type 6. Can. Med. Assoc. J. *82*:813–815, 1960.
159. Partnow, M. J., Devereaux, M. W., and Humphries, T. S.: Infectious hepatitis and the Guillain-Barré syndrome. J. Med. Soc. N. J. *77*:118–120, 1980.
160. Penney, M. D., Murphy, D., and Walters, G.: Resetting of osmoreceptor response as cause of hyponatremia in acute idiopathic polyneuritis. Br. Med. J. *2*:1474–1476, 1979.
161. Phillips, P. E.: Guillain-Barré syndrome after measles. Br. Med. J. *4*:50–57, 1972.
162. Plachy, U., Lichy, J., Horacek, J., et al.: Polyradiculoneuritis syndrome in cytomegalovirus infection. Cesk. Neurol. Neurochir. *42*:396–401, 1979.
163. Plough, J. C., and Ayerle, R. S.: The Guillain-Barré syndrome associated with acute hepatitis. N. Engl. J. Med. *249*:61–62, 1953.
164. Pollard, J. D., Westland, K. W., Harvey, G. K., et al.: Activated T cells of non-neural specificity open the blood-nerve barrier to circulating antibody. Ann. Neurol. *37*:467–475, 1995.
165. Prineas, J. W.: Acute idiopathic polyneuritis: An electron microscopic study. Lab. Invest. *26*:133–146, 1972.
166. Prineas, J. W.: Pathology of the Guillain-Barré syndrome. Ann. Neurol. *9*(Suppl.):6–19, 1981.
167. Pryor, W. M., Freiman, J. S., Gillies, M. A., et al.: Guillain-Barré syndrome associated with *Campylobacter* infection. Aust. N. Z. J. Med. *14*:687, 1984.
168. Quarles, R. H., Ilyas, A. A., and Willison, H. J.: Antibodies to gangliosides and myelin proteins in Guillain-Barré syndrome. Ann. Neurol. *27*(Suppl.):S48–S52, 1990.
169. Raman, P. T., and Taori, G. M.: Prognostic significance of electrodiagnostic studies in the Guillain-Barré syndrome. J. Neurol. Neurosurg. Psychiatry *39*:163–170, 1976.
170. Rantala, H., Cherry, J. D., Shields, W. D., et al.: Epidemiology of Guillain-Barré syndrome in children: Relationship of oral polio vaccine administration to occurrence. J. Pediatr. *124*:220–223, 1994.
170a. Raphael, J. C., Chevret, S., Hughes, R. A., and Annane, D.: Plasma exchange for Guillain-Barré syndrome. Cochrane Database Syst. Rev. CD001798, 2002.
171. Ravin, H.: The Landry-Guillain-Barré syndrome: A survey and a clinical report of 127 cases. Acta Neurol. Scand. *43*(Suppl. 30):1–64, 1967.
172. Rees, J. H., and Hughes, R. A. C.: *Campylobacter jejuni* and Guillain-Barré syndrome. Ann. Neurol. *35*:248–249, 1994.
173. Rees, J. H., Gregson, N. A., and Hughes, R. A. C.: Anti-ganglioside GM_1 antibodies in Guillain-Barré syndrome and their relationship to *Campylobacter jejuni* infection. Ann. Neurol. *38*:809–816, 1995.
174. Rees, J. H., Soudain, S. E., Gregson, N. A., et al.: *Campylobacter jejuni* infection and Guillain Barré syndrome. N. Engl. J. Med. *333*:1374–1379, 1995.
174a. Reuben, S., Mathai, A., Sumi, M.G., et al.: Significance of serum antibody to GD_{1b} ganglioside in patients with Guillain-Barré syndrome. Indian J. Med. Res. *113*:234–238, 2001.
175. Rhodes, K. M., and Tattersfield, A. E.: Guillain-Barré syndrome associated with *Campylobacter* infection. Br. Med. J. *285*:173–174, 1982.
176. Richter, R. B.: The ataxic form of polyradiculoneuritis (Landry-Guillain-Barré syndrome). J. Neuropathol. Exp. Neurol. *21*:171–184, 1962.
177. Rocklin, R. E., Sheremata, W. A., Feldman, R. G., et al.: The Guillain-Barré syndrome and multiple sclerosis: In vitro cellular responses to nervous tissue antigens. N. Engl. J. Med. *284*:803–808, 1971.
178. Ropper, A. H., and Kehne, S. M.: Guillain-Barré syndrome: Management of respiratory failure. Neurology *35*:1662–1665, 1985.
179. Ropper, A. H., and Shahani, B. T.: Pain in Guillain-Barré syndrome. Arch. Neurol. *41*:511–514, 1984.
180. Rosenberg, R. N., and Mendoza, G.: Idiopathic acute symmetrical polyradiculoneuritis: The Landry-Guillain-Barré-Strohl syndrome. West. J. Med. *120*:124–130, 1974.
181. Rossi, L. N., Mumenthaler, M., Lutschg, J., et al.: Guillain-Barré syndrome in children with special reference to the natural history of 38 personal cases. Neuropadiatrie *7*:42–51, 1976.
182. Ryberg, B.: Extra- and intrathecal production of antinerve and antibrain antibodies in Guillain-Barré syndrome: Evaluation by an antibody index. Neurology *34*:1378–1381, 1984.
183. Ryberg, B., Hindfelt, B., Nilsson, B., et al.: Antineural antibodies in Guillain-Barré syndrome and lymphocytic meningoradiculitis (Bannwarth's syndrome). Arch. Neurol. *41*:1277–1281, 1984.
184. Saeed, A. A., and Lange, L. S.: Guillain-Barré syndrome after rubella. Postgrad. Med. J. *54*:333–334, 1978.
185. Saida, T., Saida, K., Lisak, R. P., et al.: In vivo demyelinating activity of sera from patients with Guillain-Barré syndrome. Ann. Neurol. *11*:69–75, 1982.
186. Saida, T., Saida, K., Silbergerg, D. H., et al.: Transfer of demyelination by intraneural injection of experimental allergic neuritis serum. Nature *272*:639–641, 1978.
187. Sakakihara, Y., and Kamoshita, S.: Age-associated changes in the symptomatology of Guillain-Barré syndrome in children. Dev. Med. Child Neurol. *31*:611–616, 1991.
188. Samantray, S. K., Johnson, S. C., Mathai, K. V., et al.: Landry-Guillain-Barré-Strohl syndrome: A study of 302 cases. Med. J. Aust. *2*:84–91, 1977.
189. Schmitz, H., and Enders, G.: Cytomegalovirus as a frequent cause of Guillain-Barré syndrome. J. Med. Virol. *1*:21–27, 1977.
190. Schonberger, L. B., Bergman, D. J., Sullivan-Bolyai, J. Z., et al.: Guillain-Barré syndrome following vaccination in the national influenza immunization program, United States, 1976–1977. Am. J. Epidemiol. *110*:105–123, 1979.
191. Schonberger, L. B., Hurwitz, E. S., Katona, P., et al.: Guillain-Barré syndrome: Its epidemiology and associations with influenza vaccination. Ann. Neurol. *9*(Suppl.):31–38, 1981.
191a. Seneviratne, U., and Gunasekera, S.: Acute small fibre sensory neuropathy: Another variant of Guillain-Barré syndrome? J. Neurol. Sci. *196*:41–44, 2002.
192. Shahar, E., Murphy, E. G., and Roifman, C. M.: Benefit of intravenously administered immune serum globulin in patients with Guillain-Barré syndrome. J. Pediatr. *116*:141–144, 1990.
193. Sharief, M. K., McLean, B., Thompson, E. J.: Elevated serum levels of tumor necrosis factor in Guillain-Barré syndrome. Ann. Neurol. 33:591–596, 1993.
194. Sheikh, K. A., Nachamkin, I., Ho, T. W., et al.: *Campylobacter jejuni* lipopolysaccharides in Guillain-Barré syndrome: Molecular mimicry and host susceptibility. Neurology *51*:371–178, 1998.
195. Siebert, D. G., and Seals, J. E.: Polyneuropathy after herpes simplex type 2 meningitis. South. Med. J. *77*:1476, 1984.
196. Shermata, W., and Behan, P. O.: Experimental allergic neuritis: A new experimental approach. J. Neurol. Neurosurg. Psychiatry *36*:139–145, 1973.
197. Sheremata, W., Colby, S., Lusky, G., et al.: Cellular hypersensitization to peripheral nervous antigens in the Guillain-Barré syndrome. Neurology *25*:833–839, 1975.

198. Sheremata, W., Eylar, E. H., Szymanska, I., et al.: Peripheral nerve myelin P2 protein in influenza vaccine. Ann. Neurol. *10*:91–92, 1981.
199. Soffer, D., Feldman, S., and Alter, M.: Epidemiology of Guillain-Barré syndrome. Neurology *28*:686–690, 1978.
200. Stapleton, F. D., Skoglund, R. R., and Daggett, R. B.: Hypertension associated with the Guillain-Barré syndrome. Pediatrics *62*:588–590, 1978.
201. Steinberg, A. D.: Modulation of a complex immune system. Ann. Neurol. *9*(Suppl.):117–124, 1981.
202. Steiner, I., Argov, Z., Cahan, C., et al.: Guillain-Barré syndrome after epidural anesthesia: Direct nerve root damage may trigger disease. Neurology *35*:1473–1475, 1985.
203. Stewart, G. J., Pollard, J. D., McLeod, J. G., et al.: HLA antigens in the Landry-Guillain-Barré syndrome and chronic relapsing polyneuritis. Ann. Neurol. *4*:285–289, 1975.
204. Swick, H. M., and McQuillen, M. P.: The use of steroids in the treatment of idiopathic polyneuritis. Neurology *26*:205–212, 1976.
205. Tabor, E.: Guillain-Barré syndrome and other neurologic syndromes in hepatitis A, B, and non-A, non-B. J. Med. Virol. *21*:207–216, 1987.
206. Taylor, W. A., and Hughes, R. A.: T lymphocyte activation antigens in Guillain-Barré syndrome and chronic idiopathic demyelinating polyradiculoneuropathy. J. Neuroimmunol. *24*:33–39, 1989.
207. Tindall, R. S. A., Zinn, P., and Rosenberg, R. N.: Humoral immunity in the Guillain-Barré syndrome: Evidence for circulating IgG and IgM. Neurology *30*:362–363, 1980.
208. Toyka, K. V., Augspach, R., Paulus, W., et al.: Plasma exchange in polyradiculoneuropathy. Ann. Neurol. *8*:205–206, 1980.
209. Tse, K. S., Arbesman, C. E., Tomasi, et al.: Demonstration of antimyelin antibodies by immunofluorescence in Guillain-Barré syndrome. Clin. Exp. Immunol. *8*:881–887, 1971.
210. Tsukada, N., Koh, C. S., Inoue, A., et al.: Demyelinating neuropathy associated with hepatitis B virus infection: Detection of immune complexes composed of hepatitis B virus surface antigen. J. Neurol. Sci. *77*:203–216, 1987.
211. Tuck, R. R., and McLeod, J. G.: Autoimmune dysfunction in Guillain-Barré syndrome. J. Neurol. Neurosurg. Psychiatry *44*:983–990, 1981.
212. Uhari, M., Rantala, H., and Niemela, M.: Cluster of childhood Guillain-Barré cases after an oral polio vaccine campaign. Lancet *2*:440–441, 1989.
213. Usui, T., Hammada, Y., and Anta, M.: A case of Guillain-Barré associated with coxsackie. Tokushima J. Exp. Med. *21*:17–19, 1974.
214. van der Meche, F. G., and van Doorn, P. A.: Guillain-Barré syndrome. Curr. Treat. Options Neurol. *2*:507–516, 2000.
215. van der Meche, F. G.: The Guillain-Barré syndrome: Plasma exchange or immunoglobulins intravenously. J. Neurol. Neurosurg. Psychiatry *57*(Suppl.): 33–34, 1995.
216. van der Meche, F. G., and van Doorn, P. A.: Guillain-Barré syndrome and chronic inflammatory demyelinating polyneuropathy: Immune mechanisms and update on current therapies. Ann. Neurol. *37*(Suppl. 1): S14–S31, 1995.
217. Vajsar, J., Sloane, A., Wood, E., et al.: Plasmapheresis vs. intravenous immunoglobulin treatment in childhood Guillain-Barré syndrome. Arch. Pediatr. Adolesc. Med. *148*:1210–1212, 1994.
218. Vedeler, C. A., Nyland, H., and Matre, R.: Antibodies to peripheral nerve tissue in sera from patients with acute Guillain-Barré syndrome demonstrated by a mixed hemagglutination technique. J. Neuroimmunol. *2*:209–214, 1982.
219. Verma, A. K., Maheshwari, M. C., Chardhary, C., et al.: Acute ascending motor paralysis due to rabies: A clinicopathological report. Eur. Neurol. *24*:160–162, 1985.
220. Vriesendorp, F. J., Triggs, W. J., Mayer, R. F., et al.: Electrophysiological studies in Guillain-Barré syndrome: Correlation with antibodies to GM_1, GD_{1b} and *Campylobacter jejuni*. J. Neurol. *242*:460–465, 1995.
221. Vriesendorp, F. J., Mishu, B., Blasher, M. J., et al.: Serum antibodies to GM_1, GD_{1b}, peripheral nerve myelin, and *Campylobacter jejuni* in patients with Guillain-Barré syndrome and controls: Correlation and prognosis. Ann. Neurol. *34*:130–135, 1993.
222. Vyravanathan, S., and Senanayake, N.: Guillain-Barré syndrome associated with tuberculosis. Postgrad. Med. J. *59*:516–517, 1983.
223. Waksman, B. H., and Adams, R. D.: Allergic neuritis: An experimental disease of rabbits induced by the injection of peripheral nervous tissue and adjuvants. J. Exp. Med. *102*:213–235, 1955.
224. Welch, R. G.: Chickenpox and the Guillain-Barré syndrome. Arch. Dis. Child. *37*:557–559, 1962.
225. Wells, C. E. C., James, W. R. I., and Evans, A. D.: Guillain-Barré syndrome and virus of influenza A (Asian strain): Report of two fatal cases during the 1957 epidemic in Wales. Arch. Neurol. Psych. *81*:699–705, 1959.
226. Whitaker, J. N., Hirano, A., Cook, S. D., et al.: The ultrastructure of circulating immunocytes in Guillain-Barré syndrome. Neurology *20*:765–770, 1970.
227. Willison, H. J., Veitch, J., Paterson, G., et al.: Miller Fisher syndrome is associated with serum antibodies to GQ_{1b} ganglioside. J. Neurol. Neurosurg. Psychiatry *56*:204–206, 1993.
228. Winer, J. B., Hughes, R. A. C., Greenwood, R. J., et al.: Prognosis in Guillain-Barré syndrome. Lancet *1*:1202–1203, 1985.
229. Winkler, G. F.: In vitro demyelination of peripheral nerve induced with sensitized cells. Ann. N. Y. Acad. Sci. *122*:287–296, 1965.
230. Winkler, G. F., and Arnason, B. G. W.: Antiserum to immunoglobulin A: Inhibition of cell mediated demyelination in tissue culture. Science *153*:75–76, 1966.
231. Wisniewki, H., Terry, R. D., Whitaker, J. N., et al.: The Landry-Guillain-Barré syndrome: A primary demyelinating disease. Arch. Neurol. *21*:269–276, 1969.
232. Yoshii, F., and Shinohara, Y.: Lymphocyte subset proportions in Guillain-Barré syndrome patients treated with plasmapheresis. Eur. Neurol. *44*:162–167, 2000.
233. Yu, R. K., Ariga, T., Kobriyama, T., et al.: Autoimmune mechanisms in peripheral neuropathies. Ann. Neurol. *27*(Suppl.):S30–S35, 1990.
234. Yuki, N., Wim-Ang, C., Koga, M., et al.: Clinical features and response to treatment in Guillain-Barré syndrome associated with antibodies to GM_{1b} ganglioside. Ann. Neurol. *47*:314–321, 2000.
235. Yuki, N., Taki, T., Takahasi, M., et al.: Molecular mimicry between GQ_{1b} ganglioside and lipopolysaccharides of *Campylobacter jejuni* isolated from patients with Fisher's syndrome. Ann. Neurol. *36*:791–793, 1994.

SECTION V

Genitourinary Tract Infections

CHAPTER 46

Genitourinary Tract Infections

CHAPTER **46A**

Urethritis

ELLEN R. WALD

Urethritis refers to inflammation of the urethra and periurethral tissues in males and females. It may be associated with a variety of infectious and noninfectious disorders.

Epidemiology

The cause of urethritis varies with age of the patient, sexual practices, and hygienic standards.[13, 41] *Chlamydia* infections and gonorrhea are common occurrences in adolescents; fecal contamination or irritation caused by physical or chemical substances is a more usual occurrence in the preschooler. Transmission during sexual activity is the usual means of spread of *Neisseria gonorrhoeae* and *Chlamydia trachomatis* in teenagers and in sexually abused patients; however, nonvenereal transmission has been described in prepubertal children.[42] Manifestations after nonvenereal spread may include vaginitis, balanitis, and conjunctivitis in addition to urethritis.[42] The home and social environments of the prepubertal child must be examined to fully identify the pattern of spread and infection in the patient and contacts because complex psychosocial diagnoses and therapies often are involved.[33] Children with gonorrhea and chlamydial infections are concentrated in large urban centers, usually in poor socioeconomic environments.

Gonococcal infections in children 2 to 10 years of age should be considered evidence of possible sexual abuse.[18] Household contacts have been found to have positive cultures in 27 to 63 percent of such cases. Prepubertal girls infected with *N. gonorrhoeae* as a result of sexual abuse outnumber boys by a ratio of at least 3:1 and in one report 8:1.[16]

Pathophysiology

Infection caused by *N. gonorrhoeae* usually is localized to the urethra in males and to the vagina in young females; however, rectal carriage sometimes occurs in the absence of urethral colonization. Gonococcal virulence factors include pili,[47] the ability to attach to urethral epithelial cells,[49] and production of extracellular proteases that cleave IgA.[36]

Chlamydia infections are the most frequent cause of sexually transmitted disease in the United States.[9, 12] Chlamydiae are structurally complex organisms that are obligate intracellular parasites and contain both DNA and RNA. Attachment, which is not understood completely, is the first step in the infectious process of the susceptible host cell. It is followed by phagocytosis and then the failure of cellular lysosomes to fuse with the phagosome containing the elementary body, which may be mediated in part by macromolecules in the chlamydial cell envelope. After these two crucial events occur, the elementary bodies undergo biologic changes, and after approximately 72 hours, they are released from the host cell as new infective elementary bodies (Fig. 46–1).

Urethritis in younger children also may be caused by the introduction of fecal bacteria or pinworms into the urethra during the early years of toilet training, particularly in young girls. Inflammation may be related to bubble bath and other chemical and physical irritants. Edema of the mucosa and the presence of inflammation and red blood cells are common histopathologic features of urethritis that lead to dysuria, hematuria, and microscopic pyuria.

Clinical Presentation

Gonococcal urethritis is characterized by a 2- to 8-day incubation period after sexual intercourse. The onset often is sudden, with dysuria and copious urethral discharge in the male and leukorrhea in the female. The urethral discharge often is thick, profuse, and yellow. The patient usually has no fever. In prepubertal girls, leukorrhea is more prominent as a sign of gonococcal infections, and urethritis is less common. This difference may be related to the method of infection and to the different sensitivity of the vaginal epithelial surface to infection in the prepubertal child. Leukorrhea may be minimal in the adolescent girl, and dysuria may be absent.[3] Diagnosis often is made earlier in adolescent boys than in girls, perhaps because of the prominence of urethral discharge in boys and misinterpretation of the significance of leukorrhea in girls. Gonococcal urethritis also may cause asymptomatic pyuria in boys. On occasion, prepubertal patients have conjunctivitis or balanitis without significant urethritis. Clinical presentations may include systemic illness with fever, arthritis, and skin lesions secondary to bacteremia in as many as 3 percent of untreated persons with mucosal gonorrhea.[3] These lesions often begin on the extremities as small erythematous macules that progress to circular papules with an area of central necrosis.

The clinical presentation of nongonococcal urethritis may be similar to that described for gonorrhea, but it more commonly has a longer incubation period (often 8 to 14 days after sexual intercourse) and a scanty exudate, which may be clear in character and intermittent. This condition also is

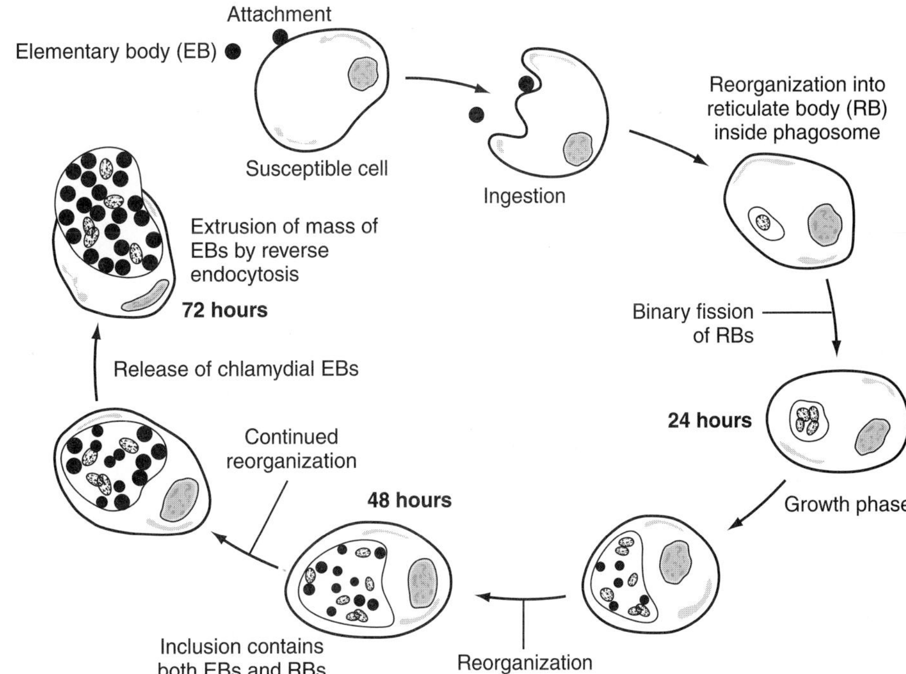

FIGURE 46–1 ■ Schematic description of the growth cycle of *Chlamydia trachomatis*. (From Batteiger, B. E., Jones, R. B.: Chlamydial infections. Infect. Dis. Clin. North Am. *1*:55–81, 1987.)

called nonspecific urethritis and may be present in association with or subsequent to gonococcal urethritis. In the latter case, the scant urethral discharge may persist after the patient has been treated for gonorrhea. Asymptomatic urethral colonization with *C. trachomatis* also is reported in males.[45]

An equivalent syndrome, acute urethral syndrome, has been described in sexually active females. The patient experiences an acute onset of dysuria and increased frequency, and pyuria (8 or more white blood cells/mm^3 of midstream urine) is a common finding. Bacterial cultures of the urine are often sterile or demonstrate less than 10^5 bacteria/mL; coliform bacteria, *Staphylococcus saprophyticus,* and *C. trachomatis* are the most common causes. Clinical expression of infection with *C. trachomatis* in adolescent girls is characterized by a yellowish, mucopurulent secretion at the cervical os.[10] However, infection with *C. trachomatis* may be asymptomatic in both sexes, an important consideration in designing effective strategies for diagnosis and management of sexual contacts.

The patient with urethritis caused by trauma may have hematuria and dysuria without fever. The trauma may be obvious or related to masturbation or introduction of foreign bodies into the urethra. Patients with urethritis secondary to bubble bath or soap usually have transient dysuria and no systemic signs. Fecal contamination of the urethra may be accompanied by hematuria, dysuria, and pyuria.

Differential Diagnosis (Table 46–1)

NONINFECTIOUS

Trauma, bubble bath, detergents found in shampoos, masturbation, radiation, and caustic substances may lead to the development of urethritis. Urethritis may also be a component of several systemic syndromes, including erythema multiforme (Stevens-Johnson syndrome), Kawasaki disease, and occasionally other forms of allergy. Reiter syndrome denotes the association of nongonococcal urethritis with conjunctivitis and arthritis.

INFECTIOUS

The most common forms of urethritis in sexually active adolescents and young adults are gonococcal and so-called nongonococcal urethritis. They may occur together or sequentially. Nongonococcal urethritis has been related causally to infections with *C. trachomatis* in approximately 30 to 50 percent of cases and with *Ureaplasma urealyticum* (T-strain mycoplasma) in approximately 25 percent of cases of nongonococcal, nonchlamydial urethritis in males.[10, 46] The remainder of cases of infectious urethritis in postpubescent, sexually active patients may be caused by a variety of pathogenic microorganisms, including *Gardnerella vaginalis, Mycoplasma hominis, Trichomonas vaginalis, Candida albicans,* herpes simplex virus type 2, *Treponema pallidum* (syphilis), and other bacteria, such as staphylococci, Enterobacteriaceae, and occasionally streptococci including group B.[17, 48]

Mycoplasma genitalium is a newly identified species, first isolated from males with urethritis.[11, 25] However, studies also have implicated a causative role in *Chlamydia*-negative

TABLE 46–1 ■ ETIOLOGY OF URETHRITIS

Infectious	Noninfectious
Sexually transmitted infections	Vasculitides
Neisseria gonorrhoeae	Reiter syndrome
Chlamydia trachomatis	Erythema multiforme
Trichomonas vaginalis	Kawasaki disease
Herpes simplex virus type 2	Mechanical
Mycoplasma species	Masturbation
Nonsexually transmitted infections	Foreign body
Staphylococcus saprophyticus	Trauma
Enterobacteriaceae	Chemical
Gardnerella vaginalis	Soaps
Streptococcus species	Detergents
Enterobius vermicularis	Drugs

nongonococcal urethritis for anaerobic organisms of the *Bacteroides* species, in particular *Bacteroides urealyticus*.

In younger children, urethritis usually has noninfectious causes as outlined earlier, although gonorrhea, *Chlamydia,* and fecal bacteria may be important as well.

Specific Diagnosis

The best method for diagnosis of gonorrhea in the sexually active male is to obtain urethral discharge by manually stripping the urethra or, if that is unproductive, by gently inserting a swab 2 to 3 cm into the distal urethra. The best culture technique for isolating *N. gonorrhoeae,* a fastidious organism, is immediate inoculation of this material onto a selective growth medium, such as regular or modified Thayer-Martin agar. Any delay in inoculation of the plates necessitates the use of a transport method with growth media in a carbon dioxide environment that will support the gonococcus at ambient temperatures. These media protect the organism from its marked susceptibility to the effects of drying, cold, and overgrowth by other bacteria. Urethral exudate from the male patient should undergo Gram staining at the same time; demonstration of typical kidney-shaped, gram-negative, intracellular diplococci is presumptively diagnostic, with a sensitivity and specificity approaching 100 percent (Fig. 46–2). Putative gonococcal colonies should be confirmed by oxidase reaction, Gram staining, sugar utilization tests, rapid enzyme tests, nucleic acid probes, or agglutination reactions with antibodies specific for *N. gonorrhoeae.* The last four tests are especially important in evaluating sites of infection or populations of patients with a low prevalence of gonorrhea.

Sexually active females with urethritis also should undergo urethral culture. Although the Gram stain of cervical secretions is only 66 percent sensitive in detecting *N. gonorrhoeae* in adolescent girls, the finding of kidney bean–shaped intracellular gram-negative diplococci is highly specific and, therefore, helpful.[50] Vaginal, cervical, and rectal swabs are recommended. Asymptomatic colonization with gonococci seems to occur most commonly in female patients, although it has been described in adolescent boys.[22] Pharyngitis, conjunctivitis, balanitis, and other less common manifestations of gonorrhea may coexist with urethritis. Samples obtained from these sites should be handled as described earlier. Blood agar and other specialized media may be indicated to identify nongonococcal causes of urethritis.

Gonococcal urethritis in prepubescent boys is diagnosed as described earlier for adolescent boys. Vaginal swabs are most useful in female patients, even though vaginal discharge may not be prominent. Endocervical cultures are not recommended for the diagnosis of gonorrhea in prepubescent girls. The yield of vaginal swabs appears adequate for most diagnostic purposes; however, rectal swabs also may be useful in female patients. Demonstration of kidney-shaped, gram-negative, intracellular diplococci in the prepubescent boy and girl is useful for a presumptive diagnosis and institution of therapy. Confirmation by culture as described for the sexually active male is necessary.

Other diagnostic approaches include the detection of gonococcal antigens in urethral or cervical specimens by enzyme-linked immunosorbent assay (ELISA), a nucleic acid probe test, and DNA amplification tests (using polymerase chain reaction and ligase chain reaction technology). None of these tests has proved superior to culture in the diagnosis of acute infection.

The emergence of penicillin-resistant strains of *N. gonorrhoeae* has increased. These isolates represent approximately 8.9 percent of the cases in the United States, with the highest percentage (71%) in New York City, Los Angeles, and Florida. One third of the cases of gonorrhea in Dade County, Florida, are caused by penicillin-resistant strains of *N. gonorrhoeae.*

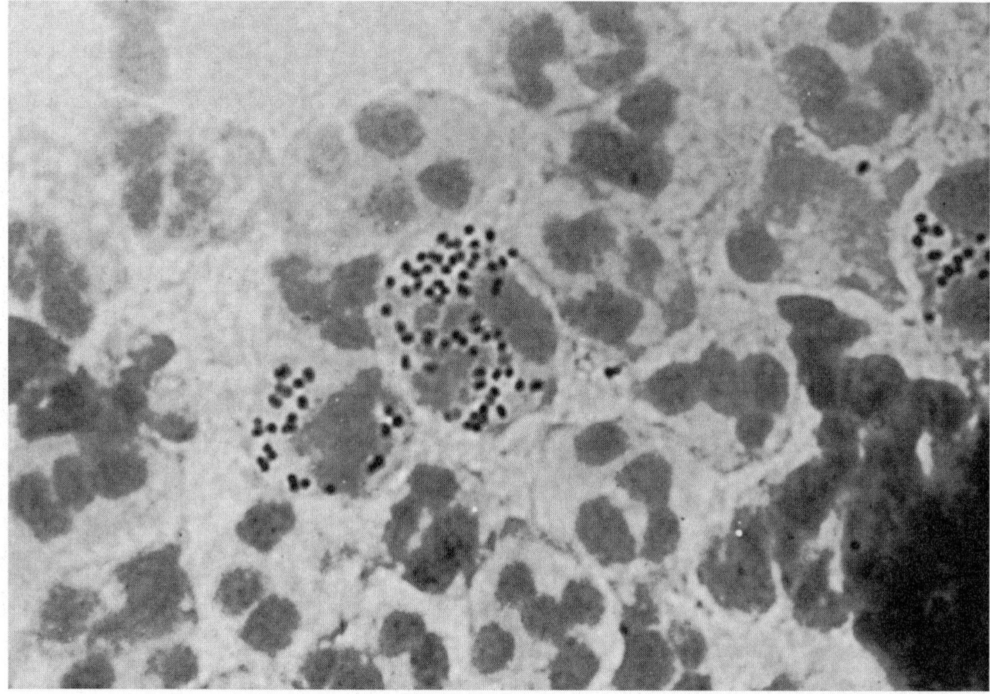

FIGURE 46–2 ■ Gram-stained smear of urethral discharge from a teenage boy with gonorrhea.

Antimicrobial resistance by *N. gonorrhoeae* may be mediated by different mechanisms:

1. Plasmid-mediated: Two plasmids are recognized: β-lactamase and tet-M. Plasmid-borne penicillin resistance results from the presence of a TEM-1 type β-lactamase gene on one of five small R factors that make up a closely related family of plasmids. Penicillinase-producing *N. gonorrhoeae* accounts for approximately 6.1 percent of the isolates in the United States. The tet-M plasmid confers resistance to tetracycline, minocycline, and doxycycline.
2. Chromosome-mediated: This is a cumulative effect of many chromosome mutations. It may confer resistance to multiple antibiotics, including β-lactams, tetracyclines, spectinomycin, and erythromycin.[23, 39] Overall, one third of strains of *N. gonorrhoeae* in the United States are resistant to penicillin, tetracycline, or both. Strains with high-level resistance to fluoroquinolones have been reported, mostly from outside the United States.[12]

Other infectious causes of urethritis may be diagnosed by specific techniques, including "wet mount" for *Trichomonas,* Gram stain and culture on Sabouraud dextrose agar for *C. albicans,* and culture for herpes simplex virus type 2, used in the patients and their contacts. New culture techniques for *Chlamydia,* such as the use of microtiter cell monolayers, have increased the recovery rates, decreased the cost, and shortened the turnaround time for the isolation of *C. trachomatis*.[6] However, the rigorous transport conditions and the small number of laboratories with cell culture techniques have limited the availability of *Chlamydia* cultures. Fortunately, noncultural methods are available. They include direct immunofluorescence staining of smears with use of monoclonal antibodies,[6, 19, 24, 29, 43] ELISA techniques, and nucleic acid probes. The immunofluorescent slide test is performed by smearing genital secretions on a slide and then fixing and staining the slide with fluorescein-conjugated monoclonal antibody that is specific for chlamydial antigens. The diagnosis is confirmed when fluorescing elementary bodies are observed. The sensitivity of this test is 70 to 85 percent compared with culture. It is a labor-intensive test, and its accuracy is directly dependent on the skill of the microscopist. The test performs best in high-risk populations. Its use as a screening tool is limited by its requirement for technical expertise and time and its insensitivity in low-risk populations.

ELISA for the detection of chlamydial antigens is another alternative to culture. The detection of *C. trachomatis* by enzyme immunoassay (Chlamydiazyme) in the sediment of a first-void urine has a sensitivity of 55 to 87 percent in men and 61 percent in women. In both sexes, it is highly specific (98%). This technique is least accurate in low-risk populations but is better suited to screening than is direct immunofluorescence. Most recently, nucleic acid probes have been developed for use in amplification assays such as ligase chain reaction and polymerase chain reaction.[7, 35, 38] These tests are the most sensitive tests for the presence of chlamydial infection and actually have surpassed culture techniques in sensitivity. Accordingly, they can be used to test for *Chlamydia* with use of urine rather than urethral or cervical specimens.[2, 5]

Ureaplasma and other genital *Mycoplasma* can be identified only by culture at this time. This test should be reserved for the evaluation of recurrent cases of urethritis with poor response to treatment.[11, 24] Selection of patients for these procedures can be facilitated by the performance of a microscopic examination of urethral secretions (>4 polymorphonuclear leukocytes per high-power field)[48] and urine (>10 white blood cells per high-power field in sediment from the initial 20 mL of void)[1] for purulence, even in asymptomatic subjects. Specimens of urethral and vaginal discharge secondary to fecal contamination, foreign bodies, and so on can be examined by conventional diagnostic bacterial techniques.

Treatment (Table 46–2)

The treatment of urethritis should include treatment of the sexual partners of the index case to avoid reinfection as well as further spread of infection. Patients with urethritis frequently have mixed infections with *N. gonorrhoeae* and the pathogens linked with nongonococcal urethritis, such as *C. trachomatis* and *U. urealyticum*. Concurrent infection with *N. gonorrhoeae* and *C. trachomatis* is documented in 20 to 40 percent of cases. Patients with gonococcal urethritis are also at risk for development of early incubating syphilis. One must consider these factors as well as the possibility of systemic infection when choosing a treatment regimen for urethritis.[31]

TABLE 46–2 ■ ANTIBIOTIC REGIMEN FOR URETHRITIS

Nongonococcal Urethritis	
Recommended regimen	Azithromycin 1 g orally in a single dose
	or
	Doxycycline 100 mg orally bid for 7 days
Alternative regimen	Erythromycin base 500 mg qid for 7 days
	or
	Erythromycin ethylsuccinate 800 mg qid for 7 days
	If patient cannot tolerate high-dose erythromycin:
	Erythromycin base 250 mg qid for 14 days
	or
	Erythromycin ethylsuccinate 400 mg qid for 14 days
Chlamydial Infection	
Recommended regimen (adults and adolescents)	Azithromycin 1 g orally in a single dose
	or
	Doxycycline 100 mg orally bid for 7 days
Alternative regimens	Ofloxacin 300 mg bid for 7 days
	Erythromycin base 500 mg qid for 7 days
	Erythromycin ethylsuccinate 800 mg qid for 7 days
Children	
<45 kg	Erythromycin 50 mg/kg/day qid for 10–14 days*
≥45 kg <8 years of age	Azithromycin 1 g orally in a single dose
>8 years of age	Use same regimen as for adults
Gonococcal Infection	
Recommended regimen (adults and adolescents)	Ceftriaxone 125 mg IM in a single dose
	or
	Cefixime 400 mg orally in a single dose
	or
	Ciprofloxacin 500 mg orally in a single dose
	or
	Ofloxacin 400 mg orally in a single dose
	plus
	Regimen effective for *Chlamydia*
Children	
<45 kg	Ceftriaxone 125 mg IM in a single dose
	If bacteremia, arthritis, or meningitis, ceftriaxone 50–100 mg/kg/day (max. 2 g/day) IV for 7–14 days
≥45 kg	Use adult regimen

***Note:** The effectiveness of treatment with erythromycin is approximately 80%; a second course of therapy may be required.

Sexual abuse is the most common cause of gonococcal infection among children 2 to 10 years of age. Anorectal and pharyngeal infections with *N. gonorrhoeae* are common occurrences and frequently asymptomatic among these patients.[32]

In 1998, the Centers for Disease Control and Prevention published treatment guidelines for sexually transmitted diseases, including urethritis (see Table 46–2). Every attempt should be made to ascertain the specific diagnosis. If doing so is not possible, the treatment regimen chosen always should be appropriate for both nongonococcal urethritis and gonococcal infection. Single-dose azithromycin for nongonococcal urethritis and either intramuscular or oral single-dose regimens for uncomplicated gonococcal infections are likely to increase compliance.[20, 21, 27, 30, 34, 37, 44, 51] Test of cure is not indicated for uncomplicated gonococcal or chlamydial infection when single-dose treatment regimens are used.[12] If these regimens fail, infections with other pathogens, such as herpes simplex virus or *T. vaginalis,* or bacterial urethritis should be considered. Appropriate testing and specific treatment should be provided when indicated.

Prognosis

Gonococcal urethritis may subside and lead to asymptomatic carriage in female patients. Such carriage may last for weeks to months in adults; however, this period is undefined in children. Untreated gonococcal urethritis also may lead to prostatitis and epididymitis in the male patient, as well as urethral stricture. Asymptomatic genital infections in women can progress to pelvic inflammatory disease with tubal scarring and infertility. Systemic complications of asymptomatic gonorrheal infections can include arthritis, endocarditis, and necrotic skin lesions.

Chlamydial infections frequently have been associated with pelvic inflammatory disease in women, resulting sometimes in infertility or ectopic pregnancy. *Chlamydia* can be transmitted to the newborn in the birth canal, which can result in conjunctivitis, pneumonia, or both.

The frequency of *U. urealyticum* is higher in sperm samples from men of infertile couples. It also has been associated in women with premature delivery and postpartum fever. In the newborn, this organism might be linked with the development of bronchopulmonary dysplasia. *Ureaplasma* central nervous system infection occasionally is reported in newborns.

Prevention

Despite substantial efforts, a specific gonococcal vaccine has not been developed. The mainstays of prevention continue to be education and screening. Prepubescent gonorrhea can be prevented from recurring only by careful family counseling and psychosocial therapy; legal intervention may be necessary.

The availability of diagnostic tests performed on urine (a noninvasive alternative to specimens obtained from the urethra or endocervix) renders extensive screening possible in nontraditional settings such as school and recreation centers.[9] Large-scale efforts that have implemented screening for all sexually active teens attending school-based clinics have been successful in reducing the prevalence of *Chlamydia* infection in boys.[14]

Prevention of noninfectious causes of urethritis usually depends on education and specific counseling of the family. Physical agents or allergens identified as a cause of urethritis must be removed.

Acknowledgments

The author acknowledges the contribution of Dr. Melvin I. Marks and Dr. Antonio C. Arrieta to the previous edition of this chapter. Many sections required minimal changes apart from addition of recently published information.

REFERENCES

1. Adger, H., Shafer, M. A., Sweet, R. L., et al.: Screening for *Chlamydia trachomatis* and *Neisseria gonorrhoeae* in adolescent males. Value of first-catch urine examination. Lancet *2*:944–945, 1984.
2. Adjei, O., and Lal, V.: Non-invasive detection of *Chlamydia trachomatis* genital infections in asymptomatic males and females by enzyme immunoassay (Chlamydiazyme). J. Trop. Med. Hyg. *98*:51–54, 1994.
3. American Academy of Pediatrics: Gonococcal infections. *In* Pickering, L. K. (ed.): 2000 Red Book: Report of the Committee on Infectious Diseases. 25th ed. Elk Grove Village, IL, American Academy of Pediatrics, 2000, p. 254.
4. Arnold, A. J., and Kleris, G. S.: The "borderline" smear in men with urethritis. J. A. M. A. *244*:157–159, 1980.
5. Backman, M., Ruden, A. K., Ringertz, O., et al.: Detection of *Chlamydia trachomatis* in urine from men with urethritis. Eur. J. Clin. Microbiol. Infect. Dis. *12*:447–449, 1993.
6. Batteiger, B. E., and Jones, R. B.: Chlamydial infections. Infect. Dis. Clin. North Am. *1*:55–81, 1987.
7. Bauwens, J. E., Clark, A. M., Loeffelholz, M. J. et al.: Diagnosis of *Chlamydia trachomatis* urethritis in men by polymerase chain reaction assay of first-catch urine. J. Clin. Microbiol. *31*:3013–3016, 1993.
8. Bowie, W. R., Alexander, E. R., Floyd, J. F., et al.: Differential responses of chlamydial and ureaplasma-associated urethritis to sulphafurazole (sulfisoxazole) and aminocyclitols. Lancet *2*:1276–1278, 1976.
9. Braverman, P. K.: Sexually transmitted diseases in adolescents. Med. Clin. North Am. *84*:869–890, 2000.
10. Brunham, R. C., Paavonen, J., Stevens, C. E., et al.: Mucopurulent cervicitis: The ignored counterpart in women of urethritis in men. N. Engl. J. Med. *311*:1–6, 1984.
11. Cassell, G. H., Davis, J. K., Waites, K. B. et al.: Pathogenesis and significance of urogenital mycoplasmal infections. Adv. Exp. Med. Biol. *224*:93–115, 1987.
12. Centers for Disease Control and Prevention: 1998 Guidelines for treatment of sexually transmitted diseases. M. M. W. R. *47*:1–111, 1998.
13. Chacko, M. R., and Lovchik, J. C.: *Chlamydia trachomatis* infection in sexually active adolescents: Prevalence and risk factors. Pediatrics *73*:836–840, 1984.
14. Cohen, D. A., Nsaumi, M., Martin, D. H., and Farley, T. A.: Repeated school-based training for sexually transmitted disease: A feasible strategy for reaching adolescents. Pediatrics *104*:1281–1285, 1999.
15. Dallabetta, G., and Hook, E. W., III: Gonococcal infections. Infect. Dis. Clin. North Am. *1*:25–54, 1987.
16. Folland, D. S., Burke, R. E., Hinman, A. R., et al.: Gonorrhea in preadolescent children: An inquiry into source of infection and mode of transmission. Pediatrics *60*:153–156, 1977.
17. Greenberg, R. N., Rein, M. F., Sanders, C. V., et al.: Urethral syndrome in women. J. A. M. A. *245*:923, 1981.
18. Hadlich, S., and Kohl, P. K.: Sexually transmitted diseases in children: A practical approach. Dermatol. Clin. *16*:859–861, 1998.
19. Hagay, Z. J., Sarov, B., and Sachs, J.: Detecting *Chlamydia trachomatis* in men with urethritis: Serology v isolation in cell culture. Genitourin. Med. *65*:166–170, 1988.
20. Hammerschlag, M. R., Golden, N. H., Oh, M. K., et al.: Single dose of azithromycin for the treatment of genital chlamydial infections in adolescents. J. Pediatr. *122*:961–965, 1993.
21. Handsfield, H. H., McCormack, W. M., Hook, E. W., et al.: A comparison of single-dose cefixime with ceftriaxone as treatment for uncomplicated gonorrhea. N. Engl. J. Med. *325*:1337–1340, 1991.
22. Hein, K., Marks, A., and Cohen, M.: Asymptomatic gonorrhea: Prevalence in a population of urban adolescents. J. Pediatr. *90*:634–635, 1977.
23. Herve, V. M. A., Georges, A. J., Massanga, M., et al.: Evaluation of a method for rapid detection of penicillinase-producing *Neisseria gonorrhoeae* in urethral exudates. J. Clin. Microbiol. *27*:227–228, 1989.
24. Hooton, T. M., and Barnes, R. C.: Urethritis in men. Infect. Dis. Clin. North Am. *1*:165–178, 1987.
25. Horner, P., Gilroy, C. B., Naidoo, B. J., and Taylor-Robinson, D.: Association of *Mycoplasma genitalium* with acute non-gonococcal urethritis. Lancet *342*:582–585, 1993.
26. Ingram, D. L., Runyan, D. K., Collins, A. D., et al.: Vaginal *Chlamydia trachomatis* infection in children with sexual contact. Pediatr. Infect. Dis. *3*:97–99, 1984.
27. Lauharanta, J., Saarinen, K., Mustonen, M. T., et al.: Single-dose oral azithromycin versus seven-day doxycycline in treatment of non-gonococcal urethritis and cervicitis. J. Antimicrob. Chemother. *31*(Suppl.):177–183, 1993.

28. Lee, H. H., Chernesky, M. A., Schachter, J., et al.: Diagnosis of *Chlamydia trachomatis* genitourinary infection in women by ligase chain reaction assay of urine. Lancet *345*:213–216, 1995.
29. Mahony, J., Castriciano, S., Sellors, J., et al.: Diagnosis of *Chlamydia trachomatis* genital infections by cell culture and two enzyme immunoassays detecting different chlamydial antigens. J. Clin. Microbiol. *27*:1934–1938, 1989.
30. Martin, D. H., Mroczkowski, T. F., Dalu, Z. A., et al.: A controlled trial of single dose of azithromycin for the treatment of chlamydial urethritis and cervicitis. N. Engl. J. Med. *327*:921–925, 1992.
31. Moran, J. S., and Levine, W. C.: Drugs of choice for the treatment of uncomplicated gonococcal infections. Clin. Infect. Dis. *20*(Suppl.): S47–S65, 1995.
32. Nair, P., Glazer-Semmel, E., Gould, C., and Ruff, E.: *Neisseria gonorrhoeae* in asymptomatic prepubertal household contacts of children with gonococcal infection. Clin. Pediatr. *25*:160–163, 1986.
33. Neinstein, L. S., Goldenring, J., and Carpenter, S.: Non-sexual transmission of sexually transmitted diseases: An infrequent occurrence. Pediatrics *74*:67–76, 1984.
34. Odugbemi, T., Oyewold, F., Isichei, C. S., et al.: Single oral dose of azithromycin for therapy of susceptible sexually transmitted diseases: A multicenter open evaluation. W. Afr. J. Med. *12*:136–140, 1993.
35. Palmer, H. M., Gilroy, C. B., Thomas, B. J., et al.: Detection of *Chlamydia trachomatis* by the polymerase chain reaction in swabs and urine from men with non-gonococcal urethritis. J. Clin. Pathol. *44*:321–325, 1991.
36. Plaut, A. G., Gilbert, J .V., Artenstein, M. S., et al.: *Neisseria gonorrhoeae* and *Neisseria meningitidis*: Extracellular enzyme cleaves human immunoglobulin A. Science *190*:1103–1105, 1975.
37. Plourde, P. J., Tyndall, M., Agoki, E., et al: Single-dose cefixime versus single-dose ceftriaxone in the treatment of antimicrobial-resistant *Neisseria gonorrhoeae* infection. J. Infect. Dis. *166*:919–922, 1992.
38. Rasmussen, S. J., Smith-Vaughan, H., Nelson, M., et al.: Detection of *Chlamydia trachomatis* in urine using enzyme immunoassay and DNA amplification. Mol. Cell. Probes *7*:425–430, 1993.
39. Rice, R. J., Biddle, J. W., JeanLouis, Y. A., et al.: Chromosomally mediated resistance in *Neisseria gonorrhoeae* in the United States: Results of surveillance and reporting, 1983–1984. J. Infect. Dis. *153*:340–345, 1986.
40. Richmond, S. J., and Sparling, P. F.: Genital chlamydial infections. Am. J. Epidemiol. *103*:428–435, 1976.
41. Shafer, M. A., Beck, A., Blain, B., et al.: *Chlamydia trachomatis*: Important relationships to race, contraception, lower genital tract infection, and Papanicolaou smear. J. Pediatr. *104*:141–146, 1984.
42. Shore, W. B., and Winkelstein, J. A.: Nonvenereal transmission of gonococcal infections to children. J. Pediatr. *79*:661–663, 1971.
43. Stamm, W. E.: Diagnosis of *Chlamydia trachomatis* genitourinary infections. Ann. Intern. Med. *108*:710–717, 1988.
44. Stamm, W. E.: Azithromycin in the treatment of uncomplicated genital chlamydial urethritis and cervicitis. Am. J. Med. *9*:195–225, 1991.
45. Stamm, W. E., Koutsky, L. A., Benedetti, J. K., et al.: *Chlamydia trachomatis* urethral infections in men. Prevalence, risk factors, and clinical manifestations. Ann. Intern. Med. *100*:47–51, 1984.
46. Steele, R. W.: Prevention and management of sexually transmitted diseases in adolescents. Adolesc. Med. *11*:315–326, 2000.
47. Swanson, J., Sparks, E., Young, D., et al.: Studies on *Gonococcus* infection. X. Pili and leukocyte association factor as mediators of interactions between gonococci and eukaryotic cells in vitro. Infect. Immunol. *11*:1352–1361, 1975.
48. Swartz, S. L., Kraus, S. J., Herrmann, K. L., et al.: Diagnosis and etiology of nongonococcal urethritis. J. Infect. Dis. *138*:445–454, 1978.
49. Tramont, E. C.: Inhibition of adherence of *Neisseria gonorrhoeae* by human genital secretions. J. Clin. Invest. *59*:117–124, 1977.
50. Wald, E. R.: Gonorrhea: Diagnosis by Gram stain in the female adolescent. Am. J. Dis. Child. *131*:1094–1096, 1977.
51. Weber, J. T., and Johnson, R. E.: New treatments for *Chlamydia trachomatis* genital infection. Clin. Infect. Dis. *20*(Suppl.):S66–S71, 1995.
52. Wilkinson, A. E., Seth, A. D., and Rodin, P.: Infection with penicillinase-producing gonococcus. Br. Med. J. *2*:1233–1235, 1976.

CHAPTER **46B**

Cystitis and Pyelonephritis

ELLEN R. WALD

Urinary tract infections (UTIs) are the most common serious bacterial infections in childhood. In several series of children evaluated for fever, UTIs account for 5 to 6 percent of infections. They are more common than are occult bacteremia, bacterial pneumonia, and bacterial meningitis. UTI is especially common as a cause of infection in white infant girls, in whom it may explain febrile episodes in nearly 20 percent of children.

Epidemiology

Infections of the urinary tract occur in all age groups and may be symptomatic or asymptomatic. The site of infection may be the bladder (cystitis), ureters, and pelvis (ureteritis and pyelitis) or the renal parenchyma (pyelonephritis). Infections in the neonate and in infancy are common occurrences. In the first 3 months of life, infections in uncircumcised boys are the most common finding.[97, 103] Beyond month 6, infections in infant girls are substantially more common than are infections in boys; the female predominance in infections of the urinary tract is maintained throughout the rest of childhood and adolescence.

RISK OF URINARY TRACT INFECTION

The risk of developing a UTI during childhood appears to have increased since the early studies by Winberg and colleagues[127] in 1960. These investigations showed that the risk of developing a UTI during the first 10 years of life was 3.0 percent in girls and 1.1 percent in boys. In a more recent retrospective study of a cohort of 3556 school entrants, 7.8 percent of girls and 1.6 percent of boys were found to have had symptomatic UTI as confirmed by significant bacteriuria.[35] In approximately half of these cases, the clinical presentation was consistent with acute pyelonephritis (APN).[33] Another population-based study was performed in Göteborg, Sweden, to describe the incidence rate of first-time symptomatic UTI in children younger than 6 years. The cumulative incidence rate during the first 6 years of life was 6.6 percent for girls and 1.8 percent for boys.[76] The apparent increase in risk almost certainly relates to an increased awareness of the diagnosis of UTI as an explanation for fever in children and the more frequent practice of culturing the urine of children who are ill.

Several studies have investigated systematically the prevalence of UTI as the explanation for fever in febrile young children presenting to the emergency department. Although the definition of significant bacteriuria has varied among studies, the overall prevalence of UTI ranges between 3.3 and 5.3 percent.[39, 106] Female and white infants had significantly more UTIs, respectively, than did male and black infants. Higher prevalences occurred in uncircumcised boys or those with abdominal or suprapubic tenderness on examination.[106] White girls with a temperature of 39° C or higher had a prevalence of UTIs of 17 percent.[39]

RISK FACTORS FOR URINARY TRACT INFECTION

Uncircumcised Boys

The common problem of UTIs in uncircumcised boys, although suspected in the 1970s, was first documented in the 1980s by Ginsburg and McCracken.[27] The strongest evidence of a causal link between an intact foreskin and UTI comes from several studies conducted by Wiswell and colleagues.[129] In their series of patients, an overall 10-fold increased incidence of UTI was found in uncircumcised compared with circumcised male infants (1.12% vs. 0.11%, $p < .001$).[129] Wiswell and other investigators have continued to document this problem.[103, 130] Where and when rates of circumcision have decreased, the frequency of UTI in boys has increased. The presence of preputial folds in uncircumcised boys encourages a high density of bacterial growth and contamination of the urethral opening.[13] Circumcision reduces meatal contamination, thereby decreasing the ascent of bacteria into the bladder.[130] The high risk of UTI in uncircumcised boys diminishes with age (as the foreskin becomes more retractable) but is still present in the toddler age group.[15a]

Dysfunctional Voiding

Dysfunctional voiding is both a risk factor for the development of UTI and an occasional consequence of UTI. Dysfunctional voiding refers to a lack of coordination between the two functions that are essential for normal voiding to occur, namely, relaxation of the urethral sphincter and contraction of the detrusor muscle of the bladder. Ordinarily, the sphincter must relax as the detrusor contracts.[3] The failure of the sphincter to relax causes an obstruction to the outflow of urine. Consequently, voiding pressures and intravesicular pressure are high, the bladder becomes overdistended, dribbling instead of a good flow occurs, and residual urine remains in the bladder after the void. This dyscoordination is termed dyssynergia.[3] Clinical manifestations range from episodes of incontinence to the development of UTI. Constipation is a common occurrence because of the inability to relax the pelvic floor musculature. The presence of dysfunctional voiding also may promote the persistence of vesicoureteral reflux (VUR) and lead to recurrence or contralateral reflux after attempts are made at surgical correction of reflux.[57]

Constipation

The distended rectum in constipated children has been suggested to press on the bladder wall and produce a bladder outflow obstruction that may cause dysfunctional voiding. Urodynamic studies have demonstrated instability of the detrusor muscle in patients with functional constipation and associated enuresis or UTI.[131] Loening-Baucke[69] studied a group of children referred with encopresis and constipation. The history indicated that many were incontinent of urine, and 11 percent had histories of UTI. When the children were prescribed a vigorous regimen to alleviate the constipation, a dramatic improvement occurred in both the enuresis and the frequency of recurrent UTI.

Prospective evaluation of the toilet habits of 77 girls and 24 boys who were evaluated after having UTI was undertaken by Wan and colleagues.[122] Parents were instructed to use a "toilet diary" to record the frequency of voiding and stooling. An abnormal voiding habit was defined as infrequent urination ($\leq$4 times daily when awake), an abnormal voiding pattern ($>$4 hours between voidings), or the practice of avoidance maneuvers (repetitive habitual squirming, crossing of legs, or sitting on heels).[122] Constipation was defined as stooling less frequently than every third day. Children with and without abnormal imaging studies were compared. Although abnormal voiding patterns and constipation were identified in both groups, only 10 percent of children with normal images were without constipation or abnormal voiding compared with 60 percent of the group with abnormal images (p = .0001). These data strongly suggest that evaluation of children with UTI should include inquiry into these functional matters.

Sexual Activity

The well-recognized association in women of acute cystitis with sexual intercourse is reflected in the popular, now perhaps outdated, term *honeymoon cystitis*.[83] This phenomenon usually is related to the new onset of sexual activity or a recent change in sexual partners. A novel study of 15 patients with a history of recurrent UTI involved daily monitoring for the presence of UTI with dipslides and calendars that recorded episodes of intercourse, menses, and the occurrence of symptoms. Eleven patients experienced 16 infections; 12 infections occurred within 24 hours of an episode of intercourse. In 12 control subjects, 3 infections occurred, all within 24 hours of an episode of intercourse. The authors concluded that in sexually active women, most UTIs are related to intercourse. These results were reinforced more recently by a large prospective study from Seattle, Washington, which confirmed that the incidence of symptomatic UTI is high in sexually active young women and that a strong and independent association exists between UTI and recent sexual intercourse, recent use of a diaphragm with spermicide, and a history of recurrent UTI.[44]

Catheters

In the hospital setting, urinary catheters are major risk factors for acquisition of nosocomial infection. In adult patients, bacteriuria develops in at least 10 to 15 percent of hospitalized patients with indwelling urethral catheters.[116] The risk of developing an infection is approximately 3 to 5 percent per day of catheterization. The usual infecting strains include *Escherichia coli, Proteus, Pseudomonas, Klebsiella,* and *Serratia*. Many of the strains of bacteria causing infection will display antibiotic susceptibilities that are more resistant than usual. The route of infection may be either intraluminal or periurethral. Bacteremia is an unusual complication of nosocomial UTI. In a study of nosocomial infections in a children's hospital, catheter-associated UTI accounted for 48 percent of the UTIs. Secondary bacteremia occurred rarely, with an incidence of 2.9 percent.[16]

Pathogenesis

BACTERIOLOGY

Most uncomplicated UTIs are caused by members of a large family of gram-negative bacteria known as Enterobacteriaceae. In most instances, the urinary tract becomes infected by the ascending route. Bacteria derived from the fecal flora colonize the periurethral area and gain access to the urethra. The most common bacterial species is *E. coli,* in both primary and recurrent infections. Other gram-negative species that commonly cause UTI are *Klebsiella, Proteus, Enterobacter,* and *Citrobacter,* although virtually any enteric organism can cause infection of the urinary tract. The gram-positive bacterial species account for approximately 5 percent of UTIs and primarily include *Staphylococcus saprophyticus* and enterococcal species. Evidence has accumulated that *S. saprophyticus* is, after *E. coli,* the most common cause of primary, nonobstructive UTI in teenagers and young adults of both sexes.[46]

Rarely, the urinary tract may become infected hematogenously in the course of a bacteremic infection. This mechanism is thought to account for at least some cases of neonatal UTI. However, increasingly, evidence indicates that even in the neonate, most infections occur by the ascending route.

VIRULENCE FACTORS

The key virulence factor for isolates of *E. coli* is the mechanism by which they attach or adhere to the uroepithelial cell.[117] Bacterial adherence is an essential initiating step in all infections. So-called uropathogenic bacteria, derived from the numerous species found in the fecal flora, can attach to specific receptor sites on the uroepithelium and can also bind in a nonspecific manner by electrostatic and hydrophobic bonds.[98] A principal means of attachment is through adhesins localized on specialized pili of the *E. coli*. These pili are referred to as P fimbriae because they can recognize and agglutinate erythrocytes of the P1 blood group; this P blood group antigen also is present on human uroepithelial cells. Evidence to support the notion of the increased pathogenicity or virulence of the P fimbriae comes from studies of *E. coli* recovered from children with infection at different levels of the urinary tract. For example, when *E. coli* strains recovered from patients with pyelonephritis are examined, 76 to 94 percent are P fimbriated; in contrast, strains of *E. coli* recovered from patients with cystitis or asymptomatic bacteriuria are 19 to 23 percent and 14 to 18 percent P fimbriated, respectively.[53, 121] Of interest, although P-fimbriated strains of *E. coli* are common in patients with pyelonephritis whose urinary tracts are completely normal, their frequency drops considerably when strains of *E. coli* are examined from patients with pyelonephritis associated with VUR. Apparently, this virulence characteristic (as well as others described later) is not necessary when reflux is present.[72]

The principal adhesin on the tip of the P fimbriae that fosters adherence to the uroepithelial cell is known as the PapG adhesin. Recently, 153 *E. coli* organisms recovered from the urinary tracts of infants and children with pyelonephritis were analyzed by polymerase chain reaction for class I, II, and III alleles of the pyelonephritis-associated adhesin gene *papG*. Strains with any class II *papG* alleles were found significantly more often in infants with normal anatomy and function or in infants with clinically insignificant abnormalities than they were in infants with significant abnormalities (90 of 119 vs. 14 of 34 infants; $p < .001$).[47] Again, this virulence factor is more important when the urinary tract is structurally normal than when anatomic features predispose to infection.

Other virulence factors related to the bacterial species causing UTI are the K antigen, hemolysins, colicins, resistance to the bactericidal action of serum, and increased iron-binding capacity. The K antigen is a capsular polysaccharide that constitutes an outer surface of the *E. coli* organism. The capsule has the capacity to impede phagocytosis and to shield the bacteria from lysis induced by complement.[45] Hemolysins are cytotoxic proteins that can damage renal tubular cells in vitro. Colicins, elaborated by "uropathogenic" strains of *E. coli,* kill other bacteria that are in their vicinity. In the presence of human serum, many bacteria are killed after activation of complement. Virulent *E. coli* organisms have the capacity to resist this bactericidal effect of serum. Another virulence factor found in bacteria is their ability to acquire and bind iron. Most bacteria require iron for optimal growth and metabolism and have developed mechanisms to acquire iron when the supply is limited. Increased iron-binding capacity, mediated by proteins such as aerobactin, which are made by some *E. coli* strains, provides additional pathogenic potential.

After reaching the bladder, P-fimbriated *E. coli* organisms can colonize the ureter even in the absence of VUR.[97] Bacterial colonization of the ureter affects ureteral peristalsis, leading to dilation and a physiologic obstruction. This dilation of the ureter and calyces favors a change in the shape of the renal papillae, which facilitates intrarenal reflux of colonizing bacteria at low pressure. APN will develop because the receptors for the P-fimbriated *E. coli* are present in the collecting duct and proximal tubules.[85, 97]

Experimental studies conducted by Roberts[97] have led to a theory of the chain of events involved in the process that ultimately leads to renal scarring. The initial event is the inoculation of the renal parenchyma with bacteria, which leads to an intense inflammatory response. This inflammation results in the release of toxic enzymes within the granulocytes and tubular lumen. Superoxide is released simultaneously, generating oxygen radicals that are toxic to the bacteria and to the tubular cells.[96] The resultant death of the tubules intensifies and extends the inflammatory process into the interstitium. At the same time, focal ischemia results from the intravascular aggregation of granulocytes and edema.[51] The tissue damage that results from the toxic enzymes, oxygen radicals, and ischemia culminates in the creation of renal scars.[97]

Clinical Presentation

CYSTITIS

Most children with cystitis present with urgency, frequency, or dysuria. Children who have the urge to urinate may have a history of difficulty in initiating the urinary stream. On occasion, children may complain of abdominal or suprapubic pain. If fever is present at all, it is low grade. Suprapubic tenderness may be present on palpation. The urine may be foul smelling and cloudy in appearance.

PYELONEPHRITIS

Many children who present with APN have impressive chills, spiking fevers, and complaints of back pain. They may have associated gastrointestinal complaints of vomiting and diarrhea, especially vomiting. Lower urinary tract symptoms such as frequency, urgency, dysuria, and suprapubic discomfort may or may not be present.

Other findings such as irritability, poor feeding, vomiting, decreased urinary output, and clinical evidence of dehydration are variable. In the youngest of children, APN usually presents as high fever without other localizing features.

PHYSICAL EXAMINATION

Features of the physical examination that should be emphasized include (1) an accurate measurement of blood pressure (hypertension may be present in patients who have chronic renal disease), general growth, and development (failure to thrive may be a sign of more chronic or recurrent UTI) and (2) a careful abdominal examination (which might reveal tenderness or a mass caused by either an enlarged bladder or an obstructed urinary tract).[119] An effort should be made to elicit the finding of costovertebral angle tenderness in children of all ages. The perineum should be inspected carefully to search for signs of irritation, scars, tears, signs of trauma, labial adhesions, or evidence of vulvovaginitis. In uncircumcised infants, the foreskin may not be retractable, leading to phimosis. A rectal examination should be considered to detect masses or poor sphincter tone, which might be associated with a neurogenic bladder.[119] The lower back should be observed for any lipoma, sinus, pigmentation, or tufts of hair that may be signs of an occult myelodysplasia. Neurologic examination of the lower extremities and evaluation of the bulbocavernosal reflex often reflect the neurologic integrity of the lower motor neuron reflex arcs. The bulbocavernosus reflex is elicited by squeezing the glans penis or clitoris and observing or feeling a reflex contraction at the external anal sphincter. Absence of this reflex is suggestive of a possible sacral lesion.[3]

ASYMPTOMATIC BACTERIURIA

A large body of work has been produced dealing with the issue of asymptomatic bacteriuria. Data were accumulated during a long-term study of the natural history of recurrent bacteriuria among schoolgirls in a well-defined community in central Virginia.[58] Girls were identified in the first grade and were observed prospectively for 10 years. Each year, approximately 0.5 percent of schoolgirls developed asymptomatic bacteriuria. The overall prevalence was 5 percent for the years between entrance to grade school and graduation from high school. Although it was billed as asymptomatic bacteriuria, approximately one third of the girls did have symptoms, and some were known to have had infection or, rarely, abnormalities of the urinary tract before the first screening. Just a few years after Kunin began his investigations, a similar study was conducted in Göteborg, Sweden. Beginning in 1970, 19,000 girls a year were screened routinely for bacteriuria in Göteborg schools at the ages of 7, 11, 14, and 16 years.[68] Once again, a substantial minority had a history of previous infection or symptoms that were referable to the urinary tract. Savage and colleagues[100] also studied covert bacteriuria in schoolgirls. In each instance, the prevalence of bacteriuria ranged from 0.7 percent[68] to 1.1 percent[58] to 1.6 percent.[100] The risks associated with asymptomatic bacteriuria are difficult to assess from these studies because patients who were truly asymptomatic were difficult to separate from those with symptoms.

Currently, physicians have relatively little enthusiasm for screening children of any age to discover the presence of asymptomatic bacteriuria. Most children clear the bacteriuria spontaneously, and treatment may be a disadvantage. The absence of pyuria in these specimens of urine provides additional evidence that the host is not perturbed by the presence of asymptomatic bacteriuria. The presence of bacteria of low virulence in the urine in asymptomatic patients seems to be protective. These strains appear to prevent invasion by other bacteria and, accordingly, provide a kind of biologic prophylaxis.[33, 54] Rather than screen asymptomatic populations of children, an appropriate approach is vigorous evaluation for the presence of UTIs in febrile children without an obvious focus of infection. In addition, health maintenance examinations should be used as an opportunity to screen for historical information that might suggest the need to collect a urine specimen for culture (Table 46–3). Items of importance include frequent episodes of unexplained fever, dribbling when urinating, enuresis, encopresis, constipation, urgency, frequency, and dysuria. In addition, of value is knowing when toilet training was accomplished, frequency of voiding, frequency of stooling, and any apparent difficulties associated with voiding such as difficulties in initiating the urinary stream. The practitioner also should inquire about so-called avoidance maneuvers (such as repetitive habitual squirming, crossing of legs, or sitting on heels)[122] and family history of UTI.

TABLE 46–3 ■ RENAL-FOCUSED HISTORY AND PHYSICAL EXAMINATION

History
Age of toilet training
Characteristics and frequency of voiding (urgency, dysuria, dribbling)
Frequency and characteristics of stooling
Family history of renal disease
Habitual squirming
Color and odor of urine
Unexplained episodes of fever

Physical Examination
Temperature
Blood pressure
Abdominal tenderness
Costovertebral angle tenderness
Suprapubic tenderness
Genital examination (irritation, scars, tears)
Rectal examination (sphincter tone, bulbocavernosus reflex)
Lower back (sinus, pigmentation, lipoma, tufts of hair)

Differential Diagnosis

INFECTIOUS

E. coli is by far the most common cause of infection in the urinary tract for both primary infections (in which *E. coli* causes 85% to 90% of infections) and recurrent infections (in which *E. coli* causes approximately 75% of infections). Virtually any other gram-negative enteric bacteria may cause infection. The more common etiologic agents include *Klebsiella, Proteus, Enterobacter, Serratia,* and *Pseudomonas. Proteus mirabilis* is a common cause of UTI in some series of boys and also in nosocomial infections of the urinary tract associated with catheterization.[55, 88] In young women, *S. saprophyticus* is second only to *E. coli* as a cause of cystitis. Rarely, *Staphylococcus epidermidis* has been reported as a cause of pyelonephritis in young boys with anatomic abnormalities of the urinary tract.[32]

In the context of bacteremia or septicemia, occasionally both the blood culture and urine culture are positive for the same bacterial species. In these instances, the kidney has been seeded as part of a hematogenous dissemination. Accordingly, any organism that is responsible for sepsis, such as *Haemophilus influenzae* type b, *Neisseria meningitidis, Neisseria gonorrhoeae, Staphylococcus aureus, Streptococcus pneumoniae,* or *Streptococcus pyogenes,* may be found in the urine.

Anaerobic infections of the urinary tract are rare occurrences in children despite the high density of gram-positive and gram-negative anaerobes in the fecal flora; this fact clearly relates to the probable lack of adherence of these bacterial species to the uroepithelium. Anaerobic infections of the urinary tract should be suspected when organisms are seen on Gram stain but do not grow in conventional culture or when the urine of symptomatic children shows no bacterial growth.[10] Another unusual infecting agent that should be suspected in instances in which the Gram stain of the urine is positive for gram-negative rods but the urine culture is negative is *H. influenzae*.[80]

Fungal infections of the urinary tract are most commonly caused by *Candida* spp. but also may be caused by *Cryptococcus neoformans*, *Aspergillus* spp., and the endemic mycoses.[115] Candiduria is an increasingly common form of nosocomial infection that may involve any level of the urinary tract.[37, 91] It often occurs in immunosuppressed patients, especially those who are receiving broad-spectrum antibiotics for treatment of documented or undocumented systemic infections. In many immunosuppressed patients, the infection is complicated by the presence of an indwelling urinary catheter.

Viruses also may cause infection of the urinary tract. For the most part, these infections involve the bladder rather than the kidney, although infection of any part of the urinary tract may occur. The principal etiologic agents are adenovirus and the enteroviruses, coxsackieviruses, and echoviruses. Mumps virus and hepatitis viruses occasionally have been implicated. Type 11 adenovirus has been the most common cause of acute hemorrhagic cystitis in school-age boys; type 21 has also been documented to be a cause of infection in this age group. In immunosuppressed patients, especially children who have undergone bone marrow transplantation or are recipients of kidney transplants, BK polyomavirus and adenovirus may cause hemorrhagic cystitis.[14, 65]

Granulomatous cystitis is the histopathologic description of cystitis caused by *Mycobacterium tuberculosis* as well as by schistosomiasis and other parasitic infections. Granulomata formed in response to certain parasites, such as *Toxocara* and microfilariae, also may contain numerous eosinophils. *Enterobius vermicularis* infection occasionally leads to signs and symptoms of cystitis and inflammatory changes of the bladder wall.

Xanthogranulomatous pyelonephritis is a rare, chronic, suppurative renal infection. Although it can occur at any age, it typically involves middle-aged women. Cases in children have been reported across all age groups, including infants.[1, 94] The patient usually presents with what appears to be an acute UTI, caused most often by *E. coli* or *Proteus* spp. Evaluation of the patient usually reveals a unilateral enlargement of the kidney, often accompanied by urolithiasis and sometimes a staghorn calculus. The differential diagnosis of the mass lesion includes neuroblastoma, Wilms tumor, tuberculosis, and renal carcinoma. The lesion is characterized histologically by granulomata, abscesses, and lipid-laden foam cells. Nephrectomy is the usual means of management.

Infectious urethritis caused by *N. gonorrhoeae* or *Chlamydia trachomatis* is a common cause of symptoms suggestive of UTI. In addition, any etiologic agents of vulvovaginitis also may cause inflammation of the distal urethra, with urgency, frequency, or dysuria; they include *Candida* spp., *Gardnerella vaginalis, Trichomonas vaginalis, S. pyogenes, S. pneumoniae, H. influenzae, C. trachomatis, Shigella* spp., and *Yersinia enterocolitica*.

NONINFECTIOUS

Urethral symptoms such as urgency, frequency, and dysuria may be caused by any factor or process that gives rise to inflammation in the lower urinary tract. Examples include mechanical irritation (that might result from insertion of foreign bodies, migration of pinworms, or masturbation) and chemical irritation (such as might arise from bubble baths or shampoos). Chemical cystitis has been reported from the inadvertent insertion of a vaginal contraceptive suppository (nonoxynol-9) into the bladder. Pharmacologic causes of urethral symptoms include cyclophosphamide and methenamine mandelate, both of which can lead to inflammatory changes in the urinary bladder. Several other agents used in the topical treatment of bladder cancer have been noted to cause cystitis.

Specific Diagnosis

COLLECTION OF A URINE SPECIMEN

Proper collection of a urine specimen is extremely important to facilitate interpretation of the culture. In toilet-trained children, a midstream clean-catch specimen is appropriate for evaluation. When this specimen is used, the definition of significant bacteriuria is 10^5 colony-forming units (CFU)/mL or more. The child is asked to void into the toilet. Straddling the commode in the opposite direction creates a natural separation between the urethra and the vulva. Cleansing of the perineum does not result in less contamination of the specimen and, therefore, no longer is encouraged.[101] The child is asked to begin voiding. A second or two after the void has been initiated, a sterile cup is passed into the stream. The hope is that the initial void will succeed in washing out the distal urethra, the site from which the urine specimen is most likely to be contaminated.

If the child is not toilet-trained, a specimen may be collected by urethral catheterization or suprapubic aspiration. When the urine is collected by urethral catheterization, the perineum is cleansed with 1 percent iodine. A properly sized catheter (10 or 12 French) or a size 5 feeding tube may be used. The catheter is lubricated and inserted into the urethra and threaded a short distance. The first few drops of urine should not be collected in the sterile container. This part of the specimen is the most likely to be contaminated with fecal flora from the distal urethra; unfortunately, these bacteria are not eliminated by the process of perineal cleansing. The remaining urine is collected in a sterile container and sent to the laboratory. When a urine specimen is collected by urethral catheterization, significant bacteriuria is defined as 50,000 CFU/mL or more. This method is preferred when only a small volume of urine in the bladder is anticipated and collecting a specimen of urine is necessary so that antibiotics can be initiated.

An alternative to the urethral catheterization is the suprapubic aspiration. Although some physicians might contend that catheterization is less traumatic than is suprapubic aspiration,[119] little evidence supports this notion. The procedure can be performed in children of any age; it has been used to obtain specimens of urine in pregnancy.[78] Urine culture specimens obtained by suprapubic aspiration are easy to interpret because the usual source of contamination, the distal urethra, has been bypassed. Accordingly, the presence of any bacteria in a specimen collected by suprapubic aspiration is significant, although most samples will contain 10^5 CFU/mL or more. The patient is in a supine position with the lower extremities flexed (Fig. 46–3 and Table 46–4). The suprapubic area is cleaned with iodine and alcohol. The symphysis pubis is located with the index finger. A 3-mL syringe is attached to a 1.5-inch, 22-gauge needle. A spinal needle (21-gauge, 2.5- or 3.0-inch) can be used in older

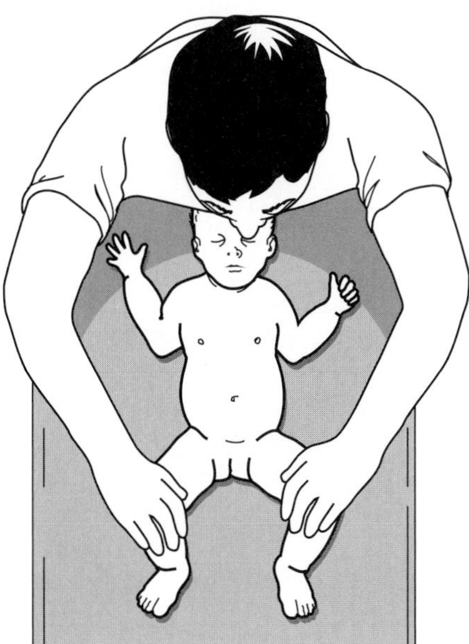

FIGURE 46–3 ■ Suprapubic aspiration technique, position of patient.

TABLE 46–4 ■ SUPRAPUBIC ASPIRATION TECHNIQUE

Step 1	Child should not have voided within 1 hour of the procedure.
Step 2	Restrain the infant in a supine, frog leg position.
Step 3	Clean the suprapubic area with povidone-iodine and alcohol.
Step 4	Identify the site of puncture at 1 to 2 cm above the symphysis pubis in the midline.
Step 5	Use a 22-gauge, 1½ inch needle (with 3-mL syringe attached to it) and puncture at 10° to 20° angle of the true vertical aiming cephalad. A second attempt can be performed at a similar angle aiming caudad.
Step 6	Exert suction gently as the needle is advanced until urine enters syringe. Aspirate urine with gentle suction. If urine is not obtained, further trials are unlikely to be successful.

patients. The needle is passed in the midline about 1.5 cm above the symphysis pubis. It is angled about 10 to 20 degrees from the vertical pointing in a slightly cephalad direction (Fig. 46–4). Negative pressure is applied while the needle is inserted. The procedure is most likely to be successful when the infant can be encouraged to drink and the diaper has been dry for at least 30 minutes before the procedure is performed. The success rate of suprapubic aspiration can be improved with the use of a portable ultrasound device.[28] If the suprapubic aspiration is unsuccessful, a catheterized specimen should be obtained. Complications of suprapubic aspiration are rare and include formation of a hematoma, perforation of the bowel, and formation of a suprapubic abscess.[92] Suprapubic aspiration is contraindicated if the patient has a bleeding diathesis.

The last method of urine collection is the bag technique. The perineum is washed with soap and water and allowed to dry. A sterile plastic bag is attached. The bag is removed as soon as the patient voids. If the patient has not voided in 20 minutes, the bag is removed, the perineum is cleaned again, and a new bag is attached. If this procedure is followed meticulously, a reasonable specimen can be collected.

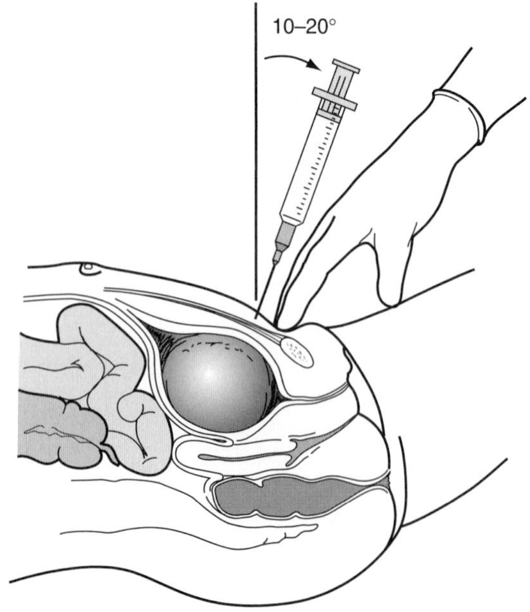

FIGURE 46–4 ■ Suprapubic aspiration technique, position of needle.

However, this specimen is susceptible to contamination from periurethral flora,[102] and, therefore, the technique is not recommended if the patient appears ill and antibiotics will need to be started immediately after the specimen of urine is collected. Furthermore, the results of the culture of a bagged specimen are useful only if they are negative. If the culture is positive, it must be repeated by a more reliable method.[2]

DIAGNOSIS OF URINARY TRACT INFECTION

The diagnosis of UTI hinges on the results of culture of a properly collected urine specimen. Unfortunately, disagreement within the literature is substantial as to the definition of significant bacteriuria.[30] As indicated in the previous section, the definition of UTI varies according to the method by which the urine is collected. This variance in definition acknowledges that, although the bladder urine is regarded as a sterile body fluid, contamination of any specimen that passes through the urethra may be present. The distal urethra frequently is colonized with coliforms derived from the gastrointestinal tract. The only urine specimen that bypasses the urethra and, therefore, is free of contamination is obtained by suprapubic aspiration. Accordingly, when a specimen is collected by this technique, any colony count of coliforms is significant. In urine that is collected by a midstream clean catch, significant bacteriuria is defined, most stringently, by the recovery of 100,000 CFU/mL or more (Table 46–5). For specimens of urine obtained by catheter, significant bacteriuria is defined as 50,000 CFU/mL or more. In each of these instances, physicians recognize that, although urine specimens containing lower colony counts may rarely represent true infection, for the most part, lower colony counts usually are the consequence of contamination of the specimen.[41]

Specimens of urine usually are inoculated onto two different kinds of solid media, one that supports the growth of only gram-negative enteric bacteria (e.g., MacConkey agar) and another that supports both gram-positive and gram-negative bacteria (e.g., 5% sheep blood agar), with use of a 0.001 calibrated loop. Colonies are counted the next day (18 hours later), and the total is multiplied by 1000 to determine the colony count. Unfortunately, the results of the urine culture are not available during the practitioner's first encounter with the ill child. Consequently, great interest is held for the development of a method that will predict the results of the urine culture so that appropriate antimicrobial therapy can be initiated presumptively at the time of the initial encounter. Both microscopic methods (to evaluate pyuria and bacteriuria) and biochemical tests (which can be evaluated with a dipstick) have been evaluated.

Microscopy

Two surrogate markers for UTI on microscopic assessment are pyuria and bacteriuria. One of the problems in assessing pyuria and bacteriuria has been the issue of the definition of significant microscopic pyuria and bacteriuria. How many

TABLE 46–5 ■ URINARY TRACT INFECTION—DEFINITIONS

Method of Collection	Colony Count (CFU/mL)
Clean catch	$\geq 10^5$
Catheter	$\geq 5 \times 10^4$
Suprapubic	Any

white blood cells (WBCs) in the urine are too many? Should the specimen of urine that is examined be centrifuged or uncentrifuged? How should the WBCs in a specimen of urine be enumerated? Should the number of WBCs on a centrifuged specimen be enumerated as the number per high-power field, or should they be enumerated on a counting chamber as the number of cells per cubic millimeter, as they would be in a sample of cerebrospinal fluid? If the urine is centrifuged, additional variables are introduced: the initial volume of urine, the duration of the spin, and the volume of urine used to resuspend the sediment. All of these variables will influence substantially the enumeration of WBCs per high-power field, especially the volume used to resuspend the sediment.

Methods to assess bacteriuria also have raised issues of definition. Should bacteriuria be assessed on a centrifuged specimen or an uncentrifuged specimen, and should the bacteria be evaluated on a wet mount or a Gram-stained specimen? Should bacteria be enumerated as the number per high-power field?

The standard definition of pyuria in the pediatric literature has been 5 WBCs per high-power field on a centrifuged specimen. Traditionally, microscopic bacteriuria has been expressed as the number of bacteria per high-power field on a Gram stain of a centrifuged specimen of urine. However, several investigations undertaken by Hoberman and colleagues[40] have shown that a so-called enhanced urinalysis has greater sensitivity, specificity, and positive predictive value than does the standard urinalysis. An enhanced urinalysis is performed on an uncentrifuged sample of urine that has been obtained by catheter. The urine is placed on a counting chamber, and the cells are enumerated as the number per cubic millimeter. A Gram stain is performed in a manner that standardizes the number of drops of urine that are assessed and the number of oil immersion fields that are reviewed. An enhanced urinalysis is considered to be positive when 10 WBCs/mm^3 or more are present and at least 1 gram-negative rod in 10 oil immersion fields is present. This definition of significant pyuria is much more sensitive than are previous definitions, and it has performed well for multiple investigators and in neonates as well as in older infants.[36, 66, 67] A systematic review of the existing literature to assess the performance of rapid diagnostic tests for UTI concluded that use of the traditional definition of pyuria (>5 WBCs per high-power field on a centrifuged specimen) is sufficiently poor that it cannot be recommended for making a presumptive diagnosis of UTI.[30]

An important note is that pyuria is not specific for UTI. In numerous other conditions, including fever, streptococcal infections, and Kawasaki disease, and after exercise, WBCs will be found in the urine. Accordingly, finding pyuria by no means ensures that an infection of the urinary tract is present. However, despite reports to the contrary, finding true UTI without pyuria is unusual.[156] In general, inflammation is expected to accompany infection. The absence of pyuria in children with UTIs is rare; it may occur when a child is being evaluated so early in the clinical course of the infection that the inflammatory response has not yet developed. It also may occur when a child is experiencing an episode of asymptomatic bacteriuria. However, the most likely explanation for significant bacteriuria by culture in the absence of pyuria is a contaminated specimen. In most cases when UTI has been reported to occur in the absence of pyuria, the definition of pyuria has been at fault. The requirement for 5 WBCs per high-power field on a centrifuged specimen corresponds to approximately 25 WBCs/mm^3; it is too stringent a requirement, with a low sensitivity for the detection of UTI in infants and children.

Urine Dipsticks

Urine dipsticks (or reagent strips) have been used to indicate the presence of leukocyte esterase (as a surrogate marker for pyuria) and urinary nitrite (which is converted from dietary nitrates by the presence of gram-negative bacteria in the urine). The conversion of dietary nitrates to nitrites by bacteria takes approximately 4 hours. The test result is most likely to be positive when the urine tested is the first morning void (representing a urine that has incubated in the bladder overnight) or a urine that has been in the bladder for at least 4 hours (e.g., obtained from an older child who may hold urine in the bladder for several hours at a time). The performance characteristics of both leukocyte esterase and nitrites will vary according to the definition used for a positive urine culture, the age and symptoms of the population being studied, and the method of urine collection. A nitrite test, although not a sensitive marker in children, is helpful when the result is positive because it is highly specific. However, a negative nitrate test result has little value in ruling out UTI.[20] The leukocyte esterase test has an average sensitivity of 83 percent.[21] However, it can have a sensitivity as high as 94 percent in settings in which UTIs are suspected clinically and a sensitivity as low as 52.9 percent when it is performed on febrile children, most of whom will not have UTI.[41] The specificity of leukocyte esterase (average 72%, with a range of 64% to 92%) generally is not as good as is the sensitivity, reflecting the nonspecificity of pyuria in general. Therefore, a positive leukocyte esterase test result should be interpreted with caution, depending in large part on the population being evaluated.[20]

Imaging

The current standard of care is to perform imaging procedures on children with a diagnosis of UTI. The categories of children for whom imaging generally is recommended are (1) any child who experiences an episode of APN, (2) boys of any age with their first UTI, (3) girls younger than 3 years with their first UTI, (4) girls older than 3 years with their second UTI, and (5) girls older than 3 years with their first UTI if an extenuating circumstance exists (Table 46–6). The extenuating circumstances include a family history of renal disease, recognition of abnormal voiding patterns, poor growth, hypertension, known abnormalities of the urinary tract, and failure to respond promptly to therapy. The imaging studies that usually are considered are renal ultrasonography, contrast voiding cystourethrography (VCUG) to detect VUR, renal cortical scintigraphy, and magnetic resonance imaging (MRI).

TABLE 46–6 ■ INDICATIONS FOR IMAGING PROCEDURES IN CHILDREN WITH URINARY TRACT INFECTION (UTI)

Any episode of acute pyelonephritis
Boys with their first UTI
Girls < 3 years with their first UTI
Girls ≥ 3 years with their second UTI
Girls ≥ 3 years with their first UTI if
- Positive family history
- Abnormal voiding patterns
- Poor growth
- Hypertension
- Abnormalities of urinary tract
- Failure to respond promptly to treatment

RENAL ULTRASONOGRAPHY

The renal ultrasound examination has replaced completely intravenous pyelography as a means to assess the gross anatomy of the urinary tract. In general, ultrasonography has been performed fairly promptly after diagnosis of the UTI. It is a noninvasive test that can describe the size and shape of the urinary tract, the presence of duplication and dilatations of the ureters, the presence of ureteroceles, and the existence of gross anatomic abnormalities such as a horseshoe kidney.[2] It is not sensitive enough, however, to signal consistently the presence of hydronephrosis, hydroureter, VUR, or renal scarring.[25] When ultrasonography was compared with intravenous pyelography for the detection of renal scars, wide interobserver variations were noted, with sensitivity ranging from 40 to 90 percent.[33]

Some investigators have questioned whether routine performance of renal ultrasonography is essential.[42] Given the current frequency with which fetal ultrasound examinations are performed during gestation, the likelihood that ultrasonography will disclose information that is not already known is small. In a study of 306 children younger than 2 years with UTIs, only one had a clinically important finding discovered by the routine performance of renal ultrasonography.[43] Most obstructions of the urinary tract are diagnosed in utero. Selective performance of renal ultrasonography is recommended for children with UTI who do not respond promptly to antibiotic therapy (i.e., have persistent fever or abdominal findings) and in those who did not have a prenatal ultrasound examination performed beyond 30 weeks of gestation at a reliable center.

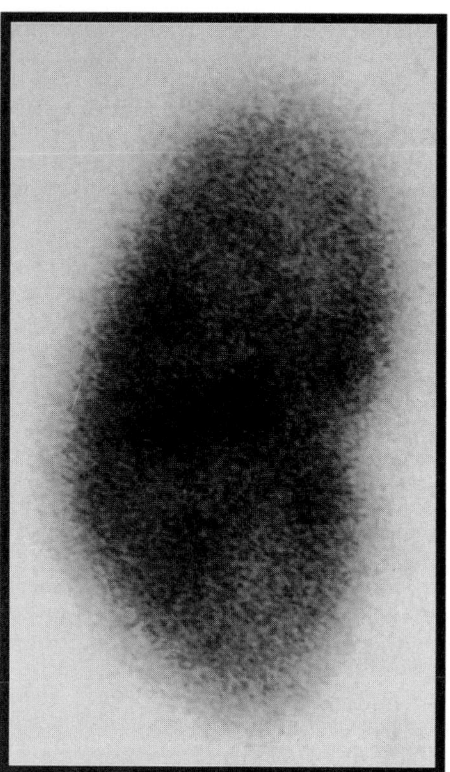

FIGURE 46–5 ■ Normal renal scintigram.

RENAL SCINTIGRAPHY

In patients with presumed APN, renal scintigraphy with technetium Tc 99m dimercaptosuccinic acid (DMSA) or glucoheptonate has been shown to be the most practical and reliable method for the detection of APN.[104] DMSA and glucoheptonate are amino acids that are cleared by the renal tubules. When these amino acids are labeled with technetium and injected intravenously, they can be used to create an image of the kidney, which reflects vascular flow and tubular function (Fig. 46–5). In experimentally induced APN in piglets, the DMSA scan had a sensitivity of 87 percent and a specificity of 100 percent in demonstrating lesions consistent with APN compared with histology as the "gold standard."[99] In most patients with APN, renal scintigraphy performed during the acute phase of the illness will show a decreased uptake of DMSA (Fig. 46–6). High-resolution pinhole images of the kidney reveal focal, multifocal, or diffuse areas of decreased uptake of isotope in the kidney without loss of volume and with the maintenance of the contour of the kidney.[104] DMSA renal scintigraphy can be used to localize the level at which the urinary tract is infected, specifically distinguishing between acute cystitis and APN with a sensitivity of a little less than 90 percent. Rarely, a patient may present with classic signs and symptoms of APN in whom renal scintigraphy does not demonstrate the usual findings.[26]

The DMSA and glucoheptonate scans also can be used to indicate the presence of renal scars that result from an episode of APN. The scar is indicated by an area in which uptake of the radioisotope is decreased (Fig. 46–7). However, in this case, the contour of the kidney is not preserved. Scarring also may be indicated by an overall reduction of the size of the kidney. Hansson and colleagues[33] prospectively observed 175 children, aged 0 to 5 years, from their first recognized nonobstructive UTI. Abnormal findings 1 year after UTI occurred in 38 percent according to DMSA scintigraphy and in 11 percent according to intravenous pyelography. Most of the additional children identified by scintigraphy

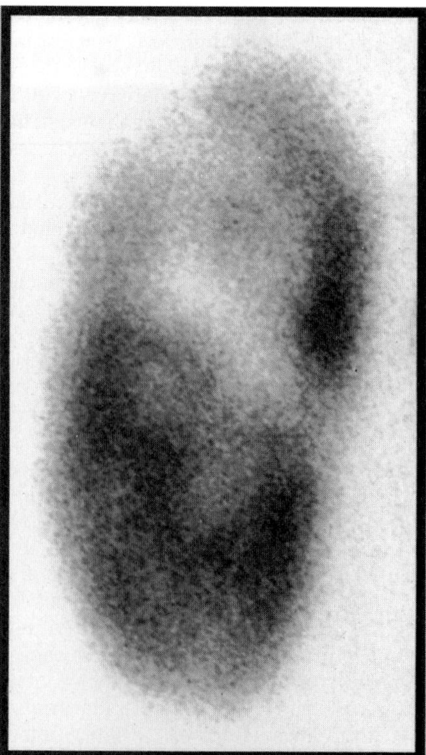

FIGURE 46–6 ■ Scintigram showing acute pyelonephritis, manifesting as a photon-deficient area in the upper pole.

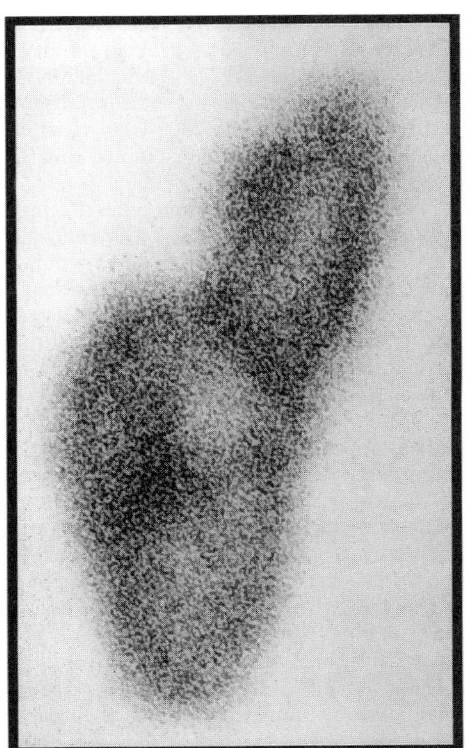

FIGURE 46–7 ■ Scintigram showing a renal scar with loss of the normal contour.

had involvement of a relatively small proportion of the kidney. Renal scintigraphy is by far the most sensitive study to indicate the presence of small renal scars that may occur after APN.

MAGNETIC RESONANCE IMAGING

MRI can be used to detect the presence of APN. Two studies by Lonergan and colleagues[73, 89] showed a sensitivity and a specificity of MRI that are equal to and perhaps even greater than those of renal scintigraphy with DMSA. In both instances, the best pulse sequence for the demonstration of areas of APN with MRI was gadolinium-enhanced fast spin-echo inversion recovery. These results have been confirmed by others.[62] However, several investigators have urged that MRI not become a screening test for children with UTI until the detection of minor changes in the renal parenchyma (by either DMSA or MR) has been proved to be of clinical importance.[62, 74]

VOIDING CYSTOURETHROGRAPHY

Two types of cystography are available for the diagnosis of VUR, fluoroscopic contrast VCUG and radionuclide cystography. Contrast VCUG has excellent anatomic resolution and provides detailed images of the bladder and the urethra. It can be used to specifically label the degree of reflux (according to the international classification)[59]; to look for trabeculations, diverticula, or ureteroceles of the bladder; and to outline the urethra (which is essential to identify posterior urethral valves causing obstruction). Radionuclide cystography provides less anatomic detail and is most useful when urethral disease is not suspected and when the patient has no history of voiding dysfunction. It is used to observe patients who are known to have reflux (to assess whether reflux is still present) and can be used for screening purposes in siblings of children with reflux and in children of adults known to have had reflux. Compared with conventional contrast VCUG, the amount of radiation exposure is reduced substantially when the radioisotope is used.

The international classification of reflux is a universally used system involving five degrees of reflux.[59] Grade I is reflux into the proximal ureter; grade II is reflux into the pelvis; and grades III, IV, and V are reflux with mild, moderate, and severe dilatation of the pelvis and calyces, respectively (Fig. 46–8).

The desire to perform VCUG on children who have experienced a symptomatic UTI is to determine the presence of VUR. Children who have VUR are at risk for developing reflux nephropathy—permanent renal damage secondary to the reflux of infected urine into the kidney. Because reflux often resolves spontaneously over several years, the purpose of identifying the child with VUR is to recommend antibiotic prophylaxis until the reflux either has resolved spontaneously or, in cases of high degrees of reflux, has been corrected surgically.

Although imaging of children with UTI is routine, little evidence exists that diagnostic imaging of children after their first UTI results in prevention of renal scarring, hypertension, or renal failure.[18] In a systematic overview of the literature using the MEDLINE database, no controlled trials or analytic studies evaluating or comparing different management strategies with regard to imaging were

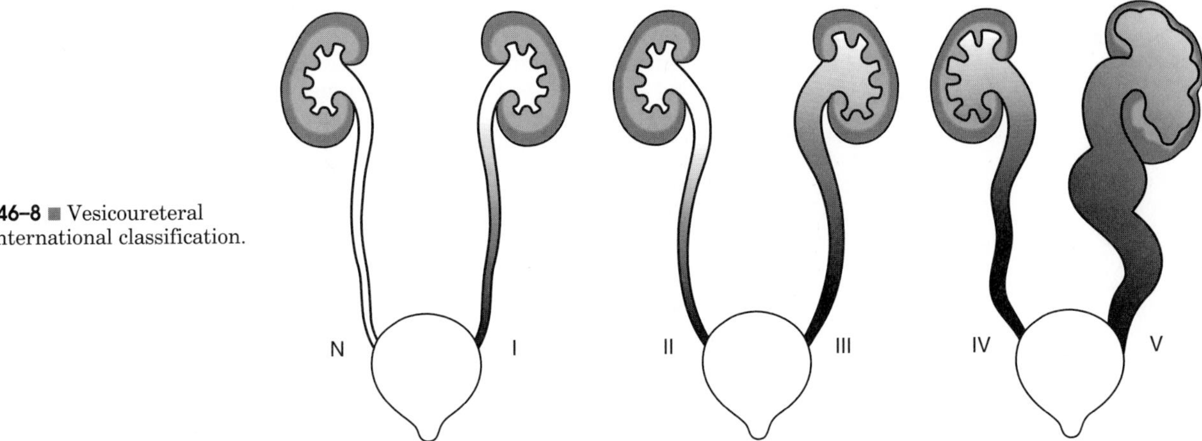

FIGURE 46–8 ■ Vesicoureteral reflux, international classification.

discovered.[18] If studies can show with certainty that antibiotic prophylaxis to prevent UTI in children with VUR is superior to placebo in the prevention of renal scarring, the necessity and import of performing VCUG will be established. Changing attitudes toward the use of antibiotics may render performing a trial of antibacterial prophylaxis compared with no prophylaxis in children with severe reflux possible.

Treatment

ANTIBIOTICS FOR TREATMENT OF THE ACUTE INFECTION

The treatment of UTI is influenced by the age of the patient, the probable site of infection (cystitis or APN), the degree of toxicity, and the likelihood of adherence to the treatment regimen. Oral antimicrobial therapy is appropriate for children with cystitis as well as for older children with suspected APN who are neither toxic nor vomiting. The more complex issue is the management of the young infant with high fever in whom the likely diagnosis is APN. These children traditionally have been admitted to the hospital for parenteral administration of antibiotics.

Numerous choices of oral antimicrobials are available for the patient who presents with presumed cystitis (Table 46–7). Alternatives include amoxicillin–potassium clavulanate; second-generation cephalosporins, such as cefuroxime and cefprozil; third-generation cephalosporins, such as cefixime, cefpodoxime, ceftibuten, and cefdinir; and the combination agent trimethoprim-sulfamethoxazole. In general, neither amoxicillin nor first-generation cephalosporins are recommended for first-line therapy because many (30% to 50%) *E. coli* now are inherently resistant to these agents. Because of some geographic variability in the prevalence of resistance, the practitioner should check with local infectious disease specialists to verify these susceptibility patterns. In the older patient who appears ill but is not toxic, a repeated visit or telephone follow-up is indicated to be sure that recovery is progressing as predicted. If fever is present, the patient generally will become afebrile within 1 or 2 days, although on occasion it may take a bit longer. If other indices of recovery, such as general well-being, appetite, and playfulness, are improving appropriately, the persistence of fever is not too alarming. If susceptibility test results are available and the organism causing infection is susceptible to the antimicrobial being used, repeating the urine culture after 24 hours is not necessary. However, urine is expected to sterilize within this time frame. The rapid sterilization of urine is a testimony to the fact that virtually all the antibiotics that are used to treat UTIs are concentrated in the kidney and excreted in the urine.

TABLE 46–7 ■ ANTIBIOTIC TREATMENT

Oral	
Amoxicillin + potassium clavulanate	45 mg/kg/day in 2 divided doses
Cefuroxime	30 mg/kg/day in 2 divided doses
Cefprozil	30 mg/kg/day in 2 divided doses
Cefixime	10 mg/kg/day in a single dose
Cefpodoxime	9 mg/kg/day in a single dose
Ceftibuten	10 mg/kg/day in a single dose
Cefdinir	14 mg/kg/day in a single dose
Trimethoprim-sulfamethoxazole	10 mg/kg/day (trimethoprim) in 2 divided doses
Parenteral	
Ampicillin + sulbactam	200 mg/kg/day in 4 divided doses
Cefuroxime	150 mg/kg/day in 3 divided doses
Cefotaxime	200 mg/kg/day in 4 divided doses
Ceftriaxone	80 mg/kg/day in a single dose
Ceftazidime	150 mg/kg/day in 3 divided doses
Gentamicin	7.5 mg/kg/day in 3 divided doses

Duration of treatment for patients who are presumed to have cystitis has been controversial. Conventional recommendations are for 7 to 10 days of antimicrobial therapy. Short courses of therapy, varying from single-dose regimens to 3- or 4-day courses, have been evaluated with mixed results. The potential advantages of short-course therapy include the likelihood of improved adherence to the drug regimen, lower cost of drug, and fewer undesirable side effects, including less alteration of normal flora.[105] In several studies comparing short-course and traditional therapies, no significant differences were found in bacteriologic cure rates. However, differences were found in rates of recurrent infections, with an increase in recurrences in the short-course therapy groups.[4, 75, 78a] In many other studies, although no differences in outcome were demonstrated, the sample size was insufficient to warrant the conclusion that the two durations of therapy were equivalent.[79, 105] Khan[56] pooled data on the same studies evaluated by others[79] and concluded that single-dose therapy was effective in patients with normal anatomy and function of the urinary tract. However, the normalcy of the urinary tract is not known at the time that antibiotics are initiated in most cases of UTI, thereby limiting the application of his recommendation. A meta-analysis (and the most comprehensive review of the data) was performed by Tran and coworkers[120] after review of 22 published trials and a total of 1279 patients. Amoxicillin in a single dose and trimethoprim-sulfamethoxazole as either a single dose or a 3-day regimen were the short-course regimens most commonly evaluated. The authors found that short-course antimicrobial therapy is less effective than is therapy of conventional duration, largely because of the ineffectiveness of single-dose amoxicillin. A 3-day course of trimethoprim-sulfamethoxazole was an effective alternative to the standard course of treatment.

Management of the young infant with presumed APN has been controversial. A study conducted by Hoberman and colleagues[43] compared oral therapy with cefixime (for 14 days) with a combination of intravenous therapy with cefotaxime (for 3 or 4 days) plus oral cefixime for 9 to 10 days. Children were eligible for this study if they were between 1 and 24 months of age and presented to their physician with temperature above 38.3°C and were found to have a positive enhanced urinalysis (≥10 WBCs/mm^3 and 1 organism per 10 oil immersion fields). After blood and urine cultures, complete blood count, C-reactive protein determination, and erythrocyte sedimentation rate were performed, the children were randomized. Outcome was evaluated with regard to the short-term measures of sterilization of the urine and time to defervescence and the long-term measures of reinfection and scarring 6 months after the initial infection. No statistically significant differences in any outcome were found. Accordingly, oral antimicrobial therapy with cefixime is recommended for the management of suspected APN in selected infants.

MANAGEMENT OF DYSFUNCTIONAL VOIDING

If a history of dysfunctional voiding is obtained, a behavioral modification approach may be helpful. The key features include frequent volitional voiding every 2 to 3 hours until the voiding pattern has been reestablished, increased water intake (1 L/day) in addition to all other fluids consumed, correction of constipation, and adequate perineal hygiene.[24] Referral to a pediatric urologist may be necessary. Children who demonstrate persistent inability to relax their sphincters may require training that involves relaxation techniques reinforced with biofeedback. Pharmacologic treatment with anticholinergics may be necessary if uninhibited bladder contractions are demonstrated with urodynamic studies.[24] Special attention must be paid to the management of constipation if anticholinergics are begun because they will exaggerate the problem.

ANTIBIOTIC PROPHYLAXIS

Although antibiotic prophylaxis commonly is recommended for children with recurrent UTIs,[63] only limited data support this position. In a review of the literature, Le Saux and colleagues[63] found sparse data of low quality to support the use of antibiotic prophylaxis in children with a normal urinary tract. A meta-analysis by Williams and colleagues[126] revealed five randomized controlled trials assessing the use of prophylactic therapy. Of these, only two trials with 71 children evaluated the effectiveness of long-term, low-dose antibiotics to prevent UTIs.[70, 108] The authors concluded that well-designed, randomized, placebo-controlled trials still are required to evaluate this commonly used intervention.

MANAGEMENT OF VESICOURETERAL REFLUX

The clinical significance of VUR as a predisposing factor for UTIs in general or APN in particular and its contribution to the formation of renal scarring have been questioned recently. As a corollary to the latter, the question also has been framed as to whether long-term antibiotic prophylaxis will prevent renal damage in patients with VUR.[26] The authors concluded that the role of VUR in UTIs needs to be redefined through well-designed, multicenter, prospective, randomized, controlled studies using state-of-the-art renal imaging techniques.

Epidemiology

The incidence of VUR in the general population is believed to be approximately 1 percent.[17] Children usually are tested for the possibility of VUR in one of two clinical situations—during the assessment of prenatally diagnosed hydronephrosis and in the evaluation of a UTI. Reflux is diagnosed in approximately 10 percent of cases of prenatally identified hydronephrosis; it often is high grade and occurs more frequently in boys than in girls in this situation.[29, 81] The incidence of reflux in girls evaluated after their first UTI is between 25 and 40 percent.[21]

An increased incidence of VUR within families suggests a genetic mode of transmission.[52] Rates for prevalence of VUR in identical and fraternal twins were 80 and 35 percent, respectively, providing evidence that this trait is transmitted in an autosomal dominant fashion. Siblings of children identified to have VUR as part of an evaluation for UTI have a much greater chance of having reflux than does the normal population.[48, 84] The presence of VUR in these siblings is accompanied by silent renal damage.[11] In addition, a girl who has reflux has a risk of having affected offspring as often as 65 percent of the time.[17] Reflux is much more common among white than black children.

Natural History of Reflux

The natural history of reflux is for spontaneous resolution to occur over time, a longer period being necessary in the more severe types of reflux. Average figures for spontaneous resolution are 80 to 86 percent for grade II reflux and 40 to 46 percent for grade III reflux during a 5-year period. In a report from Skoog and associates,[107] spontaneous resolution occurred within 1.65 years of diagnosis in patients with grade II reflux, but 1.97 years was required for resolution in patients with grade III reflux ($p < .04$). Ninety percent of patients with grades of reflux between I and III who ultimately had resolution of their reflux experienced this result within 5 years. The rate of resolution was approximately 30 to 35 percent per year, although the duration of reflux was shorter for patients in whom the diagnosis was made before 1 year of age compared with patients who were older at the time of diagnosis.[5] There is no specific age in adolescence at which one can assume reflux will not resolve. Leneghan and colleagues[60] reported cessation of reflux after 14 years of age in 27 percent of patients observed without surgical intervention.

Management of Reflux

The optimal management of children with high grades of reflux (grades III to V) has been the subject of numerous retrospective and prospective studies.[50] Since 1970, two large prospective randomized trials, the Birmingham Reflux study[7–9] and the International Reflux Study in Children,[95] have been performed to compare medical therapy (antibiotic prophylaxis) with surgical therapy (reimplantation of ureters). The International Reflux Study in Children reported results from both Europe and the United States. Because entry criteria were somewhat different, the results have been reported separately.*

In Europe and the United States, the surgical management of VUR is neither superior nor inferior to medical treatment. In both groups, new scars were acquired during the 5-year follow-up period, some in patients who did not demonstrate scarring at the time of entry. In other children, scars present at entry worsened.[90] No detectable differences were found between study groups in either renal function or renal growth. The number of episodes of infection also was similar in both groups. The only exception was a greater frequency of episodes of febrile UTIs (presumed pyelonephritis) in children receiving medical therapy. The choice of treatment, therefore, remains a value judgment governed by such local factors as preference of the parents, availability of skilled surgeons, availability of closely supervised medical treatment, and willingness to comply with prolonged periods of prophylaxis.

Does VUR predispose to pyelonephritis? Garin and associates[26] reviewed 10 studies of children with acute UTIs who underwent both DMSA scanning and VCUG. Selection of patients in at least one of the studies was biased toward the association between reflux and APN because the VCUG often was performed after the DMSA scan was reported to be abnormal. Six of 10 studies showed statistically significant results indicating that the presence of reflux definitely was associated with the occurrence of APN; all four of the remaining studies show a trend in the same direction.

*See references 22, 38, 49, 86, 95, 109, 110, 118, 123, 124.

Antimicrobial Prophylaxis

Although the use of antimicrobial prophylaxis has become routine in the management of children with VUR, substantial controversy currently surrounds this approach and an increasing literature challenges its benefit. Nonetheless, when the American Urological Association convened the Pediatric Vesicoureteral Reflux Guidelines Panel to analyze the literature about available methods for treatment of VUR, the panel recommended continuous antibiotic prophylaxis as initial treatment.[23] The panel acknowledged that the recommendation was based on limited scientific evidence. However, the opinion of the panel was that maintaining continuous urine sterility was beneficial for decreasing the risk of renal scarring and that this benefit outweighed the potential adverse effects of antibiotics. The panel also recommended surgical repair as initial therapy for patients with grade V reflux based on the opinion that such reflux is unlikely to resolve spontaneously with time, that surgery is effective for resolving severe reflux, and that these benefits outweigh the potential harms of surgery.[23]

Accepting for the moment that prophylaxis is the most effective medical therapy that can be offered to children with mild to moderate degrees of reflux, the duration of prophylaxis also is an issue. VUR spontaneously remits in most cases during the first 3 to 5 years of life. Conventional wisdom is that prophylaxis should be maintained until reflux ceases, either spontaneously or with surgical intervention. Greenfield and colleagues[31] suggest that two normal VCUGs 12 months apart are necessary before prophylactic antibiotics are discontinued. This recommendation is based on the observation that 27 percent of children will demonstrate VUR again after a single normal study. Greenfield maintains that administration of prophylactic antibiotics should continue until reflux resolves, no matter what the age. He supports this position by noting that older children with reflux may have new scars evolve when they become infected. In contrast, Belman[5] and Winberg[128] suggest that prophylaxis should be discontinued in children older than 7 years, even if low-grade reflux persists.

The only two antimicrobial agents that are recommended for prophylaxis of the urinary tract are nitrofurantoin and trimethoprim-sulfamethoxazole. Each agent is used in half the usual therapeutic dose and given before bedtime. These two agents can be used for months to years without the emergence of antibiotic resistance. In contrast, most other agents that are used for treatment of UTI are not recommended for prophylaxis. Invariably, if agents such as amoxicillin, cephalexin, and second- and third-generation cephalosporins are used for prophylaxis, infection with resistant strains will emerge within weeks.

Surgery

When antireflux surgery is undertaken, a variety of approaches are available, no one of which appears to be superior. In most cases, the surgical approach is intravesicular. Interest has been gaining in evaluation of an extravesicular approach to reimplantation of the ureters.[77] The advantage of extravesicular approaches seems to be a diminution of the intensity and frequency of bladder spasms and, therefore, less requirement for postoperative analgesia. When experienced senior surgeons embark on reimplantation of ureters, the outcome generally is successful.[22] Repeated operation for persistence or recurrence of reflux seldom is required. Rarely, when children younger than 2 years undergo surgery, ureteral obstruction may result; its persistence mandates a second operation.[95]

A new technique for the management of VUR is endoscopic correction with use of autologous chondrocytes.[12] Cartilage is harvested from the posterior auricle and grown in culture during a 6-week period. The autologous chondrocytes are injected into the ureterovesical junction of refluxing ureters by the transurethral route. In a study of 29 children (47 ureters) with grade II to grade IV VUR, endoscopic injection of chondrocytes corrected reflux in 55 percent of ureters at 3 months. Additional injections were successful in achieving an overall success rate of 86 percent. The correction of the reflux was maintained in 70 percent of the ureters and 75 percent of the patients.

Prognosis

In general, review of reports suggests that the short-term prognosis for previously normal children who experience an episode of UTI is excellent. In a large cohort of 306 children experiencing their first febrile episode of UTI, 40 percent were found to have reflux.[43] Only five (1.6%) of the children had grade IV reflux; none had grade V reflux. Most of the children with grades I, II, and III reflux can be expected to have spontaneous resolution of the process during the next several years. Although many reports indicate that recurrent UTI is common in children who have recovered from UTI, recurrence during the first 6 months after recovery from the index episode of UTI was infrequent in this cohort of children. Recurrences are most common in the early months after symptomatic or asymptomatic UTI. Symptomatic reinfections (fever, pyuria, and positive urine culture) occurred in 7 children treated orally and in 11 children treated intravenously (for a total of 5.9% of children) during the 6-month follow-up period. Asymptomatic bacteriuria (positive urine culture in the absence of fever and pyuria) occurred in one child treated orally and in two children treated intravenously (1.0%). Renal scarring occurred in 8.5 percent of all children; the average percentage of renal parenchymal involvement was 8.25 percent. In children who had an abnormal renal scintigram at the time of diagnosis, the frequency of scarring was 15.3 percent. None of the children with a normal renal scintigram at the time of diagnosis developed scars. This experience, reflecting an aggressive approach to the early diagnosis of UTI in infancy, is encouraging with regard to outcome.

When children with a diagnosis of UTI are found to have anomalies of the urinary tract, congenital dysplasias, or massive degrees of reflux, the prognosis is less optimistic. The most profound degrees of scarring are associated with advanced degrees of reflux. Reflux nephropathy is a major cause of severe hypertension in children and young adults. It occasionally progresses to chronic renal failure,[112] which accounts for approximately 25 percent of the children in the United Kingdom with end-stage renal failure requiring regular dialysis or transplantation.[64] Although surgical correction may relieve the reflux, the overall outcome for children with reflux who have undergone surgical correction has not been shown to be materially better than that for children who have been managed medically.[86, 87, 110] In the most recent investigation of this issue, Smellie and colleagues[114] undertook a randomized trial of medical management versus surgical correction in 53 children with bilateral severe VUR and bilateral nephropathy. The glomerular filtration rate of the children at enrollment was 20 mL/min per 1.73 m^2 body surface area. Children with this degree of severity of renal impairment are, fortunately, rare; recruitment to this study took 5 years. No significant differences were observed in glomerular filtration rate, renal growth, or scarring during a 10-year follow-up period. The failure to find differences may be due to the small sample size and broad heterogeneity of the study group. Nonetheless, no convincing evidence that outcome for renal function is improved by surgical correction of VUR in children with bilateral disease exists.

Prevention

Primary prevention of UTI can be accomplished in infant boys by promoting the practice of circumcision. Whether this procedure can be justified simply to prevent UTI in the context of social rituals is uncertain. However, circumcision should be recommended for selected groups of patients, including newborns with prenatal hydronephrosis who are found to have VUR in the neonatal period, boys with high grades of VUR, and boys in whom VUR is associated with unilateral renal agenesis or multicystic kidney.[13]

Other commonly recommended strategies to prevent UTI, such as the avoidance of bathing in tubs or swimming and the instruction in correct wiping techniques, are not accompanied by convincing evidence.[34] However, the relationship between constipation and UTI is well known. Effective treatment of the constipation results in normalization of bladder function and cessation of UTIs.[69]

The role of prophylactic antibiotics for patients with VUR is discussed in the section on treatment. Prophylaxis has not been shown in large, prospective, placebo-controlled, randomized trials to effectively reduce the frequency of UTI and subsequent renal scarring either in patients with reflux or in those who have experienced an episode of APN. Although definite biologic plausibility to this likelihood exists, strong evidence is lacking.

An additional preventive strategy is immunization with a potential vaccine. A small pilot study was reported from Turkey.[82] Ten otherwise healthy girls aged 5 to 11 years with recurrent UTIs were immunized with inactivated uropathogenic bacteria intramuscularly once a week for 3 consecutive weeks. A booster injection was given after 6 months. The frequency of infection was compared with that in a group of 10 age-matched girls with UTI who were not immunized. Immunization therapy caused a significant reduction in the frequency of infection and an increase in the concentration of the secretory component of IgA in the urine. Other mucosa, such as vaginal and oral surfaces, are alternative targets for vaccine delivery.

REFERENCES

1. Aia-ul-Miraj, M., and Cheema, M. A.: Xanthogranulomatous pyelonephritis presenting as a pseudotumor in a 2 month old boy. J. Pediatr. Surg. *35*:1256–1258, 2000.
2. American Academy of Pediatrics, Committee on Quality Improvement, Subcommittee on Urinary Tract Infection: Practice parameter. The diagnosis, treatment, and evaluation of the initial urinary tract infection in febrile infants and young children. Pediatrics *103*:843–853, 1999.
3. Austin, P. F., and Ritchey, M. L.: Dysfunctional voiding. Pediatr. Rev. *21*:336–340, 2000.
4. Avner, E. D., Ingelfinger, J. R., Herrin, J. T., et al.: Single-dose amoxicillin therapy of uncomplicated pediatric urinary tract infections. J. Pediatr. *102*:623–627, 1983.
5. Belman, A. B.: Vesicoureteral reflux. Pediatr. Clin. North Am. *44*:1171–1190, 1997.
6. Belman, A. F.: A perspective on vesicoureteral reflux. Urol. Clin. North Am. *22*:139, 1995.
7. Birmingham Reflux Study Group: Prospective trial of operative versus nonoperative treatment of severe vesicoureteric reflux: Two years' observation in 96 children. Br. Med. J. *287*:171–174, 1983.
8. Birmingham Reflux Study Group: A prospective trial of operative versus nonoperative treatment of severe vesicoureteric reflux: 2 years' observation in 96 children. Contrib. Nephrol. *39*:169–185, 1984.
9. Birmingham Reflux Study Group: Prospective trial of operative versus nonoperative treatment of severe vesicoureteric reflux in children: Five years' observation. Br. Med. J. *295*:237–241, 1987.
10. Brook, I.: Urinary tract infection caused by anaerobic bacteria in children. Urology *16*:596–598, 1980.
11. Buonomo, C., Treves, S. T., Jones, B., et al.: Silent renal damage in symptom-free siblings of children with vesicoureteral reflux: Assessment with technetium Tc 99m dimercaptosuccinic acid scintigraphy. J. Pediatr. *122*:721–723, 1993.
12. Caldamone, A. A., and Diamond, D. A.: Long-term results of the endoscopic correction of vesicoureteral reflux in children using autologous chondrocytes. J. Urol. *165*:2224–2227, 2001.
13. Cascio, S., Colhoun, E., and Puri, P.: Bacterial colonization of the prepuce in boys with vesicoureteral reflux who receive antibiotic prophylaxis. J. Pediatr. *139*:160–162, 2001.
14. Childs, R., Sanchez, C., Engler, H., et al.: High incidence of adeno- and polyomavirus-induced hemorrhagic cystitis in bone marrow allotransplantation for hematological malignancy following T cell depletion and cyclosporine. Bone Marrow Transplant. *22*:889–893, 1998.

15a. Craig, J. C., Knight, J. F., Sureshkuman, P., et al. Effect of circumcision on incidence of urinary tract infection in preschool boys. J. Pediatr. *128*:23–27, 1996.

15b. Crain, E., and Gershel, J. C.: Urinary tract infections in febrile infants younger than 8 weeks of age. Pediatrics *86*:363–367, 1990.

16. Davies, H. D., Jones, E. L., Sheng, R. Y., et al.: Nosocomial urinary tract infections at a pediatric hospital. Pediatr. Infect. Dis. J. *11*:349–354, 1992.
17. Decter, R. M.: Vesicoureteral reflux. Pediatr. Rev. *22*:205–210, 2001.
18. Dick, P. T., and Feldman, W.: Routine diagnostic imaging for childhood urinary tract infections: A systematic overview. J. Pediatr. *128*:15–22, 1996.
19. Djojohodipringgo, R., Abdulhamed, R. H., Thahir, S., et al.: Bladder puncture in newborns: A bacteriologic study. Paediatr. Indones. *16*:527–534, 1976.
20. Downs, S. M.: Diagnostic testing strategies in childhood urinary tract infections. Pediatr. Ann. *28*:670–676, 1999.
21. Downs, S. M.: Technical report: Urinary tract infections in febrile infants and young children. The Urinary Tract Subcommittee of the American Academy of Pediatrics Committee on Quality Improvement. Pediatrics *103*:e54, 1999.
22. Duckett, J. W., Walker, R. D., and Weiss, R.: Surgical results: International Reflux Study in Children—United States branch. J. Urol. *148*:1674–1675, 1992.
23. Elder, J. S., Peters, C. A., Arant, B. S., et al.: Pediatric Vesicoureteral Reflux Guidelines Panel summary report on the management of primary vesicoureteral reflux in children. J. Urol. *157*:1846–1851, 1997.
24. Farhat, W., and McLorie, G.: Urethral syndromes in children. Pediatr. Rev. *22*:17–20, 2001.
25. Foresman, W. H., Hulbert, W. C., Jr., and Rabinowitz, R.: Does urinary tract ultrasonography at hospitalization for acute pyelonephritis predict vesicoureteral reflux? J. Urol. *165*:2232–2234, 2001.
26. Garin, E. H., Campos, A., and Homsy, Y.: Primary vesicoureteral reflux: Review of current concepts. Pediatr. Nephrol. *12*:249–256, 1998.
27. Ginsburg, C. M., and McCracken, G. H., Jr.: Urinary tract infections in young infants. Pediatrics *69*:409–412, 1982.
28. Gochman, R. F., Karasic, R. B., and Heller, M. B.: Use of portable ultrasound to assist urine collection by suprapubic aspiration. Ann. Emerg. Med. *20*:631–635, 1991.
29. Gordon, A. C., Thomas, D. F. M., Arthur, R. J., et al.: Prenatally diagnosed reflux: A follow up study. Br. J. Urol. *65*:407–412, 1990.
30. Gorelick, M. H., and Shaw, K. N.: Screening tests for urinary tract infection in children: A meta-analysis. Pediatrics *104*:e54, 1999.
31. Greenfield, S. P., Ng, M., and Wan, J.: Experience with vesicoureteral reflux in children: Clinical characteristics. J. Urol. *158*:574–577, 1997.
32. Hall, D. E., and Snitzer, J. A., III: *Staphylococcus epidermidis* as a cause of urinary tract infections in children. J. Pediatr. *124*:437–438, 1994.
33. Hansson, S., Martinell, J., Stokland, E., et al.: The natural history of bacteriuria in childhood. Infect. Dis. Clin. North Am. *11*:499–512, 1997.
34. Hellerstein, S.: Urinary tract infections in children: Why they occur and how to prevent them. Am. Fam. Physician *57*:2440–2446, 1998.
35. Hellstrom, A., Hanson, E., Hansson, S., et al.: Association between urinary symptoms at 7 years old and previous urinary tract infection. Arch. Dis. Child. *66*:232–234, 1991.
36. Herr, S. M., Wald, E. R., Pitetti, R. D., and Choi, S. S.: Enhanced urinalysis improves identification of febrile infants ages 60 days and younger at low risk for serious bacterial illness. Pediatrics *108*:866–871, 2001.
37. Hitchcock, R. J., Pallett, A., Hall, M. A., et al.: Urinary tract candidiasis in neonates and infants. Br. J. Urol. *76*:252–256, 1995.
38. Hjalmas, K., Lohr, G., Tamminen-Mobius, T., et al.: Surgical results in the international reflux study in children (Europe). J. Urol. *148*: 1657–1661, 1992.
39. Hoberman, A., Chao, H. P., Keller, D. M., et al.: Prevalence of urinary tract infection in febrile infants. J. Pediatr. *123*:17–23, 1993.

40. Hoberman, A., Wald, E. R., Penchansky, L., et al.: Enhanced urinalysis as a screening test for urinary tract infection. Pediatrics *91*:1196–1199, 1993.
41. Hoberman, A., Wald, E. R., Reynolds, E. A., et al.: Pyuria and bacteriuria in urine specimens obtained by catheter from young children with fever. J. Pediatr. *124*:513–519, 1994.
42. Hoberman, A., and Wald, E. R.: Urinary tract infections in young febrile children. Pediatr. Infect. Dis. J. *16*:11–17, 1997.
43. Hoberman, A., Wald, E. R., Hickey, R. W., et al.: Oral versus initial intravenous therapy for urinary tract infections in young febrile children. Pediatrics *104*:79–86, 1999.
44. Hooten, T. M., Scholes, D., Hughes, J. P., et al.: A prospective study of risk factors for symptomatic urinary tract infection in young women. N. Engl. J. Med. *335*:468–474, 1996.
45. Horowitz, M. A., and Silverstein, S. C.: Influence of *Escherichia coli* capsule on complement fixation and on phagocytosis and killing by human phagocytes. J. Clin. Invest. *65*:82, 1980.
46. Hovelius, B., and Mardh, P.: *Staphylococcus saprophyticus* as a common cause of urinary tract infections. Rev. Infect. Dis. *6*:328–337, 1984.
47. Jantunen, M. E., Siitonen, A., Koskimies, O., et al.: Predominance of class II *papG* allele of *Escherichia coli* in pyelonephritis in infants with normal urinary tract anatomy. J. Infect. Dis. *181*:1822–1824, 2000.
48. Jerkins, G. R., and Noe, H. N.: Familial vesicoureteral reflux: A prospective study. J. Urol. *128*:774, 1982.
49. Jodal, U., Koskimies, O., Hanson, E., et al.: Infection pattern in children with vesicoureteral reflux randomly allocated to operation or long term antibacterial prophylaxis. J. Urol. *148*:1650–1652, 1992.
50. Jodal, U., Hansson, S., and Hjalmas, K.: Medical or surgical management for children with vesicoureteric reflux? Acta Paediatr. Suppl. *431*:53–61, 1999.
51. Kaack, M. B., Dowling, K. J., Patterson, G. M., et al.: Immunology of pyelonephritis. VIII. *E. coli* causes granulocytic aggregation and renal ischemia. J. Urol. *136*:1117–1122, 1986.
52. Kaefer, M., Curran, M., Treves, S. T., et al.: Sibling vesicoureteral reflux in multiple gestation births. Pediatrics *105*:800–804, 2000.
53. Kallenius, G., Mollby, R., Svensson, S. B., et al.: The pK antigen as receptor for the hemagglutination of pyelonephritogenic *Escherichia coli*. FEMS Microbiol. Lett. 7:297, 1980.
54. Kemper, K. J., and Avner, E. D.: The case against screening urinalyses for asymptomatic bacteriuria in children. Am. J. Dis. Child. *146*:343–346, 1992.
55. Khan, A. J., Ubriani, R. S., Bombach, E., et al.: Initial urinary tract infection caused by *Proteus mirabilis* in infancy and childhood. J. Pediatr. *93*:791–793, 1978.
56. Khan, A. J.: Efficacy of single-dose therapy of urinary tract infection in infants and children: A review. J. Natl. Med. Assoc. *86*:690–696, 1994.
57. Koff, S. A., Wagner, T. T., and Jayanthi, V. R.: The relationship among dysfunctional elimination syndromes, primary vesicoureteral reflux and urinary tract infections in children. J. Urol. *160*:1019–1022, 1998.
58. Kunin, C. M.: A ten-year study of bacteriuria in schoolgirls: Final report of bacteriologic, urologic and epidemiologic findings. J. Infect. Dis. *122*:382–393, 1970.
59. Lebowitz, R. L., Olbing, H., Parkkulainen, K. V., et al.: International system of radiographic grading of vesicoureteral reflux: International reflux study in children. Pediatr. Radiol. *15*:105–109, 1985.
60. Leneghan, D., Whitaker, J. G., Jensen, F., et al.: The natural history of reflux and long term effects of reflux on the kidney. J. Urol. *115*:728, 1976.
61. Leong, Y. Y., and Tan, K. W.: Bladder aspiration for diagnosis of urinary tract infection in infants and young children. J. Singapore Paediatr. Soc. *18*:43–47, 1976.
62. Leonidas, J. C., and Berdon, W. E.: MR imaging of urinary tract infections in children. Radiology *210*:582–583, 1999.
63. Le Saux, N., Pham, B. A., and Moher, D.: Evaluating the benefits of antimicrobial prophylaxis to prevent urinary tract infections in children: A systematic review. C. M. A. J. *163*:523–529, 2000.
64. Lewis, M.: Report of the Paediatric Renal Registry 1999. *In* Ansell, D., and Feest, T. (eds.): The Second Annual Report of the UK Renal Registry. Bristol, U. K., Renal Association, 1999, pp. 175–187.
65. Liles, W. C., Cushing, H., Holt, S., et al.: Severe adenoviral nephritis following bone marrow transplantation: Successful treatment with intravenous ribavirin. Bone Marrow Transplant. *12*:409–412, 1993.
66. Lin, D. S., Huang, F. Y., Chiu, N. C., et al.: Comparison of hemocytometer leukocyte counts and standard urinalyses for predicting urinary tract infections in febrile infants. Pediatr. Infect. Dis. J. *19*:223–227, 2000.
67. Lin, D. S., Huang, S., Lin, C., et al.: Urinary tract infection in febrile infants younger than eight weeks of age. Pediatrics *105*:e20, 2000.
68. Lindberg, U., Claesson, I., Hanson, L. A., et al.: Asymptomatic bacteriuria in schoolgirls. Clinical and laboratory findings. Acta Paediatr. Scand. *64*:425–431, 1975.
69. Loening-Baucke, V.: Urinary incontinence and urinary tract infection and their resolution with treatment of chronic constipation of childhood. Pediatrics *100*:228–232, 1997.
70. Lohr, J. A., Nunley, D. H., Howards, S. S., et al.: Prevention of recurrent urinary tract infections in girls. Pediatrics *59*:562–565, 1977.
71. Lohr, J. A., Portilla, M. G., Geuder, T. G., et al.: Making a presumptive diagnosis of urinary tract infection by using a urinalysis performed in an on-site laboratory. J. Pediatr. *122*:22–25, 1993.
72. Lomberg, L., Hellstrom, M., Jodal, U., et al.: Virulence-associated traits in *Escherichia coli* causing first and recurrent episodes of urinary tract infection in children with or without vesicoureteral reflux. J. Infect. Dis. *150*:561–569, 1984.
73. Lonergan, G. J., Pennington, D. J., Morrison, J. C., et al.: Childhood pyelonephritis: Comparison of gadolinium-enhanced MR imaging and renal cortical scintigraphy. Radiology *207*:377–384, 1998.
74. Lonergan, D. J., and Pennington, D. J.: MR imaging of urinary tract infections in children. Reply. Radiology *210*:583–584, 1999.
75. Madrigal, G., Odio, C. M., Mohs, E., et al.: Single dose antibiotic therapy is not as effective as conventional regimens for management of acute urinary tract infections in children. Pediatr. Infect. Dis. J. *7*:316–319, 1988.
76. Marild, S., and Jodal, U.: Incidence rate of first-time symptomatic urinary tract infection in children under 6 years of age. Acta Paediatr. *87*:549–552, 1998.
77. Marotte, J. B., and Smith, D. P.: Extravesical ureteral reimplantations for the correction of primary reflux can be done as outpatient procedures. J. Urol. *165*:2228–2231, 2001.
78a. McCracken, G. H., Jr., Ginsburg, C. M., Namasonthi, V., et al.: Evaluation of short-term antibiotic therapy in children with uncomplicated urinary tract infections. Pediatrics *67*:796–801, 1981.
78b. McFadyen, I. R., and Eykyn, S. J.: Supapubic aspiration of urine in pregnancy. Lancet *1*:1112–1114, 1968.
79. Moffatt, M., Embree, J., Grimm, P., et al.: Short-course antibiotic therapy for urinary tract infections in children. Am. J. Dis. Child. *142*:57–61, 1988.
80. Morgan, M. G., and Hamilton-Miller, J. M.: *Haemophilus influenzae* and *H. parainfluenzae* as urinary pathogens. J. Infect. *20*:143–145, 1990.
81. Najmaldin, A., Burge, D. M., and Atwell, J. D.: Reflux nephropathy secondary to intrauterine vesicoureteric reflux. J. Pediatr. Surg. *25*: 387–390, 1990.
82. Nayir, A., Emre, S., Sirin, A., et al.: The effects of vaccination with inactivated uropathogenic bacteria in recurrent urinary tract infections of children. Vaccine *13*:987–990, 1995.
83. Nicolle, L. E., Harding, G. K. M., Preiksaitis, J., et al.: The association of urinary tract infection with sexual intercourse. J. Infect. Dis. *146*: 579–583, 1982.
84. Noe, H. N.: The long-term results of prospective sibling reflux screening. J. Urol. *148*:1739–1742, 1992.
85. Nowicki, B., Holthofer, H., Saraneva, T., et al.: Location of adhesion sites for P-fimbriated and for O75X-positive *Escherichia coli* in the human kidney. Microb. Pathog. *1*:169–180, 1986.
86. Olbing, H., Claesson, I., Ebel, K. D., et al.: Renal scars and parenchymal thinning in children with vesicoureteral reflux: A 5-year report of the International Reflux Study in Children (European branch). J. Urol. *148*:1653–1656, 1992.
87. Olbing, H., Hirche, H., Koskimies, O., et al.: Renal growth over 10 years in a prospective study of medical or surgical treatment in children with severe vesicoureteral reflux: 10-year prospective study of medical and surgical treatment. Radiology *216*:731–737, 2000.
88. Orrett, F. A., Brooks, P. J., Richardson, E. G., et al.: Paediatric nosocomial urinary tract infection at a regional hospital. Int. Urol. Nephrol. *31*:173–179, 1999.
89. Pennington, D. J., Lonergan, G. J., Flack, C. E., et al.: Experimental pyelonephritis in piglets: Diagnosis with MR imaging. Radiology *201*:199–205, 1996.
90. Piepsz, A., Tamminen-Mobius, T., Reiners, C., et al.: Five-year study of medical or surgical treatment in children with severe vesicoureteral reflux dimercaptosuccinic acid findings. Eur. J. Pediatr. *157*:753–758, 1998.
91. Phillips, J. R., and Karlowicz, M. G.: Prevalence of *Candida* species in hospital-acquired urinary tract infections in a neonatal intensive care unit. Pediatr. Infect. Dis. J. *16*:190–194, 1997.
92. Polnay, L., Fraser, A. M., and Lewis, J. M.: Complication of suprapubic bladder aspiration. Arch. Dis. Child. *50*:80–81, 1975.
93. Pryles, C. V., Atkins, M. D., Morse, T. S., et al.: Comparative bacteriologic study of urine obtained from children by percutaneous suprapubic aspiration of the bladder and by catheter. Pediatrics *24*:983–991, 1959.
94. Quinn, F. M. J., Dick, A. C., Corbally, M. T., et al.: Xanthogranulomatous pyelonephritis in childhood. Arch. Dis. Child. *81*:483–486, 1999.
95. Report of the International Reflux Study Committee: Medical versus surgical treatment of primary vesicoureteral reflux: A prospective international reflux study in children. Pediatrics *67*:392–400, 1981.
96. Roberts, J. A., Angel, J. R., and Roth, J. K., Jr: The hydrodynamics of pyelorenal reflux. II. The effect of chronic obstructive changes on papillary shape. Invest. Urol. *18*:296–301, 1981.
97. Roberts, J. A.: Etiology and pathophysiology of pyelonephritis. Am. J. Kidney Dis. *17*:1–9, 1991.

98. Rushton, H. G.: Urinary tract infections in children: Epidemiology, evaluation, and management. Pediatr. Clin. North Am. *44*:1133–1169, 1997.
99. Rushton, H. G., Majd, M., Chandra, R., et al.: Evaluation of 99m technetium–dimercaptosuccinic acid in renal scans in experimental acute pyelonephritis in piglets. J. Urol. *140*:1169–1174, 1988.
100. Savage, D. C. L., Wilson, M. I., McHardy, M., et al.: Covert bacteriuria of childhood. A clinical and epidemiological study. Arch. Dis. Child. *48*:8–20, 1973.
101. Schlager, T. A., Smith, D. E., and Donowitz, L. G.: Perineal cleansing does not reduce contamination of urine samples from pregnant adolescents. Pediatr. Infect. Dis. J. *14*:909–911, 1995.
102. Schlager, T. A., Hendley, J. O., Dudley, S. M., et al.: Explanation for false-positive urine cultures obtained by bag technique. Arch. Pediatr. Adolesc. Med. *149*:170–173, 1995.
103. Schoen, E. J., Colby, C. J., and Ray, G. T.: Newborn circumcision decreases incidence and cost of urinary tract infections during the first year of life. Pediatrics *105*:789–793, 2000.
104. Shalaby-Rana, E., Lowe, L. H., Blask, A. N., et al.: Imaging in pediatric urology. Pediatr. Clin. North Am. *44*:1065–1089, 1997.
105. Shapiro, E. D.: Short course antimicrobial treatment of urinary tract infections in children: A critical analysis. Pediatr. Infect. Dis. J. *1*:294–297, 1982.
106. Shaw, K. N., Gorelick, M., McGowan, K. L., et al.: Prevalence of urinary tract infection in febrile young children in the emergency department. Pediatrics *102*:e16, 1998.
107. Skoog, S. J., Belman, A. B., and Majd, M.: A nonsurgical approach to the management of primary vesicoureteral reflux. J. Urol. *138*:941, 1987.
108. Smellie, J. M., Katz, G., and Gruneberg, R. N.: Controlled trial of prophylactic treatment in childhood urinary tract infection. Lancet *2*:175–178, 1978.
109. Smellie, J. M.: Commentary: Management of children with severe vesicoureteral reflux. J. Urol. *148*:1676–1678, 1992.
110. Smellie, J. M., Tamminen-Mobius, T., Olbing, H., et al.: Five year study of medical or surgical treatment in children with severe reflux: Radiological renal findings. Pediatr. Nephrol. *6*:223–230, 1992.
111. Smellie, J. M., Poulton, A., and Prescod, N. P.: Retrospective study of children with renal scarring associated with reflux and urinary infection. Br. Med. J. *308*:1193, 1994.
112. Smellie, J. M., Prescod, N. P., Shaw, P. J., et al.: Childhood reflux and urinary infection: A follow-up of 10–41 years in 226 adults. Pediatr. Nephrol. *12*:727–736, 1998.
113. Smellie, J. M.: Vesicoureteric reflux. Acta Paediatr. *88*:1182–1183, 1999.
114. Smellie, J. M., Barratt, T. M., Chantler, C., et al.: Medical versus surgical treatment in children with severe bilateral vesicoureteric reflux and bilateral nephropathy: A randomised trial. Lancet *357*:1329–1333, 2001.
115. Sobel, J. D., and Vasquez, J. A.: Fungal infections of the urinary tract. World J. Urol. *17*:410–414, 1999.
116. Stamm, W. E.: Catheter-associated urinary tract infections: Epidemiology, pathogenesis, and prevention. Am. J. Med. *91*:65S–71S, 1991.
117. Svanborg Eden, C., Hanson, L. A., Jodal, U., et al.: Variable adherence to normal human urinary-tract epithelial cells of *Escherichia coli* strains associated with various forms of urinary-tract infection. Lancet *2*:490–492, 1976.
118. Tamminen-Mobius, T., Brunier, E., Ebel, K. D., et al.: Cessation of vesicoureteral reflux for 5 years in infants and children allocated to medical treatment. J. Urol. *148*:1662–1666, 1992.
119. Todd, J. K.: Management of urinary tract infections: Children are different. Pediatr. Rev. *16*:190–196, 1995.
120. Tran, D., Muchant, D. G., and Aronoff, S. C.: Short-course versus conventional length antimicrobial therapy for uncomplicated lower urinary tract infections in children: A meta-analysis of 1279 patients. J. Pediatr. *139*:93–99, 2001.
121. Vaisanen-Rhen, V., Elo, J., Vaisanen, E., et al.: P-fimbriated clones among uropathogenic *Escherichia coli* strains. Infect. Immun. *43*:149, 1984.
122. Wan, J., Kaplinsky, R., and Greenfield, S.: Toilet habits of children evaluated for urinary tract infection. J. Urol. *154*:797–799, 1995.
123. Weiss, R., Duckett, J., and Spitzer, A.: Results of a randomized clinical trial of medical versus surgical management of infants and children with grades III and IV primary vesicoureteral reflux (United States). J. Urol. *148*:1667–1673, 1992.
124. Weiss, R., Tamminen-Mobius, T., Koskimies, O., et al.: Characteristics at entry of children with severe primary vesicoureteral reflux recruited for a multicenter, international therapeutic trial comparing medical and surgical management. J. Urol. *148*:1644–1649, 1992.
125. Wettergren, B., and Jodal, U.: Spontaneous clearance of asymptomatic bacteriuria in infants. Acta Paediatr. Scand. *79*:300–304, 1990.
126. Williams, G., Lee, A., and Craig, J.: Antibiotics for the prevention of urinary tract infection in children: A systematic review of randomized controlled trials. J. Pediatr. *138*:868–874, 2001.
127. Winberg, J., Andersen, H. J., Bergstrom, T., et al.: Epidemiology of symptomatic urinary tract infection in childhood. Acta Paediatr. Scand. *252*(Suppl.):1–20, 1974.
128. Winberg, J.: Management of primary vesicoureteric reflux in children—operation ineffective in preventing progressive renal damage. Infection *22*(Suppl. 1):S4–S7, 1994.
129. Wiswell, T. E., Smith, F. R., and Bass, J. W.: Decreased incidence of urinary tract infections in circumcised male infants. Pediatrics *75*:901–903, 1985.
130. Wiswell, T. E., and Roscelli, J. D.: Corroborative evidence for the decreased incidence of urinary tract infections in circumcised male infants. Pediatrics *78*:96–99, 1986.
131. Yazbeck, S., Schick, E., and O'Regan, S.: Relevance of constipation to enuresis, urinary tract infection and reflux. A review. Eur. Urol. *13*:318–321, 1987.

Renal Abscess

EDMOND T. GONZALES, JR. ■ SHELDON L. KAPLAN

Although acute pyelonephritis is a relatively common infection in children, the primary development of a renal abscess or progression of pyelonephritis to a renal or perinephric abscess is distinctly uncommon. In one study conducted over a 10-year period, 8 children with a renal abscess were found among 43,224 discharge diagnoses—approximately 1 case per 5400 pediatric admissions.[5] Six of the eight children were 11 years or older. Though rare, renal abscesses have been reported in neonates.[6] Renal abscess may be a primary problem—that is, one that develops in a kidney without an antecedent infection or underlying anatomic abnormality—or it may occur secondarily in a patient with previously recognized acute pyelonephritis or in a child with congenital urologic abnormalities known to predispose to the development of pyelonephritis.

A primary renal abscess is thought to develop most often after an episode of bacteremia and frequently occurs in younger children. Hematogenous spread of bacteria to the kidney usually results in a cortical abscess.[5] The most common organisms involved in these abscesses are gram-positive cocci, primarily *Staphylococcus aureus* and less often a streptococcus. In some cases, a cutaneous infection might have been present before development of the renal abscess, and this infection is thought to be the primary source for the bacteremia.[12] Most children in whom a renal abscess develops hematogenously are normal hosts.[5, 8, 16, 18] In older children and teenagers, tuberculous abscesses and caseous necrosis of the renal parenchyma also should be included in this primary classification. However, these infections tend to be indolent, although renal tuberculosis may be complicated by bacterial infection because of associated ureteral strictures and severe tuberculous cystitis. Pediatricians, though, should become familiar with this "adult" malady because of the resurgence of tuberculosis and the generally older age group for which many pediatricians now provide care.

When a renal abscess occurs in association with a recognized urologic disorder, the organism responsible most often is a gram-negative bacillus or an enterococcus, bacteria usually seen in simple urinary tract infections and pyelonephritis.[15] Examples of urologic disorders that one might encounter with these infections include congenital and acquired obstructions (e.g., ureteropelvic and ureterovesical obstruction, retrocaval ureter, ureteral stricture after surgical intervention), calculous disease (obstructing and nonobstructing), infundibular stenosis, and renal dysplasia with cystic changes. Abscesses that occur as a result of infection of the urinary tract generally are found in a corticomedullary location.[5]

Anaerobic organisms also have been implicated as a cause of renal abscess. They often are present simultaneously with the more usual aerobic bacteria, but they can cause infections and abscesses alone. These anaerobic renal infections develop most commonly in association with infections complicating bowel injury or surgery, renal transplantation, malignancy, and orodental infections.[4] The genus of the anaerobic organism may provide a clue to its source. For example, *Bacteroides fragilis* is likely to arise from an intra-abdominal source, whereas an oral site is more common for *Prevotella oralis*.[4]

Children with human immunodeficiency virus infection seem to have an increased risk for development of renal abscesses, both from the more common traditional organisms[3] and from unusual opportunistic fungal organisms, especially *Aspergillus*.[10] As expected, these children also tend to have a more fulminate course that often requires extensive surgical intervention and drainage.

The presence of a renal abscess implies the destruction and liquefaction of tissue in a confined space. Two other infectious disorders of the kidney, xanthogranulomatous pyelonephritis and acute lobar nephronia (acute focal bacterial nephritis), frequently are included in this general category, although technically, true abscesses do not always develop in these disorders.

Xanthogranulomatous pyelonephritis describes a more chronic form of severe renal parenchymal destruction that often is associated with chronic stone disease. The process may involve the whole kidney or may be focal. In children, the focal form occurs more commonly. The pathognomonic histologic finding is an accumulation of lipid-laden macrophages that coalesce into discrete yellow nodules. Small abscess cavities often are studded throughout the kidney. The organism most frequently recovered from the kidney is *Proteus,* and urinary calculi are common findings. Although these patients often have acute symptoms, the symptoms frequently are superimposed on more chronic symptoms such as weight loss, failure to thrive, and anemia. Treatment is complete or partial nephrectomy because the renal destruction generally is severe.[17]

Acute lobar nephronia describes a focal area of intense edema at the site of infection in acute pyelonephritis.[2] It usually is recognized as a mass effect on an initial screening renal ultrasonogram. Computed tomography (CT) of the kidney demonstrates poor uptake in the involved segment but no well-defined liquefaction (Fig. 47–1). Whether this edema is just an exaggerated response to infection or actually represents a pre-abscess change remains unknown. Klar and colleagues[9] described 13 children 4 months to 8 years old with acute lobar nephronia in a prospective study during a 4-year period. Bacteremia was documented in only one child. Evolution to abscess formation occurred in four (31%). Thus, these lesions generally heal satisfactorily with administration of antibiotics alone.

Clinical Findings

Children with acute renal abscess are febrile and have localized pain in the costovertebral location. Prolonged fever is a common finding, especially in older children. Most patients are febrile for longer than 7 days before the diagnosis is established. However, the initial findings generally do not differentiate between acute pyelonephritis with and without an abscess. If the abscess has spread into the perinephric region, one might be able to recognize psoas muscle irritation in the patient—that is, the patient is more comfortable with the ipsilateral leg in a position of flexion and experiences pain with full extension. A large abscess may be palpable as a flank mass.

Findings on urinalysis can be confusing. With a primary (hematogenous) abscess, the urine may be deceptively benign and culture generally is negative.[12] Blood cultures may be positive, depending on the duration of the illness when blood was obtained for culture. Abscesses associated with underlying urologic disorders can be expected to contain organisms as well as pyuria. Generally, severe leukocytosis is present. The erythrocyte sedimentation rate typically is elevated; the same probably is true for C-reactive protein.[18] All these findings, however, are nonspecific, and the diagnosis often must await further studies.

If a somewhat more indolent process is encountered, one should consider performing appropriate staining and cultures for tuberculosis.

Diagnostic Evaluation

All children admitted with a febrile urinary tract infection should undergo renal ultrasonography as soon as is reasonable after admission. The findings on this initial study can have a significant effect on the choice of therapeutic options. If both kidneys are normal and unobstructed, organism-specific therapy is satisfactory in the overwhelming majority of patients. If significant obstruction or stones are present, antibiotic therapy may not be as effective, and interventional drainage may become necessary if the response to antibiotics is inadequate. At the time of this initial screening study, findings may suggest the presence of a renal abscess. Such findings include a mass effect within the margins of the kidney along with a thickened wall and material of varying sonographic density within the mass (Fig. 47–2). Similar findings can be seen in infections accompanied by severe ureteropelvic junction obstruction or infundibular stenosis with isolated caliceal dilatation, in which case purulent material within the dilated collecting system layers out and can mimic a renal abscess (Figs. 47–3 and 47–4).

Once the diagnosis of an abscess is suspected on ultrasonography, performing CT of the involved kidney is in order.[7] CT more clearly defines the margins of the abscess, assesses whether loss of function is significant, and can screen the remainder of the kidney for small satellite abscesses.[14] If loss of function in the affected kidney appears to be significant, a dimercaptosuccinic acid renal scan should be included because it is an even more sensitive test to quantitate overall renal function. Currently, gallium 67 scintigraphy is not used frequently to diagnose an obscure

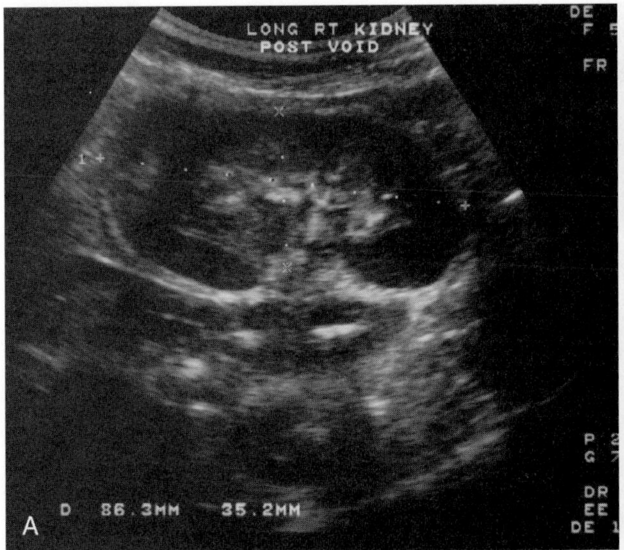

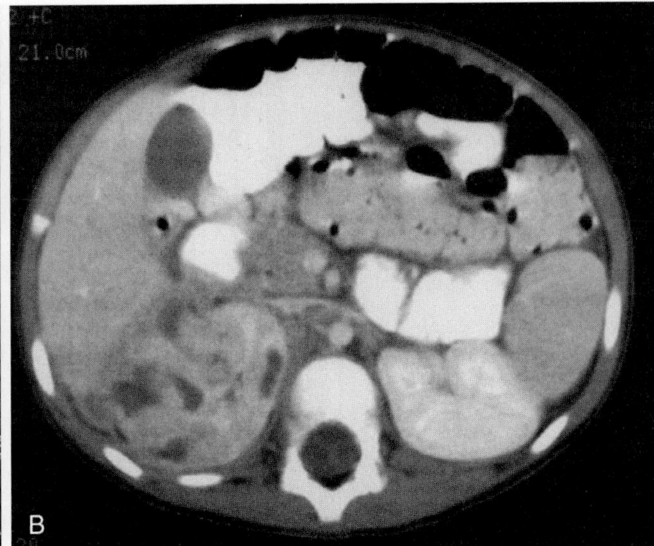

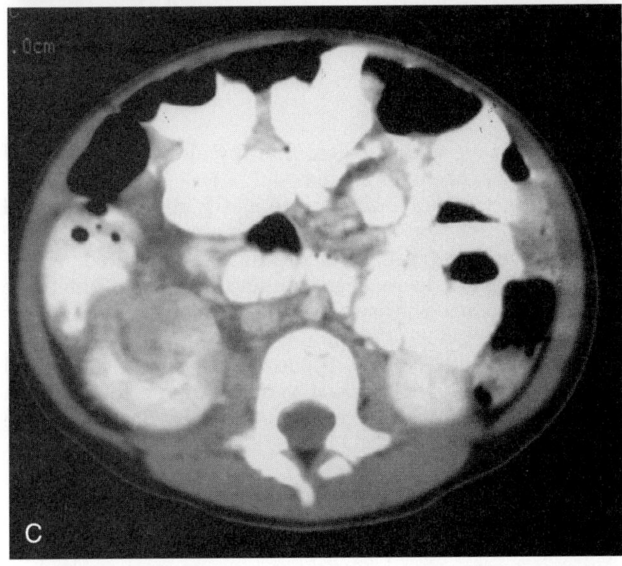

FIGURE 47–1 ■ Acute lobar nephronia in a 3-year-old girl with fever, right flank pain, and urinary tract infection. *A,* The initial renal ultrasonogram demonstrates enlargement and swelling of the right upper pole. *B,* Initial upper pole cuts by computed tomography demonstrate poor uptake of contrast media and differing tissue densities. *C,* More caudal cuts reveal better function in the right lower pole. The infection and swelling resolved completely with antibiotics alone, with no evidence of postinfectious atrophy. This case was thought to represent acute lobar nephronia.

inflammatory mass. Today, improved CT technology strongly suggests the diagnosis, and when necessary, percutaneous aspiration can confirm clearly whether an abscess is present without additional studies and, at the same time, provide material for culture.

If a child with a urinary tract infection and a previously normal result on renal ultrasonogram is taking culture-specific antibiotics and a new fever subsequently develops, ultrasonography should be repeated. A previously small, unrecognized abscess may have been treated inadequately and now may be more obvious.

Occasionally, imaging studies cannot distinguish between a renal abscess and severe acute lobar nephronia. The latter condition also may demonstrate tissues of differing density by ultrasonography or CT. In these situations, ultrasonography- or CT-guided percutaneous aspiration of the lesion may be necessary to determine whether purulent material can be obtained.

Therapeutic Considerations

Once the diagnosis of an abscess is confirmed, the choice of therapeutic options is dictated by several factors, including the overall status of the patient, the size and number of abscesses, whether the abscess appears to be unilocular or septate, associated uropathies, and the extent of renal function in the involved kidney. Included in these considerations is some insight into the responsible organism. If it is a solitary abscess in a child with unimpressive urinalysis findings and an otherwise normal kidney, one should suspect a staphylococcal abscess, which can be confirmed by percutaneous aspiration, Gram stain, and culture. If bacteremia caused by *S. aureus* possibly was nosocomial in origin or if methicillin-resistant *S. aureus* isolates are found relatively commonly in the community, antibiotics such as vancomycin or clindamycin should be included in the initial empiric regimen. Subsequent therapy is based on the antibiotic susceptibility pattern of the organism isolated. If urinalysis reveals an obvious infection, one can assume that the urine culture reflects the organism responsible for the abscess. In this situation, empiric therapy is directed against gram-negative enteric organisms. Cefotaxime, ceftriaxone, or ceftazidime plus an aminoglycoside would be suggested. The only caution is if the abscess is complicated by significant stone disease. In this situation, more than one organism may be in the urinary tract, and urine culture alone may be misleading. Again, percutaneous aspiration

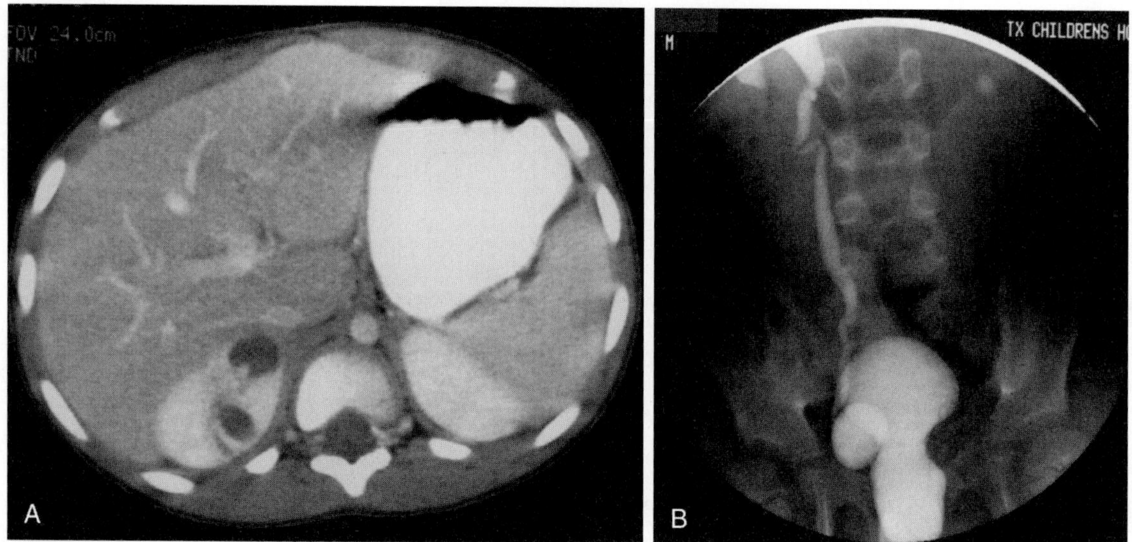

FIGURE 47–2 ■ Renal abscess (secondary) in a 6-month-old boy with a urinary tract infection. A screening renal ultrasonogram demonstrated a small mass in the right kidney. *A,* Computed tomography shows two clearly defined cystic areas consistent with small parenchymal abscesses. Treatment consisted of intravenous antibiotics only. *B,* A voiding cystogram revealed the presence of vesicoureteral reflux.

can accurately identify the organism responsible for the abscess.

Renal abscesses traditionally have been managed by open surgical drainage. With the introduction of safe percutaneous access, particularly when used with ultrasonography or CT guidance, single, unilocular lesions now can be managed effectively with percutaneous placement of an indwelling catheter that allows not only for primary drainage but also for irrigation of the cavity with appropriate antibiotic solutions.[1, 11] Small renal abscesses have been treated successfully with antibiotics alone.[13, 18] If the child does not improve with medical therapy alone, some type of drainage procedure is indicated.

When function is insufficient to justify renal salvage and ultimate nephrectomy is planned, a short course of specific antibiotics and percutaneous drainage is initiated, if the abscess is large, to decrease inflammation in the perinephric tissues and reduce the possibility of causing bacteremia at the time of surgery.

When required, surgical repair of associated congenital anomalies of the urinary tract generally is performed at a separate session after the abscess has resolved. Reconstructive

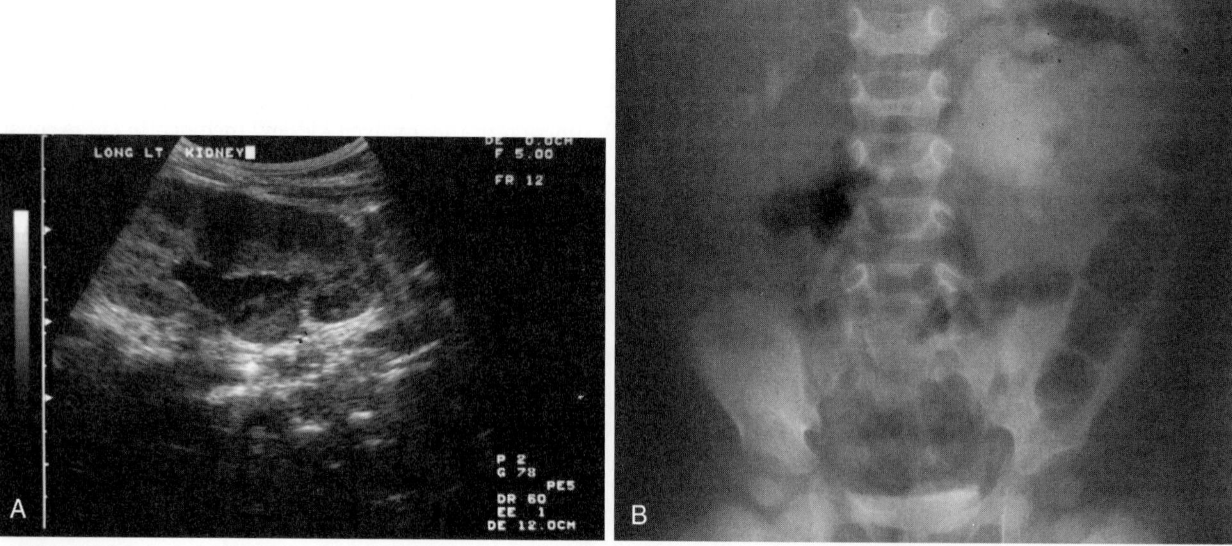

FIGURE 47–3 ■ Pyonephrosis associated with ureteropelvic junction obstruction in a 3-month-old boy with fever, left abdominal and flank tenderness, and urinary tract infection. *A,* A renal ultrasonogram demonstrates a medially placed cystic mass with layered fluids of different density consistent with purulent material. The position of the mass is most consistent with the renal pelvis. *B,* An intravenous pyelogram confirms ureteropelvic junction obstruction. This infant was treated initially with percutaneous nephrostomy drainage in addition to appropriate antibiotics.

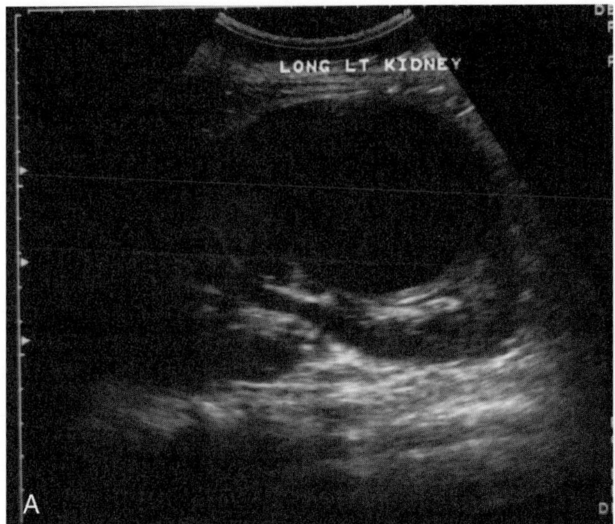

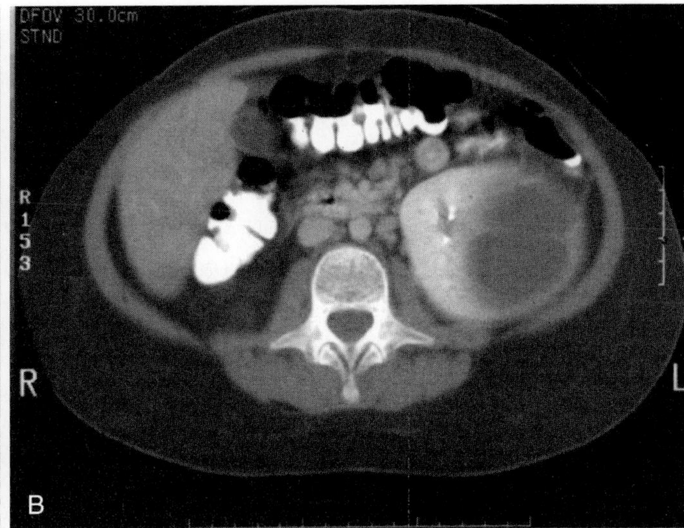

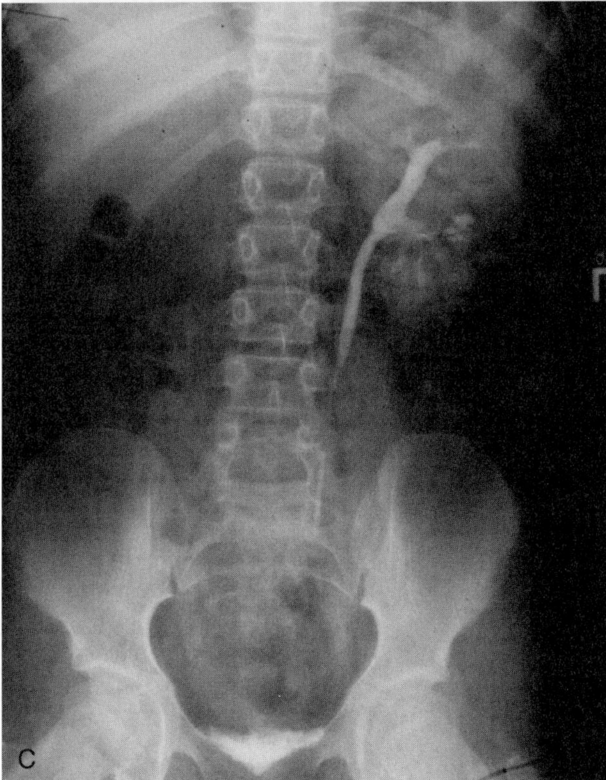

FIGURE 47–4 ■ Renal abscess complicating infundibular stenosis in a 10-year-old girl with low-grade fever, marked left costovertebral angle tenderness, leukocytosis, and pyuria but a negative urine culture (she had received outpatient antibiotics). The right kidney was absent. *A,* A sonogram of the left kidney revealed a large cystic mass with septa. *B,* The mass was confirmed by computed tomography. *C,* An intravenous pyelogram obtained after resolution of the abscess (by both percutaneous and open drainage) reveals anomalous development of the lower infundibulum and calyces.

surgery in the presence of active infection significantly increases the risk of development of surgical complications and the possibility that additional surgical procedures might be required.

Conclusions

Treatment of renal abscess today is multifaceted, and each case must be individualized. In addition to culture-specific antibiotics, treatment may include observation only, percutaneous drainage, or open surgical drainage. Diagnostic evaluation, including renal ultrasonography, CT, and percutaneous aspiration, generally can confirm that an abscess is present and assist in the decision regarding therapeutic options.

REFERENCES

1. Barker, A. P., and Ahmed, S.: Renal abscess in childhood. Aust. N. Z. J. Surg. *61*:217–221, 1991.
2. Boam, W. D., and Miser, W. F.: Acute focal bacterial pyelonephritis. Am. Fam. Physician *52*:919–924, 1995.
3. Brandels, J. M., Baskin, L. S., Kogan, B. A., et al.: Recurrent *Staphylococcus aureus* renal abscess in a child positive for the human immunodeficiency virus. Urology *46*:246–248, 1995.
4. Brook, I.: The role of anaerobic bacteria in perinephric and renal abscesses in children. Pediatrics *92*:261–264, 1994.
5. Casullo, V. A. M. C., Bottone, E., and Herold, B. C.: *Peptostreptococcus asaccharolyticus* 1 abscess: A rare cause of fever of unknown origin. Pediatrics *107*:E11, 2001. URL: *http://www.pediatrics.org/cgi/content/ full/107/1/311.*
6. Dougherty, F. E., Gottlieb, R. P., Gross, G. W., and Denison, M. R.: Neonatal renal abscess caused by *Staphylococcus aureus.* Pediatr. Infect. Dis. J. *10*:463, 1991.
7. Gerzof, S. G., and Gale, M. E.: Computer tomography and ultrasonography for diagnosis and treatment of renal and retroperitoneal abscesses. Urol. Clin. North Am. *9*:185–193, 1982.

8. Higham, M., Santos, J. I., Grodin, M., and Klein, J. O.: Renal abscess without preexisting structural abnormality. Pediatr. Infect. Dis. J. *3*:138–141, 1984.
9. Klar, A., Hurvitz, H., Berkun, Y., et al: Focal bacterial nephritis (lobar nephronia) in children. J Pediatr *128*:850–853, 1996.
10. Martinez-Jabalonas, J., Osca, J. M., Ruiz, J. L., et al.: Renal aspergillosis and AIDS. Eur. Urol. *27*:167–169, 1995.
11. Pedersen, J. F., Hancke, S., and Kristensen, J. V.: Renal carbuncle: Antibiotic therapy governed by ultrasonically guided aspiration. J. Urol. *109*:777–778, 1973.
12. Rote, A. R., Bauer, S. B., and Retik, A. B.: Renal abscess in children. J. Urol. *119*:254–258, 1978.
13. Schiff, M., Glickman, M., Weiss, R. M., et al.: Antibiotic treatment of renal carbuncle. Ann. Intern. Med. *8*:305, 1977.
14. Thornbury, J. R.: Acute renal infections. Urol. Radiol. *12*:209–213, 1991.
15. Timmons, J. W., and Perlmutter, A. D.: Renal abscess: A changing concept. J. Urol. *115*:299–301, 1976.
16. Vachvanichsanong, P., Dissaneewate, P., Patrapinyokul, S., et al.: Renal abscess in healthy children: Report of three cases. Pediatr. Nephrol. *6*:273–275, 1992.
17. Watson, A. R., Marsden, H. B., Cendon, M., et al.: Renal pseudotumors caused by xanthogranulomatous pyelonephritis. Arch. Dis. Child. *57*:635, 1982.
18. Wippermann, C. F., Schofer, O., Beetz, R., et al.: Renal abscess in childhood: Diagnostic and therapeutic progress. Pediatr. Infect. Dis. J. *10*:446–450, 1991.

CHAPTER 48 Prostatitis

EDMOND T. GONZALES, JR. ■ SHELDON L. KAPLAN

Prostatitis, a major source of chronic infection and symptoms in men, is a rare occurrence in prepubertal children. Although prostatitis may develop in postpubertal teenagers, even in this age group the diagnosis is recognized infrequently. The disorder commonly called prostatitis generally is divided into three separate clinical problems: acute prostatitis, chronic prostatitis, and prostatodynia.

Acute prostatitis is a severe infection generally associated with significant toxicity (high fever, elevated white blood cell count, systemic symptoms). Marked urinary symptoms such as frequency, dysuria, and urinary retention may be present. The urine usually is infected. On rectal examination, the prostate is enlarged, boggy (edematous), and exquisitely tender. Care must be taken when performing the rectal examination or when inserting a transurethral catheter because bacteremia can result. The organism responsible usually is one of the gram-negative pathogens that commonly cause urinary tract infection. The virulence factors of *Escherichia coli* strains recovered from men with acute prostatitis and women with urinary tract infections, such as adhesins and cytotoxins, are similar.[11] Rarely, *Trichomonas vaginalis* can cause prostatitis. Treatment generally begins with administration of broad-spectrum parenteral antibiotics, such as cefotaxime and the aminoglycosides, that are effective against gram-negative enteric organisms, pending the availability of culture-proven sensitivity results and a satisfactory clinical response. In patients older than 17 years of age, a fluoroquinolone also is recommended.

Chronic prostatitis is a more indolent infection associated with intermittent urinary tract infection, bladder irritative symptoms, and perineal discomfort. Ejaculation may be painful. Expressed prostatic secretions usually show an increase in white blood cells. Chronic prostatitis generally is recognized to occur in two different patterns: bacterial and nonbacterial. The clinical features of the two disorders are remarkably similar, including an increase in the white blood cell count in expressed prostatic secretions, but patients with chronic bacterial prostatitis usually also have recurring episodes of urinary tract infection with the same organism, most often one of the gram-negative pathogens. The diagnosis of chronic prostatitis is related in part to detecting inflammation in expressed prostatic secretions. More precise methods of determining inflammatory parameters, such as counting the white blood cells per cubic millimeter with a hemocytometer, have been proposed.[12] However, in a large cohort study, the severity of symptoms in men with chronic prostatitis did not correlate with leukocyte or bacterial counts.[16] This study suggested that the symptoms associated with chronic pelvic pain syndrome were related to factors other than leukocytes and bacteria.

As with acute infection, *E. coli* isolates associated with chronic prostatitis possess urovirulence profiles similar to those of strains from women with acute uncomplicated pyelonephritis.[1] In most studies, chronic nonbacterial prostatitis occurs more commonly than does chronic bacterial prostatitis.

The cause of nonbacterial prostatitis remains enigmatic. Prostatic secretions do not show a common organism consistently, and urinary tract infection does not recur. However, culture of prostatic secretions is notoriously unreliable because of the means by which this material is collected; these secretions are contaminated easily as they pass through the urethra.[10] A specific causal relationship has not been found for either *Ureaplasma urealyticum* or *Chlamydia trachomatis* in nonbacterial prostatitis, two organisms commonly implicated in urethritis.[17] Molecular studies have demonstrated DNA evidence of the presence of bacteria via polymerase chain reaction despite negative cultures for the typical bacteria associated with prostatitis.[5] Using these new techniques may allow greater understanding of the role of infection in the pathogenesis of prostatitis.

Treatment of chronic bacterial prostatitis is frustrating because few patients truly are cured and relapse occurs commonly after discontinuation of antibiotic therapy. Several studies have confirmed satisfactory concentrations of most common antibiotics in prostatic tissues,[4, 6, 8] but no study has provided a convincing explanation for the high treatment failure rate. Gatifloxacin and other fluoroquinolones penetrate well into seminal and prostatic fluids and reach concentrations equivalent to corresponding plasma levels.[13] Researchers have postulated that antibiotic concentrations may be inadequate within the acini of the prostatic glands and their secretions, but this theory has not been proved.[14] Normal prostatic secretions exhibit an antibacterial effect that is not present in men with chronic bacterial prostatitis. Several investigators have shown this factor to be free zinc or a zinc-based compound.[15] This antibacterial factor is depressed or absent in men with chronic prostatitis, but whether it causes or results from prostatitis remains unknown. The most successful antibiotic therapy has been with trimethoprim-sulfamethoxazole or one of the fluoroquinolones.[7] In many instances, however, low-dose maintenance chemoprophylaxis with trimethoprim-sulfamethoxazole or nitrofurantoin remains the most effective means of controlling symptoms.

A final population of patients have all the symptoms described in those with chronic (bacterial) prostatitis but no history of urinary tract infection and microscopically normal prostatic secretions. To distinguish this group of patients from those with prostatic infection, the term *prostatodynia* is used. The etiology of prostatodynia is unknown, but most investigators think that the disorder is a form of perineal and urethral muscle dysfunction with sphincter spasm, high voiding pressure within the prostatic urethra, reflux of urine into the prostatic ducts, and, ultimately, the development of chemical prostatitis.[3, 9] Treatment generally consists of the use of alpha-adrenergic blocking agents to relax the bladder neck and proximal prostatic urethra and diazepam to relax the striated muscle of the perineum. Although most patients seem to experience some benefit, the results of therapy are difficult to quantitate, and underlying psychosocial issues are thought to be responsible for the symptoms of many patients. Psychologic assessment and indicated treatment are essential parts of the total management of these patients.

In the older age group still seen in a pediatric practice, symptoms similar to those of the chronic form of prostatitis also might occur with urethritis. As noted earlier, *Chlamydia* and *Ureaplasma* commonly are found in the urethral discharge in these patients[2] and are thought to be responsible for these specific symptoms. These organisms also have been implicated as a cause of epididymitis in young men. The organisms are transmitted sexually and are treated effectively with a tetracycline (minocycline or doxycycline) or erythromycin. Therefore, to prescribe these drugs empirically for sexually active young adults with lower tract irritative symptoms and clinical findings consistent with urethritis while awaiting culture results seems reasonable.

Nonspecific urethritis is the term commonly used for the infection in men with irritative voiding symptoms and a clear mucoid discharge and in whom culture of the discharge reveals a mixture of common perineal and gram-negative organisms but without a predominant organism thought to be responsible for the infection. Undoubtedly, some of these patients have undiagnosed *Chlamydia* or *Ureaplasma* infection. Although specific treatment is empiric, a tetracycline or erythromycin appears to be a prudent first choice in most cases. Finally, one must not overlook the possibility of gonococcal urethritis.

In males, ectopic ureters can drain into the prostatic urethra or the seminal vesicle. With this anomaly, the ipsilateral renal parenchyma generally is dysplastic, the ureter is highly dilated, and the seminal vesicle may be distended markedly and form a large cyst-like structure behind the prostate, the bladder neck, and the trigone. If this anomaly becomes infected, pain in the perineum and on rectal examination generally is significant. Occasionally, frankly purulent material is passed at the urethral meatus or expressed from the urethra after rectal examination.

In most cases, the kidney drained by the ectopic ureter is highly dysplastic and shows little or no function. Ultimate management usually consists of nephroureterectomy (ureteroneocystostomy if the kidney works) and, if the seminal vesicle is unusually large, partial excision and decompression of the seminal vesicle. Even though these abnormalities are congenital and recognized easily by fetal ultrasonography, they can occur at almost any age if not identified before birth. Unless a palpable flank or lower abdominal mass is felt, infection usually is the initial symptom. Despite the severe degree of abnormality and ureteral and seminal vesicle dilation, the development of infection can be delayed well into the adult years. Infrequently, distortion at the bladder neck can result in obstruction to urinary flow.

In summary, prostatitis as it is seen and described in adults is a rare event in the population likely to be seen by a pediatrician. When it does occur, it affects pubertal adolescents, and, even in these patients, distinguishing true prostatitis from simple urethritis may be difficult.

Appropriate evaluation of an adolescent male with a lower tract urinary infection generally begins with renal ultrasonography. Special attention should be directed to the region of the bladder and prostate. With this imaging modality, one can assess the presence and normalcy of both kidneys, the degree of thickening of the bladder wall, the ability of the bladder to empty, and whether any cystic masses are located behind the bladder or prostate. Any obvious abnormality justifies obtaining a voiding cystourethrogram. A thickened detrusor or recurrence of infection suggests the possibility of urethral obstruction. Although properly performed voiding cystourethrography does image the entire urethra, other diagnostic tests might include retrograde urethrography or determination of the urinary flow rate, especially if one suspects a urethral stricture. Performing cystoscopy usually is not necessary if all imaging study results are normal, although cystoscopy may be used to confirm, and at times manage, obvious urethral obstruction.

REFERENCES

1. Andreu, A., Stapleton, A. E., Fennell, C., et al.: Urovirulence determinants in *Escherichia coli* strains causing prostatitis. J. Infect. Dis. *176*:464–469, 1997.
2. Bowie, W. R., Wang, S. P., Alexander, E. R., et al.: Etiology of nongonococcal urethritis: Evidence for *C. trachomatis* and *U. urealyticum*. J. Clin. Invest. *59*:735–742, 1977.
3. Hellstrom, W. J., Schmidt, R. A., Lue, T. F., et al.: Neuromuscular dysfunction in non-bacterial prostatitis. Urology *30*:183–188, 1987.
4. Hensle, T. W., Prout, G. R., Jr., and Griffin, P.: Minocycline diffusion into benign prostatic hyperplasia. J. Urol. *118*:609–611, 1977.
5. Krieger, J. N., and Riley, D. E.: Prostatitis: What is the role of infection? Int. J. Antimicrob. Agents *19*:475–479, 2002.
6. Larsen, E. H., Grasser, T. C., Dorflinger, T., et al.: The concentration of various quinolone derivatives in the human prostate. *In* Weidner, W., Brunner, H., Krause, W., et al. (eds.): Therapy of Prostatitis. Munich, W. Zucksweidt Verlag, 1986, pp. 40–44.
7. Meares, E. M., Jr.: Prostatitis syndromes: New perspectives about old woes. J. Urol. *123*:141–147, 1980.
8. Meares, E. M., Jr.: Prostatitis: Review of pharmacokinetics and therapy. Rev. Infect. Dis. *4*:475–483, 1982.
9. Meares, E. M., Jr.: Prostatodynia: Clinical findings and rationale for treatment. *In* Weidner, W., Brunner, H., Krause, W., et al. (eds.): Therapy of Prostatitis. Munich, W. Zucksweidt Verlag, 1986, pp. 207–212.
10. Meares, E. M., Jr., and Stamey, T. A.: Bacteriologic localization patterns in bacterial prostatitis and urethritis. Invest. Urol. *5*:492–518, 1968.
11. Mistumori, K., Terai, A., Yamamoto, S., et al.: Virulence characteristics of *Escherichia coli* in acute bacterial prostatitis. J. Infect. Dis. *180*: 1378–1381, 1999.

12. Muller, C. H., Berger, R. E., Mohr, L. E., and Krieger, J. N.: Comparison of microscopic methods for detecting inflammation in expressed prostatic secretions. J. Urol. *166*:2518–2524, 2001.
13. Naber, C. K., Steghfner, M., Kinzig-Schippers, M., et al.: Concentrations of gatifloxacin in plasma and urine and penetration into prostatic and seminal fluid, ejaculate, and sperm cells after single oral administrations of 400 milligrams to volunteers. Antimicrob. Agents Chemother. *45*:293–297, 2001.
14. Nielsen, O. S., Frimodt-Moeller, N., Maiqaard, S., et al.: Penicillanic acid derivatives in the canine prostate. Prostate *1*:79–85, 1980.
15. Parrish, R. F., Perinette, E. P., and Fair, W. R.: Evidence against a zinc binding peptide in pilocarpine-stimulated canine prostatic secretions. Prostate *4*:189–193, 1983.
16. Schaeffer, A. J., Knauss, J. S., Landis, J. R., et al.: Leukocyte and bacterial counts do not correlate with severity of symptoms in men with chronic prostatitis: The National Institutes of Health Chronic Prostatitis Cohort Study. J. Urol. *168*:1048–1053, 2002.
17. Shortliffe, L. M., and Wehner, N.: The characterization of bacterial and non-bacterial prostatitis by prostatic immunoglobulins. Medicine (Baltimore) *65*:399–414, 1986.

CHAPTER 49 Genital Infections in Childhood and Adolescence

MARIAM R. CHACKO ■ MARY A. STAAT ■ CHARLES R. WOODS

This chapter reviews the clinical aspects of genital tract infections in children and adolescents. Genital infection in males is limited to balanoposthitis. For details on other genital infections in males, such as urethritis, epididymitis, and orchitis, refer to other chapters in the section "Genitourinary Tract Infections." Genital tract infections in premenarcheal girls are, for the most part, limited to the vulva and vagina. Their clinical picture and management differ somewhat from those of similar infections in older patients. Genital infections in postmenarcheal girls, however, include all the infections found in adult women; the symptoms accompanying them are like those in adults, and their treatment essentially is the same. Genital infections associated with pregnancy are not addressed in this chapter.

Genital Tract Infections in Male Children and Adolescents

Genital tract infections in boys are uncommon occurrences at any age but can be serious when they occur. Group A streptococcal proctitis and perianal skin infections have been reported.[162, 188, 273] Perianal pruritus, erythema, and tenderness occur commonly, and abdominal pain and rectal bleeding may be present. Penile involvement occurs rarely if at all.[273]

Balanoposthitis is a condition characterized by inflammation of the prepuce (posthitis) and glans penis (balanitis). Causes of this condition have been described poorly in the literature; however, researchers have suggested that balanoposthitis results from trauma, irritation, or infection. A few cases of balanitis caused by *Streptococcus pyogenes* and *Staphylococcus aureus* have been reported.[56, 64, 75, 116, 169, 214 218]

Balanoposthitis occurs more commonly in uncircumcised than circumcised boys. In one survey, the frequency of balanitis and penile irritation was determined in 272 uncircumcised and 273 circumcised boys.[135] Balanitis was defined as redness or swelling of the entire foreskin or glans, with or without pus, and irritation was defined as redness without swelling or pus. Six percent of uncircumcised and 3 percent of circumcised boys had balanitis. Four percent of the circumcised boys were found to have irritation alone as compared with 1 percent of the circumcised boys. In another study examining penile problems in boys 0 to 8 years of age, penile inflammation developed in 8 percent of circumcised and 14 percent of uncircumcised boys.[88]

The diagnosis of balanoposthitis is made on clinical grounds. The child may have complaints of soreness, swelling, and discharge around the penis. Examination reveals redness, swelling, and discharge of the prepuce or glans penis, or both. The discharge originates from the area under the foreskin or around the glans penis and not from the urethra. Urethritis may be associated with urethral discharge, but it is not seen commonly. In a case series of 100 boys with balanitis, 100 percent had redness, 91 percent had swelling, and 73 percent had discharge on examination.[83] If an infectious etiology is suspected, Gram stain and culture of the discharge can be performed to determine the cause and guide therapy.

For nonspecific balanoposthitis, local therapy, including sitz baths, gentle cleansing, and application of hydrocortisone cream, is suggested.[257] In cases in which an infectious etiology is suspected or local therapy has not been effective, a topical or oral antibiotic with coverage against *S. pyogenes* and *S. aureus* can be used.

Circumcision or performing a dorsal slit procedure may be necessary for recalcitrant or recurrent balanoposthitis. In a study reviewing the reasons for circumcision beyond the neonatal period, 23 percent of 476 boys underwent the procedure for recurrent balanoposthitis.[300] Aside from the need for circumcision, most cases of balanoposthitis appear to be uncomplicated. However, cases resulting in necrotizing fasciitis and *Staphylococcus*-induced toxic shock have been reported.[56, 143]

Genital Tract Infections in Female Children and Adolescents

The normal vaginal microenvironment is reviewed, followed by sections on premenarcheal vulvovaginitis; other infections of the premenarcheal genital tract; issues of sexual abuse in children with genital tract infections; postmenarcheal lower genital tract infections, including infectious causes of vulvovaginitis, infections of the Bartholin ducts and glands, and vulvovaginal ulcerative disorders; infections of the cervix and uterus; infections of the uterine tubes, including pelvic inflammatory disease, salpingitis, and tubo-ovarian abscess; and ovaritis.

Information is provided regarding infections caused by specific microbes and syndromes, including trichomoniasis, candidiasis, gonorrhea, syphilis, chlamydial infections, bacterial vaginosis, herpes genitalis, condyloma acuminatum, molluscum contagiosum, lymphogranuloma venereum, granuloma inguinale, chancroid, tuberculosis, Behçet syndrome, and vulvar vestibulitis, as well as infections due to group A streptococci, *Shigella,* and other agents that occasionally cause genital tract disease. Additional information on the microbes can be found in the respective chapters dedicated to them.

Supplemental information concerning the principles of gynecologic infections in children and adolescents can be found in referenced sources.[26, 36, 37, 82, 91, 140, 246] Although the infectious complications of pregnancy are not discussed, those who provide care to adolescent patients must remain aware that pregnancy is not an uncommon occurrence in young teenage girls. Pregnancy-related infection should be considered when confronted with a septic state in an adolescent girl.

NORMAL VAGINAL FLORA

The lower female genital tract is colonized by nonpathogenic bacteria from birth. Throughout life, this colonization is dynamic and complex. A wide range of aerobic and anaerobic species have been cultured from asymptomatic girls. The results of several modern series* are summarized in Table 49–1.

Most girls harbor several organisms in the vagina at any given time. Vaginal specimens obtained for culture during anesthesia for elective surgery from 19 healthy girls 3 months to 5.7 years of age yielded a mean of 12 bacterial species.[138] Anaerobes predominated, with a mean of 8.7 species versus 3.4 aerobic species. In a series of 25 asymptomatic girls 2 months to 15 years of age, a mean of 8.7 different species (approximately 4 aerobes and 5 anaerobes) per vaginal specimen were detected.[121] Another series of adolescents and young adults 13 to 21 years of age in which only aerobic flora were evaluated noted a mean of approximately three organisms in non–sexually active subjects versus six in sexually active patients.[263] This heterogeneity in vaginal microflora during childhood and adolescence is similar to that found in adult women.[173]

Different types of bacteria are isolated at various ages. The vagina and its microbial flora form an ecosystem that changes over time from infancy to childhood to adolescence and adulthood.[137] The major forces that influence these changes are fluctuations in estrogen levels and the advent of sexual activity. Hygienic practices and medications, including oral contraceptives and antimicrobial agents, also affect the complex interactions among the various flora present in the vagina in terms of persistence, predominance, and overgrowth.

Gram-negative enteric bacteria and enterococci commonly are encountered in infants and toddlers before completion of toilet training but less frequently thereafter.[122, 138] Younger adolescents have a greater prevalence of anaerobic bacteria than do adult females. From puberty, aerobic colonization increases with age, onset of sexual activity, and parity.[174] Lactobacilli are the predominant flora in most females by the end of adolescence and may play a protective role in limiting the overgrowth of other flora.[137] In childhood, lactobacilli are present more often in girls younger than 2 years than in older prepubertal girls. The increasing presence of yeast and *Gardnerella vaginalis* from puberty to adulthood, though much less common in all ages, parallels that of lactobacilli.[122]

*See references 79, 105, 119, 121, 122, 131, 138, 173, 174, 241, 263.

TABLE 49–1 ■ VAGINAL ORGANISMS ISOLATED FROM ASYMPTOMATIC GIRLS 2 MONTHS TO 16 YEARS OF AGE

Coagulase-negative staphylococci (35–73)*
Diphtheroids (14–78)
Streptococcus viridans (13–39)
Enterococci (29–62)
Group B *Streptococcus* (5–11)
Group D *Streptococcus*
Staphylococcus epidermidis
Staphylococcus aureus
Streptococcus pneumoniae
Micrococcus species
Gaffkya (Aerococcus) species
Lactobacillus species (10–39)†
Escherichia coli (12-67)
Klebsiella species (15–52)
Enterobacter species
Proteus species (3–5)
Pseudomonas aeruginosa (5–6.5)
Citrobacter species
Haemophilus influenzae
Neisseria species other than gonococci
Moraxella (Branhamella) catarrhalis
Flavobacterium species
Alcaligenes species
Acinetobacter species
Mycoplasma hominis
Ureaplasma urealyticum
Gardnerella vaginalis‡
Peptostreptococcus species (29–56)
Peptococcus species (39–76)
Veillonella species
Eubacterium species
Propionibacterium acnes
Bacteroides fragilis
Bacteroides melaninogenicus
Other *Bacteroides* species
Prevotella species
Bifidobacterium species
Clostridium perfringens
Other *Clostridium* species
Fusobacterium species
Candida species (3–18)
Other yeasts
Actinomyces species

*Percentage range when the organism was isolated from patients in at least two studies. If no range is present, the organism was isolated from 3 to 33 percent of patients in a single study.
†Eighty-eight percent of girls were older than 11 years in one series.
‡Isolated in a number of cases without discharge.
Data from references 79, 105, 122, 131, 138, 173, 174, 185, 241.

Mycoplasma hominis and *Ureaplasma urealyticum* are present more commonly in sexually active adolescents and in girls of any age who have been sexually abused than in non–sexually active girls. However, genital mycoplasmas were found in 17 percent of one series of young girls who were not known to have suffered any sexual abuse.[125, 263]

Microbes that usually behave as commensals sometimes are associated with vulvovaginitis. The difference between colonization and disease is at least partially a function of the magnitude of the replication and, thus, the quantity of a given bacterial species. In women with bacterial vaginosis in which *G. vaginalis* is a predominant microbe, colony counts are generally greater than 10^7 colony-forming units (cfu) per gram of vaginal fluid. Asymptomatic colonization with *G. vaginalis* usually is associated with colony counts of less than 10^5 cfu/g of vaginal fluid.[174] Alteration in the vaginal microenvironment by factors such as poor hygiene, foreign bodies, hormonal fluctuations, or other events results in loss of environmental constraints on bacterial replication and thereby facilitates the overgrowth of one or more commensals.

When bacterial vaginosis occurs, typically the numbers of lactobacilli, which produce hydrogen peroxide, are decreased. When such a decrease occurs, catalase-negative microbes such as *G. vaginalis, Mobiluncus* spp., and other anaerobes can increase in number. Lactobacilli probably have mechanisms other than hydrogen peroxide production that may help restrain the growth of other microbes present on the surfaces of the lower genital tract.[174, 271]

PREMENARCHEAL VULVOVAGINITIS*

Infections and inflammation of the vulva and vagina account for 85 to 90 percent of all genital problems in premenarcheal girls. They are encountered most commonly in children between 2 and 7 years of age.[222] Infections of the vulva and vagina usually occur together and generally are discussed as one entity, vulvovaginitis. The various types of vulvovaginitis are differentiated by determining the presence or absence of specific agents associated with the inflammation in a particular case.

Genital discharge and perineal or vulvar discomfort are the most common symptoms that bring a child with vulvovaginitis to the physician.[144, 222] The discomfort may be only minor pain or soreness, or it may be intense perineal burning or pruritus. Genital erythema is the most common sign in girls with vulvovaginitis and is noted in more than 80 percent of cases. Visible discharge is present in a third of cases.[222] The discharge may be scanty serous fluid, bloody, or profuse and purulent. Infections of the vulva and vagina are more likely to be accompanied by moderate or severe inflammation and prominent discharge than is nonspecific vulvovaginitis.[152] Infection, however, can be present at times with neither discomfort nor discharge.

Genital discharge does not always indicate infection or inflammation. Most female babies have a grayish-white, somewhat mucoid discharge from the vagina during the newborn period. This discharge consists of desquamated vaginal mucosa and cervical epithelium that has undergone hypertrophy because of prenatal stimulation by placental and maternal hormones. Microscopic examination of the material reveals masses of large, superficial vaginal epithelial cells (Fig. 49–1). The condition may last for several weeks, is not pathogenic, and does not require treatment. Urinary leakage from an ectopic ureter opening into the genital tract may mimic a vaginal discharge.

A pubertal girl nearing menarche may have a copious viscous, transparent secretion that fills the vagina, bathes the vulvar tissues, and soils underclothing. The parents of such a girl may be concerned that she has a vaginal infection. In this case, the vulvar and vaginal tissues are thick and moist, a sign of increased estrogen stimulation. Microscopic examination of the vaginal fluid reveals masses of estrogenized superficial vaginal epithelial cells and few leukocytes (Fig. 49–2). Test results for pathogenic bacteria are negative. The family should be reassured that the girl does not have an infection. Frequent bathing and changes of underclothing are all that is needed.

*See references 11, 17, 61, 68, 97, 101, 131, 144, 222, 238, 290.

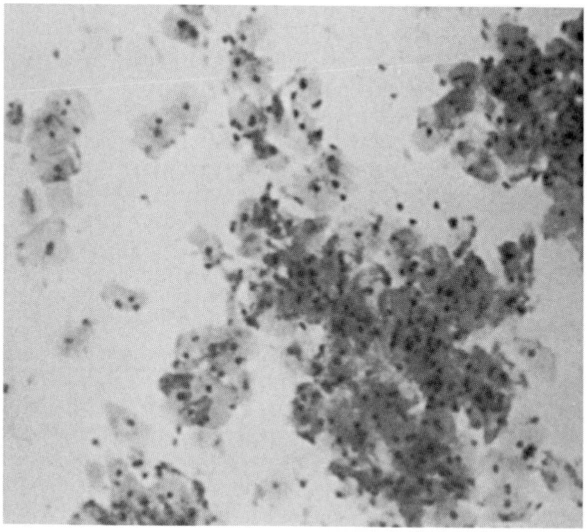

FIGURE 49–1 ■ Cytosmear from the vaginal discharge of a newborn infant.

Poor hygiene with subsequent overgrowth of a mixed aerobic and anaerobic bacterial flora is the most common cause of premenarcheal vulvovaginitis.[217] However, inflammation of the lower genitourinary tract also may be caused by a variety of specific microorganisms, chemicals, and other physical agents. Contact irritation and allergic reactions induced by soaps, detergents, and medications are frequent causes of vulvovaginitis. Some systemic diseases and focal skin disorders may mimic vulvovaginitis or allow it to develop as a secondary process when these conditions involve the vulvar or perineal tissues.[90] Anatomic abnormalities also may be associated with vulvovaginitis. An increased incidence of vulvovaginitis and urinary tract infections has been reported in girls with high posterior commissures.[297] Drainage from an ectopic ureter into the vagina can cause chronic

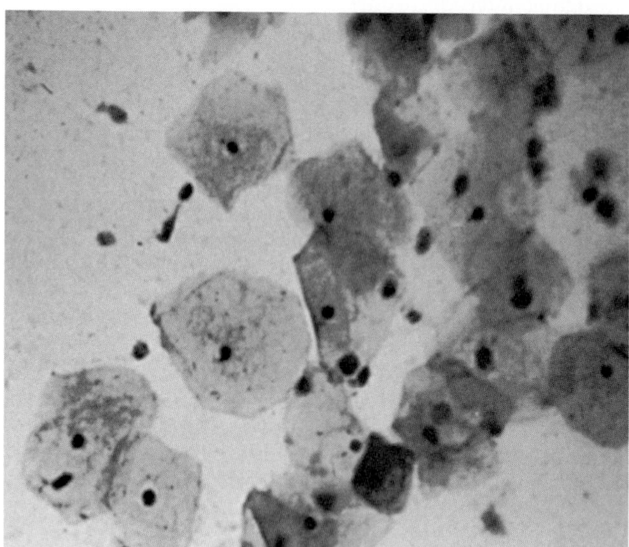

FIGURE 49–2 ■ Cytosmear from the vaginal secretion of a pubertal girl. Masses of epithelial cells and few bacteria or leukocytes attest to its nonpathologic character.

vulvovaginitis and lead to the formation of vaginal calculus. Labial adhesions were present in 7 percent of girls with vulvovaginitis in one series.[222] Table 49–2 gives an outline of the causes of vulvovaginitis in premenarcheal girls.

The history should include information about the manner and circumstances surrounding onset of the complaint, the characteristics of any discharge, the duration of symptoms, whether the problem is recurrent, and the nature of any recent treatments or medications. Information should be elicited regarding the use of bubble baths, enuresis, history of atopic dermatitis or allergies, anal pruritus (associated with pinworm infection), recent respiratory or skin infections in family members, and hygienic practices. The possibility that the child may have had or has a systemic disorder affecting the genitalia should be explored.

Sexual abuse must be considered when a child has a genital infection, regardless of the nature of the infection or the socioeconomic status of the family. This concern is particularly relevant when the child has a sexually transmissible disease, but any infectious organism can be transmitted to the genitalia by digital contact. Sexual abuse does not necessarily require penile penetration of the vagina. The history of vaginal or penile discharge in other family members should be ascertained. Behavioral changes, nightmares, fears, abdominal pain, headaches, and enuresis can be indicators of abuse or other psychosocial stressors.

TABLE 49–2 ■ ETIOLOGIC FACTORS IN PREMENARCHEAL VULVOVAGINITIS

Bacterial Infections
- Nonspecific mixed infections secondary to
  - Poor perineal hygiene
  - Foreign body in vagina
  - Respiratory tract infections
  - Skin infections (impetigo)
  - Urinary tract infection
- Specific nonvenereal infection
  - Hemolytic streptococci (groups A, B, F)
  - *Escherichia coli*
  - *Shigella flexneri, sonnei*
  - *Neisseria meningitidis, sicca*
  - *Haemophilus influenzae* type b, nontypeable strains
  - *Streptococcus pneumoniae*
  - *Corynebacterium diphtheriae*
  - *Yersinia enterocolitica*
  - *Mycobacterium tuberculosis*
  - *Moraxella (Branhamella) catarrhalis*
  - *Staphylococcus aureus*
- Specific venereal infections
  - *Neisseria gonorrhoeae*
  - *Treponema pallidum*
  - *Chlamydia trachomatis*
  - Chancroid (*Haemophilus ducreyi*)
  - Granuloma inguinale
- Bacterial vaginosis
  - *Gardnerella vaginalis*
  - *Mobiluncus* species

Fungal Infections
- *Candida albicans*
- Other yeasts
- Dermatophytes

Protozoan and Parasitic Infections
- Trichomoniasis
- Amebiasis
- *Enterobius vermicularis*
- Hirudiniasis
- Schistosomiasis
- Other parasitic infections (ascariasis, trichuriasis)

Viral Infections
- Venereal
  - Herpes simplex
  - Condyloma acuminatum (papillomavirus)
  - Molluscum contagiosum
- Involvement as part of systemic infection
  - Measles
  - Varicella
  - Mononucleosis (Epstein-Barr virus)
  - Coxsackievirus
  - Smallpox

Infestations
- Pediculosis
- Scabies

Contact Irritation or Allergic Reactions
- Bubble bath preparations
- Hair shampoos
- Vulvar deodorant sprays
- Soaps, laundry detergents
- Other medications

Vulvar or Perineal Skin Diseases
- Local
  - Seborrhea
  - Lichen sclerosus et atrophicus
  - Lichen planus
  - Lichen simplex chronicus
  - Premalignant leukoplakia
  - Erythrasma (*Corynebacterium minutissimum*)
  - Bartholinitis
  - Skenitis
- Involvement as part of a systemic disorder
  - Psoriasis
  - Bullous pemphigoid
  - Atopic dermatitis
  - Drug eruption
  - Generalized pruritus with excoriation
    - Chronic liver disease
    - Chronic renal disease
    - Metabolic errors
    - Psychosomatic
  - Crohn disease
  - Siögren syndrome
  - Henoch-Schönlein purpura
  - Histiocytosis
  - Kawasaki disease
  - Stevens-Johnson syndrome
  - Typhoid
  - Zinc deficiency

Physical Factors
- Sand (sandbox)
- Chemical or thermal trauma
- Physical trauma (accidents, abuse, masturbation)
- Nylon, rayon underclothing
- Tight garments (maceration in warm climates)
- Anatomic abnormalities
  - Neoplasms (sarcoma botryoides)
  - Polyps
  - Labial agglutination, adhesion
  - Prolapsed urethra
  - Ectopic ureter
  - Rectal fistula
  - Draining pelvic abscess via fistula

Data from references 11, 15, 79, 90, 91, 145, 172, 192, 264.

The characteristics of the discharge frequently do not help identify a specific cause. At the onset of an infection, the discharge probably is thick, purulent, and profuse. It may become scanty and seropurulent in later chronic stages of infection.[144] Discharges that are odorless and bloody or serosanguineous may result from noninfectious conditions such as vulvar irritation, trauma, precocious puberty, a foreign body, urethral prolapse, or a tumor. Vulvovaginitis caused by *Shigella* or group A streptococci also can cause bleeding. Foul-smelling discharge suggests a foreign body but also may result from a necrotic tumor. Specific diagnoses are made more often when symptoms have been present for less than 1 month.[290]

A general physical examination should precede assessment of the genital tract. The gynecologic examination begins with abdominal inspection and palpation followed by external examination of the perineum and genitalia, including the vulva, urethral meatus, clitoris, hymen, and anus. The examination should be performed with the child in a supine, frog leg position. The labia can be retracted gently to visualize the anterior of the vagina. Speculum and bimanual examinations generally are inappropriate in prepubertal children.[223] Note should be made of structural abnormalities, inflammation, sores and ulcerations, and excoriations. If complaints are those of only vulvitis and findings on external examination are limited to a scanty mucoid discharge and an erythematous introitus, further examination is generally unnecessary.[79]

If the vaginal discharge is purulent, persistent, or recurrent, thorough gynecologic assessment is warranted. Visualization of the vagina and cervix without instrumentation is possible with the child in the prone knee-chest position.[81] This method is useful in children older than 2 years. In this position, with labial traction, the vaginal muscles relax and stretch the hymenal membrane open. An otoscope head or a magnifying lens with a good wall light is used to visualize the cervix. Because the vagina of a prepubertal child is short, the presence of a foreign body or a lesion may be visualized.[78]

If visualization with instrumentation is required, the child should be examined in the supine position with the knees held apart. Vaginoscopy (Fig. 49–3) then may be performed with a pediatric cystoscope, hysteroscope, veterinary otoscope, or narrow-diameter flexible fiberoptic scope with water insufflation of the vagina. Attention to comfort of the child by allowing her to observe the examination with a mirror, asking her to assist with the examination, and having her caretaker engage her in conversation may facilitate a successful and nontraumatic examination. General anesthesia may be required for vaginoscopy in children who are small or unable to cooperate during the procedure.[78, 79]

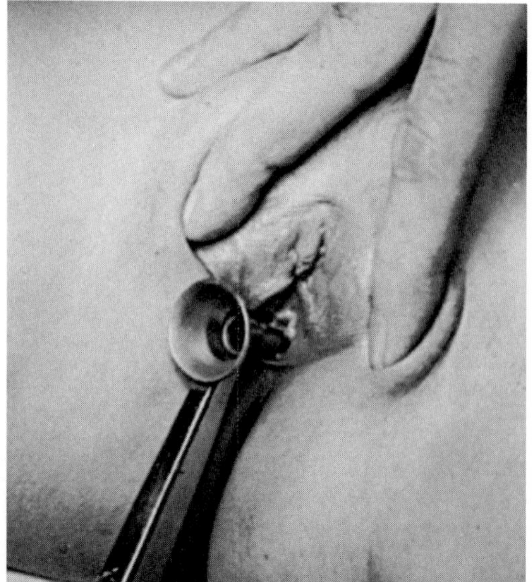

FIGURE 49–3 ■ Vaginoscopy is performed to exclude foreign bodies and tumors when a child has a vaginal discharge.

A rectal examination is important when persistent discharge, bleeding, or pelvic or abdominal pain is present. The rectal examination may help express discharge from the vagina that previously was not recognized and can permit palpation of hard foreign bodies or abnormal masses.

When a purulent, persistent, or recurrent vaginal discharge is present, samples should be obtained for culture, Gram stain, and saline (wet) and potassium hydroxide preparations. Urine analysis with microscopic examination should be performed. A complete blood cell count may be useful when pyogenic infection is suspected or bleeding has occurred.

When cultures are indicated, separate vulvar and vaginal specimens should be obtained. Material for culture from the vagina should be obtained without vulvar contamination (Table 49–3). A nasopharyngeal Calgiswab or wire Dacron swab moistened in nonbactericidal saline can be inserted easily into the vagina through the hymenal opening with minimal pain. A dry swab can be painful. The swab may be used to obtain specimens to test for gonorrhea, *Chlamydia* infection, and other nonspecific bacterial infections; it is the preferred method to test for *Chlamydia trachomatis*. When multiple samples are needed, vaginal secretions can be obtained via a catheter-within-a-catheter technique (Fig. 49–4) or an eyedropper with tubing[223, 224]. However, these aspiration methods have not been tested for their ability to obtain adequate vaginal epithelial cells, which is an important factor in the isolation of *C. trachomatis*. For the first technique, the distal 4 inches of a soft, size 12 bladder catheter and the proximal 4 inches of butterfly needle intravenous tubing are excised from their parent devices by sterile technique. The latter is attached to a tuberculin syringe that has been filled with 0.5 to 1.0 mL of sterile fluid and then is inserted into the bladder catheter. The catheter-within-a-catheter is inserted into the vagina. The fluid is flushed in and out of the upper part of the vagina several times before final aspiration into the syringe and removal of the device. Alternatively, a plastic or glass eyedropper or syringe with 4 to 5 cm of intravenous tubing attached can be used to aspirate secretions. The specimens obtained generally are adequate for wet mount, stains, cultures, and any required forensic studies.[223]

Nonspecific Vulvovaginitis

Nonspecific vulvovaginitis is identified by vaginal cultures that yield a growth of mixed bacteria not related etiologically to a specific disease. It is the premenarcheal genital

TABLE 49–3 ■ TESTS USING VAGINAL DISCHARGE OR ASPIRATE

Gram stain for bacteria and polymorphonuclear cells
Bacterial cultures (aerobic and anaerobic)
Cultures for gonococci and chlamydiae (no rapid tests)
Cultures for yeast and fungi (Nickerson medium)
Wet preparation for fungal elements (10% potassium hydroxide), white and red blood cells, vaginal epithelium (clue cells, estrogenic effect), flagellates (*Trichomonas*), parasitic ova (pinworms)

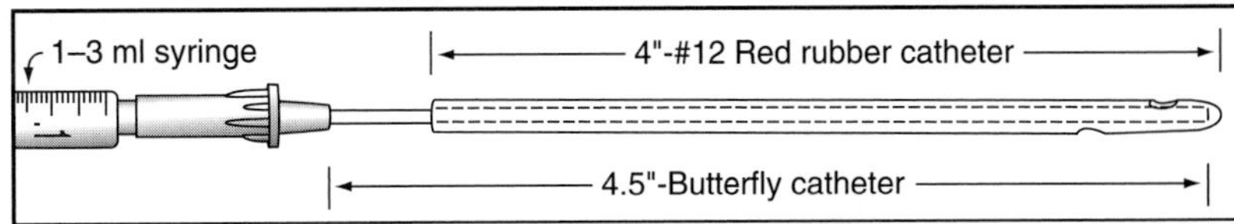

FIGURE 49–4 ■ Assembled catheter-within-a-catheter for obtaining specimens from a prepubertal child. (From Pokorny, S. F., and Stormer, L. V. N.: Atraumatic removal of secretions from the prepubertal vagina. Am. J. Obstet. Gynecol. *156*:581, 1987.)

disorder most frequently encountered[144] and is responsible for 25 to 75 percent of cases of vulvovaginitis diagnosed in this age group in referral centers.[290] In most cases, as noted in Table 49–2, identifiable secondary factors contribute to nonspecific vulvovaginitis.

Several factors other than those listed in Table 49–2 contribute to the occurrence of vulvovaginal infections in young children. The developing immature labia minora and majora flare outward as a young girl squats or sits. As a result, they do not protect the vestibular and vulvar mucosae from contamination, as occurs later in life. The nonestrogenized, prepubertal vulvar and vaginal epithelium, which consists of only a few layers of cells, is traumatized easily and infected readily; however, no evidence suggests that estrogen deficiency is a causative factor in premenarcheal vulvovaginitis. The alkaline vaginal reaction during childhood also is not as resistant to infection as is the acidic vaginal secretion of postmenarcheal females. Because children frequently do not cleanse themselves properly after defecation, the perineum and vulva are contaminated by fecal material more often than in older children. Nonabsorbent nylon garments or other tight-fitting clothes can lead to maceration, which predisposes to the development of infection.

VULVOVAGINITIS SECONDARY TO POOR PERINEAL HYGIENE

A vulvovaginal infection is considered to be secondary to poor perineal hygiene when bacteria native to the lower gastrointestinal tract are found in properly obtained cultures from the vagina. In a large series of cases of vulvovaginitis subjected to culture, *Escherichia coli* or other coliform organisms were found in 70 percent of patients in the series.[131] Other studies also have found a higher prevalence of *E. coli* in vaginal cultures from girls with vulvovaginitis than in asymptomatic controls.[79] The reappearance and disappearance of premenarcheal vulvovaginitis secondary to poor perineal hygiene are related directly to the appearance and disappearance of coliform organisms in vulvovaginal cultures. The primary role of vulvar and vaginal contamination with fecal material as a result of inadequate cleansing after defecation is supported by the observation that symptoms resolve in most cases when proper perineal hygiene is the only treatment recommended. Between 15 and 20 percent of children have recurrences, usually a month or more after resolution of the initial episode. In most instances, recurrences can be attributed to poor perineal hygiene.[131]

Children with nonspecific vulvovaginitis secondary to poor perineal hygiene do not have any uniform historical findings. If asked, the parent may be able to describe the way that the child cleanses herself after defecation. Many children wipe themselves from back to front after defecation. In girls, such practice easily results in fecal contamination of the vulvar area.

On examination, the vulvar mucosa and outer third of the vagina usually are hyperemic and covered with a scant, light gray mucoid discharge. Frequently, a clue to the cause of the infection is fecal soiling about the anus or on the perineum. Inspection of the undergarments may show fecal material in the area that comes in contact with the vulva unless, as often is the case, the girl has been bathed and dressed in clean clothes before visiting the physician.

Instructing parents regarding perineal and vulvar cleansing when the children are bathed decreases the likelihood that nonspecific vulvovaginitis will develop in their daughters. Young girls should be taught proper hygiene and that they should wash their hands both before and after urinating and defecating. Routine inspection of the perineum, vulva, hymen, and clitoris should be a part of routine physical examinations, including well-child checkups.[144]

Proper cleansing of the perineum and anus after defecation and sitz baths leads to the resolution of symptoms and infection in most cases. Sitz baths (warm water with or without Aveeno colloidal oatmeal or baking soda) 10 to 15 minutes in duration should be taken two to six times per day, depending on the severity of the vulvovaginal inflammation.[79] For intense, oozing inflammation, wet compresses with Burow solution (1 : 40) or plain water applied as often as every 3 to 4 hours may be used instead of sitz baths.[11] In mild cases, the vulva may be washed twice a day with water or a mild, unscented, nonmedicated soap (e.g., Basis, unscented Dove, Neutrogena). The perineum should be patted dry gently after baths or treatments. Complete drying may be facilitated by sitting for 10 minutes with the legs spread apart. Urinating with the labia and legs spread apart to minimize urinary reflux into the vagina may be helpful. Witch hazel pads (Tucks) may be used for cleansing after defecating and to provide mild analgesia.[80]

White cotton underpants, changed frequently to absorb discharge, and loose-fitting clothing should be worn for several days to a few weeks after the symptoms resolve. Continued wearing of such clothing also may be helpful in preventing recurrences of vulvovaginitis, especially in those living in warmer climates.

As the inflammation and exudate subside over the course of 1 to 2 days, sitz baths may be reduced in frequency and alternated two to four times a day with the application of either calamine lotion or protective ointments such as zinc oxide, Desitin, Vaseline, and A and D ointment. If pruritus is a significant symptom, an oral agent such as hydroxyzine hydrochloride (Atarax) or diphenhydramine hydrochloride (Benadryl) may be administered. Topical application of 1 percent hydrocortisone cream or triamcinolone acetonide (Mycolog) cream may be used as the inflammation resolves but should be avoided in the acute phase.[80]

Shampooing the hair while sitting in a bathtub and using harsh soaps, bubble baths, or other preparations that might lead to chemical irritation of the vulvar skin and vaginal mucosa should be avoided throughout the course of vulvovaginitis.[22, 40, 44] The application of powders should be avoided, at least until the acute symptoms have resolved.

Patients who do not improve after 2 to 3 days of hygienic measures should be re-evaluated. Specimens taken from the vagina should be sent for aerobic and anaerobic bacterial culture, if not performed initially. An intravaginal medication such as Sultrin vaginal cream, which consists of sulfathiazole, sulfacetamide, and sulfabenzamide, may be given.[2, 100] Approximately 1.0 mL is inserted into the vagina with a 5-mL Luer syringe each night for 7 nights (the applicator that comes with the tube of cream is too large to insert

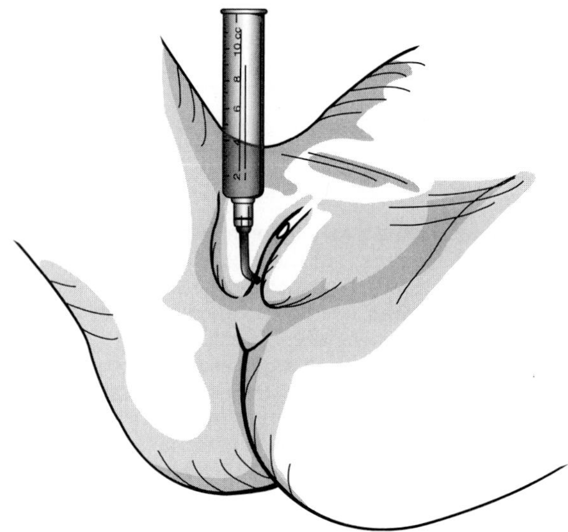

FIGURE 49–5 ■ The barrel of a Luer-type syringe and attached piece of urethral catheter are used for vaginal lavage when the patient with a vaginal infection is an older child.

into the immature vagina). A 5-cm piece of 12- or 14-French urethral catheter attached to the syringe facilitates application of the cream, if the patient is cooperative (Fig. 49–5). Parents must be warned against and instructed on how to avoid inserting the cream into the child's urethra and bladder.[131] Alternatively, the vagina may be irrigated with a 1 percent povidone-iodine (Betadine) solution with this same method and caveat.[79]

Intractable nonspecific vulvovaginal infections that are not caused by foreign bodies, intestinal parasites, or poor perineal hygiene are encountered occasionally. They are resistant to hygienic measures and topical antibiotics. Lowering vaginal pH from an alkaline or neutral to an acid reaction often helps in these difficult cases and may be achieved either by the local use of estrogen or by daily flushing of a solution of 1 mL of lactic acid, USP, in 250 mL of tap water into the child's vagina with a 10-mL Luer-type syringe and a section of a rubber or plastic urethral catheter, as shown in Figure 49–5.[131]

Estrogens cause thickening of the thin prepubertal vaginal mucosa, which lowers vaginal pH. These events generally are therapeutic. Estrogens are not recommended for the treatment of routine cases of premenarcheal vulvovaginitis for two reasons: the results do not appear to be superior to nonhormonal therapies in these cases,[131] and prolonged administration of topical estrogens may cause isosexual pseudoprecocity. For intractable cases, estrogen should be applied topically and not orally. A globule of estrogen cream (Premarin vaginal cream) measuring not more than 5 mm in diameter should be rubbed gently onto the inner surfaces of the labia minora and external surface of the hymen. This procedure is repeated daily for 2 to 4 weeks. After 7 to 10 days, the vulvar and vaginal tissues usually thicken, and a mucoid vaginal secretion may appear. The family must understand clearly that the cream must be used for no longer than instructed. The cream should be discontinued if thelarche occurs.

Oral or parenteral antibiotics may be indicated if symptoms persist for 2 to 3 weeks or if a specific pathogen that requires antibiotic treatment is isolated. When possible, selection of antibiotic agents and the route of administration should be based on susceptibility testing of organisms isolated from vaginal cultures. Nonspecific vulvovaginal infections are relatively benign, superficial, localized mucosal inflammations that usually respond to less potent chemotherapeutic agents when they are needed. Many antibiotics are absorbed through the vaginal mucosa. The indiscriminate use of vaginal, oral, or parenteral antibiotics may result in the child becoming sensitized to them.

NONSPECIFIC VULVOVAGINITIS SECONDARY TO INTESTINAL PARASITES[79]

Pinworms *(Enterobius vermicularis)* are the causative factor in many cases of recurrent or intractable nonspecific vulvovaginitis in children. Infection occurs when the worms in the lower bowel crawl out of the anus onto the perineum and migrate into the vagina, where they deposit ova. The pinworms may carry *E. coli* and other coliform bacteria into the vagina, which in turn may lead to vulvovaginitis. Other intestinal parasites seldom invade the vagina, although Huffman knew of one case in which a specimen of *Ascaris lumbricoides* was discovered in the vagina of a child.[144]

Infestation with pinworms occurs relatively commonly and does not indicate necessarily poor hygiene. Pinworm ova may be deposited in playground soil, on toys or books, and on the hands of infected persons. Infection frequently is asymptomatic.

A child with a pinworm infection and vulvovaginitis usually has a history of a chronic vaginal discharge that has recurred despite repeated attempts to eradicate it. Parents may note worms on the perineum of the child and that she awakens at night because of perineal itching. Other family members or the girl herself may have had pinworms previously.

Examination reveals a low-grade inflammation of the vulva and vagina. Excoriations from scratching may be seen on the perineum. Vaginoscopy (if indicated) shows an inflammatory reaction extending to, but not including, the cervix. Vaginal cultures produce a mixed growth of nonpathogenic bacteria, with *E. coli* and other coliform bacteria generally predominating.

The diagnosis depends on finding pinworm ova on smears from the perineum or in the vaginal discharge or a report from parents that worms are visible on the child's perianal skin. As a rule, a perineal smear is most likely to demonstrate the presence of pinworms, but pinworm ova may be detected in a wet smear of vaginal secretions (Fig. 49–6).

When a perineal smear for the ova of *E. vermicularis* is to be obtained, the parent is given a wooden tongue blade, a piece of Scotch tape, and a glass microscopic slide. The tape is attached to the tongue blade, adhesive side out (Fig. 49–7), and applied firmly to several areas about the anus. It is then removed and applied, adhesive side down, to the glass slide, which is sent to the laboratory for examination.

The type of discharge, the appearance of the vaginal mucosa, or the presence or absence of pruritus does not aid in diagnosis. A history of a previous pinworm infection in the patient, a member of the family, or a playmate is significant. Pinworms should be suspected when a child has recurrent episodes of intractable nonspecific vulvovaginitis.

Treatment consists of eradicating the pinworms. All members of the family are presumed to be infected and also must be treated. Several highly effective drugs are available for this purpose; among them are pyrantel pamoate, given as a single dose of 11 mg/kg, not to exceed 1 g, and mebendazole, 100 mg given orally as a single dose. Either treatment should be repeated after 2 weeks. Three negative perianal smears, taken at weekly intervals, should be obtained before one can assume that the worms have been eradicated.

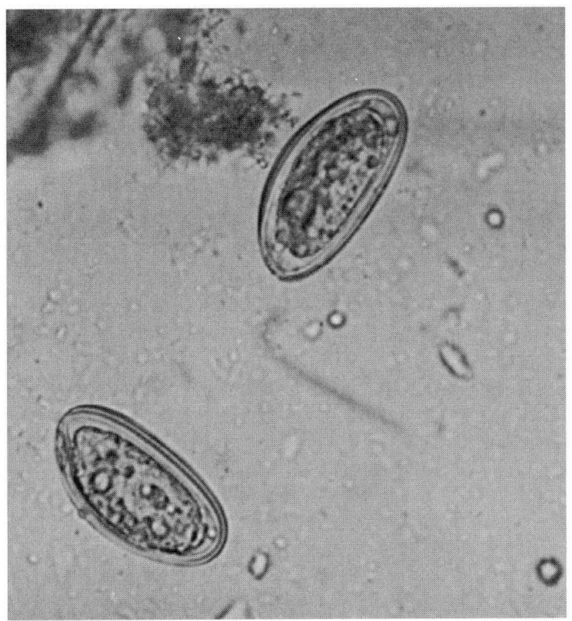

FIGURE 49–6 ■ Pinworm ova discovered in a vaginal smear from a child with intractable vulvovaginitis.

The vulvovaginitis caused by coliform organisms carried on pinworms is treated the same as other cases of nonspecific vulvovaginitis caused by poor perineal hygiene (see earlier).

NONSPECIFIC VULVOVAGINITIS SECONDARY TO VAGINAL FOREIGN BODIES

Foreign bodies account for approximately 4 percent of cases of vaginal discharge in premenarcheal girls.[11] When a foreign body remains in the vagina for some time, it inevitably causes nonspecific vulvovaginitis.

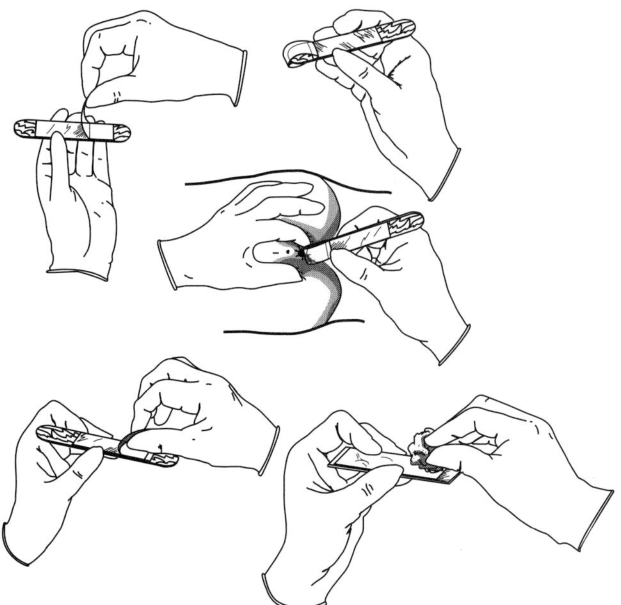

FIGURE 49–7 ■ Technique for obtaining a perianal smear for the detection of pinworm ova. Scotch tape and a tongue depressor are used.

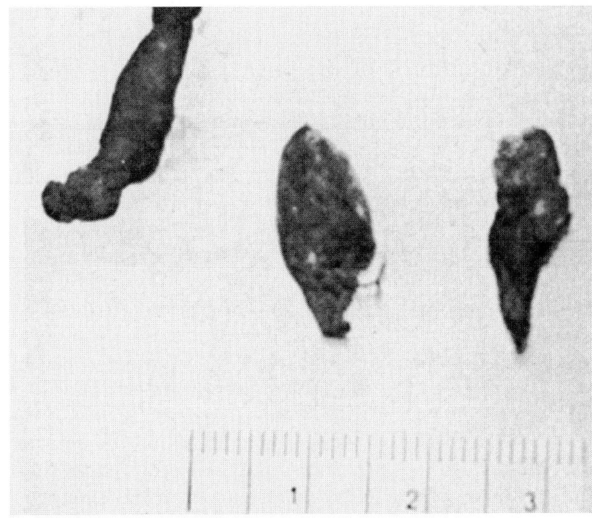

FIGURE 49–8 ■ Bits of paper or cloth are, by far, the most frequently found vaginal foreign bodies in children.

Usually, the parent is unaware that the child has inserted something into her vagina. The child is brought to a physician because of a profuse, foul-smelling, sometimes blood-tinged discharge. The presence of such a discharge is almost pathognomonic for the presence of a foreign body.

All sorts of objects, including safety pins, glass beads, coins, beans, bits of crayon, and parts of toys, have been found in children's vaginas. By far the most common objects are bits of toilet paper or shreds of cloth from nightclothes or bedding[133, 145] (Fig. 49–8).

The history does not contribute to the diagnosis unless the child has a record of having put objects in her vagina previously. Repeat episodes are common. Even without a profuse discharge or bleeding, a foul odor from the vagina suggests a foreign body. Examination reveals inflammation of the vulvar and vaginal mucosa. Although foreign material may be seen when the labia are separated, vaginoscopy is necessary to explore the full length of the vagina. Rarely, a metallic object that has been in the vagina for some time erodes the mucosa and becomes hidden in granulation tissue. When such a condition is suspected, a radiograph should be obtained. However, most foreign bodies, such as glass, plastics, paper, or cloth, are not radiopaque, and radiographic examination fails to detect the foreign material. Soft foreign bodies, such as toilet paper, can be flushed out of the vaginal canal. Vaginoscopy should be performed when a hard foreign body is suspected or when the flushing technique fails.

Extraction of a foreign body usually is a simple office procedure, but in older girls particularly, large objects may be forced into the vagina. The size of the object and edema of the vaginal mucosa from pressure may render removal a difficult task, even when the patient is anesthetized.

The nonspecific vulvovaginitis caused by a foreign body disappears gradually after removal. Recovery can be hastened by using the hygienic treatments previously described. The child should be re-examined periodically to guard against repetition of the problem.

Specific Vulvovaginal Infections

Included in this group are infections of the premenarcheal vulva and vagina by bacteria that cause specific diseases in other sites.

GONORRHEAL VULVOVAGINITIS[45, 79, 132, 261, 289, 303]

Gonococcal infections of the prepubertal genital tract are manifested as vulvovaginitis and not the endocervicitis seen in postmenarcheal females. The alkaline environment of the unestrogenized vaginal tissues of young girls appears to limit spread of infection to the upper genital tract. Gonorrhea is found less commonly in children now than in the past but must be considered whenever a girl has vulvovaginitis.

Sexual contact should be suspected strongly and almost always is the source when a child has a gonococcal infection. Whether gonococcal infection is transmitted through non-sexual contact is controversial. Researchers have suggested that transmission may occur from freshly infected bedding, towels, a toilet seat, or digital transmission from an infected adult. However, no absolute evidence exists for any of these sources of infection. Gonococcal infections in nurseries have been traced to rectal thermometers, other instruments, fomites, and attendants, but before attributing a gonococcal infection to an environmental source, the possibility of sexual transmission must be considered strongly and investigated, and supportive epidemiologic evidence should be sought (e.g., cultures of potential reservoirs).

Neisseria gonorrhoeae was the most common cause of vulvovaginal discharge among prepubertal girls in Rwanda in the late 1980s. Sexual contact was considered likely in all cases because of a cultural belief that a man with a purulent urethral discharge could be cured by rubbing his penis on the external genitalia of a prepubertal girl.[30] In a prospective study of girls 12 months to 12 years of age in the mid-1990s in Cincinnati, Ohio, who had vaginal discharge and no suspicion of sexual abuse, 4 of 43 had positive cultures for *N. gonorrhoeae*.[264] Such cases should lead to investigation for probable sexual abuse.

The acute stage of gonorrheal vulvovaginitis is characterized by inflammation and a purulent discharge. The child may complain of vulvar discomfort, dysuria, frequent urination, and pain on walking. The child usually is well otherwise. Asymptomatic vaginal infection is a rare event. On examination, the vulvar tissues are edematous, hyperemic, and covered by a profuse, thick, yellowish discharge that exudes from the vagina. The entire vaginal mucosa is inflamed.

The urethra, paraurethral glands, and the major vestibular (Bartholin) glands rarely are involved in a premenarcheal gonorrheal infection. Vulvovaginal infections, including gonorrhea, in prepubertal children rarely, if ever, affect the upper genitalia (uterus, uterine tubes, ovaries, or pelvic peritoneum). Symptoms suggestive of pelvic peritonitis have been reported in premenarcheal children who had gonorrheal vulvovaginitis; all the patients recovered promptly after the administration of penicillin.[45, 98]

The acute phase of infection lasts for a few weeks, after which most of the symptoms disappear, except the discharge. The vulvar and vaginal tissues may, in some cases, remain hyperemic and macerated. The discharge becomes scanty and seropurulent, which may persist chronically.

The diagnosis of gonorrheal vulvovaginitis and its differentiation from other types of vulvovaginitis are established by vaginal smears and cultures. Specimens from the pharynx and rectum to test for *N. gonorrhoeae* also should be obtained. Because of the potential medicolegal use of the test results for *N. gonorrhoeae* among children, standard culture systems should be used for the diagnosis of *N. gonorrhoeae* in children. DNA probes (available for vaginal and urine specimens) and other rapid tests can be used as adjunctive evidence, but they should not be performed in place of culture for the diagnosis of gonococcal infection in children. The presence of gram-negative intracellular diplococci in vaginal smears from a child with a history of exposure or with typical clinical findings is sufficient reason to start treatment, but it does not establish a definitive diagnosis. Other related species, particularly *Moraxella (Branhamella) catarrhalis* and *Neisseria sicca,* may be found in association with vulvovaginitis. A definitive diagnosis of gonorrhea is made only when *N. gonorrhoeae* is differentiated from other *Neisseria* species on the basis of glucose utilization. Additional confirmation of *N. gonorrhoeae* is recommended in children. Monoclonal fluorescent antibody tests or DNA probe confirmation tests are available. Isolates should be preserved to permit repeated or additional analyses.

Children weighing less than 45 kg with uncomplicated gonococcal vulvovaginitis, as well as urethritis, pharyngitis, or proctitis, are treated with a single dose of 125 mg of intramuscular ceftriaxone. An alternative is a single dose of intramuscular spectinomycin, 50 mg/kg (maximum, 2 g), if ceftriaxone is contraindicated. Spectinomycin is not recommended for the treatment of gonococcal pharyngitis. Treatment of children who are both 8 years or older and weigh more than 45 kg follows the guidelines for postmenarcheal females. In addition to ceftriaxone, 125 mg intramuscularly, single oral doses of cefixime (400 mg), ciprofloxacin (500 mg), or ofloxacin (400 mg) can be given to these girls. Local treatment is limited to gentle cleansing of the vulva and perineum. For hospitalized children, standard isolation precautions are recommended until 24 hours after the administration of effective parenteral therapy. Empiric therapy with erythromycin, azithromycin, or doxycycline to treat potential concomitant infection with *C. trachomatis* is given routinely to persons with gonococcal infection.[47]

Follow-up cultures should be obtained from all infected sites 2 weeks after treatment to ensure that it has been effective. If not done as part of the initial evaluation, children confirmed as having gonorrhea should be evaluated for co-infection with *C. trachomatis*, *Treponema pallidum*, *Trichomonas,* human immunodeficiency virus (HIV), and hepatitis B virus.

PREMENARCHEAL CHLAMYDIAL VAGINITIS

Although *C. trachomatis* appears to be an uncommon cause of vaginitis in prepubertal girls, vaginal infection with *C. trachomatis* can occur in children with or without a known history of sexual activity and should be considered in the evaluation of a child with vaginal symptoms. Only a few studies have evaluated young children for *C. trachomatis*. These studies have involved mostly children being evaluated for sexual abuse or vulvovaginal symptoms, or both, and some have included a control group in an attempt to control either for a history of sexual activity or for vaginal symptoms.

In studies evaluating premenarcheal children with vulvovaginitis, recovery of *C. trachomatis* has been low in both children with symptoms and healthy control groups. In one study, none of the 35 children with symptoms had *C. trachomatis,* whereas 1 of 35 without symptoms had *C. trachomatis* isolated.[217] In another study conducted in a pediatric gynecology clinic, 4 of 29 (14%) premenarcheal girls were found to have *C. trachomatis*.[42] All four had a homogeneous white discharge, and one had a bloody discharge. Sexual abuse occurred in two of the children and was considered possible in another. In a Cincinnati study evaluating vaginitis in girls younger than 12 years of age in whom sexual abuse was not suspected, none of the 87 children had a positive culture for *C. trachomatis*.[264] Similarly, in a smaller study of 11 girls with vaginitis, none were found to have *C. trachomatis*.[237]

In studies evaluating children suspected of being sexually abused, rates of recovery tend to be higher than those seen in children with vaginitis. However, in one study, a history of sexual abuse was discovered in two control children only after *C. trachomatis* was identified.[119] Initially, 2 percent of children with a history of sexual abuse versus 4 percent of healthy controls had positive vaginal cultures for chlamydiae. However, on further questioning, the two children in the control group with *C. trachomatis* were siblings who were sexually abused 3 years earlier, thus changing the rate of *C. trachomatis* vaginal infection in the sexual abuse group to 6 percent and decreasing the rate in the control group to 0 percent. This misclassification, if not discovered, would have changed the conclusion of the study, which suggested that similar rates of *C. trachomatis* infection occur in children with and without a history of sexual contact. This incidence nicely illustrates the importance of thoroughly investigating the possibility of sexual abuse whenever a sexually transmitted pathogen is isolated in a young child. In a Cincinnati study evaluating children for sexual abuse, rates were low in prepubertal girls in comparison with pubertal girls (0.8% versus 7%),[266] whereas in a study in Raleigh, North Carolina, 6 percent of sexually abused girls younger than 12 years versus 0 percent of control children had *C. trachomatis* isolated from their vagina.[150] Four of the 10 children in the later study had a vaginal discharge. The highest rates of *C. trachomatis* infection were seen in a Los Angeles study in which 47 prepubertal girls were examined for alleged sexual abuse and 17 percent had *C. trachomatis* isolated from vaginal specimens.[99] The variation in rates between studies may reflect differences in *C. trachomatis* prevalence in different communities. Although co-infection with *C. trachomatis* has not been studied well in prepubertal children, experience from adult populations has shown that it should be suspected in those with *N. gonorrhoeae* infection. In one study in prepubertal girls, 30 percent with *N. gonorrhoeae* also tested positive for *C. trachomatis*.[237]

One possibility is that a positive chlamydial culture in a young child, especially a child younger than 3 years of age, may be due to persistence of perinatal infection. Subclinical infections have been reported in 14 percent of infants of mothers with active *C. trachomatis* infection.[251] Many infants infected with *C. trachomatis* at birth remain infected for as long as 372 days in the vagina, 383 days in the rectum, and 866 days in the conjunctiva, nasopharynx, and oropharynx.[25] Persistence of perinatal infection for 18 months and as long as 6 years has been reported in other studies as well.[181, 250, 287] Although persistence of perinatal infection can occur, when *C. trachomatis* is identified in vaginal specimens, sexual abuse still must be suspected strongly.

Unlike premenarcheal gonorrhea infections, chlamydial vaginitis in children often appears to be asymptomatic. However, because of study design issues in evaluating children with *C. trachomatis* infection in which only children with a history of sexual abuse or vaginal symptoms, or both, are included, fully understanding the spectrum of symptoms seen in young children is difficult. In one study evaluating symptomatic children with *C. trachomatis* vaginal infection, 25 percent had a vaginal discharge and 12 percent had vaginal bleeding.[99]

Numerous *Chlamydia*-diagnostic methods are available.[28] Direct tissue culture isolation of *C. trachomatis* remains the gold standard and is the only test that should be used in prepubertal children or in cases in which sexual abuse is under consideration.[47] Culturing for chlamydiae requires isolation of the organism in tissue culture and confirmation of the characteristic intracytoplasmic inclusions by fluorescent monoclonal antibody staining.[47] Although the specificity of tissue culture approaches 100 percent, tissue culture is only 70 to 85 percent sensitive when compared with DNA amplification techniques.[28] The low recovery rate in studies of prepubertal children may be due to the low sensitivity of tissue culture or the use of vaginal cultures in young children. Isolation rates from the vagina usually are lower than are those of recovery from the endocervix.[184] Nonculture chlamydia tests, including enzyme immunoassays (EIAs), direct fluorescent antibody (DFA) tests, DNA hybridization, and DNA amplification tests, are available and have been investigated in cervical and urine specimens and approved for use in sexually active postmenarcheal adolescents and adults. These tests have not been field-tested for large numbers of vaginal specimens from premenarcheal girls. In addition, rectal or pharyngeal specimens have not been tested. False-positive results have been reported in vaginal specimens for some of these tests in children, and therefore, these tests should not be used in premenarcheal children.[126, 225] False-positive results probably are caused by cross-reactivity with common anogenital organisms such as group A and B streptococci, *Acinetobacter* spp., *N. gonorrhoeae, G. vaginalis, E. coli, Proteus* spp., and *Staphylococcus* spp.[165, 240, 243, 244, 286]

The treatment of choice for chlamydial infection, including vaginitis in children weighing less than 45 kg, is erythromycin, 50 mg/kg/day in four divided doses for 10 to 14 days.[47] Because erythromycin is only 80 percent efficacious, a test of cure should be considered 3 weeks after completion of treatment. A second course of therapy is recommended if the repeat culture is positive. Children weighing 45 kg or more but who are younger than 8 years of age should be treated with azithromycin as a single 1-g oral dose. For children 8 years of age and older, two regimens are recommended: azithromycin as a single 1-g dose or doxycycline at a dose of 100 mg twice a day for 7 days.[47] Because these two regimens are highly efficacious, a test of cure is recommended only if symptoms persist or reinfection is suspected.

PREMENARCHEAL VAGINAL TRICHOMONIASIS

Vaginal trichomoniasis is reported infrequently in prepubertal children. This low prevalence may be accurate or could be due to lack of appropriate testing or limitations of the diagnostic techniques used in studies in this population of children. Many diagnostic techniques are available; however, the diagnosis of *Trichomonas vaginalis* infection typically is made by identifying the motile, triflagellated trichomonads in urine or wet preparations of vaginal secretions or through culture of vaginal secretions.[14, 47] Stained smears of vaginal discharge may reveal trichomonads, but this method is the least sensitive of those available. The sensitivity of wet-mount examination of vaginal secretions is highly dependent on prompt transport of the specimen to the laboratory before the organisms lyse or lose motility and on the expertise of the person examining the specimen.[166] Although culturing of vaginal specimens is more sensitive, this method is not widely available. More sensitive techniques have allowed for the evaluation of culture and wet-mount methods. In a study examining vaginal swab samples using polymerase chain reaction (PCR), culture and wet-mount evaluations were found to have sensitivities of 70 and 36 percent, respectively.[79] A urine-based PCR enzyme-linked immunosorbent assay had a sensitivity and specificity of 91 and 93 percent, respectively, in comparison to wet mount or culture.[157] Such techniques may be promising for detection of *T. vaginalis* when vaginal specimens are not available and culture of specimens is not feasible. However, because of a lower specificity than that of culture, these techniques probably never will be recommended for use in prepubertal children in whom sexual abuse would need to be considered.

Trichomoniasis in newborn infants through the acquisition of *T. vaginalis* from the mother's vagina during delivery has been described in several case reports,[9, 54, 57, 178, 186, 226, 272] with recovery of *T. vaginalis* from urine, vaginal, and respiratory tract specimens. The prevalence of *T. vaginalis* in healthy, vaginally delivered infants of mothers with *T. vaginalis* is not known. In one study, *T. vaginalis* could not be identified in any of the 14 female babies of mothers in whom *T. vaginalis* was diagnosed.[34] The overall prevalence of *T. vaginalis* in the 868 mothers was 4 percent, but the denominator of mothers of female infants was not described. In another study of 984 female infants, direct smear or culture (or both) of infant vaginal specimens identified 3 infants with *T. vaginalis*, a prevalence of 0.3 percent.[9] Two of the three infants had a vaginal discharge. The overall prevalence of infection in the mothers of the 984 infants was not reported. Of the three infants with *T. vaginalis,* one mother had a history of vaginal discharge and a negative direct smear for *T. vaginalis,* and the other two mothers had no history of *T. vaginalis.*

Numerous reports in the literature confirm the occurrence of *T. vaginalis* outside the newborn period in prepubertal girls evaluated for vaginitis. The prevalence of *T. vaginalis* in prepubertal girls with vaginitis but no history of sexual abuse ranged from 0 to 4 percent.[113, 131, 152, 217, 264] In studies with a healthy control population,[112, 131, 152] *T. vaginalis* was not identified in any of the children in the asymptomatic control group.

T. vaginalis has been described in varying frequency in sexually abused prepubertal girls. A case report described *Trichomonas* vaginitis in two sexually abused children with vaginal discharge.[153] In two studies conducted in Raleigh, North Carolina, that described isolated pathogens in sexually abused children with a vaginal discharge, 19 percent of 52 children at risk for being sexual abused had positive wet mounts for *T. vaginalis* in one study, whereas only 2 percent of 141 children had *T. vaginalis* in the second study.[150] The variation in detection in this high-risk population cannot be explained easily. However, in studies systematically evaluating children for sexual abuse regardless of symptoms, *T. vaginalis* has not been recovered. In an Australian study evaluating 160 children younger than 10 years and 95 healthy age-matched controls, none of the children had *T. vaginalis* isolated from vaginal cultures.[103] Similarly, none of the 119 prepubertal girls evaluated for sexual abuse in a Cincinnati study had *T. vaginalis* identified by urinalysis or wet mount of vaginal secretions.[266] Without additional studies using culture techniques and conducted in diverse populations of prepubertal girls, knowing what the true prevalence of *T. vaginalis* is in prepubertal girls who have vaginitis, with or without a history of sexual abuse, is difficult.

A recent case report suggests that *T. vaginalis* could be transmitted within a family without sexual abuse or contact.[3] In this report, *Trichomonas* vaginitis was diagnosed in the mother, and her three prepubertal daughters were symptomatic with a vaginal discharge. Two of the three girls had *T. vaginalis* identified on wet-mount evaluation of their vaginal specimens. They had no history or evidence of sexual abuse, the father was asymptomatic, and microscopy of an early morning urine specimen was negative for *T. vaginalis.* Although these cases may have resulted from transmission within a family without sexual abuse, identification of *T. vaginalis* in a prepubertal child outside the newborn period should prompt further medical and social evaluation for sexual abuse. Additionally, if *T. vaginalis* is recovered from a child, the child should be evaluated for other sexually transmitted infections, including syphilis, *N. gonorrhoeae* and *C. trachomatis,* hepatitis B, and HIV infection.[14]

Metronidazole (Flagyl) is effective in the treatment of vaginal trichomoniasis in children. The recommended dose for prepubertal girls is 15 mg/kg/day in three divided doses (maximal dose, 2 g for 7 days), 500 mg twice a day for 7 days, or 40 mg/kg (maximum, 2 g) in a single dose.[14] Metronidazole can be made into a suspension for young children and has a low level of toxicity. Possible side effects are described in the discussion of trichomoniasis in adolescent girls. Metronidazole is very effective, with cure rates of 90 to 95 percent; however, if the infection does not respond to treatment, prepubertal children should be re-treated with a 7-day course as described.[4, 47] A vaginal preparation of metronidazole is available, but it is not recommended for the treatment of *T. vaginalis* infection.[47]

BACTERIAL VAGINOSIS

Bacterial vaginosis is a cause of vaginal discharge in adolescent and adult women and also may be seen in premenarcheal girls. Bacterial vaginosis is caused by a change in the relative proportions of bacteria in the vaginal flora: an overgrowth of anaerobes and *G. vaginalis* and a decrease in hydrogen peroxide–producing lactobacilli.[12] Although overgrowth of *G. vaginalis* often is found in bacterial vaginosis, identification of *G. vaginalis* by culture of the vaginal discharge is not diagnostic because *G. vaginalis* may be present in girls with or without bacterial vaginosis.[12, 47]

Two methods are used to make the diagnosis of bacterial vaginosis, Gram stain of vaginal discharge and clinical criteria,[12, 47] with clinical criteria being used most commonly. The Gram stain method is used to determine the relative concentrations of bacterial morphotypes and thereby evaluate for the overgrowth of anaerobes. This method requires an examiner with expertise in evaluating specimens for bacterial vaginosis and is less practical than is the use of clinical criteria; thus, clinical criteria are used more widely. The clinical criteria used for the diagnosis of bacterial vaginosis are the presence of three of four findings: a grayish homogeneous discharge, the presence of clue cells on a wet-mount evaluation, a pH greater than 4.5, and a positive amine test result (amine or fishy odor when vaginal secretions are mixed with 10% potassium hydroxide). Although these criteria have been used routinely in studies in postmenarcheal women, use of these criteria in premenarcheal girls has been inconsistent, thereby rendering assessment of the prevalence of bacterial vaginosis in this population difficult.

Despite the fact that the presence of *G. vaginalis* is not diagnostic of bacterial vaginosis, studies in premenarcheal girls have examined the presence of *G. vaginalis* in vaginal secretions.[21, 103, 122, 152] In a survey of vaginal flora in children without a vaginal discharge, *G. vaginalis* was isolated from 14 percent.[122] In another study, prepubertal girls with a history of sexual abuse were more likely to have *G. vaginalis* isolated from vaginal specimens (15%) than were girls with no history of sexual abuse and either genitourinary complaints (4%) or no genitourinary complaints (4%).[21] In girls with a vaginal discharge, *G. vaginalis* was isolated from 20 percent of 25 sexually abused girls versus none of the 11 girls with no history of sexual abuse. In a study examining the vaginal flora of sexually abused and nonabused 3- to 10-year-old girls, 6 percent of abused versus 1 percent of nonabused girls had *G. vaginalis* in their vaginal secretions.[103] However, in a study of premenarcheal girls older than 2 years of age with vulvovaginitis, none of the 50 girls or their age-matched controls had *G. vaginalis* isolated from vaginal specimens.[152] Because *G. vaginitis* has been isolated from symptomatic and asymptomatic girls and from girls with and without a history or evidence of sexual abuse, culture for *G. vaginitis* should not be performed in the evaluation of a child with a vaginal discharge or to determine whether sexual contact has occurred.

Bacterial vaginosis is defined poorly in premenarcheal girls. No published studies using the recommended criteria to make the diagnosis exist. However, some studies have used some of the criteria in an attempt to examine bacterial vaginosis in premenarcheal girls. In a study examining sexually transmitted infections in girls 1 to 12 years of age who were evaluated for possible sexual abuse, 99 of the 245 girls with a vaginal discharge had an amine test and were examined for clue cells.[147] Seven of the 99 girls (7%) had clue cells or a positive amine test, or both. In a similar study, 22 of 51 girls with a history of sexual contact and a vaginal discharge had an amine test performed and were evaluated for clue cells; all of them were negative for both tests.[150] In the same study, in a second group of girls defined as being at risk of having undetected previous sexual contact, 30 girls had a vaginal discharge and 10 had wet preparations performed. One had both a positive amine test and clue cells and one had a positive amine test only. In both these studies, the full criteria were not used and only a subgroup of girls with vaginal discharge were evaluated. In another study, 31 abused and 23 nonabused girls 2½ to 13 years of age had vaginal washes performed along with amine tests and testing for clue cells.[123] The abused girls had an initial visit and a follow-up visit more than 7 days after the abuse occurred. The nonabused girls had only an initial evaluation. One of the 23 nonabused girls had a positive amine test with normal examination results and was asymptomatic. Similarly, 1 of the 31 abused girls had a positive amine test on the initial visit. On follow-up evaluation, clue cells and a positive amine test developed in 4 of the 31 abused girls, and either clue cells or a positive amine test was noted in another 4 of the 31 girls. Either a new vaginal discharge or dysuria developed in five of these eight girls. Three of the eight girls were postmenarcheal. Whether the testing itself could have been responsible for the positive results is unclear because the control group did not undergo the follow-up evaluation.

Until studies using the proper and complete criteria are performed in young girls with and without a vaginal discharge, the prevalence of bacterial vaginosis will be unknown and the significance of bacterial vaginosis as a cause of vaginal discharge in premenarcheal girls will remain unclear. At this time, the presence of manifestations of bacterial vaginosis should prompt the health care provider to consider treatment of bacterial vaginosis. In addition, the possibility of sexual abuse should be contemplated because a diagnosis of bacterial vaginosis does not provide evidence of sexual abuse. Because bacterial cultures may be performed in the evaluation of a vaginal discharge in a premenarcheal girl and *G. vaginitis* may be identified, identification of *G. vaginitis* should not be considered evidence of sexual abuse or diagnostic of bacterial vaginosis.

Numerous regimens for the treatment of bacterial vaginosis exist, but no specific recommendations are available for premenarcheal girls, probably because of the infrequent diagnosis of bacterial vaginosis and the lack of clinical trials evaluating treatment of bacterial vaginosis in premenarcheal girls. Therefore, the drugs suggested for use in young girls are those recommended for postmenarcheal women, with dosages based on the child's body weight. The treatment recommended for bacterial vaginosis is with metronidazole, 500 mg orally twice a day for 7 days.[12, 47] In small children, metronidazole can be given at 35 to 50 mg/kg/day divided three times a day for 7 days.[206] Two intravaginal preparations also are available as alternative regimens for older girls. Two percent clindamycin given once a day for 7 days or 0.75 percent metronidazole gel given twice a day for 5 days can be used to treat bacterial vaginosis.[12, 47] Other alternative regimens that are known to be less effective include metronidazole in a single oral 2-g dose and clindamycin, 300 mg orally twice a day for 7 days.[12, 47] For younger girls, if clindamycin is used, a dose of 10 to 20 mg/kg/day divided three times a day for 7 days is suggested.[206]

MYCOTIC (FUNGAL) VULVOVAGINITIS

Candida albicans and other fungi can cause vulvovaginitis in infants and children. Although these infections can occur in any child, children with a history of recent antibiotic use, uncontrolled diabetes mellitus, or immunosuppression are at an increased risk for development of fungal vulvovaginitis. In children with recurrent or persistent infection, especially with no history of antibiotic use, immunosuppressive conditions such as diabetes or HIV infection should be considered. Mycotic infections are not considered sexually transmitted infections, but they are covered in this section because they can cause genital infections in young children.

Children with fungal vulvovaginitis usually complain of vulvar pruritus and burning. The burning results from urine coming in contact with desquamated or excoriated areas of the vulva. A vaginal discharge also may be present. In diapered children, an erythematous rash in the child's diaper area may be noticed.

Examination reveals findings of diffuse erythema of the vulvar mucosa that may extend onto the perineal area. The involved areas are red and shiny, and whitish plaques and edema may be found. Excoriated areas, caused by scratching, can be seen as well. If the condition has been longstanding, the edema, secondary infection, and repeated scratching may produce thickened and fissured lesions closely resembling chronic eczema or lichen sclerosis et atrophicus (Fig. 49–9). If the vagina is involved, the mucosa is dusky red, and small, whitish plaques on the vaginal surface or a scant white curdled discharge may be noted. The discharge, when present, is odorless.

The diagnosis of fungal vulvovaginitis is made by finding yeast and pseudohyphae on examination of the vaginal discharge or scraped material from the vulvar skin by Gram stain or wet preparation suspended in 10 to 20 percent

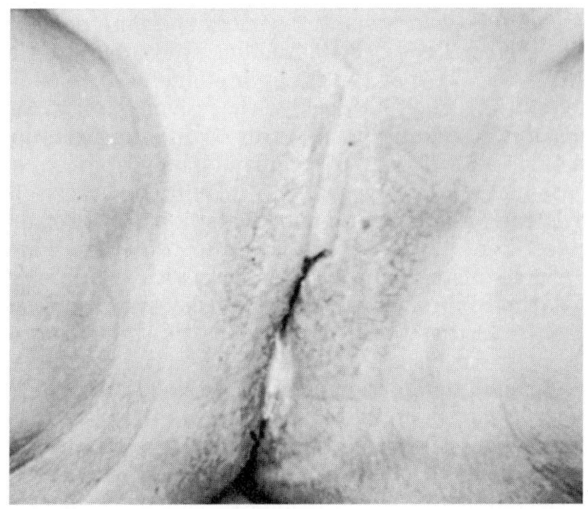

FIGURE 49–9 ■ Mycotic vulvovaginitis. The child is a diabetic.

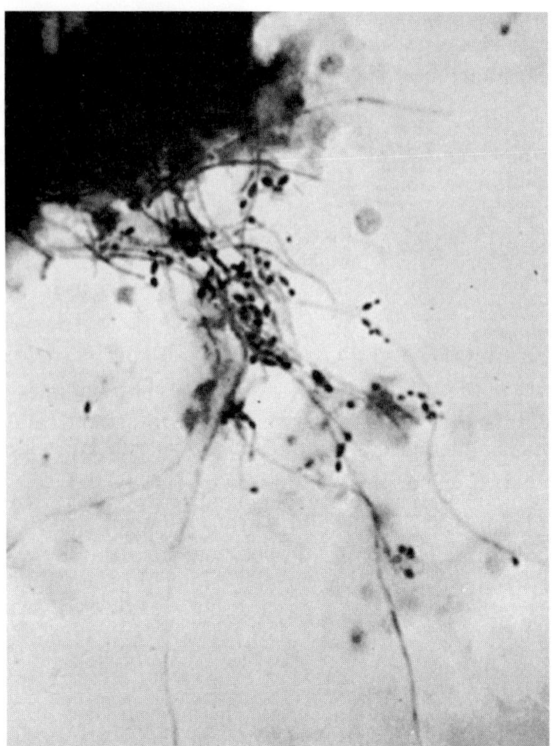

FIGURE 49–10 ■ Hyphae of *Candida albicans* discovered on a wet smear of vaginal discharge.

potassium hydroxide[13] (Fig. 49–10). Further confirmation can be made by identifying fungus by culture of material from the vagina or vulva on Sabouraud or Nickerson media.

C. albicans and other fungi have been isolated from the vagina in both asymptomatic and symptomatic girls. In a study examining the microbiology of the vagina, yeast was cultured from 48 percent of girls 2 months to 2 years of age, from 12.5 percent of girls 3 to 10 years of age, and from 35 percent of girls 11 to 15 years of age.[122] *C. albicans* (37%) and *Candida tropicalis* (26%) were the species most commonly isolated, but *Candida parapsilosis, Torulopsis glabrata,* non-*Candida* yeast species, and other *Candida* spp. were isolated as well.

In studies evaluating prepubertal girls with vulvovaginitis, fungi have been recovered at varying rates. In one study, *C. albicans* was isolated from 25 percent of 31 symptomatic prepubertal girls with an abnormal vaginal discharge or vulvovaginitis, whereas only 3 percent of asymptomatic girls had *C. albicans* isolated.[105] Another study found different results, with none of the 50 asymptomatic girls and only 2 percent of the 50 girls with vulvovaginitis having *C. albicans.*[152] Similarly, in a study evaluating girls younger than 12 years with vaginal complaints, only 3 percent of the 74 girls had *C. albicans* isolated.[264] Neither of these groups of girls had a discharge on examination, and both had been treated recently with antibiotics. In a study that examined recovery of microorganisms from girls with vaginitis, 8 percent of the 35 girls evaluated grew yeast from their vaginal culture.[112] In these latter two studies, assessing the role of yeast in their disease is difficult because they have no control population for comparison.

Several modes of therapy can be used for the management of fungal vulvovaginitis.[47] Numerous antifungal creams are available. The creams should be applied as prescribed to the affected area after cleansing. In diapered children, the cream should be applied with each diaper change.

Curing fungal infections is often difficult in children who are taking antibiotics or who receive repeated courses of antibiotic therapy. In such cases, a 1-mL dose of nystatin suspension (Mycostatin), 100,000 U/mL, can be injected into the vagina three times a day for 10 days in infants and small children. In addition, the suspension should be administered at the same dose orally four times daily. Fluconazole (Diflucan) also can be administered as a one-time oral dose. A second dose may need to be administered for severe infections.[47]

In older girls, vulvovaginal fungal infections can be treated with fungicidal vaginal creams, suppositories, or oral fluconazole as described in the section on vaginal infections in adolescent girls.[47]

NONGONORRHEAL NEISSERIAL VULVOVAGINITIS

Occasionally, other species of *Neisseria* are the causative agents in cases of premenarcheal vulvovaginitis. These gram-negative, intracellular and extracellular diplococci resemble *N. gonorrhoeae* on stained smears. *M. catarrhalis* also is identical on Gram stain. Gram-negative diplococci should be speciated completely by the microbiology laboratory to avoid misidentification of nongonococcal diplococci as gonococci and vice versa. Especially for pediatric patients, misidentification can result in serious medicolegal consequences for the family when unwarranted intervention is initiated, or it can result in failure to protect the child's welfare when appropriate measures are deemed unnecessary.[7]

N. sicca, generally considered nonpathogenic, has been isolated from children with vulvovaginal infections that clinically resembled gonorrhea.[294] *Neisseria meningitidis* also has been reported as a cause of vulvovaginitis.[85, 113] Nongonococcal *Neisseria* spp. may be considered the cause of vulvovaginal infections when isolated as the predominant flora in the setting of vaginal inflammation and discharge.

Treatment of vulvovaginitis caused by nongonococcal *Neisseria* spp. or *M. catarrhalis* is the same as for *N. gonorrhoeae.* Most nongonococcal *Neisseria* spp. are not resistant to penicillin, but the need for therapy generally is based on the Gram stain finding of gram-negative diplococci, which for therapeutic purposes should be considered gonococci pending culture results. Data are not available, but a single dose of ceftriaxone probably should be as effective for these noninvasive *Neisseria* infections as it is for gonorrhea.

Chemoprophylaxis, generally with rifampin, should be considered for family members and other contacts in cases of meningococcal vulvovaginitis.

GROUP A STREPTOCOCCAL VULVOVAGINITIS

Group A streptococci are a frequent cause of vulvovaginitis in premenarcheal girls and accounted for 9 to 20 percent of cases in several series.[70, 73, 131, 277, 290] Most cases occur in girls 2 to 7 years of age, but cases in infants and teenagers have been reported.[31, 70, 107, 277] A marked seasonal variation in incidence in some geographic regions, with peak rates in late fall and winter, may explain the low number of cases of vulvovaginitis caused by group A streptococci in some series.[89, 191] The nasopharynx appears to be the primary reservoir for group A streptococci in these girls. Infection may occur from self-inoculation by hand to nose to the vulvovaginal area.[258] The skin also may serve as the source of group A streptococcal vulvovaginitis.[107, 277] Preceding or concurrent symptoms of upper respiratory tract infection are uncommon findings, but many girls with group A streptococcal vulvovaginitis have throat cultures positive for *S. pyogenes*.[107, 277] Perineal symptoms have preceded the pharyngeal symptoms in some patients.[89] Group A streptococcal vulvovaginitis may occur during the course of scarlet fever.[31, 130, 131]

The signs and symptoms of group A streptococcal vulvovaginitis often overlap those caused by other bacterial infections, but symptoms usually are abrupt in onset.[215] Most patients seek medical care within 1 week of onset. Vaginal discharge and dysuria are the most common complaints. These girls usually are afebrile. Localized tenderness and an intense, fiery-red erythema of the vulvar tissues are frequent findings, but some cases have only mild erythema. Pruritus and excoriation may be present. The discharge usually is seropurulent but may be serosanguineous. The color may be white or green. Petechiae may be present on the vaginal mucosa, and regional papular or scarlatiniform rashes can occur.[89, 107, 258, 277] Acute poststreptococcal glomerulonephritis has been reported in association with group A streptococcal vulvovaginitis.[202] Labial abscesses caused by *S. pyogenes* have been noted rarely in prepubertal girls.[290]

Concomitant streptococcal proctitis and perianal skin infections have been reported.[89, 162, 273] Perianal pruritus, erythema, and tenderness are common findings. Abdominal pain and rectal bleeding may be present. Penile involvement occurs rarely if at all.[189]

The diagnosis of *S. pyogenes* infection may be missed if vaginal secretions are not plated onto sheep blood agar or other media that readily support the growth of streptococci.[277] The vulvovaginitis caused by group A streptococci usually responds to oral antimicrobial therapy within 24 hours. A 10-day course of oral penicillin or erythromycin generally is sufficient. A second course sometimes is necessary when perianal disease is present.[273] Adjunctive use of the hygienic measures for nonspecific vulvovaginitis hastens clinical improvement.

Group B and group F streptococci also have been isolated from girls with acute vulvovaginitis.[264]

VULVOVAGINITIS SECONDARY TO BACTERIA THAT COLONIZE THE NASOPHARYNX

Often, a history of an upper respiratory tract infection precedes the onset of vulvovaginitis by a few days. Suspicion that the two conditions are related is strengthened when vaginal cultures yield organisms that commonly colonize the nasopharynx. Vulvovaginitis is assumed to result from autoinoculation of microbes from the nasopharynx to the genitalia. The onset of vulvovaginal symptoms in these infections tends to be more acute, the inflammation and discomfort more marked, and the discharge less profuse and less purulent than in nonspecific vulvovaginitis.[144]

Haemophilus influenzae and *S. aureus* are the species isolated most commonly from cultures in this setting. *Streptococcus pneumoniae* is seen occasionally. *H. influenzae* was the organism isolated most frequently in a series of 200 girls with vulvovaginitis.[222] Acute and chronic cases of *H. influenzae* vulvovaginitis do occur, and the discharge usually is mucoid or mucopurulent, yellow, and odorless. Vulvovaginitis can be caused by serotypes a, b, and c and by nontypeable strains.[131, 187] Concurrent otitis media or urinary tract infection may be present. All three of these species occasionally are found in vaginal cultures from asymptomatic children. Their isolation in pure culture from symptomatic girls is what leads to the clinical conclusion of cause and effect.

Vulvovaginitis caused by these organisms often responds to the treatment described earlier for nonspecific vulvovaginitis secondary to poor perineal hygiene. Systemic antibiotics may be required for persistent cases or may be helpful early in severely symptomatic cases. The choice of agent depends on the anticipated or known antimicrobial susceptibilities of the specific organism.

The vagina is a well-recognized source of *S. aureus* colonization in cases of toxic shock syndrome associated with this organism. Such cases generally have occurred in adolescent and adult females in association with the use of tampons. Vulvovaginitis caused by *S. aureus* in prepubertal girls has not been reported in connection with toxic shock syndrome. Labial abscesses caused by *S. aureus* have been described in prepubertal girls.[79]

VULVOVAGINITIS SECONDARY TO SKIN INFECTIONS

Like a child with an upper respiratory tract infection, one with impetigo or an infected superficial wound may transmit bacteria from the wound to the genitalia by hand contamination. Cultures in such cases usually yield hemolytic streptococci or *S. aureus*. Treatment is the same as that described for nonspecific vulvovaginitis secondary to respiratory tract infections.

SHIGELLA VULVOVAGINITIS

Vulvovaginitis may be caused by infection with pathogens from the intestinal tract, especially when the organisms are endemic in a community. *Shigella* spp., mainly *S. flexneri* and *S. sonnei*, appear to account for most of these cases.[30, 36, 37, 63, 198] Vaginal discharge without pain, pruritus, or dysuria is the most frequent manifestation of *Shigella* vulvovaginitis. The course can be acute, but discharge that persists for 4 weeks to several months before the diagnosis is made is a common finding. Bloody discharge has been observed in approximately half the cases reported from developed countries but was not seen in any of 27 girls with *Shigella* vulvovaginitis in Rwanda between 1988 and 1991.[30] The discharge may be purulent and heavy; occasionally it is absent. The vulvar tissues usually appear inflamed.

In most instances, *Shigella* vulvovaginitis is not associated with current or recent diarrhea.[30, 198] A vaginal foreign body, which may have similar symptoms and course, was considered likely in many patients before the diagnosis of *Shigella* infection.[198]

Local application of triple-sulfa cream (Sultrin) may clear the infection in some cases. However, refractory cases were noted in two series.[63, 198] Systemic treatment with an antibiotic to which the *Shigella* isolate is susceptible is recommended. Single-dose therapy with third-generation cephalosporins is not effective; 5-day courses of oral agents generally are required.[30] Amoxicillin, trimethoprim-sulfamethoxazole, and cefixime are reasonable choices for susceptible isolates. A growing number of *Shigella* isolates are resistant to ampicillin and trimethoprim-sulfamethoxazole. As with other causes of vulvovaginitis, adjunctive use of hygienic measures may help resolve the process and prevent recurrence.

OTHER SPECIFIC CAUSES OF PREMENARCHEAL VULVOVAGINITIS[94, 172, 221]

Diphtheritic, amebic, and other types of specific vulvovaginitis in children have been reported in the literature. Most such cases have had associated primary disease elsewhere.

Diphtheritic vulvovaginitis can be the primary site of infection, but most reported cases have been secondary to nasopharyngeal infection. Although diphtheria seldom occurs today, sporadic cases occasionally appear in areas where immunization coverage is inadequate. The vulva is the most common genital site involved in diphtheria,[221] but diphtheritic lesions may occur in the vagina without vulvar involvement. The diagnosis is suspected when a child has the severe systemic symptoms produced by upper respiratory tract diphtheria and a local ulceration covered by a gray adherent membrane; it is confirmed by finding *Corynebacterium diphtheriae* in discharge from the lesion.[76] Treatment of diphtheria is the same regardless of the site of the infection and is discussed in Chapter 95.

One case of vulvovaginitis with *Yersinia enterocolitica* isolated as the predominant organism was reported in a 4-year-old girl who also had a positive stool culture and associated fever and abdominal pain but no diarrhea.[292] In other members of the community in which she lived, diarrhea developed with cultures positive for *Y. enterocolitica.* The outbreak was linked to contaminated food. Infections with this organism may be missed because special culture techniques are required for isolation.

Rarely, ulcerative vulvovaginitis caused by *Entamoeba histolytica* or related to typhoid fever has been reported. As a rule, specific genital infections with pathogenic organisms usually found in the gastrointestinal tract are the result of fecal contamination of the vulva and vagina. Treatment of infections caused by *E. histolytica* is described in Chapter 209.

OTHER INFECTIONS OF THE PREMENARCHEAL FEMALE GENITALIA

Other specific and nonspecific infections of the premenarcheal female genitalia, including herpes genitalis, condylomata acuminata, molluscum contagiosum, lymphogranuloma venereum, cervicitis, and salpingitis, are discussed in the part of this chapter devoted to genital infections in adolescents.

Pelvic inflammatory disease (i.e., infection of the uterine tubes, ovaries, and pelvic peritoneum) is extremely rare in premenarcheal girls. With the exception of gonorrhea and the inflammation caused by a foreign body, most vulvar and vaginal infections do not involve the upper third of the vagina and do not approach the cervix of premenarcheal patients. The premenarcheal cervix and endometrium apparently are barriers rather than passageways for bacteria causing all types of vulvovaginitis in children.

Reported cases of ascending pelvic infection, including gonorrhea, are most unusual, both before the advent of antibiotics and in more recent times. Girls have been described who had lower abdominal symptoms after having nonspecific or gonorrheal vulvovaginitis, but almost without exception, a causal relationship between the lower genital tract infection and that in the pelvis was not confirmed by surgical inspection or culture of the pelvic exudate.

When intrapelvic infection has been reported in premenarcheal girls, it usually has been part of either generalized primary peritonitis or peritonitis secondary to a ruptured appendix or some other intra-abdominal infection.[254]

Pelvic infection that is part of an intra-abdominal infection characteristically affects the surfaces of the uterine tubes, uterus, and ovaries and produces perisalpingitis and periovaritis; periappendicitis also is present even if the infection did not begin as appendicitis. An ascending infection from the lower genital tract, such as that caused by gonorrhea, involves the tubal mucosa and produces endosalpingitis and pyosalpingitis.

Identical bacteria should be isolated in cultures from the lower genitalia and from the pelvic exudate before an ascending infection is considered to be the cause of a pelvic infection in a specific case in which the patient is a premenarcheal child.

Sexually Transmitted Diseases in Sexually Abused Children

Isolation of a sexually transmitted disease in a child (especially a prepubertal child) places a health care provider in an awkward position of having to report the case to a children's protective service agency for investigation of sexual abuse. The possibility of nonsexual transmission of these diseases often is raised, particularly when a preliminary investigation cannot elicit a history of sexual abuse. However, the rate of eliciting evidence of sexual abuse in prepubertal children can be as high as 67 percent in those with sexually transmitted diseases.[18] The challenges involved in eliciting and validating sexual abuse in children are many. Verbal communication in children younger than 2 to 3 years of age is impossible or difficult to interpret. Fear of disclosure by children or family members, because of threats of violence, may be a major barrier to validating a case in an older child.[187]

The first step in managing such situations is for a physician to critically assess the type of diagnostic test used to detect the infection. A major problem exists with inappropriate use of nonculture tests for chlamydia testing.[6, 120] The second step is for a physician to perform a genital examination on the child to look for evidence of acute or chronic vulvar and hymenal trauma. Referral to a physician with expertise in this field would be appropriate. A brief interview of the child in a nondirected manner with open-ended questions also should be performed. Regardless of whether the child divulges any information, the case should be reported to the local children's protective service agency. The objective is for an agency caseworker to also interview the child in a nonthreatening manner. In addition, the caseworker should request that all household members be tested for sexually transmitted diseases. More than one visit and interview by the caseworker may be necessary for such testing to be accomplished. Based on a review of the literature, common sexually transmitted diseases in prepubertal children and their potential mode of transmission are presented in Table 49–4 and discussed in this section.

GONOCOCCAL INFECTION

In infants, perinatal nonsexual transmission is considered the most likely cause of gonococcal infection. Branch and Paxton found that in 1- to 11-month-old children, all the mothers were found to have gonococcal infection, and no history of sexual contact could be elicited.[35] The authors concluded that transmission of the infection was perinatal, from freshly contaminated hands, or through fomites.

Prepubertal children with gonococcal infection frequently are found to have a history of sexual contact.[147] The rate of eliciting a history of sexual contact in prepubertal children with gonorrhea ranges from 36 to 93 percent.[35, 93, 146, 149] Branch and Paxton reported that 93 percent of children 1 to 9 years of age with gonorrhea had sexual contact with relatives in the household.[35] Ingram and colleagues found that 35 percent of 1- to 4-year-old children and 100 percent of children older than 4 years of age with gonorrhea reported sexual contact with an older male family member.[146, 149] Folland and coworkers elicited a history of sexual contact from 34 percent of children with gonococcal urethritis and vaginitis.[93]

Other infected adults and children often are found in an infected child's environment.[227] Testing of household

TABLE 49–4 ■ COMMON SEXUALLY TRANSMITTED DISEASES (STDs) IN PREPUBERTAL CHILDREN AND THEIR POSSIBLE MODE OF TRANSMISSION

	Perinatal	STD Rate in Alleged Sexual Abuse Cases	Alleged Sexual Abuse Rate in STD Cases	Infected Household Members	Survival on Fomites	Other
Neisseria gonorrhoeae infection	Up to 1 yr of age[35]	5–7%[63]	35%, 1–4 yr of age[149] 100%, older than 4 yr[149] 93%, 1–9 yr of age[35]	18–29%, no history of sexual abuse elicited[6,201]	24 hr on wet fomites; 2 hr on dry fomites. None from public toilet seats[106, 223]	None
Chlamydia trachomatis infection	Up to 3 yr of age[251]	6–8%[148, 150] 4% cases vs. 7% controls[124]	75%	No data	No data	None
Trichomonas vaginalis infection	Up to 1yr of age	No data	Case report[153] History of sexual abuse not obtained in Polish studies[168]	43% fathers, 72% mothers, no history of sexual abuse elicited (Poland)[168]	Up to 6 hr on wood surface and discharge.[159] Isolated from bathing implements[205]	Bathing tanks (India).[205] Mud baths, warm mineral waters (Poland).[168] Water from toilets[44]
Syphilis	Congenital	0–5%[63]	Case reports	No data	No data	None
Bacterial vaginosis/ nonspecific vaginitis	No data	13% cases vs. 4% controls[123]	Case reports	No data	No data	None
Herpes simplex virus infection	Period unknown	No data	Case reports	Case report (mother with infected finger)[156]	2 hr on latex gloves, toilet seat[176] 24–72 hr on speculum and gauze[176]	Autoinoculation from oral lesions[200]
Human papillomavirus infection	Up to 3 yr of age[60]	No data	27–90%[51]	No data	No data	None

members can detect infected adults at a rate of 18 to 29 percent.[6, 201] In a retrospective study of 14 Native Alaskan children with gonococcal infection, 3 reported sexual contact. Seven children slept with their parents, one or both of whom had gonorrhea; the authors assumed that these children acquired the infection by nonsexual means.[265]

N. gonorrhoeae has been shown to survive for 20 to 24 hours in infected secretions on towels and handkerchiefs.[275] Although *N. gonorrhoeae* has survived on toilet seats for as long as 2 hours, no gonococci were recovered from toilet seats in public restrooms or in a clinic for sexually transmitted diseases.[106, 236] Nonsexual transmission to adults is a rare occurrence.

Nonsexual transmission conceivably occurs in children who sleep and bathe with their parents. However, sexual transmission is the more common and most likely mode of transmission.[120] An investigation for sexual abuse must be pursued in a child with gonorrhea by reporting the case to the appropriate legal authority.

CHLAMYDIAL INFECTION

C. trachomatis can be transmitted to an infant from an infected mother during the perinatal period. *C. trachomatis* has been isolated from the conjunctiva, nasopharynx, vagina, and rectum of infants born to infected mothers.[251] Perinatally acquired rectal and vaginal chlamydial infection in infants can persist for as long as 372 and 383 days, respectively. Persistent chlamydial infection of the pharynx in infants can persist for as long as 2 years.[25]

Sexual abuse as a potential mode of transmission of *C. trachomatis* infection should be considered in children older than 1 year of age.[99, 124] In a retrospective study, Ingram and associates found that 6 percent of girls who allegedly were sexually abused and no girls who denied sexual abuse had *C. trachomatis* infection. Except for one child, all the children in the control group were determined later to have been sexually abused.[148] In a prospective study, Ingram and associates found *C. trachomatis* in 8 percent of girls with a history of sexual abuse as compared with 0 percent in girls with no history of sexual abuse. In the former group, three girls also were found to have rectal and one to have pharyngeal infection.[147, 150]

In conclusion, perinatally acquired genital chlamydial infection is a strong possibility in children younger than 1 year of age. Perinatal transmission is possible in children as old as 3 years of age. After 1 year of age, however, sexual transmission should be a strong consideration in children with genital chlamydial infection. Therefore, an investigation for sexual abuse must be pursued in a child in whom genital chlamydial infection is diagnosed.[120] No studies have evaluated the presence of *C. trachomatis* on fomites and its coexistence in family members of infected children.

SYPHILIS

The prevalence of syphilis in children suspected of having been sexually abused is lower than that of infections such as gonorrhea or chlamydia. Syphilis infections not found to be acquired congenitally should be considered sexually transmitted.[108, 147] Sexually acquired infection is a strong possibility in all prepubertal children with syphilis. Syphilitic lesions and positive serologic results have been detected in alleged sexual abusers of children with syphilis.[1]

No data are available on the survival of *Treponema pallidum* on fomites. An investigation for sexual abuse must be pursued in a child in whom syphilis is diagnosed.

TRICHOMONAS VAGINALIS INFECTION

T. vaginalis has been found in the nasopharynx and vagina of newborns born to infected mothers. Therefore, transmission of *T. vaginalis* in infants as old as 1 year of age probably is perinatal. The mode of transmission in children older than 1 year is controversial. Two cases of *T. vaginalis* infection in premenarcheal girls who were sexually abused have been reported.[153] Prevalence studies either do not address the mode of transmission at all or, if they do, do not address the possibility of sexual abuse.[87, 147, 168] In addition, a vaginal wet mount for trichomonads is not performed routinely in children assessed for possible sexual abuse. A survey from Poland found one case of *T. vaginalis* infection in children 2 to 7 years of age and a significantly higher number of cases in 8- to 10-year-old girls. The numbers increased even further after 10 years of age, thus suggesting a strong association between *T. vaginalis* and the presence of an estrogenic environment, which promotes glycogen production and decreases vaginal pH.[168]

The Polish survey tested families of women infected with *T. vaginalis* and found that almost a third of their sexual partners and 8 percent of the children (mostly girls) had *T. vaginalis*. When families of men infected with *T. vaginalis* were tested, 91 percent of their sexual partners and 13 percent of the children had *T. vaginalis*. When families of children (mostly girls) infected with *T. vaginalis* were tested, 72 percent of their mothers and 43 percent of their fathers had the infection. The investigators considered that the infection in the latter group originated from mothers and the primary mode of transmission was nonsexual (beds, sponges, towels, overcrowding). Information regarding sharing of potentially infected fomites, sexual abuse, or physically intimate behavior between parents and children was not gathered in these cases.[168]

Although *T. vaginalis* has been known to survive on fomites in controlled experiments, its ability to spread by these means is not known. No cases of adults being infected by fomites have been documented. *T. vaginalis* has been found to survive for as long as 6 hours on droplets of discharge and enameled surfaces of wood blocks.[159] It has been isolated from droplets of water splashed from toilets containing the urine of an infected person.[44] *T. vaginalis* also has been found to survive in mud baths, bathing waters, and warm mineral waters and on moist bathing implements.[168, 205] In rural India, a survey found that young girls who bathed in tanks or rivers had a significantly higher risk of acquiring *T. vaginalis* than did those who used pipe or well water.[50]

In summary, *T. vaginalis* conceivably is transmitted to children nonsexually. The likelihood of perinatal transmission is high in infants younger than 1 year of age. However, a child or an infant younger than 1 year with *T. vaginalis* also may have been sexually abused. In a child older than 1 year of age, the probability of sexual abuse must be considered and the case investigated. Perinatal transmission and transmission of infection through fomites should not be assumed without an investigation for sexual abuse.

BACTERIAL VAGINOSIS

The significance of bacterial vaginosis and *G. vaginalis* and their relationship to sexual abuse in prepubertal girls are unclear. Data on the prevalence of bacterial vaginosis in children with vaginal discharge and suspected sexual abuse are limited. Based on the presence of clue cells and a positive amine test result in vaginal secretions, bacterial vaginosis has been diagnosed in 13 percent of sexually abused children versus 4 percent of girls who denied sexual abuse.[123, 147] Similar prevalence rates for *G. vaginalis* have been reported in children who have and have not been sexually abused.[21] No data are available regarding the survival of *G. vaginalis* on fomites.

In conclusion, although the prevalence of *G. vaginalis* and bacterial vaginosis is higher in sexually abused children than in nonabused children, their significance as a marker for sexual abuse is unclear. *G. vaginalis* is not the sole cause of bacterial vaginosis and is not a suitable marker of sexual activity. Therefore, the recommendation is that a child with a vaginal discharge, the presence of clue cells, and a positive amine test be questioned about sexual abuse. However, an investigation by a children's protective service agency is not necessary.

HERPES GENITALIS

Perinatal transmission of herpes simplex virus types 1 and 2 in the form of stomatitis occurs in infants. Herpes simplex virus type 2 is not a common finding. Types 1 and 2 have been isolated in the genital area in children alleging sexual abuse.[104, 147] However, no studies have reported the coexistence of herpes simplex virus genital infection in household members and infected children. Physical contact by a mother's infected finger has been reported.[156] Autoinoculation from the mouth to the genitals as a mode of transmission is possible, especially when oral herpes simplex virus infection precedes genital herpes lesions.[200] Herpes simplex virus has been known to survive for 2 hours on latex gloves and toilet seats, 24 hours on a speculum, and 72 hours on gauze.[176] However, transmission of herpes simplex virus from fomites requires direct contact of viable virus with either a mucous membrane or a break in the skin, thus rendering fomite transmission unlikely. A child with genital herpes infection should be evaluated for sexual abuse and the case reported to the authorities.

GENITAL WARTS, CONDYLOMA ACUMINATUM

Perinatal transmission of human papillomavirus (HPV) from an infected mother to her baby is well documented. The incubation period after exposure to the virus may range from 1 to 20 months.[60] Data on the presence of HPV DNA in children beyond the neonatal period are inconsistent, 1.2 to 27 percent in three different studies.[175, 229, 293] In addition, the relationship between the presence of HPV DNA and the ultimate development of disease in children is not clear either. Thus, because the exact incubation period for the development of genital lesions is not known, perinatal transmission has been found to be the most likely cause of genital warts in almost 96 percent of patients younger than 3 years of age.[60] In children 3 years of age or older, a history of sexual abuse has been elicited in 27 to 90 percent with venereal warts.[51, 134] Condylomata acuminata are acquired by children as a result of close physical contact with an infected person, by digital infection of a child's genitalia by such a person, or by sexual contact with a person who has the disease.[259] A history of condylomata in other members of the family, particularly the mother or older sisters who care for the child, sometimes may be elicited. Perinatal exposure, poor hygiene, and shared bathing have been suggested sources of infection.[278, 279] However, types 6, 11, 16, and 18 are seen in adults with anogenital warts and are the most common genital types detected in children. This finding has raised questions about warts in children resulting from sexual abuse. In many cases, however, the mode of transmission is not known.[60] Based on failure to identify sexual abuse, a report from a dermatology clinic concludes that transmission of HPV possibly occurs by fomites.[51] No reports in the literature address survival of the virus on fomites.

In conclusion, sexual abuse is the most common means of acquiring HPV infection and should be suspected and investigated in all prepubertal children older than 3 years of age who are infected. In children younger than 3 years of age, although perinatal transmission is likely, sexual abuse should be suspected all the same and investigated.

Postmenarcheal Lower Genital Tract Infections

Infections of the postmenarcheal female clitoris, urinary tract, vulva, vagina, and cervix produce a variety of overlapping symptoms, including vulvar pruritus, dysuria, and increased or altered vaginal discharge and spotting.[97, 183] As a result, distinguishing among various lower genital tract infections based solely on symptoms is difficult. The history, physical examination, and laboratory tests play an important role in assisting the clinician in diagnosing urethritis, vaginitis, or cervicitis.

DISORDERS OF THE CLITORIS

Cellulitis with induration, edema, and erythema, analogous to posthitis in males, occasionally develops in the clitoral hood. Staphylococci or streptococci are the most common etiologies. Oral antibiotics with efficacy against these organisms usually are effective. Warm soaks or sitz baths also may provide symptomatic relief.[79]

Clitorimegaly with erythema can occur with vulvovaginitis of any etiology but most often is associated with herpes simplex virus infections.[67] Edematous enlargement of the clitoris, as well as the labia, without erythema has been reported in patients with Crohn disease.[197]

POSTMENARCHEAL URETHRITIS

Urethritis is manifested clinically by dysuria or urinary urgency, or by both. Attempting to differentiate external from internal dysuria is important. External dysuria is pain from urine flowing over the vulva. Such a history suggests vulvitis and vaginitis. Internal dysuria is pain with initiation of urination and is not associated with urine flowing over the vulva. It indicates urethritis or a urinary tract infection. Thus, a careful history and examination assist the physician in differentiating urethritis from vaginitis.

Urethritis occurs commonly, particularly in sexually active postmenarcheal females. Urethritis with internal dysuria can occur as a result of sexually transmitted diseases such as *T. vaginalis, N. gonorrhoeae,* and *C. trachomatis* infections and has been implicated as an important cause of dysuria in sexually active females. It is called the acute urethral syndrome, and clinical features include dysuria, frequency, and pyuria with significant bacteriurea.[276] Urethral infection by *C. trachomatis* may occur with or without cervical infection; such infection was associated with sterile pyuria in 50 percent of females with acute-onset dysuria and frequency, and *C. trachomatis* was isolated in 31 percent of these cases.[276]

Thus, when a sexually active adolescent girl has internal dysuria, in addition to being tested for conventional uropathogens, she should be screened for common sexually transmitted diseases such as gonorrhea and *Chlamydia* and *Trichomonas* infection.[65] Urinanalysis and microscopy for the presence of leukocytes and bacteria should be performed in these patients as well. For treatment of urethritis caused by sexually transmitted organisms, the sections in this chapter on trichomoniasis, gonorrhea, and chlamydial infections should be reviewed.

PARAURETHRAL DUCT ABSCESS, BARTHOLINITIS, AND BARTHOLIN ABSCESS

The paraurethral ducts lie on each side of the urethral meatus. The Bartholin glands are small, bean-shaped glands that lie on each side of the vaginal opening, behind the hymen. Each gland opens by means of a long single duct immediately external to the hymen. Infections of the paraurethral and Bartholin ducts are found more commonly in adult women but occasionally occur in adolescent girls.

A paraurethral duct abscess creates a small, exquisitely painful swelling in the urethrovaginal septum. If the abscess is not incised and drained, it may rupture into the urethra and create a urethral diverticulum. Discharge for Gram stain should be obtained from the urethral lumen and the paraurethral ducts by downward and outward pressure on the urethrovaginal septum (Fig. 49–11).

Bartholinitis, or inflammation of the Bartholin ducts, causes pain, tenderness, and a linear ropey-shaped swelling, best palpated by holding the vulvar mucosa and labia majora between the fingers. Purulent or mucoid exudate can be expressed occasionally from the Bartholin duct.

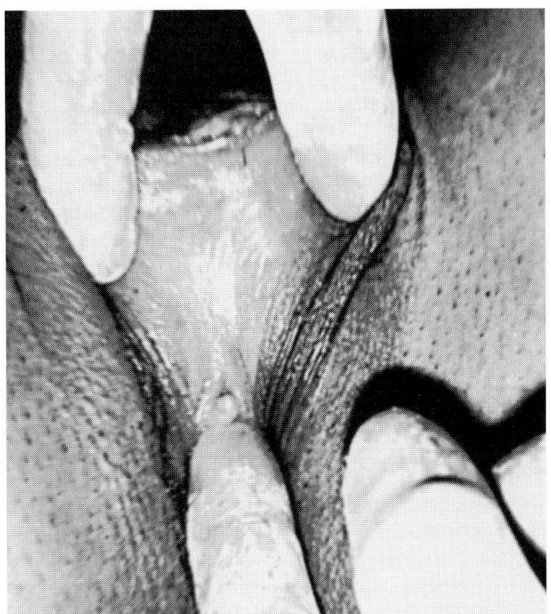

FIGURE 49–11 ■ Urethral and paraurethral duct discharge is obtained by placing downward and outward digital pressure on the distal urethrovaginal septum.

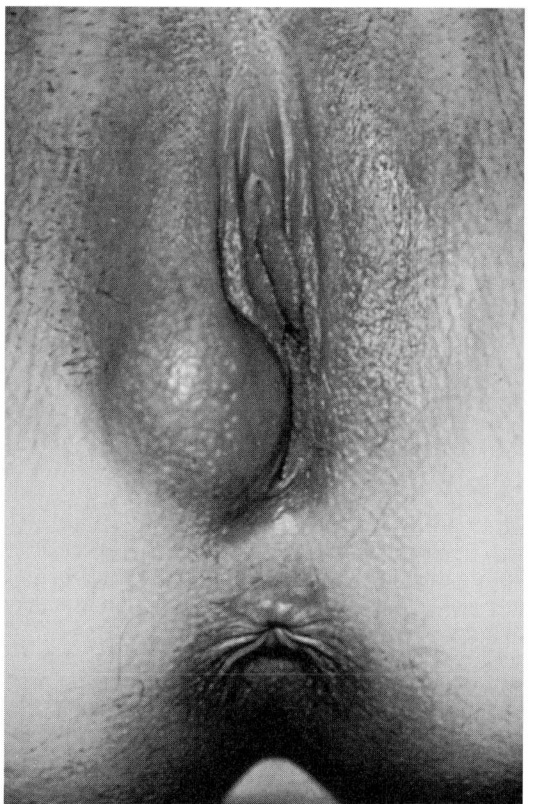

FIGURE 49–12 ■ Acute Bartholin duct abscess.

N. gonorrhoeae and *C. trachomatis* have been isolated from ductal exudate in women with bartholinitis.[59, 234] This condition should be treated with antibiotics that provide coverage for *N. gonorrhoeae, C. trachomatis,* and anaerobes. Symptomatic relief may be achieved with sitz baths.

Although a Bartholin abscess is seen most often in women 20 to 29 years of age, it does occur in sexually active adolescent girls. It also is the second most common urogenital complication of gonorrhea, after pelvic inflammatory disease, in women. Risk factors for development of Bartholin abscess are similar to those for sexually transmitted diseases.[4]

Infection of a Bartholin cyst results in a markedly tender abscess (Fig. 49–12). The abscess can rupture spontaneously and drain foul-smelling, purulent material externally through the skin. Multiple organisms are isolated from Bartholin abscesses. An early study using percutaneous aspirates from abscesses demonstrated predominantly anaerobes and facultative organisms. *N. gonorrhoeae* was isolated in 8 percent of cases and gram-negative bacilli in 16 percent. Although genital Mycoplasmataceae organisms were isolated from the duct secretions, they were not isolated directly from abscesses.[177] More recently, *Porphyromonas asaccharolyticus* (a black-pigmented, gram-negative anaerobe) and *Salmonella panama* (after an attack of *Salmonella* enteritis) have been isolated from a Bartholin abscess.[55, 74] Tuberculosis of the Bartholin gland has been reported.[69, 144, 145] Huffman encountered tuberculosis of the Bartholin gland in a 14-year-old sexually inactive female with pulmonary tuberculosis. She had painless, unilateral swelling of the left labium majus with a brown discharge exuding from a small sinus. *Mycobacterium tuberculosis* was isolated in the discharge.[144]

A Bartholin abscess should be incised and drained by applying a surface anesthetic, ethyl chloride, and making a 1- to 1½-cm, full-thickness incision on the medial aspect of the labium majus. The cavity should be probed with a sterile cotton-tipped swab to break up loculations within the abscess. To allow for further drainage, one should pack the abscess cavity with sterile gauze. Alternatively, a Word catheter can be inserted into the cavity and the balloon inflated. Clinical experience indicates that the packing method is far more painful to the patient and healing takes longer.

Antibiotic coverage for anaerobes, *N. gonorrhoeae,* and *C. trachomatis* should be provided for at least 2 weeks, and a nonsteroidal medication is recommended for inflammation and pain. Frequent sitz baths further help with drainage and healing. Close follow-up during the first week is advised. The packing or the catheter may be removed after 4 days of antibiotics. Although marsupialization frequently was used to treat recurrent Bartholin abscesses, incision plus drainage and primary suture of the abscess cavity along with administration of an antibiotic (clindamycin) has been found to lead to more rapid healing and to decrease significantly the incidence of recurrent abscesses.[16]

POSTMENARCHEAL VULVOVAGINITIS

The most common types of vulvovaginitis in postmenarcheal females are *T. vaginalis* vaginitis, vulvovaginal candidiasis, and bacterial vaginosis.

Postmenarcheal Vaginal Trichomoniasis

T. vaginalis is a triflagellated protozoan (Fig. 49–13). The organism, somewhat larger than a polymorphonuclear leukocyte, has a distinctive vibrating or whip-like movement when seen microscopically in fresh wet smears taken from the vagina. It quickly succumbs to lowering of the pH, drying, cooling, and changing the osmotic pressure of the fluid surrounding it.

Most infections are encountered in sexually active young women; the incidence increases during the early reproductive years.

Trichomoniasis frequently is asymptomatic. When it is symptomatic, patients complain of a profuse, irritating discharge. Both the discharge and the pruritus tend to be more severe just before and immediately after a menstrual period.

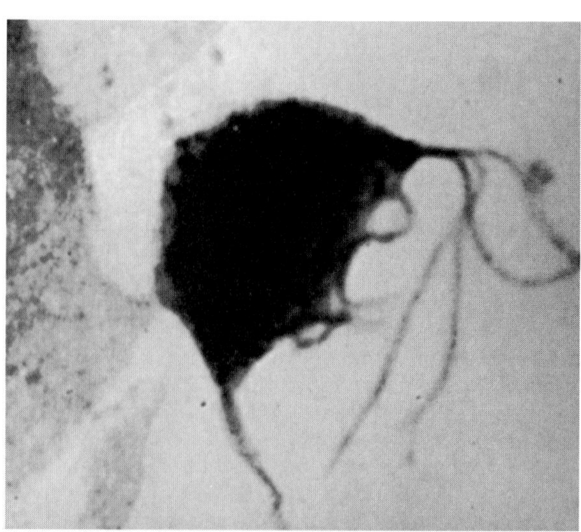

FIGURE 49–13 ■ *Trichomonas vaginalis* is a triflagellated protozoan that, when motile, is identified easily in wet smears of vaginal discharge.

Recurrent exacerbations of the infection occur commonly. Patients occasionally report dysuria and abdominal pain.

Examination reveals diffuse vulvitis with erythema and excoriations and copious leukorrhea that covers the vulvar tissues. The discharge typically is frothy or bubbly, grayish-yellow, and watery or mucopurulent. It has a pH of between 5 and 7 and an acrid or musty odor. A "strawberry"or punctate vaginal eruption with hemorrhagic spots has been described as being typical of trichomoniasis. However, such eruptions frequently are not present, even in severe cases. More often, diffuse inflammation causes the vaginal mucosa to be brilliant red.

The diagnosis of trichomoniasis most often is confirmed clinically by finding trichomonads in a wet smear of vaginal fluid. The vaginal specimen is obtained on a cotton-tipped swab and dipped into a small test tube with saline. After the solution has been stirred with the swab, one or two drops of the solution are placed with the swab on a slide. Of importance is that the slide be viewed under the microscope (dry high power) promptly because the organisms do not remain viable for long outside the vagina and are difficult to detect once they cease to be motile. The observer sees numerous ovoid-shaped, motile organisms. The sensitivity of this test ranges from 40 to 75 percent. A vaginal cytosmear including a Papanicolaou smear to detect trichomoniasis is not recommended because of the high rate of error in identifying trichomonads in stained smears. Other methods used to diagnose trichomoniasis include isolation by special culture medium, direct fluorescent immunoassay, and PCR assay. The last method is the most sensitive but is not used routinely in clinical settings yet.[241]

TREATMENT

A single 2-g oral dose of metronidazole (Flagyl) is the recommended treatment of choice. An alternative regimen is metronidazole, 500 mg orally twice daily for 7 days.[47] The cure rate is 95 percent in females. If symptoms persist and wet smears from the vagina still show trichomonads, the course of treatment is repeated. Only in unusually persistent cases is a third course necessary. Strains resistant to metronidazole are rare findings. The patient should be warned of possible gastrointestinal side effects (nausea, diarrhea). Alcohol can aggravate the side effects of metronidazole therapy and cause a disulfiram (Antabuse)-like reaction. Thus, the patient should be instructed not to consume alcoholic beverages during treatment. She should be told that trichomoniasis is a sexually transmitted disease and that her sexual partner should be treated. Reacquisition of infection should be prevented via sexual abstinence or use of condoms.

Metronidazole is not a recommended drug during the first trimester of pregnancy because of reports of spontaneous abortion, developmental anomalies, and perinatal death. A risk of preterm labor has been reported from the use of metronidazole prescribed for *Trichomonas* infection during the first trimester of pregnancy.[164] Clotrimazole vaginal suppositories, one a day for 7 days, have been found to cure two thirds of patients. Gentle vaginal douching with vinegar and water may relieve symptoms somewhat but should not be encouraged during pregnancy.[145] Metronidazole gel has not been studied for the treatment of trichomoniasis and, therefore, should not be used.

Postmenarcheal Mycotic Vulvovaginitis

Several factors play roles in causing the increased incidence of vaginal candidiasis after menarche. Menstruation, by altering vaginal pH, may offer a favorable medium for the growth of mycotic organisms. *Candida* spp. are found commonly in the intestinal tract and frequently are detected in stool cultures. Fecal contamination of the vulva during cleansing after defecation at a time when the normal vulvar and vaginal flora are depleted and not able to inhibit fungal growth would permit the development of symptomatic vulvovaginal candidiasis. Wearing tight-fitting underclothes (which keep the perineum warm and moist) is a factor that contributes to the growth of mycotic organisms. Female athletes and ballet dancers appear to be predisposed to development of candidiasis from wearing tight-fitting clothing and increased sweating. The widespread use of antibiotics that disturb the vaginal flora and the use of oral contraceptives are additional factors that increase the incidence of candidal infection. Other predisposing factors include pregnancy, obesity, uncontrolled diabetes mellitus, immunosuppressive therapy, and heroin or other drug addiction. If a patient has a recurrent unexplainable or resistant infection, a glucose tolerance test should be performed to rule out diabetes mellitus.

C. albicans and *Torulopsis glabrata* are the yeast-like fungi most often found in the vagina. *C. albicans* is responsible for 80 to 95 percent and *T. glabrata* for 3 to 16 percent of fungal infections. Other *Candida* spp. are detected less often in the vagina but can be pathogenic. *C. tropicalis,* like *C. albicans*, produces systemic infection in immunosuppressed hosts. Mycotic vulvovaginitis causes severe vulvar and vaginal itching; usually, the patient does not have an excessive discharge. The discharge is white, thick, and curdled and has a yeasty sour odor. The patient may have pain during and after voiding or external dysuria as a result of urine coming in contact with excoriated areas on the urethra and vulva.

Examination in the acute stage reveals intense inflammation of the vulva and vagina that may extend to the perineal skin. Long-standing infection can cause lichenification and hyperpigmentation of the perineal skin. During acute infection, the involved areas are shiny and beefy red with linear excoriations and edema. *C. albicans* typically forms patches of mycelia that create adherent white plaques scattered over the inflamed surfaces. Superficial, red weeping areas remain after the plaques are pulled away. Other *Candida* spp., notably *C. tropicalis,* do not form adherent plaques but produce a cottage cheese–like discharge similar to that found with *C. albicans.* Vaginal pH usually is within the normal range (below 4.5).

The diagnosis is established by microscopy and by finding hyphae and buds of the fungus in vaginal fluid (see Fig. 49–10), in the curdled discharge, in material scraped from the vulvar mucosa, or on the perineal skin. A wet smear in normal saline may suffice, but debris and cellular material may render identification of the fungus difficult. If so, a smear using 10 percent potassium hydroxide solution is helpful. After one drop of potassium hydroxide has been added to one to two drops of vaginal fluid on a slide, the slide is heated gently until bubbles appear under the coverslip. The potassium hydroxide solution dissolves other extraneous material without affecting the fungus. With an experienced microscopist, this method yields a sensitivity of 86 percent in symptomatic females. However, the yield can be as low as 40 percent. Therefore, the diagnosis frequently is based on clinical findings and can be confirmed by culture on Nickerson or Sabouraud medium. However, this diagnostic test is not performed frequently.

TREATMENT

Several vaginal preparations can be used. The antifungal creams commonly used are imidazoles (clotrimazole and miconazole) and polyenes (nystatin), but the polyenes should not be used because of increasing resistance of fungi to these compounds. A variety of imidazoles are available as vaginal creams, tablets, and coated tampons. Such agents include clotrimazole, miconazole, and terconazole. Intravaginal treatment with 100-mg vaginal tablets of clotrimazole every night for 7 days produces a cure rate of 90 percent. Comparable cure rates are observed with 100 to 200 mg of clotrimazole or miconazole (two tablets) for 3 days. The shorter regimen may result in better compliance. Creams and tablets are equally effective.[47]

Oral fluconazole, 150 mg as a single dose, is an effective preparation for the treatment of uncomplicated vulvovaginal candidiasis.[47] Low-dose prophylactic treatment also may be appropriate in these cases. Gentian violet, which has been used for many years, is considered an effective cheap treatment for vulvovaginal candidiasis in countries where the recommended pharmaceutical agents are not available.[144] Huffman described painting the cervix and the vaginal and vulvar mucosa with a 1 percent aqueous solution. Care is taken to rotate the speculum so that the anterior and posterior vaginal walls are treated. The creases between the folds of the vulvar mucosa also are covered with the dye. The speculum is reinserted, opened, and left in place for 5 minutes so that all painted surfaces will become dry. Treatment with gentian violet is repeated once weekly for 3 weeks and should include one treatment during a menstrual period. According to Huffman, Gentian violet can cause herpes-like lesions on the vulva of some patients, and it is extremely messy.

Postmenarcheal Bacterial Vaginosis

Bacterial vaginosis is a noninflammatory polymicrobial condition caused by an ecologic change in the vagina; an overgrowth of anaerobes, especially *Bacteroides* and *Mobiluncus* spp., *G. vaginalis*, and *M. hominis*; and a decrease in the concentration of lactobacilli.[15, 100, 102, 215]

Bacterial vaginosis is considered a sexually transmitted disease based on the occurrence of bacterial vaginosis with other sexually transmitted diseases and in male partners of females with this condition. However, bacterial vaginosis also has been described in adolescent girls who are not sexually active.[43]

Bacterial vaginosis has been associated with vaginal douching. It also has been noted in connection with postpartum endometritis, premature rupture of membranes, and pelvic inflammatory disease.[142]

The primary complaint is an offensive odor with moderately profuse, gray-colored leukorrhea that stains the underwear. A mild pruritus or dyspareunia may be reported. A clinician often is able to identify this condition simply by the odor of the discharge. Examination shows little or no vulvar or vaginal erythema. The urethral and vulvar glands are not involved. The vagina contains a thick, homogeneous, grayish-white discharge. The pH of vaginal secretions in bacterial vaginosis is between 5 and 6. *T. vaginalis* tends to be associated with a vaginal pH between 6 and 8.

The diagnosis is made by the presence of any three of the following four criteria: (1) a homogeneous gray malodorous discharge, (2) a pH of nonbloody vaginal secretions greater than 4.5, (3) a fishy odor caused by the release of amines when 10 percent potassium hydroxide is added to a nonbloody vaginal specimen (whiff test), and (4) the presence of clue cells in a nonbloody specimen.[15] Microscopic examination of some of the discharge mixed with normal saline solution in a wet preparation shows masses of desquamated vaginal epithelial cells and cellular debris. Clusters of bacteria adhere to the surface of many of the vaginal cells; these "clue cells" (Fig. 49–14) are characteristic of the condition. Absence of erythrocytes and leukocytes in the discharge is another characteristic finding.

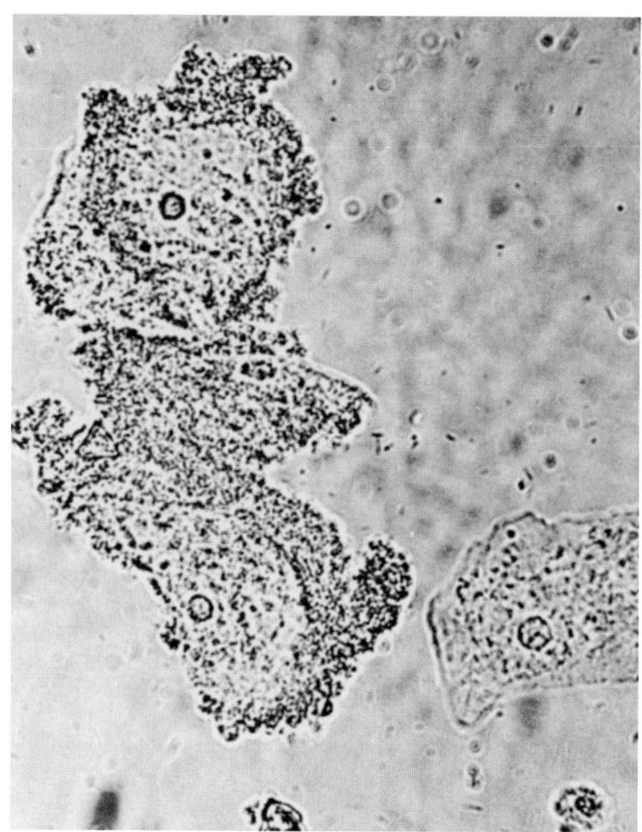

FIGURE 49–14 ■ The finding of bacteria clinging to the sides of a vaginal epithelial cell ("clue cell") is significant in bacterial vaginosis. (Courtesy of Dr. Herman L. Gardner.)

A Gram stain of vaginal secretions is considered the most reliable diagnostic test for bacterial vaginosis. A predominance of gram-variable cocci and curved rods (anaerobes) and occasional long gram-positive rods (lactobacilli) are seen.[15] A wet mount of vaginal secretions, however, is a rapid and helpful test for clue cells in a busy clinical setting. Cultures for *G. vaginalis* and anaerobes are not useful clinically in nonpregnant females.

TREATMENT

The goal of therapy for symptomatic bacterial vaginosis is to relieve vaginal symptoms and prevent an ecologic environment that predisposes to the development of pelvic inflammatory disease. Treatment of asymptomatic bacterial vaginosis may be considered before performing a surgical abortion procedure to prevent postpartum pelvic inflammatory disease. In most cases, bacterial vaginosis responds to metronidazole, 500 mg given orally twice daily for 7 days, or a 2-g oral dose repeated once at 48 hours.[47] Alternative regimens include the use of 2 percent clindamycin cream intravaginally every night for 7 days or 0.75 percent metronidazole gel intravaginally twice a day for 5 days. These regimens provide effective coverage of anaerobes and *G. vaginalis*. Bacterial vaginosis that occurs during pregnancy generally is treated during the first trimester with clindamycin cream. During the second and third trimesters of pregnancy, it can be treated with clindamycin cream or metronidazole gel. Treatment of the sexual partner has not proved to be beneficial.[47]

Postmenarcheal Nonspecific Vulvovaginitis[82, 144]

Nonspecific vulvovaginitis has several contributory factors. Vaginal foreign bodies cause discharges that are profuse, extremely malodorous, and sometimes bloody. The most frequent offender is a forgotten menstrual tampon, toilet paper, or a piece of condom. Improper or inadequate cleansing of the perineum after defecation also is responsible for many cases of chronic nonspecific vulvovaginitis, especially in mentally handicapped adolescent girls. If a male partner inserts his penis into the rectum first and then into the vagina or inadvertently touches the anal area before having vaginal intercourse, coliform organisms are carried into the vagina.

Though very rare, the possibility that a vaginal discharge is caused by a tumor always should be remembered. A discharge, with or without bleeding, may be one of the first symptoms of adenosis or adenocarcinoma of the vagina and cervix. These neoplasms are associated with prenatal exposure to diethylstilbestrol and related synthetic estrogens.

TREATMENT

Treatment of nonspecific vulvovaginitis in a postmenarcheal patient can be frustrating when no causative agent is found. Often, identification of the causative agent is impossible. In the case of a foreign body, it should be removed.

Instruction in proper perineal cleansing after defecation eradicates a major source of nonspecific vaginal infection in teenagers. Providing advice regarding sexual habits is necessary in some cases if coitus-related infections are to be avoided.

According to Huffman, in most cases, nonspecific vulvovaginitis unassociated with chronic cervicitis responds to sulfonamide (Sultrin vaginal cream) or antimicrobial creams (AVC vaginal cream) inserted at bedtime for 14 days. As a general rule, creams are preferable because they spread over a larger area of the vaginal mucosa than is treatable with suppositories.[144]

Vaginal douching sometimes may be considered helpful in the treatment of nonspecific vulvovaginitis. Recent data, however, suggest a causative relationship between vaginal douching and pelvic inflammatory disease in inner-city populations at high risk for acquiring sexually transmitted diseases.[301] Therefore, vaginal douching should be discouraged strongly.

Toxic Shock Syndrome

First recognized in the late 1970s, toxic shock syndrome is a relatively uncommon, serious, sometimes fatal acute infection most often encountered in otherwise healthy adolescent girls and young women who use menstrual tampons. It also has been reported, however, in men, children, women who do not use tampons, and nonmenstruating women. All types of tampons have been associated with it. Its incidence has decreased since women have become aware of the hazards associated with the improper use of menstrual tampons. This entity is discussed fully in Chapter 74.

Vulvovaginal Viral Infections

HERPES GENITALIS

The Premenarcheal Patient[128]

Herpes simplex virus infection of the genitalia is a rare findng in children. The mode of acquisition of the infection is not always known, but case reports describe the possibility of autoinoculation from oral lesions, physical contact by a mother's infected finger, and sexual abuse.[156] Therefore, the presence of genital herpes lesions in a child or any disease that is known to be sexually transmitted in an adult should raise a question about whether she has been subjected to some type of sexual molestation. The virus can be isolated from the pharynx or vagina of approximately 5 percent of asymptomatic adults. Such persons are carriers and may transmit the infection to susceptible contacts. One is not surprised, therefore, that children would have either herpes simplex virus type 1 or 2 genital lesions.[200]

Herpetic lesions on the vulva begin as small, erythematous spots. Papules quickly develop on the inflamed areas. The papules, in turn, become serum-filled vesicles that rupture and leave slightly eroded red areas. The latter become covered with crusts, which remain for a few days.

The lesions typically cause pruritus and burning. If they do not become secondarily infected, they heal within 2 weeks.

Herpes limited to the genitalia of a healthy child is a painful but relatively benign disease. An infection in a poorly nourished child may spread beyond the vulva and become a serious, life-endangering matter.

Treatment of genital herpes is discussed later.

The Adolescent Patient[199]

Herpes simplex virus is the most common cause of vesiculoulcerative disease of the adult genitalia. It is sexually transmitted, and its increasing frequency in teenage girls is related to their sexual activity.

As noted in Chapter 163, two types of herpes simplex virus exist and can be antigenically and culturally distinguished from each other. Type 1 is the causative agent in oronasal cold sores. Type 2 is responsible for 70 to 95 percent of genital herpes, but genital infections with type 1 have become more common (5 to 30%), probably related to increasing engagement in genital-oral sex play.[49]

Seroprevalence studies show that type 2 antibodies do not begin to appear until the early teens. The frequency gradually rises through late adulthood and is related to sexual activity, especially with multiple partners. Type 2 infections are highly contagious and may be transmitted by carriers who are asymptomatic. Approximately 9 percent of private patients and 22 percent of public clinic patients have serologic evidence of previous type 2 infection.[269] Because of its frequency and diverse clinical appearance, it should be considered in the differential diagnosis of all vulvar vesiculoulcerative lesions. It may, because of its acute symptoms, mask the presence of other venereal disease acquired concurrently; a patient with herpes genitalis always should be examined for gonorrhea and syphilis.

Three manifestations of genital disease are recognized: primary initial, nonprimary initial, and recurrent infection. Primary initial genital herpes infection develops with no preexisting herpes antibody. A nonprimary initial infection develops in a person for the first time with preexisting herpes antibody. Recurrent infection is diagnosed when a person has a history of previous similar genital infection. Patients with nonprimary initial infection have fewer lesions, less pain, fewer constitutional symptoms, shorter duration of viral shedding, and an overall shorter course of illness.[52]

A primary infection begins with sexual contact with an infected person 2 to 8 days before the onset of symptoms. The individual probably has a prodromal episode of fever, malaise, and myalgia, often accompanied by vulvar paresthesia and burning, dysuria, and tender nonsuppurative inguinal lymphadenopathy.

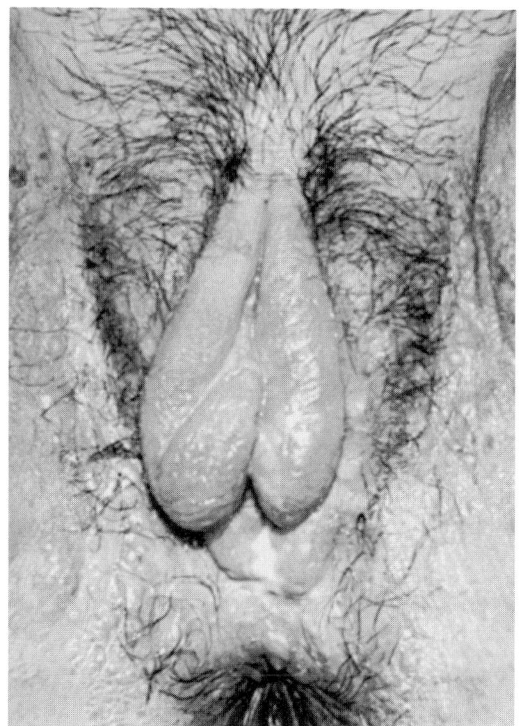

FIGURE 49–15 ■ Herpes genitalis in an adolescent patient.

Primary lesions, which often involve all the vulvar tissues, the vaginal mucosa, and the cervix, occur during a 2-week period. They first appear as papules surrounded by an erythematous zone and subsequently become vesiculopustular lesions. The vesicles enlarge and rupture, and shallow ulcerations are exposed. During the acute phase of a severe infection, more or less edema and generalized erythema of the vulvar mucosa are present (Fig. 49–15).

As a rule, the ulcers become covered with a firm yellow crust that drops off after a week or so, with a smooth, red area left behind that eventually disappears. The lesions usually are asymptomatic from 10 to 21 days, depending on the severity of the infection. Secondary bacterial infection and a coexisting immunodeficiency state, such as HIV infection, delay healing. Urethral and vesical involvement may cause severe dysuria leading to retention of urine. Proctitis may occur in females who engage in anal intercourse, although perianal ulcers also may occur without anal intercourse.

Herpes simplex virus can be cultured from the cervix in 90 percent of females with primary type 2 infection. The cervix appears abnormal in almost 90 percent of cases with positive cultures. The cervical lesions are ulcerations on the exocervix and may range from erythema to severe necrotic cervicitis. Acute cervicitis may be the only manifestation of primary herpes simplex virus infection.

Inguinal lymphadenopathy and moderate lower abdominal pain may be present, but if so, they usually occur only with the more severe first eruption. Tender inguinal lymphadenopathy is the last to resolve. If the urethra is involved, the dysuria may be sufficiently severe to cause urinary retention. Insertion of a vaginal speculum may be exquisitely painful. Extension to the perianal area may cause severe discomfort on defecation. Complete healing of lesions at all sites occurs in approximately 3 weeks. Once healed, herpetic lesions rarely leave scars.

The diagnosis of herpes genitalis is not usually difficult to make. The intense pain and the superficial vesiculo-ulcerative lesions with their irregular margins and red areolae are sufficiently characteristic to render clinical identification easy to make in a typical case. Laboratory confirmation should be attempted for all children and adolescents. Direct isolation of herpes simplex virus by tissue culture is the most reliable method and is best when the specimen is taken from a lesion within the first 48 hours of the onset of symptoms. The presence of multinucleated giant cells in a cervicovaginal smear (Papanicolaou smear) (Fig. 49–16)

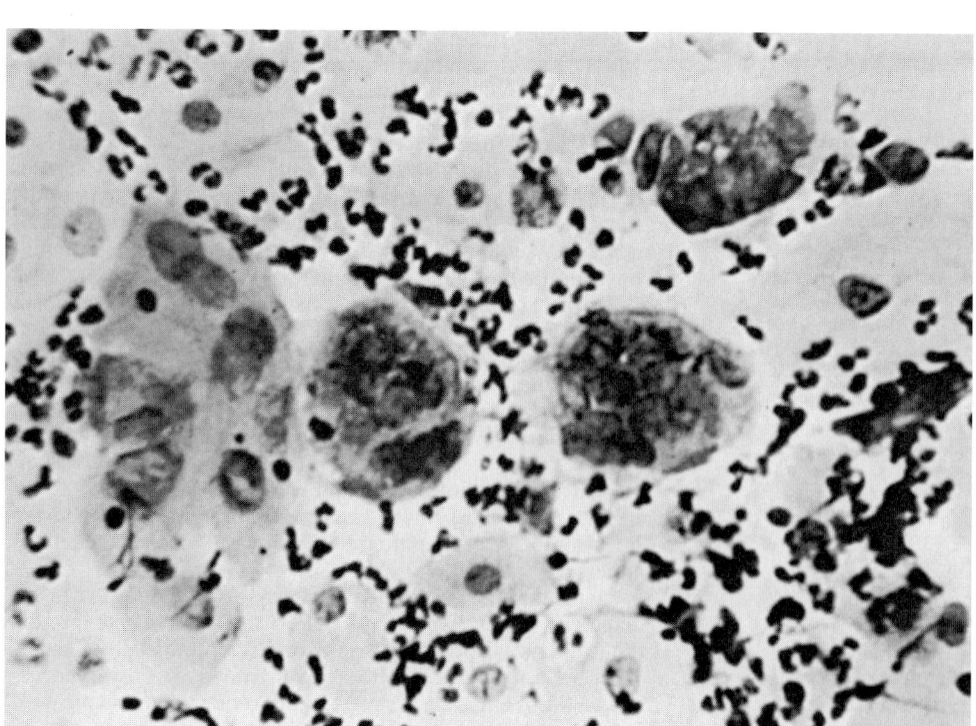

FIGURE 49–16 ■ Multinucleated giant cells in a vaginal smear are characteristic of herpes genitalis. (Courtesy of Dr. Herman L. Gardner.)

or in a herpetic fluid smear with a Tzanck preparation confirms the diagnosis for practical purposes. These tests, however, are only 40 to 50 percent sensitive in comparison with culture. Serodiagnosis with type-specific antisera by Western blot assay showing a rise in anti–herpes simplex virus titer may be useful in documenting a primary type 2 infection but has limited usefulness for recurrent infection.

For many weeks after the infection has subsided clinically and the patient appears to be cured, type 2 virus can be recovered from her cervix and vagina. The latent virus may infect others or cause recurrent infections in its host. Although the recurrence rate of herpes genitalis is unknown, recurrent episodes develop in as many as 80 percent of patients with type 2 infection, but clinical recurrence of type 1 genital infection is much less common.[52] Factors influencing recurrence rates are the severity of the initial episode and the host immune response to the disease. Emotional stress, heat, moisture, climate change, menstruation, pregnancy, oral contraceptive use, anesthesia, and trauma appear to be triggering factors. The median time from a primary infection to development of a secondary or recurrent infection is approximately 120 days.[52, 269, 295] Such recurrent episodes, though painful, usually are less severe than are primary infections. Some patients have recurrences immediately preceding or at the time of each menstrual period. Researchers have suggested that genital herpes and squamous cell carcinoma of the cervix are related.[86] Most of the evidence favoring this association originally came from seroepidemiologic studies. A much stronger association now has been observed between HPV DNA and cervical cancer. At most, herpes simplex virus may be causative or may be a cofactor in some cases of cervical cancer.[52]

Treatment

Several medications are available today for the treatment of herpes genitalis.[47] Acyclovir is the most affordable current drug on the market. For the treatment of initial genital herpes, acyclovir, one 400-mg capsule orally three times a day or one 200-mg capsule five times a day, is administered for 7 to 10 days until clinical resolution. Alternative drugs include famciclovir, one 250-mg capsule three times a day, or valacyclovir, one 1-g capsule twice a day for 7 to 10 days. These drugs are reported to shorten the time that the patient has pain, decrease the number of new lesions, hasten crusting, and reduce the time that the virus can be found in the lesions. The earlier treatment is started after the initial lesions appear, the sooner patients obtain relief. In severe primary herpes infection with marked systemic symptoms, intravenous acyclovir, 5 to 10 mg/kg/day every 8 hours for 5 to 7 days or until clinical resolution occurs, is recommended. Frequent or severe recurrent disease may benefit from medication if it is started within 2 days of the onset of lesions or at the beginning of the prodrome. Oral acyclovir may be given at 800 mg twice a day, 400 mg three times a day, or 200 mg five times a day for 5 days. Alternatively, famciclovir, 125 mg twice a day, or valacyclovir, 500 or 1000 mg twice a day for 5 days, may be prescribed. Daily suppressive treatment reduces recurrence by at least 75 percent in patients with frequent recurrences. Because of adherence problems, daily suppressive therapy may not be a practical treatment approach for adolescents. The recommended treatment is oral acyclovir, 400 mg twice a day; famciclovir, 250 mg twice a day; or valacyclovir, 500 or 1000 mg once a day for 1 year. Medication should be discontinued after 1 year to reassess the recurrence rate. The dosage regimen of medications for treating prepubertal herpes genitalis is not known, and therefore, such medications are not used commonly in this age group for mild cases. In moderate to severe cases, clinicians have prescribed approximately 50 percent of the adult dose.[47]

Recurrences can be reduced in frequency in some cases if the patients can avoid stress-inducing situations. Topical anesthetics, cold wet compresses, and sitz baths with 1 : 40 Burow solution frequently lessen local discomfort. Severe dysuria may be relieved by urinating when sitting in water. Local therapies used in the past, such as povidone-iodine solutions, photodynamic-dye light therapy, and topical surfactant, have not been found to be beneficial and are messy and potentially toxic.

Lesions caused by herpes simplex virus are relatively common in patients with HIV infection. Immunocompromised patients benefit from an increased dosage of acyclovir. For severe disease, hospitalization may be required for intravenous acyclovir treatment.[47]

CONDYLOMATA ACUMINATA

Condylomata acuminata (venereal warts) are encountered in both premenarcheal children and teenage girls. The agent causing them is HPV, a small, slow-growing virus of the papovavirus group. Several strains of HPV, including types 6, 11, 16, 18, and 31, cause exophytic genital warts and subclinical infection of the vagina and cervix. Types 16, 18, and 31 have been associated with premalignant and malignant cervical carcinoma in females.[80]

The Premenarcheal Patient

Warts in premenarcheal children may cover the entire vulva. Most often, however, warts in this population are single or scattered cauliflower-like lesions (Fig. 49–17). They have a predilection for the smooth, moist mucosa covering the inner surfaces of the labia minora and for the mucosa about the urethral meatus. The vestibular mucosa may be studded with innumerable minute excrescences as well.

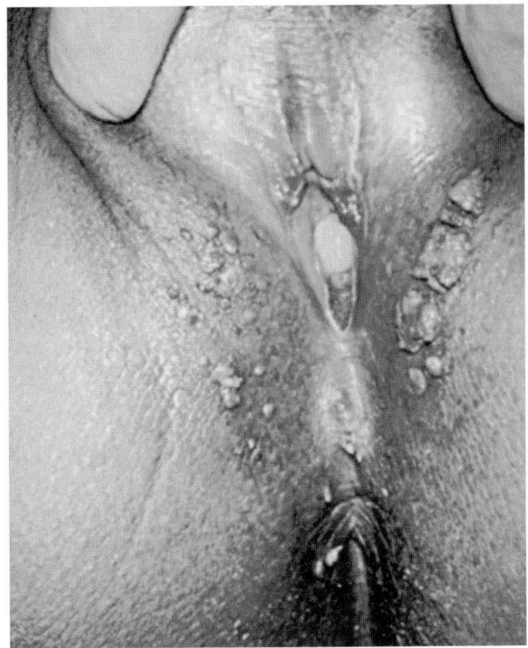

FIGURE 49–17 ■ Condylomata acuminata usually are single or scattered, relatively small warts in premenarcheal children.

Condylomata in children seldom become ulcerative, but sessile condylomata arising within the vagina may become necrotic, produce a bloody vaginal discharge, and resemble, on cursory examination, a mixed mesodermal tumor (sarcoma botryoides) of the vagina. Though not tumors, condylomata acuminata should be considered in the differential diagnosis of vaginal neoplasms. HIV infection should be considered in infants and children with severe, extensive warts.[51, 60, 80, 111]

The Adolescent Patient

Condylomata acuminata develop in adolescent girls by sexual transmission. The prevalence of HPV in adolescent and young adult females ranges from 11 to 46 percent, depending on the method of HPV DNA detection used.[80, 242] The PCR technique is more sensitive than is the dot-blot hybridization method (ViraPap; Life Technologies, Gaithersburg, MD). The prevalence of HPV in adolescents as detected by DNA isolation techniques is far higher than the prevalence of active disease. The cell-mediated or T-cell immune system appears to play an important role in whether the presence of virus results in clinically manifested disease. Cofactors of HPV infection are herpes, cervicitis, and tobacco use. Immunosuppression from a variety of conditions, including renal transplantation, Hodgkin disease, and HIV infection, is associated with a greater likelihood of development of HPV disease.[242]

In postmenarcheal girls, condylomata usually form discrete, sessile, vegetative, wart-like growths covered with folded grayish-pink epithelium. They are found most frequently on the smooth mucosa of the vulvar vestibule. Usually, they are accompanied by more or less vaginal discharge, which is increased by moisture that exudes from between the leaf-like folds of the warty masses. Most often, associated pruritus and secondary infection are present. Warts are more likely to become necrotic in adults than in children. Contact lesions frequently appear on contiguous surfaces. Huge condylomatous masses (Fig. 49–18) that completely hide the introitus are not uncommon findings in adolescent patients; if not treated, these huge growths may invade the rectum. Vaginal and cervical lesions commonly accompany those on the vulva.

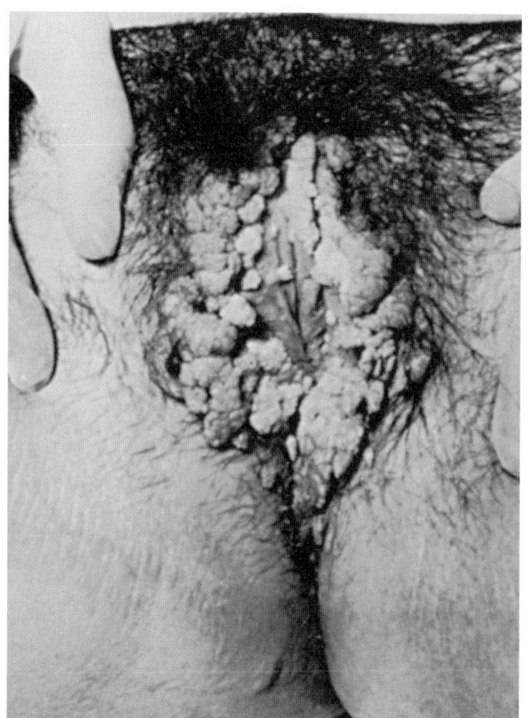

FIGURE 49–18 ■ Condylomata acuminata may form large masses covering the vulva in postmenarcheal patients.

Vulvar condylomata are associated with a 50 to 60 percent incidence of cervical disease detected by the presence of koilocytotic cells on Papanicolaou smears of the cervix. Therefore, a Papanicolaou smear is recommended twice a year in adolescents with vulvar and vaginal warts. The application of 3 to 5 percent acetic acid to suspicious areas on the cervix reveals tiny white "acetowhite" flecks. With regard to the natural history of HPV infection, Moscicki and colleagues found that over the course of a 2-year period, most (70%) cases showed regression and squamous intraepithelial lesions (LSILs) did not develop.[194, 195] Daily cigarette smoking was strongly linked to the development of LSILs.[195] Regression was more likely to be seen in young women with LSILs as opposed to high-grade squamous intraepithelial lesions (HSILs), and HSILs were more likely to develop in those with persistent positive tests demonstrating oncogenic HPV types.[194]

Treatment

The goal of treatment is removal of warts and amelioration of symptoms, not eradication of HPV. No therapy has been shown to eradicate HPV. When only a few lesions are present, they can be treated in the outpatient setting with 85 percent trichloracetic acid. In infants and children with extensive lesions, Emans and Goldstein[81] recommend carbon dioxide laser treatment with general anesthesia. It may be performed in an outpatient surgical setting when few lesions are present. Electrocautery, electrocoagulation, or laser treatment may result in deep scarring and distortion of the vulva. Older children and adolescents usually tolerate cryotherapy without general anesthesia if they know that some tingling or burning sensation will be associated with it. Liquid nitrogen may be used in the same manner as is solid carbon dioxide.

The therapeutic methods available are 22 to 94 percent effective in clearing exophytic genital warts, but recurrence rates are high, at least 25 percent within 3 months. Treatment appears to be more successful for genital warts that are small and present for less than 1 year.[47] Self-application of medication may be considered in young adults but should be discouraged for adolescents because of the risk of causing dermatologic side effects. When a few lesions are present, they can be treated with 10 to 25 percent podophyllin resin or a solution of 85 percent trichloroacetic acid. The lesions that are treated should be less than a centimeter in diameter and should not be in a confluent mass. After application of podophyllin, the treated area should be washed off in 4 hours with soap and water. The medication is applied to the wart only (not to the surrounding skin), and treatment is repeated once weekly until the lesions have disappeared (usually 3 or 4 weeks).

Urethral, anal, vaginal, and cervical lesions should not be treated with podophyllin. Both podophyllin and trichloracetic acid can cause severe irritation of normal skin and can cause ulcerations. Therefore, before application, the normal skin around a wart should be covered with K-Y jelly and a thin or narrow swab used for small warts. If excessive medication has been applied, the area should be washed immediately with soap and water, followed by the application

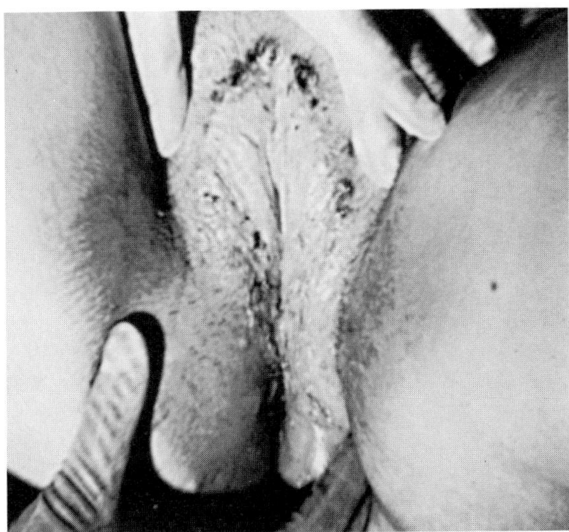

FIGURE 49–19 ■ The appearance of the vulva 10 days after electrocoagulation and surgical excision of the condylomatous mass shown in Figure 49–18.

of talcum powder or bicarbonate of soda to sooth the area.[46] Imiquimod 5 percent cream also is recommended for the treatment of warts in patients older than 18 years. This medication is self-applied to the lesions, three times a week for 16 weeks. Laser treatment or cryocautery is recommended if the lesions do not respond to chemical cautery or if they progressively increase in size. Large perianal warts may need to be removed surgically if cryotherapy does not work (Fig. 49–19). Alternative treatments for adolescents are topical 5-fluorouracil in 5 percent creams and intralesional interferon. 5-Fluorouracil is preferable for vaginal and intraurethral warts because it causes erosive dermatitis of normal surrounding skin. The use of 5-fluorouracil appears to be more effective than is the laser in treating exophytic warts in the vagina.[47, 60]

MOLLUSCUM CONTAGIOSUM

Molluscum contagiosum is a viral infection of the skin characterized by small, discrete, translucent, grayish-pink, umbilicated, wart-like papules that sometimes are surrounded by a narrow ring of erythema. The lesions, which are asymptomatic, usually are less than 5 mm in diameter and may be missed by both the patient and examiner. The disease is transmitted by close physical contact and is encountered most often in postmenarcheal patients on the inner surfaces of the thighs and perineum. Although lesions on the lower part of the abdomen and thighs have caused this infection to be classed with venereal diseases, coitus is not necessary for transmission. Pediatricians frequently encounter it on the nongenital skin of children. It can be contracted from contaminated towels, bedding, garments, and so on. Lesions of molluscum contagiosum on the lower part of the abdomen, pubis, thighs, or perineum of a child are tacit evidence of sexual contact.[140, 179]

The appearance of the lesions usually is sufficient to establish the diagnosis. It can be confirmed by finding large, intracytoplasmic inclusion bodies in a smear or biopsy specimen from a lesion.

Treatment consists of lifting off the roof of each lesion and lightly curetting its base. Cryotherapy also gives good results.[140, 179]

Vulvovaginal Granulomatous and Ulcerative Disorders

Sexually transmitted genital ulcerative diseases occur throughout the world but are found most frequently in tropical countries. Genital ulcers are a relatively common finding on evaluation of adolescent and adult patients with genital symptoms. They are less common findings in young children. Ulcers usually are secondary lesions that result from the breakdown of vesicles, papules, or pustules. By the time that many patients with genital infections seek medical attention for their symptoms, the primary lesion has proceeded to ulceration.[267] Microbial causes vary by geographic region and socioeconomic status: herpes simplex is the most common cause in Western Europe and North America, whereas chancroid is the most common one in the tropics; in the United States, syphilis and chancroid are more common occurrences in urban minority groups, whereas herpes simplex is found more commonly in more affluent groups. Complications of sexually transmitted genital ulcerative diseases also occur more commonly in developing countries and often are the reason for seeking medical care.[196]

Herpes simplex virus infection, syphilis, chancroid, lymphogranuloma venereum, granuloma inguinale, and tuberculosis all may have genital ulcers as a major clinical finding (Table 49–5). Although each of these diseases has a characteristic lesion and course, considerable overlap exists, so a diagnosis based on the history and physical appearance alone often is inaccurate. Herpetic ulcers, contrary to classic manifestations, can be painless, and syphilis chancres can be painful at times. Secondary infection of an ulcerated area may cause pain in lesions that characteristically are painless. In addition, more than one sexually transmitted disease may be present in at least 3 to 10 percent of patients with genital ulcers.

Genital ulcers also may result from infestation, fixed drug eruption, mechanical or chemical trauma, autoimmune processes (such as Behçet syndrome and Crohn disease), and neoplasia. The presence of ulcers in sites other than the genital regions or oropharynx suggests a noninfectious etiology.

In the United States, most patients with genital ulcers have herpes genitalis, syphilis, chancroid, or a combination thereof. Empiric treatment often must be given before diagnostic test results are available, and laboratory confirmation of a specific diagnosis is lacking in at least a quarter of patients with genital ulcer disease. Treatment of syphilis and chancroid should be considered in such circumstances, especially in geographic regions where chancroid morbidity is notable (see later).[47, 212] Diagnosis and treatment of the listed infectious etiologies of genital ulcers and Behçet syndrome are discussed in this chapter and elsewhere in this text.

Genital ulcers of any etiology, but especially those caused by herpes, syphilis, chancroid, and granuloma inguinale, are associated with an increased risk of acquiring HIV infection. Serologic testing for HIV infection therefore should be considered in the management of patients with genital ulcers.[47, 197] Improved treatment of sexually transmitted diseases can affect the rate of HIV seroconversion in a population: HIV seroconversion was reduced by 40 percent over the course of a 2-year follow-up period in rural communities in Tanzania where treatment programs were instituted in comparison to control communities with no programs.[114]

LYMPHOGRANULOMA VENEREUM

Lymphogranuloma venereum is a sexually transmitted disease characterized by chronicity, indolent inflammatory

TABLE 49–5 ■ DIAGNOSTIC FEATURES OF GENITAL ULCERATIONS CAUSED BY SEXUALLY TRANSMITTED DISEASES

Feature	Primary Syphilis	Genital Herpes	Chancroid	Lymphogranuloma Venereum	Granuloma Inguinale
Incubation period	9–90 days; avg., 2–4 wk	2–7 days	Range, 1–35 days; avg., 3–7 days	3 days to 3 wk; avg., 10–14 days	Precise data unavailable; probably from a few days to several months
Number of lesions	Usually one, may be multiple	Multiple; may coalesce, more with primary episodes than with recurrences	Usually 1–3, may be multiple	Usually single	Single or multiple
Description of genital ulcers	Sharply demarcated round or oval ulcer with slightly elevated edges; may be irregular, symmetric "kissing chancre"	Small, superficial, grouped vesicles, erosions, or both; lesions may coalesce and form bullae or large areas of ulceration; lesions have irregular borders	Superficial, shallow, sharply demarcated ulcer; irregular, ragged, undermined edge; size from a few millimeters to 2 cm in diameter	Papule, pustule, vesicle, or ulcer discrete and transient; frequently overlooked	Sharply defined, irregular ulcerations or hypertrophic, verrucous, necrotic, or cicatricial granulomata
Base	Red, smooth, and shiny or crusty; oozing serous exudate when squeezed	Bright red and smooth	Rough, uneven, yellow to gray	Variable	Usually friable, rough, beefy granulations; can be necrotic, verrucous, or cicatrical
Induration	Firm; does not change shape with pressure	None	Soft; changes shape with pressure	None	Firm granulation tissue
Pain	Painless; may become tender if secondarily infected	Common; more prominent with initial infection than with recurrences	Common	Variable	Rare
Inguinal lymphadenopathy	Unilateral or bilateral, firm, movable, and nontender; does not suppurate	Usually bilateral, firm, and tender; more common in primary episodes than in recurrences	Unilateral; bilateral rarely occurs; overlying erythema; matted, fixed, and tender; suppuration may occur	Unilateral or bilateral; initially movable firm, and tender; later indolent; fixed and matted; "sign of groove" may suppurate; fistulas	Pseudobuboes; subcutaneous perilymphatic granulomatous lesions that produce inguinal swellings
Constitutional symptoms	Rare	Common in primary episode; less likely in recurrences	Rare	Frequent	Rare
Course of untreated disease	Slowly (2–6 wk) resolves to latency	Recurrence is the rule	May progress to erosive lesions	Local lesions heal; systemic disease may progress; disfiguring; late complications	Worsens slowly
Diagnostic tests	Dark field examination, direct immunofluorescence, FTA-ABS, VDRL	Tzanck smear, culture, Pap smear, direct immunofluorescence, electron microscopy, direct immunoperoxidase staining, serology	Culture, biopsy (rarely used), Gram-stained smears have low specificity	Complement fixation, isolation of the microorganism by culture	"Donovan bodies" in tissue smears; biopsy

FTA-ABS, fluorescent treponemal antibody absorption test; VDRL, Venereal Disease Research Laboratory.
From Mroczkowski, T. R., and Martin, D. H.: Genital ulcer disease. Dermatol. Clin. North Am. *12*:753–764, 1994.

infiltration, granulomatous ulceration, abscess formation, and fibrotic cicatrization of the inguinal, perineal, and rectal lymphatics. The infecting agent is *C. trachomatis,* subtypes L1 to L3. It occurs more often in tropical than temperate climates.

The Premenarcheal Patient

Lymphogranuloma venereum has been reported in children.[20, 109, 296] The disease usually is acquired in childhood as a result of sexual contact, but transmission also may occur by accidental inoculation of infected material from family members, such as by handling of garments or towels that have been contaminated by drainage from ulcerative lesions or buboes. However, sexual abuse always should be considered. Little evidence suggests transplacental or perinatal transmission of the lymphogranuloma venereum serovars of *C. trachomatis*.[109]

The primary lesion, a small papule or superficial and relatively asymptomatic ulcer, seldom is seen in either children or older patients. A prodromal episode of fever, malaise, and joint pain accompanied by leukocytosis, anemia, and an increased sedimentation rate may precede the local signs. These symptoms often are mild and not diagnostically significant.

The most common manifestations in prepubertal children are inguinal lymphadenopathy and proctitis. The glands may be swollen and tender for a time and then regress spontaneously. More often, if treatment is not initiated, they progress to formation of an abscess and then rupture, with the development of draining sinuses. Rectal, anal, and deep pelvic tissue infiltration with rectal and colonic strictures is not a common occurrence in children. Arthritis, usually of the knees, and erythema nodosum occasionally occur in children, as they do in older patients.[109]

The Adolescent Patient

Adolescents usually acquire lymphogranuloma venereum through sexual activity. The primary lesion, a small papule, vesicle, or shallow ulcer on the vulva (Fig. 49–20), vaginal wall, or cervix, seldom is seen. Cervicitis is a more common finding in primary lymphogranuloma venereum, and the primary lesion often is asymptomatic, heals rapidly, and leaves no scar. The incubation period usually is 2 to 5 days after exposure, but several weeks may elapse before the primary lesion appears.[109, 144]

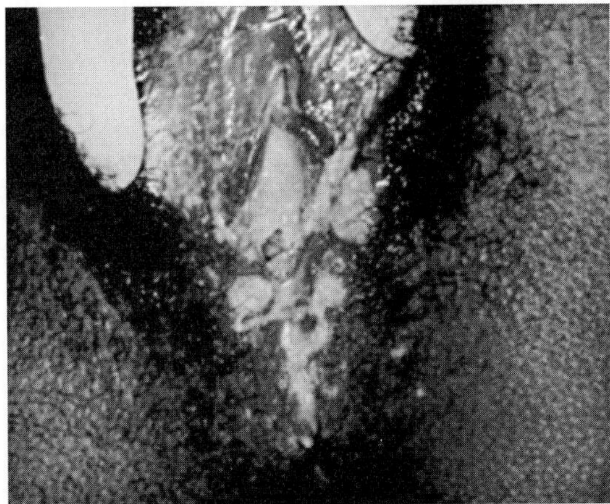

FIGURE 49–20 ■ Early lesions of lymphogranuloma venereum in the form of herpetic-like ulcers in an adolescent. The diagnosis was confirmed serologically.

Painful enlargement of the inguinal lymph nodes generally occurs after the manifestation of the initial lesions. Inguinal adenitis usually is unilateral in the early stages of infection. The perirectal lymph nodes occasionally are the first to be involved; pain on defecation is an early symptom when this condition occurs. The rectovaginal septum may become involved when the posterior vaginal area is a primary site of infection.

If the disease goes untreated, it may enter a secondary stage called the inguinal syndrome, in which the inguinal glands and the surrounding subcutaneous tissues become a brawny mass that adheres to the indurated, purplish-red overlying skin. The nodes increase in size and form abscesses (buboes). Unless aspirated, the buboes rupture and create chronically draining sinuses.[144] Enlargement of lymph nodes above and below the inguinal ligament may lead to the "groove" sign.[109] Complaints of lower abdominal pain and backache may indicate concurrent proctitis. The deep iliac nodes may be enlarged in 75 percent of cases; rupture of these nodes may cause large pelvic abscesses.

Healing of draining buboes is slow, and severe scarring occurs. In the vast majority of cases, healing of buboes indicates the end of the disease, but relapses have been reported in 20 percent of untreated cases. Disseminated disease, hepatitis, pneumonia, arthritis, erythema nodosum, erythema multiforme, and ocular infection can occur in association with the inguinal syndrome.

The anogenitorectal syndrome is a subacute manifestation of lymphogranuloma venereum. It includes proctocolitis and hyperplasia of intestinal and perirectal lymphatic tissue. Perirectal abscesses often develop and lead to ischiorectal and rectovaginal fistulas, anal fistulas, and rectal stricture or stenosis. The clinical findings consists of fever, rectal pain, and abdominal cramping. Progression of the disease causes rectal bleeding and a purulent rectal discharge. Rectal strictures lead to constipation and "pencil stools." Weight loss, bowel perforation, and peritonitis may occur. Genital elephantiasis (esthiomene), a primary infection affecting the lymphatics of the scrotum, penis, or vulva, may occur with chronic infection.

The diagnosis of lymphogranuloma venereum should be considered whenever a patient has a tender, enlarged inguinal gland or an ulcerative or granulomatous lesion of the vulva, perineum, vagina, or cervix. Acutely painful, unilateral inguinal lymphadenitis strongly suggests lymphogranuloma venereum. A definitive diagnosis is made by identification of *C. trachomatis* serotype L1, L2, or L3 in tissue cultures of material from buboes or ulcerative lesions. The sensitivity of culture for lymphogranuloma venereum is only approximately 50 percent, however.[155] Serologic tests may be used when cultures are negative or buboes are not present. Complement fixation has been available since the 1930s and 1940s. In clinical settings suggestive of lymphogranuloma venereum, a complement-fixation antibody titer of 1 : 64 or higher is considered diagnostic. Most patients with lymphogranuloma venereum have titers of 1 : 128 or higher. Titers between acute and convalescent specimens may not rise because most patients seek care well after the acute phase of the infection. Cross-reaction with other chlamydial serotypes does occur, but titers higher than 1 : 16 rarely are seen with chlamydial urethritis. Microimmunofluorescence is more specific than complement fixation and can detect IgM and IgG titers. This test is not widely available, however.[155]

Complement fixation remains the recommended test for diagnosis when the clinical findings lead to a presumptive diagnosis of lymphogranuloma venereum. If complement-fixation titers are negative, repeat testing in a few weeks may be helpful in patients who happen to be evaluated first relatively early in the course of illness. DNA probes or monoclonal antibodies specific for lymphogranuloma venereum serovars may become available in the near future.

Lymphogranuloma venereum must be differentiated from syphilis, with which it may coexist. False-positive Venereal Disease Research Laboratory (VDRL) test results may occur in 20 percent of patients with lymphogranuloma venereum. When the diagnosis is in doubt, specific tests for antitreponemal antibodies must be used to rule out syphilis. The disease is differentiated from other granulomatous and ulcerative disorders by specific tests for each, by biopsy, and by the clinical appearance of the lesions (see Table 49–4).

Treatment

The earlier the diagnosis is made and treatment started, the better the response to therapy and the less serious the tissue destruction. Fluctuant buboes are aspirated, not incised, before they rupture. The discharge from the ulcerated areas and buboes is infectious, so precautions against transmission of the disease must be taken. The patient will be more comfortable if kept in bed. Ice-cold compresses may be applied to the inguinal areas. The vulva is cleansed gently twice daily.

The preferred treatment of lymphogranuloma venereum is doxycycline, 100 mg orally twice a day for 21 days.[47] Alternatives, which are preferred in pediatric patients younger than 8 years, are erythromycin and sulfisoxazole. Either of these medications also should be given for 21 days. Because of the potential for shorter treatment courses and improved compliance, azithromycin may become a treatment option for lymphogranuloma venereum in the future. It cannot be recommended now because data are insufficient.

After treatment is initiated, patients should be monitored clinically until the signs and symptoms have resolved. Persons who have had sexual contact with a patient during the 30 days before the onset of symptoms of lymphogranuloma venereum should be examined, tested for chlamydial infection, and treated.[47]

Adolescents are likely to be treated before development of the extensive anal and rectal strictures and distorting vulvar cicatrizations, for which extensive surgery is sometimes necessary in older patients.

GRANULOMA INGUINALE

Granuloma inguinale is a chronic disease characterized by ulcerative granulomatous lesions of the skin and subcutaneous tissues (Fig. 49–21) (see Table 49–5). Common synonyms for the infection include granuloma venereum and donovanosis. The disease most often affects the external genitalia, perineum, and inguinal regions, but the vagina, cervix, and, rarely, distant extragenital sites may be involved. The disease is caused by *Calymmatobacterium granulomatis* (*Donovania granulomatis*, Donovan bodies), an encapsulated, gram-negative bacillus.[38, 72, 170, 209]

Granuloma inguinale occurs commonly in the tropical and subtropical regions of the world.[200, 210, 212] It is a relatively rare finding in developed countries. In the United States, 19 cases were reported in 1993, 4 of which involved female patients who were suspected to have been seen as a result of international travel and immigration.[71] A case in a white adolescent girl in California was reported in 1985.[115] The male-to-female ratio appears to be at least 2 : 1. The disease rarely occurs in premenarcheal children, but it should be considered in the differential diagnosis of granulomatous lesions of the genitalia in adolescents.

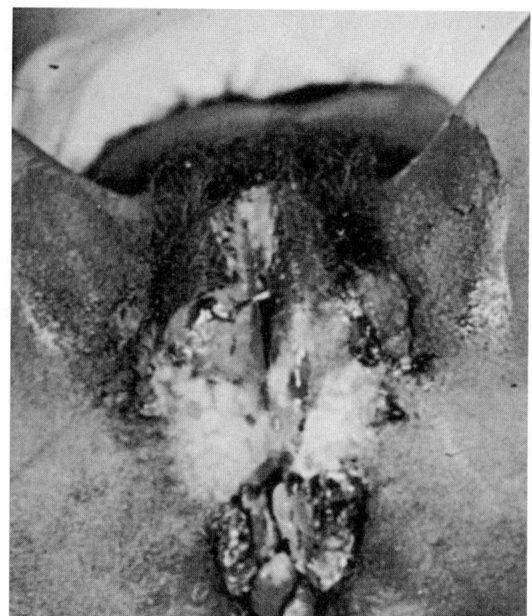

FIGURE 49–21 ■ Granuloma inguinale.

The disease clearly is transmitted to adolescents and adults during sexual intercourse. However, the close physical contact of the inguinal, perineal, and genital regions that occurs during sexual activity, and not intercourse per se, probably is more important for transmission of the infection. The organism is not highly contagious; sexual partners of patients with granuloma inguinale often do not become infected. Breaches in the integrity of the skin or mucous membranes, such as with minor trauma, may be required for an inoculum to establish a successful infection.[211] The disease apparently can be transmitted to young children by contaminated clothing or towels. Close physical contact, such as sitting on the lap of an infected parent, also has been reported as a mode of transmission to young children.[304]

The incubation period usually is less than 2 weeks but may be as long as 3 months.[211] The first manifestation of infection usually is single or multiple small, relatively painless hard nodules on the vulva or perineum that erode the skin and form ulcers. Genital tract bleeding is the next most common finding. Ulcers are shallow and have a beefy, granular base that is friable and bleeds easily. The edges are nodular, raised, and undermined. These ulcers usually are painless, unless they become infected secondarily.[209]

If left untreated, lesions progress slowly outward by eccentric expansion of the leading edge. Over time, this ulcerative stage involves large areas of the perineum, external genitalia, and surrounding skin surfaces. The central areas usually remain ulcerative but may become hypertrophic. Hypertrophic lesions consist of large, vegetating masses with overgrowth of granulation tissue. Less frequently, extensive, destructive necrosis develops in the lesions, or they are dry with sclerotic scarring, which distorts the tissues. Lymphedema of distal tissues occurs commonly during the course of the disease. Lymphatic obstruction or elephantiasis occasionally results in enlargement of the clitoris or labia.[103, 159] Subcutaneous granulation develops in approximately 5 percent of cases and may mimic the appearance of bubo formation, a condition called pseudobuboes. When true regional adenopathy occurs in the course of granuloma inguinale, it generally represents a response to a secondary infection and may be painful.

Extragenital disease may occur in as many as 6 percent of cases and usually involves the head and neck. Autoinoculation is postulated as the means of transmission of infection of these sites.[96] Occasional involvement of the liver, thorax, and bones remote from the primary genital site suggests that hematogenous spread can occur. Systemic disease is encountered more frequently in females with cervical lesions and is associated with prolonged spiking fever, anemia, and weight loss.[39, 161, 231]

Successful isolation of *C. granulomatis* rarely has proved feasible. Reliable culture techniques are not available. Therefore, the diagnosis of granuloma inguinale is based on the presence of Donovan bodies in large, histiocytic cells on crush preparations from lesions (Fig. 49–22). A portion of the granulation tissue is removed and pressed onto a clean slide, which is allowed to air-dry. The slide then is stained with Giemsa, Wright, or Warthin-Starry stain. Donovan bodies, which are pathognomonic for granuloma inguinale, are vacuolar compartments within the cytoplasm that contain up to 20 to 30 viable organisms.[72] Histopathologic study of biopsy specimens sometimes is required for diagnosis. Biopsy should be performed on very early, very sclerotic, or heavily superinfected lesions. Specimens with a scarcity of organisms and smear or crush specimens are likely to be nondiagnostic in such circumstances. Biopsy also should be performed when malignancy is thought possible or when antibiotic therapy does not lead to improvement.[155]

Complement-fixation and indirect immunofluorescence tests have been developed but have limited specificity. A more recently developed serologic test that involves indirect immunofluorescence may be helpful in the future for epidemiologic studies.[155]

The differential diagnosis of granuloma inguinale includes carcinoma, syphilis, tuberculosis, chancroid, lymphogranuloma venereum, condyloma acuminatum, blastomycosis, schistosomiasis, and other granulomatous diseases.[23, 209, 211] Sexually transmitted diseases such as syphilis may coexist with granuloma inguinale. Darkfield examination of tissue specimens and serologic tests for syphilis should be performed. Biopsy may be required to rule out neoplasia or tuberculosis.[96] Chancroid ulcers tend to be deeper and more ragged and often have associated bubo formation. Physical examination alone, however, often is not sufficient to distinguish any of these processes from the others (see Table 49–5). Granuloma inguinale also is associated with the development of carcinoma within areas that have been involved in the ulcerative process.

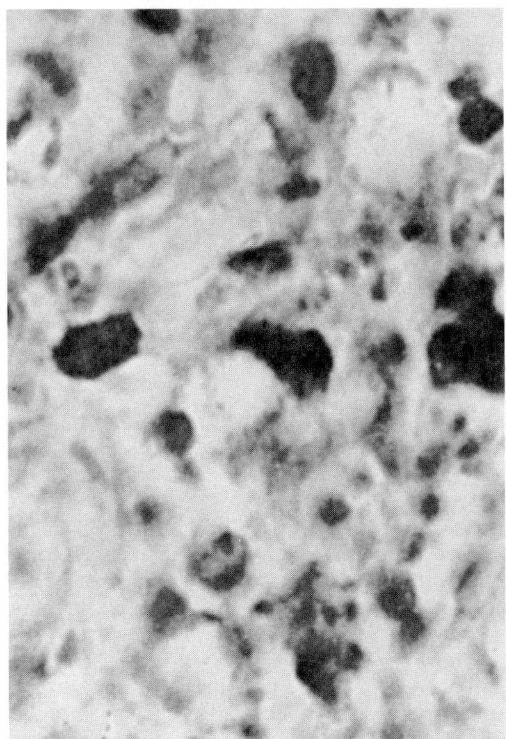

FIGURE 49–22 ■ Donovan bodies.

Treatment

Tetracycline probably is the drug of choice for the treatment of granuloma inguinale. Doxycycline is thought to be as effective and may result in improved compliance. Alternatives include trimethoprim-sulfamethoxazole and erythromycin, either of which could be administered to young children. Chloramphenicol and gentamicin also may be used.[239]

Treatment should be continued for at least 2 to 3 weeks and until the ulcerative lesions have re-epithelialized. Vulvar lesions usually heal within 2 weeks of therapy, but cervical and pelvic lesions may require longer than 3 months. Incomplete treatment can result in recurrence with extensive fibrosis and scarring.[23] The disease recurs in approximately 10 percent of cases. Surgery may be required for complications of granuloma inguinale, such as elephantiasis, strictures, and pelvic abscesses.[239]

Precautions regarding infections should be taken in the home or hospital until the lesions have healed. Sexual contacts of persons with donovanosis should be traced and examined but treated only if lesions are found.[239] Adolescent girls who have had granuloma inguinale should be kept under clinical surveillance for many years for the potential development of carcinoma in the perineum and genital tract.

CHANCROID[5, 299]

Chancroid is an acute, ulcerative disease that primarily involves the external genitalia. The causative agent, *Haemophilus ducreyi*, is a fastidious, gram-negative coccobacillus. Its only known route of transmission is sexual contact. The incubation period usually is 3 to 7 days, but may be longer. Chancroid rarely is encountered in young children but occasionally is seen in sexually active adolescents.[127, 213] It occurs far more commonly in males than females for reasons that are unclear, although asymptomatic carriage in females has been hypothesized.[29, 127, 213]

Chancroid is well established as a cofactor for transmission of HIV infection.[46, 47] As many as 10 percent of patients with chancroid may be infected with HIV. Chancroid is found more commonly in tropical and subtropical regions than in developed countries, but its frequency is increasing in many parts of the world.[213] Chancroid is endemic in the United States, and discrete outbreaks are seen occasionally. Outbreaks caused by unrelated strains occurred in New Orleans, Louisiana, and Jackson, Mississippi, in the 1990s.[129] The disease probably is under-recognized and under-reported.[46]

The first sign of infection is a small, hyperemic macule. The macule becomes a papule and then a pustule before ulceration. The ulcer is painful and usually deep, with irregular borders and undermined edges. The base is gray and covered with purulent exudate laden with the *ducreyi* bacillus. Ulcers may occur on the vulva, vaginal mucosa, cervix, or anus but usually are found on the labia minora. Dysuria is a frequent complaint. Tenesmus and rectal bleeding may be associated with anal lesions. Single ulcers are found frequently, but multiple ulcers occur more often. They may become contiguous and form large, eroded areas. Phagedenic destruction of the external genitalia may occur when treatment is not sought early in the course or a secondary infection develops in the ulcers. In such cases, scarring persists despite successful eradication of the microbe. Infection, at least experimentally, does not appear to confer protection on re-exposure to the microbe.[10]

Associated, painful inguinal adenitis occurs in a quarter to a half of cases. Adenitis occurs more commonly when genital ulcers have been present for more than 10 days. The skin overlying the nodes frequently is erythematous. Discharge from buboes and vulvar lesions is highly infectious. Constitutional symptoms are unusual, and invasiveness beyond regional lymph nodes does not seem to occur even in immunocompromised hosts.

Many patients with chancroid have concurrent infections with other sexually transmitted diseases. Patients should be tested for HIV infection and syphilis when chancroid is diagnosed. Repeat testing for both diseases should be performed in 3 months if the initial results are negative.[47]

In the United States, a probable diagnosis of chancroid is made clinically if (1) one or more painful genital ulcers are present; (2) the person has no evidence of *T. pallidum* infection by either darkfield examination of ulcer exudate or a serologic test for syphilis performed at least 7 days after the onset of ulcers; and (3) the clinical findings, appearance of the genital ulcers, and regional lymphadenopathy, if present, are typical for chancroid and a test for herpes simplex virus is negative. When present, the combination of a painful ulcer with tender inguinal adenopathy suggests chancroid. A painful genital ulcer accompanied by suppurative inguinal adenopathy is almost pathognomonic for chancroid.[47]

Definitive diagnosis of chancroid requires isolation of *H. ducreyi* on special culture media. The sensitivity of culture is at best 80 percent.[47] When culture is performed, exudate from the purulent base of the ulcer or material aspirated from buboes should be inoculated onto appropriate media. Gram-negative coccobacilli in a "school-of-fish" grouping on Gram stain suggests *H. ducreyi,* but this pattern is often not present. The diagnosis also can be based on the histologic appearance of tissue obtained by biopsy.

Rapid diagnostic tests using EIA and PCR assay have been developed but are not available for clinical use.[46, 77, 256]

Treatment

Azithromycin (1 g orally in a single dose), ceftriaxone (250 mg intramuscularly in a single dose), ciprofloxacin (500 mg orally twice a day for 3 days), and erythromycin base (500 mg orally four times a day for 7 days) are effective agents for the treatment of chancroid in adolescents and adults.[47] Trimethoprim-sulfamethoxazole no longer is recommended because of the frequency of resistant isolates of *H. ducreyi*.

Patients should be re-examined 3 to 7 days after initiation of therapy. Ulcers should improve symptomatically within 3 days and show objective improvement within 7 days if treatment is effective. If no clinical improvement occurs, one or more of the following should be considered: (1) the diagnosis may be incorrect, (2) co-infection with another sexually transmitted agent may be present, (3) the infecting strain may be resistant to the prescribed antimicrobial agent, (4) compliance with multiple-dose regimens may have been poor, or (5) the patient may have HIV infection. The time required for complete healing of ulcers is related to their size. Large ulcers may require 2 or more weeks.[47]

Resolution of fluctuant lymphadenopathy (buboes) is slower than that of ulcers. Drainage of buboes, when present, usually is required for resolution. Needle aspiration, if adequate drainage can be accomplished, is preferred over surgical incision because it results in less cicatricial scarring. Healed ulcers frequently leave significant scarring.

Persons who have had sexual contact with an individual who has chancroid during the 10 days before the onset of symptoms should be examined and treated for chancroid, even in the absence of symptoms. Patients co-infected with HIV should be monitored closely. Longer courses of therapy may be required, and healing may be slower. The optimal duration of therapy in these patients is unknown.[47]

TUBERCULOSIS[253, 280]

Even before the advent of chemotherapy for the treatment of tuberculosis, tuberculous disease of the lower genital tract was uncommon. Today, the scrofulous type is a rare finding, and primary tuberculosis of the vulva and vagina is rarer still. Most cases occur in young adult women in developing countries.

The primary lesions of vulvar tuberculosis are described as a relatively painless, slowly developing, localized, nodular thickening of the skin and subcutaneous tissues or as ulcerative lesions that are rather firm, slightly raised, reddish areas. The ulcers are demarcated sharply, with undermined edges and granular, grayish-brown bases with tubercles and areas of caseation studding their bases.

The scrofulous type is characterized by fistulous tracts and burrowing sinuses that extend from underlying tuberculous infection in the bowel, bladder, or pelvic viscera. Drainage from the ulcers and sinuses keeps the surrounding skin macerated and leads to extension of the disease.

The diagnosis is straightforward if the patient is known to have visceral tuberculosis, as most often is the case. Isolation of *M. tuberculosis* from the discharge or from lesions or examination of a biopsy specimen from the base of an ulcer is confirmatory. Primary tuberculosis of the vulva must be differentiated from other granulomatous diseases, and the scrofulous type must be distinguished from syphilis, lymphogranuloma inguinale, and Crohn disease.

Tuberculosis of the upper genital tract also is an uncommon finding but frequently leads to infertility when it does occur, probably because of scarring of the uterine tubes.[247]

Treatment

The chemotherapeutic agents used for the treatment of pulmonary and other types of systemic tuberculosis are also effective in treating the disease when it affects the genitalia. Treatment of tuberculosis is described in Chapter 101.

Vulvovaginal Ulcerative Infections

BEHÇET DISEASE[136, 160, 189, 208, 232]

In 1937, Behçet described a syndrome characterized by recurrent genital ulcers, aphthous stomatitis, and ocular inflammation. Arthritis, abnormalities of the central nervous system, a variety of skin lesions, and other systemic symptoms also may be associated with the disease. The ocular inflammation frequently is sight threatening when it occurs. Deep vein thrombosis and arterial occlusion or aneurysms can develop.[66] The onset usually occurs in patients who are between 20 and 30 years of age. Behçet disease is a rare

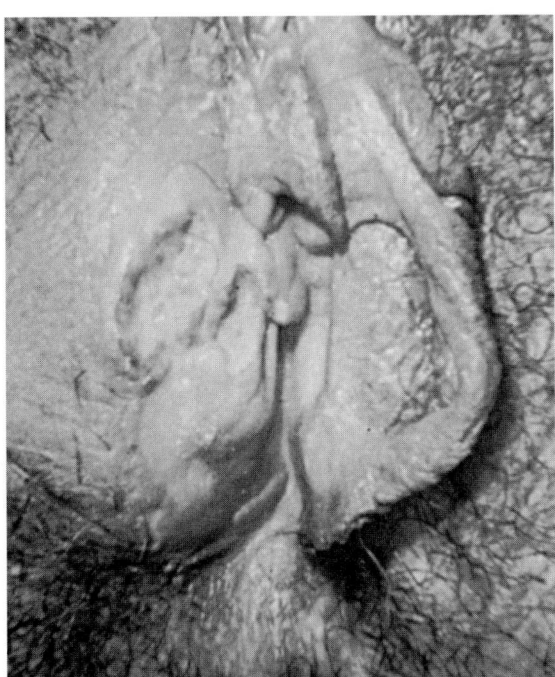

FIGURE 49–23 ■ Vulvar lesions in Behçet syndrome. (From Friedrich, E. G., Jr.: Vulvar Disease. Philadelphia, W. B. Saunders, 1976. Reproduced by permission of the author.)

condition in children and may develop more often in girls than in boys.[160] In a recent international series, 15 percent of children had a family history of Behçet disease.[163]

The cause of Behçet disease is not known, but an autoimmune basis is suspected. Herpes simplex type 1 DNA and antigens of several streptococcal species have been found in various tissues of patients with Behçet disease, and symptoms of the disease have been induced by skin tests with such antigens. Cross-reactivity of human mitochondrial and microbial heat shock proteins has been hypothesized as an immunopathogenetic mechanism for Behçet disease.[163]

The vulvar lesions take the form of destructive, deep ulcerations that, on recurrence, result in marked scarring and distortion with progressive loss of vulvar tissue (Fig. 49–23). In spite of their destructiveness, the lesions are relatively painless. The oral lesions resemble common aphthous ulcers and may precede all other manifestations of Behçet syndrome by 5 to 10 years or longer. Ocular inflammation may be manifested as iridocyclitis, chorioretinitis, or other lesions of the posterior segment. Hypopyon may be seen in some cases.

The vulvar lesions of Behçet syndrome are nonspecific in character. Diagnosis is based on associated findings and negative test results for diseases that might resemble the vulvar ulcers, notably syphilis, herpes, the granulomatous disorders, and Crohn disease. Histologic study of biopsy material from an ulcer shows only vasculitis and chronic inflammation.

Many agents, including streptococcal vaccine, chloroquine, and estrogen preparations, have been used to treat Behçet syndrome in the past. Modern treatment regimens most commonly have used systemic corticosteroids, with or without chlorambucil, colchicine, azathioprine, or thalidomide. Recent studies have suggested that cyclosporine and interferon-α may be effective.[8, 216] A randomized trial reported in 1998 of the use of colchicine plus benzathine penicillin, with or without interferon-α-2b, for the treatment of adults with Behçet disease showed a decrease in the frequency of eye involvement, episodes of arthritis, vascular events, and mucocutaneous lesions in patients treated with all three agents.[163]

Plastic surgery for correction of vaginal distortions is contraindicated because trauma may be followed by an exacerbation of the disease.

VULVAR VESTIBULITIS

A syndrome of severe and persistent superficial dyspareunia, termed vulvodynia or vulvar pain syndrome, is well recognized and may be increasing in frequency among young women in developed countries.[58, 230] The etiology is unknown and probably multifactorial. A subset of these patients have vulvar vestibulitis, which is an exquisitely tender inflammation of the vulvar vestibule.[24, 182, 228, 230] Pain and burning during intercourse, the use of tampons, or other activities that increase pressure are the most common complaints. Pain and tenderness are distinctly limited to the vulvar vestibule.[27] The physical findings are limited to vulvar erythema of varying degree.[182] Areas of focal, tender inflammation or ulceration on the vestibular mucosa that are 3 to 10 mm in size also have been described in some patients,[220] but ulceration is not a prominent feature of this entity.

Chronic inflammation of the squamous mucosa and periglandular and periductal connective tissue is the typical histopathologic finding. The infiltrate consists predominantly of T lymphocytes and plasma cells with a smaller number of B lymphocytes.[182, 228]

Subclinical infection with HPV has been suspected as an etiology, but studies can be found that support[32, 182, 248] and refute[190, 228] this hypothesis. Chronic recurrent infections (e.g., candidiasis, bacterial vaginosis), chronic alteration in vaginal pH, and the use of chemical and destructive therapeutic agents have been associated with the syndrome. One case-control study suggested a greater risk for development of vulvar vestibulitis in women who used oral contraceptives, especially if use began before they reached 17 years of age, than in those who never used them.[24] First intercourse at 15 years or younger also increased the risk relative to first intercourse at 16 years or older.

Psychosocial issues have been postulated as an explanation for vestibular vulvitis. A recent study of adult women with vulvar vestibulitis revealed more somatic symptoms than in age-matched controls, but no differences were found in their psychosocial and sexual backgrounds.[58]

Patients with acute vulvar vestibulitis should be evaluated for sexually transmitted diseases and treated for any that are found. A history of all medicinal agents or other treatment modalities used by the patient should be obtained. Any agent that might be contributing to the problem should be discontinued if possible. A variety of treatments (including steroid creams, antifungal agents, topical estrogens, interferon injections) have been tried with limited success in cases for which no specific infection could be identified.[230] If the condition is chronic and no specific etiology can be found, surgical excision may provide relief.[33, 182]

Cervicitis

PREMENARCHEAL

As a rule, the cervix is not involved when a premenarcheal child has vaginitis because most vaginal infections affect only the distal half of the vagina in children; the exception is gonococcal vaginitis, which in addition usually involves the squamous epithelium over the external cervix. Cervicitis also may occur when a vaginal foreign body is present. Endocervicitis is an unusual finding in premenarcheal females because the endocervical glands and mucosa are developed poorly before menarche, thus providing a poor environment for invading organisms.

Erosions of the cervix seldom are seen in children older than 1 year of age. So-called congenital ectopy is not the result of infection; rather, it is persistence of the fetal paramesonephric (müllerian) glandular epithelium on the outer cervix. This epithelium normally recedes into the endocervical canal as the cervix develops postnatally. Inflammation of the external cervix, which occasionally occurs with vaginitis in a premenarcheal child, need not be treated; it heals as the vaginitis improves.

POSTMENARCHEAL

The structure of the cervix during the reproductive years renders it vulnerable to infections induced by numerous factors. The long, narrow, deeply pocketed cervical canal, which is lined by open cryptic glands bathed in alkaline secretion and washed periodically by menstrual blood, is an excellent nidus for the growth of bacteria. Pathogenic bacteria in the vagina find ready access to the cervical canal. The use of oral contraceptive pills promotes cervical ectopy, thus increasing the vulnerability of endocervical cells to chlamydial infection.[141, 241]

Early recognition and aggressive treatment of cervicitis in sexually active adolescents are important to prevent serious complications, including pelvic inflammatory disease and tubo-ovarian abscess. However, some confusion tends to occur with regard to differentiating normal ectopic columnar epithelium on the exocervix (ectopy) from cervicitis. Ectopy is not an abnormal finding. When the squamocolumnar junction is exposed on the exocervix, it is called ectopy. It appears bright shiny red, in contrast to the dull pearly pink appearance of the exocervix. This area does not bleed easily when touched with a swab. During adolescence, the normal cervix may exhibit no ectopy, a small area of ectopy, or at times as much as 50 percent ectopy. When the ectopy appears edematous, raised, and friable (often with marked bleeding when touched lightly with a swab), cervicitis should be suspected.[141, 241]

Mucopurulent cervicitis primarily is endocervicitis associated with *C. trachomatis, M. hominis, U. urealyticum, N. gonorrhoeae, G. vaginalis,* and group B streptococci. In contrast, *T. vaginalis* causes an exocervicitis by extension of vaginitis. Because of the high prevalence of coexisting infections of the cervix, associating any one organism with the clinical signs and symptoms of cervicitis often is difficult. Although studies have shown a strong association between mucopurulent cervicitis and *C. trachomatis,* in most cases no organism is isolated.[141, 241, 262]

Cervicitis often is asymptomatic but should be clinically suspected if an adolescent reports a vaginal discharge and bleeding, especially after having sexual intercourse. Criteria for a clinical diagnosis of mucopurulent cervicitis include the presence of mucopurulent secretion from the endocervix, erythema of the cervix, friable ectopy, and bleeding from the cervix.[41] The mucopurulent secretion in chlamydial cervicitis is tenacious mucoid material mixed with yellow exudate and is difficult to remove from the endocervix. The ectopic area on the cervix may appear erythematous and friable. In chronic chlamydial cervicitis, the ectopic area may be swollen and irregular with a cobblestone appearance, a condition called hypertrophic cervicitis. In gonococcal cervicitis, the endocervical mucosa is swollen, intensely inflamed, and often friable as well. In contrast to the mucopurulent discharge present in chlamydial cervicitis, a profuse, yellowish-green acrid discharge is present in gonococcal cervicitis.

Cervical erosions occur in sexually active adolescents. Infections other than those listed earlier as causing mucopurulent cervicitis also can involve the cervix. A chancre, the primary lesion of syphilis, may appear on the cervix, where it forms an irregularly shaped ulcer that only remotely resembles a chancre on the vulva. Tuberculosis, herpes simplex virus, granuloma inguinale, lymphogranuloma venereum, chancroid, schistosomiasis, and actinomycosis also may affect the cervix. The cervical lesions of most of these infections are altered by the warmth and moisture of the vagina and are atypical in appearance. None of these lesions is a common finding, but all of them should be considered in the differential diagnosis when a patient has an unusual ulcerative or fungating lesion of the cervix.[144]

Treatment

The first step is to obtain good specimens from the endocervix. The cervix should be wiped with a large swab to remove vaginal secretions. Endocervical specimens then are obtained for detection of *C. trachomatis* and *N. gonorrhoeae* and a vaginal specimen for a saline wet mount and KOH preparation under microscopy. The types of tests available for chlamydial and gonococcal infection are described in this section under "Chlamydial" and "Gonococcal" cervicitis. If an endocervical Gram stain can be performed, an endocervical specimen should be obtained. This test is useful in a clinical setting. Cervicitis is suspected when an endocervical Gram-stained smear shows more than 5 to 10 polymorphonuclear cells per field under oil immersion. The presence of at least eight pairs of gram-negative intracellular diplococci in at least three polymorphonuclear cells strongly suggests gonococcal cervicitis. The absence of gram-negative intracellular diplococci but the presence of more than 5 to 10 polymorphonuclear cells per oil immersion field suggests nongonococcal cervicitis.[41, 193, 235] When cervical erosions or ulcers are seen, a specimen for culture of herpes simplex virus should be obtained. *T. vaginalis* is identified by microscopic examination of vaginal secretions in saline.

The same guidelines for the treatment of gonococcal and chlamydial cervicitis are used for the treatment of cervicitis in nonpregnant females. Current treatment of gonococcal infection is influenced by the emergence of antibiotic-resistant strains, including penicillinase-producing *N. gonorrhoeae,* fluoroquinolone-resistant strains, tetracycline-resistant strains, and chromosomally resistant strains. The high frequency of chlamydial infection in persons with gonorrhea (as high as 45% in certain populations) and the serious complications resulting from untreated gonorrhea and chlamydial infections also have influenced the treatment approach. Treatment options include cefixime, 400 mg orally in a single dose; 125 mg of intramuscular ceftriaxone in a single dose plus azithromycin, 1 g orally in a single dose; and 100 mg of doxycycline orally twice a day for 7 days.[47] In the case of penicillin allergy, a single dose of intramuscular spectinomycin (2 g) instead of cephalosporins is indicated. Azithromycin, 2 g, can be used in instead of cefixime or ceftriaxone to treat gonococcal cervicitis; however, this regimen is inadvisable because of its cost and severe gastrointestinal side effects.[47] In females older than 18 years of age not residing in Hawaii, California, or Asia, alternative regimens for gonococcal cervicitis are ciprofloxacin, 500 mg orally in a single dose, or ofloxacin, 400 mg orally in a single dose. These alternative regimens are in frequent use today because production of cefixime recently was discontinued in the United States. Pregnant females should not be treated with doxycycline or the quinolones. Azithromycin, 1 g orally in a single dose, or erythromycin base, 500 mg orally four times a day for 7 days, is recommended for presumptive *C. trachomatis* cervicitis.[47] If pharyngeal gonorrhea is suspected, the recommended treatment is intramuscular ceftriaxone or oral fluoroquinolones. When *T. vaginalis* vaginitis is diagnosed or herpes simplex virus is suspected strongly, the appropriate treatment for these infections should be given (see the sections on trichomoniasis and herpes genitalis).

Integral to treating the patient is notification, examination, and treatment of the patient's sexual partners if gonococcal or chlamydial infection (or both) is confirmed. Direct notification by the patient should be encouraged, and written information should be provided with names of diseases and medications to assist with this process. When tests are positive for gonorrhea or chlamydial infection, retesting for these infections is recommended: in 3 weeks if treated with erythromycin or if symptoms persist and in 3 months if treated with other regimens to detect reinfection from an untreated or new partner.[47]

CHLAMYDIAL

Some of the highest rates of chlamydial cervicitis (8–25%) have been reported in adolescents.[48, 92, 95, 245] It is three to four times more common than gonococcal cervicitis. *C. trachomatis* causes cervicitis by infecting the columnar and transitional epithelium of the cervix. Cervical ectopy appears to be a predisposing factor for *C. trachomatis* infection.[19]

C. trachomatis cervicitis is predominantly an asymptomatic disease in adolescent girls.[48] A clinical diagnosis is made when friable ectopy with a mucopurulent cervical discharge (mucopus) is noted. Chlamydial cervicitis is suspected when a Gram stain of an adequate endocervical smear demonstrates more than 5 to 10 polymorphonuclear cells per oil immersion field in the absence of gram-negative intracellular diplococci.[41, 195]

Numerous tests, including culture, DFA tests, EIA, nucleic acid hybridization tests, enhanced optical immunoassays, and nucleic acid amplification tests, are available today to diagnose *C. trachomatis* infection. Material from the cervix must be obtained directly from the endocervix with a sterile swab. The tissue culture method was considered the gold standard,[249] but because of the high cost of this technique, it is not used widely for adolescents and adults. However, it continues to be the gold standard for prepubertal children suspected of being infected. Overall, amplification tests are considered the most sensitive and specific tests today, and testing of urine specimens is expected to revolutionize screening and diagnosis. At present, amplification tests are being used predominantly for research purposes because of their high cost, but gradually they may become available for clinical use.

In large-volume community-based clinics, the DNA hybridization assay or DNA probe (Gen-Probe) and EIA (Abbot, Wampole, Kodak, Gen-Probe) can be used.[167, 255] Both tests perform best in clinic populations with high prevalence rates of *C. trachomatis* infection; however, the DNA probe appears to have greater sensitivity for detection of chlamydial infection and is simple to perform. The Gen-Probe is approximately 80 percent sensitive and 100 percent specific, and the EIA is 50 to 97 percent sensitive and 98 percent specific in detecting *C. trachomatis* in females. Both tests can be used as "mail-out" specimens as well.[80, 255] The DFA test or MicroTrak is considered to be suited best for low-volume laboratories and requires technical expertise. This test detects *Chlamydia* elementary bodies in cervical secretions and takes 15 to 20 minutes to perform. It has a sensitivity of 75 to 90 percent and specificity of 95 to 97 percent when compared with the culture method.[80, 255] The optical immunoassay (Biostar) has a sensitivity of 89 to 90 percent and a specificity of 90 percent. The reliability of amplification tests such as PCR, ligase chain reaction (LCR), strand displacement amplification (SDA), and transcription-mediated amplification (TMA) in detecting *C. trachomatis* appears to be equivalent for vaginal, cervical, and urine specimens as long as the urine collected is a first-catch specimen. The sensitivity of PCR, LCR, SDA, and TMA ranges from 87 to 99 percent, with specificity ranging from 97 to 100 percent.[28, 80, 252]

Treatment of chlamydial cervicitis is discussed earlier in this section "Cervicitis."

GONOCOCCAL

Gonococcal cervicitis may be symptomatic or asymptomatic. The risk of acquiring infection varies with the population. Adolescents seen in private practices in the suburbs have a significantly lower rate of gonococcal cervicitis than that noted in adolescents seen in large outpatient hospital clinics or community clinics serving inner-city populations. Although gonococcal cervicitis is estimated to be predominantly an asymptomatic condition in females, many patients, after careful questioning, are found to have symptoms. The rate of asymptomatic endocervical infection in adolescent females seen in urban settings ranges from 3 to 12 percent. Anal gonorrhea usually is secondary to discharge from gonococcal cervicitis infecting the anus. Primary anal gonorrhea as a result of anal intercourse should be suspected in a sexually active adolescent with anal discomfort. In addition, gonococcal infection should be considered in the differential diagnosis of pharyngitis in sexually active adolescents.[228] Gonococcal endocarditis, arthritis, and dermal abscesses occur but are beyond the scope of this chapter.

The initial complaints in gonococcal cervicitis include vaginal discharge, dysuria, urinary frequency, and dyspareunia. The discharge is profuse and prevalent. On examination, the vulvar tissues may be inflamed and edematous. Discharge also may be seen exuding out of the urethra and paraurethral ducts in severe cases. On speculum examination, the patient has a normal-appearing cervix, or the cervix appears erythematous and friable, with a foul-smelling purulent discharge draining from the cervical os.

Laboratory diagnosis can be made by detecting *N. gonorrhoeae* by culture technique, a gonococcal antigen-detection test (Abbott), a DNA hybridization test or DNA probe (Gen-Probe), or an amplification test. Material from the cervix must be obtained directly from the endocervix with a sterile swab. Vaginal swabs self-obtained by the adolescent also is a recommended method for amplification tests. Although the reliability of detecting gram-negative intracellular diplococci on a Gram stain of cervical secretions is low, this test can be useful in areas where more sophisticated tests are not available. The presence of at least eight pairs of gram-negative intracellular diplococci in at least three polymorphonuclear cells strongly suggests gonococcal cervicitis. Hospital-based settings continue to use the culture method. The DNA probe (Gen-Probe) can be used in hospital and community-based clinics for the same reasons described under "Chlamydial" cervicitis. This test has sensitivities ranging from 90 to 97 percent and a specificity of 99 percent. Amplification tests such as PCR, LCR, and SDA for *N. gonorrhoeae* from vaginal, cervical, and first-catch urine specimens have a sensitivity of 95 to 97 percent and a specificity of 99 to 100 percent.[80, 270]

Treatment of gonococcal cervicitis is discussed earlier in this section under "Cervicitis."

Upper Genital Tract Infections

PELVIC INFLAMMATORY DISEASE

Pelvic inflammatory disease in postmenarcheal girls is a common problem. Although salpingitis has been reported in virgins, this condition primarily occurs in sexually active adolescents at risk for acquiring sexually transmitted diseases.[82, 84]

Pelvic inflammatory disease is defined as an acute clinical syndrome (unrelated to pregnancy or surgery) attributed to the ascent of microorganisms from the vagina and endocervix to the endometrium, fallopian tubes, or contiguous structures that results in pelvic and generalized peritonitis. The use of terms specifically describing the anatomic sites involved is preferable (e.g., endometritis, salpingitis, salpingo-oophoritis, tubo-ovarian abscess). However, in most adolescents with acute severe infection, differentiating some of these entities is difficult; thus, the term *pelvic inflammatory disease* is used commonly.

Reasons for the development of pelvic inflammatory disease are physiologic and social. They include alterations in cervical mucus caused by immature and anovulatory menstrual cycles, early onset of sexual activity, and multiple sexual partners. Other factors influencing the risk of acquiring pelvic inflammatory disease are the method of contraception, a history of gonococcal or chlamydial lower genital tract infection, and uterine instrumentation, such as the use of an intrauterine device or dilatation and curettage.[158] HIV-infected patients appear to be at an increased risk for acquiring pelvic inflammatory disease and also may have serious infections. In addition, vaginal douching has been reported to be a risk factor in promoting ascending infection.[207, 298, 301]

Oral contraceptives are used commonly by adolescents. Their possible protective effect on the development of pelvic inflammatory disease has been reported. When compared with other methods of contraception, oral contraceptives have a lower risk of causing pelvic inflammatory disease.[260] Laparoscopic studies also have shown that women with pelvic inflammatory disease who were using oral contraceptive pills have significantly milder degrees of fallopian tube inflammation than do non–pill users. This finding suggests that the oral contraceptive pill may reduce potential tubal damage. Other studies, however, report that by promoting cervical ectopy, oral contraceptives are a potential risk factor for acquiring chlamydial pelvic inflammatory disease.[262, 285, 302]

Women who have had one episode of pelvic inflammatory disease have a 20 to 25 percent chance of subsequent ones. Reasons for this susceptibility may be reinfection from untreated sexual partners, an inadequately treated first infection, or increased susceptibility of the tubal epithelium to infection.[84, 298]

Pathogenic bacteria reach the endometrium and fallopian tubes by one of three routes: hematogenously, directly from a contagious site of infection, or via ascending infection from the lower genital tract. The first two routes are uncommon.[298]

The mechanism for ascending infection from the vagina and cervix to the endometrium and fallopian tubes is thought to be multifactorial. One possible factor is that cervical mucus is less viscous during menses and at midcycle and more permeable to ascending infection. In vitro experiments show that *N. gonorrhoeae, C. trachomatis, U. urealyticum,* and other aerobic and anaerobic agents can adhere to spermatozoa and migrate with them.[288] Whether this event can occur in vivo is not known. Most organisms found in nongonococcal and nonchlamydial pelvic inflammatory disease also are found in bacterial vaginosis, thus suggesting that bacterial vaginosis may be a predisposing or a precipitating factor for the development of pelvic inflammatory disease. In addition, researchers have suggested that *T. vaginalis* can act as a vector for transporting bacteria.[158] Another possible factor is upward transport of bacteria from orgasmic myometrial contractions.[298]

Endometritis

Infections of the endometrium in postmenarcheal females do not occur as rarely as previously thought. The gonococcus, on its way upward to the uterine tubes, produces a fleeting asymptomatic infection of the endometrium, or the symptoms produced are overshadowed by those of the vulvar and cervical infections. Evidence also suggests that endometritis occurs in as many as 40 percent of patients with asymptomatic endocervical chlamydial infection.[154] Symptoms specific to endometritis are not common findings. When present, they include recurrent intermittent or acute suprapubic pain and tenderness with vaginal bleeding or spotting. On bimanual examination, the uterus is tender and cervical motion tenderness may or may not be present. Endometritis in adolescents and young adult women also has been associated with postabortive and puerperal endometritis. Poor compliance with prophylactic antibiotics places an adolescent at an increased risk for development of endometritis after having an abortion. Young women who use intrauterine devices are likely to have asymptomatic, low-grade, chronic endometritis.

Endometrial tuberculosis is a rare finding in the United States and is encountered most often in patients with pulmonary tuberculosis. This entity needs to be considered in HIV-infected females and in geographic areas and regions where tuberculosis is endemic. In a recent study from a province in Iran, tuberculous endometritis was detected in 72 percent of female genital tuberculosis cases.[203] The infection is thought to reach the uterus via the gastrointestinal tract and by lymphatic spread. It is not acquired as a result of an ascending infection or through coitus with an infected male. The symptoms of endometrial tuberculosis vary from none at all to amenorrhea, pelvic pain, dysmenorrhea, and abnormal uterine bleeding. It may be an incidental finding in a patient without detectable tuberculosis in other organs who undergoes curettage for menstrual irregularity or infertility. Often, the patient has a history of healed or active pulmonary disease. Ninety percent of patients with pelvic tuberculosis have tuberculous endometritis.[247]

Endometrial tuberculosis is diagnosed by histologic study of curetted tissue or by demonstration of acid-fast *M. tuberculosis* in cultures of curettage material or menstrual blood.

Additional information on endometrial tuberculosis and the management of tuberculosis is described elsewhere in this book (see Chapter 101).

Salpingitis

The pathogenesis of salpingitis has been studied best with *N. gonorrhoeae* and *C. trachomatis*. In the fallopian tube, gonococci attach to nonciliated epithelial cells and induce sloughing of ciliated epithelial cells into the lumen. Gonococci also enter the subepithelial space, where a local inflammatory response is produced, and may reach the bloodstream. A purulent exudate is produced within the tube and may cause pelvic peritonitis. Chlamydial infection produces a similar picture, except that it causes a predominantly lymphocytic infiltrate in the submucosa, whereas with gonococcal pelvic inflammatory disease, a predominantly polymorphonuclear leukocytic infiltrate occurs in the submucosa.[219, 283, 298]

Salpingitis also is caused by several other microbial agents that have been isolated directly from the fallopian tubes. The current classification categorizes salpingitis into gonococcal, chlamydial, and nongonococcal, nonchlamydial salpingitis. The organisms most commonly recovered from the upper tract in salpingitis are mixed anaerobes (25 to 84%), followed by *N. gonorrhoeae* (25 to 40%) and *C. trachomatis* (25 to 40%). Mixed aerobic and anaerobic infections account for 25 to 60 percent of cases. The mixed anaerobes include *Bacteroides* and *Peptostreptococcus* spp. Nongonococcal, nonchlamydial pelvic inflammatory disease occurs more commonly in females with severe pelvic inflammatory disease, chronic pelvic inflammatory disease, and recurrent pelvic inflammatory disease. Pelvic inflammatory disease develops in approximately 10 to 17 percent of females with endocervical *N. gonorrhoeae* and in 10 to 30 percent with endocervical *C. trachomatis*. At first, researchers thought that *N. gonorrhoeae* initiated the infection and that superinfection with anaerobes followed. They now realize that apparently both anaerobes and aerobes can initiate pelvic inflammatory disease without *C. trachomatis* or *N. gonorrhoeae*.[80, 84, 298]

Differentiating gonococcal, chlamydial, and nongonococcal, nonchlamydial salpingitis is difficult. However, gonococcal and chlamydial salpingitis seem to occur most often within a week of menstruation.[284] The onset of nongonococcal, nonchlamydial salpingitis does not seem to be related to menses. The course of chlamydial salpingitis may be slow, with mild symptoms initially. As a result, patients delay seeking treatment. The erythrocyte sedimentation rate is elevated, and tubal damage is significant at initial evaluation in the case of chlamydial salpingitis. In contrast, gonococcal salpingitis usually has an acute manifestation with a dramatic onset of symptoms, and patients seek medical attention earlier for the condition. Fever occurs more commonly in females with gonococcal salpingitis and pelvic peritonitis than in those with chlamydial salpingitis. One report showed that adolescents with salpingitis tend to seek health care later in the course of their illness than adults do.[274]

DIAGNOSIS

The classic manifestation of acute pelvic inflammatory disease is lower abdominal pain, which usually is bilateral and continuous and may worsen with movement. After the onset of abdominal pain, fever, nausea, and vomiting develop. The temperature may reach 39 to 39.5° C (102 to 103° F). A chill seldom precedes the fever. Other common initial symptoms include vaginal discharge, irregular vaginal bleeding, and urinary symptoms.

On physical examination, the patient usually looks sick and uncomfortable. Tachycardia is present in proportion to the fever, if it develops. Abdominal examination reveals a markedly tender and often tense lower part of the abdomen. Rebound tenderness indicates generalized peritonitis. The genital examination may show a purulent vaginal discharge in the vaginal vault. Even gentle bimanual rectovaginal abdominal palpation causes great distress. Attempted mobilization of the cervix is extremely painful. The uterus is tense and tender. The adnexa may not be outlined because of discomfort produced by the examination. Palpation of the adnexa unilaterally or bilaterally may be exceptionally painful. An adnexal swelling may be palpated, but this finding is not reliable in diagnosing an adnexal mass. In a less acutely tender patient, the examination may reveal a thickened, tender tube.

Common laboratory findings in patients with pelvic inflammatory disease include a peripheral white blood cell count greater than 10,000/mm^3 and an erythrocyte sedimentation rate greater than 15 mm/hr. In addition, endocervical gonorrhea and chlamydial infection may be present simultaneously in 10 to 30 percent of cases. Ultrasonography of the pelvic cavity helps exclude adnexal masses and may detect pelvic abscesses. A study involving the use of pelvic ultrasonography in adolescents with pelvic inflammatory disease showed that the presence of fluid in the cul-de-sac was not helpful in differentiating patients with and without pelvic inflammatory disease.[110] However, almost 20 percent of patients with pelvic inflammatory disease had a tubo-ovarian abscess; in the absence of a tubo-ovarian abscess, adnexal volume was significantly larger in patients with pelvic inflammatory disease than in those without it.[110] Therefore, ultrasonography (transvaginal) can be very useful in ruling out other diagnoses and defining adnexal masses.

The clinical diagnosis of pelvic inflammatory disease is made by having a high index of suspicion of this entity. Many of the classic symptoms seen with this disease are similar to those noted in other gynecologic, urinary, and gastrointestinal tract conditions. Although these diagnoses need to be considered in a patient with an acute onset of abdominal pain, over the years, clinical criteria for the diagnosis of pelvic inflammatory disease have been developed (Table 49–6). Jacobson and Westrom[151] were the first investigators to use clinical criteria to differentiate pelvic inflammatory disease from other acute clinical conditions such as appendicitis, ovarian cysts, and ectopic pregnancy. The clinical diagnosis was confirmed by laparoscopy. Only 65 percent of cases with a clinical diagnosis of pelvic inflammatory disease were confirmed by laparoscopy, and no symptoms and signs were specific for pelvic inflammatory disease. Laparoscopy is the only means of making a definitive diagnosis. The benefits of using laparoscopy are that an accurate diagnosis can be made rapidly by direct visualization of the fallopian tubes and adjacent structures, tubal exudate can be obtained for culture, and the outcome of therapy can be evaluated.[302] This diagnostic method, however, is not without risks and adds to the cost of care and is not readily available.[281] Therefore, for practical reasons, the clinical criteria developed by Jacobson and Westrom and

TABLE 49–6 ■ CLINICAL CRITERIA FOR THE DIAGNOSIS OF ACUTE PELVIC INFLAMMATORY DISEASE

Minimal Criteria
Uterine adnexal tenderness or cervical motion tenderness

Additional Criteria to Enhance Specificity
Temperature >38.3° C (101° F)
Abnormal cervical or vaginal mucopurulent discharge
Presence of white blood cells on saline microscopy of vaginal secretions
Elevation of erythrocyte sedimentation rate
Elevated C-reactive protein; and
Laboratory documentation of cervical infection with *Neisseria gonorrheae* and/or *Chlamydia trachomatis*

Specific Criteria
Endometrial biopsy with histopathologic evidence of endometritis
Transvaginal sonography or magnetic resonance imaging technique showing thickened fluid-filled or tubo-ovarian complex
Laparoscopic abnormalities consistent with PID

revised by the Centers for Disease Control and Prevention are recommended to aid in making the diagnosis and to increase the index of suspicion for pelvic inflammatory disease. These criteria are listed in Table 49–6. The more criteria that can be met, the more likely that a tubal infection is present. However, those who use strict criteria will miss patients with mild disease.[47, 117, 151, 291]

The differential diagnosis of pelvic inflammatory disease is that of an acute abdomen. Conditions of the urinary tract that should be considered include cystitis, pyelonephritis, and urethritis. Gastrointestinal tract conditions include appendicitis, constipation, diverticulitis, gastroenteritis, inflammatory bowel disease, and irritable bowel syndrome. Gynecologic conditions include dysmenorrhea, ectopic pregnancy, endometriosis, endometritis, mittelschmerz, torsion or rupture of an ovarian cyst, ruptured follicle, septic abortion, and threatened abortion.

As in pelvic inflammatory disease, making an early diagnosis of acute appendicitis and ectopic pregnancy is important. In acute appendicitis, an adolescent is more likely to have nausea, vomiting, a short history of right lower quadrant abdominal pain, lower-grade fever, a higher leukocyte count in relation to the fever, and relatively little discomfort during pelvic examination. Occasionally, however, the appendix hangs over the pelvic brim and causes pelvic tenderness. A ruptured appendix and peritonitis may simulate pelvic inflammatory disease closely. Differentiating pelvic inflammatory disease from ectopic pregnancy is less difficult if the history suggests pregnancy. One should remember that pelvic inflammatory disease can occur during the first trimester of pregnancy. In ectopic pregnancy, the patient does not have fever or leukocytosis. The symptoms almost always are unilateral, and signs of hematoperitoneum are present if the tube is ruptured. If ectopic pregnancy is suspected, a serum pregnancy test and pelvic ultrasonography (transvaginal) for detection of a gestational sac should be performed immediately.

Treatment

The major goals of treatment of pelvic inflammatory disease are preservation of fertility and prevention of other long-term sequelae, including ectopic pregnancy. Although some data suggest that females younger than 25 years have a better fertility prognosis overall after having pelvic inflammatory disease and ectopic pregnancy, no difference exists among age groups regarding tubal infertility specifically after pelvic inflammatory disease.[298] The earlier the treatment, the lower the risk of developing infertility. Females initially evaluated after more than 3 days of abdominal pain are found to have a 2.8-fold increased risk of impaired fertility (tubal infertility or ectopic pregnancy) in comparison to those evaluated within 3 days of the onset of abdominal pain.[139] In general, the more severe the pelvic inflammatory disease, the higher the risk of future infertility occurring. In addition, the more episodes of pelvic inflammatory disease, the higher the risk of future infertility occurring. After one episode, the risk of infertility ranges from 8 to 13 percent; after two episodes, the risk is 20 to 35 percent; and after three or more episodes, it is 40 to 75 percent.[80, 282]

Therefore, to reduce the incidence of sequelae associated with this condition, of importance are early recognition of pelvic inflammatory disease, the use of broad-spectrum antibiotics to treat polymicrobial disease, careful clinical re-evaluation 48 hours after initiating antibiotic treatment to assess antibiotic response, and evaluation and treatment of sexual partners. Screening the patient for other sexually transmitted diseases, such as trichomoniasis, bacterial vaginosis, and syphilis, also is important.

TABLE 49–7 ■ AMBULATORY MANAGEMENT OF PELVIC INFLAMMATORY DISEASE

Regimen A
Ofloxacin, 400 mg PO two times a day for 14 days
with or without
Metronidazole, 500 mg PO two times a day for 14 days
An alternative regimen is amoxicillin-clavulanic acid plus doxycycline

Regimen B
Cefoxitin, 2 g IM
plus
Probenecid, 1 g PO concurrently, or ceftriaxone, 250 mg IM, or equivalent parenteral third-generation cephalosporin
plus
Doxycycline, 100 mg PO two times a day for 10–14 days
with or without
Metronidazole, 500 mg PO twice a day for 14 days

From Centers for Disease Control and Prevention: Sexually transmitted disease treatment guidelines 2002. M.M.W.R. Recomm. Rep. *51*(RR-6): 1–78, 2002.

Females with pelvic inflammatory disease often are treated on an ambulatory basis. However, because of the seriousness of the sequelae and problems with compliance in this age group, the primary reason to hospitalize an adolescent is to ensure compliance with medication when she is unable to follow or tolerate an outpatient oral regimen. Other reasons for hospitalization are an uncertain diagnosis, the presence of a tubo-ovarian abscess, pregnancy, infection with HIV, temperature above 38.5° C, nausea and vomiting precluding the use of oral medications, and lack of improvement after 48 hours of oral antibiotic treatment.

The current recommendations of the Centers for Disease Control and Prevention for the treatment of pelvic inflammatory disease in both ambulatory and hospitalized patients address antibiotic coverage for the polymicrobial etiology of this condition[47] (Tables 49–7 and 49–8). Other second- and third-generation cephalosporins, quinolones, and metronidazole may be used as alternatives for inpatient treatment of pelvic inflammatory disease. Despite concern about whether regimen B for inpatient treatment (See Table 49–8) would cover *C. trachomatis,* patients treated with clindamycin and gentamicin do experience comparable cure rates of pelvic inflammatory disease. For outpatient treatment of pelvic inflammatory disease, oral ofloxacin with or without metronidazole is a recommended regimen for

TABLE 49–8 ■ INPATIENT TREATMENT OF PELVIC INFLAMMATORY DISEASE

Regimen A
Cefoxitin, 2 g IV every 6 hr, or cefotetan, 2 g IV every 12 hr
plus
Doxycycline, 100 mg every 12 hr PO or IV
The above regimen is given for at least 48 hr after the patient clinically improves. After discharge from the hospital, doxycycline is continued at 100 mg PO two times a day for a total of 10–14 days

Regimen B
Clindamycin, 900 mg IV every 8 hr
plus
Gentamicin loading dose IV or IM (2 mg/kg) followed by a maintenance dose (1.5 mg/kg) every 8 hr
The above regimen is given for at least 48 hr after the patient improves. After discharge from the hospital, doxycycline is continued at 100 mg PO two times a day for a total of 10–14 days

From Centers for Disease Control and Prevention: Sexually transmitted disease treatment guidelines 2002. M.M.W.R. Recomm. Rep. *51*(RR-6): 1–78, 2002.

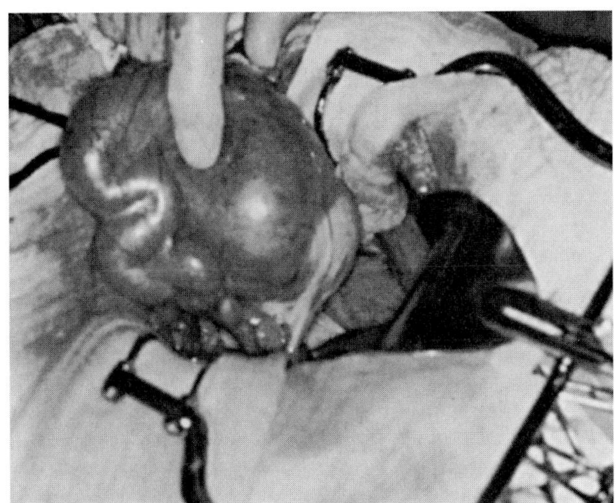

FIGURE 49–24 ■ Large hydrosalpinx, the result of gonorrheal salpingitis in an older teenage girl who had repeated gonorrheal infections. The other tube also was diseased.

those older than 18 years. The latter provides coverage of anaerobes and will also effectively treat bacterial vaginosis (frequently associated with pelvic inflammatory disease). Ofloxacin is effective against *N. gonorrhoeae* and *C. trachomatis*. In addition to antibiotic treatment, bed rest is recommended. Intravenous fluids are administered for hydration when necessary. When the diagnosis of pelvic inflammatory disease is certain, oral analgesic agents may be prescribed. Close follow-up is recommended, with a bimanual examination after 48 hours of antibiotic treatment to assess treatment response.[47]

Complications associated with pelvic inflammatory disease are perihepatitis, tubo-ovarian abscess, hydrosalpinx (obstruction of the tube caused by scarring—Fig. 49–24), chronic abdominal pain from adhesions surrounding the fallopian tubes and ovaries, recurrent pelvic inflammatory disease, ectopic pregnancy, and infertility.[82, 117]

The classic manifestation of perihepatitis, or Fitz-Hugh–Curtis syndrome,[298] is severe right upper abdominal pain that often radiates to the shoulder. Concurrent left upper abdominal pain also may be present. Lower abdominal pain and evidence of acute or subacute pelvic inflammatory disease are frequent findings. The right upper quadrant pain lasts about 48 hours. Nausea, fever, and leukocytosis are common features. Elevation of the erythrocyte sedimentation rate and liver enzymes may be present. The pathogenesis of perihepatitis is thought to be from direct spread of *N. gonorrhoeae* and *C. trachomatis* from the fallopian tubes into the peritoneal cavity, along the paracolic sulci. From there, they reach the subphrenic space and hepatic surface. However, spread from the reproductive tract also is possible via the retroperitoneal lymphatics.[298]

The diagnosis is made by having a high index of suspicion. Perihepatitis frequently mimics cholelithiasis, hepatitis, pleuritis, subphrenic abscess, perforated peptic ulcer, nephrolithiasis, appendicitis, ectopic pregnancy, abdominal trauma, and pancreatitis. Treatment of this condition is similar to that of pelvic inflammatory disease.

TUBO-OVARIAN ABSCESS

Tubo-ovarian abscess formation is a late manifestation of pelvic inflammatory disease. The incidence of tubo-ovarian abscess ranges from 14 to 38 percent in hospital-based adolescents and adults with salpingitis.[110, 117, 171, 204, 268] The abscess typically results from a mixture of facultative and anaerobic bacteria, with facultative bacteria dominating the early phase of infection and bacterial metabolic products producing an environment of low oxygen tension that favors the growth of anaerobic bacteria.[298] The most common organisms recovered from tubo-ovarian abscesses are *E. coli*, *Bacteroides fragilis*, other *Bacteroides* spp., *Peptostreptococcus*, *Peptococcus*, and aerobic streptococci.[233] Diagnosing the presence of a tubo-ovarian abscess clinically usually is difficult. Adolescents with a tubo-ovarian abscess tend to seek care later in their menstrual cycle (>18 days from the last menstrual period) than do those without a tubo-ovarian abcess.[268] Bimanual examination frequently does not demonstrate a pelvic mass.[53] Four potentially useful clinical features that suggest the presence of a pelvic abscess are pain, persistent fever, adnexal tenderness (for more than 7 days), and an erythrocyte sedimentation rate greater than 30 mm/hr.[53] Ultrasonography of the pelvis is valuable in confirming the presence of an abscess.[110]

The prompt administration of antibiotics has reduced greatly the incidence of pelvic abscess. Most of those encountered today are in patients who have not had adequate care and delay seeking treatment.[117] Adolescents are far more likely to delay seeking treatment than are young adult females.[274]

A conservative approach is favored for the treatment of a tubo-ovarian or ovarian abscess (i.e., bed rest, supportive care, intravenous antibiotics).[80] The choice of antibiotics for treating tubo-ovarian abscess should include the following considerations: effectiveness against β-lactamase–producing anaerobes, adequate coverage against resistant *Bacteroides* spp., penetration into the abscess, and ability to remain stable in an abscess environment. The antibiotic regimens for inpatient treatment of pelvic inflammatory disease fulfill these considerations and, therefore, are appropriate for the treatment of tubo-ovarian abscess (see Table 49–8). As is the case with cefoxitin, cefotetan, and clindamycin, metronidazole provides good activity against anaerobes.[233] Many hospitals prefer the use of triple antibiotics: cefoxitin and gentamicin plus clindamycin or metronidazole. A clinical response to treatment consisting of a decrease in pain, fever, and total leukocyte count should be noted in 72 hours. Pelvic ultrasonography should be repeated at this time to note any further increase in abscess size. The duration of intravenous and oral antibiotic therapy for a tubo-ovarian abscess should be at least 21 days. The patient may begin oral antibiotics once she is afebrile and asymptomatic and the size of the abscess has stabilized. The abscess either resolves without drainage or becomes an encapsulated pool of pus. The latter eventually "points" either in the cul-de-sac or anteriorly in the abdominal wall.

Surgical intervention may be needed in as many as 25 percent of cases either during the initial period or within a year, usually depending on the size of the abscess. An abscess larger than 10 cm has a 60 percent chance, a 7- to 9-cm abscess has a 35 percent chance, and a 4- to 6-cm abscess has a 20 percent chance of requiring surgical intervention. The fertility rate after treatment of tubo-ovarian abscesses may be 20 to 50 percent with conservative medical and surgical approaches.

OVARITIS

Massive inflammatory swelling of the ovary may be secondary to an acute systemic disease. It must be differentiated from an ovarian tumor. The acute exanthemas and mumps are complicated most frequently by ovaritis. Improved immunization practices, however, have decreased the prevalence of mumps ovaritis. The presence of an enlarged, tender, boggy, smooth mobile ovary in a child with mumps or one of the exanthemas is an indication for repeated examination and watchfulness. The ovary becomes less tender and gradually shrinks. Mumps ovaritis, in particular, may convert one or both ovaries into swellings 6 to 8 cm in diameter. The enlargement may persist for several months. Treatment is palliative, with analgesics given for discomfort and fever.[144]

REFERENCES

1. Ackerman, A. B., Goldfaden, G., and Cosmides, J. C.: Acquired syphilis in prepubertal children. Arch. Dermatol. 106:92–93, 1972.
2. Adams, R.: Topical therapy: A formulary for pediatric skin disease. *In* Gellis, S., and Kagan, B. (eds.): Current Pediatric Therapy 3. Philadelphia, W. B. Saunders, 1976, pp. 446–454.
3. Adu-Sarkodie, Y: *Trichomonas vaginalis* transmission in a family. Genitourin. Med. *71*:199–200, 1995.
4. Aghajanian, A., Bernstein, L., and Grimes, D. A.: Bartholin's duct abscess and cyst: A case-control study. South. Med. J. *87*:26–29, 1994.
5. Alergant, C.: Chancroid. Practitioner *209*:624–627, 1972.
6. Alexander, E. R.: Misidentification of sexually transmitted organisms in children: Medicolegal implications. Pediatr. Infect. Dis. J. *7*:1–2, 1988.
7. Alexander, W. J., Griffith, H., Housch, J. G., et al.: Infections in sexual contacts and associates of children with gonorrhea. Sex. Transm. Dis. *11*:156–158, 1983.
8. Alpsoy, E., Yilmaz, E., and Basaran, E.: Interferon therapy for Behçet disease. J. Am. Acad. Dermatol. *31*:617–619, 1994.
9. Al-Salihi, F. L., Curran, J. P., and Wang, J.: Neonatal *Trichomonas vaginalis:* Report of three cases and review of the literature. Pediatrics *53*:196–200, 1974.
10. Al-Tawfiq, J. A., Palmer, K. L., Chen, C.-Y., et al.: Experimental infection of human volunteers with *Haemophilus ducreyi* does not confer protection against subsequent challenge. J. Infect. Dis. *179*:1283–1287, 1999.
11. Altchek, A.: Vulvovaginitis, vulvar skin disease, and pelvic inflammatory disease. Pediatr. Clin. North Am. *28*:397–432, 1981.
12. American Academy of Pediatrics: Bacterial vaginosis. *In* Pickering, L. K. (ed.): 2000 Red Book: Report of the Committee on Infectious Diseases. 25th ed. Elk Grove Village, IL, American Academy of Pediatrics, 2000, pp. 183–185.
13. American Academy of Pediatrics. Candidiasis. *In* Pickering, L. K. (ed.): 2000 Red Book: Report of the Committee on Infectious Diseases. 25th ed. Elk Grove Village, IL, American Academy of Pediatrics, 2000, pp. 199–201.
14. American Academy of Pediatrics: *Trichomonas vaginalis* infection. *In* Pickering, L. K. (ed.): 2000 Red Book: Report of the Committee on Infectious Diseases. 25th ed. Elk Grove Village, IL, American Academy of Pediatrics, 2000, pp. 588–589.
15. Amsel, R., Totten, P. A., Speigel, C. A., et al.: Nonspecific vaginitis: Diagnostic criteria, microbial and epidemiologic associations. Am. J. Med. *74*:14–22, 1983.
16. Andersen, P. G., Christensen, S., Detlefsen, G. U., et al.: Treatment of Bartholin's abscess: Marsupialization versus incision, curettage and suture under antibiotic cover: A randomised study with 6 months' follow up. Acta Obstet. Gynecol. Scand. *71*:59–62, 1992.
17. Andrew, D., and Bumstead, E.: The role of fomites in the transmission of vaginitis. Can. Med. Assoc. J. *112*:1181–1183, 1975.
18. Argent, A. C., Lachman, P. I., Hanslo, D., and Bass, D.: Sexually transmitted diseases in children and evidence of sexual abuse. Child Abuse Negl. *19*:1303–1310, 1995.
19. Arya, O. P., Mallinson, H., and Goddard, A. D.: Epidemiological and clinical correlates of chlamydial infection of the cervix. Br. J. Vener. Dis. *57*:118–124, 1981.
20. Banov, L., Jr.: Rectal lesions of lymphogranuloma venereum in childhood. Am. J. Dis. Child. *83*:660–662, 1952.
21. Bartley, D. L., Morgan, L., and Rimsza, M. E.: *Gardnerella vaginalis* in prepubertal girls. Am. J. Dis. Child. *141*:1014–1017, 1987.
22. Bass, H. N.: "Bubble bath" as an irritant to the urinary tract of children. Clin. Pediatr. (Phila.) *7*:174, 1968.
23. Bassa, A. G. H., Hoosen, A. A., Moodley, J., et al.: Granuloma inguinale (donovanosis) in women: An analysis of 60 cases from Durban, South Africa. Sex. Transm. Dis. *20*:164–167, 1993.
24. Bazin, S., Bouchard, C., Brisson, J., et al.: Vulvar vestibulitis syndrome: An exploratory case-control study. Obstet. Gynecol. *83*:47–50, 1994.
25. Bell, T. A., Stamm, W. E., Wang, S. P., et al.: Chronic *Chlamydia trachomatis* infections in infants. J. A. M. A. *267*:400–402, 1992.
26. Berenson, A. B.: Adolescent gynecology. Obstet. Gynecol. Clin. North Am. *27*:1–128, 2000.
27. Bergeron, S., Binik, Y. M., Khalife, S., et al.: Vulvar vestibulitis syndrome: Reliability of diagnosis and evaluation of current diagnostic criteria. Obstet. Gynecol. *98*:45–51, 2001.
28. Black, C. M.: Current methods of laboratory diagnosis of *Chlamydia trachomatis* infections. Clin. Microbiol. Rev. *10*:160–184, 1997.
29. Blackmore, C. A., Limpakarnjanarat, K., Rigau-Perez, J. G., et al.: An outbreak of chancroid in Orange County, California: Descriptive epidemiology and disease-control measures. J. Infect. Dis. *151*:840–844, 1985.
30. Bogaerts, J., Lepage, P., De Clercq, A., et al.: *Shigella* and gonococcal vulvovaginitis in prepubertal Central African girls. Pediatr. Infect. Dis. J. *11*:890–892, 1992.
31. Boisvert, P., and Walcher, D.: Hemolytic streptococcal vaginitis in children. Pediatrics *2*:24–29, 1948.
32. Bornstein, J., Lahat, N., Sharon, A., et al.: Telomerase activity in HPV-associated vulvar vestibulitis. J. Reprod. Med. *45*:643–648, 2000.
33. Bornstein, J., Zarfati, D., Goldik, Z., and Abramovici, H.: Vulvar vestibulitis: Physical or psychosexual problem? Obstet. Gynecol. *93*:876–880, 1999.
34. Bramley, M.: Study of female babies of women entering confinement with vaginal trichomoniasis. Br. J. Vener. Dis. *52*:58–62, 1976.
35. Branch, G., and Paxton, R.: A study of gonococcal infections among infants and children. Public Heath Rep. *80*:347–352, 1965.
36. Braverman, P., and Polaneczky, M.: Adolescent gynecology, part I: Common disorders. Pediatr. Clin. North Am. *46*:489–648, 1999.
37. Braverman, P., and Polaneczky, M.: Adolescent gynecology, part II: the sexually active adolescent. Pediatr. Clin. North Am. *46*:649–829, 1999.
38. Breschi, L. C., Goldman, G., and Shapiro, S. R.: Granuloma inguinale in Vietnam. J. Am. Vener. Dis. Assoc. *1*:118–120, 1975.
39. Brigden, M., and Guard, R.: Extragenital granuloma inguinale in North Queensland. Med. J. Aust. *2*:565–567, 1980.
40. Brown, J. L.: Hair shampooing technique and pediatric vulvovaginitis. Pediatrics *83*:146, 1989.
41. Brunham, R. C., Paavonen, J., Stevens, C. E., et al.: Mucopurulent cervicitis: The ignored counterpart in women of urethritis in men. N. Engl. J. Med. *311*:1–6, 1984.
42. Bump, R. C. *Chlamydia trachomatis* as a cause of prepubertal vaginitis. Obstet. Gynecol. *65*:384–388, 1985.
43. Bump, R. C., and Buesching, W. J.: Bacterial vaginosis in virginal and sexually active adolescent females: Evidence against exclusive sexual transmission. Am. J. Obstet. Gynecol. *158*:935–939, 1988.
44. Burgess, J. A.: *Trichomonas vaginalis* infection from splashing in water closets. Br. J. Vener. Dis. *39*:248–250, 1963.
45. Burry, V.: Gonococcal vulvovaginitis and possible peritonitis in prepubertal girls. Am. J. Dis. Child. *121*:536–537, 1971.
46. Centers for Disease Control and Prevention: Chancroid detected by polymerase chain reaction—Jackson, Mississippi, 1994–1995. M. M. W. R. Morb. Mortal. Wkly. Rep. *44*(30):567, 573–574, 1995.
47. Centers for Disease Control and Prevention: Sexually transmitted disease treatment guidelines 2002. Centers for Disease Control and Prevention. M. M. W.R. Recomm. Rep. *51*(RR-6):1–78, 2002.
48. Chacko, M. R., and Lovchick, J. C.: *Chlamydia trachomatis* infection in sexually active adolescents: Prevalence and risk factors. Pediatrics *73*:836–840, 1984.
49. Chang, T.: Genital herpes, the source of infection. Int. J. Dermatol. *14*:201–202, 1975.
50. Charles, S. X.: Epidemiology of *Trichomonas vaginalis* in rural adolescent and juvenile children. J. Trop. Pediatr. *37*:90, 1991.
51. Cohen, B. A., Honig, P., and Androphy, E.: Anogenital warts in children. Arch. Dermatol. *126*:1575–1580, 1990.
52. Corey, L., and Ward, A.: Genital herpes. *In* Holmes, K. K., Sparling, P. F., and Mardh, P.-A., et al. (eds.): Sexually Transmitted Diseases. New York, McGraw-Hill, 1999, pp. 285–312.
53. Cromer, B. A., Brandstaetter, L. A., Fischer, R. A., et al.: Tubo-ovarian abscess in adolescents. Adolesc. Pediatr. Gynecol. *3*:21–24, 1990.
54. Crowther, I.: *Trichomonas* vaginitis in infancy. Lancet *1*:1074, 1962.
55. Cummins, A. J., and Atia, W. A.: Bartholin's abscess complicating food poisoning with *Salmonella panama*: A case report. Genitourin. Med. *70*:46–48, 1994.
56. Daher, A., and Fortenberry, J. D.: Staphylococcus-induced toxic shock following balanitis. Clin. Pediatr. (Phila.) *34*:172–174, 1995.
57. Danesh, I. S., Stephen, J. M., and Gorbach, J.: Neonatal *Trichomonas vaginalis* infection. J. Emerg. Med. *13*:51–54, 1995.
58. Danielsson, I., Sjoberg, I., and Wikman, M.: Vulvar vestibulitis: Medical, psychosexual and psychosocial aspects, a case control study. Acta Obstet. Gynecol. Scand. *79*:872–878, 2000.
59. Davies, J. A., Res, E., and Hobson, D.: Isolation of *Chlamydia trachomatis* from Bartholin's ducts. Br. J. Vener. Dis. *54*:409–413, 1978.
60. Davis, A. J., and Emans, S. J.: Human papilloma virus in the pediatric and adolescent patients. J. Pediatr. *115*:1–9, 1989.
61. Davis, B.: Deodorant vulvitis. Obstet. Gynecol. *36*:812, 1970.
62. Davis, T.: Chronic vulvovaginitis in children due to *Shigella flexneri*. Pediatrics *56*:41–44, 1975.
63. DeJong, A. R.: Sexually transmitted diseases in sexually abused children. Sex. Transm. Dis. *13*:123–126, 1986.
64. Deliyanni, V. A., Boniatsi, L. S, and Photinou, A. S.: Balanitis caused by group A beta-hemolytic streptococcus in an 8-year-old boy. Pediatr. Infect. Dis. J. *8*:61–62, 1989.

65. Demetriou, E., Emans, S. J., and Masland, R. P.: Dysuria in adolescent girls: Urinary tract infection or vaginitis? Pediatrics *70*:299–301, 1982.
66. Demiroglu, H., Özcebe, O. I., Barista, I., et al.: Interferon alfa-2b, colchicine, and benzathine penicillin versus colchicine and benzathine penicillin in Behçet disease: A randomised trial. Lancet *355*:605–609, 2000.
67. Dershewitz, R. A., and Levitsky, L. L.: Vulvovaginitis: A cause of clitorimegaly. Am. J. Dis. Child. *138*:887–888, 1984.
68. Dewhurst, C. J.: Practical Pediatric and Adolescent Gynecology. New York, Marcel Dekker, 1980, pp. 83–92.
69. Dhall, K., Das, S. S., and Dey, P.: Tuberculosis of Bartholin's gland. Int. J. Gynaecol. Obstet. *48*:223–224, 1995.
70. Dhar, V., Roker, K., Adhami, Z., et al.: Streptococcal vulvovaginitis in girls. Pediatr. Dermatol. *10*:366, 1993.
71. Division of STD/HIV Prevention: Sexually Transmitted Disease Surveillance, 1993. U.S. Department of Health and Human Services, Public Health Service. Atlanta, Centers for Disease Control and Prevention, 1994, pp. 55–57.
72. Dodson, R. F., Fritz, G. S., Hubler, W. R., et al.: Donovanosis: A morphologic study. J. Invest. Dermatol. *62*:611–614, 1974.
73. Donald, F. E., Slack, D. B., and Colman, G.: *Streptococcus pyogenes* vulvovaginitis in children in Nottingham. Epidemiol. Infect. *106*:459–465, 1991.
74. Duerden, B. I.: Black-pigmented gram-negative anaerobes in genitourinary tract and pelvic infections. F. E. M. S. Immunol. Med. Microbiol. *6*:223–227, 1993.
75. Duhra, P., and Ilchyshyn, A.: Perianal streptococcal cellulitis with penile involvement. Br. J. Dermatol. *123*:793–796, 1990.
76. Eigen, L.: Vaginal diphtheria. J. Med. Assoc. N. J. *29*:778–780, 1932.
77. Elkins, C., Yi, K., Olsen, B., et al.: Development of a serological test for *Haemophilus ducreyi* for seroprevalence studies. J. Clin. Microbiol. *38*:1520–1526, 2000.
78. Emans, S. J.: Office evaluation of the child and adolescent. *In* Emans, S. J. H., Laufer, M. R., and Goldstein, D. P. (eds.): Pediatric and Adolescent Gynecology. 4th ed. Philadelphia, Lippincott-Raven, 1998, pp. 1–48.
79. Emans, S. J.: Vulvovaginal problems in the prepubertal child. *In* Emans, S. J. H., Laufer, M. R., and Goldstein, D. P. (eds.): Pediatric and Adolescent Gynecology. 4th ed. Philadelphia, Lippincott-Raven, 1998, pp. 75–108.
80. Emans, S. J. H.: Sexually transmitted diseases: Gonorrhea, chlamydia, pelvic inflammatory disease and syphilis. *In* Emans, S. J., Laufer, M. R., Goldstein, D. P. (eds.): Pediatric and Adolescent Gynecology. 4th ed. New York, Lippincott-Raven, 1998, pp. 457–504.
81. Emans, S. J. H., and Goldstein, D. P.: The gynecologic examination of the prepubertal child with vulvovaginitis: Use of the knee-chest position. Pediatrics *65*:758–760, 1980.
82. Emans, S. J. H., Laufer, M. R., and Goldstein, D. P. (eds.): Pediatric and Adolescent Gynecology. 4th ed. Philadelphia, Lippincott-Raven, 1998.
83. Escala, J. M., and Rickwood, A. M.: Balanitis. Br. J. Urol. *63*:196–197, 1989.
84. Eschenbach, D. A.: Acute pelvic inflammatory disease. Urol. Clin. North Am. *11*:65–81, 1984.
85. Fallon, P., and Robinson, E. T.: Meningococcal vulvovaginitis. Scand. J. Infect. Dis. *6*:295–296, 1974.
86. FDA Drug Bulletin: Oncogenic potential of new herpes simplex therapy. F. D. A. Drug Bull. *5*:3, 1975.
87. Feo, L. G.: The incidence of *Trichomonas vaginalis* in various age groups. Am. J. Trop. Med. Hyg. *5*:786–790, 1956.
88. Fergusson, D. M., Lawton, J. M., and Shannon, F. T.: Neonatal circumcision and penile problems: An 8-year longitudinal survey. Pediatrics *81*:537–541, 1988.
89. Figueroa-Colón, R., Grunow, J. E., Torres-Pinedo, R., et al.: Group A streptococcal proctitis and vulvovaginitis in a prepubertal girl. Pediatr. Infect. Dis. J. *3*:439–442, 1984.
90. Fink, C. W.: A perineal rash in Kawasaki disease. Pediatr. Infect. Dis. *2*:140–141, 1983.
91. Fischer, G., and Rogers, M.: Vulvar disease in children: A clinical audit of 130 cases. Pediatr. Dermatol. *17*:1–6, 2000.
92. Fisher, M., Swenson, P. D., Risucci, D., et al.: *Chlamydia trachomatis* in suburban adolescents. J. Pediatr. *111*:617–620, 1987.
93. Folland, D. S., Burke, R. E., Hinman, A. R., et al.: Gonorrhea in preadolescent children: An inquiry into source of infection and mode of transmission. Pediatrics *60*:153–156, 1977.
94. Forssner, H.: Vaginaltresia mit diphtherischer pathogenese. Acta Med. Scand. *59*:690–695, 1923.
95. Frazer, J. J., Rettig, P. J., and Kaplan, D. W.: Prevalence of cervical *Chlamydia trachomatis* and *Neisseria gonorrhoeae* in female adolescents. Pediatrics *71*:333–336, 1983.
96. Freinkel, A. L.: Granuloma inguinale of cervical lymph nodes simulating tuberculous lymphadenitis: Two case reports and review of published reports. Genitourin. Med. *64*:339–343, 1988.
97. Friedrich, E.: Vulvar Disease. Philadelphia, W. B. Saunders, 1976.
98. Fuld, G.: Gonococcal peritonitis in a prepubertal child. Am. J. Dis. Child. *115*:621–622, 1968.
99. Fuster, C. D., and Neinstein, L. S.: Vaginal *Chlamydia trachomatis*: Prevalence in sexually abused pubertal girls. Pediatrics *79*:235–238, 1987.
100. Gardner, H.: The vulvovaginitides (new interpretation and treatment methods). *In* Traymor, M., and Green, T., Jr. (eds.): Progress in Gynecology. Vol. 6. New York, Grune & Stratton, 1975, p. 307.
101. Gardner, H., and Dukes, C.: *Haemophilus vaginalis* vaginitis: A newly defined specific infection previously classified "non-specific" vaginitis. Am. J. Obstet. Gynecol. *69*:962–976, 1955.
102. Gardner, H. L.: *Hemophilus vaginalis* after twenty five years. Am. J. Obstet. Gynecol. *137*:385–391, 1980.
103. Gardner, J. J.: Comparison of the vaginal flora in sexually abused and nonabused girls. J. Pediatr. *120*:872–877, 1992.
104. Gardner, M., and Jones, J. G.: Genital herpes acquired by sexual abuse of children. J. Pediatr. *104*:243–244, 1984.
105. Gerstner, G. J., Grnnberger, W., Boschitsch, E., et al.: Vaginal organisms in prepubertal children with and without vulvovaginitis. Arch. Gynecol. *231*:247–252, 1982.
106. Gilbaugh, J. H., and Fuchs, P. C.: The gonococcus and the toilet seat. N. Engl. J. Med. *301*:91–93, 1979.
107. Ginsberg, C. M.: Group A streptococcal vaginitis in children. Pediatr. Infect. Dis. J. *1*:36–37, 1982.
108. Ginsburg, C. M.: Acquired syphilis in prepubertal children. Pediatr. Infect. Dis. J. *2*:232–234, 1983.
109. Goh, B. T., and Forster, G. E.: Sexually transmitted diseases in children: Chlamydial oculo-genital infection. Genitourin. Med. *69*:213–221, 1993.
110. Golden, N., Cohen, H., Gennari, G., et al.: The use of pelvic ultrasonography in evaluation of adolescents with pelvic inflammatory disease. Am. J. Dis. Child. *141*:1235–1238, 1987.
111. Grace, D. A., Ochsner, J. A., McLain, C. R., et al.: Vulvar condylomata acuminata in prepubertal females. J. A. M. A. *201*:151–152, 1967.
112. Gray, L. A., and Kutcher, E.: Vulvovaginitis in childhood. Clin. Obstet. Gynecol. *3*:165–174, 1960.
113. Gregory, J. E., and Abramson, E.: Meningococci in vaginitis. Am. J. Dis. Child. *121*:423, 1971.
114. Grosskurth, H., Mosha, F., Todd, J., et al.: Impact of improved treatment of sexually transmitted diseases on HIV infection in rural Tanzania: Randomised controlled trial. Lancet *346*:530–536, 1995.
115. Growdon, W. A., Lebherz, T. B., Moore, J. G., et al.: Granuloma inguinale in a white teenager: A diagnosis easily forgotten, poorly pursued. West. J. Med. *143*:105–108, 1985.
116. Guerrero-Vazquez, J., Sebastian-Planes, M., Olmedo-Sanlaureno, S.: Group A streptococcal proctitis and balantitis. Pediatr. Infect. Dis. J. *9*:223, 1990.
117. Hager, W. D.: Followup of patients with tubo-ovarian abscess(es) in association with salpingitis. Obstet. Gynecol. *61*:680–684, 1983.
118. Hager, W. D., Eschenbach, D. A., Spence, M. R., et al.: Criteria for diagnosis and grading of salpingitis. Obstet. Gynecol. *61*:113, 1983.
119. Hammerschlag, M. R.: *Chlamydia trachomatis* in children. Pediatr. Ann. *23*:349–353, 1994.
120. Hammerschlag, M. R.: Sexually transmitted diseases in sexually abused children: Medical and legal implications. Sex. Transm. Infect. *74*:167–174, 1998.
121. Hammerschlag, M. R., Alpert, S., Onderdonk, A. B., et al.: Anaerobic microflora of the vagina in children. Am. J. Obstet. Gynecol. *131*:853–856, 1978.
122. Hammerschlag, M. R., Alpert, S., Rosner, I., et al.: Microbiology of the vagina in children: Normal and potentially pathogenic organisms. Pediatrics *62*:57–62, 1978.
123. Hammerschlag, M. R., Cummings, M., Doraiswamy, B., et al.: Nonspecific vaginitis following sexual abuse in children. Pediatrics *75*:1028–1031, 1985.
124. Hammerschlag, M. R., Doraiswamy, B., Alexander E. R., et al.: Are rectogenital chlamydial infections a marker of sexual abuse in children? Pediatr. Infect. Dis. *3*:100–104, 1984.
125. Hammerschlag, M. R., Doraiswamy, B., Cox, P., et al.: Colonization of sexually abused children with genital mycoplasmas. Sex. Transm. Dis. *14*:23–25, 1987.
126. Hammerschlag, M. R., Rettig, P. J., and Shields, W. E.: False-positive results with the use of chlamydial antigen detection tests in the evaluation of suspected sexual abuse in children. Pediatr. Infect. Dis. J. *7*:11–14, 1988.
127. Hammond, G. W., Slutchuk, M., Scatliff, J., et al.: Epidemiologic, clinical, laboratory, and therapeutic features of an urban outbreak of chancroid in North America. Rev. Infect. Dis. *2*:867–878, 1980.
128. Hare, M., and Mowla, A.: Genital herpesvirus infection in a prepubertal girl. Br. J. Obstet. Gynaecol. *84*:141–142, 1977.
129. Haydock, A. K., Martin, D. H., Morse, S. A., et al.: Molecular characterization of *Haemophilus ducreyi* strains from Jackson, Mississippi, and New Orleans, Louisiana. J. Infect. Dis. *179*:1423–1432, 1999.
130. Hedlund, P.: Acute vulvovaginitis in patients with streptococcal infections. Nord. Med. *49*:566–567, 1953.

131. Heller, R. H., Joseph, J. M., and Davis, H. J.: Vulvovaginitis in the premenarcheal child. J. Pediatr. *74*:370–377, 1969.
132. Hellgren, L.: Gonorre-tonsillit efter genitooral kontakt. Lakartidningen *68*:569–571, 1971.
133. Henderson, P., and Scott, R.: Foreign body vaginitis caused by toilet tissue. Am. J. Dis. Child. *111*:529–532, 1966.
134. Herman-Giddens, M. E., Gutman, L. T., and Berson, N. L.: Association of coexisting vaginal infections and multiple abusers in female children with genital warts. Sex. Transm. Dis. *1*:63–67, 1987.
135. Herzog, L. W., and Alvarez, S. R.: The frequency of foreskin problems in uncircumcised children. Am. J. Dis. Child. *140*:254–256, 1986.
136. Hewitt, A. B.: Behçet's disease. Br. J. Vener. Dis. *47*:52–53, 1971.
137. Hill, G. B., Eschenbach, D. A., and Holmes, K. K.: Bacteriology of the vagina. Scand. J. Urol. Nephrol. *86*(Suppl.):23–39, 1984.
138. Hill, G. B., St. Claire, K. K., and Gutman, L. T.: Anaerobes predominate among the vaginal microflora of prepubertal girls. Clin. Infect. Dis. *20*(Suppl. 2):269–270, 1995.
139. Hillis, S. D., Joesoef, R., Marchbanks, P. A., et al.: Delayed care of pelvic inflammatory disease as a risk factor for impaired fertility. Am. J. Obstet. Gynecol. *168*:1503–1509, 1993.
140. Holmes, K. K., Mardh, P.-A., Sparling, P. F., et al. (eds.): Sexually Transmitted Diseases. New York, McGraw-Hill, 1999.
141. Holmes, K. K., and Stamm, W. E.: Lower genital tract infection syndromes in women: *In* Holmes, K. K., Mardh, P.-A., Sparling, P. F., et al. (eds.): Sexually Transmitted Diseases. New York, McGraw-Hill, 1999, pp. 761–781.
142. Holzman, C., Leventhal, J. M., Qiu, H, et al.: Factors linked to bacterial vaginosis in nonpregnant women. Am. J. Public Health *91*:1664–1670, 2001.
143. Hsieh, W. S., Yang, P. H., Chao, H. C., and Lai, J. Y.: Neonatal necrotizing fasciitis: A report of three cases and review of the literature. Pediatrics *103*:e53, 1999.
144. Huffman, J. W.: Gynecologic infections in childhood and adolescence. *In* Feigin, R. D., and Cherry, J. D. (eds.): Textbook of Pediatric Infectious Diseases. 2nd ed. Philadelphia, W. B. Saunders, 1987, pp. 555–587.
145. Huffman, J. W., Dewhurst, C. J., and Capraro, V. J.: The Gynecology of Childhood and Adolescence. 2nd ed. Philadelphia, W. B. Saunders, 1981.
146. Ingram, D. L.: *Neisseria gonorrhoeae* in children. Pediatr. Ann. *23*:341–345, 1994.
147. Ingram, D. L., Everett, V. D., Lyna, P. R., et al.: Epidemiology of adult sexually transmitted disease agents in children being evaluated for sexual abuse. Pediatr. Infect. Dis. J. *11*:945–950, 1992.
148. Ingram, D. L., Runyan, D. K., Collins, A. D., et al.: Vaginal *Chlamydia trachomatis* infection in children with sexual contact. Pedatr. Infect. Dis. J. *3*:97–99, 1984.
149. Ingram, D. L., White, S. T., Durfee, M. F., et al.: Sexual contact in children with gonorrhea. Am. J. Dis. Child. *136*:994–996, 1982.
150. Ingram, D. L., White, S. T., Occhiuti, A. R., et al.: Childhood vaginal infections: Association of *Chlamydia trachomatis* with sexual contact. Pediatr. Infect. Dis. J. *5*:226–229, 1986.
151. Jacobson, L., and Westrom, L.: Objectivized diagnosis of acute pelvic inflammatory disease. Am. J. Obstet. Gynecol. *105*:1088–1098, 1969.
152. Jaquiery, A., Stylianopoulos, A., Hogg, G., et al.: Vulvovaginitis: Clinical features, aetiology, and microbiology of the genital tract. Arch. Dis. Child. *81*:64–67, 1999.
153. Jones, J. G., Yamauchi, T., and Lambert, B.: *Trichomonas vaginalis* infestation in sexually abused girls. Am. J. Dis. Child. *139*:846–847, 1985.
154. Jones, R. B., Mammel, J. B., Shepard, M. K., et al.: Recovery of *Chlamydia trachomatis* from the endometrium of women at risk for chlamydial infection. Am. J. Obstet. Gynecol. *155*:35–39, 1986.
155. Joseph, A. K., and Rosen, T.: Laboratory techniques used in the diagnosis of chancroid, granuloma inguinale, and lymphogranuloma venereum. Dermatol. Clin. *12*:1–8, 1994.
156. Kaplan, K. M., Fleisher, G. R., Paradise, J. E., et al.: Social relevance of genital herpes simplex in children. Am. J. Dis. Child. *138*:872–874, 1984.
157. Kaydos, S. C., Swygard, H., Wise, S. L., et al.: Development and validation of a PCR-based enzyme-linked immunosorbent assay with urine for use in clinical research settings to detect *Trichomonas vaginalis* in women. J. Clin. Microbiol. *40*:89–95, 2002.
158. Keith, L. G., Berger, G. S., Edelman, D. A., et al.: On the causation of pelvic inflammatory disease. Am. J. Obstet. Gynecol. *149*:215–224, 1984.
159. Kessel, J. F., and Thompson, C. F.: Survival of *Trichomonas vaginalis* infestation in vaginal discharge. Proc. Soc. Exp. Biol. Med. *74*:755–758, 1950.
160. Kim, D.-K., Chang, S. N., Bang, D., et al.: Clinical analysis of 40 cases of childhood-onset Behçet's disease. Pediatr. Dermatol. *11*:95–101, 1994.
161. Kirkpatrick, D. J.: Donovanosis (granuloma inguinale): A rare cause of osteolytic bone lesions. Clin. Radiol. *21*:101–105, 1970.
162. Kokx, N. P., Comstock, J. A., and Facklam, R. R.: Streptococcal perianal disease in children. Pediatrics *80*:659–663, 1987.
163. Koné-Paut, I., Yurdakul, S., Bahabri, S. A., et al.: Clinical features of Behçet disease in children: An international collaborative study of 86 cases. J. Pediatr. *132*:721–725, 1998.
164. Klebanoff, M. A., Carey, C. J. Hauth, J. C., et al.: Failure of metronidazole to prevent preterm delivery among pregnant women with asymptomatic *Trichomonas vaginalis* infection. N. Engl. J. Med. *345*:487–493, 2001.
165. Krech, T., Gerhard-Fsadni, D., Hoffman, N., et al.: Interference of *Staphylococcus aureus* in the detection of *Chlamydia trachomatis* by monoclonal antibodies. Lancet 1:1161–1162, 1985.
166. Krieger, J. N., Tam, M. R., Stevens, C. E., et al.: Diagnosis of trichomoniasis: Comparison of conventional wet mount examination with cytologic studies, cultures and monoclonal antibody staining of direct specimens. J. A. M. A. *259*:1223–1227, 1988.
167. Krowchuk, D. P., Anglin, T. M., Lembo, R. M., et al.: Use of enzyme immunoassay for the rapid diagnosis of *Chlamydia trachomatis* endocervical infection in female adolescents. J. Adolesc. Health Care *9*:296–300, 1988.
168. Kurnatowska, A., and Komorowska, A.: Urogenital trichomoniasis in children. *In* Honigsberg, B. M. (ed.): Trichomonads: Parasites in Humans. New York, Springer-Verlag, 1989, pp. 246–273.
169. Kyriazi, N. C., and Costenbader, C. L.: Group A beta-hemolytic streptococcal balanitis: It may be more common than you think. Pediatrics *88*:154–156, 1991.
170. Lal, S., and Nicholas, C.: Epidemiological and clinical features in 165 cases of granuloma inguinale. Br. J. Vener. Dis. *465*:461–463, 1970.
171. Landers, D. V., and Sweet, R. L.: Tubo-ovarian abscess: Contemporary approach to management. Rev. Infect. Dis. *5*:876–884, 1983.
172. Lang, W. R.: Pediatric vaginitis. N. Engl. J. Med. *253*:1153–1160, 1955.
173. Larsen, B., and Galask, R. P.: Vaginal microbial flora: Composition and influences of host physiology. Ann. Intern. Med. *96*:926–930, 1982.
174. Larsen, B., and Monif, G. R. G.: Understanding the bacterial flora of the female genital tract. Clin. Infect. Dis. *32*:e69–e77, 2001.
175. Larson, J., Kaye, J. N., Jewers, R. J., et al.: Perinatal transmission and persistence of human papillomavirus types 16 and 18 in infants. J. Med. Virol. *47*:209–218, 1995.
176. Larson, T., and Bryson, Y. J.: Fomites and herpes simplex virus. J. Infect. Dis. *151*:746–747, 1985.
177. Lee, Y.-H., Rankin, J. S., Alpert, S., et al.: Microbiological investigation of Bartholin's gland abscesses and cysts. Am. J. Obstet. Gynecol. *129*:150–153, 1977.
178. Littlewood, J. M., and Kohler, H. G.: Urinary tract infection by *Trichomonas vaginalis* in a newborn baby. Arch. Dis. Child. *41*:693–695, 1966.
179. Lynch, P.: Molluscum contagiosum venereum. Clin. Obstet. Gynecol. *15*:966–975, 1972.
180. Madico, G., Quinn, T. C., Rompalo, A., et al.: Diagnosis of *Trichomonas vaginalis* infection by PCR using vaginal swab samples. J. Clin. Microbiol. *36*:3205–3210, 1998.
181. Mardh, P. -A., and Stenberg, K.: Long-term vaginal carriage of chlamydia? Lancet *1*:804, 1987.
182. Marinoff, S. C., and Turner, M. L. C.: Vulvar vestibulitis syndrome: An overview. Am. J. Obstet. Gynecol. *165*:1228–1233, 1991.
183. McCormack, W. M.: Clinical spectrum of gonococcal infection in women. Lancet 2:1182–1185, 1977.
184. McCormack, W. W., Alpert, S., McComb, D. E., et al.: Fifteen-month follow-up study of women infected with *Chlamydia trachomatis*. N. Engl. J. Med. *300*:123–125, 1979.
185. McFarlane, D. E., and Sharma, D. P.: *Haemophilus influenzae* and genital tract infections in children. Acta Paediatr. Scand. *76*:363–364, 1987.
186. McLaren, L. C., Davis, L. E., Healy, G. R., and James, C. G.: Isolation of *Trichomonas vaginalis* from the respiratory tract of infants with respiratory disease. Pediatrics *71*:888–890, 1983.
187. Mishaw, C. O.: Sexual abuse and sexually transmitted diseases in prepubertal children. Semin. Pediatr. Infect. Dis. *4*:131–138, 1993.
188. Mogielnicki, N. P., Schwartzman, J. D., Elliott, J. A.: Perineal group A streptococcal disease in a pediatric practice. Pediatrics *106*:276–281, 2000.
189. Monacelli, M., and Nazzaro, P.: Behçet's Disease. New York, S. Karger, 1966.
190. Morin, C., Bouchard, C., Brisson, J., et al.: Human papillomaviruses and vulvar vestibulitis. Obstet. Gynecol. *95*:683–687, 2000.
191. Morris, C. A.: Seasonal variation of streptococcal vulvo-vaginitis in an urban community. J. Clin. Pathol. *24*:805–807, 1971.
192. Morrison, J. C., and Fish, S. A.: Adolescent genital dermatoses. South. Med. J. *69*:1136–1140, 1976.
193. Moscicki, B., Shafer, M. A., Millstein, S. G., et al.: The use and limitations of endocervical gram stains and mucopurulent cervicitis as predictors for *Chlamydia trachomatis* in female adolescents. Am. J. Obstet. Gynecol. *157*:65–71, 1987.
194. Moscicki, A. B., Hills, N., Shiboski, S., et al.: Risks for incident human papilloma virus infection and low-grade squamous intraepithelial lesion development in young females. J. A. M. A. *285*:2995–3002, 2001.

195. Moscicki, A. B., Shiboski, S., Broering, J., et al.: The natural history of human papillomavirus infection as measured by repeated DNA testing in adolescent and young women. J. Pediatr. *132*:277–284, 1998.
196. Mroczkowski, T. F., and Martin, D. H.: Genital ulcer disease. Dermatol. Clin. *12*:753–764, 1994.
197. Muram, D., Savage, M. O., Harries, J. T., et al.: Crohn's disease of the vulva in a prepubertal girl. Pediatr. Adolesc. Gynecol. *1*:189–195, 1983.
198. Murphy, T. V., and Nelson, J. D.: *Shigella* vaginitis: Report of 38 patients and review of the literature. Pediatrics *63*:511–516, 1979.
199. Nahmias, A.: Herpes simplex infection. *In* Gellis, S., and Kagan, B. (eds.): Current Pediatric Therapy 7. Philadelphia, W. B. Saunders, 1976, pp. 599–603.
200. Nahamias, A. J., Dowdle, W. R., Naib, Z. M., et al.: Genital infection with herpes virus hominis types 1 and 2 in children. Pediatrics *42*:659–666, 1968.
201. Nair, P., Glazer-Semmel, E., Gould, C., et al.: *Neisseria gonorrhoeae* in asymptomatic prepubertal household contacts of children with gonococcal infection. Clin. Pediatr. (Phila.) *25*:160–163, 1986.
202. Nair, S., and Schoeneman, M. J.: Acute glomerulonephritis with group A streptococcal vulvovaginitis. Clin. Pediatr. (Phila.) *39*:721–722, 2000.
203. Namavar, J. B., Parsanezhad, M. E., and Grane-Shirazi, R.: Female genital tuberculosis and infertility. Int. J. Gynaecol. Obstet. *75*:269–272, 2001.
204. Nebel, W. A., and Lucas, W. E.: Management of tubo-ovarian abscess. Obstet. Gynecol. *32*:382–386, 1968.
205. Neinstein, L. S., Goldenring, J., and Carpenter, S.: Nonsexual transmission of sexually transmitted diseases: An infrequent occurrence. Pediatrics *74*:67–76, 1984.
206. Nelson, J.D., and Bradley, J. S.: Nelson's Pocket Book of Pediatric Antimicrobial Therapy. 15th ed. Philadelphia, Lippincott Williams & Wilkins, 2002–2003.
207. Ness, R. B., Soper, D. E., Holley, R. L., et al.: Douching and endometritis: Results from the PID evaluation and clinical health (PEACH) study. Sex. Transm. Dis. *28*:240–245, 2001.
208. O'Duffy, J. D., Carney, J. A., and Deodhar, S.: Behçet's disease. Ann. Intern. Med. *75*:561–570, 1971.
209. O'Farrell, N.: Clinico-epidemiological study of donovanosis in Durban, South Africa. Genitourin. Med. *69*:108–111, 1993.
210. O'Farrell, N.: Global eradication of donovanosis: An opportunity for limiting the spread of HIV-1. Genitourin. Med. *71*:27–31, 1995.
211. O'Farrell, N.: Donovanosis. *In* Holmes, K. K., Mardh, P.-A., Sparling, P. F., et al. (eds.): Sexually Transmitted Diseases. New York, McGraw-Hill, 1999, pp. 525–531.
212. O'Farrell, N., Hoosen, A. A., Coetzee, K. D., et al.: Genital ulcer disease: Accuracy of clinical diagnosis and strategies to improve control in Durban, South Africa. Genitourin. Med. *70*:7–11, 1994.
213. Orellana-Diaz, O., and Hernandez-Perez, E.: Chancroid in El Salvador. Int. J. Dermatol. *27*:243–245, 1988.
214. Orden, B., Martin, R., Franco, A., et al.: Balanitis caused by group A beta-hemolytic streptococci. Pediatr. Infect. Dis. J. *15*:920–921, 1996.
215. Owen, R., Christiansen, G., Hansen, E., et al.: Reports from the working groups at the Symposium on Bacterial Vaginosis: Taxonomy of anaerobic curved rods. Scand. J. Urol. Nephrol. *86*(Suppl.):259–266, 1984.
216. Pacor, M. L., Biasi, D., Lunardi, C., et al.: Cyclosporin in Behçet's disease: Results in 16 patients after 24 months of therapy. Clin. Rheumatol. *13*:224–227, 1994.
217. Paradise, J. E., Campos, J. M., Friedman, H. M., et al.: Vulvovaginitis in premenarcheal girls: Clinical features and diagnostic evaluation. Pediatrics *70*:193–198, 1982.
218. Patrizi, A., Costa, A. M., Fiorillo, L., et al.: Perianal streptococcal dermatitis associated with guttate psoriasis and/or balanoposthitis: A study of five cases. Pediatr. Dermatol. *11*:168–171, 1994.
219. Patton, D. C.: Immunopathology and histopathology of experimental chlamydial salpingitis. Rev. Infect. Dis. *7*:746–753, 1985.
220. Peckham, B. M., Maki, D. G., Patterson, J. J., et al.: Focal vulvitis: A characteristic syndrome and cause of dyspareunia. Am. J. Obstet. Gynecol. *154*:855–864, 1986.
221. Peter, R., and Vesely, K.: Kindergynakologie. Leipzig, Germany, Georg Thieme, 1966.
222. Pierce, A. M., and Hart, C. A.: Vulvovaginitis: Causes and management. Arch. Dis. Child. *67*:509–512, 1992.
223. Pokorny, S. F.: Prepubertal vulvovaginopathies. Obstet. Gynecol. Clin. North Am. *19*:39–58, 1992.
224. Pokorny, S. F., and Stormer, J.: Atraumatic removal of secretions from prepubertal vagina. Am. J. Obstet. Gynecol. *156*:581–582, 1987.
225. Porder, K., Sanchez, N., Roblin, P. M., et al.: Lack of specificity of Chlamydiazyme for detection of vaginal chlamydial infection in prepubertal girls. Pediatr. Infect. Dis. J. 8:358–360, 1989.
226. Postethwaite, R. J.: Trichomonas vaginitis and *Escherichia coli* urinary tract infection in a newborn infant. Clin. Pediatr. (Phila.) *14*:866–867, 1975.
227. Potterat, J. J., Markewich, G. S., King, R. D., et al.: Child-to-child transmission of gonorrhea: Report of asymptomatic genital infection in a boy. Pediatrics *60*:153–156, 1977.
228. Prayson, R. A., Stoler, M. H., and Hart, W. R.: Vulvar vestibulitis: A histopathologic study of 36 cases, including human papillomavirus in situ hybridization analysis. Am. J. Surg. Pathol. *19*:154–160, 1995.
229. Puranen, M. Yliskoski, M., Saarikoski, S. et al.: Vertical transmission of human papilloma virus from infected mothers to their newborn babies and persistence of the virus in childhood. Am. J. Obstet. Gynecol. *174*:694–699, 1996.
230. Quint, E. H., and Smith, Y. R.: Vulvar disorders in adolescent patients. Pediatr. Clin. North Am. *46*:593–606, 1999.
231. Rajam, R. V., Rangiah, P. N., and Anguli, V. C.: Systemic donovaniasis. Br. J. Vener. Dis. *30*:73, 1954.
232. Rakover, Y., Adar, H., Tal, I., et al.: Behçet disease: Long-term follow-up of three children and review of the literature. Pediatrics *83*:986–992, 1989.
233. Reed, S. D., Landers, D. V., and Sweet, R. L.: Antibiotic treatment of tubo-ovarian abscess: Comparison of broad-spectrum beta-lactam agents versus clindamycin-containing regimens. Am. J. Obstet. Gynecol. *164*:1556–1561, 1991.
234. Rees, E.: Gonococcal bartholinitis. Br. J. Vener. Dis. *43*:150–156, 1967.
235. Regard, M. M., Chacko, M. R., Kozinetz, C. A., et al.: Reliability of cervical findings and endocervical polymorphonuclear cells in detecting chlamydial and gonococcal cervicitis in young women receiving contraceptive services. Adolesc. Pediatr. Gynecol. *6*:129–134, 1993.
236. Rein, M. F.: Survival of gonococci outside the body. N. Engl. J. Med. *301*:1347, 1979.
237. Rettig, P. J., and Nelson, J. D.: Genital tract infection with *Chlamydia trachomatis* in prepubertal children. J. Pediatr. *99*:206–210, 1981.
238. Rey-Stocker, I.: Vulvitis and vaginitis in the infant. Gynaecologia *168*:413–415, 1969.
239. Richens, J.: The diagnosis and treatment of donovanosis (granuloma inguinale). Genitourin. Med. *67*:441–452, 1991.
240. Riordon, T., Ellis, D. A., Mathews, P. I., et al.: False positive results with an ELISA for detection of *Chlamydia* antigen. J. Clin. Pathol. *39*:1276–1277, 1986.
241. Rosenfeld, W. D., and Clark, J.: Vulvovaginitis and cervicitis. Pediatr. Clin. North Am. *36*:489–511, 1989.
242. Rosenfeld, W., Vermund, S., Wentz, S., et al.: High prevalence rate of human papilloma virus infection and association with abnormal Papanicolaou smears in sexually active adolescents. Am. J. Dis. Child. *143*:1443–1447, 1989.
243. Rothburn, M. M., Mallinson, H., Mutton, K. J.: False-positive EIA for *Chlamydia trachomatis* recognized by atypical morphology on fluorescent staining. Lancet *2*:982–983, 1986.
244. Saikku, P., Puolakkainen M., Nissinen, A.: Cross reactivity between Chlamydiazyme and *Acinetobacter* strains. N. Engl. J. Med. *314*:922, 1986.
245. Saltz, G. R., Linneman, C. C., Brookman, R. R., et al.: *Chlamydia trachomatis* cervical infections in female adolescent. J. Pediatr. *98*:981–985, 1981.
246. Sanfilippo, J. S.: Pediatric and adolescent gynecology. Obstet. Gynecol. Clin. North Am. *19*:1–239, 1992.
247. Saracoglu, O. F., Mungan, T., and Tanzer, F.: Pelvic tuberculosis. Int. J. Gynecol. Obstet. *37*:115–120, 1992.
248. Sarma, A. V., Foxman, B., Bayirli, B., et al.: Epidemiology of vulvar vestibulitis syndrome: An exploratory case-control study. Sex. Trans. Dis. *75*:320–326, 1999.
249. Schachter, J.: Biology of *Chlamydia trachomatis*. *In* Holmes, K. K., Sparling, P. F., Mardh, P.-A., et al. (eds.): Sexually Transmitted Diseases. New York, McGraw-Hill, 1999, pp. 391–405.
250. Schachter, J., and Dattel, B. J.: Sexually transmitted diseases in victims of sexual assault. N. Engl. J. Med. *316*:1023–1024, 1987.
251. Schachter, J., Grossman, M., Sweet, R. L., et al.: Prospective study of perinatal transmission of *Chlamydia trachomatis*. J. A. M. A. *255*:3374–3377, 1986.
252. Schachter, J., Stamm, W. E., Quinn, T. C., et al.: Ligase chain reaction to detect *C. trachomatis* infection of the cervix. J. Clin. Microbiol. *32*:2540–2543, 1994.
253. Schaefer, G.: Tuberculosis of the female genital tract. Clin. Obstet. Gynecol. *13*:965–998, 1970.
254. Scheid, F.: Diseases of adnexa in children and their differentiation from appendicitis. Med. Klin. *18*:1277–1279, 1922.
255. Schubiner, H. H., Lebar, W., Jemal, C., et al.: Comparison of three new non-culture tests in the diagnosis of *Chlamydia* genital infections. J. Adolesc. Health Care *11*:505–509, 1990.
256. Schulte, J. M., and Schmid, G. P.: Recommendations for treatment of chancroid, 1993. Clin. Infect. Dis. *20*(Suppl. 1):39–46, 1995.
257. Schwartz, R. H., and Rushton, H. G.: Acute balanoposthitis in young boys. Pediatr. Infect. Dis. J. *15*:176–177, 1996.
258. Schwartz, R. H., Wientzen, R. L., and Barsanti, R. G.: Vulvovaginitis in prepubertal girls: The importance of group A *Streptococcus*. South. Med. J. *75*:446–447, 1982.
259. Seidel, J., Zonang, J., and Totten, E.: Condylomata acuminata as a sign of sexual abuse in children. J. Pediatr. *95*:553–554, 1979.

260. Senanayake, P., and Kramer, D. G.: Contraception and the etiology of pelvic inflammatory disease: New perspectives. Am. J. Obstet. Gynecol. *138*:852–860, 1980.
261. Sgroi, S.: Pediatric gonorrhea beyond infancy. Pediatr. Ann. *8*:326–336, 1979.
262. Shafer, M. A., Beck, A., Blain, B., et al.: *Chlamydia trachomatis*: Important relationships to race, contraception, lower genital tract infection, and Papanicolaou smear. J. Pediatr. *104*:141–146, 1984.
263. Shafer, M. A., Sweet, R. L., Ohm-Smith, M. J., et al.: Microbiology of the lower genital tract in postmenarcheal adolescent girls: Differences by sexual activity, contraception, and presence of nonspecific vaginitis. J. Pediatr. *107*:974–981, 1985.
264. Shapiro, R. A., Schubert, C. J., and Siegel, R. M.: *Neisseria gonorrhea* infections in girls younger than 12 years of age evaluated for vaginitis. Pediatrics *104*:e72, 1999.
265. Shore, W. B., and Winkelstein, J. A.: Nonvenereal transmission of gonococcal infections to children. J. Pediatr. *79*:661–663, 1971.
266. Siegel, R. M., Schubert, C. J., Myers, P. A., and Shapiro, R. A.: The prevalence of sexually transmitted diseases in children and adolescents evaluated for sexual abuse in Cincinnati: Rationale for limited STD testing in prepubertal girls. Pediatrics *96*:1090–1094, 1995.
267. Silber, T. J.: Genital ulcer syndrome. Semin. Adolesc. Med. *2*:155–162, 1986.
268. Slap, G. B., Forke, C. M., Cnaan, A., et al.: Recognition of tubo-ovarian abscess in adolescents with pelvic inflammatory disease. J. Adolesc. Health *18*:397–403, 1996.
269. Smith, E. W., Peutherer, J. F., Robertson, D. H., et al.: Virological studies in genital herpes. Lancet *2*:1089–1090, 1976.
270. Smith, K. R., Ching, S., Lee, M.: Evaluation of ligase chain reaction for use with urine for identification of *N. gonorrhoeae* in females attending a sexually transmitted disease clinic. J. Clin. Microbiol. *33*:455–457, 1995.
271. Sobel, J. D.: Vaginitis. N. Engl. J. Med. *337*:1896–1903, 1997.
272. Sokol, A. B., and Min, D. S.: Trichomonas cystitis in a six-week-old infant—effective treatment with metronidazole. J. Indiana State Med. Assoc. *65*:1084–1086, 1972.
273. Spear, R. M., Rothbaum, R. J., Keating, J. P., et al.: Perianal streptococcal cellulitis. J. Pediatr. *107*:557–559, 1985.
274. Spence, M. R., Adler, J., and McLellan, R.: Pelvic inflammatory disease. J. Adolesc. Health Care *11*:304–309, 1990.
275. Srivastava, A. C.: Survival of gonococci in urethral secretions with reference to the nonsexual transmission of gonococcal infection. J. Med. Microbiol. *13*:593–596, 1980.
276. Stamm, W. E., Wagner, K. F., Amsel, R., et al.: Causes of acute urethral syndrome in women. N. Engl. J. Med. *303*:409–415, 1980.
277. Straumanis, J. P., and Bocchini, J. A.: Group A beta-hemolytic streptococcal vulvovaginitis in prepubertal girls: A case report and review of the past twenty years. Pediatr. Infect. Dis. J. *9*:845–848, 1990.
278. Stringel, G., Spence, J., and Corsini, L.: Genital warts in children. Can. Med. Assoc. J. *132*:1397–1398, 1985.
279. Stumph, P. G.: Increasing occurrence of condyloma acuminata in premenarcheal children. Obstet. Gynecol. *56*:262–264, 1980.
280. Swain, V.: Tuberculous vulvovaginitis: Report of a case in infancy. Lancet *1*:868–869, 1937.
281. Sweet, R. L.: Use of laparoscopy to determine microbiologic etiology of acute salpingitis. Am. J. Obstet. Gynecol. *134*:68–74, 1979.
282. Sweet, R. L.: Pelvic inflammatory disease and infertility in women. Infect. Dis. Clin. North Am. *1*:199, 1987.
283. Sweet, R. L., Banks, J., Sung, M., et al.: Experimental chlamydial salpingitis in the guinea pig. Am. J. Obstet. Gynecol. *138*:952–956, 1980.
284. Sweet, R. L., Blankfort-Doyle, M., Robbie, M. O., et al.: The occurrence of chlamydial and gonococcal salpingitis during the menstrual cycle. J. A. M. A. *255*:2062–2064, 1986.
285. Swensson, L., Westrom, T., and Mardh, P.-A.: Contraceptives and acute salpingitis. J. A. M. A. *251*:2553–2555, 1984.
286. Taylor-Robinson, D., Thomas, B. J., and Osborn, M. F.: Evaluation of enzyme immunoassay (Chlamydiazyme) for detecting *Chlamydia trachomatis* in genital tract specimens. J. Clin. Pathol. *40*:194–199, 1987.
287. Thompson, C., Macdonald, M., and Sutherland, A.: A family cluster of *Chlamydia trachomatis* infection. B. M. J. *322*:1473–1474, 2001.
288. Toth, A., O'Leary, W. M., and Ledger, W.: Evidence for microbial transfer by spermatozoa. Obstet. Gynecol. *59*:556–559, 1982.
289. Tunnessen, W. W., Jr., and Jastremski, M.: Prepubescent gonococcal vulvovaginitis. Clin. Pediatr. (Phila.) *13*:675–676, 1974.
290. Vandeven, A. M., and Emans, J.: Vulvovaginitis in the child and adolescent. Pediatr. Rev. *14*:141–147, 1993.
291. Washington, A. E., Sweet, R. L., and Shafer, M. B.: Pelvic inflammatory disease and its sequelae in adolescents. J. Adolesc. Health Care *6*:298, 1985.
292. Watkins, S., and Quan, L.: Vulvovaginitis caused by *Yersinia enterocolitica*. Pediatr. Infect. Dis. J. *3*:444–445, 1984.
293. Watts, D. M., Koutsky, L. A., Holmes, K. K., et al.: Low risk of perinatal transmission of human papillomavirus: Results from a prospective cohort study. Am. J. Obstet. Gynecol. *178*:365–373, 1998.
294. Weaver, J.: Non-gonorrheal vulvovaginitis due to gram-negative intracellular diplococci. Am. J. Obstet. Gynecol. *60*:257–260, 1950.
295. Webb, D. H., and Fife, K. H.: Genital herpes simplex virus infection. Infect. Dis. Clin. North Am. *1*:97–122, 1987.
296. Weinstock, H., and Keesol, S.: Lymphogranuloma venereum: Report of 24 cases in children. Urol. Cutan. Rev. *50*:520–522, 1946.
297. Weissenbacher, G., and Wiltschke, H.: [Chronic urinary tract infections and vulvitis in girls with high posterior commissures.] Padiatr. Padol. *9*:60–65, 1974.
298. Westrom, L., and Eschenbach, D.: Pelvic inflammatory disease. *In* Holmes, K. K., Sparling, P. F., Mardh, P.-A., et al. (eds.): Sexually Transmitted Diseases. New York, McGraw-Hill, 1999, pp. 783–809.
299. Willcox, R.: Chancroid. *In* Morton, R. S., and Harris, J. R. (eds.): Recent Advances in Sexually Transmitted Diseases. New York, Longman, 1975.
300. Wiswell, T. E., Tencer, H. L., Welch, C. A., et al.: Circumcision in children beyond the neonatal period. Pediatrics *92*:971–973, 1993.
301. Wolner-Hanssen, P., Eschenbach, D. A., Paavonen, J., et al.: Association between vaginal douching and acute pelvic inflammatory disease. J. A. M. A. *263*:1936–1941, 1990.
302. Wolner-Hanssen, P., Svensson, L., and Mardh, P.-A.: Laparoscopic findings and contraceptive use in women with signs and symptoms suggestive of acute salpingitis. Obstet. Gynecol. *66*:233–238, 1985.
303. Woods, C. R.: Gonococcal infections in children and adolescents. Semin. Pediatr. Rev. *14*:141–147, 1993.
304. Zigas, V.: Medicine from the past: Donovanosis project in Goilala (1951–1954). Papua New Guinea Med. J. *14*:148, 1971.

Gastrointestinal Tract Infections

CHAPTER 50

Esophagitis

SUDIPTA MISRA ■ MARVIN E. AMENT

Infectious esophagitis is distinct from other gastrointestinal infections in that it is a rare event in previously healthy individuals, is predominantly of fungal and viral etiology, and is usually a harbinger of immunodeficiency caused by acquired, drug-induced, or congenital causes. Infection by multiple organisms occurs commonly in these patients. Even in normal children, infectious esophagitis is associated frequently with conditions that compromise esophageal defense mechanisms.[41]

The incidence of infectious esophagitis in children is unknown. Among patients with acquired immunodeficiency syndrome (AIDS), as many as 10 percent can have *Candida* infection.[5, 31] Seventy-one to 100 percent of patients with AIDS and both oral candidiasis and odynophagia had endoscopic evidence of esophageal candidiasis.[6, 9, 29]

Pathophysiology and Causative Organisms

The defense mechanisms of the esophagus against infection include a mucosal lining of stratified squamous epithelium that is resistant to microbial invasion, motility (continuous flow of luminal contents, which discourages colonization by microbes), and the general immune mechanism of the body. Compromise in any one or more of these factors may lead to esophageal infections. Immunosuppression (as seen in AIDS), chronic mucocutaneous candidiasis (a lymphocyte function defect), post–organ transplant immunosuppression, chemotherapy, malignancy, and prolonged steroid treatment are the most common underlying etiologic factors for fungal and viral infection of the esophagus.[3, 7, 17, 26, 31] Dysmotility of the esophagus, in addition to mucosal injury secondary to gastroesophageal reflux, can render the esophagus vulnerable to infections in immunocompetent children. The esophagus can be infected by local invasion (*Candida,* herpes simplex virus [HSV], bacteria), as a result of systemic infection (cytomegalovirus [CMV], *Candida, Pneumocystis*), or by contiguous spread from the mediastinum or neck (tuberculosis, retropharyngeal abscess).

Most the esophageal infections are caused by fungi and viruses. However, esophagitis in immunocompromised patients can be polymicrobial in origin. *Candida albicans,* HSV, and CMV are the major pathogens.[5, 31, 40, 41] Other less common pathogens include fungi such as *Aspergillus* and *Histoplasma* spp.[19, 28]; viruses such as varicella-zoster virus (VZV), Epstein-Barr virus, human immunodeficiency virus (HIV), and papillomavirus[14, 15, 30, 36]; and protozoa such as *Cryptosporidium, Pneumocystis carinii,* and *Leishmania donovani.*[8, 13, 16] Bacterial infections of the esophagus probably are underreported. As many as 10 to 16 percent of esophageal infections can have a bacterial etiology, mostly in granulocytopenic patients and as secondary infection in fungal or viral esophagitis. Gram-positive and gram-negative oropharyngeal bacterial flora and *Mycobacterium tuberculosis* are the common pathogens.[11, 37] Tubercular esophagitis, caused by both typical and atypical mycobacteria, is found mainly in immunocompromised patients in the United States. *Helicobacter pylori* has been isolated from involved tissue in Barrett esophagitis. However, this "infection" appears to be related to gastroesophageal reflux disease rather than direct invasion of the esophagus by *H. pylori.*[27]

Clinical Features

Patients with infectious esophagitis can present with esophageal, abdominal, or systemic symptoms (Table 50–1). Dysphagia (difficulty in swallowing) and odynophagia (painful swallowing) are the most common symptoms of esophagitis. Complaints also may include a sensation of food "sticking" behind the sternum or a feeling of a food or liquid bolus passing through the chest. Drooling is unusual in esophagitis per se but may be present with pharyngeal involvement. Dysphagia and odynophagia may not be apparent in small children, and esophageal involvement may be overlooked. Even in adults, only 59 to 79 percent of patients with documented esophageal infection had these symptoms. Approximately a quarter of patients with esophageal candidiasis were asymptomatic.[4]

Oral lesions may be present in 27 to 37 percent of patients with *Candida*, HSV, or HIV esophagitis, but they rarely are present with CMV infection and tuberculosis.[4] Oral thrush, however, is a common occurrence in infants and immunocompromised patients. The frequency of *Candida* esophagitis in infants with oral thrush is not known. The presence of oral thrush and esophageal symptoms does not exclude concomitant esophageal infection with pathogens other than *Candida* or the idiopathic esophageal ulcerations associated with HIV. Oropharyngeal lesions are less common findings in HSV esophagitis than in *Candida* esophagitis. A history of recurrent cold sores, vesicular lesions on the nasolabial folds, and esophageal symptoms are the typical initial features of HSV esophagitis in an immunocompetent host.

Nausea and vomiting are associated more commonly with CMV esophagitis because of the systemic nature of the illness. The abdominal pain in esophagitis may be caused by referred pain from the distal end of the esophagus, associated gastritis (as in CMV infection), or concomitant

TABLE 50–1 ■ SIGNS AND SYMPTOMS OF INFECTIOUS ESOPHAGITIS

Dysphagia
Odynophagia
Oral lesions
Nausea/vomiting
Abdominal pain
Fever
Diarrhea
Cough
Rash
Hematemesis

intra-abdominal infections in immunocompromised hosts (advanced stage of HIV infection). Fever is caused mostly by systemic (CMV) or secondary infection (mediastinal abscess or pneumonia in tuberculosis). Fever does not occur commonly in bacterial esophagitis. Cough is characteristic of tubercular infection, tracheobronchial fistulas, or high-grade esophageal obstruction. A maculopapular truncal rash and fever may be present in patients with idiopathic esophageal ulceration during acute HIV seroconversion.[30] Diarrhea can be present in CMV infection (diffuse involvement of the gastrointestinal tract) or HIV infection (opportunistic enteral infections, HIV enteropathy). Of emphasis is that most of the reported studies involve adult subjects. Symptoms, especially subjective complaints such as dysphagia and odynophagia, may differ in children. Because physicians seldom look for esophagitis in the absence of dysphagia or odynophagia, infectious esophagitis may be underdiagnosed in infants and children. In one report of fungal esophagitis in children, hematemesis was the most common initial symptom.[41]

Differential Diagnosis

Pathologic gastroesophageal reflux is the most common cause of esophagitis in children. In previously healthy children, esophageal symptoms are likely to be caused by reflux esophagitis, whereas in immunocompromised patients, the physician needs to rule out infectious esophagitis. Secondary bacterial or fungal infections can be present in reflux esophagitis, especially with severe inflammation and obstruction. Absence of reflux symptoms, such as long-standing heartburn, a water brash taste in the mouth, vomiting, spitting up (in infants), pillow wetting, and coughing, does not rule out reflux esophagitis entirely. Immunodeficiency, systemic signs, and oral lesions suggest infectious esophagitis. Endoscopy, tissue biopsy, and endoscopic brush biopsy may be required for diagnosis. Achalasia, diffuse esophageal spasm, foreign body impaction, and mediastinal or retropharyngeal abscesses can cause esophageal symptoms and may result in secondary infection.

Diagnosis

Specific diagnosis is essential for management of infectious esophagitis. Although the clinical profile, barium esophagogram, and endoscopic appearance can provide some clue, histopathology, immunohistochemistry, and culture of endoscopic and brush biopsy specimens are essential for confirmation. Viral serology may offer indirect evidence of infection in difficult cases.

BARIUM ESOPHAGOGRAPHY

The usefulness of an esophagogram in diagnosing infectious esophagitis is limited by the facts that it does not provide an etiologic diagnosis and that some patients have normal or nonspecific findings. These studies are useful for assessing motility and for excluding obstruction, perforation, and fistulas of the esophagus. Barium studies are not indicated if endoscopy is planned. Double-contrast barium esophagography with air and barium, which details the mucosal lining, is the radiologic investigation of choice. However, children may not tolerate this procedure well.[21]

Candida esophagitis generally is diffuse, whereas HSV or CMV lesions are found more frequently in the mid to distal portion of the esophagus. Discrete longitudinal plaques, a grossly irregular or "shaggy" appearance, or tiny nodular lesions with a granular appearance are characteristic of *Candida* esophagitis (Fig. 50–1). The presence of discrete superficial stellate ulcers in the mid-esophagus with normal-appearing surrounding mucosa is characteristic of HSV esophagitis. CMV lesions may mimic HSV lesions on barium esophagography. However, oval or elongated large ulcers are found mostly in CMV infection and idiopathic esophageal ulceration in HIV infection.[20, 39] Esophagograms in tuberculosis can show intramural pseudodiverticula, extrinsic compression, or esophageal displacement by mediastinal lymph nodes and sinus tracts.[10]

ESOPHAGOSCOPY

Characteristic macroscopic lesions are associated with some of the infectious agents. However, macroscopic appearances overlap considerably, and histopathologic or immunohistochemical analysis (or both) of endoscopic and brush biopsy specimens is essential for diagnosis. A diffuse esophageal lesion is characteristic of *Candida* infection, whereas CMV and HSV infections mainly involve the distal part of the esophagus. Whitish, longitudinal plaques adhering to the mucosa are characteristic of *Candida* infection.[18] Plaques from oral thrush, common findings in infants and immunocompromised children, can be washed away and reveal a nonulcerated underlying mucosa. Similar-appearing plaques, however, also may be seen in CMV, HSV, bacterial, and "pill" esophagitis and after sucralfate ingestion. Small, 1- to 3-mm vesicles are characteristic of HSV esophagitis, but by the time that endoscopy is performed, these vesicles usually slough off and reveal sharply demarcated ulcers with a raised edge, necrotic base, and normal-appearing surrounding mucosa. In progressive disease, these ulcers may coalesce to resemble *Candida* esophagitis.[1] Multiple superficial ulcers in the distal portion of the esophagus often are seen in CMV esophagitis. However, large elongated ulcers also are typical manifestations of CMV infection but may occur in idiopathic esophageal ulcerations in HIV infection as well.[20]

Complete denudation of the mucosa is an unusual finding with CMV infection.[35] Endoscopy in patients with VZV esophagitis can show vesicles, discrete ulcers, or necrotizing esophagitis, depending on the stage of the disease. Tubercular ulcers of the esophagus usually are of varying size, distinct, and shallow with a necrotic base.

BIOPSY AND BRUSHING

Endoscopic biopsy specimens should be obtained from the edge as well as the base of the lesions. In CMV infection,

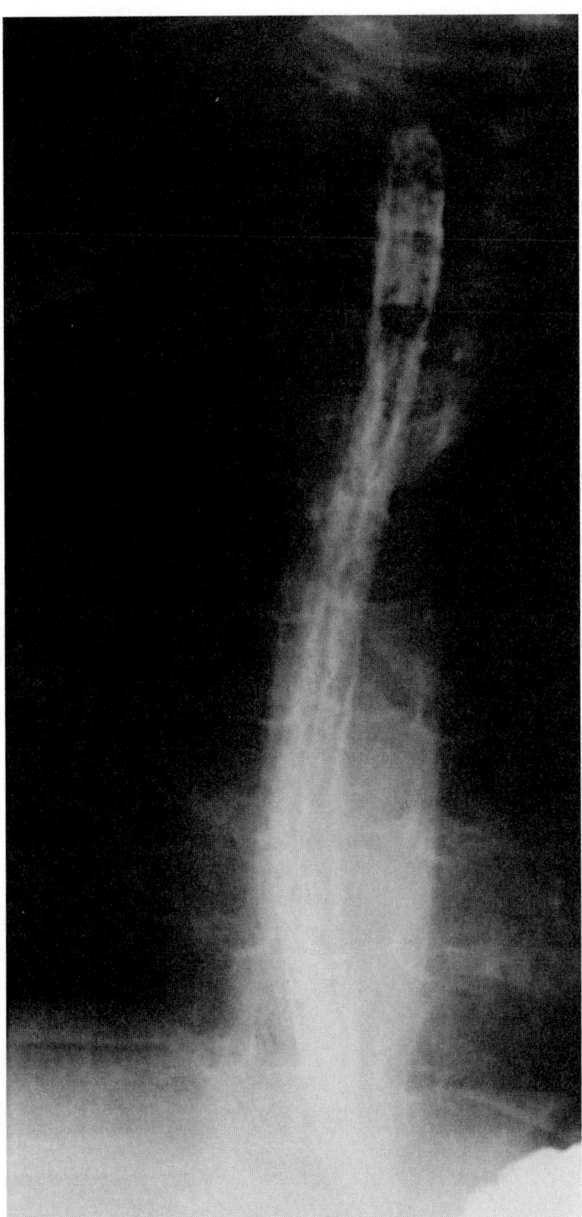

FIGURE 50–1 ■ Barium esophagogram in *Candida* esophagitis. Note the diffuse mucosal irregularity suggestive of inflammation and the longitudinal filling defects suggestive of plaques. (Courtesy of Sjirk Westra, M.D., Division of Pediatric Radiology, UCLA Medical Center, Los Angeles.)

specimens from the edge do not yield diagnostic information.[35] The pathologist should be alerted to the possibility of fungal and viral, as well as polymicrobial, infection. Appropriate fixatives should be used for routine hematoxylin and eosin stain, Gram stain, and special stains for fungi and bacteria such as *Mycobacterium*. *Candida* and *Aspergillus* can be demonstrated by silver stain, periodic acid–Schiff stain, or Gram stain (Fig. 50–2). Diagnostic histopathologic changes such as multinucleated giant cells, ballooning degeneration, intranuclear Cowdry type A inclusion bodies and margination of chromatin in HSV infection (Fig. 50–3), and amphophilic intranuclear inclusions and small multiple cytoplasmic inclusion bodies in CMV infection (Fig. 50–4) can be diagnostic. However, immunohistochemical studies

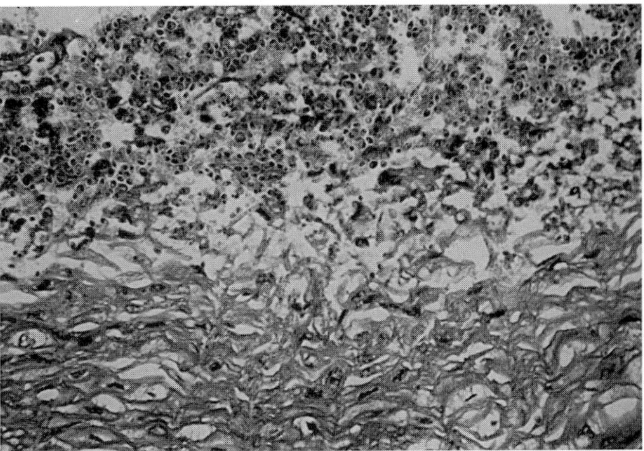

FIGURE 50–2 ■ *Candida* esophagitis: photomicrograph showing yeast-like organisms in the esophageal mucosa. Methenamine silver stain. (Courtesy of Klaus Lewin, M.D., Department of Pathology, UCLA Medical Center, Los Angeles.)

and DNA hybridization techniques often are required for diagnosis. Viral culture, with or without immunohistochemical techniques, may aid in confirmation. Material obtained by endoscopy-guided brush biopsy can reveal the features of *Candida* or viral infection described earlier. Blind brushings of the esophagus may be useful for *Candida* infection when endoscopy is not possible or is not available.[6]

If abdominal pain, fever, or other unusual symptoms are present, the possibility of disseminated or abdominal infection should be excluded by appropriate investigations.

Treatment

CANDIDA ESOPHAGITIS

Treatment depends on the severity of infection, as well as the degree of immunocompetence. Normal children and

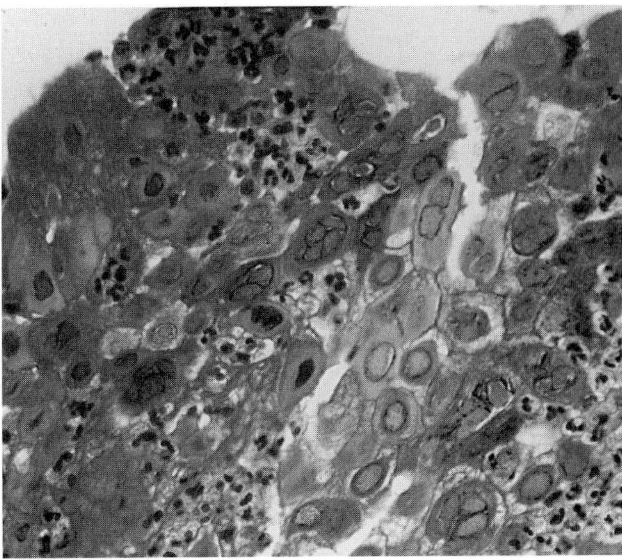

FIGURE 50–3 ■ Herpes simplex virus esophagitis: photomicrograph showing viral inclusions in squamous epithelium. Hematoxylin and eosin stain. (Courtesy of Klaus Lewin, M.D., Department of Pathology, UCLA Medical Center, Los Angeles.)

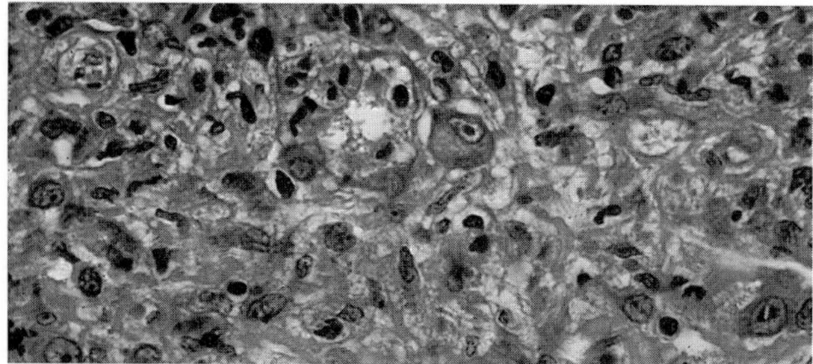

FIGURE 50–4 ■ Cytomegalovirus esophagitis: photomicrograph showing intracytoplasmic inclusion bodies in the lamina propria. Hematoxylin and eosin stain. (Courtesy of Klaus Lewin, M.D., Department of Pathology, UCLA Medical Center, Los Angeles.)

children in the early stages of HIV infection who have minimal lymphocyte dysfunction and normal granulocyte function can be treated with topical or oral antifungal agents (Table 50–2). Nystatin, ketoconazole, and fluconazole are the agents used commonly.[41] For patients with severe infection or granulocyte dysfunction, intravenous amphotericin B is used. In patients with infection confined to the esophagus, a 10- to 14-day course often suffices (Table 50–2). In those with disseminated infection, a total dose of 30 mg/kg or more may be required. Nephrotoxicity is the major toxic effect of amphotericin B. Co-administration of amphotericin B with lipid emulsions or the use of newer microsomal preparations may reduce this toxic effect.[25, 38] Intravenous fluconazole now is considered to be the drug of first choice.[24] Oral nystatin, oral amphotericin B, and fluconazole have been used with success for prophylaxis against esophageal candidiasis in patients with AIDS or organ transplants.

OTHER FUNGAL ESOPHAGITIS

Amphotericin B given intravenously is the agent of choice for treatment of aspergillosis and histoplasmosis. Itraconazole therapy also is effective treatment.

VIRAL ESOPHAGITIS

Immunocompetent children with HSV need only supportive care. However, in immunocompromised patients, intravenous acyclovir is indicated (Table 50–2). Foscarnet is an alternative agent. HSV prophylaxis with oral acyclovir has been successful in patients with solid organ and bone marrow transplantation, as well as in patients with AIDS. Valacyclovir and famciclovir are the preferred first-line agents for herpetic esophagitis because of their clinical efficacy and convenient dosing schedule.[24] Ganciclovir and foscarnet are used for CMV infection (Table 50–2). Ganciclovir, though effective, causes granulocytopenia. Foscarnet is less toxic but can only suppress CMV and does not eradicate it.

Organ transplant recipients who are seropositive for CMV or receive the graft from a CMV-seropositive donor should receive prophylaxis with intravenous acyclovir or ganciclovir[4, 33] (Table 50–2). Oral acyclovir is only partially effective in this situation. Acyclovir is the treatment of choice for VZV, and prophylaxis has effectively reduced the rate of VZV infection in post-transplantation patients. HIV-associated idiopathic ulcers do not respond to empiric antiviral or antifungal therapy. Systemic steroid therapy may improve the symptoms and ulcers in these cases.[23] However, healing is slow, treatment for more than 1 month may be required, and symptoms recur if therapy is interrupted. Topical therapy with a slurry of sucralfate and dexamethasone may be a useful alternative.[31]

BACTERIAL ESOPHAGITIS

Bacterial esophagitis should be treated with appropriate broad-spectrum antibiotics. Blood cultures always should be performed to exclude septicemia. Tuberculosis is treated with standard antituberculous drugs. Patients with AIDS respond more poorly to drug therapy than immunocompetent patients do. Surgery is required for fistulas, obstruction, and perforations.

Lack of response to appropriate therapy may indicate concomitant superinfection by other organisms or resistance to the drugs used. Fungal and bacterial superinfections

TABLE 50–2 ■ TREATMENT OF FUNGAL AND VIRAL ESOPHAGITIS

Drug	Route	Dose	Duration	Limiting Adverse Effect
Antifungal				
Nystatin[2]	Oral	5–10 × 10^6 U q3h	2–6 wk	Unpleasant taste
Amphotericin B[26]	Oral	10–100 mg q4h	2–6 wk	Unpleasant taste
Clotrimazole oral troches[12]	Oral	10 mg q4–6h	14 days	Nausea, vomiting, resistance
Ketoconazole[12]	Oral	3.3–6.6 mg/kg/day	10–14 days	Resistance, hepatotoxicity (rare)
*Fluconazole[22]	Oral	3–6 mg/kg/day	10–14 days	Resistance
Amphotericin B[35]	IV	0.5–1.0 mg/kg/day	10–14 days	Nephrotoxicity
Flucytosine[22]	Oral	50–100 mg/kg/day q6h (with amphotericin B)	Complicated *Candida* infection	Bone marrow suppression, resistance with monotherapy
Nystatin	Oral	2–5 × 10^6 U q6–8h	Prophylaxis	Unpleasant taste
Antivirals				
*Acyclovir	IV	250 mg/m² q8h	14–21 days	Neuropathy, encephalopathy
*Ganciclovir	IV	10 mg/kg/day q12h	14–21 days	Granulocytopenia
*Foscarnet	IV	60 mg/kg q8h 90 mg/kg/day maintainance	14–21 days	
*Acyclovir	Oral	10 mg/kg q6h	Prophylaxis	Gastrointestinal disturbance, headache
*Acyclovir	IV	250 mg/m² q8h	Prophylaxis	Neuropathy, encephalopathy
*Ganciclovir	IV	5 mg/kg/day	Prophylaxis	Granulocytopenia

*Dose should be adjusted for renal function.

occur commonly in viral esophagitis. Repeat endoscopy is indicated for documenting eradication of infection.

Prognosis

Candida esophagitis carries a poor prognosis for patients with AIDS. Survival is approximately 1 year after an episode of *Candida* esophagitis in children with AIDS.[5, 30] *Candida* esophagitis, if not successfully treated, can lead to strictures, obstruction, and perforation of the esophagus. Viral esophagitis usually does not have any long-term sequelae.

Acknowledgment

We are grateful to Mr. John Tse, Pharm.D., Department of Pharmacology, UCLA Medical Center, Los Angeles, California, for reviewing the drugs and dosages in Table 50–2.

REFERENCES

1. Agha, F. P., Lee, H. H., and Nostrandt, T. T.: Herpetic esophagitis: A diagnostic challenge in immunocompromised patients. Am. J. Gastroenterol. *81*:246, 1986.
2. Alexander, J. A., Brouillette, E. D., Chien, M. C., et al.: Infectious esophagitis following liver and renal transplantation. Dig. Dis. Sci. *33*:1121, 1988.
3. Ammann, J., and Hong, R.: Disorders of the T cell system. *In* Stein, E. R. (ed.): Immunologic Disorders in Infants and Children. Philadelphia, W. B. Saunders, 1989, p. 286.
4. Baehr, P. H., and McDonald, G. B.: Esophageal infections: Risk factors, presentation, diagnosis and treatment. Gastroenterology *106*:509, 1994.
5. Blanche, S., Tardieu, M., Duliege, M., et al.: Longitudinal study of 94 symptomatic infants with perinatally transmitted human immunodeficiency virus infection. Am. J. Dis. Child. *144*:1210, 1990.
6. Bonacini, M., Lane, I. L., Gal, A. A., et al.: Prospective evaluation of blind brushings in the esophagus for candida esophagitis in patients with human immunodeficiency virus infection. Am. J. Gastroenterol. *85*:385, 1990.
7. Brouilette, D. E., Alexander, J., Yoo, Y. K., et al.: T-cell population in liver transplant recipients with infectious esophagitis. Dig. Dis. Sci. *34*:92, 1989.
8. Datry, A., Similowski, T., Jais, P., et al.: AIDS-associated leishmaniasis: An unusual gastro-duodenal presentation. Trans. R. Soc. Trop. Med. Hyg. *84*:239, 1990.
9. Davitian, A., Raufman, J. B., and Rosenthal, L. E.: Oral candidiasis as a marker for esophageal candidiasis in acquired immunodeficiency syndrome. Ann. Intern. Med. *104*:54, 1986.
10. DeSilva, R., Stoopak, P. M., and Raufman, J. P.: Esophageal fistulas associated with mycobacterial infections in patients at risk for AIDS. Radiology *175*:449, 1990.
11. Eng, J., and Baratman, S.: Tuberculosis of the esophagus. Dig. Dis. Sci. *36*:536, 1991.
12. Ginsberg, C. H., Bardin, G. L., Tauber, A. I., et al.: Oral clotrimazole in the treatment of esophageal candidiasis. Am. J. Med. *71*:891, 1981.
13. Grimes, M. M., La Pook, J. D., and Barr, M. H.: Disseminated *Pneumocystis carinii* in a patient with acquired immunodeficiency syndrome. Hum. Pathol. *18*:307, 1987.
14. Hirsch, M. S.: Herpes group virus infections in the compromised host. *In* Rubin, R. H., and Young, L. S. (eds.): Clinical Approach to Infection in the Compromised Host. 2nd ed. New York, Plenum, 1988, pp. 347–366.
15. Jadven, P., and Pitman, E. R.: Squamous papilloma of esophagus. Dig. Dis. Sci. *29*:317, 1984.
16. Kazlow, P. G., Shah, K., Benkov, K. G., et al.: Esophageal cryptosporidiosis in a child with acquired immune deficiency syndrome. Gastroenterology *91*:1301, 1986.
17. Kesten, S., Hyland, R. H., Pruzanski, W. R., et al.: Esophageal candidiasis associated with beclomethasone dipropionate aerosol therapy. Drug Intell. Clin. Pharm. *22*:568, 1988.
18. Kodsi, B. E., Wickremesinghe, P. C., Kozinn, P. J., et al.: *Candida* esophagitis. A prospective study of 27 cases. Gastroenterology *71*:715, 1976.
19. Lee, J. H., Newman, D. A., and Welsh, J. D.: Disseminated histoplasmosis presenting with esophageal symptomatology. Dig. Dis. Sci. *22*:831, 1977.
20. Levin, M. S., Loerscher, G., Katzka, D. A., et al: Giant human immunodeficiency virus related ulcers in the esophagus. Radiology *180*:323, 1991.
21. Levin, M. S., Macones, J., Lauffer, I.: *Candida* esophagitis: Accuracy of radiographic diagnosis. Radiology *154*:581, 1985.
22. Mathison, R., and Dutta, S. K.: *Candida* esophagitis. Dis. Dig. Sci. *28*:365, 1983.
23. McCabe, M. C., Valenti, A. J., Howell, D. A., et al.: Odynophagia from aphthous ulcers of the pharynx esophagus in the acquired immunodeficiency. Ann. Intern. Med. *109*:338, 1988.
24. Nassar, N. N., and Gregg, C. R.: Esophageal infections: Current treatment options. Gastroenterology *1*:56–63, 1998.
25. Ng, T. T., and Dennings, D. W.: Liposomal amphotericin B (AmBisome) therapy in invasive fungal infections. Evaluation of United Kingdom compassionate data. Arch. Intern. Med. *155*:1093, 1995.
26. Nito, Y., Yoshikawa, T., Oyamada, H., et al.: Esophageal candidiasis. Gastroenterol. Jpn. *23*:363, 1988.
27. O'Connor, A. J., and Cunnane, K.: *Helicobacter pylori* and gastroesophageal reflux disease—a prospective study. Ir. J. Med. Sci. *163*:369, 1994.
28. Obrescht, W. F., Richter, J. E., Olympio, G. A., et al.: Tracheoesophageal fistula: A serious complication of infectious esophagitis. Gastroenterology *87*:1174, 1984.
29. Porro, G. B., Parente, F., and Cernushi, M.: The diagnosis of esophageal candidiasis in patients with acquired immunodeficiency syndrome. Is endoscopy always necessary? Am. J. Gastroenterol. *84*:143, 1989.
30. Rabeneck, L., Popvich, M., Gartner, S., et al.: Acute HIV infection presenting with painful swallowing and painful ulcers. J. A. M. A. *263*:2318, 1990.
31. Scott, G. B., Hutto, C., Makuck, R. W., et al.: Survival in children with perinatally acquired immunodeficiency virus type I infection. N. Engl. J. Med. *321*:1791, 1989.
32. Sokol-Anderson, M. L., Prelutsky, D. J., and Westblom, T. U.: Giant esophageal aphthous ulcers in AIDS patients: Treatment with low dose corticosteroids. A. I. D. S. *5*:1537, 1991.
33. Stratta, R. J., Schaeffer, M. S., Cushing, K. A., et al.: Successful prophylaxis of cytomegalovirus disease after primary CMV exposure in liver transplant recipients. Transplantation *51*:90, 1991.
34. Sutton, F. M., Graham, D. Y., and Goodgame, R. W.: Infectious esophagitis. Gastrointest. Endosc. Clin. N. Am. *4*:713–729, 1994.
35. Theise, N. D., Rotterdam, H., and Dieterich, D.: Cytomegalovirus esophagitis in AIDS: Diagnosis by endoscopic biopsy. Am. J. Gastroenterol. *86*:1123, 1991.
36. Tilbe, K. S., and Lloyd, D. A.: A case of viral esophagitis. J. Clin. Gastroenterol. *8*:494, 1986.
37. Ulsh, T. J., Belitos, N. J., and Hamilton, S. R.: Bacterial esophagitis in immunocompromised patient. Arch. Intern. Med. *146*:1345, 1986.
38. Vita, E., and Schroeder, D. J.: Intralipid in prophylaxis of amphotericin B nephrotoxicity. Ann. Pharmacol. *28*:1182, 1994.
39. Wall, S. D., and Jones, B.: Gastrointestinal tract in immunocompromised host, opportunistic infections and other complications. Radiology *185*:327, 1992.
40. Yolkin, R. H., Hart, W., and Berman, J.: Viral infection and gastrointestinal dysfunction in children with HIV infection. *In* Bizzo, B. A., and Wilford, C. M. (eds.): Pediatric AIDS: The Challenge of HIV in Infants, Children and Adolescents. Baltimore, Williams & Wilkins, 1991, pp. 277–287.
41. Young, C., Chang, M. H., and Chen, J. M.: Fungal esophagitis in children. Zhonghua Min Guo Xiao Er Ke Yi Xue Hui Za Zhi *34*:436, 1993.

Approach to Patients with Gastrointestinal Tract Infections and Food Poisoning

LARRY K. PICKERING ■ THOMAS G. CLEARY

The approach to treating patients with gastrointestinal (GI) tract infections begins with obtaining a thorough medical history, including information about epidemiologic factors, a physical examination, and knowledge of the pathophysiology and clinical manifestations of various enteropathogens. GI tract infections result in a wide range of symptom complexes and can be produced by a variety of enteropathogens. Most infectious diarrheal illness can be classified into one of several categories based on the causative agent, the pathophysiologic mechanism of the agent, and the clinical response. This information then can be used to determine the appropriate use of laboratory facilities and to determine therapy. All patients with diarrhea require some degree of fluid and electrolyte therapy, a few need other nonspecific support, and for some, specific antimicrobial therapy is indicated to shorten the duration of the illness and to eradicate fecal excretion of the organism. Practice guidelines for management of infectious diarrhea have been developed by the Infectious Diseases Society of America.[170] Other recommendations include a primer for physicians dealing with diagnosis and management of foodborne illnesses developed jointly by the American Medical Association, Centers for Disease Control and Prevention (CDC), Food and Drug Administration (FDA) and United States Department of Agriculture[68]; guidelines for prevention of opportunistic infections in patients with human immunodeficiency virus (HIV) developed by the United States Public Health Service (USPHS) and the Infectious Diseases Society of America[71]; management of acute gastroenteritis in young children developed by the American Association of Pediatrics[17]; and guidelines on acute diarrhea in adults.[120]

Epidemiology and Etiology

Establishing the cause of diarrhea often is difficult because of variations in host susceptibility and response to infection, geographic location, season, and complexity of laboratory techniques necessary to identify fully the wide array of causative agents. In the United States and other parts of the world, acute infectious diarrhea is caused by many enteropathogens, but on the basis of epidemiologic and etiologic considerations, numerous major categories can be differentiated (Table 51–1): (1) diarrhea in childcare centers, hospitals, and other institutional settings; (2) foodborne- or waterborne-associated diarrhea; (3) antimicrobial-associated diarrhea; (4) diarrhea of travelers; (5) diarrhea in immunosuppressed hosts, including patients with primary and secondary immune deficiencies; and (6) others, which include sporadic episodes in which the above categories do not apply. Answers to the following questions should be obtained from all patients with diarrhea: Does the patient attend or work in a childcare center or other institutional setting? Has the patient recently been hospitalized? Do other family members or acquaintances also have diarrhea? Is the patient taking or has the patient recently taken an antimicrobial agent? Has the patient traveled to or returned from a developing country within the previous week? Is the patient immunosuppressed or taking immunosuppressive agents? Is the patient infected with HIV? Does the patient have a history of chronic diarrhea or other GI tract diseases?

When a patient complains of moderate or severe diarrhea, a decision should be made as to whether he or she should be hospitalized or treated as an outpatient. The following patients with diarrhea should be considered for hospitalization: (1) infants and elderly people who appear toxic or have high temperatures; (2) patients with excessive loss of fluid and electrolytes through stools, especially when associated with vomiting; (3) patients with grossly bloody stools; and (4) patients who are immunosuppressed, including people with acquired immunodeficiency syndrome (AIDS). Once the decision has been made either to hospitalize or to treat on an outpatient basis, appropriate diagnostic procedures and therapy can be instituted.

OUTBREAKS IN CHILDCARE CENTERS OR HOSPITALS

The risk for an individual to acquire a GI tract infection varies with age, environment, season, exposure, and immune status. Clinical and epidemiologic data often guide classification of an episode of acute infectious diarrhea into one of the categories mentioned earlier. If predisposing factors are not present, the episode can be classified as sporadic. Most cases of sporadic diarrhea occur in children younger than 5 years of age, although all age groups are affected. Infants who are breastfed are relatively protected from contaminated food and water. Protection also is afforded by factors present in human milk.[341] During and after weaning, the risk for developing diarrhea increases. When an episode of acute infectious diarrhea occurs, an association with other cases should be sought, especially when highly contagious organisms, such as *Shigella* spp., *Escherichia coli* O157:H7, *Giardia lamblia, Cryptosporidium* spp., rotavirus, astrovirus, enteric adenovirus, or calicivirus are isolated and in conditions in which close contact is facilitated, such as institutions for mentally retarded people, childcare centers, hospitals, or other institutional settings.[203, 284, 316, 336, 340, 431] After respiratory tract illness, diarrhea is the second most common disease among children in childcare facilities,[203] occurring most frequently in children younger than 3 years of age.

The National Nosocomial Infectious Surveillance system of the CDC reported that from 1985 to 1991, nosocomial diarrhea occurred in general pediatric care units at a rate of 11 per 10,000 discharges, in newborn nurseries at a rate of 11 per 10,000 discharges, and in high-risk nurseries at a rate of 20 per 10,000 discharges.[287] Studies of these pediatric populations have identified viral enteropathogens as the most frequent nosocomial agents, with rotavirus being the one most frequently identified.[144]

TABLE 51–1 ■ MAJOR CATEGORIES OF ACUTE INFECTIOUS DIARRHEA

Category of Diarrhea	Epidemiologic Considerations	Most Commonly Involved Enteropathogens
Outbreaks usually due to person-to-person transmission	Child care centers, hospitals, and other institutional settings	Enteric viruses, *Cryptosporidium, Giardia lamblia,* occasionally bacteria
Foodborne or waterborne	Other people involved after common food or water exposure	See Tables 51–2 and 51–3
Antimicrobial associated	Recent administration of an antimicrobial agent	*C. difficile*
Travelers	Recent travel to a developing country	Enterotoxigenic *Escherichia coli* *Campylobacter* *Shigella* *Salmonella*
Immunosuppressed hosts	Underlying disease, including HIV infection; recent administration of an immunosuppressive drug or radiation therapy	See Table 51–4

FOODBORNE OR WATERBORNE DIARRHEA

Reporting of foodborne and waterborne diseases in the United States began in 1923 because of concern about typhoid fever and infantile diarrhea.[313] Since 1978, foodborne and waterborne outbreaks have been published in separate annual summaries. These reported outbreaks account for a small fraction of the outbreaks that occur.

An outbreak of foodborne or waterborne disease is defined as an incident in which two or more people experience a similar illness, usually involving the GI tract, after ingesting common food or water intended for drinking.[35, 313] Foodborne or waterborne disease can be produced by food or water contaminated with bacteria or a bacterial toxin, a chemical, virus, or parasite.[68, 179, 346] Table 51–2 outlines the various characteristics of foodborne and waterborne outbreaks, including outbreaks not characterized by diarrhea. Although most enteropathogens are spread by food or water, the epidemiology of outbreaks often suggests specific etiologic agents. A determination of the incubation period and the presence or absence of selected clinical findings (especially fever, vomiting, and bloody diarrhea) often leads a physician or other health care professional toward the correct diagnosis in outbreaks of foodborne or waterborne disease.[68] As a general rule, when outbreaks are divided by an incubation period of illness, those less than 1 hour usually are caused by chemical poisoning; those of 1 to 7 hours, either by *Staphylococcus aureus* or *Bacillus cereus* preformed toxins; those of 8 to 14 hours by *Clostridium perfringens* or *B. cereus* enterotoxins; and those more than 14 hours by other infectious or toxic agents (see Table 51–2). Clinical manifestations can involve the central nervous system or be systemic with little to no intestinal tract involvement.

During the period from 1993 to 1997, a total of 2751 confirmed outbreaks of foodborne disease comprising 86,058 cases were reported to the CDC from various regions of the United States.[313] Among outbreaks in which the etiology was determined, bacterial pathogens caused the largest number of outbreaks (75%) and cases (86%), with *Salmonella* serotype Enteritidis accounting for the largest number of outbreaks, cases, and deaths; most of these outbreaks were attributed to eating eggs. Chemical agents caused 17 percent of outbreaks and 1 percent of cases, with ciguatoxin, heavy metals, mushrooms, paralytic shellfish, and scombrotoxin accounting for outbreaks caused by chemical agents (Table 51–3). Viruses caused 6 percent of outbreaks and 8 percent of cases, and parasites caused 2 percent of outbreaks and 5 percent of cases. Hepatitis A and Norwalk-like viruses accounted for outbreaks caused by viruses. The etiologic agent was not detected in 68 percent of outbreaks, indicating the need for improved epidemiologic and laboratory investigations. The most common contributing factors to outbreaks were improper storage or inadequate holding temperature, followed by poor personal hygiene of a food handler and contaminated equipment.[313, 459] Outbreaks of gastroenteritis caused by caliciviruses have been associated with consumption of contaminated oysters, salads, and bakery products, and the virus has been transmitted by food handlers.[244, 291] Because 50 percent of outbreaks of unknown etiology had an incubation period of greater than or equal to 15 hours, many probably are of viral etiology.

The ingestion of raw fish (sushi or sashimi) has led to infection with *Vibrio parahaemolyticus* and various parasites from infected fish.[92] Parasites acquired through ingestion of raw fish include larval nematodes of the family Anisakidae, fish tapeworm of the species *Diphyllobothrium,* the fluke *Nanophyetus salmincola* from salmon, and many other helminths.[387, 455] Most worm infections acquired from raw fish in the United States have been acquired from dishes prepared at home and not from sushi restaurants.

Symptoms in patients with chemical poisoning generally begin within 1 to 2 hours after ingestion, although certain mushroom toxins may produce symptoms for up to 24 hours (see Table 51–3). Heavy metals, such as antimony, arsenic, cadmium, copper, mercury, thallium, tin, and zinc, cause irritation of the gastric mucosa, with nausea, vomiting, and abdominal cramps, which usually resolve 2 to 3 hours after the offending agent has been removed.[68]

The toxic syndromes acquired from fish and shellfish can be grouped clinically into two categories: the histamine-like syndrome of scombroid poisoning and the neurotoxic syndrome, which includes ciguatera, paralytic shellfish poisoning, neurotoxic shellfish poisoning, and puffer fish poisoning caused by tetrodotoxin.[124] The neurologic symptoms produced by fish, shellfish, and the Chinese restaurant syndrome agent include paresthesia, reversal of hot-cold sensations, loss of proprioception, flushing, weakness, and burning sensations. Chinese restaurant syndrome appears to be caused by excessive amounts of monosodium glutamate in foods. Fish poisoning may be caused by scombrotoxin, ciguatoxin, or tetrodotoxin. Scombroid fish poisoning is characterized by symptoms resembling those of histamine release. Shellfish poisoning can be of two types: (1) paralytic, caused by neurotoxins, including saxitoxin; and (2) neurotoxic, caused by several poorly characterized neurotoxins. Domoic acid from contaminated mussels causes acute widespread neurologic dysfunction and GI tract manifestations followed by chronic residual memory deficits and motor neuropathy or axonopathy.[327, 422]

Infectious diseases associated with consumption of raw and lightly cooked shellfish (mussels, clams, oysters, lobsters, and other mollusks) are caused by bacterial agents that are

TABLE 51–2 ■ CHARACTERISTICS OF FOODBORNE OR WATERBORNE OUTBREAKS OF DIARRHEA

Usual Incubation Periods	Clinical Illness			Causative Agent	Epidemiologic and Laboratory Diagnosis
	Fever	*Diarrhea*	*Vomiting*		
5 minutes–6 hours (usually <3 hours)	Rare	Occasional (see Table 51–3)	Common	Chemical or toxin	Demonstration of toxin or chemical from food or epidemiologic incrimination of food
1–6 hours (usually <1 hour)	Rare	Occasional	Profuse	*Staphylococcus aureus* enterotoxin *Bacillus cereus* emetic toxin	Detection of toxin in food, isolation of organisms in food (>10^5/g) or in vomitus or stool
8–16 hours	Rare	Typical	Occasional	*Clostridium perfringens* enterotoxin *B. cereus* enterotoxin	Isolation of organisms or toxin from food (>10^5g) or stools of ill persons, epidemiologic incrimination of food
16–96 hours	Common	Typical	Occasional	*Shigella* *Salmonella* *Vibrio parahaemolyticus* Enteroinvasive *Escherichia coli* *Yersinia enterocolitica*	Isolation of organisms from food or stools of ill persons
12–72 hours	Clinical syndrome compatible with botulism			*Clostridium botulinum*	Isolation of organism or toxin from food (10^5/g) or stools, demonstration of toxin in serum or food
16–96 hours	Occasional	Typical	Occasional	*E. coli* enterotoxin *V. parahaemolyticus* enterotoxin *Vibrio cholerae* enterotoxin *Y. enterocolitica* enterotoxin	Isolation of organism from food and stools of ill persons, identification of toxin, epidemiologic incrimination of food
				Listeria monocytogenes	Blood or CSF cultures, stool culture usually not helpful
1–11 days	Occasional	Common	Occasional	*Cryptosporidium parvum* *Cyclospora cayetanensis*	Request special stool examination; may need to examine water or food
2 days–weeks	Common	Typical	Frequent	*Bacillus anthracis*	Isolation of organism from blood or contaminated meat
1–7 days	Uncommon	Typical	Frequent	*E. coli* O157: H7 and other Shiga toxin–producing *E. coli*	Isolation of organism from food or stool or identification of toxin in stools of ill persons, epidemiologic incrimination of food
1–3 days	Occasional	Typical	Common	Caliciviruses (noroviruses) Rotavirus	Antigen detection (enzyme immunoassay) in stool, immune electron microscopy of stool, serology
2–5 days	Occasional	Typical	Occasional	*Campylobacter jejuni*	Isolation of organisms from food or stools of ill persons, epidemiologic incrimination of food
7–21 days	Common	Common	Rare	*Brucella abortus, melitensis,* and *suis*	Blood culture and positive serology
1–4 weeks	Rare	Common	Rare	*Giardia lamblia*	Stool for ova and parasite examination enzyme immunoassay
2 days–8 weeks	Common	Common	Common	*Trichinella spiralis*	Serology, muscle biopsy

native to the marine environment and by viral and bacterial agents from sewage effluents and other sources that contaminate environmental waters. As filter-feeding organisms, shellfish amplify public health problems associated with environmental contamination because they accumulate microbial pathogens at densities many times those found in overlying waters.

The current public health problems of greatest concern to consumers of molluscan shellfish are associated with viral pathogens. The numbers of cases and outbreaks caused by these pathogens far exceed those of all other infectious causes.[86] The *Vibrio* genus (specifically *Vibrio vulnificus*) presents the most serious problem in terms of the severity of human illness and death, especially in people with liver disease.[193]

Mushrooms produce several clinical syndromes, generally within 2 hours of ingestion[174] (see Table 51–3), except for poisoning caused by amatoxins, phallotoxins, amantin, monomethylhydrazine, and gyromitrin, which may produce symptoms, including death, up to 24 hours after ingestion.[174] Mushrooms also can be contaminated with other agents, including *S. aureus* enterotoxin A.[251]

Bacterial diseases associated with ingestion of unpasteurized milk include salmonellosis and campylobacteriosis and, less frequently, infection with *Brucella* spp., *E. coli, Listeria monocytogenes, Mycobacterium* spp., *S. aureus, Streptococcus* spp., *Streptobacillus moniliformis,* and *Yersinia enterocolitica.*[353] A nationwide outbreak of *Salmonella enteritidis* gastroenteritis involved 224,000 people in the United States and was associated with ingestion of contaminated ice cream. The origin of the outbreak was pasteurized ice cream premix that was contaminated in tanker trailers that previously had carried nonpasteurized liquid eggs containing *S. enteritidis.*[181] Consumption of raw milk has been

TABLE 51–3 ■ CHEMICAL CAUSES OF FOOD POISONING

Type of Chemical Toxin, or Poison	Food	Clinical Symptoms	Onset of Symptoms (hr)
Heavy metals*	Water (via metallic container) and food	Gastrointestinal	1
Scombrotoxin	Fish (tuna, mackerel, marlin, mahi-mahi, bluefish)	*Due to histamine:* flushing, headache, burning of mouth and throat, urticaria, rash, paresthesia	1
Ciguatera	Fish (barracuda, amberjack, snapper, grouper)	*Neurologic:* paresthesia, reversal of cold-hot sensations *Gastrointestinal:* nausea, abdominal pain, vomiting, diarrhea	1–6
Tetrodotoxin	Puffer fish	*Neurologic:* paresthesia, numbness, loss of proprioception, ascending paralysis, death	<1
Paralytic or neurotoxic compounds	Shellfish (clams, oysters, scallops, mussels, other mollusks)	Paresthesia, weakness, respiratory difficulties, dysphasia, dysphonia, gastrointestinal	1–4
Domoic acid	Shellfish (mussels)	Gastrointestinal; *acute CNS:* headache, seizures, hemiparesis, ophthalmoplegia, abnormalities of arousal; *chronic CNS:* memory deficits, motor neuropathy or axonopathy	Within 24
Monosodium glutamate	Chinese food	Burning sensation, heavy feeling in chest, pressure over face, flushing, gastrointestinal	1
Ibotenic acid, muscimol	Mushroom	*CNS:* confusion, delirium, visual disturbances, lethargy	2
Coprine	Mushroom	*Disulfiram-like effect:* nausea, vomiting, headache, hypotension, flushing, paresthesia and tachycardia	2
Muscarine	Mushroom	*Parasympathetic:* sweating, salivation, lacrimation, blurred vision, diarrhea, bradycardia, hypotension	2
Psilocybin, psilocin	Mushroom	*CNS:* hallucinations, anxiety, mood elevation, weakness	2
Diverse, mostly unknown	Mushroom	Gastrointestinal	2
Monomethylhydrazine, gyromitrin	Mushroom	Cellular destruction, gastrointestinal, loss of coordination, convulsion, coma, death	6–12
Amatoxins, phallotoxins	Mushroom	Cellular destruction, gastrointestinal, hepatic, and/or renal necrosis	6–24
Vomitoxin (deoxynivalenol)	Cereals contaminated with *Fusarium* species	Vomiting acutely; altered mucosal immunity with chronic exposure	<3

*Includes antimony, arsenic, cadium, copper, mercury, thallium, tin, and zinc.
CNS, central nervous system.

associated with a chronic diarrhea syndrome of unknown cause,[318] initially identified in Minnesota and referred to as Brainerd diarrhea. It is manifest by acute onset with marked urgency and a lack of systemic symptoms. The duration of illness is at least 9 months and generally has involved adults. Clinical and laboratory data indicate that diarrhea is caused by a secretory mechanism. No evidence of secondary transmission exists. Antimicrobial therapy has not been successful.[318] In addition, an outbreak of chronic diarrhea involving 72 people who ingested untreated drinking water was reported.[323] The cause and pathophysiologic mechanism of the illness remain unknown.

Since 1971, the number of reported waterborne outbreaks in the United States has averaged 30 per year (range, 13 to 53 years), involving approximately 7600 people annually (range, 1569 to 21,149 people).[35] During the 2-year period from 1997 to 1998, 13 states reported a total of 17 outbreaks associated with drinking water. These outbreaks caused an estimated 2038 people to become ill. This figure probably represents only a small fraction of the total number of outbreaks that occurred. Ingestion of pathogens during swimming also has been associated with outbreaks.[35] The CDC has published recommendations for management of fecal accidents in disinfected recreational water venues contaminated with formed or liquid stool.[70]

Frequencies of pathogens incriminated in waterborne outbreaks are different from those most often responsible for food poisoning. *G. lamblia* has been the pathogen most commonly documented to be spread by water,[147] and *Cryptosporidium* has produced the largest outbreak, which involved more than 403,000 people.[259] *Shigella,* hepatitis A virus, *Salmonella,* caliciviruses, *Campylobacter,* and chemicals occasionally produce disease.[147] Large outbreaks aboard passenger cruise ships continue to occur,[235] with a mean of 323 passengers involved in the 10 outbreaks investigated from 1986 to 1988.[35]

The main therapeutic modality in most patients with food poisoning is supportive care because most of these illnesses are self-limited. Exceptions include botulism, paralytic shellfish poisoning, tetrodotoxin, long-acting mushroom poisoning, and Shiga toxin–producing *E. coli* (STEC) infection, all of which may be fatal in previously healthy people. Foodborne disease caused by any agent can produce fatalities in infants, elderly people, debilitated people, or those with primary or secondary immune deficiencies. Food irradiation is an important technology that can protect the public against foodborne diseases.[417] Several websites that provide information about foodborne disease include ama-assn.org/foodborne, cdc.gov/foodnet, cdc.gov/foodsafety, and fightbac.org/main.cfm/.[346]

ANTIMICROBIAL-ASSOCIATED DIARRHEA

Diarrhea often occurs after use of an antimicrobial agent. Changes in bowel flora may result in abnormal stools in the absence of a documented enteropathogen, and discontinuation of the medication may be sufficient to eliminate symptoms. In a small number of patients with antibiotic-induced diarrhea, a severe and potentially fatal form of colitis may develop.[198]

Pseudomembranous or antimicrobial-associated colitis (AAC) refers to the presence of a pseudomembrane or of multiple plaquelike lesions in the colon induced by administration of an antimicrobial agent within the preceding 8 weeks. Pseudomembranous colitis not associated with antibiotic use occurs with *Shigella dysenteriae* serotype 1 and STEC.[228, 239] The specific cause of essentially all cases of AAC are toxins produced by *Clostridium difficile*.[390] Intestinal flora generally can prevent proliferation and production of toxins by *C. difficile;* however, administration of antibiotics to some people allows *C. difficile* to proliferate and produce sufficient toxin to cause mucosal damage. Many antimicrobial agents have been reported to cause this condition; ampicillin, the cephalosporins, clindamycin, lincomycin, erythromycin, and trimethoprim-sulfamethoxazole (TMP-SMX) have been implicated most frequently.[33] Tetracycline, metronidazole, miconazole, and chloramphenicol are rare causes of AAC, whereas vancomycin has not been reported to cause the condition. Cancer chemotherapeutic agents also have been associated with AAC. In addition, nosocomial infection with *C. difficile* occurs and can result in asymptomatic carriage or diarrhea.[275]

Patients with AAC present with watery diarrhea that often contains blood and mucus. Diarrhea may be the only manifestation of disease or may occur in association with nausea, vomiting, abdominal pain or cramps, fever, or leukocytosis. Extraintestinal *C. difficile* infections, including bacteremia, are uncommon events.[138] If not treated appropriately, GI tract symptoms may progress to toxic megacolon, colonic perforation, shock, and death. The diagnosis of AAC in a patient with diarrhea is supported by the following[263, 388]:

1. A history of ongoing or recent antimicrobial therapy. Twenty to 40 percent of episodes occur after the drug has been discontinued.
2. Finding leukocytes on a stain of fecal material.
3. Exclusion of other agents known to cause fecal leukocytes.
4. Identification of *C. difficile* toxins in stool specimens.
5. Endoscopy with rectal biopsy to identify pseudomembranes or plaques that contain mucin, fibrin, leukocytes, and sloughed epithelial cells.

Plaques or pseudomembrane not always are present in patients with AAC, but when they are, *C. difficile* usually can be presumed to be the cause of disease. Endoscopy, with or without mucosal biopsy, is the quickest way to establish the diagnosis. However, endoscopy is reserved for special situations such as when a rapid diagnosis is needed, when the patient has ileus and a stool sample is not available, or when other colonic diseases are in the differential diagnosis. The finding of *C. difficile* in feces suggests but does not confirm that *C. difficile* is the cause of the diarrhea. The finding of fecal toxin is a more useful method of diagnosing *C. difficile*–induced disease than is bacterial culture.[311] *C. difficile* and its toxins can be detected by employing a variety of tissue culture assays, enzyme immunoassays, latex agglutination, and molecular techniques.[242, 311] The toxic effect in tissue culture should be neutralized by antitoxin. This organism and the toxins may be found in the GI tract of some healthy people.[275, 285] Approximately 15 to 63 percent of neonates, up to 50 percent of infants younger than 1 year of age, and as many as 8 percent of children are asymptomatic carriers.[72]

The most important aspect of therapy in patients with AAC is discontinuation of the antimicrobial agent, after which symptoms usually resolve within 1 to 2 weeks; however, if symptoms persist or worsen or if the patient has severe diarrhea, specific therapy with metronidazole[279, 421] or oral vancomycin should be instituted. Teicoplanin, fusidic acid, and bacitracin also have been used.[198, 448] After initiation of therapy, symptoms generally resolve within several days, and fecal toxin disappears. Relapse of colitis after discontinuation of metronidazole, vancomycin, or bacitracin has been documented in 10 to 20 percent of patients, generally 1 to 4 weeks after treatment has been discontinued.[32, 421] Relapses are caused by germination of *C. difficile* spores that persist despite treatment and are not due to development of resistance. Relapses are treated with a second course of metronidazole. Other modes of therapy include dietary reduction of carbohydrates and administration of probiotics to allow normal intestinal flora to reestablish.[198, 276, 414] Both the American College of Gastroenterology and the Society of Healthcare Epidemiology have published guidelines for prevention and control of *C. difficile* infection in adults.[216] Similar guidelines have not been published for children.

TRAVELERS' DIARRHEA

Travelers' diarrhea is the most common health problem encountered by people from the United States, Northern Europe, Canada, or Australia who travel to Latin America, Asia, the Middle East, or Africa, where diarrhea is hyperendemic.[114–117, 161, 163] Half of these travelers experience diarrhea within the first few weeks after arrival. Enterotoxigenic *E. coli* (ETEC) are the most commonly identified cause of travelers' diarrhea, but the illness can be caused by a variety of bacteria, viruses, and parasites,[47, 114–116, 312, 389] including *Shigella* spp., *Campylobacter jejuni, Aeromonas* spp., *Plesiomonas shigelloides, Salmonella* spp., *V. parahaemolyticus* (in Asia), *G. lamblia,* enteroaggregative *E. coli* (EAEC), and enteric viruses. Information from existing studies concerning pathogens associated with diarrhea among children or elderly people whose travel is limited. Studies of diarrhea of travelers visiting the United States and Great Britain from developed and developing countries showed attack rates of 2 and 0.6 percent, respectively.[374]

The clinical illness varies, reflecting the diversity of causative agents. Typically, illness occurs within several weeks of arrival in a foreign country and is defined as the passage of at least three unformed stools in a 24-hour period, together with cramps, nausea, fecal urgency, tenesmus, or a combination thereof. Bloody diarrhea, vomiting, and documented elevation of temperature are less frequent symptoms. Approximately 50 percent of people who become ill have mild disease, 15 to 40 percent are forced to alter their scheduled activities, and 15 to 30 percent are confined to bed.[117] Because travelers' diarrhea is caused by a variety of enteropathogens, travelers may experience more than one episode. Travelers' diarrhea is spread by many fecally contaminated vehicles, with most studies implicating food, particularly uncooked food,[130, 426] and untreated water and ice.[187] Careful attention to food consumption with avoidance of foods that are not steaming hot, raw vegetables, fruit not peeled by the traveler, tap water, and ice is critical to prevention of disease.[117, 130, 187] Predisposing factors and host factors that increase susceptibility to travelers' diarrhea or complicate its course include young age, short duration of travel, eating in restaurants, season, reduced gastric acidity, chronic and active GI tract disease, and immunodeficiency disorders.[117, 130, 197]

Several studies have evaluated prevention and treatment of travelers' diarrhea in adults using either antidiarrheal compounds or antimicrobial agents. Compounds that have been shown to be effective chemoprophylactic agents include doxycycline, bismuth subsalicylate, TMP-SMX, fluoroquinolones, and nonabsorbable antibiotics.[4, 116, 121, 131] These compounds have been shown to offer 50 to 100 percent protection against travelers' diarrhea.[4] Potential problems with antibiotic regimens include resistance of bacteria, such as ETEC, *Salmonella* spp., *Shigella* spp., and *C. jejuni,* and side effects, such as nausea, diarrhea, and photosensitivity reactions. Large doses of bismuth subsalicylate can result in significant serum salicylate concentrations.[139, 337] The bioavailability of salicylate in 1 ounce of Pepto-Bismol is equivalent to that of one 325-mg adult aspirin tablet.[139]

Because of the uncertain risk of widespread prophylactic administration of these antimicrobial agents, including development of resistance among enteric bacteria,[161, 298] and the mildness of most cases of travelers' diarrhea, prophylactic use of antimicrobial agents generally is not recommended.[163] Instruction of travelers with regard to appropriate dietary practices as a prophylactic measure is recommended.[130, 426]

If a person becomes ill in a locale where laboratory facilities are inadequate, the choice of a therapeutic agent must be made on an empiric basis.[4] Antidiarrheal compounds as therapy for travelers' diarrhea have been used in people with nondysenteric disease. Bismuth subsalicylate has been shown to be effective in decreasing the incidence of diarrhea by up to 60 percent.[115] Loperamide should not be used in infants or older children with bloody diarrhea or fever, although it may benefit older children and adults with watery diarrhea.[17] Other nonantimicrobial compounds have been shown to be ineffective or dangerous or have not been evaluated.[17]

In episodes of travelers' diarrhea caused by bacteria that are susceptible to TMP-SMX, a 3- to 5-day course of this antibiotic may help children who develop diarrhea with 3 or more loose stools in an 8-hour period, especially if associated symptoms such as nausea, vomiting, abdominal cramps, fever, or blood in stools are present. In areas where *C. jejuni* is common or where resistance to TMP-SMX by other enteropathogens is high, ciprofloxacin, ofloxacin, levofloxacin, or azithromycin may be a better choice for treatment of adults.[4] Ciprofloxacin is equivalent to TMP-SMX in therapy of diarrhea caused by susceptible organisms and expands the coverage to resistant organisms and *C. jejuni,* which generally is resistant to TMP-SMX.[131, 279, 298] Problems with development of resistance by *C. jejuni* to fluoroquinolones may preclude its use in this situation.[303, 376, 391, 415]

Approximately 3 percent of people develop persistent diarrhea after an episode of travelers' diarrhea.[119] The differential diagnosis should include persistent infection, particularly with *Giardia, Cryptosporidium, Cyclospora,* or *Isospora* spp.; antibiotic-associated colitis; small intestinal bacterial overgrowth; transient disaccharidase deficiency; initial manifestation of ulcerative colitis or regional enteritis; postdysenteric colitis; irritable bowel syndrome; or tropical sprue.[119] An underlying immune system defect such as occurs with AIDS also should be considered.

IMMUNOCOMPROMISED HOSTS, INCLUDING PATIENTS WITH ACQUIRED IMMUNODEFICIENCY SYNDROME

Diarrheal disease often is a major problem in people with primary and secondary immunologic disorders.[21, 460] The GI tract must act as the first line of defense against a wide variety of potentially harmful organisms and toxins. Immune deficiencies can result in an increased host susceptibility to intestinal tract infections or an atypical, prolonged, or disseminated course once an organism is established.

TABLE 51–4 ■ ORGANISMS THAT CAUSE GASTROINTESTINAL TRACT INFECTIONS IN PATIENTS WITH AIDS

Area	Organisms
Esophagus	*Candida albicans**
	Cytomegalovirus (CMV)*
	Herpes simplex virus (HSV)*
Hepatobiliary	CMV
	*Cryptosporidium**
	Hepatotropic viruses
	Mycobacterium avium complex (MAC)*
Small intestine	*Campylobacter* species
	CMV*
	*Cryptosporidium**
	*Giardia lamblia**
	*Isospora belli**
	MAC*
	*Microsporidium** (*Enterocytozoon bieneusi* and *Encephalitozoon intestinalis*)
	Salmonella species*
	Strongyloides stercoralis
Large intestine	*Campylobacter* species
	Clostridium difficile
	CMV*
	Entamoeba histolytica
	HSV*
	Salmonella species*
	Shigella species

*Diseases of the gastrointestinal tract that fulfill the Centers for Disease Control and Prevention surveillance case definition of AIDS.[61]

Causes of GI tract disease in children with AIDS can be grouped under the major headings of infection, malignancy, and HIV enteropathy. The location of involvement of the GI tract by infectious agents determines the clinical symptoms and the ease with which these organisms can be diagnosed and treated (Table 51–4). Organisms and diseases of the GI tract that fulfill the CDC surveillance case definition of AIDS[61] are candidiasis, cryptosporidiosis, cytomegalovirus, herpes simplex, *Mycobacterium avium* complex, *Microsporidium,* isosporiasis, and *Salmonella* spp.[20, 109, 239, 286] In addition, the AIDS wasting syndrome (HIV infection without superimposed opportunistic enteric infection of known cause) is part of the CDC case definition for AIDS.[61] In general, HIV-infected children have the same spectrum of enteric pathogens as do uninfected children, but they require more attention because of malnutrition and comorbidity.[217] Patients with AIDS have been shown to have D-xylose malabsorption and steatorrhea, and, on jejunal and rectal biopsies, a specific pathologic process can be demonstrated in the lamina propria of the small intestine and colon.[239] A significant proportion of patients with AIDS and severe small intestinal injury have enterocyte infection, often with *Cryptosporidium* or various *Microsporidium* organisms.[162, 237] Infections with several enteropathogens in patients with AIDS occur more frequently and are more likely to be severe, recurrent, persistent, or associated with extraintestinal disease. Combination antiretroviral therapy can result in complete clinical, microbiologic, and histologic responses in patients with AIDS infected with *C. parvum* and *Enterocytozoon bieneusi*[58] and in patients with HIV enteropathy.[239] Guidelines for prevention of opportunistic infections, including those involving the GI tract, have been published.[71]

Organisms That Cause Acute Gastroenteritis

BACTERIA

Many bacterial, viral, and parasitic organisms produce diarrhea in humans. Tables 51–5 and 51–6 show the major bacterial enteric pathogens associated with acute infectious diarrhea.[81] These organisms are discussed here in alphabetical order for ease of reference. The relative importance of each organism as a cause of diarrhea varies in different populations.

Aeromonas hydrophila

Aeromonas spp. are gram-negative bacteria found in soil and fresh and brackish water worldwide. *Aeromonas* spp. are recognized as colonizers and pathogens of cold-blooded animals, including fish, reptiles, and amphibians.[15] *Aeromonas* spp. have been associated with a wide spectrum of human disease, most frequently gastroenteritis, soft tissue infection, and bacteremia, especially in immunocompromised hosts.[15, 210] Of the 14 species in the genus, five genomospecies, *Aeromonas hydrophila, Aeromonas veronii, Aeromonas caviae, Aeromonas jandaei,* and *Aeromonas schubertii,* have been associated with human disease, with the first three being defined as major pathogens and the species associated with gastroenteritis.[210] Because many clinical laboratories cannot perform precise identification, most species isolated are reported as *A. hydrophila.*

The role of *A. hydrophila* in human diarrhea remains uncertain. Despite the association of this organism with acute gastroenteritis and in some studies its more frequent isolation from patients with diarrhea than from healthy controls,[210] volunteers who have been fed the organism have not become ill.[290] *A. hydrophila* has been isolated from stools of fewer than 3 percent of healthy humans[15]; however, in Thailand, the isolation rate from healthy controls increased with age, up to 27 percent in adults.[15] *A. hydrophila* strains have been shown to produce both cytotoxin and enterotoxin, including heat-labile (cholera-like) enterotoxin and heat-stable enterotoxins.[390] Children with watery diarrhea associated with *Aeromonas* have organisms that are significantly more likely to possess genes for both a heat-labile cytotonic enterotoxin and the heat-stable cytotonic enterotoxin than are control children.[10] Other toxic or invasive properties may be important in production of disease because one fourth of patients have a dysentery-like illness.[210]

TABLE 51–5 ■ PATHOGENIC BACTERIA ASSOCIATED WITH ACUTE INFECTIOUS DIARRHEA

Agent	Epidemiologic Considerations
Aeromonas hydrophila	Water, food, or animal exposure
Bacillus cereus	Food exposure
Campylobacter jejuni	Animal or food exposure
Clostridium difficile	Exposure to antimicrobial agents
Clostridium perfringens	Food exposure
Listeria monocytogenes	Food exposure
Plesiomonas shigelloides	Water, fish, or animal exposure
Salmonella species	Exposure to carrier, food exposure
Shigella species	Exposure to an infected person or to contaminated food
Staphylococcus aureus	Food exposure
Vibrio cholerae O1	Food or water exposure
V. cholerae O139	Food or water exposure
Vibrio parahaemolyticus	Seafood exposure
Yersinia enterocolitica	Food or animal exposure

TABLE 51–6 ■ PATHOGENIC *ESCHERICHIA COLI* ASSOCIATED WITH ACUTE INFECTIOUS DIARRHEA

Class of *E. coli*	Abbreviation	Usual Presentation of Disease
Shigatoxin	STEC	Bloody diarrhea, water- and foodborne outbreaks, associated with hemorrhagic colitis and hemolytic-uremic syndrome
Enterotoxigenic	ETEC	Watery diarrhea in children living in and travelers visiting developing countries
Enteroinvasive	EIEC	Dysentery in adults and watery diarrhea, occasionally foodborne outbreaks
Enteropathogenic	EPEC	Acute and chronic diarrhea in infants in nurseries, diarrhea in children <1 year of age in developing countries
Enteroaggregative	EAEC	Acute and chronic watery diarrhea in children in developing countries

Bacillus cereus

Bacillus cereus is an aerobic, spore-forming, gram-positive bacillus that is a rare cause of food poisoning in the United States.[64, 258, 277] Although frequently present in food, *B. cereus* should be suspected as the cause of GI tract illness if appropriate symptoms are present and if incriminated food, particularly fried rice, contains 10^5 or more *B. cereus* organisms per gram.[68] Two distinct forms of GI tract illness can be produced by this organism. One is caused by production of a low-molecular-weight (1.2-kd) preformed emetic toxin, cereulide, that survives high temperatures, exposure to trypsin, and pH extremes. The other is caused by a group of three enterotoxins sensitive to high temperatures, proteolytic enzymes, and acids and is formed in vivo.[390] If the strain causing illness produces the emetic toxin, a syndrome occurs that resembles illness produced by staphylococcal enterotoxin, with nausea, vomiting, and abdominal cramps that begin within several hours of ingestion. Rarely, illness associated with the emetic toxin is followed by fulminant liver failure.[261] The diagnosis may be difficult to confirm because heating may kill the organism but leave the toxin intact. If the strain produces enterotoxins, profuse watery diarrhea and abdominal pain begin within 12 hours, with minimal or no vomiting. Some strains produce both toxins, whereas others produce only one toxin. Symptoms caused by either toxin usually resolve in less than 24 hours, and fever rarely occurs. Spores of *B. cereus* are resistant to heat and, therefore, may withstand a brief period of cooking or boiling. *B. cereus* can grow in temperatures ranging from 25° C to 40° C. *B. cereus* also has been associated with panophthalmitis, endophthalmitis, pneumonia, bacteremia, endocarditis, and meningitis.[110]

Campylobacter

Campylobacter spp. are recognized as one of the most important causes of acute diarrheal disease in humans throughout the world[13, 57, 215] and are the major bacterial cause of diarrhea in the United States.[13, 60] Most diarrheal illness in the United States caused by *C. jejuni* is foodborne.[277] Currently, 18 *Campylobacter* spp. and subspecies are recognized. *C. jejuni* and *Campylobacter coli* are the two predominant species, although the use of selective media and lack of use of stool filtration techniques may preclude isolation of other *Campylobacter* spp.[128, 215, 245, 432] Many clinical microbiology laboratories do not differentiate *C. jejuni* and *C. coli. Campylobacter fetus,* recognized as a cause of fever, bacteremia, and meningitis in immunocompromised hosts and of abortion, rarely causes diarrhea. People infected with *C. jejuni* may develop diarrhea, cramping abdominal pain, chills, and fever. Gross rectal bleeding may occur, and mucus and fecal leukocytes may be present, resembling the illness produced by *Shigella.* The clinical presentation also may mimic that of inflammatory bowel disease. Both a heat-labile enterotoxin and mucosal invasion have been incriminated in the pathogenesis. *C. jejuni* also has been associated with reactive arthritis and Guillain-Barré syndrome.[13, 14]

Phylogenetic trees have been established for *Campylobacter* and contain three distinct clades (species groups). The first consists of *Campylobacter fetus, Campylobacter hyointestinalis,* and *Campylobacter mucosalis*, all generally associated with disease in farm animals, although *C. fetus* and *C. hyointestinalis* produce human disease. The second clade consists of *C. coli, C. jejuni, Campylobacter helveticus, Campylobacter lari,* and *Campylobacter upsaliensis*; all (except *C. helveticus*) have been associated with gastroenteritis in humans. The third clade contains *Campylobacter curvus, Campylobacter concisus, Campylobacter gracilis, Campylobacter rectus, Campylobacter showae,* and *Campylobacter sputorum,* organisms generally associated with the periodontal cavity of humans and animals.

Helicobacter pylori (formerly *Campylobacter pylori)* has been isolated from the stomach and duodenum of patients with histologically confirmed type B antral gastritis, peptic ulcer disease, duodenal ulcers, and gastric lymphoma.[50] This organism is not associated with diarrhea. *Helicobacter cinaedi* and *Helicobacter fennelliae* were identified previously as *Campylobacter* spp. but have been reclassified (see Chapter 141).

Clostridium difficile

Clostridium difficile and its toxins have been shown to be the cause of pseudomembranous colitis or AAC.[33, 34] Interpretation of the finding of *C. difficile* or its toxins in stools from infants presents a special problem because both may be found without illness.[107, 285] Colitis results from production of toxin within the intestinal lumen. Both toxins appear to be important because disease has been associated with strains that produce only one toxin.[12, 381] The usual diagnostic tests detect toxin A (enterotoxin) by enzyme immunoassay and toxin B (cytotoxin) by tissue culture assay, although an enzyme immunoassay that detects both toxins is available. The toxins glucosylate the guanosine triphosphate–binding Rho protein and lead to compromise of the intestinal barrier with protein-losing enteropathy[93] and recruitment of inflammatory cells.[352] Because these toxins cause inflammation and sometimes mucosal necrosis without bacterial invasion, watery diarrhea with or without blood in feces may occur.

Clostridium perfringens

Clostridium perfringens types A, C, and D produce an enterotoxin that is implicated in the pathogenesis of disease caused by this organism.[390] Most foodborne outbreaks are caused by type A strains. *C. perfringens* causes a short-duration food poisoning syndrome.[268, 277] After ingestion of contaminated meat or poultry products, in vivo sporulation occurs in the small intestine, with release of a structural spore protein that has enterotoxic and cytotoxic properties. The heat-labile, 35-kd, single-polypeptide enterotoxin induces fluid accumulation in ileal loops in animals and produces diarrhea in humans. Within 14 hours after ingesting contaminated food, patients experience watery diarrhea and abdominal pain with minimal nausea, vomiting, or fever ensuing. Illness resolves in less than 24 hours. Fewer than 5 percent of *C. perfringens* isolates contain the chromosomal *cpe* gene encoding this toxin. *C. perfringens* type C also is associated with a rare destructive intestinal disease called *enteritis necroticans* or *pig-bel*. These strains produce three toxins (alpha-toxin, beta-toxin, and an enterotoxin) of potential pathogenetic significance.[390] This illness occurs after ingestion of undercooked pig at pork feasts in Papua New Guinea. It is characterized by vomiting, abdominal pain, bloody diarrhea, and small bowel necrosis, with peritonitis, shock, and death.[299]

Escherichia coli

Several recognized categories of *E. coli* produce diarrhea[302, 390] (see Table 51–6). *E. coli* is among the most common cause of bacterial diarrhea in humans worldwide.[335]

STEC produces bloody diarrhea, usually without fever. This hemorrhagic colitis syndrome has been recognized to be caused most often by *E. coli* O157:H7 and other STEC strains, which produce large quantities of a potent cytotoxin[224, 302, 390] similar or identical to the cytotoxin produced by *S. dysenteriae* serotype 1.[224, 310] STEC also is referred to as enterohemorrhagic *E. coli* (EHEC) and verotoxin *E. coli* (VTEC).[351] Several closely related toxins are recognized. The *E. coli* toxin that essentially is identical to Shiga toxin made by *S. dysenteriae* is called Shiga toxin 1 (Stx1, also called verotoxin 1). A structurally and functionally related toxin that is distinct immunologically is called Stx2 (or verotoxin 2). Both toxins are encoded by bacteriophages. Multiple additional variants exist that are more closely related to the second toxin.[80] STEC lacks the 140-MDa (megadalton) plasmid that is associated with the invasiveness characteristic of enteroinvasive *E. coli* (EIEC), but STEC does possess a 60-MDa plasmid.[390] *E. coli* organisms that produce high levels of cytotoxin are important clinically because, like *S. dysenteriae* 1,[310] they have been incriminated as etiologic agents of hemolytic-uremic syndrome.[79, 223, 342] These pathogens often possess adherence genes related to those of enteropathic *E. coli* (EPEC).[39]

ETEC disease is caused by heat-stable (ST) and heat-labile (LT) enterotoxins.[302, 356, 390, 420] STa and LT-I are associated with disease in humans and other animals, whereas STb is associated primarily with disease in piglets, and LT-II has been associated only with animal disease. ETEC strains from humans with diarrhea produce STa only, LT-I only, or both together. These toxins often are produced by strains that have colonization factor antigens, which are important in adherence of the organism to the GI tract.[302] ETEC strains belong to many different serogroups and cause disease in patients of all ages, especially infants and children living in developing countries, travelers from developed to developing countries, and outbreaks of foodborne disease in the United States.[356, 420]

EIEC is related antigenically and biochemically to *Shigella*[73] and causes either a dysentery-like illness or watery diarrhea. EIEC possesses a 140-MDa plasmid, which encodes for invasiveness and which contributes to dysenteric illness. This plasmid is related closely to the plasmids that are associated with *Shigella* virulence.[302] The watery diarrhea may be due to an enterotoxin referred to as EIEC enterotoxin.[290] Infections generally occur in adults; foodborne outbreaks have been reported.[277]

EPEC has been incriminated as causing both sporadic and epidemic diarrhea in infants, especially in developing countries.[104, 302] Originally, EPEC was a term used to describe all *E. coli* organisms associated with diarrheal syndromes. Currently, the term EPEC is defined more narrowly. Volunteer studies[104] and studies comparing rates of isolation from sick and healthy infants[302] have demonstrated that EPEC organisms are pathogens, although these strains rarely cause diarrhea in older children and adults. The specific mechanisms involved in production of disease may be related to adherence, which can be demonstrated in Hep-2 cells.[36, 106, 302] EPEC adherence to microvilli is known to be encoded by a gene *bfp*A, which has homology to the pilin gene of *Vibrio cholerae*.[100, 105] Some strains currently classified as EPEC have an adhesin (AIDA-I) that causes the organisms to adhere to tissue culture cells in a diffuse pattern.[302] EPEC causes a distinctive histopathologic lesion in the human intestine that involves destruction of microvilli and close adherence of bacteria to the membrane of the enterocyte, with caplike pedestals on which each bacterium rests. The classic histopathologic lesion is called the *attaching-effacing lesion*. The genes responsible for this phenotype (*EspA, EspB, EspD, Tir,* and *EaeA*) have been defined.[100] F actin, myosin, and other cytoskeletal elements are clustered beneath the attached bacteria.[390]

EAEC has been associated with acute[270, 389] and chronic[44, 136] diarrhea in developing countries and in adults with travelers' diarrhea.[5, 156] Bloody diarrhea has been described in approximately one third of patients. Chronic persistent diarrhea is especially likely to be caused by EAEC.[386, 389] Pathogenicity of EAEC in humans has been confirmed in volunteer studies and outbreak investigations.[269, 402] EAEC is defined by its aggregative or stacked brick pattern of adherence in HEp-2 cell assays,[302] the gold standard for identification. Some strains elaborate an enterotoxin (EAEC ST enterotoxin 1 [EAST1]).[302, 385] However, this toxin is not uniquely present in EAEC nor found consistently (only 40–45% of EAEC pathogens are EAST1-positive in some series).[302, 386] A plasmid-encoded enterotoxin may be important, but its role is not fully defined.[133, 304] Many EAEC pathogens have genes for aggregative adherence fimbriae (*AAF/I* or *AAF/II*).[90, 300, 362] A gene probe that appeared in initial studies to be both sensitive and specific appears to be less useful than is the original HEp-2 cell assay.[136, 362] Virulence in the EAEC remains poorly understood.

Listeria monocytogenes

The genus *Listeria* includes six species, of which two are potentially pathogenic, *Listeria monocytogenes* and *Listeria ivanovii*.[435] *L. monocytogenes* causes serious localized and generalized infection in humans. Acute febrile gastroenteritis caused by *L. monocytogenes* contamination of a variety of foods has been described.[27, 67, 91, 227] The foods most frequently implicated are soft cheeses and dairy products; pâtés and sausages; smoked fish; and industrially produced, refrigerated, ready-to-eat products that are eaten without cooking or reheating. *L. monocytogenes* tolerates high concentrations of salt and relatively low pH and is able to multiply at refrigerator temperatures. Bacteremia may complicate diarrheal illness caused by this organism,[27, 67, 378] especially in immunocompromised hosts and during pregnancy. Symptoms include fever (temperature as high as 40.3° C), chills, headache, cramps, myalgia, and diarrhea.[27] The mechanism of gastroenteritis is not fully defined, but with completion of the sequencing of the genome of *L. monocytogenes,* clarification of the molecular pathogenesis will occur.

Plesiomonas shigelloides

Plesiomonas shigelloides is a gram-negative bacillus that has been associated with opportunistic infections in immunocompromised hosts and with sporadic cases of diarrhea in immunocompetent hosts in a variety of countries.[201, 220] In some case-control studies, the organism has been found to be associated with diarrhea, whereas in others, it has not.[9] Whether a subset of *P. shigelloides* has virulence genes that make them pathogens, whereas other members of this species do not have such genes, is unclear. Organisms produce ST and HL enterotoxins, but their associations with disease are unknown.[390] The organism has been isolated from surface water and the intestines of freshwater fish and many animals, including dogs and cats.[425] *Plesiomonas* occurs commonly in tropical and subtropical areas from which most stool isolates have been reported.[201] Patients with *P. shigelloides* infection describe self-limited diarrhea, occasionally characterized by blood and mucus. The organism is a rare cause of extraintestinal illness, such as meningitis or bacteremia.[220] Appropriate antimicrobial therapy appears to shorten the duration of diarrheal illness.[201, 220] The organism has failed to produce illness when fed to volunteers, and its role as an enteric pathogen remains unknown.[184]

Salmonella

Identifying *Salmonella* spp. in the laboratory is not difficult, but understanding the various terminologies used to classify *Salmonella* spp. is confusing. Most hospital laboratories biochemically differentiate *S.* ser. Enterica and *S.* ser. Typhi, although other nomenclature schemes may be used.[53] Several clinical syndromes are caused by *Salmonella*: (1) the carrier state; (2) acute gastroenteritis; (3) bacteremia, enteric fever, or both; and (4) dissemination with localized suppuration, such as abscess, osteomyelitis, or meningitis. Although *S.* ser. Typhi is the prototype of *Salmonella* able to penetrate intestinal mucosa, reach intestinal lymphatic tissue, and disseminate, other *Salmonella* organisms occasionally behave in this manner.[199, 400] Invasion of intestinal epithelium by *S.* ser. Typhi and occasionally by nontyphoidal *Salmonella* strains is a well-known virulence trait of *Salmonella* spp. Most nontyphoidal *Salmonella* serotypes are associated with watery diarrhea; the pathogenesis of the secretory response to *Salmonella* is not understood completely.[390] *Salmonella* rarely causes an illness similar to pseudomembranous colitis.[205] *Salmonella* gastroenteritis occurs throughout life but most commonly in the first year, decreases during early childhood, and remains relatively constant throughout the adult years.[69] Reptiles, including turtles, snakes, lizards, and iguanas, are vectors for certain serotypes of *Salmonella* and have been associated with episodes of salmonellosis.[3] Numerous outbreaks of disease caused by *Salmonella* have been reported after ingestion of contaminated food products, including eggs, milk, ice cream, and sprouts.[181, 277, 353, 355] Although *Salmonella* outbreaks in childcare centers rarely occur, an outbreak of fluoroquinolone-resistant *Salmonella* caused by person-to-person transmission in adults in two nursing homes and one hospital has been reported.[314]

Shigella

Four serogroups of *Shigella,* containing more than 40 serotypes and subtypes, exist.[229] *Shigella sonnei* currently is a more common cause of bacillary dysentery in the United States and Europe than is *Shigella flexneri,* whereas

Shigella boydii and *Shigella dysenteriae* are uncommon causes of diarrhea in the United States. Patients with *Shigella* isolated from stool may present with several clinical patterns: (1) asymptomatic excretion,[333] (2) enterotoxin-like watery diarrhea, (3) bacillary dysentery,[410] (4) an arthritis similar to that seen in Reiter syndrome,[8] and (5) hemolytic-uremic syndrome occurring after infection with *S. dysenteriae* 1. The arthritis occurs 2 to 5 weeks after the dysenteric illness, characteristically in patients with histocompatibility antigen HLA-B27. Postinfectious arthritis also occurs in patients after *Salmonella, Campylobacter,* and *Y. enterocolitica* infections.[123] The molecular mechanisms by which *Shigella* organisms invade epithelial cells have been defined.[160] *S. dysenteriae* 1 produces Shiga toxin in high levels.[310] Infection by *Shigella* spp. rarely occurs in the first few months of life but is a common occurrence in children between 6 months and 10 years of age.[69]

Staphylococcus aureus

Two enteric syndromes have been associated with *S. aureus*.[277] Although previously considered a cause of AAC, whether antibiotic-associated staphylococcal enteritis actually exists as a disease entity is unclear because most antibiotic-associated diarrhea is associated with *C. difficile*.[34] The existence of the other major staphylococcal enteric syndrome is well established. Staphylococcal food poisoning is caused by ingestion of food contaminated with preformed *S. aureus* ST enterotoxin.[126, 251] Although multiple enterotoxins (A to F) have been described, only enterotoxin types A to E cause enteric disease. Type A has been responsible for more than one half of the reported outbreaks of staphylococcal food poisoning in the United States.[200, 251] All toxins are antigenically related, low-molecular-weight proteins. Illness caused by these preformed toxins begins within 1 to 6 hours after ingestion and lasts less than 12 hours. Nausea, vomiting, abdominal pain, and diarrhea occur without fever.

Vibrio cholerae

Strains of *V. cholerae* are classified according to somatic or O groups. *V. cholerae* strains are separated further into two main serotypes (Ogawa and Inaba) and two biotypes (classic and El Tor).[221] *V. cholerae* responsible for epidemic cholera belong to serogroups O1 and O139; all other *V. cholerae* strains belong to serogroups other than O1 and O139 and occasionally cause diarrhea or extraintestinal infections.[209] Cholera affects people of all ages, but children are involved disproportionately. *V. cholerae* O139 is a problem primarily in Southeast Asia. *V. cholerae* O1 is a problem primarily in Asia, Africa, and South America, although a focus is present in the Gulf Coast of the United States.[221, 257] Most clinical isolates of *V. cholerae* O1 in the United States are associated with foreign travel and less frequently with undercooked seafood, and many are resistant to antimicrobial agents.[412] Epidemic cholera appeared in Peru in January 1991 and subsequently spread throughout the Americas, including the United States.[221] The epidemic strain is biotype El Tor, serotype Inaba. This strain can be differentiated from the strain of *V. cholerae* that is endemic to the U.S. Gulf Coast by production of hemolysin and by molecular subtyping techniques.

V. cholerae O1 adheres to and multiplies on small intestinal mucosa. Diarrhea occurs after elaboration of several toxins, the most important of which is cholera toxin, an HL enterotoxin composed of one A and five B subunits.[390] The B subunits bind the toxin to the terminal galactose of the GM_1 ganglioside receptors present on intestinal mucosal cells. The A subunit adenosine 5′-diphosphate ribosylates the guanosine 5′-triphosphate–binding regulatory protein of adenylate cyclase in gut epithelium.[390] The resulting intracellular increase in cyclic adenosine monophosphate causes inhibition of sodium absorption and causes chloride and fluid secretion in the small intestine. Most non-O1 strains isolated from ill people in the United States lack cholera toxin–like activity[209] and, when tested with gene probes, are found not to possess gene sequences homologous to those of cholera toxin.[221] Two additional toxins are produced by *V. cholerae,* Zot (zonula occludens toxin) and Ace (accessory cholera enterotoxin). Strains of *V. cholerae* belonging to serotypes other than O1 and O139 are much less significant pathogens, although they can cause mild and occasionally profuse, watery diarrhea. Other *Vibrio* spp., including *Vibrio fluvialis, Vibrio mimicus, Vibrio hollisae,* and *Vibrio furnissii,* have been shown occasionally to cause GI tract disease.[209]

Vibrio parahaemolyticus

Vibrio parahaemolyticus, a common marine isolate, has been found in water, shellfish, fish, and plankton.[193] Although widely distributed in coastal waters, *V. parahaemolyticus* is an uncommon cause of diarrhea where consumption of raw seafood is common.[277] Clinical manifestations of infection with *V. parahaemolyticus* are gastroenteritis in 59 percent and include abdominal cramps, nausea, and less frequently vomiting, headache, low-grade fever, and chills; wound infection in 34 percent; and septicemia in 5 percent.[92] A dysentery-like syndrome has been described in India and Bangladesh.[206] Preexisting liver disease predisposes infected patients to septicemia and death.[193] A selective culture medium is required for isolation of the organism from stool cultures. The pathophysiology of illness is uncertain, although a 23-kd protein called *thermostable-direct hemolysin* either is responsible for the disease or is linked closely to the virulence genes.[308]

Yersinia enterocolitica

Yersinia enterocolitica is a gram-negative bacillus that appears to be a common cause of gastroenteritis among children in Europe and Canada but is a relatively uncommon cause of enteritis in the United States,[1] where *Y. enterocolitica* O8 has been the predominant clinical serotype.[49] The ingestion of contaminated milk or food such as chitterlings[1, 247] has been implicated as the mode of transmission in reported outbreaks. The clinical manifestations vary depending on the age of the person involved. Illness in children younger than 5 years of age usually is self-limited gastroenteritis. Stools may contain blood and mucus or be watery. Associated symptoms consist of fever, vomiting, and abdominal pain. Older children may present with abdominal pain associated with mesenteric adenitis that mimics acute appendicitis. Adults develop diarrhea and abdominal pain less frequently than do children but may present with polyarthritis, arthralgia, or erythema nodosum. Patients with B-thalassemia and iron overload are at an increased risk for developing severe yersiniosis.[6] Disease is caused at least in part by production of an ST enterotoxin[49, 390] and by a 42- to 44-MDa plasmid encoding for invasiveness.

The role of other bacteria in enteric infection remains speculative. Although production of enterotoxin and other potential virulence properties has been described, *Klebsiella, Citrobacter,* and *Enterobacter* spp. and *Bacteroides fragilis* have not been proved to be diarrheal pathogens.

TABLE 51–7 ■ VIRUSES ASSOCIATED WITH GASTROENTERITIS

Virus	Approximate Size (nm)
Rotavirus	70
Enteric adenovirus (types 40 and 41)	70–80
Astrovirus	20–30
Calicivirus (noroviruses)	35–39
Parvovirus	20–30
Coronavirus	80–180
Pestivirus	40–60
Breda virus	100

VIRUSES

Acute infectious diarrhea of viral origin generally is a self-limited disease characterized by various combinations of diarrhea, nausea, vomiting, abdominal cramps, headaches, myalgias, and low-grade fever.[271, 273, 274, 284, 316, 431] Bowel movements are watery and generally do not contain mucus or blood. Vomiting is the most common manifestation of this condition. Rotavirus, enteric adenovirus, astrovirus, and calicivirus are common causes of viral gastroenteritis (Table 51–7). Other viruses, including coronaviruses, Breda virus, parvoviruses, pestiviruses, picobirnaviruses, and toroviruses, have been linked to gastroenteritis in humans with varying degrees of certainty.[37, 236, 461]

Rotaviruses

Rotavirus is a 70-nm particle that on electron microscopy resembles a wheel with radiating spokes (Fig. 51–1). Rotavirus first was associated with diarrhea in children by Bishop and associates in 1973.[46] Since then, human rotavirus has been established as a major cause of acute gastroenteritis in infants, children, and various animal species worldwide. Six antigenically distinct groups of rotavirus (A through F) have been recognized. Three of these groups (A, B, and C) have been identified in humans. The group A rotaviruses are those associated with infantile diarrhea.[135] Group B rotaviruses have caused epidemics of cholera-like illness in China and sporadic cases elsewhere.[302] Group C rotaviruses have caused outbreaks of diarrhea in children in many countries.[307]

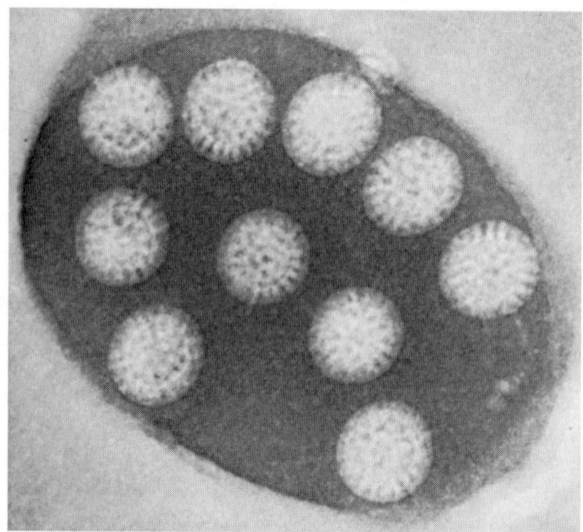

FIGURE 51–1 ■ Electron micrograph of virus particles in a fecal specimen from an infant with diarrhea. (Phosphotungstic acid, ×238,000.)

Group A rotaviruses have two outer capsid proteins, a hemagglutinin (VP4) and a glycoprotein (VP7), each of which induces neutralizing antibodies.[135] Fourteen different antigenic types of VP7 (which define serotype) and seven human serotypes of VP4 (also designated P serotypes because VP4 is protease sensitive), including two subtypes, are known. This number, combined with the ability of the gene segments to reassort independently, indicates that rotaviruses are complex antigenically.[135] In addition, rotaviruses encode an enterotoxin, NSP4, the pathophysiologic significance of which is uncertain.[29] Although 10 human rotavirus serotypes are known, VP7 (also designated G serotype) serotypes 1, 2, 3, 4 and 9 appear to be of epidemiologic importance. Epidemiologic studies indicate that these serotypes are endemic in most regions, that one serotype tends to be predominant at any particular time, that predominant serotypes differ among regions in the same country, and that predictable cycles of change of the predominant serotype may occur.[273]

Rotavirus gastroenteritis affects more than 90 percent of children by the time they are 3 years of age and may cause moderate to severe vomiting that precedes diarrhea. It accounts for 10 to 50 percent of the cases of diarrhea in children and is the most common cause of diarrhea in infants and children during winter months in colder climates. Rotavirus accounts for 35 to 50 percent of infants and young children hospitalized for acute diarrhea. In the United States, rotavirus accounts for 82,000 hospitalizations per year and 150 deaths.[272] Stools usually are watery or soft, and the presence of blood or leukocytes is rare. Asymptomatic rotavirus infections occur frequently,[316, 338] and reinfection appears to be a common event.[436, 437] The mechanism of spread is fecal to oral; whether respiratory transmission occurs is uncertain. Shedding of virus most frequently occurs from a few days before to 10 days after the onset of illness.[338] Rotavirus outbreaks in childcare centers occur commonly, usually in the colder months; are caused by a single serotype[316]; and are manifested by the fact that one half the infected children are asymptomatic.[31]

The incubation period of human rotavirus infection ranges from 2 to 4 days. Animal models suggest that whereas morphologic changes in the villous tip cells contribute to malabsorption and diarrhea, altered cell function, resulting in enzyme deficiencies, results from enterocyte immaturity and may account for the major part of the disordered physiologic findings. No specific therapy is available for children with rotavirus infection. The first rotavirus vaccine licensed in the United States was associated with an increased rate of intussusception, resulting in its withdrawal from the market within 14 months of being licensed.[297, 360] Other rotavirus vaccines are undergoing clinical trials.[282]

Astroviruses

Astroviruses, identified in 1975, are 20 to 30 nm in diameter and have a characteristic five- to six-pointed star. The virus genome is a positive-strand RNA of about 7500 nucleotides that encodes four structural proteins.[157, 442] Eight different antigenic types have been described. Astrovirus gastroenteritis occurs worldwide and has been associated with outbreaks of mild gastroenteritis in schools, childcare centers, pediatric wards, and nursing homes.[99, 157, 169, 284] Illness is restricted primarily to children and elderly people; 80 percent or more of adults have antibodies against the virus. The incubation period is 3 to 4 days.[157] Symptoms include fever and malaise, followed by watery diarrhea that may last approximately 3 days. Vomiting is an uncommon symptom. Short-term monosaccharide intolerance and more prolonged cow's milk protein intolerance have been reported after astrovirus infection.[157]

Caliciviruses

Caliciviruses include morphologically "typical" and "atypical" small, round-structured viruses that cause illness in both animals (AnCVs) and humans (HuCVs).[43, 158, 173] HuCVs cause mainly acute gastroenteritis. Multiple syndromes such as hemorrhagic pneumonia, hepatitis, abortion, mucosal infection, and gastroenteritis have been associated with AnCVs. Norwalk-like viruses (NLVs) are a group of morphologically similar but genetically and antigenically diverse HuCVs that belong in the family Calicivirida and are referred to as *noroviruses*.[212] Genetically, human NLVs can be divided into two genogroups. The NLV genogroups can be further divided into at least 15 genetic clusters based on the genetic relationships among different strains.[19] Clusters and representative strains have been identified by their genogroups and have been numbered consecutively on the basis of the date of their genetic analysis (e.g. GI/1: Norwalk virus, GI/2: Southampton virus). Many aspects of the viruses, such as host specificity, immunology, pathogenesis, and virus replication, remain unknown because HuCVs cannot be cultivated in cell culture or infect an animal model.

The major public health concern about HuCVs has been their ability to cause large outbreaks of gastroenteritis in all age groups.[165, 173] Such outbreaks usually have high attack rates and have occurred in schools, childcare centers, restaurants, summer camps, military troops, hospitals, nursing homes, hotels, and cruise ships.[168, 194, 213, 214, 359] Exposure to a common source of the virus, such as contaminated food or water, including ice, usually can be identified. Outbreaks resulting from consumption of uncooked shellfish are common occurrences. HuCVs also can be spread by person-to-person transmission. The syndrome of HuCV-associated gastroenteritis includes diarrhea, vomiting, nausea, abdominal cramps, fever, and malaise; diarrhea and vomiting occur most commonly.[173, 319]

Enteric Adenoviruses

Human adenoviruses of subgroups A to F have been identified as etiologic agents in a wide range of human diseases, including conjunctivitis, upper respiratory tract infections, and pneumonia. A subgroup of fastidious adenoviruses (group F) with a distinct set of antigenic determinants and specific tissue culture growth characteristics have been shown to be associated with acute gastroenteritis and are called *enteric adenoviruses*.[52, 240, 431] These agents fail to propagate in conventional cell lines used to grow adenoviruses but grow readily in 293 cells, an adenovirus type 5 transformed line.

The enteric adenoviruses in group F include serotypes 40 and 41.[240] Types 40 and 41 both appear to be widespread and endemic causes of diarrhea in children. Antibody prevalence to enteric adenovirus increases from 20 percent during the first 6 months of life to 50 percent or greater by the third or fourth year of life.[398] Seasonal shifts in the predominance of types 40 and 41, similar to those described for rotavirus, may occur. A 9-year study in Washington, D.C., found that enteric adenovirus types 40 and 41 circulate simultaneously all year.[52] Infection with enteric adenovirus appears to increase in the summer, although with a less marked seasonal variation than that exhibited by rotavirus, which peaks in the winter.[52] Outbreaks of enteric adenovirus diarrhea have been described in childcare centers where asymptomatic excretion is a common occurrence.[431]

PARASITES

The most important protozoa known to cause diarrhea in various populations in the United States are *Entamoeba histolytica, G. lamblia,* and spore-forming protozoa: *Cryptosporidium parvum, Isospora belli, Microsporidium* spp. *(Encephalitozoon intestinalis* and *Enterocytozoon bieneusi),* and *Cyclospora cayetanensis.* Among helminths, *Strongyloides stercoralis* and *Trichuris trichiura* may produce diarrhea. Data associating *Ascaris* or hookworm with diarrhea are lacking, but both cause abdominal pain. HIV infections have stimulated renewed interest in several of these organisms, including various *Microsporidium* spp., *C. parvum,* and *Isospora belli.*[109, 162, 163] The roles of *Blastocystis hominis, Balantidium coli,* and *Dientamoeba fragilis* as causes of diarrhea are not known. With the onset of AIDS and further development of diagnostic techniques, intestinal protozoa have emerged as major pathogens of the intestinal tract.[162]

Cryptosporidium

Cryptosporidium organisms are coccidian protozoa that invade and replicate within the microvillous region of epithelial cells lining the digestive and respiratory tracts of vertebrates.[76] *Cryptosporidium* spp. are related taxonomically to *Toxoplasma, Sarcocystis, Isospora,* and *Plasmodium* spp. A review of 38 studies that evaluated patients with diarrhea reported an overall *Cryptosporidium* prevalence of 2.1 percent in industrialized nations and 8.5 percent in developing nations.[88] Children 6 to 24 months of age appear to be at a particularly high risk for acquiring this organism.[243] Cryptosporidia have been implicated as a cause of diarrhea in travelers and of epidemics in hospitals, childcare centers, and other institutional settings worldwide.[89, 234, 267] Other groups at risk include animal handlers, travelers to foreign countries with a high prevalence of *Cryptosporidium,* and hospital personnel.[89, 111, 234, 267] Person-to-person transmission probably is the principal route of infection, although water also is important in transmission. The largest waterborne outbreak of diarrhea documented in the United States was caused by *Cryptosporidium.*[259] Volunteer studies in adults showed that 132 oocysts cause disease.[118] The incubation period in humans has been estimated to be 2 to 14 days.

Cryptosporidiosis can manifest with a wide spectrum of symptoms, including asymptomatic excretion, acute diarrhea, chronic diarrhea, epidemic diarrhea, severe life-threatening watery diarrhea, and biliary tract disease.[76, 243] Watery diarrhea is the hallmark of symptomatic infections, but few, if any, features distinguish gastroenteritis caused by *Cryptosporidium* in the immunocompetent patient from other enteric infections. Stools do not contain blood or leukocytes. Vomiting, flatulence, abdominal pain, and low-grade fever routinely accompany diarrhea.[176] Symptoms usually subside in an average of 9 days. Patients may have cholera-like illness, transient diarrhea, relapsing episodes, or a protracted clinical course with unremitting, profuse diarrhea lasting for months accompanied by profound malabsorption and weight loss. Enteritis caused by *Cryptosporidium* occurs in 10 to 15 percent of patients with AIDS in the United States and approximately 15 percent of patients with AIDS in the developing world.[264] The frequency with which *Cryptosporidium* and microsporidia are identified in stools of patients with AIDS is a reflection of the CD4 count, with identification of the organisms and symptoms being more frequent when the count is less than 100 cells/µL.[143] Antiretroviral therapy is protective against disease.[58, 264] Biliary tract infection with *Cryptosporidium* produces two syndromes: sclerosing cholangitis-type lesions that cause progressive, irregular obstruction and dilation of the intrahepatic and extrahepatic bile ducts[41] and acalculous cholecystitis caused by infection of the wall of the gallbladder.[191] Symptoms have been characterized by right upper quadrant pain, nausea, and vomiting. Pancreatitis and appendicitis also have been reported in association with *Cryptosporidium* infection.[109, 287]

Entamoeba histolytica

The life cycle of *Entamoeba histolytica* involves encystment of a trophozoite, followed by release of the trophozoite from the cyst under appropriate conditions in the GI tract.[134, 329] (Fig. 51–2) The trophozoites vary in size and are found in stools of patients with dysentery or diarrhea. The cyst is more resistant to environmental stresses and is the infective stage. Cysts are found more frequently in formed stools. The minimum period between ingestion of cysts and development of symptoms is 8 days. The incubation period ranges up to 95 days.

Certain distinct species of *Entamoeba* are morphologically identical. *Entamoeba dispar* is the more prevalent species and is associated solely with an asymptomatic carrier state. *E. histolytica,* the pathogenic species,[134] can invade intestinal mucosa, spread to other organs, and cause symptomatic disease. Species can be differentiated by zymodemes (patterns of electrophoretic mobility of certain parasitic isoenzymes), RNA and DNA probes, and antigen-detection tests such as enzyme immunoassay.[175, 329]

The clinical patterns that occur in patients with amebiasis consist of (1) *intestinal amebiasis*, with the gradual onset of colicky abdominal pain and frequent bowel movements, tenesmus, and little or no constitutional disturbance; (2) *amebic dysentery*, characterized by profuse diarrhea containing blood and mucus and the presence of constitutional signs, such as fever, dehydration, and electrolyte alterations; (3) *hepatic amebiasis*, which usually presents as abscess formation without GI tract symptoms[7]; and (4) *asymptomatic excretion*. Patients may experience tender hepatomegaly, jaundice, weight loss, fever, and anorexia. The frequency of liver abscess in patients with amebiasis is between 1 and 5 percent. The complications of intestinal amebiasis include perforation, ameboma, stricture, hemorrhage secondary to erosion into a blood vessel, intussusception, ischiorectal abscess, fistulas, and rectal prolapse. People in the third through fifth decades of life have the highest incidence of infection and clinical symptoms, although people of all ages are susceptible.

Giardia lamblia

G. lamblia, a flagellated protozoan, is an important cause of diarrhea, particularly in certain high-risk populations and in people who travel to hyperendemic areas.[66] Children appear to be more susceptible to *Giardia* than are adults. Conditions other than age that predispose to giardiasis are hypogammaglobulinemia, secretory immunoglobulin A (IgA) deficiency, peptic ulcer disease, biliary tract disease, and pancreatitis. The parasite may exist in two forms: cyst and trophozoite (Fig. 51–3). After being ingested, each cyst divides into two trophozoites, which subsequently mature. The trophozoites usually are seen in duodenal aspirates and loose stools, whereas cysts can be found in formed stools and can remain viable and infectious in water for longer than 3 months.

Individuals vary in their response to infection with *Giardia,* with the following clinical manifestations: (1) asymptomatic; (2) an acute illness with a sudden onset of explosive, watery, foul-smelling stools, flatulence, abdominal distention, nausea, anorexia, and the absence of blood and mucus; and (3) chronic diarrhea and malabsorption, with exacerbations and remissions of flatulence, abdominal distention, and abdominal pain often lasting for months.[339]

Strongyloides stercoralis

Strongyloides stercoralis is a nematode that infects humans through the intestinal tract or through skin if either comes in contact with soil that contains the larvae. About one third of people with strongyloidiasis are asymptomatic, and the remainder may have skin, pulmonary, or, more frequently, GI tract involvement.[399] People at risk include residents and travelers to endemic areas; natives and residents of the Appalachian region in the United States; institutionalized patients; and people treated with corticosteroids, cimetidine, and antacids.[152] Epigastric abdominal pain occurs and is associated with diarrhea that contains mucus and blood. Some patients may complain of nausea, vomiting, and weight loss with evidence of malabsorption. Eosinophilia and an urticarial rash are prominent features of infection. People infected with *S. stercoralis* should be treated with ivermectin or thiabendazole in an attempt to eradicate the infection.[278]

Isospora belli

Isospora was established as a cause of diarrhea in humans in the early 1900s, when sporadic cases of isosporiasis and a

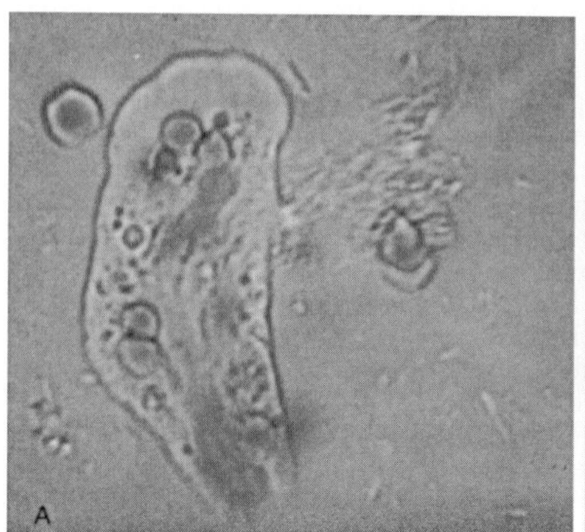

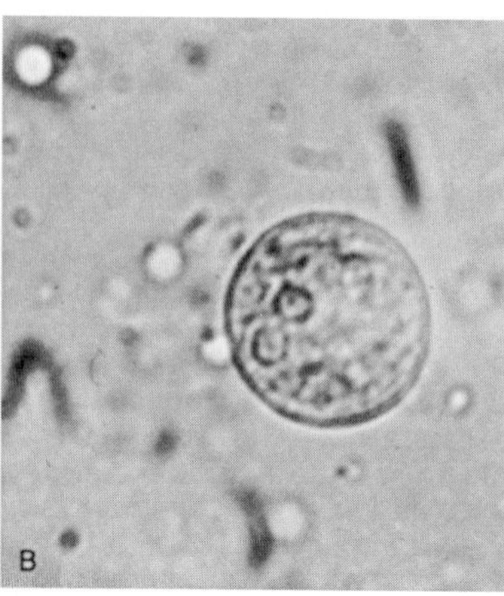

FIGURE 51–2 ■ *A,* Trophozoite of *Entamoeba histolytica* with ingested material in the cytoplasm. *B,* Cyst of *E. histolytica* seen in a merthiolate-iodine-formalin–stained preparation from a stool specimen. Note two visible nuclei. (×1000.) (From DuPont, H. L., and Pickering, L. K.: Infections of the Gastrointestinal Tract. New York, Plenum Publishing, 1980.)

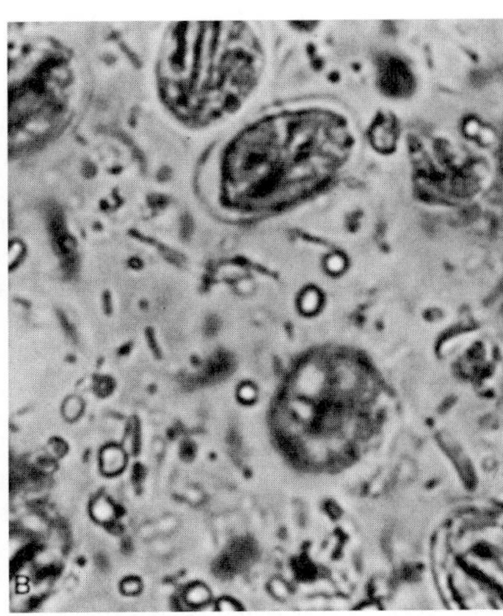

FIGURE 51–3 ■ *A,* Trophozoites of *Giardia lamblia* seen in a merthiolate-iodine-formalin–stained preparation of stool from a patient with diarrhea. (×1000.) *B,* Cysts of *G. lamblia* seen in a merthiolate-iodine-formalin–stained preparation of stool from a patient without diarrhea. (×1000.)

few clinical series were reported in the medical literature.[103] *I. belli* has gained importance with the advent of AIDS and has been shown to be an important cause of severe and prolonged gastroenteritis.[321] Humans are the only known host for *I. belli,* but the actual prevalence of this parasite is unknown. Infection can occur in adults and children and has been reported in infants with severe diarrhea.[254] *Isospora* has been encountered in 15 percent of patients with AIDS in Haiti and in 0.2 percent in the United States, although the true prevalence in this population is unknown. This organism also has been implicated as a cause of travelers' diarrhea.[154]

Transmission is fecal-oral from one human to another, but the infective dose in humans is unknown. Oocysts may be present in stools for as long as 120 days after infection. No animal reservoir of *I. belli* has been documented. Transmission is thought to occur by ingestion of oocysts contaminating food, water, or environmental surfaces.[254] *I. belli* oocysts are resistant to commonly used disinfectants and may remain viable for months in a cool, moist environment.

The clinical spectrum of disease caused by *Isospora* is indistinguishable from that described for *Cryptosporidium.* The spectrum includes asymptomatic infection, acute diarrhea in children in developing countries, and chronic diarrhea or severe protracted life-threatening diarrhea in patients with AIDS. Infection of the biliary tract in patients with AIDS by *Isospora* has been associated with acalculous cholecystitis.[40] The incubation period was 8 to 14 days in four subjects who had been exposed to the organism in the laboratory.[180] Fever, malaise, abdominal pain, and headache all have been reported. Stools are watery and do not contain blood or leukocytes. Malabsorption, steatorrhea, severe weight loss, and chronic diarrhea lasting months to years are most likely occurrences in immunocompromised hosts.[97]

Microsporidia

Microsporidia are ubiquitous, spore-forming, intracellular protozoal parasites that cause disease in a wide range of vertebrate and invertebrate hosts.[238] More than 100 genera of microsporidia have been identified. The nontaxonomic term *human microsporidia* can refer to any of the microsporidia known to cause disease in humans: *Enterocytozoon* spp., *Encephalitozoon* spp., *Pleistophora* spp., and *Nosema* spp. Of these, *Enterocytozoon bieneusi* and *Encephalitozoon intestinalis* (formerly *Septata intestinalis)* are the most important in GI tract disease of humans.[25, 145, 446] Most cases of microsporidia-related infections have occurred in patients with AIDS. Infections with these organisms have been documented in immunocompetent and immunosuppressed people from Africa, Asia, Europe, and North and South America.[394]

In animals, transmission occurs by ingestion of spores shed into the environment. The person-to-person fecal-oral route may play a role in transmission, and waterborne disease occurs.[87] The clinical spectrum appears to depend on the immune status of the host. *E. bieneusi* and *E. intestinalis* have been detected in intestinal biopsy specimens of patients with AIDS, with a clinical picture of prolonged diarrhea and weight loss.[87, 145] The primary location of all intestinal spore-forming protozoal infection is the small intestine, but colonic infection has been reported with *E. bieneusi.*[162] Infection of the biliary tract with *E. bieneusi* and *E. intestinalis* in patients with AIDS can cause sclerosing cholangitis-type lesions[350, 397, 453] and acalculous cholecystitis caused by infection of the wall of the gallbladder.[145] *E. intestinalis* can infect lamina propria macrophages, fibroblasts, and endothelial cells and can disseminate to other organs, including liver, respiratory tract, and kidney.[162, 453] Extraintestinal infection occurs after infection with other species of microsporidia.[145]

Cyclospora

Cyclospora cayetanensis (formerly cyanobacteria or blue-green algae–like bodies) is a coccidian protozoa that first was diagnosed as causing infection in humans in 1977.[317] *Cyclospora* is transmitted by the fecal-oral route; direct person-to-person transmission is unlikely to occur because excreted oocysts require days to weeks under favorable environmental conditions to sporulate and become infectious. An animal reservoir has not been described. Outbreaks of diarrhea caused by consumption of water and fresh fruits contaminated with *Cyclospora* have been described,[65, 185, 186, 260] and travelers to developing countries are at increased risk for developing diarrhea caused by *Cyclospora.*[315, 322] Most of the reported cases have occurred during the spring and summer. The mean incubation period appears to be 7 days. Clinical manifestations include asymptomatic excretion, acute watery diarrhea, and diarrhea that may be protracted from days to weeks with frequent, watery stools, which may remit and relapse.

Diagnosis

Determining the cause of an episode of acute infectious diarrhea depends on epidemiologic information, the clinical syndrome, laboratory tests, and knowledge or assessment of an organism for virulence factors. Because virulence properties determine clinical manifestations of disease, an understanding of pathophysiologic mechanisms guides the laboratory evaluation and empiric therapy. The major virulence properties of enteropathogens include adherence; production of enterotoxin, cytoskeleton-altering toxin, cytotoxin, and toxins with neural activity; and epithelial cell invasion.[390] Certain enteropathogens may produce diarrhea by other mechanisms, and enteric pathogens may possess one or several of these virulence properties (Table 51–8).

Enterotoxins are bacterial products that act on the mucosal epithelium of the small intestine, causing fluid secretion and profuse watery diarrhea without intestinal damage, so that stools are devoid of blood and leukocytes. Fluid secretion is related to enzymatic effect on intestinal cells, often through specific receptors, and increased cyclic nucleotide levels.[292] The prototype is cholera toxin produced by *V. cholerae,* which causes adenosine diphosphate ribosylation of an adenylate cyclase regulatory protein, leading to an increase in intracellular cyclic adenosine monophosphate, causing active fluid secretion and inhibition of reabsorption of salt and water. Immunologically and functionally similar HL enterotoxins are produced by *E. coli* and other enteric pathogens (see Table 51–8). Other enterotoxins produced by *E. coli, Y. enterocolitica,* and other enteric pathogens are called ST enterotoxins. These ST enterotoxins activate guanylate cyclase. Other enterotoxins act by independent mechanisms that have not been characterized.[390] Bacterial toxins are the sole cause of disease only occasionally; more frequently, they must act in concert with other virulence factors of bacteria, such as adherence mechanisms.[302]

Cytotoxins are defined by their ability to produce cell or tissue damage, usually resulting in cell death, by inhibiting protein synthesis. Cytotoxic activity is demonstrated in vitro by its effects on cells in tissue culture.[80] In vivo cytotoxins cause damage to intestinal epithelial cells and destruction of normal absorptive mechanisms, which result in intestinal hemorrhage and diarrhea containing blood. Fluid loss probably is related to impaired absorption. Unlike enterotoxins, cytotoxins do not cause active fluid secretion by the gut, nor do they leave the gut undamaged. The prototype of this group of toxins is Shiga toxin, which is produced mainly by *S. dysenteriae* serotype 1.[30, 306, 310] Functionally, immunologically, and structurally, closely related toxins (e.g., Shiga toxins 1 and 2) are produced by certain serotypes of *E. coli.* This group of toxins has been implicated in hemorrhagic colitis and plays a role in the pathogenesis of the hemolytic-uremic syndrome.[80, 223] Production of cytotoxin has been demonstrated in other pathogens, but most of them are not well characterized, and their roles in human disease need to be clarified[390] (see Table 51–8).

TABLE 51–8 ■ VIRULENCE CHARACTERISTICS OF ENTEROPATHOGENS

Organisms	Virulence Properties
Bacteria	
Aeromonas	Heat stable (ST) and heat labile (LT) enterotoxins
Bacillus cereus	Emetic toxin, diarrhea-associated enterotoxin
Campylobacter jejuni	Invasion, LT, cytotoxin, adherence
Clostridium difficile	Cytotoxin and enterotoxin
Clostridium perfringens type A	Cytotoxin
Clostridium perfringens type C	Cytotoxins (beta, alpha)
Escherichia coli	
Shiga toxin producing	Shigatoxins 1 or 2; adherence and effacing lesion
Enteropathogenic	Adherence with production of attaching and effacing lesion
Enterotoxigenic	LT, ST, adherence
Enteroinvasive	Invasion, cytotoxin
Enteroaggrative	Adherence, ST and LT toxins
Listeria monocytogenes	Invasion
Plesiomonas shigelloides	LT, ST
Salmonella	Invasion, LT, complement resistance
Shigella dysenteriae 1	Invasion, Shigatoxin
Other *Shigella*	Invasion, shigella enterotoxin (*S. flexneri*)
Staphylococcus aureus	Enterotoxins A to E, delta toxin
Vibrio cholerae	Cholera toxin, hemolysin, adherence, zona occludens toxin, accessory cholera enterotoxin
Vibrio parahaemolyticus	Thermostable direct hemolysin
Yersinia enterocolitica	ST, invasion
Parasites	
Cryptosporidium	Invade intestinal epithelial cells
Cyclospora cayetanensis	Invade intestinal epithelial cells
Encephalitozoon intestinalis	Invade intestinal epithelial and subepithelial cells
Entamoeba histolytica	Invasion, enzyme and cytotoxin production
Enterocytozoon bieneusi	Invade intestinal epithelial cells
Giardia lamblia	Adhere to mucosa by ventral suckers
Isospora belli	Invade intestinal epithelial cells
Strongyloides stercoralis	Invade intestinal epithelium with inflammatory reaction
Viruses	
Rotavirus, astrovirus, calicivirus, enteric adenovirus	Mucosal lesion, destruction of absorptive cells (villus tip cells)

Another class of enteric toxins is the cytoskeleton-altering toxins, which produce an alteration in cell shape without inducing significant cell injury, most often because of rearrangement of F actin. These toxins may be associated with evidence of net secretion in vitro or in vivo intestinal cell models of disease.[390] Many organisms, including *Aeromonas* spp., *C. jejuni, C. difficile,* EPEC, STEC, ETEC, *P. shigelloides, Salmonella* spp., *Shigella* spp., and *V. cholerae,* produce toxins with cytoskeleton-altering properties.[390]

Enteric bacteria also may produce toxins with neural activity. At least part of the secretory activity of these toxins is attributable to the release of one or more neurotransmitters from the enteric nervous system, or the toxin alters smooth muscle activity in the intestine.[166] No enteric toxin has been shown to stimulate secretion only through neural mechanisms. Organisms shown to have neural activity include *C. difficile,* ETEC, *S. aureus,* and *V. cholerae.*[390]

Invasiveness is another virulence trait of some bacteria. Bacterial invasion of GI tract epithelium is characterized clinically by fever, abdominal pain, tenesmus, and stools containing blood, mucus, and fecal leukocytes.[334] *Shigella* spp. invade and destroy epithelial cells of the GI tract, causing diffuse or focal colitis. The invasiveness of *Shigella* and EIEC is encoded by 120- to 140-MDa plasmids. Salmonella possess virulence genes closely related to those that endow shigella with invasiveness.[177, 178, 462, 463] After invading through Peyer patches, salmonella pass through gut epithelium, often with little mucosal damage to the lamina propria, where they elicit a chemotactic response resulting in an influx of polymorphonuclear leukocytes. Further invasion, resulting in systemic infection, is an infrequent occurrence, except in immunocompromised hosts and in infections caused by *S. typhi, S. paratyphi,* and *S. choleraesuis*. These organisms reach the lamina propria and elicit an influx of macrophages, which ingest the *Salmonella* organisms, drain into the mesenteric lymph nodes, and reach the bloodstream through the lymphatic system.[411] *V. parahaemolyticus* also is thought to be invasive.[209] The pathology of *Campylobacter* colitis suggests invasiveness as well as production of enterotoxin as a mechanism of disease. The fact that pathogenic *Y. enterocolitica* organisms cause a dysentery-like illness suggests invasiveness as a virulence mechanism.

Adherence, the ability of organisms to attach to and colonize gut epithelium, is the least specific virulence property in terms of associated clinical findings. The ability of ETEC to adhere to and colonize the upper small intestine in order to cause disease by production of enterotoxin has been described.[302] This capacity for adherence has been related to fimbria such as K88, K99, or multiple colonization factor antigens for piglet, calf, and human strains, respectively. The production of these adherence antigens appears to be coded genetically by transmissible plasmids.[457] These fimbriated colonization factor antigen adhesins are distinct from type 1 pili and cause mannose-resistant hemagglutination in the laboratory. *V. cholerae* organisms adhere to intestinal mucosa in the same manner. EPEC organisms are examples in which adherence appears to be a major pathogenic mechanism. EPEC colonizes the small intestine and causes a diarrheal syndrome that tends to be chronic.[77] The loss of absorptive microvillous surface that occurs with adherence of EPEC partially may explain the resulting diarrhea[368] (Fig. 51–4). EAEC also adheres and causes diarrhea without enteroinvasion.[300] The enteric protozoal pathogens adhere to and invade enterocytes and may cause symptoms of chronic malabsorption.[162]

Many enteric pathogens produce diarrhea by several mechanisms. For example, production of enterotoxin and cytotoxin occurs commonly among organisms that are invasive. Thus, shigellosis may have an early secretory diarrheal phase and a late dysenteric phase. Both host and microbiologic factors ultimately determine clinical expression in the individual patient. Not all of the recognized virulence properties of a given species are obvious clinically in each episode of disease. *Salmonella* infection, for example, may manifest clinically as mild or severe watery diarrhea with or without dysenteric symptoms.

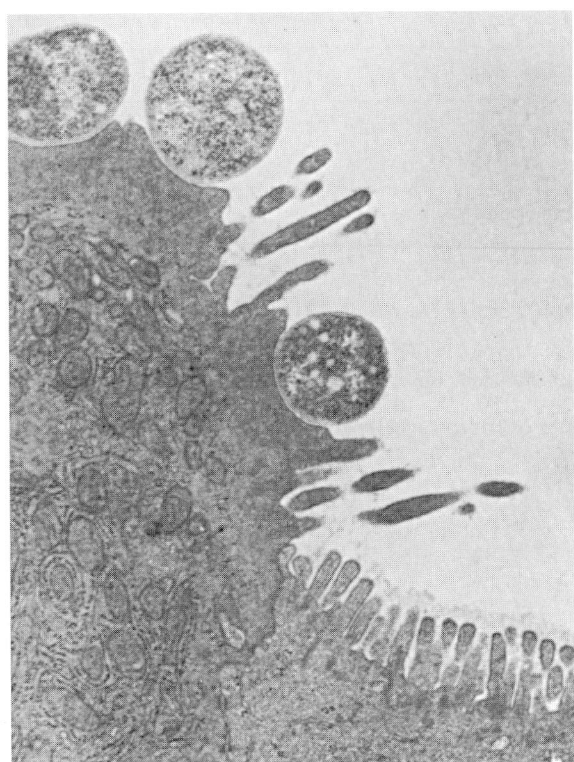

FIGURE 51–4 ■ Electron micrograph of three *Escherichia coli* organisms adherent to enterocytes that have lost their microvilli and formed pedestals on which the bacteria lie. (×25,000.) (Courtesy of Dr. R. J. Rothbaum.)

Laboratory Evaluation

Proper identification of the causative agent of an episode of acute infectious diarrhea will help facilitate initiating appropriate therapy. A gross examination of the stool specimen should be routine in all patients with diarrhea, even if no laboratory studies are performed. Diarrheal stool that is watery and without mucus or blood usually is caused by an enterotoxin, virus, or protozoan organism, or it may be caused by infection outside the GI tract. The color of stools generally conveys little information if the stool does not contain blood. Infectious causes to be considered when stools contain blood or mucus include a cytotoxin-producing bacteria; an enteroinvasive bacteria causing mucosal inflammation; or an enteric parasite associated with blood in stools, such as *E. histolytica, B. coli,* and *T. trichiura.* When present, blood usually is mixed evenly into the stool, except in the case of *E. histolytica* infections, in which blood often is on the surface of the stool, and some STEC infections, in which the stool may be blood streaked. Stools that are particularly foul smelling are consistent with *Salmonella* and other bacteria as well as *Giardia, Cryptosporidium,*

TABLE 51–9 ■ LABORATORY TESTS USED TO DETECT ENTEROPATHOGENS

Laboratory Tests	Organisms Suggested or Identified
Microscopic examination of stool	
Fecal leukocytes	Invasive or cytotoxin-producing bacteria
Trophozoites, cysts, oocysts, or spores	*Giardia lamblia, Entamoeba histolytica, Cryptosporidium, Isospora belli, Cyclospora, Enterocytozoon bieneusi, Encephalitozoon intestinalis*
Rhabditiform larva	*Strongyloides*
Spiral or S-shaped gram-negative bacilli	*Campylobacter jejuni/coli*
Stool culture	
Standard	*Escherichia coli, Shigella, Salmonella, Campylobacter jejuni*
Special	*Yersinia enterocolitica, Vibrio cholerae, Vibrio parahaemolyticus, Clostridium difficile, E. coli* O157: H7, *Listeria monocytogenes*
Stool cytotoxicity assay	*C. difficile*
Enzyme immunoassay or latex agglutination	Rotavirus, *G. lamblia, Cryptosporidium*, enteric adenovirus, *C. difficile*, STEC, *E. histolytica*
Serotyping	*E. coli* O157: H7 and other STEC, enteropathogenic *E. coli*
Latex agglutination after broth enrichment	*Salmonella, Shigella*
Tests performed in research laboratories	Toxin-producing bacteria, small round viruses, invasive *E. coli*, EAEC, gene probe or polymerase chain reaction for virulence genes

STEC, Shiga toxin–producing *E. coli*; EAEC, enteroaggregative *E. coli*.

and *Strongyloides* spp. Stools with little odor suggest an enterotoxin, such as cholera toxin or ST/HL *E. coli* or a viral enteropathogen. Laboratory tests used to detect enteropathogens are listed in Tables 51–9 and 51–10.

MICROSCOPIC EXAMINATION

Microscopic examination of stool specimens for evidence of fecal leukocytes provides information concerning the cause of diarrhea and helps to determine the anatomic location and presence of mucosal inflammation. Fecal leukocytes are produced in response to bacteria that diffusely invade the colonic mucosa and indicate that the patient has colitis. No inflammatory bacterial enteritis exists in which results of the fecal leukocyte examination are uniformly positive.[190] Thus, results of examination are more helpful when positive than when negative. When results are positive, the patient likely has an invasive or cytotoxin-producing organism, such as *Shigella, Salmonella,* or *Campylobacter* spp., invasive *E. coli,* STEC, *C. difficile,* or *Y. enterocolitica,* although ulcerative colitis and Crohn disease also are associated with fecal leukocytes. Fecal leukocytes generally are not present in stools from patients with diarrhea secondary to viruses, enterotoxin-producing bacteria, or parasites. The leukocytes seen in cytotoxin-associated and invasive bacterial diarrhea syndromes are polymorphonuclear leukocytes. The exception is infection by *S. typhi,* in which the leukocytes are mononuclear. If the fecal leukocyte examination shows evidence of inflammatory enteritis, further laboratory evaluation is indicated. The fecal lactoferrin assay has been shown to be a more accurate test than are fecal leukocytes or occult blood in patients with inflammatory diarrhea.[207]

Normally, examining stools for ova and parasites is unnecessary unless the patient has a history of recent travel to high-risk areas, stool cultures are negative for other enteropathogens, the patient is involved in an outbreak of diarrhea, diarrhea persists for longer than 1 week, or the patient is immunosuppressed. *G. lamblia* and *S. stercoralis* can be visualized microscopically in stools, duodenal fluid, and small intestinal biopsy material. Both trophozoites and cysts of *G. lamblia* and larvae of *Strongyloides* spp. can be identified on direct smears of stool specimens (see Fig. 51–3); however, the sensitivity of stool examination for most parasites can be improved by using a concentration technique and by placing stools in vials containing polyvinyl alcohol or 10 percent formalin. Trichrome and iron hematoxylin both are useful as permanent stains for *Giardia* spp. An advantage of trichrome is that it may be used in polyvinyl alcohol–preserved specimens. Pooling of preserved fecal samples is an efficient and economical procedure for detection of ova and parasites.[11]

For patients in whom giardiasis, cryptosporidiosis, isosporiasis, or strongyloidiasis is considered and in whom stools are negative, aspiration or biopsy of the duodenum or upper jejunum may be indicated. Because these organisms live in the upper intestine, this procedure is more reliable than is examination of stool specimens.[364] Duodenal biopsy is a sensitive and specific method of diagnosing giardiasis, strongyloidiasis, and spore-forming protozoa. Small intestinal biopsy should be considered in patients with characteristic clinical symptoms, negative stool and duodenal fluid specimens, and one of the following: abnormal radiographic findings such as edema and segmentation in the small intestine, abnormal lactose tolerance test results, absent secretory IgA, hypogammaglobulinemia, achlorhydria, AIDS, or severe malabsorptive diarrhea with weight loss. Electron microscopic examination of tissue sections may be useful in identifying fine structures of a parasite (Fig. 51–5).

Medications, including antibiotics, antacids, antidiarrheal compounds, and certain enema and laxative preparations, as well as contrast material for radiographic studies, can interfere with identification of an organism by altering morphology or causing a temporary disappearance of parasites from stool specimens. Patients should not receive these compounds for 48 to 72 hours before collection of stool for testing. *G. lamblia* and *Cryptosporidium* antigens in feces can be detected by use of one of several rapid and sensitive diagnostic tests.[149, 233]

E. histolytica can be diagnosed by microscopic examination of fresh stool specimens or bowel wall scrapings for cysts or trophozoites (see Fig. 51–2). A concentration technique may be helpful in demonstrating amebic cysts. Examination of several stool samples by an experienced technician may be necessary because excretion of cysts often is intermittent and making an interpretation is difficult. Confusion in differentiating amebic cysts from fecal leukocytes may occur. Microscopy can be used only as presumptive evidence of *E. histolytica* because the nonpathogen *E. dispar* is morphologically identical.[134] Monoclonal antibody–based enzyme immunoassays and polymerase chain reaction (PCR) can distinguish the pathogenic from commensal ameba.[283]

TABLE 51–10 ■ LABORATORY EVALUATION OF PATIENTS WITH PRESUMED BACTERIAL DIARRHEA

Organism	Tests
Aeromonas hydrophila	Screen colonies grown on MacConkey agar for positive oxidase test Culture on modified blood agar
Bacillus cereus	Culture food (>10^5 organisms/g), demonstrate enterotoxin in food and stool by enzyme immunoassay
Campylobacter jejuni	Stool culture using special media incubated at 42° C with 5% O_2 and 10% CO_2 Gram stain for "gull wing," like organisms, and fecal leukocytes; darkfield or phase contrast of stool for organisms with darting motility Nucleic acid probe Serology
Clostridium difficile	Culture feces anaerobically on cycloserine-cefoxitin-fructose agar Demonstrate toxins in stool by enzyme immunoassay or tissue culture cytotoxicity with neutralization with antitoxin
Clostridium perfringens	Culture food (>10^5 organisms/g) and feces; stools can be tested for enterotoxin Serotype organism
Escherichia coli	Standard stool culture for initial isolation
ETEC	
Stable toxin	Suckling mouse assay Gene probe hybridization assay
Labile toxin	Rabbit ileal loop Y-1 adrenal or Chinese hamster ovary cell assay Gene probe hybridization assay GM1, enzyme immunoassay
EPEC	Serogroup, gene probe assay Small bowel biopsy for routine microscopy and electron microscopy
EIEC	Gene probe assay Biologic assays for invasiveness (Serény or HeLa cell)
STEC	MacConkey sorbitol agar for O157:H7 Gene probe or polymerase chain reaction to detect toxin gene sequences Serotyping Toxin enzyme immunoassay Free/cytotoxin in stool by enzyme immunoassay or tissue culture Serologic responses to verotoxins or lipopolysaccharide of *E.coli* O157
EAEC	HEp-2 adherence assay, DNA probes
Listeria monocytogenes	Culture on blood agar
Plesiomonas shigelloides	Culture
Salmonella species	Standard stool culture; blood, bone marrow, and urine cultures if disseminated Serotype
Shigella species	Examine stool for fecal leukocytes Standard stool culture
Staphylococcus aureus	Culture food and skin lesions of food handlers Phage type Demonstrate enterotoxin in food, stool, and vomitus
Vibrio cholerae	Culture feces on thiosulfate citrate bile salt agar Serotype
Vibrio parahaemolyticus	Culture feces on thiosulfate citrate bile salt agar Test for Kanagawa reaction (beta-hemolysis on Wagatsuma agar), which is a marker for pathogenicity
Yersinia enterocolitica	Standard stool culture with cold enrichment; blood culture if disseminated Serology Lack of rhamnose fermentation by toxin-producing strains Suckling mouse assay for stable toxin

EAEC, enteroaggregative *E. coli*; STEC, Shiga toxin–producing *E. coli*; EIEC, enteroinvasive *E. coli*; EPEC, enteropathogenic *E. coli*; ETEC, enterotoxigenic *E. coli*.

Numerous serologic tests for amebiasis to detect different types and antibodies are available.[329] Serologic test results for amebas almost always are positive in acute amebic dysentery and hepatic amebiasis. A liver scan may indicate the presence of a liver abscess.

Diagnosis of *Cryptosporidium, Isospora, Cyclospora,* and microsporidia is based on morphology and staining of stool or histologic examination of tissue sections.[162] Among the most widely used stains to visualize oocysts of *Cryptosporidium, Isospora,* and *Cyclospora* are standard acid-fast or modified acid-fast stains, which are based on the use of reagents that enhance the penetration of fuchsin into the organism without the need for heating (modified Kinyoun acid-fast stain). Using a modified acid-fast stain, *Cryptosporidium* oocysts, which are 4 to 6 μm with four crescentic sporozoites, stain red and can be differentiated readily from yeasts that stain green.[182] Enzyme immunoassays[149, 225, 429] and fluorescent monoclonal antibody-based assays[148, 372] for detection of *Cryptosporidium* antigen in stool specimens are available. In a study of seven microscopy-based *Cryptosporidium* oocyst detection methods, false-positive results were detected by acid-fast and auramine-rhodamine stains but not by monoclonal antibody-based methods.[22] Oocysts of *I. belli* often are visualized by wet-mount preparations because of their size, which is 20 to 30 μm with four sporozoites in two sporocysts. *Cyclospora* oocysts are 8 to 10 μm in diameter and are nonrefractile spherical organisms containing two sporozoites in two sporocysts that are seen easily on wet-mount preparations and are variably acid fast.

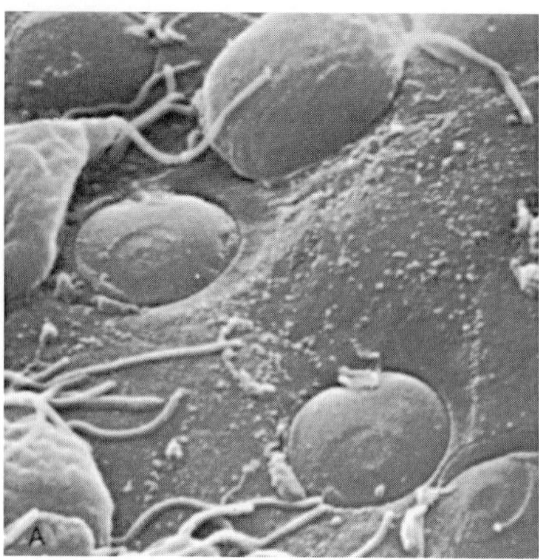
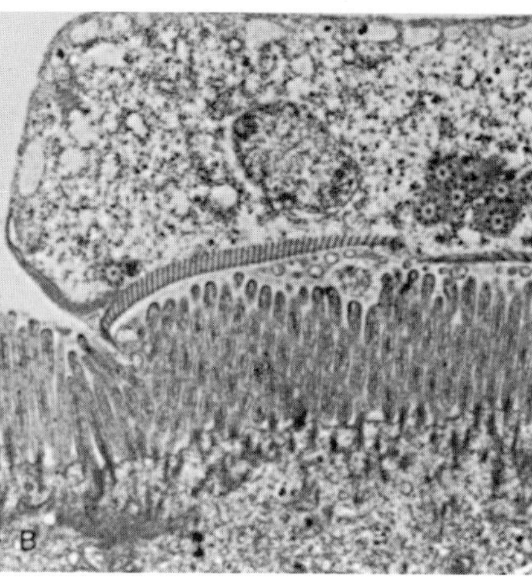

FIGURE 51–5 ■ *A,* Scanning electron micrograph of an intestinal villus revealing firm attachment of *Giardia muris* trophozoites to the microvillous border (MVB). Circular dome-shaped lesions in the MVB are produced by attachment of the adhesive disk of trophozoite. (×4600.) *B,* Transmission electron micrograph of a *G. muris* trophozoite illustrating how lesions in the MVB are produced. Note that the edges of the adhesive disk penetrate the MVB and compress the microvilli centrally. The microvilli also show some vesiculation under the adhesive disk. (×20,000.) (*A, B,* Courtesy of Dr. S. L. Erlandsen.)

Microsporidia are difficult to differentiate from bacteria and debris because of the small size of the spores, which measure 1 to 2 µm. For detection, formalin-fixed stool or duodenal fluid can be stained using a calcofluor stain, a modified trichrome stain, or a fluorescent stain.[101, 445] Gram, acid-fast, periodic acid–Schiff, and Giemsa stains also have been used to stain the organism.[394] A nonspecific fluorescence method or enzyme immunoassay may enhance speed and sensitivity and may become more useful as specific antibodies become widely available. Small bowel biopsy may be more sensitive than is stool examination for diagnosis of intestinal microsporidiosis.[38] Spores are gram positive, and parts of the internal structure are positive for acid-fast or periodic acid–Schiff stains. After preliminary identification by these stains, further examination by electron microscopy is needed to classify adequately the microsporidia into an appropriate genus. Routine histopathologic studies can provide presumptive identification in infected biopsy tissue; diagnostic confirmation requires electron microscopy. Reliable serologic tests are not available. Sensitive PCR assays are being evaluated for *E. bieneusi* and *E. intestinalis.*[94, 137, 145]

STANDARD DIAGNOSTIC STOOL CULTURES

Obtaining stool cultures cannot be justified in all patients with acute diarrhea.[190] Patients with mild, self-limited illness do not need to have stool specimens cultured. When culture is indicated, the specimen should be inoculated onto culture plate media adequate to isolate *E. coli, Shigella, Salmonella,* and *C. jejuni.* Standard stool culture media should include differential, mildly selective media, such as MacConkey or eosin methylene blue agar; selective media, such as *Salmonella-Shigella* agar, xylose-lysine-deoxycholate, or Hektoen enteric medium; a less inhibitory medium to increase the recovery of *Shigella,* such as Tergitol 7 with 1 percent triphenyltetrazolium chloride; and an enrichment broth (selenite F or GN broth) to increase the yield of *Salmonella.* For isolation of *Campylobacter,* Skirrow, Campy-BAP, or Butzler medium also should be routine. Several *Campylobacter* spp., such as *C. upsaliensis, C. hyointestinalis,* and *C. lari,* require use of selective medium and filtration techniques for identification.[128] Fecal specimens can be transported to the laboratory in a non–nutrient-holding medium, such as Cary-Blair, when immediate culture is not possible. This medium prevents drying or overgrowth of specific organisms.

E. coli grown in a hospital microbiology laboratory usually is considered to be normal flora. Proving pathogenicity is difficult because gene probe and PCR assays currently are available only in reference or research laboratories.[302] All stool specimens should be evaluated with sorbitol MacConkey medium for *E. coli* O157:H7.[51] *Shigella* organisms are identified in the standard evaluation of stool cultures. Unfortunately, volunteer studies have shown that these organisms not always are isolated in culture from patients ill with shigellosis.

Salmonella organisms routinely are isolated by clinical microbiology laboratories. Speciation is important in salmonellosis because *S.* ser. Choleraesuis and *S.* ser. Typhi cause more severe disease than do other *Salmonella* spp. *S.* ser. Enteritidis is more variable in severity. Serotyping of *S.* ser. Enteritidis usually is not helpful in the individual case, although serotyping is crucial in evaluation of an outbreak. Because so many *Salmonella* serotypes exist, isolation of an unusual serotype can be of use in the investigation of a foodborne epidemic. As with *Shigella,* isolation of a *Salmonella* sp., even without demonstration of virulence properties, is considered adequate to make an etiologic diagnosis. Serologic studies are of no value in the individual patient. DNA probes can be used to detect *S. typhi.*[370]

SPECIAL DIAGNOSTIC CULTURES

Other bacterial enteropathogens require modified laboratory procedures for identification.[190] If these agents are suspected, the laboratory should be notified so that appropriate culture methods can be used. Listeria is cultured on blood agar plates rather than on the usual enteric media.[435] *Y. enterocolitica* can be isolated from routine media, but a differential selective medium, such as cefsulodin-triclosan (Irgasan)-novobiocin agar is more effective.[49] If routine enteric media are inoculated, recovery of organisms is optimized by plating them onto MacConkey agar, followed by incubation at 25° C for 48 hours. Cold-enrichment techniques may increase the yield of the organism from contaminated specimens such as feces. Stool cultures positive for Y. enterocolitica only after prolonged cold enrichment may represent environmental strains of low virulence, unrelated to human disease. Biotyping and serotyping for 0:3, 0:8, and 0:9 are helpful in determining the clinical relevance of such isolates.

V. cholerae strains can be isolated from stool using thiosulfate-citrate-bile-salt-sucrose agar, which is the most convenient and frequently used selective medium. This medium is suitable for most enteropathogenic *Vibrio* spp., except *V. hollisae.* Placing the specimen into an enrichment broth, such as alkaline peptone water with 1 percent sodium chloride (pH 8.5) for 5 hours before placing on thiosulfate-citrate-bile-salt-sucrose agar, enhances the isolation of vibrios. Serotyping is necessary to classify organisms into those that cause typical epidemic cholera (i.e., O1 and O139 serotypes) and those that cause less severe disease (i.e., non-O1, or nonagglutinating vibrios).[221]

V. parahaemolyticus, like other vibrios, can be cultured on thiosulfate-citrate-bile-salt-sucrose agar. Strains associated with diarrhea are Kanagawa positive on Wagatsuma agar (i.e., show hemodigestion resembling beta-hemolysis), which is a marker for pathogenicity. *V. parahaemolyticus* can be serotyped based on the O and K antigens.[92]

A. hydrophila can be overlooked easily on standard stool cultures. A specialized blood agar has been suggested for isolation.[15] Oxidase testing of organisms that resemble *E. coli* can select organisms as possible *Aeromonas* spp.[15] If oxidase-positive colonies are found, they can be evaluated biochemically to determine species.

C. difficile can be isolated by anaerobic stool culture on agar containing cycloserine, cefoxitin, and fructose. For definitive diagnosis, demonstration of the presence of cytotoxin in stool specimens and neutralization with antitoxin or by use of enzyme immunoassay is necessary.[12]

C. perfringens is isolated commonly from feces of well people. Diagnosis of *C. perfringens* food poisoning requires isolation of the organisms from incriminated food in a significant quantity (more than 10^5 organisms/g) and demonstration of the same serotype of *C. perfringens* from food and feces of ill people. Stools also can be tested for enterotoxin[68] and strains tested by pulsed-field gel electrophoresis.[268]

S. aureus may be isolated from food and may not be the cause of illness because not all strains of *Staphylococcus* produce enterotoxin. Conversely, the absence of *S. aureus* from food that has been reheated just before being eaten does not exclude staphylococcal food poisoning because heating may destroy the organism without inactivating the toxin. Thus, isolation of *S. aureus* from food is only suggestive evidence of etiology. Isolation of the same phage type *S. aureus* from a skin lesion on the hands of a food handler and the food or feces of ill people can confirm the diagnosis. Stool, vomitus, and food can be tested for enterotoxin using immunologic techniques available in reference laboratories.[68]

B. cereus can be diagnosed by demonstration of greater than 10^5 organisms/g in the incriminated food. Stool culture is unreliable in the individual patient because *B. cereus* may be isolated from feces of well people. Stool and food specimens can be sent to the reference laboratory for enterotoxin identification.[68]

SEROTYPING AND TOXIN DETECTION

Certain serotypes have been associated with ETEC, EIEC, EPEC, and STEC. Studies of somatic *E. coli* antigens are not helpful in establishing the diagnosis of ETEC because more than 50 different serogroups of *E. coli* have been shown to produce ST enterotoxins, HL enterotoxins, or both.

Serogroup determination is useful for definition of EPEC. Currently, 170 distinct O and 56 H antigens are recognized. The EPEC organisms belong primarily to serogroups O26, O55, O86, O111, O114, O119, O125, O126, O127, O128, and O142.[302] Serogrouping has a role in defining outbreaks of enteritis among infants but currently is not recommended in sporadic diarrheal disease. Persistent diarrhea in an infant associated with an EPEC serogroup may warrant small bowel biopsy. Changes typical of EPEC on light microscopy of small intestine are flattening and loss of villi with chronic inflammatory changes in the lamina propria. On electron microscopy, bacteria can be seen adherent to epithelial cells that have lost their microvilli and formed "pedestals" with bacteria attached[77, 368] (see Fig. 51–4).

EIEC organisms are identified by demonstration of invasiveness in tissue culture (HeLa cells), by their ability to produce keratoconjunctivitis when inoculated into eyes of guinea pigs or rabbits (Serény test),[393] or by demonstration of the genes encoding invasiveness.[302] These dysentery-producing EIEC belong to a small number of serogroups: O28, O112, O124, O136, O143, O144, O152, O164, and O167.[73] The O antigens of EIEC are related closely to various *Shigella* O antigens. EIEC may be suspected when a nonmotile, lysine decarboxylase–negative *E. coli* strain is isolated from a patient thought clinically to have shigellosis.[427]

STEC organisms are noninvasive and produce Shiga toxins. Although *E. coli* O157:H7 is the most commonly recognized serotype associated with hemorrhagic colitis and hemolytic-uremic syndrome in the United States,[79, 80] many other serotypes have been recognized in this group. *E. coli* O157:H7 should be suspected when an *E. coli* strain that does not ferment sorbitol is isolated from a patient with the syndrome and may be identified definitively by serotyping and identification of toxin.[302] The other STEC serotypes are not distinctive biochemically and can be identified only by demonstration of production of Shiga toxin 1, 2 or 1 and 2 or by demonstration of the genes responsible for toxin production. EAEC organisms can be defined by their adherence to Hep-2 cells in tissue culture or by DNA probes.[36, 301]

VIRUS DETECTION

Rotavirus has been identified by examination of stool specimens for 70-nm particles by electron microscopy (see Fig. 51–1). Commercially available enzyme immunoassay and latex agglutination kits are available to detect rotavirus antigen in stool specimens. Assay procedures using monoclonal antibodies have improved the sensitivity and specificity to greater than 95 percent.[98, 232] Other diagnostic methods less suitable for routine use include gel electrophoresis, PCR, and viral culture. To detect non–group A rotaviruses, gel electrophoresis and electron microscopy are required because they are not detected by the commercially available assays.

Attempts at in vitro propagation of the calicivirus agents by routine techniques have been unsuccessful, and no readily available animal model has been developed for studying these viruses.[158] Hence, studying these agents by conventional neutralization test methods is difficult. The technique of immune electron microscopy has proved useful in the study of volunteers with experimentally induced Norwalk virus gastroenteritis and in the diagnosis of naturally occurring Norwalk-like agent gastroenteritis.[222] The cloning of Norwalk virus led to the development of several diagnostic assays,[212] including enzyme immunoassay based on baculovirus-expressed viral capsid proteins and reverse transcriptase PCR to detect viral RNA.[158, 212, 214, 322] The antigen enzyme immunoassays are highly specific and detect closely related strains within the same genogroup. The antibody enzyme immunoassays are relatively type specific, with low levels of cross-reaction among strains that are distinct in the antigen enzyme immunoassays. Monoclonal antibodies against the recombinant capsids have been generated and are useful for development of type-specific assays. Reverse transcriptase PCR is more broadly reactive and useful for genetic classification of the family.[158, 212, 314, 322] These assays are available only in research laboratories.

Diagnosis of enteric adenovirus can be established by immune electron microscopy of stool specimens, enzyme immunoassay of stool specimens, or propagation in a line of human embryonic kidney cells transformed by adenovirus type 5 (293 cells).[240] Restriction enzyme analysis is the definitive method for classifying individual enteric adenovirus isolates. Commercially available assays for detection of enteric adenovirus are available.[431]

Astroviruses grow well in human embryo kidney cells in the presence of trypsin. Electron microscopy, immune electron microscopy, immunofluorescence on cell culture, enzyme immunoassay, and PCR can be used as detection methods, but they are available only in reference or research laboratories.[157]

PROCTOSIGMOIDOSCOPY

When symptoms of colitis are severe or the etiology of an inflammatory enteritis syndrome remains obscure after laboratory evaluation, proctoscopic examination may help to establish the diagnosis. Table 51–11 shows the usual proctoscopic findings in the various enteric syndromes that are characterized by fever, abdominal pain, and diarrhea with mucus and blood. Inflammatory bowel disease enters the differential diagnosis when symptoms of inflammatory enteritis become chronic. Proctitis with or without diarrhea may be related to milk allergy in infants, child abuse, or sexual practices. The causes of proctitis include all of the aforementioned etiologies as well as *N. gonorrhoeae,* herpes simplex virus, lymphogranuloma venereum, and *Chlamydia trachomatis.*

Treatment

Enteric infections generally are self-limited conditions, but nonspecific therapy can provide relief for some patients, and specific therapy may shorten the duration of the illness and eradicate fecal shedding of the organism. In caring for patients with diarrhea and dehydration, several major therapeutic considerations include: (1) fluid and electrolyte therapy, (2) dietary manipulation, (3) nonspecific therapy with antidiarrheal compounds, and (4) specific therapy with antimicrobial agents. Increasing numbers of isolates resistant to antimicrobial agents and the risk for worsened illness (e.g., hemolytic-uremic syndrome occurring with Shiga toxin–producing *E. coli*) complicate antimicrobial and antimotility therapy.

FLUID AND ELECTROLYTE THERAPY

Patients who develop diarrhea lose fluid and electrolytes through the GI tract by several mechanisms: vomiting, loss of fecal fluid caused by the infecting enteropathogen, and fecal water loss in excess of sodium caused by the intraluminal osmotic effect of unabsorbed nutrients.[192] The composition and amount of lost fluid depend on the rate of stool loss and the causative agent. The higher the rate of stool loss, the greater the sodium loss, probably as a result of rapid passage of intestinal contents through the colon, where sodium-potassium exchange occurs. Stools from patients with cholera or ETEC infection contain sodium in a concentration of 80 to 120 mEq/L, whereas stools from patients with rotavirus infection have sodium concentrations of less than 50 mEq/L.[384] In secretory diarrheal disorders, loss of fluid generally is derived from the small intestine, and colonic reabsorption is overwhelmed. In viral gastroenteritis, small bowel absorptive capacity primarily is impaired, and in dysenteric or invasive diarrhea, reabsorptive capacity of the large intestine is reduced. If vomiting also is a manifestation, this loss is compounded. Continued loss of fluid or electrolytes may lead to dehydration, with potentially severe sequelae. Children, especially infants, are more susceptible to dehydration because they have greater basal fluid and electrolyte requirements per kilogram and because they depend on others to meet these needs.

TABLE 51–11 ■ PROCTOSCOPIC FINDINGS OF PERSISTENT INFLAMMATORY COLITIS

Organism or Disease	Gross Findings	Microscopic Findings
Shigella species	Diffuse erythema with loss of vascular pattern, mucopurulence, mild friability, occasional aphthoid ulcers	Edema, capillary congestion, focal hemorrhages, crypt hyperplasia, goblet cell depletion, mononuclear and polymorphonuclear leukoycte infiltrate, loss of epithelial cells with microulcerations
Salmonella species	Hyperemic, friable mucosa with petechiae and ulcerations, occasional pseudomembranous changes	Edema, inflammation, microabscesses, ulcerations
Campylobacter jejuni	Diffuse exudative edema	Inflammatory infiltrate with polymorphonuclear leukocytes, eosinophils, mononuclear cells, degeneration, loss of mucus, crypt abscesses, ulcerations
Clostridium difficile	Pseudomembranous colitis with 1- to 5-mm white-yellow nodules or plaques, minimal friability, sometimes nonspecific colitis	Fibrin, mucus, necrotic epithelial cells, leukocytes adherent to the underlying inflamed tissues
Clostridium perfringens	Rarely pseudomembranous colitis	Findings similar to those produced by *C. difficile*
Entamoeba histolytica	Discrete ulcers (mm to cm in diameter) with undermined edges amid normal mucosa	Trophozoites in flask-shaped ulcers that extend into submucosa, inflammatory cells near periphery but not near trophozoites; wet mount shows motile ameba containing erythrocytes
Ulcerative colitis	Friability, inflammatory polyps on heaped-up granulation tissue, deep linear ulcers	Mucosal ulceration extending to lamina propria, diffuse inflammation, vascular engagement, microabscesses in crypts
Crohn colitis	Hyperemic mucosa with linear ulcers	Inflammation involving all layers of bowel with lymphocytes, histiocytes, and plasma cells forming granulomas

Important factors to be considered in evaluating patients with diarrhea and possible dehydration include (1) an estimation of deficiency, (2) ongoing daily requirements, (3) continued losses and their replacement, and (4) correction of the underlying cause.[17, 192] The clinical signs and symptoms that may help in estimating deficiencies and determining the severity of dehydration include thirst, dryness of the mucous membranes, decrease in urinary output, tachycardia, loss of skin elasticity and turgor, and mottling and coolness of the skin.[17, 62] These signs may be misleading in patients who are malnourished or in those with hypertonic dehydration.

Fluids should not be withheld in the treatment of any patient with diarrheal disease. Oral therapy should consist of rapid rehydration with replacement of ongoing losses during the first 6 to 12 hours of therapy with a glucose electrolyte solution,[75, 78, 384] followed by early initiation of a modified diet.[265] If fluid and electrolyte deficits are significant, priority should be given to rehydration as rapidly as possible with oral electrolyte solutions.

Intravenous therapy is required only if the patient is in shock, is obtunded, or has ileus; otherwise, fluid and electrolyte therapy should be administered orally. Once the patient is rehydrated, an orally administered maintenance solution containing approximately 50 mEq/L of sodium should be used. Patients with mild diarrhea without clinical dehydration (less than 3% weight loss) can be managed at home by supplementing their diets with oral electrolyte solutions containing glucose. The glucose in these solutions is necessary to promote intestinal absorption of sodium and water in the small intestine.[396]

Commercial preparations of ready-to-feed glucose electrolyte solutions are available in the United States and should be used in preference to homemade solutions. The sodium and potassium contents of various commercially available preparations are outlined in Table 51–12. Gatorade and other sports drinks do not supply the quantity of electrolytes necessary to replace those lost with the continued stool losses of severe diarrhea, and they are high in carbohydrate content. High concentrations of sugar are not tolerated well because high osmotic activity may exacerbate diarrhea. The carbohydrate concentration should not exceed the sodium concentration by more than 2:1. If it does, the excess carbohydrate produces osmotic retention of water in the intestine, with subsequent loss in stool.[17] The preparation of glucose and salt solutions at home is not recommended because errors in preparing the solutions may result in hypertonic dehydration in infants.[250] The use of rice-based oral rehydration solutions that contain glucose polymers and amino acids has been shown to increase the absorption of salt, water, and glucose from the intestine and may be more beneficial than are glucose-based oral rehydration solutions.[383, 401]

Other fluids that may be consumed at home include decarbonated soda beverages, fruit juices, and Jell-O. All contain inadequate amounts of sodium and potassium and excessive carbohydrate concentrations, which may exceed the absorptive capacity of the intestine[396] and, therefore, should not be used if rehydration requires more than one or two feedings. Kool-Aid and tea are not recommended because they are low in both sodium and potassium and, thus, have little advantage over sugar and water. Soon after the child has begun drinking a fluid and electrolyte solution, feeding should be restarted.[17, 54]

DIETARY MANIPULATION

Of all common childhood illnesses, diarrhea has the most significant adverse nutritional effect. Restoration of feeding is important to reduce the nutritional defects caused by diarrhea. However, optimal conditions have not been defined in nutritional management of different diarrheal states.[54] Once rehydration is complete, food may be reintroduced while the oral electrolyte solution is continued to replace ongoing losses from stools and for maintenance. Breastfeeding in infants should be resumed as soon as possible, preferably immediately after rehydration. Some infants experience temporary lactose intolerance after diarrheal illness,[28] although most young children with acute diarrhea can be managed successfully with continued feeding of undiluted nonhuman milk.[17, 55, 265] Routine dilution of milk and routine use of lactose-free milk formula are not necessary, especially when oral rehydration therapy and early feeding are part of the approach to the clinical management of acute diarrhea.

In some children and infants, the carbohydrate fraction of milk may exacerbate diarrhea because of disaccharidase deficiency acquired as a result of diarrhea.[28] The development of lactase deficiency during a diarrheal illness may require some alteration in diet. In children with moderate or severe acute diarrhea, reducing or eliminating lactose from the diet early in the illness may be necessary to minimize the effects of lactose intolerance. Relative lactose tolerance has been shown to persist for 2 to 6 weeks after some episodes of diarrhea. Other disaccharidases may be reduced during infection, influencing the absorption of other sugars. Soybased, lactose-free formulas can be used safely during the acute phase of diarrheal illness in infants.[383] If diarrhea persists for more than 3 weeks, conditions that should be considered include not only disaccharidase deficiency but also celiac disease, cystic fibrosis, parasitic disease, allergic gastroenteropathy, bacterial overgrowth syndrome, EPEC or EAEC disease, and chronic nonspecific diarrhea.[255]

TABLE 51–12 ■ CONTENT OF REPRESENTATIVE SOLUTIONS USED FOR ORAL REHYDRATION

Solution	Sodium (mmol/L)	Potassium (mmol/L)	Carbohydrate (mmol/L)	Osmolarity (mOsm/L)
Rehydration				
World Health Organization solution*	90	20	111	310
Reduced osmolar ORS (WHO/UNICEF)	75	20	75	245
Rehydralyte (Ross)	75	20	140	301
Maintenance/Prevention				
Infalyte (Mead Johnson)	50	25	70	200
Naturalyte (Unlimited Beverage)	45	20	140	265
Pedialyte (Ross)	45	20	140	250
Pediatric electrolyte (NutraMax)	45	20	140	250

*Packets of oral rehydration salts are available in the United States from Cera Products, Columbia, MD, (410) 997-2334 and Jianas Brothers, Kansas City, MO, (816) 421-2880.

NONSPECIFIC THERAPY WITH ANTIDIARRHEAL COMPOUNDS

Many compounds are available for symptomatic treatment of patients with diarrhea. These substances are prescribed by physicians, administered by parents, or taken by patients who are eager to relieve the symptoms. Their purpose is to decrease the volume of diarrhea by increasing absorption of water and electrolytes, decrease intestinal secretion, or decrease intestinal motility. These over-the-counter and prescription preparations act on the GI tract by one or more of these mechanisms. Table 51–13 lists some commercially available antidiarrheal agents and their mechanisms of action, major value, and toxicity. Most of these compounds are not approved for children younger than 2 to 3 years of age.

Drugs that alter intestinal motility can be classified into antimuscarinics and synthetic or natural opium alkaloids.[17, 86, 113, 349] These compounds usually have a rapid onset of action. They decrease the volume of stool output and relieve abdominal cramps and pain, probably by producing segmental contractions of the intestine, which retard movement of intestinal contents responsible for diarrhea and restrict the intestinal distention that normally causes abdominal pain. Drugs that affect intestinal motility may worsen the symptoms of *Shigella*, STEC, or other invasive and cytotoxin-producing bacteria by inhibiting intestinal transit and allowing the enteropathogen to be in contact with the intestinal mucosa for a longer period of time.[113, 456] These agents may accelerate development of AAC.[309] Drugs that have central opiate-like effects can lead to overdose; fatalities in children have occurred.[153, 371, 349] Two to four doses of these compounds over a 24-hour period may be used in adolescents or adults to treat severe cramps, but prolonged therapy is not advised, and use in children is not recommended. The combination of TMP-SMX plus loperamide and the use of loperamide alone were effective in the treatment of adults with travelers' diarrhea[56, 132] and resulted in the shortest mean duration of diarrhea when compared with that in patients taking placebo or TMP-SMX alone. In infants, loperamide can cause ileus, emesis, and drowsiness.[293] The practice parameter of the American Academy of Pediatrics does not recommend this class of compounds to treat diarrhea in children.[17]

Numerous chemically inert agents are used internally as adsorbents to bind toxins and water to reduce the number and improve consistency of bowel movements. When these substances are given by mouth, they can adsorb not only bacteria and toxins but also drugs, nutrients, and enzymes. The only agents currently used widely are compounds containing activated attapulgite, which have been shown to be effective in animals by reducing diarrhea and producing formed stools,[142, 358] but studies in humans are lacking. Disadvantages include nonspecific changes in adsorption of nutrients, enzymes, and antibiotics, particularly if the absorbent is used for a prolonged period of time.

Lactobacillus preparations have been given to recolonize the intestine with saccharolytic flora and alter the intestinal pH as a way of deterring potential pathogens.[16, 82, 325, 344] Ingesting lactulose, lactobacilli, and yogurt results in an increased production of short-chain fatty acids and a decrease in pH in the intestine, which may inhibit the growth of *Salmonella* and *Shigella*. Feeding selected microorganisms, including *Bifidobacterium bifidum, Saccharomyces boulardii, Lactobacillus acidophilus,* and *Streptococcus thermophilus,* to children and adults has been shown to be effective in prevention against and treatment of intestinal disease.[127, 375] However, the lack of effect of *Lactobacillus GG* on antibiotic-associated diarrhea[424] indicates the need to better define and standardize the optimal probiotic for prevention and treatment of diarrheal disease caused by specific enteropathogens.[344]

TABLE 51–13 ■ ANTIDIARRHEAL COMPOUNDS USED AS NONSPECIFIC THERAPY FOR PATIENTS WITH ACUTE DIARRHEA

Mechanism of Action	Generic Name	Trade Name	Value	Comments
Alteration of intestinal motility	Loperamide	Imodium advanced, Imodium A-D, Maalox Antidiarrheal, Pepto Diarrhea Control	Decreases diarrhea, rapid onset of action	Numerous side effects and contraindications; not recommended or licensed for use in infants and young children; may potentiate *Shigella, Salmonella,* or STEC infections or accelerate the course of antimicrobial associated colitis
	Difenoxin and atropine	Motofen*		
	Diphenoxylate and atropine	Lomotil*		
	Tincture of opium	Paregoric*		
Alteration of secretion	Bismuth subsalicylate	Pepto-Bismol	Decreases diarrhea and cramps of travelers	Potential for salicylate and/or bismuth overdose, darkens stool
	Octreotide	Sandostatin*	Decreases diarrhea in patients with vasoactive intestinal peptide–secreting and metastatic carcinoid tumors	Used for relief of refractory AIDS-associated diarrhea; not licensed by the Food and Drug Administration for this condition
	Racecadotril	Not available	Decreases diarrhea	Decreases intestinal hypersecretion, enkephalinase inihibitor
Adsorption of toxins and water	Attapulgite	Diasorb, Donnagel, Kaopectate, Rheaban	Increases form of stool	Safe, minimally effective, decreases absorption of nutrients and drugs, causes abdominal fullness
Alteration of intestinal microflora	Probiotics (*Lactobacillus, Bifidobacterium*)	Pro-Bionate, Superdophilus	Value unproven	Safe, contraindicated in those with lactose tolerance

*Requires a prescription.
STEC, Shiga toxin–producing *Escherichia coli.*

Indomethacin, aspirin, chlorpromazine, and imidazole decrease intestinal secretion of fluid and electrolytes. Indomethacin has been shown to be effective in treating radiation-induced diarrhea, and chlorpromazine is effective in managing diarrhea caused by *V. cholerae*; however, the usefulness of these compounds in patients with various forms of acute infectious diarrhea is unknown. Laboratory studies showed that bismuth subsalicylate (Pepto-Bismol) inhibited intestinal secretion caused by *E. coli* and cholera enterotoxins,[129] reduced diarrhea in adult students who became ill in Mexico,[115] and prevented diarrhea among U.S. students traveling to Mexico.[116] Studies supporting its use in children are limited.[408, 409] Potential problems with this compound relate to the absorption of salicylate[139, 337] and bismuth.[281] Octreotide (Sandostatin) is a long-acting synthetic somatostatin analogue with pharmacologic actions mimicking those of the natural hormone somatostatin. Octreotide has been used in patients with AIDS who have severe refractory secretory diarrhea.[59]

Racecadotril (acetorphan) is an enkephalinase inhibitor that decreases intestinal hypersecretion but not motility in animals and humans by preventing breakdown of endogenous enkephalins in the GI tract. Racecadotril has been shown to decrease 48-hour stool output, median duration of diarrhea, and intake of oral rehydration solution in children with watery diarrhea.[380]

The potential immunomodulatory mechanisms involved in the interrelationships between micronutrients, including zinc and vitamin A, and infectious diseases, including diarrhea, have been reviewed.[418]

SPECIFIC THERAPY WITH ANTIMICROBIAL AGENTS

Antimicrobial therapy is administered to selected patients with gastroenteritis to abbreviate the duration of the clinical course and decrease excretion of the causative organisms.[345] A stool culture should be obtained when antibiotic treatment is anticipated, and antibiotic susceptibility testing of any suspected pathogen should be performed to ensure optimal therapy. Changing susceptibility patterns render the initial selection of an antimicrobial agent difficult.[343] Antimicrobial agents should not be used routinely or liberally for gastroenteritis of unknown etiology.

Shigella

Several antimicrobial agents have been used successfully in eradicating clinical symptoms and fecal shedding of *Shigella*. Table 51–14 outlines suggested antimicrobial therapy for children and adults who are presumed to have shigellosis or from whom *Shigella* organisms are isolated from stool.

TABLE 51–14 ■ ANTIMICROBIAL THERAPY FOR PATIENTS WITH SHIGELLOSIS

	Antimicrobial Agent
Strain of unknown susceptibility	Ceftriaxone or azithromycin or ciprofloxacin* or ofloxacin*
Trimethoprim-sulfamethoxazole (TMP-SMX)–susceptible strains	TMP-SMX
Ampicillin-susceptible strain	Ampicillin
Suspected or proven multidrug-resistant strain	Ciprofloxacin* or ofloxacin*

*Not licensed for patients younger than 18 years of age.

The history of resistance among *Shigella* strains has shown progressive acquisition of multiresistance, first to sulfonamides, shortly after their commercial availability; then to tetracycline, chloramphenicol, and streptomycin less than 10 years after they were introduced; and subsequently to ampicillin, kanamycin, and TMP-SMX.[298, 343, 416] In certain Native-American populations and in a study from Oregon, TMP-SMX resistance is a common finding, with resistance reported to TMS-SMX in 59 percent of the Oregon study population.[361] In children with known ampicillin-susceptible or TMP-SMX–susceptible strains, either drug can be given, but neither should be used as empiric therapy because of increasing resistance. Amoxicillin is not as effective as is ampicillin in the treatment of shigellosis and should not be used.[305] Parenterally and orally administered, extended-spectrum cephalosporins have been used successfully in the treatment of children with shigellosis.[24, 125, 434] Two-day[125] and 5-day[434] courses of ceftriaxone were effective in eradicating *Shigella* from stool and reducing the duration of diarrhea, but a single parenteral dose of ceftriaxone produced only a moderate reduction in diarrhea and failed to eradicate *Shigella* strains from stools.[219] Previous studies of first- and second-generation cephalosporins for treatment of shigellosis have demonstrated them to be ineffective.[345] Cefixime and ceftibuten, orally administered extended-spectrum cephalosporins, have shown good in vitro activity against various enteric pathogens and promising clinical efficacy in patients with shigellosis; cefixime, however, no longer is manufactured in the United States.[24, 354]

Ciprofloxacin, norfloxacin, and enoxacin have been used successfully to treat adults and children with shigellosis[42, 131, 231, 377, 395] and appear to be safe in children.[167] In a study evaluating dosing of ciprofloxacin in adults, 5 days of therapy were effective for patients infected with *S. dysenteriae* type 1. For other *Shigella* species, a single, 1-g dose was sufficient.[42] Ciprofloxacin is approved by the FDA for treatment of GI tract infections caused by *S. sonnei* and *S. flexneri*. In a randomized, double-blind study of 120 children 2 to 15 years of age with shigellosis, ciprofloxacin and pivmecillinam given for 5 days were successful in providing a clinical cure and eradicating the organism from stool.[377] Ciprofloxacin was not associated with development of arthropathy in children in this study. Reduced susceptibility to ciprofloxacin and ofloxacin, probably due to mutation in the DNA gyrase subunit A gene, has been noted in *S. sonnei* strains isolated from patients with dysentery.[204] A comparative study of a 5-day course of either azithromycin or ciprofloxacin in adults with shigellosis showed comparable clinical and bacteriologic responses.[231] Patients who are transient asymptomatic carriers may be managed without antimicrobial therapy if they understand and employ excellent standards of personal hygiene. Treatment of these patients, however, reduces fecal shedding of the organism and prevents spread of infection.

Salmonella

Table 51–15 shows antimicrobial therapy for patients with the various clinical manifestations of *Salmonella*. The type of syndrome produced by *Salmonella* influences the selection and duration of antimicrobial therapy. Antibiotics

TABLE 51–15 ■ ANTIMICROBIAL THERAPY FOR PATIENTS WITH *SALMONELLA* INFECTIONS

Clinical Manifestation	Antimicrobial Agent
Acute gastroenteritis*	None
Bacteremia and/or enteric fever†	Ceftriaxone or cefotaxime or ampicillin‡ or chloramphenicol‡ or trimethoprim-sulfamethoxazole‡ (TMP-SMX)
Dissemination with localized suppuration (osteomyelitis)† or bacteremia in patients with AIDS	Same as above for bacteremia
Meningitis or ampicillin-chloramphenicol and TMP-SMX-resistant organisms	Cefotaxime or ceftriaxone

*Patients with hyperpyrexia and systemic signs or symptoms should be treated empirically until bacteremia is excluded. Although of unproven efficacy, antimicrobial therapy for children in the first 3 months of life also is recommended by most authorities; a 7- to 10-day course of therapy probably is sufficient.
†Ciprofloxacin or ofloxacin can be used to treat resistant organisms in patients 18 years of age and older. Both are available for intravenous as well as oral use. Neither is recommended for pregnant women. Azithromycin has been used with success in developing countries.
‡Can be used if organism is susceptible.

should not be used in the treatment of patients who are nontyphoid *Salmonella* carriers or in most patients with mild gastroenteritis. Antimicrobial therapy may, on occasion, convert intestinal carriage into systemic disease with bacteremia,[365] prolong excretion of *Salmonella,*[23] produce a bacteriologic or symptomatic relapse,[23] or encourage development or selection of resistant strains.[294] Antimicrobial agents should be considered for patients with enterocolitis if the disease appears to be evolving into one of the systemic syndromes and for patients with a condition that impairs host resistance to infection, including neonates, young infants, and patients with hemoglobinopathies, including sickle-cell anemia, AIDS, leukemia, lymphoma, immunosuppression, congenital heart disease, valvular heart disease, prostheses, or uremia.[170] Antibiotic treatment of *Salmonella* infection should be given to all patients with typhoid fever, bacteremia caused by nontyphoidal strains, and dissemination with localized suppuration.

Despite excellent in vitro activity, several antibiotics, including first- and second-generation cephalosporins, have been ineffective in the therapy of patients with *Salmonella* infection.[227] Selection of antimicrobial agents for therapy is complicated by the emergence of *Salmonella* strains that are resistant to multiple antibiotics[2, 248, 343, 373] and by increased risk of acquiring *Salmonella* infection associated with prior antimicrobial exposure.[324]

Recommended antimicrobial agents include ampicillin, chloramphenicol, TMP-SMX, ceftriaxone, cefotaxime, or a fluoroquinolone, which is approved only for people older than 17 years of age.[279, 407] Ciprofloxacin, ofloxacin, and azithromycin are active in vitro against *Salmonella*, including *S.* ser. Typhi, and have been used clinically with success.*

*See references 26, 74, 83, 122, 146, 152, 155, 252, 280, 331, 338, 439.

In the United States, attention has focused on resistance of nontyphoidal *Salmonella* strains, which have their major reservoir in animals.[96, 151, 159, 171, 183, 288, 296] Several outbreaks of multiresistant *Salmonella* infection have been traced to animal sources in the United States and also are a major problem in other parts of the world.[96, 159, 262, 288, 295, 296] Resistant strains of *Salmonella* are common findings in retail ground meats, possibly because of use of antibiotics in animals used for food.[451] Human isolates of *Salmonella* should have susceptibility testing performed to guide therapy.

Because of the high rate of *S.* ser. Typhi transmission, together with widespread indiscriminate use of antimicrobial agents in some areas of the world, an increase in resistance patterns to ampicillin, chloramphenicol, and TMP- SMX has occurred.[369, 373] Overall in 1996 to 1997, 17 percent of *S.* ser. Typhi isolates in the United States had multiple resistance patterns to ampicillin, chloramphenicol, and TMP-SMX, with the highest rates occurring in isolates from the Indian subcontinent, Vietnam, and Tajikistan.[373] Because of this high rate of resistance in *S.* ser. Typhi strains imported by travelers,[294] empiric treatment of *S.* ser. Typhi should be provided with ceftriaxone, cefotaxime, or fluoroquinolones if the patient is older than 17 years of age. Ampicillin, chloramphenicol, and TMP-SMX should be reserved for domestically acquired cases or patients in whom susceptibility testing of the causative organism has shown susceptibility. Resistance of *S.* ser. Typhi to ceftriaxone and fluoroquinolones has been reported and occurs uncommonly but needs to be monitored.[74, 112, 296, 369] In areas of the world where *S.* ser. Typhi strains with reduced susceptibility to fluoroquinolones have been reported, azithromycin was effective for treatment of people with enteric fever,[74, 146, 155] as was cefixime.[280, 331] In a prospective, randomized study of children and adults with confirmed typhoid fever, ceftriaxone administered for 5 days was as effective and safe as was a 2- to 3-week course of chloramphenicol,[208] but in another study, short-course therapy failed.[45]

Corticosteroids can be beneficial in treating patients with typhoid fever in whom prompt relief of manifestations of toxemia might be lifesaving,[85] but corticosteroids may increase the relapse rate.[195]

Antibiotics listed in Table 51–15 can be used for treatment of *Salmonella* infections. Patients with defective host defense mechanisms, such as individuals with AIDS, should be treated with ampicillin or an expanded-spectrum cephalosporin.[406] Ciprofloxacin has been reported to be effective in treating acute diarrhea caused by *Salmonella,*[131, 332] recurrent *Salmonella* sepsis,[83] and brain abscesses in a neonate.[449] Duration of therapy is influenced by the site of infection and by the host. Patients with bacteremia without a localized infection should be treated for 14 days, whereas those with localized infection, such as osteomyelitis or endocarditis, or patients with AIDS and bacteremia, should receive at least 4 to 6 weeks of therapy.[45] In most cases, chronic carriage of *S.* ser. Typhi is associated with gallbladder disease. The presence of cholelithiasis may significantly affect the efficacy of therapy. When gallbladder disease is present, the failure rate of ampicillin is approximately 75 percent.[218] In patients without gallbladder disease, ampicillin with probenecid or amoxicillin administered for 6 weeks is the treatment of choice for chronic enteric carriers.[330] *Ciprofloxacin*[140] has been reported to be successful in eradicating *S.* ser. Typhi in adult chronic carriers. Resistance of clinical isolates and failure of treatment with ciprofloxacin have been noted in patients infected with *S.* ser. Typhi.[347] Ceftriaxone resistance of nontyphoid strains of *Salmonella* were reported in the United States at a rate of 0.5 percent in 1998.[112]

Two typhoid fever vaccines for children older than 2 years of age, adolescents, and adults are available commercially in the United States for specific situations.[63] A *Salmonella* typhi Vi conjugate vaccine has been shown to be safe, immunogenic, and 90 percent effective in children 2 to 5 years of age,[253] but this vaccine is not available commercially.

Campylobacter

C. jejuni isolates generally are susceptible to a wide variety of antimicrobial agents, including erythromycin, quinolones, furazolidone, aminoglycosides, tetracycline, chloramphenicol, imipenem, and clindamycin, whereas penicillin, ampicillin, cephalosporins, and TMP-SMX are relatively inactive. Isolation of *Campylobacter* from stool does not imply the need for antibiotics. The decision concerning therapy should be individualized, but therapy probably should be used in patients with high temperatures, bloody diarrhea, or severe diarrhea. In patients with *Campylobacter* enteritis, erythromycin or azithromycin is the agent of choice when a decision has been made to initiate therapy.[279] In a study from the United States, 3 percent of *Campylobacter* strains from human sources were resistant to erythromycin.[443] In this and other studies, a higher frequency of erythromycin resistance was noted in hog isolates, most of which were *C. coli*.[211, 376, 443] Strains of *C. jejuni* and *C. coli* that show high-level resistance to erythromycin also appear to be resistant to clarithromycin and azithromycin.[419]

Ciprofloxacin has been licensed by the FDA for treatment of *C. jejuni* enteritis in patients older than 17 years of age. Development of resistance to ciprofloxacin in *Campylobacter* spp. has been reported.[303, 376, 382, 391, 415, 464] These high rates of resistance have been related in part to the introduction of fluoroquinolones in animal feed.[403, 415] Resistance by *C. jejuni*[391] to ciprofloxacin has developed in people during therapy with ciprofloxacin. In double-blind, placebo-controlled trials of erythromycin for treatment of patients with enteritis caused by *C. jejuni*, erythromycin was shown to eradicate *C. jejuni* promptly from the feces but not to alter the clinical course when begun 4 days or more after the onset of symptoms.[18] Studies in which therapy was started early showed that *C. jejuni* was eliminated rapidly from stools, but studies gave conflicting results with regard to resolution of clinical illness.[379, 452] The treatment of choice for patients with septicemia caused by *C. jejuni* or *C. fetus* infection is gentamicin or imipenem.

Other Bacterial Agents

Antimicrobial agents have been employed frequently in attempts to treat infantile gastroenteritis caused by EPEC and as a means of controlling the spread of EPEC strains in hospital nurseries (Table 51–16). Although no definitive studies support the effectiveness of these drugs, they may be useful in certain situations, particularly when life-threatening infection occurs or when epidemic spread of the strains continues, despite the use of strict handwashing and appropriate isolation. Agents used in the treatment of mild EPEC diarrhea include oral nonabsorbable antibiotics, such as neomycin and gentamicin. TMP-SMX may be useful in the treatment of patients with diarrhea caused by EPEC, but strains may be resistant. If systemic infection is suspected, parenteral therapy should be started and modified according to antimicrobial susceptibility of the organism isolated.

Diarrhea caused by ETEC usually is limited, but studies in adults have shown that antimicrobial agents such as TMP-SMX and ciprofloxacin are effective treatments.[112] The treatment in patients with diarrhea caused by EIEC is similar to that in patients with shigellosis (see Table 51–14). Travelers infected with EAEC have shown response to ciprofloxacin.[156] Antimicrobial treatment of patients infected with STEC is not recommended.[456]

TABLE 51–16 ■ ANTIMICROBIAL THERAPY FOR BACTERIAL PATHOGENS CAUSING GASTROENTERITIS

Organism	Antibiotic Therapy
Campylobacter jejuni	
Gastroenteritis	None, or if colitis is present, erythromycin or azithromycin or ciprofloxacin
Sepsis	Aminoglycoside
Clostridium difficile (antimicrobial-associated colitis)	Metronidazole or vancomycin
Escherichia coli	
Enteropathogenic	None or trimethoprim-sulfamethoxazole (TMP-SMX)
Enterotoxigenic	None or TMP-SMX
Enteroinvasive	Same as for shigellosis (see Table 51–14)
STEC	None
Vibrio cholerae	Doxycycline or tetracycline or TMP/SMX
Vibrio parahaemolyticus	None
Yersinia enterocolitica	
Gastroenteritis	Probably none
Sepsis	TMP-SMX or an aminoglycoside or cefotaxime or ceftizoxime or ciprofloxacin*

*Licensed only for patients 18 years of age or older. STEC, Shiga toxin–producing *E. coli.*

Antimicrobial agents decrease diarrhea associated with cholera by eradicating the vibrios from the GI tract[440] and thus reducing the volume of fluid loss. Doxycycline is the drug of choice in most instances for O1 and O39 infections, including those in children, in whom the benefits of a 1- to 2-day course outweigh the risk for dental staining.[230, 357, 458] TMP-SMX can be used in children younger than 8 years of age for *V. cholerae* O1, but O139 strains often are resistant. Ampicillin probably is the safest agent for use during pregnancy. Other effective antimicrobial agents are the fluoroquinolones, azithromycin, cephems, and penems.[164, 230, 279, 458] Diarrhea caused by *V. parahaemolyticus* is self-limited, so that antimicrobial therapy shortens neither the clinical course nor the duration of excretion.[92] Antimicrobial therapy has not been proved efficacious in the treatment of uncomplicated enterocolitis caused by *Y. enterocolitica*.[49] Patients with *Y. enterocolitica*–induced septicemia or extraintestinal focal infection or compromised hosts with enterocolitis should receive TMP-SMX, a fluoroquinolone if older than 17 years of age, an aminoglycoside, cefotaxime, or cefotaxime. Table 51–16 outlines the antimicrobial therapy of these bacterial pathogens.

Protozoal Agents

Several drugs have been shown to be effective in the treatment of patients with giardiasis[95, 150, 278, 366] (Table 51–17). Metronidazole may be better tolerated than is quinacrine, is not approved for the treatment of patients with giardiasis in the United States, and is carcinogenic in animals. Quinacrine hydrochloride may produce a yellow discoloration of the skin that disappears after the drug is stopped. Quinacrine is not available commercially but as a service can be compounded (see Table 51–17). Furazolidone is the only one of these three compounds available in liquid form; like quinacrine, it is less expensive than metronidazole. Furazolidone can be used in children if compliance is a problem with quinacrine and metronidazole, both of which have an

TABLE 51–17 ■ ANTIMICROBIAL THERAPY FOR PATIENTS WITH GIARDIASIS

Antimicrobial Agent	Comments
Furazolidone (Furoxone)	Nausea, vomiting, disulfiram-like reaction with alcohol, mild hemolysis in glucose-6-phosphate dehydrogenase–deficient people, hypoglycemia, allergic reactions
Metronidazole (Flagyl)*	Metallic taste, nausea, headache, dry mouth, mutagenic in bacteria, carcinogenic in animals, disulfiram-like reaction with alcohol
Quinacrine HCl	Dizziness, headache, vomiting, diarrhea, yellow-orange skin color; not available commercially but can be obtained†
Nitazoxanide	Abdominal pain, vomiting, and headache uniformly reported. Data minimal for children younger than 12 mo or older than 11 yr and for patients with immune deficiencies
Paromomycin*	Not highly effective, proposed for use in pregnancy
Albendazole*	Anorexia, constipation; clinical trials have shown mixed results
Tinidazole	Given as one dose; not commercially available in the United States

*Not a U.S. Food and Drug Administration–licensed indication.
†Medical Center Pharmacy, New Haven, CT, (203) 785-6818, or Panorama Compounding Pharmacy, (800) 247-9767.

TABLE 51–18 ■ ANTIMICROBIAL THERAPY FOR PATIENTS WITH AMEBIASIS

Asymptomatic amebic cyst	Iodoquinol (Yodoxin) or paromomycin (Humatin) or diloxanide furoate*
Mild to moderate intestinal disease	Metronidazole (Flagyl) followed by iodoquinol or paromomycin
Severe intestinal disease, liver abscess, or other extraintestinal disease	Metronidazole followed by iodoquinol or paromomycin

*Available in the United States from the CDC Drug Service, Centers for Disease Control and Prevention, Atlanta, GA 30333; (404) 639-2888 or 3670.

objectionable taste. Clinical trials using albendazole to treat people with giardiasis have produced mixed results.[150] Treatment of children with albendazole for 5 days,[172] but not 3 days,[172, 326] has been effective. Toxicity of albendazole is low, and this compound is effective against many helminths, rendering it useful for treatment when multiple intestinal parasites are identified or suspected. Nitazoxanide has been licensed by the FDA for treatment of children with diarrhea caused by *Giardia* or *Cryptosporidium*. Tinidazole is a nitroimidazole drug similar to metronidazole, is given as a single dose, but is not available in the United States. Paromomycin is not absorbed and is not highly effective but has been proposed for use during pregnancy.[241]

In a review of comparative drug trials for the treatment of giardiasis, Davidson[95] reported that metronidazole cured 92 percent of 219 patients and furazolidone cured 84 percent of 150 patients. Approximately 7 percent of the metronidazole-treated patients and 10 percent of the furazolidone-treated patients had side effects that were serious enough to report. The drugs available in a liquid preparation are furazolidone and nitazoxanide.

In treating patients with amebiasis, iodoquinol is the best luminal amebicide presently available in the United States.[278, 329] This drug is effective against both cysts and trophozoites in the lumen of the gut but is ineffective against tissue forms of the disease. Invasive amebiasis of the intestine, liver, or other organs necessitates the additional use of tissue amebicides, such as metronidazole or paromomycin. Liver abscess or other extraintestinal forms of disease should be treated with metronidazole in the dose recommended for intestinal disease. Table 51–18 lists the recommended drugs for the treatment of children and adults with various forms of amebiasis. Nitazoxanide was effective in a double-blind study of treatment of patients with diarrhea caused by *E. histolytica,* but additional studies are needed.[366]

Patients with intestinal strongyloidiasis should receive ivermectin (200 μg/kg/day) for 1 to 2 days or thiabendazole (25 mg/kg/dose) every 12 hours for 4 doses (50 mg/kg/day; maximum, 3 g/day). Immunosuppressed patients with disseminated disease may require continued therapy for 2 to 3 weeks, but the mortality rate is high despite therapy. A thorough examination should be performed before giving immunosuppressive therapy to a patient with a past history of infection with *S. stercoralis.*

Therapeutic agents generally have not proved consistently beneficial for treatment of patients with cryptosporidiosis, and only one drug (nitazoxanide) is licensed by the FDA for this purpose. Infection is self-limited in immunocompetent patients, and therapy usually is not warranted.[188, 202, 405] In patients with persistent disease, an underlying immunodeficiency should be considered. Spiramycin has been used but is ineffective.[348, 454] Paromomycin may be effective in rapid resolution of chronic diarrhea.[141, 441, 450] Paromomycin also has been shown to inhibit *Cryptosporidium* infection of a human enterocyte cell line.[266] In a prospective, randomized, double-blind, placebo-controlled trial in the treatment of adults with AIDS and symptomatic cryptosporidiosis,[188] paromomycin was not effective, although inadequate statistical power prevented definitive rejection of the usefulness of paromomycin as therapy for this infection. Azithromycin has been shown to be effective in treatment of two children with cancer and four children with HIV infection who had severe diarrhea caused by *Cryptosporidium*.[189, 433] Combination therapy with paromomycin and azithromycin has been effective in some patients with AIDS and chronic cryptosporiodiosis.[405] In a prospective randomized, double-blind, placebo-controlled study of 50 children and 50 adults, treatment with nitazoxanide reduced the duration of diarrhea and oocyst shedding.[367] Nitazoxanide is licensed for treatment of children with diarrhea caused by cryptosporidiosis and giardiasis. The combination of clarithromycin and rifabutin, but not azithromycin alone, was highly protective against development of cryptosporidiosis in immune-suppressed HIV-infected adults.[202] The best approach to prevention of cryptosporidiosis in HIV-infected patients is maintenance of the immune system function by using highly active antiretroviral therapy (HAART) because chronic cryptosporidiosis occurs only in severely immunocompromised individuals.

Hyperimmune bovine colostrum has been used with some success in a child with agammaglobulinemia[428] and in a patient with AIDS.[430] Immune bovine colostrum has been shown to neutralize *C. parvum* sporozoites and partially to protect mice against oral challenge with *C. parvum* oocysts,[328] and oral bovine transfer factor has been used for treatment of cryptosporidiosis.[256] Nonspecific therapy with octreotide may control the severe diarrhea that occurs in patients with AIDS but has no effect on the infection[59] and is not approved for this use by the FDA.

For isosporiasis, TMP-SMX is effective and is the drug of choice.[278] In immunosuppressed patients, TMP-SMX, at a dose of 160 mg TMP and 800 mg SMX four times a day for 10 days, followed by the same dose twice a day for 3 weeks, is recommended for adults. In immunosuppressed children, use TMP 5 mg/kg with SMX 25 mg/kg four times a day for 10 days, followed by the same dose twice a day for 3 weeks. Ciprofloxacin can be used when TMP-SMX cannot be tolerated, although it is slightly less effective. Other drugs, including pyrimethamine-sulfadoxine (Fansidar), metronidazole, and furazolidone, have been reported to be successful for treating patients with isosporiasis.[320, 447] Pyrimethamine has been an effective alternative in patients allergic to sulfa drugs.[320] Problems in the treatment of isosporiasis have been encountered in patients with AIDS, in whom a high incidence of recurrence has been reported after treatment has been stopped. Continuation of therapy indefinitely with either pyrimethamine-sulfadoxine or TMP-SMX in adults has been shown to be effective in preventing recurrence of disease.[320]

Based on in vitro studies, several drugs have been used to treat microsporidial infections in humans, but successful treatment with any of them in humans is limited. Therapy with antiparasitic drugs, diet alteration, and antidiarrheal medications often fail to relieve diarrhea and malabsorption associated with microsporidiosis, although octreotide may provide symptomatic relief,[59] and diet modification to include medium-chain triglyceride-based diets has produced clinical improvement.[444] *E. intestinalis* is susceptible to albendazole,[84, 226, 363] which has been reported to stop diarrhea and weight loss, as well as promote weight gain, in patients infected with *E. intestinalis,*[48, 102, 108, 246, 289] although improvement has not been uniform. Infections caused by *E. bieneusi* are much more difficult to treat and have no acceptable treatment. Albendazole treatment of patients infected with *E. bieneusi* has produced improvement in 50 percent of patients in some studies, lower response rates in other studies, and persistence of the organism in most.[145] The use of HAART may lead to microbiologic and clinical response in HIV-infected patients with diarrhea due to microsporidia.

Patients with HIV and *Cyclospora* infection respond to TMP-SMX (TMP, 5 mg/kg, and SMX, 25 mg/kg four times daily for 10 days, then twice a day for 7 days; maximum, 160 mg/800 mg per dose), but relapses are common.[196, 260, 438] As few as 7 days of treatment may be adequate in immunocompetent children. HIV-infected patients may need higher doses and long-term maintenance.[322] Although ciprofloxacin is not as effective as is TMP/SMX, it is acceptable for patients who cannot tolerate TMP/SMX.[438]

Patients infected with *S. stercoralis* should be treated with ivermectin or alternately thiabendazole.[279] In disseminated strongyloidiasis, ivermectin or thiabendazole therapy should be continued for at least 5 days. In immunocompromised patients and patients with *Strongyloides* hyperinfection, longer duration of therapy may be necessary[249]; however, the mortality rate is high despite therapy. A thorough examination should be performed before immunosuppressive therapy is given to a patient with a history of infection with *S. stercoralis*.

The clinical significance of *B. hominis* remains unclear, few studies have considered the treatment of large numbers of patients, and case-control studies are lacking.[413] Use of metronidazole or iodoquinol in the same dose as used for mild-to-moderate intestinal disease from *E. histolytica* has been reported to be effective in uncontrolled studies,[413] and they are the recommended drugs of choice. TMP-SMX or paromomycin may be the most appropriate second-choice drug.[278] Treatment should be provided with caution, only after a thorough clinical review of other possible causes of symptoms has been performed.

REFERENCES

1. Abdel-Haq, N. M., Asmar, B. I., Abuhammour, W. M., et al.: *Yersinia enterocolitica* infection in children. Pediatr. Infect. Dis. J. *19*:954–958, 2000.
2. Ackers, M.-L., Puhr, N. D., and Tauxe, R. V.: Laboratory-based surveillance of *Salmonella* serotype typhi infections in the United States. Antimicrobial resistance on the rise. J. A. M. A. *283*:2668–2673, 2000.
3. Ackman, D. M., Drabkin, P., Birkhead, G., et al.: Reptile-associated salmonellosis in New York State. Pediatr. Infect. Dis. J. *14*:955–959, 1995.
4. Adachi, J. A., Ostrosky-Zeichner, L., DuPont, H. L., et al.: Empirical antimicrobial therapy for traveler's diarrhea. Clin. Infect. Dis. *31*:1079–1083, 2000.
5. Adachi, J. A., Jiang, Z. D., Mathewson, J. J., et al.: Enteroaggregative *Escherichia coli* as a major etiologic agent in traveler's diarrhea in 3 regions of the world. Clin. Infect. Dis. *32*:1706–1709, 2001.
6. Adamkiewicz, T. V., Berkovitch, M., Krishnan, C., et al.: Infection due to *Yersinia enterocolitica* in a series of patients with β-thalassemia: Incidence and predisposing factors. Clin. Infect. Dis. *27*:1362–1366, 1998.
7. Ahmed, L., El Rooby, A., Kassem, M. I., et al.: Ultrasonography in the diagnosis and management of 52 patients with amebic liver abscess in Cairo. Rev. Infect. Dis. *12*:330, 1990.
8. Aho, K., Ahvonen, P., Alkio, P., et al.: HLA-27 in reactive arthritis following infection. Ann. Rheum. Dis. *34*(Suppl.):29–30, 1975.
9. Albert, M. J., Faruque, A. S., Faruque, S. M., et al.: Case-control study of enteropathogens associated with childhood diarrhea in Dhaka, Bangladesh. J. Clin. Microbiol. *37*:3458–3464, 1999.
10. Albert, M. J., Ansaruzzaman, M., Talukder, K. A., et al.: Prevalence of enterotoxin genes in *Aeromonas* spp. isolated from children with diarrhea, healthy controls, and the environment. J. Clin. Microbiol. *38*:3785–3790, 2000.
11. Aldeen, W. E., Whisenant, J., Hale, D., et al.: Comparison of pooled formalin-preserved fecal specimens with three individual samples for detection of intestinal parasites. J. Clin. Microbiol. *31*:144–145, 1993.
12. Alfa, M. J., Kabani, A., Lyerly, D., et al.: Characterization of a toxin A–negative, toxin B–positive strain of *Clostridium difficile* responsible for a nosocomial outbreak of *Clostridium difficile*–associated disrrhea. J. Clin. Microbiol. *38*:2706–2714, 2000.
13. Allos, B. M.: *Campylobacter jejuni* infections: Update of emerging issues and trends. Clin. Infect. Dis. *32*:1201–1206, 2001.
14. Altekruse, S. F., Stern, N. J., Fields, P. I., et al.: *Campylobacter jejuni*—an emerging foodborne pathogen. Emerg. Infect. Dis. *5*:28–35, 1999.
15. Altwegg, M., and Geiss, H. K.: *Aeromonas* as a human pathogen. C. R. C. Crit. Rev. Microbiol. *16*:253, 1989.
16. Alvarez-Olmos, M. I., and Oberhelman, R. A.: Probiotic agents and infectious diseases: A modern perspective on a traditional therapy. Clin. Infect. Dis. *32*:1567–1576, 2001.
17. American Academy of Pediatrics, Subcommittee on Acute Gastroenteritis. Practice parameter: The management of acute gastroenteritis in young children. Pediatrics *97*:424–436, 1996.
18. Anders, B. J., Paisley, J. W., Lauer, B. A., et al.: Double-blind placebo controlled trial of erythromycin for treatment of *Campylobacter* enteritis. Lancet *1*:131–132, 1982.
19. Ando, T., Noel, J. S., and Fankhauser, R. L.: Genetic classification of "Norwalk-like viruses." J. Infect. Dis. *181*(Suppl. 2):S336–S348, 2000.
20. Angulo, F. J., and Swerdlow, D. L.: Bacterial enteric infections in persons infected with human immunodeficiency virus. Clin. Infect. Dis. *21*(Suppl. 1):S84–S93, 1995.
21. Arbo, A., and Santas, J. I.: Diarrheal disease in the immunocompromised host. Pediatr. Infect. Dis. J. *6*:894–906, 1987.
22. Arrowood, M. J., and Sterling, C. R.: Comparison of conventional staining methods and monoclonal antibody-based methods for *Cryptosporidium* oocyst detection. J. Clin. Microbiol. *27*:1490, 1989.
23. Aserkoff, B., and Bennett, J. V.: Effect of antibiotic therapy in acute salmonellosis on the fecal excretion of salmonellae. N. Engl. J. Med. *281*:636–640, 1969.
24. Ashkenazi, S., Amir, J., Waisman, Y., et al.: A randomized, double-blind study comparing cefixime and TMP/SMX in the treatment of childhood shigellosis. J. Pediatr. *123*:817–821, 1993.
25. Asmuth, D. M., DeGirolami, P. C., Federman, M., et al.: Clinical features of microsporidiosis in patients with AIDS. Clin. Infect. Dis. *18*:819–825, 1994.

26. Asperilla, M. O., Smego, R. A., Jr., and Scott, L. K.: Quinolone antibiotics in the treatment of *Salmonella* infections. Rev. Infect. Dis. *12*:873, 1990.
27. Aureli, P., Fiorucci, G. C., Caroli, D., et al.: An outbreak of febrile gastroenteritis associated with corn contaminated by *Listeria monocytogenes*. N. Engl. J. Med. *342*:1236–1241, 2000.
28. Avery, G. B., Villavicencio, O., Lilly, J. R., et al.: Intractable diarrhea in early infancy. Pediatrics *41*:712–722, 1968.
29. Ball, J. M., Tian, P., Zeng, C. O., et al.: Age-dependent diarrhea induced by a rotaviral nonstructural glycoprotein. Science *272*:101–104, 1996.
30. Bartlett, A. V., Prado, D., Cleary, T. G., et al.: Production of Shigatoxin and other cytotoxins by serogroups of *Shigella*. J. Infect. Dis. *154*:996, 1986.
31. Bartlett, A. V., Reves, R. R., and Pickering, L. K.: Rotavirus in infant-toddler day care centers: Epidemiology relevant to disease control strategies. J. Pediatr. *113*:435, 1988.
32. Bartlett, J. G., Tedesdo, F. J., Shull, S., et al.: Symptomatic relapse after oral vancomycin therapy of antibiotic-associated pseudomembranous colitis. Gastroenterology *78*:431–434, 1980.
33. Bartlett, J. G.: Antimicrobial agents implicated in *Clostridium difficile* toxin-associated diarrhea or colitis. Johns Hopkins Med. J. *149*:6–9, 1981.
34. Bartlett, J. G.: *Clostridium difficile:* History of its role as an enteric pathogen and the current state of knowledge about the organism. Clin. Infect. Dis. *18*(Suppl. 4):S265–S272, 1994.
35. Barwick, R. S., Levy, D. A., Craun, G. F., et al.: Surveillance for water-borne disease outbreaks—United States, 1997–1998. M. M. W. R. Morb. Mortal. Wkly. Rep. *49*(SS-4):1–35, 2000.
36. Baudry, B., Savarino, S. J., Vial, P., et al.: A sensitive and specific DNA probe to identify enteroaggregative *Escherichia coli,* a recently discovered diarrheal pathogen. J. Infect. Dis. *161*:1249, 1990.
37. Beards, G. M., Green, J. G., Hall, C., et al.: An enveloped virus in stools of children and adults with gastroenteritis that resembles the Breda virus of calves. Lancet *1*:1050, 1984.
38. Beauvais, B., Sarfati, C., Molina, J. M., et al.: Comparative evaluation of five diagnostic methods for demonstrating microsporidia in stool and intestinal biopsy specimens. Ann. Trop. Med. Parasitol. *87*:99–102, 1993.
39. Beebakhee, G., Louie, M., De-Azavedo, J., et al.: Cloning and nucleotide sequence of the *eae* gene homologue from enterohemorrhagic *Escherichia coli* serotype 0157:H7. F. E. M. S. Microbiol. Lett. *70*:63–68, 1992.
40. Benator, D. A., French, A. L., Beaudet, L. M., et al.: *Isospora belli* infection associated with acalculous cholecystitis in a patient with AIDS. Ann. Intern. Med. *121*:663–664, 1994.
41. Benhamou, Y., Caumes, E., Gerosa, Y., et al.: AIDS-related cholangiopathy: Critical analysis of a prospective series of 26 patients. Dig. Dis. Sci. *38*:1113–1118, 1993.
42. Bennish, M. L., Salam, M. A., Haider, R., et al.: Therapy for shigellosis. II. Randomized, double-blind comparison of ciprofloxacin and ampicillin. J. Infect. Dis. *162*:711, 1990.
43. Berke, T., and Matson, D. O.: Reclassification of the Caliciviridae into distinct genera and exclusion of hepatitis E virus from the family on the basis of comparative phylogenetic analysis. Arch. Virol. *145*:1421–1436, 2000.
44. Bhan, M. K., Raj, P., Levine, M. M., et al.: Enteroaggregative *E. coli* associated with persistent diarrhea in a cohort of rural children in India. J. Infect. Dis. *159*:1061, 1989.
45. Bhutta, A. A., Khan, I. A., and Shadmani, M.: Failure of short-course ceftriaxone chemotherapy for multidrug-resistant typhoid fever in children: A randomized controlled trial in Pakistan. Antimicrob. Agents Chemother. *44*:450–452, 2000.
46. Bishop, R. F., Davidson, G. P., Holmes, I. H., et al.: Virus particles in epithelial cells of duodenal mucosa from children with acute nonbacterial gastroenteritis. Lancet *2*:1281–1283, 1973.
47. Black, R. E.: Pathogens that cause travelers' diarrhea in Latin America and Africa. Rev. Infect. Dis. *8*:131S, 1986.
48. Blanshard, C., Ellis, D. S., Tovey, D. G., et al.: Treatment of intestinal microsporidiosis with albendazole in patients with AIDS. AIDS. *6*:311–313, 1992.
49. Bottone, E. J.: *Yersinia enterocolitica*: The charisma continues. Clin. Microbiol. Rev. *10*:257–276, 1997.
50. Bourke, B., Jones, N., and Sherman, P.: *Helicobacter pylori* infection and peptic ulcer disease in children. Pediatr. Infect. Dis. J. *15*:1–13, 1996.
51. Boyle, T. G., Pemberton, A. G., Wells, J. G., et al.: Screening for *Escherichia coli* 0157:H7: A nationwide survey of clinical laboratories. J. Clin. Microbiol. *33*:3275–3277, 1995.
52. Brandt, C. D., Kim, H. W., Rodriguez, W. J., et al.: Adenoviruses and pediatric gastroenteritis. J. Infect. Dis. *151*:437–443, 1985.
53. Brenner, F. W., Villar, R. G., Angulo, F. J., et al.: *Salmonella* nomenclature. J. Clin. Microbiol. *38*:2465–2467, 2000.
54. Brown, K. H., and McClean, W. C.: Nutritional management of acute diarrhea: An appraisal of the alternatives. Pediatrics *73*:119–125, 1984.
55. Brown, K. H., Peerson, J. M., and Fontaine, O.: Use of nonhuman milks in the dietary management of young children with acute diarrhea: A meta-analysis of clinical trials. Pediatrics *93*:17–27, 1994.
56. Caeiro, J. P., DuPont, H. L., Albrecht, H., et al.: Oral rehydration therapy plus loperamide versus loperamide alone in the treatment of traveler's diarrhea. Clin. Infect. Dis. *28*:1286–1289, 1999.
57. Calva, J. J., Ruiz-Palacios, G. M., Lopez-Vidal, A. B., et al.: Cohort study of intestinal infection with *Campylobacter* in Mexican children. Lancet *1*:503, 1988.
58. Carr, A., Marriott, D., Field, A., et al.: Treatment of HIV-1–associated microsporidiosis and cryptosporidiosis with combination antiretroviral therapy. Lancet *351*:256–261, 1998.
59. Cello, J. P., Grendell, J. H., Basuk, P., et al.: Effect of octreotide on refractory AIDS-associated diarrhea: A prospective, multicenter trial. Ann. Intern. Med. *115*:705–710, 1991.
60. Centers for Disease Control and Prevention: Preliminary FoodNet data on the incidence of foodborne illness—selected sites, United States, 2000. M. M. W. R. Morb. Mortal. Wkly. Rep. *50*:241–246, 2001.
61. Centers for Disease Control and Prevention: 1993 Revised classification system for HIV infection and expanded surveillance case definition for AIDS among adolescents and adults. M. M. W. R. Morb. Mortal. Wkly. Rep. *41*(RR-17):1–19, 1992.
62. Centers for Disease Control and Prevention: The management of acute diarrhea in children: Oral rehydration, maintenance, and nutritional therapy. M. M. W. R. Morb. Mortal. Wkly. Rep. *41*(RR-16):1–20, 1992.
63. Centers for Disease Control and Prevention: Typhoid immunization. M. M. W. R. Morb. Mortal. Wkly. Rep. *43*:1–7, 1994.
64. Centers for Disease Control and Prevention: *Bacillus cereus* food poisoning associated with fried rice at two child care centers: Virginia, 1993. M. M. W. R. Morb. Mortal. Wkly. Rep. *43*:177–178, 1994.
65. Centers for Disease Control and Prevention: Outbreaks of *Cyclospora cayetanensis* infection: United States, 1996. M. M. W. R. Morb. Mortal. Wkly. Rep. *45*:549–551, 1996.
66. Centers for Disease Control and Prevention: Giardiasis surveillance. United States, 1992–1997. M. M. W. R. Morb. Mortal. Wkly. Rep. *49*(SS-7):1–13, 2000.
67. Centers for Disease Control and Prevention: Update: Multistate outbreak of *Listeriosis*—United States, 1998–1999. M. M. W. R. Morb. Mortal. Wkly. Rep. *47*:1117–1118, 2001.
68. Centers for Disease Control and Prevention: Diagnosis and management of foodborne illnesses: A primer for physicians. M. M. W. R. Morb. Mortal. Wkly. Rep. *50*(RR-02):1–69, 2001.
69. Centers for Disease Control and Prevention: Summary of notifiable diseases, United States, 2002. M. M. W. R. Morb. Mortal. Wkly. Rep. *50*:1–108, 2003.
70. Centers for Disease Control and Prevention: Responding to fecal accidents in disinfected swimming venues. M. M. W. R. Morb. Mortal. Wkly. Rep. *50*:416–417, 2001.
71. Centers for Disease Control and Prevention: Guidelines for preventing opportunistic infections among HIV-infected persons. M. M. W. R. Morb. Mortal. Wkly. Rep. *51*(RR-8):1–52, 2002.
72. Cerquetti, M., Luzzi, I., Caprioli, A., et al.: Role of *Clostridium difficile* in childhood diarrhea. Pediatr. Infect. Dis. J. *14*:598–603, 1995.
73. Cheasty, T., and Rowe, B.: Antigenic relationships between the enteroinvasive *Escherichia coli* O antigens O28ac, O112ac, O124, O136, O143, O144, O152, and O164 and *Shigella* O antigens. J. Clin. Microbiol. *17*:681–684, 1983.
74. Chinh, N. T., Parry, C. M., Ly, N. T., et al.: A randomized controlled comparison of azithromycin and ofloxacin for treatment of multidrug-resistant or nalidixic acid–resistant enteric fever. Antimicrob. Agents Chemother. *44*:1855–1859, 2000.
75. CHOICE Study Group: Multicenter, randomized, double-blind clinical trial to evaluate the efficacy and safety of a reduced osmolarity oral rehydration salts solution in children with acute watery diarrhea. Pediatrics *107*:613–618, 2001.
76. Clark, D. P.: New insights into human cryptosporidiosis. Clin. Microbiol. Rev. *12*:554–563, 1999.
77. Clausen, C. R., and Christie, D. L.: Chronic diarrhea in infants caused by adherent enteropathogenic *Escherichia coli.* J. Pediatr. *100*:358–361, 1982.
78. Cleary, T. G., Cleary, K. R., DuPont, H. L., et al.: The relationship of oral rehydration solution to hypernatremia in infantile diarrhea. J. Pediatr. *99*:739, 1981.
79. Cleary, T. G.: Cytotoxin-producing *Escherichia coli* and hemolytic uremic syndrome. Pediatr. Clin. North Am. *35*:485, 1988.
80. Cleary, T. G., and Lopez, E. L.: The Shiga-like toxin producing *E. coli* and hemolytic uremic syndrome. Pediatr. Infect. Dis. *8*:720, 1989.
81. Cleary, T. G., Guerrant, R. L., and Pickering, L. K.: Microorganisms responsible for neonatal diarrhea. *In* Remington, J. S., Klein, J. O. (eds.): Infectious Diseases of the Fetus and Newborn Infant. 5th ed. Philadelphia, W. B. Saunders, 2000, pp. 1249–1326.
82. Clements, M. L., Levine, M. M., Black, R. E., et al.: *Lactobacillus* prophylaxis for diarrhea due to enterotoxigenic *Escherichia coli.* Antimicrob. Agents Chemother. *20*:104–108, 1981.
83. Connolly, M. J., Snow, M. H., and Ingham, H. R.: Ciprofloxacin treatment of recurrent *Salmonella* septicaemia in a patient with acquired immune deficiency syndrome. J. Antimicrob. Chemother. *18*:647, 1986.
84. Conteas, C. N., Berlin, O. G. W., Ash, L. R., et al.: Therapy for human gastrointestinal microsporidiosis. Am. J. Trop. Med. Hyg. *63*:121-127, 2000.
85. Cooles, P.: Adjuvant steroids and relapse of typhoid fever. J. Trop. Med. Hyg. *89*:229, 1986.

86. Cornett, J. W. D., Aspeling, R. L., and Mallegol, D.: A double-blind comparative evaluation of loperamide versus diphenoxylate with atropine in acute diarrhea. Curr. Ther. Res. Clin. Exp. *21*:629–637, 1977.
87. Cotte, L., Rabodonirina, M., Chapuis, F., et al.: Waterborne outbreak of intestinal microsporidiosis in persons with and without human immunodeficiency virus infection. J. Infect. Dis. *180*:2003–2008, 1999.
88. Crawford, F. G., and Vermund, S. H.: Human cryptosporidiosis. CRC Crit. Rev. Microbiol. *16*:113, 1988.
89. Current, W. L., Reese, N. C., Ernst, J. V., et al.: Human cryptosporidiosis in immunocompetent and immunodeficient persons: Studies of an outbreak and experimental transmission. N. Engl. J. Med. *308*:1252–1257, 1983.
90. Czeczulin, J. R., Balepur, S., Hicks, S., et al.: Aggregative adherence fimbria II, a second fimbrial antigen mediating aggregative adherence in enteroaggregative *Escherichia coli*. Infect Immun. *65*:4135–4145, 1997.
91. Dalton, C. B., Austin, C. C., Sobel, J., et al.: An outbreak of gastroenteritis and fever due to *Listeria monocytogenes* in milk. N. Engl. J. Med. *336*:100–105, 1997.
92. Daniels, N. A., MacKinnon, L., Bishop, R., et al.: *Vibrio parahaemolyticus* infections in the United States, 1973–1998. J. Infect. Dis. *181*:161–166, 2000.
93. Dansinger, M. L., Johnson, S., Jansen, P. C., et al.: Protein-losing enteropathy is associated with *Clostridium difficile* diarrhea but not with asymptomatic colonization: A prospective case-control study. Clin. Infect. Dis. *22*:932–937, 1996.
94. DaSilva, A. J., Schwartz, D. A., Visvesvara, G. S., et al.: Sensitive PCR diagnosis of infections by *Enterocytozoon bieneusi* (microsporidia) using primers based on the region coding for small-subunit rRNA. J. Clin. Microbiol. *34*:986–987, 1996.
95. Davidson, R. A.: Issues in clinical parasitology: The treatment of giardiasis. Am. J. Gastroenterol. *79*:256–261, 1984.
96. Davis, M. A., Hancock, D. D., Besser, T. E., et al.: Changes in antimicrobial resistance among *Salmonella enterica* serovar typhimurium isolates from humans and cattle in the northwestern United States, 1982–1997. Emerg. Infect. Dis. *5*:802–806, 1999.
97. DeHovitz, J. A., Pape, J. W., Boncy, M., et al.: Clinical manifestations and therapy of *Isospora belli* infection in patients with the acquired immunodeficiency syndrome. N. Engl. J. Med. *315*:87, 1986.
98. Dennehy, P. H., Gauntlett, D. R., and Tente, W.: Comparison of nine commercial immunoassays for the detection of rotavirus in fecal samples. J. Clin. Microbiol. *26*:1630, 1988.
99. Dennehy, P. H., Nelson, S. M., Spangenberger, S., et al.: A prospective case-control study of the role of astrovirus in acute diarrhea among hospitalized young children. J. Infect. Dis. *184*:10–15, 2001.
100. DeVinney, R., Knoechel, D. G., and Finlay, B. B.: Enteropathogenic *Escherichia coli*: Cellular harassment. Curr. Opin. Microbiol. *2*:83–88, 1999.
101. Didier, E. S., Orenstein, J. M., Aldras, A., et al.: Comparison of three staining methods for detecting microsporidia in fluids. J. Clin. Microbiol. *33*:3138–3145, 1995.
102. Dietrich, D. T., Lew, E. A., Kotler, D. P., et al.: Treatment with albendazole for intestinal disease due to *Enterocytozoon bieneusi* in patients with AIDS. J. Infect. Dis. *169*:178–183, 1994.
103. Dobell, C.: A revision of the coccidia parasitic in man. Parasitology *11*:147, 1919.
104. Donnenberg, M. D., and Kaper, J. B.: Enteropathogenic *Escherichia coli*. Infect. Immun. *60*:3953B3961, 1992.
105. Donnenberg, M. S., Yu, J., and Kaper, J. B.: A second chromosomal gene necessary for intimate attachment of enteropathogenic *E. coli* to epithelial cells. J. Bacteriol. *175*:4670–4680, 1993.
106. Donnenberg, M. S., Giron, J. A., Nataro, J. P., et al.: A plasmid-encoded type IV fimbrial gene of enteropathogenic *Escherichia coli* associated with localized ahderence. Mol. Microbiol. *6*:3427–3437, 1992.
107. Donta, S. T., and Myers, M. G.: *Clostridium difficile* toxin in asymptomatic neonates. J. Pediatr. *100*:431–434, 1982.
108. Dore, G. J., Marriott, D. J., Hing, M. C., et al.: Disseminated microsporidiosis due to *Septata intestinalis* in nine patients infected with the human immunodeficiency virus: Response to therapy with albendazole. Clin. Infect. Dis. *21*:70–76, 1995.
109. Doyle, M. G., and Pickering, L. K.: Gastrointestinal tract infections in children with AIDS. Semin. Pediatr. Infect. Dis. *1*:64, 1990.
110. Drobneiwski, F. A.: *Bacillus cereus* and related species. Clin. Microbiol. Rev. *6*:324–338, 1993.
111. Dryjanski, J., Gold, J. W., Ritchie, M. T., et al.: Cryptosporidiosis: Case report in a health team worker. Am. J. Med. *80*:751, 1986.
112. Dunne, E. F., Fey, P. D., Kludt, P., et al.: Emergence of domestically acquired ceftriaxone resistant *Salmonella* infections associated with AmpC β-lactamase. J. A. M. A. *284*:3151–3156, 2000.
113. DuPont, H. L., and Hornick, R. B.: Adverse effects of Lomotil therapy in shigellosis. J. A. M. A. *226*:1525–1528, 1973.
114. DuPont, H. L., Olarte, J., Evans, D. G., et al.: Comparative susceptibility of Latin American and United States students to enteric pathogens. N. Engl. J. Med. *295*:1520–1521, 1976.
115. DuPont, H. L., Sullivan, P., Pickering, L. K., et al.: Symptomatic treatment of diarrhea with bismuth subsalicylate among students attending a Mexican university. Gastroenterology *73*:715–718, 1977.
116. DuPont, H. L., Evans, D. G., Sullivan, P., et al.: Prevention of travelers' diarrhea (emporiatric enteritis) by prophylactic administration of bismuth subsalicylate. J. A. M. A. *243*:237–241, 1980.
117. DuPont, H. L., and Ericsson, C. D.: Prevention and treatment of traveler's diarrhea. N. Engl. J. Med. *328*:1821–1827, 1993.
118. Dupont, H. L., Chappell, C. L., Sterling, C. R., et al.: The ineffectivity of *Cryptosporidium parvum* in healthy volunteers. N. Engl. J. Med. *332*:855–859, 1995.
119. Dupont, H. L., and Capsuto, E. G.: Persistent diarrhea in travelers. Clin. Infect. Dis. *22*:124–128, 1996.
120. DuPont, H. L., and the Practice Parameters Committee of the American College of Gastroenterology: Guidelines on acute diarrhea in adults. Am. J. Gastroenterol. *92*:1962–1975, 1997.
121. DuPont, H. L., Jiang, Z.-D., Ericsson, D. D., et al.: Rifaximin versus ciprofloxacin for the treatment of traveler's diarrhea: A randomized double-blind clinical trial. Clin. Infect. Dis. *33*:1807–1815, 2001.
122. Dutta, P., Rasaily, R., Saha, M. R., et al.: Ciprofloxacin for treatment of severe typhoid fever in children. Antimicrob. Agents Chemother. *37*:1197–1199, 1993.
123. Dworkin, M. S., Shoemaker, P. C., Goldoft, M. J., et al.: Reactive arthritis and Reiter's syndrome following an outbreak of gastroenteritis caused by *Salmonella enteritidis*. Clin. Infect. Dis. *33*:1010–1014, 2001.
124. Eastaugh, J., and Shepherd, S.: Infectious and toxic syndromes from fish and shellfish consumption: A review. Arch. Intern. Med. *149*:1735, 1989.
125. Eidlitz-Marcus, T., Cohen, Y. H., Nussinovitch, M., et al.: Comparative efficacy of two- and five-day courses of ceftriaxone for treatment of severe shigellosis in children. J. Pediatr. *123*:822–824, 1993.
126. Eisenberg, M. S., Gaarslev, K., Brown, W., et al.: Staphylococcal food poisoning aboard a commercial aircraft. Lancet *2*:595–599, 1975.
127. Elmer, G. W., Surawicz, C. M., and McFarland, L. V.: Biotherapeutic agents: A neglected modality for the treatment and prevention of selected intestinal and vaginal infections. J. A. M. A. *275*:870–876, 1996.
128. Engberg, J., On, S. L. W., Harrington, C. S., et al.: Prevalence of *Campylobacter, Arcobacter, Helicobacter,* and *Sutterella* spp. in human fecal samples as estimated by a reevaluation of isolation methods for campylobacters. J. Clin. Microbiol. *28*:286–291, 2000.
129. Ericsson, C. D., DuPont, H. L., Evans, D. G., et al.: Bismuth subsalicylate inhibits activity of crude toxins of *Escherichia coli* and *Vibrio cholerae*. J. Infect. Dis. *136*:693–696, 1977.
130. Ericsson, C. D., Pickering, L. K., Sullivan, P., et al.: The role of location of food consumption in the prevention of travelers' diarrhea in Mexico. Gastroenterology *79*:812–816, 1980.
131. Ericsson, C. D., Johnson, P. C., DuPont, H. L., et al.: Ciprofloxacin or trimethoprim/sulfamethoxazole as initial therapy for travelers' diarrhea. Ann. Intern. Med. *106*:216, 1987.
132. Ericsson, C. D., DuPont, H. L., Mathewson, J. J., et al.: Treatment of travelers' diarrhea with sulfamethoxazole and trimethoprim and loperamide. J. A. M. A. *263*:257, 1990.
133. Enslava, C., Navarro-Garcia, F., Czeczulin, J. R., et al.: Pet, an autotransporter enterotoxin from enteroaggregative *Escherichia coli*. Infect. Immun. *66*:3155–3163, 1998.
134. Espinosa-Cantellano, M., and Martinez-Palomo, A.: Pathogenesis of intestinal amebiasis: From molecules to disease. Clin. Microbiol. Rev. *13*:318–331, 2000.
135. Estes, M. K., and Cohen, J.: Rotavirus gene structure and function. Microbiol. Rev. *53*:410, 1989.
136. Fang, G. D., Lima, A. A., Martins, C. V., et al.: Etiology and epidemiology of persistent diarrhea in northeastern Brazil: A hospital-based, prospective case-control study. J. Pediatr. Gastroenterol. Nutr. *21*:137–144, 1995.
137. Fedorko, D. P., Nelson, N. A., and Cartwright, C. P.: Identification of microsporidia in stool specimens by using PCR and restriction endonucleases. J. Clin. Microbiol. *33*:1739–1741, 1995.
138. Feldman, R. J., Kallich, M., and Weinstein, M. P.: Bacteremia due to *Clostridium difficile*: Case report and review of extraintestinal *C. difficile* infections. Clin. Infect. Dis. *20*:1560–1562, 1995.
139. Feldman, S., Chen, S. L., Pickering, L. K., et al.: Salicylate absorption from a bismuth subsalicylate antidiarrheal preparation. Clin. Pharmacol. Therapeut. *29*:788–792, 1981.
140. Ferreccio, C., Morriss, G., Valdivieso, C., et al.: Efficacy of ciprofloxacin in the treatment of chronic typhoid carriers. J. Infect. Dis. *157*:1235, 1988.
141. Fichtenbaum, C. J., Ritchie, D. J., and Powderly, W. G.: Use of paromomycin for treatment of cryptosporidiosis in AIDS. Clin. Infect. Dis. *16*:298–300, 1993.
142. Fioramonti, J., Droy-Lefaix, M. T., and Bueno, L.: Changes in gastrointestinal motility induced by cholera toxin and experimental osmotic diarrhoea in dogs: Effects of treatment with an argillaceous compound. Digestion *36*:230, 1987.
143. Flanigan, T., Whalen, C., and Turner, J.: *Cryptosporidium* infection and CD4 counts. Ann. Intern. Med. *116*:840–842, 1992.

144. Ford-Jones, E. L., Mindorff, C. M., Gold, R., et al.: The incidence of viral-associated diarrhea after admission to a pediatric hospital. Am. J. Epidemiol. *131*:711–718, 1990.
145. Franzen, C., and Muller, A.: Molecular techniques for detection, species differentiation, and phylogenetic analysis of microsporidia. Clin. Microbiol. Rev. *12*:243–285, 1999.
146. Frenck, R. W., Jr., Nakhla, I., Sultan, Y., et al.: Azithromycin versus ceftriaxone for the treatment of uncomplicated typhoid fever in children. Clin. Infect. Dis. *31*:1134–1138, 2000.
147. Furness, B. W., Beach, M. J., and Roberts, J. M.: Giardiasis surveillance—United States, 1992–1997. M. M. W. R. Morb. Mortal. Wkly. Rep. *49*(SS-7):1–13, 2000.
148. Garcia, L. S., Brewer, T. C., and Bruckner, D. A.: Incidence of *Cryptosporidium* in all patients submitting stool specimens for ova and parasites examination: Monoclonal antibody IFA method. Diagn. Microbiol. Infect. Dis. *11*:25, 1988.
149. Garcia, L. S., and Shimizu, R. Y.: Evaluation of nine immunoassay kits (enzyme immunoassay and direct fluorescence) for detection for *Giardia lamblia* and *Cryptosporidium parvum* in human fecal specimens. J. Clin. Microbiol. *35*:1526–1529, 1997.
150. Gardner, T. B., and Hill, D. R.: Treatment of giardiasis. Clin. Microbiol. Rev. *14*:114–128, 2001.
151. Gebreyes, W. A., Davies, P. R., Morrow, W. E. M., et al.: Antimicrobial resistance of *Salmonella* isolates from swine. J. Clin. Microbiol. *38*:4633–4636, 2000.
152. Genta, R. M.: Global prevalence of strongyloidiasis: Critical review with epidemiologic insights into the prevention of disseminated disease. Rev. Infect. Dis. *11*:755, 1989.
153. Ginsburg, C. M.: Lomotil (diphenoxylate and atropine) intoxication. Am. J. Dis. Child. *125*:241, 1973.
154. Girard, D. E., and Keefe, E. B.: *Isospora* and travelers' diarrhea. Ann. Intern. Med. *106*:908, 1987.
155. Girgis, N. I., Butler, T., Frenck, R. W., et al.: Azithromycin versus ciprofloxacin for treatment of uncomplicated typhoid fever in a randomized trial in Egypt that included patients with multidrug resistance. Antimicrob. Agents Chemother. *43*:1441–1444, 1999.
156. Glandt, M., Adachi, J. A., Mathewson, J. J., et al.: Enteroaggregative *Escherichia coli* as a cause of traveler's diarrhea: Clinical response to ciprofloxacin. Clin. Infect. Dis. *29*:335–338, 1999.
157. Glass, R. I., Noel, J., Mitchell, D., et al: The changing epidemiology of astrovirus-associated gastroenteritis. Arch. Virol. *12*(Suppl.):287–300, 1996.
158. Glass, R. I., Noel, J., Ando, T., et al.: The epidemiology of enteric caliciviruses from humans: A reassessment using new diagnostics. J. Infect. Dis. *181*:S254–S261, 2000.
159. Glynn, M. K., Bopp, D., Dewitt, W., et al.: Emergence of multidrug-resistant *Salmonella enterica* serotype typhimurium DT104 infections in the United States. N. Engl. J. Med. *338*:1333–1338, 1998.
160. Goldberg, M. B., and Sansonetti, P. J.: *Shigella* subversion of the cellular cytoskeleton: A strategy for epithelial colonization. Infect. Immun. *61*:4941–4946, 1993.
161. Gomi, H., Jiang, Z.-D., Adachi, J. A., et al.: In vitro antimicrobial susceptibility testing of bacterial enteropathogens causing traveler's diarrhea in four geographic regions. Antimicrob. Agents Chemother. *45*:212–216, 2001.
162. Goodgame, R. W.: Understanding intestinal spore-forming protozoa: Cryptosporidia, microsporidia, isospora, and cyclospora. Ann. Intern. Med. *124*:429–441, 1996.
163. Gorbach, S. L., Carpenter, C. C. J., Grayson, R., et al.: Travelers' diarrhea: Consensus conference. J. A. M. A. *253*:2700–2704, 1985.
164. Gotuzzo, E., Seas, C., Echevarria, J., et al.: Ciprofloxacin for the treatment of cholera: A randomized, double-blind controlled clinical trial of a single dose in Peruvian adults. Clin. Infect. Dis. *20*:1485–1490, 1995.
165. Gotz, H., Ekdahl, K., Lindback, J., et al.: Clinical spectrum and transmission characteristics of infection with Norwalk-like virus: Findings from a large community outbreak in Sweden. Clin. Infect. Dis. *33*:622–628, 2001.
166. Goyal, R. K., and Hirando, I.: The enteric nervous system. N. Engl. J. Med. *334*:1106–1115, 1996.
167. Green, S. D. R.: Ten years of pediatric experience with ciprofloxacin. Infect. Dis. Clin. Pract. 7(Suppl. 3):S175–S183, 1998.
168. Greenberg, H. B., Valdesuso, J., Yolken, R. H., et al.: Role of Norwalk virus in outbreaks of non-bacterial gastroenteritis. J. Infect. Dis. *139*:564, 1979.
169. Guerrero, M. L., Noel, J. S., Mitchell, D. K., et al.: A prospective study of astrovirus diarrhea of infancy in Mexico City. Pediatr. Infect. Dis. J. *17*:723–727, 1998.
170. Guerrant, R. L., Van Gilder, T., Steiner, T. S., et al.: Practice guidelines for the management of infectious diarrhea. Clin. Infect. Dis. *32*:331–350, 2001.
171. Hakaken, A., Kotilainen, P., Jalava, J., et al.: Detection of decreased fluoroquinolone susceptibility in salmonellas and validation of nalidixic acid screening text. J. Clin. Microbiol. *37*:3572–3577, 1999.
172. Hall, A., and Nahar, Q.: Albendazole as a treatment for infections with *Giardia duodenalis* in children in Bangladesh. Trans. R. Soc. Trop. Med. Hyg. *87*:84–86, 1993.
173. Hannelore, G., Ekdahl, K., Lindbäck, J., et al.: Clinical spectrum and transmission characteristics of infection with Norwalk-like virus: Findings from a large community outbreak in Sweden. Clin. Infect. Dis. *22*:622–628, 2001.
174. Hanrahan, J. P., and Gordon, M. A.: Mushroom poisoning: Case reports and a review of therapy. J. A. M. A. *251*:1057–1061, 1984.
175. Haque, R., Neville, L. M., Hahn, P., et al.: Rapid diagnosis of *Entamoeba* infection by using *Entamoeba* and *Entamoeba histolytica* stool antigen detection kits. J. Clin. Microbiol. *33*:2558–2561, 1995.
176. Hart, C. A., Baxby, D., and Blundell, N.: Gastroenteritis due to *Cryptosporidium:* A prospective survey in a children's hospital. J. Infect. *9*:264, 1984.
177. Hayward, R. D., and Koronakis, V.: Direct nucleation and bundling of actin by the SipC protein of invasive *Salmonella.* E. M. B. O. J. *18*:4926–4934, 1999.
178. Hayward, R. D., McGhie, E. J., and Koronakis, V.: Membrane fusion activity of purified SipB, a *Salmonella* surface protein essential for mammalian cell invasion. Mol. Microbiol. *37*:727–739, 2000.
179. Hedberg, C. W., MacDonald, K. L., and Osterholm, M. T.: Changing epidemiology of food-borne disease: A Minnesota prospective. Clin. Infect. Dis. *18*:671–682, 1994.
180. Henderson, A. E., Gillespie, G. W., Kaplan, P., et al.: The human *Isospora.* Am. J. Hyg. *78*:302, 1963.
181. Hennessy, T. W., Hedberg, C. W., Slutsker, L., et al.: A national outbreak of *Salmonella enteritidis* infections from ice cream. N. Engl. J. Med. *334*:1281–1286, 1996.
182. Henricksen, S. A., and Pohlenz, J. F. L.: Staining of cryptosporidia by a modified Ziehl-Neelsen technique. Acta Vet. Scand. *22*:594, 1981.
183. Herikstad, H., Hayes, P., Mokhtar, M., et al.: Emerging quinolone-resistant *Salmonella* in the United States. Emerg. Infect. Dis. *3*:371–372, 1997.
184. Herrington, D. A., Tzipori, S., Robins-Browne, R. M., et al.: In vitro and in vivo pathogenicity of *Plesiomonas shigelloides.* Infect. Immun. *55:979*, 1987.
185. Herwaldt, B. L., and Ackers, M. L.: An outbreak in 1996 of cyclosporiasis associated with imported raspberries. The Cyclospora Working Group. N. Engl. J. Med. *336*:1546–1556, 1997.
186. Herwaldt, B. L.: *Cyclospora cayetanensis*: A review, focusing on the outbreaks of cyclosporiasis in the 1990s. Clin. Infect. Dis. *31*:1040–1057, 2000.
187. Herwaldt, B. L., de Arroyave, K. R., Roberts, J. M., et al.: A multiyear prospective study of the risk factors for and incidence of diarrheal illness in a cohort of Peace Corps volunteers in Guatemala. Ann. Intern. Med. *132*:982–988, 2000.
188. Hewitt, R. G., Yiannoutsos, C. T., Higgs, E. S., et al.: Paromomycin: No more effective than placebo for treatment of cryptosporidiosis in patients with advanced human immunodeficiency virus infection. Clin. Infect. Dis. *31*:1084–1092, 2000.
189. Hicks, P., Zwiener, J., Squires, J., et al.: Azithromycin therapy for *Cryptosporidium parvum* infection in four children infected with human immunodeficiency virus. J. Infect. Dis. *129*:297–300, 1996.
190. Hines, J., and Nachamkin, I.: Effective use of the clinical microbiology laboratory for diagnosing diarrheal diseases. Clin. Infect. Dis. *23*:1292–1301, 1996.
191. Hinnant, K., Schwartz, A., Rotterdam, H., et al.: Cytomegaloviral and cryptosporidial cholecystitis in two patients with AIDS. Am. J. Surg. Pathol. *13*:57–60, 1989.
192. Hirschhorn, N.: Treatment of acute diarrhea in children: Historical and physiological perspective. J. Clin. Nutr. *33*:637–663, 1980.
193. Hlady, W. G., and Klontz, K. C.: The epidemiology of *Vibrio* infections in Florida, 1981–1993. J. Infect. Dis. *173*:1176–1183, 1996.
194. Ho, M., Glass, R. I., Monroe, S. S., et al.: Viral gastroenteritis aboard a cruise ship. Lancet *2*:961, 1989.
195. Hoffman, S. L., Punjabi, N. H., Kumala, S., et al.: Reduction of mortality in chloramphenicol-treated severe typhoid fever by high-dose dexamethasone. N. Engl. J. Med. *310*:82, 1984.
196. Hoge, C. W., Shlim, D. R., Ghimire, M., et al.: Placebo-controlled trial of co-trimoxazole for cyclospora infections among travellers and foreign residents in Nepal. Lancet *345*:691–693, 1995.
197. Hoge, C. W., Shlim, D. R., Echeverria, P., et al.: Epidemiology of diarrhea among expatriate residents living in a highly endemic environment. J. A. M. A. *275*:533–538, 1996.
198. Högenauer, C., Hammer, H. F., Krejs, G. J., et al.: Mechanisms and management of antibiotic-associated diarrhea. Clin. Infect. Dis. *27*:702–710, 1998.
199. Hohmann, E. L.: Nontyphoidal salmonellosis. Clin. Infect. Dis. *32*:263–269, 2001.
200. Holmberg, S. D., and Blake, P. A.: Staphylococcal food poisoning in the United States: New facts and old misconceptions. J. A. M. A. *251*:487–489, 1984.

201. Holmberg, S. D., Wachsmuth, I. K., Hickman-Brenner, F. W., et al.: *Plesiomonas* enteric infections in the United States. Ann. Intern. Med. *105*:690, 1986.
202. Holmberg, S. D., Moorman, A. C., Von Bargen, J. C., et al.: Possible effectiveness of clarithromycin and rifabutin for cryptosporidiosis chemoprophylaxis in HIV disease. HIV Outpatient Study (HOPS) Investigators. J. A. M. A. *279*:384–386, 1998.
203. Holmes, S. J., Morrow, A. L., and Pickering, L. K.: Child care practices: Effects of social changes on epidemiology of infectious diseases and antibiotic resistance. Epidemiol. Rev. *18*:10–28, 1996.
204. Horiuchi, S., Inagaki, Y., Yamamoto, N., et al.: Reduced susceptibilities of *Shigella sonnei* strains isolated from patients with dysentery to fluoroquinolones. Antimicrob. Agents Chemother. *37*:2486–2489, 1993.
205. Hovius, S. E. R., and Rietra, P. J.: *Salmonella* colitis clinically presenting as pseudomembranous colitis. Neth. J. Surg. *34*:81–82, 1982.
206. Hughes, J. M., Boyce, J. M., Aleem, A. R. M. A., et al.: *Vibrio parahaemolyticus* enterocolitis in Bangladesh: Report of an outbreak. Am. J. Trop. Med. Hyg. *27*:106–112, 1978.
207. Huicho, L., Campos, M., Rivera, J., et al.: Fecal screening tests in the approach to acute infectious diarrhea: A scientific overview. Pediatr. Infect. Dis. J. *15*:486–494, 1996.
208. Islam, A., Butler, T., Kabir, I., et al.: Treatment of typhoid fever with ceftriaxone for 5 days or chloramphenicol for 14 days: A randomized clinical trial. Antimicrob. Agents Chemother. *37*:1572–1575, 1993.
209. Janda, J. M., Powers, C., Bryant, R. G., et al.: Current perspectives on the epidemiology and pathogenesis of clinically significant *Vibrio* spp. Clin. Microbiol. Rev. *1*:245, 1988.
210. Janda, J. M., and Abbott, S. L.: Evolving concepts regarding the genus *Aeromonas*: An expanding panorama of species, disease presentations, and unanswered questions. Clin. Infect. Dis. *27*:332–344, 1998.
211. Jensen, L. B., and Aarestrup, F. M.: Macrolide resistance in *Campylobacter coli* of animal origin in Denmark. Antimicrob. Agents Chemother. *45*:371–372, 2001.
212. Jiang, X., Graham, D. Y., Wang, K., et al.: Norwalk virus genome cloning and characterization. Science *250*:1580–1583, 1991.
213. Jiang, X., Matson, D. O., Velazquez, F. R., et al.: A study of Norwalk-related viruses in Mexican children. J. Med. Virol. *47*:309–316, 1995.
214. Jiang, X., Turf, E., Hu, J., et al.: Outbreaks of gastroenteritis in elderly nursing homes and retirement facilities associated with human caliciviruses. J. Med. Virol. *50*:335–341, 1996.
215. Jimenez, S. G., Heine, R. G., Ward, P. B., et al.: *Campylobacter upsaliensis* gastroenteritis in childhood. Pediatr. Infect. Dis. J. *18*:988–992, 1999.
216. Johnson, S., and Gerding, D. N.: *Clostridium difficile*–associated diarrhea. Clin. Infect. Dis. *26*:1027–1036, 1998.
217. Johnson, S., Henderson, W., Crewe-Brown, H., et al.: Effect of human immunodeficiency virus infection on episodes of diarrhea among children in South Africa. Pediatr. Infect. Dis. J. *19*:972–979, 2000.
218. Johnson, W. D., Jr., Hook, E. W., Lindsey, E., et al.: Treatment of chronic typhoid carriers with ampicillin. Antimicrob. Agents Chemother. *3*:439–440, 1973.
219. Kabir, I., Butler, T., and Khanam, A.: Comparative efficacies of single intravenous doses of ceftriaxone and ampicillin for shigellosis in a placebo-controlled trial. Antimicrob. Agents Chemother. *29*:645, 1986.
220. Kain, K. C., and Kelly, M. T.: Clinical features, epidemiology, and treatment of *Plesiomonas shigelloides* diarrhea. J. Clin. Microbiol. *27*:998, 1989.
221. Kaper, J. B., Morris, J. G., Jr., and Levine, M. M.: Cholera. Clin. Microbiol. Rev. *8*:48–86, 1995.
222. Kapikian, A. Z., Wyatt, R. G., Dolin, R., et al.: Visualization by immune electron microscopy of a 27-nm particle associated with acute infectious nonbacterial gastroenteritis. J. Virol. *10*:1075–1081, 1972.
223. Karmali, M. A., Petric, M., Lim, C., et al.: The association between idiopathic hemolytic uremic syndrome and infection by verotoxin-producing *Escherichia coli*. J. Infect. Dis. *151*:775–782, 1985.
224. Karmali, M. A.: Infection by verocytotoxin-producing *Escherichia coli*. Clin. Microbiol. Rev. *2*:15, 1989.
225. Katanik, M. T., Schneider, S. K., Rosenblatt, J. E., et al.: Evaluation of colorPAC *Giardia/Cryptosporidium* rapid assay and ProSpecT *Giardia/Cryptosporidium* microplate assay for detection of *Giardia* and *Cryptosporidium* in fecal specimens. J. Clin. Microbiol. *39*:4523–4525, 2001.
226. Katiyar, S. K., and Edlind, T. D.: In vitro susceptibilities of the AIDS-associated microsporidian *Encephalitozoon intestinalis* to albendazole, its sulfoxide metabolite, 12 additioinal benzimidazole derivates. Antimicrob. Agents Chemother. *41*:2729–2732, 1997.
227. Kaye, D., Marselis, J. G., and Hook, E. W.: Susceptibility of *Salmonella* species to four antibiotics. N. Engl. J. Med. *269*:1084–1086, 1963.
228. Kelber, M., and Ament, M. E.: *Shigella dysenteriae* I: A forgotton cause of pseudomembranous colitis. J. Pediatr. *89*:595, 1976.
229. Keusch, G. T., and Bennish, M. L.: Shigellosis: Recent progress, persisting problems and research issues. Pediatr. Infect. Dis. *8*:713, 1989.
230. Khan, W. A., Bennish, M. L., Seas, C., et al.: Randomised controlled comparison of single-dose ciprofloxacin and doxycycline for cholera caused by *Vibrio cholera* 01 and 0139. Lancet *348*:296–300, 1996.
231. Khan, W. A., Seas, C., Dhar, U., et al.: Treatment of shigellosis: V. Comparison of azithromycin and ciprofloxacin. Ann. Intern. Med. *126*:697–703, 1997.
232. Knisley, C. V., Bednarz-Prashad, A. J., and Pickering, L. K.: Detection of rotavirus in stool specimens with monoclonal and polyclonal antibody-based assay systems. J. Clin. Microbiol. *23*:897–900, 1986.
233. Knisley, C. V., Englekirk, P. G., Pickering, L. K., et al.: Rapid detection of *Giardia* antigen in stool using enzyme immunoassays. Am. J. Clin. Pathol. *91*:704, 1989.
234. Koch, K. L., Phillips, D. J., Aber, R. C., et al.: Cryptosporidiosis in hospital personnel: Evidence for person-to-person transmission. Ann. Intern. Med. *102*:593, 1985.
235. Koo, D., Maloney, K., and Tauxe, R.: Epidemiology of diarrheal disease outbreaks on cruise ships, 1986 through 1993. J. A. M. A. *275*:545–547, 1996.
236. Koopmans, M. P. G., Goosen, E. S. M., Lima, A. A. M., et al.: Association of torovirus with acute and persistent diarrhea in children. Pediatr. Infect. Dis. J. *16*:504–507, 1997.
237. Kotler, D. P., Francisco, A., Clayton, F., et al.: Small intestinal injury and parasitic diseases in AIDS. Ann. Intern. Med. *113*:444, 1990.
238. Kotler, D. P., and Orenstein, J. M.: Clinical syndromes associated with microsporidiosis. Adv. Parasitol. *40*:321–349, 1998.
239. Kotler, D. P.: Characterization of intestinal disease associated with human immunodeficiency virus infection and response to antiretroviral therapy. J. Infect. Dis. *179*(Suppl.):454–456, 1999.
240. Kotloff, K. L., Losonsky, G. A., Morris, J. G., et al.: Enteric adenovirus infection and childhood diarrhea: An epidemiologic study in three clinical settings. Pediatrics *84*:219, 1989.
241. Kreutner, A. K., Del Bene, V. E., and Amstey, M. S.: Giardiasis in pregnancy. Am. J. Obstet. Gynecol. *140*:895–901, 1981.
242. Kristjansson, M., Samore M. H., Gerding, D. N., et al.: Comparison of restriction endonuclease analysis, ribotyping, and pulsed-field gel electrophoresis for molecular differentiation of *Clostridium difficile* strains. J. Clin. Microbiol. *32*:1963–1969, 1994.
243. Kuhls, T. L.: Cryptosporidiosis during childhood. Semin. Pediatr. Infect. Dis. *11*:213–219, 2000.
244. Kuritsky, J. N., Osterholm, M. T., Greenberg, H. B., et al.: Norwalk gastroenteritis: A community outbreak associated with bakery product consumption. Ann. Intern. Med. *201:519–521*, 1984.
245. Lawson, A. J., Logan, J. M. J., O'Neil, G. L., et al.: Large-scale survey of *Campylobacter* species in human gastroenteritis by PCR and PCR-enzyme–linked immunosorbent assay. J. Clin. Microbiol. *37*:3860–3864, 1999.
246. Lecuit, M., Oksenhendler, E., and Sarfati, C.: Use of albendazole for disseminated microsporidian infection in a patient with AIDS. Clin. Infect. Dis. *19*:332–333, 1994.
247. Lee, L. A., Gerber, A. R., Lonsway, D. R., et al.: *Yersinia enterocolitica* 0:3 infections in infants and children, associated with the household preparation of chitterlings. N. Engl. J. Med. *322*:984, 1990.
248. Lee, L. A., Puhr, N. D., Maloney, K., et al.: Increase in antimicrobial-resistant *Salmonella* infections in the United States. J. Infect. Dis. *170*:128–134, 1994.
249. Lessnau, K. D., Can, S., and Talavera, W.: Disseminated *Strongyloides stercoralis* in human immunodeficiency virus–infected patients: Treatment failure and a review of the literature. Chest *104*:119–122, 1993.
250. Levine, M. M., Hughes, T. P., Black, R. E., et al.: Variability of sodium and sucrose levels of simple sugar/salt oral rehydration solutions prepared under optimal and field conditions. J. Pediatr. *97*:324–327, 1980.
251. Levine, W. C., Bennett, R. W., Choi, Y., et al.: Staphylococcal food poisoning caused by imported canned mushrooms. J. Infect. Dis. *173*:1263–1267, 1996.
252. Limson, B. M., and Littana, R. T.: Ciprofloxacin vs. co-trimoxazole in *Salmonella* enteric fever. Infection *17*:105, 1989.
253. Lin, F. Y. C., Ho, V. A., Khiem, H. B., et al.: The efficacy of a *Salmonella typhi* Vi conjugate vaccine in two- to five-year-old children. N. Engl. J. Med. *344*:1263–1269, 2001.
254. Lindsay, D. S., Dubey, J. P., Blagburn, B. L.: Biology of *Isospora* spp. from humans, non-human primates, and domestic animals. Clin. Microbiol. Rev. *10*:19–34, 1997.
255. Lo, C. W., and Walker, W. A.: Chronic protracted diarrhea of infancy: A nutritional disease. Pediatrics *72*:786–800, 1983.
256. Louie, E., Barkowsky, W., and Klesius, P. H.: Treatment of cryptosporidiosis with oral bovine transfer factor. Clin. Immunol. Immunopathol. *44*:329, 1987.
257. Lowry, P. W., Pavia, A. T., McFarland, L. M., et al.: Cholera in Louisiana: Widening spectrum of seafood vehicles. Arch. Intern. Med. *149*:2079, 1989.
258. Luby, S., Jones, J., Dowda, H., et al.: A large outbreak of gastroenteritis caused by diarrheal toxin-producing *Bacillus cereus*. J. Infect. Dis. *167*:1452–1455, 1993.
259. MacKenzie, W. R., Hoxie, N. J., Proctor, M. E., et al.: A massive outbreak in Milwaukee of *Cryptosporidium* infection transmitted through the public water supply. N. Engl. J. Med. *331*:161–167, 1994.

260. Madico, G., McDonald, J., Gilman, R. H., et al.: Epidemiology and treatment of *Cyclospora cayetanensis* infection in Peruvian children. Clin. Infect. Dis. *24*:977–981, 1997.
261. Mahler, H., Pasi, A., Kramer, J. M., et al.: Fulminant liver failure in association with the emetic toxin of *Bacillus cereus*. N. Engl. J. Med. *336*:1142–1148, 1997.
262. Maiorioni, E., Lopez, E. L., Moore, R. D., et al.: Multiply resistant non-typhoidal *Salmonella* gastroenteritis in children. Pediatr. Infect. Dis. J. *12*:139–144, 1993.
263. Manabe, Y. C., Vinetz, J. M., Moore, R. D., et. al.: *Clostridium difficile* colitis: An efficient clinical approach to diagnosis. Ann. Intern. Med. *123*:835–840, 1995.
264. Manabe, Y. C., Clark, D. P., Moore, R. D., et al.: Cryptosporidiosis in patients with AIDS: Correlates of disease and survival. Clin. Infect. Dis. *27*:536–542, 1998.
265. Margolis, P. A., Litteer, T., Hare, N., et al.: Effects of unrestricted diet on mild infantile diarrhea. Am. J. Dis. Child. *144*:162, 1990.
266. Marshall, R. J., and Flanigan, T. P.: Paromomycin inhibits *Cryptosporidium* infection of a human enterocyte cell line. J. Infect. Dis. *165*:772–774, 1992.
267. Martino, P., Gentile, G., Caprioli, A., et al.: Hospital acquired cryptosporidiosis in a bone marrow transplantation unit. J. Infect. Dis. *158*:647, 1988.
268. Maslanka, S. E., Kerr, J. G., Williams, G., et al.: Molecular subtyping of *Clostridium perfringens* by pulsed-field gel electrophoresis to facilitate food-borne-disease outbreak investigations. J. Clin. Microbiol. *37*:2209–2214, 1999.
269. Mathewson, J. J., Johnson, P. C., DuPont, H. L., et al.: Pathogenicity of enteroadherent *Escherichia coli* in adult volunteers. J. Infect. Dis. *154*:524–527, 1986.
270. Mathewson, J. J., Oberhelman, R. A., DuPont, H. L., et al.: Enteroadherent *E. coli* as a cause of diarrhea among children in Mexico. J. Clin. Microbiol. *25*:1917, 1987.
271. Matson, D. O., Estes, M. K., Glass, R. I., et al.: Human calicivirus-associated diarrhea in children attending day care centers. J. Infect. Dis. *159*:71, 1989.
272. Matson, D. O., and Estes, M. K.: Impact of rotavirus infection at a large pediatric hospital. J. Infect. Dis. *162*:598, 1990.
273. Matson, D. O., Estes, M. K., Burns, J. W., et al.: Serotype variation of human group A rotaviruses in two regions of the United States. J. Infect. Dis. *162*:605, 1990.
274. Matson, D. O., Estes, M. K., Tanaka, T., et al.: Asymptomatic human calicivirus infection in a day care center. Pediatr. Infect. Dis. *9*:190, 1990.
275. McFarland, L. V., Surawicz, C. M., and Stamm, W. E.: Risk factors for *Clostridium difficile* carriage and *C. difficile*-associated diarrhea in a cohort of hospitalized patients. J. Infect. Dis. *162*:678, 1990.
276. McFarland, L. V., Surawicz, C. M., Greenberg, R. N., et al.: A randomized placebo-controlled trial of *Saccharomyces boulardii* in combination with standard antibiotics for *Clostridium difficile* disease. J. A. M. A. *271*:1913–1918, 1994.
277. Mead, P. S., Slutsker, L., Dietz, V., et al.: Food-related illness and death in the United States. Emerg. Infect. Dis. *5*:607–625, 1999.
278. Medical Letter: Drugs for parasitic infections. *In* Pickering, L. K. (ed.): 2003 Red Book: Report of the Committee on Infectious Diseases. 26th ed. Elk Grove, IL, American Academy of Pediatrics, 2003. pp. 744–770.
279. Medical Letter: The choice of antibacterial drugs. Med. Lett. Drugs Ther. *43*:69–78, 2001.
280. Memon, I. A., Billoo, A. G., and Memon, H. I.: Cefixime: An oral option for the treatment of multidrug-resistant enteric fever in children. South. Med. J. *90*:1204–1207, 1997.
281. Mendelowitz, P. C., Hoffman, R. S., and Weber, S.: Bismuth absorption and myoclonic encephalopathy during bismuth subsalicylate therapy. Ann. Intern. Med. *112*:140, 1990.
282. Midthun, K., and Kapikian, A. Z.: Rotavirus vaccines: An overview. Clin. Microbiol. Rev. *9*:423–434, 1996.
283. Mirelman, D., Nuchamowitz, Y., and Stolarsky, T.: Comparison of use of enzyme-linked immunosorbent assay–based kits and PCR amplification of rRNA genes for simultaneous detection of *Entamoeba histolytica* and *E. dispar*. J. Clin. Microbiol. *35*:2405–2407, 1997.
284. Mitchell, D. K., Monroe, S. S., Jiang, X., et al.: Virologic features of an astrovirus diarrhea outbreak in a day care center revealed by reverse transcriptase-polymerase chain reaction. J. Infect. Dis. *172*:1437–1444, 1995.
285. Mitchell, D. K., Van, R., Mason, E. H., et al.: Prospective study of toxigenic *Clostridium difficile* in children given amoxicillin/clavulanate for otitis media. Pediatr. Infect. Dis. J. *15*:514–519, 1996.
286. Mitchell, D. K., Snyder, J., and Pickering, L. K.: Gastrointestinal infections. *In* Pizzo, P. A., and Wilfert, C. M. (eds.): Pediatric AIDS: The Role of HIV Infections in Infants, Children, and Adolescents. 3rd ed. Baltimore, Williams & Wilkins, 1999, pp. 267–291.
287. Mitchell, D. K., and Pickering, L. K.: Nosocomial gastrointestinal tract infections in pediatric patients. *In* Mayhall, C. G. (ed.): Hospital Epidemiology and Infection Control. 2nd ed. Baltimore, Williams & Wilkins, 1999, pp. 629–647.
288. Molbak, K., Baggesen, D. L., Aarestrup, F. M., et al.: An outbreak of multidrug-resistant, quinolone-resistant *Salmonella enterica* serotype typhimurium DT 104. N. Engl. J. Med. *341*:1420–1425, 1999.
289. Molina, J.-M., Chastang, C., Goguel, J., et al.: Albendazole for treatment and prophylaxis of microsporidiosis due to *Encephalitozoon intestinalis* in patients with AIDS: A randomized double-blind controlled trial. J. Infect. Dis. *177*:1373–1377, 1998.
290. Morgan, D. R., Johnson, P. C., DuPont, H. L., et al.: Lack of correlation between known virulence properties of *Aeromonas hydrophila* and enteropathogenicity for humans. Infect. Immun. *50*:62, 1985.
291. Morse, D. L., Guzewich, J. J., Hanrahan, J. P., et al.: Widespread outbreaks of clam- and oyster-associated gastroenteritis: Role of Norwalk virus. N. Engl. J. Med. *314*:678–681, 1986.
292. Moss, J., Burns, D. L., Hsia, J. A., et al.: Cyclic nucleotides: Mediators of bacterial toxin action in diseases. Ann. Intern. Med. *101*:653, 1984.
293. Motala, C., Hill, I. D., Mann, M. D., et al.: Effect of loperamide on stool output and duration of acute infectious diarrhea in infants. J. Pediatr. *117*:467, 1990.
294. Mourad, A. S., Metwally, M., El Deen, A., et al.: Multiple-drug–resistant *Salmonella typhi*. Clin. Infect. Dis. *17*:135–136, 1993.
295. Munoz, P., Diaz, M. D., Rodriguez-Creixems, M., et al.: Antimicrobial resistance of *Salmonella* isolates in a Spanish hospital. Antimicrob. Agents Chemother. *37*:1200–1202, 1993.
296. Murdoch, D. A., Banatvala, N. A., Bone, A., et al.: Epidemic ciprofloxacin-resistant *Salmonella typhi* in Tajikistan. Lancet *351*:339, 1998.
297. Murphy, T. V., Gargiullo, P. M., Massoudi, M. S., et al.: Intussusception among infants given an oral rotavirus vaccine. N. Engl. J. Med. *344*:564, 2001.
298. Murray, B. E.: Problems and mechanisms of antimicrobial resistance. Infect. Dis. Clin. North Am. *3*:423, 1990.
299. Murrell, T. G. C., Egerton, J. R., Rampling, A., et al.: The ecology and epidemiology of the pig-bel syndrome in man in New Guinea. J. Hyg. *64*:375–396, 1966.
300. Nataro, J. P., Deng, Y., Maneval, D. R., et al.: Aggregative adherence fimbriae I of enteroaggregative *Escherichia coli* mediated adherence to Hep-2 cells and hemagglutination of human erythrocytes. Infect. Immun. *60*:2297–2304, 1992.
301. Nataro, J. P., Deng, Y., Cookson, S., et al.: Heterogeneity of enteroaggregative *Escherichia coli* virulence demonstrated in volunteers. J. Infect. Dis. *171*:465–468, 1995.
302. Nataro, J. P., and Kaper, J. B.: Diarrheagenic *Escherichia coli*. Microbiol. Rev. *11*:142–201, 1998.
303. Navarro, F., Miro, E., Fuentes, I., et al.: *Campylobacter* species: Identification and resistance to quinolones. Clin. Infect. Dis. *17*: 815–816, 1993.
304. Navarro-Garcia, F., Canizalez-Roman, A., Luna J., et al.: Plasmid-encoded toxin of enteroaggregative *Escherichia coli* is internalized by epithelial cells. Infect. Immun. *69*:1053–1060, 2001.
305. Nelson, J. D., and Haltalin, K. C.: Amoxicillin less effective than ampicillin against *Shigella* in vitro and in vivo: Relationship of efficacy to activity in serum. J. Infect. Dis. *129*(Suppl.):222–227, 1974.
306. Newland, J. W., and Neill, R. J.: DNA probes for Shiga-like toxins I and II and for toxin-converting bacteriophages. J. Clin. Microbiol. *26*:1292, 1988.
307. Nilsson, M., Svenungsson, B., Hedlund, K. O., et al.: Incidence and genetic diversity of group C rotavirus among adults. J. Infect. Dis. *182*:678–684, 2000.
308. Nishibuchi, M., Fasano, A., Russell, R. G., et al.: Enterotoxigenicity of *V. parahaemolyticus* with and without genes encoding thermostable direct hemolysin. Infect. Immun. *60*:3539–3545, 1992.
309. Novak, E., Lee, J. G., Seckman, C. E., et al.: Unfavorable effect of atropine-diphenoxylate (Lomotil) therapy in lincomycin-caused diarrhea. J. A. M. A. *235*:1451, 1976.
310. O'Brien, A. D., and Holmes, R. K.: Shiga and Shiga-like toxins. Microbiol. Rev. *51*:206, 1987.
311. O'Connor, D., Hynes, P., and Cormican, M.: Evaluation of methods of detection of toxins in specimens of feces submitted for diagnosis of *Clostridium difficile*–associated diarrhea. J. Clin. Microbiol. *39*:2846–2849, 2001.
312. Okhuysen, P. C.: Traveler's diarrhea due to intestinal protozoa. Clin. Infect. Dis. *33*:110–114, 2001.
313. Olsen, S. J., MacKinon, L. C., Goulding, J. S., et al.: Surveillance for foodborne disease outbreaks—United States, 1993–1997. M. M. W. R. Morb. Mortal Wkly. Rep. *49*(SS-1):1–51, 2000.
314. Olsen, S. J., DeBess, E. E., McGivern, T. E., et al.: A nosocomial outbreak of fluoroquinolone-resistant *Salmonella* infection. N. Engl. J. Med. *344*:1572–1579, 2001.
315. Ooi, W. W., Zimmerman, S. K., and Needham, C. A.: *Cyclospora* species as a gastrointestinal pathogen in immunocompetent hosts. J. Clin. Microbiol. *33*:1267–1269, 1995.
316. O'Ryan, M., Matson, D. O., Estes, M. K., et al.: Molecular epidemiology of rotaviruses in children attending day care centers in Houston. J. Infect. Dis. *162*:810, 1990.

317. Ortega, Y. R., Sterling, C. R., Gilman R. H., et al.: *Cyclospora* species: A new protozoan pathogen of humans. N. Engl. J. Med. *328*:1308–1312, 1993.
318. Osterholm, M. T., MacDonald, K. L., White, K. E., et al.: An outbreak of brainerdiasis: An outbreak of a newly recognized chronic diarrhea syndrome associated with raw milk consumption. J. A. M. A. *256*:484–490, 1986.
319. Pang, X. L., Joensuu, J., Vesikari, T., et al.: Human calcivirus-associated sporadic gasteroenteritis in Finnish children less than two years of age followed prospectively during a rotavirus vaccine trial. Pediatr. Infect. Dis. J. *18*:420–426, 1999.
320. Pape, J. W., Verdier, R., Johnson, W. D., et al.: Treatment and prophylaxis of *Isospora belli* infection in patients with the acquired immunodeficiency syndrome. N. Engl. J. Med. *320*:1044, 1989.
321. Pape, J. W., and Johnson, W. D., Jr.: *Isospora belli* infection. Prog. Clin. Parasitol. *2*:119–127, 1991.
322. Pape, J. W., Verdier, R. I., Boncy, M., et al.: *Cyclospora* infection in adults infected with HIV: Clinical manifestations, treatment and prophylaxis. Ann. Intern. Med. *121*:654–657, 1994.
323. Parsonnet, J., Trock, S. C., Bopp, C. A., et al.: Chronic diarrhea associated with drinking untreated water. Ann. Intern. Med. *110*:985, 1989.
324. Pavia, A. T., Shipman, L. D., Wells, J. G., et al.: Epidemiologic evidence that prior antimicrobial exposure decreases resistance to infection by antimicrobial-sensitive *Salmonella*. J. Infect. Dis. *161*:255, 1990.
325. Pearce, J. L., and Hamilton, J. R.: Controlled trial of orally administered lactobacilli in acute infantile diarrhea. J. Pediatr. *84*:261–262, 1974.
326. Pengsaa, K., Sirivichayakul, C., Pojjaroen-anant, C., et al.: Albendazole treatment of *Giardia intestinalis* infections in school children. Southeast Asian J. Trop. Med. Public Health *30*:78–83, 1999.
327. Perl, T. M., Bedard, L., Kosatsky, T., et al.: An outbreak of toxic encephalopathy caused by eating mussels contaminated with domoic acid. N. Engl. J. Med. *322*:1775, 1990.
328. Perryman, L. E., Riggs, M. W., Mason, P. H., et al.: Kinetics of *Cryptosporidium parvum* sporozoite neutralization by monoclonal antibodies, immune bovine serum, and immune bovine colostrum. Infect. Immun. *58*:157, 1990.
329. Petri, W. A., Jr., and Singh, U.: Diagnosis and management of amebiasis. Clin. Infect. Dis. *29*:117–125, 1999.
330. Phillips, W. E.: Treatment of chronic carriers with ampicillin. J. A. M. A. *217*:913–915, 1971.
331. Phuong, C. X. T., Kneen, R., Anh, N. T., et al.: A comparative study of ofloxacin and cefixime for treatment of typhoid fever in childen. Pediatr. Infect. Dis. J. *18*:245–248, 1999.
332. Pichler, H. E. T., Divide, G., Stickler, K., et al.: Clinical efficacy of ciprofloxacin compared with placebo in bacterial dirrhea. Am. J. Med. *82*(Suppl. 4a):329–332, 1987.
333. Pickering, L. K., DuPont, H. L., Evans, D. G., et al.: Isolation of enteric pathogens in asymptomatic students from the United States and Latin America. J. Infect. Dis. *135*:1003–1005, 1977.
334. Pickering, L. K., DuPont, H. L., Olarte, J., et al.: Fecal leukocytes in enteric infections. Am. J. Clin. Pathol. *68*:562–565, 1977.
335. Pickering, L. K., Evans, D. G., Munoz, O., et al.: Prospective evaluation of enteropathogens in children with diarrhea in Houston and Mexico. J. Pediatr. *93*:383–388, 1978.
336. Pickering, L. K., Evans, D. G., DuPont, H. L., et al.: Diarrhea caused by *Shigella*, rotavirus, and *Giardia* in day care centers: Prospective study. J. Pediatr. *99*:51–56, 1981.
337. Pickering, L. K., Feldman, S., Ericsson, C. D., et al.: Absorption of salicylate and bismuth from a bismuth subsalicylate containing compound (Pepto-Bismol). J. Pediatr. *99*:654–656, 1981.
338. Pickering, L. K., Bartlett, A. V., Reves, R. R., et al.: Asymptomatic excretion of rotavirus before and after rotavirus diarrhea in children in day care centers. J. Pediatr. *112*:361, 1988.
339. Pickering, L. K., and Engelkirk, P. G.: *Giardia lamblia*. Pediatr. Clin. North Am. *35*:565, 1988.
340. Pickering, L. K.: Bacterial and parasitic enteropathogens in day care. Semin. Pediatr. Infect. Dis. *1*:263, 1990.
341. Pickering, L. K., and Morrow, A. L.: Factors in human milk that protect against diarrhea disease. Infection *21*:355–357, 1993.
342. Pickering, L. K., Obrig, T. G., and Stapleton, F. B.: Hemolytic uremic syndrome and enterohemorrhagic *Escherichia coli*. Pediatr. Infect. Dis. J. *13*:459–475, 1994.
343. Pickering, L K.: Emerging antibiotic resistance in enteric bacterial pathogens. Semin. Pediatr. Infect. Dis. *7*:272–280, 1996.
344. Pickering, L. K.: Biotherapeutic agents and disease in infants. *In* Newburg, D. S. (ed.): Bioactive Substances in Human Milk. New York, Plenum, 2001, pp. 365–373.
345. Pickering, L. K., and Cleary, T. G.: Therapy for diarrheal illness in children. *In* Blaser, M. J., Smith, P. D., Ravdin, J. I., et al. (eds.): Infections of the Gastrointestinal Tract. New York, Raven Press, 2002, pp. 1223–1240.
346. Pickering, L. K.: Food safety. *In* Kleinman, R. E. (ed.): AAP Nutrition Handbook. 5th ed. In press.
347. Piddock, L. J. V., Griggs, D. J., Hall, M. C., et al.: Ciprofloxacin resistance in clinical isolates of *Salmonella typhimurium* obtained from two patients. Antimicrob. Agents Chemother. *37*:662–666, 1993.
348. Pilla, A. M., Rybak, M. J., and Chandrasekar, P. H.: Spiramycin in the treatment of cryptosporidiosis. Pharmacotherapy *7*:188–190, 1987.
349. Pitman, F. E.: Adverse effects of Lomotil. Gastroenterology *67*:408–410, 1974.
350. Pol, S., Romana, C. A., Richard, S., et al.: Microsporidia infection in patients with the human immunodeficiency virus and unexplained cholangitis. N. Engl. J. Med. *328*:95–99, 1993.
351. Pollard, D. R., Johnson, W. M., Lior, H., et al.: Rapid and specific detection of verotoxin genes in *Escherichia coli* by the polymerase chain reaction. J. Clin. Microbiol. *28*:540, 1990.
352. Pothoulakis, C.: Effects of *Clostridium difficile* toxins on epithelial cell barrier. Ann. N. Y. Acad. Sci. *915*:347–356, 2000.
353. Potter, M. E., Kaufmann, A. F., Blake, P. A., et al.: Unpasteurized milk: The hazards of a health fetish. J. A. M. A. *252*:2048–2054, 1984.
354. Prado, D., Lopez, E., Liu, H., et al.: Ceftibuten and trimethoprim/sulfamethoxazole for treatment of *Shigella* and enteroinvasive *Escherichia coli* disease. Pediatr. Infect. Dis. J. *11*:644–647, 1992.
355. Proctor, M. E., Hamacher, M., Tortorello, M. L., et al.: Multistate outbreak of *Salmonella* serovar Muenchen infections associated with alfalfa sprouts grown from seeds pretreated with calcium hypochlorite. J. Clin. Microbiol. *39*:3461–3465, 2001.
356. Qadri, F., Das, S. K., Faruque, A. S. G., et al.: Prevalence of toxin types and colonization factors in enterotoxigenic *Escherichia coli* isolated during a 1-year period from diarrheal patients in Bangladesh. J. Clin. Microbiol. *38*:27–31, 2000.
357. Rabbani, G. H., Islam, M. R., Butler, T., et al.: Single-dose treatment of cholera with furazolidone or tetracycline in a double-blind randomized trial. Antimicrob. Agents Chemother. *33*:1447, 1989.
358. Rateau, J. G., Morgant, G., Droy-Priot, M. T., et al.: A histological, enzymatic and water-electrolyte study of the action of smectite, a mucoprotective clay, on experimental infectious diarrhoea in the rabbit. Curr. Med. Res. Opin. *8*:233, 1982.
359. Reid, J. A., White, D. G., Caul, E. O., et al.: Role of infected food handler in hotel outbreak of Norwalk-like viral gastroenteritis: Implications for control. Lancet *2*:321, 1988.
360. Rennels, M. B.: The rotavirus vaccine story: A clinical investigator's view. Pediatrics *106*:123–125, 2000.
361. Replogle, M. L., Flemming, D. W., Cieslak, P. R.: Emergence of antimicrobial-resistant shigellosis in Oregon. Clin. Infect. Dis. *30*:515–519, 2000.
362. Rich, C., Favre-Bronte, S., Sapena, F.: Characterization of enteroaggregative *Escherichia coli* isolates. F. E. M. S. Microbiol. Lett. *173*:55–61, 1999.
363. Ridoux, O., and Drancourt, M.: In vitro susceptibilities of the microsporidia *Encephalitozoon cuniculi, Encephalitozoon hellem*, and *Encephalitozoon intestinalis* to albendazole and its sulfoxide and sulfone metabolites. Antimicrob. Agents Chemother. *42*:3301–3303, 1998.
364. Rosenthal, P., and Liebman, W. M.: Comparative study of stool examination, duodenal aspiration and pediatric Entero-test for giardiasis in children. J. Pediatr. *96*:278–279, 1980.
365. Rosenthal, S. L.: Exacerbation of *Salmonella enteritis* due to ampicillin. N. Engl. J. Med. *280*:147–148, 1969.
366. Rossignol, J.-F., Ayoub, A., Ayers, M. S.: Treatment of diarrhea caused by *Giardia intestinalis* and *Entamoeba histolytica* or *E. dispar*: A randomized double-blind, placebo-controlled study of nitazoxanide. J. Infect. Dis. *184*:381–384, 2001.
367. Rossignol, J.-F., Ayoub, A., Ayers, M. S.: Treatment of diarrhea caused by *Cryptosporidium parvum*: A prospective randomized double-blind, placebo-controlled study of nitazoxanide. J. Infect. Dis. *184*:103–106, 2001.
368. Rothbaum, R. J., Partin, J. C., Saalfield, K., et al.: An ultrastructural study of enteropathogenic *Escherichia coli* infection in human infants. Ultrastruct. Pathol. *4*:291–304, 1983.
369. Rowe, B., Ward, L. R., and Threlfall, E. J.: Multidrug-resistant *Salmonella typhi*: A worldwide epidemic. Clin. Infect. Dis. *24*(Suppl. 1): S106–S109, 1997.
370. Rubin, F. A., McWhirter, P. D., Punjabi, N. H., et al.: Use of a DNA probe to detect *Salmonella typhi* in the blood of patients with typhoid fever. J. Clin. Microbiol. *27*:1112, 1989.
371. Rumack, B. H., and Temple, A. R.: Lomotil poisoning. Pediatrics *53*:495, 1974.
372. Rusmak, J., Hadfield, T. L., Rhodes, M., et al.: Detection of *Cryptosporidium* oocysts in human fecal specimens by an indirect immunofluorescence assay with monoclonal antibodies. J. Clin. Microbiol. *27*:1135, 1989.
373. Ryan, C. A., Hargrett-Bean, N. T., and Blake, P. A.: *Salmonella typhi* infections in the United States, 1975–1984: Increasing role of foreign travel. J. Infect. Dis. *11*:1, 1989.
374. Ryder, R. W., Wells, J. G., and Gangarosa, E. J.: A study of travelers' diarrhea in foreign visitors to the United States. J. Infect. Dis. *136*:605–607, 1977.

375. Saavedra, J. M., Bauman, N. A., Oung, I., et al.: Feeding of *Bifidobacterium bifidum* and *Streptococcus thermophilus* to infants in hospital for prevention of diarrhoea and shedding of rotavirus. Lancet *344*:1046–1049, 1994.
376. Saenz, Y., Zarazaga, M., Lantero, M., et al.: Antibiotic resistance in *Campylobacter* strains isolated from animals, foods, and humans in Spain in 1997–1998. Antimicrob. Agents Chemother. *44*:267–271, 2000.
377. Salam, M. A., Dhar, U., Khan, W. A., et al.: Randomised comparison of ciprofloxacin suspension and pivmecillinam for childhood shigellosis. Lancet *353*:522–527, 1998.
378. Salamina, G. Dalle Donne, E., Niccolini, A., et al.: A foodborne outbreak of gastroenteritis involving *Listeria monocytogenes*. Epidemiol. Infect. *117*:429–436, 1996.
379. Salazar-Lindo, E., Sack, B., Chea-Woo, E., et al.: Early treatment with erythromycin of *Campylobacter jejuni* associated dysentery in children. J. Pediatr. *109*:355, 1986.
380. Salazar-Lindo, E., Santisteban-Ponce, J., Chea-Woo, E., et al.: Racecadontril in the treatment of acute watery diarrhea in children. N. Engl. J. Med. *343*:463–467, 2000.
381. Sambol, J. S. P., Merrigan, M. M., Lyerly, D., et al.: Toxin gene analysis of a variant strain of *Clostridium difficile* that causes human clinical disease. Infect. Immun. *68*:5480–5487, 2000.
382. Sanchez, R., Fernandez-Baca, V., Diaz, M. D., et al.: Evolution of susceptibilities of *Campylobacter* spp. to quinolones and macrolides. Antimicrob. Agents Chermother. *38*:1879–1882, 1994.
383. Santosham, M., Foster, S., Reid, R., et al.: Role of soy-based, lactose-free formula during treatment of acute diarrhea. Pediatrics *76*:292–298, 1985.
384. Santosham, M., and Greenough, W. B., III: Oral rehydration therapy: Global prospective. J. Pediatr. *118*:44–51, 1991.
385. Savarino, S. J., Fasano, A., Watson, J., et al.: Enteroaggregative *Escherichia coli* heat-stable enterotoxin 1 represents another subfamily of *E. coli* heat-stable toxin. Proc. Natl. Acad. Sci. U. S. A. *90*:3093–3097, 1993.
386. Scaletsky, I. C., Pedroso, M. D., Morais, M. B., et al.: Association of patterns of *Escherichia coli* adherence to Hep-2 cells with acute and persistent diarrhea. Arch. Gastroenterol. *36*:54–60, 1999.
387. Schantz, P. M.: The dangers of eating raw fish. N. Engl. J. Med. *320*:1143, 1989.
388. Schleupner, M. A., Garner, D. C., Sosnowski, K. M., et al.: Concurrence of *Clostridium difficile* toxin A enzyme-linked immunosorbent assay, fecal lactoferrin assay, and clinical criteria with *C. difficile* cytotoxin titer in two patient cohorts. J. Clin. Microbiol. *33*:1755–1759, 1995.
389. Schultssz, C., van den Ende, J., Cobelens, F., et al.: Diarrheagenic *Escherichia coli* and acute and persistent diarrhea in returned travelers. J. Clin. Microbiol. *38*:3550-3554, 2000.
390. Sears, C. L., and Kaper, J. B.: Enteric bacterial toxins: Mechanisms of action and linkage to intestinal secretion. Microbiol. Rev. *60*:167–215, 1996.
391. Segreti, J., Gootz, T. D., Goodman, L. J., et al.: High-level quinolone resistance in clinical isolates of *Campylobacter jejuni*. J. Infect. Dis. *165*:667–670, 1992.
392. Sen, A., Kobayashi, N., Das, S., et al.: The evolution of human group B rotaviruses. Lancet *357*:198–199, 2001.
393. Serény, B.: Experimental *Shigella* keratoconjunctivitis: A preliminary report. Acta Microbiol. Acad. Sci. *2*:293–296, 1955.
394. Shadduck, J. A., and Greeley, E.: *Microsporidia* and human infections. Clin. Microbiol. Rev. *2*:158, 1989.
395. Shanks, G. D., Smoak, B. L., Aleman, G. M., et al.: Single dose azithromycin or three-day course of ciprofloxacin as therapy for epidemic dysentery in Kenya. Clin. Infect. Dis. *29*:942–943, 1999.
396. Shedl, H. P., and Clifton, J. A.: Solute and water absorption by the human small intestine. Nature *199*:1264–1267, 1963.
397. Sheikh, R. A., Prindiville, T. P., Yenamandra, S., et al.: Microsporidial AIDS cholangiopathy due to *Encephalitozoon intestinalis*: Case report and review. Am. J. Gastroenterol. *95*:2364–2371, 2000.
398. Shinozaki, T., Araki, K., Ushijima, H., et al.: Antibody response to enteric adenovirus types 40 and 41 in sera from people in various age groups. J. Clin. Microbiol. *25*:1679, 1987.
399. Siddiqui, A. A., and Berk, S. L.: Diagnosis of *Strongyloides stercoralis* infection. Clin. Infect. Dis. *33*:1040–1047, 2001.
400. Sirinavin, S., Chiemchanya, S., and Vorachit, M.: Systemic nontyphoidal *Salmonella* infection in normal infants in Thailand. Pediatr. Infect. Dis. J. *20*:581–587, 2001.
401. Sloven, D. G., Jirapinyo, P., and Lebenthal, E.: Hydrolysis and absorption of glucose polymers from rice compared with corn in chronic diarrhea in infancy. J. Pediatr. *116*:876, 1990.
402. Smith, H. R., Cheasty, T., and Rowe, B.: Enteroaggregative *Escherichia coli* and outbreaks of gastroenteritis in U.K. Lancet *350*:814–815, 1997.
403. Smith, K. E., Besser, J. M., Hedberg, C. W., et al.: Quinolone-resistant *Campylobacter jejuni* infections in Minnesota, 1992–1998. N. Engl. J. Med. *340*:1525–1532, 1999.
404. Smith, M. D., Duong, N. M., Hoa, N. T. T., et al.: Comparison of ofloxacin and ceftriaxone for short-course treatment of enteric fever. Antimicrob. Agents Chemother. *38*:1716–1720, 1994.
405. Smith, N. H., Cron, S., Valdez, L. M., et al.: Combination drug therapy for cryptosporidiosis in AIDS. J. Infect. Dis. *178*:900–903, 1998.
406. Smith, P. D., Macher, A. M., Bookman, M. A., et al.: *Salmonella typhimurium* enteritis and bacteremia in the acquired immunodeficiency syndrome. Ann. Intern. Med. *102*:207, 1985.
407. Soe, G. B., and Overturf, G. D.: Treatment of typhoid fever and other systemic salmonelloses with cefotaxime, ceftriaxone, cefoperazone, and other newer cephalosporins. Rev. Infect. Dis. *9*:719, 1987.
408. Soriano-Brücher, H. E., Avendaño, P., O'Ryan, M., et al.: Use of bismuth subsalicylate in acute diarrhea in children. Rev. Infect. Dis. *12*:S51, 1990.
409. Soriano-Brücher, H., Avendaño, P., O'Ryan, M., et al.: Bismuth subsalicylate in the treatment of acute diarrhea in children: A clinical study. Pediatrics *87*:18–27, 1991.
410. Speelman, P., Kabir, I., and Islam, M.: Distribution and spread of colonic lesions in shigellosis: A colonoscopic study. J. Infect. Dis. *150*:899–903, 1984.
411. Sprinz, H. E., Gangarosa, E. J., Williams, M., et al.: Histopathology of the upper small intestine in typhoid fever: Biopsy study of experimental disease in man. Am. J. Dig. Dis. *11*:615–624, 1966.
412. Steinberg, E. B., Greene, K. D., Bopp, C. A., et al.: Cholera in the United States, 1995–2000: Trends at the end of the twentieth century. J. Infect. Dis. *184*:799–802, 2001.
413. Stenzel, D. J., and Boreham, P. F. L.: *Blastomycosis hominis* revisited. Clin. Microbiol. Rev. *9*:563–584, 1996.
414. Surawizc, C. M., McFarland, L. B., Greenberg, R. N., et al.: The search for a better treatment for recurrent *Clostridium difficile* disease: Use of high-dose vancomycin combined with *Saccharomyces boulardii*. Clin. Infect. Dis. *31*:1012–1017, 2000.
415. Talsma, E. Goettsch, W. G., Nieste, H. L. J., et al.: Resistance of *Campylobacter* species: Increased resistance to fluoroquinolones and seasonal variation. Clin. Infect. Dis. *29*:845–848, 1999.
416. Tauxe, R. V., Puhr, N. D., Wells, J. G., et al.: Antimicrobial resistance of *Shigella* isolates in the U.S.A.: The importance of international travel. J. Infect. Dis. *162*:1107, 1990.
417. Tauxe, R. V.: Food safety and irradiation: Protecting the public from foodborne infections. Emerg. Infect. Dis. *7*(Suppl. 3):516–521, 2001.
418. Taylor, C. E., and Higgs, E. S.: A workshop on micronutrients and infectious diseases. Cellular and molecular immunomodulatory mechanisms. J. Infect. Dis. *182*(Suppl.):S1–S143, 2000.
419. Taylor, D. E., and Chang, N.: In vitro susceptibilities of *Campylobacter jejuni* and *Campylobacter coli* to azithromycin and erythromycin. Antimicrob. Agents Chemother. *35*:1917–1918, 1991.
420. Taylor, W. R., Schell, W. L., Wells, J. G., et al.: A foodborne outbreak of enterotoxigenic *Escherichia coli* diarrhea. N. Engl. J. Med. *306*:1093–1095, 1982.
421. Teasley, D. G., Gerding, D. N., Olson, M. M., et al.: Prospective randomized trial of metronidazole versus vancomycin for *Clostridium difficile*-associated diarrhea and colitis. Lancet *2*:1043–1046, 1983.
422. Teitelbaum, J. S., Zatorre, R. J., Carpenter, S., et al.: Neurologic sequelae of domoic acid intoxication due to the ingestion of contaminated mussels. N. Engl. J. Med. *322*:1781, 1990.
423. Telzak, E. E., Budnick, L. D., Greenberg, M. S. Z., et al.: A nosocomial outbreak of *Salmonella enteritis* infection due to the consumption of raw eggs. N. Engl. J. Med. *323*:394, 1990.
424. Thomas, M. R., Litin, S. C., Osmon, D. R., et al.: Lack of effect of *Lactobacillus* GG on antibiotic-associated diarrhea: A randomized placebo-controlled trial. Mayo Clin. Proc. *76*:883–889, 2001.
425. Tippen, P. S., Meyer, A., Blank, E. C., et al.: Aquarium-associated *Plesiomonas shigelloides* infection: Missouri. M. M. W. R. Morb. Mortal. Wkly. Rep. *38*:617, 1989.
426. Tjoa, W. S., DuPont, H. L., Sullivan, P., et al.: Location of food consumption and travelers' diarrhea. Am. J. Epidemiol. *106*:61–66, 1977.
427. Toledo, M. R. F., and Trabulsi, L. R.: Correlation between biochemical and serological characteristics of *Escherichia coli* and results of the Serény test. J. Clin. Microbiol. *17*:419–421, 1983.
428. Tzipori, S., Roberton, D., and Chapman, C.: Remission of cryptosporidiosis in an immunodeficient child with hyperimmune bovine colostrum. B. M. J. *293*:1276, 1986.
429. Ungar, B. L.: Enzyme-linked immunoassay for detection of *Cryptosporidium* antigens in fecal specimens. J. Clin. Microbiol. *28*:2491, 1990.
430. Ungar, B. L., Ward, D. S., Fayer, R., et al.: Cessation of *Cryptosporidium*-associated diarrhea in an acquired immunodeficiency syndrome patient after treatment with hyperimmune bovine colostrum. Gastroenterology *98*:486, 1990.
431. Van, R., Wun, C. C., O'Ryan, M. L., et al.: Outbreaks of human enteric adenovirus types 40 and 41 in Houston day care centers. J. Pediatr. *120*:516–521, 1992.
432. Van Doorn, L. J., Verschuuren-van Haperen, A., Burnens, A., et al.: Rapid identification of thermotolerant *Campylobacter jejuni, Campylobacter coli, Campylobacter lari,* and *Campylobacter upsaliensis* from various geographic locations by a GTPase-based PCR-reverse hybridization assay. J. Clin. Microbiol. *37*:1790–1796, 1999.

433. Vargas, S. L., Shenep, J. L., Flynn, P. M., et al.: Azithromycin for treatment of severe *Cryptosporidium* diarrhea in children with cancer. J. Pediatr. *123*:154–156, 1993.
434. Varsano, I., Eidlitz-Marcus, T., Nassinovitch, M., et al.: Comparative efficacy of ceftriaxone and ampicillin for treatment of severe shigellosis in children. J. Pediatr. *118*:627–632, 1991.
435. Valazquez-Boland, J. A., Kuhn, M., Berche, P., et al.: *Listeria* pathogenesis and molecular virulence determinants. Clin. Microbiol. Rev. *14*:584–640, 2001.
436. Velazquez, F. R., Calva, J. J., Guerrero, M. L., et al.: Cohort study of rotavirus serotype patterns in symptomatic and asymptomatic infections in Mexican children. Pediatr. Infect. Dis. J. *12*:56–61, 1993.
437. Velazquez, F. R., Matson, D. O., Calva, J. J., et al.: Natural protection conferred by rotavirus infections: Implications for vaccine strategies. N. Engl. J. Med. *335*:1022–1028, 1996.
438. Verdier, R. I., Fitzgerald, D. W., Johnson, W. D., Jr., et al.: Trimethoprim-sulfamethoxazole compared with ciprofloxacin for treatment and prophylaxis of *Isospora belli* and *Cyclospora cayetanensis* infection in HIV-infected patients. A randomized, controlled trial. Ann. Intern. Med. *132*:885–888, 2000.
439. Vinh, H., Wain, J., Hanh, V. T. N., et al.: Two or three days of ofloxacin treatment for uncomplicated multidrug-resistant typhoid fever in children. Antimicrob. Agents Chemother. *40*:958–961, 1996.
440. Wallace, C. K., Anderson, P. N., Brown, T. C., et al.: Optimal antibiotic therapy in cholera. Bull. W. H. O. *39*:239–245, 1968.
441. Wallace, M. R., Nguyen, M.-T., and Newton, J. A., Jr.: Use of paromomycin for the treatment of cryptosporidiosis in patients with AIDS. Clin. Infect. Dis. *17*:1070–1071, 1993.
442. Walter, J. E., Briggs, J., Lourdes, G. M., et al.: Molecular characterization of a novel recombinant strain of human astrovirus associated with gastroenteritis in children. Arch. Virol. *146*:235, 2001.
443. Wang, W. L. L., Reller, L. B., and Blaser, M. J.: Comparison of antimicrobial susceptibility patterns of *Campylobacter jejuni* and *Campylobacter coli*. Antimicrob. Agents Chemother. *26*:351–353, 1984.
444. Wanke, C. A., Plesko, D., DeGirolami, P. C., et al.: A medium chain triglyceride-based diet in patients with HIV and chronic diarrhea reduces diarrhea and malabsorption: A prospective, controlled trial. Nutrition *12*:766–771, 1996.
445. Webber, R., Bryan, R. T., Owen, R. L., et al.: Improved light microscopial detection of microsporidia spores in stool and duodenal aspirates. N. Engl. J. Med. *326*:161–166, 1992.
446. Webber, R., Bryan, R. T., Schwartz, D. A., et al.: Human microsporidial infections. Clin. Microbiol. Rev. *7*:426–461, 1994.
447. Weiss, L. M., Perlman, D. C., Sherman, J., et al.: *Isospora belli* infection: Treatment with pyrimethamine. Ann. Intern. Med. *109*:474, 1988.
448. Wenisch, C., Parschalk, B., Masenhundl, M., et al.: Comparison of vancomycin, teicoplanin, metronidazole, and fusidic acid for the treatment of *Clostridium difficile*-associated diarrhea. Clin. Infect. Dis. *22*:813–818, 1996.
449. Wessalowski, R., Thomas, L., Kivit, J., et al.: Multiple brain abscesses caused by *Salmonella enteritis* in a neonate: Successful treatment with ciprofloxacin. Pediatr. Infect. Dis. J. *12*:683–688, 1993.
450. White, A. C., Chappell, C. L., Hayat, C. S., et al.: Paromomycin for cryptosporidiosis in AIDS: A prospective, double-blind trial. J. Infect. Dis. *170*:19–24, 1994.
451. White, D. G., Zhoa, S., Sudler, R., et al.: The isolation of antibiotic-resistant *Salmonella* from retail ground meats. N. Engl. J. Med. *345*:1147–1154, 2001.
452. Williams, D., Schorling, J., Barrett, L. J., et al.: Early treatment of *jejuni* enteritis. Antimicrob. Agents Chemother. *33*:248, 1989.
453. Willson, R., Harrington, R., and Stewart, B.: Human immunodeficiency virus 1–associated necrotizing cholangitis caused by infection with *Septata intestinalis*. Gastroenterology *108*:247–251, 1995.
454. Wittenberg, D. F., Miller, N. M., and Vanden Ende, J.: Spiramycin is not effective in treating *Cryptosporidium* diarrhea in infants: Results of a double-blind randomized trial. J. Infect. Dis. *159*:131, 1989.
455. Wittner, M., Turner, J. W., Jacquette, G., et al.: Eustrongylidiasis: A parasitic infection acquired by eating sushi. N. Engl. J. Med. *320*:1124, 1989.
456. Wong, C. S., Jelacic, S., Habeeb, R. L., et al.: The risk of the hemolytic uremic syndrome after antibody treatment of *Escherichia coli* 0157:H7 infections. N. Engl. J. Med. *342*:1930–1936, 2000.
457. Yamamoto, T., Honda, T., Miwatani, T., et al.: A virulence plasmid in *Escherichia coli* enterotoxigenic for humans: Intergenetic transfer and expression. J. Infect. Dis. *150*:688–698, 1984.
458. Yamamoto, T., Nair, G. B., Albert, M. J., et al.: Survey of in vitro susceptibilities of *Vibrio cholerae* 01 and 0139 to antimicrobial agents. Antimicrob. Agents Chemother. *39*:241–244, 1995.
459. Yang, S., Leff, M. G., McTague, D., et al.: Multistate surveillance for food handling, preparation and consumption behaviors associated with foodborne diseases: 1995 and 1996 BRFSS food-safety questions. M. M. W. R. Morb. Mortal. Wkly. Rep. *47*(SS-4):33–57, 1998.
460. Yolken, R. H., Bishop, C. A., Townsend, T. R., et al.: Infectious gastroenteritis in bone-marrow transplant recipients. N. Engl. J. Med. *306*:1009–1012, 1982.
461. Yolken, R., Leister, F., Dubovi, E., et al.: Infantile gastroenteritis associated with excretion of pestivirus antigens. Lancet *1*:517, 1989.
462. Zhou, D., Mooseker, M. S., and Galan, J. E.: An invasion-associated *Salmonella* protein modulates the actin-bundling activity of plastin. Proc. Natl. Acad. Sci. U. S. A. *96*:10176–10181, 1999.
463. Zhou, D., Mooseker, M. S., and Galan, J. E.: Role of the *S. typhimurium* actin-binding protein SipA in bacterial internalization. Science *283*:2092–2095, 1999.
464. Zirnstein, G., Li, Y., Swaminathan, B., et al.: Ciprofloxacin resistance in *Campylobacter jejuni* isolates: Detection of *gyrA* resistance mutations by mismatch amplification mutation assay PCR and DNA sequence analysis. J. Clin. Microbiol. *27*:3276–3280, 1999.

Antibiotic-Associated Colitis

GEORGE D. FERRY

Clostridium difficile colonization and infection accounts for 10 to 25 percent of antibiotic-associated diarrhea and is the major cause of antibiotic-associated pseudomembranous colitis.[6] Diarrhea and colitis develop when antibiotics, especially those with a broad spectrum of activity, disturb the bowel flora and allow overgrowth of *C. difficile*. Production of toxins then leads to inflammation and secretion of fluids from the colon, resulting in watery diarrhea. If inflammation progresses and pseudomembranous colitis develops, the diarrhea becomes bloody. Colitis induced by *C. difficile* has been reported without prior use of antibiotics, but it is an uncommon occurrence.

History

Pseudomembranous colitis was recognized as early as 1893[28] and derives its name from the numerous plaquelike lesions in the colon. The plaques are membranes of epithelial debris containing fibrin, mucus, and polymorphonuclear leukocytes overlying necrotic glands.[69] Not until the early 1950s was an association with antibiotics suggested. The organism that initially received the most attention as a possible cause was *Staphylococcus aureus*.[73] Stool cultures frequently were positive for *S. aureus* after antibiotic use, and autopsies showed enterocolitis with ulcers and pseudomembranes in both the small and the large bowel. The association with *C. difficile*, a gram-positive anaerobic bacillus, was shown in 1977 and 1978 with the report of production of toxins related to pseudomembranous changes in the colon.[7, 8, 49] *C. difficile* can colonize the intestine without causing diarrhea and was identified as part of the normal flora of infants and newborns in 1935.[36] Early studies suggested that *Clostridium sordellii* might be related to pseudomembranous colitis, but subsequent investigation has shown that *C. sordellii* antitoxin neutralizes *C. difficile* cytotoxicity but is not a cause of colitis.[8]

Etiology and Pathogenesis

C. difficile can be cultured in low numbers in 5 percent of healthy adults,[24, 39] but in hospitalized patients, the incidence of colonization and positive cultures reaches 20 percent or more.[55] *C. difficile* spores are viable for long periods, up to 5 months,[43] and can be cultured from flooring, toilets, and bedding as well as from the stool and hands of carriers[24, 43] (Table 52–1). Numerous studies have shown that neonates frequently are colonized with *C. difficile*.[36, 38, 86] In a London study, 2 to 52 percent of infants in three postnatal wards had positive cultures, but none developed diarrhea or colitis, and no evidence was found that infants were colonized from their mothers.[48] The rate of colonization appears to be related to the length of time infants are hospitalized.[71] In those older than 1 year, colonization decreases significantly.[35] Not only is *C. difficile* a common contaminant in hospitals,[24, 43] but person-to-person transmission between children in daycare centers also has been reported.[42] A hospital outbreak of *C. difficile* in children 18 months to 18 years was reported from a pediatric orthopedic ward.[27]

TABLE 52–1 ■ DISTRIBUTION OF *CLOSTRIDIUM DIFFICILE* ISOLATES TAKEN FROM THE ENVIRONMENT OF TWO PEDIATRIC UNITS

	No. Positive/No. Sampled (%)	
Sites Cultured	*Pediatric Ward (case-associated)*	*Newborn Intensive Care Unit (control)*
Surfaces		
Bedpan hoppers	0/25	1/15
Chart covers	0/30 (3.3)	0/20
Cribs (occupied)	2/45 (4.4)	1/20 (5)
Dust mops, dust pans on cleaning carts	2/6 (33.3)	0/4
Floors		
Bathroom	4/40 (10)	NA
Clean storage room	2/30 (6.7)	0/20
Patient's room	6/50 (12)	1/30 (3.3)
Soiled room	2/30 (6.7)	0/20
Hospital garments	0/20	0/11
Linens, blankets (clean)	0/20	0/8
Linens, blankets (in use)	5/50 (10)	3/37 (8.1)
Medical devices (e.g., stethoscopes)	0/25	0/20
Mobiles, toys	1/20 (5)	0/12
Scales	8/40 (20)	1/30 (3.3)
Washbasins, sinks, tubs	4/40 (10)	1/30 (3.3)
Air (30 cu. ft. per sample)	0/7	0/2
Total	37/478 (7.7)*	7/279 (2.5)*

*$p < .005$.

From Kim, K.-H., Fekety, R., Batts, D. H., et al.: Isolation of *Clostridium difficile* from the environment and contacts of patients with antibiotic-associated colitis. J. Infect. Dis. *143*:44–50, 1981.

Infection with *C. difficile* occurs commonly and accounts for 10 to 25 percent of cases of uncomplicated antibiotic-associated diarrhea.[6, 79] Most infections cause watery diarrhea, but 5 to 10 percent progress to pseudomembranous colitis.[6, 44] Pseudomembranous colitis can occur sporadically or in epidemics.[60, 64] In daycare centers, the incidence of *C. difficile* infection not related to antibiotics may be as high as 50 percent.[6, 42] Community-acquired diarrhea caused by *C. difficile* studied in a health maintenance organization population identified 51 cases, with an incidence of 7.7 cases per 100,000 person-years.[37] Half of these cases occurred after antibiotic use. Increased age and exposure to more than one antibiotic within a 42-day period increased the risk. *C. difficile* diarrhea was an uncommon occurrence in patients younger than 20 years. Risk factors included inflammatory bowel disease, infection with human immunodeficiency virus, and chronic treatment with antibiotics.

Virulence may differ among strains of *C. difficile;* some are highly toxigenic, and others have low virulence.[45] This difference may be related to S-layer proteins covering the surface of *C. difficile* serotypes known to cause disease.[67] Production of toxins by the organism and clinical illness are absent in 25 percent of patients with positive cultures.[25] Most toxigenic strains produce both toxin A and toxin B. Toxin B initially was thought to be a cytotoxin with little clinical effect[52, 66]; however, more recent studies have shown that it has a significant effect once tissue damage has already occurred.[67] Toxin A produces necrosis and increased cell permeability, and both toxins lead to the production of tumor necrosis factor-α and other cytokines.[67] The increased permeability is responsible for the watery diarrhea.

Studies on the epithelial cell barrier have shown two additional pathways of cell injury.[61, 65] *C. difficile* toxins disaggregate actin microfilaments in colonocytes, leading to cell destruction and opening of tight junctions. Toxin A also has a significant chemotactic effect on neutrophils, leading to local inflammation and release of inflammatory mediators.[66] Figure 52–1 illustrates these pathways. In experimental models, injection of toxin A into rabbit ileal loops results in increased fluid secretion, inflammation and necrosis of epithelial cells, and release of prostaglandin E_2 and leukotriene B_4 into the lumen.[83] Another mechanism for diarrhea may relate to decreased anaerobic flora and, subsequently, a decreased digestion of carbohydrates, leading to a decreased production of lactic acid and short-chain fatty acids and disturbed function of the colonic mucosa.[9]

Serum antibodies to *C. difficile* toxins A and B occur commonly, being found in 60 to 70 percent of patients older than 3 years.[85] In adults, specific serum IgA and IgG antibodies to toxin A have been detected in 57 to 60 percent of patients.[41] Antibodies also have been found in colonic mucosa and duodenal aspirates in 10 percent of patients. Binding of toxin A was inhibited significantly by colonic aspirates with high-IgA antitoxin-A antibody. These antibodies appear to persist throughout life, and they may have a protective role against recurrence.[46]

Protection against diarrhea and pseudomembranous colitis in newborns may be due to a lack of the intestinal receptor for toxin A[21] or prematurity of the toxin receptor. A study by Enad and colleagues[22] showed that 87 infants colonized with toxin A–positive *C. difficile* had more days of diarrhea than did those who were toxin negative. Although breast milk contains antibody against *C. difficile*, whether it influences disease activity is unclear.[87] *C. difficile* has been suggested to be a causative agent in rare cases of necrotizing enterocolitis, but this suggestion remains controversial.[12, 22]

In the normal host, many bacteria, especially lactobacilli, *Bacteroides*, group D enterococci, and *Escherichia coli,*

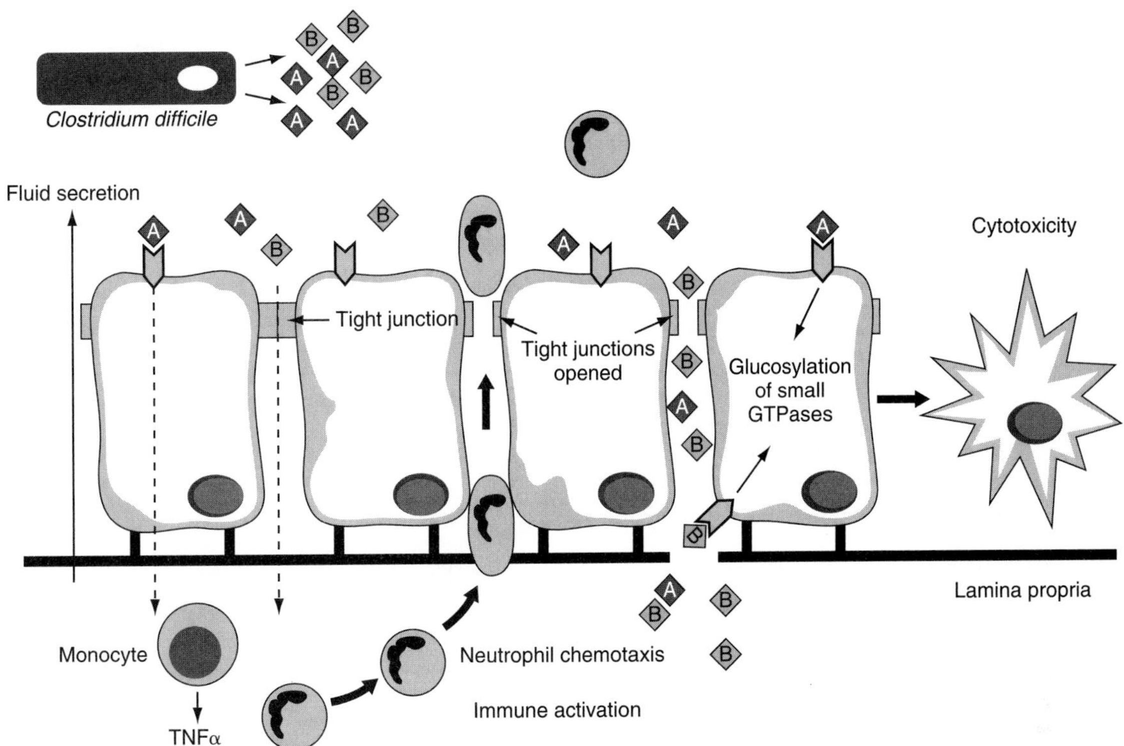

FIGURE 52–1 ■ Actions of *Clostridium difficile* toxins A and B on intestinal epithelium. (Courtesy of Ian R. Proxton, Professor of Microbial Infection and Immunity, Medical Microbiology, University of Edinburgh Medical School.)

inhibit growth of *C. difficile.*[70] Treatment with any antibiotic can result in overgrowth of *C. difficile* and lead to pseudomembranous colitis. Oral antibiotics are associated with colitis more often than are parenteral antibiotics, and broad-spectrum antibiotics are responsible for most cases. Multiple antibiotics, including clindamycin, ampicillin, cephalosporin, penicillin, chloramphenicol, gentamicin, trimethoprim-sulfamethoxazole, and rifampicin, have been implicated in antibiotic-associated diarrhea in children.[1, 58, 81] Cefixime also has been associated with pediatric pseudomembranous colitis.[34] Long-term antibiotic treatment of acne has been complicated rarely by diarrhea or colitis.[23]

C. difficile infection has been reported during chemotherapy; methotrexate is the most common precipitating agent. The spectrum of illness has been mild to fulminant colitis, just as in antibiotic-associated disease. *C. difficile* also has occurred as an outbreak with associated diarrhea in patients with acquired immunodeficiency syndrome who were admitted to the same hospital ward.[3]

Clinical Manifestations

The spectrum of clinical signs and symptoms related to *C. difficile* infection ranges from the asymptomatic carrier state to a fulminant colitis and toxic megacolon.[82] Most patients have watery diarrhea, but 10 to 15 percent have bloody stools.[44] Diarrhea most often begins 3 to 21 days after the use of antibiotics. Most children with diarrhea have a self-limited illness with watery stools, fever, and abdominal pain.[75, 81] Patients with pseudomembranous colitis present with cramping abdominal pain and fever, and watery, green, foul stools progress to bloody diarrhea.[20] Colitis often is a mild, self-limited illness once antibiotics are stopped, but it may be severe and require intensive antibiotic and supportive therapy.

Toxic megacolon, or toxic dilatation of the small bowel, may develop without preceding diarrhea. In these critically ill patients, colitis may lead to perforation and peritonitis. In a series of 201 surgical patients, toxic megacolon developed in 5, and 4 of the 5 died.[68] Confirmation of the diagnosis may depend on finding the typical pseudomembranous ulcers on colonoscopy. Response to treatment generally is rapid; symptoms clear in 50 percent of patients within 6 to 14 days and in 100 percent by 1 month.

The role of *C. difficile* infection in inflammatory bowel disease has been controversial. Some studies have shown no significant association,[56] whereas others have implicated *C. difficile* in the relapse of Crohn disease and ulcerative colitis.[14, 47] The organism has been found in 8 percent of patients in remission,[19] the same as in the general population. The presence of toxin seems to correlate with the degree of bleeding and disease activity.[33] In one study of 59 patients, toxin was found in 11 (19%). Four of the 11 had received no prior antibiotics. These patients responded promptly to treatment with vancomycin, suggesting that the flare of colitis was related to *C. difficile.*[84]

Laboratory Studies

Examination of stools often shows blood and mucus, and fecal leukocytes are present in 50 percent of patients.[25] *C. difficile* can be cultured on selective media, such as cycloserine-cefoxitin-fructose agar.[31] Stool culture is the most sensitive diagnostic tool, but it is not as specific as is assaying for *C. difficile* toxin.[32] Because not all organisms produce toxin, a causative role for *C. difficile* in diarrhea and colitis generally is based on detection of toxin in the stool rather than a positive culture.[32, 50] Only fresh, liquid stools should be tested,[18] and all specimens should be tested for both toxins A and B.[53] Production of *C. difficile* toxin can be diagnosed by a variety of techniques. The most accurate one is the assay for toxin B demonstrating its cytopathic effect on cell culture monolayers.[18, 25] The sensitivity of enzyme immunosorbent assay screening tests for toxins A and B generally is in the range of 80 to 90 percent.[25] Newer enzyme immunoassay kits are reported to have a sensitivity of 93 to 99 percent and a specificity of 93 to 100 percent.[2] An enzyme immunosorbent assay test kit combining detection of toxin A and glutamate dehydrogenase has a negative predictive value of an infection with *C. difficile* of 99.6 percent.[18]

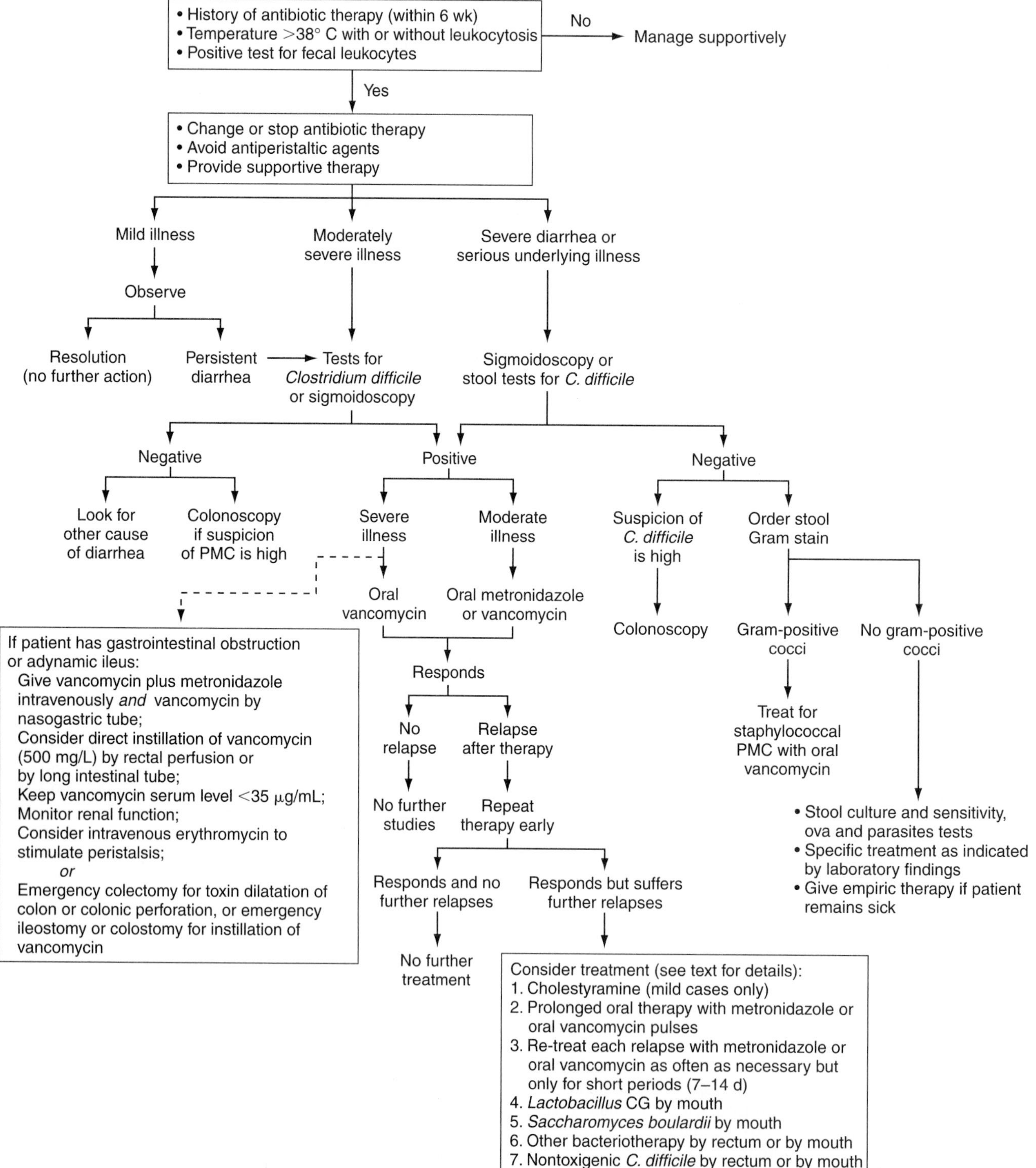

FIGURE 52–2 ■ Algorithm for management of antibiotic-associated diarrhea and colitis. PMC, pseudomembranous colitis. (From Fekety, R., and Shah, A. B.: Diagnosis and treatment of *Clostridium difficile* colitis. J. A. M. A. *269*:72, 1993.)

Glutamate dehydrogenase is found in both toxigenic and nontoxigenic strains. Polymerase chain reaction amplification of a segment of the toxin A gene also has been used to identify *C. difficile* from stool specimens in patients with antibiotic-associated diarrhea.[40] This test appears to be highly accurate compared with a stool culture and toxin assay. Latex agglutination for *C. difficile* antigen is less sensitive than is culture and not as specific as is toxin assay.[32, 63]

Leukocytosis of 15,000 is a common finding in hospitalized patients and may occur with diarrhea or with systemic symptoms of fever and toxicity before the onset of diarrhea.[15] In the appropriate setting, it may prove useful as an early marker of *C. difficile* infection, suggesting the need for testing the stool for toxins.

Endoscopic diagnosis of *C. difficile* is useful when urgent diagnosis is needed before laboratory confirmation of a positive assay for toxin is obtained (Fig. 52–2). Flexible sigmoidoscopy is a rapid diagnostic tool, but in one study of 29 patients with a positive toxin assay, only 55 percent had typical pseudomembranous colitis, 14 percent had nonspecific colitis, and 31 percent were normal.[10] In cases with a typical endoscopic appearance, *C. difficile* toxin is positive in 95 percent.[30] Flexible sigmoidoscopy will detect 90 percent of patients with colitis.[10, 79]

The colon typically appears red with raised, circular, yellow plaques.[30, 78] These pseudomembranous plaques vary from 2 to 5 mm in diameter and are scattered throughout the involved area. In the earliest stage, 1- to 2-mm ulcers may be seen but may not have an obvious membrane. Biopsy specimens of these small lesions show the same endothelial degeneration and pseudomembrane as larger lesions do.

Plain radiography of the abdomen in patients with colitis may show a variety of abnormalities, including colonic ileus, small bowel ileus, ascites, and nodular haustral thickening.[13] In severely ill patients with pseudomembranous colitis, leukocyte scintigraphy has demonstrated a constant and diffuse pattern of intense radiotracer.[59] Although not specific, this test may be useful whenever endoscopy cannot be performed.

The presence of *C. difficile* toxin A or toxin B may establish the etiology of diarrhea and colitis; the absence of toxin may not be conclusive. If symptoms are suggestive of antibiotic-associated diarrhea or colitis, studies of stools should be repeated several times before this diagnosis is ruled out.[54]

Differential Diagnosis

Bloody diarrhea occurring after recent use of antibiotics should suggest the possibility of pseudomembranous colitis. Stool specimens should be obtained for *C. difficile* toxins A and B, along with routine cultures for *Salmonella, Shigella, Campylobacter,* and type-specific *E. coli*. The possibility of inflammatory bowel disease, either ulcerative colitis or Crohn disease of the colon, always should be considered, especially if treatment fails to resolve the colitis. A hemorrhagic colitis related to penicillin has been described, but no pseudomembranes are seen on colonoscopy, and studies for *C. difficile* yield negative results.[57]

Treatment

In mild cases, discontinuing antibiotics and implementing supportive measures alone lead to gradual resolution of symptoms.[78] Antiperistaltic agents should be avoided because they may cause retention of toxins and complications.[17] Vancomycin has been the accepted treatment of choice for pseudomembranous colitis, but both vancomycin and metronidazole clear 80 to 100 percent of infections (Table 52–2), and metronidazole is considerably less expensive.[4, 5, 88] The effective oral dose of vancomycin is 40 to 50 mg/kg/day for 7 to 10 days. The adult dose is 125 mg four times daily for mild cases and up to 500 mg/dose for severe cases.[5, 26] Intravenous vancomycin is not effective. Metronidazole is effective in doses of 20 to 40 mg/kg/day; adult doses range from 250 mg four times daily up to 500 mg three times a day. One report of intravenous metronidazole, 500 mg three times daily as initial therapy, showed an excellent clinical response in 10 patients.[29] Oral bacitracin, 25,000 units four times daily, has been used in some adult patients. Systemic signs of infection generally clear within 24 to 48 hours, and diarrhea gradually subsides during 7 to 10 days.

Relapse is a major problem and occurs in 5 to 33 percent of patients treated with either vancomycin or metronidazole (see Table 52–2).[40, 76, 77] If a relapse produces severe symptoms, re-treatment generally is required.[77] In mild relapse, patients may be watched to see whether they clear the infection spontaneously. Other therapeutic regimens to treat relapse have included weaning to the point at which vancomycin or metronidazole is administered every other or every third day.[80] In some patients, administration of cholestyramine has helped to clear recurrent diarrhea.[25] One study in children showed an excellent response to immune globulin given intravenously.[51]

Probiotics also have been of interest, especially in patients who relapse. *Saccharomyces boulardii* given daily for 2 weeks produced resolution of symptoms within 1 week in 18 of 19 children with diarrhea caused by *C. difficile*.[16] Relapse occurred in 11 percent of the patients. *Lactobacillus GG* also has been effective in clearing *C. difficile* diarrhea.[11]

TABLE 52–2 ■ COMPARISON OF RESULTS OF TREATMENT WITH VARIOUS REGIMENS FOR *CLOSTRIDIUM DIFFICILE*-ASSOCIATED DIARRHEA AND COLITIS

Author	Regimen	No. Responding/Total	No. Relapsing/Total
Gerding and Brazier[32]	Metronidazole	37/39 (95%)	2/39 (5%)
	Vancomycin	45/45 (100%)	6/45 (13%)
Greenfield et al.[33]	Metronidazole	19/19 (100%)	6/19 (32%)
	Fusidic acid	20/20 (100%)	5/20 (25%)
George et al.[31]	Vancomycin	21/21 (100%)	6/18 (33%)
	Bacitracin	21/21 (100%)	5/12 (42%)
Gremse et al.[34]	Vancomycin	15/15 (100%)	3/15 (20%)
	Bacitracin	12/15 (80%)	5/15 (33%)

From Bartlett, J. G.: *Clostridium difficile*: Clinical considerations. Rev. Infect. Dis. *12*:S243–S251, 1990.

A combination of oral vancomycin and *S. boulardii* also has been effective in curing relapsed infection.[74]

Response to treatment is poor with ileus, toxic megacolon, or colonic perforation. In these cases, instillation of vancomycin by clamped nasogastric tube or direct colonic instillation can be tried.[72] The colonic dose for adults is 2000 mg initially followed by 100 mg every 6 hours.[62]

Prevention

To date, no good mechanism has evolved to prevent the spread of and colonization with *C. difficile* or to prevent antibiotic-related pseudomembranous colitis. Private rooms and enteric precautions are commonly used, but their efficacy is unknown.

REFERENCES

1. Ahmad, S. H., Kumar, P., Fakhir, S., et al.: Antibiotic associated colitis. Indian J. Pediatr. *60*:591–594, 1993.
2. Altaie, S. S., Meyer, P., and Dryja, D.: Comparison of two commercially available enzyme immunoassays for detection of *Clostridium difficile* in stool specimens. J. Clin. Microbiol. *32*:51–53, 1994.
3. Barbut, F., Mario, N., Meyohas, M. C., et al.: Investigation of a nosocomial outbreak of *Clostridium difficile*-associated diarrhoea among AIDS patients by random amplified polymorphic DNA (RAPD) assay. J. Hosp. Infect. *26*:181–189, 1994.
4. Bartlett, J. G.: Treatment of antibiotic-associated pseudomembranous colitis. Rev. Infect. Dis. *6*(Suppl. 1):S235–S241, 1984.
5. Bartlett, J. G.: *Clostridium difficile*: Clinical considerations. Rev. Infect. Dis. *12*(Suppl. 2):S243–S251, 1990.
6. Bartlett, J. G.: *Clostridium difficile*: History of its role as an enteric pathogen and the current state of knowledge about the organism. Clin. Infect. Dis. *18*(Suppl. 4):S265–S272, 1994.
7. Bartlett, J. G., Chang, T. W., Gurwith, M., et al.: Antibiotic-associated pseudomembranous colitis due to toxin-producing clostridia. N. Engl. J. Med. *298*:531–534, 1978.
8. Bartlett, J. G., Moon, N., Chang, T. W., et al.: Role of *Clostridium difficile* in antibiotic-associated pseudomembranous colitis. Gastroenterology *75*:778–782, 1978.
9. Bergogne-Berezin, E.: Treatment and prevention of antibiotic associated diarrhea. Int. J. Antimicrob. Agents *16*:521–526, 2000.
10. Bergstein, J. M., Kramer, A., Wittman, D. H., et al.: Pseudomembranous colitis: How useful is endoscopy? Surg. Endosc. *4*:217–219, 1990.
11. Biller, J. A., Katz, A. J., Flores, A. F., et al.: Treatment of recurrent *Clostridium difficile* colitis with *Lactobacillus GG*. J. Pediatr. Gastroenterol. Nutr. *21*:224–226, 1995.
12. Boccia, D., Stolfi, I., Lana, S., et al.: Nosocomial necrotising enterocolitis outbreaks: Epidemiology and control measures. Eur. J. Pediatr. *160*:385–391, 2001.
13. Boland, G. W., Lee, M. J., Cats, A., et al.: Pseudomembranous colitis: Diagnostic sensitivity of the abdominal plain radiograph. Clin. Radiol. *49*:473–475, 1994.
14. Bolton, R. P., Sherriff, R. J., and Read, A. E.: *Clostridium difficile* associated diarrhoea: A role in inflammatory bowel disease? Lancet *1*:383–384, 1980.
15. Bulusu, M., Narayan, S., Shetler, K., et al.: Leukocytosis as a harbinger and surrogate marker of *Clostridium difficile* infection in hospitalized patients with diarrhea. Am. J. Gastroenterol. *95*:3137–3141, 2000.
16. Buts, J. P., Corthier, G., and Delmee, M.: *Saccharomyces boulardii* for *Clostridium difficile*-associated enteropathies in infants. J. Pediatr. Gastroenterol. Nutr. *16*:419–425, 1993.
17. Church, J. M., and Fazio, V. W.: A role for colonic stasis in the pathogenesis of disease related to *Clostridium difficile*. Dis. Colon Rectum *29*:804–809, 1986.
18. Delmee, M.: Laboratory diagnosis of *Clostridium difficile* disease. Clin. Microbiol. Infect. *7*:411–416, 2001.
19. Dorman, S. A., Liggoria, E., Winn, W. C., Jr., et al.: Isolation of *Clostridium difficile* from patients with inactive Crohn's disease. Gastroenterology *82*:1348–1351, 1982.
20. Drapkin, M. S., Worthington, M. G., Chang, T. W., et al.: *Clostridium difficile* colitis mimicking acute peritonitis. Arch. Surg. *120*:1321–1322, 1985.
21. Eglow, R., Pothoulakis, C., Israel, E., et al.: Age-related increase in receptor binding for *Clostridium difficile* toxin A (TxA) in rabbit intestine. Gastroenterology *96*:A136, 1989.
22. Enad, D., Meislich, D., Brodsky, N. L., et al.: Is *Clostridium difficile* a pathogen in the newborn intensive care unit? A prospective evaluation. J. Perinatol. *17*:355–359, 1997.
23. Facklam, D. P., Gardner, J. S., Neidert, G. L., et al.: An epidemiologic postmarketing surveillance study of prescription acne medications. Am. J. Public Health *80*:50–53, 1990.
24. Fekety, R., Kim, K. H., Brown, D., et al.: Epidemiology of antibiotic-associated colitis; isolation of *Clostridium difficile* from the hospital environment. Am. J. Med. *70*:906–908, 1981.
25. Fekety, R., and Shah, A. B.: Diagnosis and treatment of *Clostridium difficile* colitis. J. A. M. A. *269*:71–75, 1993.
26. Fekety, R., Silva, J., Kauffman, C., et al.: Treatment of antibiotic-associated *Clostridium difficile* colitis with oral vancomycin: Comparison of two dosage regimens. Am. J. Med. *86*:15–19, 1989.
27. Ferroni, A., Merckx, J., Ancelle, T., et al.: Nosocomial outbreak of *Clostridium difficile* diarrhea in a pediatric service. Eur. J Clin. Microbiol. Infect. Dis. *16*:928–933, 1997.
28. Finney, J. M. T.: Gastroenterostomy for cicatrizing ulcer of the pylorus. Bull. Johns Hopkins Hosp. *4*:53, 1893.
29. Friedenberg, F., Fernandez, A., Kaul, V., et al.: Intravenous metronidazole for the treatment of *Clostridium difficile* colitis. Dis. Colon Rectum *44*:1176–1180, 2001.
30. Gebhard, R. L., Gerding, D. N., Olson, M. M., et al.: Clinical and endoscopic findings in patients early in the course of *Clostridium difficile*-associated pseudomembranous colitis. Am. J. Med. *78*:45–48, 1985.
31. George, W. L., Sutter, V. L., Citron, D., et al.: Selective and differential medium for isolation of *Clostridium difficile*. J. Clin. Microbiol. *9*:214–219, 1979.
32. Gerding, D. N., and Brazier, J. S.: Optimal methods for identifying *Clostridium difficile* infections. Clin. Infect. Dis. *16*(Suppl. 4):S439–S442, 1994.
33. Greenfield, C., Aguilar Ramirez, J. R., Pounder, R. E., et al.: *Clostridium difficile* and inflammatory bowel disease. Gut *24*:713–717, 1983.
34. Gremse, D. A., Dean, P. C., and Farquhar, D. S.: Cefixime and antibiotic-associated colitis. Pediatr. Infect. Dis. J. *13*:331–333, 1994.
35. Hafiz, S., and Oakley, C. L.: *Clostridium difficile*: Isolation and characteristics. J. Med. Microbiol. *9*:129–136, 1976.
36. Hall, I. C., and O'Toole, E.: Intestinal flora in newborn infants. Am. J. Dis. Child. *49*:390, 1935.
37. Hirschhorn, L. R., Trnka, Y., Onderdonk, A., et al.: Epidemiology of community-acquired *Clostridium difficile*-associated diarrhea. J. Infect. Dis. *169*:127–133, 1994.
38. Holst, E., Helin, I., and Mardh, P. A.: Recovery of *Clostridium difficile* from children. Scand. J. Infect. Dis. *13*:41–45, 1981.
39. Kato, H., Kita, H., Karasawa, T., et al.: Colonisation and transmission of *Clostridium difficile* in healthy individuals examined by PCR ribotyping and pulsed-field gel electrophoresis. J. Med. Microbiol. *50*:720–727, 2001.
40. Kato, N., Ou, C. Y., Kato, H., et al.: Detection of toxigenic *Clostridium difficile* in stool specimens by the polymerase chain reaction. J. Infect. Dis. *167*:455–458, 1993.
41. Kelly, C. P., Pothoulakis, C., Orellana, J., et al.: Human colonic aspirates containing immunoglobulin A antibody to *Clostridium difficile* toxin A inhibit toxin A-receptor binding. Gastroenterology *102*:35–40, 1992.
42. Kim, K., DuPont, H. L., and Pickering, L. K.: Outbreaks of diarrhea associated with *Clostridium difficile* and its toxin in day-care centers: Evidence of person-to-person spread. J. Pediatr. *102*:376–382, 1983.
43. Kim, K. H., Fekety, R., Batts, D. H., et al.: Isolation of *Clostridium difficile* from the environment and contacts of patients with antibiotic-associated colitis. J. Infect. Dis. *143*:42–50, 1981.
44. Knoop, F. C., Owens, M., and Crocker, I. C.: *Clostridium difficile*: Clinical disease and diagnosis. Clin. Microbiol. Rev. *6*:251–265, 1993.
45. Kuijper, E. J., Oudbier, J. H., Stuifbergen, W. N., et al.: Application of whole-cell DNA restriction endonuclease profiles to the epidemiology of *Clostridium difficile*-induced diarrhea. J. Clin. Microbiol. *25*:751–753, 1987.
46. Kyne, L., Warny, M., Qamar, A., et al.: Association between antibody response to toxin A and protection against recurrent *Clostridium difficile* diarrhoea. Lancet *357*:189–193, 2001.
47. LaMont, J. T., and Trnka, Y. M.: Therapeutic implications of *Clostridium difficile* toxin during relapse of chronic inflammatory bowel disease. Lancet *1*:381–383, 1980.
48. Larson, H. E., Barclay, F. E., Honour, P., et al.: Epidemiology of *Clostridium difficile* in infants. J. Infect. Dis. *146*:727–733, 1982.
49. Larson, H. E., and Price, A. B.: Pseudomembranous colitis: Presence of clostridial toxin. Lancet *2*:1312–1314, 1977.
50. Lashner, B. A., Todorczuk, J., Sahm, D. F., et al.: *Clostridium difficile* culture-positive toxin-negative diarrhea. Am. J. Gastroenterol. *81*:940–943, 1986.
51. Leung, D. Y., Kelly, C. P., Boguniewicz, M., et al.: Treatment with intravenously administered gamma globulin of chronic relapsing colitis induced by *Clostridium difficile* toxin. J. Pediatr. *118*(pt 1):633–637, 1991.
52. Lyerly, D. M., Krivan, H. C., and Wilkins, T. D.: *Clostridium difficile*: Its disease and toxins. Clin. Microbiol. Rev. *1*:1–18, 1988.

53. Markowitz, J. E., Brown, K. A., Mamula, P., et al.: Failure of single-toxin assays to detect *Clostridium difficile* infection in pediatric inflammatory bowel disease. Am. J. Gastroenterol. *96*:2688–2690, 2001.
54. McFarland, L. V., Brandmarker, S. A., and Guandalini, S.: Pediatric *Clostridium difficile*: A phantom menace or clinical reality? J. Pediatr. Gastroenterol. Nutr. *31*:220–231, 2000.
55. McFarland, L. V., Mulligan, M. E., Kwok, R. Y., et al.: Nosocomial acquisition of *Clostridium difficile* infection. N. Engl. J. Med. *320*:204–210, 1989.
56. Meyers, S., Mayer, L., Bottone, E., et al.: Occurrence of *Clostridium difficile* toxin during the course of inflammatory bowel disease. Gastroenterology *80*:697–700, 1981.
57. Moulis, H., and Vender, R. J.: Antibiotic-associated hemorrhagic colitis. J. Clin. Gastroenterol. *18*:227–231, 1994.
58. Nakajima, A., Yajima, S., Shirakura, T., et al.: Rifampicin-associated pseudomembranous colitis. J. Gastroenterol. *35*:299–303, 2000.
59. Nathan, M. A., Seabold, J. E., Brown, B. P., et al.: Colonic localization of labeled leukocytes in critically ill patients. Scintigraphic detection of pseudomembranous colitis. Clin. Nucl. Med. *20*:99–106, 1995.
60. Nolan, N. P., Kelly, C. P., Humphreys, J. F., et al.: An epidemic of pseudomembranous colitis: Importance of person to person spread. Gut *28*:1467–1473, 1987.
61. Nusrat, A., Eichel-Streiber, C., Turner, J. R., et al.: *Clostridium difficile* toxins disrupt epithelial barrier function by altering membrane microdomain localization of tight junction proteins. Infect. Immun. *69*:1329–1336, 2001.
62. Pasic, M., Jost, R., Carrel, T., et al.: Intracolonic vancomycin for pseudomembranous colitis. N. Engl. J. Med. *329*:583, 1993.
63. Peterson, L. R., and Kelly, P. J.: The role of the clinical microbiology laboratory in the management of *Clostridium difficile*–associated diarrhea. Infect. Dis. Clin. North Am. *7*:277–293, 1993.
64. Pierce, P. F., Jr., Wilson, R., Silva, J., Jr., et al.: Antibiotic-associated pseudomembranous colitis: An epidemiologic investigation of a cluster of cases. J. Infect. Dis. *145*:269–274, 1982.
65. Pothoulakis, C.: Effects of *Clostridium difficile* toxins on epithelial cell barrier. Ann. N. Y. Acad. Sci. *915*:347–356, 2000.
66. Pothoulakis, C., Sullivan, R., Melnick, D. A., et al.: *Clostridium difficile* toxin A stimulates intracellular calcium release and chemotactic response in human granulocytes. J. Clin. Invest. *81*:1741–1745, 1988.
67. Poxton, I. R., McCoubrey, J., and Blair, G.: The pathogenicity of *Clostridium difficile*. Clin. Microbiol. Infect. *7*:421–427, 2001.
68. Prendergast, T. M., Marini, C. P., D'Angelo, A. J., et al.: Surgical patients with pseudomembranous colitis: Factors affecting prognosis. Surgery *116*:768–774, 1994.
69. Price, A. B., and Davies, D. R.: Pseudomembranous colitis. J. Clin. Pathol. *30*:1–12, 1977.
70. Rolfe, R. D., Helebian, S., and Finegold, S. M.: Bacterial interference between *Clostridium difficile* and normal fecal flora. J Infect. Dis. *143*:470–475, 1981.
71. Sheretz, R. J., and Sarubbi, F. A.: The prevalence of *Clostridium difficile* and toxin in a nursery population: A comparison with patients with necrotizing enterocolitis and an asymptomatic group. J. Pediatr. *100*:435–439, 1982.
72. Shetler, K., Nieuwenhuis, R., Wren, S. M., et al.: Decompressive colonoscopy with intracolonic vancomycin administration for the treatment of severe pseudomembranous colitis. Surg. Endosc. *15*:653–659, 2001.
73. Speare, G. S.: *Staphylococcus* pseudomembranous enterocolitis, a complication of antibiotic therapy. Am. J. Surg. *88*:523–534, 1954.
74. Surawicz, C. M., McFarland, L. V., Greenberg, R. N., et al.: The search for a better treatment for recurrent *Clostridium difficile* disease: Use of high-dose vancomycin combined with *Saccharomyces boulardii*. Clin. Infect. Dis. *31*:1012–1017, 2000.
75. Sutphen, J. L., Grand, R. J., Flores, A., et al.: Chronic diarrhea associated with *Clostridium difficile* in children. Am. J. Dis. Child. *137*:275–278, 1983.
76. Teasley, D. G., Gerding, D. N., Olson, M. M., et al.: Prospective randomised trial of metronidazole versus vancomycin for *Clostridium difficile*–associated diarrhoea and colitis. Lancet *2*:1043–1046, 1983.
77. Tedesco, F. J.: Pseudomembranous colitis: Pathogenesis and therapy. Med. Clin. North Am. *66*:655–664, 1982.
78. Tedesco, F. J., Barton, R. W., and Alpers, D. H.: Clindamycin-associated colitis: A prospective study. Ann. Intern. Med. *81*:429–433, 1974.
79. Tedesco, F. J., Corless, J. K., and Brownstein, R. E.: Rectal sparing in antibiotic-associated pseudomembranous colitis: A prospective study. Gastroenterology *83*:1259–1260, 1982.
80. Tedesco, F. J., Gordon, D., and Fortson, W. C.: Approach to patients with multiple relapses of antibiotic-associated pseudomembranous colitis. Am. J. Gastroenterol. *80*:867–868, 1985.
81. Thompson, C. M., Jr., Gilligan, P. H., Fisher, M. C., et al.: *Clostridium difficile* cytotoxin in a pediatric population. Am. J. Dis. Child. *137*:271–274, 1983.
82. Triadafilopoulos, G., and Hallstone, A. E.: Acute abdomen as the first presentation of pseudomembranous colitis. Gastroenterology *101*:685–691, 1991.
83. Triadafilopoulos, G., Pothoulakis, C., Weiss, R., et al.: Comparative study of *Clostridium difficile* toxin A and cholera toxin in rabbit ileum. Gastroenterology *97*:1186–1192, 1989.
84. Trnka, Y. M., and LaMont, J. T.: Association of *Clostridium difficile* toxin with symptomatic relapse of chronic inflammatory bowel disease. Gastroenterology *80*:693–696, 1981.
85. Viscidi, R., Laughon, B. E., Yolken, R., et al.: Serum antibody response to toxins A and B of *Clostridium difficile*. J. Infect. Dis. *148*:93–100, 1983.
86. Viscidi, R., Willey, S., and Bartlett, J. G.: Isolation rates and toxigenic potential of *Clostridium difficile* isolates from various patient populations. Gastroenterology *81*:5–9, 1981.
87. Wada, N., Nishida, N., Iwaki, S., et al.: Neutralizing activity against *Clostridium difficile* toxin in the supernatants of cultured colostral cells. Infect. Immun. *29*:545–550, 1980.
88. Young, G. P., Ward, P. B., Bayley, N., et al.: Antibiotic-associated colitis due to *Clostridium difficile*: Double-blind comparison of vancomycin with bacitracin. Gastroenterology *89*:1038–1045, 1985.

Whipple Disease

ROBERTO A. GUERRERO ■ MARK A. GILGER

Whipple disease is a rare, systemic bacterial infection that until recently was uniformly fatal. In its most common form, Whipple disease affects white middle-aged men with diarrhea, weight loss, abdominal pain, arthralgias, and fever. Although it is an extraordinarily rare occurrence in children, its recognition may be critical. Simple treatment with appropriate antibiotics may be both curative and lifesaving.[24] The recent successful cultivation of the bacterium *Tropheryma whippelii* should allow development of a simpler and improved diagnostic test, such as serology.

History

Whipple disease was described in 1907 by George Hoyt Whipple,[70] at that time an Instructor in Pathology at The Johns Hopkins University.[6] Curiously, Whipple's description probably was not the first. Allchin and Webb appear to have described a patient with "Whipple's disease" in 1895.[43] Nonetheless, in Whipple's account, a 37-year-old medical missionary was admitted to the Johns Hopkins Hospital with low-grade fever, steatorrhea, and an abdominal mass.

The patient had a 5-year history of sporadic migratory polyarthritis. These attacks of arthritis were associated with a gradual loss of both weight and strength. His skin was pigmented with a brownish hue. Laboratory evaluation found severe anemia and an enormous number of fatty acid crystals in the stool. Explorative laparotomy revealed large, firm mesenteric lymph nodes, and a diagnosis of either Hodgkin disease or tuberculosis was made. The patient died 1 week later, and autopsy revealed marked fatty deposition within intestinal mucosa and the mesenteric and retroperitoneal lymph nodes. Other findings included polyserositis (peritonitis, pleuritis, and pericarditis) and endocarditis. Histologic examination revealed infiltration of the lamina propria of the small intestine by large, foamy mononuclear cells that did not stain for fat. Fatty acids and triglycerides were found in dilated lymph channels. Silver stains of the mesenteric lymph nodes showed "great numbers of rod-shaped organisms" that resembled the tubercle bacillus. Whipple suggested that these bacillus-like organisms in the nodes could be the cause. Whipple reported "a hitherto undescribed disease characterized anatomically by deposits of fat and fatty acids in the intestinal and mesenteric lymphatic tissues."[70] He concluded that the patient suffered from "an obscure disease of fat metabolism" and proposed the term *intestinal lipodystrophy*.[16] Whipple recognized the most important features of this disease except for the involvement of the central nervous system (CNS). In 1949, Black-Schaffer demonstrated that macrophages within the intestinal mucosa of patients with Whipple disease are stained intensely by the periodic acid–Schiff method,[31] proving that the macrophages contained glycoprotein or mucopolysaccharide, not fat, as Whipple had suggested. In 1961, Yardley and associates took tissue samples from Whipple's original patient and found them to be strongly periodic acid–Schiff positive,[60] thus confirming the diagnosis of Whipple disease.

In 1992, Relman and colleagues[54] identified a gram-positive bacillus in association with Whipple disease by use of polymerase chain reaction (PCR). They reported a unique 1321–base pair, 16S ribosomal RNA sequence amplified by PCR on intestinal and lymph node tissue from five unrelated patients with Whipple disease. They suggested that the responsible bacillus is a member of the actinomycetes. Relman concluded that the phylogenetic relations of the Whipple disease bacillus, the features of the illness, and its distinct morphologic characteristics provided sufficient grounds to propose a new genus and species name, *Tropheryma whippelii* (from the Greek *trophe*, or nourishment; *eryma*, or barrier, due to the malabsorption it causes; and *whippelii*, in honor of George Whipple).

Epidemiology

Whipple disease characteristically occurs in white middle-aged men. Its true incidence and prevalence are unknown because fewer than 1000 cases have been reported worldwide. It is an extremely rare disease in children,[1, 2, 4, 8, 30, 66] with fewer than 10 reported cases. The youngest patient was a newborn,[12] and the oldest was a person 83 years of age.[38] The peak age at presentation is 40 to 49 years.[20] In a literature review of 114 patients,[38] 88 percent were males and 12 percent were females. Most of these patients were white. The vast majority of patients reported as having Whipple disease are from continental Europe or the United States.[10] In an extensive review of 741 cases, Dobbins[15] found that most academic centers in the United States had records of three or four unreported cases. He estimated that for every published report, at least two or three unpublished cases exist, and, therefore, some 1500 to 2000 individuals probably have had Whipple disease.[16]

Etiology and Pathogenesis

Whipple disease is widely accepted as being caused by an organism known as Whipple bacillus or *T. whippelii*.[20, 38, 51, 70] However, such a bacterial etiology of Whipple disease should be confirmed by fulfilling Koch's postulates of pathogenicity, which thus far has not been possible. Many other organisms, such as *Corynebacterium* (anaerobic and aerobic), *Haemophilus* spp., *Brucella,* and atypical *Streptococcus* (alpha-hemolytic),[20, 38] have been isolated from patients with Whipple disease, but none of these organisms can be found consistently.

Despite Whipple's account of "great numbers of rod-shaped organisms,"[70] culture of the organism had been unsuccessful until recently. In 2000, Raoult and associates[51] reported that the bacterium *T. whippelii* had been cultured successfully from an aortic valve vegetation in a patient with prolonged endocarditis. The bacteria were isolated after inoculation in a human fibroblast cell line (HEL). Analysis by PCR confirmed that the 16S ribosomal RNA gene of the cultured bacterium was identical to *T. whippelii* sequence. Subcultures of the bacterium also were obtained, and high-titer polyclonal antibodies against *T. whippelii* were produced. Such antibodies potentially may allow serologic diagnosis to become a reality.

T. whippelii may be a member of the actinomycetes,[54] which are gram-positive bacteria with DNA rich in guanine and cytosine.[71] The genus consists of actinomycetes, streptomycetes, and the nocardioforms.[11] *T. whippelii* appears most closely related to the four actinobacteria *Dermatophilus congolensis, Arthrobacter globiformis, Terrabacter tumescens,* and *Micrococcus luteus*.[54] Using so-called bootstrap analysis, some researchers have argued that the Whipple bacillus is only 67 percent associated with actinobacteria, far from the level needed for scientific conclusion.[62] The Whipple bacillus may represent yet another, separate, fourth line of descent with the actinomycetes. Amplification, cloning, and sequencing of a 620–base pair fragment of *T. whippelii* heat shock protein led to the conclusion that *T. whippelii* is a member of the actinobacteria.[44]

Scant support exists for a primary humoral immune deficiency in Whipple disease,[23] but stronger evidence exists for a distinct defect in the cell-mediated immune function. Dobbins[14] reviewed data of 30 patients with HLA-A and HLA-B locus typing and 47 patients with HLA-B27 typing. He found an increased incidence of patients who were positive for HLA-B27 (28%), even with absence of concomitant sacroiliitis. Other reports have failed to confirm the increased association with the HLA-B27 antigen, however.[3] Marth and associates[40] studied 27 patients with Whipple disease. They found a significantly reduced number of cells expressing the complement receptor 3 L-chain (CD11B), a reduced proliferation to phytohemagglutinin and to sheep red blood cells, and a hypoergic skin reaction. These findings indicated a defect of cell-mediated immunity. In patients with active disease, the number of $CD8^+$ cells is increased, which results in a reduced CD4/CD8 ratio. Such defects of cellular immunity appear to persist in patients for several years, despite complete remission of the disease. Schoeden and associates[59] were able to culture *T. whippelii* in mononuclear phagocytes deactivated with interleukin-4, interleukin-10, and dexamethasone. However, interleukin-4 was found to be the critical deactivating signal that rendered monocytes permissive for intracellular multiplication of *T. whippelii*. Interleukin-4 is an immunoregulatory cytokine. Schoeden and associates suggest that host factors, such as an imbalance in the T-helper 1 and 2 immune response, may contribute to the pathogenesis of Whipple disease.

Oral acquisition of the Whipple bacillus appears most likely,[20] emphasizing greater involvement of the duodenum and proximal jejunum than the more distal small intestine. Only three reports of siblings with this disease exist; thus, contagious spread of Whipple disease seems unlikely.[28] *T. whippelii* has been identified free in the small intestine next to the glycocalyx of the enterocyte's microvilli, in epithelial cells, and in the lamina propria.[20] Even in patients with extraintestinal Whipple disease, the organism usually is identified in the small bowel.[20] The bacillus appears to spread through the lymphatics as well as through systemic circulation[20, 32, 45] and then can involve several extraintestinal organs.

T. whippelii can be seen faintly by light microscopy. The bacilli are seen best by transmission electron microscopy, which reveals a rod-shaped organism 0.2 μm wide and 1.5 to 2.5 μm long[28] (Fig. 53–1). The ultrastructure of the wall of *T. whippelii* is similar to that of other gram-positive bacteria, with the exception of an additional surface membrane. This membrane is different from the outer membrane of gram-negative bacteria because it is thinner, has a symmetric profile, and has no periodic acid–Schiff-positive components.[62] Once the bacillus has been ingested by the macrophage, the degenerative process that occurs leads to the accumulation of bacterial remnants that are resistant to degradation. The polysaccharide-containing portion of the bacillus wall correlates with these remnants, and its progressive accumulation leads to the typical intramacrophagic inclusions. These inclusions are periodic acid–Schiff positive and one of the key features in the histologic diagnosis of Whipple disease.[62]

Biopsy specimens from the small intestine in patients with Whipple disease usually show characteristic changes. The intestinal villi are preserved,[20] but distortion of the architecture occurs.[23] Usually present is a clubbed appearance of the intestinal villi[38] caused by the accumulation of foamy macrophages in the lamina propria.[20] The enterocytes may appear normal[17, 38] or may show flattening and vacuolization and occasionally appear cuboidal[17, 38] (Fig. 53–2). Lipid accumulation, with large fat droplets within the

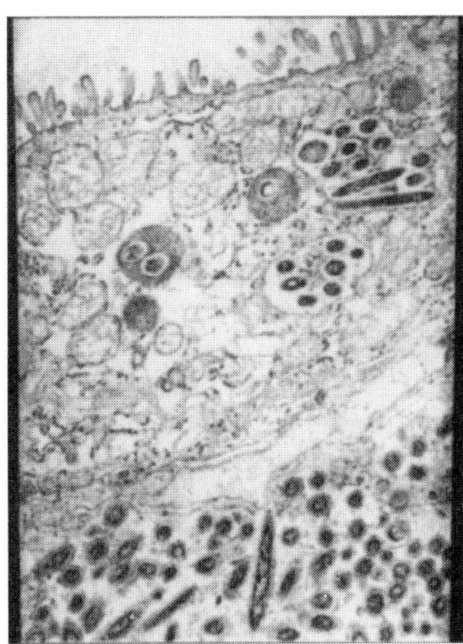

FIGURE 53–1 ■ Electron micrograph of the invasion of enterocytes by Whipple bacilli. There are numerous bacilli within the lamina propria. (Magnification ×25,000.) (From Tyor, M. P.: Whipple's disease: The Duke connection. N. C. Med. J. *55*:237–240, 1994.)

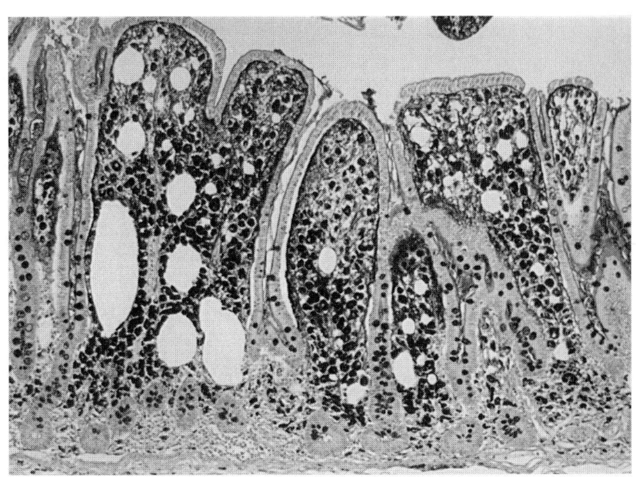

FIGURE 53–2 ■ Light microscopic photograph of intestinal mucosa from the proximal jejunum of a patient with untreated Whipple disease. The villi appear somewhat blunted and swollen with periodic acid–Schiff positive macrophages stuffed in the lamina propria. (Courtesy of Kenneth P. Batts, M. D., Mayo Clinic, Rochester, MN; Jeffrey Craver, M. D., DePaul Health Center, Bridgeton, MO; and Milton J. Finegold, M. D., Baylor College of Medicine, Houston, TX.)

lamina propria and smaller droplets within and in between the absorptive cells, occurs commonly.[38] In some instances, prominent, dilated lacteals are present.[20] Ectors and associates[17] reported reduced and even absent lactase and major histocompatibility complex class II (HLA-DR) expression. Lactase and major histocompatibility complex class II expression normalized within 3 to 6 months of starting antibiotic therapy.

The characteristic feature of Whipple disease is the presence of periodic acid–Schiff-positive, diastase-resistant macrophages.[28] These findings are not pathognomonic, however, because intestinal periodic acid–Schiff-positive macrophages can be found in other conditions,[20] such as histiocytosis, melanosis coli and *Mycobacterium avium-intracellulare* infection, and even within macrophages in healthy individuals. The macrophages in Whipple disease do not stain with Ziehl-Neelsen.[17, 28] A sickle-shaped appearance of the periodic acid–Schiff-positive granules often is present in the macrophages of patients with Whipple disease.[38] Sieracki and Fine[61] observed systemic involvement in the autopsies of five patients with Whipple disease. The sickle-shaped, periodic acid–Schiff-positive macrophages were thought to be specific for Whipple disease, demonstrating involvement of the entire gastrointestinal tract and the pancreas; diffuse involvement of the retroperitoneum and lymph nodes, the adrenals, the liver with sickle-form particles in Kupffer cells and in histiocytes, the brain, the heart, and the visceral pleura of the lungs; and minimal involvement of the genitourinary tract, skeletal muscles, and bone marrow. James and associates[32] examined the vessels of the gastrointestinal system and found abundant bacilli in the arteries of the small intestinal serosa and liver. They noted focal degeneration and fibrosis in the tunica media with arteritis and intimal proliferation. Rickman and coworkers[55] reported a case that confirmed the presence of *T. whippelii* in the vitreous of the eye.

T. whippelii produces a predominantly histiocytic inflammatory reaction, with infiltration by macrophages.[19] Noncaseating, epithelioid cell, sarcoid-like granulomata are located preferentially in peripheral lymph nodes and the liver.[13, 19] These granulomata occasionally can be seen in

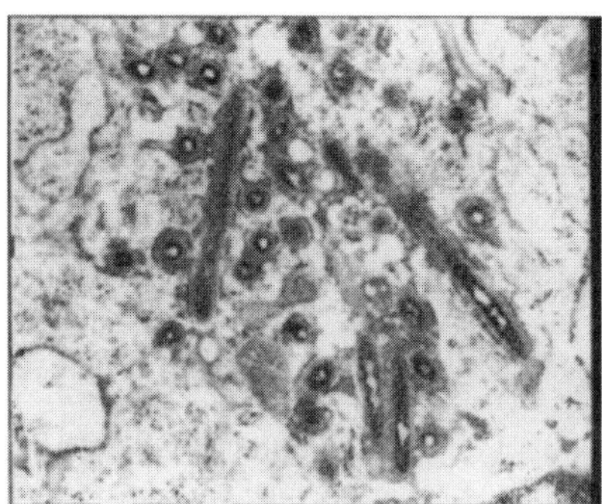

FIGURE 53–3 ■ Electron micrograph illustrating numerous rod-shaped bacilliform bodies within the cytoplasm of a macrophage. (Magnification ×13,750.) (From Tyor, M. P.: Whipple's disease: The Duke connection. N. C. Med. J. 55:237–240, 1994.)

different tissues, including three reports of granulomata in the intestinal tract.[19] Mesenteric lymph nodes often are strikingly enlarged.[10]

Electron microscopy can be useful, often revealing the presence of the rod-shaped bacterium[24] (see Fig. 53–1). Electron microscopy also demonstrates intestinal macrophages containing bacteria with signs of lysis.[62] Silva and associates[62] described steps of a degradative process of the bacillus that starts with disorganization of the surface membrane and the thick outer wall. With the loss of intracellular material, bacterial ghosts composed of the three inner layers of the envelope are present. The two electron-dense layers of the cytoplasmic membrane become disorganized and solubilized, leaving the inner dense layer of the cell wall as the final bacterial remnant (Fig. 53–3).

Clinical Manifestations

The clinical manifestations of Whipple disease vary according to the organ system involved. The disease is viewed best as a multisystemic illness, with focus on the gastrointestinal tract.[5] Malabsorption is the key feature of clinical disease, but no specific signs or symptoms for Whipple disease are known. Table 53–1 illustrates the major symptoms and signs

TABLE 53–1 ■ MAJOR SYMPTOMS AND SIGNS IN WHIPPLE DISEASE

Symptoms	Percentage of Cases
Weight loss	65-100
Chronic diarrhea	60-85
Arthralgia	65-80
Abdominal pain	60
Fever	10-55
Central nervous system-related complaints	10-40
Signs	
Malnutrition	90-95
Hypotension	70
Lymphadenopathy	55
Hyperpigmentation	45-55
Abdominal tenderness	50
Edema	30
Abdominal mass	20
Hepatomegaly	1-14
Splenomegaly	5-10
Ascites	8

Data from references 10, 23, 24, 35, 38.

of Whipple disease. In children, failure to thrive, malnutrition, and chronic diarrhea appear most commonly. Abdominal distention, abdominal pain, and generalized lymphadenopathy may be found.[2] Response to antibiotic treatment may be dramatic, with rapid weight gain and resolution of symptoms.[4]

GASTROINTESTINAL TRACT. One of the most common symptoms is weight loss, which is found in 65 to 100 percent of patients.[10, 20, 24, 38] Indeed, weight loss may be the only symptom.[8] Diarrhea is reported in 60 to 85 percent of patients.[10, 20, 24, 38] The diarrhea usually is watery or fatty in nature.[38] Several mechanisms have been proposed to explain the malabsorption and steatorrhea in Whipple disease.[20] Direct infection and secondary enterocyte dysfunction may prevent the esterification of fatty acids to triglycerides as well as inhibit the uptake of carbohydrates and amino acids. Blockage of transport of triglyceride-rich chylomicrons into lacteals may result from the deposition of foamy macrophages in the lamina propria. Lymphatic obstruction may occur by involvement of the mesenteric lymph nodes. Malabsorption and diarrhea tend to resolve within a few days after initiation of antibiotic treatment, whereas the lacteal dilatation and periodic acid–Schiff-positive macrophages can remain for months to years. Occult gastrointestinal bleeding frequently is found, but melena and gross gastrointestinal bleeding are rare findings.[20, 24, 38]

Abdominal pain is found in as many as 60 percent of patients.[10, 20, 24, 38] The pain is nonspecific, generally is epigastric, and may be worse after meals.[38] Such pain and anorexia may lead to reduced calorie intake and further weight loss.[20] Abdominal distention occurs commonly and may be secondary to intra-abdominal lymphadenopathy or to thickening of loops of diseased intestine.[20, 38] Ascites occasionally is seen and may be chylous, secondary to lymphatic obstruction.[8, 24]

JOINTS. Arthralgia, the most frequent nongastrointestinal symptom in Whipple disease,[20, 38] is present in 65 percent of adult cases.[38] Arthralgia may precede gastrointestinal symptoms by many years or even decades[20, 35] and occurs less commonly in children. In general, joint symptoms continue unchanged with the onset of gastrointestinal symptoms.[20] Acute migratory arthralgia or arthritis may last for days or weeks[24, 28, 38] and may persist as the disease progresses. The involved joints, in decreasing order of frequency, are knees, ankles, hips, fingers, wrists, elbows, hands, and spine.[20] Examination may reveal joint pain, swelling, limited range of motion, and warmth.[58] Fever sometimes is present.[20] Spondylitis, with or without sacroiliitis, may develop.[4] Permanent joint destruction and deformity are uncommon findings but can be severe.[20, 58] Arthrocentesis may reveal an inflammatory arthritis, with cell counts of 6000 to 75,000, often with a polymorphonuclear leukocyte predominance.[20] Synovial biopsy may demonstrate periodic acid–Schiff positive macrophages.[20]

CENTRAL NERVOUS SYSTEM. Whipple disease can be confined to the brain[56] but usually is accompanied by other manifestations.[24] CNS and neurologic manifestations, such as headache, diplopia, meningoencephalitis, depression, confusion, and personality changes, are uncommon occurrences[10, 20, 38] but may be significant.[10, 20, 23, 38, 48] Table 53–2 lists the spectrum of potential CNS involvement.

EYE. Indirect involvement of the CNS as well as direct involvement of the eye can produce visual problems.[20] Ophthalmoplegia and diplopia can occur with involvement of cranial nerves III, IV, and VI.[20] Reduced visual acuity and papilledema can occur with compromise of the optic nerve.[20] Numerous ophthalmologic findings, including vasculitis,

TABLE 53–2 ■ CENTRAL NERVOUS SYSTEM SYMPTOMS AND SIGNS OF WHIPPLE DISEASE

Headache
Incoordination
Mental and personality changes
Confusion
Lethargy, coma
Ataxia
Convulsions
Motor weakness
Dementia
Depression
Papilledema
Ophthalmoplegia
Visual difficulties (diplopia, blurring)
Nystagmus
Pupillary abnormalities
Ptosis
Hemiparesis
Polydipsia
Hyperphagia
Hearing loss
Sensory loss
Numbness
Slurred speech
Dizziness
Tinnitus
Loss of vibratory and position sense
Sleep disorders
Stiff neck
Facial pain
Muscle rigidity
Muscle jerks and twitches
Hyperreflexia (± Babinski sign)

vitritis, optic atrophy, uveitis, chorioretinitis, vitreous opacities, glaucoma, keratitis, retinal hemorrhages, disk edema, and lacrimal duct obstruction, have been reported.[20, 69] Rickman and associates[55] reported a case of ocular disease without marked CNS or gastrointestinal disease.

SKIN. Hyperpigmentation of the skin in sun-exposed areas occurs in roughly half of cases.[23, 38] The mechanism of hyperpigmentation is uncertain but is not related to adrenal insufficiency.[20] Subcutaneous nodules may be found and can reveal periodic acid–Schiff-positive macrophages and bacilli on electron microscopy.[27]

HEART. The heart frequently is involved in Whipple disease. Endocarditis, myocarditis, pericarditis, pancarditis, and coronary arteritis have been found.[20, 41] A blood culture–negative endocarditis may be caused by Whipple disease.[20] Chronic aortic regurgitation is the most common clinical finding of endocardial involvement.[20] Pericarditis with polyserositis (pleuritis, peritonitis) has been found.[22] The electrocardiographic abnormalities are nonspecific but include first-degree atrioventricular block, left ventricular hypertrophy, sinus tachycardia, left bundle branch block, intraventricular conduction delay, old inferior wall infarct, and short PR interval.[23] Sossai and associates[63] reported a case of regression of a right bundle branch block after treatment with antibiotics, but the block spontaneously recurred 2 years later.

SKELETAL MUSCLE. Skeletal muscle may be involved, diagnosed by electromyography or muscle biopsy.[64] Proximal muscle weakness occurs most commonly. Muscle biopsy reveals a nonspecific myopathy.

LYMPH NODES AND SPLEEN. Whipple disease may involve any lymph node in the body.[20] Mesenteric lymph nodes frequently are involved, and splenomegaly is found in 5 to 10 percent of cases.[38]

PULMONARY. Cough, pleuritic chest pain, and dyspnea have been reported.[65] Pleural involvement may appear as a pleural rub. Pleural adhesions and granulomata have been reported at autopsy.[4, 65] Chest radiography often reveals pleural thickening, parenchymal shadowing, and elevation of the diaphragm.[65] Lung function tests may demonstrate decreased lung volumes.[65]

KIDNEY. Renal involvement in Whipple disease is a rare finding.[20] However, granulomata have been found, as has focal glomerulonephritis.[34]

HEMATOLOGIC. Anemia occurs commonly and usually is of a hypochromic, microcytic variety.[20, 23, 24] Macrocytic anemia caused by malabsorption of folate also may be seen. Leukocytosis, thrombocytosis,[47] and bone marrow involvement may be found.[52] Low serum iron concentration and an elevated erythrocyte sedimentation rate frequently are seen.[23] A single case of extraintestinal lymphoma in association with Whipple disease found at autopsy has been reported.[26]

Diagnosis

No specific laboratory findings of Whipple disease have been determined. Anemia and low albumin probably are the most common ones, being found in approximately 90 percent of patients. Low serum iron and folate concentrations are seen in perhaps 30 percent of cases. Hypokalemia, hypocalcemia, low cholesterol and carotene, prolonged prothrombin time, and increased transaminases are less common findings. Elevated fecal fat is found in more than 90 percent of cases. The D-xylose malabsorption test result frequently is abnormal.

Barium x-ray studies of the small bowel may show marked thickening of the mucosal folds and separation of bowel loops, suggesting a malabsorptive disease. Such findings usually resolve completely with successful antibiotic therapy. For CNS Whipple disease, characteristic abnormalities seen on computed tomographic scans of the brain include atrophy, focal gray matter lesions, hydrocephalus, and white matter alterations.[66]

One of the key features in the histologic diagnosis of Whipple disease is the accumulation of periodic acid–Schiff-positive, diastase-resistant macrophages in the lamina propria of the small intestine.[4, 23, 39] These findings are not pathognomonic, and infection with *M. avium-intracellulare* must be excluded.[39] *T. whippelii* does not stain acid-fast,[39] whereas mycobacteria are identified readily. Small bowel involvement by *M. avium* complex can have endoscopic, histologic, and radiographic findings similar to those of Whipple disease.[50] Periodic acid–Schiff-positive macrophages occasionally can be seen in the mucosa of the large bowel and rectum in unrelated diseases, such as histiocytosis, and in benign problems, such as melanosis coli and pneumatosis intestinalis.[39] Electron microscopy can confirm the diagnosis by visualization of the characteristic bacillus.[24, 62]

Endoscopy of the small bowel may be helpful because characteristic lesions may be seen and biopsy specimens obtained. No clear data suggest where the intestinal specimens should be taken[39] because intestinal involvement usually is patchy. Random biopsy samples of the small bowel are suggested, beginning at the ligament of Treitz.[42] Endoscopic findings include yellow-white plaques and an erythematous, erosive, friable mucosa.[25]

PCR amplification may be used to detect and identify bacterial pathogens.[70] To set up a PCR, the only prerequisite information is the nucleotide sequences flanking each end of the target.[53] PCR has become an important method for the diagnosis of Whipple disease. It may be especially helpful if the histopathologic examination findings are normal or in patients with unusual extraintestinal involvement. Specific identification of *T. whippelii* can be achieved by amplification of the 1321–base pair bacterial, 16S ribosomal RNA gene isolated from infected tissue.[54] Muller and associates[45] applied this PCR technique to demonstrate *T. whippelii* in peripheral blood mononuclear cells and cells derived from pleural effusion in a patient with Whipple disease. PCR techniques have been used to detect *T. whippelii* in erythrocytes,[37] cerebrospinal fluid,[6] and resected heart valves with infective endocarditis.[8, 45]

The diagnostic utility of PCR in Whipple disease is clear, but it cannot be taken as the sole basis for diagnosis. Ehrbar and associates[18] studied the specificity of PCR for *T. whippelii*. They performed elective gastroscopy on patients without known Whipple disease. PCR analysis was positive in 4.8 percent of duodenal biopsy specimens and 11.4 percent of gastric juice samples. Compared with the "gold standard" of histology and clinical signs, the specificity of PCR for *T. whippelii* was 95.2 percent for duodenal biopsy specimen and 88.6 percent for gastric juice. These findings suggest that *T. whippelii* or a closely related bacterium may be present in some people without known Whipple disease.

Treatment

Antibiotics are the mainstay of therapy for Whipple disease.[10] However, because *T. whippelii* only recently has been cultured, no antimicrobial sensitivities are available.[20, 24] Current antibiotic treatment strategies are empirical, based only on the accumulated anecdotal experience. The successful culture of *T. whippelii* should enable researchers to develop methods for antibiotic susceptibility testing.[50] Table 53–3 illustrates several antibiotic treatments and the likelihood of relapse. In general, response to antibiotics is good and often dramatic. Symptoms such as diarrhea quickly resolve, and weight gain is rapid. Several antibiotics that have been tried alone or in combination include chloramphenicol, penicillin, streptomycin, ampicillin, trimethoprim-sulfamethoxazole (TMP-SMX), erythromycin, and doxycycline.[10, 20, 21, 24]

TABLE 53–3 ■ TREATMENT OF WHIPPLE DISEASE: INITIAL ANTIBIOTIC REGIMEN AND RELAPSE

Antibiotics	No. of Patients	Total No. of Relapses	CNS Relapses
TCN* alone	49	21	9†
PCN + STM + TCN*	15	2	0
PCN/PCN*	8	3	2
PCN + STM	5	2	0
TMP-SMX*	3	0	0
Other	8	3	2
Totals	88	31	13

*Oral therapy.

†Includes two patients treated with TCN only in whom CNS relapse was the second relapse.

CNS, central nervous system; PCN, penicillin; STM, streptomycin; TCN, tetracycline; TMP-SMX; trimethoprim-sulfamethoxazole.

Data from Keinath, R. D., Merrell, D. E., Vlietstra, R., et al.: Antibiotic treatment and relapse in Whipple's disease: Long-term follow-up of 88 patients. Gastroenterology *88*:1867–1873, 1985.

Keinath and associates[33] analyzed the antibiotic response rate of 88 patients with documented Whipple disease. Thirty-one experienced relapse, with a mean time to relapse of 4.2 years after initial diagnosis. CNS relapse occurred in 13 of 88, and all CNS and cardiac relapses were late. In addition to diagnosis, PCR also may prove useful in the monitoring of response to antibiotic therapy.[28, 48]

All patients with Whipple disease should receive antibiotics that penetrate the blood-brain barrier.[33, 57] Tetracycline and penicillin do not penetrate the blood-brain barrier well, unless the meninges are inflamed.[57] The preferred treatment in both adults and children is TMP-SMX given orally twice a day for 1 year.[57] If the small bowel is involved, repeated small bowel biopsy is suggested at least 6 months to 1 year after treatment to document the disappearance of the bacillus. For patients intolerant of TMP-SMX, penicillin or ampicillin is recommended. Levy and associates[35] described a case of acquired resistance to TMP-SMX that responded to oral penicillin. Feurle and Marth[21] noted that TMP-SMX was more efficacious than was tetracycline in inducing clinical remission of Whipple disease. However, they observed the development of aqueductal stenosis with hydrocephalus in a patient receiving TMP-SMX treatment and indicated that even TMP-SMX is no safeguard against cerebral recurrence. CNS relapse has a poor prognosis.[20, 21, 24, 33] Feurle and Marth[21] suggested an experimental therapy for CNS recurrence with a highly active bactericidal compound, such as a third-generation cephalosporin, a quinolone, or intrathecal antibiotic therapy, that readily crosses the blood-brain barrier. In adult patients, Keinath and associates[33] recommended treatment with parenteral penicillin (1.2 million units daily) plus streptomycin (1 g daily) for 10 to 14 days, followed by TMP-SMX (one double-strength tablet twice daily) for 1 year. Because of the extreme rarity of the occurrence of Whipple disease in children, prudent management dictates long-term surveillance after resolution of symptoms.

Because Whipple disease is a malabsorptive disorder, the patient's nutritional needs must be assessed carefully. Specific attention must be paid to replacement of any vitamin or mineral deficiencies. Iron, folate, vitamin D, and calcium, for example, typically are given until the steatorrhea resolves.

Conclusions

Whipple disease, despite its rare occurrence in children, deserves diagnostic consideration in any child with failure to thrive, malnutrition, and chronic diarrhea. Such findings, especially with CNS manifestations or arthralgias, should raise the specter of Whipple disease. Diagnosis of Whipple disease can be made by histology, PCR, and clinical signs. Recent success in culturing *T. whippelii* should allow new, more accurate diagnostic methods. Simple antibiotic treatment with oral TMP-SMX can result in dramatic resolution of symptoms, whereas failure to consider this rare disease can lead to catastrophic events.

REFERENCES

1. Ament, M. E.: Malabsorption syndromes in infancy and childhood. J. Pediatr. *81*:867–884, 1972.
2. Aust, C. H., and Smith, E. B.: Whipple's disease in a 3-month-old infant. Am. J. Clin. Pathol. *37*:66–74, 1962.
3. Bai, J. C., Mota, A. H., Maurino, E., et al.: Class I and class II HLA antigens in a homogeneous Argentinian population with Whipple's disease: Lack of association with HLA-B27. Am. J. Gastroenterol. *86*:992–994, 1991.

4. Barakat, A. Y., Bitar, J., and Nassar, V. H.: Whipple's disease in a seven-year-old child: Report of a case. Am. J. Proctol. *24*:312–315, 1973.
5. Bayless, T. M., and Knox, D. L.: Whipple's disease: A multisystemic infection. N. Engl. J. Med. *300*:920, 1979.
6. Birch, C. A.: Whipple's disease: George Hoyt Whipple (born 1878). Practitioner *212*(1270 spec. no.):581–582, 1974.
7. Brandle, M., Ammann, P., Spinas, G., et al.: Relapsing Whipple's disease presenting with hypopituitarism. Clin. Endocrinol. *50*:399–403, 1999.
8. Bruni, R., and Massimo, L.: Descrizione un rarissimo caso di mallatia de Whipple nel eta pediatrica. Minerva Pediatr. *11*:935–943, 1959.
9. Celard, M., De Gevigney, G., Mosnier, S., et al.: Polymerize chain reaction analysis for the diagnosis of *Tropheryma whippelii* infective endocarditis in two patients with no previous evidence of Whipple's disease. Clin. Infect. Dis. *29*:1348–1349, 1999.
10. Comer, G. M., Brandt, L. J., and Abissi, C. J.: Whipple's disease: A review. Am. J. Gastroenterol. *78*:107–114, 1983.
11. Couper, R.: Whipple's disease: The bacillus unmasked. J. Pediatr. Gastroenterol. Nutr. *17*:339–344, 1993.
12. DePra, M., Casagrande, A., and Guarino, M.: Whipple's disease: Apropos of a case demonstrating the existence of the congenital form. Minerva Pediatr. *26*:1723–1743, 1974.
13. Desmet, V. J., and Geboes, K.: Review article: Liver lesions in inflammatory bowel disorders. J. Pathol. *151*:247–255, 1987.
14. Dobbins, W. O., III: HLA antigens in Whipple's disease. Arthritis Rheum. *30*:102–105, 1987.
15. Dobbins, W. O., III: Whipple's disease. Mayo Clin. Proc. *63*:623–624, 1988.
16. Dobbins, W. O., III: Whipple's disease: An historical perspective. Q. J. Med. *56*:523–531, 1985.
17. Ectors, N. L., Geboes, K. J., DeVos, R. M., et al.: Whipple's disease: A histological, immunocytochemical and electron microscopic study of the small intestinal epithelium. J. Pathol. *172*:73–79, 1994.
18. Ectors, N., Geboes, K., Wynants, P., et al.: Granulomatous gastritis and Whipple's disease. Am. J. Gastroenterol. *87*:509–515, 1992.
19. Ehrbar, H., Bauerfeind, P., Dutly, F., et al.: PCR-positive tests for *Tropheryma whippelii* in patients without Whipple's disease. Lancet *353*:2214, 1999.
20. Feldman, M.: Southern Internal Medicine Conference: Whipple's disease. Am. J. Med. Sci. *291*:56–67, 1986.
21. Feurle, G. E., and Marth, T.: An evaluation of antimicrobial treatment for Whipple's disease: Tetracycline versus trimethoprim-sulfamethoxazole. Dig. Dis. Sci. *39*:1642–1648, 1995.
22. Finch, W.: Arthritis and the gut. Postgrad. Med. *86*:229–235, 1989.
23. Flemin, J. L., Wiesner, R. H., and Shorter, R. G.: Whipple's disease: Clinical, biochemical and histopathologic features and assessment of treatment in 29 patients. Mayo Clin. Proc. *63*:539–551, 1988.
24. Gaist, D., and Ladefoged, K.: Whipple's disease. Scand. J. Gastroenterol. *29*:97–101, 1994.
25. Geboes, K., Ectors, N., Heidbuchel, H., et al.: Whipple's disease: Endoscopic aspects before and after therapy. Gastrointest. Endosc. *36*: 247–252, 1990.
26. Gillen, C. D., Coddington, R., Montieth, P. G., et al.: Extraintestinal lymphoma in association with Whipple's disease. Gut *34*:1627–1629, 1993.
27. Good, A. E, Beals, T. F, Simmons, J. L., et al.: A subcutaneous nodule with Whipple's disease: Key to early diagnosis? Arthritis Rheum. *23*:856–859, 1980.
28. Gran, J. T., and Husby, G.: Joint manifestations in gastrointestinal diseases. Dig. Dis. *10*:295–312, 1992.
29. Gras, E., Matias, O., Guiu, X., et al.: PCR analysis in the pathological diagnosis of Whipple's disease: Emphasis on the extraintestinal involvement or atypical morphological features. J. Pathol. *188*:318–321, 1999.
30. Hamilton, J. R.: Whipple disease. *In* Behrman, R. E., Vaughn, V., and Nelson, W. E. (eds.): Textbook of Pediatrics. Philadelphia, W. B. Saunders, 1983, p. 935.
31. Harvey, A. M.: Teacher and distinguished pupil: William Henry Welch and George Hoyt Whipple. Johns Hopkins Med. J. *135*:178–190, 1974.
32. James, T. N., Bulkley, B. H., and Kent, S. P.: Case report: Vascular lesions of the gastrointestinal system in Whipple's disease. Am. J. Med. Sci. *288*:125–129, 1984.
33. Keinath, R. D., Merrell, D. E., Vlietstra, R., et al.: Antibiotic treatment and relapse in Whipple's disease: Long-term follow-up of 88 patients. Gastroenterology *88*:1867–1873, 1985.
34. Kraunz, R. F.: Whipple's disease with cardiac and renal abnormalities. Arch. Intern. Med. *123*:701–706, 1969.
35. Leirisalo-Repo, M.: Enteropathic arthritis, Whipple's disease, juvenile spondyloarthropathy and uveitis. Curr. Opin. Rheumatol. *6*:385–390, 1994.
36. Levy, M., Poyart, C., Lamarque, D., et al.: Whipple's disease: Acquired resistance to trimethoprim-sulfamethoxazole. Am. J. Gastroenterol. *95*:2390–2391, 2000.
37. Lowsky, R., Archer, G. L., Fyles, G., et al.: Brief report: Diagnosis of Whipple's disease by molecular analysis of peripheral blood. N. Engl. J. Med. *331*:1343–1346, 1994.
38. Maizel, H., Ruffin, J. M., and Dobbins, W. O., III: Whipple's disease: A review of 19 patients from one hospital and a review of the literature since 1950. Medicine (Baltimore) *49*:175–205, 1970.
39. Marbet, V. A., Stalder, G. A., and Gyr, K. E.: Whipple's disease: A multisystemic disease with changing presentation. Dig. Dis. *4*:119–128, 1986.
40. Marth, T., Roux, M., VonHerbay, A., et al.: Persistent reduction of complement receptor 3 L-chain expressing mononuclear blood cells and transient inhibitory serum factors in Whipple's disease. Clin. Immunol. Immunopathol. *72*:217–226, 1994.
41. McAllister, H. A., and Fenoglio, J. J.: Cardiac involvement in Whipple's disease. Circulation *52*:152–156, 1975.
42. Moorthy, S., Nolley, G., and Hermos, J. A.: Whipple's disease with minimal intestinal involvement. Gut *18*:152–155, 1977.
43. Morgan, A. D.: The first recorded case of Whipple's disease. Gut *2*:370–372, 1961.
44. Morgenegg, S., Dutly, F., and Altwegg, M.: Cloning and sequencing of a part of the heat shock protein 65 gene (hsp 65) of *Tropheryma whippelii* and its use for detection in clinical specimens by PDR. J. Clin. Microbiol. *38*:2248–2253, 2000.
45. Muller, C., Stain, C., and Burghuber, O.: *Tropheryma whippelii* in peripheral blood mononuclear cells and cells of pleural effusion. Lancet *341*:701, 1993.
46. Naegeli, B., Bannwart, F., and Bertel, O.: An uncommon cause of recurrent strokes: *Tropheryma whippelii* endocarditis. Stroke *31*:2002–2003, 2000.
47. Nuzum, C. T., Sandler, R. S., and Paulk, H. T.: Thrombocytosis in Whipple's disease. Gastroenterology *80*:1465–1467, 1981.
48. Ojeda, E., Redondo, J., Lapaza, J., et al.: Enfermedad de Whipple: Manifestaciones neurologicas y revision de los casos publicados en la literature nacional. Rev. Clin. Esp. *183*:1465–1467, 1981.
49. Petrides, P., Muller-Hocker, J., Fredricks, D., et al.: PCR analysis of *T. whippelii* DNA in a case of Whipple's disease: Effect of antibiotics and correlation with histology. Am. J. Gastroenterol. *93*:1579–1582, 1998.
50. Poorman, J. C., and Katon, R. M.: Small bowel involvement by *Mycobacterium avium* complex in a patient with AIDS: Endoscopic, histologic and radiographic similarities to Whipple's disease. N. Engl. J. Med. *342*:620–625, 2000.
51. Raoult, D., Birg, M. L., Scola, B. L., et al.: Cultivation of the bacillus of Whipple's disease. N. Engl. J. Med. *342*:620–625, 2000.
52. Rausing, A.: Bone marrow biopsy in diagnosis of Whipple's disease. Acta Med. Scand. *193*:5–8, 1973.
53. Relman, D. A.: Whipple's disease: A disorder associated with a visible but uncultured bacillus. J. Infect. Dis. *168*:1–8, 1993.
54. Relman, D. A., Schmidt, T. M., MacDermott, R. P., et al.: Identification of the uncultured bacillus of Whipple's disease. N. Engl. J. Med. *327*:293–300, 1992.
55. Rickman, L. S., Freeman, W. R., Green, W. R., et al.: Brief report: Uveitis caused by *Tropheryma whippelii* (Whipple's bacillus). N. Engl. J. Med. *332*:363–366, 1995.
56. Romanul, F. C. A., Radvany, J., and Rosales, R. K.: Whipple's disease confined to the brain: A case studied clinically and pathologically. J. Neurol. Neurosurg. Psychiatry *40*:901–909, 1977.
57. Ryser, R. J., Locksley, R. M., Eng, S. C., et al.: Reversal of dementia associated with Whipple's disease by trimethoprim-sulfamethoxazole, drugs that penetrate the blood-brain barrier. Gastroenterology *86*: 745–752, 1984.
58. Scheib, J. S., and Quinet, R. J.: Whipple's disease with axial and peripheral joint destruction. South. Med. J. *83*:684–687, 1990.
59. Schoeden, G., Goldenberger, D., Forrer, R., et al.: Deactivation of macrophages with interleukin-4 is the key to the isolation of *Tropheryma whippelii*. J. Infect. Dis. *176*:672–677, 1997.
60. Sharma, O. P.: Beethoven's illness: Whipple's disease rather than sarcoidosis? J. R. Soc. Med. *87*:283–285, 1994.
61. Sieracki, J. C., and Fine, G.: Whipple's disease: Observations on systemic involvement. II. Gross and histologic observations. Arch. Pathol. *67*:81–93, 1959.
62. Silva, M. T., Macedo, P. M., and Moura Nunes, J. F.: Ultrastructure of bacilli and the bacillary origin of the macrophagic inclusions in Whipple's disease. J. Gen. Microbiol. *131*:1001–1013, 1985.
63. Sossai, P., DeBoni, M., and Cielo, R.: The heart and Whipple's disease. Int. J. Cardiol. *23*:275–276, 1989.
64. Swash, M., Schwartz, M. S., Vandenberg, M. J., et al.: Myopathy in Whipple's disease. Gut. *18*:800–804, 1977.
65. Symmons, D. P. N., Shepard, A. N., Boardman, P. L., et al.: Pulmonary manifestations of Whipple's disease. Q. J. Med. *56*:497–504, 1985.
66. Tan, T., Vogel, H., Tharp, B. R., et al.: Presumed central nervous system Whipple's disease in a child: Case report. Clin. Infect. Dis. *20*:883–889, 1995.
67. Tyor, M. P.: Whipple's disease: The Duke connection. N. C. Med. J. *55*:237–240, 1994.
68. Vine, A. K.: Retinal vasculitis. Semin. Neurol. *14*:354–360, 1994.
69. von Weizsacker, F., and Blum, H. E.: Impact of molecular biology in gastroenterology. Digestion *54*:125–129, 1993.
70. Whipple, G. H.: A hitherto undescribed disease characterized anatomically by deposits of fat and fatty acids in the intestinal mesenteric lymphatic tissues. Johns Hopkins Hosp. Bull. *18*:382–391, 1907.
71. Woese, C. R.: Bacterial evolution. Microbiol. Rev. *51*:221–271, 1987.

SECTION VII

Liver Diseases

CHAPTER 54

Hepatitis

GAIL J. DEMMLER

Hepatitis is an inflammation of the liver and may be caused by a variety of infectious agents. Some agents such as hepatitis A, B, C, D, E, and G viruses are primarily hepatotropic and produce disease primarily or exclusively in the liver. Other agents such as cytomegalovirus (CMV), Epstein-Barr virus (EBV), adenovirus, and the hemorrhagic fever viruses produce hepatitis as part of a systemic or disseminated illness. With many infectious agents, hepatitis usually is subclinical or silent, and very few, if any, signs or symptoms are manifested in the patient. Symptomatic or clinical hepatitis may be acute or chronic at initial evaluation, and it may be associated with mild to severe or even fulminant or fatal disease.[63] Children of all ages, from neonates to young adults, both immunocompetent and immunocompromised, may contract infectious hepatitis, and the age and immune status of the host, as well as the exposure history, may provide clues to identification of the most likely etiologic agent. Noninfectious causes such as autoimmune, genetic, and metabolic disorders, as well as reactions to medications or drugs, also are important causes of hepatitis in children.

A general approach to a patient with hepatitis or hepatic dysfunction, from the perspective of the infectious disease specialist, is presented in this chapter. Detailed information regarding the diagnosis and management of each particular pathogen can be found in the respective chapters in the section of this textbook dedicated to infections with specific microorganisms.

History

Originally described by Hippocrates in the second century BC, hepatitis has an ancient historical perspective. The earliest descriptions of outbreaks of hepatitis in the ancient world most likely involved hepatitis A virus (HAV), and it was known as "epidemic jaundice" and "catarrhal jaundice," or "acute yellow atrophy of the liver" if the disease was severe or fulminant.[20] The earliest recorded outbreak in the United States occurred in Norfolk, Virginia, in 1812.[9] During wartimes, outbreaks of "camp jaundice" or "field jaundice" occurred and probably were caused by HAV, yellow fever, or leptospirosis. Not until 1973 was the cause of "infectious hepatitis" determined to be a 27-nm, nonenveloped viral particle, originally designated as enterovirus 72 and now known as HAV.[39] Infection with hepatitis B virus (HBV) has a relatively more recent history. It probably was described originally in the late 1880s in an epidemiologic study published by Luerman in 1885 in Germany, where an outbreak of hepatitis in shipyard and warehouse workers who received smallpox vaccine contaminated with human material was associated with a prolonged form of hepatitis.[75] Other outbreaks of "serum hepatitis" associated with percutaneous therapies, such as gold used for rheumatoid arthritis or contaminated vaccines that were stabilized with human serum have been described.[1, 12, 57] In the early 1970s, the complete HBV infectious particle identified in serum was called the *Dane particle*, and a specific serologic marker, originally called the *Australian (Au) antigen* because it was discovered first in the blood of an Australian aborigine and later designated hepatitis B surface antigen (HBsAg), also was characterized and subsequently used to diagnose *serum hepatitis* caused by HBV.[14, 74, 107] Not long thereafter, in the mid-1970s, parenterally transmitted "non-A, non-B hepatitis" was described and subsequently identified in 1989 as hepatitis C virus (HCV).[18, 58, 108, 126] The 1970s also marked the discovery of hepatitis delta virus (HDV), a "defective helper virus" that replicates only in the presence of HBV and is associated with chronic or fulminant hepatitis.[112] In the 1990s, another enterically transmitted non-A, non-B hepatitis virus was found associated with outbreaks of infectious hepatitis in developing parts of the world.[10, 51] It was characterized originally as a calicivirus-like particle and subsequently named hepatitis E virus (HEV).[110] Most recently, two other parenterally transmitted hepatitis viruses have been described, the flavivirus named hepatitis G virus (HGV) and another transfusion-transmissible virus (TTV).[3, 26, 73, 120] No doubt, as our medical knowledge evolves, even more viruses and other infectious agents associated with hepatitis will be discovered and named.

Clinical Manifestations and Evaluations

PATIENT HISTORY

The clinical approach to evaluating and managing a child with hepatitis includes careful attention to the age when first seen; evolution of the initial signs and symptoms; history of exposure to potential pathogens, toxins, or medications; the presence of underlying conditions; and a family history of liver or metabolic disorders. Initial symptoms in older children with acute hepatitis are nonspecific and may include fever, vomiting, poor feeding, anorexia or specific food aversion, indigestion, change in taste and smell, lethargy and malaise, mild weight loss, dark urine, pale stool, or jaundice, often with pruritus. Abdominal pain also is a common complaint, and it usually is mild, dull, or aching in quality; located in the right upper quadrant; and unaffected by meals, body position, or bowel movements. Often, an antecedent viral syndrome or "flulike" illness is noted

7 to 14 days before the onset of hepatitis. Rarely, a "serum sickness–like syndrome" may occur at the onset of the illness, before jaundice occurs, and is characterized by fever, rash, and arthritis. On the other hand, neonates rarely have signs and symptoms from infection with the hepatotropic viruses and are more likely to have clinical disease with agents that cause congenital or perinatal infection, such as CMV, herpes simplex virus (HSV), rubella virus, or *Treponema pallidum,* especially if extrahepatic signs such as splenomegaly, skin lesions, microcephaly, or hearing loss are present. A history of administration of blood products at any age suggests hepatitis B, C, D, or G viruses, TTV, or CMV, whereas previous attendance at summer camp or an institutional environment suggests HAV. A history of administration of antimicrobials such as the antifungal azoles, antibiotics, or isoniazid suggests drug-induced hepatitis, and exposure of older children to feral kittens suggests infection with *Bartonella henselae* or *Toxoplasma gondii.* Children receiving chemotherapy may have drug-induced hepatitis, and those who have experienced prolonged neutropenia may have fungal disease of the liver. Children with fulminant hepatitis are critically ill and initially may have persistent fever, protracted nausea and vomiting, severe abdominal pain, worsening jaundice, fluid retention with ascites, impaired clotting, and encephalopathy with seizures or coma. Patients with chronic hepatitis, on the other hand, often are clinically asymptomatic, unless complications such as cirrhosis, chronic liver failure, or primary hepatocellular carcinoma develop.

PHYSICAL FINDINGS

The physical examination of a child with hepatitis should focus on the abdomen and liver, but it also should include a careful evaluation for extrahepatic manifestations of systemic disease. Tender hepatomegaly, with or without ascites, scleral icterus, and jaundiced skin, often are present on physical examination of patients with acute hepatitis. Percussion or tapping over the right lower part of the thorax may produce right upper quadrant pain. Fever may or may not be present. Extrahepatic physical findings associated with the hepatotropic viruses, especially HAV, HBV, and HCV, include systemic vasculitis with rash or urticaria, polyarthralgia, and polyarthritis, similar to serum sickness or polyarteritis nodosa. A generalized papular rash, called infantile papular acrodermatitis (a.k.a. Gianotti disease or Gianotti-Crosti syndrome), may accompany HBV infection, especially in young children. Rarely, a patient with acute viral hepatitis may exhibit the Raynaud phenomenon, bullous lesions, or erythema nodosa. Skin excoriations may be present if the jaundice-associated pruritus is severe, and older children and adolescents may have vascular spiders or exacerbation of acne. A child who also has conjunctivitis, pneumonitis, and a maculopapular rash may have a disseminated adenovirus disease. Generalized lymphadenopathy accompanied by pharyngitis and splenomegaly, on the other hand, suggests systemic infection with CMV or EBV. The physical examination of a child with fulminant hepatitis and liver failure may actually reveal a small liver or one that is shrinking in size and a child who is confused or has had personality changes. As hepatic failure ensues, the patient may be deeply jaundiced and encephalopathic or comatose, with hyperreflexia, decerebrate posturing, involuntary movements, and asterixis. A distinctive sweetish smell (also called fetor hepaticus) from the patient also may be appreciated by an astute observer. Physical examination of a child with chronic hepatitis, in contrast, may be normal or reveal minimal enlargement of the liver.

LABORATORY DIAGNOSIS

Laboratory evaluation of a child with acute hepatitis should include a complete blood count, urinalysis, tests of hepatic function, and specific serologic tests, cultures, or detection assays for specific pathogens of interest according to the patient's history or physical findings. Patients with severe or fulminant hepatitis or hepatic failure also should have serum albumin, fibrinogen, electrolyte, and glucose determinations, as well as blood ammonia if encephalopathy is present. In many forms of viral hepatitis, the white blood cell count may be low, usually between 3000 and 4000/mm^3. Atypical lymphocytes also may be seen. If significant leukocytosis is present, sepsis or fulminant hepatitis should be considered. Urinalysis may reveal dark urine and the presence of urobilinogen. In a neonate with jaundice or hepatic dysfunction, an infectious agent such as a gram-negative enteric organism (*Escherichia coli,* for example) may be identified in the urine. Hematuria with casts or other signs of nephritis in an older child may signify an autoimmune disorder or a drug-induced process as the cause of the hepatitis. Liver enzymes, especially aspartate aminotransferase and alanine aminotransferase, will be elevated in all patients with acute hepatitis, and frequently they are elevated before the onset of clinical symptoms. Most forms of acute hepatitis will show elevations of up to 500 IU/mL. A neonate, however, with transaminase levels higher than 1000 IU/mL is likely to have infection with HSV, enteroviruses, or adenoviruses. Similarly, older children with fulminant hepatitis or hepatic necrosis may have significantly elevated transaminase levels, which gradually fall to less than 500 IU/mL as the disease progresses. Prothrombin levels usually are normal in uncomplicated acute viral hepatitis, and if they become prolonged, severe liver necrosis or fulminant hepatitis should be considered. Levels of alkaline phosphatase and γ-glutamyl transpeptidase will be elevated in acute hepatitis as well. Serum bilirubin, both conjugated and unconjugated, may be elevated, but rarely over 4 mg/dL unless fulminant hepatitis with hepatic failure is present. Exceptions to this rule include patients with underlying hemolytic states such as glucose-6-dehydrogenase deficiency or sickle-cell disease; these patients may exhibit marked jaundice and high indirect hyperbilirubinemia, even if the viral hepatitis otherwise is mild. Serum albumin often is normal in acute hepatitis, but it may be low in chronic hepatitis. Some patients will have low levels of nonspecific autoantibodies, such as an elevated homogeneous pattern of antinuclear antibodies, decreased complement levels, or false-positive VDRL (Venereal Disease Research Laboratory) test reactions. The erythrocyte sedimentation rate usually is normal or slightly increased in acute viral hepatitis.

Laboratory investigation to determine the specific etiology of the patient's hepatitis includes HBsAg, anti-HBcAg (IgM), anti-HAV (IgM), anti-HCV and HCV detection by polymerase chain reaction (PCR), anti-HDV antibody (especially if the hepatitis is fulminant), and anti-HEV antibody (if the travel history suggests exposure). Most of the non-hepatitis viruses may be identified by serologic tests that detect virus-specific IgM antibody, by fourfold rises in viral-specific IgG antibody, by isolation of the specific viral agent in cell culture, or by detection of viral nucleic acid by PCR. Bacterial pathogens may be detected by culture or, for agents associated with granulomatous hepatitis, such as *Brucella* and *Mycobacterium,* by culture, serology, or appropriate skin tests. Noninfectious causes such as autoimmune hepatitis may be identified by persistent hypergammaglobulinemia and the presence of autoantibodies. Metabolic diseases may cause hepatic dysfunction that may mimic acute hepatitis. Laboratory tests that may help differentiate these diseases include sweat chloride or genetic screening for cystic fibrosis, α_1-antitrypsin levels, serum amino acids, and urine reducing substances and organic acids for metabolic diseases. Serum ceruloplasmin and urine copper levels may help provide the laboratory diagnosis of Wilson disease. Anatomic causes of hepatic dysfunction, such as biliary atresia in infants and hepatic tumors in older children, usually require diagnostic imaging such as ultrasound or liver biopsy for diagnosis.

Infectious Causes

VIRUSES

Hepatitis Viruses

Six hepatotropic viruses are known to cause infectious viral hepatitis in children: hepatitis A, B, C, D, E, and G (Table 54–1).

HEPATITIS A VIRUS. HAV is a member of the *Picornaviridae* family and formerly was known as enterovirus 72.[79] A small, nonenveloped RNA virus with icosahedral symmetry (Fig. 54–1), HAV is transmitted by the fecal-oral route, and transplacental transmission has been documented on rare occasion.[27, 44] It is transmitted most commonly among young and school-age children cared for in group settings such as daycare, summer camp, schools, and institutions.[59] The incubation period generally is 30 days but ranges from 15 to 50 days. HAV infection in young children often is asymptomatic, and usually outbreaks in children are recognized first when symptoms occur in adult caretakers. Older children are more likely to have the classic symptoms of nausea, malaise, jaundice, and tender hepatomegaly. Rarely, HAV causes fulminant hepatitis. Acute infection with HAV is diagnosed serologically by detecting the presence of HAV IgM antibody in serum. No licensed, specific antiviral treatment is available. However, prevention may be accomplished by passive immunization with immune globulin or active immunization with licensed inactivated HAV vaccine.

HEPATITIS B VIRUS. HBV, also known as Dane particle and hepadnavirus type 1, is a member of the *Hepadnaviridae* family and is a DNA virus that is a 42-nm, nonenveloped spherical particle[79] (Fig. 54–2). It is transmitted through close contact with blood or blood-contaminated secretions, objects, or products.[44] It also has been transmitted by organ transplantation, intravenous drug use, and sexual contact. The incubation period is prolonged, usually 90 days, with ranges of 45 to 160 days reported. Neonates may acquire HBV vertically from mothers who are actively infected with HBV, especially if the mothers also are positive for hepatitis B e antigen (HBeAg). Whereas newborns rarely are symptomatic, children and adults may have mild to moderate symptoms of acute hepatitis or progress to fulminant or fatal disease. HBV also is a common cause of chronic hepatitis in children. Chronic hepatitis will develop in approximately 10 percent of older children and adults infected with HBV; the figure rises to approximately 30 percent if the infection occurs during infancy or early childhood and reaches a striking 90 to 95 percent in infants born to infected mothers who are HBeAg-positive. Acute HBV hepatitis is diagnosed serologically by the presence of HBsAg or IgM antibody to HBcAg, or both. HBV DNA also may be detected and quantified in serum by PCR during acute hepatitis. Individuals with HBeAg in their serum are highly infectious. Diagnosis

TABLE 54–1 ■ CAUSES OF HEPATITIS IN CHILDREN

Infectious
- Viral
  - Primary hepatotropic
    - Hepatitis A virus
    - Hepatitis B virus
    - Hepatitis C virus
    - Hepatitis D virus
    - Hepatitis E virus
    - Hepatitis G virus
  - DNA viruses
    - Herpes simplex viruses 1 and 2
    - Varicella-zoster virus
    - Cytomegalovirus
    - Epstein-Barr virus
    - Human herpesviruses 6, 7, and 8
    - Herpes B virus
    - Adenovirus
    - Erythrovirus
  - RNA viruses
    - Enteroviruses
    - Measles virus
    - Rubella virus
    - Hemorrhagic fever virus
    - Human immunodeficiency virus
    - Syncytial giant cell hepatitis
- Bacterial
  - Sepsis syndrome with cholestatic jaundice
  - Urinary tract infection in neonates
  - *Bartonella henselae* and *Bartonella quintana*
  - Bacille Calmette-Guérin (BCG)
  - *Mycobacterium tuberculosis*
  - Atypical mycobacteria
  - *Bacillus cereus* toxin
  - *Brucella* species
  - *Listeria monocytogenes*
- Spirochetes
  - *Treponema pallidum*
  - *Leptospira* species
- Rickettsiae
  - *Coxiella burnetii*
- Parasites
  - *Plasmodium* species
  - *Entamoeba histolytica*
  - *Toxoplasma gondii*
  - *Ascaris lumbricoides*
- Fungi
  - *Candida* species
  - *Aspergillus* species
  - *Histoplasma capsulatum*
  - *Cryptococcus neoformans*

Noninfectious
- Drugs and toxins
- Anoxic liver damage
- Kawasaki disease
- Toxic shock syndrome
- Reye syndrome
- Metabolic and genetic disorders
- Tumors
- Lymphoma
- Histiocytosis
- Hemophagocytic syndrome
- Sarcoidosis
- Biliary atresia
- Autoimmune hepatitis
- Sickle-cell crisis

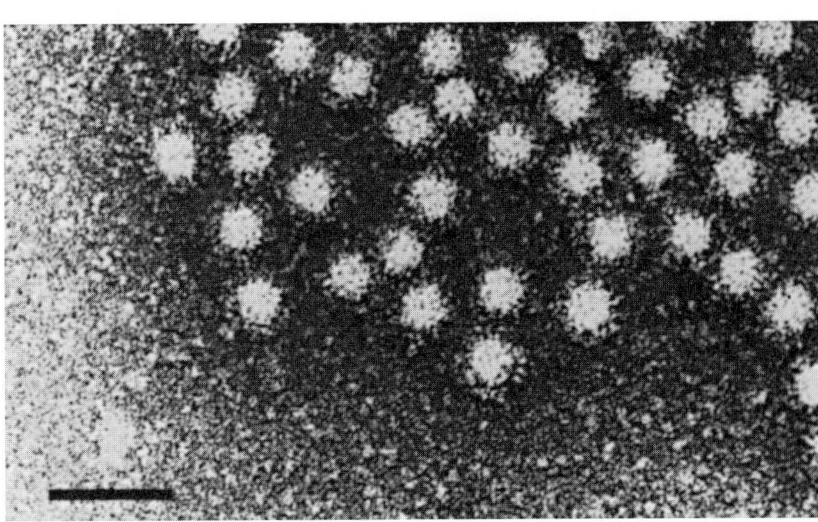

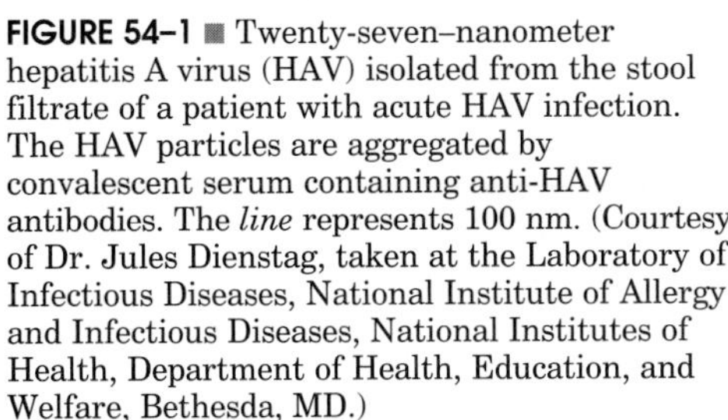

FIGURE 54–1 ■ Twenty-seven–nanometer hepatitis A virus (HAV) isolated from the stool filtrate of a patient with acute HAV infection. The HAV particles are aggregated by convalescent serum containing anti-HAV antibodies. The *line* represents 100 nm. (Courtesy of Dr. Jules Dienstag, taken at the Laboratory of Infectious Diseases, National Institute of Allergy and Infectious Diseases, National Institutes of Health, Department of Health, Education, and Welfare, Bethesda, MD.)

of chronic HBV hepatitis requires a combination of persistent clinical symptoms and laboratory abnormalities, persistence of specific serologic markers such as HBsAg over a period of at least 6 months, and histopathologic characteristics on liver biopsy. Primary hepatocellular carcinoma also is a long-term complication of infection with HBV. Successful resolution of infection with HBV is marked serologically by the presence of antibody to HBsAg. No licensed specific antiviral therapy is available for acute hepatitis caused by HBV; however, lamivudine and interferon-α may be helpful in treating chronic hepatitis. Famciclovir also has documented activity against HBV and has been used clinically in certain patients. Liver transplantation has been attempted in patients with end-stage HBV-associated cirrhosis, with variable results. Prevention is by passive immunization with hepatitis B immune globulin (HBIG) and active immunization with licensed recombinant vaccines.[56]

HEPATITIS C VIRUS. HCV is a member of the *Flaviviridae* family. It is a small RNA virus with multiple genotypes that appear to have a variable effect on the development of clinical disease and response to antiviral therapy. It is transmitted most commonly to children and adolescents who have been exposed to blood products, clotting factor concentrates before 1987, hemodialysis, organ transplantation, intravenous drug use, cocaine snorting, or tattoos and piercing procedures performed at parlors that do not practice sterile techniques. Perinatal transmission from an HCV-seropositive mother to her infant also occurs but is relatively uncommon and estimated at 5 percent.[97] Infection with HCV usually does not cause acute hepatitis; however, chronic hepatitis develops in more than 50 percent of children infected with HCV.[24] In adults, cirrhosis, end-stage liver failure, and hepatocellular carcinoma also may develop. Infection with HCV is diagnosed serologically by detecting the presence of HCV IgG antibody and by detection and quantification of HCV RNA by PCR.[68] Treatment with ribavirin plus interferon may be beneficial in some patients. Liver transplantation may be performed in patients with end-stage liver disease. Currently, no biologic products or vaccines are licensed for prevention of infection with HCV.

HEPATITIS D VIRUS. HDV, also known as the delta agent, delta virus, "helper virus," and "defective virus," is a small, 37-nm RNA virus that requires the presence of HBV, especially HBsAg, to replicate.[106] HDV can co-infect a patient at the same time or subsequent to infection with HBV. Like HBV, HDV is acquired by exposure to blood products or clotting factors, intravenous drug use, or sexual contact. It also may be transmitted by liver transplantation,

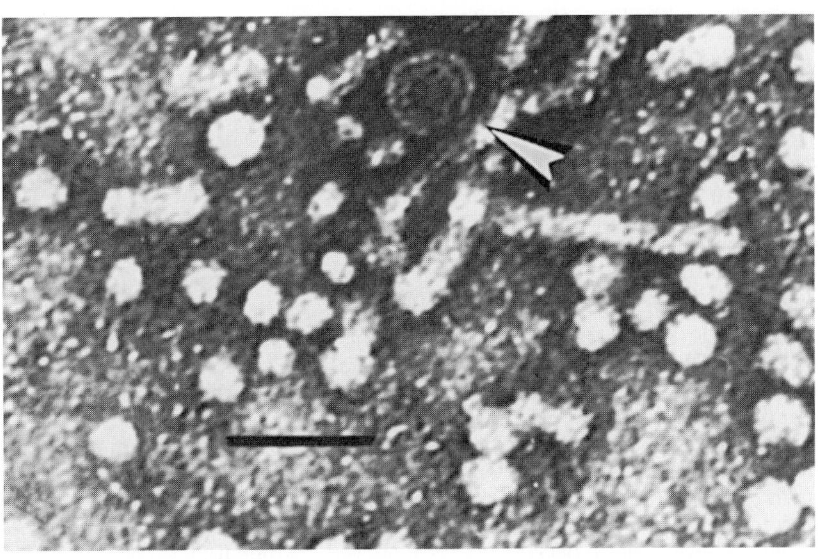

FIGURE 54–2 ■ Electron micrograph of hepatitis B virus particles. Most particles are 20 to 25 nm in diameter and consist of both spheres and tubules. A larger, 42-nm, Dane particle also is present *(arrow)*. Hepatitis B surface antigen determinants are present on the surface of all three forms.

and vertical transmission has been reported. Infection with HDV occurs more commonly in Europe, South America, Africa, and the Middle East and appears to be less common in the United States. The incubation period after superinfection is 1 to 2 months, but it is similar to HBV (90 days) if co-infection occurs simultaneously. Co-infection with HDV is associated with more severe disease or progression to fulminant hepatitis in HBV-infected patients.[111] Laboratory diagnosis is possible only at reference laboratories that can detect IgM-specific HDV antibody and HDV antigen and RNA by PCR. No specific antiviral therapy is available for HDV. Because HDV cannot be transmitted to or infect humans without HBV, prevention of HBV infection by vaccination prevents HDV infection. HDV co-infection of individuals already infected with HBV, however, cannot be prevented by any licensed biologic product or vaccine.

HEPATITIS E VIRUS. HEV is a recently described small RNA virus that is transmitted by the fecal-oral route.[10, 110] HEV infection in U.S. residents is rare, but it may be a common cause of acute, self-limited viral hepatitis in developing countries and has been linked to outbreaks associated with contaminated water supplies.[51] The incubation period is unknown. HEV appears to cause a mild to moderate, acute hepatitis, especially in adults, and may have a high case-fatality in pregnant women. Similar to HAV, HEV does not appear to cause chronic hepatitis. Laboratory diagnosis is by detection of IgM antibody to HEV in serum or detection of HEV RNA by PCR in serum or feces performed in reference laboratories or the Centers for Disease Control and Prevention. No antiviral agent is licensed for HEV, and prevention by immunoprophylaxis is not available.

HEPATITIS G VIRUS. HGV is a recently described RNA virus and, like HCV, is a member of the *Flaviviridae* family.[69] It appears to be transmitted parenterally and is found more commonly in patients who have received blood products, factor concentrates, hemodialysis, or transplants.[73] Intravenous drug use and promiscuous sexual activity are additional risk factors that have been identified, and it also may be transmitted vertically, from mother to child. Infection with HGV usually is asymptomatic. It produces high levels of viremia, but little evidence of direct hepatic involvement. It also does not appear to be associated with fulminant hepatitis or chronic disease. The incubation period is unknown at this time. The diagnosis can be made by detection of HGV RNA by PCR in serum through reference laboratories. No licensed antiviral therapy is available, and no preventive measures are known at this time.

Herpesviruses

Herpesviruses are large DNA viruses with icosahedral symmetry and a glycoprotein envelope, and they share the biologic properties of latency and reactivation. Infections with this family of viruses, the *Herpesviridae,* may be primary or recurrent. All the human herpesviruses (HHVs) and one of the primate herpesviruses (herpes B virus) can cause acute hepatitis during the course of a systemic illness, but primary hepatitis with these viral agents is an unusual event.[42]

HERPES SIMPLEX VIRUS. HSV-1 and HSV-2 most often cause mucocutaneous vesicles or ulcers, and dissemination usually occurs during periods of relative immunocompromise, such as pregnancy, the neonatal period, malnutrition, congenital or acquired immunodeficiency syndromes, or organ transplantation. Transient, "chemical hepatitis" without overt clinical signs of hepatitis may occur during acute mucocutaneous HSV disease, but fulminant hepatitis with hepatic necrosis rarely has been documented in a normal host.[38, 45, 64, 84] A special exception to this observation is HSV-associated primary hepatic necrosis and disseminated HSV disease in pregnant women.[45] Most cases occur during the late second or early third trimester, and most, but not all, cases are associated with a primary infection with HSV-2.[130] Obvious skin lesions may not be present. This disease is associated with high mortality in both the mother and infant. The neonate, especially if premature, is at risk for development of neonatal HSV hepatitis as part of a disseminated HSV disease that includes viral sepsis-like syndrome, coagulopathy, pneumonitis, and meningoencephalitis.[61] Skin lesions often are absent in this form of the disease. Neonatal HSV hepatitis develops most often in the child's first 2 weeks of life, and transaminase levels may be more than a thousand times normal. Recipients of solid organ, bone marrow, and stem cell transplants may have HSV infection with dissemination within the first 3 weeks post-transplant, most often as a result of reactivation.[43] Patients with hepatitis as a result of HSV infection may be shedding HSV from a mucocutaneous source or may be viremic, but some may require liver biopsy for confirmation. Acyclovir therapy is recommended for HSV-associated hepatitis, and post-transplant prophylaxis is very effective in preventing post-transplant HSV disease.[129] At least one case of a neonate with HSV-induced fulminant hepatic failure successfully treated by liver transplantation combined with acyclovir therapy has been reported.[31]

VARICELLA-ZOSTER VIRUS. Varicella-zoster virus also causes mucocutaneous vesicles in both immunocompetent and immunocompromised hosts. Primary infection is known as varicella (a.k.a. chickenpox) and is associated with primary and secondary viremias that often seed the visceral organs. Approximately one fourth of healthy children experiencing varicella will have a silent, "chemical hepatitis" with transaminase levels at least twice those of normal.[41, 92, 104] Fulminant hepatitis with varicella occurs rarely, however, and usually is seen in immunocompromised hosts.[5, 90, 101, 122] Patients have severe abdominal pain with little nausea or vomiting, skin lesions may or may not be present, and transaminases may be more than a thousand times normal.[89, 117, 118] Zoster in a normal host is not associated with fulminant hepatitis, but immunocompromised hosts may experience disseminated zoster with hepatitis and hepatic necrosis.[40] The diagnosis often is based on clinical findings, but viral culture of cutaneous lesions, if present, and liver biopsy also may help establish the diagnosis. Treatment with acyclovir is recommended. Varicella may be prevented or attenuated by passive immunization with varicella-zoster immune globulin or by active immunization with a licensed live virus vaccine.[16, 23]

CYTOMEGALOVIRUS. CMV infection is usually asymptomatic or "silent." However, CMV in a normal host may cause a mononucleosis-like syndrome that consists of fever, lymphadenopathy, and atypical lymphocytosis. Hepatitis occurs as part of this syndrome but often is silent or mild and rarely is accompanied by jaundice.[66, 83] Granulomatous hepatitis also may be associated with CMV.[28] Infants born congenitally infected with CMV often have hepatosplenomegaly, elevated transaminase levels, and hyperbilirubinemia.[29] The hepatitis that they experience is self-limited and usually resolves within the first few months of life. Solid organ and marrow transplant recipients and patients with acquired immunodeficiency syndrome (AIDS) and other immunodeficiency states may experience persistent fever, malaise, leukopenia, and hepatitis caused by primary or recurrent infection with CMV. Severe liver disease can occur in transplant recipients and may be associated with graft-versus-host disease or graft rejection.[35, 36] CMV-associated hepatitis may be diagnosed clinically and supported by virologic evidence of positive cultures, CMV viremia (or a viremia surrogate marker such as CMV antigenemia or CMV DNAemia), or demonstration of involvement of the end-organ by liver biopsy.[34, 94] Treatment with ganciclovir, valganciclovir, foscarnet, or cidofovir appears to be beneficial in immunocompromised hosts, and prophylaxis or preemptive therapy with antiviral agents or CMV hyperimmune globulin may prevent development of severe CMV disease in transplant recipients.[34, 37, 46]

EPSTEIN-BARR VIRUS. EBV infection also usually is asymptomatic or "silent," and it also may cause a mononucleosis-like syndrome with mild hepatitis. However, in rare patients with a genetic X-linked predisposition, a severe, often fatal lymphoproliferative syndrome with prominent liver involvement may develop.[112] Transplant recipients also may be susceptible to post-transplant lymphoproliferative disease (PTLPD) in which the liver may be involved.[6, 21] In addition, patients with tumors associated with EBV, such as lymphoma, may have hepatic involvement. The diagnosis of mononucleosis usually is clinical and supported by a positive heterophile or "Monospot" test or by specific EBV serologic tests such as VCA (viral capsid antigen) IgM antibody.[11] The immune response to EBV in immunocompromised hosts may be unusual, and the diagnosis of PTLPD is usually suspected by an increase in EBV DNA genome copies in peripheral blood, generalized adenopathy, or the presence of histopathologic features on biopsy. Treatment involves a reduction in immunosuppression, administration of rituximab (anti-CD20 monoclonal antibody), or adoptive immunotherapy.[25, 50, 99, 115] Antiviral therapy with acyclovir also may be administered, but its effectiveness is controversial.

HUMAN HERPESVIRUSES. HHV-6, HHV-7, and HHV-8 may involve the liver, especially in immunocompromised patients.[42] Hepatitis associated with HHV-6 may occur in solid organ transplant recipients. In recipients of liver transplants, infection with HHV-6, mostly reactivation, also has been associated with acute rejection, portal lymphocyte infiltration, and impaired function of the grafted liver. However, because HHV-6 is ubiquitous and commonly can be detected in blood and tissue, the role that the virus is playing in the liver disease observed in these patients is not entirely clear.[100] Normal hosts experiencing primary HHV-6 infection may have mild "chemical hepatitis" with silent elevation of aminotransferase levels. Rarely, severe disseminated disease with fulminant hepatitis has been linked to HHV-6 and HHV-7.[2, 8, 53, 80] HHV-8 (a.k.a. Kaposi sarcoma virus) causes a complex neoplasm involving skin, mucous membranes, and internal organs, most often in patients with severe immunocompromise. It rarely is seen in children but has been reported in HIV-infected children with advanced AIDS. Recipients of solid organ transplants may be infected with HHV-8. The liver is a common site of visceral disease caused by HHV-8, which most often is associated with tumors rather than hepatitis.[22] Diagnosing infection with HHV-6, HHV-7, or HHV-8 is difficult because of the ubiquity of these viruses and their viral DNA in humans, but the diagnosis is supported by serologic evidence and by detection of viral DNA in blood, in secretions, or more specifically, in tissue.[100] No licensed specific antiviral therapy is available, but these viruses may be inhibited by ganciclovir, foscarnet, and cidofovir. Response also may be noted after withdrawal or reduction of immunosuppression, and with HHV-8, chemotherapy may be indicated.

HERPES B VIRUS. Also known as herpesvirus simiae or cercopithecine herpesvirus 1, herpes B virus is an alpha-herpesvirus of monkeys that causes severe disease in humans.[128] It can be transmitted from Asian monkeys, such as rhesus and cynomolgus monkeys, to humans through bites or contact with mucous membrane secretions from infected monkeys. The human disease associated with herpes B virus involves skin vesicles at the portal of entry, regional lymphadenitis, and hemorrhagic encephalitis. The virus also may disseminate to the liver and lungs and produce hemorrhagic necrosis, with a high mortality rate. Diagnosis is made by virus isolation, and the virus is inhibited by acyclovir and ganciclovir.

Adenoviruses

Adenoviruses are small DNA viruses that are members of the viral family *Adenoviridae.* They usually are respiratory or enteric pathogens, but they also can cause disseminated disease with hepatitis and hepatic necrosis in both immunocompetent and immunocompromised hosts and neonates.[55, 91, 96] Patients often will have fever, malaise or lethargy, conjunctivitis, pharyngitis, cough, respiratory distress, vomiting and diarrhea, and a viral sepsis–like syndrome. Hepatitis is marked by hepatomegaly and elevated aminotransferases and bilirubin. A specific viral diagnosis is made by isolation of adenovirus or detection of viral DNA by PCR from respiratory secretions, blood, stool, or tissue. Adenovirus serotype 5 usually is associated with severe hepatitis, followed in frequency by types 1 and 2.[82] Viral surveillance cultures and DNA PCR testing in immunocompromised patients, such as bone marrow and stem cell transplant recipients and liver transplant recipients at high risk for acquiring severe or fatal adenovirus-associated disease, may allow early intervention before severe, disseminated disease develops.[17, 82] No licensed antiviral therapy is available, but the virus is inhibited to some extent by cidofovir, an antiviral agent with broad-spectrum activity against many DNA viruses, as well as by ribavirin and ganciclovir.[72]

Erythrovirus

Erythroviruses (i.e., human parvovirus B19) are small DNA viruses. They are members of the family *Parvoviridae* and produce a variety of illnesses, including fifth disease (i.e., erythema infectiosum), arthritis, and anemia. Liver involvement, often severe, may be seen in intrauterine infection with hydrops fetalis.[4, 81] Fulminant liver failure with massive hepatic necrosis associated with erythrovirus also has been reported in patients with aplastic anemia.[67] The diagnosis of parvovirus infection can be made by detection of virus-specific IgM antibodies or detection of viral DNA in blood, serum/plasma, bone marrow, or tissue. No specific antiviral therapy is available, but immunocompromised patients with chronic infection may benefit from intravenous immunoglobulin. Severe fetal hydrops usually requires blood transfusions for anemia.

Enteroviruses

Enteroviruses are small RNA viruses and members of the *Picornaviridae* family, along with polioviruses and rhinoviruses. The nonpolio enteroviruses usually are associated with mild respiratory or gastrointestinal illnesses, myocarditis, or aseptic meningitis, most often occurring in late summer or early fall. Significant hepatitis with hepatic necrosis, however, can occur, especially in neonates with disseminated disease. It often is accompanied by hepatomegaly, thrombocytopenia, viral sepsis syndrome, elevated aminotransferases, and elevated serum bilirubin.[86, 87] Although any serotype can cause severe liver disease, echovirus 11 is associated most commonly with severe hepatitis or hepatitic necrosis, especially in neonates.[85] Coxsackie B and echoviruses 9 and 30 also are associated with fatal disease. Enteroviruses may be transmitted to neonates perinatally from the mother or through contact with ill family members. Nosocomial nursery outbreaks with enteroviruses also have been reported.[86] Diagnosis is by isolation of the virus or detection of viral RNA by PCR in throat, stool, urine, blood, cerebrospinal fluid, or tissue samples. Treatment is supportive; however, case reports suggest that intravenous immunoglobulin, the investigational antiviral agent pleconaril, or even liver transplantation may have some clinical benefit.[19, 62, 129]

Measles Virus

Measles virus is an RNA virus that is a member of the *Paramyxoviridae* family, along with parainfluenza viruses, respiratory syncytial virus, metapneumovirus, and mumps virus. Of all the paramyxoviruses, measles virus is associated most often with hepatitis. Approximately 10 to 20 percent of children with measles will have subclinical or "chemical" hepatitis, and severe disease of the liver, lungs, and brain may occur in immunocompromised patients.[47, 93, 119] Rare reports of severe giant-cell hepatitis, often leading to liver failure, have implicated paramyxoviruses of undetermined type.[105] Measles and other paramyxoviruses may be identified by detection of virus-specific IgM antibody in serum and by isolation of virus in secretions, blood, or tissue. No specific antiviral therapy is licensed for measles virus; however, ribavirin, a broad-spectrum antiviral agent, may have some activity against the virus. Prevention is by vaccination with the live measles vaccine or postexposure administration of immunoglobulin.

Rubella Virus

Rubella virus is a member of the *Togaviridae* family of RNA viruses. Clinical disease associated with rubella virus infection usually is mild, but as many as 10 percent of children with rubella may have subclinical or "chemical" hepatitis with transient elevation of aminotransferase levels.[124] Congenital rubella syndrome caused by intrauterine infection with rubella virus is, however, associated with significant liver involvement, with hepatomegaly and jaundice noted at birth.[33, 88, 123] Congenital rubella syndrome also is associated with intrauterine growth retardation, cataracts, congenital heart disease, thrombocytopenia, purpura, and hearing loss.[65] Because isolation of the virus technically is difficult, the diagnosis of rubella most often is made serologically by detection of virus-specific IgM antibody. No specific antiviral therapy is available. Prevention, however, is by vaccination with the live rubella virus vaccine.

Hemorrhagic Fever Viruses

The hemorrhagic fever viruses are a diverse group of RNA viruses from a variety of different virus families. They include arenaviruses such as Lassa fever, bunyaviruses such as hantavirus, filoviruses such as Marburg and Ebola, and flaviviruses such as yellow fever virus and dengue. Hemorrhagic fever is characterized by fever, malaise or lethargy, headache, retro-orbital pain, myalgia, conjunctivitis, rash, and intravascular coagulation with hemorrhage. Liver involvement with hepatitis is a very common event, and elevation of aminotransferases up to 500 IU/mL occurs in almost every patient, with a thousand times the normal range in patients who are severely ill.[32] Jaundice is a significant component of yellow fever.[60] Diagnosis is by serologic means or by detection of the viral agent with electron microscopy or PCR techniques, which in most cases should be attempted only in Biosafety Level (BSL) IV reference laboratories. Treatment is supportive; however, ribavirin appears to have activity against some hemorrhagic fever viruses.[78]

BACTERIA

Nonviral acute hepatitis can be caused by bacterial illnesses[95] (see Table 54–1). Sepsis with gram-positive organisms, especially pneumococci, or with gram-negative organisms, especially gram-negative enteric bacteria, can produce hepatic dysfunction, primarily from the cholestatic effects induced by bacterial endotoxins.[95, 133] In this form of hepatic dysfunction, the patient will appear jaundiced with mild hepatomegaly, and conjugated bilirubin levels will be elevated out of proportion to the modest elevation in aminotransferase or alkaline phosphatase levels. Neonates also may have jaundice secondary to urinary tract infection with gram-negative enteric organisms. The diagnosis is made by isolation of the offending bacteria from blood, urine, or other usually sterile site. Treatment involves specific antimicrobial therapy.

Other bacterial diseases may cause chronic or granulomatous hepatitis, including actinomycosis, brucellosis, listeriosis, nocardiosis, bartonellosis (a.k.a. cat-scratch disease), and tuberculosis.[7, 98] Diseases caused by atypical mycobacteria, especially *Mycobacterium avium–intracellulare* complex (MAC complex) or *Mycobacterium mucogenicum,* may be seen, particularly in patients with congenital or acquired immunodeficiency states.[48] Rarely, disseminated disease with hepatitis may occur as a complication of vaccination with bacille Calmette-Guérin (BCG) in children or, in adults, as a complication of bladder irrigation for bladder carcinoma.[49, 71] A diagnosis of hepatitis caused by these unusual or indolent bacterial pathogens usually is accomplished by isolation of the organism from blood or the affected organ. The diagnosis may be supported by positive skin test results in the case of tuberculosis or atypical mycobacterial disease or serologically, with elevated titers to *Bartonella quintana* or *B. henselae,* in the case of hepatic involvement with cat-scratch disease. Antimicrobial therapy is guided by the susceptibility of the offending pathogen.

Bacterial toxins, such as the emetic toxin of *Bacillus cereus,* also have been linked to fulminant hepatic failure in some patients.[76]

SPIROCHETES

Acute infection with *T. pallidum,* the agent of primary or early secondary syphilis in adolescents or adults, may cause acute or granulomatous hepatitis with serum aminotransferase levels up to 5 to 10 times normal.[70] Jaundice rarely develops, but a chancre of primary disease or a rash of secondary disease is often present. Congenital syphilis also is associated commonly with hepatosplenomegaly in the newborn, along with elevated aminotransferase and bilirubin levels. Other clinical manifestations of congenital syphilis include petechiae or purpura, thrombocytopenia, osteitis, and meningitis. Laboratory diagnosis is confirmed by reactive VDRL and positive fluorescent treponemal antibody tests. Treatment with penicillin is recommended.

Leptospirosis, or infection with the pathogenic *Leptospira interrogans,* can cause acute hepatitis.[54] Leptospirosis usually is an abrupt, anicteric, "flulike" illness, but approximately 10 percent of patients will have an icteric or septicemic syndrome with a biphasic clinical course. Patients with the icteric or severe form will have jaundice, hepatomegaly, and characteristic conjunctival injection. Usually, serum bilirubin levels are elevated out of proportion to the more modest elevations in serum aminotransferases, thus suggesting a defect in bilirubin excretion rather than direct hepatic necrosis as the pathogenesis of the jaundice. Meningitis, renal failure, and even liver failure may occur in some patients. The diagnosis should be considered in older children and adolescents with a history of exposure to wild and domestic mammals, especially dogs, rats, and livestock, which may excrete *Leptospira* organisms in their urine, or with a history of exposure to contaminated water in ditches, lakes, or streams. Diagnosis is by isolation of the organisms on special media during the acute phase of illness. Serologic and PCR tests also are available in reference laboratories. Treatment with penicillin or doxycycline is recommended.

RICKETTSIAE

The rickettsial organism *Coxiella burnetii* causes Q fever, both the acute and chronic forms, in which hepatitis is a prominent feature along with persistent fever, malaise, weight loss, and pneumonitis.[13] Clinical jaundice is a rare finding, and most often the hepatitis is subclinical or "chemical." A history of exposure to mammals or birds suggests the diagnosis, which can be confirmed serologically by reference clinical laboratories. Treatment with antibiotics, usually doxycycline, is recommended.

PARASITES AND FUNGI

A variety of parasites may invade the liver and occasionally cause hepatic dysfunction or disease.[95, 131] Such parasites include *Plasmodium* spp. (malaria), *Entamoeba histolytica* (liver abscess), *T. gondii* (toxoplasmosis), and *Toxocara canis* (visceral larval migrans). *Ascaris lumbricoides* (roundworms) may invade the common bile duct and cause acute obstructive jaundice.

Fungi also may invade the liver, usually with only minimal elevation of aminotransferase levels and rarely causing jaundice or elevated bilirubin levels. Patients whose immune system is compromised may have hepatic abscesses with *Candida* spp. or abscesses or necrotic lesions with *Aspergillus* spp. Both immunocompromised and normal hosts may have liver involvement with *Histoplasma capsulatum* or *Cryptococcus neoformans*.[95]

Noninfectious Causes

An important noninfectious cause of acute hepatitis is drug-related hepatitis[132] (See Table 54–1). It can range in severity from mild, with subclinical elevation of aminotransferases, to severe, with fulminant hepatic failure.[63] A careful history of ingestion of prescription or over-the-counter medications, as well as toxin exposure, should be elicited. Although almost any drug can cause acute hepatitis, the most common agents associated with hepatitis in children include acetylsalicylic acid (i.e., aspirin), acetaminophen, isoniazid, rifampin, phenytoin, valproic acid, phenobarbital, oxacillin and other β-lactam antibiotics, sulfa drugs, and antifungal agents such as ketoconazole and fluconazole. The anesthetic drug halothane also can cause acute hepatitis with jaundice.[109] Gold and other metals used to treat arthritis have been associated with hepatitis. The amanita mushroom, if ingested, cause severe liver injury. In addition, chronic hepatitis can develop in children, especially premature infants, who receive prolonged total parenteral nutrition.

Anoxic liver injury also can resemble acute viral hepatitis.[15] It occurs in critically ill children after a period of hypotension, heart failure, or cardiopulmonary arrest. A history of such an inciting event supports the diagnosis. Anoxic liver injury is characterized by an abrupt onset of markedly elevated aminotransferases, often hundreds of times normal levels, without jaundice, and rapid recovery of enzyme elevations to normal or near-normal levels after the event has resolved.

Other diseases such as Kawasaki syndrome and toxic shock syndrome, which have been linked to or associated with infectious pathogens, may have hepatitis as part of their manifestation. Similarly, Reye syndrome, characterized by hepatomegaly with fatty infiltration of the liver and often fatal encephalopathy, may occur after a viral syndrome such as varicella or influenza.

Metabolic and genetic disorders may be manifested as hepatitis, especially in infants. Such disorders include cystic fibrosis, α_1-antitrypsin deficiency, galactosemia, glycogen storage disease, urea cycle deficiencies, organic acidemias, tyrosinemia, and lipid storage diseases such as Gaucher and Niemann-Pick disease.[102, 125] Of note, cystic fibrosis in neonates may be associated with cholestatic jaundice in the absence of pulmonary disease.[121] Disorders of metal metabolism, such as Wilson disease, may cause acute, chronic, or even fulminant hepatitis in older children.[103, 114] In addition, patients with congenital disorders of bilirubin metabolism, such as Gilbert disease, may become jaundiced without significant elevation of aminotransferases, especially during an intercurrent viral illness. Sickle-cell crisis also may be manifested as hepatitis.[116]

Tumors of the liver and infiltrative diseases such as lymphoma, histiocytosis, and hemophagocytic syndrome may have hepatitis or hepatic failure as part of the initial complaint.[52] Another multisystem disorder that may produce chronic, granulomatous hepatitis is sarcoidosis.[30]

Anatomic causes of hepatic dysfunction in children include biliary atresia, which usually develops in the first 2 months of life.[77] Autoimmune disorders with liver involvement also may be manifested as acute hepatitis, especially in older children and adolescents.[127] In these patients, hypergammaglobulinemia and autoantibodies usually are present, as are other symptoms such as rash, arthritis, malaise, and persistent fever.

REFERENCES

1. Aach, R. D., Lander, J. J., Sherman, L. A., et al.: Transfusion-transmitted viruses: Interim analysis of hepatitis among transfused and non-transfused patients. *In* Vyas, G. N., Cohen, S. N., and Schmid, R. (eds.): Viral Hepatitis. Philadelphia, Franklin Institute Press, 1978, p. 383.
2. Akashi, K., Eizuru, Y., Sumiyoshi, Y., et al.: Brief report: Severe infectious mononucleosis–like syndrome and primary human herpesvirus 6 infection in an adult. N. Engl. J. Med. *329*:168–171, 1993.
3. Alter, H. J., Nakatsuji, Y., Melpolder, J., et al.: The incidence of transfusion-associated hepatitis G virus infection and its relation to liver disease. N. Engl. J. Med. *336*:747–754, 1997.
4. Anand, A., Gray, E., Brown, T., et al.: Human parvovirus infection in pregnancy and hydrops fetalis. N. Engl. J. Med. *316*:183–186, 1987.
5. Anderson, D. R., Schwartz, J., Hunter, N. J., et al.: Varicella hepatitis: A fatal case in a previously healthy, immunocompetent adult. Report of a case, autopsy, and review of the literature. Arch. Intern. Med. *154*:2101–2106, 1994.
6. Armes, J. E., Angus, P., Southey, M. D., et al.: Lymphoproliferative disease of donor origin arising in patients after orthotopic liver transplantation. Cancer *74*:2436–2441, 1994.
7. Arisoy, E. S., Correa, A. G., Wagner, M. L., et al.: Hepatosplenic cat-scratch disease in children: Selected clinical features and treatment. Clin. Infect. Dis. *28*:778–784, 1999.

8. Asano, Y., Yoshikawa, T., Suga, S., et al.: Fatal fulminant hepatitis in an infant with human herpesvirus-6 infection. Lancet *335*:862–863, 1990.
9. Bachmann, L.: Infectious hepatitis in Europe. *In* Rodenwalt, E. (ed.): World Atlas of Epidemic Diseases. Part I. Hamburg, Germany, Falk-Verlag, 1952, p. 67.
10. Balayan, M. S., Andjaparidze, A. G., Savinskaya, S. S., et al.: Evidence for a virus in non-A/non-B hepatitis transmitted via the fecal oral route. Intervirology *20*:23–26, 1983.
11. Basson, V., and Sharp, A. A.: Monospot: A differential slide test for infectious mononucleosis. J. Clin. Pathol. *225*:324–325, 1969.
12. Beeson, P. B., Chesney, G., McFarlan, A. M., et al.: Hepatitis following injection of mumps convalescent plasma. Lancet *1*:814–816, 1944.
13. Bernstein, M., Edmondson, H. A., and Barhour, B. H.: The liver lesion in Q fever: Clinical and pathologic features. Arch. Intern. Med. *116*:491–500, 1965.
14. Blumberg, B. S., Stunick, A. I., and London, W. T.: Hepatitis and leukemia: Their relation to Australia antigen. Bull. N. Y. Acad. Med. *44*:1566–1586, 1968.
15. Bynum, T. E., Boinoit, J. K., and Maddrey, W. C.: Ischemic hepatitis. Am. J. Dig. Dis. *24*:129–135, 1979.
16. Centers for Disease Control and Prevention: Prevention of Varicella: Recommendations of the Advisory Committee on Immunization Practices (ACIP). M. M. W. R. Recomm. Rep. *45*(RR-11):1–36, 1996.
17. Chakrabarti, S., Mauther, V., Osman, H., et al.: Adenovirus infections following allogeneic stem cell transplantation: Incidence and outcome in relation to graft manipulation, immunosuppression, and immune recovery. Blood *100*:1619–1627, 2002.
18. Choo, Q.-L., Kuo, G., Weiner, A. J., et al.: Isolation of cDNA clone derived from a blood-borne non-A, non-B viral hepatitis genome. Science *244*:359–362, 1989.
19. Chuang, E., Maller, E., Hoffman, M., et al.: Successful treatment of fulminant echovirus 11 infection in a neonate by orthotopic liver transplantation. J. Pediatr. Gastroenterol. Nutr. *17*:211–214, 1993.
20. Cockayne, E. A.: Catarrhal jaundice sporadic and epidemic, and its relation to acute yellow atrophy of the liver. Q. W. J. Med. *6*:1–5, 1912.
21. Cohen, J.: Epstein-Barr virus lymphoproliferative disease with acquired immunodeficiency. Medicine (Baltimore) *70*:137–159, 1991.
22. Colina, F., Lopez-Rios, F., Lumbreras, C., et al.: Kaposi's sarcoma developing in a liver graft. Transplantation *61*:1779–1781, 1996.
23. Committee on Infectious Diseases, American Academy of Pediatrics: Varicella-zoster infections. *In* Pickering, L. K. (ed.): 1997 Red Book: Report of the Committee on Infectious Diseases. 24th ed. Elk Grove Village, IL, American Academy of Pediatrics, 1997, p. 573.
24. Committee on Infectious Diseases, American Academy of Pediatrics: Hepatitis C virus infection. Pediatrics *101*:481–485, 1998.
25. Cook, R. C., Connors, J. M., Gascoyne, R. D., et al.: Treatment of post-transplant lymphoproliferative disease with rituximab monoclonal antibody after lung transplantation. Lancet *354*:1698–1699, 1999.
26. Cossart, Y.: TTV: A common virus, but pathogenic? Lancet *2*:164,1998.
27. Cuthbert, J. A.: Hepatitis A: Old and new. Clin. Microbiol. Rev. *14*:38–58, 2001.
28. de la Serna-Higuera, C., Gonzalez-Garcia, M., Milicua, J. M., and Munoz, V.: Cytomegalovirus granulomatous hepatitis in an immunocompetent patient. Gastroenterol. Hepatol. *22*:230–231, 1999.
29. Demmler, G. J.: Summary of a Workshop on Surveillance for Congenital Cytomegalovirus Disease. Rev. Infect. Dis. *13*:315–329, 1991.
30. Devaney, K., Goodman, Z. D., Epstein, M. S., et al.: Hepatic sarcoidosis: Clinicopathologic features in 100 patients. Am. J. Surg. Pathol. *17*:1273–1280, 1993.
31. Egawa, H., Inomata, Y., Nakayama, S., et al.: Fulminant hepatic failure secondary to herpes simplex virus infection in a neonate: A case report of successful treatment with liver transplantation and perioperative acyclovir. Liver Transpl. Surg. *4*:513–515, 1998.
32. Elisaf, M., Stafanaki, S., Reparti, M., et al.: Liver involvement in hemorrhagic fever with renal syndrome. J. Clin. Gastroenterol. *17*:33–37, 1993.
33. Esterly, J., Slusser, R., and Ruebner, B.: Hepatic lesions in the congenital rubella syndrome. J. Pediatr. *71*:676–685, 1967.
34. Evans, P. C., Soin, A., Wreghitt, T. G., et al.: Qualitative and semiquantitative polymerase chain reaction testing for cytomegalovirus DNA in serum allows prediction of CMV related disease in liver transplant recipients. J. Clin. Pathol. *51*:914–921, 1998.
35. Falagas, M. E., Paya, C., Ruthazer, R., et al.: Significance of cytomegalovirus for long-term survival after orthotopic liver transplantation: A prospective derivation and validation cohort analysis. Transplantation. *66*:1020–1028, 1998.
36. Falagas, M. E., Snydman, D. R., Griffith, J., et al.: Effect of cytomegalovirus infection status on first-year mortality rates among orthotopic liver transplant recipients. The Boston Center for Liver Transplantation CMVIG Study Group. Ann. Intern. Med. *126*:275–279, 1997.
37. Falagas, M. E., Snydman, D. R., Ruthazer, R., et al.: Cytomegalovirus immune globulin (CMVIG) prophylaxis is associated with increased survival after orthotopic liver transplantation. The Boston Center for Liver Transplantation CMVIG Study Group. Clin. Transplant. *11*:432–437, 1997.
38. Farr, R. W., Short, S., and Weissman, D.: Fulminant hepatitis during herpes simplex virus infection in apparently immunocompetent adults: Report of two cases and review of the literature. Clin. Infect. Dis. *24*:1191–1194, 1997.
39. Feinstone, S. M., Kapikian, A. Z., and Purcell, R. H.: Hepatitis A: Detection by immune electron microscopy of a virus-like antigen associated with the acute illness. Science *182*:1026–1028, 1973.
40. Feldman, S., Chaudary, S., Ossi, M., et al.: A viremic phase for herpes zoster in children with cancer. J. Pediatr. *91*:597–600, 1977.
41. Feldman, S., Crout, J. D., and Andrew, M. E.: Incidence and natural history of chemically defined varicella-zoster virus hepatitis in children and adolescents. Scand. J. Infect. Dis. *29*:33–36, 1997.
42. Fingeroth, J. D.: Herpesvirus infections of the liver. Infect. Dis. Clin. North Am. *14*:1–34, 2000.
43. Fishman, J. A., and Rubin, R. H.: Infections in organ-transplant recipients. N. Engl. J. Med. *338*:1741–1751, 1998.
44. Fishman, L. N., Jonas, M. M., and Lavine, J. E.: Update on viral hepatitis in children. Pediatr. Clin. North Am. *43*:57–74, 1996.
45. Flewett, T. H., Parker, R. G., and Philip, W. M.: Acute hepatitis due to herpes simplex virus in an adult. J. Clin. Pathol. *22*:60–66, 1969.
46. Gane, E., Saliba, F., Valdecasa, G. J., et al.: Randomized trial of efficacy and safety of oral ganciclovir in the prevention of cytomegalovirus disease in liver-transplant recipients. The Oral Ganciclovir International Transplantation Study Group. Lancet *350*:1729–1733, 1997.
47. Gavish, D., Kleinman, Y., Morag, A., et al.: Hepatitis and jaundice associated with measles in young adults. Arch. Intern. Med. *143*:674–677, 1983.
48. Goldblatt, M. R., and Ribes, J. A.: *Mycobacterium mucogenicum* isolated from a patient with granulomatous hepatitis. Arch. Pathol. Lab. Med. *126*:73–75, 2002.
49. Gottke, M. U., Wong, P., Muhn, C., et al.: Hepatitis in disseminated bacillus Calmette-Guérin infection. Can. J. Gastroenterol. *14*:333–336, 2000.
50. Grillo-Lopez, A. J., White, C. A., Varns, C., et al.: Overview of the clinical development of rituximab: First monoclonal antibody approved for the treatment of lymphoma. Semin. Oncol. *26*:66–73, 1999.
51. Gust, E. D., and Purcell, R. H.: Waterborne non-A, non-B hepatitis. J. Infect. Dis. *156*:630–636, 1987.
52. Harrison, H. B., Middleton, H. M., Crosby, J. H., et al.: Fulminant hepatic failure: An unusual presentation of metastatic liver disease. Gastroenterology *80*:820–825, 1981.
53. Hashida, T., Komura, E., Yoshida, M., et al.: Hepatitis in association with human herpes virus 7 infection. Pediatrics *96*:783–785, 1995.
54. Heath, C. W., Jr., Alexander, A. D., and Galton, M. M.: Leptospirosis in the United States: Analysis of 483 cases in man 1949–1961. N. Engl. J. Med. *273*:857–867, 1965.
55. Hierholzer, J. C.: Adenoviruses in the immunocompromised host. Clin. Microbiol. Rev. *5*:262–274, 1992.
56. Hilleman, M. R.: Overview of the pathogenesis, prophylaxis, and therapeutics of viral hepatitis B, with focus on reduction to practical applications. Vaccine *19*:1837–1848, 2001.
57. Hillis, W. D.: An outbreak of infectious hepatitis among chimpanzee handlers at a United States Air Force base. Am. J. Hyg. *73*:316–320, 1961.
58. Hollinger, F. B., Gitnick, G. L., Aach, R. D., et al.: Non-A, non-B hepatitis transmission in chimpanzees: A project of the transfusion-transmitted viruses study group. Intervirology *10*:60–68, 1978.
59. Hurwitz, E. S., Deseda, C. C., Shapiro, C. N., et al.: Hepatitis infections in the day-care setting. Pediatrics *94*(Suppl.):1023–1024, 1994.
60. Ishak, K., Walker, D., Coetzer, J., et al.: Viral hemorrhagic fevers with hepatic involvement: Pathologic aspects with clinical correlations. Prog. Liver Dis. 7:495–515, 1982.
61. Jacobs, R. F.: Neonatal herpes simplex virus infections. Semin. Perinatol. *22*:64–71, 1998.
62. Johnston, J., and Overall, J.: Intravenous immune globulin in disseminated neonatal echovirus 11 infection. Pediatr. Infect. Dis. J. *8*:254–256, 1989.
63. Katelaris, P. H., and Jones, D. B.: Fulminant hepatic failure. Med. Clin. North Am. *73*:955–970, 1989.
64. Kaufman, B., Gandhi, S. A., Louie, E., et al.: Herpes simplex virus hepatitis: Case report and review. Clin. Infect. Dis. *24*:334–338, 1997.
65. Korones, S., Ainger, L., Monif, G., et al.: Congenital rubella syndrome: Study of 22 infants. Am. J. Dis. Child. *110*:434–440, 1965.
66. Lamb, S. G., and Stern, H.: Cytomegalovirus mononucleosis with jaundice as a presenting sign. Lancet *2*:1003–1006, 1966.
67. Langnas, A., Markin, R., Cattral, J., et al.: Parvovirus B19 as a possible causative agent of fulminant liver failure and associated aplastic anemia. Hepatology *22*:1661–1665, 1995.
68. Lauer, G. M., and Walker, B. D.: Hepatitis C infection. N. Engl. J. Med. *345*:41–52, 2001.
69. Leary, T. P., Myerhoff, A. S., Simons, J. N., et al.: Sequence and genomic organization of GBV-C: A novel member of the Flaviviridae associated with human non-A-E hepatitis. J. Med. Virol. *48*:60–67, 1996.

70. Lee, R. V., Thornton, G. F., and Conn, H. O.: Liver disease associated with secondary syphilis. N. Engl. J. Med. *284*:1423–1430, 1971.
71. Leebeek, F. W. G., Ouwendijk, R. J. T., Kolk, A. H. U., et al.: Granulomatous hepatitis caused by bacillus Calmette-Guérin (BCG) infection after bladder instillation. Gut *38*:616–618, 1996.
72. Legrand, F., Berrebi, D., Houhou, N., et al.: Early diagnosis of adenovirus infection and treatment with cidofovir after bone marrow transplantation in children. Bone Marrow Transplant. *27*:621–626, 2001.
73. Linnen, J., Wages, J., Jr., Zhang-Keck, Z. Y., et al.: Molecular cloning and disease association of hepatitis G virus: A transfusion-transmissible agent. Science *271*:505–508, 1996.
74. London, W. T., Sutnick, A. I., Blumberg, B. S., et al.: Australian antigen and acute viral hepatitis. Ann. Intern. Med. *70*:55–59, 1969.
75. Luerman, A.: Eine Icterusepidemie. Berl. Klin. Wochenschr. *22*:20–25, 1885.
76. Mahler, H., Pasi, A., Kramer, J. M., et al.: Fulminant liver failure in association with the emetic toxin of *Bacillus cereus.* N. Engl. M. Med. *33*:1142–1148, 1997.
77. Manolaki, B., Larcher, V. F., Mowar, A. P., et al.: The prelaparotomy diagnosis of extra-hepatic biliary atresia. Arch. Dis. Child. *58*:591–594, 1983.
78. McCormick, J. B., King, I. T., Webb, P. A., et al.: Lassa fever: Effective therapy with ribavirin. N. Engl. J. Med. *314*:20–26, 1986.
79. Melnick, J. L.: Classification of hepatitis A as enterovirus 72 and of hepatitis B virus as hepadnavirus, type 1. Intervirology *18*:105–110, 1982.
80. Mendel, I., de Matteis, M., Bertin, C., et al.: Fulminant hepatitis in neonates with human herpesvirus 6 infection. Pediatr. Infect. Dis. J. *14*:993–997, 1995.
81. Metzman, R., Anand, A., DeGiulio, P., et al.: Hepatic disease associated with intrauterine parvovirus B19 infection in a newborn premature infant. J. Pediatr. Gastroenterol. Nutr. *9*:112–114, 1989.
82. Michaels, M. G., Green, M., Wald, E. R., et al.: Adenovirus infection in pediatric liver transplant recipients. J. Infect. Dis. *165*:170–174, 1992.
83. Miguelez, M., Gonzalez, A., and Perez, F.: Severe cytomegalovirus hepatitis in a pregnant woman treated with ganciclovir. Scand. J. Infect. Dis. *30*:304–305, 1998.
84. Minuk, G. Y., and Nicolle, L. E.: Genital herpes and hepatitis in healthy young adults. J. Med. Virol. *19*:269–272, 1986.
85. Modlin, J.: Fatal echovirus 11 disease in premature neonates. Pediatrics 66:775–779, 1980.
86. Modlin, J.: Perinatal echovirus infection: Insights from a literature review of 61 cases of serious infection and 16 outbreaks in nurseries. Rev. Infect. Dis. *8*:918–926, 1986.
87. Modlin, J.: Perinatal echovirus and group B Coxsackie virus infections. Clin. Perinatol. *15*:233–245, 1988.
88. Monif, G., Asofsky, R., and Sever, J.: Hepatic dysfunction in the congenital rubella syndrome. B. M. J. *1*:1086–1088, 1966.
89. Morgan, E. R., and Smalley, L .A.: Varicella in immunocompromised children: Incidence of abdominal pain and organ involvement. Am. J. Dis. Child. *137*:883–885, 1983.
90. Morishita, K., Kodo, H., Asano, S., et al.: Fulminant varicella hepatitis following bone marrow transplantation. J. A. M. A. *253*:511–515, 1985.
91. Munoz, F., Piedra, P., and Demmler, G. J.: Disseminated adenovirus disease in immunocompromised and immunocompetent children. Clin. Infect. Dis. *27*:1194–1200, 1998.
92. Myers, M. G.: Hepatic cellular injury during varicella. Arch. Dis. Child. *57*:317–319, 1982.
93. Nickell, M., Cannady, P., and Schwitzer, G.: Subclinical hepatitis in rubeola infections in young adults. Ann. Intern. Med. *90*:354–355, 1979.
94. Niubo, J., Perez, J. L., Martinez-Lacasa, J. T., et al.: Associations of quantitative cytomegalovirus antigenemia with symptomatic infection in solid organ transplant recipients. Diagn. Microbiol. Infect. Dis. *24*:19–24, 1996.
95. Novak, D. A., Doloson, D. J.: Bacterial, parasitic, and fungal infections of the liver. *In* Suchy, F. J. (ed.): Liver Disease in Children. 1st ed. St. Louis, Mosby, 1994, pp. 550–568.
96. Odio, C., McCracken, G. H., Jr., Nelson, J. D., Jr., and Nelson, J. D.: Disseminated adenovirus infection: A case report and review of the literature. Pediatr. Infect. Dis. *3*:46–49, 1984.
97. Ohto, H., Terazawa, S., Saski, N., et al.: Transmission of hepatitis C virus from mothers to infants. N. Engl. J. Med. *330*:744–750, 1994.
98. Oliva, A., Duarte, B., Jonasson, O., and Nadimpalli, V.: The nodular form of local hepatic tuberculosis: A review. J. Clin. Gastroenterol. *12*:166–173, 1990.
99. O'Reilly, R. J., Small, T. N., Papadopoulos, E., et al.: Biology and adoptive cell therapy of Epstein-Barr virus–associated lymphoproliferative disorders in recipients of marrow allografts. Immunol. Rev. *157*:195–216, 1997.
100. Ozaki, Y., Tajiri, H., Tanaka-Taya, K., et al.: Frequent detection of the human herpesvirus 6–specific genomes in the livers of children with various liver diseases. J. Clin. Microbiol. *39*:2173–2177, 2001.
101. Patti, M. E., Selvaggi, K. J., and Kroboth, F. J.: Varicella hepatitis in the immunocompromised adult: A case report and review of the literature. Am. J. Med. *88*:77–80, 1990.
102. Perlmutter, D. H.: Alpha-1-antitrypsin deficiency. Semin. Liver Dis. *18*:217–225, 1998.
103. Perman, J. A., Werlin, S. L., Grand, R. J., et al.: Laboratory measures of copper metabolism in the differentiation of chronic active hepatitis and Wilson disease in children. J. Pediatr. *94*:564–568, 1979.
104. Pitel, P. A., McCormick, K. L., Fitzgerald, T., et al.: Subclinical hepatic changes in varicella infection. Pediatrics *65*:631–633, 1980.
105. Phillips, M. J., Blendis, L. M., Poucell, S., et al.: Syncytial giant-cell hepatitis: Sporadic hepatitis with distinctive pathologic features, a severe clinical course, and paramyxoviral features. N. Engl. J. Med. *324*:455–460, 1991.
106. Polish, L. B., Gallagher, M., Fields, H. A., et al.: Delta hepatitis: Molecular biology and clinical and epidemiologic features. Clin. Microbiol. Rev. *6*:211–229, 1993.
107. Prince, A. M.: An antigen detected in blood during the incubation period of serum hepatitis. Proc. Natl. Acad. Sci. U. S. A. *60*:814–821, 1968.
108. Prince, A. M., Brotman, B., Grady, G. F., et al.: Long-incubation, post-transfusion hepatitis without serological evidence of exposure to hepatitis B virus. Lancet *2*:241–246, 1974.
109. Ray, D. C., and Drummond, G. B.: Halothane hepatitis. Br. J. Anaesth. *67*:84–99, 1991.
110. Reyes, G. R., Purdy, M. A., Kim, J. P., et al.: Isolation of cDNA from the virus responsible for enterically transmitted non-A, non-B hepatitis. Science *247*:1335–1339, 1990.
111. Rizzetto, M.: The delta agent. Hepatology *3*:729–735, 1983.
112. Rizzetto, M., Canese, M. G., Avico, S., et al.: Immunofluorescence detection of a new antigen/antibody system (delta/anti-delta) associated with hepatitis B virus in liver and serum of HBsAg carriers. Gut *18*:977–1003, 1977.
113. Robinson, J. E., Brown, N., Andiman, W., et al.: Diffuse polyclonal B-cell lymphoma during primary infection with Epstein-Barr virus. N. Engl. J. Med. *302*:1293–1297, 1980.
114. Roche-Sicot, J., and Benhamou, J. P.: Acute intravascular hemolysis and acute liver failure associated with a first manifestation of Wilson's disease. Ann. Intern. Med. *86*:301–310, 1977.
115. Rooney, C. M., Roskrow, M. A., Smith, C. A., et al.: Immunotherapy for Epstein-Barr virus–associated cancers. J. Natl. Cancer Inst. Monogr. *23*:89–93, 1998.
116. Rosenblate, H. J., Eisenstein, R., and Holmes, A. W.: The liver in sickle cell anemia. Arch. Pathol. Lab. *90*:235–240, 1970.
117. Rowland, P., Wald, E. R., Mirro, J. R., Jr., et al.: Progressive varicella presenting with pain and minimal skin involvement in children with acute lymphoblastic leukemia. J. Clin. Oncol. *13*:1697–1703, 1995.
118. Schiller, G. J., Nimer, S. D., Gajewski, J. L., et al.: Abdominal presentation of varicella-zoster infection in recipients of allogeneic bone marrow transplantation. Bone Marrow Transplant. *7*:489–491, 1991.
119. Shalev-Zimels, H., Weizman, Z., Lotan, C., et al.: Extent of measles hepatitis in various ages. Hepatology *8*:1138–1139, 1988.
120. Simmonds, P., Davidson, F., Lycett, C., et al.: Detection of a novel DNA virus (TTV) in blood donors and blood products. Lancet *2*:191–195, 1998.
121. Sokol, R. J., and Durie, P. R.: Recommendations for management of liver and biliary tract disease in cystic fibrosis. J. Pediatr. Gastroenterol. Nutr. *28*:511–513, 1999.
122. Soriano, V., Bru, F., and Gonzalez-Laoz, J.: Fatal varicella hepatitis in a patient with AIDS. J. Infect. *25*:107–109, 1992.
123. Strauss, L., and Bernstein, J.: Neonatal hepatitis in congenital rubella. Arch. Pathol. *86*:317–327, 1968.
124. Sugaya, N., Nirasawa, M., Mitamura, K., et al.: Hepatitis in acquired rubella infection in children. Am. J. Dis. Child. *142*:817–818, 1988.
125. Svegar, T.: The natural history of liver disease in alpha-1-antitrypsin deficient children. Acta Pediatr. *77*:847–851, 1995.
126. Tabor, E., Gerety, R. J., Drucker, J. A., et al.: Transmission of non-A, non-B hepatitis from man to chimpanzees. Lancet *1*:463–466, 1978.
127. Van den Berg, A. P.: Autoimmune hepatitis: Pathogenesis, diagnosis, and treatment. Scand. J. Gastroenterol. Suppl. *225*:66–69, 1998.
128. Whitley, R. J.: Cercopithecine herpes virus 1 (B virus). *In* Fields, B. N., Knipe, D. M., Howley, P. M. (eds.): Fields Virology. ed. 3. Philadelphia, Lippincott, Williams & Wilkins, 1999, pp. 2623–2630.
129. Whitley, R. J., and Kimberlin, D. W.: Treatment of viral infections during pregnancy and the neonatal period. Clin. Perinatol. *24*:267–283, 1997.
130. Young, E. J., Chafizadek, E., Oliveira, V. L., et al.: Disseminated herpesvirus infection during pregnancy. Clin. Infect. Dis. *22*:51–58, 1996.
131. Zimmerman, H. J.: The differential diagnosis of jaundice. Med. Clin. North Am. *52*:1417–1450, 1968.
132. Zimmerman, H. J.: Hepatotoxicity: The Adverse Effects of Drugs and Other Chemicals on the Liver. New York, Appleton-Century-Crofts, 1978.
133. Zimmerman, H. J., Fang, M., Utili, R., et al.: Clinical Conference: Jaundice due to bacterial infection. Gastroenterology *77*:362–373, 1979.

CHAPTER 55

Cholangitis and Cholecystitis

JASON S. SODEN ■ SAUL J. KARPEN

Cholangitis

Cholangitis refers to any pathologic finding of inflammation of the biliary system. Clinically, it is seen most often in the presence of biliary tract disease and obstruction, and it refers to systemic sepsis secondary to biliary infection and inflammation. The diagnosis of cholangitis implies microbial colonization of the biliary tract, increased biliary pressure, and systemic signs of infection, although all these findings are not present in all patients. In general, the etiologies and treatment of infectious cholangitis are similar in adults and children. In pediatric practice, however, one specific population, those who have undergone surgery for biliary atresia, is particularly susceptible to the development of cholangitis and its sequelae. This population, as well as other patient groups at high risk of acquiring infectious cholangitis, such as those with immunodeficiency states, those who have congenital or immune-related bile duct abnormalities, or those who have undergone liver transplantation, will be highlighted in this section. Biliary tract obstruction secondary to gallstone disease will be discussed in the section on cholecystitis.

ETIOLOGY AND PATHOGENESIS

The central mechanisms leading to biliary tract infection involve both biliary colonization and stasis. Bile typically is sterile, which implies that the development of bactibilia occurs either hematogenously via the portal venous system or directly via ascending infection from the gut lumen.[16]

Much still is unknown regarding the route of bacterial infection of the biliary tree. Bacterial ascent may occur from the duodenum, most commonly in the presence of disruption at the sphincter of Oddi. In addition, bacterial invasion may occur hematogenously by way of increased gut translocation across the intestine into the portal circulation.[145] Earlier research indicates that infection of bile probably occurs via direct hematogenous spread of bacteria from portal venous flow across the gallbladder wall.[27] This pathway has not been established firmly, but the combination of transient episodes of bactibilia and biliary obstruction apparently would lead to higher concentrations of bacteria in the biliary tract. As biliary pressure increases, bacteria probably emigrate from the bile ducts into lymphatic structures and then further into the bloodstream, with subsequent development of bacteremia and clinical signs and symptoms of cholangitis.[16]

In the adult population, cholangitis typically occurs in the presence of biliary tract obstruction secondary to impaction of gallstones in the common bile duct; such obstruction leads to bile duct stasis and secondary infection. Indeed, in approximately 85 percent of cases of cholangitis in adults, evidence of a stone is found in the common bile duct.[6] In adults with documented gallstones in the common bile duct (choledocholithiasis), the incidence of positive bile cultures ranges from 30 to 90 percent.[84] Other potential causes of biliary obstruction in adults, possibly leading to a more chronic or recurrent manifestation, include neoplasm, stricture, parasitic disease, and congenital bile duct anomalies.

In pediatrics, the more common setting for acute cholangitis is in a child with biliary atresia who has undergone hepatic portojejunostomy (HPJ), or the Kasai procedure (see later). The Kasai operation provides a permissive setup for cholangitis to occur, generally secondary to baseline poor bile flow and damaged intrahepatic bile ducts in conjunction with obligate bacterial colonization of the intestinal conduit with enteric flora.[51, 52, 72, 82, 123] In this scenario, cholangitis typically occurs by reflux of jejunal flora through the HPJ (Roux-en-Y loop), directly contiguous with the hepatic porta. Cholangitis tends to occur more frequently within the first year after surgery, more so in patients with evidence of good biliary flow. However, decreased biliary and duodenal motility are associated with a higher incidence of cholangitis.[30, 147]

Microbiologic evidence of biliary tract infection ideally should involve at least 10^5 organisms per milliliter of bile.[27] Gram-negative rods, primarily *Escherichia coli* and *Klebsiella pneumoniae,* are found in infected bile, but *Enterococcus* and *Enterobacter* spp. commonly are encountered as well. Moreover, many cases of cholangitis are polymicrobial, thus lending support for the use of broad-spectrum antibiotic treatment regimens. *E. coli* stands out as the organism most commonly isolated, and it accounts for 20 to 68 percent of infections. Table 55–1 presents the range of relative frequencies of specific organisms found in both adult and pediatric studies.[51, 68, 97] Anaerobes such as *Bacteroides fragilis* and *Clostridium perfringens* also may play a significant role and have been identified in as many as 40 percent of biliary tract infections.[11] Specifically, the latter organism has been implicated in the setting of acute emphysematous cholecystitis. Despite these findings in bile, a significant majority of patients with cholangitis have *negative* blood cultures, thus leading clinicians to have a high index of suspicion for cholangitis in selected circumstances and patient populations.

In addition to bacterial infection, other pathogens, namely, viral, fungal, and parasitic, play isolated roles in reported cases of pediatric cholangitis, particularly in immunodeficient patients (primarily those with human immunodeficiency virus [HIV] infection, see later) and those with environmental exposure to parasites in endemic settings.

TABLE 55–1 ■ BACTERIAL PATHOGENS ISOLATED FROM BILE CULTURES IN CHOLANGITIS

Organism	Hitch,[51] 1978 (*N* = 283)	Lewis,[80] 1987 (*N* = 23)	Boey,[7] 1980 (*N* = 99)
Escherichia coli	230	15	46
Klebsiella	193	17	28
Enterococcus	179	6	14
Pseudomonas	150		17
Proteus	44		8
Bacteroides	28	2	
Clostridium		9	
Other species	23	10	23

Both pediatric and adult data are used.[7, 51, 68, 80] Note that many biliary cultures contained more than one bacterial species.

Cholangitis associated with viral disease has been reported in various settings. Though most commonly seen with hepatocellular disease, hepatotropic viruses, primarily hepatitis C and hepatitis B, have been associated with pathologic findings of bile duct injury with apparent clinical significance.[13] Viral cholangiopathies are associated predominantly with cytomegalovirus (CMV) infection, but they also can be a component of hepatitis B and hepatitis C infection.[13, 42, 78] Depending on the clinical setting and age of the patient, CMV can have a markedly varied manifestation, from bile duct paucity seen in congenital CMV infection to hepatomegaly and jaundice in infants and children with primary CMV infection. The role of CMV hepatitis and cholangitis is significant in immunocompromised and solid organ transplant recipients (see later).

Fungal cholangitis, specifically with *Cryptococcus neoformans* or *Candida albicans,* has been reported in both immunocompromised and immunocompetent patients, though more commonly in the former.[20]

Parasites can cause both primary and secondary infection in normal hosts. Nematodes, namely, *Ascaris* and rarely *Strongyloides,* commonly cause biliary disease in endemic regions. Migrating *Ascaris* larvae may cause either a direct inflammatory response if they pass through the biliary system or a secondary pyogenic cholangitis as a result of obstruction by the worms themselves or eggs that have been released. Liver flukes such as *Clonorchis* (now *Opisthorchis) sinensis, Opisthorchis viverrini,* and *Opisthorchis felineus* also may pass through the biliary system during their life cycle in the definitive mammalian host. Of these trematodes, *Clonorchis* is found frequently in cases of recurrent pyogenic cholangitis in Asian children.[102] Similar to worms, migration of flukes *(Fasciola hepatica)* through the biliary tree may induce primary inflammation and, later, a secondary bacterial infection. Echinococcal cholangitis has been described in the setting of obstruction secondary to cyst formation from infection with either *Echinococcus granulosus* or *Echinococcus multilocularis.*[16, 22, 70]

CLINICAL FEATURES

The classic manifestation of cholangitis, described most clearly by Charcot in 1877 and known commonly as the *Charcot triad,* consists of the clinical findings of fever, right upper quadrant pain, and jaundice, which are reported in as many as 70 percent of patients with cholangitis.[65] The "Reynold pentad" describes these findings plus septic shock and altered mental status.[81] In children, fever is the most common initial symptom and occurred in 100 percent of 105 patients with cholangitis after undergoing hepatic portoenterostomy.[30] In addition, either acholic stools or an increase in serum bilirubin concentration occurred in 68 percent of patients. Older children and teenagers with cholangitis typically report abdominal pain that may or may not be associated with meals or localized to the right upper quadrant. Patients may report new-onset pruritus as a consequence of having retained biliary constituents. Moreover, of emphasis is that the findings of cholangitis may be markedly attenuated in infants and immunocompromised patients, thus suggesting that a high index of suspicion should be maintained in the evaluation of these children at risk. For example, the findings of cholangitis in an infant with biliary atresia after undergoing Kasai portoenterostomy may be as varied as lethargy, increasing jaundice, abdominal tenderness, or fever alone. Finally, patients with ongoing hemolysis, such as those with hemoglobin SS disease, are at high risk for development of both cholecystitis and cholangitis from bilirubin stones, yet the symptoms may overlap readily with other causes of abdominal pain.

DIAGNOSTIC EVALUATION

Physical examination may reveal a varied range of toxic appearances, with vital signs suggestive of serious systemic infection (fever, tachycardia, hypotension) in more advanced cases. Icteric sclerae and a distended abdomen with tenderness localized to the mid or right upper quadrant are typical findings. The liver edge may be tender to palpation. Laboratory studies may reveal an elevated erythrocyte sedimentation rate (81%), leukocytosis, or leukopenia (56%) and increased levels of conjugated bilirubin in serum.[30] Laboratory evaluations in children should include a standard complete blood count with differential and a liver panel (alanine transaminase [ALT], aspartate transaminase [AST], alkaline phosphatase, gamma-glutamyltransferase [GGT], and fractionated bilirubin [unconjugated and conjugated]). Considerations for the differential diagnosis of fever, abdominal pain, and jaundice should include sepsis and hepatitis, and laboratory tests should be considered for these entities in appropriate circumstances. Unfortunately, no single laboratory test nor any combination of tests securely connotes the presence or absence of cholangitis.

Attempts at identifying a microbiologic agent should be made, and blood should be drawn for culture before initiation of antimicrobial therapy. Most cases are polymicrobial, with a predominance of gut-derived organisms (see Table 55–1). Blood cultures may be positive in upward of 50 percent of pediatric patients with cholangitis, as reported by Ecoffey and colleagues, but not typically in a routine pediatric practice.[30] However, other investigators have reported identification of organisms in blood in approximately 10 to 25 percent of patients, which is in keeping with our experience (see references in the article by Westphal and Brogard[161]). In patients with a history of hepatobiliary surgery, both aerobic and anaerobic cultures should be considered, and in virtually all young children with abdominal pain and jaundice, a urine culture should be considered. The role of direct testing of hepatic tissue by percutaneous biopsy is controversial but may have a place in the setting of negative blood cultures. When used along with blood cultures, hepatic cultures have been shown to increase the diagnostic yield of identifying a microbiologic organism to 75 percent, whereas histologic confirmation of cholangitis may be the only firm evidence of cholangitis in some patients.[30] In cases of gallstone-associated cholangitis that require endoscopic or surgical decompression, bile should be obtained and cultured. In a study of gallstone-associated cholangitis, bile cultures were positive in 22 of 23 adults.[80]

The initial and principal radiologic evaluation for suspected cholangitis is abdominal ultrasound, with the primary goal being to search for evidence of biliary tract obstruction—dilation of the common bile duct or intrahepatic ducts. Ultrasound examination may reveal anatomic biliary tract abnormalities (choledochal cyst), intrahepatic cysts, and hepatic or other intra-abdominal masses. Other noninvasive imaging modalities include computed tomography (CT) and scanning and magnetic resonance cholangiopancreatography (MRCP), which are increasingly able to display detailed images of the intrahepatic and biliary anatomy.[94, 120] Taken together, these noninvasive imaging techniques should be able to detect the presence of biliary tract obstruction and some congenital anatomic anomalies, although even experienced ultrasonographers may still miss small stones and sludge, especially in the common bile duct.

Ultrasound is only 80 to 85 percent sensitive in identifying biliary tract obstruction; the rate improves to approximately 90 percent with CT scanning and to 95 to 99 percent with endoscopic retrograde cholangiopancreatography (ERCP).[113]

In a biliary atresia patient who has had a Kasai portoenterostomy, imaging may be able to identify retained biliary lakes ("bilomas"), which could be infected. Nuclear medicine scans (hepatobiliary iminodiacetic acid [HIDA]) have a limited role in the evaluation of cholangitis but may be most helpful in determining whether complete obstruction of the common bile duct or an isolated obstruction of the cystic duct is present (cholecystitis, see later).

Invasive imaging has a role, especially when it may be coupled with therapeutic decompression of an obstructed and potentially infected biliary tree. ERCP has proved to be extremely useful in the evaluation and management of biliary tract obstruction and should be considered in the management of children with evidence of an obstructed common bile duct (see later and elsewhere[1, 15, 86, 136, 137, 142, 149, 166]). The role of ERCP in infants and small children is limited by the lack of experience of most pediatric gastroenterologists and should be considered in tertiary care centers that have the requisite expertise. ERCP is the most direct means of obtaining bile for microbial and chemical analysis and will provide detailed imaging of the biliary tree. In addition, ERCP may detect (and remove) small stones and sludge that are missed by ultrasound, CT, or MRCP. Moreover, it is helpful in the differential diagnosis of biliary tract diseases such as primary sclerosing cholangitis (PSC), which may be manifested similar to infectious cholangitis but may have a characteristic radiographic appearance of the biliary tree. Finally, endoscopic ultrasound recently has been used to provide detailed imaging of the pancreatic head and biliary tract, but with limited experience reported in pediatrics.[121]

DIFFERENTIAL DIAGNOSIS

The differential diagnosis for an acutely ill child with fever and clinical evidence of hyperbilirubinemia is broad, and a thorough work-up must include consideration of both infectious and noninfectious etiologies. A thorough investigation for hepatic and biliary tract pathology via blood and radiologic studies must be initiated to evaluate for stones or other obstructive processes that may cause symptoms characteristic of the Charcot triad.

Acute viral hepatitis may be manifested in any of many ways, but it often begins with nonspecific signs—fever, headache, anorexia, and jaundice. Laboratory studies more often reveal a greater elevation in transaminases (ALT and AST) than in alkaline phosphatase and GGT, the enzymes associated with the biliary tract. In a child with no other evidence of biliary tract obstruction, however, screening assays for hepatitis infection are warranted.

Pyogenic liver abscesses and amebic abscesses tend to be characterized by fever, abdominal pain, hepatomegaly, and focal right upper quadrant tenderness.[102] Laboratory findings are variable with regard to changes in liver enzymes or liver function. CT scanning is considered the most sensitive technique in evaluation.[94]

Jaundice may occur with clinical sepsis and is seen more commonly in the scenario of a critically ill infant or child. Clinical evaluation may show a predominantly direct hyperbilirubinemia with some elevation in GGT, whereas transaminases may be normal or minimally elevated. These findings are caused by hepatocellular cholestasis secondary to humoral mediators of sepsis, but they can be exacerbated by the generalized biliary sludging that accompanies septicemia. Although historically, sepsis-associated cholestasis has been linked primarily to gram-negative sepsis, it can be seen in all forms of infection.[95, 153] In some cases, radiologic work-up or biopsy is warranted to rule out ductal obstruction or biliary tract pathology. However, jaundice may occur as the sole manifestation of sepsis in infants and children.[29]

Drug-induced cholestasis tends to occur acutely with the onset of jaundice, pruritus, and other symptoms that may mimic cholangitis. Among the main classes of drugs used commonly in pediatric practice that may lead to significant hepatotoxicity are antimicrobials (mainly trimethoprim-sulfamethoxazole [TMP-SMX], amoxicillin-clavulanate, clindamycin, erythromycin, cephalosporins, isoniazid, rifampin, fluconazole), anticonvulsants (phenytoin, carbamazepine, valproate, felbamate), nonsteroidal anti-inflammatory agents (aspirin, ibuprofen), and multiple antihypertensive agents (propranolol, diltiazem).[12, 21] If the offending agent is identified in time, removal typically leads to rapid improvement. One antimicrobial agent deserves special mention because it has been linked directly to cholangitis and cholecystitis: ceftriaxone, possibly because of biliary concentration and intrinsic physicochemical properties, may precipitate in bile and lead to sludge and stones.[71]

Other systemic illnesses may be characterized by fever and evidence of biliary tract pathology. PSC is defined as a chronic inflammation of the intrahepatic or extrahepatic ducts that leads to a range of biliary tract pathology, from dilatation to obliteration and periductular fibrosis. It is seen most commonly in patients with inflammatory bowel disease (IBD) and affects males with IBD more commonly than females. Symptoms include systemic findings such as fatigue, malaise, and weight loss, as well as evidence of cholangitis, including fever. PSC must be suspected in the setting of a jaundiced patient with IBD. The diagnosis is made best by ERCP or cholangiography showing irregular narrowing and stricture of the hepatic and common bile ducts and the intrahepatic ducts.[88, 118] Patients with PSC are at risk for the development of intrahepatic and common bile duct strictures, with subsequent obstruction, sludge/stone formation, and cholangitis.

TREATMENT

Therapeutic goals in the treatment of cholangitis should be directed at general support of the patient, early initiation of appropriate antibiotic therapy, and in cases of obstruction by stones or stricture, urgent attention to decompression of the biliary obstruction via ERCP or surgery. Pediatric surgical consultation early in the course of evaluating a patient with suspected cholangitis generally is helpful. The importance of decompression and drainage of the bile tract in the face of systemic infection secondary to cholangitis cannot be overemphasized. Other potential etiologies of obstruction, such as choledochal cysts, ultimately require surgical consultation and repair.

Initial and conservative management should include appropriate inpatient monitoring, cessation of oral intake with intravenous fluid support, administration of parenteral antibiotic therapy, and pressor support if indicated. Because blood cultures tend to have a low diagnostic yield in cholangitis, antibiotic choices should be selected empirically and should not rely on culture results.

Antibiotic choices should be aimed at selecting a drug or combination of drugs with appropriate coverage of suspected or documented organisms (based on sensitivities) and the ability to achieve adequate serum and tissue concentrations.

At this point, no one perfect antibiotic or combination is recognized universally as definitive therapy for cholangitis in children. Prescriptive therapy in appropriate circumstances typically is initiated before culture results are obtained. Attention has been drawn in the past to the goal of achieving adequate biliary concentrations, although this objective may be secondary to achieving adequate serum levels.[27, 81]

Administration of parenteral antibiotics is indicated in almost all children with suspected biliary tract sepsis. Primary antibiotic choices should cover gram-negative enteric organisms, namely, *E. coli*, *Klebsiella*, and *Enterococcus*. In a child with clinical sepsis, also adding coverage for anaerobic species, particularly *Bacteroides*, is reasonable.[11] Previously, a combination of ampicillin or penicillin with an aminoglycoside was considered appropriate therapy. However, studies in adults suggest that some antipseudomonal penicillins such as mezlocillin are more effective alone than an ampicillin-gentamicin combination.[38]

The general recommendation for the treatment of a pediatric patient with suspected cholangitis is the use of a semisynthetic (e.g., piperacillin or mezlocillin) or third-generation cephalosporin, such as cefoperazone, in combination with an aminoglycoside.[75, 161] The addition of metronidazole helps cover some anaerobic gut flora. Rothenberg and associates reported a 62.7 percent success rate after treatment with imipenem-cilastatin or third-generation cephalosporins with or without aminoglycosides and 58.2 percent success with the use of semisynthetic penicillins and aminoglycosides.[123] A prospective trial involving 131 adults with biliary tract infection demonstrated "cure" in 85 percent of those treated with ampicillin and tobramycin after they had undergone a surgical procedure.[97] Though limited, a 1987 report of three patients suggests favorable results with the use of ciprofloxacin in pediatric patients with cholangitis after undergoing a Kasai procedure.[56] TMP-SMX, which achieves a high biliary-to-serum concentration ratio, also has been used successfully in similar clinical settings.[52] As previously mentioned, the use of ceftriaxone probably should be avoided because it has been associated with biliary sludging and cholecystitis.[61]

In clinical practice, the choice of antibiotic therapy often is empiric despite attempts to isolate a pathogenic organism. Therefore, antibiotic efficacy is determined by clinical parameters such as defervescence and improvement in biliary excretion. Antibiotic resistance is encountered more often in patients with repeated episodes of cholangitis.[30] The duration of antibiotic treatment varies, but a shorter course may result in recurrence.[123] The recommended course of therapy is 14 to 21 days, with longer courses recommended in special cases such as recurrent or refractory cholangitis and in the case of intrahepatic abscesses or hepatic surgery. Generally, oral antibiotic therapy has no place in the treatment of cholangitis in children, although oral ciprofloxacin has been used in some adult populations.[161]

Ultimately, if biliary obstruction persists with symptomatic cholangitis, the patient will not improve without relieving this obstruction and clearing the organism. Although antibiotic therapy may treat the septicemia, timely establishment of biliary drainage is imperative to achieve an adequate biliary concentration of antibiotics.[31] In adults with cholangitis but no documented clinical improvement after 12 to 48 hours of parenteral therapy, attempts at decompression via ERCP (or laparotomy) may be indicated; this procedure must be performed in approximately 25 percent of adults.[31, 68, 126] Initial efforts should focus on taking advantage of nonoperative options, such as ERCP or percutaneous transhepatic cholangiography, which are considered to be lower risk than is open surgical intervention.[109] These procedures can be both diagnostic, if biliary obstruction is conclusively visualized or ruled out, and therapeutic, with placement of a stent.

Management of parasitic cholangitis should include appropriate treatment of biliary parasites based on regional sensitivity results, in addition to antibiotic coverage of secondary bacterial infections. Endoscopic or surgical intervention may be required to remove worms or cysts from the biliary tree.[22]

SPECIFIC POPULATIONS AND CHOLANGITIS

Cholangitis and Biliary Atresia

In the pediatric setting, cholangitis is encountered most frequently in the setting of a patient with biliary atresia who has undergone a Kasai procedure. In 1959, Kasai and Suzuki first reported relief of biliary obstruction via hepatic portoenterostomy in children with biliary atresia.[67] The procedure, a Roux-en-Y hepatic portojejunostomy, is considered to be standard first-line surgical therapy for infants with biliary atresia, and it is associated with the highest success rates and long-term survival when performed early, usually by 60 days of life. Without this procedure, 90 percent of patients with extrahepatic biliary atresia will die before reaching the age of 3 years, the average age of death being 19 months.[66, 141]

Cholangitis remains the most frequent complication of the Kasai procedure and occurs in 40 to 60 percent of patients.[106] A subgroup of patients with the pathologic finding of cystic dilatation of the intrahepatic bile ducts seems to have the highest risk for development of postoperative cholangitis.[53] The development of cholangitis has been associated with a 50 percent worsening in the long-term prognosis of children with biliary atresia.[57] Complications of cholangitis are severe, from inflammation and scarring to alterations in biliary flow and eventual progression to biliary cirrhosis. Repeated bouts of cholangitis are associated with worsening liver function, impaired growth, and need for early transplantation. For this reason, early detection and prompt and appropriate management of cholangitis are important in this population.

Most cases of post-Kasai cholangitis occur within 1 year postoperatively. In a 1976 review of 49 children who underwent the procedure, 31 achieved good bile flow restoration. Of these, cholangitis subsequently developed in 20, with 15 cases occurring within the first postoperative month and 3 within the second month.[103] Likewise, in a study of 105 cases of cholangitis in 101 children who underwent hepatic portoenterostomy, Ecoffey and colleagues showed that 63 percent of cases occurred within 3 months after surgery, with 93 percent developing within 1 year.[30] Rarely, late cholangitis may occur and has been reported up to several years after hepatic portoenterostomy.[41]

As mentioned, the generally accepted mechanism for cholangitis that develops after the Kasai procedure is ascending bacterial colonization. This theory is reinforced by evidence that supports a significantly higher incidence of cholangitis in patients with good or partial bile flow after undergoing the Kasai procedure (78%) than in those with no obvious bile flow (13%).[30] A 1978 study of 19 patients concluded that all conduits that were bilio-enteric after the procedure were colonized within 1 month, which correlates with the high incidence of symptomatic infection at this early stage.[52] The retrograde bacterial colonization may be enhanced by overall changes in intestinal motility after the

Roux-en-Y loop.[147] Over time, the intestinal conduit from the hepatic porta to the jejunum seems to "mature" and thereby diminish the number of episodes of cholangitis. How this adaptation happens is not entirely clear; however, a persistent degree of intrahepatic biliary inflammation may cause partial obstruction during the initial 6 to 9 months. Late episodes of cholangitis, those occurring 1 to 2 years after the Kasai procedure, probably are related to mechanical obstruction such as adhesions.[82]

Gram-negative enteric organisms account for most infections. *E. coli* has been found in 50 percent of first and second cholangitis episodes and is found with decreasing frequency in further episodes.[30] Anaerobes also may be common findings and should be considered when selecting antibiotic treatment.[11] Refractory or recurrent cases occurring after surgery may warrant consideration of fungal disease, principally *Candida*.[20] Attempts to isolate an organism generally are made, but blood cultures typically produce a lower yield.[123] Bile cultures tend to reflect the multiple enteric organisms that colonize the conduit; however, they may not specify true pathogens. Success has been reported with the use of percutaneous liver biopsy to obtain specimens for culture.[104]

Attempts have been made to prevent cholangitis in the intraoperative and postoperative management of children with biliary atresia. Various modifications in the surgical configuration of the intestinal conduit have been suggested to reduce enteric reflux. Initial studies have documented a reduced incidence of ascending cholangitis in patients with a surgically placed antireflux valve. However, despite the prevention of intestinal reflux in these cases, cholangitis continues to occur.[10] Cases of refractory cholangitis may require surgical intervention, especially if obstruction of the conduit or porta hepatis is suspected.

The role of corticosteroids in improving biliary drainage is controversial and has not been subject to rigorous controlled trials. However, perioperative steroid pulses, typically a 3- to 5-day course of intravenous methylprednisolone, have been shown to be clinically beneficial by decreasing temperature, increasing bile flow, and improving liver function test results.[98, 123] In addition, some centers advocate the use of prophylactic antibiotics, typically TMP-SMX. However, the benefits of this practice are not well established.[19] In adults with recurrent cholangitis secondary to fixed obstruction, as in the case of malignancy, both TMP-SMX and ciprofloxacin have been shown to be helpful in preventing episodes.[156]

In patients with biliary atresia after undergoing the Kasai procedure, each episode of cholangitis is associated with a 1 percent mortality risk. Some studies suggest that overall, no significant clinical difference exists in the overall survival of patients after undergoing the Kasai operation who have and have not had cholangitis.[105] However, previous studies suggest an 88 percent mortality rate when cholangitis develops up to 1 month after the Kasai procedure and a 16 percent greater risk when cholangitis develops after 1 month. Recent studies suggest that the occurrence of cholangitis is related to early postoperative mortality and that the number of repeated episodes is related inversely to survival.[163]

Cholangitis after Liver Transplantation

Infection remains the most common reason for morbidity and mortality after liver transplantation, accounting for 20 to 30 percent of postoperative deaths.[125, 144] Bacterial infection after transplantation tends to occur within the first 2 months postoperatively and generally is of either respiratory tract or intra-abdominal origin. In patients with severe bacterial infections related to intra-abdominal sepsis, cholangitis and biliary tract infections occur commonly. Again, gram-negative aerobic bacteria are encountered most frequently in this setting.[128] One adult study reported that 18 percent of 284 patients receiving liver transplants had confirmed episodes of cholangitis.[157] Pediatric data suggest a 5 to 11 percent incidence of cholangitis after liver transplantation for biliary atresia. Biliary tract disease frequently occurs after the complication of hepatic artery thrombosis in liver transplant patients.[87, 91] This complication had been prevalent in the early days of pediatric liver transplantation before the use of microsurgical techniques and has been reduced in frequency ever since, but it remains a significant concern, primarily because of the nature of the small vessel anastomoses. Hepatic artery thrombosis eventually leads to bile duct damage because the blood supply of the bile ducts is exclusively from the hepatic artery, whereas the hepatic parenchyma is fed from both the portal vein and the hepatic artery. In addition, small livers and ducts are more prone to preservation injury, a complication that may lead to bile duct injury such as strictures, which set the stage for obstruction and infection in these patients. Even though many pediatric liver transplant recipients have a Roux-en-Y connection from the donor bile duct to the intestines, ascending cholangitis is a relatively rare event.

Cholangitis occurring after liver transplantation may be manifested as fever, jaundice, elevated liver enzymes, and bacteremia. However, the variable nature of an immunocompromised patient's response to infection renders the reliability of each of these signs and symptoms suspect. Distinguishing these symptoms from the sequelae of post-transplant rejection or infection (e.g., with CMV or Epstein-Barr virus) is important. For this reason, liver biopsy often is a necessary part of the evaluation of a post-transplant patient with fever and elevated liver test results.

Cholangitis in Immunocompromised Patients

Acquired immunodeficiency syndrome (AIDS)–related cholangitis is a well-known complication of AIDS that tends to occur later in the course of the illness and is more common in adults than in children. In 1989, Cello described four distinct patterns of disease in AIDS-related cholangitis, as seen on cholangiography. They included papillary stenosis, sclerosing cholangitis, combined papillary stenosis and sclerosing cholangitis, and long extrahepatic bile duct strictures.[17] The pathogenesis of these changes is unknown but may be related to biliary inflammation secondary to immunodeficiency, infiltration of the mucosa by HIV itself, or opportunistic infection by known gastrointestinal pathogens in AIDS infection. The opportunistic agents most commonly responsible are CMV, *Cryptosporidium,* Microsporida, and, uncommonly, *Mycobacterium avium–intracellulare* and *Isospora.*[100]

The clinical findings are similar to those in non–HIV-infected patients, except that jaundice tends to occur less commonly. In a series of 45 adults with AIDS-related cholangitis, abdominal pain was reported as the most common initial symptom (occurring in 64% of patients), followed by diarrhea (22%), fever (20%), and jaundice (7%). A 1995 review reports that as many as 90 percent of adults have right upper quadrant or epigastric pain. Of interest, 20 percent of patients were asymptomatic and, therefore, recognized by routine blood work alone.[28] Cholangitis has been reported as the initial manifestation of HIV infection in a small number of patients.[9, 96]

Diagnostic steps include noninvasive imaging with sonography and CT, as well as ERCP. Abdominal ultrasound is abnormal in as many as 75 percent of patients and typically shows dilatation or wall thickening of the common bile duct. These findings, along with liver function studies, may be suggestive of the disease, even in children.[124] ERCP offers the ability to further demonstrate characteristic biliary tract changes and has the added advantage of obtaining specimens for biopsy and culture and the possibility of therapeutic intervention.[164] Although AIDS-related cholangitis can be a marker for late-stage AIDS, it typically is not associated directly with mortality. However, most patients with AIDS-related cholangitis die within 1 year of its diagnosis.[85] Therapy should be aimed at alleviation of symptoms.

Cholangitis also may occur in the setting of non-AIDS immunodeficiency in children. Sclerosing cholangitis has been reported in children with primary immunodeficiency, familial T-cell deficiency, IgA/IgG deficiency, and X-linked hyper-IgM syndrome.[44, 79] Hepatobiliary infection also has been reported in the setting of a child with leukemia.[37, 73, 133, 139]

Cholangitis in Association with Congenital Anatomic Abnormalities: Choledochal Cyst and Caroli Disease

Choledochal cysts occur in 1 in 15,000 births in Western nations and in as many as 1 in 1000 live births in Japan.[102] Typically, initial signs suggesting cholestasis may include jaundice, dark urine, and acholic stools; alternatively, patients may have an abdominal mass with or without jaundice. If diagnosed late or untreated, choledochal cysts may result in severe complications secondary to biliary tract obstruction, including cholangitis. In one series of 36 Indian patients, 13 had cholangitis, which occurred more commonly in childhood as opposed to infancy.[110] Moreover, cholangitis is more likely to be the initial sign of a choledochal cyst in adult patients.[18]

Treatment of cholangitis associated with a choledochal cyst involves supportive treatment of the patient, including appropriate antibiotic treatment. In the past, cyst-enteric drainage procedures were used as temporizing treatment, and this type of repair was associated with a high rate of complications, including recurrent bouts of cholangitis, stones, and cholangiocarcinoma in the remnant duct.[117] Currently, the surgical goal is complete surgical excision, which when compared with internal drainage procedures, is associated with a lower rate of postoperative cholangitis and mortality.[127] Five types of choledochal cysts are recognized, with solitary extrahepatic cysts (type I) being encountered most frequently. After excision of this type of cyst, biliary tract reconstruction may involve a Roux-en-Y choledochojejunostomy or hepatojejunostomy. Patients who have undergone this surgery also are at risk for development of postoperative ascending cholangitis, with an incidence of 8 to 19 percent.[34, 130] Long-term follow-up is recommended to screen for the possibility of progressive liver failure as a consequence of recurrent cholangitis, but antibiotic prophylaxis typically is not used.[63]

As opposed to extrahepatic biliary obstruction caused by either biliary atresia or a choledochal cyst, Caroli disease involves congenital dilatation of the intrahepatic and extrahepatic biliary tree characterized by pure ductal ectasia.[23, 24] More commonly, dilatation of the intrahepatic ducts is attributed to ductal plate malformation in association with congenital hepatic fibrosis. Both these diseases may have clinical signs of liver disease or renal disease (or both) secondary to the associated condition of autosomal recessive polycystic kidney disease.[64, 83, 107] Dilatation of the intrahepatic bile ducts results in biliary obstruction and places the patient at increased risk for development of cholangitis, which significantly increases morbidity and mortality rates in both Caroli disease and congenital hepatic fibrosis. The diagnosis should be suspected in patients with recurrent cholangitis or portal hypertension of unknown etiology and can be confirmed by ultrasonography or cholangiography.[32] Portosystemic shunting is considered the treatment of choice. Suspicion of cholangitis, whether because of signs of infection or sepsis or because of laboratory results suggesting inflammation, should be confirmed by diagnostic liver biopsy for culture. Treating cholangitis in the setting of Caroli disease may be difficult. Recurrent episodes may occur even after administration of intensive intravenous antibiotic therapy.[158] In some cases, drainage procedures may be used for refractory or recurrent infections; orthotopic liver transplantation also may yield success.[48, 158]

Cholangitis following Endoscopic Procedures

Although at this point experience in the use ERCP in the pediatric population is limited, but growing, cholangitis is a known complication of this procedure in adults. In a series of 50 pediatric patients who underwent ERCP, low-grade fever, abdominal pain, nausea, and vomiting were reported as the most common transient complaints; one patient was treated for mild cholangitis.[149]

Cholecystitis

An understanding of cholecystitis rests first with the recognition that gallstones are the prime initiating factor. Gallstone disease is a common entity in the adult population, with more than 700,000 cholecystectomies performed each year in the United States out of approximately 20 million adults with gallstones.[77] In children, gallstones and gallstone-related complications occur much less frequently than in adults. However, in certain pediatric populations, such as those with hemolytic conditions, gallstone and gallbladder diseases are more common and, therefore, need to be considered in appropriate clinical settings.[135]

Cholelithiasis refers to the presence of gallstones, which may occur silently or in association with clinical symptoms. *Biliary colic* occurs in the setting of obstruction of either the cystic duct or the common bile duct secondary to gallstones and is associated with characteristic episodic, postprandial right upper quadrant pain. *Acute cholecystitis* involves inflammation of the gallbladder and can be seen with cholelithiasis *(calculous)* or in the absence of gallstones *(acalculous)*. In adults, acute cholecystitis almost always is associated with gallstones; indeed, as many as 90 percent of adult cases occur secondary to gallstones. In contrast, 30 to 50 percent of pediatric cases are acalculous.[154] Acalculous cholecystitis will be discussed separately at the end of this section.

ETIOLOGY AND PATHOGENESIS

In general, gallstones are classified as either pigment stones or cholesterol stones. Pigment stones can be further divided into either black or brown pigment stones. Black pigment stones occur in the face of a superabundance of unconjugated bilirubin in bile and are seen most commonly in the setting of hemolytic disease leading to the development of an increased biliary concentration of bilirubin and calcium-bilirubinate stones. Brown pigment stones occur less commonly and are associated with biliary infection or parasitic infestation or with the presence of a foreign body (e.g., retained suture material) or biliary obstruction. Cholesterol stones are the end result of biliary cholesterol supersaturation secondary to an imbalance in cholesterol–phospholipid–bile salt equilibrium or other precipitating factors.[26] These stones tend to occur in the face of either elevated production of cholesterol or decreased bile salt pools. The genetics of the formation of gallstones may provide insight into the production of cholesterol gallstones.[76]

In pediatric practice, pigment stones occur more commonly than do cholesterol stones, which is in direct contrast to adult populations, in which cholesterol stones are far more prevalent. Friesen and Roberts described 693 pediatric cases of gallstone disease, 72 percent of which were pigmented.[35] The greatest experience with pigmented gallstones in children is in those with hemolytic diseases, primarily sickle-cell anemia and thalassemia, but also in patients with hereditary spherocytosis and other red cell membrane defects, pyruvate kinase deficiency, glucose-6-phospate dehydrogenase deficiency, and autoimmune hemolytic anemia.[49, 116, 134] The prevalence of pigment gallstones in hemolytic disease increases with age. In children younger than 10 years old, the frequency is 12 to 14 percent, whereas in those between 10 and 20 years of age, the frequency increases to 36 to 42 percent.[8, 132]

Total parenteral nutrition (TPN) predisposes children to development of biliary tract disease, including gallstone formation.[114] Such disease occurs more commonly in premature neonates, especially those with enteral diseases, in whom prolonged fasting, sepsis, immaturity of the enterohepatic circulation of bile acids, and increased duration of TPN all contribute to biliary stasis and an increased prevalence of gallstones and sludge.[3, 69, 74, 131, 148, 160] The occurrence of gallstones secondary to TPN, however, does not lead necessarily to increased complications because many of these gallstones are clinically silent.

Cholesterol stones are found most commonly in adults and have an increased prevalence in females from puberty to menopause, as well as in those with obesity.[129] Indeed, some of these characteristics may translate to pediatrics as well. Although males and females have an equal incidence of gallstones at young ages, the incidence in females increases significantly after puberty, and the female preponderance of gallstone disease continues through menopause.[101] Related risk factors for the presence of cholesterol stones in children and adolescents include obesity, pregnancy, and the use of oral contraceptives. In addition, conditions associated with decreased ileal bile salt resorption predispose to the formation of stones. Included are patients who have undergone ileal resection or bypass and also those with Crohn disease.[122] Gallstones are found in as many as 28 percent of adults with cystic fibrosis at the time of autopsy.[138] The presence of gallstones in children with cystic fibrosis is well documented, but the pathogenesis probably is multifactorial. Finally, cholesterol gallstones appear to have a genetic component, with several candidate loci identified recently.[76] Table 55–2 summarizes the pediatric patient populations at risk for the development of gallstones.[36]

The probable cause of calculous cholecystitis is gallstone obstruction of the cystic duct. Such obstruction leads to increased intraluminal pressure with gallbladder distention, mucosal damage, and release of inflammatory mediators. The end result is acute inflammation of the gallbladder. Any bacterial infection probably is a secondary occurrence to biliary obstruction and the inflammatory cascade.[77]

TABLE 55–2 ■ PATIENT POPULATIONS PREDISPOSED TO GALLSTONE FORMATION

Pigment Stones	Cholesterol Stones
Hemolytic disorders	Pregnancy
Total parenteral nutrition	Obesity
Biliary tract anomalies (e.g., Caroli disease)	Rapid weight loss
Parasitic disease (*Ascaris lumbricoides*)*	Malabsorption (Crohn disease, ileal resection, etc.)
Ceftriaxone use	Genetic predisposition
Solid organ transplantation (heart, lung, kidney)	Cystic fibrosis

*Brown pigment stones.

CLINICAL FEATURES

Acute cholecystitis typically is manifested as abdominal pain and vomiting. Pain may be localized to the right upper quadrant, but this finding can be difficult to differentiate from other causes of acute abdominal pain in children. As in the model of appendicitis, initial pain with obstruction of the cystic duct tends to be visceral pain that may be epigastric and poorly localized. With gallbladder inflammation, the pain becomes parietal—more localized to the right upper quadrant and associated with some peritoneal signs such as pain with movement. With regard to the duration of pain, cholecystitis should produce pain that is more long-standing than is the case with uncomplicated biliary colic. Whereas cystic duct obstruction is associated with an acute onset of pain and resolution in 3 to 6 hours, true gallbladder inflammation may produce a more persistent pain lasting between 6 and 12 hours or longer. The presence of jaundice with right upper quadrant pain and emesis in a patient without hemolysis or the presence of increasing jaundice in hemolytic patients warrants a thorough investigation for the possibility of choledocholithiasis, as well as cholecystitis. Fever, though classically described in patients with cholecystitis, is not universally present. In a retrospective study of 198 adults who went to an emergency center with acute cholecystitis, 59 percent were afebrile.[45]

Physical examination may demonstrate a tender right upper quadrant. The examiner should try to elicit the Murphy sign, for which tenderness on palpation of the right upper quadrant worsens with palpation of the liver edge or gallbladder. It may be most apparent with deep inspiration, when the liver descends toward the examiner's hand. The patient may demonstrate voluntary guarding or peritoneal signs. A palpable mass representing the inflamed gallbladder with adjacent omentum may be present.

EVALUATION

Laboratory evaluation may show leukocytosis, although this finding is not universally present in either adults or children with cholecystitis.[45, 114] Bilirubin levels may be elevated, especially in the setting of hemolysis. Conjugated hyperbilirubinemia should cause one to be concerned about choledocholithiasis or sepsis-associated cholestasis. Transaminase as well as amylase and lipase levels frequently are ordered on initial assessment to evaluate for other etiologies of epigastric or right upper quadrant pain with vomiting or fever, such as pancreatitis and viral hepatitis. As in the evaluation of cholangitis, early consultation with a pediatric surgeon is appropriate.

Abdominal ultrasound remains the test of choice for the diagnosis of cholecystitis. Findings on ultrasound include a thickened or irregular, hyper-reflexive gallbladder wall with or without the presence of gallstones. Experienced sonographers may be able to elicit tenderness over the gallbladder, the "sonographic Murphy sign." Ultrasound is very useful for detection of gallstone disease, which is demonstrated in as many as 90 percent of patients in some cases. However, the finding of gallstones alone by sonography does not necessarily indicate cholecystitis without suspicion of gallbladder inflammation. Other false-positive studies may occur in the presence of thickened gallbladder walls in patients with hypoalbuminemia, renal failure, or heart failure.[108] Furthermore, an inability to visualize the gallbladder by ultrasound may be indicative of a diseased, chronically obstructed gallbladder.[43]

Hepatobiliary scintigraphy (HIDA scan) is extremely useful in confirming the diagnosis of acute cholecystitis. The study uses a technetium-labeled iminodiacetic agent that is excreted into the bile ducts. Subsequent images are taken and, in a normal study, should fill the gallbladder, extrahepatic ducts, and duodenum. In the case of cystic duct obstruction, a positive study fails to demonstrate filling of the gallbladder. The sensitivity and specificity of this study are high, with results approaching 90 to 100 and 90 to 95 percent, respectively.[99, 115] The test may be augmented by attempts to stimulate gallbladder contraction with a cholecystokinin analogue or the use of intravenous morphine to stimulate sphincter of Oddi contraction. Plain abdominal radiographs and oral cholecystography are tools that are used infrequently in the current clinical environment.

ACALCULOUS CHOLECYSTITIS

Acalculous cholecystitis is a rare, but important, cause of cholecystitis in pediatrics. In general, acalculous gallbladder disease in children occurs in various clinical settings, from congenital gallbladder abnormalities, to idiopathic gallbladder distention without inflammation (acute hydrops of the gallbladder), to acute or chronic cholecystitis. The exact pathogenesis of acute acalculous cholecystitis remains unclear, but stagnation of bile may be an important factor, as evident by several predisposing clinical conditions that lead to bile stasis. In addition, sphincter of Oddi spasm or dysfunction, as occurs after administration of an opiate, could lead to retrograde reflux of inflammatory enzymes or infectious agents. Alternatively, changes in gallbladder vascular supply may weaken the gallbladder mucosa and thereby allow biliary components to damage the gallbladder wall.[40] Acalculous cholecystitis has been associated with many infectious and noninfectious clinical scenarios. Bacterial, viral, and parasitic agents have been implicated in the setting of acalculous cholecystitis. In addition, gallstones or biliary microlithiasis missed by standard diagnostic evaluations may lead one to the presumptive diagnosis of acalculous cholecystitis, which ultimately turns out to be caused by stones or sludge.

Reports of true acalculous disease have been described with systemic infection by *Salmonella* strains, *Mycoplasma pneumoniae,* leptospirosis, brucellosis, and Rocky Mountain spotted fever, as well as group A *Streptococcus,* group B *Streptococcus,* and *Staphylococcus aureus* sepsis.[4, 5, 25, 50, 54, 92, 140, 150, 162] In immunosuppressed hosts, acalculous cholecystitis has been reported in fungal infections with *Candida* or *Aspergillus* or in parasitic infections with *Giardia* and *Cryptosporidium.*[100] Noninfectious systemic diseases associated with acalculous cholecystitis or hydrops include neoplastic disease, namely, leukemia, Henoch-Schönlein purpura, and Kawasaki disease.[14, 55, 90] Table 55–3 lists several conditions in which acalculous cholecystitis has been reported.[58, 60, 119, 143, 151, 152]

TABLE 55–3 ■ CONDITIONS ASSOCIATED WITH ACALCULOUS GALLBLADDER DISEASE

Critically ill intensive care unit patients
Postoperative state (e.g., cardiac surgery)
Burns
Traumatic spinal cord injury
Total parenteral nutrition
Biliary tract anomaly (e.g., choledochal cyst)
Infectious agents
Sepsis
Oncology patients undergoing chemotherapy
Bone marrow transplantation
Systemic inflammatory states
  Crohn disease, Kawasaki disease, lupus

The clinical findings are similar to those of patients with calculous disease, with right upper quadrant pain, nausea, vomiting, and fever being the most common symptoms. Leukocytosis, jaundice, or a palpable right upper quadrant mass also may be present.[154] The most common setting for acalculous disease occurs in critically ill or chronically ill patients with concurrent acute or chronic symptoms. A high degree of clinical suspicion is crucial in making the diagnosis in these populations because findings suggestive of cholecystitis often are obscured by the patient's systemic disease. The most common sonographic finding is a thickened gallbladder wall and a possible sonographic Murphy sign. Gallbladder distention, sludge, or pericholecystic fluid also may be found on ultrasound.[59] In addition to ultrasonography, the HIDA scan is an important tool in the evaluation of acalculous cholecystitis. Failure to visualize the gallbladder on scintigraphy, along with a low ejection fraction in response to a cholecystokinin analogue, is suggestive of acalculous disease.[89, 99, 112, 165]

MANAGEMENT

Management strategies for gallstone disease in children are variable and contingent on individual clinical scenarios. Silent gallstones, which are asymptomatic and often detected incidentally by ultrasound, can be monitored conservatively and sonographically without emergency or elective surgery. Despite multiple reports of conservative management of adults with asymptomatic stones, no such guidelines are available for children. Patients with hemolytic disease in whom gallstones are detected should be considered for early cholecystectomy, although this practice still is controversial.[2, 46, 62, 93, 159] In patients with sickle-cell anemia, the benefit of timely surgery may outweigh the morbidity of associated abdominal pain crises, as well as the overall morbidity and mortality of surgery in these patients, which increases with age.

In acute calculous cholecystitis, surgery is the mainstay of therapy. Patients should be admitted to the hospital for monitoring, intravenous hydration, and pain control. Antibiotic therapy often is initiated, even without clinical evidence of sepsis or perforation. The choice of antibiotics is similar to that for cholangitis and typically covers gut luminal flora, for example, a semisynthetic penicillin such as piperacillin or mezlocillin plus an aminoglycoside.[47, 161] Surgical treatment may be limited to cholecystotomy, especially in chronically ill children with a high risk for development of complications. In general, however, early cholecystectomy should be performed in patients with acute cholecystitis secondary to gallstone disease. Laparoscopic procedures are used more widely in experienced pediatric surgical centers and are associated with positive outcomes in children as well as adults.

Optimal management of acalculous cholecystitis has not been investigated fully, primarily because of the lack of a diagnostic standard and varied patient population base. This deficiency leads to an individualized approach that typically starts conservatively with observation but may involve removal of oral feeding and institution of intravenous hydration and antibiotics, or it may lead to the use of more invasive management with cholecystectomy or biliary manometrics via ERCP.[39, 59] Attempts should be made to diagnose and treat any underlying condition in such patients. A recent treatment protocol supports close monitoring of these patients with frequent examination, ultrasonography, and blood tests to determine whether the need for cholecystectomy or ERCP appears likely. If ultrasound shows improving findings, conservative management is continued with close follow-up. If biliary dyskinesia is suspected secondary to sphincter of Oddi dysfunction, ERCP offers a diagnostic and therapeutic option at experienced centers.[33, 111, 155]

COMPLICATIONS

Acute cholecystitis may lead to complications even if recognized in timely fashion. An inflamed, obstructed gallbladder may wall off and form an intraluminal abscess or empyema. Perforation of the gallbladder is the most frequent complication. A localized perforation may develop into a pericholecystic abscess that is palpable as a tender right upper quadrant mass on examination. Free perforation with peritonitis is associated with a 30 percent mortality rate but is found in only a small minority of patients, estimated at 1 to 2 percent of adult patients.[77] In each of these situations, prompt surgical intervention along with intravenous hydration and antibiotic therapy is crucial in management. Aside from gallbladder inflammation, complications of gallstone disease may include pancreatitis and choledocholithiasis. Gallstone pancreatitis was a frequent complication of gallstone disease in a series of 50 pediatric patients.[114] Choledocholithiasis with ascending cholangitis, a well-known complication of gallstones, is a rare cause of cholangitis in the pediatric population. Secondary common bile duct stones, usually originating from the gallbladder, can be found in patients with acute cholecystitis by ultrasonography, ERCP, MRCP, or intraoperative cholangiography. The possibility of choledocholithiasis should be considered in any patient with known gallstone disease who has increasing jaundice, fever, and right upper quadrant pain, and it requires urgent clinical investigation and decompression, typically via ERCP.[146]

REFERENCES

1. Allendorph, M., Werlin, S. L., Geenen, J. E., et al.: Endoscopic retrograde cholangiopancreatography in children. J. Pediatr. *110*:206–211, 1987.
2. Al-Mulhim, A. S., Al-Mulhim, F. M., and Al-Suwaiygh, A. A.: The role of laparoscopic cholecystectomy in the management of acute cholecystitis in patients with sickle cell disease. Am. J. Surg. *183*:668–672, 2002.
3. Angelico, M., and Della Guardia, P.: Review article: Hepatobiliary complications associated with total parenteral nutrition. Aliment. Pharmacol. Ther. *14*(Suppl 2):54–57, 2000.
4. Ashley, D., Vade, A., and Challapalli, M.: Brucellosis with acute acalculous cholecystitis. Pediatr. Infect. Dis. J. *19*:1112–1113, 2000.
5. Ayite, A., Etey, K., Tchatagba, K., et al.: [Acute acalculous cholecystitis of typhoid origin. A report of 5 cases.] Tunis Med. *74*:257–260, 1996.
6. Billhartz, L. E.: Gallstone disease and its complications. *In* Feldman, M. H. S., and Scharschmidt, B. F. (eds.): Sleisenger & Fordtran's Gastrointestinal and Liver Disease: Pathophysiology, Diagnosis, Management. 6th ed., Vol. 1. Philadelphia, W. B. Saunders, 1998.
7. Boey, J. H., and Way, L. W.: Acute cholangitis. Ann. Surg. *191*:264–270, 1980.
8. Bond, L. R., Hatty, S. R., Horn, M. E., et al.: Gall stones in sickle cell disease in the United Kingdom. B. M. J. *295*:234–236, 1987.
9. Bouche, H., Housset, C., Dumont, J. L., et al.: AIDS-related cholangitis: Diagnostic features and course in 15 patients. J. Hepatol. *17*:34–39, 1993.
10. Bowles, B. J., Abdul-Ghani, A., Zhang, J., et al.: Fifteen years' experience with an antirefluxing biliary drainage valve. J. Pediatr. Surg *34*:1711–1714, 1999.
11. Brook, I., and Altman, R. P.: The significance of anaerobic bacteria in biliary tract infection after hepatic portoenterostomy for biliary atresia. Surgery *95*:281–283, 1984.
12. Brown, S. J., and Desmond, P. V.: Hepatotoxicity of antimicrobial agents. Semin. Liver Dis. *22*:157–167, 2002.
13. Burgart, L. J.: Cholangitis in viral disease. Mayo Clin. Proc. *73*:479–482, 1998.
14. Buyukasik, Y., Kosar, A., Demiroglu, H., et al.: Acalculous acute cholecystitis in leukemia. J. Clin. Gastroenterol. *27*:146–148, 1998.
15. Cappell, M. S.: Endoscopic retrograde cholangiopancreatography with endoscopic sphincterotomy for symptomatic choledocholithiasis after recent myocardial infarction. Am. J. Gastroenterol. *91*:1827–1831, 1996.
16. Carpenter, H. A.: Bacterial and parasitic cholangitis. Mayo Clin. Proc. *73*:473–478, 1998.
17. Cello, J. P.: Acquired immunodeficiency syndrome cholangiopathy: Spectrum of disease. Am. J. Med. *86*:539–546, 1989.
18. Chaudhary, A., Dhar, P., Sachdev, A., et al.: Choledochal cysts—differences in children and adults. Br. J. Surg. *83*:186–188, 1996.
19. Chaudhary, S., and Turner, R. B.: Trimethoprim-sulfamethoxazole for cholangitis following hepatic portoenterostomy for biliary atresia. J. Pediatr. *99*:656–658, 1981.
20. Chen, C. C., Chang, P. Y., and Chen, C. L.: Refractory cholangitis after Kasai's operation caused by candidiasis: A case report. J. Pediatr. Surg. *21*:736–737, 1986.
21. Chitturi, S., and George, J.: Hepatotoxicity of commonly used drugs: Nonsteroidal anti-inflammatory drugs, antihypertensives, antidiabetic agents, anticonvulsants, lipid-lowering agents, psychotropic drugs. Semin. Liver Dis. *22*:169–183, 2002.
22. Chung, R. T., and Sheffer, E. C.: Case 28-2001—a 44-year-old woman with chills, fever, jaundice, and hepatic abscesses. N. Engl. J. Med. *345*:817–823, 2001.
23. Desmet, V. J.: Congenital diseases of intrahepatic bile ducts: Variations on the theme "ductal plate malformation." Hepatology *16*:1069–1083, 1992.
24. Desmet, V. J.: Ludwig symposium on biliary disorders—part I. Pathogenesis of ductal plate abnormalities. Mayo Clin. Proc. *73*:80–89, 1998.
25. Dickinson, S. J., Corley, G., Santulli, T. V.: Acute cholecystitis as a sequel of scarlet fever. Am. J. Dis. Child. *121*:331–333, 1971.
26. Donovan, J. M.: Physical and metabolic factors in gallstone pathogenesis. Gastroenterol. Clin. North Am. *28*:75–97, 1999.
27. Dooley, J. S., Hamilton-Miller, J. M., Brumfitt, W., et al.: Antibiotics in the treatment of biliary infection. Gut *25*:988–998, 1984.
28. Ducreux, M., Buffet, C., Lamy, P., et al.: Diagnosis and prognosis of AIDS-related cholangitis. AIDS *9*:875–880, 1995.
29. Dunham, E. C.: Septicemia in the newborn. Am. J. Dis. Child. *45*:229–253, 1933.
30. Ecoffey, C., Rothman, E., Bernard, O., et al.: Bacterial cholangitis after surgery for biliary atresia. J. Pediatr. *111*:824–829, 1987.
31. Elsakr, R., Johnson, D. A., Younes, Z., et al.: Antimicrobial treatment of intra-abdominal infections. Dig. Dis. *16*:47–60, 1998.
32. Fagundes-Neto, U., Schettini, S. T., Wehba, J., et al.: Caroli's disease in childhood: Report of two new cases. J. Pediatr. Gastroenterol. Nutr. *2*:708–711, 1983.
33. Fogel, E. L., Eversman, D., Jamidar, P., et al.: Sphincter of Oddi dysfunction: pancreaticobiliary sphincterotomy with pancreatic stent placement has a lower rate of pancreatitis than biliary sphincterotomy alone. Endoscopy *34*:280–285, 2002.
34. Fonkalsrud, E. W.: Choledochal cysts. Surg. Clin. North Am. *53*:1275–1281, 1973.
35. Friesen, C. A., and Roberts, C. C.: Cholelithiasis. Clinical characteristics in children. Case analysis and literature review. Clin. Pediatr. (Phila.) *28*:294–298, 1989.
36. Ganschow, R.: Cholelithiasis in pediatric organ transplantation: Detection and management. Pediatr. Transplant. *6*:91–96, 2002.
37. Garcia-Ruiz, J. C., Hernandez, I., Munoz, F., et al.: Cholangitis due to *Aspergillus fumigatus* in a patient with acute leukemia. Clin. Infect. Dis. *26*:228–229, 1998.
38. Gerecht, W. B., Henry, N. K., Hoffman, W. W., et al.: Prospective randomized comparison of mezlocillin therapy alone with combined ampicillin and gentamicin therapy for patients with cholangitis. Arch. Intern. Med. *149*:1279–1284, 1989.
39. Glenn, F.: Acute acalculous cholecystitis. Ann. Surg. *189*:458–465, 1979.
40. Glenn, F., and Becker, C. G.: Acute acalculous cholecystitis. An increasing entity. Ann. Surg. *195*:131–136, 1982.

41. Gottrand, F., Bernard, O., Hadchouel, M., et al.: Late cholangitis after successful surgical repair of biliary atresia. Am. J. Dis. Child. *145*:213–215, 1991.
42. Grant, A., Sargent, C., Weller, I. V., et al.: Disseminated cytomegalovirus infection. Genitourin. Med. *68*:75–79, 1992.
43. Greenberg, M., Kangarloo, H., Cochran, S. T., et al.: The ultrasonographic diagnosis of cholecystitis and cholelithiasis in children. Radiology *137*:745–749, 1980.
44. Gremse, D. A., Bucuvalas, J. C., and Bongiovanni, G. L.: Papillary stenosis and sclerosing cholangitis in an immunodeficient child. Gastroenterology *96*:1600–1603, 1989.
45. Gruber, P. J., Silverman, R. A., Gottesfeld, S., et al.: Presence of fever and leukocytosis in acute cholecystitis. Ann. Emerg. Med. *28*:273–277, 1996.
46. Haberkern, C. M., Neumayr, L. D., Orringer, E. P., et al.: Cholecystectomy in sickle cell anemia patients: Perioperative outcome of 364 cases from the National Preoperative Transfusion Study. Preoperative Transfusion in Sickle Cell Disease Study Group. Blood *89*:1533–1542, 1997.
47. Hanau, L. H., and Steigbigel, N. H.: Acute (ascending) cholangitis. Infect. Dis. Clin. North Am. *14*:521–546, 2000.
48. Harjai, M. M., and Bal, R. K.: Caroli syndrome. Pediatr. Surg. Int. *16*:431–432, 2000.
49. Heubi, J., Lewis, L. G., and Pohl, J.: Diseases of the gallbladder in infancy, childhood, and adolescence. *In* Frederick, J., Suchy, M. D., Ronald, J., et al. (eds.): Liver Disease in Children. 2nd ed., Vol. 1. Philadelphia, Lippincott Williams & Williams, 2001, pp. 343–362.
50. Hirata, K., Torigoe, T., Fukuda, M., et al.: [A case of acute acalculous cholecystitis due to *Salmonella.*] Nippon Shokakibyo Gakkai Zasshi *93*:137–140, 1996.
51. Hitch, D. C., and Lilly, J. R.: Identification, quantification, and significance of bacterial growth within the biliary tract after Kasai's operation. J. Pediatr. Surg. *13*:563–569, 1978.
52. Hitch, D. C., Lilly, J. R., Reller, L. B., et al.: Biliary flora and antimicrobial concentrations after Kasai's operation. J. Pediatr. Surg. *14*:648–652, 1979.
53. Honna, T., Tsuchida, Y., Kawarasaki, H., et al.: Further experience with the antireflux valve to prevent ascending cholangitis in biliary atresia. J. Pediatr. Surg. *32*:1450–1452, 1997.
54. Horii, Y., Sugimoto, T., Sakamoto, I., et al.: Acute acalculous cholecystitis complicating *Mycoplasma pneumoniae* infection. Clin. Pediatr. (Phila.) *31*:376–378, 1992.
55. Hou, J. W., Chang, M. H., Wu, M. H., et al.: Kawasaki disease complicated by gallbladder hydrops mimicking acute abdomen: A report of three cases. Zhonghua Min Guo Xiao Er Ke Yi Xue Hui Za Zhi *30*:52–60, 1989.
56. Houwen, R. H., Bijleveld, C. M., and de Vries-Hospers, H. G.: Ciprofloxacin for cholangitis after hepatic portoenterostomy. Lancet *1*:1367, 1987.
57. Houwen, R. H., Zwierstra, R. P., Severijnen, R. S., et al.: Prognosis of extrahepatic biliary atresia. Arch. Dis. Child. *64*:214–218, 1989.
58. Hyams, J. S., Baker, E., Schwartz, A. N., et al.: Acalculous cholecystitis in Crohn's disease. J. Adolesc. Health Care *10*:151–154, 1989.
59. Imamoglu, M., Sarihan, H., Sari, A., et al.: Acute acalculous cholecystitis in children: Diagnosis and treatment. J. Pediatr. Surg. *37*:36–39, 2002.
60. Imhof, M., Raunest, J., Ohmann, C., et al.: Acute acalculous cholecystitis complicating trauma: A prospective sonographic study. World J. Surg. *16*:1160–1165, 1992.
61. Jacobs, R. F.: Ceftriaxone-associated cholecystitis. Pediatr. Infect. Dis. J. 7:434–436, 1988.
62. Johna, S., Shaul, D., Taylor, E. W., et al.: Laparoscopic management of gallbladder disease in children and adolescents. J. S. L. S. *1*:241–245, 1997.
63. Joseph, V. T.: Surgical techniques and long-term results in the treatment of choledochal cyst. J. Pediatr. Surg. *25*:782–787, 1990.
64. Jung, G., Benz-Bohm, G., Kugel, H., et al.: MR cholangiography in children with autosomal recessive polycystic kidney disease. Pediatr. Radiol. *29*:463–466, 1999.
65. Kanter, M. A., and Geelhoed, G. W.: Biliary antibiotics: Clinical utility in biliary surgery. South. Med. J. *80*:1007–1015, 1987.
66. Karrer, F. M., Lilly, J. R., Stewart, B. A., et al.: Biliary atresia registry, 1976 to 1989. J. Pediatr. Surg. *25*:1076–1080, 1990.
67. Kasai, M. A., and Suzuki, S.: A new operation for "non correctable" biliary atresia: hepatic porto-enterostomy. Shujyutsu *13*:733–739, 1959.
68. Keighley, M. R., Drysdale, R. B., Quoraishi, A. H., et al.: Antibiotic treatment of biliary sepsis. Surg. Clin. North Am. *55*:1379–1390, 1975.
69. Kelly, D. A.: Liver complications of pediatric parenteral nutrition—epidemiology. Nutrition *14*:153–157, 1998.
70. Khuroo, M. S.: Ascariasis. Gastroenterol. Clin. North Am. *25*:553–577, 1996.
71. Ko, C. W., Sekijima, J. H., and Lee, S. P.: Biliary sludge. Ann. Intern. Med. *130*:301–311, 1999.
72. Kobayashi, A., Utsunomiya, T., Obe, Y., et al.: Ascending cholangitis after successful surgical repair of biliary atresia. Arch. Dis. Child. *48*:697–703, 1973.
73. Kosloske, A. M.: Acute abdomen due to acute cholangitis in a leukemic child. Pediatrics *56*:469–471, 1975.
74. Kubota, A., Yonekura, T., Hoki, M., et al.: Total parenteral nutrition–associated intrahepatic cholestasis in infants: 25 years' experience. J. Pediatr. Surg. *35*:1049–1051, 2000.
75. Kuhls, T. L., and Jackson, M. A.: Diagnosis and treatment of the febrile child following hepatic portoenterostomy. Pediatr. Infect. Dis. *4*:487–490, 1985.
76. Lammert, F., Carey, M. C., and Paigen, B.: Chromosomal organization of candidate genes involved in cholesterol gallstone formation: A murine gallstone map. Gastroenterology *120*:221–238, 2001.
77. Lee, S., and Ko, C.: Gallstones. *In* Yamada, T. (ed.): Textbook of Gastroenterology. 3rd ed., Vol. 2. Philadelphia, Lippincott Williams & Wilkins, 1999, pp. 2258–2280.
78. Lefkowitch, J. H.: Pathology of AIDS-related liver disease. Dig. Dis. *12*:321–330, 1994.
79. Levy, J., Espanol-Boren, T., Thomas, C., et al.: Clinical spectrum of X-linked hyper-IgM syndrome. J. Pediatr. *131*:47–54, 1997.
80. Lewis, R. T., Goodall, R. G., Marien, B., et al.: Biliary bacteria, antibiotic use, and wound infection in surgery of the gallbladder and common bile duct. Arch. Surg. *122*:44–47, 1987.
81. Lillemoe, K. D.: Surgical treatment of biliary tract infections. Am. Surg. *66*:138–144, 2000.
82. Lilly, J. R., and Hitch, D. C.: Postoperative ascending cholangitis following portoenterostomy for biliary atresia: Measures for control. World J. Surg. 2:581–585, 1978.
83. Lipschitz, B., Berdon, W. E., Defelice, A. R., et al.: Association of congenital hepatic fibrosis with autosomal dominant polycystic kidney disease. Report of a family with review of literature. Pediatr. Radiol. *23*:131–133, 1993.
84. Lipsett, P. A., and Pitt, H. A.: Acute cholangitis. Surg. Clin. North Am. *70*:1297–1312, 1990.
85. Liu, K. J., Atten, M. J., and Donahue, P. E.: Cholestasis in patients with acquired immunodeficiency syndrome: A surgeon's perspective. Am. Surg. *63*:519–524, 1997.
86. Livingston, E. H.: Endoscopic biliary drainage for acute cholangitis. N. Engl. J. Med. *327*:1176, 1992.
87. Lopez-Santamaria, M., Martinez, L., Hierro, L., et al.: Late biliary complications in pediatric liver transplantation. J. Pediatr. Surg. *34*:316–320, 1999.
88. MacCarty, R. L., LaRusso, N. F., Wiesner, R. H., et al.: Primary sclerosing cholangitis: Findings on cholangiography and pancreatography. Radiology *149*:39–44, 1983.
89. Mariat, G., Mahul, P., Prev t, N., et al.: Contribution of ultrasonography and cholescintigraphy to the diagnosis of acute acalculous cholecystitis in intensive care unit patients. Intensive Care Med. *26*:1658–1663, 2000.
90. McCrindle, B. W., Wood, R. A., and Nussbaum, A. R.: Henoch-Schönlein syndrome. Unusual manifestations with hydrops of the gallbladder. Clin. Pediatr. (Phila.) *27*:254–256, 1988.
91. McDiarmid, S. V.: Management of the pediatric liver transplant patient. Liver Transpl. *7*(Suppl):77–86, 2001.
92. McKiernan, J., O'Brien, D. J., and Dundon, S.: Leptospirosis and acalculous cholecystitis. Ir. Med. J. *69*:71–72, 1976.
93. Miltenburg, D. M., Schaffer, R., 3rd, Breslin, T., et al.: Changing indications for pediatric cholecystectomy. Pediatrics *105*:1250–1253, 2000.
94. Mortele, K. J., McTavish, J., and Ros, P. R.: Current techniques of computed tomography. Helical CT, multidetector CT, and 3D reconstruction. Clin. Liver Dis. *6*:29–52, 2002.
95. Moseley, R. H.: Sepsis and cholestasis. Clin. Liver Dis. *3*:465–475, 1999.
96. Mukhopadhyay, S., Monga, A., Rana, S. S., et al.: AIDS cholangiopathy as initial presentation of HIV infection. Trop. Gastroenterol. *22*:29–30, 2001.
97. Muller, E. L., Pitt, H. A., Thompson, J. E., Jr., et al.: Antibiotics in infections of the biliary tract. Surg. Gynecol. Obstet. *165*:285–292, 1987.
98. Muraji, T., and Higashimoto, Y.: The improved outlook for biliary atresia with corticosteroid therapy. J. Pediatr. Surg. *32*:1103–1106, 1997.
99. Nadel, H. R.: Hepatobiliary scintigraphy in children. Semin. Nucl. Med. *26*:25–42, 1996.
100. Nash, J. A., and Cohen, S. A.: Gallbladder and biliary tract disease in AIDS. Gastroenterol. Clin. North Am. *26*:323–335, 1997.
101. Nilsson, S.: Gallbladder disease and sex hormones. A statistical study. Acta Chir. Scand. *132*:275–279, 1966.
102. Novak: Bacterial, parasitic, and fungal infections of the liver. *In* Frederick, J., Suchy, R. J. S., and Balistreri, W. F. (eds.): Liver Disease in Children. Philadelphia, Lippincott Williams & Wilkins, 2001.
103. Odievre, M., Valayer, J., Razemon-Pinta, M., et al.: Hepatic portoenterostomy or cholecystostomy in the treatment of extrahepatic biliary atresia. A study of 49 cases. J. Pediatr. *88*:774–779, 1976.

104. Odom, F. C., Oliver, B. B., Kline, M., et al.: Gallbladder disease in patients 20 years of age and under. South. Med. J. *69*:1299–1300, 1976.
105. Oh, M., Hobeldin, M., Chen, T., et al.: The Kasai procedure in the treatment of biliary atresia. J. Pediatr. Surg. *30*:1077–1080, 1995.
106. Ohi, R.: Surgery for biliary atresia. Liver *21*:175–182, 2001.
107. Onuchic, L. F., Furu, L., Nagasawa, Y., et al.: PKHD1, the polycystic kidney and hepatic disease 1 gene, encodes a novel large protein containing multiple immunoglobulin-like plexin-transcription-factor domains and parallel beta-helix 1 repeats. Am. J. Hum. Genet. *70*:1305–1317, 2002.
108. Patriquin, H. B., DiPietro, M., Barber, F. E., et al.: Sonography of thickened gallbladder wall: Causes in children. A. J. R. Am. J. Roentgenol. *141*:57–60, 1983.
109. Pessa, M. E., Hawkins, I. F., and Vogel, S. B.: The treatment of acute cholangitis. Percutaneous transhepatic biliary drainage before definitive therapy. Ann. Surg. *205*:389–392, 1987.
110. Poddar, U., Thapa, B. R., Chhabra, M., et al.: Choledochal cysts in infants and children. Indian Pediatr. *35*:613–618, 1998.
111. Ponchon, T., and Pilleul, F.: Diagnostic ERCP. Endoscopy *34*:29–42, 2002.
112. Prevot, N., Mariat, G., Mahul, P., et al.: Contribution of cholescintigraphy to the early diagnosis of acute acalculous cholecystitis in intensive-care-unit patients. Eur. J. Nucl. Med. *26*:1317–1325, 1999.
113. Reddy, S. I., and Grace, N. D.: Liver imaging. A hepatologist's perspective. Clin. Liver Dis. *6*:297–310, ix, 2002.
114. Reif, S., Sloven, D. G., and Lebenthal, E.: Gallstones in children. Characterization by age, etiology, and outcome. Am. J. Dis. Child. *145*:105–108, 1991.
115. Rescorla, F. J.: Cholelithiasis, cholecystitis, and common bile duct stones. Curr. Opin. Pediatr. *9*:276–282, 1997.
116. Rescorla, F. J., and Grosfeld, J. L.: Cholecystitis and cholelithiasis in children. Semin. Pediatr. Surg. *1*:98–106, 1992.
117. Rha, S. Y., Stovroff, M. C., Glick, P. L., et al.: Choledochal cysts: A ten year experience. Am. Surg. *62*:30–34, 1996.
118. Roberts, E. A.: Primary sclerosing cholangitis in children. J. Gastroenterol. Hepatol. *14*:588–593, 1999.
119. Romero Ganuza, F. J., La Banda, G., Montalvo, R., et al.: Acute acalculous cholecystitis in patients with acute traumatic spinal cord injury. Spinal Cord *35*:124–128, 1997.
120. Ros, P. R., and Mortele, K. J.: Hepatic imaging. An overview. Clin. Liver Dis. *6*:1–16, 2002.
121. Roseau, G., Palazzo, L., Dumontier, I., et al.: Endoscopic ultrasonography in the evaluation of pediatric digestive diseases: Preliminary results. Endoscopy *30*:477–481, 1998.
122. Roslyn, J. J., Pitt, H. A., Mann, L. L., et al.: Gallbladder disease in patients on long-term parenteral nutrition. Gastroenterology *84*:148–154, 1983.
123. Rothenberg, S. S., Schroter, G. P., Karrer, F. M., et al.: Cholangitis after the Kasai operation for biliary atresia. J. Pediatr. Surg *24*:729–732, 1989.
124. Rusin, J. A., Sivit, C. J., Rakusan, T. A., et al.: AIDS-related cholangitis in children: Sonographic findings. A. J. R. Am. J. Roentgenol. *159*:626–627, 1992.
125. Ryckman, F. C., Alonso, M. H., Bucuvalas, J. C., et al.: Long-term survival after liver transplantation. J. Pediatr. Surg. *34*:845–849, 1999.
126. Saharia, P. C., and Cameron, J. L.: Clinical management of acute cholangitis. Surg. Gynecol. Obstet. *142*:369–372, 1976.
127. Saing, H., Han, H., Chan, K. L., et al.: Early and late results of excision of choledochal cysts. J. Pediatr. Surg. *32*:1563–1566, 1997.
128. Saint-Vil, D., Luks, F. I., Lebel, P., et al.: Infectious complications of pediatric liver transplantation. J. Pediatr. Surg. *26*:908–913, 1991.
129. Sama, C., Labate, A. M., Taroni, F., et al.: Epidemiology and natural history of gallstone disease. Semin. Liver Dis. *10*:149–158, 1990.
130. Samuel, M., and Spitz, L.: Choledochal cyst: Varied clinical presentations and long-term results of surgery. Eur. J. Pediatr. Surg. *6*:78–81, 1996.
131. Sandhu, I. S., Jarvis, C., and Everson, G. T.: Total parenteral nutrition and cholestasis. Clin. Liver Dis. *3*:489–508, viii, 1999.
132. Sarnaik, S., Slovis, T. L., Corbett, D. P., et al.: Incidence of cholelithiasis in sickle cell anemia using the ultrasonic gray-scale technique. J. Pediatr. *96*:1005–1008, 1980.
133. Scott, A. J.: Bacteria and disease of the biliary tract. Gut *12*:487–492, 1971.
134. Senaati, S., Gumruk, F. U., Delbakhsh, P., et al.: Gallbladder pathology in pediatric beta-thalassemic patients. A prospective ultrasonographic study. Pediatr. Radiol. *23*:357–359, 1993.
135. Shafer, A. D., Ashley, J. V., Goodwin, C. D., et al.: A new look at the multifactoral etiology of gallbladder disease in children. Am. Surg. *49*:314–319, 1983.
136. Shah, S. K., Mutignani, M., and Costamagna, G.: Therapeutic biliary endoscopy. Endoscopy *34*:43–53, 2002.
137. Sharma, A. K., Wakhlu, A., and Sharma, S. S.: The role of endoscopic retrograde cholangiopancreatography in the management of choledochal cysts in children. J. Pediatr. Surg. *30*:65–67, 1995.
138. Shen, G. K., Tsen, A. C., Hunter, G. C., et al.: Surgical treatment of symptomatic biliary stones in patients with cystic fibrosis. Am. Surg. *61*:814–819, 1995.
139. Sindermann, J., Foerster, E., and Kienast, J.: Severe hepatobiliary complication in a patient with acute promyelocytic leukemia treated with all-trans retinoic acid. Acta Oncol. *35*:499–501, 1996.
140. Singh, U. K., and Suman, S.: *Salmonella* cholecystitis in a neonate. Ann. Trop. Paediatr. *19*:211–213, 1999.
141. Snyder, W. A. H.: Lifespan in untreated biliary atresia. Surgery *54*:373–375, 1963.
142. Soetikno, R. M., Montes, H., and Carr-Locke, D. L.: Endoscopic management of choledocholithiasis. J. Clin. Gastroenterol. *27*:296–305, 1998.
143. Still, J., Scheirer, R., and Law, E.: Acute cholecystectomy performed through cultured epithelial autografts in a patient with burn injuries: A case report. J. Burn Care Rehabil. *17*:429–431, 1996.
144. Sudan, D. L., Shaw, B. W., Jr., and Langnas, A. N.: Causes of late mortality in pediatric liver transplant recipients. Ann. Surg. *227*:289–295, 1998.
145. Sung, J. Y., Shaffer, E. A., Olson, M. E., et al.: Bacterial invasion of the biliary system by way of the portal-venous system. Hepatology *14*:313–317, 1991.
146. Tagge, E. P., Tarnasky, P. R., Chandler, J., et al.: Multidisciplinary approach to the treatment of pediatric pancreaticobiliary disorders. J. Pediatr. Surg. *32*:158–164, 1997.
147. Takano, K., Iwafuchi, M., Uchiyama, M., et al.: Studies on intestinal motility and mechanism of cholangitis after biliary reconstruction. J. Pediatr. Surg. *24*:1225–1231, 1989.
148. Takiff, H., and Fonkalsrud, E. W.: Gallbladder disease in childhood. Am. J. Dis. Child. *138*:565–568, 1984.
149. Teng, R., Yokohata, K., Utsunomiya, N., et al.: Endoscopic retrograde cholangiopancreatography in infants and children. J. Gastroenterol. *35*:39–42, 2000.
150. Thambidorai, C. R., Shyamala, J., Sarala, R., et al.: Acute acalculous cholecystitis associated with enteric fever in children. Pediatr. Infect. Dis. J. *14*:812–813, 1995.
151. Thurston, W. A., Kelly, E. N., and Silver, M. M.: Acute acalculous cholecystitis in a premature infant treated with parenteral nutrition. C. M. A. J. *135*:332–334, 1986.
152. Toursarkissian, B., Kearney, P. A., Holley, D. T., et al.: Biliary sludging in critically ill trauma patients. South. Med. J. *88*:420–424, 1995.
153. Trauner, M., Fickert, P., and Stauber, R. E.: Inflammation-induced cholestasis. J. Gastroenterol. Hepatol. *14*:946–959, 1999.
154. Tsakayannis, D. E., Kozakewich, H. P., and Lillehei, C. W.: Acalculous cholecystitis in children. J. Pediatr. Surg. *31*:127–130, 1996.
155. Tzovaras, G., and Rowlands, B. J.: Diagnosis and treatment of sphincter of Oddi dysfunction. Br. J. Surg. *85*:588–595, 1998.
156. van den Hazel, S. J., Speelman, P., Tytgat, G. N., et al.: Successful treatment of recurrent cholangitis with antibiotic maintenance therapy. Eur. J. Clin. Microbiol. Infect. Dis. *13*:662–665, 1994.
157. Wade, J. J., Rolando, N., Hayllar, K., et al.: Bacterial and fungal infections after liver transplantation: An analysis of 284 patients. Hepatology *21*:1328–1336, 1995.
158. Waechter, F. L., Sampaio, J. A., Pinto, R. D., et al.: The role of liver transplantation in patients with Caroli's disease. Hepatogastroenterology *48*:672–674, 2001.
159. Walker, T. M., Hambleton, I. R., and Serjeant, G. R.: Gallstones in sickle cell disease: Observations from The Jamaican Cohort Study. J. Pediatr. *136*:80–85, 2000.
160. Wesdorp, I., Bosman, D., de Graaff, A., et al.: Clinical presentations and predisposing factors of cholelithiasis and sludge in children. J. Pediatr. Gastroenterol. Nutr. *31*:411–417, 2000.
161. Westphal, J. F., and Brogard, J. M.: Biliary tract infections: A guide to drug treatment. Drugs *57*:81–91, 1999.
162. Wong, M. L., Kaplan, S., Dunkle, L. M., et al.: Leptospirosis: A childhood disease. J. Pediatr. *90*:532–537, 1977.
163. Wu, E. T., Chen, H. L., Ni, Y. H., et al.: Bacterial cholangitis in patients with biliary atresia: Impact on short-term outcome. Pediatr. Surg. Int. *17*:390–395, 2001.
164. Yabut, B., Werlin, S. L., Havens, P., et al.: Endoscopic retrograde cholangiopancreatography in children with HIV infection. J. Pediatr. Gastroenterol. Nutr. *23*:624–627, 1996.
165. Ziessman, H. A.: Cholecystokinin cholescintigraphy: Clinical indications and proper methodology. Radiol. Clin. North Am. *39*:997–1006, ix, 2001.
166. Zimmon, D. S.: The management of common duct stones. Adv. Intern. Med. *31*:379–393, 1986.

CHAPTER 56

Pyogenic Liver Abscess

SHELDON L. KAPLAN

Pyogenic liver abscesses are encountered infrequently in normal children and generally have been reported in the compromised pediatric host. The rarity of liver abscesses may be explained, in part, by the rich blood supply, unique architecture, and extensive reticuloendothelial system of the liver, all of which present an effective barrier against bacterial invasion.

The precise incidence of pyogenic liver abscesses in children is unknown. Adult patients with hepatic abscesses constitute approximately 8 to 20 cases per 100,000 admissions; a 0.29 to 0.57 percent incidence of liver abscesses has been found in autopsies of adult patients.[10, 43] In an early large series of liver abscesses in children, Dehner and Kissane[9] reported a 0.38 percent incidence at autopsy in patients younger than 15 years; 11 of 27 (41%) patients were younger than 2 years, and 18 of 27 (67%) were younger than 6 years. In a review of admissions to Milwaukee Children's Hospital, Chusid[8] found five children (four of whom were younger than 6 months) with at least one hepatic abscess and estimated an incidence of three cases for every 100,000 admissions. Pineiro-Carrero and Andres[40] estimated an incidence of approximately 25 cases per 100,000 admissions in their pediatric population (11 patients older than 14 years).

Pathogenesis

Bacteria can establish an inflammatory focus in the liver by four major routes. Direct extension from contiguous structures is the most common mode in adults and precedes up to 60 percent of hepatic abscesses in adults.[6, 22, 41, 43] Biliary tract infection (cholangitis, cholecystitis), pancreatitis, and penetrating gastric or duodenal ulcer are examples of diseases associated with liver abscesses caused by extension from a contiguous focus of infection. In a review of this problem at St. Louis Children's Hospital, 3 of 27 children (11%) were considered to have a liver abscess secondary to inflammation of contiguous organs.[9] Although biliary tract disease occurs relatively uncommonly in children, ascending cholangitis is a particularly frequent complication of the hepatic portoenterostomy procedure for congenital biliary atresia and may lead to infections of the liver in such patients.[13] Liver abscesses also may develop as a complication of liver transplantation, especially if technical problems related to vascular supply or biliary drainage develop.[28]

The portal system is the second most common route by which bacteria may reach the liver in adults; 6 to 27 percent of liver abscesses in adults derive from this source.[22, 30, 43] In the newborn period, solitary liver abscesses, especially those caused by gram-negative organisms, have complicated the use of umbilical vein catheterization or have been secondary to omphalitis.[5] Prematurity and necrotizing enterocolitis also are important predisposing conditions.[12]

Portal vein inflammation and bacteremia can be associated with infections within the abdominal cavity. Appendicitis, diverticulitis, perirectal abscesses, regional enteritis, ulcerative colitis, and omphalitis are possible sources of portal vein sepsis.[9] A pyogenic liver abscess may be an unusual complication of an ingested foreign body, with subsequent portal venous bacteremia.[35] Since antibiotics have been available, portal vein inflammation or pylephlebitis has become a less common source of hepatic infection in children.

Systemic bacteremia with hematogenous spread of bacteria to the liver through the hepatic artery appears to be the most common source of liver abscess in children, but it is implicated in less than 20 percent of adult patients. In the St. Louis series, the systemic hematogenous route was responsible for 21 of 27 (78%) cases of liver abscesses.[9] In five of the patients examined before 1940, the bacteremia was associated with infection, which would be considered manageable today (pneumonia, cellulitis, and osteomyelitis). Seven of 13 patients encountered after 1940 had bacteremia associated with leukemia. Anaerobic bacteremia associated with retropharyngeal or peritonsillar abscesses presumably has preceded anaerobic liver abscesses in several children.[7] Likewise, liver abscesses in neonates may be preceded by a systemic bacteremia without evidence of portal or biliary tract involvement.[33]

Liver abscesses occur more frequently in compromised pediatric hosts than in normal children. Johnston and Baehner[23] reported that hepatic or perihepatic abscesses were present in 41 of 92 (45%) patients with chronic granulomatous disease. In a registry of 368 patients with chronic granulomatous disease from the United States, a liver abscess occurred in 27 percent of patients.[51] In addition to functional disorders of phagocytes, chronic neutropenia also predisposes to the development of liver abscesses.[39] Wintch and colleagues[52] noted that 5 of 10 children with hepatic abscesses in their institution had an underlying defect in host defense. Primary hemochromatosis predisposes to multiple liver abscesses caused by *Yersinia enterocolitica* in particular.[48]

Penetrating and nonpenetrating trauma to the liver may lead to liver abscesses, presumably caused by bacterial proliferation within small collections of blood and bile that result from the trauma. Hepatic abscess may be a rare complication of ventriculoperitoneal shunts after penetration of a peritoneal catheter into the liver.[36] This mode of infection has been reported in seven children.[20]

Unexplained or cryptogenic hepatic abscesses are encountered in most series and accounted for 40 to 50 percent of cases in many series.[22] Lee and Block[31] have proposed that these cryptogenic liver abscesses "originate from anaerobic bacterial invasion of hepatic infarcts." This theory is supported by reports that describe pyogenic liver abscesses as a complication of hepatic infarction in patients with sickle-cell anemia.[45] Normal gastrointestinal bacterial flora were isolated from 9 of 11 patients with liver abscesses at the Mayo Clinic. This finding suggested to Lazarchick and associates[30] that unrecognized intra-abdominal collections of pus were responsible. Although the reasons are unclear, diabetes mellitus also predisposes to the development of liver abscesses.[19, 41] Nematode infection with larvae migrating through the liver is thought to be another predisposing factor for the development of pyogenic abscesses in children. The larvae induce liver granulomata that trap bacteria, leading to abscess formation.[38]

Biliary tract disease generally predisposes to the development of multiple liver abscesses. In contrast, blunt trauma to the liver or portal system inflammation most commonly predisposes to a single abscess. In the neonate, liver abscesses may be solitary or multiple because of systemic bacteria.[33, 34] Solitary abscesses are the most common findings in the right lobe of the liver.[30]

Hepatic and splenic abscesses caused by *Candida* species are well described in patients with cancer.[47] Multiple abscesses are typical findings. These organs presumably are infected hematogenously, usually when the host is neutropenic.

Microbiology

Gram-negative organisms have been the predominant isolates from liver abscesses in adults. *Escherichia coli, Klebsiella, Aerobacter, Pseudomonas,* and *Proteus* spp. have been implicated most frequently. Anaerobic organisms also are important; anaerobic organisms were recovered from 45 percent of patients with liver abscesses in the UCLA series.[42] In contrast to the adult experience, Dehner and Kissane[9] reported that 33 percent of liver abscesses in children were caused by *Staphylococcus aureus*, whereas gram-negative organisms were found in only 32 percent. Two or more organisms were recovered from liver abscesses in 52 percent of children. In a review of 96 children (no neonates) with pyogenic liver abscesses, *S. aureus*, gram-negative enterics, and anaerobes were the organisms isolated most commonly, in that order.[26] In neonates, gram-negative enterics are isolated most commonly. Anaerobes, particularly *Fusobacterium necrophorum,* have been isolated from liver abscesses in children without underlying disease.[14] Human rotavirus-like particles were identified in the material aspirated from a liver abscess but were considered a secondary phenomenon and not the primary etiology of the liver abscess.[17] Fungi, particularly *Candida albicans,* have been associated with liver abscesses in children with leukemia and neutropenia who have received parenteral hyperalimentation.[2] Liver or splenic abscesses also may be an unusual complication of brucellosis.[49]

Clinical Manifestations

The clinical manifestations of pyogenic liver abscesses are nonspecific. A high index of suspicion plus an awareness of this illness is necessary to make the diagnosis. A history of preceding abdominal surgery or trauma is helpful when present, as is the knowledge that host response to infection is compromised.

Fever, nausea, vomiting, anorexia, weakness, and malaise are prominent symptoms that may last several weeks. Abdominal or pleuritic pain, weight loss, and diarrhea are less common occurrences. A history of abdominal pain and fever of unknown origin in an otherwise healthy child suggests the diagnosis of pyogenic liver abscess.[25] In contrast, fever often is not observed in the neonate.[12] Patients with a macroscopic or single abscess frequently experience a subacute to chronic course. In contrast, patients with multiple abscesses generally experience a more acute febrile illness.

Hepatomegaly occurs in 40 to 80 percent of patients; abdominal tenderness occurs less frequently. Right upper quadrant tenderness or even a mass may be subtle and not appreciated unless the physician specifically and carefully examines this region. Other physical findings include jaundice (generally associated with biliary tract disease and not liver abscesses), abdominal distention, and evidence of pleuropulmonary involvement (i.e., elevated or fixed hemidiaphragm, rales, and pleural effusion).

Diagnosis

Routine laboratory studies are of little help in attempting to establish a diagnosis. Anemia and leukocytosis are common occurrences. Liver function tests generally reflect underlying disease of the liver itself. These changes generally are not caused by the abscess. When abscesses occur secondary to biliary tract obstruction, alkaline phosphatase and bilirubin concentrations generally are elevated. Transaminase concentrations generally are normal to mildly elevated in most cases. A rapidly enlarging, tender liver in a patient with normal transaminase concentrations should alert the clinician to the possibility of liver abscess. Lazarchick and colleagues[30] found that the serum albumin concentration was the single most important test with regard to prognosis; 14 of 16 patients with a serum albumin level of less than 2 g/dL died.

Blood cultures are positive more commonly in patients with multiple abscesses than in those with solitary abscesses. Overall, however, blood cultures usually are sterile in children with pyogenic liver abscess.

More than 50 percent of adult patients have abnormalities on chest radiography. Atelectasis, pulmonary infiltrates, pleural effusion, and elevated or fixed right hemidiaphragm are the most common findings.

Computed tomography (CT) currently provides the most accurate information concerning the size, location, and number of abscesses within the liver parenchyma[24, 29, 40] (Fig. 56–1). Lesions 1 cm in diameter can be detected by CT. Multiple small abscesses may appear in clusters in a pattern suggesting early coalescence of the abscesses.[21] Liver abscesses appear as areas of low attenuation. The "target" lesions of hepatic candidiasis are not visualized by CT when the patient is neutropenic, and repeated scans may be necessary before these characteristic lesions are observed.[47] Structures contiguous with the liver also are demonstrated by CT; this information is important when a surgical

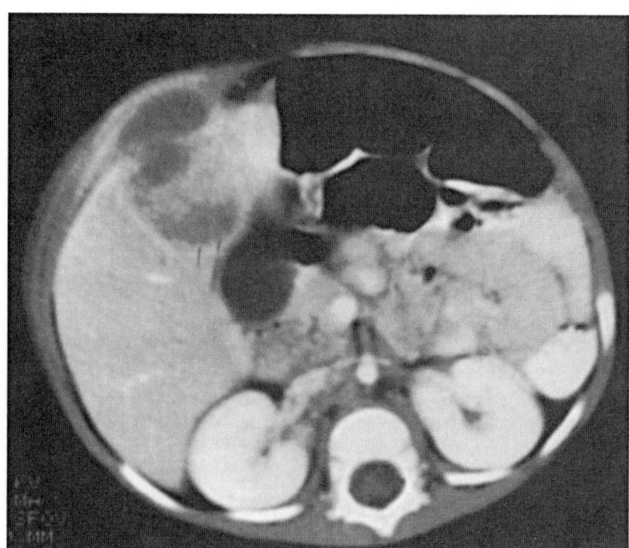

FIGURE 56–1 ■ Abdominal computed tomograph showing a 4- × 5-cm encapsulated, septate, circular mass within the liver. A low-density soft tissue mass is noted in the abdominal wall from apparent extension from the intrahepatic mass.

approach to drainage is being planned. Magnetic resonance imaging does not have any major advantages over CT for detecting or characterizing liver abscess but may demonstrate characteristic features to distinguish an abscess from other focal liver lesions in selected patients.[1, 32] Ultrasonography also is a sensitive technique for detecting liver abscesses, and because it is noninvasive and does not require exposure to radiation, it is recommended for initial evaluation.[27, 29] Hepatic angiography further defines the vascular anatomy in the area of the liver abscess and may provide information necessary for surgical management in selected cases. Nuclear medicine techniques rarely are indicated as a diagnostic method if liver abscess is suspected.

Treatment

Numerous reports have documented that patients with undiagnosed and untreated liver abscesses generally die and that surgical drainage of the solitary pyogenic liver abscess is the key to successful therapy. The choice of extraserous or transperitoneal open drainage or percutaneous closed aspiration depends on the location and size of the abscess and the experience and preference of the surgeon.[16, 22, 37, 43]

Numerous groups have described percutaneous catheter drainage of liver abscesses in adults.[3, 4, 15, 27] A catheter is placed into the cavity under CT or ultrasound guidance; material is aspirated, and once an abscess is documented, a draining catheter is placed. The cavity can be irrigated with saline initially. Criteria for the selection of patients for percutaneous drainage have been established.[15] In general, percutaneous drainage is not indicated for patients with multiple large abscesses or multiloculated abscesses.[22] The optimal route of percutaneous aspiration is directly into the abscess cavity and does not involve any uninfected organs or space. Drainage may proceed for 2 weeks or more or until drainage from the cavity is decreased, the patient is afebrile and improving, and radiography demonstrates that the cavity is becoming smaller.[18] Surgical backup is mandatory when this drainage technique is used because spillage of abscess material into the peritoneal cavity, hemorrhage, and other complications may occur. Percutaneous drainage of liver abscesses in children has been performed successfully, and this technique should be considered an alternative approach to surgical drainage of such abscesses, especially in the right lobe of the liver.[11, 40]

Appropriate antibiotic therapy initially is based on knowledge of the organisms most commonly involved, Gram stain of the purulent material, and culture and susceptibility to antibiotics of the organisms that are recovered. If a hematogenous source of infection is suspected or the host has an immune deficiency disease, *S. aureus* and streptococci are more likely. Biliary tract disease and blunt trauma are associated more frequently with gram-negative aerobic and anaerobic organisms. A logical antibiotic combination for the initial therapy of children with liver abscesses includes a penicillinase-resistant penicillin, such as nafcillin, plus an aminoglycoside. The optimal duration and route of administration of antibiotics for a child with a solitary pyogenic liver abscess that has been drained have not been determined. In general, 2 to 4 weeks of antibiotic therapy administered parenterally, followed by an appropriate oral antibiotic to complete a minimum 4-week total course, should prove adequate. Penicillin, ticarcillin-clavulanate, piperacillin-tazobactam, clindamycin, chloramphenicol, cefoxitin, or metronidazole is administered for anaerobic isolates, depending on susceptibility.

Multiple liver abscesses are more difficult to treat because complete surgical drainage usually is not possible. Prolonged antibiotic therapy plus treatment of any underlying illnesses is the keystone to effective management. Duration of treatment can be modified, depending on the evidence for resolution of the abscesses as determined by repeated ultrasound examination or CT.

Fungal liver abscesses are difficult to document by culture of the abscess material; thus, histologic evidence of a fungal infection of the liver must be sought.[2] Amphotericin B, with or without flucytosine, is administered in the treatment of fungal liver abscesses.[47] In a neutropenic rabbit model, combination therapy with amphotericin and flucytosine was superior to amphotericin B alone in clearing disseminated candidiasis.[46] The optimal duration of therapy is unknown, but prolonged therapy, guided by repeated CT scans and biopsies, should be provided until the lesions have resolved.[47] Liposomal preparations of amphotericin B may be beneficial for selected children with hepatosplenic candidiasis who are intolerant of or failing treatment with traditional amphotericin B.[50]

Complications and Prognosis

Complications of hepatic abscesses are variable and relatively common occurrences. Twenty-eight percent of the patients described by Rubin and associates[43] and 44 percent of the patients studied by Pitt and Zuidema[41] had one or more complications. Pleural and pulmonary inflammation, peritonitis, subphrenic or subhepatic abscesses, and hemobilia are just a few of the possible complications.[9, 43]

Polymicrobial bacteremia, hypoalbuminemia, multiple liver abscesses, or the presence of any complication is associated with increased mortality rates in patients with liver abscesses. The overall mortality rates largely depend on underlying pathologic processes and therefore are difficult to interpret. Mortality figures from recent reports vary between 6 and 11 percent in adults.[22] An increased awareness and suspicion of liver abscesses, in conjunction with ultrasound or CT imaging of the liver, substantially reduces the mortality of this disease.

REFERENCES

1. Balci, N. C., Semelka, R. C., Noone, T. C., et al.: Pyogenic hepatic abscesses: MRI findings on T1- and T2-weighted and serial gadolinium-enhanced gradient-echo images. J. Magn. Reson. Imaging *9*:285–290, 1999.
2. Bartley, D. L., Hughes, W. T., Parvey, L. S., et al.: Computed tomography of hepatic and splenic fungal abscesses in leukemic children. Pediatr. Infect. Dis. *1*:317–321, 1982.
3. Berger, L. A., and Osborne, D. R.: Treatment of pyogenic liver abscesses by percutaneous needle aspiration. Lancet *1*:132–134, 1982.
4. Bernardino, M. E., Berkman, W. A., Plemmons, M., et al.: Percutaneous drainage of multiseptated hepatic abscess. J. Comput. Assist. Tomogr. *8*:38–41, 1984.
5. Brans, Y. M., Ceballos, R., and Cassady, G.: Umbilical catheters and hepatic abscesses. Pediatrics *53*:264–265, 1974.
6. Branum, G. D., Tyson, G. S., Branum, M. A., et al.: Hepatic abscess: Changes in etiology, diagnosis, and management. Ann. Surg. *212*:655, 1990.
7. Brook, I., and Fraizer, E. H.: Role of anaerobic bacteria in liver abscesses in children. Pediatr. Infect. Dis. J. *12*:743, 1993.
8. Chusid, M. J.: Pyogenic hepatic abscess in infancy and childhood. Pediatrics *62*:554–559, 1978.
9. Dehner, L. P., and Kissane, J. M.: Pyogenic hepatic abscesses in infancy and childhood. J. Pediatr. *74*:763–773, 1969.
10. de la Maza, L. M., Faramary, N., and Berman, L. D.: The changing etiology of liver abscess. J. A. M. A. *227*:161–163, 1974.
11. Diament, M. J., Stanley, P., Kangarloo, H., et al.: Percutaneous aspiration and catheter drainage of abscesses. J. Pediatr. *108*:204–208, 1986.
12. Doerr, C. A., Demmler, G. J., Garcia-Pratts, J. A., et al.: Solitary pyogenic liver abscess in neonates: Report of three cases and review of the literature. Pediatr. Infect. Dis. J. *13*:64, 1994.

13. Ecoffey, C., Rothman, E., Bernard, O., et al.: Bacterial cholangitis after surgery for biliary atresia. J. Pediatr. *111*:824–829, 1987.
14. Embree, J. E., Williams, T., and Law, B. J.: Hepatic abscesses in a child caused by *Fusobacterium necrophorum*. Pediatr. Infect. Dis. *7*:359–360, 1988.
15. Gerzof, S. G., Robbins, A. H., Johnson, W. C., et al.: Percutaneous catheter drainage of abdominal abscesses: A five-year experience. N. Engl. J. Med. *305*:353–357, 1981.
16. Goldsmith, H. S., and Chen, W. F.: Management of a pyogenic abscess of the liver. Surg. Clin. North Am. *53*:711–715, 1973.
17. Grunow, J. E., Dunton, S. F., and Waner, J. L.: Human rotavirus-like particles in a hepatic abscess. J. Pediatr. *106*:73–76, 1985.
18. Hoffer, F. A., Fellows, K. E., Wyly, J. B., et al.: Therapeutic catheter procedures in pediatrics. Pediatr. Clin. North Am. *32*:1461, 1985.
19. Holt, J. M., and Spry, C. J. F.: Solitary pyogenic liver abscess in patients with diabetes mellitus. Lancet *2*:198–200, 1966.
20. Huang, L.-T., Chen, C.-C., Shih, T.-Y., et al.: Pyogenic liver abscess complicating a ventriculoperitoneal shunt. Pediatr. Surg. Int. *13*:6–7, 1998.
21. Jeffrey, R. B., Jr., Tolentino, C. S., Chang, F. C., et al.: CT of small pyogenic hepatic abscesses: The cluster sign. A. J. R. Am. J. Roentgenol. *151*:487–489, 1988.
22. Johannsen, E. C., Sifri, C. D., and Madoff, L. C.: Pyogenic liver abscesses. Infect. Dis. Clin. North Am. *14*:547–563, 2000.
23. Johnston, R. B., and Baehner, R. L.: Chronic granulomatous disease: Correlation between pathogenesis and clinical findings. Pediatrics *48*:730–739, 1971.
24. Kandel, G., and Marcon, N. E.: Pyogenic liver abscess: New concepts of an old disease. Am. J. Gastroenterol. *79*:65–71, 1984.
25. Kaplan, S. L., and Feigin, R. D.: Pyogenic liver abscess in normal children with fever of unknown origin. Pediatrics *58*:614–616, 1976.
26. Kays, D. W.: Pediatric liver cysts and abscesses. Semin. Pediatr. Surg. *1*:107, 1992.
27. Kuligowska, E., Connors, S. K., and Shapiro, J. H.: Liver abscess: Sonography in diagnosis and treatment. A. J. R. Am. J. Roentgenol. *138*:253–257, 1982.
28. Kusne, S., Dummer, J. S., Singh, N., et al.: Infections after liver transplantation: An analysis of 101 consecutive cases. Medicine (Baltimore) *67*:132–143, 1988.
29. Laurin, S., and Kaude, J. V.: Diagnosis of liver-spleen abscesses in children: With emphasis on ultrasound for the initial and follow-up examinations. Pediatr. Radiol. *14*:198–204, 1984.
30. Lazarchick, J., DeSouza, E., Silvia, N. A., et al.: Pyogenic liver abscess. Mayo Clin. Proc. *48*:349–355, 1973.
31. Lee, J. F., and Block, G. E.: The changing clinical pattern of hepatic abscesses. Arch. Surg. *104*:456–470, 1972.
32. Mendez, R. J., Schiebler, M. L., Outwater, E. K., et al.: Hepatic abscesses: MR imaging findings. Radiology *190*:431, 1994.
33. Moss, T. J., and Pysher, T. J.: Hepatic abscess in neonates. Am. J. Dis. Child. *135*:726–728, 1981.
34. Murphy, F. M., and Baker, C. J.: Solitary hepatic abscess: A delayed complication of neonatal bacteremia. Pediatr. Infect. Dis. *7*:414–416, 1988.
35. Noel, G. J., and Karasic, R. B.: Liver abscess following ingestion of a foreign body. Pediatr. Infect. Dis. *3*:342–344, 1984.
36. Paone, R. F., and Mercer, L. C.: Hepatic abscess caused by a ventriculoperitoneal shunt. Pediatr. Infect. Dis. J. *10*:338, 1991.
37. Patterson, H. C.: Open aspiration in solitary liver abscess.Am. J. Surg. *119*:326–329, 1970.
38. Pereira, F. E., Musso, C., and Castelo, J. S.: Pathology of pyogenic liver abscess in children. Pediatr. Dev. Pathol. *2*:537–543, 1999.
39. Pincus, S. H., Boxer, L. A., and Stossel, T. P.: Chronic neutropenia in childhood: Analysis of 16 cases and a review of the literature. Am. J. Med. *61*:849–861, 1976.
40. Pineiro-Carrero, V. M., and Andres, J. M.: Morbidity and mortality in children with pyogenic liver abscess. Am. J. Dis. Child. *143*:1424–1427, 1989.
41. Pitt, H. A., and Zuidema, G. D.: Factors influencing mortality in the treatment of pyogenic hepatic abscess. Surg. Gynecol. Obstet. *140*:228–234, 1975.
42. Rogers, C. A., Isenberg, J. N., Leonard, A. S., et al.: Ascending cholangitis diagnosed by percutaneous hepatic aspiration. J. Pediatr. *88*:83–86, 1976.
43. Rubin, R. H., Swartz, M. N., and Malt, R.: Hepatic abscess: Changes in clinical, bacteriologic and therapeutic aspects. Am. J. Med. *57*:601–610, 1974.
44. Sabbaj, J.: Anaerobes in liver abscess. Rev. Infect. Dis. *6*:S152–S156, 1984.
45. Shulman, S. T., and Beem, M. O.: A unique presentation of sickle cell disease: Pyogenic hepatic abscess. Pediatrics *47*:1019–1022, 1971.
46. Thaler, M., Bacher, J., O'Leary, T., et al.: Evaluation of single-drug combination antifungal therapy in an experimental model of candidiasis in rabbits with prolonged neutropenia. J. Infect. Dis. *158*:80–88, 1988.
47. Thaler, M., Pastakia, B., Shawker, T. H., et al.: Hepatic candidiasis in cancer patients: The evolving picture of the syndrome. Ann. Intern. Med. *108*:88–100, 1988.
48. Vadillo, M., Corbella, X., and Pac, V.: Multiple liver abscesses due to *Yersinia enterocolitica* discloses primary hemochromatosis: Three case reports and review. Clin. Infect. Dis. *18*:938–941, 1994.
49. Vallejo, J. G., Stevens, A. M., Dutton, R. V., et al.: Hepatosplenic abscesses due to *Brucella melitensis:* Report of a case involving a child and review of the literature. Clin. Infect. Dis. *22*:485–489, 1996.
50. Walsh, T. J., Whitcomb, P., Piscitelli, S., et al.: Safety, tolerance, and pharmacokinetics of amphotericin B lipid complex in children with hepatosplenic candidiasis. Antimicrob. Agents Chemother. *41*:1944–1948, 1997.
51. Winkestein, J. A., Marino, M. C., Johnston, R. B., et al.: Chronic granulomatous disease. Report on a national registry of 368 patients. Medicine (Baltimore) *79*:155–169, 2000.
52. Wintch, R. W., Reines, H. D., and Rambo, W. M.: Liver abscess: A changing entity. Am. J. Surg. *48*:11–15, 1982.

CHAPTER 57 Reye Syndrome

EUGENE S. HURWITZ

A syndrome involving the acute onset of encephalopathy associated with fatty metamorphosis of the liver and occurring primarily in children was described first by Reye and colleagues[8] in Australia and by Johnson and associates[7] in the United States. The similarities of these two descriptions in separate countries led to the common designation of this clinicopathologic entity as Reye-Johnson or Reye syndrome. Reye syndrome occurs most frequently after a viral illness and is characterized by the onset of severe vomiting followed by the development of encephalopathy and hepatic dysfunction. The recognition in the early 1980s that the syndrome is associated with the ingestion of aspirin during the antecedent viral illness led to public awareness of this association, a decline in aspirin use for such illnesses in children, and a dramatic decline in the occurrence of this disease in the United States.[1]

Epidemiology

In the United States, national surveillance for Reye syndrome was conducted first during the 1973 to 1974 nationwide outbreak of influenza B and influenza A (H1N1). Such surveillance led to the recognition of outbreaks of Reye syndrome regionally and nationally that were associated with outbreaks of influenza in these and subsequent years.[2] During the first 5 years of surveillance, between 250 and 550 cases were reported nationally, clearly an underestimate because it was based on voluntary reporting.[9] Population-based studies conducted in several geographic locations demonstrated that the average annual incidence of the syndrome was between 1 and 2 cases per 100,000 children younger than 18 years. Adults rarely were affected. Case-fatality rates reported through national surveillance, initially as high as 40 percent, declined to between 20 and 30 percent in later years when the syndrome was prevalent, although this rate undoubtedly was an overestimate because of the tendency to report more severe and fatal cases through this system.

Between 1980 and 1982, four case-control studies reported an association between Reye syndrome and the ingestion of aspirin during an antecedent respiratory or chickenpox illness.[3, 11, 12] The results of these studies subsequently were confirmed in the Public Health Service Pilot and Main Studies of Reye Syndrome and Medications.[4, 5] In these studies, more than 90 percent of patients with Reye syndrome versus 40 to 70 percent of controls had received aspirin for the antecedent respiratory or chickenpox illness; reported odds ratios were between 11.5 and 40. After these studies were reported, publicity and recommendations from various expert panels, including those issued by the Food and Drug Administration in 1985, led to a decline in the use of aspirin and a decline in the incidence of Reye syndrome, particularly in the age group that had been affected most, children between 5 and 15 years of age.[1]

Clinical Illness and Laboratory Findings

Reye syndrome is described classically as an illness characterized by the abrupt onset of severe vomiting and progressive encephalopathy in a child who is just recovering from a viral illness, the most common of which are influenza and chickenpox. The onset of these symptoms typically occurs within several days after the onset of the viral illness and commonly during a period when the child appears to be recovering from this illness. In association with severe—often projectile—vomiting, which occurs for a transient period, are progressive encephalopathic changes that may follow stages from delirium through confusion, agitation, and lethargy to coma if untreated.

The definition used by the Centers for Disease Control and Prevention (CDC) and widely adopted for clinical purposes includes (1) evidence of acute encephalopathy manifested by alterations in consciousness and documented, when available, by cerebrospinal fluid (CSF) with less than 9×10^6/L leukocytes or by biopsy or autopsy evidence of cerebral edema without perivascular or meningeal inflammation in histologic sections of the brain; (2) evidence of liver involvement to include either biopsy or autopsy findings of fatty metamorphosis of the liver if available or, in the absence of such specimens, elevations in liver enzymes (alanine transaminase, aspartate transaminase, or serum ammonia) that typically are more than three times normal levels; and (3) no other more reasonable explanation for the cerebral or hepatic abnormalities. The last requirement emphasizes that Reye syndrome is a diagnosis of exclusion and that every effort should be undertaken to identify other possible causes for the clinical and laboratory abnormalities.

Liver biopsy or autopsy findings are considered characteristic and include panlobular microvesicular fat and mitochondrial abnormalities on electron-microscopic examination demonstrating peroxisome swelling and enlarged pleomorphic mitochondria with loss of dense granules. Additional findings include normal bilirubin levels and absence of jaundice. Most patients also have hypoglycemia and a prolonged prothrombin time. The typically elevated CSF pressure in patients leads to progressive stages of coma.

Staging criteria for the syndrome have been used to define the level of encephalopathy. Patients have been reported with liver involvement but without evidence of encephalopathy. These patients have been described as having stage 0 encephalopathy, and, although they do not meet the CDC criteria for Reye syndrome, they are considered to have mild disease. Patients with stage I encephalopathy are difficult to arouse and lethargic, whereas those with stage II are delirious and combative with some movement. Patients with higher stages of encephalopathy (III to V) cannot be aroused and have progressively deeper stages of coma. These patients have a poor prognosis, with a mortality rate approaching 50 percent for those admitted with stage III or greater and 90 percent for those admitted with stage V.

Exclusion of other diseases that may resemble Reye syndrome, such as salicylate toxicity, is essential in patients with symptoms resembling this entity. Accordingly, intensive laboratory investigations should be undertaken to exclude such disorders. In young children, particularly those younger than 3 years of age, inherited metabolic disorders frequently may mimic Reye syndrome and must be excluded. Such metabolic disorders include disorders of fatty acid oxidation, urea cycle disorders, carnitine transport defects, and organic acidemias. Laboratory studies must be performed for the younger age group to exclude these disorders before a diagnosis of Reye syndrome is made, particularly because some of these disorders can be treated effectively. With the declining incidence of Reye syndrome in the typical age group (5 to 15 years) after virtual elimination of the use of aspirin in children, an increasing number of patients with features of Reye syndrome are in this younger age group and ultimately are found, after careful evaluation, to have one of the many metabolic disorders that mimic this syndrome.

Treatment and Prevention

The mainstay of treatment of Reye syndrome is early recognition of disease and supportive care focusing on various measures to control intracranial pressure (ICP) and electrolyte and other abnormalities. Patients should have glucose levels monitored, and early infusion of glucose is considered by many physicians to improve outcome. Comatose patients should be transferred to tertiary care centers that have experience in caring for such patients and can monitor and treat elevated ICP. When such measures were undertaken before the decline in incidence of this disease, they were associated with improved outcome and decreased mortality. Other therapeutic measures that have been used include efforts to reduce ammonia levels, such as exchange transfusions, peritoneal dialysis, and total-body washout via cardiopulmonary bypass. With advances in supportive care, the mortality rate declined to 10 to 20 percent in later years before the syndrome became extremely rare.

Since recognition of the association between Reye syndrome and aspirin, aspirin no longer is recommended or used for the treatment of febrile illnesses in children. Alternative antipyretics, including nonsteroidal anti-inflammatory agents and acetaminophen (Tylenol), have replaced aspirin as the primary therapy for such illnesses. These medications have not been associated with an increased risk for development of this syndrome. Children with some disorders, including juvenile rheumatoid arthritis and Kawasaki syndrome, continue to be given aspirin to treat these disorders. Efforts to reduce the risk of development of Reye syndrome in these children have included influenza vaccination annually, as well as vaccination against chickenpox. Careful monitoring of these children also is necessary to ensure early recognition and treatment of Reye syndrome should it occur.

REFERENCES

1. Belay, E. D., Bresee, J. S., Holman, R. C., et al.: Reye's syndrome in the United States from 1981 through 1997. N. Engl. J. Med. *340*:1377–1382, 1999.
2. Corey, L., Rubin, R. J., Hattwick, M. A., et al.: Nationwide outbreak of Reye's syndrome: Its epidemiologic relationship to influenza B. Am. J. Med. *61*:615–625, 1976.
3. Halpin, T. J., Holtzhauer, F. J., Campbell, R. J., et al.: Reye's syndrome and medication use. J. A. M. A. *248*:687–691, 1982.
4. Hurwitz, E. S., Barrett, M. J., Bregman, D., et al.: Public Health Service study on Reye's syndrome and medications: Report of the pilot phase. N. Engl. J. Med. *313*:849–857, 1985.
5. Hurwitz, E. S., Barrett, M. J., Bregman, D., et al.: Public Health Service study of Reye's syndrome and medications: Report of the main study. [Erratum, J. A. M. A. *257*:3366, 1987.] J. A. M. A. *257*:1905–1911, 1987.
6. Hurwitz, E. S., Nelson, D. B., Davis, C., et al.: National surveillance for Reye syndrome: A five-year review. Pediatrics *70*:895–900, 1982.
7. Johnson, G. M., Scurletis, T. D., and Carroll, N. B.: A study of sixteen fatal cases of encephalitis-like disease in North Carolina children. N. C. Med. J. *24*:464–473, 1963.
8. Reye, R. D. K., Morgan, G., and Baral, J.: Encephalopathy and fatty degeneration of the viscera: A disease entity in childhood. Lancet *2*:749–752, 1963.
9. Reye syndrome surveillance—United States, 1987 and 1988. M. M. W.R. Morb. Mortal. Wkly. Rep. *38*(18):325–327, 1989.
10. Rowe, P. C., Valle, D., and Brusilow, S. W.: Inborn errors of metabolism in children referred with Reye's syndrome: A changing pattern. J. A. M. A. *260*:3167–3170, 1988.
11. Starko, K. M., Ray, C. G., Dominguez, L. B., et al.: Reye's syndrome and salicylate use. Pediatrics *66*:859–864, 1980.
12. Waldman, R. J., Hall, W. N., McGee, H., and Van Amburg, G.: Aspirin as a risk factor in Reye's syndrome. J. A. M. A. *247*:3089–3094, 1982.

SECTION VIII

Other Intra-abdominal Infections

CHAPTER 58

Appendicitis and Pelvic Abscess

THOMAS L. KUHLS

The ability to diagnose appendicitis accurately in a child continues to be one of the most fundamental skills that a pediatric surgeon has to master, although making the diagnosis often is difficult in young patients. The surgeon ultimately is responsible for deciding whether a child is taken to the operating room for appendectomy; however, a primary care physician often is the first person to evaluate the patient who complains of abdominal pain. Pediatricians with expertise in infectious diseases frequently are involved in the care of children who present with subtle or atypical manifestations of appendicitis, have unusual microorganisms recovered from their appendices, or have complications as a result of appendiceal rupture, such as the development of wound infections, sepsis, peritonitis, intra-abdominal abscesses, and pelvic abscesses.

History

As early as the 16th century, physicians began describing patients with clinical manifestations suggestive of perforated appendicitis. Until the late 1800s, the inflammatory process was called *typhlitis* or *perityphlitis* because the illness was thought to originate from the cecum. In 1886, Reginald Fitz recognized that the source of the inflammation was the appendix and suggested that a laparotomy be performed early in the course of the illness.[48] Shortly afterward, Charles McBurney reported that in patients with appendicitis, tenderness is greatest 2 inches from the anterior iliac spine on a line drawn to the umbilicus.[93] Despite intensive research and refinement of our understanding of appendicitis during the past century, the rates of removing nondiseased appendices or finding already perforated appendices at laparotomy both remain at about 20 percent.

Despite the continued difficulties in diagnosing appendicitis, the mortality rate from appendicitis has greatly decreased since Fitz reported a 40 percent operative mortality rate. In 1936, Bancroft and Skoluda reported a mortality rate of 8 percent and a complication rate of 11 percent for appendicitis, most likely because of the availabilities of general anesthesia and better aseptic surgical techniques.[12] The second major improvement in outcome occurred in the 1940s, when sulfonamides and banked blood became widely available.[91] Not until the 1970s were anaerobes, such as *Bacteroides fragilis*, found to cause postoperative infections frequently in patients with appendicitis and was treating these microorganisms found to reduce further the rate of postoperative complications.[76] Currently, death from appendicitis is a rare event in the United States.

Epidemiology

The reported incidences of acute appendicitis vary widely, depending on where the studies were performed and what methodologies were used. The consensus is that the number of cases of acute appendicitis has been decreasing during the past few decades.[2, 94] In the United States, 1.5 million appendectomies were performed for acute appendicitis during the years 1979 to 1984.[2] In California,[25, 41] appendectomies (1 per 1000 residents) were performed for acute appendicitis in 1984.[83] Although appendicitis occurs in all age groups, the highest incidence occurs during the second decade of life.[2, 84] Appendicitis is an uncommon occurrence in children younger than 5 years of age and occurs extremely rarely in infants younger than 6 months of age. Researchers have suggested that patients with acquired immunodeficiency syndrome (AIDS) have a higher incidence of appendicitis than does the normal population.[73]

Most studies show a modest increase in incidence of appendicitis in males compared with females.[2, 84] An estimated lifetime risk for developing appendicitis is 8.6 percent for males, whereas in females, it is 6.7 percent.[2] In a study of acute appendicitis in California, the rate of appendicitis in whites was twice that of blacks and Asians.[84] Other studies from the United States and South Africa have revealed similar findings.[2, 159] Whether the reported racial differences are due to errors of measurement, sociodemographic factors, environmental factors, factors related to body constitution, or genetic factors remains unknown. Children with appendicitis more frequently have a history of having family members who previously have had appendicitis, suggesting that genetic background plays a role in the susceptibility to appendicitis.[14] Decreased dietary fiber and ingestion of refined carbohydrates also have been suggested to increase the risk for developing appendicitis.

Numerous studies have demonstrated that the peak rates of appendicitis occur during the summer months, whereas the lowest rates occur during the winter months.[2, 84] The reasons for this seasonal pattern are unknown, but changes in diet and exposure to allergens have been suggested as explanations.[84] Also, enteric infections occur most commonly during the summer months and may play a role in raising the incidence of appendicitis during that particular time of the year.

Pathophysiology

The initial event in the development of most cases of appendicitis is thought to be obstruction of the appendiceal lumen.[139] Only occasionally do microorganisms invade the appendiceal mucosa and initiate the inflammatory process. Appendiceal obstruction can be caused by inspissated feces (fecalith), hypertrophied lymphoid tissue that develops during a systemic viral infection or bacterial enterocolitis, infestation by parasites, appendiceal wall hemorrhage associated with anaphylactic purpura, inspissated barium, or ingested seeds. Continued production of mucus by the appendiceal mucosa distal to the obstruction causes the appendix to distend. Vascular congestion and ischemia occur as the increased intraluminal pressure of the appendix becomes greater than the venous pressure, and edema develops as lymphatic flow becomes obstructed. Stasis of intestinal flow and intestinal ischemia allow the microorganisms in the appendix to invade the tissues, enhancing the already developing inflammatory response. Bacteria then may translocate across the appendiceal wall and reach the peritoneal cavity.[13] If the process is severe and arteriolar blood flow to the appendix is obstructed, transmural infarction occurs, and the appendix ruptures. Microorganisms then are liberated into the peritoneal cavity, causing generalized peritonitis and formation of an abscess. Animal studies have suggested that synergism occurring between enteric aerobes, such as *Escherichia coli,* and anaerobes, such as *B. fragilis*, is important in the development of intra-abdominal and pelvic abscesses after perforation.[30, 51] Similarly, an association between the development of an abscess after appendiceal perforation and the presence of *Streptococcus milleri* appears to exist.[56, 63]

As the appendix distends in the early stages of appendicitis, the visceral afferent autonomic nerves that enter the spinal cord at T-8 to T-10 are stimulated, thus referring the pain to the epigastric and periumbilical areas of the abdomen.[139] When the inflammatory response reaches the serosal surface of the appendix, the parietal peritoneum is stimulated, and the pain intensifies in the right lower quadrant. If perforation occurs, the peritoneal inflammatory response causes more generalized abdominal tenderness.

Although appendiceal obstruction may play an important role in the early stages of most cases of appendicitis, not all obstructed appendices become inflamed. Ten percent of normal appendices removed during abdominal surgical procedures contain inspissated fecal material. Also, children may develop recurrent, crampy abdominal pain, possibly from intermittent appendiceal obstruction.[133]

The classic description of the pathophysiology of appendicitis does not explain easily many epidemiologic features of this disease, including its peak incidence during adolescence, its low incidence in newborns and infants, its higher incidence in males, and its higher incidences in certain races. The amount and reactivity of the lymphoid tissue in the wall of the appendix have been suggested to be key determinants to the development of appendicitis.[84] The amount of lymphoid tissue in the appendix is greatest during adolescence, and the amount most likely is controlled genetically. In a case-control study from Italy, prolonged breast-feeding during infancy was associated with a decreased risk for developing acute appendicitis later in life.[117] The investigators hypothesized that breast-feeding may have decreased the amount of stimulation to intestinal lymphocytes by microbial and food antigens early in life, so that appendiceal lymphoid tissues were less reactive to antigenic challenge during adolescence and adulthood.

Clinical Manifestations

In school-age children and adolescents with appendicitis, the median duration of symptoms before the time of hospital admission is 24 to 28 hours.[122] Pain in the right iliac fossa is the most common sign of appendicitis, occurring in 88 to 99 percent of patients.[122, 126] Pain shifts from the periumbilical area to the right lower quadrant of the abdomen in approximately two thirds of pediatric patients with appendicitis. In three fourths of the children, the pain becomes worse during movement. Importantly, the characteristics of the abdominal pain do not always predict accurately which children have appendicitis. Twenty-five percent of children found to have mesenteric adenitis at laparotomy report a shift in their abdominal pain to the right iliac fossa, and 33 percent experience worsening of their pain during movement.[122]

Nausea and vomiting are found in 86 to 96 percent of children with appendicitis.[122, 126] Vomiting usually occurs after the onset of abdominal pain but may precede the pain in nearly 20 percent of cases. If only nausea or vomiting is present, the child less likely has appendicitis.[122] Anorexia occurs less commonly in children than in adults, occurring in 47 to 91 percent of cases of appendicitis. Because 50 percent of children found to have normal appendices at surgery complain of anorexia, differentiating appendicitis from other causes of right iliac fossa pain is not always a helpful clinical finding. Similarly, complaints of diarrhea (9–16%), constipation (5–28%), and dysuria (7%) occasionally can be elicited from children with appendicitis.[122, 129] Fever may be helpful as a clinical sign of appendicitis if it is present (temperature >37.5° C in 68–96% of cases), but absence of fever does not exclude the possibility of acute appendicitis. Very high temperatures (>39° C) suggest that perforation already has occurred or that another intra-abdominal process is present.[139] Rarely, children present with erythema and tenderness of the scrotum as the only manifestation of acute appendicitis.[169]

During the physical examination, the child frequently lies quietly on the examination table with the right hip flexed. Tenderness in the right iliac fossa is the most sensitive sign of appendicitis, occurring in 93 to 100 percent of cases of appendicitis.[122, 126] If the psoas muscle is irritated from the inflamed appendix, the child feels increased pain when the right hip is flexed actively. Likewise, if the obturator internus muscle is involved, pain is elicited when the flexed thigh is rotated internally.[139] Guarding is found in 80 to 91 percent of cases of appendicitis, compared with 50 percent of cases of mesenteric adenitis and 8 percent of cases of nonspecific abdominal pain.[122] Similarly, rebound tenderness is found in 56 to 83 percent of cases of appendicitis, 33 percent of cases of acute mesenteric adenitis, and 1 percent of cases of nonspecific abdominal pain.[122] The development of diffuse abdominal tenderness and the absence of bowel sounds usually indicate perforation. Extremely hyperactive bowel sounds suggest that the patient may not have appendicitis. Occasionally, a mass can be palpated in the right lower quadrant of the abdomen in children with appendicitis who are relaxed or well sedated. Rectal tenderness is present more commonly in children with appendicitis (44–68%) than in those with other causes of abdominal pain (12%); however, findings during the rectal examination seldom alter the clinical decision of the surgeon.[122]

In preschool-age children, the diagnosis of appendicitis becomes more difficult to make because of the relative inability of young children to express their symptoms and because they often do not cooperate during the physical examination.[164, 165] Most young children with appendicitis are seen early in the course of their symptoms and are prescribed antibiotics, antihistamines, or antipyretics. By the time one realizes that the child has appendicitis, the appendix usually is perforated (50–90%).[164, 165] Unlike with older children, vomiting is the initial symptom of appendicitis most frequently observed, and abdominal pain may be absent or may never localize in the right iliac fossa.[122] Sleep disturbances, irritability, restlessness, and crying are common manifestations of appendicitis in this age group. The preschool-age child is more likely to have a palpable inflammatory mass at presentation.[139]

During the newborn period, appendicitis is an extremely uncommon event.[8, 138] The symptoms of neonatal appendicitis include abdominal distention; vomiting; irritability; diarrhea; erythema, edema, or cellulitis of the abdominal wall; gastrointestinal hemorrhage; abdominal rigidity; lethargy; and jaundice. Usually, the symptoms of neonatal appendicitis are indistinguishable from those of necrotizing enterocolitis. Underlying conditions, such as total colonic Hirschsprung disease, meconium plugs, or hernias, may predispose the newborn to developing this condition.

In children who are undergoing chemotherapy for leukemia, acute appendicitis may present with only vague abdominal pain, abdominal distention, lack of abdominal guarding, fever, dehydration, diarrhea, or such unusual symptoms as gastrointestinal bleeding.[5] The symptoms of appendicitis may be identical to those of typhlitis.

The differential diagnosis of acute abdominal pain in children is extensive. Conditions that can present with symptoms suggestive of acute appendicitis are outlined in Table 58–1.

TABLE 58–1 ■ DIFFERENTIAL DIAGNOSIS OF ACUTE APPENDICITIS IN CHILDREN

Cecal and Colonic Diseases
Crohn disease
Intestinal obstruction
Typhlitis (leukemia patients)
Infectious colitis (bacterial, parasitic)
Necrotizing enterocolitis (newborns)
Constipation
Small Intestinal Diseases
Gastroenteritis (including mesenteric adenitis)
Duodenal ulcers (acute and perforated)
Intestinal obstruction
Intussusception
Meckel diverticulitis
Volvulus
Intestinal duplication
Hepatobiliary and Pancreatic Diseases
Cholecystitis
Hepatitis
Hydrops of the gallbladder
Pancreatitis
Other Diseases
Spontaneous peritonitis
Pneumonia
Omental torsion
Psoas abscess
Reproductive Tract Diseases
Intrauterine and ectopic pregnancy
Ovarian torsion
Ovarian cysts
Pelvic inflammatory disease
Testicular torsion
Urinary Tract Diseases
Hydronephrosis
Pyelonephritis
Urolithiasis
Wilms tumor
Urachal abscess
Systemic Illnesses
Anaphylactoid purpura
Lymphoma (Burkitt)
Rocky Mountain spotted fever
Tuberculosis
Cytomegalovirus infection (in patients with AIDS)
Diabetic ketoacidosis
Porphyria
Sickle-cell disease

Diagnosis

The diagnosis of acute appendicitis should be established without laboratory studies when a child complains of abdominal tenderness in the right lower quadrant that initially started in the periumbilical area, develops nausea and vomiting, and has rebound tenderness in the right lower quadrant with guarding during an abdominal examination.[139] The child should be taken to the operating room for an appendectomy as soon as possible before perforation occurs. Many children, however, do not have all of the classic clinical manifestations of appendicitis; thus, a great emphasis has been placed on using various laboratory tests to help clinicians accurately diagnose the disease.

For decades, physicians have valued peripheral blood leukocyte counts, neutrophil counts, C-reactive protein concentrations, and erythrocyte sedimentation rates to help them distinguish appendicitis from other noninflammatory causes of abdominal pain. When properly evaluated, however, these tests have been found to be too insensitive to use as reliable tools for diagnosing appendicitis.[39, 63, 114, 127] Although these tests help to confirm a physician's suspicions when results are positive, normal results clearly do not rule out the possibility that the child has appendicitis. Certain groups of patients commonly have normal leukocyte counts despite having acute appendicitis. Black patients with acute appendicitis frequently do not develop leukocytosis.[77, 90, 106] Similarly, patients with AIDS who develop appendicitis often do not have elevated white blood cell counts.[21, 103]

The role of routine radiologic studies in the diagnosis of appendicitis remains controversial. A chest radiograph often is obtained because right lower lobe pneumonia can cause severe abdominal pain in children. Although radiographs of the abdomen frequently are obtained in children complaining of abdominal pain, there are no sensitive or specific signs of appendicitis.[25, 53] Abnormalities described in association with acute appendicitis include an abnormal bowel gas pattern, a mass, a fecalith, and obliteration of normal fat planes in the right lower quadrant. Gas in the appendiceal lumen is thought to be diagnostic of acute appendicitis but may occur rarely in its absence.

Before the use of ultrasonography and computed tomography (CT) to diagnose appendicitis, barium enema was used to evaluate patients with right lower quadrant abdominal pain.[44] Findings suggestive of acute appendicitis include partial or absent visualization of the appendix, pressure defects on the cecum, and irritability of the cecum or terminal ileum as demonstrated by fluoroscopy. Five to 10 percent of normal appendices, however, cannot be visualized during the procedure. Also, changes consistent with acute appendicitis have been found in patients with small bowel obstruction, acute enterocolitis, pelvic hemorrhage, pelvic inflammatory disease, hemorrhagic ovarian cysts, and torsion of the ovary. Examination results have been normal in a few patients with histologically proven acute appendicitis.

Graded compression ultrasonography has become the diagnostic procedure of choice in many institutions when evaluating a patient with possible appendicitis.[142, 143, 167] The transducer is used to apply gradual pressure to the abdomen. The technician must make sure that all gas and fluid contents from the loops of bowel are expressed for the examination to be adequate. A noncompressible, enlarged (>6 mm in diameter in adolescents) appendix or a fecalith is the major criterion used for diagnosing appendicitis by ultrasonography.[168] Interruption in the continuity of the echogenic submucosa suggests necrosis of the appendiceal wall and impending perforation. An echogenic periappendiceal mass indicates inflammation of the mesenteric or omental fat. Loculated or generalized fluid collections suggest that perforation already has occurred.

Most studies of graded compression ultrasonography have demonstrated that the procedure is 70 to 90 percent sensitive and greater than 90 percent specific in diagnosing acute appendicitis in adults and children.[168] False-positive ultrasonographic results occur in obese patients who have noncompressible appendices because of overlying fat and in children who have inflamed appendices caused by Crohn disease, ulcerative colitis, or adjacent salpingitis. False-negative results occur if retrocecally located appendices are not visualized properly, if the cecum is filled with gas or feces and is not compressed adequately, or if perforation has occurred, allowing the appendix to be compressible. In one study, a noncompressible appendix was identified in only 38 percent of pediatric patients with perforated appendicitis, thus rendering the other ultrasonographic findings of appendicitis important in diagnosing the disease.[118] When a normal appendix is found during the ultrasonographic evaluation, the examination should be turned to diagnose other causes of abdominal pain that can mimic appendicitis.

CT also has been used to diagnose appendicitis when diagnosis cannot be made on clinical grounds alone.[20] However, intravenous contrast agents and high-resolution, thin-section scanning techniques must be used to visualize the appendix adequately. An enlarged appendix with a circumferentially and symmetrically thickened bowel wall is the most common CT finding in appendicitis. Periappendiceal inflammatory reaction or fluid collections may be identified. If the appendix is not well visualized, the presence of a fecalith, along with pericecal inflammatory changes, strongly suggests appendicitis. However, fecaliths can be visualized in normal appendices by CT and are of no clinical significance unless other inflammatory changes are present. In a study comparing high-resolution CT with graded compression ultrasonography in evaluating patients with suspected appendicitis, CT had higher sensitivity, accuracy, and negative predictive value than did ultrasonography; however, the specificity and positive predictive values were similar.[11]

In recent years, helical CT scanning techniques that are focused only to the right lower quadrant using rectal or no contrast have been shown to be very accurate in diagnosing appendicitis in children.[45, 82, 115] By using a focused approach, CT scans may be completed within 5 minutes. Because of the high accuracy rates in diagnosing appendicitis, some physicians have suggested that all children with suspected disease should have a focused CT scan.[116] In most community hospitals and medical centers, waiting for a CT scan may delay a surgical consultation and increase the rate of perforation before surgery.[75] Radiolabeled autologous leukocyte scans also have been used to diagnose appendicitis in children; however, this modality should be reserved for atypical presentations of disease when localizing signs are not present.[58]

Microbiology

Numerous microorganisms have been implicated as a cause of acute appendicitis; however, considerable debate has ensued as to whether simply isolating an organism from the appendiceal lumen is sufficient proof to define causation[1] (Table 58–2).

TABLE 58–2 ■ MICROORGANISMS ASSOCIATED WITH ACUTE APPENDICITIS IN CHILDREN

Parasites
Ascaris lumbricoides
Enterobius vermicularis
Taenia species
Anisakis species
Trichuris trichiura
Strongyloides stercoralis
Schistosoma species
Angiostrongylus costaricensis
Balantidium coli
Entamoeba histolytica
Cryptosporidium parvum
Viruses
Coxsackieviruses B
Adenoviruses
Epstein-Barr virus
Measles
Cytomegalovirus (in patients with AIDS)
Anaerobes
Bacteroides species
Bilophilia wadsworthia
Peptostreptococcus species
Fusobacterium species
Clostridium species
Pigmented bile-resistant, gram-negative rod
Enteric Aerobes and Facultative Anaerobes
Escherichia coli
Streptococcus milleri group
Enterococcus species
Citrobacter species
Klebsiella species
Enterobacter species
Proteus species
Morganella morganii
Providencia rettgeri
Shigella species
Salmonella species
Campylobacter species
Yersinia species
Other Bacteria
Pseudomonas species
Eikenella corrodens
Staphylococcus species
Streptococcus pneumoniae
Haemophilus species
Pasteurella multocida
Streptococcus pyogenes
Actinomyces species
Atypical mycobacteria (in patients with AIDS)

PARASITES

Roundworms, such as *Ascaris lumbricoides*, plausibly may obstruct the appendiceal lumen on occasion and initiate the cascade of inflammatory events leading to perforated appendicitis.[87, 110] Parasites such as *Enterobius vermicularis* can be identified in the lumen of 1 to 12 percent of surgically removed appendices obtained from patients living in highly endemic areas.[22, 33, 99] However, pinworms have been found more frequently in appendices with no evidence of appendiceal inflammation in some studies, suggesting that pinworms probably are a part of the normal appendiceal flora in some children and do not play a role in the pathogenesis of appendicitis.[33, 162] Whether some parasites may cause abdominal pain that mimics the symptoms of appendicitis necessitating surgical intervention remains unclear. Scattered reports from mostly developing nations describe other worms, including *Taenia* spp., *Anisakis* spp., *Trichuris trichiura, Strongyloides stercoralis, Schistosoma* spp., and *Angiostrongylus costaricensis*, that have been identified in the lumen of appendices from patients with appendicitis.[3, 6, 40, 54, 81, 104] Similarly, protozoa such as *Balantidium coli, Entamoeba histolytica,* and *Cryptosporidium parvum* have been found in inflamed appendices, but whether they play a role in the pathogenesis of disease is unknown.[36, 89, 104, 121]

VIRUSES

The role that viruses play in causing appendicitis also is controversial, although one suggestion is that a systemic viral infection may induce hypertrophied lymphoid aggregates that obstruct the appendiceal lumen. In the 1960s, elevated levels of antibodies against coxsackieviruses B and adenoviruses were found in the sera of some children with appendicitis.[149] A later study, however, could not confirm this finding.[100] Six adolescents with infectious mononucleosis have developed appendicitis.[80] Other children have had histologic evidence of measles virus infection in the wall of inflamed appendices.[111] Because of the rarity of documented simultaneous viral infections and appendicitis, whether these viruses play a major role in the pathogenesis of acute appendicitis is doubtful.

BACTERIA

In most cases of appendicitis, bacteria do not appear to be involved directly in the initial stages of the inflammatory process. However, microorganisms that normally inhabit the appendix are liberated into the peritoneal cavity when appendiceal perforation occurs or when translocation through the inflamed tissues is present; thus, one is not surprised that polymicrobial infections develop as a complication of the disease process.[16, 148] In a study of 30 adolescents and adults with nonperforated and perforated appendicitis, 223 different anaerobes and 82 aerobes were recovered from cultures of their appendiceal tissues, peritoneal fluid, and contents of abscesses.[16] An average of 10 different organisms were isolated per specimen collected.

In most microbiologic studies of appendiceal tissues and peritoneal fluid specimens from patients with appendicitis, *B. fragilis* is the strict anaerobe most frequently isolated, occurring in more than 70 percent of patients.[16, 124] Other anaerobes that are isolated frequently include *Bacteroides* spp., *Bilophila wadsworthia*, *Peptostreptococcus* spp., *Fusobacterium* spp., and *Clostridium* spp. In more recent studies, a gram-negative anaerobic rod that develops a pigment in culture and is bile resistant also has been identified frequently.[123, 124]

E. coli is the aerobic or facultative anaerobic bacteria most frequently isolated from children with appendicitis.[16, 124] It can be found in more than 75 percent of patients. Researchers have suggested that certain *E. coli* strains with type 1C fimbriae may contribute to the development of appendiceal inflammation.[132] Enterohemorrhagic *E. coli* O157:H7 and O111:H have been isolated infrequently from the stools and peritoneal fluid of children with appendicitis.[149, 153, 158]

Viridans streptococci of the *S. milleri* group, including *Streptococcus anginosus,* can be found in more than 60 percent of cultures from children with appendicitis.[64, 86, 124] Group D streptococci are isolated in approximately 20 to 30 percent of patients with appendicitis, whereas *Pseudomonas* spp. are isolated slightly less commonly.[18, 124] Other aerobes or facultative anaerobes that can be isolated from appendiceal tissues or abscesses include *Citrobacter* spp.; *Klebsiella* spp.; *Enterobacter* spp.; *Proteus* spp.; *Morganella morganii*; *Providencia rettgeri*; *Eikenella corrodens*; groups C, F, and G beta-hemolytic streptococci; and staphylococci.[38, 65, 119, 124, 148] Rarely, encapsulated organisms, such as *Streptococcus pneumoniae, Haemophilus influenzae,* and *Haemophilus segnis*, have been isolated from appendiceal tissues or peritoneal fluid of young children with appendicitis, and often these organisms have been isolated in pure culture.[9, 57, 105, 124] Very rarely, organisms such as *Pasteurella multocida, Streptococcus pyogenes, Candida albicans,* and *Actinomyces* spp. have been cultured from immunocompetent patients with appendicitis.[120, 131, 134, 152] *Shigella, Salmonella, Campylobacter,* and *Yersinia* spp. also have been isolated occasionally from appendiceal tissues or peritoneal fluid of patients with nonperforated and perforated appendicitis; but again, whether they played a role in the pathogenesis of disease is unknown.[17, 68, 97, 156] Much more commonly, these organisms cause enterocolitis or mesenteric adenitis, with symptoms mimicking appendicitis.[156]

Adults and children with appendicitis usually are not bacteremic at the time of diagnosis, especially if the appendix is not perforated. Occasionally, *Klebsiella pneumoniae, E. coli, B. fragilis,* and *B. wadsworthia* are isolated from the blood of patients with nonperforated appendicitis.[18, 112, 130] In a review of 1000 children and adults with appendicitis, 10 percent of patients with perforation had positive blood cultures, whereas none of the patients without perforation had bacteremia.[77] A higher rate of bacteremia may occur when laparoscopic surgery is performed because of the air that is forced into the peritoneum, although the clinical significance of the induced bacteremia is unknown.[109]

In immunocompromised patients who develop appendicitis, the microorganisms that are isolated from appendiceal tissues or peritoneal cultures usually are identical to those found in immunocompetent patients.[103] In adults infected with human immunodeficiency virus, however, appendicitis has been caused by cytomegalovirus infection and neoplastic obstruction of the base of the appendix by Kaposi sarcoma.[29, 107] Patients with AIDS who have gastrointestinal *Mycobacterium avium* complex or *Mycobacterium tuberculosis* infections may develop symptoms that mimic appendicitis.[35, 157] Atypical mycobacteria have been isolated from an appendiceal abscess from a child with AIDS.[42]

Treatment

NONPERFORATED APPENDICITIS

In previously healthy children with signs of acute appendicitis and no clinical evidence of perforation, nasogastric suctioning should be established, and imbalances in fluid and electrolyte concentrations should be corrected quickly. The child should be taken to the operating room as soon as possible for exploratory laparotomy and appendectomy. Although some controversy still remains, most studies have demonstrated that prophylactic antibiotics given perioperatively decrease the rate of postoperative wound infection, even in noncomplicated cases of childhood appendicitis.[52, 69, 108, 150] No consensus exists concerning the appropriate antimicrobial agent or agents that should be used or the appropriate duration of treatment required after surgery to reduce the complication rate. Although most surgeons continue the antibiotics for 1 to 3 days after surgery, one prospective, randomized study demonstrated that a single perioperative dose of gentamicin or metronidazole was as effective as continuing both medications for 24 hours.[151]

Few data support the routine intraoperative collection of peritoneal fluid cultures in children with nonperforated appendicitis, although 5 to 20 percent of cultures grow enteric aerobes, anaerobes, or both.[19, 95] Immunocompromised patients, however, should undergo intraoperative cultures, including cultures for mycobacteria and cytomegalovirus.

Interest in performing laparoscopic appendectomies in children with nonperforated and perforated appendicitis has been increasing.[28, 41] Although the procedure must be performed by a surgeon experienced in laparoscopic techniques, the advantages of the procedure are a reduction in scarring, a shorter hospital stay, and an earlier return to normal activity. However, the mean total cost of a laparoscopic appendectomy is similar to that of the more commonly performed open appendectomy, and recent studies in pediatric patients have determined that the advantages may be minimal.[74] The use of smaller laparoscopic instruments may improve the speed of recovery of children in the future.[101]

PERFORATED APPENDICITIS

Some controversy remains as to whether immediate appendectomy should be performed on children in whom a palpable mass is associated with their appendicitis or who show evidence of appendiceal rupture with or without abscess formation at the time of presentation.[139] Most surgeons consider that early intervention is preferred, despite the high complication rate, to prevent severe complications such as death, fistula formation, and abscess rupture.[85] If a laparotomy is performed, debate also ensues as to whether the wound should be closed primarily and whether transperitoneal drains should be placed at the time of surgery.[26, 32, 85] During the surgical procedure, most surgeons irrigate the peritoneal cavity with copious amounts of saline or antibiotics to lower the quantity of bacteria in the abdomen.[85] Whether the addition of antibiotics to the lavage fluid further decreases the rate of postoperative complications in children with perforated appendicitis who are receiving systemic antibiotics remains unclear.[92]

Researchers have demonstrated that more than 70 percent of children with palpable masses respond to conservative, nonoperative management consisting of administration of intravenous fluids and broad-spectrum antibiotics.[139] If the child does not improve or a walled-off abscess develops, drainage of the area and appendectomy should be performed. If the child responds to conservative management, an interval appendectomy should be performed 6 to 8 weeks after resolution of the symptoms. Proponents of initial conservative management consider that the complication rate after interval appendectomy is significantly lower than that after procedures performed during the acute stage of disease.

Antimicrobial agents should be administered routinely to children when perforation or appendiceal abscess is suspected or discovered during surgery. Antibiotics active against aerobes and anaerobes that normally inhabit the intestinal tract have been effective in treating children with perforated appendicitis. Treatment failures occur most commonly when *B. fragilis* or *Pseudomonas* spp. are isolated from intraoperative cultures and antimicrobial agents without activity against these organisms are used.[59] Controversy continues as to the value of obtaining routine intraoperative peritoneal cultures in cases of perforated appendicitis.[19, 37, 67, 71, 145]

The antimicrobial combination of ampicillin, gentamicin, and clindamycin has been the gold standard of therapy since the 1970s.[85, 136] The importance of including ampicillin in the regimen for adequate enterococcal coverage continues to be controversial. Animal studies and clinical trials using antibiotics with poor enterococcal activity have shown that ampicillin probably is not required in the treatment of perforated appendicitis.[51] Because of the increasing problem of ampicillin resistance in enterococcal strains, ampicillin probably should be reserved for the rare child with enterococcal bacteremia or with persistent intra-abdominal infection in which enterococci have been isolated. Some medical centers use metronidazole instead of clindamycin because of the former's broader activity against enteric anaerobes, whereas other institutions substitute cefotaxime for gentamicin.[136]

In recent years, efforts have been made to determine whether single antibiotics are effective in treating perforated appendicitis. To date, the only agents that have been shown to be effective in treating children with perforated appendicitis are cefoxitin, imipenem-cilastatin, ticarcillin-clavulanate, piperacillin-tazobactam, ampicillin-sulbactam, and meropenem.[47, 67, 140, 141, 154, 166] In a few medical centers, nearly 50 percent of *B. fragilis* isolates are resistant to cefoxitin, thus raising the question as to whether cefoxitin should be used routinely as a single agent in these institutions.[49] In general, the convenience of monotherapy does not outweigh the potential development of resistance to these broad-spectrum agents and their associated increased costs.[67] They may be useful in the treatment of appendicitis in children with renal disease or hearing loss when avoiding the use of gentamicin is prudent.

Most patients with perforated appendicitis are treated with intravenous antibiotics for 5 to 10 days. If complications occur, such as the development of an intra-abdominal abscess, phlegmon, wound infection, or enterocutaneous fistula, another surgical procedure often is performed, and antibiotic treatment is prolonged. In recent years, efforts have been made to shorten the hospital stay of children with perforated appendicitis. Some institutions have set criteria for hospital discharge and discontinuation of antibiotics, such as absence of fever for 24 hours, ability to eat well, and less than 3 percent band forms on the white blood cell differential.[60] Providing home antimicrobial therapy also can reduce costs and hasten hospital discharge in selected children with perforated appendicitis.[147] Single antimicrobial drug therapy may simplify the home care for these patients.[47]

Prognosis and Early Complications

Currently in the United States, the risk of dying of appendicitis is very low. The estimated mortality rate for nonperforated and perforated appendicitis in California during the 1980s was 0.02 percent.[83] In smaller series of children and adults reported in the 1990s, the mortality rate was 0 percent.[85, 91] One statement that has been made is that the risk of death from appendicitis should be the risk of death from general anesthesia.[91] However, the mortality rate appears higher in the rare newborn or premature infant who develops appendicitis. Also, factors contributing to the death of children rarely may include delay in diagnosis, inadequate fluid replacement, immunodeficiency, and postoperative vascular or infectious complications.

The most predictive factor of postoperative morbidity occurring from appendicitis is perforation.[125] Age, obesity, duration of the surgical procedure, and nutritional status also are risk factors for the development of complications.[69] Wound infection rates in children who receive at least perioperative antibiotics have ranged between 0 and 7 percent.[151] The microorganisms that cause wound infections usually are the same organisms that are isolated in cultures obtained during the appendectomy. Occasionally, children develop peritonitis, intra-abdominal abscesses, psoas abscesses, fistulas, pylophlebitis of the portal vein, scrotal abscesses, or pneumoperitoneum during the course of treatment of appendicitis.[10, 55, 61, 128] The next section focuses on pelvic abscess as an early complication of appendicitis because the topic is not discussed elsewhere in this textbook.

Pelvic Abscess

The pelvic area is a common site for development of abscesses because it is the most dependent portion of the peritoneal cavity. Pelvic abscesses most commonly occur in children in whom intestinal perforations have occurred after appendicitis, who have suffered penetrating abdominal or retroperitoneal injury, or who have undergone an abdominal surgical procedure.[4, 50] Occasionally, adolescents with pelvic inflammatory disease or Crohn disease develop a pelvic abscess.[135]

In children with perforated appendicitis, a coexisting pelvic abscess often is diagnosed at the time of laparotomy. In patients who recently have had penetrating trauma to the abdomen or pelvic inflammatory disease or who have undergone gastrointestinal surgery, a pelvic abscess should be suspected when they have continued fever or complain of abdominal pain despite receiving adequate treatment of the initial disease process. Symptoms may not develop until days to months after therapy is terminated. No characteristic physical findings are associated with a pelvic abscess, although abdominal palpation or rectal examination may elicit tenderness, or signs of intestinal obstruction may be present.

If a pelvic abscess is suspected, ultrasonographic and usually CT evaluation of the pelvis should be completed.[50] The bladder should be filled before the procedure so that it can displace bowel loops from the pelvis, act as an anatomic marker, and act as a standard of fluidity against which an abscess cavity can be compared. Walled-off fluid collections in the pelvis can be identified, and sometimes the rectum, sigmoid colon, or bladder is compressed because of mass effect from the abscess cavity.[50] Because most pelvic abscesses develop as complications of intestinal or pelvic infections, enteric aerobes and anaerobes are the organisms most commonly isolated from the abscess cavity. Only rarely do yeasts cause pelvic abscesses.[155, 163] An *Actinomyces* spp.–related pelvic abscess developed in an adult who had an intrauterine device.[113] Rarely, tuberculous abscesses can develop as a complication of genital tuberculosis.[161]

When a pelvic abscess is identified, antibiotics covering intestinal aerobes and anaerobes, such as clindamycin and gentamicin, should be started and the abscess contents should be drained. In most situations, reaching the abscess cavity by an anterior approach is difficult. In recent years, considerable interest has developed in using CT or ultrasonography to guide percutaneous drainage of pelvic abscesses by transgluteal, transrectal, transparacoccygeal, or transvaginal approaches.[4, 15, 27, 43, 46, 78, 79] Although placement of a transgluteal catheter is easiest, the sciatic nerve and gluteal vessels must be avoided.[88] Also, an increased risk for development of a wound infection may occur because microorganisms may track along the outside of the catheter to the skin. Many surgeons prefer the transrectal approach because it often is the most direct route to the abscess. However, transvaginal drainage has been used with good results in young women. Most often, drainage catheters can be removed after 7 to 10 days of treatment.

Abscesses also may develop within the muscles of the pelvic girdle, including the psoas and internal obturator muscles.[23, 144, 146] Similar to true pelvic abscesses, pelvic muscle abscesses usually cause fever in children, who occasionally have abdominal complaints. However, most children begin to limp, refuse to walk, or complain of pain in the buttocks, thigh, or groin.[23, 144] Often, a suppurative hip infection is suspected initially. A pelvic muscle abscess is diagnosed by ultrasonography, CT, or magnetic resonance imaging. Labeled leukocyte scans sometimes are useful in localizing the infection to within the pelvis, especially when the child has no symptoms other than fever or refusing to walk.

Pelvic muscle abscesses (psoas abscesses) usually develop as a complication of Crohn disease or appendicitis; however, they also may develop after an episode of bacteremia. *Staphylococcus aureus* is the most common cause of a primary pelvic muscle abscess.[23, 144, 146] *S. pneumoniae, H. influenzae* type b, *E. coli, Enterococcus faecalis, S. milleri* group, *Yersinia enterocolitica, Salmonella* spp., *Proteus mirabilis*, and *Actinomyces* spp. also have been reported to cause hematogenously acquired abscesses.[23, 24, 31, 34, 62, 66, 70, 137] Bacteremia secondary to intravenous drug abuse or the presence of central lines occasionally predisposes patients to developing this type of infection.[72, 160] Rarely, tuberculous psoas abscesses develop as a complication of vertebral osteomyelitis.

Pelvic muscle abscesses usually are drained by a percutaneous or surgical approach, and antibiotic therapy is based on Gram stain and culture results. Successful therapy with antibiotics alone has been reported.[146] The duration of treatment is individualized and depends on the child's response and the drainage techniques used.

Late Complications

Most children who have undergone appendectomy or drainage of a pelvic abscess do not have late complications. Occasionally, patients later develop signs of bowel obstruction from peritoneal adhesions. Some studies have suggested that the future risk for infertility is greater in women who have perforated appendices or pelvic abscesses, presumably because of adhesion formation that impairs the migration of ova in the reproductive tract.[102] Although some retrospective studies have suggested that patients with appendectomies have a higher rate of developing malignancies later in life, prospective and controlled studies have failed to demonstrate this association.[96, 98] Patients who have had appendicitis have been reported to be three times more likely to develop right inguinal hernias than are people who have not undergone removal of the appendix.[7]

REFERENCES

1. Addiss, D. G,, and Juranek, D. D.: Lack of evidence for a causal association between parasitic infections and acute appendicitis. J. Infect. Dis. *164*:1036–1037, 1991.
2. Addiss, D. G., Shaffer, N., Fowler, B. S., et al.: The epidemiology of appendicitis and appendectomy in the United States. Am. J. Epidemiol. *132*:910–925, 1990.
3. Adebamowo, C. A., Akang, E. E. U., Ladipo, J. K., et al.: Schistosomiasis of the appendix. Br. J. Surg. *78*:1219–1221, 1991.
4. Alexander, A. A., Eschelman, D. J., Nazarian, L. N., et al.: Transrectal sonographically guided drainage of deep pelvic abscesses. A. J. R. Am. J. Roentgenol. *162*:1227–1230, 1994.
5. Angel, C. A., Rao, B. N., Wrenn, E., et al.: Acute appendicitis in children with leukemia and other malignancies: Still a diagnostic dilemma. J. Pediatr. Surg. *27*:476–479, 1992.
6. Arenal Vera, J. J., Marcos Rodriquez, J. L., Borrego Pintado, M. H., et al.: Anisakiasis as a cause of acute appendicitis and rheumatologic picture: The first case in medical literature. Revista Espanola de Enfermedades Digestivas *79*:355–358, 1991.
7. Arnbjornsson, E.: Development of right inguinal hernia after appendectomy. Am. J. Surg. *143*:174–175, 1982.
8. Arora, N. K., Deorari, A. K., Bhatnagar, V., et al.: Neonatal appendicitis: A rare cause of surgical emergency in preterm babies. Indian Pediatr. *28*:1330–1333, 1991.
9. Astagneau, P., Goldstein, F. W., Francoual, S., et al.: Appendicitis due to both *Streptococcus pneumoniae* and *Haemophilus influenzae*. Eur. J. Clin. Microbiol. Infect. Dis. *11*:559–560, 1992.

10. Babcock, D. S.: Ultrasound diagnosis of portal vein thrombosis as a complication of appendicitis. A. J. R. Am. J. Roentgenol. *133*:317–319, 1979.
11. Balthazar, E. J., Birnbaum, B. A., Yee, J., et al.: CT and sonography correlation in acute appendicitis: Prospective evaluation of 100 patients. Radiology *190*:31–35, 1994.
12. Bancroft, F. W., and Skoluda, E. R.: Appendicitis: A study of 596 cases. N. Y. State J. Med. *36*:507–509, 1936.
13. Baron, E. J., Bennion, R., Thompson, J., et al.: Microbiological comparison between acute and complicated appendicitis. Clin. Infect. Dis. *14*:227–231, 1992.
14. Basta, M., Morton, N. E., Mulvihill, J. J., et al.: Inheritance of acute appendicitis: Familial aggregation and evidence of polygenic transmission. Am. J. Hum. Genet. *46*:377–382, 1990.
15. Bennett, J. D., Kozak, R. I., Taylor, B. M., et al.: Deep pelvic abscesses: Transrectal drainage with radiologic guidance. Radiology *185*:825–828, 1992.
16. Bennion, R. S., Baron, E. J., Thompson, J. E., et al.: The bacteriology of gangrenous and perforated appendicitis revisited. Ann. Surg. *211*:165–171, 1990.
17. Bennion, R. S., Thompson, J. E., Gil, J., et al.: The role of *Yersinia enterocolitica* in appendicitis in the southwestern United States. Am. Surg. *57*:766–768, 1991.
18. Bernard, D., Verschraegen, G., Claeys, G., et al.: *Bilophila wadsworthii* bacteremia in a patient with gangrenous appendicitis. Clin. Infect. Dis. *18*:1023–1024, 1994.
19. Bilik, R., Burnweit, C., Shandling, B., et al.: Is abdominal cavity culture of any value in appendicitis? Am. J. Surg. 175:267–270, 1998.
20. Birnbaum, B. A., and Balthazar, E. J.: CT of appendicitis and diverticulitis. Radiol. Clin. North. Am. *32*:885–898, 1994.
21. Bova, R., and Meagher, A.: Appendicitis in HIV-positive patients. Aust. N. Z. J. Surg. *68*:337–339, 1998.
22. Bredesen, J., Lauritzen, A. F., Kristiansen, V. B., et al.: Appendicitis and enterobiasis in children. Acta Chir. Scand. *154*:585–587, 1988.
23. Bresee, J. S., and Edwards, M. S.: Psoas abscess in children. Pediatr. Infect. Dis. J. *9*:201–206, 1990.
24. Brooks, D. J., Cant, A. J., Lambert, H. P., et al.: Recurrent *Salmonella* septicaemia with aortitis, osteomyelitis and psoas abscess. J. Infect. *7*:156–158, 1983.
25. Brooks, D. W., and Killen, D. A.: Roentgenographic findings in acute appendicitis. Surgery *57*:377–384, 1965.
26. Burnweit, C., Bilik, R., and Shandling, B.: Primary closure of contaminated wounds in perforated appendicitis. J. Pediatr. Surg. *26*:1362–1365, 1991.
27. Butch, R. J., Mueller, P. R., Ferrucci, J. T., et al.: Drainage of pelvic abscesses through the greater sciatic foramen. Radiology *158*:487–491, 1986.
28. Canty, T. G., Sr., Collins, D., Losasso, B., et al.: Laparoscopic appendectomy for simple and perforated appendicitis in children: The procedure of choice? J. Pediatr. Surg. *35*:1582–1585, 2000.
29. Chetty, R., Slavin, J. L., and Miller, R. A.: Kaposi's sarcoma presenting as acute appendicitis in an HIV-1 positive patient. Histopathology *23*:590–591, 1993.
30. Cimolai, N., Anderson, J. D., Bhanji, N. M., et al.: *Escherichia coli* 0157:H7 infections associated with perforated appendicitis and chronic diarrhoea. Eur. J. Pediatr. *149*:259–260, 1990.
31. Coakham, H. B., and Ashby, E. C.: Actinomycosis in recurrent psoas abscess. Proc. R. Soc. Med. *65*:880, 1972.
32. Curran, T. J., and Muenchow, S. K.: The treatment of complicated appendicitis in children using peritoneal drainage: Results from a public hospital. J. Pediatr. Surg. *28*:204–208, 1993.
33. Dahlstrom, J. E., and Macarthur, E. B.: *Enterobius vermicularis*: A possible cause of symptoms resembling appendicitis. Aust. N. Z. J. Surg. *64*:92–94, 1994.
34. Davies, D., King, S. M., Parekh, R. S., et al.: Psoas abscess caused by *Haemophilus influenzae*, type b. Pediatr. Infect. Dis. J. *10*:411–412, 1991.
35. Dezfuli, M. G., Oo, M. M., Jones, B. E., et al.: Tuberculosis mimicking acute appendicitis in patients with human immunodeficiency virus infection. Clin. Infect. Dis. *18*:650–651, 1994.
36. Dodd, L. G.: *Balantidium coli* infestation as a cause of acute appendicitis. J. Infect. Dis. *163*:1392, 1991.
37. Dougherty, S. H.: Antimicrobial culture and susceptibility testing has little value for routine management of secondary bacterial peritonitis. Clin. Infect. Dis. 25(Suppl 2):S258–S261, 1997.
38. Dougherty, S. H., Saltzstein, E. C., Peacock, J. B., et al.: Perforated or gangrenous appendicitis treated with aminoglycosides. Arch. Surg. *124*:1280–1283, 1989.
39. Dueholm, S., Bagi, P., and Bud, M.: Laboratory aid in the diagnosis of acute appendicitis: A blinded, prospective trial concerning diagnostic value of leukocyte count, neutrophil differential count, and C-reactive protein. Dis. Colon Rectum *32*:855–859, 1989.
40. Duong, T. H., Dumon, H., Quilici, M., et al.: Taenia et appendicite, ou appendicite a taenia. Presse Med. *15:*2020, 1986.
41. El Ghoneimi, A., Valla, J. S., Limonne, B., et al.: Laparoscopic appendectomy in children: Report of 1,379 cases. J. Pediatr. Surg. *29*:786–789, 1994.
42. Enami, M. A., Frayha, H. H., and Halim, M. A.: An appendiceal abscess due to *Mycobacterium kansasii* in a child with AIDS. Clin. Infect. Dis. *27*:891–892, 1998.
43. Eschelman, D. J., and Sullivan, K. L.: Use of a colapinto needle in US-guided transvaginal drainage of pelvic abscesses. Radiology *186*:893–894, 1993.
44. Fedyshin, P., Kelvin, F. M., and Rice, R. P.: Nonspecificity of barium enema findings in acute appendicitis. A. J. R. Am. J. Roentgenol. *143*:99–102, 1984.
45. Fefferman, N. R., Roche, K. J., Pinkney, L. P., et al.: Suspected appendicitis in children: Focused CT technique for evaluation. Radiology *220*:691–695, 2001.
46. Feld, R., Eschelman, D. J., Sagerman, J. E., et al.: Treatment of pelvic abscesses and other fluid collections: Efficacy of transvaginal sonographically guided aspiration and drainage. A. J. R. Am. J. Roentgenol. *163*:1141–1145, 1994.
47. Fishman, S. J., Pelosi, L., Klavon, S. L., et al.: Perforated appendicitis: Prospective outcome analysis for 150 children. J. Pediatr. Surg. *35*:923–926, 2000.
48. Fitz, R. H.: Perforating inflammation of the vermiform appendix, with special reference to its early diagnosis and treatment. Am. J. Med. Sci. *92*:321–346, 1886.
49. Fraulin, F. O. G., and Thurston, O. G.: Value of cultures of tissue samples taken at operation for lower intestinal perforation. Can. J. Surg. *36*:261–265, 1993.
50. Gazelle, G. S., and Mueller, P. R.: Abdominal abscess: Imaging and intervention. Radiol. Clin. North Am. *32*:913–932, 1994.
51. Gorbach, S. L.: Intra-abdominal infections. Clin. Infect. Dis. *17*:961–967, 1993.
52. Gorecki, W. J., and Grochowski, J. A.: Are antibiotics necessary in nonperforated appendicitis in children? A double blind randomized controlled trial. Med. Sci. Monit. *7*:289–292, 2001.
53. Graham, A. D., and Johnson, H. F.: The incidence of radiographic findings in acute appendicitis compared to 200 normal abdomens. Milit. Med. *131*:272–276, 1966.
54. Gupta, S. C., Gupta, A. K., Keswani, N. K., et al.: Pathology of tropical appendicitis. J. Clin. Pathol. *42*:1169–1172, 1989.
55. Haas, G. P., Shumaker, B. P., and Haas, P. A.: Appendicovesical fistula. Urology *24*:604–609, 1984.
56. Hardwick, R. H., Taylor, A., Thompson, M. H., et al.: Association between *Streptococcus milleri* and abscess formation after appendicitis. Ann. R. Coll. Surg. Engl. *82*:24–26, 2000.
57. Heltberg, O., Korner, B., and Schouenborg, P.: Six cases of acute appendicitis with secondary peritonitis caused by *Streptococcus pneumoniae*. Eur. J. Clin. Microbiol. *3*:141–143, 1984.
58. Henneman, P. L., Marcus, C. S., Inkelis, S. H., et al.: Evaluation of children with possible appendicitis using technetium 99m leukocyte scan. Pediatrics *85*:838–843, 1990.
59. Heseltine, P. N. R., Yellin, A. E., Appleman, M. D., et al.: Perforated and gangrenous appendicitis: An analysis of antibiotic failures. J. Infect. Dis. *148*:322–329, 1983.
60. Hoelzer, D. J., Zabel, D. D., and Zern, J. T.: Determining duration of antibiotic use in children with complicated appendicitis. Pediatr. Infect. Dis. J. *18*:979–982, 1999.
61. Hoffer, F. A., Ablow, R. C., Gryboski, J. D., et al.: Primary appendicitis with an appendico-tuboovarian fistula. A. J. R. Am. J. Roentgenol. *138*:742–743, 1982.
62. Humphreys, H., Keane, C. T., Marron, P., et al.: Infective sacroiliac arthritis and psoas abscess caused by *Streptococcus milleri*. J. Infect. *19*:77–78, 1989.
63. Hyman, P., and Westring, D. W.: Leukocytosis in acute appendicitis: Observed racial difference. J. A. M. A. *229*:1630–1632, 1974.
64. Jackson, D. S., Welch, D. F., Pickett, D. A., et al.: Suppurative infections in children caused by non-beta-hemolytic members of the *Streptococcus milleri* group. Pediatr. Infect. Dis. J. *14*:80–82, 1995.
65. Jakobsen, J., Andersen, J. C., and Klausen, I. C.: Beta-haemolytic streptococci in acute appendicitis. Acta Chir. Scand. *154*:301–303, 1988.
66. Kahn, F. W., Glasser, J. E., and Agger, W. A.: Psoas muscle abscess due to *Yersinia enterocolitica*. Am. J. Med. *76*:947–949, 1984.
67. Kaplan, S.: Antibiotic usage in appendicitis in children. Pediatr. Infect. Dis. J. *17*:1047–1048, 1998.
68. Kazlow, P. G., Freed, J., Rosh, J. R., et al.: *Salmonella typhimurium* appendicitis. J. Pediatr. Gastroenterol. Nutr. *13*:101–103, 1991.
69. Kizilcan, F., Tanyel, F. C., Buyukpamukcu, N., et al.: The necessity of prophylactic antibiotics in uncomplicated appendicitis during childhood. J. Pediatr. Surg. *27*:586–588, 1992.
70. Knobel, B., Sommer, I., and Schwartz, G.: Primary psoas abscess three years after ipsilateral nephrectomy. Infection *13*:27–28, 1985.
71. Kokoska, E. R., Silen, M. L., Tracy, T. F., et al.: The impact of intraoperative culture on treatment and outcome in children with perforated appendicitis. J. Pediatr. Surg. *34*:749–753, 1999.
72. Kwok, T., and Coles, J.: Psoas abscess as a complication of subclavian venous catheterization. Postgrad. Med. J. *66*:771–772, 1990.
73. LaRaja, R. D., Rothenberg, R. E., Odom, J. W., et al.: The incidence of intra-abdominal surgery in acquired immunodeficiency syndrome: A statistical review of 904 patients. Surgery *105*:175–179, 1989.
74. Lavonius, M. I., Liesjarvi, S., Ovaska, J., et al.: Laparoscopic versus open appendectomy in children: A prospective randomized study. Eur. J. Pediatr. Surg. *11*:235–238, 2001.

75. Lee, S. L., Walsh, A. J., and Ho, H. S.: Computed tomography and ultrasonography do not improve and may delay the diagnosis and treatment of acute appendicitis. Arch. Surg. *136*:556–562, 2001.
76. Leigh, D. A., Simmons, K., and Normal, E.: Bacterial flora of the appendix fossa in appendicitis and postoperative wound infection. J. Clin. Pathol. *27*:997–1000, 1974.
77. Lewis, F., Holcroft, J., Boey, J., et al.: Appendicitis in critical review of diagnosis and treatment in 1000 cases. Arch. Surg. *110*:677–684, 1975.
78. Lomas, D. J., Dixon, A. K., Thomson, H. J., et al.: CT-guided drainage of pelvic abscesses: The perianal transrectal approach. Clin. Radiol. *45*:246–249, 1992.
79. Longo, J. M., Bilbao, J. I., deVilla, V. H., et al.: CT-guided paracoccygeal drainage of pelvic abscesses. J. Comput. Assist. Tomogr. *17*:909–914, 1993.
80. Lopez-Navidad, A., Domingo, P., Cada Falch, G.: Acute appendicitis complicating infectious mononucleosis: Case report and review. Rev. Infect. Dis. *12*:297–302, 1990.
81. Loria-Cortes, R., and Lobo-Sanahuja, J. F.: Clinical abdominal angiostrongylosis. Am. J. Trop. Med. Hyg. *29*:538–544, 1980.
82. Lowe, L. H., Penney, M. W., Stein, S. M., et al.: Unenhanced limited CT of the abdomen in the diagnosis of appendicitis in children: Comparison with sonography. A. J. R. Am. J. Roentgenol. *176*:31–35, 2001.
83. Luckmann, R.: Incidence and case fatality rates for acute appendicitis in California: A population-based study of the effects of age. Am. J. Epidemiol. *129*:905–918, 1989.
84. Luckmann, R., and Davis, P.: The epidemiology of acute appendicitis in California: Racial, gender, and seasonal variation. Epidemiology *2*:323–330, 1991.
85. Lund, D. P., and Murphy, E. U.: Management of perforated appendicitis in children: A decade of aggressive treatment. J. Pediatr. Surg. *29*:1130–1134, 1994.
86. Madden, N. P., and Hart, C. A.: *Streptococcus milleri* in appendicitis in children. J. Pediatr. Surg. *20*:6–7, 1985.
87. Malde, H. M., and Chadha, D.: Roundworm obstruction: Sonographic diagnosis. Abdom. Imaging *18*:274–276, 1993.
88. Malden, E. S., and Picus, D.: Hemorrhagic complication of transgluteal pelvic abscess drainage: Successful percutaneous treatment. J. Vasc. Interv. Radiol. *3*:323–328, 1992.
89. Malik, A. K., Hanum, N., and Yip, C. H.: Acute isolated amoebic appendicitis. Histopathology *24*:87–88, 1994.
90. Marrero, R. R., Barnwell, S., and Hoover, E. L.: Appendicitis in children: A continuing clinical challenge. J. Natl. Med. Assoc. *84*:850–852, 1992.
91. Maxwell, J. M., and Ragland, J. J.: Appendicitis: Improvements in diagnosis and treatment. Am. Surg. *57*:282–285, 1991.
92. McAllister, T. A., Fyfe, A. H., Young, D. G., et al.: Cefotaxime lavage in children undergoing appendicectomy. Drugs *35*(Suppl. 2):127–132, 1988.
93. McBurney, C.: Experience with early operative interference in cases of disease of the vermiform appendix. N. Y. State Med. J. *50*:676, 1889.
94. McCahy, P.: Continuing fall in the incidence of acute appendicitis. Ann. R. Coll. Surg. Engl. *76*:282–283, 1994.
95. McNamara, M. J., Pasquale, M. D., and Evans, S. R. T.: Acute appendicitis and the use of intraperitoneal cultures. Surg. Gynecol. Obstet. *177*:393–397, 1993.
96. McVay, J. R.: The appendix in relation to neoplastic disease. Cancer *17*:929–937, 1964.
97. Miron, D., Sochotnick, I., Yardeni, D., et al.: Surgical complications of shigellosis in children. Pediatr. Infect. Dis. J. *19*:898–900, 2000.
98. Moertel, C. G., Nobrega, F. T., Elveback, L. R., et al.: A prospective study of appendectomy and predisposition to cancer. Surg. Gynecol. Obstet. *138*:549–553, 1974.
99. Mogensen, K., Pahle, E., and Kowalski, K.: *Enterobius vermicularis* and acute appendicitis. Acta Chir. Scand. *151*:705–707, 1985.
100. Morrison, J. D.: *Yersinia* and viruses in acute non-specific abdominal pain and appendicitis. Br. J. Surg. *68*:284–286, 1981.
101. Mostafa, G., Matthews, B. D., Sing, R. F., et al.: Mini-laparoscopic versus laparoscopic approach to appendectomy. B. M. C. Surg. 1:1–4, 2001.
102. Mueller, B. A., Daling, J. R., Moore, D. E., et al.: Appendectomy and the risk of tubal infertility. N. Engl. J. Med. *315*:1506–1508, 1986.
103. Mueller, G. P., and Williams, R. A.: Surgical infections in AIDS patients. Am. J. Surg. *169* (Suppl. 5A):34S–38S, 1995.
104. Nadler, S., Cappell, M. S., Bhatt, B., et al.: Appendiceal infection by *Entamoeba histolytica* and *Strongyloides stercoralis* presenting like acute appendicitis. Dig. Dis. Sci. *35*:603–608, 1990.
105. Namnyak, S. S., Martin, D. H., Ferguson, J. D. M., et al.: *Haemophilus segnis* appendicitis. J. Infect. *23*:339–341, 1991.
106. Natesha, R., Barnwell, S., Weaver, W., et al.: Is there evidence for a racial difference in the misdiagnosis in patients explored for appendicitis? J. Natl. Med. Assoc. *81*:269–271, 1989.
107. Neumayer, L. A., Makar, R., Ampel, N. M., et al.: Cytomegalovirus appendicitis in a patient with human immunodeficiency virus infection. Arch. Surg. *128*:467–468, 1993.
108. Nguyen, B-L., Raynor, S., and Thompson, J. S.: Selective versus routine antibiotic use in acute appendicitis. Am. Surg. *5*:280–283, 1992.
109. Nordentoft, T., Bringstrup, F. A., Bremmelgaard, A., et al.: Effect of laparoscopy on bacteremia in acute appendicitis: A randomized controlled study. Surg. Laparosc. Endosc. Percutan. Tech. *10*:302–304, 2000.
110. Ochoa, B.: Surgical complications of ascariasis. World J. Surg. *15*:222–227, 1991.
111. Pancharoen, C., Ruttanamongkol, P., Suwangool, P., et al.: Measles-associated appendicitis: Two case reports and literature review. Scand. J. Infect. Dis. *33*:632–633, 2001.
112. Park, J.: *Escherichia coli* septicemia associated with acute appendicitis. South Med. J. *84*:667–668, 1991.
113. Pearlman, M., Frantz, A. C., Floyd, W. S., et al.: Abdominal wall *Actinomyces* abscess associated with an intrauterine device. J. Reprod. Med. *36*:398–402, 1991.
114. Peltola, H., Ahlqvist, J., Rapola, J., et al.: C-reactive protein compared with white blood cell count and erythrocyte sedimentation rate in the diagnosis of acute appendicitis in children. Acta Chir. Scand. *152*:55–58, 1986.
115. Pena, B. M. G., Mandl, K. D., Kraus, S. J., et al.: Ultrasonography and limited computed tomography in the diagnosis and management of appendicitis in children. J. A. M. A. *282*:1041–1046, 1999.
116. Pena, B. M. G., Taylor, G. A., Lund, D. P., et al.: Effect of computed tomography on patient management and costs in children with suspected appendicitis. Pediatrics *104*:440–446, 1999.
117. Pisacane, A., de Luca, U., Impagliazzo, N., et al.: Breast feeding and acute appendicitis. Br. Med. J. *310*:836–837, 1995.
118. Quillin, S. P., Siegel, M. J., and Coffin, C. M.: Acute appendicitis in children: Value of sonography in detecting perforation. A. J. R. Am. J. Roentgenol. *159*:1265–1268, 1992.
119. Raffensperger, J.: *Eikenella corrodens* infections in children. J. Pediatr. Surg. *21*:644–646, 1986.
120. Raffi, F., David, A., Mouzard, A., et al.: *Pasteurella multocida* appendiceal peritonitis: Report of three cases and review of the literature. Pediatr. Infect. Dis. *5*:695–698, 1986.
121. Ramsden, K., and Freeth, M.: Cryptosporidial infection presenting as an acute appendicitis. Histopathology *14*:209–211, 1989.
122. Rasmussen, O., and Hoffmann, J.: Assessment of the reliability of the symptoms and signs of acute appendicitis. J. R. Coll. Surg. Edinb. *36*:372–377, 1991.
123. Rautio, M., Lonnroth, M., Saxen, H., et al.: Characteristics of an unusual anaerobic pigmented gram-negative rod isolated from normal and inflamed appendices. Clin. Infect. Dis. *25*(Suppl. 2):S107–S110, 1997.
124. Rautio, M., Saxen, H., Siitonen, A., et al.: Bacteriology of histopathologically defined appendicitis in children. Pediatr. Infect. Dis. J. *19*:1078–1083, 2000.
125. Reid, R. I., Dobbs, B. R., and Frizelle, F. A.: Risk factors for post-appendicectomy intra-abdominal abscess. Aust. N. Z. J. Surg. *69*:373–374, 1999.
126. Reynolds, S. L., and Jaffe, D. M.: Diagnosing abdominal pain in a pediatric emergency department. Pediatr. Emerg. Care *8*:126–128, 1992.
127. Rodriguez-Sanjuan, J. C., Martin-Parra, J. I., Seco, I., et al.: C-reactive protein and leukocyte count in the diagnosis of acute appendicitis in children. Dis. Colon Rectum *42*:1325–1329, 1999.
128. Robertson, F. M., Olsen, S. B., Jackson, M. R., et al.: Inguinal-scrotal suppuration following treatment of perforated appendicitis. J. Pediatr. Surg. *28*:267–268, 1993.
129. Rothrock, S. G., Skeoch, G., Rush, J. J., et al.: Clinical features of misdiagnosed appendicitis in children. Ann. Emerg. Med. *20*:45–50, 1991.
130. Ruff, M. E., Friedland, I. R., and Hickey, S. M.: *Escherichia coli* septicemia in nonperforated appendicitis. Arch. Pediatr. Adolesc. Med. *148*:853–855, 1994.
131. Sabbe, L. J. M., Van De Merwe, D., Schouls, L., et al.: Clinical spectrum of infections due to the newly described *Actinomyces* species *A. turicensis, A. radingae,* and *A. europaeus*. J. Clin. Microbiol. *37*:8–13, 1999.
132. Saxen, H., Tarkka, E., Hannikainen, P., et al.: *Escherichia coli* and appendicitis: Phenotypic characteristics of *E. coli* isolates from inflamed and noninflamed appendices. Clin. Infect. Dis. *23*:1038–1042, 1996.
133. Schisgall, R. M.: Appendiceal colic in childhood: The role of inspissated casts of stool within the appendix. Ann. Surg. *192*:687–693, 1980.
134. Schmidt, P., Koltai, J. L., and Weltzien, A.: Actinomycosis of the appendix in childhood. Pediatr. Surg. Int. *15*:63–65, 1999.
135. Schratter-Sehn, A. U., Lochs, H., Handl-Zeller, L., et al.: Endosonographic features of the lower pelvic region in Crohn's disease. Am. J. Gastroenterol. *88*:1054–1057, 1993.
136. Schropp, K. P., Kaplan, S., Golladay, E. S., et al.: A randomized clinical trial of ampicillin, gentamicin and clindamycin versus cefotaxime and clindamycin in children with ruptured appendicitis. Surgery *172*:351–356, 1991.
137. Scott, B. D., and Schmidt, J. H.: Pneumococcal meningitis due to psoas abscess. South. Med. J. *82*:1310–1311, 1989.
138. Sharma, A. K., Shukla, A. K., Agarwal, L. D., et al.: Appendicitis in the newborns. Indian Pediatr. *29*:1293–1294, 1992.
139. Silen, M. L., and Tracy, T. F.: The right lower quadrant "revisited." Pediatr Clin North Am *40*:1201–1211, 1993.
140. Sirinek, K. R., and Levine, B. A.: Antimicrobial management of surgically treated gangrenous or perforated appendicitis: Comparison of cefoxitin and clindamycin-gentamicin. Clin. Ther. *9*:420–428, 1987.

141. Sirinek, K. R., and Levine, B. A.: A randomized trial of ticarcillin and clavulanate versus gentamicin and clindamycin in patients with complicated appendicitis. Surg. Gynecol. Obstet. *172*:30–35, 1991.
142. Sivit, C. J.: Diagnosis of acute appendicitis in children: Spectrum of sonographic findings. A. J. R. Am. J. Roentgenol. *161*:147–152, 1993.
143. Sivit, C. J., Newman, K. D., Boenning, D. A., et al.: Appendicitis: Usefulness of US in diagnosis in a pediatric population. Radiology *185*:549–552, 1992.
144. Snook, M. E., and LiPuma, J. J.: Pelvic muscle abscess: An unusual cause of gait disturbance in young children. Clin. Pediatr. *32*:298–299, 1993.
145. Soffer, D., Zait, S., Klausner, J., et al.: Peritoneal cultures and antibiotic treatment in patients with perforated appendicitis. Eur. J. Surg. *167*:214–216, 2001.
146. Souid, A. K., Sadowitz, P. D., Weiner, L., et al.: Obturator internus muscle abscess: A case report and review of the literature. Am. J. Dis. Child. *147*:1278–1279, 1993.
147. Stovroff, M. C., Totten, M., and Glick, P. L.: PIC lines save money and hasten discharge in the care of children with ruptured appendicitis. J. Pediatr. Surg. *29*:245–247, 1994.
148. Thadepalli, H., Mandal, A. K., Chuah, S. K., et al.: Bacteriology of the appendix and the ileum in health and in appendicitis. Am. Surg. *57*:317–322, 1991.
149. Tobe, I.: Inapparent virus infection as a trigger of appendicitis. Lancet *1*:1343–1346, 1965.
150. Tonz, M., Schmid, P., and Kaiser, G.: Antibiotic prophylaxis for appendectomy in children: Critical appraisal. World J. Surg. *24*:995–998, 2000.
151. Tsang, T. M., Tam, P. K. H., and Saing, H.: Antibiotic prophylaxis in acute non-perforated appendicitis in children: Single dose of metronidazole and gentamicin. J. R. Coll. Surg. Edinb. *37*:110–112, 1992.
152. Tufariello, J. M., Kaleya, R. N., and Klein, R. S.: Group A streptococcal appendicitis in a patient with AIDS. Diagn. Microbiol. Infect. Dis. *38*:171–172, 2000.
153. Uchimura, M., Tsuruoka, Y., Hukuda, T., et al.: Isolation of vero toxin-producing *Escherichia coli* (enterohemorrhagic *E. coli*) 0111:H- from 2 cases diagnosed as appendicitis. Kansenshogaku Zasshi *65*:905–908, 1991.
154. Uhari, M., Seppanen, J., and Heikkinen, E.: Imipenem-cilastatin vs. tobramycin and metronidazole for appendicitis-related infections. Pediatr. Infect. Dis. J. *11*:445–450, 1992.
155. Urizar, R. E., Lepow, M., Neumann, M., et al.: Fungal peritonitis with splenic-pelvic abscess in a patient on continuous ambulatory peritoneal dialysis. Peritoneal Dialysis Int. *13*:162–163, 1993.
156. Van Noyen, R., Selderslaghs, R., Bekaert, J., et al.: Causative role of *Yersinia* and other enteric pathogens in the appendicular syndrome. Eur. J. Clin. Microbiol. Infect. Dis. *10*:735–741, 1991.
157. Visvanathan, K., Jones, P. D., and Truskett, P.: Abdominal mycobacterial infection mimicking acute appendicitis in an AIDS patient. Aust. N. Z. J. Surg. *63*:558–560, 1993.
158. Volinsky, J. B., Karrer, F. M., Todd, J. K.: Hemolytic-uremic syndrome caused by *Escherichia coli* 0157:H7 after perforated appendix. Pediatr. Infect. Dis. J. *17*:846–847, 1998.
159. Walker, A. R., and Walker, B. F.: Appendicitis in South Africa inter-ethnic school pupils. Am. J. Gastroenterol. *82*:219–222, 1987.
160. Walsh, T. R., Reilly, J. R., Hanley, E., et al.: Changing etiology of iliopsoas abscess. Am. J. Surg. *163*:413–416, 1992.
161. Wehner, J. H., De Bruyne, K., Kagawa, F. T., et al.: Pulmonary tuberculosis, amenorrhea, and a pelvic mass. West. J. Med. *161*:515–518, 1994.
162. Wiebe, B. M.: Appendicitis and *Enterobius vermicularis*. Scand. J. Gastroenterol. *26*:336–338, 1991.
163. Wiesenfeld, H. C., Berg, S. R., and Sweet, R. L.: *Torulopsis glabrata* pelvic abscess and fungemia. Obstet. Gynecol. *83*:887–889, 1994.
164. Williams, N., and Kapila, L.: Acute appendicitis in the preschool child. Arch. Dis. Child. *66*:1270–1272, 1991.
165. Williams, N., and Kapila, L.: Acute appendicitis in the under 5-year-old. J. R. Coll. Surg. Edinb. *39*:168–170, 1994.
166. Wilson, S. E.: Results of a randomized, multicenter trial of meropenem versus clindamycin/tobramycin for the treatment of intra-abdominal infections. Clin. Infect. Dis. *24*(Suppl. 2):S197–S206, 1997.
167. Wong, M. L., Casey, S. O., Leonidas, J. C., et al.: Sonographic diagnosis of acute appendicitis in children. J. Pediatr. Surg. *29*:1356–1360, 1994.
168. Yacoe, M. E., and Jeffrey, R. B.: Sonography of appendicitis and diverticulitis. Radiol. Clin. North Am. *32*:899–912, 1994.
169. Yasumoto, R., Kawano, M., Kawanishi, H., et al.: Left acute scrotum associated with appendicitis. Int. J. Urol. *5*:108–110, 1998.

Pancreatitis

THOMAS L. KUHLS

Before 1980, pancreatitis was thought to be a rare cause of abdominal pain in children and a disease primarily of adults.[66] Because of better recognition of symptoms in children and the more frequent use of medications that cause pancreatic inflammation, pancreatitis currently is being diagnosed more frequently in pediatric practices. Pancreatitis develops in an estimated 1 in 50,000 children, a figure nearly 10 times higher than noted in previous decades.[35] The mortality rate for children with pancreatitis is 14 percent.[79]

When compared with causes of pancreatitis in adults—primarily alcoholism, cholelithiasis, and trauma—causes of childhood pancreatitis are more diverse. Microorganisms account for a significant proportion of cases of pancreatitis in children. In addition, antimicrobial agents have been associated with severe and occasionally fatal episodes of pancreatitis, and bacterial infections may complicate the natural history of acute and chronic pancreatitis. Thus, pediatricians who care for children with pancreatitis must have expertise in the diagnosis and treatment of infectious diseases.

Clinical Manifestations

More than 80 percent of children with pancreatitis complain of abdominal pain.[58, 134, 141] However, only 30 percent of pediatric patients have epigastric pain as usually described by adults.[134] In children, other sites of tenderness or diffuse pain include the right upper quadrant of the abdomen, the periumbilical area, the entire abdomen, and, less commonly, the right lower quadrant of the abdomen. The onset of pain usually is rapid and increases to a maximal intensity in a few hours. Usually, it is described as sharp and excruciating in nature. Only one third of children complain of pain that radiates to other areas, including the back, lower part of the abdomen, upper abdominal quadrants, and anterior chest wall. In school-age children, the pain often intensifies after meals.

Most children with pancreatitis have nausea and vomiting. Children younger than 5 years occasionally experience vomiting without abdominal tenderness.[141] Fever is present in only 30 percent of children with pancreatitis, but temperatures higher than 38.5°C are observed occasionally.[134]

On physical examination, children usually are found lying quietly on their sides with their knees flexed. They have epigastric tenderness to palpation and decreased or absent bowel sounds. Abdominal distention is found in 30 percent of children with pancreatitis and occurs more commonly in preschool-age children.[134, 141] Occasionally, rebound tenderness, guarding of the epigastrium, jaundice, an abdominal mass, or ascites is detected. Rarely, ecchymoses of the flanks (Grey Turner sign) or the umbilical area (Cullen sign) can be identified but usually only when life-threatening hemorrhagic pancreatitis is present.

Laboratory Diagnosis

The single most common useful laboratory test for the clinical diagnosis of pancreatitis in children is measurement of serum amylase, but the level correlates poorly with the severity of the disease.[35, 58, 66] The serum concentration rises quickly within hours after symptoms in more than 90 percent of children with pancreatitis. High serum amylase concentrations, however, can be observed in numerous other illnesses, including acute cholecystitis, intestinal obstruction, perforated abdominal organs, appendicitis, salpingitis, ruptured ectopic pregnancy, and salivary gland disease. The serum amylase concentration can return to normal in 24 to 72 hours after the onset of symptoms, and, therefore, the diagnosis of pancreatitis can be missed. In this situation, the urine amylase concentration can remain elevated for at least 1 week.

Rarely, serum amylase concentrations are not elevated during the course of pancreatitis in children.[107] In addition, marked hyperlipidemia may interfere with the laboratory measurement of amylase.[16] Serum lipase is useful in these situations; however, high serum concentrations often are not detected until 24 hours after the beginning of the illness. Because lipase is produced only in the pancreas and intestinal cells, measurement of its serum concentration helps distinguish children with high serum amylase concentrations of pancreatic as opposed to salivary origin. Measurement of serum trypsinogen may be the most sensitive and specific way of detecting acute pancreatitis, but it is not available in most clinical laboratories.[134]

Nonspecific laboratory findings in children with pancreatitis can include leukocytosis with increased immature polymorphonuclear leukocytes and an elevated erythrocyte sedimentation rate. In children with fulminant hemorrhagic pancreatitis, anemia develops quickly. Other associated findings include hyperglycemia, hypertriglyceridemia, hypoalbuminemia, and hypocalcemia. Elevated transaminases and alkaline phosphatase generally are observed only when the episode of pancreatitis is caused by biliary obstruction, such as in gallstone-related disease.

The radiographic features of childhood pancreatitis also are nonspecific. Radiographs of the abdomen may demonstrate localized ileus of the jejunum in the midepigastric or left upper quadrant region adjacent to the pancreas (sentinel loop), a distended transverse colon without visualization of the descending colon because of adjacent pancreatic inflammation (colon cutoff sign), duodenal distention with air-fluid levels, or loss of the left psoas shadow.[58] Occasionally, chest radiography reveals an elevated left hemidiaphragm or pleural effusion.

In recent years, the ability to diagnose pancreatitis in children has been improved greatly by ultrasonography.[36] Normally, the echodensity of the pancreas is equal to or greater than that of the left lobe of the liver. During acute pancreatitis, edema causes the gland to enlarge and become less dense than the liver. These two findings can aid in making the diagnosis of pancreatitis, and such complications as abscesses and pseudocysts can be identified. Visualization of the pancreas by ultrasonography may be obscured because of overlying bowel gas. In such cases, computed tomography (CT) is useful in detecting pancreatic size and density. Often, CT imaging is helpful in complicated cases of pancreatitis, especially when surgery is being considered. In recent years, magnetic resonance cholangiopancreatography has been used as a noninvasive technique for evaluating children with pancreatitis.[9]

Endoscopic retrograde cholangiopancreatography is difficult to perform in children but occasionally should be considered for those with pancreatitis to exclude gallstones, pseudocysts, strictures, or ascaris infection.[102]

Noninfectious Etiologies

An etiology for childhood pancreatitis can be determined in more than 90 percent of cases if diagnostic evaluation is thorough.[141] However, the frequency of each specific cause is highly dependent on the patient population of the particular medical center. For instance, 33 percent of children with pancreatitis at Children's Hospital of Michigan have biliary tract–related disease because of their large sickle-cell anemia patient population.[141] At Yale–New Haven Hospital, on the other hand, drug-related pancreatitis accounts for 30 percent of the total cases of childhood pancreatitis because of the frequent use of immunosuppressive and cancer chemotherapeutic agents in this hospital setting.[58]

TRAUMA

Table 59–1 outlines the most common noninfectious causes of pancreatitis in children. In most series, trauma is the leading cause of acute pancreatitis. Because the pancreas is immobilized by the stomach, duodenum, and vertebrae and because the organ is highly vascular, it is susceptible to blunt and penetrating trauma. The less developed abdominal wall musculature in pediatric patients may enhance their susceptibility to pancreatic injury after episodes of blunt trauma. Child abuse has been recognized increasingly as a cause of trauma-related pancreatitis. Postoperative pancreatitis occurs most commonly after abdominal or cardiac surgery.[43] Pancreatitis also may be associated with traumatic brain injury in children.[126]

MEDICATIONS

Medications used in pediatric practice increasingly are causing episodes of pancreatitis in children. Azathioprine, steroids, 6-mercaptopurine, and L-asparaginase have been associated with cases of childhood pancreatitis, and other immunosuppressive agents most likely play a role in post-transplantation pancreatitis.[71, 80, 100, 114, 137] Valproic acid is a pediatric anticonvulsant that is used commonly and that can cause pancreatitis.[33, 134] Diuretics, including hydrochlorothiazide and furosemide, have been associated with disease.[80] Acute pancreatitis recently has been associated with growth hormone therapy and sulfasalazine treatment of inflammatory bowel disease.[48, 81] Alcohol consumption is an uncommon cause of pancreatitis in younger children; however, it can cause illness occasionally in the adolescent population.

TABLE 59–1 ■ NONINFECTIOUS CAUSES OF CHILDHOOD PANCREATITIS

Trauma
Blunt
Penetrating
Postoperative
Brain injury

Drugs
Immunosuppressives (azathioprine, steroids, asparaginase, 6-mercaptopurine, tacrolimus)
Diuretics (thiazides, furosemide, ethacrynic acid)
Valproic acid
Growth hormone
Ethyl alcohol
Antimicrobials (pentamidine, antimonials, interferon-α, sulfonamides, tetracycline, rifampin, metronidazole, dapsone, nitrofurantoin, erythromycin, ceftriaxone, 2′, 3′-dideoxyinosine)

Obstructive Diseases
Cholelithiasis
Anatomic abnormalities

Genetic and Metabolic Diseases
Hyperlipoproteinemia types I, IV, V
Cystic fibrosis
Diabetes mellitus
Hyperparathyroidism
Aminoacidurias
Glycogen storage disease type 1
Recurrent hereditary pancreatitis
Chronic idiopathic pancreatitis

Vasculitic Diseases
Kawasaki syndrome
Henoch-Schönlein purpura
Systemic lupus erythematosus

Miscellaneous
Crohn disease
Scorpions of Trinidad and Israel
Reye syndrome
Anticholinesterase insecticide intoxication
Lymphoma
Orthotopic liver transplantation

Physicians with expertise in the management of infectious diseases are becoming more aware of drug-induced pancreatitis because many antimicrobial agents can cause pancreatic inflammation. Pentamidine isethionate is used in the treatment of *Pneumocystis carinii* pneumonia, African trypanosomiasis, and leishmaniasis. It may cause hypoglycemia because of toxicity to pancreatic islet cells and is associated with severe and occasionally fatal episodes of pancreatitis.[86, 90, 142] In children and adults, aerosolized pentamidine prophylaxis for *P. carinii* pneumonia also has been associated with severe cases of pancreatitis in patients with acquired immunodeficiency syndrome (AIDS).[53, 86] Similarly, pentavalent antimonials such as sodium stibogluconate and meglumine antimonate used for the treatment of visceral leishmaniasis can induce pancreatic inflammation.[10, 75]

Sulfonamides, including trimethoprim-sulfamethoxazole, have been implicated on occasion as a cause of acute pancreatitis in adults.[4, 8] Symptoms have recurred when patients have been re-exposed to the medication. The abdominal pain often is accompanied by a hypersensitivity-type rash. Tetracycline-induced pancreatitis has been described in children with and without overt liver disease.[41, 122] In addition, metronidazole, erythromycin, rifampin, dapsone, and nitrofurantoin have been added to the list of agents that can cause pancreatitis in previously healthy persons.[15, 28, 34, 93, 101] Recently, an adolescent who was receiving ceftriaxone developed pancreatitis secondary to obstruction of the biliary tract from gallstones.[82]

Pancreatitis has been a major dose-limiting toxic effect of the human immunodeficiency virus (HIV)-inhibiting drug 2′,3′-dideoxyinosine in adult and pediatric patients with AIDS.[24, 25] Most episodes of pancreatitis occur when the dose is 360 mg/m^2/day or more, and usually the pancreatic inflammation resolves when the medication is discontinued. Concomitant administration of pentamidine with 2′,3′-dideoxyinosine possibly increases the risk of developing pancreatitis. In pediatric patients with AIDS, serum amylase concentrations often are elevated in those without pancreatic symptoms, whereas children with pancreatitis can have normal serum amylase concentrations. Thus, the serum lipase concentration is useful in evaluating HIV-infected children for possible pancreatic inflammation.[25, 86] Increased liver transaminase or lipase concentrations before the administration of 2′,3′-dideoxyinosine may be helpful in predicting the children in whom pancreatitis will develop.[25] In all children with symptoms consistent with pancreatitis, 2′,3′-dideoxyinosine should be withheld pending the results of a lipase assay, and it should be discontinued if the concentration is elevated. Similarly, 2′,3′-dideoxyinosine should be discontinued for 1 week after treatment with pentamidine for *P. carinii* pneumonia.[46]

Interferon-α, which is used in the treatment of chronic hepatitis and malignancies, also has been associated with the development of pancreatitis.[117]

OBSTRUCTIVE DISEASES

Obstruction of the common bile duct, pancreatic duct, or sphincter of Oddi may cause pancreatitis.[5, 97] Gallstones or congenital anatomic malformations, including an annular pancreas, pancreas divisum, choledochal cysts, and intrapancreatic duplication cysts, can cause pancreatitis by obstructing normal pancreatic flow.

GENETIC AND METABOLIC DISEASES

Metabolic diseases often are associated with recurrent episodes of pancreatitis. Such diseases include hyperlipoproteinemias, cystic fibrosis, diabetes mellitus, hyperparathyroidism, aminoacidurias, and glycogen storage disease type I.[58, 67, 115] Recurrent hereditary pancreatitis usually occurs in an autosomal dominant pattern, with onset taking place between infancy and adolescence.[108] It has been linked to chromosome 7q35. The mutation allows trypsinogen to become activated to trypsin within the pancreas. Other children and adults with chronic idiopathic pancreatitis have been shown to have mutations in the cystic fibrosis transmembrane regulator (CFTR) gene similar to individuals with cystic fibrosis.[31, 111, 124]

VASCULITIC DISEASES

Pancreatitis also can occur in syndromes in which vasculitis is a major component of the disease process. It has been associated with common pediatric diseases, including Kawasaki syndrome, Henoch-Schönlein purpura, and systemic lupus erythematosus.[29, 58, 119]

MISCELLANEOUS CAUSES

Other pediatric diseases that have been associated with pancreatitis include Crohn disease and Reye syndrome.[49, 110] The venom of the scorpions *Tityus trinitatus* and *Leiurus quinquestriatus* can cause pancreatitis in patients who have been stung; however, these species do not live naturally in the United States.[13, 116] The gastrointestinal symptoms observed in children with anticholinesterase insecticide poisoning may be caused by pancreatitis.[135] Rarely, primary pancreatic lymphoma may be manifested during childhood as acute pancreatitis.[40]

Although a much less common occurrence than in adults, acute pancreatitis after orthotopic liver transplantation is severe in children and often results in death.[120, 121] The cause of pancreatitis in liver transplant recipients most likely is multifactorial but probably involves traumatic injury, biliary obstruction, and immunosuppressive therapy.

Infectious Etiologies

Infections caused by various microorganisms have been demonstrated by culture, histologic examination, or antibody titer rise during the course of acute pancreatitis in humans (Table 59–2). However, a true causal relationship usually is not demonstrated. Although not all of the following infectious agents have been shown to be associated with childhood pancreatitis, they must be considered as possible etiologic agents because adult patients with infectious pancreatitis have been described.

VIRAL INFECTIONS

Mumps virus and group B coxsackieviruses are the best documented causes of pancreatitis in children. Usually, mumps pancreatitis occurs in the presence of parotitis; however, abdominal pain and vomiting may occur for days before the development of salivary swelling.[132] Rarely, mumps virus can cause pancreatitis without other common clinical manifestations.[91] Because more than 80 percent of children with mumps parotitis have elevated serum amylase concentrations, the diagnosis of pancreatitis should be aided by ultrasonography and serum lipase concentrations.[52] An estimated 15 percent of children with mumps virus infection have abdominal tenderness and vomiting suggestive of the diagnosis of pancreatitis.[58] Only in a single report has the pancreatitis been hemorrhagic and severe.[44] Occasionally, chronic or recurring pancreatitis develops after mumps infection.[139]

Pancreatitis has been caused by group B coxsackieviruses in children. Associated clinical manifestations include aseptic meningitis, mild diarrhea, rash, and myocarditis.[26, 61] How commonly these enteroviruses cause pancreatic inflammation is unknown. Thirty-one percent of patients with aseptic meningitis during an epidemic of group B coxsackievirus infection had increased serum amylase concentrations in one epidemiologic study.[92] Multiple studies have demonstrated coxsackievirus-induced damage to pancreatic acinar cells in mouse models of infection.[17, 130] Coxsackievirus B strains have been isolated from pancreatic biopsy samples of patients with chronic pancreatitis.[112]

Researchers previously thought that acute pancreatitis occurred in cases of viral hepatitis only when fulminant liver disease developed. Increasingly, however, children with mild hepatitis A infection and pancreatitis are being described.[1, 77, 87] Additionally, an adolescent with acute hepatitis and pancreatitis was found to have hepatitis E viral infection.[87] Hepatitis B viral antigens have been detected in the pancreatic glandular cells of patients with severe acute hemorrhagic pancreatitis.[129] The role of hepatitis B virus in the pathogenesis of pancreatic inflammation in these patients is unknown.

Human herpesviruses are uncommon causes of childhood pancreatitis. Occasionally, pancreatitis develops in children and adolescents with infectious mononucleosis.[73, 89] Acute pancreatitis and occasionally pseudocyst formation also have been reported in immunocompetent individuals with varicella infection.[72, 123] In addition, an immunocompetent 22-year-old patient developed pancreatitis during a period in which seroconversion to cytomegalovirus was documented.[69]

Viral pancreatitis also occurs in immunocompromised patients. Cytomegalovirus has been identified in pancreatic specimens from autopsies of AIDS, transplant, and cancer chemotherapy patients.[62, 64] Moreover, the symptoms of pancreatitis have resolved in a few patients with AIDS treated with ganciclovir or foscarnet.[32] Adenovirus has caused hemorrhagic pancreatitis and death in a child who received a bone marrow transplant, and varicella-zoster virus has caused pancreatitis and death in a patient with AIDS.[45, 95] Disseminated parainfluenza virus infection in an infant with severe combined immunodeficiency was temporally associated with the

TABLE 59–2 ■ MICROORGANISMS ASSOCIATED WITH EPISODES OF ACUTE PANCREATITIS

Viruses
Mumps virus
Group B coxsackieviruses
Hepatitis A virus
Hepatitis B virus
Hepatitis E virus
Epstein-Barr virus
Varicella-zoster virus
Cytomegalovirus
Adenoviruses
Parainfluenza viruses
Human immunodeficiency virus
Measles virus
Rubella virus
Rotavirus
Parasites
Ascaris lumbricoides
Clonorchis sinensis
Fasciola hepatica
Taenia saqinata
Echinococcus granulosus
Wuchereria bancrofti
Cryptosporidium parvum
Toxoplasma gondii
Plasmodium falciparum
Mycoplasmas and Bacteria
Mycoplasma pneumoniae
Escherichia coli
Salmonella species
Campylobacter jejuni
Yersinia species
Legionella species
Mycobacterium tuberculosis
Leptospira species
Brucella melitensis
Fungi
Aspergillus species
Candida species
Cryptococcus neoformans

development of pancreatitis; however, no attempt was made to culture the virus from postmortem pancreatic tissue.[47]

Whether HIV directly causes pancreatitis is unclear. Laboratory-diagnosed episodes of pancreatitis in adults and children with AIDS do occur, but whether the pancreatic inflammation is caused by HIV or an unrecognized opportunistic pathogen is unknown.[140] However, HIV-infected children frequently have elevated amylase and lipase levels with no correlation to antiviral therapy.[27]

Interstitial pancreatitis also occurs relatively commonly in children with congenital rubella syndrome.[88] In addition, severe pancreatitis has been identified in immunocompetent and immunocompromised patients with fatal measles virus infection.[127] One case of an adolescent with rotavirus gastroenteritis in whom pancreatitis developed has been reported.[38]

PARASITE INFESTATIONS AND INFECTIONS

Ascaris lumbricoides can migrate in the intestines to the ampulla of Vater and subsequently to the pancreatic duct or common bile duct. Obstruction of the biliary or pancreatic duct can cause acute pancreatitis.[11, 70] Ascariasis is diagnosed when adult roundworms are identified in the duodenum by radiographs of the upper gastrointestinal tract (Fig. 59–1) or more commonly by ultrasonography or retrograde cholangiopancreatography. Often, a history of seeing worms in the feces can be elicited. The flukes *Clonorchis sinensis* and *Fasciola hepatica* and the cestode *Taenia saginata* also can migrate to the pancreatic and biliary drainage systems and cause pancreatitis.[18, 113, 128] Rarely, hepatic hydatid cysts can obstruct biliary drainage and cause pancreatic inflammation.[20, 84] *Wuchereria bancrofti* occasionally has been found to cause chronic pancreatitis.[63] Parasitic infestations should be considered as a cause of pancreatitis, particularly in immigrant children and patients who have traveled to developing nations.

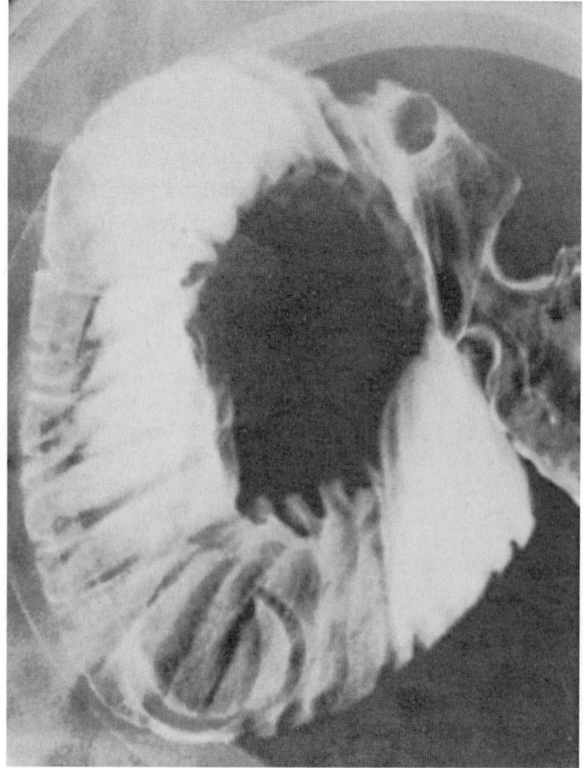

FIGURE 59–1 ■ An ascaris close to the ampulla of Vater, the body and tail lying in the second and third parts of the duodenum. The patient is a 9-year-old girl with acute pancreatitis.

The protozoan *Cryptosporidium parvum* has been identified in the bile of a patient with AIDS and with elevated serum amylase and right upper quadrant abdominal pain.[50] Cholangiopancreatography demonstrated biliary and pancreatic ductal disease, but no other opportunistic pathogens could be isolated. *Cryptosporidia* also have been observed in the interlobular pancreatic ducts of experimentally infected immunocompromised mice.[125] Whether cryptosporidial infection causes pancreatitis in immunocompetent patients is unknown; however, a previously healthy adolescent developed pancreatitis after having a bout of cryptosporidial diarrhea.[54] *Toxoplasma gondii* cysts have been found in the postmortem pancreatic tissue of patients with AIDS.[2, 59] Rarely, pancreatitis occurs during acute episodes of falciparum malaria.[65] Other systemic manifestations of malaria that often are present include high fever, hepatitis, intestinal malabsorption, encephalitis, and pulmonary insufficiency.

MYCOPLASMAL AND BACTERIAL INFECTIONS

In adolescents and adults, moderately severe symptoms of pancreatitis have occurred just before or during the course of atypical pneumonia.[56, 83] In these cases, most patients have had cold agglutinins in their sera, and all have had significant changes in *Mycoplasma pneumoniae* antibody titer. Some controversy has ensued over whether *M. pneumoniae* can cause acute pancreatitis without evidence of pneumonia. Although complement-fixing IgM antibodies against *M. pneumoniae* often increase significantly during the course of acute pancreatitis, researchers have argued that pancreatic cellular antigenic components similar to *Mycoplasma* lipid antigens are exposed during the disease process and that the antibodies elicited cross-react in *Mycoplasma* serologic assays.[76]

Generally accepted is that common pyogenic bacteria do not cause acute pancreatitis. However, secondary invasion of inflamed pancreatic tissue does occur. Some evidence exists that circulating endotoxin from *Escherichia coli* can cause extrahepatic cholestasis and pancreatitis.[39] Acute pancreatitis also has been seen in children with hemolytic-uremic syndrome.[21, 105] Occasionally, pancreatitis occurs during acute episodes of enteritis. *Salmonella typhimurium, Salmonella typhosa, Campylobacter jejuni, Yersinia enterocolitica,* and *Yersinia pseudotuberculosis* all have been reported to cause clinically evident and laboratory-confirmed cases of pancreatitis.[7, 37, 57, 109]

Along with *M. pneumoniae* infection, legionnaires' disease must be considered when acute pancreatitis develops along with pneumonia.[85, 138] In addition, miliary tuberculosis can cause symptoms of pancreatitis.[42, 106] The prognosis of patients with tuberculous pancreatitis generally is poor.

Pancreatitis has been reported in children with leptospirosis.[14, 96] *Brucella melitensis* also has been added to the list of uncommon causes of acute pancreatitis.[3]

FUNGAL INFECTIONS

Fungal infections have not been reported to cause acute pancreatitis in immunocompetent patients. However, *Aspergillus* has caused fatal hemorrhagic pancreatitis in an adult patient with cancer who was undergoing chemotherapy.[51] *Candida* spp. and *Cryptococcus neoformans* have been isolated from the pancreatic tissue of patients with AIDS, but whether they cause clinical symptoms of pancreatitis is unknown.[140]

Pathogenesis

Enzymes for polysaccharides, fats, and proteins are produced and stored in pancreatic acinar cells. They exist intracellularly in an inactive precursor form. After cholecystokinin-pancreozymin stimulation, the proenzymes are released into the pancreatic ducts and flow into the duodenum. The enzymes normally do not become enzymatically active until they reach the intestinal lumen.

When proteolytic enzymes are activated within the pancreas, pancreatitis results from autodigestion and inflammation of the gland.[16] The specific mechanisms that activate pancreatic enzymes during specific pathologic processes have not been well elucidated. Drug-induced and infectious causes of pancreatitis are thought to be due to direct toxic effects on acinar cells. Gallstones, ascaris infection, and congenital abnormalities are thought to damage acinar cells by obstructing pancreatic flow. Traumatic pancreatitis probably occurs as a result of direct injury to the glandular cells, whereas vasculitis may cause changes in pancreatic blood flow, thereby eliciting premature activation of proteolytic enzymes.

Autodigestion of the pancreas causes inflammation. The inflammatory response can be relatively mild, as occurs commonly in episodes of infectious pancreatitis, or be more severe with hemorrhagic necrosis, as occurs typically in adults after the consumption of alcohol.

Treatment

Despite our increasing recognition of cases of childhood pancreatitis, no major advances have been made in treatment of the disease since the mid-1970s.[78] Animal data have demonstrated that such medications as glucagon, aprotinin, 5-fluorouracil, and somatostatin may be useful in the treatment of pancreatitis; however, trials in adults have not substantiated their efficacy.[30, 118] The continuing main objectives of treatment are to relieve abdominal pain, reduce pancreatic exocrine secretion, and aggressively treat systemic manifestations such as shock, electrolyte abnormalities, and anemia.[66] Meperidine continues to be the medication most commonly used for controlling pain.

In the past, children were kept in the fasted state and nasogastric suction was applied to decrease duodenal acid–stimulated secretin release. Feeding with carbohydrate solutions was not restarted until all symptoms had resolved. Recent studies in adults, however, have demonstrated that jejunal feeding with a low-fat elemental diet decreases the complication rate of treating patients with acute pancreatitis and now is considered the treatment of choice over total parenteral nutrition.[104, 136] Intravenous fluids and colloids are used during the acute episode to maintain intravascular volume. During the entire course of acute pancreatitis, the hematologic and biochemical parameters of the child must be monitored closely.

If the episode of pancreatitis is drug induced, use of the medication should be curtailed immediately. Often, the symptoms recur if the medication is restarted. Pancreatitis caused by *M. pneumoniae* or bacteria should be treated with proper antimicrobials. Obstructions to pancreatic flow (e.g., gallstones, roundworms, congenital abnormalities) may have to be removed or altered surgically or endoscopically.[22, 74, 102]

Complications

During the acute episode of pancreatitis, renal, hematologic, central nervous system, pulmonary, and cardiovascular complications can occur as a result of shock.

In 12 percent of children with pancreatitis, an inflammatory mass develops in the first weeks after the onset of illness.[131] Continued or increasing abdominal pain, nausea, or vomiting often accompanies the development of a phlegmon, abscess, or pseudocyst. An inflammatory phlegmon usually develops into a thin-walled pseudocyst of the lesser sac but may become secondarily infected and induce the formation of an abscess. Patients in whom an inflammatory mass develops must be monitored closely with frequent physical examinations and serial ultrasound studies. In children with pseudocysts, acute abdominal pain accompanied by hypotension often signifies bleeding into the pseudocyst or rupture of the pseudocyst into the peritoneum. Slowly leaking pseudocysts may cause pancreatic ascites. Pseudocysts either are resected surgically or are drained externally when complications occur. Approximately 33 percent of pseudocysts resolve spontaneously within 6 weeks.[103]

The development of fever and leukocytosis during the course of pancreatitis should suggest an infected pseudocyst or pancreatic abscess. The role of prophylactic antibiotics in preventing the suppurative complications of acute pancreatitis is controversial; prophylactic antibiotics should be considered only when pancreatic necrosis is severe.[19, 98, 99] Infections, when they do occur after the administration of prophylactic antimicrobials, often are caused by bacteria that are resistant to the antimicrobials commonly used. In adults, infectious complications account for 80 percent of deaths associated with acute pancreatitis.[23] Isolates from pancreatic abscesses have yielded intestinal flora, including anaerobes, in more than 90 percent of cases, but *Candida* spp. are becoming more common findings in many medical centers.[6, 133] Even with early diagnosis and surgical intervention, the death rate from pancreatic abscesses reaches 22 to 57 percent.[58, 60] Performing percutaneous catheter drainage under CT guidance may reduce the mortality rate associated with treating pancreatic abscesses.[12] Rarely, fistulas from pseudocysts or abscesses to other abdominal organs may develop.[55]

Osteolytic lesions resembling osteomyelitis may develop weeks to months after an acute episode of pancreatitis.[68, 94] One hypothesis is that elevated serum lipase causes intramedullary fat necrosis in the bone. Usually, the lesions are asymptomatic and resolve spontaneously without therapy.

REFERENCES

1. Agarwal, K. S., Puliyel, J. M., Mathew, A., et al.: Acute pancreatitis with cholestatic hepatitis: An unusual manifestation of hepatitis A. Ann. Trop. Paediatr. *19*:391–394, 1999.
2. Ahuja, S. K., Ahuja, S. S., Thelmo, W., et al.: Necrotizing pancreatitis and multisystem organ failure associated with toxoplasmosis in a patient with AIDS. Clin. Infect. Dis. *16*:432–434, 1993.
3. Al-Awadhi, N. Z., Ashkenani, F., and Khalaf, E. S.: Acute pancreatitis associated with brucellosis. Am. J. Gastroenterol. *84*:1570–1574, 1989.
4. Alberti-Flor, J. J., Hernandez, M. E., Ferrer, J. P., et al.: Fulminant liver failure and pancreatitis associated with the use of sulfamethoxazole-trimethoprim. Am. J. Gastroenterol. *84*:1577–1579, 1989.
5. Albu, E., Buiumsohn, A., Lopez, R., et al.: Gallstone pancreatitis in adolescents. J. Pediatr. Surg. *22*:960–962, 1987.
6. Aloia, T., Solomkin, J., Fink, A. S., et al.: *Candida* in pancreatic infection: A clinical experience. Am. Surg. *60*:793–796, 1994.
7. Andrén-Sandberg, A., and Höjer, H.: Necrotizing acute pancreatitis induced by *Salmonella* infection. Int. J. Pancreatol. *15*:229–230, 1994.
8. Antonow, D. R.: Acute pancreatitis associated with trimethoprim sulfamethoxazole. Ann. Intern. Med. *104*:363–365, 1986.

9. Arcement, C. M., Meza, M. P., Arumanla, S., et al.: MRCP in the evaluation of pancreaticobiliary disease in children. Pediatr. Radiol. *31*:92–97, 2001.
10. Aronson, N. E., Wortman, G. W., Johnson, S. C., et al.: Safety and efficacy of intravenous sodium stibogluconate in the treatment of leishmaniasis: Recent U.S. experience. Clin. Infect. Dis. *27*:1457–1464, 1998.
11. Baldwin, M., Eisenman, R. E., Prelipp, A. M., et al.: *Ascaris lumbricoides* resulting in acute cholecystitis and pancreatitis in the Midwest. Am. J. Gastroenterol. *88*:2119–2121, 1993.
12. Baril, N. B., Ralls, P. W., Wren, S. M., et al.: Does an infected peripancreatic fluid collection or abscess mandate operation? Ann. Surg. *23*:361–367, 2000.
13. Bartholomew, C.: Acute scorpion pancreatitis in Trinidad. B. M. J. *1*:666–668, 1970.
14. Bell, M. J., Ternberg, J. L., and Feigin, R. D.: Surgical complications of leptospirosis in children. J. Pediatr. Surg. *13*:325–330, 1978.
15. Berger, T. M., Cook, W. J., O'Marcaigh, A. S., et al.: Acute pancreatitis in a 12-year-old girl after an erythromycin overdose. Pediatrics *90*:624–626, 1992.
16. Blake, R. L.: Acute pancreatitis. Primary Care *15*:187–199, 1988.
17. Blay, R., Simpson, K., Leslie, K., et al.: Coxsackie-virus–induced disease, $CD4^+$ cells initiate both myocarditis and pancreatitis in DBA/2 mice. Am. J. Pathol. *135*:899–907, 1989.
18. Bouteloup, C., Michel, P., Desechalliers, J.-P., et al.: Pancréatite aiguë récidivante a *Taenia saginata*. Gastroenterol. Clin. Biol. *16*:818–820, 1992.
19. Bradley, E. L.: Antibiotics in acute pancreatitis: Current status and future directions. Am. J. Surg. *158*:472–477, 1989.
20. Braithwaite, P. A., and Brodribb, R. K.: Hepatic hydatid disease presenting as pancreatitis. Med. J. Aust. *2*:369–370, 1983.
21. Brandt, J. R., Joseph, M. W., Fouser, L. S., et al.: Cholelithiasis following *Escherichia coli* O157:H7-associated hemolytic uremic syndrome. Pediatr. Nephrol. *12*:222–225, 1998.
22. Brown, C. W., Werlin, S. L., Geenen, J. E., et al.: The diagnosis and therapeutic role of endoscopic retrograde cholangiopancreatography in children. J. Pediatr. Gastroenterol. Nutr. *17*:19–23, 1993.
23. Buggy, B. P., and Nostrant, T. T.: Lethal pancreatitis. Am. J. Gastroenterol. *78*:810–814, 1983.
24. Butler, K. M., Husson, R. N., Balis, F. M., et al.: Dideoxyinosine in children with symptomatic human immunodeficiency virus infection. N. Engl. J. Med. *324*:137–144, 1991.
25. Butler, K. M., Venzon, D., Henry, N., et al.: Pancreatitis in human immunodeficiency virus–infected children receiving dideoxyinosine. Pediatrics *91*:747–751, 1993.
26. Capner, P., Lendrum, R., Jeffries, D. J., et al.: Viral antibody studies in pancreatic disease. Gut *16*:866–870, 1975.
27. Carroccio, A., Fontana, M., Spagnuolo, M. I., et al.: Serum pancreatic enzymes in human immunodeficiency virus–infected children. Scand. J. Gastroenterol. *33*:998–1001, 1998.
28. Celifarco, A., Warschauer, C., and Burakoff, R.: Metronidazole-induced pancreatitis. Am. J. Gastroenterol. *84*:958–964, 1989.
29. Cheung, K. M., Mok, F., Lam, P., et al.: Pancreatitis associated with Henoch-Schönlein purpura. J. Paediatr. Child. Health. *37*:311–313, 2001.
30. Choi, T. K., Mok, F., Zhan, W. H., et al.: Somatostatin in the treatment of acute pancreatitis: A prospective randomized controlled trial. Gut *30*:223–227, 1989.
31. Cohn, J. A., Friedman, K. J., Noone, P. G., et al.: Relation between mutations of the cystic fibrosis gene and idiopathic pancreatitis. N. Engl. J. Med. *339*:653–658, 1998.
32. Colebunders, R., Van den Abbeele, K., Fleerackers, Y., et al.: Two AIDS patients with life-threatening pancreatitis successfully treated, one with ganciclovir, the other with foscarnet. Acta Clin. Belg. *49*:229–232, 1994.
33. Cooper, M. A., and Groll, A.: A case of chronic pancreatic insufficiency due to valproic acid in a child. Can. J. Gastroenterol. *15*:127–130, 2001.
34. Corp, C. C., and Ghishan, F. K.: The sulfone syndrome complicated by pancreatitis and pleural effusion in an adolescent receiving dapsone for treatment of acne vulgaris. J. Pediatr. Gastroenterol. Nutr. *26*:103–105, 1998.
35. Cox, K. L.: Pancreatitis in children. Pediatric case reports in gastrointestinal diseases. Ross Laboratories *6*:1–7, 1986.
36. Cox, K. L., Ament, M. E., Sample, W. F., et al.: The ultrasonic and biochemical diagnosis of pancreatitis in children. J. Pediatr. *96*:407–411, 1980.
37. de Bois, M. H. W., Schoemaker, M. C., van der Werf, S. D. J., et al.: Pancreatitis associated with *Campylobacter jejuni* infections: Diagnosis by ultrasonography. B. M. J. *298*:1004, 1989.
38. De La Rubia, L., Herrera, M. I., Cebrero, M., et al.: Acute pancreatitis associated with rotavirus infection. Pancreas *12*:98–99, 1996.
39. Dev, G., Sikka, M., Sehgal, S., et al.: *Escherichia coli* infection producing pancreatitis and extrahepatic cholestasis. Indian Pediatr. *24*:249–253, 1987.
40. Eisenhuber, E., Schoefl, R., Wiesbauer, P., et al.: Primary pancreatic lymphoma presenting as acute pancreatitis in a child. Med. Pediatr. Oncol. *37*:53–54, 2001.
41. Elmore, M. F., and Rogge, J. D.: Tetracycline-induced pancreatitis. Gastroenterology *81*:1134–1136, 1981.
42. Fan, S. T., Yan, K. W., Lau, W. Y., et al.: Tuberculosis of the pancreas: A rare cause of massive gastrointestinal bleeding. Br. J. Surg. *73*:373, 1986.
43. Feiner, H.: Pancreatitis after cardiac surgery: A morphologic study. Am. J. Surg. *131*:684–688, 1976.
44. Feldstein, J. D., Johnson, F. R., Kallick, C. A., et al.: Acute hemorrhagic pancreatitis and pseudocyst due to mumps. Ann. Surg. *180*:85–88, 1974.
45. Fernàndez, R. A., Varona, T. L., Jaquotot, J. M. K., et al.: Pancreatitis aguda asociada a infeccin por virus de la varicela-zoster en un paciente con sindrome de immunodeficiencia adquirida. Med. Clin. (Barc.) *98*:339–341, 1992.
46. Foisy, M. M., Slayter, K. L., Hewitt, R. G., et al.: Pancreatitis during intravenous pentamidine therapy in an AIDS patient with prior exposure to didanosine. Ann. Pharmacother. *28*:1025–1028, 1994.
47. Frank, J. A., Warren, R. W., Tucker, J. A., et al.: Disseminated parainfluenza infection in a child with severe combined immunodeficiency. Am. J. Dis. Child. *137*:1172–1174, 1983.
48. Garau, P., Orenstein, S. R., Neigut, D. A., et al.: Pancreatitis associated with olsalazine and sulfasalazine in children with ulcerative colitis. J. Pediatr. Gastroenterol. Nutr. *18*:481–485, 1994.
49. Glassman, M., Tahan, S., Hillemeier, C., et al.: Pancreatitis in patients with Reye's syndrome. J. Clin. Gastroenterol. *3*:165–169, 1981.
50. Gross, T. L., Wheat, J., Bartlett, M., et al.: AIDS and multiple system involvement with *Cryptosporidium*. Am. J. Gastroenterol. *81*:456–458, 1986.
51. Guice, K. S., Lynch, M., and Weatherbee, L.: Invasive aspergillosis: An unusual cause of hemorrhagic pancreatitis. Am. J. Gastroenterol. *82*:563–565, 1987.
52. Haddock, G., Coupar, G., Youngson, G. G., et al.: Acute pancreatitis in children: A 15-year review. J. Pediatr. Surg. *29*:719–722, 1994.
53. Hart, C. C.: Aerosolized pentamidine and pancreatitis. Ann. Intern. Med. *111*:691, 1989.
54. Hawkins, S. P., Thomas, R. P., and Teasdale, C.: Acute pancreatitis: A new finding in *Cryptosporidium* enteritis. B. M. J. *294*:483–484, 1987.
55. Henderson, J. M., and MacDonald, J. A. E.: Fistula formation complicating pancreatic abscess. Br. J. Surg. *63*:233–234, 1976.
56. Herbaut, C., Tielemans, C., Burette, A., et al.: *Mycoplasma pneumoniae* infection and acute pancreatitis. Acta Clin. Belg. *38*:186–188, 1983.
57. Hermans, P., Gerard, M., Van Laethem, Y., et al.: Pancreatic disturbances and typhoid fever. Scand. J. Infect. Dis. *23*:201–205, 1991.
58. Hillemeier, C., and Gryboski, J. D.: Acute pancreatitis in infants and children. Yale J. Biol. Med. *57*:149–159, 1984.
59. Hofman, P., Michiels, J.-F., Mondain, V., et al.: Pancréatite aiguë toxoplasmique. Gastroenterol. Clin. Biol. *18*:895–897, 1994.
60. Hurley, J. E., and Vargish, T.: Early diagnosis and outcome of pancreatic abscesses in pancreatitis. Am. Surg. *53*:29–33, 1987.
61. Imrie, C. W., Ferguson, J. C., and Sommerville, R. G.: Coxsackie and mumps virus infection in a prospective study of acute pancreatitis. Gut *18*:53–56, 1977.
62. Iwasaki, T., Tashiro, A., Satodate, R., et al.: Acute pancreatitis with cytomegalovirus infection. Acta Pathol. Jpn. *37*:1661–1668, 1987.
63. Jesudason, S. R. B., Mathai, V., Muthusami, J. C., et al.: *Wuchereria bancrofti* induced pancreatitis. Trop. Gastroenterol. *13*:115–118, 1992.
64. Joe, L., Ansher, A. F., and Gordin, F. M.: Severe pancreatitis in an AIDS patient in association with cytomegalovirus infection. South. Med. J. *82*:1444–1445, 1989.
65. Johnson, R. C., DeFord, J. W., and Carlton, P. K.: Pancreatitis complicating falciparum malaria. Postgrad. Med. *61*:181–183, 1977.
66. Jordan, S. C., and Ament, M. E.: Pancreatitis in children and adolescents. J. Pediatr. *91*:211–216, 1977.
67. Kahler, S. G., Sherwood, W. G., Woolf, D., et al.: Pancreatitis in patients with organic acidemias. J. Pediatr. *124*:239–243, 1994.
68. Keating, J. P., Shackelford, G. D., Shackelford, P. G., et al.: Pancreatitis and osteolytic lesions. J. Pediatr. *81*:350–353, 1972.
69. Keidar, S., Porath, E. B., Naftali, V., et al.: Acute pancreatitis associated with rising cytomegalovirus titer. Isr. J. Med. Sci. *23*:296–297, 1987.
70. Khuroo, M. S., Zargar, S. A., Yattoo, G. N., et al.: *Ascaris*-induced acute pancreatitis. Br. J. Surg. *79*:1335–1338, 1992.
71. Kirschner, B. S.: Safety of azathioprine and 6-mercaptopurine in pediatric patients with inflammatory bowel disease. Gastroenterology *115*:813–821, 1998.
72. Kirschner, S., and Raufman, J. P.: Varicella pancreatitis complicated by pancreatic pseudocyst and duodenal obstruction. Dig. Dis. Sci. *33*:1192–1195, 1988.
73. Koutras, A.: Epstein-Barr virus infection with pancreatitis, hepatitis, and proctitis. Pediatr. Infect. Dis. *2*:312–313, 1983.
74. Kozarek, R. A., Christie, D., and Barclay, G.: Endoscopic therapy of pancreatitis in the pediatric population. Gastrointest. Endosc. *39*:665–669, 1993.
75. Kuyucu, N., Kara, C., Bakirtac, A., et al.: Successful treatment of visceral leishmaniasis with allopurinol plus ketoconazole in an infant who developed pancreatitis caused by meglumine antimonate. Pediatr. Infect. Dis. J. *20*:455–457, 2001.
76. Leinikki, P. O., Panzar, P., and Tykka, H.: Immunoglobulin M antibody response against *Mycoplasma pneumoniae* lipid antigen in patients with acute pancreatitis. J. Clin. Microbiol. *8*:113-118, 1978.

77. Lopez Morante, A., Rodriquez de Lope, C., San Miguel, G., et al.: Acute pancreatitis in hepatitis A infection. Postgrad. Med. J. *62*:407–408, 1986.
78. Löser, C., and Fölsch, U. R.: A concept of treatment in acute pancreatitis: Results of controlled trials, and future developments. Hepatogastroenterology *40*:569–573, 1993.
79. Mader, T. J., and McHugh, T. P.: Acute pancreatitis in children. Pediatr. Emerg. Care *8*:157–161, 1992.
80. Mallory, A., and Kern, F.: Drug-induced pancreatitis: A critical review. Gastroenterology *78*:813–820, 1980.
81. Malozowski, S., Hung, W., Scott, D. C., et al.: Acute pancreatitis associated with growth hormone therapy for short stature. N. Engl. J. Med. *332*:401–402, 1995.
82. Maranan, M. C., Gerber, S. I., and Miller, G. G.: Gallstone pancreatitis caused by ceftriaxone. Pediatr. Infect. Dis. J. *17*:662–663, 1998.
83. Mardh, P. A., and Ursing, B.: The occurrence of acute pancreatitis in *Mycoplasma pneumoniae* infection. Scand. J. Infect. Dis. *6*:167–171, 1974.
84. Mathai, V., Jesudason, S. R. B., Muthusami, J. C., et al.: Chronic pancreatitis caused by intraductal hydatid cysts of the pancreas. Br. J. Surg. *81*:1029, 1994.
85. Michel, O., Naeije, N., Csoma, M., et al.: Acute pancreatitis in legionnaires' disease. Eur. J. Respir. Dis. *66*:62–64, 1985.
86. Miller, T. L., Winter, H. S., Luginbuhl, L. M., et al.: Pancreatitis in pediatric human immunodeficiency virus infection. J. Pediatr. *120*:223–227, 1992.
87. Mishra, A., Saigal, S., Gupta, R., et al.: Acute pancreatitis associated with viral hepatitis: A report of six cases with review of literature. Am. J. Gastroenterol. *94*:2292–2295, 1999.
88. Monif, G. R. G.: Rubella virus and the pancreas. Med. Chir. Dig. *3*:195–197, 1974.
89. Mor, R., Pitlik, S., Dux, S., et al.: Parotitis and pancreatitis complicating infectious mononucleosis. Isr. J. Med. Sci. *18*:709–710, 1982.
90. Murphey, S. A., and Josephs, A. S.: Acute pancreatitis associated with pentamidine therapy. Arch. Intern. Med. *141*:56–58, 1981.
91. Naficy, K., Nategh, R., and Ghadimi, H.: Mumps pancreatitis without parotitis. B. M. J. *1*:529–533, 1973.
92. Nakao, T., Nitta, T., Miura, R., et al.: Clinical and epidemiological studies on an outbreak of aseptic meningitis caused by Coxsackie B5 and A9 viruses in Aomori in 1961. Tohoku J. Exp. Med. *83*:94–102, 1964.
93. Nelis, G. F.: Nitrofurantoin-induced pancreatitis: Report of a case. Gastroenterology *84*:1032–1034, 1983.
94. Neuer, F. S., Roberts, F. F., and McCarthy, V.: Osteolytic lesions following traumatic pancreatitis. Am. J. Dis. Child. *131*:738–740, 1977.
95. Niemann, T. H., Trigg, M. E., Winick, N., et al.: Disseminated adenoviral infection presenting as acute pancreatitis. Hum. Pathol. *24*:1145–1148, 1993.
96. O'Brien, M. M., Vincent, J. M., Person, D. A., et al.: Leptospirosis and pancreatitis: A report of ten cases. Pediatr. Infect. Dis. J. *17*:436–438, 1998.
97. Patamasucon, P., Pillsbury, H. L., and Colon, A. R.: Childhood pancreatitis with biliary calcareous disease. J. Pediatr. Surg. *17*:189–190, 1982.
98. Pederzoli, P., Bassi, C., Vesentini, S., et al.: A randomized multicenter clinical trial of antibiotic prophylaxis of septic complications in acute necrotizing pancreatitis with imipenem. Surg. Gynecol. Obstet. *176*:480–483, 1993.
99. Pederzoli, P., Bassi, C., Vesentini, S., et al.: Antibiotics in acute pancreatitis: The debate revisited. Am. J. Gastroenterol. *90*:666–667, 1995.
100. Penn, I., Durst, A. L., Machado, M., et al.: Acute pancreatitis and hyperamylasemia in renal homograft recipients. Arch. Surg. *105*:167–172, 1972.
101. Perry, W., Jenkins, M. V., and Stamp, T. C. B.: Lysosomal enzymes and pancreatitis during rifampicin therapy. Lancet *1*:492, 1979.
102. Poddar, U., Thapa, B. R., Bhasin, D. K., et al.: Endoscopic retrograde cholangiopancreatography in the management of pancreaticobiliary disorders in children. J. Gastroenterol. Hepatol. *16*:927–931, 2001.
103. Pollak, E. W., Michas, C. A., and Wolfman, E. F.: Pancreatic pseudocyst: Management in 54 patients. Am. J. Surg. *135*:199–201, 1978.
104. Pupelis, G., Selga, G., Austrums, E., et al.: Jejunal feeding, even when instituted late, improves outcomes in patients with severe pancreatitis and peritonitis. Nutrition *17*:91–94, 2001.
105. Robitaille, P., Gonthier, M., Grignon, A., et al.: Pancreatic injury in the hemolytic-uremic syndrome. Pediatr. Nephrol. *11*:631–632, 1997.
106. Rushing, J. L., Hanna, C. J., and Selecky, P. A.: Pancreatitis as the presenting manifestation of miliary tuberculosis. West. J. Med. *129*:432–436, 1978.
107. Ruzena, S.: Normal serum amylase in acute pancreatitis. Dig. Dis. Sci. *34*:960–961, 1989.
108. Sakorafas, G. H., and Tsiotou, A. G.: Etiology and pathogenesis of acute pancreatitis. J. Clin. Gastroenterol. *30*:343–356, 2000.
109. Schulz, T. B.: Association of pancreas infection and yersiniosis. Acta Med. Scand. *205*:255–256, 1979.
110. Seidman, E. G., Deckelbaum, R. J., Owen, H., et al.: Relapsing pancreatitis in association with Crohn's disease. J. Pediatr. Gastroenterol. Nutr. *2*:178–182, 1983.
111. Sharer, N., Schwarz, M., Malone, G., et al.: Mutations of the cystic fibrosis gene in patients with chronic pancreatitis. N. Engl. J. Med. *339*:645–652, 1998.
112. Shirobokov, V. P., Zhurba, T. B., and Zemlyansky, V. V.: Properties of the Coxsackie viruses isolated from pancreatic tissue of patients with chronic pancreatitis. Mikrobiol. Z. *50*:78–81, 1988.
113. Shugar, R. A., and Ryan, J. J.: *Clonorchis sinensis* and pancreatitis. Am. J. Gastroenterol. *65*:400–403, 1975.
114. Sindhi, R., Webber, S., Venkataramanan, R., et al.: Sirolimus for rescue and primary immunosuppression in transplanted children receiving tacrolimus. Transplantation *72*:851–855, 2001.
115. Slyper, A. H., Wyatt, D. T., and Brown, C. W.: Clinical and/or biochemical pancreatitis in diabetic ketoacidosis. J. Pediatr. Endocrinol. *7*:261–264, 1994.
116. Sofer, S., Shalev, H., Weizman, Z., et al.: Acute pancreatitis in children following envenomation by the yellow scorpion *Leiurus quinquestriatus*. Toxicon *29*:125–128, 1991.
117. Sotomatsu, M., Shimoda, M., Ogawa, C., et al.: Acute pancreatitis associated with interferon-α therapy for chronic myelogenous leukemia. Am. J. Hematol. *48*:211–212, 1995.
118. Steinberg, W. M., and Schlesselman, S. E.: Treatment of acute pancreatitis: Comparison of animal and human studies. Gastroenterology *93*:1420–1427, 1987.
119. Stoler, J., Biller, J. A., and Grand, R. J.: Pancreatitis in Kawasaki disease. Am. J. Dis. Child. *141*:306–308, 1987.
120. Tissieres, P., Durand, P., Chardot, C., et al.: Acute pancreatitis after orthotopic liver transplantation in children. Liver Transplant. Surg. *3*:430–432, 1997.
121. Tissieres, P., Simon, L., Debray, D., et al.: Acute pancreatitis after orthotopic liver transplantation in children: Incidence, contributing factors, and outcome. J. Pediatr. Gastroenterol. Nutr. *26*:315–320, 1998.
122. Torosis, J., and Vender, R.: Tetracycline-induced pancreatitis. J. Clin. Gastroenterol. *9*:580–581, 1987.
123. Torre, J. A. C., Martin, J. J. D., Garcia, C. B., et al.: Varicella infection as a cause of acute pancreatitis in an immunocompetent child. Pediatr. Infect. Dis. J. *19*:1218–1219, 2000.
124. Truninger, K., Malik, N., Ammann, R. W., et al.: Mutations of the cystic fibrosis gene in patients with chronic pancreatitis. Am. J. Gastroenterol. *96*:2657–2661, 2001.
125. Ungar, B. L. P., Burris, J. A., Quinn, C. A., et al.: New mouse models for chronic *Cryptosporidium* infection in immunodeficient hosts. Infect. Immun. *58*:961–969, 1990.
126. Urban, M., Splaingard, M., and Werlin, S. L.: Pancreatitis associated with remote traumatic brain injury in children. Childs Nerv. Syst. *10*:388–391, 1994.
127. Vargas, P. A., Bernardi, F. D. C., Alves, V. A. F., et al.: Uncommon histopathological findings in fatal measles infection: Pancreatitis, sialoadenitis and thyroiditis. Histopathology *37*:141–146, 2000.
128. Veerappan, A., Siegel, J. H., Podany, J., et al.: *Fasciola hepatica* pancreatitis: Endoscopic extraction of live parasites. Gastrointest. Endosc. *37*:473–475, 1991.
129. Vital Durand, D., Trepo, C., Bouletreau, P., et al.: Hepatite fulminante a virus HB avec pancreatite aigue: Deux observations. Ann. Med. Interne *132*:120–123, 1981.
130. Vuorinen, T., Kallajoki, M., Hyypia, T., et al.: Coxsackie B3–induced acute pancreatitis: Analysis of histopathological and viral parameters in a mouse model. Br. J. Exp. Pathol. *70*:395–403, 1989.
131. Warner, R. L., Othersen, H. B., and Smith, C. D.: Traumatic pancreatitis and pseudocyst in children: Current management. J. Trauma. *29*:597–601, 1989.
132. Warren, W. R.: Serum amylase and lipase in mumps. Am. J. Med. Sci. *230*:161–168, 1955.
133. Warshaw, A. L.: Pancreatic abscesses. N. Engl. J. Med. *287*:1234–1236, 1972.
134. Weizman, Z., and Durie, P. R.: Acute pancreatitis in childhood. J. Pediatr. *113*:24–29, 1988.
135. Weizman, Z., and Sofer, S.: Acute pancreatitis in children with anticholinesterase insecticide intoxication. Pediatrics *90*:204–206, 1992.
136. Werlin, S. L.: Disorders of the pancreas in children. Curr. Opin. Pediatr. *10*:505–511, 1998.
137. Werlin, S. L., Casper, J., Antonson, D., et al.: Pancreatitis associated with bone marrow transplantation in children. Bone Marrow Transplant. *10*:65–69, 1992.
138. Westblom, T. U., and Hamory, B. H.: Acute pancreatitis caused by *Legionella pneumophila*. South Med. J. *81*:1200–1201, 1988.
139. Wood, C. B., Bradbrook, R. A., Blumgart, L. H.: Chronic pancreatitis in childhood associated with mumps virus infection. Br. J. Clin. Pract. *28*:67–69, 1974.
140. Zazzo, J. F., Pichon, F., and Regnier, B.: HIV and the pancreas. Lancet *2*:1212–1213, 1987.
141. Ziegler, D. W., Long, J. A., Philippart, A. I., et al.: Pancreatitis in childhood: Experience with 49 patients. Ann. Surg. *207*:257–261, 1988.
142. Zuger, A., Wolf, B. Z., El-Sadr, W., et al.: Pentamidine-associated fatal acute pancreatitis. J. A. M. A. *256*:2383–2385, 1986.

CHAPTER 60

Peritonitis and Intra-abdominal Abscess

JUDITH R. CAMPBELL ■ JOHN S. BRADLEY

Intra-abdominal infection can be a life-threatening condition that occurs spontaneously or as a result of intra-abdominal disease, injury, or surgery. Given the compartmental anatomy and physiology of the abdominal cavity, intra-abdominal infection frequently is categorized as peritonitis, intraperitoneal abscess, retroperitoneal abscess, and visceral abscess.[3] In this chapter, peritonitis and intra-abdominal abscess are reviewed; liver abscess and retroperitoneal abscess are reviewed in Chapters 56 and 61, respectively.

Peritonitis

ANATOMY

Knowledge of the anatomic relationships within the abdomen is important for understanding the source and routes of spread of infection. The peritoneal cavity extends from the undersurface of the diaphragm to the pelvis. In males, it is a closed space, whereas in females, the ends of the fallopian tubes penetrate into the peritoneal cavity. The transverse mesocolon and greater omentum separate the upper and lower peritoneal cavity. Peritoneal reflections further divide the intraperitoneal space into several compartments: the lesser sac, the paracolic gutters, and the subhepatic and subphrenic spaces (Fig. 60–1). The most dependent area of the peritoneal cavity is the pelvis. However, exudate can extend to any of the recesses within the peritoneal cavity distant from the original source and cause diffuse inflammation.[3] When inflamed, the anterior parietal peritoneum, which is supplied by somatic afferent nerves, gives the sensation of localized pain. Stimulation of the visceral peritoneum causes dull, poorly localized pain.

PATHOGENESIS

Peritonitis is defined as inflammation of the serosal lining of the abdominal cavity or the peritoneum and may be caused by any agent, chemical or infectious, that irritates the peritoneal surfaces. Noninfectious peritonitis is caused by extravasation of irritants such as gastric juice, bile, urine, blood, pancreatic secretions, or the contents of a ruptured cyst into the peritoneal cavity. Although chemical peritonitis generally is aseptic, it may be an important antecedent event to the development of infectious peritonitis.

After peritoneal contamination has occurred, the first mechanism of host defense is lymphatic clearance. In experimental peritonitis, this clearance is so efficient that peritonitis and abscess formation will occur only if adjuvant substances such as hemoglobin or necrotic tissue are present.[23, 24, 46] In the first hours after bacterial contamination, local resident macrophages are the predominant phagocytic cells. The macrophages then are cleared by the lymphatic system. After bacterial proliferation occurs, polymorphonuclear leukocytes become more numerous in the peritoneal cavity and inflammation ensues. These peritoneal defense mechanisms also have adverse effects. Fibrin is deposited, which potentially entraps bacteria into a sequestered environment. An increase in splanchnic blood flow causes exudation of fluid into the peritoneal space, further impairing host defenses by diluting important peritoneal opsonins.[23, 24] These host responses serve as a means of containing infection, but they also may contribute to the formation of abscesses.

Infectious peritonitis is subdivided into primary and secondary peritonitis based on the pathophysiology of the infection. Peritonitis that is associated with peritoneal dialysis or the presence of a ventriculoperitoneal shunt is a unique form of peritonitis that also will be reviewed. The microbial etiologies of peritonitis vary with the underlying cause and are summarized in Table 60–1.

Primary Peritonitis

Primary, or spontaneous, bacterial peritonitis is a rare infection defined as bacterial peritonitis in the absence of intra-abdominal findings such as intestinal perforation. The incidence of spontaneous peritonitis in children is unknown; however, in the early 20th century, 8 to 10 percent of abdominal emergencies requiring surgical intervention were due to spontaneous peritonitis.[17, 70] Freij and colleagues conducted a 22-year review of children with primary peritonitis in Dallas, Texas. Primary peritonitis was diagnosed in 7 previously healthy children, as compared with 1840 cases of appendicitis during the same period.[29] Currently, 1 to 2 percent of abdominal emergencies requiring surgical intervention are due to primary peritonitis.[37, 40] However, now that this condition frequently is recognized clinically with the assistance of computed tomography (CT), the diagnosis often is made without exploratory laparotomy. The peak incidence of spontaneous peritonitis in children occurs between 5 and 9 years of age. In children, the most common predisposing factor is nephrotic syndrome, but this form of peritonitis also occurs in children with postnecrotic cirrhosis.[3, 17, 31, 37, 41, 45, 70, 71] Spontaneous peritonitis rarely develops in previously healthy individuals without underlying conditions.[32, 47]

The exact pathophysiologic mechanism for primary peritonitis is unknown; however, hematogenous inoculation is thought to be the most likely mechanism because the same organism frequently is recovered from cultures of blood and peritoneal fluid.[17, 31, 37] Alternative mechanisms include peritoneal seeding via the lymphatics, transmural migration through edematous bowel, and ascending infection from the female genitourinary tract.[31, 37] In certain cases, impaired host defenses allow proliferation of bacteria that invade the peritoneal cavity, but a few children with primary peritonitis have no apparent impaired defense. Ascitic fluid from patients with nephrotic syndrome or cirrhosis contains lower levels of complement and immunoglobulin than does peritoneal fluid from a healthy host.[17, 70] Deficiency of these important opsonins diminishes the natural clearance of organisms from the peritoneal cavity. Proliferation of organisms then triggers the influx of phagocytes, release of inflammatory mediators, and the localized or diffuse peritoneal irritation that gives rise to symptoms of abdominal pain and fever.

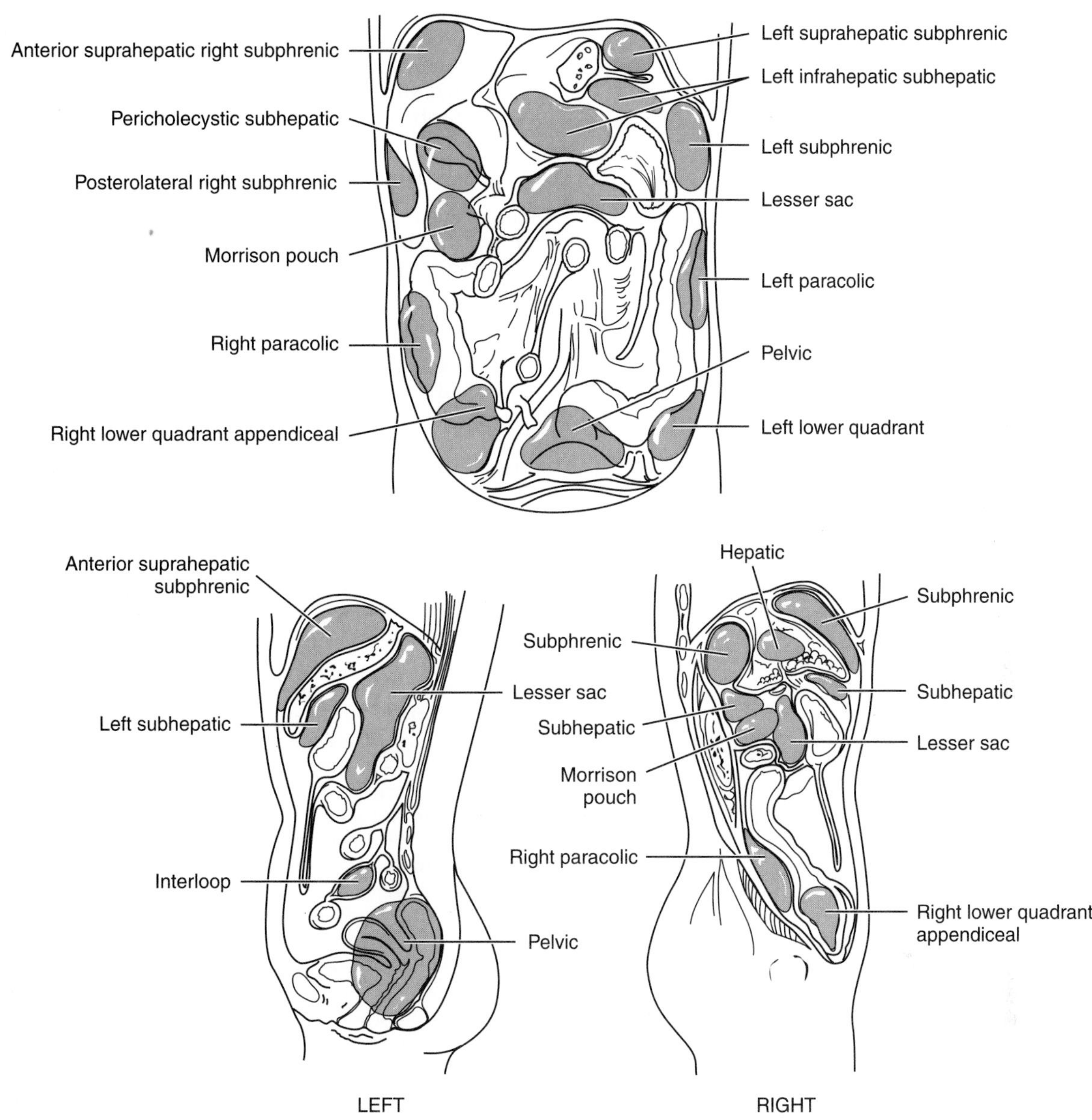

FIGURE 60–1 ■ Anterior and sagittal views of the peritoneal cavity. (From Altemeier, W. A., Culbertson, W. R., and Fullen, W. D.: Intra-abdominal sepsis. Adv. Surg. *5*:281–333, 1971.)

Since the pre-antibiotic era, researchers have recognized that primary peritonitis frequently is caused by *Streptococcus pneumoniae,*[31] *Streptococcus pyogenes,*[32] and *Staphylococcus aureus.*[17] Rarely, primary peritonitis in prepubescent girls is caused by extension of upper genital tract *S. pneumoniae* infection.[37, 66] Since the 1960s, the bacteriology of primary peritonitis has shifted to include an increased proportion of infections caused by gram-negative enteric organisms such as *Escherichia coli* and *Klebsiella* spp.[17, 37, 41, 71] In some instances, primary *E. coli* peritonitis may occur concurrently with bacteremic urinary tract infection. Tuberculous peritonitis may be caused by *Mycobacterium tuberculosis* or *Mycobacterium bovis*. It may occur as a complication of primary mycobacteremia or be caused by reactivation of latent intra-abdominal infection within lymphoid tissue, but only rarely does it appear to occur as a function of the ingestion of swallowed organisms from a pulmonary primary focus.[35, 65, 75] Peritoneal infection with *M. bovis,* which is clinically similar to *M. tuberculosis* peritonitis, is acquired from unpasteurized dairy products and has been reported in children living along the border between the United States and Mexico. These organisms may cause peritonitis from either mycobacteremia or erosion of organisms through the mesenteric lymph nodes or bowel wall into the peritoneal cavity.[20] *Salmonella* spp. rarely cause primary peritonitis and have been reported primarily in patients with underlying conditions.[47]

Secondary Peritonitis

Secondary peritonitis, the most common form of peritonitis, arises as a complication of intra-abdominal injury or disease when microorganisms, secretions, and the particulate material of an intra-abdominal organ enter the peritoneal cavity. Congenital or acquired conditions that result in ischemia, inflammation, or perforation of abdominal viscera may be complicated by secondary peritonitis.[46] In premature infants, necrotizing enterocolitis is the most common cause

TABLE 60–1 ■ MOST COMMONLY IDENTIFIED ETIOLOGIC AGENTS

Primary Peritonitis	Secondary Peritonitis
Streptococcus pnueumoniae (30%–50%)	Aerobes
Escherichia coli (25%–40%)	*E. coli*
Staphylococcus aureus (2%–4%)	*Enterococcus*
Other streptococci (alpha- and beta-hemolytic)	*Klebsiella*
Klebsiella	*Pseudomonas aeruginosa*
Other enteric gram-negative bacilli	*Enterobacter*
Neisseria meningitidis	*Serratia*
Haemophilus influenzae type b	Anaerobes
Mycobacterium tuberculosis	*Bacteroides fragilis* group
Mycobacterium bovis	*Peptostreptococcus*
CAPD–Associated Peritonitis	**VP Shunt–Associated Peritonitis**
Coagulase-negative staphylococci	Coagulase-negative staphylocci
S. aureus	*S. aureus*
Enteric gram-negative bacilli	*E. coli*
Pseudomonas	*Klebsiella*
Stenotrophomonas	*Enterobacter*
Candida	*Pseudomonas*
Other fungi	
Mycobacterium	

CAPD, continuous ambulatory peritoneal dialysis; VP, ventriculoperitoneal.

of secondary peritonitis.[51] In infants and children, appendicitis is the most common cause; however, it also may occur with volvulus, intussusception, incarcerated hernia, or rupture of a Meckel diverticulum.[51] Although less common in children than in adults, peritonitis also occurs as a complication of mucosal diseases such as peptic ulcer, ulcerative colitis, Crohn disease, and pseudomembranous colitis.[51]

Rupture of or injury to an intra-abdominal viscus results in spillage of the luminal contents and contamination of the peritoneal cavity with bacteria, gastrointestinal secretions, and debris. Thus, both chemical and infectious sources of inflammation are introduced. The stomach and upper gastrointestinal tract contents contain only 10^3 to 10^4 or fewer organisms per gram because of the low pH of gastric secretions. Gram-negative aerobic organisms colonize the upper gastrointestinal tract. In contrast, the colonic contents have predominantly anaerobes, with as many as 10^{11} anaerobes and 10^8 aerobes per gram.[11, 37, 64] Secondary peritonitis usually is a polymicrobial infection, with as many as 5 to 10 different bacterial species of anaerobes and facultative gram-negative bacilli. Synergy among the various bacterial species enhances bacterial proliferation.[11] Members of the *Bacteroides fragilis* group and *Peptostreptococcus* spp. are the anaerobic organisms reported most commonly in secondary peritonitis. Of the aerobic organisms, *E. coli, Klebsiella* spp., *Pseudomonas aeruginosa,* and *Enterococcus* spp. are isolated most often. Recently *P. aeruginosa* has been noted to be present in 20 to 30 percent of children with complicated ruptured appendicitis.[8, 38] When secondary peritonitis occurs in patients with a history of prolonged hospitalization, underlying chronic conditions, or recent antibiotic therapy, the etiology may include nosocomial pathogens that have colonized the gastrointestinal tract, such as *P. aeruginosa*, *Enterobacter* spp., *Acinetobacter* spp., or other antibiotic-resistant organisms.

Focal suppurative infection may be present within an intra-abdominal or retroperitoneal solid organ or within intra-abdominal lymphoid tissue. Organisms then spread from this purulent focus through the capsule of the organ or lymphoid tissue and enter the peritoneal cavity, with the subsequent development of peritonitis. The intra-abdominal organ or lymphoid tissue may be inoculated via bacteremia (e.g., *S. aureus* and renal infection) or be inoculated as a complication of the normal function of the organ (e.g., *E. coli* and renal infection or *Yersinia* and mesenteric adenitis).[13, 36, 42]

Peritonitis and Implanted Devices

Peritonitis is the most significant infectious complication of chronic peritoneal dialysis. Contamination of the dialysis tubing, migration of skin flora from the exit site, or contamination of the dialysate may lead to peritonitis in patients undergoing continuous ambulatory peritoneal dialysis (CAPD). In each instance, a single pathogen usually is isolated. Gram-positive organisms, coagulase-negative staphylococci, and *S. aureus* account for 30 to 45 percent of peritonitis episodes in children during CAPD. Twenty to 30 percent of CAPD-associated peritonitis episodes are caused by Enterobacteriaceae.[26] In these instances, contamination of the catheter site with fecal material most often occurs in young children who wear diapers and those with incontinence, an open urogenital sinus, or nephrostomy tubes. The water-borne pathogens *Pseudomonas* and *Acinetobacter* account for 6 percent and 4 percent of peritonitis episodes in children receiving CAPD, respectively. *Pseudomonas* peritonitis is especially difficult to treat with the dialysis catheter in situ and may recur despite appropriate antimicrobial therapy.[26] Fungal peritonitis is another complication of CAPD that is difficult to treat successfully without removal of the catheter. Although fungal pathogens have accounted for only 2 percent of peritonitis episodes in children undergoing CAPD, this problem is occurring more commonly.[15, 25, 26, 48, 56, 76] Most patients with fungal peritonitis have had previous episodes of bacterial peritonitis and antibiotic therapy. The most common fungal pathogens are *Candida* spp.[25, 26]; however, rare fungi such as *Curvularia* spp.,[15] *Fusarium* spp.,[26] *Trichosporon asahii,*[48] and *Aspergillus* spp.[26] have been reported.[56, 76] Other rare causes of CAPD-associated peritonitis include *Mycobacterium fortuitum* and *Mycobacterium chelonae.*[77]

Intra-abdominal infectious complications develop on average in less than 5 percent of infants and children who undergo ventriculoperitoneal shunt placement or revision for hydrocephalus.[43, 55, 68] Rarely does peritonitis, peritoneal pseudocyst, or perforation of the bowel by the abdominal catheter occur in children with such shunts.[5, 30, 33, 60, 61, 63, 67, 72] Cerebrospinal fluid (CSF) in the peritoneal cavity may be seeded during transient bacteremia or a febrile illness or after abdominal trauma. In addition, peritonitis may develop as a complication of infection within the ventricles being drained[68] as organisms descend into the peritoneal cavity via the distal tubing. A peritoneal pseudocyst containing CSF is the most common manifestation of peritoneal inflammation in patients with ventriculoperitoneal shunts. These patients often have a history of symptoms compatible with a shunt infection before the formation of a pseudocyst and may have signs of peritoneal inflammation and a palpable abdominal mass. The microbial etiology of ventriculoperitoneal shunt–associated peritonitis is varied and reflects the pathogenesis of infection. Infections occurring within months of surgery often are caused by skin flora, *Staphylococcus epidermidis* and *S. aureus*.[30, 60] The microbiology of late shunt-associated peritonitis is similar to that of spontaneous bacterial peritonitis and may include gram-negative enteric organisms, as well as gram-positive cocci.[60] Peritonitis caused by colonic flora also rarely has been associated with bowel perforation by the distal end of the ventriculoperitoneal shunt.[33, 60, 67]

CLINICAL MANIFESTATIONS

The initial signs and symptoms of primary bacterial peritonitis include nausea, vomiting, diarrhea, and diffuse abdominal pain.[37, 40, 41] These signs and symptoms are similar to those of secondary peritonitis caused by a ruptured appendix.

Rupture of the appendix is the most common cause of secondary peritonitis in children; hence, the initial symptoms of anorexia, vomiting, and localized abdominal pain frequently precede the signs and symptoms of diffuse peritoneal inflammation. In both primary and secondary peritonitis, patients typically lie very still because any movement exacerbates the abdominal pain. Physical findings include fever, tachycardia, abdominal distention, hypoactive bowel sounds, abdominal tenderness, rebound tenderness, abdominal wall rigidity, and tenderness on rectal or vaginal examination. Peritoneal inflammation is associated with an increase in splanchnic blood flow, capillary permeability, and a shift of fluid into the peritoneal space, which, in addition to systemic absorption of endotoxin and bacteria, may lead to intravascular hypovolemia and shock.[46]

Fever and abdominal pain in any child undergoing peritoneal dialysis should be evaluated carefully. Turbid dialysate fluid raises the suspicion of CAPD-associated peritonitis. Similarly, symptomatic children with ventriculoperitoneal shunts should be evaluated for shunt-associated peritonitis.[61, 68, 80] In a retrospective report of 19 children with ventriculoperitoneal shunts and peritonitis, Reynolds and associates noted that fever and abdominal pain were the symptoms most commonly present in 14 of their patients.[61] Stamos and colleagues found that fever, lethargy, nausea, and vomiting were the symptoms most frequently reported in a review of 23 children with gram-negative infection of ventriculoperitoneal shunts.[68]

Primary tuberculous peritonitis is usually gradual in onset and associated with weight loss, malaise, and night sweats.[35, 37, 65] The degree of tenderness is less than that present with acute pyogenic peritonitis and may be nonexistent. Palpation of the abdomen may reveal an extensive, irregular collection of masses, often described as "doughy," caused by widespread granulomatous inflammation.[37]

DIAGNOSIS

Laboratory findings in a child with peritonitis often are nonspecific. The white blood cell (WBC) count usually is elevated and between 16,000 and 25,000 cells/mm^3 or greater with a predominance of polymorphonuclear leukocytes and an increase in immature forms.[37] The hematocrit may be elevated because of dehydration and hemoconcentration. Mild pyuria is noted occasionally because of irritation of the urinary bladder or ureters.

Diagnostic imaging studies can be useful in evaluating intra-abdominal infections. Upright and lateral decubitus radiographs of the abdomen may demonstrate distended adynamic loops of bowel suggestive of ileus, as well as obliteration of the peritoneal fat lines and psoas shadows. Free intraperitoneal air below the diaphragm indicates a ruptured viscus. The presence of a fecalith or right lower quadrant mass may be consistent with appendicitis. Abdominal ultrasound and CT may reveal an underlying cause of the peritonitis.[47, 51]

Analysis of peritoneal fluid aspirate or lavage material may be helpful in differentiating primary from secondary peritonitis. Free air, blood, or bile indicates peritonitis secondary to intestinal perforation. In peritonitis, the leukocyte count in peritoneal fluid usually is greater than 250 to 300 WBCs/mm^3 and sometimes as high as 3000 to 5000 WBCs/mm^3, with granulocytes predominating in 80 percent of cases.[37, 45, 70] A total protein content greater than 1 g/dL, a glucose level less than 50 mg/dL, or an elevated lactate dehydrogenase concentration ($>$25 mg/dL) is consistent with secondary peritonitis.[17, 31, 37, 70] If a Gram stain of peritoneal fluid shows only gram-positive cocci, primary peritonitis is most likely. The presence of gram-negative bacilli is consistent with primary or secondary peritonitis, but the presence of many different organisms on Gram stain is diagnostic of secondary peritonitis. Bacteremia occurs in as many as 75 percent of patients with primary peritonitis. Thus, specimens of both peritoneal fluid and blood should be sent for culture.[37] Similarly, secondary peritonitis also can be associated with bacteremia, again suggesting the need for obtaining cultures of blood in addition to peritoneal fluid. Specimens of peritoneal fluid should be processed to optimize the recovery of aerobic and anaerobic organisms, and the use of specific transport tubes or an airless, capped syringe is required.[11, 37] The wide variety of pathogens isolated from intra-abdominal infections along with the variable antibiotic susceptibility of these pathogens supports taking an aggressive approach to obtaining samples for microbiologic evaluation.

A child undergoing CAPD who is suspected of having peritonitis should have dialysate sent for cell count, Gram stain, and culture for bacterial, mycobacterial, and fungal pathogens. If a child with a ventriculoperitoneal shunt is suspected of having peritonitis, CSF from the proximal portion of the shunt should be sent for culture, cell count, and determination of glucose and protein levels in addition to Gram stain and culture of peritoneal fluid.[30] Abdominal imaging by ultrasound or CT is useful in identifying a peritoneal pseudocyst and the location of distal tubing.

Differential Diagnosis

Other infectious diseases that may mimic primary or secondary bacterial peritonitis include mesenteric adenitis, gastroenteritis, hepatitis, streptococcal pharyngitis, lower lobe pneumonia, pyelonephritis, and pelvic inflammatory disease. Noninfectious diseases to be considered in the differential diagnosis are pancreatitis, diabetic ketoacidosis, Henoch-Schönlein purpura, ovarian torsion, sickle-cell pain crisis, and lead poisoning.[51]

TREATMENT

Optimal management of peritonitis involves prompt and aggressive physiologic support, surgical consultation, and antimicrobial therapy. Correction of fluid and electrolyte imbalances and hemodynamic stabilization should be initiated as soon as the diagnosis of peritonitis is suspected. Spontaneous bacterial peritonitis usually is managed medically unless the diagnosis is uncertain, in which case exploratory laparotomy or laparoscopy is performed. Before the emergence of resistant strains of *S. pneumoniae*, primary peritonitis in children was treated with aqueous penicillin G.[17, 31] Given the increased prevalence of *S. pneumoniae* with reduced susceptibility to penicillin, third-generation cephalosporins such as cefotaxime or ceftriaxone are recommended until susceptibility results are available.[45, 71] If primary peritonitis is caused by gram-negative organisms, cefotaxime or ceftriaxone, an aminoglycoside, a carbapenem, ticarcillin-clavulanate, or piperacillin-tazobactam is appropriate empiric therapy pending completion of culture and susceptibility testing. Patients with secondary peritonitis may require either immediate surgery to control the source of contamination and to remove necrotic tissue, blood, and intestinal contents from the peritoneal cavity or a drainage procedure if a limited number of large abscesses can be demonstrated.[43, 47, 52, 79] In cases of phlegmon, or extensive inflammatory edema, surgery usually is not performed acutely because of the child's unstable metabolic state and friable intra-abdominal tissues. Surgery is delayed for several hours or weeks to allow the inflammation to resolve. Surgery also may be postponed indefinitely.[6, 14, 74]

Empiric antimicrobial therapy for secondary peritonitis should have activity against anaerobes, especially the *B. fragilis* group and enteric gram-negative aerobes.[7] Although controversial, some regimens also include an antibiotic effective against enterococci. Thus, the "gold standard" for antimicrobial therapy historically has been clindamycin or metronidazole, gentamicin, and ampicillin.[7, 11, 27, 43, 46, 52, 62] Alternative efficacious regimens, as single or combination therapy, include aztreonam, cefotaxime, cefoxitin, imipenem-cilastatin, meropenem, piperacillin-tazobactam, and ticarcillin-clavulanate.[7, 43, 46, 52, 79] Rates of resistance to cefoxitin and clindamycin among the *B. fragilis* group have increased and are reported to be as high as 49 percent; thus, in some institutions, alternative regimens are used routinely.[2, 46]

Other studies have examined the use of a single broad-spectrum antibiotic, which allows a portion of the therapy to be delivered less expensively on an outpatient basis. Fishman and coworkers prospectively evaluated the clinical outcomes of 150 children with perforated appendicitis treated postoperatively with a 10-day course of piperacillin-tazobactam. They compared the outcome with that of historical controls treated with a 10-day course of ampicillin, gentamicin, and clindamycin. Rates of postoperative infectious complications were similar in both groups.[27] Bradley and colleagues prospectively identified 87 children with complicated appendicitis in five pediatric centers, also comparing costs and outcomes with historical controls. Although inpatient treatment courses were reduced by an average of 42 percent in meropenem-treated children, outcome measures again were equivalent to those of historical controls.[8] Table 60–2 summarizes randomized trials of monotherapy versus combination therapy for ruptured appendicitis in children. Although no differences in outcome were observed, the potential of emerging resistance to broad-spectrum agents versus the convenience of monotherapy must be considered and balanced against the possible decreased risk of developing nosocomial infection among children who can receive a substantial component of parenteral therapy in the home.[38]

Empiric antibiotic treatment of CAPD-associated peritonitis should be effective against gram-positive and gram-negative organisms until culture results are available. Intraperitoneal antibiotics, with or without concomitant intravenous antibiotics, achieve adequate serum and dialysate concentrations. Vancomycin is used for empiric therapy for gram-positive infections, but if staphylococcal organisms are susceptible to β-lactam agents, treatment with cefazolin is effective.[26] Aminoglycosides (gentamicin or tobramycin) or cephalosporins are used for gram-negative infections; however, because most intraperitoneal antibiotics are absorbed into the systemic circulation, serum aminoglycoside or vancomycin concentrations should be monitored for possible toxicity. Therapy for fungal peritonitis usually is intravenous amphotericin B, although successful use of the newer azole antifungal agents or intraperitoneal amphotericin B has been reported.[26, 56] Indications for removal of a dialysis catheter include persistent infection with *S. aureus* or *Pseudomonas,* tunnel infection, or fungal peritonitis.[26]

Treatment of peritonitis associated with ventriculoperitoneal shunts usually requires externalization of the distal end of the catheter in addition to institution of antibiotic therapy.[30] Empiric antibiotic therapy should include an antistaphylococcal agent active against both coagulase-positive and coagulase-negative staphylococci. Coagulase-negative staphylococci are a common cause of ventriculoperitoneal shunt infection; thus, vancomycin should be administered pending culture and susceptibility results. If Gram stain of ventricular CSF or peritoneal fluid reveals gram-negative organisms, cefotaxime, ceftriaxone, ceftazidime, or meropenem should be added.[5, 61]

The duration of antibiotic therapy for peritonitis should be dictated by the clinical course of the patient inasmuch as no single regimen or treatment course is accepted universally.[37] Indicators of sufficient therapy include resolution of fever and abdominal pain and return of the leukocyte and differential counts to normal.[37, 52, 69] Primary peritonitis caused by streptococci is treated successfully with a 10- to 14-day course of antibiotics.[17, 37] Primary peritonitis with gram-negative organisms may require 10 days to 3 weeks of antibiotic treatment.[17] The duration of therapy for secondary peritonitis after adequate surgery usually is 5 to 10 days, but it depends on the clinical response to therapy.[37, 52, 69] Short-course therapy for 5 days has been shown to be efficacious in some patients,[37, 52] but longer courses are required if persistence of fever or abdominal signs and symptoms are present.

Standard therapy for tuberculous peritonitis consists of a minimum of two antituberculous drugs. As with other forms of extrapulmonary tuberculosis in children, empiric therapy with isoniazid, rifampin, and pyrazinamide is advised pending culture and susceptibility results. Although *M. bovis* is resistant to pyrazinamide, most strains are susceptible to isoniazid and rifampin, as well as to ethambutol.

TABLE 60–2 ■ MONOTHERAPY VERSUS COMBINATION THERAPY FOR RUPTURED APPENDICITIS IN CHILDREN

			Number of Patients		Complications*	
Study	**Monotherapy (A)**	**Combination Therapy (B)**	A	B	A (%)	B (%)
Meller et al.[49]	Cefoxitin	Clindamycin/gentamicin	29	27	1 (3)	4 (15)
Dougherty et al.[22]	Ticarcillin-clavulanate	Clindamycin/gentamicin ± ampicillin	79	45	14 (18)	5 (11)
Uhari et al.[73]	Imipenem-cilastatin	Metronidazole/tobramycin	9	10	2 (22)	1 (10)
Collins et al.[19]	Ampicillin-sulbactam ± aminoglycoside	Ampicillin/clindamycin ± aminoglycoside	75	39	2 (1)	1 (3)
Fishman et al.,[27] Lund & Murphy[43]	Pipercillin-tazobactam	Ampicillin/gentamicin/clindamycin	150	373	14 (9)	24 (6)
Bradley et al.[8]	Meropenem	Cefotaxime ± amikacin or tobramycin, clindamycin or metronidazole	22	13	2 (9)	1 (8)

*Wound infections, intra-abdominal abscess, or rehospitalization.
Modified from Kaplan, S. L.: Antibiotic usage in appendicitis in children. Pediatr. Infect. Dis. J. *17*:1047–1048, 1998.

COMPLICATIONS

Acute complications associated with peritonitis include septic shock, adult respiratory distress syndrome, septic thrombophlebitis of the portal vein, acute renal failure, and multiorgan system failure.[46] Postoperative complications include wound infection, adhesions, bowel obstruction, formation of a fistula, and formation of an intra-abdominal or retroperitoneal abscess.

Recurrent peritonitis (tertiary peritonitis) is an entity described as occurring late in the course of therapy for secondary peritonitis.[37, 44, 79] Patients with this condition continue to have symptoms despite appropriate antimicrobial therapy, and peritoneal fluid reveals persistent inflammation. Bacterial cultures often are negative or may yield an organism of low virulence. Multiorgan system failure and a poor outcome frequently are associated with tertiary peritonitis. The mechanism of ongoing peritoneal inflammation is unknown; however, some investigators have proposed that immunoregulatory dysfunction and poor nutrition are contributing factors.

Intra-abdominal Abscess

Intra-abdominal abscesses often are categorized as intraperitoneal, visceral, or retroperitoneal (reviewed in Chapter 61).[4, 10] In children, intraperitoneal abscesses are the most common. The most common underlying conditions associated with an intra-abdominal abscess in children are appendicitis and trauma.[10, 51] Reviews of gangrenous or perforated appendicitis in children indicate that 2 to 20 percent of cases are complicated by the formation of an abscess.[52, 62] Two basic mechanisms exist for the development of an intraperitoneal abscess. In the first mechanism, diffuse peritonitis may cause loculations of purulent material to form in the areas anatomically most dependent, typically the pelvic, subphrenic, and paracolic regions (see Fig. 60–1). The second mode of formation of an abscess involves a localized focus related to contiguous disease or injury in which host defenses and the inflammatory response prevent diffuse spread and peritonitis.[4] The microbiology of intraperitoneal abscesses is polymicrobial and reflects that of the intestinal flora. In a review of intra-abdominal abscess in 36 children, Brook noted that the predominant organisms were the *B. fragilis* group, *Peptostreptococcus, E. coli,* and other Enterobacteriaceae.[10, 11]

The most common sites of visceral abscess in children are the liver (discussed in Chapter 56), pancreas, and spleen. Underlying conditions that may lead to the development of a pancreatic abscess include pancreatic injury, pancreatitis, and biliary obstruction. Pancreatitis or surgical or accidental injury to the pancreas causes the release of pancreatic enzymes and focal necrosis.[28] Reflux of contaminated bile into the pancreatic duct is hypothesized to be the mechanism by which enteric organisms gain access to the injured pancreas and proliferate. Thus, a pancreatic abscess usually is a polymicrobial infection caused by aerobic (*E. coli*, *K. pneumoniae*, group D streptococci) or anaerobic (peptostreptococci, *B. fragilis* group) organisms that inhabit the gastrointestinal tract. Rare instances of *S. aureus* pancreatic abscess occur as a result of bacteremia.[12, 13]

Splenic abscesses are unusual findings in infants and children. Before the 1970s, most reports involved solitary pyogenic abscesses. Since then, the number of reports of multiple splenic abscesses has increased.[16, 39, 58] Splenic abscess usually is associated with one of five underlying conditions: endocarditis, injury, hemoglobinopathy, immunodeficiency, or adjacent infection. Given the filtering function of the spleen, an abscess can form as a result of any metastatic hematogenous infection, such as endocarditis. Though rare, splenic abscess can be a delayed complication of the nonoperative management of splenic injuries. Splenic infarcts associated with hemoglobinopathies such as sickle-cell disease may become secondarily infected and form an abscess.[16] The more recent literature cites immunodeficiency, such as malignancy or acquired immunodeficiency syndrome, as a significant risk factor for the development of multiple splenic abscesses.[39, 53, 58] Rarely, infection or disease in a contiguous focus may extend to the spleen. In a review of 56 children with splenic abscesses, 7 (12.5%) were cryptogenic with no apparent cause.[39] In most instances, a single pathogen is isolated, with *S. aureus,* streptococci, *E. coli,* and *Salmonella* spp. being the most common. Fungi, most often *Candida* spp., have been isolated from splenic abscesses primarily in immunocompromised hosts.[39, 53, 58]

CLINICAL MANIFESTATIONS

The typical clinical features of an intra-abdominal abscess include fever, abdominal pain, and tenderness over the involved area. Subphrenic abscesses also may be manifested as referred pain or pulmonary or pleuritic symptoms. Pancreatic abscess may be associated with a palpable epigastric mass and elevated serum lipase and amylase.[12] Splenomegaly or a splenic mass may be noted in approximately half of patients with splenic abscesses.[39] In postoperative patients, persistence of abdominal symptoms or fever warrants evaluation for an intraperitoneal abscess.[3] Leukocytosis in the range of 20,000 to 50,000 cells/mm^3 frequently is present in children with an intra-abdominal abscess.[3, 37]

DIAGNOSIS

Imaging studies are helpful in making the diagnosis of an intra-abdominal abscess. Plain radiographs remain useful as an initial procedure and may show an extraintestinal air-fluid level, right lower quadrant mass, or localized ileus.[1] Chest radiographs should be obtained because subphrenic abscesses often are associated with a pleural effusion. In a series of 27 children with splenic abscesses, chest radiographs were abnormal in 20 cases, with the most common findings being left pleural effusion and an elevated left hemidiaphragm.[39] Ultrasonography is a useful noninvasive technique that can detect abdominal and pelvic abscesses. However, the quality of the images depends on the examiner. In addition, conditions such as ileus, postoperative drains, or dressings may hinder ultrasonic detection of an abscess.[1, 47, 50] CT is the most sensitive tool for detection of an intra-abdominal abscess, and it provides good anatomic resolution. Disadvantages of CT are the radiation and, if used, exposure to intravenous, oral, or rectal contrast material.[1, 47, 50] Although recent experience with the use of magnetic resonance imaging (MRI) for the detection of an intraperitoneal abscess has been described in the literature,[54] MRI should be considered in children only when an abscess may not be detected more easily by other methods or in patients who should not have exposure to radiation.[54] Gallium scanning is a sensitive technique for the diagnosis of an abscess, but it is relatively nonspecific, particularly in the abdomen.[1]

TREATMENT

Management of an intra-abdominal abscess includes physiologic and nutritional support, antimicrobial therapy, and drainage. After obtaining blood cultures, empiric antibiotic therapy should be instituted with agents effective against anaerobes, Enterobacteriaceae, and other enteric flora as discussed earlier for peritonitis. Antibiotic therapy usually is begun before surgery to minimize any complications of bacteremia during the procedure. Abscess material should be obtained for culture of aerobic, anaerobic, fungal, and mycobacterial pathogens. Effective surgical management depends on accurate localization of the abscess, discrimination between single and multiple abscesses, and early and adequate drainage.[3, 4, 46] Traditional therapy for intraperitoneal abscesses has relied on open surgical drainage, although drainage of intraperitoneal abscesses percutaneously under ultrasound or CT guidance now is used often.[1, 18, 21, 46, 50, 59] In instances of multiple intraperitoneal abscesses or if the source of peritoneal contamination has not been controlled, laparotomy is indicated.[46] Pancreatic abscesses require intensive surgical and medical therapy. Antimicrobial therapy for mixed aerobic and anaerobic infection is suggested,[12] but splenectomy remains the definitive treatment of bacterial splenic abscesses. However, in selected patients, percutaneous drainage or splenotomy has the advantage of preserving splenic function.[39, 53, 58] Multiple small splenic abscesses and fungal lesions generally are treated medically.[39] Antibiotic therapy for a pyogenic splenic abscess should be guided by the pathogens associated with the child's underlying condition. Therapy should include antibiotics effective against *S. aureus*, streptococci, and gram-negative enteric bacilli. Specific therapy then should be revised after culture and susceptibility results are available.

COMPLICATIONS

Intraperitoneal and visceral abscesses, if not adequately drained, may be associated with significant complications, including ongoing spread of the infectious process and, for splenic or pancreatic abscesses, a high mortality rate. Fistula formation, adhesions, and bowel obstruction may be late complications of intra-abdominal infection.

REFERENCES

1. Afshani, E.: Computed tomography of abdominal abscesses in children. Radiol. Clin. North Am. *19*:515–526, 1981.
2. Aldridge, K. E., Ashcraft, D., Cambre, K., et al.: Multicenter survey of the changing in vitro antimicrobial susceptibilities of clinical isolates of *Bacteroides fragilis* group, *Prevotella, Fusobacterium, Porphyromonas,* and *Peptostreptococcus* species. Antimicrob. Agents Chemother. *45*:1238–1243, 2001.
3. Alteimeier, W. A., Culbertson, W. R., and Fullen, W. D.: Intra-abdominal sepsis. Adv. Surg. *5*:281–333, 1971.
4. Altemeier, W. A., Culbertson, W. R., Fuller, W. D., et al.: Intra-abdominal abscesses. Am. J. Surg. *125*:70–79, 1973.
5. Baird, C., O'Connor, D., and Pittman, T.: Late shunt infections. Pediatr. Neurosurg. *31*:269–273, 1999.
6. Blakely, M. L., Spurbeck, W. W., and Lobe, T. E.: Current status of laparoscopic appendectomy in children. Semin. Pediatr. Surg. *7*:225–227, 1998.
7. Bohnen, J. M., Solomkin, J. S., Dellinger, E. P., et al.: Guidelines for clinical care: Anti-infective agents for intra-abdominal infection: A Surgical Infection Society policy statement. Arch. Surg. *127*:83–89, 1992.
8. Bradley, J. S., Behrendt, C. E., Arrieta, A. C., et al.: Convalescent phase outpatient parenteral antiinfective therapy for children with complicated appendicitis. Pediatr. Infect. Dis. J. *20*:19–24, 2001.
9. Bradley, J. S., Faulkner, K. L., and Klugman, K. P.: Efficacy, safety and tolerability of meropenem as empiric antibiotic therapy in hospitalized pediatric patients. Pediatr. Infect. Dis. J. *15*:749–757, 1996.
10. Brook, I.: Intra-abdominal abscess in children: A 13 year experience. Hosp. Pract. *25*:20–23, 1990.
11. Brook, I.: Intra-abdominal infections in children: Pathogenesis, diagnosis and management. Drugs *46*:53–62, 1993.
12. Brook, I., and Frazier, E. H.: Microbiological analysis of pancreatic abscess. Clin. Infect. Dis. *22*:384–385, 1996.
13. Brook, I., and Frazier, E. H.: Aerobic and anaerobic microbiology of retroperitoneal abscesses. Clin. Infect. Dis. *26*:938–941, 1998.
14. Bufo, A. J., Shah, R. S., Li, M. H., et al.: Interval appendectomy for perforated appendicitis in children. J. Laparoendosc. Adv. Surg. Tech. A *8*:209–214, 1998.
15. Canon, H. L., Buckingham, S. C., Wyatt, R. J., et al.: Fungal peritonitis caused by *Curvularia* species in a child undergoing peritoneal dialysis. Pediatr. Nephrol. *16*:35–37, 2001.
16. Chun, C. H., Raff, M. J., Contreras, L., et al.: Splenic abscess. Medicine (Baltimore) *59*:50–65, 1980.
17. Clark, J. H., Fitzgerald, J. F., and Kleiman, M. B.: Spontaneous bacterial peritonitis. J. Pediatr. *104*:495–500, 1984.
18. Clark, R. A., and Towbin, R.: Abscess drainage with CT and ultrasound guidance. Radiol. Clin. North Am. *21*:445–459, 1983.
19. Collins, M. D., Dajani, A. S., Kim, K. S., et al.: Comparison of ampicillin/sulbactam plus aminoglycoside vs. ampicillin plus clindamycin plus aminoglycoside in the treatment of intraabdominal infections in children. Pediatr. Infect. Dis. J. *17*(Suppl.):15–18, 1998.
20. Dankner, W. M., and Davis, C. E.: *Mycobacterium bovis* as a significant cause of tuberculosis in children residing along the United States–Mexico border in the Baja California region. Pediatrics 105/6/e79.
21. Diament, M. J., Stanley, P., Kangarloo, H., and Donaldson, J. S.: Percutaneous aspiration and catheter drainage of abscesses. J. Pediatr. *108*:204–208, 1986.
22. Dougherty, S. H., Sirinek, K. R., Schauer, P. R., et al. Ticarcillin/clavulanate compared with clindamycin/gentamicin (with or without ampicillin) for the treatment of intra-abdominal infections in pediatric and adult patients. Am. Surg. *61*:297–303, 1995.
23. Dunn, D. L., Barke, R. A., Ahrenholz, D. H., et al.: The adjuvant effect of peritoneal fluid in experimental peritonitis: Mechanism and clinical implications. Ann. Surg. *199*:37–43, 1984.
24. Dunn, D. L., Barke, R. A., Knight, N. B., et al.: Role of resident macrophages, peripheral neutrophils, and translymphatic absorption in bacterial clearance from the peritoneal cavity. Infect. Immun. *49*:257–264, 1985.
25. Enriquez, J. L., Kalia, A., and Travis, L. B.: Fungal peritonitis in children on peritoneal dialysis. J. Pediatr. *117*:830–832, 1990.
26. Feinstein, E. I., Chesney, R. W., and Zelikovic, I.: Peritonitis in childhood renal disease. Am. J. Nephrol. *8*:147–165, 1988.
27. Fishman, S. J., Pelosi, L., Klavon, S. L., et al.: Perforated appendicitis: Prospective outcome analysis for 150 children. J. Pediatr. Surg. *35*:923–926, 2000.
28. Ford, E. G., Hardin, W. D., Mahour, G. H., et al.: Pseudocysts of the pancreas in children. Am. Surg. *56*:384–387, 1990.
29. Freij, B. J., Votteler, T. P., and McCracken, G. H.: Primary peritonitis in previously healthy children. Am. J. Dis. Child. *138*:1058–1061, 1984.
30. Gaskill, S. J., and Marlin, A. E.: Spontaneous bacterial peritonitis in patients with ventriculoperitoneal shunts. Pediatr. Neurosurg. *26*:115–119, 1997.
31. Gorensek, M. J., Lebel, M. H., and Nelson, J. D.: Peritonitis in children with nephrotic syndrome. Pediatrics *81*:849–856, 1988.
32. Graham, J. C., Moss, P. J., and McKendrick, M. W.: Primary group A streptococcal peritonitis. Scand. J. Infect. Dis. *27*:171–172, 1995.
33. Grosfeld, J. L., Cooney, D. R., Smith, J., et al.: Intra-abdominal complications following ventriculoperitoneal shunt procedures. Pediatrics *54*:791–796, 1974.
34. Gurkan, F., Ozates, M., Bosnak, M., et al.: Tuberculous peritonitis in 11 children: Clinical features and diagnostic approach. Pediatr. Int. *41*:510–513, 1999.
35. Jakubowski, A., Elwood, R. K., and Enarson, D. A.: Clinical features of abdominal tuberculosis. J. Infect. Dis. *158*:687–692, 1988.
36. Jelloul, L., Fremond, B., Dyon, J. F., et al.: Mesenteric adenitis caused by *Yersinia pseudotuberculosis* presenting as an abdominal mass. Eur. J. Pediatr. Surg. *7*:180–283, 1997.
37. Johnson, C. C., Baldessarre, J., and Levison, M. E.: Peritonitis: Update on pathophysiology, clinical manifestations, and management. Clin. Infect. Dis. *24*:1035–1047, 1997.
38. Kaplan, S. L.: Antibiotic usage in appendicitis in children. Pediatr. Infect. Dis. J. *17*:1047–1048, 1998.
39. Keidl, C. M., and Chusid, M. J.: Splenic abscesses in childhood. Pediatr. Infect. Dis. J. *8*:368–373, 1989.
40. Kimber, C. P., and Hutson, J. M.: Primary peritonitis in children. Aust. N. Z. J. Surg. *66*:169–170, 1996.
41. Krensky, A. M., Ingelfinger, J. R., and Grupe, W. E.: Peritonitis in childhood nephrotic syndrome. Am. J. Dis. Child. *136*:732–736, 1982.
42. Lamps, L. W., Madhusukhan, K. T., Greenson, J. K., et al.: The role of *Yersinia enterocolitica* and *Yersinia pseudotuberculosis* in granulomatous appendicitis: A histologic and molecular study. Am. J. Surg. Pathol. *25*:508–515, 2001.

43. Lund, D. P., and Murphy, E. U.: Management of perforated appendicitis in children: A decade of aggressive treatment. J. Pediatr. Surg. *29*:1130–1134, 1994.
44. Malangoni, M. A.: Evaluation and management of tertiary peritonitis. Am. Surg. *66*:157–161, 2000.
45. Markenson, D. S., Levine, D., and Schacht, R.: Primary peritonitis as a presenting feature of nephrotic syndrome: A case report and review of the literature. Pediatr. Emerg. Care *15*:407–409, 1999.
46. McClean, K. L., Sheehan, G. J., and Harding, G. K. M.: Intraabdominal infection: A review. Clin. Infect. Dis. *19*:100–116, 1994.
47. McConkey, S. J., McCarthy, N. D., and Keane, C. T.: Primary peritonitis due to nonenteric salmonellae. Clin. Infect. Dis. *29*:211–212, 1999.
48. Melez, K. A., Cherry, J., Sanchez, C., et al.: Successful outpatient treatment of *Trichosporon beigelii* peritonitis with oral fluconazole. Pediatr. Infect. Dis. J. *14*:1110–1113, 1995.
49. Meller, J. L., Reyes, H. M., Loeff, D. S., et al.: One drug versus two-drug antibiotic therapy in pediatric perforated appendicitis: A prospective randomized study. Surgery *110*:764–768, 1991.
50. Montgomery, R. S., and Wilson, S. E.: Intraabdominal abscesses: Image-guided diagnosis and therapy. Clin. Infect. Dis. *23*:28–36, 1996.
51. Neblett, W. W., Pietsch, J. B., and Holcomb, G. W., Jr.: Acute abdominal conditions in children and adolescents. Surg. Clin. North Am. *68*:415–430, 1988.
52. Neilson, I. R., Laberge, J. M., Nguyen, L. T., et al.: Appendicitis in children: Current therapeutic recommendations. J. Pediatr. Surg. *25*:1113–1116, 1990.
53. Nelken, N., Ignatius, J., Skinner, M., et al.: Changing clinical spectrum of splenic abscess: A multicenter study and review of the literature. Am. J. Surg. *154*:27–34, 1987.
54. Noone, T. C., Semelka, R. C., Worawattanakul, S., et al.: Intraperitoneal abscesses: Diagnostic accuracy of and appearances at MR imaging. Radiology *208*:525–528, 1998.
55. Odio, C., McCracken, G. H., and Nelson, J. D.: CSF shunt infections in pediatrics. A seven-year experience. Am. J. Dis. Child. *138*: 1103–1108,1984.
56. Oh, S. H., Conley, S. B., Rose, G. M., et al.: Fungal peritonitis in children undergoing peritoneal dialysis. Pediatr. Infect. Dis. J. *4*:62–66, 1985.
57. Olika, D., Yamini, D., Udani, V. M., et al.: Nonoperative management of perforated appendicitis without periappendiceal mass. Am. J. Surg. *179*:177–181, 2000.
58. Phillips, G. S., Radosevich, M. D., and Lipsett, P. A.: Splenic abscess: Another look at an old disease. Arch. Surg. *132*:1331–1336, 1997.
59. Ramakrishnan, M. R., and Sarathy, T. K. P.: Percutaneous drainage of splenic abscess: Case report and review of literature. Pediatrics *79*:1029–1031, 1987.
60. Rekate, H. L., Yonas, H., White, R. J., et al.: The acute abdomen in patients with ventriculoperitoneal shunts. Surg. Neurol. *11*:442–445, 1979.
61. Reynolds, M., Sherman, J. O., and Mclone, D. G.: Ventriculoperitoneal shunt infection masquerading as an acute surgical abdomen. J. Pediatr. Surg. *18*:951–955, 1983.
62. Schwartz, M. Z., Tapper, D., and Solenberger, R. I.: Management of perforated appendicitis in children: The controversy continues. Ann. Surg. *197*:407–411, 1983.
63. Sells, C. J., and Loeser, J. D.: Peritonitis following perforation of the bowel: A rare complication of a ventriculoperitoneal shunt. J. Pediatr. *83*:823–824, 1973.
64. Simon, G. L., and Gorbach, S. L.: Intestinal flora in health and disease. Gastroenterology *86*:174–193, 1984.
65. Sioson, P. B., Stechenberg, B. W., Courtney, R., et al.: Tuberculous peritonitis in a three-year-old boy: Case report and review of the literature. Pediatr. Infect. Dis. J. *11*:409–411, 1992.
66. Sirotnak, A. P., Eppes, S. C., and Klein, J. D.: Tuboovarian abscess and peritonitis caused by *Streptococcus pneumoniae* serotype 1 in young girls. Clin. Infect. Dis. *22*:993–996, 1996.
67. Snow, R. B., Lavyne, M. H., and Fraser, R. A. R.: Colonic perforation by ventriculoperitoneal shunts. Surg. Neurol. *25*:173–177, 1986.
68. Stamos, J. K., Kaufman, B. A., and Yogev, R.: Ventriculoperitoneal shunt infections with gram-negative bacteria. Neurosurgery *33*:858–862, 1993.
69. Stone, H. H., Bourneuf, A. A., and Stinson, L. D.: Reliability of criteria for predicting persistent or recurrent sepsis. Arch. Surg. *120*:17–20, 1985.
70. Such, J., and Runyon, B. A.: Spontaneous bacterial peritonitis. Clin. Infect. Dis. *27*:669–676, 1998.
71. Tain, Y. L., Lin, G. J., and Cher, T. W.: Microbiological spectrum of septicemia and peritonitis in nephrotic children. Pediatr. Nephrol. *13*:835–837, 1999.
72. Tchirkow, G., and Verhagen, A. D.: Bacterial peritonitis in patients with ventriculoperitoneal shunt. J. Pediatr. Surg. *14*:182–184, 1979.
73. Uhari, M., Seppanen, J., and Heikkinen, E.: Imipenem-cilastatin vs. tobramycin and metronidazole for appendicitis-related infections. Pediatr. Infect. Dis. J. *11*:445–450, 1992.
74. Vargas, H. I., Averbook, A., and Stamos, M. J.: Appendiceal mass: Conservative therapy followed by interval laparoscopic appendectomy. Am. Surg. *60*:753–758, 1994.
75. Veeragandham, R. S., Lynch, F. P., Canty, T. G., et al.: Abdominal tuberculosis in children: Review of 26 cases. J. Pediatr. Surg. *31*:170–176, 1996.
76. Warady, B. A., Bashir, M., and Donaldson, L. A.: Fungal peritonitis in children receiving peritoneal dialysis: A report of the NAPRTCS. Kidney Int. *58*:384–389, 2000.
77. White, R., Abreo, K., Flanagan, R., et al.: Nontuberculous mycobacterial infections in continuous ambulatory peritoneal dialysis patients. Am. J. Kidney Dis. *22*:581–587, 1993.
78. Wilfert, C. M., and Katz, S. L.: Etiology of bacterial sepsis in nephrotic children 1963–1967. Pediatrics *42*:840–843, 1968.
79. Wittmann, D. H., Schein, M., and Condon, R. E.: Management of secondary peritonitis. Ann. Surg. *224*:10–18, 1996.
80. Younger, J. J., Simmons, J. C. H., and Barrett, F. F.: Occult distal ventriculoperitoneal shunt infections. Pediatr. Infect. Dis. J. *4*: 557–558,1985.

Retroperitoneal Infections

ALICE PONG ■ JOHN S. BRADLEY

Retroperitoneal infections consist primarily of suppurative bacterial infections that originate within the retroperitoneal structures or as an extension from another primary site. In children, these infections are much less common than are intra-abdominal infections; however, they can lead to significant morbidity if missed. Making a diagnosis can be difficult because symptoms often are indolent and poorly localized.

The retroperitoneal structures are separated from the intra-abdominal organs by the posterior peritoneal fascia (Fig. 61–1). Structures posterior to this fascia layer, in the anterior retroperitoneal space, include the duodenum, pancreas, and parts of the colon. The kidneys and ureters are encased further by the renal fascia. The iliopsoas and psoas muscles lie at the posterior aspect of the retroperitoneal space and are separated from the other retroperitoneal structures by the transversalis fascia. Pelvic structures, including the bladder, uterus, and rectum, that lie inferior to the pelvic peritoneum constitute the pelvic portion of the retroperitoneal space. The fascial layers limit the spread of

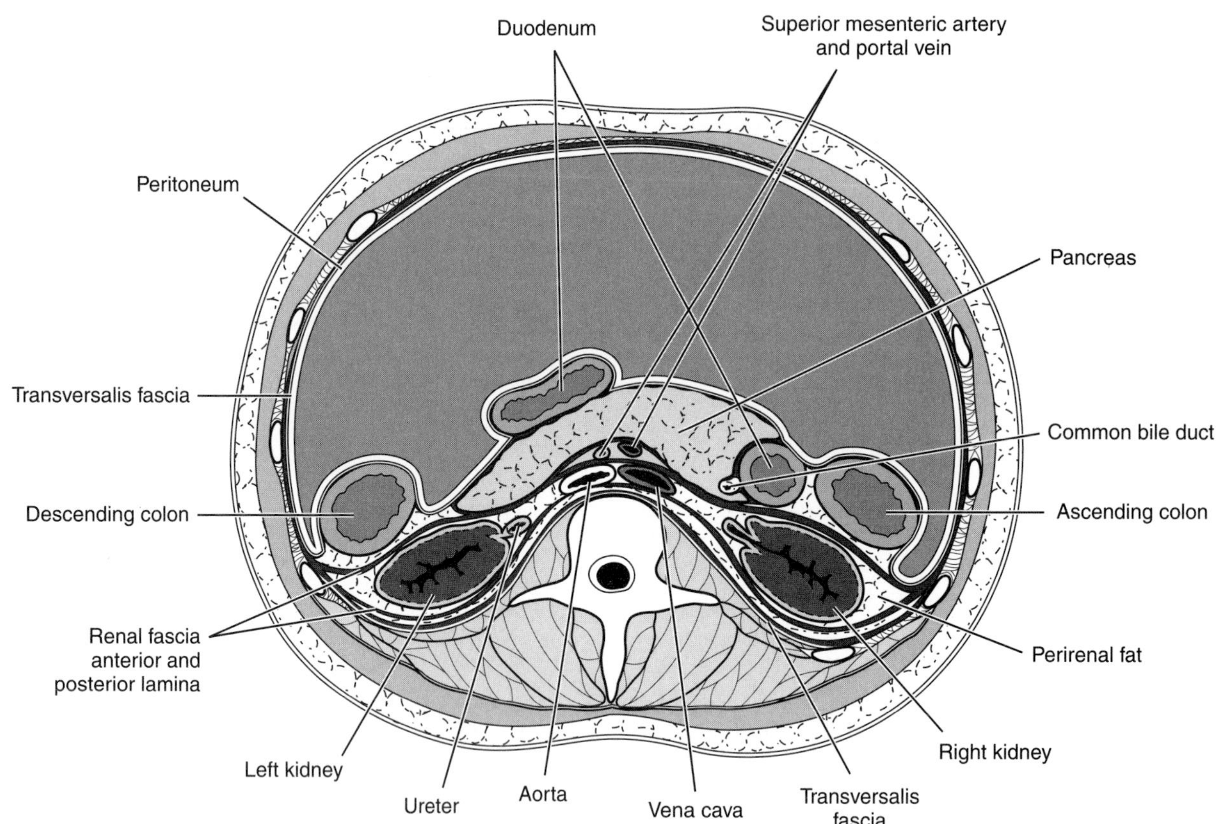

FIGURE 61–1 ■ A cross section of abdomen at L2 shows the structures within the retroperitoneal space. (From Altemeier, W. A, and Alexander, J. W.: Retroperitoneal abscess. Arch. Surg. *83*:515, 1961, with permission.)

retroperitoneal infections. However, the deep location can be difficult to assess by physical examination.

Etiology and Pathogenesis

Retroperitoneal infections in children arise in numerous anatomic structures. Brook reviewed cases of retroperitoneal infections from five U.S. hospitals from 1974 to 1994. Forty-one children were identified. Twenty-one had infections in the anterior retroperitoneal space related to the pancreas (4) and intestines (13), six perinephric abscesses, seven iliopsoas abscesses, and seven pelvic retroperitoneal abscesses.[5]

Primary infection of the retroperitoneal space can be hematogenous in origin or complicate an ascending urinary tract infection. Secondary infections occur as a direct extension from gastrointestinal perforations arising from ruptured appendices or are related to Crohn disease.[5, 15, 16] Greenstein and associates reported retroperitoneal abscesses in 12 of 231 patients with Crohn disease.[15] Retroperitoneal infections also can develop secondary to primary infections of the vertebral spine, pelvic bones, and sacroiliac joint.[17, 25, 28] Suppurative iliac or retroperitoneal lymph nodes are another suspected source of retroperitoneal infections. Prior surgery has been associated with perinephric abscesses[6, 14] and in vascular grafts in adults.[7] Pancreatic abscesses are seen more commonly in adult patients and are associated with underlying biliary tract disease, alcoholism, surgery, and trauma.[8]

Infections of the perinephric retroperitoneal space include those involving the kidney and adrenal glands. Adrenal abscesses are reported more frequently in neonates than in older children and are suspected to be related to adrenal hemorrhages that become secondarily infected.[22] Perinephric abscesses can result from bacteremic inoculation of renal tissue or as a consequence of an ascending urinary tract infection. Nephronia (i.e., focal bacterial nephritis) is thought to be an intermediate stage of renal infection between pyelonephritis and renal abscess, resulting from an ascending infection of the urinary tract.[23]

Iliopsoas abscesses may develop in relation to hematogenous seeding of the muscle or with trauma as a predisposing factor.[16, 24] Although primary infection occurs most commonly,[4] the iliopsoas muscle extends from the rib and lumbar vertebrae to its insertion on the femur and is exposed to the risk of contiguous extension of infection from numerous adjacent structures. Psoas abscesses have developed from vertebral infections, intestinal perforations, and genitourinary sources and as an extension of primary pelvic osteomyelitis.[16, 18, 24, 25]

Complications of retroperitoneal abscesses include rupture into the intraperitoneal space and extension of the infection along fascial planes to adjacent muscles that extend from origins in the pelvis and trunk to insertion sites on the femur. Rupture into the thoracic cavity also has been reported.[1] Other complications include pneumonia, recurrent abscess, renal failure, and venous and arterial thrombosis.[11]

Microbiology

The microbiology of retroperitoneal infections is determined by the source of the infection and the retroperitoneal compartment involved. Most primary infections thought to result from bacteremia are caused by *Staphylococcus aureus*.

Secondary infection related to the gastrointestinal tract is caused by mixed bowel flora. Common pathogens include *Escherichia coli*, other gram-negative enteric bacteria, *Pseudomonas* spp., and gastrointestinal anaerobes, particularly *Bacteroides fragilis* and *Peptostreptococcus*.[5] Most infections in the anterior retroperitoneal space are associated with a gastrointestinal source and may be polymicrobial.

Ascending infections from the urinary tract usually are caused by *E. coli*; however, perinephric abscesses also are reported as a complication of renal infection caused by *S. aureus*, group B *Streptococcus*, and *Salmonella*.[14, 30, 31]

S. aureus is the leading pathogen isolated in iliopsoas abscesses unless the infection results from erosion of a primary gastrointestinal focus. In this situation, gram-negative enteric bacteria and anaerobes are more likely to be the causative agents.[4, 24] Retroperitoneal necrotizing fasciitis from group A *Streptococcus* also has been reported.[12]

Tuberculosis caused by *Mycobacterium tuberculosis* or *Mycobacterium bovis* may involve the retroperitoneal space, particularly as an extension of vertebral tuberculous osteomyelitis.[1, 13, 18] Abdominal tuberculosis usually manifests as an intraperitoneal infection but can produce retroperitoneal adenopathy.

Clinical Presentation

Children with retroperitoneal infections present clinically in a variety of ways, ranging from nonspecific fever to overwhelming sepsis. The most common clinical symptoms associated with retroperitoneal infections include fever and pain in the hip, back, and abdomen.[11, 21] Psoas abscesses often manifest with the child limping or refusing to walk.[4] Neonates with a retroperitoneal abscess may present with an abdominal mass.[26] Symptoms often are vague, and pain is not well localized. Patients often have been evaluated previously for fevers and have been treated with antibiotics before a diagnosis has been made.[4, 20, 25] A delay in the diagnosis is not uncommon.

Differential Diagnosis

Retroperitoneal infections can be confused with a variety of other infections caused by poorly localized and often misleading symptoms. Pyogenic arthritis of the hip and infection of the sacroiliac joint and pelvic bones are the leading diagnoses for patients presenting with a limp and fever. Intra-abdominal infections, including appendicitis and intra-abdominal abscesses, are seen more commonly in patients with abdominal pain and fever. Noninfectious processes, including trauma and malignancy, are more frequent causes of retroperitoneal masses compared with infectious causes and should be considered.

Specific Diagnosis

Laboratory tests often are nonspecific and of minimal benefit. Sedimentation rates and leukocyte counts often are elevated.[4, 6, 24, 25] Pyuria often is absent in children with perinephric and renal abscesses, and the urine culture result may be negative.[6, 14, 29, 30] However, in patients with nephronia, pyuria and positive urine cultures are more likely.[20, 23] Blood cultures may be helpful in identifying a bacterial pathogen. Brook reported that 40 percent of blood cultures were positive for children with retroperitoneal infections compared with 23 percent for a mixed population of adults and children.[5, 7] For children with psoas abscesses, Santaella[24] reported that 71 percent of blood cultures were positive, and Bresee[4] reported that 55 percent of blood cultures were positive.

Imaging studies are the most useful diagnostic tools. Ultrasound can be used to diagnose perinephric infections[6, 29] and has been used to diagnose abscesses of the iliopsoas muscle.[16] Computed tomography (CT) with contrast enhancement appears to be the most helpful[10, 11, 24] because of superior delineation of organ involvement and the extent of infection. CT also can provide clues about the primary focus of the infection, thereby helping to guide empirical antibiotic therapy. Abscess fluid is seen on CT as areas of low attenuation, possibly with an enhancing rim.[10, 19, 30] Alternative diagnoses also can be evaluated with CT,[27] although hematomas and certain tumors may not be easily distinguished radiographically from infection. Nuclear medicine studies and magnetic resonance imaging scans may be more helpful if bone involvement or vascular tumors are suspected.

Treatment

Percutaneous or open surgical drainage should be considered for all retroperitoneal infections for diagnostic and treatment purposes. Culture of the aspirated fluid for aerobic and anaerobic bacteria, mycobacteria, and fungi is vital to selecting appropriate antimicrobial therapy. Reports of percutaneous drainage of perinephric abscesses and iliopsoas abscesses are increasing.[4, 18] These procedures usually are performed with ultrasound or CT guidance. Treatment of patients with antibiotics without surgical drainage may not be effective, particularly in cases involving larger abscesses.[1, 10]

Initial antimicrobial therapy of retroperitoneal infections should be directed by the presumed source of the infection with definitive therapy guided by microbiologic culture results. Infections related to gastrointestinal perforation should include coverage for enteric gram-negative bacteria and gastrointestinal anaerobes such as β-lactamase–producing *B. fragilis*. Coverage for *Pseudomonas* and *Enterococcus* spp. also should be considered. Antibiotic combinations such as ampicillin for enterococcus, metronidazole or clindamycin for anaerobes, and a third-generation cephalosporin or aminoglycoside for gram-negative bacteria have been used. Carbapenems such as meropenem or imipenem as single agents may be more cost effective, particularly if any outpatient antibiotic therapy is being considered. The β-lactam and β-lactamase inhibitor combinations (e.g., ticarcillin-clavulanate, piperacillin-tazobactam), with or without an aminoglycoside, also may be effective.

Infections of renal origin, usually caused by *E. coli* or other gram-negative enteric organisms, can be treated with cephalosporins such as ceftriaxone or cefotaxime or with aminoglycosides such as gentamicin or tobramycin. The activity of aminoglycosides may be compromised by the acidic environment of abscess cavities and may lead to clinical failures despite in vitro susceptibility of the organism.[9] Increasing resistance to ampicillin by *E. coli*[2, 3] renders it less reliable for empirical use in severe urinary tract infections. *Pseudomonas* is not an uncommon pathogen in children with anatomic genitourinary problems.[2] *Pseudomonas* spp. usually are resistant to ceftriaxone; extended spectrum cephalosporins such as ceftazidime or cefepime may be needed. Urine culture and susceptibility results help to focus the antibiotic choice to the most narrow-spectrum agent required.

Psoas abscesses and primary perinephric abscesses caused by *S. aureus* should be treated with an antistaphylococcal agent such as nafcillin (or oxacillin or methicillin) or a first-generation cephalosporin such as cefazolin. Clindamycin and vancomycin also may be effective in treating the patient who is unable to tolerate penicillin or cephalosporin antibiotics or for the treatment of methicillin-resistant *S. aureus*.

Infections originating in the vertebrae may be pyogenic, usually *S. aureus*, or result from tuberculosis. Empirical antistaphylococcal therapy can be started, but culture and histologic examination of tissue are needed to direct appropriate therapy. For the child with risk factors for tuberculosis and a negative Gram stain result, consideration of empirical therapy with three or four antituberculous antibiotics is recommended. Mantoux skin testing should be performed, as should a chest radiograph to look for evidence of pulmonary tuberculosis.

After adequate drainage is achieved, the duration of antimicrobial therapy depends on several factors, including the organism, the site and extent of infection, and clinical improvement. Most drained retroperitoneal bacterial abscesses of renal or muscular origin are treated for 2 to 3 weeks with initial parenteral and follow-up oral antibiotics. Infections involving bone may require 6 to 8 weeks or longer, depending on how quickly the infection responds to treatment. Radiographic studies, erythrocyte sedimentation rate, and C-reactive protein measurements can be helpful to monitor recovery. Tuberculous infections typically take as long as a year to treat, particularly if bone is involved.

Prognosis

Historically, retroperitoneal abscesses are reported to have high morbidity and mortality rates. However, with modern imaging techniques enabling more timely diagnoses, the overall prognosis is good, and most children with no underlying disease recover without sequelae.

REFERENCES

1. Altemeier, W. A., and Alexander, J. W.: Retroperitoneal abscess. Arch. Surg. *83*:512–524, 1961.
2. Ashkenazi, S., Even-Tov, S., Samra, Z., et al.: Uropathogens of various childhood populations and their antibiotic susceptibility. Pediatr. Infect. Dis. J. *10*:742–746, 1991.
3. Bonadio, W. A., Smith, D. S., Madagame, E., et al.: *Escherichia coli* bacteremia in children. Am. J. Dis. Child. *145*:671–674, 1991.
4. Bresee, J. S., Edwards, M. S.: Psoas abscess in children. Pediatr. Infect. Dis. J. *9*:201–206, 1990.
5. Brook, I: Microbiology of retroperitoneal abscesses in children. J. Med. Microbiol. *48*:697–700, 1999.
6. Brook, I.: The role of anaerobic bacteria in perinephric and renal abscesses in children. Pediatrics. *93*:261–264, 1994.
7. Brook, I., and Frazier, E. H.: Aerobic and anaerobic microbiology of retroperitoneal abscesses. Clin. Infect. Dis. *26*:938–941, 1998.
8. Brook, I., and Frazier, E. H.: Microbiological analysis of pancreatic abscess. Clin. Infect. Dis. *22*:384–385, 1996.
9. Bryant, R. E., Fox, K., Oh, G., and Morthland, V. H.: β-Lactam enhancement of aminoglycoside activity under conditions of reduced pH and oxygen tension that may exist in infected tissues. J. Infect. Dis. *165*: 676–682, 1992.
10. Chen, W. C., Huang, J. K., Chen, K. K., et al.: Retroperitoneal abscesses. Chin. Med. J. *46*:208–212, 1990.
11. Crepps, J. T., Welch, J. P., and Orlando, R., III: Management and outcome of retroperitoneal abscesses. Ann. Surg. *205*:276–281, 1987.
12. Devin, B., McCarthy, A., Mehran, R., and Auger, C.: Necrotizing fasciitis of the retroperitoneum: an unusual presentation of group A *Streptococcus* infection. Can. J. Surg. *41*:156–160, 1998.
13. Dinc, H., Onder, C., Turhan, A. U., et al.: Percutaneous catheter drainage of tuberculous and nontuberculous psoas abscesses. Eur. J. Radiol. *23*:130–134, 1996.
14. Edelstein, H., and McCabe, R. E.: Perinephric abscess in pediatric patients: Report of six cases and review of the literature. Pediatr. Infect. Dis. J. *8*:167–170, 1989.
15. Greenstein, A. J., Dreiling, D. A., Aufses, A. H., Jr.: Crohn's disease of the colon. Am J Gastroenterol. *64*:306–318, 1975.
16. Hoffer, F. A., Shamberger, R. C., and Teele, R. L.: Ilio-psoas abscess: Diagnosis and management. Pediatr. Radiol. *17*:23–27, 1987.
17. Holliday, P. O., III, Davis, C. H., Jr., and Shaffner, L. S: Intervertebral disc space infection in a child presenting as a psoas abscess: Case report. Neurosurgery 7:395–397, 1980.
18. Kang, M., Gupta, S., Gulati, M., and Suri, S.: Ilio-psoas abscess in the paediatric population: Treatment by US-guided percutaneous drainage. Pediatr. Radiol. *28*:478–481, 1998.
19. Kuhns, L. R.: Computed tomography of the retroperitoneum in children. Radiol. Clin. North Am. *19*:495–501, 1981.
20. Kline, M. W., Kaplan, S. L., and Baker, C. J.: Acute focal bacterial nephritis: Diverse clinical presentations in pediatric patients. Pediatr. Infect. Dis. J. 7:346–349, 1988.
21. March, A. W., Riley, L. H., and Robinson, R. A.: Retroperitoneal abscess and septic arthritis of the hip in children. J. Bone Joint Surg. *54-A*:67–74, 1972.
22. Mondor, C., Gauthier, M., Garel, L., et al.: Nonsurgical management of neonatal adrenal abscess. J. Pediatr. Surg. *23*:1048–1050, 1988.
23. Rathore, M. H., Barton, L. L., and Luisiri, A.: Acute lobar nephronia: A review. Pediatrics. *87*:728–734.
24. Santaella, R. O., Fishman, E. K., and Lipsett, P. A.: Primary vs secondary iliopsoas abscess. Arch. Surg. *130*:1309–1313, 1995.
25. Schwaitzberg, S. D., Pokorny, W. J., Thurston, R. S., et al.: Psoas abscess in children. J. Pediatr. Surg. *20*:339–342, 1985.
26. Sedaghatian, M. R., Barkhordar, J., and Gerami, S.: Retroperitoneal abscess presenting as an abdominal mass in neonate. J. Pediatr. Surg. *13*:544–545, 1978.
27. Siegel, M. J., Balfe, D. M., McClennan, B. L., and Levitt, R. G.: Clinical utility of CT in pediatric retroperitoneal disease: 5 years' experience. Am. J. Roentgenol. *138*:1011–1017, 1982.
28. Simons, G. W., Sty, J. R., and Starshak, R. J.: Retroperitoneal and retrofascial abscesses. J. Bone Joint Surg. Am. *65*:1041–1058, 1983.
29. Vachvanichsanong, P., Dissaneewate, P., Patrapinyokul, S., et al.: Renal abscess in healthy children: Report of three cases. Pediatr. Nephrol. *6*:273–275, 1992.
30. Wippermann, C. F., Schofer, O., Beetz, R., et al.: Renal abscess in childhood: diagnostic and therapeutic progress. Pediatr. Infect. Dis. J. *10*:446–450, 1991.
31. Woods, C. R., and Edwards, M. S.: Renal abscess caused by group B *Streptococcus*. Clin. Infect. Dis. *18*:662–663, 1994.

SECTION IX

Musculoskeletal Infections

CHAPTER 62

Osteomyelitis and Septic Arthritis

PAUL KROGSTAD

OSTEOMYELITIS

Osteomyelitis denotes inflammation of bone and marrow but generally implies the presence of infection. Although bacteria are the most common cause, fungi, parasites, and other microorganisms also may cause osteomyelitis.[99] Acute osteomyelitis, if not treated adequately, may result in a chronic lesion, often with devastating consequences.

The incidence of osteomyelitis in normal children has been examined in several populations during the past 40 years. Estimates have varied from as low as 1 in 20,000 adolescent females in New Zealand to as high as 1 in 1000 Australian aboriginals.[24, 76] Males appear to be at greater risk and contract the disease 1.2 to 3.7 times more often than do females.[76, 144, 175] The incidence of osteomyelitis is highest in the first 2 decades of life. Approximately 25 percent of children with osteomyelitis are younger than 2 years, and 50 percent are younger than 5 years.[111, 140, 200] The incidence is increased in patients with sickle-cell disease and in some other immunocompromised patients (see the section on special populations).

Microorganisms can be introduced into bone in three ways: (1) by direct inoculation (usually traumatic, but also during surgery), (2) by local invasion from a contiguous focus of infection (usually cellulitis), and (3) by hematogenous delivery (bacteremia). In children, osteomyelitis generally is of hematogenous origin. Regardless of the route of infection, the common denominator is microscopic bone death.

Usual Microbial Etiology

Staphylococcus aureus, the primary pathogen in immunocompetent children, is incriminated in as many as 89 percent of cases.[157, 193, 198] Group A streptococci are next in frequency. Before the development of effective vaccines, *Haemophilus influenzae* was reported consistently in pediatric case series and caused approximately 5 to 8 percent of cases[111, 140, 157, 197] (Table 62–1). As with other invasive *H. influenzae* infections, osteomyelitis caused by this organism usually occurs in children between 3 months and 6 years of age.[57, 65, 79, 185] With the advent of effective immunization, cases of *H. influenzae* osteomyelitis are noticeably absent from recent case series.[104, 122] *Streptococcus pneumoniae* has been a cause of osteomyelitis in all large published series; protein conjugate vaccines also are likely to diminish markedly the incidence of pneumococcal osteomyelitis. In contrast, *Kingella kingae,* a fastidious gram-negative organism, is being identified increasingly in children as a cause of osteoarticular infection, including osteomyelitis, diskitis, and septic arthritis.[42, 78, 122, 211]

Hematogenous osteomyelitis caused by *Pseudomonas aeruginosa* most often is associated with a history of injecting illicit drugs.[92, 116, 208] *Salmonella* spp. are an infrequent cause of osteomyelitis in immunocompetent patients but are the single most common organism found in cases of osteomyelitis in patients with sickle-cell disease (see later). The microbiologic peculiarities of other immunocompromised patients and special populations are discussed further in later sections. Osteomyelitis caused by other gram-negative organisms is seen less commonly and generally occurs in neonates and young infants.

Four distinct clinical entities of infection caused by anaerobic bacteria are recognized: bacteremic seeding of previously normal bones in children and young adults, superinfection of a fracture site already infected with *S. aureus,* indolent (months to years after surgery) infection of a prosthetic device, and contiguous chronic infection,[187] which most often occurs in the skull and the extremities. *Bacteroides* spp. are found most commonly and are associated with paranasal, sinus, or mastoid infection. In most cases, a foul odor is noted when the bone is incised or the focus is opened; trauma often has been an inciting influence.[117]

Isolation of multiple bacteria from bone pus is uncommon in acute osteomyelitis in children.[140, 148] Polymicrobial infection generally reflects spread of infection from contiguous infectious foci and most often occurs in the skull, face, hands, or feet. Distal extremities compromised by vascular insufficiency or immobilized because of peripheral neuropathy also are sites of polymicrobial osteomyelitis (including paraplegia caused by spina bifida).

Osteomyelitis caused by fungal and atypical bacterial pathogens is discussed in greater detail later.

Hematogenous Osteomyelitis

PATHOGENESIS[36, 103, 195]

In long tubular bones, the infection begins in the metaphysis, the broad cancellous end of the bone shaft adjacent to the epiphyseal growth plate. The cartilaginous epiphyseal growth plate (the physis) is nourished by diffusion of nutrients from a narrow plexus of capillaries fed by the metaphyseal branches of the nutrient artery; these capillaries drain into a large sinusoidal plexus that ultimately joins the large sinusoidal veins in the bone marrow[90] (Fig. 62–1). Trauma or emboli lead to occlusion of the slow-flowing sinusoidal

TABLE 62–1 ■ ETIOLOGY OF ACUTE HEMATOGENOUS OSTEOMYELITIS IN CHILDREN

	Number of Bacteriologically Confirmed Cases			
Organisms	Nelson[140] (*n* = 296)	LaMont et al.[111] (*n* = 90)	Unkila-Kallio et al.[198] (*n* = 44)	Roine et al.[157] (*n* = 38)
Gram-positive bacteria				
Staphylococcus aureus	67%	70%	89%	89%
Coagulase-negative staphylococci	3%	1%		
Streptococcus pneumoniae	2%	5%	2%	
Other streptococci	12%	16%	2%	1%
Gram-negative bacteria				
Haemophilus influenzae	4%	8%	7%	8%
Pseudomonas aeruginosa	3%			
Salmonella species	2%			
Escherichia coli	<1%			
Kingella kingae	<1%			
Mixed or unusual organisms	4%			

vessels, thereby establishing a nidus for infection. Blood-borne bacteria then can seed the poorly perfused area and proliferate.

The high frequency of *S. aureus* in osteomyelitis may reflect specific pathogenic properties of the organism. It has the ability to adhere to type I collagen of bone fibrils via a ligand that is distinct from the fibronectin receptor.[30] Once *S. aureus* binds to collagen, bacterial replication gives rise to microcolonies surrounded by a glycocalyx.[84] Continued injury, elicited by *S. aureus* exoproducts and the host cellular inflammatory response to the injury, causes the accumulation of exudate under pressure. The pressure compresses blood vessels of bone and produces focal bone necrosis. The low ratio of surface area to mass, combined with the blood vessel anatomy described earlier, interferes with reabsorption of necrotic cortical bone[36, 103] and the effectiveness of host defense mechanisms.

The very early stages of osteomyelitis may be aborted by appropriate chemotherapy. In the absence of therapy, necrosis of cortical bone and marrow continues. The exudate under pressure is forced through the haversian systems and Volkmann canals and into the cortex (see Fig. 62–1). Given this complex pathogenesis, that osteomyelitis usually involves only a single bone is not surprising; only 7 percent in one series had more than one bone involved at the time of diagnosis.[140]

SIGNS AND SYMPTOMS

The clinical manifestations of osteomyelitis are age-dependent (Fig. 62–2). In newborn infants, the relatively thin cortex and loosely applied periosteum are poor barriers to the spread of infection. Consequently, the purulence rapidly ruptures through both these structures into the contiguous muscle bed. With progression of the infection, the purulent material often dissects the muscle bundles, with the swollen, discolored limb taking the appearance of a sausage. In addition, the nutrient metaphyseal capillaries perforate the epiphyseal growth plate in newborn infants. Moreover, in infants, the capsule of the diarthrodial joints frequently extends to or is slightly distal to the epiphyseal plate. These anatomic

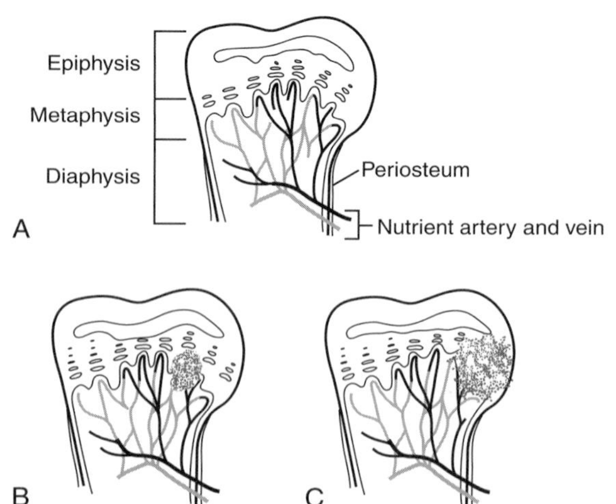

FIGURE 62–1 ■ *A,* The sluggish blood flow in the sinusoidal venous connections located at the metaphyseal-epiphyseal junction predisposes to the development of traumatic thrombosis and infarction. *B,* Bacteremic seeding of the relatively avascular area initiates the infection, which then spreads through the Volkmann canals and the haversian systems and causes septic thrombosis. *C,* Infection tends to spread laterally through the cortex and elevates or ruptures through the periosteum.

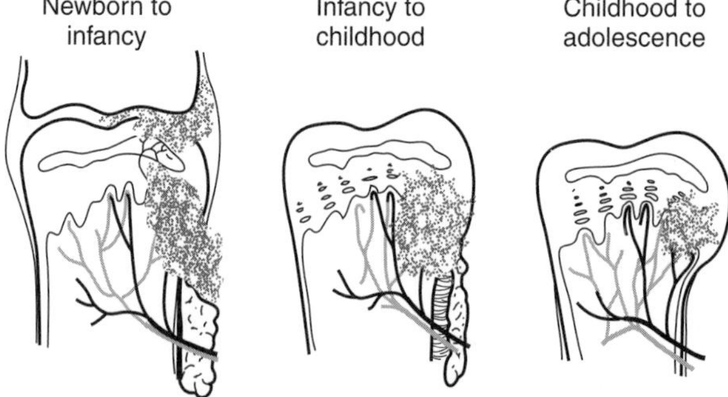

FIGURE 62–2 ■ In young infants and neonates, particularly in the hip where the epiphyseal growth plate is traversed by nutrient vessels terminating in the distal ossification center, septic thrombophlebitis of the nutrient vessels can lead to growth discrepancies. With the capsule of the joint extending to the metaphysis, rupture of the infection through the cortex leads to the development of septic arthritis. Because of the thin cortex and loose periosteum, the osteomyelitis may come to medical attention as a deep soft tissue abscess. In older infants and young children, the thicker cortex and denser periosteum are a greater barrier to the infection. Local tenderness from subperiosteal edema or abscess is the rule. In late childhood and adolescence, the lesion is extremely well localized and rarely penetrates the bony cortex. In this age group, performing invasive procedures such as windowing or drilling is necessary to obtain infected material.

characteristics permit an infection arising in the metaphysis to involve the epiphysis and perforate into the adjacent joint cavity. In older infants, the cortex (see Fig. 62–2) is thicker and the periosteum is slightly more dense. Consequently, the infection rarely spreads to the soft tissues of the extremity. Subperiosteal abscess and contiguous edema, however, readily develop. In children in this age group, the nutrient metaphyseal capillaries are atrophic, which, though recently disputed,[145] is thought to decrease the risk of spread of infection into the adjacent joint space. The subperiosteal purulence almost always is at the metaphysis, the area in which the cortex is the thinnest.[81] In children and adolescents (4 to 16 years of age), the metaphyseal cortex is considerably thicker, with a dense, fibrous periosteum. The pathogenesis of the infection is the same in this age group, but the infection rarely ruptures and spreads to the outer cortical lamellae. As a result, the signs and symptoms of this illness tend to be very focal.

The bacteremic phase of hematogenous osteomyelitis may be entirely subclinical and associated only with malaise and low-grade fever, or it may be characterized by severe constitutional symptoms with a temperature as high as 40° C. No correlation exists between the magnitude of these signs and symptoms and the severity of subsequent osteomyelitis, but the mode of infection is influenced somewhat by the organisms involved. For example, osteoarticular infections caused by *Kingella* spp. generally have an indolent course, with limb pain being present for longer than a week before initial medical evaluation is made.[122] Osteomyelitis caused by *H. influenzae* appears to occur primarily in the upper extremities.[56, 57, 79, 185]

A newborn infant usually is irritable when the affected extremity is touched or moved. Pseudoparalysis may occur, and if the disease remains untreated, massive swelling of the extremity may be seen. Obtaining a plain radiograph is invaluable in this age group: most of these patients have changes consistent with osteomyelitis on the initial radiograph.[108, 133, 205]

In infants and young children, pain usually is present, as well as a limp because osteomyelitis occurs more commonly in the lower extremities. The child refuses to use the affected extremity and displays variable constitutional symptoms. The hallmark of the disease is the marked focal nature of symptoms; point tenderness and well-localized pain suggest the diagnosis. Percussion of the long bone away from the area of point tenderness often elicits pain at the site of osteomyelitis. In late childhood and adolescence, less restriction of function of the extremity is present. The point tenderness is circumscribed more sharply and may be found only as a small area of discomfort at rest. This disease most often affects the lower extremities and produces a mild limp. Most commonly, tubular bones are involved, but infection in other bones occurs as well (Table 62–2). Deep venous thrombophlebitis also has been associated with osteomyelitis in these older patients and may be the initial symptom. Some suggestion exists that this process is associated with a contiguous periosteal abscess.[102] A diagnosis of osteomyelitis should be entertained in any child with deep thrombophlebitis who has not had that extremity immobilized either in bed or with a cast.[93]

DIFFERENTIAL DIAGNOSIS

Osteomyelitis can be confused with many other diseases associated with fever, pain, and tenderness in an extremity. Such diseases include rheumatic fever, septicemia, septic arthritis, cellulitis, Ewing sarcoma, leukemia, reflex neurovascular dystrophy, thrombophlebitis, bone infarction secondary to sickle-cell or Gaucher disease, and toxic synovitis.

TABLE 62–2 ■ SITE OF INVOLVEMENT IN ACUTE HEMATOGENOUS OSTEOMYELITIS

Bone Type	Percent
Tubular	
Femur	25
Tibia	24
Humerus	13
Phalanges	5
Fibula	4
Radius	4
Ulna	2
Metatarsal	2
Clavicle	0.5
Metacarpal	0.5
Cuboidal	
Calcaneus	5
Talus	0.8
Carpals	0.5
Cuneiform	0.5
Cuboid	0.3
Irregular	
Ischium	4
Ilium	2
Vertebra	2
Pubis	0.8
Sacrum	0.8
Flat	
Skull	1
Rib	0.5
Sternum	0.5
Scapula	0.5
Maxilla	0.3
Mandible	0.3

The bone classification is according to Jaffe.[99] Data from Nelson.[140]

DIAGNOSIS

Microbiology

The cornerstone of the diagnosis of osteomyelitis is isolation of bacteria or other microbes from bone or from anatomic structures contiguous to bone. Overall, such cultures (bone, subperiosteal exudate, or joint fluid) provide a bacteriologic diagnosis in 66 to 76 percent of cases. Blood cultures are rewarding less frequently; an organism was recovered from blood in only 36 to 74 percent of patients in three series.[140, 193, 197]

In neonates, needle aspiration of soft tissue or incision and drainage of bone may yield the offending organism. In infants and young children, subperiosteal needle aspiration can be performed if the point tenderness is localized easily. In older children and adolescents, noninvasive culturing of the bone is less rewarding. In this age group, windowing or drilling to drain pus from the bone yields valuable material for culture but is controversial; some orthopedic surgeons consider the risk of causing epiphyseal damage and subsequent length discrepancy secondary to the procedure too great. Thus, greater reliance is placed on blood cultures and noninvasive methods.

Radiology

PLAIN RADIOGRAPHS. Conventional radiographs play an irreplaceable role in the diagnosis of pediatric osteomyelitis and always should be obtained.[86] Because bone density must decrease 50 percent to be detected by radiographs,[7] changes in the less ossified bones of neonates are detected more readily than are those in older children. In

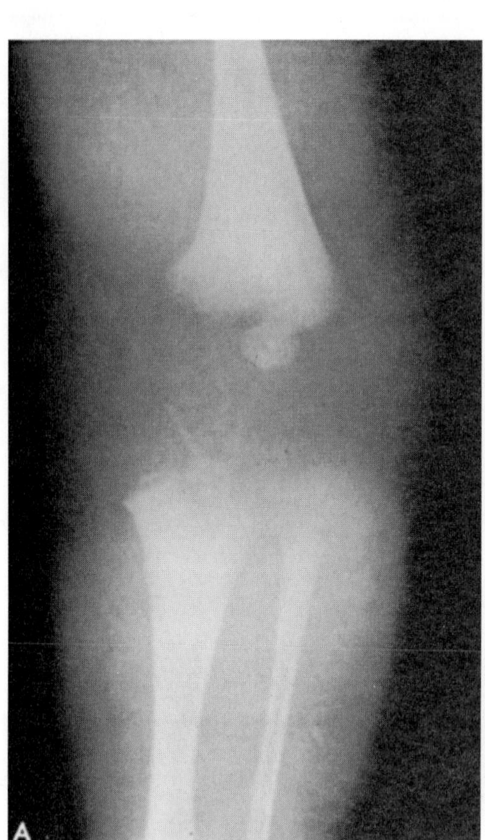

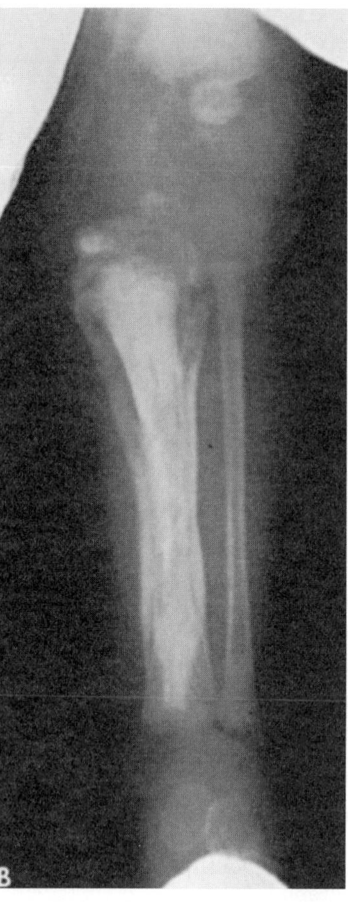

FIGURE 62–3 ■ *A*, The left knee of an infant shows diffuse soft tissue swelling around the proximal ends of the tibia and fibula. *B*, Six weeks later, subcutaneous fat lines between the muscles and the skin can be seen, as can an involucrum involving almost all the tibia.

contrast, Waldvogel and Papageorgiou[201] found in adults that plain radiographs were of no diagnostic value in 23 percent and were misleading in an additional 16 percent.

Radiographic changes occur in three stages.[32] The first stage, which occurs approximately 3 days after the onset of symptoms, is the formation of a small area of localized, deep soft tissue swelling, usually in the region of the metaphysis (Fig. 62–3). Thus, when early diagnosis of osteomyelitis is sought, examination of the radiograph should be directed to the soft tissue rather than the bone. During the second stage, which occurs 3 to 7 days after the onset of symptoms, swelling of the muscles with obliteration of the interposed translucent fat planes can be noted. It is caused by continued spread of edema fluid and can progress, particularly in neonates and young infants, to superficial soft tissue edema; the skin may take on an orange-peel texture.

Radiographic evidence of bone destruction usually is not detected until 10 to 21 days after the onset of symptoms. The variability depends on the specific bone involved: in general, long tubular bones tend to show bone destruction and periosteal new bone formation 2 to 3 weeks earlier than do membranous or irregular bones.

MAGNETIC RESONANCE IMAGING. Magnetic resonance imaging (MRI) is becoming the imaging modality of choice when additional imaging is needed. The major advantage of MRI is that without using ionizing radiation it accurately delineates subperiosteal or soft tissue collections of pus that might require surgical drainage, and it can identify sinus tracts for removal[63, 150, 183] (Fig. 62–4). Thus, it often provides more specific anatomic information than does computed tomography (CT) or plain radiography. In acute osteomyelitis, bone marrow edema caused by the accumulation of purulent material leads to decreased signal on T1-weighted images. On T2-weighted images of the same area, increased signal is seen. With commonly used sequences, the sensitivity of MRI for the detection of acute osteomyelitis may approach 100 percent.[127] Fat-suppression sequences, including short-tau inversion recovery, decrease the signal from fat. Inversion recovery sequences thus allow more sensitive detection of bone marrow edema. MRI may have a particular advantage in the diagnosis of spinal osteomyelitis because clear distinction can be made between the vertebral body and the adjacent disk. Loss of this border is one of the first abnormalities detected by MRI in spinal osteomyelitis. The need for sedation in most infants and children and the cost of MRI are the major disadvantages.

COMPUTED TOMOGRAPHY. CT is used occasionally in the diagnosis and management of osteomyelitis because it provides excellent definition of cortical bone and high spatial resolution. CT abnormalities commonly found in osteomyelitis include increased density of bone marrow caused by the accumulation of purulent material, as well as periosteal new bone formation and purulence. CT is particularly useful in detecting sequestra and delineating subperiosteal abscesses. It previously has been used to define infections of the spine. However, MRI has replaced CT for this indication.

RADIONUCLIDE IMAGING. Radionuclide scanning historically has been a valuable adjunct to the diagnosis of osteomyelitis.[51] Bone imaging using technetium 99m

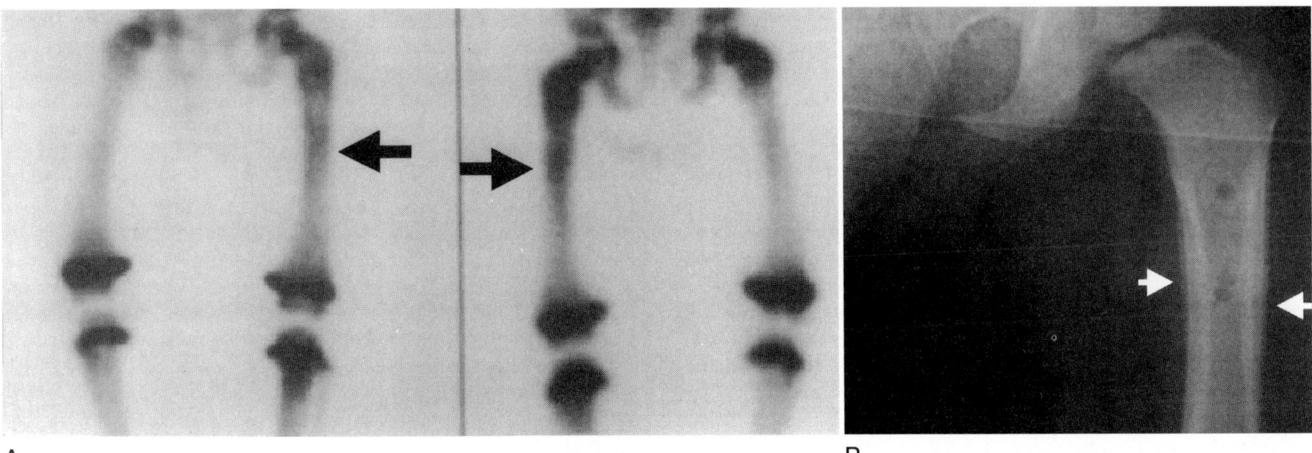

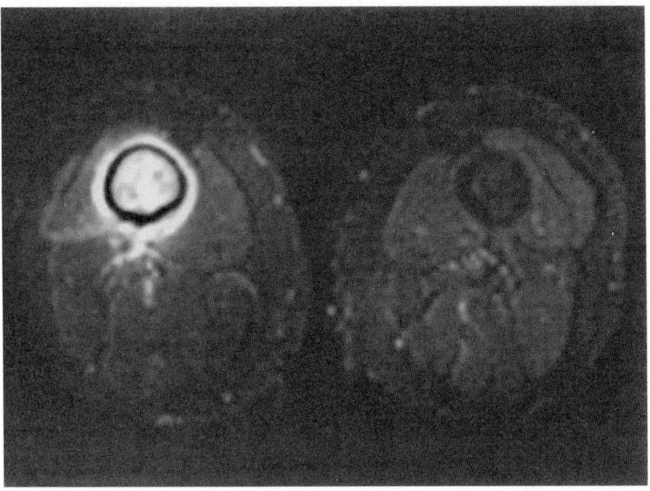

FIGURE 62–4 ■ Acute osteomyelitis. *A,* Technetium bone scan of a 2-year-old boy with fever and a limp. Moderately increased tracer activity is seen in the proximal end of the left femur because of the increased bone turnover. *B,* Plain radiograph taken 3 weeks later. Unilamellar periosteal new bone formation is seen along the femoral shaft *(arrows).* The circular radiolucencies seen are the result of cortical drilling to allow diagnostic aspiration; the culture yielded *Streptococcus pyogenes. C,* An axial T2-weighted magnetic resonance image of the thigh from a different patient shows abnormally high signal intensity throughout the marrow cavity. The band of high signal surrounding the cortex represents periostitis. (Courtesy of Dr. Leanne Seeger.)

(Tc 99m) diphosphonate compounds is based on initial flow through the bone and adsorption of covalently bonded Tc 99m phosphate adduct to the surface of the hydroxyapatite crystal in bone. Tc 99m is concentrated in the cement line located at the junction of osteoid and mineralized bone.[190]

Most institutions perform a three-phase bone scan for evaluation of infection. Shortly after injection (2 to 5 seconds), a nuclear angiogram (flow phase) of the area of suspected osteomyelitis is obtained. The second phase (the blood pool phase) consists of a single image obtained 5 to 10 minutes after injection. The third image is obtained 2 to 4 hours after injection. In this later phase, specificity of the diphosphonate compounds for the bone is revealed. Anything increasing local blood flow to the area, particularly if accompanied by inflammation, results in increased general uptake in the first two phases, but osteomyelitis results in focal uptake in the third phase, with the intensity of the signal detected reflecting the level of osteoblastic activity.[34, 44, 46, 51, 74, 109, 166] Although localization of a lesion near the growth plate can complicate interpretation of the study, the overall accuracy of a Tc 99m image in revealing osteomyelitis in non-neonates exceeds 90 percent (see Fig. 62–4). Osteomyelitis clearly can be diagnosed by a Tc 99m scan and treated successfully before evidence of bone changes is noted on plain radiographs.[192] Serial bone scans have been performed in children with osteomyelitis.[168] In general, changes on the nuclide scan are more characteristic when patients have had an illness of longer duration.

However, bone scans that use Tc 99m may be nondiagnostic in neonates.[5, 65] Destruction of cortical bone occurs, and periosteal new bone formation often is present on plain-film radiographs of bones with normal Tc 99m uptake. The false-negative result of bone scans probably is due to the paucity of mineralization in neonates' bones. Ischemia of bone, probably caused by infarction, also has been noted on the initial bone scan.[133] Overall, the sensitivity of bone scans in neonates is uncertain but may be as low as 30 percent.[65]

Older infants with osteomyelitis and a nondiagnostic Tc 99m bone scan also have been described.[15, 85] In such instances, a gallium 67 scan may be of value. Gallium 67 is a transition metal that, like iron, is bound to plasma proteins; the unbound portion, 10 to 25 percent, is excreted in urine. It localizes in inflammatory foci because of increased capillary permeability (leaking plasma proteins), in vivo leukocyte labeling, binding to lactoferrin in the lesion, and perhaps direct bacterial uptake. Because of the slower elimination of gallium from blood, its uptake in an inflammatory focus is less dependent on blood flow. Delayed elimination, however, often results in poor contrast of bone to soft tissue and delays reliable interpretation for 24 to 72 hours after injection.[91] Fifteen of 16 cases of osteomyelitis with a nondiagnostic Tc 99m scan had changes on gallium

67 scan typical of osteomyelitis.[174] Combined evaluation with both gallium imaging and Tc 99m bone scanning may lead to greater diagnostic certainty when the studies are not conclusively diagnostic.[171]

Numerous studies have been conducted to examine the utility of indium 111–labeled leukocyte scans for the diagnosis of osteomyelitis. This method involves removing leukocytes and injecting them back into the patient after in vitro labeling. A sensitivity of approximately 86 percent has been ascribed to this method.[163] The sensitivity appears to be best for the detection of lesions in long bones. False-positive scans can result from a variety of processes, including fracture and infarction. Enthusiasm for this modality also is limited by the higher organ absorption of the radiation dose.[67] Numerous other scintigraphic methods for the detection of osteomyelitis, including Tc 99m hexamethylpropyleneamine oxime–labeled leukocytes and monoclonal antibodies, have been examined. At present, these methods do not offer any advantage over MRI and older radionuclide imaging approaches.

TREATMENT

The need for surgical therapy also must be evaluated. Subperiosteal and soft tissue abscesses and intramedullary purulence should be drained. Sequestra, if present, should be removed. If contiguous infectious foci are present, they should be débrided adequately and treated with effective antimicrobial therapy. Immobilization of the affected extremity or splinting may afford relief from pain and sometimes is used to prevent the development of pathologic fractures when extensive bone involvement is detected by plain radiography.

Initial antimicrobial therapy always should have potent activity against *S. aureus* and group A streptococci. Acute bacterial hematogenous osteomyelitis should be treated initially with parenteral anti-infective agents. *S. aureus* is prone to disseminate to other organs and tissues. One should keep in mind that in the pre-antibiotic era, the mortality rate in *S. aureus* osteomyelitis in children was 20 percent.[81] Proliferation of this organism needs to be stopped as quickly as possible. Moreover, the concomitant physiologic changes resulting from bacteremia in acute osteomyelitis are not conducive to the absorption of oral antibiotics. Thus, initial therapy should consist of penicillinase-resistant, semisynthetic penicillin such as nafcillin or oxacillin administered parenterally in a dosage of 150 to 200 mg/kg/day in four divided doses.[80, 96, 157] In areas where methicillin-resistant *S. aureus* (MRSA) is a common community pathogen, vancomycin or clindamycin (if >90% of community-acquired MRSA isolates are susceptible) should be included in the initial empiric therapy. Cefuroxime, a second-generation cephalosporin, also has been used for empiric therapy, with good results.[140] In addition, antimicrobial coverage for *H. influenzae* should be considered for younger children, particularly those who have not been immunized adequately. In these circumstances, the use of cefuroxime or the addition of a third-generation cephalosporin (such as cefotaxime) or chloramphenicol to oxacillin or nafcillin might be warranted. Other agents may be administered when epidemiologic factors suggest the possible presence of other pathogens: ampicillin, chloramphenicol, or third-generation cephalosporins for *Salmonella* osteomyelitis; ceftazidime and aminoglycosides for *P. aeruginosa*; ampicillin and aminoglycosides for enteric gram-negative organisms; and clindamycin for suspected anaerobic infections.[58, 156]

When an organism is isolated or identified by other means, antimicrobial therapy can be chosen with greater specificity. Staphylococci should be treated with penicillin G if they are susceptible to this antibiotic. In most cases, staphylococci must be treated with a penicillinase-resistant penicillin (oxacillin or nafcillin). Ceftriaxone should be used with great caution for the treatment of staphylococcal osteomyelitis; numerous treatment failures have been described. Infection with methicillin-resistant strains of *S. aureus* should be treated with vancomycin, 40 to 45 mg/kg/day administered every 6 hours. Oxazolidinone and streptogramin drugs have been used with success for the treatment of osteomyelitis in some adults with methicillin-resistant and methicillin-sensitive *S. aureus,*[49] as well as for the treatment of vancomycin-resistant enterococci. They may prove useful in cases of pediatric osteomyelitis caused by *S. aureus* with decreased susceptibility to vancomycin. Osteomyelitis caused by *S. pneumoniae* strains with decreased susceptibility to penicillin have been managed successfully with a variety of agents, including ceftriaxone, vancomycin, and clindamycin.[22] β-Lactam antibiotics, including oxacillin, nafcillin, and cephalosporins, have been used successfully in the treatment of *K. kingae* infection.[42, 78, 211]

Once controversial, sequential use of the intravenous and oral routes of administration of antibiotics has gained acceptance for the treatment of pediatric osteomyelitis. Completing treatment with oral therapy avoids the cost, pain, inconvenience, and hazards of long-term intravenous antibiotic administration. In most series in which oral therapy was used,[27, 47, 140, 189, 202] treatment was continued with intravenous antibiotics until the patient was afebrile, until local signs and symptoms of infection were reduced considerably, and until the patient was maintaining caloric and fluid balances by the oral route. In severe or complicated cases, an advisable approach is to delay switching to the oral route until the peripheral leukocyte count has normalized and the erythrocyte sedimentation rate has decreased by 20 percent or more or until a marked decrease in the concentration of C-reactive protein has occurred.[157, 197] Oral therapy is most likely to succeed, and oral therapy is an acceptable option when the following criteria are met: the patient has the ability to swallow and retain medication, an etiologic agent has been established, the laboratory is able to monitor the degree of antibiotic absorption, and the patient has a clear clinical response to intravenously administered antibiotics.[140, 142]

Antibiotics administered orally for osteomyelitis must be given in doses higher than those used for the treatment of other infections and higher than those listed on package inserts.[7, 141, 189] Specific antibiotics and the recommended starting doses are listed in Table 62–3. Dosages of β-lactams often can be increased to 200 mg/kg/day without having serious adverse side effects. Diarrhea, an infrequent complication of high-dose oral β-lactam therapy, can be mitigated by a reduction in dose and the administration of probenecid (40 mg/kg/day, every 6 hours; maximal dose, 2 g/day).[27, 140, 189] The assumption implicit in successful oral therapy is that the antibiotic reaches an effective concentration at the focus of infection. Compliance with the prescribed dose and frequency and absorption into the bloodstream are necessary to fulfill this assumption. Patient (or parent) education and a continuing time commitment by a physician or nurse are essential to maintaining the compliance required for successful treatment.

Although eschewed by some physicians,[125, 144] therapeutic drug monitoring generally is recommended to demonstrate that adequate absorption of orally administered antibiotics is occurring.[141] Rare patients will have inadequate serum

TABLE 62–3 ■ INITIAL ANTIBIOTIC DOSAGES FOR ORAL TREATMENT OF OSTEOMYELITIS

Drug	Dosage (mg/kg/day)	Interval between Doses (hr)
Amoxicillin	100	6
Cefaclor	150	6
Cephalexin	150	6
Chloramphenicol	75	8
Clindamycin	40	8
Cloxacillin	125	6
Dicloxacillin	100	6
Penicillin V	125	4

Data from refs. 27, 70, 140, 189.

levels despite high oral dosages.[189] If bacteria have been isolated from the patient, a peak serum bactericidal titer of 1 : 8 or greater is sought.[151, 189] A disadvantage of assessing serum bactericidal activity is the difficulty of performing the test when other antibiotics are present in the serum sample. For example, nafcillin administered intravenously would interfere with evaluating the bioactivity of dicloxacillin. Chemical assays of a specific agent circumvent this problem. Dicloxacillin, for example, can be administered orally and adjustment of the dose based on dicloxacillin measurements before the intravenous administration of another β-lactam has been discontinued. This procedure avoids several days of inadequate therapy should the dosage of the oral agent need to be adjusted.

The duration of appropriate therapy is as important a factor in outcome as is the specific antimicrobial agent chosen. Treatment failure and complications of osteomyelitis have been linked repeatedly to a short duration of therapy. Harris noted that 4 of 45 patients with acute hematogenous osteomyelitis who experienced relapse had been treated for 4 to 10 days.[87] Likewise, Dich and colleagues[47] noted a 19 percent failure rate in 37 patients treated for 3 weeks or less; the rate was 2 percent in 48 patients treated for 21 to 50 days. Similar data were provided by Blockey and Watson.[19] Thus, the minimal duration of therapy for hematogenous osteomyelitis to minimize the risk of recurrence appears to be 4 to 6 weeks. A conservative approach would be to administer antibiotics until the erythrocyte sedimentation rate is within the normal range.[140–142, 182] During successful treatment of osteomyelitis, this rate generally increases during the first several days and then declines in the weeks that follow.[197] Failure of the erythrocyte sedimentation rate to decrease during the second week of treatment may indicate a need for surgical drainage or the development of chronic osteomyelitis.[182] Measurement of C-reactive protein also has been used to monitor the response to therapy for osteoarticular infections. In one study, C-reactive protein returned to normal levels more rapidly in children with an uneventful clinical course than it did in children whose treatment was complicated by prolonged fever, pain, or signs of inflammation or who required repeated surgical drainage.[157] A slow decline in C-reactive protein has been associated with more extensive radiographic changes or persistent symptoms 1 to 2 months after discharge from the hospital.

SPECIAL MANIFESTATIONS OF HEMATOGENOUS OSTEOMYELITIS

Epiphyseal Osteomyelitis[72, 121, 194]

Rarely, hematogenous osteomyelitis may arise in the epiphysis of the tubular bones of young children. Although the pathogenesis is not clear, it may involve delivery of microorganisms to the epiphysis by transphyseal vessels. After the child reaches 15 to 18 months of age, these vessels are lost and the physis acts as a physical barrier to the spread of infection from the metaphysis. However, the vascular anatomy of the epiphysis is very similar to that of the metaphysis, and in some cases infection may occur when bacteria are delivered to venous sinusoids by terminal branches of the epiphyseal arteries. Hematogenous epiphyseal osteomyelitis may be acute or subacute. In the acute manifestation,septic arthritis initially may be diagnosed when joint swelling occurs and abnormal fluids are removed by diagnostic aspiration. In cases with a more indolent course, pain, limp, or other symptoms prompt an evaluation for the possibility of an osteoarticular infection. The correct diagnosis typically is made when a radionuclide bone scan or plain radiographs taken weeks later show evidence of increased bone turnover or the lytic changes characteristic of osteomyelitis. Administration of appropriate therapy for epiphyseal osteomyelitis has been followed by complete recovery without apparent sequelae 2 to 6 years after diagnosis.

Involvement of Nontubular Bones

Less than 20 percent of all cases of osteomyelitis involve nontubular bones. Infection of the calcaneus appears to be the most common.[140] In patients with hematogenous infection, destruction occurs just under the epiphyseal line in the metaphysis posteriorly and medially, where the blood supply is greatest. It is present in all patients, in addition to destruction of the adjacent epiphysis, particularly in its middle to superior portion. Periosteal new bone formation occurs very late, with 3 to 4 months required for re-ossification. Osteomyelitis in the other cuboidal bones rarely occurs.

Almost equal in frequency to infection of the calcaneus is infection of the bones of the pelvis.[140] Of the bones of the pelvis, the ischium is involved most commonly. The next most frequently involved bone is the ilium, followed by the sacroiliac joint. The pubis is involved in only 20 percent of cases of pelvic osteomyelitis.[89, 138] Pelvic osteomyelitis causes an increase in the erythrocyte sedimentation rate in nearly all patients, and two thirds have a peripheral leukocyte count greater than 10,000 cells/mm^3.[138] The most common organism causing pelvic osteomyelitis is *S. aureus,* which is isolated from either blood or an aspirate from the bone lesions in approximately 80 percent of cases. Making the diagnosis of pelvic osteomyelitis often is difficult. Most patients are judged to have disease in the hip at the time that medical attention is sought. Most often, patients with pelvic osteomyelitis have hip pain and a gait abnormality but allow their hips to be put through a range of motion passively. Point tenderness at the site of the lesion can be elicited in approximately 50 percent of these patients. Sacroiliitis frequently is difficult to identify by clinical examination. Pressing down on the pelvis, which stresses the sacroiliac joint, produces local pain. Tenderness in the buttocks or the sciatic notch, if present, is an invaluable diagnostic finding.[1, 35, 50, 134, 206] Pelvic osteomyelitis can mimic appendicitis and urinary tract infection[206]; it occurs more frequently in individuals with inflammatory bowel disease. In most patients, plain films of the pelvis are not rewarding, whereas Tc 99m bone scans indicate the diagnosis in approximately 90 percent.[123, 138] CT has revealed infection not evident by bone scanning. MRI also is likely to reveal abnormalities.[196] Antibiotic therapy alone is adequate in most cases of pelvic osteomyelitis. Only when a lack of response to antimicrobial therapy occurs is surgery indicated. Osteomyelitis in the pelvic bones has a uniformly good

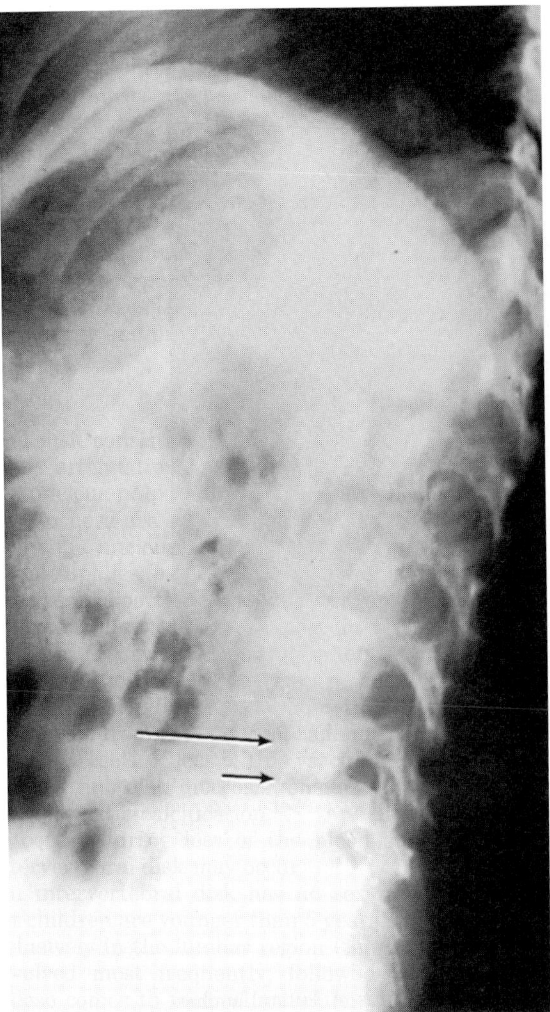

FIGURE 62–6 ■ Vertebral osteomyelitis. The *large arrow* indicates the lytic lesion with some anterior sclerosis in the lumbar vertebra. A *small arrow* indicates involvement of the adjacent lower vertebra and narrowing of the disk space. (Courtesy of Dr. Joel Blumhagen.)

Most cases of vertebral osteomyelitis are caused by *S. aureus*. Organisms causing urinary tract infection can cause osteomyelitis, presumably by local spread through the Batson plexus.[25, 88, 114] However, urinary tract infection rarely precedes the development of vertebral osteomyelitis, and only approximately 2 percent of all cases can be shown to be related to infection of the urinary tract.[71] The best method of establishing the diagnosis is through examination of bone biopsy specimens and cultures.[139] *P. aeruginosa* also has been recognized as a pathogen in vertebral osteomyelitis. All patients were intravenous drug abusers, and the organisms presumably were inoculated along with the illicit drug. Not surprisingly, younger heroin addicts have been found to have *P. aeruginosa* infection in their intervertebral disks.[26, 167] In areas of the world where brucellosis is endemic, spinal osteomyelitis caused by *Brucella* spp. needs to be considered.[118] Fungal pathogens causing vertebral osteomyelitis include *Coccidioides immitis* in endemic areas and *Candida* spp. (often in immunocompromised patients).[130] *Bartonella henselae* also has been found to cause vertebral osteomyelitis.[60]

Therapy for spinal osteomyelitis includes immobilization. Whether it should be accomplished by simple bed rest or with a body cast is controversial. Administration of an antibiotic always is indicated. The average duration of treatment of bacterial vertebral osteomyelitis is 2 months; however, no data are available that can be used for determining the most appropriate duration of therapy. The need for surgical drainage in some cases should not be overlooked because spinal cord compression caused by an epidural or subdural abscess can lead to permanent paraplegia. A paraspinal mass may rupture into the abdominal cavity or erode the aorta; both events are catastrophic complications.[66] The optimal therapy for fungal infection of the vertebra is not clear.

Brodie Abscess[177]

Some patients have a subacute form of osteomyelitis that results in the formation of intraosseous abscesses. These patients most often are adolescents with complaints of long bone pain and tenderness. A bony defect with sclerotic margins is detected by plain radiography in most patients. A distinctive "target" lesion has been described in MRI studies of Brodie abscesses.[126] Concentric layers are seen and reflect a central abscess cavity surrounded by an inner ring of granulation tissue, an outer ring of fibrotic reaction, and a peripheral rim of endosteal reaction that is hypointense on T1-weighted images.

The erythrocyte sedimentation rate usually is normal. Treatment consists of surgical drainage and curettage followed by antimicrobial therapy, as for other forms of hematogenous osteomyelitis. A variety of organisms, including *H. influenzae,* have been isolated from these lesions,[110] but *S. aureus* and other gram-positive cocci are the pathogens usually involved. The prognosis generally is good, although deformities occur in some cases.

HEMATOGENOUS OSTEOMYELITIS IN SPECIAL POPULATIONS

Osteomyelitis in the Newborn[6, 45]

Infection of the bones of newborns has distinct physiologic and clinical features that merit emphasis.[6] Though a rare event, neonatal osteomyelitis may occur in individuals with certain risk factors such as prematurity, skin infections, and complicated delivery.[66, 108] As indicated earlier, the epiphyseal-metaphyseal junction frequently is within the joint capsule, and blood vessels that penetrate the epiphysis are common findings, particularly in the hip, shoulder, and knee of the newborn. In newborns, osteomyelitis in the long tubular bones frequently (50–70% of cases) is accompanied by contiguous septic arthritis. Fever is present in one third to one half of the newborns; of these, one half have a "septic" or "toxic" appearance. One half the infants have multiple bones involved. Antecedent infections are present in one half the cases and usually are nosocomial; infection of heel puncture sites, arterial cannulae, lungs, and cut-down sites and cephalhematoma have been described.[6] *S. aureus* is the etiologic agent in more than 90 percent of cases; gram-negative bacilli cause a minority of cases.

Group B streptococci have been found consistently,[53] and infants with such infection are older (2 to 4 weeks of age), have no recognized preceding infection, and have only a single bone involved, often the right tibia or humerus.[6]

Osteomyelitis in the skull, an uncommon disease, can occur in neonates. Frequently it is associated with a cephalhematoma, with or without loss of skin integrity,[113] but it can be caused by fetal monitoring without a cephalhematoma.[128] Numerous bacteria have been isolated from such lesions; as one might expect, most of these bacteria have been present as vaginal flora. Radiographic changes (i.e., bony erosion) are a late finding, but CT of the skull appears to assist in the diagnosis. Infection of a cephalhematoma should be considered if it is enlarging, if it is inflamed, or if laboratory evidence of infection is present, such as an increased C-reactive protein concentration or leukocyte count. In most cases, the lesion is drained and treated with an antibiotic appropriate for the infecting organism.

In older series of neonatal osteomyelitis, sequelae were common. However, in more recent series,[108, 209] approximately three fourths of all cases have had good outcomes, even when the hip has been involved. When seen, sequelae include avascular necrosis of the femoral head, bony deformities, and shortening of the involved limb.[147]

Chronic Hemodialysis Patients

Patients undergoing chronic hemodialysis, with multiple invasions of their vascular compartment, appear to be at greater risk for development of hematogenous osteomyelitis.[115] Their indwelling intravenous cannulas can be colonized with coagulase-negative staphylococci or *S. aureus,* and osteomyelitis may develop. The thoracic spine and ribs are the bones most commonly involved; other tubular and cuboidal bones that have been traumatized also can become infected.

Osteomyelitis in Children with Hemoglobinopathies

After pneumonia, osteomyelitis is the most common serious infection in children with sickle-cell disease.[10] Patients at risk are those with hemoglobin SS, hemoglobin S-Thal, or hemoglobin SO-Arab and certain children with hemoglobin SC disease.[83, 172] The clinical manifestations of osteomyelitis are similar to those of other children, but a propensity for simultaneous involvement of multiple sites, a tendency toward recurrence, and a greater frequency in children 18 to 48 months of age have been observed.

As noted earlier, the microbiology of osteomyelitis in children with sickle-cell disease is complex and dominated by *Salmonella* spp.[10, 29] Seventy percent of all lesions or blood cultures in children with hemoglobinopathy and presumptive osteomyelitis yield *Salmonella* microorganisms; 10 percent contain *S. aureus*; and aerobic gram-negative rods, including *Shigella sonnei,*[159] *Escherichia coli,*[82] *Serratia* spp.,[64] and *Arizona hinshawii,*[94] are isolated in 7 percent. Although *Salmonella* osteomyelitis occurs in less than 1 percent of normal patients with *Salmonella* bacteremia,[207] the frequency of *Salmonella* osteomyelitis in sickle-cell disease is several hundred times that occurring in the general population, with an incidence estimated at 0.36 percent per annum.[10, 48, 149] Many factors probably contribute to the greater incidence of osteomyelitis in patients with sickle-cell hemoglobinopathy. Injuries to the intestinal mucosa from local thrombosis during a thrombotic crisis may facilitate the entrance of *Salmonella* and other enteric organisms into the bloodstream.[29, 207] Once infection of the bloodstream occurs, the splenic dysfunction in these patients may allow a prolonged period or greater magnitude of bacteremia. Evidence of impaired production of opsonic antibodies also exists. Whether bacteria lodge in infarcted bone or whether a different pathogenesis exists is not clear. Infarction occurs in the capital femoral epiphysis, hands, feet, and vertebrae, whereas osteomyelitis involves the metaphyseal-diaphyseal junction of long tubular bones.[55, 149]

Infants with the hand and foot syndrome are not distinguished easily from those with osteomyelitis of the phalanges of the hands or tarsal bones of the feet.[14, 37, 204] The changes caused by osteomyelitis that are seen on plain radiographs are more severe than are those expected in uncomplicated sickle-cell disease. The most common radiographic findings are a longitudinal intracortical diaphyseal fissure and overabundant periosteal new bone formation. The cortical fissures are thought to represent a layer of purulent exudate in and between the periosteal new bone and dead bone.[48]

Radionuclide scans also are used frequently to help differentiate osteomyelitis from bone infarction. In theory, bone infarction should have decreased uptake of Tc 99m in the early “blood pool” phase of the scan; increased uptake would be found only as the lesion healed.[105] However, in one series with 34 sites of infarction, increased Tc 99m uptake occurred in 10, normal uptake in 9, and decreased uptake surrounded by zones of increased concentration in the remaining 15 sites.[75] Gallium 67 or bone marrow scans of lesions with technetium sulfur colloid also may be of value in differentiating infarction from infection; increased uptake of the radionuclide is seen more frequently with infection than with infarction.[152] Acute infarction and osteomyelitis cannot be differentiated by MRI, perhaps because of preexisting abnormalities in bone marrow. However, MRI may be useful for presurgical evaluation. Ultrasonographic imaging also has been used to distinguish osteomyelitis and sickle-cell crisis and, if confirmed, may prove to be a useful adjunct to other imaging modalities.[20]

Generally, patients with bony infarcts have had dactylitis as an infant and multiple episodes; their temperature usually is less than 39° C. Children with hemoglobinopathy and osteomyelitis may lack this history and have a modest leukocytosis of immature granulocytes.[96] If fever, leukocytosis, and local symptoms persist despite hydration and other supportive measures, needle aspiration of the area must be considered. Identification of an infectious pathogen is particularly important because of the large number of possible organisms involved.

Osteomyelitis in Human Immunodeficiency Virus Infection[95, 129, 176]

Although recurrent invasive bacterial infections often complicate human immunodeficiency virus (HIV) infection in children and adults, few reports of osteomyelitis in these patients exist. Many of the existing reports involve patients with recent intravenous drug use, which probably acted as a predisposing factor. *S. aureus* was recovered most commonly, although *E. coli, Salmonella enteritidis, Cryptococcus neoformans, Mycobacterium kansasii, Histoplasma capsulatum,* and other organisms also were seen in individual cases. To date, no evidence supports the view that the initial signs and symptoms or treatment needed for recovery from osteomyelitis is affected by co-infection with HIV.

Osteomyelitis after Closed Fractures

Acute hematogenous osteomyelitis sometimes occurs after closed fractures of tubular bones.[31, 203] The diagnosis generally is not recognized until fluctuation is apparent at the fracture site. However, a clue to its diagnosis is that after the initial post-fracture pain has subsided, the pain of osteomyelitis appears. It begins as early as 1 week and as late as 6 weeks after the injury occurs. The pain differs from that associated with the fracture by being progressive, and it is not relieved by immobilization. When the cast is removed, local erythema and warmth are apparent and are increased when these findings would seem to be resolving if they were secondary to the fracture. Patients are febrile and may be thought to have another focus of infection before osteomyelitis is discovered. Anaerobic superinfection of staphylococcal osteomyelitis at the fracture site has been recognized.[187] Adequate débridement, administration of appropriate antibiotics, and external fixation have been used in such cases. The outcome, however, is variable.

Osteomyelitis in Patients with Chronic Granulomatous Disease

The phagocytes of patients with chronic granulomatous disease fail to kill intracellular organisms, and infection with catalase-positive bacteria and fungi is a frequent complication. Although staphylococci are a common cause of cutaneous infection and formation of an abscess, osteomyelitis is caused most often by *Serratia* and *Aspergillus* spp. Osteomyelitis is attributed less often to staphylococci, *Pseudomonas, Burkholderia, Nocardia,* and other bacterial and fungal species.[210]

Nonhematogenous Osteomyelitis

Nonhematogenous infections of the bone arise either through inoculation or from a contiguous focus of infection.

PUNCTURE WOUND OSTEOMYELITIS

Inoculation osteomyelitis most often involves either the patella or the bones of the foot. Soft tissue infections occur after puncture wounds of the foot approximately 15 percent of the time, and osteomyelitis occurs in 1.5 percent of these injuries.[62] Osteomyelitis of the foot that develops after puncture wounds in children should be termed osteochondritis because it commonly includes infection of the articular cartilage in the metatarsals. Most patients are between 9 and 18 years of age. After the initial pain of the puncture wound subsides (in 24 to 48 hours), the signs of osteochondritis appear after another 48 to 72 hours. Typically, joint tenderness as well as localized swelling, erythema, and pain over the puncture wound entrance are present. Fever is an infrequent event, and seldom does the patient have any other constitutional symptoms. No peripheral leukocytosis is noted, and the erythrocyte sedimentation rate is increased minimally. Although the offending organism most commonly is *P. aeruginosa* (90% of the time), staphylococci, streptococci, *Stenotrophomonas maltophilia,*[8] and *Serratia marcescens*[137] also have been isolated.[23, 62, 97, 98, 100] In some series,[98] as many as 20 percent of the cases involved infection with both *P. aeruginosa* and *S. aureus.* The predominance of *Pseudomonas* can be explained partially on the basis of the mechanism of injury. *Pseudomonas* is not found commonly in surveys of the microbial flora of the skin of the feet,[77, 131, 184] but often it is found by culture of the sponge liner from children's sneakers.[61] In addition, many patients in whom *P. aeruginosa* osteochondritis develops have received prophylactic treatment with oral antibiotics that have activity against gram-positive bacteria. A semisynthetic penicillinase-resistant penicillin and an aminoglycoside or ceftazidime often are used as initial therapy.[97, 98]

Surgical débridement of necrotic cartilage is a key element of treatment because foreign material frequently is found embedded in the soft tissue; débridement also provides the opportunity to identify organisms resistant to the initial antibiotic agents. Four to 5 days after adequate débridement is performed, the local signs and symptoms of infection usually resolve and allow the patient to bear weight on the foot. In contrast, antibiotic therapy alone after diagnostic aspiration may need to be continued 6 to 8 weeks before weight bearing is possible. Long-term follow-up of *P. aeruginosa* osteochondritis indicates that many patients have asymptomatic, radiographic abnormalities.[12] Radiographic abnormalities are found more commonly in patients in whom an adjacent joint was involved initially.[12]

Osteomyelitis also has been described repeatedly after puncture wounds from stepping on wooden toothpicks. In these cases, *Eikenella corrodens,* a member of the human oral flora, has been found with other organisms. Surgical débridement to remove toothpick fragments and drain local abscesses is essential.[154]

Osteomyelitis of the patella is a disease of children between 5 and 15 years of age, the time in life in which the patella is vascularized. By adulthood, the vessels are almost completely atrophied. In almost all cases, the diagnosis shows the cause to be by inoculation, such as kneeling on a needle. The most common etiologic agent is *S. aureus;* signs of osteomyelitis appear 1 week after the puncture occurs. No constitutional symptoms occur, but extension of the leg produces pain over the anterior aspect of the patella. The diagnosis is made by isolation of the organism from the patella. Radiographic confirmation of the diagnosis often requires 2 to 3 weeks. Because the bone lacks periosteum, no periosteal elevation is present, but rarefaction and sclerosis may be seen on the profile view or on tomograms. Treatment of this disease is similar to that for other forms of osteomyelitis.

OSTEOMYELITIS CAUSED BY SPREAD OF INFECTION FROM A CONTIGUOUS FOCUS

In children, osteomyelitis related to an infected contiguous focus is a rare finding. Almost all cases of osteomyelitis from a contiguous source in childhood are nosocomial or are caused by an infected burn wound. The probability of postoperative osteomyelitis developing is a function of the surgeon's experience, the technique, the length of time that the wound was open, and whether prophylactic antibiotics were administered.[178] The interval between the precipitating event and pain and the appearance of persistent sinus drainage or ulceration is 2 to 4 weeks. The peripheral white blood cell count is often normal, as is the erythrocyte sedimentation rate. More than one half the cases are caused by multiple organisms. When small draining sinuses are present, correlation between sinus culture and bone biopsy findings is good. However, with large open areas, organisms obtained by culture of the wound may not be important etiologically, and obtaining a bone biopsy specimen is necessary for making a definitive bacteriologic diagnosis. Staphylococci and streptococci predominate; however, nosocomial gram-negative organisms often are seen.

ORTHOPEDIC FIXATOR DEVICES

Infection involving the wires or pins used for orthopedic stabilization represents a diagnostic and therapeutic challenge. Osteomyelitis is suspected when evidence of inflammation or infection is noted near these materials, but it seldom can be proved.[18] Plain radiographs are essential because they may reveal bone destruction at the site of entry of fixation pins. No controlled studies of treatment are available. Soft tissue débridement and removal of necrotic bone should be performed as soon as possible, but fixation devices generally are left in place.[9, 146] Prolonged therapy usually is given, guided by the susceptibility pattern of any organisms recovered from local cultures.[146]

Unusual Microbial Causes of Osteomyelitis

ACTINOMYCES

More than one half of all such actinomycotic infections involve the facial or cervical area. The most common site of actinomycotic bone infection is the jaw, the mandible being involved more frequently than the maxilla. Local signs and symptoms of fever and discharge from a sinus indicate the presence of the disease. Radiographically, periosteal elevation is followed by lytic changes. Often, several "eggshell" areas of new bone are present.

Forty percent of all actinomycotic infections occur in the vertebral bodies. In this illness, the infection almost always is associated with a focus elsewhere; the condition comes to medical attention because of mild pain, tenderness, and some stiffness. It can be distinguished from tuberculosis radiographically by the diffuse honeycombing of the vertebral bodies and the periosteal reaction; large lytic lesions usually are absent. Although no controlled trials of therapy have been performed, long-term (>3 months) penicillin G therapy is indicated at dosages of 150,000 U/kg of body weight per day (i.e., approximately 100 mg/kg/day). Extensive débridement may be needed and has been linked to successful short-term treatment of mandibular actinomycosis.[11]

Brucella spp. can produce abscesses in the vertebral bodies or long bones, although they are not striking features of the disease. Malaise, headaches, night sweats, and minimally tender cervical adenopathy with hepatosplenomegaly predominate.

FUNGI

Osteomyelitis may be caused by numerous endemic and opportunistic fungal agents, including *Coccidioides immitis* and species of *Candida, Blastomyces,* and *Aspergillus*.

Coccidioidomycosis may be characterized by cough, chest pain, night sweats, and anorexia and often is associated with erythema nodosum or erythema multiforme. This disease commonly is found in the southwestern part of the United States. Extrapulmonary involvement is suggested by persistent high temperature and toxicity. *C. immitis* primarily occurs in cancellous bone (e.g., the vertebral bodies, distal tubular bones, and the skull).[153] These lesions are not radiographically distinct from those seen in osteomyelitis from other causes.[169] Débridement of bone lesions often is needed initially, and years of therapy are required. Oral triazole agents generally are recommended.[68]

Blastomycosis may mimic coccidioidomycosis, but the pulmonary involvement is much more varied, and fusion of the vertebral bodies rarely occurs. A propensity for the development of verrucous, reddened, weeping skin lesions has been noted, and prostate involvement may be seen. Bone involvement occurs frequently, with the skull and vertebral bodies being infected most often. Distinguishing this from other forms of osteomyelitis is impossible by radiographic examination.

Aspergillus osteomyelitis is being recognized with increasing frequency.[33] Most commonly, it is a disease of immunosuppressed patients, with *Aspergillus* pneumonia seen initially followed by disseminated disease. However, bone disease occurring by hematogenous spread has developed in normal individuals[39, 158] without intravenous inoculation, such as that associated with drug abuse. Penetrating trauma also has produced *Aspergillus* osteomyelitis.

Rhizopus osteomyelitis of the femur without direct introduction has been reported in an immunocompromised adolescent.[52]

Disseminated *C. neoformans* may be seen in 5 to 10 percent of patients with pulmonary disease. Slowly destructive, very discrete bone lesions may be part of the dissemination. They occur primarily in the long tubular bones without marginal sclerosis. This radiologic reaction is confused most commonly with tumor and, occasionally, with tuberculosis.[28, 120]

Chronic Osteomyelitis

Chronic osteomyelitis often is the result of bone infection after a surgical procedure or major trauma.[195] Inadequate treatment of acute hematogenous osteomyelitis also can lead to the development of chronic osteomyelitis. The diagnosis of chronic osteomyelitis usually is straightforward; patients generally have a painful, nonfunctional extremity and may have chronically draining sinuses. Cultures of the purulent exudate or necrotic bone usually reveal *S. aureus*. Gram-negative bacteria, including *H. influenzae*,[110] may be isolated from the intraosseous abscess. Plain radiographs, CT, and MRI all play roles in medical and surgical management by revealing details of the bony and soft tissue involvement, including the formation of abscesses[150] and sequestra (Fig. 62–7).

Treatment of chronic osteomyelitis involves the removal of devitalized bone, management of soft tissue disease, and the long-term administration of appropriate antibiotics. Few controlled trials comparing different modes of therapy have been performed. Antimicrobial regimens for chronic staphylococcal osteomyelitis that have been studied include oral cloxacillin plus probenecid for 6 to 12 months; 9 of 19 patients apparently were treated successfully.[11, 13] In another study, the outcome of a 6-week course of nafcillin was compared with that of nafcillin and oral rifampin. No statistically significant differences were observed with the addition of rifampin, but most (10/17) of the patients showed no evidence of disease activity 2 years after the cessation of treatment with antibiotics.[143]

The high failure rate in these and other studies has led to investigation of a variety of adjunctive measures to improve the outcome of chronic osteomyelitis. Local irrigation with antibiotic solutions, with[124] and without[3] added detergents, has been examined. The use of surgically implanted polymethylmethacrylate beads impregnated with an antibiotic (usually gentamicin) has been compared with conventional antibiotic therapy and with therapy with both.[17] No differences were seen among the three groups in a preliminary analysis. Hyperbaric oxygen also has been suggested as an aid to therapy, but no comparative studies have been performed.[41, 136] Because perpetuation of chronic infection appears to be caused by the presence of avascular bone and tissue, advances such as the use of laser Doppler flowmetry ultimately may improve the outcome of this disease.[181] Surgical approaches to close open wounds after débridement and improve blood flow with mobilized tissue flaps also appear to bring about prolonged remission in some patients.[4] Meticulous surgical technique is essential to avoid thermal injury and retain the vascular supply to compromised areas.[188] Complications of chronic osteomyelitis include secondary amyloidosis and local sarcomatosis or carcinomatous changes at the site of infection. The high

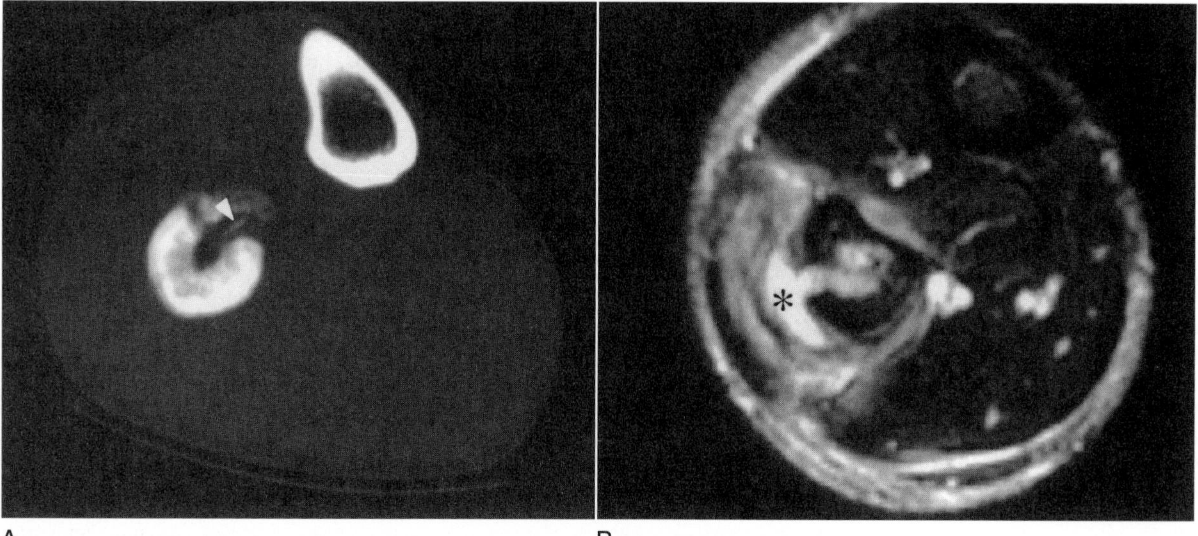

FIGURE 62–7 ■ Chronic osteomyelitis. *A,* Computed tomography reveals thickening of the fibular cortex and a sinus tract that contains a sequestrum *(arrow). B,* T2-weighted axial magnetic resonance imaging from a different level shows a lateral sinus tract through the cortex communicating with a soft tissue abscess *(asterisk).* Edema is surrounding the entire fibula. (Courtesy of Dr. Leanne Seeger.)

likelihood of a poor outcome in chronic osteomyelitis must be kept in mind during treatment of acute hematogenous osteomyelitis. Failure to comply with a regimen of oral therapy may result in chronic infection.[182]

CHRONIC RECURRENT MULTIFOCAL OSTEOMYELITIS

Chronic recurrent multifocal osteomyelitis, an illness characterized by chronic focal, multiple inflammatory lesions in bone with periodic exacerbation and remission, moderate bone pain, and sterile lesions, first was described by Giedion and coworkers.[73, 199] Initially, this disease is difficult to distinguish from pyogenic osteomyelitis; the only difference appears to be the apparent absence of an infecting agent. Repeated biopsy of lesions that prove to be sterile usually leads to the diagnosis. It occurs more commonly in girls younger than 10 years of age. At initial evaluation, slightly more than 50 percent of the patients have fever, and virtually all have an increased erythrocyte sedimentation rate (or increased C-reactive protein). The lesions primarily occur in the distal femoral, distal tibial, and proximal tibial regions. Virtually all tubular bones can be involved.[165] Patients may have from 1 to 18 lesions at a time, which on biopsy show a nonspecific chronic inflammatory process. Occasionally, a predominance of plasma cells is present, which erroneously leads to this disease being called plasma-cell osteomyelitis. In the first reported cases, the lesions were symmetric. However, this feature has not been present consistently as more cases have been described. Many of the cases are in children of northern European origin.[16, 107] Approximately 20 percent of patients have a pustular eruption of the palms and soles at the same time that they come to medical attention with bone lesions; this illness is called pustulosis palmaris et plantaris. Some patients also may have Sweet syndrome, in which painful, indurated, cutaneous plaques are accompanied by fever and leukocytosis. Sweet syndrome and pustulosis palmaris et plantaris may well be variations of the same illness. In addition, Sweet syndrome and congenital dyserythropoietic anemia also have been associated with chronic recurrent multifocal osteomyelitis.[54] The long-term outlook in children with this disease is good.[16] Glucocorticoids and nonsteroidal anti-inflammatory agents have been administered to children with this disease. All appear to afford transient relief. However, patients usually have a recurrence of symptoms and lesions when these agents are discontinued. Treatment with interferon-γ also has been reported to be helpful.[69]

REFERENCES

1. Ailsby, R. L., and Staheli, L. T.: Pyogenic infections of the sacroiliac joint in children. Radioisotope bone scanning as a diagnostic tool. Clin. Orthop. *100*:96–100, 1974.
2. Ambrose, G. B., Alpert, M., and Neer, C. S.: Vertebral osteomyelitis. A diagnostic problem. J. A. M. A. *197*:619–622, 1966.
3. Anderson, L. D., and Horn, L. G.: Irrigation-suction technic in the treatment of acute hematogenous osteomyelitis, chronic osteomyelitis, and acute and chronic joint infections. South. Med. J. *63*:745–754, 1970.
4. Anthony, J. P., and Mathes, S. J.: Update on chronic osteomyelitis. Clin. Plast. Surg. *18*:515–523, 1991.
5. Ash, J. M., and Gilday, D. L.: The futility of bone scanning in neonatal osteomyelitis: Concise communication. J. Nucl. Med. *21*:417–420, 1980.
6. Asmar, B. I.: Osteomyelitis in the neonate. Infect. Dis. Clin. North Am. *6*:117–132, 1992.
7. Babaiantz, L.: Les osteopathies atrophiques. J. Radiol. Radiother. Nucl. Med. *19*:333, 1948.
8. Baltimore, R. S., and Jenson, H. B.: Puncture wound osteochondritis of the foot caused by *Pseudomonas maltophilia*. Pediatr. Infect. Dis. J. *9*:143–144, 1990.
9. Barret, J. P., Desai, M. H., and Herndon, D. N.: Osteomyelitis in burn patients requiring skeletal fixation. Burns *26*:487–489, 2000.
10. Barrett-Connor, E.: Bacterial infection and sickle cell anemia. An analysis of 250 infections in 166 patients and a review of the literature. Medicine (Baltimore) *50*:97–112, 1971.
11. Bartkowski, S. B., Zapala, J., Heczko, P., and Szuta, M.: Actinomycotic osteomyelitis of the mandible: Review of 15 cases. J. Craniomaxillofac. Surg. *26*:63–67, 1998.
12. Barton, L. L., Hoddy, D. M., Rathore, M. H., et al.: Long-term radiologic outcome of *Pseudomonas* osteomyelitis of the foot. Pediatr. Infect. Dis. J. *9*:476–478, 1980.
13. Bell, S. M.: Further observations on the value of oral penicillins in chronic staphylococcal osteomyelitis. Med. J. Aust. *2*:591–593, 1976.
14. Bennett, O. M.: *Salmonella* osteomyelitis and the hand-foot syndrome in sickle cell disease. J. Pediatr. Orthop. *12*:534–538, 1992.
15. Berkowitz, I. D., and Wenzel, W.: 'Normal' technetium bone scans in patients with acute osteomyelitis. Am. J. Dis. Child. *134*:828–830, 1980.

16. Bjorksten, B., Gustavson, K. H., Eriksson, B., et al.: Chronic recurrent multifocal osteomyelitis and pustulosis palmoplantaris. J. Pediatr. *93*:227–231, 1978.
17. Blaha, J. D., Calhoun, J. H., Nelson, C. L., et al.: Comparison of the clinical efficacy and tolerance of gentamicin PMMA beads on surgical wire versus combined and systemic therapy for osteomyelitis. Clin. Orthop. *295*:8–12, 1993.
18. Blasier, R. D., Aronson, J., and Tursky, E. A.: External fixation of pediatric femur fractures. J. Pediatr. Orthop. *17*:342–346, 1997.
19. Blockey, N. J., and Watson, J. T.: Acute osteomyelitis in children. J. Bone Joint Surg. Br. *52*:77–87, 1970.
20. Booz, M. M.: The value of ultrasound and aspiration in differentiating vaso-occlusive crisis and osteomyelitis in sickle cell disease patients. Clin. Radiol. *54*:636–639, 1999.
21. Boston, H. C., Jr., Bianco, A. J., Jr., and Rhodes, K. H: Disk space infections in children. Orthop. Clin. North Am. *6*:953–964, 1975.
22. Bradley, J. S., Kaplan, S. L., Tan, T. Q., et al.: Pediatric pneumococcal bone and joint infections. The Pediatric Multicenter Pneumococcal Surveillance Study Group (PMPSSG). Pediatrics *102*:1376–1382, 1998.
23. Brand, R. A., and Black, H.: *Pseudomonas* osteomyelitis following puncture wounds in children. J. Bone Joint Surg. Am. *56*:1637–1642, 1974.
24. Bremnet, A., and Neligan, G.: Pyogenic osteitis. In Gairdner D (ed): Recent Advances in Pediatrics, 2nd ed. London, TA Churchill Ltd, 1958.
25. Bruno, M. S., Silverberg, T. N., and Goldstein, D. H.: Embolic osteomyelitis of the spine as a complication of infection of the urinary tract. Am. J. Med. *19*:865–878, 1960.
26. Bryan, V., Franks, L., and Torres, H.: *Pseudomonas aeruginosa* cervical diskitis with chondro-osteomyelitis in an intravenous drug abuser. Surg. Neurol. *1*:142–144, 1973.
27. Bryson, Y. J., Connor, J. D., LeClerc, M., and Giammona, S. T.: High-dose oral dicloxacillin treatment of acute staphylococcal osteomyelitis in children. J. Pediatr. *94*:673–675, 1979.
28. Burch, K. H., Fine, G., Quinn, E. L., and Eisses, J. F.: *Cryptococcus neoformans* as a cause of lytic bone lesions. J. A. M. A. *231*:1057–1059, 1975.
29. Burnett, M. W., Bass, J. W., and Cook, B. A.: Etiology of osteomyelitis complicating sickle cell disease. Pediatrics *101*:296–297, 1998.
30. Buxton, T. B., Rissing, J. P., Horner, J. A., et al.: Binding of a *Staphylococcus aureus* bone pathogen to type I collagen. Microb. Pathog. *8*:441–448, 1990.
31. Canale, S. T., Puhl, J., Watson, F. M., and Gillespie, R.: Acute osteomyelitis following closed fractures. Report of three cases. J. Bone Joint Surg. Am. *57*:415–418, 1975.
32. Capitanio, M. A., and Kirkpatrick, J. A: Early roentgen observations in acute osteomyelitis. A. J. R. Am. J. Roentgenol. *108*:488–496, 1970.
33. Casscells, S. W.: *Aspergillus* osteomyelitis of the tibia. A case report. J. Bone Joint Surg. Am. *60*:994–995, 1978.
34. Charkes, N. D.: Skeletal blood flow: Implications for bone-scan interpretation. J. Nucl. Med. *21*:91–98, 1980.
35. Chung, S. M., and Borns, P.: Acute osteomyelitis adjacent to the sacroiliac joint in children. Report of two cases. J. Bone Joint Surg. Am. *55*:630–634, 1973.
36. Collin, D. H.: Pathology of Bone. London, Butterworths, 1966.
37. Constant, E., Green, R. L., and Wagner, D. K.: *Salmonella* osteomyelitis of both hands and the hand-foot syndrome. Arch. Surg. *102*:148–151, 1971.
38. Conventry, M. B., Ghormley, R. K., and Kernohan, J. W.: Intervertebral disc: Its microscopic anatomy and pathology. J. Bone Joint Surg. *27*:105–112, 1945.
39. Corrall, C. J., Merz, W. G., Rekedal, K., and Hughes, W. T.: *Aspergillus* osteomyelitis in an immunocompetent adolescent: A case report and review of the literature. Pediatrics *70*:455–461, 1982.
40. Cushing, A. H.: Diskitis in children. Clin. Infect. Dis. *17*:1–6, 1993.
41. Davis, J. C., Heckman, J. D., DeLee, J. C., and Buckwold, F. J.: Chronic non-hematogenous osteomyelitis treated with adjuvant hyperbaric oxygen. J. Bone Joint Surg. Am. *68*:1210–1217, 1986.
42. de Groot, R., Glover, D., Clausen, C., et al.: Bone and joint infections caused by *Kingella kingae:* Six cases and review of the literature. Rev. Infect. Dis. *10*:998–1004, 1988.
43. Delorimier, A. A., Haskin, D., and Massie, F. S.: Mediastinal mass caused by vertebral osteomyelitis. Am. J. Dis. Child. *111*:639–643, 1966.
44. Demopulos, G. A., Bleck, E. E., and McDougall, I. R.: Role of radionuclide imaging in the diagnosis of acute osteomyelitis. J. Pediatr. Orthop. *8*:558–565, 1988.
45. Deshpande, P. G., Wagle, S. U., Mehta, S. D., et al.: Neonatal osteomyelitis and septic arthritis. Indian Pediatr. *27*:453–457, 1990.
46. Deutsch, S. D., Gandsman, E. J., and Spraragen, S. C.: Quantitative regional blood-flow analysis and its clinical application during routine bone-scanning. J. Bone Joint Surg. Am. *63*:295–305, 1981.
47. Dich, V. Q., Nelson, J. D., and Haltalin, K. C.: Osteomyelitis in infants and children. A review of 163 cases. Am. J. Dis. Child. *129*:1273–1278, 1975.
48. Diggs, L. W.: Bone and joint lesions in sickle-cell disease. Clin. Orthop. *52*:119–143, 1967.
49. Drew, R. H., Perfect, J. R., Srinath, L., et al.: Treatment of methicillin-resistant *Staphylococcus aureus* infections with quinupristin-dalfopristin in patients intolerant of or failing prior therapy. For the Synercid Emergency-Use Study Group. J. Antimicrob. Chemother. *46*:775–784, 2000.
50. Dunn, E. J., Bryan, D. M., Nugent, J. T., and Robinson, R. A.: Pyogenic infections of the sacro-iliac joint. Clin. Orthop. *118*:113–117, 1976.
51. Duszynski, D. O., Kuhn, J. P., Afshani, E., and Riddlesberger, M. M., Jr.: Early radionuclide diagnosis of acute osteomyelitis. Radiology *117*:337–340, 1975.
52. Echols, R. M., Selinger, D. S., Hallowell, C., et al.: *Rhizopus* osteomyelitis. A case report and review. Am. J. Med. *66*:141–145, 1979.
53. Edwards, M. S., Baker, C. J., Wagner, M. L., et al.: An etiologic shift in infantile osteomyelitis: The emergence of the group B streptococcus. J. Pediatr. *93*:578–583, 1978.
54. Edwards, T. C., Stapleton, F. B., Bond, M. J., and Barrett, F. F.: Sweet's syndrome with multifocal sterile osteomyelitis. Am. J. Dis. Child. *140*:817–818, 1986.
55. Epps, C. H., Jr., Bryant, D. D., 3rd, Coles, M. J., and Castro, O.: Osteomyelitis in patients who have sickle-cell disease. Diagnosis and management. J. Bone Joint Surg. Am. *73*:1281–1294, 1991.
56. Farr, H.: Acute hematogenous osteomyelitis due to type B *Haemophilus* osteomyelitis and arthritis. Lancet *1*:517–518, 1966.
57. Farrand, R. J., Johnstone, J. M., and McCabe, A. F.: *Haemophilus* osteomyelitis and arthritis. B. M. J. *2*:334–336, 1968.
58. Feigin, R. D., Pickering, L. K., Anderson, D., et al.: Clindamycin treatment of osteomyelitis and septic arthritis in children. Pediatrics *55*:213–223, 1975.
59. Ferguson, W. R.: Some observations on circulation in fetal and infant spine. J. Bone Joint Surg. *32*:640–648, 1950.
60. Fernandez, M., Carrol, C. L., and Baker, C. J.: Discitis and vertebral osteomyelitis in children: An 18-year review. Pediatrics *105*:1299–1304, 2000.
61. Fisher, M. C., Goldsmith, J. F., and Gilligan, P. H.: Sneakers as a source of *Pseudomonas aeruginosa* in children with osteomyelitis following puncture wounds. J. Pediatr. *106*:607–609, 1985.
62. Fitzgerald, R. H., Jr., and Cowan, J. D.: Puncture wounds of the foot. Orthop. Clin. North Am. *6*:965–972, 1975.
63. Fletcher, B. D., Scoles, P. V., and Nelson, A. D.: Osteomyelitis in children: Detection by magnetic resonance: Work in progress. Radiology *150*:57–60, 1984.
64. Fonk, J., and Coonrod, J. D.: *Serratia* osteomyelitis in sickle cell disease. J. A. M. A. *217*:80–81, 1970.
65. Fox, L., and Sprunt, K.: Neonatal osteomyelitis. Pediatrics *62*:535–542, 1978.
66. Freehafer, A. A., Furey, J. G., and Pierce, D. S.: Pyogenic osteomyelitis of the spine resulting in spinal paralysis. J. Bone Joint Surg. *44*:710–716, 1962.
67. Gainey, M. A., Siegel, J. A., Smergel, E. M., and Jara, B. J.: Indium-111–labeled white blood cells: Dosimetry in children. J. Nucl. Med. *29*:689–694, 1988.
68. Galgiani, J. N., Ampel, N. M., Catanzaro, A., et al.: Practice guideline for the treatment of coccidioidomycosis. Infectious Diseases Society of America. Clin. Infect. Dis. *30*:658–661, 2000.
69. Gallagher, K. T., Roberts, R. L., MacFarlane, J. A., and Stiehm, E. R.: Treatment of chronic recurrent multifocal osteomyelitis with interferon gamma. J. Pediatr. *131*:470–472, 1997.
70. Geddes, A. M., Finch, R. S., Goodall, A. C., et al.: The treatment of pediatric infections with clindamycin. *In* Hejzlar, M., Simonsky, M., and Masak, S. (eds.): Advances in Antimicrobial and Antineoplastic Chemotherapy. Baltimore, University Park Press, 1972.
71. Genster, H. G., and Andersen, J. J. F.: Spinal osteomyelitis complicating urinary tract infection. J. Urol. *107*:109–111, 1971.
72. Gibson, W. K., Bartosh, R., and Timperlake, R.: Acute hematogenous epiphyseal osteomyelitis. Orthopedics *14*:705–707, 1991.
73. Giedion, A., Holthusen, W., Masel, L. F., and Vischer, D.: [Subacute and chronic "symmetrical" osteomyelitis.] Ann. Radiol. (Paris) *15*:329–342, 1972.
74. Gilday, D. L., Paul, D. J., and Paterson, J.: Diagnosis of osteomyelitis in children by combined blood pool and bone imaging. Radiology *117*:331–335, 1975.
75. Gilfand, M. J., and Harcke, H. T.: Skeletal imaging in sickle cell disease. J. Nucl. Med. *19*:698–709, 1978.
76. Gillespie, W. J.: Epidemiology in bone and joint infection. Infect. Dis. Clin. North Am. *4*:361–376, 1990.
77. Goldstein, E. J., Ahonkhai, V. I., Cristofaro, R. L., et al.: Source of *Pseudomonas* in osteomyelitis of heels. J. Clin. Microbiol. *12*:711–713, 1980.
78. Goutzmanis, J. J., Gonis, G., and Gilbert, G. L.: *Kingella kingae* infection in children: Ten cases and a review of the literature. Pediatr. Infect. Dis. J. *10*:677–683, 1991.
79. Granoff, D. M., Sargent, E., and Jolivette, D.: *Haemophilus influenzae* type b osteomyelitis. Am. J. Dis. Child. *132*:488–490, 1976.
80. Green, J. H.: Cloxacillin in treatment of acute osteomyelitis. B. M. J. *2*:414–416, 1967.

81. Green, W. T.: Osteomyelitis of infants: A disease different from osteomyelitis of older children. Arch. Surg. *32*:462–493, 1936.
82. Greenberg, L. W., and Haynes, R. E.: *Escherichia coli* osteomyelitis in an infant with sickle cell disease. Clin. Pediatr. (Phila.) *9*:436–438, 1990.
83. Griesemer, D. A., Winkelstein, J. A., and Luddy, R.: Pneumococcal meningitis in patients with a major sickle hemoglobinopathy. J. Pediatr. *92*:82–84, 1978.
84. Gristina, A. G., Oga, M., Webb, L. X., and Hobgood, C. D.: Adherent bacterial colonization in the pathogenesis of osteomyelitis. Science *228*:990–993, 1985.
85. Handmaker, H., and Giammona, S. T.: Improved early diagnosis of acute inflammatory skeletal-articular diseases in children: A two-radiopharmaceutical approach. Pediatrics *73*:661–669, 1984.
86. Harcke, H. T.: Role of imaging in musculoskeletal infections in children. J. Pediatr. Orthop. *15*:141–143, 1995.
87. Harris, N. H.: Some problems in the diagnosis and treatment of acute osteomyelitis. J. Bone Joint Surg. *42*:535–542, 1960.
88. Henson, F. W., Jr., and Coventry, M. B.: Osteomyelitis of the vertebrae as a result of infection of the urinary tract. Surg. Gynecol. Obstet. *102*:207–214, 1956.
89. Highland, T. R., and LaMont, R. L.: Osteomyelitis of the pelvis in children. Pediatrics *73*:661–669, 1984.
90. Hobo, T.: Zur Pathogenese der Vitalfarbungalehre. Acta Sch. Med. Univ. Kioto *4*:1–29, 1921.
91. Hoffer, P.: Gallium and infection. J. Nucl. Med. *21*:484–488, 1980.
92. Holzman, R. S., and Bishko, F.: Osteomyelitis in heroin addicts. Ann. Intern. Med. *75*:693–696, 1971.
93. Horvath, F. L., Brodeur, A. E., and Cherry, J. D.: Deep thrombophlebitis associated with acute osteomyelitis. J. Pediatr. *79*:815–818, 1971.
94. Hruby, M. A., Honig, G. R., Lolekha, S., and Gotoff, S. P.: *Arizoni hinshawii* osteomyelitis in sickle cell anemia. Am. J. Dis. Child. *125*:867–868, 1973.
95. Hughes, R. A., Rowe, I. F., Shanson, D., and Keat, A. C.: Septic bone, joint and muscle lesions associated with human immunodeficiency virus infection. Br. J. Rheumatol. *31*:381–388, 1992.
96. Jackson, M. A., and Nelson, J. D.: Etiology and medical management of acute suppurative bone and joint infections in pediatric patients. J. Pediatr. Orthop. *2*:313–323, 1982.
97. Jacobs, R. F., Adelman, L., Sack, C. M., and Wilson, C. B.: Management of *Pseudomonas* osteochondritis complicating puncture wounds of the foot. Pediatrics *69*:432–435, 1982.
98. Jacobs, R. F., McCarthy, R. E., and Elser, J. M.: *Pseudomonas* osteochondritis complicating puncture wounds of the foot in children: A 10-year evaluation. J. Infect. Dis. *160*:657–661, 1989.
99. Jaffe, H. L.: Degenerative and Inflammatory Diseases of the Bones and Joints. Philadelphia, Lea & Febiger, 1972.
100. Johanson, P. H.: *Pseudomonas* infections of the foot following puncture wounds. J. A. M. A. *204*:262–264, 1968.
101. Jordan, M. C., and Kirby, W. M.: Pyogenic vertebral osteomyelitis. Treatment with antimicrobial agents and bed rest. Arch. Intern. Med. *128*:405–410, 1971.
102. Jupiter, J. B., Ehrlich, M. G., Novelline, R. A., et al.: The association of septic thrombophlebitis with subperiosteal abscesses in children. J. Pediatr. *101*:690–695, 1982.
103. Kahn, D. S., and Pritzker, K. P.: The pathophysiology of bone infection. Clin. Orthop. *96*:12–19, 1973.
104. Karwowska, A., Davies, H. D., and Jadavji, T.: Epidemiology and outcome of osteomyelitis in the era of sequential intravenous-oral therapy. Pediatr. Infect. Dis. J. *17*:1021–1026, 1998.
105. Keeley, K., and Buchanan, G. R.: Acute infarction of long bones in children with sickle cell anemia. J. Pediatr. *101*:170–175, 1982.
106. Kemp, H., Jackson, J., and Jeremia, J.: Pyogenic infections occurring primarily in intervertebral discs. J. Bone Joint Surg. *55*:698–714, 1963.
107. King, S. M., Laxer, R. M., Manson, D., and Gold, R.: Chronic recurrent multifocal osteomyelitis: A noninfectious inflammatory process. Pediatr. Infect. Dis. J. *6*:907–911, 1987.
108. Knudsen, C. J., and Hoffman, E. B.: Neonatal osteomyelitis. J. Bone Joint Surg. Br. *72*:846–851, 1990.
109. Kozin, F., Carrera, G. F., Ryan, L. M., et al.: Computed tomography in the diagnosis of sacroiliitis. Am. J. Dis. Child. *134*:828–830, 1980.
110. Kurlandsky, L. E., Quinn, P. H., and Sills, E. M.: *Haemophilus influenzae* as a cause of Brodie's abscess in an infant. Johns Hopkins Med. J. *144*:15–17, 1979.
111. LaMont, R. L., Anderson, P. A., Dajani, A. S., and Thirumoorthi, M. C.: Acute hematogenous osteomyelitis in children. J. Pediatr. Orthop. *7*:579–583, 1987.
112. Lascari, A. D., Graham, M. H., and MacQueen, J. C.: Intervertebral disk infection in children. J. Pediatr. *70*:751–757, 1967.
113. Lee, P. Y.: Infected cephalhaematoma and neonatal osteomyelitis. J. Infect. *21*:191–193, 1990.
114. Leigh, T. F., Kelly, R. P., and Weens, H. S.: Spinal osteomyelitis associated with urinary tract infections. Radiology *65*:334–342, 1955.
115. Leonard, A., Comty, C. M., Shapiro, F. L., and Raij, L.: Osteomyelitis in hemodialysis patients. Ann. Intern. Med. *78*:651–658, 1973.
116. Lewis, R., Gorbach, S., and Altner, P.: Spinal *Pseudomonas* chondro-osteomyelitis in heroin users. N. Engl. J. Med. *286*:1303, 1972.
117. Lewis, R. P., Sutter, V. L., and Finegold, S. M.: Bone infections involving anaerobic bacteria. Medicine (Baltimore) *57*:279–305, 1978.
118. Lifeso, R. M., Harder, E., and McCorkell, S. J.: Spinal brucellosis. J. Bone Joint Surg. Br. *67*:345–351, 1985.
119. Light, R. W., and Dunham, T. R.: Vertebral osteomyelitis due to *Pseudomonas* in the occasional heroin user. J. A. M. A. *228*:1272, 1974.
120. Littman, M. L., and Walter, J. E.: Cryptococcosis: Current status. Am. J. Med. *45*:922–932, 1968.
121. Longjohn, D. B., Zionts, L. E., and Stott, N. S.: Acute hematogenous osteomyelitis of the epiphysis. Clin. Orthop. *316*:227–234, 1995.
122. Lundy, D. W., and Kehl, D. K.: Increasing prevalence of *Kingella kingae* in osteoarticular infections in young children. J. Pediatr. Orthop. *18*:262–267, 1998.
123. Majeed, H. A., Kalaawi, M., Mohanty, D., et al.: Congenital dyserythropoietic anemia and chronic recurrent multifocal osteomyelitis in three related children and the association with Sweet syndrome in two siblings. J. Pediatr. *115*:730–734, 1989.
124. Makin, M., Geller, R., Jacobs, J., and Sacks, T.: Non-toxic detergent irrigation of chronic infections. An experimental evaluation. Clin. Orthop. *92*:320–324, 1973.
125. Marshall, G. S., Mudido, P., Rabalais, G. P., and Adams, G.: Organism isolation and serum bactericidal titers in oral antibiotic therapy for pediatric osteomyelitis. South. Med. J. *89*:68–70, 1996.
126. Marti-Bonmati, L., Aparisi, F., Poyatos, C., and Vilar, J.: Brodie abscess: MR imaging appearance in 10 patients. J. Magn. Reson. Imaging *3*:543–546, 1993.
127. Mazur, J. M., Ross, G., Cummings, J., et al.: Usefulness of magnetic resonance imaging for the diagnosis of acute musculoskeletal infections in children. J. Pediatr. Orthop. *15*:144–147, 1995.
128. McGregor, J. A., and McFarren, T.: Neonatal cranial osteomyelitis: A complication of fetal monitoring. Obstet. Gynecol. *73*:490–492, 1989.
129. Medina, F., Fuentes, M., Jara, L. J., et al.: *Salmonella* pyomyositis in patients with the human immunodeficiency virus. Br. J. Rheumatol. *34*:568–571, 1995.
130. Miller, D. J., and Mejicano, G. C.: Vertebral osteomyelitis due to *Candida* species: Case report and literature review. Clin. Infect. Dis. *33*:523–530, 2001.
131. Miller, E. H., and Semian, D. W.: Gram-negative osteomyelitis following puncture wounds of the foot. Medicine (Baltimore) *57*:279–305, 1978.
132. Modic, M. T., Feiglin, D. H., Piraino, D. W., et al.: Vertebral osteomyelitis: Assessment using MR. Radiology *157*:157–166, 1985.
133. Mok, P. M., Reilly, B. J., and Ash, J. M.: Osteomyelitis in the neonate. Clinical aspects and the role of radiography and scintigraphy in diagnosis and management. Radiology *145*:677–682, 1982.
134. Morgan, A., and Yates, A. K.: The diagnosis of acute osteomyelitis of the pelvis. Postgrad. Med. J. 42:74–78, 1966.
135. Morrey, B. F., Bianco, A. J., and Rhodes, K. H.: Hematogenous osteomyelitis at uncommon sites in children. Mayo Clin. Proc. *53*:707–713, 1978.
136. Morrey, B. F., Dunn, J. M., Heimbach, R. D., and Davis, J.: Hyperbaric oxygen and chronic osteomyelitis. Clin. Orthop. *144*:121–127, 1979.
137. Murray, M. M., Welch, D. F., and Kuhls, T. L.: *Serratia* osteochondritis after puncture wounds of the foot. Pediatr. Infect. Dis. J. *9*:523–525, 1990.
138. Mustafa, M. M., Saez-Llorens, X., McCracken, G. H., Jr., and Nelson, J. D.: Acute hematogenous pelvic osteomyelitis in infants and children. Pediatr. Infect. Dis. J. *9*:416–421, 1990.
139. Nagal, D. A., Albright, J. A., and Keggi, K. J.: Closer look at spinal lesions: Open biopsy of vertebral lesions. J. A. M. A. *191*:975–978, 1965.
140. Nelson, J. D.: Acute osteomyelitis in children. Infect. Dis. Clin. North Am. *4*:513–522, 1990.
141. Nelson, J. D.: Toward simple but safe management of osteomyelitis. Pediatrics *99*:883–884, 1997.
142. Nelson, J. D., Bucholz, R. W., Kusmiesz, H., and Shelton, S.: Benefits and risks of sequential parenteral-oral cephalosporin therapy for suppurative bone and joint infections. J. Pediatr. Orthop. *2*:255–262, 1982.
143. Norden, C. W., Bryant, R., Palmer, D., et al.: Chronic osteomyelitis caused by *Staphylococcus aureus:* Controlled clinical trial of nafcillin therapy and nafcillin-rifampin therapy. South. Med. J. *79*:947–951, 1986.
144. Peltola, H., Unkila-Kallio, L., and Kallio, M. J.: Simplified treatment of acute staphylococcal osteomyelitis of childhood. The Finnish Study Group. Pediatrics *99*:846–850, 1997.
145. Perlman, M. H., Patzakis, M. J., Kumar, P. J., and Holtom, P.: The incidence of joint involvement with adjacent osteomyelitis in pediatric patients. J. Pediatr. Orthop. *20*:40–43, 2000.
146. Perry, J. W., Montgomerie, J. Z., Swank, S., et al.: Wound infections following spinal fusion with posterior segmental spinal instrumentation. Clin. Infect. Dis. *24*:558–561, 1997.
147. Peters, W., Irving, J., and Letts, M.: Long-term effects of neonatal bone and joint infection on adjacent growth plates. J. Pediatr. Orthop. *12*:806–810, 1992.

148. Pichichero, M. E., and Friesen, H. A.: Polymicrobial osteomyelitis: Report of three cases and review of the literature. Rev. Infect. Dis. *4*:86–96, 1982.
149. Piehl, F. C., Davis, R. J., and Prugh, S. I.: Osteomyelitis in sickle cell disease. J. Pediatr. Orthop. *13*:225–227, 1993.
150. Poyhia, T., and Azouz, E. M.: MR imaging evaluation of subacute and chronic bone abscesses in children. Pediatr. Radiol. *30*:763–768, 2000.
151. Prober, C. G., and Yeager, A. S.: Use of the serum bactericidal titer to assess the adequacy of oral antibiotic therapy in the treatment of acute hematogenous osteomyelitis. J. Pediatr. *95*:131–135, 1979.
152. Rao, S., Solomon, N., Miller, S., and Dunn, E.: Scintigraphic differentiation of bone infarction from osteomyelitis in children with sickle cell disease. J. Pediatr. *107*:685–688, 1985.
153. Rhangos, W. C., and Chick, E. W.: Mycotic infections of bone. South. Med. J. *57*:664–674, 1964.
154. Robinson, L. G., and Kourtis, A. P.: Tale of a toothpick: *Eikenella corrodens* osteomyelitis. Infection *28*:332–333, 2000.
155. Rocco, H. D., and Eyring, E. J.: Intervertebral disk infections in children. Am. J. Dis. Child. *123*:448–451, 1972.
156. Rodriguez, W., Ross, S., Khan, W., et al.: Clindamycin in the treatment of osteomyelitis in children: A report of 29 cases. Am. J. Dis. Child. *131*:1088–1093, 1977.
157. Roine, I., Faingezicht, I., Arguedas, A., et al.: Serial serum C-reactive protein to monitor recovery from acute hematogenous osteomyelitis in children. Pediatr. Infect. Dis. J. *14*:40–44, 1995.
158. Roselle, G. A., and Baird, I. M.: *Aspergillus flavipes* group osteomyelitis. Arch. Intern. Med. *139*:590–592, 1995.
159. Rubin, H. M., Eardley, W., and Nichols, B. L.: *Shigella sonnei* osteomyelitis and sickle-cell anemia. Am. J. Dis. Child. *116*:83–87, 1968.
160. Rubin, R. C., Jacobs, G. B., Cooper, P. R., and Wille, R. L.: Disc space infections in children. Childs Brain *3*:180–190, 1977.
161. Salahuddin, N. I., Madhavan, T., Fisher, E. J., et al.: *Pseudomonas* osteomyelitis. Radiologic features. Radiology *109*:41–47, 1973.
162. Sapico, F. L., and Montgomerie, J. Z.: Pyogenic vertebral osteomyelitis: Report of nine cases and review of the literature. Rev. Infect. Dis. *1*:754–776, 1979.
163. Schauwecker, D. S.: Osteomyelitis: Diagnosis with In-111–labeled leukocytes. Radiology *171*:141–146, 1989.
164. Schechter, L. S., Smith, A., and Pearl, M.: Intervertebral disk calcification in childhood. Am. J. Dis. Child. *123*:608–611, 1972.
165. Schultz, C., Holterhus, P. M., Seidel, A., et al.: Chronic recurrent multifocal osteomyelitis in children. Pediatr. Infect. Dis. J. *18*:1008–1013, 1999.
166. Scoles, P. V., Hilty, M. D., and Sfakianakis, G. N.: Bone scan patterns in acute osteomyelitis. Clin. Orthop. *153*:210–217, 1980.
167. Selby, R. C., and Pillay, K. V.: Osteomyelitis and disc infection secondary to *Pseudomonas aeruginosa* in heroin addiction. Case report. J. Neurosurg. *37*:463–466, 1972.
168. Sfakianakis, G. N., Scoles, P., Welch, M., et al.: Evolution of bone imaging findings in osteomyelitis. J. Nucl. Med. *199*:706, 1978.
169. Smith, C. E., Beard, R. R., Whiting, E. G., et al.: Varieties of coccidioidal infection in relation to epidemiology and control of the disease. Am. J. Public Health *36*:1394–1402, 1946.
170. Smith, R. F., and Taylor, T. K.: Inflammatory lesions of intervertebral discs in children. J. Bone Joint Surg. Am. *49*:1508–1520, 1967.
171. Sorsdahl, O. A., Goodhart, G. L., Williams, H. T., et al.: Quantitative bone gallium scintigraphy in osteomyelitis. Skeletal Radiol. *22*:239–242, 1993.
172. Specht, E. E.: Hemoglobinopathic *Salmonella* osteomyelitis. Orthopedic aspects. Clin. Orthop. *79*:110–118, 1971.
173. Spiegel, P. G., Kengla, K. W., Isaacson, A. S., and Wilson, J. C., Jr.: Intervertebral disc-space inflammation in children. J. Bone Joint Surg. Am. *54*:284–296, 1972.
174. Staab, E. V., and McCartney, W. H.: Role of gallium 67 in inflammatory disease. Semin. Nucl. Med. *8*:219–234, 1978.
175. Starr, C. L.: Acute hematogenous osteomyelitis. Arch. Surg. *4*:567–587, 1922.
176. Steinbach, L. S., Tehranzadeh, J., Fleckenstein, J. L., et al.: Human immunodeficiency virus infection: Musculoskeletal manifestations. Radiology *186*:833–838, 1993.
177. Stephens, M. M., and MacAuley, P.: Brodie's abscess. A long-term review. Clin. Orthop. *234*:211–216, 1988.
178. Stevens, J.: Post-operative orthopedic infections. J. Bone Joint Surg. *46*:96, 1964.
179. Stone, D. B., and Bonfiglio, M.: Pyogenic vertebral osteomyelitis: A diagnostic pitfall for the internists. Arch. Intern. Med. *112*:491–500, 1963.
180. Swick, H. M.: Calcification of intervertebral discs in childhood. J. Pediatr. *86*:364–369, 1975.
181. Swiontkowski, M. F.: Surgical approaches in osteomyelitis. Use of laser Doppler flowmetry to determine nonviable bone. Infect. Dis. Clin. North Am. *4*:501–512, 1990.
182. Syrogiannopoulos, G. A., and Nelson, J. D.: Duration of antimicrobial therapy for acute suppurative osteoarticular infections. Lancet *1*:37–40, 1988.
183. Tang, J. S., Gold, R. H., Bassett, L. W., and Seeger, L. L.: Musculoskeletal infection of the extremities: Evaluation with MR imaging. Radiology *166*:205–209, 1988.
184. Taplin, D.: Environmental influences on the microbiology of the skin. Arch. Environ. Health *11*:546, 1968.
185. Taylor, J. C., and Fallon, R. J.: Osteomyelitis due to *Hemophilus influenzae*. Lancet *1*:715, 1966.
186. Taylor, J. R.: Growth of human intervertebral discs and vertebral bodies. J. Anat. *120*:49–68, 1975.
187. Templeton, W. C., 3rd, Wawrukiewicz, A., Melo, J. C., et al.: Anaerobic osteomyelitis of long bones. Rev. Infect. Dis. *5*:692–712, 1983.
188. Tetsworth, K., and Cierny, G., 3rd.: Osteomyelitis débridement techniques. Clin. Orthop. *360*:87–96, 1999.
189. Tetzlaff, T. R., McCracken, G. H., Jr., and Nelson, J. D.: Oral antibiotic therapy for skeletal infections of children. II. Therapy of osteomyelitis and suppurative arthritis. J. Pediatr. *92*:485–490, 1978.
190. Tilden, R. L., Jackson, J., Jr., Enneking, W. F., et al.: 99m Tc-polyphosphate: Histological localization in human femurs by autoradiography. J. Nucl. Med. *14*:576–578, 1973.
191. Torda, A. J., Gottlieb, T., and Bradbury, R.: Pyogenic vertebral osteomyelitis: Analysis of 20 cases and review. Clin. Infect. Dis. *20*:320–328, 1995.
192. Treves, S., Khettry, J., Broker, F. H., et al.: Osteomyelitis: Early scintigraphic detection in children. Pediatrics *57*:173–186, 1976.
193. Trobs, R., Moritz, R., Buhligen, U., et al.: Changing pattern of osteomyelitis in infants and children. Pediatr. Surg. Int. *15*:363–372, 1999.
194. Trueta, J.: The three types of acute hematogenous osteomyelitis. J. Bone Joint Surg. *41*:671–680, 1959.
195. Tsukayama, D. T.: Pathophysiology of posttraumatic osteomyelitis. Clin. Orthop. *360*:22–29, 1999.
196. Unger, E., Moldofsky, P., Gatenby, R., et al.: Diagnosis of osteomyelitis by MR imaging. A. J. R. Am. J. Roentgenol. *150*:605–610, 1988.
197. Unkila-Kallio, L., Kallio, M. J., Eskola, J., and Peltola, H.: Serum C-reactive protein, erythrocyte sedimentation rate, and white blood cell count in acute hematogenous osteomyelitis of children. Pediatrics *93*:59–62, 1994.
198. Unkila-Kallio, L., Kallio, M. J., and Peltola, H.: Acute haematogenous osteomyelitis in children in Finland. Finnish Study Group. Ann. Med. *25*:545–549, 1993.
199. Van Howe, R. S., Starshak, R. J., and Chusid, M. J.: Chronic, recurrent multifocal osteomyelitis. Case report and review of the literature. Clin. Pediatr. (Phila.) *28*:54–59, 1989.
200. Vaughan, P. A., Newman, N. M., and Rosman, M. A.: Acute hematogenous osteomyelitis in children. J. Pediatr. Orthop. *7*:652–655, 1987.
201. Waldvogel, F. A., and Papageorgiou, P. S.: Osteomyelitis: The past decade. N. Engl. J. Med. *303*:360–370, 1980.
202. Walker, S. H.: Staphylococcal osteomyelitis in children. Success with cephaloridine-cephalexin therapy. Clin. Pediatr. (Phila.) *12*:98–100, 1973.
203. Watson, F. M., and Whitesides, T. E., Jr.: Acute hematogenous osteomyelitis complicating closed fractures. Clin. Orthop. *203*:296–302, 1976.
204. Watson, R. J., Burko, H., Megas, H., et al.: The hand-foot syndrome in sickle cell disease in young children. Pediatrics *31*:505–509, 1963.
205. Weissberg, E. D., Smith, A. L., and Smith, D. H.: Clinical features of neonatal osteomyelitis. Pediatrics *53*:505–510, 1974.
206. Weld, P. W.: Osteomyelitis of the ileum, masquerading as acute appendicitis. J. A. M. A. *173*:634–636, 1960.
207. Widen, A. L., and Cardon, L.: *Salmonella typhimurium* osteomyelitis with sickle cell hemoglobin C disease: A review and case report. Ann. Intern. Med. *54*:510–521, 1961.
208. Wiesseman, G. J., Wood, V. E., Kroll, L. L., and Linda, L.: *Pseudomonas* vertebral osteomyelitis in heroin addicts. Report of five cases. J. Bone Joint Surg. Am. *55*:1416–1424, 1973.
209. Williamson, J. B., Galasko, C. S., and Robinson, M. J.: Outcome after acute osteomyelitis in preterm infants. Arch. Dis. Child. *65*:1060–1062, 1990.
210. Winkelstein, J. A., Marino, M. C., Johnston, R. B., Jr., et al.: Chronic granulomatous disease. Report on a national registry of 368 patients. Medicine (Baltimore) *79*:155–169, 2000.
211. Yagupsky, P., Howard, C. B., Einhorn, M., and Dagan, R.: *Kingella kingae* osteomyelitis of the calcaneus in young children. Pediatr. Infect. Dis. J. *12*:540–541, 1993.

SEPTIC ARTHRITIS

This section deals with acute infection of the joints caused by bacteria, fungi, and viruses. Bacterial infections occur most frequently. The terms *septic arthritis, acute suppurative pyarthrosis,* and *infectious arthritis* are used interchangeably with regard to bacterial infections; they refer to the presence of organisms in the joint space.

Epidemiology

Septic arthritis occurs most commonly in childhood. The overall incidence of septic arthritis in children has been estimated as 5.5 to 12 cases per 100,000 individuals.[29] Describing the age distribution of septic arthritis is difficult because of the varying age intervals selected by authors of different studies. However, in a review from the pre-antibiotic era, one half the patients were younger than 20 years of age.[40] In a later study, performed after antibiotics became available for systemic use, 31 of 66 patients (47%) also were younger than 20 years of age.[5] Males are affected more often than females by ratios of 1.2 to 2.0.[9, 48, 51, 68, 81]

Pathophysiology

Synovial joints, also termed diarthrodial joints, are freely movable articulations containing synovia. Synovia is a transparent viscous fluid that lubricates the joint and nourishes the avascular articular cartilage. The synovium, a connective tissue layer interposed between the fibrous joint capsule and the fluid-filled synovial cavity, is responsible for formation of the joint fluid. Synovium contains a prominent capillary supply embedded in a connective tissue network containing at least two types of cells. One morphologic type (type A) appears to be related to mononuclear phagocytes, whereas fibroblast-like type B cells appear to be responsible for the synthesis of hyaluronic acid. Joint fluid (synovia) is formed by filtration through the capillary network (i.e., the net balance of back-diffusion into the capillary bed and diffusion into the joint space). Diarthrodial joints normally contain small amounts of fluid (e.g., 0.5 to 3 mL in the knee),[73] with glucose and electrolyte concentrations equal to those in plasma. An oxygen partial pressure of 60 to 70 mm Hg, an albumin concentration of 10 to 20 g/L, and an IgG content of 500 mg/L are typical.[20, 22, 27, 73]

Diffusion from the joint space is increased by any mechanism that increases pressure (distention with injected solution, active or passive motion, or external massage). Particulate material is removed from the joint space by synovial membrane macrophages and free monocytes (the latter are usually present in concentrations of $<60 \times 10^6$/L).[66] The viscosity of joint fluid is due to hyaluronic acid; enzymatic depolymerization produces a viscosity approximately equivalent to that of water. With the loss of hyaluronidase from the synovia, the articular cartilage, with continued use, becomes eroded and sclerotic.[8] The vasculature of the synovial membrane is innervated, which has two consequences: joint pain is localized poorly because it results from stretching of the fibrous joint capsule, and inflammation within the joint cavity elicits an axon reflex leading to vasodilation and warmth over an infected joint. Lymphatic channels are present in all the joint tissues except cartilage; they drain to the regional lymph nodes.

Microorganisms can enter the joint space by hematogenous spread, direct inoculation, or extension of a contiguous focus of infection. The synovial membrane has been shown to have high effective blood flow, approximately equal to that of the brain (if one assumes that 1 g of synovial membrane is in an adult knee joint). Thus, a large number of bacteria in blood potentially are delivered to the synovial membrane during transient bacteremia. A history of trauma often is cited as a predisposing factor for bacterial arthritis, but the significance of such a history is unclear in view of the great frequency of minor trauma in childhood. Upper respiratory tract infections frequently precede the development of septic arthritis caused by *Haemophilus influenzae* and *Kingella kingae,* and, like traumatic injuries, they are presumed to increase the likelihood of bacteremia occurring.[9, 81] Septic arthritis also may develop after joint surgery and joint injections. Gram-negative organisms are the most frequent pathogens when septic arthritis occurs after surgery or instrumentation of the urinary or intestinal tracts. *Salmonella* septic arthritis may develop during the course of *Salmonella* bacteremia in a normal host, but it occurs with increased frequency in patients with sickle-cell disease and related hemoglobinopathies. Although septic arthritis occurs in children and adults infected with human immunodeficiency virus (HIV),[50] as yet no data have substantiated that HIV increases the incidence of musculoskeletal infections in children. Septic arthritis has been described during varicella, presumably caused by bacteremia resulting from infection of skin lesions. It must be differentiated from the apparent ability of varicella-zoster virus to cause joint inflammation on its own.[53, 65] Arthritis also occurs during acute infection with other viruses (e.g., variola, Epstein-Barr virus, Erythrovirus [parvovirus] B19, mumps, measles, and enteroviruses).

Inoculation arthritis occurs after invasion of the joint by a contaminated object. In one series, 5 of 35 cases of septic arthritis were caused by such a mechanism. Not surprisingly, a predilection for the knee exists; four of five cases cited in this study were secondary to kneeling on sewing needles.[68]

Aside from joint involvement during osteomyelitis, contiguous extension of an infection into the joint space rarely occurs. In one series, 10 of 77 patients with septic arthritis had disease originating from a contiguous focus.[16] None of them involved the joints of the foot, and eight occurred before the availability of many antibiotics (1951). This surprisingly high frequency of septic arthritis caused by spread of infection from a contiguous focus has not been seen in more recent studies.

Etiology

Staphylococcus aureus is the most common agent causing septic arthritis. Streptococci (especially group A beta-hemolytic organisms and pneumococci) have been responsible for most other gram-positive infections (Table 62–4). *Haemophilus influenzae* type b (Hib) historically has been an important cause of septic arthritis in children younger than 2 years of age but now is seen only rarely in areas with widespread immunization.[12, 36, 48, 70] Arthritis caused by *Streptococcus pneumoniae* also generally occurs in these younger children and may diminish in frequency with broader use of protein conjugate vaccines. *K. kingae* has been recognized increasingly as a cause of septic arthritis,[23, 48, 52, 81] perhaps because of improvements in laboratory methods.[82] In one series from Israel, *Kingella* was the most common bacterial isolate (48% of cases), and *S. aureus* was not found.[81] In a small number of cases, septic arthritis is seen with acute *Neisseria meningitidis* infection. In newborns and sexually active adolescents with suspected septic arthritis, *Neisseria gonorrhoeae* should be considered.[31, 45, 46]

Salmonella spp. cause approximately 1 percent of the total cases of septic arthritis. Beyond the newborn period, infections with other enteric gram-negative bacteria are rare events in pediatric septic arthritis and often are associated with inoculation, instrumentation, or an

TABLE 62–4 ■ BACTERIAL ETIOLOGY OF SEPTIC ARTHRITIS IN CHILDREN

	Gram-Positive Bacteria				Gram-Negative Bacteria							
Year of Report	*Staphylococcus aureus*	Streptococci	*Streptococcus pneumoniae*	CNS	*Haemophilus influenzae*	*Kingella kingae*	*Neisseria meningitidis*	*Salmonella*	Non-*Salmonella Enterobacteriaceae*	*Neisseria gonorrhoeae*	**Other**	**Total Cases**
1941[40]	50	45	2	10	0	0	0	0	0	14	0	121
1958[68]	18	8	5	2	3	0	0	0	2	0	1	38*
1972[55]	40	20	8	5	37	0	4	2	7	13	11	146*
1975[51]	37	10	0	5	14	0	0	0	2	0	7	75
1987[9]	40	8	5	0	20	0	4	0	2	2	9	90
1995[81]	0	2	3	0	8	19	1	1	1	0	5	40
1999[48]	10	5	2	2	1	3	3	0	4	2	1	33
Total	195	98	25	24	83	22	12	3	18	31	34	543
Percentage of all isolates	36%	18%	5%	4%	15%	4%	2%	1%	3%	6%	6%	

*Two isolates in one case each.
CNS, coagulase-negative staphylococci.

immunocompromised state.[31] Infections with *Serratia, Aeromonas, Enterobacter, Bacteroides,* and *Campylobacter* generally occur in patients with malignancy who are immunosuppressed.[1, 5, 17, 31, 49, 55, 59] *Pseudomonas aeruginosa* infections are associated with arthritis in infants, with infection of puncture wounds, or with injectable drug use.[51, 55, 75] Other rare bacterial causes of septic arthritis include *Propionibacterium acnes,*[83] *Corynebacterium pyogenes,*[59] and *Pasteurella multocida.*[34] *Streptobacillus moniliformis* infection of joints may become evident 2 to 3 days after a rat bite; a macular rash commonly is present at initial evaluation. Discussion of Lyme arthritis is beyond the scope of this chapter, but intermittent, inflammatory arthritis is seen in many patients after *Borrelia burgdorferi* is transmitted by a tick bite.[44, 72] *Brucella* and mycobacteria (*Mycobacterium tuberculosis* and "atypical" species), as well as *Nocardia asteroides,* may cause a chronic monarticular arthritis with a granulomatous reaction.

Diagnosis

CLINICAL FINDINGS

Almost all patients have fever and constitutional symptoms within the first few days of infection with the most common bacterial pathogens.[28] The frequency of specific joint involvement in hematogenous septic arthritis of childhood is indicated in Table 62–5. Lower extremity (knee, hip, and ankle) infections consistently account for approximately 80 percent of all cases.[40, 51, 55, 68] Focal findings in the joint involved almost always are present. In infants, in whom the hip is one of the most frequent joints involved, swelling, tenderness, and heat may be absent. Most commonly, the infant lies with the involved leg abducted and externally rotated. Often, dislocation occurs.[57] When the capsule of the joint can be examined, swelling is noted; effusion was present in 22 of 24 cases in one series.[78] Because pain fibers are located in the capsule, any maneuver that increases intracapsular pressure also produces pain. In the hip, this pain can be elicited by compression of the head of the femur into the acetabulum. A portal of entry almost never is apparent, and bilateral hip joint infection occurs in a small number of cases.[61] Pyogenic sacroiliitis often is accompanied by tenderness detected by pressure applied over the sacrum during a digital rectal examination and by pain experienced during simultaneous flexion, abduction, and external rotation at the hip.[2]

Gonococcal arthritis in newborns has nonspecific prodromal symptoms: poor feeding, irritability, and fever. The portal of entry is unknown, and the joints below the hip usually are involved (knee, ankle, and metatarsal). During adolescence, gonococcal arthritis occurs as a manifestation of sepsis with fever, chills, rash, and multiple small joint involvement, often with tenosynovitis.[26] The illness frequently follows the onset of menses by a few days.

RADIOLOGIC FINDINGS

Findings on plain-film radiographs are due to capsular swelling. In the joints readily accessible to physical examination, radiographs add little to the diagnostic evaluation, but when septic arthritis of the hip is suspected in a child, they are a valuable adjunct and may identify other causes of hip pain such as Legg-Calvé-Perthes disease, slipped capital femoral epiphysis, and fracture. Films of the hip should be made with the child in the "frog leg position," as well as with the legs extended at the knee and slightly internally rotated. The early signs of septic arthritis are caused by swelling of the capsule, which displaces the fat lines. One of the oldest signs is the obturator sign: as the tendon of the obturator internus passes over the capsule of the hip joint, the margins of this muscle are displaced medially into the pelvis[41] (Fig. 62–8). With continued swelling of the hip joint capsule, the femoral head is displaced laterally and upward.[18] One of the most consistent findings is obliteration or lateral displacement of the gluteal fat lines[80] (see Fig. 62–8). Coincident with filling of the capsule with exudate, the femoral portion of the Shenton line is raised and its arc is widened.[80] If a technetium bone scan is performed, increased uptake on either side of the joint is seen during the "blood pool" phase of the scan.[77] Ultrasound evaluation has proved useful in evaluation of septic arthritis of the hip.[43, 84] In a series of 96 patients, none of the 40 patients with normal sonographic findings had septic arthritis.[84] Bacterial infections causing pyogenic sacroiliitis may be particularly difficult to diagnose; CT appears to be the diagnostic radiologic method of choice.[2]

LABORATORY EVALUATION

Diagnostic evaluation for suspected septic arthritis generally includes determination of the erythrocyte sedimentation rate (or C-reactive protein) and the peripheral blood leukocyte count and differential. However, they may be only mildly elevated in cases of proven infection.[24, 84] Blood for culture always should be obtained because blood cultures sometimes may yield the pathogen when joint fluid cultures do not.

Joint fluid should be collected in a heparinized syringe so that the large clot that usually forms in fluid obtained from patients with septic arthritis or juvenile rheumatoid arthritis does not preclude enumeration of leukocytes. Fluid aspirated from joint fluid should have a cell and differential count performed, and it must be Gram-stained and cultured. Identification of organisms in joint fluid is the primary

TABLE 62–5 ■ JOINTS INVOLVED IN SEPTIC ARTHRITIS OF CHILDREN

Reference	Knee	Hip	Ankle	Wrist	Elbow	Shoulder	Small Diathrodial Joints
40	40	50	13	3	8	9	2
79	8	13	2	6	9	2	3
68	8	19	2	0	6	3	0
55	103	48	38	12	35	10	4
28	37	41	13	2	3	3	0
81	16	6	13	1	2	3	1
Total	212	177	81	23	63	30	10
Percentage of all cases	36%	30%	14%	4%	11%	5%	2%

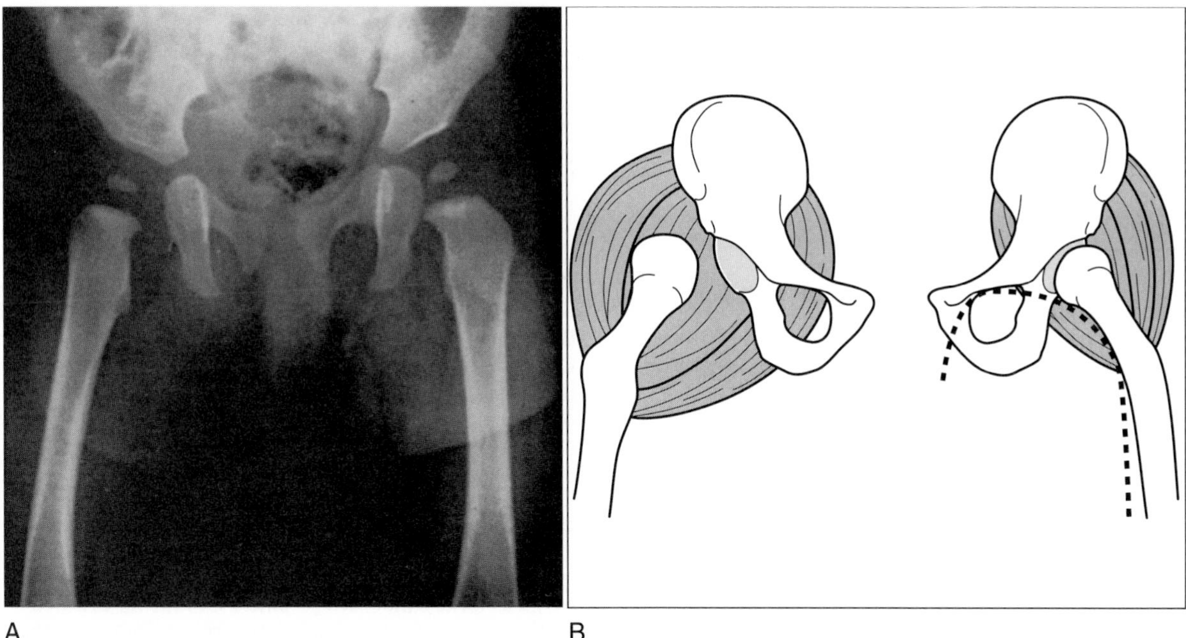

FIGURE 62–8 ■ The obturator sign in the hip is one of the oldest signs of septic arthritis. Another consistent finding is obliteration or lateral displacement of the gluteal fat lines and loss of continuity of the Shenton line. These findings are illustrated radiographically *(A)* and schematically *(B)*.

criterion for diagnosis of septic arthritis. The need to carefully examine a Gram-stained smear of joint fluid aspirates must be emphasized because joint fluid exerts a bacteriostatic effect on microorganisms and organisms that can be seen but may not grow in culture. Approximately 35 percent of joint aspirates are sterile in patients with other clinical and laboratory findings of a septic joint, including positive blood cultures.[9, 55] Joint fluid should be cultured both aerobically and under anaerobic conditions. The use of cell lysis culture bottles may enhance the recovery of *K. kingae* and other organisms.[82] *N. gonorrhoeae* is a highly fastidious organism, and oropharyngeal, rectal, and urogenital cultures or detection of gonococcal DNA in urine may be needed to confirm the diagnosis of gonococcal arthritis.

The median synovial fluid leukocyte count in bacterial arthritis in one study was 60.5 x 10^9 cells/L.[71] In this and other surveys,[66] polymorphonuclear leukocytes accounted for 75 to 90 percent of the white blood cells. Cell density generally is lower in fluid obtained from patients with acute rheumatic fever, juvenile rheumatoid arthritis, and other inflammatory causes of arthritis[7, 66, 71] (Table 62–6). The glucose concentration often is decreased in septic arthritis, but it may be normal.[71, 78] It also may be depressed in rheumatoid arthritis and other conditions. One should remember that a joint fluid leukocyte density of 5 to 8 x 10^9 cells/L has been found in joint fluid from patients ultimately proved to have septic arthritis.[66] Thus, minimally turbid fluid with a seemingly low number of cells still should be processed for bacterial culture and Gram stain. Examination of the fluid for uric acid and other types of crystals should be considered in certain children (e.g., those with hyperuricemia).

DIFFERENTIAL DIAGNOSIS

Although bacterial infections are the most common cause of septic arthritis, other microorganisms, including viruses (varicella-zoster, Erythrovirus [parvovirus] B19, rubella, togaviruses, variola, vaccinia, certain enteroviruses, others), mycobacteria, and fungi (*Coccidioides immitis, Sporothrix schenckii, Blastomyces dermatitidis, Candida* spp.), may be involved. The differential diagnosis includes obturator internus muscle abscess,[76] epiphyseal osteomyelitis, traumatic arthritis, bacterial endocarditis, villonodular synovitis, leukemia, deep cellulitis, serum sickness, ulcerative colitis, granulomatous colitis, Schönlein-Henoch purpura, traumatic arthritis, fracture, Legg-Calvé-Perthes disease, slipped femoral capital epiphysis, and metabolic diseases affecting joints (e.g., ochronosis in adults with alkaptonuria). Toxic synovitis (also referred to as irritable hip, reactive synovitis, and transient synovitis) frequently is seen in children. Nearly all patients are afebrile and have a normal erythrocyte sedimentation rate at the time of evaluation.[24, 84] Septic (suppurative) bursitis, though a rare event

TABLE 62–6 ■ JOINT FLUID FINDINGS IN CHILDHOOD ARTHRITIDES

Diagnosis	Spontaneous Clotting	Mucin Clot	Leukocytes Cells/mL	% PMN	Glucose as Percentage of Blood Value
Septic arthritis	Rapid formation of large clot	Curdled milk	73,000	90	30
Rheumatic fever	Small to absent	Tightrope	18,000	60	75
Juvenile rheumatoid arthritis	Large clot	Small, friable masses	15,000	60	75

PMN, polymorphonuclear leukocytes.
From Ropes, M.: Joint fluid findings in disease. Bull. Rheum. Dis. 7(Suppl.): 21, 1957.

in childhood, can be difficult to distinguish from septic arthritis. Children with septic bursitis frequently have a history of recent trauma and fever along with limitation of joint movement.[39, 62] Careful physical examination and aspiration of bursal fluid allow the entities to be differentiated.

Treatment

ANTIBIOTIC THERAPY

Antibiotic treatment of septic arthritis should target the most common pathogens. In children beyond the neonatal period, *S. aureus* and other gram-positive organisms currently predominate.[12, 48, 55] Although the risk of acquiring invasive *H. influenzae* infection is low in areas with effective immunization, cases continue to be reported. Children younger than 2 years of age who have not been immunized against Hib should be treated initially with a regimen that contains a penicillinase-resistant penicillin (such as nafcillin) and an agent active against this organism (such as cefotaxime). Cefuroxime, which is active against *S. aureus* (and other gram-positive pathogens) and *H. influenzae*, is a useful alternative. As with osteomyelitis, vancomycin or clindamycin should be included in the empiric treatment regimen in areas where community-acquired, methicillin-resistant *S. aureus* is a concern. At present, no regimen is preferred for the treatment of penicillin-nonsusceptible *S. pneumoniae*, but ceftriaxone, cefotaxime, and clindamycin have been used successfully.[13] If the β-lactam resistance continues to increase in *S. pneumoniae* and *S. aureus*, other regimens that target highly resistant gram-positive organisms may be needed. Ceftriaxone and cefotaxime are appropriate for the treatment of gonococcal infection.

All antibiotics that have been studied penetrate into joint fluid readily; soon after administration, at the time of peak serum levels, the joint fluid concentration averages 30 percent of the serum value.[4, 6, 54, 64] However, the efflux of antibiotic from joint fluid back to serum is slow. Immediately before the next systemic dose is administered, joint fluid antibiotic concentrations frequently exceed those present in serum. Thus, antibiotics, whether administered orally or parenterally, can achieve efficacious concentrations in joint fluid.

Injecting antibiotics into the joint space usually is unnecessary because of their excellent penetration. Moreover, many antibiotics (such as cephalothin) are capable of evoking an intense inflammatory reaction, much as they do if they are infiltrated beneath the skin. Tetzlaff and associates[74] have demonstrated that septic arthritis can be treated for 1 week (or less) parenterally, with the balance of the drug given orally. These investigators caution that the drug dosage should be adjusted for each patient to ensure a peak serum bactericidal titer of at least 1 : 8 and that the patient should remain hospitalized so that compliance can be ensured. They considered the minimal duration of therapy to be 3 weeks.

The adequacy of antibiotic therapy can be assessed by serial joint fluid examinations, leukocyte density, and culture results.[78] Not surprisingly, the time required for resolution of joint symptoms and the time for the synovia to become sterile are proportional to the duration of symptoms before the initiation of appropriate antibiotic therapy.[42] In one study, some patients still had cultures yielding bacteria after undergoing a week of therapy. In these patients, cellular density ranged from 25 to 253 $\times$ 10^9 cells/L (mean, 109 $\times$ 10^9 cells/L) at the beginning of therapy; 92 percent of the cells were polymorphonuclear leukocytes. By the end of 2 weeks of therapy, all cultures were sterile and leukocyte density ranged from 4.9 to 23 $\times$ 10^9 cells/L, with a mean of 12.3.[78] Similar studies of the rate of resolution of indicators of inflammation in joint fluid have suggested that after receiving 9 days of treatment, patients who ultimately recovered completely had a density of 5 $\times$ 10^9 cells/L; however, in those with recrudescent infection or a poor outcome, the density was 6 $\times$ 10^{10} cells/L.[31] When an effusion re-accumulates, one should remove it by arthrocentesis, not only to make the patient more comfortable but also to permit serial assessment of therapy. In general, disease caused by *S. aureus* and Enterobacteriaceae requires longer treatment than does that caused by *H. influenzae* or meningococci. Radiographs should be obtained during therapy to seek bone changes indicating that osteomyelitis may have been present. Osteomyelitis may require surgical intervention or more prolonged antibiotic therapy.

SURGICAL TREATMENT

In infants, septic arthritis in the hips or shoulders is a surgical emergency; these joints should be drained as soon as the diagnosis is apparent to prevent bony destruction.[61] In a study in adults, the outcome of septic arthritis was better in patients treated by repeated needle aspiration than in those treated by surgical drainage.[32, 33] Eighty percent of the patients treated by needle aspiration were thought to have a good outcome versus 47 percent treated by surgical drainage. All wrist joint infections in this series were treated only by needle aspiration; in treatment of septic arthritis of the knee, however, the outcome was almost equivalent. Similar findings have been reported by others.[10] The investigators suggested that surgical drainage should be performed in any joint whenever the presence of large amounts of fibrin, tissue debris, or loculation prevents adequate drainage by needle aspiration.

Prognosis

Sequelae, including hip dislocation, are more likely to develop in infants and those with longer durations of symptoms.[78, 79] In one study, seven of eight patients in whom "permanent" hip dislocation developed had symptoms for 7 or more days before receiving treatment.[79] Similarly, all patients with spontaneous ankylosis had symptoms longer than 7 days.[79] Comparable data were obtained by Samilson and colleagues.[68] Eight of 10 patients with pathologic dislocation of the hip had symptoms for longer than 7 days. A detailed analysis of factors affecting satisfactory outcomes in hematogenous septic arthritis of childhood showed no significant difference in the joint when arthrotomy, with or without irrigation, was compared with repeated aspiration.[51] Likewise, the specific antibiotic used had no effect on outcome as long as it was effective against the infecting organism. The literature does suggest that septic arthritis caused by Enterobacteriaceae is associated with more frequent sequelae than when cause by other pathogens.[33, 56] *S. aureus* is more likely to cause sequelae than is *H. influenzae*.[9]

Special Problems

NEONATAL SEPTIC ARTHRITIS

Neonatal septic arthritis is a problem that deserves special attention because of its subtle signs and symptoms,[19] its potential for catastrophic consequences of untreated disease,[60] and the unusual organisms occasionally seen.

Any newborn who has swelling in the region of the thigh and the buttock and holds that leg flexed with slight abduction and external rotation at the hip should be suspected of having femoral-acetabular septic arthritis. It can occur from 1 to 28 days after femoral venipuncture (in most newborns, 5 to 9 days) and should not be confused with femoral vein thrombosis.[3, 15] In most newborns, no toxemia, fever, or leukocytosis is present. More than one joint may be involved when initially evaluated. The progression of disease in newborns can be so indolent that the hip spontaneously drains along the obturator internus and the condition is manifested as a lower abdominal mass just above the inguinal canal.[25] Problems in recognizing the disease in newborn infants undoubtedly contribute to the poor outcome. In one series, the delay from onset to diagnosis was an average of 1 week; only two of the nine infants in this series had a normal hip examination at follow-up.[60]

In most series, the causative agents are staphylococci and streptococci,[3, 11, 15, 19, 60] but gram-negative organisms often are found. More importantly, arthritis caused by *Candida albicans* has been described,[21] and the gonococcus should not be forgotten. In gonococcal arthritis, the symptoms, which usually become apparent between 1 and 5 weeks of age, generally are polyarthritic (more than one joint involved).[30] As previously noted, other symptoms of neonatal gonococcal arthritis are no different from those caused by other pathogens.

Initial antibiotic therapy for neonatal septic arthritis should be directed toward *S. aureus* and the nosocomial gram-negative bacteria that are prevalent in the nursery. Antibiotic therapy can be altered when the susceptibility of the causative bacterium is known. As noted earlier, the usual duration of therapy is 3 to 4 weeks, and radiography should be performed toward the end of treatment. Oral therapy has been used successfully to complete treatment of septic arthritis in the newborn,[63] but absorption of antibiotics in this age range is unpredictable.[69] Consequently, either intravenous therapy or measurement of serum bactericidal activity should be used to verify absorption.[74]

FUNGAL ARTHRITIS

Fungal arthritis is a rare occurrence in children but may be seen with pathogens of endemic mycoses such as *Histoplasma capsulatum, C. immitis*, and *B. dermatitidis* and with opportunistic fungal pathogens (*Candida* spp., *Cryptococcus neoformans*, and others).[48, 55] These pathogens usually manifest after an indolent course.

JOINT INFECTIONS DURING RHEUMATOID ARTHRITIS

Joint infections that occur during a case of rheumatoid arthritis appear to occur more frequently in adults with rheumatoid arthritis than in children. In one series, only 2 of 17 patients were younger than 10 years.[5] Its notable features are that the hips generally are not involved and infection of multiple joints (17 of 44 patients had more than one joint involved) frequently occurs. Because of the preexisting joint disease, the diagnosis often is delayed and the outcome usually is poor. Septic arthritis should be considered if an unusual worsening of one joint occurs during a flare-up of rheumatoid arthritis.

REACTIVE ARTHRITIS

After infections with *Shigella*,[14, 58] *Chlamydia trachomatis, Salmonella*,[38] and *Yersinia* spp., a reactive arthritis can occur.[47] This postinfectious joint inflammation appears to develop with greater frequency in individuals who are carriers of the histocompatibility antigen HLA-B27, perhaps as a result of molecular similarities between bacterial antigens and the human protein. In addition, during the initial infection, bacterial antigens apparently may be deposited in the synovium and may persist for a long period and lead to pathogenic inflammation.[35, 47] In general, the onset of joint symptoms takes place a few days to several weeks after a transient and often mild episode of diarrhea. The arthritis may mimic rheumatic fever and is characterized by daily low-grade fever and an increased erythrocyte sedimentation rate. Reactive arthritis generally can be distinguished from septic arthritis by analysis of synovial fluid; infectious arthritis usually is associated with high white blood cell fluid numbers.[7] Resolution of joint symptoms in reactive cases takes 7 to 10 days.

Similarly, reactive arthritis also may occur after acute infections with *N. meningitidis*[37] and *H. influenzae*.[67] Symptoms and signs of joint inflammation often appear a week or more after the acute septic episode and resolve without sequelae.

REFERENCES

1. Ament, M. E., and Gaal, S. A.: *Bacteroides* arthritis. Am. J. Dis. Child. *114*:427–428, 1967.
2. Aprin, H., and Turen, C.: Pyogenic sacroiliitis in children. Clin. Orthop. *287*:98–106, 1993.
3. Asnes, R. S., and Arendar, G. M.: Septic arthritis of the hip: A complication of femoral venipuncture. Pediatrics *38*:837–841, 1966.
4. Baciocco, E. A., and Iles, R. L.: Ampicillin and kanamycin concentrations in joint fluid. Clin. Pharmacol. Ther. *12*:858–863, 1971.
5. Baitch, A.: Recent observations of acute suppurative arthritis. Clin. Orthop. *22*:153–165, 1962.
6. Balboni, V., Shapiro, I. M., and Kydd, D. M.: The penetration of penicillin into joint fluid following intramuscular administration. Am. J. Med. Sci. *210*:588–591, 1945.
7. Baldassare, A. R., Chang, F., and Zuckner, J.: Markedly raised synovial fluid leucocyte counts not associated with infectious arthritis in children. Ann. Rheum. Dis. *37*:404–409, 1978.
8. Barnett, C., Davies, D. V., and MacConcill, M. A.: Synovial Joints. Springfield, IL, Charles C. Thomas, 1961.
9. Barton, L. L., Dunkle, L. M., and Habib, F. H.: Septic arthritis in childhood. A 13-year review. Am. J. Dis. Child. *141*:898–900, 1987.
10. Betz, R. R., Cooperman, D. R., Wopperer, J. M., et al.: Late sequelae of septic arthritis of the hip in infancy and childhood. J. Pediatr. Orthop. *10*:365–372, 1990.
11. Bodganovitich, A.: Neonatal arthritis due to *Proteus vulgaris*. Arch. Dis. Child. *23*:65–66, 1948.
12. Bowerman, S. G., Green, N. E., and Mencio, G. A.: Decline of bone and joint infections attributable to *Haemophilus influenzae* type b. Clin. Orthop. *341*:128–133, 1997.
13. Bradley, J. S., Kaplan, S. L., Tan, T. Q., et al.: Pediatric pneumococcal bone and joint infections. The Pediatric Multicenter Pneumococcal Surveillance Study Group (PMPSSG). Pediatrics *102*:1376–1382, 1998.
14. Calin, A., and Fries, J. F.: An "experimental" epidemic of Reiter's syndrome revisited. Follow-up evidence on genetic and environmental factors. Ann. Intern. Med. *84*:564–566, 1976.
15. Chacha, P. B.: Suppurative arthritis of the hip joint in infancy. A persistent diagnostic problem and possible complication of femoral venipuncture. J. Bone Joint Surg. Am. *53*:538–544, 1971.
16. Chartier, Y., Martin, W. J., and Kelly, P. J.: Bacterial arthritis: Experiences in the treatment of 77 patients. Ann. Intern. Med. *50*:1462–1472, 1959.
17. Chmel, H., and Armstrong, D.: Acute arthritis caused by *Aeromonas hydrophilia:* Clinical and therapeutic aspects. Arthritis Rheum. *19*:169–172, 1976.
18. Chont, L.: Roentgen sign of early suppurative arthritis of the hip in infancy. Radiology *38*:708–714, 1942.
19. Chung, S. M., and Pollis, R. E.: Diagnostic pitfalls in septic arthritis of the hip in infants and children. Clin. Pediatr. (Phila.) *14*:758–761, 1975.
20. Curtiss, P.: Joint infections: Pathophysiology. Clin. Orthop. *96*:129, 1973.

21. Dan, M.: Septic arthritis in young infants: Clinical and microbiologic correlations and therapeutic implications. Rev. Infect. Dis. *6*:147–155, 1984.
22. Daniel, D., Akeson, W., Amiel, D., et al.: Lavage of septic joints in rabbits: Effects of chondrolysis. J. Bone Joint Surg. Am. *58*:393–395, 1976.
23. de Groot, R., Glover, D., Clausen, C., et al.: Bone and joint infections caused by *Kingella kingae:* Six cases and review of literature. Rev. Infect. Dis. *10*:998–1004, 1988.
24. Del Beccaro, M. A., Champoux, A. N., Bockers, T., et al.: Septic arthritis versus transient synovitis of the hip: The value of screening laboratory tests. Ann. Emerg. Med. *21*:1418–1422, 1992.
25. Freiberg, J. A., and Perlman, R.: Pelvic abscesses associated with acute purulent infection of the hip joint. J. Bone Joint Surg. *18*:417–427, 1936.
26. Garcia-Kutzbach, A., and Masi, A. T.: Acute infectious agent arthritis (IAA): A detailed comparison of proved gonococcal and other blood-borne bacterial arthritis. J. Rheumatol. *1*:93–101, 1974.
27. Gardner, E. D.: Physiology of joints. J. Bone Joint Surg. *45*:152–159, 1963.
28. Gillespie, R.: Septic arthritis of childhood. Clin. Orthop. *96*:152–159, 1973.
29. Gillespie, W. J.: Epidemiology in bone and joint infection. Infect. Dis. Clin. North Am. *4*:361–376, 1990.
30. Glaser, S., Boxerbaum, B., and Kennell, J. H.: Gonococcal arthritis in the newborn. Report of a case and review of the literature. Am. J. Dis. Child. *112*:185–188, 1966.
31. Goldenberg, D. L., Brandt, K. D., Cathcart, E. S., and Cohen, A. S.: Acute arthritis caused by gram-negative bacilli: A clinical characterization. Medicine (Baltimore) *53*:197–208, 1974.
32. Goldenberg, D. L., Brandt, K. D., Cohen, A. S., and Cathcart, E. S.: Treatment of septic arthritis: Comparison of needle aspiration and surgery as initial modes of joint drainage. Arthritis Rheum. *18*:83–90, 1975.
33. Goldenberg, D. L., and Cohen, A. S.: Acute infectious arthritis. A review of patients with nongonococcal joint infections (with emphasis on therapy and prognosis). Am. J. Med. *60*:369–377, 1976.
34. Gomez, R., Shah, M., Gorevic, P., et al.: *Pasteurella multocida* arthritis: Case report. J. Bone Joint Surg. Am. *62*:1212–1213, 1980.
35. Granfors, K., Jalkanen, S., von Essen, R., et al.: *Yersinia* antigens in synovial-fluid cells from patients with reactive arthritis. N. Engl. J. Med. *320*:216–221, 1989.
36. Granoff, D. M., Sargent, E., and Jolivette, D.: *Haemophilus influenzae* type b osteomyelitis. Am. J. Dis. Child. *132*:488–490, 1978.
37. Greenwood, B. M., Whittle, H. C., and Bryceson, A. D.: Allergic complications of meningococcal disease. II. Immunological investigations. B. M. J. *2*:737–740, 1973.
38. Hakansson, U., Low, B., Eitrem, R., and Winblad, S.: HLA-B27 and reactive arthritis in an outbreak of salmonellosis. Tissue Antigens *6*:366–367, 1975.
39. Harwell, J. I., and Fisher, D.: Pediatric septic bursitis: Case report of retrocalcaneal infection and review of the literature. Clin. Infect. Dis. *32*:E102–E104, 2001.
40. Heberling, J. A.: A review of two hundred and one cases of suppurative arthritis. J. Bone Joint Surg. *23*:917–921, 1941.
41. Hefke, H. W, and Turner, V. C.: The obturator sign as the earliest roentgenographic sign in the diagnosis of septic arthritis and tuberculosis of the hip. J. Bone Joint Surg. *24*:857–869, 1942.
42. Ho, G., Jr., and Su, E. Y.: Therapy for septic arthritis. J. A. M. A. *247*:797–800, 1982.
43. Jamillo, D., Treves, S. T., Kasser, J. R., et al.: Osteomyelitis and septic arthritis in children: Appropriate use of imaging to guide treatment. A. J. R. Am. J. Roentgenol. *165*:339–403, 1995.
44. Kalishm, R.: Lyme disease. Rheum. Dis. Clin. North Am. *19*:399–426, 1993.
45. Kleiman, M. B., and Lamb, G. A.: Gonococcal arthritis in a newborn infant. Pediatrics *52*:285–287, 1973.
46. Kohen, D. P.: Neonatal gonococcal arthritis: Three cases and review of the literature. Pediatrics *53*:436–440, 1974.
47. Koopman, W. J.: Host factors in the pathogenesis of arthritis triggered by infectious organisms. Overview. Rheum. Dis. Clin. North Am. *19*:279–292, 1993.
48. Luhmann, J. D., and Luhmann, S. J.: Etiology of septic arthritis in children: An update for the 1990s. Pediatr. Emerg. Care *15*:40–42, 1999.
49. Martin, C. M., Merrill, R. H., and Barrett, O., Jr.: Arthritis due to *Serratia*. J. Bone Joint Surg. Am. *52*:1450–1452, 1970.
50. Merchan, E. C., Magallon, M., Manso, F., and Martin-Villar, J.: Septic arthritis in HIV positive haemophiliacs. Four cases and a literature review. Int. Orthop. *16*:302–306, 1992.
51. Morrey, B. F., Bianco, A. J., Jr., and Rhodes, K. H.: Septic arthritis in children. Orthop. Clin. North Am. *6*:923–934, 1975.
52. Morrison, V. A., and Wagner, K. F.: Clinical manifestations of *Kingella kingae* infections: Case report and review. Rev. Infect. Dis. *11*:776–782, 1989.
53. Mulhern, L. M., Friday, G. A., and Perri, J. A.: Arthritis complicating varicella infection. Pediatrics *48*:827–829, 1971.
54. Nelson, J. D.: Antibiotic concentrations in septic joint effusions. N. Engl. J. Med. *284*:349–353, 1971.
55. Nelson, J. D.: The bacterial etiology and antibiotic management of septic arthritis in infants and children. Pediatrics *50*:437–440, 1972.
56. Newman, J. H.: Review of septic arthritis throughout the antibiotic era. Ann. Rheum. Dis. *35*:198–205, 1976.
57. Nicholson, J.: Pyogenic arthritis with pathologic dislocation of the hip in infants. J. A. M. A. 141, 1949.
58. Noer, H. R.: An "experimental" epidemic of Reiter's syndrome. J. A. M. A. *198*:693–698, 1966.
59. Norenberg, D. D., Bigley, D. V., Virata, R. L., and Liang, G. C.: *Corynebacterium pyogenes* septic arthritis with plasma cell synovial infiltrate and monoclonal gammopathy. Arch. Intern. Med. *138*:810–811, 1978.
60. Obletz, B.: Acute suppurative arthritis of the hip in the neonatal period. J. Bone Joint Surg. Am. *42*:23–30, 1960.
61. Obletz, B.: Suppurative arthritis of the hip joint in infants. Clin. Orthop. *22*:27–33, 1962.
62. Paisley, J. W.: Septic bursitis in childhood. J. Pediatr. Orthop. *2*:57–61, 1982.
63. Perkins, M. D., Edwards, K. M., Heller, R M., and Green, N. E.: Neonatal group B streptococcal osteomyelitis and suppurative arthritis. Outpatient therapy. Clin. Pediatr. (Phila.) *28*:229–230, 1989.
64. Plott, M. A., and Roth, H.: Penetration of clindamycin into synovial fluid. Clin. Pharmacol. Ther. *11*:577–580, 1970.
65. Priest, J. R., Urick, J. J., Groth, K. E., and Balfour, H. H., Jr.: Varicella arthritis documented by isolation of virus from joint fluid. J. Pediatr. *93*:990–992, 1978.
66. Ropes, M.: Joint fluid findings in disease. Bull. Rheum. Dis. *7*(Suppl.):21, 1957.
67. Rush, P. J., Shore, A., Inman, R., Gold, R., et al.: Arthritis associated with *Haemophilus influenzae* meningitis: Septic or reactive? J. Pediatr. *109*:412–415, 1986.
68. Samilson, R. L., Bersani, F. A., and Watkins, M. B.: Acute suppurative arthritis in infants and children: The importance of early diagnosis and surgical drainage. Pediatrics *21*:798–803, 1958.
69. Schwartz, G. J., Hegyi, T., and Spitzer, A.: Subtherapeutic dicloxacillin levels in a neonate: Possible mechanisms. J. Pediatr. *89*:310–312, 1976.
70. Schwartz, R. H., and Reing, C. M.: Acute hematogenous osteomyelitis secondary to *Haemophilus influenzae.* J. Pediatr. Orthop. *1*:385–389, 1981.
71. Shmerling, R. H., Delbanco, T. L., Tosteson, A. N., and Trentham, D. E.: Synovial fluid tests. What should be ordered? J. A. M. A. *264*:1009–1014, 1990.
72. Steere, A. C.: Lyme disease. N. Engl. J. Med. *345*:115–125, 2001.
73. Stravino, V. D.: The synovial system. Am. J. Phys. Med. *51*:312–320, 1972.
74. Tetzlaff, T. R., McCracken, G. H., Jr., and Nelson, J. D.: Oral antibiotic therapy for skeletal infections of children. II. Therapy of osteomyelitis and suppurative arthritis. J. Pediatr. *92*:485–490, 1978.
75. Tindel, J. R., and Crowder, J. G.: Septic arthritis due to *Pseudomonas aeruginosa.* J. A. M. A. *218*:559–561, 1971.
76. Viani, R. M., Bromberg, K., and Bradley, J. S.: Obturator internus muscle abscess in children: Report of seven cases and review. Clin. Infect. Dis. *28*:117–122, 1999.
77. Volberg, F. M., Sumner, T. E., Abramson, J. S., and Winchester, P. H.: Unreliability of radiographic diagnosis of septic hip in children. Pediatrics *74*:118–120, 1984.
78. Ward, J., Cohen, A. S., and Bauer, W.: The diagnosis and therapy of acute suppurative arthritis. Arthritis Rheum. *3*:522–525, 1960.
79. Watkins, M. B., Similson, R. L., and Winter, D. M.: Acute suppurative arthritis. J. Bone Joint Surg. Am. *38*:1313–1320, 1956.
80. White, H.: Roentgen findings of acute infectious disease of the hip in infants and children. Clin. Orthop. *2*:34–42, 1962.
81. Yagupsky, P., Bar-Ziv, Y., Howard, C. B., and Dagan, R.: Epidemiology, etiology, and clinical features of septic arthritis in children younger than 24 months. Arch. Pediatr. Adolesc. Med. *149*:537–540, 1995.
82. Yagupsky, P., and Press, J.: Use of the isolator 1.5 microbial tube for culture of synovial fluid from patients with septic arthritis. J. Clin. Microbiol. *35*:2410–2412, 1997.
83. Yocum, R. C., McArthur, J., Petty, B. G., et al.: Septic arthritis caused by *Propionibacterium acnes.* J. A. M. A. *248*:1740–1741, 1982.
84. Zawin, J. K., Hoffer, F. A., Rand, F. F., and Teele, R. L.: Joint effusion in children with an irritable hip: US diagnosis and aspiration. Radiology *187*:459–463, 1993.

CHAPTER 63 Pyomyositis and Bacterial Myositis

CHARLES GROSE

Myositis is not a common manifestation of bacterial infection, but when it occurs, the consequences to the patient may be severe or even fatal. *Staphylococcus aureus* and group A streptococci are the most likely causative organisms. Myositis also has been associated with several other infectious agents, including clostridia, viruses, fungi, and parasites. These pathogens have been listed in Table 63–1; they are not discussed further herein because the muscle diseases caused by these agents are described thoroughly in the chapters on the specific microorganisms. This discussion focuses on two forms of pyogenic myositis, designated as acute bacterial myositis and tropical pyomyositis. The former is caused primarily by group A streptococci and the latter by *S. aureus*. Tropical (or staphylococcal) pyomyositis is by far the more common of the two bacterial diseases and should be considered a distinct nosologic entity.

Pyomyositis

The pathologic entity called *spontaneous acute myositis* was recognized by Virchow in the mid-19th century, but the first clinical description of suppurative myositis generally is attributed to the Japanese surgeon Scriba.[20] In 1904, another Japanese surgeon, Miyake,[17] extensively reviewed the subject of skeletal muscle abscesses and added an additional 33 cases. As the British and French expanded their colonial empires at the turn of the 20th century, the disease was recognized with increasing frequency in the native populations, as well as in the soldiers who lived in the tropical areas of Asia and Africa (reviewed by Traquair[26]). It, therefore, acquired the name by which it now is known widely, *tropical pyomyositis*.[9, 10]

The suitability of this designation was confirmed by an epidemiologic study in East Africa, which discovered that the disease was found commonly only in regions with a truly tropical climate (i.e., a fairly constant high temperature and high relative humidity) at an altitude below 4000 ft.[15] However, pyomyositis has been described in children from geographic regions of the United States as diverse as New England,[9] northern California,[2] Iowa,[16] and Texas.[11, 21] A large number of reported cases within the continental United States have occurred in and around San Antonio, Texas.[5] In a 10-year chart review, one or two cases of pyomyositis per 4000 pediatric admissions occurred annually. All of the cases occurred during the warmest months of May through October, when San Antonio experiences a modified subtropical climate—which underscores the original appellation of *tropical* pyomyositis. In contrast, a review of consultations of pediatric infectious diseases at the University of Iowa Hospital disclosed fewer cases of pyomyositis among children younger than 16 years of age.[7] Pyomyositis appears to occur more commonly in children who live in the southernmost regions of the United States (e.g., San Antonio at latitude 29° N) than in those who live in the northern regions (e.g., Iowa City at latitude 41° N).

TABLE 63–1 ■ INFECTIOUS CAUSES OF MYOSITIS

Bacterial
Tropical pyomyositis
Acute bacterial myositis
Clostridial myonecrosis
Viral
Coxsackievirus myositis
Postinfluenza myositis
Fungal
Disseminated candidiasis
Parasitic
Trichinosis
Toxoplasmosis
Cysticercosis

PATHOPHYSIOLOGY

The etiologic agent of the skeletal muscle abscesses in more than 90 percent of the cases is *S. aureus*. Phage typing of many isolates in different countries has not identified a particular staphylococcal strain that is more likely to cause pyomyositis.[11] The second most common bacteriologic isolate is *Streptococcus,* including group A and nonhemolytic strains. Whether more virulent streptococcal infections are occurring at the beginning of the 21st century is an issue that remains unresolved.

The experimental conditions under which staphylococci cause muscle abscesses were studied extensively by Miyake.[17] When healthy rabbits were given boluses of staphylococci intravenously, they occasionally developed small abscesses in the kidney, liver, or spleen but never in the skeletal muscles. However, when specific muscles were damaged by mechanical pinching or electrical current 24 or 48 hours before the intravenous injection of bacteria, small abscesses developed within 2 to 28 days at some of the injured sites in nearly one half of the animals. Abscesses were not found in healthy muscle tissue.

The role of trauma received further support from a study of pyomyositis in the British Army.[3] After physicians found this disease to be a common problem in Gurkha army recruits, they investigated 32 cases and made several observations: two thirds of the men recalled having experienced trauma at the affected site, the incidence of abscesses increased as the severity of physical training increased, and the abscesses occurred three times more commonly on the dominant (right) side of the body. In an analysis of 78 cases in Uganda, abscesses also were found more commonly on the right side of the body.[15]

From experimental evidence and clinical observations, two conditions appear to be necessary for pyomyositis to occur: muscle injury and bacteremia, usually staphylococcal. A reported case is illustrative.[11] A 12-year-old girl caught her left foot in the wheel of a moving bicycle and tumbled to the

TABLE 63–2 ■ PYOMYOSITIS AND TRAUMA

Case	Sex	Age (yr)	Source of Trauma	Circumstances of Trauma	Extent of Disease
1*	F	12	Bicycle accident	Thrown from bicycle onto street after foot was caught in the wheel	Right deltoid/right chest wall/left thigh/right groin
2	M	3	Fall while running	Fell while running on street	Left calf/right scapula/right buttock
3	M	11	Hay bale accident	Struck in abdomen by bale of hay thrown from a hay baler	Abdominal wall musculature
4	M	6	Blunt trauma to abdomen	Struck in abdomen during mock fistfight with sibling	Abdominal wall musculature
5	F	17	Aerobics exercises	Injured while instructing others in aerobics exercises	Left thigh
6	M	7	Bicycle accident	Fell from fast-moving bicycle onto street	Left calf
7	F	13	Volleyball accident	Fell several times diving for volleyball during training exercises	Left iliopsoas

*Cases 1 and 2 from reference 11, cases 3 and 4 from reference 5, cases 5 and 6 from reference 7, and case 7 from reference 16.

ground. One week later, she developed a furuncle of the foot, and within the next 2 weeks, she developed painful lumps in muscles of the thigh, shoulder, and chest wall (which had been injured during the original accident). Cultures from the furuncle and blood, as well as from the incised muscle abscesses, grew *S. aureus*. All isolates were identified as phage type 94. The initial episode of trauma resulted in a staphylococcal skin lesion and, presumably, a bacteremia that seeded sites of previously bruised muscle. Since the 1978 report, I have cared for six additional children with pyomyositis (Table 63–2). An analysis of all seven cases clearly illustrates the association of pyomyositis with trauma. The sources of muscle trauma have ranged from bicycle accidents to strenuous aerobic exercises. These cases also may explain the predilection of the disease to occur in warmer climates; concomitant skin infections and muscle trauma are more likely to occur in a climate in which children can play or work outside wearing fewer clothes for most of the year.

In tropical countries, pyomyositis is said to occur in individuals who are malnourished and who have multiple parasitic infections. However, this association has not been confirmed in the children with pyomyositis seen in the United States or Australia.[5, 7, 13] The children have not been malnourished or vitamin deficient, nor have they had parasitic infestation or marked eosinophilia. Extensive immunologic evaluations also have been normal; the tests included quantitative immunoglobulins, enumeration of T-lymphocyte subpopulations, total hemolytic complement levels, and leukocyte function as tested by reduction of nitroblue tetrazolium.

CLINICAL PRESENTATION

Pyomyositis often is considered a disease of adolescents and young adults, even though it occurs in individuals of all ages, including infants and young children.[2, 6, 13] Boys are affected more often than are girls. However, as more girls enter competitive sporting activities, pyomyositis is being reported in female athletes.[16] Most children with pyomyositis have a solitary lesion, but multiple lesions are not rare findings. The most common site of abscess formation is the thigh, followed by the calf, buttock, arm, scapula, and chest wall. The muscle lesions are firm or "woody" to palpation, with a well-defined border. The sign of fluctuation may be difficult to elicit. Erythema and warmth often are not apparent because of the deep location of the masses, although diffuse tenderness usually occurs. When a muscle in an extremity is involved, the entire limb may be swollen. Occasionally, none of the abscess is palpable, and the patient has only fever and vague muscle pain of a few weeks' duration.

The American children with pyomyositis, who ranged from 2 years of age through the teenage years, generally had similar presenting complaints.[7, 11] Many had incurred a recent accidental injury (often involving a leg) that usually was not considered serious. After a few days, the children developed low-grade fever (38.3° C to 39.0° C), muscle pain, and, occasionally, an impaired gait. These symptoms persisted from a few days to a few weeks until a mass appeared. When first examined, many of the patients were considered to have only a contusion or a hematoma; occasionally, a child was diagnosed as having a rhabdomyosarcoma. Although the disease usually occurs in individuals who are otherwise healthy, pyomyositis has been reported in patients with malignancy. Pyomyositis also may develop in children with acquired immunodeficiency syndrome (AIDS).[19] However, the pathophysiology of pyogenic muscle abscess may not be the same in immunodeficient individuals with increased susceptibility to bacterial infection. Most children with pyomyositis have no definable immunologic abnormalities.

An unusual clinical presentation is acute abdominal pain. Beck and Grose[5] described two children with pyomyositis whose initial complaints were confined to the abdominal wall. One patient, a 6-year-old child, had been struck in the abdomen in a mock fistfight with an older sibling. One week later, he developed a low-grade fever and began to walk with a stoop; after another week, his mother detected a "knot" in his right mid-abdominal wall. The second case involved the 11-year-old son of a rancher who was struck in the abdomen by a bale of hay tossed from a hay baler. When he subsequently developed symptoms of abdominal pain, the diagnosis of appendicitis was entertained. When a mass later became palpable in his abdominal wall, rhabdomyosarcoma was suspected. A correct diagnosis was made after the use of scintigraphy and sonography, as described later.[5] A review from Nigeria found muscle abscesses in the anterior abdominal wall to be rather common.[2]

DIAGNOSIS

The diagnosis of pyomyositis should be considered in any child with fever and muscle pain, especially if a recent history of trauma exists. When a child has visible masses at commonly involved sites, such as the thigh, the diagnosis of pyomyositis can be made by needle aspiration of a mass.

If a febrile child complains of myalgia in an extremity but has no palpable masses, the differential diagnosis must include the more common inflammatory and infectious conditions of the bone or joint. A definitive diagnosis usually depends on one or more radiologic procedures. Plain films may demonstrate a soft tissue swelling or even a widened fascial plane suggestive of a mass lesion. A combination of plain roentgenography and radionuclide (technetium 99m phosphate) bone scintigraphy often can exclude osteomyelitis and pyoarthritis. If the diagnosis still is in question, scanning with gallium or indium can localize a muscle abscess precisely and can visualize other intramuscular abscesses too small to palpate (Fig. 63–1). Alternatively, ultrasonography also can detect muscle abscesses and may be preferable as an initial procedure because it avoids the radiation exposure from computed tomography (CT) or scintigrams (Fig. 63–2). Nonetheless, gallium 67 citrate scanning remains a sensitive diagnostic procedure for detection of small muscle abscesses.[5, 14] Because of the intensity of the signal, the scan often can be completed within 1 to 4 hours after injection of the isotope.

Magnetic resonance imaging (MRI) can be very helpful in delineating the extent of a muscle abscess. In many cases, the abscess is much larger than suspected by physical symptoms and signs. The MRI scans of an illustrative case are presented in Figure 63–3. The patient was a 17-year-old girl with a swollen left lower thigh. She worked part time as an attendant in an athletic club, where she participated in some of the vigorous exercise programs. Radiographs of the knee were normal, whereas a technetium bone scan showed slightly increased radionuclide uptake in the soft tissues around the distal left femur. MRI of the left and right thighs demonstrated a large fluid collection extending from the middle to distal left femur. Surgical exploration identified extensive abscess formation around the posterior aspect of the femur; the culture grew *S. aureus*. The affected muscle groups included the vastus medialis, vastus intermedius, vastus lateralis, and biceps femoris. The bone was not involved. For the reasons described, MRI has become the preferred procedure for diagnosis of pyomyositis.[22, 27]

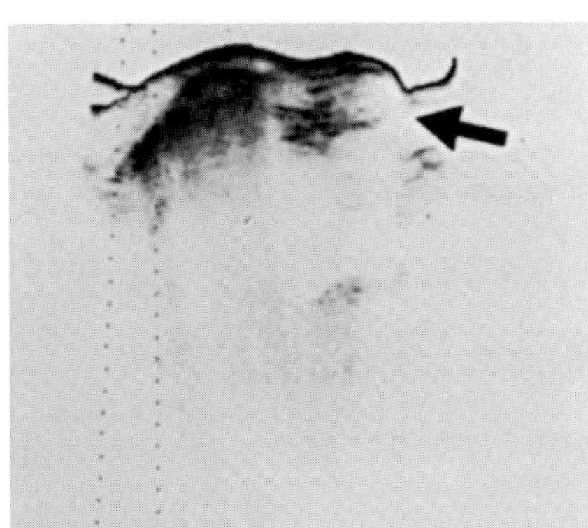

FIGURE 63–2 ■ Sonogram of the abdominal wall of a patient with pyomyositis. The transverse view of the abdomen shows an abscess cavity in the right belly of the rectus abdominis muscle (*arrow*).

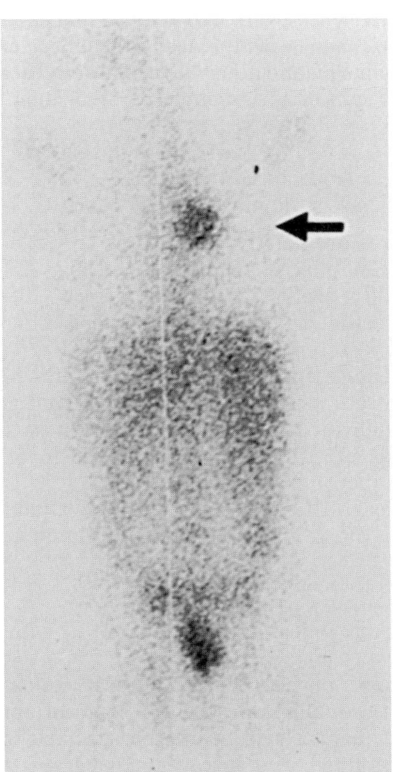

FIGURE 63–1 ■ Scintigram of a patient with pyomyositis. The posterior gallium 67 citrate scan shows abnormally high uptake over the right scapula (*arrow*), where an abscess cavity was located within the muscle. Increased radioactivity also is observed in the bladder, which is a normal finding.

TREATMENT

Because pyomyositis is an abscess of skeletal muscle, the treatment is surgical incision and drainage.[2] However, several physicians have seen that smaller lesions resolve spontaneously, even before the antibiotic era. An important role for systemic antibiotics is to prevent the formation of further muscle abscesses, especially in a patient with proven bacteremia. Because *S. aureus* is the most likely agent, a semisynthetic penicillinase-resistant penicillin is the preferred antibiotic. Usually, nafcillin or oxacillin is administered intravenously every 6 hours at a total daily dosage of 150 to 200 mg/kg. When pyomyositis occurs in a patient with penicillin hypersensitivity, clindamycin (40 mg/kg/day, divided every 8 hours) can be substituted because of its excellent coverage of gram-positive cocci. Parenteral therapy is continued until clinical improvement is evident, usually within a few days after surgical drainage. Thereafter, the antibiotics can be given orally at a reduced dosage for an additional 2 to 3 weeks. A penicillin derivative (dicloxacillin at 25 mg/kg/day or cefadroxil at 30 mg/kg/day) or clindamycin (20 to 30 mg/kg/day) is acceptable.

Acute Bacterial Myositis

Far less common than tropical pyomyositis is the condition of acute bacterial myositis, usually caused by group A streptococci. In this condition, the bacterial infection often is not confined to distinct abscesses within the muscle but instead extends diffusely through one or more muscle groups. As with pyomyositis, the disease occurs more commonly in males than in females and usually is associated with prior physical exertion and perhaps minor trauma. Unlike pyomyositis, most published cases of acute bacterial myositis

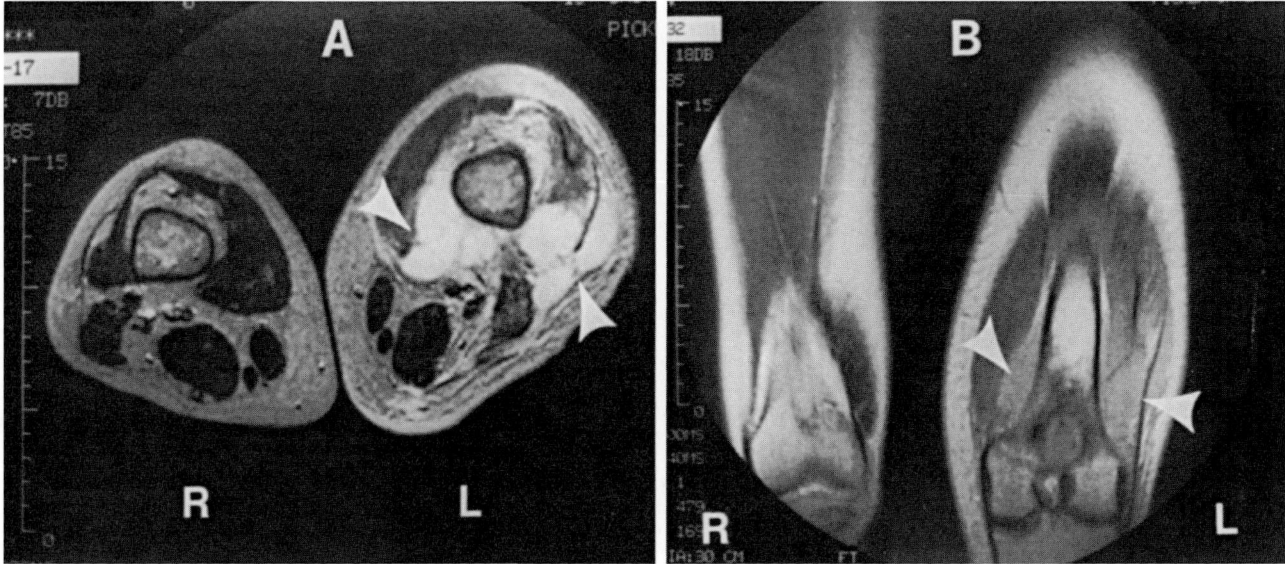

FIGURE 63–3 ■ Magnetic resonance imaging of the thighs of a patient with pyomyositis. *A,* Axial images of the right (R) and left (L) thighs. *B,* Coronal images around the distal femoral shafts and femoral condyles. The scans demonstrate several well-defined areas of extremely high intensity in the muscle bundles and fascial planes from the middle to distal left femur (*arrows*). The high signal intensity suggests a fluid collection (e.g., an abscess) rather than a neoplastic process. Edema of the subcutaneous tissues also is evident in the lateral aspect of the swollen left thigh. There are no abnormal signals within the bone.

have occurred in adults and not in children.[4] The disease has been divided by Svane into the following four main types[25]:

1. A malignant form with septicemia and a uniformly fatal outcome
2. An acute form with a more protracted clinical course, as well as other foci of suppuration such as the bones, joints, or viscera
3. A subacute form with a better clinical prognosis
4. A benign type associated with more distinct muscle abscesses

The benign type of acute bacterial myositis by the Svane classification is the same disease process as described in the preceding section on pyomyositis.

CLINICAL PRESENTATION

The main clinical difference between the acute myositis syndrome and the pyomyositis syndrome is the virulence of the former disease, especially the malignant type. A case in a San Antonio native is illustrative. The patient was a muscular, 23-year-old jackhammer operator who was admitted because of high fever, malaise, and pains in his arms. On examination, both upper extremities were tender to palpation, and faint erythema was visible over the same areas. He soon became incoherent, and his general condition quickly deteriorated. Death followed within 24 hours. Blood cultures drawn before death grew group A streptococci, and cultures of the biceps muscles obtained at autopsy grew the same organism. This case is similar to others described in the literature.[4, 25] The patient worked as a jackhammer operator, who presumably would incur considerable minor trauma to the muscles of the upper arms and shoulders. Two reported cases of streptococcal myositis in children involved the left thigh and the left paravertebral muscles, respectively.[18] The first child developed septic shock and required intensive care for 27 days before a definitive diagnosis was made by CT.

A case of generalized myositis with staphylococcal septicemia has been described in a 15-year-old boy.[1] The patient presented with signs of fever and very diffuse muscle swelling and tenderness. All muscle groups of the extremities appeared inflamed and markedly tender; the creatine phosphokinase enzyme levels were markedly elevated. Culture of a muscle biopsy grew *S. aureus*, as did previously drawn blood cultures. The patient experienced a stormy hospital course with severe hypotension and shock syndrome, requiring treatment with intravenous fluids, corticosteroids, dopamine, heparin, and assisted ventilation. He also received a total of 4 weeks of antistaphylococcal antibiotic therapy.

DIAGNOSIS

Blood cultures are positive most often in patients with the most significant clinical symptoms. Cultures of muscle biopsies may yield a profuse growth of bacteria. In rare circumstances, myositis has occurred as a delayed complication of chickenpox, often together with fasciitis.[12, 17, 24] In this situation, bacteremia may not be documented because the bacterial process usually is the result of contiguous spread from a secondarily infected pock lesion. These streptococcal complications of chickenpox often occur in an extremity, which may become swollen and painful. Under these circumstances, MRI can be an extremely valuable diagnostic tool to gauge the depth and extent of inflammation.[27]

TREATMENT AND THE EAGLE EFFECT

The treatment of acute streptococcal or staphylococcal myositis of the malignant type is a medical emergency. As soon as the diagnosis is suspected, bacteriologic cultures should be obtained, and intravenous therapy with a high-dose semisynthetic penicillin (e.g., nafcillin given at a dosage of 50 mg/kg every 6 hours) should be initiated. If the cultures yield group A streptococci rather than *Staphylococcus*, the antibiotic can be switched to penicillin G at an equivalent high dosage. Surgical consultation is required to evaluate the need for débridement and drainage. MRI may be advisable to document the extent of the disease and the response to antibiotic therapy. In severe cases of bacterial myositis, the total duration of hospitalization can exceed 4 weeks.[1, 18]

The apparent resurgence of serious streptococcal infection has led to an increased interest in what has been called the *Harry Eagle effect*, named after the scientist who first described the failure of penicillin to eradicate group A streptococcal infection in a mouse model.[8] Eagle inoculated mice intramuscularly with group A streptococci and observed a markedly retarded bactericidal action of penicillin on organisms in the older abscesses, even though the bacteria remained highly sensitive to the antibiotic. Even massive doses of penicillin 10,000 times greater than the minimum inhibitory concentration were not effective at eradicating the bacteria. Subsequent studies by other investigators confirmed the existence of the Eagle effect and disclosed that clindamycin demonstrated superior efficacy to penicillin in treatment of streptococcal myositis in the mouse model.[23] In an editorial comment, Stevens[24] observed that penicillin most likely fails to kill stationary-phase streptococci in muscle infections, an explanation for the Eagle effect. He suggested that streptococcal myositis or fasciitis be treated with intravenous clindamycin (40 mg/kg/day) if the condition fails to respond to penicillin therapy.

REFERENCES

1. Adamski, G. B., Garin, E. H., Ballinger, W. E., et al.: Generalized nonsuppurative myositis with staphylococcal septicemia. J. Pediatr. *96*:694–697, 1980.
2. Ameh, E. A.: Pyomyositis in children: Analysis of 31 cases. Ann. Trop. Paediatr. *19*:263–265, 1999.
3. Ashken, M. H., and Cotton, R. E.: Tropical skeletal muscle abscesses (pyomyositis tropicans). Br. J. Surg. *50*:846–852, 1963.
4. Barrett, A. M., and Gresham, G. A.: Acute streptococcal myositis. Lancet *1*:347–351, 1958.
5. Beck, W., and Grose, C.: Pyomyositis presenting as acute abdominal pain. Pediatr. Infect. Dis. *3*:445–448, 1984.
6. Chacha, P. B.: Muscle abscesses in children. Clin. Orthop. *70*:174–180, 1970.
7. Diamandakis, V., and Grose, C.: Bad consequences of bicycle accidents. Pediatr. Infect. Dis. J. *13*:422–425, 1994.
8. Eagle, H.: Experimental approach to the problem of treatment failure with penicillin. I. Group A streptococcal infection in mice. Am. J. Med. *13*:389–399, 1952.
9. Echeverria, P., and Vaughn, M. C.: Tropical pyomyositis: A diagnostic problem in temperate climates. Am. J. Dis. Child. *129*:856–857, 1975.
10. Goldberg, J. S., London, W. L., and Nagel, D. M. Tropical pyomyositis: A case report and review. Pediatrics. *63*:298–300, 1979.
11. Grose, C.: Staphylococcal pyomyositis in south Texas. J. Pediatr. *93*:457–458, 1978.
12. Grose, C.: Varicella-zoster virus infections: Chickenpox, shingles, and varicella vaccine. *In* Glaser, R., and Jones, J. F. (eds.): Herpesvirus Infections. New York, Marcel Dekker, 1994, pp. 117–185.
13. Gubbay, A. J., and Issacs, D.: Pyomyositis in children. Pediatr. Infect. Dis. J. *19*:1009–1012, 2000.
14. Hirano, T., Srinivasan, G., Janakiraman, N., et al.: Gallium 67 citrate scintigraphy in pyomyositis. J. Pediatr. *97*:596–598, 1980.
15. Marcus, R. T., and Foster, W. D.: Observations on the clinical features, aetiology and geographic distribution of pyomyositis in East Africa. East Afr. Med. J. *45*:167–176, 1968.
16. Meehan, J., Grose, C., Soper, R. T., and Kimura, K. Pyomyositis in an adolescent female athlete. J. Pediatr. Surg. *30*:127–128, 1995.
17. Miyake, H.: Beitrage zur kenntnis der sogenannten myositis infectiosa. Mitt. Grenageb. Med. Chir. *13*:155–198, 1904.
18. Moore, D. L., Delage, G., Labelle, H., et al.: Peracute streptococcal pyomyositis: Report of two cases and review of the literature. J. Pediatr. Orthop. *6*:232–235, 1986.
19. Raphael, S. A., Wolfson, B. J., Parker, P., et al.: Pyomyositis in a child with acquired immunodeficiency syndrome. Am. J. Dis. Child. *143*: 779–781, 1989.
20. Scriba, J.: Beitrag zur aetiologie der myositis acuta. Dtsch. Z. Chir. *22*:497–502, 1885.
21. Sirinavin, S., and McCracken, G. H.: Primary suppurative myositis in children. Am. J. Dis. Child. *133*:263–265, 1979.
22. Solar, R., Rodriguez, E., Aguiler, C., and Fernandez, R. Magnetic resonance imaging of pyomyositis in 43 cases. Eur. J. Radiol. 35:59–64, 2000.
23. Stevens, D. L., Gibbons, A. E., Bergstrom, R., and Winn, V.: The Eagle effect revisited: Efficacy of clindamycin, erythromycin, and penicillin in the treatment of streptococcal myositis. J. Infect. Dis. *158*:23–28, 1988.
24. Stevens, D. L.: Editorial response: Varicella gangrenosa with toxic shock-like syndrome. Clin. Infect. Dis. *20*:1061–1062, 1995.
25. Svane, S.: Peracute spontaneous streptococcal myositis. Acta Chir. Scand. *137*:155–163, 1971.
26. Traquair, R. N.: Pyomyositis. J. Trop. Med. Hyg. *50*:81–89, 1947.
27. Zittergruen, M., and Grose, C.: Magnetic resonance imaging for early diagnosis of necrotizing fasciitis. Pediatr. Emerg. Care *9*:26–28, 1993.

Miscellaneous Causes of Myositis

BERNHARD L. WIEDERMANN

In addition to the many gram-positive and gram-negative bacteria that may cause pyogenic and nonpyogenic myositis, a host of other infectious agents have been implicated in acute and chronic inflammatory diseases of muscle. The pathophysiology of these disorders varies with the etiologic agent, but three basic categories exist. First, the microorganism can cause muscle injury by direct invasion of skeletal muscle. This injury is demonstrated most commonly for some of the parasitic causes of myositis, such as trichinosis, but it also has been seen rarely with viral causes. The second and probably most common mechanism of myositis is a postinfectious syndrome. Patients with this syndrome present with symptoms of muscle inflammation in the convalescent stage of a (usually) minor respiratory infection. The mechanism of this process has not been determined, but an autoimmune basis is suspected. Third, systemic infections that result in diffuse vasculitis may manifest with severe myalgias; dengue, Rocky Mountain spotted fever, and leptospirosis are examples.

The major clinical syndromes encompassed by the nonbacterial causes of myositis are discussed here. Chapters on the specific pathogens offer a more complete discussion of the etiologic agents.

Benign Acute Childhood Myositis

Benign acute childhood myositis originally was described in Lundberg's classic 1957 report of 74 cases of "myalgia cruris epidemica."[49] As more cases have been described,

TABLE 64–1 ■ MISCELLANEOUS (NONPYOGENIC) CAUSES OF MYOSITIS

Benign Acute Childhood Myositis and Myoglobinuric Myositis
Influenza viruses A and B[11, 14, 18, 20, 21, 32, 46, 57, 59–61, 68, 72, 77, 79, 80, 82, 92]
Parainfluenza viruses 2 and 3[84, 93]
Echoviruses 6 and 9[41, 43, 70]
Coxsackieviruses[11]
Rotavirus[35]
Measles virus[1]
Rubella virus (immunization)[34]
Adenovirus 7[73]
Adenovirus 21[58, 90]
Varicella-zoster virus[67]
Cytomegalovirus[37, 64]
Epstein-Barr virus[30, 43, 74]
Herpes simplex virus type 2[74]
Mycoplasma pneumoniae[9, 10]
Hantaviruses[36, 47]
Pleurodynia
Coxsackieviruses A and B[6, 22, 42]
Many echoviruses[42]
Parasitic Myositis
Trichinella spiralis[5, 31, 62]
Cysticercus cellulosae (*Taenia solium*)[13, 53]
Toxoplasma gondii[33, 83]
Toxocara species[88]
Microsporidia[15, 16, 28, 48, 50]
Sarcocystis[3, 7]
Wucheria bancrofti[63, 69]
Plasmodium falciparum[19, 78]
Spirochetal Myositis
Borrelia burgdorferi[4, 23, 71, 75, 76]
Leptospira species[27]
Chronic Polymyositis
Hepatitis C virus[86]
Human immunodeficiency virus type 1[25, 39, 89,]
Human T-cell lymphotrophic virus type 1[24, 66]
Coxsackieviruses (?)[13]

a prototype clinical picture has emerged.* Typically, school-age children are affected, with a male-to-female ratio of 2 : 1. They usually have an initial upper respiratory illness with resolution of symptoms over a period of days. During this resolution, a relatively abrupt presentation of calf pain and tenderness occurs. The pain can be severe enough to interfere with normal ambulation. Examination reveals muscle tenderness that primarily involves the gastrocnemius and soleus muscles. Muscle swelling occurs uncommonly, and the patient usually has no findings of systemic illness. Other muscle groups in the lower extremities, upper extremities, and neck have been reported to be involved. Marked elevation of serum creatinine phosphokinase and other muscle enzyme levels occurs. Myoglobinuria usually is absent, distinguishing this entity from the more severe myositides, which cause extensive destruction of muscle tissue. Many different viruses, including influenza A and B, parainfluenza viruses, enteroviruses, adenoviruses, measles, and mumps, as well as *Mycoplasma pneumoniae*, have been implicated as etiologic agents (Table 64–1).

Histologic examination of muscle biopsy specimens generally shows edema and acute inflammatory infiltrates. Occasionally, scattered areas of necrosis are evident, with minimal perivascular inflammation. In general, examinations for viral particles by electron microscopy or indirect fluorescent antibody staining have been negative, suggesting an autoimmune mechanism for this disease.

No specific treatment for benign acute childhood myositis is needed. The illness resolves spontaneously, usually within several days.

Myositis with Myoglobinuria

Myositis with myoglobinuria probably is not distinct from benign acute childhood myositis but instead represents a more severe form of the acute myositis continuum. The presence of myoglobinuria in a child with myositis implies a more severe degree of muscle destruction than that seen with typical benign acute childhood myositis. The differences in clinical manifestations are more reflective of the host than of the specific infectious agent, but from a clinical standpoint, discussing this group of patients separately is useful. Influenza A virus infection seems to be the organism implicated most commonly in myoglobinuric myositis.[11, 17, 18, 20, 60, 61, 77, 92] In general, these patients may be more likely than those with benign acute childhood myositis to present with muscle pain during the acute phase of the precipitating infection, and their muscle pain is more severe and more generalized. The offending microorganism may be demonstrable more readily in muscle tissue. However, none of these features can distinguish these entities clearly in any patient, and a urinalysis is the most important test to obtain in this regard.

Patients with myoglobinuria have positive results of tests for urinary occult blood by dipstick but have no demonstrable erythrocytes on microscopic urine examination. The diagnosis can be confirmed by specific myoglobin determination in urine. After this diagnosis is made, monitoring renal function in these individuals is important because of the risk of developing myoglobinuric renal failure. Patients with severe myoglobinuria may have an underlying disorder of muscle, such as carnitine palmityl transferase deficiency or paroxysmal rhabdomyolysis, which should be considered.[26, 45]

No specific therapy exists for this disorder. Providing supportive care, including that appropriate for patients with renal failure, is most important. Amantadine therapy for patients with early influenza A infection may be effective but has not been evaluated in this clinical situation.

Epidemic Pleurodynia

Epidemic pleurodynia (i.e., Bornholm disease) is an acute viral syndrome most commonly seen with coxsackievirus B infection in children and young adults (see Chapter 170).[6, 22, 42] The typical syndrome consists of fever and pain involving the chest and upper abdomen. Tenderness without muscle swelling occurs in the affected areas, and pain may be aggravated by sudden movement with coughing or deep inspiration. The symptoms may mimic those of acute appendicitis in the younger child. The patient may have upper respiratory and gastrointestinal symptoms suggestive of viral illness. A pleural friction rub may be heard on examination, but chest radiographs and routine laboratory tests generally are unrewarding. Clinical manifestations usually wane after 2 to 3 days but may reappear several days later. No specific therapy is available.

Parasitic Myositis

Myositis resulting from parasitic disease usually occurs with tissue invasion by the pathogen. Most affected individuals,

*See references 2, 9, 14, 51, 54, 55, 59, 72, 82, 91.

therefore, have significant eosinophilia as the primary diagnostic clue.

TRICHINOSIS

Trichinella spiralis is the most common cause of trichinosis, resulting from ingestion of the encysted larvae in undercooked meat, primarily pork and wild game.[5] Initially, patients present with fever, diarrhea, and abdominal pain during the intestinal phase of infection. In the second week of illness, these symptoms are replaced with signs and symptoms related to dissemination through the bloodstream and invasion of skeletal muscle. Fever, malaise, eyelid edema, and pain, tenderness, and swelling of muscles are the predominant symptoms.[31, 62] The sites most frequently involved are in the upper body and include extraocular muscles, muscles of mastication, neck, deltoids, intercostals, and diaphragm. Untreated, the illness resolves slowly, with calcification developing in affected muscle tissue after several months. Trichinosis occurring in natives of northern Canada may manifest with less prominent or no symptoms of myositis.[52] These individuals manifest a persistent diarrheal illness, perhaps related to secondary *Trichinella nativa* infection in previously sensitized patients.[52a]

A history of ingestion of undercooked meat or an outbreak of myositis in the community accompanied by the finding of eosinophilia in the patient strongly suggests a diagnosis of trichinosis. Muscle biopsy is the most direct and accurate method of confirming the diagnosis, but obtaining serologic tests may be helpful.[40, 87]

Administration of mebendazole or albendazole may be effective treatment for trichinosis.[56] Systemic corticosteroids have been helpful in alleviating severe symptoms.

CYSTICERCOSIS

Cysticercosis occurs with human ingestion of eggs of the pork tapeworm, *Taenia solium*, in material from a human source (i.e., feces or vomitus). Cysticercosis is not a common occurrence in the United States but frequently is found in Mexico, Central and South America, and parts of Africa. After ingestion occurs, virtually any organ system in the body can be infected, but skeletal muscle is one of the most common sites.[13, 53] Typically, muscular involvement is asymptomatic, although fever, myalgias, and eosinophilia can be seen. More commonly, cysticercal myositis is diagnosed incidentally in a patient with central nervous system involvement or by histologic examination of subcutaneous nodules that are present occasionally. Calcific densities in skeletal muscle, in a classic "puffed rice" appearance, are highly suggestive of the diagnosis. Granulomatous reactions in tissue commonly are observed. Treatment with praziquantel has resulted in resolution of the subcutaneous nodules; the effects of treatment on muscular involvement, which normally has a benign course, are difficult to judge.[53] Individuals with cysticercal myositis should have careful neurologic and ophthalmologic evaluations performed for detection of potentially more serious manifestations of the disease.

OTHER PARASITES

Myalgias are a frequent complaint in acquired *Toxoplasma gondii* infection, and toxoplasmosis rarely may manifest with a polymyositis-like syndrome.[33, 83] *Toxocara* myositis was diagnosed in two previously healthy children by clinical and serologic means.[88] Both children had resolution of symptoms within 72 hours and received no specific therapy. Microsporidiosis reportedly caused myositis in a young man with acquired immunodeficiency syndrome (AIDS), as well as in another adult patient with a nonspecific immunodeficiency.[16, 48, 50] The diagnoses were made by demonstration of microsporidia in biopsy material. *Sarcocystis* and *Wucheria bancrofti* have been reported to cause inflammatory muscle disease.[7, 63, 69]

Spirochetal Myositis

Although spirochetes are classified correctly as bacteria, the clinical presentation of myositis caused by spirochetes has more similarities to viral myositis than to overt bacterial pyomyositis. These entities are discussed briefly here.

BORRELIA BURGDORFERI

Muscular pain is a common complaint of patients with acute Lyme disease, and several patients with Lyme disease who had myositis as a major feature at initial presentation have been reported.[4, 23, 71, 75] Lyme myositis primarily is a feature in stage II Lyme disease, appearing 2 to 5 months after infection. Clinically, proximal muscles, particularly the thigh muscles, are involved, with a rather painful swelling that may wax and wane over the course of several months. Orbital myositis, usually considered an idiopathic condition, has been associated with Lyme disease in a 5-year-old girl.[76] Typically, biopsy specimens show chronic inflammation surrounding intramuscular veins. Spirochetes can be demonstrated in tissue, and antibiotic treatment for Lyme disease appears to result in a favorable response in most individuals with Lyme myositis.[4, 71, 75]

LEPTOSPIROSIS

Myalgia often is a prominent and severe component in the initial manifestation of leptospirosis.[27] That the histologic changes in muscle are not more prominent is, therefore, somewhat surprising. Most commonly, only minimal changes (of cytoplasmic vacuoles in the myofibrillar cells) are seen, with occasional acute inflammatory infiltrates. With resolution of the infection, healing of muscle occurs without fibrosis.

Retroviral Myositis

Published reports of muscle involvement related to primary infection with human immunodeficiency virus type 1 (HIV-1) or human T-cell lymphotrophic virus type 1 (HTLV-1) suggest a role for these retroviruses in the production of a relatively chronic form of myositis.

HUMAN IMMUNODEFICIENCY VIRUS TYPE 1

Myalgia is a frequent finding in patients with HIV-1 infection. Generalized disease usually is present, and muscular atrophy may be prominent. However, to ascribe all of these changes to HIV-1 infection is difficult because these individuals usually have multiple medical problems that could contribute to muscle wasting. The p24 antigen has been demonstrated in affected muscle tissue, and virus-like particles have been seen,[24, 66] but immunohistologic studies do not suggest direct infection of muscle fibers by HIV-1. Intravenous immunoglobulin therapy may have benefited one adult with HIV-1–associated polymyositis.[85]

HUMAN T-CELL LYMPHOTROPHIC VIRUS TYPE 1

The association between HTLV-1 infection and a polymyositis-like syndrome is more clear-cut than is the case with HIV-1 disease. Although more prominently a cause of tropical spastic paraparesis, a myelopathy primarily involving the lower extremities, some studies strongly suggest an etiologic role in some cases of polymyositis.[25, 39, 88] Initially, seroepidemiologic data implicated HTLV-1 in this syndrome, and specific virologic data in individual cases have strengthened this contention. One patient with combined infection with HTLV-1 and HIV-1 and diffuse muscle weakness had evidence of HTLV-1 in muscle biopsy specimens demonstrated by in situ hybridization and by immunocytochemistry.[25] No evidence of HIV-1 material was found in the biopsy by those methods.

Although these cases of retroviral myopathy occurred in adults, the clinical entity should be recognized so that the cases of infants and children with polymyositis-like symptoms and risk factors for HIV-1 or HTLV-1 disease can be evaluated appropriately for these infections.

Other Forms of Chronic Polymyositis

Limited data may suggest a causal role for other infectious agents, primarily enteroviruses and mumps virus, in idiopathic polymyositis. Virus-like particles have been observed in muscle tissue sections from patients with chronic myositis, and coxsackievirus A9 has been isolated from the muscle of an individual with polymyositis.[81] Coxsackievirus B antigen has been demonstrated by in situ hybridization in patients with polymyositis and with acute and chronic dermatomyositis but not in normal controls or samples from muscular dystrophy patients.[12] However, another study showed no link between picornaviruses and chronic inflammatory myopathies.[8] Mumps long has been suspected as an etiologic agent of inclusion-body myositis because the structure of abnormal muscle filaments bears some resemblance to mumps virus nucleoproteins.[65] However, no evidence of mumps antigen was detected by hybridization or immunocytochemical means in muscle tissues of 20 patients with such myositis[65] or by polymerase chain reaction in another 18 patients.[29] Further studies are necessary before a true link can be established between chronic, idiopathic myositis and viral infections.

REFERENCES

1. Ando, T., Suzuki, M., and Sato, T.: A case of myoglobinuria associated with measles. Shonika. *15*:981, 1974.
2. Antony, J. H., Procopis, P. G., and Ouvrier, R. A.: Benign acute childhood myositis. Neurology. *29*:1068, 1979.
3. Arness, M. K., Brown, J. D., Dubey, J. P., et al.: An outbreak of acute eosinophilic myositis attributed to human *Sarcocystis* parasitism. Am. J. Trop. Med. Hyg. *61*:548, 1999.
4. Atlas, E., Novak, S. N., Duray, P. H., et al.: Lyme myositis: Muscle invasion by *Borrelia burgdorferi*. Ann. Intern. Med. *109*:245, 1988.
5. Bailey, T. M., and Schantz, P. M.: Trichinosis surveillance, United States, 1986. Morb Mortal Wkly Rep CDC Surveill Summ *37*(SS-5):1, 1988.
6. Bain, H. N., McLean, D. M., and Walker, S. J.: Epidemic pleurodynia (Bornholm disease) due to coxsackie B-5 virus: The interrelationship of pleurodynia, benign pericarditis, and aseptic meningitis. Pediatrics. *27*:889, 1961.
7. Beaver, P. C., Gadgil, R. K., and Morera, P.: *Sarcocystis* in man: A review and report of five cases. Am. J. Trop. Med. Hyg. *28*:819, 1979.
8. Behan, W. M., Gow, J. W., Simpson, K., et al.: Search for picornaviruses at onset of inflammatory myopathy. J. Clin. Pathol. *49*:592, 1996.
9. Belardi, C., Roberge, R., Kelly, M., et al.: Myalgia cruris epidemica (benign acute childhood myositis) associated with a *Mycoplasma pneumoniae* infection. Ann. Emerg. Med. *16*:579, 1987.
10. Berger, R. P., and Wadowksy, R. M.: Rhabdomyolysis associated with infection by *Mycoplasma pneumoniae*: A case report. Pediatrics. *105*:433, 2000.
11. Berlin, B. S., Simon, N. M., and Bovner, R. N.: Myoglobinuria precipitated by viral infection. J. A. M. A. *227*:1414, 1974.
12. Bowles, N. E., Sewry, C. A., Dubowitz, V., et al.: Dermatomyositis, polymyositis, and coxsackie-B-virus infection. Lancet *1*:1004, 1987.
13. Brown, W. J., and Voge, M.: Cysticercosis: A modern day plague. Pediatr. Clin. North Am. *32*:953, 1985.
14. Buchta, R. M.: Myositis and influenza. Pediatrics. *60*:761, 1977.
15. Cali, A., Takvorian, P. M., Lewin, S., et al.: *Brachiola vesicularum*, n. g., n. sp., a new microsporidium associated with AIDS and myositis. J. Eukaryot. Microbiol. *45*:240–251, 1998.
16. Chupp, G. L., Alroy, J., Adelman, L. S., et al.: Myositis due to *Pleistophora* (Microsporidia) in a patient with AIDS. Clin. Infect. Dis. *16*:15, 1993.
17. Christenson, J. C., and San Joaquin, V. H.: Influenza-associated rhabdomyolysis in a child. Pediatr. Infect. Dis. J. *9*:60, 1990.
18. Cunningham, E., Kohli, R., and Venuto, R. C.: Influenza-associated myoglobinuric real failure. J. A. M. A. *242*:2428, 1979.
19. De Silva, H. J., Goonetilleke, A., K., E., Senaratna, N., et al.: Skeletal muscle necrosis in severe falciparum malaria. Br. Med. J. *296*:1039, 1988.
20. DiBona, F. J., and Morens, D. M.: Rhabdomyolysis associated with influenza: Report of a case with unusual fluid and electrolytes abnormalities. J. Pediatr. *91*:943, 1977.
21. Dietzman, D. E., Schaller, J. G., Ray, C. G., et al.: Acute myositis associated with influenza B infection. Pediatrics. *57*:255, 1967.
22. Disney, M. E., Howard, E. M., and Wood, B. S. B.: Bornholm disease in children. Br. Med. J. *1*:1351, 1953.
23. Duray, P. H.: Clinical pathologic correlations of Lyme disease. Rev. Infect. Dis. *11*:S1487, 1989.
24. Espinoza, L. R., Aguilar, J. L., Berman, A., et al.: Rheumatic manifestations associated with human immunodeficiency virus infection. Arthritis Rheum. *32*:1615, 1989.
25. Evans, B. K., Gore, I., Harrell, L. E., et al.: HTLV-I–associated myelopathy and polymyositis in a US native. Neurology. *39*:1572, 1989.
26. Favara, B. E., Vawter, G. F., Wagner, R., et al.: Familial paroxysmal rhabdomyolysis in children: A myoglobinuric syndrome. Am. J. Med. *42*:196, 1967.
27. Feigin, R. D., and Anderson, D. C.: Human leptospirosis. CRC. Crit. Rev. Clin. Lab. Sci. *5*:413, 1975.
28. Field, A. S., Marriott, D. J., Milliken, S. T., et al.: Myositis associated with a newly described microsporidian, *Trachipleistophora hominis*, in a patient with AIDS. J. Clin. Microbiol. *34*:2803, 1996.
29. Fox, S. A., Ward, B. K., Robbins, P. D., et al.: Inclusion body myositis: Investigation of the mumps virus hypothesis by polymerase chain reaction. Muscle Nerve. *19*:23, 1996.
30. Friedman, B. I., and Libby, R.: Epstein-Barr virus infection associated with rhabdomyolysis and acute renal failure. Clin. Pediatr. *25*:228, 1986.
31. Gould, S. E.: Clinical manifestations. A. Symptomatology. *In* Gould, S. E. (ed.): Trichinosis in Man and Animals. Springfield, Charles C. Thomas, 1970, p. 269.
32. Greco, T. P., Askenase, P. W., and Kashgarian, M.: Postviral myositis: Myxovirus-like structures in affected muscles. Ann. Intern. Med. *86*:193, 1977.
33. Greenlee, J. E., Johnson, W. D., Campa, J. F., et al.: Adult toxoplasmosis presenting as polymyositis and cerebral ataxia. Ann. Intern. Med. *82*:367, 1975.
34. Hanissian, A. S., Martinez, A. J., Jabbour, J. T., et al.: Vasculitis and myositis secondary to rubella vaccination. Arch. Neurol. *28*:202, 1973.
35. Hattori, H., Torii, S., Nagafuji, H., et al.: Benign acute myositis associated with rotavirus gastroenteritis. J. Pediatr. *121*:748, 1992.
36. Hjelle, B., Goade, D., Torrez-Martinez, N., et al.: Hantavirus pulmonary syndrome, renal insufficiency, and myositis associated with infection by Bayou hantavirus. Clin. Infect. Dis. *23*:495, 1996.
37. Hughes, G. S., and Hunt, R.: Cytomegalovirus infection with rhabdomyolysis and myoglobinuria. Ann. Intern. Med. *101*:276, 1984.
38. Illa, I., Nath, A., and Dalakas, M.: Immunocytochemical and virological characteristics of HIV-associated inflammatory myopathies: Similarities with seronegative polymyositis. Ann. Neurol. *29*:474, 1991.
39. Ishii, K., Yamato, K., Iwahara, Y., et al: Isolation of HTLV-1 from muscle of a patient with polymyositis. Am. J. Med. *90*:267, 1991.
40. Ivanoska, D., Cuperlovi, K., Gamble, H. R., et al.: Comparative efficacy of antigen and antibody detection tests for human trichinellosis. J. Parasitol. *75*:38, 1989.
41. Jehn, U. W., and Fink, M. K.: Myositis, myoglobinemia, and myoglobinuria associated with enterovirus echo 9 infection. Arch. Neurol. *37*:457, 1980.
42. Johnson, K. M., Bloom, H. H., Forsyth, B., et al.: The role of enteroviruses in respiratory disease. Am. Rev. Respir. Dis. *88*:240, 1963.

43. Josselson, J., Pula, T., and Sadler, J. H.: Acute rhabdomyolysis associated with an echovirus 9 infection. Arch. Intern. Med. *140*:1671, 1980.
44. Kantor, R. J., Norden, C. W., and Wein, T. P.: Infectious mononucleosis associated with rhabdomyolysis and renal failure. South. Med. J. *71*:346, 1978.
45. Kelly, K. J., Garland, J. S., Tang, T. T., et al.: Fatal rhabdomyolysis following influenza infection in a girl with familial carnitine palmityl transferase deficiency. Pediatrics. *84*:312, 1989.
46. Kessler, H. A., Trenholme, G. M., Harris, A. A., et al.: Acute myopathy associated with influenza A/Texas/1/77 infection. J. A. M. A. *243*:461, 1980.
47. Khan, A. S., Gaviria, M., Rollin, P. E., et al.: Hantavirus pulmonary syndrome in Florida: association with the newly identified Black Creek Canal virus. Am. J. Med. *100*:46, 1996.
48. Ledford, D. K., Overman, M. D., Gonzalvo, A., et al.: Microsporidiosis myositis in a patient with the acquired immunodeficiency syndrome. Ann. Intern. Med. *102*:628, 1985.
49. Lundberg, A.: Myalgia cruris epidemica. Acta Paediatr. *46*:18, 1957.
50. Macher, A. M., Neafie, R., Angritt, P., et al.: Microsporidial myositis and the acquired immunodeficiency syndrome (AIDS): A four-year follow-up. Ann. Intern. Med. *109*:343, 1988.
51. Mackay, M. T., Kornberg, A. J., Shield, L. K., et al.: Benign acute childhood myositis: Laboratory and clinical features. Neurology. *53*:2127, 1999.
52. MacLean, J. D., Viallet, J., Law, C., et al.: Trichinosis in the Canadian Arctic: Report of five outbreaks and a new clinical syndrome. J. Infect. Dis. *160*:513, 1989.
52a. MacLean, J. D., Poirier, L., Gyorkos, T. W., et al.: Epidemiologic and serologic definition of primary and secondary trichinosis in the Arctic. J. Infect Dis. *165*:908, 1992.
53. Manson-Bahr, P. E. C., and Bell, D. R. (eds.): Tapeworms (cestodes). *In* Manson's Tropical Diseases. 19th ed. Philadelphia, Baillieres Tindall, 1987, p. 521.
54. Mason, W., and Keller, E.: Acute transient myositis with influenza-like illness. J. Pediatr. *86*:813, 1975.
55. McKinlay, I. A., and Mitchell, I.: Transient acute myositis in childhood. Arch. Dis. Child. *51*:135, 1979.
56. Medical Letter on Drugs and Therapeutics: Drugs for parasitic infections. Med. Lett. online: Available at http://www.medicalletter.com, 2000.
57. Mejlszenkier, J. D., Safran, A. P., Healy, J. J., et al.: The myositis of influenza. Arch. Neurol. *29*:441, 1973.
58. Meshkinpour, H., and Vaziri, M. D.: Acute rhabdomyolysis associated with adenovirus infection. J. Infect. Dis. *143*:133, 1981.
59. Middleton, P. J., Alexander, R. M., and Szymanski, M. T.: Severe myositis during recovery from influenza. Lancet *2*:533, 1970.
60. Minow, R. A., Gorbach, S., Johnson, B. L., et al.: Myoglobinuria associated with influenza A infection. Ann. Intern. Med. *80*:359, 1980.
61. Morgensen, J. L.: Myoglobinuria and renal failure associated with influenza. Ann. Intern. Med. *80*:362, 1974.
62. Most, H.: Trichinosis: Preventable yet still with us. N. Engl. J. Med. *298*:1178, 1978.
63. Narasimhan, C., George, T. J., Thomas George, K., et al.: *W. bancrofti* as a causal agent of polymyositis. J. Assoc. Physicians India *40*:471, 1992.
64. Naylor, C. D., Jevnikar, A. M., and Witt, N. J.: Sporadic viral myositis in two adults. Can. Med. Assoc. J. *137*:819, 1987.
65. Nishino, H., Engel, A. G., and Rima, B. K.: Inclusion body myositis: The mumps hypothesis. Ann. Neurol. *25*:260, 1989.
66. Nordstrom, D. M., Petropolis, A. A., Giorno, R., et al.: Inflammatory myopathy and acquired immunodeficiency syndrome. Arthritis Rheum. *32*:475, 1989.
67. Norris, F. H., Jr., Dramov, B., Calder, C. D., et al.: Virus-like particles in myositis accompanying herpes zoster. Arch. Neurol. *21*:25, 1969.
68. Partin, J. C., Schubert, W. K., Partin, J. S., et al.: Isolation of influenza virus from liver and muscle biopsy specimens from a surviving case of Reye's syndrome. Lancet. *2*:599, 1976.
69. Poddar, S. K., Misra, S., and Singh, N. K.: Acute polymyositis associated with *W. bancrofti*. Acta Neurol. Scand. *89*:225, 1994.
70. Poels, P., Ewals, J., Joosten, E., et al.: Rhabdomyolysis associated with simultaneous Epstein-Barr virus infection and isolation of echovirus 6 from muscle: A dual infection. J. Neurol. Neurosurg. Psychiatry. *52*:412, 1989.
71. Reimers, C. D., Pongratz, D. E., Neubert, U., et al.: Myositis caused by *Borrelia burgdorferi*: Report of four cases. J. Neurol. Sci. *91*:215, 1989.
72. Ruff, R. L., and Secrist, D.: Viral studies in benign acute childhood myositis. Arch. Neurol. *39*:261, 1982.
73. Sakata, H., Taketazu, G., Nagaya, K., et al.: Outbreak of severe infection due to adenovirus type 7 in a paediatric ward in Japan. J. Hosp. Infect. *39*:207, 1998.
74. Schlesinger, M. J. J., Gandara, D., and Bensch, K. G.: Myoglobinuria associated with herpes-group viral infection. Arch. Intern. Med. *138*:422, 1978.
75. Schoenen, J., Sianard-Gainko, J., Carpentier, M., et al.: Myositis during *Borrelia burgdorferi* infection (Lyme disease). J. Neurol. Neurosurg. Psychiatry *52*:1002, 1989.
76. Seidenberg, K. B., and Leib, M. L.: Orbital myositis with Lyme disease. Am. J. Ophthalmol. *109*:13, 1990.
77. Simon, N. M., Rovner, R. N., and Berlin, B. S.: Acute myoglobinuria associated with type A2 (Hong Kong) influenza. J. A. M. A. *212*:1704, 1970.
78. Sinniah, R., and Lye, W.: Acute renal failure from myoglobinuria secondary to myositis from severe falciparum malaria. Am. J. Nephrol. *20*:339, 2000.
79. Stang, H.: Acute transient myositis associated with influenza virus infection. Pediatr. Infect. Dis. J. *8*:257, 1989.
80. Stevens, D., Burman, D., Clarke, S. K. R., et al.: Temporary paralysis in childhood after influenza B. Lancet *2*:1354, 1974.
81. Tang, T. T., Sedmak, G. V., Siegesmund, K. A., et al.: Chronic myopathy associated with coxsackievirus type A9: A combined electron microscopical and viral isolation study. N. Engl. J. Med. *292*:608, 1975.
82. Tepperberg, J.: Transient acute myositis in children. J. A. M. A. *238*:27, 1977.
83. Teutsch, S. M., Juranek, D. D., Sulzer, A., et al.: Epidemic toxoplasmosis associated with infected cats. N. Engl. J. Med. *300*:695, 1979.
84. Ueda, K., Robbins, D. A., Itaka, K., et al.: Fatal rhabdomyolysis associated with parainfluenza type 3 infection. Hiroshima J. Med. Sci. *27*:99, 1978.
85. Viard, J. P., Vittecoq, D., Lacroix, C., et al.: Response of HIV-1–associated polymyositis to intravenous immunoglobulin. Am. J. Med. *92*:580, 1992.
86. Villanova, M., Caudai, C., Sabatelli, P., et al.: Hepatitis C virus infection and myositis: a polymerase chain reaction study. Acta. Neuropathol. (Berl.) *99*:271, 2000.
87. Walls, K. W.: Serodiagnostic tests for parasitic diseases. *In* Lennette, E. H., Balows, A., Hausler, W. J., et al. (eds.): Manual of Clinical Microbiology. 4th ed. Washington, D.C., American Society for Microbiology, 1985, p. 945.
88. Walsh, S. S., Robson, W. J., and Hart, C. A.: Acute transient myositis due to *Toxocara*. Arch. Dis. Child. *63*:1087, 1988.
89. Wiley, C. A., Nerenberg, M., Cros, D., et al.: HTLV-I polymyositis in a patient also infected with the human immunodeficiency virus. N. Engl. J. Med. *320*:992, 1989.
90. Wright, J., Couchonnal G., and Hodges, G. R.: Adenovirus type 21 infection: Occurrence with pneumonia, rhabdomyolysis, and myoglobinuria in an adult. J. A. M. A. *241*:2420, 1979.
91. Zafeiriou, D. I., Katzos, G., Gombakis, N., et al.: Clinical features, laboratory findings and differential diagnosis of benign acute childhood myositis. Acta Paediatr. *89*:1493, 2000.
92. Zamkoff, K., and Rosen, N.: Influenza and myoglobinuria in brothers. Neurology. *29*:340, 1979.
93. Zvolanek, J. R.: Benign acute childhood myositis associated with parainfluenza type 2 infection. Pediatr. Infect. Dis. *3*:594, 1984.

SECTION X

Skin Infections

CHAPTER 65

Cutaneous Manifestations of Systemic Infections

JAMES D. CHERRY ■ RAVI JHAVERI

Many illnesses caused by infectious agents have associated cutaneous manifestations. In some cases, the exanthem may be the hallmark of the disease, and in others, it may be only a vague indicator of a more significant underlying process. When an exanthem occurs, it often offers important clues to the etiology of a patient's illness. Although most exanthematous illnesses in children are benign, their differential diagnosis is critical because the early manifestations of potentially fatal bacterial and rickettsial diseases frequently have cutaneous findings.

History

Exanthematous manifestations of infectious illnesses have been important since medical antiquity. Major epidemics of both measles and smallpox occurred in the Roman Empire and in China at the beginning of the Christian era.[22, 125] Scarlet fever was recognized as a distinct entity in the 17th century, and chickenpox and rubella were identified in the 18th and 19th centuries, respectively.[46]

In the writings of the early 20th century, maculopapular exanthematous illnesses of children frequently were referred to by number. Scarlet fever and measles historically were the first two classic maculopapular exanthems of childhood. Which one had the honor of being the "first disease" is unknown today. The "third disease" was rubella, which was recognized by the beginning of the 20th century as a distinct entity.[64, 66, 83, 152, 172–174] In 1900, Dukes[64] described an exanthematous illness with the characteristics of both rubella and scarlet fever, which he suggested was a "fourth disease." The general opinion today is that his disease was not a distinct entity. Shaw[174] suggested that Dukes' cases had mild atypical scarlet fever, and Powell[152] raised the possibility that the illness resulted from epidermolytic toxin–producing staphylococci. Most probably, rubella and scarlet fever both were epidemic in the student population under Dr. Dukes' care; combined infections led to the confusion.

Erythema infectiosum (see Chapter 158) commonly is referred to as the "fifth disease," and roseola infantum (see Chapter 66) qualifies as the "sixth disease."[173]

During the last 50 years, interest in exanthematous diseases has been renewed because a large number of previously unknown viruses and other infectious agents that cause cutaneous manifestations have been discovered. In addition, the pattern of disease caused by classic exanthem-producing agents has changed; smallpox has been eradicated, the epidemiology of measles and rubella has been altered by immunization, and ecologic changes have resulted in differences in bacterially induced rashes.

Etiologic Agents

Many different types of viruses, chlamydiae, rickettsiae, mycoplasmas, bacteria, fungi, and protozoan and metazoan agents cause illnesses with associated cutaneous manifestations. Although this chapter is devoted to systemic infectious diseases with cutaneous manifestations, the demarcation between exanthematous disease of systemic and local origin is not always readily apparent. For example, the recurrent cold sore caused by herpes simplex virus (HSV) infection frequently is considered a local problem, although its nature and pathogenesis involve central virus latency and host systemic immune functions. Similarly, superficial fungal diseases and other local infections, such as warts, may be quite dependent on more general immunologic functions of the host. The exanthems of enteroviral infections frequently are confused with those caused by insect bites and allergic problems.

Table 65–1 presents viruses that have cutaneous manifestations in humans. Erythema infectiosum is caused by human parvovirus B19.[5, 198] This virus also is an important cause of the papular-purpuric gloves and socks syndrome that is an uncommon occurrence and mainly affects young adults.[47, 81, 178] Human parvovirus B19 also has been associated with a vesiculopustular exanthem, erythema multiforme, and other petechial and purpuric rashes. Adenovirus types 1, 2, 3, 4, 7, and 7a have been isolated from children and young adults with exanthem.[46, 105, 201, 202] The overall clinical expression rate of exanthem in adenovirus infection rarely has been studied. Fukumi and associates[75] noted that rash occurred in 2 percent of adenoviral infections; Hope-Simpson and Higgins[93] indicated a rate of about 8 percent.

Eight species in the *Herpesvirus* genus have cutaneous manifestations associated with infection, but clinical expression rates vary greatly. Nearly all primary varicella infections are associated with exanthem, whereas exanthem with acquired cytomegalovirus infection is rare.[16, 19, 46, 160, 183, 201] The incidence of exanthem in Epstein-Barr virus infection varies from 3 to nearly 100 percent, depending on whether concomitant ampicillin is administered.[13, 25, 90, 99, 106, 141, 153, 190, 191] Although firm data are lacking, probably less than 10 percent of primary infections with HSV type 1 are associated with cutaneous manifestations. Erythema multiforme occasionally occurs with recurrent HSV virus infections.[33, 72, 102, 139]

TABLE 65–1 ■ CLINICAL CHARACTERISTICS OF VIRAL INFECTIONS WITH CUTANEOUS MANIFESTATIONS

Virus	Disease or Syndrome	Incubation Period (Days)	Main Season	Clinical Characteristics	Exanthem		Usual Duration (Days)
					Lesions	Distribution	
Parvovirus (see Figs. 65–6 to 65–8)	Erythema infectiosum	7–17	Winter and spring	Biphasic illness with mild prodromal period with headache and malaise for 2–3 days, then 7-day symptom-free period, followed by typical exanthem	Three-stage exanthem: initially, rash on cheeks (slapped-cheek appearance) and then erythematous maculopapular rash on trunk and limbs. Finally, rash develops a recticular pattern	Starts on face. More prominent on extensor surfaces of extremities	7–21
Wart	Warts		Nonseasonal	Local cutaneous disease	Papular or nodular isolated lesions	Most common on extremities	100+
Adenovirus types 1, 2, 3, 4, 7, and 7a		6–9	Winter and spring	Fever and signs and symptoms or respiratory illness. Occasionally, rash occurs after defervescence (roseola-like)	Most commonly erythematous, maculopapular, and discrete (rubelliform), but occasionally confluent (morbilliform); rarely, erythema multiforme and Stevens-Johnson syndrome	Usually starts on face and spreads downward to trunk and extremities	3–5
Herpes simplex types 1 and 2 (see Fig. 65–5)	Cold sores, genital herpes, neonatal herpes, or other	2–12	Nonseasonal	Primary disease associated with fever and systemic symptoms. Recurrent disease caused by exogenous and endogenous infections	Singular or grouped vesicular lesions varying in size from 2 to 10 mm, frequently on a mildly erythematous base. Occasionally, erythema multiforme, Stevens-Johnson syndrome, and erythema nodosum	Lesions in primary infection with type 1 virus are mainly in and around the mouth. Recurrent type 1 lesions usually perioral. Primary and recurrent type 2 lesions usually on genitals	7–14
Human herpesvirus-6 (HHV-6)	Roseola infantum		Nonseasonal	Fever 3–5 days in duration, rapid defervescence, and then the appearance of rash	Erythematous macular or maculopapular	Most prominent on neck and trunk. Face and extremities may be affected	1–2
Human herpesvirus-7 (HHV-7)	Roseola infantum		Nonseasonal	Fever 3–5 days in duration, rapid defervescence, and then the appearance of rash	Erythematous macular or maculopapular	Most prominent on neck and trunk. Face and extremities may be affected	1–2
Human herpesvirus-8 (HHV-8)	Kasopi sarcoma	Months to years	Nonseasonal	Asymptomatic infection. Most commonly noted in AIDS patients, but occurs in other immunodeficiency states	Purple to blue nodular, raised lesions	Any epidermal or mucosal surface	Months to years
Varicella-zoster (see Fig. 65–4)	Chickenpox (varicella)	12–20	Late fall, winter, and spring	Malaise and fever of 5–6 days' duration	Basic lesion is vesicular, but lesions go through stages: macules, papules, vesicles, and crusts Lesions occur in crops	Lesions more profuse on trunk than on extremities. Proximal end of extremities more involved than distal end	8–10
	Herpes zoster		Nonseasonal	Endogenous infection. Pain and paresthesia with dermatome distribution	Basic lesion is vesicular, but lesions go through stages: macules, papules, vesicles, and crusts	Lesions localized to area of skin innervated by a single sensory ganglion	10–28
Epstein-Barr	Infectious mononucleosis	28–49	Nonseasonal	Fever, pharyngitis, and lymphadenopathy. Exanthem occurs in 3–13% of cases. If ampicillin administered, then exanthem in 50% of cases	Most commonly erythematous, macular, maculopapular, and discrete (rubelliform). In association with ampicillin administration, the rash may be more vivid. Erythema multiforme and urticaria may occur	Mainly on trunk and proximal end of extremities	2–7

Continued

TABLE 65–1 ■ CLINICAL CHARACTERISTICS OF VIRAL INFECTIONS WITH CUTANEOUS MANIFESTATIONS—cont'd

Virus	Disease or Syndrome	Incubation Period (Days)	Main Season	Clinical Characteristics	Exanthem		Usual Duration (Days)
					Lesions	Distribution	
Cytomegalovirus	Cytomegalovirus mononucleosis		Nonseasonal	Acquired: Mild febrile illness with lymphadenopathy Congenital: Disseminated disease	Erythematous, maculopapular, and discrete. Vesicular or petechial in congenital infection	Located mainly on trunk and proximal end of extremities	2–7
Vaccinia	Roseola vaccinatum, eczema vaccinatum, vaccination "take," or disseminated vaccinia		Nonseasonal	Illness caused by direct exposure via vaccination or exposure to a vaccinee	Vaccination and eczema vaccinatum: Lesions go through stages: papule, vesicle, pustule, and scab. Roseola vaccinatum: erythematous maculopapular lesions. Occasionally erythema multiforme. Disseminated vaccinia: papular or vesicular lesions	Lesions in roseola vaccinatum, eczema vaccinatum, and disseminated vaccinia are generalized	7–14
Variola	Smallpox	8–17	Seasonal by geographic area	Abrupt onset of high fever, headache, and muscle and joint pain. Rash appears 2–4 days after onset	Basic lesion is vesicular, but lesions go through stages: macules, papules, vesicles, pustules, and crusts	Most prominent on exposed body surfaces. Starts on extremities and face. Spreads centripetally	12–20
Monkeypox				Similar to mild smallpox. Exposure to monkeys. No human-to-human spread	Similar to mild smallpox	Similar to mild smallpox	
Orf	Ecthyma contagiosum	4–7	Spring	Disease of sheep acquired by humans	Initially erythematous papule. Becomes umbilicated, nodular, and then vesicular. Occasionally erythema multiforme	Solitary lesion, usually on hands	30–40
Molluscum contagiosum	Molluscum contagiosum			Local cutaneous disease	Umbilicated nodular lesions: singular or clusters	Most common on face, inner aspect of thigh, breasts, and genitalia	100+
Paravaccinia	Milker nodules	4–7		Human infection acquired from infected calves	Nodular lesion. Occasionally erythema multiforme	Solitary lesion, usually on hands	30–40
Tanapox				A virus of monkeys. Human infection associated with fever and regional lymphadenopathy	Umbilicated vesicular lesion	Upper part of body. Solitary lesion	35–56
Coxsackieviruses A2, A4, A5, A7, A9, A10, and A16; coxsackieviruses B1–B5; echoviruses 1–7, 9, 11–14, 16–19, 22, 24, 25, 30, and 33; enterovirus 71 (see Figs. 65-9 through 65-16)		4–7	Summer and fall	Fever and mild to moderate pharyngitis. Occasionally, herpangina, meningitis, and other manifestations of systemic viral infection. Exanthem occurs in 5–50% of infections, depending on virus type. Rash may occur during fever or after defervescence. Hand, foot, and mouth syndrome	Most commonly erythematous, maculopapular, and discrete. May have macular, petechial, vesicular, and urticarial components. Rarely erythema multiforme	Usually starts on face and spreads downward to trunk and extremities. May have peripheral distribution (hand, foot, and mouth syndrome)	3–7

Rhinoviruses (many types)		2–4	Fall, winter, and spring	Mild fever and signs and symptoms of respiratory illness. Exanthem occurs in about 5% of cases	Erythematous, maculopapular, and discrete	Starts on face and spreads downward to trunk and extremities	1–4
Foot and mouth		3–4		Direct animal contact. Fever, sore mouth, and lymphadenopathy. Vesicles and ulcers within the mouth	Vesicular lesions	Hands and feet	3–6
Colorado tick fever		3–5	Summer	Fever, chills, eye pain, myalgia, and headache. Diphasic course. Rash in only about 10% of cases	Occasionally maculopapular but usually petechial	Maculopapular rash is generalized. Petechial rash most prominent on arms, legs, and trunk	2–7
Reovirus 2 and 3		4–7	Summer	Fever, mild pharyngitis, and cervical adenopathy	Erythematous or maculopapular. Discrete or confluent. Occasionally vesicular	Starts on face and spreads downward to trunk and extremities	3–9
Rotavirus		2–4	Fall, winter, and spring	Gastroenteritis	Petechial and morbilliform	Generalized	7–14
Chikungunya, O'nyong-nyong, Ross River, Sindbis			During periods of arthropod prevalence	Fever, headache, eye pain, and marked myalgia, arthralgia, and arthritis. Geographically localized diseases	Rubelliform and morbilliform. Frequently vesicular and petechial	Starts on face and spreads downward to trunk and extremities	4–7
Rubella (see Fig. 65–3)	Rubella (German measles)	15–21	Winter and spring	Mild symptoms with onset 1–5 days before rash. Fever usually <38.5°C (101.5°F). Headache, malaise, and suboccipital and postauricular lymphadenopathy	Erythematous, maculopapular, and discrete	Starts on face and spreads downward to trunk and extremities	3–5
West Nile				Sudden onset of fever, chills, and drowsiness. Rash may appear during or after fever. Geographically localized disease	Erythematous, macular, and maculopapular	Starts on trunk and spreads to extremities	3–6
Dengue and Kunjin		7	During periods of specific arthropod prevalence	Sudden onset of high fever, then severe headache, myalgia, arthralgia, abdominal pain, and marked diaphoresis. Fever lasts 5–6 days and ends by crisis. Rash appears within 48 hours of onset of fever. Geographically localized disease	Initially, macular, flushed appearance, then erythematous, maculopapular rash. May be scarlatiniform. Frequently becomes petechial and purpuric. Small vesicles occur in Kunjin virus infection	Initial macular rash is more prominent centrally. Maculopapular rash may start on hands and feet and spread to trunk	3–10
Influenza A and B		2–5	Fall, winter, and spring	Fever, cough, headache, and muscle aches and pains. Usually in young children. Rash an occasional occurrence	Erythematous, maculopapular, and discrete (rubelliform). Rarely erythema multiforme	Starts on face and trunk and spreads to extremities	1–3
Respiratory syncytial		2–5	Fall, winter, and spring	Fever, coryza, and respiratory distress (bronchitis, bronchiolitis, or pneumonia). Usually in children <2 years of age	Erythematous, maculopapular, and discrete (rubelliform)	Starts on face and trunk and spreads to extremities	1–3
Parainfluenza 1–3		2–5	Fall, winter, and spring	Fever, coryza, nasopharyngitis, croup, and bronchitis. Usually in young children	Erythematous, maculopapular, and discrete (rubelliform)	Starts on face and trunk and spreads to extremities	1–3
Mumps	Mumps	14–21	Fall, winter, and spring	Fever, headache, and salivary gland swelling	Erythematous, maculopapular, and discrete. Also, urticaria and vesicles. Rarely, erythema multiforme	Most prominent on trunk	2–5

Continued

TABLE 65–1 ■ CLINICAL CHARACTERISTICS OF VIRAL INFECTIONS WITH CUTANEOUS MANIFESTATIONS—cont'd

Virus	Disease or Syndrome	Incubation Period (Days)	Main Season	Clinical Characteristics	Exanthem: Lesions	Exanthem: Distribution	Usual Duration (Days)
Measles (see Figs. 65–1 and 65–2)	Measles	8–12	Winter and spring	Onset with fever, cough, coryza, and conjunctivitis. About 2 days after onset, appearance of enanthem (Koplik spots), and 2 days later, onset of exanthem	Erythematous, maculopapular, and confluent. Develops a brownish appearance, and fine desquamation occurs	Starts behind ears and on forehead. Spreads downward over body. Confluence most prominent on face, trunk, and proximal end of extremities	5–7
Lassa	Lassa fever			Sudden onset of fever, chills, headache, and sore throat. Progresses to pneumonia and renal failure. Geographically localized outbreaks	Macular and sometimes petechial	Localized or general	
Hepatitis B	Papular acrodermatitis of childhood	50–180		Insidious onset with arthralgia, arthritis, and rash occurring before jaundice	Maculopapular, macular, and/or urticarial. In young children, papular (Gianotti-Crosti syndrome or papular acrodermatitis of childhood) Rarely, erythema multiforme	Generalized	4–10
Hepatitis C	Mixed cryoglobulinemia (not reported in children)	7–14	Nonseasonal	Acute hepatitis followed by chronic infection. Skin findings occur late in disease	Palpable purpura	Mostly buttocks, lower extremities	Variable
Marburg		5–7		Headache, conjunctivitis, photophobia, myalgia, vomiting, diarrhea, and fever (biphasic). Exposure to vervet monkeys	Initially erythematous macular, then discrete maculopapular, and, finally, confluent maculopapular. Exfoliation occurs. Occasionally purpura	Generalized	2–14
Ebola	Hemorrhagic fever	5–10	Occurs in outbreaks	Febrile illness that progresses to hemorrhage, shock, and coma	Maculopapular rash that appears toward end of first week of illness	Lateral sides of trunk, groin, and axillae. Can become generalized but spares the face	14–60
Hantavirus	Hemorrhagic fever with renal syndrome (nephropathia epidemica)		Spring and summer outbreaks	Febrile illness with hemorrhagic and renal manifestations	Flushing and petechial rash	Face (flushing), skin folds (petechiae)	14–28
HIV		14–60	Nonseasonal	Fever, pharyngitis, myalgia, arthralgias, adenopathy, and rash	Macular	Mainly chest and abdomen	7
Human T-lymphotropic virus	Infective dermatitis		Nonseasonal	Acute onset of eczema	Severe exudative eczema with a crusting, generalized fine papular rash	Scalp, eyelid margins, perinasal skin, retroauricular areas, axillae, and groin	Months to years

Data from references 1–3, 5–9, 13, 16, 19, 23, 33, 36, 39, 41, 43, 45–47, 49, 54, 55, 57, 59, 61, 72–75, 81, 90, 92, 93, 97, 99, 101, 106, 109, 111, 112, 116, 121, 130, 132–136, 139, 141, 145, 147, 158, 160, 161, 163–165, 168, 169, 178, 182, 186, 190, 191, 195, 198, 200–202, 209, 210.

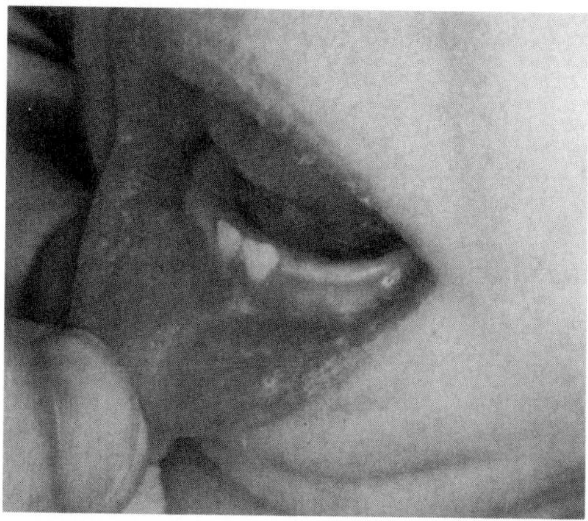

FIGURE 65–1 ■ Koplik spots with involvement of the buccal and lower labial mucosa.

Human herpesvirus–6 (HHV-6) is a major cause of roseola infantum.[8, 198, 210] HHV-7 also is a cause of roseola infantum[7]; in addition, some evidence suggests that this virus may play a role in pityriasis rosea.[62] HHV-8 infection is necessary for the development of Kaposi sarcoma in patients with acquired immunodeficiency syndrome (AIDS) and other immunodeficiency states.[97, 109, 130]

At present, human illnesses with cutaneous manifestations caused by poxviruses rarely occur. Because smallpox as a disease has ceased to exist, the use of vaccinia virus for immunization has decreased dramatically. However, the terrorist events of 2001 raised concern regarding the possible use of smallpox virus as a terrorist weapon. Because of this potential danger, smallpox vaccines are being produced and used again. With the increased use of these vaccines, cutaneous complications of vaccinia virus infection can be expected. Monkeypox, orf, and paravaccinia (milker's nodules) continue to occur as isolated events in exposed individuals.[164, 201, 202] Human infection with tanapox virus is a geographically related illness occurring in limited areas of Kenya.

In the present era, enteroviruses are the leading cause of infection-related exanthematous diseases.[48, 52, 104, 201, 202] Thirty-seven types have been associated with rash illnesses. The clinical expression rate varies greatly among the different types; it is as high as 50 percent in children with coxsackievirus A16 and echovirus 9 infections. Only approximately 15 percent of individuals infected with echovirus 4 have exanthem, and rash is a rare occurrence in echovirus 6 infection. Hope-Simpson and Higgins[93] noted exanthem in approximately 5 percent of patients with rhinoviral respiratory illness.

A young adult research worker had a flulike illness and a hand, foot, and mouth syndrome–like rash caused by infection with a calicivirus (San Miguel sea lion virus serotype 5) of oceanic origin.[177]

Two percent of patients with Colorado tick fever encephalitis have exanthem.[48] Although infection with reoviruses occurs commonly, exanthem has been noted on only nine occasions.[48, 116] A morbilliform rash has been observed in one adult with a rotavirus infection, and a 4-year-old boy was noted to have a petechial rash in association with a rotaviral illness.[57, 161]

Of the *Togaviridae* family of viruses, rubella virus is the most important as a worldwide cause of exanthematous disease. Several alphaviruses also frequently cause exanthems.[103, 136, 201, 202] Each of these viruses has a marked geographic distribution. Similarly, flaviviruses also have exanthem as part of their clinical expression, and they too have specific geographic boundaries.[201, 202] In the New York City area outbreak of West Nile virus infection in 1999, 19 percent of patients had exanthem.[133] The rash was erythematous macular, papular, or morbilliform.

Exanthem generally is not considered to be a manifestation of influenza virus infection, but Hope-Simpson and Higgins[93] noted exanthem in approximately 8 percent of patients from whom influenza B virus was isolated and in 1 or 2 percent of those infected with influenza A virus. Measles virus is the most notable of the *Paramyxoviridae* family with an associated exanthem. However, exanthem occurs rather frequently in young children infected with parainfluenza virus types 1, 2, and 3 and also in those with respiratory syncytial virus (RSV) illnesses.[77, 88, 89, 192, 195] Hope-Simpson and Higgins[93] noted a 15 percent incidence of rash in RSV infection and an approximately 15 percent incidence in parainfluenza virus infection. Exanthem also has been noted on rare occasion with mumps virus infection.[49]

Lassa fever virus, Marburg virus, Ebola virus, and hepatitis B virus all have been associated with exanthem on occasion.[39, 43, 59, 71, 147, 201] Hepatitis B virus is the main cause of papular acrodermatitis (Gianotti-Crosti syndrome) in children.[43, 165, 169] Chronic hepatitis C virus infection occasionally causes systemic vasculitis and cryoglobulinemia in adults, with purpuric lesions concentrated on the lower extremities.[2, 92] Other cutaneous manifestations of chronic hepatitis C virus infection include urticaria, erythema nodosum, lichen planus, and nodular prurigo.[101, 209]

Hantaviruses cause two major syndromes throughout the world: hemorrhagic fever with renal syndrome and hantavirus pulmonary syndrome.[3, 36, 145, 168] Exanthem (facial flushing and petechial lesions in skin folds) occurs in approximately 30 percent of patients with hemorrhagic fever with renal syndrome, but rash is not reported in the hantavirus pulmonary syndrome. A macular rash has been noted in association with acute infection with human immunodeficiency virus type 1 (HIV-1).[132, 134, 135, 182] Several reports have associated human T-lymphotropic virus type 1 (HTLV-1) with an atypical form of eczema called infective dermatitis. This exanthem has an acute onset and is somewhat recalcitrant to treatment.[111, 112, 121]

Chlamydiae, rickettsiae, and mycoplasmas associated with cutaneous manifestations are listed in Table 65–2. Of the chlamydiae, only *Chlamydia psittaci* has been associated with exanthem. In contrast, all rickettsiae that infect humans, with the exception of *Coxiella burnetii,* usually display some cutaneous manifestations as part of their systemic disease.[28, 65, 80, 110, 117, 138, 142, 167] Approximately 4 to 7 percent of adults with Q fever have exanthem.[37, 180] Of the mycoplasmas that infect humans, only *Mycoplasma pneumoniae* is associated with exanthem.[10, 48, 50] In epidemics, exanthem occurs in approximately 15 percent of persons with respiratory illness.

In Table 65–3, bacterial agents for which cutaneous manifestations are part of the clinical illness are presented (see Chapter 67). The clinical expression of exanthem varies tremendously among the different etiologic agents, as do the conditions associated with a specific infection. For example, infection with phage group II staphylococci usually results in cutaneous disease in young infants, whereas in adults, the same organisms rarely cause illness. Symptomatic infection with *Streptococcus pneumoniae* is associated with cutaneous manifestations only occasionally; on the other hand, similar systemic disease with *Neisseria meningitidis* virtually always is associated with the characteristic petechial exanthem. Of the other bacterial agents listed in Table 65–3, exanthem is most important in the following: *Neisseria*

TABLE 65–2 ■ CLINICAL CHARACTERISTICS OF CHLAMYDIAL, RICKETTSIAL, AND MYCOPLASMAL INFECTIONS WITH CUTANEOUS MANIFESTATIONS

Agent	Disease or Syndrome	Incubation Period (Days)	Main Season	Clinical Characteristics	Exanthem		Usual Duration (Days)
					Lesions	Distribution	
Chlamydia psittaci	Psittacosis	7–14	Nonseasonal	Fever, chills, headache, and cough. Respiratory distress	Erythematous macules. Occasionally erythema multiforme or erythema nodosum	Mainly on trunk	2–7
Rickettsia akari	Rickettsialpox	7–14	Nonseasonal	Fever, chills, headache, backache, and malaise 4–7 days after onset of primary lesion at site of mite bite. Geographically localized disease	Initial lesion at site of mite bite is papular and then vesicular, and finally an eschar forms. Two days after onset of fever, erythematous maculopapular discrete rash occurs. Lesions progress to small vesicles and later to scabs	Most prominent on trunk and proximal end of extremities	7–10
Rickettsia typhii	Endemic, murine typhus	7–14	Nonseasonal	Fever and headache. Rash appears on 4th–7th day. Geographically localized disease	Initially discrete macules and then erythematous maculopapular. May become purpuric	Initially upper part of trunk and axilla. Progresses to entire body except face, palms, and soles	7–21
Rickettsia prowazekii	Epidemic typhus	10–14	Nonseasonal	Sudden onset of fever, chills, headache, and myalgias. Rash appears on 4th–7th day. Geographically localized disease	Initially discrete macules and then progresses to maculopapular and petechial lesions. Sometimes purpuric	Appears first on trunk and spreads to extremities. Spares palms and soles	7–14
Rickettsia tsutsugamushi	Scrub typhus	7–21	Nonseasonal	Sudden onset of chills, fever, and headache	Local lesion at site of chigger bite is present at onset of symptoms; characterized by vesicle, ulcer, and eschar. Maculopapular rash occurs 5–8 days after onset of fever	Maculopapular rash first occurs on trunk and then becomes generalized	7–14
Rickettsia rickettsii	Rocky Mountain spotted fever	3–12	Summer	Abrupt onset of fever, chills, and headache. Rash appears 2–4 days after onset	Early maculopapular, then petechial, and sometimes purpuric	Rash starts on distal end of extremities. Rarely involves the trunk	7–14
Other tick-borne *Rickettsiae*			Tick seasons	Similar to mild Rocky Mountain spotted fever	Similar to Rocky Mountain spotted fever; eschar at site of tick bite	Similar to Rocky Mountain spotted fever	7–14
R. siberica	North Asian tick-borne rickettsiosis						
R. australis	Queensland tick typhus						
R. conorii	Boutonneuse fever						
R. africae	African tick fever						
Coxiella burnetii	Q fever	20–40	Nonseasonal	Acute febrile illness with chills, headache, and myalgia	Fine discrete macular rash occuring during febrile illness. Transient urticarial rash also noted	Mainly on trunk	2–7
Ehrlichia species	Ehrlichiosis	14–28	Tick seasons	Similar to Rocky Mountain spotted fever, but rash usually not on palms and soles	Similar to endemic typhus	Similar to endemic typhus	7–14
Mycoplasma pneumoniae		21	All seasons	Gradual onset of fever, malaise, headache, and cough	Maculopapular rash occurs in 5–15% of cases. Vesicular and bullous lesions common (Stevens-Johnson syndrome); more common in males. Papular, petechial, and urticarial lesions also noted. Erythema multiforme common	Rash most prominent on trunk and proximal end of extremities	7–14

Data from references 10, 11, 15, 28, 32, 37, 48, 50, 65, 80, 87, 110, 117, 124, 131, 138, 142, 154, 167, 180, 208.

TABLE 65–3 ■ BACTERIA ASSOCIATED WITH CUTANEOUS MANIFESTATIONS

Agent	Disease or Syndrome	Clinical Characteristics	Exanthem: Lesions	Exanthem: Distribution
Gram-Positive Cocci				
Staphylococcus aureus exfoliative toxin-producing (mainly phage group 2) (see Figs. 65–17 and 65–18)	Bullous impetigo	Usually occurs in neonates. May be epidemic	Rapid progression from vesicles to bullous lesions	Most common in diaper area
	Scalded skin syndrome. Toxic epidermal necrolysis (Ritter disease in infants <4 months of age; Lyell syndrome in older children)	Usually occurs in infants and children 1 month–5 years of age. Mucopurulent nasal and eye discharge. Fever	Scarlatiniform eruption with exfoliation. Positive Nikolsky sign. Crusty appearance around eyes and under nose	Generalized. Most marked on trunk
	Staphylococcal scarlet fever or staphylococcal scarlatiniform eruption	Fever and staphylococcal infection in throat, but no evidence of pharyngitis	Scarlet fever–like rash with desquamation. Pastia lines present	Generalized
Staphylococcus aureus (non–exfoliative toxin producing)	Septicemic disease	Severe septicemia with osteomyelitis, arthritis, endocarditis, or pneumonia	Diffuse, erythematous, confluent, and macular rash (flush). With endocarditis, may have petechiae and splinter hemorrhages. Osler nodes. Janeway spots	Trunk and proximal end of extremities
Staphylococcus aureus (toxin-1 (TSST-1)-producing)	Toxic shock syndrome	Fever, intense myalgias, vomiting, and diarrhea. Mental confusion and hypotension	Erythematous, deep red (sunburn-like) rash. Desquamation occurs	Generalized
Staphylococcus aureus (non–exfoliative toxin producing)	Folliculitis, furuncles, or carbuncles	See Primary Skin Infections, Chapter 67		
Streptococcus pyogenes	Scarlet fever	Fever, pharyngitis, and cervical lymphadenitis. Rash onset within 2 days of first symptoms. Incubation period 3–4 days	Diffuse erythematous and fine maculopapular (looks and feels like red sandpaper). Rash darker in skin folds (Pastia lines). Desquamation occurs	Circumoral pallor. Generalized rash, with trunk and proximal end of extremities being most involved
	Erysipelas	Fever, headache, and vomiting. Localized infection.	Circumscribed area that is raised and erythematous. Advancing edge is irregular	Anywhere
	Impetigo	Localized superficial pyoderma. See Primary Skin Infections, Chapter 67	Discrete and coalescent lesions of a vesicular nature. Quickly becomes more pustular and then crusts over with a yellowish-brown appearance	Forearms, legs, and face
	Septicemia	Fever and systemic foci of infection	Petechiae	Diffuse
	Miscellaneous skin manifestations of *S. pyogenes* infections		Erythema multiforme, erythema nodosum, and erythema marginatum	
Streptococcus pneumoniae	Septicemia	Fever	Petechiae	Diffuse
Enterococcal and viridans group streptococci	Endocarditis	Endocarditis	Petechiae, splinter hemorrhages, Osler nodes, and Janeway spots	
Gram-Negative Cocci				
Neisseria gonorrhoeae	Gonococcemia	Fever and polyarthralgias	Papular, petechial, purpuric, pustular, and/or necrotic lesions	Most common on extremities. Extensor surfaces over joints
Neisseria menigitidis	Meningococcemia	Fever and pharyngitis. Sudden onset of rash	Characteristic rash is petechial or purpuric. Early lesions may be erythematous, maculopapular, or urticarial	Generalized
Moraxella catarrhalis	Bacteremia	Fever and pharyngitis	Maculopapular and petechial	Generalized
Gram-Positive Bacilli				
Bacillus anthracis	Anthrax	Fever, headache, malaise, and joint pain	Initially, macular, pruritic lesion. Later, a papule forms and then vesiculation. Vesicles last 2–6 days, and then eschar forms	Usually, single lesion initially at point of exposure. Secondary lesions in area develop later

Continued

TABLE 65–3 ■ BACTERIA ASSOCIATED WITH CUTANEOUS MANIFESTATIONS—cont'd

Agent	Disease or Syndrome	Clinical Characteristics	Exanthem	
			Lesions	Distribution
Listeria monocytogenes	Listeriosis	Neonatal meningitis with hepatosplenomegaly	Maculopapular, discrete lesions. Pustules	Trunk and legs
Erysipelothrix rhusiopathiae	Crab or fishnet dermatitis	Fever and local pain	Erysipeloid lesion (violet or red)	Hands
Corynebacterium diphtheriae	Cutaneous diphtheria	Secondary infection in cutaneous wounds	Impetigo or ecthyma-like. Rarely, erythema multiforme	Exposed surfaces
Arcanobacterium hemolyticum	Scarlet fever–like illness	Fever and pharyngitis	Scarlet fever–like rash. Occasionally, rubelliform	Generalized rash with peripheral predominance
Enteric Gram-Negative Bacilli				
Salmonella typhi	Typhoid fever	Malaise, headache, and marked fever. Rash onset 10 days after onset of fever	Rose spots. 2–4 mm macular lesions	Discrete lesions on abdomen
Other *Salmonella* species	Septicemic salmonellosis	Similar to mild typhoid fever	Similar to typhoid fever	Similar to typhoid fever
Shigella sonnei	Shigellosis	Diarrhea	Urticaria	Diffuse
Campylobacter species		Gastroenteritis	Skin pustules and erythema nodosum	Lower part of legs
Other Gram-Negative Bacilli				
Francisella tularensis	Tularemia	Chills, fever, headache, and localized lymphadenopathy	Initial papula that later ulcerates	Site of inoculation
Haemophilus ducreyi	Chancroid	Local pain and tenderness	Pustular lesions that ulcerate	External genitalia
Haemophilus influenzae	Septicemia	Fever	Petechiae. Reddish-purple cellulitis	Diffuse. Cellulitis mainly on cheeks and extremities
Streptobacillus moniliformis	Rat-bite fever	Fever, chills, malaise, headache, and polyarthritis	Erythematous, maculopapular rash that may become petechial	Most prominent on extremities, including palms and soles
Yersinia pestis	Septicemic plague	Sudden onset of fever	Initial generalized erythema followed by petechiae and purpura	Generalized
Yersinia pseudotuberculosis		Mesenteric lymphadenitis	Erythema nodosum and scarlatiniform eruption	Lower part of legs and generalized
Yersinia enterocolitica	Yersiniosis	Enterocolitis	Erythema nodosum and urticaria	Lower part of legs and generalized
Bartonella bacilliformis	Bartonellosis, Carrion disease, or Oroya fever	Initially, intermittent fever, malaise, and myalgias. 30–60 days after initial fever, exathem appears	Erythematous maculopapular. Later recurrent nodules	Face and extensor surface of extremities
Bartonella quintana	Trench fever	Usually, mild fever, headache, chills, and tibial bone pain	Mascular rash	Mainly on trunk
Calymmatobacterium granulomatis	Granuloma inguinale	See *Calymmatobacterium granulomatis*, Chapter 135	Nodular, ulcerovegetative, hypertrophic, or cicatricial lesions	Genitals
Pseudomonas aeruginosa	Ecthyma gangrenosa	Septicemia (usually in immunocompromised patients)	Initially, vesicular and then hemorrhagic. Become ulcerated with central black necrotic eschar	Anywhere
	Pseudomonas folliculitis (health spa dermatitis)	Headache, malaise, and fatigue	Papular and pustular	Generalized

Burkholderia mallei	Glanders, melioidosis	Fever, malaise, chills, arthralgia, and muscle pains	Nodule or ulcer at site of inoculation and then widespread papules, bullae, and pustules	Generalized
Brucella species	Brucellosis	Acute or subacute febrile illness. Exanthem in 8% of cases	Erythematous and maculopapular. Occasionally vesicles	Generalized
Legionella pneumophila	Legionnaires' disease	Severe pneumonia	Maculopapular	Anterior of trunk
Bartonella henselae	Cat-scratch fever	Subacute regional lymphadenitis	Erythematous maculopapular, morbilliform, petechial, erythema nodosum, erythema multiforme, and erythema marginatum. May be pruritic	Generalized
Acid-Fast Bacilli				
Mycobacterium tuberculosis	Lupus vulgaris	Usually, associated with other manifestations of tuberculosis	Reddish-brown nodular or scaling lesions	Mainly on face and neck
	Papulonecrotic tuberculids	Associated with disseminated tuberculosis	Initially, vesicular. Become pustules, umbilical, and ulcerated and then form scabs and leave scars	Single or multiple lesions anywhere
Atypical mycobacteria			Granulomatous and ulcerative lesions at site of superficial injury	Usually on hands
Mycobacterium leprae	Erythema nodosum leprosum	General findings of lepromatous leprosy	Erythematous nodular lesions	Disseminated. Most prominent on face and extremities
Spirochetes				
Treponema pallidum	Primary syphilis	Chancre	Large ulcers with indurated edges	Genitals
	Secondary syphilis		Erythematous maculopapules that frequently are scaly (psoriasiform)	Generalized, including palms and soles
Treponema pertenue	Yaws		Papular lesions at sites of inoculations. Lesions ulcerate, leaving a wart-like appearance	Anywhere
Borrelia burgdorferi	Lyme disease (erythema chronicum migrans)	Skin, cardiac, neurologic, and joint abnormalities	Expanding erythematous, annular lesions	Thighs, buttocks, or axillae
Treponema carateum	Pinta		Initially, erythematous, papular lesions. Increase in size over 1-month period and become scaly	Exposed surfaces of body
Spirillum minus	Rat-bite fever	Fever and chills	Discrete, macular rash	Trunk and extremities, including palms and soles
Leptospira species	Leptospirosis	Fever, conjunctivitis, and anorexia. Rash rarely noted	Erythematous maculopapular rash	Mainly on trunk
Borrelia species	Relapsing fever	Relapsing fever, headache, myalgia, and photophobia	Morbilliform and petechial. Erythema multiforme	Generalized

Data from references 4, 14, 18, 21, 26, 27, 29–31, 34, 35, 38, 51, 56, 60, 65, 67, 70, 82, 84, 86, 95, 96, 98, 100, 107, 108, 113, 118, 120, 123, 127, 137, 140, 144, 146, 148, 150, 151, 155, 156, 162, 166, 171, 181, 183–185, 187–189, 194, 197, 199, 204, 206, 207, 211.

gonorrhoeae, Salmonella typhi, Streptobacillus moniliformis, Spirillum minus, Pseudomonas aeruginosa, and *Treponema pallidum.*

Fungal, protozoan, and metazoan agents associated with cutaneous manifestations in humans are listed in Tables 65–4, 65–5, and 65–6, respectively. These agents and their diseases, discussed more completely in other chapters, are included here for completeness of the differential diagnosis.

Epidemiology

Tables 65–1 through 65–6 clearly show that exanthematous disease has many possible etiologic agents; hence, no unified epidemiology exists. Epidemiologic events related to specific agents are considered in the appropriate sections throughout this text. Each agent with exanthem as a clinical manifestation has a unique epidemiologic pattern that, if understood, separates it from many of the other agents that cause otherwise identical clinical illnesses. In the evaluation of all patients with rash, exposure, season, and incubation period are important aspects of the diagnostic process.

Pathophysiology and Pathology of Exanthems

Even though the skin can respond in only a limited number of ways, what is obvious from the extensive number of etiologic agents is that multiple pathogenic mechanisms must occur. In many sections of this book, the pathology and pathophysiology of specific agents are presented in detail. An overview is presented here.

Small vessel vasculitis (leukocytoclastic vasculitis) is a leading event in most exanthematous illnesses caused by infectious agents.[179] The cutaneous manifestations of systemic diseases can be separated into three broad categories. The first category involves dissemination of infectious agents by blood (viremia, bacteremia, and so on), which results in secondary infection at the cutaneous site. The clinical cutaneous findings in this type of infection can be the direct result of infectious agents in the epidermis, dermis, or dermal capillary endothelium or can be the result of an immune response between the organism and antibody or cellular factors in the cutaneous location. The possible events in the skin with this type of infection are presented in Table 65–7. Chickenpox, many enteroviral infections, and meningococcemia are examples of diseases in which infectious agents have reached the skin via the blood and are causing the cutaneous findings without the additional contribution of host immune factors. In illnesses such as measles, rubella, and gonococcemia, the timing, histologic picture, and difficulty of direct recovery of the agent by culture suggest both a direct effect and an immune-mediated response.

The second category of pathogenesis relates to the dissemination of known specific toxins of infectious agents. The infection is in a localized area of the body, but the toxin liberated by the infectious agents reaches the skin by bloodborne dissemination. Three examples of toxin-mediated exanthematous disease are streptococcal scarlet fever, staphylococcal scalded skin syndrome, and toxic shock syndrome.

The third category of pathogenesis in systemic disease with exanthem is poorly understood but appears to have an immunologic basis. Most important in this category are the clinical pictures of erythema multiforme, erythema multiforme exudativum (Stevens-Johnson syndrome), and erythema nodosum. In erythema multiforme associated with *M. pneumoniae* and HSV infection, the respective organisms have been isolated or identified at the skin site. In most

TABLE 65–4 ■ FUNGI ASSOCIATED WITH CUTANEOUS MANIFESTATIONS

Agent	Disease or Syndrome	Clinical Characteristics	Exanthem	
			Lesions	Distribution
Dermatophytic fungi	Tinea capitis, tinea cruris, tinea pedis, or tinea circinata		Localized, brownish, maculopapular lesions that are scaly. Erythema nodosum	
Candida albicans	Congential cutaneous candidiasis	Congenital infection	Discrete vesicular lesions	Generalized
	Chronic mucocutaneous candidiasis	Immunodeficiency disease	Confluent, erythematous, and exudative lesions	Generalized, including scalp
	Acquired candidiasis		Confluent, fiery red lesions	Most common in diaper area
Candida spp.	Systemic candidiasis	Severe opportunistic infection	Erythematous nodular lesions	Generalized
Histoplasma capsulatum	Histoplasmosis	Primary respiratory infection	Erythema nodosum, erythema multiforme, and erythematous maculopapular	
Cryptococcus neoformans	Cryptococcosis	Primary respiratory infection	Erythema nodosum and acneiform eruptions	
Coccidioides immitis	Coccidioidomycosis	Primary respiratory infection	Initially, erythematous, maculopapular rash. Later, erythema multiforme and erythema nodusum	Generalized maculopapular rash
Sporotrichum schenckii	Sporotrichosis	Cutaneous inoculation	Nodular lesions that ulcerate	Usually, hands, arms, and legs
Blastomyces dermatitidis	Blastomycosis	Primary respiratory infection	Nodular lesions that ulcerate Erythema nodosum	
Scedosporium spp.	No specific syndrome	Severe opportunistic infection	Nodular or necrotic skin lesions	Generalized
Fusarium spp.	No specific syndrome	Severe opportunistic infection	Nodular skin lesions, abscesses	Generalized
Aspergillus spp.	No specific syndrome	Severe opportunistic infection	Nodular and purpuric lesions	Generalized

Data from references 11, 12, 20, 24, 40, 65, 69, 76, 78, 122, 126, 157, 176, 196, 205.

TABLE 65–5 ■ CUTANEOUS MANIFESTATIONS OF PROTOZOAN AND HELMINTHIC INFECTIONS

Agent	Disease or Syndrome	Cutaneous Manifestations
Plasmodium spp.	Malaria	Occasionally generalized urticaria in chronic infection
Toxoplasma gondii	Acquired toxoplasmosis	Occasionally generalized erythematous, maculopapular rash
	Congenital toxoplasmosis	Generalized petechial rash
Giardia lamblia	Giardiasis	Rarely urticaria
Entamoeba histolytica	Amebiasis	Rarely urticaria
Leishmania tropica	Oriental sore	Red nodular lesion that ulcerates. Lasts 2–3 months
Leishmania braziliensis and *mexicana*	American cutaneous leishmaniasis	Erythematous papular lesion that vesiculates and ulcerates
Trypanosoma gambiense	African trypanosomiasis	Red nodular lesion at site of bite, followed by generalized, pruritic, erythema multiforme-like rash
Trypanosoma cruzi	American trypanosomiasis or Chagas disease	Nodular lesion at site of bite. Generalized, recurrent, erythematous, maculopapular rash
Trichomonas vaginalis	Vulvovaginalis	Rarely urticaria and erythema multiforme
Ascaris lumbricoides	Roundworm infestation	Erythema nodosum
Enterobius vermicularis	Pinworm infestation	Rarely urticaria
Necator americanus	Hookworm disease	Papules and papulovesicles on exposed surfaces (feet). Generalized urticaria
Trichinella spiralis	Trichinosis	Urticaria common. Also, generalized maculopapular rash may occur. Petechiae frequently develop
Strongyloides stercoralis	Strongyloidiasis. Also, creeping eruption (cutaneous larva migrans)	Erythematous, maculopapular lesions on feet. Creeping eruption
Ancylostoma braziliense	Creeping eruption (cutaneous larva migrans)	Creeping eruption
Dermatobia hominis	Cutaneous myiasis	Creeping eruption, subacute draining lesions
Schistosoma haematobium, mansoni, and *japonicum*	Schistosomiasis	Pruritic papular eruption where exposed, generalized urticaria, and granulomatous lesions
Trichobilharzia ocellata, physellae, and *stagnicolae*	Swimmer's itch or collector's itch	Initial erythema and urticaria, followed by papules and vesiculation. Pruritic
Wuchereria bancrofti	Filariasis	Localized erythema, urticaria, and erythema nodosum
Onchocerca volvulus	Onchocerciasis	Chronic, papular, scaly rash
Echinococcus granulosus and *multilocularis*	Echinococcosis	Frequent urticaria

Data from references 11, 17, 40, 53, 65, 68, 79, 85, 128.

TABLE 65–6 ■ CUTANEOUS MANIFESTATIONS OF ARTHROPOD BITES AND STINGS

Agent	Disease	Cutaneous Manifestations
Spiders		
Loxosceles reclusa	Recluse spider bite or brown spider bite	Erythema followed by blister and necrosis
Ticks	Tick bite	Initial pruritus at site; becomes ulcerated and granulomatous
Mites		
Sarcoptes scabiei	Scabies	Pruritic burrows in body creases and generalized. Become erythematous and then papular urticaria
Trombicula irritans	Chigger bite	Marked pruritus and then papular urticaria
Other mites: Food, grain, murine, and fowl		Marked pruritus and then papular urticaria
Lice		
Pediculus humanus	Body lice or pediculosis	Erythematous, maculopapular, pruritic lesions. Sometimes urticaria
Phthirus pubis	Crabs	Pruritus and erythema under pubic hair
Bedbugs and kissing bugs		
Cimex lectularius	Bedbug bite	Pruritic papular urticaria
Triatoma sanguisuga	Kissing bug bite	Papular urticaria. Occasionally hemorrhagic nodular lesions
Gypsy moth caterpillar		
Lymantria dispar	Gypsy moth rash	Pruritic blotchy erythema and maculopapular
Moths		
Hylesia alinda	Moth-associated dermatitis	Erythema and pruritis. Feeling of warmth in area of rash. May have vesicular lesions
Ants		
Solenopsis saevissima	Fire ant bite	Painful papular urticarial lesions that become pustular and then nodular
Fleas		
Pulex irritans (human flea) and fleas of many animals	Flea bite	Papular urticaria
Flies and mosquitoes	Fly and mosquito bite	Papular, nodular, and urticarial lesions in sensitive persons

Data from references 42, 44, 58, 65, 91, 143, 159, 170, 175.

TABLE 65–7 ■ ASPECTS OF PATHOGENESIS IN EXANTHEMS ASSOCIATED WITH BLOOD-BORNE DISSEMINATION OF THE INFECTIOUS AGENT

Anatomic Location	Spread of Agent	Histology	Clinical Expressions	Pathophysiology
Blood	Free in plasma → Infection; Associated with leukocytes → Infection			
Dermal capillary endothelium	Infection →	Damage to vessel, endothelial swelling, perivascular edema, cellular infiltration, hemorrhage	Macule, papule, petechia	Direct effect of agent or immune reaction with pathologic consequences
	Free in plasma: To dermis through breaks in basement membrane (secondary to trauma) → Dermis; Infection: Contiguous spread → Dermis; Associated with leukocytes: To dermis by diapedesis → Dermis			
Dermis	Infection → Contiguous spread → Epidermis	Edema: cellular infiltration, hemorrhage, microscopic visualization of organism	Papule, urticaria, purpura, vesicle	Direct effect of agent or immune reaction with pathologic consequences; histamine release
Epidermis	Infection	Cytopathic effects (inclusions, ballooning, vacuolation, necrosis, nuclear disruption); microscopic visualization of organism	Papule, vesicle, ulcer	Direct effect of agent

Modified from Cherry, J. D.: Newer viral exanthems. Adv. Pediatr. *16*:233–286, 1969.

instances, however, neither antigen localization nor disseminated toxin has been identified.

Important clinical aspects of exanthematous diseases are the distribution and progression of the lesions, yet little is known of the cause of these aspects. Differences in skin thickness, vascularity, proliferation rate, temperature, and metabolic activity are important in animal diseases with cutaneous manifestations.[48, 71, 119, 129, 149] In humans, similar factors must be important but obviously affect the various etiologic agents differently (e.g., the more central exanthem of chickenpox versus that of the hand, foot, and mouth syndrome of coxsackievirus A16 infection).

Clinical Manifestations

The clinical findings in exanthematous diseases resulting from systemic infections are varied and depend on the inciting pathogens. By examination of skin alone, differentiating an exanthematous disease resulting from systemic infection (e.g., coxsackievirus A9, rubella virus infection) from primary cutaneous diseases of infectious and noninfectious origin (insect bites, acne, and contact with poison ivy) frequently is difficult. In Tables 65–1 through 65–6, the clinical characteristics of viral, chlamydial, rickettsial, bacterial, fungal, parasitic, and arthropod-induced illnesses with primary or secondary cutaneous manifestations are presented. In Tables 65–8 through 65–17, etiologic agents and clinical manifestations are presented on the basis of the more pronounced cutaneous manifestations or syndrome

TABLE 65–8 ■ INFECTIOUS AGENTS ASSOCIATED WITH ILLNESS IN WHICH A MACULAR EXANTHEM HAS BEEN OBSERVED

Infectious Agent	Illness
Human herpesvirus-6, -7	Roseola infantum
Epstein-Barr virus	Infectious mononucleosis
Coxsackieviruses B1, B2, B5	—
Echoviruses 2, 4, 5, 14, 17–19, 30	—
Enterovirus 71	—
Dengue virus	Dengue fever
Lassa virus	Lassa fever
Marburg virus	Marburg fever
Parvovirus	Erythema infectiosum
HIV-1	Manifestation of acute infection
Hantavirus	Hemorrhagic fever with renal syndrome
Chlamydia psittaci	Psittacosis
Rickettsia typhi	Murine typhus
Rickettsia prowazekii	Epidemic typhus
Rickettsia quintana	Trench fever
Coxiella burnetii	Q fever
Mycoplasma pneumoniae	—
Staphylococcus aureus	Septicemia and toxic shock syndrome
Streptococcus pyogenes	Scarlatina and septicemia
Bacillus anthracis	Anthrax
Salmonella typhi	Typhoid fever
Salmonella species	Septicemic salmonellosis
Spirillum minus	Rat-bite fever
Leptospira species	Leptospirosis
Yersinia pestis	Plague

TABLE 65–9 ■ INFECTIOUS AGENTS ASSOCIATED WITH ILLNESSES IN WHICH MACULOPAPULAR EXANTHEMS OCCUR

		Character of Rash	
Infectious Agent	**Illness**	**Discrete**	**Confluent**
Parvovirus	Erythema infectiosum	+++	+
Adenoviruses 1, 2, 3, 4, 7, 7a		+++	+
Human herpesvirus-6	Roseola infantum	+++	+
Epstein-Barr virus	Infectious mononucleosis	+++	+
Cytomegalovirus		++++	
Vaccinia virus	Roseola vaccinatum	+++	+
Coxsackieviruses A2, A4, A5, A7, A9, A10, A16		+++	+
Coxsackieviruses B1–B5		+++	+
Echoviruses 1–7, 9, 11, 13, 14, 16–19, 22, 25, 30, 33		+++	+
Enterovirus 71		++++	
Rhinoviruses (many types)		++++	
Colorado tick fever virus	Colorado tick fever	++++	
Reoviruses 2, 3		++	++
Rotavirus		++++	
Alphaviruses: Chikungunya, Sindbis, O'nyong-nyong fever, Ross River		++	++
Rubella virus	Rubella (German measles)	+++	+
Flavivirus: Dengue, Kunjin, West Nile	Dengue, Kunjin fever	++	++
Influenza viruses A, B		++++	
Respiratory syncytial virus		++++	
Parainfluenza viruses 1–4		++++	
Mumps virus	Mumps	++++	
Measles virus	Measles	+	+++
Hepatitis B virus		++++	
Marburg virus	Marburg fever	++	++
Ebola virus	Ebola hemorrhagic fever	+++	+
Rickettsia akari	Rickettsialpox	++++	
Rickettsia typhi	Murine typhus	+++	+
Rickettsia prowazekii	Epidemic typhus	+++	+
Rickettsia tsutsugamushi	Scrub typhus	+++	+
Rickettsia rickettsii	Rocky Mountain spotted fever	+	+++
Ehrlichia species	Ehrlichiosis	+++	+
Mycoplasma pneumoniae		++	++
Staphylococcus aureus (exfoliative toxin producing)	Staphylococcal scarlet fever		++++
Streptococcus pyogenes	Scarlet fever		++++
Arcanobacterium hemolyticum		++	++
Neisseria meningitidis	Meningococcemia	++++	
Moraxella catarrhalis		++++	
Listeria monocytogenes	Listeriosis	++++	
Streptobacillus moniliformis	Rat-bite fever	+++	+
Yersinia pseudotuberculosis			++++
Bartonella bacilliformis	Bartonellosis	++++	
Brucella species	Brucellosis	++++	
Legionella pneumophila	Legionnaires' disease	++++	
Bartonella henselae	Cat-scratch fever	+++	+
Treponema pallidum	Secondary syphilis	+++	+
Leptospira species	Leptospirosis	++++	
Borrelia species	Relapsing fever		++++
Coccidioides immitis	Coccidioidomycosis	+++	+
Toxoplasma gondii	Toxoplasmosis	++++	
Strongyloides stercoralis	Strongyloidiasis	++++	

associations. The clinician must keep in mind that other aspects of an illness (e.g., exposure, season, incubation period, geographic location, patient age, associated signs and symptoms) may be more important in determining the underlying etiologic agent. Clinical manifestations of specific exanthematous diseases are presented in greater detail in other chapters of this book.

ERYTHEMATOUS MACULAR EXANTHEMS

When all infectious diseases with exanthems are taken into consideration, the occurrence of illnesses in which the lesions are just macular is rare. However, many important, severe diseases have a transitory erythematous macular rash early in their course, and recognition of this fact can be lifesaving. Infectious agents associated with illnesses in which macular exanthems have been observed are presented in Table 65–8.

The most common rash in infectious mononucleosis is erythematous and maculopapular, but rarely (most often in association with the administration of ampicillin), the exanthem is generalized, confluent, fiery red, and macular. Blotchy or diffuse erythematous macular rashes have been caused specifically by 12 different enterovirus types. Most of these descriptions involve neonates, other very young

TABLE 65–10 ■ INFECTIOUS AGENTS ASSOCIATED WITH ILLNESSES IN WHICH VESICULAR EXANTHEMS OCCUR

Infectious Agent	Illness
Human parvovirus B19	
Herpes simplex virus types 1 and 2	Cold sores, genital herpes, or neonatal herpes
Varicella-zoster virus	Chickenpox (varicella) or herpes zoster
Vaccinia virus	Disseminated vaccinia or eczema vaccinatum
Variola virus	Smallpox
Monkeypox virus	
Orf virus	Ecthyma contagiosum
Tanapox virus	
Coxsackieviruses A4, A5, A8, A10, A16	
Coxsackieviruses B1–B3	
Echoviruses 6, 9, 11, 17	
Enterovirus 71	
Reovirus 2	
Calicivirus of oceanic origin	
Alphaviruses: Chikungunya, O'nyong-nyong fever, Ross River, Sindbis	
Kunjin virus	
Mumps virus	Mumps
Measles virus	Atypical measles
Rickettsia akari	Rickettsialpox
Rickettsia tsutsugamushi	
Mycoplasma pneumoniae	
Streptococcus pyogenes	Impetigo
Pseudomonas aeruginosa	
Brucella species	Brucellosis
Bacillus anthracis	Anthrax
Mycobacterium tuberculosis	Papulonecrotic tuberculids
Candida albicans	Congenital cutaneous candidiasis
Leishmania braziliensis	American cutaneous leishmaniasis
Necator americanus	Hookworm disease

infants, and adults; children in the peak ages for enteroviral exanthematous diseases do not seem to have solely macular lesions. In neonates, enteroviral disease with a blotchy macular rash in association with fever and lethargy usually is confused with bacterial sepsis.

Patients with dengue, Lassa, and Marburg viral infections frequently have a macular, flushed appearance before other cutaneous manifestations develop. Similarly, in both murine and epidemic typhus, the initial skin manifestations are macular but progress rapidly to more pronounced findings.

Bacterial septicemia with both common and exotic organisms is associated frequently with a generalized flush. In staphylococcal disease, it is particularly apparent in endocarditis and osteomyelitis. The most famous disease with a macular rash is typhoid fever. Rose spots occur most commonly on the abdomen, but they also are seen on the chest and back. They are erythematous, macular lesions 2 to 4 mm in size. Lesions likewise have been noted in leptospirosis and psittacosis. In addition, rose spots are seen occasionally in septicemic illnesses caused by other *Salmonella* spp.

The slapped-cheek appearance in erythema infectiosum (Fig. 65–6, Color Plate I) is caused by an erythematous macular flush of the cheeks. The full-blown rash in streptococcal scarlet fever is maculopapular, but frequently in mild cases and in those altered by antibiotic therapy, the exanthem is only macular in character (scarlatina).

TABLE 65–11 ■ INFECTIOUS AGENTS ASSOCIATED WITH ILLNESS IN WHICH PETECHIAL AND/OR PURPURIC EXANTHEMS OCCUR

Infectious Agent	Illness
Human parvovirus B19	Glove and socks syndrome
Varicella-zoster virus	Hemorrhagic chickenpox
Cytomegalovirus	Congenital cytomegalovirus infection
Variola virus	Hemorrhagic smallpox
Coxsackieviruses A4, A9	
Coxsackieviruses B2–B4	
Echoviruses 4, 7, 9	
Colorado tick fever virus	Colorado tick fever
Rotavirus	
Alphaviruses: Chikungunya, O'nyong-nyong fever, Ross River, Sindbis	
Rubella virus	Rubella (German measles) or congenital rubella
Respiratory syncytial virus	
Measles virus	Hemorrhagic (black measles) or atypical measles
Lassa virus	Lassa fever
Marburg virus	
Hepatitis C virus	Mixed cryoglobulinemia
Hantavirus	Hemorrhagic fever with renal syndrome
Rickettsia typhi	Murine typhus
Rickettsia prowazekii	Epidemic typhus
Rickettsia rickettsii and other tick-borne rickettsiae	Rocky Mountain spotted fever
Ehrlichia species	Ehrlichiosis
Mycoplasma pneumoniae	
Streptococcus pyogenes	Scarlet fever or septicemia
Streptococcus pneumoniae	Pneumococcal septicemia
Enterococcal and viridans group streptococci	Endocarditis
Neisseria gonorrhoeae	Gonococcemia
Neisseria meningitidis	Meningococcemia
Moraxella catarrhalis	
Haemophilus influenzae	*H. influenzae* septicemia
Pseudomonas aeruginosa	Ecthyma gangrenosa
Streptobacillus moniliformis	
Yersinia pestis	Septicemic plague (Black Death)
Bartonella henselae	Cat-scratch fever
Treponema pallidum	Congenital syphilis
Borrelia species	Relapsing fever
Toxoplasma gondii	Congenital toxoplasmosis
Trichinella spiralis	Trichinosis

ERYTHEMATOUS MACULOPAPULAR EXANTHEMS

An erythematous maculopapular rash is the most common cutaneous manifestation of systemic infection (Figs. 65–2, 65–8, 65–10, and 65–13 and Color Plates I to III). It also is an exceedingly common occurrence in allergic conditions. However, all too frequently the rash of an infectious illness is ascribed to an allergic reaction to an administered drug rather than correctly to the disease process. The converse—an allergic rash illness that is attributed mistakenly to an infectious agent—rarely occurs. Infectious agents associated with illnesses in which maculopapular exanthems occur are presented in Table 65–9.

Both by the number of possible etiologic agents and by total infections, viruses account for the vast majority of illnesses with maculopapular eruptions. Although the distribution and progression of rashes are important aspects relating to the differential diagnosis, the single most important point is whether the lesions are discrete (rubelliform) or

TABLE 65–12 ■ INFECTIOUS AGENTS ASSOCIATED WITH ILLNESS IN WHICH URTICARIAL EXANTHEMS OCCUR

Infectious Agent	Illness
Epstein-Barr virus	Infectious mononucleosis
Coxsackieviruses A9, A16, B4, B5	
Echovirus 11	
Mumps virus	Mumps
Hepatitis B virus	
Hepatitis C virus	
Mycoplasma pneumoniae	
Neisseria meningitidis	Meningococcemia
Shigella sonnei	Shigellosis
Yersinia enterocolitica	Yersiniosis
Borrelia burgdorferi	Lyme disease
Plasmodium species	Malaria
Coxiella burnetii	Q fever
Giardia lamblia	Giardiasis
Entamoeba histolytica	Amebiasis
Trichomonas vaginalis	Vulvovaginalis
Enterobius vermicularis	Pinworm infestation
Necator americanus	Hookworm disease
Trichinella spiralis	Trichinosis
Schistosoma species	Schistosomiasis
Trichobilharzia species	Swimmer's itch or collector's itch
Wuchereria bancrofti	Filariasis
Echinococcus species	Echinococcosis
Sarcoptes scabiei	Scabies
Trombicula irritans	Chigger bites
Other mites	Mite bites
Pediculus humanus	Pediculosis
Bedbugs, kissing bugs, ants, fleas, flies, and mosquitoes	Bites and stings

TABLE 65–13 ■ INFECTIOUS AGENTS ASSOCIATED WITH PAPULAR, NODULAR, AND ULCERATIVE LESIONS

Agent	Illness*
Wart virus	Warts (P and N)
Orf virus	Ecthyma contagiosum (N)
Molluscum contagiosum virus	Molluscum contagiosum (P and N)
Hepatitis B virus	Gianotti-Crosti syndrome (P)
Paravaccinia virus	Milker's nodules (N)
Francisella tularensis	Tularemia (U)
Haemophilus ducreyi	Chancroid (U)
Bartonella bacilliformis	Bartonellosis (N)
Calymmatobacterium granulomatis	Granuloma inguinale (N and U)
Pseudomonas aeruginosa	Ecthyma gangrenosa (U)
Pseudomonas aeruginosa	*Pseudomonas* folliculitis (P)
Burkholderia mallei	Glanders (N and U)
Mycobacterium tuberculosis	Lupus vulgaris (N) Papulonecrotic tuberculids (U)
Atypical mycobacteria	(U)
Mycobacterium leprae	(N)
Treponema pallidum	Chancre (U)
Treponema pertenue	Yaws (P and U)
Sporotrichum schenckii	Sporotrichosis (U)
Blastomyces dermatitidis	Blastomycosis (N and U)
Fusarium species	Opportunistic infection (N)
Scedosporium species	Opportunistic infection (N)
Candida albicans	Systemic candidiasis (N)
Leishmania tropica	Oriental sore (N and U)
Leishmania braziliensis and *mexicana*	American cutaneous leishmaniasis (P and U)
Trypanosoma species	Trypanosomiasis (N)
Necator americanus	Hookworm disease (P)
Schistosoma species	Schistosomiasis (P)
Trichobilharzia species	Swimmer's itch or collector's itch (P)
Onchocerca volvulus	Onchocerciasis (P)
Loxosceles reclusa	Recluse spider bites (U)
Ticks	Tick bites (U)
Sarcoptes scabiei	Scabies (P)
Trombicula irritans	Chigger bites (P)
Other mites	Mite bites (P)
Cimex lectularius	Bedbug bites (P)
Triatoma sanguisuga	Kissing bug bites (P and N)
Solenopsis saevissima	Fire ant bites (P and N)
Fleas	Flea bites (P)
Flies and mosquitoes	Fly and mosquito bites (P)

*N, nodular; P, papular; U, ulcerative.

confluent (morbilliform). Adenoviruses are not uncommon causes of erythematous maculopapular eruptions. In most instances, signs and symptoms of upper respiratory infection are present. Most commonly, the lesions are discrete, but occasionally, a confluent morbilliform rash is present. A roseola infantum picture—occurrence of rash after the fever falls by crisis—frequently occurs. As a rule, the exanthem in adenoviral infections starts on the head and spreads to the trunk and extremities.

Enteroviruses account for the greatest number of erythematous maculopapular rash illnesses; 36 different serologic types have been implicated. The enteroviral types most commonly associated with maculopapular exanthems are coxsackieviruses A9 and B5 and echoviruses 4, 9, and 16. Echovirus 9 has been the most frequent cause of enteroviral exanthem for the last 35 years (see Fig. 65–13, Color Plate III). Although morbilliform rashes do occur, the more usual cutaneous manifestation is one suggestive of rubella. The exanthem usually starts on the head and upper part of the trunk and spreads to the extremities.

Though not common manifestations of respiratory viruses (rhinoviruses, influenza A and B viruses, RSV, and parainfluenza viruses types 1 through 4), exanthems probably occur more often than generally realized. Because children infected with these agents frequently are given antibiotics, confusion often occurs between an allergic and an infectious etiology. With all the respiratory viruses, the signs and symptoms of respiratory illness (cough, coryza, croup, bronchiolitis, and so on) are prominent. The exanthems are virtually always discrete and rubelliform in character.

In dengue, the exanthem goes through several stages. Initially, it is macular, then erythematous maculopapular, and finally hemorrhagic. Similarly, the exanthems in the rickettsial diseases go through stages that vary in relation to the specific agent (see Table 65–2). In Rocky Mountain spotted fever, the rash starts on the distal ends of extremities. Although the hallmark of meningococcemia is a petechial or purpuric rash, in the initial stages the exanthem may be erythematous and maculopapular. In addition, maculopapular eruptions are observed in chronic meningococcemia. The most notable cutaneous lesion in coccidioidomycosis is erythema nodosum, but a rubelliform rash early in infection is not an unusual manifestation.

VESICULAR EXANTHEMS

The three main categories of vesicular exanthems are single or localized lesions, generalized lesions in greatest concentration on the trunk and head, and generalized lesions with the greatest concentration on the extremities

TABLE 65–14 ■ INFECTIOUS AGENTS ASSOCIATED WITH ERYTHEMA MULTIFORME

Agent	Illness
Human parvovirus B19	Erythema infectiosum
Adenovirus 7	Respiratory infection
Herpes simplex virus type 1	Perioral or respiratory infection
Epstein-Barr virus	Infectious mononucleosis
Varicella virus	Chickenpox
Coxsackieviruses A10, A16, B5	Enterovirus syndrome
Echovirus 6	Enterovirus syndrome
Poliomyelitis virus	Poliomyelitis
Vaccinia virus	Smallpox vaccination
Variola virus	Smallpox
Orf virus	Ecthyma contagiosum
Paravaccinia virus	Milker's nodules
Influenza A virus	Influenza
Mumps	Mumps
Hepatitis B virus	Serum hepatitis
Chlamydia psittaci	Psittacosis
Chlamydia trachomatis	Lymphogranuloma venereum
Mycoplasma pneumoniae	Respiratory symptoms
Staphylococcus aureus	Septicemia
Streptococcus pyogenes	Respiratory symptoms
Neisseria gonorrhoeae	Gonorrhea
Corynebacterium diphtheriae	Diphtheria
Pseudomonas aeruginosa	Septicemia
Salmonella species	Gastroenteritis
Francisella tularensis	Tularemia
Yersinia species	Gastrointestinal symptoms
Vibrio parahaemolyticus	Gastroenteritis
Treponema pallidum	Syphilis
Bartonella henselae	Cat-scratch fever
Mycobacterium tuberculosis	Tuberculosis
Mycobacterium leprae	Leprosy
Coccidioides immitis	Coccidioidomycosis
Histoplasma capsulatum	Histoplasmosis
Trichomonas vaginalis	Vulvovaginalis

TABLE 65–15 ■ INFECTIOUS AGENTS ASSOCIATED WITH ERYTHEMA NODOSUM

Agent	Illness
Herpes simplex virus	Perioral or respiratory infection
Epstein-Barr virus	Infectious mononucleosis
Chlamydia psittaci	Psittacosis
Chlamydia trachomatis	Lymphogranuloma venereum
Streptococcus pyogenes	Respiratory infection
Neisseria meningitidis	Meningococcemia
Corynebacterium diphtheriae	Diphtheria
Campylobacter species	Gastroenteritis
Haemophilus ducreyi	Chancroid
Salmonella species	Salmonellosis
Yersinia species	Gastrointestinal symptoms
Brucella species	Brucellosis
Treponema pallidum	Syphilis
Bartonella henselae	Cat-scratch fever
Mycobacterium tuberculosis	Tuberculosis
Mycobacterium leprae	Leprosy
Trichophyton species	Kerion of scalp
Histoplasma capsulatum	Histoplasmosis
Cryptococcus neoformans	Cryptococcosis
Coccidioides immitis	Coccidioidomycosis
Blastomyces dermatitidis	Blastomycosis
Ascaris lumbricoides	Roundworm infestation
Wuchereria bancrofti	Filariasis

TABLE 65–16 ■ INFECTIOUS AGENTS ASSOCIATED WITH EXANTHEM AND MENINGITIS

Agent	Illness
Herpes simplex virus type 2	Recurrent genital herpes
Coxsackieviruses A2, A9, B1, B4, B5	Enterovirus syndrome
Echoviruses 4, 6, 9, 11, 14, 17, 25, 33	Enterovirus syndrome
Colorado tick fever virus	Colorado tick fever
Reovirus 2	Respiratory infection
West Nile virus	Meningoencephalitis
Neisseria meningitidis	Meningococcemia
Borrelia burgdorferi	Lyme disease
Listeria monocytogenes	Listeriosis
Toxoplasma gondii	Toxoplasmosis

(Figs. 65–4, 65–5, and 65–9 and Color Plates I and II). Infectious agents associated with illnesses in which vesicular rashes develop are presented in Table 65–10. The exanthem in primary or recurrent HSV infection is localized, as it is in recurrent endogenous varicella-zoster infection (herpes zoster), ecthyma contagiosum, tanapox, scrub typhus, anthrax, and papulonecrotic tuberculids (see Fig. 65–5 and Color Plate I).

The vesicular exanthematous disease that occurs most commonly in children today is chickenpox (see Fig. 65–4, Color Plate I). It should be a readily recognizable disease, but all too frequently it is confused with enteroviral infections or insect bites and allergic conditions. Chickenpox has a long incubation period (16 days) and is associated with mild fever and an exanthem that starts on the head and upper part of the trunk and spreads to the extremities. The rash always is more prominent on the trunk than on the extremities. At any time during the first few days of the rash, lesions in all stages (macules, papules, and vesicles) can be seen. Individual lesions in chickenpox form scabs that persist for approximately 7 days.

In contrast to that of chickenpox, the exanthem in enteroviral infections frequently is peripheral in distribution, and the lesions generally heal without scabs. The incubation period (5 days) is much shorter than that of chickenpox. The hand, foot, and mouth syndrome is a

TABLE 65–17 ■ INFECTIOUS AGENTS ASSOCIATED WITH EXANTHEM AND PULMONARY INVOLVEMENT

Agent	Illness
Adenoviruses 7, 7a	Respiratory infection
Herpes simplex virus type 1	Respiratory infection
Varicella-zoster virus	Chickenpox pneumonia
Epstein-Barr virus	Infectious mononucleosis
Coxsackievirus A9	Enterovirus syndrome
Echovirus 11	Enterovirus syndrome
Reovirus 3	Respiratory infection
Measles virus	Measles pneumonia and atypical measles
Chlamydia psittaci	Psittacosis
Mycoplasma pneumoniae	*M. pneumoniae* pneumonia
Neisseria meningitidis	Meningococcal pneumonia
Mycobacterium tuberculosis	Tuberculosis
Histoplasma capsulatum	Histoplasmosis
Cryptococcus neoformans	Cryptococcosis
Coccidioides immitis	Coccidioidomycosis

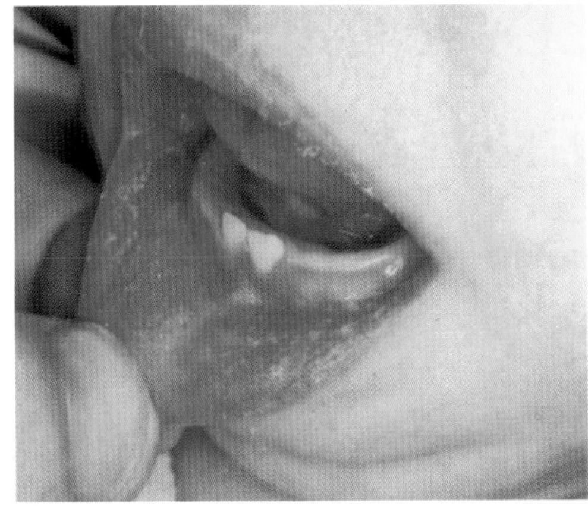

FIGURE 65–1

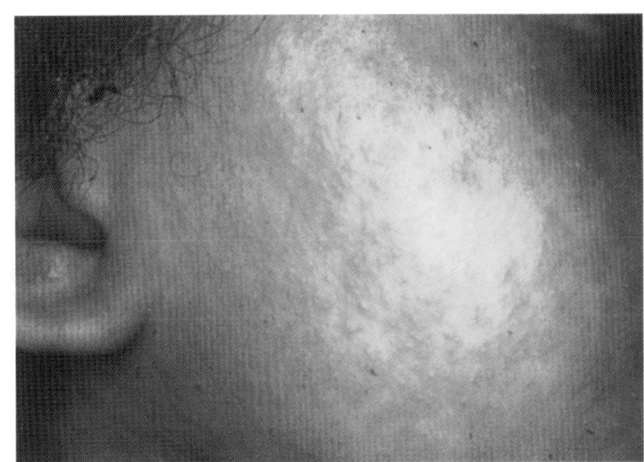

FIGURE 65–2

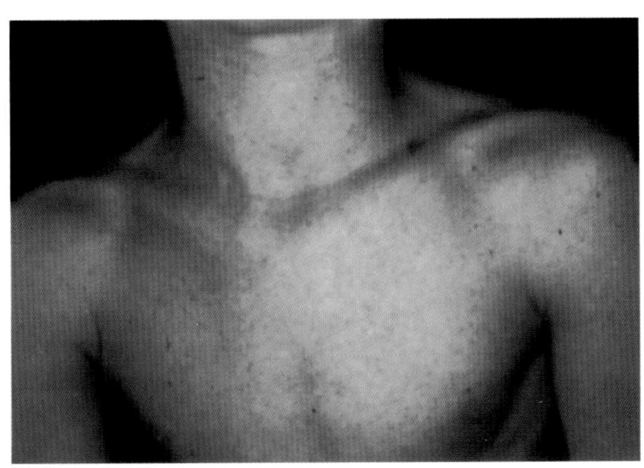

FIGURE 65–3

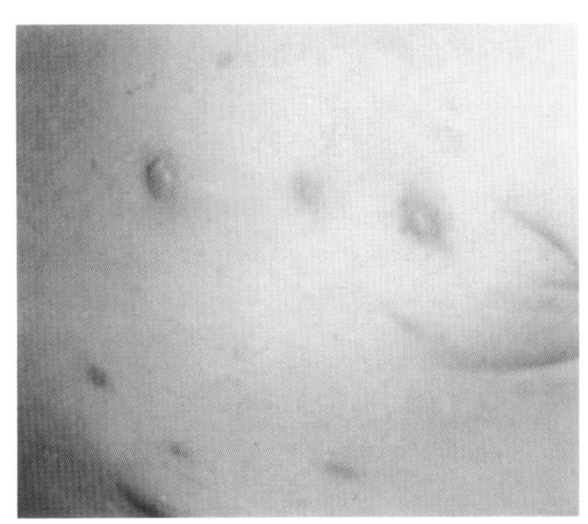

FIGURE 65–4

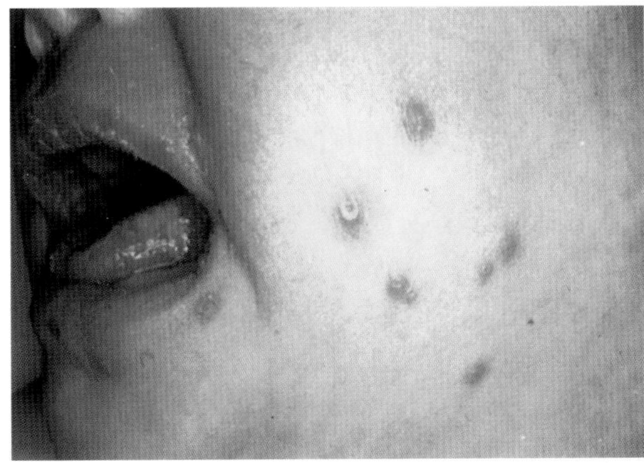

FIGURE 65–5

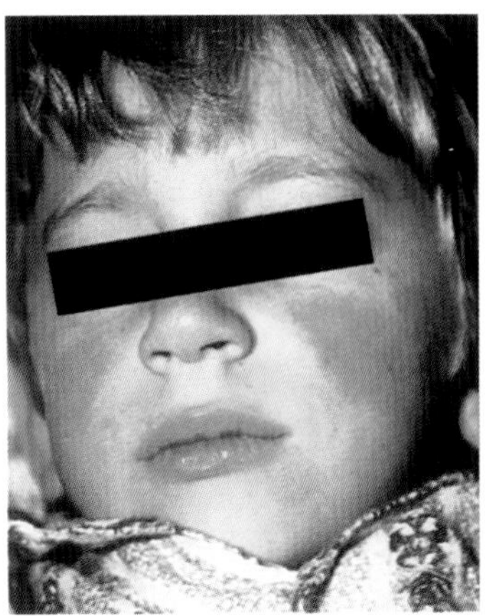

FIGURE 65–6

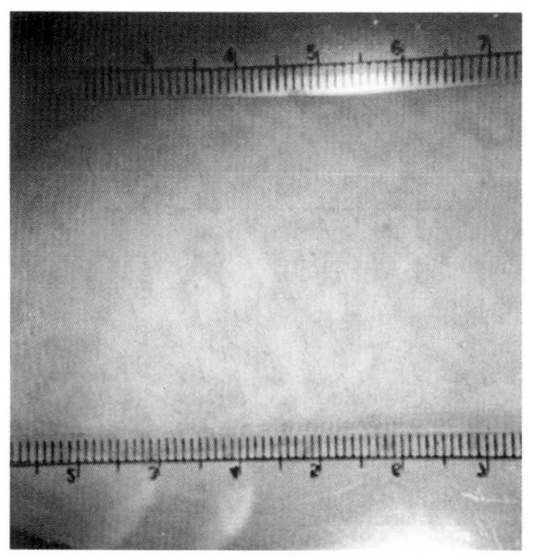

FIGURE 65–7

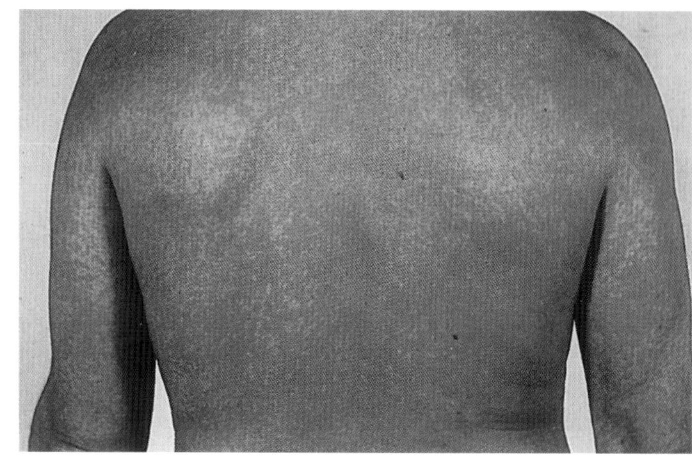

FIGURE 65–8

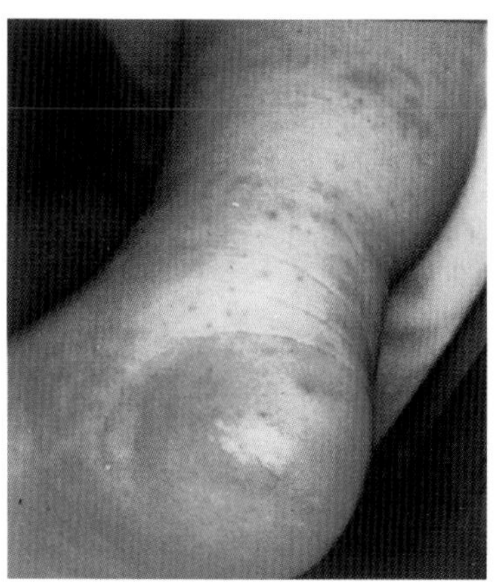

FIGURE 65–9

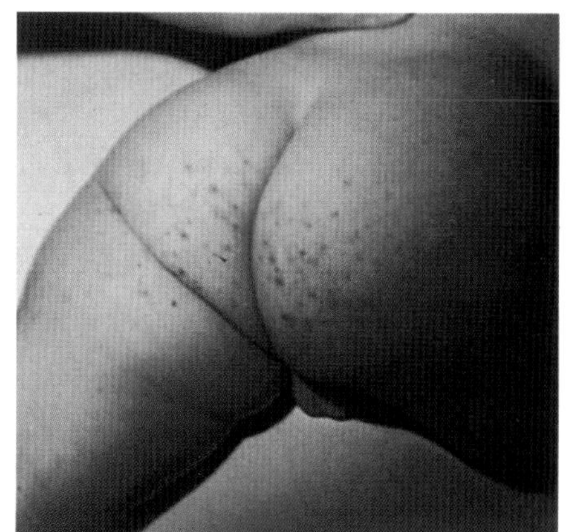

FIGURE 65–10

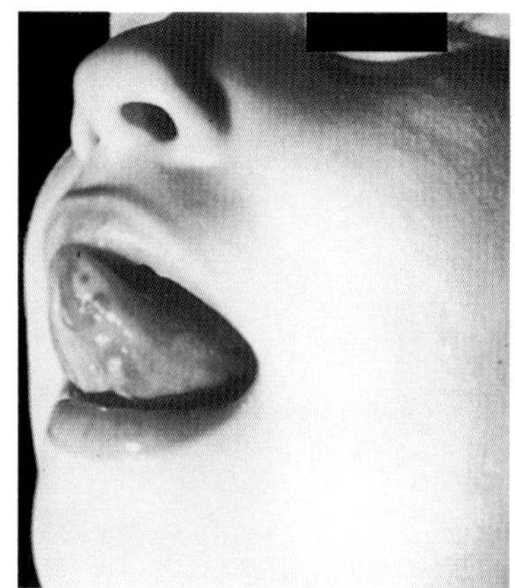

FIGURE 65–11

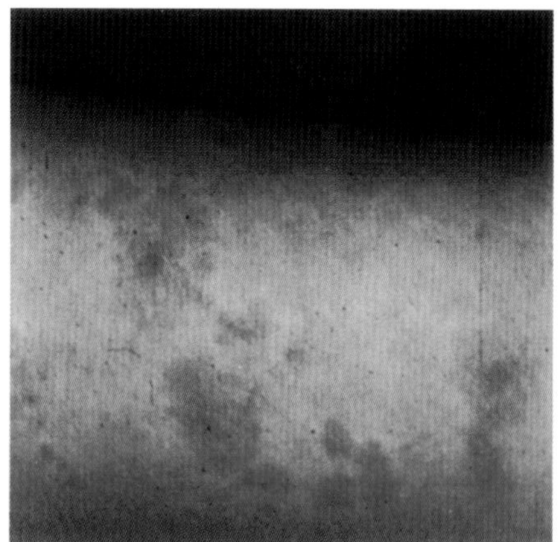

FIGURE 65–12

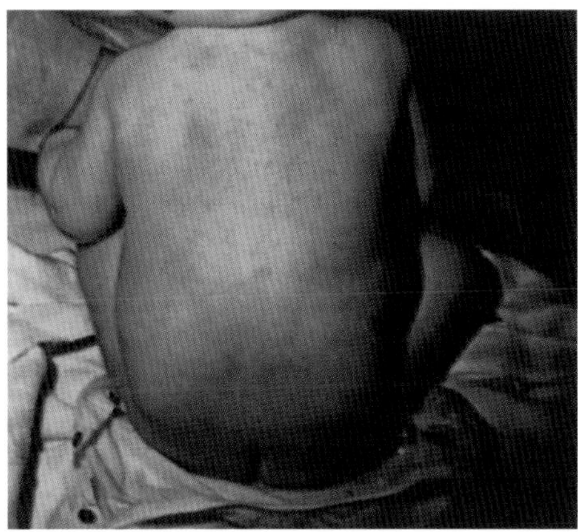
FIGURE 65–13

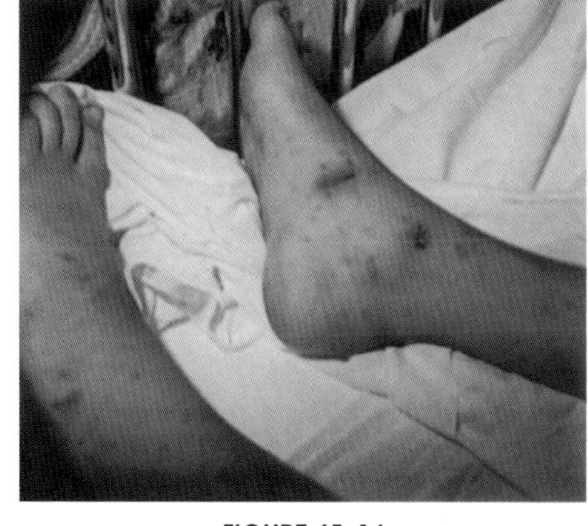
FIGURE 65–14

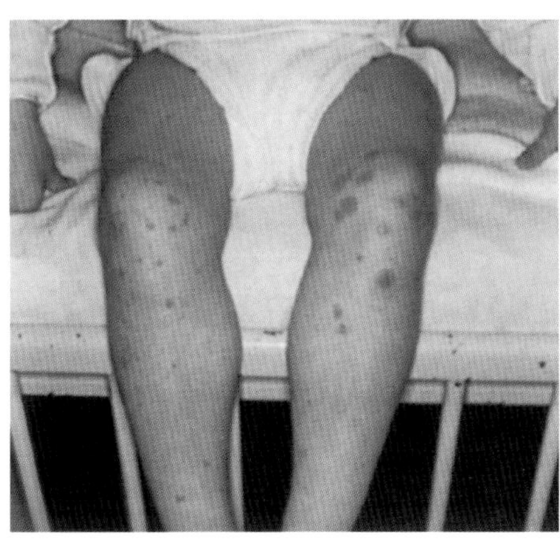
FIGURE 65–15

FIGURE 65–16

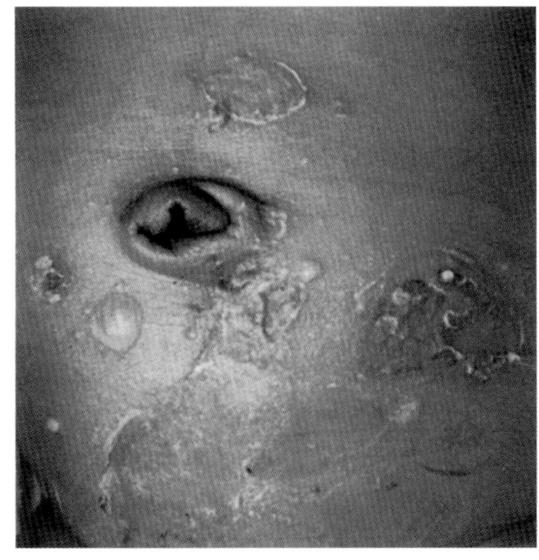
FIGURE 65–17

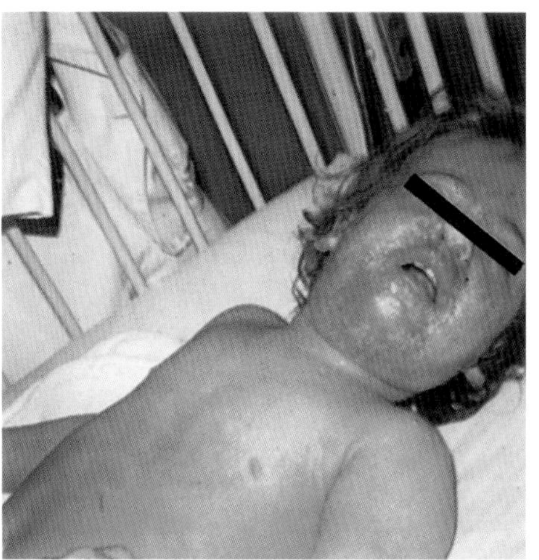
FIGURE 65–18

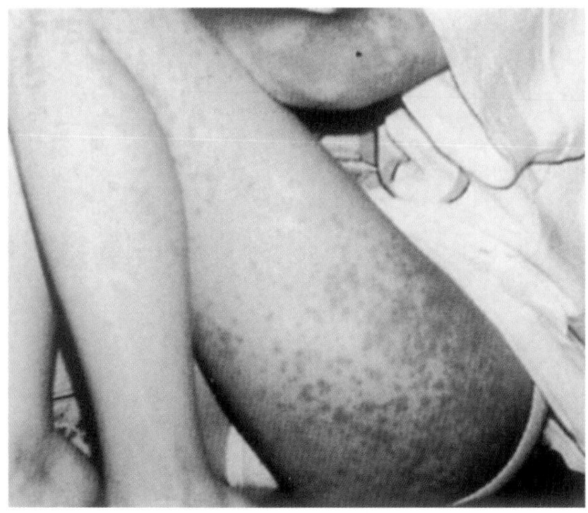

FIGURE 65–19

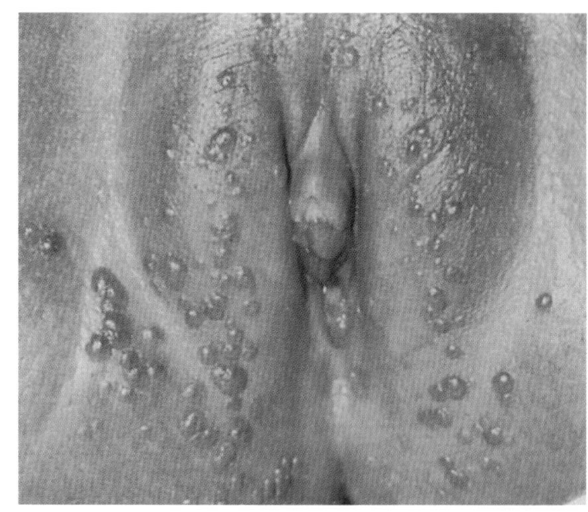

FIGURE 65–20

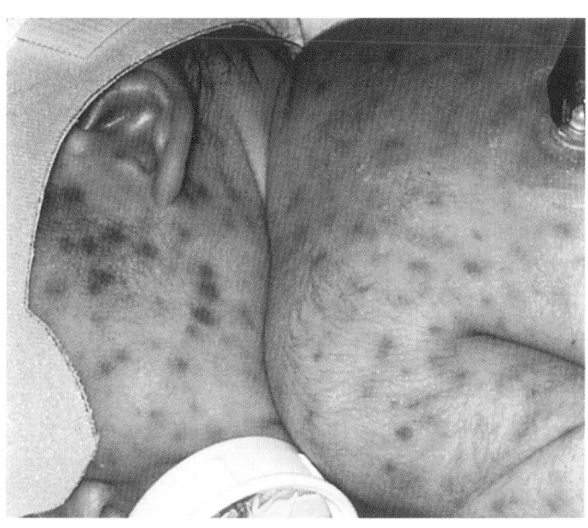

FIGURE 65–21

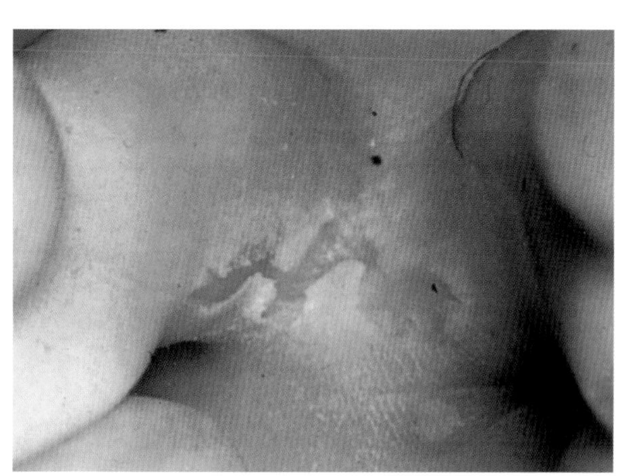

FIGURE 65–22

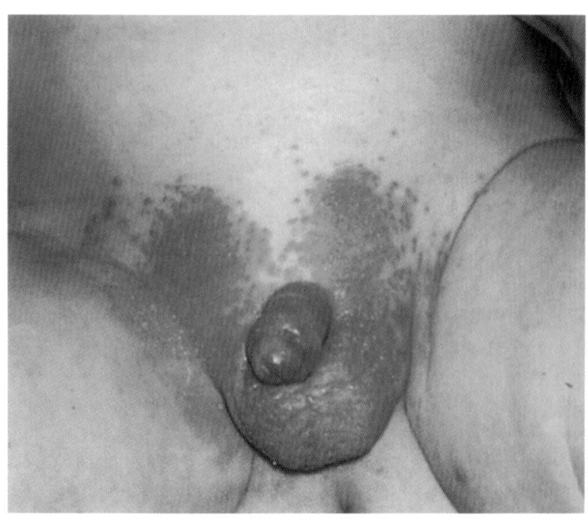

FIGURE 65–23

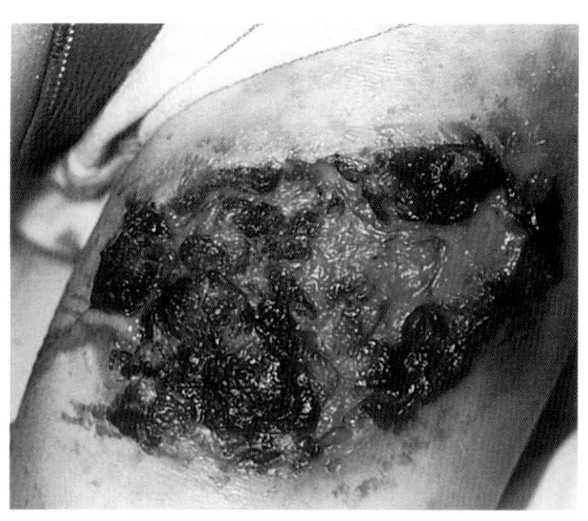

FIGURE 65–24

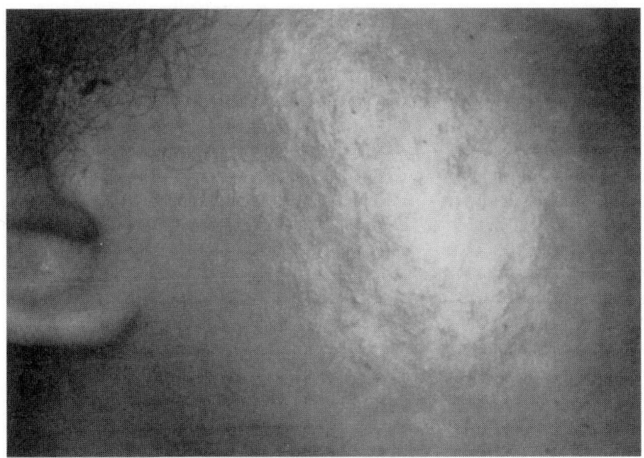

FIGURE 65–2 ■ Measles exanthem. Note the generalized erythematous confluent base supporting small papular and microvesicular lesions.

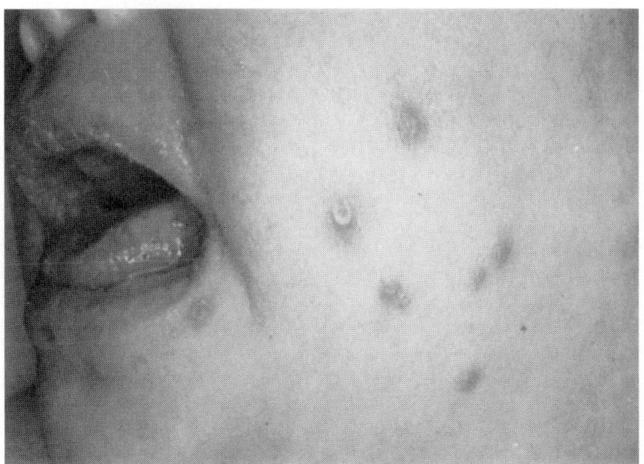

FIGURE 65–5 ■ Primary herpes simplex virus infection in an infant. Note the severe stomatitis and papulovesicular and vesicular lesions under the lower lip and on the cheek.

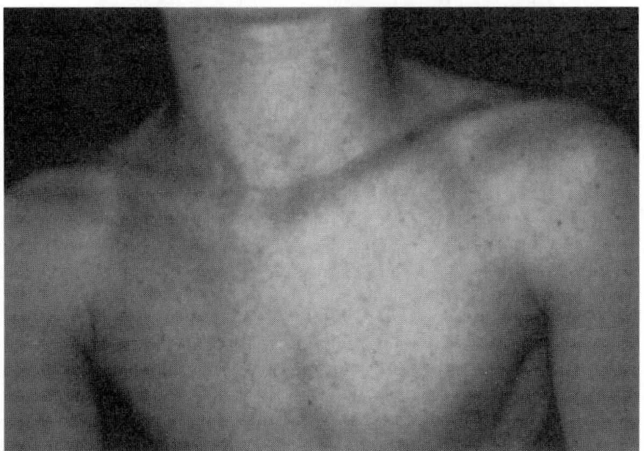

FIGURE 65–3 ■ Rubella exanthem. The rash is erythematous, maculopapular, and discrete. (From Cherry, J. D.: Newer viral exanthems. Adv. Pediatr. *16*:233–286, 1969.)

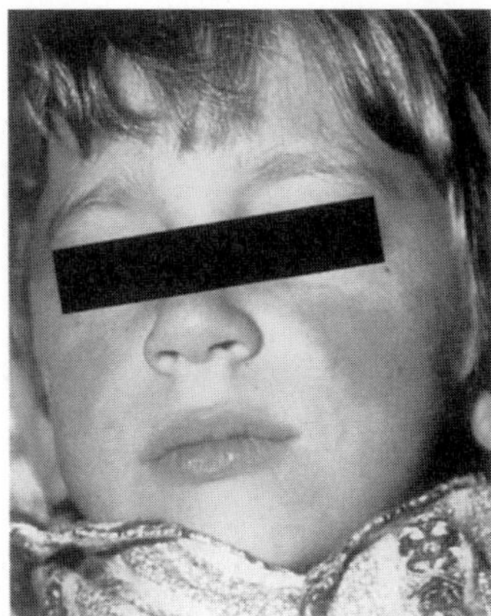

FIGURE 65–6 ■ Slapped-cheek appearance with a relative circumoral maculopapular rash in erythema infectiosum.

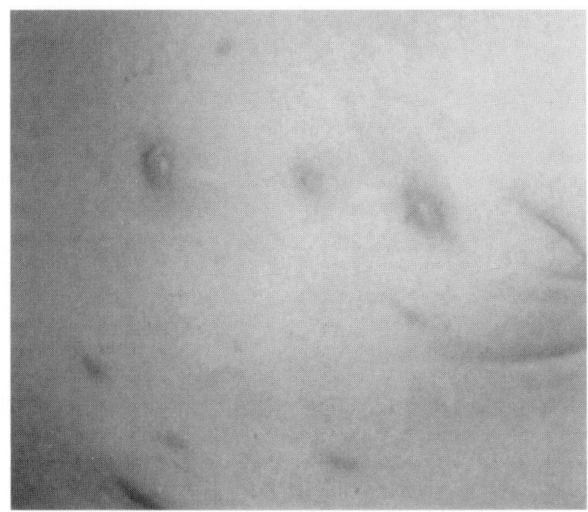

FIGURE 65–4 ■ Chickenpox exanthem. Typical lesions in all stages: Vesicles, papulovesicles, and papules. (From Cherry, J. D.: Newer viral exanthems. Adv. Pediatr. *16*:233–286, 1969.)

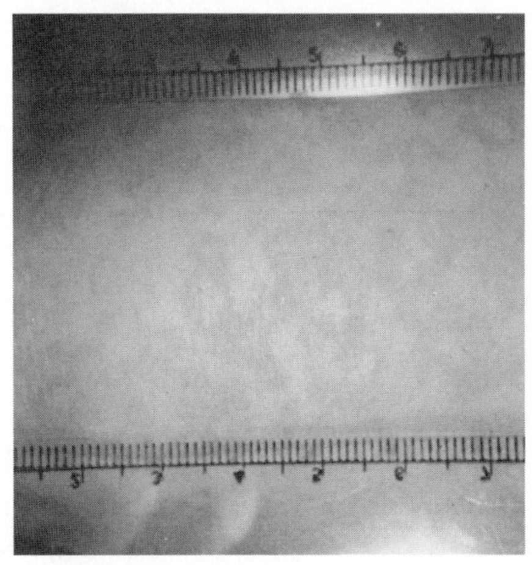

FIGURE 65–7 ■ Rash with a lacelike, or reticular, pattern in erythema infectiosum.

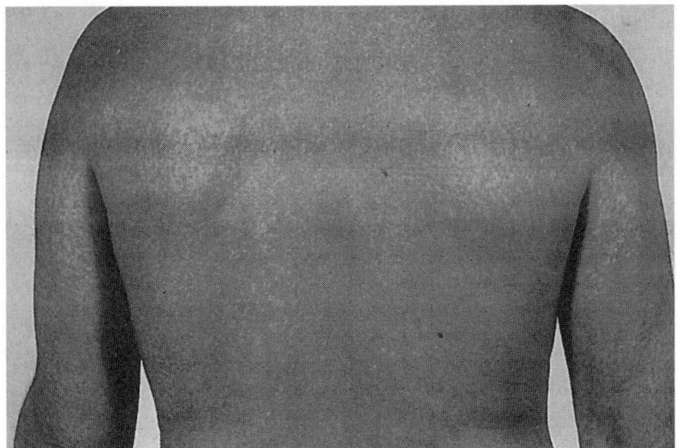

FIGURE 65–8 ■ Confluent exanthem in a patient with human parvovirus infection.

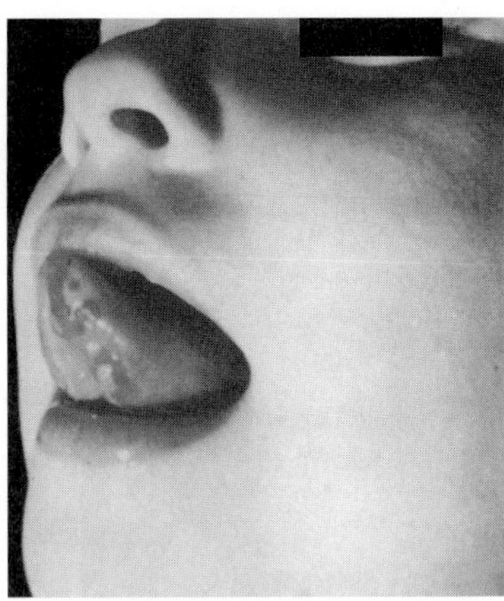

FIGURE 65–11 ■ Two large ulcerative lesions on the underside of the tongue in a patient with hand, foot, and mouth syndrome caused by coxsackievirus A16.

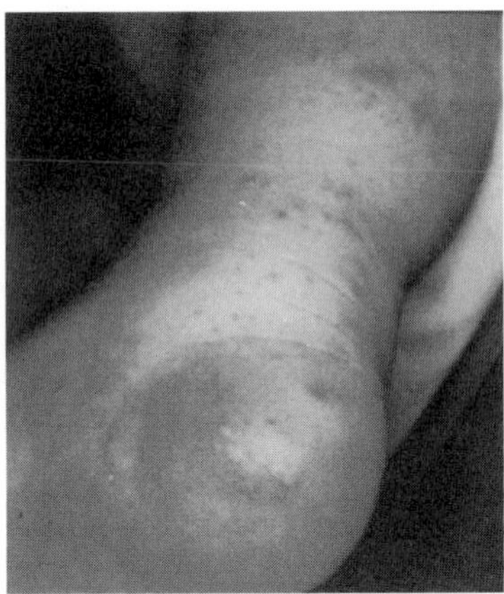

FIGURE 65–9 ■ Vesicular and maculopapular lesions on the foot and lower part of the leg as part of the hand, foot, and mouth syndrome caused by coxsackievirus A16. (From Cherry, J. D., and Jahn, C. L.: Hand, foot, and mouth syndrome: Report of six cases due to coxsackievirus, group A, type 16. Pediatrics *37*:637, 1966. Copyright American Academy of Pediatrics 1966.)

FIGURE 65–12 ■ Papulo-urticarial lesions in coxsackievirus A9 infection. (From Cherry, J. D.: Newer viral exanthems. Adv. Pediatr. *16*:233–286, 1969.)

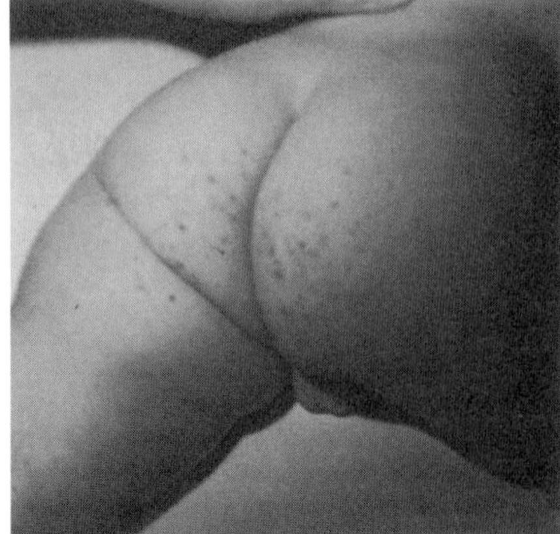

FIGURE 65–10 ■ Erythematous maculopapular lesions on the buttocks as part of the hand, foot, and mouth syndrome caused by coxsackievirus A16. (From Cherry, J. D., and Jahn, C. L.: Hand, foot, and mouth syndrome: Report of six cases due to coxsackievirus, group A, type 16. Pediatrics *37*:637, 1966. Copyright American Academy of Pediatrics 1966.)

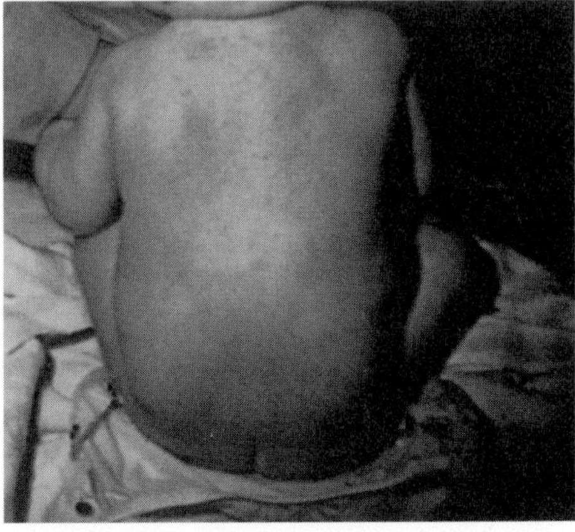

FIGURE 65–13 ■ Erythematous, discrete, maculopapular, and petechial rash of echovirus 9 infection. (From Cherry, J. D.: Newer viral exanthems. Adv. Pediatr. *16*:233–286, 1969.)

common manifestation of enteroviral vesicular rash illnesses (see Figs. 65–9 to 65–11 and Color Plate II). The most frequent etiologic agent in the hand, foot, and mouth syndrome is coxsackievirus A16, but the syndrome also has been attributed to coxsackieviruses A5, A9, A10, B1, and B3 and enterovirus 71.

Enteroviral infections with vesicular exanthems in which the hand, foot, and mouth distribution is not present are diagnosed erroneously as insect bites or poison ivy quite frequently.

PETECHIAL AND PURPURIC EXANTHEMS

A large number of infectious agents are associated with petechial and purpuric skin manifestations (Figs. 65–14 and 65–15 and Color Plate III). They are listed in Table 65–11. Infectious diseases with hemorrhagic rash can be fulminant fatal events or relatively benign illnesses. On a worldwide basis, meningococcemia is perhaps the most important and feared, though not the most prevalent of the petechial and purpuric exanthematous diseases. The relatively sudden onset of fever and a petechial rash must be considered and treated as meningococcemia unless another etiology can be established with absolute certainty. The most important of the differential diagnostic problems is exanthem caused by enteroviral infection. Many different enterovirus illnesses have a sudden onset with accompanying fever and petechial rash. In addition, the situation frequently is complicated further by the occurrence of meningitis. The most important enterovirus in its ability to mimic meningococcemia is echovirus 9.

Purpuric and petechial lesions in infectious illnesses can result from a direct or indirect (immunologic) effect of the infectious agent at the cutaneous site or from the occurrence of thrombocytopenia. Thrombocytopenia is noted most commonly in acquired rubella virus infections.

URTICARIAL EXANTHEMS

The occurrence of urticaria all too frequently leads the physician to suspect an allergic or dermatologic condition[192, 193] (Figs. 65–12 and 65–16 and Color Plates II and III). However, what has become quite evident in recent years is that when urticaria develops in association with an acute febrile illness, the cutaneous reaction is a direct effect of an infectious agent, and its mediation does not require an allergic response. Listed in Table 65–12 are infectious agents associated with urticarial exanthems.

Papular urticaria occurs very commonly in children in the summer and fall and most frequently is the result of insect bites (see Table 65–6). However, virtually identical lesions occur in infections with coxsackievirus A, as well as other enteroviruses (see Fig. 65–12 and Color Plate II). The main point for differentiation is the fact that fever regularly develops in the virus-induced exanthems but is not a characteristic associated with insect bites.

Early in the course of meningococcemia, the exanthem can be urticarial, so an illness of sudden onset with fever and this cutaneous manifestation never should be taken lightly.

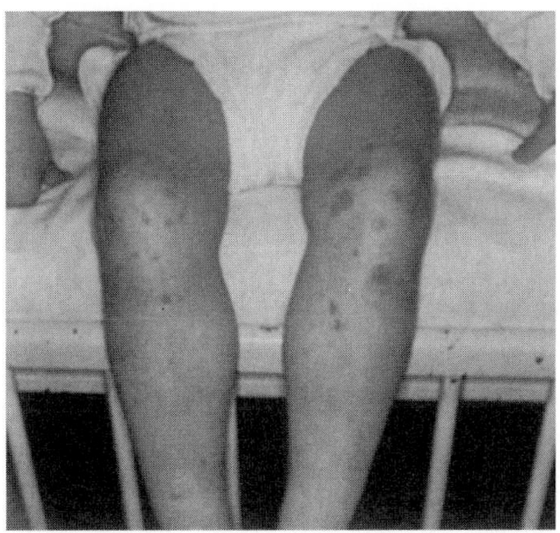

FIGURE 65–15 ■ Erythematous, papular, papulovesicular, and petechial lesions suggestive of anaphylactic purpura in a child with coxsackievirus A4 infection.

PAPULAR, NODULAR, AND ULCERATIVE LESIONS

In many instances, the lesions in this category occur as single events at the site of primary inoculation. Specific illnesses and etiologic agents are listed in Table 65–13.

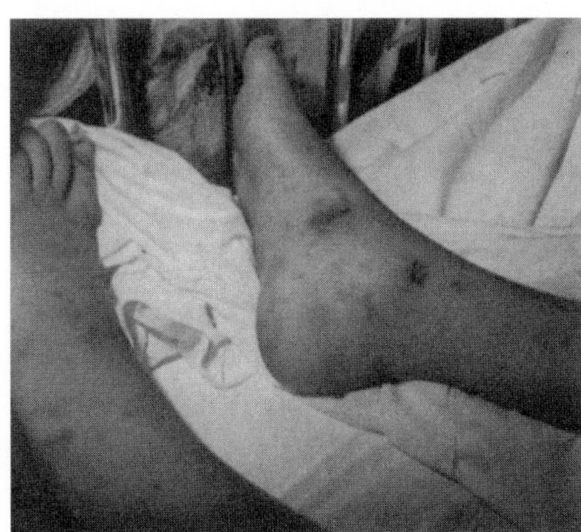

FIGURE 65–14 ■ Petechial and purpuric rash in a child with coxsackievirus A9 infection.

FIGURE 65–16 ■ Acute urticaria in a child with hand, foot, and mouth syndrome caused by coxsackievirus A16 infection.

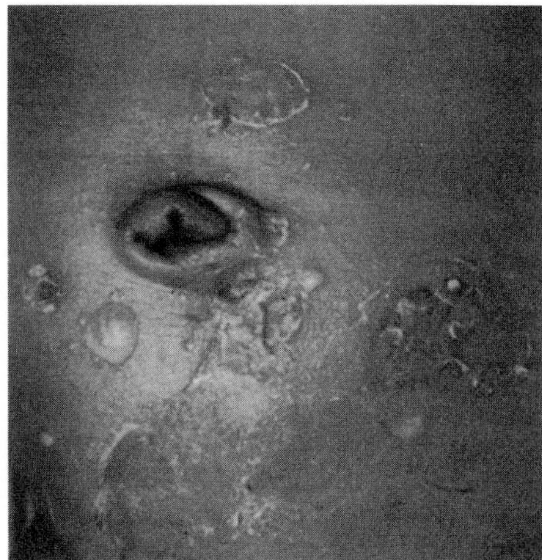

FIGURE 65–17 ■ Bullous impetigo in a newborn infant caused by exfoliative toxin–producing *Staphylococcus aureus.*

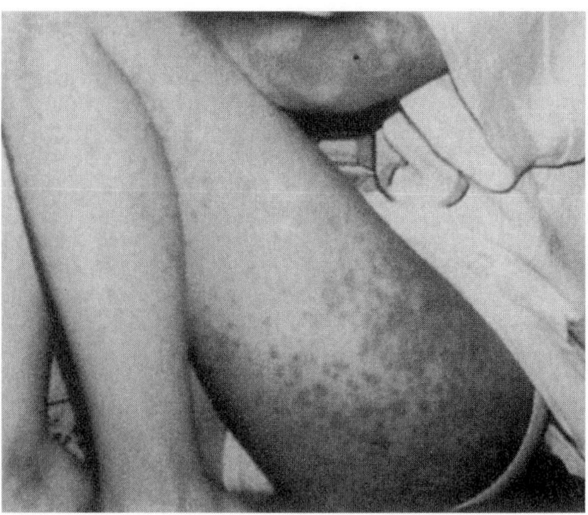

FIGURE 65–19 ■ An erythematous maculopapular discrete and confluent rash on the thigh and arm of a 16-year-old girl with pharyngitis and *Arcanobacterium haemolyticum* isolated from her throat. (From Mackenzie, A., Fuite, L. A., Chan, F. T. H., et al.: Incidence and pathogenicity of *Arcanobacterium haemolyticum* during a 2-year study in Ottawa. Clin. Infect. Dis. *21*:177–181, 1995.)

DISTINCTIVE CLINICAL FEATURES OR SYNDROMES

(Figs. 65–19 to 65–24 and Color Plate IV)

Erythema Multiforme

Erythema multiforme is a self-limited skin eruption that is erythematous and characterized by distinctive target or iris lesions, or both. Small vesicles and urticarial areas also may develop. Occasionally, the disease is severe and associated with mucosal involvement and genital lesions. In this latter illness—the Stevens-Johnson syndrome, bullous erythema multiforme, erythema multiforme exudativum major—severe ulcerative, oral, and genital lesions occur; generalized exanthems become bullous; and conjunctivitis is present. The illness is associated with fever and general distress.

Although the pathogenesis of erythema multiforme is unknown, what is clear is that multiple factors, including infectious agents, are responsible for its occurrence. Infectious agents associated with erythema multiforme are listed in Table 65–14. The single most important infectious cause of erythema multiforme and Stevens-Johnson syndrome is *M. pneumoniae.* When *M. pneumoniae* is the instigating agent, the patient nearly always has concomitant pneumonia.

HSV frequently has been recovered from the throats of persons with erythema multiforme, but the cause-and-effect relationship in many cases must be questioned. However, in a recent study, HSV DNA was found in the skin lesions of 11 of 31 patients with erythema multiforme.[55]

Erythema Nodosum

Erythema nodosum most commonly occurs on the anterior aspect of the lower part of the legs but may be seen anywhere on the body. The lesions are raised, erythematous, and painful to touch. Their usual size is approximately 2 to 4 cm, with a duration of 2 to 6 weeks.

Erythema nodosum occurs less commonly today than it did 4 decades ago, and the frequency of specific associated infectious agents also is different. In the past, streptococcal

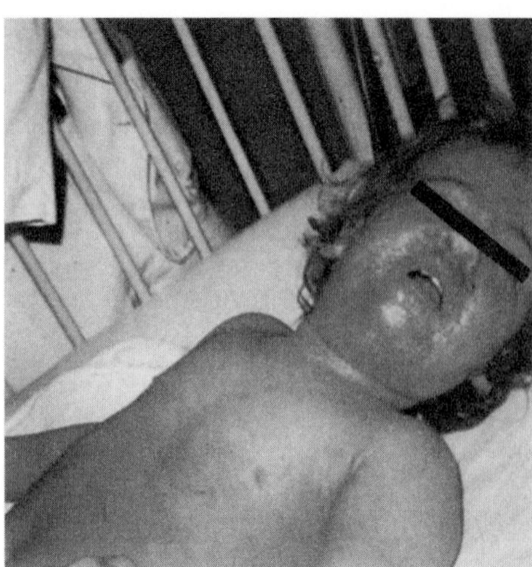

FIGURE 65–18 ■ Scalded skin syndrome caused by exfoliative toxin–producing *Staphylococcus aureus.*

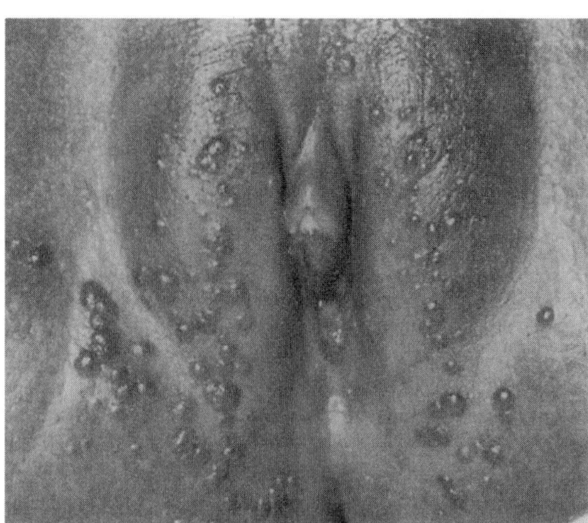

FIGURE 65–20 ■ Numerous flat-topped and dome-shaped, slightly erythematous papules over the skin of the perineum of a young girl with bowenoid papulosis.

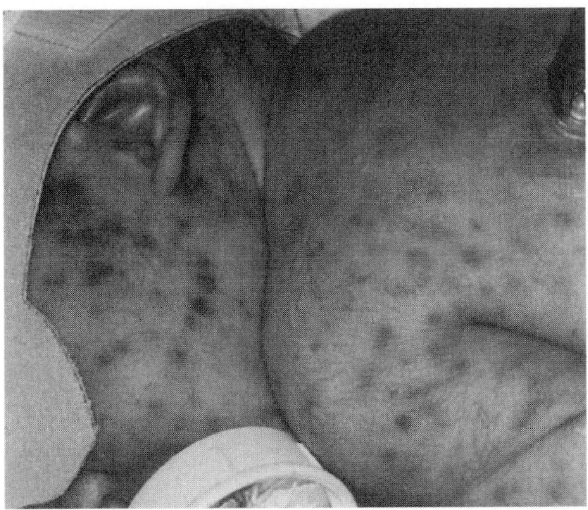

FIGURE 65–21 ■ Numerous isolated purple papules of dermal erythropoiesis overlying the icteric skin of a neonate with congenital cytomegalovirus infection.

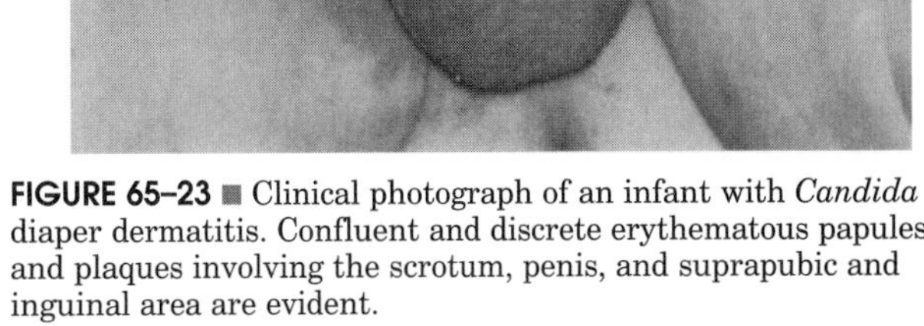

FIGURE 65–23 ■ Clinical photograph of an infant with *Candida* diaper dermatitis. Confluent and discrete erythematous papules and plaques involving the scrotum, penis, and suprapubic and inguinal area are evident.

and mycobacterial infections were the agents most commonly related. Now, the exanthem most often is associated with respiratory infection with *Histoplasma capsulatum, Cryptococcus neoformans,* and *Coccidioides immitis.* Infectious agents associated with erythema nodosum are listed in Table 65–15.

Hand, Foot, and Mouth Syndrome

The hand, foot, and mouth syndrome is a clearly recognizable viral illness characterized by vesicular lesions in the anterior of the mouth and on the hands and feet in association with fever. Although several enteroviruses (coxsackieviruses A5, A9, A10, A16, B1, and B3 and enterovirus 71) have been implicated, as have HSV and foot and mouth disease virus, most of these cases are caused by coxsackievirus A16.

Roseola-like Illness

Roseola infantum is a classic pediatric illness characterized by fever of 3 to 5 days' duration, rapid defervescence, and then the appearance of an erythematous macular or maculopapular rash that persists for 1 to 2 days. Roseola is an age-related response to infection with many viruses. Recent studies suggest that a leading cause of roseola infantum is primary infection with HHV-6. The following other viruses have been noted in association with roseola: adenoviruses 1, 2, 3, and 14; coxsackieviruses A6, A9, B1, B2, B4, and B5; echoviruses 9, 11, 16, 25, 27, and 30; parainfluenza virus type 1; and measles vaccine virus.

Rocky Mountain Spotted Fever–like Illness

Rocky Mountain spotted fever is a clinical illness characterized by fever and a petechial rash located mainly on the distal ends of extremities. The illness is caused by *Rickettsia rickettsii* and is prevalent in many areas of North America; the infectious agent is transmitted to humans by ticks. In other areas of the world, other tick-borne *rickettsiae (Rickettsia siberica, Rickettsia australis, Rickettsia conorii)* produce similar human illness. Infection with *Ehrlichia canis* also can cause an illness similar to Rocky Mountain spotted fever.

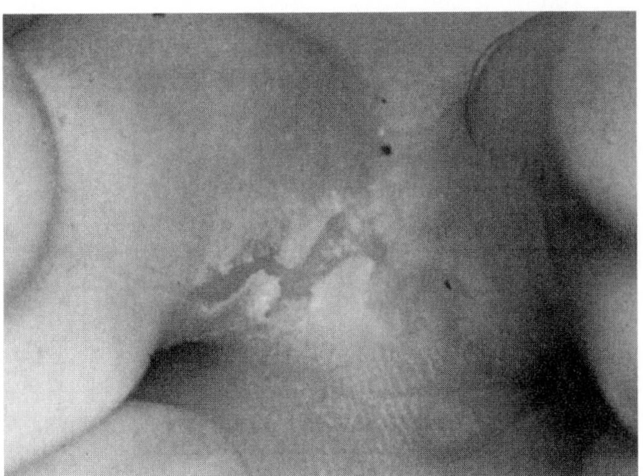

FIGURE 65–22 ■ Tinea pedis. Peeling, macerations, and fissuring in the fourth interdigital space of the foot are characteristic of dermatophytic infections.

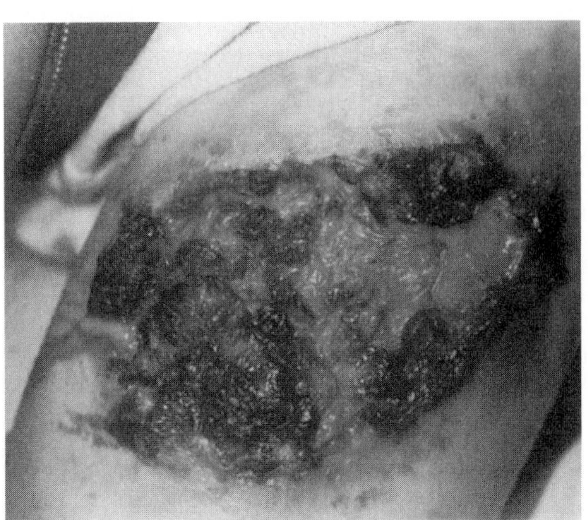

FIGURE 65–24 ■ An extensive crusted erosion on the left thigh of a child with a cryptococcal skin infection.

The most important illness confused with Rocky Mountain spotted fever is atypical measles (see Chapter 183). This illness, which has both the constitutional symptoms of Rocky Mountain spotted fever and a rash most prominent on the extremities, occurs almost exclusively after exposure to measles virus in some persons previously immunized with inactivated (killed) measles vaccine.

Rat-bite fever caused by *S. moniliformis* also has been misdiagnosed as Rocky Mountain spotted fever.[151]

Exanthem and Meningitis

Aseptic and also bacterial meningitis frequently are characterized by both exanthem and symptoms and signs of neurologic involvement. Infectious agents associated with exanthem and meningitis are presented in Table 65–16. Of most importance in this category is the differential diagnosis of enteroviral syndromes and meningococcemia.

Exanthem and Pulmonary Involvement

Infectious agents associated with exanthem and pulmonary involvement are listed in Table 65–17. In patients older than 5 years, the leading cause of exanthem and pneumonia is *M. pneumoniae* infection. In younger children, adenoviruses are the most important etiologic agents. With the exception of enteroviral infections, which are more likely to involve young children, most of the illnesses listed in Table 65–17 occur in older children and young adults.

Gianotti-Crosti Syndrome (Papular Acrodermatitis)

Gianotti-Crosti syndrome is a distinct clinical entity characterized by a papular (lichenoid) exanthem, generalized lymphadenopathy, hepatomegaly, and acute anicteric hepatitis.[43, 164, 167] In most instances, this illness has been associated with hepatitis B virus infection. The syndrome also has been noted in association with Epstein-Barr virus, cytomegalovirus, coxsackievirus B virus, and RSV infections.[61, 106, 165, 186]

Cutaneous Manifestations Associated with Infections in Immunocompromised Patients

All infectious agents that cause exanthems in immunologically normal children can cause infections in immunocompromised children. However, the clinical manifestations may be different. For example, measles virus infection in a child who is T-cell deficient may be associated with a severe, progressive pneumonia but not the typical rash. Other viral exanthems that are self-limited in normal children, such as varicella, may be progressive and develop into hemorrhagic skin lesions with disseminated organ involvement in children with T-cell deficiency.

Of particular concern are bacterial and fungal infections, which are rarely a problem in normal children but are rapidly fatal in granulocytopenic children. These patients have characteristic skin lesions resulting from disseminated infections. Of importance are ecthyma gangrenosa resulting from *Pseudomonas aeruginosa* septicemia and the nodular and purpuric lesions of disseminated fungal infections caused by *Aspergillus, Candida,* and other less common agents.

Diagnosis

DIFFERENTIAL DIAGNOSIS

The diagnosis of infectious exanthems frequently is considered an impossible task by many physicians. Other physicians glibly call the first maculopapular exanthem of childhood "roseola" and the first vesicular rash "chickenpox" without consideration of more appropriate choices. The hallmark of diagnosis in exanthematous disease is careful elicitation of historic data. Differential diagnosis requires the consideration of noninfectious etiologies, as well as different infectious agents. Listed in Table 65–18 are the major considerations in the diagnosis of diseases with cutaneous manifestations.

TABLE 65–18 ■ IMPORTANT ASPECTS IN THE DIAGNOSIS OF EXANTHEMATOUS ILLNESS

Exposure	Types of rash
Season	Distribution of rash
Incubation period	Progession of rash
Age	Exanthem
Previous exanthems	Other associated symptoms
Relationship of rash to fever	Laboratory tests
Adenopathy	

From Cherry, J. D.: Newer viral exanthems. Adv. Pediatr. *16*: 233–286, 1969.

A history of exposure is most important in making a differential diagnosis. For example, was the patient exposed to poison ivy, insects, or a person ill with a specific disease? In infectious illnesses with high clinical expression rates (measles, chickenpox, rubella), proper questioning usually reveals a contact case or at least other cases in the community. On the other hand, in illnesses with low rates of clinical expression of exanthem, such as adenoviral and some enteroviral infections, the source may not be apparent.

Consideration of the seasonal occurrence of different infectious agents, as well as insects, is particularly useful in making a differential diagnosis. In temperate climates, enteroviral and arthropod-mediated diseases occur in the summer and fall. Exanthems with measles, varicella-zoster, and rubella viruses occur most often in the winter and spring. The diagnosis of rubella is important because of fetal consequences. All too frequently, rubella is overdiagnosed and underdiagnosed, both of which can be avoided if its seasonal prevalence is understood.

The incubation period is important in separating the exanthem caused by rubella, varicella-zoster, or measles viruses from rash illnesses caused by enteroviruses or common respiratory viruses. The former have long incubation periods, whereas in the others, the period from exposure to the onset of illness is less than 1 week. Age can be useful. Today in the United States, measles and rubella often are illnesses of adolescents and young adults. Enteroviral exanthem frequency is related inversely to age.

Questioning to obtain a pertinent history of previous exanthems can give useful information if it is done with care. For example, if patients are asked whether they had rubella, the answer is quite unreliable. However, if the past illness is documented by year, season, and symptomatology, accurate information often is obtained. The relationship of rash to fever is most significant in the diagnosis of roseola. The presence or absence of fever is important in separating exanthems of infectious and noninfectious etiology. Frequently, insect bites are diagnosed as chickenpox by parents and physicians as well. Chickenpox rarely occurs without fever.

The type and distribution of exanthem obviously are important. They virtually are diagnostic in hand, foot, and mouth syndrome, Rocky Mountain spotted fever, and atypical measles. Enanthem can lead to a specific diagnosis (Koplik spots in measles) or a category diagnosis (herpangina in enteroviral infections). Other characteristics, such as those listed in Tables 65–8 through 65–17, obviously are useful in delineating a specific illness.

SPECIFIC DIAGNOSIS

As with other infectious diseases, specific diagnosis depends on the acquisition of proper cultures, serologic tests, and microscopic study of secretions or histologic or cytologic preparations. These techniques are discussed in other chapters of this book.

Vesicular lesions always should be scraped for cytologic study or direct antigen identification (varicella, herpes simplex), and, frequently, petechial lesions should be scraped and stained in a search for infectious agents (meningococci). The etiology of viral infections can be established by isolation of virus, direct antigen detection, or serologic methods. In most instances, a virus recovered from the throat indicates acute infection and is the probable cause of a particular illness. Serologic study without culture is useful in diagnosing rickettsial diseases, some viral infections, and a few illnesses of bacterial origin. Serologic study without virus isolation generally is not useful in diagnosing enteroviral illnesses.

Treatment, Prognosis, and Prevention

The treatment, prognosis, and prevention of exanthematous diseases are presented in appropriate chapters throughout this text.

REFERENCES

1. Africk, J. A., and Halprin, K. M.: Infectious mononucleosis presenting as urticaria. J. A. M. A. *209*:1524–1525, 1969.
2. Agnello, V., and Abel, G.: Localization of hepatitis C virus in cutaneous vasculitic lesions in patients with type II cryoglobulinemia. Arthritis Rheum. *40*:2007–2015, 1997.
3. Ahlm, C., Settergren, B., Gothfors, L., et al.: Nephropathia epidemica (hemorrhagic fever with renal syndrome) in children: Clinical characteristics. Pediatr. Infect. Dis. J. *13*:45–49, 1994.
4. Ahvonen, P.: Human yersiniosis in Finland. II. Clinical features. Ann. Clin. Res. *4*:39–48, 1972.
5. Anderson, M. J., Lewis, E., Kidd, I. M., et al.: An outbreak of erythema infectiosum associated with human parvovirus infection. J. Hyg. (Lond.) *93*:85–93, 1984.
6. Arkwright, J. A.: Foot-and-mouth disease in man. Lancet *1*:1191–1192, 1928.
7. Asano, Y., Suga, S., Yoshikawa, T., et al.: Clinical features and viral excretion in an infant with primary human herpesvirus 7 infection. Pediatrics *95*:187–190, 1995.
8. Asano, Y., Yoshikawa, T., Suga, S., et al.: Viremia and neutralizing antibody response in infants with exanthem subitum. J. Pediatr. *114*: 535–539, 1989.
9. Athreya, B. H., and Coriell, L. L.: Erythema multiforme exudativum major: A review and report of four cases. Clin. Pediatr. (Phila.) *3*:68–74, 1964.
10. Azimi, P. H., Chase, P. A., and Petru, A. M.: Mycoplasmas: Their role in pediatric disease. Curr. Probl. Pediatr. *14*:7–46, 1984.
11. Baer, R. L.: Erythema multiforme—1976.Am. J. Med. Sci. *271*:119–120, 1976.
12. Baley, J. E., Kliegman, R. M., and Fanaroff, A. A.: Disseminated fungal infections in very low-birth weight infants: Clinical manifestations and epidemiology. Pediatrics *83*:144–152, 1984.
13. Balfour, H. H., Jr., Forte, F. A., Simpson, R. B., et al.: Penicillin-related exanthems in infectious mononucleosis identical to those associated with ampicillin. Clin. Pediatr. (Phila.) *11*:417–421, 1972.
14. Baron, J., and Shapiro, E. D.: Unsuspected bacteremia caused by *Branhamella catarrhalis*. Pediatr. Infect. Dis. *4*:100–101, 1985.
15. Barrett, P. K. M., and Greenberg, M. J.: Outbreak of ornithosis. B. M. J. *2*:206–207, 1966.
16. Baumgartner, J. D., Glauser, M. P., Burgo-Black, A. L., et al.: Severe cytomegalovirus infection in multiply transfused, splenectomised, trauma patients. Lancet *2*:63–66, 1982.
17. Beall, G. N.: Urticaria: A review of laboratory and clinical observations. Medicine (Baltimore) *43*:131–151, 1964.
18. Benoit, F. L.: Chronic meningococcemia: Case report and review of the literature. Am. J. Med. *35*:103–112, 1963.
19. Berant, M., Naveh, Y., and Weissman, I.: Papular acrodermatitis with cytomegalovirus hepatitis. Arch. Dis. Child. *58*:1024–1025, 1983.
20. Berenguer, J., Rodriguez-Tudela, J. L., Richard, C., et al.: Deep infections caused by *Scedosporium prolificans*. Medicine (Baltimore) *76*:256–265, 1997.
21. Berger, B. W.: Erythema chronicum migrans of Lyme disease. Arch. Dermatol. *120*:1017–1021, 1984.
22. Black, F. L.: Measles. *In* Evans, A. S. (ed.): Viral Infections of Humans: Epidemiology and Control. New York, Plenum, 1976, pp. 297–316.
23. Blatt, J., Kastner, O., and Hodes, D. S.: Cutaneous vesicles in congenital cytomegalovirus infection. J. Pediatr. *92*:509, 1978.
24. Bodey, G. P., and Fainstein, V.: Systemic candidiasis. *In* Bodey, G. P., and Fainstein, V. (eds.): Candidiasis. New York, Raven Press, 1985, pp. 135–168.
25. Boughton, C. R.: Glandular fever: A study of hospital series in Sydney. Med. J. Aust. *2*:529–535, 1970.
26. Bowmer, E. J., McKiel, J. A., Cockcroft, W. H., et al.: *Listeria monocytogenes* infections in Canada. Can. Med. Assoc. J. *109*:125–135, 1973.
27. Bowmer, M. I., Leggat, I., and Barrowman, J. A.: Disseminated gonococcal infection. Can. Med. Assoc. J. *126*:1188–1190, 1982.
28. Bradford, W. D., and Hawkins, H. K.: Rocky Mountain spotted fever in childhood. Am. J. Dis. Child. *131*:1228–1232, 1977.
29. Breese, B. B.: Streptococcal pharyngitis and scarlet fever. Am. J. Dis. Child. *132*:612–616, 1978.
30. Breese, B. B.: Pharyngitis and scarlet fever. *In* Breese, B. B., and Hall, C. B. (eds.): Beta Hemolytic Streptococcal Diseases. Boston, Houghton Mifflin, 1978, pp. 65–78.
31. Breese, B. B.: Streptococcal skin infections. *In* Breese, B. B., and Hall, C. B. (eds.): Beta Hemolytic Streptococcal Diseases. Boston, Houghton Mifflin, 1978, pp. 176–211.
32. Brettman, L. R., Lewin, S., Holzman, R. S., et al.: Rickettsialpox: Report of an outbreak and a contemporary review. Medicine (Baltimore) *60*:363–372, 1981.
33. Brody, I.: Topical treatment of recurrent herpes simplex and postherpetic erythema multiforme with low concentrations of zinc sulphate solution. Br. J. Dermatol. *104*:191–194, 1981.
34. Browne, S. G.: Mycobacterial diseases: Leprosy. *In* Fitzpatrick, T. B., Eisen, A. Z., Wolff, K., et al. (eds.): Dermatology in General Medicine. New York, McGraw-Hill, 1979, pp. 1492–1505.
35. Bruhn, F. W.: Lyme disease. Am. J. Dis. Child. *138*:467–470, 1984.
36. Bruno, P., Harrison Hassell, L., Brown, J., et al.: The protean manifestations of hemorrhagic fever with renal syndrome: A retrospective review of 26 cases from Korea. Ann. Intern. Med. *113*:385–391, 1990.
37. Buckley, B.: Q fever epidemic in Victorian general practice. Med. J. Aust. *1*:593–595, 1980.
38. Burnett, J. W.: Uncommon bacterial infections of the skin. Arch. Dermatol. *86*:597–607, 1962.
39. Bwaka, M. A., Bonnet, M. J., Calain, P., et al.: Ebola hemorrhagic fever in Kitwit, Democratic Republic of the Congo: Clinical observations of 103 patients. J. Infect. Dis. *179*(Suppl.):1–7, 1999.
40. Caputo, R. V., and Solomon, L. M.: Vascular reactive diseases. *In* Solomon, L. M., Esterly, N. B., and Loeffel, E. D. (eds.): Adolescent Dermatology. Philadelphia, W. B. Saunders, 1978, pp. 404–432.
41. Carlstrom, G., Alden, J., Belfrage, S., et al.: Acquired cytomegalovirus infection. B. M. J. *2*:521–525, 1968.
42. Carslaw, R. W.: Skin infestation. Practitioner *216*:154–158, 1976.
43. Castellano, A., Schweitzer, R., Tong, M. J., et al.: Papular acrodermatitis of childhood and hepatitis B infection. Arch. Dermatol. *114*:1530–1532, 1978.
44. Centers for Disease Control and Prevention: Moth-associated dermatitis—Cozumel, Mexico. M. M. W. R. Morb. Mortal. Wkly. Rep. *39*(13):219–220, 1990.
45. Chanarin, I., and Walford, D. M.: Thrombocytopenic purpura in cytomegalovirus mononucleosis. Lancet *2*:238–239, 1973.
46. Cherry, J. D.: Newer viral exanthems. Adv. Pediatr. *16*:233–286, 1969.
47. Cherry, J. D.: Parvovirus infections in children and adults. Adv. Pediatr. *46*:245–269, 1999.
48. Cherry, J. D., Hurwitz, E. S., and Welliver, R. C.: *Mycoplasma pneumoniae* infections and exanthems. J. Pediatr. *87*:369–373, 1975.
49. Cherry, J. D., and Jahn, C. L.: Exanthem and enanthem associated with mumps virus infection. Arch. Environ. Health *12*:518–521, 1966.
50. Cherry, J. D., and Welliver, R. C.: *Mycoplasma pneumoniae* infections of adults and children. West. J. Med. *125*:47–55, 1976.
51. Chesney, P. J., Davis, J. P., Purdy, W. K., et al.: Clinical manifestations of toxic shock syndrome. J. A. M. A. *246*:741–748, 1981.
52. Chonmaitree, T., Menegus, M. A., and Powell, K. R.: The clinical relevance of "CSF viral culture": A two-year experience with aseptic meningitis in Rochester, New York. J. A. M. A. *247*:1843–1847, 1982.
53. Clark, R. F.: Localized urticaria due to *Enterobius vermicularis*. Arch. Dermatol. *84*:1026, 1961.
54. Cowdrey, S. C., and Reynolds, J. S.: Acute urticaria in infectious mononucleosis. Ann. Allergy *27*:182–187, 1969.
55. Darragh, T. M., Egbert, B. M., Berger, T. G., et al.: Identification of herpes simplex virus DNA in lesions of erythema multiforme by the polymerase chain reaction. J. Am. Acad. Dermatol. *24*:23–36, 1991.

56. Daye, S., McHenry, J. A., and Roscelli, J. D.: Pruritic rash associated with cat scratch disease. Pediatrics *81*:559–561, 1988.
57. Delage, G., McLaughlin, B., and Berthiaume, L.: A clinical study of rotavirus gastroenteritis. J. Pediatr. *93*:455–457, 1978.
58. Derbes, V. J.: Arthropod bites and stings. *In* Fitzpatrick, T. B., Eisen, A. Z., Wolff, K., et al. (eds.): Dermatology in General Medicine. New York, McGraw-Hill, 1979, pp. 1656–1668.
59. Dienstag, J. L., Rhodes, A. R., Bhan, A. K., et al.: Urticaria associated with acute viral hepatitis type B: Studies of pathogenesis. Ann. Intern. Med. *88*:34–40, 1978.
60. Dooley, J. R.: Haemotropic bacteria in man. Lancet *2*:1237–1239, 1980.
61. Draelos, Z. K., Hansen, R. C., and James, W. D.: Gianotti-Crosti syndrome associated with infections other than hepatitis B. J. A. M. A. *256*:2386–2388, 1986.
62. Drago, F., Ranieri, E., Malaguti, F., et al.: Human herpesvirus 7 in pityriasis rosea. Lancet *349*:1367–1368, 1997.
63. Dryer, R. F., Goellner, P. G., and Carney, A. S.: Lyme arthritis in Wisconsin. J. A. M. A. *241*:498–499, 1979.
64. Dukes, C.: On the confusion of two different diseases under the name of rubella (rose-rash). Lancet *2*:89–94, 1900.
65. Duncan, W. C.: Cutaneous manifestations of infectious diseases. *In* Hoeprich, P. D. (ed.): Infectious Diseases: A Modern Treatise of Infectious Processes. Hagerstown, MD, Harper & Row, 1977, pp. 68–74.
66. Editor's Reply: First, second, third, fourth and fifth diseases. Am. J. Dis. Child. *108*:440–441, 1964.
67. Ellis, M. E., Pope, J., Mokashi, A., et al.: *Campylobacter* colitis associated with erythema nodosum. B. M. J. *285*:937, 1982.
68. Farah, F. S.: Protozoan and helminth infections. *In* Fitzpatrick, T. B., Eisen, A. Z., Wolff, K., et al. (eds.): Dermatology in General Medicine. New York, McGraw-Hill, 1979, pp. 1635–1656.
69. Fass, R. J., and Saslaw, S.: Earth day histoplasmosis: A new type of urban pollution. Arch. Intern. Med. *128*:588–590, 1971.
70. Fell, H. W. K., Nagington, J., Naylor, G. R. E., et al.: *Corynebacterium haemolyticum* infections in Cambridgeshire. J. Hyg. (Lond.) *79*:269–275, 1977.
71. Fenner, F.: The clinical features and pathogenesis of mouse-pox (infectious ectromelia of mice). J. Pathol. Bacteriol. *60*:529–552, 1948.
72. Fiumara, N. J., and Solomon, J.: Recurrent herpes simplex virus infections and erythema multiforme: A report of three patients. Sex. Transm. Dis. *10*:144–146, 1983.
73. Flaum, A.: Foot-and-mouth disease in man. Acta Pathol. Microbiol. Scand. *16*:197–213, 1939.
74. Formenty, P., Hatz, C., Le Guenno, B., et al.: Human infection due to Ebola virus, subtype Cote d'Ivoire: Clinical biologic presentation. J. Infect. Dis. *179*(Suppl.):48–53, 1999.
75. Fukumi, H., Nishikawa, F., Kokubu, Y., et al.: Isolation of adenovirus from an exanthematous infection resembling roseola infantum. Jpn. J. Med. Sci. Biol. *10*:87–91, 1957.
76. Game, M. A., Owen, W. C., and Mitchell, D. K.: Cutaneous manifestations of disseminated fungal infection in an immunocompromised child. J. Pediatr. *133*:466, 1998.
77. Gardner, S. D.: The isolation of parainfluenza 4 subtypes A and B in England and serological studies of their prevalence. J. Hyg. (Camb.) *67*:545–550, 1969.
78. Goodwin, R. A., Loyd, J. E., and Des Prez, R. M.: Histoplasmosis in normal hosts. Medicine (Baltimore) *60*:231–266, 1981.
79. Gordon, P. M., Hepburn, N. C., Williams, A. E., et al.: Cutaneous myiasis due to *Dermatobia hominis:* A report of six cases. Br. J. Dermatol. *132*:811–814, 1995.
80. Griffith, G. L., and Luce, E. A.: Massive skin necrosis in Rocky Mountain spotted fever. South. Med. J. *71*:1337–1340, 1978.
81. Grilli, R., Izquierdo, M. J., Farina, M. C., et al.: Papular-purpuric "gloves and socks" syndrome: Polymerase chain reaction demonstration of parvovirus B19 DNA in cutaneous lesions and sera. J. Am. Acad. Dermatol. *41*:793–796, 1999.
82. Gustafson, T. L., Band, J. D., Hutcheson, R. H., Jr., et al.: *Pseudomonas* folliculitis: An outbreak and review. Rev. Infect. Dis. *5*:1–8, 1983.
83. Hall, C. B.: The exanthematous family tree: Diseases one, two, three and five? Am. J. Dis. Child. *131*:816, 1977.
84. Halliday, H. L., and Hirata, T.: Perinatal listeriosis: A review of twelve patients. Am. J. Obstet. Gynecol. *133*:405–410, 1979.
85. Hamrick, H. J., and Moore, G. W.: Giardiasis causing urticaria in a child. Am. J. Dis. Child. *137*:761–763, 1983.
86. Hannuksela, M., and Ahvonen, P.: Skin manifestations in human yersiniosis. Ann. Clin. Res. *7*:368–373, 1975.
87. Harrison, D. L.: A case of human ornithosis presenting as an obscure febrile illness associated with macular rash. Practitioner *190*:245–246, 1963.
88. Herrmann, E. C., Jr., and Hable, K. A.: Experiences in laboratory diagnosis of parainfluenza viruses in routine medical practice. Mayo Clin. Proc. *45*:177–188, 1970.
89. Hilleman, M. R., Hamparian, V. V., Ketler, A., et al.: Acute respiratory illnesses among children and adults: Field study of contemporary importance of several viruses and appraisal of the literature. J. A. M. A. *180*:445–453, 1962.
90. Hoagland, R. J.: The clinical manifestations of infectious mononucleosis: A report of two hundred cases. Am. J. Med. Sci. *240*:55–62, 1960.
91. Honig, P. J.: Bites and parasites. Pediatr. Clin. North Am. *30*:563–581, 1983.
92. Hoofnagle, J. H.: Hepatitis C: the clinical spectrum of disease. Hepatology. *26*(Suppl.):15–20, 1997.
93. Hope-Simpson, R. E., and Higgins, P. G.: A respiratory virus study in Great Britain: Review and evaluation. Prog. Med. Virol. *11*:354–407, 1969.
94. Horton, J. M., and Blaser, M. J.: The spectrum of relapsing fever in the Rocky Mountains. Arch. Intern. Med. *145*:871–875, 1985.
95. Humphrey, T., Sanders, S., and Stadius, M.: Leptospirosis mimicking MLNS. J. Pediatr. *91*:853–854, 1977.
96. Jacobs, R. F., Hsi, S., Wilson, C. B., et al.: Apparent meningococcemia: Clinical features of disease due to *Haemophilus influenzae* and *Neisseria meningitidis.* Pediatrics *72*:469–472, 1983.
97. Jaffe, H. W., and Pellett, P. E.: Human herpesvirus 8 and Kaposi's sarcoma—some answers, more questions. N. Engl. J. Med. *340*: 1912–1913, 1999.
98. Johnson, R. A.: Atypical mycobacteria. *In* Fitzpatrick, T. B., Eisen, A. Z., Wolff, K., et al. (eds.): Dermatology in General Medicine. New York, McGraw-Hill, 1979, pp. 1505–1508.
99. Joncas, J., Chiasson, J. P., Turcotte, J., et al.: Studies on infectious mononucleosis. III. Clinical data, serologic and epidemiologic findings. Can. Med. Assoc. J. *98*:848–854, 1968.
100. Kalis, P., LeFrock, J. L., Smith, W., et al.: Listeriosis. Am. J. Med. Sci. *271*:159–169, 1976.
101. Kanazawa, K., Yaoita, H., Tsuda, F., et al.: Hepatitis C virus infection in patients with urticaria. J. Am. Acad. Dermatol. *35*:195–198, 1996.
102. Kazmierowski, J. A., Peizner, D. S., and Wuepper, K. D.: Herpes simplex antigen in immune complexes of patients with erythema multiforme: Presence following recurrent herpes simplex infection. J. A. M. A. *247*:2547–2550, 1982.
103. Kennedy, A. C., Fleming, J., and Solomon, L.: Chikungunya viral arthropathy: A clinical description. J. Rheumatol. *7*:231–236, 1980.
104. Kennett, M. L., Birch, C. J., Lewis, F. A., et al.: Enterovirus type 71 infection in Melbourne. Bull. World Health Organ. *51*:609–615, 1974.
105. Kiernan, J. P., Schanzlin, D. J., and Leveille, A. S.: Stevens-Johnson syndrome associated with adenovirus conjunctivitis. Am. J. Ophthalmol. *92*:543–545, 1981.
106. Konno, M., Kikuta, H., Ishikawa, N., et al.: A possible association between hepatitis B antigen–negative infantile papular acrodermatitis and Epstein-Barr virus infection. J. Pediatr. *101*:222–224, 1982.
107. Krause, V. W., Embree, J. E., MacDonald, S. W., et al.: Congenital listeriosis causing early neonatal death. Can. Med. Assoc. J. *127*:36–38, 1982.
108. Krober, M. S., Bass, J. W., and Barcia, P. J.: Scarlatiniform rash and pleural effusion in a patient with *Yersinia pseudotuberculosis* infection. J. Pediatr. *102*:879–881, 1983.
109. Kusenbach, G., Rubben, A., Schneider, E. M., et al.: Herpes virus (KSHV) associated Kaposi sarcoma in a 3-year-old child with non–HIV-induced immunodeficiency. Eur. J. Pediatr. *156*:440–443, 1997.
110. Lackman, D. B.: A review of information on rickettsialpox in the United States. Clin. Pediatr. (Phila.) *2*:296–301, 1963.
111. La Grenade, L., Hanchard, B., Feltcher, V., et al.: Infective dermatitis of Jamaican children: A marker for HTLV-I infection. Lancet. *336*: 1345–1347, 1990.
112. La Grenade, L., Hanchard, B., Feltcher, V., et al.: Clinical, pathologic, and immunologic features of human T-lymphotropic virus type I–associated infective dermatitis in children. Arch. Dermatol. *134*: 439–444, 1998.
113. Lambie, J. A., and Gustafson, A. A.: Contagious ecthyma in man: Report of two cases with laboratory studies. Lancet *87*:400–402, 1967.
114. Le, C. T.: Tick-borne relapsing fever in children. Pediatrics *66*:963–966, 1980.
115. Leavell, U. W., Jr., McNamara, M. J., Meulling, R. J., et al.: Ecthyma contagiosum (orf). South. Med. J. *58*:239–243, 1965.
116. Lerner, A. M., Cherry, J. D., Klein, J. O., et al.: Infections with reoviruses. N. Engl. J. Med. *267*:947–952, 1962.
117. Linnemann, C. C., Jr., and Janson, P. J.: The clinical presentations of Rocky Mountain spotted fever: Comments on recognition and management based on a study of 63 patients. Clin. Pediatr. (Phila.) *17*:673–679, 1978.
118. Litt, I. F., Edberg, S. C., and Finberg, L.: Gonorrhea in children and adolescents: A current review. J. Pediatr. *85*:595–607, 1974.
119. Liu, C., and Coffin, D. L.: Studies on canine distemper infection by means of fluorescein-labeled antibody. I. The pathogenesis, pathology, and diagnosis of the disease in experimentally infected ferrets. Virology *3*:115–131, 1957.
120. Maki, M., Vesikari, T., Rantala, I., et al.: *Yersinia* in children. Arch. Dis. Child. *55*:861–865, 1980.

121. Maloney, E. M., Hisada, M., Palmer, P., et al.: Human T-cell lymphotropic virus type-I associated infective dermatitis in Jamaica: A case report of clinical and biologic correlates. Pediatr. Infect. Dis. J. *19*:560–565, 2000.
122. Martinez-Roig, A., Llorens-Terol, J., and Torres, J. M.: Erythema nodosum and kerion of the scalp. Am. J. Dis. Child. *136*:440–442, 1982.
123. Mast, W. E., and Burrows, W. M.: Erythema chronicum migrans in the United States. J. A. M. A. *236*:859–860, 1976.
124. McDade, J. E.: Ehrlichiosis: A disease of animals and humans. J. Infect. Dis. *161*:609–617, 1990.
125. McNeill, W. H.: Plagues and Peoples. Garden City, New York, Anchor Press–Doubleday, 1976, pp. 105, 119.
126. Medeiros, A. A., Marty, S. D., Tosh, F. E., et al.: Erythema nodosum and erythema multiforme as clinical manifestations of histoplasmosis in a community outbreak. N. Engl. J. Med. *274*:415–420, 1966.
127. Melish, M. E., and Glasgow, L. A.: Staphylococcal scalded skin syndrome: The expanded clinical syndrome. J. Pediatr. *78*:958–967, 1971.
128. Milder, J. E., Walzer, P. D., Kilgore, G., et al.: Clinical features of *Strongyloides stercoralis* infection in an endemic area of the United States. Gastroenterology *80*:1481–1488, 1981.
129. Mims, C. A.: Pathogenesis of rashes in virus diseases. Bacteriol. Rev. *30*:739–760, 1966.
130. Moore, P. S.: The emergence of Kaposi's sarcoma–associated herpesvirus (human herpesvirus 8). N. Engl. J. Med. *343*:1411–1413, 2000.
131. Moraga, F. A., Martinez-Roig, A., Alonso, J. L., et al.: Boutonneuse fever. Arch. Dis. Child. *57*:149–151, 1982.
132. Myskowski, P., and Ahkami, R.: Dermatologic complications of HIV infection. Med. Clin. North Am. *80*:P1415–P1435, 1996.
133. Nash, D., Mostashari, F., Fine, A., et al.: The outbreak of West Nile virus infection in the New York City area in 1999. N. Engl. J. Med. *344*:1807–1814, 2001.
134. Needlestick transmission of HTLV-III from a patient infected in Africa. Lancet *2*:1376–1377, 1984.
135. Neisson-Vernant, C., Arfi, S., Mathez, D., et al.: Needlestick HIV seroconversion in a nurse. Lancet *2*:814, 1986.
136. Niklasson, B., Espmark, A., LeDuc, J. W., et al.: Association of a Sindbis-like virus with Ockelbo disease in Sweden. Am. J. Trop. Med. Hyg. *33*:1212–1217, 1984.
137. Nussbaum, M., Scalettar, H., and Shenker, I. R.: Gonococcal arthritis-dermatitis (GADS) as a complication of gonococcemia in adolescents. Clin. Pediatr. (Phila.) *14*:1037–1040, 1975.
138. Older, J. J.: The epidemiology of murine typhus in Texas, 1969. J. A. M. A. *214*:2011–2017, 1970.
139. Orton, P. W., Huff, J. C., Tonnesen, M. G., et al.: Detection of a herpes simplex viral antigen in skin lesions of erythema multiforme. Ann. Intern. Med. *101*:48–50, 1984.
140. Patamasucon, P., Schaad, U. B., and Nelson, J. D.: Melioidosis. J. Pediatr. *100*:175–182, 1982.
141. Patel, B. M.: Skin rash with infectious mononucleosis and ampicillin. Pediatrics *40*:910–911, 1967.
142. Paterson, P. Y., and Taylor, W.: Rickettsialpox. Bull. N. Y. Acad. Med. *42*:579–587, 1966.
143. Perlman, F.: Arthropod sensitivity. *In* Criep, L. H. (ed.): Dermatologic Allergy. Philadelphia, W. B. Saunders, 1967, pp. 222–244.
144. Peter, G.: Leptospirosis: A zoonosis of protean manifestations. Pediatr. Infect. Dis. *1*:282–288, 1982.
145. Pether, J. V. S., and Lloyd, G.: The clinical spectrum of human hantavirus infection in Somerset, UK. Epidemiol. *111*:171–175, 1993.
146. Pfister, L. E., Gallagher, M. V., Potterfield, T. G., et al.: *Neisseria catarrhalis:* Bacteremia with meningitis. J. A. M. A. *193*:399–401, 1965.
147. Pittsley, R. A., Shearn, M. A., and Kaufman, L.: Acute hepatitis B simulating dermatomyositis. J. A. M. A. *239*:959, 1978.
148. Place, E. H., and Sutton, L. E.: Erythema arthriticum epidemicum (Haverhill fever). Arch. Intern. Med. *54*:659–684, 1934.
149. Platt, H.: The susceptibility of the skin and epidermoid mucous membranes to virus infection in man and other animals. J. Pathol. Bacteriol. *76*:479–497, 1948.
150. Pollowitz, J. A.: Acute urticaria associated with shigellosis: A case report. Ann. Allergy *45*:302–303, 1980.
151. Portnoy, B. L., Satterwhite, T. K., and Dyckman, J. D.: Rat bite fever misdiagnosed as Rocky Mountain spotted fever. J. South. Med. Assoc. *72*:607–609, 1979.
152. Powell, K. R.: Filatow-Dukes' disease: Epidermolytic toxin-producing staphylococci as the etiologic agent of the fourth childhood exanthem. Am. J. Dis. Child. *133*:88–90, 1979.
153. Pullen, H., Wright, N., and Murdoch, J. M.: Hypersensitivity reactions to antibacterial drugs in infectious mononucleosis. Lancet *2*:1176–1178, 1967.
154. Raoult, D., Fournier, P. E., Fenollar, F., et al.: *Rickettsia africae,* a tick-borne pathogen in travelers to sub-Saharan Africa. N. Engl. J. Med. *344*:1504–1510, 2001.
155. Rasmussen, J. E., and Graves, W. H.: *Pseudomonas aeruginosa,* hot tubs, and skin infections. Am. J. Dis. Child. *136*:553–554, 1982.
156. Resnick, S. D.: Toxic shock syndrome: Recent developments in pathogenesis. J. Pediatr. *116*:321–328, 1990.
157. Richter, H. S.: Coccidioidomycosis: A report of 300 new cases. G. P. *39*:89–92, 1969.
158. Robbins, F. C.: Measles: Clinical features. Am. J. Dis. Child. *103*: 266–273, 1962.
159. Rook, A.: Papular urticaria. Pediatr. Clin. North Am. *8*:817–833, 1961.
160. Rustgi, V. K., Sacher, R. A., O'Brien, P., et al.: Fatal disseminated cytomegalovirus infection in an apparently normal adult. Arch. Intern. Med. *143*:372–373, 1983.
161. Ruzicka, T., Rosendahl, C., and Braun-Falco, O.: A probable case of rotavirus exanthem. Arch. Dermatol. *121*:253–254, 1985.
162. Saari, T. N., and Triplett, D. A.: *Yersinia pseudotuberculosis* mesenteric adenitis. J. Pediatr. *85*:656–659, 1974.
163. Sabin, A. B.: Research on dengue during World War II. Am. J. Trop. Med. *1*:30–50, 1952.
164. Sanchez, R. L., Hebert, A., Lucia, H., et al.: Orf: A case report with histologic, electron microscopic, and immunoperoxidase studies. Arch. Pathol. Lab. Med. *109*:166–170, 1985.
165. San Joaquin, V. H., and Marks, M. I.: Gianotti disease or Gianotti-Crosti syndrome? J. Pediatr. *101*:216–217, 1982.
166. Saslaw, S.: Chronic meningococcemia: Report of a case. N. Engl. J. Med. *266*:605–607, 1962.
167. Schaffner, W.: The rickettsioses. *In* Fitzpatrick, T. B., Eisen, A. Z., Wolff, K., et al. (eds.): Dermatology in General Medicine. New York, McGraw-Hill, 1979, pp. 1563–1570.
168. Schmaljohn, C., and Hjelle, B.: Hantaviruses: A global disease problem. Emerg. Infect. Dis. *3*:95–104, 1997.
169. Schneider, J. A., Poley, J. R., Millunchick, E. W., et al.: Papular acrodermatitis (Gianotti-Crosti syndrome) in a child with anicteric hepatitis B, virus subtype adw. J. Pediatr. *101*:219–222, 1982.
170. Shama, S. K., Etkind, P. H., Odell, T. M., et al.: Gypsy-moth-caterpillar dermatitis. N. Engl. J. Med. *306*:1300–1301, 1982.
171. Shanson, D. C., Gazzard, B. G., Midgley, J., et al.: *Streptobacillus moniliformis* isolated from blood in four cases of Haverhill fever: First outbreak in Britain. Lancet *2*:92–94, 1983.
172. Shapiro, L.: The numbered diseases: First through sixth. J. A. M. A. *194*:210, 1965.
173. Shapiro, L.: On the numbered exanthemata. Clin. Pediatr. (Phila.) *6*:611–612, 1967.
174. Shaw, E. B.: Fifth disease. Am. J. Dis. Child. *131*:816, 1977.
175. Shelley, E. D., Shelley, W. B., Pula, J. F., et al.: The diagnostic challenge of nonburrowing mite bites: *Cheyletiella yasguri.* J. A. M. A. *251*:2690–2691, 1984.
176. Siewers, C. M. F., and Cramblett, H. G.: Cryptococcosis (torulosis) in children: A report of four cases. Pediatrics *34*:393–400, 1964.
177. Smith, A. W., Berry, E. S., Skilling, D. E., et al.: In vitro isolation and characterization of a calicivirus causing a vesicular disease of the hands and feet. Clin. Infect. Dis. *26*:434–439, 1998.
178. Smith, P. T., Landry, M. L., Carey, H., et al.: Papular-purpuric gloves and socks syndrome associated with acute parvovirus B19 infection: Case report and review. Clin. Infect. Dis. *27*:164–168, 1998.
179. Somer, T., and Finegold, S. M.: Vasculitides associated with infections, immunization, and antimicrobial drugs. Clin. Infect. Dis. *20*:1010–1036, 1995.
180. Spelman, D. W.: Q fever: A study of 111 consecutive cases. Med. J. Aust. *1*:547–553, 1982.
181. Steere, A. C., Broderick, T. F., and Malawista, S. E.: Erythema chronicum migrans and Lyme arthritis: Epidemiologic evidence for a tick vector. Am. J. Epidemiol. *108*:312–321, 1978.
182. Stricof, R. L., and Morse, D. L.: HTLV-III/LAV seroconversion following a deep intramuscular needlestick injury. N. Engl. J. Med. *314*:1115, 1986.
183. Strong, W. B.: Petechiae and streptococcal pharyngitis. Am. J. Dis. Child. *117*:156–160, 1969.
184. Swartz, M. N., and Weinberg, A. N.: Infections due to gram-positive bacteria. *In* Fitzpatrick, T. B., Eisen, A. Z., Wolff, K., et al. (eds.): Dermatology in General Medicine. New York, McGraw-Hill, 1979, pp. 1426–1445.
185. Swartz, M. N., and Weinberg, A. N.: Miscellaneous bacterial infections with cutaneous manifestations. *In* Fitzpatrick, T. B., Eisen, A. Z., Wolff, K., et al. (eds.): Dermatology in General Medicine. New York, McGraw-Hill, 1979, pp. 1459–1473.
186. Taieb, A., Plantin, P., DuPasquier, P., et al.: Gianotti-Crosti syndrome: A study of 26 cases. Br. J. Dermatol. *115*:49–59, 1986.
187. Taylor, P. R., Weinstein, W. M., and Bryner, J. H.: *Campylobacter fetus* infection in human subjects: Association with raw milk. Am. J. Med. *66*:779–783, 1979.
188. Tertti, R., Granfors, K., Lehtonen, O. P., et al.: An outbreak of *Yersinia pseudotuberculosis* infection. J. Infect. Dis. *149*:245–250, 1984.
189. Thomas, P., Moore, M., Bell, E., et al.: *Pseudomonas* dermatitis associated with a swimming pool. J. A. M. A. *253*:1156–1159, 1985.
190. Timar, L., Budai, J., Gero, A., et al.: Rare complications and unusual syndromes associated with Epstein-Barr virus. Pediatr. Infect. Dis. *4*:212–213, 1985.

191. Timar, L., Budai, J., and Koller, M.: A prospective study on infectious mononucleosis in childhood: Symptoms, serology, Epstein-Barr virus specific leukocyte migration inhibition. Infection *10*:139–143, 1982.
192. Toth, M., Barna, M., and Voltay, B.: Aetiology of acute respiratory diseases in infants and children. Acta Paediatr. Hung. *6*:367–374, 1966.
193. Tudor, R. B.: Urticaria in childhood. Lancet *82*:273–274, 1962.
194. Turner, T. W., and Wilkinson, D. S.: *Pasteurella pseudotuberculosis* as a cause of erythema nodosum. Br. J. Dermatol. *81*:823–826, 1969.
195. Unger, A., Tapia, L., Minnich, L. L., et al.: Atypical neonatal respiratory syncytial virus infection. J. Pediatr. *100*:762–764, 1982.
196. Utz, J. P., and Shadomy, H. J.: Deep fungus infections. *In* Fitzpatrick, T. B., Eisen, A. Z., Wolff, K., et al. (eds.): Dermatology in General Medicine. New York, McGraw-Hill, 1979, pp. 1533–1563.
197. Van Arsdall, J. A., Wunderlich, H. F., Melo, J. C., et al.: The protean manifestations of legionnaires disease. J. Infect. Dis. *7*:51–62, 1983.
198. Ware, R.: Human parvovirus infection. J. Pediatr. *114*:343–348, 1989.
199. Weinberg, A. N., and Swartz, M. N.: Gram-negative coccal and bacillary infections. *In* Fitzpatrick, T. B., Eisen, A. Z., Wolff, K., et al. (eds.): Dermatology in General Medicine. New York, McGraw-Hill, 1979, pp. 1445–1459.
200. Weller, T. H.: The cytomegaloviruses: Ubiquitous agents with protean clinical manifestations. I and II. N. Engl. J. Med. *285*:203–214, 267–274, 1971.
201. Wenner, H. A.: Virus diseases associated with cutaneous eruptions. Prog. Med. Virol. *16*:269–336, 1973.
202. Wenner, H. A., and Lou, T. Y.: Virus diseases associated with cutaneous eruptions. Prog. Med. Virol. *5*:219–294, 1963.
203. Whiteford, S. F., Taylor, J. P., and Dumler, J. S.: Clinical, laboratory, and epidemiology features of murine typhus in 97 Texas children. Arch. Pediatr. Adolesc. Med. *155*:396–400, 2001.
204. Wiesenthal, A. M., and Todd, J. K.: Toxic shock syndrome in children aged 10 years or less. Pediatrics *74*:112–117, 1984.
205. Winn, W. A., Levine, H. B., Broderick, J. E., et al.: A localized epidemic of coccidioidal infection: Primary coccidioidomycosis occurring in a group of ten children infected in a backyard playground in the San Joaquin Valley of California. N. Engl. J. Med. *268*:867–870, 1963.
206. Wolff, K.: Mycobacterial diseases: Tuberculosis. *In* Fitzpatrick, T. B., Eisen, A. Z., Wolff, K., et al. (eds.): Dermatology in General Medicine. New York, McGraw-Hill, 1979, pp. 1473–1492.
207. Wong, M. L., Kaplan, S., Dunkle, L. M., et al.: Leptospirosis: A childhood disease. J. Pediatr. *90*:532–537, 1977.
208. Woodward, T. E.: Rocky mountain spotted fever: Epidemiological and early clinical signs are keys to treatment and reduced mortality. J. Infect. Dis. *150*:465–468, 1984.
209. Yamamoto, T., and Yokoyama, A.: Hepatitis C virus infection and nodular prurigo. Br. J. Dermatol. *135*:489–504, 1996.
210. Yamanishi, K., Shiraki, K., Kondo T., et al.: Identification of human herpesvirus-6 as a causal agent for exanthem subitum. Lancet *1*:1065–1067, 1988.
211. Young, E. J.: Human brucellosis. Rev. Infect. Dis. *5*:821–842, 1983.

CHAPTER 66 Roseola Infantum (Exanthem Subitum)

JAMES D. CHERRY

Roseola infantum (i.e., exanthem subitum, pseudorubella, exanthem criticum, sixth disease, or 3-day fever) is a common, acute illness of young children characterized by a fever of 3 to 5 days' duration, rapid defervescence, and then the appearance of an erythematous macular or maculopapular rash that persists for 1 to 2 days.

History

Zahorsky[74] generally is given credit for the original description of roseola infantum. However, in his writings, he pointed out that the syndrome was described in earlier pediatric and dermatology texts.[75–77] Altschuler[1] observed that a British dermatologist, Robet Willan, presented a description of the illness in his 1809 book *On Cutaneous Diseases*. The descriptions in the older literature did not separate the syndrome from the known exanthematous diseases (i.e., measles, rubella, and scarlet fever), an omission that Zahorsky corrected.

In 1921, Veeder and Hempelmann[70] described the syndrome further and noted that leukopenia and relative lymphocytosis occurred. These investigators objected to the name *roseola infantum*, which in the past had been used to describe a large group of diseases of indefinite causes. They suggested the term *exanthem subitum* because it was "descriptive of the most striking clinical symptom, namely, the sudden, unexpected appearance of the eruption on the fourth day." Currently, the term roseola is used most commonly to describe the syndrome.

From 1920 through 1940, many excellent clinical descriptions of the syndrome were published.* From 1940 through 1988, papers relating to roseola were concerned with unusual manifestations and complications[8, 11–13, 22, 31, 45–47, 51, 54, 60] and attempts to recover an etiologic agent.[26, 29, 39, 44, 61] In 1988, Yamanishi and associates[72] identified human herpesvirus–6 in the blood of infants with roseola, and since then, this virus and disease association has been confirmed on many occasions.† Human herpesvirus–7 has been found to be the cause of many cases of roseola.[3, 14, 30, 64, 66, 67, 69]

Epidemiology

In his original paper, Zahorsky[74] reported that roseola occurred most commonly in the fall. In his second paper, a year-round incidence was observed[75]; in 1925, he pointed out that most cases occurred in the spring, summer, and fall.[76] Breese[10] noted that the greatest number of cases occurred in the summer and early fall. In contrast, 55 percent of Clemens' cases occurred in February, March, and April; 16 percent were seen in October.[17] In a review of 243 cases during a 10-year period, Juretic[37] observed that the peak month was May. Juretic also reviewed the seasonal incidence

*See references 6, 7, 10, 17, 18, 20, 24, 25, 35, 77, 78.
†See references 2–5, 9, 19, 21, 27, 28, 32–34, 38, 40–43, 52, 55, 57, 62–65.

in 10 other studies and found only minor variations by month. Prevalence was greatest in March, April, and October and least in December. One epidemic of roseola in a maternity hospital occurred in the summer,[35] another epidemic in an infants' home occurred in the fall,[6] and a hospital outbreak occurred in the winter.[18]

Roseola predominantly is an illness of young children. It is a rare occurrence in infants younger than 3 months of age or children older than 4 years of age. In a review of 1462 cases, the peak age range prevalence was from 7 to 13 months of age; 55 percent of the cases occurred within the first year of life and 90 percent within the first 2 years of life.[37] Occasionally, cases have been seen in older children, adolescents, and young adults, as well as in neonates and other infants younger than 6 months of age.[25, 35]

Although Faber and Dickey[20] found twice as many girls as boys with the syndrome, the sex ratio in most large studies has been equal.[7, 10, 17, 25, 44] Although three epidemics have been reported and cases frequently occur in groups by season, most cases occur sporadically without known exposure. The syndrome, when seen sporadically, generally is considered to be noncontagious, but secondary cases have been reported occasionally.[6, 10, 18, 35] The incubation period range in epidemics is 5 to 15 days.[6, 10, 18]

Surprisingly, the attack rate of roseola has not been well studied. Berenberg and associates[7] state that roseola is the exanthem most commonly encountered in children younger than 2 years of age. Breese[10] found that 16 percent of a group of infants that he followed for the first 12 months of life had definite roseola. He estimated that 30 percent of children would have clinical roseola. Juretic[37] looked at the frequency of roseola in 6735 children; the yearly attack rate during a 10-year period varied from 1 to 10 percent, with a mean of 3.3 percent.

Etiology

In 1941, Breese[8] reported rather vigorous attempts to isolate a filterable virus from three children with pre-eruptive roseola. These studies included extensive animal inoculations, but no viral agents were uncovered. In 1950, Kempe and associates[39] reported the passage of the illness to a 6-month-old susceptible infant by the intravenous injection of serum from an 18-month-old child with pre-eruptive roseola. Febrile illnesses without exanthem also were produced in monkeys with serum and throat washings from a child with the syndrome. In similar experiments, Hellström and Vahlquist[29] produced the syndrome in three children 6 to 9 days after the intramuscular administration of blood from typical roseola cases.

In electron microscopic studies, Reagan and associates[58] observed uniform virus-like particles (100 to 110 nm) in the blood of an 18-month-old child with the syndrome. Febrile illness was produced in two monkeys after inoculation of the concentrated virus-containing material.

Since the advent of modern diagnostic virology in the early 1950s, numerous viral agents have been recovered from children with roseola. In 1951, Neva and associates[50] studied an epidemic exanthematous illness (i.e., Boston exanthem) caused by echovirus 16, in which many of the illnesses were characteristic of roseola. In 1954, Neva[48] observed additional cases of roseola-like illness associated with echovirus 16 infection. In 1974, Hall and colleagues[27] reported four additional echovirus 16 infections with clinical manifestations of roseola. The reporting of roseola in Rochester, New York, nearly doubled during the time of echovirus 16 activity in the area. Roseola-like illnesses that also have been associated with these enteroviruses are caused by coxsackievirus A6, A9, B1, B2, B4, and B5 and echovirus 9, 11, 25, 27, and 30.[15, 16, 27, 62, 71] Outbreaks of roseola that occur in the summer and fall probably are caused by enteroviral infections.

In addition to enteroviruses, adenovirus types 1, 2, 3, and 14 and parainfluenza type 1 virus have been recovered from children with roseola.[23, 36, 49, 71] Saitoh and associates[61] detected rotavirus capsomeres in fecal specimens of nine children with roseola. In contrast with these findings, Gurwith and colleagues[26] studied fecal specimens from five children with roseola, and in none were viral particles identified. One of 13 children in this study did develop antibody to rotavirus around the time of illness, however.

In addition to the occurrence of roseola associated with a large number of natural viral infections, its pattern (i.e., fever and then rash with defervescence) was observed frequently in recipients of Edmonton B measles vaccine.[15]

In 1988, Yamanishi and associates[72] isolated human herpesvirus–6 from four infants with roseola, and all four had significant titer rises for this virus. Shortly after this finding was reported, several other investigators noted similar findings.[2, 4, 19, 32, 41, 65, 68] The implication from these studies, as suggested by the various investigators, is that human herpesvirus–6 is the cause of roseola. This viewpoint obviously overlooks or ignores the past experience in which other viral agents have been associated with the clinical syndrome. Subsequent studies indicate that human herpesvirus–6 is a major cause of roseola and the cause of acute febrile illness without exanthem in infants.* Since 1993, human herpesvirus–7 has been accepted as an additional causative agent in roseola.[3, 14, 30, 64, 66]

In a study of 1653 infants and young children with acute febrile illnesses, Hall and colleagues[27] found that 160 (9.7%) had primary human herpesvirus–6 infections; 27 (17%) of the children who were infected with human herpesvirus–6 had roseola. In a study of clinical roseola, Okada and associates[52] found that 81 percent had serologic evidence of human herpesvirus–6 infection and that 8 percent had an echovirus-18 infection. In a study of roseola in Italy, Braito and Uberti[9] found serologic evidence of human herpesvirus–6 infection in only 30 percent of the cases. In 33 percent of the remaining cases, they attributed the illnesses to another infectious agent. In 1994, Hidaka and associates[30] estimated that 73.5 percent, 10.2 percent, and 16.3 percent of their roseola cases were caused by human herpesvirus–6, human herpesvirus–7, and other viruses, respectively. Human herpesvirus–6 appears to be the major cause of roseola.

Pathophysiology

The pathophysiologic process of roseola is unknown. Watson[71] has suggested that roseola is not an infection caused by one particular pathogen but is the result of an immunizing reaction against many different viruses. He also suggests that the rash is caused by the neutralization of virus in the skin at the end of the period of viremia.

Because viremia is a common occurrence in human herpesvirus–6, human herpesvirus–7, enteroviral, and adenoviral infections, a reasonable conclusion is that the rash in roseola is related to an immunologic event resulting from the virus that is localized in the skin. Why the pattern of fever and then rash with defervescence is so clearly age

*See references 5, 9, 27, 33, 40, 43, 52, 55, 57, 63.

dependent is unknown. Most of the viruses that in the past have been associated with roseola cause other exanthematous manifestations in older patients.[15]

Clinical Presentation

The basic clinical pattern of roseola is a febrile period of 3 to 5 days, defervescence, and the appearance of a rash that persists for 1 to 2 days. Because the syndrome is caused by many different viruses, the illness apparently may be associated with a large number of other symptoms and signs. The major manifestations have been reviewed on several occasions.[7, 10, 17, 25, 37, 75]

Illness usually occurs with the apparent abrupt onset of fever. Slight irritability and malaise occur frequently, but more commonly, the child's temperature is taken because a parent notices that the child feels warm. The temperature commonly is in the range of 38.9° C to 40.6° C (102° F to 105° F). Despite the high fever, the child usually is active, alert, and generally unphased. The fever is constant or intermittent, with its greatest degree in the early evening. Restlessness and irritability occur with higher temperatures. The usual duration of fever is 3 to 5 days, but it has persisted for 9 days. The temperature most often returns to normal by crisis, but in some cases, temperature "lysis" occurs over 24 to 36 hours.

Mild cough and coryza are seen frequently in cases occurring in the winter and spring, and headache and abdominal pain are reported in older children, mainly in the summer and fall. Vomiting and diarrhea are infrequent occurrences.

On initial physical examination during the febrile period, most children appear to be happy, alert, and playful. However, with high temperatures, some children are irritable; occasionally, a child appears to be sick, which suggests more serious illness, such as meningitis or septicemia. Examination within the oral cavity frequently reveals one or more abnormalities. Mild inflammation of the pharynx and tonsils occurs most commonly. Occasionally, small exudative follicular lesions are noted on the tonsils. In other cases, small ulcerative lesions on the soft palate, uvula, and tonsillar pillars are observed. Usually, the lesions on the soft palate consist of only erythematous macules and maculopapules, presumably because of lymphoid hyperplasia.

Mild injection of the tympanic membranes occurs commonly. Enlargement of the suboccipital, posterior cervical, and postauricular lymph nodes is a common occurrence, but the degree is not particularly remarkable.

Berliner[8] noticed that children with roseola had palpebral edema. He suggested that the "heavy eyelids" or "droopy" or "sleepy" appearance resulting from this edema was diagnostic of the syndrome before the appearance of the rash. Bulging of the anterior fontanelle also has been observed in roseola.[54]

Appearance of the rash in roseola usually coincides with the subsidence of fever, but it may occur after an afebrile interlude of several hours to 2 days. When defervescence occurs by lysis, onset of the exanthem can occur before the temperature has returned entirely to a normal level. However, by definition, to call an illness roseola if the fever and rash are truly concomitant is incorrect.

Zahorsky[74, 75] originally described the rash as morbilliform, but his use of *morbilliform* was not the same as ours is today (i.e., measles-like, erythematous, maculopapular with confluence). The rash is erythematous and macular or maculopapular, and the lesions are discrete. The lesions are 2 to 5 mm in diameter, and they blanch on pressure. Frequently, individual lesions are surrounded by a whitish ring. The rash is most prominent on the neck and trunk, but the proximal extremities and the face also may be affected. Although they have been reported,[17, 24] pruritus and desquamation usually do not occur. The rash usually persists for 24 to 48 hours. In occasional cases, well-documented rashes have been observed to appear and resolve within 2 to 4 hours. Yoshida and associates[73] described a 7-month-old boy with human herpesvirus–6 infection and typical roseola initially. However, on the ninth day of illness, vesicular lesions appeared on the face and limbs. These lesions persisted for 12 days.

Except for the white blood cell count, routine laboratory studies are of little use in roseola. The total white blood cell count usually is low. However, early in the febrile period, high counts occasionally are found. The total count drops to its lowest level at the third to the sixth day of illness and then gradually returns to normal over the ensuing 7 to 10 days. During the same time frame, the percentage of lymphocytes increases from a normal value of about 50 percent to 60 to 80 percent on days 3 to 10 and then returns to normal over the course of the next 7 days. Frequently, extreme counts in the range of 3000 cells/mm^3 with 90 percent lymphocytes are found, which raises the consideration of a granulocytic defect.

Clinical Complications

The most important complications of roseola are convulsions and other neurologic symptoms.* The incidence of convulsions has varied widely among reports. Juretic[37] found not one instance of convulsions in the 243 cases in his study. Breese[10] did not report convulsions in any of 100 roseola attacks that he studied. In contrast, Greenthal[25] noted convulsions in 6 percent of his cases, and Faber and Dickey[20] found seizures in 8 of 26 cases of roseola. Möller[46] observed that 8 percent of children admitted to the hospital because of febrile convulsions eventually were diagnosed with roseola infantum.[46]

Möller[46] also reported cerebrospinal fluid evaluations in 29 cases of roseola and febrile convulsions. In six instances, the pressure was elevated; in two, there were 5 white blood cells/mm^3; and in another instance, there were 9 white blood cells/mm^3. In most other cerebrospinal fluid examinations, the findings have been within normal limits, but mild pleocytosis with mononuclear cells has been identified occasionally.[7, 31] A surprising number of cases of encephalitis associated with roseola have been reported,[13, 22, 31, 34] and residua have been common occurrences. Hemiplegia has occurred after illness,[13, 22, 56, 59] and permanent paresis and mental retardation have occurred in some affected patients.

Thrombocytopenic purpura has been seen in five children with roseola; all of these patients recovered.[51] Okafugi and colleagues[53] described an 8-month-old boy with roseola caused by human herpesvirus–6 infection who had the syndrome of inappropriate secretion of antidiuretic hormone (SIADA).

Diagnosis

Although detecting leukopenia with relative lymphocytosis is fortuitous, the only necessity in establishing the diagnosis of a roseola is to document the fever, defervescence, and exanthem pattern. All too frequently, however, the first exanthematous illness that a child has is called roseola, regardless of whether the exanthem and the fever are concomitant or the child has no febrile period at all.

*See references 4, 7, 11–13, 20, 22, 25, 31, 34, 42, 46, 56, 59, 60.

The only problem in the differential diagnosis occurs when a febrile child is receiving antibiotics and a rash follows defervescence. This event occurs fairly frequently, and, unfortunately, the child usually is labeled allergic to the antibiotic rather than suspected of having roseola. In most instances of drug allergy, the exanthem lasts longer than roseola does, and in allergic cases, pruritus and fever may accompany the rash.

Treatment and Prognosis

No specific treatment for roseola exists. When fever is a problem, it may be treated with acetaminophen. Acetaminophen can alter the temperature curve, possibly obscuring the correct diagnosis. Febrile seizures and other neurologic complications should be treated vigorously.

In most cases, the outlook is excellent. When encephalitis occurs, the prognosis must be guarded. Because roseola is the result of infection with multiple different viruses, no practical way to prevent it exists.

REFERENCES

1. Altschuler, E. L.: Oldest description of roseola and implications for the antiquity of human herpesvirus 6. Pediatr. Infect. Dis. *19*:903, 2000.
2. Asano, Y., Yoshikawa, T., Suga, S., et al.: Viremia and neutralizing antibody response in infants with exanthem subitum. J. Pediatr. *114*:535–539, 1989.
3. Asano, Y., Suga, S., Yoshikawa, T., et al.: Clinical features and viral excretion in an infant with primary human herpesvirus 7 infection. Pediatrics. *95*:187–190, 1995.
4. Asano, Y., Nakashima, T., Yoshikawa, T., et al.: Severity of human herpesvirus-6 viremia and clinical findings in infants with exanthem subitum. J. Pediatr. *118*:891–895, 1991.
5. Asano, Y., Yoshikawa, T., Suga, S., et al.: Clinical features of infants with primary human herpesvirus 6 infection (exanthem subitum, roseola infantum). Pediatrics. *93*:104–108, 1994.
6. Barenberg, L. H., and Greenspan, L.: Exanthema subitum (roseola infantum). Am. J. Dis. Child. *58*:983–993, 1939.
7. Berenberg, W., Wright, S., and Janeway, C. A.: Roseola infantum (exanthem subitum). N. Engl. J. Med. *241*:253–259, 1949.
8. Berliner, B. C.: A physical sign useful in diagnosis of roseola infantum before the rash. Pediatrics. *25*:1034, 1960.
9. Braito, A., and Uberti, M.: Roseola infantum and its correlation with HHV6. Eur. J. Pediatr. *153*:209, 1994.
10. Breese, B. B., Jr.: Roseola infantum (exanthem subitum). N. Y. State J. Med. *41*:1854–1859, 1941.
11. Broberger, A. O.: Exanthema subitum och feberkramper. Nord. Med. *59*:523–525, 1958.
12. Brunner, V. N.: 172 Fälle von exanthema subitum aus praxis und klinik. Helv. Paediatr. Acta. *14*:408–425, 1959.
13. Burnstine, R. C., and Paine, R. S.: Residual encephalopathy following roseola infantum. Am. J. Dis. Child. *98*:144–152, 1959.
14. Caserta, M. T., Hall, C. B., Schnabel, K., et al.: Primary human herpesvirus 7 infection: A comparison of human herpesvirus 7 and human herpesvirus 6 infections in children. J. Pediatr. *133*:386–389, 1998.
15. Cherry, J. D.: Newer viral exanthems. Adv. Pediatr. *16*:233, 1969.
16. Cherry, J. D., Lerner, A. M., Klein, J. O., et al.: Coxsackie B5 infections with exanthems. Pediatrics. *31*:455–462, 1963.
17. Clemens, H. H.: Exanthem subitum (roseola infantum): Report of eighty cases. J. Pediatr. *26*:66–77, 1945.
18. Cushing, H. B.: An epidemic of roseola infantum. Can. Med. Assoc. J. *17*:905–906, 1927.
19. Enders, G., Biber, M., Meyer, G., et al.: Prevalence of antibodies to human herpesvirus 6 in different age groups, in children with exanthema subitum, other acute exanthematous childhood diseases, Kawasaki syndrome, and acute infections with other herpesviruses and HIV. Infection. *18*:12–15, 1990.
20. Faber, H. K., and Dickey, L. B.: The symptomatology of exanthem subitum. Arch. Pediatr. *44*:491–496, 1927.
21. Fox, J. D., Ward, P., Briggs, M., et al.: Production of IgM antibody to HHV6 in reactivation and primary infection. Epidemiol. Infect. *104*:289–296, 1990.
22. Friedman, J. H., Golomb, J., and Aronson, L.: Hemiplegia associated with roseola infantum (exanthem subitum). N. Y. State J. Med. *50*:1749–1750, 1950.
23. Fukumi, H., Nishikawa, F., Kokubu, Y., et al.: Isolation of adenovirus from an exanthematous infection resembling roseola infantum. Jpn. J. Med. Sci. Biol. *10*:87–91, 1957.
24. Greenthal, R. M.: An unusual exanthem occurring in infants. Am. J. Dis. Child. *23*:63–65, 1922.
25. Greenthal, R. M.: Roseola infantum (exanthem subitum). Wis. Med. J. *40*:25–27, 1941.
26. Gurwith, M., Gurwith, D., Wenman, W., et al.: Exanthem subitum not associated with rotavirus. N. Engl. J. Med. *305*:174–175, 1981.
27. Hall, C. B., Cherry, J. D., Hatch, M. H., et al.: The return of Boston exanthem: Echovirus 16 infections in 1974. Am. J. Dis. Child. *131*:323–326, 1977.
28. Hall, C. B., Long, C. E., Schnabel, K. C., et al.: Human herpesvirus-6 infection in children: A prospective study of complications and reactivation. N. Engl. J. Med. *331*:432–438, 1994.
29. Hellström, B., and Vahlquist, B.: Experimental inoculation of roseola infantum. Acta Paediatr. *40*:189–197, 1951.
30. Hidaka, Y., Okada, K., Kusuhara, K., et al.: Exanthem subitum and human herpesvirus 7 infection. Pediatr. Infect. Dis. *13*:1010–1011, 1994.
31. Holliday, P. B., Jr.: Pre-eruptive neurological complications of the common contagious diseases: Rubella, rubeola, roseola, and varicella. J. Pediatr. *36*:185–198, 1950.
32. Huang, L. M., Lee, C. Y., Chen, J. Y., et al.: Primary human herpesvirus 6 infections in children: A prospective serologic study. J. Infect. Dis. *165*:1163–1164, 1992.
33. Irving, W. L., Chang, J., Raymond, D. R., et al.: Roseola infantum and other syndromes associated with acute HHV6 infection. Arch. Dis. Child. *65*:1297–1300, 1990.
34. Ishiguro, N., Yamada, S., Takahashi, T., et al.: Meningoencephalitis associated with HHV-6–related exanthem subitum. Acta Paediatr. Scand. *79*:987–989, 1990.
35. James, U., and Freier, A.: Roseola infantum: An outbreak in a maternity hospital. Arch. Dis. Child. *23–24*:54–58, 1948–1949.
36. Jansson, E., Wager, O., Forssell, P., et al.: An exanthema subitumlike rash in patients with adenovirus infection. Ann. Paediatr. Fenn. *7*:3–11, 1961.
37. Juretic, M.: Exanthema subitum: A review of 243 cases. Helv. Paediatr. Acta. *18*:80–95, 1963.
38. Kawaguchi, S., Suga, S., Kozawa, T., et al.: Primary human herpesvirus-6 infection (exanthem subitum) in the newborn. Pediatrics. *90*:628–630, 1992.
39. Kempe, C. H., Shaw, E. B., Jackson, J. R., et al.: Studies on the etiology of exanthema subitum (roseola infantum). J. Pediatr. *37*:561–568, 1950.
40. Knowles, W., and Gardner, S.: High prevalence of antibody to human herpesvirus 6 and seroconversion associated with rash in 2 infants. Lancet. *2*:912–913, 1988.
41. Kodo, S., Kondo, K., Kondo, T., et al.: Detection of human herpesvirus 6 DNA in throat swabs by polymerase chain reaction. J. Med. Virol. *32*:139–142, 1990.
42. Kondo, K., Nagafuji, H., Hata, A., et al.: Association of human herpesvirus 6 infection of the central nervous system with recurrence of febrile convulsions. J. Infect. Dis. *167*:1197–1200, 1993.
43. Kusuhara, K., Ueda, K., Okada, K., et al.: Do second attacks of exanthema subitum result from human herpesvirus-6 reactivation or reinfection? Pediatr. Infect. Dis. J. *10*:468–469, 1991.
44. Letchner, A.: Roseola infantum: A review of fifty cases. Lancet. *2*:1163–1165, 1955.
45. McEnery, J. T.: Postoccipital lymphadenopathy as a diagnostic sign in roseola infantum (exanthem subitum). Clin. Pediatr. *9*:512–514, 1970.
46. Möller, K. L.: Exanthema subitum and febrile convulsions. Acta Paediatr. *45*:534–540, 1956.
47. Moore, W. F., Jr.: Roseola infantum. Hawaii Med. J. *22*:431–434, 1963.
48. Neva, F. A.: A second outbreak of Boston exanthem disease in Pittsburgh during 1954. N. Engl. J. Med. *254*:838, 1956.
49. Neva, F. A., and Enders, J. F.: Isolation of a cytopathogenic agent from an infant with a disease in certain respects resembling roseola infantum. J. Immunol. *72*:315–321, 1954.
50. Neva, F. A., Feemster, R. F., and Gorback, I. J.: Clinical and epidemiological features of an unusual epidemic exanthem. J. A. M. A. *155*:544, 1954.
51. Nishimura, K., and Igarashi, M.: Thrombocytopenic purpura associated with exanthem subitum. Pediatrics. *60*:260, 1977.
52. Okada, K., Ueda, K., Kusuhara, K., et al.: Exanthema subitum and human herpesvirus 6 infection: Clinical observations in fifty-seven cases. Pediatr. Infect. Dis. J. *12*:204–208, 1993.
53. Okafuji, T., Uchiyama, H., Okabe, N., et al.: Syndrome of inappropriate secretion of antidiuretic hormone associated with exanthem subitum. Pediatr. Infect. Dis. *16*:532–533, 1997.
54. Oski, F. A.: Roseola infantum: Another case of bulging fontanel. Am. J. Dis. Child. *101*:376–378, 1961.
55. Portolani, M., Cermelli, C., Moroni, A., et al.: Human herpesvirus-6 infections in infants admitted to hospital. J. Med. Virol. *39*:146–151, 1993.
56. Posson, D. D.: Exanthem subitum (roseola infantum) complicated by prolonged convulsions and hemiplegia. J. Pediatr. *35*:235–236, 1949.
57. Pruksananonda, P., Hall, C. B., Insel, R. A., et al.: Primary human herpesvirus 6 infection in young children. N. Engl. J. Med. *326*:1445–1450, 1992.
58. Reagan, R. L., Chang, S. C., Moolten, S. E., et al.: Electron microscopic studies of the roseola infantum (exanthem subitum) virus. Tex. Rep. Biol. Med. *13*:929–933, 1955.
59. Rosenblum, J.: Roseola infantum (exanthem subitum) complicated by hemiplegia. Am. J. Dis. Child. *69*:234–236, 1945.

60. Rothman, P. E., and Naiditch, M. J.: Nervous complications of exanthem subitum. Calif. Med. J. *88*:39–44, 1958.
61. Saitoh, Y., Matsuno, S., and Mukoyama, A.: Exanthem subitum and rotavirus. N. Engl. J. Med. *304*:845, 1981.
62. St. Geme, J. W., Jr., Prince, J. T., Scherer, W. F., et al.: A clinical study of an exanthem due to ECHO virus type 9. J. Pediatr. *54*:459–467, 1959.
63. Suga, S., Yazaki, T., Kajita, Y., et al.: Detection of human herpesvirus 6 DNAs in samples from several body sites of patients with exanthem subitum and their mothers by polymerase chain reaction assay. J. Med. Virol. *46*:52–55, 1995.
64. Suga, S., Yoshikawa, T., Nagai, T., et al.: Clinical features and virological findings in children with primary human herpesvirus 7 infection. Pediatrics. Available at *http://www.pediatric.org/cgi/content/full/99/3/e4*, 1997.
65. Takahashi, K., Sonoda, S., Kawakami, K., et al.: Human herpesvirus 6 and exanthem subitum. Lancet. *1*:1463, 1988.
66. Tanaka, K., Kondo, T., Torigoe, S., et al.: Human herpesvirus 7: Another causal agent for roseola (exanthem subitum). J. Pediatr. *125*:1–5, 1994.
67. Torigoe, S., Kumamoto, T., Koide, W., et al.: Clinical manifestations associated with human herpesvirus 7 infection. Arch. Dis. Child. *72*:518–519, 1995.
68. Ueda, K., Kusuhara, K., Hirose, M., et al.: Exanthem subitum and antibody to human herpesvirus-6. J. Infect. Dis. *159*:750–752, 1989.
69. Ueda, K., Kusuhara, K., Okada, K.: Primary human herpesvirus 7 infection and exanthem subitum. Pediatr. Infect. Dis. J. *13*:167–168, 1994.
70. Veeder, B. S., and Hempelmann, T. C.: A febrile exanthem occurring in childhood (exanthem subitum). J. A. M. A. *77*:1787–1789, 1921.
71. Watson, G. I.: The roseolar reaction. Br. Med. J. *4*:719–720, 1974.
72. Yamanishi, K., Okuno, T., Shiraki, K., et al.: Identification of human herpesvirus-6 as a causal agent for exanthem subitum. Lancet. *1*:1065–1067, 1988.
73. Yoshida, M., Fukui, K., Orita, T., et al.: Exanthem subitum (roseola infantum) with vesicular lesions. Br. J. Dermatol. *132*:614–616, 1995.
74. Zahorsky, J.: Roseola infantilis. Pediatrics. *22*:60–64, 1910.
75. Zahorsky, J.: Roseola infantum. J. A. M. A. *61*:1446–1450, 1913.
76. Zahorsky, J.: Roseola infantum: The rose rash of infants. Arch. Pediatr. *42*:610–613, 1925.
77. Zahorsky, J.: Roseola infantum: A critical survey of some recent literature. Arch. Pediatr. *57*:405–409, 1940.
78. Zahorsky, J.: Roseola infantum, a critical survey of recent literature. Arch. Pediatr. *64*:579–583, 1947.

Skin Infections

MARY ANNE JACKSON

Normal Skin

ANATOMY

The epidermal skin layer provides both the primary barrier to invasion by microorganisms and an interface between the body and the environment. Hair follicles, sebaceous glands, nails, and sweat glands are considered epidermal appendages and as such may be involved in skin infection. A dermal layer composed of collagen and elastic fibers gives skin its elasticity; however, other cell elements that are present, including mast cells, blood and lymph vessels, and cutaneous nerves, may be involved in the inflammatory process in response to infection. The subcutaneous fat layer resides just beneath the dermis and contributes primarily to thermal stability, but it also may be involved when infection extends beyond the epidermal-dermal layer.

FLORA

Colonization is defined as the presence of a microorganism on the skin without either clinical signs or symptoms of infection at the time of isolation. Normal bacterial skin colonization is divided into resident and transient flora. Resident flora predominates and includes typical nonpathogens such as *Staphylococcus epidermidis* and *Propionibacterium acnes*, in addition to other anaerobic diphtheroids and micrococci. Transient flora includes pathogenic organisms such as *Staphylococcus aureus,* streptococci, gram-negative enterics, and *Candida albicans*; these pathogens usually are present in smaller numbers than is the resident flora and may be removed by skin cleansing.

Acutely or chronically damaged skin, contact with animate and inanimate environmental sources, and exposure to antimicrobial agents or indwelling devices can modify the skin flora and predispose to infection by either resident or acquired transient flora.[75, 81]

Cutaneous Infection and Dermatologic Manifestations of Systemic Disease

Dermatologic manifestations of infection can occur when the skin is infected primarily or as a secondary phenomenon. Prompt diagnosis and treatment of certain systemic or disseminated diseases may be made when the secondary dermatologic manifestations are recognized. Empiric treatment of systemic diseases such as endocarditis (septic emboli) or septicemia caused by bacterial pathogens such as *Neisseria meningitidis* or *Pseudomonas aeruginosa* (purpura fulminans, ecthyma gangrenosum) is possible when the dermatologic manifestations are noted. Generalized viral infections may be heralded by pathognomonic skin findings such as occur in varicella or measles. Alternatively, skin manifestations may be mediated by toxin (staphylococcal scalded skin syndrome or toxic shock syndrome [TSS]) or by immunologic mechanisms (gonococcemia).

The list of bacterial infectious agents associated with skin infections is extensive (Table 67–1). This chapter focuses on the bacterial skin infections most frequently encountered by practicing clinicians and the more common superficial fungal infections.

Impetigo

NONBULLOUS OR SIMPLE SUPERFICIAL IMPETIGO

The bacterial skin infection most commonly encountered in children is nonbullous impetigo, which accounts for more than 70 percent of impetigo cases in children. This superficial infection is seen predominantly in the summer months, with insect bites, cutaneous injuries, and primary dermatitis serving as the portal of entry.[42, 57]

Nonbullous impetigo, sometimes called thick crusted impetigo, is characterized by the appearance of erythematous

TABLE 67–1 ■ BACTERIAL INFECTIOUS AGENTS ASSOCIATED WITH CUTANEOUS MANIFESTATIONS

Anthrax	*Bacillus anthracis*
Blistering dactylitis*	*Streptococcus pyogenes* *Streptococcus agalactiae* *Staphylococcus aureus*
Cellulitis	*S. pyogenes* *Staphylococcus aureus* *Haemophilus influenzae* type b *Streptococcus pneumoniae*
Chancroid	*Haemophilus ducreyi*
Diphtheria	*Corynebacterium diphtheriae*
Ecthyma gangrenosum	*Pseudomonas aeruginosa*
Erysipelas	*S. pyogenes* *S. agalactiae*; group C, G streptococci *S. pneumoniae*
Erysipeloid	*Erysipelothrix rhusiopathiae*
Folliculitis	*S. aureus* Coagulase-negative staphylococci *Klebsiella* spp. *Enterobacter* spp. *Escherichia coli* *Pseudomonas aeruginosa* *Proteus* spp.
Erythrasma	*Corynebacterium minutissimum*
Furunculosis	*S. aureus*
Hidradenitis suppurativa	*S. aureus* *Streptococcus milleri* *Escherichia coli* Anaerobic streptococci
Granuloma inguinale	*Calymmatobacterium granulomatis*
Impetigo	
Simple superficial	*S. aureus* *S. pyogenes*
Bullous	*S. aureus*
Lymphogranuloma venereum	*Chlamydia trachomatis*
Melioidosis	*Burkholderia pseudomallei*
Necrotizing fasciitis	*S. pyogenes* Polymicrobial
Nocardiosis	*Nocardia brasiliensis* *Nocardia asteroides*
Paronychia	Polymicrobial
Perianal dermatitis	*S. pyogenes*
Pitted keratolysis	Coryneform bacteria
Syphilis	*Treponema pallidum*

*Note: Entries in bold are discussed in the text.

maculopapules that rapidly evolve from a vesicular to a pustular stage. Centrally crusted plaques range in size from a few millimeters to a centimeter and are surrounded by a distinct margin of erythema. The honey-colored crust is a classic feature, and removal of the crust results in the re-accumulation of fresh exudate. Regional lymphadenopathy can occur and often is the reason that the patient seeks medical attention. Spread to exposed areas, usually the face, neck, and limbs, occurs frequently. Still, this form of pyoderma often is associated with a 2- to 3-week delay in making the diagnosis because the lesions are slow to progress, only mildly tender at the site of the lesion, and generally not associated with systemic signs or symptoms.

Nonbullous impetigo classically has been associated with infection caused by group A beta-hemolytic streptococcus (GABHS); however, recent data underscore the importance of *S. aureus*, which now accounts for most cases of nonbullous impetigo in the United States.[6, 46]

Primarily a disease of children, nonbullous impetigo is spread within families and by close physical contact. It is prevalent during warm, humid seasons and is seen year-round in tropical regions. Endemic disease occurs in the southeastern part of the United States, as well as Hawaii.

Epidemics of streptococcal impetigo have been associated with postinfectious glomerulonephritis, and streptococcal strains, including types 2, 31, 49, 53, 55, 56, 57, and 60, have been implicated in such outbreaks.[12, 63] Studies published in the 1950s and 1960s from the Red Lake Indian Reservation in Minnesota first confirmed the association of impetigo in children of school age with a postinfectious nephritis that occurred 18 to 21 days after the onset of impetigo and implicated the so-called Red Lake strain, M-type 49.[5] Further studies in this population performed in the early 1970s found that GABHS was isolated from normal skin in 23 of 31 high-risk children a mean of 10 days before the development of impetigo.[31] Local trauma and other environmental factors appeared to explain the predilection of exposed skin to streptococcal infection, especially the skin of the legs, where 62 percent of the total lesions were noted. Secondary acquisition of streptococcal isolates in other family members occurred a mean of 5 days after the primary case, a time frame that was noted to be significantly shorter than that of secondary respiratory acquisition.[48] Rheumatic fever does not occur as a postinfectious sequela of streptococcal skin infection.

Cutaneous botryomycosis, an indolent infection reminiscent of crusted impetigo, usually is caused by *S. aureus*. Characterized by plaque-like lesions with superficial pustules and crusts, this entity has a predilection for patients with altered immune function.[22] Histologic examination may suggest the diagnosis of actinomycosis if a granulomatous lesion with granules resembling those seen with *Actinomyces* is noted. Successful treatment can be accomplished after the bacterial pathogen has been identified.

BULLOUS IMPETIGO

Bullous impetigo is diagnosed when the primary lesion begins as small vesicles and later appears as flaccid, painless bullae, generally measuring greater than 1 cm. Initially filled with clear fluid, the lesions eventually may demonstrate a purulent fluid level. Rupture of the thin bullae usually reveals a moist, erythematous base that dries to a shiny lacquer-like appearance, sometimes described as a varnished finish (Fig. 67–1). Systemic toxicity is not seen, except in neonates, in whom disseminated disease may occur.

In contrast to thick, crusted impetigo, in virtually all cases of bullous impetigo, staphylococci are isolated in pure culture from aspirated bulla fluid. Other bullous dermatitides of childhood, such as pemphigus or Stevens-Johnson syndrome, may be excluded by isolation of the organism. Occasionally, biopsy is performed in cases in which extensive bullae or an atypical clinical appearance is noted. Confirmation of a cleavage plane high in the epidermis with gram-positive organisms and polymorphonuclear leukocytes present is a definitive diagnosis of bullous staphylococcal disease.

Infection generally is caused by phage group II strains, particularly phage type 71, but also 3A, 3C, and 55, which are noted to elaborate epidermolytic toxins A and B. Pathologically, these toxins act by disrupting the intercellular attachment of epidermal cells of the stratum granulosum. The toxin is thought to function as a protease in separating the upper layers of the epidermis of both adult and infant human skin. Production of antibody to epidermolytic toxin occurs with age; however, it does not protect against the development of new bullous lesions during the localized impetiginous stage of this staphylococcal disease.

Epidemiologically, large outbreaks of bullous impetigo have been traced most notably to hospital nurseries, where

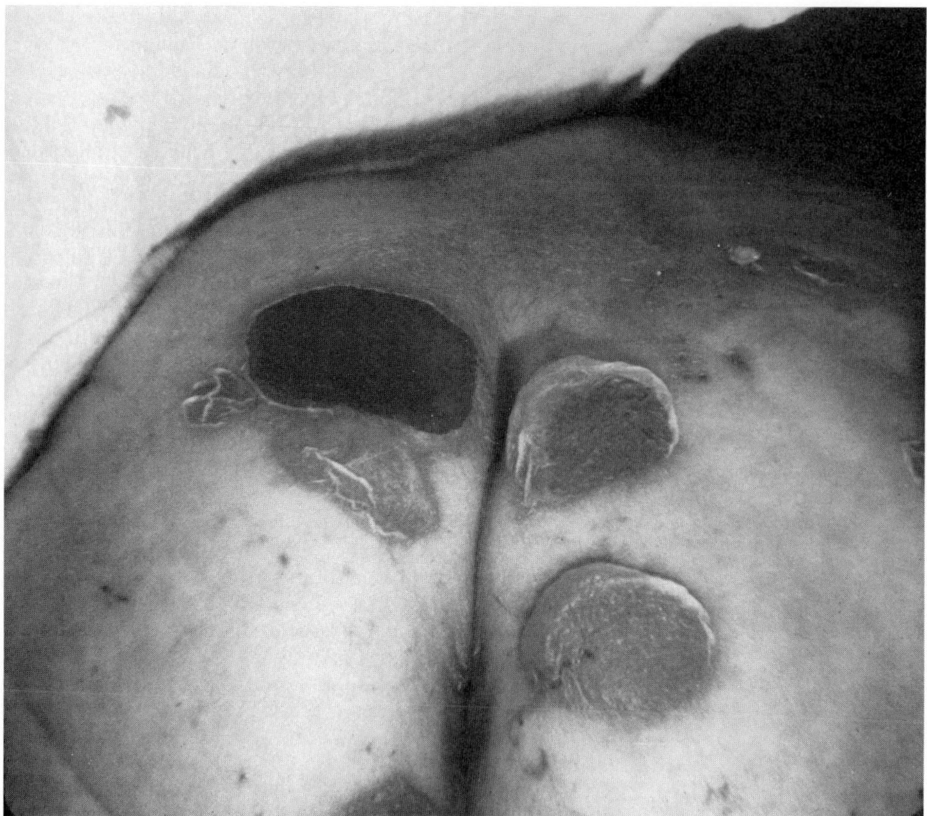

FIGURE 67–1 ■ Flaccid bullae and shiny lacquer base of staphylococcal impetigo.

identification of infected infants always occurs within the first month of life but after the infant has been sent home. A more severe, generalized form of the epidermolytic toxin–mediated disease (Ritter disease) may be seen in a few infants during one of these outbreaks, thus underscoring the importance of infection control surveillance practices in recognizing such an outbreak (Fig. 67–2).

TREATMENT OF IMPETIGO

Topical mupirocin may be used in cases of nonbullous impetigo in which adequate coverage of the affected sites can be ensured.[18, 30, 89] In other cases, systemic treatment with an oral antistaphylococcal antimicrobial agent such as cephalexin should be used.[34, 35, 41, 99] As in other staphylococcal diseases, an increase in community-acquired, methicillin-resistant *S. aureus* (MRSA) cases has been noted in the last decade.[58, 59, 68, 112] In cases for which traditional antistaphylococcal agents are unsuccessful or in patients with recurrent disease, culture should be performed to identify the bacterial strain and susceptibility pattern. At the current time, most community-acquired MRSA isolates remain susceptible to clindamycin.[17, 23]

Perianal Streptococcal Dermatitis

Formerly called perianal cellulitis, perianal streptococcal dermatitis, a commonly recognized superficial skin infection, is characterized by the presence of marked, well-demarcated, perirectal erythema with associated swelling, pruritus, and tenderness but an absence of systemic symptoms or progressive disease. Approximately one half of patients complain of significant rectal pain on defecation, and a third note blood in their stools.[4, 27, 66, 88]

Heavy growth of GABHS is seen on perianal culture, and in one study, isolation of a specific T-type streptococcus (T 28) raised the question of whether certain streptococcal strains have tropism for the perineal region.[94] Asymptomatic patients were evaluated in two studies and had only sparse growth of GABHS in 6 percent of cases.

Perianal streptococcal dermatitis is treated with oral penicillin agents, and topical mupirocin has been used successfully. Recurrences are noted commonly, however. In one large series of patients, one third had recurrent disease.[79] Intrafamilial spread of disease occurs commonly and may provide a vector for recurrence. For those with recurrent or persistent disease, clindamycin or a β-lactam agent plus rifampin may be used, and identification and treatment of other affected family members may be necessary.

Blistering Distal Dactylitis

Most commonly identified in school-age children, blistering distal dactylitis is a distinctive superficial skin infection classically associated with GABHS.[13] Bullae up to 2 cm in diameter develop over the anterior fat pad of the distal phalanges, sometimes extending to involve the nail folds. Involvement of the proximal phalanges or the palms occasionally is noted. Frankly pustular lesions may occur, but the lesions themselves usually are asymptomatic or only mildly tender. A thin purulent exudate generally is apparent on incision and drainage.[67]

The diagnosis is confirmed by recovery of the etiologic agent on culture, most commonly GABHS, although group B streptococci and *S. aureus* also have been noted.[54] Concurrent recovery of GABHS in the pharynx has been reported in a few cases.

Treatment includes a 10-day course of an oral β-lactam agent, usually penicillin or amoxicillin, in addition to incision and drainage of any tense bullae.

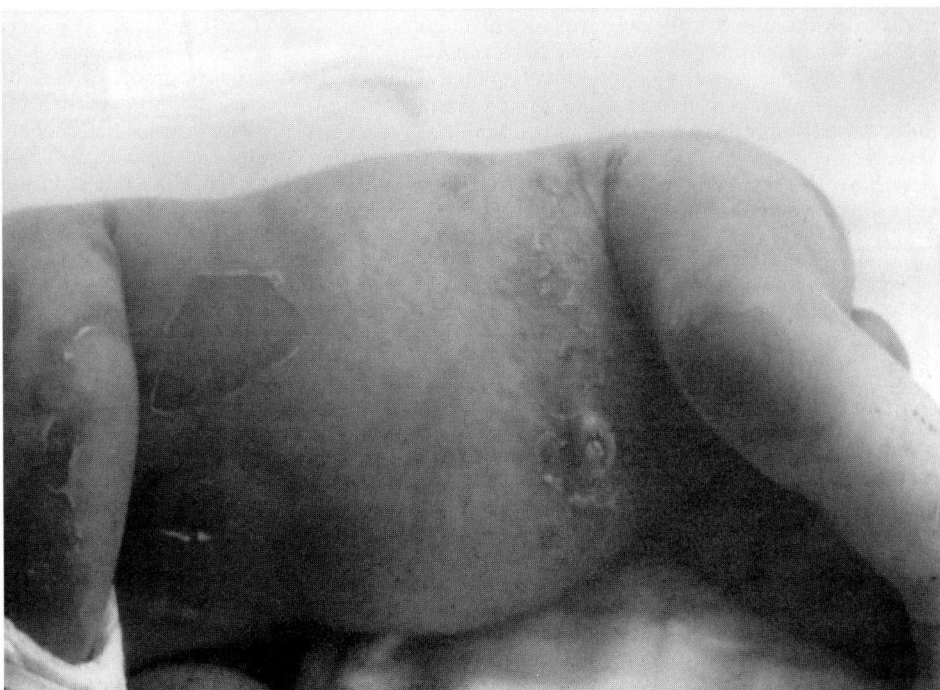

FIGURE 67–2 ■ Typical appearance of a neonate with Ritter disease.

Erysipelas

This superficial cellulitis, referred to as St. Anthony's fire in the Middle Ages, is characterized by the appearance of a bright erythematous plaque with a distinct, elevated border that sharply demarcates affected from unaffected skin. The lesion most often involves the face or lower extremity, although extensive involvement of the trunk has been noted. The involved skin is warm and tender and may have a *peau d'orange* appearance. Large tension bullae may be seen in the erythematous zone.[61] The patient generally appears toxic and is highly febrile, and rapid extension of the affected skin may occur over the course of hours.[29, 62, 120]

Histopathologic findings include intense edema with vascular dilatation of the dermis and uppermost subcutaneous tissue. Involvement of lymphatic channels and tissue spaces with polymorphonuclear leukocytes is a typical finding.

Surgical wounds, the umbilicus of the neonate, or any break in skin may serve as the portal of entry; however, the initial lesion may be inapparent. Localized edema, such as occurs from a renal or lymphatic source, is a predisposing factor, and antecedent respiratory infection often is reported. An increased risk for development of erysipelas has been noted in patients with hypogammaglobulinemia, certain malignancies such as lymphoma, or lymphedema complicating radiation therapy.

The diagnosis generally is recognized on clinical grounds, and GABHS traditionally has been isolated by aspiration of the advancing margin of the lesion. A few case reports have identified other streptococci (including group B, C, G), *Moraxella* spp., *Haemophilus influenzae,* and *Streptococcus pneumoniae* as etiologic agents.[15, 28, 38, 80, 92, 111, 121]

A combination of intravenous penicillin and clindamycin should be used until the results of culture are available. Erysipelas has a classic clinical appearance, and appropriate diagnosis and therapy result in a prompt clinical response in most cases. Penicillin prophylaxis may be considered for patients with recurrent erysipelas, particularly those with underlying risk factors.[16, 36]

Ecthyma

Ecthyma gangrenosa is a deep-seated infectious process manifested as a necrotic ulcer covered by a black eschar. Usually, the initial lesion, a vesicopustule, sits on an erythematous base; it eventually erodes through the epidermis to the dermis, where it forms a crusted ulcer with heaped-up borders and then becomes frankly necrotic.[60]

It can occur as a primary cutaneous infection in an immunocompetent host, and etiologic agents that have been confirmed include *S. aureus, Aeromonas hydrophila,* and GABHS.[44, 53, 69, 76, 86, 95, 118] A similar appearing lesion is seen with cutaneous anthrax; however, extensive nonpitting edema of the surrounding soft tissues is an important clue to this diagnosis. Ecthymatous-like lesions have been seen in patients with herpes simplex infection.[77]

In contrast, when an ecthymatous lesion is noted in a febrile neutropenic host, it generally signals disseminated infection. *P. aeruginosa* is the etiologic pathogen identified most commonly in such cases, but other gram-negative pathogens and fungi, including *Enterobacter, Escherichia coli, Morganella, Pseudomonas cepacia, Serratia marcescens, Stenotrophomonas maltophilia, Aspergillus, Mucor, Fusaria,* and *C. albicans*, have been implicated in ecthyma gangrenosum in compromised hosts.[32, 47, 49, 87, 97, 102, 105, 110] Ecthyma has been seen as the heralding manifestation of acute lymphoblastic leukemia in children.[101] Empiric antimicrobial therapy for ecthyma gangrenosum in a neutropenic host should include intravenous therapy with an anti-*Pseudomonas* agent plus an aminoglycoside. Biopsy of the lesion may provide more specific etiologic information and allow for confirmation of antimicrobial susceptibility.

Folliculitis, Furunculosis, and Carbuncles

Folliculitis, furunculosis, and carbuncles represent a group of infections characterized by their origin in the hair follicles and the formation of abscesses. Virtually always caused by *S. aureus,* these infections were seen commonly in the 1950s in disease that often involved multiple family members. Outbreaks among athletes likewise have been reported.[116]

By definition, these infections involve sites where body hair is present, including the axilla, breast area, perineum, neck, and extremities. Lesions of folliculitis represent abscesses of a single hair follicle with limited surrounding tissue involvement. When deeper inflammatory nodules are associated with tissue edema, furunculosis is diagnosed. When several interconnecting furuncles are present, the lesion is referred to as a carbuncle.

Generally, older children and adolescents are predisposed to the development of follicular infections, and those with diabetes mellitus, abnormal neutrophil chemotaxis, and impaired circulation may have recurrent disease.

Although *S. aureus* nearly always is the cause of folliculitis as in the past, outbreaks of so-called hot tub folliculitis have been described and almost always are caused by *P. aeruginosa;* rarely, other gram-negative organisms have been reported.[25, 26] Folliculitis in an immunocompromised host often is caused by unusual fungal pathogens.[3, 104, 113] Though typically associated with hot tubs and whirlpools, a large outbreak of *Pseudomonas* folliculitis reported in 1984 involved 117 individuals after swimming in an indoor pool. An incubation period of 24 to 30 hours could be ascertained, and a typical follicular, pustular eruption was noted. The mean duration of the folliculitis, 15 days, is consistent with other reports, but some patients continued to complain of rash for weeks, and recurrent pustules appearing months later have been reported in other studies.[52]

Recognition of the typical skin lesion usually is sufficient to make the diagnosis. Unless the patient has a history of exposure to a hot tub or whirlpool, a regimen of antistaphylococcal therapy should be sufficient. Systemic agents should be used for 7 to 10 days in those with extensive disease or associated cellulitis. Large lesions should be incised and drained, and culture should be performed in such cases. In some patients, hematogenous metastatic spread may occur, and a search for foci in the heart, bones, joints, deep tissues, or brain should be performed in patients with significant systemic toxicity.

For patients in whom recurrent disease develops, chronic dermatoses such as eczema should be identified, and in obese adolescents, the diagnosis of diabetes mellitus should be considered.[7] The patient should be cautioned to refrain from sharing washcloths or towels, and skin trauma and use of irritants such as deodorants should be avoided. Rarely, children with white blood cell defects may have recurrent staphylococcal skin abscesses, and tests of white blood cell function may be considered in specific patients. Data suggest that vitamin C may be beneficial in cases of recurrent folliculitis.[83, 84]

Hidradenitis Suppurativa

Hidradenitis suppurativa, a chronic, debilitating condition, is a disorder of the apocrine glands that primarily involves skin in the axilla and anogenital region, although scalp, umbilical, and breast involvement has been reported. Seen mainly in adolescents, this androgen-dependent condition is manifested by the development of multiple painful nodules and the formation of deep abscesses in the skin in areas where apocrine glands are present. The formation of fistulas, ulcers, and contracted scars may complicate the course, and recurrent relapses may be noted. Infection usually is polymicrobial, and pathogens to consider include *S. aureus*, gram-negative enterics, and anaerobes. Drainage of abscesses and institution of systemic antimicrobial therapy may be necessary. When fistulas associated with anogenital disease develop, adjacent structures, including the urethra, bladder, and rectum, may be involved. Surgery usually is required for cure.

Cellulitis

The diagnosis of cellulitis is made when the subcutaneous tissues and dermis are involved in a clinical process manifested as localized edema, erythema, warmth, and tenderness of the tissues. The leading edge of the involved site may be notable, but it is not raised and well demarcated as in erysipelas.

Infection usually is caused by coagulase-positive staphylococci and GABHS; however, infection also is caused by group B streptococci (neonates) and *S. pneumoniae*, and in the past, *H. influenzae* type b cellulitis was described.[117]

Streptococcal and staphylococcal cellulitis can involve patients of any age and any site, although the extremity is noted most often. Frequently, the patient has a history of antecedent trauma at the site of involvement, but the injury may not have appeared significant. Some researchers advocate culture of the cellulitic site, but in practice, it rarely is performed. Blood cultures are of value in individuals with disease caused by group B streptococci, *S. pneumoniae*, and *H. influenzae* type b.[71]

Group B streptococcal cellulitis occurs in neonates and generally is seen as part of invasive, late-onset disease. Unilateral involvement of the face or submandibular sites occurs most commonly, but inguinal, scrotal, and prepatellar involvement has been described.[10, 65] When cellulitis occurs in an infant younger than 3 months, group B streptococcal bacteremia should be suspected, even in the absence of other signs of systemic infection.

Pneumococcal soft tissue infections are not uncommon findings.[100] Patients with connective tissue disorders, such as systemic lupus erythematosus, seem especially prone, although these infections can occur in healthy infants and children. Sites of involvement can include the head, neck, leg, and torso.

H. influenzae type b cellulitis often involves the face of infants (Fig. 67–3). A violaceous hue of the cellulitic area, which some researchers thought to be pathognomonic, might be observed. This process nearly always was the result of hematogenous seeding by *H. influenzae* type b, and meningitis occurred in 15 to 20 percent of such patients.[64, 115, 123] As has been the case with other forms of *H. influenzae* type b disease, almost complete eradication has been achieved in the last decade with the use of conjugate vaccine.

Treatment of simple cellulitis in patients with a clear-cut area of preceding trauma should include an agent that is active against *S. aureus* and GABHS, such as cephalexin or clindamycin. In infants with buccal or periorbital involvement or in those with soft tissue involvement but without a clear-cut focus of infection, a third-generation cephalosporin such as cefotaxime or ceftriaxone should be included with clindamycin.

Necrotizing Fasciitis

Necrotizing fasciitis (NF) is a rapidly progressive bacterial infection of the soft tissues associated with a fulminant course and a high mortality rate. This infection spreads rapidly in the plane between the subcutaneous tissue and superficial muscle fascia and causes widespread necrosis. Prompt and aggressive medical and surgical management is necessary to ensure a good outcome.

In children, NF usually is caused by GABHS; traumatic lesions involving the skin, including varicella, burns, or eczema, may predispose to this aggressive process.[19, 43, 51, 55, 72, 98, 107, 108, 125] An association has been noted among varicella, ibuprofen use, and invasive GABHS infection, although no data convincingly link this triad to necrotizing

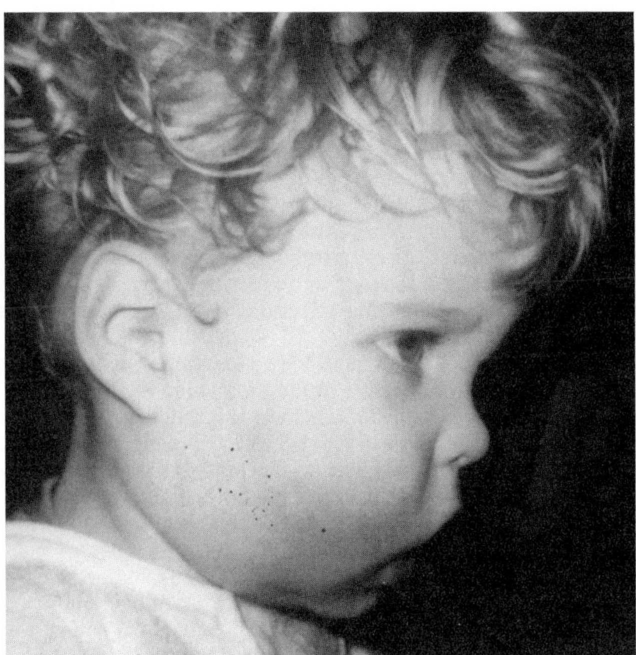

FIGURE 67–3 ■ Buccal involvement in an infant with invasive *Haemophilus influenzae* type b disease.

infection.[50, 82, 126] Patients with congenital or acquired immunodeficiencies are at greater risk for the development of NF, and in neonates, omphalitis and circumcision are predisposing conditions.

CLINICAL MANIFESTATIONS

The child generally has a high fever and is fussy. In infants, the irritability may be profound and may not appear to be localized to an involved site, unless the clinician is meticulous in conducting the examination. An extremity most commonly is involved, and older infants and children often refuse to bear weight or move the affected extremity. Swelling of soft tissue usually is noted, but the erythema may be subtle. The hallmark tip-off on examination is the finding of intense pain on manipulation of the involved site that is out of proportion to the cutaneous signs. Skin changes that occur during the subsequent 24 to 48 hours include blistering with bleb formation, and a dusky appearance of the involved site is noted as vessels are thrombosed and cutaneous ischemia develops. Skin necrosis is a late sign and indicates a poor prognosis[74, 119] (Fig. 67–4).

Recognition of the manifestations of TSS is critical because mortality rates of 60 percent have been reported in patients with associated fasciitis. Multisystem complaints, including vomiting, diarrhea, and severe myalgia, are present when GABHS fasciitis is associated with streptococcal TSS. Tachycardia out of proportion to fever and altered mental status may be early signs of TSS. Renal and hepatic dysfunctions occur typically, and symptoms and signs of adult respiratory distress syndrome often are identified.

DIAGNOSIS

The diagnosis cannot be based on the appearance of the involved site because none of the early findings of NF are pathognomonic. Plain radiographs usually are normal and of no value in the diagnosis. Magnetic resonance imaging (MRI) is the preferred technique to detect soft tissue involvement, and it permits visualization of the soft tissue edema infiltrating the fascial planes.[21, 103, 127] However, although MRI may be helpful, it should not delay surgical intervention. Waiting for a radiographic procedure to be performed to confirm the diagnosis may only serve to delay implementing definitive surgical therapy and to increase the risk for development of systemic complications, thereby further contributing to the increased morbidity and mortality rates. In the typical clinical scenario in which the index of suspicion for NF is high, surgical exploration is appropriate, even in the presence of "normal" MRI findings.

Laboratory manifestations of streptococcal TSS should be sought in any pediatric patient with fasciitis. Typically, the white blood cell count is normal; however, most patients have a significant increase in band forms (>50%) noted on the peripheral blood smear. Thrombocytopenia and evidence of coagulopathy are found commonly, and marked hypoalbuminemia with hypocalcemia is a typical finding. Laboratory findings associated with renal failure, myocardial dysfunction, and adult respiratory distress syndrome may develop during the first 48 to 72 hours.

A microbiologic diagnosis can be made by isolating bacteria from blood, tissue, or wound culture. In some cases, a polymicrobial etiology has been noted, particularly in patients with so-called Fournier gangrene or NF of the perineum.[45, 70] In these cases, *S. aureus,* GABHS, and one or more anaerobes, including *Peptostreptococcus, Prevotella, Bacteroides fragilis,* and *Porphyromonas,* have been implicated in infection.[20] Fasciitis caused by *P. aeruginosa* or *Clostridium septicum* has been seen in neutropenic patients. In the last decade, however, GABHS has been reported widely as a single pathogen and is the etiologic agent in most cases of pediatric fasciitis. As in other cases of invasive disease caused by GABHS, virulence is related to certain structural characteristics of the organism and to its ability to produce biologically active substances, some of which facilitate invasion and spread of the pathogen.

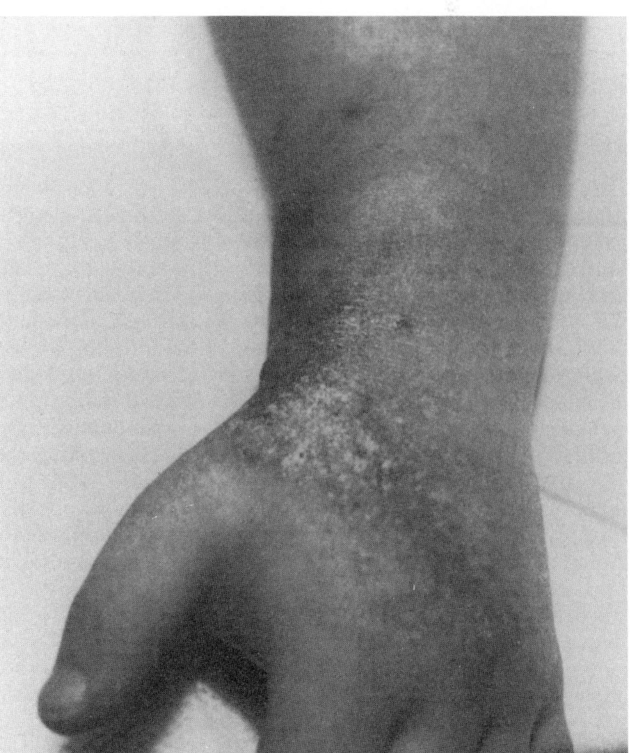

FIGURE 67–4 ■ Necrotizing fasciitis in a toddler with varicella.

TREATMENT

Surgical débridement of necrotic tissue is the key to managing NF, and increased mortality rates have been observed when the débridement is delayed more than 24 hours.[96] Mandatory return to the operating room for examination and repeat débridement should occur during the following 24 to 48 hours. Careful management of fluids, attention to pain control, anticipation and management of multisystem organ failure, and administration of appropriate parenteral antimicrobial therapy should be initiated promptly. The use of intravenous immunoglobulin may be considered in cases of TSS-associated fasciitis.[24]

Appropriate therapy includes intravenous penicillin, 150,000 U/kg/day divided into four to six doses, and clindamycin, 40 mg/kg/day divided into four doses. The use of additional coverage with agents active against *P. aeruginosa* and gram-negative enterics should be considered in neutropenic patients.

Response to therapy is assessed by careful serial examination. Control of pain is critical in such patients, while keeping in mind that persistent, severe pain is suggestive of ongoing tissue necrosis and may signal the need for further surgical intervention. Careful attention to nutritional support should be maintained throughout the child's hospital stay. Physical therapy is necessary for most patients, especially those who require amputation, skin grafting, or extensive reconstructive surgery, and giving attention to the psychosocial needs of the child and the family is imperative.

Contaminated Wounds

Although staphylococci and streptococci are the most likely causes of infection after traumatic skin lesions, the list of etiologies may be extensive, depending on the nature of the injury. Specific pathogens should be considered when infections develop after human or animal bites, soil or water contamination, or various types of injury. Management of such infections is dependent on recognition of infection patterns and careful culture for identification of the specific organism or organisms involved (Table 67–2).

HUMAN BITES (See also Chapter 246)

The two types of human bites that are described are occlusional and clenched fist. Occlusional bites are related most commonly to child abuse, although in a pediatric patient, a biting toddler may be the culprit. Accidental bites may occur during sporting activities, and generally they involve the face of a teammate. Clenched-fist injuries are associated with the most prevalent and severe infections that occur after human bites. Rapidly progressive infection may follow despite the patient's receiving early medical attention.[11] When clenched-fist injuries are associated with bite wounds, laceration and puncture wounds commonly occur along the dorsal aspect of the third metacarpophalangeal joint, and bone, joint capsule, or tendon structures may be involved.

Polymicrobial infection is the usual finding, and as such, broad-spectrum empiric antimicrobial coverage should be initiated promptly, after adequate drainage has been performed.[106] *Eikenella corrodens* commonly is involved in human bite infections and is intrinsically resistant to clindamycin and cephalosporins. Ampicillin with clavulanate given orally (simple infections) or ampicillin-sulbactam given intravenously for more complicated infections may be used as a single agent.

ANIMAL BITES (See also Chapter 246)

Animal bite wounds occur commonly, with more than 4 million reported annually in the United States. Children account for more than one half of those who go to emergency departments for care of bite wounds.[2] Although one survey has revealed that rodents and lagomorphs are the biting animals most commonly reported, wounds related to these bites infrequently are associated with infection. By contrast, cats and dogs together account for approximately 40 percent of bites, and their bites are associated more frequently with morbidity. The etiology of animal bite infections is often related to the species of animal involved[37, 40, 73, 85] (see Table 67–2).

Approximately 1000 emergency department visits related to dog bites occur each day, at a cost of more than $100 million dollars per year.[114] The incidence of infection related to dog bites has been estimated at 3 to 17 percent.[9, 33]

Cat bites are most likely to become infected, probably because of the puncture-like nature of the injury. One study suggests that one half of cat bites will result in infection, thus prompting recommendations for prophylaxis of such bites, especially if they involve the face or hands. In the presence of infection, exploration plus débridement of devitalized tissue is necessary, and purulent collections should be drained.

Although *Pasteurella multocida* is implicated most frequently, a number of other pathogens that are associated with dog and cat bites include *S. aureus, Capnocytophaga canimorsus,* and other aerobic and anaerobic bacteria. Depending on the depth of the wound's penetration, underlying structures such as bones, joints, and tendons may be involved in such infections.[56] The wound itself may not appear significant, particularly in the case of puncture wounds, but several clinical features should influence treatment decisions. The presence of tissue edema and point tenderness on palpation over the site should signal that deeper structures may be involved. Soft tissue imaging may be necessary, and appropriate drainage or débridement of involved sites should be pursued.

As with human bites, oral amoxicillin-clavulanate may be used for prophylaxis or treatment of simple infections. Indications for prophylaxis of bite wounds include bites associated with a crush or puncture injury and those involving the face, hands, feet, and genitalia. Wounds in the immunocompromised, especially asplenic, individuals should be considered for prophylaxis. Intravenous ampicillin-sulbactam or ticarcillin-clavulanate can be used for more serious infections. For individuals who have a history of anaphylaxis with penicillin or cephalosporins, a combination of clindamycin plus trimethoprim-sulfamethoxazole or ciprofloxacin can be used.[103, 104] Antimicrobial therapy may be modified further depending on the biting animal and suspected pathogen[14] (see Table 67–2).

Appropriate tetanus prophylaxis should be considered for all bites. Hepatitis B clearly can be transmitted by human bites, and appropriate management should be ensured for susceptible patients. Rabies vaccine should be administered after bat, skunk, or raccoon bites; public health information should be accessed to decide whether rabies vaccine is indicated for other animal bites.

SOIL- AND WATER-CONTAMINATED WOUNDS

Four factors that must be considered in the acute care of contaminated wounds include the mechanism of injury, the length of time that transpires from injury to treatment, the type of pathogens that occur in the environment, and the presence of underlying disease in the host.[39]

TABLE 67–2 ■ INFECTIONS ASSOCIATED WITH ANIMAL BITES

Nature of Injury	Pathogens Involved
Human bites	Staphylococci Anaerobic and aerobic streptococci *Eikenella corrodens*
Animal bites	
Dog/cat	*Pasteurella* species *Staphylococcus aureus* Streptococci Anaerobes *Capnocytophaga canimorsus, Capnocytophaga cynodegmi* *Moraxella* *Corynebacterium* *Neisseria* species
Reptile	Enteric gram-negatives Anaerobes
Horse and sheep	*Actinobacillus, Pasteurella*
Pig	*Flavobacterium, Actinobacillus, Pasteurella aerogenes*
Rat	*Streptobacillus moniliformis, S. aureus*

TABLE 67–3 ■ INFECTIONS ASSOCIATED WITH SOIL- OR WATER-CONTAMINATED WOUNDS

Soil-contaminated wounds	*Staphylococcus aureus* Group A beta-hemolytic streptococci Many gram-negative enterics *Enterobacter cancerogenus* Anaerobes *Nocardia asteroides, Nocardia otitidis-caviarum* *Mycobacterium fortuitum, Mycobacterium abscessus* *Actinomyces* *Aspergillus* spp. *Enterococcus* spp.
Water-contaminated wounds	*Aeromonas hydrophila* *Pseudomonas* Many gram-negative enterics *Edwardsiella tarda* (catfish injury) *Mycobacterium marinum*

When a traumatic wound becomes infected, a polymicrobial etiology is typical, and common pathogens such as *S. aureus,* gram-negative enterics, and anaerobes characteristically are involved.[1] Unusual and rare organisms such as nontuberculous mycobacteria, *Nocardia, Actinomyces*, fungi including *Aspergillus* spp., and unusual gram-negative organisms occasionally may be encountered[78, 90, 91, 93, 122] (Table 67–3). *A. hydrophila* has been implicated in infections associated with injuries contaminated by fresh water and may produce rapidly progressive wound infection with fascia, tendon, muscle, bone, or joint involvement.[109]

Managing wounds contaminated by soil or water is difficult, especially if the mechanism of injury is a catastrophic event with complex bone and soft tissue injuries. In the acute setting of such an event, complete exploration and thorough débridement with copious irrigation are performed primarily, and signs of infection generally are not present. Days later, the clinician often is faced with the dilemma of a patient who is receiving antimicrobial prophylaxis with broad-spectrum agents and in whom new signs or symptoms develop acutely. Separating infectious from noninfectious complications often is difficult; however, the onset of fever in such a patient, especially in the setting of an open fracture or dural tear, should prompt further evaluation. Careful serial examination of the site of injury is necessary, and more extensive evaluation generally is indicated. Such assessment may include radiographic imaging and specific evaluation of body fluids with appropriate cultures. Infections associated with foreign bodies such as wood generally cannot be cured until the foreign body is identified and removed.[124] Puncture wounds should be explored carefully, and further débridement of necrotic tissue or drainage of involved sites such as joints may be necessary.[8]

Treatment of simple wound infections associated with soil or water contamination should include an agent such as ciprofloxacin, although of importance is that deeper tissue infection may develop after a seemingly innocuous injury, and tissue débridement may be necessary. Determining the appropriate therapy for a patient with infection involving extensive soft tissue injury and open fractures is problematic. Administration of an empiric regimen with an agent such as piperacillin-tazobactam, imipenem, or a fluoroquinolone plus vancomycin may be reasonable after evaluation and appropriate culturing have been conducted.

Fungal Infections

Most infections caused by fungi involving the skin are superficial in nature. Such infections generally are due to dermatophytes, yeasts, or (rarely) the dermatiaceous fungi.

DERMATOPHYTE INFECTIONS

Dermatophytosis describes infection with organisms belonging to the *Trichophyton*, *Microsporum*, or *Epidermophyton* genus. Infections with these agents generally manifest with skin involvement. The most common dermatophytes are anthropophilic and can be passed from human to human. The zoophilic agents, although seen in humans, generally infect animals. Lastly, the geophilic dermatophytes came from the soil and can infect both humans and animals. Dermatophyte infections are described using the designation *tinea* with the body site involved (e.g., tinea capitis = scalp, tinea pedis = foot, tinea manum = hand).

In the general population, tinea corporis is seen with greater frequency than is either tinea pedis or tinea unguium.

In North and South America, infection of the scalp with fungi generally is due to *Trichophyton tonsurans*. Tinea capitis is seen primarily in prepubertal children. Its clinical presentation may be that of a diffusely distributed seborrheic-like scaling of the scalp, focal areas of scaling with or without alopecia, alopecia with only black dots representative of broken hairs in affected individuals, or with a kerion representing a hypersensitivity response by the host to the dermatophyte. Kerions more often are seen with either zoophilic or geophilic fungi owing to the inflammatory nature of these organisms. "Id" reactions may be seen in some individuals with particularly inflammatory lesions. These represent inflammatory lesions on the skin seen adjacent to or distant from the primary infection. Id reactions are thought to be another immune response to the dermatophyte infections. Tinea corporis refers to fungal infection of the trunk or extremities with a dermatophyte. Clinically, annular scaling patches or plaques (with the scale being present at the periphery or advancing margin of a lesion) are seen. The more central area generally is free of scale. Erythema is distributed throughout such a lesion. In addition, one may see pustules, papules, or nodules in cases of tinea corporis. Infection with *Microsporum canis*, *Trichophyton rubrum*, *Epidermophyton floccosum*, and other organisms may prove to be the cause of cases of tinea corporis. Tinea pedis describes infection of the feet with any of a variety of dermatophytes. Most isolates, however, are *T. rubrum* or *Trichophyton mentagrophytes*. Scaling, fissuring, and maceration between toes with erythema surrounding the area of involvement commonly are seen (see Fig. 65–22). In addition, some patients may present with a moccasin-like distribution of tinea pedis involving the soles of the feet. Children and adults also may present with tense, deeply situated vesicles over the instep of the feet. Tinea cruris describes infection of the groin area with any of a variety of dermatophytes. Clinically, affected patients will complain of some discomfort in the involved area and, on examination, will reveal erythema and maceration in the skin folds with a scaling advancing margin to the area of inflammation.

DIAGNOSIS. Examination of suitable clinical material (e.g., affected scalp hairs, skin scrapings from the advancing margin of lesions on the body, nails) with potassium hydroxide by standard light microscopy should reveal branching hyphae in cases of tinea corporis or tinea unguium. With suspected cases of tinea capitis, however, branching hyphae generally are not seen. Rather, multiple spores in or around infected hairs should be demonstrated. To perform a potassium hydroxide examination, the clinical material is placed on a glass slide, onto which either 10 or 20 percent potassium hydroxide is applied. After a coverslip is placed over the sample, the epithelial cells will "clear" after a period of 10 to 15 minutes. The specimen then is examined under the 20× or 40× objective to reveal hyphae or spores.

Suitable clinical material can be inoculated easily onto Sabouraud dextrose agar medium. Chloramphenicol and cycloheximide sometimes are added to Sabouraud to inhibit bacterial or saprophytic growth. Lastly, biopsy of representative skin lesions occasionally may be required.

TREATMENT. Whitfield ointment, which is a mixture of salicylic acid and benzoic acid, may be useful on dry lesions, such as these found in uncomplicated cases of tinea pedis. Tolnaftate has moderate utility in treating cases of tinea pedis and, perhaps, mild cases of tinea corporis or tinea cruris. Undecylenic acid is available in a variety of preparations and offers only mild to moderate success in the treatment of tinea pedis.

The imidazole class of antifungals offers significantly more effective treatment of dermatophyte infections than do any of the previously mentioned products. Some relatively newer imidazole compounds, such as econazole, sulconazole, ketoconazole, and oxiconazole, have been shown to offer similar efficacy with shorter treatment schedules than the over-the-counter imidazole compounds. These compounds are useful against dermatophytes, yeasts, and dermatiaceous fungi.

Naftifine and terbinafine offer fungicidal activity against dermatophytes with only limited utility for infections due to yeast.

Systemic therapy is indicated for widespread cases of tinea corporis, tinea unguium, and tinea capitis. Griseofulvin, used at a dose of 15 to 20 mg/kg/day in the liquid microsized form or 10 mg/kg/day in the ultramicrosized tablet form, continues to be the treatment of choice for most cases of tinea capitis. The drug (in either form) is effective for the treatment of tinea capitis and should be continued for 6 to 8 weeks. Routine testing of blood counts and liver functions is not needed in patients who are not receiving hepatotoxic drugs and who have no history of liver disease. Like griseofulvin, ketoconazole has been shown to have utility in treating widespread or resistant cases of tinea corporis. It is less useful than griseofulvin for treating tinea capitis, although some studies have shown its utility for treating resistant cases of tinea unguium. In children, long-term use should include monitoring of liver functions. In addition, there may be some concern in children owing to its effect on sterol biosynthesis.

Fluconazole is a biosynthesis product, that is, it is an azole product with a spectrum of activity similar to that of the other compounds in its class. It is unique in that its oral absorption is good and is not affected by gastric acidity. Another azole compound, itraconazole, has proved to be very useful against dermatophyte infections. Some studies have suggested its superiority to griseofulvin in the treatment of dermatophyte infections at a variety of sites on the body. It has shown to be of particular utility in the treatment of tinea unguium, in which it can be utilized for shorter courses of therapy than griseofulvin. Lastly, terbinafine demonstrates excellent activity against the wide variety of dermatophyte infections. Like itraconazole, this drug should prove to be particularly useful in view of its ability to clear tinea unguium with shorter courses of therapy than those currently required for griseofulvin.

TINEA VERSICOLOR

A distinctive yeast infection of the skin caused by *Malassezia furfur* can occur. In spite of its name, tinea versicolor is not due to dermatophyte infection. Hyper- or hypopigmented scaling patches or plaques are seen characteristically over the upper chest, back, face, or neck. Such lesions generally are asymptomatic, although some patients may complain of mild pruritus. Infections due to *M. furfur* may manifest with follicular papules or pustules affecting the same areas.

DIAGNOSIS. As with other fungal infections, potassium hydroxide examination of appropriate clinical material (involved skin or nails) generally demonstrates yeastlike structures. *Candida* is seen as budding yeast with hyphae or pseudohyphae, whereas *M. furfur* is seen as typical "spaghetti and meatballs." *Candida* grows readily on routine culture media, whereas culture of *M. furfur* requires special media.

TREATMENT. The allylamines, terbinafine, and to a lesser extent naftifine have some utility topically in the management of candidiasis.

Selenium sulfide shampoo applied as a lotion for limited periods is of proven utility in the management of this chronic disorder. Any of the azole compounds are useful as well. Although the newer oral azole compounds (itraconazole, fluconazole) are effective against this infection, they should not be considered to be of primary indication. Ketoconazole, however, has been utilized in a very short-term (bolus) form for the treatment of very widespread disease that is resistant to topical therapy.

DERMATIACEOUS FUNGAL INFECTIONS

Tinea nigra represents a superficial fungal infection most commonly involving the hands, but any areas of the body may be involved. Dark brown to black macules or patches may be seen. This infection is due to *Exophiala werneckii*, which can be cultured easily on Sabouraud agar.

Chromoblastomycosis may manifest as primarily cutaneous disease, with the organism being visualized within lesions as darkly pigmented flecks. Infiltrated inflammatory plaques, nodules, or tumors may be seen. More deeply situated skin infection may be due to chromoblastomycosis. Most cases of chromoblastomycosis are due to *Fonsecaea pedrosoi*. Diagnosis of suspected lesions can be made by potassium hydroxide examination, which reveals the characteristic bodies. Culture is indicated to diagnose the causative agent specifically.

Treatment of chromoblastomycosis is difficult. Surgical excision, when feasible, probably represents the primary line of therapy. Systemic therapy with ketoconazole or itraconazole shows some utility. Amphotericin B also has shown limited success in the management of chromoblastomycosis.

REFERENCES

1. Abbott, S. L., and Janda, J. M.: *Enterobacter cancerogenus ("Enterobacter taylorae")* infections associated with severe trauma or crush injuries. Am. J. Clin. Pathol. *107*:359–361, 1997.
2. Aghabian, R. V., and Conte, J. E., Jr.: Mammalian bite wounds. Ann. Emerg. Med. *9*:79–83, 1980.
3. Alves, E. V., Martins, J. E., Ribeiro, E. B., et al.: *Pityrosporum* folliculitis: Renal transplantation case report. J. Dermatol. *27*:49–51, 2000.
4. Amren, D. P., Anderson, A. S., and Wannamaker, L. W.: Perianal cellulitis associated with group A streptococci. Am. J. Dis. Child. *112*:546–552, 1966.
5. Anthony, B. F., Perlman, L. V., and Wannamaker, L. W.: Skin infections and acute nephritis in American Indian children. Pediatrics *39*:263–279, 1967.
6. Aranow, H., and Wood, W. B.: Staphylococcal infections simulating scarlet fever. J. A. M. A. *119*:1491–1495, 1942.
7. Aroni, K., Aivaliotis, M., and Davaris, P.: Disseminated and recurrent infundibular folliculitis (D. R. I. F.): Report of a case successfully treated with isotretinoin. J. Dermatol. *25*:51–53, 1998.
8. Ashford, R. U., Sargeant, P. D., and Lum, G. D.: Septic arthritis of the knee caused by *Edwardsiella tarda* after a catfish puncture wound. Med. J. Aust. *168*:443–444, 1998.
9. Avner, J. R., and Baker, M. D.: Dog bites in urban children. Pediatrics *88*:55–57, 1991.
10. Baker, C. J.: Group B streptococcal cellulitis-adenitis in infants. Am. J. Dis. Child. *136*:631–633, 1982.
11. Baker, M. D., and Moore, S. E.: Human bites in children: A six-year experience. Am. J. Dis. Child. *141*:1285–1290, 1987.
12. Baraff, L. J., Fine, R. N., and Knutson, D. W.: Poststreptococcal acute glomerulonephritis: Fact and controversy. Ann. Intern. Med. *91*:76–86, 1979.
13. Barnett, B. O., and Frieden, I. J.: Streptococcal skin diseases in children. Semin. Dermatol. *11*:3–10, 1992.
14. Benaoudia, F., Escande, F., and Simonet, M.: Infection due to *Actinobacillus lignieresii* after a horse bite. Eur. J. Clin. Microbiol. Infect. Dis. *13*:439–440, 1994.
15. Binnick, A. N., Klein, R. B., and Baughman, R. D.: Recurrent erysipelas caused by group B streptococcus organisms. Arch. Dermatol. *116*:798–799, 1980.
16. Bitnun, S.: Prophylactic antibiotics in recurrent erysipelas. Lancet *1*:345, 1985.
17. Bratcher, D.: Methicillin-resistant *Staphylococcus aureus* in the community. Pediatr. Infect. Dis. J. *20*:1167–1168, 2001.
18. Britton, J. W., Fajardo, J. E., and Krafte-Jacobs, B.: Clinical and laboratory observations: Comparison of mupirocin and erythromycin in the treatment of impetigo. J. Pediatr. *117*:827–829, 1990.
19. Brogan, T. V., Nizet, V., Waldhausen, J. H., et al.: Group A streptococcal necrotizing fasciitis complicating primary varicella: A series of fourteen patients. Pediatr. Infect. Dis. J. *14*:588–594, 1995.
20. Brook, I., and Frazier, E. H.: Clinical and microbiological features of necrotizing fasciitis. J. Clin. Microbiol. *33*:2382–2387, 1995.
21. Brothers, T. E., Tagge, D. U., Stutley, J. E., et al.: Magnetic resonance imaging differentiates between necrotizing and non-necrotizing fasciitis of the lower extremity. J. Am. Coll. Surg. *187*:416–421, 1998.
22. Buescher, E. S., Hebert, A., and Rapini, R. P.: *Staphylococcal botryomycosis* in a patient with the hyperimmunoglobulin E–recurrent infection syndrome. Pediatr. Infect. Dis. J. *7*:431–433, 1988.
23. Bukharie, H. A., Abdelhadi, M. S., Saeed, I. A., et al.: Emergence of methicillin-resistant *Staphylococcus aureus* as a community pathogen. Diagn. Microbiol. Infect. Dis. *40*:1–4, 2001.
24. Cawley, M. J., Briggs, M., Haith, L. R., et al.: Intravenous immunoglobulin as adjunctive treatment for streptococcal toxic shock syndrome associated with necrotizing fasciitis: Case report and review. Pharmacotherapy *19*:1094–1098, 1999.
25. Chandrasekar, P. H., Rolston, K. V. I., Kannangara, W., et al.: Hot tub–associated dermatitis due to *Pseudomonas aeruginosa:* Case report and review of the literature. Arch. Dermatol. *120*:1337–1340, 1984.
26. Chastain, M. A.: A cycle: Recurrent gram-negative folliculitis with *Citrobacter diversus (koseri)* following eradication of recurrent staphylococcal pyoderma. Arch. Dermatol. *136*:803, 2000.
27. Combs, J. T.: Perianal streptococcal disease. Clin. Pediatr. (Phila.) *39*:500, 2000.
28. Cox, N. H., Knowles, M. A., and Porteus, I. D.: Pre-septal cellulitis and facial erysipelas due to *Moraxella* species. Clin. Exp. Dermatol. *19*:321–323, 1994.
29. Crickx, B., Chevron, F., Sigal-Nahum, M., et al.: Erysipelas: Epidemiological, clinical and therapeutic data (111 cases). Ann. Dermatol. Venereol. *118*:545–546, 1991.
30. Dagan, R., and Bar-David, Y.: Double-blind study comparing erythromycin and mupirocin for treatment of impetigo in children: Implications of a high prevalence of erythromycin-resistant *Staphylococcus aureus* strains. Antimicrob. Agents Chemother. *36*:287–290, 1992.
31. Dajani, A. S., Ferrieri, P., and Wannamaker, L. W.: Natural history of impetigo: II. Etiologic agents and bacterial interactions. J. Clin. Invest. *51*:2863–2871, 1972.
32. Del Pozo, J., Garcia-Silva, J., Almagro, M., et al.: Ecthyma gangrenosum–like eruption associated with *Morganella morganii* infection. Br. J. Dermatol. *139*:520–521, 1998.
33. de Melker, H. E., and de Melker, R. A.: Dog bites: Publications on risk factors, infections, antibiotics, and primary wound closure. Ned. Tijdschr. Geneeskd. *140*:709–713, 1996.
34. Demidovich, C. W., Wittler, R. R., Ruff, M. E., et al.: Impetigo: Current etiology and comparison of penicillin, erythromycin, and cephalexin therapies. Am. J. Dis. Child. *144*:1313–1315, 1990.
35. Dillon, H. C.: The treatment of streptococcal skin infections. J. Pediatr. *76*:676–684, 1970.
36. Duvanel, T., Merot, Y., Harms, M., et al.: Prophylactic antibiotics in erysipelas. Lancet *1*:1401, 1985.
37. Ejlertsen, T., Gahrn-Hansen, B., Sogaard, P., et al.: *Pasteurella aerogenes* isolated from ulcers or wounds in humans with occupational exposure to pigs: A report of 7 Danish cases. Scand. J. Infect. Dis. *28*:567–570, 1996.
38. Eriksson, B. K.: Anal colonization of group G beta-hemolytic streptococci in relapsing erysipelas of the lower extremity. Clin. Infect. Dis. *29*:1319–1320, 1999.
39. Eron, L. J.: Targeting lurking pathogens in acute traumatic and chronic wounds. J. Emerg. Med. *17*:189–195, 1999.
40. Escande, F., Bailly, A., Bone, S., et al.: *Actinobacillus suis* infection after a pig bite. Lancet *348*:888, 1996.
41. Esterly, N. B., and Markowitz, M.: The treatment of pyoderma in children. J. A. M. A. *212*:1667–1670, 1970.
42. Esterly, N. B., Nelson, D. B., and Dunne, W. M., Jr.: Impetigo. Am. J. Dis. Child. *145*:125–126, 1991.
43. Falcone, P. A., Pricolo, V. E., and Edstrom, L. E.: Necrotizing fasciitis as a complication of chickenpox. Clin. Pediatr. (Phila.) *27*:339–343, 1988.
44. Farber, S., and Vawter, G. F.: Clinical pathological conference: The Children's Hospital Medical Center, Boston, Mass. J. Pediatr. *69*:485–489, 1966.
45. Farrell, L. D., Karl, S. R., Davis, P. K., et al.: Postoperative necrotizing fasciitis in children. Pediatrics *82*:874–879, 1988.
46. Feldman, C. A.: Staphylococcal scarlet fever. N. Engl. J. Med. *267*:877–878, 1962.
47. Fergie, J. E., Patrick, C. C., and Lott, L.: *Pseudomonas aeruginosa* cellulitis and ecthyma gangrenosum in immunocompromised children. Pediatr. Infect. Dis. J. *10*:496–500, 1991.
48. Ferrieri, P., Dajani, A. S., Wannamaker, L. W., et al.: Natural history of impetigo: I. Site sequence of acquisition and familial patterns of spread of cutaneous streptococci. J. Clin. Invest. *51*:2851–2862, 1972.
49. Fine, J. D., Miller, J. A., Harrist, T. J., et al.: Cutaneous lesions in disseminated candidiasis mimicking ecthyma gangrenosum. Am. J. Med. *70*:1133–1135, 1981.
50. Forbes, N., and Rankin, A. P.: Necrotizing fasciitis and non-steroidal anti-inflammatory drugs: A case series and review of the literature. N. Z. Med. J. *114*:3–6, 2001.
51. Ford, L. M., and Waksman, J.: Necrotizing fasciitis during primary varicella. Pediatrics *103*:783–790, 1999.
52. Fox, A. B., and Hambrick, G. W.: Recreationally associated *Pseudomonas aeruginosa* folliculitis. Arch. Dermatol. *120*:1304–1307, 1984.
53. Francis, Y. F., Richman, S., Hussain, S., et al.: *Aeromonas hydrophila* infection: Ecthyma gangrenosum with aplastic anemia. N. Y. State J. Med. *82*:1461–1464, 1982.
54. Frieden, I. J.: Blistering dactylitis caused by group B streptococci. Pediatr. Dermatol. *6*:300–302, 1989.
55. Givner, L. B., Abramson, J. S., and Wasilauskas, B.: Apparent increase in the incidence of invasive group A beta-hemolytic streptococcal disease in children. J. Pediatr. *118*:341–346, 1991.
56. Goldstein, E. J.: Current concepts on animal bites: Bacteriology and therapy. Curr. Clin. Top. Infect. Dis. *19*:99–111, 1999.
57. Gonzalez, A., Schachner, L. A., Cleary, T., et al.: Pyoderma in childhood. Adv. Dermatol. *4*:127–141, 1989.
58. Gorak, E. J., Yamada, S. M., and Brown, J. D.: Community-acquired methicillin-resistant *Staphylococcus aureus* in hospitalized adults and children without known risk factors. Clin. Infect. Dis. *29*:797–800, 1999.
59. Gosbell, I. B., Mercer, J. L., Neville, S. A., et al.: Non-multiresistant and multiresistant methicillin resistant *Staphylococcus aureus* in community-acquired infections. Med. J. Aust. *174*:627–630, 2001.
60. Greene, S. L., Su, W. P., and Muller, S. A.: Ecthyma gangrenosum: Report of clinical, histopathologic, and bacteriologic aspects of eight cases. J. Am. Acad. Dermatol. *11*:781–787, 1984.
61. Guberman, D., Gilead, L. T., Zlotogorski, A., et al.: Bullous erysipelas: A retrospective study of 26 patients. J. Am. Acad. Dermatol. *41*:733–737, 1999.

62. Gucluer, H., Ergun, T., and Demircay, Z.: Ecthyma gangrenosum. Int. J. Dermatol. *38*:299–302, 1999.
63. Hall, W. D., Blumberg, R. W., and Moody, M. D.: Studies in children with impetigo: Bacteriology, serology, and incidence of glomerulonephritis. Am. J. Dis. Child. *125*:800–806, 1973.
64. Halperin, S. A.: *Haemophilus influenzae* type b and its role in diseases of the head and neck. J. Otolaryngol. *19*:169–174, 1990.
65. Hauger, S. B.: Facial cellulitis: An early indicator of group B streptococcal bacteremia. Pediatrics *67*:376–377, 1981.
66. Hayden, G. F.: Skin diseases encountered in a pediatric clinic: A one-year prospective study. Am. J. Dis. Child. *139*:36–38, 1985.
67. Hays, G. C., and Mullard, J. E.: Blistering distal dactylitis: A clinically recognizable streptococcal infection. Pediatrics *56*:129–131, 1975.
68. Herold, B. C., Immergluck, L. C., Maranan, M. C., et al.: Community-acquired methicillin-resistant *Staphylococcus aureus* in children with no identified predisposing risk. J. A. M. A. *279*:593–598, 1998.
69. Hewitt, W. D., and Farrar, W. E.: Bacteremia and ecthyma caused by *Streptococcus pyogenes* in a patient with acquired immunodeficiency syndrome. Am. J. Med. Sci. *295*:52–54, 1988.
70. Hirn, M., and Niinikoski, J.: Management of perineal necrotizing fasciitis (Fournier's gangrene). Ann. Chir. Gynaecol. *78*:277–281, 1989.
71. Ho, P. W., Pien, F. D., and Hamburg, D.: Value of cultures in patients with acute cellulitis. South. Med. J. *72*:1402–1403, 1979.
72. Hoeger, P. H., Lenz, W., Boutonnier, A., et al.: Staphylococcal skin colonization in children with atopic dermatitis: Prevalence, persistence, and transmission of toxigenic and nontoxigenic strains. J. Infect. Dis. *165*:1064–1068, 1992.
73. Hsieh, S., and Babl, F. E.: *Serratia marcescens* cellulitis following an iguana bite. Clin. Infect. Dis. *28*:1181–1182, 1999.
74. Jackson, M. A., Colombo, J., and Boldrey, A.: Streptococcal fasciitis with toxic shock syndrome in the pediatric patient. Orthop. Nurs. *22*:4–8, 2003.
75. Jarvis, W. R.: The epidemiology of colonization. Infect. Control Hosp. Epidemiol. *17*:47–52, 1996.
76. Kelly, C., Taplin, D., and Allen, A. M.: Streptococcal ecthyma: Treatment with benzathine penicillin G. Arch. Dermatol. *103*:306–310, 1971.
77. Kimyai-Asadi, A., Tausk, F. A., and Nousari, H. C.: Ecthyma secondary to herpes simplex virus infection. Clin. Infect. Dis. *29*:454–455, 1999.
78. Kocher, M. S., Coombs, C. J., and Upton, J., 3rd: Actinomycetoma of the phalanx in an immunocompromised patient: A case report. J. Hand Surg. [Am.] *21*:515–517, 1996.
79. Kokx, N. P., Comstock, J. A., and Facklam, R. R.: Streptococcal perianal disease in children. Pediatrics *80*:659–663, 1987.
80. Lacroix, J., Cau, D., Pascal, C., et al.: A case of erysipelas caused by *Haemophilus influenzae.* Union Med. Can. *112*:272, 1983.
81. Larson, E. L., Hughes, C. A., Pyrek, J. D., et al.: Changes in bacterial flora associated with skin damage on hands of health care personnel. Am. J. Infect. Control *26*:513–521, 1998.
82. Lesko, S. M., O'Brien, K. L., Schwartz, B., et al.: Invasive group A streptococcal infection and nonsteroidal antiinflammatory drug use among children with primary varicella. Pediatrics *107*:1108–1115, 2001.
83. Levy, R., and Schlaeffer, F.: Successful treatment of a patient with recurrent furunculosis by vitamin C: Improvement of clinical course and of impaired neutrophil functions. Int. J. Dermatol. *32*:832–834, 1993.
84. Levy, R., Shriker, O., Porath, A., et al.: Vitamin C for the treatment of recurrent furunculosis in patients with impaired neutrophil functions. J. Infect. Dis. *173*:1502–1505, 1996.
85. Lion, C., Conroy, M. C., Dupuy, M. L., et al.: *Pasteurella* "SP" group infection after a guinea pig bite. Lancet *346*:901–902, 1995.
86. Loebl, E. C., Marvin, J. A., Curreri, P. W., et al.: Survival with ecthyma gangrenosum, a previously fatal complication of burns. J. Trauma 14:370–377, 1974.
87. Mandell, I. N., Feiner, H. D., Price, N. M., et al.: *Pseudomonas cepacia* endocarditis and ecthyma gangrenosum. Arch. Dematol. *113*:199–202, 1977.
88. Marks, V. J., and Maksimak, M.: Perianal streptococcal cellulitis. J. Am. Acad. Dermatol. *18*:587–588, 1988.
89. McLinn, S.: A bacteriologically controlled, randomized study comparing the efficacy of 2% mupirocin ointment (Bactroban) with oral erythromycin in the treatment of patients with impetigo. J. Am. Acad. Dermatol. *22*:883–885, 1990.
90. Meredith, F. T., and Sexton, D. J.: *Mycobacterium abscessus* osteomyelitis following a plantar puncture wound. Clin. Infect. Dis. *23*:651–653, 1996.
91. Mereghetti, L., van der Mee-Marquet, N., Dubost, A. F., et al.: *Nocardia otitidis-caviarum* infection of a traumatic skin wound. Eur. J. Clin. Microbiol. Infect. Dis. *16*:383–384, 1997.
92. Milstein, P., and Gleckman, R.: Pneumococcal erysipelas: A unique case in an adult. Am. J. Med. *59*:293–296, 1975.
93. Miron, D., El, A. L., Zuker, M., et al.: *Mycobacterium fortuitum* osteomyelitis of the cuboid after nail puncture wound. Pediatr. Infect. Dis. J. *19*:483–485, 2000.
94. Mogielnicki, N. P., Schwartzman, J. D., and Elliott, J. A.: Perineal group A streptococcal disease in a pediatric practice. Pediatrics *106*:276–281, 2000.
95. Moyer, C. D., Sykes, P. A., and Rayner, J. M.: *Aeromonas hydrophila* septicaemia producing ecthyma gangrenosum in a child with leukaemia. Scand. J. Infect. Dis. *9*:151–153, 1977.
96. Murphy, J. J., Granger, R., Blair, G. K., et al.: Necrotizing fasciitis in childhood. J. Pediatr. Surg. *30*:1131–1134, 1995.
97. Murphy, O., Marsh, P. J., Gray, J., et al.: Ecthyma gangrenosum occurring at sites of iatrogenic trauma in pediatric oncology patients. Med. Pediatr. Oncol. *27*:62–63, 1996.
98. O'Brien, K., Schwartz, B., Lesko, S. M., et al.: Necrotizing fasciitis during primary varicella. Pediatrics *103*:783–790, 1999.
99. Ohana, N., Keness, J., Verner, E., et al.: Skin-isolated, community-acquired *Staphylococcus aureus:* In vitro resistance to methicillin and erythromycin. J. Am. Acad. Dermatol. *21*:544–546, 1989.
100. Patel, M., Ahrens, J. C., Moyer, D. V., et al.: Pneumococcal soft-tissue infections: A problem deserving more recognition. Clin. Infect. Dis. *19*:149–151, 1994.
101. Pouryousefi, A., Foland, J., Michie, C., et al.: Ecthyma gangrenosum as a very early herald of acute lymphoblastic leukaemia. J. Paediatr. Child Health *35*:505–506, 1999.
102. Rabinowitz, R., and Lewin, E. B.: Gangrene of the genitalia in children with *Pseudomonas* sepsis. J. Urol. *124*:431–432, 1980.
103. Rahmouni, A., Chosidow, O., Mathieu, D., et al.: MR imaging in acute infectious cellulitis. Radiology *192*:493–496, 1994.
104. Rhie, S., Turcios, R., Buckley, H., et al.: Clinical features and treatment of *Malassezia* folliculitis with fluconazole in orthotopic heart transplant recipients. J. Heart Lung Transplant. *19*:215–219, 2000.
105. Rodot, S., Lacour, J. P., van Elslande, L., et al.: Ecthyma gangrenosum caused by *Klebsiella pneumoniae.* Int. J. Dermatol. *34*:216–217, 1995.
106. Rolle, U.: *Haemophilus influenzae* cellulitis after bite injuries in children. J. Pediatr. Surg. *35*:1408–1409, 2000.
107. Roujeau, J. C.: Necrotizing fasciitis: Clinical criteria and risk factors. Ann. Dermatol. Venereol. *128*:376–381, 2001.
108. Schwarz, G., Sagy, M., and Barzilay, Z.: Multifocal necrotizing fasciitis in varicella. Pediatr. Emerg. Care *5*:31–33, 1989.
109. Semel, J. D., and Trenholme, G.: *Aeromonas hydrophila* water-associated traumatic wound infections: A review. J. Trauma *30*:324–327, 1990.
110. Sevinsky, L. D., Viecens, C., Ballesteros, D. O., et al.: Ecthyma gangrenosum: A cutaneous manifestation of *Pseudomonas aeruginosa* sepsis. J. Am. Acad. Dermatol. *29*:104–106, 1993.
111. Shama, S., and Calandra, G. B.: Atypical erysipelas caused by group G streptococci in a patient with cured Hodgkin's disease. Arch. Dermatol. *118*:934–936, 1982.
112. Shopsin, B., Mathema, B., Martinez, J., et al.: Prevalence of methicillin-resistant and methicillin-susceptible *Staphylococcus aureus* in the community. J. Infect. Dis. *182*:359–362, 2000.
113. Smith, K. J., Neafie, R., Yeager, J., et al.: *Micrococcus folliculitis* in HIV-1 disease. Br. J. Dermatol. *141*:558–561, 1999.
114. Smith, P. F., Meadowcroft, A. M., and May, D. B.: Treating mammalian bite wounds. J. Clin. Pharm. Ther. *25*:85–99, 2000.
115. Sokol, R. J., and Bowden, R. A.: An erysipelas-like scalp cellulitis due to *Haemophilus influenzae* type b. J. Pediatr. *96*:60–61, 1980.
116. Sosin, D. M., Gunn, R. A., Ford, W. L., et al.: An outbreak of furunculosis among high school athletes. Am. J. Sports Med. *17*:828–832, 1989.
117. Stone, L., Codère, F., and Ma, S. A.: Streptococcal lid necrosis in previously healthy children. Can. J. Ophthalmol. *26*:386–390, 1991.
118. Turnbull, D., and Parry, M. F.: Ecthyma-like skin lesions caused by *Staphylococcus aureus.* Arch. Intern. Med. *141*:689, 1981.
119. Umbert, I. J., Winkelmann, R. K., Oliver, G. F., et al.: Necrotizing fasciitis: A clinical, microbiologic, and histopathologic study of 14 patients. J. Am. Acad. Dermatol. *20*:774–781, 1989.
120. Vaillant, L.: Diagnostic criteria for erysipelas. Ann. Dermatol. Venereol. *128*:326–333, 2001.
121. Varghese, R., Melo, J. C., Chun, C. H., et al.: Erysipelas-like syndrome caused by *Streptococcus pneumoniae*. South. Med. J. *72*:757–758, 1979.
122. Wenger, P. N., Brown, J. M., McNeil, M. M., et al.: *Nocardia farcinica* sternotomy site infections in patients following open heart surgery. J. Infect. Dis. *178*:1539–1543, 1998.
123. Wilfert, C. M.: Epidemiology of *Haemophilus influenzae* type b infections. Pediatrics *85*:631–635, 1990.
124. Zentner, J., Hassler, W., and Petersen, D.: A wooden foreign body penetrating the superior orbital fissure. Neurochirurgia *34*:188–190, 1991.
125. Zerr, D. M., Alexander, E. R., Duchin, J. S., et al.: A case-control study of necrotizing fasciitis during primary varicella. Pediatrics *105*:1372–1373, 2000.
126. Zerr, D. M., and Rubens, C. E.: NSAIDs and necrotizing fasciitis. Pediatr. Infect. Dis. J. *18*:724–725, 1999.
127. Zittergruen, M., and Grose, C.: Magnetic resonance imaging for early diagnosis of necrotizing fasciitis. Pediatr. Emerg. Care *9*:26–28, 1993.

SECTION XI

Ocular Infections

CHAPTER 68

Ocular Infectious Diseases

DAVID K. COATS ■ THOMAS S. CAROTHERS ■ KATHRYN BRADY-MCCREERY ■ EVELYN A. PAYSSE

The eye may be affected by a wide spectrum of infections and infestations that manifest as primary disease or as part of a larger systemic process. Many infections are vision threatening, and others have important implications affecting the generalized disease process. Findings in the eye, for example, can aid in narrowing the differential diagnosis in some cases of systemic disease such as congenital viral infections. A helpful approach to delineating the ophthalmic manifestations of infectious diseases is use of an anatomic scheme that considers the primary site of involvement. This chapter proceeds systematically from infections involving the eyelids and ocular surface to those involving intraocular structures, concluding with a discussion of infections involving deeper tissues in the orbit. Some overlap and duplication are unavoidable because disease involvement that is truly isolated to a single anatomic component of the eye or orbit is an unusual occurrence. Most infectious processes involving the eye can be diagnosed accurately with a careful history and ophthalmic screening examination. Simple tools such as a penlight and a direct ophthalmoscope facilitate making a diagnosis in most cases, although special ophthalmologic testing is required in some cases.

Infections of the Eyelids

Despite being only 2 mm thick, the eyelid anatomy is complex and elegant. The eyelids are composed of dense connective tissue, hair follicles, sweat and sebaceous glands, smooth and striated muscles, sensory and motor nerves, and vascular elements. The skin covering the eyelids is the thinnest of the entire body. The internal surface of the eyelid, that part adjacent to the eye, is covered by conjunctiva. In this location, it is known as the palpebral conjunctiva; bulbar conjunctiva covers the surface of the globe itself. Sebaceous glands, known as the glands of Zeis, are associated with hair follicles. Meibomian glands, located within the tarsal plates of the eyelids, also are sebaceous. They drain at the posterior aspect of the lid margin.

Infection of the eyelids may be generalized or focal. Involvement of the skin by an infectious agent is referred to as dermatoblepharitis. *Staphylococcus aureus* and *Staphylococcus epidermidis* infections predominate. The exception is angular blepharitis, characterized by inflammation in the lateral canthal region, which frequently is caused by *Moraxella* spp. Impetigo or erysipelas of the eyelids may be caused by *Streptococcus pyogenes*. A variety of infestations, including *Demodex folliculorum*, *Sarcoptes scabiei* (scabies), *Pediculus capitis*, and the pubic louse *Phthirus pubis*, may involve the eyelids.

Although more commonly found in adults, lid margin infection does occur in children. The anterior lid margin infections most frequently encountered include bacterial blepharitis, molluscum contagiosum, and parasitic diseases. Posterior lid margin infections include those associated with chronic meibomian gland dysfunction. Herpes simplex virus (HSV) and herpes zoster virus (HZV) may involve the lid and lid margin and are discussed elsewhere in this chapter.

ANTERIOR EYELID INFECTION

Staphylococcal Blepharitis

Staphylococcal eyelid infection may be an acute or chronic condition. The chronic form of the disease typically manifests as crusting of the lid margins, especially on awakening. Thickening of the lid margin, seen most easily on slit-lamp examination, is a frequent manifestation. Mild, chronic conjunctival infection often occurs as a spillover phenomenon caused by local reaction to materials secreted by the infecting organism. A child with staphylococcal blepharitis may be completely asymptomatic or may complain of ocular discomfort, burning, or foreign body sensation. Lid hygiene typically is all that is required to treat the condition. Eyelid scrubs, with attention to the lid margin, are recommended twice daily using warm water on a clean washcloth or a 50:50 mixture of baby shampoo and warm water. Both procedures are effective in reducing the concentration of local bacterial flora and symptoms from chronic staphylococcal infection. A 2- to 4-week course of erythromycin or bacitracin ophthalmic ointment applied twice daily may hasten resolution and reduce exacerbation and recurrence.

Molluscum Contagiosum Infection

Molluscum contagiosum is a member of the family *Poxviridae*. Eyelid infection typically is unilateral. Infection may be transmitted by skin-to-skin contact or fomites or by autoinoculation. Epidemics among people who use public pools and in closed communities have been reported.[129] Eyelid manifestations typically include an isolated nodule or nodules with mild surrounding inflammation. The nodules vary in size but typically are 1 to 3 mm in diameter. Older lesions often become umbilicated, developing a white or waxy core. Mild conjunctival injection often accompanies lesions on or near the eyelid margin. The associated conjunctivitis occasionally can be severe and chronic. In chronic cases, corneal epithelial disease, including subepithelial infiltrates, may develop.

Molluscum infection is considered to be self-limiting, with most lesions spontaneously resolving within a few months. However, the infection can be recalcitrant and problematic in immunocompromised patients and usually requires treatment.[183, 190] Despite the self-limited nature of the disease in immunocompetent individuals, treatment often is advocated to prevent auto-inoculation that may prolong the course of the disease. Treatment also may be offered to provide symptomatic relief. Mechanical treatments such as cryotherapy, expression or curettage of the central core, excision, and cautery have been effective.[37] Medical treatments that have been effective against molluscum infection remote from the eye include 1% imiquimod cream[166] and podophyllotoxin.[165] These agents are not recommended for treatment of periocular lesions because of the possibility of injury to the eye if the agent comes into contact with it.

PARASITIC EYELID DISEASE

Phthirus pubis Infestation

The crab louse, *Phthirus pubis,* is a tiny insect well adapted to living in coarse, widely spaced hair. Infestation most commonly involves pubic, axillary, and body hair. The organism is transmitted by direct person-to-person contact and possibly by fomite transmission.[155] Eyelid infestation often is a marker for sexually transmitted diseases in adult patients.[155] Affected patients typically present with a unilateral, chronic blepharoconjunctivitis, although some may be asymptomatic. Although unmagnified ocular examination may reveal signs of the disease, diagnosis is facilitated by slit-lamp examination that offers a magnified view of the eyelid margins and eyelashes. Slit-lamp examination reveals adult lice firmly adherent to the eyelashes and egg cases (i.e., nits) attached to the proximal ends of hair shafts. Reddish-brown flecks of louse excreta often are found at the bases of the lashes.[36]

Treatment can be facilitated by simple mechanical removal of the lice and associated nits under magnification offered by the slit-lamp or other devices. Medical treatment often is preferred for young children because of their inability to tolerate mechanical removal. The organisms can be smothered by application of a bland ointment such as petrolatum jelly applied four times each day to the eyelids. Mercuric oxide eye ointment has been used in the past and probably is directly toxic to the louse. The use of this preparation now is considered outmoded by some physicians.[29] Physostigmine ophthalmic ointment, an anticholinesterase agent, is a treatment commonly preferred by ophthalmologists. The agent, which inhibits nerve transmission in the insect, is applied to the eyelid margin twice daily. If it comes into contact with the eye, it has several significant side effects, the most bothersome of which is stimulation of accommodation, which can produce blurred vision that may last for several hours. Medical treatments should be continued for as long as 2 weeks to ensure treatment of lice that emerge from the nits during the normal life cycle of the organism.[36]

Patients also should undergo general physical examination to assess for involvement of other body regions. Lindane shampoo scrubs of the scalp, pubic hair, and body are recommended if these areas are found to be infested. Clothing and bed linens should be laundered, and family members should be examined and treated as necessary. Follow-up 4 to 6 weeks after treatment is recommended to detect reinfestation.

Demodex Infection

Demodex folliculorum and *Demodex brevis* are mites that frequently infest hair follicles in humans, including the hair follicles of the eyelids.[54] The organisms generally are considered nonpathogenic parasites, although they have been postulated to cause obstruction of sebaceous glands in the eyelids that leads to increased hordeola formation. Rosacea-like eruptions also have been attributed to *Demodex,* and one pathologic report demonstrated a granulomatous dermal inflammation associated with *Demodex* infection.[133] Because of the frequency of infestation and the paucity of definitive disease caused by the organism, treatment often is considered unnecessary.

POSTERIOR EYELID INFECTION

Hordeolum

A hordeolum (i.e., stye) is an infection of the sebaceous glands in the eyelids. When the glands of Zeis are involved, the term *external hordeolum* is used. The lesion typically points to the skin surface. When meibomian glands are involved, the term *internal hordeolum* is used. An internal hordeolum may point toward the skin or toward the palpebral conjunctiva. *S. aureus* is the most common causal agent in cases of internal and external hordeola.

Patients with disease of the lid margin, such as those with chronic blepharitis, seborrhea, and rosacea, are prone to develop recurrent hordeolum, especially during the first decade of life. Hordeola manifest as erythematous, elevated, tender nodules. The nodules typically are 5 to 10 mm in diameter and usually are solitary. Occasionally, they may be multiple or bilateral. Patients with a history of recurrent hordeolum may present with hordeola in various stages of evolution or resolution.

The condition usually is self-limiting and typically resolves within 5 to 7 days with spontaneous drainage of the abscess. Warm compresses may hasten resolution and improve comfort. Parents should be advised to place a clean washcloth soaked in warm tap water on the involved eyelid for 10 to 15 minutes several times each day. Only warm tap water should be used, and parents should be advised to ensure that the water is not hot enough to result in a burn. For significant coexisting blepharitis, a topical antibiotic such as erythromycin ointment may prove useful by reducing the normal bacterial skin flora of the eyelid and reducing the risk of recurrence. Systemic antibiotics rarely are indicated for acute hordeolum. Children with frequent recurrences, however, may benefit from a short course of systemic antibiotics such as erythromycin (younger than 12 years old) or tetracycline (older than 12 years old). These agents further decrease the bacterial flora on the eyelid and may further reduce the risk of recurrences. Lid hygiene efforts, as described for the treatment of staphylococcal blepharitis, should be instituted. Long-term lid hygiene efforts should be maintained for children with recurrent hordeola. Surgical drainage of a hordeolum usually is unnecessary.

Chalazion

A chalazion is a lipogranuloma of a meibomian gland that develops as a foreign body reaction to secretions produced by the gland that have been extruded into the surrounding tissues. A chalazion may develop after resolution of an internal hordeolum, in which case it is preceded by an acute stage, or it may develop primarily, without a preceding acute inflammatory phase. A typical chalazion manifests as a round, nontender nodule within the substance of the eyelid. Multiple and bilateral chalazions may occur in susceptible patients. The lesion typically is 2 to 10 mm in diameter and occasionally larger.

Spontaneous resolution of smaller chalazions can be anticipated after a period of observation without treatment, sometimes as long as several months. Larger lesions, particularly those more than 10 mm in diameter, frequently do not resolve without specific treatment. For cases with an acute or chronic inflammatory component, application of warm compresses may be beneficial. Surgical intervention may be warranted to treat medium- to large-sized chalazions that are cosmetically objectionable, that cause astigmatism by pressing on the cornea, that produce mechanical ptosis, or that cause other symptoms. The most common surgical treatment offered is incision and curettage through an internal incision on the palpebral conjunctival surface. Surgery is highly effective but unfortunately requires general anesthesia when done for most young children. Because of the need for general anesthesia, we typically recommend deferring surgical treatment until several months have elapsed without spontaneous resolution, when possible. Earlier intervention is recommended if the chalazion is particularly large, if pigmentary changes have developed in the overlying skin, or if astigmatism or ptosis is present in a young child at risk for development of amblyopia.

Intralesional steroid injection alone,[48, 135] or in combination with excision and drainage,[56] has been reported to accelerate resolution of a chalazion. The major drawback of intralesional steroid injection is the risk of complications developing for an otherwise relatively benign condition. Steroid injection rarely can result in sterile abscess formation or eyelid necrosis. Intralesional injections are done best with a chalazion clamp in place to protect the underlying globe from accidental needle trauma occurring during injection. This device places a metal plate between the chalazion and the eye.

DACRYOADENITIS

Dacryoadenitis is an uncommon ophthalmic condition. Even in a busy ophthalmology practice, dacryoadenitis was diagnosed only in approximately 1 of every 10,000 patient visits.[141] The clinical presentation is variable.

Localized tenderness and swelling of the temporal aspect of the upper eyelid usually occurs, often producing an S-shaped deformity of the lid margin. Pain often is a predominant feature. Associated signs and symptoms include fever, follicular conjunctivitis, mucopurulent discharge, limited extraocular movements, and proptosis.[141] Before the era of widespread immunization, mumps was a leading cause of dacryoadenitis. Bacteria such as staphylococci, streptococci, and gonococci also have been implicated. Exceedingly rare organisms such as *Brucella* occasionally are implicated in bacterial cases.[10] Epstein-Barr virus (EBV) has been implicated as the etiologic agent in a large proportion of nonsuppurative cases. Marked regional lymphadenopathy may be a distinguishing feature of EBV dacryoadenitis.[141]

Appropriate laboratory evaluation includes Gram stain and culture of mucopurulent discharge from the eye. Neuroimaging is indicated when the patient has severe inflammation, proptosis, limitation of extraocular movements, or other orbital signs to rule out a more generalized orbital process. Biopsy of the lacrimal gland may be required in cases not responding to standard medical treatment or when atypical features are identified on clinical examination or radiographic studies. Blood cultures are indicated for patients with signs of systemic toxicity.

Intravenous nafcillin or vancomycin is a reasonable initial antibiotic choice for severe dacryoadenitis caused by gram-positive organisms. Oral antistaphylococcal agents may be used for less severe cases. For gram-negative cases, ceftazidime or other similar agents should be considered. For suppurative cases without Gram-stain guidance, intravenous nafcillin or vancomycin should be considered as initial therapy in severe cases, and oral antistaphylococcal agents are used in less acute cases. Therapy in the form of warm compresses and oral analgesics are indicated for nonsuppurative dacryoadenitis. Serum testing for evidence of EBV infection should be considered in patients with regional lymphadenopathy.[141] Noninfectious causes of dacryoadenitis include sarcoidosis, Sjögren syndrome, leukemia, lymphoma, eosinophilic granuloma, and orbital pseudotumor. Noninfectious cases of dacryoadenitis sometimes can be difficult to distinguish from infectious cases. Lacrimal gland biopsy and neuroimaging usually are necessary to establish a diagnosis in noninfectious cases.[107]

DACRYOCYSTITIS

Dacryocystitis may result from congenital or acquired lacrimal outflow obstruction. Simple membranous nasolacrimal duct obstruction occurs in as many as 6 percent of the newborn population, and intermittent, mild, self-limiting bacterial infection is a commonly associated feature. More severe infection of the lacrimal sac results in dacryocystitis. It manifests as an acute episode of erythema, pain, and swelling in the medial canthal region. Swelling typically is located below the medial canthal tendon. Marked epiphora (i.e., increased tearing) is a common finding, and a mucopurulent discharge frequently can be expressed through the lacrimal punctum if the proximal aspect of the lacrimal drainage system is not obstructed. If the infection has resulted in or from an obstruction proximal and distal to the lacrimal sac, the overlying skin may become tense as the nasolacrimal sac distends in response to the infectious process. Formation of a fistula to the overlying skin may occur, and surgical excision of the fistula tract often is needed after the acute process has resolved. Dacryocystitis is a particularly common finding in neonates who present with a dacryocele, with as many as 60 percent of affected neonates developing dacryocystitis.[131]

Aerobic and anaerobic bacteria and fungi may produce dacryocystitis.[25–27] In one study, *S. epidermidis* and *Pseudomonas* spp. were the aerobic organisms most commonly identified, and *Peptostreptococcus* spp. and *Propionibacterium* spp. were the anaerobes most commonly isolated. Less common agents include *Escherichia coli, Pseudomonas* spp., *Haemophilus influenzae, Pasteurella multocida,* and various anaerobes.

Laboratory investigation should include aerobic and anaerobic culture of mucopurulent discharge from the lacrimal sac. Mild massage of the lacrimal sac may be used to facilitate expression of material for Gram stain and culture. Sepsis work-up should be considered for children who are acutely ill and for young infants.

Intravenous nafcillin or vancomycin or both agents are good initial therapeutic choices for serious gram-positive infections. Mild cases in older children can be treated with oral agents. Intravenous ceftazidime is a reasonable initial antibiotic choice for gram-negative dacryocystitis. Oral ciprofloxacin is useful for less severe cases in adult patients, but the drug is not approved for use in children. Intravenous nafcillin or vancomycin typically provides good initial empirical therapy in patients without Gram-stain guidance.

Ophthalmologic consultation should be requested in all cases of acute dacryocystitis. Decompression of the lacrimal sac by aspiration, incision and drainage, or probing the proximal lacrimal drainage system may be needed to hasten resolution. Probing of the distal lacrimal system (i.e., lacrimal duct) often is deferred until the acute infection has subsided, although probing during the acute infection has been reported to be a safe and effective adjunct to treatment.[136] Mucopurulent material aspirated or obtained during surgical decompression should be sent for appropriate cultures.

PRESEPTAL (PERIORBITAL) CELLULITIS

The term *preseptal cellulitis* refers to an infectious process in the eyelids that is isolated to regions anterior to the orbital septum. The orbital septum is a thin layer of fascia that extends vertically from the periosteum of the orbital rim to the tarsal plate within the eyelids. Although the septum is penetrated by nerves and vascular structures, it provides a barrier that slows the spread of infectious agents into deeper orbital and retro-orbital structures.[161] Typical signs and symptoms of preseptal cellulites include erythema and edema of the eyelids. Distinctively absent are signs of deeper orbital involvement such as restricted ocular motility, pain with eye movements, and proptosis. Preseptal cellulitis may occur after trauma or result from the spread of infection from adjacent structures, such as adjacent skin and upper respiratory system.[181]

Post-traumatic Preseptal Cellulitis

Post-traumatic preseptal cellulitis occurs after puncture wounds of the lids, face, or scalp. It also may occur after blunt trauma with no obvious entry wound. The etiologic agents most commonly identified are *S. aureus* and *S. pyogenes,* and polymicrobial infections occur. Other bacterial causes include non–spore-forming anaerobes, such as *Peptococcus, Peptostreptococcus,* and *Bacteroides.* Infection by aerobic gram-negative bacilli is an uncommon finding.[8] *Pasteurella multocida* is the organism most commonly producing post-traumatic preseptal cellulitis after dog and cat bites.[102, 132]

Clinical signs and symptoms are determined in large part by the severity of the injury, the interval since injury, and the infecting organisms. The involved lids are edematous, erythematous, and typically quite tender. Fluctuation of the subcutaneous tissues may be seen if an abscess has developed. Swelling of the uninvolved contralateral eyelids may occur as a result of lymphedema. As with any form of isolated preseptal cellulitis, vision is unaffected, and proptosis and eye movement disturbances are absent. On rare occasions, eyelid edema may be sufficiently severe to preclude evaluation of the eye. Neuroimaging is required in such cases to assess the globe and to rule out involvement of structures posterior to the orbital septum. Ophthalmologic consultation is critical in cases of severe post-traumatic preseptal cellulitis because of the potential for a concurrent globe injury.

Laboratory analysis includes Gram stain and aerobic and anaerobic cultures of mucopurulent material to aid with therapeutic decisions. Amoxicillin-clavulanate or a related agent is the drug of choice for treating post-traumatic cellulitis caused by a dog bite because of the high prevalence of *P. multocida.* Tetanus prophylaxis should be considered as guided by standard recommendations. Surgical drainage of large abscesses may be required if a rapid response to antimicrobial therapy does not occur.

Nontraumatic Preseptal Cellulitis

The clinical features of nonsuppurative, nontraumatic preseptal cellulitis depend to a large degree on the causative agent. Erythema and swelling of the involved eyelids are typical occurrences and often are accompanied by pain. Signs of orbital infection, such as altered vision, proptosis, and eye movement abnormalities, are absent.

Before the advent of the *H. influenzae* type b vaccine (Hib vaccine), the organism was a frequent cause of nonsuppurative preseptal cellulitis in children. The agent is seen infrequently as a cause of preseptal cellulitis today.[44] It was a particularly dangerous agent because of a high risk of spread to the central nervous system (CNS), which occurred in as many as 2 to 3 percent of patients. Although they seldom occur today, Hib infections still may be encountered. Like many other infecting organisms, Hib gains access to the subcutaneous tissues through infected nasal passages.

Streptococcus pneumoniae is now the most common bacterial cause of preseptal cellulitis in the pediatric age group.[44] It occurs in association with upper respiratory tract infection, although constitutional symptoms usually are less pronounced than are those associated with Hib infection. A variety of other bacterial agents may cause preseptal cellulitis, but they are seen less commonly.

Adenovirus is another particularly common cause of preseptal cellulitis in children. Adenovirus is an important consideration in the differential diagnosis of childhood preseptal cellulitis because, although the condition is self-limiting, it can occasionally mimic bacterial infection. Adenovirus can be recognized by its characteristic copious discharge, which may be serous. Swelling of the lid may be prominent, but erythema usually is minimal. Preauricular lymphadenopathy often occurs in older children, and marked conjunctival hyperemia with or without chemosis and subconjunctival hemorrhage may be present. Photophobia also may be noticed in cases of concurrent punctate keratopathy. A history of having had recent contact with other infected individuals usually is noted and should be sought. Care should be taken to avoid spreading the infection to family members, medical personnel, and other contacts.

Hospital admission should be considered for bacterial preseptal cellulitis in children younger than 1 year of age. Hospitalization also is important for children with signs of systemic toxicity and children with inadequate immunization to *H. influenzae.* Sepsis work-up is indicated for children with signs of systemic toxicity and for extremely young children. Ophthalmologic consultation is recommended if orbital involvement is suspected or if clinical examination is inconclusive. Computed tomography (CT) scanning usually is unnecessary for isolated preseptal cellulitis. Cultures of blood obtained from patients with preseptal cellulitis usually are negative but are more likely to be positive in children younger than 2 years of age.[44] Culture of conjunctival discharge often is done but rarely has significant diagnostic benefit.

Antibacterial treatment should include intravenous agents for young children and for those with signs of serious systemic infection. Intravenous cefuroxime or a combination of nafcillin plus cefotaxime or ceftriaxone is recommended frequently for empirical therapy. Outpatient treatment with intramuscular or oral antibiotics is reasonable for older, less acutely ill children. Systemic antibiotics should be continued for 7 to 10 days. Patients initially started on intravenous antibiotics can be converted to an oral antibiotic after they have been afebrile for at least 24 hours, unless the possibility of development of sepsis or meningitis remains a concern.

Orbital Cellulitis

Bacterial infection of orbital structures posterior to the orbital septum is the most common cause of acute orbital inflammation. Orbital cellulitis occurs more commonly in children and more frequently during cold weather, a time when sinusitis is more prevalent.

Presenting signs and symptoms can vary from mild inflammation to severe and fulminant orbital disease. Cardinal signs and symptoms of infectious orbital cellulitis include proptosis, limited eye movements (including total ophthalmoplegia), and pain with eye movements. Decreased vision or even blindness can occur as the most serious ophthalmic complication. Elevated intraocular pressure and chemosis of the conjunctiva are common ancillary signs. Preseptal cellulitis often coexists with orbital cellulitis but is not a prerequisite.

Most cases of orbital cellulitis result from spread of infection from an adjacent infected sinus.[33] Ethmoid sinusitis is the most common predisposing factor. Rare cases are caused by penetrating orbital trauma or skin infection involving the face, with spread of organisms into the orbit. Orbital cellulitis may occur infrequently after orbital, ocular, or periocular surgery.[187] Orbital cellulitis and cavernous sinus thrombosis have been reported to occur after dental infections and dental surgery.[28]

Comprehensive evaluation of the patient with confirmed or suspected orbital cellulitis includes ophthalmologic and systemic examinations. Assessment of visual acuity in both eyes is important in excluding vision loss and in establishing a baseline to aid in following the progression of the disease or the effects of therapy. Assessing optic nerve dysfunction by examining the pupils for an afferent pupillary defect is important before pupillary dilation is performed for evaluation of the retina. Careful evaluation of extraocular movements should be performed in all extreme positions of gaze to identify restriction of ocular ductions and to elicit pain on eye movements. The presence or absence of proptosis can be assessed clinically by viewing the eyes from above (bird's-eye view) or below (worm's-eye view) and by comparing their relative positions within the orbits. In severe cases of orbital cellulitis, funduscopic examination may reveal dilation of the retinal venules and signs of compressive optic neuropathy such as optic disk edema. Central retinal artery occlusion has been reported occasionally.[91] Systemic evaluation includes determination of temperature, which usually is in the range of 39° C to 40° C (102° F to 104° F). Sinus examination, a screening neurologic examination, and evaluation for signs and symptoms of sepsis and meningitis should be performed.

In any case of clinically definite or suspected orbital cellulitis, CT scanning of the orbit and brain is indicated. CT can establish or confirm the diagnosis of orbital cellulitis, and it provides critical information needed to manage the patient in the immediate setting. Imaging of the brain is important because orbital cellulitis can evolve into a brain abscess, meningitis, or cavernous sinus thrombosis.

Microbiologic studies often are acutely unhelpful for the routine patient with orbital cellulitis. Nonetheless, baseline studies remain important because critical information is acquired sometimes. Blood cultures should be obtained at a minimum, and a lumbar puncture with culture of the cerebrospinal fluid should be considered in extremely young children and in those with signs of CNS infection. Cultures of the ocular, nasal, and nasopharyngeal mucous membranes are of limited value and can be omitted from the work-up. However, cultures should be obtained of any material removed during surgery.

Optimal management of the child with orbital cellulitis requires a multidisciplinary approach. In addition to evaluation and management by an experienced pediatrician, ophthalmologic and otolaryngologic consultations should be obtained as soon as possible. A neurosurgical consultation is required when involvement of the CNS is diagnosed or suspected. In atypical cases and those not responding to treatment, consultation with an infectious disease specialist is warranted.

The most common offending etiologic bacteria are *S. aureus*, *Streptococcus* spp., and *Haemophilus* spp. (other than *H. influenzae*). *S. pneumonia* also is implicated frequently, and a variety of less common organisms have been reported. Hib orbital cellulitis rarely has occurred since widespread use of the Hib vaccine was implemented.[3, 44] Fungal infection of the orbit occasionally is encountered, typically in immunocompromised individuals.

The differential diagnosis of orbital inflammation in childhood includes a broad range of noninfectious conditions, including cavernous sinus thrombosis, idiopathic inflammatory orbital pseudotumor, Wegener granulomatosis, sarcoidosis, leukemic infiltration, lymphoma, rhabdomyosarcoma, necrotic retinoblastoma, metastatic carcinoma, and histiocytosis X. Thyroid ophthalmopathy also can manifest as an acute orbital inflammatory process, although its onset usually is slow and insidious.

Treatment of all patients with orbital cellulitis requires hospitalization, with initiation of intravenous antibiotics as soon as possible after cultures have been obtained. Infection with penicillin-resistant organisms is a common occurrence and must be considered during treatment.[31] Appropriate initial antibiotic therapy may include nafcillin, metronidazole, and cefotaxime as combination therapy. Other antimicrobial agents may be useful, and local susceptibility patterns should guide the choice of initial antimicrobial therapy. Antibiotic coverage should be modified based on the clinical course and the culture results. If the patient fails to respond to antibiotic treatment within 24 to 48 hours, consultation with an infectious disease specialist should be considered strongly and a repeat CT scan considered to look for development of an orbital abscess. The mean hospital stay for uncomplicated cases of orbital cellulitis is 10 to 14 days, and oral antibiotics after discharge should be prescribed for 7 to 10 days. A nasal decongestant commonly is prescribed at the time of diagnosis to aid in opening the sinus ostia, promoting drainage of the infected sinus, and speeding resolution. Nasal decongestants should be continued for 7 to 10 days after initiation.

Children with orbital cellulitis require diligent follow-up while in the hospital and should be seen at least twice each day during the acute phase of the disease. Vision should be assessed at the bedside at least twice daily; results may be more accurate if a single examiner routinely performs vision assessment on a given patient. Rapid progression and rapid deterioration can occur, justifying examination twice a day at a minimum. Pupillary examination for an afferent pupillary defect (APD) should be performed at each examination. Development of an APD indicates compromise of the optic nerve and warrants escalation of treatment, usually requiring urgent surgical intervention. Reduction of vision, development of an APD, onset of CNS signs, or a worsening of the systemic status should prompt emergent repeat neuroimaging of the brain and orbit with further intervention as dictated by the scan. The close anatomic relationship of the orbit to the brain, with the orbital venous system freely anastomosing with the facial venous plexus and cranial venous sinus system through a series of valveless veins, seriously increases the potential for spread of infection to contiguous structures, including the brain.

Acute surgical intervention to decompress the orbit or drain an orbital or subperiosteal abscess is indicated if vision loss or an APD is identified at any point during treatment. Immediate neurosurgical consideration is indicated if CNS involvement is documented. Most patients who do not have evidence of vision loss, optic nerve dysfunction, or CNS involvement can be successfully managed medically. The surgical adage that all abscesses should be subjected to incision and drainage does not apply necessarily to abscesses associated with orbital cellulitis. Most subperiosteal abscesses located in the medial orbit can be managed successfully with medical therapy alone.[70, 146] Formation of an abscess within the substance of the orbit (as opposed to a subperiosteal abscess) seldom occurs. Guidelines for surgical drainage are similar to those for subperiosteal abscesses,[146] although such abscesses are more likely to require surgical intervention because of treatment failures or spread of infection to contiguous structures.[70] Provided clinical improvement continues, no worrisome signs or symptoms of CNS involvement develop, and the patient's overall clinical status does not worsen, repeat neuroimaging of the patient with an orbital abscess is unnecessary. Short-term resolution of an orbital abscess often is not obvious on CT scan. The radiographic appearance of the abscess typically remains unchanged on early follow-up scans, although it may no longer contain viable organisms.

Garcia and Harris[64] recommended that surgical intervention for a subperiosteal abscess be considered if any of the following develops: vision loss or APD, absence of defervescence within 36 hours, clinical deterioration after 48 hours, or absence of clinical improvement after 72 hours of medical therapy. Surgical management includes drainage and culture of abscesses and decompression of the orbit by removing surrounding bone in cases of acute compressive optic neuropathy or retinal vascular compromise. Sinus drainage by the otolaryngologist frequently is required to hasten resolution. Formation of an abscess is not a prerequisite for surgical intervention, and orbital cellulitis without such formation may progress to the point of requiring surgery. Despite prompt and appropriate treatment, serious complications such as permanent vision loss and brain abscess can occur. Most patients, however, can be treated effectively, with no permanent sequelae.

Orbital cellulitis caused by fungal infection has a course and prognosis markedly different from those of bacterial orbital cellulitis, particularly those caused by mucormycosis and aspergillosis. Fungal orbital cellulitis typically occurs in patients who are immunocompromised or those who have a metabolic acidosis, such as patients with poorly controlled diabetes. Orbital cellulitis may manifest as a subacute or chronic process. Orbital apex syndrome is considered to be the most severe form, with loss of function of all cranial nerves traversing the orbital apex into the orbit (i.e., cranial nerves II, III, IV, V, and VI). A black eschar-like lesion may form in the oropharynx or nasopharynx.

Aspergillus orbital infections (most commonly caused by *Aspergillus flavus*, *Aspergillus fumigatus*, or *Aspergillus oryzae*) are rare findings in children and may take a slow, chronic course over the course of months or years. No clear predisposing factors exist, and most cases occur in otherwise healthy individuals, with a predilection for humid climates. Signs and symptoms of orbital infections caused by *Aspergillus* spp. include loss of vision, constant dull pain, decreased or absent ocular motility, and proptosis with firm resistance to retropulsion. Palate and nasopharyngeal lesions occur but rarely. Biopsy is required for the diagnosis.[72]

Effective treatment of orbital fungal infection requires correction of systemic and metabolic disturbances and administration of intravenous antifungal agents, such as amphotericin B. Surgical débridement of the orbit or adjacent infected sinuses often is required. Treatment often is unsuccessful, and fatalities are not uncommon, particularly with mucormycosis.

The larva of *Echinococcus granulosus* can produce a hydatid cyst in the orbit. The dog is the definitive host animal, although the organism also may live in the intestines of sheep, goats, cattle, pigs, and other animals. The disease is endemic in the Middle East, Africa, and Asia. Humans become infected by eating contaminated food, typically meat, and infection may occur in any age group. Affected patients present with noninflammatory proptosis, decreased ocular motility, and dull orbital pain. Surgical excision is required for treatment. The cyst may be injected with hypertonic saline to kill the parasite, followed by excision.[119]

Conjunctival Infections

The conjunctiva is the mucous membrane covering the inner surfaces of the eyelids and the anterior surface of the eye, except the cornea. The mucous membrane lining the inner surface of the eyelids is called the *palpebral conjunctiva,* and the mucous membrane covering the globe is called the *bulbar conjunctiva.* The conjunctiva contains numerous small glands that produce most of the aqueous component of tears and the mucin component of tears that is responsible for effecting a smooth, uniform tear film over the cornea. The conjunctiva may become infected by a wide variety of bacterial and viral agents. It also may have inflammation caused by noninfectious allergic and toxic agents.

Patients with conjunctivitis may complain of burning or itching and occasionally of a foreign body sensation. Significant itching usually signifies an allergic or viral cause. The affected eyes are infected, with most of the conjunctival erythema located away from the cornea. Conjunctival infection concentrated adjacent to the cornea (i.e., limbal or ciliary flush) suggests keratitis (i.e., inflammation of the cornea), iritis, or iridocyclitis (i.e., inflammation of the iris, ciliary body, or both). When the eye is severely infected, however, such a differentiating pattern may not be discernible. Conjunctivitis usually is accompanied by a discharge that has some important diagnostic properties. Purulence suggests a bacterial cause, a mucoid discharge most often is seen with viral infections, and a serous discharge usually is seen with viral or allergic causes. Patients with isolated conjunctivitis do not have any significant alteration of vision. Conjunctivitis with poor vision warrants search for another diagnosis.[66, 113]

BACTERIAL CONJUNCTIVITIS

Bacterial conjunctivitis is a common form of infectious conjunctivitis in childhood. It is characterized by a purulent discharge and commonly is unilateral. To divide bacterial conjunctivitis into mild and severe forms is useful clinically.

Mild Bacterial Conjunctivitis

The agents most commonly causing mild bacterial conjunctivitis in children 5 years of age or older are *S. pneumoniae* and *Moraxella* spp.[66] *H. influenzae* was a prominent causative agent before the availability of the Hib vaccine. *S. aureus* conjunctivitis is seen most frequently after trauma or surgical manipulation. Conjunctival stains and cultures usually are not necessary because the disease is self-limited or responds rapidly to topical antibiotics. The eye often has returned to normal by the time the culture results are finalized.

Many appropriate topical antimicrobial agents for treatment of bacterial conjunctivitis are readily available and include topical erythromycin, tobramycin, gentamicin, ciprofloxacin, norfloxacin, sulfacetamide, and combination antibodies. Aminoglycoside-containing compounds such as neomycin occasionally can cause a dramatic allergic blepharoconjunctivitis that may be much worse than the original problem. The choice of drops or ointment often is best left to the person who will be instilling the medication at home because neither has any proven therapeutic advantage. A typical regimen for treatment of mild conjunctivitis is 1 drop or a 0.25-inch bead of ointment into the inferior conjunctival fornix 3 to 6 times daily for 3 to 5 days. The infection should be resolved by this time. Persistent infection should prompt the parent or patient to return to the physician for reconsideration of the diagnosis. Mild bacterial conjunctivitis usually resolves spontaneously in 7 to 14 days, even without treatment.[66, 67]

Severe Bacterial Conjunctivitis

Severe bacterial conjunctivitis, characterized by pronounced conjunctival injection and copious purulent discharge, usually is caused by *Neisseria gonorrhoeae, Neisseria meningitidis, S. aureus, S. pneumoniae,* and, in children younger than 5 years of age, *H. influenzae.* A hyperpurulent state, in which the copious purulent discharge reaccumulates in a matter of minutes, is characteristic of infection with *N. gonorrhoeae.*[79, 157]

Severe conjunctivitis demands a comprehensive microbiologic evaluation consisting of stains and cultures. Samples from both eyes should be cultured separately, even if only one eye is involved, allowing the uninvolved eye to serve as a useful control.[168] Gram stains of conjunctival scrapings should be done at the time of culture. A useful culture technique includes the use of a cotton or calcium alginate swab (Calgiswab, Spectrum, Houston, TX) gently rubbed against the palpebral conjunctiva of the lower lid and inoculated onto blood and chocolate agar. If *N. gonorrhoeae* is suspected, culture for *Chlamydia* also is indicated because concurrent infection with both organisms is a common finding.

Treatment of severe bacterial conjunctivitis is based initially on the results of the stains and later modified based on culture and sensitivities. If *Neisseria* is strongly suspected, the patient should be treated as if he or she has the disease, even if the laboratory results are not confirmatory. Ocular *N. gonorrhoeae* infection is a vision- and life-threatening disease. These organisms can penetrate the intact cornea, causing microbial keratitis, corneal perforation, and endophthalmitis in addition to conjunctivitis. *N. gonorrhoeae* conjunctivitis should be considered in three patient groups: neonates after passage through an infected birth canal; sexually active individuals; and victims of suspected sexual abuse. Pediatric infection with *N. gonorrhoeae* requires hospital admission and administration of a systemic antibiotic. Because of the prevalence of penicillin-resistant strains, an extended-spectrum (third-generation) cephalosporin, such as ceftriaxone, is the most appropriate choice of antibiotic.[74] Adjunctive topical treatment of *N. gonorrhoeae* conjunctivitis with erythromycin ointment or, preferably, simple saline irrigation for the first 1 to 2 days of systemic treatment can be useful, but topical agents should *never* be used as isolated treatment.[79]

Conjunctivitis caused by gram-positive cocci can be treated with topical erythromycin ointment or ciprofloxacin drops. Nafcillin or cefuroxime can be added as needed. Ciprofloxacin drops have not been approved for use in the pediatric population. Gram-negative bacterial conjunctivitis can be treated with topical erythromycin ointment or an aminoglycoside drip such as gentamicin or tobramycin. Systemic antibiotics can be added if needed.[168]

VIRAL CONJUNCTIVITIS

Adenoviral Conjunctivitis

Viruses are another common cause of infectious conjunctivitis in childhood. Most pediatric cases of viral conjunctivitis are caused by the adenovirus. Serotypes 1, 2, 3, 4, 7, and 10 produce an acute form of conjunctivitis with prominent conjunctival follicles. Serotypes 3 and 7 also may cause pharyngoconjunctival fever. This entity is characterized by conjunctivitis, fever, and pharyngitis.[18] Serotypes 8, 19, and 37 primarily can cause epidemic keratoconjunctivitis, which is characterized by a combination of conjunctivitis and keratitis.[168] The keratitis is characterized by a combination of a punctate epithelial keratitis and an immune response that results in subepithelial infiltrates. Vision may be decreased markedly, and photophobia is a prominent feature. Epidemic keratoconjunctivitis commonly is associated with pharyngitis and rhinitis, which may precede or coexist with the conjunctivitis.

Adenoviral conjunctivitis is highly contagious. It is transmitted easily from the infected individual to others at home or school. The incubation period is 5 to 10 days but may be as long as 21 days. The virus is shed from the infected conjunctiva for 7 to 12 days after the onset of infection. Often, a prodromal upper respiratory infection occurs with fever, pharyngitis, or otitis media.[168] Ocular signs and symptoms include photophobia (with corneal involvement), foreign body sensation, epiphora, bulbar and palpebral conjunctival infection and chemosis (edema), and subconjunctival hemorrhage.[82] Formation of grayish-pink friable membranes on the palpebral conjunctiva is a hallmark of the disease and may result in bleeding when removed. Preauricular lymphadenopathy is a common feature in older children and adults. Keratitis may be prolonged, with mild to moderate reduction of vision lasting weeks to months.[82, 113]

The diagnosis of adenoviral conjunctivitis usually is clinical. Rarely is laboratory confirmation necessary. Viral cultures are specific when indicated, and a rapid enzyme immunoassay test is available.[185] Treatment of adenoviral conjunctivitis is aimed at reducing symptoms. Cool compresses and acetaminophen are helpful, and removal of conjunctival membranes with a cotton swab may relieve the foreign body sensation. A small amount of bleeding often occurs after removal of these membranes, and the membranes can recur after several days. If corneal subepithelial infiltrates cause significant discomfort or an unacceptable decrease in vision, treatment with a short course of topical steroids may provide symptomatic relief and speed resolution. The use of steroid preparations requires careful monitoring,[113, 168] and they should be prescribed only by an ophthalmologist.

The clinician should wear gloves when examining patients with suspected adenovirus infection. Careful hand-washing is essential after any direct contact. Instruments or equipment used in examining an infected patient should be cleaned with 10 percent sodium hypochlorite solution or other solutions known to eradicate adenovirus. Mini-epidemics have originated in physicians' offices.[93] At home, families should exercise caution, separating the towels and bed clothes of the patient from those of others in the household. Children of school age should be kept home for 7 to 14 days to reduce the risk of infecting classmates.[168]

External Ocular Infections Caused by Herpes Simplex Virus

HSV conjunctivitis may occur as a primary or secondary infection. Ocular infection usually is caused by HSV-1, except in newborns, in whom HSV-2 predominates.[35] Typical presenting signs of HSV conjunctivitis include a serous discharge, scant conjunctival follicle formation on the inferior palpebral conjunctiva, and preauricular lymphadenopathy. Eighty percent of cases are unilateral. Eyelid vesicles often occur in primary infections. Bulbar conjunctival ulceration is an unusual occurrence, but when present, it is virtually pathognomonic of primary HSV-1 infection. Keratitis occurs in as many as 50 percent of primary cases and is characterized by mild epithelial irregularities. Reactivated HSV keratitis manifests with the characteristic dendritic pattern of epithelial disease. Lid vesicles usually do not occur in reactivated HSV infection.[95]

Primary HSV dermatoblepharitis is seen most commonly in children younger than 6 years of age, but it may occur at any age. The initial episode may be associated with an upper respiratory infection, and recurrences are common. Clinical signs include an eyelid vesicular reaction, mild follicular conjunctivitis, preauricular lymphadenopathy, and occasionally, atypical epithelial keratitis. Secondary bacterial infection can occur. Systemic acyclovir is a safe and effective treatment, although the disease itself is self-limited and does not necessarily require treatment.[95]

The diagnosis of HSV keratoconjunctivitis usually is made on the basis of the clinical appearance alone. Antigen detection tests or viral cultures can be used when the diagnosis is in doubt.[113] Viral cultures, when necessary, require a special handling.[168] In primary HSV infection, after swabbing the skin surface with an alcohol sponge, a tuberculin syringe with a 30-gauge needle is used to aspirate fluid from an intact vesicle. If no vesicles are present, a Dacron swab is wiped on the palpebral conjunctiva of the lower lid. In either case, the viral transport medium then is inoculated, taken to the laboratory, and chilled on ice but not frozen.

Treatment of HSV conjunctivitis alone (in the absence of corneal epithelial disease) is somewhat controversial. Oral acyclovir may be used for severe cases of primary HSV infection.[152, 164] Three topical antiviral agents are available: iododeoxyuridine (IDU), vidarabine (ARA-A), and trifluridine (TFT).

When epithelial HSV keratitis is reactivated and the typical dendritic (branched) epithelial lesions are seen, the cornea typically is hypesthetic. Iritis commonly is associated with HSV keratitis and is characterized by miosis, photophobia, ocular pain, and foreign body sensation. Vision may be decreased if the epithelial disease involves the visual axis.[168] Epithelial HSV may be atypical, more severe, or more complicated in patients receiving topical steroids and in immunocompromised patients.

Treatment with topical trifluridine or vidarabine is indicated in all cases of HSV keratitis. Topical steroid is effective in decreasing corneal scarring caused by HSV stromal keratitis. When using a topical steroid, coverage with a topical antiviral agent, such as vidarabine, always should be used to reduce the risk of development of recurrent active viral proliferation during steroid treatment. Oral acyclovir is not effective for treating active HSV keratitis, but it may be useful in treating HSV uveitis.[164] Ancillary treatments include cycloplegic eyedrops to dilate the pupil and pain medications.

Although not useful for treating acute epithelial disease, chronic suppression with oral acyclovir is effective in reducing the number of recurrences of HSV epithelial and stromal keratitis, especially in patients with stromal keratitis.[164, 168] Interferon also significantly adds to the efficacy of topical antiviral therapy, but the adverse side effects of interferon must be weighed against its potential benefits.[164]

Varicella-Zoster Virus External Ocular Infections

Childhood varicella infection (chickenpox) commonly is accompanied by conjunctivitis. Vesicles, ulcers, or both occur occasionally on the bulbar or palpebral conjunctiva. Conjunctivitis associated with varicella infection does not result in permanent visual sequelae. Corneal involvement rarely occurs and typically heals without sequelae. Occasionally, it may result in stromal scarring, producing irregular astigmatism and reduced vision.

After primary varicella infection, the virus may persist in latent form in the trigeminal nerve ganglia. Herpes zoster ophthalmicus occurs when the ophthalmic division of the trigeminal nerve is affected by a reactivation of the virus. The condition occurs more commonly in immunocompromised patients, and recurrences are infrequent events except in immunocompromised patients.

The diagnosis of herpes zoster ophthalmicus almost always is made on the basis of the characteristic clinical features of a painful, tender vesicular eruption in the V1 dermatome. Ocular involvement may include keratitis and uveitis. Corneal epithelial lesions may appear dendritic-like, with or without subepithelial infiltrates. Uveitis may occur with or without an associated keratitis. Usually, it is mild, but occasionally, it may be severe, with the formation of a hypopyon or hyphema. Immunofluorescence testing of vesicular base scrapings or viral cultures may be helpful if the presentation is atypical or the diagnosis is in doubt.[104]

Treatment of herpes zoster ophthalmicus involves administration of oral or intravenous acyclovir. Treatment is most effective when initiated within 72 hours of the appearance of vesicles. Keratitis and uveitis do not respond to topical antiviral therapy.[164] Topical steroids sometimes can be helpful in treating varicella keratitis and uveitis, but this treatment should be administered under the direction of an ophthalmologist.[113]

Chlamydial Conjunctivitis and Trachoma

Chlamydia spp. can cause conjunctivitis and trachoma. *Chlamydia psittaci* rarely causes ocular disease in humans. *Chlamydia trachomatis*, however, has numerous serotypes that affect the eye. Serotypes A, B, Ba, and C cause trachoma, and serotypes B, C, D, Da, D–, E, F, G, H, I, Ia, J, and K cause inclusion conjunctivitis, including neonatal inclusion conjunctivitis. Neonatal chlamydial conjunctivitis is discussed in the Neonatal Conjunctivitis section.

Inclusion conjunctivitis in older children and adults manifests as subacute or chronic inflammation of the conjunctiva.

The condition may be unilateral or bilateral. A mucopurulent discharge occurs typically as do follicles on the bulbar and perilimbal conjunctiva. Preauricular lymphadenopathy is a common finding. Punctate epithelial keratitis with subepithelial infiltrates and a superior micropannus (i.e., vascular growth on the cornea) may develop.[41]

The differential diagnosis of inclusion conjunctivitis is sizable and includes viral and bacterial conjunctivitis, molluscum contagiosum, and toxic keratoconjunctivitis from chronic administration of topical agents. Laboratory testing may be necessary for diagnostic confirmation. Giemsa staining of conjunctival scrapings may demonstrate the classic intracytoplasmic inclusions. A fluorescent antibody detection test or enzyme immunoassay is used to make a rapid diagnosis.[168] Chlamydial cultures rarely are needed except when the diagnosis remains in doubt.

Treatment consists of oral erythromycin or doxycycline if systemic infection is suspected. Topical erythromycin or tetracycline ointment alone four times each day for 7 days is effective treatment for infection limited to the conjunctiva.[41, 168]

Trachoma remains a leading cause of blindness worldwide, ranking second or third, depending on the region studied. It is a disease of impoverished populations, exacerbated by inadequate supplies of water and by poor hygiene. Trachoma seldom is seen in developed countries. In the United States, it is encountered on Native American reservations in the Southwest and in individuals arriving in the endemic areas of the United States. Eye-seeking flies play an important role in transmission of *Chlamydia* from one person to another.[168]

Trachoma causes blindness by producing a chronic inflammation of the palpebral conjunctiva of the upper eyelid with secondary scar formation. Contracture of the palpebral conjunctiva scar produces entropion of the eyelid and trichiasis. Eventually, this situation leads to corneal opacification and vision loss.[167, 168] Less commonly, the cornea may be infected directly. The complete course of the disease from initial infection to blindness usually takes decades.

The diagnosis of trachoma almost always is made on the basis of clinical findings alone. The disease passes through characteristic stages, from simple inflammation to scarring to ultimate entropion and trichiasis. Multiple stages may coexist in various parts of the eyelids. The World Health Organization classification characterizes the stages of trachoma as follows: TF, trachomatous follicular response; TI, diffuse trachomatous conjunctival inflammation; TS, trachomatous scarring of the palpebral conjunctiva; TT, trachomatous trichiasis; and TO, trachomatous corneal opacification. In the pediatric population, physicians usually encounter only stages TI and TF.[175] The scars on the palpebral conjunctiva, referred to as the Arlt lines, are linear and multidirectional. Slit-lamp examination may reveal a superior limbal micropannus and Herbert pits (i.e., hollowed-out areas in the superior limbus), which represent the sites of resolved follicles.

Treatment of trachoma consists of topical tetracycline or erythromycin ointment instilled twice daily for 2 months and, more importantly, improved sanitation and hygiene to prevent recurrences.[168] Trachoma often is self-limited if hygiene alone is improved.[167] In patients who do not respond promptly to topical treatment or in those with severe disease, systemic antimicrobial agents should be instituted. For those older than 8 years of age, doxycycline should be administered orally daily for 40 days. Erythromycin can be substituted in younger children or in patients intolerant of doxycycline.

Neonatal Conjunctivitis

Neonatal conjunctivitis, also known as ophthalmia neonatorum, is a common, vision-threatening disorder throughout the world, although it has been relegated to a position of secondary importance in the industrialized world where screening and prophylactic measures are in widespread use. It remains a significant cause of childhood ocular morbidity in developing countries.

Dilute topical silver nitrate solution instilled just after birth for prophylaxis against ophthalmia neonatorum was the first treatment used. It was responsible for reducing the prevalence of gonococcal ophthalmia neonatorum from 10 to 0.17 percent of live births in Europe.[168] A mild, self-limited chemical conjunctivitis is associated with the use of silver nitrate.[124] It lasts 2 to 4 days and resolves with no special treatment. Topical erythromycin largely has replaced silver nitrate in developed countries because it is effective without producing a chemical conjunctivitis.[77] In the developing world, regional conflicts, political instability, and burgeoning refugee populations often result in underusing these simple prophylactic measures.[63, 76]

The causes of neonatal conjunctivitis are highly variable among populations. In areas that use silver nitrate drops for prophylaxis, chemical conjunctivitis is the most common cause of neonatal conjunctivitis.[124] Infectious conjunctivitis occurs in 0.5 to 6.0 percent of live births in the United States. The leading infection is *C. trachomatis*.[12, 81, 148, 168] Neonatal infection is caused by ocular exposure to contaminated maternal discharge during normal birth, although it may occur in infants born by cesarean section, especially if the membranes ruptured prematurely. Other important infectious agents that may cause ophthalmia neonatorum are *N. gonorrhoeae* and *S. aureus*.[62, 157] Bacteria that normally reside in the vaginal or gastrointestinal tracts occasionally are implicated in ophthalmia neonatorum. They include *Streptococcus* spp., *Haemophilus* spp., *Pseudomonas aeruginosa, Moraxella* spp., *Moraxella catarrhalis, N. meningitidis, E. coli*, and *Enterobacter cloacae*.[149, 163]

Viruses occasionally produce neonatal conjunctivitis. HSV rarely may produce keratoconjunctivitis.[63] It is associated with distinctive vesicular skin changes and systemic signs, and the diagnosis seldom is in doubt.[7] Life-threatening HSV meningoencephalitis is a serious potential complication of HSV ophthalmia neonatorum.[122] Other viruses occasionally implicated include adenovirus, coxsackievirus A9, cytomegalovirus (CMV), and echovirus.[162]

Certain clinical features may help establish the specific etiologic diagnosis in cases of ophthalmia neonatorum (Table 68–1), but considerable overlap in presentation exists, and the physician cannot rely on history and physical

TABLE 68–1 ■ CLINICAL CHARACTERISTICS OF NEONATAL CONJUNCTIVITIS CAUSED BY VARIOUS AGENTS

Agent	Onset Day of Life	Discharge
Silver nitrate	1 (0–2)	Serous
Chlamydia trachomatis	7 (1–21)	Mucopurulent
Staphylococcus aureus	5 (1–21)	Mucopurulent
Other bacteria	7 (1–21)	Mucopurulent
Neisseria gonorrhoeae	3 (0–21)	Purulent
Herpes simplex virus	5 (0–21)	Serosanguineous
Other viruses	Not established	Probably serous

examination alone to make a definitive diagnosis. Even when all appropriate investigative modalities are used, the cause may remain in doubt in some cases.

Variations in the time of onset after birth, severity of inflammation, and character of the ocular discharge are common findings, and none is considered pathognomonic of a specific infectious process, but general considerations are worth reviewing.[149] Silver nitrate conjunctivitis typically begins during the first 48 hours of life and produces a watery discharge with mild inflammation. It is self-limited and resolves within 48 to 72 hours of appearance.[124] *C. trachomatis* conjunctivitis typically begins 1 to 21 days after birth, usually manifesting by day 7. A moderately copious, mucopurulent discharge may be present but can be variable.[81, 120] *S. aureus* conjunctivitis also begins during the first 3 weeks of life and can produce a moderately profuse, mucopurulent discharge. Many other bacterial agents produce an overlapping clinical picture. Conjunctivitis caused by *N. gonorrhoeae* ordinarily begins somewhat earlier, usually by the third day of life, but it may appear as late as 3 weeks after birth. The hallmark is a copious, hyperpurulent discharge that can reaccumulate in a matter of minutes after it is removed. *N. gonorrhoeae* can penetrate an initially intact cornea, resulting in perforation of the eye and endophthalmitis.[79, 151, 162]

Viral neonatal conjunctivitis is a rare occurrence. HSV infection may begin during the first 3 weeks of life and usually produces a serous or serosanguineous discharge.[63, 122] Other viruses have highly variable characteristics, but a serous discharge is a common finding.

The differential diagnosis of neonatal conjunctivitis includes congenital glaucoma dacryostenosis with or without dacryocystitis. Dacryostenosis manifests with epiphora and a watery or purulent discharge. Occasionally, conjunctivitis may develop. Because epiphora caused by congenital dacryostenosis ordinarily is not seen until the second or third week of life, it rarely is a serious consideration. Newborns with congenital glaucoma often are photophobic and irritable.[180] They may exhibit increased tearing, conjunctival injection, and corneal edema. The presence of photophobia is strong evidence of isolated conjunctivitis.

Laboratory testing is important in establishing a specific diagnosis. Laboratory testing should include Gram and Giemsa stains, a *Chlamydia* immunoassay, and cultures for aerobic and anaerobic bacteria. Cotton-tipped swabs should be used to obtain material for cultures from the conjunctival fornices. Viral and *Chlamydia* cultures and immunoassays can be considered but usually are unnecessary.[11, 170] Gonococcal immunoassay and HSV immunochemical tests are available but are not in widespread use.

The initial treatment of neonatal conjunctivitis depends on the suspected infectious agent. Broad-spectrum treatment should be considered if the diagnostic possibilities cannot be narrowed. Silver nitrate–induced conjunctivitis is self-limited and does not require treatment. *C. trachomatis* conjunctivitis is treated with tetracycline (1%) or erythromycin (0.5%) ointment four times daily for 3 weeks and with systemic erythromycin for 2 to 3 weeks to prevent or to treat *Chlamydia* pneumonia. Sulfonamides can be used to treat *Chlamydia* conjunctivitis if erythromycin is not tolerated. Topical antibiotics alone are insufficient for the treatment of neonatal *Chlamydia* infection.[69, 78, 81] Staphylococcal conjunctivitis can be treated with erythromycin ointment or a variety of other topical antimicrobial agents every 4 to 6 hours for 3 to 7 days. Appropriate systemic antibiotic treatment should be considered if the infection is particularly severe.[168]

N. gonorrhoeae infection requires systemic treatment in all cases. Aqueous penicillin G can be considered if resistant strains are unlikely. However, 1 dose of intramuscular ceftriaxone is the treatment of choice because it is effective against all gonorrhoeae strains.[74, 138] Eyes should be irrigated with saline every hour until the discharge clears and then in reduced frequency as necessary to reduce the risk of development of corneal infection. This interval usually is 24 to 48 hours after initiation of systemic treatment. Penicillin G drops are recommended by some ophthalmologists, but the drops do not appear to improve the overall prognosis or the speed of recovery.

HSV neonatal conjunctivitis is treated with systemic acyclovir in appropriate doses for as long as 3 weeks.[63] Treatment should be instituted on an emergent basis because of the potential for development of serious neurologic sequelae and death if treatment is delayed. Vidarabine ophthalmic ointment also should be applied to the eyes four times daily for 2 to 3 weeks.

Prevention of ophthalmia neonatorum is simple, requiring only instillation of an antibiotic or antiseptic agent within the first hour after birth. Silver nitrate drops (1%), erythromycin ointment (0.5%), and tetracycline ointment (1%) have been effective treatment against *N. gonorrhoeae* and *C. trachomatis*.[78, 168] A 5 percent solution of povidone-iodine also has been effective and economical in prophylaxis against a variety of agents, including gonococcal neonatal conjunctivitis. It may be particularly useful in developing countries.[90] As with other sexually transmitted diseases, neonatal conjunctivitis caused by *N. gonorrhoeae, C. trachomatis*, or HSV should be addressed according to standard public health policies, with reporting, investigative, and case identification as required by local law.

Keratitis: Corneal Infection

The cornea, with its overlying tear film, is the major refracting component of the human eye. Keratitis means inflammation of the cornea. Any irregularity of the corneal surface or an opacity involving the central visual axis of the cornea may impair vision.

The cornea is composed of five distinct layers: epithelium, Bowman membrane, stroma, Descemet membrane, and endothelium. The epithelium is several layers thick and, when healthy, can regenerate without scarring after an insult. The Bowman membrane lies beneath the epithelium. It does not regenerate and, when injured, heals with a scar. The stroma, measuring approximately 0.5 mm thick, is the thickest part of the cornea. It is composed of regularly arranged collagen fibrils embedded in a matrix of mucoproteins and glycoproteins. The arrangement of the fibrils is more regular in the posterior aspect of the stroma. Like the Bowman membrane, the stroma heals with scarring. The Descemet membrane is the basement membrane of the corneal endothelium. It can regenerate after an insult and does not opacify. The innermost layer, the endothelium, is derived from neuroectoderm. It consists of a single layer of cells that does not have significant regenerative capacity. The cornea is an avascular structure that is kept clear by virtue of the regular arrangement of collagen fibers in the stroma and by the pumping action of the endothelium, which keeps the stroma relatively dehydrated. The cornea will become edematous and opacify if the endothelium is significantly damaged or diseased.

The external corneal surface is protected from injury and exposure by the eyelids. Reflex tearing in response to mechanical irritation provides further protection. The blink response to threat and the antimicrobial properties of the normal tear film further protect the cornea from injury and infection.

The term *keratitis* refers to inflammatory reactions and to infectious processes of the cornea. The diagnosis of keratitis is based on the presence of corneal epithelial or stromal infiltrate. Persons with keratitis usually have erythema of the perilimbal bulbar conjunctiva and eye pain. Vision may be impaired if the process involves the visual axis. A grayish-white corneal infiltrate may have indistinct borders. The infiltrate can be extremely difficult to see in uncooperative infants and young children. Ideally, the patient is examined with a slit lamp; sedation sometimes is required for adequate examination of uncooperative children.

Expertise with slit-lamp examination and maneuvers needed to obtain appropriate stains and cultures are required, and an ophthalmologist should be consulted promptly. Rarely, a biopsy of the cornea is needed to obtain material for culture, and corneal transplantation occasionally is required to halt the progression of an infection or to treat corneal perforation. Etiologic diagnosis is based on clinical presentation and examination of stains and cultures.

ISOLATED EPITHELIAL KERATITIS

Keratitis can be classified further according to the layer of the cornea involved. Most infections involve the epithelium or stroma. Isolated epithelial keratitis usually is caused by one of several viruses: HSV, varicella-zoster virus, adenovirus, EBV, and measles virus (rubeola). The first three organisms are discussed in an earlier section.

EBV causes HSV-like dendritic corneal epithelial lesions. Stromal disease also may occur. The lesions are self-limiting and do not respond to antiviral therapy.[114] When measles involves the cornea, it usually does so in the context of transient epithelial infiltrates, which resolve without permanent sequelae.[95] In malnourished children with vitamin A deficiency, however, measles represents a serious threat to life and to vision. Deep corneal ulcers may develop during the first few days of measles infection. Rapid progression culminating in corneal perforation and ultimate loss of the eye may occur.[17, 59] Whether the ulcers are caused by direct measles virus infection, by keratomalacia of vitamin A deficiency, or by some combination of these factors long has been debated. Measles immunization programs and vitamin A administration programs can reduce significantly the prevalence of childhood blindness in developing nations.

STROMAL KERATITIS

Syphilis and unique parasitic and viral infections can cause a nonsuppurative keratitis isolated to the corneal stroma. Congenital syphilis produces interstitial (stromal) keratitis in childhood, although the condition usually does not manifest until late in the first decade of life. An indolent, peripheral corneal haze develops and slowly progresses centrally. Ghost vessels, devoid of blood flow, are seen in the corneal stroma on slit-lamp examination.[169] The condition is bilateral in 80 percent of cases and is accompanied by iritis, iridocyclitis, or scleritis at some point in the course of the disease. When ocular syphilis is diagnosed, systemic infection is present by definition. The systemic disease should be treated according to accepted guidelines.

BACTERIAL KERATITIS

Bacterial keratitis (i.e., corneal ulcer) most often occurs after trauma that disrupts normal integrity of the corneal epithelium. The trauma can be mild and occult, such as that caused by lens wear. *S. aureus, S. pneumoniae, P. aeruginosa,* and *Moraxella* spp. are the most common bacterial causes of severe necrotizing bacterial keratitis.[6, 103] Other organisms, such as *S. epidermidis, Actinomyces* spp., *S. viridans* streptococci, and a variety of others, have been implicated in less severe cases.

Accurate identification of the offending organism facilitates treatment. A specimen is obtained by scraping the edge of the ulcer with a sterile platinum spatula. Smears should be fixed in 70 percent methanol, not by heat, and Gram stains for bacteria and acridine orange stain for fungi and *Acanthamoeba* are recommended. The yield of culture-positive cases is higher in laboratories skilled in handling corneal cultures. Material for cultures should be inoculated onto fresh media, such as blood and chocolate agar (aerobes and facultative anaerobes), Sabouraud agar (fungi), and thioglycolate broth (anaerobic bacteria). Thayer-Martin agar should be plated if *N. gonorrhoeae* is suspected. Initial treatment is based on the resulting stains (Table 68–2) and modified pending cultures (Table 68–3).[14, 105]

Medical treatment of bacterial keratitis includes fortified topical antibiotics and, occasionally, subconjunctival antibiotic injection (see Table 68–2).[168] Antibiotics are administered as often as every 15 to 30 minutes initially. Systemic antibiotics only are required for gonococcal, chlamydial, and onchocercal keratitis. Systemic antibiotics also are indicated for actual or threatened perforation of the cornea, extension of the infection to the sclera, or worsening of the process while on topical, periocular, or both regimens. Topical steroids are useful if the resulting inflammation threatens to destroy the mechanical or optical integrity of the cornea, but steroids never are used as isolated treatment.[168]

FUNGAL KERATITIS

Fungal keratitis may occur after trauma and usually is caused by *Candida, Aspergillus,* or *Fusarium,* although almost any fungus can infect the traumatized cornea. Soft

TABLE 68–2 ■ TREATMENT OF KERATITIS BASED ON SMEAR MORPHOLOGY

	Antibiotic	
Organism	Ocular	Systemic‖
Gram-positive cocci, gram-positive bacilli	Cefazolin*	Nafcillin, IV
Gram-positive filaments	Amikacin†	Trimethoprim-sulfamethoxazole, IV
Gram-negative cocci	Ceftriaxone* or ciprofloxacin†, ‡	Ceftriaxone, IV or IM
Gram-negative bacilli	Tobramycin*	Tobramycin, IV
Acid-fast bacilli	Amikacin†	
Hyphal fragments	Natamycin†, fluconazole§	Fluconazole, PO
Yeasts	Amphotericin B†, fluconazole§	Fluconazole, PO
Cysts, trophozoites	Polyhexamethylene biguanide,† paromomycin,† and propamidine isethionate†	Itraconazole, PO

*Topical and periocular use only.
†Topical use only.
‡Use in children 12 years of age or older.
§Periocular use only.
‖Standard age-appropriate mg/kg dosages.
IM, intramuscularly; IV, intravenously; PO, orally.

TABLE 68–3 ■ TREATMENT BASED ON IDENTIFICATION OF ORGANISMS

Organism	Antibiotic	
	Ocular	**Systemic**
Micrococcus, *Staphylococcus* (penicillin-resistant)	Cefazolin*	Nafcillin, IV
Micrococcus, *Staphylococcus* (methicillin-resistant)	Vancomycin*	Vancomycin, IV
Streptococcus	Penicillin G*	Penicillin G, IV
Enterococcus	Vancomycin* and gentamicin*	Vancomycin, IV, and gentamicin, IV
Anaerobic gram-positive coccus	Penicillin G*	Penicillin G, IV
Corynebacterium species	Penicillin G*	Penicillin G, IV
Mycobacterium fortuitum-chelonae	Amikacin†	Amikacin, IV,* or clarithromycin, PO
Nocardia	Amikacin†	Trimethoprim-sulfamethoxazole, IV
Neisseria gonorrhoeae	Ceftriaxone*	Ceftriaxone, IV or IM
Pseudomonas species	Ceftazidime* Tobramycin*	Ceftazidime, IV or IM
Other aerobic, gram-negative bacilli	Ceftazidime* Tobramycin*	Ceftazidime, IV or IM
Filamentous fungi	Natamycin† Fluconazole‡	Fluconazole, PO
Candida species	Amphotericin B† Fluconazole‡	Fluconazole, PO
Acanthamoeba	Polyhexamethylene biguanide,† paromomycin,† and propamidine isethionate†	Itraconazole, PO

*Topical and/or periocular use only.
†Topical use only.
‡Periocular use only.
IM, intramuscularly; IV, intravenously.

contact lens wearers are at increased risk for developing microbial keratitis. Fungal keratitis tends to be relatively indolent compared with bacterial microbial keratitis. Typically, white stromal infiltrates with irregular and indistinct borders are detected. Satellite lesions, independent of the main lesion, may be evident. A mild concurrent iritis is a common finding. Severe iritis with a hypopyon can occur but is an infrequent occurrence in fungal corneal disease.[126] An acridine orange stain is recommended, and culture on a Sabouraud agar plate is indicated. Hyphal fungi are treated with topical natamycin, topical fluconazole, or systemic fluconazole or some combination of these medications. Yeasts are treated with topical or systemic amphotericin B, fluconazole, or both agents.[60]

PROTOZOAN KERATITIS

Protozoan keratitis represents a particularly serious, vision-threatening process. It usually is caused by *Acanthamoeba* and occurs more frequently among soft contact lens wearers. Use of homemade saline solutions is a significant risk factor and should be discouraged.[27] Amebae are ubiquitous organisms in soil, water, and air. They have been identified in hot tubs and in the feces of domestic animals.[112] People living in rural areas may be at special risk.

Acanthamoeba corneal ulcers are pleomorphic.[89] Older lesions may exhibit a ringlike infiltrate around a central ulcer. Iritis or iridocyclitis may be intense, and severe pain is a hallmark of the disease. Acridine orange and calcofluor white stains aid in making an early diagnosis of the condition. Tandem scanning confocal microscopy of corneal specimens may increase the accuracy of diagnosis, and the organism may grow on blood and chocolate agar.[27, 109, 111, 115, 134]

Treatment of *Acanthamoeba* keratitis is complex and suboptimal. Topical application of polyhexamethylene biguanide (2%), chlorhexidine (2%), paromomycin (10 mg/mL), or propamidine isethionate (Brolene) drops may be effective. Oral itraconazole (Sporanox) has been used successfully in adults.[101, 109, 115] Cycloplegic agents are recommended to improve the patient's comfort, and pain medications often are required. Corneal transplantation is needed if the infection progresses despite treatment, if perforation occurs, or if significant corneal opacification remains after the disease is eradicated.

Onchocerca volvulus is a filarial parasite that causes river blindness (i.e., onchocerciasis). The disease is endemic in sub-Saharan West Africa and in areas of Central and South America. The organism is transmitted by the bite of a blackfly in the family *Simuliidae*.[144] Larvae migrate to the subcutaneous tissue and pass through several molts to become adult worms. The adult worms encapsulate in nodules and produce microfilariae that pass into the blood, skin, and other organs, including the eyes. The conjunctiva, cornea, aqueous humor, vitreous, retina, uveal tract, sclera, and optic nerve all may be infested. Corneal involvement can lead to vision loss caused by corneal opacification, although most severe vision loss is caused by choroidal, retinal, and optic nerve disease.[75] Although children often are infected, blindness usually does not occur until they reach the third or fourth decade of life.[174, 179]

The current treatment for onchocercal infection is ivermectin every 6 to 12 months to all individuals living in endemic areas. Ivermectin kills the microfilariae but not the adult worms, which remain until their death.[172] The adult worm may live 10 years or more. Because of the long life span, ivermectin should be taken every 6 months for at least 10 years to treat microfilariae as they develop.

Infections Primarily Involving the Uvea

The uveal tract is the vascular middle coat of the eye. It is situated between the sclera and the retina. Its major function is to provide nourishment for the intraocular tissues, including the retina, the lens, and the cornea. The uveal tract is composed of the iris, the ciliary body, and the choroid.

Uveitis is a nonspecific term for inflammation of the uvea. If the inflammatory process primarily affects the iris, it is called *iritis*. If the ciliary body is involved, the process is called *cyclitis*. If these two structures together are involved, the process is called *iridocyclitis* (i.e., anterior uveitis). The term *intermediate uveitis* (i.e., pars planitis) applies to inflammation in the region of the ciliary body and peripheral (anterior) retina. The term *posterior uveitis* usually applies to combined inflammation of the retina and choroid, which sometimes is called *chorioretinitis*. If the choroid alone is involved, it is called *choroiditis*; inflammation of the retina alone is called *retinitis*. Because of the thinness and close apposition of these two tissue layers, inflammation in one layer frequently "spills over" into the other. The vitreous body occupies the central area of the eye behind the lens. It is composed of water, mucopolysaccharide, and collagen. Although transparent in the normal, healthy eye, it is subject to inflammation (i.e., vitritis) that usually results from inflammation in adjacent retinal tissue or in the pars plana.

The causes of uveitis are numerous but can be categorized into two main groups: infectious and noninfectious causes. Infectious causes are discussed in this chapter. Uveitis in any localization may result in pain, conjunctival or episcleral hyperemia, photophobia, lacrimation, and decreased vision, although these symptoms vary relative to the site and the aggressiveness of the inflammation.

With slit-lamp examination, the hallmark of anterior uveitis is the finding of hazy, proteinaceous aqueous humor, called *flare*, and the presence of leukocytes in the anterior chamber. The cell and flare components are graded independently on a 1+ to 4+ scale. If present in sufficiently great numbers, the leukocytes can precipitate into a mass (with location depending on gravity) called a *hypopyon*. The cells can aggregate on the back of the cornea to create fine, medium, and large precipitates known as keratic precipitates. The conjunctiva usually is infected or hyperemic. With chronic inflammation, the pupil border often adheres to the anterior surface of the lens. Such adhesions are called *posterior synechiae* and may cause the pupil to have an irregular shape and size and poor reactivity to light. Chronic or recurrent anterior segment inflammation may lead to formation of a cataract. Iris nodules or atrophy may develop with longstanding inflammation. Anterior vitreous cells may occur as a spillover phenomenon in the setting of prolonged or vigorous anterior chamber reaction. Although inflammatory effects on the ciliary body generally compromise its aqueous humor production and thereby reduce intraocular pressure, cellular and proteinaceous debris can occlude the aqueous humor outflow channels and lead to elevated intraocular pressure.

Inflammation primarily involving the posterior segment of the eye often leads to decreased vision, which may be the presenting symptom. Pain may be minimal or absent. Inflammatory lesions of the retina and choroid also may lead to development of cellular debris in the vitreous, causing the patient to perceive "floaters." The borders of the retinal or choroidal inflammatory focus often are indistinct and cream colored. In the healing phase, the borders of these lesions become increasingly distinct, and a defined, partially pigmented scar results. Inflammatory perivascular sheathing of the retinal vessels may occur. Involvement of the macula with edema or exudates may result from inflammation of the posterior segment; long-standing edema may evolve into a cystoid configuration, causing loss of central visual acuity. The optic nerve may exhibit an inflammatory response; if the optic disk is so involved, the response is called *papillitis*. Inflammatory debris also may be found in the vitreous.[4, 128, 189]

Under normal circumstances, the amount of immune traffic within the eye, especially in the anterior chamber, is held to a minimum by a group of immunomodulatory pathways that together form the anterior chamber–associated immune deviation (ACAID). Chief among these deviations is the active suppression of delayed hypersensitivity; distinctive ocular antigen-presenting cells migrate to the spleen, where they generate an immune response deficient in $CD4^+$ cells but high in $CD8^+$ cells. These regulatory T cells return to the eye to suppress the $CD4^+$ populace, minimizing the arm of inflammation most likely to impair visual clarity.[58, 163]

EPIDEMIOLOGY

In the United States, most uveitis cases have noninfectious causes. Large samples demonstrate a predominance of anterior, rather than posterior, uveitis. The most common category of anterior uveitis is idiopathic; the most common infectious cause of anterior uveitis is herpetic keratouveitis (simplex and zoster). Posterior uveitis most commonly is caused by *Toxoplasma gondii*. In developing nations, infectious uveitis plays a proportionately larger role. In West Africa, *T. gondii* probably accounts for most cases of intraocular inflammation.[142, 143]

VIRAL UVEITIS

Herpes Simplex Virus

Most of the uveal inflammation associated with HSV (typically iridocyclitis) results from the corneal disease. Occasionally, a case demonstrates iritis as an isolated finding, but most cases of ocular HSV demonstrate conjunctivitis, keratitis, chorioretinitis, or retinal vasculitis, as described in the following section. The iritis may require treatment with topical steroids and a "cover" of topical antivirals to prevent corneal epithelial disease.[177, 189]

Varicella-Zoster Virus

Occasionally, varicella infection (i.e., chickenpox) may be associated with a transient iritis that requires no treatment. Although rare, cases of unifocal choroiditis causing visual loss responsive to acyclovir in children with primary varicella have been reported.[118]

Herpes zoster may cause an iridocyclitis during the acute stage of the disease; the anterior chamber reaction can persist or recur long after the resolution of the cutaneous component of the condition. Herpes zoster always should be considered in the differential diagnosis of chronic unilateral iridocyclitis. Topical steroids are indicated for iritis, with the addition of oral or intravenous acyclovir for severe cases. Segmental iris atrophy is a characteristic sequela of herpes zoster uveitis. Glaucoma, hyphema, retinitis, vasculitis, and extraocular muscle palsies occasionally occur in patients with herpes zoster ophthalmicus. In the profoundly immunosuppressed patient, varicella zoster can cause a devastating retinitis known as progressive outer retinal necrosis (PORN).[104]

Varicella-zoster virus (VZV) and HSV-2 have been implicated as causes of the acute retinal necrosis syndrome. Patients diagnosed with this syndrome range from 13 to 71 years of age, with an average age of 43 years. This syndrome typically occurs in healthy patients. The virus causes a triad of acute vitritis, retinal vasculitis, and peripheral necrotizing retinitis and is bilateral in 33 percent of patients. Treatment is intravenous acyclovir. Prophylactic laser photocoagulation may prevent retinal detachment. The visual prognosis is guarded.[19, 104]

Epstein-Barr Virus

Ocular involvement with EBV has been reported primarily in patients with infectious mononucleosis. A follicular conjunctivitis may be diagnosed in 2 to 40 percent of patients. Corneal stromal inflammation, iritis, episcleritis, optic neuritis, and chorioretinitis occur less commonly. Systemic corticosteroids and acyclovir may be useful in treating cases of sight-threatening complications of chronic intraocular inflammation from EBV infection.[113] A postinfectious uveitis also has been described and is discussed later.

Enteroviruses

Coxsackievirus A24 and enterovirus 70 may cause a painful follicular conjunctivitis called *acute hemorrhagic conjunctivitis*. Rarely, chorioretinitis may be diagnosed. The treatment for these infections primarily is supportive.[128]

Rubella Virus

Rubella virus can cause congenital and acquired infections. Ocular manifestations of acquired rubella include conjunctivitis in 70 percent of patients, superficial keratitis, and iritis. Rarely, retinitis has been reported.

Congenital rubella syndrome can manifest with cataracts, glaucoma, microphthalmia, and retinitis. Cataracts occur in 15 percent of the patients and glaucoma in 10 percent. Retinal examination reveals a "salt and pepper fundus" because of the alternating pattern of hypopigmentation and hyperpigmentation of the retinal pigment epithelium. The prognosis for patients with retinitis alone usually is good, with vision between 20/20 and 20/40. Glaucoma resulting from rubella commonly requires surgery, as do the cataracts. Iritis is reported less commonly.[20, 113]

Mumps Virus

Results of ocular involvement by the mumps virus include dacryoadenitis, conjunctivitis, iritis, optic neuritis, and keratitis. Retinitis also has been reported. Prognosis for visual recovery from the retinitis is good, and sequelae of the iritis are rare occurrences.[61, 113]

Measles Virus

The measles virus can cause congenital and acquired infections. In congenital infections, a "salt and pepper" retinopathy and cataract formation may occur, similar to that found in rubella. Ocular manifestations in acquired measles include conjunctivitis and, much less commonly, retinitis, retinal vasculitis, and optic nerve edema.[9, 128]

Subacute Sclerosing Panencephalitis

Between 30 and 75 percent of patients with subacute sclerosing panencephalitis (SSPE; i.e., Dawson encephalitis) have ocular findings. SSPE is caused by a variant of the measles virus, differing from the wild-type virus by alterations or absence of viral M protein. Optic nerve edema, inflammation, and subsequent optic atrophy have been reported. Macular retinitis is a common finding; the contiguous non-neural tissues (vitreous and choroid) almost never are involved. The visual prognosis of survivors is poor.[125, 128]

Creutzfeldt-Jakob Disease

The most common ocular manifestation of Creutzfeldt-Jakob disease is cortical blindness. Optic atrophy may result from degeneration of the neurons of the optic nerve.[128]

Human Immunodeficiency Virus and Acquired Immunodeficiency Syndrome

As many as 75 percent of patients with advanced acquired immunodeficiency syndrome (AIDS) have ocular findings. Cotton-wool spots occur in more than 50 percent of the patients and are bilateral in more than 80 percent. Cotton-wool patches represent focal infarctions of the neural layer of the retina and are the most common ocular finding in patients with AIDS. They generally produce no symptoms and do not decrease vision. These spots are white and fluffy and occur most commonly in the macular portion of the retina. They resolve in 4 to 6 weeks with no residual scars. Occasionally, flame-shaped hemorrhages also are detected. The retina and choroid in these patients may become infected with HSV, CMV, VZV, syphilis, tuberculosis, ocular histoplasmosis, *Candida*, toxoplasmosis, and *Pneumocystis*, although in the highly active anti-retroviral therapy (HAART) era, the incidence of CMV retinitis has declined, and its advance in existing cases has been slowed or halted. Symptomatic anterior uveitis in the absence of the aforementioned pathogens occurs rarely in patients with AIDS and may be caused by the human immunodeficiency virus (HIV) itself.[13, 92]

Cytomegalovirus Infection

CMV infections may occur in preterm neonates and immunosuppressed patients, especially patients with AIDS. In neonates demonstrating symptoms of CMV infection (i.e., low birth weight, microcephaly, jaundice, thrombocytopenia, hepatosplenomegaly, or petechial rash), congenital CMV infection[15] (i.e., prenatal transmission) may be manifested in the fundus by chorioretinal scars (21%) and optic atrophy (7%).[34]

Approximately 30 percent of adult patients with AIDS,[45] usually those with $CD4^+$ counts less than 50/mm^3, develop CMV retinitis. In the pediatric AIDS population, $CD4^+$ counts of less than 20/mm^3 may be required for appearance of the retinitis.[46] The disease is less common in pediatric patients with AIDS. Patients with CMV retinitis have no external ocular signs but may complain of vision loss. Children may not complain of vision loss, and the problem may become apparent only after bilateral severe vision loss has occurred.[46] The retinal lesions of CMV typically are yellow-white and often are associated with hemorrhage. The retinitis typically follows a perivascular distribution. The retina becomes necrotic and eventually atrophies, leaving a gliotic scar. CMV optic neuritis also may develop. Treatment consists of intravenous or intravitreal ganciclovir, intravenous or intravitreal cidofovir, or intravenous foscarnet.[46, 189]

Parvovirus Infection

Unilateral anterior uveitis has been associated with parvovirus B19 infection.[108]

Human T-Cell Lymphotrophic Virus Infection

The human T-cell lymphotrophic virus (HTLV) is endemic in several regions of the globe: Japan, the Caribbean islands, and parts of central Africa. It probably is responsible for several cases of self-limited, occasionally recurrent uveitides in those regions.[123]

Lymphocytic Choriomeningitis Virus Infection

Lymphocytic choriomeningitis virus (LCMV) is an arenavirus endemic in mice, also reported in hamsters, and occasionally transmitted to humans by direct contact with the rodent or through aerosolization of their feces or urine. Postnatal exposure results in asymptomatic seroconversion or an aseptic meningitis, but intrauterine infection can have devastating consequences; spontaneous abortion, congenital hydrocephalus, psychomotor retardation, and chorioretinitis have been documented. Diffuse chorioretinal scarring identified postnatally may bode a grim visual prognosis. LCMV may be an underdiagnosed cause of unexplained congenital chorioretinitis. Diagnosis is confirmed by elevated LCMV antibody titers. A survey of severely retarded, visually disabled children revealed immunologic evidence pointing to LCMV as the cause of the visual loss in approximately one half of those surveyed.[116, 117]

BACTERIAL UVEITIS

Syphilis

Syphilis *(Treponema pallidum)* should be considered as a possible cause in all cases of intraocular inflammation. Any patient with confirmed syphilitic uveitis should undergo a lumbar puncture to rule out asymptomatic neurosyphilis.

Ocular manifestations of congenital syphilis include interstitial keratitis; a mottled, "salt and pepper" fundus; and chorioretinal scarring. Acute interstitial keratitis occurs as a late manifestation of congenital syphilis (ages 5 to 25 years) and is thought to be a hypersensitivity response to treponemal antigen in the cornea. Patients present with pain and photophobia and have a diffusely opaque cornea and an anterior uveitis. Blood vessels invade the inflamed cornea and eventually are obliterated, leaving ghost vessels in the corneal stroma. Glaucoma may occur. A unilateral presentation of interstitial keratitis suggests a postnatally acquired lues.

Secondary syphilis may involve any layer of the eye. Episcleritis; scleritis; acute, chronic, or recurrent iridocyclitis; iris capillary dilatation (i.e., iris roseata); vascular papules of the iris (i.e., iris papulosa); inflammatory nodules (i.e., iris nodosa); choroiditis; chorioretinitis; and retinal vasculitis all have been reported, as have optic neuritis and subsequent atrophy.

Tertiary syphilis may have associated gummata of the iris and an Argyll Robertson pupil (i.e., miotic, irregularly shaped pupil with loss of response to light but preservation of the near response). Intraocular inflammation seldom occurs at this stage.

Ocular inflammation secondary to syphilis should be treated as neurosyphilis. With the appropriate doses of penicillin G, the inflammation typically resolves rapidly. Occasionally, topical regional steroids are required to control local inflammation. Treatment of ocular syphilis may lead, at least initially, to a vigorous local and systemic inflammatory response, presumably caused by liberation of spirochetal antigens or toxins. Topical oral corticosteroids may be required to quell this response (i.e., Jarisch-Herxheimer reaction).[4, 110, 128]

Lyme Disease

A mild follicular conjunctivitis occurs in 11 percent of patients with stage 1 Lyme disease, caused by *Borrelia burgdorferi*. During the second and third stages, neuro-ophthalmic manifestations, including cranial neuropathies (most often cranial nerves 3, 4, 6, and 7), optic neuritis, bilateral keratitis, bilateral iridocyclitis, diffuse choroiditis, vasculitis, intermediate uveitis, and Parinaud oculoglandular syndrome, may be seen. The most frequent manifestation of late Lyme disease is arthritis. Ocular inflammation occurs in approximately 4 percent of children with Lyme arthritis.[88] Early, localized Lyme disease may be treated with doxycycline (ages 8 years and up) or amoxicillin. More advanced or persistent disease is treated best with intravenous ceftriaxone.[5] Antibiotic treatment early in the course of the disease carries a better prognosis than does therapy initiated at later stages.[16]

Leptospirosis

Leptospirosis may cause an anterior uveitis that occurs months after the acute infection. Leptospirosis is identified as an important cause of epidemic panuveitis in southern India; the most common posterior segment manifestations in this group are vasculitis and vitritis.[32]

Tuberculosis

Any structure of the eye may be affected by tuberculosis. Allergic and infectious processes have been implicated as important causes of tuberculous uveitis. An anterior uveitis with or without keratitis has been ascribed to tuberculosis. Choroiditis, optic neuritis, and orbital infections have been detected in cases of miliary tuberculosis. The most frequent manifestations of ocular tuberculosis are choroidal nodules and scars; anterior uveitis is an uncommon occurrence.[23]

Treatment should be undertaken with the appropriate antituberculous medications. Corticosteroids often are necessary in conjunction with the antimicrobial therapy.

Leprosy

Because *Mycobacterium leprae,* the cause of leprosy, grows best at lower temperatures, corneal infections predominate. Corneal infection is associated with prominence of the corneal nerves, interstitial keratitis, and corneal hypoesthesia. Secondary spread to the iris and ciliary body may lead to anterior uveitis.

Brucella Infection

Ocular manifestations of *Brucella* infection are rare but include iritis, focal nodular choroiditis, and panophthalmitis.[128]

Cat-Scratch Disease

Bartonella henselae is a gram-negative rod transmitted to humans by the bite or scratch of an infected animal, often a young cat or kitten. Regional lymphadenopathy is the predominant nonocular finding. A striking stellate neuroretinitis is the most easily identifiable complication of ocular infection and is characterized by swelling of the optic nerves and lipid deposition in the retina. Other manifestations include intermediate uveitis, optic disk swelling, multifocal choroiditis, and serous macular detachment. The discrete foci of multifocal choroiditis are the most common findings in the posterior segment. The role of antibiotics in this condition is debated.[97, 158]

FUNGAL UVEITIS

Histoplasmosis

Diagnosis of the presumed ocular histoplasmosis syndrome is based on the clinical picture of disseminated retinal "histo spots," atrophic retinal changes around the optic nerve, and a clear vitreous. Later in the course of the disease, subretinal hemorrhages and retinal detachment may occur. Ocular histoplasmosis often is bilateral and can result in legal blindness from the loss of macular vision. Presumed ocular histoplasmosis syndrome may occur after an episode of benign systemic histoplasmosis during childhood. Active inflammation and vitreous cells usually are not seen in this syndrome, although case series have documented active chorioretinal inflammation as new-onset lesions and as reactivation of previously quiescent lesions.[30, 94] The hallmark histoplasmosis spots appear as white, punched-out, well-demarcated chorioretinal scars and represent healed fungal lesions. Usually, they first appear during adolescence, do not reduce vision, and do not require treatment. Macular disease, which may reduce vision, does not develop until after the patient reaches the second decade of life. Subretinal neovascularization may develop at the site of a macular histoplasmosis spot, with fluid, blood, and lipid accumulating in the subretinal space. This process plus local scarring can result in a marked reduction in central vision.

Macular neovascularization may be treated suitably with laser photocoagulation in an attempt to salvage the remaining central vision. Antifungal drugs may play a role in the unusual setting of demonstrated active histoplasmosis choroiditis.[147]

Candidiasis

Candida spp., including *C. albicans*, are fungi with yeast and filamentous forms. Candidiasis is encountered in immunocompromised patients and in situations involving indwelling catheters, intravenous therapy, chronic antibiotic use, poorly controlled diabetes, and intravenous drug abuse. Candidal chorioretinitis develops in approximately 9 percent of patients with blood cultures positive for the fungus.[43]

In the eye, *Candida* infection usually begins in the choroid and eventually causes multifocal white chorioretinal lesions. If the fungus proliferates unchecked, it may break through the retina into the vitreous, producing the classic, white, snowball-like "fungus ball." Candidal infection that progresses to an endophthalmitis is an exceedingly rare occurrence if appropriate intravenous antifungals are started promptly on notice of a positive blood culture.

Intravenous amphotericin B is the drug of choice. Other antifungal agents, such as fluconazole, flucytosine, and miconazole, also may be effective, but none is dramatically so. The surgical treatment of intraocular *Candida* disease is discussed in the section on endophthalmitis.

Aspergillosis

Aspergillus spp. can infest the choroid, retina, and vitreous of immunocompromised individuals. One group of investigators found a high rate (7%) of these unusual infections on reviewing records of deceased liver transplant recipients.[87]

Coccidioidomycosis

Coccidioides spp. have yeast and filamentous forms. Ocular disease consists of a multifocal chorioretinitis that develops during the course of systemic coccidioidomycosis. The lesions initially appear similar to those seen in histoplasmosis; in severe cases, endophthalmitis results, and a vitrectomy may need to be performed. In less severe cases, the lesions may respond to intravenous amphotericin B.

Cryptococcosis

Cryptococcus neoformans is a yeast-like fungus that can cause a multifocal chorioretinitis and endophthalmitis. Most patients with cryptococcosis are severely immunocompromised; many have AIDS. The CNS and eye commonly are involved, and elevated intracranial pressure may cause papilledema and sixth cranial nerve palsies. Intravenous amphotericin B in combination with oral flucytosine is the treatment regimen of choice.[5, 98]

Sporotrichosis

The dimorphic fungus *Sporothrix schenckii* commonly is encountered in rotting vegetable matter, wood, and soil. The fungus gains access to the host by traumatic implantation or inhalation. It has been reported to be responsible for anterior uveitis in the setting of a suggestive lesion on a finger of the dominant hand, with presumed hand-to-eye transmission.[178]

PROTOZOAL UVEITIS

Leishmaniasis

Ocular leishmaniasis has been described. Manifestations include conjunctivitis, blepharitis, and anterior uveitis. This trio of findings responds to systemic treatment with sodium stibogluconate.[52]

HELMINTHIC UVEITIS

Toxocariasis

Toxocara canis causes visceral larval migrans, which is not associated with ocular disease. In the retina, larvae get trapped in small capillaries and burrow into surrounding tissues; the dead larvae incite an intense eosinophilic abscess. Ocular toxocariasis has three classic clinical presentations, almost always involving one eye only.

One form occurs in children 2 to 9 years of age and causes an indolent endophthalmitis and leukocoria (i.e., white pupil). Tractional retinal detachment may occur. The eye typically shows little or no external evidence of inflammation, and the patient experiences no pain.

A second form appears in children between 4 and 14 years of age. These patients present with reduced vision but little or no external inflammation and no pain. The reduced vision may cause strabismus, which may be the first sign. An inflammatory granuloma is seen in the macula.

The third form of ocular toxocariasis occurs in patients between 6 and 40 years of age but may not be recognized until years later. The patients have good vision, but a peripheral retinal granuloma is seen on routine eye examination. Vision may be affected if a traction band from the granuloma distorts the macula.

Inactive *Toxocara* granulomas do not respond to medication. When active intraocular inflammation exists in such a magnitude as to pose a further threat to vision, administration of periocular or systemic steroids may be necessary. Anthelminthic agents eradicate migrating larvae, but their effect on "residing" larvae is questionable. When giving antihelminthics, one should combine them with a short course of corticosteroids because the death of the larvae may incite vigorous inflammation. Cryotherapy and laser therapy may be useful when the *Toxocara* granuloma is located away from the macula and optic nerve. Vitrectomy may be helpful if significant traction on the retina occurs. Antihelminthic drugs should not be administered after the patient has undergone posterior segment surgery. Visual prognosis is poor if the macula is involved.[128, 150, 153, 186]

Onchocerciasis

Onchocerciasis often causes a severe choroiditis with an overlying retinitis. The various ocular manifestations of infestation with *O. volvulus* are discussed in the section on keratitis.

Loiasis

The loa loa worm can migrate through the tissues of the eye and cause conjunctivitis, iridocyclitis, vitritis, and chorioretinitis. The disease is transmitted by a mango fly bite. Vascular obstruction, with intraretinal hemorrhage and retinal exudation, also may occur. Medical treatment with diethylcarbamazine can kill the adult worms and the microfilariae. The adult also can be removed from the eye surgically.[128]

Cysticercosis

The tapeworm *Taenia solium* causes cysticercosis. When the larva gains access to the eye, cysts form in the vitreous or subretinal space in 13 to 46 percent of patients. The living worm may be seen undulating in these spaces. With death of the organism, severe panuveitis can occur. Orbital and subconjunctival involvement occurs less commonly.

Surgical removal of the intraocular cysts may prevent the severe inflammation that occurs with the death of the worm. Praziquantel can kill the organism, but the ensuing increase in inflammation may be dramatic.[128]

UVEITIS CAUSED BY INSECT-INDUCED DISEASE

Ophthalmomyiasis is the ocular disorder caused by infestation with fly larvae, most commonly the larval form of the sheep botfly, *Oestrus ovis*. Maggots may be seen in the conjunctival fornix (cul-de-sac) or inside the eye. Internal ophthalmomyiasis can manifest with a motile larva in the anterior chamber, vitreous, or subretinal space. The maggot may leave behind trails ("railroad tracks") throughout the retina. A mild inflammatory response in the anterior chamber (e.g., iritis, iridocyclitis) or vitreous may occur.

The treatment is surgical removal of the larva. Corticosteroids may be used to treat the accompanying intraocular inflammation.[49, 128]

POSTINFECTIOUS UVEITIS

Increasingly, attention is being given to the role of bacterial and viral systemic illness in the eventual development of sterile intraocular inflammation. This type of uveitis is thought to be caused by an autoimmune response that occurs between sensitized lymphocytes and host tissues that bear some antigenic similarity to the recently cleared pathogen. Disruption of the ACAID probably is a prerequisite for the development of these postinfectious syndromes. Several reports exist of anterior uveitis occurring weeks or months after streptococcal infections. These uveitides may be associated with other poststreptococcal findings (e.g., arthritis, glomerulonephritis) or may be the sole manifestation. Treatment with cycloplegics and topical corticosteroids is sufficient for the ocular manifestations.[13, 188]

Uveitis, predominantly of the anterior type, has been reported to occur after illnesses caused by gram-negative enteric bacteria such as *Klebsiella*, *Salmonella*, and *Yersinia*. These gram-negative–induced uveitides are much more likely to occur in the setting of HLA-B27 positivity. The ocular findings often parallel development of arthritis, suggesting that parallel immunologic processes are occurring in both of these mesenchymal cavities (i.e., the joint space and the anterior chamber). An association between recent EBV infection and acute tubulointerstitial nephritis and anterior uveitis (TINU) has been described, with the onset of the renal and ocular inflammation occurring several months after the characteristic acute EBV infection.[71]

Infections Involving Primarily the Retina

The TORCHS complex is a group of congenital and perinatal infections that may cause severe systemic and ophthalmic abnormalities. The effect of infection with one of the TORCHS organisms—*T. gondii*, rubella virus, CMV, HIV, varicella virus, and syphilis—may be evident at birth or manifest later in childhood or adulthood. Diagnosis cannot always be made on clinical grounds alone, and neonatal and maternal serologic tests must be obtained to confirm the clinical suspicion.

TOXOPLASMOSIS

T. gondii is an obligate intracellular parasite that has an affinity for the CNS and retina. The parasite has three forms: tachyzoite, bradyzoite, and sporozoite or oocyst. Human infection may be congenital or acquired. Acquired infection results from ingestion of undercooked meat contaminated with oocysts or from exposure to feces of an infected cat, the definitive host. The oocysts release tachyzoites, which multiply intracellularly and result in cell death. In adults, primary acquired infection usually is asymptomatic. The immune response then transforms the tachyzoite into the bradyzoite, which encysts and remains dormant in tissues for years. These cysts have the propensity to rupture sometime later and cause an inflammatory response resulting in recurrent infection.

Congenital infection is transmitted through the transplacental route. In the United States, the reported incidence of congenital toxoplasmosis infection is 1 case in 1000 to 10,000 births.[7, 38] Congenital infection is most severe when acquired in the first trimester and can result in chorioretinitis, intracranial calcifications, microcephaly, mental retardation, and deafness.[38, 55, 57] Symptomatic neonates with disseminated disease have hepatosplenomegaly, lymphadenopathy, jaundice, fever, anemia, pneumonitis, and a poor prognosis. Other ocular manifestations include strabismus, microphthalmia, nystagmus, and ptosis. In a prospective study, 15 percent of infected newborns had chorioretinal scars, indicating infection in utero; 4 percent had active chorioretinitis; and 10 percent developed retinal lesions by 1 to 2 years of age. Long-term follow-up studies have found that between 82 and 85 percent of children with subclinical *Toxoplasma* infection developed chorioretinal lesions, some with severe visual loss. Infants with asymptomatic toxoplasmosis should have regular ophthalmologic examinations because retinal involvement can occur later in childhood or adulthood.[24, 55, 99] Some researchers have suggested that all cases of toxoplasmosis in the neonate should receive drug therapy even if asymptomatic.[55]

Toxoplasmosis is the leading cause of acquired necrotizing retinitis and, in many cases, represents reactivation of congenitally acquired infection. Clinically, an area of active retinochoroiditis is adjacent to the border of a chorioretinal scar.[57, 140] Associated choroiditis and vitritis may be present. Primary acquired ocular toxoplasmosis, which manifests as retinochoroiditis, also is well documented, and reports suggest that this route of infection may be more common than originally thought.[24, 85] Recurrent ocular disease with postnatally acquired *Toxoplasmosis* infection has been reported.[22]

T. gondii causes a focal necrotizing retinitis with a secondary choroiditis and vitritis. Patients may present with floaters, blurred vision, and photophobia. Those with macular involvement can suffer significant visual loss. After the inflammation has resolved, a flat, pigmented chorioretinal scar develops. Visual loss depends on the location of the retinal lesion, peripheral lesions result in little or no visual disturbance, and macular lesions can produce profound visual loss.

Toxoplasma retinochoroiditis is an emerging problem in patients with AIDS and may be the initial manifestation of this disease.[182] The clinical appearance often is atypical.[156] Chronic suppressive therapy is necessary because infection recurs with discontinuation of treatment. A combination of pyrimethamine and clindamycin has been reported to be most effective as prophylaxis.[182]

The diagnosis of *Toxoplasma* retinochoroiditis usually is presumptive, based on clinical appearance and serologic testing. The standard serologic diagnosis is based on the presence of anti-*Toxoplasma* IgM in any sample or demonstration of a significant antibody titer rise in paired sera taken 4 to 6 weeks apart. However, in reactivated congenital infections, which many cases are, *Toxoplasma* IgM results are not positive. The demonstration of any antibodies in the serum is considered essential to the diagnosis, and antibody levels do not reflect activity of disease. The antibody tests most commonly used are indirect immunofluorescent assay (IFA) and enzyme linked immunosorbent assay (ELISA). False-positive results can occur with both tests in the presence of rheumatoid factor. If clinical infection is suspected strongly and initial testing results are negative, repeat testing or an alternative testing technique should be considered.

Standard treatment for *Toxoplasma* retinochoroiditis is triple therapy with sulfadiazine (100–200 mg/kg/day in four divided doses [maximum 1.5 g]), pyrimethamine (2 mg/kg/day for 3 days, then 1 mg/kg/day [maximum 25 mg/day]), and folinic acid (10–25 mg given orally daily for 6 weeks). Folinic acid prevents leukopenia and thrombocytopenia that may result from pyrimethamine therapy. Weekly complete blood counts are required for these patients to monitor toxicity from therapy. Alternative therapy with clindamycin (40 mg/kg/day in four divided doses [maximum 2.4 g] for 6 weeks), rather than sulfadiazine, has also been effective.[171] This therapy is less toxic than is triple therapy and therefore is better tolerated. In cases with severe intraocular inflammation, systemic corticosteroids can be used with concurrent antimicrobial therapy.

RUBELLA INFECTION

The rubella virion is an RNA virus of the family *Togaviridae* that causes a febrile exanthem. Before the advent of the rubella vaccine in 1969, rubella or "German measles" epidemics occurred every 6 to 9 years. With immunization programs of preschool children, most primary cases reported now occur in individuals between 15 and 24 years of age. Transmission occurs by aerosolized droplet inhalation in the nasopharynx. Primary infection in adults results in a mild febrile illness associated with lymphadenopathy and a rash. Susceptibility of nonimmunized women of child-bearing age ranges from 10 to 25 percent. Fetal infection occurs transplacentally, and the likelihood of transmission occurring from mother to fetus is highest in the first trimester; it can produce severe fetal damage that may result in spontaneous abortion, stillbirth, or multiple congenital anomalies.

The classic congenital rubella syndrome is characterized by cardiac defects, ocular abnormalities, and hearing deficits. The incidence of ocular and cardiac defects is higher with exposure early in the first trimester; hearing deficits appear associated with exposure late in the first trimester. Givens and associates[68] reported that 88 percent had multiorgan involvement. The most common cardiac defects are a patent ductus arteriosus, pulmonary artery stenosis, and pulmonary valve stenosis. Other features include microcephaly, thrombocytopenia, hepatosplenomegaly, and mental retardation.

Ocular involvement occurs in approximately 50 percent of infants.[65] Pigmentary retinopathy (i.e., "salt and pepper" retinopathy) is the most common ophthalmic manifestation of the congenital rubella syndrome. The retina has a mottled appearance most frequently observed in the posterior pole; the optic nerve and vessels usually are normal unless the patient also has glaucoma.

Nuclear cataracts, affecting between 15 and 27 percent of patients, are the second most frequent ocular complication. Glaucoma is seen in approximately 10 percent of eyes; the combination of cataracts and glaucoma is an uncommon finding. Microphthalmia (which occurs in 10 to 63 percent of affected individuals), iris atrophy, and iritis also have been reported.[20]

Retinopathy associated with rubella usually is asymptomatic and does not necessitate treatment. In some cases, it can be complicated by subretinal neovascularization that may require laser or macular surgery. Cataracts cause most visual morbidity. Visual rehabilitation depends on early cataract extraction to prevent deprivation amblyopia, correction of aphakia with spectacles or contact lenses, and careful follow-up. Glaucoma in infants and children can be temporized with topical medications, but most cases require glaucoma surgery.

Congenital rubella has long-term consequences for all organs involved. Nearly two thirds of infants with no manifestations at birth subsequently develop hearing loss or psychomotor deficits. From the ophthalmic standpoint, individuals with congenital rubella need continued follow-up.[68]

CYTOMEGALOVIRUS INFECTION

CMV is an enveloped DNA virus of the family *Herpesviridae*. An estimated 80 percent of adults have been infected by the time they reach 40 years of age.[160] In immunocompetent adults, infection is asymptomatic or can cause a mononucleosis syndrome. Individuals can shed virus in saliva, urine, and other body fluids for months to years after initial infection. Transmission occurs through exposure to body fluids, sexual contact, blood transfusions, organ transplantation, or transplacentally. Primary infection acquired in the birth canal is not likely to result in serious disease.

Congenital CMV is the most common congenital virus in humans[159] and can result from exposure to the virus in utero or in the birth canal. Only in utero infection produces serious disease. Infection occurs in 1 percent of all live births. Maternal infection may be primary or recurrent, but primary infection carries the greatest risk (30% to 40%) for transmission of symptomatic CMV disease in the newborn.[160] Only 5 percent of infants with congenital CMV infection are symptomatic. Blood transfusions from CMV antibody-positive donors also can result in severe CMV infections in the newborn.

In symptomatic congenital CMV infection, the retina is the primary site of ocular involvement. Cytomegalic inclusion bodies are seen in all layers of the retina. Patchy white areas of necrotic retina with hemorrhage and vascular sheathing are seen in the peripheral retina, although the posterior pole can be affected as well.[106] Nonhemorrhagic retinitis also may be seen, and most affected infants do not have active retinitis at birth, although scars may be visible as evidence of previous disease.[34] Resolution of the retinitis results in an atrophic scar with areas of hyperpigmentation. If retinitis involves the retinal periphery, vision may be normal. However, visual loss may occur if the posterior pole is involved or if optic atrophy or retinal detachment occurs. CMV retinopathy develops in 5 to 30 percent of infants with clinically apparent disease.[50] Microphthalmia, optic nerve hypoplasia, optic nerve colobomas, anophthalmia, and anterior segment dysgenesis also have been associated with congenital CMV infection.[83]

The diagnosis of CMV retinitis is based on the clinical appearance and the constellation of systemic symptoms and signs. Recovery of the virus from urine, maternal cervical secretions, saliva, or aqueous humor can confirm the diagnosis. Complement fixation can identify IgM antibodies to CMV and does not cross-react with other herpesviruses. Immunofluorescence techniques are more sensitive but less specific than is complement fixation.[106]

Treatment of neonatal or pediatric CMV retinitis is based on the results of treatment of adults with CMV retinitis. Ganciclovir has been shown to stabilize and prevent the spread of the disease in infants. Maintenance therapy is not required, but continued follow-up is necessary to detect recurrence of the disease. Granulocytopenia and thrombocytopenia can result. Retinal detachment requires vitrectomy, membrane peel, and silicone oil to tamponade the detached retina.[84]

HERPES SIMPLEX VIRUS

HSV is an enveloped DNA virus. Both subtypes, HSV-1 and HSV-2, cause a vesicular skin eruption. HSV-1 typically is isolated from oral-facial infections; HSV-2 usually is isolated from genital infections. After primary infection, HSV can maintain latency in neuronal ganglion cells and reactivate. Transmission occurs by exposure to infected body fluids, such as saliva, and the risk of transmission is higher when the individual is symptomatic.[122]

Maternal-fetal transmission occurs through infected genital secretions in the birth canal (HSV-2) or exposure to infected individuals with oral-facial herpetic disease (HSV-1) in the postnatal period. In active genital disease, the risk of transmission to the neonate with vaginal delivery is 50 percent. Most series report that between 70 and 80 percent of neonatal HSV infection is caused by HSV-2. Neonatal HSV infection is life-threatening, and without treatment, the mortality rate is 80 percent.[184]

Less than 1 percent of immunocompetent adults with HSV infection develop ocular sequelae. In contrast, 17 to 40 percent of affected neonates have ocular disease.[113, 160] Ocular involvement can range from mild conjunctivitis to severe bilateral necrotizing retinitis and may be unilateral or bilateral. Conjunctivitis is the most common manifestation. Conjunctivitis, keratitis, and occasionally retinitis manifest 2 to 14 days after birth. Keratitis may be diffuse, geographic, or dendritic in configuration and can result in corneal scarring. HSV retinitis causes punctate, white-yellow lesions in the periphery and the posterior pole accompanied by choroiditis, vascular sheathing, hemorrhage, and vitritis. Chorioretinal atrophic scars with variable amounts of pigmentation around the border result after resolution of acute infection.[86, 139] Visual prognosis depends on the severity of disease, macular scarring, optic atrophy, or CNS involvement of the visual pathways. Severe chorioretinitis and cortical blindness are the usual sequelae of HSV infection acquired through transplantation, a rare mode of transmission.

El Azazi and colleagues[51] examined individuals with serologically proven HSV infection 1 to 15 years after neonatal exposure and found a higher prevalence of chorioretinal scars than that noted in previous reports (28% compared with 4%). This finding suggests that HSV remains dormant in the retina and reactivates later in childhood or adulthood. Chorioretinitis, cataracts, optic atrophy, and microphthalmia have been reported.[73] Acute retinal necrosis from reactivation of HSV-2 also has occurred.[173]

Ocular HSV infection can be seen in conjunction with a vesicular rash or with disseminated disease. The differential diagnosis for the ophthalmic complications of HSV include infection with any of the TORCHS complex organisms. Identification of neonatal IgM antibody to HSV confirms the diagnosis of in utero infection. Demonstration of intranuclear inclusions and multinucleated giant cells in skin, conjunctiva, and oral and genital lesions may be diagnostic.

Acyclovir is the drug of choice to treat neonatal HSV infection. Conjunctival and corneal disease also can be treated with débridement and topical antivirals, such as vidarabine. In neonatal HSV infection, systemic acyclovir should be given, regardless of topical treatment. Early diagnosis and treatment can reduce ocular morbidity.

VARICELLA-ZOSTER VIRUS INFECTION

VZV is a DNA virus of the family *Herpesviridae*; enveloped virions are the infectious agents. Primary infection results in chickenpox, a highly communicable, febrile illness with a vesicular rash that appears after 48 to 72 hours of incubation. VZV can remain dormant in sensory ganglion neurons and reactivate as herpes zoster, a painful rash in the dermatomal distribution of the sensory ganglion.

Congenital varicella syndrome is considered a rare entity. One prospective series reported a 24 percent incidence of congenital varicella with serologic or clinical confirmation of maternal infection during pregnancy. Mortality rates can be high if maternal infection develops 5 days before delivery to 2 days after delivery. Systemic complications of VZV infection include cranial nerve palsies, hemiparesis, cicatricial skin lesions, intrauterine growth retardation, developmental delay, seizures, neurogenic bladder, and learning difficulties.[100, 130]

Ocular abnormalities in congenital VZV infection include chorioretinitis, cataract, Horner syndrome, optic nerve hypoplasia, retinal coloboma, and microphthalmia. The chorioretinal scars of VZV infection have a deeply pigmented center with depigmented borders or a gliotic white center with hyperpigmented edges. The neurotropic nature of VZV infection may explain the association of Horner syndrome. Ocular involvement can be unilateral or bilateral. VZV chorioretinitis affects the macula, periphery, or both.

Serologic testing for IgG and IgM antibodies to VZV, history of maternal infection during pregnancy, and the constellation of systemic findings help make the diagnosis. Because active infection may occur early in the pregnancy, the neonate may have IgG but no detectable IgM antibodies to VZV by the time of delivery. The persistence of elevated IgG antibodies beyond 6 months of age, when passive immunity through maternal antibodies has waned, without evidence of primary VZV infection postnatally, is a helpful indication of infection in utero.

SYPHILIS

Syphilis is caused by the spirochete *T. pallidum*. Acquired syphilis is a sexually transmitted chronic disease and has three stages of infection. Primary infection is characterized by painless, indurated chancres of the skin or mucous membranes at the site of inoculation. The secondary stage appears as a maculopapular rash, classically involving the palms and soles. Generalized lymphadenopathy, fever, malaise, sore throat, headache, and arthralgias can accompany the rash. Hypertrophic lesions (i.e., condyloma lata) occur in moist mucous membranes. Approximately one third of untreated cases progress to the tertiary stage, which occurs after a variable latent period that may have occasional recurrences of secondary syphilis. Transmission to the fetus can occur with maternal syphilis in any stage of the disease.[169]

Pigmentary retinopathy is the most common early ocular manifestation of congenital syphilis. Diffuse mottling in the periphery (i.e., salt and pepper retinopathy) is indicative of chorioretinitis in utero. Pigment clumping in the periphery usually has no effect on vision, but macular involvement can cause decreased vision. Retinal changes can appear later in adulthood, suggesting that inflammatory changes caused by congenital infection can occur after birth. Salt and pepper retinopathy is evidence of previous inflammation, and no treatment is required. Interstitial keratitis (see the Stromal Keratitis section) is the hallmark of congenital syphilis and occurs in 75 percent of these patients.[169] It usually is not detected until late in the first decade of life. Other reported ocular manifestations include optic neuritis and iritis.

Testing the serum by nontreponemal and treponemal methods confirms the diagnosis of congenital infection. The American Academy of Pediatrics recommends physical examination, quantitative nontreponemal serologic testing, cerebrospinal fluid VDRL test, long bone radiographs, and anti-treponemal IgM testing, as specified by the Centers for Disease Control and Prevention. Treatment is with intravenous penicillin G for 10 to 14 days.[5, 110]

Endophthalmitis

Endophthalmitis is an infection within the eye that may be endogenous during septicemia or exogenous from accidental or surgical trauma.[145, 154] Sixty-two percent of cases occur after intraocular surgery, 20 percent after penetrating trauma, and 10 percent after glaucoma surgery; 8 percent result from metastatic infection.[43, 137] The patient usually presents with severe ocular pain and visual loss. Rarely, patients may be asymptomatic. Signs of endophthalmitis include conjunctival injection, vitritis, uveitis, hypopyon, and intraocular membrane formation.

Endophthalmitis constitutes an ophthalmic emergency and necessitates immediate evaluation of aqueous and vitreous cultures and institution of intravitreal antibiotic therapy. Any significant delay in recognition and treatment of endophthalmitis can result in permanent vision loss.

Postsurgical endophthalmitis occurs in 0.086 percent of cataract operations.[2] The source of postsurgical infection may be from the eyelids, conjunctiva, contaminated instruments and irrigating solutions, or contamination by operating room personnel. The routine use of subconjunctival antibiotics after intraocular surgery does not prevent all cases of postoperative endophthalmitis. Vitreous loss, which may occur occasionally as a complication of cataract surgery, increases the risk of developing infection. Patients who have undergone glaucoma filtering surgery are particularly prone to endophthalmitis primarily because sclerostomy is performed routinely as part of this procedure, and the only remaining protection the eye has from infective organisms is a thin layer of conjunctiva overlying the sclerostomy. Local antimetabolites, often used in conjunction with glaucoma filtering procedures, predispose the conjunctiva to bleb leaks that allow direct access of microorganisms into the eye.

Endogenous (metastatic) endophthalmitis should be suspected when ocular inflammation occurs in a septicemic patient, particularly if the patient is immunocompromised or has an underlying systemic illness, such as diabetes or leukemia.[21, 121, 127]

Post-traumatic endophthalmitis should be considered in any patient with a history of injury and visual loss. A history of a high-velocity projectile presents a great concern for a penetrating injury, and an apparently minor accidental ocular trauma may represent a globe perforation with or without a retained foreign body. The likelihood of post-traumatic endophthalmitis occurring increases directly with the extent of the injury and the degree of intraocular contamination.

After the diagnosis is suspected, immediate referral to an ophthalmologist is necessary. After the patient has been examined, a vitreous and aqueous aspirate is obtained under general anesthesia and material is evaluated with Gram and Giemsa stains. Stains with calcofluor white or acridine orange are performed if fungal infection is a concern. The material is cultured on blood and chocolate agar, thioglycolate broth, and Sabouraud agar. Vancomycin (1 mg) to cover gram-positive organisms and ceftazidime (2.5 mg) to cover gram-negative organisms are injected into the vitreous cavity. If fungal infection is suspected, intravitreal amphotericin B is given. Occasionally, the ophthalmologist uses intravitreal dexamethasone to control associated, intense intraocular inflammation. Gram stain results often are inconsistent with cultures.

The role of vitrectomy in postoperative endophthalmitis has been addressed in the Endophthalmitis Vitrectomy Study (EVS).[53] In eyes with better than light-perception vision at the time of patient presentation, the outcome measurements were equal between the vitrectomy group and the vitreous tap or biopsy group. In eyes with light-perception-only vision, the EVS found that patients who underwent immediate pars plana vitrectomy did significantly better than did those who had vitreous tap or biopsy alone.

The most common infectious agents in endophthalmitis are *S. epidermidis*, *Bacillus* spp., *Streptococcus* spp., *S. aureus*, and various fungi. *Bacillus cereus* is isolated in 30 to 40 percent of cases and can cause severe ocular morbidity.[1, 39, 40, 42, 80]

S. epidermidis is the predominant organism in postoperative cases, and *Streptococcus* spp. with filtering blebs and *B. cereus* are the organisms associated most frequently with penetrating trauma. Approximately 65 percent of cases are culture positive.

Fungal endophthalmitis has become a relatively common form of endophthalmitis in childhood because of the prolonged hospital care required for severely ill immunocompromised children. The most common organism is *C. albicans*. Children with a central line catheter or receiving prolonged intravenous therapy of any type are particularly prone to infection. In patients with *Candida* endophthalmitis, the vitreous may be hazy, and small, white "snowball" localizations of infected material may appear in the vitreous or on the surface of the retina. Daily careful observation may be required during intravenous amphotericin B therapy. If the endophthalmitis clears, no ocular surgical intervention is indicated. If the infection is not adequately controlled with intravenous therapy, a vitrectomy with injection of intravitreal amphotericin may be required.

REFERENCES

1. Alfaro, D. V., Roth, D., and Liggett, P. E.: Posttraumatic endophthalmitis: Causative organisms, treatment, and prevention. Retina. *14*:206–211, 1994.
2. Allen, H. F., Mangiaracine, A. B.: Bacterial endophthalmitis after cataract extraction. II. Incidence in 36,000 consecutive operations with special reference to preoperative topical antibiotics. Arch. Ophthalmol. *91*:3–7, 1974.
3. Ambati, B. K., Ambati, J., Azar, N., et al.: Periorbital and orbital cellulitis before and after the advent of haemophilus influenzae type B vaccination. Ophthalmology. *107*:1450–1453, 2000.
4. American Academy of Ophthalmology: Basic and Clinical Science Course, Section 9: Intraocular Inflammation and Uveitis. San Francisco, American Academy of Ophthalmology, 1995, pp. 57–61.
5. American Academy of Pediatrics: 1997 Red Book: Report of the Committee on Infectious Diseases. 24th ed. Elk Grove Village, American Academy of Pediatrics, 1997.
6. Asbell, P., and Stenson, S.: Ulcerative keratitis, survey of 30 years laboratory experience. Arch. Ophthalmol. *100*:77–80, 1982.
7. Bale, J. F., Jr., and Murphy, J. R.: Congenital infections and the nervous system. Pediatr. Clin. North Am. *39*:669–690, 1982.
8. Barkin, R. M., Todd, J. K., and Amer, J.: Periorbital cellulitis in children. Pediatrics. *62*:390–392, 1978.
9. Bedrossian, R. H.: Neuroretinitis following measles. J. Pediatr. *46*:329–331, 1955.
10. Bekir, N. A., Gungor, K., and Namiduru, M.: *Brucella melitensis* dacryoadenitis: A case report. Eur. J. Ophthalmol. *10*: 259–261, 2000.
11. Bell, T. A., Kuo, C., Stamm, W. E., et al.: Direct fluorescent monoclonal antibody stain for rapid detection of infant *Chlamydia trachomatis* infections. Pediatrics. *74*:224–228, 1984.
12. BenEzra, D.: Ocular Inflammation: Basic and Clinical Concepts. London, Martin Dunitz, 1999, pp. 427–444.
13. Benjamin, A., Tufail, A., and Holland, G. N.: Uveitis as the only clinical manifestation of poststreptococcal syndrome. Am. J. Ophthalmol. *123*:259–260, 1997.
14. Benson, W. H., and Lanier, J. D.: Current diagnosis and treatment of corneal ulcers. Curr. Opin. Ophthalmol. *9*:45–49, 1998.
15. Berenberg, W., and Nankervis, G.: Long-term follow-up cytomegalic inclusion disease of infancy. Pediatrics. *46*:403, 1970.
16. Bertuch, A. W., Rocco, E., and Schwartz, E. G.: Lyme disease: Ocular manifestations. Ann. Ophthalmol. *20*:376–378, 1988.
17. Bhaskaram, P., Mathur, R., Rao, V., et al.: Pathogenesis of corneal lesions in measles. Hum. Nutr. Clin. Nutr. *40*:197–204, 1986.
18. Birenbaum, E., Linder, N., Varsano, N., et al.: Adenovirus type 8 conjunctivitis outbreak in a neonatal intensive care unit. Arch. Dis. Child. *68*:610–611, 1993.
19. Blumenkranz, M., Clarkson, J., Culbertson, W. W., et al.: Visual results and complications after retinal reattachment in the acute retinal necrosis syndrome: The influence of operative technique. Retina. *9*:170–174, 1989.
20. Boniuk, M. M., and Zimmerman, L. E.: Ocular pathology in the rubella syndrome. Arch. Ophthalmol. *77*:455–473, 1967.
21. Borne, M. J., Shields, J. A., Shields, C. L., et al.: Bilateral viral endophthalmitis as the presenting sign of severe combined immunodeficiency. Arch. Ophthalmol. *112*:1280–1281, 1994.
22. Bosch-Driessen, E. H., and Rothova, A.: Recurrent ocular disease in postnatally acquired toxoplasmosis. Am. J. Ophthalmol. *128*:421–425, 1999.
23. Bouza, E., Merino, P., Sanchez-Carrillo, C., et al.: Ocular tuberculosis: A prospective study in a general hospital. Medicine (Baltimore). *76*:53–61, 1997.
24. Brezin, A. P., Kasner, L., Thulliez, P., et al.: Ocular toxoplasmosis in the fetus: Immunohistochemistry analysis and DNA amplification. Retina. *14*:19–26, 1994.
25. Brook, I.: Dacryocystitis caused by anaerobic bacteria in the newborn. Pediatr. Infect. Dis. J. *17*:172–173, 1998.
26. Brook, I., and Frazier, E. H.: Aerobic and anaerobic microbiology of dacryocystitis. Am. J. Ophthalmol. *125*:552–554, 1998.
27. Buck, S. L., Rosenthal, R. A., and Schlech, B. A.: Methods used to evaluate the effectiveness of contact lens care solutions and other compounds against *Acanthamoeba*: A review of the literature. CLAO. J. *26*:72–84, 2000.
28. Bullock, J. D., and Fleishman, J. A.: Orbital cellulitis following dental extraction. Trans. Am. Ophthalmol. Soc. *82*:111–133, 1984.
29. Burns, D. A.: The treatment of *Phthirus pubis* infestation of the eyelashes. Brit. J. Dermatol. *117*: 741–743, 1987.
30. Callanan, D., Fish, G. E., and Anand, R.: Reactivation of inflammatory lesions in ocular histoplasmosis. Arch. Ophthalmol. *116*:470–484, 1998.
31. Chang, C. H., Lai, Y. H., Wang, H. Z., et al.: Antibiotic treatment of orbital cellulitis: An analysis of pathogenic bacteria and bacterial susceptibility. J. Ocul. Pharmacol. Ther. *16*:75–79, 2000.
32. Chu, K. M., Rathinam, R., Namperumalsamy, P., et al.: Identification of *Leptospira* species in the pathogenesis of uveitis and determination of clinical ocular characteristics in south India. J. Infect. Dis. *177*: 1314–1321, 1998.
33. Clary, R., Weber, A. L., Eavey, R., et al.: Orbital cellulitis with abscess formation caused by sinusitis. Ann. Otol. Rhinol. Laryngol. *97*:211–212, 1988.
34. Coats, D. K., Demmler, G. J., Paysse, E. A., et al.: Ophthalmologic findings in children with congenital cytomegalovirus infection. J. AAPOS. *4*:110–116, 2000.
35. Corey, L.: Herpes simplex viruses. *In* Braunwald, E., Isselbacher, K. J., Petersdorf, R. G., et al. (eds.): Harrison's Principles of Internal Medicine. 14th ed. New York, McGraw-Hill, 1998, pp. 1080–1086.
36. Couch, J. M., Green, W. R., Hirst, L. W., et al.: Diagnosing and treating *Phthirus pubis* palpebrarum. Surv. Ophthalmol. *26*:219–225, 1982.
37. Credo, B. V., and Dyment, P. G.: Molluscum contagiosum. Adolesc. Med. *7*:57–62, 1996.
38. Daffos, F., Forestier, F., Capella-Pavlovsky, M., et al.: Prenatal management of 746 pregnancies at risk for congenital toxoplasmosis. N. Engl. J. Med. *318*:271–275, 1988.
39. Davey, R. T., and Tauber, W. B.: Post traumatic endophthalmitis: The emerging role of *Bacillus cereus* infection. Rev. Infect. Dis. *9*:110–124, 1987.
40. David, D. B., Kirkby, G. R., and Noble, B. A.: *Bacillus cereus* endophthalmitis. Br. J. Ophthalmol. *78*:577–580, 1994.
41. Dawson, D. R., and Sheppard, J. D.: Follicular conjunctivitis. *In* Tasman, W., and Jaeger, E. A. (eds.): Duane's Clinical Ophthalmology. Philadelphia, Lippincott, 1990, pp. 16–18.
42. Diamond, J. G.: Intraocular management of endophthalmitis. Arch. Ophthalmol. *99*:96–99, 1981.
43. Donahue, S. P., Greven, C. M., et al.: Intraocular candidiasis in patients with candidemia. Ophthalmology. *101*:1302–1309, 1994.
44. Donahue, S. P., and Schwartz, G.: Preseptal and orbital cellulitis in childhood. A changing microbiologic spectrum. Ophthalmology. *105*: 1902–1905, 1998.
45. Drew, W. L.: Cytomegalovirus infection in patients with AIDS. J. Infect. Dis. *158*:449–456, 1988.
46. Du, L. T., Coats, D. K., Paysse, E. A., et al.: Incidence of presumed cytomegalovirus retinitis in HIV-infected pediatric patients. J. AAPOS. *3*:245–249, 1999.
47. Dua, H. S., and Nilawar, D. V.: Nonsurgical therapy of chalazion. Am. J. Ophthalmol. *94*:424–425, 1982.
48. Duke-Elder, S. S., and Leigh, A. G.: Diseases of the Outer Eye. System of Ophthalmology Series. Vol. 8. St. Louis, C. V. Mosby, 1965, p. 790.
49. Edwards, K. M., Meredith, T. A., Hager, W. S., et al.: Ophthalmomyiasis interna causing visual loss. Am. J. Ophthalmol. *97*:605–610, 1984.
50. Eichenwald, H. F., and Shinefield, H. R.: Viral infections of the fetus and of the premature and newborn infant. Adv. Pediatr. *12*:249, 1962.
51. El Azazi, M., Malm, G., and Forsgren, M.: Late ophthalmologic manifestations of neonatal herpes simplex virus infection. Am. J. Ophthalmol. *109*:1–7, 1990.
52. El Hassan, A. M., Khalil, E. A., el Sheikh, E. A., et al.: Post kala-azar ocular leishmaniasis. Trans. R. Soc. Trop. Med. Hyg. *92*:177–179, 1998.
53. Endophthalmitis Vitrectomy Study Group: Results of the endophthalmitis vitrectomy study: A randomized trial of immediate vitrectomy and of intravenous antibiotics for the treatment of postoperative bacterial endophthalmitis. Arch. Ophthalmol. *113*:1479–1496, 1995.
54. English, F. P., and Nutting, W. B.: Demodicosis of ophthalmic concern. Am. J. Ophthalmol. *91*:362–372, 1981.
55. Engstrom, R. E., Holland, G. N., Nussenblatt, R. B., et al.: Current practices in the management of ocular toxoplasmosis. Am. J. Ophthalmol. *111*:601–610, 1991.

56. Epstein, G. A., and Putterman, A. M.: Combined excision and drainage with intralesional corticosteroid injection in the treatment of chronic chalazia. Arch. Ophthalmol. *106*:514–516, 1988.
57. Fair, J. R.: Clinical eye findings in congenital toxoplasmosis. Surv. Ophthalmol. *6*:923–935, 1961.
58. Feltkamp, T. E. W., and Ringrose, J. H.: Acute anterior uveitis and spondyloarthropathies. Curr. Opin. Rheumatol. *10*:314–318, 1998.
59. Foster, A., and Sommer, A.: Corneal ulceration, measles, and childhood blindness in Tanzania. Br. J. Ophthalmol. *71*:331–343, 1987.
60. Foster, C. S.: Fungal keratitis. Infect. Dis. Clin. North Am. *6*:851–857, 1992.
61. Foster, R. E., Lowder, C. Y., Meisler, D. M., et al.: Mumps neuroretinitis in an adolescent. Am. J. Ophthalmol. *110*:91–93, 1990.
62. Fox, K. R., and Golomb, H. S.: Staphylococcal ophthalmia neonatorum and the staphylococcal scalded skin syndrome. Am. J. Ophthalmol. *88*:1052–1055, 1979.
63. Friendly, D. S.: Ophthalmia neonatorum. Pediatr. Clin. North Am. *30*:1033–1042, 1983.
64. Garcia, G. H., and Harris, G. J.: Criteria for nonsurgical management of subperiosteal abscess of the orbit: Analysis of outcomes, 1988–1998. Ophthalmology. *107*:1454–1456, 2000.
65. Geltzer, A. I., Guber, D., and Sears, M. L.: Ocular manifestations of the 1964–65 rubella epidemic. Am. J. Ophthalmol. *63*:221–229, 1967.
66. Gigliotti, F., Williams, W. T., Hayden, F. G., et al.: Etiology of acute conjunctivitis in children. J. Pediatr. *98*:531–536, 1981.
67. Gigliotti, F., Hendley, J. O., Morgan, J., et al.: Efficacy of topical antibiotic therapy in acute conjunctivitis in children. J. Pediatr. *104*:623–626, 1984.
68. Givens, K. T., Lee, D. A, and Ilstrup, D. M.: Congenital rubella syndrome: Ophthalmic manifestations and associated systemic disorders. Br. J. Ophthalmol. *77*:358–363, 1993.
69. Goscienski, P. J.: Inclusion conjunctivitis in the newborn infant. J. Pediatr. *77*:19–26, 1970.
70. Greenberg, M. F., and Pollard, Z. F.: Medical treatment of pediatric subperiosteal orbital abscess secondary to sinusitis. J. AAPOS. *2*:351–355, 1998.
71. Grefer, J., Santer, R., Ankermann, T., et al.: Tubulointerstitial nephritis and uveitis in association with Epstein-Barr virus infection. Pediatr. Nephrol. *13*:336–339, 1999.
72. Green, W. R., Font, R. L., and Zimmerman, L. E.: Aspergillosis of the orbit. Arch. Ophthalmol. *82*:302–313, 1969.
73. Hagler, W. S., Walters, P. V., and Nahmias, A. J.: Ocular involvement in neonatal herpes simplex virus infection. Arch. Ophthalmol. *82*:109–176, 1969.
74. Haimovici, R., and Roussel, T. J.: Treatment of gonococcal conjunctivitis with a single-dose intramuscular ceftriaxone. Am. J. Ophthalmol. *107*:511–514, 1989.
75. Hall, L. R., and Pearlman, E.: Pathogenesis of onchocercal keratitis. Clin. Microbiol. Rev. *12*:445–453, 1999.
76. Hammerschlag, M. R.: Neonatal conjunctivitis. Pediatr. Ann. *22*:346–351, 1993.
77. Hammerschlag, M. R., Chandler, J. W., Alexander, E. R., et al.: Erythromycin ointment for ocular prophylaxis of neonatal chlamydial infection. J. A. M. A. *244*:2291–2293, 1980.
78. Hammerschlag, M. R., Cummings, C., Roblin, P. M., et al.: Efficacy of neonatal ocular prophylaxis for the prevention of chlamydial and gonococcal conjunctivitis. N. Engl. J. Med. *320*:769–772, 1989.
79. Hansen, T., Burns, R. P., and Allen, A.: Gonorrheal conjunctivitis: An old disease returned. J. A. M. A. *195*:1156, 1966.
80. Hemady, R., Zaltas, M., Paton, B., et al.: *Bacillus*-induced endophthalmitis: New series of 10 cases and review of the literature. Br. J. Ophthalmol. *74*:26–29, 1990.
81. Hess, D. L.: *Chlamydia* in the neonate. Neonatal Netw. *12*:9–12, 1993.
82. Hierholzer, J. C., and Hatch, M. H.: Acute hemorrhagic conjunctivitis. *In* Darnell, R. W. (ed.): Viral Diseases of the Eye. Philadelphia, Lea & Febiger, 1985, pp. 165–196.
83. Holland, G. N.: Infectious diseases. *In* Isenberg, S. (ed.): The Eye in Infancy. Chicago, Yearbook Medical Publishers, 1989, pp. 387–416.
84. Holland, G. N.: An update on AIDS-related cytomegalovirus retinitis. *In* Focal Points: Clinical Modules for Ophthalmologists. Vol. 9, Module 5. San Francisco, American Academy of Ophthalmology, 1991.
85. Holland, G. N.: Reconsidering the pathogenesis of ocular toxoplasmosis. Am. J. Ophthalmol. *128*:502–505, 1999.
86. Honda, Y., Nakazawa, Y., and Chihara, E.: Necrotizing chorioretinitis induced by herpes simplex virus infection in the neonate. Metab. Pediatr. Syst. Ophthalmol. *7*:147–152, 1983.
87. Hunt, K. E., and Glasgow, B. J.: Aspergillus endophthalmitis: An unrecognized endemic disease in orthotopic liver transplantation. Ophthalmology. *103*:757–767, 1996.
88. Huppertz, H.-I., Munchmeier, D., Lieb, W.: Ocular manifestations in children and adolescents with Lyme arthritis. Br. J. Ophthalmol. *83*:1149–1152, 1999.
89. Illingworth, C. D., and Cook, S. D.: *Acanthamoeba* keratitis. Surv. Ophthalmol. *42*:493–508, 1998.
90. Isenberg, S. J., Apt, L., and Wood, M.: A controlled trial of povidone-iodine as prophylaxis against ophthalmia neonatorum. N. Engl. J. Med. *332*:562–566, 1995.
91. Jarrett, W. H., and Gutman, F. A.: Ocular complications of the paranasal sinuses. Arch. Ophthalmol. *81*:683, 1969.
92. Jabs, D. A., Green, W. R., Fox, R., et al.: Ocular manifestations of AIDS. Ophthalmology. *96*:1092–1099, 1989.
93. Jones, D. B.: Viral and chlamydial conjunctivitis. *In* Symposium on Medical and Surgical Diseases of the Cornea: Transactions of the New Orleans Academy of Ophthalmology. St. Louis, CV Mosby, 1980, pp. 497–523.
94. Katz, B. J., Scott, W. E., and Folk, J. C.: Acute histoplasmosis choroiditis in 2 immunocompetent brothers. Arch. Ophthalmol. *115*:1470–1472, 1997.
95. Kaufman, H. E.: Treatment of viral diseases of the cornea and external eye. Prog. Retin. Eye Res. *19*:69–85, 1998.
96. Kayikcioglu, O., Kir, E., Soyler, M., et al.: Ocular findings in a measles epidemic among young adults. Ocul. Immunol. Inflamm. *8*:59–62, 2000.
97. Kerkhoff, F. T., Ossewaarde, J. M., de Loos, W. S., et al.: Presumed ocular bartonellosis. Br. J. Ophthalmol. *83*:270–275, 1999.
98. Kestelyn, P., Taelman, H., Bogaerts, J., et al.: Ophthalmic manifestations of infections with *Cryptococcus neoformans* in patients with the acquired immunodeficiency syndrome. Am. J. Ophthalmol. *116*: 721–727, 1993.
99. Koppe, J. G., Kloosterman, G. J., de Roever-Bonnet, H., et al.: Toxoplasmosis and pregnancy, with a long-term follow-up of the children. Eur. J. Obstet. Gynecol. Reprod. Biol. *4*:101–110, 1974.
100. Laforet, E. G., and Lynch, C. L.: Multiple congenital defects following maternal varicella. Report of a case. N. Engl. J. Med. 236:534, 1947.
101. Larkin, D. F. P., Kilvington, S., and Dart, J. K. G.: Treatment of *Acanthamoeba* keratitis with polyhexamethylene biguanide. Ophthalmology. *99*:185–191, 1992.
102. Lewis, K. T., and Stiles, M.: Management of cat and dog bites. Am. Fam. Physician. *52*:479–485, 489–490, 1995.
103. Liesegang, T. J., and Forster, R. K.: Spectrum of microbial keratitis in south Florida. Am. J. Ophthalmol. *90*:338–347, 1980.
104. Liesegang, T. J.: Diagnosis and therapy of herpes zoster ophthalmicus. Ophthalmology. *98*:1216–1229, 1991.
105. Liesegang, T. J.: Bacterial keratitis. Infect. Dis. Clin. North Am. *6*:815–829, 1992.
106. Lonn, L. I.: Neonatal cytomegalic inclusion disease chorioretinitis. Arch. Ophthalmol. *88*:434–438, 1972.
107. Mafee, M. F., Deepak, P., Edward, D. P., et al.: Lacrimal gland tumors and simulating lesions: Clinicopathologic and MR imaging features. Radiol. Clin. North Am. *37*:219–239, 1999.
108. Maini, R., and Edelsten, C.: Uveitis associated with parvovirus infection. Br. J. Ophthalmology. *83*:1403–1404, 1999.
109. Mannis, M. J., Tamaru, R., Roth, A. M., et al.: *Acanthamoeba* sclerokeratitis: Determining diagnostic criteria. Arch. Ophthalmol. *104*: 1313–1317, 1986.
110. Margo, C. E., and Hamed, L. M.: Ocular syphilis. Surv. Ophthalmol. *37*:203–220, 1992.
111. Marines, H. M., Osato, M. S., and Font, R. L.: The value of calcofluor white in the diagnosis of mycotic and acanthamoeba infections of the eye and ocular adnexa. Ophthalmology. *94*:23–26, 1987.
112. Mathers, W. D., Sutphin, J. E., Folberg, R., et al.: Outbreak of keratitis presumed to be caused by *Acanthamoeba*. Am. J. Ophthalmol. *121*:129–142, 1996.
113. Matoba, A. Y.: Ocular viral infections. Pediatr. Infect. Dis. *3*:358–368, 1984.
114. Matoba, A. Y.: Ocular disease associated with Epstein-Barr virus infection. Surv. Ophthalmol. *35*:145–150, 1990.
115. McCulley, J. P., Alizadeh, H., and Niederkorn, J. Y.: The diagnosis and management of *Acanthamoeba* keratitis. CLAO. J. *26*:47–51, 2000.
116. Mets, M. B., Bechtel, R. T., Haught, K. A., et al.: Lymphocytic choriomeningitis virus: A new addition to the TORCH evaluation. Arch. Ophthalmol. *115*:680–681, 1997.
117. Mets, M. B.: Childhood blindness and visual loss: An assessment at two institutions including a "new" cause. Trans. Am. Ophthalomol. Soc. *97*:653–696, 1999.
118. Moinfar, N., Wagner, D. G., Chrousos, G. A., et. al.: Paediatric varicella choroiditis. Br. J. Ophthalmol. *82*:1092–1093, 1998.
119. Morales, A. G., Croxatto, J. O., Crovetto, L., et al.: Hydatid cysts of the orbit: A review of 35 cases. Ophthalmology. *95*:1027–1032, 1988.
120. Mordhorst, C. H., and Dawson, C.: Sequelae of neonatal inclusion conjunctivitis and associated disease in parents. Am. J. Ophthalmol. *71*:861–867, 1971.
121. Nagelberg, H. P., Petashnick, D. E., and To, K. W.: Group B streptococcal metastatic endophthalmitis. Am. J. Ophthalmol. *117*:498–500, 1994.
122. Nahmias, A. J., and Visintine, A. M.: Eye infections with herpes simplex viruses in neonates. Surv. Ophthalmol. *21*:100–105, 1976.
123. Nakao, K., Ohba, N., Nakagawa, M., et al.: Clinical course of HTLV-1-associated uveitis. Jpn. J. Ophthalmol. *43*:404–409, 1999.
124. Nishida, H., and Risemberg, H. M.: Silver nitrate ophthalmic solution and chemical conjunctivitis. Pediatrics. *56*:368–373, 1975.
125. Obenour, L. C.: Subacute sclerosing panencephalitis. Int. Ophthal. Clin. *12*:215–223, 1972.

126. O'Day, D. M., and Head, W. S.: Advances in the management of keratomycosis and *Acanthamoeba* keratitis. Cornea. *19*:681–687, 2000.
127. Okada, A. A., Johnson, R. P., and Liles, W. C.: Endogenous bacterial endophthalmitis: Report of a ten-year retrospective study. Ophthalmology. *101*:832–838, 1994.
128. Opremcak, E. M.: Uveitis: A Clinical Manual for Ocular Inflammation. New York, Springer-Verlag, 1994, pp. 1–183.
129. Oren, B., and Wende, S. O.: An outbreak of molluscum contagiosum in a kibbutz: Relationship to swimming. Infection. *19*:159–161, 1991.
130. Paryani, S. G., and Arvin, A. M.: Intrauterine infection with varicella-zoster virus after maternal varicella. N. Engl. J. Med. *314*:1542–1546, 1986.
131. Paysse, E. A., Coats, D. K., Bernstein, J. M., et al.: Management and complications of congenital dacryocele with concurrent intranasal mucocele. J. AAPOS. *4*:46–53, 2000.
132. Peal, M. M.: Dog-associated bacterial infections in humans: Isolates submitted to an Australian reference laboratory, 1981–1992. Pathology. *25*:379–384, 1993.
133. Pena, G. P., and Andrade, F. J. S.: Is *Demodex* really non-pathogenic? Rev. Inst. Med. Trop. Sao Paulo. *42*:171–173, 2000.
134. Pfister, D. R., Cameron, J. D., Krachmer, J. H., et al.: Confocal microscopy findings of *Acanthamoeba* keratitis. Am. J. Ophthalmol. *121*:119–128, 1996.
135. Pizzarello, L. D., Jakobiec, F. A., Hofeldt, A. J., et al.: Intralesional corticosteroid therapy of chalazia. Am. J. Ophthalmol. *85*:818–821, 1978.
136. Pollard, Z. F.: Treatment of acute dacryocystitis in neonates. J. Pediatr. Ophthalmol. Strabismus. *28*:341–343, 1991.
137. Puliafito, C. A., Baker, A. S., Haaf, J., et al.: Infectious endophthalmitis. Ophthalmology. *89*:921–929, 1982.
138. Raucher, H. S., Newton, M. J., and Stearn, R. H.: Ophthalmia neonatorum caused by penicillinase-producing *Neisseria gonorrhoeae.* J. Pediatr. *100*:925–926, 1982.
139. Reersted, P., and Hansen, B.: Chorioretinitis of the newborn with herpes simplex virus type 1. Acta Ophthalmol. 57:1096–1100, 1979.
140. Remington, J. S., and Desmonts, G.: Toxoplasmosis. *In* Remington, J. S., and Klein, J. O. (eds.): Infectious Diseases of the Fetus and Newborn. 3rd ed. Philadelphia, W. B. Saunders, 1990, pp. 89–105.
141. Rhem, M. N., Wilhelmus, K. R., and Jones, D. B.: Epstein Barr virus dacryoadenitis. Am. J. Ophthalmol. *129*:372–375, 2000.
142. Rodriguez, A., Calonge, M., Petroza-Sers, M., et al.: Referral patterns of uveitis in a tertiary eye care center. Arch. Ophthalmol. *114*:593–599, 1996.
143. Ronday, M. J., Stilma, J. S., Barbe, R. F., et al.: Aetiology of uveitis in Sierra Leone, West Africa. Br J Ophthalmol *80*:956–961, 1996.
144. Rowe, S. G., and Durand, M.: Blackflies and white water: Onchocerciasis and the eye. Int. Ophthalmol. Clin. 38:231–240, 1998.
145. Rowsey, J. J., Jensen, H., and Sexton, D. J.: Clinical diagnosis of endophthalmitis. Int. Ophthalmol. Clin. *27*:82–88, 1987.
146. Rubin, S. E., Rubin, L. G., Zito, J., et al.: Medical management of orbital subperiosteal abscess in children. J. Pediatr. Ophthalmol. Strabismus. *26*:21–26, 1989.
147. Ryan, S. J., Jr.: De novo subretinal neovascularization in the histoplasmosis syndrome. Arch. Ophthalmol. *94*:321–327, 1976.
148. Sandstrom, K. I., Bell, T. A., Chandler, J. W., et al.: Diagnosis of neonatal purulent conjunctivitis caused by *Chlamydia trachomatis* and other organisms. *In* Marah, P. A., Holmes, K. K., Oriel, J. D., et al. (eds.): Chlamydial Infections. Amsterdam, Elsevier Biomedical Press, 1982, pp. 217–220.
149. Sandstrom, K. I., Bell, T. A., Chandler, J. W., et al.: Microbial causes of neonatal conjunctivitis. J. Pediatr. *105*:706–711, 1984.
150. Schantz, P. M., and Glickman, L. T.: *Toxocara* visceral larva migrans. N. Engl. J. Med. *298*:436–439, 1978.
151. Schneider, G.: Silver nitrate prophylaxis. Can. Med. Assoc. J. *131*:193–197, 1984.
152. Schwab, I. R.: Oral acyclovir and the management of herpes simplex ocular infections. Ophthalmology. *95*:423–430, 1988.
153. Shields, J. A.: Ocular toxocariasis: A review. Surv. Ophthalmol. *28*:361–381, 1984.
154. Shrader, S. K., Band, J. D., and Lauter, C. B.: The clinical spectrum of endophthalmitis: Incidence, predisposing factors, and features influencing outcome. J. Infect. Dis. *162*:115–120, 1990.
155. Skinner, C. J., Viswalingam, N. D., and Goh, P. T.: *Phthirus pubis* infestation of the eyelids: A marker for sexually transmitted diseases. Int. J. STD. AIDS. *6*: 451–452, 1995.
156. Smith, R. E.: Toxoplasmic retinochoroiditis as an emerging problem in AIDS patients. Editorial. Am. J. Ophthalmol. *106*:738–739, 1988.
157. Snowe, R. J., and Wilfert, C. M.: Epidemic reappearance of gonococcal ophthalmia neonatorum. Pediatrics. *51*:110–114, 1973.
158. Solley, W. A., Martin, D. F., Newman, N. J., et al.: Cat scratch disease: Posterior segment manifestations. Ophthalmology. *106*:1546–1553, 1999.
159. Stagno, S., and Whitley, R. J.: Herpesvirus infections of pregnancy. Part I. Cytomegalovirus and Epstein-Barr virus infections. N. Engl. J. Med. *313*:1270–1274, 1985.
160. Stagno, S.: Cytomegalovirus. *In* Remington, J. S., Kelin, J. O. (eds): Infectious Diseases of the Fetus and Newborn Infant. 3rd ed. Philadelphia, W. B. Saunders, 1990.
161. Steinkuller, P. G., and Jones, D. B. Microbial preseptal and orbital cellulitis. *In* Duane, T. D. (ed.): Clinical Ophthalmology. Vol. 4. Hagerstown, Md., Harper & Row, 1997, p. 8.
162. Stenson, S., Newman, R., and Fedukowicz, H.: Conjunctivitis in the newborn: Observations on the incidence, cause, and prophylaxis. Ann. Ophthalmol. *13*:329–334, 1981.
163. Streilein, J. W.: Anterior chamber associated immune deviation: the privilege of immunity in the eye. Surv. Ophthalmol. *35*:67–73, 1990.
164. Sudesh, S., and Laibson, P. R.: The impact of the herpetic eye disease studies on the management of herpes simplex virus ocular infections. Curr. Opin. Ophthalmol. *10*:230–233, 1999.
165. Syed, T. A., Ludin, S., and Ahmad, M.: Topical 0.3% and 0.5% podophyllotoxin cream for self-treatment of molluscum contagiosum in males. Dermatology. *189*:65–68, 1994.
166. Syed, T. A., Goswami, J., Ahmadpour, O. A., et al.: Treatment of molluscum in males with an analog of imiquimod 1% in cream: A placebo-controlled, double mask study. J. Dermatol. *25*:309–313, 1998.
167. Tabbara, K. F.: Trachoma: Have we advanced in the last 20 years? Int. Ophthalmol. Clin. *30*:23–27, 1990.
168. Tabbara, K. F., and Hyndiuk, R. A.: Infections of the Eye. 2nd ed. Boston, Little, Brown and Co., 1996, pp. 323–347, 361–385, 423–431, 433–478, 603–606.
169. Taber, L. H.: Syphilis. *In* Kaplan, S. L. (ed.): Current Therapy in Pediatric Infectious Disease. 3rd ed. St. Louis, Mosby, 1993, pp. 243–245.
170. Talley, A. R., Garcia-Ferrer, F., and Laycock, K. A., et al.: Comparative diagnosis of neonatal chlamydial conjunctivitis by polymerase chain reaction and McCoy cell culture. Am. J. Ophthalmol. *117*:50–57, 1994.
171. Tate, G. W., and Martin, R. G.: Clindamycin in the treatment of human ocular toxoplasmosis. Can. J. Ophthalmol. *12*:188–195, 1977.
172. Taylor, H. R., and Dax, E. M.: Ocular onchocerciasis. *In* Tabbara, K. F., and Hyndiuk, R. A. (eds.): Infections of the Eye. 2nd ed. Boston, Little, Brown and Co., 1996, pp. 673–683.
173. Thompson, W. S., Culbertson, W. W., Smiddy, W. E., et al.: Acute retinal necrosis caused by reactivation of herpes simplex virus type 2. Am. J. Ophthalmol. *118*:205–211, 1994.
174. Thylefors, B.: Onchocerciasis: An overview. Int. Ophthalmol. Clin. *30*:21–22, 1990.
175. Thylefors, B., Dawson, C. R., Jones, B. R., et al.: A simple system for the assessment of trachoma and its complications. Bull. World Health Organ. *65*:477–483, 1987.
176. Touboul, J. P., et al.: Uveites au cours de la syphilis acquise. J. Fr. Ophthalmol. *8*:321–331, 1985.
177. Van der Lelij, A., Ooijman, F. M., Kijlstra, A., and Rothova, A.: Anterior uveitis with sectoral iris atrophy in the absence of keratitis. Ophthalmology. *107*:1164–1170, 2000.
178. Vieira-Dias, D., Sena, C. M., Orefice, F., et al.: Ocular and concomitant cutaneous sporotrichosis. Mycoses. *40*:197–201, 1997.
179. von Noorden, G. K., and Buck, A. A.: Ocular onchocerciasis: An ophthalmological and epidemiological study in an African village. Arch. Ophthalmol. *80*:26–34, 1968.
180. Wagner, R. S.: Glaucoma in childhood. Pediatr. Clin. N. Amer. *40*:855–867, 1993.
181. Weiss, A., Friendly, D., Eglin, K., et al.: Bacterial periorbital and orbital cellulitis in childhood. Ophthalmology. *90*:195–203, 1983.
182. Weiss, A., Margo, C. E., Ledford, D. K., et al.: Toxoplasmic retinochoroiditis as an initial manifestation of the acquired immune deficiency syndrome. Am. J. Ophthalmol. *101*:248–249, 1986.
183. Wheaton, A. F., Timothy, N. H., Dossett, J. H., et al.: The surgical treatment of molluscum contagiosum in a pediatric AIDS patient. Ann. Plast. Surg. *44*:651–655, 2000.
184. Whitley, R. J.: Herpes simplex virus infections. *In* Remington, J. S., and Klein, J. O. (eds.): Infectious Diseases of the Fetus and Newborn Infant. 3rd ed. Philadelphia, W. B. Saunders, 1990.
185. Wiley, L., Springer, D., Kowalski, R. P., et al.: Rapid diagnostic test for ocular adenovirus. Ophthalmology. *95*:431–433, 1988.
186. Wilkinson, C. P., and Welch, R. B.: Intraocular *Toxocara*. Am. J. Ophthalmol. *71*:921–930, 1971.
187. Wilson, M. E., and Paul, T. O.: Orbital cellulitis following strabismus surgery. Ophthalmic Surg. *18*:92–94, 1987.
188. Wirostko, W. J., Connor, T. B., and Wagner, P. F.: Recurrent poststreptococcal uveitis. Arch. Ophthalmol. *117*:1649–1650, 1999.
189. Yoser, S. L., Forster, D. J., and Rao, N. A.: Systemic viral infections and their retinal and choroidal manifestations. Surv. Ophthalmol. *37*:313–352, 1993.
190. Yoshinaga, I. G., Conrado, L. A., Schainberg, S. C., et al.: Recalcitrant molluscum contagiosum in a patient with AIDS: Combined treatment with CO_2 laser, trichloroacetic acid, and pulsed dye laser. Lasers Surg. Med. *27*:291–294, 2000.

SECTION XII

Systemic Infectious Diseases

CHAPTER 69 Bacteremia and Septic Shock

SHELDON L. KAPLAN

One of the most serious and potentially life-threatening infectious diseases in childhood is a bacteremic illness. Bacteremia may be caused by a wide variety of gram-positive or gram-negative microorganisms, and it may or may not be associated with a specific focus of infection, such as pneumonia or meningitis. Some bacteremias are transient and self-limited, and they are not discussed in this chapter. The incidence of bacteremia in children has been studied in hospital and ambulatory settings. In otherwise normal children, beyond the newborn age group, *Streptococcus pneumoniae, Haemophilus influenzae* type b (in unimmunized children), *Staphylococcus aureus,* group A *Streptococcus, Salmonella* spp., and *Neisseria meningitidis* are the most common microorganisms causing bacteremia.[203, 227] Children with underlying illnesses that depress the host response to infection may develop illnesses caused by these same microorganisms; however, in this population of children, especially when hospitalized, Enterobacteriaceae, *S. aureus,* coagulase-negative staphylococci, and fungi are the most important organisms commonly isolated from the blood cultures.[3, 151, 192] Indwelling vascular lines, urinary catheters, and endotracheal tubes, as well as other foreign material, further predispose already compromised children to nosocomial infections. The diagnosis of septicemia has increased since the late 1970s, in part related to improved medical technology and the greater numbers of individuals with immunocompromising conditions who previously would not have survived.[143]

Gray and colleagues[76] reported that the incidence of bloodstream infections in a pediatric intensive care unit (ICU) during a 3-year period was 39 cases per 1000 admissions. Sixty-four percent of the episodes were acquired in the ICU, and 20.6 percent were community-acquired infections. Gram-positive and gram-negative organisms accounted for 62 percent and 31 percent of the isolates, respectively. Yeast were isolated in 5.6% of episodes. In a 1-year prospective surveillance study of bloodstream infections in children with cancer conducted among 18 hematology centers in Italy, 191 episodes of bacteremias were reported.[214] Sixty-four percent occurred in neutropenic patients. Gram-positive cocci, gram-negative rods, and fungi accounted for 45 percent, 41 percent, and 9 percent of episodes, respectively. A central venous catheter was associated with infection in 55 percent of the non-neutropenic patients and 20 percent of the neutropenic patients. Children with acquired immunodeficiency syndrome (AIDS) or severe immunosuppression caused by human immunodeficiency virus (HIV) infection also are at increased risk for developing bacteremias caused by gram-negative bacilli, especially *Pseudomonas aeruginosa.*[175]

One potential consequence of bacteremia is septic shock, a state characterized by inadequate tissue perfusion that is associated frequently with endotoxemia. Although most children with septic shock have infections caused by gram-negative enteric bacteria, *P. aeruginosa,* or *N. meningitidis,* organisms with endotoxin or lipopolysaccharide within cell walls, it also is associated with disease caused by gram-positive bacteria (especially *S. aureus, Streptococcus pyogenes,* and viridans streptococci), viruses, rickettsiae, and fungi.

The incidence of septic shock in children is unknown. In adults, the frequency of septic shock is thought to be approximately 20-fold that of two decades ago. Dupont and Spink[55] reviewed the cases of 172 children, 30 days to 16 years of age, who were hospitalized at the University of Minnesota Medical Center with gram-negative bacteremia. Shock occurred in 25 percent of the children, and 98 percent of those with shock died. In contrast, 42 percent of children with bacteremia but without shock survived. In meningococcal infections, 11 to 40 percent of children develop hypotension.[56, 228] During a 10-month study period, Naqvi and colleagues[140] reported that shock occurred in 5 of 39 (13%) episodes of gram-negative bacillary sepsis, with three deaths. Jacobs and associates[94] reviewed the admissions of previously normal children to a pediatric ICU in a large children's hospital for a 30-month period. Hypotension or evidence of peripheral hypoperfusion occurred in 143 children with confirmed bacterial sepsis or apparent meningococcemia (Table 69–1). The overall mortality rate for children with proven sepsis and septic shock was 9.8 percent (14 of 143). However, in this series, the most common organism was *H. influenzae* type b, which rarely causes systemic infections in the infant or child who has received at least 2 doses of a conjugate *H. influenzae* type b vaccine.[176] Among 1058 consecutive admissions of 916 children to a pediatric ICU in Canada from July 1, 1991, to July 31, 1992, 25 episodes (2%) of septic shock occurred.[163] During a 12-month period, 140 episodes of septicemia (135 bacterial and 5 fungal) were documented in 100 pediatric hematology-oncology patients.[5] Septic shock occurred in 19 percent. Early-onset group B streptococcal infections in neonates and overwhelming *S. pneumoniae* infections in the child with splenic dysfunction or asplenia are associated with shock in a high percentage of cases. *S. aureus* or group A *Streptococcus* may cause hypotension in a child with or without other manifestations of toxic shock syndrome.[191, 203]

During the past decade, many advances in our understanding of the pathogenesis and pathophysiology of septic shock with respect to the host response to infection have

TABLE 69–1 ■ CONFIRMED ETIOLOGY AND MORTALITY OF SEPTIC SHOCK IN CHILDREN*

Organism	Number	Mortality
Haemophilus influenzae type b	59	1 (1.7%)
Neisseria meningitidis	26	3 (11.5%)
Apparent meningococcemia	3	3 (100%)
Streptococcus pneumoniae	16	1 (6.3%)
Group B *Streptococcus*	8	1 (12.5%)
Staphylococcus aureus	7	2 (29%)
Gram-negative enteric	8	2 (25%)
Other	16	1 (6.3%)

*Arkansas Children's Hospital (9/84 to 4/87); oncology, burn, and primary immunodeficiency patients excluded from analysis.

Modified from Jacobs, R. F., Sowell, M. K., Moss, M. M., et al.: Septic shock in children: Bacterial etiologies and temporal relationships. Pediatr. Infect. Dis. J. 9:196–200, 1990.

required that more precise clinical definitions of sepsis and expanded syndromes be developed. Much of the impetus for this effort is related to the ability to identify more readily patients with infections who may benefit from newer (expensive) adjunctive measures. An American College of Chest Physicians and Society of Critical Care Medicine Consensus Conference in 1991 developed new terminology to define sepsis and its sequelae.[23] The terminology may not apply directly to the pediatric population, and modifications for use in children have been proposed[83, 181, 182] (Table 69–2).

Pathophysiology

The pathophysiology of bacteremia is highly variable and depends on the specific microorganism isolated; the nature of the immune status of the host; and other factors, such as the locations of indwelling lines. Highly encapsulated organisms, such as *S. pneumoniae, N. meningitidis,* and *H. influenzae* type b, normally may reside in the nasopharynx

TABLE 69–2 ■ TERMINOLOGY OF SEPSIS AND ITS SEQUELAE

Bacteremia—positive blood culture indicating viable bacteria in the blood

Systemic inflammatory response syndrome (SIRS)—severe clinical insult leading to a systemic inflammatory response manifested by ≥2 of the following conditions: (1) temperature >38° C or <36° C; (2) heart rate >2 standard deviations above normal for age; (3) respiratory rate >2 standard deviations above normal for age; (4) peripheral white blood cell count <4000/mm^3, >12,000/mm^3, or >10 percent immature forms

Sepsis—SIRS due to an infection

Severe sepsis—sepsis plus organ dysfunction, hypoperfusion, or hypotension. Evidence of hypoperfusion may include oliguria, lactic acidosis, and acute alteration in mental status

Septic shock—sepsis associated with hypotension despite adequate fluid resuscitation in addition to evidence of hypoperfusion as defined under severe sepsis. Patients may not be hypotensive at the time perfusion abnormalities are noted if they are receiving inotropic or vasopressor agents.

Sepsis-induced hypotension—systolic blood pressure measurement >2 standard deviations below the mean for age in the absence of other causes for hypotension

Multiple organ dysfunction syndrome (MODS)—presence of altered organ function in an acutely ill patient such that homeostasis cannot be maintained without intervention

and, for reasons that are poorly understood, are capable of invading beyond mucosal barriers into the bloodstream. A preceding viral upper respiratory tract infection may play some role in alterations in local host defense mechanisms that result in bacteremia.[101, 128]

Using human columnar nasopharyngeal tissue in organ cultures, Stephens and colleagues[198] demonstrated that *N. meningitidis* organisms were ingested by the columnar cells, then found within phagocytic vacuoles and later observed within subepithelial tissues, which suggests that the meningococci had penetrated the epithelial layer. In this same model, *H. influenzae* type b organisms attach to nonciliated columnar epithelial cells and subsequently are found in the intercellular spaces in association with a preceding disruption of the tight junctions of epithelial cells.[57] Once past the mucosal barriers, *H. influenzae* type b may enter the bloodstream directly through pharyngeal blood vessels.[179] Pneumococci adhere to specific ligands on respiratory cells. The generation of inflammatory factors during viral infections upregulate platelet-activating factor receptor on respiratory cells to which the pneumococci adhere more avidly and subsequently invade.[212] Pili or adhesins of gram-negative enteric organisms appear to be important in attachment and adherence of these microorganisms to specific receptor sites on epithelial surfaces.

The placement of an endotracheal tube unmasks a greater number of these receptor sites, presumably through increased protease activity of secretions and decreased cell-bound fibronectin, and leads to colonization of the upper respiratory tract with gram-negative organisms, which are ubiquitous in the environment of an ICU.[230] By mechanisms that are related in part to altered host defenses, these organisms are able to move beyond epithelial surfaces and cause bacteremia.

The gastrointestinal and genitourinary tracts are major sources of gram-negative organisms responsible for bacteremia. These organisms first may cause localized abscesses or peritonitis if intestinal perforation occurs, or they may translocate the intestinal mucosa, particularly when the mucosa is affected by antineoplastic agents. Viridans streptococci can cause bacteremia in the neutropenic patient, with severe mucositis occurring after the patient undergoes chemotherapy.[194] Microorganisms within the bladder may ascend the genitourinary tract and presumably enter the bloodstream through the kidneys. *S. aureus* and *S. pyogenes* are common inhabitants of the skin and skin structures. Any skin wound or foreign matter within the skin tissue renders the skin more susceptible to bacterial invasion. Staphylococci have a unique capability of adhering to solid surfaces, such as catheters, which may be an important prerequisite to colonization and subsequent line-related bacteremia.[157]

The pathophysiology of septic shock is very complex. Septic shock associated with gram-negative organisms has been studied most extensively, especially with respect to endotoxin, which has multiple biologic effects. Bacterial lipopolysaccharide or endotoxin has three basic components:

1. Terminal side chains, which consist of repeating oligosaccharides that differ from strain to strain and are responsible for the antigenic specificity of the O antigens
2. A core lipopolysaccharide, which also consists of oligosaccharides but has less diversity in structure among strains than do the terminal side chains
3. Lipid A, which is very similar among the different strains and is responsible for most of the biologic activity of endotoxin

Endotoxin shock has been the subject of intensive animal research, and much of what is known about the pathogenesis of endotoxin shock has been derived from animal models. Although septic shock in humans is not simulated precisely in these animal models because the animals do not have underlying host defense defects, much of what has been learned about endotoxin shock in animals has been corroborated in the human host.

ENDOTOXIN SHOCK IN ANIMALS

Most animal models of endotoxin shock employ infusions of live gram-negative bacteria, usually *Escherichia coli*, or purified endotoxin, after which observations are made. The effects of purified endotoxin depend in part on the species of animal being studied. The effects of endotoxin in animal models are summarized in Table 69–3.

That several circulating mediators induced by endotoxin play a pivotal role in the pathogenesis of endotoxin shock is clear. Tumor necrosis factor (TNF) or cachectin, a polypeptide hormone, appears to be one of the key cytokines mediating septic shock.[208] The tissue injury induced by TNF largely is a result of other mediators that are stimulated by TNF, including interleukin-1, interleukin-6, eicosanoids, and platelet-activating factor.[53, 89, 206, 209] TNF is synthesized by a wide variety of cells (including monocytes/macrophages, natural killer cells, microglial cells, hepatic Kupffer cells) after stimulation by lipopolysaccharides, C5a, viruses, and enterotoxins, among other agents. It initiates a cascade of events leading eventually to endothelial cell injury, an enhanced inflammatory response, and ultimately to the characteristic findings of endotoxic shock.

Nitric oxide (i.e., endothelium-derived relaxing factor) is the final pathway by which endogenous vasodilators stimulated by endotoxin result in hypotension from altered control of microcirculation. Endotoxin through the release of cytokines induces a form of the enzyme nitric oxide synthase, which leads to increased production of nitric oxide.[135] Inhibitors of nitric oxide synthase, such as N^G-monomethyl-L-arginine, can reverse or prevent hypotension in animals after administration of endotoxin.[127] Cardiac myocytes also can produce significant amounts of TNF-α after endotoxin stimulation, which may play some role in the development of myocardial dysfunction in animal models.[98] Toll-like receptors are involved in signaling cytokine production induced by endotoxin within the heart.[15]

The sequence of events that occurs in the pathophysiology of septic shock caused by gram-positive bacteria is very similar to that described for gram-negative organisms.[159, 196] Cell wall components such as peptidoglycan and teichoic acid promote proinflammatory activity but are less potent than is endotoxin.

ENDOTOXIN SHOCK IN HUMANS

The pathophysiology of septic shock is highly complex and is related predominantly to actions of endogenous mediators released as part of the systemic inflammatory response to an infection. The cascade of events is intertwining, with production of one cytokine stimulating the synthesis of others; synergistic in that the activities of certain cytokines act in concert; and sometimes antagonistic, with the production of other molecules to inhibit or compete with various cytokines. This complicated response to an infectious stimulus has been studied best for lipopolysaccharide, but a similar series of events occurs in response to gram-positive infections.

Lipopolysaccharide stimulates numerous different cells to increase production of cytokines, especially mononuclear phagocytes. Mononuclear cells have a surface receptor (CD14) that recognizes and binds a complex of lipopolysaccharide and lipopolysaccharide-binding protein, a glycoprotein that opsonizes lipopolysaccharide and is an acute-phase reactant increased during sepsis.[221, 231] The lipopolysaccharide and lipopolysaccharide-binding protein complex

TABLE 69–3 ■ ENDOTOXIN SHOCK IN ANIMAL MODELS

Effects	Mediators
Cardiovascular Effects	
Decreased peripheral vascular resistance[141]	Histamine, bradykinin,[108] serotonin, complement activation, prostaglandins, anaphylatoxins
Lowered cardiac output[5, 8, 167]	
Depressed myocardial function[119]	
Decreased systemic blood pressure	
Metabolic Effects	
Hyperglycemia[35, 45]	Hypoinsulinemia
Hypoglycemia[50]	
Increased adrenocorticotropic hormone, growth hormone, and antidiuretic hormone[193, 226]	
Decreased calcium[201]	
Increased triglycerides[84, 176]	
Decreased iron, transferrin, and zinc	
Pulmonary Effects	
Congestive atelectasis[29]	Polymorphonuclear leukocytes
Increased capillary permeability[26, 71, 87]	Polymorphonuclear leukocytes
Vasoconstriction	Thromboxane, prostacyclin
Bronchoconstriction[18]	Leukotrienes
Central Nervous System Effects	
Decreased regional and total cerebral blood flow[140]	
Increased cerebral oxygen consumption[140, 166]	

interaction with CD14 leads to a signal transduction through transmembrane toll-like receptors (TLR4). The lipopolysaccharide–lipopolysaccharide-binding protein–TLR4 complex also involves another small protein, MD-2, on the cell surface[18, 92] (Fig. 69–1). The resulting signal promotes mononuclear phagocytes to produce reactive oxygen molecules, cytokines, and arachidonic acid metabolites, including prostaglandin and leukotrienes. A counterregulatory protein is a bactericidal, permeability-increasing protein that is stored in the granules of polymorphonuclear leukocytes and inhibits the effects of lipopolysaccharide.[67]

TNF is responsible largely for the biologic effects of lipopolysaccharide in humans, including fever, shock, myocardial suppression, capillary leak (i.e., endothelial damage), coagulation alterations, and metabolic changes.[31, 32, 129, 161, 207] In children, including neonates, the role of cytokines in sepsis caused by a variety of organisms, but especially *N. meningitidis*, is well documented.[28, 47, 70, 201, 216] Lipopolysaccharide and TNF each can induce the synthesis of other proinflammatory cytokines, such as interleukin-1β and interleukin-6.[54] Interleukin-6 levels in plasma correlate with mortality. Interleukin-8 plasma concentrations also are increased after infusion of lipopolysaccharide or interleukin-1β.[54, 79]

The "anti-inflammatory" cytokine interleukin-10 is produced after injection of lipopolysaccharide and inhibits the production of TNF-α, interleukin-1β, and interleukin-6.[122] Naturally occurring inhibitors of TNF or interleukin-1β are measurable in patients with the sepsis syndrome.[50, 51, 72] Interleukin-1 receptor antagonist (interleukin-1ra) binds competitively to the interleukin-1 receptor to block the action of interleukin-1. Soluble TNF receptors bind to circulating TNF, which prevents its proinflammatory actions (see Fig. 69–1).

In humans, gram-negative bacteremia is followed by a decrease in systemic vascular resistance and mean blood pressure and an increase in cardiac output.[19, 222] Decreased systemic vascular resistance may be accompanied by activation of the complement and kinin systems.[130] After this early phase, the blood pressure decreases further without change in the central venous pressure. Certain patients are able to maintain their cardiac output and index, and this ability may be associated with increased rates of survival. When peripheral resistance is measured within 12 to 24 hours of the onset of shock, its decrease is significant in patients who survive compared with those who die.[145] In contrast, cardiac output is reduced significantly in other patients; this decrease is associated with increased concentration of blood lactate, decreased arterial blood pH, and decreased rates of survival.

Depression of myocardial function has been demonstrated in adult and pediatric patients in septic shock.[36, 60] These patients have a reduced ejection fraction and left ventricular dilatation and significantly altered ventricular performance in response to infusion of volume.[147] However, this depression of myocardial function is transient in survivors, reverting to normal within 1 to 4 days.[60, 148] Parker and colleagues[149] found that patients who did not survive septic shock did not have left ventricular dilatation or reduction in the ejection fraction. When the systemic vascular resistance index was averaged over time, nonsurvivors had a significantly ($p < 0.05$) lower index than did survivors of septic shock. This study included three children who were 9 to 17 years of age. Abraham and associates[1] sequentially monitored hemodynamic and oxygen transport measurements in 33 patients with septic shock. In the 24-hour period before the onset of hypotension, the survivors demonstrated significantly greater cardiac index, left cardiac work index, oxygen delivery, and oxygen consumption than did the nonsurvivors.

The pathogenesis of the myocardial depression in septic shock may be related to some humoral factor. By infusing plasma from patients with septic shock into the coronary arteries of healthy dogs, McConn and colleagues[119] caused a marked decline in the left ventricular work index and found two different patterns of myocardial depression in an early and a late phase. By employing an in vitro preparation of newborn rat heart cell cultures that beat spontaneously, Parrillo and colleagues[150] demonstrated a circulation of myocardial depressant substance in humans with septic shock. Serum from 20 patients with septic shock (including three patients 9 to 15 years of age) decreased the extent and velocity of myocardial cell shortening during contraction. In a subsequent study in patients with septic shock, those with myocardial depressant substance-positive assays had lower mean lowest ejection fractions and greater pulmonary artery wedge pressures and peak lactic acid concentrations than

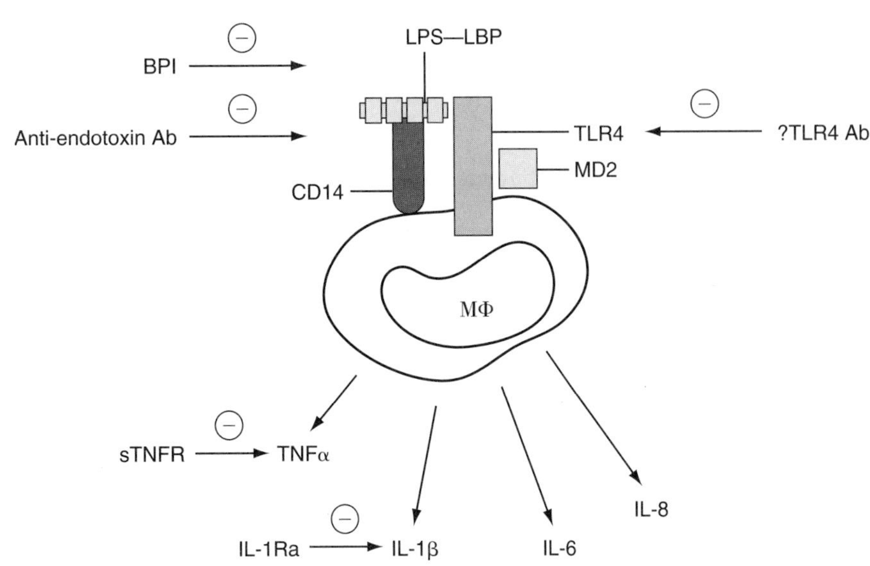

FIGURE 69–1 ■ Activation of the cytokine network by lipopolysaccharide-lipopolysaccharide binding protein complex binding to the CD14 receptor of mononuclear phagocytes with signal transduction through the toll-like receptor 4. IL-1ra, interleukin-1 receptor antagonist; sTNFr, soluble tumor necrosis factor receptor; TLR4, toll-like receptor 4; ⊖, antagonistic effect.

did patients with negative assays.[168] The myocardial depressant substance has a molecular mass of more than 10,000 daltons. This same group has shown that the infusion of purified *E. coli* endotoxin into normal volunteers results in a depression of left ventricular function and a cardiovascular state similar to that observed in clinical septic shock, which suggests that endotoxin is the major mediator of the cardiovascular dysfunction in gram-negative septic shock.[200]

In children, the most comprehensive investigation of myocardial dysfunction has been in meningococcal septic shock. Thiru and coworkers[202] measured serum concentrations of the cardiac muscle-specific protein cardiac troponin I (cTnI), which is released from injured cardiac myocytes, in 101 children with meningococcal septicemia. Minimum left ventricular ejection fraction was inversely related to peak cTnI levels. The degree of myocardial dysfunction, as determined by inotrope measurement, was related directly to peak cTnI concentrations. Their results suggested that myocardial cell death might be responsible in part for the cardiac dysfunction of meningococcal septic shock.

Hematologic changes, such as leukocytosis, leukopenia, and thrombocytopenia, have been observed in human volunteers after receiving an infusion of endotoxin. Thrombocytopenia commonly occurs in association with septicemia of any cause.[41] Septic shock is one of the most common causes of disseminated intravascular coagulation in children. Hageman factor (i.e., factor XII), which initiates the coagulation cascade, can be activated directly by endotoxin or through endothelial damage induced by bacteria.[125] In bacterial shock, concentrations of Hageman factor, prekallikrein, high-molecular-weight kininogen, and factor VII are decreased in part through consumption.[44, 97] Similarly, levels of inactivators of clotting factors, such as C1 esterase inhibitor, α_2-macroglobulin, and antithrombin III, also are diminished. Corrigan and Jordan[44] diagnosed disseminated intravascular coagulation in 24 of 26 children with septic shock and found that improvement in coagulation parameters appeared to be related most to restoration of blood pressure. Gram-negative bacteremia may be associated with a coagulopathy that is not disseminated intravascular coagulation but is characterized by prolongation of the prothrombin and partial thromboplastin times caused by a reduction in the vitamin K–dependent coagulation factors.[43]

Lipopolysaccharide or cell wall components of gram-positive organisms through cytokine stimulation activates blood coagulation predominantly through the extrinsic pathway. The procoagulant state is enhanced further by decreased protein C activity, which is an important inhibitor of coagulation factors Va and VIIIa. The fibrinolytic system also is altered by endotoxemia mediated by plasminogen activator inhibitor 1–induced suppression. The coagulopathy associated with septic shock is characterized by a procoagulant state and inhibition of fibrinolysis.[109, 114] Protein C has anti-inflammatory properties. The antithrombotic, profibrinolytic, and anti-inflammatory actions of activated protein C counteract the consequences of cytokine activation, but a deficiency of protein C may be acquired during severe sepsis. Low levels of protein C have been associated with increased morbidity and mortality in patients with severe sepsis and septic shock.[64] For meningococcal disease in particular, dysfunction of the protein C activation pathway is a key factor in the development of the thrombosis of purpura fulminans. Down-regulation of the endothelial thrombomodulin-endothelial protein C receptor pathway appears to be the mechanism for impaired activation of protein C during an episode of severe meningococcal sepsis.[58]

Endotoxin can activate the complement cascade by the classic or the alternate pathways. Significantly depressed concentrations of C3 occur in human patients with bacteremia and hypotension compared with normal individuals or with patients with uncomplicated bacteremia, and C3 is activated primarily by the alternate pathway.[59, 97, 115] In patients with bacteremia and hypotension, C1, C4, and C2 levels were not depressed significantly from values found in normal controls or in normotensive patients with bacteremia. In contrast, C3, C5, C6, C9, properdin, and factor B levels were decreased significantly ($p < 0.05$) in bacteremic patients with shock. In children with meningococcal disease, Tubbs[211] found a mean C3 concentration (as a percentage of normal values) of 132 ± 21 percent for survivors versus 91 ± 21 percent for nonsurvivors. The C3 levels did not correlate with endotoxin levels in sera. Complement activation also occurs during episodes of group B streptococcal sepsis in newborns.[61]

Many metabolic alterations have been documented in the human host during endotoxin shock. Hyperglycemia followed by hypoglycemia can complicate the shock state induced by sepsis.[62, 131] Whole-body use of glucose is increased during sepsis, which probably is cytokine mediated.[132] Glycolysis and gluconeogenesis are increased, but insulin resistance occurs in skeletal muscle. Children with underlying liver disease or with reduced glycogen stores are most likely to develop hypoglycemia during septic shock. Lactic acidosis develops as a result of poor tissue perfusion and cellular hypoxia. Lactic acid concentrations are increased in nonsurvivors and those patients with poor or low-flow cardiac output during sepsis. In clinical studies, Clowes and associates[39] identified a subgroup of patients with low-flow septic shock in whom concentrations of serum insulin were lower than those in a control population.

Hypocalcemia and decreased serum ionized calcium concentrations occur frequently during bacterial sepsis. In one study, 12 (20%) of 60 critically ill adults with bacterial sepsis had hypocalcemia.[234] The mortality rate in the hypocalcemic patients was 50 percent, compared with 30 percent in the patients who were normocalcemic. Cardenas-Rivero and associates[34] studied calcium homeostasis in 145 children admitted to an ICU. Of eight children with confirmed sepsis or meningitis (or both) not caused by *H. influenzae* type b, seven had hypocalcemia, and six of seven had ionized hypocalcemia. Five of the six children with ionized hypocalcemia had inappropriately normal concentrations of parathyroid hormone, which suggests that transient hypoparathyroidism occurs in some children with sepsis. Hypocalcemia also occurs commonly in patients with toxic shock syndrome.[225] In women with toxic shock syndrome and hypocalcemia, serum concentrations of calcitonin are elevated by mechanisms that are unknown.[37] Hypocalcemia and elevated calcitonin concentrations also have been documented in children with fulminant meningococcemia.[121] Procalcitonin levels are elevated in several conditions associated with systemic inflammatory response syndrome (SIRS), including sepsis.[82, 105] These changes in calcium levels especially are critical because the level of ionized calcium and cardiac output in septic shock can be correlated.[229] Other metabolic changes may occur during septic shock in humans:

1. Increased concentrations of cortisol and growth hormone[217] (including in neonates[204])
2. Depression of T_3 and T_4 levels related to poor nutrition[172]
3. Elevations in total concentrations of amino acid in plasma and the preferential use of branched-chain amino acids as an energy source for skeletal muscle[132]

4. Muscle proteolysis, possibly induced by one or more circulating agents in the plasma of patients with serious infections[38]

5. Elevations in concentrations of plasma thromboxane, which are observed in nonsurvivors of septic shock[170]

6. Elevation in concentrations of triglycerides and free fatty acid during gram-negative bacteremia[68, 102]

Liver dysfunction is an important aspect of endotoxin shock in adults. Banks and colleagues[11] found that clinical jaundice was apparent in 63 percent of their patients with septic shock, that it was found more commonly in nonsurvivors than survivors, and that the degree of biochemical liver abnormalities was related to the duration of shock. Postmortem findings included focal liver necrosis, Kupffer cell hyperplasia, portal tract inflammation, venous congestion, and intrahepatic cholestasis.

Adult respiratory distress syndrome (ARDS), or shock lung, is a major complication of septic shock in children.[90, 160] The lungs of children with ARDS have characteristic changes consisting of increased lung weight reflecting congestion and atelectasis, alveoli lined with hyaline membranes, microthrombi, hemorrhage, and interstitial edema.[90] Increased capillary permeability and intrapulmonary shunts have been documented in patients with shock lung.[7, 46] C5a, a potent chemotactic factor, causes aggregation of polymorphonuclear neutrophils, is elevated in the sera of patients who ultimately develop ARDS, and is found in increased concentrations in bronchoalveolar lavage fluid obtained from patients with ARDS.[80, 173] Leukocyte aggregates are thought to be trapped in lung tissue and may cause damage to the endothelium of the pulmonary microvasculature through the release of oxygen radicals, lysosomal enzymes, and products of arachidonic acid metabolism. Although neutrophils clearly play a critical role in the pathogenesis of ARDS, other factors also are important, considering that ARDS can develop in patients who are neutropenic.[146, 223] Thromboxane, platelet-activating factor, fibrin, and other substances contribute to the lung injury in ARDS.[177]

The effects of endotoxin shock on the central nervous system have not been studied carefully in humans; however, a study by Graham and associates[75] is particularly intriguing. The brains of six adult patients with septic shock caused by gram-negative bacteremia and neurologic dysfunction, predominantly coma, demonstrated an acute hemorrhagic leukoencephalitis on histologic examination. Microscopic findings included necrosis of vessel walls, perivascular tissue destruction, perivascular edema (especially of white matter), polymorphonuclear leukocyte infiltration into abnormal areas of the brain, and ball or ring hemorrhages. The investigators postulated that these histologic findings could be caused by a Shwartzman reaction mediated by endotoxin. The encephalopathy associated with sepsis appears to be caused in part by altered phenylalanine metabolism; concentrations of phenylalanine and its metabolite, phenylacetic acid, are increased in the sera and cerebrospinal fluid of septic adults who are stuporous or comatose.[133]

Endotoxin has been implicated in the pathogenesis of acute renal failure associated with septicemia. Wardle[219, 220] showed that 12 of 16 patients with acute tubular necrosis had endotoxemia. Renal arterial blood flow and renal vascular resistance are decreased significantly in baboons 2 to 4 hours after infusion of endotoxin. Inadequate perfusion pressure was associated with renal ischemia and negligible urine output in these animals shortly after administration of endotoxin.[185] Pathologic examination of the kidneys revealed focal necrosis of the proximal tubular epithelium, eosinophilic casts within proximal and distal tubules, and microthrombi in the glomerular capillaries. Endothelin, a potent vasoconstrictor peptide produced by endothelial cells, is elevated in concentration in the plasma of patients with septic shock. Because endothelin contributes to the regulation of regional blood flow, elevated levels suggest that it may relate to renal vasoconstriction and dysfunction.[215]

Endotoxin can be measured in the plasma of patients with gram-negative bacteremia; the presence of circulating endotoxin, however, does not necessarily mean that bacteremia is present or ever has occurred because endotoxin presumably may be "absorbed or leak" into the circulation from the gastrointestinal tract.[111, 199, 210] However, endotoxemia may be a valid indicator of impending gram-negative septicemia in febrile patients.[52] Preformed antibody to lipopolysaccharide or lipid A is associated with protection against shock and death caused by gram-negative bacteremia in adults. McCartney and colleagues[117] detected endotoxin in the blood (after chloroform extraction) of patients with gram-negative septic shock; all 18 patients with persistently positive endotoxin assays died. In contrast, nine patients who initially had endotoxemia but subsequently had negative assays survived. Other studies confirm the association between endotoxemia and outcome.[106] Evidence exists that human endotoxin is cleared from the circulation by the liver and can be detoxified by neutrophil enzymes (i.e., acyloxacyl hydrolases).[126, 137]

The sequence of events in the evolution of endotoxin shock has been outlined by several investigators.[142] Bacteria, endotoxin, or other bacterial products stimulate the production of TNF and other cytokines, which in concert with endotoxin set off a whole series of events. Potent mediators, including C3a, C5a, eicosanoids, platelet-activating factor, histamine, and myocardial depressant substance, are released. Potent vasodilators cause peripheral vasodilation, and decreased systemic peripheral resistance leads to pooling of blood and decreased venous return to the heart. Mean blood pressure may be low, or it may be normal if cardiac output increases sufficiently to compensate for these alterations despite depression of ventricular function. The central venous pressure, which partially depends on myocardial competence, may be low or in the normal range.

If intravascular volume is increased by the administration of sufficient fluids, shock may be prevented or corrected. However, continued hypotension and diminished perfusion pressure may lead to cellular hypoxia and increased production of lactic acid from pyruvate. The microcirculation is altered by local tissue acidosis. Capillary beds become congested, and intravascular fluid may leak into the interstitial spaces. Increased secretion of catecholamine leads to arteriolar and venular constriction and increased peripheral resistance. Pooling of blood is enhanced, which leads to a further diminution in venous return and a reduction of cardiac output. Oliguria, coagulation abnormalities, and additional metabolic alterations indicate multiple organ system failure and presage the death of the patient.

Clinical Presentation and Diagnosis

The symptoms and signs of bacteremia are highly variable, greatly depending on the age and underlying disease of the patient, the duration of illness, and the specific microorganisms. Young, otherwise healthy children between 3 months and 3 years of age may present with fever and evidence of an upper or lower respiratory tract infection or no focus of infection and yet have unsuspected bacteremia. Most studies have indicated that the risk of developing bacteremia increases as the body temperature rises and that, after the temperature exceeds 41° C, almost 25 percent of these children may be bacteremic.[14] In the previously healthy child, the persistence of irritability and the inability to console the infant despite optimal environmental conditions have been proposed as key points in the physical examination that should alert the clinician to the possibility of a serious infection, such as bacteremia or meningitis.[116, 193] Underlying illnesses with splenic dysfunction place the child at increased risk for acquisition of infections caused by encapsulated organisms, whereas children with leukemia or other immunosuppressive diseases or children in the ICU are more likely to be infected with gram-negative bacilli or *S. aureus*. A history of diarrhea may suggest *Salmonella* spp. as a possible cause of illness. Preceding skin infections or wounds are important clues to infection caused by *S. aureus* or group A streptococcal organisms. An indwelling vascular catheter may precipitate overlying erythema in the patient with evidence of phlebitis proximally. Gram-positive cocci and gram-negative bacilli can be associated with catheter-related sepsis.[188] Toxic shock syndrome should be considered in a hypotensive girl or woman with a recent menstrual period and history of tampon use, although toxic shock also is associated with *S. aureus* sepsis in males and nonmenstruating females. Intra-abdominal sources of infection increase the likelihood of developing anaerobic bacteremia. Petechiae may be associated with many microorganisms, especially invasive disease caused by *N. meningitidis*.[144] Purpura is an ominous finding and frequently is associated with overwhelming infection caused by *N. meningitidis, S. pneumoniae,* and *H. influenzae* type b. *P. aeruginosa* is associated specifically with erythema gangrenosum. Other skin and soft tissue manifestations of gram-negative sepsis include bullous lesions, cellulitis, fasciitis, thrombophlebitis, and symmetrical peripheral gangrene with disseminated intravascular coagulation.[138] Signs of meningeal irritation or increased intracranial pressure are important because they may modify the approach to fluid management of the child in shock.

The onset of bacteremia may be heralded by chills, fever, nausea, vomiting, diarrhea, rashes, and petechiae. Initially, the skin feels warm and appears flushed. A change or impairment in mental status may be the first clue to the presence of shock. Hyperventilation also may occur before the onset of clinical shock, which can alert the physician to impending circulatory insufficiency.[20] In time, cold, clammy extremities; a weak pulse; tachycardia; tachypnea; hypotension; and oliguria may occur. The skin over the extremities, the tip of the nose, and the earlobes especially are prone to cyanosis. Auscultation of the lungs may reveal rales, indicating pneumonia or pulmonary edema. Abnormal distention or tenderness to palpation and guarding may be evidence of peritonitis. Costovertebral angle tenderness suggests acute pyelonephritis as a source of bacteremias.

The physician must distinguish between the three main types of shock in children[154]:

1. *Hypovolemic shock*, such as occurs with blood loss, fluid and electrolyte loss, adrenal insufficiency, or other causes
2. *Cardiogenic shock*, which is associated with drug intoxication, cardiac surgery, arrhythmias, and pericardial tamponade, among other causes
3. *Distributive shock*, which indicates abnormal distribution of blood flow leading to inadequate tissue perfusion (e.g., septic shock, anaphylaxis)

The laboratory evaluation of the child with bacteremia, septic shock, or both conditions should provide information concerning the cause and the data required for optimal supportive management. Several studies have demonstrated that a total white blood cell (WBC) count exceeding 15,000 cells/mm^3 in a 3- to 36-month-old child with a fever exceeding 39° C to 40° C and without a focus of infection is an indication that the child is at increased risk for developing bacteremia.[12] An erythrocyte sedimentation rate greater than 30 mm/hr and C-reactive protein levels also have been suggested as useful screening tools for detecting serious bacterial infections. A low peripheral WBC count also may suggest septicemia and commonly is observed during episodes of overwhelming bacteremic illnesses. Procalcitonin levels are elevated in bacteremic children and are related to the severity of illness such as organ failure and even mortality.[82, 105] Rapid measurement of concentrations of procalcitonin is available in some countries by using commercial kits. The hemoglobin and hematocrit results should help differentiate between septic and hemorrhagic shock. Examination of the peripheral smear may disclose evidence of splenic dysfunction (i.e., Howell-Jolly bodies) or fragmented red blood cells, as seen in disseminated intravascular coagulation. Thrombocytopenia, prolongation of prothrombin time and partial prothrombin time, and the presence of fibrin split products are consistent with disseminated intravascular coagulation.[42] Hyponatremia is a common finding. Concentrations of serum bicarbonate may be depressed, which may signify a state of metabolic acidosis. Elevated lactic acid concentrations result from inadequate tissue perfusion and in some reports have been significantly greater in nonsurvivors or those with low-flow states than in survivors or patients with high-flow shock.[39] In pediatric studies, serial lactate levels showing normalization are associated with recovery.[30] Hyperglycemia or hypoglycemia may be encountered. Transaminase levels may be elevated and presumably reflect cellular injury. Serum calcium concentrations (preferably ionized calcium levels) should be checked periodically because hypocalcemia may interfere with optimal myocardial function.

Arterial blood gases obtained early in the course of endotoxin shock usually reveal hypocapnia and normal to elevated pH.[20, 21] At this point, the patient has a mixed metabolic acidosis and respiratory alkalosis. If the shock state progresses, the metabolic acidosis becomes so severe that respiratory compensation is ineffective, and the patient becomes acidotic. In some patients, respiratory acidosis accompanies metabolic acidosis. In either case, decompensated metabolic acidosis in the patient with septic shock is associated with a grave prognosis. A major consequence of ARDS is hypoxemia. For patients with ARDS, the chest radiograph characteristically shows bilateral and diffuse hazy infiltrates; opacification of all lung fields usually is seen during the late phases of ARDS.

Concentrations of blood urea nitrogen and serum creatinine may be elevated. Jones and Weil[96] found that the ratio of urine to plasma osmolality was the most valuable indicator of renal impairment in adult patients with shock. When this ratio was greater than 1.5, the likelihood of developing progressive renal failure was remote. A urine osmolality value greater than 400 mOsm/kg also indicated adequate renal function. Many WBCs or WBC casts in the urine may suggest the genitourinary tract as the source of bacteremia. If one or more gram-negative rods are seen on the Gram stain of unspun urine, more than 10^5 colony-forming units per milliliter of bacteria are likely to be present.

Isolating the organism responsible for bacteremia or septic shock is important for documenting the infection and for providing optimal antimicrobial therapy. With instruments that continuously monitor growth in the blood culture bottles, growth can be detected sooner than if the bottles are inspected just once or twice daily. Many authorities recommend that a blood culture be obtained in the 3- to 36-month-old child with fever higher than 39° C to 40° C and a total WBC count greater than or equal to 15,000 cells/mm^3 and without a specific focus of infection. In this way, instances of "unsuspected" or "outpatient" bacteremia can be identified. In an outpatient setting, almost 90 percent of blood cultures growing true pathogens were positive within 24 hours of incubation using a continuously monitored system.[120] Because most children with occult bacteremia have pneumococcal bacteremia, this approach may be less useful in the era of pneumococcal conjugate vaccine administration to young infants. In the infant who has received 3 or more doses of the conjugate pneumococcal vaccine, the likelihood of developing invasive pneumococcal infection is reduced approximately 90 percent. The proportion of children with high fever without localizing findings and a WBC count of 15,000/mm^3 or greater who might have occult pneumococcal bacteremia may be less than 1 percent, a level that no longer justifies this approach. Studies addressing this issue are necessary before firm recommendations can be made for this change in approach.[108]

When appropriate, cerebrospinal fluid, urine, and other pertinent sites should be cultured before initiating antibiotic therapy, if possible. When an intra-abdominal source of infection is likely, blood and other cultures should be processed anaerobically. Gram stain or acridine orange stain of a buffy coat smear of peripheral blood may reveal evidence of the causative microorganism, especially in an overwhelming infection.[103] Gram stain of material obtained from petechial or purpuric lesions may show gram-negative diplococci suggestive of meningococcus. Polymerase chain reaction for detecting *N. meningitidis* is available in selected laboratories and may be the only method by which infection is documented when cultures are sterile. Bacterial polysaccharide antigens can be detected rapidly in many body fluids by latex agglutination tests. Unfortunately, rapid diagnostic procedures for evaluating outpatients with suspected bacteremia are not reliable. Pneumococcal antigenuria is not detected readily when bacteremia occurs without a specific focus of infection. The value of assays for detecting circulating endotoxin is unclear.

Treatment

The initial selection of antibiotics for administration to a child with suspected bacteremia is based on the clinical situation (Table 69–4). If untreated initially, children with occult bacteremia are at risk of developing serious complications, such as meningitis or pneumonia.[124, 139] Empirical antibiotic therapy for children who are selected carefully and followed, therefore, seems reasonable.[12] However, two prospective studies of empirical administration of antibiotics in this situation reached different conclusions. Carroll and associates[35] randomly treated children with suspected occult bacteremia with no antibiotic or with 25,000 U/kg of penicillin G benzathine and 25,000 U/kg of penicillin G procaine administered intramuscularly, followed by oral penicillin V (100 mg/kg/day in 3 or 4 doses). Four of five children with bacteremia in the expectant treatment group compared with none of five untreated bacteremic children were improved at follow-up ($p < 0.05$). Four of the five untreated children subsequently developed a local infection, which included meningitis in two of them. In the second study, Jaffe and colleagues[95] randomly treated children with possible occult bacteremia with a placebo or oral amoxicillin. No differences in the incidence of major infectious morbidity associated with bacteremia occurred between the two groups. Differences in the type of expectant antibiotic therapy administered may explain in part the opposite conclusions of these studies. Ceftriaxone has been compared with amoxicillin or amoxicillin-clavulanate in two large studies involving children 3 to 36 months of age. Ceftriaxone was marginally superior at best to the oral agents with regard to efficacy.[14, 65]

One approach has been to obtain a blood culture from children 3 to 36 months of age with a temperature of 39° C or higher who have no focal findings and whose peripheral WBC count is greater than or equal to 15,000/mm^3. In such patients, the decision to administer antibiotics expectantly may be based on several factors, especially the ability of the parents to observe the child and communicate this information back to the physician in a timely manner. Ceftriaxone given parenterally; an oral agent, such as amoxicillin and amoxicillin-clavulanate (if the child has not received two or more conjugate *H. influenzae* type b vaccines); or other oral antibiotics can be administered. If treatment is initiated, a properly collected urine specimen for urinalysis or urine culture also should be obtained so that a urinary tract infection will not be treated inadvertently. Occult bacteremia caused by *S. pneumoniae* intermediate or resistant to penicillin or intermediate to ceftriaxone in an otherwise normal child should resolve with any of the options noted earlier.[100] This approach probably is less useful in the infant or child who has received 3 or more doses of the conjugate pneumococcal vaccine.

Children who subsequently are determined to have *S. pneumoniae* bacteremia and who have been treated with antibiotics expectantly need to be reevaluated as soon as the results of the blood cultures are known. If the child appears well and has been afebrile for at least 24 hours and if the

TABLE 69–4 ■ EMPIRICAL ANTIBIOTIC REGIMENS FOR SEPTIC SHOCK IN INFANTS AND CHILDREN UNDER SELECTED CLINICAL CIRCUMSTANCES

Circumstances	Antibiotics
Normal Child	
Skin findings suggesting meningococcemia or preceding skin trauma or varicella	Cefotaxime or ceftriaxone + vancomycin ± nafcillin
Urinary tract source	Cefotaxime or ceftriaxone + aminoglycoside
Intra-abdominal source	Clindamycin + gentamicin + ampicillin or piperacillin or piperacillin-tazobactam
Immunocompromised Child	
Malignancy or immunodeficiency or neutropenia or central line	Vancomycin + aminoglycoside + ticarcillin-clavulanate piperacillin-tazobactam or ceftazidime
Asplenia or splenic dysfunction	Vancomycin + cefotaxime or ceftriaxone

parents can observe the child carefully and are able to communicate frequently with the physician, outpatient management can be continued. For children who were not treated initially, who remain febrile, and who are called back to be reevaluated for a positive blood culture, a parenteral dose of antibiotics is recommended.[10] Close contact with the parents and patient is mandatory no matter how these children are managed initially. Hospitalization for intravenous antibiotics is indicated if the child appears "toxic" or has other signs suggesting a serious infection.

For children with suspected bacteremia who are ill and require admission to the hospital, antibiotics are selected to cover the most serious organisms causing that infection. In normal children 3 months of age or older, a combination of nafcillin (150 to 200 mg/kg/day) or another semisynthetic antistaphylococcal penicillin plus cefotaxime (150 to 200 mg/kg/day) or ceftriaxone (75 to 100 mg/kg/day) covers most of the likely pathogens (e.g., *S. pneumoniae, S. aureus, S. pyogenes, N. meningitidis, H. influenzae* type b). In areas of the country where community-acquired methicillin-resistant *S. aureus* (MRSA) is a problem, an agent effective against MRSA should be included in the initial empirical regimen.[85] Vancomycin (40 to 60 mg/kg/day) is the gold standard for treating infections caused by MRSA. For most community-acquired MRSA isolates, clindamycin (40 mg/kg/day in 4 divided doses) also is an effective antibiotic. Treatment of bacteremia associated with a genitourinary or gastrointestinal source requires antibiotics to which gram-negative enterics are susceptible. In such cases, initial therapy could consist of an aminoglycoside with an additional antibiotic active against anaerobes such as clindamycin, metronidazole, ticarcillin-clavulanate, or piperacillin-tazobactam for a gastrointestinal focus of infection. Extended-spectrum cephalosporins, such as cefotaxime or ceftriaxone, are possible alternative drugs for treating serious gram-negative enteric infections.[99] Optimal management of intra-abdominal or other abscesses usually requires surgical drainage, which should be undertaken as soon as the child's condition allows.

Immunosuppressed children or children with serious illnesses in intensive care settings require a different initial approach to suspected bacteremia. Gram-negative enterics, *P. aeruginosa, S. aureus,* and coagulase-negative staphylococcus are very likely to be isolated from these patients.[3] Empirical therapy of nosocomial infection is based on the current antibiotic susceptibility pattern within the hospital.[205] *E. coli, Klebsiella* spp., and *Enterobacter* spp. are among the most common organisms causing bacteremia in the patient in the pediatric ICU.[171] *E. coli* and *Klebsiella* spp. frequently produce β-lactamases that lead to resistance to ticarcillin or piperacillin. In general, a combination of an antistaphylococcal semisynthetic penicillin or vancomycin (if a central line is present) or, if MRSA is a relatively common nosocomial pathogen, an aminoglycoside, and an extended-spectrum penicillin (e.g., ticarcillin-clavulanate, piperacillin-tazobactam) is administered initially until a specific pathogen is isolated.[91] Broad-spectrum penicillins and aminoglycosides frequently exhibit synergy in vitro against gram-negative organisms, especially against *P. aeruginosa*.[107, 187] In the critically ill patient, a synergistic combination of antibiotics is beneficial for treating bacteremia caused by *P. aeruginosa* or *Klebsiella* spp.[70, 86, 104]

After a specific organism is identified and antibiotic susceptibilities are known, the most appropriate agent is selected. If *E. coli* or *Klebsiella* spp. are isolated, these organisms can produce extended-spectrum β-lactamases (ESBL), and the isolates should be tested for this possibility.[153] An ESBL-producing organism may appear susceptible to the extended-spectrum cephalosporins with minimal inhibitory concentrations of 2 to 8 μg/mL, but treatment failures may occur. If an ESBL-producing organism is identified, treatment with an extended-spectrum cephalosporin (e.g., cefotaxime, ceftriaxone, ceftazidime) is not recommended.[152] In this case, a carbapenem such as imipenem-cilastatin or meropenem is suggested. *Enterobacter* spp. may hyperproduce β-lactamase enzymes or be induced to hyperproduce these enzymes and are resistant or can become resistant to the extended-spectrum cephalosporins.[158] In many institutions, more than 30 percent of *Enterobacter cloacae* isolates are resistant to ceftazidime.[29] Cefepime may be more active than is ceftazidime or cefotaxime against *Enterobacter* spp. and other Amp C, β-lactamase enzyme–producing, gram-negative bacilli.[183] A carbapenem with an aminoglycoside is the treatment regimen recommended for treating infections caused by *Enterobacter* spp. resistant to ceftazidime.

In these patients, rapidly achieving therapeutic aminoglycoside levels in the plasma is important.[136] Serum concentrations of the aminoglycoside should be measured within 24 hours of initiation of therapy to ensure that therapeutic concentrations have been reached.

The management of septic shock is directed toward three main objectives: control of the infectious process, restoration of adequate tissue perfusion, and maintenance of efficient respiratory function. Details of management have been the subject of numerous reports.[30, 155]

Antibiotics should be administered as soon as the diagnosis of septic shock is suspected. The selection of antibiotics is the same as that for bacteremia. However, if *S. aureus* is suspected among the potential causes of septic shock, antibiotic therapy is complicated by two factors: MRSA may make up 50 percent of community-acquired isolates,[184] and nafcillin or oxacillin may be superior to vancomycin for the treatment of serious infections caused by methicillin-susceptible *S. aureus*.[74] Nafcillin or oxacillin plus an aminoglycoside may be synergistic against staphylococci. Some authorities include nafcillin or oxacillin plus vancomycin plus gentamicin in the initial empirical therapy of patients with life-threatening infections possibly caused by *S. aureus*.[6]

Restoration of adequate tissue perfusion requires infusions of fluids intravenously. Initially, an isotonic solution, such as 5 percent dextrose and normal saline or 5 percent dextrose and lactated Ringer solution, should be infused rapidly at 20 to 40 mL/kg over 15 to 30 minutes. In one study of children presenting in septic shock, the administration of fluid in excess of 40 mL/kg in the first hour in the emergency department was associated with improved survival, decreased occurrence of persistent hypovolemia, and no increased risk of developing ARDS.[33] Current guidelines call for 60 mL/kg of fluid resuscitation in the first hour of therapy. Unless the initial fluid administration returns perfusion to normal, all children should have central venous pressure measured to help guide fluid therapy. Urine output should be monitored carefully by catheterization of the bladder. If hypoproteinemia is documented, albumin or fresh-frozen plasma should be considered with careful monitoring of the central venous pressure. If no improvement in blood pressure, urine output, or mental status occurs after the infusion and the central venous pressure has risen less than 5 cm H_2O, additional fluid should be administered. Infusion of isotonic fluids (blood if the hematocrit is less than 30%) should be continued at rates sufficient to maintain systolic blood pressure at greater than 80 mm Hg and a urine output greater than 300 mL/m^2/24 hours.

Improvement in mental status usually accompanies administration of fluid. The efficacy of administering sodium bicarbonate to correct the metabolic acidosis is controversial. A nasogastric tube is inserted so that gastric bleeding can be recognized easily.

When expansion of the extracellular space with administration of fluid is not followed by improvement, when central venous pressure increases to more than 5 cm above its initial value or to an absolute value greater than 10 to 15 cm H_2O, or when pulmonary edema develops, the use of vasoactive agents, such as dopamine and dobutamine, may be considered.[156] When such agents are used, optimal management requires careful monitoring of the central venous pressure and possibly the pulmonary capillary wedge pressure and cardiac output through pulmonary artery catheterization. More detailed information is available in general reviews or studies of the use of vasoactive agents in children.[13, 36, 123, 164, 186]

The benefits of therapy with high doses of corticosteroids in the treatment of endotoxin shock remain unproved. Extensive experimental data document the salutary hemodynamic, metabolic, microcirculatory, and cellular effect of steroids in laboratory models of endotoxin shock. Pretreated animals or tissue preparations have been used for most of these studies; thus, extrapolating these data to clinical situations is difficult. Hinshaw and associates[88] have shown that the combination of methylprednisolone (15 to 30 mg/kg) and gentamicin leads to greater survival ($p < 0.025$) than does gentamicin alone or no therapy in baboons injected with 2 to 3×10^{10} live *E. coli* organisms. In this experiment, therapy was not administered until after the *E. coli* had been infused.

In a prospective, controlled study, Sprung and colleagues[195] evaluated high-dose corticosteroids in patients with septic shock. Patients in septic shock were assigned randomly to one of three treatment groups: methylprednisolone sodium succinate (30 mg/kg); dexamethasone sodium phosphate (6 mg/kg); and no steroid preparation. If shock persisted, the same dose of steroid was administered in 4 hours. Steroid therapy did result in a greater likelihood of reversal of shock in the first 24 hours after administration of drug (26% for steroid-treated patients versus 0 in controls, $p < 0.05$). By 133 hours after the drugs were administered, 40 percent (17 of 43 patients) of steroid-treated patients versus 69 percent (11 of 16 patients) of the control group had died ($p < 0.05$). However, the overall survival rate was not changed by the steroid therapy. Although superinfections did occur significantly ($p < 0.05$) more frequently in corticosteroid-treated patients than in controls, the number of patients at risk for developing superinfection was diminished in the control group, especially 2 days after administration of the study drugs.

Two other randomized, controlled, multicenter clinical trials of administration of high-dose methylprednisolone in adults with severe sepsis, septic shock, or both conditions have been conducted. In both studies, the placebo or corticosteroids were to be administered within 2 hours of the time the patient was considered to have met the entry criteria. In one study, methylprednisolone was administered as a 30 mg/kg dose given every 6 hours for 4 doses.[25] In the other study, methylprednisolone was administered as an initial 30 mg/kg bolus over 15 minutes followed by a 5 mg/kg/hr constant infusion for 9 hours.[213] In both studies, methylprednisolone did not alter the mortality rates of severe sepsis or septic shock. Reversal or prevention of shock also was not affected. Children were not included in any of these studies.

On the basis of these studies, the routine use of high-dose corticosteroids in patients with severe sepsis or septic shock is not recommended. Later, results of small studies enrolling adults suggested that lower stress doses of hydrocortisone might be beneficial in managing patients with septic shock.[22, 27] In one of these trials, placebo was compared with a 100-mg loading dose of hydrocortisone followed by a continuous infusion of 0.18 mg/kg/hr with a reduction of the infusion after shock had been reversed. Twenty patients were randomized to each treatment arm. Infusion of stress doses of hydrocortisone reduced the time to discontinuing the vasopressor therapy and was associated with a trend to earlier resolution of sepsis-induced organ dysfunction. However, overall reversal of shock and mortality rates were not changed. Randomized studies are needed to clarify the role of stress doses of hydrocortisone in children with septic shock.

Every effort should be expended to ensure an adequate airway, which may require periodic suctioning if the patient is unable to clear pooled secretions. A chest radiograph may reveal underlying pneumonia or other pulmonary pathology. Humidified oxygen in concentrations required to maintain an adequate partial pressure of oxygen should be provided early. The method of oxygen administration (e.g., mask, ventilator) depends on the clinical state of the patient. Intubation and assisted ventilation are indicated if the child shows evidence of impending respiratory failure.

Shock lung, usually appearing within 2 days after the onset of shock, may complicate the respiratory and fluid management.[90] Pulmonary edema, atelectasis, decreased pulmonary compliance, and ventilation-perfusion abnormalities are some of the factors that can lead to inadequate oxygenation. Administration of excessive fluids may contribute to shock lung. The central venous pressure may remain normal, despite the presence of pulmonary edema. Positive end-expiratory pressure, oxygen, and careful attention to cardiovascular parameters are the mainstays of therapy for ARDS.[90, 160, 178] Steroids are not beneficial after ARDS has been diagnosed.

The general supportive care of the child with septic shock includes attention to nutritional and metabolic requirements.[169] Administration of fluids containing 10 percent glucose may be necessary to prevent development of hypoglycemia. Parenteral alimentation may be the only means by which to provide nutrition, although the optimal amount and composition of elemental nutrients for children with septic shock are unknown. Hypocalcemia should be corrected. Platelet transfusions or fresh-frozen plasma may be necessary to correct coagulopathies. Continuous venovenous hemofiltration with or without dialysis may be instituted for complications of renal failure, such as fluid overload with pulmonary edema or hyperkalemia.[73]

INVESTIGATIVE THERAPIES

Based on the evolving understanding of the pathophysiology of septic shock, many large, randomized, double-blind, multicenter trials have been conducted to assess the efficacy of agents that neutralize or counteract toxins or cytokines that are important in the evolution of septic shock.

Antibody to Lipopolysaccharide

Endotoxemia frequently can be documented in patients with gram-negative sepsis. Endotoxin is released when bacteria are killed by bactericidal antibiotics.[189, 190] This release may help explain why some patients develop shock after parenteral antibiotics are administered.[78] Because endotoxin is responsible directly or through mediators for many of the adverse effects of gram-negative bacteremia, attempts to neutralize endotoxin have been undertaken. One problem with this approach is that only patients with septic shock caused by endotoxin-producing organisms may benefit from this treatment, and on patient presentation, distinguishing a gram-positive from gram-negative infection is not possible.

The *E. coli* J5 is a mutant strain that lacks side chains to the core polysaccharide. The J5 lipopolysaccharide, therefore, consists of lipid A and other core determinants that are surface exposed. Antibody to the J5 *E. coli* is thought to be broadly reactive with the lipopolysaccharide of a wide variety of gram-negative bacteria, although some studies have questioned the broad-spectrum cross-reactivity by J5 antisera.[78]

Human antisera to *E. coli* J5 mutant harvested from volunteers immunized with *E. coli* J5 in phenol proved to be efficacious in preventing mortality in adults with bacteremia and hypotension or profound shock.[236] However, the antibody titer to *E. coli* J5 was not related conclusively to prevention of mortality. Moreover, human antisera to *E. coli* J5 did not affect the course or mortality of severe infectious purpura (predominantly caused by *N. meningitidis*) in children.[93]

Murine and human immunoglobulin monoclonal antibodies to the core–lipid A region of lipopolysaccharide have been developed using *E. coli* J5 and appear to be broadly reactive with lipid A from other gram-negative organisms.[162] E-5 (XMMEN-OEJ, XOMA Corp., Berkeley, CA) is a murine monoclonal antibody that has a serum half-life in humans of 10 to 18 hours, depending on the dose.[81] In a randomized, multicenter trial, patients with gram-negative sepsis received E-5 or placebo in addition to antibiotics.[77] Mortality was reduced significantly only for patients with gram-negative sepsis without shock. However, a follow-up study focusing on patients with gram-negative sepsis with non-refractory shock did not demonstrate efficacy.[24] Another multicenter study compared a different human monoclonal antibody against lipid A HA-1A (Centoxin, Centocor, Malvern, PA) with human serum albumin in patients with a presumptive diagnosis of gram-negative sepsis with hypotension or systemic manifestations of infection.[235] Mortality was reduced significantly for patients with gram-negative bacteremia with or without shock who received HA-1A. A larger second study of patients with gram-negative bacteremia and septic shock found no efficacy for HA-1A and suggested a greater mortality for patients without gram-negative bacteremia in association with HA-1A.[118] Children were not included in either study, although the pharmacokinetics and safety of HA-1A have been established in children.[174] In the one study performed, HA-1A did not reduce mortality in children with meningococcal disease.[48]

Other Potential Adjunctive Therapies

Antibody to TNF-α, anti-TNF receptor, soluble TNF receptor, antiplatelet activating factor, recombinant IL-1ra, antibradykinin, nitric oxide synthase inhibitor, and other therapies have undergone evaluation in large clinical trials of adjunctive therapy for adults with sepsis syndrome. Unfortunately, none has proved beneficial.[2, 9, 63] Some combination of therapies may provide significant benefit in humans with gram-negative septic shock, as has been demonstrated in animals.[180] Using recombinant soluble CD14 is another approach for blocking the action of endotoxin.[84]

Recombinant bactericidal/permeability-increasing protein ($rBPI_{23}$), a human-derived recombinant protein that expresses the amino-terminal half of the whole bactericidal, permeability-increasing protein molecule, has been studied in children with severe meningococcal sepsis.[134] Preliminary evaluation of $rBPI_{23}$ in 26 children with severe meningococcal sepsis in an open-label phase I/II trial was associated with fewer cases of mortality than in historical control patients.[71] A subsequent large, multicenter, randomized, double-blind trial in which 395 children were enrolled was conducted in 22 centers throughout the United States and the United Kingdom.[110] Mortality rates (7.4%) were not diminished significantly in the $rBPI_{23}$ group because the mortality rate in the control group was only 9.9 percent, a rate much less than anticipated. Children receiving $rBPI_{23}$ did have fewer amputations and a better functional outcome than did those receiving placebo. Further studies may be required before $rBPI_{23}$ is approved for adjunctive treatment of severe meningococcal disease. Meningococcal disease also may become less common after conjugate meningococcal vaccines become administered routinely to young children.[165]

Based on the complex interaction of the inflammatory and procoagulation responses of the host to infection as outlined in the pathophysiology section, recombinant human activated protein C (drotrecogin alpha activated [rhAPC]) was evaluated for adjunctive treatment of severe sepsis in patients 18 years old and older. In a multicenter, double-blind, placebo-controlled study conducted in several countries, placebo or rhAPC was infused at a rate of 24 μg/kg/hr for 96 hours to patients with severe sepsis.[17] Selected demographic and clinical characteristics of the patients demonstrated that the patients were matched well. The mortality rate at 28 days was 30.8 percent for the 840 patients in the placebo group and 24.7 percent for the patients receiving rhAPC (p = 0.005). The relative risk of mortality was reduced in the rhAPC group by 19.4 percent (95% confidence interval, 6.6 to 30.5). The major difference in serious adverse effects was for serious bleeding, which occurred in 3.5 percent and 2.0 percent of the rhAPC and placebo patients, respectively.

Protein C concentrate has been administered to several children with fulminant meningococcemia and thought to be associated with enhanced survival and decreased amputations.[4, 224] These findings support the continued evaluation of rhAPC in the adjunctive treatment of septic shock in children. Phase I and II studies have evaluated the pharmacokinetics and safety of rhAPC in children with severe sepsis.[113] An infusion rate of 24 μg/kg/hr resulted in mean serum concentrations of 67 ng/mL in 43 infants and children. (The mean concentration found in adults was 52 ng/mL.) rhAPC did not accumulate during a 96-hour infusion. The estimated half-life was 0.91 hours, and plasma clearance was 0.49 L/hr/kg. Compassionate use of rhAPC is being conducted in children with purpura fulminans. Of the 83 children who have received rhAPC in pediatric studies, a 14-year-old patient had an intracranial hemorrhage that was possibly related to this drug. Recombinant human activated protein C has been approved for use in adults by the U.S. Food and Drug Administration.

Polymyxin B is an antibiotic that can neutralize endotoxin possibly through a detergent-like action. In experimental models, polymyxin B moderates some of the cardiovascular, metabolic, and lethal consequences of *E. coli* sepsis in rabbits and overwhelming *H. influenzae* type b disease in infant rats.[66, 218] Clinical studies of polymyxin B have not been conducted in humans with sepsis or septic shock.

Pentoxifylline is a phosphodiesterase inhibitor that has anti-inflammatory properties, including the ability to suppress endotoxin-induced mononuclear cell production of TNF. Pentoxifylline decreases endotoxin or TNF-induced lung injury and increases survival in animals infected with *E. coli* or infused with endotoxin.[112] In a study of human volunteers, a 500-mg dose of pentoxifylline infused 30 minutes before a 100-ng injection of endotoxin from *Salmonella abortus equi* blunted the TNF response but did not affect interleukin-6 serum levels after administration of endotoxin.[232] Clinical effects, such as fever, myalgia, and headache, were not affected by pentoxifylline. In one small study of

51 patients, a continuous infusion of pentoxifylline was associated with improvement in organ dysfunction scores, PaO_2/FIO_2 ratio, and the pressure-adjusted heart rate compared with placebo-treated patients.[197] Larger clinical studies of pentoxifylline or similar agents are warranted for the adjunctive treatment of sepsis and septic shock.

Plasmapheresis, exchange transfusions, and extracorporeal membrane oxygenation are heroic measures that appear to be beneficial in selected patients not responding to standard management.[16, 49, 69, 233] These procedures may be considered for such patients when, in the opinion of experienced clinicians, their use is justified and they are the last hope for a successful outcome.

Prognosis

The morbidity and mortality rates for septic shock in children vary with age, the presence or absence of underlying diseases, and the specific microorganisms responsible for the septicemic state. Dupont and Spink[55] reported a 98 percent mortality rate in their series of children with septic shock and gram-negative bacteremia. Jacobs and colleagues[94] reported a 9.8 percent case-fatality rate for otherwise normal children with septic shock. In the pediatric HA-1A study, the overall mortality rate for severe sepsis or septic shock was 31 percent.[174] As with many infections, prevention is more desirable than is treatment. Careful attention to sterile techniques for insertion and maintenance of intravascular or other lines, as well as other procedures, is critically important and may prevent some episodes of bacteremia and septic shock.

REFERENCES

1. Abraham, E., Bland, R. D., Cobo, J. C., et al.: Sequential cardiorespiratory patterns associated with outcome in septic shock. Chest *85*:75–80, 1984.
2. Abraham, E., Wunderink, R., Silverman, H., et al.: Efficacy and safety of monoclonal antibody to human tumor necrosis factor α in patients with sepsis syndrome: A randomized, controlled, double-blind, multicenter clinical trial. J. A. M. A. *273*:934–941, 1995.
3. Albano, E. A., and Pizzo, P. A.: Infectious complications in childhood acute leukemias. Pediatr. Clin. North Am. *35*:873–901, 1988.
4. Alberio, L., Lämmle, B., Esmon, C. T.: Protein C replacement in severe meningococcemia: Rationale and clinical experience. Clin. Infect. Dis. *32*:1338–1346, 2001.
5. Aledo, A., Heller, G., Gardner, S., et al: Septicemia and septic shock in pediatric patients: 140 consecutive cases on a pediatric hematology-oncology service. J. Pediatr. Hematol. Oncol. *20*:215–221, 1998.
6. American Academy of Pediatrics Staphylococcal infections. *In* Pickering, L. K. (ed.): 2000 Red Book: Report of the Committee on Infectious Diseases. 25th ed. Elk Grove Village, IL, American Academy of Pediatrics, 2000, pp. 514–526.
7. Anderson, R. R., Holliday, R. L., Driedger, A. A., et al.: Documentation of pulmonary capillary permeability in the adult respiratory distress syndrome accompanying human sepsis. Am. Rev. Respir. Dis. *119*:869–877, 1979.
8. Archer, L. T., Benjamin, B. A., Beller-Todd, B. K., et al.: Does LD_{100} *E. coli* shock cause myocardial failure? Cir. Shock *9*:7–16, 1982.
9. Astiz, M. E., and Rackow, E. C.: Septic shock. Lancet *351*:1501–1505, 1998.
10. Bachur, R., and Harper, M. B.: Reevaluation of outpatients with *Streptococcus pneumoniae* bacteremia. Pediatrics *105*:502–509, 2000.
11. Banks, J. G., Foulis, A. K., Ledingham, I. M., et al.: Liver function in septic shock. J. Clin. Pathol. *35*:1249–1252, 1982.
12. Baraff, L. J., Bass, J. W., Fleisher, G. R., et al.: Practice guideline for the management of infants and children 0 to 36 months of age with fever without source. Pediatrics *92*:1–12, 1993.
13. Barton, P., Garcia, J., Kouatli A., et al.: Hemodynamic effects of IV milrinone lactate in pediatric patients with septic shock. A prospective, double-blinded, randomized, placebo-controlled, interventional study. Chest. *109*:1302–1312, 1996.
14. Bass, J. W., Steele, R. W., Wittler, R. R., et al.: Antimicrobial treatment of occult bacteremia: A multicenter cooperative study. Pediatr. Infect. Dis. J. *12*:466–473, 1993.
15. Baumgarten, G., Knuefermann, P., Nozaki, N., et al.: In vivo expression of proinflammatory mediators in the adult heart after endotoxin administration: The role of toll-like receptor-4. J. Infect. Dis. *183*:1617–1624, 2001.
16. Beca, J., and Butt, W.: Extracorporeal membrane oxygenation for refractory septic shock in children. Pediatrics *93*:726–729, 1994.
17. Bernard, G. R., Vincent, J.-L., Laterre, P.-F., et al.: Efficacy and safety of recombinant human activated protein C for severe sepsis. N. Engl. J. Med. *344*:699–709, 2001.
18. Beutler, B., and Poltorak, A.: Sepsis and evolution of the innate immune response. Crit. Care Med. *29*(Suppl 1):S2–S6, 2001.
19. Blain, C. M., Anderson, T. O., Pietras, R. J., et al.: Immediate hemodynamic effects of gram-negative vs. gram-positive bacteremia in man. Arch. Intern. Med. *126*:260–265, 1970.
20. Blair, E.: Hypocapnea and gram-negative bacteremic shock. Am. Surg. J. *119*:433–438, 1970.
21. Blair, E.: Acid-base balance in bacteremic shock. Arch. Intern. Med. *127*:731–739, 1971.
22. Bollaert, P. E., Charpentier, C., Levy, S., et al.: Reversal of late septic shock with supraphysiologic doses of hydrocortisone. Crit. Care Med. *26*:645–650, 1998.
23. Bone, R. C., Balk, R. A., Cerra, F. B., et al.: Definitions for sepsis and organ failure and guidelines for the use of innovative therapies in sepsis. Chest. *101*:1644–1655, 1992.
24. Bone, R. C., Balk, R. A., Fein, A. M., et al.: A second large controlled clinical study of E5, a monoclonal antibody to endotoxin: Results of a prospective, multicenter, randomized, controlled trial: The E5 sepsis study group. Crit. Care Med. *23*:994–1006, 1995.
25. Bone, R. C., Fisher, C. J., Jr., Clemmer, T. P., et al.: A controlled clinical trial of high-dose methylprednisolone in the treatment of severe sepsis and septic shock. N. Engl. J. Med. *317*:653–658, 1987.
26. Brigham, K. L., and Meyrick, B.: Endotoxin and lung injury. Am. Rev. Respir. Dis. *133*:913–927, 1986.
27. Briegel, J., Forst, H., Haller, M., et. Al.: Stress doses of hydrocortisone reverses hyperdynamic septic shock: A prospective, randomized, double-blind, single-center study. Crit. Care Med. 27:723–732, 1999.
28. Buck, C., Bundschu, J., Gallati, H., et al.: Interleukin-6: A sensitive parameter for early diagnosis of neonatal bacterial infection. Pediatrics *93*:54–58, 1994.
29. Burwen, D. R., Banerjee, S. N., Gaynes, R. P., and the National Nosocomial Infections Surveillance System: Ceftazidime resistance among selected nosocomial gram-negative bacilli in the U.S. J. Infect. Dis. *170*:1622–1625, 1994.
30. Butt, W.: Septic shock. Pediatr. Clin. North Am. *48*:601–625, 2001.
31. Calandra, T., Baumgartner, J. D., Grau, G. E., et al.: Prognostic values of tumor necrosis factor/cachectin, interleukin-1, interferon-alpha, and interferon-gamma in the serum of patients with septic shock. J. Infect. Dis. *161*:982–987, 1990.
32. Cannon, J. G., Tompkins, R. G., Gelfand, J. A., et al.: Circulating interleukin-1 and tumor necrosis factor in septic shock and experimental endotoxin fever. J. Infect. Dis. *161*:79–84, 1990.
33. Carcillo, J. A., Davis, A. L., and Zaritsky, A.: Role of early fluid resuscitation in pediatric septic shock. J. A. M. A. *266*:1242–1245, 1991.
34. Cardenas-Rivero, N., Chernow, B., Stoiko, M. A., et al.: Hypocalcemia in critically ill children. J. Pediatr. *114*:946–951, 1989.
35. Carroll, W. L., Farrell, M. K., Singer, J. L., et al.: Treatment of occult bacteremia: A prospective randomized clinical trial. Pediatrics *72*:608–612, 1983.
36. Ceneviva, G., Paschall, J. A., Maffei, F., and Carcillo, J. A.: Hemodynamic support in fluid-refractory pediatric septic shock. Pediatrics *102*:e19, 1998.
37. Chesney, R. W., McCarron, D. M., Haddad, J. G., et al.: Pathogenic mechanisms of the hypocalcemia of the staphylococcal toxic-shock syndrome. J. Lab. Clin. Med. *101*:576–585, 1983.
38. Clowes, G. H. A., George, B. C., Villee, C. A., et al.: Muscle proteolysis induced by a circulating peptide in patients with sepsis or trauma. N. Engl. J. Med. *308*:545–552, 1983.
39. Clowes, G. H. A., O'Donnell, T. F., Ryan, V. T., et al.: Energy metabolism in sepsis: Treatment based on different patterns in shock and high output stage. Ann. Surg. *179*:684–696, 1974.
40. Coalson, J. J., Archer, L. T., Hall, N. K., et al.: Prolonged shock in the monkey following live *E. coli* organism infusion. Circ. Shock *6*:343–355, 1979.
41. Corrigan, J. J.: Thrombocytopenia: A laboratory sign of septicemia in infants and children. J. Pediatr. *85*:219–221, 1974.
42. Corrigan, J. J.: Disseminated intravascular coagulopathy. Pediatrics *64*:37–45, 1979.
43. Corrigan, J. J.: Vitamin K–dependent coagulation factors in gram-negative septicemia. Am. J. Dis. Child. *138*:240–242, 1984.
44. Corrigan, J. J., and Jordan, C. M.: Heparin therapy in septicemia with disseminated intravascular coagulation. N. Engl. J. Med. *283*:778–782, 1970.
45. Cryer, P. E., Coran, A. G., Soda, J., et al.: Lethal *Escherichia coli* septicemia in the baboon: Alpha-adrenergic inhibition in insulin secretion and its relationship to the duration of survival. J. Lab. Clin. Med. *79*:622–638, 1972.

46. Dantzsker, D. R., Brook, C. J., Hebart, P., et al.: Ventilation-perfusion distributions in the adult respiratory distress syndrome. Am. Rev. Respir. Dis. *120*:1039–1052, 1979.
47. DeBont, E. S. J. M., Raan, M. J., Samson, G., et al.: Tumor necrosis factor-α, interleukin-1β, and interleukin-6 plasma levels in neonatal sepsis. Pediatr. Res. *33*:330–383, 1993.
48. Derkx, B., Wittes, J., McCloskey, R., and the European Pediatric Meningococcal Septic Shock Trial Study Group: Randomized placebo-controlled trial of HA-1A, a human monoclonal antibody to endotoxin in children with meningococcal septic shock.Clin. Infect. Dis. *28*:770–770, 1999.
49. Deuren, M., Santman, F. W., Dalen, R., et al.: Plasma and whole blood exchange in meningococcal sepsis. Clin. Infect. Dis. *15*:424–430, 1992.
50. Deuren, M., Ven-Jongekrijg, J., Bartelink, A. K. M., et al.: Correlation between proinflammatory cytokines and antiinflammatory mediators and severity of disease in meningococcal infections. J. Infect. Dis. *172*: 433–439, 1995.
51. Deuren, M., Ven-Jongekrijg, J., Demacker, P. N. M., et al.: Differential expression of proinflammatory cytokines and their inhibitors during the course of meningococcal infections. J. Infect. Dis. *169*:157–161, 1994.
52. Deventer, S. J. H. V., Bulter, H. R., Cate, J. W. T., et al.: Endotoxaemia: An early predictor of septicaemia in febrile patients. Lancet *1*:605–609, 1988.
53. Dinarello, C. A.: Interleukin-1 and its biologically related cytokines. Adv. Immunol. *44*:153–203, 1989.
54. Dinarello, C. A., and Wolff, S. M.: The role of interleukin-1 in disease. N. Engl. J. Med. *328*:106–113, 1993.
55. Dupont, H. L., and Spink, W. W.: Infections due to gram-negative organisms: An analysis of 860 patients with bacteremia at the University of Minnesota Medical Center, 1958–1966. Medicine (Baltimore). *48*: 307–332, 1969.
56. Edwards, M. S., and Baker, C. J.: Complications and sequelae of meningococcal infections in children. J. Pediatr. *99*:540–545, 1981.
57. Farley, M. M., Stephens, D. S., Mulks, M. H., et al.: Pathogenesis of IgA1 protease producing and non producing *Haemophilus influenzae* in human nasopharyngeal organ cultures. J. Infect. Dis. *154*:752–759, 1986.
58. Faust, S. N., Levin, M., Harrison, O. B., et al.: Dysfunction of endothelial protein C activation in severe meningococcal sepsis. N. Engl. J. Med. *345*:408–416, 2001.
59. Fearson, D. T., Ruddy, S., Schur, P. H., et al.: Activation of the properdin pathway of complement in patients with gram-negative bacteremia. N. Engl. J. Med. *292*:937–940, 1975.
60. Feltes, T. F., Pignatelli, R., Kleinert, S., and Mariscalco, M.: Quantitated left ventricular systolic mechanics in children with septic shock utilizing noninvasive wall-stress analysis. Crit. Care Med. *22*:1647–1648, 1994.
61. Fenton, L. J., and Strunk, R. C.: Complement activation and group B streptococcal infection in the newborn: Similarities to endotoxin shock. Pediatrics *60*:901–907, 1977.
62. Filkins, J. P., and Cornell, R. P.: Depression of hepatic gluconeogenesis and the hypoglycemia of endotoxin shock. Am. J. Physiol. *227*:778–781, 1974.
63. Fisher, C. J., Dhainaut, J.-F. A., Opal, S. M., et al.: Recombinant human interleukin 1 receptor antagonist in the treatment of patients with sepsis syndrome: Results from a randomized, double-blind, placebo-controlled trial. J. A. M. A. *271*:1836–1843, 1995.
64. Fisher, C. J., Jr., and Yan, S. B.: Protein C levels as a prognostic indicator of outcome in sepsis and related diseases. Crit. Care Med. *28*:S49–S56, 2000.
65. Fleisher, G. R., Rosenberg, N., Vinci, R., et al.: Intramuscular versus oral antibiotic therapy for the prevention of meningitis and other bacterial sequelae in young, febrile children at risk for occult bacteremia. J. Pediatr. *124*:504–512, 1994.
66. Flynn, P. M., Shenep, J. L., Stokes, D. C., et al.: Polymyxin B moderates acidosis and hypotension in established experimental gram-negative septicemia. J. Infect. Dis. *156*:706–712, 1987.
67. Froon, A. H. M., Dentener, M. A., Greve, J. W. M., et al.: Lipopolysaccharide toxicity-regulating proteins in bacteremia. J. Infect. Dis. *171*: 1250–1257, 1995.
68. Gallin, J. I., Kaye, D., and O'Leary, W. M.: Serum lipids in infections. N. Engl. J. Med. *281*:1081–1086, 1969.
69. Garlund, B., Sjölin, J., Nilsson, A., et al.: Plasmapheresis in the treatment of primary septic shock in humans. Scand. J. Infect. Dis. *25*:757–761, 1993.
70. Girardin, E., Grau, G. E., Dayer, J. M., et al.: Tumor necrosis factor and interleukin-1 in the serum of children with severe infectious purpura. N. Engl. J. Med. *319*:397–400, 1988.
71. Giroir, B. P., Quint, P. A., Barton, P., et al.: Preliminary evaluation of recombinant amino-terminal bactericidal/permeability-increasing protein in children with severe meningococcal sepsis. Lancet *350*:1439–1443, 1997.
72. Goldie, A. S., Fearon, K. C. H., Ross, J. A., et al.: Natural cytokine antagonists and endogenous antiendotoxin core antibodies in sepsis syndrome. J. A. M. A. *274*:172–177, 1995.
73. Goldstein, S. L., Currier, H., Graf, J. M., et al.: Outcome in children receiving continuous venovenous hemofiltration. Pediatrics *107*:1309–1312, 2001.
74. Gonzalez, C., Rubio, M., Romero-Vivas, J., et al.: Bacteremic pneumonia due to *Staphylococcus aureus*: A comparison of disease caused by methicillin-resistant and methicillin-susceptible organisms. Clin. Infect. Dis. *29*:1171–1177, 1999.
75. Graham, D. L., Behan, P. O., and More, I. A. R.: Brain damage complicating septic shock: Acute hemorrhagic leukoencephalitis as a complication of the generalized Schwartzman reaction. J. Neurol. Neurosurg. Psychiatr. *42*:19–28, 1979.
76. Gray, J., Gossain, S., and Morris, K.: Three-year survey of bacteremias and fungemia in a pediatric intensive care unit. Pediatr. Infect. Dis. J. *20*:416–421, 2001.
77. Greenman, R. L., Schein, R. M., Martin, M. A., et al.: A controlled clinical trial of E5 murine monoclonal IgM antibody to endotoxin in the treatment of gram-negative sepsis. J. A. M. A. *266*:1097–1102, 1991.
78. Greisman, S. E., and Johnston, C. A.: Failure of antisera to J5 and R595 rough mutants to reduce endotoxemic lethality. J. Infect. Dis. *157*:54–64, 1988.
79. Hack, C. E., Hart, M., Strack, R. J. M., et al.: Interleukin-8 in sepsis: Relation to shock and inflammatory mediators. Infect. Immun. *60*:2835–2842, 1992.
80. Hammerschmidt, D. E., Weaver, L. J., Hudson, L. D., et al.: Association of complement activation and elevated plasma-C5a with adult respiratory distress syndrome: Pathophysiologic relevance and possible prognostic value. Lancet *1*:947–949, 1980.
81. Harkonen, S., Scannon, P., Mischak, R. P., et al.: Phase I study of a murine monoclonal antilipid A antibody in bacteremic and nonbacteremic patients. Antimicrob. Agents Chemother. *32*:710–716, 1988.
82. Hatherill, M., Tibby, S. M., Turner, C., Ratnavel, N., and Murdoch, I. A.: Procalcitonin and cytokine levels: Relationship to organ failure and mortality in pediatric septic shock. Crit. Care Med. *28*:2591–2594, 2000.
83. Hayden, W. R.: Sepsis terminology in pediatrics. J. Pediatr. *124*:657–658, 1993.
84. Haziot, A., Rong, G. W., Lin, X.-Y., et al.: Recombinant soluble CD14 prevents mortality in mice treated with endotoxin (lipopolysaccharide). J. Immunol. *154*:6529–6532, 1995.
85. Herold, B. C., Immergluck, L. C., Maranan, M. C., et al: Community-acquired methicillin-resistant *Staphylococcus aureus* in children with no identified predisposing risks. J. A. M. A. *279*:593–598, 1998.
86. Hilf, M., Yu, V. L., Sharp, J., et al.: Antibiotic therapy for *Pseudomonas aeruginosa* bacteremia: Outcome correlations in a prospective study of 200 patients. Am. J. Med. *87*:540–546, 1989.
87. Hill, S. L., Eblings, V. B., and Lewis, F. R.: Changes in lung water and capillary permeability following sepsis and fluid overload. J. Surg. Res. *28*:140–150, 1980.
88. Hinshaw, L. B., Beller-Todd, B. K., Archer, L. T., et al.: Effectiveness of steroid/antibiotic treatment in primates administered LD_{100} *Escherichia coli*. Ann. Surg. *194*:51–56, 1981.
89. Hinshaw, L. B., Tekamp-Olson, P., Chang, A. C. K., et al.: Survival of primates in LD_{100} septic shock following therapy with antibody to tumor necrosis factor (TNF). Circ. Shock. *30*:279–292, 1990.
90. Holbrook, P. R., Taylor, G., Pollack, M. M., et al.: Adult respiratory distress syndrome in children. Pediatr. Clin. North Am. *27*:677–685, 1980.
91. Hughes, W. T., Armstrong, D., Bodey, G. P., et al.: Guidelines for the use of antimicrobial agents in neutropenic patients with unexplained fever. J. Infect. Dis. *161*:381–396, 1990.
92. Ingalls, R. R., Heine, H., Lien, E., et al.: Lipopolysacchaide recognition, CD14, and lipopolysaccharide receptors. Infect. Dis. Clin. North Am. *13*:341–353, 1999.
93. J5 Study Group: Treatment of severe infectious purpura in children with human plasma from donors immunized with *Escherichia coli* J5: A prospective double-blind study. J. Infect. Dis. *165*:695–701, 1992.
94. Jacobs, R. F., Sowell, M. K., Moss, M. M., et al.: Septic shock in children: Bacterial etiologies and temporal relationships. Pediatr. Infect. Dis. J. *9*:196–200, 1990.
95. Jaffe, D. M., Tanz, R. R., Davis, A. T., et al.: Antibiotic administration to treat possible occult bacteremia in febrile children. N. Engl. J. Med. *317*:1175–1180, 1987.
96. Jones, L. W., and Weil, M. H.: Water, creatinine and sodium excretion following circulatory shock with renal failure. Am. J. Med. *51*:314–318, 1971.
97. Kalter, E. S., Daha, M. R., Cate, J. W. T., et al.: Activation and inhibition of Hageman factor-dependent pathways and the complement system in uncomplicated bacteremia or bacterial shock. J. Infect. Dis. *151*:1019–1027, 1985.
98. Kapadia, S., Torre-Amione, G., Birdsall, H. H., et al.: Tumor necrosis factor-a gene and protein expression in adult feline myocardium after endotoxin administration. J. Clin. Invest. *96*:1042–1052, 1995.
99. Kaplan, S. L.: Serious pediatric infections. Am. J. Med. *88*(Suppl.4A): 18S–24S, 1990.
100. Kaplan, S. L., Mason, E. O., Jr., Barson, W. J., et al.: Outcome of invasive infections outside the central nervous system caused by *Streptococcus pneumoniae* isolates nonsusceptible to ceftriaxone in children treated with beta-lactam antibiotics. Pediatr. Infect. Dis. J. *20*:392–396, 2001.

101. Kaplan, S. L., Taber, L. H., Frank, A. L., et al.: Nasopharyngeal viral isolates in children with *Haemophilus influenzae* type b meningitis. J. Pediatr. *99*:591–593, 1981.
102. Kaufmann, R. L., Matson, C. F., and Beisel, W. R.: Hypertriglyceridemia produced by endotoxin: Role of impaired triglyceride disposal mechanisms. J. Infect. Dis. *133*:548–555, 1976.
103. Kleiman, M. B., Reynolds, J. K., Schreiner, R. L., et al.: Rapid diagnosis of neonatal bacteremia with acridine orange-stained buffy coat smears. J. Pediatr. *105*:419–421, 1984.
104. Korvick, J. A., Bryan, C. S., Farber, B., et al.: Prospective observational study of *Klebsiella* bacteremia in 230 patients: Outcome for antibiotic combinations versus monotherapy. Antimicrob. Agents Chemother. *36*:2639–2644, 1992.
105. Lacour, A. G., Gervaix, A., Zamora, S. A., et al: Procalcitonin, IL-6, IL-8, IL receptor antagonist and C-reactive protein as identificators of serious bacterial infections in children with fever without localizing signs. Eur. J. Pediatr. *160*:95–100, 2001.
106. Langevelde, P. V., Joop, K., Loon, J. V., et al.: Endotoxin, cytokines, and procalcitonin in febrile patients admitted to the hospital: Identification of subjects at high risk of mortality. Clin. Infect. Dis. *31*:1343–1348, 2000.
107. Lau, W. K., Young, L. S., Black, R. E., et al.: Comparative efficacy and toxicity of amikacin/carbenicillin versus gentamicin/carbenicillin in leukopenic patients: A randomized prospective trial. Am. J. Med. *62*: 959–966, 1977.
108. Lee, G. M., Fleisher, G. R., and Harper, M. B.: Management of febrile children in the age of the conjugate pneumococcal vaccine: A cost-effectiveness analysis. Pediatrics *108*:835–844, 2001.
109. Levi, M., ten Cate, H., Poll, T., et al.: Pathogenesis of disseminated intravascular coagulation in sepsis. J. A. M. A. *270*:975–979, 1993.
110. Levin, M., Quint, P. A., Goldstein, B., et al.: Recombinant bactericidal/permeability-increasing protein ($rBPI_{23}$) as adjunctive treatment for children with severe meningococcal sepsis: A randomized trial. Lancet *356*:961–967, 2000.
111. Levin, J., Poore, T. E., Young, N. S., et al.: Gram-negative sepsis: Detection of endotoxemia with the Limulus test. Ann. Intern. Med. *76*:1–7, 1972.
112. Lilly, C. M., Sandhu, J. S., Ishizaka, A., et al.: Pentoxifylline prevents tumor necrosis factor–induced lung injury. Am. Rev. Respir. Dis. *139*: 1361–1368, 1989.
113. Lilly research Laboratories: Briefing document for XIGRIS™ for the treatment of severe sepsis. FDA Anti-Infective Drugs Advisory Committee, 12 September 2001. Available at www.fda.gov/ohrms/dockets/ac/01/briefing/3787b1_01_Sponsor.pdf
114. Lorente, J. A., Garcia-Frade, L. J., Landin, L., et al.: Time course of hemostatic abnormalities in sepsis and its relation to outcome. Chest *103*:1536–1542, 1993.
115. McCabe, M. R.: Serum complement levels in bacteremia due to gram-negative organisms. N. Engl. J. Med. *288*:21–23, 1973.
116. McCarthy, P. L.: Controversies in pediatrics: What tests are indicated for the child under 2 with fever? Pediatr. Rev. *1*:51–56, 1979.
117. McCartney, A. C., Banks, J. G., Clements, G. B., et al.: Endotoxemia in septic shock: Clinical and post-mortem correlations. Intensive Care Med. *9*:117–122, 1983.
118. McCloskey, R. V., Straube, R. C., Sanders, C., et al.: Treatment of septic shock with human monoclonal antibody HA-1A: A randomized, double-blind, placebo-controlled trial. Ann. Intern. Med. *121*:1–5, 1994.
119. McConn, R., Greineder, J. K., Wasserman, F., et al.: Is there a humoral factor that depresses ventricular function in sepsis? Circ. Shock *1*(Suppl.):9–27, 1979.
120. McGowan, K. L., Foster, J. A., and Coffin, S. E.: Outpatient pediatric blood cultures: Time to positivity. Pediatrics *106*:251–255, 2000.
121. Mallet, E., Lanse, X., Devaux, A. M., et al.: Hypercalcitoninaemia in fulminant meningococcaemia in children. Lancet *1*:294, 1983.
122. Marchant, A., Devière, J., Byl, B., et al.: Interleukin-10 production during septicemia. Lancet *343*:707–708, 1994.
123. Marik, P. E., and Mohedin, M.: The contrasting effects of dopamine and norepinephrine on systemic and splanchnic oxygen utilization in hyperdynamic sepsis. J. A. M. A. *272*:1354–1357, 1994.
124. Marshall, R., Teele, D. W., and Klein, J. O.: Unsuspected bacteremia due to *Haemophilus influenzae*: Outcome in children not initially admitted to hospital. J. Pediatr. *95*:690–695, 1979.
125. Mason, J. W., Kleeberg, V., Dolan, P., et al.: Plasma kallikrein and Hageman factor in gram-negative bacteremia. Ann. Intern. Med. *73*:545–551, 1970.
126. Matuschak, G. M., and Rinaldo, J. E.: Organ interactions in the adult respiratory distress syndrome during sepsis: Role of the liver in host defense. Chest *94*:400–406, 1988.
127. Meyer, J., Traber, L. D., Nelson, S., et al.: Reversal of hyperdynamic response to continuous endotoxin administration by inhibition of NO synthesis. J. Appl. Physiol. *73*:324–328, 1992.
128. Michaels, R. H., Myerowitz, R. L., and Klaw, R.: Potentiation of experimental meningitis due to *Haemophilus influenzae* by influenza A virus. J. Infect. Dis. *135*:641–645, 1977.
129. Michie, H. R., Manoque, K. R., Spriggs, D. R., et al.: Detection of circulating tumor necrosis factor after endotoxin administration. N. Engl. J. Med. *318*:1481–1486, 1988.
130. Miller, R. L., Reichgott, M. J., and Melmon, K. L.: Biochemical mechanisms of generation of bradykinin by endotoxin. J. Infect. Dis. *128*(Suppl.):144–156, 1973.
131. Miller, S. I., Wallace, R. J., Musher, D. M., et al.: Hypoglycemia as a manifestation of sepsis. Am. J. Med. *68*:649–654, 1980.
132. Mizock, B.: Metabolic derangements in sepsis and septic shock. Crit. Care Clin. *16*:319–336, 2000.
133. Mizock, B. A., Sabelli, H. C., Dubin, A., et al.: Septic encephalopathy. Evidence for altered phenylalanine metabolism and comparison with hepatic encephalopathy. Arch. Intern. Med. *150*:443–449, 1990.
134. Möhlen, M. A. M., Kimmings, A. N., Wedel, N. I., et al.: Inhibition of endotoxin-induced cytokine release and neutrophil activation in humans by use of recombinant bactericidal/permeability-increasing protein. J. Infect. Dis. *172*:144–151, 1995.
135. Moncada, S., and Higgs, A.: The L-arginine-nitric oxide pathway. N. Engl. J. Med. *329*:2002–2012, 1993.
136. Moore, R. D., Smith, C. R., and Lietman, P. S.: The association of aminoglycoside plasma levels with mortality in patients with gram-negative bacteremia. J. Infect. Dis. *199*:443–448, 1984.
137. Munford, R. S., and Hall, C. L.: Detoxification of bacterial lipopolysaccharides (endotoxins) by a human neutrophil enzyme. Science *234*: 203–205, 1986.
138. Musher, D. M.: Cutaneous and soft-tissue manifestations of sepsis due to gram-negative enteric bacilli. Rev. Infect. Dis. *2*:854–866, 1980.
139. Myers, M. G., Wright, P. F., Smith, A. L., et al.: Complications of occult pneumococcal bacteremia in children. J. Pediatr. *84*:656–660, 1974.
140. Naqvi, S. H., Chundu, K. R., and Friedman, A. D.: Shock in children with gram-negative bacillary sepsis and *Haemophilus influenzae* type b sepsis. Pediatr. Infect. Dis. *5*:512–515, 1986.
141. Natanson, C., Fink, M. P., Ballantyne, H. K., et al.: Gram-negative bacteremia produces both severe systolic and diastolic cardiac dysfunction in a canine model that simulates human septic shock. J. Clin. Invest. *78*:259–270, 1986.
142. Natanson, C., Hoffman, W. D., Suffredini, A. F., et al.: Selected treatment strategies for septic shock based on proposed mechanisms of pathogenesis. Ann. Intern. Med. *120*:771–783, 1994.
143. National Center for Health Statistics: Increase in national hospital discharge survey rates for septicemia: United States, 1979–1987. M. M. W. R. Morb. Mortal. Wkly. Rep. *39*:31–34, 1990.
144. Nguyen, Q. V., Nguyen, E. A., and Weiner, L. B.: Incidence of invasive bacterial disease in children with fever and petechiae. Pediatrics *74*:77–80, 1984.
145. Nishijima, J., Weil, M. H., Subin, H., et al.: Hemodynamic and metabolic studies on shock associated with gram-negative bacteremia. Medicine (Baltimore). *52*:287–294, 1973.
146. Ognibene, F. P., Martin, S. E., Parker, M. M., et al.: Adult respiratory distress syndrome in patients with severe neutropenia. N. Engl. J. Med. *315*:547–551, 1986.
147. Ognibene, F. P., Parker, M. M., Natanson, C., et al.: Depressed left ventricular performance: Response to volume infusion in patients with sepsis and septic shock. Chest *93*:903–910, 1988.
148. Parker, M. M., and Parillo, J. E.: Septic shock: Hemodynamics and pathogenesis. J. A. M. A. *250*:3324–3327,1983.
149. Parker, M. M., Shelhamer, J. H., Bacharach, S. L., et al.: Profound but reversible myocardial depression in patients with septic shock. Ann. Intern. Med. *100*:483–490,1984.
150. Parrillo, J. E., Burch, C., Shelhamer, J. H., et al.: A circulating myocardial depressant substance in humans with septic shock: Septic shock patients with a reduced ejection fraction have a circulating factor that depresses *in vitro* myocardial cell performance. J. Clin. Invest. *76*: 1539–1553, 1985.
151. Patrick, C. C.: Coagulase-negative staphylococci: Pathogens with increasing clinical significance. J. Pediatr. *116*:497–507, 1990.
152. Patterson, D. L., Ko, W.-C., Gottberg, A. V., et al.: Outcome of cephalosporin treatment for serious infections due to apparently susceptible organisms producing extended-spectrum β-lactamases: Implications for the clinical laboratory. J. Clin. Microbiol. *39*:2206–2212, 2001.
153. Patterson, D. L., and Yu, V. L.: Editorial response: Extended-spectrum β-lactamases: A call for improved detection and control. Clin. Infect. Dis. *29*:1419–1422, 1999.
154. Perkin, R. M., and Levin, D. L.: Shock in the pediatric patient. Pt. I. J. Pediatr. *101*:163–169, 1982.
155. Perkin, R. M., and Levin, D. L.: Shock in the pediatric patient. Pt. II. Therapy. J. Pediatr. *101*:319–332, 1982.
156. Perkin, R. M., Levin, D. L., Webb, R., et al.: Dobutamine: A hemodynamic evaluation in children with shock. J. Pediatr. *101*:977–983, 1982.
157. Peters, G., Locci, R., and Pulverer, G.: Adherence and growth of coagulase-negative staphylococci on surfaces of intravenous catheters. J. Infect. Dis. *146*:479–482, 1982.

158. Pfaller, M., A., Jones, R., N., Marshall, S. A., et al.: Inducible Amp C β-lactamase producing gram-negative bacilli from bloodstream infections: Frequency, antimicrobial susceptibility, and molecular epidemiology in a national surveillance program (SCOPE). Diagn. Microbiol. Infect. Dis. *28*:211–219, 1997.
159. Pfeffer, K., Matsuyama, T., Kundig, T. M., et al.: Mice deficient for the 55-kD tumor necrosis factor receptor are resistant to endotoxic shock, yet succumb to *L. monocytogenes* infection. Cell *73*:457–467, 1993.
160. Pfenniger, J., Gerber, A., Tschappeler, H., et al.: Adult respiratory distress syndrome in children. J. Pediatr. *101*:352–357, 1982.
161. Poll, T. V. D., Büller, H. R., Cate, H. T., et al.: Activation of coagulation after administration of tumor necrosis factor to normal subjects. N. Engl. J. Med. *322*:1622–1627, 1990.
162. Pollack, M., Raubitschek, A. A., and Larrick, J. W.: Human monoclonal antibodies that recognize conserved epitopes in the core-lipid A region of lipopolysaccharides. J. Clin. Invest. *79*:1421–1430, 1987.
163. Proulx, F., Fayon, M., Farrell, C. A., et al.: Epidemiology of sepsis and multiple organ dysfunction syndrome in children. Chest *109*: 1033–1037, 1996.
164. Quezado, Z. M. N., and Natanson, C.: Systemic hemodynamic abnormalities and vasopressor therapy in sepsis and septic shock. Am. J. Kidney Dis. *20*:214–222, 1992.
165. Ramsay, M. E., Andrews, N., Kaczmarski, E. B., et al.: Efficacy of meningococcal serogroup C conjugate vaccine in teenagers and toddlers in England. Lancet *357*:195–196, 2001.
166. Raymond, R. M., and Emerson, T. E.: Cerebral metabolism during endotoxin shock in the dog. Circ. Shock *5*:407–414, 1978.
167. Reichgott, M. L., Melmon, K. L., Forsyth, R. P., et al.: Cardiovascular and metabolic effects of whole or fractionated gram-negative bacterial endotoxin in the unanesthetized rhesus monkey. Circ. Res. *33*:346–352, 1973.
168. Reilly, J. M., Cunnion, R. E., Burch-Whitman, C., et al.: A circulating myocardial depressant substance is associated with cardiac dysfunction and peripheral hypoperfusion (lactic acidemia) in patients with septic shock. Chest *95*:1072–1080, 1989.
169. Reimer, S. L., Michener, W. M., and Steiger, E.: Nutritional support of the critically ill child. Pediatr. Clin. North Am. *27*:647–660, 1980.
170. Reines, H. D., Cook, J. A., Halushka, P. V., et al.: Plasma thromboxane concentrations are raised in patients dying with septic shock. Lancet *11*:174–175, 1982.
171. Richards, M. J., Edwards, J. R., Culver, D. H., et al.: Nosocomial infections in the pediatric intensive care units in the United States. Pediatrics *103*:e39, 1999.
172. Richmond, D. A., Molitch, M. E., and O'Donnell, T. F.: Altered thyroid hormone levels in bacterial sepsis: The role of nutritional adequacy. Metabolism *29*:936–942, 1980.
173. Robbins, R. A., Russ, W. D., Rasmussen, J. K., et al.: Activation of the complement system in the adult respiratory distress syndrome. Am. Rev. Respir. Dis. *135*:651–658, 1987.
174. Romano, M. J., Kearns, G. L., Kaplan, S. L., et al.: Single-dose pharmacokinetics and safety of HA-1A, a human IgM anti-lipid-A monoclonal antibody, in pediatric patients with sepsis syndrome. J. Pediatr. *122*:974–981, 1993.
175. Rongkavilit, C. Rodriguez, Z. M., Gomez-Marin, O., et al.: Gram-negative bacillary bacteremia in human immunodeficiency virus type 1-infected children. Pediatr. Infect. Dis. J. *19*:122–128, 1998.
176. Rothbrock, G., Vugia, D., Waterman, S., et al.: Progress toward elimination of *Haemophilus influenzae* type b disease among infants and children—United States, 1987–1997. M. M. W. R. Morb. Mortal. Wkly. Rep. *47*:993–998, 1998.
177. Royall, J. P., and Levin, D. L.: Adult respiratory distress syndrome in pediatric patients. 1. Clinical aspects, pathophysiology, pathology, and mechanisms of lung injury. J. Pediatr. *112*:169–180, 1988.
178. Royall, J. A., and Levin, D. L.: Adult respiratory distress syndrome in pediatric patients. II. Management. J. Pediatr. *112*:335–347, 1988.
179. Rubin, L. G., and Moxon, E. R.: Pathogenesis of bloodstream invasion with *Haemophilus influenzae* type b. Infect. Immun. *41*:280–284, 1983.
180. Russell, D. A., Tucker, K. K., Chinookoswong, N., et al.: Combined inhibition of interleukin-1 and tumor necrosis factor in rodent endotoxemia: Improved survival and organ function. J. Infect. Dis. *171*:1528–1538, 1995.
181. Sáez-Llorens, X., and McCracken, G. H., Jr.: Sepsis syndrome and septic shock in pediatrics: Current concepts of terminology, pathophysiology, and management. J. Pediatr. *123*:497–508, 1993.
182. Saez-Llorens, X., Vargas, S., Guerra, F., et al.: Application of new sepsis definitions to evaluate outcome of pediatric patients with severe systemic infections. Pediatr. Infect. Dis. J. *14*:557–561, 1995.
183. Sanders, C. C.: Cefepime: The next generation? Clin. Infect. Dis. *17*:369–379, 1993.
184. Sattler, C. A., Mason, E. O., Jr., and Kaplan, S. L.: Prospective comparison of risk factors and demographic and clinical characteristics of community-acquired methicillin resistant vs. methicillin susceptible *Staphylococcus aureus* infection in children. Pediatr. Infect. Dis. J. *21*:910–916, 2002.
185. Schmyer, J. P., Reynolds, D. G., and Swan, K. G.: Renal blood flow during endotoxin shock in the subhuman primate. Surg. Gynecol. Obstet. *137*:3–6, 1973.
186. Seri, I.: Cardiovascular, renal, and endocrine actions of dopamine in neonates and children. J. Pediatr. *126*:333–344, 1995.
187. Shales, D. M., and Bass, S. N.: Combination antimicrobial therapy. Pediatr. Clin. North Am. *30*:121–134, 1983.
188. Shapiro, E. D., Wald, E. R., Nelson, K. A., et al.: Broviac catheter-related bacteremia in oncology patients. Am. J. Dis. Child. *136*:679–681, 1982.
189. Shenep, J. L., Barton, R. P., and Mogan, K. A.: Role of antibiotic class in the rate of liberation of endotoxin during therapy for experimental gram-negative bacterial sepsis. J. Infect. Dis. *151*:1012–1018, 1985.
190. Shenep, J. L., Flynn, P. M., Barrett, F. F., et al.: Serial quantitation of endotoxemia and bacteremia during therapy for gram-negative bacterial sepsis. J. Infect. Dis. *157*:565–568, 1988.
191. Shulman, S. T., and Ayoub, E. M.: Severe staphylococcal sepsis in adolescents. Pediatrics *58*:59–66, 1976.
192. Siber, G. R.: Bacteremias due to *Haemophilus influenzae* and *Streptococcus pneumoniae*: Their occurrence and course in children with cancer. Am. J. Dis. Child. *134*:668–672, 1980.
193. Smith, A. L.: Commentary: The febrile infant. Pediatr. Rev. *1*:35–36, 1979.
194. Sotiropoulos, S. V., Jackson, M. A., Woods, G. M., et al.: Alpha-streptococcal septicemia in leukemic children treated with continuous or large dosage intermittent cytosine arabinoside. Pediatr. Infect. Dis. J. *8*:755–758, 1989.
195. Sprung, C. L., Caralis, P. V., Marcial, E. H., et al.: The effects of high-dose corticosteroids in patients with septic shock: A prospective, controlled study. N. Engl. J. Med. *311*:1137–1143, 1984.
196. Sriskandan, S., Cohen, J.: Gram-positive sepsis. Mechanisms and differences from gram-negative sepsis. Infect. Dis. Clin. North Am. *13*:392–412, 1999.
197. Staubach, K. H., Schroder, L., Stuber, F., et al.: Effect of pentoxifylline in severe sepsis: Results of a randomized, double-blind, placebo-controlled study. Arch. Surg. *133*:94–100, 1998.
198. Stephens, D. S., Hoffman, L. H., and McGee, Z. A.: Interaction of *Neisseria meningitidis* with human nasopharyngeal mucosa: Attachment and entry into columnar epithelial cells. J. Infect. Dis. *148*:369–376, 1983.
199. Stumacher, R. J., Kovnat, M. J., and McCabe, W. R.: Limitations of the usefulness of the Limulus assay for endotoxin. N. Engl. J. Med. *288*:1261–1264, 1973.
200. Suffredini, A. F., Fromm, R. E., Parker, M. M., et al.: The cardiovascular response of normal humans to the administration of endotoxin. N. Engl. J. Med. *321*:280–287, 1989.
201. Sullivan, J. S., Kilpatrick, L., Costarino, A. T., et al.: Correlation of plasma cytokine elevations with mortality rate in children with sepsis. J. Pediatr. *120*:510–515, 1992.
202. Thiru, Y., Pathan, N., Bignall, S., et al.: A myocardial cytotoxic process is involved in the cardiac dysfunction of meningococcal septic shock. Crit. Care Med. *28*:2979–2983, 2000.
203. Todd, J., Fishant, M., Kapral, F., et al.: Toxic-shock syndrome associated with phage-group I staphylococci. Lancet *2*:1116–1118, 1978.
204. Togari, H., Sugiyama, S., Ogino, T., et al.: Interactions of endotoxin with cortisol and acute phase proteins in septic shock neonates. Acta Paediatr. Scand. *75*:69–74, 1986.
205. Toltzis, P., and Blumer, J. L.: Antibiotic-resistant gram-negative bacteria in the critical care setting. Pediatr. Clin. North Am. *42*:687–702, 1995.
206. Tracey, K. J., Beutler, B., Lowry, S. F., et al.: Shock and tissue injury induced by recombinant human cachectin. Science *234*:470–474, 1986.
207. Tracey, K. J., and Cerami, A.: Tumor necrosis factor: An updated review of its biology. Crit. Care Med. *21*:5415–5422, 1993.
208. Tracey, K. J., Lowry, S. F., and Cerami, A.: Cachectin: A hormone that triggers acute shock and chronic cachexia. J. Infect. Dis. *157*:413–420, 1988.
209. Tracey, K. J., Vlassara, H., and Cerami, A.: Cachectin/tumor necrosis factor. Lancet *1*:1122–1126, 1989.
210. Triger, D. R., Boyer, T. D., and Levin, J.: Portal and systemic bacteremia and endotoxaemia in liver disease. Gut *19*:935–939, 1978.
211. Tubbs, H. R.: Endotoxin in meningococcal infections. Arch. Dis. Child. *55*:808–819, 1980.
212. Tuomanen, E. I.: The biology of pneumococcal infections. Pediatr. Res. *42*:253–258, 1997.
213. Veterans Administration Systemic Sepsis Cooperative Study Group: Effect of high-dose glucocorticoid therapy on mortality in patients with clinical signs of systemic sepsis. N. Engl. J. Med. *317*:659–665, 1987.
214. Viscoli, C., Castagnola, E., Giacchino, M., et al.: Bloodstream infections in children with cancer: A multicentre surveillance study of the Italian Association of Paediatric Haematology and Oncology. Supportive Therapy Group-Infectious Diseases Section. Eur. J. Cancer *35*:770–774, 1999.

215. Voerman, H. J., Stehouwer, C. D. A., Kamp, G. J., et al.: Plasma endothelin levels are increased during septic shock. Crit. Care Med. *20*:1097–1101, 1992.
216. Waage, A., Brandtzaeg, P., Halstensen, A., et al.: The complex pattern of cytokines in serum from patients with meningococcal septic shock. Association between interleukin 6, interleukin 1, and fatal outcome. J. Exp. Med. *169*:333–338, 1989.
217. Wajchenberg, B., Leme, C. E., Tambascia, M., et al.: The adrenal response to exogenous adrenocorticotrophin in patients with infections due to *Neisseria meningitidis*. J. Infect. Dis. *138*:387–391, 1978.
218. Walterspiel, J. W., Kaplan, S. L., and Mason, E. O., Jr.: Protective effect of subinhibitory polymyxin B alone and in combination with ampicillin for overwhelming *Haemophilus influenzae* type b infection in the infant rat: Evidence for in vivo and in vitro release of free endotoxin after ampicillin treatment. Pediatr. Res. *20*:237–241, 1986.
219. Wardle, E. N.: Endotoxin and acute renal failure. Nephron *14*:321–332, 1975.
220. Wardle, E. N.: Acute renal failure in the 1980's: The importance of septic shock and of endotoxaemia. Nephron *30*:193–200, 1982.
221. Watson, R. W. G., Redmond, H. P., and Bouchier-Hayes, D.: Role of endotoxin in mononuclear phagocyte-mediated inflammatory responses. J. Leuk. Biol. *56*:95–103, 1994.
222. Weil, M. H., and Nishijima, H.: Cardiac output in bacterial shock. Am. J. Med. *64*:920–922, 1978.
223. Weiland, J. E., Davis, W. B., Holter, J. F., et al.: Lung neutrophils in the adult respiratory distress syndrome: Clinical and pathophysiologic significance. Am. Rev. Respir. Dis. *133*:218–225, 1986.
224. White, B., Livingston, W., Murphy, C., et al.: An open-label study of the role of adjuvant hemostatic support with protein C replacement therapy in purpura fulminans-associated meningococcemia. Blood *96*:3719–3724, 2000.
225. Wiesenthal, A. M., and Todd, J. K.: Toxic shock syndrome in children aged 10 years or less. Pediatrics *74*:112–117, 1984.
226. Wilson, M. D., Brackett, D. J., Hinshaw, L. B., et al.: Vasopressin release during sepsis and septic shock in baboons and dogs. Surg. Gynecol. Obstet. *153*:869–872, 1981.
227. Winchester, P. D., Todd, J. K., and Roe, M. H.: Bacteremia in hospitalized children. Am. J. Dis. Child. *131*:753–758, 1977.
228. Wong, V. K., Hitchcock, W., and Mason, W. H.: Meningococcal infections in children: A review of 100 cases. Pediatr. Infect. Dis. J. *8*:224–227, 1989.
229. Woo, P., Carpenter, M. A., and Trunkey, D.: Ionized calcium: The effect of septic shock in the human. J. Surg. Res. *26*:605–610, 1979.
230. Woods, D. E., Strauss, D. C., Johanson, W. G., Jr., et al.: Role of salivary protease activity in adherence of gram-negative bacilli to mammalian buccal epithelial cells in vivo. J. Clin. Invest. *68*:1435–1440, 1981.
231. Wright, S. D., Ramos, R. A., Tobias, P. S., et al.: CD14, a receptor for complexes of lipopolysaccharide (LPS) and LPS binding protein. Science *249*:1431–1433, 1990.
232. Zabel, P., Schönharting, M. M., Wolter, D. T., et al.: Oxpentifylline in endotoxaemia. Lancet *2*:1474–1477, 1989.
233. Zaeg, P. B., Sirnes, K., Folsland, B., et al.: Plasmapheresis in the treatment of severe meningococcal or pneumococcal septicemia with DIC and fibrinolysis: Preliminary data on eight patients. Scand. J. Clin. Lab. Invest. *45*(Suppl. 178):53–55, 1985.
234. Zaloga, G. P., and Chernow, B.: The multifactorial basis for hypocalcemia during sepsis: Studies of the parathyroid hormone-vitamin D axis. Ann. Intern. Med. *107*:36–41, 1987.
235. Ziegler, E., Fisher, C., Sprung, C., et al.: Treatment of gram-negative bacteremia and septic shock with HA-1A human monoclonal antibody against endotoxin. N. Engl. J. Med. *324*:429–436, 1991.
236. Ziegler, E. J., McCutchan, J. A., Fierer, J., et al.: Treatment of gram-negative bacteremia and shock with human antiserum to a mutant *Escherichia coli*. N. Engl. J. Med. *307*:1225–1230, 1982.

Fever without Source and Fever of Unknown Origin

MARTIN I. LORIN ■ RALPH D. FEIGIN

Petersdorf and Beeson[70] proposed in 1961 that the term *fever of unknown origin* (FUO) be reserved for persons with an illness persisting for 3 or more weeks and accompanied by temperatures higher than 38.4° C (101.2° F) on at least several occasions. They further specified that the cause of the fever should remain undetermined after at least 1 week of investigation in the hospital. Although this definition was arbitrary, it was useful at that time, when many of the diagnostic tests now in routine use were unknown. The purpose of their precise definition was to explore the cause of fever in this select group of adult patients and to permit comparison of data from different investigations. This exacting definition likely never was applied rigorously in pediatric practice.

Many investigators prefer using the term *fever without source* (FWS) for fever of recent onset with no adequate explanation determined by history or on physical examination. The term FUO should be reserved for fever in children of at least 8 days' duration and for which no diagnosis is apparent after the initial work-up in the hospital or as an outpatient.

The distinction between FUO and FWS is of more than academic interest for several reasons. First, although overlap exists, the differential diagnoses of these two clinical conditions are distinct, and the most frequent causes of one are different from the most frequent causes of the other. Second, the child with fever of recent onset generally warrants more immediate evaluation than does a child with FUO. The latter usually does not present as an emergency and requires timely, but not urgent, diagnostic or therapeutic intervention. Third, although expectant antibiotic treatment of children with FUO usually is not indicated, expectant treatment of a select group of infants with FWS generally is recommended.

Fever without Source

A convenient definition for FWS is the occurrence of fever for 1 week or less in a child in whom careful history and physical examination fail to reveal a probable cause of the fever. An estimated 5 to 10 percent of children presenting with fever have no localizing signs or symptoms,[49] although in some series, this figure has been as high as 22 percent.[90] Stein[79] found the peak incidence to occur during the second year of life. On the basis of a review of private pediatric practices in upstate New York, Hoekelman and colleagues[39] predicted that every 4 to 5 days a practicing pediatrician would see one child between 1 and 24 months of age with FWS.

Most children with fever of recent onset have acute infectious diseases, most of which are self-limited.[90] A few of these patients have serious acute infectious diseases, including meningitis and bacteremia, and a very few have acute noninfectious diseases or chronic disorders. For example, an occasional patient presenting with FWS is discovered to have a disorder such as heat illness, drug poisoning, malignancy, or connective tissue disease. However, these occurrences are so infrequent that most series of patients with FWS include no such patients.[9, 28, 58, 60, 83] The physician faced with a child with FWS should consider the possibility of a noninfectious cause or the onset of a chronic disease, but unless a clinical clue suggests one of these entities, investigation in this direction is not warranted. Kawasaki disease, a disease of unknown but presumably infectious cause, can manifest as FWS.

Many children with FWS are in the prodromal stages of an acute infectious illness, and they develop evidence of specific infection, such as pharyngitis, otitis media, or pneumonia, within hours to days of first being seen by a physician. Fever may precede the appearance of specific signs and symptoms by as long as 3 days, as in measles, Rocky Mountain spotted fever, and leptospirosis. In some infections, such as roseola, viral hepatitis, infectious mononucleosis, typhus, typhoid fever, and Kawasaki disease (presumably an infectious disease), the interval between the onset of fever and the appearance of specific findings often is more than 3 days.

OCCULT BACTEREMIA

One major concern regarding the young child with FWS is the possibility that the child has occult bacteremia. The patient does not look very ill, is judged clinically well enough to be managed as an outpatient, and does not have an infection commonly associated with bacteremia such as pneumonia, but the blood culture yields a pathogenic bacteria, most commonly *Streptococcus pneumoniae* and less commonly *Neisseria meningitidis, Haemophilus influenzae, Salmonella*, or *Staphylococcus aureus*. The incidence of occult bacteremia in children with FWS is approximately 3 to 5 percent.[9, 21, 53, 66, 83, 90] In most series, occult bacteremia has been found to occur more commonly in children with FWS than in febrile children of the same age with infections such as pharyngitis, otitis media, or upper respiratory tract infection. For example, McCarthy and associates[53] found the incidence of bacteremia among febrile children without an obvious source of infection to be 9.9 percent, compared with 3.3 percent in children with otitis media, upper respiratory tract infection, or flulike syndrome. Teele and colleagues[83] found an incidence of bacteremia of 3.9 percent among children with FWS and 1.5 percent in comparably febrile children with otitis media or pharyngitis.

Occult bacteremia is a problem among all pediatric populations. Baron and Fink,[9] showed that occult bacteremia occurred with approximately the same frequency in patients in a private office as in urban emergency centers, and a study in Chicago found an incidence of occult bacteremia of 3.5 percent for febrile children seen at an inner-city hospital outpatient department, 1.9 percent for children at a suburban hospital emergency room, and 5.9 percent for predominantly white middle-class children in the offices of pediatricians in private practice.[28] These differences were not statistically significant.

The risk of occult bacteremia occurring in a child with FWS is age related, with most cases occurring in children younger than 24 months old. Numerous studies have demonstrated an especially high risk for developing bacteremia or other serious bacterial infections (SBIs) in the febrile infant younger than 3 months of age.[53, 58, 75, 81] In a group of children with clinically unsuspected meningococcemia reported by Dashefsky and associates,[27] all 12 patients who initially looked well enough to be treated as outpatients were younger than 24 months of age. Bonadio and coworkers[16] found the incidence of positive bacterial cultures to be 12 percent among febrile infants younger than 4 weeks of age, compared with 6 percent for those between 4 and 8 weeks old.

The risk of occult bacteremia and other SBIs increases with the severity of fever. In a prospective study of bacteremia in children seen in the outpatient department, McCarthy and colleagues[53] identified a small but statistically significant difference in the incidence of bacteremia between children with temperatures of 40° C (104° F) or higher and those with temperatures of 40.5° C (104.9° F) or higher. In a prospective study in which blood cultures were obtained from all febrile children younger than 2 years of age seen in a walk-in clinic, Teele and colleagues[83] found no positive blood cultures among 44 children with FWS and rectal temperatures of less than 38.9° C (102° F) and five (3.9%) positive blood cultures among 129 FWS children with rectal temperatures equal to or greater than 38.9° C (102° F). Other series have reported similar findings.[9, 58] Several series of children with fevers of 41° C (105.8° F) or higher found a relatively high prevalence of bacteremia and other SBIs, especially meningitis and pneumonia.[15, 59, 73] However, even in this group of children with very high fever, most of those older than 2 or 3 months who looked well did not have an SBI.

The white blood cell (WBC) count has been studied extensively as a potential tool in the diagnosis of occult bacteremia. In 1974, on the basis of a study of hospitalized children, Todd[84] reported that the absolute number of polymorphonuclear leukocytes and the absolute number of nonsegmented polymorphonuclear leukocytes were more sensitive than was the total WBC count, the percentage of polymorphonuclear leukocytes, or the percentage of nonsegmented polymorphonuclear leukocytes. However, whether information based on hospitalized children—presumably all of whom had serious localized infections or looked ill enough to warrant hospitalization—can be applied to the child with FWS who looks well enough to be treated on an ambulatory basis is questionable.

Considerable debate continues over the usefulness of the WBC count in febrile children seen in the outpatient setting. McCarthy and associates[60] concluded that a WBC count equal to or greater than 15,000/mm^3 was helpful in identifying patients at greatest risk for developing bacteremia. Dershewitz[28] found a direct relationship between total leukocyte count and the prevalence of bacteremia and stated that "knowledge of the count was a helpful but limited predictor of patients with positive blood cultures." McGowan and associates[62] found that the incidence of bacteremia increased with increased WBC counts and that bacteremia most commonly occurred in patients with counts of 20,000/mm^3 or higher.

Other studies have examined the utility of the WBC count specifically in children with FWS who look well enough to be treated on an outpatient basis. One such study by Teele and colleagues[83] found a sensitivity of 1.0 and a positive predictive value of 0.11 for a total WBC of 15,000/mm^3. Using a WBC of 20,000/mm^3 would have decreased the sensitivity to 0.4 while increasing positive predictive value to only 0.13. In the Baron and Fink series,[9] the sensitivity for a WBC of 15,000/mm^3 was 0.87 with a specificity of 0.73. McGowan and colleagues[62] provided data for a total WBC of 20,000/mm^3, which had a sensitivity of 0.35 and positive predictive value of 0.12. Kline and coworkers[44] found that a WBC count of 15,000/mm^3 was more sensitive for *S. pneumoniae* bacteremia than for *H. influenzae* bacteremia. Although a total WBC of 15,000/mm^3 does not accurately predict which child is or is not bacteremic, it is helpful in dividing the population of children with FWS into high- and low-risk groups.

Some investigators have found the erythrocyte sedimentation rate to be no more useful than the WBC count in predicting bacteremia in ambulatory febrile patients.[60] Others have reported that the serum concentration of C-reactive protein may be more accurate than the complete blood count or erythrocyte sedimentation rate in distinguishing bacterial from viral infections,[54, 69] but its role in detecting occult bacteremia in FWS has not been determined.

Other hematologic findings that suggest bacteremia include thrombocytopenia,[25] Döhle inclusion bodies, toxic granulations, and vacuolization of neutrophils. In one study, peripheral blood smears of children younger than 24 months of age with acute febrile illnesses were reviewed the following day by a single investigator to determine whether vacuolization and toxic granulations were present; when both abnormalities were present, the positive predictive value for bacteremia was 0.76.[46] The presence of these findings should be considered when estimating the risk of bacteremia.[1, 25, 65]

Several studies have examined the response to acetaminophen and found no difference between bacteremic and nonbacteremic children regarding the rate of reduction of temperature or the improvement in clinical appearance.[6, 85, 92] Mazur and associates,[52] however, found that febrile children 2 months to 6 years of age who did not respond to a dose of acetaminophen by at least 0.8° C in 2 hours had a statistically significant increased risk of developing occult bacteremia compared with those who did respond.

The most important aspects of assessment of the febrile child are a careful history and physical examination. Laboratory data are secondary and should be ordered on the basis of the clinical assessment. By definition, the child with FWS has no localizing signs to explain the fever or indicate a site of infection. Many physicians suggest that a general impression can indicate whether the child has occult bacteremia. Some physicians have suggested that careful clinical judgment, based on extensive experience, can identify most, if not all, children with serious illnesses.[14] McCarthy and colleagues,[55–57] in a series of carefully designed studies, elucidated those variables of history and observation most useful in assessing febrile children. They found that the observation variable *playfulness* had the strongest correlation with overall assessment.[56] However, they observed that even the experienced attending pediatrician could identify only 57 percent of seriously ill children by initial impression before performing a full physical examination. Dershewitz[28] found that private pediatricians were no more accurate than were pediatric residents in identifying children with occult bacteremia and that, in the private office, pediatricians were no better at predicting bacteremia in familiar patients than in first-time patients.

In a study of 292 consecutive febrile children seen in an emergency department, Waskerwitz and Berkelhammer[87] identified a subgroup of patients who had no localizing signs and who looked so well that they were predicted not to have bacteremia. The physicians were assisted in their assessment by a functional scale that gave 0 to 2 points for the child's eating, drinking, sleeping, and play activities, with a best possible score of 8. The group of patients with functional scores equal to or greater than 5, with no localized infection and predicted clinically not to have bacteremia, were free of bacteremia, whereas 14 of 202 patients with functional scores of 4 or less were bacteremic. In this study, the physicians were not able to identify which patients had bacteremia and which did not; rather, they were able to identify one subgroup at high risk for having bacteremia and another at very low risk. Teach and Fleisher[82] found that, although the Yale Observation Scale scores were higher among patients with bacteremia than among those without, the difference was not clinically useful in detecting bacteremia in well-looking febrile children without a discernible focus of infection. The clinician's overall assessment of the degree of illness of the child appears to be a valuable, but not infallible, tool in estimating the risk of occult bacteremia being present in children with FWS.

CLINICAL MANAGEMENT OF FEVER WITHOUT SOURCE

Approximately 3 to 5 percent of children with FWS are bacteremic. Numerous studies (all performed before the institution of routine use of *H. influenzae* vaccine) showed that if these children were not treated with antibiotics at the time of the initial clinical encounter, 5 to 10 percent would return with bacterial meningitis, 10 percent with localized bacterial infection, and another 30 percent with continued fever and persistent bacteremia.[9, 17, 39, 51, 53, 60, 62, 83] In all of these retrospective studies, patients initially treated with antibiotics fared better than did those not treated initially, although the decision of whether or not to treat always was at the discretion of the treating physician and not randomized.

In a prospective, randomized investigation, Carroll and associates[21] studied 96 children who were between the ages of 6 and 24 months and who had FWS and a temperature higher than 40° C (104° F). Of 10 patients who were bacteremic, five were treated initially with antibiotics on an outpatient basis and five were not treated. The difference in outcome between the two groups was statistically significant in favor of the treatment group; four of the five treated patients were improved clinically, whereas none of the five untreated patients was improved clinically. None of the treated patients developed bacterial meningitis, whereas two of the five untreated patients developed bacterial meningitis. In a prospective, randomized, placebo-controlled study of empirical treatment with amoxicillin in children at risk for developing occult bacteremia, Jaffee and colleagues[41] showed no difference between treatment and nontreatment groups. However, the power of this study was low, and a true difference in outcome easily could have been missed.[4] The dosage of amoxicillin used was 125 mg three times daily for children who weighed 10 kg or less and 250 mg three times daily for those weighing more than 10 kg, so some children may have received as little as 37.5 mg/kg/day. Although this dosage is close to the usual recommended dosage of 40 mg/kg/day for infections such as otitis media, Baron and coworkers[11] suggested that considerably higher doses might be required to treat occult bacteremia. In a retrospective study of a private pediatric practice, these investigators found that none of 11 infants with FWS and bacteremia who initially received 150 mg/kg/day or more of amoxicillin developed complications ($p = 0.03$). In contrast, 5 of 12 such infants not treated or treated with less than 100 mg/kg/day of amoxicillin developed complications. A study of the outcome of outpatient management of febrile children who proved to have pneumococcal bacteremia found that those not treated with antibiotics and those still febrile on reevaluation were most likely to have persistent bacteremia.[12]

One should not be dogmatic about the management of children with FWS. One reasonable approach, based on a careful history, thorough physical examination, and overall clinical impression, is to classify these children as being at low or high risk for development of occult bacteremia and other SBIs. For the low-risk group, no laboratory investigation is required routinely. For the high-risk group, a complete blood count and blood culture should be obtained. A lumbar puncture, chest radiograph, urinalysis, and urine culture are considered on an individual basis. If the patient appears ill, admission to the hospital may be justified, even if all test results are negative. When high-risk children look well enough to be sent home, they are reasonable candidates for expectant antibiotic therapy, pending the outcome of the blood culture. For those patients clinically considered at moderate risk (not clearly high or low risk), the physician has the option of obtaining a WBC count and using the results to decide whether to draw blood for culture and prescribe antibiotics expectantly.

Table 70–1 lists risk factors for development of occult bacteremia. Current information is not sufficient to warrant the use of scoring systems except as part of investigational series. In the final analysis, the clinician's judgment, taking into account all available clinical and laboratory data about each patient, is the guide to selecting which children require diagnostic work-up and expectant therapy with antibiotics.

If the physician elects to prescribe antibiotics while awaiting the results of the blood culture, such antibiotic therapy should provide adequate coverage for *S. pneumoniae, N. meningitidis,* and *H. influenzae,* although the frequency of *H. influenzae* has decreased dramatically with current immunization practice. In geographic areas where ampicillin-resistant *H. influenzae* is common, the physician may wish to use an antibiotic that covers this organism as well. A reasonable choice is amoxicillin-clavulanate (45 to 90 mg/kg based on amoxicillin content). A single injection of 75 mg/kg of ceftriaxone given while awaiting the results of blood culture has been successful in resolving fever, clearing bacteremia, and preventing meningitis and was found to be superior to oral regimens in several series.[8, 10, 34] However, the decreasing frequency of *H. influenzae* type b (Hib) disease may lessen the need for this drug.[48] A study of bacteremia in febrile infants and children between 1993 and 1996 showed an absence of cases caused by *H. influenzae* and an overall decrease in the prevalence of occult bacteremia compared with that before the Hib immunization era.[2] For the patient with a significant history of penicillin allergy for whom a cephalosporin is not considered appropriate, trimethoprim-sulfamethoxazole, in a dosage of 8 mg of trimethoprim per kilogram per day, may be an acceptable alternative. Children for whom the blood culture is positive should be recalled for reevaluation, even if they are afebrile.

Because *S. pneumoniae* is the dominant cause of occult bacteremia, the routine use of pneumococcal vaccine is expected to diminish the occurrence of occult bacteremia significantly. Children who have been immunized against both *H. influenzae* and *S. pneumoniae* should be considered at relatively low risk for development of occult bacteremia and may require less work-up, unless they appear ill or have a very high fever.

Infants younger than 90 days of age pose a special problem because they have an increased risk of developing an SBI, the clinical evaluation is more difficult, and a broader spectrum of invading organisms (e.g., group B *Streptococcus, Escherichia coli, Listeria monocytogenes*) exists. Baker and coworkers[5] showed the safety of outpatient management without antibiotics of selected infants 30 to 90 days of age who were low-risk patients (i.e., normal WBC, urinalysis, lumbar puncture, chest roentgenogram, and, if diarrhea was present, negative smear for fecal leukocytes). Jaskiewicz and coworkers[42] found the Rochester criteria (WBC count between 5000 and 15,000/mm^3, band count < 1500/mm^3, spun urine specimen < 10 WBC/high-power field, stool specimen [if diarrhea] < 5 WBC/high-power field) to have a 98.9 percent negative predictive value in well-appearing, previously healthy infants younger than 90 days of age with no focal infections. One reasonable practice guideline for managing infants with FWS is to hospitalize and treat all who appear toxic and all younger than 28 days of age. Those between 28 and 90 days of age may be managed as outpatients if they look well and the blood count, urinalysis, and cerebrospinal fluid analysis are within normal limits.[7]

Fever of Unknown Origin

Considerable disagreement ensues about the exact definition of FUO, and series in the pediatric literature differ in their criteria for inclusion. Brewis[18] defined FUO in children as the presence of temperature equal to or greater than 38.3° C (101° F) for 5 to 7 consecutive days without localizing signs or symptoms. In sharp contrast, McClung[61] and Lohr and Hendley[47] considered children with fever for at least 3 weeks on an outpatient basis or 1 week in the hospital to have FUO. Pizzo and associates,[72] however, required only that the fever be present for 2 weeks, with no distinction made between outpatient or in-hospital status. A reasonable working definition of FUO for clinical purposes is the presence of fever for 8 or more days in a child for whom a careful and thorough history and physical examination and preliminary laboratory data fail to reveal a probable cause for the fever.

Most cases of FUO in children are caused by relatively common diseases. In four series of FUO, totaling 418 children, only five patients would be considered to have rare disorders (i.e., Behçet syndrome, ichthyosis, variant of "blue diaper" syndrome, diencephalic seizure disorder, and "possible chronic lead and/or arsenic intoxication").[18, 47, 61, 72]

TABLE 70–1 ■ RISK FACTORS FOR OCCULT BACTEREMIA

Factor	High Risk	Low Risk
Age	≥ 24 mo	> 36 mo
Magnitude of fever	≥ 40° C (104° F)	≤ 39.4° C (103° F)
White blood cell count	≥ 15,000/mm^3	< 15,000/mm^3
Peripheral blood smear	Toxic granulation or vacuolization of polymorphonuclear leukocytes; thrombocytopenia	
Underlying chronic disorder	Sickle-cell disease, immunodeficiency, malnutrition	None
History of contact with bacterial disease	Contact with *Neisseria meningitidis* or *Haemophilus influenzae*	No known contact
Clinical appearance	Appears ill, "toxic," or unhappy; inconsolable; irritable or lethargic; not eating or drinking enough	Looks well; playful; eating normally; not irritable

The adage that an FUO is more likely to be caused by an unusual manifestation of a common disorder than by a common manifestation of a rare disorder certainly is true in pediatrics. The three most common discernible causes of FUO in children, in order of decreasing frequency, are infectious diseases, connective tissue diseases, and neoplasms. In approximately 10 to 20 percent of cases, a definitive diagnosis never is established.

In the United States, the systemic infectious diseases diagnosed most frequently in children with FUO include tuberculosis, brucellosis, tularemia, salmonellosis, and infections caused by rickettsia, spirochetes (e.g., leptospirosis), Epstein-Barr virus, cytomegalic inclusion virus, human immunodeficiency virus, hepatitis viruses, and other viruses. The most common causes of localized infection are upper respiratory tract infections (e.g., sinusitis, otitis, tonsillitis), urinary tract infection, osteomyelitis, and occult abscesses, including hepatic and pelvic abscesses.

The connective tissue disease most commonly manifesting as FUO in children is juvenile rheumatoid arthritis, accounting for more than 90 percent of connective tissue diseases in most series, followed by systemic lupus erythematosus and then by undefined vasculitis.[47, 61, 64, 72] Frequently, the definitive diagnosis of juvenile rheumatoid arthritis can be made only after an extended period of observation because physical examination may yield no findings and because the results of specific serologic studies generally are normal or negative.

Malignancy is a less frequent cause of FUO in children than in adults and usually is the third-largest group, after infectious diseases and connective tissue diseases. Malignancy accounted for 7 percent of the cases in the series of Pizzo and associates[72] and for 13 percent in the Lohr and Hendley[47] series. Leukemia and lymphoma are responsible for most cases of cancer manifesting as FUO in children. Other tumors less commonly reported as causing FUO include neuroblastoma, hepatoma, sarcoma, and atrial myxoma.

Although the prognosis for children with FUO is better than that for adults and although most children with FUO have treatable or self-limited diseases, the overall prognosis is far from benign. The mortality rate was 9 percent in the series of Pizzo and associates[72] and 6 percent in Lohr and Hendley's series.[47] The prognosis for children in whom a definitive diagnosis is not established during the initial hospitalization is mixed. In most cases, fever eventually resolves.[33] In some patients, a specific diagnosis is made, whereas other patients continue to have fever without definitive diagnosis. McClung[61] described 11 such patients, most of whom appeared to do well despite having recurrent episodes of fever.

DIAGNOSTIC APPROACH TO THE CHILD WITH FEVER OF UNKNOWN ORIGIN

A child with FUO is admitted to the hospital for more than simply laboratory investigation. Hospitalization provides an opportunity to observe the child, repeat the history and physical examination, analyze all available data, and follow up on every potential diagnostic lead. In the Lohr and Hendley[47] series of 54 children with FUO, an incomplete history delayed the diagnosis in nine cases, and physical findings that were ignored delayed the diagnosis in four cases. In McClung's[61] report of 99 pediatric cases of FUO, errors in the history or physical examination obscured the correct diagnosis for at least 10 patients. Failure to use existing laboratory data correctly is another common factor preventing early diagnosis of children with FUO.[47, 72]

Clinical Evaluation

The first and most important step in the diagnostic work-up of the child with FUO is obtaining a complete and detailed history and conducting a physical examination. The clinical evaluation must be thorough and careful, and it must be repeated frequently. Often, a patient or parent eventually recalls information that was omitted or forgotten when the initial history was obtained. Physical findings change, and abnormalities not originally present may appear subsequently. In the series by Lohr and Hendley,[47] more than 25 percent of children admitted to the hospital with FUO developed significant physical findings not present at the time of admission.

A detailed history should be obtained regarding contact with infected or otherwise ill persons and any exposure to animals, including pets and wild animals. The number of children with zoonotic infections is increasing each year. Immunization against leptospirosis of domestic animals, such as the dog, may prevent canine disease, but it does not prevent the carriage, excretion, and transmission of this infection. A history of travel extending back to birth must be elicited. Reemergence of histoplasmosis, coccidioidomycosis, blastomycosis, or malaria years after visiting or living in an endemic area is well known. Inquiring about prophylactic immunizations, precautions taken against the ingestion of contaminated food or water, and malarial prophylaxis is important. Questioning should include the possibility that rocks, soil, or artifacts from geographically distant regions may have been brought into the home, as well as the possibility of having contact with persons who have visited distant countries. Even contact with insects can be important. Tick bites can be a clue to Rocky Mountain spotted fever or tick-borne relapsing fever. North American mosquitoes and some ticks carry a variety of arboviruses.

The physician should determine if the patient has eaten game meat, raw meat, or raw shellfish. A history of pica should be sought routinely. Ingestion of dirt may suggest a diagnosis of visceral larva migrans, toxoplasmosis, or other infectious diseases. A detailed history regarding all medications, including topical agents and nonprescription items, must be elicited carefully. Any history of surgical procedures should be explored carefully.

Questions designed to determine the genetic or ethnic background of the patient may reveal information that specifically suggests or largely excludes diagnoses such as nephrogenic diabetes insipidus (found in Ulster Scots), familial Mediterranean fever (found in Armenians, Arabs, and Sephardic Jews), and familial dysautonomia (found in Jews).

The history should be exacting regarding the duration, height, and pattern of the fever, as well as the circumstances under which temperature elevation occurs, whether the child appears ill or develops any signs or symptoms, and how well the fever responds to antipyretic drugs. A history of "fever" occurring only after exercise or late in the afternoon may indicate parental concern about normal variations in body temperature. A history of high fevers occurring in the absence of malaise or other generalized signs may be a clue to factitious fever. The physician also should take a careful history regarding how well the fever has been documented. Has a thermometer been used, by whom, and in whose presence? A history of sweating and heat intolerance may indicate hyperthyroidism, whereas a history of heat intolerance with the absence of sweating may be a clue to ectodermal dysplasia.

In the series of Lohr and Hendley[47] and Pizzo,[72] neither the pattern of fever nor its duration was useful in pointing to or establishing a diagnosis in children with FUO. However, occasionally, the character of the fever can be helpful. *Intermittent fever* is characterized by the return of temperature to normal at least once daily. If the peak of fever is high and the rate of defervescence quick, this pattern often is referred to as hectic or spiking. Intermittent fevers suggest pyogenic infections but also occur with tuberculosis, lymphoma, and juvenile rheumatoid arthritis. In *remittent fever*, the temperature fluctuates but does not return to normal. A *sustained fever* pattern is characterized by persistent fever with little or no fluctuation and may occur in typhoid fever or typhus. Antipyretic agents can make a remittent or sustained fever appear intermittent. *Relapsing fever* refers to a pattern in which the patient is afebrile for 1 or more days between episodes of fever and may be seen in malaria, ratbite fever, infection with the *Borrelia* organism, and lymphomas. Recurrent episodes of fever of more than a year's duration should suggest metabolic defects, central nervous system abnormalities of temperature control, and immunodeficient states.

The general activity and appearance of the patient should be observed, vital signs checked, and growth parameters measured. Weight loss is an important, although nonspecific, finding. Impairment of linear growth or short stature may be a clue to inflammatory bowel disease, an intracranial lesion involving the pituitary gland, or a longstanding, chronic disease. Examining the patient during an episode of fever, observing the presence or absence of sweating, the effect of the fever on the heart and respiratory rate, the presence or absence of malaise or other symptoms, and the appearance of "toxicity," is helpful. The rash of juvenile rheumatoid arthritis characteristically is evanescent and may be present only during periods of temperature elevation.

Some special aspects of the physical examination merit mention. Hypohidrosis, anomalous dentition, and sparse hair, particularly of the eyebrows and eyelashes, suggest anhidrotic ectodermal dysplasia. Palpebral conjunctivitis may be a clue to the presence of infectious mononucleosis, Newcastle disease, or lupus erythematosus, whereas predominantly bulbar conjunctivitis may suggest leptospirosis or Kawasaki disease. Phlyctenular conjunctivitis may signal tuberculosis.

Absence of the pupillary constrictor response may be caused by a deficiency of the constrictor sphincter muscle of the eye. This muscle, derived from ectoderm rather than mesoderm, develops embryologically at the same time that hypothalamic structures and function are undergoing differentiation. The absence of this muscle may suggest that elevation of temperature is the result of hypothalamic or autonomic dysfunction. Careful funduscopic examination may disclose evidence of miliary tuberculosis, vasculitis, or toxoplasmosis. Lack of tears, absence of corneal reflexes, and a smooth tongue with absence of the fungiform papillae would indicate familial dysautonomia.

Purulent or persistent nasal discharge may be a sign of sinusitis. The physician should palpate for tenderness over the sinuses.

Hyperemia of the pharynx, even in the absence of exudate or specific symptoms, may be a clue to the diagnosis of infectious mononucleosis, cytomegalic inclusion disease, toxoplasmosis, tularemia, or leptospirosis. Gingival hypertrophy or inflammation and loosening or loss of teeth may indicate leukemia or Langerhans cell histiocytosis.

The bones and muscles should be palpated carefully. Tenderness over a bone may be found in cases of osteomyelitis or marrow invasion of neoplastic disease. Muscle tenderness may be associated with trichinosis, dermatomyositis, polyarteritis, or various arboviral infections.

The search for skin lesions and rashes must be careful, extensive, and repeated. Petechiae may indicate endocarditis or other sources of bacteremia but also may occur with viral and rickettsial infections. A seborrheic rash may be a sign of histiocytosis.

A careful rectal examination is imperative for patients of all ages and may reveal pararectal tenderness or a mass, indicating a pelvic abscess or tumor. A test for occult blood should be performed on any stool found on the examining finger. Examination of the external genitalia should be completed on patients of all ages, and sexually active adolescent females should undergo pelvic examination.

Laboratory Evaluation

The extent of laboratory investigation depends on the age of the patient, duration of fever, and history and physical examination. Laboratory studies should be directed, as much as possible, toward the most likely diagnostic possibilities. The tempo of the diagnostic evaluation should be adjusted to the severity of the illness. In a critically ill child, speed is important. If the patient is less severely ill, however, the evaluation can proceed more slowly; the clinician sometimes may be rewarded by the disappearance of fever without apparent explanation before a definitive diagnosis can be established and before any invasive diagnostic procedures have been undertaken.

A complete blood count and careful examination of the peripheral smear are indicated for all patients. Anemia should be detected and attention paid to thrombocytosis, as well as thrombocytopenia. Although mild or moderate changes in the total WBC count or differential count usually are of no help, in some series, children with more than 10,000 polymorphonuclear leukocytes or 500 nonsegmented neutrophils/mm^3 were found to have a high chance of having a severe bacterial infection.[79, 84] Atypical lymphocytes generally indicate viral infections, whereas bizarre or immature forms may suggest leukemia. Although the erythrocyte sedimentation rate is of no specific diagnostic value, it is a general indicator of inflammation and can help in ruling out factitious fever, determining the need for further evaluation, and following the progress of the disease process.

Blood cultures should be obtained aerobically and anaerobically from all patients. In select cases, media appropriate for the isolation of *Francisella* organisms, *Leptospira,* and *Spirillum* also should be employed.

Urine analysis and culture should be obtained for all patients. In one series of FUO in children, failure to perform urinalysis and failure to investigate pyuria adequately were the most common laboratory errors.[61] Radiographic study of the urinary tract, however, should be performed only when indicated.

All patients should undergo radiographic examination of the chest. Diagnostic imaging of the nasal sinuses, mastoids, and gastrointestinal tract are ordered initially only for specific indications but should be done eventually in all children whose fever persists without explanation for a long period. Persistent fever and elevation of the erythrocyte sedimentation rate, with or without anemia, abdominal complaints, anorexia, and weight loss, are sufficient indications for radiographic study to rule out inflammatory bowel disease.

All patients should have an intradermal tuberculin skin test. Control skin tests with antigens such as *Candida* are of limited value because anergy may be specific for tuberculosis rather than universal for all skin-testing materials.[50, 63, 67, 68]

A positive control test result and negative tuberculin test result still do not rule out tuberculosis.

Bone marrow examination is most useful in diagnosing cancer (especially leukemia), histiocytic disorders, and hemophagocytic disease. It is less useful in determining infection. Hayani and associates[37] reviewed the results of 414 bone marrow examinations for FUO in children. In only one case was an organism (*Salmonella* group D) recovered from the marrow not also recovered from blood or another source. Noninfectious causes of FUO were found in 8 percent of specimens: malignancy (6.7%), hemophagocytic syndromes (0.7%), histiocytosis (0.5%), and hypoplastic anemia (0.2%). In most of these cases, the diagnosis had been suspected clinically before the bone marrow examination was done.

All patients should undergo a serum test for human immunodeficiency virus infection. Other appropriate serologic tests can help to establish a diagnosis of salmonellosis, brucellosis, tularemia, Epstein-Barr virus infections, cytomegalic inclusion virus infection, and other viral infections, toxoplasmosis, and certain fungal infections.

Hepatic enzymes and serum chemistries, including electrolytes, urea nitrogen, and creatinine, should be determined in all patients. Serum antinuclear antibody should be measured in those older than 5 years of age. Serum hepatitis antigens, electrocardiography, electroencephalography, echocardiography, and stool culture and examination for ova and parasites generally should be performed in selected cases. Other tests to be considered for individual patients include ophthalmologic examination by slit lamp, radiographic bone survey, technetium bone scan, liver-spleen scan, and abdominal imaging by ultrasonography or computed tomography.[20, 71] Computed tomographic scanning, gallium scanning, and indium 111 scanning[33] can detect inflammatory lesions and tumors. Such scanning procedures offer a relatively noninvasive technique for screening patients with FUO for a variety of disorders. Although Steele and associates[78] found that radionucleotide scans seldom led to unsuspected diagnoses in children and suggested that they not be used indiscriminately, gallium scanning has been helpful in diagnosing adult patients with FUO,[36] and it may be a reasonable test for selected children. Lymph node biopsy, liver biopsy, and exploratory laparoscopy are reserved for patients with evidence of involvement of these organs.

In general, antibiotics or other medications should not be administered empirically as a diagnostic measure in children with FUO. Exceptions include the use of nonsteroidal agents in children with presumed juvenile rheumatoid arthritis and the use of antituberculous drugs in critically ill children thought to have disseminated tuberculosis. Empirical trials of broad-spectrum antibiotics generally do more to obscure than illuminate and may mask or delay diagnosis of infections such as meningitis, parameningeal infection, endocarditis, or osteomyelitis.

Examples of disorders that can manifest as FUO in children are listed in Table 70–2. A few of these disorders are discussed briefly in the following sections.

INFECTIOUS CAUSES OF FEVER OF UNKNOWN ORIGIN

Infectious causes of FUO can be divided into systemic and localized. Immunodeficient states may be considered under the general classification of infections.

TABLE 70–2 ■ CAUSES OF FEVER OF UNKNOWN ORIGIN IN CHILDREN

Infectious Diseases
Bacterial
Bacterial endocarditis
Brucellosis
Cat-scratch disease
Leptospirosis
Liver abscess
Mastoiditis (chronic)
Osteomyelitis
Pelvic abscess
Perinephric abscess
Pyelonephritis
Salmonellosis
Sinusitis
Subdiaphragmatic abscess
Tuberculosis
Tularemia
Viral
Cytomegalovirus
Hepatitis viruses
Epstein-Barr virus (infectious mononucleosis)
Chlamydial
Lymphogranuloma venereum
Psittacosis
Rickettsial
Q fever
Rocky Mountain spotted fever
Fungal
Blastomycosis (nonpulmonary)
Histoplasmosis (disseminated)
Parasitic
Malaria
Toxoplasmosis
Visceral larva migrans
Unclassified
Sarcoidosis

Collagen Vascular Diseases
Juvenile rheumatoid arthritis
Polyarteritis nodosa
Systemic lupus erythematosus

Malignancies
Hodgkin disease
Leukemia/lymphoma
Neuroblastoma

Miscellaneous
Central diabetes insipidus
Drug fever
Ectodermal dysplasia
Factitious fever
Familial dysautonomia
Granulomatous colitis
Infantile cortical hyperostosis
Nephrogenic diabetes insipidus
Pancreatitis
Periodic fever
Serum sickness
Thyrotoxicosis
Ulcerative colitis

Generalized Infections

BRUCELLOSIS

The manifestation of this disease as FUO is explained by the nonspecific symptoms it engenders and by the chronicity of untreated infection. Many physicians, particularly in urban areas, tend to ignore the possibility of this disease and neglect to ask for a history of exposure to animals or animal products, especially the eating of unpasteurized goat milk cheese (see Chapter 133).

CAT-SCRATCH DISEASE

During recent years, many children presenting with FUO have proved to be infected with *Bartonella henselae*. Cat-scratch disease is one of the most common causes of FUO in patients presenting to the infectious disease service at Texas Children's Hospital in Houston, Texas.[3] Most of the children with this manifestation of cat-scratch disease have hepatosplenic involvement. Jacobs and Schutze[40] reported that *B. henselae* infection was the cause of 4.8 percent of all cases of FUO at the Arkansas Children's Hospital and 10.9 percent of the cases of FUO of an infectious cause. *B. henselae* infection can be diagnosed by biopsy of lesions (e.g., lymph nodes, liver, bone marrow) and by serologic evaluation (i.e., immunofluorescence assay that detects serum antibody to *B. henselae*). Rifampin or rifampin plus gentamicin or trimethoprim-sulfamethoxazole therapies have been used successfully in the treatment of this disease. In particular, rifampin in a dose of 20 mg/kg/day in two divided doses for 14 days has been particularly efficacious.[3] Fluoroquinolones and macrolides also may be a consideration in the treatment of cat-scratch disease in the future.

LEPTOSPIROSIS

Leptospirosis is caused by a single family of organisms composed of multiple serotypes; it is one of the most widespread zoonoses in the world. Transmission of infection from animal to human may occur by direct contact with the blood, tissue, organs, or urine of infected animals or indirectly by exposure to an environment that has been contaminated by leptospires. The organism also may be acquired from soil or from fresh water after ingestion. Reports indicate that leptospirosis is not a rare disease, that most infections no longer are associated with occupational exposure, and that urban and suburban cases are more prevalent than are cases reported from rural areas.[22] Clinical manifestations of leptospirosis usually are not specific. A variety of laboratory aids are available, but specimens must be collected and handled properly. In some cases, establishing a definitive diagnosis may be impossible; negative cultures or failure to demonstrate a rise in antibody titer does not exclude the possibility that the patient has active infection because the organism may not be in the specimens that have been cultured, the antibody titer may have peaked before an acute phase specimen was collected, and antibiotic therapy may suppress the development of positive titers or delay their appearance (see Chapter 148).

TOXOPLASMOSIS

Toxoplasmosis should be considered in any child with persistent fever. Cervical or supraclavicular adenopathy is present in most cases, but occasionally fever is the only manifestation. The diagnosis is established by demonstration of a rising serologic titer; antibody to *Toxoplasma gondii* is so prevalent that demonstration of a high titer alone is not diagnostic of acute infection. Demonstration of *Toxoplasma* in tissue sections or body fluid is highly suggestive, although the organism may persist in tissue for years. Isolation of the parasite is not absolutely diagnostic of recent infection (see Chapter 222).

MALARIA

Malaria also should be considered in children with FUO. In addition to fever, splenomegaly usually is present. A history of travel to endemic areas should be sought, although malaria has occurred in patients who never left the United States. The disease can become apparent even in persons who have taken antimalarial drugs when they visited the endemic region. A hiatus of several months may occur between development of infection and onset of symptoms. The infection may be transmitted from a person who has visited an endemic area to one who has not when an appropriate mosquito vector is present. Malaria also may be acquired by blood transfusion or by the use of needles and syringes contaminated by the parasite. Demonstration of malarial organisms on appropriately stained thin or thick smears of blood is diagnostic (see Chapter 218).

SALMONELLOSIS

Salmonella organisms are contaminants in many food products. In view of the nonspecific signs and symptoms with which salmonellosis may occur, its association with FUO in children is not surprising. Repetitive blood and stool cultures are most helpful in establishing a diagnosis. Serologic evidence of infection also should be sought (see Chapter 115).

TUBERCULOSIS

Tuberculosis is an important cause of FUO in children as well as in adults. Nonpulmonary tuberculosis manifests as FUO more frequently than does pulmonary tuberculosis, which usually is evident on routine chest radiographs. FUO occurs most commonly with disseminated tuberculosis or infection of the liver, peritoneum, pericardium, or genitourinary tract. Active disseminated tuberculosis has been well documented in children with negative results on chest radiography and tuberculin tests.[68, 80] A high index of suspicion and a careful history for possible contacts can be the best diagnostic tools. Funduscopic examination may reveal choroid tubercles. Liver and bone marrow frequently are involved in children with miliary tuberculosis; liver biopsy specimens and bone marrow aspirates should be obtained and processed for morphologic evaluation and culture. If the chest radiograph yields abnormal results, cultures of gastric aspirates, sputum, or both should be obtained. Because nontuberculous mycobacteria (i.e., atypical organisms) are present in the gastric contents of normal individuals, demonstration of acid-fast organisms on smears of gastric secretion does not indicate disease necessarily. Rarely, a patient with tuberculous pericarditis presents with fever, weight loss, and weakness but without precordial pain or other specific cardiac complaints. Disseminated infection with atypical mycobacteria generally is seen in patients with human immunodeficiency virus infections (see Chapter 101).

TULAREMIA

Failure to consider tularemia in children with FUO generally may be attributed to a lack of appreciation of the many sources of infection and the various routes of inoculation. The organism may be acquired from contact with a variety of animal species, as well as from ticks, mosquitoes, lice, fleas, flies, and contaminated water. The organism can penetrate mucous membranes and broken or unbroken skin, or it may be inhaled or swallowed. The patients and parents should be questioned about animal contact and about ingestion of rabbit or squirrel meat (see Chapter 138).

VIRAL INFECTIONS

Infection by most viruses produces an illness that is relatively brief. Exceptions to this rule include cytomegalovirus, Epstein-Barr virus, hepatitis viruses, and certain arboviruses. In all of these diseases, symptoms are extremely variable, and signs and symptoms frequently are nonspecific. Diagnosis can be established by appropriate cultures and serologic studies (see Section 17 and Chapters 244 and 245).

IMMUNODEFICIENCY

A variety of congenital and acquired immunodeficient states can manifest as FUO. Patients with immunoglobulin deficiencies (e.g., Bruton agammaglobulinemia) may have a long history of recurrent fevers, with or without evident infections, whereas patients with abnormalities of lymphocyte function are more likely to have prolonged fever caused by persistent viral or parasitic infection.

Localized Infections

BACTERIAL ENDOCARDITIS

Infective endocarditis is an infrequent cause of FUO in children. Acute bacterial endocarditis tends to be explosive in onset, but the subacute form begins insidiously, generally at the site of a preexisting cardiac lesion. Subacute bacterial endocarditis is a rare occurrence in infants and increases in frequency with advancing age. The organisms most commonly encountered are viridans streptococci, enterococci, *S. aureus,* and *Staphylococcus epidermidis.* The absence of a cardiac murmur does not exclude the possibility of endocarditis, especially when the infection is limited to the right side of the heart. Endocarditis also may occur in the absence of positive blood cultures, especially in association with the following factors: use of antibiotics for an undefined febrile illness; right-sided cardiac lesions; prolonged duration of disease; infection by unusual organisms, such as *Brucella* or *Coxiella burnetii;* and inadequate culture methods for the detection of infection with anaerobic organisms. Frequently associated laboratory findings include anemia, leukocytosis, and an elevated erythrocyte sedimentation rate. Several blood cultures (aerobic and anaerobic) should be obtained before starting antibiotics. Echocardiography and gallium scan may reveal vegetations, but negative results do not rule out endocarditis (see Chapter 32).

BONE AND JOINT INFECTIONS

Infections of the bones and joints usually can be diagnosed clinically but occasionally manifest as FUO. This manifestation occurs commonly in young children who cannot explain where they hurt and is more likely to occur with osteomyelitis than with septic arthritis. Infection of the pelvic bones most often is implicated in this regard. Radioisotopic bone scan and whole-body gallium scan are more sensitive than are plain radiographs of the bones (see Chapter 64).

INTRA-ABDOMINAL ABSCESSES

Subphrenic, perinephric, and pelvic abscesses may manifest as FUO. A history of prior intra-abdominal disease or abdominal surgery or a history of vague abdominal complaints should heighten suspicion of an intra-abdominal collection of pus. The organisms involved most commonly are *S. aureus,* streptococci, *E. coli,* and anaerobic flora. Fever may be the only sign of a pelvic, perinephric, or psoas abscess. Urinalysis generally yields normal results, but the mass can be demonstrated by ultrasound examination, gallium scan, or computed tomography.

LIVER ABSCESS AND OTHER HEPATIC INFECTIONS

Pyogenic liver abscesses are encountered most frequently in the immunocompromised pediatric patient but may be seen in the otherwise normal child.[43] In some patients, persistent fever is the only finding. Blood cultures usually are sterile, and serum levels of liver enzymes generally are close to or within normal limits. Many patients have hepatomegaly and right upper quadrant abdominal tenderness. Diagnosis can be established by examination of the liver by ultrasonography, radioisotope scan, or computed tomography; a body gallium scan also may yield positive results. Bacterial hepatitis and bacterial cholangitis can occur in the absence of jaundice and other specific signs of liver dysfunction.[88, 91] Granulomatous hepatitis is not a specific disease but rather a syndrome characterized by granuloma formation within the liver. A specific cause cannot always be determined. Although most reported cases have been in adults,[76] pediatric cases do occur, particularly with Epstein-Barr virus infection and with cat-scratch disease. The diagnosis can be made by ultrasound or other diagnostic imaging (see Chapter 58).

UPPER RESPIRATORY TRACT INFECTIONS

Frequently, infections of the upper respiratory tract and related organs manifest as FUO.[47, 61, 72] Although obvious signs or symptoms would be expected, the complaints often appear trivial and may be ignored. Reported cases of FUO in children have included mastoiditis, sinusitis, chronic or recurrent otitis media, chronic or recurrent pharyngitis, tonsillitis, peritonsillar abscess, and nonspecific upper respiratory tract infection. A parapharyngeal inflammatory pseudotumor manifesting as FUO has been reported in a 3-year-old girl who also developed anemia and weight loss. The cause never was discerned, but the symptoms resolved after surgical removal of the inflammatory mass.[23]

A syndrome of periodic fever has been associated with recurrent aphthous stomatitis, pharyngitis, and cervical adenitis. Symptoms recur at 4- to 6-week intervals, generally beginning abruptly and resolving spontaneously in 4 to 5 days. The cause of this syndrome remains unknown.[31]

NONINFECTIOUS CAUSES OF FEVER OF UNKNOWN ORIGIN

Central Nervous System Dysfunction

Children with severe brain damage may have dysfunction of thermoregulation, and some of these patients may run elevated body temperatures for months. Cases of otherwise neurologically normal children who have had fever as a result of central dysfunction also have been reported. Berger[13] discussed a 16-year-old child with recurrent episodes of fever that were thought to represent a form of epilepsy and that disappeared when treatment with phenytoin was begun. Wolff and associates[89] reported a 14-year-old child with cyclic episodes of fever, nausea, vomiting, and emotional disturbance caused by a central nervous system lesion.

Diabetes Insipidus

Central and nephrogenic diabetes insipidus can cause FUO in infants and young children. Polyuria and polydipsia may not be appreciated during infancy. Hyperthermia, weight loss, and peripheral vascular collapse may ensue. Signs of dehydration or an increased serum concentration of sodium suggests the diagnosis. Diagnosis is established by simultaneous measurements of urine and serum electrolytes and osmolality during periods of normal hydration and after carefully controlled periods of water deprivation. Serum levels of antidiuretic hormone also may be measured by radioimmunoassay.

Drug Fever

Nearly any medication can be associated with an allergic reaction, including fever. The offending agent may be a prescribed drug, an over-the-counter preparation, or a street drug, such as amphetamine or PCP. Atropine, whether taken systemically or used topically as eyedrops, can cause elevation of temperature. Phenothiazines and anticholinergic drugs can inhibit sweating and impair regulation of temperature. Epinephrine and related compounds may affect thermoregulatory control mechanisms and produce fever. Generally, drug fever is low grade but may be high and spiking. Fever may be continuous or intermittent. Discontinuation of the drug generally is followed by disappearance of fever within 48 hours, but the fever sometimes persists for as long as a month as a result of slow excretion of the offending agent.

Factitious Fever

A parent or patient may report the presence of fever that does not exist, or the reading of the thermometer may be increased by immersing the bulb in hot liquids or by rinsing the mouth with hot liquid immediately before inserting the thermometer. Clues to a factitious fever include absence of tachycardia, malaise, or discomfort despite a markedly elevated temperature; apparent rapid defervescence unaccompanied by diaphoresis; failure of the temperature curve to follow the normal diurnal variation of body temperature; hyperpyrexia; and normal temperature reading when the temperature is obtained rectally by someone who remains in attendance during the procedure. The presence of fever also may be confirmed or excluded by measuring the temperature of a freshly voided urine specimen. The current use of electronic thermometers in most hospitals decreases the possibility of factitious fever in that setting because the nurse or aide usually brings in the thermometer and stays in attendance during the relatively brief period of insertion. In more unusual cases, the patient or parent may induce fever by the injection of infective or foreign materials.

Familial Dysautonomia

Familial dysautonomia (Riley-Day syndrome), an autosomal recessive disorder, is characterized by autonomic and peripheral sensory nerve dysfunction. Eighty percent of patients have been children of Jewish parentage, particularly Ashkenazi Jews. Defective regulation of temperature may result in hypothermia or hyperthermia.[26]

A careful history and physical examination may reveal the following: poorly coordinated swallowing movements, which lead to recurrent aspiration and pneumonia; recurrent episodes of vomiting; excessive salivation; excessive or diminished sweating; diminished formation of tears; periods of hypotension, hypertension, or both; and erythema or blanching of the skin. The fungiform papillae of the tongue are absent or diminished in number, and the sensation of taste is deficient.[77] Self-mutilation or multiple sites of skin trauma may reflect diminished or absent pain sensation peripherally. Deep tendon reflexes are diminished; corneal reflexes are impaired; and mental deficiency, dysarthria, and emotional lability are common findings.

Vanillylmandelic acid excretion in urine may be diminished, and homovanillic acid excretion may be increased. Administration of histamine intradermally may produce a wheal but no flare or pain at the site of injection. Placement of methacholine (2.5%) into the conjunctival sac produces pupillary constriction in children with familial dysautonomia but no response in the normal child. Intravenous infusion of norepinephrine is followed by an exaggerated pressor response, and the hypotensive response to infusion of methacholine is increased.

Inflammatory Bowel Disease

Fever is a prominent feature in many children with inflammatory bowel disease.[24, 45, 86] A greater percentage of children than adults with regional enteritis have fever. Appropriate radiographic contrast studies of the intestines should be undertaken in children with prolonged FUO, even in the absence of findings specifically referable to the gastrointestinal tract, especially if the erythrocyte sedimentation rate is elevated and if the patient has anemia, weight loss, failure of linear growth, or a positive stool guaiac test.

Ulcerative colitis may manifest as FUO, although less commonly than does regional enteritis. In patients with ulcerative colitis, symptoms referable to the gastrointestinal tract generally are present at the time the patient is febrile.

Infantile Cortical Hyperostosis

The cause of infantile cortical hyperostosis (i.e., Caffey disease) is unknown. Decreased frequency in recent years has suggested an infectious, possibly viral, cause. Spontaneous hyperplasia of the subperiosteal bone begins during infancy and is associated with swelling of the overlying tissues. The skull, mandible, clavicles, scapula, and ribs are affected most frequently, but in some children, the long bones and even the metatarsal bones may be involved. Most patients have persistent fever, sometimes as high as 40° C (104° F). Tenderness over the affected regions, irritability, elevated erythrocyte sedimentation rate, and leukocytosis are common findings. The diagnosis is established by the clinical picture in conjunction with radiographically demonstrated periosteal involvement.

Juvenile Rheumatoid Arthritis

Juvenile rheumatoid arthritis is a chronic inflammatory disorder that usually manifests as one of three distinct syndromes: the systemic form, characterized by high, spiking temperatures (generally once or twice each day), evanescent rash, and lymphadenopathy; a polyarticular form; and a monarticular or pauciarticular form. Fever is associated with all three manifestations but occurs most commonly in the systemic form, in which case it is present in nearly 100 percent of patients. This form also is the one most likely to manifest as FUO.[19] Arthritis may not develop for months to years after the onset of fever. The diagnosis often needs to be made by exclusion because serologic tests generally are negative.

Periodic Fevers

Familial Mediterranean fever is characterized by episodic fever and abdominal pain.[30] This disease, found in persons of Mediterranean ancestry, is inherited as an autosomal recessive trait. The pattern of recurrent fever, however, is irregular, with varying periods of normality between episodes of fever.

Reimann[74] called attention to a group of patients with recurrent episodes of fever at regular intervals, usually 7 to 21 days. Some of the patients had leukopenia and abdominal or thoracic pain. The reasons for the fever and its periodicity remain unknown. Patients with cyclic neutropenia frequently have fever during acute episodes, but not all the patients reported by Reimann had neutropenia. Cases of children with periodic fever and hyperimmunoglobulinemia D, with or without chills, cervical lymphadenopathy, and occasionally abdominal pain have been reported,[29, 35] primarily from Europe. The cause of the syndrome remains unknown.

REFERENCES

1. Adams, K. C., Dixon, J. H., and Eichner, E. R.: Clinical usefulness of polymorphonuclear leukocyte vacuolization in predicting septicemia in febrile children. Pediatrics *62*:67–70, 1978.
2. Alpern, E. R., Alessandrin, E. A., Bell, L. M., et al.: Occult bacteremia from a pediatric emergency department: Current prevalence, time to detection and outcome. Pediatrics *106*:505–511, 2000.
3. Arisoy, E. S., Correa, A. G., Wagner, M. L., and Kaplan, S. L.: Hepatosplenic cat-scratch disease in children: Selected clinical features and treatment. Clin. Infect. Dis. *28*:778–784, 1999.
4. Ayus, C. J., Krothapalli, R. K., and Arieff, A. I.: Occult bacteremia in febrile children. N. Engl. J. Med. *318*:1338–1339, 1988.
5. Baker, M. D., Bell, L. M., Avner, J. R.: The efficacy of routine outpatient management without antibiotics of fever in selected infants. Pediatrics *103*:627–631, 1999.
6. Baker, R. C., Tiller, T., Bausher, J. C., et al.: Severity of disease correlated with fever reduction in febrile infants. Pediatrics *83*:1016–1019, 1989.
7. Baraff, L. J., Bass, J. W., Fleisher, G. R., et al.: Practice guidelines for the management of infants and children 0 to 36 months of age with fever without source. Pediatrics *92*:1–12, 1993.
8. Baraff, L. J., Oslund, S., and Prather, M.: Effect of antibiotic therapy and etiologic microorganism on the risk of bacterial meningitis in children with occult bacteremia. Pediatrics *92*:140–143, 1993.
9. Baron, M. A., and Fink, H. D.: Bacteremia in private pediatric practice. Pediatrics *66*:171–175, 1980.
10. Bass, J. W., Steel, R. W., Wittler, R. R., et al.: Antimicrobial treatment of occult bacteremia: A multicenter cooperative study. Pediatr. Infect. Dis. J. *12*:466–473, 1993.
11. Baron, M. A., Fink, H. D., and Cicchetti, D. V.: Blood cultures in private pediatric practice: An eleven-year experience. Pediatr. Infect. Dis. *8*:2–7, 1989.
12. Bachur, R., Harper, M.: Reevaluation of outpatients with *Streptococcus pneumoniae* bacteremia. Pediatrics *105*:502–509, 2000.
13. Berger, H.: Fever: An unusual manifestation of epilepsy. Postgrad. Med. *40*:479–481, 1966.
14. Bloom, H. R.: Must we teach clinical judgment? Pediatrics *67*:745–746, 1981.
15. Bonadio, W. A.: Systemic bacterial infections in children with fever greater than 41°C. Pediatr. Infect. Dis. J. *8*:120–121; 1989.
16. Bonadio, W. A., Webster, H., Wolfe, A., and Gorecki, D. Correlating infectious outcome with clinical parameters of 1130 consecutive febrile infants aged zero to eight weeks. Pediatr. Emerg. Care. *9*:84–86, 1993.
17. Bratton, L., Teele, D. W., and Klein, J. O.: Outcome of unsuspected pneumococcemia in children not initially admitted to the hospital. J. Pediatr. *90*:703–706, 1977.
18. Brewis, E. C.: Undiagnosed fever. Br. Med. J. *1*:107–110, 1965.
19. Calabro, J. J., and Marchesano, J. M.: Juvenile rheumatoid arthritis. N. Engl. J. Med. *277*:746–749, 1967.
20. Carey, B. M., Williams, C. E., and Arthur, R. J.: Ultrasound demonstration of pericardial empyema in an infant with pyrexia of undetermined origin. Pediatr. Radiol. *18*:349–350, 1988.
21. Carroll, W. L., Farrell, M. K., Singer, J. I., et al.: Treatment of occult bacteremia: A prospective randomized clinical trial. Pediatrics *72*: 608–611, 1983.
22. Centers for Disease Control: Annual Survey of Leptospirosis for 1972. Atlanta, Centers for Disease Control, 1974.
23. Chan, Y. F., Ma, L. T., Yeung, L. T., et al.: Parapharyngeal inflammatory pseudotumor presenting as fever of unknown origin in a 3-year-old girl. Pediatr. Pathol. *8*:195–203, 1988.
24. Chron, B. B., and Yarnis, H.: Continuous fever of intestinal origin. Ann. Intern. Med. *26*:858–862, 1947.
25. Corrigan, J. J.: Thrombocytopenia: Laboratory sign of septicemia in infants and children. J. Pediatr. *85*:219–223, 1974.
26. Dancis, J., and Smith, A. A.: Familial dysautonomia. N. Engl. J. Med. *274*:207–209, 1966.
27. Dashefsky, B., Teele, D. W., and Klein, J. O.: Unsuspected meningococcemia. J. Pediatr. *102*:69–72, 1983.
28. Dershewitz, R. A.: A comparative study of the prevalence, outcome and prediction of bacteremia in children. J. Pediatr. *103*:352–358, 1983.
29. Drenth, J. P. H., Haagsma, C. J., van Der Meer, J. W. H.: Hyperimmunoglobulinemia D and periodic fever syndrome. Medicine (Baltimore) *73*:133–144, 1994.
30. Ehrenfeld, E. N., Eliakin, M., and Rachmilewitz, M.: Recurrent polyserositis (familial Mediterranean fever, periodic disease): A report of 55 cases. Am. J. Med. *31*:107–123, 1961.
31. Feder, H. M. J., and Bialecki, C. A.: Periodic fever associated with aphthous stomatitis, pharyngitis and cervical adenitis. Pediatr. Infect. Dis. *8*:186–189, 1989.
32. Feigin, R. D., and Shearer, W. T.: Fever of unknown origin in children. Curr. Probl. Pediatr. *6*:2–57, 1976.
33. Fineman, D. S., Palestno, C. J., Kim, C. K., et al.: Detection of abnormalities in febrile AIDS patients with In-111–labelled leukocyte and Ga-67 scintigraphy. Radiology *170*:677–680, 1989.
34. Fleishner, G. R., Rosenberg, N., Vinci, R., et al.: Intramuscular versus oral antibiotic therapy for the prevention of meningitis and other bacterial sequela in young febrile children at risk for occult bacteremia. J. Pediatr. *124*:504–512, 1994.
35. Gross, C., Schnetzer, J. R., Ferrante, A., and Vladutiu, A. O.: Children with hyperimmunoglobulinemia D and periodic fever syndrome. Pediatr. Infect. Dis. J. *15*:72–77, 1996.
36. Habibian, M. R., Staab, E. V., and Matthews, H. A.: Gallium citrate Ga 67 scans in febrile patients. J. A. M. A. *233*:1073–1076, 1975.
37. Hayani, A., Mahoney, D. H., and Fernback, D. J.: Role of bone marrow examination in the child with prolonged fever. J. Pediatr. *116*:919–920, 1990.
38. Heldrich, F. J.: *Diplococcus pneumoniae* bacteremia. Am. J. Dis. Child. *119*:12–17, 1970.
39. Hoekelman, R., Lewin, E. B., and Shapira, M. D., et al.: Potential bacteremia in pediatric practice. Am. J. Dis. Child. *133*:1017–1019, 1979.
40. Jacobs, R. F., and Schutze, G. E.: *Bartonella henselae* as a cause of prolonged fever and fever of unknown origin in children. Clin. Infect. Dis. *26*:80–84.
41. Jaffee, D. M., Tanz, R. R., Davis, T., et al.: Antibiotic administration to treat possible occult bacteremia in febrile children. N. Engl. J. Med. *317*:1175–1180, 1987.
42. Jaskiewicz, J. A., McCarthy, C. A., Richardson, A. C., et al.: Febrile infants at low risk for serious bacterial infection—An appraisal of the Rochester criteria and implications of management. Pediatrics *94*:390–396, 1994.
43. Kaplan, S. L., and Feigin, R. D.: Pyogenic liver abscess in normal children with fever of unknown origin. Pediatrics. *58*:614–616, 1976.
44. Kline, M. W., Smith, E. O., Kaplan, S. L., et al.: Effects of causative organism and presence or absence of meningitis on white blood cell counts in children with bacteremia. J. Emerg. Med. *6*:33–35, 1988.
45. Lee, F. I., and Davies, D. M.: Crohn's disease presenting as pyrexia of unknown origin. Lancet *1*:1205–1206, 1961.
46. Liu, C., Lehan, C., Speer, M. E., et al.: Early detection of bacteremia in an outpatient clinic. Pediatrics *75*:827–831, 1985.
47. Lohr, J. A., and Hendley, J. O.: Prolonged fever of unknown origin: Record of experience with 54 childhood patients. Clin. Pediatr. *16*:768–773, 1977.
48. Long, S. S.: Antibiotic therapy in febrile children: "Best laid schemes..." J. Pediatr. *124*:585–588, 1994.
49. Lorin, M. I.: The Febrile Child: Clinical Management of Fever and Other Types of Pyrexia. New York, John Wiley & Sons, 1982, p. 70.
50. Margolis, M. T.: Specific anergy in tuberculosis. N. Engl. J. Med. *309*:1388, 1983.
51. Marshall, R., Teele, D. W., and Klein, J. O.: Unsuspected bacteremia due to *Haemophilus influenzae:* Outcome in children not initially admitted to hospital. J. Pediatr. *95*:690–695, 1979.
52. Mazur, L. J., Jones, T., and Kozinetz, C. A.: Temperature response to acetaminophen and risk of occult bacteremia: A case control study. J. Pediatr. *115*:888–891, 1989.
53. McCarthy, P. L., Grundy, G. W., Spiesel, S. Z., et al.: Bacteremia in children: An outpatient review. Pediatrics *57*:861–868, 1976.

54. McCarthy, P. L., Frank, A. L., Ablow, R. C., et al.: Creative protein test in the differentiation of bacterial and viral pneumonia. J. Pediatr. *92*:454–459, 1978.
55. McCarthy, P. L., Jekel, J. F., Stashwick, C. A., et al.: History and observation variables in assessing febrile children. Pediatrics *65*:1090–1095, 1980.
56. McCarthy, P. L., Jekel, J. F., Stashwick, C. A., et al.: Further definition of history and observation variables in assessing febrile children. Pediatrics *67*:687–693, 1981.
57. McCarthy, P. L., Sharpe, M. R., Spiesel, S. Z., et al.: Observation scales to identify serious illness in febrile children. Pediatrics *70*:802–809, 1982.
58. McCarthy, P. L., and Dolan, T. F.: Hyperpyrexia in children: Eight-year emergency room experience. Am. J. Dis. Child. *130*:849–851, 1976.
59. McCarthy, P. L., and Dolan, T. F.: Hyperpyrexia in children. Am. J. Dis. Child. *130*:849–851, 1976.
60. McCarthy, P. L., Jekel, J. F., and Dolan, T. F.: Temperature greater than or equal to 40°C in children less than 24 months of age: A prospective study. Pediatrics *59*:663–668, 1977.
61. McClung, H. J.: Prolonged fever of unknown origin in childhood. Am. J. Dis. Child. *124*:544–550, 1972.
62. McGowan, J. E., Bratton, L., Klein, J. O., et al.: Bacteremia in febrile children seen in a walk-in pediatric clinic. N. Engl. J. Med. *288*:1309–1312, 1973.
63. McMurray, D. N., and Echeverri, A.: Cell-mediated immunity in anergic patients with pulmonary tuberculosis. Am. Rev. Respir. Dis. *118*:827–834, 1978.
64. Miller, M. L., Szer, I., Yogev, R., and Bernstein, B: Fever of unknown origin. Pediatr. Clin. North Am. *42*:999–1011, 1995.
65. Morens, D. W.: WBC and differential: Value in predicting bacterial disease in children. Am. J. Dis. Child. *133*:25–27, 1979.
66. Murray, D. L., Zonana, J., Seidel, J. S., et al.: Relative importance of bacteremia and viremia in the course of acute fevers of unknown origin in outpatient children. Pediatrics *68*:157–160, 1981.
67. Nash, D. R., and Douglas, J. E.: Anergy in active pulmonary tuberculosis: A comparison between positive and negative reactors and an evaluation of 5 TU and 250 TU skin test doses. Chest *77*:32–37, 1980.
68. Ostrow, J. H.: Tuberculin negative tuberculosis. Am. Rev. Respir. Dis. *107*:882–883, 1973.
69. Peltola, H.: C-reactive protein in rapid differentiation of acute epiglottitis from spasmodic croup and acute laryngotracheitis: Preliminary report. J. Pediatr. *102*:713–715, 1983.
70. Petersdorf, R. G., and Beeson, P. B.: Fever of unexplained origin: Report on 100 cases. Medicine (Baltimore) *40*:1–30, 1961.
71. Picus, D., Siegel, M. J., and Balfe, D. M.: Abdominal computed tomography in children with unexplained prolonged fever. J. Comput. Assist. Tomogr. *8*:851–856, 1984.
72. Pizzo, P. A., Lovejoy, F. H., and Smith, D. H.: Prolonged fever in children: Review of 100 cases. Pediatrics *55*:468–473, 1975.
73. Press, S.: Association of hyperpyrexia with serious disease in children. Clin. Pediatr. *33*:19–25, 1994.
74. Reimann, H. A.: Periodic disease, periodic fever, periodic abdominalgia, cyclic neutropenia, intermittent arthralgia, angioneurotic edema, anaphylactoid purpura and periodic paralysis. J. A. M. A. *141*:175–183, 1949.
75. Roberts, K. B., and Borzy, M. S.: Fever in the first eight weeks of life. Johns Hopkins Med. J. *141*:9–13, 1977.
76. Simon, H. B., and Wolff, S. M.: Granulomatous hepatitis and prolonged fever of unknown origin: A study of 13 patients. Medicine (Baltimore) *52*:1–21, 1973.
77. Smith, A. A., Farbman, A., and Dancis, J.: Tongue in familial dysautonomia. Am. J. Dis. Child. *110*:152–153, 1965.
78. Steele, R. W., Jones S. M., Lowe, B. A., et al.: Usefulness of scanning procedures for diagnosis of fever of unknown origin in children. J. Pediatr. *119*:526–530, 1991.
79. Stein, R. C.: The white blood cell count in fevers of unknown origin. Am. J. Dis. Child. *124*:60–63, 1972.
80. Steiner, P., and Portuguleza, C.: Tuberculous meningitis in children. Am. Rev. Respir. Dis. *107*:22–29, 1973.
81. Strickland, A. D.: Serious implications of fever in the young infant. Presentation at Grand Rounds, Ben Taub Hospital, Houston, September 1978.
82. Teach, S. J., Fleisher, G. R.: Efficacy of an observation scale in detecting bacteremia in febrile children three to thirty six months of age, treated as outpatients. J. Pediatr. *126*:877–881, 1995.
83. Teele, D. W., Pelton, S. I., Grant, M. J., et al.: Bacteremia in febrile children under 2 years of age: Results of cultures of blood of 600 consecutive febrile children in a "walk-in" clinic. J. Pediatr. *87*:227–230, 1975.
84. Todd, J. K.: Childhood infections: Diagnostic value of peripheral white blood cell and differential cell counts. Am. J. Dis. Child. *127*:810–816, 1974.
85. Torrey, S. B., Henretig, F., Fleisher, G., et al.: Temperature response to antipyretic therapy in children. Am. J. Emerg. Med. *3*:190–192, 1985.
86. Walker, S. H.: Periodic fever in juvenile regional enteritis. J. Pediatr. *60*:561–565, 1962.
87. Waskerwitz, S., and Berkelhammer, J. E.: Outpatient bacteremia: Clinical findings in children under two years with initial temperatures of 39.5° C or higher. J. Pediatr. *99*:231–233, 1981.
88. Weinstein, L.: Bacterial hepatitis: A case report on an unrecognized cause of fever of unknown origin. N. Engl. J. Med. *299*:1052–1054, 1978.
89. Wolff, S. M., Ward, S. B., and Landy, M.: A syndrome of periodic hypothalamic discharge. Am. J. Med. *36*:956–966, 1964.
90. Wright, P. F., Thompson, J., McKee, K. T., Jr., et al.: Patterns of illness in the highly febrile young child: Epidemiologic, clinical and laboratory correlates. Pediatrics *67*:694–700, 1981.
91. Wyllie, R., and Fitzgerald, J. F.: Bacterial cholangitis in a 10-week-old infant with fever of undetermined origin. Pediatrics *65*:164–167, 1980.
92. Yamamoto, L. T., Wigder, H. N., Fligner, D. J., et al.: Relationship of bacteremia to antipyretic therapy in febrile children. Pediatr. Emerg. Care. *3*:223–226, 1987.

CHAPTER 71 Toxic Shock Syndrome

P. JOAN CHESNEY ■ JEFFREY P. DAVIS

Much has been learned about the pathogenesis and pathophysiology of toxic shock syndrome (TSS) since the initial description in 1978 by Dr. James K. Todd. The clinical illness is defined by the criteria listed in the case definition formulated for epidemiologic studies (Table 71–1). Although often confused with septic shock, TSS has unique clinical manifestations not generally noted in septic shock, including diffuse erythroderma, delayed desquamation of the palms and soles, conjunctival and pharyngeal hyperemia, muscle injury, rapidly accelerated renal failure, and gastrointestinal symptoms. The capillary leak syndrome, or rapid and massive loss of fluid from capillaries into the interstitial space, loss of peripheral vascular resistance, and subsequent multisystem end-organ failure further characterize this entity. The histopathologic findings are minimal and nonspecific, with extensive interstitial edema of all tissues and minimal perivascular mononuclear cellular infiltrates. TSS can recur after both menstrual and nonmenstrual cases. The highest

TABLE 71–1 ■ TOXIC SHOCK SYNDROME CLINICAL CASE DEFINITION

Fever:	Temperature ≥ 38.9° C
Rash:	Diffuse macular erythroderma
Desquamation:	1–2 wk after onset of illness, particularly on palms, soles, fingers, and toes
Hypotension:	Systolic blood pressure ≤90 mm Hg for adults; <5th percentile by age for children <16 yr old; orthostatic drop in diastolic blood pressure ≥15 mm Hg from lying to sitting; orthostatic syncope or orthostatic dizziness

Involvement of three or more of the following organ systems:
Gastrointestinal: vomiting or diarrhea at onset of illness
Muscular: severe myalgia or creatinine phosphokinase level greater than twice the upper limit of normal for laboratory
Mucous membrane: vaginal, oropharyngeal, or conjunctival hyperemia
Renal: BUN or serum creatinine greater than twice the upper limit of normal or ≥5 white blood cells per high-power field in the absence of a urinary tract infection
Hepatic: total bilirubin, AST, or ALT greater than twice the upper limit of normal for the laboratory
Hematologic: platelets <100,000/mm^3
Central nervous system: disorientation or alterations in consciousness without focal neurologic signs when fever and hypotension are absent

Negative results on the following tests, if obtained:
Blood, throat, or cerebrospinal fluid cultures; blood culture may be positive for *Staphylococcus aureus*
Serologic tests for Rocky Mountain spotted fever, leptospirosis, or measles

Case Classification
Probable: A case with 5 of the 6 clinical findings described above
Confirmed: A case with all 6 of the clinical findings described above, including desquamation, unless the patient dies before desquamation could occur

ALT, alanine transaminase; AST, aspartate transaminase; BUN, blood urea nitrogen.
From Wharton, M., Chorba, T. L., Vogt, R. L., et al.: Case definitions for public health surveillance. M. M. W. R., Recomm. Rep. 39(RR-13): 1–43, 1990.

recurrence rate of 65 percent was described in a subset of untreated women with menstrual TSS who continued to use tampons during menses.

When first described, TSS had unique geographic, age, sex, and racial characteristics. It was associated with menses, particularly tampon use, as well as with a phenotypically distinctive type of *Staphylococcus aureus*. In 1994, at least 42 percent of reported cases of TSS were nonmenstrual. *S. aureus* exotoxins now are recognized to be "superantigens," and the endogenous mediators produced by these exotoxins appear to mediate the manifestations of the disease.

TSS toxin I (TSST-I) and the staphylococcal enterotoxins are extremely potent stimuli for the in vitro macrophage production of interleukin-1 (IL-1) and tumor necrosis factor–α (TNF-α) and the T-lymphocyte production of IL-2, lymphotoxin (TNF-β), and interferon-γ. These staphylococcal exotoxins are functionally bivalent mitogens that highly selectively bind to the major histocompatibility complex (MHC) class II receptors on antigen-processing cells and to selected V_β elements of the T-cell receptor (TCR) specific for each toxin. They now are known as superantigens.

History

Illnesses resembling TSS and associated with *S. aureus* have been reported since 1927,[7, 88, 99, 271, 300] but the initial description of the illness as a disease of children was published in 1978.[281] A Kawasaki-like syndrome described in adults subsequently was recognized to be TSS.[185] The first 12 cases of TSS identified in Wisconsin and Minnesota between July 1979 and January 1980 were reported by state epidemiologists to the Centers for Disease Control and Prevention (CDC) in January 1980.[70, 257, 288] All 12 cases had occurred in women, and a possible association with menses was noted. The probable recurrent nature of the illness also was reported.[70, 288] In May 1980, the CDC reported findings of the first 55 nationally reported cases,[288] 95 percent of which occurred in women. Of 40 patients for whom a menstrual history was obtained, 38 (95%) had onset during menstruation. Thirteen patients had experienced recurrent episodes of TSS.

By June 1980, case-control studies statistically linking the occurrence of menstrual TSS with tampons had been completed by the Wisconsin Division of Health[70] and the CDC,[257] and similar trends had been noted by the Utah Department of Health.[149] In September 1980, the CDC reported that although TSS had been associated with many tampon brands, women using one particular brand of tampon, Rely (Procter & Gamble), were at greater risk. This brand was withdrawn immediately and voluntarily from the market by the manufacturer.[22, 110, 246] Subsequent frequent updates by the CDC documented a decrease in reported cases.[289, 290, 296]

Microbiologic studies have established that most patients with menses-associated TSS (menstrual TSS) had vaginal or cervical colonization with *S. aureus*.[20] These strains of *S. aureus* made a characteristic marker protein or toxin initially called staphylococcal enterotoxin F (SEF)[21] and pyrogenic exotoxin C[252] and now known as TSST-I.

Epidemiology

SURVEILLANCE AND INCIDENCE

Statewide surveillance for cases of TSS began in Wisconsin[72] and Minnesota[212] in January 1980, in Utah in February 1980,[161] and in other states after the national communications about TSS in the spring of 1980. In 1982, TSS became a nationally notifiable disease. During the years 1983 through 1994, the CDC had received reports of 4192 cases of TSS through the National Electronic Telecommunications System for Surveillance (NETSS).[274] The National Center for Infectious Diseases at the CDC maintains a database of cases meeting the TSS case definition. This database includes cases reported before 1983. Since 1983, a continued downward trend in passively reported cases has been noted (Fig. 71–1).[305]

Of 2509 confirmed cases reported to the CDC through April 1984, 95 percent were in females.[231] Among the 2295 women with known menstrual histories, 89 percent had an onset of TSS associated with menstruation. Of 1716 menses-associated cases for which information related to catamenial product use was available, 99 percent occurred in tampon users, 1 percent occurred with the exclusive use of napkins or minipads, and 1 case occurred after the use of a sea sponge.

The results of an active surveillance study conducted by the CDC in 1986 and 1987 in five states and Los Angeles County confirmed the trends previously noted in the CDC passive surveillance system.[117] The incidence of menstrual TSS was found to be 1 case per 100,000 women 15 to 44 years of age. This rate is a substantial reduction from the reported rates of 2.4 to 12.3 cases per 100,000 women of

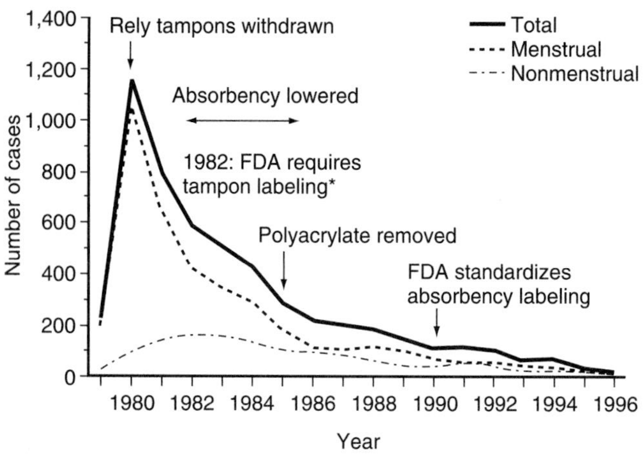

*FDA, Food and Drug Administration, including definite and probable toxic shock syndrome cases

FIGURE 71–1 ■ Menstrual and nonmenstrual toxic shock syndrome cases reported to the Centers for Disease Prevention and Control by year, 1979 to 1996. (From Hajjeh, R. A., Reingold, A., Weil, A., et al.: Toxic-shock syndrome in the United States: Surveillance update, 1979–1996. Emerg. Infect. Dis. *5*:807–810, 1999.)

menstruating age in 1980.[70, 161, 212, 223] Only 55 percent of the cases detected in the 1986 and 1987 study were in women, and 45 percent of all cases were menstrually associated.[36, 117] In 1986 and 1987, the incidence of nonmenstrual, nonvaginal TSS in women (0.25 case per 100,000 women) and TSS in males (0.16 case per 100,000 men) had changed little since 1980. In 1994, only 192 cases of TSS were reported to the CDC through the NETSS. The overall passive reported incidence of TSS was 0.1 case per 100,000 population. Among confirmed cases, 42 percent were nonmenstrual.[274] The proportion of nonmenstrual cases reported after surgical procedures increased from 14 percent during 1979 to 1986 to 27 percent during 1987 to 1996.[122]

The principal reasons for the striking reduction in the incidence of menstrual TSS include a decrease in tampon absorbency, changes in tampon composition and usage patterns during the 1980s, and the impact of publicity on the early reporting during 1980.[72, 73, 211, 230, 254] Other factors may have contributed to the significant decrease in incidence.[230, 254] With enhanced recognition of symptoms of TSS, women may seek medical help sooner, thus obviating development of the severe syndrome. In addition, proportionately fewer women now may use tampons continuously or at all.[102]

The nationally reported TSS-related mortality rate for menstrual cases decreased from 5.5 percent in 1979 and 1980 to 2.8 percent in 1981 to 1986, to 1.8 percent in 1987 to 1996 (chi-square for linear trend, $p = .0001$).[122] During the years 1980 to 1986, an increased mortality rate was observed in nonmenstrual case patients. The increase in mortality rate was noticeable particularly in men (17.1%) and women (13.2%) older than 45 years of age in comparison to men (9.5%) or women with nonmenstrual TSS (4.3%) who were between 15 and 44 years of age. Overall, no significant change in the case-fatality ratio for nonmenstrual cases has occurred: 8.5 percent for 1979 and 1980, 5.3 percent for 1981 to 1986, and 6 percent for 1987 to 1996.[36, 122]

Although cases in the United States have been reported in all 50 states and the District of Columbia, significant differences in incidence were noted among the states through 1983.[231] Through mid-1983, the five states of Wisconsin, Minnesota, Colorado, Utah, and California accounted for 44 percent of the total reported cases but represented only 16 percent of the U.S. population.[285] Although intensified surveillance may have been a factor, regional differences in the degree of immunity to TSS-associated *S. aureus* toxins and in the distribution of toxin-producing organisms may have been important factors.[297] Geographic differences in occurrence of TSS continue to exist, even with the increase in the relative proportion of nonmenstrual cases.[36]

RISK FACTORS FOR MENSTRUAL TOXIC SHOCK SYNDROME

From early 1980 through 1990, most reported cases of TSS occurred in previously healthy, young white menstruating women who were using tampons at the time of onset of illness (Table 71–2). The explanation for this combination of risk factors is complex.

Age

The mean age of patients with confirmed menstrual TSS (22.6 years in 1980, 23 years in 1986) has varied little since 1980.[117, 122, 231] Roughly one third of cases occur in adolescents 15 to 19 years of age[231] (Fig. 71–2). The mean age of patients with nonmenstrual TSS (27 years through 1982, 30 years in 1986) is significantly higher than that for menses-associated cases.[117, 232] The precise reason for the increased incidence of TSS in adolescent girls is not known; however, a lower prevalence of antibody to TSST-I may increase susceptibility in this age group.[299]

TABLE 71–2 ■ RISK FACTORS FOR NONMENSTRUAL TOXIC SHOCK SYNDROME

I. Colonization with toxin-producing *Staphylococcus aureus*
II. Absence of protective antitoxin antibody
III. Infected site
  A. Primary *S. aureus* infection

Carbuncle	Peritonitis
Cellulitis	Peritonsillar abscess
Dental abscess	Pneumonia
Empyema	Pyarthrosis
Endocarditis	Pyomyositis
Folliculitis	Sinusitis
Mastitis	Tracheitis
Osteomyelitis	

  B. After surgery: wound infection

Abdominal	Ear, nose, and throat
Breast	Genitourinary
C-section	Neurosurgery
Dermatologic	Orthopedic

  C. Skin or mucous membrane disruption
    Burns (chemical, scald, etc.)
    Dermatitis
    Postpartum (vaginal delivery)
    Superficial/penetrating trauma (insect bite, needle-stick)
    Viral infection
      Influenza
      Pharyngitis
      Varicella
  D. After surgical or nonsurgical foreign body placement
    Augmentation mammoplasty
    Catheters
    Diaphragm
    Sponge (contraceptive)
    Surgical prostheses/stents/packing material/sutures
  E. No obvious focus of infection (vaginal or pharyngeal colonization)

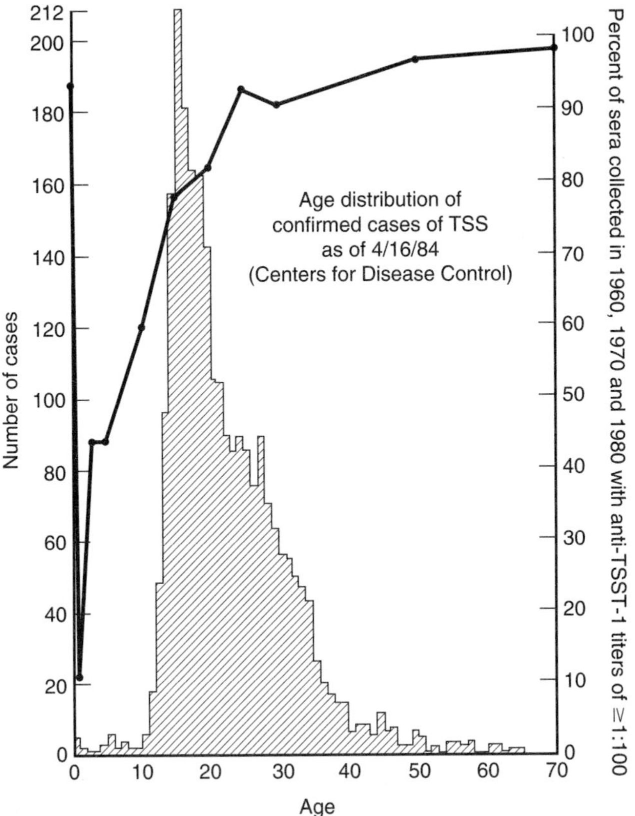

FIGURE 71–2 ■ Age distribution of patients with confirmed toxic shock syndrome reported to the Centers for Disease Control and Prevention before April 16, 1984. The age-specific prevalence of antibodies to toxic shock syndrome toxin I in a normal population in Wisconsin in the years 1960, 1970, and 1980 is indicated by the *solid connected line.* (Data from Vergeront, J. M., Stolz, S. J., Crass, B. A., et al.: Prevalence of serum antibody to staphylococcal enterotoxin F among Wisconsin residents: Implications for toxic shock syndrome. J. Infect. Dis. *148*:692–698, 1983.)

Race

A striking race-ethnicity distribution is present for menstrual TSS; 97 percent of such cases have occurred in whites, who make up 83 percent of the U.S. population. This distribution is not as striking for nonmenstrual TSS because 87 percent of nonmenstrual cases have occurred in whites. The reasons for racial differences are not clear and only partially explained by differences in menses-related practices.[102, 231, 232] Racial differences in antibody to TSST-I may explain partially the differences in the distribution of cases.[297]

Menstruation and Tampon Use

The initial observations in 1980 that a high proportion of patients with TSS had an onset during menses now has been documented well. The use of tampons as a significant risk factor for the development of TSS was established clearly in six case-control studies conducted in 1980[70, 126, 149, 210, 246, 257] and one conducted in 1987.[117] Even though these studies varied in design and methodologic technique, all demonstrated that at least 97 percent of case individuals used tampons during menstrual periods associated with disease onset. Although 76 to 89 percent of matched control individuals used tampons during temporally comparable menstrual periods, the use of tampons was associated with menstrual TSS in each of these studies, with odds ratios ranging from 11 to 18.[36]

Despite the fact that TSS has occurred and continues to occur with the use of all brands of tampons, the second CDC case-control study demonstrated a greater relative risk for menstrual TSS with the use of one tampon brand, Rely.[110, 246] The Tri-State (Minnesota, Wisconsin, and Iowa) TSS Study established that tampons of increasing absorbency were associated with an increasing relative risk for development of menstrual TSS and that the risk of menstrual TSS associated with Rely tampons was greater than that predicted by absorbency alone.[210]

Reasons listed earlier for the striking reduction in incidence of menstrual TSS may be the decrease in tampon absorbency and changes in tampon composition.[230] In 1980, very high absorbency products were used by 42 percent of tampon users.[212] By 1983, this proportion had decreased to 18 percent and, by 1986, to 1 percent.[230] Overall, the absorbency of available tampon brand styles, as measured by the Syngina test,[201] ranged from 10.3 to 20.5 g in 1980 to less than 6 to 15 g in 1990, indicative of an industry-wide decrease in tampon absorbency. Tampon composition also has changed since 1980. Tampons currently available are composed of cotton or cotton and rayon combinations. In 1980, tampon additives included polyacrylate, polyester foam, cross-linked carboxymethylcellulose, and several surfactants, including Pluronic L-92.[249] Whether these additives enhanced the risk of developing TSS independently or in combination with their increasing absorbency is unclear.[22, 210, 246]

Two subsequent case-control studies conducted by the CDC and involving patients with an onset of TSS in 1983 and 1984 (CDC III) and 1986 and 1987 (CDC IV) confirmed the Tri-State TSS Study results of a linear increasing TSS risk related to increasing tampon absorbency; for each 1-g increase in absorbency, the TSS risk increased by 34 to 37 percent.[22, 106] In addition, the Tri-State TSS Study and the CDC III study both suggested that the effects of tampon absorbency and chemical composition on TSS risk were independent.[22, 36, 210]

Continuous use of tampons was associated with a greater risk for development of TSS than was noncontinuous use in one case-control study[257]; however, this finding was not confirmed in a subsequent investigation.[210] No association between TSS and the frequency of changing tampons has been demonstrated.

As a result of these studies demonstrating the importance of tampons in menses-associated TSS, as well as the voluntary withdrawal of Rely, several other changes in tampon manufacture, labeling, and distribution have occurred. After a request by the Food and Drug Administration (FDA) in November 1980 that tampon manufacturers place warnings on tampon packages, on June 22, 1982, an FDA regulation required that information on TSS and tampon-associated risks appear on tampon packages.[83] In April 1985, two additional tampon manufacturers withdrew their superabsorbent tampons containing polyacrylate from the market on the basis of an in vitro study[192] and a judicial decision.[205] In 1990, the FDA published the in vitro rating system to be used by manufacturers to inform the public about tampon absorbency.[167, 201, 277]

RISK FACTORS FOR NONMENSTRUAL TOXIC SHOCK SYNDROME

Before 1986, less than 20 percent of confirmed cases of TSS reported to the CDC were nonmenstrual. In the 1986 and 1987 multistate active surveillance study (CDC IV),

54 percent of cases were found to be nonmenstrual.[117] Although the mean age of nonmenstrual cases is higher than that of menstrual cases and the ratio of males to females with nonmenstrual TSS is closer to that in the general population, the clinical findings and complications of nonmenstrual TSS are the same as those occurring in menstrual TSS. The number of confirmed cases of TSS reported in children younger than 10 years of age is surprisingly low, particularly in light of their demonstrated low antibody titers to TSST-I and the increased prevalence of nasal colonization (10%) with TSST-I–positive strains.[36, 140, 299, 309]

Data on risk factors (see Table 71–2) were obtained for 559 nonmenstrual TSS cases reported to the CDC through 1986.[36] Associated infections or procedures included nonsurgical cutaneous and subcutaneous infections, 22 percent; childbirth or abortion, 15 percent; infections after a wide variety of surgical procedures, 15 percent; vaginal infections occurring at times other than during menses, 6 percent; vaginal contraceptive sponge use, 5 percent[68]; diaphragm use, 6 percent; and other or unknown sources of infection, 31 percent. The proportion of all nonmenstrual cases reported after surgical procedures increased from 14 percent during 1979 to 1986 to 27 percent during 1987 to 1996. The proportion of female nonmenstrual case patients using barrier contraceptives was significantly less in 1987 to 1996 (6%) than in 1979 to 1986 (14%).[122]

In 1994, nonmenstrual cases accounted for at least 42 percent of all cases of TSS reported to the CDC through the passive surveillance system.[274] The three risk factors necessary for the acquisition of nonmenstrual disease include colonization (or acquisition) of a toxin-producing strain of *S. aureus,* absence of protective antitoxin antibody, and an infected site. TSS has been reported in association with *S. aureus* infections of almost every type, including primary staphylococcal infections and those occurring after surgery, infections associated with disruption of skin or a mucous membrane, and infections occurring after placement of a foreign body[20] (see Table 71–2). Numerous patients with TSS have been reported for whom no obvious focus of infection was found.[36, 232] Trauma or surgery at areas of the body frequently colonized with *S. aureus* (nose, skin, vagina) places individuals at enhanced risk for acquiring infection and TSS.

HOST RISK FACTORS: GENERAL

Colonization with Exotoxin *Staphylococcus aureus*

For TSS to develop, an individual must be colonized with or acquire a strain of *S. aureus* that produces TSST-I or one of the staphylococcal enterotoxins. Evidence that SEB alone and uncommonly SEA or SEC alone as well as TSST-I may be responsible for the manifestations of TSS is compelling. Although many genotypically different strains of *S. aureus* possess the *tst*H gene, one clone has been isolated from 88 percent of menstrual cases and 54 percent of nonmenstrual cases.[198] Colonization with this clone, particularly for menstruating women, clearly provides a significant risk factor. Future work may identify other clones with unique adherence properties for other mucosal or skin sites.

Absence of Protective Antibody Levels

A necessary factor for the development of TSS is the absence of protective antibody levels for the toxin (TSST-I or enterotoxin) produced by the isolate associated with TSS. Thus, more than 90 percent of women with menstrual TSS associated with TSST-I–positive strains have antibody titers of 1:10 or lower, whereas a titer of 1:100 or higher is considered protective.[20] Because most adults acquire these antibodies without disease developing, absent antibody levels may be the result of a lack of exposure to a toxin-producing organism or a lacunar inability to respond to the toxin. The failure of most patients, menstrual and nonmenstrual, to form antibody during convalescence may reflect this lacunar nonrecognition of staphylococcal protein antigen, or it may be a reflection of the superantigenic nature of these proteins and failure of the toxin proteins to be presented to the TCR as conventional antigens. In mice and in one patient with TSS, in vivo TSST-I–induced proliferation was followed by hyporesponsiveness of TSST-I–responsive $V_{\beta}2^{+}$ T cells.[166]

Interruption of a Mucosal or Skin Surface

Primary deep-tissue staphylococcal infections (e.g., osteomyelitis, pyarthrosis, pyomyositis,[4] endocarditis,[224, 306] renal carbuncles, bacteremia) rarely are associated with TSS. Most nonmenstrual cases occur in patients with an altered skin or mucosal surface. Examples of skin disruption associated with TSS include burns, insect bites, needlesticks, surgical incisions, and varicella. Examples of mucous membrane disruption can be divided into those associated with respiratory and those associated with genital mucosae. Damaged respiratory mucosa may appear after nasal or other surgery, particularly with placement of stents or packing, in association with a viral respiratory infection such as influenza or as a primary sinusitis, tracheitis, or parapharyngeal abscess. Heavy colonization of the pharynx also has been associated with TSS. The vaginal mucosa may be damaged in numerous ways, including placement of tampons or barrier contraceptives,[96, 255, 286] postpartum,[20, 216] or after genital surgery or genital mucosal damage.[97, 214, 239] Heavy colonization of the vagina without any other apparent risk factor also has been associated with TSS.[232] These mucosal infections may provide the right conditions for production of TSST-I, including an aerobic environment, a high carbon dioxide concentration, a neutral pH, high protein and low glucose concentrations, and low to normal magnesium concentrations.[284]

Presence of a Foreign Body

Tampons create an aerobic environment in the vagina, which normally is anaerobic. Tampons of three different types have been shown in humans to change the partial pressure of oxygen of the vaginal wall from an anaerobic environment to that of atmospheric air throughout the 90-minute interval after insertion.[301] Because oxygen is required for production of TSST-I, researchers have suggested that tampons of enhanced absorbency allow the introduction of increasing concentrations of oxygen to enhance toxin production.

Several alternative explanations for the role of tampons have been proposed. Tampons may remove vaginal substrates that normally inhibit the growth of *S. aureus.*[20] Another suggested role for tampons is that of inducing cervicovaginal ulcerations. These ulcers have been suggested to enhance bacterial growth or toxin absorption and expose submucosal fibronectin for *S. aureus* binding.[64, 66, 304] Tampons can induce chronic cervicovaginal ulcers after long-term continuous use or superficial micro-ulcerations after a brief insertion in otherwise healthy women. However, vaginal ulcerations of the type typically seen in TSS have been found during postmortem examination in women who had never used tampons. This finding suggests that vaginal ulcerations, such as those seen in the esophagus and bladder in TSS, may be induced by TSST-I.[160]

Investigations to determine whether individual tampon components can induce or amplify the production of TSST-I in vitro have provided conflicting data, in part because no consensus exists regarding how best to test tampons and their components to determine their potential to increase risk for the development of TSS. In one setting, although bacterial growth was unaffected, production of TSST-I varied from undetectable levels to levels of 300 μg/mL, depending on the particular brand and style of tampon studied.[20] Other investigators have found that most tampons tested were inhibitory to both bacterial growth and production of TSST-I and that none consistently increased the production of TSST-I.[20]

Two studies clearly have demonstrated the enhanced production of TSST-I in vitro by the Rely tampon composed of cross-linked carboxymethylcellulose and polyester foam.[220, 250] The polyacrylate rayon included in two tampons now removed from the market increased the production of TSST-I under certain conditions,[192] as did the surfactant Pluronic L-92 used in at least one tampon.[250] Neither cotton nor rayon amplifies the production of TSST-I in vitro, nor do cotton tampons adsorb TSST-I or prevent its production.[220, 250] Thus, cotton tampons cannot be claimed to be safer than cotton/rayon combinations, although this contention has been disputed.[279] The role of magnesium in controlling the production of TSST-I in the presence of tampons is unclear.[192]

Implanted foreign material such as sutures, central venous lines, and metallic or polymeric implants has been documented repeatedly to enhance the risk of acquiring bacterial infection.[20, 142] These infections are characterized by limited spread beyond the tissues in immediate contact with the implants, poor response to antibiotics, and poor healing without removal of the foreign material. Two important differences between TSS and other *S. aureus* infections related to foreign material are the added ability of the organism to produce a toxin that readily disseminates and the limited ability of these strains to produce inflammation.[98] Researchers have suggested that the increased number of surgically associated TSS cases may be related to the number of implanted materials.[122]

The enhanced risk of acquiring infection by *S. aureus* in the presence of foreign material has been defined experimentally in animals. Rats remained asymptomatic after the subcutaneous injection of more than 1×10^6 colony-forming units of *S. aureus,* whereas 3×10^2 colony-forming units invariably led to infection in the presence of a suture. In addition, the ability of the sutured tissue to resist infection varies with the kind of material implanted, particularly its physical or chemical configuration. For example, bacterial adherence is eightfold higher for braided sutures of silk, silicone-heated blue polyester, and absorbable polyglycolic acid than for monofilament nylon.[142]

In addition to sutures, other foreign materials associated with TSS-related wound infection are Teflon splints, gauze packing, and mammary implants.[20]

OTHER POTENTIAL HOST RISK FACTORS

Other factors have been examined in an attempt to identify individuals who may be at increased risk for development of TSS.[75] Some of these factors have included HLA typing,[20] neutrophil function,[128] adherence of *S. aureus* to vaginal epithelial cells,[20] alteration of the cervicovaginal flora,[20] hormonal factors, and personal hygiene practices.[75] Of all these factors, those of potential importance included the cervicovaginal flora and hormonal factors.

Vaginal co-colonization with *S. aureus* and one of the Enterobacteriaceae has been postulated to enhance the risk of development of TSS.[52] Prospective examination of 495 healthy women revealed a 7 percent vaginal colonization rate for *S. aureus* TSST-I–positive strains. Women who were colonized with toxin-producing *S. aureus* also were colonized with *E. coli* or other Enterobacteriaceae statistically significantly more often than were women colonized with non–toxin-producing or no *S. aureus. E. coli* isolation rates were 54 percent in women with TSST-I–positive isolates, 15 percent in women with TSST-I–negative isolates, and 11 percent in women with no *S. aureus.* Co-isolation of *E. coli* was the only identified factor associated with vaginal carriage of TSST-I–positive *S. aureus*. Additionally, among the 14 patients with TSS monitored in this study, 9 had *E. coli* as well as TSST-I–positive *S. aureus* co-isolated during the acute TSS episode. The significance of these observations and their relationship to postulated roles for endotoxin in TSS is not clear.

The results of early case-control studies suggested that oral contraceptive steroids may have an effect on vaginal *S. aureus* organisms that may produce or release TSS-associated toxins[70, 210] and that this effect was protective. However, one case-control study found no protective effect or enhanced risk associated with oral contraceptive use.[117] Hormonal control is known to be responsible for numerous cycle changes in the vaginal pH and flora; however, the role of hormonal factors in the pathogenesis of TSS has not been well examined.

Histopathology[1, 26, 34, 160, 213, 308]

The histopathologic findings found on postmortem examination support the concept that TSS is a toxin-mediated disease. Striking histopathologic similarities exist between patients with TSS and those with "scarlet fever" reported in 1936.[34] Typically, a total absence of tissue invasion by bacteria and minimal evidence of an inflammatory reaction in most organs are noted. Findings thought to be due to a direct effect of the toxin or mediators (or both) and unrelated to hypoperfusion have included subepidermal ulcerations in the cervix, vagina, esophagus, and bladder; lymphocyte depletion in the lymph nodes; a subepidermal cleavage plane in the skin; and mild inflammatory changes in the kidney, liver, heart, and muscle.

Cervicovaginal ulcerations are the only characteristic lesions noted in the genital tract of patients with fatal menstrual TSS and also were found in a patient with menstrual TSS who had never used tampons.[160, 216] The ulcerations are superficial. Capillary vasodilation and thrombosis with inflammation of the mucosa are present, but no deep-tissue bacterial invasion is seen. The layer of vacuolization and separation in the ulcers occurs beneath the basal layer. The same type of ulcer also has been found in the bladder and the esophagus, which suggests that these ulcerations may be caused by the toxins or mediators and not by the use of tampons.

Although the myocardium was described as normal in one postmortem series of TSS, in another series of eight fatal cases, all patients had evidence of focal round-cell infiltration with variable degrees of congestion, edema, and hemorrhage.[160, 213] Myxoid degeneration was found in all heart valves from four patients in one series. Sections of skeletal muscle have demonstrated only congestion, edema, focal hemorrhage or fiber necrosis, and a mild acute inflammatory infiltrate.

Varying degrees of triaditis or periportal lymphocytic inflammation have been the most consistent findings in the liver; centrilobular congestion with necrosis and mild cellular degeneration also has been described.[137] In the kidney, toxin-mediated mononuclear interstitial nephritis may result from perivasculitis of the adventitia of the renal venules, lesions that probably precede the development of hypotension-induced acute tubular necrosis. The most characteristic findings in the spleen and lymph nodes have been lymphocyte depletion; inactive hypocellular, hypoplastic lymphoid follicles with edema; marked histiocytosis in the interfollicular areas; and hemophagocytosis.

Perivascular lymphocytic infiltrates and bullae that separate at the basement membrane are characteristic of the early skin changes in TSS.[8, 10, 128] No evidence of vasculitis has been reported.

Clinical Spectrum

ACUTE PHASE: MODERATE TO SEVERE DISEASE[44, 53, 71, 104–106, 127, 176, 257, 281, 292]

Multisystem end-organ damage secondary to loss of peripheral vascular resistance, loss of intravascular volume as a result of endothelial damage and the capillary leak syndrome, and interstitial edema constitute the most important mediator-induced changes of TSS. Prolonged hypotension, interstitial edema, and vascular congestion additionally may result in ischemic organ damage.

The onset of illness in moderate to severe disease is abrupt, with symptoms and signs including fever, chills, malaise, headache, sore throat, myalgia, muscle tenderness, fatigue, vomiting, diarrhea, abdominal pain, and orthostatic dizziness or syncope (Figs. 71–3 and 71–4).

During the first 24 to 48 hours, diffuse erythroderma, severe watery diarrhea often with incontinence, decreased urine output, cyanosis, and edema of the extremities may be noted. Cerebral ischemia and edema rapidly result in somnolence, confusion, irritability, agitation, and, occasionally, hallucinations, even in individuals without hypotension. Patients with TSS have had signs and symptoms of encephalopathy, cerebral infarct, meningismus,[15, 25, 124, 164, 262] and the cauda equina syndrome.[8]

During initial physical examination of a moderately to severely ill patient, fever, tachycardia, tachypnea, a low or unobtainable blood pressure, erythroderma (generally not seen in patients with severe hypotension or in patients without T cells)[146] (see Fig. 71–4*A*), and muscle tenderness are noted in conjunction with peripheral cyanosis and edema, conjunctival hyperemia, subconjunctival hemorrhages (see Fig. 71–4*B*), beefy red edematous mucous membranes, somnolence, disorientation, and agitation. In menstrual TSS, edema and erythema of the inner aspect of the thighs and the perineum may be noted in conjunction with a normal uterine and adnexal examination. In nonmenstrual cases, vaginitis or another focus of infection will be present. In most postoperative cases, the surgical wound is not inflamed. If erythroderma is present, it will be most intense surrounding the infected focus.

Surgical wounds and some abscesses colonized or infected with *S. aureus* and responsible for postoperative or nonmenstrual TSS may have minimal or no signs of inflammation.[6, 17, 86, 232] The production of TNF-α by macrophages in response to TSST-I inhibits neutrophil mobilization in vitro,[98] which may provide an explanation for the absence of signs of inflammation. The incubation period for postoperative or postpartum TSS may be as short as 12 to 48 hours. Relatively few cases have been associated with deep-tissue infections.[20]

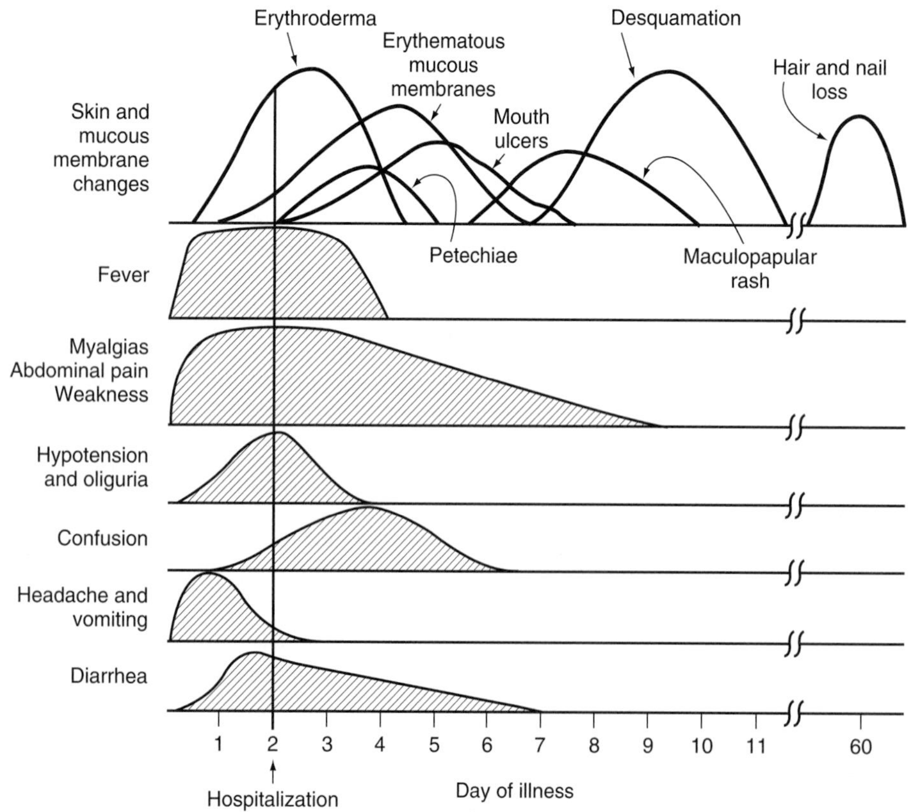

FIGURE 71–3 ■ Composite drawing of the major systemic skin and mucous membrane manifestations of toxic shock syndrome. (From Chesney, P. J., Davis, J. P., Purdy, W. K., et al.: The clinical manifestations of toxic shock syndrome. J. A. M. A. *246*:741–748, 1981. Copyright 1981, American Medical Association.)

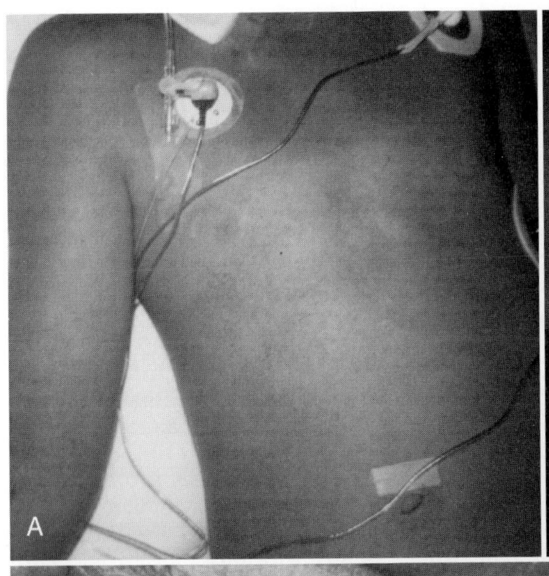

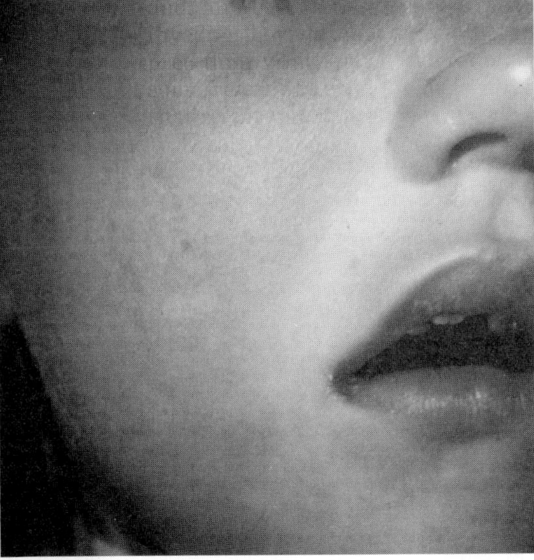

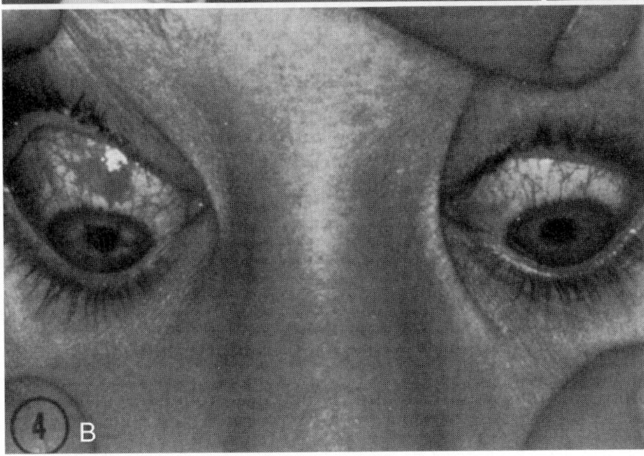

FIGURE 71–4 ■ Skin and mucous membrane manifestations present at the onset of toxic shock syndrome (TSS). *A,* Diffuse erythroderma in a 7-year-old child with nonmenstrual TSS associated with osteomyelitis of the fibula. *B,* Bulbar conjunctival infection and subconjunctival hemorrhage in a 24-year-old woman with nonmenstrual TSS. *(B* from Bach, M. C.: Dermatologic signs in toxic shock syndrome: Clues to diagnosis. J. Am. Acad. Dermatol. *8*:343–347, 1983.)

LABORATORY CHANGES

Abnormalities in clinical laboratory tests will reflect the endogenous cytokine release, shock, and organ failure. Leukocytosis may not be present, but the total proportion of mature and immature neutrophils generally exceeds 90 percent. The proportion of immature neutrophils usually is 25 to 50 percent of the total number of neutrophils and is associated with a profound and absolute lymphopenia. Thrombocytopenia and anemia are present during the first few days and frequently are accompanied by prolonged prothrombin and partial thromboplastin times. Disseminated intravascular coagulation may be present. Sterile pyuria and a cerebrospinal fluid pleocytosis are indicative of generalized involvement of the mucous membranes and serosal surfaces. Elevated blood urea nitrogen and creatinine levels reflect kidney damage,[47] abnormalities in tests of liver function reflect liver damage and acute cholestasis,[119, 137] and profound hypocalcemia may reflect both hypoproteinemia and high serum levels of a calcitonin-like material.[48, 265] Muscle involvement is noted by an elevated creatine phosphokinase level, and the hypophosphatemia that occurs despite impaired renal function is unexplained.[14, 48, 295] Most of these tests will return to normal within 7 to 10 days of disease onset. *S. aureus* will be cultured from the cervix or vagina in more than 85 percent of patients with menstrual TSS and from the focus of infection in patients with nonmenstrual TSS. Positive blood culture results are rare findings.[65] Antibody to TSST-I or the staphylococcal enterotoxins will be absent at the onset of disease in more than 85 percent of patients.[21, 31, 62, 241, 272, 307]

TREATMENT

The four general principles of treatment of TSS (Table 71–3) are (1) identification and drainage of the focus of toxin production, (2) identification and susceptibility testing of the organism, (3) antimicrobial therapy to block the synthesis of toxin and to kill *S. aureus,* and (4) management of the systemic multiorgan actions of the toxins or mediators.*

Location and Drainage of the Infected Site

The focus of infection should be identified rapidly, any foreign bodies should be removed, and the site should be drained or irrigated completely, even if it does not appear to be inflamed. Performing this procedure is of utmost importance because perpetuation of even a small, undrained focus of infection may result in serious clinical consequences. If TSS occurs in the immediate postoperative period, the wound should be assumed to be the source of infection, regardless of its benign appearance.

*See references 44, 53, 70, 71, 104, 106, 127, 176, 246, 280, 292.

TABLE 71–3 ■ THERAPEUTIC PRINCIPLES FOR MANAGEMENT OF TOXIC SHOCK SYNDROME

Identify focus of infection: débride and irrigate extensively and remove any foreign material
Isolate organism for antimicrobial susceptibility studies
Parenteral antimicrobial therapy
- Stop enzyme/toxin production with protein synthesis inhibitor (e.g., clindamycin, erythromycin, gentamicin)

  and
- Eradicate organism with bacterial cell wall inhibitor (e.g., β-lactamase–resistant antistaphylococcal antimicrobial agent)

Consider intravenous immunoglobulin to provide antitoxin antibodies for a subset of patients, including those with
- Disease refractory to initial fluid replacement and several hours of vasopressor support
- A focus of infection that cannot be drained
- Persistent oliguria in spite of massive fluid replacement and in the presence of pulmonary edema

Consider methylprednisolone to suppress cytokine production and the inflammatory response
Fluid therapy to maintain adequate venous return and cardiac filling pressures and to prevent end-organ damage
Anticipatory management of multisystem organ failure

Identification and Susceptibility Testing of the Organism

Community-acquired methicillin-resistant *S. aureus* (MRSA) infections have increased dramatically during the past 5 years.[129] These MRSA strains differ from the long-standing hospital-acquired MRSA strains in that they are acquired in the community by well individuals with no risk factors and are not multiresistant. Most strains are susceptible to clindamycin. Because MRSA strains are fully capable of producing TSST-I,[253] a reasonable assumption is that in the future, community-acquired menstrual and nonmenstrual cases of TSS may be caused by either community or multiresistant hospital-acquired strains of MRSA. To date, vancomycin-resistant strains of *S. aureus* are rare findings.[131, 267] Thus, every effort should be made to obtain the organism for susceptibility testing.

Antimicrobial Agents

Antistaphylococcal antibiotics are indicated to eradicate organisms and prevent recurrences.[70, 71] The infection may be a superficial or deep-tissue infection and may be associated with *S. aureus* bacteremia or bacteriuria. The antistaphylococcal antimicrobial agents should be used intravenously at maximal doses for age and should be initiated as soon as possible.

Once the patient is stable, no longer vomiting or having diarrhea, and able to take food by mouth, high doses of an oral antimicrobial agent to which the organism is susceptible can be given to complete a total course of 10 to 14 days.

Subinhibitory concentrations of the protein synthesis inhibitors clindamycin, lincomycin, erythromycin, clarithromycin, kanamycin, gentamicin, and tetracycline have been shown to suppress TSST-I production in vitro.[82, 219, 251] In one study, clindamycin concentrations 1/64th the minimal inhibitory concentration (MIC) were effective in totally blocking TSST-I production.[219] In a mouse model of myositis caused by *Streptococcus pyogenes*, another superantigen-producing organism, clindamycin and erythromycin were more efficacious than was penicillin.[89, 268, 270]

Data suggest that subinhibitory concentrations of β-lactam antibiotics actually may *increase* TSST-I production by *S. aureus*. At a concentration one half the MIC, nafcillin can *increase* toxin production 10-fold more than control conditions.[5] A similar effect has been described for nafcillin and the staphylococcal alpha-toxin.[150] The effect is not seen with vancomycin, another cell wall–active drug, thus suggesting a specificity beyond merely a cell wall effect. The co-administration of a protein synthesis inhibitor with a β-lactam antibiotic blocks the effect.[5]

The choice of initial empirical antimicrobial therapy has become more complex as a result of an increase in the number of community-acquired MRSA infections and the spread of multiresistant MRSA strains in hospitals.[148] The severity of TSS warrants initiating maximally effective therapy. Once the susceptibilities of the organism are available, therapy can be adjusted appropriately. In the past, the most effective initial empirical therapy was a combination of a β-lactamase–resistant penicillin and clindamycin. For hospital-acquired nonmenstrual TSS, consideration should be given to initiating therapy with vancomycin and clindamycin. This situation clearly is difficult because most patients with TSS have a degree of renal failure. In addition, if the organism is methicillin-susceptible, the β-lactamase–resistant penicillins generally are more efficacious than is vancomycin. An infectious disease consultation should be considered to help with the management of these patients.

Most community-acquired MRSA infections are susceptible to clindamycin.[129] Thus, for these infections, a β-lactamase–resistant penicillin plus clindamycin should provide adequate initial empirical coverage. For patients allergic to penicillin, a first- or second-generation cephalosporin could be used as an alternative, with recognition of the 10 percent cross-reactivity between cephalosporins and penicillins.

Fluid Replacement

The most important aspect of the nonspecific treatment of symptomatic patients is fluid replacement.[280] Intravascular volume and cardiac filling pressures must be restored rapidly to achieve adequate tissue perfusion. Because of the ongoing capillary leakage, this fluid replacement may far exceed the estimated fluid requirements based on calculated maintenance and fluid deficit volumes. Some adults have required vasopressors and as much as 12 L of fluid during the first 24 hours to stabilize the circulating blood pressure. Pleural, pericardial, and peritoneal effusions and interstitial edema inevitably occur as a result of the continued vascular capillary fluid leak. Close monitoring in an intensive care unit will facilitate determination of when the correct intravascular volume has been achieved, as well as detection and appropriate monitoring and treatment of myocardial dysfunction, hemodynamic derangements, pulmonary edema, adult respiratory distress syndrome, acute renal failure, encephalopathy, and disseminated intravascular coagulation.

Corticosteroids

Short courses of methylprednisolone or dexamethasone, if given early in the course of the disease, have been associated with a reduction in the duration of fever and the severity of illness but no reduction in mortality rates.[283] In vitro, dexamethasone has been shown to down-regulate TSST-I–induced cytokine production.[154] Because no controlled prospective study has demonstrated efficacy, the use of steroids probably should be restricted to hypotensive patients unresponsive to fluid resuscitation, antimicrobial agents, and intravenous immunoglobulin (IVIG).

Intravenous Immunoglobulin

Not surprisingly, given the high prevalence of antibodies to TSST-I in adults,[299] high levels of antibody to TSST-I are present in IVIG preparations.[43, 49, 179, 216, 276] Through use of the rabbit subcutaneous Wiffle ball or tampon model of TSS, human IVIG given at the time of inoculation of TSST-I–positive *S. aureus* prevented the development of TSS. When IVIG was administered 8 hours later, it decreased the mortality rate from 90 percent in control rabbits to 16 percent. When IVIG was given 29 hours after TSST-I administration, the increase in survival rates among the IVIG-treated animals still was significant. No adverse reactions were noted in the treated animals, and no evidence was found of disease mediated by the formation of antigen-antibody complexes.[179, 181, 183, 184] Monoclonal antibodies to TSST-I can prevent the development of manifestations of TSS in the rabbit model completely.[32, 218, 256]

High concentrations of antibodies to TSST-I and the staphylococcal enterotoxins (SEA; SEB; SEC types 1, 2, and 3; SED; and SEE) have been demonstrated in pooled IVIG.[43, 49, 216, 276] These antibodies may inhibit the binding of toxins to the MHC class II antigen-processing cells or interfere with toxin presentation by these cells to the TCR. As a result, production of TNF-α and TNF-β is inhibited by these antibodies in vitro in an apparent toxin-specific manner.[276] In vitro down-regulation of lymphokine production induced by streptococcal pyrogenic exotoxin A by IVIG also has been demonstrated.[199, 260]

The results of these in vitro studies have led to the suggestion that IVIG may be valuable in patients with both streptococcal and staphylococcal TSS.[235] Anecdotal case reports have indicated a beneficial effect for both streptococcal[16, 199, 312] and staphylococcal[2, 49, 57, 204, 216] TSS in humans. Until more information is available and because IVIG is expensive and most patients respond rapidly once standard therapeutic measures are initiated, most authors would reserve IVIG use for patients with an inaccessible focus of infection or those who continue to deteriorate after receiving fluid and vasopressor support for several hours (see Table 71–3). The dose most often used has been 400 mg/kg given as a single dose over the course of several hours. This dose results in a serum antibody titer of greater than 1:100, much higher than that appearing to provide immunity to TSST-I.[216] Because early administration of IVIG possibly could blunt the immune response to TSST-I or other toxins and increase the possibility of a recurrent episode, the potential risks and benefits of this form of therapy must be considered for each patient.

The role of endotoxin in the pathogenesis of TSS is unclear. The failure of polymyxin B and anti-J5 antiserum to alter the course of TSST-I–positive TSS in a rabbit model suggests that endotoxin may not be an important mediator of TSS in humans.[182]

Early and sporadic case reports of TSS have suggested therapeutic benefits of naloxone,[55] calcium,[216] and exchange transfusion in severely ill patients unresponsive to the usual forms of therapy.

SUBACUTE PHASE: AFTER TREATMENT IS INITIATED

Once treatment is initiated, the response usually is rapid. The temperature returns to normal within 48 hours. The hemodynamic changes are observed initially as tachycardia, decreased systemic vascular resistance, decreased central venous pressure, hypovolemia, a normal pulmonary artery wedge pressure, and an increased cardiac index.[13, 38, 63, 104, 107] Once aggressive fluid therapy has been initiated, myocardial edema and potential failure along with pulmonary and cerebral edema in the face of renal failure become the most critical management issues. The reasons for the myocardial failure are unclear but probably are related to perivascular inflammation of the coronary vessels, edema, and postulated myocardial depressant factors.[160, 213] TSST-I has been shown to inhibit systolic function in isolated rabbit atria, though at higher than usual circulating concentrations.[207] Arrhythmias may result from myocardial damage or electrolyte abnormalities.[177, 237] An endomyocardial biopsy from one patient with severe global hypokinesis of the left ventricle revealed no substantial inflammatory infiltrate but a mild to moderate number of T cells scattered diffusely throughout the biopsy specimen.[63]

During the decompensated stage of myocardial dysfunction, the cardiac index falls and pulmonary wedge pressure increases, with both left atrial and ventricular and diastolic diameters at the upper limits of normal.[104] Reversible electrocardiographic findings include sinus tachycardia, diffuse loss of voltage, flattened T waves, and diffuse nonspecific ST-T wave changes. If a fatal arrhythmia does not occur during the decompensated stage, the toxic cardiomyopathy is reversible and rarely results in permanent changes. This process is similar to "stunned myocardium," a transient, postischemic myocardial dysfunctional state.[63]

Pulmonary edema and adult respiratory distress syndrome occur commonly in severe disease when massive fluid replacement is necessary and the capillary leak syndrome continues in the lungs. Pulmonary edema appears rapidly once fluid replacement is initiated and often necessitates intubation and respirator management for several days.[280]

Forms of TSS-associated acute renal failure include prerenal azotemia and both nonoliguric and oliguric renal failure.[47] The form of renal failure manifested may be dependent on the degree of intravascular volume depletion. Unless severe acute tubular necrosis necessitates temporary hemodialysis, repletion of intravascular volume usually results in rapid restoration of renal function and, ultimately, diuresis. Permanent renal damage is an extremely rare event.[43]

The gastrointestinal, musculoskeletal, and hepatic changes resolve rapidly. Sequelae associated with these changes are rare, except for prolonged muscle weakness.[43, 74] Joint manifestations generally are self-limited.[20, 109]

Management of fluids, electrolytes, and metabolic acidosis in a patient with TSS is complex. Although tetany is a rare occurrence, this common severe hypocalcemia may be life-threatening and should be corrected.[48, 216, 265] Most patients require potassium replacement and management of metabolic acidosis. The use of colloid for fluid replacement and removal of the toxin stimulus for capillary leak syndrome ultimately correct the hypoproteinemia.

The typical dermatologic manifestations follow a predictable sequence (see Fig. 71–3). A dandruff-like flaky desquamation begins on the trunk and extremities 5 to 7 days after the onset of symptoms. From days 10 to 12 and for as long as a month, the characteristic full-thickness desquamation of the fingers, toes, palms, and soles takes place (Fig. 71–5). A variety of atypical dermatologic manifestations, including petechiae and subepidermal bullae, have been described.[10, 93, 134]

Early in the acute phase, many patients have desquamation of the mucous membranes, which is particularly painful when the oral mucous membranes are involved.[44] In addition, a small number of patients will have reactivated herpes simplex virus type 1 or 2 lesions with the acute illness.[44] A late-onset pruritic maculopapular rash with edema and

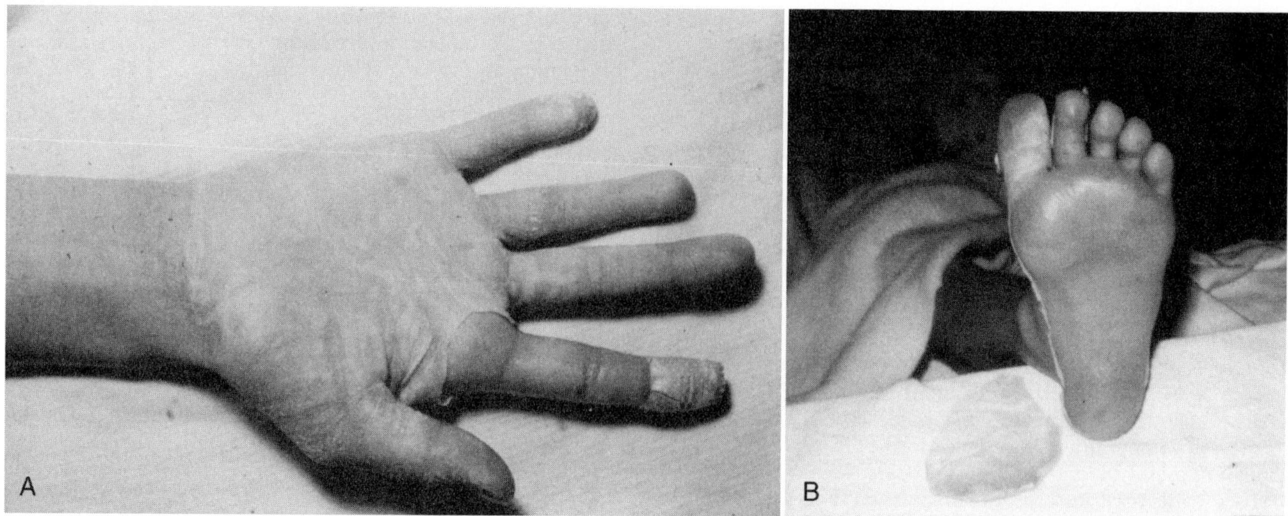

FIGURE 71–5 ■ Universal full-thickness desquamation of the hands *(A)* and feet *(B)* first noted 7 to 14 days after disease onset and with persistence for up to 30 days.

low-grade fever probably unrelated to antimicrobial therapy occurs in more than 50 percent of menses-associated cases within 7 to 14 days of disease onset.[44, 79] The cause of this late-onset rash is unknown.

Telogen effluvium, a common sequela, is a nonspecific response to severe trauma, sepsis, or stress that results in disturbed metabolism and keratinization of the hair follicles and nails. The hair follicles appear to transform prematurely from the growth, or anlagen, phase to the telogen, or resting, phase. Hair and nail loss occurs 4 to 16 weeks after the onset of illness, with restoration in 5 to 6 months.[20, 24, 44]

The hematologic system seldom is involved with major complications in TSS. Although disseminated intravascular coagulation may be present, gastrointestinal, uterine, or cerebral bleeding rarely occurs. Thrombocytopenia may be present initially in patients with disseminated intravascular coagulation; thrombocytosis is characteristic of the recovery phase. Mild to moderate normocytic, normochromic anemia, which probably is dilutional and a result of suppressed red blood cell synthesis, develops in virtually all moderately to severely ill patients with TSS and resolves during convalescence.[44, 46] Hypoferrinemia occurs commonly.[46]

The relatively common toxic or ischemic encephalopathy, rarely complicated by seizures, resolves slowly during the first 4 to 5 days of hospitalization.

OUTCOME AND SEQUELAE

Death associated with TSS usually occurs within the first few days of hospitalization, but it may occur as late as 15 days after admission. Fatalities have been attributed to refractory cardiac arrhythmias, cardiomyopathy, irreversible respiratory failure, and, rarely, bleeding caused by coagulation defects.[160, 213] The duration of circulation of toxins and mediators and the associated hypotension may be the best predictors of the severity of the end-organ damage.

After discharge, prolonged fatigue, muscle weakness, and pain are noted by most patients.[43] Sequelae attributed to TSS that appear to be related to a prolonged period of hypotension have included chronic renal failure, gangrene, and telogen effluvium.[74, 145, 186, 240, 244] Other sequelae, such as neuropsychologic abnormalities, prolonged myalgia and weakness, carpal tunnel syndrome, chronic dermatitis, Raynaud syndrome, new allergies, and recurrences, are explained less easily. Abnormalities such as impaired memory and poorly sustained concentration have been found in patients who did not require any therapy other than intravenous fluids to restore their blood pressure.[240] In one center, patients with nonmenstrual TSS had more serious short- and long-term neuropsychologic complications than did patients with menstrual TSS.[145] Sequelae related primarily to the neuromuscular system have resulted in speculation that the TSS-associated toxin may have a direct effect on nerve or muscle tissue. In one patient with TSS, a cauda equina syndrome with partial paralysis developed after lumbar laminectomy and staphylococcal meningitis, thus suggesting a neurotoxic effect of the intrathecally produced SEC.[8]

One study compared the sequelae and other long-term effects in 183 (174 menstrual cases) women with TSS and 366 control women hospitalized for appendicitis and appendectomy and matched for age, race, and duration of follow-up.[74] Each subject completed two comprehensive phone interviews. When compared with controls, women with TSS were significantly more likely to report sequelae involving fatigue, the integument (hair loss and nail changes), mental and cognitive skills (problems with concentration, reading difficulty, and memory loss), emotions (menses attitude and emotional changes), and multiple organ systems (conditions involving the joint, cardiac, muscle, and genitourinary systems). In addition, women with TSS were significantly more likely than were controls to report persistence of symptoms. Fertility patterns and pregnancy outcomes were similar in controls and women with TSS, both before and after the index illness.[74]

Recurrences

One of the most puzzling aspects of the pathophysiology of TSS is the high rate of recurrence in patients with inadequately treated menstrual or nonmenstrual disease.[6, 44, 70, 71, 175, 176] A small number of patients with menstrual disease and repeated tampon exposure have experienced as many as 6 to 12 recurrences. Recurrences associated with menstrual disease have no predictable pattern. In most patients, the first episode is the most severe. However, asymptomatic menses may occur between symptomatic episodes, and the most severe episode may occur after one or more milder episodes.[71] The use of antistaphylococcal antimicrobial therapy to which the organism is susceptible in doses recommended for serious infections for 10 to 14 days and discontinuation of tampon use can be expected to reduce the rate of recurrence significantly.[71] Recurrences after nonmenstrual TSS are well described and usually also associated with inadequate initial therapy.[6, 145, 216] Cisplatin administration resulting in significant hypomagnesemia precipitated several recurrent episodes of TSS in an immunocompromised adult.[23]

The absent or delayed antibody response to TSST-I found in both menstrual and nonmenstrual TSS patients probably accounts for the continued susceptibility to TSS and for the high recurrence rate.[20, 31, 166, 241, 272, 307] The fact that superantigenic toxins are not processed by antigen-processing cells and T lymphocytes as conventional antigens may provide an explanation for the poor convalescent antibody response to these antigens.[153]

Culture-negative, menses-associated, recurrent episodes of TSS continue to occur in a small number of patients despite discontinuation of tampon use and the administration of appropriate antimicrobial therapy during the acute episode.[71] Administration of an oral β-lactamase–resistant antistaphylococcal antimicrobial agent during menses has been tried in an attempt to prevent these recurrences but is not always successful. In recurrent cases resistant to this form of prophylaxis, consideration could be given to the untested and empirical use of rifampin, clindamycin, erythromycin, or IVIG (if the patient has no antibody to TSST-I) or to the use of an oral contraceptive.[175]

ATYPICAL MANIFESTATIONS

Mild Disease

Recognition of mild episodes of TSS is particularly important in patients with menstrual TSS because repeated use of tampons and the risk for recurrence are episodic.[45, 80, 291] Patients with mild or severe menstrual TSS typically do not form antibody to TSST-I during convalescence[20, 31, 241, 272, 307] and, without appropriate therapy, may have one or more recurrences. Such recurrences may be mild or severe.[70, 71, 176] Patients with nonmenstrual TSS also do not form antibodies in convalescence. A mild episode may be recognized only in retrospect, after desquamation or a recurrent episode (or both) develop.[216]

The presence of any combination of fever, headache, sore throat, diarrhea, vomiting, orthostatic dizziness, syncope, and myalgia in a menstruating woman or an individual with a potential *S. aureus* infection, no matter how trivial, should raise suspicion of TSS. A specific laboratory test to confirm the clinical diagnosis is not available. A bacterial culture positive for *S. aureus* may be helpful but is not diagnostic for menstrual cases because *S. aureus* may be cultured from the cervix or vagina of as many as 33 percent of menstruating women.[171, 221]

Other laboratory data usually do not reflect multisystem involvement in mild disease, and assays for TSST-I in body fluids are investigational.[178, 298] Diagnostic support for the theory that the patient's signs and symptoms represent mild TSS often depends on the constellation of findings, including subsequent typical desquamation of the palms, soles, toes, or fingers; demonstration that *S. aureus* isolates from the site of infection produce TSST-I or an enterotoxin; absence of antibody to TSST-I or enterotoxins in an acute-phase serum; and recurrent disease, if it develops.

Recalcitrant, Erythematous Desquamating Disorder

An atypical, subacute variant of TSS has been described in patients with acquired immunodeficiency syndrome (AIDS) and labeled the recalcitrant, erythematous, desquamating disorder. *S. aureus* strains producing TSST-I, SEA, or SEB have been isolated from patients with AIDS and prolonged erythema, extensive cutaneous desquamation, hypotension, tachycardia, and multiple and variable organ involvement.[57, 84, 151] The illness is recalcitrant, prolonged, and characterized by multiple recurrences. In one patient, elevated levels of TNF and IL-6 were found during severe episodes. When antitoxin antibodies have been measured during recurrence, they have been undetectable. Two patients responded well to IVIG.[57, 151] Patients with the combined cellular and humoral immunodeficiencies of AIDS may be at particular risk for development of severe, frequent, and prolonged recurrent episodes of TSS.[57, 84, 103, 151, 263] TSST-I and the enterotoxins may activate human immunodeficiency virus type 1 (HIV-1) gene expression in vivo, as has been observed in vitro.[113]

Nonmenstrual Disease

The incidence of postoperative cases of TSS after all types of surgery has been estimated to be 3 per 100,000 population.[120] For ear, nose, and throat surgery, the incidence is higher (16.5/100,000 population).[139] A striking feature of most postoperative cases with rapid onset is the absence of any signs of wound infection.[17, 120, 228, 242] The mean time from surgery to the onset of symptoms is 2 to 4 days.[16] Nosocomial acquisition of TSST-I–positive organisms rarely has been documented for postoperative cases.[9, 155, 196] A wide variety of types of surgery have been associated with TSS.[20, 40, 195, 206, 234, 258, 261]

Burn wounds provide a particularly rich environment for *S. aureus* growth and the production of toxins.* In burn centers, TSS occurs predominantly in young children with small burns.[90] In one large pediatric burn center, *S. aureus* normally was not cultured from any site on admission.[49] However, it was acquired within a few days of admission and became the most common wound pathogen. Of all wound isolates of *S. aureus*, only 16 percent produced TSST-I. Only 50 percent of the children had antibodies to TSST-I on admission, which reflects the low prevalence of antibodies in this population.[299] Of administered blood products, 76 percent had antibodies to TSST-I, and seroconversion occurred in children receiving these products. A TSS-like syndrome developed in 13 percent (7/53) of children, only 1 of whom had TSST-I–producing *S. aureus* isolated from the wound. SEA and SEB were produced by isolates from three patients. In burn patients, issues regarding the use of prophylactic antibiotics, occlusive dressings, and enhancement of production of TSST-I by topical antimicrobial agents are unsettled.[91] The mortality rate associated with TSS in children with burns may be as high as 57 percent.[112] Skin disrupted in any way, including by varicella or a tattoo, also may be a focus for TSS.[20, 35, 61]

Patients who have colonization of the anterior nares by *S. aureus* are at particular risk for the development of TSS when the respiratory mucosa is disrupted by surgery, trauma, or a respiratory infection such as influenza.[20, 59, 165, 287, 293] TSS has been reported in association with sinusitis,[20, 100] pharyngitis,[20, 245] parapharyngeal abscesses,[245] tracheitis,[20, 67, 85, 115, 202] pneumonia,[20, 69] rubeola,[275] and submandibular space abscesses. TSS occurring after ear, nose, and throat

*See references 11, 49, 56, 90, 112, 114, 118, 130, 168, 172, 303.

surgery has been associated with the use of nasal splints and packing materials and in part may be the result of interruption of the ciliary blanket.[3, 20, 111, 191, 313]

After orthopedic procedures or in association with bone and joint infections, the clinical manifestation of TSS may be confusing as a result of the intense and generalized myalgias associated with TSS, which may be misinterpreted as postoperative musculoskeletal symptoms. The wounds usually appear to be benign.[20, 190, 222, 278, 294] Infected abrasions under casts may be focal sites of TSST-I production.[264]

In one center, when cases of nonmenstrual TSS were compared with menstrual cases, patients with nonmenstrual disease were found to have a delayed onset of symptoms after the precipitating event, more frequent central nervous system manifestations, less frequent musculoskeletal involvement (myalgia and arthralgia), and a higher degree of anemia.[145] Recurrences occurred in both groups in untreated patients, and mortality rates were not different. Clinical differences between the two categories are suggested to be related to differences in the types of toxins produced. TSST-I was produced with comparable frequency in both groups. SEA was produced less often by nonmenstrual isolates, and menstrual isolates more often produced both TSST-I and SEA. SEB was produced more often by nonmenstrual isolates.

Several patients with TSS have been reported to have simultaneous infection with *S. aureus* and *S. pyogenes*.[92] Determining which infection primarily was responsible for the manifestations or whether an amplified effect of exotoxins from both organisms was present was not possible.

Streptococcal Toxic Shock–like Syndrome

An increase in the incidence and severity of invasive *S. pyogenes* infections has occurred during the last decade. Manifestations of severe disease have included septicemia with or without a focus of infection; severe, painful cellulitis; necrotizing fasciitis; and, in some cases, a streptococcal toxic shock–like syndrome with or without a focus of infection. Streptococcal toxic shock–like syndrome is similar to staphylococcal TSS in that it appears to be mediated by superantigenic toxins and results in endothelial damage, hypotension, and multisystem organ involvement. Streptococcal toxic shock–like syndrome differs from staphylococcal TSS in numerous respects, including a slower onset over several days; usual absence of vomiting, profuse diarrhea, and conjunctival infection; frequent absence of erythroderma or the presence of only a sandpaper-like rash; severe generalized hyperesthesia; extreme pain at the site of skin involvement; and a mortality rate of 40 to 50 percent.[58, 269]

UNIQUE MANIFESTATIONS

Work with superantigens suggests that the pathophysiologic events observed in TSS are the result of release of endogenous mediators after monocyte and T-cell activation by TSST-I or the staphylococcal enterotoxins.

The physiologic changes induced by this dysregulation of the immune system are striking in their rapidity of onset and progression and the involvement of almost all body tissues and organs. The consequent functional disorders of many organs appear to be the result of extensive endothelial damage and loss of peripheral vascular resistance. The generalized decrease in vasomotor tone results in pooling of blood in the peripheral vasculature, vascular congestion, and probable relaxation of the microcirculation. Rapid, nonhydrostatic leakage of fluid from the intravascular to the interstitial space, or "second spacing," does occur and is manifested as extensive generalized anasarca-like, nonpitting edema. The universal hypoproteinemia and hypoalbuminemia in patients with TSS suggest that the fluid that leaks from the vasculature is high in protein.

Unique clinical manifestations include the profuse vomiting and diarrhea often associated with incontinence; generalized erythroderma; intense erythema of mucous membranes, including conjunctival injection and subconjunctival hemorrhages; absence of inflammation in surgical wounds and other focal sites of infection; absence of bacteremia; severe hypocalcemia and hypophosphatemia; rapidly accelerated renal dysfunction; universal desquamation of the palms, soles, fingers, and toes; and risk for recurrent disease and long-term cognitive sequelae.

Diagnosis

Application of the case definition for a single episode[305] or recurrent episodes[71] to the patient's illness is currently the only way to confirm the diagnosis (see Table 71–1). Aggressive attempts that always should be made to find the focus of *S. aureus* replication include taking cultures of the cervix and vagina in patients with menses-associated illness and other potentially infected sites that may not obviously appear to be infected in patients with nonmenstrual illness. *S. aureus* isolates could be examined, when possible, for their ability to produce TSST-I, although such testing seldom is indicated. This test is of limited usefulness for nonmenstrual cases because TSST-I is produced by only 40 to 60 percent of *S. aureus* isolates from such patients.[116] Isolates from these patients could be examined for the presence of the other enterotoxins. Acute and convalescent sera can be tested for the presence of antibodies to TSST-I and the other enterotoxins.[132] Elevated levels of anti–TSST-I in the acute-phase serum of a patient with menstrual-associated TSS would be highly unusual.

In most instances, toxin detection tests are of value only for research or for the rare patient with chronic recurrent or otherwise puzzling disease. Genes for TSST-I and the enterotoxins have been detected in *S. aureus* strains by polymerase chain reaction[144] and hybridization techniques.[143, 200, 209] A noncompetitive enzyme-linked immunosorbent assay allows quantitation of TSST-I in clinical samples.[178, 193] Reversed passive latex agglutination has been used in hospital laboratories to detect TSST-I and in research laboratories to detect enterotoxins.[78, 95]

Differential Diagnosis

The differential diagnosis of TSS includes clinical entities in which a rapid onset of fever, erythroderma-like rash, hypotension, and multisystem involvement are observed[39, 101, 194, 216, 223, 225] (Table 71–4).

Prevention and Prophylaxis

To decrease the risk of development of menstrual TSS, in 1982 the Institute of Medicine Committee on TSS recommended that women, particularly adolescents, minimize their use of high-absorbency tampons.[226] The committee also recommended that women who have had TSS not use tampons because of the increased risk of recurrence and that postpartum women be informed that the use of tampons might increase their risk for development of TSS.

TABLE 71–4 ■ DIFFERENTIAL DIAGNOSIS OF TOXIC SHOCK SYNDROME BASED ON CLINICAL MANIFESTATIONS

Diagnosis	Fever	Exanthem	Shock
Severe invasive *Streptococcus pyogenes* infections	+	+	+
Meningococcemia	+	+	+
Rocky Mountain spotted fever	+	+	±
Ehrlichioisis	+	+	±
Kawasaki disease	+	+	−
Staphylococcal scalded skin syndrome	+	+	−
Toxic epidermal necrolysis	+	+	−
Viral syndromes	+	+	−
Leptospirosis	+	+	−
Systemic lupus erythematosus	+	+	−
Erythema multiforme	+	+	−
Septic shock	+	−	+
Hantavirus pulmonary syndrome	+	−	+
Salmonella infections	+	−	±
Gastroenteritis	+	−	−
Urinary tract infection	+	−	−
Drug reactions			
Phenytoin (Dilantin)	+	+	±
Cocaine	+	+	±
Pseudoephedrine	+	+	±
Inhalational mercury	+	+	±
Quinidine	+	+	−
Sulfonamides	+	+	−
β-Lactam antibiotics	+	+	−
Quinolones	+	+	−

Although the frequency of changing tampons during a menstrual period has not been associated with risk for development of TSS, the use of an individual tampon for no more than 12 hours at a time might decrease the risk of development of menstrual TSS. Women using intravaginal contraceptive devices also should be informed of the potential increase in risk for developing TSS.[255]

Although postoperative TSS is a rare event, it generally occurs in healthy people. As a result of the unexpected and potentially severe consequences of TSS, issues regarding surgical antimicrobial prophylaxis for prevention have been raised. Perioperative systemic antistaphylococcal antibiotics did not prevent TSS in four patients[33, 242] and do not eradicate nasal carriage of *S. aureus*.[141] TSS with onset after 48 hours of amoxicillin therapy was reported in two patients after endonasal sinus surgery.[2] Topical bacitracin ointment on nasal packing does not prevent the development of TSS.[33, 81, 139, 141]

Most authors think that the rare risk of development of postoperative TSS is comparable to the risk of having a severe antimicrobial reaction and that perioperative antimicrobial prophylaxis is not indicated for clean procedures of short duration.[120, 228] Effort should be intensified to recognize postoperative cases early; to open, explore extensively, and irrigate wounds; and to provide immediate antimicrobial and supportive therapy for suspected TSS.

Characteristics of Toxic Shock Syndrome–Associated *Staphylococcus aureus* Isolates

The ability to produce TSST-I, a previously uncharacterized protein, is the single most distinguishing characteristic of TSS-associated *S. aureus* strains. More than 90 percent of *S. aureus* isolates from patients with menstrual TSS[21, 252] and 40 to 60 percent of isolates from patients with nonmenstrual disease[116] produce TSST-I as compared with less than 20 percent of non-TSS strains.

S. aureus strains isolated from patients with TSS are phenotypically different from other strains of *S. aureus*.[20, 282] They produce less beta-hemolysis on sheep blood agar and less frequently harbor plasmids than control strains do. An increase in protease production and proteolytic activity by TSS-associated strains has been noted.[282] Next to TSST-I production, production of protease is the most characteristic marker for these strains.

Unlike non-TSS *S. aureus* strains, most TSST-I–positive strains of *S. aureus* require tryptophan for growth and production.[54] In one study, 91 percent of 27 TSST-I–positive vaginal *S. aureus* isolates were tryptophan auxotrophs as compared with 6 percent of 32 TSST-I–negative vaginal *S. aureus* isolates. Eight of 22 TSST-I–producing tryptophan auxotrophs were blocked at the tryptophan synthetase B locus, which suggests that the TSST-I gene cluster may have been inserted into this locus and disrupted its function.

Additional differences between TSS and non-TSS strains of *S. aureus* include the resistance of TSS strains to cadmium, arsenate, and penicillin, characteristics that usually are plasmid-mediated but, in TSS strains, are chromosomally mediated. As such, these traits must be the result of heterologous insertions. These characteristics are not cotransferred with and, therefore, presumably not closely linked to the gene segment responsible for TSST-I production.[20, 282] TSST-I production is unrelated to methicillin susceptibility or resistance.[253]

Roles of the Staphylococcal Exotoxin TSST-I and the Enterotoxins in Toxic Shock Syndrome

ROLE OF TSST-I

TSST-I appears to be an important toxin in TSS. Factors supporting this statement include (1) the observation that more than 90 percent of isolates from patients with TSS produce TSST-I, (2) the absence of acute-phase antibody to TSST-I in more than 90 percent of patients with menstrual TSS, (3) the increase in anti–TSST-I antibody during recovery in nonmenstrual cases, (4) absent or low levels of antibody in patients with recurrent menstrual TSS, (5) comparable illness inducible with TSST-I in in vivo animal models, and (6) neutralization of IL-1 stimulation and response to TSST-I by antibody to TSST-I.

Most convincing are experiments in which the ability to cause TSS followed bacteriophage-mediated transfer of the TSST-I–positive chromosomal segment into a recipient *S. aureus* strain without the segment.[77, 216] Experiments demonstrating the effectiveness of monoclonal antibodies to TSST-I in reversing the effects of TSST-I provide additional strong support.[157]

ROLES OF ENTEROTOXINS

Because 40 to 60 percent of nonmenstrual TSS *S. aureus* isolates and 5 to 10 percent of menstrual TSS isolates do not produce TSST-I, a role for other staphylococcal exotoxins, including the enterotoxins, has been proposed.[20, 62, 163, 174, 217, 248, 311] Patients with nonmenstrual disease infected with TSST-I–negative strains may have a higher mortality rate.[116] Significant increases in the titer of antibody to the staphylococcal enterotoxins during convalescence strongly suggest a role for these proteins in the pathogenesis of TSS.[12]

In rabbit models, morbidity and mortality occurring after the injection of TSST-I–negative TSS isolates were comparable to those occurring after infection with TSST-I–positive strains and significantly greater than after inoculation with TSST-I–negative non-TSS isolates.[116] Administration of staphylococcal enterotoxins to animals results in many of the manifestations characteristic of TSS.[19, 94]

When large numbers of isolates from patients with TSS have been examined, production of TSST-I alone is the toxin pattern identified most commonly.[20, 62, 169] Other patterns identified include production of TSST-I in combination with one or more of the identified enterotoxins, production of enterotoxins *only* (one or more), and nonproduction of TSST-I and enterotoxins. Of the TSS strains producing TSST-I, 60.6 percent also produce an enterotoxin.[62, 169] SEA is co-expressed with TSST-I frequently, particularly in menstrual isolates. A clone producing both TSST-I and SEA is associated with 88 percent of menstrual TSS cases and may account for as many as 54 percent of isolates from nonmenstrual TSS cases.[41] Seroconversion to SEA occurs more commonly in TSS than in non-TSS *S. aureus* infection, further suggesting a role for SEA. TSST-I and SEA have a common MHC class II–binding domain and share overlapping domains critical for superantigenic and lethal activities. A monoclonal antibody to TSST-I inhibits these SEA-induced activities.[158]

The third most common pattern of toxin production by TSS isolates is that of TSST-I plus SEC. These isolates have been associated with both menstrual and nonmenstrual cases and particularly with severe respiratory tract TSS-associated infections.[62]

The fourth most common pattern of toxin production is that of SEB alone. In one study, strains producing SEB alone accounted for 38 percent of all nonmenstrual TSS isolates.[163, 248] This prevalence is significantly higher than for isolates from non-TSS *S. aureus* infections (15%) or asymptomatic carriers (13%). SEB never is co-expressed with TSST-I. Even though all TSST-I–positive isolates contain the SEB genetic determinant, none produces SEB. SEB is produced only by isolates that have the SEB gene and no TSST-I gene. Given that production of both toxins is mutually exclusive and both genes are located close together on the chromosome, researchers have suggested that the TSST-I genetic determinant may have a preferred site of insertion within the SEB genetic element. Because the TSST-I gene is associated with a variable genetic element and such mobile genetic elements are known to be capable of gene disruption, the gene possibly was inserted within the SEB gene or in a position to interfere with its transcription.[78]

TSS isolates producing TSST-I plus two other enterotoxins in combination are the fifth most common combination, and isolates producing no known toxins are the sixth. The identification of new enterotoxins[233, 273] capable of producing a TSS-like disease in rabbits may account for isolates previously identified as producing no toxins. Isolates producing a non-SEB enterotoxin alone are the least common.

Prevalence of Exotoxin-Producing *Staphylococcus aureus* Strains and Antibody to the Exotoxins

PREVALENCE OF EXOTOXIN-PRODUCING ORGANISMS

TSST-I–positive strains of *S. aureus* have been present since at least 1957, and antibody to TSST-I was as prevalent in a general population in 1960 as it was in 1983.[299] Thus, the increase in incidence of TSS from 1980 to 1985 is assumed to have been the result of newly introduced cofactors rather than the result of an increase in the prevalence of TSST-I–positive organisms.

At any given time, *S. aureus* is present in 20 to 40 percent of cultures from the anterior nasal vestibule of adults and in as many as 33 percent of nasal cultures from children.[138] In women, the prevalence of *S. aureus* in vaginal cultures is higher during menses than at midcycle.[171, 208] Vaginal carriage rates vary from 7 percent in premenarcheal and nonmenstruating women to 33 percent in menstruating women.[221] TSST-I–positive *S. aureus* is present in 1 to 5 percent of vaginal cultures in women, 7 percent of nasal cultures in hospitalized patients, and 18 percent of nasal cultures in children. In prospective studies of *S. aureus* isolates from healthy individuals and from specimens received for other purposes, 14 to 39 percent of all isolates produced TSST-I and 7 to 14 percent produced SEB.[80, 216] Overall, between 1 and 4 percent of healthy individuals at any given time are colonized at a mucosal site with TSST-I–positive *S. aureus*.

Of 60 *S. aureus* isolates from blood cultures of patients who did not have TSS, 28 percent produced TSST-I.[43] Presumably, these patients had circulating antibody to TSST-I that prevented the development of TSS despite an *S. aureus* infection. Adults and children who have persistent nasal carriage with a TSST-I–positive strain have high levels of antibody to TSST-I.[236]

Evidence suggests that a single clone of *S. aureus* causes most cases of TSS.[41, 198] Multilocus enzyme electrophoresis has demonstrated that the TSST-I gene *tst*H is distributed widely over the whole spectrum of *S. aureus* genotypes. Of 315 *S. aureus* strains collected from around the world, 88 percent of menstrual TSS strains and 53 percent of nonmenstrual strains were indistinguishable by multilocus enzyme electrophoresis. The same clone also was found in 28 percent of vaginal isolates from asymptomatic women. This remarkable phenomenon may reflect the unique ability of this clone to colonize the urogenital epithelium or the unique capability of this clone to cause disease. Although TSS strains are similar in gene content, indicative of a common ancestor, their considerable heterogeneity indicates that the common ancestor was not recent in evolutionary time.[108] Thus, the TSS outbreak was the result of a change in the host environment and not the geographic dissemination of a new "hypervirulent" strain.[108]

Even though TSST-I–positive strains may cluster within families, living units, and hospital settings, the occurrence of TSS clusters is a rare event.[155, 196] Probable TSS has developed within 24 hours in a husband and wife[105] and in two mother-daughter pairs. Nosocomial acquisition and transmission of TSST-I–positive organisms have been described.[9, 155, 196]

PREVALENCE OF ANTIBODY TO EXOTOXINS

The prevalence of antibody to TSST-I in 689 Wisconsin residents was found to be 47 percent at 1 year of age, 58 percent at 5 years, 70 percent at 10 years, 88 percent at 20 years, and 96 percent for ages 30 to 50 during the years 1960 to 1983 (see Fig. 71–2).[299] The presence of transplacentally acquired antibody in more than 90 percent of infants also was demonstrated. No significant gender differences were found in antibody prevalence. Mucosal colonization with TSST-I–positive *S. aureus* strains is assumed to result in antibody formation[236] because more than 90 percent of adults have antibody to TSST-I and have never had TSS. This assumption is supported by data from a burn unit staffed by a nurse in whom recurrent TSS developed. Personnel in the unit were demonstrated to be colonized by TSST-I–positive strains and to form antibody to TSST-I but not acquire TSS during a period of several months.[9] Subclinical and mild, unrecognized disease[45] also may result in the formation of antibodies.

The acquisition of antibodies to the enterotoxins also is age related. By the age of 10 years, the percentage of children with antibody titers of 1:100 or higher is 15 percent for SEA, 65 percent for SEB, 30 percent for SEC, 5 percent for SED, and 20 percent for SEE. By 22 years of age, the numbers increase to 55 percent for SEA, 77 percent for SEB, and 98 percent for SEC.[20]

The prevalence of antibody varies from one area of the country to another. During 1982, of 1017 serum samples obtained from U.S. Air Force recruits between the ages of 17 and 26 years, 35 percent from the Mountain and Pacific states were serosusceptible to TSST-I versus 3 percent from the south Atlantic states and 5 percent from the east south central states. Because low titers appear to indicate susceptibility, the findings in this study suggest that differences in TSS incidence between states and regions were explained in part by differences in host susceptibility.[297]

Sera randomly selected from 87 control women were seronegative more frequently for antibody to TSST-I (24%) than were those from 66 control men (9%), which led to the suggestion that women may be more susceptible to TSS than men are.[241] Patients in whom TSS develops have significantly lower levels of antibody to SEB and SEC, as well as to TSST-I, than does the general population.[20, 62]

As noted in the discussion on recurrence, acute-phase sera of patients with TSS uniformly demonstrate absent or low levels of antibody to TSST-I. The antibody response to TSST-I is absent or delayed in both menstrual and nonmenstrual TSS.[216, 272]

Physicochemical and Biologic Characteristics of TSST-I

PHYSICOCHEMICAL PROPERTIES

The mature secreted TSST-I protein is a single polypeptide chain with a molecular weight of 22,000 d and an isoelectric point of 7.2. It is resistant to proteolytic digestion by trypsin but is hydrolyzed by pepsin at pH 4.5. In sterile solution at neutral pH, it is stable for months. When lyophilized, it is a white powder easily dissolved in distilled water. No loss of serologic activity of the lyophilized powder occurs for at least a year. TSST-I can be heated to 100° C for longer than an hour without loss of biologic activity.[27]

Purification of TSST-I has yielded diffraction-quality crystals that have led to an understanding of its three-dimensional structure.[27] The molecule is folded into two closely associated domains that create two major grooves, the front and backside grooves. The backside groove is larger and more exposed to the external environment. The crystal structures of all the protein superantigens have striking similarity in the two-domain conformational architecture, even though the primary protein segments are different.[173]

REGULATION OF PRODUCTION

S. aureus is highly adaptable and able to live and grow in extremes of temperature, pH, and oxygen concentration. TSST-I production, however, is controlled tightly. TSST-I is not produced in unfavorable conditions, including an anaerobic environment, pH values less than 6.0 and greater than 8.0, concentrations of clindamycin below the MIC of the organism, glucose concentrations greater than 3 percent, and temperatures less than 37° C or greater than 40° C.[20, 27, 310] Conditions and factors that enhance TSST-I production include uniform aeration of medium through shaking or a roller apparatus, complex medium containing animal protein and low glucose concentrations, a neutral pH, incubation in 5 percent carbon dioxide (under some in vitro conditions), and temperatures of 37 to 40° C. The role of magnesium is unclear.[82] Twice as much toxin is produced at 40° C as at 37° C. The addition of blood to media does not increase TSST-I production reliably. Depending on in vitro growth conditions, most strains of TSST-I–negative *S. aureus* produce 3 μg/mL of TSST-I, but some may produce up to 30 μg/mL.

Under optimal in vitro growth conditions, TSST-I production lags behind but parallels bacterial growth. Like other *S. aureus* exotoxins, TSST-I is made primarily during the postexponential phase of growth, when nutrients are scarce and cell density is great.[80] Levels of TSST-I remain stable throughout the stationary phase, even after the organisms begin to die. Under less than optimal conditions, synchronous production of TSST-I and growth of *S. aureus* do not occur. For example, bacterial growth may be reduced only twofold in an anaerobic environment, whereas TSST-I production is inhibited. Likewise, clindamycin at concentrations below the MIC for the organism will inhibit the production of toxins without altering growth.[251]

Most strains of *S. aureus* do not have the genes for TSST-I or the enterotoxins. TSST-I is, thus, not necessary for bacterial homeostasis, and its production is a variable genetic trait.

The gene *tst*H is encoded by a transposon-like mobile genetic element.[54, 78, 135, 156] The chromosomal fragment with the structural gene for production of TSST-I is a 10.6-kb unit that has been cloned in *Escherichia coli*. *tst*H has been sequenced and encodes a 234–amino acid protein that is converted by the removal of a signal peptide of 40 amino acids to the mature exotoxin of 194 amino acids.[27, 80, 156] *tst*H has been inserted in the chromosome to disrupt both the tryptophan synthetase B and SEB genes, thereby preventing the production of both proteins.[54, 78]

The production of TSST-I and other postexponential-phase virulence factors is regulated by three separate genetic loci: the accessory gene regulator *(agr)*, the staphylococcal accessory regulator *(sar)*, and the extracellular protein regulator *(xpr)*.[12, 27, 80] All three regulators affect gene expression primarily at the level of transcription. During the late log phase of bacterial growth, they activate the expression of TSST-I, alpha- and gamma-hemolysins, serine protease, and nuclease and down-regulate the expression of cell wall–associated proteins, fibronectin-binding protein, protein A, and coagulase. Beta-hemolysin, SEB, SEC, and exfoliative toxin A are regulated less tightly by *agr* than is TSST-I. SEA appears to be independent of *agr* in some strains. This complex regulation of exoprotein synthesis probably is the result of a complex interaction between environmental factors and gene products.[27, 80] These regulatory functions explain why the production of TSST-I is stimulated under some conditions without SEA or SEC stimulation.[310]

Glyceryl monolaurate is a mild surfactant and emulsifier commonly used in the food and cosmetic industries. It is capable of inhibiting the production of staphylococcal and streptococcal exotoxins at concentrations subinhibitory to growth.[37, 180, 227, 249] As a lipophilic compound, the mechanism of action appears to be that of insertion into the cell membrane with resulting interruption of signal transduction. Other surfactants used in the tampon industry have been found to both inhibit and enhance[250] the production of TSST-I in vitro.

KINETICS OF DISTRIBUTION

Detecting TSST-I in body fluids is difficult. In humans, nanogram quantities have been detected by radioimmunoassay in the breast milk of a woman with TSS,[136, 298] in serum early during illness in two of four patients,[178] in urine, and in vaginal washings in a small number of patients.[178] By means of the rabbit subcutaneous Wiffle ball abscess model, TSST-I can be detected first in the abscess fluid 4 hours after *S. aureus* has been inoculated into the Wiffle ball and can be detected in urine until 48 hours after inoculation.[178]

For further examination of in vivo target tissues for TSST-I activity, purified TSST-I radiolabeled with iodine 139 has been injected intravenously into rabbits. Measurement of plasma clearance demonstrated a half-life of 1.5 hours. Within 15 minutes of injection, TSST-I was concentrated fourfold in blood cells in comparison to plasma. Toxin persisted in the cellular compartment, and plasma concentrations fell. After 3 hours, most of the radiolabel was found in the spleen.

Recent studies provide evidence that TSST-I, SEA, and SEB can cross epithelial membranes intact and in a fully functional form. Whether such transport is mediated by a receptor-facilitated or nonspecific mechanism is not clear.[123]

CELLULAR INTERACTIONS

TSST-I has been shown to inhibit systolic function in isolated rabbit atria.[207] It also can bind directly to human and porcine endothelial cells and is cytotoxic for porcine endothelial cells because it permits leakage across endothelial cell monolayers.[159, 162] However, the concentrations of TSST-I needed to induce these and other diverse cytotoxic changes in vitro are higher than the usual tissue and serum levels are. The interactions of TSST-I and the enterotoxins with T lymphocytes and antigen-processing cells are described in the next section.

BIOLOGIC FUNCTIONS

Animal Models

Much information regarding pathogenesis has been obtained from both the subcutaneous Wiffle ball and the vaginal tampon rabbit models and a primate model.[76] Rabbits, primates, and other species have been examined for sensitivity to TSST-I or TSS-associated strains of *S. aureus*.[215] Rabbits and baboons exhibit clinical and laboratory changes most consistent with the human syndrome, including pyrogenicity and lethality.* The signs and symptoms observed in these animals after the intravenous injection of purified TSST-I include skin erythema, conjunctivitis, diarrhea, lethargy, tachypnea, respiratory distress, central nervous system changes, and increased capillary permeability, as demonstrated by the skin bluing technique. A variety of laboratory abnormalities consistent with those described in human TSS have been described for these models.

*See references 29, 30, 76, 77, 179, 180, 182, 184, 217, 229, 252, 256.

Immunoregulatory Activities

The absence of in vitro cytotoxicity of TSST-I[20, 215] despite potent in vivo biologic effects has suggested an important role for endogenous mediators in TSS. The ability of SEB to induce dramatic T-cell proliferation was recognized a decade ago.[147, 153, 170] Subsequent work has shown it to be a feature of other bacterial exotoxins, including TSST-I, the staphylococcal enterotoxins, the streptococcal pyrogenic exotoxins A and C, a new streptococcal superantigen, and a streptococcal M surface protein.[153] Since the late 1980s, activation of T cells by these bacterial components or products has become an area of intense interest. The term *superantigen* was coined in 1989 to describe antigens that at concentrations lower than those of conventional antigens (picomolar concentrations) can stimulate proliferation of a large percentage of T cells bearing a TCR beta-chain variable (V_β) sequence or sequences specific for each superantigen. Such activation and proliferation of T cells result in profound alterations in immune system homeostasis by inducing the release of large quantities of both monokines (IL-1, TNF-α) and lymphokines (IL-2, TNF-β).[153, 259, 315]

T cells are activated to produce lymphokines as a result of TCR-antigen binding and activation of signal transduction.[42, 266] Antigens can bind to the TCR in one of two forms: as conventional antigens or superantigens. Conventional antigens enter antigen-processing cells by endocytosis. They are broken into small peptides in the lysosomal compartments of the antigen-processing cell and targeted to small vesicles, where they form complexes with one of the allele-restricted MHC class II molecules (HLA-DQ, HLA-DP, and HLA-DR).[259] The complex then is transported to the cell surface, where it is bound in the groove on the heavy chain formed by the alpha and beta chains of the class II molecule. Certain amino acids in residues at critical points in the peptide's sequence anchor the peptides in the groove, and this interaction is moderately specific for each different allelic form of the MHC molecule.[259] This complex of peptide and MHC molecule of the same allelic type as the T cell is recognized by the TCR.

The TCR is composed of both alpha and beta glycoprotein chains, each of which is composed of variable (V) and joining (J) segments. The beta chain has an additional diversity (D) segment. As many as 50 V_β and 32 V_α segments are present on human T cells. The $V_{\alpha\beta\alpha\beta\beta}$ segments each are encoded by different genes that undergo gene rearrangement to give more than 10,000 possible combinations to recognize conventional antigenic peptides presented by the antigen-processing cells.[16, 259] Conventional antigens presented as peptides must be recognized by a specific combination of these elements. Thus, one peptide will activate only 1 in 10^4 to 10^6 T cells, and only $CD4^+$ T cells respond to conventional antigens.

In contrast, superantigens are presented to T lymphocytes in a very different fashion. They bind first as intact proteins (small fragments are inactive) to most allelic forms of MHC class II molecules in an unrestricted fashion at a site outside the peptide-binding groove. They then react with the TCR only through the V_β element or elements specific for that molecule and will react with all T cells carrying that V_β element.[133] Because only 25 to 50 major families of V_β genes exist in humans, each superantigen can interact with 5 to 20 percent of resting T cells, depending on the frequency of T cells expressing that V_β family in each individual's repertoire. Both $CD4^+$ and $CD8^+$ T cells are activated. Features unique to the presentation of superantigens to the TCR V_β receptor thus include the requirement for initial superantigen binding to the MHC class II molecule (even if unrestricted and not self) outside the antigen-presenting groove and the requirement for an intact superantigen protein.

Once the T cell has recognized the superantigen,[121] both antigen-processing cell and T-cell activation by signal transduction[42] results in cytokine release by the antigen-processing cell (IL-1, TNF-α) and the lymphocyte (IL-2, TNF-β). In mice and possibly also in humans, the initial T-cell activation occurs in lymph nodes.[189] Within hours of T-cell activation by superantigens, cytokines are detected in vitro and in serum in vivo.

TSST-I binds only to the $V_\beta2$ element.[238] In humans with TSS caused by TSST-I–secreting *S. aureus*, within 10 to 14 days 30 to 70 percent of the circulating T-cell population will be T cells bearing the $V_\beta2$ element.[50, 51] The number of circulating $V_\beta2$ T cells does not return to normal for several months. In contrast, patients with TSS caused by *S. pyogenes* have a consistent pattern of depletion of certain V_β T-cell types after T-cell activation.[153, 203, 302] In mice, such depletion is thought to be the result of programmed cell death (apoptosis).[187, 188]

Thus, activation of T cells by superantigens may result in massive cytokine release with subsequent selected V_β T-cell expansion, T-cell deletion, or apoptosis, depending on the superantigen and species. The fact that superantigens bind only to selected and specific V_β elements distinguishes them from the nondiscriminating mitogens.

Activation of monocytes and lymphocytes by superantigens involves signal transduction. Activation of both src protein tyrosine kinases and protein kinase C occurs in a manner common to that of other immunoglobulin supergene family members. MHC class II cells also are expressed on beta, endothelial, and dendritic cells. In some instances, superantigens may activate these cells uniquely.

Convincing evidence from the mouse model supports a central role for T-lymphocyte activation in superantigen-mediated disease. Mice that have received cyclosporine to block T-cell activation and lymphokine production or mice with severe combined immunodeficiency disease are protected against SEB-induced lethal shock. Repopulation with T cells results in susceptibility to SEB. The same mice are not protected against endotoxin-induced shock because lipopolysaccharide activates only monocytes.[187–189]

Mononuclear production of IL-1 and TNF-α is central to shock induced by endotoxin. Production of these two cytokines in addition to production of the lymphokines IL-2, IFN-α, and TNF-β may explain the enhanced severity of superantigen-associated TSS.[28, 121, 153] These powerful effects on the immune system may account for the tenacity of shock in otherwise healthy individuals. If more than one superantigen is produced by an organism (e.g., TSST-I plus one or more enterotoxins), different V_β specificities would result in an even greater number of T cells being activated, with the potential for development of enhanced disease severity and mortality.

Once superantigens have resulted in monokine and lymphokine release, the subsequent pathophysiologic events appear to be related to the many and complex interactions of these cytokines,[28, 125, 314] with the ultimate result being profound endothelial damage. TNF-α and TNF-β and the complex interaction of cytokines, leukotrienes, prostaglandins, adhesion molecules, nitric oxide, platelet-activating factor, complement components, neutrophils, platelets, and endothelium-derived factors appear to be responsible for the extensive endothelial damage and resulting capillary fluid leakage and decrease in peripheral vascular resistance.[28, 125, 243, 314] In a different setting of antineoplastic therapy, high doses of IL-2 and lymphokine-activated killer cells induce the capillary leak syndrome, which is characterized by rapid weight gain, anasarca, pulmonary edema, hypoalbuminemia, and multiple organ dysfunctions in humans.[60, 152]

Endotoxin Enhancement

A striking property of TSST-I is its marked ability to enhance the susceptibility of some animals to lethal endotoxin shock.[27, 247, 252] Intravenous administration of TSST-I to rabbits at less than 1/20th the median lethal dose (LD_{50}) followed 2 hours later by endotoxin at less than 1/500th the LD_{50} results in 50 to 100 percent mortality, a 10,000-fold enhancement. In vitro, endotoxin enhances IL-1 production by TSST-I–stimulated monocytes.[18] Whether enhanced endotoxin susceptibility plays any role in human disease is not clear.[52]

STRUCTURE-FUNCTION RELATIONSHIPS

Effort to understand the molecular actions of TSST-I has focused on separating regions that interact with the TCR from those required for lethality.[27, 29, 30, 197] Through the use of TSST-I variants (TSST-ovine and TSST-bovine) and TSST-I molecules with single amino acid mutations, the areas responsible for binding of TSST-I to both the TCR and to the macrophage class II MHC molecule have been defined.[27] In animal models, lethality, induction of fever, and endotoxin susceptibility do not depend on T-cell proliferation as measured by superantigenic activity but must involve interaction of toxin with other host-cell receptors in the body.[27]

Most secreted bacterial superantigens are small, compact globular proteins of 20 to 30 kd.[27] They are protease-, heat-, and acid-resistant and share immunologic, biologic, and functional properties. However, they do not share sequence homology. Although they do not share obvious structural features that would predict their superantigen properties, they may share a common conformational structure.[153] The secreted exotoxins can be divided into two groups based on their amino acid sequence homology. In group 1, SEA, SED, and SEE share 54 to 90 percent homology. In group 2, streptococcal pyrogenic exotoxin A, SEB, and SEC-1, SEC-2, and SEC-3 share 46 to 68 percent homology. In group 3, TSST-I, the exfoliative toxins, and streptococcal pyrogenic exotoxin show no significant homology to each other or to any of the members of group 1 or 2. However, all the secreted superantigens may share a three-dimensional conformation that allows them to interact simultaneously with two different receptors on two different cell types.[27, 153]

The structure and binding sites of SEB to the MHC class II molecule have been determined by crystallographic conformation. Two different MHC class II binding sites for SEB exist. The amino-terminal domain forms most of the contact, but residues at the carboxy-terminal domain also contact the MHC class II molecule as well as the TCR. Although TSST-I is very similar to SEB on the basis of crystallographic structure, the two proteins do not compete with each other for the same MHC class II HLA-DR sites. Likewise, SEA and SEE have greater than 90 percent amino acid sequence homology but quite distinct patterns of V_β specificity. TSST-I and the exfoliative toxins A and B are unrelated structurally but have the same $V_\beta2$ specificity.[153, 170]

REFERENCES

1. Abdul-Karim, F. W., Lederman, M. M., Carter, J. R., et al.: Toxic shock syndrome: Clinicopathologic findings in a fatal case. Hum. Pathol. *12*:16–22, 1981.

2. Abram, A. C., Bellian, K. T., Giles, W. J., et al.: Toxic shock syndrome after functional endonasal sinus surgery: An all or none phenomenon? Laryngoscope *104*:927–931, 1994.
3. Allen, S. T., Liland, J. B., Nichols, C. G., et al.: Toxic shock syndrome associated with use of latex nasal packing. Arch. Intern. Med. *150*:2587–2588, 1990.
4. Alsoub, H.: Toxic shock syndrome associated with pyomyositis. Postgrad. Med. J. *70*:309–312, 1994.
5. Andrews, M. M., Giacobbe, K. D., and Parsonnet, J.: Induction of toxic shock syndrome toxin-1 (TSST-1) and beta-lactamase by subinhibitory concentrations of beta-lactam antibiotics. Abstract N-IN-0011. Presented at Biomedicine '96, May 3–6, 1996, Washington, DC.
6. Andrews, M. M., Parent, E. M., Barry, M., and Parsonnet, J.: Recurrent nonmenstrual toxic shock syndrome: Clinical manifestations, diagnosis, and treatment. Clin. Infect. Dis. *32*:1470–1479, 2001.
7. Aranow, H., Jr., and Wood, W. B., Jr.: Staphylococcic infection simulating scarlet fever. J. A. M. A. *119*:1491–1495, 1942.
8. Arend, S. M., Steenmeyer, A. V., Mosmans, P. C. M., et al.: Postoperative cauda syndrome caused by *Staphylococcus aureus.* Infection *21*:248–250, 1993.
9. Arnow, P. M., Chou, T., Weil, D., et al.: Spread of a toxic-shock syndrome–associated strain of *Staphylococcus aureus* and measurement of antibodies to staphylococcal enterotoxin F. J. Infect. Dis. *149*:103–107, 1984.
10. Bach, M. C.: Dermatologic signs in toxic shock syndrome: Clues to diagnosis. J. Am. Acad. Dermatol. *8*:343–347, 1983.
11. Bacha, E. A., Sheridan, R. L., Donohue, G. A., et al.: Staphylococcal toxic shock syndrome in a paediatric burn unit. Burns *20*:499–502, 1994.
12. Balaban, N., and Novick, R. P.: Autocrine regulation of toxin synthesis by *Staphylococcus aureus.* Proc. Natl. Acad. Sci. U. S. A. *92*:1619–1623, 1995.
13. Bannister, B., and Platts, A. J.: Some cardiological findings in toxic shock syndrome. J. Infect. *3*:293–294, 1981.
14. Baracos, V., Rodemann, P., Dinarello, C. A., et al.: Stimulation of muscle protein degradation and prostaglandin E2 release by leucocytic pyrogen (interleukin-1). N. Engl. J. Med. *308*:553–558, 1983.
15. Barrett, J. A., and Graham, D. R.: TSS presenting as encephalopathy. J. Infect. *12*:276, 1986.
16. Barry, W., Hudgins, L., Donta, S. T., et al.: Intravenous immunoglobulin therapy for toxic-shock syndrome. J. A. M. A. *267*:3315–3317, 1992.
17. Bartlett, P., Reingold, A. L., Graham, D. R., et al.: Toxic shock syndrome associated with surgical wound infections. J. A. M. A. *247*:1448–1450, 1982.
18. Beezhold, D. H., Best, G. K., Bonventre, P. F., et al.: Endotoxin enhancement of TSST-1–induced secretion of interleukin-1 by murine macrophages. Rev. Infect. Dis. *11*(Suppl.):289–293, 1989.
19. Beisel, W. R.: Pathophysiology of staphylococcal enterotoxin, type B, (SEB) toxemia after the intravenous administration to monkeys. Toxicon *10*:433, 1972.
20. Bergdoll, M. S., and Chesney, P. J.: Toxic-Shock Syndrome. Boca Raton, FL, CRC Press, 1991.
21. Bergdoll, M. S., Crass, B. A., Reiser, R. F., et al.: A new staphylococcal enterotoxin, enterotoxin F, associated with toxic-shock syndrome *Staphylococcus aureus* isolates. Lancet *1*:1017–1021, 1981.
22. Berkley, S. F., Hightower, A. W., Broome, C. W., et al.: The relationship of tampon characteristics to menstrual toxic-shock syndrome. J. A. M. A. *258*:917–920, 1987.
23. Berman, A. C., and Boly, L. R.: Cisplatin therapy–associated recurrent toxic shock syndrome. West. J. Med. *155*:415–416, 1991.
24. Bernstein, G. M., Crollick, J. S., and Hassett, J. M., Jr.: Post febrile telogen effluvium in critically ill patients. Crit. Care Med. *16*:98–99, 1988.
25. Black, D. A., and Maw, D. S.: Toxic shock syndrome presenting as cerebral infarct. Corres. J. Neurol. Neurosurg. Psychiatry *47*:568, 1984.
26. Blair, J. D., Livingston, D. G., and Vongsnichakul, R.: Tampon-related toxic-shock syndrome: Histopathologic and clinical findings in a fatal case. Am. J. Clin. Pathol. *78*:372–376, 1982.
27. Bohach, G. A., Dinges, M. M., Mitchell, D. T., et al.: Staphylococcal exotoxins. *In* Leung, D. Y. M., Huber, B. T., and Schlievert, P. M. (eds.): Superantigens: Molecular Biology, Immunology and Relevance to Human Disease. New York, Marcel Dekker, 1997.
28. Bone, R. C.: The pathogenesis of sepsis. Ann. Intern. Med. *115*:457–469, 1991.
29. Bonventre, P. F., Heeg, H., Cullen, C., et al.: Toxicity of recombinant toxic shock syndrome toxin 1 and mutant toxins produced by *Staphylococcus aureus* in a rabbit infection model of toxic shock syndrome. Infect. Immun. *61*:793–799, 1993.
30. Bonventre, P. F., Heeg, H., Edwards, C. K., III, et al.: A mutation at histidine residue 135 of toxic shock syndrome toxin yields an immunogenic protein with minimal toxicity. Infect. Immun. *63*:509–515, 1995.
31. Bonventre, P. F., Linnemann, C., Weckback, L. S., et al.: Antibody responses to toxic-shock-syndrome (TSS) toxin by patients with TSS and by healthy staphylococcal carriers. J. Infect. Dis. *150*:662–666, 1984.
32. Bonventre, P. F., Thompson, M. R., Adinolfi, L. E., et al.: Neutralization of TSST-1 by monoclonal antibodies in vitro and in vivo. Infect. Immun. *50*:135, 1987.
33. Breda, S. D., Jacobs, J. B., Lebowitz, A. S., et al.: Toxic shock syndrome in nasal surgery: A physiochemical and microbiologic evaluation of Merocel and NuGauze nasal packing. Laryngoscope *97*:1388, 1987.
34. Brody, H., and Smith, L. W.: The visceral pathology in scarlet fever and related *Streptococcus* infections. Am. J. Pathol. *12*:373, 1936.
35. Brook, M. G., and Bannister, B. A.: Staphylococcal enterotoxins in scarlet fever complicating chicken pox. Postgrad. Med. J. *67*:1013–1014, 1991.
36. Broome, C. V.: Epidemiology of TSS in the United States: Overview. Rev. Infect. Dis. *11*(Suppl.):14–21, 1989.
37. Brown-Skrobot, S. K., Irving, M. M., and Wojnarowicz, L.: Tampon additives and toxic shock syndrome toxin-1 (TSST-1) production. Abstract B18. Presented at the 91st General Meeting of the American Society of Microbiology, Chicago, 1991, p. 28.
38. Burns, J. R., and Menpace, F. J.: Acute reversible cardiomyopathy complicating toxic shock syndrome. Arch. Intern. Med. *142*:1032–1034, 1982.
39. Cavanah, D. K., and Ballas, Z. K.: Pseudoephedrine reaction presenting as recurrent toxic shock syndrome. Ann. Intern. Med. *119*:302–303, 1993.
40. Cederna, J. P.: Toxic shock syndrome after transverse rectus abdominis musculocutaneous flap breast reconstruction. Ann. Plast. Surg. *34*:73–75, 1995.
41. Chang, A. H., Musser, J. M., and Chow, A. W.: A single clone which produces both TSST-1 and SEA causes the majority of menstrual toxic shock syndrome. Abstract. Clin. Res. *39*:36, 1991.
42. Chatila, T., and Geha, R. S.: Signal transduction by microbial superantigens via MHC class II molecules. Immunol. Rev. *131*:43–59, 1993.
43. Chesney, P. J., Crass, B. A., and Polyak, M. B., et al.: Toxic-shock syndrome: Management and long-term sequelae. Ann. Intern. Med. *96*:847–851, 1982.
44. Chesney, P. J., Davis, J. P., Purdy, W. K., et al.: The clinical manifestations of toxic shock syndrome. J. A. M. A. *246*:741–748, 1981.
45. Chesney, P. J., Slama, S. L., Hawkins, R. L., et al.: Outpatient diagnosis and management of toxic-shock syndrome. N. Engl. J. Med. *304*:1426, 1981.
46. Chesney, P. J., and Zimmerman, J. J.: Hypoferrinemia in toxic-shock syndrome (TSS). Abstract. Pediatr. Res. *20*:306, 1986.
47. Chesney, R. W., Chesney, P. J., Davis, J. P., et al.: Renal manifestations of the staphylococcal toxic-shock syndrome. Am. J. Med. *71*:583–588, 1981.
48. Chesney, R. W., McCarren, D. M., Haddad, J. G., et al.: Pathogenic mechanisms of the hypocalcemia of the staphylococcal toxic-shock syndrome. J. Lab. Clin. Med. *101*:576–585, 1983.
49. Childs, C., Edwards-Jones, V., Healthcote, D. M., et al.: Patterns of *Staphylococcal aureus* colonization, toxin production, immunity and illness in burned children. Burns *20*:514–521, 1994.
50. Choi, Y., Kotzin, B., Herron, L., et al.: Interaction of *Staphylococcus aureus* toxin "superantigens" with human T cells. Proc. Natl. Acad. Sci. U. S. A. *86*:8941–8945, 1989.
51. Choi, Y., Lafferty, J. A., Clements, J. R., et al.: Selective expansion of T cells expressing V beta 2 in toxic-shock syndrome. J. Exp. Med. *172*:981–984, 1990.
52. Chow, A.: Microbiology of toxic shock syndrome: Overview. Rev. Infect. Dis. *1*:55–60, 1989.
53. Chow, A. W., Wong, C. K., MacFarlane, A. M., et al.: Toxic shock syndrome: Clinical and laboratory findings in 30 patients. Can. Med. Assoc. J. *130*:425–430, 1984.
54. Chu, M. C., Kreiswirth, B. N., Pattee, P. A., et al.: Association of toxic shock toxin-1 determinant with a heterologous insertion at multiple loci in the *Staphylococcus aureus* chromosome. Infect. Immun. *56*:2702–2708, 1988.
55. Cohen, K. R., Emmons, K. M., and Goldstein, M. F.: Naloxone treatment of toxic shock syndrome. Arch. Intern. Med. *143*:1072, 1983.
56. Cole, R. P., and Shakespeare, P. G.: Toxic-shock syndrome in scalded children. Burns *16*:221–224, 1990.
57. Cone, L. A., Woodward, D. R., Byrd, R. G., et al.: A recalcitrant, erythematous, desquamating disorder associated with toxin-producing staphylococci in patients with AIDS. J. Infect. Dis. *165*:638–643, 1992.
58. Cone, L. A., Woodard, D. R., Schlievert, P. M., et al.: Clinical and bacteriologic observations of a toxic-shock–like syndrome due to *Streptococcus pyogenes.* N. Engl. J. Med. *317*:146–149, 1987.
59. Conway, E. E., Jr., Haber, R. S., Gumprecht, J., et al.: Toxic shock syndrome following influenza A in a child. Crit. Care Med. *19*:123–125, 1991.
60. Cotran, R. S., Proba, J. S., Gimbrone, M. A., et al.: Endothelial activation during IL-2 immunotherapy: A possible mechanism for the vascular leak syndrome. J. Immunol. *139*:1883, 1987.
61. Cowan, R. K., and Martens, M. G.: Toxic shock syndrome mimicking pelvic inflammatory disease presumably resulting from tattoo. South. Med. J. *86*:1427–1431, 1993.
62. Crass, B. A., and Bergdoll, M. S.: Toxin involvement in toxic shock syndrome. J. Infect. Dis. *153*:918–926, 1986.
63. Crews, J. R., Harrison, J. K, Corey, G. R., et al.: Stunned myocardium in the toxic shock syndrome. Ann. Intern. Med. *117*:912–913, 1992.
64. Crowder, W. E., and Shannon, F. C.: Colposcopic diagnosis of vaginal ulcerations in toxic-shock syndrome. Obstet. Gynecol. *61*:505–535, 1983.
65. Crowther, M. A., and Ralph, E. D.: Menstrual toxic shock syndrome complicated by persistent bacteremia: Case report and review. Clin. Infect. Dis. *16*:288–289, 1993.

66. Danielson, R. W.: Vaginal ulcers caused by tampons. Am. J. Obstet. Gynecol. *146*:547–549, 1983.
67. Dann, E. J., Weinberger, M., Gillis, S., et al.: Bacterial laryngotracheitis associated with toxic-shock syndrome in an adult. Clin. Infect. Dis. *18*:437–439, 1994.
68. Dart, R. C., and Levitt, M. A.: Toxic-shock syndrome associated with the use of the vaginal contraceptive sponge. J. A. M. A. *253*:1877, 1985.
69. Davidson, A. C., Creach, M., and Cameron, I. R.: Staphylococcal pneumonia, pneumatoceles, and the toxic shock syndrome. Thorax *45*:639–640, 1990.
70. Davis, J. P., Chesney, P. J., Wand, P. J., et al.: Toxic shock syndrome: Epidemiologic features, recurrences, risk factors and prevention. N. Engl. J. Med. *303*:1429–1435, 1980.
71. Davis, J. P., Osterholm, M. T., Helms, C. M., et al.: Tristate toxic-shock syndrome study. II. Clinical and laboratory findings. J. Infect. Dis. *145*:441–448, 1982.
72. Davis, J. P., and Vergeront, J. M.: The effect of publicity on the reporting of toxic-shock syndrome in Wisconsin. J. Infect. Dis. *145*:449–457, 1982.
73. Davis, J. P., and Vergeront, J. M.: A review of toxic shock syndrome surveillance in Wisconsin: The effect of media publicity and laboratory services on reporting of illness. Ann. Intern. Med. *96*:883–886, 1982.
74. Davis, J. P., Vergeront, J. V., Amsterdam, L. E., et al.: Long-term effects of TSS in women: Sequelae, subsequent pregnancy, menstrual history, and long-term trends in catamenial product use. Rev. Infect. Dis. *11*(Suppl.):50, 1989.
75. Davis, J. P., Vergeront, J. M., and Chesney, P. J.: Possible host-defense mechanisms in toxic shock syndrome. Ann. Intern. Med. *96*:986–991, 1982.
76. de Azavedo, J. C. S.: Animal models for toxic-shock syndrome: Overview. Rev. Infect. Dis. *11*(Suppl.):205–209, 1989.
77. de Azavedo, J. C. S., Foster, T. J., Hartigan, J., et al.: Expression of the cloned toxic shock syndrome toxin 1 gene *(tst)* in vivo with a rabbit uterine model. Infect. Immun. *50*:304–309, 1985.
78. De Boer, M. L., and Chow, A. W.: Toxic shock syndrome toxin 1–producing *Staphylococcus aureus* isolates contain the staphylococcal enterotoxin B genetic element but do not express staphylococcal enterotoxin B. J. Infect. Dis. *170*:818–827, 1994.
79. Deetz, T. R., Reves, R., and Septimus, E.: Secondary rash in toxic shock syndrome. N. Engl. J. Med. *304*:174, 1981.
80. Deresiewicz, R. L.: Staphylococcal toxic shock syndrome. *In* Leung, D. Y. M., Huber, B. T., and Schlievert P. M. (eds.): Superantigens: Molecular Biology, Immunology and Relevance to Human Disease. New York, Marcel Dekker, 1997.
81. deVries, N., and Vander Baan, S.: Toxic shock syndrome after nasal surgery: Is prevention possible? A case report and review of literature. Rhinology *27*:125–128, 1989.
82. Dickgiesser, N. and Wallach, U.: Toxic shock syndrome toxin-1 (TSST-1): Influence of its production by subinhibitory antibiotic concentrations. Infection *15*:351–353, 1987.
83. Donawa, M. E., Schmid, G. R., and Osterholm, M. T.: Toxic shock syndrome: Chronology of state and federal epidemiologic studies and regulatory decision-making. Public Health Rep. *99*:342–350, 1984.
84. Dondorp, A. M., Veenstra, J., vanderPoll, T., et al.: Activation of the cytokine network in a patient with AIDS and the recalcitrant erythematous desquamating disorder. Clin. Infect. Dis. *18*:942–945, 1994.
85. Donnelly, B. W., McMillan, J. A., and Weiner, L. B.: Bacterial tracheitis: Report of eight new cases and a review. Rev. Infect. Dis. *12*:729–735, 1990.
86. Dornan, K. J., Thompson, D. M., Conn, A. R., et al.: Toxic shock syndrome in the postoperative patient. Surg. Gynecol. Obstet. *154*:65–68, 1982.
87. Driessen, C., Hirv, K., Kirchner, H., et al.: Zinc regulates cytokine induction by superantigens and lipopolysaccharide. Immunology *84*:272–277, 1995.
88. Dunnet, U. B., and Schallibaum, E. M.: Scarlet fever–like illness due to staphylococcal infection. Lancet *2*:1227–1229, 1960.
89. Eagle, H.: Experimental approach to the problem of treatment failure with penicillin. I. Group A streptococcal infection in mice. Am. J. Med. *13*:389–399, 1952.
90. Edwards-Jones, V., Dawson, M. M., and Childs, C.: A survey into toxic shock syndrome (TSS) in UK burn units. Burns *26*:323–333, 2000.
91. Edwards-Jones, V., and Foster, H. A.: The effect of topical antimicrobial agents on the production of toxic shock syndrome toxin-1. J. Med. Microbiol. *41*:408–413, 1994.
92. Ejlertsen, T., and Porsborg, P. A.: Toxic-shock syndrome related to simultaneous *Staphylococcus aureus* epiglottic abscess and group A streptococcal pharyngitis with bacteremia. A. P. M. I. S. *102*:956–959, 1994.
93. Elbaum, D. J., Wood, C., Abuabara, F., et al.: Bullae in a patient with toxic shock syndrome. J. Am. Acad. Dermatol. *10*:267–272, 1984.
94. Elsberry, D. D., Rhoda, D. A., and Beisel, W. R.: Hemodynamics of staphylococcal B enterotoxemia and other types of shock in monkeys. J. Appl. Physiol. *27*:164, 1969.
95. Espersen F., Baek, L., Kjaeldgaard, P., et al.: Detection of staphylococcal toxic shock syndrome toxin 1 by a latex agglutination kit. Scand. J. Infect. Dis. *20*:449–450, 1988.
96. Faich, G., Pearson, K., and Fleming, D., et al.: Toxic-shock syndrome and the vaginal contraceptive sponge. J. A. M. A. *255*:216–218, 1986.
97. Farley, D. E., Katz, V. L., and Dotters, D. J.: Toxic shock syndrome associated with vulvar necrotizing fasciitis. Obstet. Gynecol. *82*:660–662, 1993.
98. Fast, D. J., Schlievert, P. M., and Nelson, R. D.: Nonpurulent response to toxic shock syndrome toxin-1–producing *Staphylococcus aureus*. J. Immunol. *140*:949–953, 1988.
99. Feldman, C. A.: Staphylococcal scarlet fever. N. Engl. J. Med. *267*:877–888, 1962.
100. Ferguson, M. A., and Todd, J. K.: Toxic-shock syndrome associated with *Staphylococcus aureus* sinusitis in children. J. Infect. Dis. *161*:953–955, 1990.
101. Fichtenbaum, C. J., Peterson, L. R. and Weil, G. J.: Ehrlichiosis presenting as a life-threatening illness with features of the toxic shock syndrome. Am. J. Med. *95*:351–357, 1993.
102. Finkelstein, J. W., and von Eye, A.: Sanitary product use by white, black and Mexican American women. Public Health Rep. *105*:491, 1990.
103. Finkelstein, S., and Hyland, R. H.: Toxic shock syndrome as the AIDS defining diagnosis. Chest *104*:950–951, 1993.
104. Fisher, C. J., Jr., Horowitz, Z., and Albertson, T. E.: Cardiorespiratory failure in toxic shock syndrome: Effect of dobutamine. Crit. Care Med. *13*:160–165, 1985.
105. Fisher, C. J., Jr., Horowitz, B. Z., and Nolan, S. M.: The clinical spectrum of toxic shock syndrome. West. J. Med. *15*:175–182, 1981.
106. Fisher, R. F., Goodpasture, H. C., Peterie, J. D., et al.: Toxic shock syndrome in menstruating women. Ann. Intern. Med. *94*:156–163, 1981.
107. Fitz, J. D., Weeks, K. D., and Duff, P.: Left ventricular dysfunction in a patient with toxic shock syndrome. Am. J. Obstet. Gynecol. *146*:467–468, 1983.
108. Fitzgerald, J. R., Sturdevant, D. E., Mackie, S. M., et al.: Evolutionary genomics of *Staphylococcus aureus:* Insights into the origin of methicillin-resistant strains and the toxic shock syndrome epidemic. Proc. Natl. Acad. Sci. U. S. A. *98*:8821–8826, 2001.
109. Foley-Nolan, D., Coughlan, R. J., and Sugrue, D.: Toxic shock syndrome associated arthropathy. *Staphylococcus aureus:* A further triggering event in reactive arthritis? Ann. Rheum. Dis. *48*:331, 1989.
110. Follow-up on toxic-shock syndrome—United States. M. M. W. R. Morb. Mortal. Wkly. Rep. *29*:441–445, 1980.
111. Fornadley, J. A., Gomez, P. J., Crane, R. T., et al.: Toxic shock syndrome following submandibular gland excision. Head Neck *12*:66–68, 1990.
112. Frame, J. D., Eve, M. D., Hackett, M. E., et al.: The toxic shock syndrome in burned children. Burns *11*:234–241, 1985.
113. Fuleihan, R., Trede, N., Chatila, T., et al.: Superantigens activate HIV-1 gene expression in monocytic cells. Clin. Immunol. Immunopathol. *72*:357–361, 1994.
114. Galea, P., and Goel, K. M.: Toxic shock syndrome (TSS) in children. Scott. Med. J. *32*:28–29, 1987.
115. Gallagher, P. G., and Myer, C. M.: An approach to the diagnosis and treatment of membranous laryngotracheobronchitis in infants and children. Pediatr. Emerg. Care 7:337–342, 1991.
116. Garbe, P. L., Arko, R. J., and Reingold, A. L., et al.: *Staphylococcus aureus* isolates from patients with non-menstrual toxic shock syndrome: Evidence for additional toxins. J. A. M. A. *253*:2538–2542, 1985.
117. Gaventa, S., Reingold, A. L., Hightower, A. W., et al.: Active surveillance for TSS in the United States. Rev. Infect. Dis. *11*(Suppl.):28–34, 1989.
118. Glazowski, M. J., Ostergaard, G. Z., Arpi, M., et al.: Toxic shock sydrome: A case of a child with burns. Ugeskr. Laeger *154*:868–869, 1992.
119. Gourley, G. R., Chesney, P. J., Davis, J. P., et al.: Acute cholestasis in patients with toxic-shock syndrome. Gastroenterology *81*:928–931, 1981.
120. Graham, D. R., O'Brien, M., Hayes, J. M., et al.: Postoperative toxic shock syndrome. Clin. Infect. Dis. *20*:895–899, 1995.
121. Hackett, S. P., and Stevens, D. L.: Superantigens associated with staphylococcal and streptococcal toxic shock syndrome are potent inducers of tumor necrosis factor β synthesis. J. Infect. Dis. *168*:232–235, 1993.
122. Hajjeh, R. A., Reingold, A., Weil, A., et al.: Toxic shock syndrome in the United States: Surveillance update, 1979–1996. Emerg. Infect. Dis. *5*:807–810, 1999.
123. Hamad, A. R. A., Marrach, P., and Kappler, J. W.: Transcytosis of staphylococcal superantigen toxins. J. Exp. Med. *185*:1447–1454, 1997.
124. Hanafiah, S. R., and Chong, S. K. F.: Toxic shock syndrome presenting as an acute encephalopathy and diarrhoea. J. R. Soc. Med. *84*:48–49, 1991.
125. Hauschildt, S., Bessler, W. G., and Scheipers, P.: Engagement of major histocompatibility complex class II molecules leads to nitrite production in bone marrow–derived macrophages. Eur. J. Immunol. *23*:2988–2992, 1993.
126. Helgerson, S. D., and Foster, L. R.: Toxic shock syndrome in Oregon: Epidemiologic findings. Ann. Intern. Med. *96*:909–911, 1982.
127. Helms, C. M., Lengeling, R. W., Pinsky, R. L., et al.: Toxic shock syndrome: A retrospective study of 25 cases from Iowa. Am. J. Med. Sci. *282*:50–60, 1981.

128. Hensler, T., Koller, M., Geoffroy, C., et al.: *Staphylococcus aureus* toxic shock syndrome toxin 1 and *Streptococcus pyogenes* erythrogenic toxin A modulate inflammatory mediator release from human neutrophils. Infect. Immun. *61*:1055–1061, 1993.
129. Herold, B. C., Immergluck, L. C., Maranan, M. C., et al.: Community-acquired methicillin-resistant *Staphylococcus aureus* in children. Pediatr. Infect. Dis. J. *279*:593–598, 1998.
130. Heywood, A. J., and al-Essa, S.: Toxic shock syndrome in child with only 2% burn. Lancet *335*:867, 1990.
131. Hiramatsu, K.: Vancomycin-resistant *Staphylococcus aureus:* A new model of antibiotic resistance. Lancet Infect. Dis. *1*:147–155, 2001.
132. Hirose-Kumagai, A., Whipple, F. H., Ikejima, T., et al.: A comparison of neutralizing and antigen-binding assays for human antibodies against toxic-shock-syndrome 1. J. Infect. Dis. *150*:788, 1984.
133. Hurley, J. M., Shimonkevitz, R., Hanagan, A., et al.: Identification of class II major histocompatibility complex and T cell receptor binding sites in the superantigen toxic shock syndrome toxin 1. J. Exp. Med. *181*:2229, 1995.
134. Hurwitz, R. M., and Ackerman, A. B.: Cutaneous pathology of the toxic shock syndrome. Am. J. Dermatopathol. *7*:563, 1985.
135. Iandolo, J. J.: Genetic analysis of extracellular toxins of *Staphylococcus aureus.* Annu. Rev. Microbiol. *43*:375–402, 1989.
136. Ikejima, T., and Dinarello, C. A.: Distribution of radiolabeled toxic shock syndrome toxin: Implications for the pathogenesis of interleukin-1 mediated-toxic shock syndrome. J. Leukoc. Biol. *37*:714, 1985.
137. Ishak, K. G., and Rogers, W. A.: Cryptogenic acute cholangitis: Association with toxic shock syndrome. Am. J. Clin. Pathol. *76*:619–626, 1981.
138. Jacobson, J. A., Kasworm, E. M., and Bolte, R. G., et al.: Prevalence of nasal carriage of toxigenic *Staphylococcus aureus* and antibody to TSST-1 in Utah children. Rev. Infect. Dis. *11*(Suppl.):324–325, 1989.
139. Jacobson, J. A., Kasworm, E., and Daly, J. A.: Risk of developing TSS associated with TSST-1 following nongenital staphylococcal infection. Rev. Infect. Dis. *11*(Suppl.):8–13, 1989.
140. Jacobson, J. A., Kasworm, E. M., Reiser, R. F., et al.: Low incidence of toxic shock syndrome in children with staphylococcal infection. Am. J. Med. Sci. *294*:403–407, 1987.
141. Jacobson, J. A., Stevens, M. H., and Kasworm, E. M.: Evaluation of single-dose cefazol in prophylaxis for toxic-shock syndrome. Arch. Otolaryngol. Head Neck Surg. *114*:326–327, 1988.
142. James, R. C., and MacLeod, C. J.: Induction of staphylococcal infections in mice with small inocula introduced on sutures. Br. J. Exp. Pathol. *42*:266, 1961.
143. Jaulhac, B., Bes, M., Bornstein, N., et al.: Synthetic DNA probes for detection of genes for enterotoxins A, B, C, D, E and for TSST-1 in staphylococcal strains. J. Appl. Bacteriol. *72*:386–392, 1992.
144. Johnson, W. M., Tyler, S. D., Ewan, E. P., et al.: Detection of genes for enterotoxins, exfoliative toxins, and toxic shock syndrome toxin 1 in *Staphylococcus aureus* by the polymerase chain reaction. J. Clin. Microbiol. *29*:426–430, 1991.
145. Kain, K. C., Schulzer, M., and Chow, A. W.: Clinical spectrum of nonmenstrual toxic shock syndrome (TSS): Comparison with menstrual TSS by multivariate discriminant analyses. Clin. Infect. Dis. *16*:100–106, 1993.
146. Kamel, N. S., Banks, M. C., Dosik, A., et al.: Lack of mucocutaneous signs of toxic shock syndrome when T cells are absent: *S. aureus* shock in immunodeficient adults with multiple myeloma. Clin. Exp. Immunol. *128*:131–129, 2002.
147. Kappler, J., Kotzin, B., Herron, L., et al.: Vβ-specific stimulation of human T-cells by staphylococcal toxins. Science *244*:811–813, 1989.
148. Kato, K., and Tanaka, T.: MRSA infection and toxic shock syndrome in burn patients. Jpn. J. Clin. Med. *50*:1104–1111, 1992.
149. Kehrberg, M. W., Latham, R. H., Haslam, B. T., et al.: Risk factors for staphylococcal toxic-shock syndrome. Am. J. Epidemiol. *114*:873–879, 1981.
150. Kernodle, D. S., McGraw, P. A., Barg, N. L., et al.: Growth of *Staphylococcus aureus* with nafcillin in vitro induces α-toxin production and increases the lethal activity of sterile broth filtrates in a murine model. J. Infect. Dis. *172*:410–419, 1995.
151. Kline, M. W., and Dunkle, L. M.: Toxic shock syndrome and the acquired immunodeficiency syndrome. Pediatr. Infect. Dis. J. *7*:736–738, 1988.
152. Kotasek, D., Vercelloti, G. M., Ochoa, A. C., et al.: Mechanism of cultured endothelial injury induced by lymphokine activated killer cells. Cancer Res. *48*:5528, 1988.
153. Kotb, M.: Bacterial pyrogenic exotoxins as superantigens. Clin. Microbiol. Rev. *8*:411–426, 1995.
154. Krakauer, T.: Inhibition of toxic shock syndrome toxin-1–induced cytokine production and T cell activation by interleukin-10, interleukin-4 and dexamethasone. J. Infect. Dis. *172*:988–992, 1995.
155. Kreiswirth, B. N., Kravitz, G. R., Schlievert, P. M., et al.: Nosocomial transmission of a strain of *Staphylococcus aureus*, causing toxic shock syndrome. Ann. Intern. Med. *105*:704, 1986.
156. Kreiswirth, B. N., Projan, S. J., Schlievert, P. M., et al.: Toxic shock syndrome toxin 1 is encoded by a variable genetic element. Rev. Infect. Dis. *11*(Suppl.):83–88, 1989.
157. Ku, W. W. S., and Chow, A. W.: Monoclonal antibodies (MAb5 and MAb4) protect against the lethal effect of toxic shock syndrome toxin-1 in the D-galactosamine sensitized mouse mode. Abstract. J. Invest. Med. *110*:68, 1996.
158. Kum, W. W., and Chow, A. W.: Inhibition of staphylococcal enterotoxin A–induced superantigenic and lethal activities by a monoclonal antibody to toxic shock syndrome toxin-1. J. Infect. Dis. *183*:1739–1748, 2001.
159. Kushnaryov, V. M., MacDonald, H. S., Reiser, R. F., et al.: Reaction of TSST-1 with endothelium of human umbilical cord vein. Rev. Infect. Dis. *11*(Suppl.):282–287, 1989.
160. Larkin, S. M., Williams, D. N., Osterholm, M. T., et al.: Toxic shock syndrome: Clinical, laboratory, and pathologic findings in nine fatal cases. Ann. Intern. Med. *96*:858–864, 1982.
161. Latham, R. H., Kehrberg, M. W., Jacobson, J. A., et al.: Toxic shock syndrome in Utah: A case-control and surveillance study. Ann. Intern. Med. *96*:906–908, 1982.
162. Lee, P. K., Vercellotti, G. M., Deringer, J. R., et al.: Effects of staphylococcal toxic shock syndrome toxin 1 on aortic endothelial cells. J. Infect. Dis. *164*:711–719, 1991.
163. Lee, V. T. P., Chang, A. H., and Chow, A. W.: Detection of staphylococcal enterotoxin B among toxic-shock syndrome (TSS) and non-TSS associated *Staphylococcus aureus* isolates. J. Infect. Dis. *166*:911–915, 1992.
164. Lund, L., Nielsen, D., and Anderson, E. S.: Meningismus as the main symptom in toxic shock syndrome. Acta Obstet. Gynecol. Scand. *67*:395, 1988.
165. MacDonald, K. L., Osterholm, M. T., Hedberg, C. W., et al.: Toxic shock syndrome: A newly recognized complication of influenza and influenza like illness. J. A. M. A. *257*:1053–1058, 1987.
166. Malknecht, U., Hunter, M., Hoffmann, M. K., et al.: The toxic shock syndrome toxin-1 induces anergy in human T cells in vivo. Hum. Immunol. *45*:42–45, 1996.
167. Marlowe, D. E., Weigle, R. M., and Stauffenberg, R. S.: Measurement of Tampon Absorbency: Evaluation of Tampon Brands. Rockville, MD, FDA Bureau of Biologics, 1981.
168. Marodi, L., Kaposzta, R., Rozgonyi, F., et al.: Staphylococcal enterotoxin A involvement in the illness of a 20-month-old burn patient. Pediatr. Infect. Dis. J. *14*:632–634, 1995.
169. Marples, R. R., and Wienecke, A. A.: Enterotoxins and toxic-shock syndrome-1 in non-enteric staphylococcal disease. Epidemiol. Infect. *110*:477–488, 1993.
170. Marrack, P., and Kappler, J.: The staphylococcal enterotoxins and their relatives. Science *248*:705–711, 1990.
171. Martin, R. R., Buttram, V., Besch, P., et al.: Nasal and vaginal *Staphylococcus aureus* in young women: Quantitative studies. Ann. Intern. Med. *96*:951–953, 1982.
172. McAllister, R. M., Mercer, N. S., Morgan, B. D., et al.: Early diagnosis of staphylococcal toxemia in burned children. Burns *19*:22–25, 1993.
173. McCormick, J. K., Yarwood, J. M., and Schlievert, P. M.: Toxic shock syndrome and bacterial superantigens: An update. Annu. Rev. Microbiol. *55*:77–104, 2001.
174. McGann, V. G., Rollins, J. B., and Mason, D. W.: Evaluation of resistance to staphylococcal enterotoxin B: Naturally acquired antibodies of man and monkey. J. Infect. Dis. *124*:206–213, 1971.
175. McIvor, M. E., and Levin, M. L.: Treatment of recurrent toxic shock syndrome with oral contraceptive agents. Md. Med. J. *31*:56–57, 1982.
176. McKenna, U. G., Meadows, J. A., III, Brewer, N. S., et al.: Toxic shock syndrome, a newly recognized disease entity: Report of 11 cases. Mayo Clin. Proc. *55*:663–672, 1980.
177. McMahon, W. S., Patrenos, M. E., McConnell, M. E., et al.: Complete heart block in toxic shock syndrome. Am. J. Dis. Child. *144*:748, 1990.
178. Melish, M. E., Chen, F. S., and Murata, M. S.: Quantitative detection of toxic shock marker protein in human and experimental toxic shock syndrome. Abstract. Clin. Res. *31*:122, 1983.
179. Melish, M. E., Frogner, K. S., Hirata, S. A., et al.: Use of IVGG for therapy in the rabbit model of TSS. Abstract. Clin. Res. *35*:220, 1987.
180. Melish, M., Murata, S., Frogner, K., et al.: Glyceryl monolaurate (GML) in model toxic shock syndrome (TSS). Abstract B19. Presented at the 91st General Meeting of the American Society of Microbiology, Chicago, 1991, p. 28.
181. Melish, M. E., Murata, S., Fukunaga, C., et al.: Corticosteroid and immunoglobulin therapy in toxic shock syndrome (TSS). Abstract. Clin. Res. *36*:781, 1988.
182. Melish, M. E., Murata, S., Fukunaga, C., et al.: Endotoxin is not an essential mediator in TSS. Rev. Infect. Dis. *11*(Suppl.):219–228, 1989.
183. Melish, M. E., Murata, S., Fukunaga, C., et al.: Vaginal tampon model for toxic shock syndrome. Rev. Infect. Dis. *11*(Suppl.):238–246, 1989.
184. Melish, M. E., Murata, S., Fukunaga, C., et al.: Corticosteroid and immunoglobulin therapy in TSS. Rev. Infect. Dis. *11*(Suppl.):332–333, 1989.
185. Michels, T. C.: Mucocutaneous lymph node syndrome in adults: Differentiation from toxic shock syndrome. Am. J. Med. *80*:724, 1986.
186. Michie, C. A., Davis, T., and MacAllister, M.: The sequelae of toxic shock syndrome. Abstract. Pediatr. Res. *39*:179, 1996.

187. Miethke, T., Duschek, K., Wahl, C., et al.: Pathogenesis of the toxic shock syndrome: T-cell–mediated lethal shock caused by the superantigen TSST-1. Eur. J. Immunol. *23*:1494–1500, 1993.
188. Miethke, T., Wahl, I. C., Heeg, K., et al.: T-cell–mediated lethal shock triggered in mice by the superantigen staphylococcal enterotoxin B: Critical role of tumor necrosis factor. J. Exp. Med. *175*:91–98, 1992.
189. Miethke, T., Wahl, C., Regele, D., et al.: *Staphylococcus aureus* mediated shock: A cytokine release syndrome. Immunobiology *189*:270–284, 1993.
190. Miller, S. D.: Postoperative toxic shock syndrome after lumbar laminectomy in a male patient. Spine *19*:1182–1185, 1994.
191. Miller, W., and Stankiewicz, J. A.: Delayed toxic shock syndrome in sinus surgery. Otolaryngol. Head Neck Surg. *111*:121–123, 1994.
192. Mills, J. T., Parsonnet, J., Hickman, R. K., et al.: Control of production of toxic-shock syndrome toxin-1 (TSST-1) by magnesium ion. J. Infect. Dis. *151*:1158–1161, 1985.
193. Miwa, K., Fukuyama, M., Kunitomo, T., et al.: Rapid assay for detection of toxic shock syndrome toxin 1 from human sera. J. Clin. Microbiol. *32*:539–542, 1994.
194. Mohan, S. B., Tamilarasan, A., and Buhl, M.: Inhalational mercury poisoning masquerading as toxic shock syndrome. Anaesth. Intensive Care *22*:305–306, 1994.
195. Mohsenipour, M., Deusch, E., Twerdy, K., et al.: Toxic shock syndrome in transsphenoidal neurosurgery. Acta Neurochir. *128*:169–170, 1994.
196. Moyer, M. A., Edwards, L. D., and Bergdoll, M. S.: Nosocomial toxic shock syndrome in two patients after knee surgery. Am. J. Infect. Control *11*:83–87, 1983.
197. Murray, D. L., Earhart, C. A., Mitchell, D. T., et al.: Localization of biologically important regions on toxic shock syndrome toxin-1. Infect. Immun. *64*:371–374, 1996.
198. Musser, J. M., Schlievert, P. M., Chow, A. W., et al.: A single clone of *Staphylococcus aureus* causes the majority of cases of toxic-shock syndrome. Proc. Natl. Acad. Sci. U. S. A. *87*:225–229, 1990.
199. Nadal, D., Lauener, R. P., Braegger, C. P., et al.: T-cell activation and cytokine release in streptococcal toxic shock–like syndrome. J. Pediatr. *122*:727–729, 1993.
200. Neill R. J., Fanning G. R., Delahoz F., et al.: Oligonucleotide probes for detection and differentiation of *Staphylococcus aureus* strains containing genes for enterotoxins A, B, and C and toxic shock syndrome toxin 1. J. Clin. Microbiol. *28*:1514–1518, 1990.
201. Nightingale, S. L.: New requirements for tampon labeling. Am. Fam. Physician *41*:999, 1990.
202. Nijssen-Jordan, C., Donaldson, J. D., and Halperin, S. A.: Bacterial tracheitis associated with respiratory syncytial virus infection and toxic-shock syndrome. Can. Med. Assoc. J. *142*:233–234, 1990.
203. Norrby-Teglund, A., Pauksens, K., Holm, S. E., et al.: Relation between low capacity of human sera to inhibit streptococcal mitogens and serious manifestation of disease. J. Infect. Dis. *170*:585–591, 1994.
204. Ogawa, M., Ueda, S., Anzai, N., et al.: Toxic shock syndrome after staphylococcal pneumonia treated with intravenous immunoglobulin. Vox Sang. *68*:59–60, 1995.
205. O'Gilvie vs. International Playtex, No. 83-1845, Vol. 37 (DC Kansas March 21, 1985, post-trial motions and court findings).
206. Olesen, L. L., Ejlertsen, T., and Nielsen, J.: Toxic shock syndrome following insertion of breast prostheses. Br. J. Surg. *78*:585–586, 1991.
207. Olson, R. D., Stevens, D. L., and Melish, M. E.: Direct effects of purified staphylococcal TSST-1 on myocardial function of isolated rabbit atria. Rev. Infect. Dis. *11*(Suppl.):313–315, 1989.
208. Onderdonk, A. B., Delaney, M. L., Zamarchi, G. R., et al.: Normal vaginal microflora during use of various forms of catamenial protection. Rev. Infect. Dis. *11*(Suppl.):61–67, 1989.
209. Orden, J. A., Goyache, J., Hernandez, F. J., et al.: Detection of staphylococcal enterotoxin and toxic shock syndrome toxin-1 (TSST-1) by immunoblot combined with a semiautomated electrophoresis system. J. Immunol. Methods *144*:197–202, 1991.
210. Osterholm, M. T., Davis, J. P., Gibson, R. W., et al.: Tri-state toxic-shock syndrome study. I. Epidemiologic findings. J. Infect. Dis. *145*:431–440, 1982.
211. Osterholm, M. T., Davis, J. P., Gibson, R. W., et al.: Toxic shock syndrome: Relation to catamenial products, personal health and hygiene, and sexual practices. Ann. Intern. Med. *96*:954–958, 1982.
212. Osterholm, M. T., and Forfang, J. C.: Toxic-shock syndrome in Minnesota: Results of an active-passive surveillance system. J. Infect. Dis. *145*:458–464, 1982.
213. Paris, A. L., Herwaldt, L. A., Blum, D., et al.: Pathologic findings in twelve fatal cases of toxic-shock syndrome. Ann. Intern. Med. *96*:852–857, 1982.
214. Parkin, D. E.: Fatal toxic shock syndrome following endometrial resection. Br. J. Obstet. Gynaecol. *102*:163–164, 1995.
215. Parsonnet, J.: Mediators in the pathogenesis of TSS: Overview. Rev. Infect. Dis. *11*(Suppl.):263–269, 1989.
216. Parsonnet, J.: Nonmenstrual toxic shock syndrome: New insights into diagnosis, pathogenesis and treatment. Curr. Clin. Top. Infect. Dis. *16*:1–20, 1996.
217. Parsonnet, J., Gillis, Z. A., and Pier, G. B.: Induction of interleukin-1 by strains of *Staphylococcus aureus* from patients with non-menstrual toxic shock syndrome. J. Infect. Dis. *154*:55–63, 1986.
218. Parsonnet, J., Gillis, Z. A., Thompson, M. R., et al.: Effects of monoclonal antibody on biologic function of TSST-1 in vitro and in vivo. Rev. Infect. Dis. *11*(Suppl.):318–319, 1989.
219. Parsonnet, J., Modern, P. A., and Giacobbe, K.: Effect of subinhibitory concentrations of antibiotics on production of toxic shock syndrome toxin-1 (TSST-1). Abstract 29. Presented at the 32nd Annual Meeting of the Infectious Disease Society of America, 1994, Washington, DC.
220. Parsonnet, J., Modern, P. A., and Giacobbe, K. D.: Effect of tampon composition on production of toxic shock syndrome toxin-1 by *Staphylococcus aureus* in vitro. J. Infect. Dis. *173*:98–103, 1996.
221. Parsonnet, J., Tosteson, A., Modern, P., et al.: Antibody to toxic shock syndrome toxin-1 (TSST-1) and vaginal colonization by TSST-1 producing *S. aureus* among adolescent women. Abstract 1327. Presented at the 33rd Interscience Conference on Antimicrobial Agents and Chemotherapy, American Society for Microbiology, 1993, Washington, DC.
222. Paterson, M. P., Hoffman, E. B., and Roux, P.: Severe disseminated staphylococcal disease associated with osteitis and septic arthritis. J. Bone Joint Surg. Br. *72*:94–97, 1990.
223. Petitti, D. B., Reingold, A., and Chin, J.: The incidence of toxic shock syndrome in northern California: 1972 through 1983. J. A. M. A. *255*:368–372, 1986.
224. Pokriefka, R., Rabah, M., Saravolatz, L., et al.: Toxic shock syndrome in an injection drug user with *Staphylococcus aureus* endocarditis. Infect. Med. *11*:34–36, 48–49, 1994.
225. Potter, T., DiGregorio, F., Stiff, M., et al.: Dilantin hypersensitivity syndrome imitating staphylococcal toxic shock. Arch. Dermatol. *130*:856–858, 1994.
226. Prevention and Recognition of TSS: Institute of Medicine: Toxic Shock Syndrome: Assessment of Current Information and Future Research Needs. Washington, DC, National Academy Press, 1982, pp. 85–86.
227. Projan, S. J., Brown-Skrobot, S., and Schlievert, P. M.: Glycerol monolaurate inhibits the production of beta-lactamase, toxic shock toxin-1, and other staphylococcal exoproteins by interfering with signal transduction. J. Bacteriol. *176*:4204–4209, 1994.
228. Raab, M. G., O'Brien, M., Hayes, J. M., et al.: Postoperative toxic shock syndrome. Am. J. Orthop. *24*:130–136, 1995.
229. Rasheed, J. K., Arko, R. J., Feeley, J. C., et al.: Acquired ability of *Staphylococcus aureus* to produce toxic shock–associated protein and resulting illness in a rabbit model. Infect. Immun. *47*:598–604, 1985.
230. Reduced incidence of menstrual toxic-shock syndrome—United States, 1980–1990. M. M. W. R. Morb. Mortal. Wkly. Rep. *39*(25):421–423, 1990.
231. Reingold, A. L.: Epidemiology of toxic-shock syndrome, United States, 1960–1984. M. M. W. R. CDC Surveill. Summ. *33*(3):19SS–22SS, 1984.
232. Reingold, A. L., Hargrett, N. T., Dan, B. B., et al.: Nonmenstrual toxic shock syndrome: A review of 130 cases. Ann. Intern. Med. *96*:871–874, 1982.
233. Ren, K., Bannan, J. D., Pancholi, V., et al.: Characterization and biological properties of a new staphylococcal exotoxin. J. Exp. Med. *180*:1675–1683, 1994.
234. Rhee, C. A., Smith, R. J., and Jackson, I. T.: Toxic shock syndrome associated with suction-assisted lipectomy. Aesthetic Plast. Surg. *18*:161–163, 1994.
235. Rich, R. R.: Intravenous IgG: Supertherapy for superantigens. J. Clin. Invest. *91*:378, 1993.
236. Ritz, H. L., Kirkland, J. J., Bond, G. G., et al.: Association of high levels of serum antibody to staphylococcal toxic shock antigen with nasal carriage of toxic shock antigen–producing strains of *Staphylococcus aureus*. Infect. Immun. *43*:954–958, 1984.
237. Rolston, R. D., Yabek, S. M., Florman, A. L., et al.: Severe cardiac conduction abnormalities associated with atypical toxic-shock syndrome. J. Pediatr. *117*:89, 1990.
238. Romagne, F., Besnardeau, L., and Malissen, B.: A versatile method to produce antibodies to human T cell receptor V beta segments: Frequency determination of human V beta 2+ T cells that react with toxic-shock syndrome toxin-1. Eur. J. Immunol. *22*:2749–2752, 1992.
239. Rose, P. G., and Wilson, G.: Advanced cervical carcinoma presenting with toxic shock syndrome. Gynecol. Oncol. *52*:264–266, 1994.
240. Rosene, K. A., Copass, M. K., Kastner, L. S., et al.: Persistent neuropsychological sequelae of toxic shock syndrome. Ann. Intern. Med. *96*:865–870, 1982.
241. Rosten, P. M., Bartlett, K. H., and Chow, A. W.: Serologic responses to toxic shock syndrome (TSS) toxin-1 in menstrual and nonmenstrual TSS. Clin. Invest. Med. *11*:187–192, 1988.
242. Rovner, R. A., Baird, R. A., and Malerich, M. M.: Fatal toxic-shock syndrome as a complication of orthopedic surgery. J. Bone Joint Surg. Am. *66*:952–954, 1984.
243. Royall, J. A., Berkow, R. L., Beckman, J. S., et al.: Tumor necrosis factor and interleukin 1α increase vascular endothelial cell permeability. Am. J. Physiol. *257*:L399–L410, 1989.
244. Sahs, A. L., Helms, C. M., and DuBois, C.: Carpal tunnel syndrome: Complication of toxic shock syndrome. Arch. Neurol. *40*:414–415, 1983.

245. Sales, J. H., Kennedy, K. S., Galantich, P. T., et al.: Toxic shock syndrome associated with pharyngitis and submandibular space abscess. Ann. Otol. Rhinol. Laryngol. *100*:540–543, 1991.
246. Schlech, W. F., III, Shands, K. N., Reingold, A. L., et al.: Risk factors for development of toxic shock syndrome: Association with a tampon brand. J. A. M. A. *7*:835–839, 1982.
247. Schlievert, P. M.: Enhancement of host susceptibility to lethal endotoxin shock by staphylococcal pyrogenic exotoxin type C. Infect. Immun. *36*:123–128, 1982.
248. Schlievert, P. M.: Staphylococcal enterotoxin B and toxic-shock syndrome toxin-1 are significantly associated with non-menstrual TSS. Lancet *1*:1149, 1986.
249. Schlievert, P. M.: Comparison of cotton and cotton/rayon tampons for effect on production of toxic shock syndrome toxin. J. Infect. Dis. *172*:1112–1114, 1995.
250. Schlievert, P. M., Deringer, J. R., Kim, M. H., et al.: Effect of glycerol monolaurate on bacterial growth and toxin production. Antimicrob. Agents Chemother. *36*:626–632, 1992.
251. Schlievert, P. M., and Kelly, J. A.: Clindamycin-induced suppression of toxic-shock syndrome–associated exotoxin production. J. Infect. Dis. *149*:471, 1984.
252. Schlievert, P. M., Shands, K. N., Dan, B. B., et al.: Identification and characterization of exotoxin from *Staphylococcus aureus* associated with toxic shock syndrome. J. Infect. Dis. *143*:509–516, 1981.
253. Schmitz, F. J., Mackenzie, C. R., Geisel, R., et al.: Enterotoxin and toxic shock syndrome toxin-1 production of methicillin resistant and methicillin sensitive *Staphylococcus aureus* strains. Eur. J. Epidemiol. *13*:699–708, 1997.
254. Schuchat, A., and Broome, C. V.: Toxic shock syndrome and tampons. Epidemiol. Rev. *13*:99–112, 1991.
255. Schwartz, B., Gaventa, S., Broome, C. V., et al.: Nonmenstrual TSS associated with barrier contraceptives: Report of a case-control study. Rev. Infect. Dis. *11*(Suppl.):43–48, 1989.
256. Scott, D. F., Best, G. K., Kling, J. M., et al.: Passive protection of rabbits infected with TSS associated strains of *Staphylococcus aureus* by monoclonal antibody to TSST-1. Rev. Infect. Dis. *11*(Suppl.):214–217, 1989.
257. Shands, K. N., Schmid, G. P., Dan, B. B., et al.: Toxic-shock syndrome in menstruating women: Association with tampon use and *Staphylococcus aureus* and clinical features in 52 cases. N. Engl. J. Med. *303*:1436–1442, 1980.
258. Shlasko, E., Harris, M. T., Benjamin, E., et al.: Toxic shock syndrome after pilonidal cystectomy: Report of a case. Dis. Colon Rectum *34*:502–505, 1991.
259. Sissons, J. G.: Superantigens and infectious disease. Lancet *341*:1627–1629, 1993.
260. Skansen-Saphir, U., Andersson, J., Bjork, L., et al.: Lymphokine production induced by streptococcal pyrogenic exotoxin A is selectively down regulated by pooled human IgG. Eur. J. Immunol. *24*:916–922, 1994.
261. Slingluff, C. L., Jr., Burns, W. W., and Cooperberg, C.: Toxic shock syndrome after inguinal hernia repair: Report of a case with patient survival. Am. Surg. *56*:610–612, 1990.
262. Smith, D. B., and Gulinson, J.: Fatal cerebral edema complicating toxic shock syndrome. Neurosurgery *22*:598–599, 1988.
263. Sparano, J., and Ferranti, E.: The acquired immunodeficiency syndrome and non-menstrual toxic shock syndrome. Ann. Intern. Med. *105*:300–301, 1986.
264. Spearman, P. W., and Barson, W. J.: Toxic shock syndrome occurring in children with abrasive injuries beneath casts. J. Pediatr. Orthop. *12*:169–172, 1992.
265. Sperber, S. J., Blevins, D. D., and Francis, J. B.: Hypercalcitonemia, hypocalcemia, and toxic-shock syndrome. Rev. Infect. Dis. *12*:736–739, 1990.
266. Spertini, F., Spits, H., and Geha, R. S.: Staphylococcal exotoxins deliver activation signals to human T-cell clones via major histocompatibility complex class II molecules. Proc. Natl. Acad. Sci. U. S. A. *88*:7533–7537, 1991.
267. *Staphylococcus aureus* resistant to vancomycin—United States, 2002. M. M. W. R. Morb. Mortal. Wkly. Rep. *51*(26):565–567, 2002.
268. Stevens, D. L., Gibbons, A. E., Bergstrom, R., et al.: The eagle effect revisited: Efficacy of clindamycin, erythromycin, and penicillin in the treatment of streptococcal myositis. J. Infect. Dis. *158*:23–28, 1988.
269. Stevens, D. L., Tanner, M. H., Winship, J., et al.: Severe group A streptococcal infections associated with a toxic shock–like syndrome and scarlet fever toxin A. N. Engl. J. Med. *321*:1–7, 1989.
270. Stevens, D. L., Yan, S., and Bryant, A. E.: Penicillin-binding protein expression at different growth stages determines penicillin efficacy in vitro and in vivo: An explanation for the inoculum effect. J. Infect. Dis. *167*:1401–1405, 1993.
271. Stevens, F. A.: The occurrence of *Staphylococcus aureus* infection with a scarlatiniform rash. J. A. M. A. *18*:1957–1958, 1927.
272. Stolz, S. J., Davis, J. P., Vergeront, J. M., et al.: Development of serum antibody to toxic shock toxin among individuals with toxic shock syndrome in Wisconsin. J. Infect. Dis. *151*:883–889, 1985.
273. Su, Y. C., and Wong, A. C.: Identification and purification of a new staphylococcal enterotoxin, H. Appl. Environ. Microbiol. *61*:1438–1443, 1995.
274. Summary of notifiable diseases, United States, 1994. M. M. W. R. Morb. Mortal. Wkly. Rep. *43*(53):1–80, 1994.
275. Swift, J. D., Barruga, M. C., Perkin, R. M., et al.: Respiratory failure complicating rubeola. Chest *104*:1786–1787, 1993.
276. Takei, S., Arora, Y. K., and Walker, S. M.: Intravenous immunoglobulin contains specific antibodies inhibitory to activation of T cells by staphylococcal toxin superantigens. J. Clin. Invest. *91*:602–607, 1993.
277. Tampon packages carry TSS information. F. D. A. Drug Bull. *3*(3):19–20, 1982.
278. Thompson, T. D., and Friedman, A. L.: Simultaneous occurrence of *Staphylococcus aureus*–associated septic arthritis and toxic shock syndrome. Clin. Pediatr. (Phila.) *33*:243–245, 1994.
279. Tierno, P. M., Jr., and Hanna, B. A.: Propensity of tampons and barrier contraceptives to amplify *Staphylococcus aureus* toxic shock syndrome toxin-1. Infect. Dis. Obstet. Gynecol. *2*:140–145, 1994.
280. Todd, J. K.: Therapy of toxic shock syndrome. Drugs *39*:856–861, 1990.
281. Todd, J. K., Fishaut, M., and Kapral, F., et al.: Toxic-shock syndrome associated with phage-group-1 staphylococci. Lancet *2*:1116–1118, 1978.
282. Todd, J. K., Franco-Buff, A., Lawellin, D. W., et al.: Phenotypic distinctiveness of *Staphylococcus aureus* strains associated with toxic shock syndrome. Infect. Immun. *45*:339–344, 1984.
283. Todd, J. K., Ressman, M., Caston, S. A., et al.: Corticosteroid therapy for patients with toxic shock syndrome. J. A. M. A. *252*:3399–3402, 1984.
284. Todd, J. K., Todd, B. H., Franco-Buff, A., et al.: Influence of focal growth conditions on the pathogenesis of toxic shock syndrome. J. Infect. Dis. *155*:673–681, 1987.
285. Todd, J. K., Weisenthal, A. M., Ressman, M., et al.: Toxic shock syndrome. II. Estimated occurrence in Colorado as influenced by case ascertainment methods. Am. J. Epidemiol. *22*:857–867, 1985.
286. Toxic-shock syndrome and the vaginal contraceptive sponge. M. M. W. R. Morb. Mortal. Wkly. Rep. *33*(4):43–44, 49, 1984.
287. Toxic shock syndrome following influenza—Oregon, United States; update on influenza activity—United States. M. M. W. R. Morb. Mortal. Wkly. Rep. *36*(5):64–65, 1987.
288. Toxic-shock syndrome—United States. M. M. W. R. Morb. Mortal. Wkly. Rep. *29*:229–230, 1980.
289. Toxic-shock syndrome—United States, 1970–1980. M. M. W. R. Morb. Mortal. Wkly. Rep. *30*(3):25–28, 33, 1981.
290. Toxic-shock syndrome, United States, 1970–1982. M. M. W. R. Morb. Mortal. Wkly. Rep. *31*(16):201–204, 1982.
291. Tofte, R. W., and Williams, D. N.: Toxic shock syndrome: Evidence of a broad clinical spectrum. J. A. M. A. *246*:2163–2167, 1981.
292. Tofte, R. W., and Williams, D. N.: Clinical and laboratory manifestations of toxic shock syndrome. Ann. Intern. Med. *96*:843–847, 1982.
293. Tolan, R. W., Jr.: Toxic shock syndrome complicating influenza A in a child: Case report and review. Clin. Infect. Dis. *17*:43–45, 1993.
294. Tracey, K. J., Lowry, S. F., Beutler, B., et al.: Cachectin/tumor necrosis factor mediates changes of skeletal muscle plasma membrane potential. J. Exp. Med. *164*:1368–1373, 1986.
295. Turker, R., Lubicky, J. P., and Vogel, L. C.: Toxic shock syndrome in patients with external fixators. J. Pediatr. Orthop. *12*:658–662, 1992.
296. Update: Toxic shock syndrome—United States. M. M. W. R. Morb. Mortal. Wkly. Rep. *32*(30):398–400, 1983.
297. Vergeront, J. M., Blouse, L. E., Crass, B. A., et al.: Regional differences in the prevalence of serum antibody to toxic-shock toxin (anti-TST). Abstract 610. Presented at the 24th Interscience Conference on Antimicrobial Agents and Chemotherapy, Atlanta, 1984, p. 193.
298. Vergeront, J. M., Evenson, M. L., Crass, B. A., et al.: Recovery of staphylococcal enterotoxin F from the breast milk of a woman with toxic-shock syndrome. J. Infect. Dis. *146*:456–459, 1982.
299. Vergeront, J. M., Stolz, S. J., Crass, B. A., et al.: Prevalence of serum antibody to staphylococcal enterotoxin F among Wisconsin residents: Implications for toxic shock syndrome. J. Infect. Dis. *148*:692–698, 1983.
300. Vic-Dupont, M. P., Duval, P., and Kamaliv, S. R.: Scarlatiniform staphylococcal diseases. Soc. Med. Hop. Paris *116*:51, 1965.
301. Wagner, G., Bohr, L., Wagner, P., et al.: Tampon-induced changes in vaginal oxygen and carbon dioxide tensions. Am. J. Obstet. Gynecol. *148*:147–150, 1984.
302. Watanabe-Ohnishi, R., Low, D. E., McGeer, A., et al.: Selective depletion of Vβ-bearing T cells in patients with severe invasive group A streptococcal infections and streptococcal toxic shock syndrome. J. Infect. Dis. *171*:74–84, 1995.
303. Weinzweig, J., Gottlich, L. J., and Krizek, T. J.: Toxic shock syndrome associated with the use of Biobrane in a scald burn victim. Burns *20*:180–181, 1994.
304. Weissberg, S. M., and Dodson, M. G.: Recurrent vaginal and cervical ulcers associated with tampon use. J. A. M. A. *250*:1430–1431, 1983.
305. Wharton, M., Chorba, T. L., Vogt, R. L., et al.: Case definitions for public health surveillance. M. M. W. R. Recomm. Rep. *39*(RR-13):1–43, 1990.
306. Whitby, M., Fraser, S., Gemmell, C. G., et al.: Toxic shock syndrome and endocarditis. B. M. J. *286*:1613, 1983.

307. Whiting, J. L., Rosten, P. M., and Chow, A. W.: Determination by Western blot (immunoblot) of serconversions to toxic shock syndrome (TSS) toxin 1 and enterotoxin A, B, or C during infection with TSS- and non–TSS-associated *Staphylococcus aureus*. Infect. Immun. *57*:231–234, 1989.
308. Wick, M. R., Bahn, R. C., and McKenna, U. G.: Toxic shock syndrome: A fatal case with autopsy findings. Mayo Clin. Proc. *57*:583–589, 1982.
309. Wiesenthal, A. M., and Todd, J. K.: Toxic shock syndrome in children aged 10 years or less. Pediatrics *74*:112–117, 1984.
310. Wong, A. C. L., and Bergdoll, M. S.: Effect of environmental conditions on production of toxic shock syndrome toxin 1 by *Staphylococcus aureus*. Infect. Immun. *58*:1026–1029, 1990.
311. Yagoob, M., McClelland, P., Murray, A. E., et al.: Staphylococcal enterotoxins A and C causing toxic shock syndrome. J. Infect. *20*:176–178, 1990.
312. Yong, J. M.: Necrotising fasciitis. Lancet *343*:1427, 1994.
313. Younis, R. T., Gross, C. W., and Lazar, R. H.: Toxic shock syndrome following functional endonasal sinus surgery: A case report. Head Neck *13*:247–248, 1991.
314. Zembowicz, A., and Vane, J. R.: Induction of nitric oxide synthase activity by toxic shock syndrome toxin 1 in a macrophage-monocyte cell line. Proc. Soc. Natl. Acad. Sci. U. S. A. *89*:2051–2055, 1992.
315. Zumla, A.: Superantigens, T cells and microbes. Clin. Infect. Dis. *15*:313–320, 1992.

CHAPTER 72

Adult Respiratory Distress Syndrome in Children

CHRISTOPHER M. OERMANN ■ PETER W. HIATT

Ashbaugh and associates first used the term adult respiratory distress syndrome (ARDS) in a case series that they reported in 1967.[7] In it, they described a clinical syndrome of diverse etiologies that was characterized by the development of fulminant respiratory failure associated with rapidly progressive bilateral pulmonary infiltrates in the absence of cardiac failure. Although mortality in their patients was 67 percent, four individuals treated with continuous positive airway pressure and high positive end-expiratory pressure (PEEP) survived. Postmortem examination of the lungs from nonsurvivors revealed significant pulmonary edema and hyaline membrane formation. They assumed that the presence of hyaline membranes and the favorable response to positive pressure indicated an acquired surfactant deficiency. The term "adult respiratory distress syndrome" was used as an analogy to neonatal respiratory distress syndrome (hyaline membrane disease) caused by insufficient surfactant production.

ARDS now is recognized as a relatively common sequela of a variety of local or systemic diseases that result in damage to the vascular endothelium, alveolar epithelium, and alveolar-capillary membrane. Compromise of these structures leads to the final common pathway of ARDS: pulmonary vascular leak, noncardiogenic pulmonary edema, and respiratory failure. The clinical syndrome is composed of tachypnea, dyspnea, and marked hypoxemia caused by edema and reduced total lung compliance. Radiographs demonstrate diffuse bilateral opacities. Although considerable research has been conducted in an attempt to identify factors predisposing individuals to ARDS and even more in therapeutic trials, ARDS remains poorly understood and therapy is primarily supportive. Even though mortality in adults has decreased during the past 20 years, ARDS remains a life-threatening disease.[46, 62, 76]

ARDS initially was described in adults, but it has been recognized as a leading cause of mortality in pediatric critical care unit patients. More than 500 cases have been reported in children ranging from 2 weeks to 17 years of age.* The true incidence of pediatric ARDS is unknown but has been estimated to be between 8.5 and 10.4 cases per 100 pediatric intensive care unit (ICU) admissions.[65] The prevalence rate of ARDS in pediatric ICU patients has been reported as 0.6 to 7.2 percent.[13, 15] As in adults, ARDS in children can result from a variety of injuries that all lead to increased vascular permeability, pulmonary edema, and clinical respiratory failure. As in adults, ARDS develops in most children as a result of sepsis, although viral pneumonitis and inhalation or aspiration events also are common occurrences.[15, 57] Even though advances in supportive therapy for ARDS have improved outcomes in adults, these improvements have resulted in little change in the mortality rates in children during the past 20 years. Overall mortality has remained higher than 50 percent, whereas mortality rates in children with sepsis is up to 65 percent, and it is 90 percent for those in whom ARDS develops after cardiopulmonary resuscitation.[15, 17]

*See references 9, 13, 15, 17, 27, 31, 40, 52, 56, 65, 67–69, 81.

Definition

Defining ARDS has been the source of much confusion and, at times, heated debate. Initially, ARDS signified a disease of adults, but the reporting of numerous cases in children prompted the use of *acute* rather than *adult* respiratory distress syndrome. Although both terms occasionally appear, acute respiratory distress syndrome currently is the preferred designation. Early attempts at defining ARDS resulted in the use of criteria proposed by the National Heart, Lung, and Blood Institute that included (1) acute and rapidly progressing pulmonary disease of a noncardiac nature; (2) progressive, diffuse, bilateral pulmonary infiltrates on chest radiographs; and (3) hypoxemia, defined as an arterial oxygen tension/fractional concentration of inspired oxygen (Pa_{O_2}/F_{IO_2}) ratio less than 150 without PEEP or less than 200 with PEEP. Continued interest in the systematic study of ARDS from epidemiologic and therapeutic standpoints, combined with continued difficulty in comparing data because of differences in definition, led to the formation of an international discussion group. The European-American Consensus Committee on ARDS then published a unifying definition of ARDS that included (1) impaired oxygenation with a Pa_{O_2}/F_{IO_2} ratio less than 200, regardless of PEEP; (2) bilateral densities demonstrated on chest radiographs; and (3) a pulmonary artery wedge pressure less than 18 mm Hg and no evidence of left atrial hypertension.[10]

Pathophysiology

The pathophysiologic abnormalities that are associated with ARDS, though extensively studied since the original description of the syndrome in 1967, remain incompletely understood. A host of seemingly unrelated systemic diseases and local insults to the respiratory tract have been reported to result in ARDS. Despite efforts to elucidate the precise chain of events that lead from these initial triggers to massive cellular injury and rapidly progressive respiratory failure, much of the process remains a mystery. Nevertheless, certain cellular and biochemical markers, as well as physiologic characteristics associated with ARDS, have been identified. In addition, the histologic findings seen in ARDS follow a characteristic pattern that has been well described. These pathophysiologic events and findings generally correlate with the clinical findings seen in ARDS.

As mentioned earlier, a wide variety of apparently unrelated disorders and injuries have been associated with the development of ARDS[15, 17, 40, 57, 65] and include a broad spectrum of infections (bacterial, viral, and other), inhalation/aspiration injuries, sepsis syndromes, trauma, drug reactions and metabolic disorders, and malignancies, among other causes (Tables 72–1 and 72–2). Although the mechanism or mechanisms of injury that unite this group are unknown, clearly, underlying damage to the vascular endothelium, alveolar epithelium, or alveolar-capillary membrane (or any combination of such damage) must be present. Several hypotheses have been proposed and are summarized in review articles.[63, 68] These hypotheses include activation of the complement cascade, excessive neutrophil and macrophage activity, and others.

Complement activation occurs after trauma, pancreatic damage, endothelial damage, endotoxin exposure, and other systemic and respiratory injuries.[61] By-products of complement activation then cause recruitment and activation of neutrophils, which in turn escalate the inflammatory cycle and damage the pulmonary parenchyma through the release of oxygen radicals, proteolytic enzymes, and eicosanoids. A strong association has been demonstrated between complement activation and the development of ARDS.[25] However, other investigators have reported that complement activation is nonspecific in predicting the development of ARDS.[21, 35, 51, 88] Additional evidence suggests that the combination of circulating endotoxin and complement activation is potentially more important in the development of ARDS than is complement activation alone.[50]

Significant, though again not conclusive, evidence suggests a key role for neutrophils in the genesis of ARDS.[80] Once activated, neutrophils can damage the lung parenchyma by the release of proteolytic enzymes, generation of toxic oxygen radicals, and initiation of arachidonic acid metabolism. Numerous studies have indicated potential roles for superoxide radicals in the development of ARDS or the presence of elevated concentrations of peroxide in the breath of ARDS patients.[28, 77, 78] Patients with ARDS similarly have elevated concentrations of elastase and collagenase and increased leukotriene B_4 in bronchoalveolar lavage fluid, findings consistent with neutrophil degranulation.[77] Although neutrophils are capable of causing widespread parenchymal lung damage, are characteristically found in ARDS, and probably play some role in the pathogenesis or propagation of ARDS (or both), the occurrence of ARDS in severely neutropenic individuals suggests that they are not essential or singly responsible for its development.[48, 72]

Alveolar macrophages may play a critical role in the pathogenesis of ARDS. They are found in abundance in normal airways, and when stimulated by endotoxin or endogenous proinflammatory cytokines, alveolar macrophages synthesize and release tumor necrosis factor and interleukin-1.[68] Both products promote neutrophil chemotaxis, degranulation, and release of oxygen metabolites, thereby creating a cycle of inflammation within the pulmonary parenchyma. Administration of tumor necrosis factor to animals in experimental models produces pulmonary edema, decreased pulmonary compliance, increased cellularity, and increased lung water, the primary physiologic markers of ARDS.[75, 83, 84] Conversely, anti–tumor necrosis factor antibody offered protection from ARDS in a baboon septicemia model.[85]

TABLE 72–1 ■ NONINFECTIOUS CONDITIONS ASSOCIATED WITH ADULT RESPIRATORY DISTRESS SYNDROME

Direct Injury to the Lung	Secondary Injury to the Lung
Inhalation	Anaphylaxis
NO_2	Shock—any cause
Cl_2	Sepsis
SO_2	Trauma
NH_3	Multiple trauma
Phosgene	Fractures
Smoke	Burns
Oxygen toxicity	Head trauma
Aspiration	Blood disorders
Foreign body	Diffuse intravascular coagulation
Gastric fluid (especially if pH <2.5)	Massive blood transfusion
	Drug overdose
Near drowning (fresh or salt water)	Heroin
	Methadone
Hydrocarbons	Barbiturates
Emboli	Ethchlorvynol
Air	Salicylates
Fat	Propoxyphene
Amniotic fluid	Deferoxamine
Pulmonary contusion	Metabolic disorders
Radiation pneumonitis	Diabetic ketoacidosis
Asphyxiation/strangulation	Uremia
	Pancreatitis
	Increased intracranial pressure
	Post-cardiopulmonary bypass
	Post-hemodialysis
	Post-cardioversion
	Paraquat ingestion
	Malignancy/lymphoproliferative disorder

From Royall, J. A., and Levin, D. L.: Adult respiratory distress syndrome in pediatric patients. I. Clinical aspects, pathophysiology, pathology, and mechanisms of lung injury. J. Pediatr. *112*:169–180, 1988.

In his review article, Royall also discusses putative roles for oxygen radicals, platelet-derived eicosanoids, proteolytic enzymes, fibrin and its degradation products, and other processes that may be involved in the pathogenesis of ARDS.[63] Likewise, secondary injuries, such as acquired surfactant deficiency, oxygen toxicity, and barotrauma, are thought to contribute to pulmonary damage. As is noted in the same article, a single mediator or mechanism probably is not responsible for all the findings seen in ARDS, and simultaneous activity on several fronts probably occurs.

The physiologic hallmark of ARDS is damage to the capillary endothelium and alveolar epithelial barriers leading to disruption of the alveolar-capillary membrane, increased permeability, and noncardiogenic pulmonary edema.[65] Increasing fluid within the alveoli and interstitial spaces leads to decreased total lung compliance, decreased functional residual capacity, increased airway resistance, and increased dead space. The resultant ventilation-perfusion mismatch creates the large intrapulmonary shunt responsible for the profound hypoxemia seen clinically.[34] Additional physiologic derangements seen in ARDS include alterations

TABLE 72–2 ■ INFECTIOUS CONDITIONS ASSOCIATED WITH ADULT RESPIRATORY DISTRESS SYNDROME IN CHILDREN

Author	Year	No. of Patients	Mortality	Viral Isolates	Bacterial Isolates	Fungal	Other
Lyrene[40]	1981	15	9/15 (60%)	0	*Enterococcus*	0	0
Pfenninger[57]	1982	20	8/20 (40%)	0	Intra-abdominal process, 7/20, NS	0	0
Nussbaum[47a]	1983	7	2/7 (29%)	0	*Haemophilus influenzae* type b	0	0
Katz[31]	1984	23	8/23 (35%)	2/23, NS	*Pneumococcus*	0	0
Tamburro[79a]	1991	37	19/37 (51%)	Adenovirus, cytomegalovirus, varicella	*Stapyhlococcus aureus*	0	0
DeBruin*[17]	1992	100	72/100 (72%)	HIV, cytomegalovirus, respiratory syncytial virus	Septic shock syndrome, 64/100, NS *Bordetella pertussis*	5/100, NS	*Pneumocystis carinii*, 14/100
Davis[15]	1993	60	37/60 (62%)	Respiratory syncytial virus, influenza virus, cytomegalovirus, varicella	Sepsis syndrome, 22/60, NS	4/60, NS	0

*Children with malignancy and/or compromised immunity.
NS, organism not specified.

in peripheral oxygen delivery and consumption, pulmonary hypertension with right ventricular compromise, and end-organ (liver, kidney, intestine, bone marrow) damage.[12, 68, 86]

The histologic findings seen at postmortem examination of patients dying as a result of ARDS are very consistent and have been well described.[8, 32, 59, 82] Historically, three interrelated and overlapping phases are described. They correlate well with clinical progression of the syndrome and include the exudative, proliferative, and fibrotic phases. The early exudative phase typically is recognized from 12 to 96 hours after the onset of respiratory failure.[65, 68, 82] It is characterized by increased fluid in the alveoli and interstitium and hemorrhagic alveolitis. Grossly, the lungs are rigid, dusky, red-blue, and very heavy.[82] The alveolar fluid is protein-rich, often hemorrhagic, and associated with hyaline membranes.[59] A combined neutrophilic and monocytic infiltrate is observed in the pulmonary capillaries, interstitium, and alveoli (Fig. 72–1*A*). Although capillaries also contain fibrin plugs and microthrombi, endothelial cells show only subtle abnormalities when compared with the alveolar surfaces, which undergo degeneration and sloughing.[65]

The proliferative phase occurs 3 to 10 days after the onset of ARDS and is characterized by organization of the alveolar and interstitial exudates acquired during the exudative phase.[82] Gross examination reveals the lungs to be solid, pale gray, and slippery because of the generation of connective tissue. The proliferation of type II cuboidal epithelial cells occurs as early as 3 days after onset, with fibrosis visible by 10 days. Type II pneumocytes are metabolically active and responsible for the production of surfactant, and they evolve into the type I epithelial cells that line the alveolar spaces (see Fig. 72–1*B*). Within the alveolar walls, fibroblasts and myofibroblasts also proliferate and migrate through the basement membrane into the alveolar space. In addition, early resolution of the hyaline membranes and pulmonary edema begins. This phase is considered to be reparative in nature.

Phase III, the fibrotic stage, begins to develop 7 to 10 days after the onset of respiratory failure and is characterized by progressive fibrosis that distorts the primary acinar architecture of the lung. The lungs appear pale and spongy with a cobblestone surface. Cellularity is reduced, alveolar fluid organizes, and fibrosis develops in and around the terminal respiratory units (see Fig. 72–1*C*). Airspaces are irregularly enlarged and separated by thick bands of collagenous connective tissue. Extensive fibrosis appears to be related to irreversible respiratory failure.[8]

Clinical Manifestations

The clinical features of ARDS are a reflection of the pathophysiologic changes previously discussed and generally follow a typical course regardless of the initiating event or injury. The syndrome progresses through four stages: the acute injury, a latent period, acute respiratory failure, and a period of severe physiologic derangement.[63, 65, 68] During the period of acute injury, the physical, laboratory, and radiographic findings associated with the causative disease or injury generally overshadow those associated with ARDS itself. Disorders associated with primary lung injury (e.g., aspiration pneumonitis or inhalation injury) may demonstrate significant physical or radiographic findings, whereas individuals with trauma or sepsis syndromes may have entirely normal auscultative or radiographic examinations of the chest.

The latent period is said to occur from 6 to 48 hours after the onset of ARDS and is characterized by cardiopulmonary stabilization or even improvement in the patient's condition. Subtle physical examination findings (mild tachypnea), radiographic findings (fine reticular infiltrates), and laboratory abnormalities (increased Pa_{CO_2}, increased pulmonary vascular resistance, decreased tissue oxygen delivery, increased serum von Willebrand factor antigen) may suggest the development of ARDS during this phase.[1, 66, 71]

The diagnosis of ARDS generally is made during the period of acute respiratory failure and is based on appropriate clinical and laboratory findings supportive of the diagnosis combined with a preexisting condition known to be associated with ARDS. The physical examination is remarkable for tachypnea, tachycardia, dyspnea, and cyanosis. The chest generally is quiet, but fine crackles may be present. Hypoxemia refractory to supplemental oxygen therapy is one of the hallmarks of the syndrome. Chest radiographs demonstrate diffuse, bilateral infiltrates suggestive of both interstitial fluid and alveolar filling or atelectasis (Fig. 72–2). Computed tomography may be helpful in characterizing the nature of the pulmonary infiltrates or even distinguishing the cause of the ARDS.[19] Respiratory failure and profound hypoxemia require intubation. The hypoxemia often worsens rapidly despite assisted ventilation, and many patients

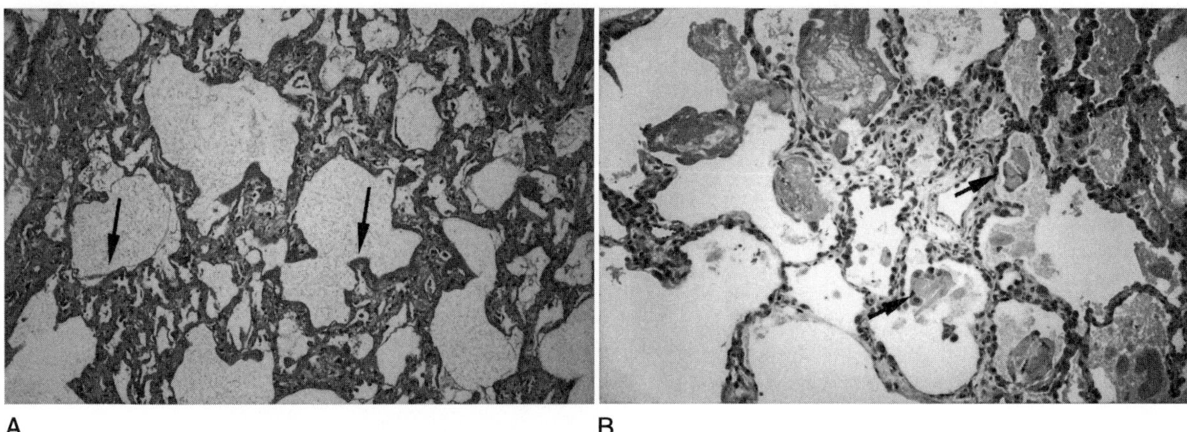

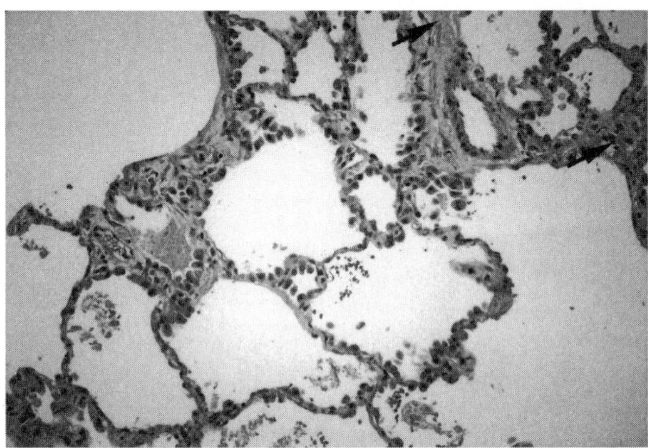

FIGURE 72–1 ■ *A,* Exudative phase of adult respiratory distress syndrome (ARDS). Acute lung injury is demonstrated with diffuse alveolar and interstitial edema. Hyaline membranes are visible within the alveoli (↓). *B,* Proliferative phase of ARDS. Early repair is evident with residual hyaline membranes surrounded by macrophages (↑), early fibroblast activation, and epithelial hyperplasia. *C,* Late proliferative to early fibrotic phase of ARDS. Epithelial proliferation and hyperplasia persists with increasing evidence of fibroblast activation (↑).

progress to the phase of severe physiologic abnormalities. During this stage, hypoxemia and hypercapnia refractory to high levels of ventilatory support often denote an irreversible pulmonary process. Multiorgan system failure often ensues at this point. The clinical course thereafter depends on the severity and character of the initial illness and the development of complications such as sepsis, disseminated intravascular coagulation, and pulmonary air leak syndromes.

Treatment

Although tremendous energy and resources have been invested in research aimed at defining the mechanism of lung injury in ARDS, a definitive answer and, thus, definitive therapeutic interventions have remained elusive. For this reason, management of ARDS historically has been primarily supportive. The traditional goals of therapy have been to treat the underlying or predisposing condition, to maintain adequate end-organ oxygenation through the use of oxygen and supportive ventilation, and to minimize complications of therapy or acute/chronic illness (oxygen toxicity, barotrauma, nosocomial infections, negative nitrogen balance, and multisystem organ dysfunction).[64, 68] Only in the past decade have significant advances been made in improving supportive care and attempts made to treat some of the underlying pathologies encountered in ARDS.

Both Sarnaik and Royall have stressed the importance of adequate monitoring for patients with ARDS. Invasive and noninvasive monitoring modalities allow an assessment of pulmonary mechanics, the adequacy of peripheral oxygen delivery and consumption, cardiac function, and other critical physiologic parameters. Pulse oximetry, arterial catheters, and central venous pressure monitors are suggested as a minimum, with the use of pulmonary artery catheters as indicated by the patient's clinical status.

The historical approach to the respiratory management of ARDS has focused on the use of oxygen and PEEP. Hypoxemia is profound in patients with ARDS and is refractory to supplemental oxygen given by face mask. The vast majority of patients require intubation and supportive mechanical ventilation. Once the patient is intubated, high concentrations of supplemental oxygen and high levels of PEEP often are needed. PEEP improves pulmonary function in ARDS by reducing ventilation-perfusion mismatch and decreasing intrapulmonary shunting,[14, 70] which is accomplished by increasing functional residual capacity by enlarging open alveoli and recruiting atelectatic airspaces. PEEP additionally reduces the repetitive expansion and collapse of terminal airways and redistributes alveolar fluid. Improved lung compliance and decreased ventilation-perfusion mismatch may allow a reduction in FIO_2, thereby decreasing the potential for oxygen toxicity and potentially protecting the lung.[55, 89]

Although PEEP significantly improves ventilation-perfusion mismatch, it can affect cardiac output. Decreased venous return to the heart and a shift in the interventricular cardiac septum can occur with high pressures. These complications are treated by a reduction in left ventricular afterload. PEEP should be used to maximize oxygen delivery at the lowest pressure that achieves this goal. Peak inspiratory pressure should be limited to 50 cm H_2O, if possible, to reduce barotrauma.

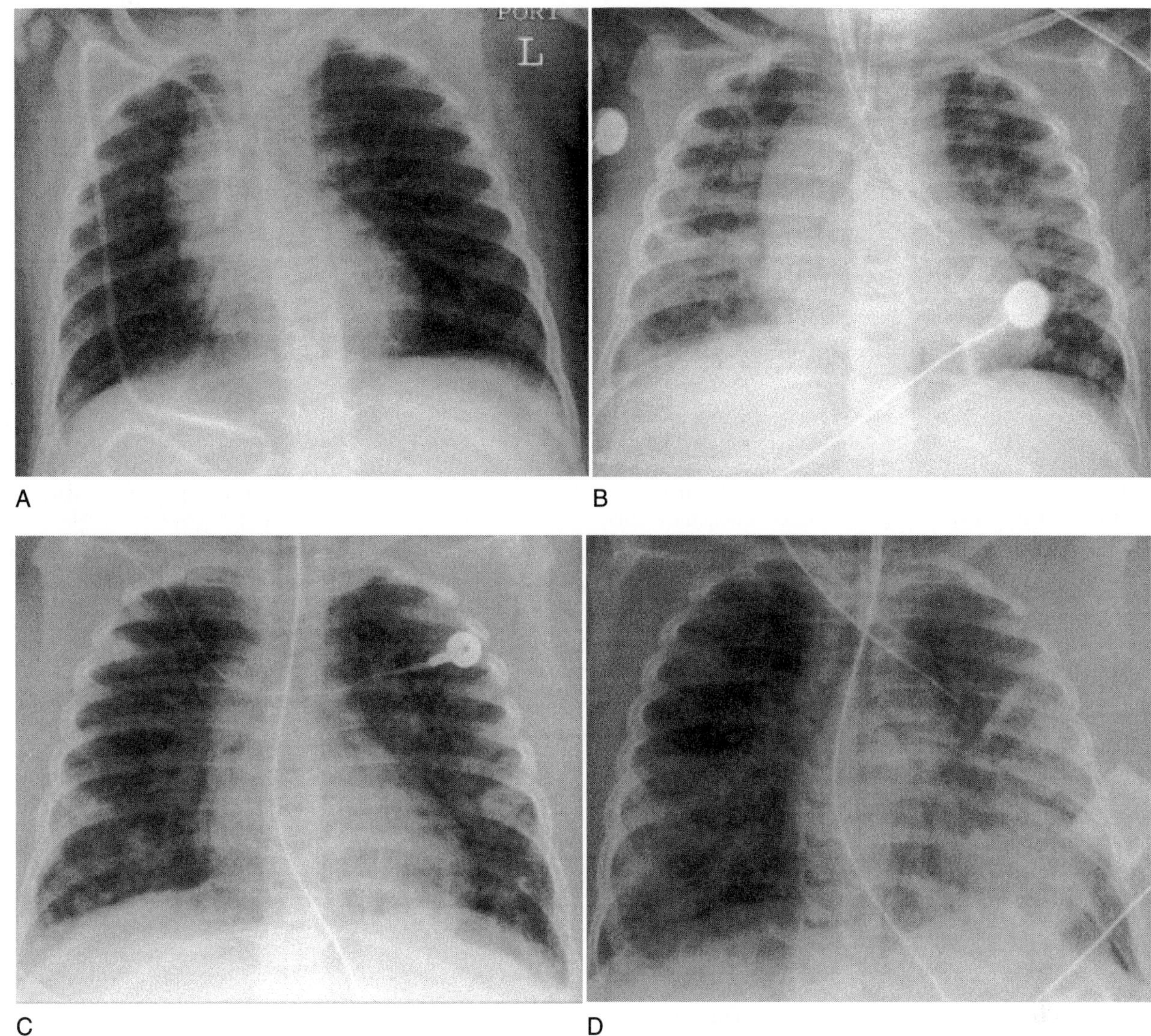

FIGURE 72–2 ■ Chest radiographs from a 4-year-old with central line sepsis and adult respiratory distress syndrome. Note the diffuse bilateral infiltrates suggestive of alveolar filling, interstitial fluid, and atelectasis. The time from *A* to *B* was 24 hours, but the intervals from *B* to *C* and from *C* to *D* were several days.

Many of the predisposing conditions associated with ARDS result in cardiovascular instability. Cardiovascular function should be monitored and maintained with additional therapies (e.g., inotropic agents, fluids) as needed. Colloid or crystalloid is used for volume resuscitation. Once patients are hemodynamically stable, fluids are restricted to decrease vascular leak and subsequent pulmonary edema. Patients frequently are given diuretics to reduce fluid in the interstitium and alveolus. Positive inotropic support with dopamine or dobutamine may be required.

The overall goal of cardiopulmonary management of ARDS is to maintain good cardiac output and optimize oxygen delivery to the periphery. Other important aspects of the supportive care required for management of ARDS include maintenance of adequate nutrition, avoidance or treatment of complications related to therapy (barotrauma and oxygen toxicity) or prolonged illness (infection), and support of other organ systems.[64] Poor nutrition is common in critically ill children and results in poor tissue repair, multiple organ system dysfunction, respiratory muscle weakness, and immune deficiency.[58, 74] Hence, nutritional support is of paramount importance in ARDS and must be maintained.[60] The related issues of oxygen toxicity and barotrauma are considered later. Infection is both a common precipitating event in ARDS and an important factor in the course and outcome.[64] Infections typically take the form of bacteremia/sepsis or nosocomial pneumonia. Organisms frequently isolated from the lower respiratory tract are *Klebsiella* and *Pseudomonas*; however, *Escherichia coli, Candida albicans*, and *Staphylococcus epidermidis* are not uncommon isolates.[68] A high index of suspicion and a low threshold for therapy should be maintained. Finally, prevention, detection, and treatment of multisystem organ dysfunction or complications are critical in the overall management of children with ARDS.

As suggested earlier, many of the innovations in the supportive care of ARDS have come in the arena of ventilatory support. Pressure-limited ventilation with a reversed inspiratory-to-expiratory ratio, permissive hypercapnia, high-frequency ventilation (positive pressure, jet, and oscillating), liquid ventilation, and extracorporeal membrane oxygenation have been reported.[4, 6, 24, 26, 29, 33, 36, 38, 52, 53] Patients unresponsive to conventional mechanical ventilation may benefit, in terms of improved oxygenation, from any of these methods. Additionally, patients may benefit from lower FiO_2 and peak airway pressure to decrease the potential oxygen toxicity and barotrauma. Although many of these newer forms of ventilation for children with ARDS show promise, none has been shown conclusively to be superior to another, and all will require more research and clinical experience. At present, many of them are considered "rescue therapy."

Numerous pharmacologic agents have been used for the treatment of ARDS during the past decade. Therapeutic trials with corticosteroids, vasodilators, and prostaglandin E_1 have been reported.[5, 11, 44, 64, 87] Small trials with a host of other agents have failed to identify universally effective therapies.[33, 43] Among the many pharmacologic agents studied, only exogenous surfactant and inhaled nitric oxide (NO) have been evaluated in large, multicenter trials and currently show promise.

The relative or acquired surfactant deficiency seen in ARDS renders surfactant replacement therapy an attractive area of investigation. In 1993, Lewis and Jobe presented a comprehensive review of the rationale behind surfactant use in ARDS.[37] Theoretically, replacement of endogenous surfactant by exogenous material would increase total lung compliance, decrease atelectasis, and improve pulmonary mechanics, thereby leading to decreased ventilation-perfusion mismatch, improved oxygenation, and less potential oxygen toxicity and barotrauma. The results of several trials have been reported in recent years and appear to offer some hope of improving outcomes in children with ARDS.[22, 39, 41, 73, 79, 90] Problems with surfactant therapy include difficulty with delivery and inactivation by lung fluid proteins. As the aforementioned references suggest, solutions to these and other issues related to surfactant therapy for ARDS are being sought aggressively, and researchers hope that surfactant will prove to be a valuable therapy in the future.

Another area of active research for the treatment of ARDS is the use of inhaled NO. NO has been shown to be a potent vasodilator and has been used in numerous settings for infants and children with a variety of cardiopulmonary diseases.[3, 30] Numerous clinical trials have suggested a potential role for NO in the treatment of ARDS.[2, 16, 18, 20, 45, 47, 49] Nonetheless, the results of many of these trials fail to provide conclusive arguments for the use of NO, and several authors have questioned its use altogether.[42, 54] Obviously, additional study is required to answer questions regarding the many problems that remain about NO therapy for ARDS.

Prognosis

Despite the huge investments of time, money, energy, and talent that have gone into research on the basic pathophysiologic mechanisms involved in the development of ARDS and equal amounts into potential therapies, many questions remain unanswered and mortality has not changed appreciably in the 15 to 20 years since this disease first was described in children. Mortality rates remain high, from 40 to 70 percent (see Table 72–2). New supportive and therapeutic interventions have failed to provide the "magic bullet" that has been sought for treating ARDS, but some hold promise for the future. Most children who survive ARDS eventually have normal radiographic results, and pulmonary function improves gradually with only a mild reduction in forced vital capacity.[23] Long-term physiologic abnormalities show a strong correlation with the severity of acute illness and the degree of support required in the acute phase of ARDS. The search for innovative therapies to decrease the acuity of illness during the acute phase of the disease and decrease iatrogenic complications holds some hope for the future.

REFERENCES

1. Aberle, D. R., and Brown, K.: Radiologic considerations in the adult respiratory distress syndrome. Clin. Chest Med. *11*:737–754, 1990.
2. Abman, S. H., Griebel, J. L., Parker, D. K., et al.: Acute effects of inhaled nitric oxide in children with severe hypoxemic respiratory failure. J. Pediatr. *124*:881–888, 1994.
3. Abman, S. H., and Kinsella, J. P.: Inhaled nitric oxide therapy for pulmonary disease in pediatrics. Curr. Opin. Pediatr. *10*:236–242, 1998.
4. Amato, M. B., Barbas, C. S., Medeiros, D. M., et al.: Effect of a protective-ventilation strategy on mortality in the acute respiratory distress syndrome. N. Engl. J. Med. *338*:347–354, 1998.
5. Annest, S. J., Rhodes, G. R., Stratton, H. H., et al.: Increased intrapulmonary shunt following infusion of nitroglycerine or nitroprusside in patients with posttraumatic respiratory distress. Surg. Forum *30*:22–24, 1979.
6. Arnold, J. H., Harrison, J. H., Toro-Figuero, L. O., et al.: Prospective, randomized comparison of high frequency oscillatory ventilation and conventional mechanical ventilation in pediatric respiratory failure. Crit. Care Med. *22*:1530–1539, 1994.
7. Ashbaugh, D. G., Bigelow, D. B., Petty, T. L., et al.: Acute respiratory distress in adults. Lancet *2*:319–323, 1967.
8. Bachofen, M., and Weibel, E. R.: Structural alterations of lung parenchyma in the adult respiratory distress syndrome. Clin. Chest Med. *3*:35–56, 1982.
9. Beaufils, F., Mercier, J. C., Farnoux, C., et al.: Acute respiratory distress syndrome in children. Curr. Opin. Pediatr. *9*:207–212, 1997.
10. Bernard, G. R., Artigas, A., Brigham, K. L., et al.: The American-European Consensus Conference on ARDS. Definitions, mechanisms, relevant outcomes, and clinical trial coordination. Am. J. Respir. Crit. Care Med. *149*:818–824, 1994.
11. Bernard, G. R., Luce, J. M., Sprung, C. L., et al.: High-dose corticosteroids in patients with the adult respiratory distress syndrome. N. Engl. J. Med. *317*:1565–1570, 1987.
12. Clarke, C., Edwards, J. D., Nightingale, P., et al.: Persistence of supply dependency of oxygen uptake at high levels of delivery in adult respiratory distress syndrome. Crit. Care Med. *19*:497–502, 1991.
13. Costil, J., Cloup, M., Leclerc, F., et al.: Acute respiratory distress syndrome (ARDS) in children: Multicenter Collaborative Study of the French Group of Pediatric Intensive Care. Pediatr. Pulmonol. Suppl. *11*:106–107, 1995.
14. Dantzker, D. R.: Gas exchange in the adult respiratory distress syndrome. Clin. Chest Med. *3*:57–67, 1982.
15. Davis, S. L., Furman, D. P., and Costarino, A. T.: ARDS in children: Associated disease, clinical course, and predictors of death. J. Pediatr. *123*:35–45, 1993.
16. Day, R. W., Allen, E. M., and Witte, M. K.: A randomised, controlled study of the 1-hour and 24-hour effects of inhaled nitric oxide therapy in children with acute hypoxemic respiratory failure. Chest *112*:1324–1331, 1997.
17. DeBruin, W., Notterman, D., Magid, M., et al.: Acute hypoxemic respiratory failure in infants and children: Clinical and pathologic characteristics. Crit. Care Med. *20*:1223–1234, 1992.
18. Dellinger, R. P., Zimmerman, J. L., Taylor, R. W., et al.: Effects of inhaled nitric oxide in patients with acute respiratory distress syndrome: Results of a randomized phase II trial. Inhaled Nitric Oxide in ARDS Study Group. Crit. Care Med. *26*:15–23, 1998.
19. Desai, S. R., and Hansell, D. M.: Lung imaging in the adult respiratory distress syndrome: Current practice and new insights. Intensive Care Med. *23*:7–15, 1997.
20. Dobyns, E. L., Cornfield, D. N., Anas, N. G., et al.: Multicenter randomized controlled trial of the effects of inhaled nitric oxide therapy on gas exchange in children with acute hypoxemic respiratory failure. J. Pediatr. *134*:406–412, 1999.
21. Duchateau, J., Haas, M., Schreyen, H., et al.: Complement activation in patients at risk of developing the adult respiratory distress syndrome. Am. Rev. Respir. Dis. *130*:1058–1064, 1984.
22. Evans, D. A., Wilmott, R. W., and Whitsett, J. A.: Surfactant replacement therapy for adult respiratory distress syndrome in children. Pediatr. Pulmonol. *21*:328–336, 1996.
23. Fanconi, S., Kraemer, R., Weber, J., et al.: Long-term sequelae in children surviving adult respiratory distress syndrome. J. Pediatr. *106*:218–222, 1985.
24. Gauger, P. G., Pranikoff, T., Schreiner, R. J., et al.: Initial experience with partial liquid ventilation in pediatric patients with the acute respiratory distress syndrome. Crit. Care Med. *24*:16–22, 1996.
25. Hammerschmidt, D. E., Weaver, L. J., Hudson, L. D., et al.: Association of complement activation and elevated plasma-C5a with adult respiratory distress syndrome. Lancet *1*:947–949, 1980.
26. Hickling, K. G., Walsh, J., Henderson, S., et al.: Low mortality rate in adult respiratory distress syndrome using low-volume, pressure limited ventilation with permissive hypercapnia: A prospective study. Crit. Care Med. *22*:1568–1578, 1994.
27. Holbrook, P. R., Taylor, G., Pollack, M. M., et al.: Adult respiratory distress syndrome in children. Pediatr. Clin. North Am. *27*:677–685, 1980.
28. Holman, R. G., and Maier, R. V.: Superoxide production by neutrophils in a model of adult respiratory distress syndrome. Arch. Surg. *123*:1491–1495, 1988.

29. Kallas, H. J.: Non-conventional respiratory support modalities applicable in the older child. High frequency ventilation and liquid ventilation. Crit. Care Clin. *14*:655–683, 1998.
30. Kass, L. J., and Apkon, M: Inhaled nitric oxide in the treatment of hypoxemic respiratory failure. Curr. Opin. Pediatr. *10*:284–290, 1998.
31. Katz, R., Pollack, M., and Spady, D.: Cardiopulmonary abnormalities in severe acute respiratory failure. J. Pediatr. *104*:357–364, 1984.
32. Katzenstein, A. L., Bloor, C. M., and Leibow, A. A.: Diffuse alveolar damage—the role of oxygen, shock, and related factors. Am. J. Pathol. *85*:209–228, 1976.
33. Kollef, M. H.: Rescue therapy for the acute respiratory distress syndrome (ARDS). Chest *111*:845–846, 1997.
34. Lamy, M., Fallat, R. J., Koeniger, E., et al.: Pathologic features and mechanisms of hypoxemia in adult respiratory distress syndrome. Am. Rev. Respir. Dis. *114*:267–284, 1976.
35. Langlois, P. F., and Gawryl, M. S.: Complement activation occurs through both classical and alternative pathways prior to onset and resolution of adult respiratory distress syndrome. Clin. Immunol. Immunopathol. *47*:152–163, 1988.
36. Lewandowski, K.: Extracorporeal membrane oxygenation for severe acute respiratory failure. Crit. Care *4*:156–168, 2000.
37. Lewis, J. F., and Jobe, A. H: Surfactant and the adult respiratory distress syndrome. Am. Rev. Respir. Dis. *147*:218–233, 1993.
38. Linden, V., Palmer, K., Reinhard, J., et al.: High survival in adult patients with acute respiratory distress syndrome treated by extracorporeal membrane oxygenation, minimal sedation, and pressure supported ventilation. Intensive Care Med. *26*:1630–1637, 2000.
39. Lopez-Herce, J., de Lucas, N., Carrillo, A., et al.: Surfactant treatment for acute respiratory distress syndrome. Arch. Dis. Child. *80*:248–252, 1999.
40. Lyrene, R. K., and Troug, W. E.: Adult respiratory distress syndrome in a pediatric intensive care unit: Predisposing conditions, clinical course, and outcome. Pediatrics *67*:790–795, 1981.
41. Marraro, G. A., Luchetti, M., Galassini, E. M., et al.: Natural surfactant supplementation in ARDS in paediatric age. Minerva Anestesiol. *65*(Suppl.):92–97, 1999.
42. Matthay, M. A., Pittet, J. F., and Jayr, C.: Just say NO to inhaled nitric oxide for the acute respiratory distress syndrome. Crit. Care Med. *26*:1–2, 1998.
43. McIntyre, R. C., Jr., Pulido, E. J., Bensard, D. D., et al.: Thirty years of clinical trials in acute respiratory distress syndrome. Crit. Care Med. *28*:3314–3331, 2000.
44. Meduri, G. U.: Levels of evidence for the pharmacologic effectiveness of prolonged methylprednisolone treatment in unresolving ARDS. Chest *116*(Suppl.):116–118, 1999.
45. Michael, J. R., Barton, R. G., Saffle, J. R., et al.: Inhaled nitric oxide versus conventional therapy: Effect on oxygenation in ARDS. Am. J. Respir. Crit. Care Med. *157*:1372–1380, 1998.
46. Milberg, J. A., Davis, D. R., Steinberg, K. P., et al.: Improved survival of patients with acute respiratory distress syndrome (ARDS): 1983–1993. J. A. M. A. *273*:306–309, 1995.
47. Nakagawa, T. A., Morris, A., Gomez, R. J., et al.: Dose response to inhaled nitric oxide in pediatric patients with pulmonary hypertension and acute respiratory distress syndrome. J. Pediatr. *131*:63–69, 1997.
47a. Nussbaum, E.: Adult type respiratory distress syndrome in children. Clin. Pediatr. *22*:401–406, 1983.
48. Ognibene, F. P., Martin, S. E., Parker, M. M., et al.: Adult respiratory distress syndrome in patients with severe neutropenia. N. Engl. J. Med. *315*:547–551, 1986.
49. Okamato, K., Hamaguchi, M., Kukuta, K., et al.: efficacy of inhaled nitric oxide in children with ARDS. Chest *114*:827–833, 1998.
50. Parsons, P. E., and Giclas, P. C.: The terminal complement complex (sC5b-9) is not specifically associated with the development of the adult respiratory distress syndrome. Am. Rev. Respir. Dis. *141*:98–103, 1990.
51. Parsons, P. E., Worthen, G. S., Moore, E. E., et al.: The association of circulating endotoxin with the development of the adult respiratory distress syndrome. Am. Rev. Respir. Dis. *140*:294–301, 1989.
52. Paulson, T. E., Spear, R. M., and Peterson, B. M.: New concepts in the treatment of children with acute respiratory distress syndrome. J. Pediatr. *127*:163–175, 1995.
53. Paulson, T. E., Spear, R. M., Silva, P. D., et al.: High-frequency pressure-control ventilation with high positive end-expiratory pressure in children with acute respiratory distress syndrome. J. Pediatr. *129*: 566–573, 1996.
54. Payen, D. M.: Is nitric oxide inhalation a "cosmetic" therapy in acute respiratory distress syndrome? Am. J. Respir. Crit. Care Med. *157*: 1361–1362, 1998.
55. Pepe, P. E., Hudson, L. D., and Carrico, C. J.: Early application of positive end-expiratory pressure in patients at risk for the adult respiratory-distress syndrome. N. Engl. J. Med. *311*:281–286, 1984.
56. Pfenninger, J.: Acute respiratory distress syndrome (ARDS) in neonates and children. Paediatr. Anaesth. *6*:173–181, 1996.
57. Pfenninger, J., Gerber, A., Tschäppeler, H., et al.: Adult respiratory distress syndrome in children. J. Pediatr. *101*:352–357, 1982.
58. Pingleton, S. K., and Harmon, G. S.: Nutritional management in acute respiratory failure. J. A. M. A. *257*:3094–3099, 1987.
59. Pratt, P. C., Vollmer, R. T., Shelburne, J. D., et al.: Pulmonary morphology in a multihospital collaborative extracorporeal membrane oxygenation project. I. Light microscopy. Am. J. Pathol. *95*:191–214, 1979.
60. Reimer, S. L., Michener, W. M., and Steiger, E.: Nutritional support of the critically ill child. Pediatr. Clin. North Am. *27*:647–660, 1980.
61. Rinaldo, J. E., and Christman, J. W.: Mechanisms and mediators of the adult respiratory distress syndrome. Clin. Chest Med. *11*:621–632, 1990.
62. Rocco, T. R., Jr., Reinert, S. E., Cioffi, W., et al.: A 9-year, single-institution, retrospective review of death rate and prognostic factors in adult respiratory distress syndrome. Ann. Surg. *233*:414–422, 2001.
63. Royall, J. A.: Adult respiratory distress syndrome in children. Semin. Respir. Med. *11*:223–234, 1990.
64. Royall, J. A., and Levin, D. L.: Adult respiratory distress syndrome in pediatric patients. 1. Clinical aspects, pathophysiology, pathology, and mechanisms of lung injury. J. Pediatr. *112*:169–180, 1988.
65. Royall, J., and Levin, D. L.: Adult respiratory distress syndrome in pediatric patients. II. Management. J. Pediatr. *112*:335–347, 1988.
66. Rubin, D. B., Wiener-Kronish, J. P., Murray, J. F., et al.: Elevated von Willebrand factor antigen is an early plasma predictor of acute lung injury in nonpulmonary sepsis syndrome. J. Clin. Invest. *86*:474–480, 1990.
67. Sachdeva, R. C., and Guntupalli, K. K.: Acute respiratory distress syndrome. Crit. Care Clin. *13*:503–521, 1997.
68. Sarnaik, A. P., and Lieh-Lai, M.: Adult respiratory distress syndrome in children. Pediatr. Clin. North Am. *41*:337–363, 1994.
69. Scannell, G., Waxman, K., and Tominagam G. T.: Respiratory distress in traumatized and burned children. J. Pediatr. Surg. *30*:612–614, 1995.
70. Shapiro, B. A., Cane, R. D., and Harrison, R. A.: Positive end-expiratory pressure therapy in adults with special reference to acute lung injury: A review of the literature and suggested clinical correlations. Crit. Care Med. *12*:127–141, 1984.
71. Shoemaker, W. C., Appel, P., Czerm L. S., et al.: Pathogenesis of respiratory failure (ARDS) after hemorrhage and trauma: I. Cardiorespiratory patterns preceding the development of ARDS. Crit. Care Med. *8*:504–512, 1980.
72. Sivan, Y., Mor, C., al-Jundi, S., et al.: Adult respiratory distress syndrome in severely neutropenic children. Pediatr. Pulmonol. *8*:104–108, 1990.
73. Spragg, R. G.: Surfactant replacement therapy. Clin. Chest Med. *21*:531–541, 2000.
74. Steffee, W. P.: Malnutrition in hospitalized patients. J. A. M. A. *244*:2630–2635, 1980.
75. Stephens, K. E., Ishizaka, A., Larrick, J. W., et al.: Tumor necrosis factor causes increased pulmonary permeability and edema: Comparison to septic acute lung injury. Am. Rev. Respir. Dis. *137*:1364, 1988.
76. Suchyta, M. R., Clemmer, T. P., Elliot, C. G., et al.: The adult respiratory distress syndrome. A report of survival and modifying factors. Chest *101*:1074–1079, 1992.
77. Swank, D. W., and Moore, S. B.: Roles of the neutrophil and other mediators in adult respiratory distress syndrome. Mayo Clin. Proc. *64*:1118–1132, 1989.
78. Sznajder, J. I., Fraiman, A., Hall, J. B., et al.: Increased hydrogen peroxide in the expired breath of patients with acute hypoxemic respiratory failure. Chest *96*:606–612, 1989.
79. Taeusch, H. W.: Treatment of acute (adult) respiratory distress syndrome. The holy grail of surfactant therapy. Biol. Neonate *77*(Suppl.):2–8, 2000.
79a. Tamburro, R. F., Bugnitz, M. C., and Stidham, G. L.: Alveolar-arterial oxygen gradient as a predictor of outcome in patients with non-neonatal pediatric respiratory failure. J. Pediatr. *119*:935–938, 1991.
80. Tate, R. M., and Repine, J. E.: Neutrophils and the adult respiratory distress syndrome. Am. Rev. Respir. Dis. *128*:552–559, 1983.
81. Timmons, O. D., Dean, J. M., and Vernon, D. D.: Mortality rates and prognostic variables in children with adult respiratory distress syndrome. J. Pediatr. *119*:896–899, 1991.
82. Tomashefski, J. F., Jr.: Pulmonary pathology of the adult respiratory distress syndrome. Clin. Chest Med. *11*:593–619, 1990.
83. Tracey, K. J., Beutler, B., Lowry, S. F., et al.: Shock and tissue injury induced by recombinant human cachectin. Science *234*:470–474, 1986.
84. Tracey, K. J., Fong, Y., Hessem D. G., et al.: Anti-cachectin/TNF monoclonal antibodies prevent septic shock during lethal bacteraemia. Nature *330*:662–664, 1987.
85. Tracey, K. J., Lowry, S. F., Fahey, T. J., III, et al.: Cachectin/tumor necrosis factor induces lethal shock and stress hormone responses in the dog. Surg. Gynecol. Obstet. *164*:415, 1987.
86. Weg, J. G.: Oxygen transport in adult respiratory distress syndrome and other acute circulatory problems: Relationship of oxygen delivery and oxygen consumption. Crit. Care Med. *19*:650–657, 1991.
87. Weigelt, J. A., Norcross, J. F., Borman, K. R., et al.: Early steroid therapy for respiratory failure. Arch. Surg. *120*:536–540, 1985.
88. Weinberg, P. F., Matthay, M. A., Webster, R. O., et al.: Biologically active products of complement and acute lung injury in patients with the sepsis syndrome. Am. Rev. Respir. Dis. *130*:791–796, 1984.
89. Weisman, I. M., Rinaldo, J. E., Rogers, R. M.: Current concepts: Positive end-expiratory pressure in adult respiratory failure. N. Engl. J. Med. *307*:1381–1384, 1982.
90. Wiswell, T. E., Smith, R. M., Katz, L. B., et al.: Bronchopulmonary segmental lavage with Surfaxin (KL(4)-surfactant) for acute respiratory distress syndrome. Am. J. Respir. Crit. Care Med. *160*:1188–1195, 1999.

SECTION **XIII**

Viral and Miscellaneous Infections of the Fetus and Newborn

CHAPTER 73 Viral Infections of the Fetus and Neonate

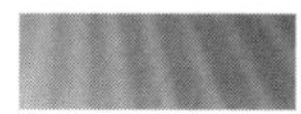

CHAPTER **73A**

General Aspects of Viral Infections

PABLO J. SÁNCHEZ

The fetus and newborn infant are highly susceptible to many different viruses, which in most instances cause little or no disease in older age groups. However, relatively few of the hundreds of viruses to which humans constantly are exposed are ever transmitted to the fetus or cause infection in newborn infants. Nevertheless, viral infections are an important cause of neonatal morbidity and mortality. The cumulative frequency of viral infections in the fetus or newborn infant may be as high as 6 to 8 percent of all live births, whereas systemic bacterial disease occurs in only 1 to 2 percent of neonates.[421]

Contributing to the frequency of viral infections in this age group is that the infection can be acquired at several different periods during intrauterine and neonatal life: in utero (congenital infection), at the time of birth (natal infection), or after birth but during the neonatal period (postnatal infection). In addition, numerous different outcomes of infection are possible. Congenital infections can result in resorption of the embryo; abortion; stillbirth; congenital malformation; prematurity; intrauterine growth restriction; acute disease apparent in utero, at birth, or shortly thereafter; asymptomatic infection in the neonatal period, but a persistent postnatal infection with neurologic sequelae later in life; or a normal infant without apparent sequelae. Natal or postnatal infections can cause acute systemic illness leading to death, persistent infection with late sequelae, self-limited disease with no discernible damage, or asymptomatic infection.

Recent developments in the fields of diagnostic virology, epidemiology, and viral immunology have expanded our knowledge tremendously and modified our understanding of fetal and neonatal viral infections and their contribution to disease, not only in the neonatal period but also later in life. In addition, the development of rubella vaccine and antiviral drugs effective against a few of the agents offers hope for prevention or control of these infections. This chapter provides the physician with an approach to diagnosis and management of, as well as prognostic information about, viral infections that occur in the fetus and newborn infant. Human immunodeficiency virus (HIV), an important perinatal viral pathogen, is covered in Chapter 193. For more detailed information and more extensive bibliographies, the reader can consult several excellent recent reviews, monographs or chapters, and textbooks.[31, 143, 176, 194, 212, 421]

PATHOGENESIS

Congenital Viral Infections

Congenital viral infections occur secondary to exposure of the fetus during maternal viral infection. Evidence from both humans and experimental animals indicates that fetal infection is preceded by a systemic viral infection in the mother, with hematogenous spread of the virus to the placenta and subsequently to the fetus (Fig. 73–1). Most viral infections that occur in the mother during pregnancy appear to be limited to the respiratory or gastrointestinal tract and, therefore, do not pose a risk to the fetus. Even if viremia does occur in the mother, maternal host defense mechanisms and the placenta appear to provide a protective barrier for the fetus. With most viruses known to cause fetal infection—cytomegalovirus (CMV), rubella virus, herpes simplex virus (HSV), varicella-zoster virus (VZV), and vaccinia virus—placental involvement by the virus also has been documented.[58] Viruses may reach the fetal circulation by (1) replication through the layers of the placenta, (2) production of virus-induced vascular lesions in the placenta resulting in abnormal communications between the maternal and fetal circulation, or (3) diapedesis of virus-infected maternal leukocytes through the layers of the placenta to the fetal circulation.[58, 380, 505] Damage to the fetus also may occur in the absence of actual fetal viral infection as a result of severe systemic illness in the mother or alteration of placental function (e.g., abortion or stillbirth in maternal measles, influenza). Viruses demonstrated to have caused congenital infection are listed in Table 73–1. Proof of congenital infection usually consists of the presence of disease caused by the virus or demonstration of the pathogen in the neonate at birth or shortly thereafter.[212, 421]

The effect that congenital infection with various viruses can have on the fetus is shown in Table 73–2.[421, 461–463] Abortion or stillbirth usually occurs when the mother is infected very early in gestation (e.g., rubella) or when the systemic illness in the mother is severe (e.g., measles, influenza). The reasons that premature birth occurs in congenital viral infection are not well understood. Infants with congenital viral infection who are small for gestational age have intrauterine growth restriction, usually the result of decreased numbers of cells in organs.[356, 357]

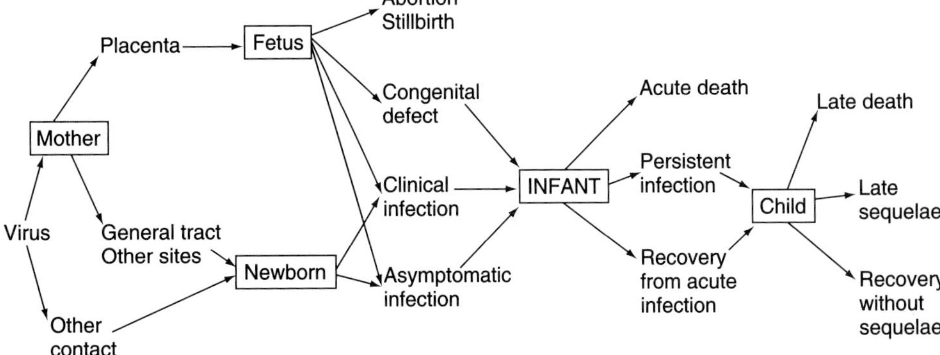

FIGURE 73–1 ■ Pathogenesis of viral infections in the fetus and newborn.

Developmental malformations result from infection of the fetus with the virus (see Table 73–2). Rubella virus is the classic known teratogen; that is, it causes disturbances in organogenesis. VZV has been shown to cause limb hypoplasia and developmental malformations of the eye.[187] The other viruses that result in congenital defects, CMV and HSV, cause inflammatory, destructive lesions of already developed organs.[212] Type B coxsackieviruses have been associated with a variety of congenital malformations of the heart,[73–75] and mumps has been linked to endocardial fibroelastosis,[470] but these associations require further substantiation before a causative role can be assigned.

In Table 73–2, congenital disease refers to any manifestation of illness present at birth or shortly thereafter that is secondary to transplacental infection with the virus. Some of the viruses that result in congenital disease cause a chronic persistent infection (CMV, rubella, and hepatitis B), whereas others cause acute, self-limited, or fatal infection (echovirus, coxsackievirus B, poliovirus, measles, vaccinia, smallpox, western equine encephalitis, and human parvovirus B19). HSV and VZV can cause chronic persistent intrauterine infection, as well as acute transplacental infection at the time of delivery. With one virus, HSV, congenital infection has occurred by other than the transplacental route. Ascending amniotic infection with HSV, in association with premature rupture of membranes and maternal genital herpes infection, has resulted in acute disease at birth because of the short incubation period in the neonate.

TABLE 73–1 ■ PERIOD OF TRANSMISSION OF SELECTED VIRUSES TO THE FETUS OR NEWBORN INFANT

Viruses	Congenital	Natal	Postnatal
Cytomegalovirus	++	++	++
Rubella	++	–	–
Hepatitis A	–	++	+
Hepatitis B	+	++	+
Hepatitis C	+	++	–
Herpes simplex	+	++	+
Varicella-zoster	++	–	–
Echoviruses	+	+	+
Type B coxsackieviruses	+	+	+
Polioviruses	+	–	–
Mumps	+	–	–
Measles	+	–	–
Vaccinia	+	–	–
Smallpox	+	–	–
Influenza	(+)	–	–
Western equine encephalitis	+	–	–
Epstein-Barr	+	–	–
Human parvovirus B19	+	–	–
Lymphocytic choriomeningitis virus	++	–	–
Human immunodeficiency virus	+	++	+

++, major demonstrated route; +, minor demonstrated route; (+), suggested route, few supporting data; –, route not demonstrated.

Viruses and Congenital Malformation

The role of viruses as etiologic agents in congenital malformations merits special mention. After the recognition by Gregg[195] in 1941 that congenital cataracts and other defects occurred in the offspring of mothers with German measles, the concept of an infectious origin for congenital malformations was established firmly. Major malformations occur in 2 to 3 percent of all live births.[212] Although great strides have been made in the diagnosis and management of these defects, their etiologic basis remains largely undefined. Approximately 10 percent are caused by environmental agents such as infections, drugs, or radiation. Another 10 percent have genetic origin and result from familial inheritance or demonstrable chromosomal abnormalities.[380] The remaining 80 percent are of unknown etiology. Most congenital defects may not be caused by environmental or genetic factors acting individually but rather in concert with one another. A genetically predisposed fetus is exposed to the appropriate environmental factor at a particular stage during organogenesis, which then leads to the development of malformations.[212] Because control of the genetic factors contributing to fetal malformation is unlikely to be developed to the point of practical application in the near future, efforts to identify environmental factors that are amenable to control appear warranted.

For several reasons, viruses have been considered to be likely contributors to the 80 percent of malformations that are of unknown etiology. First, the precedent is established that rubella virus and VZV infections during pregnancy do cause congenital defects. Second, most women are expected to have one or more viral infections at some time during pregnancy,[453] so the potential exposure rate is high. Third, a viral infection could be unrecognized in the mother yet produce significant disease in the fetus, which could lead to the occurrence of a "congenital defect of unknown etiology." Fourth, viruses are known to multiply readily in rapidly dividing immature cells, with resultant cell destruction or altered cell function.[342] In the case of more destructive viruses (e.g., measles, vaccinia), fetal death with abortion or stillbirth may occur, whereas with less cytolytic agents (e.g., rubella, CMV), the fetus may survive but defects are

TABLE 73–2 ■ EFFECT OF SPECIFIC VIRUSES ON THE FETUS AND NEWBORN INFANT

	Abortion, Stillbirth	Prematurity	Small for Gestational Age	Developmental Malformations	Congenital Disease	Acute Postnatal Disease	Persistent Postnatal Infection
Cytomegalovirus	+	+	+	+	+(C)	+	+
Rubella	+	+	+	+	+(C)	–	+
Hepatitis B	–	+	–	–	+(C)	+	+
Herpes simplex	+	+	+	+	+(C,A)	+	+
Varicella-zoster	–	+	+	+	+(C,A)	+	+
Echoviruses	–	–	–	–	+(A)	+	–
Type B coxsackieviruses	+	–	–	(+)	+(A)	–	–
Polioviruses	+	+	–	–	+(A)	–	–
Mumps	+	–	–	(+)	–	–	–
Measles	+	+	–	–	+(A)	–	–
Vaccinia	+	+	–	–	+(A)	–	–
Smallpox	+	+	–	–	+(A)	–	–
Influenza	+	–	–	–	–	(+)	–
Western equine encephalitis	–	–	–	–	+(A)	–	–
Epstein-Barr	–	–	+	+	+(C)	–	+
Parvovirus B19	+	–	–	–	+(C,A)	+	+

+, effect established; –, effect not established; (+), effect suggested, but not proved; (A), acute fatal or self-limited infection; (C), chronic persistent infection.

produced. Finally, experimental animals provide numerous examples of infection with a virus resulting in little or no disease in the pregnant mother, yet the fetuses are aborted or the newborn offspring are deformed.[160] Therefore, physicians caring for newborn infants should not only be familiar with the patterns of congenital defects currently known to be caused by viruses (CMV, rubella, HSV, and VZV) but also be aware that additional viruses may be added to the list of causative agents in the future.

Natal Viral Infections

Natal viral infections are the result of exposure of the newborn to virus replicating in the genital tract (CMV, HSV, hepatitis B virus [HBV]) or to fecal virus contaminating genital secretions (enteroviruses) (see Fig. 73–1 and Table 73–1). Because the incubation periods of HSV and enteroviruses are short, acute postnatal disease may appear in the neonate within 5 to 7 days after natal infection with these agents (see Table 73–2). In contrast, the incubation periods of CMV and HBV are long, and clinically apparent disease, if it occurs, may not be observed for several weeks or even months after birth (see Table 73–2). Persistent postnatal infection can occur after natal infection with CMV, HSV, and HBV.

Postnatal Viral Infections

The source of exposure for postnatal infections of a newborn infant often is the mother, but other sources have been observed, such as personnel or other infants in the nursery or newborn intensive care unit and family members (see Fig. 73–1). Outbreaks of enterovirus[345] and respiratory syncytial virus[204] infection have occurred in nurseries, and nosocomial HSV infections[206, 252, 390, 434, 518] have been reported (see Table 73–1). Although the maternal respiratory and gastrointestinal tracts are the most common sites from which virus can be transmitted to the neonate postnatally, HIV, CMV,[220] and HBV[306] have been recovered from breast milk. Finally, HIV, CMV,[559] and HBV[154] have been transmitted to newborn infants by blood transfusion.[152, 554] Although most postnatal infections are acute, self-limited processes, fatalities have been reported, and persistent postnatal infection may occur with CMV and HBV (see Table 73–2).

EPIDEMIOLOGY

Factors Influencing the Frequency of Infection

Many factors can influence the frequency of infections in the fetus and newborn infant (Table 73–3). Because the mother is the source of the virus causing fetal and neonatal infection in most instances, factors influencing the frequency of maternal infection are of major importance. Except for CMV infection, most congenital infections of the fetus occur after primary viral infection in the mother. Congenital CMV infection may occur as frequently in mothers known to be seropositive before conception as in seronegative mothers.[478] Congenital rubella, on the other hand, occurs only rarely in immune mothers.[212, 426] Transplacental HBV infection occurs much more often in mothers with acute, primary, symptomatic infection, whereas natal infection is the primary route of transmission in chronic carrier mothers.[377, 443]

TABLE 73–3 ■ FACTORS INFLUENCING FREQUENCY AND SEVERITY OF VIRAL INFECTIONS IN THE FETUS AND NEWBORN INFANT

	Time of Fetal or Neonatal Infection		
Factors	Congenital	Natal	Postnatal
Primary infection in mother	++	++	++
Maternal age	++	+	++
Gestational age of fetus	++	+	+
Absence of vaccine	++	–	–
Presence of epidemic in community	++	+	++
Season of year	++	+	++
Geographic location	++	++	++
Socioeconomic status	++	++	++
Sexual promiscuity	+	++	–
Method of case indentification	++	++	++

++, major influence; +, minor influence; –, little or no influence.

Perinatal enteroviral infections acquired from the mother almost always are the result of primary maternal infection. In contrast, natal infections with CMV, HBV, and HSV may result from persistent or recurrent genital infections in the mother. The frequency of primary viral infection in mothers is influenced by maternal age because susceptibility is related inversely to the age of the mother.

The evidence is clear that the time during pregnancy at which the mother is infected (the gestational age of the fetus) is a major factor influencing both the frequency and the severity of congenital rubella. One hundred percent of infants who have congenital infection during the first 11 weeks of pregnancy have malformations associated with congenital rubella syndrome, 30 percent who have congenital infection from 12 to 20 weeks have malformations, and no malformations develop with infections occurring after 20 weeks.[338] The same phenomenon occurs with congenital CMV and VZV infections.[225, 391, 473] In contrast, transplacental HBV infection appears to develop more frequently when the acute, symptomatic maternal infection occurs in the third trimester rather than the first or second.[564] With viruses such as polio, measles, vaccinia, and smallpox, early-gestation maternal disease results in abortion or stillbirth, whereas late-gestation infection results in congenital disease with acute symptoms in the early neonatal period (see Table 73–2).

Several social and environmental factors may influence the likelihood of development of maternal infection and thereby affect the frequency of infection in the fetus and neonate. The development of rubella vaccine and its licensure in 1969 reduced the incidence of congenital rubella syndrome significantly.[41, 379] The successful eradication of smallpox worldwide and discontinuation of the need for smallpox vaccine (vaccinia virus) have eliminated fetal infection with these viruses. Although measles and mumps vaccines have reduced the frequency of occurrence of these diseases in childhood significantly, whether waning immunity in women of child-bearing age who were vaccinated as infants will predispose to reinfection in pregnant women and subsequent fetal or neonatal disease remains unclear. The presence of epidemics in the community, such as those caused by rubella or enteroviruses, certainly can influence the frequency of maternal and, therefore, congenital, natal, and postnatal infections. The incidence of infection with some viruses (e.g., rubella, primary VZV, enteroviruses, measles, mumps, influenza) clearly is higher during certain months of the year, so the season can influence maternal and neonatal infection rates. In contrast, other viruses causing congenital or natal infection (CMV, HBV, HSV) do not occur in an epidemic or seasonal fashion. Geographic location also can be influential, probably because of differences in the ethnic (and, therefore, genetic) origin of populations in different locations. Rates of chronic carriage of hepatitis B surface antigen (HBsAg) in mothers and the frequency of congenital and natal HBV infection in neonates are much higher in Taiwanese than in U.S. residents.[564] The incidence of numerous maternal viral infections is known to be higher in populations with a lower socioeconomic status, thereby influencing the frequency of congenital, natal, and postnatal infections. Other social factors such as drug abuse, which is associated with higher rates of HBV infection, also can affect the frequency of congenital and natal infections. Because CMV, HBV, and HSV all have been shown to be transmitted venereally, sexual promiscuity in the mother can influence the frequency of these infections in the neonate.

Though listed last in Table 73–3, the method of case identification is a major factor that can have some bearing on the frequency of recognized infection in the neonate. Because most neonates with congenital CMV, rubella virus, or HBV infection are asymptomatic, the use of clinical case-finding methods alone significantly underestimates the true frequency of these infections. Epidemiologic observations (e.g., rubella or enterovirus epidemic in the community), clinical or laboratory information about the mother (e.g., viral illness with a rash or the presence of HBsAg in serum), or screening tests in the newborn (e.g., elevated quantitative IgM in umbilical cord blood) often have been used to select a group of neonates at high risk of contracting congenital infection. The performance of additional laboratory tests in these high-risk neonates to identify potential specific causative agents often has led to the demonstration of infection rates much higher than previously suspected.

Frequency of Infection in the Mother and Neonate

Table 73–4 shows the approximate frequency of the most common viral infections in the mother during pregnancy and in the newborn infant.[31, 212, 421] Although the figures have been obtained by a variety of laboratory methods and some are based on a relatively small or nonrepresentative population sample, they do provide an estimate of the relative frequency of the infections. In many studies, prospective screening of mothers for viral infection during pregnancy or screening of infants for elevated cord blood serum IgM levels was done to select a population of neonates at high risk of acquiring congenital infection for more detailed virologic investigation.

CMV clearly is the most common cause of viral infection, both in the mother and in the neonate. Surveys in the United States indicate that 30 to 110 per 1000 women excrete virus in urine during pregnancy and that 60 per 1000

TABLE 73–4 ■ APPROXIMATE FREQUENCY OF INFECTIONS IN THE MOTHER DURING PREGNANCY AND IN THE NEWBORN INFANT

Viruses	Mother (No./1000 Pregnancies)	Neonate (No./1000 Live Births)
Cytomegalovirus		
During pregnancy, congenital	30–120	6–24
At delivery, natal	80–130	20–60
After delivery, postnatal	130–280	140–210
Rubella		
1964 epidemic	20–40	3–7
Interepidemic prevaccine	0.1–2.0	0.1–0.7
Postvaccine	0.15–0.3	0.03
Hepatitis B	1–160	0–61
Enteroviruses	90–600	2–38
Herpes simplex	1–7	0.1–0.6

are excreters at the time of delivery.[173, 226, 268, 350, 364, 423] Isolation from cervical swabs is even more common: 80 to 120 per 1000 women during pregnancy and 110 to 130 per 1000 at delivery.[98, 268, 350, 423] Most maternal CMV infections during pregnancy are recurrent rather than primary.[475] Extrapolation from data obtained at the same institution[423, 475, 480] suggests that two thirds to three quarters of CMV shedding in the cervix or urine during pregnancy is the result of recurrent rather than primary CMV infection in the mother. The frequency of primary CMV infection during pregnancy averages 20 to 25 per 1000 (range, 10 to 40), with higher rates occurring in populations with a larger percentage of susceptible persons (seronegative at the beginning of pregnancy).[196, 473] Several factors are known to be associated with increased rates of recurrent urine or cervical shedding: (1) sampling on several occasions rather than a single time; (2) collection of specimens during the third rather than the first trimester because shedding rates are known to increase as gestation progresses; (3) Asian, black, or Native American versus white populations; (4) younger maternal age; (5) lower socioeconomic status; (6) a greater number of lifetime sexual partners; and (7) a history of sexually transmitted diseases.[98, 268, 364, 481] An even more important source for transmission of CMV to the neonate may be breast milk. Postpartum shedding from colostrum or breast milk, the cervix, urine, or saliva was demonstrated in 130 to 280 per 1000 unselected women, and breast milk was the most common site by far.[155, 473, 480, 482] Because maternal CMV infection usually is asymptomatic, estimating the frequency of clinical disease is not possible.

Congenital CMV infection has been documented in 6 to 24 per 1000 live births, as determined by isolation of virus from the urine of the neonate within the first few days of life.[57, 425, 478] In contrast to rubella, congenital infection with CMV occurs in mothers with either primary or recurrent infections during pregnancy.[478] Congenital CMV infection rates are significantly higher in lower socioeconomic groups (1.6%) than in middle to upper ones (0.6%).[475] However, among low-income mothers, the status of immunity to CMV is high (82%), and most congenital infections (81%) are associated with recurrent CMV infection during pregnancy. In contrast, seroimmunity to CMV in middle- to upper-income women is lower (55%), and the frequency of congenital infection associated with recurrent maternal CMV also is lower (47%). Although the rate of total congenital CMV infection is lower in mid- to high-income mothers, the proportion of infants born after primary CMV infection is acquired during pregnancy is higher (53 versus 19%). Pooled data from several studies indicate that 30 to 40 percent of mothers with primary CMV infection during pregnancy (range, 20 to 52% in various studies) deliver congenitally infected infants.[10, 11, 196, 290, 473, 475] Congenitally infected babies born to mothers with primary rather than recurrent CMV infection during pregnancy have a greater frequency of symptoms of CMV disease at birth, higher levels of IgM in cord serum, higher titers of virus in urine, and a greater likelihood of having neurologic sequelae at follow-up.[9, 10, 473, 475] The time during gestation when maternal primary CMV infection occurs does not appear to influence the rate of fetal infection, but fetal damage seems to occur more frequently and to be more severe after the acquisition of maternal infection during the first half than during the second half of pregnancy.[9, 196, 408, 473]

The frequency of natal and postnatal acquisition of CMV by newborn infants is far greater than that of congenital infection. Natally acquired CMV infection occurs at an incidence of 20 per 1000 live births.[423, 480] Because approximately one half the infants born to mothers known to be cervical excreters at the time of delivery acquire natal infection[423] and because as many as 130 per 1000 mothers from a low socioeconomic group are excreting CMV at this time,[423] the actual rate of natally acquired CMV infection may be as high as 60 per 1000 live births. A more frequent source for infection of the neonate with CMV is postnatal consumption of virus-infected colostrum or breast milk. In two studies, 58 to 69 percent of infants of nursing mothers who excreted CMV in milk acquired infection.[155, 480] Maternal shedding occurred most frequently between 2 and 12 weeks post partum, and the onset of infant viruria usually occurred when the infants were between 1 and 6 months of age. The aforementioned rates of postnatal infection would project to between 140 and 210 infections per 1000 live births in the United States. These rates, of course, would be affected by all the factors mentioned earlier that influence maternal CMV infection rates, as well as the frequency and duration of breast-feeding.

Yet another source for transmission of CMV to neonates is blood transfusion in infants in neonatal intensive care units. Risk factors include birth weight less than 1250 g, a CMV-seronegative mother, hospitalization for a period longer than 4 weeks, receipt of multiple blood transfusions or a total volume of more than 50 mL, and receipt of blood from a CMV-seropositive donor.[8, 39, 175, 559] The infection rate in high-risk infants may be high: 24 to 31 percent. Morbidity and mortality rates with these infections also are high: clinical disease developed in 88 percent of 34 reported cases, and 24 percent died (CMV believed to be causal or contributory).

In summary, several factors contribute to the high rates of fetal and neonatal CMV infection: (1) virus can be transmitted from both immune mothers (recurrent infection) and nonimmune mothers (primary infection); (2) virus may be shed or carried in many different sites in the mother—blood (for transplacental infection), urine, cervix, breast milk, and saliva; (3) infection may occur at different times—congenitally, natally, and postnatally; and (4) infection may come from sources other than the mother (e.g., hospital-acquired infection from blood transfusion).

The use of rubella vaccine has modified the epidemiologic patterns of this disease in the United States,[41, 379] and incidence data from periods before licensure of the vaccine in 1969 are not applicable. In addition, rates of maternal and congenital rubella during the 1964 epidemic were many times higher than in interepidemic periods. Nonetheless, a comparison of the incidence during the 1964 epidemic, the rates during prevaccine interepidemic periods, and what may be happening currently provides useful information. The frequency of serologically proven clinical rubella among 30,000 pregnant women in the Collaborative Perinatal Research Study was approximately 1 per 1000 during the interepidemic years before vaccine licensure but rose to 22 per 1000 during the epidemic.[353] The total figure for rubella during pregnancy is likely to be at least two times higher because as many as one half to two thirds of maternal rubella infections are subclinical or not diagnosed as rubella.[451] An incidence of congenital rubella of 0.7 per 1000 live births was demonstrated during the interepidemic period in a study screening cord blood sera for the presence of rubella-specific IgM antibody.[13] During the 1964 epidemic, an estimated 20,000 babies were born with congenital rubella syndrome in the United States among approximately 4 million live births, an incidence of 5 per 1000 live births.[366] During 1980 to 1982, an average of 11 cases of confirmed congenital rubella syndrome were reported to the Centers for Disease Control and Prevention (CDC) each year.[379] Correcting for under-reporting and missed cases yielded an annual estimate of 110 cases.[379]

With an annual national birth rate of 3.5 million per year, this figure projects to 0.03 cases of congenital rubella syndrome per 1000 live births currently in the United States. Assuming a 10 to 20 percent rate of congenital rubella infection during pregnancy,[212] the current estimate is thought to be 0.15 to 0.3 cases of maternal rubella per 1000 pregnancies. Importantly, however, a resurgence in acquired and congenital rubella, particularly in unvaccinated women in correctional institutions and unimmunized communities,[89, 332] emphasizes the need for continued surveillance for rubella disease and proper use of the vaccine.

HBV infection during pregnancy may result in acute clinical disease in the mother or, more commonly, may result in an asymptomatic chronic carrier state.[444] The frequency of HBsAg in the serum of pregnant women varies highly and is influenced by geographic location, ethnic origin, socioeconomic status, and other social factors such as illicit drug use and sexual promiscuity. An incidence of 1 to 160 per 1000 pregnancies has been reported in several series.* The frequency of HBV infection in the neonate is even more variable, for several reasons. First, transmission of the virus to the fetus or neonate may occur by several routes: (1) transplacental; (2) natal, from the genital tract; (3) postnatal, by intrafamilial spread through unknown mechanisms; and (4) postnatal, by blood transfusion. Second, infants born to mothers with hepatitis B may follow one of the following courses: (1) serum from the infant remains negative for HBsAg, and hepatitis B never develops; (2) umbilical cord blood is positive for HBsAg, but the antigenemia clears and no disease is evident, presumably representing transplacental transmission of antigen only or insufficient virus to cause true infection in the neonate; (3) umbilical cord blood is HBsAg-positive, and clinical or subclinical infection develops with or without persistent hepatitis B antigenemia; or (4) cord blood is antigen-negative but infection occurs, sometimes not until several months after birth, and persistent antigenemia may or may not develop. Third, because exposed infants may follow one of several courses and because HBV infection may be demonstrable at various times after birth, serial blood specimens must be obtained for evaluation of the true frequency of neonatal infection. Serial blood specimens are difficult to obtain in this age group, and published reports may have based their estimates of infection on one or two blood specimens per infant. Fourth, transplacental infection occurs much more commonly in mothers with acute, symptomatic hepatitis, particularly during the second or third trimester of pregnancy, than it does in mothers who are chronic carriers.[444] Finally, even in these mothers, true differences in the rate of transplacental transmission occur: Asians have a much higher incidence than whites do,[564] and mothers who are hepatitis B e antigen (HBeAg)-positive are much more likely to transmit infection than are mothers who have anti-HBe antibody or lack e-antigen markers.[376] Therefore, the incidence of HBV infection in the neonate varies from 0 to 61 per 1000 live births in different reports.†

Data from several studies indicate that perinatal enteroviral infections occur much more frequently than previously realized.[129, 244, 249, 345, 348, 351, 429] Serologic surveys indicate a surprisingly high rate of seroconversion to at least one enterovirus during pregnancy (first serum at the time of enrollment for obstetric care, second serum at delivery): 90 to 600 per 1000 pregnancies.[73–75, 279, 450] Several factors complicate arriving at an interpretation of the data concerning the frequency of occurrence of maternal enteroviral infections. First, only 2 to 13 of the almost 70 nonpolio enterovirus serotypes were used for antibody testing, thereby resulting in an underestimate of the true frequency for all enteroviruses. Second, the data are reported as the total number of enteroviral infections for a group of pregnant women rather than the percentage of pregnancies complicated by at least one enteroviral infection. Use of these data for calculating the number of pregnancies per 1000 complicated by enteroviral infection would result in an overestimation because more than 25 percent of women may have more than one enteroviral infection during the 9 months of pregnancy.[73] Nonetheless, these data represent the best estimates of the frequency of enteroviral infection during pregnancy.

Data concerning the actual frequency of neonatal enteroviral infection are also difficult to summarize because of differences in the study designs used in the various published results. Modlin and associates[348] reported four echovirus 11 infections among 158 consecutive neonates who had stool samples taken when they were 3 days and 2 weeks of age during the 3-week period of an outbreak of echovirus 11 infection in Boston. Assuming that live births are distributed evenly throughout the year and that no additional cases of enteroviral infection occurred during the remainder of the year, this incidence translates into two enteroviral infections per 1000 live births. These calculations probably underestimate the true frequency markedly because only echovirus 11 was sought in the diagnostic virology laboratory evaluation of these 158 infants and, obviously, enteroviral infections occur for more than a 3-week period of the year. A prospective study of all enteroviral infections acquired during the patient's first month of life in Rochester, New York, during the peak enterovirus season (June to October) demonstrated 75 (12.8%) nonpolio enteroviral infections in 586 infants.[244] Fourteen (18.7%) of these 75 infected infants were hospitalized for "suspected sepsis." By using the estimated number of live births per year in the Rochester area and assuming that no additional cases of neonatal enteroviral infection occurred during the remaining 7 months of the year, the authors projected a rate of 7 neonatal enteroviral infections serious enough to require hospitalization per 1000 live births. If one considered the total 75 enteroviral infections (14 hospitalized and 61 not hospitalized), the rate would be 38 per 1000 live births. A survey by Kaplan and associates[249] of 77 cases of coxsackievirus B infection occurring during the first 3 months of life in infants hospitalized at the Nassau County Medical Center between 1970 and 1979 yielded an estimated rate of 0.5 per 1000 live births. Because group B coxsackieviruses account for only 45 percent of all enteroviral infections during early infancy[351] and because only 18 to 19 percent of all enterovirus-infected infants may require hospitalization,[244] the actual rate for all enteroviral infections may be 6 per 1000 live births. Despite the variation in estimates, enteroviral infections are clearly a frequent cause of maternal and neonatal infection.

As mentioned earlier, the infected genital tract of the mother is the source of virus for most neonatal HSV infections. Other sources, however, such as nongenital sites in the mother, family members, and even other infants in the nursery (through the hands of personnel) have been implicated. Both genital and neonatal herpes have increased in frequency in recent years.[52, 497] Current estimates are that culture-positive genital herpes may occur during pregnancy at a rate of 1 to 7 per 1000[59, 60, 76–78, 362] and at the time of delivery at a rate of 1 to 4 per 1000.[76, 78, 361, 412, 502] However, culture is not the most sensitive method to detect genital

*See references 25, 51, 139, 153, 274, 306, 376, 389, 444, 489, 551.
†See references 25, 51, 139, 153, 274, 306, 376, 389, 444, 457, 489, 551.

HSV-2 infection. Seroprevalence studies have demonstrated HSV-2–specific antibody in 32 percent of women in private obstetric practices,[288] and polymerase chain reaction (PCR) detected HSV DNA in 9 percent of asymptomatic women in labor.[114] Higher rates are associated with lower socioeconomic status, increased numbers of sexual partners, and occurrence of other sexually transmitted diseases. Rates of neonatal herpes have been estimated at 0.1 to 0.6 per 1000 live births.[76, 362, 497, 534] The greatest risk of acquiring neonatal infection occurs when the mother has an initial genital infection at the time of vaginal delivery.

The frequency of infection with the other viruses listed in Tables 73–1 and 73–2 is so low that numeric estimates per 1000 pregnancies or live births are not possible.

APPROACH TO DIAGNOSIS

The usual set of circumstances leading one to consider the diagnosis of viral infection in a newborn infant is the presence of clinical or laboratory features in the neonate that suggest this possibility (Table 73–5). The observation of congenital defects, icterus, petechiae, or hepatosplenomegaly at the time of birth or shortly thereafter in a small-for-gestational-age infant points toward a chronic viral infection. On the other hand, acute viral infection in this age group usually comes to mind in an infant with suspected sepsis when cultures of blood, spinal fluid, and urine fail to yield a bacterial or fungal agent.

TABLE 73–5 ■ COMMON MANIFESTATIONS OF VIRAL INFECTIONS IN THE NEWBORN INFANT

Asymptomatic Infection	
Chronic Infection (Early Gestation to Midgestation Congenital)	
General Characteristics	
Manifestations present at birth or shortly thereafter	
Presence of congenital defects	
Specific Features	
General	Small for gestational age
Central nervous system	Microcephaly, seizures, cerebral calcification, hypertonia or hypotonia, cerebrospinal fluid pleocytosis, encephalitis
Skin	Icterus, petechiae, purpura, vesicles, hypopigmentation
Eye	Chorioretinitis, cataracts, glaucoma, microphthalmos, optic atrophy
Heart	Patent ductus arteriosus, pulmonary artery stenosis
Abdomen	Hepatosplenomegaly, hepatitis
Lung	Pneumonitis
Musculoskeletal	Bone lesions, limb hypoplasia
Acute Infection (Late Gestation Congenital, Natal, or Postnatal)	
General Characteristics	
Manifestations usually appear several days to weeks after birth	
Absence of congenital defects	
Specific Features	
General	Hyperthermia or hypothermia, irritability, lethargy, jitters, poor feeding, vomiting
Central nervous system	Seizures, hypertonia or hypotonia, full fontanelle, meningitis, encephalitis
Skin	Icterus, petechiae, purpura, vesicles, maculopapular rash
Eye	Conjunctivitis, keratitis
Heart	Myocarditis
Abdomen	Hepatosplenomegaly, hepatitis
Lung	Pneumonitis, respiratory distress, cyanosis

Evaluation of the Mother

Once the suspicion of a viral infection in a newborn infant has been raised, one should proceed with an evaluation of the mother for features that might add further evidence to this possibility. For example, the occurrence of maternal viral illness with an associated maculopapular rash suggests rubella or enterovirus infection in the neonate, whereas ulcerative genital lesions point toward HSV and heterophile-negative infectious mononucleosis is suggestive of CMV. One should note, however, that most maternal viral infections that lead to fetal or neonatal infection (almost all cases of CMV and HBV infection[486, 551] and one half to two thirds of rubella virus and HSV infections[361, 451, 534, 539]) are asymptomatic in the mother. Therefore, the absence of a history of viral infection in the mother certainly does not rule out the possibility of such infection in her neonate.

Specimens from the mother for isolation or detection of the viral agent usually are not available. However, the presence of HBsAg in maternal serum or isolation of CMV or HSV from the genital tract or an enterovirus from the stool at the time of delivery certainly should lead one to consider these agents in her newborn infant. Serologic documentation of a specific viral illness in the mother during pregnancy requires serum specimens that bracket the illness. Unfortunately, these specimens rarely are available when the pediatrician is considering the possibility of a congenital viral illness in the neonate. Routine antibody determinations on a single specimen obtained from the mother after the birth of an abnormal child with suspected congenital viral infection are not likely to yield useful information, except if the mother lacks IgG antibody to the pathogen in question. Such a finding in the face of a symptomatic infant would rule out that organism as the cause of the infant's disease. Although the presence of specific IgM antibody against CMV,[198, 214, 483] rubella virus,[190] or HSV[358] in a single maternal serum specimen is highly suggestive of recent infection, IgM tests are known to produce false-positive results and need to be interpreted accordingly. On the other hand, if the maternal viral infection occurs near the time of delivery (e.g., enterovirus meningitis, coxsackievirus B pleurodynia, initial genital herpes), acute and convalescent serum specimens may be obtained from the mother that do demonstrate the diagnostic fourfold or greater rise in antibody titer against a specific agent. Documentation of a particular causative agent in the mother does not constitute proof that the same agent is causing disease in the neonate, but it certainly does provide strong suggestive evidence. Definitive proof, therefore, must come from studies in the newborn infant.

Clinical Features in the Neonate

Certain clinical manifestations of viral disease in the neonate may provide helpful clues to the specific etiologic agent. However, most viral infections are asymptomatic in neonates: more than 95 percent of CMV, two thirds of rubella virus, and most HBV infections. In contrast, less than 1 percent of HSV infections in the neonate are subclinical.[362] To complicate the effort to pinpoint the diagnosis further, the clinical and laboratory manifestations of symptomatic disease caused by numerous agents often have similar patterns (see Table 73–5; Figs. 73–2 and 73–3). However, infants whose congenital viral infections were incurred in early gestation to midgestation have manifestations of

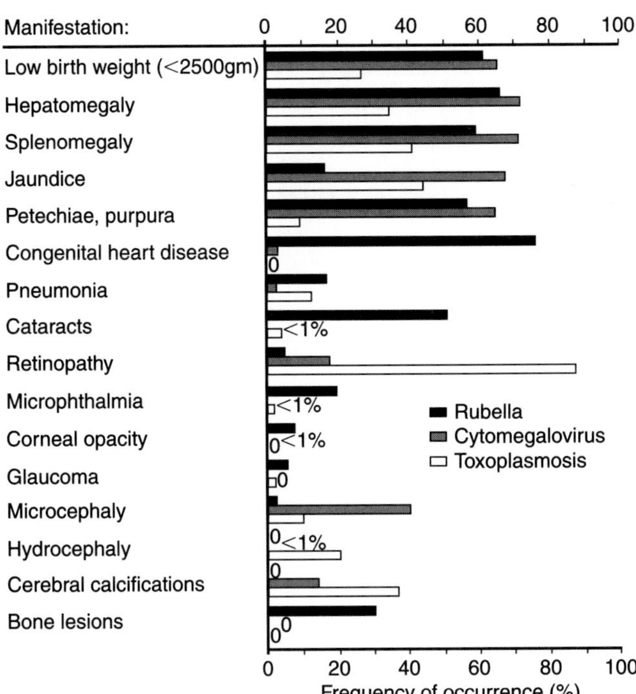

FIGURE 73–2 ■ Manifestations of symptomatic congenital rubella virus and cytomegalovirus infections and toxoplasmosis.

disease at birth or shortly thereafter, whereas infants with late-gestation congenital infections or natal or postnatal infections usually do not exhibit signs and symptoms for several days to several weeks after birth (see Table 73–5). In addition, newborn infants who acquire congenital infections in early gestation to midgestation exhibit congenital defects and intrauterine growth retardation, whereas neonates who acquire viral infections near the time of birth have acute disease resembling bacterial sepsis or the viral syndrome typically seen in older children (e.g., enterovirus exanthem, chickenpox) (see Table 73–5). Because the viral agents that commonly cause chronic intrauterine infections are different from those that result in acute neonatal diseases (see Tables 73–1 to 73–3), recognition of these two different patterns helps define a specific etiologic agent.

The most common manifestations of congenital CMV and rubella infection in symptomatic newborn infants are shown in Figure 73–2. Also shown in this figure are the features observed in infants with congenital toxoplasmosis because this infection is important to consider in the differential diagnosis. (Infection with *Toxoplasma gondii* is covered in Chapter 222.) Note that many nonspecific manifestations, such as low birth weight caused by intrauterine growth retardation, hepatomegaly, splenomegaly, jaundice, and petechiae/purpura, occur with a similar frequency in the three infections. However, certain specific findings may be helpful in the differential diagnosis. The presence of cataracts, congenital heart disease, bone lesions, or microphthalmos is highly suggestive of rubella, whereas chorioretinitis, cerebral calcifications, and hydrocephaly are findings against this diagnosis. In congenital CMV infection, microcephaly, cerebral calcifications, and sensorineural hearing loss are relatively common findings, but congenital heart disease, eye abnormalities, and bone lesions rarely occur. Chorioretinitis, cerebral calcifications, or hydrocephaly should suggest toxoplasmosis. The cerebral calcifications in CMV infection tend to be periventricular, whereas those in toxoplasmosis are scattered through the parietal lobes of the cerebrum. An important note is that some manifestations may not be evident for several months after birth: congenital heart disease, chorioretinitis, microcephaly, hydrocephaly, and cerebral calcifications.

The most frequent findings in the common acute viral infections of the neonate—HSV and enterovirus infections—are shown in Figure 73–3. Because the features in infants with these two kinds of viral infection resemble those associated with bacterial sepsis, the manifestations in neonates with septicemia also are presented. Again, the more common nonspecific features, such as fever or hypothermia, respiratory distress, cyanosis, anorexia or vomiting, and hepatomegaly, occur at a relatively similar frequency in the three infections. Lethargy, irritability, and central nervous system (CNS) signs are found more commonly in HSV and enterovirus infections, probably because encephalitis and meningitis, respectively, occur more frequently in these two infections. Features that suggest a diagnosis of HSV infection are a vesicular rash and keratitis, conjunctivitis, or chorioretinitis, whereas those that bring to mind enterovirus infection include diarrhea and abdominal distention. The rash in enterovirus infection usually is erythematous and maculopapular, but petechiae can occur with overwhelming infection. The skin lesions in bacterial sepsis generally are pustules, abscesses, cellulitis, or purpura.

Differential Diagnosis in the Neonate

The differential diagnosis in a newborn infant with a suspected viral infection is extensive.[212] Many of the manifestations shown in Figures 73–2 and 73–3, such as lethargy, irritability, respiratory distress, cyanosis, and anorexia, can be caused by the most common diseases occurring in sick newborn infants—hyaline membrane disease, prematurity, intraventricular hemorrhage, metabolic disturbances, and bacterial sepsis.[53] In infants with low birth weight caused by intrauterine growth restriction (small for gestational age), one should consider congenital malformations, chromosomal abnormalities, placental insufficiency, and inborn errors of metabolism. Hepatosplenomegaly usually is caused by one of the infectious diseases of the neonate. In infants with jaundice, ABO and Rh hemolytic disease and physiologic jaundice should be considered. Noninfectious causes of petechiae/purpura include idiopathic or drug-induced (including transplacental passage) thrombocytopenia, erythroblastosis fetalis, and disseminated intravascular coagulation.

Little firm evidence indicates that infectious agents other than rubella can cause congenital heart disease. Diffuse pulmonary infiltrates early in the neonatal period most commonly are caused by hyaline membrane disease, but in older neonates one should consider bronchopulmonary dysplasia and chlamydial infection. Causes of cataracts other than congenital rubella, HSV, and VZV infection include congenital galactosemia and the oculocerebrorenal (Lowe) syndrome. Chorioretinitis or retinopathy usually is caused by infection with *T. gondii* or with viruses such as HSV, CMV, rubella, or lymphocytic choriomeningitis virus. Microcephaly also can be caused by infection with HSV or VZV; noninfectious causes include Down syndrome, perinatal anoxia, phenylketonuria, and maternal irradiation. Hydrocephalus generally is caused by a congenital malformation of the ventricular aqueductal or subarachnoid space system. In an infant with manifestations of an acute infection, the major diagnostic consideration is a serious bacterial infection such as sepsis, meningitis, urinary tract infection, or pneumonia. After appropriate samples for culture have been

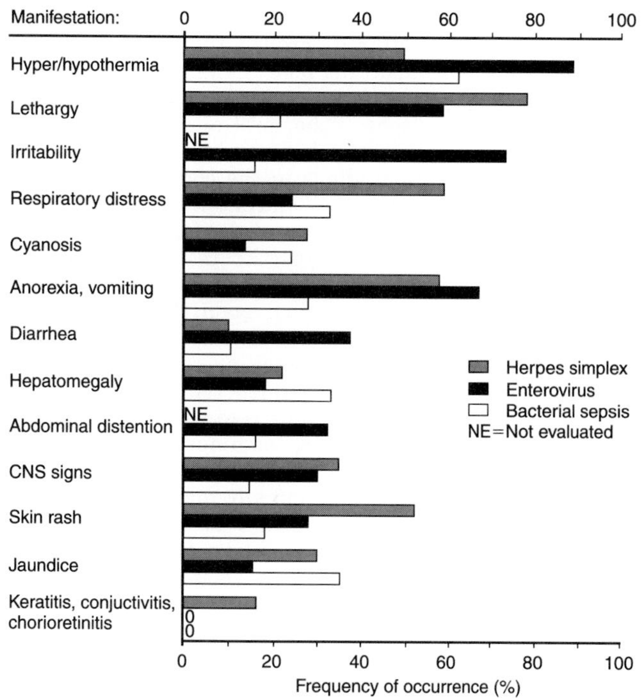

FIGURE 73–3 ■ Manifestations of herpes simplex virus and enterovirus infections and bacterial sepsis in the neonate.

obtained from the infant, antibiotics should be administered until a bacterial infection has been ruled out.

Laboratory Diagnosis

Because the clinical manifestations in the various neonatal viral infections frequently overlap, a specific etiologic diagnosis usually depends on the laboratory. Unfortunately, general laboratory tests such as the peripheral white blood cell count, urinalysis, and blood chemistry panels are not helpful in this regard. The approach to the specific laboratory diagnosis of viral infection in a newborn infant is outlined in Table 73–6. Details of the various methods for each virus are covered in the respective chapters for these agents; only general comments relevant to the diagnosis of infection in the neonate are presented here.

Routine histopathologic methods include examination of stained cells from urine for CMV inclusions or examination of cells scraped from the base of a vesicle or from the conjunctivae for multinucleated giant cells with intranuclear inclusions characteristic of HSV or VZV. In addition, tissue obtained by biopsy or at postmortem examination may reveal intranuclear inclusions and multinucleated giant cells characteristic of the herpesviruses. Except for the propensity to involve certain organs (e.g., rubella virus, the heart; HBV, the liver), the pathologic changes induced by viruses other than the herpes group rarely are sufficiently specific to enable one to make an etiologic diagnosis. Even for the herpesviruses, the routine histopathologic methods are only one half to two thirds as sensitive as is isolation of the virus.

The most direct and preferred method of establishing the diagnosis is isolation of the agent from an appropriate site in the infant. The following sites generally are used: urine and saliva for CMV; throat and occasionally spinal fluid or urine for rubella; skin vesicles, buffy coat, cerebrospinal fluid (CSF), conjunctivae, throat, stool, and urine for HSV;

TABLE 73–6 ■ LABORATORY DIAGNOSIS OF VIRAL INFECTION IN THE NEWBORN INFANT

Procedure	Details, Comments
Routine histopathologic methods	Urine cells stained for inclusions Scraping of vesicle base or conjunctiva for multinucleated giant cells Examination of biopsy or autopsy tissue
Isolation or detection of infectious agents	Isolation of infectious agent in cell culture or animals Detection of viral particles by electron microscopy Detection of viral antigen by immunologic methods Detection of viral nucleic acid by DNA probes, often after amplification by PCR
IgG antiviral antibody	Persistence of antibody in serum of infant beyond age of normal decline in maternal transplacental antibody—usually 4–6 mo Variety of methods available (CF, neut, HI, IHA, IFA, ELISA, etc.)—sensitivity of method varies according to specific virus
IgM-specific antiviral antibody	IgM not normally passed transplacentally, presence in cord blood or neonatal serum diagnostic IgM-specific antibodies not always present in neonate False-positive and false-negative results
Quantitative IgM level	Not a specific diagnostic test, suggests intrauterine infection

CF, complement fixation; ELISA, enzyme-linked immunosorbent assay; HI, hemagglutination inhibition; IFA, immunofluorescent assay; IHA, indirect hemagglutination; neut, neutralization; PCR, polymerase chain reaction. Modified from Hanshaw, J. B., Dudgeon, J. A., and Marshall. W. C.: Viral Diseases of the Fetus and Newborn. 2nd ed. Philadelphia, W. B. Saunders, 1985.

throat, stool, CSF, or serum/buffy coat for enteroviruses; and skin vesicles for VZV. In addition, isolation of virus can be attempted from biopsy material or sterile specimens obtained at autopsy. Recovery of a virus from internal body fluids (buffy coat, CSF, urine), vesicle fluid, or tissue from organs is strong evidence of an etiologic association. However, one should interpret the isolation of agents from throat swabs or stool specimens cautiously, particularly enteroviruses. In the latter instance, viral isolation data must be considered in conjunction with the clinical picture and serologic studies. Electron-microscopic examination of vesicle fluid can demonstrate typical herpesvirus particles in both HSV and VZV infection but cannot distinguish between the two. Immunofluorescence and immunoperoxidase methods are available for many of the viruses and can demonstrate viral antigen in cells scraped from lesions or in biopsy material. HBsAg is demonstrable in serum by radioimmunoassay or enzyme-linked immunosorbent assay (ELISA).

Methods for amplifying a particular segment of a viral genome, such as PCR, followed by detection of the particular amplified gene by probe or gel electrophoresis, are available for CMV, HBV, HSV, VZV, and the enteroviruses.[384] In general, PCR and other amplification methods are more sensitive than is virus isolation and are quite specific and have become widely available.

Though not as sensitive, immediate, or direct as is isolation or detection of the viral agent, serologic studies are a readily available means for laboratory diagnosis of viral infection in a newborn infant. They should be used only when isolation of the organism is not possible. The TORCH screen for

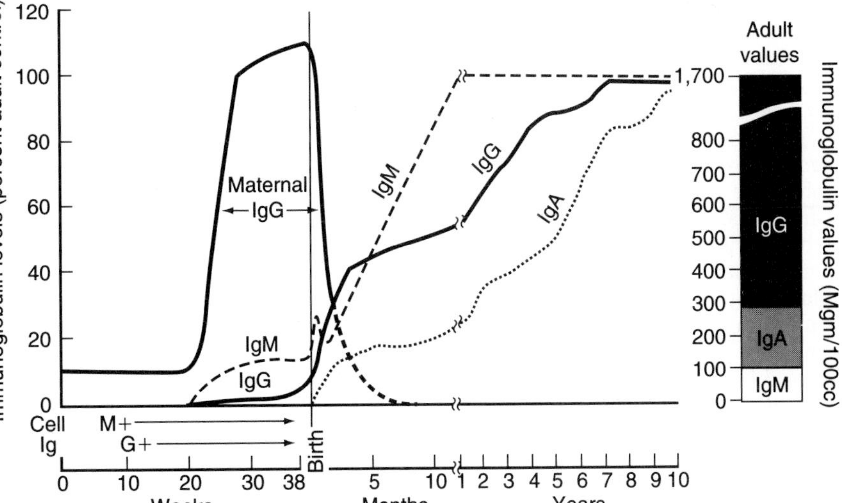

FIGURE 73–4 ■ Kinetics of fetal and neonatal immunoglobulins. (From Alford, C. A.: Immunoglobulin determinations in the diagnosis of fetal infection. Pediatr. Clin. North Am. *18*:99–113, 1971.)

antibodies (*Toxoplasma,* other, rubella, cytomegalovirus, and herpes simplex) was developed for this purpose. However, proper interpretation of serologic tests in newborn infants requires an understanding of the kinetics of the humoral immune response in the fetus and newborn infant, as well as an appreciation of the transplacental passage of antibodies from mother to fetus. Figure 73–4 illustrates the pattern of immunoglobulin concentrations in the serum of the fetus and newborn infant, as well as older infants and children. Maternal IgG, which contains antibody against viruses to which the mother has been exposed, passes transplacentally, beginning at midgestation. Peak levels are reached in fetal serum at the time of birth (umbilical cord blood); they decline to undetectable levels by the time that the infant reaches 6 to 12 months of age. However, the use of more sensitive assays for IgG antibody detection, such as immunoblotting, has demonstrated that maternal IgG antibody may persist for as long as 15 to 18 months.

In contrast, maternal IgM antibody normally is not passed transplacentally. Because the fetus is in a "protected" environment and usually does not receive an antigenic challenge in utero, fetal immunoglobulin levels remain low and do not begin to rise until after birth, when exposure to a variety of antigens occurs. However, the fetus is capable of mounting a humoral immune response when exposed to an antigen (a virus) in utero. Elevated levels of fetal immunoglobulins, therefore, can be detected at birth in umbilical cord blood. Because maternal IgG is present in such high concentration in cord blood serum, assays for IgM are performed. A fetus challenged in utero with a virus can have specific IgM antibodies against the viral agent, as well as elevated levels of the total IgM fraction. Typically, three approaches can be used to make a serologic diagnosis of viral infection in a newborn infant: (1) assay of maternal serum and serum specimens from the infant at birth and at 5 to 6 months of age for antiviral antibody (predominantly IgG activity), (2) assay of neonatal serum for IgM antibody against a specific viral agent,and (3) assay of neonatal serum for quantitative IgM levels, a nonspecific indication of antigenic challenge in utero.

For purposes of illustration, the rubella hemagglutination-inhibition titers of two mother/infant pairs are shown in Table 73–7. Both mothers were exposed to someone with a rubella-like rash during pregnancy. The first mother was susceptible; subclinical rubella developed, and she delivered an infant with congenital rubella, whereas the second mother was immune and delivered an uninfected normal infant. The serum specimen obtained from the first mother at the time of exposure showed no detectable hemagglutination-inhibition titer, whereas the serum at delivery and 6 months post partum showed high titers indicative of acute rubella virus infection during pregnancy. Both serum specimens from her infant, at birth and at 6 months of age, demonstrated rubella virus hemagglutination-inhibition antibodies at approximately the same level, thus indicating the persistence of antibody formed by the infant and substantiating the occurrence of congenital infection. In the second mother, the rubella hemagglutination-inhibition titers remained unchanged in all three specimens. Her infant had evidence of transplacental maternal antibody in serum obtained at birth but no detectable antibody at 6 months of age. Similar results could be expected from serologic studies with the other viral agents listed in Tables 73–1 and 73–2, not only for congenital infections but also for natal and postnatal infections in which primary viral infection occurred in the mother. Even with natal infections in immune mothers and postnatal infections from nonmaternal sources, the serologic responses in the neonate would be similar to those shown in Table 73–7.

Although the presence of IgM antibodies in neonatal serum against a specific virus usually is considered to be diagnostic of infection with that agent, both false-positive and false-negative results can occur. False-positive findings can result from cross-reaction between viruses, especially the herpesviruses,[369] and the presence of rheumatoid factor (IgM antibody that binds to the Fc portion of IgG) in

TABLE 73–7 ■ MOTHER AND INFANT SEROLOGIC RESPONSE IN CONGENITAL RUBELLA

Serum Specimens	Rubella Hemagglutination-Inhibition Antibody Titers			
	Mother A	Infant A	Mother B	Infant B
At exposure	<8	—	128	—
At birth	1024	1024	128	256
6 mo postpartum	1024	2048	250	<8
Comment	Congenital rubella		Passive transfer of antibody; no congential rubella	

serum.[97] False-negative results can occur because of a poor or delayed humoral immune response in the fetus/neonate. For example, CMV IgM antibody was present in the serum of only 70 percent of congenitally infected infants, as proved by isolation of virus from urine in the first few days of life.[483]

Determination of a quantitative IgM level in cord blood serum often has been recommended as a screening test for congenital viral infection. Values above 20 mg/dL are considered to be abnormal,[16] but the normal values in local laboratories should be used as a guide. Unfortunately, contamination of cord blood serum samples by maternal blood may occur in one half to two thirds of specimens.[13, 341] Contamination is determined by demonstrating that the concentration of cord blood serum IgA, which also is not passed transplacentally, is higher than the IgM level. If one excludes contaminated specimens, the incidence of congenital infection in infants with an elevated IgM level is many times higher than that in infants with normal levels. However, as many as 50 percent of infants with a proven congenital infection, particularly those with asymptomatic infection, have a normal IgM level.[212] In two thirds of infants with elevated IgM, infection with a specific etiologic agent could not be diagnosed.[13, 16] Therefore, a high rate of both false-positive and false-negative results occurs. Finally, an elevated IgM level does not enable a specific etiologic diagnosis; it merely provides strong evidence for an intrauterine infection of some type.

The similarities in the clinical signs and physical findings associated with congenital and perinatal infection have led to the recommendation that for appropriate diagnosis of these infections, submission of maternal and neonatal serum specimens for the TORCH screen or, in selected instances, a single neonatal specimen for specific IgM antibodies is best. The use of a TORCH battery of serologic tests, however, cannot be recommended because of poor diagnostic return; these tests are difficult to interpret because of transplacental passage of maternal IgG antibodies, and IgM assays may result in false-positive findings. Instead, the laboratory test or tests that should be performed must be dictated by which congenital infection or infections one is trying to diagnose or rule out. As seen in Table 73–6, the variety of tests that are available for the diagnosis of any of the multitude of different potential congenital pathogens renders a TORCH assay, and by inference the term TORCH itself, obsolete by current standards. Finally, if a congenital infection is suspected in the delivery room, the placenta should be sent for histopathologic studies.

Cytomegalovirus Infection

CMV is a ubiquitous agent that usually causes asymptomatic infection in a normal infant, child, or adult. However, patients with immature or impaired host defenses, such as a fetus, newborn infant, or immunosuppressed patient, may exhibit a variety of clinical manifestations during the acute infection and have a greater potential for long-term neurologic sequelae[15, 137, 175, 211, 363] (see also Chapter 164).

MICROBIOLOGY AND EPIDEMIOLOGY

CMV is a member of the herpesvirus group, which includes HSV, VZV, and Epstein-Barr virus. Several strains of CMV differ antigenically, and an individual can have more than one CMV infection.[15, 137, 175] Human CMV is limited to the human host and grows only in human cells in tissue culture.[212] Its distribution is worldwide, and no predilection for either sex or a particular season of the year exists.[15, 137, 175, 524] Studies of antibody prevalence and virus isolation have indicated two peak ages for acquisition of infection: (1) infancy and early childhood and (2) early adulthood (in the sexually active).[175, 561] Infection rates are higher and exposure to the virus occurs earlier in life in developing countries, lower socioeconomic groups in industrial nations, and Asian populations.[175] The major source of infection of young infants is the mother, whereas transmission in the daycare setting is an important source for older infants and toddlers.[393, 474] Approximately 50 percent of susceptible children between the ages of 1 to 3 years who are in group daycare acquire CMV, mostly by transfer of virus present in saliva on hands and toys. Within 3 to 7 months of their acquiring CMV infection in the daycare center, as many as 33 percent of their seronegative mothers become infected.[5] Transmission of CMV from a child in daycare to his mother and her fetus has been confirmed. Thus, CMV infection in young children in daycare has become an important source of maternal and fetal infection.[394] In young adults, intimate interpersonal contact appears to be necessary for transmission, and an infected sexual partner also may be the source of infection for a pregnant woman and her fetus.

The usual sites for isolation of virus are the urine, cervix, and saliva,[175] but CMV also has been recovered from amniotic fluid,[133] semen,[301, 302] breast milk,[155, 220] feces,[123] and autopsy and biopsy tissue.[212] Excretion of virus in urine, saliva, or the cervix may be prolonged after primary infection, particularly with congenital disease.[15, 137, 212, 478, 481] Intermittent, recurring shedding also may occur in a significant proportion of seropositive young adults.[423, 478, 481] Despite this prevalence of virus excretion, CMV seems to be of low communicability.[175] Beyond the neonatal period, infection appears to require prolonged or intimate contact and presumably is transmitted through oropharyngeal or genital secretions.[212] Researchers have assumed that CMV may be transmitted sexually because of the frequency of isolation of virus from genital secretions and because the prevalence of antibody is higher in sexually active populations.[15, 137] Finally, transmission of CMV by blood transfusion has been documented, particularly in the event of multiple seropositive blood donors.[8, 175]

Prenatal transmission of CMV to the fetus presumably is associated with maternal viremia and transplacental passage of the virus, perhaps within virus-infected leukocytes.[15, 137, 212] An important observation is that congenital CMV infection occurs in the infants of mothers known to be immune to CMV, thus indicating that transplacental transmission is possible despite circulating antibody in maternal serum.[475, 478] In addition, mothers have delivered more than one congenitally infected infant in successive pregnancies.[478, 479] Analysis of CMV isolates obtained from the same mothers on repeated occasions are antigenically and genetically identical, whereas strains from different mothers are not.[238] In addition, strains obtained from pairs of mothers and their congenitally infected infant pairs, as well as congenitally infected siblings, usually are identical. These results suggest that most CMV transmission from immune mothers to their fetuses or newborns is the result of reactivated latent infection. Recently, however, Boppana and colleagues[65] have documented that acquisition of a new strain of CMV by pregnant immune women can lead to symptomatic congenital CMV infection in their offspring. Concern also exists about the potential role of maternal HIV infection in facilitating fetal infection with CMV.[148, 355, 442] Symptomatic congenital CMV infection has been documented in a preterm infant who died of disseminated CMV infection and was born to an HIV-infected, CMV-immune mother with acquired immunodeficiency syndrome (AIDS).[442] Among HIV-infected,

CMV-immune women without advanced HIV disease, the rate of congenital CMV infection in their infants was similar to that of a comparison group of infants born to CMV-immune, HIV-uninfected mothers.[355] In another study, among a cohort of infants born to HIV-infected mothers, infants who were infected with HIV were significantly more likely to have congenital CMV infection than were non–HIV-infected infants, 21 versus 4 percent, respectively.[148] Importantly, HIV-infected infants who are co-infected with CMV appear to have greater immunosuppression and disease progression than do those infected with HIV alone.[148, 280, 370]

Natal transmission of CMV results from exposure of the neonate to infected genital secretions at the time of delivery.[15, 423, 424] If the mother is excreting virus at the time of delivery, 40 to 50 percent of exposed infants become infected.[423] The level of maternal antibody did not influence the frequency or time of onset of infection in the neonate. The usual incubation period for natal infection is 5 to 6 weeks.[424]

The importance of breast milk and blood transfusion as sources for postnatal acquisition of CMV was mentioned earlier in the section "Frequency of Infection in the Mother and Neonate." Although nosocomial transmission of CMV from baby to baby via fomites or health care workers' hands in the neonatal intensive care unit has been documented,[468] it rarely occurs.[6, 168]

PATHOGENESIS AND PATHOLOGY

Congenital infection results from transplacental transmission during maternal viremia.[15, 212] However, CMV placentitis may occur without transplacental transmission of virus.[221] After transplacental transmission occurs, the virus spreads through the fetus by the hematogenous route. The severity of congenital disease in the neonate probably correlates with intrauterine infection at an earlier gestational age.[473] With the exception of blood transfusion–associated infection, natal and postnatal infection with CMV usually is acquired secondary to challenge of the nasopharynx or oropharynx of the infant with virus from infected maternal genital secretions or breast milk.[15, 137, 212] Replication of virus in the neonate occurs in the mucosa of the respiratory or gastrointestinal tract, with subsequent viremic spread to target organs. With blood transfusion–associated infection, virus is inoculated directly into the bloodstream. The major target organs are the CNS, eyes, lungs, liver, and kidneys.[15, 212] Of interest is that overt disease in the neonate appears to be associated more commonly with the hematogenous route of inoculation: transplacental infection or infection secondary to blood transfusion.

CMV appears to have a particular affinity for epithelial cells, for ependymal cells lining the ventricles of the brain, and for the organ of Corti and neurons of the eighth nerve.[212, 477] The characteristic pathologic features of CMV infection are cytolysis, focal necrosis and an inflammatory response, the formation of enlarged cells with intranuclear inclusions (cytomegalic cells), and the production of multinucleated giant cells.[212] Healing results in fibrosis and often calcifications, which cause structural damage to the fetal developing organs. Damage may continue after birth because of persistent postnatal viral replication.[15] Replication of CMV in the epithelial cells of blood vessels may result in vascular damage and secondary structural defects. The intrauterine growth restriction associated with symptomatic congenital infection appears to be the result of a reduction in the numbers of cells in various organs rather than a diminution in cell size.[356] Abnormalities resulting from faulty organogenesis secondary to CMV infection are limited primarily to the brain and include microcephaly, optic atrophy, aplasia of various parts of the brain, and microphthalmos.[209, 212] Although a variety of congenital malformations outside the CNS have been observed in infants with congenital CMV infection, they probably are coincidental rather than true teratogenic effects of the virus.[209] Such malformations include a variety of heart lesions, clubfoot deformities, indirect inguinal hernias, high arched palate, dental defects, and hypospadias.[15, 209] Other than inguinal hernia in male infants and tooth enamel defects, the extraneural defects in infants with congenital CMV infection have been infrequent, sporadic, and diverse occurrences.

The fetus is capable of mounting a humoral immune response to CMV, as evidenced by the presence of elevated IgM levels and specific CMV IgM antibody in cord serum.[15, 212, 425, 483] Excessive production of IgM and IgG in the presence of virus replication during the early postnatal course of congenital CMV has resulted in the formation of circulating immune complexes and rheumatoid factor, thereby providing a potential risk for tissue damage by immune complexes.[484] The factors contributing to prolonged replication and excretion of CMV in involved infants are not understood fully, but it does not appear to be a matter of immunologic tolerance because infants do produce specific antibody against CMV.[15]

However, abnormalities in other aspects of the immune response of congenitally infected infants, including decreased lymphocyte blastogenesis and immune interferon production in response to CMV antigen,[422, 487] a decreased percentage of T cells in peripheral blood,[438] and a diminished interferon response in leukocytes challenged with Newcastle disease virus in vitro, have been observed.[162] The degree of suppression of these responses appears to correlate with the presence and amount of virus excretion and the severity of the disease.[422, 487] Further investigations are needed to determine the contribution of these immunologic aberrations to the pathogenesis of congenital CMV infection. The clinical relevance of these immunologic impairments is uncertain. Infants with congenital CMV infection do not have a higher incidence or severity of bacterial infections, although three fatal cases of overwhelming sepsis secondary to *Staphylococcus epidermidis* have been described in CMV-infected, low-birth-weight infants.[291] Recently, *Pneumocystis carinii* pneumonia was reported in a 4-month-old infant who had congenital CMV infection; this infant was not infected with HIV but was severely malnourished.[311]

CLINICAL MANIFESTATIONS

From 90 to 95 percent of neonates with congenital CMV infection are asymptomatic in the neonatal period. Babies born to mothers with primary CMV infection during pregnancy are much more likely to be symptomatic as neonates than are newborns of mothers with recurrent infection.[9, 15, 137, 178, 409, 475] The clinical manifestations present in those with overt disease in the neonatal period are shown in Figure 73–2. These features may occur singly or in combination. The constellation of findings seen in infants with multiorgan disease that primarily affects the reticuloendothelial system and CNS has been referred to as "cytomegalic inclusion disease."

Typical clinical features include hepatomegaly, splenomegaly, jaundice, petechiae or purpura, pneumonia, microcephaly, chorioretinitis, and cerebral calcifications (see Figs. 65–21 and 164–3). The enlargement of the liver and spleen is caused by mild hepatitis, a reticuloendothelial response to chronic infection, and extramedullary hematopoiesis.[212] Hepatitis is associated with direct- and indirect-reacting hyperbilirubinemia and mild elevation of liver enzymes.[212] Liver biopsy specimens have revealed local infiltration and necrosis, multinucleated giant cells, large inclusion-bearing cells, cholangitis, fatty metamorphosis, interstitial fibrosis, and bile stasis.[15, 137, 139] Although hepatomegaly and mild alteration in liver function test results may persist for several months after birth, severe chronic liver disease with cirrhosis rarely occurs.[212] Splenomegaly is a common event and may be the only abnormality present at birth. Petechiae and purpura are the result of thrombocytopenia, which usually resolves within a few weeks or months but may persist through the first year of life.[212] Thrombocytopenia may the only manifestation of CMV infection. "Blueberry muffin spots" are discrete, well-circumscribed lesions often mistaken for purpura; they represent dermal erythropoiesis in the more severely affected infants. A diffuse interstitial pneumonitis occurs in less than 1 percent of newborns with symptomatic disease. Congenital CMV infection also has been associated with defective enamelization of the deciduous teeth.[476]

Involvement of the CNS by CMV results in the most severe sequelae of the disease. CMV infection of the brain causes encephalitis and periependymitis, with resultant gliosis and calcification. The cerebral calcifications typically are periventricular, a pattern that may be distinguished from the more diffuse pattern observed in congenital toxoplasmosis. In addition, linear calcifications along the lenticulostriate vessels within the basal ganglia and thalamus have been associated with CMV infection; they are visualized best by cranial ultrasonography.[96] As many as 70 percent of symptomatic infants have neurologic findings, with the most common being microcephaly. Microcephaly may not be present at birth but may become apparent when the child is 1 year of age or older, a period in which differences in growth rates between the brain and somatic tissues are observed. When associated with cerebral calcification, microcephaly carries a high probability of psychomotor retardation. On occasion, microcephaly is associated with obstruction of the fourth ventricle, with subsequent development of hydrocephalus.

The most common ocular abnormalities are chorioretinitis, strabismus, and optic atrophy.[212] Although microphthalmos, cataracts, and other eye abnormalities have been observed, they are rare occurrences.[209] The associated chorioretinitis cannot be differentiated from that caused by congenital toxoplasmosis, either in appearance or in location in the retina.[212]

Sensorineural hearing loss occurs in approximately 50 percent of symptomatic infants and 7 percent of those with asymptomatic infection. Urine or saliva culture for the diagnosis of CMV infection should be performed on newborns who fail their hearing screens. Among those with hearing loss detected in the neonatal period, approximately 50 percent will have further deterioration in hearing up through adolescence.[177] Approximately 20 percent of infants with congenital CMV will not manifest hearing loss until after reaching 1 year of age. Deafness probably is the most common sequela of congenital CMV infection.

Most naturally acquired natal and postnatal CMV infections in full-term newborn infants are asymptomatic and not associated with late neurologic sequelae such as hearing loss and psychomotor retardation. Most of these infections result from reactivation of latent maternal CMV, and infants are born with transplacentally acquired maternal IgG antibody that ameliorates the disease. However, mostly pneumonitis, but also hepatosplenomegaly and lymphadenopathy, has been noted in some infants.[292, 472, 535, 560] Severe disease manifested also by neutropenia and thrombocytopenia has been reported predominantly in preterm infants and is associated with the development of chronic lung disease.[560] In addition, exacerbation of congenital CMV infection has been documented in premature infants receiving corticosteroid therapy for chronic lung disease of prematurity.[515] Similarly, postnatal acquisition of CMV through breast-feeding nearly always is an asymptomatic infection in full-term infants because of the presence of maternal antibodies. In recent studies, however, CMV infection acquired through breast milk by premature infants with a birth weight of 1000 g or less has been associated with a sepsis-like illness consisting of apnea and bradycardia, hepatosplenomegaly, a distended bowel, pallor, thrombocytopenia, and elevated liver function test results.[207, 521]

Transfusion-acquired CMV infection is an important clinical syndrome associated with multiple blood transfusions from seropositive donors to very-low-birth-weight infants in neonatal intensive care units.[8, 39, 554, 559] Eighty-eight percent of babies had hepatosplenomegaly, a "septic" appearance, deterioration in respiratory status, a peculiar gray pallor, and atypical lymphocytosis approximately 4 to 12 weeks after receiving transfusions.[8, 39, 559] The illness lasted 2 to 3 weeks in most infants, although 24 percent died.

DIAGNOSIS AND DIFFERENTIAL DIAGNOSIS

The definitive means of diagnosing CMV infection in the mother is isolation of virus from the cervix or urine. However, primary infection cannot be differentiated from recurrent infection unless serologic studies are performed. Because most maternal CMV infections are asymptomatic, acute and convalescent sera bracketing an "illness" rarely are available. Primary CMV infection occurring during pregnancy has been documented by demonstration of IgG seroconversion with sera obtained before or during early pregnancy and at delivery or by detection of anti-CMV IgM in a single specimen.[10, 11, 198, 290, 364, 408, 483] Caution, however, must be exercised when analyzing the results of CMV IgM tests. Even with the best commercially available assays, at least 5 percent of positive serum IgM tests represent false-positive results. On the other hand, a negative CMV IgG antibody test in the mother of an infant in whom the diagnosis of CMV infection is in question would exclude congenital transmission as a possible source of CMV.

Because the signs and symptoms of symptomatic CMV infection in newborns so often overlap with those in other diseases during this period of life, definitive diagnosis requires the use of laboratory tests. Isolation of virus from infants within their first 2 weeks of life is considered proof of congenital infection and is the most sensitive and recommended means of diagnosis.[15, 137] The usual specimens for isolation of CMV are urine and saliva,[38] but virus has been recovered from CSF, buffy coat, and biopsy and postmortem tissue.[212] Congenitally infected infants are known to excrete virus for several years after birth.[212] Isolation of virus in an infant beyond 2 or 3 weeks of age does not, by itself, differentiate between natal or postnatal infection and congenital infection, unless negative cultures have been obtained previously. Recently, detection of CMV DNA by PCR in such body fluids as urine, saliva, blood,[181, 246] or CSF also has confirmed congenital infection, although the sensitivity and specificity of PCR performed on urine are less than those for viral culture.[138, 367] On the other hand, PCR is preferred for detection of CMV in CSF because CMV culture usually is negative.[156, 291, 512] The presence of CMV DNA by PCR in the CSF of congenitally infected infants has correlated with abnormal neurologic outcome.[512] Similarly, the finding of a positive serum CMV PCR in infants with congenital CMV infection has been associated with the development of hearing loss.[67]

Serologic tests performed for specific antibody determination in neonates rarely are helpful and are not recommended for establishing a diagnosis of congenital infection. If serologic tests that predominantly measure IgG are used, serial serum specimens from birth are required to differentiate congenital from natal or postnatal infection. One observes maintenance of a stable antibody titer during the first 6 months of life in infants with a congenital infection. In contrast, with natal and postnatal infection, a drop in antibody titer occurs during the first 2 to 3 months of life as maternal passive antibody declines, followed by a rise by the time the infant reaches 5 to 6 months of age.[424, 482] If the infant is not evaluated until several months of age and serum specimens from earlier life are not available, determining whether the infection is congenital, natal, or postnatal in origin may not be possible.

Detection of CMV antigenemia in blood can be achieved by means of an assay that uses monoclonal antibodies to pp65, a tegument protein of the virus that is present in infected polymorphonuclear leukocytes.[144] This assay has been useful in diagnosing CMV disease in both normal and immunocompromised adults. Its relevance in congenital CMV infection requires further study. Its major use may be for evaluation of a symptomatic infant who has natally or postnatally acquired CMV infection, for which making a differentiation between congenital and acquired CMV infection is difficult at best and the finding of a positive urine CMV culture may be only incidental.

Examination for inclusion-bearing cells in urine may be performed, but this test yields positive results in only 20 to 50 percent of known virus-positive cases.[15, 137] Typical intranuclear inclusions may be seen in biopsy tissue or in megakaryocytes of bone marrow aspirates,[15, 137, 212] but virus may be isolated from tissue when these pathologic findings are absent.

The major diseases to consider in the differential diagnosis include congenital syphilis, congenital rubella, congenital toxoplasmosis, erythroblastosis fetalis, disseminated HSV infection, neonatal sepsis, and enterovirus infection.[212] Congenital syphilis is suggested by the presence of osteochondritis and periostitis on radiographs of the long bones in an infant born to a mother with reactive serologic tests for syphilis. Darkfield examination of spirochete-laden nasal secretions in infants with rhinitis confirms the diagnosis. The presence of congenital heart disease and cataracts suggests rubella, and chorioretinitis, hydrocephalus, and intracranial calcifications suggest toxoplasmosis, but a definitive diagnosis depends on the laboratory findings. In uncomplicated erythroblastosis, the direct bilirubin and liver function study results remain normal. Vesicular skin lesions suggest HSV or VZV infection. Positive blood cultures confirm the diagnosis of neonatal sepsis. Congenital CMV infection seldom is complicated by bacterial sepsis in a newborn.[212] Neonatal enterovirus infections are seasonal; associated with maternal symptoms of enteroviral disease; and characterized by aseptic meningitis, hepatitis, myocarditis, or gastroenteritis.

TREATMENT

Although treatment with idoxuridine,[113] 5-fluorodeoxyuridine,[405] cytosine arabinoside,[283, 326, 405] adenine arabinoside,[43, 105] interferon inducers,[405] human interferon,[33, 163] and acyclovir[404] has been tried in infants with congenital CMV infection, the only effect was a transient alteration in viral excretion. Little or no effect on the clinical course of the disease was achieved. Foscarnet has been approved for the treatment of CMV retinitis, and in adults, cidofovir also is efficacious for the treatment of CMV retinitis. Because these agents have appreciable side effects, they should not be used for the treatment of CMV disease in neonates. Neither standard nor CMV hyperimmune intravenous immunoglobulin has a role in the treatment of congenital CMV infection.

Ganciclovir has been licensed for the treatment of life- or sight-threatening CMV disease in immunosuppressed adults.[80] The combination of ganciclovir plus CMV hyperimmune intravenous immunoglobulin has reduced mortality rates in CMV pneumonitis.[161, 418] The use of ganciclovir to treat infants with congenital CMV disease has been reported,[228, 371, 515] but routine administration of this drug is not recommended by the Committee on Infectious Diseases of the American Academy of Pediatrics.[22] Ganciclovir acts as a chain terminator during elongation of newly synthesized viral DNA, and in laboratory animals, it is a teratogen and carcinogen, as well as a cause of gonadal atrophy and decreased spermatogenesis.

Recent studies, however, support the use of ganciclovir in selected neonates. A phase II study of intravenous ganciclovir (4 or 6 mg/kg per dose every 12 hours for 6 weeks) in 47 neonates with congenital CMV infection involving the CNS found that the preferred dose was 12 mg/kg/day.[536] Adverse effects of ganciclovir included neutropenia in 16 (34%) infants and increases in aspartate aminotransferase in 6 (13%) and direct hyperbilirubinemia in 3 (6%). Hearing was improved or stabilized in 16 percent of infants at 6 months or longer of follow-up, thus suggesting efficacy.

Subsequently, a phase III, multicenter randomized study of ganciclovir therapy for infants with congenital CMV infection involving the CNS was performed by the Collaborative Antiviral Study Group (CASG) from 1991 to 1999.[262] This study evaluated the safety and efficacy of intravenous ganciclovir (6 mg/kg per dose every 12 hours for 6 weeks) versus no therapy in 100 CMV-infected neonates (≥32 weeks of gestation, birth weight ≥1200 g). Among only 47 evaluable infants, those who received ganciclovir were significantly more likely to have either improved or normal hearing at 6 months than were untreated infants, and none of the ganciclovir-treated infants had worse hearing. At 1 year or longer, those who received ganciclovir also were significantly less likely to have worse hearing than were those in the untreated group. Other beneficial effects of ganciclovir therapy included a significant decrease in the median time to normalization of alanine transaminase, as well as improved weight gain and head circumference after 6 weeks of therapy, but no change in mortality rates. Neutropenia developed in 63 percent of ganciclovir recipients. Unfortunately, no neurodevelopmental assessments were performed in this study to know whether ganciclovir therapy had an impact on the long-term prognosis in these high-risk infants.

Currently, offering ganciclovir therapy to CMV-infected neonates with CNS disease seems reasonable; more than 90 to 95 percent of these infants will have significant neurologic sequelae. Extrapolating from the effects on hearing, for which ganciclovir was most effective in preventing hearing deterioration rather than improving hearing function, the beneficial effects of ganciclovir may be in prevention of further damage to the CNS. Deciding which neonate should receive ganciclovir therapy certainly may become an ethical decision; the brain injury that has occurred in utero in some infants is so severe that no antiviral therapy would be expected to dramatically reverse the damage and exert a beneficial impact on outcome. Moreover, 6 weeks of therapy may not be sufficient because infants with congenital CMV infection shed virus for years, possibly contributing to further neurologic deterioration. A phase I/II pharmacokinetic evaluation of oral valganciclovir in neonates with CMV infection of the CNS is ongoing, with the hope that in the future, infants may receive prolonged suppressive oral therapy.

Ganciclovir also may be beneficial in treating critically ill neonates with life-threatening CMV disease manifested by pneumonitis, hepatitis, or encephalitis and particularly that acquired intrapartum or postnatally in premature infants. It has been used in steroid-associated CMV disease in preterm infants, in whom it may be combined with CMV immunoglobulin because these infants have low transplacentally acquired CMV IgG antibodies. Ganciclovir prophylaxis should be considered in CMV-infected preterm infants who require steroid therapy for severe chronic lung disease. Further studies in these areas are needed.

PROGNOSIS

The major long-term sequelae of neonatal CMV infection are mental retardation, hearing loss, and microcephaly.[178, 213, 293, 425, 433, 477] The worst prognosis occurs in neonates born to mothers with primary CMV infection during pregnancy; in infants with symptoms at birth, particularly those of the CNS; in infants with microcephaly, intracranial calcification, or both; and in neonates who have elevated quantitative IgM or in whom CMV-specific IgM is present.[15, 137, 178, 197, 212, 293] The duration of CMV urinary excretion has not been associated with abnormalities in growth or neurodevelopmental deficits.[373] The best predictor of future neurodevelopmental abnormalities is an abnormal head computed tomography (CT) scan in the neonatal period.[63, 542] Overall, 25 percent of infants born to mothers with primary CMV infection during pregnancy will have at least one sequela, versus 8 percent of those born to mothers with recurrent infection.[178] Of symptomatic, congenitally infected neonates, approximately 30 percent die during infancy, with most deaths occurring in the neonatal period and usually caused by severe multisystem organ involvement and pneumonitis.[64] Six percent of these symptomatic infants die after the neonatal period, and death often is caused by progressive liver disease and failure to thrive. Death beyond infancy is a result of malnutrition, aspiration pneumonia, or overwhelming infection. Of survivors with symptomatic congenital CMV disease, as many as 90 percent have some evidence of CNS abnormality, such as microcephaly, impaired intellect or development, neuromuscular disorders (seizures, cerebral palsy, spasticity, hemiparesis), sensorineural hearing loss, and ocular abnormalities (usually chorioretinitis).[112, 178, 395, 471, 543] Neurologic sequelae of congenital CMV disease, especially sensorineural hearing loss, may progress after the first year of life.[62] For this reason, the recommendation is that CMV-infected newborns have close audiologic and neurodevelopmental follow-up through childhood and adolescence. Cochlear transplantation at 18 to 24 months of age has been used successfully in some infants who have profound bilateral hearing loss.

Ninety to 95 percent of infants with congenital CMV infection are asymptomatic in the neonatal period. Several long-term follow-up studies have indicated that at least 10 percent of these infants may suffer neurologic damage as a result of their infection. The following abnormalities were noted in infected infants when compared with matched control children: IQ less than 90 (32 versus 16%), significant hearing loss (23 versus 9%), predicted school failure (36 versus 14%), and microcephaly (15 versus 5%).[213, 425] In addition, approximately 2 percent of infants with asymptomatic congenital infection will have chorioretinitis.

As many as one third of neonates who acquire CMV natally from maternal cervical secretions may have acute disease associated with the onset of viruria, regardless of birth weight.[292, 560] However, birth weight and age of onset of viral excretion appear to influence the development of neurologic sequelae significantly. Full-term neonates with natally acquired CMV do not have significantly altered behavioral, neurologic, audiologic, speech, and language examinations on long-term follow-up when compared with uninfected controls.[293] In contrast, infants with birth weight less than 2000 g and onset of CMV excretion before they reach 8 weeks of age have associated severe cardiopulmonary disease during the neonatal intensive care unit stay (perhaps because of CMV worsening the pulmonary disease) and a significantly greater percentage of severe handicaps on long-term follow-up than do matched controls.[392] The relationships among low birth weight, early onset of CMV excretion, lower levels of transplacental antibody, and more severe cardiopulmonary disease and their contribution to neurologic sequelae require further evaluation, but natal acquisition of CMV appears to contribute to the development of sequelae in selected situations. CMV disease acquired from blood transfusion in very-low-birth-weight infants also may contribute to neurologic sequelae.[8, 15, 559]

Infants with congenital CMV infection have many special needs. These infants and children require physical, occupational, and speech therapy, as well as audiologic follow-up, to assess their need for hearing aids and cochlear transplantation. Ophthalmologic follow-up also is necessary because strabismus and, rarely, chorioretinitis may develop and affect visual acuity. Failure to thrive secondary to swallowing dysfunction, such as microaspiration and gastroesophageal reflux, often is present in the more severely affected infants, which renders the need for gastrostomy tube feeding essential for survival. This decision often becomes an ethical issue, as is establishment of resuscitation orders. Severely affected children also may have sleep disorders that may require the use of nighttime sedatives. In less severely affected children, school function must be assessed carefully. Finally, all these issues bring stress to the family unit, and the need for family support cannot be overemphasized.

PREVENTION

Routine serologic screening of pregnant women is not recommended because no prophylactic or therapeutic interventions are available during pregnancy. Meticulous adherence to standard precautions, especially handwashing after exposure to urine or saliva from young infants and toddlers, is the most effective means of preventing transmission of CMV infection to pregnant women.

Because of the frequency of congenital, natal, and postnatal CMV infection in infants and because of prolonged excretion of the virus in urine and saliva, concern has been raised about potential nosocomial spread of this agent among hospital personnel and hospitalized infants. However, the rate of transmission of CMV in the hospital setting appears to be low,[175] and prolonged or intimate contact seems to be necessary for spread.[15, 137, 175, 555] Health care workers do not have higher rates of seroconversion than control subjects do. For this reason and because of the ubiquity of the virus, pregnant women are not excluded routinely from caring for patients infected with CMV.[22] Adherence to standard precautions for all patients will prevent nosocomial transmission to patients and health care workers.

Blood transfusion–associated CMV infection in low-birth-weight infants in neonatal intensive care units virtually has been eliminated by the use of CMV-seronegative blood donors,[4, 69, 300, 310] frozen deglycerolized red cells,[69, 501] removal of the buffy coat, and filtration to remove white blood cells. Pasteurization of breast milk effectively kills CMV, although freezing at −20° C significantly reduces but does not eliminate infectivity. If donor breast milk is provided to premature infants or full-term infants born to nonimmune mothers, only that from a seronegative mother should be used.

Two live attenuated CMV vaccines (AD-169 and Towne strains) have been developed and evaluated clinically.[7] However, many questions remain to be answered before these vaccines can be considered for use in preventing congenital or natal CMV infection.[15, 137, 212] First, the attenuated live virus vaccine strains could be oncogenic. Second, the duration of protection by vaccine-induced immunity against infection with the wild virus is not known. Third, whether the vaccine virus itself could be passed transplacentally and cause congenital infection in humans is not known. In addition, concern exists that the vaccine virus could result in latent infection and subsequently reactivate with transmission to the fetus. Fourth, because congenital infection is known to occur in the fetuses of mothers with natural immunity, vaccine-induced immunity also probably will not provide full protection. Some of these potential problems may be circumvented by using a subunit vaccine.[71] Such a vaccine using CMV glycoprotein gB, a principal target of the neutralizing antibody response, has been developed and awaits immunogenicity and efficacy trials.

Rubella

Rubella usually is a mild, often subclinical disease involving school-age children and young adults. However, rubella virus also can cross the placenta, infect the fetus, and cause fetal death or congenital malformations. Since the original observations made by the Australian ophthalmologist Norman McAlister Gregg[195] in which maternal rubella was associated with the birth of offspring with defects of the eye and heart, rubella has been the prototype for congenital viral infection (see also Chapter 177).

MICROBIOLOGY AND EPIDEMIOLOGY

Rubella virus is an enveloped RNA virus in the family *Togaviridae* and has only a single antigenic type.[117] Rubella virus grows in tissue culture from a variety of animal species, but commonly, African green monkey kidney cells are used for isolation in the diagnostic virology laboratory.[102] Several serologic tests, including complement fixation, hemagglutination inhibition, immunofluorescence, radioimmunoassay, and enzyme immunoassay (EIA), are available.[102, 212, 224] Although hemagglutination inhibition[493] has been the gold standard, many diagnostic virology laboratories now use more sensitive tests such as ELISA, latex agglutination, or fluorescent assay kits.[102]

Rubella is worldwide in distribution. Human beings are the only host, and transmission occurs from person to person.[117, 545] In the era before rubella vaccine was available, epidemics occurred at 6- to 9-year intervals, and pandemics occurred every 10 to 20 years.[545] Since licensure of the vaccine in 1969, this epidemic pattern has been interrupted; the last major outbreak in the United States was in 1964.[41, 379] The peak seasonal incidence is in the spring.[545] In the prevaccine era, the peak age incidence was between 5 and 14 years of age,[545] but in the mid-1970s, the peak age was 15 to 19 years.[379] Currently, no peak age exists. Approximately 5 to 25 percent of women of child-bearing age lack rubella antibody and are susceptible to primary infection.[41, 89, 212] The attack rate for rubella in susceptible populations with prolonged intimate exposure is high—95 to 100 percent.[117, 545] The frequency of transmission after brief exposure, however, is low.[117, 545] The frequency of subclinical infections is much higher in adults than in children, although some serologically diagnosed infections in adults actually may be reinfections rather than primary disease.[234, 235, 449]

The incubation period for acquired rubella ranges from 14 to 23 days but usually is 16 to 18 days.[449] Virus may be isolated from the throat from 1 week before to 2 weeks after the onset of rash. Rubella virus infection may be subclinical in one third to a half of children and in half to two thirds of adults.[234, 449] Rubella hemagglutination-inhibition antibody is detectable in serum within 2 to 3 days after the onset of rash, with peak titers being reached in 3 to 4 weeks.[102, 212] Complement-fixation antibody rises more slowly, with peak titers noted 4 to 6 weeks after the rash appears.[212] Primary rubella virus infection is associated with an initial response in IgM-specific antibody, followed by an increase in IgG antibody.[212] Reinfection with rubella virus is known to occur, and rates are higher in vaccine-immune than in naturally immune subjects.[234] The vast majority of congenital rubella virus infections occur after primary infection, but a few cases have been reported after reinfection.[99, 158, 212, 426] If no evidence of rubella-specific IgM can be found in mothers with subclinical reinfection during pregnancy, the fetus is unlikely to be at risk.[212]

PATHOGENESIS AND PATHOLOGY

Transplacental infection of the fetus with rubella virus occurs secondary to maternal viremia during the course of primary infection.[12, 14, 276] Fetal infection appears to result from embolization of pieces of necrotic placental vascular endothelium.[336] However, involvement of the placenta with rubella virus does not always result in fetal infection, particularly after the first trimester.[14, 212] After maternal immunity, the next most critical factor determining the frequency of fetal infection and the severity of disease in neonates is the time during gestation that rubella virus infection occurs.[212] Studies of the frequency of fetal infection and congenital defects according to gestational age at the time of maternal infection have used more sensitive methods to detect maternal and neonatal infection and long-term follow-up to detect abnormalities that were not apparent during infancy.[338] These studies indicated higher fetal infection rates than previously realized: 90 percent during the first 11 weeks, 50 percent during weeks 11 to 20, 37 percent from 20 to 35 weeks, and 100 percent during the last month. The congenital defect rate was 100 percent for the first 11 weeks, 30 percent during weeks 11 to 20, and none thereafter. Neonatal purpura and cataracts or glaucoma are observed when maternal rubella occurs during the first 2 months of gestation; congenital heart disease, during the first 3 months; deafness and neurologic deficit, during the first 4 months; and retinopathy, during the first 5 months.[212, 338, 513]

Excretion of rubella virus from the throat of congenitally infected infants may continue for several months after birth; approximately 10 to 20 percent of infected infants shed virus in nasopharyngeal secretions at 6 months of age. A small number will continue to shed virus for 1 year or more, and the virus has been recovered from tissues up to several years later.[14, 119, 212] Persistence of viral replication after birth may result in continuing damage to involved tissues. In fact, hearing loss and neurologic deficits may appear long after birth in children previously considered well, or the clinical severity of these sequelae actually may worsen as the child's condition is being monitored.[104, 119, 140, 212]

Rubella virus is a proven teratogenic viral agent—that is, one that results in congenital malformations.[380] Hence, knowledge of the mechanisms by which rubella virus causes deformities may lead to a basic understanding of the pathogenesis of these malformations. Rubella virus is noncytolytic in certain tissues in that it does not destroy the cells in which it replicates. This characteristic, if manifested in the fetus, would tend to allow survival but result in disordered function of cells, tissues, and organs. On the other hand, selective cell destruction also may occur in fetal tissues.

In studies of the pathology of therapeutically aborted, rubella-infected fetuses, scattered foci of necrotic cellular damage without inflammatory infiltrates were noted in the endothelial cells of blood vessels and in myocardial cells.[505] These rubella-induced defects could result in defective formation or function of developing tissues by direct cellular destruction or by hypoxic damage secondary to blood vessel obliteration. For example, alteration of the elastic or muscle fibers in the ductus arteriosus could result in failure of postnatal ductus closure. Studies of tissue obtained from infants with rubella syndrome and maintained in culture showed that the cells were infected with rubella virus persistently and had a decreased growth rate and shortened survival time.[417] Naeye and Blanc[357] noted that the growth retardation of infants with rubella syndrome was the result of decreased numbers of cells in organs. This impaired cellular growth, if it occurred during a crucial phase in cardiac development, for example, could result in such cardiac anomalies as septal defects.

Increased numbers of chromosome breaks have been noted in leukocyte cultures of children with congenital rubella.[374] This chromosomal injury possibly results in cell loss during rapid organ development and is, in part, responsible for the congenital anomalies. Persistence of virus possibly results in continuing cell destruction or immunopathologic damage to tissues.[212] In addition, two studies have demonstrated circulating rubella antigen-antibody complexes in 10 infants with congenital rubella and late-onset manifestations such as interstitial pneumonia, hepatosplenomegaly, rash, lymphocytic meningitis, and rapid neurologic deterioration.[61, 500] IgG levels were low and IgM levels were elevated, with a diminished number of T cells and an increased proportion of B cells. Delayed maturation of the immune response in congenital rubella was postulated to predispose possibly to persistent antigenemia complexed with IgM and deposition of circulating immune complexes in tissues. Finally, antibodies against thyroid microsomes or thyroglobulin were found in a much larger percentage of children with congenital rubella syndrome than in control subjects.[108] A significant number of the patients with congenital rubella and thyroid antibodies also had thyroid dysfunction. These observations suggest that autoimmunity, induced in some way by persistent infection with rubella virus, plays a role in the late-onset endocrine dysfunction that occurs in children and young adults with congenital rubella syndrome.

Specific pathologic lesions in infants with congenital rubella depend on the gestational age at the time of infection and the particular organs involved. One common finding is necrosis of vascular endothelium, which may be accompanied by damage to organs secondary to vascular obstruction.[336, 505] Diffuse intimal changes have been observed in the pulmonary and systemic arteries, as well as the ductus arteriosus.[336] Focal inflammation and necrosis have been seen in the myocardium[278] and structures of the inner ear.[212]

The fetus is capable of an immune response to rubella virus: specific IgM and, occasionally, IgA have been observed in fetal and cord blood specimens.[212] In fact, hypergammaglobulinemia may be observed during early life in some infants with congenital rubella.[208] On the other hand, hypogammaglobulinemia has been noted in a few infants.[208, 403] In 10 to 20 percent of infants with congenital rubella, hemagglutination-inhibition antibody declines to undetectable levels when they reach 1 to 4 years of age.[119, 215] Several of these infants failed to respond to immunization with rubella vaccine.[116, 212] In fact, infants with congenital rubella have been reinfected with rubella virus later in life.[334] Several defects in cell-mediated immunity, including diminished responsiveness of peripheral blood leukocytes to phytohemagglutinin and diminished lymphocyte transformation, interferon production, and synthesis of leukocyte migration inhibitory factor in response to challenge with rubella virus antigen, have been observed in infants with congenital rubella.[81, 378] Normal responses were observed in healthy, seropositive children and adults. Researchers have presumed, but have not proved, that these abnormalities in cell-mediated immunity play a role in persistent viral excretion in congenitally infected infants.

CLINICAL MANIFESTATIONS

Although the typical clinical features of rubella may occur in pregnant women, as many as one half to two thirds of these infections are subclinical.[212, 451] Typical features that might occur in symptomatic postpubertal women include fever, rash, posterior auricular and postoccipital adenopathy, and arthralgia or arthritis.[212]

As many as two thirds of infants with proven congenital rubella may be asymptomatic in the neonatal period.[439] However, evidence of long-term sequelae was noted in almost three quarters of such infants within the first 5 years of life.[439] The clinical manifestations of congenital rubella syndrome vary highly, not only with regard to specific features but also in relation to the age during which the specific feature occurs. The collected features may be divided into three broad categories: (1) transient—those that are present in the neonatal period and clear after a few months, such as thrombocytopenia and hepatitis; (2) permanent—major malformations that persist and may even worsen as the child grows older, such as congenital heart lesions, cataracts, or hearing loss; and (3) developmental—aspects that do not emerge until childhood or young adulthood, such as behavioral disorders or endocrine dysfunction.[116, 212, 452] This categorization of abnormal features may be useful in determining the prognosis and management of these children.

The manifestations of congenital rubella that are symptomatic in the neonatal period, compiled from several series,[118, 233, 277, 316, 432] are illustrated in Figure 73–2. The low birth weight of infants with rubella syndrome results from intrauterine growth restriction; even when born prematurely, the infant often is small for gestational age. The frequency of purpura in most series ranges from 15 to 50 percent. Thrombocytopenia almost always was present in association with the purpura and usually resolved spontaneously in the first month of life. Neonatal thrombocytopenic purpura is a poor prognostic sign because it generally occurs in severely affected infants with multiple manifestations. Thirty-five percent of 58 patients with purpura in one series[118] died during the first year, in contrast to a mortality rate of only 13 percent during the first 18 months for patients from the entire series. Although the thrombocytopenia frequently was profound, death rarely was caused by hemorrhage.

Direct involvement of the liver by rubella virus results in neonatal hepatitis, as evidenced by hepatomegaly, predominantly direct-reacting hyperbilirubinemia, and elevation of liver enzymes.[167] Pathology studies usually demonstrate hepatocellular disease with necrosis, giant-cell formation, bile stasis, and fibrosis, but extrahepatic biliary obstruction also has been demonstrated.[494]

Congenital heart disease occurs frequently and generally is detectable in the neonatal period, although specific lesions may not be defined until later in life. The most common lesions in 87 catheterized patients with congenital rubella were patent ductus arteriosus in 78 percent, right pulmonary artery stenosis in 70 percent, left pulmonary artery stenosis in 56 percent, valvular pulmonic stenosis in 40 percent, mild aortic valvular stenosis in 14 percent, aberrant subclavian artery in 11 percent, and ventricular septal defect in 10 percent.[119] Evidence of active myocardial disease has been noted in some infants.[278]

Interstitial pneumonia with cough, tachypnea, and breathlessness as the major manifestation of congenital rubella has been reported.[400] Six of seven patients with this syndrome died in the first year of life as a result of their pulmonary disease. Cardiac abnormalities also were present but were thought to not be significant either clinically or from autopsy findings. Microscopic studies revealed acute to subacute chronic interstitial pneumonitis. Rubella virus was isolated from all of the four lung specimens cultured.

Although cataracts are the most characteristic ocular lesion in rubella syndrome, they may not be visualized until after the neonatal period. The retinopathy is described as widespread, with mottled or blotchy, black pigmentary deposits of variable size and location: the "salt and pepper" retinitis.[284] Retinal function usually is not affected adversely. The frequency of retinopathy in the combined data from six series of children monitored for several years was 36 percent.

Bone lesions are another finding in congenital rubella in the neonatal period. Radiographic studies reveal small linear areas of radiolucency and increased bone density in the longitudinal axis of the metaphyseal area of the long bones of the lower and upper extremities.[432] The abnormality results from disturbances in deposition and calcification of osteoid and usually resolves by the time the child is 2 to 3 months of age.

Involvement of the CNS frequently is evident in symptomatic infants. Lethargy, irritability, disturbances in tone, and a bulging fontanelle are common findings. One or more seizures developed in 27 of 100 infants in one series.[140, 141] However, they usually occurred after the neonatal period. In most infants with CNS involvement, CSF protein is elevated, but increased cell counts are seen less frequently. Rubella virus may be isolated from the CSF; in one series, 25 percent of 99 CSF specimens obtained during the first 3 months of life from patients with CNS symptoms were positive.[140, 141] The extent of impairment at 18 months of age was not readily predictable on the basis of clinical symptoms or isolation of virus in the first few weeks of life. However, severe involvement was found more frequently in infants with seizures and high levels of CSF protein in the first few months of life.[140, 141] An important emphasis is the chronic nature of congenital rubella infection, and one should note that although most infants may be asymptomatic in the neonatal period, evidence of disease was seen on follow-up examination in as many as 70 percent.[212]

DIAGNOSIS AND DIFFERENTIAL DIAGNOSIS

Because many maternal rubella cases are subclinical and other diseases may mimic symptomatic rubella, definitive diagnosis in the mother depends on the laboratory. Although rubella virus may be isolated from the throat during the acute phase of the illness, such culture frequently is not a practical means of establishing the diagnosis. The tissue culture cells required for isolation of rubella virus are not always available in routine virology laboratories. Widely used serologic tests include hemagglutination inhibition, ELISA, and fluorescent assay.[95, 102] Susceptible persons lack IgG antibody. Detectable antibody is present in the blood within a few days after onset of the rash, and peak titers are reached within 2 to 3 weeks. If serum specimens are not available until some time after the onset of illness, complement-fixation antibody titers may be useful because peak titers are not reached for 4 to 6 weeks after the rash is manifested.[212] If only a single specimen is available, rubella-specific IgM antibody may be demonstrable by ELISA or immunofluorescence methods.[102, 224] These antibodies peak 3 to 6 weeks after infection occurs and persist for several months.[212] Although culturing of amniotic fluid for virus and sampling of fetal blood for antibody have been used in an attempt to make an antenatal diagnosis of congenital rubella, both false-positive (viral infection but no fetal damage) and false-negative results may be obtained. PCR on chorionic villi samples also has been used for prenatal diagnosis.

The most characteristic clinical features of congenital rubella are congenital heart disease, cataracts, microphthalmos, corneal opacity, glaucoma, and radiolucent bone lesions. In infants with these classic features, the clinical diagnosis correlates with laboratory confirmation of congenital rubella 80 percent of the time.[212] However, many of the features, such as low birth weight, hepatosplenomegaly, icterus, and petechiae/purpura, overlap with those found in other infectious diseases of the newborn, and definitive diagnosis requires laboratory confirmation. The diagnosis of congenital rubella is confirmed by isolation of virus from the throat or urine; in addition, virus has been recovered from cataracts, conjunctivae, CSF, feces, bone marrow, and circulating leukocytes.[212] The lens is an excellent site for recovery of virus, especially because cataracts are removed from these infants within the first few weeks of life. The diagnosis of congenital rubella also can be made by serologic means. Because rubella IgG antibody is passed transplacentally, serum levels determined early in the neonatal period mimic those of the mother. Stable or rising serum concentrations of rubella-specific IgG antibody in the serum of infants during their first 4 to 6 months of life can be considered diagnostic of congenital rubella when the clinical picture is compatible.[212] The presence of specific IgM antibody in a single serum specimen obtained from an infant early in life also can be diagnostic, but false-positive test results have been reported. Whenever possible, viral isolation should be performed for definitive diagnosis. PCR performed on nasopharyngeal secretions ultimately may aid in making the diagnosis.[136, 523]

The finding during pregnancy that a mother is immune to rubella is not sufficient to exclude the diagnosis because reinfection may have occurred or maternal infection may have developed before the screen was performed. If the diagnosis of congenital rubella is suspected clinically when the mother is thought to be immune, the infant should be screened with rubella-specific IgM ELISA and viral culture or PCR of appropriate clinical specimens. The diagnosis of congenital rubella infection can be eliminated if the mother is nonimmune when the infant manifests clinical signs of possible congenital infection.

The principal diseases to consider in the differential diagnosis include congenital CMV infection, congenital toxoplasmosis, erythroblastosis fetalis, disseminated herpes simplex, neonatal sepsis, and congenital syphilis. Infants with congenital CMV infection more commonly have chorioretinitis and microcephaly, whereas congenital heart disease and eye malformations are unusual findings. Infants with symptomatic congenital toxoplasmosis have chorioretinitis, hydrocephaly, and cerebral calcifications, but not congenital heart disease, cataracts, or glaucoma. In uncomplicated erythroblastosis, the direct bilirubin and liver function studies remain normal. Disseminated herpes simplex should be differentiated on the basis of the characteristic vesicular skin lesions or the presence of keratoconjunctivitis. Positive blood cultures identify neonatal sepsis. The bone lesions in congenital syphilis are associated with periosteal new bone formation; rhinitis and lesions of the skin and mucous membranes also are seen. Because of overlapping clinical features, however, definitive diagnosis requires laboratory confirmation.

TREATMENT

No specific antiviral therapy exists for congenital rubella. Although amantadine hydrochloride inhibits rubella virus in vitro, treatment with this drug was not shown to alter the clinical or virologic course of the disease.[403]

PROGNOSIS

The most common long-term sequelae of congenital rubella are listed in Table 73–8. Deafness is the most frequent finding and may not be apparent for several months to several years after birth. In 15 to 20 percent of children, it may be the only abnormality detectable.[119, 212] Approximately one half the children may have absent or hyporeactive responses to tests of vestibular function.[340] The hearing loss may be profound and, thus, a major contributor to speech impairment and learning disability. In approximately 50 percent of children with mental retardation, the deficiency is moderate to severe. Although retinopathy is present in a significant proportion of infants, it does not appear to interfere with vision. Cataracts, of course, certainly can interfere with the development of vision, and they should be removed surgically in the first few weeks of life. Most fatalities from congenital rubella occur in the first year of life and are associated with severe congenital heart disease and general debility from multiple defects.[119]

Long-term follow-up evaluation of children with congenital rubella syndrome is available.[104, 140, 141, 334, 452] Among 205 children examined at 8 to 9 years of age, 26 percent had severe mental retardation, 18 percent had reactive behavior disorder, 12 percent showed behavior disorder with neurologic damage, and 6 percent displayed autism. Of 29 children with neurologic manifestations of congenital rubella between birth and 18 months of age but with normal intelligence, 93 percent had hearing loss when examined at 9 to 12 years of age; 61 percent, poor balance; 54 percent, muscular weakness; 52 percent, learning deficits; 48 percent, behavioral disturbance; and 41 percent, deficits in tactile perception. Head circumference appears to correlate poorly with intellectual function in patients with congenital rubella.[322] Diabetes mellitus has been observed in 15 to 20 percent of adults with congenital rubella.[335] Onset usually occurs in the second or third decade of life. Other late manifestations[452] of congenital rubella syndrome include chronic lymphocytic thyroiditis,[565] thymic hypoplasia,[182] abnormal dermatoglyphics,[119] chromosomal abnormalities,[27] pancreatic insufficiency,[145] and progressive panencephalitis.[511, 527] As one might expect, the severity of long-term sequelae appears to correlate with the number of defects observed in early life.[104, 119]

TABLE 73–8 ■ FREQUENCY OF DEFECTS IN CHILDREN WITH CONGENITAL RUBELLA

Defect	Percentage of Cases
No defect	19
Deafness	67
Congenital heart disease	48
Psychomotor retardation	45
Retinopathy	39
Cataracts	29
Neonatal purpura	23
Glaucoma	3
Deaths	16

Data from 376 children studied in the New York Rubella Birth Defect Project. Modified from Cooper, L. Z., Ziring, P. R., Ockerse, A. B., et al.: Rubella: Clinical manifestations and management. Am. J. Dis. Child. *118*: 18–29, 1969.

PREVENTION

Active immunization with live, attenuated rubella virus vaccine is the most effective means of preventing congenital rubella syndrome. The development and use of rubella vaccine in the United States clearly have reduced the frequency of congenital rubella.[41, 227, 379] The target population in the United States has been preschool- and school-age children, whereas in Great Britain, selective vaccination of 11- to 14-year-olds and women immediately after delivery has been the goal. The strategy used in the United States is more effective in decreasing the incidence of congenital rubella syndrome. More recently, immunization programs in the United States have emphasized the need to vaccinate susceptible women of child-bearing age.[41, 227, 379] Moreover, routine prenatal screening for rubella immunity should be performed, and all nonimmune women should be vaccinated during the immediate postpartum period and before discharge. Breast-feeding is not a contraindication to postpartum immunization. Although the vaccine virus may be transmitted in breast milk, the infection in the neonate is asymptomatic. Immunization with rubella vaccine, however, is contraindicated during pregnancy, and physicians recommend that a woman not conceive during the 3-month period after being immunized.[76, 294] Data collected by the CDC from more than 500 pregnancies show that vaccine viruses can cross the placenta and infect the fetus but do not produce the defects associated with congenital rubella syndrome. The rate of isolation of vaccine virus from the products of conception is only 3 percent for the currently used RA 27/3 vaccine. Thus, inadvertent administration of rubella vaccine during the first trimester of pregnancy is not an indication for termination of pregnancy.

Chapter 177 provides more detailed information about rubella vaccine. Continuing concerns with regard to rubella include reinfection with wild rubella virus in vaccine-immune subjects[234]; failure of rubella herd immunity during an epidemic[267]; arthralgia and arthritis as side effects of the vaccine in children and particularly postpubertal women, even though the risk of developing chronic arthropathy is not increased[257, 526]; waning immunity that is more profound after immunization than after natural infection[41, 227, 379]; and, more recently, outbreaks of rubella among unvaccinated pregnant women in custodial institutions, immigration camps in border states, or selected communities.[87, 89, 332]

Although administration of gamma-globulin to women during pregnancy may reduce the frequency of symptomatic disease in the mother, it appears to have little effect on the frequency or severity of fetal and neonatal disease.[72, 327] Infants with congenital rubella syndrome are considered to be contagious and are maintained with contact precautions until they are at least 1 year of age, unless repeated nasopharyngeal and urine cultures after 3 months of age are negative for rubella virus.[212] Health care workers are required to report all cases of congenital rubella to their local health department.

Hepatitis

Since the late 1970s, a veritable explosion of information concerning infection with hepatitis A virus (HAV), HBV, hepatitis C virus (HCV), hepatitis D virus (HDV), and hepatitis E virus (HEV) has occurred.* HAV has been grown in cell cultures, and two purified viral glycoprotein vaccines have been licensed and recommended for use in high-risk individuals 2 years and older.[109, 230, 308, 309] HBV and HCV are discussed later. HDV is a defective virus that infects only persons with acute or chronic HBV infection.[406] The major cause of enterically transmitted non-A, non-B (NANB) hepatitis, a problem confined largely to developing countries,[519] has been shown to be HEV, an RNA virus of the family *Calicivirus*.[281, 504] Epidemic NANB hepatitis occurs more frequently during pregnancy and can result in fulminant hepatic failure in these women.

HAV and HDV rarely cause infection of the fetus and newborn.[488, 564] Natal transmission of hepatitis A to the newborn can occur if the mother has jaundice or had acute hepatitis within the 2 weeks before and 1 week after delivery. Although most infants are asymptomatic, researchers have recommended that exposed infants receive 0.02 mL/kg of immunoglobulin intramuscularly as soon as possible after delivery. The infant should be maintained with contact precautions for 6 weeks, or for 1 week after the onset of symptoms. Preterm infants may excrete HAV antigen and RNA for several months after acquiring acute infection. Nosocomial transmission of hepatitis A within nurseries has been documented. A report from India indicated a relatively high rate of vertical transmission among eight women with third-trimester HEV infection[255]; more investigations are needed to determine the true significance of maternal HEV infection for the fetus and newborn infant in the United States. The following section focuses on HBV and HCV.

See also Chapters 54, 162, 172, and 180 on hepatitis viruses.

MICROBIOLOGY AND EPIDEMIOLOGY

HBV, a double-stranded DNA virus with a DNA polymerase, is the prototype member of the family *Hepadnaviridae*.[237, 273] Seroepidemiologic investigation of HBV infection has been enhanced by the identification and development of three major antigen systems, antibody systems, or both: surface antigen (HBsAg and anti-HBs), core antigen (total anti-HBc and IgM anti-HBc), and e antigen (HBeAg and anti-HBe).[237, 273] Tests for HBsAg are used widely for the diagnosis of acute or chronic infection with HBV, anti-HBc is a marker of continuing viral replication in the liver, IgM anti-HBc is present during acute but not chronic HBV infection, and HBeAg is a more specific indicator of infectivity than HBsAg is.[91, 229, 237, 273, 455]

*See references 82, 84, 91, 127, 192, 232, 237, 273, 282, 287, 406, 455, 491, 517.

HBV accounts for 40 to 50 percent of all the cases of hepatitis in the United States and 10 percent of those associated with blood transfusion.[91, 455] Between 5 and 10 percent of patients infected with HBV become chronic carriers, and many of them have benign chronic persistent hepatitis or the more serious chronic active hepatitis.[237, 273, 319, 455] A strong association, particularly in Asian males, has been noted between chronic carriage of HBsAg and death from cirrhosis or primary hepatocellular carcinoma.[21, 47, 330] The age at which HBV infection occurs has a significant effect on the occurrence of clinically overt hepatitis and the development of a chronic carrier state.[185] The vast majority of neonates who acquire HBV from their mothers have subclinical infection, but 60 to 95 percent of infected infants become chronic carriers, particularly when the mother is HBeAg-positive.[45, 46, 51, 139, 186, 376, 488, 492, 550]

In the United States, the frequency of surface antigenemia (HBsAg in serum) in the general population is 0.2 to 0.9 percent.[88] The highest prevalence of HBV antigenemia in the United States is in Asian immigrants/refugees (13%), Alaska Natives/Pacific Islanders (5–15%), clients in institutions for the developmentally disabled (10–20%), users of illicit parenteral drugs (7%), sexually active homosexual men (6%), household contacts of HBV chronic carriers (3–6%), and patients in hemodialysis units (3–10%).[88] Only 10 to 15 percent of persons reactive for HBsAg have a history of contracting hepatitis. In chronic carriers of HBsAg, antigen has been detected in saliva, feces, urine, wound exudates, vaginal secretions, breast milk, amniotic fluid, and semen.[237, 273, 455] The prevalence of anti-HBs in the general population is approximately 11 percent; this frequency increases with advancing age and is related inversely to socioeconomic status.[88]

Among children and adults, HBV is transmitted by the parenteral route (blood transfusion, needle-sticks), but infection by nonparenteral routes also occurs.[44, 48, 455, 507] Hepatitis B is not transmitted by the fecal-oral route. In the United States, transmission by blood and blood products now is a rare event because of routine screening of blood donors and viral inactivation of certain blood products.

Clustering of HBV infections in families is known to occur; family members of a known antigen-positive index case have a 10-fold higher prevalence of HBsAg or anti-HBs than do control families of the same ethnic background.[499] Although this clustering within families initially was considered to have a genetic basis,[499] "vertical" transmission of HBV infection from the mother to the infant may be a source.[139, 186, 376] However, person-to-person spread clearly occurs, but the exact mechanism is not known.[44, 507, 564] It has been seen in household settings from child to child, but not in daycare centers.

Moreover, transmission of HBV has occurred in children born to HBsAg-negative mothers who immigrated to the United States from countries where HBV infection is endemic.[44, 507, 564] The incubation period for the onset of HBV antigenemia after parenteral inoculation is 2 weeks to 2 months, depending on the dose of virus received. In nonparenteral exposure, the incubation period for antigenemia is 2 to 3 months. The onset of elevated liver enzymes and clinical symptoms follows the onset of antigenemia by 2 weeks to 2 months.[273]

In the fetus and neonate, transmission by the following routes has been suggested: transplacental, either during pregnancy or at the time of delivery secondary to placental leaks; natal, by exposure to HBsAg in amniotic fluid, cervical and vaginal secretions, or maternal blood; and postnatal, by contact with household members who are infected or are chronic carriers or, rarely, by transfusion of blood or blood products. Ninety-five percent of infections occur at the time of delivery, whereas only 5 percent occur in utero. The fetus or newborn infant, therefore, can be infected by hematogenous (transplacental, blood transfusion) or nonparenteral (contamination of the oropharynx or breaks in the skin) routes. Differences in the time of exposure (congenital, natal, postnatal) and in the route of viral inoculation (parenteral, nonparenteral) may account for the wide variation in time of onset of antigenemia in the neonate after birth. The usual age at onset of antigenemia in neonates born to chronic carrier mothers is 2 to 5 months,[25, 139, 153, 306, 377, 457, 489] which is consistent with exposure at the time of birth. Infections secondary to blood transfusion in the neonatal period also are associated with the onset of antigenemia at younger than 2 months of age.[154] Infants with an onset of antigenemia at younger than 2 months of age presumably were exposed to HBV in utero.[153, 186, 306, 377, 443, 457] In general, infants of mothers with acute hepatitis near the time of birth have antigenemia at an earlier age (1 to 2 months), thus suggesting transplacental transmission of HBV.[186, 443] Infants with an onset of antigenemia after they reach 6 months of age can be assumed to have had postnatal exposure,[443] but the exact source of virus in these infants is unclear.

In summary, evidence is good that infection with HBV can occur transplacentally, at the time of birth, and postnatally by blood transfusion or contamination of the oropharynx with infected secretions.[488] Several studies indicate that transmission by breast milk is a rare occurrence.[50, 139, 551] Further substantiation for the mother as the primary source of virus for the neonate comes from observations that the HBV serotype almost always is the same in infants and their carrier mothers.[186, 377, 489]

From 0.1 to 15.6 percent of pregnant women are asymptomatic chronic carriers of HBsAg. The lowest rates occur in the United States and in northern European populations,[139, 153, 465, 551] and the highest rates occur in Chinese, regardless of geographic location.[25, 51, 139, 306, 489] Intermediate rates are observed in Japanese,[376, 457] African,[139, 551] South Asian,[139, 551] and Mediterranean populations.[389] Rates of transmission of HBsAg from infected mothers to neonates vary highly and are influenced by the sensitivity of the HBsAg assay system used in the study, whether neonatal serum is examined for anti-HBs as well as for HBsAg, the frequency of bleeding and length of follow-up of infants, and the e antigen/antibody status of the mother. In general, HBsAg in a cord blood specimen is not a reliable indicator of neonatal infection because of the possibility of contamination with antigen-positive maternal blood or vaginal secretions and because of the possibility of transient noninfectious antigenemia from the mother.[139, 306, 388, 551] Demonstration of HBsAg in the serum of the infant during the first several months of life can be considered diagnostic of infection with HBV in the absence of immunization with hepatitis B vaccine. HBsAg may be detected for up to 1 week after the administration of a dose of vaccine. Most infants demonstrate antigenemia by the time that they are 6 months of age, with peak acquisition at 3 to 4 months of age.[25, 186, 306, 457]

Factors known to be associated with higher rates of HBV transmission to neonates include the presence of HBeAg and the absence of anti-HBe in maternal serum—attack rates of 80 to 95 percent[51, 139, 158, 306, 376, 388, 551]; an Asian racial origin, particularly Chinese—attack rates of 40 to 70 percent[25, 139, 306, 457, 489]; maternal acute hepatitis in the third trimester of pregnancy or the immediate postpartum period—attack rates of 60 to 70 percent[186, 443, 444]; a higher titer of HBsAg in maternal serum—attack rates parallel the titer[51, 306, 489]; and the presence of antigenemia in older siblings.[25, 376, 489] Factors *not* related to transmission include the presence or absence of breast-feeding,[50, 139, 551] the particular HBV subtype in the mother,[186, 377, 489] the presence or absence of HBsAg in amniotic fluid,[306] and the presence or absence of anti-HBc in cord blood.[139, 153, 186] Data conflict regarding the significance of HBsAg in cord blood. Some studies have found no relationship between its presence or absence and subsequent infection of the neonate, whereas others have found a correlation. The reasons for this difference are not understood.[139, 306, 388, 489, 551]

From 75 to 100 percent of infants in whom HBsAg develops in serum within the first several months of life have persistent or chronic antigenemia.[25, 139, 186, 376, 377, 457, 489] In some infants, anti-HBs may develop after transient carriage of HBsAg, and in a few (usually those born to asymptomatic carrier mothers), anti-HBs may develop without the infant ever having detectable antigen.[388, 457]

Transmission of HBV to infants in successive pregnancies of the same mother has been documented,[146, 152] and such transmission has, on occasion, been associated with the development of fatal hepatitis.

PATHOGENESIS AND PATHOLOGY

HBV transmitted to the neonate by the hematogenous route probably seeds the liver directly, whereas nonparenteral exposure requires replication at the portal of entry before spread to the liver through the bloodstream. Electron-microscopic studies of liver biopsy specimens from chronic carrier infants indicate that replication of HBV appears to occur in the nuclei of hepatocytes and that 50 to 100 percent of cells are involved.[151, 443] Histopathologic examination demonstrates a diffuse hydropic appearance of the liver cells, with effacement of the normal cord pattern and the creation of a "cobblestone appearance" in the liver lobule.[443] Only small foci of hepatocytolysis surrounded by macrophages and lymphocytes are present. Infants with symptomatic acute hepatitis have more widespread hepatic necrosis with surrounding inflammatory infiltrates, including giant cells.[152, 250] In fulminant disease, massive necrosis with little or no inflammatory response is present.[152, 250] In some infants with symptomatic hepatitis, the disease may progress to chronic persistent hepatitis, chronic active hepatitis, cirrhosis, or hepatocellular carcinoma.[66, 154, 250, 323, 506, 514, 553]

CLINICAL MANIFESTATIONS

Although clinically typical acute hepatitis may occur in mothers of infants in whom HBV infection develops, most are asymptomatic chronic carriers of HBsAg. Therefore, routine screening of serum for antigen in all pregnant women is necessary for the identification of infants at risk for development of HBV infection. Maternal HBV infection has not been associated with abortion, stillbirth, congenital malformations, or intrauterine growth retardation.[139, 154, 457] However, prematurity has been observed, particularly when the mother has acute hepatitis during pregnancy.[443]

A fetus or newborn infant exposed to HBV may follow one of several courses: (1) asymptomatic transient hepatitis B antigenemia, followed by the production of anti-HBs[153, 388]; (2) asymptomatic persistent antigenemia, variably associated with mild and fluctuating elevations in liver enzymes[25, 153, 186, 443, 457]; (3) symptomatic hepatitis with recovery and clearance of the antigen[153, 154]; (4) symptomatic hepatitis that becomes chronically persistent or chronically active with continued presence of hepatitis B antigenemia[152, 154, 250, 553]; (5) acute fulminant hepatitis with death[154, 171]; and (6) asymptomatic neonatal/infant infection with progression to cirrhosis or liver cancer.[66, 506, 514] Most infants with HBsAg in their serum become asymptomatic chronic carriers. However, liver function studies may be abnormal in some of these infants, and liver biopsy specimens usually show evidence of mild, unresolved hepatitis.[139, 154, 186, 443, 457] The long-term significance of these persistent abnormalities in asymptomatic chronic carrier infants is unknown. The factors that determine which pattern of HBV infection occurs in a given newborn infant and the mechanisms responsible for chronic carriage of HBsAg in many infants are not understood.

The source of virus for 29 infants with symptomatic HBV infection in the first few months of life was blood transfusion in 15 (52%), a chronic carrier mother in 9 (31%), and unknown in 5 (17%).[154] The type of clinical disease in these infants was acute, self-limited hepatitis in 16 (55%), severe or fulminant hepatitis in 9 (31%), chronic persistent hepatitis in 2 (7%), chronic active hepatitis in 1, and an asymptomatic chronic carrier state in 1. Most patients with fulminant hepatitis died.

DIAGNOSIS AND DIFFERENTIAL DIAGNOSIS

HBV infection in an infant generally is diagnosed by the demonstration of HBsAg in serum. If positive, infants also should be tested for HBeAg and anti-HBc IgM. In addition, PCR is available for detecting HBV DNA in blood. The major diseases to be considered in the differential diagnosis include biliary atresia and acute hepatitis caused by other viruses—HAV, CMV, rubella virus, and HSV.

TREATMENT

Treatment with human interferon has resulted in the termination or transient cessation of hepatitis B antigenemia in chronic hepatitis of adults,[193, 232, 399] but experience in children has been limited.[251, 296, 365] Lamivudine also is licensed for the treatment of chronic infection in adults. Treatment of established disease in infants with hepatitis B immunoglobulin (HBIG) has not altered the course of illness.[152, 171] Therefore, treatment of neonatal HBV infection primarily is supportive.

PROGNOSIS

The long-term outcome of asymptomatic infants with persistent antigenemia is guarded because chronic active and progressive hepatitis occur, as do death from cirrhosis, liver failure, and hepatocellular carcinoma. Death from fulminant HBV infection in neonates or young infants is a rare event but has occurred, particularly in successive children born to the same chronic carrier mother.[146, 171]

PREVENTION

Remarkable advances have occurred in the prophylaxis of neonates born to mothers with HBV infection. Initial studies in infants born to HBeAg-positive, chronic carrier mothers demonstrated that administration of HBIG significantly reduced the development of a chronic carrier state.[46, 49, 146, 245, 274, 419] The most successful regimens were those that began as soon as possible after birth and used multiple doses of HBIG. Anti-HBs developed in most infants who were protected against becoming chronic carriers, thus indicating that passive/active immunization had occurred. However, protection against persistent antigenemia was only 50 to 75 percent effective. Twenty to 30 percent of infants became infected during the second and third years after the protective effects of their passive immunoglobulin subsided.[46, 49] This finding suggests that the risk of developing infection continues beyond the time of birth and that active immunization would be necessary to provide long-term protection.

Hepatitis B vaccine (Heptavax B, licensed but no longer produced in the United States) then was demonstrated to be both safe and effective in inducing protective levels of anti-HBs in 95 percent or more of infants receiving three doses of the vaccine.[40, 307] Because passive/active immunization (HBIG plus three doses of HBV vaccine) in adults was shown to be safe and as effective in inducing long-term protective titers of anti-HBs as was a dosage of three doses of vaccine alone,[562] this regimen was tried in infants. Several investigations have demonstrated 85 to 96 percent efficacy in preventing chronic antigenemia with the combined HBIG/vaccine regimen.[45, 320, 492, 549] Persistent antibody against HBsAg developed in virtually all protected infants. Vaccine failures were thought to occur in babies who already were infected with HBV in utero and, hence, could not be protected by the HBIG/vaccine regimen initiated at birth. Subsequent studies using recombinant DNA vaccines (Recombivax HB, Engerix-B) showed them to be safe and highly immunogenic in neonates (>95%), with an efficacy of 90 to 95 percent.[407, 490]

The concentration of HBsAg protein differs in the two vaccines; the pediatric formulation of Recombivax HB contains 10 μg/mL, whereas Engerix-B has 20 mg/mL. The two vaccines are interchangeable, and neither one contains thimerosal.

Because most chronic carrier mothers are asymptomatic, serologic screening during pregnancy would be required to identify neonates needing prophylaxis beginning at birth. Initial recommendations suggested screening during pregnancy in populations with high-risk factors: (1) Asian, Alaskan, or Pacific Island descent; (2) birth in Haiti, sub-Saharan Africa, Eastern Europe, the Middle East, the Caribbean, or Central or South America; (3) acute or chronic liver disease; (4) work or treatment in a dialysis unit; (5) work or residence in an institution for the mentally retarded; (6) rejection as a blood donor; (7) blood transfusion on repeated occasions; (8) frequent occupational exposure to blood in medical or dental settings; (9) household contact with an HBV carrier or hemodialysis patient; (10) multiple episodes of sexually transmitted disease; or (11) percutaneous use of illicit drugs.[84, 88, 466] Because routine prenatal history to screen for these risk factors will miss one half to two thirds of asymptomatic chronic carrier mothers,[126, 289] the current recommendation is to screen *all* pregnant women for HBsAg early in pregnancy.[29, 30, 85, 90, 491] Testing should be repeated late in pregnancy for women who are negative initially and at high risk for acquiring HBV infection or who have had clinical hepatitis since the screening was performed.[94]

Perinatal transmission is prevented in more than 90 percent of cases by the intramuscular administration of 0.5 mL of HBIG and hepatitis B vaccine to both term and preterm infants of HBsAg-positive mothers as soon as possible but within 12 hours of delivery.[88] HBIG efficacy decreases markedly if treatment is delayed beyond 48 hours. HBV vaccine is administered intramuscularly at a separate site at birth (preferably) or within 7 days, and in infants with a birth weight of 2 kg or more, administration is repeated at 1 to 2 months and 6 months after administration of the first dose. In infants with a birth weight less than 2 kg, the initial dose of hepatitis B vaccine does not count toward completion of the hepatitis B vaccine series, and administration of three additional doses of hepatitis B vaccine should commense when the infant is 1 month of age.[93] By the chronologic age of 1 month, all premature infants, regardless of initial birth weight or gestational age, are likely to respond as adequately as do older and larger infants.[258, 291, 321, 397] Testing for HBsAg and anti-HBs is recommended at 1 to 3 months after completion of the vaccine series. The presence of anti-HBs along with the absence of HBsAg indicates successful prophylaxis and immunization. An HBsAg-positive result indicates failure of prophylaxis or in utero infection. Infants who are negative for anti-HBs and HBsAg should receive three additional doses of vaccine at a 0-, 1-, and 6-month schedule, followed by retesting for anti-HBs 1 month after the third dose. Alternatively, additional doses of vaccine (one to three) can be administered and the infant tested for anti-HBs 1 month after each dose has been administered to determine whether subsequent doses are needed. Household members and sexual contacts of HBsAg-positive mothers should be screened, and if no evidence of previous HBV infection is noted, they also should be immunized.

Infants delivered by HBsAg-positive women are bathed as soon as possible after delivery to remove all maternal blood and secretions. Intramuscular injections should be delayed until bathing is completed; if such bathing is not possible, meticulous cleaning of the site with alcohol is necessary. These infants require standard precautions. Infants who have received both active and passive prophylaxis may be breast-fed.

In 1991, the Advisory Committee on Immunization Practices of the CDC[90] and, in 1992, the Committee on Infectious Diseases of the American Academy of Pediatrics[111] recommended the universal use of hepatitis B vaccine in all infants as the optimal strategy for prevention of HBV infection.[491] For infants with a birth weight of 2 kg or greater and born to mothers whose HBsAG status is negative, the first dose of HBV vaccine should be administered at or soon after birth, the second dose at 1 month or more after the first dose, and the third dose at 6 to 18 months of age. The minimal interval between the second and third doses is 2 months, and the third dose should not be given before 6 months. For infants who receive their first dose after they have reached 2 months of age, the minimal interval between the first and third doses is 4 months. An alternative schedule of the three doses administered at 2, 4, and 6 to 18 months of age concurrently with other routine vaccines may be used for HBsAg-negative infants not vaccinated at birth.

Seroconversion rates in premature infants who have a birth weight less than 2 kg and are vaccinated shortly after birth are lower than those in larger preterm infants and full-term infants vaccinated at birth.[305] For this reason, for premature infants weighing less than 2 kg at birth and born to HBsAg-negative mothers, initiation of the vaccination series is delayed until they are 1 month of age.[93] The schedule for follow-up doses is the same as for other infants.

Infants with a birth weight of 2 kg or more and born to mothers whose HBsAg status is unknown should receive the first dose of vaccine within 12 hours of birth. Blood should be drawn from the mother at delivery to determine her HBsAg status. If it is positive, HBIG should be given as soon as possible, but no later than when the infant is 1 week of age. If the infant's birth weight is less than 2 kg, HBIG in addition to vaccine should be given within 12 hours of birth. This initial vaccine dose should not be counted as part of the three-dose schedule. The subsequent vaccine schedule is based on the mother's HBsAg status. If it remains unknown, the infant should be treated as though the mother had been HBsAg-positive.

Because the rate of perinatal transmission is greatest in mothers who are HBeAg-positive or those who are negative for both HBeAg and anti-HBe, some researchers have suggested administering prophylaxis to neonates born only to this group of mothers.[428, 458] However, the occurrence of several cases of hepatitis in babies born to mothers with anti-HBe[135, 464] and the demonstration that measurements such as HBV DNA polymerase or HBV DNA by PCR may be more accurate indicators of infectivity than are measurements of HBe antigen or antibody[223, 507] indicate that prophylaxis should be given to neonates of all chronic carrier mothers, regardless of their e antigen/antibody status. Because the combined HBIG/vaccine regimen results in effective and long-term protection, breast-feeding is allowed and encouraged in chronic carrier mothers. These significant developments in prophylaxis against perinatal transmission of hepatitis B should reduce the frequency of chronic carriers strikingly and thereby decrease the number of cases of chronic active or progressive hepatitis and death from cirrhosis, liver failure, and hepatocellular carcinoma.

HEPATITIS C VIRUS INFECTION

The remarkable molecular biology effort to isolate and clone the gene of HCV[107] and to express a major nonstructural protein[294] led to the demonstration that HCV is the predominant cause of NANB hepatitis and a major contributor to chronic hepatitis in developed countries[18–20, 92, 127, 517] (see also Chapter 180). Rates of HCV seroprevalence are highest (60–90%) in those with repeated exposure to blood or blood products (e.g., injection drug users, hemophilia patients), intermediate (20%) in those with repeated or inapparent percutaneous exposure (e.g., hemodialysis patients), lower (1–10%) in those with high-risk sexual behavior or household contacts of infected persons, and lowest (0.5–1%) in blood donors.[19, 127, 517]

Among studies of infants born to anti-HCV–positive women, an average of 5 percent (range, 0–25%) of infants were persistently positive for second-generation assay anti-HCV antibody or HCV RNA during a follow-up period of a least 10 months.* The risk of vertical transmission correlated with higher concentrations of plasma HCV RNA[314, 375]; with HIV-1 co-infection, especially in those with advanced stages of AIDS; with the specific genotype of HCV; and possibly, with the vaginal route of delivery. HCV RNA has been detected in the breast milk of infected women, but transmission by breast milk has not been documented, and HCV infection is not a contraindication to breast-feeding.[315]

HCV infection can be diagnosed by antibody titers and molecular methods to detect and quantitate viral RNA. Antigen-detection tests and IgM assays are not available. Antibody titers in infants are confounded by maternal transplacental antibody; this effect presumably is gone by the time that the infant reaches 12 months of age. Antibody testing involves a screening EIA, with repeat positive results confirmed by a recombinant immunoblot assay (RIBA), analogous to what is done for the serologic diagnosis of HIV infection. The second-generation EIA (EIA-2) and RIBA are 95 percent sensitive and 97 percent specific.[199] Infants born to HCV antibody–positive mothers should be screened for anti-HCV with the EIA-2 after they are 12 months of age. RIBA may be used as a supplemental test for specificity; both the EIA-2 and RIBA measure IgG antibody to recombinant HCV antigens. PCR to detect HCV RNA in infant blood is available commercially through national reference laboratories.[199] Infants who are infected perinatally should have

*See references 299, 314, 324, 372, 375, 420, 431, 503, 528, 529, 563.

annual screening of liver enzymes, even if they remain asymptomatic.

Controlled trials of interferon therapy in children with chronic hepatitis C are limited,[110] and this drug is not approved by the Food and Drug Administration for use in persons younger than 18 years of age. The long-term prognosis for HCV infection in infants and children is not clear, but 85 percent of adults become chronically infected, and HCV is known to be associated with cirrhosis and hepatocellular carcinoma.[19, 127, 517]

The development of a successful vaccine for hepatitis C must overcome several obstacles, including multiple genotypes of the virus, lack of cross-protective immunity among the genotypes, lack of long-term protection with the same genotype, and lack of successful cultivation of the virus in cell culture.[19, 127] In February 1994, the Advisory Committee on Immunization Practices reviewed the available data and concluded that no support was found for the use of immunoglobulin for postexposure prophylaxis. Immunoglobulin is not protective because blood from anti-HCV–positive donors is excluded from the pool used for preparation and no neutralizing antibody for HCV has been identified as yet. Routine screening of all pregnant women for HCV infection cannot be recommended at this time, but screening should be considered in those with known risk factors. Infants who received 1 U or more of blood or blood products before 1992 should be screened for anti-HCV. The U.S. Public Health Service also has recommended that infants who received Gammagard (also called Polygam, Baxter Healthcare Corp., Glendale, CA) between April 1, 1993, and February 23, 1994, be offered screening (alanine aminotransferase and anti-HCV) for HCV infection. This intravenous immunoglobulin product was implicated in an outbreak of HCV infection in 1994.

Herpes Simplex

HSV, the etiologic agent of cold sores, keratitis, encephalitis, and genital ulcers in older children and adults, causes serious disease in neonates, with high mortality rates and severe neurologic sequelae (see also Chapter 163).

MICROBIOLOGY AND EPIDEMIOLOGY

The two types of HSV, type 1 and type 2, may be distinguished by antigenic, biochemical, and biologic differences.[121, 531] HSV-1 (the oral strain) causes mouth lesions, eye infections, and encephalitis and is transmitted nonvenereally, whereas HSV-2 (the genital strain) is associated with genital infection and sexual transmission.[121, 531] However, from 8 to 50 percent of genital disease is caused by HSV-1,[381] perhaps reflecting an increase in orogenital sex.

Antiviral collaborative studies indicate that 4 percent of neonatal herpes cases are acquired in utero, 86 percent natally, and 10 percent postnatally.[532] Three quarters of natal/postnatal cases of neonatal herpes are caused by HSV-2, and the remainder are caused by HSV-1 strains.[362, 385] Virtually all neonatal HSV-2 infections are acquired from mothers with an active genital herpes infection at the time of delivery.[362, 382, 497, 532, 539, 557] Importantly, however, 60 to 80 percent of these mothers have no signs or symptoms of genital herpes at the time of labor and delivery and have a negative past history of genital herpes or sexual contact with a partner who had a genital vesicular rash.[532, 533, 538] In a study of 140 pregnant women with cytologically diagnosed genital herpes, only 36 percent had clinically recognized herpetic lesions.[361] Twenty-one percent had nonspecific abnormal findings, and 43 percent were asymptomatic. In addition, 20 to 40 percent of nonpregnant women from whose genital secretions HSV is isolated are asymptomatic.[243, 544] The use of more sensitive techniques, such as PCR, detects genital HSV shedding in asymptomatic women even more frequently.[114]

Neonates with HSV-1 infection can acquire the virus from several sources: maternal genital, oral, or breast lesions[150, 313, 496, 557]; oral herpes in the father or other family members[147, 497, 557]; or nosocomial transmission from other infected babies.[206, 317] Although HSV-1 cold sores and asymptomatic oral shedding may be common findings in nursery personnel,[218, 219] transmission to a neonate from this source rarely occurs.[334, 362, 518] If one needs to identify the source clearly, HSV from the infected neonate and from the suspected contact should be typed and examined by molecular techniques.[427, 532]

Because most fetal and neonatal HSV infections are transmitted from the mother, a summary of several aspects of herpes infection during pregnancy is appropriate. Fulminant or disseminated primary HSV disease may occur in pregnancy, but whether it develops more often than in nonpregnant women is not clear. A review[398] of seven such cases revealed (1) infection during the third trimester in all; (2) four beginning as a genital HSV infection and three as oral disease; (3) hepatitis in six, encephalitis in two, and pancreatitis in two; (4) maternal death in three (43%)—two from hepatitis and one from encephalitis; and (5) three instances of fetal death—each secondary to severe maternal systemic illness rather than direct infection with HSV. Evidence of visceral disease in a pregnant woman with either genital or oral HSV infection is an indication for providing systemic antiviral therapy.[295]

An increased rate of spontaneous abortion occurs in women with primary genital herpes during early pregnancy, regardless of socioeconomic status.[216, 217, 361, 385] Premature delivery does not occur more commonly in prospectively monitored women with recurrent genital herpes,[217, 385, 522, 546] but most reports of neonatal herpes cases find a greater preponderance of premature infants than in the general population.[385, 533, 539, 557] This finding, however, may reflect a higher susceptibility of premature infants to HSV infection secondary to a lack of transplacentally acquired IgG neutralizing antibodies rather than being a cause of the prematurity. Recurrent genital herpes in middle-class pregnant women is no more severe or frequent than in nonpregnant ones,[216, 522, 546] but older studies demonstrated more frequent and longer episodes in women of lower socioeconomic groups.[361, 368] Between 74 and 88 percent of middle-class pregnant women with a history of genital herpes had at least one clinical recurrence during an observed pregnancy.[216, 522, 546] A mean of 2.7 to 3.0 episodes occurred during gestation, and HSV was isolated from lesions in 56 to 75 percent of the recurrences and in 0.6 to 12 percent of concomitant cervical cultures obtained during the recurrence. Asymptomatic shedding of HSV from the cervix, either between clinical recurrences or in a history-positive woman with no episodes during the observed pregnancy, was detected in 0.5 to 2.3 percent of the cultures obtained. Importantly, the presence of HSV shedding during the latter weeks of pregnancy was not predictive of shedding at the time of delivery.[32, 546]

The number of cases of neonatal herpes occurring in the United States each year is far less than one would expect from the probable number of pregnancies complicated by genital herpes. Of the 3.5 million annual pregnancies, from 7000 to 200,000 of these women have genital herpes at some time during the pregnancy, and 3500 to 14,000 have positive HSV cultures at the time of delivery.[59, 200, 217, 362, 502, 522, 546] The actual number of cases of neonatal herpes per year in Seattle and Atlanta (0.1 and 0.3 per 1000 live births, respectively) would project to a national estimate of 350 to 1050 per year in the United States.[362, 497] Because asymptomatic HSV infection of the neonate rarely occurs,[362] subclinical cases or missed diagnoses probably do not account for the differences between the estimated number of maternal and neonatal infections. More likely, neonatal infection rates in the babies of mothers with genital herpes are far lower than currently assumed, possibly because of the preventive measures used. The estimated infection rates quoted most often are currently (1) a 33 to 50 percent rate for infants vaginally delivered by mothers with primary genital herpes, (2) a 3 to 5 percent rate for infants vaginally delivered by mothers with recurrent lesions, and (3) less than 3 percent for those delivered by mothers with recurrent asymptomatic shedding at the time of delivery.[59, 76, 120, 385, 546] In the early 1970s, Nahmias and associates[361] reported the following neonatal infection rates in babies born to mothers with genital herpes during pregnancy: (1) 33 percent in mothers with primary disease after the 32nd week of gestation, (2) 3 percent in mothers with recurrent episodes after 32 weeks, and (3) 42 percent in mothers with virus-positive lesions at the time of delivery (primary versus recurrent episodes not specified). More recent studies have examined the risk of neonatal herpes occurring in babies born to mothers with asymptomatic shedding at the time of vaginal delivery: 33 percent with subclinical first episodes[76] and 0 to 3 percent with recurrent shedding.[76, 386, 410] Accurate knowledge of the actual neonatal infection risk is important for making decisions about management (e.g., cesarean section, prophylactic antiviral therapy).

Several factors influence the risk of acquiring neonatal herpes and the severity of neonatal disease once the infection develops. The greater risk of transmitting neonatal infection by mothers with primary, as opposed to recurrent, lesions at the time of delivery has been mentioned already. In turn, a woman with virus-positive recurrent lesions at the time of delivery is likely to be a greater risk than is an asymptomatic shedder identified by only HSV surveillance cultures. Other aspects of the anatomic site and the severity of maternal genital herpes also would be associated with a greater risk of development of neonatal disease: (1) cervical as opposed to vulvar or buttock skin involvement—resulting in more virus being shed into vaginal secretions; (2) multiple as opposed to single lesions—again, more virus from multiple lesions; (3) higher titer of virus in vaginal secretions—cultures positive sooner or more intensely positive in the diagnostic virology laboratory; and (4) longer duration of fetal exposure to infected vaginal secretions because of prolonged rupture of membranes.[120, 362, 383, 385]

Investigations by Yeager and associates[557, 558] indicate that no anti-HSV antibody or a low titer of such antibody in maternal and neonatal serum is associated with a greater risk of acquisition of neonatal infection and more serious disease and that high-titer antibody is associated with a lower risk. Studies of HSV antibody titers in neonates enrolled in the CASG trial do not show an association between antibody titer and disease outcome.[540] More investigations are required, therefore, to determine the potential protective role of maternal transplacental anti-HSV antibody.

Premature infants have accounted for 40 to 50 percent of cases of neonatal herpes,[362, 532, 533, 540] in contrast to the usual prematurity rates of 6 to 7 percent for whites and 17 to 18 percent for nonwhites. Whether the increased frequency of prematurity among neonates with herpes indicates a greater propensity of mothers with genital herpes to deliver prematurely or a greater susceptibility of premature infants to HSV infection is not known. Premature infants are more likely to have a fatal outcome.[533, 534]

Instrumentation of the neonate, particularly scalp electrodes for fetal monitoring, is known to increase the risk of acquiring neonatal HSV infection.[157, 252, 362, 390] Mortality appears to be higher in neonates with HSV-1 than in those with HSV-2 infection, probably because of the greater proportion of HSV-1–infected babies with dissemination.[534] In neonatal herpes survivors, neurologic damage occurs much more frequently with HSV-2 than with HSV-1 infection.[122, 534] Finally, the body sites of involvement in the neonate clearly influence outcome. Babies with disseminated infection (liver, lungs, adrenals), with or without CNS involvement, have the highest mortality rates (70–80%); those with encephalitis have only intermediate rates (30–40%); and those with infection limited to the skin, eye, or mouth have the lowest rates (0%).[362, 532, 540] The factors that are discussed in this paragraph and that are associated with a higher risk of acquisition of neonatal infection (e.g., the type and severity of maternal genital infection, fetal instrumentation) should be kept in mind in the management approach to an infant determined postnatally to have been delivered through a virus- or lesion-positive birth canal. Babies delivered in a high-risk situation might be given anticipatory antiviral chemotherapy after appropriate cultures have been obtained, whereas those in low-risk situations might be cultured and observed closely for evidence of neonatal herpes.[385, 386]

PATHOGENESIS AND PATHOLOGY

As mentioned previously, HSV may be transmitted to the neonate in utero either by a transplacental (congenital infection) or ascending route, at the time of birth (natal infection), or after birth (postnatal infection). Congenital infection probably results from transplacental transmission of virus secondary to leukocyte-associated viremia in a mother with genital herpes, but no direct evidence supports this hypothesis. HSV-2 viremia has been documented in two women with primary genital herpes.[124] A report of 13 neonates with intrauterine HSV infection indicated that primary genital herpes was present during pregnancy in four mothers, recurrent disease was present in one, and no history of genital herpes was elicited in the remaining eight.[241] In the fetus, HSV appears to be transmitted directly from the placenta through the bloodstream to target organs. Because of the known tropism of HSV for the CNS, one is not surprised that most infants with congenital infection have evidence of brain involvement at birth.[241] Intrauterine infection also may occur by an ascending route from an infected maternal genital tract, and such transmission is supported by the development of clinical signs of HSV infection in the first 5 days of life.

The natal infection presumably is acquired secondary to aspiration of infected vaginal secretions into the upper respiratory tract of the infant. Other portals of entry for natal infection include the eyes, scalp, skin, and umbilical cord.[362, 385, 532, 533] In postnatal HSV infection, no evidence supports the genital tract as a source of virus. Most postnatally acquired infections appear to result from contact with saliva from persons with oral herpes or with virus carried on the hands of personnel.[313, 532, 533, 557] After natal or postnatal acquisition of HSV, initial replication of the virus occurs at the portal of entry, with subsequent viremic dissemination to viscera. Involvement of the CNS occurs either from hematogenous spread to the brain in infants with disseminated disease, which results in multiple areas of cortical hemorrhagic necrosis, or from retrograde axonal transport of the virus to the CNS from superficial replication in the skin, eye, or mouth.[254, 363, 532, 533]

Characteristic pathologic features of neonatal herpes include involvement primarily of the brain, liver, adrenals, and lungs, as manifested by necrosis, eosinophilic intranuclear inclusions, and multinucleated giant cells. An important note is that virus may be isolated from tissue that does not show evidence of inclusions or giant cells.[362]

CLINICAL MANIFESTATIONS

The clinical features of genital herpes in women have been discussed in detail elsewhere.[77, 120, 360, 381] Women with initial or primary infections may have extensive vesicular and ulcerative lesions involving the cervix, vagina, vulva, and skin of the perineal region. With the appearance of lesions, severe pain and tenderness develop. In addition, patients may complain of inguinal or pelvic pain that is caused by associated lymphadenopathy. Systemic symptoms consisting of fever, malaise, and myalgia are usually present. The total duration of pain is 10 days to 2 weeks, whereas the total duration of lesions may be 2 to 3 weeks. Peak lesion virus titers, from 10^4 to 10^5 plaque-forming units per milliliter, occur during the first week of illness.[77] The total duration of viral shedding lasts from 10 to 14 days.[77, 120] Lesions on dry skin progress through the well-defined vesicle, ulcer, crust, and healed stages described for herpes simplex labialis.[469] On moist mucous membranes, vesicles quickly rupture to form shallow ulcers that persist for days and gradually heal from the periphery.[77]

Recurrent genital herpes in women is milder and of shorter duration, the lesions are more circumscribed and fewer in number, and the disease appears to be limited largely to the external genitals.[77] Peak lesion virus titers occur during the first few days and are lower, 10^3 to 10^4 plaque-forming units per milliliter. The total duration of pain is 5 to 9 days, that of lesions is 8 to 11 days, and the duration of viral shedding is 5 to 8 days.[77, 120] Importantly, women with both primary or initial and recurrent genital herpes may be asymptomatic.[76]

The clinical spectrum in infants with congenital HSV infection is different from that observed in babies with natal or postnatal disease. The most prominent features summarized from 30 cases of congenital infection reported in the literature are shown in Table 73–9.* A vesicular rash or bullae present at birth or within a few days of birth were noted in almost all infants. In some cases, the extent and severity of these lesions resulted in an initial diagnosis of epidermolysis bullosa. Two thirds of the infants demonstrated some evidence of extensive involvement of the CNS at birth, either clinically or from autopsy findings: diffuse brain damage, microcephaly, or intracranial calcifications. In many infants, eye findings more commonly observed in congenital CMV and rubella infections were noted: chorioretinitis, microphthalmos, retinal dysplasia, and cataracts.

As indicated in Figure 73–3, infants with natal or postnatal herpes commonly have a clinical picture resembling that of bacterial sepsis: alterations in temperature, lethargy, respiratory distress, anorexia or vomiting, and cyanosis.[210, 532, 538, 539] The three general patterns of infection are categorized by the extent of disease: (1) disseminated infection with or without CNS involvement, present in 25 percent of cases; (2) infection localized to the CNS in 30 percent of cases; and (3) infection localized to the skin, eye, or mouth in 45 percent of cases.[261, 532]

*See references 149, 174, 231, 241, 275, 303, 343, 349, 454, 460, 467, 495.

TABLE 73–9 ■ CONGENITAL HERPES SIMPLEX VIRUS INFECTION: FEATURES IN 30 CASES*

Feature	Number	Percentage
Low birth weight	22/26	85
Small for gestational age	9/25	36
Microcephaly, seizures, diffuse brain damage, intracranial calcification	20/30	67
Chorioretinitis, microphthalmos	17/30	57
Culture-positive vesicles or bullae	28/30	93
HSV-2	24/27	89
Other features: retinal dysplasia, scars on skin or digits, cataracts, pneumonitis, hepatomegaly		

*Features present at birth or shortly thereafter.
From Hutto, C., Arvin, A., Jacob, R., et al: Intrauterine herpes simplex virus infections. J. Pediatr. *110*:97–101, 1987.

The frequency of disseminated disease has decreased from a high of 51 percent in the years 1973 to 1981; this decrease probably represents earlier diagnosis and treatment of localized infection before dissemination occurs.[537] The disseminated form of infection develops in infants between 9 and 11 days of age and usually involves the liver, where it causes fulminant hepatitis with disseminated intravascular coagulation, and the adrenal glands, and it most closely resembles the picture of bacterial sepsis.[222, 510, 532] Disseminated infection can affect multiple organs, including the brain, larynx, trachea, lungs, esophagus, stomach, lower gastrointestinal tract, spleen, kidneys, pancreas, and heart. Pneumonia occurs in 37 percent of infants. Elevated transaminase levels and direct hyperbilirubinemia are common findings. Approximately 60 to 75 percent of infants with disseminated disease have CNS involvement, as manifested by irritability, a bulging fontanelle, localized or generalized seizures, flaccid or spastic paralysis, opisthotonos, decerebrate rigidity, or coma.[362, 532] Importantly, 39 percent of infants with disseminated disease do not have skin vesicles at initial evaluation, and vesicles do not develop during the acute HSV disease; only 56 percent initially have fever.[261]

CNS disease from axonal transmission of virus occurs when the infant is 11 to 17 days of age, though on occasion as old as 4 to 6 weeks of age. Typically, these infants have focal seizures that subsequently generalize. Examination of CSF demonstrates pleocytosis with a predominance of lymphocytes, a moderately low glucose concentration, and elevated protein levels. A normal cell count and protein concentration, however, may be found on the initial lumbar puncture. An elevated red blood cell count secondary to hemorrhagic brain involvement may be present but by itself is an unreliable sign. Fever is present at initial evaluation in only 44 percent of infants with HSV encephalitis, and 32 percent of infants do not have skin vesicles either initially or during the course of their illness.

Localized skin, eye, or mouth disease develops within the infant's first 7 to 10 days of life. Approximately 83 percent of neonates have skin lesions: usually single vesicles, occasionally vesicle clusters, and rarely a zoster-like rash.[354, 532] As many as 46 to 80 percent of neonates with skin lesions have 1 to 12 recurrences during the first 6 to 12 months of age.[236, 264, 534] Approximately 13 to 25 percent of infants have eye involvement; disease is limited to only the eye in one third of these cases.[362] Common manifestations include conjunctivitis, keratitis, and chorioretinitis.[202, 359] As many as 83 percent of infants are afebrile initially. Although one third of all infants have evidence of herpetic mouth lesions, involvement of this site alone rarely occurs.

DIAGNOSIS AND DIFFERENTIAL DIAGNOSIS

Importantly, more than 80 percent of infants have classic features that would suggest herpes simplex, such as skin vesicles, mouth ulcers, or keratoconjunctivitis. One half of the remaining 15 to 20 percent have either (1) focal or diffuse encephalitis or (2) a sepsis syndrome with pneumonitis, hepatitis, encephalitis, and frequently, disseminated intravascular coagulopathy.[385, 532] A clinical picture of encephalitis certainly should suggest HSV infection; the combination of pneumonitis, hepatitis, and encephalitis seldom is seen in bacterial sepsis/meningitis. Nonetheless, as many as 32 percent of all HSV-infected neonates do not have vesicular skin lesions that would prompt a rapid diagnosis. Kimberlin and colleagues[261] with the CASG compared the clinical characteristics of neonates with HSV disease in two multicenter studies that they conducted, one from 1981 to 1988 and the other from 1989 to 1997. They found that no progress has been made in decreasing the time interval between the onset of HSV symptoms and the initiation of antiviral therapy; the mean time between the earliest manifestation of an HSV symptom and initiation of acyclovir therapy was between 5 and 7 days. Even though acyclovir should not be part of routine antibiotic therapy for neonates with presumed sepsis, intravenous acyclovir should be provided promptly if the diagnosis likely is HSV.

The most definitive means of establishing a diagnosis of HSV infection in a neonate is isolation or identification of the virus in clinical or autopsy specimens. Samples for isolation of virus in cell culture may be obtained from the skin vesicles, nares, throat, nasopharynx, conjunctivae, stool, urine, peripheral blood buffy coat, CSF, brain tissue, and liver biopsy and autopsy material.[142] HSV has been isolated from CSF in as many as 25 to 40 percent of cases of encephalitis. HSV also has been isolated from duodenal aspirates of infants with hepatitis. Ideally, specimens should be processed immediately or frozen at −70° C if testing cannot be performed until later. However, HSV is stable for 2 to 3 days at 4° C in trypticase soy broth or brain-heart infusion broth.[556] In cell culture, the typical HSV cytopathic effect often is evident within 1 to 2 days after inoculation. Studies using centrifugation of the specimen onto a cell monolayer at the bottom of a shell vial, followed by staining for HSV antigen the next day, yielded 99 percent sensitivity and 100 percent specificity.[384] Typing of HSV should be performed because recent evidence suggests that neurologic outcomes are significantly worse with neonatal infection caused by HSV-2 than with infection caused by HSV-1. Moreover, it might help in determining the mode of transmission.

Immunofluorescent or immunoperoxidase techniques are available to demonstrate HSV-1 or HSV-2 antigens in cells scraped from the base of vesicles or the conjunctivae or in biopsy or autopsy material.[252, 441] Scraping from the base of a vesicle reveals intranuclear inclusions and multinucleated giant cells by the Tzanck test or Wright stain in 60 to 70 percent of cases. Detection of specific HSV antigen from mucocutaneous lesions by immunofluorescence is preferred and can be accomplished in 70 to 80 percent of cases. Direct detection of HSV antigen by commercial EIA has variable reliability compared with that of traditional cell culture.[520]

The diagnosis of HSV encephalitis has been improved greatly by the development of PCR for detection of HSV DNA in CSF.[259, 260, 298] PCR has supplanted the need for biopsy testing of brain tissue for diagnostic purposes. It has a sensitivity of 48 to 98 percent and a specificity of 94 to 100 percent. HSV DNA can be detected by PCR in most culture-positive CSF even after 1 week of acyclovir therapy. PCR also has been used on infant serum to document HSV infection.[260, 485] Other tests that aid in the detection of CNS abnormalities include electroencephalography, CT, and magnetic resonance imaging (MRI). The characteristic electroencephalographic abnormality is a periodic slow and sharp wave discharge; more commonly, multiple independent foci of periodic activity are present. CT scanning may be normal early in the course of the disease, with characteristic abnormalities appearing 3 to 5 days later. The findings most frequently observed in the acute phase are (1) patchy areas of low attenuation in both cerebral hemispheres or (2) hemorrhage or calcification in the thalamus, insular cortex, and periventricular white matter and along the corticomedullary junction. Late findings include multicystic encephalomalacia and ventriculomegaly as a result of brain atrophy and destruction. MRI is more sensitive in detecting early abnormalities in the periventricular white matter and in defining the extent of parenchymal lesions. Because of the improved diagnostic yield seen with MRI, technetium brain scanning rarely is used today. When abnormal, it demonstrated increased perfusion to the abnormal area. Positive findings in any neurodiagnostic study provide sufficient evidence to initiate antiviral therapy.

In most circumstances, serologic assays are not useful for the diagnosis of maternal or neonatal herpes during the acute phase of the disease. Emphasis must be placed on obtaining appropriate specimens for HSV culture and PCR.[142] Antibody assays may be used for documenting initial or primary genital herpes infection in the mother, as well as for determining whether the mother has a past history of HSV-2 infection. New serologic assays are available that reliably detect serum HSV-2 IgG antibodies.[94] The lack of such antibody in a mother when her infant has clinical evidence of possible HSV infection would rule out HSV-2 as the cause of the infant's symptoms. However, the possibility of the infection being caused by HSV-1 remains. Immunofluorescent techniques to quantify HSV-specific IgM antibodies have been developed, but these antibodies usually are not detected in serum for 2 or more weeks after onset of the infection in neonates.[358]

The major diseases to be considered in the differential diagnosis include bacterial sepsis, enterovirus infection, and, to a lesser extent, congenital infection with CMV, rubella virus, and VZV. Inquiry about illness in the mother and other epidemiologic features may be helpful. For example, mothers of neonates with HSV infection may have a history of having had genital lesions or sexual contact with someone who has genital herpes. Infants with sepsis usually have associated factors known to predispose to bacterial infection, such as maternal peripartum infection, premature rupture of membranes, and procedures performed in the intensive care unit or nursery. Enterovirus infection of infants tends to occur in the summer and fall and is associated with signs and symptoms of enterovirus disease in the mother.

TREATMENT

Studies conducted by the CASG of the National Institute of Allergy and Infectious Diseases (NIAID) have shown that antiviral therapy for neonatal HSV disease significantly improves mortality rates and long-term outcomes of infected neonates. Vidarabine was the first commercially available drug for the treatment of neonatal HSV disease.[106] Placebo-controlled trials demonstrated that adenine arabinoside (vidarabine, ara-A) at doses of 15 or 30 mg/kg/day given as a 12-hour infusion significantly reduced the mortality rate from 62 percent in historic cases and placebo controls to 35 percent in treated cases and increased the percentage of normal survivors from 19 to 43 percent.[540] Results were best in infants with disseminated infection and disease localized to the CNS, with the mortality rate reduced from 70 to 40 percent and the percentage of normal survivors increased from 10 to 30 percent. No difference was found between the 15-mg and the 30-mg dose in side effects, but the higher dose appeared to inhibit more effectively the progression of disease from skin-eye-mouth involvement to disseminated or CNS disease.[538] None of the 49 treated patients had significant adverse clinical reactions or laboratory abnormalities attributable to the drug. On the negative side, 21 percent of infants progressed to more serious disease while receiving therapy, and serious neurologic sequelae developed in 27 percent of the total. Fifteen percent of babies with disseminated or CNS disease continued to excrete HSV in the throat after 10 days of therapy.

The results of a vidarabine-acyclovir comparison trial in the treatment of neonatal herpes did not show any difference in efficacy and safety between the two drugs.[533] When the results with vidarabine and vidarabine-acyclovir were combined, the mortality rate was reduced from 49 percent in untreated historical controls[362] to 17 percent in treated patients (Table 73–10). Normal survivors increased from 26 to 67 percent. Although the results in the total group of patients are encouraging, the outcome in the group of patients with disseminated disease is not: a mortality rate of 54 percent in treated patients versus 76 percent in untreated historical controls and normal development in 59 percent of treated survivors versus 54 percent of controls (see Table 73–10). Factors that predicted mortality and their relative risk are as follows: disseminated disease, 33; CNS disease, 5.8; semicoma or coma, 5.2; disseminated intravascular coagulation, 3.8; prematurity, 3.7; and pneumonitis, 3.6.[534] Factors significantly associated with neurologic sequelae in survivors and their relative risk are as follows: skin-eye-mouth disease with three or more recurrent skin lesions after completion of acute therapy, 21; skin-eye-mouth disease caused by HSV-2, 14; HSV-2 infection, regardless of disease category, 4.9; CNS disease, 4.4; and seizures, 3.0. Specifically, in infants with HSV disease limited to the skin, eye, or mouth, those with HSV-1 infection were all normal developmentally at 1 year of age as compared with 86 percent of those with HSV-2 infection. Among the latter infants, those with impaired neurologic outcome were significantly more likely to have had three or more skin recurrences in the first 6 months of life.

Because of greater ease of administration, intravenous acyclovir has supplanted vidarabine as the drug of choice for the treatment of neonatal HSV infection. Vidarabine no longer is available commercially. Because mortality and morbidity in neonates with HSV infection remain high, the CASG evaluated intermediate (45 mg/kg/day) and high-dose (60 mg/kg/day) intravenous acyclovir for 21 days in 79 neonates with neonatal HSV infection.[262] Data were compared with those of a previous CASG study in which all infants received standard doses of acyclovir (30 mg/kg/day) for 10 days. Overall, after stratification for disease category, the survival rate for patients treated with high-dose acyclovir was significantly higher than that for patients treated with the standard dose. Specifically, in neonates who received high-dose acyclovir, those with disseminated disease but not encephalitis had a significantly higher survival rate. The mortality rate at 24 months for patients with disseminated disease who received 21 days of high-dose acyclovir was 31 percent, as opposed to 57 percent for patients who received an intermediate dose for 21 days and 61 percent for those who received the standard dose for 10 days in the earlier CASG trial. For encephalitis, the mortality rate of infants at 24 months was 6 percent with high-dose acyclovir, 20 percent with the intermediate dose, and 19 percent with the standard dose. In addition, recipients of high-dose acyclovir had less morbidity than did historical control infants who received the standard dose of acyclovir. Patients treated with high-dose acyclovir were 6.6 times as likely to have normal development at 12 months of age. Among infants with encephalitis, however, 31 percent of high-dose acyclovir recipients were developing normally at 12 months as compared with 29 percent of patients treated with the standard dose. With respect to toxicity in the high-dose acyclovir recipients, 21 percent had a transient neutropenia that resolved either during continuation of high-dose acyclovir or after its cessation. Nephrotoxicity occurred in four (6%) infants who had disseminated disease. Because acyclovir is eliminated by the kidneys, the dose should be adjusted for renal disease.[166] Finally, high-dose acyclovir did not impede the development of an adequate antibody response to HSV in infected infants.

These studies have led to the current recommendation for the use of intravenous acyclovir at a dose of 60 mg/kg/day for 21 days to treat neonatal CNS and disseminated HSV disease and for 14 days for skin, eye, or mouth (SEM) disease.[23] In addition, infants with ocular involvement should receive a topical ophthalmic drug (1% to 2% trifluridine, 1% idoxuridine, or 3% vidarabine). Intravenous immunoglobulin has no role in the treatment of neonatal HSV infection. All patients with CNS disease should have a repeat lumbar puncture performed at the completion of acyclovir therapy to determine whether the CSF specimen is PCR-negative. A positive CSF HSV PCR at this time is an indication for continuing intravenous acyclovir therapy and for performing neuroimaging studies to evaluate the extent of CNS damage.

TABLE 73–10 ■ NEONATAL HERPES: ANTIVIRAL THERAPY

Outcome	Total	Skin, Eyes, Mouth	Encephalitis	Disseminated
Mortality				
ACV, Ara-A*	17%	0	14%	54%
Historical controls†	49%	7%	37%	76%
Development Normal				
ACV, Ara-A*	67%	94%	36%	59%
Historical controls†	26%	73%	19%	54%

*Data from Whitley, R., Arvin, A., Prober, C., et al.: A controlled trial comparing vidarabine with acyclovir in neonatal herpes simplex virus infection. N. Engl. J. Med. *324*:444–449, 1991.
†Data from Nahmias, A. J., Keyserling, H.L., and Kerrick, G. M.: Herpes simplex. *In* Remington, J. S., and Klein, J. O. (eds.): Infectious Diseases of the Fetus and Newborn Infant. 2nd ed. Philadelphia, W.B. Saunders, 1983, pp. 636–678.
ACV, acyclovir; Ara-A, vidarabine (adenine arabinoside).

Concern has been raised that some infants may have progressive neurologic injury after acquiring neonatal herpes encephalitis.[201] In addition, infants who have three or more skin recurrences with HSV-2 in the first 6 months of life have been shown to be at increased risk for having neurodevelopmental abnormalities at follow-up, whether as a consequence of previously undetected CNS infection or because of CNS dissemination during skin reactivation.[534] Suppression of HSV skin reactivation can be accomplished with the administration of acyclovir (300 mg/m^2 per dose given orally three times daily) for 6 months, although Kimberlin and coworkers[263] documented that such therapy resulted in neutropenia in 50 percent of treated infants and emergence of an acyclovir-resistant HSV isolate in one infant. Foscarnet has been used to treat HSV infection resistant to acyclovir. An ongoing study of acyclovir suppression in neonates with HSV encephalitis and SEM disease currently is being performed by the CASG. Until the results of this study are available, acyclovir suppression should be considered after the initial recurrence of skin lesions in the first 2 to 3 months of age or after a recurrent episode of HSV encephalitis. In both situations, evaluation of CSF by HSV PCR should be performed to detect and document possible CNS dissemination or reactivation that would warrant initiation of intravenous acyclovir therapy. Acyclovir suppression also has been used after development of HSV eye infection in which reactivation might imperil vision.

General supportive measures, such as maintenance of fluid and electrolyte balance, correction of hypoglycemia, management of disseminated intravascular coagulation and shock, control of seizures with anticonvulsants, mechanical support of the respiratory system, nutritional support, and antimicrobial therapy for complicating bacterial infections, also are critical in improving the outcome for neonates with HSV infection.

PROGNOSIS

As indicated in Table 73–10, the overall mortality rate from untreated neonatal HSV infection is 49 percent, and only 26 percent of survivors develop normally. The worst prognosis is in infants with a natal infection that is disseminated or localized to the CNS. The development of pneumonia is a particularly poor prognostic sign. Between 50 and 60 percent of infants with HSV infection limited to the skin, eye, and mouth progress to CNS or disseminated disease. As shown in Table 73–10, neurologic sequelae develop in an appreciable proportion of survivors. All infants with neonatal herpes, therefore, require antiviral chemotherapy, regardless of the mildness of disease at initial evaluation.

The major sequelae in infants surviving neonatal herpes involve the CNS. Diffuse brain damage, seizures, microcephaly, spasticity, paralysis, growth retardation, and chorioretinitis with visual loss all have been observed.[532, 540] Serial CT or MRI of the head may be useful in these infants and can provide prognostic information.[532, 538] Most infants with skin involvement have recurrent lesions in subsequent months, usually beginning in the week after discontinuation of intravenous acyclovir therapy.[362]

PREVENTION

The major approaches to the prevention of neonatal herpes involve interruption of transmission from sites of HSV infection at the time of delivery and postnatally from a variety of potential sources. Because congenital infection occurs so infrequently[533] and predicting the occurrence of congenital infection during pregnancy is not possible,[241] no prophylaxis is available.

Cesarean section within 4 hours of rupture of fetal membranes in a mother with active genital herpes at the time of delivery is the major means used to prevent natal infection. Because serial vaginal cultures during the latter stages of pregnancy have failed to predict shedding at the time of delivery,[32, 56, 546] such monitoring has been abandoned and cesarean section is recommended only for women with active lesions at the time of delivery.[36, 188, 217, 385, 410, 445] Cesarean section is not 100 percent protective, even if the membranes are intact.[217, 362, 385, 410, 445] As many as 33 percent of neonates with HSV infection are delivered by cesarean section. The cost-effectiveness of performing a cesarean section in women with recurrent lesions at delivery has been questioned, although in the United States, it remains the standard of care.[416] Acyclovir suppressive therapy has been used with some success in pregnant women with a history of genital herpes to prevent clinical HSV recurrence at delivery and thereby prevent the necessity of performing a cesarean section.[446, 447] No adverse effect has been seen in infants exposed to maternal acyclovir during pregnancy. Further studies are under way to evaluate the effect of both acyclovir and valaciclovir on the newborn after maternal administration. The use of a fetal scalp electrode monitor, forceps, and maneuvers that might cause a break in the infant's skin during delivery should be avoided.

The results of antenatal genital HSV cultures from pregnant women with a history of genital herpes do not predict the infant's risk of exposure to HSV at delivery. Because 60 to 80 percent of mothers of babies with neonatal herpes are asymptomatic or have unrecognized infection,[532] the optimal approach is to perform a screening test to identify women shedding or likely to shed HSV at the time of delivery. Although HSV rapid antigen-detection tests continue to be developed commercially,[384] their sensitivity in *asymptomatic* women still is only 60 to 75 percent. PCR ultimately may allow rapid identification of these women, but studies are not available, and at this time, it is not a feasible option. Screening of pregnant women for non–type-specific HSV antibody would be confounded by the presence of HSV-1 antibody, which is present in 60 to 80 percent of the population.[381] The presence of HSV-1 antibody probably represents oral herpes, which poses little risk to the neonate. Although type-specific antibody assays are available to identify pregnant women infected with HSV-2,[94, 247] such an approach would miss women with genital HSV-1 infection[120, 410] or those with asymptomatic primary HSV-2 infection near the time of delivery before antibody is detectable.[76, 410] Its use has been recommended in identifying discordant couples, that is, women with no history of having genital HSV infection but whose sexual partner has had previous infection, so barrier precautions may be used before delivery to decrease the chance of a maternal primary infection that poses a greater risk to her infant.[94] Culturing the genital tract of women at the time of vaginal delivery would identify infants exposed to HSV and allow anticipatory management.[383, 385, 410] However, because infection rates are only 0.1 to 0.4 percent,[76, 361, 412] this approach likely would not be cost-effective for *all* women. Culturing of *selected* women at delivery could focus on (1) those identified by HSV-2 serologic tests, (2) those with a history of genital herpes in themselves or their sexual partners, and (3) those with a history of another sexually transmitted disease or multiple sexual partners. Further investigation is required to determine whether screening of pregnant women to prevent neonatal herpes is practical and cost-effective.[132]

No studies have been conducted on the optimal management of asymptomatic infants exposed to maternal HSV infection at delivery, although some guidelines on obtaining viral cultures and prophylactic or anticipatory antiviral therapy are recommended widely.[23, 383–386, 410, 445] In general, appropriate cultures for HSV should be performed for all infants born to mothers with active genital HSV infection at delivery. In asymptomatic infants, cultures of the conjunctiva, throat, rectum, and possibly urine should be done at 24 to 36 hours of age. Cultures obtained at birth may indicate only contaminating virus, whereas those obtained 1 to 2 days after birth probably represent HSV newly replicating in the mucous membranes. If the infant is delivered by cesarean section within 4 hours of rupture of membranes, no prophylactic antiviral therapy is indicated. If the infant is born vaginally or by cesarean section performed more than 4 hours after rupture of membranes, further management is dependent on the presence of other risk factors. If the mother has primary infection at delivery, a situation in which the neonatal infection rate may be as high as 30 to 50 percent, intravenous acyclovir (60 mg/kg/day) should be initiated. If the mother has recurrent infection, in which the risk of neonatal disease occurring after vaginal delivery is probably less than 3 percent, acyclovir can be withheld pending the results of culture or the development of clinical illness in the neonate that could be caused by HSV. Situations that increase the risk of neonatal transmission despite maternal recurrent disease include prematurity, the use of a scalp electrode monitor, or skin lacerations; prophylactic acyclovir should be considered in these instances if the infant has been delivered vaginally or by cesarean section more than 4 hours after rupture of membranes. In all instances, acyclovir can be discontinued when HSV cultures are negative at 48 to 72 hours and the infant has remained well. All infants should be monitored closely for any clinical evidence of HSV infection. Any positive culture or the occurrence of signs or symptoms suggesting HSV infection in the neonate requires full virologic evaluation, including CSF analysis for HSV by PCR, as well as antiviral therapy. Neonates with positive HSV cultures of mucosal sites should not be assessed as being merely colonized; all require intravenous acyclovir therapy. The duration of therapy, however, probably can be shortened to 7 or 10 days if no other site of infection is found and the infant remains asymptomatic. Breast-feeding is contraindicated only if the mother has a vesicular lesion on her breast. Physicians also have recommended that circumcision be delayed for 1 month in infants at highest risk of transmission.

Prevention of postnatally acquired neonatal infection needs to take into account the potential sources of HSV: (1) maternal oral herpes or breast lesions, (2) paternal or other close contact with oral herpes, and (3) nosocomial transmission from other infected babies.[147, 206, 317, 496, 497, 557] Transmission to the neonate from oral herpes lesions can be interrupted by education and commonsense personal hygiene, including handwashing, and nosocomial spread can be interrupted by conventional isolation and infection control measures.[256, 266]

Personnel with herpetic whitlow should not have direct patient care responsibilities until the lesion has healed. Infants with HSV infection should be placed in contact isolation for the duration of the illness.[23] The median duration of viral shedding from skin vesicles and mucosal sites in infants receiving acyclovir is approximately 5 to 8 days.[262] Asymptomatic, but high-risk infants born to mothers with herpes at delivery also should be in contact isolation; alternatively, they may room-in with the mother in a private room.

Enterovirus Infections

The enteroviruses are members of the family *Picornaviridae* and include the polioviruses, coxsackieviruses A and B, and echoviruses. Enteroviruses are limited to the human host, infections develop commonly, and a wide spectrum of clinical manifestations occur in children and adults, as well as in neonates (see Chapter 170). Coxsackievirus and echovirus infections are fairly common events in young infants and, as with other viral agents, often result in more severe disease in neonates. Neonatal poliomyelitis, however, is a rare occurrence in the United States and is not covered in this section.

MICROBIOLOGY AND EPIDEMIOLOGY

Twenty-three types of type A coxsackieviruses, 6 types of type B coxsackieviruses, 30 types of echoviruses, and 5 types of enteroviruses (68 to 72) are recognized.[333] Most strains grow in tissue culture, but some, particularly type A coxsackieviruses, require inoculation in suckling mice. Because no common or group antigens for the enteroviruses exist, separate antibody titration must be performed for each virus. Therefore, to make a laboratory diagnosis of enteroviral infection by serologic means alone is not practical. However, antibody titers can be performed after a specific enterovirus has been isolated from the patient or when a concurrent epidemic with a known virus occurs in the community.

The attack rate for enteroviral infections is highest during infancy and early childhood.[3, 128–130, 285, 325, 345, 351, 548] In addition, severe disease occurs much more commonly in neonates than in older children or adults.[345, 548] Sixty to 70 percent of infected neonates are males.[249, 297, 345, 351, 415] The enteroviruses are worldwide in distribution, and in temperate climates, infections occur predominantly during the summer and fall months, with peaks in July, August, and September.[83, 244, 333] The incubation period for enteroviral infections in children and adults usually is 5 to 8 days, with a range of 2 to 12 days.[435, 530] Of the cases reported to the CDC from 1970 to 1979, echoviruses accounted for 57 percent; type B coxsackieviruses, 25 percent; polioviruses, 9 percent; type A coxsackieviruses, 8 percent; and enterovirus types 68 to 71, 0.1 percent.[83] In infants younger than 2 months of age, echoviruses accounted for 51 percent of infections; type B coxsackieviruses, 45 percent; and type A coxsackieviruses, 4 percent.[318, 351] In any given year in the United States, usually an epidemic occurs that is caused by a few enterovirus types: echovirus 11 and coxsackieviruses B2 and B4 in 1979, echoviruses 9 and 4 in 1978, echovirus 6 in 1977, coxsackievirus B4 in 1976, and echovirus 9 in 1975.[83] Outbreaks of enteroviral disease have occurred in normal nurseries and in neonatal intensive care units.*

Acute enteroviral infection in a newborn infant may be acquired congenitally, natally, or postnatally.[103, 429] However, confusion concerning the incubation period and source of virus for neonatal infection often has ensued. Late-gestation congenital infection is presumed to occur in infants with an onset of illness at birth or within the first few days of life, when their mothers had symptoms of enteroviral disease just before or immediately after delivery.[3, 101, 134, 297, 345, 401] Further evidence of congenital infection is the observation that viremia with echoviruses and coxsackieviruses is known to occur in pregnant women,[103] and virus has been isolated from the placenta of infants with an onset of disease

*See references 34, 70, 100, 125, 170, 304, 325, 345, 379, 429, 498.

early in life.[70, 345] Infants with an onset of enteroviral disease between 3 and 8 to 10 days of age probably acquired the infection from their mothers at the time of birth (natal infection), whereas those with illness appearing after this time probably acquired it postnatally. The source of virus for most cases in nurseries appears to be the mother because the age of the infants at the time that the first symptoms appear is usually less than 10 days.[3, 297, 304, 345, 415, 498] However, in some cases and outbreaks, the infection clearly appears to be nosocomial in origin, presumably through spread of virus from other infected neonates by the hands of personnel or from infected personnel themselves.[125, 328, 345]

Some investigations indicate that enteroviral infections acquired in the community are a common cause of hospitalization for a febrile illness in young infants.[128–130, 244, 285] Enteroviral infections were estimated to account for 20,000 to 40,000 hospitalizations per year in young infants in the United States. In one study of 182 infants younger than 3 months of age and hospitalized for fever over the course of a year, viral pathogens were isolated in 41 percent and bacteria in only 15 percent.[285] Enteroviruses accounted for 85 percent of the viral isolates. Among a cohort of 586 newborns prospectively monitored during the enteroviral season in Rochester, New York, 24 (4%) were hospitalized during the first month of life.[244] Two thirds of these 24 were infected with enteroviruses. Risk factors associated with development of infection and more severe enteroviral disease included a particular serotype of virus (e.g., echovirus 22, presumably a more virulent strain); lower socioeconomic status, probably with associated crowding and an increased rate of transmission; bottle feeding (absence of passive antibody in breast milk); and absence of antibody in cord serum.[129, 244, 345, 348]

Evidence suggests that coxsackieviral infections in early pregnancy may cause congenital malformations in the fetus. Brown and colleagues[74, 75] demonstrated a significant association between serologic evidence of coxsackievirus A9, B2, B3, or B4 infection in mothers during pregnancy and the birth of infants with anomalies of the cardiovascular, urogenital, and digestive systems. However, specific viral isolation and antibody studies were not performed on the involved infants, and no seasonal distribution was noted in their births. In addition, the observations of Brown and colleagues[74, 75] have not been confirmed by others.[159, 279, 402] The association between maternal infection with coxsackieviruses and congenital malformations, therefore, remains suggestive but not proven. Moreover, no conclusive evidence supports any relationship between maternal infection with type B coxsackieviruses and congenital CNS malformations.[159]

PATHOGENESIS AND PATHOLOGY

Our knowledge of the pathogenesis of congenital enteroviral infection is incomplete because its occurrence is relatively infrequent in humans. However, studies in gravid mice support the transplacental passage of enteroviruses with resultant fetal infection.[1, 246, 291, 387] By inference from these studies and our understanding of congenital CMV and rubella virus infections, transplacental transmission secondary to maternal viremia probably occurs. Virus then is transmitted through fetal blood to target organs, principally the CNS, liver, heart, lungs, kidneys, and adrenal glands. In congenital infections that are fatal in the early neonatal period, type B coxsackieviruses involve primarily the heart, CNS, liver, and lungs,[183, 249, 297, 548] and echoviruses involve the liver, adrenals, kidneys, CNS, and lungs.[101, 203, 239, 286, 344, 345, 401] Histopathologic findings have consisted of focal myocardial necrosis with type B coxsackieviruses[183, 548]; massive hepatic necrosis with echoviruses[239, 286, 345, 401]; and evidence of disseminated intravascular coagulation and adrenal, pulmonary, and renal hemorrhage with both virus groups.[101, 183, 239, 286, 297, 345, 401, 548] Of interest is that the onset of illness in most neonates with fatal coxsackievirus B and echovirus infection occurred at birth or within the first few days of life, thus suggesting that transplacental infections carry a worse prognosis.[3, 101, 239, 286, 297, 345, 401] In addition, lack of transplacental transfer of maternal antibody before delivery could play a role.[344, 345] Only a few isolated cases of congenital coxsackievirus A infection have been reported.[103]

Natal infection presumably occurs secondary to aspiration and swallowing of enterovirus-contaminated vaginal secretions at the time of birth. Postnatal acquisition is the result of fecal-oropharyngeal spread of the virus on the hands of the mother, other family members, or hospital personnel.[103, 345] The pathogenesis of natal and postnatal infection is similar to that observed in older infants and children (see Chapter 170). Because most infants with postnatal infection survive, the pathologic features are not well characterized.

CLINICAL MANIFESTATIONS

The clinical features in 134 neonates and very young infants with echoviral and coxsackieviral infections are shown in Figure 73–3. The most common findings, hyperthermia or hypothermia, anorexia or vomiting, and lethargy, are relatively nonspecific findings and are encountered with similar frequency in neonates with other viral infections or bacterial sepsis. Features that appear to be characteristic of enteroviral infection include signs and symptoms of aseptic meningitis and meningoencephalitis (irritability, CNS signs, including seizures), gastroenteritis (anorexia, vomiting, diarrhea, abdominal distention), and an erythematous, maculopapular exanthem. In addition, neonates may manifest a mild, nonspecific febrile illness, a severe sepsis-like disease, respiratory illness, hepatitis that may be fulminant with resultant hepatic necrosis and death, and cardiovascular manifestations secondary to myocarditis. Enteroviral DNA also has been detected by PCR in the respiratory tract of infants with sudden death.[189]

Infants with more serious disease may have a biphasic course that begins as a mild illness with slight elevation of temperature, coryza, anorexia, and diarrhea. After an apparent recovery period lasting 1 to 5 days, infants may have more severe symptoms of aseptic meningitis, myocarditis (tachycardia, tachypnea, respiratory distress, cyanosis), or disseminated infection (abdominal distention, hepatomegaly, petechial rash, disseminated intravascular coagulation).

Milder forms of disease, such as pneumonitis, undifferentiated febrile illness, exanthematous illness, or gastroenteritis lasting only a few days, also occur.[242, 297] In a survey of 338 infants younger than 2 months of age with enteroviral infections reported to the CDC, 74 percent had severe disease and 26 percent had mild disease.[351] Five (1%) of these infants died, all in the group with severe disease. Asymptomatic infections in neonates have been detected during outbreaks in nurseries or when routine virologic surveillance was being performed in a nursery.[70] An outbreak of neonatal herpangina caused by coxsackievirus A5 was observed in Thailand.[100]

DIAGNOSIS AND DIFFERENTIAL DIAGNOSIS

The major epidemiologic and clinical features that suggest a diagnosis of enteroviral infection in a neonate are listed in Table 73–11. Because the signs and symptoms in neonates

TABLE 73–11 ■ CHARACTERISTICS ASSOCIATED WITH ENTEROVIRAL INFECTION IN NEONATES

Seasonal occurrence—summer and fall
Presence of known enteroviral epidemic in the community
History of maternal viral illness near the time of delivery
Absence of factors predisposing to bacterial sepsis
Nursery outbreak of infectious illness with negative bacterial cultures
Development of culture-negative sepsis or aseptic meningitis in the neonate
Development of myocarditis, hepatitis, or erythematous maculopapular exanthem in the neonate

with enteroviral disease often mimic those of bacterial sepsis and meningitis, antibiotic therapy generally should be initiated until a bacterial etiology is ruled out. In addition to sepsis and meningitis, the major diseases to be considered in the differential diagnosis include HSV infection and, to a lesser extent, congenital infection with CMV and rubella virus. HSV infection is nonseasonal, endemic, and associated with genital ulcerative lesions in the mother. Symptomatic congenital CMV and rubella infections are associated with intrauterine growth retardation and a chronic rather than an acute infectious clinical picture in the infant.

The most direct means of establishing a diagnosis of enteroviral infection in neonates is isolation of the virus in tissue culture or suckling mice.[384] Virus may be recovered from throat swab, stool, CSF, serum or buffy coat, and biopsy and autopsy tissue. Ideally, specimens should be processed immediately, but enteroviruses may remain stable at 4°C for several days if testing cannot be performed until later. Isolation of virus from CSF, blood, or tissue can be considered diagnostic. A throat or stool isolate also can be considered etiologic in most neonatal illnesses. PCR performed for detection of enterovirus RNA in CSF is more sensitive and rapid than is isolation of virus[429] and is the preferred method for diagnosing enteroviral meningitis.[437, 440] PCR also has been performed on blood, urine, and tissue such as myocardium with excellent results.

TREATMENT

No licensed and effective antiviral chemotherapy exists for enteroviruses. Pleconaril administered orally on a compassionate basis to neonates with severe disseminated enteroviral disease has resulted in clinical recovery.[28, 253, 430] In adults, pleconaril has decreased the duration of clinical symptomatology in aseptic meningitis significantly, and in immunocompromised individuals, it has resulted in cessation of viral shedding. Studies of pleconaril in neonatal sepsis syndrome with liver or cardiac involvement are in progress through the NIAID CASG. Intravenous immunoglobulin often is recommended, but few data support its routine use.[2, 131, 205, 248] Anecdotal reports suggest that infusion of large doses of intravenous immunoglobulin, which contains high titers of antibody to enteroviruses,[131] may improve survival.[248]

PROGNOSIS

The outcome is influenced by several factors: the enterovirus serotype causing the infection, the route of transmission of virus to the neonate, the age at acquisition of the infection, prematurity, and severity of the disease in the neonate. Mortality rates are highest for coxsackievirus B infections, intermediate for echovirus infections, and lowest for coxsackievirus A infections.[103, 183, 249, 297, 345] Most of the neonatal deaths caused by enteroviruses reported in recent years have occurred in infants whose onset of disease was at or within a few days of birth and who, therefore, had congenital disease.[101, 239, 286, 297, 345, 401] Infection and mortality rates both appear to be higher for premature infants.[70, 345] Death is most likely to occur in infants with myocarditis, encephalitis, or hepatitis.[103, 345] Neurologic sequelae have been observed to occur after meningoencephalitis in the neonatal period,[169, 448, 541] although most infants who survive enteroviral meningitis have an excellent long-term prognosis.[55] Long-term cardiac sequelae do not appear to follow myocarditis.[183]

PREVENTION

Polio vaccine has reduced maternal and neonatal poliomyelitis to an extremely rare occurrence. No prospects exist for vaccines for the echoviruses or coxsackieviruses. With the appearance of a case of enteroviral disease in a newborn nursery or intensive care unit, initiation of vigorous infection control measures involving contact precautions, including such measures for suspected cases and renewed emphasis on handwashing and exclusion of personnel with symptoms of enteroviral disease, is indicated. Of emphasis is that infection control measures applied in the nursery do not prevent congenital or natal transmission of virus from the mother to the infant. The continued appearance of cases in neonates younger than 8 to 10 days of age may reflect a persistent epidemic among pregnant women rather than a failure of nursery infection control measures and spread within the nursery.[498]

Varicella-Zoster Virus Infection

VZV causes both chickenpox, the result of primary exposure to the virus, and zoster, caused by reactivation of latent virus.[184, 187, 381] VZV infection of a pregnant woman results in three separate and distinct syndromes that become apparent in neonates and infants: (1) congenital defects secondary to intrauterine VZV infection, (2) congenital chickenpox, and (3) zoster in infants.[164, 165, 184, 187, 212, 396] Transmission to the fetus occurs as a consequence of maternal viremia.[184, 187] For a discussion of postnatally acquired VZV infections, see Chapter 167.

MATERNAL VARICELLA

Knowledge of several features of chickenpox in the mother is necessary to understand the pathogenesis of VZV infection in the fetus and neonate. Because antibody to VZV is present in approximately 90 percent of women of child-bearing age,[187] one would expect chickenpox in pregnancy to be a rare occurrence. In fact, maternal chickenpox has been reported to occur in only 0.7 per 1000 pregnancies.[453] The incubation period for chickenpox (from exposure to the onset of rash) usually is between 14 and 16 days, with a range of 10 to 21 days.[184, 187]

CONGENITAL VARICELLA SYNDROME

In several large prospective studies, no increase in anomalies was apparent in the offspring of women who had VZV infection during pregnancy.[68, 461–463] However, a prospective study[331] of 43 pregnancies complicated by varicella indicated that (1) 21 percent of the women experienced appreciable morbidity, (2) 24 percent of 33 infants tested had clinical or immunologic evidence of intrauterine VZV infection, and (3) congenital varicella syndrome occurred in 9 percent of 11 women with first-trimester varicella. Pooling of results from several prospective studies indicates an approximate 2 percent risk of fetal malformations caused by maternal varicella during the first 20 weeks of pregnancy.[165, 337, 396] Of the reported cases of congenital varicella syndrome, 93 percent have occurred after maternal chickenpox and only 7 percent after maternal zoster. Seven percent of reported cases occurred after maternal varicella at less than the 20th week, with the latest being at 28 weeks of gestation.[17]

The abnormalities present in 77 infants with congenital varicella syndrome are summarized in Table 73–12. The defects apparently are the result of VZV replication in and destruction of developing fetal ectodermal tissue: skin, peripheral nerves, cervical and lumbosacral spinal cord, brain, and eye.[35] Diagnosis of the syndrome essentially is clinical: a history of chickenpox in the mother and recognition of the characteristic defects in the neonate. Virus has not been isolated from these infants, and serologic studies often have been inconclusive.[179, 187] However, detection of varicella-zoster DNA by PCR has been used to confirm the syndrome in some cases.[353, 413, 436] Infants with varicella embryopathy do not require isolation. Damage to the infants has been severe; many died in infancy.[179, 187] Fortunately, the syndrome is a relatively rare event. Prenatal diagnosis remains difficult; fetal ultrasound, specific VZV IgM determination in fetal blood, and detection of VZV DNA in amniotic fluid have been used but are neither specific nor sensitive for differentiation of congenital varicella syndrome from benign congenital chickenpox. Universal varicella immunization should decrease the importance of this virus in congenital and neonatal disease.

CONGENITAL CHICKENPOX

Congenital varicella syndrome refers to the onset of chickenpox within the first 10 days of life. The incubation period, defined as the interval between the onset of rash in the mother and onset in the fetus or neonate, usually is 9 to 15 days, with a range between 1 and 16 days. Congenital varicella syndrome occurs when a pregnant woman suffers from chickenpox during the last 1 to 2 weeks of pregnancy or within the first few days post partum. The attack rate is approximately 25 to 50 percent. As indicated in Table 73–13, the timing of the onset of disease in the mother and the neonate is a critical factor influencing the outcome in the infant. If disease onset occurs in the mother 5 or more days before delivery or in the neonate during the first 4 days of life, the infection is mild. In contrast, if disease onset in the mother is within 4 days before delivery or in the neonate between 5 and 10 days of age, the infection usually is disseminated and fulminant, and approximately one third of the infants die.[187, 339] Other investigations have found that the risk period of the onset of maternal rash extends from 7 days before to 7 days after delivery.[411] The generally accepted explanation for this observation is that when illness in the mother occurs more than 5 days before delivery or when illness in the baby occurs during the first 4 days of life, maternal antibody has time to pass transplacentally and provide passive protection for the infant. However, passive protection does not have time to occur when illness in the mother occurs within 4 days of delivery. Presumably, the immune responses of the neonate are insufficient to retard the growth and dissemination of VZV after intravenous inoculation via the placenta, and disseminated disease results.

The milder form of neonatal chickenpox resembles the disease in normal, older children, whereas the disseminated variety is similar to that seen in immunosuppressed, leukemic children. In the latter, diffuse pneumonia, severe hepatitis, and meningoencephalitis are the most common clinical manifestations. The diagnosis usually can be made clinically from the characteristic appearance of skin vesicles, and VZV antigen can be demonstrated by immunofluorescence testing of vesicular fluid. Less commonly, VZV may be isolated from vesicular fluid by tissue culture during the first 3 days of the rash, but VZV is difficult to isolate in commercial virology laboratories.[212, 384] VZV DNA can be demonstrated in vesicular fluid by PCR.[240] The major disease to consider in the differential diagnosis is disseminated neonatal HSV infection. With HSV infection, usually a history of maternal genital herpes exists; characteristic keratoconjunctivitis, mouth lesions, or both may be present in the infant, and growth of the virus in cell culture is markedly

TABLE 73–12 ■ ABNORMALITIES IN 77 INFANTS WITH CONGENITAL VARICELLA SYNDROME

Features	Percentage
Skin scars*	61
Eye abnormalities	56
Chorioretinitis	27
Horner syndrome/anisocoria	16
Microphthalmos	19
Cataract	19
Nystagmus	13
Abnormal limb†	47
Hypoplasia	36
Equinovarus	14
Abnormal/absent digits	10
Cortical atrophy/mental retardation	40
Prematurity, low birth weight	36
Early death	26
Dysphagia/aspiration	19
Gastrointestinal tract abnormalities	12
Urinary tract abnormalities	10

*Cicatricial in 37 (79%).
†Eleven of 28 (39%) with a hypoplastic limb had mental retardation or early death.
Data from Gershon, A. A.: Chickenpox, measles and mumps. *In* Remington, J. S., and Klein, J. O. (eds.): Infectious Diseases of the Fetus and Newborn Infant. Philadelphia, W. B. Saunders, 2001, p. 698.

TABLE 73–13 ■ CONGENITAL VARICELLA SYNDROME: OUTCOME IN RELATION TO RASH ONSET IN MOTHER AND NEONATE

		Neonatal Deaths	
Day of Rash Onset	Neonatal Cases	Number	Percentage
Mother, antepartum			
5 or more	23	0	0
0 to 4	13	4	31
Neonate, after delivery			
0 to 4	22	0	0
5 to 10	19	4	21

Modified from Gershon, A. A.: Chickenpox, measles and mumps. *In* Remington, J. S., and Klein, J. O. (eds.): Infectious Diseases of the Fetus and Newborn Infant. Philadelphia, W. B. Saunders, 1990, pp. 395–445, as modified from Meyers, J. D.: Congenital varicella in term infants: Risk reconsidered. J. Infect. Dis. *129*:215–217, 1974, with permission from the University of Chicago.

different.[381, 384] Immunofluorescence testing of vesicular lesions with commercially available specific monoclonal antibodies will rapidly differentiate the two.

Varicella-zoster immunoglobulin (VZIG), 125 U intramuscularly, should be given to a neonate born to a mother with an onset of chickenpox rash between 5 days before delivery and 2 days after delivery.[411] VZIG should be administered as soon as possible after birth. Breakthrough severe varicella has occurred in neonates properly treated with VZIG, however.[37] These infants still must be considered potentially infective and are maintained on airborne precautions in a negative-pressure room for 16 days after maternal onset of rash because the incubation period with in utero exposure is decreased. If the newborn is exposed to maternal varicella at delivery, airborne precautions are extended until 21 days after exposure (28 days when VZIG is given) if hospitalization is required. Exposed infants do not need to be separated from their mothers; on the contrary, rooming-in may be preferable to preclude nosocomial spread. If breakthrough occurs despite VZIG therapy and the neonatal varicella appears to be becoming severe (extensive skin lesions, high fever and toxicity, hepatitis, pneumonitis), treatment with intravenous acyclovir at 1500 mg/m^2/day or 45 mg/kg/day divided every 8 hours should be instituted.[456]

Infants born to mothers with zoster do not require VZIG prophylaxis because they already have high levels of transplacentally acquired maternal VZV IgG antibody. No special precautions are indicated except that the maternal lesions should be covered and good handwashing when handling the infant must be stressed.

ZOSTER IN INFANCY AND CHILDHOOD

Epidemiologic and serologic evidence indicates that zoster is a reactivated latent, rather than an exogenously acquired infection with VZV.[184, 381] Persons with zoster, therefore, have had a previous episode of chickenpox. The vast majority of zoster occurs in older adult patients. The occurrence of zoster in infants and children is somewhat of a paradox because many of these patients have a negative history of having had chickenpox.[79, 187, 329] However, with several of these cases of childhood zoster, particularly those occurring in infants and young children, the mother had a history of chickenpox during pregnancy.[79, 165, 184, 312] The presumption is that fetal VZV infection occurred, with recovery and no evidence of disease in the neonate at birth. In a few other instances, an infant born to a VZV-immune mother may be exposed to chickenpox or zoster during early life at a time when maternal transplacental antibody still would be present. This passive antibody could provide protection against chickenpox and modify the disease to a subclinical or mild form that was not recognized.[172] Both situations could result in a patient with (1) an unrecognized episode of varicella and (2) the occurrence of zoster as the first overt manifestation of VZV infection.

Again, the major disease in the differential diagnosis is HSV infection. Patients with neonatal herpes may have a clinical picture resembling that of zoster,[354] and laboratory evaluation is required to differentiate the two diseases. Both neonatal chickenpox and childhood zoster are contagious, and appropriate isolation procedures should be used when the patient is hospitalized. In addition to standard precautions, airborne and contact precautions are recommended for patients with varicella for a minimum of 5 days after the onset of rash and as long as the rash remains vesicular. For immunocompetent individuals with zoster, contact precautions are indicated, whereas in immunocompromised patients with localized zoster and individuals with disseminated zoster, airborne and contact precautions should be used.

Human Parvovirus B19 (Erythrovirus) Infection

Human parvovirus B19 (erythrovirus) is the cause of erythema infectiosum, or fifth disease, a mild exanthematous illness in school-age children[26] (see Chapter 158). Concern about parvovirus B19 infection in pregnant women has been great because of the known associated occurrence of abortion, stillbirth, and nonimmune hydrops fetalis secondary to transplacental passage of the virus.[24, 265, 269, 272, 459, 508, 516, 525, 547] A summary of 22 published case reports of parvovirus fetal infection revealed that (1) only half the mothers had parvovirus-like clinical illness 4 to 13 weeks before fetal death, (2) all fetuses had hydrops fetalis and probable myocarditis, and (3) 19 died in utero at 16 to 26 weeks and the remaining 3 died within 24 hours of delivery.[26] Laboratory evidence of parvovirus infection included (1) maternal parvovirus IgM antibody, (2) elevated maternal alpha-fetoprotein, and (3) the presence of parvovirus DNA in amniotic fluid.[26, 508, 509] Hydrops fetalis occurs from replication of parvovirus in the bone marrow and resultant profound fetal anemia, with myocarditis playing a potential secondary role.[26]

Importantly, not all pregnancies complicated by parvovirus infection result in fetal infection, and hydrops does not develop in all infected fetuses. A British study of 186 pregnant women who had parvovirus IgM antibody and were monitored to term demonstrated that fetal loss occurred in 16 percent (no data on fetal loss rates in a control population) and that 43 percent of 14 fetal tissues tested showed parvovirus DNA.[86, 413] Extrapolation from these figures yielded a maximal parvovirus-associated adverse fetal outcome of 7 percent in pregnancies with laboratory-proven parvovirus infection. Extrapolation to the community level yielded the following estimates of fetal death in a pregnant woman exposed to active parvovirus infection: 1.8 percent with home exposure and 1.1 percent or less with school exposure.[86, 413] The figures used in this estimate include the 7 percent fetal death rate with documented maternal infection cited earlier. Furthermore, only approximately 50 percent of women of child-bearing age are seronegative and, therefore, susceptible, and infection rates after exposure to parvovirus infection are 50 percent in the home and 30 percent with a *widespread* school outbreak. More recent studies have indicated a total fetal infection rate of 25 to 50 percent, but an adverse fetal outcome rate of less than 1 to 2 percent.[191, 270–272, 516]

Overall, after an acute parvovirus B19 infection during pregnancy, the vertical transmission rate is approximately 30 to 50 percent, the risk of fetal death is between 2 and 6 percent, and most infected newborns are asymptomatic. In addition, maternal parvovirus B19 infection during pregnancy has not been associated with congenital anomalies. These data indicate that most intrauterine parvovirus infections are benign and self-limited. However, CNS abnormalities have been reported in a few infants with in utero infection.[115] These abnormalities consisted of cerebral atrophy, ventricular enlargement, basal ganglia and periventricular calcifications, and diffuse cortical dysplasia, with hypotonia and later development of cerebral palsy and developmental delay. These findings could be secondary to parvovirus infection of the fetal brain; alternatively, they could be a result of the profound anemia that can occur in the fetus.

Fetal infection is diagnosed best by demonstration of parvovirus B19 DNA in amniotic fluid, and fetal hydrops is readily detectable by antenatal ultrasound.[525] PCR also has been used on fetal blood and tissues, as well as on infant blood and CSF. Assays for detection of human parvovirus B19 IgG and IgM antibodies are available commercially. Many infected newborns lack specific parvovirus IgM antibody at birth but will demonstrate persistence of parvovirus B19 IgG antibody beyond infancy, thus documenting infection.

No specific therapy is available. Intravenous immunoglobulin therapy has suppressed or controlled parvovirus-associated chronic anemia in immunosuppressed patients,[180] although no evidence indicates that it would be beneficial in pregnant women with parvovirus infection. Intrauterine transfusions have been used in cases of fetal hydrops associated with severe anemia, although some cases of hydrops resolve spontaneously.

Prevention consists largely of the rational use of infection control measures, including handwashing and disposal of used facial tissues. To isolate or quarantine otherwise normal children who have the rash of erythema infectiosum makes no sense because viral shedding has ceased by the time that the rash appears.[26] On the other hand, hemoglobinopathy patients with parvovirus-induced aplastic crisis or immunosuppressed patients with parvovirus-associated chronic anemia are highly infectious,[54] so droplet precautions should be instituted.

Lymphocytic Choriomeningitis Virus

Lymphocytic choriomeningitis virus (LCMV) is an RNA virus and a member of the *Arenaviridae* family. It causes a chronic infection with virus excretion in rodents, but it also may infect humans worldwide, especially in Europe, Africa, and the Americas. LCMV most commonly causes a nonspecific febrile illness, aseptic meningitis, or encephalitis. In adults, it also has been associated with nonbacterial orchitis, parotitis, and sudden-onset deafness. On rare occasion, congenital infection and disease have been documented.[42] The incidence of congenital infection with this virus, however, has not been studied systematically, and some experts suggest that it may be under-recognized as a pathogen of the fetus and newborn.[552] Congenital infection with LCMV appears to be a common cause of ocular abnormalities such as chorioretinitis, chorioretinal scars, and optic atrophy. Rarely, microphthalmos and cataracts have been observed. Other neurologic abnormalities noted at birth include microcephaly, hydrocephalus, and periventricular calcifications. Sequelae such as cognitive delays, major motor disabilities, seizures, and vision loss have been seen in these infants. In contrast to other congenital viral infections, signs such as hydrops, hepatosplenomegaly, skin lesions, thrombocytopenia, and hearing loss are uncommon findings in children born with congenital LCMV infection.

The diagnosis of congenital LCMV infection should be suspected in an infant who appears to have a congenital viral infection or congenital toxoplasmosis, but the laboratory evaluation does not confirm these infections. Supporting evidence includes a mother with prenatal exposure to wild, pet, or laboratory rodents such as mice, hamsters, or gerbils. The laboratory diagnosis of LCMV most commonly is established serologically, and detection of LCMV-specific IgG and IgM antibodies in serum or CSF supports the diagnosis. Detection of the virus by culture or reverse transcription PCR–based methods may be available in reference laboratories. Currently, management is supportive because antiviral therapy has not been evaluated in clinical trials. Prevention of congenital LCMV infection includes minimizing exposure of pregnant women to rodents in the home and workplace.

REFERENCES

1. Abzug, M. J.: Maternal factors affecting the integrity of the late gestation placental barrier to murine enterovirus infection. J. Infect. Dis. *176*:41–49, 1997.
2. Abzug, M. J., Keyerling, H. L., Lee, M. L., et al.: Neonatal enterovirus infection: Virology, serology, and effects of intravenous immune globulin. Clin. Infect. Dis. *20*:1201–1206, 1995.
3. Abzug, M. J., Levin, M. J., and Rotbart, H. A.: Profile of enterovirus-disease in the first two weeks of life. Pediatr. Infect. Dis. J. *12*:820–824, 1993.
4. Adler, S. P.: Transfusion-associated cytomegalovirus infections. Rev. Infect. Dis. *5*:977–993, 1983.
5. Adler, S. P.: Molecular epidemiology of cytomegalovirus: Viral transmission among children attending a day care center, their parents, and caretakers. J. Pediatr. *112*:366–372, 1988.
6. Adler, S. P., Baggett, J., Wilson, M., et al.: Molecular epidemiology of cytomegalovirus in a nursery: Lack of evidence for nosocomial transmission. J. Pediatr. *108*:117–123, 1986.
7. Adler, S. P., Hempfling, S. H., Starr, S. E., et al.: Safety and immunogenicity of the Towne strain cytomegalovirus vaccine. Pediatr. Infect. Dis. J. *17*:200–206, 1998.
8. Adler, S. P., Tattamangalam, C., Lawrence, L., et al.: Cytomegalovirus infections in neonates acquired by blood transfusions. Pediatr. Infect. Dis. *2*:114–118, 1983.
9. Ahlfors, K., Forsgren, M., Ivarsson, S. A., et al.: Congenital cytomegalovirus infection: On the relation between type and time of maternal infection and infant's symptoms. Scand. J. Infect. Dis. *15*:129–138, 1983.
10. Ahlfors, K., Ivarsson, S. A., Harris, S., et al.: Congenital cytomegalovirus infection and disease in Sweden and the relative importance of primary and secondary maternal infections. Scand. J. Infect. Dis. *16*:129–137, 1984.
11. Ahlfors, K., Ivarsson, S. A., Johnsson, T., et al.: Primary and secondary maternal cytomegalovirus infections and their relation to congenital infection. Acta Paediatr. *71*:109–113, 1982.
12. Alestig, K., Bartsch, F. K., Nilsson, L.-A., et al.: Studies of amniotic fluid in women infected with rubella. J. Infect. Dis. *129*:79–81, 1974.
13. Alford, C. A., Jr., Foft, J. W., Blankenship, W. J., et al.: Subclinical central nervous system disease of neonates: A prospective study of infants born with increased levels of IgM. J. Pediatr. *75*:1167–1178, 1969.
14. Alford, C. A., Jr., Neva, F. A., and Weller, T. H.: Virologic and serologic studies on human products of conception after maternal rubella. N. Engl. J. Med. *271*:1275–1281, 1964.
15. Alford, C. A., Stagno, S., Pass, R. F., et al.: Congenital and perinatal cytomegalovirus infections. Rev. Infect. Dis. *12*(Suppl. 7):745–753, 1990.
16. Alford, C. A., Jr., Stagno, S., and Reynolds, D. W.: Diagnosis of chronic perinatal infections. Am. J. Dis. Child. *129*:455–463, 1975.
17. Alkalay, A. L., Pomerance, J. J., and Rimoin, D. L.: Fetal varicella syndrome. J. Pediatr. *111*:320–323, 1987.
18. Alter, H. J., Purcell, R. H., Shih, J. W., et al.: Detection of antibody to hepatitis C virus in prospectively followed transfusion recipients with acute and chronic non-A, non-B hepatitis. N. Engl. J. Med. *321*:1492–1500, 1989.
19. Alter, M. J.: The detection, transmission, and outcome of hepatitis C virus infection. Infect. Agents Dis. *2*:155–166, 1993.
20. Alter, M. J., Hadler, S. C., Judson, F. N., et al.: Risk factors for acute non-A, non-B hepatitis in the United States and association with hepatitis C virus infection. J. A. M. A. *264*:2231–2235, 1990.
21. Alward, W. L. M., McMahon, B. J., Hall, D. B., et al.: The long-term serological course of asymptomatic hepatitis B virus carriers and the development of primary hepatocellular carcinoma. J. Infect. Dis. *151*:604–609, 1985.
22. American Academy of Pediatrics. Cytomegalovirus. *In* Pickering, L. K. (ed.): 2000 Red Book: Report of the Committee on Infectious Diseases. 25th ed. Elk Grove Village, IL, American Academy of Pediatrics, 2000, pp. 227–230.
23. American Academy of Pediatrics. Herpes simplex. *In* Pickering, L. K. (ed.): 2000 Red Book: Report of the Committee on Infectious Diseases. 25th ed. Elk Grove Village, IL, American Academy of Pediatrics, 2000, pp. 309–318.
24. Anand, A., Gray, E. S., Brown, T., et al.: Human parvovirus infection in pregnancy and hydrops fetalis. N. Engl. J. Med. *316*:183–186, 1987.
25. Anderson, K. E., Stevens, C. E., Tsuei, J. J., et al.: Hepatitis B antigen in infants born to mothers with chronic hepatitis B antigenemia in Taiwan. Am. J. Dis. Child. *129*:1389–1392, 1975.
26. Anderson, L. J.: Human parvoviruses. J. Infect. Dis. *161*:603–608, 1990.
27. Ansari, B. M., and Mason, M. K.: Chromosomal abnormality in congenital rubella. Pediatrics *59*:13–15, 1977.
28. Aradottir, E., Alonso, E. M., Shulman, S. T.: Severe neonatal enteroviral hepatitis treated with pleconaril. Pediatr. Infect. Dis. J. *20*:457–459, 2001.
29. Arevalo, J. A.: Hepatitis B in pregnancy. West. J. Med. *150*:668–674, 1989.

30. Arevalo, J. A., and Washington, A. E.: Cost-effectiveness of prenatal screening and immunization for hepatitis B virus. J. A. M. A. *259*:365–369, 1988.
31. Arvin, A. M., and Alford, C. A., Jr.: Chronic intrauterine and perinatal infections. *In* Galasso, G. J., Whitley, R. J., and Merigan, T. C. (eds.): Antiviral Agents and Viral Diseases of Man. 3rd ed. New York, Raven Press, 1990, pp. 497–580.
32. Arvin, A. M., Hensleigh, P. A., Prober, C. G., et al.: Failure of antepartum maternal cultures to predict the infant's risk of exposure to herpes simplex virus at delivery. N. Engl. J. Med. *315*:796–800, 1986.
33. Arvin, A. M., Yeager, A. S., and Merigan, T. C.: Effect of leukocyte interferon on urinary excretion of cytomegalovirus by infants. J. Infect. Dis. *133*(Suppl.):A205–A210, 1976.
34. Bacon, C. J., and Sims, D. G.: Echovirus 19 infection in infants under six months. Arch. Dis. Child. *51*:631–633, 1976.
35. Bai, P. V. A., and John, T. J.: Congenital skin ulcers following varicella in late pregnancy. J. Pediatr. *94*:65–67, 1979.
36. Baker, D. A.: Herpes and pregnancy: New management. Clin. Obstet. Gynecol. *33*:253–257, 1990.
37. Bakshi, S. S., Miller, T. C., Kaplan, M., et al.: Failure of varicella-zoster immunoglobulin in modification of severe congenital varicella. Pediatr. Infect. Dis. *5*:699–702, 1986.
38. Balkarek, K. B., Warren, W., Smith, R. J., et al.: Neonatal screening for congenital cytomegalovirus infection by detection of virus in saliva. J. Infect. Dis. *167*:1433–1436, 1993.
39. Ballard, R. A., Drew, W. L., Hufnagle, K. G., et al.: Acquired cytomegalovirus infection in preterm infants. Am. J. Dis. Child. *133*:482–485, 1979.
40. Barin, F., Goudeau, A., Denis, F., et al.: Immune response in neonates to hepatitis B vaccine. Lancet *1*:251–253, 1982.
41. Bart, K. J., Orenstein, W. A., Preblud, S. R., et al.: Elimination of rubella and congenital rubella from the United States. Pediatr. Infect. Dis. *4*:14–21, 1985.
42. Barton, L. L., and Mets, M. B.: Congenital lymphocytic choriomeningitis virus infection: Decade of rediscovery. Clin. Infect. Dis. *33*:370–374, 2001.
43. Baublis, J. V., Whitley, R. J., Ch'ien, L. T., et al.: Treatment of cytomegalovirus infection in infants and adults. *In* Pavan-Langston, D., and Buchanan, R. A. (eds.): Adenine Arabinoside: An Antiviral Agent. New York, Raven Press, 1975, pp. 247–260.
44. Beasley, R. P., and Hwang, L.-Y.: Postnatal infectivity of hepatitis B surface antigen-carrier mothers. J. Infect. Dis. *147*:185–190, 1983.
45. Beasley, R. P., Hwang, L.-Y., Lee, G. C.-Y., et al.: Prevention of perinatally transmitted hepatitis B virus infections with hepatitis B immune globulin and hepatitis B vaccine. Lancet *2*:1099–1102, 1983.
46. Beasley, R. P., Hwang, L.-Y., Lin, C.-C., et al.: Hepatitis B immune globulin (HBIG) efficacy in the interruption of perinatal transmission of hepatitis B virus carrier state. Lancet *2*:388–393, 1981.
47. Beasley, R. P., Hwang, L.-Y., Lin, C.-C., et al.: Hepatocellular carcinoma and hepatitis B virus: A prospective study of 22,707 men in Taiwan. Lancet *2*:1129–1133, 1981.
48. Beasley, R. P., Hwang, L.-Y., Lin, C.-C., et al.: Incidence of hepatitis B virus infections in preschool children in Taiwan. J. Infect. Dis. *146*:198–204, 1982.
49. Beasley, R. P., Hwang, L.-Y., Stevens, C. E., et al.: Efficacy of hepatitis B immune globulin for prevention of perinatal transmission of the hepatitis B virus carrier state: Final report of a randomized double-blind, placebo-controlled trial. Hepatology *3*:135–141, 1983.
50. Beasley, R. P., Shiao, I.-S., Stevens, C. E., et al.: Evidence against breastfeeding as a mechanism for vertical transmission of hepatitis B. Lancet *2*:740–741, 1975.
51. Beasley, R. P., Trepo, C., Stevens, C. E., et al.: The e antigen and vertical transmission of hepatitis B surface antigen. Am. J. Epidemiol. *105*:94–98, 1977.
52. Becker, T. M., Blount, J. H., and Guinan, M. E.: Genital herpes infections in private practice in the United States, 1966 to 1981. J. A. M. A. *253*:1601–1603, 1985.
53. Behrman, R. E.: The high-risk infant. *In* Vaughan, V. C., III, McKay, R. J., Jr., and Behrman, R. E. (eds.): Nelson Textbook of Pediatrics. Philadelphia, W. B. Saunders, 1979, pp. 398–414.
54. Bell, L. M., Naides, S. J., Stoffman, P., et al.: Human parvovirus B19 infection among hospital staff members after contact with infected patients. N. Engl. J. Med. *321*:485–491, 1989.
55. Bergman, I., Painter, M. J., Wald, E. R., et al.: Outcome in children with enteroviral meningitis during the first year of life. J. Pediatr. *110*:705–709, 1987.
56. Binkin, N. J., Koplan, J. P., and Cates, W., Jr.: Preventing neonatal herpes: The value of weekly viral cultures in pregnant women with recurrent genital herpes. J. A. M. A. *251*:2816–2821, 1984.
57. Birnbaum, G., Lynch, J. I., Margileth, A. M., et al.: Cytomegalovirus infections in newborn infants. J. Pediatr. *75*:789–795, 1969.
58. Blanc, W. A.: Pathology of the placenta and cord in some viral infections. *In* Hanshaw, J. B., and Dudgeon, J. A. (eds.): Viral Diseases of the Fetus and Newborn. Philadelphia, W. B. Saunders, 1978, pp. 237–258.
59. Boehm, F. H., Estes, W., Wright, P. F., et al.: Management of genital herpes simplex virus infection occurring during pregnancy. Am. J. Obstet. Gynecol. *141*:735–740, 1981.
60. Bolognese, R. J., Corson, S. L., Fuccillo, D. A., et al.: Herpesvirus hominis type II infections in asymptomatic pregnant women. Obstet. Gynecol. *48*:507–510, 1976.
61. Boner, A., Wilmott, R. W., Dinwiddie, R., et al.: Desquamative interstitial pneumonia and antigen-antibody complexes in two infants with congenital rubella. Pediatrics *72*:835–839, 1983.
62. Boppana, S., Amos, C., Britt, W., et al.: Late onset and reactivation of chorioretinitis in children with congenital cytomegalovirus infection. Pediatr. Infect. Dis. J. *13*:1139–1142, 1994.
63. Boppana, S. B., Fowler, K. B., Vaid, Y., et al.: Neuroradiographic findings in the newborn period and long-term outcome in children with symptomatic congenital cytomegalovirus infection. Pediatrics *99*:409–414, 1997.
64. Boppana, S., Pass, R. F., Britt, W. S., et al.: Symptomatic congenital cytomegalovirus Infection: Neonatal morbidity and mortality. Pediatr. Infect. Dis. J. *11*:93–99, 1992.
65. Boppana, S. B., Rivera, L. B., Fowler, K. B., et al.: Intrauterine transmission of cytomegalovirus to infants of women with preconceptional immunity. N. Engl. J. Med. *344*:1366–1371, 2001.
66. Bortolotti, F., Caizia, R., Cadrobbi, P., et al.: Liver cirrhosis associated with chronic hepatitis B virus infection in childhood. J. Pediatr. *108*:224–227, 1986.
67. Bradford, R. D., Kimberlin, D. W., Lakeman, F. D., et al.: Baseline viremia in congenital cytomegalovirus (CMV) infection correlates with clinical outcome. Abstract 37. Oral Presentation at the 39th Annual Meeting of the Infectious Diseases Society of America, October 25–28, 2001, San Francisco.
68. Bradford-Hill, A., Doll, R., Galloway, T. M., et al.: Virus diseases in pregnancy and congenital defects. Br. J. Prev. Soc. Med. *12*:1–7, 1958.
69. Brady, M. T., Milam, J. D., Anderson, D. C., et al.: Use of deglycerolized red blood cells to prevent posttransfusion infection with cytomegalovirus in neonates. J. Infect. Dis. *150*:334–339, 1984.
70. Brightman, V. J., Scott, T. F. M., Westphal, M., et al.: An outbreak of Coxsackie B-5 virus infection in a newborn nursery. J. Pediatr. *69*:179–192, 1966.
71. Britt, W. J.: Vaccines against human cytomegalovirus: Time to test. Trends Microbiol. *4*:34–38, 1996.
72. Brody, J. A., Sever, J. L., and Schiff, G. M.: Prevention of rubella by gamma globulin during an epidemic in Barrow, Alaska, in 1964. N. Engl. J. Med. *272*:127–129, 1965.
73. Brown, G. C.: Maternal virus infection and congenital anomalies. Arch. Environ. Health *21*:362–365, 1970.
74. Brown, G. C., and Evans, T. N.: Serologic evidence of coxsackievirus etiology of congenital heart disease. J. A. M. A. *199*:183–187, 1967.
75. Brown, G. C., and Karunas, R. S.: Relationship of congenital anomalies and maternal infection with selected enteroviruses. Am. J. Epidemiol. *95*:207–217, 1972.
76. Brown, Z. A., Benedetti, J., Ashley, R., et al.: Neonatal herpes simplex virus infection in relation to asymptomatic maternal infection at the time of labor. N. Engl. J. Med. *324*:1247–1252, 1991.
77. Brown, Z. A., Kern, E. R., Spruance, S. L., et al.: Clinical and virologic course of herpes simplex genitalis. West. J. Med. *130*:414–421, 1979.
78. Brown, Z. A., Vontver, L. A., Benedetti, J., et al.: Effects on infants of a first episode of genital herpes during pregnancy. N. Engl. J. Med. *317*:1246–1251, 1987.
79. Brunell, P. A., Miller, L. H., and Lovejoy, F.: Zoster in children. Am. J. Dis. Child. *115*:432–437, 1968.
80. Buhles, W. C., Jr., Mastre, B. J., Tinker, A. J., et al.: Ganciclovir treatment of life- or sight-threatening cytomegalovirus infection: Experience in 314 immunocompromised patients. Rev. Infect. Dis. *10*(Suppl. 3):495–506, 1988.
81. Buimovici-Klein, E., Lang, P. B., Ziring, P. R., et al.: Impaired cell-mediated immune response in patients with congenital rubella: Correlation with gestational age at time of infection. Pediatrics *64*:620–626, 1979.
82. Centers for Disease Control and Prevention: Immune globulins for protection against viral hepatitis. M. M. W. R. Morb. Mortal. Wkly. Rep. *30*(34):423–428, 433–435, 1981.
83. Centers for Disease Control and Prevention: Enterovirus surveillance report, 1970–1979. Issued November 1981.
84. Centers for Disease Control and Prevention: Recommendations for protection against viral hepatitis. M. M. W. R. *34*(22):313–324, 329–335, 1985.
85. Centers for Disease Control and Prevention: Prevention of perinatal transmission of hepatitis B virus: Prenatal screening of all pregnant women for hepatitis B surface antigen. M. M. W. R. *37*(22):341–346, 351, 1988.
86. Centers for Disease Control and Prevention: Risks associated with human parvovirus B19 infection. M. M. W. R. Morb. Mortal. Wkly. Rep. *38*(6):81–88, 93–97, 1989.
87. Centers for Disease Control and Prevention: Rubella vaccination during pregnancy: United States, 1971–1988. M. M. W. R. Morb. Mortal. Wkly. Rep. *38*(17):289–293, 1989.

88. Centers for Disease Control and Prevention: Protection against viral hepatitis. Recommendations of the Immunization Practices Advisory Committee (ACIP). M. M. W. R. Recomm. Rep. *39*(RR-2):1–26, 1990.
89. Centers for Disease Control and Prevention: Increase in rubella and congenital rubella syndrome—United States, 1988–1990. M. M. W. R. Morb. Mortal. Wkly. Rep. *40*(6):93–99, 1991.
90. Centers for Disease Control and Prevention: Hepatitis B virus: A comprehensive strategy for eliminating transmission in the United States through universal childhood vaccination. Recommendations of the Immunization Practices Advisory Committee (ACIP). M. M. W. R. Recomm. Rep. *40*(RR-13):1–25, 1991.
91. Centers for Disease Control and Prevention: Hepatitis surveillance report No. 55, 1994, pp. 1–34.
92. Centers for Disease Control and Prevention: Recommendations for prevention and control of hepatitis C virus (HCV) infection and HCV-related chronic disease. M. M. W. R. Recomm. Rep. *47*(RR-19): 1–39, 1998.
93. Centers for Disease Control and Prevention: General recommendations on immunization. Recommendations of the Advisory Committee on Immunization Practices (ACIP) and the American Academy of Family Physicians (AAFP). M. M. W. R. Recomm. Rep. *51*(RR-2):1–35, 2002.
94. Centers for Disease Control and Prevention: Sexually transmitted diseases treatment guidelines 2002. M. M. W. R. Recomm. Rep. *51*(RR-6):1–78, 2002.
95. Chairez, R., Cesario, A. J., Barrett, J. E., et al.: Evaluation of CMV antibody EIA: An enzyme immunoassay for detection of antibodies to cytomegalovirus. Diagn. Microbiol. Infect. Dis. *3*:403–410, 1985.
96. Chamnanvanakij, S., Rogers, C. G., Luppino, C., et al.: Linear hyperechogenicity within the basal ganglia and thalamus of preterm infants. Pediatr. Neurol. *23*:129–133, 2000.
97. Champsaur, H., Fattal-German, M., and Arranhado, R.: Sensitivity and specificity of viral immunoglobulin M determination by indirect enzyme-linked immunosorbent assay. J. Clin. Microbiol. *26*:328–332, 1988.
98. Chandler, S. H., Alexander, E. R., and Holmes, K. K.: Epidemiology of cytomegaloviral infection in a heterogeneous population of pregnant women. J. Infect. Dis. *2*:249–256, 1985.
99. Chang, T. W.: Rubella reinfection and intrauterine involvement. J. Pediatr. *84*:617–618, 1974.
100. Chawareewong, S., Kiangsiri, S., Lokaphadhana, K., et al.: Neonatal herpangina caused by Coxsackie A-5 virus. J. Pediatr. *93*:492–494, 1978.
101. Cheeseman, S. H., Hirsch, M. S., Keller, E. W., et al.: Fatal neonatal pneumonia caused by echovirus type 9. Am. J. Dis. Child. *131*:1169, 1977.
102. Chernesky, M. A., and Mahony, J. B.: Rubella virus. *In* Murray, P. R., Barron, E. J., Pfaller, M. A., et al.: (eds.): Manual of Clinical Microbiology. Washington, D.C., American Society of Microbiology, 1995, pp. 968–973.
103. Cherry, J. D.: Enteroviruses. *In* Remington, J. S., and Klein, J. O. (eds.): Infectious Diseases of the Fetus and Newborn Infant. 5th ed. Philadelphia, W. B. Saunders, 2001, pp. 477–518.
104. Chess, S., Fernandez, P., and Korn, S.: Behavioral consequences of congenital rubella. J. Pediatr. *93*:699–703, 1978.
105. Ch'ien, L. T., Cannon, N. J., Whitley, R. J., et al.: Effect of adenine arabinoside on cytomegalovirus infections. J. Infect. Dis. *130*:32–39, 1974.
106. Ch'ien, L. T., Whitley, R. J., Nahmias, A. J., et al.: Antiviral chemotherapy and neonatal herpes simplex virus infection: A pilot study—Experience with adenine arabinoside (ARA-A). Pediatrics *55*:678–685, 1975.
107. Choo, Q.-L., Kuo, G., Weiner, A. J., et al.: Isolation of a cDNA clone derived from a blood-borne non-A, non-B viral hepatitis genome. Science *244*:359–362, 1989.
108. Clarke, W. L., Shaver, K. A., Bright, G. M., et al.: Autoimmunity in congenital rubella syndrome. J. Pediatr. *104*:370–373, 1984.
109. Clemens, R., Safary, A., Hepburn A., et al.: Clinical experience with an inactivated hepatitis A vaccine. J. Infect. Dis. *171*(Suppl. 1):44–49, 1995.
110. Clemente, M. G., Congia, M., Lai, M. E., et al.: Effect of iron overload on the response to recombinant interferon-alfa treatment in transfusion dependent patients with thalassemia major and chronic hepatitis C. J. Pediatr. *125*:123–128, 1994.
111. Committee on Infectious Diseases: Universal hepatitis B immunization. Pediatrics *89*:795–800, 1992.
112. Conboy, T. J., Pass, R. F., Stagno, S., et al.: Early clinical manifestations and intellectual outcome in children with symptomatic congenital cytomegalovirus infection. J. Pediatr. *111*:343–348, 1987.
113. Conchie, A. F., Barton, B. W., and Tobin, J. O.: Congenital cytomegalovirus infection treated with idoxuridine. B. M. J. *4*:162–163, 1968.
114. Cone, R. W., Hobson, A. C., Brown, Z., et al.: Frequent detection of genital herpes simplex virus DNA by polymerase chain reaction among pregnant women. J. A. M. A. *272*:792–796, 1994.
115. Conry, J. A., Török, T., Andrews, P. I.: Perinatal encephalopathy secondary to in utero human parvovirus B-19 (HPV) infection. Abstract 736S. Neurology *43*(Suppl):346, 1993.
116. Cooper, L. Z.: The history and medical consequences of rubella. Rev. Infect. Dis. *7*(Suppl. 1):2–10, 1985.
117. Cooper, L. Z., and Alford, C. A., Jr.: Rubella. *In* Remington, J. S., and Klein, J. O. (eds.): Infections of the Fetus and Newborn Infant. Philadelphia, W. B. Saunders, 5th ed., 2001, pp. 347–388.
118. Cooper, L. Z., Green, R. H., Krugman, S., et al.: Neonatal thrombocytopenic purpura and other manifestations of rubella contracted in utero. Am. J. Dis. Child. *110*:416–427, 1965.
119. Cooper, L. Z., Ziring, P. R., Ockerse, A. B., et al.: Rubella: Clinical manifestations and management. Am. J. Dis. Child. *118*:18–29, 1969.
120. Corey, L., Adams, H. G., Brown, Z. A., et al.: Genital herpes simplex virus infections: Clinical manifestations, course, and complications. Ann. Intern. Med. *98*:958–972, 1983.
121. Corey, L., and Spear, P. G.: Infections of herpes simplex viruses. N. Engl. J. Med. *314*:686–691, 749–757, 1986.
122. Corey, L., Whitley, R. J., Stone, E. F., et al.: Difference between herpes simplex virus type 1 and type 2 neonatal encephalitis in neurological outcome. Lancet *1*:1–4, 1988.
123. Cox, F., and Hughes, W. T.: Fecal excretion of cytomegalovirus in disseminated cytomegalic inclusion disease. J. Infect. Dis. *129*:732–736, 1974.
124. Craig, C. P., and Nahmias, A. J.: Different patterns of neurologic involvement with herpes simplex virus types 1 and 2: Isolation of herpes simplex virus type 2 from the buffy coat of two adults with meningitis. J. Infect. Dis. *127*:365–372, 1973.
125. Cramblett, H. G., Haynes, R. E., Azimi, P. H., et al.: Nosocomial infection with echovirus type 11 in handicapped and premature infants. Pediatrics *51*:603–607, 1973.
126. Cruz, A. C., Frentzen, B. H., and Behnke, M.: Hepatitis B: A case for prenatal screening of all patients. Am. J. Obstet. Gynecol. *156*:1180–1183, 1987.
127. Cuthbert, J. A.: Hepatitis C: Progress and problems. Clin. Microbiol. Rev. *7*:505–552, 1994.
128. Dagan, R., Hall, C. B., Powell, K. R., et al.: Epidemiology and laboratory diagnosis of infection with viral and bacterial pathogens in infants hospitalized for suspected sepsis. J. Pediatr. *115*:351–356, 1989.
129. Dagan, R., Jenista, J. A., and Menegus, M. A.: Clinical, epidemiological, and laboratory aspects of enterovirus infection in young infants. *In* de la Maza, L. M., and Peterson, E. M. (eds.): Medical Virology IV. Hillsdale, NJ, L. Erlbaum Associates, 1985, pp. 123–151.
130. Dagan, R., Jenista, J. A., Prather, S. L., et al.: Viremia in hospitalized children with enterovirus infections. J. Pediatr. *106*:397–401, 1985.
131. Dagan, R., Prather, S. L., Powell, K. R., et al.: Neutralizing antibodies to non-polio enteroviruses in human immune serum globulin. Pediatr. Infect. Dis. *2*:454–456, 1983.
132. Daling, J. A., and Wolf, M. E.: The role of decision and cost analyses in the treatment of pregnant women with recurrent genital herpes. J. A. M. A. *251*:2828–2829, 1984.
133. Davis, L. E., Tweed, G. V., Chin, T. D. Y., et al.: Intrauterine diagnosis of cytomegalovirus infection: Viral recovery from amniocentesis fluid. Am. J. Obstet. Gynecol. *109*:1217–1219, 1971.
134. De Backer, S., Samule, K., Carton, D., et al.: Neonatal Coxsackie B3 sepsis. Acta Paediatr. Belg. *29*:55–57, 1976.
135. Delaplane, D., Yogev, R., Crussi, F., et al.: Fatal hepatitis B in early infancy: The importance of identifying HBsAg-positive pregnant women and providing immunoprophylaxis to their newborns. Pediatrics *72*:176–180, 1983.
136. Del Mar Mosquera, M., de Ory, F., Moreno, M., and Echevarria, J. E.: Simultaneous detection of measles virus, rubella virus, and parvovirus B19 by using multiplex PCR. J. Clin. Microbiol. *40*:111–116, 2002.
137. Demmler, G. J.: Summary of a workshop on surveillance for congenital cytomegalovirus disease. Rev. Infect. Dis. *13*:315–329, 1991.
138. Demmler, G. J., Buffone, G. J., Schimbor, C. M., et al.: Detection of cytomegalovirus in urine from newborns by using polymerase chain reaction DNA amplification. J. Infect. Dis. *158*:1177–1184, 1988.
139. Derso, A., Boxall, E. H., Tarlow, M. J., et al.: Transmission of HBsAg from mother to infant in four ethnic groups. B. M. J. *1*:949–952, 1978.
140. Desmond, M. M., Fisher, E. S., Vorderman, A. L., et al.: The longitudinal course of congenital rubella encephalitis in nonretarded children. J. Pediatr. *93*:584–591, 1978.
141. Desmond, M. M., Wilson, G. S., and Melnick, J. L.: Congenital rubella encephalitis. J. Pediatr. *71*:311–331, 1967.
142. Diamond, C., Mohan, K., Hobson, A., et al.: Viremia in neonatal herpes simplex virus infections. Pediatr. Infect. Dis. J. *18*:487–489, 1999.
143. Dickinson, J., and Gonik, B.: Teratogenic viral infections. Clin. Obstet. Gynecol. *33*:242–252, 1990.
144. Dodt, K. K., Jacobsen, P. H., Hofmann, B., et al.: Development of cytomegalovirus (CMV) disease may be predicted in HIV-infected patients by CMV polymerase chain reaction and the antigenemia test. A. I. D. S. *11*:F21–F28, 1997.
145. Donowitz, M., and Gryboski, J. D.: Pancreatic insufficiency and the congenital rubella syndrome. J. Pediatr. *87*:241–243, 1975.
146. Dosik, H., and Jhaveri, R.: Prevention of neonatal hepatitis B infection by high-dose hepatitis B immune globulin. N. Engl. J. Med. *298*: 602–603, 1978.
147. Douglas, J. M., Schmidt, O., and Corey, L.: Acquisition of neonatal HSV-1 infection from a paternal source contact. J. Pediatr. *103*:908–910, 1983.

148. Doyle, M., Atkins, J. T., and Rivera-Matos, I. R.: Congenital cytomegalovirus infection in infants infected with human immunodeficiency virus type 1. Pediatr. Infect. Dis. J. *15*:1102–1106, 1996.
149. Dublin, A. B., and Merten, D. F.: Computed tomography in the evaluation of herpes simplex encephalitis. Radiology *125*:133–134, 1977.
150. Dunkle, L. M., Schmidt, R. R., and O'Connor, D. M.: Neonatal herpes simplex infection possibly acquired via maternal breast milk. Pediatrics *63*:250–251, 1979.
151. Dunn, A. E. G., Peters, R. L., Schweitzer, I. L., et al.: Virus-like particles in livers of infants with vertically transmitted hepatitis. Arch. Pathol. *94*:258–264, 1972.
152. Dupuy, J. M., Frommel, D., and Alagille, D.: Severe viral hepatitis type B in infancy. Lancet *1*:191–194, 1975.
153. Dupuy, J. M., Giraud, P., Dupuy, C., et al.: Hepatitis B in children. II. Study of children born to chronic HBsAg carrier mothers. J. Pediatr. *92*:200–204, 1978.
154. Dupuy, J. M., Kostewicz, E., and Alagille, D.: Hepatitis B in children. I. Analysis of 80 cases of acute and chronic hepatitis B. J. Pediatr. *92*:17–20, 1978.
155. Dworsky, M., Yow, M., Stagno, S., et al.: Cytomegalovirus infection of breast milk and transmission in infancy. Pediatrics *72*:295–299, 1983.
156. Dzierzahowska, D., Augustynowicz, F., Gyzl, A., et al.: Application of polymerase chain reaction (PCR) for the detection of DNA-HCMV in cerebrospinal fluid of neonates and infants with cytomegalovirus infection. Neurol. Neurochir. Pol. *31*:447–462, 1997.
157. Echeverria, P., Miller, G., Campbell, A. G. M., et al.: Scalp vesicles within the first week of life: A clue to early diagnosis of herpes neonatorum. J. Pediatr. *83*:1062–1064, 1973.
158. Eilard, T., and Strannegard, Ö.: Rubella reinfection in pregnancy followed by transmission to the fetus. J. Infect. Dis. *129*:594–596, 1974.
159. Elizan, T. S., Ajero-Froehlich, L., Fabiyi, A., et al.: Viral infection in pregnancy and congenital CNS malformations in man. Arch. Neurol. *20*:115–119, 1969.
160. Elizan, T. S., and Fabiyi, A.: Congenital and neonatal anomalies linked with viral infections in experimental animals. Am. J. Obstet. Gynecol. *106*:147–165, 1970.
161. Emanuel, D., Cunningham, I., Jules-Elysee, K., et al.: Cytomegalovirus pneumonia after bone marrow transplantation successfully treated with the combination of ganciclovir and high-dose intravenous immune globulin. Ann. Intern. Med. *109*:777–782, 1988.
162. Emodi, G., and Just, M.: Impaired interferon response of children with congenital cytomegalovirus disease. Acta Paediatr. *63*:183–187, 1974.
163. Emodi, G., O'Reilly, R., Müller, A., et al.: Effect of human exogenous leukocyte interferon in cytomegalovirus infections. J. Infect. Dis. *133*(Suppl.):A199–A203, 1976.
164. Enders, G.: Varicella-zoster virus infection in pregnancy. Prog. Med. Virol. *29*:166–196, 1984.
165. Enders, G., Miller, E., and Cradock-Watson, J.: Consequences of varicella and herpes zoster in pregnancy: Prospective study of 1379 cases. Lancet *343*:1547–1560, 1994.
166. Englund, J. A., Courtney, F. V., and Balfour, H. H.: Acyclovir therapy in neonates. J. Pediatr. *119*:129–135, 1991.
167. Esterly, J. R., Slusser, R. J., and Ruebner, B. H.: Hepatic lesions in the congenital rubella syndrome. J. Pediatr. *71*:676–685, 1967.
168. Faix, R. G.: Survival of cytomegalovirus on environmental surfaces. J. Pediatr. *106*:649–652, 1985.
169. Farmer, K., MacArthur, B. A., and Clay, M. M.: A follow-up study of 15 cases of neonatal meningoencephalitis due to coxsackievirus B5. J. Pediatr. *87*:568–571, 1975.
170. Faulkner, R. S., and van Rooyen, C. E.: Echovirus type 17 in the neonate. Can. Med. Assoc. J. *108*:878–882, 1973.
171. Fawaz, K. A., Grady, G. F., Kaplan, M. M., et al.: Repetitive maternal-fetal transmission of fatal hepatitis B. N. Engl. J. Med. *293*:1357–1359, 1975.
172. Feldman, G. V.: Herpes zoster neonatorum. Arch. Dis. Child. *27*:126–127, 1952.
173. Feldman, R. A.: Cytomegalovirus infection during pregnancy. Am. J. Dis. Child. *117*:517–521, 1969.
174. Florman, A. L., Gershon, A. A., Blackett, P. R., et al.: Intrauterine infection with herpes simplex virus. J. A. M. A. *225*:129–132, 1973.
175. Forbes, B. A.: Acquisition of cytomegalovirus infection: An update. Clin. Microbiol. Rev. *2*:204–216, 1989.
176. Forbes, B. A.: Perinatal viral infections. Clin. Microbiol. Newsl. *14*:169–173, 1992.
177. Fowler, K. B., McCollister, F. P., Dahle, A. J., et al.: Progressive and fluctuating sensorineural hearing loss in children with asymptomatic congenital cytomegalovirus infection. J. Pediatr. *130*:624–630, 1997.
178. Fowler, K. B., Stagno, S., and Pass, R. F., et al.: The outcome of congenital cytomegalovirus infection in relation to maternal antibody status. N. Engl. J. Med. *326*:663–667, 1992.
179. Frey, H. M., Bailkin, G., and Gershon, A. A.: Congenital varicella: Case report of a serologically proved long-term survivor. Pediatrics *59*: 110–112, 1977.
180. Frickhofen, N., Abkowitz, J. L., Safford, M., et al.: Persistent B19 parvovirus infection in patients infected with human immunodeficiency virus type-1 (HIV-1): A treatable cause of anemia in AIDS. Ann. Intern. Med. *113*:926–933, 1990.
181. Funato, T., Satou, N., Abukawa, D., et al.: Quantitative evaluation of cytomegalovirus DNA in infantile hepatitis. J. Viral Hepat. *8*:217–222, 2001.
182. Garcia, A. G. P., Olinto, F., and Fortes, T. G. O.: Thymic hypoplasia due to congenital rubella. Arch. Dis. Child. *49*:181–185, 1974.
183. Gear, J. H. S., and Measroch, V.: Coxsackievirus infections of the newborn. Prog. Med. Virol. *15*:42–62, 1973.
184. Gelb, L. D.: Varicella-zoster virus. *In* Fields, B. N., and Knipe, D. M. (eds.): Virology. New York, Raven Press, 1990, pp. 2011–2054.
185. Gerety, R. J., Hoofnagle, J. H., Markenson, J. A., et al.: Exposure to hepatitis B virus and development of the chronic HBAg carrier state in children. J. Pediatr. *84*:661–665, 1974.
186. Gerety, R. J., and Schweitzer, I. L.: Viral hepatitis type B during pregnancy, the neonatal period, and infancy. J. Pediatr. *90*:368–374, 1977.
187. Gershon, A. A.: Chickenpox, measles and mumps. *In* Remington, J. S., and Klein, J. O. (eds.): Infectious Diseases of the Fetus and Newborn Infant. 5th ed. Philadelphia, W. B. Saunders, 2001, pp. 683–732.
188. Gibbs, R. S., Amstey, M. S., Sweet, R. L., et al.: Management of genital herpes infection in pregnancy. Obstet. Gynecol. *71*:779–780, 1988.
189. Grangeot-Keros, L., Broyer, M., Briand, E., et al.: Enterovirus in sudden unexpected deaths in infants. Pediatr. Infect. Dis. *15*:123–128, 1996.
190. Grangeot-Keros, L., Pillot, J., Daffos, F., et al.: Prenatal and postnatal production of IgM and IgA antibodies to rubella virus studied by antibody capture immunoassay. J. Infect. Dis. *158*:138–143, 1988.
191. Gratacos, E., Torres, P.-J., Vidal, J., et al.: The incidence of human parvovirus B19 infection during pregnancy and its impact on perinatal outcome. J. Infect. Dis. *171*:1360–1363, 1995.
192. Greenberg, D. P.: Pediatric experience with recombinant hepatitis B vaccines and relevant safety and immunogenicity studies. Pediatr. Infect. Dis. J. *12*:438–445, 1993.
193. Greenberg, H. B., Pollard, R. B., Lutwick, L. L., et al.: Effect of human leukocyte interferon on hepatitis B virus infection in patients with chronic active hepatitis. N. Engl. J. Med. *295*:517–522, 1976.
194. Greenough, A., Osborne, J., and Sutherland, S.: Congenital, Perinatal and Neonatal Infections. Edinburgh, Churchill Livingstone, 1992.
195. Gregg, N. M.: Congenital cataract following German measles in the mother. Trans. Ophthalmol. Soc. Aust. *3*:35–46, 1941.
196. Griffiths, P. D., and Baboonian, C.: A prospective study of primary cytomegalovirus infection during pregnancy: Final report. Br. J. Obstet. Gynaecol. *91*:307–315, 1984.
197. Griffiths, P. D., Stagno, S., Pass, R. F., et al.: Congenital cytomegalovirus infection: Diagnostic and prognostic significance of the detection of specific immunoglobulin M antibodies in cord serum. Pediatrics *69*:544–549, 1982.
198. Griffiths, P. D., Stagno, S., Pass, R. F., et al.: Infection with cytomegalovirus during pregnancy: Specific IgM antibodies as a marker of recent primary infection. J. Infect. Dis. *145*:647–653, 1982.
199. Gross, J. B., Jr., and Persing, D. H.: Hepatitis C: Advances in diagnosis. Mayo Clin. Proc. *70*:296–297, 1995.
200. Grossman, J. H., III: Herpes simplex virus (HSV) infections. Clin. Obstet. Gynecol. *25*:555–561, 1982.
201. Gutman, L. T., Wilfert, C. M., and Eppes, S.: Herpes simplex virus encephalitis in children: Analysis of cerebrospinal fluid and progressive neurodevelopmental deterioration. J. Infect. Dis. *154*:415–421, 1986.
202. Hagler, W. S., Walters, P. V., and Nahmias, A. J.: Ocular involvement in neonatal herpes simplex virus infection. Arch. Ophthalmol. *82*:169–176, 1969.
203. Halfon, N., and Spector, S. A.: Fatal echovirus type 11 infections. Am. J. Dis. Child. *135*:1017–1020, 1981.
204. Hall, C. B., Douglas, R. G., Jr., Gelman, J. M., et al.: Nosocomial respiratory syncytial virus infections. N. Engl. J. Med. *293*:1343–1346, 1975.
205. Hammond, G. W., Lukes, H., Wells, B., et al.: Maternal and neonatal neutralizing antibody titers to selected enteroviruses. Pediatr. Infect. Dis. J. *4*:32, 1985.
206. Hammerberg, O., Watts, J., Chernesky, M., et al.: An outbreak of herpes simplex virus type I in an intensive care nursery. Pediatr. Infect. Dis. *2*:290–294, 1983.
207. Hamprecht, K., Maschmann, J., Vochem, M., et al.: Epidemiology of transmission of cytomegalovirus from mother to preterm infant by breastfeeding. Lancet *357*:513–518, 2001.
208. Hancock, M. P., Huntley, C. C., and Sever, J. L.: Congenital rubella syndrome with immunoglobulin disorder. J. Pediatr. *72*:636–645, 1968.
209. Hanshaw, J. B.: Developmental abnormalities associated with congenital cytomegalovirus infection. Adv. Teratol. *4*:64–93, 1970.
210. Hanshaw, J. B.: Herpesvirus hominis infections in the fetus and the newborn. Am J. Dis. Child. *126*:546–555, 1973.
211. Hanshaw, J. B.: Congenital cytomegalovirus infection. Pediatr. Ann. *23*:124–128, 1994.
212. Hanshaw, J. B., Dudgeon, J. A., and Marshall, W. C.: Viral Diseases of the Fetus and Newborn. 2nd ed. Philadelphia, W. B. Saunders, 1985.
213. Hanshaw, J. B., Scheiner, A. P., Moxley, A. W., et al.: School failure and deafness after "silent" congenital cytomegalovirus infection. N. Engl. J. Med. *295*:468–470, 1976.

214. Hanshaw, J. B., Steinfeld, H. J., and White, C. J.: Fluorescent-antibody test for cytomegalovirus macroglobulin. N. Engl. J. Med. *279*:566–570, 1968.
215. Hardy, J. B., Sever, J. L., and Gilkeson, M. R.: Declining antibody titers in children with congenital rubella. J. Pediatr. *75*:213–220, 1969.
216. Harger, J. H.: Indications for antepartum HSV screening cultures. Infect. Surg. *8*:24–33, 1989.
217. Harger, J. H., Pazin, G. J., Armstrong, J. A., et al.: Characteristics and management of pregnancy in women with genital herpes simplex virus infection. Am. J. Obstet. Gynecol. *145*:784–791, 1983.
218. Hatherley, L. I., Hayes, K., Hennessy, E. M., Jack, I.: Herpesvirus in an obstetric hospital. I. Herpetic eruptions. Med. J. Aust. *2*:205–208, 1980.
219. Hatherley, L. I., Hayes, K., and Jack, I.: Herpesvirus in an obstetric hospital. II. Asymptomatic virus excretion in staff members. Med. J. Aust. *2*:273–275, 1980.
220. Hayes, K., Danks, D. M., Gibas, H., et al.: Cytomegalovirus in human milk. N. Engl. J. Med. *287*:177–178, 1972.
221. Hayes, K., and Gibas, H.: Placental cytomegalovirus infection without fetal involvement following primary infection in pregnancy. J. Pediatr. *79*:401–405, 1971.
222. Haynes, R. E., Azimi, P. H., and Cramblett, H. G.: Fatal herpesvirus hominis (herpes simplex virus) infections in children: Clinical, pathologic, and virologic characteristics. J. A. M. A. *206*:312–319, 1968.
223. Heijtink, R. A., Boender, P. J., Schalm, S. W., et al.: Hepatitis B virus DNA in serum of pregnant women with HBsAg and HBeAg or antibodies to HBe. J. Infect. Dis. *150*:462, 1984.
224. Herrmann, K. L.: Available rubella serologic tests. Rev. Infect. Dis. *7*(Suppl. 1):108–112, 1985.
225. Higa, K., Dan, K., and Manabe, H.: Varicella-zoster virus infections during pregnancy: Hypothesis concerning the mechanisms of congenital malformations. Obstet. Gynecol. *69*:214–222, 1987.
226. Hildebrandt, R. J., Sever, J. L., Margileth, A. M., et al.: Cytomegalovirus in the normal pregnant woman. Am. J. Obstet. Gynecol. *98*:1125–1128, 1967.
227. Hinman, A. R.: Prevention of congenital rubella infection: Symposium summary. Pediatrics *75*:1162–1165, 1985.
228. Hocker, J. R., Cook, L. N., Adams, G., et al.: Ganciclovir therapy of congenital cytomegalovirus pneumonia. Pediatr. Infect. Dis. J. *9*:743–745, 1990.
229. Hollinger, F. B.: Serologic evaluation of viral hepatitis. Hosp. Pract. *22*:101–114, 1987.
230. Holzer, B R., and Egger, M.: Hepatitis A vaccine. Curr. Opin. Infect. Dis. *8*:186–190, 1995.
231. Honig, P. J., and Brown, D.: Congenital herpes simplex virus infection initially resembling epidermolysis bullosa. J. Pediatr. *101*:958–959, 1982.
232. Hoofnagle, J. H.: Therapy of acute and chronic viral hepatitis. Adv. Intern. Med. *39*:241–275, 1994.
233. Horstmann, D. M., Banatvala, J. E., Riordan, J. T., et al.: Maternal rubella and the rubella syndrome in infants: Epidemiologic, clinical, and virologic observations. Am. J. Dis. Child. *110*:408–415, 1965.
234. Horstmann, D. M., Liebhaber, H., Le Bouvier, G. L., et al.: Rubella: Reinfection of vaccinated and naturally immune persons exposed in an epidemic. N. Engl. J. Med. *283*:771–778, 1970.
235. Horstmann, D. M., Pajot, T. G., and Liebhaber, H.: Epidemiology of rubella: Subclinical infection and occurrence of reinfection. Am. J. Dis. Child. *118*:133–136, 1969.
236. Hovig, D. E., Hodgman, J. E., Mathies, A. W., Jr., et al.: Herpesvirus hominis (simplex) infection: With recurrences during infancy. Am. J. Dis. Child. *115*:438–444, 1968.
237. Hsu, H. H., Feinstone, S. M., and Hoofnagle, J. H.: Acute viral hepatitis. *In* Mandell, G. L., Bennett, J. E., and Dolin, R. (eds.): Principles and Practice of Infectious Diseases. 4th ed. New York, Churchill Livingstone, 1995, pp. 1136–1153.
238. Huang, E.-S., Alford, C. A., Reynolds, D. W., et al.: Molecular epidemiology of cytomegalovirus infections in women and their infants. N. Engl. J. Med. *303*:958–962, 1980.
239. Hughes, J. R., Wilfert, C. M., Moore, M., et al.: Echovirus 14 infection associated with fatal neonatal hepatic necrosis. Am. J. Dis. Child. *123*:61–67, 1972.
240. Hughes, P., LaRusso, P. S., Pearce, J. M., et al.: Transmission of varicella-zoster virus from a vaccinee with underlying leukemia, demonstrated by polymerase chain reaction. J. Pediatr. *124*:932, 1994.
241. Hutto, C., Arvin, A., Jacob, R., et al.: Intrauterine herpes simplex virus infections. J. Pediatr. *110*:97–101, 1987.
242. Jahn, C. L., and Cherry, J. D.: Mild neonatal illness associated with heavy enterovirus infection. N. Engl. J. Med. *274*:394–395, 1966.
243. Jeansson, S., and Molin, L.: On the occurrence of genital herpes simplex virus infection: Clinical and virological findings and relation to gonorrhoea. Acta Derm. Venereol. (Stockh.) *54*:479–485, 1974.
244. Jenista, J. A., Powell, K. R., and Menegus, M. A.: Epidemiology of neonatal enterovirus infection. J. Pediatr. *104*:685–690, 1984.
245. Jhaveri, R., Rosenfeld, W., Salazar, J. D., et al.: High titer multiple dose therapy with HBIG in newborn infants of HBsAg positive mothers. J. Pediatr. *97*:305–308, 1980.
246. Johansson, P. J. H., Jonsson, M., Ahlfors, K., et al.: Retrospective diagnosis of congenital cytomegalovirus infection performed by polymerase chain reaction in blood stored on filter paper. Scand. J. Infect. Dis. *29*:465–468, 1997.
247. Johnson, R. E., Nahmias, A. J., Magder, L. S., et al.: A seroepidemiologic survey of the prevalence of herpes simplex virus type 2 infection in the United States. N. Engl. J. Med. *321*:7–12, 1989.
248. Johnston, J. M., and Overall, J. C., Jr.: Intravaneous immunoglobulin in disseminated neonatal echovirus 11 infection. Pediatr. Infect. Dis. J. *8*:254–256, 1989.
249. Kaplan, M. H., Klein, S. W., McPhee, J., and Harper, R. G.: Group B Coxsackie infections in infants younger than three months of age: A serious childhood illness. Rev. Infect. Dis. *5*:1019–1032, 1983.
250. Kattamis, C. A., Demetrios, D., and Matsaniotis, N. S.: Australia antigen and neonatal hepatitis syndrome. Pediatrics *54*:157–164, 1974.
251. Kay, M. H., Wyllie, R., Deimler, C., et al.: Alpha interferon therapy in children with chronic active hepatitis B and delta virus infection. J. Pediatr. *123*:1001–1004, 1993.
252. Kaye, E. M., and Dooling, E. C.: Neonatal herpes simplex meningoencephalitis associated with fetal monitor scalp electrodes. Neurology *31*:1045–1047, 1981.
253. Kearns, G. L., Bradley, J. S., Jacobs, R. F., et al.: Single dose pharmacokinetics of pleconaril in neonates. Pediatr. Infect. Dis. J. *19*:833–839, 2000.
254. Kern, E. R., Overall, J. C., Jr., and Glasgow, L. A.: Herpesvirus hominis infection in newborn mice. I. An experimental model and therapy with iododeoxyuridine. J. Infect. Dis. *128*:290–299, 1973.
255. Khuroo, M. S., Kamili, S., and Jameel, S.: Vertical transmission of hepatitis E virus. Lancet *345*:1025–1026, 1995.
256. Kibrick, S.: Herpes simplex infection at term: What to do with mother, newborn, and nursery personnel. J. A. M. A. *243*:157–160, 1980.
257. Kilroy, A. W., Schaffner, W., Fleet, W. F., Jr., et al.: Two syndromes following rubella immunization: Clinical observations and epidemiological studies. J. A. M. A. *214*:2287–2292, 1980.
258. Kim, S. C., Chung, E. K., Hodinka, R. L., et al.: Immunogenicity of hepatitis B vaccine in preterm infants. Pediatrics *99*:534–536, 1997.
259. Kimberlin, D. W., Lakeman, F. D., Arvin, A. M., et al.: Application of the polymerase chain reaction to the diagnosis and management of neonatal herpes simplex virus disease. J. Infect. Dis. *174*:1162–1167, 1996.
260. Kimberlin, D. W., Lin, C.-Y., Jacobs, R. F., et al.: Natural history of neonatal herpes simplex virus infections in the acyclovir era. Pediatrics *108*:223–229, 2001.
261. Kimberlin, D. W., Lin, C.-Y., Jacobs, R. F., et al.: Safety and efficacy of high-dose intravenous acyclovir in the management of neonatal herpes simplex virus infections. Pediatrics *108*:230–238, 2001.
262. Kimberlin, D. W., Lin, C.-Y., Sanchez, P. J., et al.: Ganciclovir treatment of symptomatic congenital cytomegalovirus (CMV) infections: Results of a phase III randomized trial. Oral presentation at the 40th Interscience Conference on Antimicrobial Agents and Chemotherapy, September 17–20, 2000, Toronto (ICAAC Program Committee Award recipient in the area of Therapy of Microbial Diseases).
263. Kimberlin, D., Powell, D., Gruber, W., et al.: Administration of oral acyclovir suppressive therapy after neonatal herpes simplex virus disease limited to the skin, eyes, and mouth: Results of a phase I/II trial. Pediatr. Infect. Dis. J. *15*:247–254, 1996.
264. Kimura, H., Futamara, M., Kito, H., et al.: Detection of viral DNA in neonatal herpes simplex virus infections: Frequent and prolonged presence in serum and cerebrospinal fluid. J. Infect. Dis. *164*:289–293, 1991.
265. Kinney, J. S., Anderson, L. J., Farrar, J., et al.: Risk of adverse outcomes of pregnancy after human parvovirus B19 infection. J. Infect. Dis. *157*:663–667, 1988.
266. Kleiman, M. B., Schreiner, R. L., Eitzen, H., et al.: Oral herpesvirus infection in nursery personnel: Infection control policy. Pediatrics *70*: 609–612, 1982.
267. Klock, L. E., and Rachelefsky, G. S.: Failure of rubella herd immunity during an epidemic. N. Engl. J. Med. *288*:69–72, 1973.
268. Knox, G. E., Pass, R. F., Reynolds, D. W., et al.: Comparative prevalence of subclinical cytomegalovirus and herpes simplex virus infections in the genital and urinary tracts of low-income, urban women. J. Infect. Dis. *140*:419–422, 1979.
269. Koch, W. C., and Adler, S. P.: Human parvovirus B19 infections in women of childbearing age and within families. Pediatr. Infect. Dis. J. *8*:83–87, 1989.
270. Koch, W. C., and Adler, S. P.: Detection of human parvovirus B19 DNA by using the polymerase chain reaction. J. Clin. Microbiol. *28*:65, 1990.
271. Koch, W. C., Adler, S., P., and Harger, J.: Intrauterine parvovirus B19 infection may cause an asymptomatic or recurrent postnatal infection. Pediatr. Infect. Dis. J. *12*:747–750, 1993.
272. Koch, W. C., Harger, J. H., Barnstein, B., and Adler, S. P.: Serologic and virologic evidence for frequent intrauterine transmission of human parvovirus B19 with a primary maternal infection during pregnancy. Pediatr. Infect. Dis. J. *17*:489–494, 1998.
273. Koff, R. S.: Hepatitis B today: Clinical and diagnostic overview. Pediatr. Infect. Dis J. *12*:428–432, 1993.
274. Kohler, P. F., Dubois, R. S., Merrill, D. A., et al.: Prevention of chronic neonatal hepatitis B virus infection with antibody to the hepatitis B surface antigen. N. Engl. J. Med. *291*:1378–1380, 1974.

275. Komorous, J. M., Wheeler, C. E., Briggaman, R. A., et al.: Intrauterine herpes simplex infections. Arch. Dermatol. *113*:918–922, 1977.
276. Kono, R., Hayakawa, Y., Hibi, M., et al.: Experimental vertical transmission of rubella virus in rabbits. Lancet *1*:343–347, 1969.
277. Korones, S. B., Ainger, L. E., Monif, G. R. G., et al.: Congenital rubella syndrome: New clinical aspects with recovery of virus from affected infants. J. Pediatr. *67*:166–181, 1965.
278. Korones, S. B., Ainger, L. E., Monif, G. R. G., et al.: Congenital rubella syndrome: Study of 22 infants. Myocardial damage and other new clinical aspects. Am. J. Dis. Child. *110*:434–440, 1965.
279. Koskimies, O., Lapinleimu, K., and Saxen, L.: Infections and other maternal factors as risk indicators for congenital malformations: A case-control study with paired serum samples. Pediatrics *61*:832–837, 1978.
280. Kovacs, A., Schluchter, M., Easley, K., et al.: Cytomegalovirus infection and HIV-1 disease progression in infants born to HIV-1–infected women. N. Engl. J. Med. *341*:77–84, 1999.
281. Krawczynski, K., and Bradley, D. W.: Enterically transmitted non-A, non-B hepatitis: Identification of virus-associated antigen in experimentally infected cynomolgus macaques. J. Infect. Dis. *159*:1042–1049, 1989.
282. Krawitt, E. L.: Chronic hepatitis. *In* Mandell, G. L., Bennett, J. E., and Dolin, R. (eds.): Principals and Practice of Infectious Diseases. 4th ed. New York, Churchill Livingstone, 1995, pp. 1153–1159.
283. Kraybill, E. N., Sever, J. L., Avery, G. B., et al.: Experimental use of cytosine arabinoside in congenital cytomegalovirus infection. J. Pediatr. *80*:485–487, 1972.
284. Krill, A. E.: The retinal disease of rubella. Arch. Ophthalmol. *77*:445–449, 1967.
285. Krober, M. S., Bass, J. W., Powell, J. M., et al.: Bacterial and viral pathogens causing fever in infants less than 3 months old. Am. J. Dis. Child. *139*:889–892, 1985.
286. Krous, H. F., Dietzman, D., and Ray, C. G.: Fatal infections with echovirus types 6 and 11 in early infancy. Am. J. Dis. Child. *126*: 842–846, 1973.
287. Krugman, S.: Viral hepatitis: A, B, C, D and E infection. Pediatr. Rev. *13*:203–212, 1992.
288. Kulhanjian, J. A., Soroush, V., Au, D. S., et al.: Identification of women at unsuspected risk of primary infection with herpes simplex virus during pregnancy. N. Engl. J. Med. *326*:916–920, 1992.
289. Kumar, M. L., Dawson, N. V., McCullough, A. J., et al.: Should all pregnant women be screened for hepatitis B? Ann. Intern. Med. *107*:273–277, 1987.
290. Kumar, M. L., Gold, E., Jacobs, I. B., et al.: Primary cytomegalovirus infection in adolescent pregnancy. Pediatrics *74*:493–500, 1984.
291. Kumar, M. L., Jensen, H. B., and Dahms, B. D.: Fatal *Staphylococcal epidermidis* infections in very low-birth-weight infants with cytomegalovirus infection. Pediatrics *76*:110, 1985.
292. Kumar, M. L., Nankervis, G. A., Cooper, A. R., et al.: Postnatally acquired cytomegalovirus infections in infants of CMV-excreting mothers. J. Pediatr. *104*:669–673, 1984.
293. Kumar, M. L., Nankervis, G. A., Jacobs, I. B., et al.: Congenital and postnatally acquired cytomegalovirus infections: Long-term follow-up. J. Pediatr. *104*:674–679, 1984.
294. Kuo, G., Choo, Q.-L., Alter, H. J., et al.: An assay for circulating antibodies to a major etiologic virus of human non-A, non-B hepatitis. Science *244*:362–364, 1989.
295. Lagrew, D. C., Jr., Furlow, T. G., Harger, W. D., et al.: Disseminated herpes simplex virus infection in pregnancy: Successful treatment with acyclovir. J. A. M. A. *252*:2058–2059, 1984.
296. Lai, C.-L., Lin, H.-J., Yeoh, E.-K., et al.: Placebo-controlled trial of recombinant α_2-interferon in Chinese HBsAg-carrier children. Lancet *2*:877–880, 1987.
297. Lake, A. M., Lauer, B. A., Clark, J. C., et al.: Enterovirus infections in neonates. J. Pediatr. *89*:787–791, 1976.
298. Lakeman, F. D., and Whitley, R. J.: Collaborative Antiviral Study Group: Diagnosis of herpes simplex encephalitis: Application of polymerase chain reaction to cerebrospinal fluid from brain-biopsied patients and correlation with disease. National Institute of Allergy and Infectious Diseases. J. Infect. Dis. *171*:857–863, 1995.
299. Lam, J. P. H., McOmish, F., Burns, S. M., et al.: Infrequent vertical transmission of hepatitis C virus. J. Infect. Dis. *167*:572–576, 1993.
300. Lamberson, H. V., Jr., McMillan, J. A., Weiner, L. B., et al.: Prevention of transfusion-associated cytomegalovirus (CMV) infection in neonates by screening blood donors for IgM to CMV. J. Infect. Dis. *157*:820–823, 1988.
301. Lang, D. J., and Kummer, J. F.: Cytomegalovirus in semen: Observations in selected populations. J. Infect. Dis. *132*:472–473, 1975.
302. Lang, D. J., Kummer, J. F., and Hartley, D. P.: Cytomegalovirus in semen: Persistence and demonstration in extracellular fluids. N. Engl. J. Med. *291*:121–124, 1974.
303. Lapinleimu, K., Cantell, K., Koskimies, O., et al.: Association between maternal herpesvirus infections and congenital malformations. Lancet *1*:1127–1129, 1974.
304. Lapinleimu, K., and Hakulinen, A.: A hospital outbreak caused by echovirus type 11 among newborn infants. Ann. Clin. Res. *4*:183–187, 1972.
305. Lau, Y. L., Tam, A. Y., Ng, K. W., et al.: Response of preterm infants to hepatitis B vaccine. J. Pediatr. *121*:962–965, 1992.
306. Lee, A. K. Y., Ip, H. M. H., and Wong, V. C. W.: Mechanisms of maternal-fetal transmission of hepatitis B virus. J. Infect. Dis. *138*:668–671, 1978.
307. Lee, G. C.-Y., Hwang, L.-Y., Beasley, R. P., et al.: Immunogenicity of hepatitis B virus vaccine in healthy Chinese neonates. J. Infect. Dis. *148*:526–529, 1983.
308. Lemon, S. M.: Type A viral hepatitis: New developments in an old disease. N. Engl. J. Med. *313*:1059–1067, 1985.
309. Lemon, S. M.: Inactivated hepatitis A vaccines. J. A. M. A. *271*: 1363–1364, 1994.
310. Lentz, E. B., Dock, N. L., McMahon, C. A., et al.: Detection of antibody to cytomegalovirus-induced early antigens and comparison with four serologic assays and presence of viruria in blood donors. J. Clin. Microbiol. *26*:133–135, 1988.
311. Leung, T. F., Ng, P. C., Fok, T. F., et al.: *Pneumocystis carinii* pneumonia in an immunocompetent infant with congenital cytomegalovirus infection. Infection *28*:184–186, 2000.
312. Lewkonia, I. K., and Jackson, A. A.: Infantile herpes zoster after intrauterine exposure to varicella. B. M. J. *3*:149, 1973.
313. Light, I. J.: Postnatal acquisition of herpes simplex by the newborn infant: A review of the literature. Pediatrics *63*:480–482, 1979.
314. Lin, H.-H., Kao, J.-H., Hsu, H.-Y., et al.: Possible role of high titered maternal viremia in perinatal transmission of hepatitis C virus. J. Infect. Dis. *169*:638–641, 1994.
315. Lin, H.-H., Kao, J.-H., Hsu, H.-Y., et al.: Absence of infection in breast-fed infants born to hepatitis C virus–infected mothers. J. Pediatr. *126*:589–591, 1995.
316. Lindquist, J. M., Plotkin, S. A., Shaw, L., et al.: Congenital rubella syndrome as a systemic infection: Studies of affected infants born in Philadelphia, U. S. A. B. M. J. 2:1401–1406, 1965.
317. Linnemann, C. C., Jr., Light, I. J., Buchman, T. G., et al.: Transmission of herpes simplex virus type 1 in a nursery for the newborn identification of viral isolates by D.N.A. "fingerprinting." Lancet *1*:964–966, 1978.
318. Linnemann, C. C., Jr., Steichen, J., Sherman, W. G., et al.: Febrile illness in early infancy associated with ECHO virus infection. J. Pediatr. *84*:49–54, 1974.
319. Lo, K.-J., Tong, M. J., Chien, M.-C., et al.: The natural course of hepatitis B surface antigen–positive chronic active hepatitis in Taiwan. J. Infect. Dis. *146*:205–210, 1982.
320. Lo, K.-J., Tsai, Y.-T., Lee, S.-D., et al.: Immunoprophylaxis of infection with hepatitis B virus in infants born to hepatitis B surface antigen–positive carrier mothers. J. Infect. Dis. *152*:817–822, 1985.
321. Losonsky, G. A., Wasserman, S. S., Stephens, I., et al.: Hepatitis B vaccination of premature infants: A reassessment of current recommendations for delayed immunization. Pediatrics *103*:e14, 1999.
322. Macfarlane, D. W., Boyd, R. D., Dodrill, C. B., et al.: Intrauterine rubella, head size, and intellect. Pediatrics *55*:797–801, 1975.
323. Maggiore, G., De Giacomo, C., Marzani, D., et al.: Chronic viral hepatitis B in infancy. J. Pediatr. *103*:749–752, 1983.
324. Manzini, P., Saracco, G., Cerchier, A., et al.: Human immunodeficiency virus infection as risk factor for mother-to-child hepatitis C virus transmission: Persistence of anti-hepatitis C virus in children is associated with mother's anti–hepatitis C virus immunoblotting pattern. Hepatology *21*:328–332, 1995.
325. Marier, R., Rodriguez, W., Chloupek, R. J., et al.: Coxsackievirus B5 infection and aseptic meningitis in neonates and children. Am. J. Dis. Child. *129*:321–325, 1975.
326. McCracken, G. H., Jr., and Luby, J. P.: Cytosine arabinoside in the treatment of congenital cytomegalic inclusion disease. J. Pediatr. *80*:488–495, 1972.
327. McDonald, J. C., and Peckham, C. S.: Gammaglobulin in prevention of rubella and congenital defect: A study of 30,000 pregnancies. B. M. J. *3*:633–637, 1967.
328. McDonald, L. L., St. Geme, J. W., Jr., and Arnold, B. H.: Nosocomial infection with echovirus type 31 in a neonatal intensive care unit. Pediatrics *47*:995–999, 1971.
329. McKendrick, G. D. W., and Raychoudhury, S. C.: Herpes zoster in childhood. Scand. J. Infect. Dis. *4*:23–25, 1972.
330. McMahon, B. J., Alberts, S. R., Wainwright, R. B., et al.: Hepatitis B–related sequelae: Prospective study in 1400 hepatitis B surface antigen–positive Alaska native carriers. Arch. Intern. Med. *150*:1051–1054, 1990.
331. McMahon, B. J., Alward, W. L. M., Hall, D. B., et al.: Acute hepatitis B virus infection: Relation of age to the clinical expression of disease and subsequent development of the carrier state. J. Infect. Dis. *151*:599–603, 1985.
332. Mellinger, A. K., Cragan, J. D., Atkinson, W. L., et al.: High incidence of congenital rubella syndrome after a rubella outbreak. Pediatr. Infect. Dis. J. *14*:573–578, 1995.
333. Melnick, J. L.: Enteroviruses: Polioviruses, coxsackieviruses, echoviruses, and newer enteroviruses. *In* Fields, B. N., and Knipe, D. M. (eds.): Virology. 2nd ed. New York, Raven Press, 1990, pp. 549–605.
334. Menser, M. A., Dods, L., and Harley, J. D.: A twenty-five year follow-up of congenital rubella. Lancet *2*:1347–1350, 1967.

335. Menser, M. A., Forrest, J. M., and Bransby, R. D.: Rubella infection and diabetes mellitus. Lancet *1*:57–60, 1978.
336. Menser, M. A., and Reye, R. D. K.: The pathology of congenital rubella: A review written by request. Pathology *6*:215–222, 1974.
337. Meyers, J. D.: Congenital varicella in term infants: Risk reconsidered. J. Infect. Dis. *129*:215–217, 1974.
338. Miller, E., Cradock-Watson, J. E., and Pollock, T. M.: Consequences of confirmed maternal rubella at successive stages of pregnancy. Lancet *2*:781–784, 1982.
339. Miller, E., Cradock-Watson, J. E., and Ridehalgh, M. K. S.: Outcome in newborn babies given anti–varicella-zoster immunoglobulin after perinatal maternal infection with varicella-zoster virus. Lancet *2*: 371–373, 1989.
340. Miller, M. H., Rabinowitz, M. A., Frost, J. O., and Seager, G. M.: Audiological problems associated with maternal rubella. Laryngoscope *79*: 417–426, 1969.
341. Miller, M. J., Sunshine, P. J., and Remington, J. S.: Quantitation of cord serum IgM and IgA as a screening procedure to detect congenital infection: Results of 5006 infants. J. Pediatr. *75*:1287–1291, 1969.
342. Mims, C. A.: Pathogenesis of viral infections of the fetus. Prog. Med. Virol. *10*:194–237, 1968.
343. Mitchell, J. E., and McCall, F. C.: Transplacental infection by herpes simplex virus. Am. J. Dis. Child. *106*:207–209, 1963.
344. Modlin, J. F.: Fatal echovirus 11 disease in premature neonates. Pediatrics *66*:775–780, 1980.
345. Modlin, J. F.: Perinatal echovirus infection: Insights from a literature review of 61 cases of serious infection and 16 outbreaks in nurseries. Rev. Infect. Dis. *8*:918–926, 1986.
346. Modlin, J. F., and Crumpacker, C. S.: Coxsackievirus B infection in pregnant mice and transplacental infection of the fetus. Infect. Immunol. *37*:222, 1982.
347. Modlin, J. F., Herrmann, K., Brandling-Bennett, A. D., et al.: Risk of congenital abnormality after inadvertent rubella vaccination of pregnant women. N. Engl. J. Med. *294*:972–974, 1976.
348. Modlin, J. F., Polk, B. F., Horton, P., et al.: Perinatal echovirus infection: Risk of transmission during a community outbreak. N. Engl. J. Med. *305*:368–371, 1981.
349. Montgomery, J. R., Flanders, R. W., and Yow, M. D.: Congenital anomalies and herpesvirus infection. Am. J. Dis Child. *126*:364–366, 1973.
350. Montgomery, R., Youngblood, L., and Medearis, D. N., Jr.: Recovery of cytomegalovirus from the cervix in pregnancy. Pediatrics *49*:524–530, 1972.
351. Morens, D. M.: Enteroviral disease in early infancy. J. Pediatr. *92*:374–377, 1978.
352. Moseley, R. C., Corey, L., Benjamin, D., et al.: Comparison of viral isolation, direct immunofluorescence, and indirect immunoperoxidase techniques for detection of genital herpes simplex virus infection. J. Clin. Microbiol. *13*:913–918, 1981.
353. Mouly F., Mirlesse, V., Meritet, J. F., et al.: Prenatal diagnosis of fetal varicella-zoster virus infection with polymerase chain reaction of amniotic fluid in 107 cases. Am. J. Obstet. Gynecol. *177*:894, 1997.
354. Music, S. T., Fine, E. M., and Togo, Y.: Zoster-like disease in the newborn due to herpes-simplex virus. N. Engl. J. Med. *284*:24–26, 1971.
355. Mussi-Pinhata, M. M., Yamamoto, A. Y., Figueiredo, L. T. M., et al.: Congenital and perinatal cytomegalovirus infection in infants born to mothers infected with human immunodeficiency virus. J. Pediatr. *132*:285–290, 1998.
356. Naeye, R. L.: Cytomegalic inclusion disease: The fetal disorder. Am. J. Clin. Pathol. *47*:738–744, 1967.
357. Naeye, R. L., and Blanc, W.: Pathogenesis of congenital rubella. J. A. M. A. *194*:1277–1283, 1965.
358. Nahmias, A. J., Dowdle, W. R., Josey, W. E., et al.: Newborn infection with herpesvirus hominis types 1 and 2. J. Pediatr. *75*:1194–1203, 1969.
359. Nahmias, A. J., and Hagler, W. S.: Ocular manifestations of herpes simplex in the newborn (neonatal ocular herpes). Int. Ophthalmol. Clin. *12*:191–213, 1972.
360. Nahmias, A. J., Josey, W. E., and Naib, Z. M.: Significance of herpes simplex virus infection during pregnancy. Clin. Obstet. Gynecol. *15*:929–938, 1972.
361. Nahmias, A. J., Josey, W. E., Naib, Z. M., et al.: Perinatal risk associated with maternal genital herpes simplex virus infection. Am. J. Obstet. Gynecol. *110*:825–836, 1971.
362. Nahmias, A. J., Keyserling, H. L., and Kerrick, G. M.: Herpes simplex. *In* Remington, J. S., and Klein, J. O. (eds.): Infectious Diseases of the Fetus and Newborn Infant. 2nd ed. Philadelphia, W. B. Saunders, 1983, pp. 636–678.
363. Nankervis, G. A.: Cytomegaloviral infections: Epidemiology, therapy, and prevention. Pediatr. Rev. *7*:169–175, 1985.
364. Nankervis, G. A., Kumar, M. L., Cox, F. E., et al.: A prospective study of maternal cytomegalovirus infection and its effect on the fetus. Am. J. Obstet. Gynecol. *149*:435–440, 1984.
365. Narkiewicz, M. R., Smith, D., Silverman, A., et al.: Clearance of chronic hepatitis B virus infection in young children after alpha interferon treatment. J. Pediatr. *127*:815–818, 1995.
366. National Communicable Disease Center: Rubella Surveillance, June 1969.
367. Nelson, C. T., Istas, A. S., Wilkerson, M. K., and Demmler, G. J.: PCR detection of cytomegalovirus DNA in serum as a diagnostic test for congenital cytomegalovirus infection. J. Clin. Microbiol. *33*:3317–3318, 1995.
368. Ng, A. B. P., Reagan, J. W., and Yen, S. S. C.: Herpes genitalis. Obstet. Gynecol. *36*:645–651, 1970.
369. Nielsen, C. M., Hansen, K., Andersen, H. M. K., et al.: An enzyme labeled nuclear antigen immunoassay for detection of cytomegalovirus IgM antibodies in human serum: Specific and nonspecific reaction. J. Med. Virol. *7*:111–113, 1987.
370. Nigro, G., Krzysztofiak, A., Gattinara, G. C., et al.: Rapid progression of HIV disease in children with cytomegalovirus DNAemia. A. I. D. S. *10*:1127–1133, 1996.
371. Nigro, G., Scholz, H., and Bartmann, U.: Ganciclovir therapy for symptomatic congenital cytomegalovirus infection in infants: A two-regimen experience. J. Pediatr. *124*:318–322, 1994.
372. Novati, R., Thiers, V., Monforte, A. D., et al.: Mother-to-child transmission of hepatitis C virus detected by nested polymerase chain reaction. J. Infect. Dis. *165*:720–723, 1992.
373. Noyola, D. E., Demmler, G. J., Williamson, W. D., et al.: Cytomegalovirus urinary excretion and long term outcome in children with congenital cytomegalovirus infection. Congenital CMV Longitudinal Study Group. Pediatr. Infect. Dis. J. *19*:505–510, 2000.
374. Nusbacher, J., Hirschhorn, K., and Cooper, L. Z.: Chromosomal abnormalities in congenital rubella. N. Engl. J. Med. *276*:1409–1413, 1967.
375. Ohto, H., Terazawa, S., Sasaki, N., et al.: Transmission of hepatitis C virus from mothers to infants. N. Engl. J. Med. *330*:744–750, 1994.
376. Okada, K., Kamiyama, I., Inomata, M., et al.: e Antigen and anti-e in the serum of asymptomatic carrier mothers as indicators of positive and negative transmission of hepatitis B virus to their infants. N. Engl. J. Med. *294*:746–749, 1976.
377. Okada, K., Yamada, T., Miyakawa, Y., et al.: Hepatitis B surface antigen in the serum of infants after delivery from asymptomatic carrier mothers. J. Pediatr. *87*:360–363, 1975.
378. Olson, G. B., Dent, P. B., Rawls, W. E., et al.: Abnormalities of in vitro lymphocyte responses during rubella virus infections. J. Exp. Med. *128*:47–68, 1968.
379. Orenstein, W. A., Bart, K. J., Hinman, A. R., et al.: The opportunity and obligation to eliminate rubella from the United States. J. A. M. A. *251*:1988–1994, 1984.
380. Overall, J. C., Jr.: Intrauterine virus infections and congenital heart disease. Am. Heart J. *84*:823–833, 1972.
381. Overall, J. C., Jr.: Dermatologic viral diseases. *In* Galasso, G. J., Merigan, T. C., and Buchanan, R. A. (eds.): Antiviral Agents and Viral Diseases of Man. 2nd ed. New York, Raven Press, 1984, pp. 247–312.
382. Overall, J. C., Jr.: Genital and perinatal herpes simplex virus infections. *In* de la Maza, L. M., and Peterson, E. M. (eds.): Medical Virology. IV. Hillsdale, NJ, L. Erlbaum Associates, 1985, pp. 253–304.
383. Overall, J. C., Jr.: Empiric therapy with acyclovir for suspected neonatal herpes simplex infections. Pediatr. Infect. Dis. J. *8*:808–809, 1989.
384. Overall, J. C., Jr.: Diagnostic virology. *In* McClatchy, K. D. (ed.): Clinical Laboratory Medicine. Baltimore, Williams & Wilkins, 1994, pp. 1359–1385.
385. Overall, J. C., Jr.: Herpes simplex virus infection of the fetus and newborn. Pediatr. Ann. *23*:131–136, 1994.
386. Overall, J. C., Jr., Whitley, R. J., Yeager, A. S., et al.: Prophylactic or anticipatory antiviral therapy for newborns exposed to herpes simplex infection. Pediatr. Infect. Dis. *3*:193–195, 1984.
387. Palmer, A., L., Rotbart, H. A., Tyson, R. W., et al.: Adverse effects of maternal enterovirus infection on the fetus and placenta. J Infect. Dis. *176*:1437–1444, 1997.
388. Papaevangelou, G., and Hoofnagle, J. H.: Transmission of hepatitis B virus infection by asymptomatic chronic HBsAg carrier mothers. Pediatrics *63*:602–605, 1979.
389. Papaevangelou, G., Hoofnagle, J., and Kremastinou, J.: Transplacental transmission of hepatitis-B virus by symptom-free chronic carrier mothers. Lancet *2*:746–748, 1974.
390. Parvey, L. S., and Ch'ien, L. T.: Neonatal herpes simplex virus infection introduced by fetal-monitor scalp electrodes. Pediatrics *65*:1150–1153, 1980.
391. Paryani, S. G., and Arvin, A. M.: Intrauterine infection with varicella-zoster virus after maternal varicella. N. Engl. J. Med. *314*:1542–1546, 1986.
392. Paryani, S. G., Yeager, A. S., Hosford-Dunn, H., et al.: Sequelae of acquired cytomegalovirus infection in premature and sick term infants. J. Pediatr. *107*:451–456, 1985.
393. Pass, R. F., August, A. M., Dworsky, M., et al.: Cytomegalovirus infection in a day-care center. N. Engl. J. Med. *307*:477–479, 1982.
394. Pass, R. F., Little, E. A., Stagno, S., et al.: Young children as a probable source of maternal and congenital cytomegalovirus infection. N. Engl. J. Med. *316*:1366–1370, 1987.
395. Pass, R. F., Stagno, S., Myers, G. J., et al.: Outcome of symptomatic congenital cytomegalovirus infection: Results of long-term longitudinal follow-up. Pediatrics *66*:758–762, 1980.

396. Pastuszak, A. L., Levy, M., Schick, B., et al.: Outcome after maternal varicella infection in the first 20 weeks of pregnancy. N. Engl. J. Med. *330*:901–905, 1994.
397. Patel, D. M., Butler, J., Feldman, S., et al.: Immunogenicity of hepatitis B vaccine in healthy very low birth weight infants. J. Pediatr. *131*:641–643, 1997.
398. Peacock, J. E., Jr., and Sarubbi, F. A.: Disseminated herpes simplex virus infection during pregnancy. Obstet. Gynecol. *61*(Suppl.):13–18, 1983.
399. Perrillo, R. P., Schiff, E. R., Davis, G. L., et al.: A randomized, controlled trial of interferon alpha-2b alone and after prednisone withdrawal for the treatment of chronic hepatitis B. N. Engl. J. Med. *323*:295–301, 1990.
400. Phelan, P., and Campbell, P.: Pulmonary complications of rubella embryopathy. J. Pediatr. *75*:202–212, 1969.
401. Philip, A. G. S., and Larson, E. J.: Overwhelming neonatal infection with ECHO 19 virus. J. Pediatr. *82*:391–397, 1973.
402. Plager, H., Beebe, R., and Miller, J. K.: Coxsackie B-5 pericarditis in pregnancy. Arch. Intern. Med. *110*:735–738, 1962.
403. Plotkin, S. A., Klaus, R. M., and Whitely, J. P.: Hypogammaglobulinemia in an infant with congenital rubella syndrome: Failure of 1-adamantanamine to stop virus excretion. J. Pediatr. *69*:1085–1091, 1966.
404. Plotkin, S. A., Starr, S. E., and Bryan, C. K.: In vitro and in vivo responses of cytomegalovirus to acyclovir. Am. J. Med. *73*(Suppl. 1A): 257–261, 1982.
405. Plotkin, S. A., and Stetler, H.: Treatment of congenital cytomegalic inclusion disease with antiviral agents. Antimicrob. Agents Chemother. *9*:372–379, 1969.
406. Polish, L. B., Gallagher, M., Fields, H. A., et al.: Delta hepatitis: Molecular biology and clinical and epidemiologic features. Clin. Microbiol. Rev. *6*:211–229, 1993.
407. Poovorawan, Y., Sanpavat, S., Pongpunlert, W., et al.: Protective efficacy of a recombinant DNA hepatitis B vaccine in neonates of HBe antigen–positive mothers. J. A. M. A. *261*:3278–3281, 1989.
408. Preece, P. M., Blount, J. M., Glover, J., et al.: The consequences of primary cytomegalovirus infection in pregnancy. Arch. Dis. Child. *58*: 970–975, 1983.
409. Preece, P. M., Pearl, K. N., and Peckham, C. S.: Congenital cytomegalovirus infection. Arch. Dis. Child. *59*:1120–1126, 1984.
410. Prober, C. G., Corey, L., Brown, Z. A., et al.: The management of pregnancies complicated by genital infection with herpes simplex virus. Clin. Infect. Dis. *15*:1031–1038, 1992.
411. Prober, C. G., Gershon, A. A., Grose, C., et al.: Consensus: Varicella-zoster infections in pregnancy and the perinatal period. Pediatr. Infect. Dis. J. *9*:865–869, 1990.
412. Prober, C. G., Hensleigh, P. A., Boucher, F. D., et al.: Use of routine viral cultures at delivery to identify neonates exposed to herpes simplex virus. N. Engl. J. Med. *318*:887–891, 1988.
413. Public Health Laboratory Service Working Party on Fifth Disease: Prospective study of human parvovirus B19 infection in pregnancy. B. M. J. *300*:1166–1170, 1990.
414. Puchhammer-Stockl, E., Kunz, C., Wagner, G., and Enders, G.: Detection of varicella-zoster virus (VZV) in fetal tissue by polymerase chain reaction. J. Perinat. Med. *22*:65, 1994.
415. Purdham, D. R., Purdham, P. A., Wood, B. S. B., et al.: Severe echo 19 virus infection in a neonatal unit. Arch. Dis. Child. *51*:634–636, 1976.
416. Randolph, A. G., Washington, A. E., and Prober, C. G.: Cesarean delivery for women presenting with genital herpes lesions: Efficacy, risks, and costs. J. A. M. A. *270*:77–82, 1993.
417. Rawls, W. E., and Melnick, J. L.: Rubella virus carrier cultures derived from congenitally infected infants. J. Exp. Med. *123*:795–816, 1966.
418. Reed, E. C., Bowden, R. A., Dandliker, P. S., et al.: Treatment of cytomegalovirus pneumonia with ganciclovir and intravenous cytomegalovirus immunoglobulin in patients with bone marrow transplants. Ann. Intern. Med. *109*:783–788, 1988.
419. Reesink, H. W., Reerink-Brongers, E. E., Lafeber-Schut, B. J. T., et al.: Prevention of chronic HBsAg carrier state in infants of HBsAg-positive mothers by hepatitis B immunoglobulin. Lancet *2*:436–438, 1979.
420. Reinus, J. F., Leikin, E. L., Alter, H. J., et al.: Failure to detect vertical transmission of hepatitis C virus. Ann. Intern. Med. *117*:881–886, 1992.
421. Remington, J. S., and Klein, J. O. (eds.): Infectious Diseases of the Fetus and Newborn Infant. 5th ed. Philadelphia, W. B. Saunders, 2001.
422. Reynolds, D. W., Dean, P. H., Pass, R. F., et al.: Specific cell-mediated immunity in children with congenital and neonatal cytomegalovirus infection and their mothers. J. Infect. Dis. *140*:493–499, 1979.
423. Reynolds, D. W., Stagno, S., Hosty, T. S., et al.: Maternal cytomegalovirus excretion and perinatal infection. N. Engl. J. Med. *289*:1–5, 1973.
424. Reynolds, D. W., Stagno, S., Reynolds, R., et al.: Perinatal cytomegalovirus infection: Influence of placentally transferred maternal antibody. J. Infect. Dis. *137*:564–567, 1978.
425. Reynolds, D. W., Stagno, S., Stubbs, G., et al.: Inapparent congenital cytomegalovirus infection with elevated cord IgM levels. N. Engl. J. Med. *290*:291–296, 1974.
426. Robinson, J., Lemay, M., and Vaudry, W. L.: Congenital rubella after anticipated maternal immunity: Two cases and a review of the literature. Pediatr. Infect. Dis. J. *13*:812–815, 1994.
427. Roizman, B., and Buchman, T.: The molecular epidemiology of herpes simplex viruses. Hosp. Pract. *14*:95–104, 1979.
428. Rosendahl, C., Kochen, M. M., Kretschmer, R., et al.: Avoidance of perinatal transmission of hepatitis B virus: Is passive immunisation always necessary? Lancet *1*:1127–1129, 1983.
429. Rotbart, H. A.: Human Enterovirus Infections. Washington, D.C., ASM Press, 1995.
430. Rotbart, H. A., and Webster, A.D.: Treatment of potentially life-threatening enterovirus infections with pleconaril. Clin. Infect. Dis. *32*:228–235, 2001.
431. Roudot-Thoraval, F., Pawlotsky, J.-M., Thiers, V., et al.: Lack of mother-to-infant transmission of hepatitis C virus in human immunodeficiency virus–seronegative women: A prospective study with hepatitis C virus RNA testing. Hepatology *17*:772–777, 1993.
432. Rudolph, A. J., Singleton, E. B., Rosenberg, H. S., et al.: Osseous manifestations of the congenital rubella syndrome. Am. J. Dis. Child. *110*:428–433, 1965.
433. Saigal, S., Lunyk, O., Larke, R. P. B., et al.: The outcome in children with congenital cytomegalovirus infection: A longitudinal follow-up study. Am. J. Dis. Child. *136*:896–901, 1982.
434. Sakaoka, H., Saheki, Y., Uzuki, K., et al.: Two outbreaks of herpes simplex virus type 1 nosocomial infection among newborns. J. Clin. Microbiol. *24*:36–40, 1986.
435. Sanford, J. P.: Coxsackievirus and echovirus infections. *In* Hoeprich, P. D. (ed.): Infectious Diseases. New York, Harper & Row, 1977, pp. 1107–1117.
436. Sauerbrai, A., Muller, D., Eichhorn, U., and Wutzler, P.: Detection of varicella-zoster virus in congenital varicella syndrome: A case report. Obstet. Gynecol. *88*:687, 1996.
437. Sawyer, M. H., Holland, D., Aintablian, N., et al.: Diagnosis of enteroviral central nervous system infection by polymerase chain reaction during a large community outbreak. Pediatr. Infect. Dis. J. *13*:177–182, 1994.
438. Schauf, V., Strelkauskas, A. J., and Deveikis, A.: Alteration of lymphocyte subpopulations with cytomegalovirus infection in infancy. Clin. Exp. Immunol. *26*:478–483, 1976.
439. Schiff, G. M., Sutherland, J., and Light, I.: Congenital rubella. *In* Thalhammer, O. (ed.): Prenatal Infections. Stuttgart, Germany, Georg Thieme Verlag, 1971, pp. 31–36.
440. Schlesinger, Y., Sawyer, M. H., Storch, G. A.: Enteroviral meningitis in infancy: Potential role for polymerase chain reaction in patient management. Pediatrics *94*:157–162, 1994.
441. Schmidt, N. J., Dennis, J., Devlin, V., et al.: Comparison of direct immunofluorescence and direct immunoperoxidase procedures for detection of herpes simplex virus antigen in lesion specimens. J. Clin. Microbiol. *18*:445–448, 1983.
442. Schwebke, K., Henry, K., Balfour, H. H., Jr., et al.: Congenital cytomegalovirus infection as a result of nonprimary cytomegalovirus disease in a mother with acquired immunodeficiency syndrome. J. Pediatr. *126*:293–295, 1995.
443. Schweitzer, I. L., Dunn, A. E. G., Peters, R. L., et al.: Viral hepatitis B in neonates and infants. Am. J. Med. *55*:762–771, 1973.
444. Schweitzer, I. L., Mosley, J. W., Ashcaval, M., et al.: Factors influencing neonatal infection by hepatitis B virus. Gastroenterology *65*:277–283, 1973.
445. Scott, L. L.: Perinatal herpes: Current status and obstetric management strategies. Pediatr. Infect. Dis. J. *14*:827–832, 1995.
446. Scott, L. L., Hollier, L. M., McIntire, D., et al.: Acyclovir suppression to prevent recurrent genital herpes at delivery. Infect. Dis. Obstet. Gynecol. *10*:71–77, 2002.
447. Scott, L. L., Sánchez, P. J., Jackson, G. L., et al.: Acyclovir suppression to prevent cesarean delivery after first-episode genital herpes. Obstet. Gynecol. *87*:69–73, 1996.
448. Sells, C. J., Carpenter, R. L., and Ray, C. G.: Sequelae of central-nervous-system enterovirus infections. N. Engl. J. Med. *293*:1–4, 1975.
449. Sever, J. L., Brody, J. A., Schiff, G. M., et al.: Rubella epidemic on St. Paul Island in the Pribilofs, 1963. II. Clinical and laboratory findings for the intensive study population. J. A. M. A. *191*:624–626, 1965.
450. Sever, J. L., Huebner, R. J., Castellano, G. A., et al.: Serologic diagnosis "en masse" with multiple antigens. II. Am. Rev. Respir. Dis. *88*:342–359, 1963.
451. Sever, J. L., Nelson, K. B., and Gilkeson, M. R.: Rubella epidemic, 1964: Effect on 6000 pregnancies. I. Preliminary clinical and laboratory findings through the neonatal period: A report from the Collaborative Study on Cerebral Palsy. Am. J. Dis. Child. *110*:395–407, 1965.
452. Sever, J. L., South, M. A., and Shaver, K. A.: Delayed manifestations of congenital rubella. Rev. Infect. Dis. *7*(Suppl. 1):164–169, 1985.
453. Sever, J., and White, L. R.: Intrauterine viral infections. Annu. Rev. Med. *19*:471–486, 1968.
454. Shackelford, G. D., and Kirks, D. R.: Neonatal hepatic calcification secondary to transplacental infection. Radiology *122*:753–757, 1977.
455. Shapiro, C. N.: Epidemiology of hepatitis B. Pediatr. Infect. Dis. J. *12*:433–437, 1993.
456. Shepp, D. H., Dandliker, P. S., and Meyers, J. D.: Treatment of varicella-zoster virus infection in severely immunocompromised patients: A randomized comparison of acyclovir and vidarabine. N. Engl. J. Med. *314*:208–212, 1986.

457. Shiraki, K., Yoshihara, N., Kawana, T., et al.: Hepatitis B surface antigen and chronic hepatitis in infants born to asymptomatic carrier mothers. Am. J. Dis. Child. *131*:644–647, 1977.
458. Shiraki, K., Yoshihara, N., Sakurai, M., et al.: Acute hepatitis B in infants born to carrier mothers with the antibody to hepatitis B e antigen. J. Pediatr. *97*:768–770, 1980.
459. Shmoys, S., and Kaplan, C.: Parvovirus and pregnancy. Clin. Obstet. Gynecol. *33*:268–275, 1990.
460. Sieber, O. F., Fulginiti, V. A., Brazie, J., et al.: In utero infection of the fetus by herpes simplex virus. J. Pediatr. *69*:30–34, 1966.
461. Siegel, M.: Congenital malformations following chickenpox, measles, mumps, and hepatitis: Results of a cohort study. J. A. M. A. *226*:1521–1524, 1973.
462. Siegel, M., and Fuerst, H. T.: Low birth weight and maternal virus diseases: A prospective study of rubella, measles, mumps, chickenpox, and hepatitis. J. A. M. A. *197*:680–681, 1966.
463. Siegel, M., Fuerst, H. T., and Peress, N. S.: Comparative fetal mortality in maternal virus diseases: A prospective study on rubella, measles, mumps, chickenpox, and hepatitis. N. Engl. J. Med. *274*:768–771, 1966.
464. Sinatra, F. R., Shah, P., Weissman, J. Y., et al.: Perinatal transmitted acute icteric hepatitis B in infants born to hepatitis B surface antigen–positive and anti–hepatitis Be–positive carrier mothers. Pediatrics *70*:557–559, 1982.
465. Skinhoj, P., Sardemann, H., Cohn, J., et al.: Hepatitis-associated antigen (HAA) in pregnant women and their newborn infants. Am. J. Dis. Child. *123*:380–381, 1972.
466. Snydman, D. R.: Hepatitis in pregnancy. N. Engl. J. Med. *313*:1398–1401, 1985.
467. South, M. A., Tompkins, W. A. F., Morris, C. R., et al.: Congenital malformation of the central nervous system associated with genital type (type 2) herpesvirus. J. Pediatr. *75*:13–18, 1969.
468. Spector, S. A.: Transmission of cytomegalovirus among infants in hospital documented by restriction-endonuclease-digestion analyses. Lancet *1*:378–381, 1983.
469. Spruance, S. L., Overall, J. C., Jr., Kern, E. R., et al.: The natural history of recurrent herpes simplex labialis: Implications for antiviral therapy. N. Engl. J. Med. *297*:69–75, 1977.
470. St. Geme, J. W., Jr., Noren, G. R., and Adams, P., Jr.: Proposed embryopathic relation between mumps virus and primary endocardial fibroelastosis. N. Engl. J. Med. *275*:339–346, 1966.
471. Stagno, S.: Cytomegalovirus. *In* Remington, J. S., and Klein, J. O. (eds.): Infectious Diseases of the Fetus and Newborn Infant. 5th ed. Philadelphia, W. B. Saunders, 2001, pp. 389–424.
472a. Stagno, S., Brasfield, D. M., Brown, M., C., et al.: Infant pneumonitis associated with cytomegalovirus, *Chlamydia, Pneumocystis* and *Ureaplasma*—a prospective study. Pediatics *68*:322–329, 1981.
473. Stagno, S., Pass, R. F., Cloud, G., et al.: Primary cytomegalovirus infection in pregnancy: Incidence, transmission to fetus, and clinical outcome. J. A. M. A. *256*:1904–1908, 1986.
474. Stagno, S., Pass, R. F., Dworsky, M. E., et al.: Congenital and perinatal cytomegalovirus infections. Semin. Perinatol. 7:31–42, 1983.
475. Stagno, S., Pass, R. F., Dworsky, M. E., et al.: Congenital cytomegalovirus infection: The relative importance of primary and recurrent maternal infection. N. Engl. J. Med. *306*:945–949, 1982.
476. Stagno, S., Pass, R. F., Thomas, J. P., et al.: Defects of tooth structure in congenital cytomegalovirus infection. Pediatrics *69*:646–648, 1982.
477. Stagno, S., Reynolds, D. W., Amos, C. S., et al.: Auditory and visual defects resulting from symptomatic and subclinical congenital cytomegalovirus and *Toxoplasma* infections. Pediatrics *59*:669–678, 1977.
478. Stagno, S., Reynolds, D. W., Huang, E.-S., et al.: Congenital cytomegalovirus infection: Occurrence in an immune population. N. Engl. J. Med. *296*:1254–1258, 1977.
478. Stagno, S., Reynolds, D. W., Lakeman, A., et al.: Congenital cytomegalovirus infection: Consecutive occurrence due to viruses with similar antigenic compositions. Pediatrics *52*:788–794, 1973.
480. Stagno, S., Reynolds, D. W., Pass, R. F., et al.: Breast milk and the risk of cytomegalovirus infection. N. Engl. J. Med. *302*:1073–1076, 1980.
481. Stagno, S., Reynolds, D., Tsiantos, A., et al.: Cervical cytomegalovirus excretion in pregnant and nonpregnant women: Suppression in early gestation. J. Infect. Dis. *131*:522–527, 1975.
482. Stagno, S., Reynolds, D. W., Tsiantos, A., et al.: Comparative serial virologic and serologic studies of symptomatic and subclinical congenitally and natally acquired cytomegalovirus infections. J. Infect. Dis. *132*:568–577, 1975.
483. Stagno, S., Tinker, M. K., Elrod, C., et al.: Immunoglobulin M antibodies detected by enzyme-linked immunosorbent assay and radioimmunoassay in the diagnosis of cytomegalovirus infections in pregnant women and newborn infants. J. Clin. Microbiol. *21*:930–935, 1985.
484. Stagno, S., Volanakis, J. E., Reynolds, D. W., et al.: Immune complexes in congenital and natal cytomegalovirus infections of man. J. Clin. Invest. *60*:838–845, 1977.
485. Stanberry, L. R., Floyd-Reising, S. A., Connelly, B. L., et al.: Herpes simplex viremia: Report of eight pediatric cases and review of the literature. Clin. Infect. Dis. *18*:401–407, 1994.
486. Starr, J. G.: Cytomegalovirus infection in pregnancy. N. Engl. J. Med. *282*:50–51, 1970.
487. Starr, S. E., Tolpin, M. D., Friedman, H. M., et al.: Impaired cellular immunity to cytomegalovirus in congenitally infected children and their mothers. J. Infect. Dis. *140*:500–505, 1979.
488. Stevens, C. E.: In utero and perinatal transmission of hepatitis viruses. Pediatr. Ann. *23*:152–158, 1994.
489. Stevens, C. E., Beasley, R. P., Tsui, J., et al.: Vertical transmission of hepatitis B antigen in Taiwan. N. Engl. J. Med. *292*:771–774, 1975.
490. Stevens, C. E., Taylor, P. E., Tong, M. J., et al.: Yeast-recombinant hepatitis B vaccine: Efficacy with hepatitis B immune globulin in prevention of perinatal hepatitis B transmission. J. A. M. A. *257*:2612–2616, 1989.
491. Stevens, C. E., Toy, P. T., Taylor, P. E., et al.: Prospects for control of hepatitis B virus infection: Implications of childhood vaccination and long-term protection. Pediatrics *90*:170–173, 1992.
492. Stevens, C. E., Toy, P. T., Tong, M. J., et al.: Perinatal hepatitis B virus transmission in the United States: Prevention by passive-active immunization. J. A. M. A. *253*:1740–1745, 1985.
493. Stewart, G. L., Parkman, P. D., Hopps, H. E., et al.: Rubella-virus hemagglutination-inhibition test. N. Engl. J. Med. *276*:554–557, 1967.
494. Strauss, L., and Bernstein, J.: Neonatal hepatitis in congenital rubella. Arch. Pathol. *86*:317–327, 1968.
495. Strawn, E. Y., and Scrimenti, R. J.: Intrauterine herpes simplex infection. Am. J. Obstet. Gynecol. *115*:581–582, 1973.
496. Sullivan-Bolyai, J. Z., Fife, K. H., Jacobs, R. F., et al.: Disseminated neonatal herpes simplex virus type 1 from a maternal breast lesion. Pediatrics *71*:455–457, 1983.
497. Sullivan-Bolyai, J. Z., Hull, H. F., Wilson, C., et al.: Neonatal herpes simplex virus infection in King County, Washington: Increasing incidence and epidemiologic correlates. J. A. M. A. *250*:3059–3062, 1983.
498. Swender, P. T., Shott, R. J., and Williams, M. L.: A community and intensive care nursery outbreak of coxsackievirus B5 meningitis. Am. J. Dis. Child. *127*:42–45, 1974.
499. Szmuness, W., Harley, E. J., and Prince, A. M.: Intrafamilial spread of asymptomatic hepatitis B. Am. J. Med. Sci. *270*:292–304, 1975.
500. Tardieu, M., Grospierre, B., Durandy, A., et al.: Circulating immune complexes containing rubella antigens in late-onset rubella syndrome. J. Pediatr. *97*:370–373, 1980.
501. Taylor, B. J., Jacobs, R. F., Baker, R. L., et al.: Frozen deglycerolyzed blood prevents transfusion-acquired cytomegalovirus infections in neonates. Pediatr. Infect. Dis. *5*:188–191, 1986.
502. Tejani, N., Klein, S. W., and Kaplan, M.: Subclinical herpes simplex genitalis infections in the perinatal period. Am. J. Obstet. Gynecol. *135*:547, 1979.
503. Thaler, M. M., Park, C.-K., Landers, D. V., et al.: Vertical transmission of hepatitis C virus. Lancet *338*:17–18, 1991.
504. Ticehurst, J.: Hepatitis E virus. *In* Murray, P. R., Baron, E. J., Pfaller, M. A., et al. (eds.): Manual of Clinical Microbiology. 6th ed. Washington, D.C., ASM Press, 1995, pp. 1056–1067.
505. Tondury, G., and Smith, D. W.: Fetal rubella pathology. J. Pediatr. *68*:867–879, 1966.
506. Tong, M. J., and Govindarajan, S.: Primary hepatocellular carcinoma following perinatal transmission of hepatitis B. West. J. Med. *148*:205–208, 1988.
507. Tong, M. J., Thursby, M. W., Lin, J.-H., et al.: Studies on the maternal-infant transmission of the hepatitis B virus and HBV infection within families. Prog. Med. Virol. *27*:137–147, 1981.
508. Torok, T. J.: Human parvovirus B19 infections in pregnancy. Pediatr. Infect. Dis. J. *9*:772–776, 1990.
509. Torok, T. J., Wang, Q.-Y., Gary, G. W., Jr., et al.: Prenatal diagnosis of intrauterine infection with parvovirus B19 by the polymerase chain reaction technique. J. Infect. Dis. *14*:149–155, 1992.
510. Torphy, D. E., Ray, C. G., McAlister, R., et al.: Herpes simplex virus infection in infants: A spectrum of disease. J. Pediatr. *76*:405–408, 1970.
511. Townsend, J. J., Baringer, J. R., Wolinsky, J. S., et al.: Progressive rubella panencephalitis: Late onset after congenital rubella. N. Engl. J. Med. *292*:990–993, 1975.
512. Troendle-Atkins, J., Demmler, G. J., Williamson, W. D., et al.: Polymerase chain reaction to detect cytomegalovirus DNA in the cerebrospinal fluid of neonates with congenital infection. J. Infect. Dis. *169*:1334–1377, 1994.
513. Ueda, K., Nishida, Y., Oshima, K., et al.: Congenital rubella syndrome: Correlation of gestational age at time of maternal rubella with type of defect. J. Pediatr. *94*:763–765, 1979.
514. Vajro, P., Hadchouel, P., Hadchouel, M., et al.: Incidence of cirrhosis in children with chronic hepatitis. J. Pediatr. *117*:392–396, 1990.
515. Vallejo, J. G., Englund, J. A., Garcia-Prats, J. A., et al.: Ganciclovir treatment of steroid-associated cytomegalovirus disease in a congenitally-infected neonate. Pediatr. Infect. Dis. J. *13*:239–241, 1994.
516. Valeur-Jensen, A., Pedersen, C. B., Westergaard, T., et al.: Risk factors for parvovirus B19 infection in pregnancy. J. A. M. A. *281*:1099–1105, 1999.
517. Van der Poel, C. L., Cuypers, H. T., and Reesink, H. W.: Hepatitis C virus 6 years on. Lancet *344*:1475–1479, 1994.

518. Van Dyke, R. B., and Spector, S.: Transmission of herpes simplex virus type 1 to a newborn infant during endotracheal suctioning for meconium aspiration. Pediatr. Infect. Dis. *3*:153–156, 1984.
519. Velazquez, O., Stetler, H. C., Avila, C., et al.: Epidemic transmission of enterically transmitted non-A, non-B hepatitis in Mexico, 1986–1987. J. A. M. A. *263*:3281–3285, 1990.
520. Verano, L., and Michalski, F. J.: Herpes simplex virus antigen direct detection in standard virus transport medium by DuPont Herpchek enzyme-linked immunosorbent assay. J. Clin. Microbiol. *28*:2555–2558, 1990.
521. Vochem, M., Hamprecht, K., Jahn, G., and Speer, C. P.: Transmission of cytomegalovirus to preterm infants through breast milk. Pediatr. Infect. Dis. J. *17*:53–58, 1998.
522. Vontver, L. A., Hickok, D. E., Brown, Z., et al.: Recurrent genital herpes simplex virus infection in pregnancy: Infant outcome and frequency of asymptomatic recurrences. Am. J. Obstet. Gynecol. *143*:75–84, 1982.
523. Vyse, A. J., and Jin, L.: An RT-PCR assay using oral fluid samples to detect rubella virus genome for epidemiological surveillance. Mol. Cell. Probes *16*:93–97, 2002.
524. Waner, J. L., Weller, T. H., and Kevy, S. V.: Patterns of cytomegaloviral complement-fixing antibody activity: A longitudinal study of blood donors. J. Infect. Dis. *127*:538–543, 1973.
525. Wattre, P., Deilde, A., Subtil, D., et al.: A clinical and epidemiological study of human parvovirus B19 infection in fetal hydrops using PCR Southern blot hybridization and chemiluminescence detection. J. Med. Virol. *54*:140–144, 1998.
526. Weibel, R. E., Stokes, J., Jr., Buynak, E. B., et al.: Rubella vaccination in adult females. N. Engl. J. Med. *280*:682–685, 1969.
527. Weil, M. L., Itabashi, H. H., Cremer, N. E., et al.: Chronic progressive panencephalitis due to rubella virus simulating subacute sclerosing panencephalitis. N. Engl. J. Med. *292*:994–998, 1975.
528. Weinstock, H. S., Bolan, G., Reingold, A. L., et al.: Hepatitis C virus infection among patients attending a clinic for sexually transmitted diseases. J. A. M. A. *269*:392–394, 1993.
529. Wejstal, R., Widell, A., Mansson, A.-S., et al.: Mother-to-infant transmission of hepatitis C virus. Ann. Intern. Med. *117*:887–890, 1992.
530. Wenner, H. A.: Viral meningitis. *In* Hoeprich, P. D. (ed.): Infectious Diseases. New York, Harper & Row, 1977, pp. 881–888.
531. Whitley, R. J.: Herpes simplex viruses. *In* Fields, B. N., and Knipe, D. M. (eds.): Virology. 2nd ed. New York, Raven Press, 1990, pp. 1843–1887.
532. Whitley, R. J., and Arvin, A. M.: Herpes simplex virus infections. *In* Remington, J. S., and Klein, J. O. (eds.): Infectious Diseases of the Fetus and Newborn Infant. 4th ed. Philadelphia, W. B. Saunders, 1995, pp. 354–376.
533. Whitley, R., Arvin, A., Prober, C., et al.: A controlled trial comparing vidarabine with acyclovir in neonatal herpes simplex virus infection. N. Engl. J. Med. *324*:444–449, 1991.
534. Whitley, R., Arvin, A., Prober, C., et al.: Predictors of morbidity and mortality in neonates with herpes simplex virus infections. N. Engl. J. Med. *324*:450–454, 1991.
535. Whitley, R. J., Brasfield, D., Reynolds, D. W., et al.: Protracted pneumonitis in young infants associated with perinatally acquired cytomegaloviral infection. J. Pediatr. *89*:16–22, 1976.
536. Whitley, R. J., Cloud, G., Gruber, W., et al.: Ganciclovir treatment of symptomatic congenital cytomegalovirus infection: Results of a phase II study. J. Infect. Dis. *175*:1080–1086, 1997.
537. Whitley, R. J., Corey, L., Arvin, A., et al.: Changing presentation of herpes simplex virus infection in neonates. J. Infect. Dis. *158*:109–116, 1988.
538. Whitley, R. J., and Hutto, C.: Neonatal herpes simplex virus infections. Pediatr. Rev. *7*:119–126, 1985.
539. Whitley, R. J., Nahmias, A. J., Visintine, A. M., et al.: The natural history of herpes simplex virus infection of mother and newborn. Pediatrics *66*:489–494, 1980.
540. Whitley, R. J., Yeager, A., Kartus, P., et al.: Neonatal herpes simplex virus infection: Follow-up evaluation of vidarabine therapy. Pediatrics *72*:778–785, 1983.
541. Wilfert, C. M., Thompson, R. J., Sunder, T. R., et al.: Longitudinal assessment of children with enteroviral meningitis during the first three months of life. Pediatrics *67*:811–815, 1981.
542. Williamson, W. D., Demmler, G. J., Percy, A. K., et al.: Progressive hearing loss in infants with asymptomatic congenital cytomegalovirus infection. Pediatrics *90*:862–865, 1992.
543. Williamson, W. D., Desmond, M. M., LaFevers, N., et al.: Symptomatic congenital cytomegalovirus: Disorders of language, learning, and hearing. Am. J. Dis. Child. *136*:896–901, 1982.
544. Willmott, F. E., and Mair, H. J.: Genital herpesvirus infection in women attending a venereal diseases clinic. Br. J. Vener. Dis. *54*:341–343, 1978.
545. Witte, J. J., Karchmer, A. W., Herrmann, K. L., et al.: Epidemiology of rubella. Am. J. Dis. Child. *118*:107–111, 1969.
546. Wittek, A. E., Yeager, A. S., Au, D. S., et al.: Asymptomatic shedding of herpes simplex virus from the cervix and lesion site during pregnancy: Correlation of antepartum shedding with shedding at delivery. Am. J. Dis. Child. *138*:439–442, 1984.
547. Woernle, C. H., Anderson, L. J., Tattersall, P., et al.: Human parvovirus B19 infection during pregnancy. J. Infect. Dis. *156*:17–20, 1987.
548. Wong, S. N., Tam, A. Y. C., Ng, T. H. K., et al.: Fatal Coxsackie B1 virus infection in neonates. Pediatr. Infect. Dis. J. *8*:638–641, 1989.
549. Wong, V. C. W., Ip, H. M. H., Reesink, H. W., et al.: Prevention of the HBsAg carrier state in newborn infants of mothers who are chronic carriers of HBsAg and HBeAg by administration of hepatitis-B vaccine and hepatitis-B immunoglobulin. Lancet *1*:921–926, 1984.
550. Wong, V. C. W., Lee, A. K. Y., and Ip, H. M. H.: Transmission of hepatitis B antigens from symptom free carrier mothers to the fetus and the infant. Br. J. Obstet. Gynaecol. *87*:958–965, 1980.
551. Woo, D., Cummins, M., Davies, P. A., et al.: Vertical transmission of hepatitis B surface antigen in carrier mothers in two west London hospitals. Arch. Dis. Child. *54*:670–675, 1979.
552. Wright, R., Johnson, D., Neumann, M., et al.: Congenital lymphocytic choriomeningitis virus syndrome: A disease that mimics congenital toxoplasmosis and cytomegalovirus infection. Pediatrics *100*:e9–e14, 1997.
553. Wright, R., Perkins, J. R., Bower, B. D., et al.: Cirrhosis associated with the Australia antigen in an infant who acquired hepatitis from her mother. B. M. J. *4*:719–721, 1970.
554. Yeager, A. S.: Transfusion-acquired cytomegalovirus infection in newborn infants. Am. J. Dis. Child. *128*:478–483, 1974.
555. Yeager, A. S.: Longitudinal, serological study of cytomegalovirus infections in nurses and in personnel without patient contact. J. Clin. Microbiol. *2*:448–452, 1975.
556. Yeager, A. S.: Storage and transport of cultures for herpes simplex virus type 2. Am. J. Clin. Pathol. *72*:977–979, 1979.
557. Yeager, A. S., and Arvin, A. M.: Reasons for the absence of a history of recurrent genital infections in mothers of neonates infected with herpes simplex virus. Pediatrics *73*:188–193, 1984.
558. Yeager, A. S., Arvin, A. M., Urbani, L. J., et al.: Relationship of antibody to outcome in neonatal herpes simplex virus infections. Infect. Immun. *29*:532–538, 1980.
559. Yeager, A. S., Grumet, F. C., Hafleigh, E. B., et al.: Prevention of transfusion-acquired cytomegalovirus infections in newborn infants. J. Pediatr. *98*:281–287, 1981.
560. Yeager, A. S., Palumbo, P. E., Malachowski, N., et al.: Sequelae of maternally derived cytomegalovirus infections in premature infants. J. Pediatr. *102*:918–922, 1983.
561. Yow, M. D., White, N. H., Taber, L. H., et al.: Acquisition of cytomegalovirus infection from birth to 10 years: A longitudinal serologic study. J. Pediatr. *110*:37–42, 1987.
562. Zachoval, R., Jilg, W., Lorbeer, B., et al.: Passive/active immunization against hepatitis B. J. Infect. Dis. *150*:112–117, 1984.
563. Zanetti, A. R., Tanzi, E., Paccagnini, S., et al.: Mother-to-infant transmission of hepatitis C virus. Lancet *345*:289–291, 1995.
564. Zeldis, J. B., and Crumpacker, C. S.: Hepatitis. *In* Remington, J. S., and Klein, J. O. (eds.): Infectious Diseases of the Fetus and Newborn Infant. 4th ed. Philadelphia, W. B. Saunders, 1995, pp. 805–834.
565. Ziring, P. R., Gallo, G., Finegold, M., et al.: Chronic lymphocytic thyroiditis: Identification of rubella virus antigen in the thyroid of a child with congenital rubella. J. Pediatr. *90*:419–420, 1977.

CHAPTER **73B**

Chlamydia trachomatis Infection

PABLO J. SÁNCHEZ

Chlamydiae are obligate intracellular bacterial parasites that depend on the host cell for high-energy compounds such as adenosine triphosphate. Of the three species, *Chlamydia psittaci, Chlamydia pneumoniae,* and *Chlamydia trachomatis,* only the last is a genital pathogen associated with neonatal infection.[48] *C. trachomatis* has 14 serotypes that are divided into two groups: oculogenital serovars A to K and lymphogranuloma serovars L-1 to L-3. The oculogenital serovars are divided further into trachoma serovars A to C, which cause hyperendemic blinding trachoma in the Far East, and genital serovars D to K, which result in genital and neonatal infections.

C. trachomatis is the most common sexually transmitted pathogen in the United States.[11, 23, 47, 56, 67] The rate of cervical infection with *C. trachomatis* during pregnancy varies from 1 to 37 percent, with the highest rates occurring in young, unmarried, nonwhite women of lower socioeconomic status.[23] Characteristically, genital chlamydial infection in women results in mucopurulent cervicitis,[11] although infection often is asymptomatic. Chlamydial infection also has been associated with pelvic inflammatory disease, ectopic pregnancy, and tubal infertility.[12] Pregnant women with cervical chlamydial infection who have IgM antibody against *C. trachomatis* may be at increased risk for having premature rupture of amniotic membranes and delivery of low-birth-weight infants.[21, 30]

Transmission

Transmission of *C. trachomatis* from an infected mother to her newborn can result in neonatal inclusion conjunctivitis, as well as respiratory tract disease, including pneumonia.[23, 48] Chlamydial infection of the newborn occurs most often intrapartum during vaginal delivery by passage through an infected cervix. After delivery by an infected mother, 53 percent of infants born vaginally and 19 percent of infants delivered by cesarean section are colonized.[7] Neonatal infection after delivery by cesarean section reflects an ascending route of infection. It usually occurs after prolonged rupture of fetal membranes, but neonatal infection has been described in infants delivered by cesarean section with intact membranes at delivery.[22, 35, 57] Transplacental transmission probably does not occur because *C. trachomatis* is not associated with the abnormalities present at birth that are characteristic of other congenital infections and because IgM antibody directed against *C. trachomatis* has not been detected in umbilical cord blood.

Schachter and associates[51] reported that IgM antibody develops in approximately two thirds of infants delivered vaginally by mothers infected with *C. trachomatis* or that infants exhibit a persistence or rise in IgG antibodies to *C. trachomatis* beyond 9 to 12 months of age. Approximately 25 to 50 percent of exposed infants are colonized in the conjunctivae, 25 to 50 percent in the nasopharynx or throat, 10 to 20 percent in the vagina, and 20 percent in the rectum.[48, 50, 52] Initial colonization with *C. trachomatis* occurs in the conjunctiva and pharynx, and the rectum and vagina usually become colonized in the second through sixth months of life. Colonization at these sites may persist for as long as 28 months.[8] Of exposed infants, conjunctivitis develops in 25 to 50 percent and pneumonia in 5 to 20 percent.[24]

Nosocomial transmission has not been reported.

Clinical Manifestations

Many infected infants have no clinical signs or symptoms suggestive of chlamydial infection.[52] The most common clinical manifestations are conjunctivitis and pneumonia.

CONJUNCTIVITIS

C. trachomatis is the most common cause of ophthalmia neonatorum in developed countries, where it causes 6 to 74 percent (mean, 29%) of cases of neonatal conjunctivitis.[15, 18, 20, 45] Its onset usually occurs 5 to 14 days after birth. Conjunctivitis is a rare occurrence on the first day of life but can occur after prolonged rupture of fetal membranes.

Clinical illness varies from a mild mucoid or watery eye discharge without significant conjunctival erythema to profuse, purulent bilateral discharge with severe chemosis and red, friable conjunctivae. In the most severe cases, the clinical findings are indistinguishable from those associated with *Neisseria gonorrhoeae* infection. Pseudomembranes may occur as inflammatory exudate adheres to the inflamed surface of the conjunctiva. Subconjunctival lymphoid hypertrophy and follicular conjunctivitis rarely occur in the neonatal period because most newborns lack lymphoid follicles. Approximately 19 to 83 percent of infants with conjunctivitis have nasopharyngeal carriage of *C. trachomatis* when first examined.

Untreated chlamydial conjunctivitis usually resolves spontaneously after several weeks to months, although ocular carriage of the organism may persist for as long as 2.5 years.[8] Persistent conjunctivitis can occur and may result in mild conjunctival scars with punctate keratitis and micropannus.[41] Normal visual acuity is preserved in most cases.

PNEUMONIA

In 1977, *C. trachomatis* was recovered from lung biopsy specimens, thus proving its ability to infect and cause pneumonia.[19] The organism is thought to gain access to the lower respiratory tract possibly by drainage of infected conjunctival secretions or direct inoculation of the nasopharynx or airway during birth. No evidence supports the possibility of bloodstream invasion.

C. trachomatis accounts for 15 to 73 percent of cases of afebrile pneumonia in infants between 2 and 19 weeks of age, but it usually occurs between 3 and 11 weeks.[1, 3, 31, 53, 63] The child has a history of conjunctivitis (80%) or mucoid rhinorrhea or nasal congestion (80%), followed by gradually worsening tachypnea and a characteristic staccato cough.[3, 31, 63] Most infants are afebrile or have only mild temperature elevation. On occasion, apnea may be present in the absence of other signs of respiratory involvement, or it may develop during the course of the pneumonia.[10, 17] Auscultation of the chest reveals diffuse rales, but only 16 percent of infants have expiratory wheezes. On chest roentgenogram, hyperexpansion and diffuse bilateral interstitial infiltrates are present; lobar consolidation and pleural effusion are unusual findings but have been reported.[61] Blood gas values may show mild hypoxia, but carbon dioxide retention seldom occurs. Approximately one half of infected infants will have middle ear abnormalities, with *C. trachomatis* isolated from some middle ear aspirates.[27] The total leukocyte count generally is normal, but 50 to 70 percent of infants have eosinophil counts greater than 300/mm^3. Serum levels of IgM, IgG, and IgA usually are elevated. Untreated infants gradually improve after 24 to 61 days, with an average of 43 days.

Chlamydial pneumonia in premature infants may be severe, require mechanical ventilatory support, and result in chronic lung disease.[2, 38, 60] An increased risk for long-term pulmonary sequelae, such as reactive airway disease, chronic cough, and abnormal pulmonary function tests, has been noted in children who require hospitalization for chlamydial pneumonia in early infancy.[68]

OTHER

Chlamydia is an uncommon cause of myocarditis[43] and otitis media.[27] Isolation of *Chlamydia* from the nasopharynx has been associated with rhinitis, nasopharyngitis, and nasal congestion without rhinorrhea that last for weeks or months.[48, 58] The clinical significance of vaginal and rectal colonization with *C. trachomatis* in infancy remains unknown.

Diagnosis

The diagnosis of chlamydial infection is confirmed by inoculation of McCoy cells in tissue culture with conjunctival scrapings, nasopharyngeal secretions, pleural fluid, or lung tissue and subsequent demonstration of the characteristic intracytoplasmic inclusions by immunofluorescence microscopy. Although tissue culture is the gold standard for diagnosis of chlamydial infection and is particularly useful for the diagnosis of pneumonia, rapid detection tests for chlamydial antigen are available for accurate diagnosis of conjunctivitis.[9, 44]

Polymerase chain reaction (PCR) and ligase chain reaction have been developed for the diagnosis of chlamydial infection in infants[29, 34, 62] and adults.[14, 36, 40, 54, 59] These tests amplify a region of a plasmid that is present in virtually all strains of *C. trachomatis* and a region of the genome coding for a chlamydial outer-membrane protein. They have yielded excellent sensitivity and specificity on infant conjunctival and nasopharyngeal samples and adult urine and cervical specimens. The hope is that these tests will provide a convenient method for screening high-risk populations and help identify women with chlamydial infection so that they receive treatment before delivery. Performance of these tests within 3 weeks after completion of appropriate therapy is not recommended because positive results could be caused by continued excretion of dead organisms.[14]

CONJUNCTIVITIS

Chlamydial conjunctivitis is diagnosed by sampling the inflamed lower conjunctiva and not the purulent drainage because the organism resides within the epithelial cells of the conjunctiva. Gram stain examination of the ocular discharge reveals both polymorphonuclear leukocytes and mononuclear cells. Giemsa staining of a conjunctival scraping that contains a large number of epithelial cells detects chlamydial inclusions in the cytoplasm of the epithelial cells in approximately 40 percent of cases. A monoclonal antibody directed against chlamydial elementary bodies in a direct immunofluorescent stain of conjunctival scraping has shown a sensitivity and specificity of 100 percent.[5, 48] A second method is an enzyme-linked immunoassay that offers the advantage of semi-automation and has demonstrated a sensitivity and specificity of 93 and 97 percent, respectively, in examination of conjunctival smears.[28] Because of their ease of performance and their general availability in most clinical laboratories, these rapid tests have become the preferred methods for diagnosing chlamydial conjunctivitis. Recently, PCR of ocular specimens from infants with conjunctivitis has shown a sensitivity and specificity of 92 and 100 percent, respectively.[29]

A microimmunofluorescence test for detection of both IgG and IgM antibodies is available.[42, 49, 65, 69] However, serologic evaluation is not useful in the diagnosis of chlamydial conjunctivitis because specific IgM antibodies do not develop in most infants and their antichlamydial IgG is of maternal origin.

PNEUMONIA

The diagnosis of pneumonia often is made on the basis of a typical clinical syndrome, although an attempt should be made in all cases to establish the infection either by tissue culture or rapid tests or by serology. Confirmation will allow identification of an infected mother and sexual partner and lead to treatment before complications occur.[56]

Rapid antigen testing of nasopharyngeal specimens for the diagnosis of pneumonia often is not helpful; direct antigen-detection assays have a sensitivity of 85 percent and specificity of 75 percent.[42, 48] The best approach is to perform tissue culture on available clinical specimens (e.g., nasopharyngeal and endotracheal secretions, lung tissue, pleural fluid) for optimal recovery of the organism. PCR ultimately may prove to be the most useful rapid test for diagnosing chlamydial pneumonia. Hammerschlag and colleagues[29] showed that PCR of nasopharyngeal specimens from 75 infants with conjunctivitis compared favorably with culture for detection of chlamydial infection; the sensitivity and specificity were 100 and 97 percent, respectively.

Schachter and Grossman[48] reported that infants with chlamydial pneumonia have a specific IgM antibody response as detected by microimmunofluorescence technique, with a titer greater than 1:64 being diagnostic of chlamydial pneumonia. They reported a sensitivity and specificity of 100 percent with the use of this test.[49] Its general lack of availability has limited the usefulness of this test in clinical practice, however.

Treatment

The recommended treatment of both chlamydial conjunctivitis and pneumonia is a 14-day course of either erythromycin base or ethylsuccinate (50 mg/kg body weight per day in four divided doses) administered orally.[4, 14] The advantage of orally administered erythromycin for the treatment of chlamydial conjunctivitis is eradication of *C. trachomatis* from the nasopharynx in infants. Moreover, a shorter clinical course with lower relapse rates has been reported after oral therapy for conjunctivitis. Topical therapy alone has been associated with a failure rate of greater than 50 percent. Topical therapy in addition to oral erythromycin is not necessary because therapeutic levels of the drug are achieved in tears after oral administration. The efficacy of oral erythromycin therapy for conjunctivitis and pneumonia has been estimated at 80 percent, so a second course may be necessary. Oral erythromycin has been associated with hypertrophic pyloric stenosis in infants younger than 6 weeks of age.[13, 32, 36, 37, 46, 47] Alternative regimens include sulfisoxazole (150 mg/kg/day) and clarithromycin, which at a dosage of 7.5 mg/kg every 12 hours for 21 days showed an efficacy of 95 percent for conjunctival and nasopharyngeal chlamydial infection. Hammerschlag and colleagues[26] administered azithromycin (20 mg/kg once daily for 3 days) to eight infants with chlamydial conjunctivitis and reported a clinical and culture cure rate of 86 percent in seven evaluable infants. When azithromycin was administered as a single dose to five infants with chlamydial conjunctivitis, two infants remained mildly symptomatic and culture-positive 2 weeks after therapy. These investigators attributed the treatment failures to the infants not receiving the full dose of drug. The optimal dosage and duration of azithromycin therapy for chlamydial conjunctivitis and pneumonia remain to be determined.

Treatment of the mother and her sexual partner with azithromycin (1 g orally in a single dose) or doxycycline (100 mg twice a day for 7 days) is recommended at the time of diagnosis of the infant's infection.[14, 39]

Prevention

Current ophthalmic prophylaxis at birth does not prevent the acquisition of chlamydial conjunctivitis reliably, and it does not eliminate nasopharyngeal carriage and prevent the development of pneumonia.[6, 16, 25, 70] Hammerschlag and associates[25] reported that ophthalmic prophylaxis at birth with 1 percent silver nitrate, 0.5 percent erythromycin ointment, or 1 percent tetracycline ointment resulted in a 20, 14, and 11 percent incidence, respectively, of chlamydial eye infection in 230 infants born to *Chlamydia*-infected mothers. Infants born to mothers known to have untreated chlamydial infection should be monitored closely for the development of signs and symptoms suggestive of chlamydial infection; prophylactic antibiotic therapy is not indicated because its efficacy is unknown.[14] Standard precautions are recommended for infants with chlamydial infection.

Identification as well as treatment of pregnant women infected with *C. trachomatis* and their sexual partners is thought to be the most efficacious method of preventing infection and disease in neonates.[33, 55, 64, 66] The Centers for Disease Control and Prevention recommends that a test for *C. trachomatis* be performed at the first prenatal visit.[14] High-risk women (younger than 25 years, new or multiple sexual partners) should be retested during the third trimester. In women infected with *N. gonorrhoeae,* presumptive therapy for chlamydial infection also should be provided because as many as 50 percent of such individuals will have concomitant infection with *C. trachomatis.*[14]

REFERENCES

1. Arth, C., Von Schmidt, B., Grossman, M., et al.: Chlamydial pneumonitis. J. Pediatr. *93*:447, 1978.
2. Attenburrow, A. A., and Barker, C. M.: Chlamydial pneumonia in the low-birthweight neonate. Arch. Dis. Child. *60*:1169, 1985.
3. Beem, M. O., and Saxon, E. M.: Respiratory tract colonization and a distinctive pneumonia syndrome in infants infected with *Chlamydia trachomatis*. N. Engl. J. Med. *296*:306, 1977.
4. Beem, M. O., Saxon, E. M., and Tipple, M.: Treatment of chlamydial pneumonia in infancy. Pediatrics *63*:198, 1979.
5. Bell, T. A., Kuo, C. C., Stamm, W. E., et al.: Direct fluorescent monoclonal antibody stain for rapid detection of infant *Chlamydia trachomatis* infections. Pediatrics *74*:224, 1984.
6. Bell, T. A., Sandstrom, K. I., Gravett, M. G., et al.: Comparison of ophthalmic silver nitrate solution and erythromycin ointment for prevention of natally acquired *Chlamydia trachomatis*. Sex. Transm. Dis. *14*:195, 1987.
7. Bell, T. A., Stamm, W. E., Kuo, C. C., et al.: Risk of perinatal transmission of *Chlamydia trachomatis* by mode of delivery. J. Infect. *29*:165, 1994.
8. Bell, T. A., Stamm, W. E., Wang, S. P., et al.: Chronic *Chlamydia trachomatis* infections in infants. J. A. M. A. *267*:400, 1992.
9. Black, C. M.: Current methods of laboratory diagnosis of *Chlamydia trachomatis* infections. Clin. Microbiol. Rev. *10*:160, 1997.
10. Brayden, R. M., Paisley, J. W., Lauer, B. A., et al.: Apnea in infants with *Chlamydia trachomatis* pneumonia. Pediatr. Infect. Dis. J. *6*:423, 1987.
11. Brunham, R. C., Paavonen, J., Stevens, C. E., et al.: Mucopurulent cervicitis: The ignored counterpart in women of urethritis in men. N. Engl. J. Med. *311*:1, 1984.
12. Cates, W., Jr., Rolfs, R. T., Jr., and Aral, S. O.: Sexually transmitted disease, pelvic inflammatory disease, and infertility: An epidemiologic update. Epidemiol. Rev. *12*:199, 1990.
13. Centers for Disease Control and Prevention: Hypertrophic pyloric stenosis in infants following pertussis prophylaxis with erythromycin—Knoxville, Tennessee, 1999. M. M. W. R. Morb. Mortal. Wkly. Rep. *48*(49):1117, 1999.
14. Centers for Disease Control and Prevention: Sexually transmitted diseases treatment guidelines 2002. M. M. W. R. Recomm. Rep. *51*(RR-6):32, 2002.
15. Chandler, W. J., Alexander, E. R., Pheiffer, T. A., et al.: Ophthalmia neonatorum associated with maternal chlamydial infections. Trans. Am. Acad. Ophthalmol. Otolaryngol. *83*:302, 1977.
16. Chen, J.-Y.: Prophylaxis of ophthalmia neonatorum: Comparison of silver nitrate, tetracycline, erythromycin and no prophylaxis. Pediatr. Infect. Dis. J. *11*:1026, 1992.
17. Cohen, S. D., Azimi, P. H., and Schachter, J.: *Chlamydia trachomatis* associated with severe rhinitis and apneic episodes in a one-month-old infant. Clin. Pediatr. (Phila.) *21*:498, 1982.
18. Dannevig, L., Straume, B., and Melby, K.: Ophthalmia neonatorum in northern Norway. II. Microbiology with emphasis on *Chlamydia trachomatis*. Acta Ophthalmol. (Copenh.) *70*:19, 1992.
19. Frommell, G. T., Bruhn, F. W., and Schwartzman, J. D.: Isolation of *Chlamydia trachomatis* from infant lung tissue. N. Engl. J. Med. *296*:1150, 1977.
20. Frommell, G. T, Rothenberg, R., Wang, S.-P., et al.: Chlamydial infection of mothers and their infants. J. Pediatr. *95*:28, 1979.
21. Gencay, M., Koskiniemi, M., Saikku, P., et al.: *Chlamydia trachomatis* seropositivity during pregnancy is associated with perinatal complications. Clin. Infect. Dis. *21*:424, 1995.
22. Givner, L. B., Rennels, M. B., Woodward, C. L., et al.: *Chlamydia trachomatis* infection in an infant delivered by cesarean section. Pediatrics *68*:420, 1981.
23. Hammerschlag, M. R.: Chlamydial infections. J. Pediatr. *114*:727, 1989.
24. Hammerschlag, M. R., Anderka, M., Semine, D. Z., et al.: Prospective study of maternal and infantile infection with *Chlamydia trachomatis*. Pediatrics *64*:142, 1979.
25. Hammerschlag, M. R., Cummings, C., Roblins, P. M., et al.: Efficacy of neonatal ocular prophylaxis for the prevention of chlamydial and gonococcal conjunctivitis. N. Engl. J. Med. *320*:769, 1989.
26. Hammerschlag, M. R., Gelling, M., Roblin, P. M., et al.: Treatment of neonatal chlamydial conjunctivitis with azithromycin. Pediatr. Infect. Dis. J. *17*:1049, 1998.
27. Hammerschlag, M. R., Hammerschlag, P. E., and Alexander, E. R.: The role of *Chlamydia trachomatis* in middle ear effusions in children. Pediatrics *66*:615, 1980.
28. Hammerschlag, M. R., Herrmann, J. E., Cox, P., et al.: Enzyme immunoassay for diagnosis of neonatal chlamydial conjunctivitis. J. Pediatr. *107*:741, 1985.
29. Hammerschlag, M. R., Roblin, P. M., Gelling, M., et al.: Use of polymerase chain reaction for the detection of *Chlamydia trachomatis* in ocular and nasopharyngeal specimens from infants with conjunctivitis. Pediatr. Infect. Dis. J. *16*:293, 1997.
30. Harrison, H. R., Alexander, E. R., Weinstein, L., et al.: Cervical *Chlamydia trachomatis* and mycoplasmal infections in pregnancy. J. A. M. A. *250*:1721, 1983.
31. Harrison, H. R., English, M. G., Lee, C. K., et al.: *Chlamydia trachomatis* infant pneumonitis: Comparison with matched controls and other infant pneumonitis. N. Engl. J. Med. *298*:702, 1978.
32. Honein, M. A., Paulozzi, L. J., Himelright, I. M., et al.: Infantile hypertrophic pyloric stenosis after pertussis prophylaxis with erythromycin: A case review and cohort study. Lancet *354*:2101–2105, 1999.
33. Jain, S.: Perinatally acquired *Chlamydia trachomatis* associated morbidity in young infants. J. Matern. Fetal. Med. *8*:130, 1999.
34. Khan, M. A., and Potter, C. W.: The nPCR detection of *Chlamydia pneumoniae* and *Chlamydia trachomatis* in children hospitalized for bronchiolitis. J. Infect. *33*:173, 1996.
35. La Scolea, L. J., Jr., Paroski, J. S., Burzynski, L., et al.: *Chlamydia trachomatis* infection in infants delivered by cesarean section. Clin. Pediatr. (Phila.) *23*:118, 1984.
36. Lee, H. H., Chernesky, M. A., Schachter, J., et al.: Diagnosis of *Chlamydia trachomatis* genitourinary infection in women by ligase chain reaction assay of urine. Lancet *345*:213, 1995.
37. Mahon, B. E., Rosenman, M. B., and Kleiman, M. B.: Maternal and infant use of erythromycin and other macrolide antibiotics as risk factors for infantile hypertrophic pyloric stenosis. J. Pediatr. *139*:380, 2001.

38. Mardh, P. A., Johansson, P. J. H., and Svenningsen, N.: Intrauterine lung infection with *Chlamydia trachomatis* in a premature infant. Acta Paediatr. *73*:569, 1984.
39. Martin, D. H., Mroczkowski, T. F., Dalu, Z. A., et al.: A controlled trial of a single dose of azithromycin for the treatment of chlamydial urethritis and cervicitis: The Azithromycin for Chlamydial Infections Study Group. N. Engl. J. Med. *327*:921, 1992.
40. Martin, J. L., Alexander, S. Y., Selwood, T. S., et al.: Use of the polymerase chain reaction for the detection of *Chlamydia trachomatis* in clinical specimens and its comparison to commercially available tests. Genitourin. Med. *71*:169, 1995.
41. Mordhorst, C. H., and Dawson, C.: Sequelae of neonatal inclusion conjunctivitis and associated disease in parents. Am. J. Ophthalmol. *71*:861, 1971.
42. Paisley, J. W., Lauer, B. A., Melinkovich, P., et al.: Rapid diagnosis of *Chlamydia trachomatis* pneumonia in infants by direct immunofluorescence microscopy of nasopharyngeal secretions. J. Pediatr. *109*:653, 1986.
43. Ringel, R. E., Givner, L. B., Brenner, J. I., et al.: Myocarditis as a complication of infantile *Chlamydia trachomatis* pneumonitis. Clin. Pediatr. (Phila.) *22*:631, 1983.
44. Roblin, P. M., Gelling, M., Kutlin, A., et al.: Evaluation of a new optical immunoassay for diagnosis of neonatal chlamydial conjunctivitis. J. Clin. Microbiol. *35*:515, 1997.
45. Rowe, S., Aicardi, E., Dawson, C. R., Schachter, J.: Purulent ocular discharge in neonates: Significance of *Chlamydia trachomatis*. Pediatrics *63*:628, 1979.
46. SanFilippo, A.: Infantile hypertrophic pyloric stenosis related to ingestion of erythromycin estolate: A report of five cases. J. Pediatr. Surg. *11*:177, 1976.
47. Schachter, J.: Chlamydial infections. N. Engl. J. Med. *298*:428, 1978.
48. Schacter, J. and Grossman, M.: *Chlymadia. In* Remington, J. S., and Klein, J. O. (eds.): Infectious Diseases of the Fetus and Newborn Infant. 5th ed. Philadelphia, W. B. Saunders, 2001, pp. 769–778.
49. Schachter, J., Grossman, M., and Azimi, P. H.: Serology of *Chlamydia trachomatis* in infants. J. Infect. Dis. *146*:530, 1982.
50. Schachter, J., Grossman, M., Holt, J., et al.: Infection with *Chlamydia trachomatis:* Involvement of multiple anatomic sites in neonates. J. Infect. Dis. *139*:232, 1979.
51. Schachter, J., Grossman, M., Holt, J., et al.: Prospective study of chlamydial infection in neonates. Lancet *2*:377, 1979.
52. Schachter, J., Grossman, M., Sweet, R. L., et al.: Prospective study of perinatal transmission of *Chlamydia trachomatis.* J. A. M. A. *255*:3374, 1986.
53. Schachter, J., Lum, L., Gooding, C. A., et al.: Pneumonitis following inclusion blennorrhea. J. Pediatr. *87*:779, 1975.
54. Schachter, J., Stamm, W. E., Quinn, T. C., et al.: Ligase chain reaction to detect *Chlamydia trachomatis* infection of the cervix. J. Clin. Microbiol. *32*:2540, 1994.
55. Schachter, J., Sweet, R. L., Grossman, M., et al.: Experience with the routine use of erythromycin for chlamydial infections in pregnancy. N. Engl. J. Med. *314*:276, 1986.
56. Scholes, D., Stergachis, A., Heidrich, F. R., et al.: Prevention of pelvic inflammatory disease by screening for cervical chlamydial infection. N. Engl. J. Med. *334*:1362, 1996.
57. Shariot, H., Young, M., and Abedin, M.: An interesting case presentation: A possible new route for perinatal acquisition of *Chlamydia.* J. Perinatol. *12*:300, 1992.
58. Shinkwin, C. A., and Gibbin, K. P.: Neonatal upper airway obstruction caused by chlamydial rhinitis. J. Laryngol. Otol. *109*:58, 1995.
59. Skulnick, M., Chua, R., Simor, A. E., et al.: Use of the polymerase chain reaction for the detection of *Chlamydia trachomatis* from endocervical and urine specimens in an asymptomatic low-prevalence population of women. Diagn. Microbiol. Infect. Dis. *20*:195, 1994.
60. Sollecito, D., Midulla, M., Bavastrelli, M., et al.: *Chlamydia trachomatis* in neonatal respiratory distress of very preterm babies: Biphasic clinical picture. Acta Paediatr. *81*:788, 1992.
61. Stutman, H. R., Rettig, P. H., and Reyes, S.: *Chlamydia trachomatis* as a cause of pneumonitis and pleural effusion. J. Pediatr. *104*:588, 1984.
62. Talley, A. R., Garcia-Ferrer, F., Laycock, K. A., et al.: Comparative diagnosis of neonatal chlamydial conjunctivitis by polymerase chain reaction and McCoy cell culture. Am. J. Ophthalmol. *117*:50, 1994.
63. Tipple, M., Beem, M. O., and Saxon, E.: Clinical characteristics of the afebrile pneumonia associated with *Chlamydia trachomatis* infection in infants less than 6 months of age. Pediatrics *63*:192, 1979.
64. Turrentine, M. A., and Newton, E. R.: Amoxicillin or erythromycin for the treatment of antenatal chlamydial infection: A meta-analysis. Obstet. Gynecol. *86*:1021, 1995.
65. Wang, S.-P., Grayston, J. T., Alexander, E. R., et al.: Simplified microimmunofluorescence test with trachoma-lymphogranuloma venereum *(Chlamydia trachomatis)* antigens for use as a screening test for antibody. J. Clin. Microbiol. *1*:250, 1975.
66. Weber, J. T., and Johnson, R. E.: New treatments for *Chlamydia trachomatis* genital infection. Clin. Infect. Dis. *20*(Suppl. 1):66, 1995.
67. Weinstock, H., Dean, D., and Bolan, G.: *Chlamydia trachomatis* infection. Infect. Dis. Clin. North Am. *8*:797, 1994.
68. Weiss, S. G., Newcomb, R. W., and Beem, M. O.: Pulmonary assessment of children after chlamydial pneumonia in infancy. J. Pediatr. *108*:659, 1986.
69. Yong, E. C., Chinn, J. S., Caldwell, H. D., et al.: Reticulate body as a single antigen in *Chlamydia trachomatis* serology with microimmunofluorescence. J. Clin. Microbiol. *10*:351, 1979.
70. Zanoni, D., Isenberg, S. J., and Apt, L.: A comparison of silver nitrate with erythromycin for prophylaxis against ophthalmia neonatorum. Clin. Pediatr. (Phila.) *31*:295, 1992.

CHAPTER **73C**

Mycoplasma and *Ureaplasma* Infections

PABLO J. SÁNCHEZ

The genital mycoplasmas consist of *Mycoplasma hominis, Mycoplasma fermentans, Mycoplasma genitalium,* and *Ureaplasma urealyticum* (T-strain *Mycoplasma),* with only *M. hominis* and *U. urealyticum* being of clinical significance in neonatal disease.[22] Mycoplasmas are the smallest free-living microorganisms and are characterized by lack of a cell wall. Serologic studies have demonstrated seven serotypes of *M. hominis* and 14 serotypes of *U. urealyticum.* Based on polymerase chain reaction (PCR) studies of four different genes and genetic regions of the 14 serovars of *U. urealyticum,* this organism has been divided into two distinct species, namely, *Ureaplasma parvum* (biovar 1) and *U. urealyticum* (T960, biovar 2).[61, 79, 80] Recently, the complete genome of *U. urealyticum* (parvum biovar) has been sequenced; except for *M. genitalium,* it has the smallest sequenced prokaryotic genome.[55]

M. hominis and *U. urealyticum* are sexually transmitted organisms that account for female urogenital colonization rates of 20 to 50 percent and 40 to 80 percent, respectively.[15, 92, 134] Colonization rates are similar in pregnant and nonpregnant women. Colonization has been associated with younger age, lower socioeconomic status, sexual activity with multiple partners, black ethnicity, and oral contraceptive use.

In general, cervicovaginal colonization with *U. urealyticum* and *M. hominis* is not predictive of such adverse pregnancy outcomes as prematurity, low birth weight, and spontaneous abortion.[25, 42] High-density genital ureaplasmal colonization recently has been associated with chorioamnionitis and preterm delivery.[3] Both *U. urealyticum* and *M. hominis* appear to be capable of invading the upper genital tract, as evidenced by their isolation from the endometrium,[82] placenta,[40, 81] amniotic fluid,[21, 24, 44, 57, 67, 136, 154, 155] and even blood[18] in a subpopulation of women. *U. urealyticum* has been associated strongly with histologic chorioamnionitis, postpartum fever, and endometritis.[8, 9, 20, 24, 25, 128] *M. hominis* is a recognized cause of pelvic inflammatory disease, postpartum septicemia, and endometritis.[22, 39, 74, 93, 98] It also has been associated with surgical wound infection after cesarean delivery.[87, 114] The role of these organisms in causing spontaneous abortion and premature birth, however, remains controversial and currently unproved.[41]

Transmission

Vertical transmission of *U. urealyticum* and *M. hominis* from a colonized mother to her newborn occurs in utero or during delivery.[5, 7, 56, 118] The relative frequency of occurrence at each time point is not known fully. In utero transmission occurs either transplacentally or by an ascending route from a colonized maternal genital tract. Such transmission is supported by isolation of mycoplasmas from maternal blood at the time of delivery; by isolation of mycoplasmas from umbilical cord blood, amniotic fluid, endometrium, chorioamnion, placenta, and aborted fetal tissue; and by detection of a specific IgM antibody response in neonatal serum. Mycoplasmas also have been isolated from the mucosal surfaces of newborn infants delivered by cesarean section performed before the onset of labor and rupture of amniotic membranes.[121, 132] Acquisition of mycoplasmas by newborn infants also can occur at the time of delivery through contact with a colonized birth canal. Postpartum or nosocomial transmission probably occurs, but definitive proof is lacking. It has been suggested by the finding of initial ureaplasmal colonization at 3 to 4 weeks of age in some infants who previously had been shown not to be colonized with *U. urealyticum* while in a neonatal intensive care unit (NICU).[121]

The rate of vertical transmission of *U. urealyticum* ranges from 0.9 to 45 to 55 percent in full-term infants and 8.5 to 58 percent in preterm infants, depending on the number and type of mucosal surfaces sampled.[7, 26, 99, 118, 120, 121, 132] Similar data are scarce for *M. hominis;* it has been isolated from the nasopharyngeal aspirates and gastric secretions of 30 to 42 percent[26, 27] and 8 percent,[56] respectively, of infants born to colonized mothers. The rate of vertical transmission of *U. urealyticum* is not affected by the method of delivery or the duration of time after rupture of membranes; colonization of infants occurs despite cesarean delivery with intact fetal membranes. Vertical transmission is increased significantly in the presence of chorioamnionitis and intra-amniotic infection.[37, 125] Colonization of newborn infants increases with decreasing gestational age and birth weight,[7] and it is highest in infants weighing less than 1000 g at birth.[121] Female newborns also are more likely than are males to be colonized with *U. urealyticum* because the vagina is a common site of colonization.[45, 120]

Colonization with *U. urealyticum* persists through early infancy; 68, 33, and 37 percent of full-term newborns colonized in the throat, eye, and vagina, respectively, still are colonized at 3 months of age.[132] However, most lose colonization by 2 years of age.[45] Among preterm infants, 65 percent remain colonized at discharge from the NICU or at 28 days of life.[121] Overall, the prevalence of ureaplasmal colonization varies from 2 to 86 percent among infants admitted to NICUs, and as many as 14 to 41 percent of infants have endotracheal aspirate cultures positive for *U. urealyticum*.[35, 38, 62, 70, 106, 118] Ultimately, however, mycoplasmal colonization of newborns depends on the prevalence of maternal colonization in that population.

Clinical Manifestations

The roles of *U. urealyticum* and *M. hominis* in neonatal disease continue to be investigated and defined. *M. hominis* and *U. urealyticum* have been recovered from the lungs, brain, heart, and viscera of aborted fetuses and stillborn infants, with histologic findings of bronchopneumonia present in the lungs of these fetuses.[88, 133] The genital mycoplasmas also have been isolated from the blood, urine, cerebrospinal fluid (CSF), and lung tissue of newborn infants with clinical signs of infection. Because these organisms frequently colonize the mucosal surfaces of newborns,[76, 120] ascribing disease often is difficult. However, isolation from normally sterile body fluids has led to their recognition as neonatal pathogens.

The following clinical associations with *U. urealyticum* have been made: (1) isolation of *U. urealyticum* from blood in as many as 34 percent of infants younger than 34 weeks' gestational age[104] and 26 percent of preterm infants with positive endotracheal aspirate cultures for *U. urealyticum*[23]; (2) fatal neonatal pneumonia in a term infant documented by isolation of the organism from lung tissue at autopsy and demonstration of elevated serum IgG and IgM titers to *U. urealyticum* in the infant[112]; (3) pneumonia and persistent pulmonary hypertension in five infants from whom *U. urealyticum* was isolated from blood, endotracheal aspirates, pleural fluid, or lung tissue (or any combination of these sites) at autopsy[143]; (4) afebrile pneumonitis in infants younger than 3 months[129]; (5) development of chronic lung disease in low-birth-weight infants whose respiratory tracts are colonized with *U. urealyticum* in the first week of life*; (6) isolation of *U. urealyticum* from the lung biopsy tissue of four infants with chronic lung disease[149]; (7) isolation of *U. urealyticum* from the CSF of both preterm and full-term infants[49, 64, 96, 130, 138, 144, 146]; (8) osteomyelitis of the femur in association with isolation of *U. urealyticum* from blood in a preterm infant[52]; (9) nonimmune hydrops fetalis in a newborn at 32 weeks' gestation in which *U. urealyticum* was isolated from bronchial secretions and lung and brain tissue at autopsy[102]; and (10) scalp abscess at the site of an internal fetal electrode monitor.[59]

The potential role of *U. urealyticum* in neonatal pneumonia[16, 47, 53, 107] has been strengthened by the demonstration of histologic evidence of pneumonia in the lungs of newborn mice and premature baboons; ureaplasmal isolates were obtained from the pleural fluid, lung biopsy specimens, and lung tissue of these experimental pneumonia models.[22, 115, 148] Crouse and colleagues[29] demonstrated that pneumonia is produced in newborn mice, but significantly less often in mice older than 14 days, and is potentiated by oxygen therapy. *U. urealyticum* has been shown to induce ciliostasis and mucosal lesions in human fetal tracheal organ cultures.[22] In addition, *U. urealyticum* can induce production of alveolar macrophage proinflammatory cytokine in vitro,[83] and both *U. urealyticum* and *M. hominis* stimulate the production of tumor necrosis factor–α (TNF-α) and inducible nitric oxide synthase from murine macrophages.[30]

Isolation of *U. urealyticum* from endotracheal secretions, the nasopharynx, the throat, or gastric aspirates (or any combination of these specimens) also has been associated with chronic lung disease of prematurity. A meta-analysis performed by Wang and associates[153] involving 17 publications supported a significant association between ureaplasmal colonization and the subsequent development of chronic lung disease, even with the use of surfactant therapy for respiratory distress syndrome. In 1997, Van Waarde and colleagues[139] questioned this association because preterm infants who are at highest risk for development of chronic lung disease (i.e., those of lowest gestational age and birth

*See references 1, 6, 7, 11, 22, 48, 60, 66, 69, 72, 73, 107, 109, 110, 119, 127, 150, 151.

weight) also are the ones most likely to be colonized with *U. urealyticum*. Nevertheless, Crouse and coworkers[31, 32] showed that among infants who weigh 1250 g at birth or less and who have respiratory disease, those colonized with *U. urealyticum* in their tracheal secretions have radiographic evidence of more severe pulmonary disease than do those who are not colonized. These findings were not supported by Cordero and colleagues,[28] who did not detect any specific radiographic abnormalities in 183 infants with a birth weight of 1250 g or less and who had endotracheal colonization with *U. urealyticum,* gram-negative cocci, or gram-negative bacilli. However, Ollikainen and collaborators[105] found that preterm infants colonized with *U. urealyticum* required high-frequency oscillatory ventilation more often than did those not colonized. In addition, the isolation by Walsh and associates[149] of *U. urealyticum* from the lungs of infants with chronic lung disease implies an invasive bacterial process as part of the pathogenesis of lung injury.

The possibility that ureaplasmal colonization of the respiratory tract induces an inflammatory response without direct pulmonary invasion and infection cannot be excluded.[58, 85] It has been supported by the finding of elevated levels of TNF-α, interleukin-6 (IL-6), IL-8, and monocyte chemoattractant protein-1 (MCP-1) in the tracheal secretions of colonized infants,[11, 22, 89, 131] as well as by elevated white blood cell counts and eosinophilia in infants with respiratory tract colonization by *U. urealyticum*.[101, 105, 108] Finally, the contribution of the two recently described species of *U. urealyticum, U. urealyticum* and *U. parvum,* was evaluated by Heggie and colleagues.[62] Both species colonized preterm infants with a birth weight less than 1500 g; however, no association was seen between endotracheal colonization with either species and the development of chronic lung disease.

M. hominis has been associated with neonatal septicemia,[22, 137] meningitis,[50, 51, 65, 75, 90, 94, 126, 146] pneumonia,[137] pericarditis,[95] and conjunctivitis.[71] Other manifestations of infection with *M. hominis* are brain and scalp abscesses, ventriculitis, submandibular adenitis, and abscesses of subcutaneous tissue.[54, 111, 117]

Both *U. urealyticum* and *M. hominis* have been isolated from the CSF of both full-term and preterm infants. Their repeated isolation from CSF and their ability to result in a CSF pleocytosis consisting of a polymorphonuclear or mononuclear cellular response, hypoglycorrhachia, and elevated protein content in predominantly preterm infants with suspected meningitis support their role in causing neonatal meningitis. Waites and coworkers[146] noted hemiplegia, hydrocephalus, and developmental delay in survivors. Isolation of *U. urealyticum* from the CSF of preterm infants also has been associated with severe intraventricular hemorrhage.[2, 103, 146] However, primarily in full-term infants, isolation of *U. urealyticum* and *M. hominis* often has been associated with minimal if any CSF abnormalities, and these infants do well without specific antimicrobial therapy.[63, 96, 124, 138, 144] In these instances, their isolation remains of unclear clinical significance, and their role in producing disease is questionable.

The clinical significance of the isolation of genital mycoplasmas from urine obtained by suprapubic bladder aspiration in infants remains to be determined.[84] In such instances, analysis of the urinary sediment has been normal.

Diagnosis

The diagnosis of mycoplasmal infection is made by isolation of the organism from a normally sterile body fluid or suppurative focus. Because colonization of newborn infants with mycoplasmas occurs frequently, an etiologic role for these agents cannot be supported by isolation from mucosal surfaces only. Genital mycoplasmas may be isolated on special broth and solid media that are available commercially. Shepard 10 broth and A8 agar have been used successfully for cultivation of both *U. urealyticum* and *M. hominis*.[22] Cultures generally become positive within 2 to 5 days. *M. hominis* but not *U. urealyticum* may be identified presumptively on blood agar as tiny pinpoint colonies.

Cassell and associates[19, 22] recommended that mucosal specimens be obtained with a Dacron or calcium alginate swab and placed in a specific mycoplasmal transport medium such as Shepard 10B broth. Specimens should be refrigerated at 4° C until transported to the laboratory and protected from drying. Alternatively, specimens in appropriate transport media can be frozen at −70° C because both *U. urealyticum* and *M. hominis* are stable for long periods under these conditions. Specimens should be diluted serially in 10B broth to at least 10^{-3} (preferably to 10^{-5}) to overcome any potential inhibitory substances or metabolites, and an aliquot of the original sample and dilution should be plated directly onto A8 agar. Body fluids (e.g., blood, CSF, pleural fluid) should be inoculated into 10B broth in an approximate 1:10 ratio (usually 0.1 mL of fluid per 0.9 mL of 10B broth). Blood should be collected free of anticoagulants. Broth cultures and agar plates are incubated under 95 percent nitrogen and 5 percent carbon dioxide. The presence of mycoplasmal growth in 10B medium is indicated by a color change from yellow to pink, which is caused by an alkaline shift in the media as a result of either the urease activity of ureaplasmas or arginine hydrolysis by *M. hominis*. Growth of mycoplasmas in broth culture as indicated by a color change should be confirmed by inoculation of a broth specimen onto A8 agar. Characteristic colonies of *U. urealyticum* and *M. hominis* can be identified readily on A8 agar after 24 to 72 hours of incubation.

Serologic tests have been used to measure antibody to genital mycoplasmas. Such tests include the metabolic inhibition assay, enzyme-linked immunosorbent assay, mycoplasmacidal test, indirect hemagglutination, indirect immunofluorescence, and IgG and IgM immunoblotting.[22, 36, 46, 113] Use of these tests for the diagnosis of mycoplasmal infection in infants remains problematic and is not well established. None are available commercially, and in newborns, the diagnosis rests on culture results.

PCR involving the urease structural gene or the multiple-banded (MB) ureaplasmal surface antigen has been used to detect *U. urealyticum* in neonatal clinical specimens.[4, 5, 12, 34, 85, 86, 97, 123, 135] On endotracheal secretions, Blanchard and associates[12] reported a sensitivity of 100 percent and a specificity of 99 percent in comparison to ureaplasmal culture. PCR also is available for *M. hominis*.[4, 86] Ultimately, PCR may aid in identifying colonized or infected infants more readily and reliably given the fastidious nature of these organisms and the scarcity of microbiology laboratories that routinely perform mycoplasmal cultures.

Treatment

The decision to treat an infant for possible mycoplasmal infection should be based on clinical symptomatology and culture results. In general, isolation of mycoplasmas from a normally sterile site in an ill neonate is an indication for consideration of treatment. However, no large randomized clinical trials have determined the efficacy of treatment in neonates, and experience on which to base treatment decisions, the choice of drug, and the duration of therapy is very limited.[152]

In preterm infants with clinical evidence of sepsis in whom routine bacterial and viral cultures are sterile and the infant is not responding to antibacterial or antiviral therapy, the diagnosis should be suspected and appropriate samples obtained for culture of mycoplasmas. In addition, CSF from neonates who have abnormal indices but whose cultures are sterile should be cultured for mycoplasmas. Recovery of mycoplasmas from endotracheal secretions is not diagnostic of pneumonia, and most of these infants do not require any antimycoplasmal therapy. However, if pneumonia is suspected and the infant's clinical condition is deteriorating, a therapy trial may be indicated, although the efficacy of treatment remains unknown. Treating very-low-birth-weight infants who have respiratory tract colonization with *U. urealyticum* in order to prevent chronic lung disease cannot be recommended at present.[17] Steroid therapy for chronic lung disease has been administered to colonized infants without resulting in disseminated ureaplasmal infection.

Mycoplasmas are not susceptible to the antimicrobial agents routinely used to treat neonatal infections.[14, 141, 142, 145] Because mycoplasmas lack a cell wall, they are insensitive to penicillins, cephalosporins, polymyxins, sulfonamides, and vancomycin. Although they may have moderate sensitivity to the aminoglycosides, the minimal inhibitory concentrations (MICs) of these agents for genital mycoplasmas usually are too high for therapeutic use. The drugs of choice for the treatment of infection caused by *M. hominis* are chloramphenicol, clindamycin, doxycycline, and tetracycline; for the treatment of ureaplasmal infections, erythromycin, doxycycline, tetracycline, and chloramphenicol are recommended.[77, 91, 141, 147] Whenever possible, antibiotic susceptibility testing should be performed on all clinically significant isolates because multidrug resistance occurs.

M. hominis is resistant to erythromycin, but high-level resistance of *U. urealyticum* to erythromycin (MIC ≥32 mg/mL) is found very infrequently. Cardiac toxicity consisting of acute cardiorespiratory deterioration possibly secondary to cardiac arrhythmias has been reported in neonates treated with intravenous erythromycin lactobionate for presumed ureaplasmal pneumonia.[43] Ototoxicity also has been seen in adults but not in neonates.[33] Oral erythromycin has been associated with hypertrophic pyloric stenosis in infants younger than 6 weeks of age.[68] Although the exact duration of therapy is not known, a 10- to 14-day course seems reasonable when associated clinical improvement and microbiologic eradication are observed during that period.

Azithromycin and clarithromycin are active in vitro against *U. urealyticum* but not *M. hominis*.[78, 116, 140] Their use in neonates has not been evaluated. When given orally to very-low-birth-weight infants colonized with *U. urealyticum*, serum levels of clarithromycin at a dose of 7.5 mg/kg every 12 hours were subtherapeutic.[122] For this reason, a dose of 15 mg/kg every 12 hours is recommended.

Prevention

Erythromycin administered between 26 and 35 weeks' gestation to pregnant women colonized with *U. urealyticum* was not effective in reducing adverse outcomes such as preterm delivery, low birth weight, or premature rupture of membranes.[42] Because erythromycin therapy does not eliminate *U. urealyticum* from the lower genital tract, it most likely also will not prevent neonatal ureaplasmal colonization.[100] Its effect on prevention of neonatal disease has not been evaluated fully.[10] Administration of erythromycin to preterm infants with *U. urealyticum* reduced respiratory tract colonization but did not decrease the duration of supplemental oxygen therapy[73] or chronic lung disease.[13, 85] Whether administration of an anti-ureaplasmal agent such as erythromycin to very-low-birth-weight infants colonized with *U. urealyticum* will prevent or ameliorate chronic lung disease of prematurity is not known.

REFERENCES

1. Abele-Horn, M., Genzel-Boroviczeny, O., Uhlig, T., et al.: *Ureaplasma urealyticum* colonization and bronchopulmonary dysplasia: A comparative prospective multicentre study. Eur. J. Pediatr. *157*:1004, 1998.
2. Abele-Horn, M., Peters, J., Genzel-Boroviczeny, O., et al.: Vaginal *Ureaplasma urealyticum* colonization: Influence on pregnancy outcome and neonatal morbidity. Infection *25*:286, 1997.
3. Abele-Horn, M., Scholz, M., Wolff, C., et al.: High-density vaginal *Ureaplasma urealyticum* colonization as a risk factor for chorioamnionitis and preterm delivery. Acta. Obstet. Gynecol. Scand. *79*:973, 2000.
4. Abele-Horn, M., Wolff, C., Dressel, P., et al.: Polymerase chain reaction versus culture for detection of *Ureaplasma urealyticum* and *Mycoplasma hominis* in the urogenital tract of adults and the respiratory tract of newborns. Eur. J. Clin. Microbiol. Infect. Dis. *15*:595, 1996.
5. Abele-Horn, M., Wolff, C., Dressel, P., et al.: Association of *Ureaplasma urealyticum* biovars with clinical outcome for neonates, obstetric patients, and gynecological patients with pelvic inflammatory disease. J. Clin. Microbiol. *35*:1199, 1997.
6. Agarwal, P., Rajadurai, V. S., Pradeepkumar, V. K., and Tan, K. W.: *Ureaplasma urealyticum* and its association with chronic lung disease in Asian neonates. J. Paediatr. Child Health *36*:487, 2000.
7. Alfa, M. J., Embree, J. E., Degagne, P., et al.: Transmission of *Ureaplasma urealyticum* from mothers to full and preterm infants. Pediatr. Infect. Dis. J. *14*:341, 1995.
8. Andrews, W., Shah, S., Goldenberg, R., et al.: Post-cesarean endometritis: Role of asymptomatic antenatal colonization of the chorioamnion with *Ureaplasma urealyticum*. Am. J. Obstet. Gynecol. *170*:416, 1994.
9. Andrews, W. W., Shah, S. R., Goldenberg, R. L., et al.: Association of post–cesarean delivery endometritis with colonization of the chorioamnion by *Ureaplasma urealyticum*. Obstet. Gynecol. *85*:509, 1995.
10. Antsaklis, A., Daskalakis, G., Michalas, S., et al.: Erythromycin treatment for subclinical *Ureaplasma urealyticum* infection in preterm labor. Fetal Diagn. Ther. *12*:89, 1997.
11. Baier, R. J., Loggins, J., and Kruger, T. E.: Monocyte chemoattractant protein-1 and interleukin-8 are increased in bronchopulmonary dysplasia: Relation to isolation of *Ureaplasma urealyticum*. J. Invest. Med. *49*:362, 2001.
12. Blanchard, A., Hentschel J., Duffy, L., et al.: Detection of *Ureaplasma urealyticum* by polymerase chain reaction in the urogenital tract of adults, in amniotic fluid, and in the respiratory tract of newborns. Clin. Infect. Dis. *17*(Suppl. 1):148, 1993.
13. Bowman, E. D., Dharmalingam, A., Fan, W. Q., et al.: Impact of erythromycin on respiratory colonization of *Ureaplasma urealyticum* and the development of chronic lung disease in extremely low birth weight infants. Pediatr. Infect. Dis. J. *17*:615, 1998.
14. Braun, P., Klein, J. O., and Kass, E. H.: Susceptibility of *Mycoplasma hominis* and T-strains to 14 antimicrobial agents. Appl. Microbiol. *19*:62, 1970.
15. Braun, P., Klein, J. O., Lee, Y. H., et al.: Methodologic investigations and prevalence of genital mycoplasmas in pregnancy. J. Infect. Dis. *121*:391, 1970.
16. Brus, F., van Waarde, W. M., Schoots, C., et al.: Fatal ureaplasmal pneumonia and sepsis in a newborn infant. Eur. J. Pediatr. *150*:782, 1991.
17. Buhrer, C., Hoehn, T., and Hentschel, J.: Role of erythromycin for treatment of incipient chronic lung disease in preterm infants colonised with *Ureaplasma urealyticum*. Drugs *61*:1893, 2001.
18. Caspi, E., Herczeg, E., Solomon, F., et al.: Amnionitis and T strain mycoplasmemia. Am. J. Obstet. Gynecol. *111*:1102, 1971.
19. Cassell, G. H., Blanchard, A., Duffy, L., et al.: Mycoplasmas. *In* Howard B. J., Klaas, J., III, Rubin S. J., et al. (eds.): Clinical and Pathogenic Microbiology. St. Louis, Mosby–Year Book, 1994, pp. 491–502.
20. Cassell, G. H., Clyde, W. A., Kenny, G. E., et al.: Ureaplasmas of humans with emphasis on maternal and neonatal infections. Pediatr. Infect. Dis. J. *6*(Suppl.):221, 1986.
21. Cassell, G. H., Davis, R. O., Waites, K. B., et al.: Isolation of *Mycoplasma hominis* and *Ureaplasma urealyticum* from amniotic fluid at 16–20 weeks gestation. Potential effect on pregnancy outcome. Sex. Transm. Dis. *10*:294, 1983.
22. Cassell, G. H., Waites, K. B., and Crouse, D. T.: Mycoplasmal infections. *In* Remington, J. S., and Klein, J. O. (eds.): Infectious Diseases of the Fetus and Newborn Infant. 5th ed. Philadelphia, W. B. Saunders, 2001, pp. 733–767.

23. Cassell, G. H., Waites, K. B., Crouse, D. T., et al.: Association of *Ureaplasma urealyticum* infection of the lower respiratory tract with chronic lung disease and death in very low birthweight infants. Lancet *2*:240, 1988.
24. Cassell, G. H., Waites, K. B., Gibbs, R. S., et al.: The role of *Ureaplasma urealyticum* in amnionitis. Pediatr. Infect. Dis. J. *5*(Suppl.):247, 1986.
25. Cassell, G. H., Waites, K. B., Watson, H. L., et al.: *Ureaplasma urealyticum* intrauterine infection: Role in prematurity and disease in newborns. Clin. Microbiol. Rev. *6*:69, 1993.
26. Chua, K. B., Ngeow, Y. F., Lim, C. T., et al.: Colonization and transmission of *Ureaplasma urealyticum* and *Mycoplasma hominis* from mothers to full and preterm babies by normal vaginal delivery. Med. J. Malaysia *54*:242, 1999.
27. Chua, K. B., Ngeow, Y. F., Ng, K. B., et al.: *Ureaplasma urealyticum* and *Mycoplasma hominis* isolation from cervical secretions of pregnant women and nasopharyngeal secretions of their babies at delivery. Singapore Med. J. *39*:300, 1998.
28. Cordero, L., Coley, B. D., Miller, R. L., et al.: Bacterial and *Ureaplasma* colonization of the airway: Radiologic findings in infants with bronchopulmonary dysplasia. J. Perinatol. *17*:428, 1997.
29. Crouse, D. T., Cassell, G. H., Waites, K. B., et al.: Hyperoxia potentiates *Ureaplasma urealyticum* pneumonia in newborn mice. Infect. Immun. *58*:3487, 1990.
30. Crouse, D. T., English, B. K., Livingston, L., and Meals, E. A.: Genital mycoplasmas stimulate tumor necrosis factor-alpha and inducible nitric oxide synthase production from a murine macrophage cell line. Pediatr. Res. *44*:785, 1998.
31. Crouse, D. T., Odrezin, G. T., Cutter, G. R., et al.: Radiographic changes associated with tracheal isolation of *Ureaplasma urealyticum* in a neonatal intensive care population. J. Paediatr. Child Health *29*:295, 1993.
32. Crouse, D. T., Odrezin, G. T., Cutter, G. R., et al.: Radiographic changes associated with tracheal isolation of *Ureaplasma urealyticum* from neonates. Clin. Infect. Dis. *17*(Suppl. 1):122–130, 1993.
33. Crouse, D. T., Waites, K. B., Geerts, M. H., et al.: Parenteral erythromycin is not associated with hearing loss in preterm infants. Abstract. Clin. Res. *39*:832, 1991.
34. Cunliffe, N. A., Fergusson, S., Davidson, F., et al.: Comparison of culture with the polymerase chain reaction for detection of *Ureaplasma urealyticum* in endotracheal aspirates of preterm infants. J. Med. Microbiol. *45*:27, 1996.
35. DaSilva, O., Gregson, D. and Hammerberg, O.: Role of *Ureaplasma urealyticum* and *Chlamydia trachomatis* in development of bronchopulmonary dysplasia in very low birth weight infants. Pediatr. Infect. Dis. J. *16*:364, 1997.
36. Dinsmoor, M. J., Ramamurthy, R. S., Cassell, G. H., et al.: Neonatal serologic response at term to the genital mycoplasmas. Pediatr. Infect. Dis. J. *8*:487, 1989.
37. Dinsmoor, M. J., Ramamurthy, R. S., and Gibbs, R. S.: Transmission of genital mycoplasmas from mother to neonate in women with prolonged membrane rupture. Pediatr. Infect. Dis. J. *8*:483, 1989.
38. Dyke, M. P., Grauaug, A., Kohan, R., et al.: *Ureaplasma urealyticum* in a neonatal intensive care population. J. Paediatr. Child Health *29*:295, 1993.
39. Edelin, K. C., and McCormack, W. M.: Infection with *Mycoplasma hominis* in postpartum fever. Lancet *2*:1217, 1980.
40. Embree, J. E., Krause, V. W., Embil, J. A., et al.: Placental infection with *Mycoplasma hominis* and *Ureaplasma urealyticum:* Clinical correlation. Obstet. Gynecol. *56*:475, 1980.
41. Eschenbach, D. A.: *Ureaplasma urealyticum* and premature birth. Clin. Infect. Dis. *17*(Suppl. 1):100, 1993.
42. Eschenbach, D. A., Nugent, R. P., Rao, A. V., et al.: A randomized placebo-controlled trial of erythromycin for the treatment of *Ureaplasma urealyticum* to prevent premature delivery. Am. J. Obstet. Gynecol. *164*:734, 1991.
43. Farrar, H. C., Walsh-Sukys, M. C., Pharmd, K. K., et al.: Cardiac toxicity associated with intravenous erythromycin lactobionate: Two case reports and a review of the literature. Pediatr. Infect. Dis. J. *12*:688, 1993.
44. Foulon, W., Naessens, A., Dewaele, M., et al.: Chronic *Ureaplasma urealyticum* amnionitis associated with abruptio placentae. Obstet. Gynecol. *68*:280, 1986.
45. Foy, H. M., Kenny, G. E., Levinsohn, E. M., et al.: Acquisition of mycoplasmata and T-strains during infancy. J. Infect. Dis. *121*:579, 1970.
46. Gallo, D., Dupuis, K. W., Schmidt, N. J., et al.: Broadly reactive immunofluorescence test for measurement of immunoglobulin M and G antibodies to *Ureaplasma urealyticum* in infant and adult sera. J. Clin. Microbiol. *17*:614, 1983.
47. Gannon, H.: *Ureaplasma urealyticum* and its role in neonatal lung disease. Neonat. Network *12*:13, 1993.
48. Garland, S. M. and Bowman, E. D.: Role of *Ureaplasma urealyticum* and *Chlamydia trachomatis* in lung disease in low birth weight infants. Pathology *28*:266, 1996.
49. Garland, S., and Murton, L. J.: Neonatal meningitis caused by *Ureaplasma urealyticum.* Pediatr. Infect. Dis. J. *6*:868, 1987.
50. Gewitz, M., Dinwiddle, R., Rees, L., et al.: *Mycoplasma hominis:* A cause of neonatal meningitis. Arch. Dis. Child. *54*:231, 1979.
51. Gilbert, G. L., Law, F., and Macinnes, S. J.: Chronic *Mycoplasma hominis* infection complicating severe intraventricular hemorrhage in a premature neonate. Pediatr. Infect. Dis. *5*:285, 1973.
52. Gjuric, G., Prislin-Muskic, M., Nikolic, E., et al.: *Ureaplasma urealyticum* osteomyelitis in a very low birth weight infant. J. Perinat. Med. *22*:79, 1994.
53. Gjuric, G., Prislin-Muskic, M., Zurga, B., et al.: *Ureaplasma urealyticum* infection in newborns: Three case reports. Eur. J. Pediatr. *152*:599, 1993.
54. Glaser, J. B., Engelbert, M., and Hammerschlag, M.: Scalp abscess associated with *Mycoplasma hominis* infection complicating intrapartum monitoring. Pediatr. Infect. Dis. J. *2*:468, 1983.
55. Glass, J. I., Lefkowitz, E. J., Glass, J. S., et al.: The complete sequence of the mucosal pathogen *Ureaplasma urealyticum.* Nature *407*:757, 2000.
56. Grattard, F., Soleihac, B., de Barbeyrac, B., et al.: Epidemiologic and molecular investigations of genital mycoplasmas from women and neonates at delivery. Pediatr. Infect. Dis. J. *14*:853, 1995.
57. Gray, D. J., Robinson, H. B., Malone, J., et al.: Adverse outcome in pregnancy following amniotic fluid isolation of *Ureaplasma urealyticum.* Prenat. Diagn. *12*:111, 1992.
58. Groneck, P., Goetze-Speer, B., and Speer, C. P.: Inflammatory bronchopulmonary response of preterm infants with microbial colonization of the airways at birth. Arch. Dis. Child. Fetal Neonatal Ed. *74*:F51, 1996.
59. Hamrick, H. J., and Mangum, M. E.: *Ureaplasma urealyticum* abscess at site of an internal fetal heart rate monitor. Pediatr. Infect. Dis. J. *12*:410, 1993.
60. Hannaford, K., Todd, D. A., Jeffery, H., et al.: Role of *Ureaplasma urealyticum* in lung disease of prematurity. Arch. Dis. Child. Fetal Neonatal Ed. *81*:F162, 1999.
61. Harasawa, R., and Kanamoto, Y.: Differentiation of two biovars of *Ureaplasma urealyticum* based on the 16S-23S rRNA intergenic spacer region. J. Clin. Microbiol. *37*:4135, 1999.
62. Heggie, A. D., Bar-Shain, D., Boxerbaum, B., et al.: Identification and quantification of ureaplasmas colonizing the respiratory tract and assessment of their role in the development of chronic lung disease in preterm infants. Pediatr. Infect. Dis. J. *20*:854, 2001.
63. Heggie, A. D., Jacobs, M. R., Butler, V. T., et al.: Frequency and significance of isolation of *Ureaplasma urealyticum* and *Mycoplasma hominis* from cerebrospinal fluid and tracheal aspirate specimens from low birth weight infants. J. Pediatr. *124*:956, 1994.
64. Hentschel, J., Abele-Horn, M., and Peters, J.: *Ureaplasma urealyticum* in the cerebrospinal fluid of a premature infant. Acta Paediatr. *82*:690, 1993.
65. Hjelm, E., Jousell, E., Linglof, T., et al.: Meningitis in a newborn infant caused by *Mycoplasma hominis.* Acta Paediatr. *68*:415, 1980.
66. Horowitz, S., Landau, D., Shinwell, E. S., et al.: Respiratory tract colonization with *Ureaplasma urealyticum* and bronchopulmonary dysplasia in neonates in southern Israel. Pediatr. Infect. Dis. J. *11*:847, 1992.
67. Horowitz, S., Mazor, M., Romero, R., et al.: Infection of the amniotic cavity with *Ureaplasma urealyticum* in the midtrimester of pregnancy. J. Reprod. Med. *40*:375, 1995.
68. Hypertrophic pyloric stenosis in infants following pertussis prophylaxis with erythromycin—Knoxville, Tennessee, 1999. M. M. W. R. Morb. Mortal. Wkly. Rep. *48*(49):1117, 1999.
69. Iles, R., Lyon, A., Ross, P., and McIntosh, N.: Infection with *Ureaplasma urealyticum* and *Mycoplasma hominis* and the development of chronic lung disease in preterm infants. Acta. Paediatr. *85*:482, 1996.
70. Izraeli, S., Samra, Z., Sirota, L., et al.: Genital mycoplasmas in preterm infants: Prevalence and clinical significance. Eur. J. Pediatr. *150*:804, 1991.
71. Jones, D. M., and Tobin, B.: Neonatal eye infections due to *Mycoplasma hominis.* B. M. J. *2*:467, 1968.
72. Jonsson, B., Karell, A. C., Ringertz, S., et al.: Neonatal *Ureaplasma urealyticum* colonization and chronic lung disease. Acta Paediatr. *83*:927, 1994.
73. Jonsson, B., Rylander, M., and Faxelius, G.: *Ureaplasma urealyticum,* erythromycin and respiratory morbidity in high-risk preterm neonates. Acta Paediatr. *87*:1079, 1998.
74. Kelly, V. N., Garland, S. M., and Gilbert, G. L.: Isolation of genital mycoplasmas from the blood of neonates and women with pelvic infection using conventional SPS-free blood culture media. Pathology *19*:277, 1987.
75. Kirk, N., and Kovar, I.: *Mycoplasma hominis* meningitis in a preterm infant. J. Infect. *15*:109, 1987.
76. Klein, J. O., Buckland, D. O., and Finland, M.: Colonization of newborn infants by mycoplasmas. N. Engl. J. Med. *20*:1025, 1969.
77. Knausz, M., Niederland, T., Dosa, E. and Rozgonyi, F.: Meningoencephalitis in a neonate caused by maternal *Mycoplasma hominis* treated successfully with chloramphenicol. J. Med. Microbiol. *51*:187, 2002.
78. Kober, M. B., and Mason, B. A.: Colonization of the female genital trace by resistant *Ureaplasma urealyticum* treated successfully with azithromycin. Clin. Infect. Dis. *27*:401, 1998.
79. Kong, F., James, G., Ma, Z., et al.: Phylogenetic analysis of *Ureaplasma urealyticum*—support for the establishment of a new species, *Ureaplasma parvum.* Int. J. Syst. Bacteriol. *49*:1879, 1999.

80. Kong, F., Ma, Z., James, G., et al.: Species identification and subtyping of *Ureaplasma parvum* and *Ureaplasma urealyticum* using PCR-based assays. J. Clin. Microbiol. *38*:1175, 2000.
81. Kundsin, R. B., Driscoll, S. G., Monson, R. R., et al.: Association of *Ureaplasma urealyticum* in the placenta with perinatal morbidity and mortality. N. Engl. J. Med. *310*:941, 1984.
82. Lamey, J. R., Foy, H. M., and Kenny, G. E.: Infection with *Mycoplasma hominis* and T-strains in the female genital tract. Obstet. Gynecol. *44*:703, 1974.
83. Li, Y. H., Brauner, A., Jonsson, B., et al.: *Ureaplasma urealyticum*–induced production of proinflammatory cytokines by macrophages. Pediatr. Res. *48*:114, 2000.
84. Likitnukul, S., Kusmiesz, H., Nelson, J. D., et al.: Role of genital mycoplasmas in young infants with suspected sepsis. J. Pediatr. *109*:971, 1986.
85. Lyon, A. J., McColm, J., Middlemist, L., et al.: Randomised trial of erythromycin on the development of chronic lung disease in preterm infants. Arch. Dis. Child. Fetal Neonatal Ed. *78*:F10, 1998.
86. Luki, N., Lebel, P., Boucher, M., et al.: Comparison of polymerase chain reaction assay with culture for detection of genital mycoplasmas in perinatal infections. Eur. J. Clin. Microbiol. Infect. Dis. *17*:255, 1998.
87. Maccato, M., Faro, S., and Summers, K. L.: Wound infections after cesarean section with *Mycoplasma hominis* and *Ureaplasma urealyticum:* A report of three cases. Diagn. Microbiol. Infect. Dis. *13*:363, 1990.
88. Madan, E., Meyer, M. P., and Amortegui, A. J.: Isolation of genital mycoplasmas and *Chlamydia trachomatis* in stillborn and neonatal autopsy material. Arch. Pathol. Lab. Med. *112*:749, 1988.
89. Manimtim, W. M., Hasday, J. D., Hester, L., et al.: *Ureaplasma urealyticum* modulates endotoxin-induced cytokine release by human monocytes derived from preterm and term newborns and adults. Infect. Immun. *69*:3906, 2001.
90. Mardh, P. A.: *Mycoplasma hominis* infection of the central nervous system in newborn infants. Sex. Transm. Dis. *10*:332, 1983.
91. Matlow, A., Th'ng, C., Kovach, D., et al.: Susceptibilities of neonatal respiratory isolates of *Ureaplasma urealyticum* to antimicrobial agents. Antimicrob. Agents Chemother. *42*:1290, 1998.
92. McCormack, W. M., Rosner, B., Alpert, S, et al.: Vaginal colonization with *Mycoplasma hominis* and *Ureaplasma urealyticum.* Sex. Transm. Dis. *134*:67, 1986.
93. McCormack, W. M., Rosner, B., Lee, Y. H., et al.: Isolation of genital mycoplasmas from blood obtained shortly after vaginal delivery. Lancet *1*:596, 1975.
94. McDonald, J. C.: *Mycoplasma hominis* meningitis in a premature infant. Pediatr. Infect. Dis. J. 7:795, 1988.
95. Miller, T. C., Baman, S. I., and Albers, W. H.: Massive pericardial effusion due to *Mycoplasma hominis* in a newborn. Am. J. Dis. Child. *136*:271, 1982.
96. Neal, T. J., Roe, M. F., and Shaw, N. J.: Spontaneously resolving *Ureaplasma urealyticum* meningitis. Eur. J. Pediatr. *153*:342, 1994.
97. Nelson, S., Matlow, A., Johnson, G., Th'ng, C., Dunn, M., and Quinn, P.: Detection of Ureaplasma urealyticum in endotracheal tube aspirates from neonates by PCR. J. Clin. Microbiol. *36*:1236, 1998.
98. Neman-Simha, V., Renaudin, H., de Barbeyrac, B., et al.: Isolation of genital mycoplasmas from blood of febrile obstetrical-gynecologic patients and neonates. Scand. J. Infect. Dis. *24*:317, 1992.
99. Ogasawara, K. K., and Goodwin, T. M.: The efficacy of prophylactic erythromycin in preventing vertical transmission of *Ureaplasma urealyticum.* Am. J. Perinatol. *14*:233, 1997.
100. Ogasawara, K. K., and Goodwin, T. M.: Efficacy of azithromycin in reducing lower genital *Ureaplasma urealyticum* colonization in women at risk for preterm delivery. J. Matern. Fetal Med. *8*:12, 1999.
101. Ohlsson, A., Wang, E., and Vearncombe, M.: Leukocyte counts and colonization with *Ureaplasma urealyticum* in preterm neonates. Clin. Infect. Dis. *17*(Suppl. 1):144, 1993.
102. Ollikainen, J., Hiekkaniemi, H., Korppi, M., et al.: Hydrops fetalis associated with *Ureaplasma urealyticum.* Acta Paediatr. *81*:851, 1992.
103. Ollikainen, J., Hiekkaniemi, H., Korppi, M., et al.: *Ureaplasma urealyticum* cultured from brain tissue of preterm twins who die of intraventricular hemorrhage. Scand J. Infect. Dis. *25*:528, 1993.
104. Ollikainen, J., Heikkaniemi, H., Korppi, M., et al.: *Ureaplasma urealyticum* infection associated with acute respiratory insufficiency and death in premature infants. J. Pediatr. *122*:756, 1993.
105. Ollikainen, J., Heiskanen-Kosma, T., Korppi, M., et al.: Clinical relevance of *Ureaplasma urealyticum* colonization in preterm infants. Acta. Paediatr. *87*:1075, 1998.
106. Ollikainen, J., Korppi, M., Heiskanen-Kosma, T., and Heinonen, K.: Chronic lung disease of the newborn is not associated with *Ureaplasma urealyticum.* Pediatr. Pulmonol. *32*:303, 2001.
107. Pacifico, L., Panero, A., Roggini, M., et al.: *Ureaplasma urealyticum* and pulmonary outcome in a neonatal intensive care population. Pediatr. Infect. Dis. J. *16*:579, 1997.
108. Panero, A., Pacifico, L., Rossi, N., et al.: *Ureaplasma urealyticum* as a cause of pneumonia in preterm infants: Analysis of the white cell response. Arch. Dis. Child. Fetal Neonatal Ed. *73*:F37–F40, 1995.
109. Payne, N. R., Steinberg, S., Stefan, H., et al.: New prospective studies of the association of *Ureaplasma urealyticum* colonization and chronic lung disease. Clin. Infect. Dis. *17*(Suppl. 1):117, 1993.
110. Perzigian, R. W., Adams, J. T., Weiner, G. M., et al.: *Ureaplasma urealyticum* and chronic lung disease in very low birth weight infants during the exogenous surfactant era. Pediatr. Infect. Dis. J. *17*:620, 1998.
111. Powell, D. A., Miller, K., and Clyde, W. A., Jr.: Submandibular adenitis in a newborn caused by *Mycoplasma hominis.* Pediatrics *63*:789, 1979.
112. Quinn, P. A., Gillian, J. E., Markestad, T., et al.: Intrauterine infection with *Ureaplasma urealyticum* as a cause of fatal neonatal pneumonia. Pediatr. Infect. Dis. J. *4*:538, 1985.
113. Quinn, P. A., Li, H. C., Th'ng, C., et al.: Serological response to *Ureaplasma urealyticum* in the neonate. Clin. Infect. Dis. *17*(Suppl. 1):136, 1993.
114. Roberts, S., Maccato, M., Faro, S., et al.: The microbiology of post-cesarean wound morbidity. Obstet. Gynecol. *81*:383, 1993.
115. Rudd, P. T., Cassell, G. H., Waites, K. B., et al.: Experimental production of *Ureaplasma urealyticum* pneumonia and demonstration of age-related susceptibility. Infect. Immun. *57*:918, 1989.
116. Rylander, M., and Hallander, H. O.: In vitro comparison of the activity of doxycycline, tetracycline, erythromycin and a new macrolide, CP 62993, against *Mycoplasma pneumoniae, Mycoplasma hominis* and *Ureaplasma urealyticum.* Scand. J. Infect. Dis. Suppl. *53*:12–17, 1988.
117. Sacker, I., and Brunnell, P. A.: Abscess in newborn infants caused by *Mycoplasma.* Pediatrics *46*:303, 1970.
118. Sánchez, P. J.: Perinatal transmission of *Ureaplasma urealyticum*: Current concepts based on review of the literature. Clin. Infect. Dis. *17*(Suppl. 1):107, 1993.
119. Sánchez, P. J., and Regan, J. A.: *Ureaplasma urealyticum* colonization and chronic lung disease in low birth weight infants. Pediatr. Infect. Dis. J. *78*:542, 1988.
120. Sánchez, P., and Regan, J. A.: Vertical transmission of *Ureaplasma urealyticum* in full term infants. Pediatr. Infect. Dis. J. *6*:825, 1988.
121. Sánchez, P. J., and Regan, J. A.: Vertical transmission of *Ureaplasma urealyticum* in preterm infants. Pediatr. Infect. Dis. J. *9*:398, 1990.
122. Sánchez, P. J., Zeray, F., Priest, C., et al.: Pharmacokinetic analysis of clarithromycin in very-low-birth-weight infants colonized with *Ureaplasma urealyticum.* Abstract 110. Poster presented at the 37th Interscience Conference on Antimicrobial Agents and Chemotherapy, Toronto, September 28–October 1, 1997.
123. Scheurlen, W., Frauendienst, G., Schrod, L., et al.: Polymerase chain reaction–amplification of urease genes: Rapid screening for *Ureaplasma urealyticum* infection in endotracheal aspirates of ventilated newborns. Eur. J. Pediatr. *151*:740, 1992.
124. Shaw, N. J., Pratt, B. C., and Weindling, A. M.: *Ureaplasma* and *Mycoplasma* infections of the central nervous system in preterm infants. Lancet *23*:1530, 1989.
125. Shurin, P. A., Alpert, S., Rosner, B., et al.: Chorioamnionitis and colonization of the newborn infant with genital mycoplasmas. N. Engl. J. Med. *293*:5, 1975.
126. Siber, G. R., Alpert, S., Smith, D. L., et al.: Neonatal central nervous system infection due to *Mycoplasma hominis.* J. Pediatr. *90*:625, 1977.
127. Smyth, A. R., Shaw, N. J., Pratt, B. C., et al.: *Ureaplasma urealyticum* and chronic lung disease. Eur. J. Pediatr. *152*:931, 1993.
128. Sompolinsky, D., Solomon, F., Leiba, H., et al.: Puerperal sepsis due to T-strain *Mycoplasma.* Isr. J. Med. Sci. *7*:745, 1971.
129. Stagno, S., Brasfield, D. M., Brown, M. B., et al.: Infant pneumonitis associated with cytomegalovirus, *Chlamydia, Pneumocystis,* and *Ureaplasma:* A prospective study. Pediatrics *68*:322, 1981.
130. Stahelin-Massik, J., Levy, F., Friderich, P., et al.: Meningitis caused by *Ureaplasma urealyticum* in a full term neonate. Pediatr. Infect. Dis. J. *13*:419, 1994.
131. Stancombe, B. B., Walsh, W. F., Derdak, S., et al.: Induction of human neonatal pulmonary fibroblast cytokines by hyperoxia and *Ureaplasma urealyticum.* Clin. Infect. Dis. *17*(Suppl. 1):154, 1993.
132. Syrogiannopoulos, G. A., Kapatais-Zoumbox, K., Decavalas, G. O., et al.: *Ureaplasma urealyticum* colonization of full term infants: Perinatal acquisition and persistence during early infancy. Pediatr. Infect. Dis. J. *9*:236, 1990.
133. Tafari, N., Ross, S., Naeye, R. L., et al.: *Mycoplasma* "T" strains and perinatal death. Lancet *1*:108, 1976.
134. Taylor-Robinson, D., and McCormack, W. M.: The genital mycoplasmas. N. Engl. J. Med. *302*:1003, 1980.
135. Teng, L. J., Zheng, X., Glass, J. I., et al.: *Ureaplasma urealyticum* biovar specificity and diversity are encoded in multiple-banded antigen gene. J. Clin. Microbiol. *32*:1464–1469, 1994.
136. Thomsen, A. C., Taylor-Robinson, D., Hanson, K. B., et al.: The infrequent occurrence of mycoplasmas in amniotic fluid from women with intact fetal membranes. Acta Obstet. Gynecol. Scand. *3*:425, 1983.
137. Unsworth, P. F., Taylor-Robinson, D., Sho, E. E., et al.: Neonatal mycoplasmemia: *Mycoplasma hominis* as a significant cause of disease? J. Infect. *10*:163, 1985.
138. Valencia, G. B., Banzon, F., Cummings, M., et al.: *Mycoplasma hominis* and *Ureaplasma urealyticum* in neonates with suspected infection. Pediatr. Infect. Dis. J. *12*:571, 1993.

139. Van Waarde, W. M., Brus, F., Okken, A., and Kimpen, J. L.: *Ureaplasma urealyticum* colonization, prematurity and bronchopulmonary dysplasia. Eur. Respir. J. *10*:886, 1997.
140. Waites, K. B., Cassell, G. H., Canupp, K. C., et al.: In vitro susceptibilities of mycoplasmas and ureaplasmas to new macrolides and arylfluoroquinolones. Antimicrob. Agents Chemother. *32*:1500, 1988.
141. Waites, K. B., Crouse, D. T., and Cassell, G. H.: Antibiotic susceptibilities and therapeutic options for *Ureaplasma urealyticum* infections in neonates. Pediatr. Infect. Dis. J. *11*:23, 1992.
142. Waites, K. B., Crouse, D. T., and Cassell, G. H.: Therapeutic consideration for *Ureaplasma urealyticum* infections in neonates. Clin. Infect. Dis. *17*(Suppl. 1):208, 1993.
143. Waites, K. B., Crouse, D. T., Phillips, J. G., et al.: *Ureaplasma* pneumonia and sepsis associated with persistent pulmonary hypertension of the newborn. Pediatrics *83*:84, 1991.
144. Waites, K. B., Duffy, L. B., Crouse, D. T., et al.: Mycoplasmal infection of cerebrospinal fluid in newborn infants from a community hospital population. Pediatr. Infect. Dis. J. *9*:241, 1990.
145. Waites, K. B., Figarola, T. A., Schmid, T., et al.: Comparison of agar versus broth dilution techniques for determining antibiotic susceptibilities of *Ureaplasma urealyticum*. Diagn. Microbiol. Infect. Dis. *14*:265, 1991.
146. Waites, K. B., Rudd, P. T., Crouse, D. T., et al.: Chronic *Ureaplasma urealyticum* and *Mycoplasma hominis* infections of central nervous systems in preterm infants. Lancet *2*:17, 1988.
147. Waites, K. B., Sims, P. J., Crouse, D. T., et al.: Serum concentrations of erythromycin after intravenous infusion in preterm neonates treated for *Ureaplasma urealyticum* infection. Pediatr. Infect. Dis. J. *13*:287, 1994.
148. Walsh, W. F., Butler, J., Coalson, J., et al.: A primate model of *Ureaplasma urealyticum* infection in the premature infant with hyaline membrane disease. Clin. Infect. Dis. *17*(Suppl. 1):158, 1993.
149. Walsh, W. F., Stanley, S., Lally, K. P., et al.: *Ureaplasma urealyticum* demonstrated by open lung biopsy in newborns with chronic lung disease. Pediatr. Infect. Dis. J. *10*:823, 1991.
150. Wang, E. L., Cassell, G. H., Sánchez, P., et al.: *Ureaplasma urealyticum* and chronic lung disease of prematurity: Critical appraisal of the literature on causation. Clin. Infect. Dis. *17*(Suppl. 1):112, 1993.
151. Wang, E. E., Frayha, H., Watts, J., et al.: The role of *Ureaplasma urealyticum* and other pathogens in the development of chronic lung disease of prematurity. Pediatr. Infect. Dis. J. *7*:547, 1988.
152. Wang, E. E., Matlow, A. G., Ohlsson, A., and Nelson, S. C.: *Ureaplasma urealyticum* infections in the perinatal period. Clin. Perinatol. *24*:91, 1997.
153. Wang, E. E. L., Ohlsson, A., and Kellner, J. D.: Association of *Ureaplasma urealyticum* colonization with chronic lung disease of prematurity: Results of a metaanalysis. J. Pediatr. *127*:640, 1995.
154. Yoon, B. H., Romero, R., Kim, M., et al.: Clinical implications of detection of *Ureaplasma urealyticum* in the amniotic cavity with the polymerase chain reaction. Am. J. Obstet. Gynecol. *183*:1130, 2000.
155. Yoon, B. H., Romero, R., Park, J. S., et al.: Microbial invasion of the amniotic cavity with *Ureaplasma urealyticum* is associated with a robust host response in fetal, amniotic, and maternal compartments. Am. J. Obstet. Gynecol. *179*:1254, 1998.

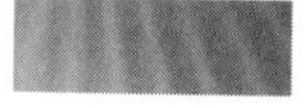

CHAPTER **73D**

Candida Infections

PABLO J. SÁNCHEZ

The improved survival of preterm infants since the early 1980s has resulted in the emergence of *Candida* as a significant neonatal pathogen.[5, 10, 18, 44, 53, 59, 104] *Candida* spp. account for approximately 9 percent of nosocomial infections in the neonatal intensive care unit (NICU), and they infect approximately 1 to 6 percent of infants with a birth weight less than 1500 g and 10 percent of infants with a birth weight less than 1000 g; the case-fatality rate is 30 percent.[18, 109] The species most frequently isolated is *Candida albicans*,[5, 18, 109] which represents approximately 40 to 60 percent of isolates. Non-*albicans* species, however, have become increasingly more prevalent, and in many NICUs, they are isolated more frequently than is *C. albicans*.[31, 65, 69, 71, 83, 90] Among these organisms, *Candida parapsilosis* is the most common,[34, 69] although *Candida tropicalis*,[5, 71] *Candida glabrata*,[31] *Candida guilliermondii*,[90, 92, 93] and *Candida lusitaniae*[94] also cause neonatal infection. Manifestations of disease range from the commonly encountered and relatively benign oral and cutaneous candidiasis to the more severe and even fatal congenital and systemic candidiasis. The latter, representing a disseminated form of candidal infection, remains one of the most vexing infectious problems in the NICU. Delay in recognition of infection and institution of antifungal therapy often leads to significant morbidity and mortality in high-risk infants.[5]

Transmission

Candida may be transmitted to the fetus in utero by an ascending route from the colonized vagina of the mother. Transplacental infection has not been described. In utero transmission results in either a pulmonary or mucocutaneous infection termed congenital candidiasis.[27, 48, 52, 54, 70, 72, 105, 106] More commonly, transmission to the newborn occurs during birth from contact with an infected birth canal,[4] which results in the development of oral candidiasis, or thrush, in the infant.[2] Subsequent colonization of the gastrointestinal tract and its presence in stool lead to superficial cutaneous infection primarily involving the perineal area.[4] In high-risk neonates, gastrointestinal colonization also may lead to bloodstream dissemination, particularly if the integrity of the intestinal mucosal lining is disrupted by surgery, ischemia, or enterocolitis.[15, 18, 29] In addition, the immature skin of extremely-low-birth-weight infants may predispose them to the acquisition of invasive candidal infection. Candidal dissemination in neonates is aided further by abnormal neonatal leukocyte function, as demonstrated by an impaired ability of polymorphonuclear leukocytes to adhere to, ingest, and kill *Candida* and a reduced capacity of lymphocytes to inhibit candidal growth.[101, 109]

Candida also may be acquired by the infant during breast-feeding if the mother's skin is colonized, as well as from inadequate sterilization of feeding bottles and nipples.[32] Nosocomial transmission occurs and has resulted in nursery outbreaks; infant-to-infant transmission probably occurs via the hands of health care workers.*

Candidal colonization of the neonatal oropharynx is a common finding that occurs in approximately 4 to 19 percent of infants in the first few days of life. Baley and colleagues[4] in 1986 studied 146 infants with a birth weight less than 1500 g during an 11-month period. They performed fungal cultures of the pharynx, rectum, and endotracheal aspirates within 24 hours of birth and then weekly while the infant was in the NICU. The overall colonization rate was 27 percent, although by the time that they reached 2 weeks of age, 85 percent of the infants were colonized, primarily with *Candida* spp. Mucocutaneous disease developed in 28 percent of the colonized infants, and systemic candidiasis was seen in 8 percent. Gastrointestinal colonization with *Candida* occurs before the development of candidemia in most preterm infants.[92, 93] In addition, Rowen and colleagues[88]

*See references 10, 11, 46, 68, 85, 91, 93, 102, 115, 116, 121.

showed that very-low-birth-weight infants with endotracheal colonization by *Candida* had a sixfold increased risk for development of invasive disease.

Clinical Manifestations

ORAL CANDIDIASIS

Oral candidiasis is the most common form of infection.[73] Lesions on the mucous membranes of the mouth and oropharynx usually appear on the 7th to 10th day of life as whitish-gray plaques that can be scraped easily from the mucosa to expose an erythematous base but no blood. Persistent infection may be caused by the continued use of bottle nipples and pacifiers that have been used before initiation of antifungal therapy because *Candida* may be recovered readily from these sources. However, the need to consider immunodeficiency states, including infection with human immunodeficiency virus, when oral thrush fails to clear cannot be overemphasized.

CUTANEOUS CANDIDIASIS

Cutaneous candidiasis typically is manifested by erythematous, vesiculopustular lesions found primarily on the skin of the perineum, axilla, and intertriginous areas, but the periumbilical area also can be involved.[73] So-called satellite lesions are common findings, and the peak incidence occurs at 3 to 4 months of age.

CONGENITAL CANDIDIASIS

Congenital candidal infection is manifested at birth or within 24 hours of life as a widespread, erythematous maculopapular or vesiculopustular rash with or without pneumonia.[27, 48, 52, 54, 70, 72, 105, 106] A presumptive diagnosis can be made with potassium hydroxide preparations or Gram stain of the pustular or vesicular contents. *Candida* can be isolated from these skin lesions. Pneumonia as a sole manifestation of congenital candidiasis has been reported. Histologic chorioamnionitis and funisitis also may be present. Risk factors include a maternal history of vaginitis, antibiotic use, cervical cerclage, and prolonged rupture of fetal membranes, although often none of these factors is present. Poor prognostic factors include the presence of pneumonia and prematurity. At autopsy, *Candida* has been isolated only from the lungs, gastrointestinal tract, and skin; hematogenous dissemination is an uncommon finding except in preterm, low-birth-weight infants.

SYSTEMIC CANDIDIASIS

Systemic candidiasis refers to the isolation of *Candida* or its histopathologic demonstration in a normally sterile body site. Butler and Baker[18] proposed two forms of this clinical syndrome: (1) catheter-associated sepsis in which *Candida* is isolated from the blood of infants who have central venous catheters but no evidence of focal infection or disseminated disease and (2) disseminated candidiasis in which fungemia is present in association with other foci of infection irrespective of whether the infant has a central venous catheter. Several risk factors have been associated with systemic candidiasis,* the most common being prematurity, very low birth weight with its attendant impairment of host defense mechanisms, and prolonged use of broad-spectrum antimicrobial therapy, in particular, third-generation cephalosporins.[92] Antibiotics have a suppressive effect on normal gastrointestinal flora, with the concomitant overgrowth of *Candida*.[99] Gastrointestinal surgery or illness (or both) can further facilitate passage of the fungus across the bowel mucosa and into the bloodstream. Prolonged use of intravascular catheters and the use of hyperalimentation solutions also play a role in the development of systemic candidiasis. Other risk factors associated with the development of candidal infections include malnutrition, prolonged endotracheal intubation, and the use of corticosteroids and H_2 blockers.[93] The early use of steroids for the treatment of hypotension has been associated with the development of fungal infections in extremely-low-birth-weight infants.[16, 87] Although aminophylline is able to inhibit the candicidal activity of human granulocytes, its use has not been associated with the development of neonatal fungal infection. Recently, in vitro studies by Hostetter have found the use of heparin to be another predisposing factor; this finding will need confirmation in the clinical setting.[44a]

The clinical and laboratory signs of systemic candidiasis usually are nonspecific and resemble those seen with bacterial sepsis.[10, 18] Respiratory deterioration (74%), apnea and bradycardia (60%), carbohydrate intolerance (56%), skin manifestations (53%),[8, 87] abdominal distention (49%), temperature instability (35%), guaiac-positive stools (26%), and hypotension (21%) are the signs and symptoms most commonly seen.[18] The sites most commonly involved include blood (60–80%), the central nervous system (CNS) (meningitis, 25–60%),[32, 33, 36, 64] the lungs (pneumonia, 70%),[5, 56, 79] the kidneys (renal candidiasis, 60%),[5, 28, 33, 37, 60, 78, 80] and the eyes (endophthalmitis, 30%).[3, 77] Other less common but significant manifestations include brain abscess, intracranial calcifications, endocarditis,[35, 38, 50, 81, 95, 124] osteoarthritis,[1, 42, 64, 111, 119] peritonitis,[9, 51] liver abscess, and even cataract.[100, 112] Systemic candidemia in preterm infants also has been associated with retinopathy of prematurity.[74]

Diagnosis

The diagnosis of systemic candidiasis is established by isolation of *Candida* spp. in culture from a normally sterile body fluid or site. No reliable, sensitive, or specific rapid antigen or serologic test is available to aid in the diagnosis. Therefore, that systemic candidiasis is diagnosed in as many as 20 to 50 percent of infants at autopsy is not surprising.[5] Similarly, a mean delay of 11 days has been reported between the onset of symptomatic disease and the initiation of antifungal therapy.

The diagnosis often is made when a routine blood culture from an infant evaluated for possible bacterial sepsis yields a *Candida* organism. *Candida* will demonstrate growth in routine blood cultures processed in the automated sytems used by most clinical laboratories, such as the BacT/Alert Microbial Detection System. The use of such blood culture systems has detected *Candida* spp. as early as after 4 hours of incubation. However, for optimal recovery of more fastidious fungi, specific fungal blood cultures should be initiated and held in the laboratory for as long as 4 weeks. On occasion, yeast may be detected in smears of blood even before being incubated in culture media.[82] Reddy and colleagues[84] reported the usefulness of buffy coat smear and culture for detection of fungal infection in high-risk neonates. These

*See references 5, 6, 10, 18, 33, 65, 71, 88, 92, 93, 120.

tests had a sensitivity of 62 and 85 percent, respectively, and excellent specificity when compared with recovery of fungi from routine blood culture.

In the evaluation of an infant for possible candidemia, blood for culture should be obtained from a peripheral vein or artery, as well as through all intravascular catheters in place at the time.[89] Isolation of *Candida* from blood obtained through any vascular catheter requires prompt removal of that device.[25, 30, 107] *Candida* is difficult to eradicate from such catheters. Moreover, the longer these infected devices remain in place, the greater the likelihood that fungal dissemination to other body sites will occur and the greater the morbidity and mortality rates. Examination and culture of cerebrospinal fluid (CSF) also should be performed, although normal CSF indices do not exclude the presence of CNS involvement. Fernandez and associates,[36] in a 10-year review of candidal meningitis in 23 infants in an NICU, reported that pleocytosis occurred in only 39 percent of infants, hypoglycorrhachia in 25 percent, and a positive CSF culture for *Candida* in 74 percent of infants. However, abnormal CSF analysis, when present, may be the only indicator of fungal invasion of the CNS.[33]

Urine obtained by suprapubic bladder aspiration is an excellent source for recovery of *Candida*.[80] Bag specimens of urine should not be used because of the high rate of perineal candidal colonization in infants. Catheterized urine specimens, though preferable to those obtained by bag, may be contaminated from improper cleansing of the perineum and penis. The need for obtaining an adequate urine sample from the bladder, even if by ultrasound guidance, cannot be overemphasized because results of urine cultures will help determine the duration of antifungal therapy. Fungal culture of urine may yield candidal growth when other body fluids such as blood and CSF are sterile. A potassium hydroxide preparation of freshly obtained urine may show evidence of fungi, thereby leading to a presumptive diagnosis and early initiation of antifungal therapy.

In addition to cultures of blood, CSF, and urine, cultures of all involved sites such as joints, bones, catheter exit sites, catheter tips, and abscesses should be performed. The peritoneal fluid from infants with necrotizing enterocolitis who require surgical intervention should be examined. In addition, biopsy of skin lesions for fungal culture and histopathologic examination may be needed and should be performed if the diagnosis is in question. If these cultures are positive, antifungal therapy should be instituted. Endotracheal fungal cultures are of questionable value because of frequent candidal colonization of the neonatal respiratory tract. Thrombocytopenia is a frequent early finding in infants with systemic candidiasis. Additional laboratory tests, such as a complete blood cell count, liver function tests, and determination of serum glucose, blood urea nitrogen, and creatinine, may be helpful in assessing the degree of systemic involvement.

Infants whose cultures yield *Candida* should have further evaluation performed to detect any evidence of dissemination that will influence the prognosis and duration of antifungal therapy. Ultrasonographic evaluation of the abdomen should be performed to assess for possible liver or splenic abscesses, as well as ultrasonography of the kidneys and bladder to detect evidence of fungal balls. Cranial ultrasound may be a useful screen for CNS pathology such as hydrocephalus.[17, 62, 63] However, in infants with a positive CSF candidal culture or evidence of meningitis, computed tomography of the head is preferred for the detection of possible abscess or infarction[55] and intracerebral calcifications presumably secondary to parenchymal granulomata.[40] Careful ophthalmologic examination will detect endophthalmitis. Infants with a central venous catheter or persistent candidemia should have an echocardiogram performed for possible endocarditis.[95]

Treatment

Thrush is treated with oral nystatin suspension or gentian violet. Superficial cutaneous candidiasis is treated with topical nystatin cream. When the diaper area is involved, oral nystatin therapy may be administered as well in an attempt to eliminate the yeast from the gastrointestinal tract. Congenital candidiasis generally does not require treatment—or requires only topical antifungal therapy—except in preterm infants and those with pulmonary involvement, who are at greater risk for dissemination and a poor outcome.[18, 73] In these instances, amphotericin B should be used for approximately 5 to 10 days until the clinical signs and symptoms have resolved.

Amphotericin B deoxycholate remains the drug of choice for systemic candidiasis.[5, 7, 10, 18, 19, 36, 108] In general, it is tolerated better in neonates than in older children and adults. The dose is 1 mg/kg/day infused over the course of 2 to 4 hours. No initial test dose, slow escalation of dosing, or premedication is necessary. The duration of therapy varies with the severity and type of candidal infection. For catheter-associated candidiasis in which prompt removal of the intravascular device results in rapid clinical and laboratory improvement, a cumulative dose of 7 to 10 mg/kg is sufficient.[18] However, for disseminated infection, cumulative doses of at least 25 mg/kg often are necessary.[18, 19] Specifically for meningitis, a 30-mg/kg cumulative dose is preferred, whereas for endocarditis, cumulative doses as high as 40 to 50 mg/kg have been administered.[95] Intrathecal amphotericin B has been used for the treatment of candidal meningitis, but it rarely is needed. The initial intrathecal dose is 0.01 mg, which is increased gradually over the course of 5 to 7 days to 0.1 mg given every other or every third day. Adverse effects of amphotericin B include nephrotoxicity manifested by oliguria, azotemia, and an elevated serum creatinine concentration.[5, 21, 108] Hypokalemia occurs commonly and reflects tubular injury resulting in increased urinary excretion of potassium.[18, 19] Hepatic enzyme abnormalities, anemia, and thrombocytopenia[20] have been reported but rarely occur in neonates. Similarly, neonates do not experience the fever, chills, and vomiting that are common manifestations in older individuals.

The addition of oral 5-fluorocytosine (5-FC, 100 to 150 mg/kg/day divided every 6 hours) to amphotericin B therapy has been advocated when candidemia, meningitis,[22] or endocarditis[95] persists. Synergy of 5-FC with amphotericin B has been documented.[76] Moreover, 5-FC is well absorbed from the gastrointestinal tract and diffuses well into the CSF.[13, 22] Approximately 4 to 8 percent of *Candida* isolates, mostly *C. tropicalis* and *Candida krusei,* are resistant to 5-FC. Side effects include hepatotoxicity, bone marrow suppression, and gastrointestinal intolerance, as well as hemorrhagic enterocolitis.[13, 57, 95] These effects usually are the result of elevated serum levels in excess of 100 μg/mL. Because of the potential for significant toxicity and the need for oral administration and monitoring of drug levels, as well as the excellent clinical experience with amphotericin B monotherapy,[19] routine use of 5-FC has been discouraged. It generally is used only for persistent candidemia despite the removal of all foreign material such as central venous catheters.

Fluconazole (6 mg/kg/day), an azole agent, has been used in neonates and has compared favorably with amphotericin B.[14, 26, 47, 86, 96, 98, 122] It has excellent penetration of CSF and has been used successfully to treat some infants with candidal meningitis.[47] For these reasons, fluconazole rather than 5-FC has become the second-line agent after amphotericin B when candidemia persists beyond 5 days after the initiation of therapy. Breakthrough candidemia occurring while the patient was receiving fluconazole therapy has been described.[66, 75] Although fluconazole resistance is rare in *C. albicans,* Rowen and colleagues[90] have demonstrated fluconazole resistance in neonatal isolates of *C. glabrata, C. tropicalis,* and *C. guilliermondii.* Antifungal susceptibility testing should be performed if fluconazole therapy is used for severe infections.[45, 90]

Lipid preparations of amphotericin B such as liposomal amphotericin B, amphotericin B lipid complex, amphotericin B colloidal dispersion, and lipid emulsion (10 to 20% Intralipid combined with amphotericin B) have been used successfully in neonates and older children, but because of limited experience and expense, they are not recommended for routine use in neonates.[39, 41, 43, 49, 67, 97, 118, 123] In general, lipid preparations are used when toxicity, primarily renal, occurs during the course of conventional amphotericin B therapy. Of the lipid preparations, AmBisome, a liposomal amphotericin B agent, has improved CNS penetration. Because these preparations preferentially accumulate in organs of the reticuloendothelial system, they may be more useful for the treatment of hepatic or splenic candidal abscesses.

Itraconazole and miconazole have been used to treat systemic candidiasis in neonates.[12, 23, 110, 113, 114] Itraconazole is preferred for infections caused by *Aspergillus* spp. No data are available on the treatment of neonates with the new azole preparations such as voriconazole or on treatment with echinocandin agents.

Prevention

Because of the high frequency and significant morbidity and mortality rates associated with candidal infection in premature infants, preventive strategies using antifungal agents have been studied. Oral nystatin reduced fungal colonization and disease in preterm infants with a birth weight less than 1250 g, and it has been used to control a nursery outbreak of candidal infection.[24, 103] Miconazole oral gel decreased rectal fungal colonization, a predisposing factor for the development of systemic candidiasis, when compared with placebo in infants with a birth weight less than 1750 g.[117] Most recently, Kaufman and coworkers[58] demonstrated that fluconazole administered during the first 6 weeks of age to mechanically ventilated preterm infants with a birth weight of 1000 g or less significantly reduced fungal colonization and disease. However, in another randomized trial of fluconazole versus placebo, Kicklighter and colleagues[61] showed a significant reduction in rectal colonization but not disease in 103 preterm infants with a birth weight of 1500 g or less. The development of fluconazole resistance is a major concern with the routine use of such prophylaxis in NICUs. Any preventive strategy must include minimizing exposure to the known risk factors associated with systemic candidiasis, as well as limiting the duration of such exposure in preterm infants. Ultimately, benchmarking studies and rational antimicrobial use will be required in all NICUs.

REFERENCES

1. Adler, S., Randall, J., and Plotkin, S. A.: Candidal osteomyelitis and arthritis in a neonate. Am. J. Dis. Child. *123*:595, 1972.
2. Anderson, N. A., Sage, D. N., and Spaulding, E. H.: Oral moniliasis in newborn infants. Am. J. Dis. Child. *67*:450, 1944.
3. Baley, J. E., Annable, W. L., and Kliegman, R. M.: *Candida* endophthalmitis in the premature infant. J. Pediatr. *98*:458, 1981.
4. Baley, J. E., Kliegman, R. M., Boxerbaum, B., et al.: Fungal colonization in the very low birth weight infant. Pediatrics *78*:225, 1986.
5. Baley, J. E., Kliegman, R. M., and Fanaroff, A. A.: Disseminated fungal infections in very low birth weight infants: Clinical manifestations and epidemiology. Pediatrics *73*:144, 1984.
6. Baley, J. E., Kliegman, R. M., and Fanaroff, A. A.: Disseminated fungal infections in very low birth weight infants: Therapeutic toxicity. Pediatrics *73*:152, 1984.
7. Baley, J. E., Meyers, C., Kliegman, R. M., et al.: The pharmacokinetics, outcome and toxicity of amphotericin B and 5-fluorocytosine in neonates. J. Pediatr. *116*:791, 1990.
8. Baley, J. E., and Silverman, R. A.: Systemic candidiasis: Cutaneous manifestations in low birth weight infants. Pediatrics *82*:211, 1988.
9. Bayer, A. S., Blumenkrantz, M. J., Montgamerie, J. Z., et al.: *Candida* peritonitis: Report of 22 cases and review of the English literature. Am J. Med. *61*:832, 1976.
10. Bendel, C. M., and Hostetter, M. K.: Systemic candidiasis and other fungal infections in the newborn. Semin. Pediatr. Infect. Dis. *5*:35, 1994.
11. Benjamin, D. K., Jr., Ross, K., McKinney, R. E., Jr., et al.: When to suspect fungal infection in neonates: A clinical comparison of *Candida parapsilosis* fungemia with coagulase-negative staphylococcal bacteremia. Pediatrics *106*:712, 2000.
12. Bhandari, V., Narang, A., Kumar, B., et al.: Itraconazole therapy for disseminated candidiasis in very low birth weight neonate. J. Pediatr. Child Health *28*:323, 1992.
13. Block, E. R., and Bennett, J. E.: Pharmacological studies with 5-fluorocytosine. Antimicrob. Agents Chemother. *1*:476, 1972.
14. Bode, S., Pederson-Bjergaard, L., and Hjelt, K.: *Candida albicans* septicemia in a premature infant successfully treated with oral fluconazole. Scand. J. Infect. Dis. *24*:673, 1992.
15. Bond, S., Stewart, D. L., and Bendon, R. W.: Invasive *Candida* enteritis of the newborn. J. Pediatr. Surg. *35*:1496, 2000.
16. Botas, C. M., Kurlat, I., Young, S. M., et al.: Disseminated candidal infections and intravenous hydrocortisone in preterm infants. Pediatrics *95*:883, 1995.
17. Boxynski, M. E., Naglie, R. A., and Russell, E. J.: Real-time ultrasonographic surveillance in the detection of CNS involvement in systemic candidiasis. Pediatr. Radiol. *16*:235, 1986.
18. Butler, K. N., and Baker, C. J.: *Candida*: An increasingly important pathogen in the nursery. Pediatr. Clin. North Am. *35*:543, 1988.
19. Butler, K. M., Rench, M. A., and Baker, C. J.: Amphotericin B as a single agent in the treatment of systemic candidiasis in neonates. Pediatr. Infect. Dis. J. *9*:51, 1990.
20. Chan, C. S., Tuazon, C. U., and Lessin, L. S.: Amphotericin-B–induced thrombocytopenia. Ann. Intern. Med. *96*:332, 1982.
21. Cherry, J. D., Lloyd, C. A., Quilty, J. F., et al.: Amphotericin B therapy in children. J. Pediatr. *75*:1063, 1969.
22. Chesney, P. J., Teets, K. C., Mulvihill, J. J., et al.: Successful treatment of *Candida* meningitis with amphotericin B and 5-fluorocytosine in combination. J. Pediatr. *89*:1017, 1976.
23. Clarke, M.., and Davies, D. P.: Neonatal systemic candidiasis treated with miconazole. B. M. J. *281*:354, 1980.
24. Damjanovic, V., Connolly, C. M., van Saene, F., et al.: Selective decontamination with nystatin for control of a *Candida* outbreak in a neonatal intensive care unit. J. Hosp. Infect. *24*:245, 1993.
25. Dato, V. M., and Dajani, A. S.: Candidemia in children with central venous catheters: Role of catheter removal and amphotericin B therapy. Pediatr. Infect. Dis. J. *9*:309, 1990.
26. Driessen, M., Ellis, J. B., Cooper, P. A., et al.: Fluconazole vs. amphotericin B for the treatment of neonatal fungal septicemia: A prospective randomized trial. Pediatr. Infect. Dis. J. *15*:1107, 1996.
27. Dvorak, A. M., and Gavaller, B.: Congenital systemic candidiasis. N. Engl. J. Med. *10*:540, 1966.
28. Eckstein, C. J., and Kass, E. J.: Anuria in a newborn secondary to bilateral uteropelvic fungus balls. J. Urol. *127*:109, 1982.
29. Ekenna, O., and Sherertz, R. J: Factors affecting colonization and dissemination of *Candida albicans* from the gastrointestinal tract of mice. Infect. Immun. *55*:1558, 1987.
30. Eppes, S. C., Troutman, J. L., and Gutman, L. T.: Outcome of treatment of candidemia in children whose central catheters were removed or retained. Pediatr. Infect. Dis. J. *8*:99, 1989.
31. Fairchild, K. D., Tomkoria, S., Sharp, E. C., et al.: Neonatal *Candida glabrata* species: Clinical and laboratory features compared with other *Candia* species. Pediatr. Infect. Dis. J. *21*:39, 2002.
32. Faix, R. G.: *Candida parapsilosis* meningitis in premature infant. Pediatr. Infect. Dis. *2*:462, 1983.
33. Faix, R. G.: Systemic *Candida* infections in infants in intensive care nurseries. High incidence of central nervous system involvement. J. Pediatr. *105*:616–522, 1984.
34. Faix, R. G.: Invasive neonatal candidiasis: Comparison of *albicans* and *parapsilosis* infection. Pediatr. Infect. Dis. J. *11*:88, 1992.
35. Faix, R. G., Feick, H. J., Frommelt, P., et al.: Successful medical treatment of *Candida parapsilosis* endocarditis in a premature infant. Am J. Perinatol. 7:272, 1990.

36. Fernandez, M., Moylett, E. H., Noyola, D. E., et al.: Candidal meningitis in neonates: A 10-year review. Clin. Infect. Dis. *31*:458, 2000.
37. Fisher, J. F., Chew, W. H., Shadomy, S., et al.: Urinary tract infections due to *Candida albicans*. Rev. Infect. Dis. *4*:1107, 1982.
38. Foker, J. E., Bass, J. L., Thompson, T., et al.: Management of intracardiac fungal masses in premature infants. J. Thorac. Cardiovasc. Surg. *87*:244, 1984.
39. Friedlich, P. S., Steinberg, I., Fujitani, A., et al.: Renal tolerance with the use of intralipid-amphotericin B in low-birth-weight neonates. Am. J. Perinatol. *14*:377, 1997.
40. Goldsmith, L. S., Rubenstein, S. D., Wolfson, B. J., et al.: Cerebral calcifications in a neonate with candidiasis. Pediatr. Infect. Dis. J. *9*:451, 1990.
41. Groll, A. H., Giri, N., Petraitis, V., et al.: Comparative efficacy and distribution of lipid formulations of amphotericin B in experimental *Candida albicans* infection of the central nervous system. J. Infect. Dis. *182*:274, 2000.
42. Harris, M. C., Pereira, G. R., Myers, M.. D., et al.: Candidal arthritis in infants previously treated for systemic candidiasis during the newborn period: Report of three cases. Pediatr. Emerg. Care. *16*:249, 2000.
43. Hiemenz, J. W., and Walsh, T. J.: Lipid formulations of amphotericin B: Recent progress and future directions. Clin. Infect. Dis. *22*(Suppl):133, 1996.
44. Ho, N. K.: Systemic candidiasis in premature infants. Aust. Pediatr. J. *20*:127, 1984.
44a. Hostetter, M. K.: Integrin-like proteins in *Candida* spp. and other microorganisms. Fungal Genet. Biol. *21*:1212–1284, 2001.
45. Huang, Y. C., Kao, H. T., Lin, T. Y., et al.: Antifungal susceptibility testing and the correlation with clinical outcome in neonatal candidemia. Am. J. Perinatol. *18*:141, 2001.
46. Huang, Y. C., Lin, T. Y., Leu, H. S., et al.: Outbreak of *Candida parapsilosis* fungemia in neonatal intensive care units: Clinical implications and genotyping analysis. Infection *27*:97, 1999.
47. Huttova, M., Hartmanova, I., Kralinsky, K., et al.: *Candida* fungemia in neonates treated with fluconazole: Report of forty cases, including eight with meningitis. Pediatr. Infect. Dis. J. *17*:1012, 1998.
48. Jahn, C. L., and Cherry, J. D.: Congenital cutaneous candidiasis. Pediatrics *33*:440, 1966.
49. Jarløv, J. O., Born, P., and Bruun, B.: *Candida albicans* meningitis in a 27 weeks premature infant treated with liposomal amphotericin B (AmBisome). Scand. J. Infect. Dis. *27*:419, 1995.
50. Johnson, D. E., Bass, J. L., Thompson, T. R., et al.: *Candida* septicemia and right atrial mass secondary to umbilical vein catheterization. Am. J. Dis. Child. *135*:275, 1981.
51. Johnson, D. E., Conroy, M. M., Foker, J. E., et al.: *Candida* peritonitis in the newborn infant. J. Pediatr. *97*:298, 1980.
52. Johnson, D. E., Thompson, T. R., and Ferrieri, P.: Congenital candidiasis. Am. J. Dis. Child. *135*:273, 1981.
53. Johnson, D. E., Thompson, T. R., Green, T. P., et al.: Systemic candidiasis in very low-birth-weight infants (<1500 grams). Pediatrics *73*:138, 1984.
54. Kam, L. A., and Giaoia, G. P.: Congenital cutaneous candidiasis. Am. J. Dis. Child. *129*:1215, 1975.
55. Kamitsuka, M. D., Nugent, N. A., Conrad, P. D., et al.: *Candida albicans* brain abscesses in a premature infant treated with amphotericin B, flucytosine and fluconazole. Pediatr. Infect. Dis. J. *14*:329, 1995.
56. Kassner, E. G., Kauffman, S. L., Yoon, J. J., et al.: Pulmonary candidiasis in infants: Clinical, radiologic and pathologic features. A. J. R. Am. J. Roentgenol. *137*:707, 1981.
57. Kauffman, C. A., and Frame, P. T.: Bone marrow toxicity associated with 5-fluorocytosine therapy. Antimicrob. Agents Chemother. *11*:244, 1977.
58. Kaufman, D., Boyle, R., Hazen, K. C., et al.: Fluconazole prophylaxis against fungal colonization and infection in preterm infants. N. Engl. J. Med. *345*:1660, 2001.
59. Keller, M. A., Sellers, B. B., Melish, M. E., et al.: Systemic candidiasis in infants. Am. J. Dis. Child. *131*:1260, 1977.
60. Khan, M. Y.: Anuria from *Candida* pyelonephritis and obstructing fungal balls. Urology *21*:421, 1983.
61. Kicklighter, S. D., Springer, S. C., Cox, T., et al.: Fluconazole for prophylaxis against candidal rectal colonization in the very low birth weight infant. Pediatrics *107*:293, 2001.
62. Kintanar, C., Cramer, B. C., Reid, W. D., et al.: Neonatal candidiasis: Sonographic diagnosis. A. J. R. Am. J. Roentgenol. *147*:801, 1986.
63. Kirpekar, M., Abiri, M. M., Hilfer, C., et al.: Ultrasound in the diagnosis of systemic candidiasis (renal and cranial) in very low birth weight premature infants. Pediatr. Radiol. *16*:17, 1986.
64. Klein, J. D., Yamauchi, T., and Horlick, S. P.: Neonatal candidiasis, meningitis and arthritis: Observations and a review of the literature. J. Pediatr. *81*:31, 1972.
65. Kossoff, E. H., Buescher, E. S., and Karlowicz, M. G.: Candidemia in a neonatal intensive care unit: Trends during fifteen years and clinical features of 111 cases. Pediatr. Infect. Dis. J. *17*:504, 1998.
66. Krcmery, V., Huttova, M., Mateicka, F., et al.: Breakthrough fungaemia in neonates and infants caused by *Candida albicans* and *Candida parapsilosis* susceptible to fluconazole in vitro. J. Antimicrob. Chemother. *48*:521, 2001.
67. Lackner, H., Schwinger, W., Urban, C., et al.: Liposomal amphotericin-B (AmBisome) for treatment of disseminated fungal infections in two infants of very low birth weight. Pediatrics *89*:1259, 1992.
68. Leibovitz, E., Iuster-Reicher, A., Amitai, M., et al.: Systemic candidal infections associated with the use of peripheral venous catheters in neonates: A 9-year experience. Clin. Infect. Dis. *14*:485, 1992.
69. Levy I., Rubin L. G., Vasishtha S., et al.: Emergence of *Candida parapsilosis* as the predominant species causing candidemia in children. Clin. Infect. Dis. *26*:1086, 1998.
70. Lopez, E. R., and Aterman, K.: Intra-uterine infection by *Candida*. Am. J. Dis. Child. *115*:663, 1968.
71. Makhoul, I. R., Kassis, I., Smolkin, T., et al.: Review of 49 neonates with acquired fungal sepsis: Further characterization. Pediatrics *107*:61, 2001.
72. Mamlok, R. J., Richardson, C. J., Mamlok, V., et al.: A case of intrauterine pulmonary candidiasis. Pediatr. Infect. Dis. *4*:692, 1985.
73. Miller, M. J: Fungal infections. *In* Remington, J. S., and Klein, J. O. (eds.): Infectious Diseases of the Fetus and Newborn Infant. 5th ed. Philadelphia, W. B. Saunders, 2001, pp. 813–853.
74. Mittal, M., Dhanireddy, R., and Higgins, R. D.: *Candida* sepsis and association with retinopathy of prematurity. Pediatrics *101*:654, 1998.
75. Mogyorosy, G., Soos, G., and Nagy, A.: *Candida* endocarditis in a premature infant. J. Perinat. Med. *28*:407, 2000.
76. Montgomery, J. A., Edwards, J. E., and Guze, L. B.: Synergism of amphotericin B and 5-fluorocytosine for *Candida* species. J. Infect. Dis. *132*:82, 1975.
77. Noyola, D. E., Fernandez, M., Moylett, E. H., and Baker, C. J.: Ophthalmologic, visceral, and cardiac involvement in neonates with candidemia. Clin. Infect. Dis. *32*:1018, 2001.
78. Pappu, L. D., Purohit, D. M., Bradford, B. F., et al.: Primary renal candidiasis in two preterm neonates. Am. J. Dis. Child. *138*:923, 1984.
79. Patriquin, H., Lebowitz, R., Perreault, G., et al.: Neonatal candidiasis: Renal and pulmonary manifestations. A. J. R. Am. J. Roentgenol. *135*:1205, 1980.
80. Phillips, J. R., and Karlowicz, M. G.: Prevalence of *Candida* species in hospital-acquired urinary tract infections in a neonatal intensive care unit. Pediatr. Infect. Dis. J. *16*:190, 1997.
81. Picarelli, D., Surraco, J., Zuniga, C., et al.: Surgical management of active infective endocarditis in a premature neonate weighing 950 grams. J. Thorac. Cardiovasc. Surg. *119*:380, 2000.
82. Portnoy, J., Wolf, P. L., Webb, M., et al.: *Candida* blastospores and pseudohyphae in blood smears. N. Engl. J. Med. *285*:1010, 1971.
83. Rangel-Fausto, M. S., Wiblin, T., Blumberg, H. M., et al.: National Epidemiology of Mycosis Survey (NEMIS): Variations in rates of bloodstream infections due to *Candida* species in 7 surgical intensive care units and 6 neonatal intensive care units. Clin. Infect. Dis. *29*:253, 1999.
84. Reddy, T. C. S., Chakrabarti, A., Singh, M., et al.: Role of buffy coat examination in the diagnosis of neonatal candidemia. Pediatr. Infect. Dis. J. *15*:718, 1996.
85. Reef, S. E., Lasker, B. A., Butcher, D. S., et al.: Nonperinatal nososcomial transmission of *Candida albicans* in a neonatal intensive care unit: Prospective study. J. Clin. Microbiol. *36*:1255, 1998.
86. Robinson, L. G., Jain, L., and Kourtis, A. P.: Persistent candidemia in a premature infant treated with fluconazole. Pediatr. Infect. Dis. J. *18*:735, 1999.
87. Rowen, J. L., Atkins, J. T., Levy, M. L., et al.: Invasive fungal dermatitis in the #1000-gram neonate. Pediatrics *95*:682, 1995.
88. Rowen, J. L., Rench, M. A., Kozinetz, C. A., et al.: Endotracheal colonization with *Candida* enhances risk of systemic candidiasis in very low birth weight neonates. J. Pediatr. *124*:789, 1994.
89. Rowen, J. L., and Tate, J. M.: Management of neonatal candidiasis. Neonatal Candidiasis Study Group. Pediatr. Infect. Dis. J. *17*:1007, 1998.
90. Rowen, J. L., Tate, J. M., Nordoff, N., et al.: Candida isolates from neonates: Frequency of misidentification and reduced fluconazole susceptibility. J. Clin. Microbiol. *11*:3735, 1999.
91. Ruiz-Diez, B., Martinez, V., Alvarez, M., et al.: Molecular tracking of *Candida albicans* in a neonatal care unit: Long-term colonization versus catheter-related infections. J. Clin. Microbiol. *35*:3032, 1997.
92. Saiman, L., Ludington, E., Dawson, J. D., et al.: Risk factors for *Candida* species colonization of neonatal intensive care unit patients. Pediatr. Infect. Dis. J. *20*:1119, 2001.
93. Saiman, L., Ludington, E., Pfaller, M., et al.: Risk factors for candidemia in neonatal intensive care unit patients. Pediatr. Infect. Dis. J. *19*:319, 2000.
94. Sanchez, P. J., and Cooper, B. H.: *Candida lusitaniae:* Sepsis and meningitis in a neonate. Pediatr. Infect. Dis. *6*:758, 1987.
95. Sanchez, P. J., Siegel, J. D., and Fishbein, J.: *Candida* endocarditis: Successful medical management in three preterm infants and review of the literature. Pediatr. Infect. Dis. J. *10*:239, 1991.
96. Saxen, H., Hoppu, K., and Pohjavuori, M.: Pharmacokinetics of fluconazole in very low birth weight infants during the first two weeks of life. Clin. Pharmacol. Ther. *54*:269, 1993.
97. Scarcella, A., Pasquariello, M. B., Giugliano, B., et al.: Liposomal amphotericin B treatment for neonatal fungal infections. Pediatr. Infect. Dis. J. *17*:146, 1998.

98. Schwarze, R., Penk, A., and Pittow, L.: Treatment of candidal infections with fluconazole in neonates and infants. Eur. J. Med. Res. *5*:203, 2000.
99. Seelig, M. S.: The role of antibiotics in the pathogenesis of *Candida* infections. Am J. Med. *40*:887, 1966.
100. Shah, G. J., Vander, J., and Eagle, R. C.: Intralenticular *Candida* species abscess in a premature infant. Am. J. Ophthalmol. *129*:390, 2000.
101. Shareef, M. J., Myers, T. F., Mathews, H. L., et al.: Reduced capacity of neonatal lymphocytes to inhibit the growth of *Candida albicans*. Biol. Neonate *75*:31, 1999.
102. Sherertz, R. J., Gledhill, K. S., Hampton, K. D., et al.: Outbreak of *Candida* bloodstream infections associated with retrograde medication administration in a neonatal intensive care unit. J. Pediatr. *120*:455, 1992.
103. Sims, M. E., Yoo, Y., You, H., et al.: Prophylactic oral nystatin and fungal infections in very-low-birth-weight infants. Am. J. Perinatol. *5*:33, 1988.
104. Smith, H., and Congdon, P.: Neonatal systemic candidiasis. Arch. Dis. Child. *60*:365, 1985.
105. Sonnenschein, H., Clark, H. L., and Taschdjian, C. L.: Congenital cutaneous candidiasis in a premature infant. Am. J. Dis. Child. *99*:81, 1960.
106. Sonnenschein, H., Taschdjian, C. L., and Clark, D. H.: Congenital cutaneous candidiasis in a premature infant. Am. J. Dis. Child. *107*:260, 1964.
107. Stamos, J. K., and Rowley, A. H.: Candidemia in a pediatric population. Clin. Infect. Dis. J. *20*:571, 1995.
108. Starke, J. R., Mason, E. O., Kramer, W. G., et al.: Pharmacokinetics of amphotericin B in infants and children. J. Infect. Dis. *155*:766, 1987.
109. Stoll, B. J., Gordon, T., Korones, S. B., et al.: Late-onset sepsis in very low birth weight neonates: A report from the National Institute of Child Health and Human Development Neonatal Research Network. J. Pediatr. *129*:63, 1996.
110. Sung, J. P., Rajani, K., Chopra, D. R., et al.: Miconazole therapy for systemic candidiasis in conjoined (Siamese) twin and a premature newborn. Am. J. Surg. *138*:688, 1979.
111. Svirsky-Fein, S., Langer, L., Milbauer, B., et al.: Neonatal osteomyelitis caused by *Candida tropicalis*. J. Bone Joint Surg. Am. *61*:455, 1979.
112. Todd Johnston, W., and Cogen, M. S.: Systemic candidiasis with cataract formation in a premature infant. J. Am. Assoc. Pediatr. Ophthalmol. Strabismus *4*:386, 2000.
113. Tuck, S.: Neonatal systemic candidiasis treated with miconazole. Arch. Dis. Child. *55*:903, 1980.
114. van den Anker, J. N.: Treatment of neonatal *Candida albicans* septicemia with itraconazole. Pediatr. Infect. Dis. J. *11*:684, 1992.
115. Vaudry, W. L., Tierney, A. J., and Wenman, W. M.: Investigation of a cluster of systemic *Candida albicans* infections in a neonatal intensive care unit. J. Infect. Dis. *158*:1375, 1988.
116. Waggoner-Fountain, L. A., Walker, M. W., Hollis, R. J., et al.: Vertical and horizontal transmission of unique *Candida* species to premature newborns. *22*:803, 1996.
117. Wainer, S., Cooper, P. A., Funk, E., et al.: Prophylactic miconazole oral gel for the prevention of neonatal fungal rectal colonization and systemic infection. Pediatr. Infect. Dis. J. *11*:713, 1992.
118. Walsh, T. J., Seibel, N. L., Arndt, C., et al.: Amphotericin B lipid complex in pediatric patients with invasive fungal infections. Pediatr. Infect. Dis. J. *18*:702, 1999.
119. Ward, R. M., Sattler, R. F., and Dalton, A. S.: Assessment of antifungal therapy in an 800 gram infant with candidal arthritis and osteomyelitis. Pediatrics *72*:234, 1983.
120. Weese-Mayer, D. E., Fondriest, D. W., Brouillette R. T., et al.: Risk factors associated with candidemia in the neonatal intensive care unit: A case-control study. Pediatr. Infect. Dis. J. *6*:190, 1987.
121. Welbel, S. F., McNeil, M. M., Kuykendall, R. J., et al.: *Candida parapsilosis* bloodstream infections in neonatal intensive care unit patients: Epidemiologic and laboratory confirmation of a common source outbreak. Pediatr. Infect. Dis. J. *15*:998, 1996.
122. Wenzl, T. G., Schefels, J., Hörnchen, H., et al.: Pharmacokinetics of oral fluconazole in premature infants. Eur. J. Pediatr. *157*:661, 1998.
123. Wong-Beringer, A., Jacobs, R. A., and Guglielmo, B. J.: Lipid formulations of amphotericin B: Clinical efficacy and toxicities. Clin. Infect. Dis. *27*:603, 1998.
124. Zenker, P. N., Rosenberg, E. M., Van Dyke, R. B., et al.: Successful medical treatment of presumed *Candida* endocarditis in critically ill infants. J. Pediatr. *119*:472, 1991.

CHAPTER **73E**

Congenital Toxoplasmosis

PABLO J. SÁNCHEZ

Congenital toxoplasmosis results from placental infection and subsequent hematogenous infection of the fetus by the obligate intracellular protozoan parasite *Toxoplasma gondii.*[62] *Toxoplasma* is a coccidian that is ubiquitous in nature, with the cat family being the definitive host.[27] The organism exists in three forms: (1) an oocyst that produces sporozoites, (2) a proliferative form that formerly was referred to as a trophozoite but more recently as an endozoite or tachyzoite, and (3) a tissue cyst that has an intracystic form termed a cystozoite or bradyzoite. Nonfeline mammals or birds ingest infective oocysts from contaminated soil. Tissue cysts then accumulate in the organs and skeletal muscle of these animals. Possible routes of transmission from animal to human are direct contact with cat feces, ingestion of undercooked meat containing infective cysts, and ingestion of fruits or vegetables that have been in contaminated soil.

The prevalence of antibody to *T. gondii* in women of child-bearing age in the United States varies from approximately 3 to 30 percent, depending on the region of the country.[5, 62] The lowest seroprevalence rates have been found in the Mountain and Pacific states, and the highest rates have been noted in the northeastern and southeastern states. In contrast, the seropositivity rate for women in Paris is as high as 70 percent. These widely disparate seroprevalence rates in different adult populations throughout the world have been explained by differences in eating and sanitation practices that contribute to the acquisition of infection.

The prevalence of congenital infection in the United States has been documented to be 0.08 per 1000 births by IgM screening of blood specimens collected on filter paper from newborns in Massachusetts and New Hampshire.[34] This figure compares with a rate of 3 to 10 per 1000 live births in Paris and Vienna. In Massachusetts, a case-control study involving 14 years of newborn screening for congenital toxoplasmosis found that birth of the mother outside the United States, particularly in Cambodia and Laos, and the educational level and higher gravidity of the mother were strongly predictive of congenital infection.[39]

Transmission

Infection of the fetus occurs during maternal parasitemia, with subsequent infection of the placenta by tachyzoites.[5, 62] Placental infection represents an important intermediary step between maternal and fetal infection. A delay of as long as 16 weeks between placental infection and subsequent infection of the fetus has been noted and is termed the prenatal incubation period.[62] Fetal infection occurs as a consequence of maternal primary infection during pregnancy or, rarely, just before conception.[75] Reactivation of latent *Toxoplasma* infection during pregnancy does not lead to fetal infection except in immunocompromised women, such as those infected with human immunodeficiency virus (HIV).[7, 44, 52, 56, 62, 82] In these instances, congenital infection has been documented, although the risk is very low.[17, 21] On the other hand, maternal reinfection leading to congenital toxoplasmosis has been reported.[22, 30, 36] Congenital toxoplasmosis has

TABLE 73–14 ■ VERTICAL TRANSMISSION OF CONGENITAL TOXOPLASMOSIS BY THE TIMING OF MATERNAL INFECTION DURING PREGNANCY

	Fetal	Infection	Rate
Trimester of Pregnancy	1st	2nd	3rd
Overall transmission rate	15%	30%	60%
Rate by disease severity			
Subclinical	18%	67%	90%
Mild	6%	18%	10%
Severe	41%	8%	0
Stillborn/perinatal death	35%	7%	0

occurred in twins[11, 70] and triplets.[81] In monozygotic twins, the clinical manifestations usually are similar, whereas in dizygotic twins, discrepancies in clinical findings are frequent.

The overall fetal infection rate from untreated maternal infection during pregnancy is approximately 40 percent, although the rate depends on when in pregnancy the mother became infected[18, 62, 82] (Table 73–14). Although the actual rate of fetal infection increases as pregnancy advances, the severity of clinical manifestations is greatest when maternal infection is acquired during the first trimester.

Transmission during breast-feeding in humans has not been demonstrated, although the organism has been detected in human milk.

Clinical Manifestations

Acute maternal infection, usually acquired early in pregnancy, may lead to fulminant fetal infection and result in stillbirth, nonimmune fetal hydrops, preterm birth, and perinatal death.[42, 82] On the other hand, chronic *Toxoplasma* infection only rarely has been associated with sporadic abortion.[63]

Most infants born with congenital *Toxoplasma* infection are asymptomatic in the neonatal period, with clinical signs and symptoms being present in only approximately 25 percent of infants.[1, 2, 34] However, long-term follow-up of these asymptomatically infected infants reveals eye or neurologic disease, or both, in as many as 80 to 90 percent by adulthood.[8, 10, 49, 69, 79] The clinical manifestations of congenital toxoplasmosis in the newborn generally are indistinguishable from those associated with other agents of congenital infection such as cytomegalovirus (CMV) and *Treponema pallidum.* The most characteristic clinical findings, frequently referred to as the classic triad of congenital toxoplasmosis, are chorioretinitis, intracranial calcifications, and hydrocephalus.[5, 19, 62] They are seen in approximately 86, 37, and 20 percent of symptomatic infants, respectively. Moreover, they often are accompanied by a combination of such signs and symptoms as anemia (59%), jaundice (43%), splenomegaly (41%), seizures (41%), fever (40%), hepatomegaly (34%), lymphadenopathy (32%), microcephaly (9%), and eosinophilia (9%).[5, 19]

Involvement of the central nervous system is a hallmark of congenital *Toxoplasma* infection.[16, 47, 62] Hydrocephalus usually is obstructive and often requires ventriculoperitoneal shunting.[46, 47] It may be the only manifestation of disease. Abnormalities in cerebrospinal fluid (CSF) occur in approximately 63 percent of infected infants; characteristically, they consist of lymphocytic pleocytosis and an elevated protein content. The markedly high protein concentrations in ventricular fluid, often exceeding 1 g/100 mL, and hydrocephalus are explained by periaqueductal and periventricular vasculitis with necrosis, which are associated specifically with toxoplasmosis.[62] Inflammation and necrosis involving the hypothalamus have resulted in both hypothermia and hyperthermia. When microcephaly is present, it is indicative of severe brain damage. Intracranial calcifications may be single or multiple but typically are generalized and located in the caudate nucleus, choroid plexus, meninges, and subependyma.[53] Periventricular calcifications similar to those associated with CMV also have been described. They are visualized best by computed tomography,[47] although ultrasonography also has been helpful. The calcifications may resolve with appropriate antimicrobial therapy.[47] Neurologic sequelae from untreated congenital toxoplasmosis include mental retardation (87%), seizures (82%), spasticity and palsies (71%), and deafness (15%).[19, 38, 43, 47] *Toxoplasma* has been detected in the inner ear and mastoid, with the associated inflammation resulting in deafness. An ascending flaccid paralysis with myelitis also has been reported.[6]

Chorioretinitis caused by *Toxoplasma* at any age is considered to be a result of congenital infection.[62] In infants, the most common manifestation is strabismus, whereas in older children and adults, defects in visual acuity predominate. The characteristic lesion consists of a focal necrotizing retinitis that often is bilateral. Organisms are present in the retina, and they have a predilection for the macula, with resultant loss of vision. Involvement of the optic nerve also may occur. Other complications include iridocyclitis and cataracts.[47]

Other manifestations of congenital toxoplasmosis include nonspecific maculopapular or petechial rash, myocarditis, pneumonitis, thrombocytopenia, nephrotic syndrome, and abnormalities in immunoglobulin production.[19, 62] Bony abnormalities consisting of metaphyseal radiolucencies similar to those seen in congenital syphilis also have been reported.[51] A variety of endocrine abnormalities, including hypothyroidism, diabetes insipidus,[57, 83] precocious puberty, and growth hormone deficiency, may occur. All these abnormalities are related to the fact that the organism is capable of widespread dissemination throughout the body, with involvement of virtually all organ systems.

Diagnosis

The diagnosis of congenital toxoplasmosis can be established by isolation of the organism from infected body fluids and tissues such as the placenta, amniotic fluid, fetal blood obtained by cordocentesis, umbilical cord blood, infant blood, and CSF.[25, 62, 82] Such isolation involves inoculation of the specimen intraperitoneally into laboratory mice and requires approximately 4 to 6 weeks for confirmation. Though not a practical method, it is available at the *Toxoplasma* Serology Laboratory, Palo Alto Medical Foundation (860 Bryant St., Palo Alto, CA 94301; 415-326-8120). Alternatively, a diagnosis can be made by histopathologic examination of the placenta in which tachyzoites are revealed. Polymerase chain reaction (PCR) has been used successfully to detect *Toxoplasma* DNA in amniotic fluid, placenta, CSF, and fetal and infant blood.[25, 28, 32, 33, 35, 37, 40, 68] PCR performed on amniotic fluid obtained by amniocentesis is the preferred method of confirming in utero infection. A negative amniotic fluid PCR result, however, does not always rule out congenital infection.[68] In addition, interlaboratory variability in performance of PCR assays has been documented.[35]

The most practical and usual method of making the diagnosis is by serologic techniques.* The major problems

*See references 4, 5, 13–15, 23, 34, 45, 54, 55, 60, 61, 64, 65, 71, 73, 80, 82, 84.

associated with serologic diagnosis are determining the acuity of the maternal infection and differentiating endogenous from transplacentally acquired antibodies in neonatal/fetal infection. Because of this difficulty, a battery of serologic tests must be used. They are available commercially at the *Toxoplasma* Serology Laboratory. Tests that detect *T. gondii*–specific IgG include the Sabin-Feldman dye test, which is considered to be the gold standard but requires live organisms/tachyzoites; the indirect immunofluorescent antibody test; IgG enzyme-linked immunosorbent assay (ELISA); and direct agglutination. An AC/HS differential agglutination test has been developed as a confirmatory test to differentiate acute and chronic maternal infection.[13, 45] This test compares the IgG serologic titer obtained with the use of formalin-fixed tachyzoites (HS antigen) with those obtained with acetone- or methanol-fixed tachyzoites (AC antigen). The latter preparation contains stage-specific *Toxoplasma* antigens that are recognized by IgG antibodies only during early infection. Recently, Zufferey and colleagues[84] reported that an enzyme-linked immunofiltration assay (ELIFA) that compares the immunologic profile of the mother's antibody response and that of her child at delivery allowed discrimination between IgG antibodies of maternal origin and IgG synthesized by the fetus, with a sensitivity of 94 percent and a specificity of 99 percent.

Tests that detect *T. gondii*–specific IgM include (1) the double-sandwich IgM ELISA, which has a sensitivity of 75 percent and a specificity of 100 percent[34]; (2) the IgM immunosorbent agglutination assay, which is the most sensitive test but should not be performed on umbilical cord blood because even small quantities of maternal IgM antibodies contaminating the specimen will result in a falsely positive test result[5]; and (3) the IgM immunofluorescent antibody test, which is not recommended because of lower sensitivity than either the IgM ELISA or IgM immunosorbent agglutination assay and poor specificity secondary to rheumatoid factors and antinuclear antibodies contributing to false-positive test results. Other tests that remain under research investigation include a *T. gondii*–specific IgA ELISA and IgA immunofiltration assay; a *T. gondii*–specific IgE immunofiltration assay; and IgG, IgM, and IgA immunoblotting tests.[14, 23, 54, 65, 71, 73]

Evaluation of a pregnant woman and fetus is prompted initially by either seroconversion or the finding of an elevated *Toxoplasma* IgG titer.[9, 12] Because the latter may reflect only chronic infection, the acuity of the maternal infection is best determined serologically by means of the AC/HS differential agglutination test. If recent maternal infection is documented, the fetus should be evaluated by ultrasound, and amniotic fluid should be tested for specific *Toxoplasma* DNA by PCR. The latter has supplanted the need for cordocentesis, and a positive result confirms fetal infection.[37] Postnatally, serologic testing of paired maternal and infant sera should be performed at a reliable laboratory that will include assays for IgG and IgM antibodies. Subinoculation of placental tissue, amniotic fluid, and umbilical cord blood into mice should be considered. If the results of these tests suggest possible infection, the newborn should be evaluated fully by a complete blood cell count and platelet determination, liver function tests, CSF evaluation (including tests for IgG and IgM antibodies and PCR),[76] ophthalmologic examination, and computed tomography of the head. The presence of neonatal IgM antibody in serum or CSF or a positive PCR in serum or CSF is indicative of congenital infection. In addition, at-risk infants should have serologic follow-up to detect increasing serum IgG titers during the first year of life or persistent IgG antibody beyond 12 to 15 months of age, which would be indicative of congenital infection.[66] Uninfected infants have a continuous decline in *Toxoplasma* IgG titer, with no detectable IgM or IgA antibodies.

Low IgG titers and an AC/HS differential agglutination test that indicates remote maternal infection do not require further evaluation of the mother or infant unless the mother is infected with HIV. Because fetal infection has occurred during chronic *Toxoplasma* infection in HIV-infected pregnant women, their infants should be evaluated serologically at birth for evidence of congenital infection. A suggestion is that HIV-infected pregnant women who have low CD4 counts and who are seropositive for *Toxoplasma* antibody receive empirical therapy to prevent fetal infection.[3, 82] However, at present, insufficient data are available for routine recommendation of such therapy.

Treatment

Pregnant women with acute toxoplasmosis and infants with congenital toxoplasmosis, even if they have no clinical signs or symptoms, should receive treatment.* Based on comparison with historical controls, the outcome is improved substantially by maternal and fetal treatment. Nonetheless, because of the lack of randomized clinical studies, the importance of antenatal treatment recently has been questioned.[31, 59, 77] Neonatal treatment has resulted in a reduction in sensorineural hearing loss[48] and neurodevelopmental and visual handicaps.[47] Current therapies, however, are not effective against encysted bradyzoites and, therefore, do not prevent reactivation of chorioretinitis and neurologic disease.[62] Table 73–15 shows the recommended guidelines for the treatment of congenital toxoplasmosis. In infants with congenital toxoplasmosis, treatment consists of pyrimethamine, sulfadiazine, and folinic acid.[5, 47, 50, 62] The duration of treatment should be at least 1 year.[62, 74] Complete blood cell and platelet counts need to be monitored closely while the patient is receiving therapy because granulocytopenia, thrombocytopenia, and megaloblastic anemia may occur. They usually improve quickly once an increased dosage of folinic acid is administered or pyrimethamine and sulfadiazine are discontinued temporarily. In France, spiramycin has been used in alternate months in place of the aforementioned regimen.

Indications for corticosteroid therapy with prednisone (0.5 mg/kg twice a day) are a CSF protein concentration of 1 g/dL or greater or chorioretinitis that threatens vision, and it is continued until these findings are resolved.

Prevention

The focus of prevention should be on education of women of child-bearing age to avoid ingesting oocysts in cat feces, fruits, or vegetables and encysted bradyzoites in raw meat.[20, 24, 41, 62, 78] Routine serologic screening of women during pregnancy has been an effective means of prevention in France and Austria, and it has been advocated in other areas where the incidence of congenital toxoplasmosis remains high. Neonatal screening for IgM antibody also has been advocated so that asymptomatic infants can be detected and treated before neurologic symptoms develop.[34, 58] This strategy, however, has been hampered by the lack of readily available and reliable IgM test kits. Moreover, it will not

*See references 9, 12, 26, 29, 38, 43, 46–48, 53, 67, 72, 82.

TABLE 73–15 ■ TREATMENT GUIDELINES FOR CONGENITAL TOXOPLASMOSIS

Manifestations of Disease	Therapy	Dosage (Oral Unless Specified)	Duration
In pregnant women with acute toxoplasmosis			
First 21 wk of gestation or until term if fetus not infected	Spiramycin*	1 g q8h without food	Until fetal infection documented or excluded at 21 wk; if documented, replace with pyrimethamine, leucovorin, and sulfadiazine
If fetal infection confirmed after 18th wk of gestation or if infection acquired in last few weeks of gestation	Pyrimethamine *and*	Loading dose: 100 mg/day in 2 divided doses for 2 days, followed by 50 mg/day	Until delivery
	Sulfadiazine* *and*	Loading dose: 75 mg/kg/day in 2 divided doses (maximum, 4 g/day) for 2 days, then 100 mg/kg/day in 2 divided doses (maximum, 4 g/day)	Until delivery
	Leucovorin†	10–20 mg/day	Until delivery
Congenital *Toxoplasma* infection in infant	Pyrimethamine *and*	Loading dose: 2 mg/kg/day for 2 days, then 1 mg/kg/day for 2 or 6 mo then this on each Mon, Wed, and Fri	≥1 yr
	Sulfadiazine* *and*	100 mg/kg/day in 2 daily divided doses	≥1 yr
	Leucovorin† (folinic acid)	10 mg 3 times weekly	≥1 yr
	Corticosteroids (prednisone)‡	1 mg/kg/day in 2 daily divided doses	Until resolution of elevated (≥1 g/dL) CSF protein or active chorioretinitis that threatens vision

*Available only on request from the Food and Drug Administration (301-827-2127; fax, 301-927-2475).
†Monitor blood counts and platelets weekly, and adjust for megaloblastic anemia, granulocytopenia, or thrombocytopenia.
‡Corticosteroids should be continued until signs of inflammation (high CSF protein: ≥1 g/dL) or active chorioretinitis that threatens vision have subsided; the dosage then can be tapered and discontinued. Use only in conjunction with pyrimethamine, sulfadiazine, and leucovorin.
Modified from Boyer, K. M., and McAuley, J. B.: Congenital toxoplasmosis. Semin. Pediatr. Infect. Dis. *5*:42, 1994; and Remington, J. S., McLeod, R., Thulliez, P., and Desmonts, G.: Toxoplasmosis. *In* Remington, J. S., and Klein, J. O. (eds.): Infectious Diseases of the Fetus and Newborn Infant. 5th ed. Philadelphia, W. B. Saunders, 2001, p. 293.

detect approximately 25 percent of infected infants who lack anti-*Toxoplasma* IgM antibody. Further studies involving cost analyses are needed to define the best preventive strategy for congenital toxoplasmosis in specific populations, regions, and countries.

REFERENCES

1. Alford, C. A., Jr., Foft, J. W., Blanckenship, W. J., et al.: Subclinical central nervous system disease of neonates: A prospective study of infants born with increased levels of IgM. J. Pediatr. *75*:1167, 1969.
2. Alford, C. A., Jr., Stagno, S., and Reynolds, D. W.: Congenital toxoplasmosis: Clinical, laboratory and therapeutic considerations, with special reference to subclinical disease. Bull. N. Y. Acad. Med. *50*:160, 1974.
3. Beaman, M. H., Luft, B. J., and Remington, J. S.: Prophylaxis for toxoplasmosis in AIDS. Ann. Intern. Med. *117*:163, 1992.
4. Boyer, K. M.: Diagnostic testing for congenital toxoplasmosis. Pediatr. Infect. Dis. J. *20*:59, 2001.
5. Boyer, K. M., and McAuley, J. B.: Congenital toxoplasmosis. Semin. Pediatr. Infect. Dis. *5*:42, 1994.
6. Campbell, A. L., Sullivan, J. E., and Marshall, G. S.: Myelitis and ascending flaccid paralysis due to congenital toxoplasmosis. Clin. Infect. Dis. *33*:1778, 2001.
7. Cohen-Addad, N. E., Joshi, V. V., Sharer, L. R., et al.: Congenital acquired immunodeficiency syndrome and congenital toxoplasmosis: Pathologic support for a chronology of events. J. Perinatol. *8*:328, 1988.
8. Couvreur, J., and Desmonts, G.: Congenital and maternal toxoplasmosis: A review of 300 congenital cases. Dev. Med. Child Neurol. *4*:519, 1962.
9. Couvreur, J., Desmonts, G., and Thulliez, P.: Prophylaxis of congenital toxoplasmosis. Effect of spiramycin on placental infection. J. Antimicrob. Chemother. *22*:193, 1988.
10. Couvreur, J., Desmonts, G., Tournier, G., et al.: Study of a homogeneous series of 210 cases of congenital toxoplasmosis in infants aged 0 to 11 months detected prospectively. Ann. Pediatr. *31*:815, 1984.
11. Couvreur J., Thulliez P., Daffos F., et al.: Six cases of toxoplasmosis in twins. Ann. Pediatr. (Paris) *38*:63, 1991.
12. Daffos, F., Forestier, F., Capella-Pavlovsky, M., et al.: Prenatal management of 746 pregnancies at risk for congenital toxoplasmosis. N. Engl. J. Med. *318*:271, 1988.
13. Dannemann, B. R., Vaughan, W. C., Thurlliez, P., et al.: Differential agglutination test for diagnosis of recently acquired infection with *Toxoplasma gondii*. J. Clin. Microbiol. *28*:1928, 1990.
14. Decoster, A., Darcy, F., Caron, A., et al.: IgA antibodies against P30 as markers of congenital and acute toxoplasmosis. Lancet *2*:1104, 1988.
15. Desmonts, G., Naot, Y., and Remington, J. S.: Immunoglobulin M–immunosorbent agglutination assay for diagnosis of infectious diseases: Diagnosis of acute congenital and acquired *Toxoplasma* infections. J. Clin. Microbiol. *11*:186, 1981.
16. Diebler, C., Dusser, A., and Dulac, O.: Congenital toxoplasmosis: Clinical and neuroradiologic evaluation of the cerebral lesions. Neuroradiology *27*:125, 1985.
17. Dunn D., Newell M. L., and Gilbert R.: Low risk of congenital toxoplasmosis in children born to women infected with human immunodeficiency virus. Pediatr. Infect. Dis. J. *16*:84, 1997.
18. Dunn D., Wallon M., Peyron F., et al.: Mother-to-child transmission of toxoplasmosis: Risk estimates for clinical counselling. Lancet *353*:1829, 1999.
19. Eichenwald, H. G.: A study of congenital toxoplasmosis, with particular emphasis on clinical manifestations, sequelae, and therapy. *In* Siim, J. C. (ed.): Human Toxoplasmosis. Copenhagen, Munksgaard, 1960, pp. 41–49.
20. Eskild, A., Oxman, A., Magnus, P., et al.: Screening for toxoplasmosis in pregnancy: What is the evidence of reducing a health problem? J. Med. Screen. *3*:188, 1996.
21. European Collaborative Study and Resaerch Network on Congenital Toxoplasmosis: Low incidence of congenital toxoplasmosis in children born to women infected with human immunodeficiency virus. Eur. J. Obstet. Gynecol. Reprod. Biol. *68*:93, 1996.
22. Fortier, B., Aissi, E., Ajana, F., et al.: Spontaneous abortion and reinfection by *Toxoplasma gondii*. Lancet *338*:444, 1991.

23. Foudrinier, F., Marx-Chemla, C., Aubert, D., et al.: Value of specific immunoglobulin A detection by two immunocapture assays in the diagnosis of toxoplasmosis. Eur. J. Clin. Microbiol. Infect. Dis. *14*:585, 1995.
24. Foulon, W., Naessens, A., and Ho-Yen, D.: Prevention of congenital toxoplasmosis. J. Perinat. Med. *28*:337, 2000.
25. Foulon, W., Pinon, J. M., Stray-Pederson, B., et al.: Prenatal diagnosis of congenital toxoplasmosis: A mulitcenter evaluation of different diagnostic parameters. Am. J. Obstet. Gynecol. *181*:843, 1999.
26. Foulon, W., Villena, I., Stray-Pederson, B., et al.: Treatment of toxoplasmosis during pregnancy: A multicenter study of impact on fetal transmission and children's sequelae at age 1 year. Am. J. Obstet. Gynecol. *180*:410, 1999.
27. Frenkel, J. K.: Toxoplasmosis: Parasite life cycle, pathology and immunology. *In* Hammond, D. M. (ed.): The Coccidia. Baltimore, University Park Press, 1973, pp. 343–410.
28. Fricker-Hidalgo, H., Pelloux, H., Racinet, C., et al.: Detection of *Toxoplasma gondii* in 94 placentae from infected women by polymerase chain reaction, in vivo, and in vitro cultures. Placenta *19*:545, 1998.
29. Friedman, S., Ford-Jones, L. E., Toi, A., et al.: Congenital toxoplasmosis: Prenatal diagnosis, treatment and postnatal outcome. Prenat. Diagn. *19*:330, 1999.
30. Gavinet M. F., Robert F., Firtion G., et al.: Congenital toxoplasmosis due to maternal reinfection during pregnancy. J. Clin. Micrbiol. *35*:1276, 1997.
31. Gilbert, R. E., Gras, L., Wallon, M., et al.: Effect of prenatal treatment on mother to child transmission of *Toxoplasma gondii:* Retrospective cohort study of 554 mother-child pairs in Lyon, France. Int. J. Epidemiol. *30*:1303, 2001.
32. Gratzl, R., Hayde, M., Kohlhauser, C., et al.: Follow-up of infants with congenital toxoplasmosis detected by polymerase chain reaction analysis of amniotic fluid. Eur. J. Clin. Microbiol. Infect. Dis. *17*:853, 1998.
33. Grover, C. M., Thulliez, P., Remington, J. S., et al.: Rapid prenatal diagnosis of congenital *Toxoplasma* infection by using polymerase chain reaction and amniotic fluid. J. Clin. Microbiol. *28*:2297, 1990.
34. Guerina, N. G., Hsu, H.-W., Meissner, H. C., et al.: Neonatal serologic screening and early treatment for congenital *Toxoplasma gondii* infection. N. Engl. J. Med. *330*:1858, 1994.
35. Guy, E. C., Pelloux, H., Lappalainen, M., et al.: Interlaboratory comparison of polymerase chain reaction for the detection of *Toxoplasma gondii* DNA added to samples of amniotic fluid. Eur. J. Clin. Microbiol. Infect. Dis. *15*:836, 1996.
36. Hennequin, C., Dureau, P., N'Guyen, L., et al.: Congenital toxoplasmosis acquired from an immune woman. Pediatr. Infect. Dis. J. *16*:75, 1997.
37. Hohlfeld, P., Daffos, F., Costa, J.-M., et al.: Prenatal diagnosis of congenital toxoplasmosis with a polymerase-chain-reaction test on amniotic fluid. N. Engl. J. Med. *331*:695, 1994.
38. Hohlfeld, P., Daffos, F., Thurlliez, P., et al.: Fetal toxoplasmosis: Outcome of pregnancy and infant follow-up after in utero treatment. J. Pediatr. *115*:765, 1989.
39. Jara, M., Hsu, H. W., Eaton, R. B., and Demaria, A., Jr.: Epidemiology of congenital toxoplasmosis identified by population-based newborn screening in Massachusetts. Pediatr. Infect. Dis. J. *20*:1132, 2001.
40. Jenum, P. A., Holberg-Petersen, M., and Melby, K. K.: Diagnosis of congenital *Toxoplasma gondii* infection by polymerase chain reaction (PCR) on amniotic fluid samples. The Norwegian experience. A. P. M. I. S. *106*:680, 1998.
41. Jones, J. L., Lopez, A., Wilson, M., et al.: Congenital toxoplasmosis: A review. Obstet. Gynecol. Surv. *56*:296, 2001.
42. Kimball, A. C., Dean, B. H., and Fuchs, F.: The role of toxoplasmosis in abortion. Am. J. Obstet. Gynecol. *111*:219, 1971.
43. Koppe, J. G., Loewer-Sieger, D. H., and DeRoever-Bonnet, H.: Result of 20-year follow-up of congenital toxoplasmosis. Lancet *1*:254, 1986.
44. Langer, H.: Repeated congenital infection with *Toxoplasma gondii.* Obstet. Gynecol. *21*:318, 1983.
45. Lappalainen, M., Koskela, P., Koskiniemi, M., et al.: Toxoplasmosis acquired during pregnancy: Improved serodiagnosis based on avidity of IgG. J. Infect. Dis. *167*:691, 1993.
46. Martinovic, J., Sibalic, D., Djordjevic, M., et al.: Frequency of toxoplasmosis in the appearance of congenital hydrocephalus. J. Neurosurg. *56*:830, 1982.
47. McAuley, J., Boyer, K. M., Patel, D., et al.: Early and longitudinal evaluations of treated infants and children and untreated historical patients with congenital toxoplasmosis: The Chicago collaborative treatment trial. Clin. Infect. Dis. *18*:38, 1994.
48. McGee, T., Wolters, C., Stein, L., et al.: Absence of sensorineural hearing abnormalities in treated infants with congenital toxoplasmosis. Otolaryngol. Head Neck Surg. *106*:75, 1992.
49. McLeod R., Boyer K., Roizen N., et al.: The child with congenital toxoplasmosis. Curr. Clin. Top. Infect. Dis. *20*:189, 2000.
50. McLeod, R., Mack, D., Foss, R., et al.: The Toxoplasmosis Study Group: Levels of pyrimethamine in sera and cerebrospinal and ventricular fluids from infants treated for congenital toxoplasmosis. Antimicrob. Agents Chemother. *36*:1040, 1992.
51. Milgram, J. W.: Osseous changes in congenital toxoplasmosis. Arch. Pathol. *97*:150, 1974.
52. Mitchell, C. D., Erlich, S. S., Mastrucci, M. T., et al.: Congenital toxoplasmosis occurring in infants perinatally infected with human immunodeficiency virus 1. Pediatr. Infect. Dis. *9*:512, 1990.
53. Müssbichler, H.: Radiologic study of intracranial calcifications in congenital toxoplasmosis. Acta Radiol. *7*:369–379, 1968.
54. Naessens, A., Jenum, P. A., Pollak, A., et al.: Diagnosis of congenital toxoplasmosis in the neonatal period: A multicenter evaluation. J. Pediatr. *135*:714, 1999.
55. Naot, Y., Desmonts, G., and Remington, J. S.: IgM enzyme-linked immunosorbent assay test for the diagnosis of congenital *Toxoplasma* infection. J. Pediatr. *98*:32,1991.
56. O'Donohoe, J. M., Brueton, M. J., and Holliman, R. E.: Concurrent congenital human immunodeficiency virus infection and toxoplasmosis. Pediatr. Infect. Dis. J. *10*:627, 1991.
57. Oygur, N., Yilmaz, G., Ozkaynak, C., and Guven, A. G.: Central diabetes insipidus in a patient with congenital toxoplasmosis. Am. J. Perinatol. *15*:191, 1998.
58. Peterson, E., and Eaton, R. B.: Control of congenital infection with *Toxoplasma gondii* by neonatal screening based on detection of specific immunoblobulin M antibodies eluted from phenylketonuria filter-paper blood-spot samples. Acta Paediatr. Suppl. *88*:36, 1999.
59. Peyron, F., Wallon, M.: Options for the pharmacotherapy of toxoplasmosis during pregnancy. Expert Opin. Pharmacother. *2*:1269, 2001.
60. Pinon, J. M., Dumon, H., Chemla, C., et al.: Strategy for diagnosis of congenital toxoplasmosis: Evaluation of methods comparing mothers and newborns and standard methods for postnatal detection of immunoglobulin G, M, and A antibodies. J. Clin. Microbiol. *39*:2267, 2001.
61. Remington, J., Araujo, F. G., and Desmonts, G.: Recognition of different toxoplasma antigen by IgM and IgG antibodies in mothers and their congenitally infected newborns. J. Infect. Dis. *152*:1020, 1985.
62. Remington, J. S., McLeod, R., Thulliez P., and Desmonts, G.: Toxoplasmosis. *In* Remington, J. S., and Klein, J. O. (eds.): Infectious Diseases of the Fetus and Newborn Infant. 5th ed. Philadelphia, W. B. Saunders, 2001, pp. 205–346.
63. Remington, J. S., Newell, J. W., and Cavanaugh, E.: Spontaneous abortion and chronic toxoplasmosis. Report of a case, with isolation of the parasite. Obstet. Gynecol. *24*:25, 1964.
64. Robert-Gangneux, F.: Contribution of new techniques for the diagnosis of congenital toxoplasmosis. Clin. Lab. *47*:135, 2001.
65. Robert-Gangneux, F., Commerce, V., Tourte-Schaefer, C., and Dupouy-Camet, J.: Performance of a Western blot assay to compare mother and newborn anti-*Toxoplasma* antibodies for the early neonatal diagnosis of congenital toxoplasmosis. Eur. J. Microbiol. Infect. Dis. *18*:648, 1999.
66. Robert-Gangneux, F., Gavinet, M. F., Ancelle, T., et al.: Value of prenatal diagnosis and early postnatal diagnosis of congenital toxoplasmosis: Retrospective study of 110 cases. J. Clin. Microbiol. *37*:2893, 1999.
67. Roizen, N., Swisher, C. N., Stein, M. A., et al.: Neurologic and developmental outcome in treated congenital toxoplasmosis. Pediatrics *95*:11, 1995.
68. Romand, S., Wallon, M., Franck, J., et al.: Prenatal diagnosis using polymerase chain reaction on amniotic fluid for congenital toxoplasmosis. Obstet. Gynecol. *97*:296, 2001.
69. Saxon, S. A., Knight, N., Reynolds, D. W., et al.: Intellectual deficits in children born with subclinical congenital toxoplasmosis: A preliminary report. J. Pediatr. *82*:792, 1973.
70. Sibalic, D., Djurkovic-Djakovic, O., and Nikolic, R.: Congenital toxoplasmosis in premature twins. Folia Parasitol. (Praha) *33*:1, 1986.
71. Stepick-Bick, P., Thulliez, P., Araujo, F. G., and Remington, J. S: IgA antibodies for diagnosis of acute congenital and acquired toxoplasmosis. J. Infect. Dis. *162*:270, 1990.
72. Vergani, P., Ghidini, A., Ceruti, P., et al.: Congenital toxoplasmosis: Efficacy of maternal treatment with spiramycin alone. Am. J. Reprod. Immunol. *39*:335, 1998.
73. Villena, I., Aubert, D., Brodard, V., et al.: Detection of specific immunoglobulin E during maternal, fetal, and congenital toxoplasmosis. J. Clin. Microbiol. *37*:3487, 1999.
74. Villena, I., Aubert, D., Leroux, B., et al.: Pyrimethamine-sulfadoxine treatment of congenital toxoplasmosis: Follow-up of 78 cases between 1908 and 1997. Reims Toxoplasmosis Group. Scand. J. Infect. Dis. *30*:295, 1998.
75. Villena, I., Chemla, C., Quereux, C., et al.: Prenatal diagnosis of congenital toxoplasmosis transmitted by an immunocompetent woman infected before conception. Prenat. Diagn. *18*:1079, 1998.
76. Wallon, M., Caudie, C., Rubio, S., et al.: Value of cerebrospinal fluid cytochemical examination for the diagnosis of congenital toxoplasmosis at birth in France. Pediatr. Infect. Dis. J. *17*:705, 1998.
77. Wallon, M., Liou, C., Garner, P., and Peyron, F.: Congenital toxoplasmosis: Systematic review of evidence of efficacy of treatment in pregnancy: B. M. J. *318*:1511, 1999.
78. Wilson, C. B., and Remington, J. S.: What can be done to prevent congenital toxoplasmosis? Am. J. Obstet. Gynecol. *138*:357, 1980.

79. Wilson, C. B., Remington, J. S., Stagno, S., et al.: Development of adverse sequelae in children born with subclinical congenital *Toxoplasma* infection. Pediatrics *66*:767, 1980.
80. Wilson, M., and McAuley, J. B.: Laboratory diagnosis of congenital toxoplasmosis. Clin. Lab. Med. *11*:923, 1991.
81. Wiswell, T. E., Fajardo, J. E., Bass, J. W., et al.: Congenital toxoplasmosis in triplets. J. Pediatr. *105*:59, 1984.
82. Wong, S.-Y., and Remington, J. S.: Toxoplasmosis in pregnancy. Clin. Infect. Dis. *18*:853, 1994.
83. Yamakawa, R., Yamashita, Y., Yano, A., et al.: Congenital toxoplasmosis complicated by central diabetes insipidus in an infant with Down syndrome. Brain Dev. *18*:75, 1996.
84. Zufferey, J., Hohlfeld, P., Bille, J., et al.: Value of the comparative enzyme-linked immunofiltration assay for early neonatal diagnosis of congenital *Toxoplasma* infection. Pediatr. Infect. Dis. J. *18*:971, 1999.

CHAPTER 74 Perinatal Bacterial Diseases

XAVIER SÁEZ-LLORENS ■ GEORGE H. McCRACKEN, JR.

In this chapter, we update relevant information on neonatal bacterial infections, with emphasis on epidemiology, pathogenesis, diagnosis, treatment, and prevention strategies. Those aspects of the clinical manifestations, laboratory features, and management that are peculiar to the newborn infant are stressed. More complete descriptions of the bacterial pathogens, host-parasite relationships, and spectrum of diseases in older infants and children are presented elsewhere in the text.

Antibiotic Dosage Schedules for Neonates

Much has been written about the irrational use of antimicrobial agents in newborn infants. The "therapeutic misadventures" (i.e., the gray syndrome of chloramphenicol, kernicterus associated with sulfisoxazole, enamel hypoplasia after tetracycline therapy, and deafness from streptomycin and kanamycin) of past decades primarily resulted from the lack of knowledge about pharmacologic concepts in neonates. Dosage recommendations for babies were calculated from simplified formulas that pared down the usual dosage for adults or from armchair reasoning based on information obtained from healthy men and women. In either case, the amount of antibiotic administered to neonates was as often subtherapeutic as it was toxic.

Physicians have come to realize that many of the physiologic and metabolic processes of the newborn constantly change during the first few days of life and that these alterations profoundly affect pharmacokinetics of antibiotics. During the past *25* years, systematic investigations of these drugs have produced a clearer understanding of the factors influencing absorption, distribution, metabolism, and excretion of antimicrobials in newborn infants. As a result, the dosage and intervals of administration for the drugs most commonly used have been defined (Table 74–1).[228, 317] These dosage schedules are offered as a guide to safe and effective use of antibiotics in newborn infants. The suggested regimens must be modified in premature babies weighing less than 1200 g at birth, in patients with reduced renal or hepatic function, and in infants with altered metabolic or physiologic states (e.g., congestive heart failure, shock, hypothyroidism, during exchange transfusions and extracorporeal membrane oxygenation treatment) in whom the volume of drug distribution in the body may be affected profoundly. Under such circumstances, the most effective means of prescribing antibiotics is to monitor serum concentrations and to adjust the dosage accordingly.

Epidemiology and Pathogenesis

Throughout pregnancy and until the membranes rupture, the infant's environment usually is sterile. Not until delivery and in the immediate neonatal period is the infant exposed to many microorganisms. The human birth canal is host to large numbers of aerobic and anaerobic bacteria, *Mycoplasma, Ureaplasma, Chlamydia*, fungi, yeast, and viruses. *Staphylococcus epidermidis*, lactobacilli, diphtheroids, and alpha-hemolytic streptococci are found in 50 to 100 percent of the vaginal cultures of pregnant women and constitute the predominant aerobic flora.[34, 200, 362] Significant but less common isolates include *Gardnerella vaginalis*, *Proteus* and *Klebsiella* spp., and group B and D streptococci; miscellaneous organisms, such as *Citrobacter, Acinetobacter*, and the *Campylobacter* group, are identified even less commonly.

Obligate anaerobes are present in most vaginal cultures of normal, healthy women.[141] Commonly, multiple anaerobic and aerobic species are present in the same host. Approximately 85 percent of women with genital colonization by anaerobes harbor *Bacteroides* spp., including *Bacteroides fragilis* in one third of cases. Anaerobic streptococci, *Peptostreptococcus* and *Peptococcus*, are found in approximately 40 percent of women, and *Clostridium* is found in 20 percent. Uncommon anaerobic isolates include *Veillonella, Bifidobacterium*, and *Eubacterium*. Vaginal cultures of pregnant women also yield mixed aerobic and anaerobic species, but the number of anaerobes decreases from early pregnancy to delivery.[200]

During the process of delivery, encounters with some of these bacteria initiate colonization of the infant's respiratory and gastrointestinal tracts. In most infants, the microbial flora is established without incident; however, disease caused by one of these organisms develops occasionally in an infant. The factors influencing conversion from colonization to disease are not understood well.

The incidence of neonatal sepsis ranges from 1 to 10 case per 1000 live births. This rate varies from country to country,

TABLE 74–1 ■ ANTIBIOTIC DOSAGE SCHEDULES IN NEONATES

		Individual Dose (mg/kg) and Frequency of Administration									
		Weight <1200 g		Weight 1200–2000 g				Weight >2000 g			
Antibiotics	**Route**	*Ages: 0–4 Weeks*		*0–7 Days*		*>7 Days*		*0–7 Days*		*>7 Days*	
Amikacin	IV, IM	7.5	q12h	7.5	q12h	7.5	q8h	10	q12h	10	q8h
Ampicillin*	IV, IM	25	q12h	25	q12h	25	q8h	25	q8h	25	q6h
Cefazolin	IV, IM	20	q12h	20	q12h	20	q12h	20	q12h	20	q8h
Cefotaxime	IV, IM	50	q12h	50	q12h	50	q8h	50	q12h	50	q8h
Ceftazidime	IV, IM	50	q12h	50	q12h	50	q8h	50	q12h	50	q8h
Ceftriaxone	IV, IM	50	q24h	50	q24h	50	q24h	50	q24h	75	q24h
Cephalothin	IV	20	q12h	20	q12h	20	q8h	20	q8h	20	q6h
Ciprofloxacin†	IV	—	—	—	—	10–20	q24h	—	—	20–30	q12h
Clindamycin	IV, IM, PO	5	q12h	5	q12h	5	q8h	5	q8h	5	q6h
Erythromycin	PO	10	q12h	10	q12h	10	q8h	10	q12h	10	q8h
Gentamicin	IV, IM	2.5	q18h	2.5	q12h	2.5	q8h	2.5	q12h	2.5	q8h
Imipenem	IV, IM	—	—	20	q12h	20	q12h	20	q12h	20	q8h
Meropenem	IV, IM	—	—	20	q12h	20	q12h	20	q12h	20	q8h
Metronidazole	IV, PO	7.5	q48h	7.5	q24h	7.5	q12h	7.5	q12h	7.5	q8h
Mezlocillin	IV, IM	7.5	q12h	7.5	q12h	7.5	q8h	7.5	q12h	7.5	q8h
Nafcillin*	IV	25	q12h	25	q12h	25	q8h	25	q8h	25	q6h
Netilmicin	IV, IM	2.5	q18h	2.5	q12h	2.5	q8h	2.5	q12h	2.5	q8h
Oxacillin*	IV, IM	25	q12h	25	q12h	25	q8h	25	q8h	25	q6h
Penicillin G (units/kg)*	IV	25,000	q12h	25,000	q12h	25,000	q8h	25,000	q8h	25,000	q6h
Piperacillin	IV, IM	75	q12h	75	q12h	75	q8h	75	q8h	75	q6h
Ticarcillin	IV, IM	75	q12h	75	q12h	75	q8h	75	q8h	75	q6h
Tobramycin	IV, IM	2.5	q18h	2	q12h	2	q8h	2	q12h	2	q8h
Vancomycin	IV	15	q24h	10	q12h	10	q12h	10	q8h	10	q8h

*For meningitis, double the recommended dosage.
†Doses based on anecdotic clinical experience.

nursery to nursery, and within the same nursery at different times. The incidence also varies according to conditions that predispose to infection, prominent among which are prematurity and low birth weight. Between 1962 and 1987, the overall incidence of neonatal sepsis in Panorama City, California, was 2.2 cases per 1000 live births; it was 18.6 for infants with birth weights less than 2500 g, compared with 1.2 for those with birth weights equal to or greater than 2500 g.[193] In the same study, the incidence of meningitis was 0.3 case per 1000 live births and 2.8 and 0.07 for those with birth weights less than and greater than 2500 g, respectively. The highest age-specific incidence of bacterial meningitis occurs during the first month of life.[192]

Socioeconomic factors appear to be important in determining whether infants are at risk of developing infection. Premature infants and infants with low birth weight are born more frequently to mothers of low socioeconomic class than to those of average or high socioeconomic class.

Although no noticeable sex predilection has been observed for infants with intrauterine infections, a male predominance is reported in almost all studies. The greater susceptibility of male infants is more evident in cases of sepsis caused by gram-negative enteric bacilli. The reasons behind this male predominance are unknown but may be related to sex-linked factors in host susceptibility.

The bacterial cause of neonatal sepsis and meningitis varies from one geographic area to another. Although the bacterial causes of neonatal sepsis in countries of western Europe are similar to those in the United States, a different pattern has been identified in other countries, such as Saudi Arabia,[263] Nigeria,[30] Mexico,[86] and Panama.[243] In these countries, gram-negative enteric bacilli are the predominant organisms causing neonatal sepsis and meningitis. The worldwide prevalence of group B streptococcal genital colonization among pregnant women varies from 5 to 30 percent, but group B streptococci are reported more frequently as a cause of neonatal sepsis in developed countries than in developing areas. In a report from Panama,[243] only 5 percent of poor pregnant women seen in a public hospital were colonized by group B streptococci, and approximately 2 percent of documented neonatal sepsis cases were caused by these organisms; in contrast, almost 20 percent of "septic" neonates born to mothers with better socioeconomic status and higher vaginal colonization (seen in a hospital that is only 5 miles away) had group B streptococcal disease.[318a] Possibly, better hygienic practices contribute to eradication of many microorganisms from vaginal sites, allowing group B streptococci to colonize the vagina without interference by other microbes.

The bacterial pathogens that cause infections that occur in the nursery are different from those encountered when the infant arrives home. In the nursery, besides organisms acquired vertically from mothers, staphylococci (coagulase positive and negative) and gram-negative bacilli constitute the predominant etiologic agents causing nosocomial disease. At home, the infant is exposed to a different environment and to members and pets of the household, which provides opportunity for infection in the newborn and probably in the household from the newborn.

The three most common bacterial pathogens of the neonatal period are group B beta-hemolytic streptococci, *Escherichia coli*, and *Listeria monocytogenes*. These three organisms account for approximately 65 to 70 percent of all systemic neonatal bacterial diseases. The bacteria usually are acquired from the mother during the intrapartum period. The acute septicemic form of group B streptococcal disease can be caused by any of the group B types (B_{I} to B_{VIII}), and the specific B type causing disease in the infant usually is found in the maternal vaginal tract.[18, 19] Epidemiologic studies have shown that approximately 35 percent of pregnant women in the United States are colonized vaginally, rectally, or both with group B streptococci.[100] Vertical transmission from mother to infant occurs in 40 to 70 percent of women colonized with this organism.[1, 29, 119, 399] Infants born to heavily colonized women are more likely to harbor the organism, frequently at multiple sites, than are those born to lightly colonized women.[10, 180, 274] Some mothers of infants who are infected with group B *Streptococcus* are at high risk of having babies in the future who are infected similarly. A low titer of serum antibodies to the type of infecting group B *Streptococcus* and persistence of the organism in the mother have been demonstrated.[72]

Although intrapartum mother-to-infant transfer is the initial mode of acquisition of group B streptococci for the newborn, it is not the sole way in which the baby becomes colonized.[1, 12, 29, 273] In a Houston nursery, infant colonization rates increased from 20 to 25 percent at 1 day of age to 60 to 65 percent at 3 to 5 days of age without a concomitant increase in parturient colonization rates.[273] Nosocomial spread of organisms from the hands of nursery personnel to the infant probably explains the remarkable increase in colonization rates in this nursery. Analysis of serotype distribution of group B streptococci discloses no significant differences among parturients, 1-day-old infants, nursery personnel, and infants at hospital discharge.

The major sites of colonization in infants are the skin, nasopharynx, and rectum. The group B *Streptococcus* persists in the nasopharynx for weeks to months, whereas its cutaneous location usually is lost by several weeks of age. For every 100 infants colonized with group B streptococci, an estimated one or two infants will develop disease caused by this organism.

Group B streptococcal meningitis is caused almost exclusively by the B_{III} organism.[19] These organisms may be acquired from nonmaternal sites. Clusters of three or four cases of group B streptococcal meningitis have occurred in nurseries during short intervals, suggesting nosocomial acquisition.[1, 23, 354]

E. coli is the second most common agent implicated in neonatal bacterial disease, with an annual incidence of approximately 1 case per 1000 live births. The *Escherichia* genus is antigenically complex, comprising at least 160 somatic (O), 100 capsular (K), and 50 flagellar (H) antigens. The epidemiology of this agent in relation to newborn infection was defined more clearly with the discovery of the association between the K1 capsular polysaccharide antigen and invasive disease.[300] Strains with K1 antigen are responsible for approximately 75 percent of neonatal meningitis cases caused by *E. coli* and 40 percent of sepsis cases.[244, 322] K1 strains are associated with more severe disease than are non-K1 strains.[229]

The explanation for the association between *E. coli* K1 strains and neonatal meningitis is unknown. Animal studies have demonstrated that *E. coli* strains with K1 are highly virulent for mice and that this lethal effect can be prevented completely by pretreatment of mice with minute amounts of specific K1 antibody.[300] The proclivity of K1 strains for the meninges also has been demonstrated in infant rats, in which oral feedings of *E. coli* K1 strains resulted in septicemia and meningitis in approximately 20 percent of experimental animals.[137] Similar feeding experiments with *E. coli* K92 and K100 strains did not cause disease in this animal model.

The highest prevalence rates for rectal colonization with *E. coli* K1 strains are found in pregnant and nonpregnant women who are 16 to 31 years of age. Approximately 45 to 50 percent of this population have K1 organisms on rectal culture.[322] Studies of pediatric populations have disclosed colonization rates of 20 to 30 percent for newborns on the second day of life, 40 percent for infants 4 weeks to 1 year of age, and 35 percent for children 1 year to 16 years of age. As expected, the organism is dispersed widely among hospital personnel, who have rectal carriage rates of approximately 40 percent.

Vertical (mother-to-infant) and horizontal (nursery staff–to-infant, infant-to-infant) modes of transmission have been documented for *E. coli* K1 infections.[48, 322] Approximately 70 percent of infants born to culture-positive women acquire *E. coli* K1 strains during the first 48 hours of life; in these instances of vertical transmission, serologic concordance exists for O and H types of the *E. coli* cultured from mother and baby. Approximately 10 to 15 percent of infants colonized with K1 strains are born to K1-negative mothers. For this group of babies, *E. coli* is acquired at a later age (3 to 4 days), presumably from horizontal transmission. Vertical acquisition of K1 organisms has been documented in approximately three fourths of neonates with *E. coli* K1 meningitis. Based on a colonization rate of approximately 200 to 300 infants per 1000 live births and an attack rate of 1 per 1000 live births, the colonization-to-disease ratio for *E. coli* is approximately 200:1 to 300:1.

Our knowledge of the epidemiology of *Listeria* remains relatively incomplete. It is a ubiquitous soil organism, and although the animal reservoir for this organism is large, transfer from animals to humans is a rare event and occurs in high-risk persons, such as farmers and veterinarians.[271] Epidemiologic information implicating food as a vehicle for transmission of listeriosis from animals to humans now appears to be established firmly. Food-borne outbreaks have been traced to cabbage, dairy products, and vegetables. In an outbreak in Canada,[330] *Listeria*-contaminated sheep manure was used to fertilize locally grown cabbage that was stored for the winter in the cold, where the organism is known to survive for long periods. Clinical disease occurred among pregnant women who consumed the processed cabbage months after its original contamination. In 1985, the first well-documented outbreak of listeriosis in humans through contaminated milk products was reported.[125] The milk, which came from a group of farms where listeriosis among dairy cattle was known to have occurred, was well pasteurized, which indicated that pasteurization might not be sufficient to eradicate a large inoculum of *L. monocytogenes*. Linnan and associates[213] reported a large outbreak of perinatal listeriosis in Southern California that appeared to be caused by Mexican-style cheese contaminated with raw milk. In a report from Costa Rica, a nosocomial outbreak of listeriosis was associated with the use of contaminated mineral oil for bathing neonates.[333]

Several large prospective epidemiologic studies have demonstrated that few women are colonized with *Listeria* strains during pregnancy and that the organism is cultured infrequently from healthy premature and term infants or from stillborn fetuses.[171, 391] These studies suggest that human carriage of this bacterium does not appear to be of the same magnitude as that for group B *Streptococcus* and *E. coli* K1, but asymptomatic colonization with *Listeria* does occur. *Listeria* has been found occasionally in the genitourinary tracts of pregnant women, in the throats of children, and in the noses of adult males.[147] *L. monocytogenes* rectal carriage rates of from 1 to 30 percent of all pregnant or nonpregnant women have been reported.[205] The possible venereal nature of listerial colonization has been suggested.[146]

Since the 1980s, epidemic and endemic colonization and disease of the newborn infant with methicillin-resistant *Staphylococcus aureus* (MRSA) have been reported with increasing frequency in the United States and Europe. Table 74–2 demonstrates the relative frequency of infections

TABLE 74–2 ■ ETIOLOGY AND OUTCOME OF NEONATAL BACTERIAL SYSTEMIC INFECTIONS AT PARKLAND MEMORIAL HOSPITAL FROM 1969 TO 1989

Organisms	No.	(%)	Death	(%)
Group B *Streptococcus*	277	(37)	47	(17)
Escherichia coli	127	(17)	43	(34)
Other coliforms	76	(10)	28	(37)
*Staphylococcus aureus**	94	(13)	20	(21)
Enterococci	79	(10)	6	(8)
Coagulase-negative *Staphylococcus*	56	(7)	3	(5)
Pseudomonas aeruginosa	17	(2)	13	(76)
Listeria monocytogenes	5	(1)	1	(20)
Streptococcus pneumoniae	4	(1)	0	
Haemophilus influenzae type b	3	(1)	1	(33)
Nontypeable *H. influenzae*	5	(1)	1	(20)
Neisseria meningitidis	1	(0)	0	
Miscellaneous	5	(1)	2	(40)
Polymicrobial†	50	(6)	15	(30)
Totals	799	(100)	180	(23)

*51 (54%) of *S.aureus* strains exhibited methicillin resistance.
†Mostly caused by gram-negative rods and anaerobes.

caused by MRSA compared with those caused by other common neonatal pathogens in nurseries at Parkland Memorial Hospital in Dallas, Texas. Epidemics of disease caused by MRSA have been reported in the United States and in several other countries. Risk factors associated with development of MRSA infections include lengthy hospitalization, previous antibiotic administration, overcrowding and understaffing, and the presence of predisposing factors, such as indwelling central venous catheters, cerebrospinal shunts, mechanical ventilation, and prematurity.[194]

Potential reservoirs of MRSA in the hospital environment include colonized or infected neonates, hospital personnel, and the hospital inanimate environment. Although chronic nasal carriage of MRSA by hospital personnel has been implicated in several hospital outbreaks, it generally is an uncommon event and is not necessary for initiation or propagation of hospital outbreaks.[366] Limited data suggest that the hospital inanimate environment may become contaminated with MRSA, possibly sustaining outbreaks of infection.[366] Colonized patients without clinical disease contribute substantially to the inpatient reservoir of MRSA.

Coagulase-negative staphylococci also have been increasingly important neonatal pathogens. They are the most common species of the normal flora on the skin, nasal mucosa, and umbilicus of the newborn. With sensitive culture techniques, colonization rates with coagulase-negative staphylococci of the nose, umbilicus, gastrointestinal tract, and cutaneous areas of the neonate can be as high as 83 percent at 4 days of age.[345] The ubiquitous presence of the organisms and their tolerance to drying and temperature changes contribute to the increased presence of coagulase-negative staphylococci in neonates. In some neonatal intensive care units, disease caused by coagulase-negative staphylococci exceeds that of group B streptococci and *E. coli*.[288]

Prematurity, high rates of colonization, and aggressive treatment of the newborn infant in intensive care units (e.g., placement of umbilical catheters, central venous catheters, intravenous parenteral nutrition, mechanical ventilation) account for coagulase-negative staphylococci becoming important invasive nosocomial pathogens. Despite plausible evidence of their increasing prevalence as neonatal pathogens, distinguishing between infection and contamination of blood cultures by these organisms often is difficult.[155]

Group D streptococci are normal inhabitants of the gastrointestinal tract and can cause invasive disease. From 1969 to 1989,[312] approximately 10 percent of neonatal infections in nurseries at Parkland Memorial Hospital in Dallas were caused by group D streptococci (see Table 74–2). Dobson and Baker[103] reported an increase in the number of blood culture isolates of enterococci from neonates in Jefferson Davis Hospital in Houston, Texas, and described differences in incidence rates for early-onset and late-onset diseases. The increased incidence between 1973 and 1986 was attributed to infections in infants older than 1 week of age. In support of this finding is our experience at Parkland Memorial Hospital, where 80 percent of enterococcal infections occurred in infants older than 1 week of age. Outbreaks of bacteremia and meningitis related to *Streptococcus faecium* were reported from the neonatal intensive care units at the Medical College of Virginia and Children's Hospital of Denver, Colorado.[89] These organisms have become resistant to ampicillin and vancomycin in many hospitals. Disease caused by these multidrug-resistant enterococci often is difficult to treat.

Maternal, environmental, and host factors determine which infants exposed to a potentially pathogenic organism will develop invasive bacterial infections. The presence of any of the following factors can be associated with a 10-fold or greater increased risk of developing systemic infection: premature onset of labor, prolonged rupture of fetal membranes, chorioamnionitis, and maternal fever. Twin pregnancy remains an independent risk factor for acquisition of group B *Streptococcus* infection and other organisms after correction for low birth weight. The first-born twin is at a higher risk of contracting ascending intrauterine infection than is the second-born. Infection developed in 3 of 56 twin births, or 54 per 1000 live births, compared with 7 infections in 603 single births, or 12 per 1000 live births.[275] The basis for increased risk of acquisition of infection in twins includes the common features of virulent organisms, absence of protective antibody, and similar genetic heritage. Substance abuse by the mother (e.g., heroin) has been shown to alter significantly T-cell activity in the neonate that persists through the first year of life.[90] Although numerous microorganisms have been documented to cause maternal bacteremia before delivery, infants born to mothers with bacteremia usually remain well. This phenomenon most likely is explained by a balance among the presence of maternal antibody, the virulence of the organism, and the effectiveness of the placenta in preventing transmission of the organism to the fetus.

All arms of the defense system are relatively immature (i.e., lack of prior experience with microorganisms) in the healthy neonate and are impaired further by conditions such as prematurity, hypoxia, acidosis, jaundice, and metabolic derangements. Infants with galactosemia particularly are susceptible to developing sepsis by gram-negative enteric bacilli.[208] *E. coli* is by far the organism most commonly encountered as a cause of sepsis and meningitis in these infants. The umbilical stump may serve as the portal of entry of microorganisms to the bloodstream. Closure of the umbilical vessels and the subsequent aseptic necrosis of the cord, which begins soon after birth, result in an ideal environment for microorganisms to multiply and invade deeper tissues, with resultant omphalitis. Complications of omphalitis include septic umbilical arteritis, suppurative thrombophlebitis of the umbilical or portal vein, peritonitis, liver abscess, and endocarditis.

Of the various microbial virulence factors, the polysaccharide capsule has been studied most thoroughly. Bloodstream infections in infant rats and mice caused by *E. coli*

K1 or any of the group B streptococcal serotypes can be prevented by pretreatment with type-specific capsular polysaccharide antibody. In infants, mortality and long-term sequelae have been increased in cases of meningitis caused by *E. coli* K1 strains compared with those caused by non-K1 strains.[163] K1 capsular polysaccharide has been detected in cerebrospinal fluid (CSF) by counterimmunoelectrophoresis in higher concentrations and for longer durations in patients who died or were impaired neurologically compared with those who were normal survivors.[163] Concentrations and persistence of K1 capsular polysaccharide in the CSF of neonates with *E. coli* meningitis have been correlated with concentrations and persistence of endotoxin and interleukin-1β in CSF.[227] *E. coli* strains also have been found to resist phagocytosis by normal adult polymorphonuclear leukocytes, resulting in delayed clearance of bacteria from the bloodstream. This delay allows the organism to multiply and achieve the concentration of 1000 colony-forming units per milliliter of blood or more, an inoculum that generally is considered essential for invasion of the meninges. The presence of K1 antigen alone, however, does not appear to account fully for an organism's virulence because nonpathogenic *E. coli* K12 strains that are transformed by plasmid containing the cloned K1 antigen gene do not become virulent on expression of the K1 antigen.[344] Because clones of pyelonephritis strains in which specific K types are associated with O antigens, pili, and an alphahemolysin have been identified, the virulence of an organism appears to be multifactorial, and certain infections, specific K types, in conjunction with other bacterial properties determine pathogenicity.

Detailed studies of the type III group B *Streptococcus* demonstrated that the quantity of sialic acid residues in the capsular polysaccharide and the spatial conformation of the antigenic molecule determine the antiphagocytic properties of this organism. A gene sequence that is specific for type III group B *Streptococcus* has been identified and cloned. Strains with multiple copies of the gene sequence repeated within the chromosome have a lower lethal dose required to kill 50 percent of the infected animals (LD_{50}) in the infant rat model of disease and are more resistant to opsonophagocytosis than are strains that do not contain the gene structure or have only one or two copies of that sequence.[308]

Studies in children and adults have demonstrated clearly that protection from disease caused by bacteria (i.e., *Haemophilus influenzae* type b, *Neisseria meningitidis*, and *Streptococcus pneumoniae*) possessing polysaccharide capsules is afforded by specific antibody directed against these structures.[240, 331] Resistance to bloodstream clearance probably relates in part to relative complement resistance of the encapsulated organisms. The capsule may protect the deep somatic antigen structures capable of activating the alternative complement pathway. Opsonization is essential for phagocytosis and intracellular killing of these organisms and depends primarily on anticapsular antibody. Studies indicate that levels of B_{III} antibody correlate with in vitro opsonic activity[11] and with in vivo protection in animals experimentally infected with group B streptococci.[376] The lack of type-specific maternal opsonizing antibody is a significant risk factor for the development of systemic disease caused by group B streptococcal organisms in the mother and infant.[23, 166]

Most pregnant women colonized with group B_{III} organisms have increased concentrations of antibody in the circulation that pass transplacentally to the fetus. Both mother and baby in this instance are protected against disease by that specific B type. Conversely, infants born to mothers with undetectable concentrations of antibody are susceptible to invasion by the group B organisms. In one study, protective B_{III} antibody titers were detected in 73 percent of women whose newborns were well, compared with 17 percent of mothers whose newborn infants developed group B streptococcal sepsis or meningitis.[21] The same study documented lower concentrations of B_{III} antibody in sick neonates compared with those in healthy infants born to mothers with vaginal colonization. Other studies have shown that premature infants have lower concentrations of B_{Ia}, B_{II}, and B_{III} antibody, compared with term neonates.[59, 78] This finding may explain in part the higher incidence and larger case-fatality rates of group B streptococcal disease observed for premature infants. Probably, a lack of K1 antibody in the sera of neonates predisposes them to *E. coli* K1 disease as well.[230] Mouse protection studies lend credence to this contention.[300]

Strong parallels exist between the host-parasite relationships found with the group B *Streptococcus* and with *E. coli*. Both organisms possess immunochemical structures as components of the surface polysaccharide capsule that appear to confer virulence. In both cases, neonatal immunity is mediated, at least in part, by maternally derived serum antibody. For both organisms, asymptomatic infection (i.e., colonization) occurs commonly and clinical disease rarely (i.e., colonization-to-disease ratios of 100:1 to 200:1). Questions concerning the precise role of the complement system in opsonization of these and other bacterial pathogens, the exact concentration of antibody that confers protection, and the feasibility of screening large populations for absence of antibody need further investigation. The role of local immunity in determining invasion of these bacteria from their sites of colonization (i.e., respiratory and gastrointestinal tracts) needs clarification.

The meninges can be invaded directly from an infected adjacent site, such as skin lesions, meningomyelocele, or a skull fracture. Most cases of meningitis, however, result from bacteremia. After gaining access to the blood, bacteria probably enter the CSF space through the choroid plexus of the lateral ventricle and then spread to the subarachnoid space along normal paths of CSF flow. Because of the absence of antibody and complement in the subarachnoid space, bacteria multiply logarithmically, and as many as 10^8 colony-forming units/mL can be cultured from lumbar CSF. The larger the number of bacteria in CSF, the poorer the prognosis.

As a response to the interaction of bacteria or their cell wall components with central nervous system (CNS) tissues, the local production of inflammatory mediators, such as tumor necrosis factor and interleukin-1β, is an initial step in the cascade of events leading to inflammation and tissue destruction.[248, 295, 316] Experiments in animals demonstrated that interleukin-1β, tumor necrosis factor, and other mediators can act synergistically in altering the function of the cerebral capillary endothelium (i.e., blood-brain barrier) and in promoting attachment of leukocytes through the expression of adhesion receptors.[316, 328] The net result is injury and increased permeability of the usually highly efficient blood-brain barrier that allows transendothelial passage of phagocytic cells and low-molecular-weight serum proteins, including complement. Despite this influx, the opsonic activity of the CSF remains low; as a result, phagocytosis is inefficient, allowing continued bacterial growth and meningeal inflammation.

Accumulation of inflammatory exudate and inflammation of the arachnoid villi can alter CSF flow, which, coupled with loss of autoregulation of cerebral blood flow, can result in increased intracranial pressure. Hydrocephalus results from aqueductal obstruction by fibrinous debris or from reduced CSF outflow caused by inflammation of the arachnoid villi. The raised intracranial pressure, occlusion of blood vessels traversing the subarachnoid space, and edema of vascular endothelial cells can result in cerebral ischemia and possibly in cerebral infarction. Anaerobic glycolysis by poorly perfused cerebral tissues results in increased CSF lactate concentrations and hypoglycorrhachia, which further potentiate swelling of glial and neuronal cells through failure of the adenosine triphosphate–dependent sodium pump, which results in accumulation of intracellular sodium. Inappropriate secretion of antidiuretic hormone also can contribute to cerebral edema.

Sepsis Neonatorum

Sepsis neonatorum is a bacterial disease of infants 30 days of age or younger. It involves primarily the bloodstream, although spread to the meninges or other organs occurs in a substantial portion of affected infants. No obvious focus of infection of the bloodstream can be found in most cases. The presence of clinical and laboratory findings distinguishes this condition from the transient bacteremia observed in some healthy neonates. Newer terminology guidelines have been proposed[314, 315] to classify infants and children with a systemic inflammatory response syndrome resulting from an infectious process; the terms *sepsis, severe sepsis, septic shock,* and *multiple organ dysfunction syndrome* have been validated in large retrospective reviews.[314] Their application to septic newborns, however, needs careful assessment.

The incidence of sepsis neonatorum ranges from 1 to 10 cases per 1000 live births.[340] This rate varies from nursery to nursery and depends on conditions predisposing to infection.

PREDISPOSING FACTORS

Many prepartum and intrapartum obstetric complications are associated with an increased risk of acquisition of infection in newborn infants. Among these complications are premature onset of labor, prolonged rupture of the fetal membranes, uterine inertia with high forceps extraction, and maternal pyrexia.[43, 231, 269]

Sophisticated equipment for respiratory and nutritional support combined with invasive techniques provides life support to the ill infant. Arterial and venous umbilical catheters, central venous catheters, peripheral arterial and venous cannulas, urinary indwelling catheters, and tracheal intubation provide enormous opportunity for relatively nonvirulent pathogens to establish infection and to invade the host.[3, 27, 62, 85, 163, 178, 197, 358] The frequency of these infections varies and usually is sporadic. Recognizing these opportunistic infections may be difficult because of the severe underlying illnesses requiring intensive therapy and the frequent use of antimicrobial agents in these infants.

CLINICAL MANIFESTATIONS

The newborn infant responds to many varieties of noxious stimuli (e.g., infectious, metabolic, respiratory, traumatic) with a limited repertoire of stereotyped reactions. As a result, many of the manifestations of sepsis have their counterparts in hypoglycemia, hypocalcemia, hypoxemia, hemolytic blood disorders, drug reactions, and surgical events. Most infectious problems in infants cannot be differentiated from other neonatal disorders on the basis of the presenting clinical manifestations. The major signs and symptoms of sepsis relate to disturbances of thermoregulation, respiration, and gastrointestinal function.[105, 231, 260, 346]

Abnormalities of temperature regulation frequently are observed as initial complaints. They may take the form of hyperthermia (approximately 40% of cases) or, less commonly, hypothermia.[91, 111, 377] With the introduction of isolette care of the premature infant to maintain an optimal thermic environment, thermoregulatory disturbances commonly become obvious when the nurse reports the need to make frequent changes in the isolette's thermostat to accommodate the infant's loss of regulatory control. Fever can result from a variety of noninfectious causes, such as dehydration, elevation in ambient temperature, and hematomas, or fever can result from central origins from neonatal conditions such as anoxia, CNS hemorrhage, and kernicterus.

Another frequent mode of presentation is respiratory distress manifested as tachypnea, grunting respirations, cyanosis, intercostal and substernal retractions, and apnea. A heart rate persistently in excess of 160 beats per minute can be a sensitive indicator of early-onset neonatal sepsis.[145] Although these findings particularly are indicative of early-onset group B streptococcal disease, they have been associated with infection caused by all of the pathogens commonly encountered in the neonatal period.

Approximately one third of infants have gastrointestinal findings, including poor feeding, regurgitation, vomiting, weak suck, abdominal distention, diarrhea, and, rarely, gallbladder distention.[278] Although in most cases conditions other than sepsis explain these findings, bacterial disease always must be considered. In most patients, ruling out sepsis on clinical grounds alone is impossible. Appropriate laboratory studies and therapeutic intervention frequently are necessary in the assessment of these nonspecific clinical manifestations.

Only a small percentage of infants show cutaneous findings (except for jaundice). They include cellulitis, impetiginous lesions, furunculosis, papular lesions (i.e., listeriosis), vascular lesions (i.e., *Pseudomonas*), and exfoliative dermatitis (i.e., phage group II staphylococcal disease). Jaundice occurs in approximately one third of infants with sepsis and can occur in infants with urinary tract infection. Occasionally, jaundice is the only sign of infection and occurs in septic infants, regardless of the type of bacterial pathogen.

In utero infection is identified by the presence of bacteria in blood obtained at delivery. Signs of fetal distress may be the first indication of infection in the newborn. Schiano and associates[329] suggested fetal tachycardia in the second stage of labor as a sign of intrauterine infection. Pneumonia or sepsis occurred in 3 of 8 infants with fetal heart beats of more than 180 per minute, in 7 of 32 infants with 160 to 179 beats per minute, and in 1 of 167 infants with lower heart rates.

One report suggests that infants with documented sepsis or with a sepsis-like illness have abnormal heart rate characteristics for as long as 24 hours preceding their clinical signs. The abnormalities included reduced baseline variability and short-lived decelerations in heart rate. If these findings are confirmed, monitoring of these parameters in neonates at risk for developing sepsis may lead to earlier suspicion of disease and initiation of more effective and prompt therapy.[150]

ETIOLOGY

Since the middle of the 20th century, a shift has occurred in the microorganisms responsible for neonatal septicemia and meningitis.[105, 129, 138, 231, 260] In the 1930s and 1940s, the predominant organism was the group A beta-hemolytic *Streptococcus*. It was replaced in the 1950s by the phage group I *S. aureus* and by coliform organisms. From the late 1950s to the present, *E. coli* and group B beta-hemolytic streptococci have accounted for approximately 60 to 70 percent of all infections. *S. epidermidis* has emerged as an important pathogen for neonates and is responsible for a large proportion of cases of sepsis in newborn intensive care facilities.[33, 73, 245] In a survey of high-risk nurseries participating in the National Nosocomial Infection Surveillance System of the Centers for Disease Control and Prevention (CDC) conducted from October 1986 through September 1994, the pathogen most commonly reported as the cause of nosocomial bacteremia was coagulase-negative staphylococci, which accounted for 51 percent of isolates.[132] The apparent increased incidence of *S. epidermidis* sepsis has been associated with increased survival of very small premature infants and the introduction of invasive procedures.[155] MRSA also has emerged as a nosocomial pathogen of major importance in some nurseries. The prevalence rates for a specific bacterial pathogen vary from nursery to nursery and may change abruptly in any one unit.[32, 35, 129, 138, 166] Knowledge of the bacteria most commonly isolated in a nursery or intensive care unit, as well as the antimicrobial susceptibility of these organisms, is invaluable in treating infants with suspected sepsis neonatorum.

Table 74–3 presents the bacterial agents responsible for neonatal sepsis in three nurseries from different areas of the world.[167, 243, 312] Group B *Streptococcus* has remained the most common single etiologic agent of neonatal sepsis and meningitis in Dallas, Texas; it was the second most frequent one in Mallorca, Spain; and it was isolated uncommonly in Panama City, Panama. The etiologic agents of neonatal sepsis and meningitis at Parkland Memorial Hospital in Dallas, Texas, for 1987 through 1999 are shown in Table 74–4.

Coliform bacteria, including *E. coli, Klebsiella* spp., and *Enterobacter* spp., were recovered more frequently in Panama and Mallorca than in Dallas. *S. aureus* was recovered relatively commonly in the three nurseries; a large percentage of the strains isolated in the United States were methicillin resistant, which underscores the importance of these organisms in some neonatal units. Coagulase-negative staphylococci also were recovered frequently in infants with neonatal sepsis. Anaerobes were responsible for a small percentage of cases of septicemia. Because special techniques for isolation of these relatively fastidious organisms were not used, the actual contribution of these bacteria in causing sepsis may have been underestimated considerably.

H. influenzae, S. pneumoniae, and *N. meningitidis* are occasional causes of neonatal sepsis. Viridans streptococci are being isolated with increased frequency and, in one series, were the major pathogens in neonates with streptococcal septicemia. From 1987 to 1989, viridans streptococci were recovered from the blood of 20 of 273 infants with neonatal sepsis in nurseries at Parkland Memorial Hospital in Dallas.

The changing distribution of etiologic agents over time has been demonstrated in developed and in developing countries.[215, 265, 348] In nurseries in the United States, gram-negative enteric organisms were the isolates most frequently recovered 2 decades ago; gram-positive bacteria (mostly group B streptococci and staphylococci) constitute the predominant pathogens today. In the largest public hospital of Panama during an 18-year period (1975 to 1992), the proportional incidence of gram-negative infections also declined with time, whereas that of gram-positive infections increased.[243]

SPECIFIC CLINICAL SYNDROMES

Group B Beta-Hemolytic Streptococcal Infection

Group B streptococcal infection may become evident in a variety of ways, ranging from asymptomatic bacteremia to septicemia, pneumonia, and meningitis. Skin infections, such as impetigo, cellulitis, erythema nodosum–like lesions, adenitis, breast abscess, and scalp abscesses, also may occur.[16, 173, 253] Group B streptococci may present first as conjunctivitis, orbital cellulitis, otitis media, or ethmoiditis. These organisms are responsible for an increasing proportion of suppurative arthritis and osteomyelitis cases during the newborn period and have been incriminated in unusual infections such as retropharyngeal cellulitis, pleural empyema, endocarditis, peritonitis, and adrenal abscess.[14, 74, 173, 379, 386]

TABLE 74–3 ■ CAUSES OF BACTERIAL SEPSIS IN NEWBORNS FROM THREE DIFFERENT AREAS OF THE WORLD

	Number and Percentage of Isolates		
Organisms	Dallas (U.S.) (1969–1989) n = 744	Mallorca (Spain) (1977–1991) n = 332	Panama (Panama) (1975–1992) n = 577
Gram-negative	229 (30%)	151 (45%)	361 (63%)
Escherichia coli	17%	10%	14%
Klebsiella species	7%	15%	20%
Other enteric rods	3%	10%	20%
Pseudomonas species	2%	6%	6%
Haemophilus influenzae	1%	1%	<1%
Others	<1%	3%	2%
Gram-positive	515 (70%)	181 (55%)	216 (37%)
Group B *Streptococcus*	37%	22%	2%
Coagulase-negative *Staphylococcus*	9%	15%	20%
S. aureus	12%	8%	12%
Enterococci	10%	7%	1%
Listeria monocytogenes	1%	2%	<1%
S. pneumoniae	<1%	<1%	<1%
Others	<1%	<1%	<1%

TABLE 74–4 ■ PRINCIPAL ETIOLOGIC AGENTS ISOLATED FROM BLOOD AND CEREBRAL SPINAL FLUID OF NEONATES WITH SUSPECTED SEPSIS ACCORDING TO AGE OF ONSET AND TIME PERIOD*

	1987–1994		1995–1999	
Etiologic Agents	Early Onset	Late Onset	Early Onset	Late Onset
Gram-positive bacteria	290	426	39	161
Streptococcus agalactiae	233	61	32	5
Enterococci	13	42	1	17
Other streptococci	25	12	2	1
Staphylococcus aureus	8	100	2	22
Coagulase-negative *Staphylococcus*	10	210	0	116
Listeria monocytogenes	1	0	2	0
Gram-negative bacteria	49	80	18	56
Escherichia coli	23	34	13	28
Klebsiella species	3	16	1	13
Enterobacter species	3	18	1	8
Pseudomonas species	1	4	0	2
Acinetobacter species	1	2	0	0
Others	18	6	3	5
Total live births	117,478		67,869	
Rate of GBS infection†				
Early onset (≤3 days)	2		0.5	
Late onset (>3 days)	0.5		0.1	

*Parkland Memorial Hospital, Dallas, Texas. 1987–1999. Data provided by Sithembiso Velaphi, M.D. Intrapartum prophylaxis was used routinely in the 1995–1999 period.
†Cases per 1000 live births.

Two clinically and epidemiologically distinct forms of illness have been described.[20, 31, 127, 173] The early- or acute-onset form is seen in the first 5 days of life (usually within the first 6 to 12 hours) and is characterized by a high incidence of maternal complications. These infants usually are very ill within hours of delivery and exhibit unexplained apnea or tachypnea, respiratory distress, hypoxemia, and shock. Chest radiographs reveal a diffuse pulmonary infiltrate similar to that seen after aspiration or findings indistinguishable from those of hyaline membrane disease. One of the major diagnostic problems associated with the acute-onset syndrome is its clinical differentiation from respiratory distress syndrome. Several features of early-onset group B streptococcal disease may be helpful in differentiating it from the respiratory distress syndrome. Obstetric complications are encountered commonly in mothers of infants with group B streptococcal disease, whereas they seldom occur in mothers of infants with respiratory distress syndrome.[31, 127] Evidence indicates that prenatal complications may protect the infant from respiratory distress syndrome because of increased corticosteroid secretion by the mother.

Compared with infants with respiratory distress syndrome, infants with streptococcal disease usually are sicker early in the course of illness, and apnea, shock, or both occur within 12 to 24 hours of onset of infection. Infants with respiratory distress syndrome experience a more gradual evolution of events. In some infants with group B streptococcal disease, rapid progression to respiratory failure and death occurs within 12 hours. This situation is an unusual occurrence in the infants with uncomplicated respiratory distress syndrome. The peak inspiratory pressures required to ventilate babies with streptococcal disease are said to be lower than those necessary for infants with respiratory distress syndrome.[2] In preterm infants, leukopenia with increased numbers of band forms occurs commonly in the infected cases.[2, 218]

The chest radiograph may be helpful in differentiating these two illnesses. Neonatal pneumonia is found in approximately 40 percent of infants with group B streptococcal disease. In the others, a diffuse reticulogranular pattern with air bronchograms is seen and cannot be distinguished from that observed in infants with the respiratory distress syndrome. Hyaline membranes are seen pathologically in both illnesses.

The second major form of neonatal group B streptococcal disease is the late-onset syndrome. In contrast to the acute fulminant disease of the first day of life, the late-onset syndrome has an insidious onset after the infant reaches 5 to 7 days of age, although it occasionally may be fulminant.[20, 176] The disease almost invariably involves the meninges. Most infants present in the second through fourth weeks of life, but documented cases have occurred at up to 12 weeks of age. A history of maternal obstetric complications usually is lacking, and the infants almost always have an unremarkable early neonatal history, although late-onset disease does occur occasionally among premature infants.[101] The case-fatality rate is low, on the order of 5 to 15 percent.

In contrast to the uniform distribution of all five major serotypes causing early-onset disease, the group B_{III} organism is responsible for approximately 90 percent of all late-onset cases[19] (irrespective of clinical manifestation) and of cases of infants with meningitis (irrespective of age of onset). This apparently virulent effect of type III strains, which account for two thirds of group B streptococcal infections in infants, appears to be restricted to young infants. In contrast, type II strains are predominant among isolates from adults with meningitis, but this serotype rarely is isolated from the CSF of infants with meningitis. The mode of acquisition is uncertain because the B_{III} organism usually cannot be recovered from maternal sites at the onset of the infant's illness. Horizontal transmission of the pathogen from nursery personnel, caregivers at home, and other individuals to the newborn has been proposed as the most reasonable mode of acquisition.[1, 19, 276]

The clinical features of illness are indistinguishable from those of the other forms of purulent meningitis of this age group. An exception to the normal pattern for late-onset infection is the intensive care unit setting, where nosocomially acquired clusters of disease among low-birth-weight infants have been reported.[259, 385] In such circumstances, the spectrum of clinical expression is similar to that of early-onset disease, although serotype III still predominates.[259]

Other Streptococcal Disease

Group A beta-hemolytic streptococcal disease does not occur as frequently now as in previous decades. Disease caused by this organism varies from a low-grade chronic omphalitis to fulminant septicemia and meningitis. Because of the explosive nature of this organism in nursery settings, constant surveillance for colonized infants and prompt recognition of illness are mandatory to avert a nursery outbreak of group A streptococcal disease.[134]

Groups D and G streptococci have been reported to cause an illness indistinguishable from early-onset group B streptococcal sepsis.[106, 339] Viridans streptococci usually cause a less severe illness with a lower incidence of respiratory distress, shock, and white blood cell (WBC) count abnormalities.[349] Dobson and Baker,[103] in a review of 56 neonates with enterococcal septicemia from a single hospital in Houston, Texas, from 1977 through 1986, described two distinct clinical syndromes. Infants older than 7 days were more premature, had lower birth weights and, in most cases, had infections characterized by a nosocomial origin. Compared with early-onset disease (5 days of age or younger), which was characterized by mild illness with respiratory distress or diarrhea without focal infection, the late-onset enterococcal sepsis was heralded by severe apnea, bradycardia, circulatory collapse, and increased ventilation requirements. Focal infections, such as meningitis, pneumonia, scalp abscess, and catheter-related illnesses, were common occurrences.

Staphylococcus Infection

In the mid-1950s, phage group I *S. aureus* was the most common bacterial agent causing serious bacterial diseases in newborn infants. Its unique invasive properties caused disseminated disease, including mastitis, furunculosis, suppurative arthritis, osteomyelitis, septicemia, and meningitis, with widespread manifestations. Because bloodstream infection usually occurs after local invasion, the primary focus must be searched for carefully in all septic babies. Changes in the epidemiologic characteristics of the organism, coupled with intensified microbial surveillance and infection control measures, have reduced colonization and disease rates caused by the phage group I *Staphylococcus*.

Coagulase-positive staphylococcal disease in nurseries also has been caused by phage group II organisms.[233] These organisms produce an exotoxin (i.e., exfoliatin) that results in intraepidermal cleavage through the granular cell layer because of the disruption of desmosomes.[234] Clinical disease may take one of several forms, including bullous impetigo, toxic epidermal necrolysis (i.e., Ritter disease), and non-streptococcal scarlatina. The initial finding in Ritter disease is intense, painful erythema followed by bulla formation that, when ruptured, leaves a tender, weeping erythematous area. A characteristic desquamation of large epidermal sheets occurs approximately 3 to 5 days after the onset of disease. A fine desquamation is observed commonly in the perioral region. Bullous impetigo has been the disease associated most commonly with nursery outbreaks of group II staphylococcal infections.[6]

In the 1980s, MRSA emerged as a nosocomial pathogen of considerable importance. MRSA demonstrates resistance to the penicillinase-resistant penicillin class of antibiotics, which includes methicillin, nafcillin, oxacillin, cloxacillin, and dicloxacillin. The mechanism of resistance involves in part alteration of penicillin-binding proteins in the periplasm of the bacterium, resulting in a decrease in affinity for those antibiotics. The spectrum of clinical disease that is caused by MRSA is similar to that caused by methicillin-susceptible *S. aureus,* except that patients with MRSA bacteremia were reported to be less likely to have bone or joint infection.[357] Of 44 cases of MRSA infections in the nurseries of Parkland Memorial Hospital in Dallas, Texas, from 1987 to 1990, the organism was recovered from the blood in 35, from CSF in 4, from peritoneal fluid in 4, and from joint fluid in 1. Of the 35 patients with bacteremia, 7 had pneumonia, 2 had meningitis, 2 had arthritis or osteomyelitis, 1 had urinary tract infection, and 1 had a soft tissue abscess (J. D. Siegel, personal communication, 1991).

Coagulase-negative staphylococci are being identified more often in blood cultures of neonates with signs and symptoms of sepsis[32, 124] but frequently are dismissed as contaminants. The isolation of these organisms should be considered significant when they grow in aerobic and anaerobic blood culture bottles, when growth occurs within 72 hours, or when they are isolated from two or more sites or from the same site at different times.[33, 245, 258] *S. epidermidis* disease tends to occur as a late-onset infection (i.e., nosocomial acquisition) and is associated with the usual signs and symptoms of sepsis. WBC count abnormalities are found in approximately one half of all infected infants. Major risk factors include prematurity, low birth weight, invasive procedures, central venous catheters, and total parenteral nutrition. Exposure to intravenous lipid emulsions was the major determinant of bacteremia caused by coagulase-negative staphylococci in very-low-birth-weight infants in one case-control study.[128] These infections frequently are associated with colonization of the central venous catheters and involvement of other sites, such as the CNS. The patients usually are not very ill and respond well to antimicrobial therapy, but frequently the central venous catheters must be removed to prevent further seeding of the bloodstream. The mortality rate is low and ranges between 0 and 15 percent in different series.[33, 124, 245, 258]

Escherichia coli Infection

E. coli strains are the most common gram-negative bacteria causing septicemia during the neonatal period. Annual incidence rates for the past 15 years in Dallas, Texas, have remained reasonably constant at 0.5 to 1.5 cases per 1000 live births.[173] This etiologic agent remains the single most frequent cause of neonatal sepsis and meningitis in many developing countries (*Klebsiella* spp. is more common in some countries).[243] Unlike illnesses caused by group B streptococci and *L. monocytogenes, E. coli* infections do not fit into distinct clinical syndromes of early- and late-onset disease. Approximately 40 percent of *E. coli* strains causing septicemia possess K1 capsular antigen.[322] The clinical features of *E. coli* sepsis generally are similar to those observed in infants with disease caused by other pathogens. Localized *E. coli* infections have included breast abscess, cellulitis, meningitis, pneumonia, lung abscess, empyema, osteomyelitis, septic arthritis, urinary tract infection, ascending cholangitis, and otitis media.

Listeria monocytogenes Infection

The pathogenesis and clinical spectrum of diseases caused by *L. monocytogenes* are similar to those caused by group B streptococci. Because the most common foci for neonatal infection are lung and gut, the fetus probably is infected by the mother's swallowing of contaminated liquor and through the transplacental route. Chorioamnionitis diagnosed by transabdominal amniocentesis in pregnant women with intact fetal membranes has been reported,[280] favoring the blood-borne route of infection. Nonetheless, an ascending pathway from the lower genital tract is a possible route. Early gestational *Listeria* can be associated with abortion or stillbirth. Premature labor in mothers with *Listeria* infection is a common occurrence; in approximately 70 percent of cases, delivery occurs before 35 weeks' gestation.

Evidence of preceding maternal illness often is described in infants with early-onset disease. Symptoms in mothers can be vague (i.e., malaise and myalgia) or distinctive (i.e., fever and chills) and may alert the physician to a risk of *Listeria* infection. Blood cultures often (35%) are positive for *Listeria* in such mothers. A fulminant, disseminated disease (i.e., granulomatosis infantisepticum) may occur during the first several days of life. The pathogen is acquired transplacentally[374] or by aspiration at the time of vaginal delivery; multiple organ systems are involved.[36] The infant frequently has hypothermia, is lethargic, and feeds poorly.[334] A characteristic rash consisting of small, salmon-colored papules scattered primarily on the trunk may be observed in some infants.

Listeria infection should be suspected in premature infants with early passage of meconium. Because meconium is an extremely unusual finding in premature infants younger than 32 weeks of gestational age, if it is present, the physician should suspect *Listeria* infection. Chest radiographs show parenchymal infiltrates suggesting aspiration pneumonitis in most infants. A miliary type of bronchopneumonia also can be seen in some cases. No cases of acute-onset listeriosis mimicking the radiographic picture of hyaline membrane disease have been reported. *Listeria* serotypes Ia, Ib, and IVb produce the early-onset disease, whereas serotype IVb is the predominant type in late-onset meningitic disease.[7]

A delayed form of neonatal listeriosis occurs during the second through the eighth week of life and involves the meninges in almost all cases. The infected infant usually is the term product of an uncomplicated labor and delivery. Onset of symptoms and signs is relatively insidious, and it is indistinguishable from those observed with meningitis caused by other pathogens. Acute *Listeria* encephalitis, which usually is fatal within a few days, is a rare disease in humans. Other clinical forms of disease at this age include *Listeria*-induced colitis with associated diarrhea and sepsis without meningitis. The bacteriology laboratory should be forewarned of the clinical suspicion of listerial meningitis because these microorganisms frequently are discarded as contaminants because of their tinctorial and morphologic similarities with diphtheroids. Overnight refrigeration of spinal fluid specimens frequently enhances growth of this organism.

The peripheral WBC count usually shows a brisk leukocytosis with a predominance of polymorphonuclear leukocytes in the differential count. A significant elevation in the number of monocytes to 7 to 21 percent of the total WBC count has been documented on admission laboratory evaluation of infected infants.[375] Likewise, a monocytosis of this magnitude can be demonstrated in most remaining infants on repetitive testing of the peripheral WBC count. In contrast, monocytes are not found typically in the spinal fluid of infants infected with *L. monocytogenes*. Polymorphonuclear leukocytes predominate in approximately 75 percent of cases, with a relative lymphocytosis detected in the remaining 25 percent. As with other pyogenic meningitides, hypoglycorrhachia and elevated protein concentrations are frequent findings. Examination of the stained smear of spinal fluid has not been rewarding in more than 50 percent of cases, a reflection of the relatively low concentrations of organisms in the fluid,[118] the atypical morphology, and the variable decoloration resulting from the Gram staining procedure, which may result in organisms appearing as gram-negative rods or gram-positive cocci.

Pseudomonas aeruginosa Infection

Pseudomonas septicemia may show a characteristic violaceous papular lesion or lesions, in which central necrosis develops after several days (i.e., ecthyma gangrenous). Noma (i.e., gangrenous lesions of the nose, lips, and mouth) has been associated with bacteremia caused by *P. aeruginosa*. It is caused by a suppurative vasculitis, and deep-seated abscess formation is common.[298] The neonate who is treated with broad-spectrum antimicrobial agents while in an environment potentially contaminated by "water bugs" (e.g., respirators, moist oxygen) particularly is prone to acquisition of disease caused by *Pseudomonas* spp. or other fastidious commensals. The organism usually is a cause of late-onset disease.[204] Stevens and associates,[356] however, reported nine cases of *Pseudomonas* sepsis, four of which presented in the first 72 hours of life. The clinical and radiologic findings in these four infants were similar to those of hyaline membrane disease.

DIAGNOSIS

The diagnosis of sepsis neonatorum relies heavily on the clinical judgment and diagnostic acumen of the physician. Signs and symptoms may be vague and frequently misleading. Bacterial infection may masquerade as metabolic disease, respiratory distress, environmental stress, and other noninfectious conditions. The physician confronted by an infant with possible sepsis must be guided by a complete perinatal history eliciting factors that place the infant at high risk, by a thorough physical examination attentive to signs suggestive of infection, and by clinical experience. When infection is likely, a laboratory work-up is indicated. When infection is unlikely and not substantiated by history, physical examination, and clinical judgment, investigation for an infectious process usually is unnecessary. If doubt exists, as frequently is the case, a good practice is to proceed with a laboratory work-up.

Recovery of an organism from a meaningful site, such as blood, CSF, urine, abscesses, pleural and peritoneal spaces, joints, bones, and middle ear cavities, substantiates the clinical impression of systemic bacterial disease. Isolation of an organism from mucocutaneous sites, such as skin, ear canal, nasopharynx, gastric aspirate, and rectum, usually does not reflect the microbiologic status of normally sterile body fluids or tissues.[121] A point of emphasis is that the colonization-to-disease ratio for the major pathogens of the neonate is approximately 100:1 to 200:1. For every infant with documented systemic bacterial disease, 100 or more infants are colonized superficially with this organism but are free of systemic bacterial disease.

Several sites for sampling blood for culture give reliable results: peripheral vein, umbilical artery, and capillary blood. The preferred site is the peripheral vein. Venipuncture should be performed after the skin has been prepared properly by cleansing with an iodine-containing solution.[110] A two-phase antisepsis procedure using 70 percent isopropyl alcohol followed by chlorhexidine or povidone-iodine has been shown to be superior to one using chlorhexidine or povidone-iodine alone in reducing skin colonization by *S. epidermidis*.[75] The theoretical minimal amount of blood needed for detecting bacteremia is a function of the number of organisms circulating at any given time. Infants with *E. coli* sepsis have 5 to more than 1000 colony-forming units per milliliter of blood.[98] Culturing as little as 0.2 mL of blood should be sufficient for detecting *E. coli* bacteremia in these patients. On the basis of experimental *E. coli* sepsis in rabbits, a cultured volume of blood of 0.2 mL is as sensitive as 1 mL in detecting bacteremia at a threshold level of 5 organisms per milliliter of circulating blood.[122] Similar data for the other pathogens of neonatal sepsis are not available. Until additional studies have been reported, a prudent procedure is to obtain 0.5 to 1 mL of blood for culture. Optimal results are obtained when the cultured volume of blood is 5 to 10 percent of the total amount of liquid growth medium to be inoculated.

Bacterial growth is evidenced in most blood cultures within 48 hours. With the use of conventional culture techniques and subcultures at 4 and 14 hours, only 4 percent of cultures that had positive results required more than 48 hours of incubation.[285] With the use of radiometric technique, 98 percent of cultures growing group B *Streptococcus* and *E. coli* were identified within 24 hours.[307] The number of blood cultures required to document sepsis in newborn infants is unknown. We generally recommend one or two blood cultures before initiating antibiotic therapy. Urine and CSF should be obtained for examination and culture before starting therapy.

Many laboratory tests have been recommended for the evaluation of suspected bacterial diseases in neonates. The WBC count is a simple, readily available test that can help in the early detection of sepsis.[40, 218, 219] Elevated total WBC counts, absolute neutrophil counts, and absolute band counts usually are not helpful singly as indicators of sepsis. Although neutropenia in neonates most often is caused by infection, it frequently is associated with other conditions, such as birth asphyxia and pregnancy-induced hypertension.[112]

The usefulness of abnormal WBC counts in the detection of sepsis is enhanced by measurement of the immature-to-total neutrophil ratio; a ratio of 0.2 or greater is a relatively sensitive indicator of neonatal sepsis.[79, 281, 282] Numerous studies that have evaluated the immature-to-total neutrophil ratio have shown that the ratio is too unreliable to achieve more than limited clinical usefulness. Sensitivities ranging from 90 to 60 percent or less have been reported.[46, 47] Elevated ratios caused by a variety of perinatal conditions have been seen in 25 to 50 percent of noninfected, ill infants.[133, 190] The ratio's greatest value is thought to be in its good negative predictive value; if the ratio is normal, the likelihood that infection is absent is very high.[133, 190] An immature-to-total ratio of 0.8 or greater indicates depletion of bone marrow neutrophil reserves and is a poor prognostic indicator. A combination of all these laboratory findings (i.e., hematologic scoring system), rather than those of any test alone, increases the diagnostic specificity of a bacterial infection.[302] This scoring system is of limited value in late-onset, coagulase-negative staphylococcal infections.[94]

Taking a repeat WBC count and immature-to-total ratio determination 6 to 8 hours after performing the initial evaluation is important because studies in animals and human infants have demonstrated that the WBC count can be normal at the onset of group B streptococcal sepsis and abnormal 4 to 8 hours later. Morphologic changes in neutrophils, such as vacuolization and toxic granulation, suggest the presence of infection. The degree of these degenerative changes in neutrophils of infected neonates has no implication as to the severity or potential outcome of the illness.[214] Identical morphologic findings can occur as artifacts in citrated blood samples stored for longer than 1 hour before smears are made. The platelet count is unreliable for establishing the diagnosis of bacterial infection during the neonatal period.

The erythrocyte sedimentation rate in infected patients usually is elevated above the normal range of 1 to 2 mm/hr at 12 hours of age to 17 to 20 mm/hr at 14 days of age.[4] Elevated rates usually are not observed until 24 to 48 hours after clinical signs of disease first occur. Other acute-phase reactants, such as C-reactive protein, haptoglobin, prealbumin, orosomucoid, and transferrin, may be useful in the diagnosis of neonatal sepsis and in following the course of the infection.[283] The most extensively studied of these acute-phase reactants is the C-reactive protein. Concentrations of this protein increase significantly within a few hours of the onset of infection. In general, other perinatal events have little impact on C-reactive protein neonatal values.[332] C-reactive protein concentrations decrease rapidly in infected neonates who respond to therapy and, conversely, persistently are elevated in neonates whose infections fail to respond to therapy.[321] Reliance on a single C-reactive protein determination as an early indicator of neonatal bacterial infections is not recommended. Serial determinations are helpful, especially in combination with other hematologic tests, when making a decision to stop antimicrobial therapy safely.[52, 284]

Fibronectin is a glycoprotein that has been identified on cell surfaces and in extracellular fluids. The concentration of it in fetal plasma increases with gestational age to values at term of approximately one half of those found in healthy adults. Plasma concentrations fall significantly during sepsis[133] but may decrease in noninfectious neonatal conditions, such as perinatal asphyxia and respiratory distress syndrome.[398] More data are needed for determining the value of fibronectin concentrations as indicators of bacterial sepsis.

Detection of interleukin-6 in plasma samples of newborns has been suggested as a reliable early indicator of sepsis.[65, 151, 164] Interleukin-6 is a pleiotropic cytokine involved in many aspects of the immune system. It is synthesized and released in response to inflammatory stimuli by monocytes, endothelial cells, and fibroblasts after production of tumor necrosis factor and interleukin-1. Interleukin-6 is the major inducer of hepatic protein synthesis including C-reactive protein, fibrinogen, and other acute-phase reactants. Its sensitivity in the diagnosis of sepsis and necrotizing enterocolitis appears to be high.[164] One study suggests that measuring serum concentration of platelet-activating factor can identify septic infants at risk for developing necrotizing enterocolitis.[292] An analysis of all studies published indicates that the main diagnostic importance of measuring interleukin-6 in neonates appears to relate to its very high negative predictive value. An initial interleukin-6 value below 20 pg/mL excludes possibility of sepsis in more than 90 percent of infants; if still below this value when repeated several hours later, its usefulness as a negative predictor of sepsis is even stronger.[120, 185, 216] More studies are needed, however, to evaluate the precise role of interleukin-6 measurement in guiding physicians to a better diagnostic approach of systemic neonatal infections.

The detection of bacterial antigens in blood, urine, or CSF confirms the presence of systemic bacterial disease. Diagnostic techniques include countercurrent immunoelectrophoresis, latex particle agglutination, and coagglutination procedures. Countercurrent immunoelectrophoresis is specific but has low sensitivity and can be used to detect infections caused by *E. coli* K1 and group B streptococci.[25, 162] Latex particle agglutination and coagglutination tests are more sensitive than is countercurrent immunoelectrophoresis, but they have been associated with a small percentage of false-positive and false-negative reactions.[130, 162] They can be used for the detection of disease caused by group B streptococci, *N. meningitidis*, *S. pneumoniae*, and *Haemophilus influenzae* type b. The highest yield is achieved by testing concentrated heat-treated urine specimens and CSF. The sensitivity of this test is 90 to 98 percent, with an average false-positive rate of 2 to 6 percent. Perineal contamination may cause false-positive results in healthy colonized infants in the absence of invasive disease when the urine tested is obtained by bag collection.[319] The absence of antigen does not rule out infection. A positive result in the urine antigen test with negative results in the blood culture can imply occult infection (e.g., osteomyelitis), partial treatment by intrapartum antibiotic therapy, or a false-positive result. The *E. coli* K1 antigen is identical immunologically to the *N. meningitidis* group B antigen and, therefore, can be detected by *N. meningitidis* group B kits. The usefulness of this test is much decreased, however, by its low sensitivity and the high contamination rates of urine collected by bag with *E. coli* from the gastrointestinal tract.

Direct examination of Gram-stained or methylene blue buffy coat smears can help in the early detection of neonatal bacteremia if bacteria engulfed by neutrophils are visualized.[115] Some physicians consider only those smears with intragranulocytic bacteria to be positive. Bacteria are seen more readily when acridine orange stain is used.[191] This technique requires a smaller volume of blood but cannot distinguish between gram-positive and gram-negative bacteria. Identification of bacteria on Gram-stained smears of tracheal secretions obtained in the first 12 hours of life from infants who require intubation is associated with bacteremia in approximately one half of these cases.[335]

Endotoxin elaborated from gram-negative bacteria circulates in blood and is present in urine for considerable periods after these fluids have been sterilized. Detection of endotoxin by the *Limulus* amebocyte lysate assay may be helpful in the early identification of infected infants.[186, 327] Endotoxin may be present in blood of septic-appearing infants who have sterile blood cultures. Transient endotoxemia possibly is responsible for "clinical sepsis" in these infants. The source of endotoxin may be the gram-negative bacterial flora of the bowel. Endotoxin possibly enters the circulation through an injured and permeable gastrointestinal mucosa.

Several serologic tests for the diagnosis of listeriosis have been described, but none has become an established means of routine diagnosis. Agglutination reactions, complement fixation, enzyme-linked immunosorbent assay, precipitin, indirect hemagglutination, and antigen fixation tests are available and may help occasionally. Caution is warranted, however, in attempts to use these tests for diagnostic purposes. Genetic studies showed that an extracellular hemolysin, listeriolysin O, is essential for intracellular multiplication of *Listeria*.

In one study,[41] French investigators examined whether detection of specific antilisteriolysin O could be used for serodiagnosis of human listeriosis. Sera from 28 patients (13 were newborn) infected with *L. monocytogenes* and 101 controls were tested by dot-blot titration with purified listeriolysin O. Twenty-seven patients (96%) with *Listeria* infection produced specific antilisteriolysin O, which was detected in low titers in 16 percent of healthy controls and in 12 percent of persons who had various bacterial, fungal, and viral infections. Anti-listeriolysin O could be detected soon after infection and persisted for at least several months. Although this test might be useful for epidemiologic surveys and for serodiagnosis of listeriosis, more data are needed before it can be used routinely for serodiagnosis of human listeriosis.

TREATMENT

After the diagnosis of sepsis is suspected or established and the appropriate cultures have been obtained, antibiotic therapy should be instituted. When the infant's condition prompts an evaluation for sepsis, initiating empirical parenteral antibiotic treatment usually is prudent, despite the fact that only 5 to 10 percent of blood cultures are positive. For practical purposes, we have summarized recommended empirical antimicrobial treatment for the various bacterial infections occurring during the neonatal period based on the published etiologic organisms identified; therapeutic alternatives also are provided (Table 74–5).

Infants with suspected sepsis should be treated with a combination that includes a penicillin and an aminoglycoside. The choice of antibiotics must be based on the historic experience of the nursery, the antimicrobial susceptibilities of bacteria recently isolated from sick and healthy neonates, the likely etiologic agent, CSF penetration of antibiotics, and the infant's hepatic and renal functions. Factors that

TABLE 74–5 ■ RECOMMENDED EMPIRIC ANTIMICROBIAL TREATMENT OF SEVERAL NEONATAL BACTERIAL INFECTIONS ON THE BASIS OF LIKELY ETIOLOGIC MICROORGANISMS

Bacterial Infection	Recommendation	Alternatives	Observations
Sepsis			
Early onset (<5 days)	AMPI + GENTA	AMPI + CEFO	
Late onset	AMPI + GENTA	AMPI + CEFO	Readmission of neonate at term
Nosocomial	OXA/NAF + GENTA or AMIK	VAN + CEFTA	Consider AMPHO
Meningitis	AMPI + CEFO	AMPI + GENTA	
Otitis media	AMOX/CLAV	CEFUROXIME	Given orally unless systemic signs
Urinary infection	AMPI + GENTA	AMPI + CEFO	
Osteoarticular infection	OXA/NAF + CEFO	VAN + CEFO	Consider AMPHO
Cellulitis/fasciitis/funisitis/omphalitis	OXA/NAF or CLIN + GENTA or AMIK	VAN + CEFTA	Surgery
Pneumonia			
Early onset (<5 days)	AMPI + GENTA	AMPI + CEFO	
Nosocomial	OXA/NAF + GENTA or AMIK	VAN + CEFTA	Consider macrolide

AMIK, amikacin; AMOX/CLAV, amoxicillin/clavulanate; AMPHO, amphotericin B; AMPI, ampicillin; CEFO, cefotaxime; CEFTA, ceftazidime; GENTA, gentamicin; NAF, nafcillin; OXA, oxacillin; VAN, vancomycin.

determine the likely infecting organism include patient age and birth weight; environment (home versus hospital); prior antibiotic therapy; perinatal or nosocomial exposure to pathogens (e.g., MRSA); presence of central lines, drains, or endotracheal tube; and identification of specific infections, such as meningitis, necrotizing enterocolitis, peritonitis, thrombophlebitis, pneumonia, and soft-tissue infections.

For treating early-onset sepsis neonatorum, we recommend ampicillin and gentamicin. Ampicillin is effective in vitro and clinically against group B streptococci, *Listeria, Proteus*, and most enterococci and is active against approximately 50 percent of *E. coli* strains. The aminoglycosides have broader antimicrobial activity against many Enterobacteriaceae, including most *E. coli, Klebsiella-Enterobacter*, and *Proteus* strains, and with the exception of kanamycin, against *P. aeruginosa*. Although gentamicin frequently is used, the choice of the aminoglycoside (e.g., amikacin, tobramycin, netilmicin) should be based on antimicrobial susceptibilities of nosocomial bacteria within individual nurseries. For infections caused by gentamicin-resistant coliforms, amikacin or third-generation cephalosporins, such as cefotaxime and ceftazidime, should be used.[174, 182, 325]

Cephalosporins are not active against *Listeria* or enterococci and should not be used without concomitant administration of ampicillin. Moreover, when used with ampicillin, cephalosporins do not offer the advantage of synergism that aminoglycosides do against strains of enterococci. Staphylococci, nosocomial gram-negative organisms, and fungi rarely are encountered in early-onset sepsis neonatorum, and empirical coverage for them usually is not required. When the epidemiologic experience of the nursery or cutaneous lesions suggest *Pseudomonas*, an extended-spectrum penicillin (i.e., ticarcillin or piperacillin) or ceftazidime combined with an aminoglycoside should be used (see Table 74–1 for dosages). Therapeutic drug monitoring is recommended when aminoglycosides are used, especially in low-birth-weight neonates, and adjustment of the dosage is essential in infants with impaired renal function. Recent interest has focused on evaluating the use of extended intervals for aminoglycoside administration in the neonatal period[264]; guidelines for drug monitoring in these circumstances need to be evaluated carefully.

Because late-onset sepsis neonatorum is more heterogeneous in its epidemiology than is early-onset disease and may reflect maternal, family, community, or nosocomial sources for the infecting pathogen, the organisms involved cover a broad taxonomic spectrum. As a result, empirical antimicrobial regimens vary. In the previously healthy infant who already has been discharged from the hospital, ampicillin and an aminoglycoside or cefotaxime are recommended unless staphylococcal infection is highly suspected, in which case an antistaphylococcal agent (e.g., oxacillin, nafcillin) should replace ampicillin. Selection of empirical antibiotic regimens can be more difficult for a septic premature infant who has had a prolonged hospitalization, previous antibiotic administration, possible prolonged tracheal intubation, and placement of a central or peripheral intravascular catheter.

In these patients, major pathogens include coagulase-negative and -positive staphylococci (including MRSA), aminoglycoside-resistant coliforms, highly resistant opportunistic organisms (e.g., *Pseudomonas, Serratia*), fungi, and possibly enterococci. As a result, empirical regimens in this situation should be individualized. Examples include ampicillin, amikacin, and clindamycin for suspected necrotizing enterocolitis, vancomycin and an aminoglycoside or cefotaxime for patients with indwelling central vascular lines, and nafcillin and an aminoglycoside for babies with skin infection. Avoiding empirical vancomycin therapy seems to be a reasonable approach to treating late-onset sepsis because coagulase-negative staphylococci are common contaminants of blood cultures and are associated with a very low frequency of fulminant infection.[184] For infants who fail antimicrobial therapy or have superficial cultures positive for *Candida albicans*, empirical use of amphotericin should be considered. Ceftazidime and cefotaxime should not be used routinely in neonatal units because of the potential for emergence of resistant *Enterobacter* and *Serratia* spp.

After the culture and susceptibility studies are available, changes in therapy may be necessary. Ampicillin alone is preferred for enterococcal and *Listeria* infections, whereas ampicillin or penicillin can be used for group B streptococcal disease. Infants infected with these organisms usually receive the combination of ampicillin and an aminoglycoside for the first 3 to 5 days, followed by ampicillin for the balance of 7 to 10 days. The minimal inhibitory concentration and minimal bactericidal concentration of ampicillin or penicillin against streptococci and of nafcillin or oxacillin against *S. aureus* should be considered for the purpose of detecting tolerant strains of these organisms.[189, 304, 311, 343] Tolerant strains are inhibited but not killed by concentrations of these antibiotics that usually can be achieved in body fluids and are treated best by the addition of an aminoglycoside to ampicillin or nafcillin. The clinical significance of tolerance is uncertain. For *S. epidermidis* infections, vancomycin is the drug of choice unless the isolate demonstrates in vitro susceptibility to nafcillin or oxacillin; most are resistant to these latter drugs. In selected neonates, the addition of rifampin to vancomycin therapy may be beneficial in clearing a persistent bacteremia caused by coagulase-negative *Staphylococcus*.[361]

Central venous catheters or other foreign bodies frequently must be removed to eliminate the source of these organisms. If a gram-negative enteric isolate is susceptible to ampicillin and aminoglycosides, treatment with either antibiotic alone can be adequate, but we prefer treatment with both drugs for at least a portion of the treatment period. For *Pseudomonas* infections, combined therapy with ticarcillin, piperacillin, or ceftazidime and an aminoglycoside should be used for the total duration of therapy. In certain circumstances, antibiotics not approved for infants (i.e., cefepime, imipenem or meropenem, ciprofloxacin) need to be used for treatment of an infection caused by a multidrug-resistant gram-negative isolate. Few anecdotal reports have been published suggesting successful outcome of treated neonates.[54, 187, 198, 249]

Although the third-generation cephalosporins have attractive features for therapy of sepsis neonatorum, such as excellent in vitro activity against group B streptococci and gram-negative enteric bacilli, provision of high serum and CSF concentrations, and no dose-related toxicity, we do not recommend their routine use in the nursery. Clinical studies suggest that they are comparable with but not superior to ampicillin and gentamicin and that gram-negative enteric bacilli rapidly can become resistant when the third-generation cephalosporins are used for presumptive therapy of neonatal sepsis.

In a 1991 survey of directors of programs in pediatric infectious disease in the United States and Canada, most physicians favored the traditional regimen of ampicillin and gentamicin for initial empirical treatment of sepsis and meningitis.[397] Use of a cephalosporin (cefotaxime in most cases) in combination with ampicillin was considered to be appropriate alternative therapy when meningitis was diagnosed. Antibiotics, such as ceftriaxone and sulfonamides, that have the potential of displacing bilirubin from albumin-binding sites should be avoided in the newborn period.[246] Currently, no rationale exists for routine use of chloramphenicol in newborn infants because of the individual variations in pharmacokinetics in neonates that are associated with increased risk of developing toxicity and that necessitate monitoring serum drug concentrations, its bacteriostatic action against most gram-negative enteric pathogens in vitro, antagonism with ampicillin against enteric gram-negative rods and group B streptococci, and the availability of equally potent and safer β-lactam antibiotics.

The duration of antimicrobial therapy for neonatal sepsis usually is 7 to 10 days or for approximately 5 to 7 days after clinical signs and symptoms of infection have disappeared. Delayed clinical improvement or persistently positive blood cultures during therapy may indicate that inappropriate antibiotics have been selected or that occult sites of infection (e.g., endocarditis, abscesses, infected foreign bodies) exist.

Blood cultures in bacteremic neonates become positive in 96 percent of infants by 48 hours and in 98 percent by 72 hours.[285] For infants whose initial bacterial cultures are sterile after 48 to 72 hours of incubation, antimicrobial therapy can be stopped. If no pathogen has been isolated but bacterial sepsis cannot be excluded, a negative C-reactive protein test at 72 hours can help support the decision to discontinue antibiotics.[351] Because postmortem blood cultures can be negative (in 18 percent of patients in one study[350]) in infants with unequivocal evidence of sepsis, blood cultures from septic infants likely are sterile in some at the time of initial evaluation.

Careful attention to fluid and electrolyte balances; correction of hypoxia, acidosis, hypoglycemia, and other metabolic abnormalities; and nutritional support all are critical for a good outcome. The use of fresh-frozen plasma and exchange transfusions as adjunctive therapy in severe neonatal sepsis has not been studied adequately, and no recommendations for their use can be made.[384] The infusion of intravenous immunoglobulin with functional activity against group B streptococci to neonates produces a significant increase in group B *Streptococcus*-specific immunoglobulin G that is sustained for several days.[123] The potential therapeutic benefits of intravenous immunoglobulin include enhanced chemotaxis and opsonophagocytosis and improved bactericidal activity of neonatal sera for these organisms. In animal models, a therapeutic effect is achieved only when immunoglobulins are given early in the course of disease.[297]

Experience with human immunoglobulin for intravenous use in septic neonates is limited, but such use appears safe. In a double-blind, placebo-controlled study, Weisman and associates[390] evaluated the effect of intravenous immunoglobulin (500 mg/kg) in the outcome of 31 premature infants with early-onset sepsis. During the first 7 days after therapy, 5 (30%) of 17 albumin-treated patients and none of 14 patients treated with intravenous immunoglobulin died ($p < 0.05$). The survival rate at 56 days of age, however, was not improved significantly. Very large doses of intravenous immunoglobulin may cause a blockade of the neutrophil receptors that are necessary for opsonophagocytosis of group B streptococci. Additional studies are required to demonstrate efficacy, safety, and optimal dosage before immunoglobulin therapy can be recommended confidently.

The efficacy of granulocyte transfusions in reducing mortality from severe neonatal sepsis has been reported by several researchers.[69, 80, 201] Christensen and associates[80] conducted a randomized, prospective, controlled trial of granulocyte transfusions in 16 septic neonates with depleted bone marrow reserves. None of seven infants receiving the transfusions died, whereas only one of nine neonates survived among those not receiving granulocyte transfusions. Cairo and coworkers[69] evaluated the early administration of granulocyte transfusions to neonates with clinical sepsis. Of 23 infants in their study, only 3 had depleted neutrophil storage pools. These researchers also found that survival was improved in neonates with sepsis who received these transfusions, compared with control neonates. Only infants with granulocyte-depleted storage pools are likely to benefit from receiving transfusions. Neither clinical severity nor the degree of neutropenia predicted neutrophil storage pool depletion in septic infants; bone marrow aspiration is required for determining the granulocyte storage pool.[28]

Although these studies are encouraging, they involve a small number of patients, and larger, carefully designed studies are needed. Currently, this strategy is used sporadically in a few nurseries around the world. The granulocytes normally are obtained from healthy adult volunteers by leukapheresis and then irradiated for prevention of graft-versus-host disease. Approximately 0.5 to 1×10^9 granulocytes per kilogram of recipient body weight are transfused in 20 to 30 minutes.[384] These transfusions usually are tolerated well by neonates, but potential risks include blood group sensitization, graft-versus-host disease, transmission of cytomegalovirus and hepatitis viruses, and volume overload from hydroxyethyl starch.

A more practical and safe approach to reverse sepsis-associated neonatal neutropenia and potentially improve survival is the use of recombinant human granulocyte-macrophage colony-stimulating factors (rhGM-CSF). Several small studies have documented that a subcutaneous injection of rhGM-CSF (5 to 10 μg/kg/day for 5 to 7 consecutive days) to septic infants with neutropenia significantly increases the number of various phagocytic cells and decreases mortality rates.[49, 61, 196, 352] Large trials are needed to confirm these benefits before administration of these hematopoietic factors can be recommended routinely.

Other nonconventional therapeutic approaches that are being evaluated include extracorporeal membrane oxygenation of neonates with early-onset group B streptococcal disease,[169] administration of colony-stimulating factors to neutropenic infants,[70] and immunomodulating strategies (e.g., anti-cytokine agents, steroids, pentoxifylline, nitric oxide inhibitors).[315] The precise role, if any, of these approaches for management of newborns with systemic infections needs to be demonstrated in rigorous, carefully designed, double-blind clinical studies.

PREVENTION

Chemoprophylaxis

Studies on the prevention of neonatal infections have focused on those caused by group B *Streptococcus* because of its greater prevalence and immunogenicity compared with other common neonatal pathogens. Methods proposed for the prevention of neonatal group B streptococcal disease are aimed at decreasing the likelihood of exposure of the infant to group B *Streptococcus* by use of antibiotic chemoprophylaxis or at decreasing the susceptibility of the exposed infant through improved host defenses by passive or active immunoprophylaxis.

The efficacy of antepartum, intrapartum, or postpartum administration of ampicillin or penicillin has been evaluated in numerous studies. The results have established that selective intrapartum chemoprophylaxis can prevent colonization and disease caused by group B streptococci in the first days of life and prevent postpartum maternal infection caused by this organism.

Many investigators have attempted to eradicate group B streptococcal colonization from pregnant women during the last trimester. In a prospective, randomized study of women known to be colonized with group B *Streptococcus*, Hall and associates[156] demonstrated that treatment with ampicillin (500 mg four times daily for 1 week) briefly reduced maternal colonization, but no difference was found in maternal or infant colonization at the time of delivery. Reinfection from the untreated sexual partner or re-emergence of group B *Streptococcus* from an undetectably low population of organisms remaining after antibiotic treatment probably explains failure of antepartum chemoprophylaxis. Gardner and associates[131] treated colonized women in the last trimester of pregnancy and their husbands simultaneously with oral penicillin for 12 to 14 days. Before therapy, 63 percent of husbands also were colonized with group B *Streptococcus* in the genital tract with concordance of isolated serotypes in 88 percent of colonized couples. Such treatment was found to have no effect on the colonization rate of the maternal genital tract at delivery. Other studies also demonstrated that antibiotic therapy had little effect on carriage of group B *Streptococcus*.

In contrast, Merenstein and associates[236] demonstrated that treatment of colonized pregnant women with 500 mg of penicillin four times daily at 38 weeks' gestation until delivery resulted in a significant reduction in maternal and infant colonization. Such an approach may eliminate colonization in infants delivered after 38 weeks' gestation; however, because 30 percent of infants with early-onset disease are preterm, the timing of such treatment is inappropriate. The bulk of evidence indicates that antepartum oral antibiotic prophylaxis generally is unacceptable for prevention of early-onset group B streptococcal disease.

The parenteral administration of antibiotics during labor has been examined in an attempt to overcome the potential shortcomings of antibiotic administration during pregnancy. In the first published study of intrapartum therapy, 34 women with group B streptococcal genital colonization early in the third trimester were treated at term with intravenously administered ampicillin (500 mg every 6 hours until delivery) at hospital admission.[400] This approach uniformly interrupted vertical transmission of the organism to the infants of treated mothers, which would be expected in approximately 50 percent of infants born to genitally colonized women. Easmon and associates[107] conducted a prospective, controlled trial of 87 colonized parturient patients based on vaginal and anorectal cultures obtained at 36 weeks' gestation. Intrapartum prophylaxis with benzyl penicillin during labor significantly reduced the rate of transmission of group B *Streptococcus* from mothers to their babies from 45 percent (untreated controls) to 3 percent ($p < 0.001$). Allerdice and associates[9] identified prospectively 57 women with prenatal colonization with group B *Streptococcus* and treated them intrapartum with ampicillin. Seven percent of infants born to treated women acquired group B streptococcal colonization, and none had invasive disease; 46 percent of infants born to untreated women acquired colonization, and 7 percent had invasive disease.

Intrapartum chemoprophylaxis given to women with proven group B *Streptococcus* colonization reliably prevents colonization of the newborn in the postpartum period. Universal prophylaxis given to all pregnant women with group B *Streptococcus* colonization, however, would result in a large number of pregnant women being treated unnecessarily and clearly is unacceptable. Realizing this limitation, researchers started to investigate the feasibility of providing selective, rather than universal, intrapartum chemoprophylaxis.

Boyer and Gotoff[58] were the first to document the efficacy of maternal chemoprophylaxis in high-risk parturients for the prevention of neonatal sepsis. Infants born to women with prenatal cultures positive for group B *Streptococcus* and gestation of less than 37 weeks, rupture of amniotic membranes more than 12 hours before delivery, or both, were studied. Eighty women were randomized to receive ampicillin (2 g intravenously and then 1 g every 4 hours until delivery) or no therapy. Infants whose mothers had received ampicillin also were given ampicillin (50 mg/kg body weight every 12 hours intramuscularly for 4 days). Only 1 (2%) of 43 infants born to treated mothers was colonized, compared with 13 (35%) of 37 born to untreated mothers. Boyer and associates,[57, 58] in a randomized controlled trial of selective intrapartum chemoprophylaxis using the same selection criteria, demonstrated the efficacy of this approach in prevention of neonatal sepsis and postpartum maternal febrile morbidity.[56] None of the 85 infants born to mothers in the treatment group versus 5 (6%) of 79 infants born to mothers in the untreated control group developed group B streptococcal bacteremia ($p = 0.024$). None of the parturient women developed an intrapartum temperature of more than 37.5° C in the ampicillin-treated group compared with four in the control group ($p < 0.01$). The investigators estimated that their approach had the potential to eliminate more than 50 percent of early-onset group B streptococcal disease and 75 percent of associated deaths in the United States.

A prospective epidemiologic study of early-onset group B *Streptococcus* disease for a 9-year period has provided additional data regarding risk factors for development of early-onset disease.[57] In this study, the relative risk of developing early-onset disease was 7.3 for infants whose birth weight was 2500 g or less (compared with those weighing more than 2500 g), 7.2 for infants delivered more than 18 hours after rupture of membranes, and 4.0 for those born to women with intrapartum fever. Overall, 74 percent of the 61 infants had one of those perinatal risk factors at the time the pregnant women were admitted to the hospital in labor. In Finland, Tupperainen and associates,[371] using a rapid latex agglutination test, selected patients solely on the basis of healthy intrapartum colonization. Seven (12%) of 58 babies born to mothers who did not receive penicillin developed early-onset group B streptococcal sepsis, whereas only 1 (3%) of 36 infants whose mothers received penicillin developed infection. That one infant had intrauterine pneumonia thought probably to be caused by group B *Streptococcus*.

Morales and associates[242] selected patients in labor who had positive results on serial coagglutination tests on vaginal secretions performed prenatally. Patients were stratified according to whether their test results were positive after 5 hours' preincubation, which indicated heavy colonization, or after 20 hours' preincubation, which indicated light colonization. None of the infants born to treated, highly colonized mothers was colonized at birth, compared with 35 percent of the control babies ($p < 0.001$). No infant in either group developed group B streptococcal invasive disease. None of the infants born to treated, heavily colonized mothers was colonized at birth or developed early-onset disease, compared with 80 percent colonization of the control babies whose mothers were untreated ($p < 0.001$), and three control infants developed early-onset group B streptococcal disease ($p = 0.08$). In another study by the same group,[241] only preterm patients who had premature rupture of membranes were studied again with the use of the results of a rapid coagglutination test on vaginal secretions obtained at the time of hospital admission. Ampicillin treatment of 36 women resulted in no cases of chorioamnionitis or neonatal sepsis, whereas 23 percent of untreated mothers developed chorioamnionitis, and 27 percent of babies developed early-onset group B streptococcal sepsis.

Together, these studies establish the efficacy of selective treatment with chemoprophylaxis to prevent early-onset group B streptococcal disease in neonates and postpartum infections in their mothers. Despite endorsement of this approach by the American Academy of Pediatrics and the American College of Obstetricians and Gynecologists, many physicians involved in the management of mothers and their infants are not aware of or do not follow widely published guidelines to prevent group B streptococcal disease.[177]

Chemoprophylaxis also has been targeted to neonates at birth. The observation in 1978 that infants born at Mount Sinai Hospital in New York who received intramuscular penicillin at birth for the prevention of development of gonococcal ophthalmia did not develop early-onset group B streptococcal disease prompted two prospective, randomized studies using this regimen. Siegel and associates[341, 342] studied preterm and term infants and demonstrated the efficacy of a single dose of penicillin administered at birth. The population in this study was characterized by group B streptococcal infections, mostly in term infants who acquired infection at the time of delivery, as evidenced by the delayed onset of symptoms. Because blood cultures were not obtained before administration of penicillin, whether some infections were suppressed inadvertently was unknown. The other study of chemoprophylaxis at birth was reported by Pyati and associates.[289] They studied only infants weighing 2000 g or less at birth and found no beneficial effect of penicillin administered at birth. These infants were infected in utero, as evidenced by the presence of positive blood cultures at the time of delivery in 21 of 24 infants with group B streptococcal disease. Infection had been established before the administration of penicillin at delivery. The population in each of these studies had unique characteristics, and the results, therefore, may not be broadly applicable to all nurseries.

Intrapartum ampicillin prophylaxis coupled with a dose of penicillin to the neonate immediately after birth has been used for years in Dallas. This policy has resulted in approximately 75 percent reduction of group B streptococcal infection in neonates (see Table 74–4) without altering incidence of infections caused by other pathogens. The substantial decline of neonatal, group B streptococcal, early-onset sepsis related to routine intrapartum prophylaxis also has been documented by the CDC and other U.S. institutions.[38, 217] In our Dallas, Texas, series, the incidence of late-onset group B streptococcal sepsis also has declined.

Three special circumstances merit chemoprophylaxis. The first one is the asymptomatic twin of an infant with group B streptococcal disease. This twin has an approximately 25-fold increased risk for the development of invasive group B streptococcal disease.[108] Cultures of blood and CSF should be obtained from the twin, and close observation in the hospital with or without treatment is indicated until cultures have been sterile for 72 hours. The second situation is chemoprophylaxis for the pregnant woman who previously has delivered an infant with invasive group B streptococcal disease. Starting at the end of the second trimester, rectal and vaginal cultures are recommended on three occasions at regular intervals for isolation of group B streptococci. If cultures are negative and delivery occurs at term in the absence of maternal risk factors for neonatal infection, prophylaxis can be withheld. If one or more cultures are positive or delivery occurs before 37 weeks' gestation, intrapartum ampicillin should be administered intravenously. The condition of the newborn infant should be assessed; clinical findings and maternal obstetric factors may warrant further laboratory evaluation and antimicrobial therapy. To initiate chemoprophylaxis in all women colonized with group B *Streptococcus* who have two or more risk factors for invasive infection of the neonate seems prudent.[22, 135, 290]

Several studies[120, 207, 235, 363, 370] have indicated that routine administration of prophylactic ampicillin during labor to women with risk factors for group B *Streptococcus*–associated infections has facilitated the proliferation of resistant gram-negative bacteria in the vaginal and rectal maternal mucosa, resulting in increased incidence of neonatal sepsis caused by these organisms, particularly by *E. coli*. Based on these findings, switching to an exclusive use of intrapartum penicillin for prevention of early group B streptococcal sepsis in neonates seems reasonable.

Prevention of early sepsis caused by gram-negative bacilli is important for areas of the world where these organisms are prevalent. Unfortunately, no evidence-based medicine guidelines on the epidemiology, risk factors, and prophylactic approaches exist for making a clear recommendation. Empirical use of aminoglycosides during labor frequently is used in Latin American countries, but no published reports have demonstrated its usefulness. We demonstrated that a single, 1-g parenteral injection of ceftriaxone given to high-risk Panamanian pregnant women (i.e., gestations of less than 37 weeks, prolonged rupture of membranes of more than 12 hours, or both) during labor is associated with decreased bacterial colonization and early-onset infection caused by gram-negative enteric bacilli and possibly by group B streptococci.[313] Although this prophylactic strategy seems safe and attractive, cost-effective analysis and careful evaluation of potential emergence of ceftriaxone-resistant organisms must be done before recommending it for routine use in selected mothers.

Immunoprophylaxis

Effective immunoprophylaxis would be preferable to chemoprophylaxis because of the limitations of antibiotic prophylaxis and because an immunologic approach is more likely to prevent early- and late-onset group B streptococcal disease in neonates and postpartum febrile morbidity in the pregnant woman. The underlying principle is that IgG antibody directed against the type-specific polysaccharide antigen critical to protection against invasive group B streptococcal disease would be provided by passive or active immunization. Group B *Streptococcus* type-specific polysaccharide vaccines have been developed and were found to be associated with low rates of side effects.[24] However, the immune response was unsatisfactory in as many as 40 percent of nonimmune pregnant women who received type III polysaccharide vaccine. These nonresponders did not develop specific antibody, even after repeated vaccine challenges.[24] Response to vaccine possibly is determined genetically, and some of the women in whom antibodies do not respond to vaginal colonization by group B streptococci may be the same women in whom the vaccine will fail. Pregnant women with the highest risk may not benefit from vaccination. A second-generation vaccine consisting of polysaccharide antigen conjugated to a protein carrier likely will be immunogenic, as observed with *H. influenzae* vaccines in young infants. Maternal immunization, however, no matter how successful, does not prevent disease in neonates who are born so prematurely (<32 weeks) that sufficient amounts of antibody would not have passed transplacentally. Administration of hyperimmunoglobulin to newborns, provided they are not already seriously ill at birth, may help these infants.

Prevention of late-onset infection, compared with early-onset disease, in neonates by the administration of intravenous immunoglobulin to preterm babies has undergone intense clinical scrutiny.[17, 26, 116, 388] Premature babies, particularly those born before 32 weeks' gestation, are relatively hypogammaglobulinemic at birth and become more so during the first several weeks of life. Because these same infants are at high risk for developing infection beyond the first week of life (late onset), intravenous immunoglobulin infusions may provide opsonizing antibody to prevent late-onset infections. Three of the five early clinical trials that examined the efficacy of intravenous immunoglobulin administration in preventing infection in neonates demonstrated significant favorable responses.[77, 83, 154, 353] Problems with these studies included a small sample size, definition of infection, and the lack of a blind design.

A well-controlled, multicenter study demonstrated efficacy of intravenous immunoglobulin infusions in reducing late-onset infection rates.[17] Study infants received intravenous immunoglobulin (500 mg/kg) or placebo at 3 to 7 days of age, 1 week later, and every 2 weeks for a total of five infusions or until hospital discharge. Infusions were tolerated well. Although no significant differences in mortality or reduction of infections in infants weighing more than 1500 g occurred, bacterial infections were reduced significantly in infants weighing less than 1500 g at birth, and the duration of hospitalization was significantly shorter among intravenous immunoglobulin recipients. Most infections were bacterial in origin, and approximately 70 percent of them were caused by gram-positive organisms, primarily staphylococci. In contrast with the beneficial effect found in this study, two larger, multicenter, well-designed trials showed no significant differences in the rate of nosocomial infection or in the mortality rate between control and treated groups.[116, 388] At this time, intravenous immunoglobulin cannot be recommended as routine prophylaxis for low-birth-weight infants. Investigations now are directed at evaluating the usefulness of pathogen-specific hyperimmunoglobulin for the prevention and treatment of sepsis caused by the most common etiologic agents.[389]

Purulent Meningitis

As many as one fourth of neonates with bacterial sepsis have a simultaneous meningeal infection. The incidence of neonatal meningitis varies greatly among institutions in North America. Rates are approximately 0.2 to 0.4 cases per 1000 live births but may be as high as 1 case per 1000 live births in some nurseries. In general, group B beta-hemolytic streptococci and *E. coli* strains account for two thirds of all cases of neonatal meningitis in North America. Gram-negative enteric bacilli predominate in many developing areas of the world (Table 74–6).

Information about the bacteria isolated from CSF cultures of 257 neonates with meningitis treated at Children's Medical Center or Parkland Memorial Hospital in Dallas, Texas, from 1969 to 1989 is presented in Table 74–6. One hundred thirty-six (53%) of these 257 infants had disease caused by group B streptococci. An additional 49 infants (19%) had meningitis caused by *E. coli* strains. *L. monocytogenes* added an additional 7 percent of cases. These three agents accounted for 79 percent of cases seen during the 20-year period. *E. coli* and *Klebsiella-Enterobacter* strains accounted for 77 percent of gram-negative organisms causing meningitis. For an etiologic comparison, the distribution of meningeal pathogens in a developing setting[243] also is displayed in the same table.

TABLE 74–6 ■ ETIOLOGIC AGENTS OF NEONATAL MENINGITIS IN NURSERIES FROM A DEVELOPED AND DEVELOPING COUNTRY

	Isolation Rate (%) in	
Organisms	*Dallas (U.S.) (1969–1989) n = 257*	*Panama (Panama) (1975–1992) n = 105*
Gram-negative bacteria	88 (35%)	68 (64%)
Escherichia coli	19%	16%
Klebsiella species	8%	25%
Other gram-negative rods	4%	16%
Pseudomonas aeruginosa	2%	5%
Haemophilus influenzae	1%	1%
Neisseria meningitidis	1%	1%
Gram-positive bacteria	169 (65%)	37 (36%)
Group B *Streptococcus*	53%	5%
Coagulase-negative *Staphylococcus*	<1%	18%
Staphylococcus aureus	2%	10%
Listeria monocytogenes	7%	1%
Enterococci	2%	1%
Streptococcus pneumoniae	1%	<1%

PATHOLOGY

The pathologic findings are similar, regardless of bacterial cause. Studies of the fulminant, early-onset form of group B streptococcal disease have shown primarily a bronchopneumonia with or without hyaline membranes and usually no histologic evidence of meningeal involvement. The most consistent finding at necropsy of meningitis cases is a purulent exudate of the meninges and ependymal surfaces of the ventricles.[46] The inflammatory response of neonates is similar to that observed in adults with meningitis, with the exception that babies have a scarcity of plasma cells and lymphocytes during the subacute stage of meningeal reactions. Some patients also have perivascular inflammation. Hydrocephalus and a noninfectious encephalopathy can be demonstrated in approximately 50 percent of infants dying of meningitis.

Subdural effusions occur rarely in neonates. In contrast, effusions are observed commonly (i.e., by computed tomography or magnetic resonance imaging) in infants with meningitis who are 3 to 12 months of age. Various degrees of phlebitis and arteritis of intracranial vessels can be found in all infants. Thrombophlebitis with occlusions of veins may occur in the subependymal zone. K1 antigen has been demonstrated in brain tissue of infants succumbing to *E. coli* K1 infection.[322] High concentrations of interleukin-1β have been detected in brain and meningeal tissues of infants succumbing to meningitis.[28]

CLINICAL MANIFESTATIONS

The early signs and symptoms of neonatal meningitis frequently are indistinguishable from those of septicemia and other disorders occurring in the neonatal period. The most frequent signs are temperature instability, respiratory distress, irritability, lethargy, and poor feeding or vomiting. Group B *Streptococcus* occasionally has been reported to present as hydrocephalus without other signs of infection. Signs suggestive of meningeal involvement, such as stiff neck, bulging fontanelle, convulsions, and opisthotonus, are the exception in neonates with meningitis. The frequency of these findings as culled from the literature is 17 percent for bulging fontanelle, 33 percent for opisthotonos, 23 percent for stiff neck, and 12 percent for convulsions.[46, 231, 269] The sensitivity of these findings to distinguish infection of the pia-arachnoid is poor. All newborns being evaluated for sepsis should undergo examination of the CSF, especially if antimicrobial therapy is to be instituted.

DIAGNOSIS

Interpretation of CSF values in newborn infants may be difficult. During the first several days of life, the mean WBC count is 15 ± 30 (95% limit, 12 to 18 cells/mm^3) in the CSF of healthy or high-risk uninfected babies.[268, 323] Approximately 60 percent of these cells are polymorphonuclear leukocytes. During the first week of life, the cell count slowly diminishes in term infants and increases in premature infants. Cell counts in the range of 0 to 10 cells/mm^3 (median, 4 cells/mm^3) are observed at approximately 2 to 4 weeks of age. The WBC count is uncertain when bleeding occurs after the lumbar puncture. The fixed relationship between the number of WBCs in CSF and peripheral blood has been disputed. A repeat lumbar puncture in 12 to 24 hours may be necessary to resolve the ambiguity of the traumatic lumbar puncture.

The mean cerebrospinal protein concentration in the first month of life is 64 ± 24 mg/dL, although individual values can be as great as 170 mg/dL, especially in low-birth-weight, premature infants. The percentage ratio of cerebrospinal glucose to blood glucose is 60 to 70 percent and can be greater than 100 percent in term and preterm infants.[323] The upper normal limits of cellular and chemistry values are higher in very-low-birth-weight, uninfected infants.[53]

These data indicate that CSF values must be interpreted in relation to these normal findings if an early diagnosis of neonatal meningitis is to be made. Comparisons of the results of initial CSF evaluations obtained from newborns with proven bacterial meningitis with those from normal or high-risk infants revealed considerable overlap in the findings.[323] For example, approximately 30 percent of infants with group B streptococcal meningitis had normal spinal fluid leukocyte counts (<32 cells/mm^3), whereas only 4 percent of neonates with meningitis caused by gram-negative organisms had normal counts.[324] The ratio of CSF to blood glucose was normal in 45 percent and 15 percent of patients with streptococcal and coliform meningitis, respectively. However, when the total CSF evaluation (including Gram-stained smears) was considered, fewer than 1 percent of babies with bacteriologically proven meningitis had a totally normal CSF on initial lumbar tap. The likelihood of suppurative meningitis is diminished greatly but not impossible if the evaluation of CSF discloses no abnormalities. In some patients in whom the diagnosis is obscured, a repeat CSF examination performed 4 to 6 hours after the initial tap (whether or not therapy has been instituted in the interim) may help establish the diagnosis. In premature infants with meningitis caused by *S. epidermidis*, the CSF analysis can be only mildly abnormal, despite compatible clinical findings.[152]

Examining carefully the stained smears of CSF from every infant with suspected meningitis is important. Grossly clear fluid may contain few WBCs and many bacteria. The stained smears from approximately 20 percent of neonates with proven meningitis are interpreted as showing no bacteria. Because of the low concentrations of organisms, most Gram-stained smears of CSF from infants with *L. monocytogenes* meningitis do not reveal bacteria. The CSF findings in the infant with a brain abscess may have a pleocytosis of up to a few hundred cells with a predominance of mononuclear cells and with an elevated protein concentration. Bacteria may not be seen in a Gram-stained smear of CSF if meningitis is not present. Ventriculitis is diagnosed on the basis of elevated WBC count (>100 cells/mm^3), identification of organism by culture, Gram-stained smear antigen detection, increased intraventricular pressure, and dilated ventricles. A cranial computed tomogram with contrast material may show enhancement of the lining tissue of the ventricles.

Several techniques to diagnose bacterial meningitis rapidly have been described. The first, counterimmunoelectrophoresis, is used to detect bacterial capsular antigens in CSF and other body fluids. Depending on the source of antisera used in this method, meningitis can be diagnosed with counterimmunoelectrophoresis in almost all patients with *H. influenzae* type b and meningococcal groups B and C meningitis if spinal fluid, serum, and urine are tested.[117] Approximately 70 percent of infants with *E. coli* K1 meningitis have detectable K1 antigen in CSF, serum, or both.[219] Group B_{III} streptococcal antigen has been detected in CSF, serum, and urine of approximately 90 percent of infected infants.[25] Quantitation of antigen is a helpful means of establishing the prognosis of infants with *E. coli* K1 and type III group B streptococcal meningitis.[25, 229]

Latex particle agglutination and staphylococcal coagglutination tests have been developed for detection of bacterial antigens in body fluid. The latex particle agglutination method has been found useful in detecting antigen in the CSF of older infants and children with meningitis caused by *H. influenzae* type b; *N. meningitidis* groups A, B, and C; and *S. pneumoniae*.[257, 392] This method is more sensitive than is counterimmunoelectrophoresis for measuring capsular antigen of *H. influenzae*.[382] The staphylococcal coagglutination test has not been used extensively in pediatric patients. The polyribose phosphate antigen of *H. influenzae* has been detected in body fluids by this method.[359] Both methods can be used for the detection of group B streptococcal infection.

The *Limulus* lysate test detects the presence of endotoxin, a soluble lipopolysaccharide constituent of the cell wall of gram-negative bacteria.[206] Endotoxin can be measured in the CSF of patients with meningitis caused by coliform bacteria, *H. influenzae,* and *N. meningitidis*.[225] Endotoxin has been detected in initial CSF specimens obtained from infants with meningitis caused by *E. coli* and other coliforms. Both counterimmunoelectrophoresis and the *Limulus* lysate techniques require approximately 1 hour to run and can be established in most hospital laboratories. If both methods are used, approximately 80 percent of neonates with coliform meningitis can be identified as having disease within an hour of the initial lumbar tap. However, these results are no better than those obtained from a carefully prepared and examined stained smear of CSF, in which bacteria can be identified in approximately 80 percent of patients with documented bacterial meningitis.[323]

TREATMENT

Selection of appropriate antibiotic therapy for meningitis is based in part on achievable CSF concentrations of these drugs in relation to the susceptibility of the pathogens causing disease. The highest concentrations of penicillin or ampicillin in CSF are at least 10 to 100 times greater than the susceptibilities (i.e., minimal inhibitory concentrations) of group B streptococci and *L. monocytogenes*. As a result, sufficient activity remains in CSF for at least 40 to 60 percent of the dosing interval, and most infants with meningitis caused by these two organisms respond promptly to ampicillin or penicillin therapy. CSF cultures usually are sterile within 24 to 36 hours of initiation of therapy. In contrast, the concentrations of the aminoglycosides (i.e., kanamycin, gentamicin, tobramycin, and amikacin) in CSF usually are equal to or several times greater than the minimal inhibitory concentrations for coliform organisms and *P. aeruginosa*. Because killing of bacteria by the aminoglycosides is concentration dependent, requiring drug concentrations in the CSF at least fourfold to eightfold the minimal bactericidal concentration, cultures of CSF from infants with meningitis caused by these organisms often remain positive for 2 or 3 days or longer. Documenting bacteriologic cure in patients with meningitis is important because outcome is correlated with the time necessary to eradicate the bacterial pathogen.

Ampicillin and gentamicin or cefotaxime are recommended for initial empirical therapy of neonatal meningitis (for dosages, see Table 74–1). All infants should undergo repeat CSF examination and culture at 24 to 36 hours after initiation of therapy. If organisms are observed on methylene blue– or Gram-stained smears of fluid, modification of the therapeutic regimen should be considered. For many years, physicians have attempted to increase antibiotic concentrations in CSF by instilling drugs directly into the lumbar intrathecal space. The first Neonatal Meningitis Cooperative Study evaluated 117 prospectively enrolled, randomly treated infants to determine the role of intrathecal gentamicin therapy in the management of neonatal meningitis caused by coliform bacilli.[225] No statistically significant differences were seen in mortality, long-term morbidity, or days that CSF cultures remained positive among infants who received lumbar intrathecal gentamicin plus systemic therapy and those who were treated with systemic drugs only.

Data from the Neonatal Meningitis Cooperative Study and from adult neurosurgical patients with meningitis demonstrated that lumbar CSF concentrations of aminoglycosidic drugs administered locally usually exceed the minimal inhibitory concentration values for coliform organisms by 10 to 50 times.[225, 293] However, lumbar instillation does not result consistently in diffusion of these drugs to the level of the cisterna or into ventricular fluid. In contrast, instillation of aminoglycosides into unobstructed ventricles results in rapid and uniform distribution of drug throughout the CSF space.

Data obtained from the second Neonatal Meningitis Cooperative Study demonstrated ventricular fluid gentamicin concentrations of 10 to 130 μg/mL at 1 to 6 hours after administration of a 2.5-mg intraventricular dose and from 1 to 24 μg/mL 16 to 24 hours later.[224, 226] The concentrations in lumbar CSF at comparable intervals after intraventricular administration were 8 to 85 μg/mL and 1.8 to 4.2 μg/mL, respectively. However, results of the intraventricular regimen were inferior to those obtained with systemic therapy alone. The mortality rate was significantly higher in infants who had meningitis and ventriculitis and who received intraventricular gentamicin and systemic antibiotics (43%) than in those who were given systemic therapy only (12.5%). The duration of positive CSF cultures was 1 day shorter in those receiving intraventricular therapy. Using serial CSF samples from patients enrolled in this study, we demonstrated some years later that intraventricular gentamicin therapy, which resulted in higher gentamicin CSF concentrations, was associated with higher ventricular CSF endotoxin and interleukin-1β concentrations and greater CNS inflammation (i.e., higher CSF leukocyte count, higher protein concentration, and lower glucose concentration), most likely as a result of lysis of organisms.[247] This finding possibly could explain the poor outcome in those patients compared with that in infants who received parenteral antibiotic therapy only.[247]

On the basis of the findings from the second Neonatal Meningitis Cooperative Study, intraventricular therapy cannot be recommended for the routine management of neonatal meningitis caused by gram-negative enteric bacilli. A controlled study[232] found that ampicillin and moxalactam therapy (a broad-spectrum cephalosporin no longer available) in neonatal coliform meningitis was as effective as was a conventional regimen of ampicillin and amikacin. In that study, moxalactam achieved greater CSF and ventricular fluid concentrations, and the bactericidal titers were considerably greater than those achieved with conventional therapy, but this increase did not translate into more rapid sterilization of the CSF, lower case-fatality rates, or improved neurologic outcomes for survivors. Although no large controlled trials have evaluated the use of cefotaxime, clinical experience indicates that it can be used safely and effectively for the treatment of gram-negative meningitis in neonates. CSF examination and culture should be repeated 48 to 72 hours after initiation of therapy. If the results still are positive, computed tomography should be performed to rule out the possibility of subdural empyema, brain abscess, or ventriculitis. In all cases caused by *Citrobacter diversus*, cranial computed tomograms should be obtained early because of the frequent association with brain abscess. The duration of antibiotic therapy should be extended, depending on clinical evolution and resolution of the lesion based on repeated tomography. A neurosurgeon should be consulted early for needle aspiration or excision of the abscess. Aminoglycosides probably should not be used because of decreased activity in abscess cavities that have a low pH and anaerobic conditions.

Third-generation cephalosporins possess attractive features for therapy of bacterial meningitis in newborn infants, which include lower minimal inhibitory concentrations for gram-negative enteric bacilli than for aminoglycosides, good penetration into CSF in the presence of inflamed meninges, and a wide therapeutic index. These agents are active against most streptococci but inactive against *L. monocytogenes* and enterococci. Only ceftazidime provides adequate activity against *P. aeruginosa*. Among these agents, cefotaxime is preferred for therapy of neonatal meningitis because of the extensive experience with this drug in the neonatal period and because it does not alter substantially the bowel flora. Cefotaxime can be used singly or in combination with an aminoglycoside. Ceftazidime has been shown to be effective in treating patients with *P. aeruginosa* meningitis. Because of high biliary excretion and marked alteration of the normal intestinal flora and because of potential concern for displacement of bilirubin, we do not recommend routine use of ceftriaxone during the neonatal period. A prospective study of neonatal bacterial meningitis conducted in England indicated that treatment with third-generation cephalosporins has been associated with a decrease in mortality rates from disease seen during the past decade, especially that related to gram-negative bacillary infection.[165]

For premature infants hospitalized in the nursery for prolonged periods, staphylococci, enterococci, and gentamicin-resistant gram-negative organisms are potential pathogens; an alternative antimicrobial regimen should be considered for initial empirical treatment. A combination of nafcillin or oxacillin and amikacin or ceftazidime or cefotaxime could be used as initial empirical therapy. When MRSA or *S. epidermidis* is a potential cause of infection, vancomycin and amikacin or cefotaxime can be used initially. Imipenem, meropenem, cefepime, and ciprofloxacin have been used to treat neonatal meningitis caused by multiresistant gram-negative bacteria. Greater experience is required before they can be recommended for routine use. For neonatal meningitis caused by *Flavobacterium meningosepticum* isolates, the combined use of parenteral vancomycin and rifampin has been suggested as the best therapeutic option.[102]

After the pathogen has been identified and susceptibility studies are available, the single drug or combination of drugs that is most effective should be used. In general, penicillin G or ampicillin is preferred for group B streptococcal meningitis, ampicillin for *L. monocytogenes* and enterococci, ampicillin plus an aminoglycoside or cefotaxime for coliforms, and ceftazidime or ticarcillin and an aminoglycoside for *Pseudomonas* infections. The duration of systemic therapy in neonatal meningitis depends on the causative agent and the time necessary to sterilize CSF cultures. As a rule, therapy is given for approximately 2 weeks after bacteriologic cure has been achieved. For meningitis caused by group B streptococci or *Listeria,* approximately 2 weeks of therapy usually is satisfactory. Because delayed sterilization is common in infants with gram-negative enteric disease, systemic therapy is given for a minimum of 3 weeks and in some babies for many additional weeks. Final judgment about when to stop therapy must be based on the clinical course of illness and on CSF findings at the time this decision is to be made.

Despite the beneficial effects of dexamethasone found in several prospective, randomized, double-blind studies for the treatment of infants and children with bacterial meningitis,[316] especially that caused by *H. influenzae,*[326] no such data are available for its use in newborns; the use of steroids in neonatal meningitis cannot be recommended. A prospective trial performed in Jordan found lack of effectiveness of dexamethasone in neonatal meningitis in terms of mortality and sequelae rates compared with the nonsteroid group.[93] Because this study was small (not sufficient statistical power), not blinded, and without a placebo group, additional studies are required to determine whether dexamethasone has a beneficial effect in neonatal meningitis.

PROGNOSIS

The acute complications of bacterial meningitis include communicating and noncommunicating hydrocephalus, subdural effusions (approximately 1% of patients), deafness, and blindness. Ventriculitis occurs in approximately 70 percent of neonates with coliform meningitis and usually is detected at the time of initial diagnosis. Brain abscess is an infrequent complication except in infants with *C. diversus* meningitis, in whom it develops approximately 70 percent of the time.[144, 225, 226, 232] Although gross retardation and neurologic deficits may be obvious in some infants at discharge, most babies appear "well" at this time. Only after prolonged and careful follow-up do the perceptual difficulties, behavioral problems, and other subtle neurologic signs become apparent. Within 4 to 6 weeks of recovering from meningitis, hearing should be evaluated by evoked response audiometry.

The case-fatality rates in neonates with meningitis range from 15 to more than 30 percent.[231, 269] A mortality rate of 30 percent was observed in 117 neonates with coliform meningitis enrolled in the first Neonatal Meningitis Cooperative Study.[225] In this project, term infants had a significantly lower rate (18%) than that observed in low-birth-weight (<2500 g) babies (45%) and in infants older than 30 days of age (48%). Poor outcome after gram-negative enteric meningitis is correlated directly with the presence of ventriculitis, the persistence of positive CSF cultures, the presence and persistence of elevated endotoxin and interleukin-1β concentrations in CSF, CSF cell count of more than 10,000/mm^3, and a CSF protein concentration of more than 500 mg/dL.[188] When meningitis is caused by *E. coli* K1, poor outcome is associated with persistence of large quantities of K1 capsular polysaccharide antigen in CSF.[227, 229]

In a 20-year period, the mortality rate of neonatal meningitis at Parkland Memorial Hospital and Children's Medical Center in Dallas, Texas, did not change appreciably. Approximately 15 percent of infants died during the 4-year periods of 1956 to 1959, 1969 to 1972, and 1973 to 1976. During the 8 years from 1969 to 1976, 17 (14%) of 123 neonates with bacterial meningitis died, and this rate did not change appreciably through 1984.[224] The first 24 hours of management are critical; the case-fatality rate for infants who survive the first 24 hours of therapy is approximately 5 percent.

Long-term follow-up studies of babies with coliform meningitis enrolled in the Neonatal Meningitis Cooperative Study have revealed that approximately 65 percent of survivors were normal at 3 to 7 years after illness. An additional 30 percent were classified as having mild to moderate neurologic sequelae. Many of these latter patients had only slightly abnormal neurologic or psychologic evaluations and were considered normal on routine physical examination. Approximately 5 to 10 percent of survivors had severe neurologic or mental impairment requiring custodial care. Approximately 15 to 20 percent of survivors of group B streptococcal meningitis have major sequelae, including spastic quadriplegia, profound mental retardation, hemiparesis, deafness, and blindness.[80] Hydrocephalus develops in 11 percent, and 13 percent have a seizure disorder. The survivors without major sequelae on physical examination, however, appear to function within normal limits and comparably with their siblings.

Edwards and associates[109] reported a 21 percent morbidity rate after having group B streptococcal meningitis. Of the survivors, 29 percent had severe neurologic sequelae, 21 percent had minor deficits, and 50 percent were functioning normally. Factors associated with death or severe disability at presentation included coma, decreased perfusion, CSF protein greater than 300 mg/dL, an absolute neutrophil count of less than 1000, and a total leukocyte count of less than 5000/mm^3. A report from Canada noted that duration of seizures for more than 72 hours, presence of coma, use of inotropes, and leukopenia were the most important predictors of adverse outcome.[195] Our experience with gram-negative enteric bacillary meningitis in 98 identified neonates managed from 1969 through 1989 had a case-fatality rate of 17 percent; 61 percent of survivors had long-term sequelae that included seizure disorders, hydrocephalus, physical disability, developmental delay, and hearing loss.[373]

Otitis Media

Otitis media (see Chapter 19) is diagnosed infrequently in neonates because of the paucity of clinical findings and the difficulty in examining the infant's tympanic membrane. The external canal is narrow and tortuous and often is filled with debris. Because the healthy baby's membrane may appear thickened and dull, mobility of the drum determined by pneumatoscopy should be used as the single most reliable indicator of middle ear abnormalities. The examiner must beware of mistaking the movement of the distal interior canal wall for movement of the tympanic membrane. Movement of the normal membrane is seen best in the posterior portion. A reddish or reddish-orange color of the tympanic membrane usually indicates infection, provided that the infant is not crying.

The exact incidence of disease is unknown, but a prospective study found that 34 percent of 70 infants followed from birth developed their first episode of otitis media before reaching 2 months of age.[220] Otitis media occurs more commonly in premature than in term infants and occurs almost exclusively in bottle-fed babies. It is a frequent finding in neonates receiving intensive care, especially those with prolonged nasotracheal intubation.[47] The ears of 127 infants with birth weights of less than 2300 g were examined by Warren and Stool[383] three times weekly until discharge from the nursery; only 3 patients (2%) developed otitis media. In contrast, in a study of 125 premature infants in a neonatal intensive care unit, Berman and associates[47] found that 38 infants (30%) had middle ear fluid compatible with the diagnosis of otitis media; this finding was confirmed by tympanocentesis in 13 patients in whom the procedure was done. Development of otitis media was correlated significantly with nasotracheal intubation for longer than 7 days.

Meconium staining of amniotic fluid and prolonged rupture of membranes are two other risk factors for subsequent development of middle ear disease.[279] Neonates with cleft palate, Down syndrome, or maxillofacial anomalies are at high risk for development of chronic middle ear disease. Onset of illness is insidious, and the most common manifestations are rhinorrhea, irritability, and failure to thrive. Fever greater than 38° C is a rare finding. The presence of lethargy, hypotonia, hypothermia, high fever, or jaundice suggests septic complications, such as bacteremia or meningitis.

The cause of neonatal otitis media is similar to that observed in older infants and children. *S. pneumoniae, H. influenzae,* and *Moraxella catarrhalis* account for more than 50 percent of cases.[50, 338, 364] The important difference from disease in older patients is that 10 to 15 percent of neonates have disease caused by coliforms, group B streptococci, or *S. aureus.* Pathogens isolated from middle ear fluid of 169 infants 6 weeks of age or younger were *S. pneumoniae* in 18 percent of cases, *H. influenzae* in 12 percent, *S. aureus* in 8 percent, *E. coli* in 6 percent, *Klebsiella-Enterobacter* spp. in 5 percent, *M. catarrhalis* in 5 percent, group A or B streptococci in 3 percent, and *P. aeruginosa* in 2 percent; no pathogen was isolated in 32 percent.[51] We occasionally have encountered neonates with otitis media associated with septicemia and pneumonia or meningitis. Group B streptococci or coliform organisms were the causative agents in these cases.

The importance of establishing the diagnosis and cause of otitis media in neonates and of employing appropriate therapy cannot be overemphasized. When the otologic examination demonstrates middle ear disease, the infant should be examined carefully for other sites of infection. If none is found, which is the usual case, the infant can be treated on an outpatient basis. Because a small percentage of these cases are caused by coliform bacilli or *S. aureus,* drugs that include those organisms in their spectrum of activity (i.e., second-generation cephalosporin or amoxicillin-clavulanate) are preferable to the aminopenicillins. The patient's condition should be reevaluated 8 to 72 hours after initiation of therapy to determine whether clinical improvement has occurred and whether middle ear infection is resolving. In patients demonstrating no improvement, tympanocentesis should be performed for examination of stained smears of middle ear fluid and for culture of the contents. Alteration of therapy should be based on the findings of these examinations. If gram-negative organisms or staphylococci are observed, the infant probably is managed best in the hospital by means of parenteral therapy, with an aminoglycoside if coliforms are suspected or with an antistaphylococcal penicillin for *S. aureus.* If organisms are not observed in infants with unresolving disease, nafcillin and gentamicin or cefuroxime can be used until results of cultures and susceptibility studies are available. A CSF examination should be performed before initiation of parenteral therapy.

All infants with otitis media should be followed carefully for many months after illness. Misdiagnosis or improper therapy may result in chronic middle ear disease and, occasionally, in extension of infection to adjacent structures, such as the mastoid or CNS. Infants who develop their first episode of otitis media before reaching 2 months of age may require 3 to 4 months to clear the effusions, and a third of them are said to develop recurrent or chronic otitis media.[220]

Diarrheal Disease

Although diarrheal disease during the neonatal period usually is brief and self-limited, it may cause significant morbidity in some infants and represents a potential danger to other infants in the nursery. The advent of modern sterilization practices and increased emphasis on hospital infection control measures have reduced significantly the incidence of nosocomial diarrheal disease.

Numerous factors contribute to an increased susceptibility of neonate enteric infections and include underdevelopment of local and systemic immune responses; lack of a fully developed aerobic and anaerobic enteric flora, which protects the gastrointestinal tract of older infants and children; a less effective gastric bactericidal barrier; less intestinal mucus; and less motility.[263] The infant may have been fed powdered formula that could have been mixed with contaminated water, or the critically ill newborn may have received a broad-spectrum antibiotic in intensive care, in which case highly resistant nosocomial flora pose a special risk.

The importance of breast feeding in prevention of diarrheal diseases in infants cannot be overemphasized. The protective effects of breast feeding have been confirmed in surveys of sporadic gastroenteritis, in community epidemics, and in outbreaks in newborn nurseries. Antibacterial and antiviral factors in breast milk, including lactoferrin, lysozyme, phagocytes, specific secretory immunoglobulins, and lymphocytes sensitive to organisms such as *E. coli, Salmonella, Shigella, Clostridium difficile* toxins A and B, and rotavirus, are well documented.[147, 157, 263] Breast-fed infants are less susceptible to diarrheal diseases than are bottle-fed infants.[153, 263]

ETIOLOGY AND PATHOGENESIS

The most common cause of diarrhea in young infants is alteration of diet and feeding practices rather than specific bacterial or viral pathogens. Diarrhea can be a nonspecific symptom of sepsis or urinary tract infection in the newborn infant. Of the infectious causes, rotaviruses are important in infantile diarrheal disease.[238, 310] They have been associated with nursery outbreaks of gastroenteritis and necrotizing enterocolitis.[82, 305] Studies from France have shown that approximately one third of all neonates shed rotavirus in their stools; of these infants, only 29 percent have associated diarrhea.[76]

The transplacental transfer of rotaviral group-specific or type-specific maternal antibodies to neonates appears to have little effect on the incidence of infection or illness by the rotaviruses.[100, 101, 261] The essential pathogenic feature of rotavirus infection is destruction of the absorptive cells lining the duodenum, the jejunum, and possibly the ileum.[237]

Lactase, which exists only in the brush borders of the differentiated epithelial cells at these sites, has been suggested to act as a combined receptor and uncoating enzyme for the virus, which may explain why rotavirus infection occurs less commonly in infants of fewer than 32 weeks' gestation than in more mature infants.[71] In infants of between 26 and 34 weeks' gestation, the lactase activity is approximately 30 percent of that found in term infants.[203]

Enteropathogenic *E. coli* serotypes once were considered the most common bacterial agents responsible for diarrhea in young infants. Failure to demonstrate on rectal cultures specific serotypes of *E. coli* designated as enteropathogenic does not rule out coliform disease. Enterotoxigenic strains of *E. coli* possessing nonenteropathogenic serotypes have been identified in nursery outbreaks of diarrheal disease.[60, 266] These organisms inhabit the small bowel, where they attach to but do not invade the intestinal mucosa. The enterotoxin produced by these organisms stimulates cyclic adenosine monophosphate, which inhibits sodium and chloride transport across the intestinal wall. As a result, these salts are lost into the lumen of the upper bowel, followed passively by water, which causes a net loss of stools containing high concentrations of electrolytes. *Vibrio cholerae,* some *E. coli* serotypes (almost exclusively nonenteropathogenic strains), *Vibrio parahaemolyticus, Aeromonas,* and possibly some *Campylobacter* and *Yersinia* strains are examples of bacteria that cause diarrhea by this mechanism.

The importance of recognizing this form of diarrheal disease was emphasized in a nursery outbreak in the southwestern United States. Severe, watery diarrhea was observed in 59 infants during a 9-month period; in the 7 percent of infants who died, death resulted from altered hepatic function and a hemorrhagic diathesis.[60] An O142/K86/H6 *E. coli* strain was responsible for the outbreak. Because this organism is not a classic enteropathogenic serotype, it was not identified as a pathogen, which thereby delayed definitive diagnosis and institution of proper infection control techniques. Only by special laboratory techniques was this *E. coli* strain shown to produce labile enterotoxin.

A second mechanism involved in development of bacterial diarrhea is invasion of the intestinal mucosa. *Shigella* dysentery is the classic example of this disease. Colonic invasion with subsequent destruction of the mucosa causes an outpouring of polymorphonuclear cells and mucus. The resultant diarrhea usually is bloody and contains mucus and pus. *Salmonella* spp. also invade the intestinal mucosa, but destruction is not extensive. The epithelial lining is left intact, and the organisms reach the lamina propria, where an inflammatory response is elicited.[360] *Campylobacter, Yersinia, Aeromonas* spp., and *C. difficile* also can cause bloody diarrhea.

Although serotyping of *E. coli* to identify the traditional enteropathogenic strains no longer is available routinely, the epidemiologic evidence is strong enough to support a pathogenic role for these strains, even though the mechanism of pathogenicity is unknown. When an index case of diarrhea caused by enteropathogenic *E. coli* or other pathogens is recognized in a nursery, secondary cases are likely to occur. In any nursery infant with diarrhea, a potentially communicable disease should be suspected. For all infants in proximity to the index case, rectal swabs should be tested by culture or by fluorescent antibody technique, which is more sensitive for identifying asymptomatic carriers of enteropathogenic *E. coli.* Ill and healthy colonized infants should be segregated and treated with orally administered neomycin (100 mg/kg/day in three or four divided doses) or with colistin sulfate (15 mg/kg/day in three or four divided doses) for 5 days. Neomycin causes rapid disappearance of the organism and abbreviates the period of diarrhea, but approximately 20 percent of infants revert to an asymptomatic carrier state (J. D. Nelson, personal communication, 1990). Repeated surveillance of infants is necessary until the pathogenic strain has been eliminated from the nursery. A report from Yugoslavia identified a multiresistant strain of enteroaggregative *E. coli* (O4 serogroup) associated with an outbreak of transient, self-limited diarrhea in a neonatal nursery ward.[84]

Campylobacter, a curved, gram-negative bacterium, has been recognized increasingly as a common cause of enteritis. Of the 14 known species, *Campylobacter fetus* and *Campylobacter jejuni* cause human disease most frequently. *C. fetus* causes prenatal and neonatal infections that result in abortion, premature delivery, bacteremia, and meningitis. Infections caused by *C. fetus* appear to be the most common type of *Campylobacter* infection in the first 3 weeks of life and are associated with a high incidence of fetal and neonatal morbidity.[153] In contrast, the most common syndrome produced by a *Campylobacter* spp. is enteritis caused by *C. jejuni*. Unlike the serious neonatal disease caused by *C. fetus,* infections with *C. jejuni* usually result in mild gastroenteritis, although meningitis occurs rarely. Nursery outbreaks of gastroenteritis caused by *C. jejuni* have been documented well.[153]

Although some diarrheal episodes in neonates likely can be caused by *C. difficile*, the diagnostic criteria used in older children and adults are inadequate to establish a definitive diagnosis in this age group. *C. difficile* is a gram-positive anaerobic bacillus that produces an enterotoxin (i.e., toxin A) that causes fluid secretion and a cytotoxin that damages cells (i.e., toxin B).[67, 209] *C. difficile* colonic overgrowth and toxin production can result from the selective pressure of antibiotic therapy. A wide variety of antibiotic, antifungal, and antituberculous agents have been associated with *C. difficile* colitis.[153] Although healthy children older than 1 year of age and healthy adults rarely carry the organisms, as many as two thirds of neonates can be demonstrated to have both *C. difficile* and its cytotoxins in their stools.[153] This high frequency of colonization and the presence of cytotoxin have led to skepticism about the pathogenic potential of this organism in the neonate.

CLINICAL MANIFESTATIONS

Although the cause of diarrhea in infants and children may be suspected on clinical grounds, this usually is not possible in newborn infants. As a general rule, diarrhea caused by enteropathogenic strains of *E. coli* is insidious in onset; is associated with 7 to 10 green, watery stools daily; and usually is without blood or mucus. The infants do not appear to be acutely ill. Complications rarely occur and primarily are related to dehydration and electrolyte disturbances. *Shigella* infection seldom occurs, usually is episodic in neonates, and usually does not spread within nurseries.[158] Shigellosis in the newborn may occur as a diarrheic or dysenteric syndrome or may be evidenced only by a septic or toxic infant. Suppurative complications are rare events, but dehydration and electrolyte disturbances are common occurrences and need immediate and constant attention. *C. jejuni* infection typically involves the gastrointestinal tract, producing watery diarrhea or a dysentery-like illness with fever and bloody mucoid stools. Extraintestinal infections related to *C. jejuni,* other than bacteremia, are rare occurrences but include cholecystitis, urinary tract infection, and meningitis.[153] The clinical manifestations in neonates with *C. fetus* infection are similar to those caused by the common neonatal pathogens.[153] *C. jejuni* has been reported to cause bloody diarrhea in otherwise asymptomatic neonates.[66]

A useful procedure for differentiating enteroinvasive from enterotoxigenic diarrhea is examination of fecal material for polymorphonuclear cells. Feces from many patients with dysentery show significant numbers of polymorphonuclear leukocytes, whereas those from patients with enterotoxigenic disease usually show few neutrophils.

TREATMENT

The most important aspect of therapy for diarrheal disease of newborn infants is maintenance of hydration and electrolyte balance. As a rule, parenteral solutions containing appropriate electrolytes should be administered during the time of active diarrhea, and the infant should be examined and weighed frequently to ensure proper rehydration and to prevent development of complications. Estimation of fluid loss from diarrhea and vomiting should be recorded carefully and used as a basis for replacement therapy.

Selection of appropriate antimicrobial therapy depends in part on the mechanism of diarrhea. In general, an orally administered, absorbable antibiotic, such as ampicillin and trimethoprim-sulfamethoxazole, is indicated for disease caused by invasive bacteria (e.g., shigellosis), whereas orally administered, nonabsorbable drugs, such as neomycin and colistin sulfate, are used for noninvasive organisms that produce enterotoxin (e.g., some *E. coli*).

Antimicrobial therapy for *Salmonella* gastroenteritis is controversial. We do not recommend antibiotics for most infants and children with uncomplicated *Salmonella* disease because such therapy does not shorten the course of illness and can be associated with an increased likelihood of prolonged asymptomatic excretion of the organism. However, neonates and infants younger than 3 or 4 months of age should be treated with a 7-day course of amoxicillin because of their propensity to develop a protracted illness or bloodstream invasion with distant foci of infection.[96] Trimethoprim-sulfamethoxazole is a suitable alternative for ampicillin-resistant strains. The asymptomatic carrier state requires no therapy.

Ampicillin formerly was the antibiotic of choice for shigellosis, but in recent years, significant resistance to this agent has been observed in many areas of the country. Some strains are susceptible to trimethoprim-sulfamethoxazole in a daily dosage of 10 mg of trimethoprim and 50 mg of sulfamethoxazole/kg/day in two divided doses. Sulfa drugs are contraindicated in newborns with jaundice. For multiresistant *Shigella* strains, some authorities recommend third-generation cephalosporins given parenterally (e.g., ceftriaxone) or orally (e.g., cefixime).

Erythromycin is the preferred drug for treating symptomatic *C. jejuni* enteritis. Often, if erythromycin therapy is initiated within the first 4 days of illness, excretion of the organism is reduced and symptoms resolve rapidly. An aminoglycoside is the drug of choice for treating *C. fetus* infections; chloramphenicol is an alternative.

Any infant with diarrhea must be isolated from the other babies in the nursery. Surveillance of all infants in contact with the index case and institution of infection control measures are mandatory, as discussed earlier.

Urinary Tract Infections

The incidence of bacteriuria in newborn infants ranges from 0.5 to 1 percent for term infants and is approximately 3 percent for premature infants.[256] Urinary tract infections occur more commonly in babies born to bacteriuric mothers and in boys during the neonatal period. The latter observation contrasts with the predominance in girls beyond the first months of life. The frequencies of urinary tract infection and bacteremia are significantly higher in uncircumcised male neonates and young infants.[395] Circumcision reduces the frequency of urinary tract infection by approximately 90 percent. Bacterial colonization of both the prepuce and female perineum may occur because of the presence of maternal urinary tract infection. This prevalence was shown in a study in which 24 percent of infants were bacteriuric when delivered to mothers who had bacteriuria, whereas control infants whose mothers had not been bacteriuric had no bacteriuria. Clinical pyelonephritis occurred in 3 percent of these bacteriuric infants, whereas only 0.2 percent of 500 control infants of nonbacteriuric mothers had pyelonephritis.[277]

ETIOLOGY

E. coli is the most common etiologic agent of urinary tract infections, accounting for approximately 90 percent of acute infections and 70 to 80 percent of recurrent disease. Approximately 70 percent of *E. coli* strains belong to one of eight common somatic (O) antigen groups similar to those found in older persons. Several capsular polysaccharide antigens (K1, K2, K12, and K13) are found more often in children with upper tract disease than in those with cystitis.[183, 393] The association between K1 antigen and upper tract disease is found significantly more often in newborn and young infants than in older infants and children with *E. coli* urinary tract infections.[393] Fimbriated *E. coli* can attach to specific receptors or uroepithelial cells. Glycolipids of the P blood group constitute a specific receptor that is thought to be associated with pyelonephritis in patients who do not have reflux. Compared with asymptomatic bacteriuric infants, those with febrile urinary tract infections were found to have significantly increased inflammatory signs (e.g., C-reactive protein value, microsedimentation rate) and attaching *E. coli*.[222] This finding suggests that bacterial properties determine not only the location of urinary tract infection but also the severity of inflammation in individual patients.

Proteus, Klebsiella, and *Pseudomonas* spp. are encountered in patients with recurrent disease, particularly those receiving prolonged antimicrobial prophylaxis. Gram-positive bacteria, with the exception of enterococci, rarely are encountered as pathogens for the urinary tract. Only a few neonatal cases of renal abscess have been reported in the literature. *S. aureus* and coliforms were the predominant etiologic agents.[347]

CLINICAL MANIFESTATIONS

Most infants with significant bacteriuria are asymptomatic or have nonspecific signs and symptoms. The neonate may appear septic or may have decreased activity, feeding problems, and the other constitutional signs that are seen with infections of other organ systems. Jaundice, hepatomegaly, and thrombocytopenia may be observed in a few infants with urinary tract infection; these findings are associated with septicemia or cholestatic hepatitis in some babies.[44] Localizing signs suggesting urinary tract involvement are unusual findings. When present, they usually consist of a weak urinary stream on voiding or an abdominal tumor from bladder distention, hydronephrosis, or both.

DIAGNOSIS

The diagnosis of urinary tract infection is confirmed by examination and culture of urine. The results of these tests depend largely on the method of urine collection. Most pediatricians obtain urine with a sterile, plastic receptacle applied to the cleansed perineum. However, urine obtained by this method may have an elevated cell count because of recent circumcision, vaginal reflux of urine, or contamination from the perineum. Neonatal asphyxia also may increase the urine cell count. WBCs must be differentiated from round epithelial cells, which appear in the urine in significant numbers during the early days of life. Although pyuria commonly accompanies significant bacteriuria, cells can be few or absent. Direct microscopic examination of uncentrifuged, fresh urine is useful. If bacteria are seen readily in each high-power field, they generally number greater than 10^5 cells/mL. Glitter cells are thought by many physicians to be diagnostic of urinary tract infections.

Quantitative urine cultures from infants with documented disease usually contain more than 100,000 colonies/mL of a single bacterial species. Any number of bacteria in a urine specimen obtained by percutaneous needle puncture of the bladder should be considered significant. This latter procedure is the single best source of urine for culture and is safe in most newborn infants.[256] The procedure should not be performed in infants who are dehydrated or have bleeding problems. Minor, transient hematuria is an uncommon occurrence, and serious problems from hemorrhage or perforation of the bowel have been rare events. If a "bagged urine specimen" contains fewer than 100,000 colonies/mL of a single species of bacteria or if the culture yields a mixed bacterial population, a repeat urine specimen should be obtained for culture by suprapubic bladder aspiration or catheterization.

Examination of the urinary sediment for antibody-coated bacteria has been found useful in differentiating upper tract disease from cystitis in adult patients.[181] Some reports have suggested, however, that this technique is not applicable to infants and children.[393] These studies have demonstrated false-positive and false-negative rates of approximately 30 percent. Because acute pyelonephritis is associated with enlargement of the kidneys resulting from edema and acute inflammatory infiltrate of the medulla and the pelvis, ultrasound volume measurements of the kidneys provide a noninvasive method for identifying the probable site of urinary tract infection.[179] Fifteen of 18 children with upper urinary tract infection had volume increases of 30 percent or more in at least one kidney, whereas only 4 of 21 children with lower urinary tract infection had increases of greater than 30 percent ($p < 0.005$).

TREATMENT

Blood and urine cultures should be obtained from all newborn infants with suspected or proven urinary tract infection before antimicrobial therapy is initiated. Antibiotics initially are administered parenterally because sepsis is associated with urinary tract infection in 20 to 30 percent of infants,[136] and antibiotic absorption after oral administration is erratic in some babies. Therapy is initiated with an aminoglycoside and ampicillin to provide antibacterial coverage for the anticipated coliforms, enterococci, and group B streptococci. If the patient has renal impairment, ampicillin and cefotaxime constitute an alternative empirical regimen. Because urine concentrations of these drugs exceed many times the minimal inhibitory concentration values of the urinary pathogens, the usual dosages may be reduced after septicemia has been ruled out.[228] Infants with renal or perineal abscesses require percutaneous drainage under sonographic guidance or open surgical drainage if the former fails.

A repeat urine culture taken 48 to 72 hours after initiation of appropriate therapy should be sterile or show a substantial reduction in the bacterial count. Infants with persistent bacteriuria should be evaluated for the possibility of inappropriate therapy, obstruction, or perinephric abscess. In uncomplicated disease, therapy usually is continued for a period of 7 to 10 days. Approximately 1 week after discontinuance of therapy, a repeat urine culture is obtained.

All infants with documented infection should undergo radiologic evaluation of the urinary tract. An intravenous pyelogram or renal sonograph is obtained during the course of therapy to rule out the possibility of gross congenital abnormalities of the urinary system. Renal sonography is preferred over intravenous pyelography in the acute phase of disease. Congenital malformations are unusual findings in the first week of life but may be found in a significant portion of infants with urinary tract infections after this age. If obstruction is demonstrated, urologic procedures to ensure proper drainage are mandatory if therapy is to be successful. A voiding cystourethrogram or a radionuclide cystourethrogram should be obtained several weeks after therapy is stopped. Radiologic abnormalities are found in approximately 45 percent of infants, especially in girls.[55, 136]

Physicians have the responsibility of ascertaining that neonates with urinary tract infections do not have congenital abnormalities of the urinary system.[299] In these patients, recurrent urinary tract infections are common events, and physical growth may be retarded until definitive surgery has been performed. Every infant with urinary tract infection should undergo long-term follow-up studies for detection of recurrent infections, many of which are asymptomatic.

Infants identified to have anatomic abnormalities (e.g., vesicoureteral reflux) must be protected from reinfection by prophylactic administration of trimethoprim-sulfamethoxazole or nitrofurantoin, and urine cultures or urinary nitrite tests should be performed soon thereafter for children. Although no absolute medical indication exists for routine circumcision of the newborn, cumulative data suggest that circumcision protects against urinary tract infections during early infancy.[396] Compared with complications of urinary tract infections, short-term complications of circumcision are rare occurrences and mostly minor.[395]

Suppurative Arthritis and Osteomyelitis

Osteomyelitis and suppurative arthritis rarely occur in the first 4 weeks of life. The incidence has not changed for many years and is estimated to be 1 to 3 cases of bone or joint infections per 1000 nursery admissions. According to the Dallas experience, 18 cases (3%) of neonatal arthritis and 18 cases (5%) of osteomyelitis occurred among 632 arthritis and 365 osteomyelitis cases in infants and children managed from 1959 to 1986.[251] Male infants are affected more often than are female (1.6:1), and the incidence is higher for premature than term infants.

Bone and joint infections can be difficult to detect in neonates and young infants. Early diagnosis and appropriate management are vital to prevent orthopedic abnormalities later in life.

ETIOLOGY AND PATHOGENESIS

The infecting organisms in osteomyelitis and septic arthritis vary, but the predominant ones are *S. aureus,* group B *Streptococcus*, and gram-negative enteric organisms, such as *Klebsiella, Proteus,* and *E. coli.* In neonates in Dallas,

S. aureus was the etiologic agent in 50 and 44 percent of cases of osteomyelitis and arthritis, respectively, whereas streptococci were responsible for 6 and 22 percent of such cases, respectively. Group B *Streptococcus* has become the single most common agent associated with arthritis in many areas of the United States.[126] Osteomyelitis and arthritis caused by gram-negative enteric bacilli have remained uncommon events, despite the frequency of neonatal bacteremia caused by these organisms. Coliforms caused 11 percent of cases in Dallas, Texas, and 5 percent in a children's hospital in Stockholm.[39] In Africa and Asia, rates as high as 45 percent have been reported.[199] We reported that coliforms and *S. aureus* accounted for two thirds of isolates in neonates with osteoarticular infections in Panama.[318] Gonococcal arthritis and tenosynovitis were common occurrences in previous decades, but they are seen only occasionally today.[87] Other causative agents associated infrequently with newborn infection are *Salmonella, Pseudomonas*, and *C. albicans*.[92, 287]

Osteomyelitis and arthritis have been reported after several invasive procedures in newborns, including heel puncture, femoral venipuncture, exchange transfusions, fetal monitoring using electrodes, serial lumbar punctures, and umbilical artery catheterization.[15, 42, 211, 250, 270, 287, 291] Osteomyelitis of cranial bones has complicated infected cephalohematomas. The use of peripheral and central intravascular catheters in neonates has been associated with bacterial and fungal osteomyelitis.[112] Septic embolization from catheter tip thrombi together with local hypoxia from partial occlusion of the vessel by the catheter may explain this association.[126, 212] A very strong correlation exists between the site of the catheter and localization of infection in the limb; for example, the knees and hips are involved in most cases associated with aortic catheters.[212] Usually, the origin is unknown and presumed to be hematogenous.

During the infant's first month of life, the epiphyseal plate is traversed by multiple small transepiphyseal vessels that provide a direct communication between the articular space and the metaphysis of the long bones.[262] As a result, infection of the metaphysis (i.e., osteomyelitis) can spread across the growth plate to penetrate the epiphysis or enter the joint space. Because the perforating vessels disappear when the child is approximately 1 year of age, septic arthritis usually is not associated with osteomyelitis in older infants and children. The two exceptions to this rule are osteomyelitis of the proximal femur and of the proximal humerus. The capsule of the hip and shoulder attaches below the proximal metaphysis of the femur and humerus, respectively. Infection of the epiphyseal cartilage may rupture through the periosteum and enter the joint space, producing purulent arthritis. Because the capsular articulation of the hip and shoulder is permanent, osteomyelitis and septic arthritis may coexist, rendering the origin of infection difficult to establish.

The large vascular spaces and thin spongy structure of the metaphyseal cortex in infants permit early decompression of the primary abscess into the subperiosteal space. The abscess then dissects rapidly between the loosely attached periosteum. As pressure increases from the accumulating pus, a subcutaneous abscess can form that may point and drain spontaneously through the skin, forming a sinus tract. Free communication between the original site of osteomyelitis and subperiosteal space prevents the necrosis and extensive spread of infection within bone that occurs frequently in older children and adults.

CLINICAL MANIFESTATIONS

Two distinct clinical syndromes that may be associated with osteomyelitis in the newborn period have been described.[97, 149, 367] The first is a benign form in which the earliest sign of bone and joint infections of newborns is failure to move an extremity spontaneously or apparent pain on movement without systemic evidence of infection. Swelling, erythema, and heat localized to the affected part are late findings. Multiple bones or joints can be involved, especially when disease is caused by *S. aureus*. The striking feature of this form is the satisfactory general condition of the infant despite the intensity of the local process. The fatality rate is exceedingly low, and healing is prompt. The second syndrome, a severe form, is characterized by systemic manifestations of sepsis; only later are multiple sites of bone and visceral involvement noted.

Two other clinical entities unique to the newborn are maxillary bone involvement and osteomyelitis caused by group B *Streptococcus*. Maxillitis or osteomyelitis of the superior maxilla is an unusual form of bone infection in newborn infants.[210, 211] More than 85 percent of all maxillary infections in infants occur in the first 3 months of life, with the peak incidence occurring in the second to fourth weeks.[221] Swelling of the cheek, associated with unilateral nasal discharge of pus, and swelling of the alveolar ridge of the maxilla should alert the physician to this entity. Initially, dacryocystitis or orbital cellulitis may be suspected. The etiologic agent usually is *S. aureus*. Septicemia and death occur commonly in untreated cases.

Group B streptococcal osteomyelitis manifests during the third and fourth weeks of life (i.e., late onset) and is caused predominantly by type III strains. It affects girls more often than boys, and the humerus is the most common site of involvement. In contrast with the fulminant onset and poor outcome that occur in some infants with late-onset meningitis, group B streptococcal bone and joint infection has an indolent nature and an almost uniformly good outcome. Occasionally, a diagnosis of Erb palsy may be entertained when inflammatory signs are minimal and diminished use of an arm is marked. Manipulations known to predispose neonates to bone and joint infections caused by other organisms have not been reported among infants with group B streptococcal arthritis or osteomyelitis.[221]

DIAGNOSIS

Conventional radiography remains the most useful way of establishing the diagnosis in patients with suspected suppurative arthritis; radiographs may be normal or show enlargement of the joint space. Later in the course of disease, subluxation and destruction of the joint are common occurrences. In early osteomyelitis, the normal radiographic water markings of tissues adjacent to the affected bone may be obliterated, indicating deep tissue inflammation and swelling. Lifting of the periosteum also may be observed, but cortical bone destruction seldom occurs before the second week of illness. A complete skeletal survey should be performed because of the frequent involvement of multiple sites.[126, 239] In approximately 10 percent of patients, radiographic abnormalities are not seen during the course of disease. Although radionuclide bone scans are useful in early diagnosis of osteomyelitis in infants and children, they can be normal in newborn and young infants with confirmed infection. A report indicates a sensitivity of 90 percent for three-phase bone scintigraphy to diagnose neonatal osteomyelitis.[5] Magnetic resonance imaging has been used successfully for diagnosis of osteomyelitis in the newborn period.

Blood cultures should be obtained from all infants with osteomyelitis or septic arthritis. Considering the varied etiologic bacteria, getting specimens of bone or a joint aspirate for culture is imperative, as is percutaneous needle aspiration of intra-articular pus in patients with suspected suppurative arthritis or of sequestrum in those with suspected osteomyelitis. If pus is obtained, the material should be Gram stained and cultured.

TREATMENT

Selection of initial antimicrobial therapy is guided by preliminary identification of the pathogen from stained smears of material obtained from needle aspirations. If no microorganisms are seen, initiating treatment with two drugs, a penicillinase-resistant penicillin (e.g., nafcillin, oxacillin) and cefotaxime, is advisable. Use of an aminoglycoside with the antistaphylococcal penicillin does not provide adequate coverage for group B *Streptococcus*. Definitive treatment is based on culture and susceptibility results. Direct instillation of an antibiotic into the joint space is unnecessary because most drugs penetrate the inflamed synovium, and adequate concentrations are achieved in purulent material.[252] The same applies to treatment of osteomyelitis; direct instillation of antibiotics into acutely inflamed bone is unnecessary.[365]

Surgical removal of infected material is an integral part of treatment. Open drainage is essential for managing septic hip disease. Inflammation in osteomyelitis or in septic arthritis can occupy the epiphyseal and metaphyseal sides of the growth plate, resulting in ischemia and necrosis of the plate and in permanent orthopedic damage. For other joints, repeated daily evacuation of fluid with needle and syringe usually is adequate. In patients with osteomyelitis, the subperiosteal space and the metaphysis should be drained if pus is obtained during diagnostic aspiration. If only a small amount of bloody material is obtained at aspiration, immediate surgery does not need to be performed, and the patient usually can be managed with antibiotic therapy alone as long as local and systemic signs resolve. If improvement is unsatisfactory, repeat aspirations or open surgical drainage may need to be performed.

Antimicrobial therapy of neonatal musculoskeletal infections caused by staphylococci or coliform organisms is continued for a minimum of 3 weeks. Group B streptococcal infection is treated with penicillin G or ampicillin for at least 2 weeks. Ten days of therapy usually is adequate for treating gonococcal infection. Use of oral antibiotics as a substitute for parenteral therapy during the second and third weeks of treatment is unwise unless compliance can be ensured and serum bactericidal activity or antibiotic concentration is satisfactory, indicating adequate absorption of the orally administered drug. Parenteral antibiotic therapy can be administered at home if the infant can be assessed routinely by a physician.

As a general rule, systemic symptoms disappear within several days of initiation of therapy and of adequate surgical drainage, although such local signs as heat, erythema, and swelling may persist for 4 to 7 days. Full range of motion may not return to the involved limb for several months. The erythrocyte sedimentation rate is a useful guide for determining duration of therapy. The rate usually returns to within the normal range within 2 to 4 weeks compared with the C-reactive protein value that becomes normal sooner. As reported for older infants and children, serial determinations of C-reactive protein may be valuable in assessing the clinical course, but experience is inadequate to use this test in guiding duration of antimicrobial therapy in neonatal osteoarticular infections.[303] Complete resolution of the radiographic changes may take several months.

Physical therapy to ensure full range of motion should be started as soon as pain has abated. Assessing residual joint abnormalities and abnormal bone growth patterns in infants frequently is difficult until many months or years have passed. Maintaining good long-term follow-up after treatment has been concluded is important.

Conjunctivitis and Orbital Cellulitis

Infections of the eye of the newborn can be caused by a variety of microorganisms, including *Neisseria gonorrhoeae, Chlamydia trachomatis, S. aureus,* and *P. aeruginosa.* From a review of more than 300 cases of eye infections in newborns at Grady Memorial Hospital in Atlanta, Georgia,[13] researchers determined that 29 percent were caused by *Chlamydia,* 14 percent by gonococci, 10 percent by staphylococci, 2 percent by chemical reactions, and 1 percent by mixed gonococcal and chlamydial infections. The remaining 44 percent were of uncertain cause. A prospective, controlled study found that the major microbial causes of neonatal conjunctivitis were *Haemophilus* spp. in 17 percent, *S. aureus* in 17 percent, *C. trachomatis* in 14 percent, *S. pneumoniae* in 11 percent, and enterococci in 8 percent.[320] Other less frequently encountered organisms included *M. catarrhalis, Pasteurella multocida, N. meningitidis,* and herpes simplex virus.

The incidence of ophthalmia neonatorum has not paralleled the large increase in gonococcal disease rates among adolescent and young adults, almost certainly a result of universal neonatal prophylaxis with 1 percent silver nitrate solution, antibiotic ointment, or systemic penicillin G. Today, we rarely see the invasive, destructive ophthalmitis described so vividly in the early literature.[224]

Numerous agents have been shown to be effective prophylactically against gonococci. The largest series was published by Greenberg and Vandow[148] and involved 250,000 infants treated with 1 percent silver nitrate. A failure rate of 6.6 per 100,000 infants treated with silver nitrate compared favorably with the 22.5 per 100,000 rate in 86,000 infants who received no prophylaxis. Of the topical antimicrobial agents, tetracycline or erythromycin appears to be comparable in efficacy to silver nitrate and has the advantage of causing fewer cases of chemical conjunctivitis.[267] Penicillin applied topically or given intramuscularly also is effective, although the ointment no longer is available commercially. Bacitracin ointment is ineffective.[81, 223] Ceftriaxone as a single dose of 50 mg/kg (for low-birth-weight infants, 25 to 50 mg/kg) can be useful for prophylaxis when the risk is high. Infants born to mothers with active gonorrhea should receive a single 125-mg dose of ceftriaxone intravenously or intramuscularly. Ceftriaxone should be given cautiously to hyperbilirubinemic infants, especially premature infants.

A study by Hammerschlag and associates[158] showed that neonatal ocular prophylaxis with erythromycin or tetracycline ophthalmic ointment does not reduce significantly the incidence of chlamydial conjunctivitis in the offspring of mothers with *Chlamydia* infection, compared with silver nitrate. The investigators concluded that better management of maternal *Chlamydia* infection is required if the incidence of conjunctivitis caused by this organism is to be reduced. They suggested that a small but appreciable incidence of neonatal gonococcal ophthalmia could be prevented by performing better prenatal screening and treating maternal gonococcal infections.

DIAGNOSIS

Any infant with a conjunctival discharge should be evaluated carefully to determine the cause. Three tests should be performed: Gram and methylene blue stain of the exudate; culture of the exudate; and Giemsa stain and culture for *Chlamydia,* if available, of scrapings made from the lower palpebral conjunctiva after exudate has been removed. The results of the stained smears determine the appropriate therapy. Direct detection of chlamydial antigens in eye scrapings now is possible by means of a commercially available enzyme-linked immunoassay (e.g., Chlamydiazyme). Limited experience in neonates suggests that it is a sensitive and specific test that can provide rapid and reliable results.[160]

DIFFERENTIAL DIAGNOSIS

Conjunctivitis occurring in the first days of life can be chemical or bacterial. Chemical irritants, such as silver nitrate, cause transient conjunctival hyperemia and a watery discharge that rarely turns purulent.

Gonococcal ophthalmia usually becomes apparent within the first 5 days of life and is characterized initially by a clear watery discharge. Conjunctival hyperemia and chemosis are associated with a copious discharge of thick, white, purulent material. Both eyes usually are involved, although not necessarily to the same degree. Untreated gonococcal ophthalmia may extend to involve the cornea (i.e., keratitis) and the anterior chamber of the eye. Corneal perforation and blindness can result. Before the introduction of adequate prophylactic measures, ophthalmia neonatorum was the most frequent cause of acquired blindness in the United States.

If gram-negative rods are seen in the stained exudate, the greatest concern is *P. aeruginosa* because of the virulent necrotizing endophthalmitis that can result. In this condition, a relatively mild conjunctivitis can progress to infection of the entire globe within 12 to 24 hours. Invasion of the cornea by small blood vessels (pannus) is characteristic of *Pseudomonas* conjunctivitis. Perforation of the cornea may occur, and blindness from corneal opacity occurs commonly. The ophthalmic disease occasionally can be followed by bacteremia and septic foci in other organs.[68] Prompt diagnosis and immediate institution of appropriate antimicrobial therapy are mandatory.[68]

Conjunctivitis during the second or third week of life can be caused by viral, bacterial, or chlamydial agents. Viral conjunctivitis frequently is associated with other symptoms of respiratory tract disease, such as rhinorrhea, cough, and rash, and several individuals in the family or nursery may have disease simultaneously. The discharge in viral conjunctivitis usually is watery or mucopurulent but rarely purulent. A hemorrhagic discharge can be seen with adenoviral infection. Preauricular adenopathy is a common finding. Staphylococci, streptococci, *Haemophilus,* and occasionally, gonococci cause conjunctivitis in this age group. A smear of purulent material helps to differentiate these bacterial agents. However, the presence of bacteria on a Gram-stained smear of exudate is not necessarily related etiologically to the conjunctivitis. The exudate may contain normal inhabitants of the skin and mucous membranes, such as staphylococci, diphtheroids, and *Neisseria* spp.

Chlamydial eye infection may begin in the first days of life but usually does not come to the attention of the physician until the second or third week. Clinical manifestations of chlamydial infection (inclusion blennorrhea) vary from mild conjunctivitis to intense inflammation and swelling of the lids, associated with copious purulent discharge.[142, 306] Pseudomembrane formation and a diffuse "matte" injection of the tarsal conjunctiva are common findings. The cornea rarely is affected, and preauricular adenopathy is an unusual occurrence. In the early stages of disease, one eye may appear more swollen and infected than the other, but both eyes almost invariably are involved.

Diagnosis is made by scraping the tarsal conjunctiva and looking for typical cytoplasmic inclusions within epithelial cells (not in the exudate). Specially prepared tissue culture cells for *Chlamydia* are available in some centers, and immunoassays are available commercially for a rapid and specific diagnosis. The obtained conjunctival material is layered carefully onto a microscope slide and stained by the Giemsa method. Without treatment, the acute inflammation continues for several weeks, merging into a subacute phase of slight conjunctival infection with scant purulent material. Occasionally, chronicity develops; some cases persist for longer than a year. The polymerase chain reaction (PCR) method is used comparably to culture for detection of *C. trachomatis* in conjunctival and nasopharyngeal specimens from infants with conjunctivitis.[161]

TREATMENT

Initial therapy is based on the results of stained smears of exudate and epithelial cells. If gonococci are seen, parenteral penicillin or ceftriaxone therapy is employed. If staphylococci are seen, nafcillin or another penicillinase-resistant penicillin analogue is used. The necessity for using topical antibiotics in these two bacterial infections is dubious. In the presence of acute inflammation, ample antibiotic is present in eye secretions to inhibit bacteria.

Since the beginning of the 1980s, gonococci resistant to penicillin have appeared in the United States and other parts of the world.[104, 296] These strains are susceptible to spectinomycin, erythromycin, and the new-generation cephalosporins (e.g., ceftriaxone, cefotaxime). Experience in treating gonococcal ophthalmia with these drugs is limited, as are pharmacologic data for spectinomycin in the newborn. Infants with documented gonococcal infections at any site, including the eye, should be examined for disseminated gonococcal infection. This investigation should include a careful physical examination, especially of the joints, and evaluation of blood and CSF cultures. Infants with gonococcal ophthalmia should be treated for 4 to 7 days with ceftriaxone (50 mg/kg given intravenously or intramuscularly every 24 hours). Limited data suggest that uncomplicated gonococcal ophthalmia in infants can be cured with a single injection of ceftriaxone (50 mg/kg, up to 125 mg). If the gonococcal isolate is susceptible to penicillin, crystalline penicillin G can be given. The dose is 100,000 units/kg/day given in two doses (or four doses in infants older than 1 week of age). The eye should be irrigated with buffered saline solution until eye discharge has cleared. In patients who do not respond satisfactorily, co-infection with *Chlamydia* should be considered. The mother and infant should be tested routinely for *Chlamydia* infection.

Pseudomonas eye infection always should be treated with parenteral therapy consisting of ticarcillin or ceftriaxone and gentamicin. Gentamicin ophthalmic drops are used for simple *Pseudomonas* conjunctivitis, and subtenon injections of gentamicin may be indicated for endophthalmitis.[140]

Orally administered erythromycin is superior to topically applied tetracycline or sodium sulfacetamide in the therapy of chlamydial conjunctivitis. Topical therapy suppresses chlamydial growth only, whereas erythromycin eradicates the organism in most patients. Topical and oral erythromycin regimens have comparable efficacies, but oral therapy has the advantage of eradicating nasopharyngeal carriage of *Chlamydia*.[276] Although infantile hypertropic pyloric stenosis has been associated with erythromycin administered orally in infants younger than 6 months of age, erythromycin remains the antibiotic of choice for treatment of *C. trachomatis* disease in infants.[170] Eight infants with documented chlamydial conjunctivitis were treated with azithromycin (20 mg/kg, once daily for 3 days); failure to eradicate the organism occurred in 3 patients, but compliance was doubtful in these cases.[159] Most cases heal without residua.[143] Approximately 25 percent of infants with gonococcal ophthalmia have concomitant infection with *Chlamydia* that requires therapy.

Patients with gonococcal ophthalmia should be segregated, and strict handwashing techniques should be employed because the exudate is highly contagious.

Cutaneous and Glandular Infections

PUSTULAR AND VESICULAR LESIONS

Superficial pustular staphylococcal disease (i.e., impetigo neonatorum) is the most common skin infection of neonates. The lesions tend to concentrate in the periumbilical and diaper areas and rarely become invasive, except when extensive areas are involved or when monitoring devices, catheters, or other invasive devices are used in the gravely ill infant. The lesions respond to simple topical measures; systemic antibiotic treatment usually is not indicated unless extensive involvement of the skin occurs. The organisms should be phage typed (they usually belong to group I) so that if additional cases are encountered in the same nursery the infected infants and their cohorts can be evaluated for the possibility of nosocomial staphylococcal disease. If these infections are caused by the same staphylococcal phage type, prompt measures should be instituted to determine the source and extent of infection to prevent further colonization and disease.

A second form of staphylococcal disease has been recognized with increased frequency in recent years. The disease takes one of several clinical forms, including bullous impetigo, the most common manifestation, and Ritter disease, the eponymic equivalent in newborns of toxic epidermal necrolysis of older infants.[233] These illnesses usually are caused by phage group II staphylococci, which produce an exotoxin (i.e., exfoliatin) that causes intraepidermal cleavage through the granular cell layer resulting from disruption of desmosomes.[234] The initial finding in Ritter disease is intense, painful erythema, not unlike a severe sunburn. During the next hours, bullous formations occur, and when they rupture, they leave a tender, weeping, erythematous area. A characteristic desquamation of large epidermal sheets occurs approximately 3 to 5 days after onset of illness. A finer desquamation commonly is seen periorally.

Bacteremic complications occur more commonly in neonates than in older infants with the scalded skin syndrome. Treatment is with systemically administered, penicillinase-resistant penicillin because most phage group II staphylococci are resistant to penicillin. Because the cleavage plane in this syndrome is very superficial in the epidermis, little risk of development of superinfection exists. Steroids are contraindicated. Maceration may occur in intertriginous areas, which should be treated by local soaks with Burow solution.

CELLULITIS AND FASCIITIS

Group A streptococci are the usual cause of diffuse, well-demarcated cellulitis (or erysipelas), although we have seen the same diseases also caused by group B organisms. The involved skin usually is intensely red, hot, and moderately indurated. Occasionally, streptococci can be recovered from material aspirated from the lesion, but the blood culture rarely is positive. Parenteral therapy is with penicillin G, and although the borders continue to advance for the first 12 to 24 hours, stabilization of body temperature and improvement in general appearance of the infant give reassurance that the diagnosis and therapy are correct.

Necrotizing fasciitis is a virulent form of cellulitis that is a relatively rare event in newborns. Initially, it resembles uncomplicated cellulitis, but the baby rapidly becomes "toxic," the lesion advances progressively, and the central portion becomes discolored and anesthetic. The lesion has borders that usually are indistinct compared with erysipelas, in which the borders are raised and palpated easily. The disease may be associated with surgical procedures, birth trauma, previous omphalitis, fetal monitoring, or cutaneous infection and has been reported after the infant has undergone circumcision. The abdominal wall is the usual site of involvement, but other areas such as thorax, back, scalp, and the extremities also can be involved.[175] Causative agents include several streptococci, *S. aureus, P. aeruginosa, E. coli,* and anaerobic bacteria.[294, 387, 394] In this condition, subcutaneous tissues, including muscle layers, are invaded, and the organism spreads along the fascial planes. Extensive surgery involving resection of destroyed tissue is imperative in treating necrotizing fasciitis.[394] Blood and tissue cultures should be obtained, and initial antibiotic therapy should be with a penicillinase-resistant penicillin or clindamycin and an aminoglycosidic drug, pending results of these cultures. Hypocalcemia and hypoproteinemia may complicate the illness. If the infant survives the first days, extensive skin grafting usually is necessary. In a retrospective review, the overall mortality rate for 66 neonatal cases was 59 percent.[175] High index of suspicion, prompt aggressive surgery, appropriate antibiotics, and optimal supportive care are the mainstays of management.[63, 113, 175] The role of adjuvant hyperbaric oxygen is controversial, and very limited information is available.

FUNISITIS AND OMPHALITIS

The umbilical cord may be colonized with numerous different potential bacterial pathogens, some of which may have significant epidemiologic importance. Hexachlorophene was used in many institutions in an attempt to reduce or eliminate staphylococci that were responsible for nursery epidemics in the late 1950s and early 1960s. Although this antiseptic is effective in reducing staphylococcal colony counts, the agent is not effective in controlling nosocomial staphylococcal disease in nursery units. Its widespread use occasionally has been associated with CNS spongiform degeneration, particularly in premature infants.[337] A single application of triple dye to the cord results in significant reduction of all bacteria, particularly staphylococci, streptococci, and coliforms.[255, 286] Mupirocin ointment applied to the cord or the nasal mucosa also is effective in eradicating staphylococcal carriage.[168]

Group A streptococci may colonize the umbilical cord and be important as a focal point for epidemic streptococcal disease in a nursery. Unlike staphylococci, they tend to cause an inflammatory reaction.[99, 255] Streptococcal funisitis (i.e., inflammation of the cord) is mild and is characterized by a wet, malodorous umbilical stump with minimal inflammation. Disseminated disease is an uncommon occurrence, but when present, it results from bloodstream invasion or direct extension to the peritoneal cavity by way of the umbilical vessels. Treatment is with systemic penicillin G and topical therapy with antibiotic ointment or with triple dye.

Local therapy is provided for epidemiologic reasons to eliminate surface colonization. Identification of a single infant with group A streptococcal disease in a nursery necessitates immediate institution of infection control measures for identification and segregation of all colonized persons. When a nursery outbreak is suspected, specific M and T typing of the organism is useful in defining the source and spread of infection. A single injection of benzathine penicillin G is satisfactory for mild superficial infection or for elimination of the organism from colonized persons.[134, 255]

Omphalitis, or infection of the umbilicus, has many causes and occurs more frequently in low-birth-weight infants and in those with complicated deliveries. The incidence is estimated to be approximately 2 percent, and symptoms start at an average age of 3 days. Culture and susceptibility test results are necessary for the selection of an appropriate antibiotic.

BREAST ABSCESS

Breast abscesses are encountered most frequently during the second or third week of life and are more common findings in girls, particularly those older than 2 weeks of age.[309] The disease does not occur in premature infants, presumably because of underdevelopment of the mammary glands in these infants. Bilateral disease is a rare event, but a case caused by group B streptococci has been reported.[253]

The major clinical finding is swelling of the affected breast with or without accompanying erythema and warmth. Systemic manifestations are uncommon occurrences, and only one fourth of patients have low-grade fever. The disease sometimes can progress rapidly and involve breast tissue and the entire subcutaneous tissue beyond the breast's anatomic area.[336] This condition is associated with considerable toxicity and systemic signs and symptoms. *S. aureus* is the major pathogen, but coliform bacteria and group B streptococci have become more common causes in the past decade.[309, 355] Mixed infection rarely occurs. In 36 infants with mastitis seen in Dallas, Texas, during a 16-year period, 32 cases were caused by *S. aureus*, 1 case by *E. coli*, 2 cases by *Salmonella* spp., and 1 case by both *S. aureus* and *E. coli*.

Breast abscess is diagnosed by examination of stained purulent material obtained from gentle manipulation of the nipple or by needle aspiration of the abscess. If gram-positive cocci are identified, nafcillin or another penicillinase-resistant penicillin is given. For gram-negative bacilli, an aminoglycoside or cefotaxime is appropriate. When no organisms are seen, nafcillin and an aminoglycoside or cefotaxime should be used initially until results of the culture are available. Bacteremia is a rare finding in this condition.

If the patient has only mild cellulitis and no discernible fluctuance, antibiotic treatment alone may suffice. We have managed successfully several patients with group B streptococcal mastitis in this fashion. In most instances, however, surgical incision and drainage by a skilled surgeon are required. Duration of treatment depends on the rate of response. It generally is rapid, and we have found that healing is complete within 5 to 7 days in most instances. Long-term follow-up studies suggest that some girls will have diminished breast tissue on the affected side.[309]

SUPPURATIVE PAROTITIS

Suppurative parotitis of the newborn usually is easy to recognize, although occasionally it is confused with infection of a preauricular or superior anterior cervical lymph node. We have encountered one instance in which delay in initiating therapy was caused by attributing the swelling to trauma from obstetric forceps. Infection occurs more commonly in low-birth-weight infants than in term infants and in boys. Dehydration predisposes to stasis of parotid secretions and subsequent infection. Bilateral infection is a rare event.

Although *S. aureus* accounts for most cases, disease may be caused by coliform bacteria, *Pseudomonas*, pneumococci, and group A streptococci.[95, 202] The clinical manifestations include fever, anorexia, irritability, and failure to gain weight. Erythema, swelling, and tenderness over the involved gland may occur. Diagnosis can be confirmed by expressing pus through the parotid duct or by needle aspiration of a fluctuant area. Gram staining of this material helps identify the causative agent; however, one should recognize that material expressed from the duct may be contaminated by mouth microflora.

Selection of antimicrobial therapy should be based on interpretation of the Gram-stained smear of expressed pus. If gram-positive cocci are seen, nafcillin or another penicillinase-resistant penicillin should be used. Gram-negative organisms are treated best with an aminoglycoside, cefotaxime, or ceftazidime to cover both coliform bacteria and *Pseudomonas*. If no organisms are seen in the purulent material, a combination of nafcillin and gentamicin or cefotaxime should be used until results of the culture are available. In most cases, antibiotic therapy alone suffices, and surgical incision and drainage are unnecessary. The gland should not be extirpated. Response to therapy generally is rapid. Most patients require only 7 to 10 days of therapy until healing is complete.

SCALP ABSCESS

Scalp abscesses usually are a complication of fetal monitoring using scalp electrodes.[64, 378] The number of vaginal examinations, use of more than one electrode, and fetal scalp blood sampling are risk factors for its development. Pathogens incriminated include staphylococci, gonococci, and gram-negative enteric bacteria. A polymicrobial flora, including anaerobic organisms, frequently is isolated in scalp abscesses resulting from electronic fetal monitoring electrodes. Incision and drainage of the infected site usually are sufficient. If an associated cellulitis occurs, antibiotics are used and are continued for 5 to 7 days.

Lower Respiratory Tract Infections

Neonatal lower respiratory tract infections may be acquired congenitally or postnatally. Perinatal infection results from transplacental transfer of the agent (i.e., congenital infection) or inhalation of infected amniotic fluid (usually associated with prolonged rupture of membranes) or of infected vaginal secretions during delivery. Viruses, bacteria, *Chlamydia,* and spirochetes are the most common causative agents that produce perinatal pneumonias. The common viral agents include cytomegalovirus, rubella, and herpes simplex virus. The common bacterial agents are group B streptococci, *L. monocytogenes*, and coliform bacilli. *Chlamydia* organisms have been implicated as the cause of a chronic interstitial pneumonitis of early infancy (i.e., eosinophilic pertussis-like pneumonia).[37] *Treponema pallidum* produces a severe, sometimes fatal, pneumonitis, and mycoplasmas have caused a rare form of fatal congenital pneumonia. We also have seen in Panama in the last 4 years a few cases of congenital pneumonia caused by *Candida* spp. (unpublished observation).

Perinatal lower respiratory tract disease usually becomes apparent clinically in infants from birth to 7 days, occasionally up to 2 weeks of age. Of emphasis is that inhalation of amniotic fluid or of maternal vaginal secretions usually is not associated with infection, nor is meconium inhalation, in which the pneumonitis has a chemical cause. Only a small percentage of inhalation pneumonias are bacterial in origin; the pathogens most commonly encountered in such cases are group B streptococci and coliform organisms. The clinical signs of inhalation pneumonia are caused by obstruction, chemical inflammation, or both.

The second category of pneumonias is acquired postnatally and usually beyond the first week of life. These diseases may be caused by viral or bacterial agents and most frequently are bronchopneumonic in type. Viral disease may be sporadic or occur as part of a nosocomial nursery outbreak. The respiratory syncytial virus is the most important pathogen of lower respiratory tract disease in young infants.[45] This agent causes particularly severe disease in infants with congenital heart disease. The parainfluenza viruses and adenoviruses also cause bronchiolitis and pneumonia during early infancy. An obliterating, necrotizing bronchiolitis may be caused by adenoviruses and result in radiographic hyperlucency of a segment or a lobe in later infancy and childhood.[139]

Documented nursery outbreaks of lower respiratory tract disease have been associated with respiratory syncytial virus, adenoviruses, echoviruses, influenza A and B viruses, and parainfluenza virus infections. During these outbreaks, many infants are colonized with the epidemic strains, but only a few have clinical disease.

The common bacterial pathogens causing postnatally acquired pneumonia are *S. aureus*, coliform bacilli, and *Pseudomonas*. These infections occur sporadically or epidemically and often are of nosocomial origin. They may be rapidly progressive, necrotic pneumonias that result in pyogenic complications (e.g., empyema, pulmonary abscesses) and metastatic disease in the bones or meninges.

CLINICAL MANIFESTATIONS

The early signs of respiratory disease in the neonate and young infant frequently are nonspecific and include change in feeding status, listlessness or irritability, and poor color. More specific findings that may not be present at the onset of illness are tachypnea, dyspnea, cyanosis, alteration of temperature (i.e., hypothermia or fever), cough, and grunting. Accentuation of the normal irregularity of breathing is a common finding in neonates.

The physical findings of pneumonia are variable. Flaring of the alae nasi, rapid respirations, and sternal and subcostal retractions are common findings. Coughing indicates lower respiratory tract involvement; brassy coughing is found frequently in viral disease. Percussion dullness is difficult to demonstrate, but when present, it indicates consolidation or effusion. Breath sounds also may be diminished over the affected area. Crackles or wheezes usually can be heard on deep inspiration (or when the baby is crying) but may be absent early in disease. The clinician frequently is surprised by the meager clinical signs in the face of clearly demonstrable and sometimes extensive radiographic findings of pneumonitis.

DIAGNOSIS

The WBC count usually does not help to differentiate viral from bacterial pneumonia. An exception is seen in premature infants with acute respiratory distress syndrome caused by group B streptococci. In these patients, the WBC count often reveals a leukopenia with an increased proportion of band forms.[224]

Cultures of blood and material from the trachea frequently help in defining the etiologic agent of neonatal pneumonia. Results of cultures from the ear canal, throat, and other external sites usually are unreliable in defining the cause of pneumonia; more often, they are misleading. Lung puncture should be considered for severely ill infants with consolidated pneumonia when the cause is unknown or for an infant who fails to respond to conventional antimicrobial therapy. Material obtained by needle aspiration is Gram stained for direct visualization and cultured.

A chest radiograph should be obtained for all babies with suspected lower respiratory tract disease. Radiographic evidence of pneumonia may not exist in the absence of specific physical findings. Although the cause of neonatal pneumonia usually can be determined from a radiograph, certain radiologic patterns are associated with specific diseases. With acute-onset group B streptococcal disease, the radiograph may mimic one showing hyaline membrane disease. A consolidating bronchopneumonia with pneumatoceles with or without empyema suggests staphylococcal disease. When a lobar infiltrate is associated with expansion of the lobe, *Klebsiella pneumoniae* infection should be considered. A miliary type of bronchopneumonia in a septic neonate is characteristic of listeriosis.

SPECIFIC CLINICAL SYNDROMES

Staphylococcal Pneumonia

Primary staphylococcal pneumonia occurs quite frequently in young infants. Epidemics of staphylococcal disease caused by phage group I organisms are rare events today. In the epidemic setting, many infants are colonized with a virulent strain, but only a few have disease. Concomitant viral respiratory tract infections possibly play a role in promoting dissemination of staphylococci among infants and in converting colonization to disease, but such has not been established.

Staphylococci cause a confluent bronchopneumonia consisting of extensive areas of hemorrhagic necrosis and irregular areas of cavitation. The pleural surface usually is covered by a thick layer of fibrinopurulent exudate. Multiple, small abscesses are scattered throughout the affected lung. Rupture of a small subpleural abscess may result in a pyopneumothorax. If erosion into a large bronchus occurs, a bronchopleural fistula results.

Most patients with staphylococcal pneumonia have radiographic evidence of bronchopneumonia early in the illness. The infiltrate may be patchy and limited in extent or dense and homogeneous, involving an entire lobe or hemithorax. Bilateral disease occurs in one half of the patients. Pleural effusion or empyema is detected in most infants. Pneumatoceles of various sizes are common findings. Although no radiographic picture can be considered absolutely diagnostic, progression over the course of a few hours from bronchopneumonia to empyema or pyopneumothorax, with or without pneumatoceles, strongly suggests staphylococcal disease.

Klebsiella pneumoniae Pneumonia

Primary *K. pneumoniae* infection is an unusual event in infants and young children. However, nursery epidemics of *Klebsiella* infection have been reported. During these epidemics, colonization rates are high, but most infants remain asymptomatic. Contaminated fomites are the primary source of nosocomial infection with this organism.

K. pneumoniae pneumonia may be difficult to distinguish clinically from pneumonia caused by other causes. The disease may have a fulminant course characterized by copious, thick, purulent secretions and the formation of pulmonary abscesses and cavitation. The case-fatality rate in sporadic cases is approximately 50 percent but is considerably lower during epidemics.

Pertussis

Based on approximately 400 confirmed cases in Dallas, Texas, from 1959 to 1977, the annual incidence of pertussis has decreased more than 50 percent, but the proportion of cases in infants younger than 3 months of age has doubled from 15 to 30 percent.[254] More recently, approximately 35 percent of cases have occurred in infants younger than 6 months and 50 percent in those younger than 12 months of age. Although infants formerly acquired disease from siblings, in the past 10 to 15 years, infection usually has been acquired from one or both parents whose illnesses have not been diagnosed correctly as pertussis. The reason for these epidemiologic changes most likely is better vaccination in schoolchildren. Because immunity starts to wane in adolescence, parents of young infants are susceptible to infection. The infants of these women also are susceptible to development of infection because of the lack of transplacental immunity.

The onset of disease usually is in the second to sixth weeks of life; the earliest onset reported was at 10 days of age. Most young infants do not have a characteristic whoop. Pertussis should be suspected when an infant has a paroxysmal cough with excessive mucus. Because apneic spells are common occurrences in these infants, as they are also in those with respiratory syncytial virus, *Chlamydia*, or influenza virus infection, all infants with pertussis are admitted to the hospital for management. Fluorescent antibody testing provides a means of making a rapid diagnosis, but false-negative and false-positive results are common occurrences. Cultures for *Bordetella* should be performed in all infants. PCR-based testing may become the most sensitive means to document *B. pertussis* in the future. Mucus for examination is obtained from patients with a nasopharyngeal flexible wire swab or by nasopharyngeal washing or aspiration.

The greatest hazards to an infant with pertussis are asphyxia and secondary bacterial pneumonias. Supportive care is essential. Excessive mucus must be suctioned, and equipment for emergency airway intubation should be at hand. Administration of fluid therapy is necessary, and maintaining adequate nutritional intake may present the greatest challenge. Infants with pertussis should not be placed in mist tents. Mist therapy provides no substantial amelioration of paroxysmal coughing episodes, and it increases the risk of development of secondary infection with *P. aeruginosa* (or with other commensals).

Atelectasis caused by mucus plugs is a common complication of pertussis in small babies. After the infant has passed the stage of severe paroxysms, chest physiotherapy can be employed. In almost all cases, atelectasis resolves within 2 to 3 weeks.

Chlamydial Pneumonia

Chlamydial pneumonia manifests between the 4th and 11th weeks of life in most infants.[368] Infants typically are afebrile and tachypneic, and they have a characteristic staccato cough. Only one half of the patients have a history of conjunctivitis. On chest auscultation, rales may be heard, but wheezes are uncommon findings. The chest radiograph reveals hyperexpanded lungs with bilateral interstitial infiltrates. Approximately one half of the infants have peripheral eosinophilia. A definitive diagnosis made by isolating the organism from the respiratory tract is not possible in many institutions. The role of immunologic techniques to identify *Chlamydia* in throat swabs is yet to be determined. Serologic testing more readily is available. These infants usually respond to therapy with erythromycin. The clinical course and duration of nasopharyngeal shedding of *Chlamydia* are shortened by treatment with this antibiotic. If left untreated, these infants remain sick for several weeks but do not become acutely ill. Death from this infection seldom occurs.

TREATMENT

Initial antibiotic therapy of suspected bacterial pneumonia should be with ampicillin or nafcillin and an aminoglycoside or cefotaxime. The most suitable combination of these drugs depends on the clinical features of illness and the recent historical experience with bacterial diseases in the local nursery or community. For patients in whom the cause never is defined and staphylococcal disease cannot be ruled out, therapy with nafcillin or vancomycin and an aminoglycoside or cefotaxime is indicated. If the organism is identified, the single most effective drug should be used. Penicillin G or ampicillin is effective against group B streptococci and penicillin-susceptible staphylococci, ampicillin against *Listeria*, and nafcillin or another suitable anti-staphylococcal penicillin against penicillinase-producing *S. aureus*. Vancomycin should be used for disease caused by MRSA or coagulase-negative staphylococci. For pneumonia caused by gram-negative bacilli (e.g., *K. pneumoniae* and others), an aminoglycoside or a third-generation cephalosporin should be used. *Pseudomonas* pneumonia is treated best with ticarcillin or ceftazidime in combination with an aminoglycoside. Therapy is continued for 10 to 14 days for disease caused by group B streptococci and *Listeria* and for a minimum of 3 weeks for pneumonia caused by staphylococci or gram-negative bacilli.

Nosocomial pneumonia is a relatively frequent condition of mechanically-ventilated premature infants and can be caused by a vast array of microorganisms. Accordingly, treatment with an empirical regimen of broad-spectrum antibiotics is advised until microbial identification. Nonetheless, the physician should realize that isolation of bacteria from tracheal aspirates usually represents airway colonization and not necessarily the etiologic agents. For a reliable etiologic approach, a combination of clinical, radiographic, laboratory, and microbiologic findings is recommended. An important matter to recognize is that antimicrobial therapy commonly fails to eradicate microorganisms from the airway of ventilated infants despite clinical and radiographic resolution of pneumonia.[88]

Empyema is managed best with closed drainage, using chest tubes of the largest possible caliber. Generally, placement of one tube high and anteriorly and a second tube low and posterolaterally is necessary for optimal drainage. Pyopneumothorax is another indication for immediate insertion of a catheter into the pleural space. After the infant has improved clinically and the amount of drainage is minimal, the tubes should be removed. In general, they should not remain in the chest for more than 5 to 7 days. The instillation of antimicrobial agents or enzymes into the pleural space does not help control infection or promote drainage.

Pneumonia may be one manifestation of generalized congenital viral infection. Distinguishing these infections from congenital syphilis and bacterial pneumonias resulting from inhalation is important.

Most infants with inhalation pneumonia do not require antimicrobial therapy. Differentiating infants inhaling sterile fluid from those inhaling infected materials frequently is difficult. If doubt exists, therapy with ampicillin and an aminoglycoside should be initiated and continued until results of cultures are available.

Therapy for pertussis is with erythromycin administered orally. Antibiotic therapy may lessen the symptoms of pertussis if administered early in the paroxysmal stage and is valuable for rendering the patient noncontagious. Hyperimmune serum probably is not beneficial.

An association between bronchopulmonary dysplasia and respiratory colonization by species of *Ureaplasma* or *Mycoplasma* has received considerable attention.[389] In a prospective cohort study, isolation of *Ureaplasma urealyticum* from respiratory tract secretions was associated with radiographic evidence of pneumonia within 7 days of birth, precocious development of bronchopulmonary dysplasia, and severe pulmonary outcome.[272] A few case reports have suggested that eradication of *Ureaplasma* with erythromycin contributes to faster resolution of symptoms or to better outcome for neonates with this chronic disease.[8, 172, 381] Controlled studies are needed to verify these preliminary observations. No experience with the use of newer macrolides in neonates exists.

Recognition of the role of endogenous surfactant inactivation in the pathogenesis of bacterial pneumonia suggests that therapy with exogenous surfactant, in conjunction with antimicrobial drugs, could be potentially beneficial for management of affected infants. Large, prospective, placebo-controlled, randomized trials are needed to explore the effect of surfactant therapy for neonatal bacterial pneumonia.[301]

REFERENCES

1. Aber, R. C., Allen, N., Howell, J. T., et al.: Nosocomial transmission of group B streptococci. Pediatrics *58*:346, 1976.
2. Ablow, R. C., Driscoll, S. G., Effmann, E. L., et al.: A comparison of early-onset group B streptococcal neonatal infection and the respiratory-distress syndrome of the newborn. N. Engl. J. Med. *294*:65, 1976.
3. Adams, J. M., Speer, M. E., and Rudolph, A. J.: Bacterial colonization of radial artery catheters. Pediatrics *65*:94, 1980.
4. Adler, S. M., and Denton, R. L.: The erythrocyte sedimentation rate in the newborn period. J. Pediatr. *86*:942, 1975.
5. Aigner, R. M., Fueger, G. F., and Ritter, G.: Results of three-phase bone scintigraphy and radiography in 20 cases of neonatal osteomyelitis. Nucl. Med. Commun. *17*:20–28, 1996.
6. Albert, S., Baldwin, R., Czekajewski, S., et al.: Bullous impetigo due to group II *Staphylococcus aureus*: An epidemic in a normal newborn nursery. Am. J. Dis. Child. *120*:10, 1970.
7. Albritton, W. L., Wiggins, G. L., and Feeley, J. C.: Neonatal listeriosis: Distribution of serotypes in relation to age at onset of disease. J. Pediatr. *88*:481, 1976.
8. Alfa, M. J., Embree J. E., Degagne P., et al.: Transmission of *Ureaplasma urealyticum* from mothers to full and preterm infants. Pediatr. Infect. Dis. J. *14*:341, 1995.
9. Allerdice, J. G., Baskett, T. F., Seshia, M. M. K., et al.: Perinatal group B streptococcal colonization and infection. Am. J. Obstet. Gynecol. *142*:617, 1982.
10. Ancona, R. J., Ferrieri, P., and Williams, P. P.: Maternal factors that enhance the acquisition of group B streptococci by newborn infants. J. Med. Microbiol. *13*:273, 1980.
11. Anderson, D. C., Edwards, M. S., and Baker, C. J.: Luminol-enhanced chemiluminescence for evaluation of type III group B streptococcal opsonins in human sera. J. Infect. Dis. *141*:370, 1980.
12. Anthony, B. F., Okada, D. M., and Hobel, C. J.: Epidemiology of the group B *Streptococcus*: Maternal and nosocomial sources for infant acquisitions. J. Pediatr. *95*:431, 1979.
13. Armstrong, J. H., Zacarias, F., and Rein, M. F.: Ophthalmia neonatorum: A chart review. Pediatrics *57*:884, 1976.
14. Asmar, B. I.: Neonatal retropharyngeal cellulitis due to group B *Streptococcus*. Clin. Pediatr. *26*:183, 1987.
15. Asnes, R. S., and Arendar, G. M.: Septic arthritis of the hip: A complication of femoral venipuncture. Pediatrics *38*:837, 1966.
16. Baker, C. J.: Group B streptococcal cellulitis-adenitis in infants. Am. J. Dis. Child. *136*:631, 1982.
17. Baker, C. J., and the Neonatal IVIG Collaborative Study Group: Multicenter trial of intravenous immunoglobulin (IVIG) to present late-onset infection in preterm infants: Preliminary results. Pediatr. Res. *25*:275A, 1989. Abstract.
18. Baker, C. J., and Barrett, F. F.: Transmission of group B streptococci among parturient women and their neonates. J. Pediatr. *83*:919, 1973.
19. Baker, C. J., and Barrett, F. F.: Group B streptococcal infections in infants: The importance of the various serotypes. J. A. M. A. *230*:1158, 1974.
20. Baker, C. J., Barrett, F. F., Gordon, R. C., et al.: Suppurative meningitis due to streptococci of Lancefield group B: A study of 33 infants. J. Pediatr. *82*:724, 1973.
21. Baker, C. J., Edwards, M. S., and Kasper, D. L.: Role of antibody to native type III polysaccharide of group B *Streptococcus* in infant infection. Pediatrics *68*:544, 1981.
22. Baker, C. J., and Edwards, M. S.: Group B streptococcal infections. *In* Remington, J. S., and Klein, J. O. (eds.): Infectious Diseases of the Fetus and Newborn Infants. 3rd ed. Philadelphia, W. B. Saunders, 1990, pp. 742–811.
23. Baker, C. J., and Kasper, D. L.: Correlation of maternal antibody deficiency with susceptibility to neonatal group B streptococcal infection. N. Engl. J. Med. *294*:753, 1976.
24. Baker, C. J., and Kasper, D. L.: Group B streptococcal vaccines. Rev. Infect. Dis. *7*:458, 1985.
25. Baker, C. J., Webb, B. J., Jackson, C. V., et al.: Counter-current immunoelectrophoresis in the evaluation of infants with group B streptococcal disease. Pediatrics *65*:1110, 1980.
26. Baker C. J., Melish M. E., Hall R. T., et al.: Intravenous immune globulin for the prevention of nosocomial infection in low-birth-weight neonates. N. Engl. J. Med. *327*:213, 1992.
27. Balagtas, R. C., Bell, C. E., Edwards, L. D., et al.: Risk of local and systemic infections associated with umbilical vein catheterization: A prospective study in 86 newborn patients. Pediatrics *48*:359, 1971.
28. Baley, J. E., Stork, E. K., Warkentin, P. I., et al.: Buffy coat transfusions in neutropenic neonates with presumed sepsis: A prospective, randomized trial. Pediatrics *80*:712, 1987.
29. Band, J. D., Clegg, H. W., II, Hayes, P. S., et al.: Transmission of group B streptococci: Traced by use of multiple epidemiologic markers. Am. J. Dis. Child. *135*:355, 1981.
30. Barclay, N.: High frequency of *Salmonella* species as a cause of neonatal meningitis in Ibadan, Nigeria: A review of thirty-eight cases. Acta Paediatr. Scand. *60*:540, 1971.
31. Barton, L. L., Feigin, R. D., and Lins, R.: Group B beta hemolytic streptococcal meningitis in infants. J. Pediatr. *82*:719, 1973.
32. Battisti, O., Mitchison, R., and Davies, P. A.: Changing blood culture isolates in a referral neonatal intensive care unit. Arch. Dis. Child. *56*:775, 1981.
33. Baumgart, S., Hall, S. E., Campos, J. M., et al.: Sepsis with coagulase-negative staphylococci in critically ill newborns. Am. J. Dis. Child. *137*:461, 1983.
34. Beargie, R., Lynd, P., Tucker, E., et al.: Perinatal infection and vaginal flora. Am. J. Obstet. Gynecol. *122*:31, 1975.
35. Beck-Sague, C. M., Azimi P., Fonseca, S. N., et al.: Bloodstream infections in neonatal intensive care unit patients: Results of a multicenter study. Pediatr. Infect. Dis. J. *13*:1110, 1994.
36. Becroft, D. M. O., Farmer, K., Seddon, R. J., et al.: Epidemic listeriosis in the newborn. Br. Med. J. *3*:747, 1971.
37. Beem, M. O., and Saxon, E. M.: Respiratory-tract colonization and a distinctive pneumonia syndrome in infants with *Chlamydia trachomatis*. N. Engl. J. Med. *296*:306, 1977.
38. Benitz, W. E., Gould, J. B., and Druzin, M. L.: Antimicrobial prevention of early-onset group B streptococcal sepsis: Estimates of risk reduction based on a critical literature review Pediatrics *103*:e78, 1999.
39. Bennet, R., Eriksson, M., and Zetterström, R.: Increasing incidence of neonatal septicemia: Causative organisms and predisposing risk factors. Acta Paediatr. Scand. *70*:207, 1981.
40. Benuck, I., and David, R. J.: Sensitivity of published neutrophil indexes in identifying newborn infants with sepsis. J. Pediatr. *103*:961, 1983.
41. Berche, P., Reich, K. A., Bonnichon, M., et al.: Detection of anti-listeriolysin O for serodiagnosis of human listeriosis. Lancet *335*:624, 1990.
42. Bergman, I., Wald, E. R., Meyer, J. D., et al.: Epidural abscess and vertebral osteomyelitis following serial lumbar punctures. Pediatrics *72*:476, 1983.
43. Bergqvist, G., Eriksson, M., and Zetterström, R.: Neonatal septicemia and perinatal risk factors. Acta Paediatr. Scand. *68*:337, 1979.
44. Bergstrom, T., Larson, H., Lincoln, K., et al.: Studies of urinary tract infections in infancy and childhood. XII. Eighty consecutive patients with neonatal infection. J. Pediatr. *80*:858, 1972.

45. Berkovich, S., and Taranko, L.: Acute respiratory illness in the premature nursery associated with respiratory syncytial virus infections. Pediatrics *34*:753, 1964.
46. Berman, P. H., and Banker, B. Q.: Neonatal meningitis: A clinical and pathological study of 29 cases. Pediatrics *38*:6, 1966.
47. Berman, S. A., Balkany, T. J., and Simmons, M. A.: Otitis media in the neonatal intensive care unit. Pediatrics *62*:198, 1978.
48. Bettelheim, K. A., and Lennox-King, S. M. J.: The acquisition of *Escherichia coli* by new-born babies. Infection *4*:174, 1976.
49. Bilgin, K., Yaramis, A., Haspolak, K., et al. A randomized trial of granulocyte-macrophage colony-stimulating factor in neonates with sepsis and neutropenia. Pediatrics *107*:36–41, 2000.
50. Bland, R. D.: Otitis media in the first six weeks of life: Diagnosis, bacteriology, and management. Pediatrics *49*:187, 1972.
51. Bluestone, C. D., and Klein, J. O.: Otitis Media in Infants and Children. Philadelphia, W. B. Saunders, 1988.
52. Bomela H. N., Ballot, D. E.; Cory, B. J., et al.: Use of C-reactive protein to guide duration of empiric antibiotic therapy in suspected early neonatal sepsis. Pediatr. Infect. Dis. J. *19*:531–535, 2000.
53. Bonadio, W. A., Stanco, L., Bruce, R., et al.: Reference values of normal cerebrospinal fluid composition in infants ages 0 to 8 weeks. Pediatr. Infect. Dis. J. *11*:589, 1992.
54. Boswald, M., Dobig, C., Kandler, C., et al.: Pharmacokinetic and clinical evaluation of serious infections in premature and newborn infants under therapy with imipenem/cilastatin. Infection *27*:299–304, 1999.
55. Bourchier, D., Abbott, G. D., and Maling, T. M. J.: Radiological abnormalities in infants with urinary tract infections. Arch. Dis. Child. *59*:620, 1984.
56. Boyer, K. M., Gadzala, C. A., Kelly, P. D., et al.: Selective intrapartum chemoprophylaxis of neonatal group B streptococcal early-onset disease. III. Interruption of mother-to-infant transmission. J. Infect. Dis. *148*:810, 1983.
57. Boyer, K. M., Gadzala, C. A., Burd, L. I., et al.: Selective intrapartum chemoprophylaxis of neonatal group B streptococcal early-onset disease. I. Epidemiologic rationale. J. Infect. Dis. *148*:795, 1983.
58. Boyer, K. M., and Gotoff, S. P.: Prevention of early-onset neonatal group B streptococcal disease with selective intrapartum chemoprophylaxis. N. Engl. J. Med. *314*:1665, 1986.
59. Boyer, K. M., Papierniak, C. K., Gadzala, C. A., et al.: Transplacental passage of IgG antibody to group B *Streptococcus* serotype Ia. J. Pediatr. *104*:618, 1984.
60. Boyer, K. M., Petersen, N. J., Farzaneh, I., et al.: An outbreak of gastroenteritis due to *E. coli* 0142 in a neonatal nursery. J. Pediatr. *86*:919, 1975.
61. Bracho, F., Goldman, S., and Cairo, M. S.: Potential use of granulocyte colony-stimulating factor and granulocyte-macrophage colony-stimulating factor in neonates. Curr. Opin. Hematol. *5*:215–220, 1998.
62. Brans, Y. W., Ceballos, R., and Cassady, G.: Umbilical catheters and hepatic abscesses. Pediatrics *53*:264, 1974.
63. Brook, I.: Microbiology of necrotizing fasciitis associated with omphalitis in the newborn infant. J. Perinatol. *18*:28–30, 1998.
64. Brook I., and Frazier, E. H.: Microbiology of scalp abscess in newborns. Pediatr. Infect. Dis. J. *11*:766, 1992.
65. Buck, C., Bundschu, J., Gallati, H., et al.: Interleukin-6: A sensitive parameter for the early diagnosis of neonatal bacterial infection. Pediatrics *93*:54, 1994.
66. Buck, G. E., Kelly, M. T., Pichanick, A. M., et al.: *Campylobacter jejuni* in newborns: A cause of asymptomatic bloody diarrhea. Am. J. Dis. Child. *136*:744, 1982.
67. Burdon, D. W., Thompson, H., Candy, D. C. A., et al.: Enterotoxin(s) of *Clostridium difficile.* Lancet *2*:258, 1981.
68. Burns, R. P., and Rhodes, D. H., Jr.: *Pseudomonas* eye infection as a cause of death in premature infants. Arch. Ophthalmol. *65*:517, 1961.
69. Cairo, M. S., Rucker, R., Bennetts, G. A., et al.: Improved survival of newborns receiving leukocyte transfusions for sepsis. Pediatrics *74*:887, 1984.
70. Cairo, M. S.: Review of G-CSF and GM-CSF effects on neonatal neutrophil kinetics. Am. J. Pediatr. Hematol. Oncol. *11*:238, 1989.
71. Cameron, D. J. S., Bishop, R. F., Veenstra, A., et al.: Nonculturable viruses and neonatal diarrhea: Fifteen-month survey in a newborn special care nursery. J. Clin. Microbiol. *8*:93, 1978.
72. Carstensen, H., Christensen, K. K., Grennert, I., et al.: Early-onset neonatal group B streptococcal septicemia in siblings. J. Infect. *17*:201, 1988.
73. Centers for Disease Control: Nosocomial infection surveillance, 1980–1982. MMWR CDC Surveill Summ. *32*:1SS, 1983.
74. Chadwick, E. G., Shulman, S. T., and Yogev, R.: Peritonitis as a late manifestation of group B streptococcal disease in newborns. Pediatr. Infect. Dis. *2*:142, 1983.
75. Champagne, S., Fussell, S., and Scheifele, D.: Evaluation of skin antisepsis prior to blood culture in neonates. Infect. Control. *5*:489, 1984.
76. Champsaur, H., Questiaux, E., Prevot, J., et al.: Rotavirus carriage, asymptomatic infection, and disease in the first two years of life. I. Virus shedding. J. Infect. Dis. *149*:667, 1984.
77. Chirico, G., Rondini, G., Plebani, A., et al.: Intravenous gammaglobulin therapy for prophylaxis of infection in high-risk neonates. J. Pediatr. *110*:437, 1987.
78. Christensen, K. K., Christensen, P., Duc, G., et al.: Correlation between serum antibody-levels against group B streptococci and gestational age in newborns. Eur. J. Pediatr. *142*:86, 1984.
79. Christensen, R. D., Bradley, P. P., and Rothstein, G.: The leukocyte left shift in clinical and experimental neonatal sepsis. J. Pediatr. *98*:101, 1981.
80. Christensen, R. D., Rothstein, G., Anstall, H. B., et al.: Granulocyte transfusions in neonates with bacterial infection, neutropenia, and depletion of mature marrow neutrophils. Pediatrics *70*:1, 1982.
81. Christian, J. R.: Comparison of ocular reactions with the use of silver nitrate and erythromycin ointment in ophthalmia neonatorum prophylaxis. J. Pediatr. *57*:55, 1960.
82. Chrystie, I. L., Totterdell, B., Baker, M. J., et al.: Rotavirus infections in a maternity unit. Lancet *2*:79, 1975.
83. Clapp, D. W., Kliegman, R. M., Baley, J. E., et al.: The use of intravenously administered immune globulin to prevent nosocomial sepsis in low birth weight infants: Report of a pilot study. J. Pediatr. *115*:973, 1989.
84. Cobeljic, M., Miljkovic-Selimovic, B., Paunovic-Todosijevic, D., et al.: Enteroaggregative *Escherichia coli* associated with an outbreak of diarrhoea in a neonatal nursery ward. Epidemiol. Infect. *117*:11–16, 1996.
85. Cochran, W. D., Davis, H. T., and Smith, C. A.: Advantages and complications of umbilical artery catheterization in the newborn. Pediatrics *42*:769, 1968.
86. Collado, M., Kretschmer, R. R., Becker, I., et al.: Colonization of Mexican pregnant women with group B *Streptococcus*. J. Infect. Dis. *143*:134, 1981.
87. Cooperman, M. B.: *Gonococcus* arthritis in infancy: A clinical study of forty-four cases. Am. J. Dis. Child. *33*:932, 1927.
88. Cordero, L., Sananes, M., and Ayers, L. W.: Failure of systemic antibiotics to eradicate gram-negative bacilli from the airway of mechanically ventilated very low-birth-weight infants. Am. J. Infect. Control. *28*:286–290, 2000.
89. Coudron, P. E., Mayhall, C. G., Fracklam, R. R., et al.: *Streptococcus faecium* outbreak in a neonatal intensive care unit. J. Clin. Microbiol. *20*:1044, 1984.
90. Culver, K. W., Ammann, A. J., Partridge, J. C., et al.: Lymphocyte abnormalities in infants born to drug-abusing mothers. J. Pediatr. *111*:230, 1987.
91. Dagan, R., and Gorodischer, R.: Infections in hypothermic infants younger than 3 months old. Am. J. Dis. Child. *138*:483, 1984.
92. Dan, M.: Septic arthritis in young infants: Clinical and microbiologic correlations and therapeutic implications. Rev. Infect. Dis. *6*:147, 1984.
93. Daoud, A. S., Batieha, A., Al-Sheyyab, M., et al.: Lack of effectiveness of dexamethasone in neonatal bacterial meningitis. Eur. J. Pediatr. *158*:230–233, 1999.
94. DaSilva, O., and Hammerberg, O.: Diagnostic value of leukocyte indices in late neonatal sepsis. Pediatr. Infect. Dis. J. *13*:409, 1994.
95. David, R. B., and O'Connell, E. J.: Suppurative parotitis in children. Am. J. Dis. Child. *119*:332, 1970.
96. Davis, R. C.: *Salmonella* sepsis in infancy. Am. J. Dis. Child. *135*:1096, 1981.
97. Dennison, W. M.: Haematogenous osteomyelitis of the newborn. Lancet *2*:474, 1955.
98. Dietzman, D. E., Fischer, G. W., and Schoenknecht, F. D.: Neonatal *Escherichia coli* septicemia: Bacterial counts in blood. J. Pediatr. *85*:128, 1974.
99. Dillon, H. C., Jr.: Group A type 12 streptococcal infection in a newborn nursery: Successfully treated neonatal meningitis. Am. J. Dis. Child. *112*:177, 1966.
100. Dillon, H. C., Jr., Gray, E., Pass, M. A., et al.: Anorectal and vaginal carriage of group B streptococci during pregnancy. J. Infect. Dis. *145*:794, 1982.
101. Dillon, H. C., Jr., Khane, S., and Gary, B. M.: Group B streptococcal carriage and disease: A 6-year prospective study. J. Pediatr. *110*:31, 1987.
102. Di Pentima, M. C., Mason, E. O., and Kaplan, S. L.: In vitro antibiotic synergy against *Flavobacterium meningosepticum*: implications for therapeutic options. Clin. Infect. Dis. *26*:1169–1176, 1998.
103. Dobson, S. R. M., and Baker, C. J.: Enterococcal sepsis in neonates: Features by age at onset and occurrence of focal infection. Pediatrics *85*:165, 1990.
104. Doraiswamy, B., Hammerschlag, M. R., Pringle, G. F., et al.: Ophthalmia neonatorum caused by β-lactamase–producing *Neisseria gonorrhoeae*. J. A. M. A. *250*:790, 1983.
105. Dunham, E. C.: Septicemia in the new-born. Am. J. Dis. Child. *45*:229, 1933.
106. Dyson, A. E., and Read, S. E.: Group G streptococcal colonization and sepsis in neonates. J. Pediatr. *99*:944, 1981.
107. Easmon, C. S. F., Hastings, M. J. G., Deeley, J., et al.: The effect of intrapartum chemoprophylaxis on the vertical transmission of group B streptococci. Br. J. Obstet. Gynaecol. *90*:633, 1983.
108. Edwards, M. S., Jackson, C. V., and Baker, C. J.: Increased risk of group B streptococcal disease in twins. J. A. M. A. *245*:2044, 1981.
109. Edwards, M. S., Rench, M. A., Haffar, A. A. M., et al.: Long-term sequelae of group B streptococcal meningitis in infants. J. Pediatr. *106*:717, 1985.

110. Eitzman, D. V., and Smith, R. T.: The significance of blood cultures in the newborn period. Am. J. Dis. Child. *94*:601, 1957.
111. El-Radhi, A. S., Jawad, M. H., Mansor, N., et al.: Infection in neonatal hypothermia. Arch. Dis. Child. *58*:143, 1983.
112. Engle, W. D., and Rosenfeld, C. R.: Neutropenia in high-risk neonates. J. Pediatr. *105*:982, 1984.
113. Epps, C., and Brown, M.: Necrotizing fasciitis: A case study. Neonatal Netw. *16*:19–25, 1997.
114. Evanston, R. T., and Maunsell, H.: A Practical Treatise on the Management and Diseases of Children [first American edition from the first Irish edition in 1836]. Philadelphia, Haswell, Barrington, & Haswell, 1838, p. 115.
115. Faden, H. S.: Early diagnosis of neonatal bacteremia by buffy-coat examination. J. Pediatr. *88*:1032, 1976.
116. Fanaroff, A. A., Korones, S. B., Wright, L. L., et al.: Controlled trial of intravenous immune-globulin to reduce nosocomial infections in very low-birth-weight infants. N. Engl. J. Med. *330*:1107–1113, 1994.
117. Feigin, R. D., Wong, M., Shackelford, P. G., et al.: Countercurrent immunoelectrophoresis of urine as well as of CSF and blood for diagnosis of bacterial meningitis. J. Pediatr. *89*:773, 1976.
118. Feldman, W. E.: Relation of concentrations of bacteria and bacterial antigen in cerebrospinal fluid to prognosis in patients with bacterial meningitis. N. Engl. J. Med. *296*:433, 1977.
119. Ferrieri, P., Cleary, P. P., and Seeds, A. E.: Epidemiology of group-B streptococcal carriage in pregnant women and newborn infants. J. Med. Microbiol. *10*:103, 1977.
120. Figueroa-Damian, R., Arrendondo-García, J. L., Mancilla-Ramírez, J.: Amniotic fluid interleukin-6 and the risk of early-onset sepsis among preterm infants. Arch. Med. Res. *30*:198–202, 1999.
121. Finelli, L., Livengood, J. R., and Saiman, L.: Surveillance of pharyngeal colonization: Detection and control of serious bacterial illness in low birth weight infants. Pediatr. Infect. Dis. J. *13*:854, 1994.
122. Fischer, G. W., Crumrine, M. H., and Jennings, P. B.: Experimental *Escherichia coli* sepsis in rabbits. J. Pediatr. *85*:117, 1974.
123. Fischer, G. W., Weisman, L. B., Hemming, V. G., et al.: Intravenous immunoglobulin in neonatal group B streptococcal disease: Pharmacokinetic and safety studies in monkeys and humans. Am. J. Med. *76*(Suppl. 3A):117, 1984.
124. Fleer, A., Senders, R. C., Visser, M. R., et al.: Septicemia due to coagulase-negative staphylococci in a neonatal intensive care unit: Clinical and bacteriological features and contaminated parenteral fluids as a source of sepsis. Pediatr. Infect. Dis. *2*:426, 1983.
125. Fleming, D. W., Cochi, S. L., MacDonald, K. L., et al.: Pasteurized milk as a vehicle of infection in an outbreak of listeriosis. N. Engl. J. Med. *312*:404, 1985.
126. Fox, L., and Sprunt, K.: Neonatal osteomyelitis. Pediatrics *62*:535, 1978.
127. Franciosi, R. A., Knostman, J. D., and Zimmerman, R. A.: Group B streptococcal neonatal and infant infections. J. Pediatr. *82*:707, 1973.
128. Freeman, J., Goldmann, D. A., Smith, N. E., et al.: Association of intravenous lipid emulsion and coagulase-negative staphylococcal bacteremia in neonatal intensive care units. N. Engl. J. Med. *323*:301–308, 1990.
129. Freedman, R. M., Ingram, D. L., Gross, I., et al.: A half century of neonatal sepsis at Yale: 1928 to 1978. Am. J. Dis. Child. *135*:140, 1981.
130. Friedman, C. A., Wender, D. F., and Rawson, J. E.: Rapid diagnosis of group B streptococcal infection utilizing a commercially available latex agglutination assay. Pediatrics *73*:27, 1984.
131. Gardner, S. E., Yow, M. D., Leeds, L. J., et al.: Failure of penicillin to eradicate group B streptococcal colonization in the pregnant woman: A couple study. Am. J. Obstet. Gynecol. *135*:1062, 1979.
132. Gaynes, R. P., Edwards, J. R., Jarvis, W. R., et al.: Nosocomial infections among neonates in high-risk nurseries in the United States. Pediatrics *98*:357–361, 1996.
133. Gerdes, J. S., and Polin, R. A.: Sepsis screen in neonates with evaluation of plasma fibronectin. Pediatr. Infect. Dis. J. *6*:443, 1987.
134. Gezon, H. M., Schaberg, M. J., and Klein, J. O.: Concurrent epidemics of *Staphylococcus aureus* and group A *Streptococcus* disease in a newborn nursery: Control with penicillin G and hexachlorophene bathing. Pediatrics *51*:383, 1973.
135. Gibbs, R. S., Hall, R. T., Yow, M. D., et al.: Consensus: Perinatal prophylaxis for group B streptococcal infection. Pediatr. Infect. Dis. J. *11*:179, 1992.
136. Ginsburg, C. M., and McCracken, G. H., Jr.: Urinary tract infections in young infants. Pediatrics *69*:409, 1982.
137. Glode, M. P., Sutton, A., Moxon, E. R., et al.: Pathogenesis of neonatal *Escherichia coli* meningitis: Induction of bacteremia and meningitis in infant rats fed *E. coli* K1. Infect. Immun. *16*:75, 1977.
138. Gluck, L., Wood, H. F., and Fousek, M. D.: Septicemia of the newborn. Pediatr. Clin. North Am. *13*:1131, 1966.
139. Gold, R., Wilt, J. C., Adhikari, P. K., et al.: Adenoviral pneumonia and its complications in infancy and childhood. J. Can. Assoc. Radiol. *20*:218, 1969.
140. Golden, B.: Subtenon injection of gentamicin for bacterial infections of the eye. J. Infect. Dis. *124*:S271, 1971.
141. Gorbach, S. L., Menda, K. B., Thadepalli, H., et al.: Anaerobic microflora of the cervix in healthy women. Am. J. Obstet. Gynecol. *117*:1053, 1973.
142. Goscienski, P. J.: Inclusion conjunctivitis in the newborn infant. J. Pediatr. *77*:19, 1970.
143. Goscienski, P. J., and Sexton, R. R.: Follow-up studies in neonatal inclusion conjunctivitis. Am. J. Dis. Child. *124*:180, 1972.
144. Graham, D. R., Anderson, R. L., Ariel, F. E., et al.: Epidemic nosocomial meningitis due to *Citrobacter diversus* in neonates. J. Infect. Dis. *144*:203, 1981.
145. Graves, G. R., and Rhodes, P. G.: Tachycardia as a sign of early onset neonatal sepsis. Pediatr. Infect. Dis. *3*:404, 1984.
146. Gray, M. L.: Genital listeriosis as a cause of repeated abortion. Lancet *2*:315, 1960.
147. Gray, M. L.: Epidemiological aspects of listeriosis. Am. J. Public Health. *53*:554, 1963.
148. Greenberg, M., and Vandow, J. E.: Ophthalmia neonatorum: Evaluation of different methods of prophylaxis in New York City. Am. J. Public Health. *51*:836, 1961.
149. Greengard, J.: Acute hematogenous osteomyelitis in infancy. Med. Clin. North Am. *30*:135, 1946.
150. Griffin, M. P., and Moorman, J. R.: Toward the early diagnosis of neonatal sepsis and sepsis-like illness using novel heart rate analysis. Pediatrics *107*:97–104, 2001.
151. Groll, A. H., Meiser, A., Weise, M., et al.: Interleukin-6 as early mediator in neonatal sepsis. Pediatr. Infect. Dis. J. *11*:496, 1992.
152. Gruskay, J., Harris, M. C., Costarino, A. T., et al.: Neonatal *Staphylococcus epidermidis* meningitis with unremarkable CSF examination results. Am. J. Dis. Child. *143*:580, 1989.
153. Guerrant, R. L., Cleary, T. G., and Pickering, L. K.: Microorganisms responsible for neonatal diarrhea. *In* Remington, J. S., and Klein, J. O. (eds.): Infectious Diseases of the Fetus and Newborn Infant. 3rd ed. Philadelphia, W. B. Saunders, 1990, pp. 901–989.
154. Hague, K. N., Zaidi, M. H., Hazne, S. K., et al.: Intravenous immunoglobulin for prevention of sepsis in preterm and low birth weight infants. Pediatr. Infect. Dis. J. *5*:622, 1986.
155. Hall, S. L.: Coagulase-negative staphylococcal infections in neonates. Pediatr. Infect. Dis. J. *10*:57, 1991.
156. Hall, R. T., Barnes, W., Krishnan, et al.: Antibiotic treatment of parturient women colonized with group B streptococci. Am. J. Obstet. Gynecol. *124*:630, 1976.
157. Haltalin, K. C.: Neonatal shigellosis: Report of 16 cases and review of the literature. Am. J. Dis. Child. *114*:603, 1967.
158. Hammerschlag, M. R., Cummings, C., Roblin, P. M., et al.: Efficacy of neonatal ocular prophylaxis for the prevention of *Chlamydia* and gonococcal conjunctivitis. N. Engl. J. Med. *320*:769, 1989.
159. Hammerschlag, M. R., Gelling, M., Roblin, P. M., et al.: Treatment of neonatal chlamydial conjunctivitis with azithromycin. Pediatr. Infect. Dis. J. *17*:1049–1050, 1998.
160. Hammerschlag, M. R., Herrmann, J. E., Cox, P., et al.: Prospective comparison of Chlamydiazyme to chlamydial cultures for the diagnosis of neonatal conjunctivitis. Presented at the Twenty-Fourth Interscience Conference on Antimicrobial Agents and Chemotherapy, Washington, D. C., October, 1984.
161. Hammerschlag, M. R., Roblin, P. M., Gelling, M., et al.: Use of polymerase chain reaction for the detection of *Chlamydia trachomatis* in ocular and nasopharyngeal specimens from infants with conjunctivitis. Pediatr. Infect. Dis. J. *16*:293–297, 1997.
162. Hamoudi, A. C., Marcon, M. J., Cannon, H. J., et al.: Comparison of three major antigen detection methods for the diagnosis of group B streptococcal sepsis in neonates. Pediatr. Infect. Dis. *2*:432, 1983.
163. Harris, H., Wirtschafter, D., and Cassady, G.: Endotracheal intubation and its relationship to bacterial colonization and systemic infection of newborn infants. Pediatrics *58*:816, 1976.
164. Harris, M. C., Costarino, A. T., Sullivan, J. S., et al.: Cytokine elevations in critically ill infants with sepsis and necrotizing enterocolitis. J. Pediatr. *124*:105, 1994.
165. Harvey, D., Holt, D. E., and Bedford, H. Bacterial meningitis in the newborn: A prospective study of mortality and morbidity. Semin. Perinatol. *23*:218–225, 1999.
166. Hemming, V. G., Hall, R. T., Rhodes, P. G., et al.: Assessment of group B streptococcal opsonins in human and rabbit serum by neutrophil chemiluminescence. J. Clin. Invest. *58*:1379, 1976.
167. Hervás, J. A., Alomar, A., Salvá, F., et al.: Neonatal sepsis and meningitis in Mallorca, Spain, 1977–1991. Clin. Infect. Dis. *16*:719, 1993.
168. Hitomi, S., Kubota, M., Nori, N., et al.: Control of a methicillin-resistant *Staphylococcus aureus* outbreak in a neonatal intensive care unit by unselective use of nasal mupirocin ointment. J. Hosp. Infect. *46*:123–129, 2000.
169. Hocker, J. R., Simpson, P. M., Rabalais, G. P., et al.: Extracorporeal membrane oxygenation and early-onset group B streptococcal sepsis. Pediatrics *89*:1, 1992.
170. Honein, M. A., Paulozzi, L. J., Himelright, I. M., et al.: Infantile hypertrophic pyloric stenosis after pertussis prophylaxis with erythromycin: A case review and cohort study. Lancet *354*:2101–2105, 2000.
171. Hood, M.: Listeriosis as an infection of pregnancy manifested in the newborn. Pediatrics *27*:390, 1961.

172. Horowitz, S., Landau, D., Shinwell, E. S., et al.: Respiratory tract colonization with *Ureaplasma urealyticum* and bronchopulmonary dysplasia in neonates in southern Israel. Pediatr. Infect. Dis. J. *11*:847, 1992.
173. Howard, J. B., and McCracken, G. H., Jr.: The spectrum of group B streptococcal infections in infancy. Am. J. Dis. Child. *128*:815, 1974.
174. Howard, J. B., and McCracken, G. H., Jr.: Reappraisal of kanamycin usage in neonates. J. Pediatr. *86*:949, 1975.
175. Hsieh, W. S., Yang, P. H., Chao, H. C., et al.: Neonatal necrotizing fasciitis: A report of three cases and review of the literature. Pediatrics *103*:e53, 1999.
176. Isaacman, S. H., Heroman, W. M., and Lightsey, A. L.: Purpura fulminans following late-onset group B β-hemolytic streptococcal sepsis. Am. J. Dis. Child. *138*:915, 1984.
177. Jafari, H. S., Schuchat, A., Hildson, R., et al.: Barriers to prevention of perinatal group B streptococcal disease. Pediatr. Infect. Dis. J. *14*:662, 1995.
178. Johns, A. W., Kitchen, W. H., and Leslie, D. W.: Complications of umbilical vessel catheters. Med. J. Aust. *2*:810, 1972.
179. Johnson, C. E., DeBaz, B. P., Shurin, P. A., et al.: Renal ultrasound evaluation of urinary tract infection in children. Pediatrics *78*:871, 1986.
180. Jones, D. E., Kanarek, K. S., and Lim, D. V.: Group B streptococcal colonization patterns in mothers and their infants. J. Clin. Microbiol. *20*:438, 1984.
181. Jones, S. R., Smith, J. W., and Sanford, J. P.: Localization of urinary-tract infections by detection of antibody-coated bacteria in urine sediment. N. Engl. J. Med. *290*:591, 1974.
182. Kafetzis, D. A., Brater, D. C., Kapiki, A. N., et al.: Treatment of severe neonatal infections with cefotaxime: Efficacy and pharmacokinetics. J. Pediatr. *100*:483, 1982.
183. Kaijser, B., Hanson, L. A., Jodal, U., et al.: Frequency of *E. coli* K antigens in urinary-tract infections in children. Lancet *1*:663, 1977.
184. Karlowicz, M. G., Buescher, E. S., and Surka, A. E.: Fulminant late-onset sepsis in a neonatal intensive care unit, 1988–1997, and the impact of avoiding empiric vancomycin therapy. Pediatrics *106*:1387–1390, 2000.
185. Kashlan, F., Smulian, J., Shen-Schwarz, S., et al.: Umbilical vein interleukin 6 and tumor necrosis factor alpha plasma concentrations in the very preterm infant. Pediatr. Infect. Dis. J. *19*:238–243, 2000.
186. Kelsey, M. C., Lipscomb, A. P., and Mowles, J. M.: *Limulus* amoebocyte lysate endotoxin test: An aid to the diagnosis in the septic neonate? J. Infect. *4*:69, 1982.
187. Khaneja, M., Naprawa, J., Kumar, A., et al.: Successful treatment of late-onset infection due to resistant *Klebsiella pneumoniae* in an extremely low birth weight infant using ciprofloxacin. J. Perinatol. *19*:311–314, 1999.
188. Klinger, G., Chin, C. N., Beyene, J., et al.: Predicting the outcome of neonatal bacterial meningitis. Pediatrics *106*:477–482, 2000.
189. Kim, K. S., and Anthony, B. F.: Penicillin tolerance in group B streptococci isolated from infected neonates. J. Infect. Dis. *144*:411, 1981.
190. King, J. C., Berman, E. D., and Wright, P. F.: Evaluation of fever in infants less than 8 weeks old. South. Med. J. *80*:948, 1987.
191. Kleiman, M. B., Reynolds, J. K., Schreiner, R. L., et al.: Rapid diagnosis of neonatal bacteremia with acridine orange-stained buffy coat smears. J. Pediatr. *105*:419, 1984.
192. Klein, J. O., Feigin, R. D., and McCracken, G. H., Jr.: Report of the task force on diagnosis and management of meningitis. Pediatrics *78*(Suppl.):959, 1986.
193. Klein, J. O., and Marcy, S. M.: Bacterial sepsis and meningitis. *In* Remington, J. S., and Klein, J. O. (eds.): Infectious Diseases of the Fetus and Newborn Infant. 3rd ed. Philadelphia, W. B. Saunders, 1990, p. 60.
194. Kline, M. W., and Mason, E. O., Jr.: Methicillin-resistant *Staphylococcus aureus*: Pediatric perspective. Pediatr. Clin. North Am. *35*:613, 1988.
195. Klinger, G., Chin, C. N., Beyene, J., et al.: Predicting the outcome of neonatal bacterial meningitis. Pediatrics *106*:477–482, 2000.
196. Kocherlakota, P., and La Gamma, E. F.: Preliminary reports: rhG-CSF may reduce the incidence of neonatal sepsis in prolonged preeclampsia-associated neutropenia. Pediatrics *102*:1107–1111, 1998.
197. Krauss, A. N., Albert, R. F., and Kannan, M. M.: Contamination of umbilical catheters in the newborn infant. J. Pediatr. *77*:965, 1970.
198. Krcmery, V., Filka, J., Uher, J. et al.: Ciprofloxacin in treatment of nosocomial meningitis in neonates and in infants: report of 12 cases and review. Diagn. Microbiol. Infect. Dis. *35*:75–80, 1999.
199. Kumari, S., Bhargava, S. K., Baijal, V. N., et al.: Neonatal osteomyelitis: A clinical and follow-up study. Indian Pediatr. *15*:393, 1978.
200. Larsen, B., and Galask, R. P.: Vaginal microbial flora: Practical and theoretic relevance. Obstet. Gynecol. *55*:100S, 1980.
201. Laurenti, F., Ferro, R., Isacchi, G., et al.: Polymorphonuclear leukocyte transfusion for the treatment of sepsis in the newborn infant. J. Pediatr. *98*:118, 1981.
202. Leake, D., and Leake, R.: Neonatal suppurative parotitis. Pediatrics *46*:203, 1970.
203. Lebenthal, E.: Lactose malabsorption and milk consumption in infants and children. Am. J. Dis. Child. *133*:21, 1979.
204. Leigh, L., Stoll, B. J., Rahman M., et al.: *Pseudomonas aeruginosa* infection in very low birth weight infants: A case-control study. Pediatr. Infect. Dis. J. *14*:367, 1995.
205. Lennon, D., Lewis, B., Mantell, C., et al.: Epidemic perinatal listeriosis. Pediatr. Infect. Dis. *3*:30, 1984.
206. Levin, J., and Bang, F. B.: Clottable protein in *Limulus*: Its localization and kinetics of its coagulation by endotoxin. Thromb. Diath. Haemorrh. *19*:186, 1968.
207. Levine, E. M., Ghai, V., Barton, J. J., et al. Intrapartum antibiotic prophylaxis increases the incidence of gram-negative neonatal sepsis. Infect. Dis. Obstet. Gynecol. 7:210–213, 1999.
208. Levy, H. L., Sepe, S. J., Shih, V. E., et al.: Sepsis due to *Escherichia coli* in neonates with galactosemia. N. Engl. J. Med. *297*:1403, 1977.
209. Libby, J. M., Donta, S. T., and Wilkins, T. D.: *Clostridium difficile* toxin A in infants. J. Infect. Dis. *148*:606, 1983.
210. Lieberman, H., and Brem, J.: Syndrome of acute osteomyelitis of the superior maxilla in early infancy. N. Engl. J. Med. *260*:318, 1959.
211. Lilien, L. D., Harris, V. J., Ramamurthy, R. S., et al.: Neonatal osteomyelitis of the calcaneus: Complication of heel puncture. J. Pediatr. *88*:478, 1976.
212. Lim, M. O., Gresham, E. L., Franken, E. A., Jr., et al.: Osteomyelitis as a complication of umbilical artery catheterization. Am. J. Dis. Child. *131*:142, 1977.
213. Linnan, M. J., Mascola, L., Lou, X. D., et al.: Epidemic listeriosis associated with Mexican-style cheese. N. Engl. J. Med. *319*:823, 1988.
214. Liu, C.-H., Lehan, C., Speer, M. E., et al.: Degenerative changes in neutrophils: An indicator of bacterial infection. Pediatrics *74*:823, 1984.
215. MacFarlane, D. E.: Neonatal group B streptococcal septicemia in a developing country. Acta Pediatr. Scand. *76*:470, 1987.
216. Magudumana, M. O., Ballot, D. E., Cooper, P. A., et al.: Serial interleukin 6 measurements in the early diagnosis of neonatal sepsis. J. Trop. Pediatr. *46*:267–271, 2000.
217. Main, E. K., and Slagle, T.: Prevention of early-onset invasive neonatal group B streptococcal disease in a private hospital setting: The superiority of culture-based protocols. Am. J. Obstet. Gynecol. *182*:1344–1354, 2000.
218. Manroe, B. L., Rosenfeld, C. R., Weinberg, A. G., et al.: The differential leukocyte count in the assessment and outcome of early-onset neonatal group B streptococcal disease. J. Pediatr. *91*:632, 1977.
219. Manroe, B. L., Weinberg, A. G., Rosenfeld, C. R., et al.: The neonatal blood count in health and disease. I. Reference values for neutrophilic cells. J. Pediatr. *95*:89, 1979.
220. Marchant, C. D., Shurin, P. A., Turczyk, V. A., et al.: Course and outcome of otitis media in early infancy: A prospective study. J. Pediatr. *104*:826, 1984.
221. Marcy, S. M.: Bacterial infections of the bones and joints. *In* Remington, J. S., and Klein, J. O. (eds.): Infectious Diseases of the Fetus and Newborn Infant. 3rd ed. Philadelphia, W. B. Saunders, 1990, p. 674.
222. Marild, S., Wettergren, B., Hellstrom, M., et al.: Bacterial virulence and inflammatory response in infants with febrile urinary tract infection or screening bacteriuria. J. Pediatr. *112*:348, 1988.
223. Mathieu, P. L.: Comparison study: Silver nitrate and oxytetracycline in newborn eyes: A comparison of the incidence of conjunctivitis following the instillation of silver nitrate or oxytetracycline into the eyes of newborn infants. Am. J. Dis. Child. *95*:609, 1958.
224. McCracken, G. H., Jr.: Intraventricular treatment of neonatal meningitis due to gram-negative bacilli. J. Pediatr. *91*:1037, 1977.
225. McCracken, G. H., Jr., and Mize, S. G.: A controlled study of intrathecal antibiotic therapy in gram-negative enteric meningitis of infancy: Report of the Neonatal Cooperative Study Group. J. Pediatr. *89*:66, 1976.
226. McCracken, G. H., Jr., Mize, S. G., and Threlkeld, N.: Intraventricular gentamicin therapy in gram-negative bacillary meningitis of infancy: Report of the Second Neonatal Meningitis Cooperative Study Group. Lancet *1*:787, 1980.
227. McCracken, G. H., Jr., Mustafa, M. M., Ramilo, O., et al.: Cerebrospinal fluid interleukin-1β and tumor necrosis factor concentrations and outcome from neonatal gram-negative enteric bacillary meningitis. Pediatr. Infect. Dis. J. *8*:155, 1989.
228. McCracken, G. H., Jr., and Nelson, J. D.: Antimicrobial Therapy for Newborns. 2nd ed. New York, Grune & Stratton, 1983.
229. McCracken, G. H., Jr., Sarff, L. D., Glode, M. P., et al.: Relation between *Escherichia coli* K1 capsular polysaccharide antigen and clinical outcome in neonatal meningitis. Lancet *2*:246, 1974.
230. McCracken, G. H., Jr., Sarff, L. D., Robbins, J. B., et al.: Ontogeny of serum and secretory K1 antibodies. Presented to the American Pediatric Society, St. Louis, April, 1976.
231. McCracken, G. H., Jr., and Shinefield, H. R.: Changes in the pattern of neonatal septicemia and meningitis. Am. J. Dis. Child. *112*:33, 1966.
232. McCracken, G. H., Jr., Threlkeld, N., Mize, S., et al.: Moxalactam therapy for neonatal meningitis due to gram-negative enteric bacilli: A prospective controlled evaluation. J. A. M. A. *252*:1427, 1984.
233. Melish, M. E., and Glasgow, L. A.: Staphylococcal scalded skin syndrome: The expanded clinical syndrome. J. Pediatr. *78*:958, 1971.

234. Melish, M. E., Glasgow, L. A., and Turner, M. D.: The staphylococcal scalded-skin syndrome: Isolation and partial characterization of the exfoliative toxin. J. Infect. Dis. *125*:129, 1972.
235. Mercer, B. M., Carr, T. L., Beazley, D. D. et al.: Antibiotic use in pregnancy and drug-resistant infant sepsis. Am. J. Obstet. Gynecol. *181*:16–21, 1999.
236. Merenstein, G. B., Todd, W. A., Brown, G., et al.: Group B β-hemolytic *Streptococcus:* Randomized controlled treatment study at term. Obstet. Gynecol. *55*:315, 1980.
237. Middelton, P. J.: Pathogenesis of rotaviral infection. J. Am. Vet. Med. Assoc. *173*:544, 1978.
238. Middelton, P. J., Szymanski, M. T., and Petric, M.: Viruses associated with acute gastroenteritis in young children. Am. J. Dis. Child. *131*:733, 1977.
239. Mok, P. M., Reilly, B. J., and Ash, J. M.: Osteomyelitis in the neonate. Radiology. *145*:677, 1982.
240. Monto, A. S., Brandt, B. L., and Artenstein, M. S.: Response of children to *Neisseria meningitidis* polysaccharide vaccines. J. Infect. Dis. *127*:394, 1973.
241. Morales, W. J., and Lim, D. V.: Reduction of group B streptococcal maternal and neonatal infections in preterm pregnancies with premature rupture of membranes through a rapid identification test. Am. J. Obstet. Gynecol. *157*:13, 1987.
242. Morales, W. J., Lim, D. V., and Walsh, A. F.: Prevention of neonatal group B streptococcal sepsis by the use of rapid screening test and selective intrapartum chemoprophylaxis. Am. J. Obstet. Gynecol. *155*:979, 1986.
243. Moreno, M. T., Vargas, S., Poveda, R., et al.: Neonatal sepsis and meningitis in a developing Latin American country. Pediatr. Infect. Dis. J. *13*:516, 1994.
244. Mulder, C. J. J., van Alphen, L., and Zanen, H. C.: Neonatal meningitis caused by *Escherichia coli* in the Netherlands. J. Infect. Dis. *150*:935, 1984.
245. Munson, D. P., Thompson, T. R., Johnson, D. E., et al.: Coagulase-negative staphylococcal septicemia: Experience in a newborn intensive care unit. J. Pediatr. *101*:602, 1982.
246. Mustafa, M. M., and McCracken, G. H., Jr.: Antimicrobial agents in Pediatrics Infect. Dis. Clin. North Am. *3*:491, 1989.
247. Mustafa, M. M., Mertsola, J., Ramilo, O., et al.: Increased endotoxin and interleukin-1β concentrations in cerebrospinal fluid of infants with coliform meningitis and ventriculitis associated with intraventricular gentamicin therapy. J. Infect. Dis. *160*:891, 1989.
248. Mustafa, M. M., Ramilo, O., Olsen, K. D., et al.: Tumor necrosis factor in mediating experimental *Haemophilus influenzae* type b meningitis. J. Clin. Invest. *84*:1253, 1989.
249. Nejjari, N., Benomar, S., and Lahbabi, M. S.: Nosocomial infections in neonatal and pediatric intensive care: The appeal of ciprofloxacin. Arch. Pediatr. *7*:1268–1273, 2000.
250. Nelson, D. L., Hable, K. A., and Matsen, J. M.: *Proteus mirabilis* osteomyelitis in two neonates following needle puncture: Successful treatment with ampicillin. Am. J. Dis. Child. *125*:109, 1973.
251. Nelson, J. D.: Duration of neomycin therapy for enteropathogenic *Escherichia coli* diarrheal disease: A comparative study of 113 cases. Pediatrics *48*:248, 1971.
252. Nelson, J. D.: Antibiotic concentrations in septic joint effusions. N. Engl. J. Med. *284*:349, 1971.
253. Nelson, J. D.: Bilateral breast abscess due to group B *Streptococcus*. Am. J. Dis. Child. *130*:567, 1976.
254. Nelson, J. D.: The changing epidemiology of pertussis in young infants: The role of adults as reservoirs of infection. Am. J. Dis. Child. *132*:371, 1978.
255. Nelson, J. D., Dillon, Jr., H. C., and Howard, J. B.: A prolonged nursery epidemic associated with a newly recognized type of group A *Streptococcus*. J. Pediatr. *89*:792, 1976.
256. Nelson, J. D., and Peters, P. C.: Suprapubic aspiration of urine in premature and term infants. Pediatrics *36*:132, 1965.
257. Newman, R. B., Stevens, R. W., and Gaafar, H. A.: Latex agglutination test for the diagnosis of *Haemophilus influenzae* meningitis. J. Lab. Clin. Med. *76*:107, 1970.
258. Noel, G. J., and Edelson, P. J.: *Staphylococcus epidermidis* bacteremia in neonates: Further observations and the occurrence of focal infection. Pediatrics *74*:832, 1984.
259. Noya, F. J. D., Rench, M. N., Metzger, T. A., et al.: Unusual occurrence of an epidemic of type Ib/c group B streptococcal sepsis in a neonatal intensive care unit. J. Infect. Dis. *115*:1135, 1987.
260. Nyhan, W. L., and Fousek, M. D.: Septicemia of the newborn. Pediatrics *22*:268, 1958.
261. Offit, P. A., and Clarke, H. F.: Protection against rotavirus-induced gastroenteritis in a murine model by passively acquired gastrointestinal but not circulatory antibodies. J. Virol. *54*:58, 1985.
262. Ogden, J. A., and Lister, G.: The pathology of neonatal osteomyelitis. Pediatrics *55*:474, 1975.
263. Ogra, P. L., and Fishaut, M.: Human breast milk. *In* Remington, J. S., and Klein, J. O. (eds.): Infectious Diseases of the Fetus and Newborn Infant. 3rd ed. Philadelphia, W. B. Saunders, 1990, pp. 68–88.
264. Ohler, K. H., Menke, J. A., and Fuller, L.: Use of higher dose extended interval aminoglycosides in a neonatal intensive care unit. Am. J. Perinatol. *17*:285–290, 2000.
265. Ohlsson, A., Baily, T., and Takiedine, F.: Changing etiology and outcome of neonatal septicemia in Riyadh, Saudi Arabia. Acta Paediatr. Scand. *75*:540, 1986.
266. Olarte, J., and Ramos-Alvares, M.: Epidemic diarrhea in premature infants: Etiologic significance of a newly recognized type of *Escherichia coli* (0142:K86[B]:H6). Am. J. Dis. Child. *109*:436, 1965.
267. Oriel, J. D.: Ophthalmia neonatorum: Relative efficacy of current prophylactic practices and treatment. J. Antimicrob. Chemother. *14*:209, 1984.
268. Otila, E.: Studies on the cerebrospinal fluid in premature infants. Acta Paediatr. *35*(Suppl. 8):9, 1948.
269. Overall, J. C., Jr.: Neonatal bacterial meningitis: Analysis of predisposing factors and outcome compared with matched control subjects. J. Pediatr. *76*:499, 1970.
270. Overturf, G. D., and Balfour, G.: Osteomyelitis and sepsis: Severe complications of fetal monitoring. Pediatrics *55*:244, 1975.
271. Owen, C. R., Meis, A., Jackson, J. W., et al.: A case of primary cutaneous listeriosis. N. Engl. J. Med. *262*:1026, 1960.
272. Pacifico, L., Panero, A., Roggini, M., et al.: *Ureaplasma urealyticum* and pulmonary outcome in a neonatal intensive care population. Pediatr. Infect. Dis. J. *16*:579–586, 1997.
273. Paredes, A., Wong, P., Mason, E. O., Jr., et al.: Nosocomial transmission of group B streptococci in a newborn nursery. Pediatrics *59*:679, 1977.
274. Pass, M. A., Gray, B. M., Khare, S., et al.: Prospective studies of group B streptococcal infections in infants. J. Pediatr. *95*:437, 1979.
275. Pass, M. A., Khare, S., and Dillon, H. C., Jr.: Twin pregnancies: Incidence of group B streptococcal colonization and disease. J. Pediatr. *97*:635, 1980.
276. Patamasucon, P., Rettig, P. J., Faust, K. L., et al.: Oral *v* topical erythromycin therapies for chlamydial conjunctivitis. Am. J. Dis. Child. *136*:817, 1982.
277. Patrick, M. J.: Influence of maternal renal infection on the fetus and infant. Arch. Dis. Child. *42*:208, 1967.
278. Peevy, K. J., and Wiseman, H. J.: Gallbladder distension in septic neonates. Arch. Dis. Child. *57*:75, 1982.
279. Pestalozza, G.: Otitis media in newborn infants. Int. J. Pediatr. Otorhinolaryngol. *8*:109, 1984.
280. Petrilli, E. S., d'Ablaig, G., and Ledger, W. J.: *Listeria monocytogenes* chorioamnionitis: Diagnosis by transabdominal amniocentesis. Obstet. Gynecol. *55*:5S, 1980.
281. Philip, A. G. S.: Decreased use of antibiotics using a neonatal sepsis screening technique. J. Pediatr. *98*:795, 1981.
282. Philip, A. G. S.: Detection of neonatal sepsis of late onset. J. A. M. A. *247*:489, 1982.
283. Philip, A. G. S.: Acute-phase proteins in neonatal infection. J. Pediatr. *105*:940, 1984.
284. Philip, A. G., and Mills, P. C.: Use of C-reactive protein in minimizing antibiotic exposure: Experience with infants initially admitted to a well-baby nursery. Pediatrics *106*:E4, 2000.
285. Pichichero, M. E., and Todd, J. K.: Detection of neonatal bacteremia. J. Pediatr. *94*:958, 1979.
286. Pildes, R. S., Ramamurthy, R. S., and Vidyasagar, D.: Effect of triple dye on staphylococcal colonization in the newborn infant. J. Pediatr. *82*:987, 1973.
287. Pittard, W. B., III, Thullen, J. D., and Fanaroff, A. A.: Neonatal septic arthritis. J. Pediatr. *88*:621, 1976.
288. Placezek, M. M., and Whitelaw, A.: Early and late septicemia. Arch. Dis. Child. *58*:728, 1983.
289. Pyati, S. P., Pildes, R. S., Jacobs, N. M., et al.: Penicillin in infants weighing two kilograms or less with early-onset group B streptococcal disease. N. Engl. J. Med. *308*:1383, 1983.
290. Pylipow, M., Gaddis, M., and Kinney, J. S.: Selective intrapartum prophylaxis for group B *Streptococcus* colonization: Management and outcome of newborns. Pediatrics *93*:631, 1994.
291. Qureshi, M. E., and Puri, S. P.: Osteomyelitis after exchange transfusion. Br. Med. J. *2*:28, 1971.
292. Rabinowitz, S. S., Dzakpasu, P., Piecuch, S., et al.: Platelet-activating factor in infants at risk for necrotizing enterocolitis. J. Pediatr. *138*:81–86, 2001.
293. Rahal, J. J., Jr., Hyams, P. J., Simberkoff, M. S., et al.: Combined intrathecal and intramuscular gentamicin for gram-negative meningitis: Pharmacologic study of 21 patients. N. Engl. J. Med. *290*:1394, 1974.
294. Ramamurthy, R. S., Srinivasan, G., and Jacobs, N. M.: Necrotizing fasciitis and necrotizing cellulitis due to group B *Streptococcus*. Am. J. Dis. Child. *131*:1169, 1977.
295. Ramilo, O., Mertsola, J., Mustafa, M. M., et al.: Interleukin-1β appears to mediate CSF inflammation in rabbits. Abstract No. 708. Presented at the 29th Interscience Conference on Antimicrobial Agents and Chemotherapy, Houston, September, 1989.
296. Raucher, H. S., Newton, M. J., and Stern, R. H.: Ophthalmia neonatorum caused by penicillinase-producing *Neisseria gonorrhoeae*. J. Pediatr. *100*:925, 1982.

297. Redd, H., Christensen, R. D., and Fisher, C. W.: Circulating and storage neutrophils in septic neonatal rats treated with immunoglobulin. J. Infect. Dis. *157*:705, 1988.
298. Reed, R. K., Larter, W. E., Sieber, O. F., et al.: Peripheral nodular lesions in *Pseudomonas* sepsis: The importance of incision and drainage. J. Pediatr. *88*:977, 1976.
299. Reid, B. S., Binder, T. M.: Radiographic evaluation of children with urinary tract infections. Radiol. Clin. North Am. *26*:933, 1988.
300. Robbins, J. B., McCracken, G. H., Jr., Gotschlich, E. C., et al.: *Escherichia coli* K1 capsular polysaccharide associated with neonatal meningitis. N. Engl. J. Med. *290*:1216, 1974.
301. Rodriguez, R. J., and Martin, R. J.: Exogenous surfactant therapy in newborns. Respir. Care Clin. North Am. *5*:595–616, 1999.
302. Rodwell, R. L., Faims, K., Taylor, K., et al.: Hematologic scoring system in early diagnosis of sepsis in neutropenic newborns. Pediatr. Infect. Dis. J. *12*:372, 1993.
303. Roine, I., Faingezicht, I., Arguedas, A., et al.: Serial serum C-reactive protein to monitor recovery from acute hematogenous osteomyelitis in children. Pediatr. Infect. Dis. J. *14*:40, 1995.
304. Rolston, K. V. I., Chandrasekar, P. H., and LeFrock, J. L.: Antimicrobial tolerance in group C and group G streptococci. J. Antimicrob. Chemother. *13*:389, 1984.
305. Rotbart, H. A., Levin, M. J., Yolken, R. H., et al.: An outbreak of rotavirus-associated neonatal necrotizing enterocolitis. J. Pediatr. *103*:454, 1983.
306. Rowe, D. S., Aicardi, E. Z., Dawson, C. R., et al.: Purulent ocular discharge in neonates: Significance of *Chlamydia trachomatis*. Pediatrics *63*:628, 1979.
307. Rowley, A. H., and Wald, E. R.: Incubation period necessary to detect bacteremia in neonates. Pediatr. Infect. Dis. J. *5*:590, 1986.
308. Rubens, C. E., Heggan, L., and Wessels, M.: A genetic marker for virulence of the type III group B streptococci Pediatr. Res. *23*:380A, 1988. Abstract 1076.
309. Rudoy, R. C., and Nelson, J. D.: Breast abscess during the neonatal period: A review. Am. J. Dis. Child. *129*:1031, 1975.
310. Ryder, R. W., McGowan, J. E., Hatch, M. H., et al.: Reovirus-like agent as a cause of nosocomial diarrhea in infants. J. Pediatr. *90*:698, 1977.
311. Sabath, L. D., Wheeler, N., Laverdiere, M., et al.: A new type of penicillin resistance of *Staphylococcus aureus*. Lancet *1*:443, 1977.
312. Sáez-Llorens, X., and Siegel, J. D.: Neonatal septicemia, meningitis, and pneumonia. *In* Gellis & Kagan's Current Pediatric Therapy. 14th ed. Philadelphia, W. B. Saunders, 1993, pp. 544–549.
313. Sáez-Llorens, X., Ah Chu, M. S., Casta-Zo, E., et al.: Intrapartum prophylaxis with ceftriaxone decreases rates of bacterial colonization and early-onset infection in newborns. Clin. Infect. Dis. *21*:876, 1995.
314. Sáez-Llorens, X., Vargas, S., Guerra, F., et al.: Application of new sepsis definitions to evaluate outcome of pediatric patients with severe systemic infections. Pediatr. Infect. Dis. J. *14*:557, 1995.
315. Sáez-Llorens, X., and McCracken, G. H.: Sepsis syndrome and septic shock in pediatrics: Current concepts on terminology, pathophysiology, and management. J. Pediatr. *123*:497, 1993.
316. Sáez-Llorens, X., Ramilo, O., Mustafa, M., et al.: The molecular pathophysiology of bacterial meningitis: Current concepts and therapeutic implications. J. Pediatr. *116*:671, 1990.
317. Sáez-Llorens, X., and McCracken, G. H.: Clinical pharmacology of antibacterial agents. *In* Remington, J. S., and Klein, J. O. (eds.): Infectious Diseases of the Fetus and Newborn Infant. 4th ed. Philadelphia, W. B. Saunders, 1995, pp. 1287–1336.
318. Sáez-Llorens, X., Velarde, J., and Cantón, C.: Pediatric osteomyelitis in a developing country. Clin. Infect. Dis. *19*:323, 1994.
318a. Sáez-Llorens, X., Espino, R. T., Moreno, M. T., and Vargas, S.: Sepsis neonatal: Diferencias en la epidemiologia y microbiologia de dos unidades materno-infantiles metropolitanas (1975–1992). Bol. Soc. Panam. Pediatr. *24*:26–33, 1995.
319. Sánchez, P. J., Siegel, J. D., Cushion, N. B., et al.: Significance of a positive urine group B streptococcal latex agglutination test in neonates. J. Pediatr. *116*:601, 1990.
320. Sandström, K. I., Bell, T. A., Chandler, J. W., et al.: Microbial causes of neonatal conjunctivitis. J. Pediatr. *105*:706, 1984.
321. Sann, L., Bienvenu, F., Bienvenu, J., et al.: Evolution of serum prealbumin, C-reactive protein, and orosomucoid in neonates with bacterial infection. J. Pediatr. *105*:977, 1984.
322. Sarff, L. D., McCracken, G. H., Jr., Schiffer, M. S., et al.: Epidemiology of *Escherichia coli* K1 in healthy and diseased newborns. Lancet *1*:1099, 1975.
323. Sarff, L. D., Platt, L. H., and McCracken, G. H., Jr.: Cerebrospinal fluid evaluation in neonates: Comparison of high-risk infants with and without meningitis. J. Pediatr. *88*:473, 1976.
324. Sarman, G., Moise, A. A., and Edwards, M. S.: Meningeal inflammation in neonatal gram-negative bacteremia. Pediatr. Infect. Dis. J. *14*:701, 1995.
325. Schaad, U. B., McCracken, G. H., Jr., Threlkeld, N., et al.: Clinical evaluation of a new broad-spectrum oxa-beta-lactam antibiotic, moxalactam, in neonates and infants. J. Pediatr. *98*:129, 1981.
326. Schaad, U. B., Kaplan, S. L., and McCracken, G. H.: Steroid therapy for bacterial meningitis. Clin. Infect. Dis. *20*:685, 1995.
327. Scheifele, D. W., Melton, P., and Whitchelo, V.: Evaluation of the *Limulus* test for endotoxemia in neonates with suspected sepsis. J. Pediatr. *98*:899, 1981.
328. Scheld, W. M., Quagliarello, V. J., and Wispelwey, B.: The potential role of host cytokines in *Haemophilus influenzae* lipopolysaccharide-induced blood-brain barrier permeability. Pediatr. Infect. Dis. J. *8*:910, 1989.
329. Schiano, M. A., Hauth, J. C., and Gilstrap, L. C.: Second-stage fetal tachycardia and neonatal infection. Am. J. Obstet. Gynecol. *148*:779, 1984.
330. Schlech, W. F., III, Lavigne, P. M., Bortolussi, R., et al.: Epidemic listeriosis: Evidence of transmission by food. N. Engl. J. Med. *308*:203, 1983.
331. Schneerson, R., Rodrigues, L. P., Parke, J. C., Jr., et al.: Immunity to disease caused by *Hemophilus influenzae* type b. II. Specificity and some biologic characteristics of "natural," infection-acquired, and immunization-induced antibodies to the capsular polysaccharide of *Hemophilus influenzae* type b. J. Immunol. *107*:1081, 1971.
332. Schouten-Van Meeteren, N. Y., Rietveld, A., Moolenaar, A. J., et al.: Influence of perinatal conditions on C-reactive protein production. J. Pediatr. *120*:621, 1992.
333. Schuchat, A., Lizano, C., Broome, C. V., et al.: Outbreak of neonatal listeriosis associated with mineral oil. Pediatr. Infect. Dis. J. *10*:183, 1991.
334. Seeliger, H. P. R.: Listeriosis. New York, Hafner, 1961.
335. Sherman, M. P., Chance, K. H., and Goetzman, B. W.: Gram's stains of tracheal secretions predict neonatal bacteremia. Am. J. Dis. Child. *138*:848, 1984.
336. Shinefield, H. R.: Staphylococcal infections. *In* Remington, J. S., and Klein, J. O. (eds.): Infectious Diseases of the Fetus and Newborn Infant. 3rd ed. Philadelphia, W. B. Saunders, 1990, pp. 866–900.
337. Shuman, R. M., Leech, R. W., and Alvord, E. C., Jr.: Neurotoxicity of hexachlorophene in the human. I. A clinicopathologic study of 248 children. Pediatrics *54*:689, 1974.
338. Shurin, P. A., Howie, V. M., Pelton, S. I., et al.: Bacterial etiology of otitis media during the first six weeks of life. J. Pediatr. *92*:893, 1978.
339. Siegel, J. D., and McCracken, G. H., Jr.: Group D streptococcal infections. J. Pediatr. *93*:542, 1978.
340. Siegel, J. D., and McCracken, G. H., Jr.: Sepsis neonatorum. N. Engl. J. Med. *304*:642, 1981.
341. Siegel, J. D., McCracken, G. H., Jr., Threlkeld, N., et al.: Single-dose penicillin prophylaxis against neonatal group B streptococcal infection. N. Engl. J. Med. *303*:769, 1980.
342. Siegel, J. D., McCracken, G. H., Jr., Threlkeld, N., et al.: Single-dose penicillin prophylaxis of neonatal group-B streptococcal disease: Conclusion of a 41 month controlled trial. Lancet *1*:1426, 1982.
343. Siegel, J. D., Shannon, K. M., and DePasse, B. M.: Recurrent infection associated with penicillin-tolerant group B streptococci: A report of two cases. J. Pediatr. *99*:920, 1981.
344. Silver, R. P., Finn, C. W., Vann, W. F., et al.: Molecular cloning of the K1 capsular polysaccharide genes of *E. coli*. Nature. *289*:696, 1981.
345. Simpson, R. A., Spencer, A. F., Speller, D. C. E., et al.: Colonization by gentamicin-resistant *Staphylococcus epidermidis* in a special care baby unit. J. Hosp. Infect. *7*:108, 1986.
346. Smith, R. T., Platou, E. S., and Good, R. A.: Septicemia of the newborn: Current status of the problem. Pediatrics *17*:549, 1956.
347. Sood, K., Mulvihill, D., and Daum, R. S.: Intrarenal abscess caused by *Klebsiella pneumoniae* in a neonate: Modern management and diagnosis. Am. J. Perinatol. *6*:367, 1989.
348. Speer, C. P., Hauptmann, D., Stubbe, P., et al.: Neonatal septicemia and meningitis in Göttingen, West Germany. Pediatr. Infect. Dis. *4*:36, 1985.
349. Spigelblatt, L., Saintonge, J., Chicoine, R., et al.: Changing pattern of neonatal streptococcal septicemia. Pediatr. Infect. Dis. *4*:56, 1985.
350. Squire, E., Favara, B., and Todd, J.: Diagnosis of neonatal bacterial infection: Hematologic and pathologic findings in fatal and nonfatal cases. Pediatrics *64*:60, 1979.
351. Squire, E. N., Jr., Reich, H. M., Merenstein, G. B., et al.: Criteria for the discontinuation of antibiotic therapy during presumptive treatment of suspected neonatal infection. Pediatr. Infect. Dis. *1*:85, 1982.
352. Sreenan, C., and Osiovich, H.: Myeloid colony-stimulating factors: Use in the newborn. Arch. Pediatr. Adolesc. Med. *153*:984–988, 1999.
353. Stabile, A., Miceli Sopo, S., Romanelli, V., et al.: Intravenous immunoglobulin for prophylaxis of neonatal sepsis in premature infants. Arch. Dis. Child. *63*:441, 1988.
354. Steere, A. C., Aber, R. C., Warford, L. R., et al.: Possible nosocomial transmission of group B streptococci in a newborn nursery. J. Pediatr. *87*:784, 1975.
355. Stetler, H., Martin, E., Plotkin, S., et al.: Neonatal mastitis due to *Escherichia coli*. J. Pediatr. *76*:611, 1970.
356. Stevens, D. C., Kleiman, M. B., and Schreiner, R. L.: Early onset *Pseudomonas* sepsis of the neonate. Perinatol. Neonatol. *6*:75, 1982.
357. Storch, G. A., and Rajagopalan, L.: Methicillin-resistant *Staphylococcus aureus* bacteremia in children. Pediatr. Infect. Dis. J. *5*:59, 1986.
358. Storm, W.: Transient bacteremia following endotracheal suctioning in ventilated newborns. Pediatrics *65*:487, 1980.

359. Suksanong, M., and Dajani, A. S.: Detection of *Haemophilus influenzae* type b antigens in body fluids, using specific antibody-coated staphylococci. J. Clin. Microbiol. *5*:81, 1977.
360. Szanton, V. L.: Epidemic salmonellosis: A 30-month study of 80 cases of *Salmonella oranienburg* infection. Pediatrics *20*:794, 1957.
361. Tan, T. Q., Mason, E. O., Jr., Ou, C. N., and Kaplan, S. C.: Use of intravenous rifampin in neonates with persistent staphylococcal bacteremia. Antimicrob. Agents Chemother. *37*:2401–2406, 1993.
362. Tashjian, J. H., Coulam, C. B., and Washington, J. A.: II. Vaginal flora in asymptomatic women. Mayo Clin. Proc. *51*:557, 1976.
363. Terrone, D. A., Rinehart, B. K., Einstein, M. H., et al.: Neonatal sepsis and death caused by resistant *Escherichia coli*: Possible consequences of extend maternal ampicillin administration. Am. J. Obstet. Gynecol. *180*:1345–1348, 1999.
364. Tetzlaff, T. R., Ashworth, C., and Nelson, J. D.: Otitis media in children less than 12 weeks of age. Pediatrics *59*:827, 1977.
365. Tetzlaff, T. R., Howard, J. B., McCracken, G. H., Jr., et al.: Antibiotic concentrations in pus and bone of children with osteomyelitis. J. Pediatr. *92*:135, 1978.
366. Thompson, R. L., Cabezudo, I., and Wenzel, R. P.: Epidemiology of nosocomial infections caused by methicillin-resistant *Staphylococcus aureus*. Ann. Intern. Med. *97*:309, 1982.
367. Thomson, J., and Lewis, I. C.: Osteomyelitis in the newborn. Arch. Dis. Child. *25*:273, 1950.
368. Tipple, M. A., Beem, M. O., and Saxon, E. M.: Clinical characteristics of the afebrile pneumonia associated with *Chlamydia trachomatis* infection in infants less than 6 months of age. Pediatrics *63*:192, 1979.
369. Totterdell, B. M., Chrystie, I. L., and Banatvala, J. E.: Cord blood and breast milk antibodies in neonatal rotavirus infection. Br. Med. J. *1*:828, 1980.
370. Towers, C. V., Carr, M. H., Padilla, G., et al.: Potential consequences of widespread antepartal use of ampicillin. Am. J. Obstet. Gynecol. *179*:879–883, 1998.
371. Tupperainen, N., Osterlund, K., and Hallman, M.: Selective intrapartum penicillin prophylaxis of early onset group B streptococcal disease. Pediatr. Res. *20*:403A, 1986.
372. Umaña, M. A., Odio, C. M., Salas, J. L., et al.: Comparative evaluation of aztreonam/ampicillin versus amikacin/ampicillin in neonates with bacterial infections. Presented at the 27th Interscience Conference on Antimicrobial Agents and Chemotherapy, New York, October, 1987.
373. Unhanand, M., Mustafa, M. M., McCracken, G. H., et al.: Gram-negative enteric bacillary meningitis: A twenty-one-year experience. J. Pediatr. *122*:15, 1993.
374. Vawter, G. F.: Perinatal listeriosis. *In* Rosenberg, H. S., and Bernstein, J. (eds.): Perspectives in Pediatric Pathology. Vol. 6. New York, Masson Publishing, 1981, p. 153.
375. Visintine, A. M., Oleske, J. M., and Nahmias, A. J.: *Listeria monocytogenes* infection in infants and children. Am. J. Dis. Child. *131*:393, 1977.
376. Vogel, L. C., Kretschmer, R. R., Boyer, K. M., et al.: Human immunity to group B streptococci measured by indirect immunofluorescence: Correlation with protection in chick embryos. J. Infect. Dis. *140*:682, 1979.
377. Voora, S., Srinivasan, G., Lilien, L. D., et al.: Fever in full-term newborns in the first four days of life. Pediatrics *69*:40, 1982.
378. Wagener, M. M., Rycheck, R. R., Yee, R. B., et al.: Septic dermatitis of the neonatal scalp and maternal endomyometritis with intrapartum internal fetal monitoring. Pediatrics *74*:81, 1984.
379. Walker, K. M., and Coyer, W. F.: Suprarenal abscess due to group B *Streptococcus*. J. Pediatr. *94*:970, 1979.
380. Walsh, W. F., Stanley, S., Lally, K. P., et al.: *Ureaplasma urealyticum* demonstrated by open lung biopsy in newborns with chronic lung disease. Pediatr. Infect. Dis. J. *10*:823, 1991.
381. Wang, E. L., Cassell, G. H., Sánchez, P. J., et al.: *Ureaplasma urealyticum* and chronic lung disease of prematurity: Critical appraisal of the literature on causation. Clin. Infect. Dis. *17*:S112, 1993.
382. Ward, J. I., Siber, G. R., Scheifele, D. W., et al.: Rapid diagnosis of *Hemophilus influenzae* type b infections by latex particle agglutination and counterimmunoelectrophoresis. J. Pediatr. *93*:37, 1978.
383. Warren, W. S., and Stool, S. E.: Otitis media in low-birth weight infants. J. Pediatr. *79*:740, 1971.
384. Wasserman, R. L.: Unconventional therapies for neonatal sepsis. Pediatr. Infect. Dis. *2*:421, 1983.
385. Weems, J. J., Jr., Jarvis, W. R., and Colman, G.: A cluster of late onset group B streptococcal infections in low birth weight premature infants: No evidence of horizontal transmission. Pediatr. Infect. Dis. J. *5*:715, 1986.
386. Weinberg, A. G., and Laird, W. P.: Group B streptococcal endocarditis detected by echocardiography. J. Pediatr. *92*:335, 1978.
387. Weinberger, M., Haynes, R. E., and Morse, T. S.: Necrotizing fasciitis in a neonate. Am. J. Dis. Child. *123*:591, 1972.
388. Weissman, C. L. E., Stoll, B. J., Kueser, T. J., et al.: Intravenous immune globulin prophylaxis of late-onset sepsis in premature neonates. J. Pediatr. *125*:922, 1994.
389. Weissman C. L. E., Anthony B. F., Hemming, V. G., et al.: Comparison of group B streptococcal hyperimmune globulin and standard intravenously administered immune globulin in neonates. J. Pediatr. *122*:929, 1993.
390. Weissman, C. L. E., Stoll, B. J., Kueser, T. J., et al.: Intravenous immune globulin therapy for early-onset sepsis in premature neonates. J. Pediatr. *121*:434, 1992.
391. Welshimer, H. J., and Winglewish, N. G.: Listeriosis: Summary of seven cases of *Listeria* meningitis. J. A. M. A. *171*:1319, 1959.
392. Whittle, H. C., Tugwell, P., Egler, L. J., et al.: Rapid bacteriological diagnosis of pyogenic meningitis by latex agglutination. Lancet *2*:619, 1974.
393. Wientzen, R. L., McCracken, G. H., Jr., Petruska, M. L., et al.: Localization and therapy of urinary tract infections of childhood. Pediatrics *63*:467, 1979.
394. Wilson, H. D., and Haltalin, K. C.: Acute necrotizing fasciitis in childhood: Report of 11 cases. Am. J. Dis. Child. *125*:591, 1973.
395. Wiswell, T. E., and Geschke, D. W.: Risk from circumcision during the first month of life compared with those for uncircumcised boys. Pediatrics *83*:1011, 1989.
396. Wiswell, T. E., and Roscelli, J. D.: Corroborative evidence for the decreased incidence of urinary tract infections in circumcised male infants. Pediatrics *78*:96, 1986.
397. Word, B. M., and Klein, J. O.: Therapy of bacterial sepsis and meningitis in infants and children: 1989 poll of directors of programs in pediatric infectious diseases. Pediatr. Infect. Dis. J. *8*:635, 1989.
398. Yoder, M. C., Douglas, S. D., Gerdes, J., et al.: Plasma fibronectin in healthy newborn infants: Respiratory diseases syndrome and perinatal asphyxia. J. Pediatr. *102*:777, 1983.
399. Yow, M. D., Leeds, L. J., Thompson, P. K., et al.: The natural history of group B streptococcal colonization in the pregnant woman and her offspring. I. Colonization studies. Am. J. Obstet. Gynecol. *137*:34, 1980.
400. Yow, M. D., Mason, E. O., Leeds, L. J., et al.: Ampicillin prevents intrapartum transmission of group B *Streptococcus*. J. A. M. A. *241*:1245, 1979.

Infections of the Compromised Host

CHAPTER 75

Primary Immunodeficiencies

JAVIER CHINEN ■ MARK W. KLINE ■ WILLIAM T. SHEARER

The term *primary immunodeficiency* encompasses a broad range of congenital and hereditary disorders having in common a principal defect of the immune system development or function and, therefore, having a predisposition to recurrent or unusual infections. These disorders are present from birth, although clinical manifestations may not be evident until much later in life. The primary immunodeficiency disorders manifest with a wide range of severity, and milder variants may be subtle and difficult to diagnose. The secondary immunodeficiencies are acquired disorders, with immune dysfunction occurring as a result of exogenous factors or along with some other primary disease process. Causes of secondary immunodeficiency include infection (e.g., human immunodeficiency virus [HIV]), medications (e.g., corticosteroid administration), malnutrition, and neoplastic or metabolic diseases (e.g., Hodgkin disease, diabetes mellitus). Many secondary immunodeficiency disorders are far more common than are the primary immunodeficiencies.

Children generally are referred for immunologic evaluation because of unusually frequent or severe infections or because of infections caused by unusual organisms (Table 75–1). Only a small percentage of children who undergo evaluation have demonstrable immunodeficiency. This chapter focuses on the medical history and physical examination findings that can differentiate the few children with immunodeficiency from the many other children with normal immune function. Screening laboratory tests that are useful in excluding clinically significant immune dysfunction are discussed, and some of the most common or distinctive primary antibody, cellular, complement, and phagocyte deficiencies are described. When known, the genetic and molecular defects are reported in the sense of understanding the clinical expression of the resulting diseases.

Initial Evaluation for Suspected Immunodeficiency

MEDICAL HISTORY

Minor infections occur commonly throughout childhood. For example, otherwise healthy children younger than 5 years of age average between three and eight episodes of upper respiratory infection annually.[11, 14, 33] By 1 year of age, 62 percent of children have had at least one episode of acute otitis media, and 17 percent have had three or more episodes.[91] By 3 years of age, more than 80 percent of children have had at least one episode of acute otitis media, and 46 percent have had three or more episodes. Approximately 2 percent of children 1 to 5 years of age develop symptomatic urinary tract infection.[80] The incidence of gastroenteritis among children in the United States is approximately two to three episodes per child-year, with rates as high as five episodes per child-year among children attending daycare centers.[12, 37] Occurrence of these infections during infancy or early childhood is the result of several factors, including immunologic immaturity or naïveté (lack of prior exposure to infectious agents), poor hygiene, mouthing behavior, allergic disease, and frequent exposure to ill contacts in the home, school, or daycare settings.

TABLE 75–1 ■ WHEN TO SUSPECT AN IMMUNODEFICIENCY DISORDER

Increased number of infections
Increased severity of infectious disease
Poor response to antibiotic therapy
Unusual organisms (opportunistic infections)
Failure to thrive
Poor wound healing
Cold *Staphylococcus* infection
Recurrent periodontitis

Medical history is the key element in distinguishing children with immunodeficiency from those with frequent infections but normal immune function. Children with immunodeficiency often have a history of frequent and severe infections (e.g., pneumonia, meningitis, septicemia, osteomyelitis, abscess of soft tissue or an internal organ). The course of individual episodes of infection may be unusually prolonged or associated with unexpected complications (e.g., lung abscess in a child with pneumonia or skull bone osteomyelitis as a complication of sinusitis). In general, infections over time at multiple body sites are more suggestive of immunodeficiency than are infections occurring at only one site (e.g., recurrent otitis media). In the latter circumstance, a mechanical or anatomic explanation for the infections (e.g., foreign body or occult tracheoesophageal fistula in the child with recurrent pneumonia, congenital fistulous tract to the middle ear in the child with recurrent bacterial meningitis) should be considered.

A history of recurrent infections of defined cause may be more meaningful than one of frequent, self-limited infections of presumed viral cause (Table 75–2). Children with primary antibody deficiencies typically experience infections caused by extracellular bacteria with polysaccharide capsules (e.g., *Streptococcus pneumoniae, Haemophilus*

TABLE 75–2 ■ COMMON PATHOGENS IN CHILDREN WITH PRIMARY IMMUNODEFICIENCY

Immunodeficiency	Common Pathogens
Antibody deficiencies	*Streptococcus pneumoniae, Haemophilus influenzae, Staphylococcus aureus, Pseudomonas aeruginosa, Mycoplasma, Salmonella, Shigella, Campylobacter*, rotavirus, enteroviruses, *Giardia*
Cellular and combined immune deficiencies	Mycobacteria, *S. pneumoniae, P. aeruginosa, Candida*, Herpesviruses, *Pneumocystis carinii*
Complement deficiencies	*S. pneumoniae, H. influenzae, Neisseria meningitidis*
Phagocyte deficiencies	*S. aureus, Nocardia* species, *P. aeruginosa, Serratia*, enteric gram-negative bacilli, *Candida, Aspergillus*

influenzae type b). In contrast, children with primary cellular immunodeficiencies often have infections with unusual or opportunistic viruses, fungi, protozoa, and mycobacteria. Because of the impairment of T-cell–dependent antibody responses, infections with common bacteria also may be observed. Children with primary deficiencies of complement components typically have recurrent neisserial infections, and those with phagocyte deficiencies have infections with a variety of catalase-positive bacterial (e.g., *Staphylococcus aureus, Pseudomonas aeruginosa, Serratia marcescens*) and fungal (e.g., *Candida* spp., *Aspergillus* spp.) organisms. Severe infections with atypical mycobacteria often indicate a defect in interleukin-12 or gamma-interferon mediated responses.

In addition to the microbial cause of infections, several other items of historical information may help to define the risk for and possible nature of a primary immunodeficiency. Because young infants are afforded some protection by the presence of maternal IgG, children with primary antibody deficiencies generally have an initial period of relative well-being, with onset of infections occurring when they are between 3 and 18 months of age. On the other hand, children with severe T-cell, complement, or phagocyte deficiencies may have onset of infections in the first days or weeks of life. Omphalitis and poor wound healing suggest phagocyte deficiency. Hypocalcemic seizures in the neonatal period and congenital heart disease may be clues to the presence of DiGeorge syndrome. Severe disease associated with live vaccines (e.g., BCG, measles, poliomyelitis, varicella) may be observed in children with primary immunodeficiencies. The absence of potential causes for secondary immunodeficiency should be established.

Family history can offer important clues to the presence of a primary immunodeficiency. A history of consanguinity or deaths from infection or unexplained causes during infancy or early childhood should be sought. Many of the better-defined immunodeficiency syndromes have X-linked inheritance patterns (Table 75–3), resulting in an overall male-to-female ratio of 5:1 among children with primary immunodeficiency.

PHYSICAL EXAMINATION

The physical examination in children with primary immunodeficiency often is unrevealing. Short stature is a feature of some of these congenital disorders (e.g., chronic granulomatous disease), and wasting or failure to thrive is observed because of recurrent infections or chronic intestinal malabsorption. Oral candidiasis, omphalitis, and multiple skin abscesses may indicate an underlying immune disorder. A paucity of lymphoid tissues (e.g., tonsils, lymph nodes) suggests X-linked agammaglobulinemia.

Several congenital immunodeficiency syndromes are associated with highly characteristic physical stigmata. For example, children with DiGeorge syndrome often have characteristic facial features (Fig. 75–1) and cardiac malformations. Telangiectasia of the bulbar conjunctivae (Fig. 75–2), nasal bridge, ears, and flexor surfaces of the extremities, with or without ataxia, suggest ataxia telangiectasia. Chronic eczema is observed in the hyperimmunoglobulinemia E and Wiskott-Aldrich syndromes, and severe gingivitis and periodontitis with loss of alveolar bone and dentition can occur in children with leukocyte adhesion deficiency (Fig. 75–3).

TABLE 75–3 ■ X-LINKED PRIMARY IMMUNODEFICIENCY DISORDERS

X-linked agammaglobulinemia (Bruton disease)
Immunodeficiency with hyper-IgM (CD40 ligand deficiency)
X-linked lymphoproliferative syndrome
Severe combined immune deficiency (common gamma-chain deficiency)
Properdin deficiency
Wiskott-Aldrich syndrome
X-linked chronic granulomatous disease (most cases)

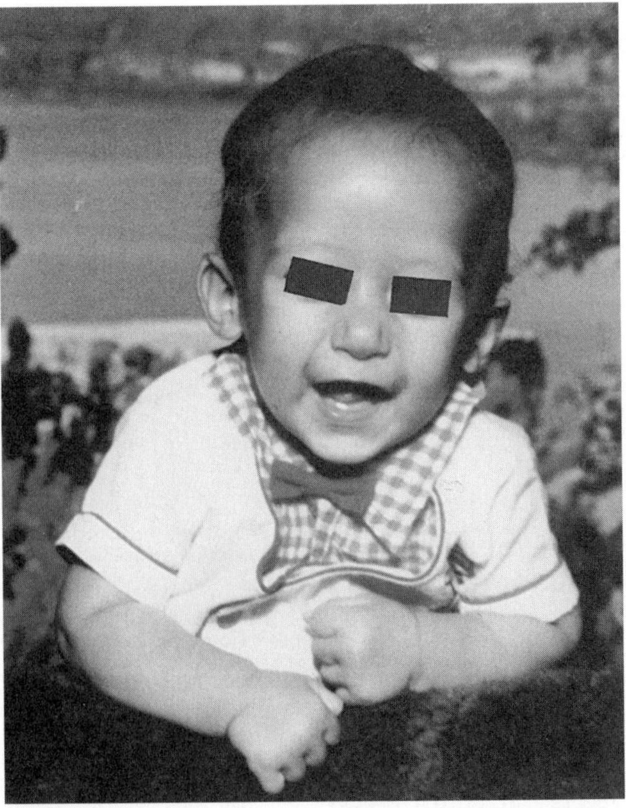

FIGURE 75–1 ■ Typical facial appearance of a child with DiGeorge anomaly. Notice the microstomia, hypertelorism, upturned nose, and posteriorly rotated and small, low-set ears.

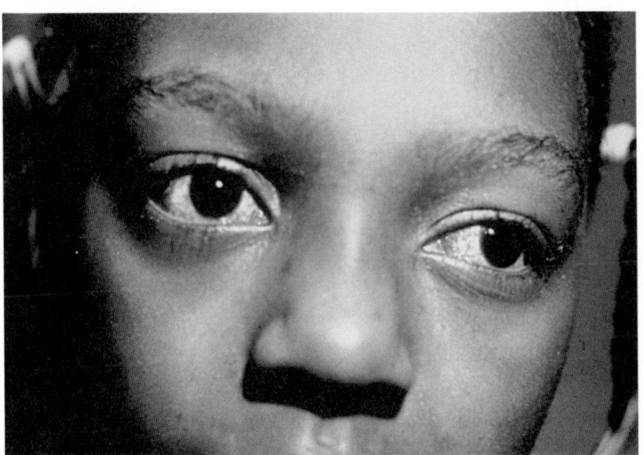

FIGURE 75–2 ■ Telangiectases of the bulbar conjunctivae in a child with ataxia telangiectasia. (Courtesy of Dr. Martin Lorin, Texas Children's Hospital, Houston, TX.)

TABLE 75–4 ■ SCREENING TESTS FOR SUSPECTED PRIMARY IMMUNODEFICIENCY

Immunodeficiency	Screening Tests
All types	Complete blood count Peripheral blood smear
Antibody deficiency	Quantitative serum immunoglobulins Postimmunization antibody titers Isohemagglutinins
Cellular immunodeficiency	Delayed hypersensitivity skin tests Chest radiography
Complement deficiency	Total hemolytic complement (CH_{50}) assay
Phagocyte deficiency	Nitroblue tetrazolium (NBT) dye test Neutrophil $CD11_{a,b,c}$/CD18 expression

LABORATORY TESTS

A screening evaluation for immunodeficiency employs generally available, relatively inexpensive laboratory tests to exclude common and serious disorders (Table 75–4). If possible, the evaluation should be targeted to the type of immunodeficiency (e.g., primary antibody deficiency) suggested by the child's medical history and physical examination findings. Laboratory test results must be interpreted in the context of the child's age.

The initial evaluation for immune deficiency should include a complete blood count and examination of the peripheral blood smear. Because 50 to 70 percent of circulating lymphocytes are T cells, children with severe cellular (e.g., DiGeorge syndrome) or combined (e.g., severe combined immunodeficiency [SCID]) immunodeficiencies may have lymphopenia. Children with Wiskott-Aldrich syndrome have reduced numbers of platelets, which are small (i.e., decreased mean platelet volume). Large neutrophil cytoplasmic granules are observed in children with Chediak-Higashi syndrome. A complete blood count also is useful in excluding congenital neutropenia. Children with leukocyte adhesion deficiency often have markedly increased neutrophil and total white blood cell counts. The presence of Howell-Jolly bodies, with or without thrombocytosis, suggests anatomic or functional asplenia. Other tests to rule out malnutrition or metabolic disorders as causes of secondary immunodeficiency should be considered.

Evaluation of Humoral Immunity

Screening evaluation of the child with suspected antibody deficiency should include quantitative measurement of serum immunoglobulins and functional assessment of specific antibody production. Most children with primary antibody deficiencies have abnormalities of serum immunoglobulin concentrations. Measurement of serum IgG, IgA, and IgM concentrations can identify children with panhypogammaglobulinemia and those with deficiency of a particular immunoglobulin isotype, such as selective IgA deficiency. Because of marked age-related changes in serum immunoglobulin concentrations, use of age-appropriate normal values for comparison purposes is important.

Functional antibody production usually is assessed by measuring antibody titers generated in response to immunization with diphtheria and tetanus toxoids. Antibody responses to polysaccharide antigens do not require T-cell cooperation and are evaluated separately using the pneumococcal polysaccharide (Pneumovax 23, Merck & Co., West Point, PA) immunization, after 24 months of age. Infants are thought to present a functional immaturity in the ability to respond to this class of antigens. Alternatively, because ABO blood group antigens are polysaccharides and cross-reacting environmental antigen epitopes are ubiquitous,

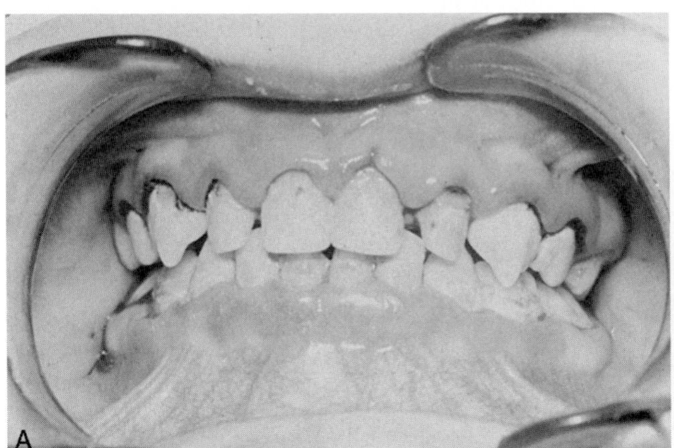

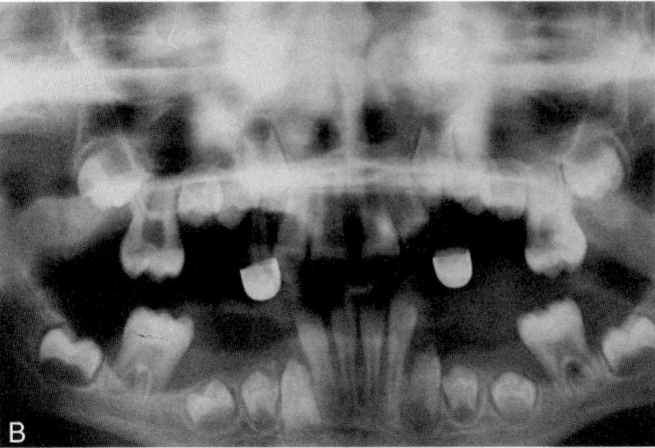

FIGURE 75–3 ■ *A,* Chronic periodontitis in a boy with leukocyte adhesion deficiency. *B,* Radiograph of the same patient shows extensive alveolar bone loss. (Courtesy of Dr. Bruce Carter, Texas Children's Hospital, Houston, TX.)

anti-polysaccharide antibody production can be assessed by measuring serum isohemagglutinin titers. Children with blood type AB do not form isohemagglutinins. The conjugated pneumococcal (Prevnar, Wyeth-Ayerst, Philadelphia, PA) and *H. influenzae* type b (several brand names) vaccines are not suitable for the assessment of antipolysaccharide antibody responses because they are not pure polysaccharides. Patients vaccinated with the conjugated pneumococcal vaccine still can be evaluated for antipolysaccharide antibody production because the pneumococcal polysaccharide vaccine contains serotype antigens against which the conjugated vaccine does not protect.

Measurement of serum IgG subclasses may be indicated in children with apparent abnormalities in functional antibody production. Further evaluation of children whose screening tests indicate significant quantitative and functional antibody abnormalities should include enumeration of T and B cells in the peripheral blood and in vitro studies of mitogen- or antigen-induced B-cell proliferation. The antibody response to neo-antigens (e.g., bacterial phages) may be useful for the evaluation of patients receiving immunoglobulin therapy.

Evaluation of Cellular Immunity

The screening evaluation for primary cellular immunodeficiency generally consists of delayed hypersensitivity skin tests and, in the young infant, posteroanterior and lateral chest radiographs for the assessment of the thymic shadow (Fig. 75–4).

Delayed hypersensitivity skin tests are performed using vaccine or microbial antigens to which the child has had prior exposure. Commonly used antigens include tetanus toxoid and *Candida albicans*. Standard initial dilutions are 1:100 for both antigens, but a *C. albicans* dilution of 1:10 may be more appropriate for children 5 years of age or younger because they are less likely to have been exposed to this antigen. The diluted antigen is administered intradermally and read at 24 and 48 hours for the presence of wheal formation.

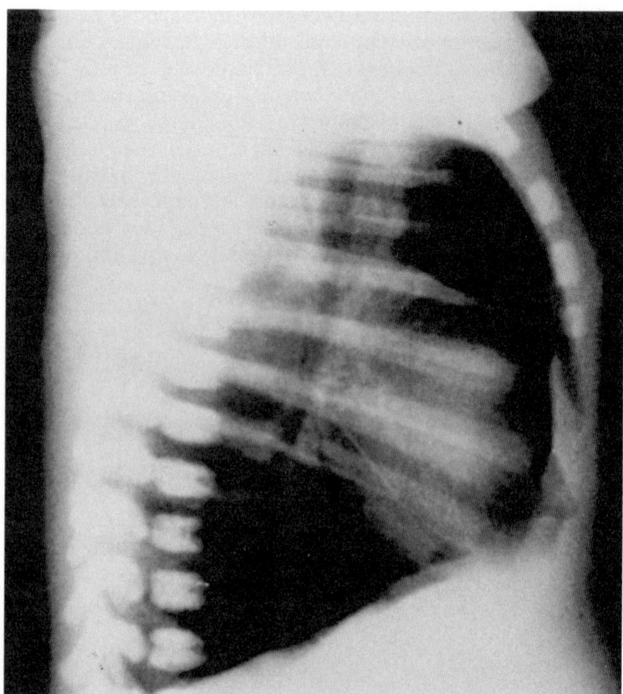

FIGURE 75–4 ■ Lateral chest radiograph of an infant with severe combined immune deficiency. Notice absence of the normal thymic shadow.

Unfortunately, delayed hypersensitivity skin test responses have low specificity and often are absent in children younger than 2 years of age. Enumeration of peripheral blood T cells, T-cell subset analysis (i.e., $CD4^+$ or $CD8^+$ lymphocyte counts), and mitogen- and antigen-induced lymphocyte proliferation studies may be needed for a reliable determination of cellular immune function.

Evaluation of the Complement System

Primary deficiencies of components of the classic complement pathway can be detected with the total serum hemolytic complement (CH_{50}) assay. This test measures the ability of fresh patient serum to lyse antibody-coated sheep erythrocytes and reflects the activity of all numbered components of the classic complement pathway from C1 through C9. Complete deficiency of any of these components results in a CH_{50} approaching zero. Complement component levels and function should be investigated only when this result is obtained because deficiencies are rare findings.

Evaluation of Phagocyte Function

A variety of assays are available for assessment of phagocyte function. The nitroblue tetrazolium (NBT) dye test uses the reduction of NBT to formazan by activated phagocytes to measure the oxidative metabolic responses that accompany phagocytosis. Children with chronic granulomatous disease (CGD) show very little dye reduction (less than 10% of cells are formazan positive); carriers of X-linked CGD typically have between 20 and 90 percent formazan-positive cells. More sophisticated tests, including chemiluminescence and assays of chemotaxis, phagocytosis, and bactericidal activity, may be performed when the NBT test results are abnormal and when high clinical suspicion of a phagocyte disorder exists.[10]

Enumeration of $CD11_{a,b,c}{}^+/CD18^+$ white blood cells is indicated when diagnosis of leukocyte adhesion deficiency is suspected.

Genetic Testing

Several gene defects responsible for immunodeficiency disorders have been identified (Table 75–5). However, testing for the defects is available only in a few specialized laboratories. Genetic testing is indicated for the affected patient who is ill, for prenatal diagnosis of an unborn child with an affected sibling, or for an individual who may have inherited or is a carrier of a known immunodeficiency gene defect. Genetic testing is used most often to confirm the DiGeorge syndrome, in which a deletion in chromosome 22 is identified by fluorescent in situ hybridization (FISH) or by the less sensitive chromosome banding analysis. Genetic evaluation and counseling are recommended for the families of patients with primary immunodeficiencies.

Management

Management of the immunodeficient patient requires specialist care that can indicate different recommendations according to the specific diagnosis. For example, intravenous

TABLE 75–5 ■ GENE DEFECTS IN SELECTED PRIMARY IMMUNODEFICIENCIES

Immunodeficiency	Gene Defect	Chromosome
Antibody Deficiency		
Agammaglobulinemia	Immunoglobulin heavy-chain	14q23
	Bruton tyrosine kinase	Xq22
	Activation-induced cytidine deaminase	12p13
Hyper-IgM syndrome	CD40 ligand (CD154)	Xq26
Cellular Immunodeficiency		
DiGeorge syndrome	Unknown	22q11.2, 10p13
Severe combined immunodeficiency	*RAG1, RAG2*	11p13
	JAK3	19p13.1
	Adenosine deaminase	20q13.11
	Common gamma chain	Xq13.1
Ataxia telangiectasia	ATM, DNA kinase	11q22.3
Wiskott-Aldrich	*WASP*, cytoskeleton protein	Xp11.23
Phagocyte Deficiency		
Chronic granulomatous disease	gp67phox	1q25
	gp47phox	7q11.23
	gp22phox	16q24
	gp91phox	Xp21.1
Leukocyte adhesion deficiency type I	CD18	21q22

immunoglobulins are recommended for patients with proven deficiency of immunoglobulin G synthesis. Recommendations that apply to all patients with immunodeficiency include the avoidance of contact with sick persons and avoidance of live vaccines[7]; the use of irradiated, leukocyte-depleted, cytomegalovirus-negative blood products when needed; and the prompt diagnosis and early treatment of infections (Table 75–6).

TABLE 75–6 ■ KEY CONCEPTS IN THE MANAGEMENT OF PRIMARY IMMUNODEFICIENCIES

1. ***Immune function.*** T- and B-cell number and function should be assessed periodically.
2. ***Immunoglobulin G therapy.*** For patients with low IgG levels or poor antibody function.
3. ***Immunizations.*** Live vaccines should not be administered to immunodeficiency patients, except for complement deficiency and selective IgA deficiency. Patients with complement deficiency may benefit from receiving the pneumococcal and meningococcal vaccines because of their increased susceptibility to encapsulated organisms. Household contacts of children with immunodeficiency should not receive oral poliovirus vaccines because of the risk of transmission to the immunodeficient child. Other live vaccines (BCG, MMR and varicella vaccine) may be administered to the household contact. If the vaccine recipient develops a rash, contact with the immunodeficient child should be avoided.[7]
4. ***Blood products.*** When needed, patients with immunodeficiencies should receive only irradiated, cytomegalovirus-negative, leukocyte-depleted blood products.
5. ***Antibiotic prophylaxis.*** T-cell–deficient patients should take antibiotic prophylaxis for *Pneumocystis carinii.* Antibiotic prophylaxis is recommended for dental and surgical procedures.
6. ***Infectious diseases.*** Infections should be recognized promptly, and unusual pathogens should be considered. Antibiotic therapy should be started early and discontinued cautiously.
7. ***Diet and activity.*** Patients with immunodeficiency should have a regular diet and lifestyle but should be instructed to avoid eating raw food and playing in environments potentially highly contaminated with pathogens, including daycare centers. Strict handwashing and reverse isolation may be indicated for patients with poor T-cell function.

Primary Antibody Deficiencies

X-LINKED AGAMMAGLOBULINEMIA

Clinical Features

Boys with X-linked agammaglobulinemia (i.e., Bruton disease) often are healthy during the first months of life because of the protective presence of transplacentally acquired maternal IgG. As maternal immunoglobulin disappears, chronic or recurrent infections develop.[16, 22a, 41, 50] Otitis media, sinusitis, pneumonia, and diarrhea are the most common findings, but infections are not limited to mucosal surfaces, and bacteremia, meningitis, and osteomyelitis also may occur. The mean age at diagnosis in a retrospective study of 96 patients with X-linked agammaglobulinemia was 2.5 years when there was a family history of the disease and 3.5 years when there was not.[50]

S. pneumoniae, *H. influenzae* type b, *S. aureus*, and *P. aeruginosa* are bacterial pathogens observed commonly in the setting of X-linked agammaglobulinemia. *Mycoplasma* spp. infections also occur with increased frequency. These organisms have been implicated as a cause of a subacute, destructive arthritis.[41, 51, 71] Gastrointestinal infections may be caused by *Salmonella*, *Shigella*, *Campylobacter*, or rotavirus.[41, 51, 71] Chronic giardiasis with intestinal malabsorption has been described.[67]

Children with X-linked agammaglobulinemia are susceptible to chronic enteroviral meningoencephalitis.[41, 59] Diverse signs and symptoms, including fever, headache, altered mental status, seizures, ataxia, myoclonus, paresthesias, peripheral neuropathy, aphasia or dysarthria, and visual disturbances, are observed. Treatment with intrathecal and intravenous immunoglobulin (IVIG) therapy has been attempted, but most reported cases have had a fatal outcome. Increased incidence of vaccine-associated paralytic poliomyelitis also has been reported.[41]

Pathogenesis

X-linked agammaglobulinemia results from developmental arrest of B-cell maturation. As a consequence, blood, lymph nodes, and bone marrow contain markedly diminished numbers of B cells and plasma cells, resulting in hypogammaglobulinemia. Other components of the immune system are normal.

The defective gene maps to the midportion of the long arm of the X chromosome. The gene encodes a cytoplasmic protein-tyrosine kinase, the normal function of which is necessary for expansion of B-cell populations during their maturation.[95, 98] Inactivating mutations of the gene have been found in all affected individuals studied.

Diagnosis

Because of the confounding presence of transplacentally acquired maternal IgG, use of quantitative serum immunoglobulin determinations for diagnosis of X-linked agammaglobulinemia in the child's first 6 months of life is problematic. Infants with X-linked agammaglobulinemia also have low concentrations of other immunoglobulin isotypes (e.g., IgA, IgM), but defining values that clearly differentiate between infants with the disease and normal infants is difficult. Definitive diagnosis during early infancy generally relies on immunophenotyping by flow cytometry to demonstrate absence of B cells in peripheral blood. After the infant reaches 6 months of age, serum IgG concentrations usually are less than 100 mg/dL, and concentrations of other immunoglobulin isotypes are low or undetectable. Iso-hemagglutinins are absent, and specific antibodies are not produced in response to immunization or natural infection.

Treatment and Prognosis

Lifetime replacement therapy with IVIG is indicated for all patients with X-linked agammaglobulinemia.[17] It decreases the frequency of serious infections, reduces the need for hospitalization, and may help to prevent chronic bronchiectasis.[55] The dose and frequency of administration of IVIG are adjusted to produce serum IgG trough concentrations of at least 500 mg/dL. For most patients, IVIG doses of 400 to 600 mg/kg, given every 3 or 4 weeks, are required.

Acute infections should be treated aggressively in patients with X-linked agammaglobulinemia. Minor middle ear, sinus, and skin infections usually respond to oral antibiotics. Pneumonia and other serious focal or systemic infections should be treated initially with intravenous antibiotics. Empirical antibiotic therapy is directed against common bacterial pathogens, including *S. pneumoniae*, *H. influenzae*, and *S. aureus*. If possible, etiologic diagnosis should be obtained, particularly in cases of severe or chronic infection. Because serum IgG concentrations often decrease during acute infection, the serum IgG concentration should be measured, and additional doses of IVIG may be indicated.

Chronic pulmonary disease with bronchiectasis is an important cause of death of patients with X-linked agammaglobulinemia. Long-term antibiotic therapy, similar to that employed in patients with cystic fibrosis, may be helpful in individual cases. Long-term survivors of X-linked agammaglobulinemia are at increased risk for developing lymphoreticular malignancies.[83]

IMMUNOGLOBULIN DEFICIENCY WITH INCREASED IMMUNOGLOBULIN M

Clinical Features

Most cases of immunoglobulin deficiency with increased IgM (i.e., hyper-IgM syndrome) are associated with X-linked transmission, but autosomal recessive and dominant inheritance patterns also have been reported. Patients with this disorder develop recurrent pyogenic infections during infancy as transplacentally acquired IgG wanes. Respiratory tract infections and chronic diarrhea with failure to thrive are common occurrences; septicemia, meningitis, and other serious systemic infections also occur.[66] *Pneumocystis carinii* pneumonia, an unusual infection in children with other primary antibody deficiencies, has been reported.

One half of patients with hyper-IgM syndrome have neutropenia. It can be intermittent but lacks the precise periodicity of cyclic neutropenia. Aphthous ulcers occur commonly. Perirectal ulcers and abscesses also have been reported. Hyperplasia of superficial and deep lymph nodes is a common occurrence. Intestinal nodular lymphoid hyperplasia may lead to malabsorption and protein-losing enteropathy. Diffuse lymphoid infiltration of other organs also may occur. Autoimmune conditions, including arthritis and nephritis, have been described, and the incidence of lymphoreticular malignancies is increased.

Pathogenesis

Males with hyper-IgM syndrome have mutations of a gene on the X chromosome that encodes the T-cell ligand (CD154) for the B-cell surface molecule CD40.[3, 9] Several patients with normal expression of the CD40 ligand and defects in the B-cell CD40 signaling pathway also have been described.[23] Interaction of CD40 with the CD40 ligand is essential to B-cell proliferation, isotype switching, and terminal differentiation of B cells to antibody-secreting plasma cells. Mutations in the activation-induced cytidine deaminase gene have been found in patients with the autosomal recessive form of the hyper-IgM syndrome.[61]

Diagnosis

Patients with this disorder have a characteristic increase in serum IgM concentrations in association with low to absent concentrations of serum IgA and IgG. Serum IgM concentrations may exceed 1000 mg/dL. Circulating B cells expressing surface IgM are found in normal numbers, but few cells bearing IgA or IgG circulate. Antibody responses to immunization often are present but consist predominantly or exclusively of IgM; isotype switching does not occur.

Evaluation of boys with suspected immunoglobulin deficiency with increased IgM should include a determination of activated T cells binding to CD40, which is done by flow cytometry using a recombinant CD40 fusion protein.[3, 9]

Treatment and Prognosis

Replacement therapy with IVIG is indicated. Reports of two patients successfully treated with HLA-identical bone marrow transplantation have been published.[53, 92] Patients with hyper-IgM syndrome usually have a worse clinical course than do patients with X-linked agammaglobulinemia. Causes of mortality include infection, severe liver disease, and malignancy.[53]

COMMON VARIABLE IMMUNODEFICIENCY

Clinical Features

The term *common variable immunodeficiency* (CVID) includes a heterogeneous group of disorders having in common hypogammaglobulinemia, abnormal antibody production, recurrent infections, and a propensity for autoimmune conditions with low or normal numbers of B cells. Onset can occur at any time from infancy to old age, but symptoms frequently begin during the second or third decades of life.

The clinical manifestations of CVID are similar to those of X-linked agammaglobulinemia, with recurrent infections of the respiratory tract, bacteremia, meningitis, osteomyelitis, and septic arthritis. Frequently, patients develop bronchiectasis and chronic lung disease. The most common infecting organisms are *S. pneumoniae*, *H. influenzae*, and *S. aureus*.

Many individuals with CVID suffer from chronic diarrhea and intestinal malabsorption that have an infectious or autoimmune basis.[24, 25, 40] These conditions may exacerbate the underlying hypogammaglobulinemia. Organisms implicated in these gastrointestinal infections include *Giardia*, *Campylobacter*, *Salmonella*, and *Cryptosporidium*. Bacterial overgrowth syndrome commonly occurs. Ulcerative colitis and Crohn disease are present with increased frequency in persons with CVID, as are atrophic gastritis with achlorhydria, viral or autoimmune chronic active hepatitis, and cholelithiasis.

Approximately 22 percent of individuals with CVID develop autoimmune conditions, which include a chronic arthritis resembling juvenile rheumatoid arthritis; scleroderma, a lupus-like syndrome; hypothyroidism; and neutropenia, anemia, and thrombocytopenia.[24, 25, 40]

A pseudolymphoma syndrome with lymphoid hyperplasia of the lung (i.e., lymphoid interstitial pneumonia) and intestine (i.e., nodular lymphoid hyperplasia), massive splenomegaly, and mediastinal adenopathy occurs in patients with CVID. Malignancies, including lymphomas and gastric carcinoma, are common findings among adults with CVID.[25, 26, 81]

Pathogenesis

The pathogenesis of CVID is poorly defined and may correspond to several different genetic defects that result in impaired antibody secretion. B-cell maturation is intact, and normal or low numbers of B cells are present in peripheral blood and lymph nodes, but production of antibody is impaired.[25, 85] Many patients with CVID appear to have an intrinsic B-cell defect that impairs the ability of these cells to differentiate into immunoglobulin-secreting plasma cells, but a variety of T-cell functional abnormalities also have been described. They include decreased lymphocyte proliferation to mitogens and antigens and reduced expression of cytokines.[25, 85]

Diagnosis

Quantitative immunoglobulin determination generally reveals a serum IgG concentration persistently less than 250 mg/dL, with comparable decreases in other immunoglobulin isotypes. Immunophenotyping of peripheral blood lymphocytes demonstrates presence of mature B cells expressing surface immunoglobulin. Antibody responses to immunization are subnormal or absent.

Treatment and Prognosis

Treatment of patients with CVID is similar to that of patients with X-linked agammaglobulinemia. Replacement therapy with IVIG is indicated.[18a] Because of enteric protein losses, patients with enteropathy may require unusually large doses of IVIG to maintain thorough serum IgG concentrations of 500 mg/dL or higher. Chronic lung disease with bronchiectasis resulting from multiple pneumonias is the most frequent cause of morbidity and mortality.[25]

IMMUNOGLOBULIN A DEFICIENCY

Clinical Features

Most individuals with selective IgA deficiency are clinically asymptomatic. Some patients have frequent, noninvasive viral and bacterial infections of the respiratory tract. Chronic diarrhea may occur, with *Giardia* being a pathogen commonly implicated. Infections in patients with IgA deficiency usually are less severe than those observed in patients with X-linked agammaglobulinemia or CVID. Individuals with more severe or chronic infections often have another associated immune deficiency, such as IgG subclass deficiency[68] or, rarely, ataxia telangiectasia.

Patients with IgA deficiency have a higher incidence of atopy than does the general population. Autoimmune disorders, including systemic lupus erythematosus, rheumatoid arthritis, and pernicious anemia, and lymphoreticular and gastrointestinal malignancies are more prevalent in this population.[74]

Pathogenesis

The pathogenesis of IgA deficiency has clear parallels with that of CVID. The fundamental defect in both disorders is a failure of B cells to differentiate into immunoglobulin-secreting plasma cells. Rare alleles of complement genes within major histocompatibility complex III on chromosome 6 have been associated strongly with the development of selective IgA deficiency and CVID, suggesting that these two disorders may be related.[100] Some individuals with selective IgA deficiency subsequently develop CVID.

Diagnosis

Selective IgA deficiency is diagnosed by a quantitative serum immunoglobulin determination showing subnormal concentration or absence of circulating IgA. In interpreting test results, an important consideration is that serum IgA concentrations can be undetectable in normal infants younger than 6 to 9 months of age because of a possible maturational delay. The diagnosis is reliable only after the child reaches 4 years of age.

Treatment and Prognosis

IVIG generally is not recommended in the management of patients with selective IgA deficiency. Because IgA is a new antigen for IgA-deficient patients and most blood products, including IVIG, contain trace amounts of IgA, IgA-deficient patients are at risk for developing IgE-mediated anaphylactic reactions if the patient is sensitized and blood products containing IgA are administered.[18]

Sinopulmonary infections in individuals with IgA deficiency often require unusually long courses of antibiotic therapy for cure. Parenteral antibiotic therapy sometimes is necessary for refractory cases of sinusitis or pneumonia.

IMMUNOGLOBULIN G SUBCLASS DEFICIENCY

Clinical Features

Commonly reported IgG subclass deficiencies include IgG2, sometimes in association with deficiency of IgG4 or

IgA, and IgG3, which may occur in association with IgG1 deficiency.[78, 96] Many individuals with IgG subclass deficiencies are asymptomatic; others have recurrent or chronic bacterial infections, usually of the respiratory tract. Commonly implicated pathogens include *S. pneumoniae*, *H. influenzae* type b, and other encapsulated bacteria. Children with selective IgG subclass deficiency usually do not have problems with intestinal malabsorption or autoimmunity.

Pathogenesis

The pathogenesis of IgG subclass deficiency is unknown. Genetic factors have been implicated by studies showing linkage to certain immunoglobulin allotypes.[39] T-cell immunity generally is intact in patients with IgG subclass deficiency.

Diagnosis

A diagnosis of IgG subclass deficiency is supported by finding a marked decrease from age-adjusted normal values in the serum concentrations of one or more IgG subclasses, together with evidence of a functional impairment in antibody production. The total serum IgG concentration may be normal, decreased, or even elevated as a result of a compensatory increase in production of unaffected IgG subclasses.

Some children with IgG2 subclass deficiency respond poorly to pure polysaccharide vaccines (e.g., pneumococcal vaccine).[78, 79, 96] Responses to protein antigens (e.g., tetanus toxoid) and protein-conjugated polysaccharide vaccines (e.g., *H. influenzae* type b conjugate vaccines) also may be abnormal.[78, 79] In contrast, patients with IgG3 subclass deficiency may respond poorly to protein antigens, but responses to polysaccharides generally are normal.[96] Assessment of the patient's antibody responses to vaccination with polysaccharide and protein antigens can help to establish the functional significance of an IgG subclass deficiency. Because of the age-dependent nature of antipolysaccharide antibody responses, such testing is not feasible in children younger than 2 years of age.

Treatment and Prognosis

Antibiotic prophylaxis of recurrent sinopulmonary infections and aggressive treatment of infections form the cornerstone of management for symptomatic IgG subclass deficiency. IVIG replacement therapy is reserved for patients with abnormal antibody responses and a demonstrated propensity for frequent or chronic infections. The perceived effectiveness and continued need for IVIG should be reassessed at least annually. IVIG must be administered with caution to patients who have concomitant IgG subclass and IgA deficiency.

TRANSIENT HYPOGAMMAGLOBULINEMIA OF INFANCY

Clinical Features

Transient hypogammaglobulinemia of infancy is a developmental disorder with a delay in the physiologic maturation of immunoglobulin synthesis, resulting in prolongation of the relative hypogammaglobulinemia observed in most normal infants at 4 or 5 months of age. Many of these infants come to medical attention because of recurrent respiratory tract infections (e.g., otitis media, sinusitis). Septicemia, meningitis, and other serious systemic infections are rare.

Pathogenesis

Patients with transient hypogammaglobulinemia of infancy do not appear to have any inherent defects of B-cell maturation or function.[28]

Diagnosis

Transient hypogammaglobulinemia of infancy is a diagnosis that can be made with certainty only in retrospect. Serum immunoglobulin concentrations may remain low in children until they are up to several years of age in some cases.[58] Circulating mature B cells numbers are normal and generate normal antibody responses to diphtheria, tetanus, and pertussis vaccines.

Treatment and Prognosis

Infants with suspected transient hypogammaglobulinemia should be followed clinically, and serial serum immunoglobulin concentration measurements should be performed. Some of these children eventually are diagnosed as having CVID, selective IgA deficiency, or another disorder. Because it is self-limited and specific antibody production usually is normal, replacement therapy with IVIG is not indicated. Antibiotic prophylaxis for recurrent respiratory infections occasionally is indicated.

Primary Cellular and Combined Immune Deficiencies

DiGEORGE SYNDROME

Clinical Features

The DiGeorge syndrome includes facial, cardiac, parathyroid, and thymic defects.[49] Patients with DiGeorge anomaly may present early in infancy with findings unrelated to immunodeficiency. Neonatal hypoparathyroidism occurs in almost all infants with DiGeorge anomaly, and hypocalcemic tetany is the most common presenting feature. Congenital heart disease, particularly truncus arteriosus and interrupted aortic arch, also are detected in the first few weeks of life.[97] Characteristic facial features include microstomia; hypertelorism; upturned nose; arched palate; posteriorly rotated and small, low-set ears with notched pinnae; and antimongoloid slant of the eyes (see Fig. 75–1). Hypothyroidism, esophageal atresia, tracheoesophageal fistula, and bifid uvula have been described.

Clinical manifestations may include predisposition to a wide variety of common and opportunistic infectious diseases. Recurrent or chronic pneumonias; chronic diarrhea; and candidiasis of the skin, mouth, or esophagus are common findings. Recurrent or severe herpesvirus infections (e.g., herpes simplex virus, cytomegalovirus); *P. carinii* pneumonia; and other opportunistic viral, fungal, protozoal, and mycobacterial infections occasionally are observed. Fatal graft-versus-host disease may occur if infants receive blood products containing viable lymphocytes during surgical correction of their heart defects. Only a minority of patients with DiGeorge syndrome have clinically significant immunodeficiency. Most patients develop adequate T-cell numbers and function by 1 year of age and do not have an increased incidence of opportunistic infections.[88] At Texas Children's Hospital, 20 percent of patients with DiGeorge syndrome and mild T-cell deficiency present with an increased incidence of sinopulmonary infections.

Pathogenesis

The syndrome is classified as a developmental field defect resulting from faulty embryologic development of the third and fourth branchial arches and their derivatives, including parathyroid glands, aortic arch structures, and thymus gland.[49] Partial deletions of chromosome 22 and 10 are found in more than 90 percent of patients. Working with mice models, three groups of investigators have reproduced all the characteristic features of DiGeorge syndrome with the hemizygous deletion of *tbx-1*, a gene within the chromosome 22 critical region.[45]

Diagnosis

Hypocalcemia, congenital heart disease, and characteristic facies may lead to suspicion of DiGeorge syndrome in the newborn period. A deletion in chromosome 22q is detected by FISH analysis. Lymphopenia is variable, and severe T-cell deficiency is a rare event. Determination of T-cell number and a proliferative response to mitogens discriminate between patients with or without immunodeficiency. Quantitative serum immunoglobulin determinations often are normal, but antibody responses after immunization usually are poor. Chest X-ray examination may show absence of the thymic shadow.

Treatment and Prognosis

Initial management should focus on the treatment of hypocalcemia and the surgical correction of congenital heart disease. Children with $CD4^+$ lymphopenia or evidence of cellular immune dysfunction should receive *P. carinii* pneumonia prophylaxis. Infections should be recognized early and treated promptly. Only irradiated, cytomegalovirus-negative blood products and inactivated vaccines should be administered. Severe immunodeficiency may require bone marrow or thymus transplantation.[29]

WISKOTT-ALDRICH SYNDROME

Clinical Features

Wiskott-Aldrich syndrome is an X-linked disorder classically characterized by recurrent infection, bleeding, and eczema. However, only a minority of patients has this classic triad of features, and some patients have infectious manifestations alone.[89] Patients commonly present with recurrent otitis media or pneumonia caused by encapsulated bacteria (e.g., *S. pneumoniae, H. influenzae*). Septicemia, meningitis, and other serious systemic bacterial infections also may occur. Common opportunistic pathogens include *Candida*, cytomegalovirus and other herpesviruses, and *P. carinii*.

Individuals with Wiskott-Aldrich syndrome often have depressed platelet counts. A unique feature is the presence of small platelets in approximately 50 percent of cases. As a consequence, gastrointestinal bleeding in the first months of life is a common presenting feature of Wiskott-Aldrich syndrome. Life-threatening gastrointestinal or intracranial hemorrhage also may occur. Eczematous lesions are generalized and prone to superinfection.

Patients with Wiskott-Aldrich syndrome have a high incidence of autoimmune disorders. Hemolytic anemia, a juvenile rheumatoid arthritis-like condition, and large- or small-vessel vasculitis have been reported. Some patients develop autoimmune thrombocytopenia as their disease progresses. Lymphoreticular malignancies, especially non-Hodgkin lymphomas involving the brain, are common occurrences.

Pathogenesis

The gene *(WASP)* that is mutated in individuals with Wiskott-Aldrich syndrome[27] maps to the X chromosome. This gene encodes a 501–amino-acid product that is expressed in lymphocytes and platelets and is involved in cytoskeletal organization and formation of pseudopodia. This defect results in failure to provide adequate T-cell help to B cells. T-cell morphologic and membrane abnormalities and signal transduction defects have been described.[62] X-linked thrombocytopenia without or with only mild immunodeficiency and eczema has been found to be caused by *WASP* mutations.[99]

Diagnosis

Wiskott-Aldrich syndrome should be suspected in a boy with thrombocytopenia and small platelets. Presence of eczema supports the diagnosis. Serum immunoglobulin concentrations are variable, with the most typical pattern showing normal IgG, increased IgA and IgE, and decreased IgM. Antibody responses to protein antigens (e.g., tetanus) usually are normal, but responses to polysaccharides (e.g., *S. pneumoniae*, *H. influenzae* type b, isohemagglutinins) are absent.

Patients with Wiskott-Aldrich syndrome are anergic on delayed hypersensitivity skin testing. They have near-normal numbers of circulating T cells, and in vitro proliferative responses to mitogens are normal. However, responses to specific antigens are decreased. Monocytes exhibit abnormal chemotaxis and poor antibody-dependent cellular cytotoxicity.

Treatment and Prognosis

Bone marrow transplantation results in normalization of cellular immunity, specific antibody responses, and platelet count. It is the definitive treatment of choice.

Splenectomy is indicated for severe thrombocytopenia and may improve quality of life. Daily antibiotic prophylaxis directed against *S. pneumoniae* and *H. influenzae* may be indicated for patients who have undergone splenectomy. Aspirin is contraindicated. Acute infections should be treated aggressively. IVIG is indicated for patients with recurrent bacterial infections, but high-dose IVIG only rarely improves platelet count.

The prognosis of Wiskott-Aldrich syndrome has improved in recent years, with some patients surviving to adulthood.[89] Infection, malignancy, and hemorrhage are the leading causes of death.

ATAXIA TELANGIECTASIA

Clinical Features

Ataxia telangiectasia is characterized by cerebellar ataxia, oculocutaneous telangiectases, variable immunodeficiency with frequent infections, and a high incidence of malignancy.[102] Neurologic signs and symptoms dominate the clinical picture. Ataxia usually becomes evident when the child is approximately 1 year of age. Progressive choreoathetosis, myoclonic jerking movements, and oculomotor abnormalities subsequently develop, resulting in severe disability. Telangiectases appear on the bulbar conjunctivae, usually in patients between 2 and 5 years of age (see Fig. 75–2). They subsequently appear on the nasal bridge, ears, and other areas of sun exposure or trauma. Other cutaneous manifestations include café-au-lait spots, vitiligo, and prematurely gray hair. Recurrent infections are a major feature of ataxia telangiectasia in most patients. Sinopulmonary infections predominate. Organisms commonly implicated include *S. pneumoniae* and *H. influenzae*. As many as 15 percent of patients with ataxia telangiectasia develop neoplasias. Non-Hodgkin lymphomas and leiomyomas occur most frequently. Carcinomas (especially of the stomach) occur commonly among adults with ataxia telangiectasia.

Pathogenesis

Ataxia telangiectasia is inherited in an autosomal recessive manner. The defective gene *(ATM)* responsible for the disorder has been identified and maps to chromosome 11.[47, 72, 90] One domain of the ATM protein resembles the phosphatidylinositol-3 kinases, which appear to be important in numerous cellular responses, including cytokine signaling. Another region of the protein is involved in DNA repair. Disease manifestations result from a major defect in one or more DNA repair mechanisms. Breakage and rearrangements of the T-cell receptor genes and immunoglobulin heavy-chain genes on chromosomes 7 and 14 may explain the observed immunodeficiency.

Diagnosis

A clinical diagnosis of ataxia telangiectasia is possible when the disease is fully manifested. However, laboratory studies usually are needed for early diagnosis. Increased serum alpha-fetoprotein concentrations are observed in essentially all patients older than 6 months of age. Most patients have deficiencies in serum IgA and IgE. Specific antibody responses usually decline as the patient ages. Most patients have serum IgM in a monomeric 7S form rather than the pentameric 19S molecule usually observed. Common manifestations of immunodeficiency include delayed hypersensitivity skin test anergy and decreased lymphocyte proliferative responses to mitogens and antigens.

Treatment and Prognosis

No specific treatment exists for ataxia telangiectasia. Infections should be treated aggressively with oral or parenteral antibiotics. Continuous prophylactic antibiotic therapy may be of benefit to individual patients. Replacement therapy with IVIG is reserved for patients with recurrent infections and abnormal specific antibody responses.

The clinical course and prognosis of ataxia telangiectasia are variable. Death from chronic pulmonary disease or malignancy occurs commonly.

SEVERE COMBINED IMMUNE DEFICIENCY

Clinical Features

Infants with SCID generally present during the first few months of life with recurrent infections.[86] In their first weeks of life, they may present with a rash produced by a graft-versus-host reaction induced by maternal lymphocytes. Recurrent pneumonias, other respiratory tract infections, and persistent oral and cutaneous candidiasis are common occurrences, as are chronic diarrhea and failure to thrive. Septicemia and other serious systemic bacterial infections also occur. Causative organisms include routine pathogens (e.g., *S. pneumoniae, H. influenzae* type b) and more unusual organisms, such as *P. aeruginosa*. Life-threatening opportunistic infections, including *P. carinii* pneumonia, sometimes occur early in infancy. Fatal Epstein-Barr virus–associated lymphocyte proliferative disease has been observed in bone marrow transplant recipients and untreated patients with SCID.[32]

Pathogenesis

The term *SCID* encompasses a heterogeneous group of disorders having in common defects that lead to profound immunodeficiency with failure of cellular and humoral immune function. Various types of SCID have been defined on the basis of enzymatic, genetic, and immunologic criteria (Table 75–7), including reticular dysgenesis, with impaired lymphoid, myeloid, and erythroid differentiation; absence of T-cell and B-cell differentiation; selective absence of T-cell differentiation; and purine metabolism defects (e.g., adenosine deaminase deficiency [ADA]). Autosomal and X-linked recessive inheritance patterns have been recognized. Individuals with X-linked SCID have a defect in the gamma chain of the interleukin-2 receptor, and it is the genetic defect of SCID patients most frequently identified.[16, 65] This same protein also is a

TABLE 75–7 ■ TYPES OF SEVERE COMBINED IMMUNODEFICIENCY

Type	Defect
T^-B^-	
Reticular dysgenesis	Stem cell defect
RAG1, RAG2 deficiency, Ommen syndrome	Deficient rearrangement of B- and T-cell receptor
T^-B^+	
X-linked SCID (common gamma-chain deficiency)	Deficient signaling for interleukins 2, 4, 7 and 15 (most frequent cause of SCID)
JAK3 deficiency	Deficient cytokine signaling
Interleukin-7 (IL-7) receptor deficiency	Deficient signaling for IL-7
Enzymatic defect	
Adenosin deaminase deficiency	Metabolite (dATP) toxicity to lymphocytes
Purine nucleoside phosphorylase deficiency	Metabolite (dGTP) toxicity to lymphocytes
Major histocompatibility complex deficiency	
MHC class I deficiency	Defect in transporter proteins TAP-1, TAP-2
MHC class II deficiency	Defects in transcription factors RFXAP, RFX5, RFXANK, and transactivator CIITA

functional component of the interleukin-4, interleukin-7, interleukin-9, and interleukin-15 receptors.[52, 65, 70] These findings help to explain why this defect has such a profound effect on lymphoid development and function.

Diagnosis

Infants with SCID typically lack palpable lymph nodes, visible tonsils, and radiographic evidence of a thymus gland. Lymphopenia often is identified.[86] Some patients have panhypogammaglobulinemia, whereas others have depressed concentrations of only one or two immunoglobulin isotypes. Antibody responses almost always are profoundly impaired or absent. Lymphocyte monoclonal phenotyping may reveal the presence of circulating mature B cells. Particularly in boys with X-linked SCID, B cells may account for all circulating lymphocytes.

Circulating T-cell counts are diminished (<10% of normal) in most patients with SCID. Delayed hypersensitivity skin test anergy is identified, and lymphocyte proliferative responses to mitogens and antigens are severely depressed. Testing for specific genetic defect may be pursued, and a genetic evaluation of immediate relatives for carrier status is recommended. Biochemical tests for ADA and purine nucleoside phosphorylase (PNP) levels and enzymatic activities are available in specialized laboratories.

Treatment and Prognosis

Stem cell transplantation is the treatment of choice for most patients with SCID. Prognosis is poor for patients without therapy. French investigators reported success in a gene therapy trial for X-linked SCID. Using autologous $CD34^+$ stem cells corrected with the gene, they were able to restore humoral and cellular immunity in three affected patients.[20] Enzyme replacement[42] and gene therapy[13] have been used for treatment of SCID resulting from ADA. Although genetically corrected lymphocytes were shown to persist in the periphery, attempts to withdraw exogenous ADA have been unsuccessful.[13]

MISCELLANEOUS CELLULAR IMMUNE DEFICIENCIES

Many other disorders of cellular immunity have been described. Four cellular immune deficiencies are particularly noteworthy. The X-linked lymphoproliferative syndrome represents a defect in control of Epstein-Barr virus infection. A candidate gene product, SAP, involved in the signal transduction of T cells has been identified. The absence of this protein affects the interaction of T and B cells, leading to an inability to control B-cell proliferation caused by Epstein-Barr virus infection.[36, 73] Patients may present with severe and often fatal infectious mononucleosis or with B-cell lymphoma.

Chronic mucocutaneous candidiasis is a condition characterized by chronic, severe candidal infection of mucous membranes, skin, and nails, often in association with autoimmune polyendocrinopathy.[1] T-cell numbers and function usually are normal, but most patients do not manifest delayed hypersensitivity skin test responses to *Candida*, and their lymphocytes fail to proliferate in response to *Candida* antigen in vitro.

Mutations in the interferon-γ receptor genes have been recognized in patients with severe infections caused by atypical mycobacteria.[46] Patients with a mutation in the interleukin-12 receptor β_2-chain gene or in the gene for interleukin-12 40-kd chain also show increased susceptibility to mycobacterial disease and disseminated nontuberculous mycobacterial infection.[4]

NEMO deficiency is a newly recognized primary immunodeficiency caused by specific missense mutations in the *IKKG* (also known as *NFκB* enhancing modulator, or NEMO) gene, located in the chromosome Xq28. NEMO participates in signal transduction mediated by *NFκB*. Most mutations in the NEMO gene are lethal for male fetuses, and female carriers of these mutations may present with incontinentia pigmenti. The surviving male patients with specific missense mutations present with anhydrotic ectodermal dysplasia, low IgG, low IgA, normal or increased IgM levels, and poor T-cell proliferative responses to mitogen and antigen stimuli.[80a, 103a]

Primary Complement Deficiencies

CLINICAL FEATURES

Three types of complement deficiency can cause increased susceptibility to infections: deficiency of opsonic activity of complement proteins, deficiency of the complement lytic proteins, and deficiency of the mannose-binding lectin pathway.[101] Patients with deficiencies of early-acting complement components (e.g., C3, C1, C4, C2) are particularly susceptible to infection with encapsulated bacteria, including *S. pneumoniae* and *H. influenzae*. *Neisseria meningitidis* is the most important bacterial pathogen observed in patients with deficiencies of terminal complement components (C5 through C9). Recurrent episodes of septicemia and meningitis are especially common occurrences.[31, 48, 69] Although patients with deficiencies of late-acting complement components are at increased risk for developing meningococcal septicemia and meningitis, they appear to suffer lower rates of morbidity and mortality than do immunologically normal individuals with systemic meningococcal infection. The frequency of primary complement deficiencies among patients with invasive meningococcal disease is approximately 5 to 10 percent,[31] although the likelihood of having complement deficiency increases dramatically (31 percent) among individuals who have had more than one episode of invasive disease.[60] A deficiency of opsonization in children with recurrent pyogenic infections and failure to thrive led to the recognition of the mannose-binding lectin pathway deficiencies. The clinical characteristic of these patients is the increased frequency of pyogenic infections.[87]

PATHOGENESIS

Various heterozygous and homozygous gene defects are responsible for the many distinct primary complement deficiencies. The particular bacteria that cause infection may indicate the missing component in host defense. For example, C3b, the major cleavage product of C3, is an important opsonic ligand that promotes ingestion and killing of bacteria. As a consequence, patients with C3 deficiency have increased susceptibility to infection with bacteria (e.g., *S. pneumoniae, H. influenzae*), for which opsonization is the primary mechanism of host defense.[31, 69] Individuals with deficiencies of C1, C4, or C2 also have increased susceptibility to these same encapsulated bacteria because these components are necessary for activation of C3 through the classic pathway. Activation of terminal complement components C5, C6, C7, C8, and C9 results in assembly of the membrane attack complex C5b-9, a multicomponent macromolecule capable of bactericidal activity. Only gram-negative bacteria are susceptible to this bactericidal effect. Infections in patients with deficiencies of terminal complement components are limited to gram-negative bacteria, such as *N. meningitidis*.[31, 69]

DIAGNOSIS

The screening test used most commonly for primary complement deficiencies is the CH_{50} assay, which reflects the activity of all numbered components of the classic complement pathway from C1 through C9. Specific immunochemical and functional testing can be performed for identifying the deficient component.

TREATMENT AND PROGNOSIS

No specific therapy exists for primary complement deficiencies. Meningococcal vaccine is recommended for children with terminal complement component deficiencies.[6] Antibiotic prophylaxis is of doubtful benefit.

Primary Phagocyte Deficiencies

The primary phagocyte deficiencies are a heterogeneous group of disorders having in common a propensity for frequent infections, resulting from a decreased number of phagocytic cells (e.g., neutropenia) or because of impaired adhesion, chemotaxis, opsonization and phagocytosis, or intracellular killing (Table 75–8). Infections resulting from quantitative or qualitative phagocyte deficiencies tend to be prolonged and recurrent, with a response to antibiotic therapy that is slower than expected. Common pathogens include *S. aureus*, *P. aeruginosa*, enteric gram-negative bacteria, and certain fungi (e.g., *Candida* spp., *Aspergillus* spp.).

QUANTITATIVE PHAGOCYTE ABNORMALITIES

Primary quantitative phagocyte deficiencies can be observed as solitary defects or in association with other disorders (e.g., Schwachman syndrome). Infantile agranulocytosis (i.e., Kostmann syndrome) is an autosomal recessive disorder characterized by arrest of granulocyte maturation, markedly decreased numbers of circulating granulocytes, and severe infection. The more benign familial granulocytopenia syndrome manifests at various ages from infancy to adulthood, usually with indolent infections of the skin and soft tissues.

TABLE 75–8 ■ PRIMARY PHAGOCYTE DEFICIENCIES

Quantitative Defects
Infantile agranulocytosis
Familial granulocytopenia
Cyclic neutropenia

Qualitative Defects

Adhesion defects
Leukocyte adhesion deficiency
  Type I, integrin deficiency
  Type II, E- and P- selectin ligand deficiency

Intracellular killing defects
Chronic granulomatous disease
Glucose-6-phosphate dehydrogenase deficiency
Myeloperoxidase deficiency
Chediak-Higashi syndrome
Griscelli syndrome

Cyclic neutropenia is an autosomal dominant defect of myelopoiesis in which periodic disappearance of granulocytes from the circulation occurs.[82] Early granulocyte precursors are present in the bone marrow during periods of granulocytopenia, suggesting transient maturation arrest. Periods of granulocytopenia usually last 5 to 7 days and occur at 14- to 35-day intervals. The length of the cycle generally is constant for any given individual. Fever, malaise, aphthous stomatitis, and skin and soft tissue infections often are observed during periods of granulocytopenia.

Some of the primary quantitative phagocyte deficiencies, particularly familial granulocytopenia and cyclic neutropenia, respond to therapy with recombinant granulocyte colony-stimulating factor.[34, 38, 44] Alternate-day corticosteroid therapy also has been used with some success in cyclic neutropenia.[103]

CHRONIC GRANULOMATOUS DISEASE

Clinical Features

The physical findings of patients with chronic granulomatous disease (CGD) are nonspecific. Lymphadenopathy and hepatomegaly are common occurrences, and patients may have aphthous stomatitis. Infections often begin during infancy and recur throughout the patient's life. Occasionally, patients have a relatively mild disease course and come to medical attention only during adolescence or adulthood.[75] Suppurative lymphadenitis, soft tissue abscesses, pneumonia, lung abscess, hepatic abscess, and osteomyelitis are especially common occurrences. Perirectal abscesses may occur during early infancy. Infections in patients with CGD may progress with few symptoms, and the erythrocyte sedimentation rate may be useful to detect active infection.

Patients with CGD generally have infections caused by catalase-positive bacteria and fungi.[22, 63] *S. aureus* accounts for almost one third of all infections of determined cause. *Nocardia*, *Serratia marcescens*, *Pseudomonas* spp., *Burkholderia cepacia*,[84] and certain enteric gram-negative bacilli also are common findings. *S. marcescens* osteomyelitis particularly is suggestive of the diagnosis of CGD. Fungi, especially *Aspergillus*, account for nearly one fifth of all defined infections in CGD patients (Fig. 75–5).

Patients with CGD often have poor wound healing. Granulomatous obstructive lesions of the urinary[2] and gastrointestinal[5] tracts have been reported. Corticosteroid therapy may be effective in relieving these sometimes life-threatening obstructions.[21] Granulomatous bowel involvement may resemble Crohn disease. Boys with X-linked CGD occasionally have the McLeod blood phenotype, which results in difficult transfusion cross-matching and the potential for hemolytic transfusion reactions.[15]

Pathogenesis

X-linked and autosomal recessive forms of CGD have been described. The various gene defects result in abnormalities of membrane or cytosolic components of the nicotinamide adenine dinucleotide phosphate oxidase complex system.[77] Despite the genetic heterogeneity, all individuals with CGD have in common the failure of the cellular respiratory burst, which ordinarily accompanies phagocytosis and various

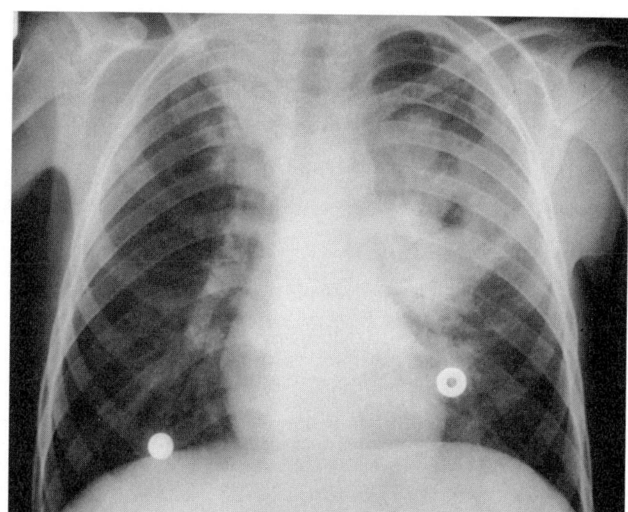

FIGURE 75–5 ■ Chest radiograph of a 10-year-old boy with chronic granulomatous disease shows a left-sided pulmonary infiltrate and cavitary lung lesion. Biopsy revealed an *Aspergillus fumigatus* infection.

soluble stimuli. As a consequence, oxygen-derived microbicidal factors are not formed, and intracellular killing of phagocytized microorganisms is severely impaired. Catalase-negative microorganisms are killed normally because hydrogen peroxide can accumulate within the phagocytic vacuole.

Diagnosis

The diagnosis of CGD usually is made with the NBT dye test.[10] Neutrophils are stimulated in the presence of NBT, a soluble yellow dye that is reduced by cellular superoxide to formazan, an insoluble blue precipitate. Neutrophils from normal individuals show 100 percent reduction of NBT, asymptomatic carriers show 20 to 90 percent reduction, and patients with CGD show essentially no dye reduction. In patients with mild forms of the disease, the NBT test result may be negative. More sensitive methods, including chemiluminescence and flow cytometry to measure hydrogen peroxide production, are recommended when the clinical suspicion is high.[76]

Treatment and Prognosis

Specific microbiologic diagnosis of infections should be established whenever possible. Empirical therapy is directed against the organisms known to be common causes of infection: *S. aureus*, *Pseudomonas*, and enteric gram-negative bacilli. Surgical drainage or débridement of sites of infection often is required. Anecdotal reports suggest beneficial effects of granulocyte transfusions in patients with CGD and serious bacterial or fungal infections.[22] Stem cell transplantation has been used successfully,[54] and gene therapy trials in humans are ongoing. Corrected granulocytes have been detectable more than 6 months after infusion of autologous stem cells carrying the normal gene.[56]

Antibiotic prophylaxis with cotrimoxazole reduces the frequency of bacterial infections in patients with CGD.[57] Itraconazole also may be effective for the prevention of *Aspergillus* infections.[64] Interferon-γ, given by subcutaneous injection three times weekly, reduces the incidence of serious infections in CGD by as much as two thirds without causing major deleterious side effects.[43] The prognosis of CGD has improved remarkably during the past several decades, and most patients survive to adulthood.

LEUKOCYTE ADHESION DEFICIENCY

Clinical Features

Patients with leukocyte adhesion deficiency (LAD) suffer severe and recurrent bacterial infections of the skin and soft tissues, mucosal surfaces, and gastrointestinal tract, often beginning during early infancy.[94] Common causative microorganisms include staphylococci and *Pseudomonas* spp. Moderate and severe phenotypes are recognized.[8] Infants with the severe phenotype may have delayed separation of the umbilical cord with omphalitis. Cutaneous infections may become necrotic, resembling ecthyma gangrenosum or pyoderma gangrenosum. Poor wound healing also is observed. Individuals surviving infancy typically develop severe gingivitis and periodontitis with progressive alveolar bone loss (see Fig. 75–3).

Marked granulocytosis is a hallmark of LAD. Circulating granulocyte counts may range between 15,000/mm^3 and 75,000/mm^3, even in the absence of infection, and counts of 100,000/mm^3 or greater are common findings during episodes of infection. Despite this granulocytosis, formation of pus is poor.

Pathogenesis

LAD type I is an autosomal recessive disorder that maps to chromosome 21. Neutrophils from individuals with LAD are defective in their expression of several surface glycoproteins known as the leukocyte integrin (CD11/CD18) complex. These molecules are critical for adhesion-dependent functions, and their absence is responsible for defects in leukocyte adherence, chemotaxis, and phagocytosis. The severity of infectious complications of LAD is related directly to the degree of CD18 expression.[8] Patients with the severe clinical phenotype have undetectable expression of CD11/CD18 complexes on their phagocytes, whereas individuals with the moderate phenotype generally have 2 to 8 percent expression.

A second form of LAD has been described in two patients with craniofacial dysmorphism, neurologic deficits, recurrent respiratory infections, and marked granulocytosis.[30, 35] Both individuals manifested the Bombay (hh) blood phenotype. Unlike those of patients with LAD type I, neutrophils from patients with LAD type II had normal surface expression of CD18. The molecular basis for the phagocyte dysfunction is a glycosylation defect influencing the expression of sialyl-Lewis X, a carbohydrate ligand for the endothelial adhesion molecules E-selectin and P-selectin.

Diagnosis

The diagnosis of LAD type I is made by flow cytometry using fluorescence-labeled monoclonal anti-CD11/CD18 antibody. In vitro studies reveal abnormalities of phagocyte adherence, chemotaxis, and phagocytosis. Individuals with LAD type II have similar phagocyte function abnormalities, with normal expression of CD18.

Treatment and Prognosis

Intercurrent bacterial infections in patients with LAD must be treated aggressively with prolonged courses of parenteral antibiotics. Although survival to adulthood is described, almost one half of affected individuals die before reaching

2 years of age. Bone marrow transplantation offers the best hope for long-term survival.[93]

OTHER PRIMARY PHAGOCYTE DEFICIENCIES

A variety of other defects of phagocyte chemotaxis, phagocytosis, and intracellular killing have been described. The Chediak-Higashi syndrome is a rare autosomal recessive disorder characterized by partial oculocutaneous albinism, rotatory nystagmus, and peripheral neuropathy. Affected individuals develop recurrent serious or life-threatening infections caused by a wide variety of bacteria. In the accelerated phase of the illness, hepatosplenomegaly, lymphadenopathy, lymphocytic infiltration of multiple body organs, and unexplained febrile illnesses are common occurrences. Giant granules are found in numerous different cell types, including leukocytes, in the body. Neutrophils exhibit defective chemotaxis and abnormal bactericidal activity.

Hyperimmunoglobulinemia E with impaired chemotaxis (i.e., Job syndrome) is characterized by markedly elevated serum IgE levels, eczema, recurrent staphylococcal abscesses, sinusitis, and otitis media. Coarse facial features are common findings. In addition to staphylococcal abscesses, recurrent pneumonia with bronchiectasis and pneumatoceles and mucocutaneous candidiasis are common occurrences. Other observed features include delay of shedding of primary dentition, recurrent bone fractures, scoliosis, and joint hyperextensibility. Patients also have a variable neutrophil chemotactic defect. A candidate gene locus has been identified in chromosome 4q.[19, 76]

REFERENCES

1. Ahonen, P., Myllarniemi, S., Sipila I., et al.: Clinical variations of autoimmune polyendocrinopathy-candidiasis-ectoderm dystrophy (APECED) in a series of 68 patients. N. Engl. J. Med. *322*:1829–1836, 1990.
2. Aliabadi, H., Gonzalez, R., and Quie, P. G.: Urinary tract disorders in patients with chronic granulomatous disease. N. Engl. J. Med. *321*:706–708, 1989.
3. Allen, R. C., Armitage, R. J., Conley, M. E., et al.: CD40 ligand gene defects responsible for X-linked hyper-IgM syndrome. Science *259*:990–993, 1993.
4. Altare F., Durandy, A., Lammas, D., et al.: Impairment of mycobacterial immunity in human interleukin-12 receptor deficiency. Science *280*:1432–1435, 1998.
5. Ament, M. E., and Ochs, H. D.: Gastrointestinal manifestations of chronic granulomatous disease. N. Engl. J. Med. *288*:382–387, 1973.
6. American Academy of Pediatrics: Meningococcal infections. *In* Pickering, L. K. (ed.): 2000 Red Book: Report of the Committee on Infectious Diseases. 25th ed. Elk Grove Village, IL, American Academy of Pediatrics, 2000, pp. 400–401.
7. American Academy of Pediatrics: Active and passive immunization. *In* Pickering, L. K. (ed.): 2000 Red Book: Report of the Committee on Infectious Diseases. 25th ed. Elk Grove Village, IL, American Academy of Pediatrics, 2000, pp. 56–60.
8. Anderson, D. C., Schmalstieg, F. C., Finegold, M. J., et al.: The severe and moderate phenotypes of heritable MAC-1, LFA-1, P150,95 deficiency: Their quantitative definition and relation to leukocyte dysfunction and clinical features. J. Infect. Dis. *152*:668–689, 1985.
9. Aruffo, A., Farrington, M., Hollenbaugh, D., et al.: The CD40 ligand, gp39, is defective in activated T cells from patients with X-linked hyper-IgM syndrome. Cell 72:291–300, 1993.
10. Axtell, R. A.: Evaluation of the patient with a possible phagocytic disorder. Hematol. Oncol. Clin. North Am. *2*:1–12, 1988.
11. Badger, G. F., Dingle, J. H., Feller, A. E., et al.: A study of illness in a group of Cleveland families. II. Incidence of the common respiratory diseases. Am. J. Hyg. *58*:31, 1953.
12. Bartlett, A. V., Moore, M., Gary, G. W., et al.: Diarrheal illness among infants and toddlers in day care centers. II. Comparison with day care homes and households. J. Pediatr. *107*:503–509, 1985.
13. Bordignon, C., Notarangelo, L. D., Nobili, N., et al.: Gene therapy in peripheral blood lymphocytes and bone marrow for adenosine deaminase immunodeficient patients. Science *270*:470–474, 1995.
14. Brimblecombe, F. S. W., Cruickshank, R., Masters, P. L., et al.: Family studies of respiratory infections. Br. Med. J. *1*:119, 1958.
15. Brzica, S. M., Jr., Pineda, A. A., Taswell, H. F., et al.: Chronic granulomatous disease and the McLeod phenotype: Successful treatment of infection with granulocyte transfusions resulting in subsequent hemolytic transfusion reaction. Mayo Clin. Proc. *52*:153–156, 1977.
16. Buckley, R. H.: Primary Immunodeficiency diseases due to defects in lymphocytes. N. Engl. J. Med. *343*:1313–1324, 2000.
17. Buckley, R. H., and Schiff, R. I.: The use of intravenous immune globulin in immunodeficiency diseases. N. Engl. J. Med. *325*:110–117, 1991.
18. Burks, A. W., Sampson, H. A., and Buckley, R. H.: Anaphylactic reactions after gamma globulin administration in patients with hypogammaglobulinemia: Detection of IgE antibodies to IgA. N. Engl. J. Med. *314*:560–564, 1986.
18a. Busse, P. J., Razvi, S., and Cunningham-Rundles, C.: Efficacy of intravenous immunoglobulin in the prevention of pneumonia in patients with common variable immunodeficiency. J. Allergy Clin. Immunol. *109*:1001–1004, 2002.
19. Candotti, F. The potential for therapy of immune disorders with gene therapy. Pediatr. Clin. North Am. *47*:1389–1407, 2000.
20. Cavazzano-Calvo, M., Hacein-Bey, B., deSaint Basile, G., et al.: Gene therapy of human severe combined immunodeficiency (SCID) X-l disease. Science *288*:669–673, 2000.
21. Chin, T. W., Stiehm, E. R., Falloon, J., et al.: Corticosteroids in treatment of obstructive lesions of chronic granulomatous disease. J. Pediatr. *111*:349–352, 1987.
22. Cohen, M. S., Isturiz, R. E., Malech, H. L., et al.: Fungal infection in chronic granulomatous disease: The importance of the phagocyte in defense against fungi. Am. J. Med. *71*:59–66, 1981.
22a. Conley, M. E., and Howard, V.: Clinical findings leading to the diagnosis of X-linked agammaglobulinemia. J. Pediatr. *141*:566–571, 2002.
23. Conley, M. E., Larche, M., Bonagura, V. R., et al.: Hyper IgM syndrome associated with defective CD40-mediated B cell activation. J. Clin. Invest. *94*:1404–1409, 1994.
24. Conley, M. E., Park, C. L., and Douglas, S. D.: Childhood common variable immunodeficiency with autoimmune disease. J. Pediatr. *108*:915–922, 1986.
25. Cunningham-Rundles, C., Bodian, C.: Common Variable Immunodeficiency: Clinical and Immunological features of 248 patients. Clin. Immunol. *92*:34–38, 1999.
26. Cunningham-Rundles, C., Siegal, F. P., Cunningham-Rundles, S., et al.: Incidence of cancer in 98 patients with common varied immunodeficiency. J. Clin. Immunol. *7*:294–299, 1987.
27. Derry, J. M. J., Ochs, H. D., and Francke, U.: Isolation of a novel gene mutated in Wiskott-Aldrich syndrome. Cell *78*:635–644, 1994.
28. Dressler, F., Peter, H. H., Muller, W., et al.: Transient hypogammaglobulinemia of infancy. Acta Paediatr. Scand. *78*:767–774, 1989.
29. Driscoll, D. A., and Sullivan, K. E.: DiGeorge syndrome: A chromosome 22q11.2 deletion syndrome. *In* Ochs, H. D. (ed.): Primary Immunodeficiency Diseases. New York, Oxford University Press, 1999, pp. 198–208.
30. Etzioni, A., Frydman, M., Pollack, S., et al.: Brief report: Recurrent severe infections caused by a novel leukocyte adhesion deficiency. N. Engl. J. Med. *327*:1789–1792, 1992.
31. Figueroa, J. E., and Densen, P.: Infectious diseases associated with complement deficiencies. Clin. Microbiol. Rev. *4*:359–395, 1991.
32. Filipovich, A. H., Mathur, A., Kamat, D., et al.: Lymphoproliferative disorders and other tumors complicating immunodeficiencies. Immunodeficiency *5*:91–112, 1994.
33. Fox, J. P., Hall, C. E., Cooney, M. K., et al.: The Seattle virus watch. II. Objectives, study population and its observation, data processing and summary of illnesses. Am. J. Epidemiol. *96*:270–285, 1972.
34. Frampton, J. E., Lee, C. R., and Faulds, D.: Filgrastim: A review of its pharmacological properties and therapeutic efficacy in neutropenia. Drugs *48*:731–760, 1994.
35. Frydman, M., Etzioni, A., Eidlitz-Markus, T., et al.: Rambam-Hasharon syndrome of psychomotor retardation, short stature, defective neutrophil motility, and Bombay phenotype. Am. J. Med. Genet. *44*:297–302, 1992.
36. Grierson, H., and Purtilo, D. T.: Epstein-Barr virus infections in males with the X-linked proliferative syndrome. Ann. Intern. Med. *106*:538–545, 1987.
37. Guerrant, R. L., Lohr, J. A., and Williams, E. K.: Acute infectious diarrhea. I. Epidemiology, etiology, and pathogenesis. Pediatr. Infect. Dis. *5*:353–359, 1986.
38. Hammond, W. P., IV, Price, T. H., Souza, L. M., et al.: Treatment of cyclic neutropenia with granulocyte colony-stimulating factor. N. Engl. J. Med. *320*:1306–1311, 1989.
39. Hanson, L. A., Soderstrom, R., Nilssen, D. E., et al.: IgG subclass deficiency with or without IgA deficiency. Clin. Immunol. Immunopathol. *61*:S70–S77, 1991.
40. Hausser, C., Virelizier, J. L., Buriot, D., et al.: Common variable hypogammaglobulinemia in children: Clinical and immunologic observations in 30 patients. Am. J. Dis. Child. *137*:833–837, 1983.

41. Hermaszewski, R. A., and Webster, A. D.: Primary hypogammaglobulinemia: A survey of clinical manifestations and complications. Q. J. Med. *86*:31–42, 1993.
42. Hershfield, M. S.: Adenosine deaminase deficiency: Clinical expression, molecular basis and therapy. Semin. Hematol. *35*:291–297, 1998.
43. International Chronic Granulomatous Disease Cooperative Study Group: A controlled trial of interferon gamma to prevent infection in chronic granulomatous disease. N. Engl. J. Med. *324*:509–516, 1991.
44. Jayabose, S., Tugal, O., Sandoval, C., et al.: Recombinant human granulocyte colony stimulating factor in cyclic neutropenia: Use of a new 3-day-a-week regimen. Am. J. Pediatr. Hematol. Oncol. *16*:338–340, 1994.
45. Jerome, L. A., and Papaioanouve, V. E.: DiGeorge syndrome phenotype in mice mutant for the T-box gene *tbx1*. Nat. Genet. *27*:286–291, 2001.
46. Jouanguy, E., Lanhamedi-Cherradi, S., Lammas, D., et al.: A human IFNGR1 small deletion hotspot associated with dominant susceptibility to mycobacterial infection. Nat. Genet *21*:370–380, 1999.
47. Kapp, L. N., Painter, R. B., Yu, L. C., et al.: Cloning of a candidate gene for ataxia-telangiectasia group D. Am. J. Hum. Genet. *51*:45–54, 1992.
48. Kline, M. W.: Recurrent bacterial meningitis. Antibiot. Chemother. *45*:254–261, 1992.
49. Lammer, E. J., and Opitz, J. M.: The DiGeorge anomaly as a developmental field defect. Am. J. Med. Genet. *2*(Suppl.):113–127, 1986.
50. Lederman, H. M., and Winkelstein, J. A.: X-linked agammaglobulinemia: An analysis of 96 patients. Medicine (Baltimore). *64*:145–156, 1985.
51. Lee, A. H., Levinson, A. I., and Schumacher, H. R.: Hypogammaglobulinemia and rheumatic disease. Semin. Arthritis Rheum. *22*:252–264, 1993.
52. Leonard, W. J., Noguchi, I. M., Russell, S. M., et al.: The molecular basis of X-linked severe combined immunodeficiency: The role of interleukin-2 receptor gamma chain is a common gamma chain. Immunol. Rev. *138*:61–64, 1994.
53. Levy, J., Espanol-Boren, T., Thomas, C., et al.: The clinical spectrum of X-linked hyper-IgM syndrome. J. Pediatr. *131*:47–54, 1997.
54. Leung, T., Chik, K., Li, C., et al.: Bone marrow transplantation for chronic granulomatous disease: Long-term follow up and review of the literature. Bone Marrow Transplant. *24*:567–570, 1999.
55. Liese, J. G., Wintergerst, J., Tympner, K. D., et al.: High- vs low-dose immunoglobulin therapy in the long-term treatment of X-linked agammaglobulinemia. Am. J. Dis. Child. *146*:335–339, 1992.
56. Malech, H. L., Maples, P. B., Whitting-Theobald, N., et al.: Prolonged production of NADPH oxidase-corrected granulocytes after gene therapy of chronic granulomatous disease. Proc. Natl. Acad Sci. U. S. A. *94*:12133–12138, 1997.
57. Margolis, D. M., Melnick, D. A., Alling, D. W., et al.: Trimethoprim-sulfamethoxazole prophylaxis in the management of chronic granulomatous disease. J. Infect. Dis. *162*:723–726, 1990.
58. McGeady, S. J.: Transient hypogammaglobulinemia of infancy: Need to reconsider name and definition. J. Pediatr. *110*:47–50, 1987.
59. McKinney, R. E., Jr., Katz, S. L., and Wilfert, C. M.: Chronic enteroviral meningoencephalitis in agammaglobulinemic patients. Rev. Infect. Dis. *9*:334–356, 1987.
60. Merino, J., Rodriguez-Valverde, V., Lamelas, J. A., et al.: Prevalence of deficits of complement components in patients with recurrent meningococcal infections. J. Infect. Dis. *148*:331, 1983.
61. Minegishi, Y., Lavoie, A., Cunningham-Rundles, C., et al.: Mutations in activation-induced cytidine deaminase in patients with hyper IgM syndrome. Clin. Immunol. *97*:203–210, 2000.
62. Molina, I. J., Kenney, D. M., Rosen, F. S., et al.: T cell lines characterize events in the pathogenesis of the Wiskott-Aldrich syndrome. J. Exp. Med. *176*:867–874, 1992.
63. Mouy, R., Fischer, A., Vilmer, E., et al.: Incidence, severity, and prevention of infections in chronic granulomatous disease. J. Pediatr. *114*:555–560, 1989.
64. Mouy, R., Veber, F., Blanche, S., et al.: Long-term itraconazole prophylaxis against *Aspergillus* infections in thirty-two patients with chronic granulomatous disease. J. Pediatr. *125*:998–1003, 1994.
65. Noguchi, M., Nakamura, Y., Russell, S. M., et al.: Interleukin-2 receptor gamma chain: A functional component of the interleukin-7 receptor. Science *262*:1877–1880, 1993.
66. Notarangelo, L. D., Duse, M., and Ugazio, A. G.: Immunodeficiency with hyper-IgM (HIM). Immunodefic. Rev. *3*:101–121, 1992.
67. Ochs, H. D., Ament, M. E., and Davis, S. D.: Giardiasis with malabsorption in X-linked agammaglobulinemia. N. Engl. J. Med. *287*:341–342, 1972.
68. Oxelius, V. A., Laurell, A. B., Lindquist, B., et al.: IgG subclasses in selective IgA deficiency: Importance of IgG2-IgA deficiency. N. Engl. J. Med. *302*:1476–1477, 1981.
69. Ross, S. C., and Densen, P.: Complement deficiency states and infection: Epidemiology, pathogenesis and consequences of neisserial and other infections in an immune deficiency. Medicine (Baltimore) *63*:243–273, 1984.
70. Russell, S. M., Keegan, A. D., Harada, N., et al.: Interleukin-2 receptor gamma chain: A functional component of the interleukin-4 receptor. Science *262*:1880–1883, 1993.
71. Saulsbury, F. T., Winkelstein, J. A., and Yolken, R. H.: Chronic rotavirus infection in immunodeficiency. J. Pediatr. *97*:61–65, 1980.
72. Savitsky, K., Bar-Shira, A., Gilad, S., et al.: A single ataxia-telangiectasia gene with a product similar to PI-3 kinase. Science *268*:1749–1753, 1995.
73. Sayos, J., Wu, C., Morra, M., et al.: The X-linked lymphoproliferative disease gene product SAP regulates signal induced through the coreceptor SLAM. Nature *395*:462–469, 1998.
74. Schaffer, F. M., Monteiro, R. C., Volanakis, J. E., et al.: IgA deficiency. Immunodefic. Rev. *3*:15–44, 1991.
75. Schapiro, B. L., Newburger, P. E., Klempner, M. S., et al.: Chronic granulomatous disease presenting in a 69-year-old man. N. Engl. J. Med. *325*:1786–1790, 1991.
76. Segal, B. H., Holland, H. M.: Primary phagocytic disorders of childhood. Pediatr. Clin. North Am. *47*:1311–1338, 2000.
77. Segal, B. H., Leto, T. L., Gallin J. I., et al.: Genetic, biochemical and clinical features of chronic granulomatous disease. Medicine (Baltimore) *79*:170–200, 2000.
78. Shackelford, P. G., Granoff, D. M., Polmar, S. H., et al.: Subnormal serum concentrations of IgG2 in children with frequent infections associated with varied patterns of immunologic dysfunction. J. Pediatr. *116*:529–538, 1990.
79. Shackelford, P. G., Polmar, S. H., Mayus, J. L., et al.: Spectrum of IgG2 subclass deficiency in children with recurrent infections: Prospective study. J. Pediatr. *108*:647–653, 1986.
80. Siegel, S. R., Siegel, B., Sokoloff, B. Z., et al.: Urinary tract infection in infants and preschool children. Am. J. Dis. Child. *134*:369–372, 1980.
80a. Smahi, A., Courtois, G., Vabres, P., et al.: Genomic rearrangement in NEMO impairs NF-kappaB activation and is a cause of incontinentia pigmenti. The International Incontinentia Pigmenti (IP) Consortium. Nature *405*:466–472, 2000.
81. Sneller, M. C., Strober, W., Eisenstein, E., et al.: New insights into common variable immunodeficiency. Ann. Intern. Med. *118*:720–730, 1993.
82. Souid, A. K.: Congenital cyclic neutropenia. Clin. Pediatr. *34*:151–155, 1995.
83. Spector, B. D., Perry, G. S., III, and Kersey, J. H.: Genetically determined immunodeficiency disease (GDID) and malignancy: Report from the Immunodeficiency–Cancer Registry. Clin. Immunol. Immunopathol. *11*:12–29, 1978.
84. Speert, D. P., Bond, M., Woodman, R. C., et al.: Infection with *Pseudomonas cepacia* in chronic granulomatous disease: Role of nonoxidative killing by neutrophils in host defense. J. Infect. Dis. *170*: 1524–1531, 1994.
85. Spickett, G. P., Webster, A. D., and Farrant, J.: Cellular abnormalities in common variable immunodeficiency. Immunodefic. Rev. *2*:199–219, 1990.
86. Stephan, J. L., Vlekova, V., Le Deist, F., et al.: Severe combined immunodeficiency: A retrospective single-center study of clinical presentation and outcome in 117 cases. J. Pediatr. *123*:564–572, 1993.
87. Summerfield, J. A., Sumya, M., Levin, M., and Turner, M. W.: Association of mutations in mannose binding protein gene with childhood infection in consecutive hospital series. B. M. J. *314*:1229–1232, 1997.
88. Sullivan, K. E., McDonald-McGinn, D., Driscoll, D. A., et al.: Longitudinal analysis of lymphocyte function and numbers in the first year of life in chromosome 22q11.2 deletion syndrome (DiGeorge syndrome/ velocardiofacial syndrome). Clin. Diagn. Lab. Immunol. *6*:906–911, 1999.
89. Sullivan, K. E., Mullen, C. A., Blaese, R. M., et al.: A multi-institutional survey of the Wiskott-Aldrich syndrome. J. Pediatr. *125*:876–885, 1994.
90. Taylor, A. M., Jaspers, N. G., and Gatti, R. A.: Fifth International Workshop on Ataxia-Telangiectasia. Cancer Res. *53*:438–441, 1993.
91. Teele, D. W., Klein, J. O., Rosner, B., et al.: Epidemiology of otitis media during the first seven years of life in children in greater Boston: A prospective cohort study. J. Infect. Dis. *160*:83–94, 1989.
92. Thomas, C., deSaint Basile, G., Le Deist, F., et al.: Correction of X-linked hyper IgM syndrome by allogeneic bone marrow transplantation. N. Engl. J. Med. *333*:426–429, 1995.
93. Thomas, C., Le Deist, F., Cavazzana-Calvo, M., et al.: Results of allogeneic bone marrow transplantation in patients with leukocyte adhesion deficiency. Blood *86*:1629–1635, 1995.
94. Todd, R. F., III, and Freyer, D. R.: The CD11/18 leukocyte glycoprotein deficiency. Hematol. Oncol. Clin. North Am. *2*:13–31, 1988.
95. Tsukada, S., Saffran, D. C., Rawlings, D. J., et al.: Deficient expression of a B cell cytoplasmic tyrosine kinase in human X-linked agammaglobulinemia. Cell *72*:279–290, 1993.
96. Umetsu, D. T., Ambrosino, D. M., Quinti, I., et al.: Recurrent sinopulmonary infection and impaired antibody response to bacterial capsular polysaccharide antigen in children with selective IgG-subclass deficiency. N. Engl. J. Med. *313*:1247–1251, 1985.
97. Van Mierop, L. H., and Kutsche, L. M.: Cardiovascular anomalies in DiGeorge syndrome and importance of neural crest as a possible pathogenetic factor. Am. J. Cardiol. *58*:133–137, 1986.
98. Vetrie, D., Vorechovsky, I., Sideras, P., et al.: The gene involved in X-linked agammaglobulinemia is a member of the *src* family of protein-tyrosine kinases. Nature *316*:226–233, 1993.
99. Villa, A., Notarangelo, L., Mach, P., et al.: X-linked thrombocytopenia and Wiskott-Aldrich syndrome are allelic diseases with mutations in the WASP gene. Nat Genet. *9*:414–417, 1995.

100. Volanakis, J. E., Zhu, Z. B., Schaffer, F. M., et al.: Major histocompatibility complex class III genes and susceptibility to immunoglobulin A deficiency and common variable immunodeficiency. J. Clin. Invest. *89*:1914–1922, 1992.
101. Walport, M. J.: Complement. N. Engl. J. Med. *344*:1058–1066, 2001.
102. Woods, C. G., and Taylor, A. M.: Ataxia-telangiectasia in the British Isles: The clinical and laboratory features of 70 affected individuals. Q. J. Med. *82*:169–179, 1992.
103. Wright, D. G., Fauci, A. S., Dale, D. C., et al.: Correction of human cyclic neutropenia and prednisolone. N. Engl. J. Med. *298*:295–300, 1978.
103a. Zonana, J., Elder, M. E., Schneider, L. C., et al.: A novel X-linked disorder of immune deficiency and hypohidrotic ectodermal dysplasia is allelic to incontinentia pigmenti and due to mutations in IKK-gamma (NEMO). Am. J. Hum. Genet. *67*:1555–1562, 2000.

Opportunistic Infections in Hematopoietic Stem Cell Transplantation

JORGE LUJÁN-ZILBERMANN ■ CHRISTIAN C. PATRICK

Hematopoietic stem cell transplantation (HSCT) involves the infusion of stem cells from a donor to a recipient who has received a special conditioning regimen for the procedure. In recent years, the term HSCT has replaced the traditional term bone marrow transplantation (BMT) because hematopoietic stem cells can be obtained from bone marrow, umbilical cord blood, and peripheral blood.[70, 93] HSCT has become the standard treatment for many patients with hematologic malignancies and solid tumors as well as nonmalignant conditions, such as primary immunodeficiencies, hemoglobinopathies, bone marrow failure syndromes, and a variety of genetic conditions, including inherited metabolic disorders.[5, 16, 48, 58, 60, 73, 107, 127]

HSCT can be classified as syngeneic, autologous, or allogeneic depending on the genetic match of the donor to the recipient of the stem cells. Syngeneic HSCT is the transplantation of stem cells from an identical twin. In an autologous HSCT, the patient's own stem cells harvested before ablative chemotherapy are transplanted. Autologous HSCTs are used for patients who require marrow ablative chemotherapy to treat the underlying malignancy but have a healthy bone marrow.[79] Allogeneic HSCT involves the transplantation of stem cells from a human leukocyte antigen (HLA)-matched sibling, an HLA-partially matched family member, or an HLA-matched unrelated donor.[79] In general, engraftment is faster for syngeneic and autologous transplantations when a total HLA match between the recipient and the donor exists. Allogeneic HSCT has a higher chance of success when completely matched HLA sibling donors are used.

Infectious complications occurring after HSCT are somewhat predictable based on the underlying primary disease and the acquired immunodeficiencies that occur after the transplantation.[105] Patients undergoing HSCT are at increased risk for developing infectious complications secondary to the acquired immunodeficiencies that occur after the procedure or secondary to medications (e.g., cyclosporine, steroids used to treat complications of the transplantation).[79] Infections are a major cause of morbidity and mortality and represent the most significant barrier to both immediate and long-term survival after HSCT.

The recovery of immune function after HSCT is a gradual process that takes place over the course of several months to years. Immune reconstitution after HSCT follows the normal pattern of immune ontogeny, developing from immature to mature immune functions. The general early immune mechanisms, such as phagocytic and cytotoxic functions, recover first, usually by post-transplantation day 100, but the specialized functions of T and B lymphocytes may remain impaired for a year or even longer.[26, 96]

These immune defects and the gradual recovery of host defenses cause infections to occur in three predictable time periods, as shown in Table 76–1. The first or pre-engraftment period begins with the onset of the conditioning regimen and continues until engraftment, about 30 days after transplantation. This phase is characterized by profound neutropenia that lasts 3 to 4 weeks. Treatment with colony-stimulating factors can shorten the duration of this phase.[69] The middle or early engraftment period starts after resolution of the neutropenia with transplant engraftment and lasts until approximately 100 days after HSCT. The last or late engraftment period starts about 100 days after the transplantation and is associated with selected deficits in both cellular and humoral immune responses and reticuloendothelial function.[105]

Epidemiology

Several risk factors place the HSCT recipient at increased risk for acquiring infectious complications; however, significant differences in the relative risks for infection after HSCT exist, depending on the type of transplantation. The degree of immunosuppression is less with autologous HSCT because no risk for graft-versus-host disease (GVHD) exists. Preventive therapy against GVHD, which can include cyclosporine, methotrexate, steroids, and purging of T cells from the graft, increases the risk for development of infection. All these agents enhance the infection rate by depressing the cell-mediated immune response and, in the case of methotrexate, by disrupting the mucosal barriers. The presence of GVHD increases the infection rate because it is associated with a delay in the return of normal immune function, prolonged immunodeficiency, and ulceration of the gastrointestinal tract.[5, 38] The conditioning regimens for most allogeneic HSCT

TABLE 76–1 ■ TEMPORAL ASSOCIATION OF INFECTIONS AND PREDOMINANT ETIOLOGIC AGENTS AFTER HSCT

Phase	Predominant Host Defect	Bacterial Infections	Fungal Infections	Viral Infections
Pre-engraftment (0–30 days)	Neutropenia	*Staphylococcus aureus* *Staphylococcus epidermidis* Viridans streptococci *Pseudomonas aeruginosa* Enterobacteriaceae *Escherichia coli* *Klebsiella pneumoniae* *Enterobacter* species	*Candida* species *Aspergillus* species	Herpes simplex virus
Early engraftment (31–100 days)	Cytotoxic and phagocytic functions	*S. aureus* *S. epidermidis* Viridans streptococci *P. aeruginosa* Enterobacteriaceae	*Candida* species *Aspergillus* species *Pneumocystis jiroveci*	Cytomegalovirus Adenovirus Respiratory viruses
Late engraftment (>100 days)	Cellular and humoral immunity	*Haemophilus influenzae* *Streptococcus pneumoniae*	*Candida* species	Varicella-zoster virus

patients include concomitant total-body irradiation that compromises the immune system and can cause severe mucositis. Diarrhea also is a very frequent complication in the first week after irradiation.

The serologic statuses of the donor and the recipient also are important because many infections in transplant recipients are caused by reactivation of previous infections. Serologic evaluation for cytomegalovirus (CMV), Epstein-Barr virus (EBV), hepatitis B virus (HBV), hepatitis C virus, human immunodeficiency virus, and toxoplasmosis should be performed for both donor and recipient before the transplantation[79, 116] (Table 76–2).

All HSCT recipients have a central venous catheter in place for administration of blood products, nutritional supplements, and medications, adding a potential site for infection.[98] The presence of other indwelling medical devices, such as a Foley catheter or a cerebrospinal fluid shunt, is associated with increased risk for development of infection.

Knowledge of the epidemiology of the hospital and the transplantation unit allows an assessment of risk for acquiring environmental organisms. Infection rates can be reduced by preventive strategies that inhibit aerosolization of organisms, such as the use of laminar air-flow rooms or high-efficiency particulate air (HEPA)-filtered rooms.

Clinical Manifestations and Approach

The clinical approach to infections in the patient with HSCT is based on understanding the type of transplantation and the natural history of the infections that can occur during each of the different at-risk periods based on the immune reconstitution after transplantation. This knowledge provides the framework for matching possible etiologic agents with the clinical syndromes at presentation.[105]

TABLE 76–2 ■ DIAGNOSTIC EVALUATIONS FOR PATIENTS UNDERGOING HSCT

Complete blood count with differential
Serology for Epstein-Barr virus, cytomegalovirus, human immunodeficiency virus, hepatitis B virus surface antigen, hepatitis C virus, rapid plasma reagin, and toxoplasmosis
Liver function tests
Renal function tests
Stool for ova and parasites
Skin testing with Mantoux purified protein derivative
Posteroanterior and lateral chest x-rays

INFECTIONS DURING THE PRE-ENGRAFTMENT PHASE

The pre-engraftment phase begins with the conditioning regimen, usually 7 to 10 days before the time of stem cell infusion, and continues to stem cell engraftment, usually 3 to 4 weeks after transplantation. A profound neutropenia is the major immune defect present during this stage of transplantation.[105]

Bacterial Infections

During the neutropenic period, bacterial infections are the most frequent infectious complication in HSCT recipients. The patients are at high risk for acquiring bacterial infection, similar to that of patients with cancer who develop chemotherapy-induced neutropenia.[22] Most infections result from invasion of the patient's endogenous flora colonizing the oral mucosa, the gastrointestinal tract, or the skin.[89]

Catheter-related infections are common occurrences, and the spectrum of etiologic agents is similar to that in other chemotherapy-induced neutropenic patients. Among the gram-positive organisms, *Staphylococcus aureus* and *Staphylococcus epidermidis* are the most frequently isolated, with other gram-positive bacteria, such as *Stomatococcus mucilaginosus,* also implicated.[55] Infections with *S. epidermidis* and other coagulase-negative staphylococci continue to occur as long as the central venous catheter remains in place.[27, 34, 98] Infections with viridans streptococci are associated with mucositis after chemotherapy and antibiotic prophylaxis with quinolones and in some series have replaced *Staphylococcus* spp. as the most common cause of bacteremia.[13, 22, 103, 114, 121]

Gram-negative rod infections occur after mucosal damage with bacterial translocation from the intestinal lumen into the bloodstream. The organisms most frequently involved from this group are *Pseudomonas aeruginosa* and Enterobacteriaceae, including *Escherichia coli, Klebsiella* spp., and *Enterobacter* spp., although other gram-negative organisms have been identified. *Enterobacter* spp. are especially worrisome because they display a high rate of an inducible β-lactamase, limiting the effect of front-line drugs such as the cephalosporins.

Fungal Infections

Fungal infections, predominantly with *Candida* spp., occur frequently in this phase.[67] *Aspergillus* spp. represent the second most common fungal infection during this time.[61] Less frequently, infections occur with the agents of mucormycosis (*Mucor, Rhizopus,* and *Absidia* spp.), *Trichosporon* spp., *Fusarium* spp., and other saprophytic fungi.[123] Fungal infections usually occur after a period of antibiotic therapy and correlate with the degree and duration of neutropenia.[46, 87, 88, 124]

Candida spp. colonizing the gastrointestinal tract disseminate after mucosal injury, usually between 2 and 4 weeks after the transplantation. The seeding of the portal circulation leads to hepatosplenic candidiasis manifested as fever and hepatosplenomegaly. Ultrasound or computed tomography reveals multiple round defects in the liver and spleen ("bull's eye" lesions). Candidal infections also can involve the lungs, kidneys, and the central nervous system, leading to meningitis or brain abscess.[67] Although *Candida albicans* is the most frequent *Candida* spp. causing candidemia, *Candida tropicalis* may be more aggressive.[46, 124] Other *Candida* spp., including *Candida krusei,* have emerged as pathogens because of their resistance to the antifungal agent fluconazole that is used as prophylaxis.[59, 131]

Aspergillus spp., *Fusarium* spp., and the agents of mucormycosis have the respiratory tract as their portal of entry and usually are associated with sinopulmonary disease and dissemination to other sites, including the central nervous system.[1, 15, 30, 41, 87, 88]

Viral Infections

Herpes simplex virus (HSV) infection usually is the result of reactivation in seropositive patients undergoing HSCT and is one of the most common viral infections in patients after HSCT.[82, 128] Reactivation generally occurs with oral and genital lesions. Oral lesions can be difficult to diagnose because lip involvement rarely occurs and mucosal ulcers are similar to the mucositis caused by the conditioning regimen. HSV reactivation can be complicated by esophagitis, pneumonitis, and bacterial superinfection of skin lesions. Mortality is a rare event, and rapid diagnosis allows for timely administration of therapy. The use of acyclovir prophylaxis in HSV-seropositive patients has decreased the incidence of this complication.[37]

Diarrhea after transplantation is related mostly to noninfectious causes, especially total-body irradiation, GVHD, and chemotherapy-related toxicity.[24, 94] Viral gastroenteritis can occur throughout the transplant period. Etiologic agents to consider are rotavirus, coxsackievirus, and enteric adenovirus.[24, 39, 51] Generally, the enteric viruses are seasonal in their presentation. The course of these enteric infections can be very prolonged, especially with the adenoviruses. Approximately 5 percent of HSCT recipients develop adenovirus infection that can become latent in lymphoid and renal tissues.[24]

Hemorrhagic cystitis can occur throughout the transplantation period. This condition has several infectious and noninfectious etiologies[104] (Table 76–3). Chemotherapy-induced cystitis (e.g., high-dose cyclophosphamide) occurs soon after the conditioning regimen. Later in the transplantation period, GVHD can be a contributing cause. The most common infectious etiologies of hemorrhagic cystitis are adenovirus or the polyomaviruses BK or JC.[2, 21, 57] Adenoviral infections can be systemic with associated pneumonitis, hepatitis, and renal insufficiency.[62] Allogeneic transplantation and the use of total-body irradiation are risk factors for adenovirus infection.[51] Shedding of polyomaviruses in the urine may occur in as many as 44 percent of HSCT patients without any clinical symptoms. HSV and CMV also have been associated with hemorrhagic cystitis.

TABLE 76–3 ■ DIFFERENTIAL DIAGNOSIS OF HEMORRHAGIC CYSTITIS AFTER HSCT

Infectious Etiologies
Bacterial
Mainly gram-negative enteric rods associated with urinary tract infection
Fungal
Urinary tract infection
Fungus ball
Viral
Adenovirus
Polyomaviruses BK and JC
Herpesviruses: cytomegalovirus, herpes simplex virus
Noninfectious Etiologies
Chemotherapy induced (e.g., cyclophosphamide)
Graft-versus-host disease
Mechanical trauma from Foley catheter

INFECTIONS DURING THE EARLY ENGRAFTMENT PHASE

The risk for infection decreases after stem cell engraftment occurs. However, severe abnormalities in host defense still exist. The general early immune functions, such as phagocytic and cytotoxic cells, recover first, followed by the cellular and humoral arms of the immune system.[96, 105] Another factor that influences immunologic recovery is the presence of acute GVHD.

Bacterial Infections

Bacterial infections continue to occur in this phase as a complication of indwelling central venous catheters or as a complication of acute GVHD, with skin and gastrointestinal tract breakdown. The same organisms that cause illness during the neutropenic phase can produce illness in this phase.[13, 34]

Fungal Infections

Fungal infections still occur during this phase, with *Candida* spp. and *Aspergillus* spp. the prominent pathogens. Systemic candidal infections usually occur earlier than does aspergillosis.[30, 46, 124]

Development of brain abscess after HSCT usually occurs during this phase and, in contrast to immunocompetent hosts, is caused mainly by fungal pathogens. The most common etiologic agents of brain abscess in transplant recipients are *Aspergillus* and *Candida* spp. Despite initiation of aggressive antifungal and surgical therapy, the outcome of this complication after HSCT is very poor.[50]

In the past, *Pneumocystis jiroveci* pneumonia occurred in 5 to 10 percent of allogeneic HSCT recipients during this phase.

However, the routine use of trimethoprim-sulfamethoxazole prophylaxis has decreased its incidence significantly. Patients with *P. jiroveci* pneumonia usually present with hypoxemia, dyspnea, cough, fever, and bilateral infiltrates.[120] The treatment of choice is trimethoprim-sulfamethoxazole.

Viral Infections

In the past, CMV infections predominated during this phase, but their incidence has decreased since the routine use of prophylactic ganciclovir was initiated. CMV infection usually occurs between 40 and 50 days after the transplantation. Most commonly, it results from reactivation in seropositive patients, but it also can occur in seronegative patients who receive their stem cells from a seropositive donor. The clinical manifestations of CMV infection vary from asymptomatic infection to the constellation of fever, hepatitis, and leukopenia to life-threatening diseases such as esophagitis, interstitial pneumonitis, and encephalitis.[36, 135]

Pneumonia continues to be a common problem after HSCT, and the outcome continues to be poor.[31] Pulmonary infiltrates in the HSCT recipient must be distinguished from infectious processes or noninfectious pulmonary complications after HSCT (Table 76–4). Diffuse alveolar hemorrhage presents with gradually worsening dyspnea and is characterized by repeated bloody aspirates from bronchoscopic examinations. Idiopathic interstitial pneumonitis is a process of widespread alveolar damage characterized clinically by varying degrees of respiratory failure and diffuse interstitial infiltrates in the absence of infection. Idiopathic interstitial pneumonitis occurs in two peaks, one in the first few weeks and the other near the end of the early engraftment period. It is thought to be related to the chemotherapy and total-body irradiation used with the conditioning regimen and has a high mortality rate.

Viral respiratory infections may occur throughout the transplantation period but are more severe during the early engraftment period. Etiologic agents include respiratory syncytial virus, human parainfluenza viruses 1 to 4, influenza viruses A and B, adenovirus, rhinoviruses, and nonpolio enteroviruses.* Distinctive features of respiratory viral infections among immunocompromised hosts include a high frequency of nosocomial acquisition, prolonged persistence of infection, a higher frequency of progression to pneumonia, and a high mortality rate in association with the infection.[80]

Respiratory viral infections occur throughout the year in HSCT recipients; although seasonal variations in the type of respiratory viral infection are similar to those seen in the general pediatric population, with respiratory syncytial virus and influenza viruses predominating during the winter and human parainfluenza viruses during the spring and summer.[80]

The differential diagnosis of jaundice and increase in liver enzymes after HSCT is very broad (Table 76–5) and presents a challenge in distinguishing the infectious from the noninfectious etiologies of hepatic disease. Two major noninfectious causes of liver disease after HSCT are GVHD of the liver and hepatic veno-occlusive disease.[38, 86] The latter is a complication related to the conditioning regimen that presents with weight gain, hepatomegaly, and direct hyperbilirubinemia without elevation in liver enzymes.[86] The differential diagnosis of infectious etiologies includes viral hepatitis with any of the hepatitis viruses from A through C and also includes other hepatotropic viruses such as CMV, EBV, adenovirus, HSV, and varicella-zoster virus (VZV).[40, 51, 64, 68]

EBV can reactivate after HSCT and cause EBV-associated lymphoproliferative disease. This disease presents as fever, hepatosplenomegaly, and lymphadenopathy and can progress to lymphoma. These EBV lymphomas are of donor origin and can occur in patients receiving HSCT for as long as 6 months after transplantation.[78]

TABLE 76–4 ■ DIFFERENTIAL DIAGNOSIS OF PNEUMONITIS AFTER HSCT

Infectious Etiologies	Noninfectious Etiologies
Bacterial	Radiation
Enterobacteriaceae	Chemotherapy (e.g., bleomycin)
Legionella pneumophila	Bronchiolitis obliterans organizing pneumonia
Staphylococcus aureus	Underlying malignancy
Chlamydia trachomatis	Pulmonary edema
Mycoplasma hominis	Diffuse alveolar hemorrhage
Fungal	Idiopathic interstitial pneumonitis
Aspergillus spp.	Pulmonary vascular disease
Candida spp.	
Pneumocystis jiroveci	
Mucormycosis	
Viral	
Cytomegalovirus	
Human parainfluenza viruses 1 to 4	
Respiratory syncytial virus	
Influenza viruses A and B	
Adenovirus	
Rhinovirus	
Nonpolio enteroviruses	

TABLE 76–5 ■ DIFFERENTIAL DIAGNOSIS OF HEPATITIS AFTER HSCT

Infectious Etiologies	Noninfectious Etiologies
Bacterial	Acute graft-versus-host disease
Cholestatic liver injury secondary to sepsis	Veno-occlusive disease
	Chemotherapy (e.g., cyclosporine)
Viral	Drug-induced (e.g., acetaminophen)
Hepatitis viruses A–D	Parenteral hyperalimentation
Herpes simplex virus	
Epstein-Barr virus	
Cytomegalovirus	
Adenovirus	
Varicella-zoster virus	
Echovirus	

Protozoan Infections

Toxoplasmosis is an infrequent but almost always fatal infection after HSCT. It usually occurs 2 to 6 months after transplantation and in most cases is the result of reactivation of a previous infection. The brain is the organ most frequently affected. Cerebral toxoplasmosis manifests with neurologic focal signs, fever, seizures, headache, and altered mental status. Imaging of the central nervous system typically shows multiple lesions in both hemispheres and basal ganglia with peripheral enhancement after contrast medium infusion.[84, 85, 112]

*See references 7, 9, 42, 44, 53, 76, 80, 128, 129, 130.

TABLE 76–6 ■ DIFFERENTIAL DIAGNOSIS OF SKIN RASHES AFTER HSCT

Infectious Etiologies	Noninfectious Etiologies
Bacterial	Graft-versus-host disease
Embolic lesions of systemic gram-negative bacteremia	Chemotherapy
Cellulitis of central venous catheter exit site or tunnel infections	Drug-induced (e.g., β-lactam antibiotics)
Fungal	Radiation for conditioning therapy
Focal dermatitis (*Candida* species and superficial dermatophytes)	
Embolic lesions of systemic fungal disease (*Aspergillus* and *Fusarium* species)	
Viral	
Varicella-zoster virus	
Herpes simplex virus	
Human herpesvirus type 6	
Human parvovirus B19	

Dermatologic Manifestations

Skin rashes are a common symptom after HSCT that can occur in any phase after transplantation. The differential diagnosis is broad, with infectious and noninfectious etiologies (Table 76–6). Noninfectious causes include acute GVHD, chemotherapy-induced toxicity, and drug eruptions, most commonly caused by the β-lactam antibiotics used for empiric treatment of febrile neutropenia. Because the etiology of these lesions usually is indistinguishable on a clinical basis, a skin biopsy is useful in determining the diagnosis.

Infectious skin disorders in the HSCT recipient may be secondary to bacterial, fungal, and viral etiologies (see Table 76–6). Embolic lesions can be a manifestation of systemic bacterial or fungal infection, especially *C. tropicalis* and *Aspergillus* spp. and *Fusarium* spp.[15, 108] Lesions are tender and usually papular but can be purpuric, nodular, or necrotic, scattered on the trunk and extremities.

Primary infection with human herpesvirus type 6 after HSCT usually is associated with self-limited clinical symptoms, including a diffuse maculopapular rash. Asymptomatic reactivation with human herpesvirus type 6 appears to be a common occurrence after allogeneic HSCT. Human herpesvirus type 6 might have a possible role in pneumonitis, meningoencephalitis, and bone marrow dysfunction after HSCT.[20, 23, 65] Human parvovirus B19 is another cause of erythroderma in HSCT recipients as well as a rare cause of anemia.[109]

INFECTIONS DURING THE LATE ENGRAFTMENT PHASE

The late engraftment period is characterized by decreased risk for development of infection, especially in autologous transplant recipients because they have a more rapid recovery of immune function. During this phase, the central venous catheter usually is removed, and immunosuppressive therapy to prevent GVHD is discontinued. Most recipients are outpatients at this point, and educating the recipients and their families to avoid environmental exposures to opportunistic pathogens is very important.

Serious infections can still occur, especially in patients with chronic GVHD or inadequate stem cell engraftment. Chronic GVHD predisposes the patient to infections by delaying the recovery of the immune system and its effects on target organs and by the patient receiving steroid therapy. Also, the cellular and humoral arms of the immune system are not recovered fully at this stage, placing the patient at risk for development of infection. Most defects in immune function resolve by 1 year after transplantation.[92, 102]

Bacterial Infections

Encapsulated bacteria, including *Haemophilus influenzae* type b, *Neisseria* spp., and *Streptococcus pneumoniae*, are the predominant causes of bacterial infection not related to catheters during this phase. These infections are secondary to deficient opsonization activity and decreased function of the reticuloendothelial system.[91]

Viral Infections

The predominant viral infection contracted during this period is caused by VZV, which occurs in 25 to 40 percent of pediatric HSCT recipients. Most infections represent reactivation, and risk factors include both acute and chronic GVHD as well as allogeneic transplantation. VZV infection usually presents as localized vesicles in a dermatomal distribution. Disseminated infection occurs more frequently with VZV than with HSV, especially in patients with GVHD.[52, 72, 82]

Diagnosis and Laboratory Findings

The most important diagnostic evaluation is a complete physical exam because it can identify a site of infection that may be missed by laboratory tests. Sites requiring special attention include the skin; the oral mucosa, looking for ulcers and thrush; the nares, looking for necrotic lesions suggestive of invasive mold infection; the sinuses, looking for tenderness; the chest; the abdomen; and the perianal area. All suspicious lesions should be cultured. Signs of infection may be subtle in patients who are neutropenic because inflammation is minimal.

The diagnostic approach should be guided by the knowledge of which organisms are frequent pathogens during the specific phase after the transplantation (see Table 76–1). Except for microbiologic evaluations, laboratory tests are of limited value. Blood cultures for bacteria, fungi, and viruses should be obtained for any febrile episode. The use of the Wampole isolator blood culture system (Wampole Laboratories, Cranbury, NJ) may increase the yield of fungal pathogens and can help in the diagnosis of central-line infections by the use of quantitative cultures. Urine cultures are indicated in the presence of hemorrhagic cystitis or if the patient has a Foley catheter in place. Evaluation of the cerebrospinal fluid should be reserved for patients with neurologic signs and symptoms.

Diagnosis of mold infections depends on tissue histology and culture of samples obtained by bronchoscopy, bronchoalveolar lavage, paranasal sinus washings, lung biopsy, or skin biopsy because these organisms are not recovered routinely from blood cultures. Fungal surveillance cultures are not indicated for asymptomatic HSCT patients.[100] Additionally, Gram stain, acid-fast stains, and other special stains can be useful in identifying microorganisms early in the infectious process.

Nasopharyngeal swabs or washes for viral culture and direct fluorescent antibody testing are useful for identifying respiratory viruses in the patient with upper respiratory tract symptoms. Shell vial assays are a rapid viral diagnostic technique for a variety of viruses, including CMV, adenovirus, and respiratory viruses. The base of vesicular skin lesions should be scraped and the cells examined by direct fluorescent antibody stain with specific monoclonal antibodies to confirm the diagnosis of either HSV or VZV infection.

Nucleic acid detection, such as polymerase chain reaction, has shown usefulness in the rapid diagnosis of certain pathogens, including adenovirus, CMV, EBV, human herpesvirus type 6, and parvovirus B19.[11, 20, 23, 71] Additionally, quantitation of viruses has allowed evaluation of the response to therapy. Blood assays to detect viral antigens such as pp65 also have been used in the diagnosis of CMV infection.[10, 12]

Serologic testing is useful for the diagnosis of toxoplasmosis, *Bartonella henselae,* and fungal infections such as histoplasmosis and blastomycosis. However, serologic assays have a limited value because patients are immunosuppressed and immunoglobulin therapy is administered to most patients.

Other laboratory tests are of limited value. Complete blood counts are useful to determine the engraftment status. Liver and renal function tests can provide evidence of disease from an infectious agent or can indicate noninfectious causes of hepatic or renal disease such as chemotherapy or GVHD.

Radiologic studies should be performed based on the assessment of the patient. A chest x-ray should be part of the work-up of a febrile neutropenic patient and any patient with respiratory symptoms. Computed tomography scans of the paranasal sinuses, chest, and abdomen are useful in evaluating and following patients with invasive fungal disease.[30] Ultrasound examination can be used to diagnose abdominal problems such as typhlitis. Neuroimaging studies should be reserved for the patients with neurologic signs and symptoms.

Management and Therapy

The initial management of HSCT recipients with fever and neutropenia is similar to that of cancer patients with chemotherapy-induced fever and neutropenia.[63] The use of a standardized antibiotic regimen should be developed to ensure adequate coverage of organisms identified by the hospital's environment and to allow the hospital's staff to compare outcomes of patients. Empirical antibiotic therapy directed against the predominant pathogens should be started after obtaining appropriate cultures.[63] One approach consists of an empirical antibiotic regimen of ceftazidime with or without vancomycin, a combination providing adequate therapy for gram-positive cocci and gram-negative bacteria. If *P. aeruginosa* is suspected, an aminoglycoside should be added.

The choice of any specific antimicrobial therapy should take into account the transplantation center's spectrum of organisms, the patient's surveillance isolates, and the antibiotic susceptibility pattern within the community and the hospital. If the patient persists febrile after 3 or more days, reevaluation of the patient may lead to a modification of the antibiotic regimen.[63]

THERAPY FOR FUNGAL INFECTIONS

Empirical amphotericin B to treat occult fungal disease is recommended in the patient who remains persistently febrile for 5 to 7 days of antibiotic therapy, without identification of a bacterial cause.[63]

Amphotericin B remains the drug of choice for treatment of invasive mold infections; however, lipid formulations of amphotericin B can be substituted if infusion-related toxicity or nephrotoxicity with the use of conventional amphotericin B is noted.[115, 125, 134] Itraconazole has been shown to have some efficacy in the treatment of invasive aspergillosis in immunocompromised hosts.[115] However, interaction with other drugs may impair its use in HSCT recipients. Combination therapy may be of potential benefit, but the efficacy of any of these combinations has not been established. Fluconazole has activity against most *Candida* spp. and exhibits good penetration of the central nervous system.[31]

Surgery plays a prominent role in the treatment of mold infections, especially in the neutropenic patient. However, the outcome for invasive mold infections in HSCT patients remains dismal.

THERAPY FOR VIRAL INFECTIONS

Treatment of viral infections is started once the diagnosis is established, if therapy is available. Acyclovir is the recommended therapy for both HSV and VZV infections. Famciclovir and valacyclovir also can be used to treat HSV infections, but they are available only for oral administration. CMV pneumonitis is treated with a combination of intravenous gamma-globulin and ganciclovir. In the case of acyclovir-resistant HSV or ganciclovir-resistant CMV infections, foscarnet is the drug of choice.[90] Cidofovir also has been used for CMV infection.[77]

Respiratory syncytial virus infections have been treated with aerosolized ribavirin and more recently with respiratory syncytial virus immunoglobulin.[28, 29, 35] Aerosolized ribavirin also has been used for the treatment of human parainfluenza virus infections.[32, 35]

Intravenous ribavirin has been used for therapy of adenovirus hemorrhagic cystitis with anecdotal success.[18] More recently, cidofovir treatment was associated with clinical improvement as well as viral clearance in cultures and polymerase chain reaction analysis.[14, 71]

The recommended therapy for influenza A virus infections includes oral amantadine or rimantadine. Their efficacy, particularly in the treatment of severe disease, has not been established in the immunocompromised host. Both drugs also are useful as prophylaxis of influenza A virus infection.[54] Zanamivir and oseltamivir, both neuraminidase inhibitors, appear promising for the treatment of both influenza A and B virus infections, but data are lacking regarding their use in pediatric immunocompromised patients.[54]

Adoptive immunotherapy by transferring virus-specific cytotoxic T lymphocytes to patients after allogeneic HSCT has proved to be useful to treat CMV and EBV infections and to reconstitute immune dysfunction selectively against these viruses.[56, 101, 126]

Prevention of Infections after Transplantation

Measures to prevent infectious complications are a high priority for all HSCT recipients. Regular handwashing remains the best strategy for prevention of infections in HSCT recipients. Every HSCT recipient should have a dental evaluation before conditioning to assess the oral health and to perform any needed dental procedures to decrease the risk for developing oral complications and infections after transplantation.[25, 103] A strong effort should be made to enforce published guidelines for preventing indwelling catheter-related infections.[98]

The Centers for Disease Control and Prevention recently published extensive guidelines for the prevention of opportunistic infections in HSCT recipients that go beyond the scope of this chapter.[19] A brief review of preventive strategies, including targeted antimicrobial prophylaxis, prevention of exposure, enhancement of immune reconstitution by using colony-stimulating factors, and active and passive immunization, is presented here.

ANTIMICROBIAL PROPHYLAXIS

Antimicrobial prophylaxis must be weighed against the toxicity and the drug interactions of the prophylactic agent. Prophylaxis against *P. carinii* infection with trimethoprim-sulfamethoxazole is started after engraftment and is given orally three times a week until 6 months after transplantation. For patients with intolerance to sulfa-containing medications, other options for prophylaxis include atovaquone, dapsone, or inhaled pentamidine.[74, 81]

The administration of fluconazole for 75 days after HSCT was associated with persistent protection against disseminated candidal infections and candidiasis-related death, resulting in an overall survival benefit in allogeneic HSCT recipients in a randomized, placebo-controlled trial.[83] However, the emergence of resistant pathogens such as *C. krusei* and some strains of *C. albicans* has complicated the routine use of fluconazole.[18] Low-dose amphotericin B is similar in efficacy to fluconazole in preventing fungal infections, but the latter is tolerated better.[133] The use of aerosolized amphotericin B to prevent *Aspergillus* spp. infection needs further study.[58, 111]

Antiviral prophylaxis is directed to prevent infections with herpesviruses during high-risk periods. Acyclovir has been used to prevent reactivation of HSV in seropositive transplant recipients during the neutropenic phase after the transplantation. This strategy can reduce the incidence of reactivation of HSV in seropositive recipients from 80 to 5 percent during the first month after transplantation.

Strategies used to prevent CMV infection include prophylactic and preemptive therapy. Prophylactic therapy is administered to all recipients at risk for acquiring CMV infection and is used routinely for allogeneic transplant recipients when the donor is CMV seropositive.[47, 110] Ganciclovir is the agent of choice for prophylaxis of CMV infection.[45, 47] Ganciclovir usually is given for 3 to 4 months after engraftment; however, its use has been associated with neutropenia.[47, 106] Preemptive therapy is administered only to the recipients who have evidence of CMV replication based on plasma polymerase chain reaction or pp65 antigenemia.[10, 12] Primary CMV infection also can be prevented in CMV-seronegative HSCT recipients by transfusing blood products that are leukocyte filtered and seronegative for CMV.[117]

ISOLATION MEASURES

The use of laminar air-flow protection for HSCT patients is controversial, and although some studies have proved its effectiveness, it is very expensive. HEPA filtration is associated with similar efficacy to laminar air flow in preventing airborne pathogens such as *Aspergillus* spp. Major indications for strict isolation of patients include colonization with resistant bacteria, viral respiratory infections, and disseminated VZV infection.[12, 99]

COLONY-STIMULATING FACTORS

The use of granulocyte and granulocyte-macrophage colony-stimulating factors in stem cell transplant recipients is safe and effective in reducing the period of neutropenia after HSCT.[4, 69, 119] However, whether this response translates into a reduction in the number of infections or duration of antimicrobial use remains controversial.[4, 91] They also appear to be safe and effective in transplant recipients who do not show engraftment, 3 to 4 weeks after transplantation.

ACTIVE IMMUNIZATION

Immunizations should be part of the routine follow-up care of HSCT recipients. Most allogeneic and a large proportion of autologous and syngeneic transplant recipients lose their immunity to vaccine-preventable diseases. Also, transplant recipients are at increased risk for acquiring infections with encapsulated bacteria, such as *H. influenzae* type b and *S. pneumoniae*, for which vaccines are available.[8, 43] For all these reasons, reimmunizing HSCT recipients between the first and second year after transplantation is very important.[75, 113] When immunizing transplant recipients, recent administration of immunoglobulin must be kept in mind because it may interfere with the response to vaccinations.

However, an optimal schedule for administering vaccinations after HSCT in pediatric patients has not been established. A schedule for immunization of HSCT recipients based on the recommendations of the Centers for Disease Control and Prevention Advisory Committee on Immunization Practices and the Infectious Diseases Committee of the American Academy of Pediatrics is presented in Table 76–7.[3, 19] Specific recommendations likely will change as further data become available.

Immunizations after HSCT can be started 12 months after the transplantation as long as the patient has no chronic complications, such as chronic GVHD, and is not receiving immunosuppressive therapy. Immunization is started with diphtheria and tetanus toxoids (dT); if the patient is younger than 7 years of age, DTaP or DT can be used.[95, 122] Inactivated polio vaccine (IPV), *H. influenzae* type b vaccine (Hib), and hepatitis B vaccine also are included in the first round of immunizations after HSCT. Boosters of these vaccines are given at 14 and 24 months after transplantation.[8, 49, 97, 122]

TABLE 76–7 ■ IMMUNIZATIONS IN PATIENTS AFTER HSCT

Recommended Time after HSCT	Immunizations
12 mo	dT,* IPV, Hib, pneumococcal and hepatitis B
14 mo	dT, IPV, Hib, pneumococcal and hepatitis B
24 mo	Measles-mumps-rubella†

*DtaP if the patient is younger than 7 years of age.
†DO NOT use live virus vaccines for patients who have active chronic graft-versus-host disease or who are receiving immunosuppressive therapy. dT, diphtheria and tetanus toxoids; Hib, *Haemophilus influenzae* type b vaccine; IPV, inactivated polio vaccine.

The 23-valent pneumococcal vaccine is recommended at 12 and 24 months after transplantation.[3, 6, 19] The second dose is not a booster dose but provides a second opportunity for immunization for patients who failed to respond to the first dose.[3]

The measles-mumps-rubella (MMR) vaccine should be given 24 months after transplantation to both autologous and allogeneic HSCT patients. It should not be given to patients with chronic GVHD or to patients receiving steroids or any other form of immunosuppressive therapy.[66] The live attenuated varicella vaccine should be avoided in HSCT recipients.[3]

The influenza vaccine should be given yearly in early autumn to HSCT recipients. Children younger than 9 years of age receiving influenza vaccination for the first time require two doses given 1 month apart. Children younger than 12 years of age should receive only split-virus influenza vaccine. Those older than 12 years of age may receive whole or split-virus vaccine.[3, 19, 33, 54]

Vaccination for hepatitis A is not recommended routinely but may be considered 12 months or more after HSCT for patients with chronic liver disease or chronic GVHD, for those living in areas endemic for hepatitis A, and for those in areas experiencing outbreaks. Hepatitis A immunization is given in two doses 6 to 12 months apart.[3, 19]

Health care workers and household contacts of HSCT recipients should have immunity to or be immunized against hepatitis A, influenza, polio, measles, mumps, rubella, and varicella.[3, 19, 113]

PASSIVE IMMUNIZATION

Administration of intravenous immunoglobulin commonly is employed in the first months after allogeneic HSCT to prevent infections and acute GVHD.[17] The use of intravenous immunoglobulin after transplantation has been shown to decrease the incidence of CMV pneumonia and systemic bacterial infections as well as interstitial pneumonia.[118, 132] The optimal dose is not known. However, prolonged administration of intravenous immunoglobulin can be associated with delayed immune reconstitution and an increased incidence of infections after its discontinuation.

The indications for passive immunization with specific immune globulin preparations such as hepatitis B, rabies, and tetanus vaccines in transplant recipients are similar to those in otherwise healthy individuals.[3, 19] Patients with tetanus-prone wounds sustained during the first year after transplantation should be given tetanus immunoglobulin, regardless of their tetanus immunization status.[3] Passive immunization with varicella-zoster immune globulin is recommended for susceptible patients with known exposure to varicella.[3]

REFERENCES

1. Abbasi, S., Shenep, J. L., Hughes, W. T., et al.: *Aspergillus* in children with cancer: A 34-year experience. Clin. Infect. Dis. *29*:1210–1219, 1999.
2. Akiyama, H., Kurosu, T., Sakashita, C., et al.: Adenovirus is a key pathogen in hemorrhagic cystitis associated with bone marrow transplantation. Clin. Infect. Dis. *32*:1325–1330, 2001.
3. American Academy of Pediatrics: Immunization in special clinical circumstances: Transplant recipients. *In* Pickering, L. (ed.): 2000 Red Book: Report of the Committee on Infectious Diseases. 25th ed. Elk Grove Village, IL: American Academy of Pediatrics, 2000, pp. 62–64.
4. American Society for Clinical Oncology: Recommendations for the use of hematopoietic colony-stimulating factors: Evidence-based, clinical practice guidelines. J. Clin. Oncol. *12*:2471–2508, 1994.
5. Armitage, J. O.: Bone marrow transplantation. N. Engl. J. Med. *330*:827–838, 1994.
6. Avanzini, M., Carra, A., Maccario, R., et al.: Antibody response to pneumococcal vaccine in children receiving bone marrow transplantation. J. Clin. Immunol. *15*:137–144, 1995.
7. Baldwin, A., Kingman, H., Darville, M., et al.: Outcome and clinical course of 100 patients with adenovirus infection following bone marrow transplantation. Bone Marrow Transplant. *26*:1333–1338, 2000.
8. Barra, A., Cordonnier, C., Presiosi, M., et al.: Immunogenicity of *Haemophilus influenzae* type B conjugate vaccine in allogeneic bone marrow recipients. J. Infect. Dis. *166*:1021–1028, 1992.
9. Biggs, D. D., Toorkey, B. C., Carrigan, D. R., et al.: Disseminated echovirus infection complicating bone marrow transplantation. Am. J. Med. *88*:421–425, 1990.
10. Boeckh, M., Gooley, T. A., Myerson, D., et al.: Cytomegalovirus pp65 antigenemia-guided early treatment with ganciclovir versus ganciclovir at engraftment after allogeneic bone marrow transplantation: A randomized double-blind study. Blood *10*:4063–4071, 1996.
11. Boeckh, M., Gallez-Hawkins, G. M., Myerson, D., et al.: Plasma polymerase chain reaction for cytomegalovirus DNA after allogeneic bone marrow transplantation: Comparison with polymerase chain reaction using peripheral blood leukocytes, pp65 antigenemia, and viral culture. Transplantation *64*:108–113, 1997.
12. Boeckh, M., Bowden, R. A., Gooley, T., et al.: Successful modification of a pp65 antigenemia-based early treatment for prevention of cytomegalovirus disease in allogeneic marrow transplant recipients. Blood *93*:1781–1782, 1999.
13. Bochud, P-Y., Eggiman, P. H., Calandra, T., et al.: Bacteremia due to viridans streptococcus in neutropenic patients with cancer: Clinical spectrum and risk factors. Clin. Infect. Dis. *18*:25–31, 1994.
14. Bordigoni, P., Carret, A-S., Venard, V., et al.: Treatment of adenovirus infections in patients undergoing allogeneic hematopoietic stem cell transplantation. Clin. Infect. Dis. *32*:1290–1297, 2001.
15. Boutati, E. I., and Anaissie, E. J.: *Fusarium*, a significant emerging pathogen in patients with hematologic malignancy: Ten years' experience at a cancer center and implications for management. Blood *90*:999–1008, 1997.
16. Buckley, R. H., Schiff, S. E., Schiff, R. I., et al.: Hematopoietic stem-cell transplantation for the treatment of severe combined immunodeficiency. N. Engl. J. Med. *340*:508–516, 1999.
17. Casper, J. T., Sedmak, G., and Harrie, R. E.: Intravenous immunoglobulin: Use in pediatric bone marrow transplantation. Semin. Hematol. *29*(Suppl. 2):S100–S105, 1992.
18. Cassano, W. F.: Intravenous ribavirin therapy for adenovirus cystitis after allogeneic bone marrow transplantation. Bone Marrow Transplant. *7*:247–248, 1991.
19. Centers for Disease Control and Prevention: Guidelines for preventing opportunistic infections among hematopoietic stem cell transplant recipients. M. M. W. R. Morb. Mortal. Wkly. Rep. *49*:1–128, 2000.
20. Chan, P. K. S., Peiris, J. S. M., Yuen, K. Y., et al.: Human herpesvirus-6 and human herpesvirus-7 infections in bone marrow transplant recipients. J. Med. Virol. *53*:295–305, 1997.
21. Childs, R., Sanchez, C., Engler, H., et al.: High incidence of adeno- and polyomavirus-induced hemorrhagic cystitis in bone marrow allotransplantation for hematological malignancy following T cell depletion and cyclosporine. Bone Marrow Transplant. *22*:889–893, 1998.
22. Collin, B. A., Leather, H. L., Wingard, J. R., and Ramphal, R: Evolution, incidence and susceptibility of bacterial bloodstream isolates from 519 bone marrow transplant patients. Clin. Infect. Dis. *33*:947–953, 2001.
23. Cone, R. W., Huang, M-L. W., Corey, L., et al.: Human herpes virus 6 infections after bone marrow transplantation: Clinical and virologic manifestations. J. Infect. Dis. *179*:311–318, 1999.
24. Cox, G. J., Matsui, S. M., Lo, R. S., et al.: Etiology and outcome of diarrhea after marrow transplantation: A prospective study. Gastroenterology *107*:1398–1407, 1994.
25. da Fonseca, M. A.: Pediatric bone marrow transplantation: oral complications and recommendations for care. Pediatric Dentistry *20*:386–394, 1998.
26. de Vries, E., van Tol, M. J. D., Langlois van den Bergh, R., et al.: Reconstitution of lymphocyte subpopulations after pediatric bone marrow transplantation. Bone Marrow Transplant. *25*:267–275, 2000.

27. Dell'Orto, M. G., Rovelli, A., Barzaghi, A., et al.: Febrile complications in the first 100 days after bone marrow transplantation in children: A single center's experience. Pediatr. Hematol. Oncol. *14*:335–347, 1997.
28. DeVincenzo, J. P., Leombuno, D., Soiffer, R. J., and Siber, G. R.: Immunotherapy of respiratory syncytial virus pneumonia following bone marrow transplantation. Bone Marrow Transplant. *17*:1051–1056, 1996.
29. DeVincenzo, J. P., Hirsch, R. L., Fuentes, R. J., and Top, F. H., Jr.: Respiratory syncytial virus immune globulin treatment of lower respiratory tract infection in pediatric patients undergoing bone marrow transplantation: A compassionate use experience. Bone Marrow Transplant. *25*:161–165, 2000.
30. Drakos, P. E., Nagler, A., Or, R., et al.: Invasive fungal sinusitis in patients undergoing bone marrow transplantation. Bone Marrow Transplant. *12*:203–208, 1993.
31. Edwards, J. E. Jr., Bodey, G. P., Bowden, R. A., et al.: International Conference for the development of a consensus on the management and prevention of severe candidal infections. Clin. Infect. Dis. *25*:43–59, 1997.
32. Elizaga, J., Olavarria, E., Apperley, J. F., et al.: Parainfluenza virus 3 infection after stem cell transplant: Relevance to outcome of rapid diagnosis and ribavirin treatment. Clin. Infect. Dis. *32*:413–418, 2001.
33. Engelhard, D., Nagler, A., Hardan, I., et al.: Antibody response to a two-dose regimen of influenza vaccine in allogeneic T cell-depleted and autologous BMT recipients. Bone Marrow Transplant. *11*:1–5, 1993.
34. Engelhard, D., Elishoov, H., Strauss, N., et al.: Nosocomial coagulase-negative staphylococcal infections in bone marrow transplantation recipients with central vein catheter: A 5-year prospective study. Transplantation *61*:430–434, 1996.
35. Englund, J. A., Piedra, P. A., and Whimbey, E.: Prevention and treatment of respiratory syncytial virus and parainfluenza viruses in immunocompromised patients. Am. J. Med. *102*(3A):S61–S70, 1997.
36. Enright, H., Haake, R., Weisdorf, D., et al.: Cytomegalovirus pneumonia after bone marrow transplantation. Transplantation *55*:1339–1346, 1993.
37. Epstein, J. B., Ransier, A., Sherlock, C. H., et al.: Acyclovir prophylaxis of oral herpes virus during bone marrow transplantation. Eur. J. Cancer B. Oral. Oncol. *32*:158–162, 1996.
38. Ferrara, J. L. M., and Deeg, H. J.: Graft versus host disease. N. Engl. J. Med. *324*:667–674, 1991.
39. Flomenberg, P., Babbitt, J., Drobyski, W. R., et al.: Increasing incidence of adenovirus disease in bone marrow transplant recipients. J. Infect. Dis. *169*:775–781, 1994.
40. Frickhofen, N., Wiesneth, M., Jainta, C., et al.: Hepatitis C virus infection is a risk factor for liver failure from veno-occlusive disease after bone marrow transplantation. Blood *83*:1998–2004, 1994.
41. Gamis, A. S., Gudnason, T., Giebink, G. S., et al.: Disseminated infection with *Fusarium* in recipients of bone marrow transplants. Rev. Infect. Dis. *13*:1077–1088, 1991.
42. Ghosh, S., Champlin, R., Couch, R., et al.: Rhinovirus infections in myelosuppressed adult blood and marrow transplant recipients. Clin. Infect. Dis. *29*:528–532, 1999.
43. Giebink, G. S., Warkentin, P. I., Ramsay, N. K. C., et al.: Titers of antibody to pneumococci in allogeneic bone marrow transplant recipients before and after vaccination with pneumococcal vaccine. J. Infect. Dis. *166*:1021–1028, 1992.
44. González, Y., Martino, R., Badell, I., et al.: Pulmonary enterovirus infections in stem cell transplant recipients. Bone Marrow Transplant. *23*:511–513, 1999.
45. Goodrich, J. M., Mori, M., Gleaves, C. A., et al.: Early treatment with ganciclovir to prevent cytomegalovirus disease after allogeneic bone marrow transplantation. N. Engl. J. Med. *325*:1601–1607, 1991.
46. Goodrich, J. M., Reed, E. C., Mori, M., et al.: Clinical features and analysis of risk factors for invasive candidal infection after marrow transplantation. J. Infect. Dis. *164*:731–740, 1991.
47. Goodrich, J. M., Bowden, R. A., Fisher, L., et al.: Ganciclovir prophylaxis to prevent cytomegalovirus disease after allogeneic marrow transplant. Ann. Intern. Med. *118*:173–178, 1993.
48. Gratwohl, A., Hermans, J., Baldomero, H., et al.: Indications for haematopoietic precursor cell transplants in Europe. Br. J. Haematol. *92*:35–43, 1996.
49. Guinan, E. C., Molrine, D. C., Antin, J. H., et al.: Polysaccharide conjugate vaccine response in bone marrow transplant recipients. Transplantation *57*:677–684, 1994.
50. Hagensee, M. E., Bauwens, J. E., Kjos, B., et al.: Brain abscess following marrow transplantation: Experience at the Fred Hutchinson Cancer Research Center, 1984–1992. Clin. Infect. Dis. *19*:402–408, 1994.
51. Hale, G. A., Heslop, H. E., Krance, R. A., et al.: Adenovirus infection after pediatric bone marrow transplantation. Bone Marrow Transplant. *23*:277–282, 1999.
52. Han, C. S., Miller, W., Haake, R., et al.: Varicella zoster infection after bone marrow transplantation: Incidence, risk factors and complications. Bone Marrow Transplant. *13*:277–283, 1994.
53. Harrington, R. D., Hooton, T. M., Hackman, R. C., et al.: An outbreak of respiratory syncytial virus in a bone marrow transplant center. J. Infect. Dis. *165*:987–993, 1992.
54. Hayden, F. G.: Prevention and treatment of influenza in immucompromised patients. Am. J. Med. *102*(3A):S55–S60, 1997.
55. Henwick, S., Koehler, M., and Patrick, C. C.: Complications of bacteremia due to *Stomatococcus mucilaginosus* in neutropenic children. Clin. Infect. Dis. *17*:667–671, 1993.
56. Heslop, H. E., Ny, C. Y. C., Li, C., et al.: Long-term restoration of immunity against Epstein-Barr virus by infection by adoptive transfer of gene-modified virus-specific T lymphocytes. Nat. Med. *2*:551–555, 1996.
57. Hierholzer, J. C.: Adenovirus in the immunocompromised host. Clin. Microbiol. Rev. *5*:262–274, 1992.
58. Hong, R.: Bone marrow transplantation. Adv. Pediatr. *40*:101–124, 1993.
59. Hoppe, J. E., Klingebiel, T., and Niethammer, D.: Selection of *Candida glabrata* in pediatric bone marrow transplant recipients receiving fluconazole. Pediatr. Hematol. Oncol. *11*:207–210, 1994.
60. Horwitz, M. E.: Stem-cell transplantation for inherited immunodeficiency disorders. Pediatr. Clin. North Am. *47*:1371–1387, 2000.
61. Hovi, L., Saarinen-Pihkala, U. M., Vettenranta, K., and Saxen, I. L.: Invasive fungal infections in pediatric bone marrow transplant recipients: Single center experience of 10 years. Bone Marrow Transplant. *9*:999–1004, 2000.
62. Howard, D. S., Phillips, G. L. III, Reece, D. E., et al.: Adenovirus infections in hematopoietic stem cell transplant recipients. Clin. Infect. Dis. *29*:1494–1501, 1999.
63. Hughes, W. T., Armstrong, D., Bodey, G. P., et al.: 1997 Guidelines for the use of antimicrobial agents in neutropenic patients with unexplained fever. Clin. Infect. Dis. *25*:551–573, 1997.
64. Johnson, J. R., Egaas, S., Gleaves, C. A., et al.: Hepatitis due to herpes simplex virus in marrow transplant recipients. Clin. Infect. Dis. *14*:38–45, 1992.
65. Kadakia, M. P., Rybka, W. B., Stewart, J. A., et al.: Human herpes virus 6: Infection and disease following autologous and allogeneic bone marrow transplantation. Blood *87*:5341–5354, 1996.
66. King, S. M., Saunders, E. F., Petric, M., and Gold, R.: Responses to measles, mumps and rubella vaccine in paediatric bone marrow transplant recipients. Bone Marrow Transplant. *17*:633–636, 1996.
67. Klingspor, L., Stintzing, G., Fasth, A., and Tollemar, J.: Deep *Candida* infection in children receiving allogeneic bone marrow transplants: Incidence, risk factors and diagnosis. Bone Marrow Transplant. *17*:1043–1049, 1996.
68. Kolho, E., Ruutu, P., and Ruutu, T.: Hepatitis C in BMT patients. Bone Marrow Transplant. *11*:119–123, 1993.
69. Lau, A. S., Lehman, D., Geertsma, F. R., et al.: Biology and therapeutic uses of myeloid hematopoietic growth factors and interferons. Pediatr. Infect. Dis. J. *15*:563–575, 1996.
70. Laughlin, M. J.: Umbilical cord blood for allogeneic transplantation in children and adults. Bone Marrow Transplant. *27*:1–6, 2001.
71. Legrand, F., Berrebi, D., Houhou, N., et al.: Early diagnosis of adenovirus infection and treatment with cidofovir after bone marrow transplantation in children. Bone Marrow Transplant. *27*:621–625, 2001.
72. Leung, T. F., Chik, K. W., Li, C. K., et al.: Incidence, risk factors and outcome of varicella-zoster virus infection in children after haematopoietic stem cell transplantation. Bone Marrow Transplant. *25*:167–172, 2000.
73. Leung, W., Pitts, N., Burnette, K., et al.: Allogeneic bone marrow transplantation for infants with acute leukemia or myelodysplastic syndrome. Bone Marrow Transplant. *27*:717–722, 2001.
74. Link, H., Vöhringer, H-F., Wingen, F., et al.: Pentamidine aerosol prophylaxis of *Pneumocystis carinii* pneumonia after BMT. Bone Marrow Transplant. *11*:403–406, 1993.
75. Ljungman, P., Cordonnier, C., de Bock, R., et al.: Immunizations after bone marrow transplantation: Results of the European group for blood and marrow transplantation. Bone Marrow Transplant. *15*:455–460, 1995.
76. Ljungman, P.: Respiratory virus infections in bone marrow transplant recipients: The European perspective. Am. J. Med. *102*(3A):S44–S47, 1997.
77. Ljungman, P., Deliliers, G. L., Platzbecker, U., et al.: Cidofovir for cytomegalovirus infection and disease in allogeneic stem cell transplant recipients. Blood *97*:388–392, 2001.
78. Lucas, K. G., Pollok, K. E., and Emanuel, D. J.: Post-transplant EBV induced lymphoproliferative disorders. Leuk. Lymphoma *25*:1–8, 1996.
79. Luján-Zilbermann, J., and Patrick, C. C.: Infections in patients undergoing hematopoietic stem cell transplantation. *In* Patrick, C. C. (ed.): Clinical Management of Infections in Immunocompromised Infants and Children. Philadelphia, Lippincott Williams & Wilkins, 2001, pp. 195–211.
80. Luján-Zilbermann, J., Benaim, E., Tong, X., et al.: Respiratory virus infections in pediatric hematopoietic stem cell transplantation. Clin. Infect. Dis. *33*:962–968, 2001.
81. Maltezou, H. C., Petropoulos, D., Choroszy, M., et al.: Dapsone for *Pneumocystis carinii* prophylaxis in children undergoing bone marrow transplantation. Bone Marrow Transplant. *20*:879–881, 1997.
82. Maltezou, H. C., Kafetzis, D. A., Abisaid, D., et al.: Viral infections in children undergoing hematopoietic stem cell transplant. Pediatr. Infect. Dis. J. *19*:307–312, 2000.
83. Marr, K. A., Seidel, K., Slavin, M. A., et al.: Prolonged fluconazole prophylaxis is associated with persistent protection against candidiasis-related death in allogeneic marrow transplant recipients: Long-term follow-up of a randomized, placebo-controlled trial. Blood *96*:2055–2061, 2000.

84. Martino, R., Maertens, J., Bretagne, S., et al.: Toxoplasmosis after hematopoietic stem cell transplantation. Clin. Infect. Dis. *31*:1188–1194, 2000.
85. Maschke, M., Dietrich, U., Prumbaum, M., et al.: Opportunistic CNS infections after bone marrow transplantation. Bone Marrow Transplant. *23*:1167–1176, 1999.
86. McDonald, G. B., Hinds, M. S., Fischer, L. D., et al.: Veno-occlusive disease of the liver and multiorgan failure after bone marrow transplantation: A cohort study of 335 patients. Ann. Intern. Med. *118*:255–267, 1993.
87. Morrison, V. A., Haake, R. J., and Weisdorf, D. J.: The spectrum of non-*Candida* fungal infections following bone marrow transplantation. Medicine *72*:78–89, 1993.
88. Morrison, V. A., and McGlave, P. B.: Mucormycosis in the BMT population. Bone Marrow Transplant. *11*:383–388, 1993.
89. Mullen, C. A., Nair, J., Sandesh, S., and Chan, K. W.: Fever and neutropenia in pediatric hematopoietic stem cell transplant patients. Bone Marrow Transplant. *25*:59–65, 2000.
90. Naik, H. R., Siddique, N., and Chandrasekar, P. H.: Foscarnet therapy for acyclovir-resistant herpes simplex virus 1 infection in allogeneic bone marrow transplant recipients. Clin. Infect. Dis. *21*:1514–1515, 1995.
91. Nemunaitis, J., Rabinowe, S. N., Singer, J. W., et al.: Recombinant granulocyte-macrophage colony-stimulating factor after autologous bone marrow transplantation for lymphoid cancer. N. Engl. J. Med. *324*:1773–1778, 1991.
92. Ochs, L., Shu, X. O., Miller, J., et al.: Late infections after allogeneic bone marrow transplantation: Comparison of incidence in related and unrelated donor transplant recipients. Blood *86*:3979–3986, 1995.
93. Ottinger, H. D., Beelen, D. W., Scheulen, B., et al.: Improved immune reconstitution after allotransplantation of peripheral blood stem cells instead of bone marrow. Blood *88*:2775–2779, 1996.
94. Papadopoulou, A., Nathavitharana, K. A., Williams, M. D., et al.: Diarrhea and weight loss after bone marrow transplantation in children. Pediatr. Hematol. Oncol. *11*:601–611, 1994.
95. Parkkali, T., Olander, R., Ruutu, T., et al.: A randomized comparison between early and late vaccination with tetanus toxoid vaccine after allogeneic BMT. Bone Marrow Transplant. *19*:933–938, 1997.
96. Parkman, R., and Weinberg, K.: Immunological reconstitution following bone marrow transplantation. Immunol. Rev. *157*:73–78, 1997.
97. Pauksen, K., Hammarström, V., Ljungman, P., et al.: Immunity to poliovirus and immunization with inactivated poliovirus vaccine after autologous bone marrow transplantation. Clin. Infect. Dis. *18*:547–552, 1994.
98. Pearson, M. L.: Guidelines for prevention of intravascular device-related infections. Part I. Intravascular device-related infections: An overview. Am. J. Infect. Control *24*:262–293, 1996.
99. Raad, I., Abbas, J., and Whimbey, E.: Infection control of nosocomial respiratory viral disease in the immunocompromised host. Am. J. Med. *102*(3A):S48–S52, 1997.
100. Riley, D. K., Pavia, A. T., Beatty, P. G., and Denton, D.: Surveillance cultures in bone marrow transplant recipients: Worthwhile or wasteful? Bone Marrow Transplant. *15*:469–473, 1995.
101. Rooney, C. M., Smith, C., Ng, C. Y., et al.: Use of gene modified virus specific T lymphocytes to control Epstein-Barr-virus-related lymphoproliferation. Lancet *345*:9–13, 1995.
102. Roy, V., Ochs, L., Weisdorf, D.: Late infections following allogeneic bone marrow transplantation: Suggested strategies for prophylaxis. Leuk. Lymphoma *26*:1–15, 1997.
103. Ruescher, T. J., Sodeifi, A., Scrivani, S. J., et al.: The impact of mucositis on alpha-hemolytic streptococcal infection in patients undergoing autologous bone marrow transplantation for hematologic malignancies. Cancer *82*:2275–2281, 1998.
104. Russell, S. J., Vowels, M. R., and Vale, T.: Hemorrhagic cystitis in pediatric bone marrow transplant patients: An association with infective agents, GVHD and prior cyclophosphamide. Bone Marrow Transplant. *13*:533–539, 1994.
105. Sable, C. A., and Donowitz, G. R.: Infections in bone marrow transplant recipients. Clin. Infect. Dis. *19*:273–284, 1994.
106. Salzberger, B., Bowden, R. A., Hackman, R. C., et al.: Neutropenia in allogeneic marrow transplant recipients receiving ganciclovir for prevention of cytomegalovirus disease: Risk factors and outcome. Blood *90*:2502–2508, 1990.
107. Sanders, J. E.: Bone marrow transplantation for pediatric malignancies. Pediatr. Clin. North Am. *44*:1005–1020, 1997.
108. Schimmelpfennig, C., Naumann, R., Zuberbier, T., et al.: Skin involvement as the first manifestation of systemic aspergillosis in patients after allogeneic hematopoietic cell transplantation. Bone Marrow Transplant. *27*:753–755, 2001.
109. Schleuning, M., Jager, G., Holler, E., et al.: Human parvovirus B19-associated disease in bone marrow transplantation. Infection *27*:114–117, 1999.
110. Schmidt, G. M., Horak, D. A., Niland, J. C., et al.: A randomized, controlled trial of prophylactic ganciclovir for cytomegalovirus pulmonary infection in recipients of allogeneic bone marrow transplants. N. Engl. J. Med. *324*:1005–1011, 1991.
111. Schwartz, S., Behre, G., Heinemann, V., et al.: Aerosolized amphotericin B inhalations as prophylaxis of invasive *Aspergillus* infections during prolonged neutropenia: Results of a prospective randomized multicenter trial. Blood *93*:3654–3661, 1999.
112. Slavin, M. A., Meyers, J. D., Remington, J. S., et al.: *Toxoplasma gondii* infection in bone marrow transplant recipients: A 20-year experience. Bone Marrow Transplant. *13*:549–557, 1994.
113. Singhal, S., and Mehta, J.: Reimmunization after blood or marrow stem cell transplantation. Bone Marrow Transplant. *23*:637–646, 1999.
114. Steiner, M., Villablanca, J., Kersey, J., et al.: Viridans streptococcal shock in bone marrow transplant patients. Am. J. Hematol. *42*:354–358, 1993.
115. Stevens, D. A., Kan, V. L., Judson, M. A., et al.: Practice guidelines for diseases caused by *Aspergillus*. Clin. Infect. Dis. *30*:696–709, 2000.
116. Strasser, S. I., and McDonald, G. B.: Hepatitis viruses and hematopoietic stem cell transplantation: A guide to patient and donor management. Blood *93*:1127–1136, 1999.
117. Strauss, R. G.: Leukocyte-reduction to prevent transfusion-transmitted cytomegalovirus infections. Pediatr. Transplant. *3*(1):S19–S22, 1999.
118. Sullivan, K. M., Kopecky, K. J., Jocom, J., et al.: Immunomodulatory and antimicrobial efficacy of intravenous immunoglobulin in bone marrow transplantation. N. Engl. J. Med. *323*:705–712, 1990.
119. Trigg, M. E., Peters, C., and Zimmerman, M. B.: Administration of recombinant human granulocyte-macrophage colony-stimulating factor to children undergoing allogeneic marrow transplantation: A prospective, randomized, double-masked, placebo-controlled trial. Pediatr. Transplant. *4*:123–131, 2000.
120. Tuan, I. Z., Dennison, D., and Weisdorf, D. J.: *Pneumocystis carinii* pneumonitis following bone marrow transplantation. Bone Marrow Transplant. *10*:267–272, 1992.
121. Valteau, D., Hartmann, O., Brugieres, L., et al.: Streptococcal septicaemia following autologous bone marrow transplantation in children treated with high-dose chemotherapy. Bone Marrow Transplant. *7*:415–419, 1991.
122. Vance, E., George, S., Guinan, E. C., et al.: Comparison of multiple immunization schedules for *Haemophilus influenzae* type b-conjugate and tetanus toxoid vaccines following bone marrow transplantation. Bone Marrow Transplant. *22*:735–741, 1998.
123. Vartivarian, S. E., Anaissie, E. J., and Bodey, G. P.: Emerging fungal pathogens in immunocompromised patients: Classification, diagnosis and management. Clin. Infect. Dis. *17*(2):S487–S491, 1993.
124. Verfaille, C., Weisdorf, D. J., Haake, R. J., et al.: *Candida* infections in bone marrow transplant recipients. Bone Marrow Transplant. *8*:177–184, 1991.
125. Walsh, T. J., Finberg, R. W., Arndt, C., et al.: Liposomal amphotericin B for empirical therapy in patients with persistent fever and neutropenia. N. Engl. J. Med. *340*:764–771, 1999.
126. Walter, E. A., Greenberg, P. D., Gilbert, M. J., et al.: Reconstitution of cellular immunity against cytomegalovirus in recipients of allogeneic bone marrow by transfer of T-cell clones from the donor. N. Engl. J. Med. *333*:1038–1044, 1995.
127. Walters, M. C., Patience, M., Leisenring, W., et al.: Bone marrow transplantation for sickle cell disease. N. Engl. J. Med. *330*:827–838, 1996.
128. Wasserman, R., August, C. S., and Plotkin, S. A.: Viral infections in pediatric bone marrow transplant patients. Pediatr. Infect. Dis. J. *7*:109–115, 1988.
129. Wendt, C. H., Weisdorf, D. J., Jordan, M. C., et al.: Parainfluenza virus respiratory infection after bone marrow transplantation. N. Engl. J. Med. *326*:921–926, 1992.
130. Whimbey, E., Champlin, R. E., Couch, R. B., et al.: Community respiratory virus infections among hospitalized adult bone marrow transplant recipients. Clin. Infect. Dis. *22*:778–782, 1996.
131. Wingard, J. R., Merz, W. G., Rinaldi, M. G., et al.: Increase in *Candida krusei* infection among patients with bone marrow transplantation and neutropenia treated prophylactically with fluconazole. N. Engl. J. Med. *325*:1274–1277, 1991.
132. Winston, D. J., Ho, W. G., Lin, C-H., et al. Intravenous immunoglobulin for prevention of interstitial pneumonia after bone marrow transplantation. Ann. Intern. Med. *106*:12–18, 1987.
133. Wolff, S. N., Fay, J., Stevens, D., et al.: Fluconazole *vs* low-dose amphotericin B for the prevention of fungal infections in patients undergoing bone marrow transplantation: A study of the North American Marrow Transplant Group. Bone Marrow Transplant. *25*:853–859, 2000.
134. Wong-Beringer, A., Jacobs, R. A., and Guglielmo, B. J.: Lipid formulations of amphotericin B: Clinical efficacy and toxicities. Clin. Infect. Dis. *27*:603–618, 1998.
135. Zaia, J. A.: Epidemiology and pathogenesis of cytomegalovirus disease. Semin. Hematol. *27*(1):S5–S10, 1990.

Infection in Pediatric Heart Transplant Recipients

SHELDON L. KAPLAN

Each year in the United States more than 300 children undergo heart transplantation,[57] and infection is an important cause of morbidity and some mortality in these patients. The Pediatric Heart Transplant Study Group prospectively collected data from 22 pediatric centers in the United States from January 1993 to December 1994 on 332 children younger than 18 years (mean age, 5.5 years) who had undergone heart transplantation.[107] One or more infections (276 total) occurred in 41 percent of the patients (mean follow-up time, 11.8 months) for an average of 0.84 infections per patient; 22 percent had 1 infection, 8 percent had 2 infections, and 11 percent had 3 or more infections during the study period (Table 77–1). In a similar multicenter study in adults who had undergone heart transplantation between January 1990 and June 1991, infections developed in 31 percent of 814 patients, with 22 percent having 1 infection and 9 percent having 2 or more infections.[78] Bacterial infections were the most common type of infection occurring after transplantation in both pediatric and adult patients.

Immunosuppressive therapy for children who have undergone heart transplantation usually consists of some combination of cyclosporine, azathioprine, and corticosteroids. Induction immunosuppression may include antithymocyte globulin or monoclonal OKT3, and some centers administer tacrolimus instead of cyclosporine; in addition, mycophenolate mofetil may be substituted for azathioprine.[23] Cyclosporine and tacrolimus predominantly block the effect of interleukin-2 on T cells, an action resulting in a diminished T-cell response to mitogen stimulation.[45] The infections seen in heart transplant patients outside the postoperative period generally are a result of this block in T-cell function. Because the types of infection seen in these patients vary with the time elapsed since transplantation, this chapter is organized in such a manner.

TABLE 77–1 ▪ TYPES OF INFECTIONS ENCOUNTERED IN 332 CHILDREN AFTER HEART TRANSPLANTATION IN A MULTI-INSTITUTIONAL STUDY*

Type	Number
Bacterial (total)	164
Coagulase-negative staphylococci	25
Enterobacter species	21
Pseudomonas aeruginosa	16
Cytomegalovirus	51
Varicella-zoster	11
Respiratory syncytial virus	10
Herpes simplex	6
Other viruses	8
Fungal	19
Candida species	12
Pneumocystis carinii	7

*Two hundred seventy-six infections in 136 patients.

Data from Schowengerdt, K. O., Naftel, D., Seib, P. M., et al.: Infection after pediatric heart transplantation; results of a multiinstitutional study. J. Heart Lung Transplant. *16*:1207–1216, 1997.

Pretransplantation Evaluation

Several infectious agents may be transmitted to the patient via the transplanted organ or can become "reactivated" after transplantation. Thus, determining the antibody status of the recipient, as well as the donor, against selected microorganisms (cytomegalovirus [CMV], Epstein-Barr virus [EBV], *Toxoplasma gondii*) helps anticipate or diagnose infections that develop subsequent to transplantation. A reasonable pretransplant evaluation for children is outlined in Table 77–2. The child's immunization status is documented, and vaccinations are completed when possible (i.e., hepatitis B vaccine or *Streptococcus pneumoniae*). The Committee on Infectious Diseases of the American Academy of Pediatrics (AAP) recommends that for immunized children older than 12 months who are scheduled to undergo solid organ transplantation, serologic tests be performed for rubeola, mumps, rubella, and varicella to determine whether protective titers are present.[3] If possible, appropriate vaccines should be administered at least 1 month before the patient undergoes transplantation. Evidence of selected active infections is a contraindication for transplantation. Chemoprophylaxis should be considered strongly for children with a positive tuberculin skin test (purified protein derivative). Dental status also is assessed.

In addition to having the routine pretransplant evaluation as outlined in Table 77–2, each patient should be screened carefully for selected infections appropriate to the individual circumstances. If surgery is planned during the respiratory disease season and the patient has respiratory symptoms just before surgery, screening for influenza virus

TABLE 77–2 ▪ EVALUATION OF CHILDREN BEFORE HEART TRANSPLANTATION

Serology
- Cytomegalovirus
- Epstein-Barr virus
- *Toxoplasma gondii*
- Human immunodeficiency virus
- Hepatitis A, B, and C
- Rubeola, mumps, rubella, varicella*

Cultures
- Nasopharyngeal, stool, or tracheal aspirates†

Skin tests
- Purified protein derivative

Freezing of an extra aliquot of serum

Review of the child's immunization status

*For children who are older than 12 months and previously immunized.
†See text for an explanation.

or respiratory syncytial virus (RSV) by rapid techniques may facilitate prescribing antiviral therapy postoperatively. In areas where community-acquired methicillin-resistant *Staphylococcus aureus* (MRSA) is an important cause of infection, performing surface cultures to detect MRSA colonization may modify the choice of antibiotics for surgical prophylaxis.[55] Children from resource-poor countries may harbor *Salmonella* or intestinal parasites asymptomatically, and these organisms can cause serious infection after the child undergoes transplantation. Preoperative stool cultures for enteropathogens and examination of the stool for parasites may alert the clinicians that these pathogens are present and could be the etiology of postoperative infections. If the patient is being mechanically ventilated before undergoing transplantation, review of recent tracheal aspirate cultures may help in the selection of empiric antibiotics for initial treatment of suspected nosocomial sepsis or pneumonia. Pretransplant infections associated with procedures such as implantation of ventricular assist devices may require prolonged antibiotic therapy after transplantation is performed.[72] These infections typically are caused by common nosocomial pathogens and are not a contraindication to undergoing heart transplantation.

Surgical Prophylactic Antibiotics

Prophylactic antibiotics typically are administered to patients undergoing heart transplantation surgery. For each institution, selection of prophylactic antibiotics should be based, in part, on the organisms isolated from postoperative wound infections in that center and the antimicrobial susceptibility of these organisms. Cefazolin generally is a reasonable choice for prophylaxis unless MRSA is a nosocomial pathogen of concern, in which case vancomycin is suggested. Furthermore, in areas where MRSA is a common community pathogen, vancomycin or some other antibiotic active against MRSA should be considered rather than cefazolin, as determined by preoperative surveillance cultures. Routine use of extended-spectrum cephalosporins is to be discouraged because it may lead to colonization of the patient by antibiotic-resistant gram-negative organisms that hyperproduce β-lactamase, such as *Enterobacter cloacae.* Recommendations for the duration of prophylactic antibiotic treatment in these patients are not definite, but some centers continue prophylactic antibiotics for 2 to 5 days or more postoperatively or until all lines and chest tubes have been removed.

Immediate Postoperative Infections

COMMON INFECTIONS

During the month after the patient undergoes heart transplantation, the types of infections encountered are the same as those complicating major thoracic surgery. Pneumonia and bacteremia are the most common postoperative infections. The frequency of bacteremia and the distribution of organisms are similar in children and adults after undergoing heart transplantation.[78, 107] In a multi-institutional study, the risk of development of any infection was 25 percent 1 month after transplantation. Overall, 60 episodes of bacteremia occurred in the 136 patients who became infected, and the bloodstream was the most common site of bacterial infection.[107] Lung abscesses and mediastinitis are seen less frequently. Familiarity with the organisms and the antimicrobial susceptibility of isolates recovered from other children in the intensive care units (ICUs) in which these patients receive care helps direct the initial selection of empiric antibiotics.

Postoperative bacteremia is related predominantly to the indwelling lines required for monitoring and infusion of medication. *S. aureus*, coagulase-negative staphylococci, *Enterococcus* spp., and gram-negative enteric organisms such as *Enterobacter* spp., *Pseudomonas aeruginosa*, *Klebsiella* spp., and *Escherichia coli* are the most common causes of nosocomial bacteremia in the pediatric ICU.[97] Other foci of infection, such as pneumonia or mediastinitis, also may result in bacteremia.[126] Vancomycin plus an aminoglycoside is a typical empiric antibiotic combination for suspected bacteremia in patients with central lines in place and without focal evidence of infection. Vancomycin therapy should be discontinued as soon as possible if an organism requiring the administration of vancomycin is not isolated.[94] A bacterial line infection may be eradicated successfully without removing the line, but the line should be removed if blood cultures remain positive or the patient's clinical condition deteriorates.[105] Fungemia, generally with *Candida albicans* or other *Candida* spp., also may be associated with line-related infections. Central lines complicated by fungemia should be removed immediately.[32] Moreover, centrally placed lines must be removed as soon as practical so that catheter-associated infections can be prevented.

As in other critically ill children, pneumonia is a particularly common occurrence in heart transplant patients because of the operative site and requirements for intubation and mechanical ventilation. During the first postoperative week, definite bacterial pneumonia developed in 3 of 22 children (14%) in an early study from Pittsburgh.[49] In the pediatric multi-institutional study, 56 bacterial lung infections were identified, 24 of which developed in patients maintained on a ventilator at the time of transplantation.[107] Nosocomial pneumonia caused by gram-negative bacilli such as *Pseudomonas* and *Enterobacter* or *S. aureus* is an especially common development in this setting.[97] Daily chest radiographs taken until the patient is out of intensive care may identify pneumonitis before it is clinically suspected. Gram stain and culture of a tracheal aspirate can help guide therapy for lobar pneumonia. A broad-spectrum combination of antibiotics such as an extended-spectrum penicillin with a β-lactamase inhibitor (i.e., piperacillin-tazobactam or ticarcillin-clavulanate) plus an aminoglycoside usually is initiated until a pathogen or pathogens are identified. However, empiric therapy should be based on the antibiotic susceptibility patterns of the common nosocomial pathogens in the specific ICU in which the patient is receiving care. Vancomycin again also should be considered if MRSA is part of the resident flora in the ICU. Computed tomography (CT) of the chest may detect basilar and retrocardiac pneumonia that may not be visualized readily by conventional chest radiographs. CT or ultrasound generally is helpful in assessing the size or characteristics of pleural effusions that may require drainage.

If interstitial pneumonitis is encountered, a more aggressive approach to determining an etiology is warranted. Bronchoscopy with bronchoalveolar lavage should be considered strongly. In children with pulmonary infiltrates after heart transplantation, flexible bronchoscopy is more useful for establishing a fungal or viral etiology as opposed to a bacterial cause of pneumonia because most patients have received broad-spectrum antibiotics before undergoing the procedure.[119] Lavage fluid is pooled and processed for bacteria, including mycobacteria, and for viruses, fungi, and protozoa by using culture techniques as well as special stains. *Legionella* may be an important consideration in some centers.[16, 95] Noninfectious causes of pulmonary infiltrates in these children include pulmonary edema, atelectasis, hemorrhage, and adult respiratory distress syndrome.

Urinary tract infections (UTIs) also are common occurrences in the month after heart transplantation. Urinary catheterization, as well as the immunosuppressive agents, contributes to the risk for developing UTI. Gram-negative enteric organisms (*E. coli, K. pneumoniae, P. aeruginosa,* and *Enterobacter* spp.), enterococci, and *Candida* spp. are isolated most commonly. Removal of the catheter as soon as possible minimizes the potential for development of a UTI, which has occurred in approximately 10 percent of adults. In the multicenter pediatric study, the urinary tract was the site of 16 bacterial infections.[107] In addition, UTI developed in three children (14%) in Pittsburgh during the 2 to 3 weeks after they underwent transplantation.[49] The broad-spectrum antibiotics used to treat the bacterial complications of transplantation promote *Candida* infection of the urinary tract. Along with removal of the urinary catheter, short-course intravenous amphotericin B for 10 days or less or fluconazole with careful dosing because of drug interactions with cyclosporine and tacrolimus is an option for treating candidal cystitis.[22, 35, 64] In some patients, a urine culture positive for *Candida* is a clue that a disseminated *Candida* infection is present and that further investigation is necessary to exclude the involvement of other organs, especially the kidneys.

Risk factors for early infection in the pediatric multi-institutional study were younger recipient age (particularly <6 months), mechanical ventilation at the time of transplantation, positive donor CMV serology with a CMV-negative recipient, and longer donor ischemic time.[107]

STERNAL WOUNDS AND MEDIASTINITIS

Sternal wound infections and mediastinitis occur in less than 5 percent of adult patients receiving modern immunosuppressive therapy for heart transplantation.[60, 78, 79] Most of these infections occur during the first postoperative month, usually within the first 2 weeks, and are superficial. Almost all are caused by bacteria. Staphylococci and other gram-positive bacteria generally are responsible for 50 percent of cases, and the remainder are caused by a variety of gram-negative bacilli.[81] Surgical wound infections developed in eight children in the pediatric multi-institution study, although the site of the infection was not noted.[107] Postoperative bleeding requiring re-exploration is a risk factor for development of mediastinitis. Fever, incisional pain, and an unstable sternum suggest mediastinitis; however, patients may have no specific evidence of infection, including fever. The white blood cell count may be elevated. A pericardial effusion frequently is detected with the development of mediastinitis, and pericardiocentesis may yield purulent material. CT of the chest may demonstrate a fluid collection or abscess within the mediastinum and can detect sternal osteomyelitis. Most cases of mediastinitis are caused by *S. aureus*, coagulase-negative staphylococci, or gram-negative bacteria. Median sternotomy wound infections after repair of a congenital heart lesion occur in less than 1 percent of children in large centers. Mediastinitis caused by gram-negative bacilli in association with pneumonia and bacteremia developed in 3 of the 22 children in the Pittsburgh series; each occurred within 2 weeks postoperatively.[49] Two of the three patients died.

A superficial median sternotomy wound infection not associated with an unstable sternum can be treated by local drainage of the infected subcutaneous tissue and appropriate antibiotics.[28] A more aggressive approach is required for more serious infections associated with an unstable sternum, mediastinitis, or osteomyelitis of the sternum.[19, 28, 60] Adequate drainage and débridement of the area are crucial, and any involved wires should be removed. Mediastinal drains usually are kept in place for several days. Some authorities recommend irrigating the drains with povidone-iodine, but the duration of irrigation is uncertain. Performing a reoperation after the initial drainage procedure may be necessary. Pending culture results, antibiotic therapy is directed against *S. aureus* and gram-negative bacilli. A 4- to 6-week course of antibiotics usually is recommended. Careful attention to surgical technique to minimize postoperative bleeding and early withdrawal of chest and mediastinal tubes placed intraoperatively decrease the incidence of these potentially fatal infections.

OTHER INFECTIONS ENCOUNTERED DURING THE FIRST POSTOPERATIVE MONTH

Herpes Simplex

Herpes simplex infections of the oral mucosa and other superficial surfaces are relatively common events after heart transplantation. Oral herpes simplex was observed in 21 percent (11/53) of children undergoing transplantation at Stanford.[12] In the pediatric multi-institutional study, only six episodes of herpes simplex infection were noted. Visceral involvement is an unusual occurrence, although it may develop.[68] Herpes simplex infections typically occur approximately 13 days (range, 0 to 4 months) after transplantation and are reactivation processes, not newly acquired infections.[91] A decrease in lymphocyte transformation in response to viral antigen in vitro may explain the increased rate of infection that occurs in the first 12 weeks post-transplantation.

Antiviral therapy for herpes simplex infection is warranted in these immunocompromised patients. The most common antiviral agent for herpes simplex is acyclovir, which can be administered orally or intravenously. Valacyclovir dosing in children has not been established, and a suspension is not available.

Some authorities recommend prophylactic acyclovir for heart transplant patients who are seropositive for herpes simplex.[44] Acyclovir is given intravenously during the perioperative period and then orally for 30 days. Other physicians suggest that because labial or oral herpes simplex is treated so easily, a prophylactic approach is not warranted. In view of concern related to toxicity, drug interactions, and the possibility of resistance developing, I favor the approach that targets treatment once a mucocutaneous lesion is noted.

Legionella pneumophila

L. pneumophila infection should be included in the differential diagnosis for fever, respiratory symptoms, and pulmonary infiltrates that develop after heart transplantation.[21] *Legionella* pneumonia can develop during the first postoperative month, but the frequency at which this infection occurs varies among transplant centers. Although legionnaires' disease is not a common occurrence in children, nosocomial infections have been documented in a children's hospital, and immunosuppression is a risk factor.[16, 18] Appropriate cultures and direct fluorescent antibody stains for *Legionella* should be performed on sputum, other respiratory secretions (obtained by invasive techniques), pleural fluid, or lung tissue to detect this pathogen in a timely fashion. A *Legionella* urinary antigen test is available for serogroup 1 antigens and is quite sensitive.[120] Macrolides should be contemplated for empiric therapy if *Legionella* is a serious consideration in children with nosocomial pneumonia. Erythromycin or azithromycin is provided for 2 weeks to complete therapy. However, macrolides interact with many of the immunosuppressive agents administered to these patients. Quinolones also are quite active against *Legionella* and avoid many of these interactions; in adult transplant patients they have become the agents of choice.[120] The use of quinolones should be considered for pediatric organ transplant patients in whom infection with *L. pneumophila* is suspected. In hospitals caring for transplant patients, routine surveillance culture of the hospital water supply is recommended.

Respiratory Syncytial Virus

Ten episodes of RSV infection were noted in the pediatric multi-institutional study.[107] RSV can be acquired in the hospital soon after undergoing transplantation or can be acquired in the community before undergoing surgery or after discharge. Too few patients in whom RSV infection developed after they underwent heart transplantation have been described to comment on the clinical features. Two children in the early Pittsburgh study were noted to be infected with RSV, both occurring on postoperative day 10. Rapidly progressive patchy infiltrates on chest radiographs developed in one child after heart-lung transplantation was performed, and the second child had only mild upper respiratory symptoms.[49] Tachypnea, cough, fever, wheezing, and the use of accessory muscles occurred commonly in the 18 pediatric liver transplant recipients from Pittsburgh with RSV infection.[90] Radiographic changes included interstitial and lobar infiltrates, atelectasis, and pleural effusion in 12 patients. Two patients required mechanical ventilation after the onset of symptoms related to RSV infection; three others were intubated before acquiring RSV infection and subsequently had complicated courses. Morbidity and mortality rates related to RSV infection are increased in otherwise immunocompetent children with congenital heart disease, especially when associated with pulmonary hypertension.[71] Because RSV can be acquired in the hospital, RSV infection should be considered in a young transplant patient with respiratory symptoms and fever, especially during the colder months.[51] RSV infection is documented by culture or by rapid detection of RSV infection by enzyme-linked immunosorbent assay or fluorescent antibody testing of respiratory secretions.

The decision to administer ribavirin to these patients is based primarily on the severity of the illness. In a small group of children with underlying bronchopulmonary dysplasia or congenital heart disease, aerosolized ribavirin appeared to be associated with more rapid improvement than that in patients given placebo.[52] Administration of aerosolized ribavirin to a heart transplant patient with proved or suspected moderate to severe RSV infection is reasonable. However, as is the case with children requiring mechanical ventilation because of severe RSV lower respiratory tract infection, the efficacy of ribavirin in this situation is unknown.[116] The Committee on Infectious Disease of the AAP recommends that ribavirin therapy be considered in infants and children with organ transplants who are at high risk for acquiring serious RSV disease and that such therapy be based on the particular clinical circumstance and the experience of the treating physicians.[6, 93]

No specific recommendations have been made regarding the use of palivizumab, a humanized mouse monoclonal antibody, in children who have undergone heart or other organ transplantation.[87, 92] The combination of ribavirin and RSV immune globulin (RSV-IG) has been administered to pediatric bone marrow transplant recipients with RSV lower respiratory tract infection.[25] The outcome in these patients was improved over that of historical controls, but no randomized trials have been conducted. Furthermore, RSV-IG was not efficacious in treating RSV lower respiratory tract infection in children with congenital heart disease who were younger than 2 years of age.[98] Although palivizumab reduced the concentration of RSV in the tracheal aspirates of children with respiratory failure caused by RSV, its efficacy in treatment is unknown.[73]

Infections between the First and Sixth Postoperative Months

CYTOMEGALOVIRUS

CMV is the virus that most frequently infects immunosuppressed cardiac transplant patients. Asymptomatic or symptomatic infections are noted most commonly between the first and sixth months after transplantation and rarely after the seventh month. In adult series, 12 to 90 percent of patients had evidence of CMV infection postoperatively.[27, 47, 78] In the multi-institutional pediatric study, 51 episodes of CMV infection occurred in 332 patients and accounted for 60 percent of the viral infections, with a peak occurrence in the second month after transplantation.[107] CMV infection occurred more frequently in older children than in infants. In another study, infants younger than 120 days had CMV infection and disease less commonly than those older than 120 days did after undergoing heart transplantation.[38] Maternal antibody to CMV may have been protective in the younger infants. In the Pittsburgh series, 7 children (32%) had CMV infections with onset at a mean of 33 days posttransplant (range, 23 to 43 days).

CMV infection in transplant recipients occurs in three or four possible settings. In a seronegative recipient, primary CMV infection is acquired through the transplanted heart, through blood transfusions from seropositive donors, or from the community. Seropositive recipients can have reactivation of latent CMV infection or be reinfected with a second strain of CMV from the heart or from blood products derived from seropositive donors.[20] The exact site within the donor heart where CMV may reside in a latent form is not known, but it may be either cardiac cells or leukocytes that remain within the donor heart. However, when primary CMV infection is acquired from the donor organ, CMV disease tends to be more severe than if CMV infection is acquired from blood or blood products.[128]

Several risk factors for development of CMV infection after undergoing organ transplantation are recognized. Donor and recipient serologic status and the immunosuppressive regimen are the most significant risk factors for acquiring CMV infection after undergoing heart transplantation. Gorensek and colleagues[47] found that positive recipient CMV serology before transplantation and a larger than average dose of corticosteroids were significant risk factors for acquiring CMV infection. Among the group of patients with CMV infection, positive recipient serology was associated with asymptomatic infection, and excessive steroid dosing was a risk factor for acquiring symptomatic CMV infection.

The clinical manifestations of CMV infection are quite variable. Patients may seroconvert or a latent infection may be reactivated, as determined by positive cultures, but these patients have no symptoms attributable to the CMV infection. Fever, leukopenia, and thrombocytopenia are common postoperative manifestations of systemic CMV infection. Patients may complain of arthralgias, myalgias, and nonspecific abdominal pain. Atypical lymphocytes are noted more commonly in adult than pediatric patients. CMV infection can cause hepatitis, pneumonitis, retinitis, myocarditis, and gastrointestinal disease, including colitis.[27, 33, 34, 46, 47, 59, 112] The retinitis may be asymptomatic or be associated with complaints such as floaters or scotomata. Thus, ophthalmologic screening for CMV retinitis is recommended for all patients 3 to 4 months after cardiac transplantation.[34]

Of the tissues invaded by CMV, involvement of the lung leads to the greatest mortality, 13 percent in one study.[63] CMV pneumonitis is characterized by fever, hypoxemia, and, usually, diffuse interstitial infiltrates, although lobar consolidation may occur.[111] Pulmonary infections with other viruses or with bacteria or *Pneumocystis carinii,* as well as other pathologic processes (infarction), may coexist with CMV pneumonitis. Gastritis, gastric ulceration, duodenitis, esophagitis, pyloric perforation, and colonic hemorrhage can be documented by endoscopy. In the multi-institutional pediatric study, the lung or gastrointestinal tract was the site of CMV infection in 13 and 6 episodes, respectively.[107] Death related to CMV in the pediatric study occurred in 6 percent.

The diagnosis of CMV infection can be based on changes in antibody titer to CMV in paired sera run in parallel with the use of established tests or on changes in CMV IgM results. Isolation of CMV or detection of CMV DNA from a variety of sources such as urine, blood, bronchial washings, or tissues also establishes that CMV infection is present. In a seronegative recipient, the possibility of active CMV infection can be anticipated by periodic monitoring of CMV serology and cultures. Whether the CMV infection is causing a symptomatic or invasive illness is more difficult to establish. Histopathologic evidence of CMV infection, such as typical viral inclusions or detection of antigen in tissue by special stains, is required to confirm organ involvement by CMV, although this criterion often is not considered a requirement for clinical trials of preventive measures for CMV disease. Cultures of the buffy coat are positive more frequently in patients with symptomatic than in those with asymptomatic CMV infection; in patients with primary CMV infection and lung involvement, CMV cultures tend to be positive earlier in the postoperative period than in those who do not have lung involvement.[47] CMV antigen–positive leukocytes detected by monoclonal antibodies to the early antigen of CMV were found 10 to 28 days before increases in CMV antibody in five patients with active CMV infection.[125] Polymerase chain reaction (PCR) can detect DNA from CMV in blood and other tissues readily and with great sensitivity.[37] The antigen and PCR techniques have been used for early detection of CMV infection so that preemptive antiviral therapy can be initiated.[29]

In addition to the CMV infection syndromes, CMV infection itself appears to affect the transplant recipient adversely in other ways. Symptomatic or asymptomatic CMV infection is associated with a higher rate of graft rejection or graft loss, a greater risk of fungal infection, and more frequent and earlier graft atherosclerosis, as well as a significantly lower survival rate, than in patients who do not experience CMV infection.[37, 100] In the multi-institutional study, positive donor CMV serology in conjunction with CMV-negative recipient serology was a risk factor for the acquisition of earlier infection with any organism.[107]

CMV infection of the wide variety of cells that it invades leads to the activation of protein synthesis and the production of multiple immunologically active molecules, including cytokines, especially tumor necrosis factor–α, which adds to the immune deficits induced by the immunosuppressive agents.[37, 65] Allograft injury or rejection may be associated with CMV infection of the transplanted organ itself.[37]

Successful treatment or suppression of visceral CMV disease by ganciclovir, a nucleoside analogue active in vitro against CMV, requires a timely diagnosis. Ganciclovir has been shown to alter CMV disease favorably in heart transplant patients, along with allowing a reduction in immunosuppressive therapy, when possible.[61] The standard approach for treating symptomatic CMV infection is 2 to 3 weeks of intravenous ganciclovir, although the optimal duration of this therapy and the need for maintenance oral doses are not clear.[101] The dose is 5 mg/kg every 12 hours with careful monitoring of hematologic parameters and renal function if renal function initially is normal. Modification of the dose is necessary if renal function is impaired. Viremia should be cleared before discontinuing therapy.[37] The most common adverse reactions to ganciclovir are neutropenia, thrombocytopenia, impaired renal function, seizures, and other central nervous system (CNS) abnormalities.

The role of CMV hyperimmune globulin in treating CMV infection in these patients requires further study. After bone marrow transplantation, the addition of CMV immune globulin to ganciclovir may be superior to ganciclovir alone in treating CMV pneumonia.[31, 96]

In one pediatric study, symptomatic CMV disease developed in five children after they had undergone heart transplantations; each had blood cultures and PCR positive for CMV.[40] Four were treated with ganciclovir for 14 days; one received ganciclovir for 30 days. All received CMV-IgG (150 mg/kg) weekly for 3 weeks. Symptomatic CMV disease was treated successfully in each case.

If possible, prevention of CMV infection in heart transplant recipients is optimal. Only seronegative blood should be used for transfusions when both the recipient and the donor are seronegative. Careful control of immunosuppressive therapy, especially with corticosteroids, may help avoid the acquisition of some infections. In a seronegative recipient of a heart from a seropositive donor, prophylactic administration of CMV immune globulin may be useful in some patients. In one study involving the prevention of CMV disease, ganciclovir was compared with CMV immune globulin (misoprostol [Cytotec]) in 31 CMV-seropositive heart transplant recipients in whom OKT3 monoclonal antibody was used for early immunoprophylaxis.[1] CMV disease and visceral involvement occurred more frequently in the CMV immune globulin group (40%) than in the ganciclovir group (6%; $p = .03$). However, CMV-IgG would be expected to be more beneficial in recipients who are CMV-seronegative.

In one large randomized double-blind, placebo-controlled trial of CMV-seropositive transplant recipients, ganciclovir significantly reduced CMV illness during the first 120 days after heart transplantation (9% versus 46% in controls, $p < .001$).[76] No differences were noted between the study groups for seronegative recipients. Combining ganciclovir and CMV-IgG for prophylaxis of high-risk seronegative recipients of hearts from seropositive donors has resulted in mixed findings. Avery found that the combination was not particularly effective; symptomatic CMV syndrome developed in 50 percent of patients.[10] Gajarski and associates[40] provided CMV-IgG (150 mg/kg intravenously at weeks 0, 2, 4, 6, and 8 and then 100 mg/kg intravenously at weeks 12 and 16) plus ganciclovir (5 mg/kg every 12 hours intravenously for weeks 1 and 2 and then 6 mg/kg/day intravenously in weeks 3 and 4) to 19 children who were recipients of heart transplants from CMV-seropositive donors. CMV disease occurred in 3 of the 10 children who were CMV-seronegative and in 1 of the 10 recipients who were seropositive. Adverse effects of these agents were not reported.

In the study from Stanford, high-risk recipients received CMV-IgG immediately after undergoing transplantation (150 mg/kg administered within 72 hours after transplantation, followed by 100 mg/kg at weeks 2, 4, 6, and 8 and 50 mg/kg at weeks 12 and 16).[123, 124] In addition, ganciclovir was administered intravenously immediately after transplantation at a dose of 5 mg/kg every 12 hours for 14 days, followed by 6 mg/kg/day for the next 2 weeks. These patients were compared with a historical control group at the same institution that received ganciclovir in the 2 to 3 years before CMV-IgG was used. The 27 recipients treated prophylactically with both ganciclovir and CMV-IgG had a higher disease-free incidence of CMV, a lower incidence of rejection, and a higher survival rate than did the historical cohort treated with ganciclovir alone. The combination looks promising for prevention of CMV disease in high-risk heart transplant recipients but requires a randomized trial before the combination can be routinely recommended.

CMV resistant to ganciclovir may emerge as a result of ganciclovir prophylaxis or treatment.[11] Foscarnet or cidofovir is an alternative agent in this situation.

EPSTEIN-BARR VIRUS

EBV may cause a spectrum of diseases in pediatric heart transplant recipients, including a mononucleosis-like syndrome, polyclonal lymphoproliferation, or monoclonal lymphoproliferation, usually of B cells. The transplanted organ is thought to be the source of EBV most frequently. Posttransplantation lymphoproliferative disorders (PTLDs) refer to B-cell expansion that may be localized, nodal, extranodal, or widely disseminated. The largest series of children who have undergone heart transplantation is from Pittsburgh; in this series, PTLD developed in 7.7 percent (6/78) of pediatric heart transplant recipients.[15] A major risk factor for the subsequent development of PTLD was being seronegative for EBV before undergoing transplantation. PTLD developed in one third of the seronegative recipients of thoracic organs who acquired primary EBV infection (10/30). In none of the children who were seropositive before transplantation did PTLD develop. Almost all these cases occurred within 1 year of transplantation. In another series, 19 children were EBV-seropositive and 31 were EBV-seronegative before undergoing heart transplantation. PTLD developed in 1 of 19 patients who were seropositive pretransplant and in 12 of 19 who became seropositive after undergoing transplantation.[130] It did not develop in any of the 12 recipients who remained EBV-seronegative. In contrast to the Pittsburgh experience, the mean time to confirmation of PTLD was 29 months (range, 3 to 72 months).

Symptoms of PTLD may include fever, malaise, sore throat, and lymphadenopathy. Some children may have splenomegaly, CNS symptoms such as lethargy or seizures, or gastrointestinal complaints.[13, 15] Concurrent opportunistic infections are common occurrences. Nodules in the lung may be noted on chest radiographs.

The diagnosis of PTLD requires biopsy of involved tissue showing lymphoid proliferation with an immunoblastic component. Molecular techniques typically detect EBV nucleic acids in tissue. EBV serology also is helpful. Quantitative measurement of EBV DNA and RNA in peripheral blood is being used to detect primary infection or reactivation at a very early time point, as well as to monitor viral loads serially over time to detect PTLD in the most timely manner.[99] When reported as EBV copies per 10^5 peripheral blood lymphocytes, patients with PTLD typically have viral loads between 500 and 5000, which are much greater than the loads detected in normal latency.

Management generally involves decreasing the immunosuppressive regimen or discontinuing it temporarily. Anti-CD20 antibody (rituximab) is a commercially available monoclonal antibody that specifically binds to the CD20 antigen of normal and malignant B cells and results in antibody- and complement-dependent cytotoxicity. Rituximab has been administered to children with PTLD after they have undergone solid organ transplantation, with some success.[110] Antiviral therapy with acyclovir or ganciclovir also is administered. Some centers administer ganciclovir, acyclovir, or intravenous gamma-globulin for prevention of PTLD, although no prospective studies have confirmed that such an approach is efficacious.[48]

TOXOPLASMA GONDII

An increased incidence of toxoplasmosis is apparent in recipients of heart transplants in comparison to other organ transplants, although it remains an uncommon infection after heart transplantation.[117] In the pediatric multi-institutional study, toxoplasmosis was not mentioned. *T. gondii* has a predilection for muscle and can be transmitted to the recipient from the heart of a seropositive donor. Active *T. gondii* infections may occur in donor hearts.[102] Less commonly, reactivation of old infection occurs in the recipient. The greatest risk for acquisition of toxoplasmosis occurs in a seronegative recipient of a heart from a seropositive donor. Clinical symptoms usually develop after the first postoperative month and generally within 3 months of transplantation.[53, 70, 77] Fever alone may be the only clinical manifestation. Dissemination of the parasite to the CNS may lead to signs and symptoms of meningoencephalitis, such as lethargy, seizures, coma, and hemiparesis. Chorioretinitis may result in diminished visual acuity. A sepsis-like picture, pneumonia, or cutaneous lesions are unusual manifestations.[9] CT or magnetic resonance imaging of the brain may detect ring-enhancing mass lesions, which typically are multiple and in periventricular locations. Definitive diagnosis of CNS toxoplasmosis requires the demonstration of tachyzoites or cysts in tissue by biopsy or at necropsy. Serologic tests help monitor seronegative patients for seroconversion and allow a more aggressive approach to the early diagnosis of toxoplasmosis.[115] *T. gondii* has been seen on endomyocardial biopsy specimens routinely obtained to monitor for rejection.[69]

Therapy for toxoplasmosis with pyrimethamine and sulfadiazine may lead to recovery; these drugs also should be administered if the patient seroconverts.[39] Prophylactic administration of pyrimethamine to seronegative recipients of hearts from seropositive donors is recommended.[129] Prophylactic trimethoprim-sulfamethoxazole also appears to be protective in this high-risk situation.[81] Spiramycin is not a useful prophylactic agent.[115]

ASPERGILLUS FUMIGATUS

A. fumigatus is the non-*Candida* fungal infection most commonly reported outside the immediate postoperative period in most series and may be noted first at necropsy.[88] In an early Stanford series, *Aspergillus* infections (four pulmonary, four disseminated) occurred in 8 of 72 (11%) cyclosporine-treated patients between 12 and 45 days postoperatively.[56] In a follow-up report, 54 *Aspergillus* infections developed in 620 consecutive heart transplant recipients between 1980 and 1996.[81] Most commonly, the *Aspergillus* infections were in the lung (n = 31) or were disseminated (n = 17). The median time to onset was 52 days. Disseminated aspergillosis was the single most common infectious episode responsible for the highest mortality rates in this series. One child in Pittsburgh had disseminated aspergillosis.[49] In the multi-institutional study, seven non-*Candida* fungal infections occurred: *Aspergillus* spp., two; *Cryptococcus, Rhizopus,* and *Rhizomucor,* one each; and unspecified, two. All patients with disseminated infection died.

CNS invasion occurs in many patients with pulmonary aspergillosis, and aspergillosis is the most common cause of brain abscess in organ transplant recipients.[53, 80, 114] Alterations in mental status occur most frequently, and seizures may occur in 40 percent of cases. On CT scans of the head, multifocal lesions are seen commonly and show a predilection for the junction of the gray and white matter.

Although isolation of *Aspergillus* from respiratory secretions in a patient with pneumonitis does not establish a diagnosis, aspergillosis is so difficult to establish firmly and is so frequently fatal that based on this culture alone, administration of amphotericin B should be considered seriously. The combination of amphotericin B plus flucytosine is recommended for invasive aspergillosis. Liposomal amphotericin B may provide an alternative therapy for patients failing treatment with or intolerant of conventional amphotericin B.[30, 127] The role of itraconazole for aspergillosis in heart transplant recipients is not clear. In one small study, amphotericin B was superior to itraconazole at a dose of 200 mg twice daily.[83] Caspofungin also may be beneficial in some patients, but the dose and safety of this agent have not been established in children.[8] Performing surgical drainage and débridement is important for managing most infections.[24] Some type of drainage procedure is indicated if CNS aspergillosis is documented or suspected, although the response to therapy with amphotericin B generally is dismal. In some centers, inhalation of aerosolized amphotericin B (20 mg in sterile water three times per day) has been used prophylactically throughout the hospital stay to prevent the acquisition of invasive aspergillosis.[81]

Infections after the Sixth Postoperative Month

NOCARDIA ASTEROIDES

A dry cough, fever, and the presence of a solitary pulmonary nodule or abscess on a chest radiograph are characteristic of infection with *N. asteroides*.[67, 113] Although pulmonary nodules are characteristic of *Nocardia, Aspergillus* and CMV can be associated with nodules as well.[82] Some patients are asymptomatic despite an abnormal chest radiograph. Infection with *Nocardia* was noted in only 3 percent of the cyclosporine-treated patients in the early Stanford series.[56] The median time to the onset of infection was 225 days. A similar incidence of lung nodules or masses secondary to *Nocardia* was noted in a series from New York.[54] In the follow-up Stanford series, 23 episodes of *Nocardia* infection (3.7%) occurred, 19 in the lung.[81] The median onset of infection in the second series was 147 days. *Nocardia* infections are very unusual events in pediatric heart transplant recipients.

Nocardia is isolated best from direct lung tissue specimens, but it may be cultured from bone, skin, or other sites of involvement as well. If a cutaneous skin lesion of *Nocardia* is recognized, other sites should be evaluated promptly for involvement.[43] The formation of single or multiple abscesses in the CNS may result from hematogenous dissemination.[53] Seizures may develop after invasion of brain parenchyma.

The drug of choice for treating *N. asteroides* infection is a sulfonamide. Prolonged administration (average of 10 months) generally leads to clearing of the pulmonary lesions. Minocycline is an alternative therapy.[89] The incidence of *Nocardia* infection has declined with the introduction of routine prophylaxis with trimethoprim-sulfamethoxazole.

PNEUMOCYSTIS CARINII

P. carinii pneumonia has been reported in approximately 3 to 4 percent of heart transplantation recipients during the postcyclosporine era.[36, 50, 56] In the multi-institutional study, *P. carinii* was noted in 7 children (2.1%).[107] Fever, a nonproductive cough, and tachypnea are typical symptoms; hypoxemia is characteristic. The chest radiograph classically shows a diffuse interstitial infiltrate that can progress rapidly. The most expeditious method of documenting *P. carinii* pneumonia in children is methenamine silver or specific antibody staining of fluid or tissue obtained by bronchoalveolar lavage or lung biopsy. Co-infection with CMV or other pathogens occurs commonly.

Treatment of *Pneumocystis* pneumonia in a pediatric heart transplant recipient is identical to that for other immunocompromised children. Use of trimethoprim-sulfamethoxazole prophylaxis for at least 4 months after transplantation has decreased markedly the incidence of this infection in recipients of heart transplants.[85]

STREPTOCOCCUS PNEUMONIAE

S. pneumoniae is an important community-acquired pathogen in heart transplantation recipients, who are at increased risk for acquiring this organism.[2] In the multi-institutional pediatric study, two episodes of pneumococcal infection were recorded.[107] During a 10-year period, 9 (11%) of 80 cardiac transplant patients in Little Rock, Arkansas, had 12 episodes of pneumococcal bacteremia.[121] In the follow-up series from Stanford, seven pulmonary infections with *S. pneumoniae* were reported.[81] In an eight-center pediatric surveillance study spanning 5 years, pneumococcal infection developed in 10 patients after a median time from transplantation of 17 months (range, 5 to 76 months).[109] Three of the 10 patients had two episodes, and 1 patient had three episodes of pneumococcal infection. The median age of the 10 patients at the time of the first pneumococcal infection was 26 months (range, 15 to 89 months). The pneumococcal serotypes of the isolates from these patients were the same as noted in normal children and generally would be covered by the 23-valent pneumococcal vaccine or the 7-valent pneumococcal conjugate vaccine.

OTHER VIRUSES

Influenza and parainfluenza viruses can cause serious infections at any time after transplantation, but especially in the immediate postoperative period.[7, 74] Additional risk factors for development of severe disease leading to death are young age and augmentation of immunosuppression. Fever, cough, rhinorrhea, and pharyngitis are typical symptoms of upper respiratory infections. More serious manifestations include adult respiratory distress syndrome, a requirement for intubation and mechanical ventilation, a sepsis-like picture, or CNS symptoms such as headache, photophobia, and lethargy. Viral infection may enhance the likelihood of allograft rejection occurring.

For influenza A infection, amantadine or rimantadine should be considered in younger children with a heart transplant because of their enhanced predisposition for severe or complicated influenza infection.[4] However, experience with either of these agents in patients with solid organ transplants is limited.[103] In older children, zanamivir or oseltamivir is indicated.

Parvovirus B19 infection is recognized to cause severe anemia associated with low or no reticulocytes in recipients of heart transplants, similar to the red blood cell suppression in other immunosuppressed patients.[84] In one child, severe pneumonia developed in association with fever and a blanching maculopapular rash involving the face, trunk, and extremities.[58] The parvovirus B19 genome also has been detected in myocardial biopsy specimens of children experiencing cardiac allograft rejection. Of six children described in one report, one had a diffuse rash and two had persistent rejection despite receiving aggressive therapy.[108] Intravenous immune globulin is beneficial for the treatment of anemia related to parvovirus B19, but its efficacy in treating pneumonia or possible allograft rejection is unknown.

Varicella virus infection remains a common childhood illness that can cause life-threatening disease in immunocompromised children. In a group of 28 children younger than 10 years at the time of heart transplantation who had been monitored for at least 1 year between 1986 and 1999, 14 cases of primary infection with varicella-zoster virus were identified.[26] The mean time post-transplant was 3 years (range, 9 months to 7.5 years). All were seronegative at the time of transplantation. These children were treated successfully with either parenteral followed by oral acyclovir or oral valacyclovir (mean dose, 77 mg/kg/day) for 7 days. Only one child had recurrent varicella, and none had zoster. Presumably, routine administration of varicella vaccine to young children would preclude most concerns about varicella developing after organ transplantation.

Cyclosporine and Antibiotics

Cyclosporine and tacrolimus have improved the success of organ transplantation considerably. In general, the incidence of infection appears to be less since the introduction of cyclosporine than with the earlier immunosuppressive regimens, although morbidity and morality rates remain high in heart transplant recipients.[62] Cyclosporine serum levels are monitored carefully to ensure that concentrations associated with optimal immunosuppression and minimal adverse effects are maintained. Some antibiotics interfere with the pharmacokinetics of cyclosporine, which may lead to an increase or decrease in cyclosporine levels.[17, 66, 86, 104, 106, 118, 122] Table 77–3 outlines these interactions. Because cyclosporine is nephrotoxic, the antimicrobial agents (amphotericin B, aminoglycosides, acyclovir, ceftazidime) administered to heart transplantation recipients may be additive; therefore, renal function must be monitored carefully.

TABLE 77–3 ■ EFFECT OF VARIOUS ANTIBIOTICS ON CYCLOSPORINE LEVELS

Increase Cyclosporine Level	Decrease Cyclosporine Level
Clarithromycin	Sulfadiazine
Azithromycin	Rifampin
Erythromycin	Trimethoprim-sulfamethoxazole
Ketoconazole	? Nafcillin
Fluconazole	? Isoniazid
Itraconazole	? Ciprofloxacin (counteracts immunosuppression)
Caspofungin	

Immunizations

No specific guidelines exist for the immunization of children after receiving a heart transplant, although studies examining the immunogenicity of selected vaccines in this population are being conducted. A prudent approach is to follow the recommendations that the Committee on Infectious Diseases of the AAP has developed for immunizing immunosuppressed children.[3] Ideally, the patient will have received the recommended routine vaccines before undergoing transplantation. Hepatitis A vaccine is recommended for patients who reside in areas with an increased incidence of this disease. Children who have received transplants before reaching 2 to 3 years of age do not respond to the pneumococcal polysaccharide vaccine as well as do children who are older when they receive their transplanted heart, even though the vaccine is administered several years after the transplant.[42] An impairment in immunoglobulin isotype switching from IgM to IgG and especially IgG2 appears to result from the immunosuppressive therapy that these children are receiving.[41] The conjugate pneumococcal vaccine is recommended for all children younger than 24 months, as well as for those as old as 60 months. Although no data related to antibody response to the pneumococcal conjugate vaccine in pediatric heart transplant recipients exist, I also recommend that before transplantation a single dose of the conjugate pneumococcal vaccine be administered to children older than 60 months. Ideally, the 23-valent pneumococcal vaccine is administered to children 2 months after completion of the conjugate series and before transplantation, if possible.[5] Ongoing immunosuppression appears to prevent maturation of the response to polysaccharide antigens in younger children, which it is hoped that the conjugate vaccine can overcome. The 23-valent pneumococcal vaccine is less immunogenic in adults after they have undergone heart transplantation than in healthy controls. Antibodies to the influenza vaccine will develop in most children, but previous exposure predicts a better response.[75] Annual administration of influenza vaccine appears safe and immunogenic in children after they have undergone solid organ transplantation. In one study, low-level histologic rejection occurred after the administration of influenza vaccine.[14] Depending on the time of year and the approximate date of transplantation, influenza vaccination is appropriate for the patient, as well as all household contacts and health care workers to whom the patient might be exposed.

After transplantation has been performed and after immunosuppressive therapy has been initiated, administration of live viral vaccines is contraindicated. The enhanced inactivated polio vaccine should be given to the child as well as to normal siblings. Measles, mumps, rubella, and varicella vaccines can be given to the siblings. Diphtheria, tetanus, and acellular pertussis inactivated vaccines should be given at the routine booster schedule, although antibody responses may not be equivalent to those observed in normal children. However, varicella vaccine should be administered before performing transplantation if varicella antibody is not detected at the pretransplant evaluation in a child 12 months of age or older. Whether the antibody response data generated in children with leukemia during maintenance chemotherapy can be applied to heart transplant recipients who must continue daily immunosuppressive therapy is unclear. Passive immunization with varicella-zoster immune globulin is indicated as recommended for other immunocompromised children.

REFERENCES

1. Aguado, J. M., Gomez-Sanchez, M. A., Lumbreras, C., et al.: Prospective randomized trial of efficacy of ganciclovir versus that of anti-cytomegalovirus (CMV) immunoglobulin to prevent CMV disease in CMV-seropositive heart transplant recipients treated with OKT3. Antimicrob. Agents Chemother. *39*:1643–1645, 1995.
2. Amber, I. J., Gilbert, E. M., Schiffman, G., and Jacobson, J. A.: Increased risk of pneumococcal infections in cardiac transplant recipients. Transplantation *49*:122–125, 1990.
3. American Academy of Pediatrics: Immunization in special circumstances. *In* Pickering, L. K. (ed.): 2000 Red Book: Report of the Committee on Infectious Diseases. 25th ed. Elk Grove Village, IL, American Academy of Pediatrics, 2000, p. 64.
4. American Academy of Pediatrics: Influenza. *In* Pickering, L. K. (ed.): 2000 Red Book: Report of the Committee on Infectious Diseases. 25th ed. Elk Grove Village, IL, American Academy of Pediatrics, 2000, p. 351.
5. American Academy of Pediatrics. Pneumococcal infections. *In* Pickering, L. K. (ed.): 2000 Red Book: Report of the Committee on Infectious Diseases. 25th ed. Elk Grove Village, IL, American Academy of Pediatrics, 2000, p. 452.
6. American Academy of Pediatrics: Respiratory syncytial virus. *In* Pickering, L. K. (ed.): 2000 Red Book: Report of the Committee on Infectious Diseases. 25th ed. Elk Grove Village, IL, American Academy of Pediatrics, 2000, p. 485.
7. Apalsch, A. M., Green, M., Ledesma-Medina, J., et al.: Parainfluenza and influenza virus infections in pediatric organ transplant recipients. Clin. Infect. Dis. *20*:394–399, 1995.
8. Arkin, S., Lozano-Chui, M., Paetnick, V., and Rex, J. H.: In vitro synergy of caspofungin and amphotericin B against *Aspergillus* and *Fusarium* spp. Antimicrob. Agents Chemother. *46*:245–247, 2002.
9. Arnold, S. J., Kinney, M. C., McCormick, S., et al.: Disseminated toxoplasmosis. Unusual presentation in the immunocompromised host. Arch. Pathol. Lab. Med. *121*:869–873, 1997.
10. Avery, R. K.: Prevention and treatment of cytomegalovirus infection and disease in heart transplant recipients. Curr. Opin. Cardiol. *13*:122–129, 1998.
11. Baldanti, F., Simoncini, L., Sarasini, A., et al.: Ganciclovir resistance as a result of oral ganciclovir in a heart transplant recipient with multiple human cytomegalovirus strains in blood. Transplantation *66*:324–329, 1998.
12. Baum, D., Bernstein, D., Starnes, V. A., et al.: Pediatric heart transplantation at Stanford: Results of a 15-year experience. Pediatrics *88*:203–214, 1991.
13. Bernstein, D., Baum, D., Berry, G., et al.: Neoplastic disorders after pediatric heart transplantation. Circulation *88*:230–237, 1993.
14. Blumberg, E. A., Fitzpatrick, J., Stutman, P. C., et al.: Safety of influenza vaccine in heart transplant recipients. J. Heart Lung Transplant. *17*:1075–1080, 1998.
15. Boyle, G. J., Michaels, M. G., Webber, S. A., et al.: Transplantation lymphoproliferative disorders in pediatric thoracic organ recipients. J. Pediatr. *131*:309–313, 1997.
16. Brady, M. T.: Nosocomial legionnaires' disease in a children's hospital. J. Pediatr. *115*:46–50, 1989.
17. Campana, C., Regazzi, M. B., Buggia, I., and Molinaro, M.: Clinically significant drug interactions with cyclosporine. An update. Clin. Pharmacokinet. *30*:141–179, 1996.
18. Carlson, N. C., Kuskie, M. R., Dobyns, E. L., et al.: Legionellosis in children: An expanding spectrum. Pediatr. Infect. Dis. J. *9*:133–137, 1990.
19. Carrier, M., Hudon, G., Paquet, E., et al.: Mediastinal and pericardial complications after heart transplantation. Not-so-unusual postoperative problems? Cardiovasc. Surg. *2*:395–397, 1994.
20. Chou, S.: Cytomegalovirus infection and reinfection transmitted by heart transplantation. J. Infect. Dis. *155*:1054–1056, 1987.
21. Chow, J. W., and Yu, V. L.: *Legionella:* A major opportunistic pathogen in transplant recipients. Semin. Respir. Infect. *13*:132–139, 1998.
22. Como, J. A., and Dismukes, W. E.: Oral azole drugs as systemic antifungal therapy. N. Engl. J. Med. *330*:263–272, 1994.
23. Deng, M. C.: Cardiac transplantation. Heart *87*:177–184, 2002.
24. Denning, D. W., and Stevens, D. A.: Antifungal and surgical treatment of invasive aspergillosis: Review of 2,121 published cases. Rev. Infect. Dis. *12*:1147–1201, 1990.
25. DeVincenzo, J. P., Hirsch, R. L., Fuentes, R. J., and Top, F. H., Jr.: Respiratory syncytial virus immune globulin treatment of lower respiratory tract infection in pediatric patients undergoing bone marrow transplantation—a compassionate use experience. Bone Marrow Transplant. *25*:161–165, 2000.
26. Dood, D. A., Burger, J., Edwards, K. M., and Dummer, J. S.: Varicella in a pediatric heart transplant population on nonsteroidal maintenance immunosuppression. Pediatrics 2001;108(5). URL: http:/www.pediatrics.org/cgi/content/full/108/5/e80.
27. Dummer, J. S., White, L. T., Ho, M., et al.: Morbidity of cytomegalovirus infection in recipients of heart or heart-lung transplants who received cyclosporine. J. Infect. Dis. *152*:1182–1191, 1985.
28. Edwards, M. S., and Baker, C. J.: Median sternotomy wound infections in children. Pediatr. Infect. Dis. *2*:105–109, 1983.
29. Egan, J. J., Lomax, J., Barber, L., et al.: Preemptive treatment for the prevention of cytomegalovirus disease in lung and heart transplant recipients. Transplantation *65*:747–752, 1998.
30. Ellis, M., Spence, D., de Pauw, B., et al.: An EORTC international multicenter randomized trial (EORTC Number 19923) comparing two dosages of liposomal amphotericin B for treatment of invasive aspergillosis. Clin. Infect. Dis. *27*:1406–1412, 1998.
31. Emanuel, D., Cunningham, I., Jules-Elysee, K., et al.: Cytomegalovirus pneumonia after bone marrow transplantation successfully treated with the combination of ganciclovir and high-dose intravenous immune-globulin. Ann. Intern. Med. *109*:777–782, 1988.
32. Epps, S. C., Troutman, J. L., and Gutman, L. T.: Outcome of treatment of candidemia in children whose central catheters were removed or retained. Pediatr. Infect. Dis. J. *8*:99–104, 1989.
33. Etheridge, S. P., Bolman, R. H., and Braunlin, E. A.: Cytomegalovirus colitis in a pediatric heart transplant patient. Clin. Transplant. *8*:409–412, 1994.
34. Fishburne, B. C., Mitrani, A. A., and Davis, J. L.: Cytomegalovirus retinitis after cardiac transplantation. Am. J. Ophthalmol. *125*:104–106, 1998.
35. Fisher, J. F., Chew, W. H., Shadomy, S., et al.: Urinary tract infections due to *Candida albicans.* Rev. Infect. Dis. *4*:1107–1118, 1982.
36. Fishman, J. A.: *Pneumocystis carinii* and parasitic infections in transplantation. Infect. Dis. Clin. North Am. *9*:1005–1074, 1995.
37. Fishman, J. A., and Rubin, R. H.: Infection in organ-transplant recipients. N. Engl. J. Med. *338*:1741–1751, 1998.
38. Fukushima, N., Gundry, S. R., Razzouk, A. J., and Bailey, L. L.: Cytomegalovirus infection in pediatric heart transplantation. Transplant. Proc. *25*:1423–1425, 1993.
39. Gallino, A., Maggiorini, M., Kiowoski, W., et al.: Toxoplasmosis in heart transplant recipients. Eur. J. Clin. Microbiol. Infect. Dis. *15*:389–393, 1996.
40. Garjarski, R. J., Rosenblatt, H. M., Denfield, S. W., et al.: Outcomes among pediatric heart transplant recipients after dual-therapy cytomegalovirus prophylaxis. Tex. Heart Inst. J. *24*:97–104, 1997.
41. Gennery, A. R., Cant, A. J., Baldwin, C. I., and Calvert, J. E.: Characterization of the impaired antipneumococcal polysaccharide antibody production in immunosuppressed pediatric patients following cardiac transplantation. J. Clin. Immunol. *21*:43–50, 2001.
42. Gennery, A. R., Cant, A. J., Spickett, G. P., et al.: Effect of immunosuppression after cardiac transplantation in early childhood on antibody response to polysaccharide antigen. Lancet *351*:1778–1781, 1998.
43. Gentry, L. O., Zeluff, B., and Kielhofner, M. A.: Dermatologic manifestations of infectious diseases in cardiac transplant patients. Infect. Dis. Clin. North Am. *8*:637–654, 1994.
44. Gold, D., and Corey, L.: Acyclovir prophylaxis for herpes simplex virus infection. Antimicrob. Agents Chemother. *31*:361–367, 1987.
45. Goldman, M. H., Barnhart, G., Mohanakumar, T., et al.: Cyclosporine in cardiac transplantation. Surg. Clin. North Am. *65*:637–659, 1985.
46. Gonwa, T. A., Capehart, J. E., Pilcher, J. W., and Alivizatos, P. A.: Cytomegalovirus myocarditis as a cause of cardiac dysfunction in a heart transplant recipient. Transplantation *47*:197, 1989.
47. Gorensek, M. J., Stewart, R. W., Keys, T. F., et al.: A multivariate analysis of the risk of cytomegalovirus infection in heart transplant recipients. J. Infect. Dis. *157*:515–522, 1988.
48. Green, M., Reyes, J., Webber, S., and Rowe, D.: The role of antiviral and immunoglobulin therapy in the prevention of Epstein-Barr virus infection and post-transplant lymphoproliferative disease following solid organ transplantation. Transpl. Infect. Dis. *3*:97–103, 2001.
49. Green, M., Wald, E. R., Fricker, F. J., et al.: Infections in pediatric orthotopic heart transplant recipients. Pediatr. Infect. Dis. J. *8*:87–93, 1989.
50. Gryzan, S., Paradis, I. L., Zeevi, A., et al.: Unexpectedly high incidence of *Pneumocystis carinii* infection after lung heart transplantation. Implications for lung defense and allograft survival. Am. Rev. Respir. Dis. *137*:1268–1274, 1988.
51. Hall, C. B., Douglas, R. G., Jr., Geiman, J. M., and Messner, M. K.: Nosocomial respiratory syncytial virus infections. N. Engl. J. Med. *293*:1343–1346, 1975.
52. Hall, C. B., McBride, J. T., Gala, C. L., et al.: Ribavirin treatment of respiratory syncytial viral infection in infants with underlying cardiopulmonary disease. J. A. M. A. *254*:3047–3051, 1985.

53. Hall, W. A., Martinez, A. J., Dummer, J. S., et al.: Central nervous system infections in heart and heart-lung transplantation recipients. Arch. Neurol. *46*:173–177, 1989.
54. Haramati, L. B., Schulman, L. L., and Austin, J. H.: Lung nodules and masses after cardiac transplantation. Radiology *188*:491–497, 1993.
55. Herold, B. C., Immergluck, L. C., Maranan, M. C., et al.: Community-acquired methicillin-resistant *Staphylococcus aureus* in children with no identifying predisposing risk. J. A. M. A. *279*:593–598, 1998.
56. Hofflin, J. M., Potasman, I., Baldwin, J. C., et al.: Infectious complications in heart transplant recipients receiving cyclosporine and corticosteroids. Ann. Intern. Med. *106*:209–216, 1987.
57. International Society for Heart and Lung Transplantation Registry. 18th Annual Report. www.ishlt.org.
58. Janner, D., Bork, J., Baum, M., and Chinnock, R.: Severe pneumonia after heart transplantation as a result of human parvovirus B19. J. Heart Lung Transplant. *13*:336–338, 1994.
59. Kaplan, C. S., Peterson, E. A., Icenogle, T. B., et al.: Gastrointestinal cytomegalovirus infection in heart and heart-lung transplant recipients. Arch. Intern. Med. *149*:2095–2100, 1989.
60. Karwande, S. V., Renlund, D. G., Olsen, S. L., et al.: Mediastinitis in heart transplantation. Ann. Thorac. Surg. *54*:1039–1045, 1992.
61. Keay, S., Petersen, E., Icenogle, T., et al.: Ganciclovir treatment of serious cytomegalovirus infection in heart and heart-lung transplant recipients. Rev. Infect. Dis. *10*(Suppl. 3):563–572, 1988.
62. Kim, J. H., and Perfect, J. R.: Infection and cyclosporine. Rev. Infect. Dis. *11*:677–690, 1989.
63. Kirklin, J. K., Naftel, D. C., Levine, T. B., et al.: Cytomegalovirus after heart transplantation. Risk factors for infection and death: A multiinstitutional study. J. Heart Lung Transplant. *13*:394–404, 1994.
64. Kohn, D. B., Uehling, D. T., Peters, M. E., et al.: Short-course amphotericin B therapy for isolated candiduria in children. J. Pediatr. *10*:310–313, 1987.
65. Koskinen, P. K., Kallio, E. A., Tikkanen, J. M., et al.: Cytomegalovirus infection and cardiac allograft vasculopathy. Transpl. Infect. Dis. *1*:115–126, 1999.
66. Kramer, M. R., Marshall, S. E., Denning, D. W., et al.: Cyclosporine and itraconazole interaction in heart and lung transplant recipients. Ann. Intern. Med. *113*:327–329, 1990.
67. Krick, J. A., Stinson, E. B., and Remington, J. S.: *Nocardia* infection in heart transplant patients. Ann. Intern. Med. *82*:18–26, 1975.
68. Kusne, S., Schwartz, M., Breinig, M. K., et al.: Herpes simplex virus hepatitis after solid organ transplantation in adults. J. Infect. Dis. *163*:1001–1007, 1991.
69. Luft, B. J., Billingham, M., and Remington, J. S.: Endomyocardial biopsy in the diagnosis of toxoplasmic myocarditis. Transplant. Proc. *83*:1871–1873, 1986.
70. Luft, B. J., Naot, Y., Araujo, F. G., et al.: Primary and reactivated *Toxoplasma* infection in patients with cardiac transplants, clinical spectrum and problems in diagnosis in a defined population. Ann. Intern. Med. *99*:27–31, 1983.
71. MacDonald, N. E., Hall, C. B., Suffin, S. C., et al.: Respiratory syncytial viral infection in infants with congenital heart disease. N. Engl. J. Med. *307*:397–400, 1982.
72. Malani, P. N., Dyke, D. B. S., Pagini, F. D., and Chenoweth, C. E.: Nosocomial infections in left ventricular device recipients. Clin. Infect. Dis. *34*:1295–1300, 2002.
73. Malley, R., DeVincenzo, J., Ramilo, O., et al.: Reduction of respiratory syncytial virus (RSV) in tracheal aspirates in intubated infants by use of humanized monoclonal antibody to RSV F protein. J. Infect. Dis. *178*:1555–1561, 1998.
74. Mauch, T. J., Bratton, S., Myers, T., et al.: Influenza B virus infection in pediatric solid organ transplant recipients. Pediatrics *94*:225–229, 1994.
75. Mauch, T. J., Crouch, N. A., Freese, D. K., et al.: Antibody response of pediatric solid organ transplant recipients to immunization against influenza virus. J. Pediatr. *127*:957–960, 1995.
76. Merigan, T. C., Renlund, D. G., Keay, S., et al.: A controlled trial of ganciclovir to prevent cytomegalovirus disease after heart transplantation. N. Engl. J. Med. *326*:1182–1186, 1992.
77. Michaels, M. G., Wald, E. R., Fricker, F. J., et al.: Toxoplasmosis in pediatric recipients of heart transplants. Clin. Infect. Dis. *14*:847–851, 1992.
78. Miller, L. W., Naftel, D. C., Bourge, R. C., et al.: Infection after heart transplantation. A multi-institutional study. J. Heart Lung Transplant. *13*:981–993, 1994.
79. Miller, R., Ruder, J., Karwande, S. V., and Burton, N. A.: Treatment of mediastinitis after heart transplantation. J. Heart Transplant. *5*:477–479, 1986.
80. Montero, C. G., and Martinez, A. J.: Neuropathy of heart transplantation: 23 cases. Neurology *36*:1149–1154, 1986.
81. Montoya, J. G., Giraldo, L. F., Efron, B., et al.: Infectious complications among 620 consecutive heart transplant patients at Stanford University Medical Center. Clin. Infect. Dis. *33*:629–640, 2001.
82. Muñoz, P., Palomo, J., Guembe, P., et al.: Lung nodular lesions in heart transplant recipients. J. Heart Lung Transplant. *19*:660–667, 2000.
83. Nanas, J. N., Saroglou, G., Anastasion-Nana, M. I., et al.: Itraconazole for the treatment of pulmonary aspergillosis in heart transplant recipients. Clin. Transplant. *12*:30–34, 1998.
84. Nour, B., Green, M., Michaels, M., et al.: Parvovirus B 19 infection in pediatric transplant patients. Transplantation *56*:835–838, 1993.
85. Olsen, S. L., Renlund, D. G., O'Connell, J. B., et al.: Prevention of *Pneumocystis carinii* pneumonia in cardiac transplant recipients by trimethoprim-sulfamethoxazole. Transplantation *56*:359–362, 1993.
86. Osowski, C. L., Dix, S. P., Lin, S. L., et al.: Evaluation of the drug interaction between intravenous high-dose fluconazole and cyclosporine or tacrolimus in bone marrow transplant patients. Transplantation *61*:1268–1272, 1996.
87. Palivizumab, a humanized respiratory syncytial virus monoclonal antibody, reduces hospitalization from respiratory syncytial virus infection in high-risk infants. The IMpact-RSV Study Group. Pediatrics *102*:531–537, 1998.
88. Paya, C. V.: Fungal infections in solid-organ transplantation. Clin. Infect. Dis. *16*:677–688, 1993.
89. Peterson, E. A., Nash, M. L., Mammana, R. B., and Copeland, J. G.: Minocycline treatment of pulmonary nocardiosis. J. A. M. A. *250*: 930–932, 1983.
90. Pohl, C., Green, M., Wald, E. R., and Ledesma-Medina, J.: Respiratory syncytial virus infections in pediatric liver transplant recipients. Clin. Infect. Dis. *165*:166–169, 1992.
91. Pollard, R. B., Arvin, A. M., Gambert, P., et al.: Specific cell-mediated immunity and infections with herpes viruses in cardiac transplant recipients. Am. J. Med. *73*:679–687, 1982.
92. Prevention of respiratory syncytial virus infections: Indications for the use of palivizumab and update on the use of RSV-IGIV. American Academy of Pediatrics and Committee on Infectious Diseases and Committee on Fetus and Newborn. Pediatrics *102*:1211–1216, 1998.
93. Reassessment of the indications for ribavirin therapy in respiratory syncytial virus infections. American Academy of Pediatrics Committee on Infectious Diseases. Pediatrics *97*:137–140, 1996.
94. Recommendation for preventing the spread of vancomycin resistance. Hospital Infection Control Practices Advisory Committee (PICPAC). Infect. Control Hosp. Epidemiol. *16*:105–113, 1995.
95. Redd, S. C., Schuster, D. M., Quan, J., et al.: Legionellosis in cardiac transplant recipients: Results of a nationwide study. J. Infect. Dis. *158*:651–653, 1988.
96. Reed, E. C., Bowden, R. A., Dandliker, P. S., et al.: Treatment of cytomegalovirus pneumonia with ganciclovir and intravenous cytomegalovirus immunoglobulin in patients with bone marrow transplants. Ann. Intern. Med. *109*:783–788, 1988.
97. Richards, M. J., Edwards, J. R., Culver D. H., et al.: Nosocomial infections in pediatric intensive care units in the United States. Pediatrics www.pediatrics.org/cgi/content/full/103/4/e39.
98. Rodriguez, W. J., Gruber, W. C., Welliver, R. C., et al.: Respiratory syncytial virus (RSV) immune globulin intravenous therapy for RSV lower respiratory tract infection in infants and young children at high risk for severe RSV infections. Pediatrics *99*:454–461, 1997.
99. Rowe, D. T., Webber, S., Schauer, E. M., et al.: Epstein-Barr virus load monitoring: Its role in the prevention and management of post-transplant lymphoproliferative disease. Transpl. Infect. Dis. *3*:79–87, 2001.
100. Rubin, R. H.: The indirect effects of cytomegalovirus infection on the outcome of organ transplantation. J. A. M. A. *261*:3607–3609, 1989.
101. Rubin, R. H.: Prevention and treatment of cytomegalovirus disease in heart transplant patients. J. Heart Lung Transplant. *19*:731–735, 2000.
102. Ryning, F. W., McLeod, R., Maddox, J. C., et al.: Probable transmission of *Toxoplasma gondii* by organ transplantation. Ann. Intern. Med. *90*:47–49, 1979.
103. Sable, C. A., and Hayden, F. G.: Orthomyxoviral and paramyxoviral infections in transplant patients. Infect. Dis. Clin. North Am. *9*:987–1003, 1994.
104. Sadaba, B., Lopez de Ocariz, A., Jr., Quiroga, J., and Cienfuegos, J. A.: Concurrent clarithromycin and cyclosporine A treatment. J. Antimicrob. Chemother. *42*:393–395, 1998.
105. Salzman, M. B., and Rubin, L. G.: Intravenous catheter–related infections. Adv. Pediatr. Infect. Dis. *10*:337–368, 1995.
106. Sands, M., and Brown, R. B.: Interactions of cyclosporine with antimicrobial agents. Rev. Infect. Dis. *11*:691–697, 1989.
107. Schowengerdt, K. O., Naftel, D., Seib, P. M., et al.: Infection after pediatric heart transplantation: Results of a multiinstitutional study. The Pediatric Heart Transplant Study Group. J. Heart Lung Transplant. *16*:1207–1216, 1997.
108. Schowengerdt, K. O., Ni, J., Denfield, S. W., et al.: Association of parvovirus B19 genome in children with myocarditis and cardiac allograft rejection. Diagnosis using the polymerase chain reaction. Circulation *96*:3549–3554, 1997.
109. Schutze, G. E., Mason, E. O., Jr., Wald, E. R., et al.: Pneumococcal infections in children after transplantation. Clin. Infect. Dis. *33*:16–21, 2001.
110. Serinet, M. O., Jacquemin, E., Habes, D., et al.: Anti-CD20 monoclonal antibody (rituximab) treatment for Epstein-Barr virus–associated, B-cell lymphoproliferative disease in pediatric liver transplant recipients. J. Pediatr. Gastroenterol. Nutr. *34*:389–393, 2002.
111. Shulman, L. L.: Cytomegalovirus pneumonitis and lobar consolidation. Chest *91*:558–601, 1978.

112. Shuster, L. D., Cox, G., Bhatia, P., and Miner, P. B., Jr.: Gastric mucosal nodules due to cytomegalovirus infection. Dig. Dis. Sci. *34*:103–107, 1989.
113. Simpson, G. L., Stinson, E. B., Egger, M. J., and Remington, J. S.: Nocardial infections in the immunocompromised host: A detailed study in a defined population. Rev. Infect. Dis. *3*:492–508, 1981.
114. Singh, N., and Husain, S.: Infections of the central nervous system in transplant recipients. Transpl. Infect. Dis. *2*:101–111, 2000.
115. Sluiters, J. F., Balk, A. H. M. M., Essed, C. E., et al.: Indirect enzyme-linked immunoassay for immunoglobulin G and four immunoassays for immunoglobulin M to *Toxoplasma gondii* in a series of heart transplantation recipients. J. Clin. Microbiol. *27*:529–535, 1989.
116. Smith, D. W., Frankel, L. R., Mathers, L. H., et al.: A controlled trial of aerosolized ribavirin in infants receiving mechanical ventilation for severe respiratory syncytial virus infection. N. Engl. J. Med. *325*:24–29, 1991.
117. Spiers, G. E., Hakim, M., Calne, R. Y., and Wreghitt, T. G.: Relative risk of donor-transmitted *Toxoplasma gondii* infection in heart, liver and kidney transplant recipients. Clin. Transplant. *2*:257–260, 1988.
118. Stamatakis, M. K., and Richards, J. G.: Interaction between quinupristin/dalfopristin and cyclosporine. Ann. Pharmacother. *31*:576–578, 1997.
119. Stokes, D. C., Shenep, J. L., Parham, D., et al.: Role of flexible bronchoscopy in the diagnosis of pulmonary infiltrates in pediatric patients with cancer. J. Pediatr. *115*:561–567, 1989.
120. Stout, J. E., and Yu, V. L.: Legionellosis. N. Engl. J. Med. *337*:682–687, 1997.
121. Stovall, S. H., Ainley, K. A., Mason, E. O., Jr., et al.: Invasive pneumococcal infections in pediatric cardiac transplant patients. Pediatr. Infect. Dis. J. *20*:946–950, 2001.
122. Theisen, K.: Sulfadiazine therapy for toxoplasmosis in heart transplant recipients decreases cyclosporine concentration. Clin. Invest. *70*: 752–754, 1992.
123. Valantine, H. A.: Prevention and treatment of cytomegalovirus disease in thoracic organ transplant. Evidence for a beneficial effect of hyperimmune globulin. Transplant. Proc. *27*(Suppl. 1):49–57, 1995.
124. Valantine, H. A., Luikart, H., Doyle, R., et al.: Impact of cytomegalovirus hyperimmune globulin on outcome after cardiothoracic transplantation: A comparative study of combined prophylaxis with CMV hyperimmune globulin plus ganciclovir versus ganciclovir alone. Transplantation *72*:1647–1652, 2001.
125. Van der Bij, W., Van Dijk, R. B., Van Son, W. J., et al.: Antigen test for early diagnosis of active cytomegalovirus infection in heart transplant recipients. J. Heart Transplant. *7*:106–109, 1988.
126. Wagener, M. W., and Yu, V. L.: Bacteremia in transplant recipients: A prospective study of demographics, etiologic agents, risk factors and outcomes. Am. J. Infect. Control *20*:239–247, 1992.
127. Walsh, T. J., Hiemenz, J. W., Seibel, N. L., et al.: Amphotericin B lipid complex for invasive fungal infections: Analysis of safety and efficacy in 556 cases. Clin. Infect. Dis. *26*:1383–1396, 1998.
128. Wreghitt, T.: Cytomegalovirus infections in heart and heart-lung transplant recipients. J. Antimicrob. Chemother. *23*(Suppl. E):49–60, 1989.
129. Wreghitt, T. G., Gray, J. J., Pavel, P., et al.: Efficacy of pyrimethamine for the prevention of donor-acquired *Toxoplasmosis gondii* infection in heart and heart-lung transplant patients. Transplant. Int. *5*:197–200, 1992.
130. Zangwill, S. D., Hsu, D. T., Kichuk, M. R., et al.: Incidence and outcome of primary Epstein Barr virus infection and lymphoproliferative disease in pediatric heart transplant recipients. J. Heart Lung Transplant. *17*:1161–1166, 1998.

Opportunistic Infections in Liver Transplantation

MICHAEL GREEN

Liver transplantation has gained increasing acceptance as treatment for children with end-stage liver disease. Improved surgical techniques and the availability of new and more potent immunosuppressive regimens have led to enhanced short- and long-term survival rates that now approach or exceed 80 percent. In response to these excellent results, more children are being referred for liver transplantation. To accommodate the increasing number of children on transplant waiting lists, newer procedures, including reduced graft, split-liver graft, and living-related donor liver transplantation, have been developed to increase the donor pool and make this lifesaving procedure more widely available.

Infectious complications have been a significant cause of morbidity and mortality in children undergoing liver transplantation since this procedure gained its initial acceptance in the 1980s. However, expanding experience of liver transplantation in children, along with the increasing availability of new antimicrobial agents and diagnostic tools, has resulted in improved treatment regimens. More recently, emphasis has begun to focus on the development of strategies aimed at the prevention of infectious complications in children undergoing liver transplantation. This chapter provides a general overview of the problem of infections that develop in children after they have undergone liver transplantation.

Predisposing Factors

Liver transplantation is associated with a set of technical and medical conditions that predispose to a unique set of infectious complications. The most common site of infection in patients undergoing this procedure is the abdomen,[21] almost certainly because of the occurrence of local ischemic injury and bleeding as well as potential soilage with contaminated material.[45] Additional factors predisposing to infection can be divided into those that exist before transplantation and those secondary to intraoperative and post-transplantation activities.

PRETRANSPLANTATION FACTORS

The underlying illnesses leading to transplantation may be associated with intrinsic risk factors for infection. Some disorders may require palliative surgery, which increases the technical difficulty of the transplantation and may be associated with an enhanced risk of developing post-transplantation infections.[19] Some palliative procedures (e.g., Kasai procedure [choledochojejunostomy] as a treatment for biliary atresia) may predispose to recurrent infections before transplantation, increasing the likelihood of colonization with multiple antibiotic-resistant bacteria, which can cause infection after liver transplantation. Complications of end-stage liver disease also may predispose to development of infection after transplantation. For example, a history of one or more episodes of spontaneous bacterial peritonitis before transplantation in patients with ascites has been associated with an increased rate of bacterial infections after liver transplantation.[87]

Age, another important pretransplantation factor, is a major determinant of susceptibility to certain agents, severity of expression of infection, and immune maturation. Young children undergoing liver transplantation may experience moderate to severe infection with certain viral (e.g., respiratory syncytial virus [RSV]) or bacterial (coagulase-negative staphylococci) pathogens compared with more mild illness experienced by adult recipients infected with these pathogens. In contrast, certain pathogens, such as *Cryptococcus neoformans*, uncommonly manifest as infections in patients before they reach young adulthood.[90] Age also is an important factor governing clinical expression of infection with cytomegalovirus (CMV) and Epstein-Barr virus (EBV). When transplantations are performed in young patients, the likelihood is high that these patients will be seronegative for CMV and EBV and, therefore, susceptible to primary infections, which are more severe than are infections caused by reactivation.[9, 46]

Donor-related issues represent another set of pretransplantation factors. Transplant recipients are at risk for acquiring infections that may be active or latent within the donor at the time of organ harvesting. Perhaps the best example is CMV, historically the most frequent and important viral pathogen among transplant recipients.[8] Other pathogens that are established as causing donor-associated infections include EBV,[14] human immunodeficiency virus (HIV),[22] and histoplasmosis.[91]

INTRAOPERATIVE FACTORS

Operative factors unique to liver transplantation also may predispose to development of infectious complications. For example, patients undergoing Roux-en-Y choledochoduodenostomy experience more infectious episodes than do those who undergo a choledochocholedochostomy with T-tube drainage.[53, 74] However, only the former option usually is performed in children undergoing liver transplantation because of the small size of their bile ducts. Prolonged operative time (>12 hours) during the initial transplantation has been associated with an increased risk for development of infection after transplantation[27, 53] and is likely a surrogate marker for the technical difficulty of the surgery. Finally, intraoperative events, such as contamination of the operative field, clearly predispose to postoperative infections.

POST-TRANSPLANTATION FACTORS

Technical problems, immunosuppression, presence of indwelling cannulas, and nosocomial exposures are major postoperative risk factors for infectious complications. Thrombosis of the hepatic artery is the most serious technical problem and predisposes to areas of necrotic liver and development of hepatic abscesses and bacteremia.[71, 74] Bile duct strictures, developing as a sequela of thrombosed hepatic artery and ischemia or caused by technical difficulties, may predispose to cholangitis.[74]

Immunosuppression is the critical postoperative factor predisposing to infection in transplant recipients. Immunosuppressive regimens have evolved in an attempt to achieve more specific control of rejection with the least impairment of immunity. Thus, this evolution is aimed not only at improved control of rejection but also at decreased morbidity and mortality rates from infections. The use of cyclosporine-based regimens resulted in a decreased incidence of infections in renal and cardiac transplant recipients.[21, 47, 65] More recently, the introduction of tacrolimus (FK 506) has allowed many patients to be managed without steroids.[37, 85] Although reported rates of infection have been similar in patients treated with tacrolimus compared with those receiving cyclosporine, an apparent decrease in morbidity and mortality rates, especially from viral pathogens, has been noted with tacrolimus.[2, 37] In contrast to these results, some centers have reported an increased rate of EBV-associated post-transplantation lymphoproliferative disease (PTLD) in patients receiving tacrolimus.[18] However, recent data from the University of Pittsburgh suggest that the short- and long-term incidence of EBV-associated PTLD appears to be similar in pediatric liver transplant recipients treated with either cyclosporine or tacrolimus.[11]

The treatment of rejection with additional or higher doses of immunosuppressants increases the risk for acquiring invasive and potentially fatal infection. Of particular concern is the use of antilymphocyte preparations, especially OKT3, which often is indispensable in the management of rejection that is refractory to steroids.[8, 27, 53] Use of newer antilymphocyte antibodies (e.g., thymoglobulin) also is likely to be associated with an increased risk of developing infection.

The prolonged use of indwelling cannulas at any site is an important cause of infection throughout the postoperative course. The presence of central venous catheters is a cause of bacteremia after transplantation. Similarly, urinary tract infections and bacterial pneumonia are associated with the use of urethral catheters and prolonged nasotracheal or endotracheal intubation, respectively.[27, 53]

Nosocomial exposures constitute the final group of postoperative risk factors. Transplant recipients, especially children, may be exposed to many common viral pathogens (e.g., rotavirus, RSV, or influenza virus) while in the hospital. In addition, all transplant recipients are at risk for exposure to transfusion-associated pathogens (e.g., hepatitis B and C, HIV). Finally, the presence in the hospital of heavy areas of contamination with pathogenic fungi, such as *Aspergillus* spp., may increase the risk for acquisition of invasive fungal disease in these patients.

Timing of Infections

The time of onset of infection with various pathogens after transplantation tends to be predictable. Most clinically important infections occur within the first 180 days after transplantation.[34, 53] The timing of infections can be divided into three intervals: early (0 to 30 days after transplantation), intermediate (30 to 180 days after transplantation), and late (greater than 180 days after transplantation). Additionally, some infections may occur throughout the postoperative course. These divisions, although arbitrary, generally are useful in approaching a patient with fever after transplantation and can be used as a guide to differential diagnosis. An overview of the infectious complications occurring during each of these time periods is provided in Tables 78–1 through 78–3 (presented later) and is summarized in the following sections.

EARLY INFECTIONS (0 TO 30 DAYS)

Early infections tend to be associated with preexisting conditions and surgical manipulation (Table 78–1). In general,

TABLE 78–1 ■ DIFFERENTIAL DIAGNOSIS OF INFECTIOUS COMPLICATIONS DURING THE EARLY PERIOD (0–30 DAYS) AFTER LIVER TRANSPLANTATION: CHILDREN'S HOSPITAL OF PITTSBURGH

Clinical Syndrome	Associated Pathogens
Wound infection	*Staphylococcus aureus*
Superficial	Enterococci
Deep	Enterobacteriaceae
	Candida species
Intra-abdominal infection	Enterobacteriaceae
Peritonitis	Enterococci
Intra-abdominal abscess	*Candida* species
Intrahepatic abscess with or without bacteremia	
Bloodstream infection associated with	
Central venous catheters	Coagulase-negative staphylococci
	Enterococci
	S.aureus
	Candida species
Hepatic artery thrombosis	Enterobacteriaceae
	Enterococci
	Candida species
Bacterial cholangitis	Enterobacteriaceae
	Enterococci
	Candida species
Urinary tract infection	Enterobacteriaceae
	Enterococci
	Candida species
Ventilator-associated pneumonia	Enterobacteriaceae
	Enterococci
	S. aureus
	Candida species
Nosocomial acquisition of common community pathogens	Respiratory syncytial virus
	Parainfluenza virus
	Influenza virus
	Rotavirus
Noninfectious causes	Rejection
	Drug fever

From Green, M.: Infectious complications of liver transplantation in children. *In* Patrick, C. C. (ed.): Clinical Management of Infections in Immunocompromised Infants and Children. Philadelphia, Lippincott Williams & Wilkins, 2001, p. 167.

TABLE 78–2 ■ DIFFERENTIAL DIAGNOSIS OF INFECTIOUS COMPLICATIONS DURING THE INTERMEDIATE PERIOD (31–180 DAYS) AFTER LIVER TRANSPLANTATION: CHILDREN'S HOSPITAL OF PITTSBURGH

Clinical Syndrome	Associated Pathogens
Viral syndrome: fever, leukopenia, thrombocytopenia with or without atypical lymphocytosis	CMV
	EBV
Hepatitis	CMV
	EBV
	Adenovirus
	Hepatitis B
	Hepatitis C
Enteritis	CMV
	EBV
	Rotavirus
	Adenovirus
	Clostridium difficile
PTLD	EBV
Bacterial cholangitis*	Enterobacteriaceae
	Enterococci
	Candida species
Pneumonia	*Streptococcus pneumoniae*
	CMV
	Adenovirus
	Respiratory syncytial virus
	Parainfluenza virus
	Influenza virus
	Pneumocystis carinii
	Aspergillus fumigatus
Adenopathy	EBV and PTLD
Pulmonary nodules	EBV and PTLD
	Aspergillus fumigatus

*Usually associated with the presence of technical complication (e.g., biliary stricture).
CMV, cytomegalovirus; EBV, Epstein-Barr virus; PTLD, post-transplantation lymphoproliferative disease.
From Green, M: Infectious complications of liver transplantation in children. *In* Patrick, C. C. (eds.): Clinical Management of Infections in Immunocompromised Infants and Children. Philadelphia, Lippincott Williams & Wilkins, 2001, p. 167.

they are caused by either bacteria or yeast. As many as one half of these early infectious complications may develop in the first 2 weeks after liver transplantation.[7] Cholangitis or spontaneous bacterial peritonitis presenting at or near the time of liver transplantation may lead to intraabdominal infection after the transplantation. Herpes simplex infection can reactivate and cause early symptomatic disease,[53] although it seldom occurs in children. Technical difficulties (e.g., thrombosis of the hepatic artery or portal vein, biliary strictures) predispose to early bacterial infections. Likewise, development of bile leaks and bowel perforations are associated with polymicrobial intraabdominal infections, primarily consisting of enteric bacteria and *Candida* spp., in the first month after transplantation.[29] Finally, re-exploration of the abdomen is associated with increased rate of fungal infection.[53]

INTERMEDIATE PERIOD (31 TO 180 DAYS)

The intermediate period is the typical time of onset of infections associated with donor transmission (either organ or blood products), reactivated viruses, and opportunistic infections (Table 78–2). CMV peaks in incidence of infection during this time,[8, 53] when many patients also begin to present with EBV-associated PTLD[46] and *Pneumocystis carinii* pneumonia.[53]

LATE INFECTIONS (MORE THAN 180 DAYS)

Late infections after liver transplantation are less well characterized than are those of other periods because patients usually have been discharged from the transplantation center to home, which often is quite far away (Table 78–3). Hence, accumulating accurate data on these late infections is difficult. Nonetheless, problems such as recurrent episodes of bacterial cholangitis (typically associated with underlying problems of the biliary tree) and PTLD[57] occur in this time period and usually require the patient to return to the transplantation center for definitive diagnosis and management.

INFECTIONS OCCURRING THROUGHOUT THE POSTOPERATIVE COURSE

Iatrogenic factors are an important cause of bacterial and fungal infections at all times but predominate in the early

TABLE 78–3 ■ DIFFERENTIAL DIAGNOSIS OF INFECTIOUS COMPLICATIONS DURING THE LATE PERIOD (MORE THAN 180 DAYS) AFTER LIVER TRANSPLANTATION: CHILDREN'S HOSPITAL OF PITTSBURGH

Clinical Syndrome	Associated Pathogens
Bacterial cholangitis*	Enterobacteriaceae Enterococci *Candida* species
Post-transplantation lymphoproliferative disease	Epstein-Barr virus
Varicella-zoster virus infection	Varicella-zoster virus

*Usually associated with the presence of technical complication (e.g., biliary stricture).

From Green, M Infectious complications of liver transplantation in children. *In* Patrick, C. C. (eds.): Clinical Management of Infections in Immunocompromised Infants and Children. Philadelphia, Lippincott Williams & Wilkins, 2001, p. 167.

transplantation period. Central venous lines are maintained for a variable time; the risk of developing infection persists for the entire period that the catheter remains in place. Similarly, the presence of urethral catheters and endotracheal tubes also increases the risk for acquiring infections whenever they are in use.

Nosocomial acquisition of community viruses, such as RSV, rotavirus, and influenza A or B, can occur at any time after transplantation. These viruses spread easily in hospital environments from personnel or other hospitalized patients to transplant recipients. Therefore, modifying diagnostic considerations according to local epidemiologic considerations is important.

Bacterial and Fungal Infections

Bacterial and fungal infections are a frequent and early problem after liver transplantation.[17, 27, 53, 74, 96] Rates for bacterial infection of 40 to 70 percent[27, 34, 53, 57, 74] and for fungal infection of up to 63 percent[3, 17, 29, 43] have been reported from multiple series. Bacteremia is a frequent problem and may be seen in association with central venous catheters or intraabdominal infection or without an obvious source. Enteric gram-negative organisms account for more than 50 percent of episodes.[9, 17, 53] However, the use of oral selective intestinal decontamination may be associated with an increased prevalence of infections caused by gram-positive bacteria.[7] Bacterial infection involving the abdomen or wound occurs frequently in most series. Infectious complications of the transplanted liver also occur.[16] The most important of them is the development of a hepatic abscess associated with hepatic artery or portal vein thrombosis[53] that may be accompanied by refractory bacteremia. Urgent retransplantation, in addition to antimicrobial therapy, is necessary if the patient is to survive.[74, 96] However, percutaneous drainage of the intrahepatic abscess may allow stabilization of patients before retransplantation.[71]

Another common infection seen after transplantation is ascending cholangitis, usually associated with biliary abnormalities. This diagnosis typically is made on clinical grounds in a patient with fever and biochemical evidence of bile duct disease. Empiric antibiotic treatment is chosen to include enteric gram-negative bacteria and enterococcal species.

Of increasing concern is the importance of antimicrobial resistance among the bacterial pathogens infecting children undergoing liver transplantation. Outbreaks of colonization and disease caused by vancomycin-resistant *Enterococcus faecium* and ceftazidime-resistant *Klebsiella pneumoniae* have been reported among pediatric liver transplant recipients.[30, 31] These multiple antibiotic–resistant bacteria have been transmitted from patient to patient, prompting the imposition of strict infection control procedures. Reports of multiple antibiotic–resistant strains of *Enterobacter cloacae* associated with de-repression of a chromosomally located broad-spectrum β-lactamase enzyme have identified this very resistant organism as an important pathogen after liver transplantation.[15] The increasing prevalence of these multiple antibiotic–resistant organisms limits the therapeutic options available for the treatment of bacterial infections after liver transplantation; in some cases, effective antimicrobials may be unavailable to treat these complications.

Candida spp. are the most common fungal pathogens to occur after liver transplantation in children and usually are associated with intra-abdominal or catheter-associated infections. As many as one-third of children undergoing orthotopic liver transplantation may experience a significant candidal infection.[17, 29] Infections caused by *Candida* spp. usually are recognized in the first month after transplantation, with candidal peritonitis most likely presenting in the first 2 weeks after orthotopic liver transplantation in association with a bile leak or bowel perforation. Other risk factors associated with the development of candidal infection include duration of intubation after transplantation, hepatic artery thrombosis, volume of blood transfused, and exposure to steroids within the 3 months before transplantation. The recovery of *Candida* spp. from a J-P drain in the early postoperative period may be the first indication of either of these two technical complications and may occur before the onset of clinical symptoms of intra-abdominal infection.[29] Accordingly, recovery of *Candida* spp. alone or in combination with enteric bacteria should prompt an initiation of antimicrobial therapy and an aggressive evaluation for the presence of these complications. Early initiation of treatment is particularly important given an attributable mortality rate of up to 33 percent for candidal infections in pediatric liver transplant recipients.[29] The availability of newer azole antifungal agents (e.g., fluconazole) increases the number of therapeutic options for the treatment of candidal infections. However, acquired or inherent resistance to the azoles is an increasing concern, as are the drug–drug interactions between azoles and both cyclosporine and tacrolimus.

Episodes of invasive aspergillosis occur infrequently in pediatric liver transplant recipients.[38] Although uncommon, *Aspergillus* spp. are very important because infections with these pathogens frequently are fatal. A summary of a suggested approach to the diagnosis and management of fungal infections after liver transplantation in children is provided in Table 78–4.

Viral Infections

CYTOMEGALOVIRUS

CMV continues to be the most common and one of the most important viral pathogens causing infection after liver transplantation in children. CMV infection can be asymptomatic or symptomatic and may be caused by primary infection (either from the donor graft or blood products), reactivation of latent infection, or superinfection with a different CMV strain in a previously seropositive child. Before the use of prophylaxis, the incidence of symptomatic CMV infection was reported to be as high as 22 percent in adult[53]

TABLE 78–4 ■ OVERVIEW OF DIAGNOSIS AND MANAGEMENT OF FUNGAL INFECTIONS AFTER LIVER TRANSPLANTATION IN CHILDREN

	***Candida* species: Noninvasive (mucositis, dermatitis and cystitis)**	***Candida* species: Invasive**	***Aspergillus* species**	***Cryptococcus* species**	**Other species (e.g., *Histoplasma, Mucor, Fusarium, Blastomycetes, Altenaria*)**
Frequency	Common*	Common*	Uncommon*	Rare*	Rare*
Diagnostic tests	Clinical examination Culture Gram stain	Culture Gram stain Histology	Culture Gram stain Histology Radiographic staging**	Culture Antigen test India ink stain Histology CSF examination	Culture Histology Antigen testing (when appropriate)
Treatment Primary	Nystatin* Clotrimazole	Amphotericin B§ Fluconazole	Amphotericin B§	Amphotericin B§ Fluconazole‡, ‖	Amphotericin B§
Secondary	Topical amphotericin B†	5-Flucytosine¶	Itraconazole‡,††,‡‡ 5-Flucytosine¶	5-Flucytosine¶	Azole therapy (for susceptible organisms)‡
Adjunctive	Fluconazole‡,‖	Removal of central lines	Surgical resection		Surgical débridement
Duration of therapy	Dependent on the rate of clearance	Dependent on the rate of clearance: minimum of 14 days	Dependent on the rate of clearance: minimum of 4 weeks, usually 8–12 weeks	Minimum of 6–8 weeks Many would continue with fluconazole indefinitely	Dependent on rate of clearance
Follow-up	Clinical examination Repeat urine analysis and cultures	Dependent on clinical scenario	Dependent on clinical scenario	Clinical examination Antigen testing Repeat culture of appropriate source (sputum, CSF, urine) Radiographs if relevant	Clinical examination Antigen testing Repeat culture of appropriate source (sputum, CSF, urine) Radiographs if relevant

*Common, >5%; uncommon, 1%–5%; rare, <1%.
†Topical amphotericin B for bladder wash for noninvasive candiduria—ultrasound of kidneys recommended to determine that no invasive disease is present.
‡Azole use must be accompanied by close follow-up of levels of cyclosporine or tacrolimus. In general, tacrolimus dosing should be cut in half when using a standard dose of fluconazole.
§Amphotericin B dosed at 0.75–1.0 mg/kg/day; lipid formulations are used if renal failure is present.
‖Fluconazole is alternative first-line drug for invasive disease if the species is known to be sensitive to fluconazole and the patient is clinically stable. Fluconazole is dosed at 6–12 mg/kg/day based on severity of infection.
¶5-Flucytosine should not be used alone but is synergistic when used in conjunction with amphotericin B. Flucytosine is dosed at 100–150 mg/kg/day divided every 6 hours.
**Radiographic staging includes computed tomography of head, chest, and abdomen.
††Itraconazole can be used long-term for patients who have been treated for invasive aspergillus but in general is not recommended as first-line therapy.
‡‡Itraconazole absorption can be erratic. Accordingly, monitoring of itraconazole levels is recommended. Itraconazole is dosed at 3–5 mg/kg/day as a single dose. Dosing adjustment based on monitoring of levels is recommended. Adjustment of cyclosporine or tacrolimus dosing should be individualized.
From Green, M: Infectious complications of liver transplantation in children. *In* Patrick, C. C. (eds.): Clinical Management of Infections in Immunocompromised Infants and Children. Philadelphia, Lippincott Williams & Wilkins, 2001, p. 169.

and 40 percent in pediatric[8] liver transplant recipients. Use of ganciclovir prophylaxis has resulted in a decreased rate and severity of CMV disease.[32]

Primary CMV infection, typically acquired from the donor organ (or passenger donor leukocytes that accompany the organ), is associated with the greatest degree of morbidity and mortality.[32, 39] Accordingly, CMV-seronegative recipients of organs from CMV-seropositive donors are considered at high risk of developing CMV disease. Reactivation of or superinfection with CMV tends to result in milder illness.[9] CMV disease appears more likely to develop in CMV-seropositive recipients of CMV-seropositive donors than in seropositive recipients of seronegative donors.[39] Patients treated with unusually high doses of immunosuppressants, especially antilymphocyte antibody preparations, experience an increased rate of CMV disease, regardless of previous immunity.[8, 53]

Symptomatic CMV disease typically presents between 1 and 3 months after transplantation. An important note is that the use of prophylactic regimens may delay onset of CMV disease. A characteristic constellation of fever (which may be high-grade, prolonged, and hectic) and hematologic abnormalities (including leukopenia, atypical lymphocytosis, and thrombocytopenia) frequently is seen. This "CMV syndrome" occurs in 25 to 50 percent of patients with symptomatic CMV infection. Invasive CMV disease manifests with visceral organ involvement; common sites include the gastrointestinal tract, liver, and lungs. CMV hepatitis appears to be the most common site among liver transplant recipients. CMV chorioretinitis is a rare occurrence in organ transplant recipients.

Diagnosis of CMV disease may be confirmed by positive buffy coat culture, by pp65 antigenemia assay,[84] or by detecting the presence of CMV DNA in the blood of a patient with a compatible clinical syndrome. However, clinicians must be aware that results of viral cultures of the urine and even bronchoalveolar lavage specimens are difficult to interpret because patients frequently shed CMV asymptomatically in these secretions. Similarly, the presence of pp65 antigen and CMV DNA in the blood can be misleading because these assays often are positive in asymptomatic patients. The specificity of this approach may be improved by quantitative determination of the pp65 antigen or CMV DNA. Because of the lack of specificity of these assays, histologic examination of involved organs to confirm the presence of CMV is critical when the diagnosis of invasive CMV is being entertained.

Antiviral agents with activity against CMV (e.g., ganciclovir, foscarnet, and cidofovir) have improved the survival rates of transplant recipients with CMV disease. Fatal, disseminated CMV disease occurred in 19 percent of infected children[8] and 5 percent of infected adults undergoing liver transplantation in the era before ganciclovir.[77] For clinical CMV disease, ganciclovir therapy is given in conjunction with reduction of immunosuppression unless evidence of rejection is present. Clinical response usually occurs 5 to 7 days after initiation of therapy. Baseline immunosuppression levels typically are restored at the time of initial clinical response or upon recognition of rejection. Although some experts advocate prolonged treatment courses, we have found a course of 14 to 21 days to be sufficient in most cases. The role of CMV hyperimmunoglobulin in combination with ganciclovir in the treatment of CMV disease is controversial, although some evidence for improved outcome has been reported in the treatment of CMV pneumonia in adult liver transplant recipients.[28] Finally, because of the relatively high rates of nephrotoxicity associated with their use, foscarnet and cidofovir should be restricted to patients with apparent or proven resistance to ganciclovir.

Approximately 25 percent of patients treated with ganciclovir for an initial episode of symptomatic CMV develop one or more episodes of recurrent CMV disease.[76, 82] Recurrences are observed approximately 1 month after the initial infectious episode and may be associated with invasive disease. More commonly, however, these recurrent episodes tend to be milder than the initial episode. Factors associated with an increased risk for experiencing recurrent CMV disease include being a CMV-seronegative recipient of a CMV-seropositive donor, having disseminated CMV disease, and having a history of multiple treatment courses for rejection.[76] In addition, one center has demonstrated a correlation between the height of the CMV viral load in peripheral blood leukocytes before and at the end of treatment and the likelihood of developing recurrent CMV disease.[76] Accordingly, some centers have begun to use serial measurements of the CMV viral load (as measured by pp65 early antigen or quantitative CMV DNA polymerase chain reaction [PCR]) as a marker of clinical response to antiviral therapy. However, little data are available describing the course of CMV pp65 antigenemia in patients treated for symptomatic CMV disease; studies evaluating the effect of prolonging treatment to achieve low or nondetectable CMV viral loads on the likelihood of developing recurrent CMV disease have not been published. Thus, the use of either of these tools as a guide to the appropriate duration of antiviral therapy requires further study before it can be fully endorsed. A summary of my suggested approach to the diagnosis and management of CMV infection is provided in Table 78–5.

EPSTEIN-BARR VIRUS

EBV infection, including EBV-associated PTLD, is an important cause of morbidity and mortality after liver transplantation.[46, 81, 86, 95] PTLD is a more common occurrence after primary EBV infection, placing seronegative recipients (particularly those who receive organs from seropositive donors) at the highest risk for developing complications. As many as 80 percent of children who are EBV-seronegative before liver transplantation develop a primary EBV infection after undergoing this procedure.[79, 80] Although primary infection occurs in the vast majority of seronegative patients, clinical disease develops in less than one third of these children.[79, 80] Exposure to augmented levels of immunosuppression, particularly antilymphocyte preparations (e.g., OKT3), and age younger than 2 years at the time of transplantation have been identified as risk factors for development of EBV disease and PTLD. Some centers also have found patients receiving tacrolimus-based immunosuppression to be at a greater risk of developing these complications compared with those on cyclosporine-based regimens.[18, 80] However, many of the patients in these reports were placed on tacrolimus as part of "rescue" protocols for refractory rejection and had been treated previously with high levels of cyclosporine, high-dose steroids, and OKT3. Another potential explanation for these differences is that EBV disease and PTLD tend to occur earlier in patients treated with tacrolimus than in those on cyclosporine-based regimens.[10, 12, 13, 95] Thus, whereas short-term follow-up might suggest an increased risk of developing EBV disease in patients receiving tacrolimus, in my experience, long-term rates have been similar between the two treatment groups.[12]

Infection with EBV can result in a broad clinical spectrum ranging from subclinical infection to symptomatic EBV disease. A wide range of clinical manifestations is observed among those patients developing symptomatic disease. The classification scheme I favor categorizes the spectrum of EBV disease as nonspecific viral illness, mononucleosis, PTLD, and lymphoma. As many as one half of all cases of symptomatic EBV infection may fall into the less well-defined categories of nonspecific viral illness, which include a febrile syndrome (fever, malaise, leukopenia, and atypical lymphocytosis), enteritis, and hepatitis. Although these syndromes do not meet the classic criteria for EBV-associated PTLD, they are being recognized increasingly as an important cause of morbidity after transplantation and may represent "early" manifestations of EBV before progression to the more ominous (and perhaps neoplastic) PTLD. Accordingly, diagnosing these EBV-associated syndromes is important not only to determine the cause of illness in febrile transplant recipients but also to intervene before the infection progresses to a neoplastic manifestation.

An EBV-associated syndrome should be considered in patients presenting with a febrile illness lasting longer than 3 days, particularly if it is associated with exudative tonsillitis, peripheral adenopathy, and abnormalities of the complete blood count (including leukopenia, atypical lymphocytosis, and thrombocytopenia). The diagnosis of EBV also should be considered in children with unexplained gastrointestinal symptoms, prolonged diarrhea (particularly if it is associated with gross or microscopic blood), or hepatitis. The diagnosis of EBV disease is made on the basis of clinical, laboratory, and histologic examination. Diagnostic evaluation of children presenting with one or more of these symptoms should include a search for other pathogens (including CMV) and performance of computed tomography scans of the chest and abdomen to look for occult lesions. Serologic diagnosis often is confounded by the presence of passive antibody acquired at the time of transplantation or during subsequent transfusions. The detection of increased EBV viral load in the peripheral blood identified by quantitative or semiquantitative EBV PCR recently has been introduced and is gaining wide acceptance as an assay to predict risk for the presence of EBV and PTLD.[52, 70, 72] These assays often are elevated in asymptomatic patients. Accordingly, every effort should be made to confirm the diagnosis of EBV and PTLD histologically. Palpable nodes or lesions (or both) identified by radiographic surveillance should undergo

TABLE 78–5 ■ OVERVIEW OF DIAGNOSIS AND MANAGEMENT OF VIRAL INFECTIONS AFTER LIVER TRANSPLANTATION IN CHILDREN

	Cytomegalovirus (CMV)	Epstein-Barr Virus (EBV)	Respiratory Syncytial Virus (RSV)	Influenza Virus	Parainfluenza Virus	Adenovirus
Frequency*	Common	Common	Uncommon	Uncommon	Uncommon	Uncommon
Diagnostic tests	Culture pp65 Antigen Histology	EBV PCR Histology Serology	NP aspirate for antigen detection and culture	NP aspirate for antigen detection and culture	NP aspirate for culture	Viral culture Histology
Treatment						
Primary	Ganciclovir (5 mg/kg bid)	Decrease IS	Supportive care	Supportive care	Supportive care	Decrease IS
Secondary	Foscarnet[†] Cidofovir		Aerosolized ribavirin	Amantadine Rimantadine Zanamivir Oseltamivir		IV ribavirin
Adjunctive	Decrease IS CMV IVIG	Ganciclovir IVIG	RSV IVIG Decreased IS	Decrease IS	Decreased IS	IVIG
Duration of therapy	Site dependent	Individualized	Individualized	Individualized	Individualized	Individualized
Follow-up	Monitor pp65 Ag	Monitor EBV PCR Repeat imaging studies if positive at outset	None	None	None	None

*Uncommon, frequency ~ 1%–5%; common, frequency ~ >5%; rare, frequency <1%.

[†]Foscarnet is used for CMV infection when ganciclovir resistance is suspected or proven. Experience from patients with human immunodeficiency virus suggests that a synergistic benefit will be obtained from the combined use of both of these agents when ganciclovir resistance is present.

PCR, polymerase chain reaction; NP, nasopharyngeal; IS, immune suppression; IVIG, intravenous immune globulin.

From Green, M: Infectious complications of liver transplantation in children. *In* Patrick, C. C. (eds.): Clinical Management of Infections in Immunocompromised Infants and Children. Philadelphia, Lippincott Williams & Wilkins, 2001, p. 171.

biopsy. Endoscopy should be considered for patients with diarrheic illnesses and elevated EBV viral loads because a high incidence of PTLD of the intestinal tract has been found in these children.[13]

Histologic classification generally describes whether the lesions are polymorphic or monomorphic. Special stains are used to demonstrate the presence of EBV within a lesion. Studies of gene rearrangement are used to determine the clonality of PTLD lesions (e.g., polyclonal, oligoclonal, or monoclonal). The histology of a lesion, as well as its clonality, is helpful in differentiating between EBV-associated hyperplastic and neoplastic disease. This differentiation may be of value in considering therapeutic options for EBV in organ transplant recipients.

The management of PTLD is controversial.[10, 35, 66] Reduction or withdrawal of immunosuppression is recommended.[46, 57, 96] Antiviral agents are used widely, although their roles have not been studied formally.[41] The potential impact of monoclonal antibodies,[24] interferon,[75] and chemotherapy[26] awaits formal clinical trials. Resection of tumor also may be of value for patients with localized disease or lymphoma. A summary of my suggested approach and management of EBV and PTLD is provided in Table 78–5.

OTHER HERPESVIRUSES

Other herpesviruses also can be hazardous after transplantation. Herpes simplex can reactivate early after surgery or after augmentation of immunosuppression. Prophylaxis with acyclovir has been beneficial in these situations. A summary of the suggested approach to the diagnosis and management of HSV is provided in Table 78–5. Varicella in nonimmune transplant recipients can lead to disseminated, fatal disease[61] and should be treated early and aggressively with intravenous acyclovir.

Interest has focused on determining what role, if any, the recently recognized human herpesvirus type 6 (HHV-6) and human herpesvirus type 7 (HHV-7) may play in causing disease in organ transplant recipients in general and liver transplant recipients in particular. Several groups of investigators have identified a potential interaction between the development of HHV-6 and HHV-7 and CMV infection in organ transplant recipients.[50, 62] Reactivation of HHV-6 infection after liver transplantation has been associated with the development of an increased CMV viral load in the peripheral blood as well as a greater likelihood of developing symptomatic CMV disease.[50] More recently, some or all of the symptoms typically associated with the CMV syndrome (e.g., fever, leukopenia) in patients with confirmed CMV infection have been suggested to be attributable possibly in part to HHV-6 or HHV-7. Studies in children have suggested that infection caused by HHV-6 alone is a relatively common cause of unexplained fever in pediatric liver transplant recipients.[93, 94] Interest also has begun to focus on what role, if any, human herpesvirus type 8 (HHV-8) may have in causing infection and disease in organ transplant recipients. The full spectrum of disease of these newer viruses and their potential therapies remain to be determined.

ADENOVIRUS

Adenovirus has been reported to be the third most important virus affecting pediatric liver transplant recipients, occurring in 10 percent of our series of 484 children undergoing liver transplantation under cyclosporine-based immunosuppression.[63] Symptomatic disease (ranging from self-limited fever, gastroenteritis, or cystitis to devastating illness with necrotizing hepatitis or pneumonia) occurred in more than 60 percent of infected patients. Infection occurred within the first 3 months after transplantation. The frequency of invasive adenovirus infection after pediatric liver transplantation appears to have decreased markedly with the use of tacrolimus-based immunosuppression.[37]

Presumptively diagnosing infection caused by adenovirus in pediatric liver transplant recipients is very difficult because fever, hepatitis, or pneumonia may be caused by a variety of other pathogens. The presence of high-grade fevers and symptoms suggestive of adenovirus infection should prompt taking serial cultures for viruses (including adenovirus) from the buffy coat, stool, throat, and urine. Unexplained elevations in hepatocellular enzymes suggestive of hepatitis should warrant consideration of a liver biopsy. Histologic examination for the presence of adenoviral inclusions, as well as the use of immunohistochemical stains, helps to confirm this diagnosis in most cases.

Unfortunately, no definitive treatment for adenoviral infection exists at this time. The most important component of therapy is supportive care along with a decrease in immunosuppression. The role of antiviral agents is not known. A small number of case reports describe the use of ribavirin[6, 51, 56, 64] and ganciclovir[92] in treating single patients with adenoviral infection after solid organ or bone marrow transplantation. In vitro evidence supports the theoretical role of ribavirin but not that of ganciclovir in the treatment of these infections. In addition to these published reports, an adult lung transplant recipient with disseminated adenovirus type 7 improved after treatment with cidofovir (HPMPC) and pooled, high-titered immunoglobulin against RSV (RespiGam) along with decreased immunosuppression.[33] Other case reports have been published describing the successful use of cidofovir for the treatment of adenoviral disease in a bone marrow transplant recipient and in a patient with acquired immunodeficiency syndrome.[42, 69] A single case report also suggested the possible role of intravenous immunoglobulin as treatment for adenovirus infection.[20] Unfortunately, no conclusive evidence of the efficacy of these antiviral agents or immunoglobulin therapy can be drawn from these reports. A summary of a suggested approach to the diagnosis and management of adenovirus infection is provided in Table 78–5.

COMMON COMMUNITY-ACQUIRED VIRUSES

Although the course of illness has not been documented well, most children who undergo liver transplantation experience the usual respiratory viruses and gastrointestinal illness without significant problems. However, infections caused by influenza, parainfluenza, or RSV virus lead to more severe disease in young children, especially if infection occurs soon after transplantation and during periods of maximal immunosuppression.[4, 67] A summary of suggested strategies for the diagnosis and management of these community-acquired viruses can be found in Table 78–5.

OTHER VIRUSES

Other viruses, including nosocomially acquired viral infection (e.g., hepatitis B and C viruses) and community acquired viral pathogens (e.g., enterovirus), are relatively uncommon causes of infection after liver transplantation. Suggested approaches to the diagnosis and management of each of these viral pathogens are provided in Table 78–5.

Opportunistic Infections

P. carinii is a well-documented cause of pneumonia in immunocompromised patients, including liver transplant recipients. Prophylactic trimethoprim-sulfamethoxazole is safe, inexpensive, and effective.[49] The use of this strategy has eliminated *P. carinii* pneumonia in these patients at our center. Alternative prophylactic regimens for the sulfa-allergic patient include aerosolized pentamidine (for patients older than 5 years of age)[54] and dapsone.[48]

Tuberculosis (TB) is a particular concern in immunosuppressed hosts, including recipients of liver transplantation. The incidence of TB after liver transplantation in Europe and the United States has been reported to range from 0.9 to 2.3 percent, with most reported cases in adults.[78, 88] In contrast, as many as 15 percent of organ transplant recipients in areas of high-level endemnicity may develop TB.[78] However, development of TB after pediatric liver transplantation is an extremely uncommon occurrence, with only 11 cases reported to date.[59, 78, 88] Development of TB among solid organ transplant recipients is associated with mortality rates ranging from 25 to 40 percent, with additional morbidity and mortality associated with development of rejection in patients receiving antituberculosis therapy.[78, 88]

Diagnosis of TB in transplant recipients is complicated by the fact that extrapulmonary disease occurs frequently, and purified protein derivative (PPD) testing is likely to be unreliable after transplantation. Management of TB in liver transplant recipients is difficult because of the side effects of antituberculosis agents and their potential interactions with immunosuppressive agents.[78, 88] Limited published experience in pediatric liver transplant recipients suggests that most infections caused by *Mycobacteria tuberculosis* most likely are caused by a primary infection, often associated with family contacts who have positive skin tests.[59, 88] In contrast, experience with adult transplant recipients suggests that development of TB is more likely caused by reactivation of latent TB.[44, 78, 83] Although only limited published information is available describing TB in these patients, transplant recipients known to have a positive PPD or who come from an area endemic for TB appear to be at increased risk for developing symptomatic reactivation after transplantation.[44, 83] Additional factors predisposing to the development of TB after transplantation include severe hepatic failure at the time of transplantation, aggressive antirejection therapy, and concurrent HIV infection.[44, 83]

Experience among adult renal transplant recipients suggests that, although the risk appears greatest in patients who received inadequate or no prior TB therapy,[55, 58] TB also can occur in patients who received appropriate anti-TB therapy in the pretransplantation period.[55, 58, 68] Although TB has been encountered only rarely among pediatric liver transplant recipients,[88] screening for TB by history and placement of a PPD, along with review of a chest radiograph for lesions consistent with healed TB, is recommended highly. Patients with a positive TB history or a positive PPD should receive isoniazid for 6 to 12 months after transplantation, although some experts recommend continuing it indefinitely while patients remain on immunosuppression. Attempts at a more definitive diagnosis are indicated for patients from endemic areas with a negative PPD but suspicious chest radiograph. Careful evaluation for evidence of side effects, particularly hepatotoxicity, is recommended, and isoniazid is discontinued if unacceptable toxicity is identified.

Additional potential opportunistic infections include cryptococcosis, coccidiomycosis, and histoplasmosis, although these pathogens have not been reported frequently among pediatric liver transplant recipients. Prior infection with these pathogens is common in geographic areas where they are endemic. Because patients often travel to transplantation centers distant to their homes, transplant physicians must be aware of the local environmental risks for each patient. Experience with coccidiomycosis in transplant recipients suggests that a minimum of 4 months of antifungal therapy, such as fluconazole, should be administered to transplant recipients with this history.[40] Similarities between coccidiomycosis and other fungal pathogens suggest that similar strategies may be necessary for patients with a positive history of prior fungal infection with pathogens known to recur after resolution of primary infection.

Management

PRETRANSPLANTATION EVALUATION

A pretransplantation evaluation is helpful in the management of infectious complications in liver transplant recipients. A complete history and physical examination should be performed, with particular attention given to previous infections, immunizations, and drug allergies. An intermediate-strength tuberculin skin test should be performed in all patients.

We recommend obtaining serologies for CMV; EBV; varicella; herpes simplex virus; hepatitis A, B, and C; and HIV in all candidates. Serologic tests on the donor should include HIV, hepatitis B and C, CMV, and EBV. Donors positive for HIV or hepatitis B should be excluded. The use of organs from donors who are positive for hepatitis C is controversial, although experience suggests that the use of hepatitis C–positive renal donors may be acceptable in hepatitis C–positive children requiring renal transplantation. Knowledge of donor and recipient status for these viruses allows one to anticipate infection, identifying patients who might benefit from prophylactic regimens and guiding in the diagnostic evaluation of fever.

PROPHYLACTIC REGIMENS

Prophylactic regimens vary among transplantation centers. These strategies have been divided into perioperative and long-term prophylaxis and often evolve to reflect the infectious complications seen at individual institutions.

Perioperative prophylaxis is used to prevent intraoperative sepsis and wound infection. It is based on individual patient characteristics and expected normal flora. A combination of ampicillin and cefotaxime, or alternatively piperacillin and tazobactam, is appropriate for perioperative prophylaxis. If sepsis is suspected in the donor, antibiotics are chosen to cover those organisms identified from the donor, and treatment usually is extended to a therapeutic course of 10 to 14 days. In the absence of proven or suspected infection in the donor, perioperative prophylaxis usually is limited to the first 48 hours after transplantation.

Considerations regarding long-term prophylaxis against infections occurring beyond the perioperative period include the risk and severity of infection as well as the toxicity, cost, and efficacy of a given prophylactic strategy. Nystatin is recommended for all pediatric transplant recipients in an effort to prevent oropharyngeal candidiasis. Trimethoprim-sulfamethoxazole is used to prevent *P. carinii* pneumonia. Although some centers recommend using this drug for only the first 6 months after liver transplantation, anecdotal experience with patients presenting with *P. carinii* pneumonia long after transplantation and the relative safety of this agent have led me to recommend its use indefinitely after liver transplantation in children.

The frequency and severity of CMV infection in transplant recipients prompts consideration of prophylactic strategies. Although acyclovir was used initially,[5] many centers now use ganciclovir, which has greater in vitro activity against CMV. Winston and colleagues demonstrated a decline in CMV disease to 1 percent of adult liver transplant recipients who received intravenous ganciclovir for the first 100 days after transplantation.[89] More recently, the efficacy of 14 weeks of oral ganciclovir in adult liver transplant recipients was evaluated compared with a placebo.[25] These investigators were able to demonstrate a decline in CMV disease from 19 to 5 percent among those receiving oral ganciclovir therapy. Although these results are encouraging, applying them to pediatric liver transplant recipients may be confounded by the poor absorption of oral ganciclovir in children. Further, similar rates of prevention might be obtained with the use of shorter courses of either intravenous or oral ganciclovir. Several centers also have evaluated intravenous immunoglobulin (both high-titer anti-CMV and commercially available products) in the prevention of CMV disease in liver transplant recipients.[5, 23, 73] Unfortunately, this strategy has tended to be less effective in preventing CMV disease in high-risk, donor-recipient mismatched patients. Finally, the excellent outcome of children receiving only 2 weeks of intravenous ganciclovir as CMV prophylaxis at my center emphasizes the need for performing clinical trials to determine the most cost-effective and safe strategy to prevent CMV disease as well as those children who are likely to benefit from it.

An alternate approach to the prevention of CMV has been to monitor the rise of CMV pp65 antigenemia as a marker of increasing risk for subsequent symptoms in patients at risk for developing CMV disease.[84] In this preemptive strategy, patients are begun on intravenous ganciclovir when results of the CMV pp65 antigenemia assay exceed predetermined cutoffs. Unfortunately, despite fairly broad acceptance of this approach, few published data confirm the effectiveness of this strategy or determine acceptable cutoffs for treatment of CMV-seronegative and CMV-seropositive transplant recipients. Monitoring the quantitative CMV PCR as an alternative measure of the CMV viral load is another potential approach to preemptive therapy. However, as noted earlier, the limited amount of published data describing the use of this test for this purpose prevents making any comparison of these two approaches at this time. Additional studies are necessary before protocols using either CMV pp65 or CMV PCR can be recommended or compared.

Finally, the increasing attention on the importance of EBV disease and PTLD in pediatric liver transplant recipients has prompted efforts to prevent these problems. The prolonged use of oral acyclovir as chemoprophylaxis against EBV failed to prevent PTLD in pediatric liver transplant recipients.[32] Similar to preemptive strategies against CMV, EBV viral loads as measured by EBV PCR assays of peripheral blood lymphocytes have been used by several sets of investigators in an attempt to guide preemptive management of EBV. Unfortunately, the complicated nature of EBV infection of B cells limits the likelihood that an antiviral therapeutic approach using a nucleoside analogue will be effective. However, these investigators have used additional strategies, including the reduction of immunosuppression[60] and the use of intravenous immunoglobulin, effectively.[36] Unfortunately, neither of these approaches has been subject to controlled trials. Finally, a third approach of immunoprophylaxis using regular infusions of intravenous immunoglobulin from the time of transplantation is supported by the SCID mouse model of EBV-associated lymphoma[1] and is now under study in pediatric liver transplant recipients.

Summary

Infections after liver transplantation remain an important problem. Knowledge of the type, timing, and predisposing risk factors for these infectious complications allows for their timely and appropriate diagnosis and management.

REFERENCES

1. Abedi, M. R., Linde, A., Christensson, B., et al.: Preventive effect of IgG from EBV-seropositive donors on the development of posttransplant lymphoproliferative disease in SCID mice. Int. J. Cancer *71*:624–629, 1997.
2. Alessiani, M., Kusne, S., Martin, F. M., et al.: Infections with FK 506 immunosuppression: Preliminary results with primary therapy. Transplant. Proc. *22*:44–46, 1990.
3. Andrews, W., Fyock, B., Gray, S., et al.: Pediatric liver transplantation: The Dallas experience. Transplant. Proc. *19*:3267–3276, 1987.
4. Apalsch, A. M., and Green, M.: Influenza and parainfluenza virus infections in pediatric organ transplant recipients. Clin. Infect. Dis. *20*:394–399, 1995.
5. Balfour, H. H., Chace, B. A., Stapleton, J. T., et al.: A randomized, placebo controlled trial of oral acyclovir for the prevention of cytomegalovirus disease in recipients of renal allografts. N. Engl. J. Med. *320*:1381–1387, 1989.
6. Boger-Arav, R., Echavarria, M., Forman, M., et al.: Clearance of adenoviral hepatitis with ribavirin therapy in a pediatric liver transplant recipient. Pediatr. Infect. Dis. J. *19*:1097–1100, 2000.
7. Bouchut, J. C., Stamm, D., Boillot, O., et al.: Postoperative infectious complications in paediatric liver transplantation: A study of 48 transplants. Paediatr. Anaesth. *11*:93–98, 2001.
8. Bowman, J. S., Green, M., Scantlebury, V. P., et al.: OKT3 and viral disease in pediatric liver transplant recipients. Clin. Transplant. *5*: 294–300, 1991.
9. Breinig, M. K., Zitelli, B., Starzl, T. E., and Ho, M.: Epstein-Barr virus, cytomegalovirus, and other viral infections in children after liver transplantation. J. Infect. Dis. *156*:273–279, 1987.
10. Cacciarelli, T. V., Green, M., Jaffe, R., et al.: Management of posttransplant lymphoproliferative disease in pediatric liver transplant recipients receiving primary tacrolimus (FK506) therapy. Transplantation *66*:1047–1052, 1998.
11. Cacciarelli, T. V., Jaffe, R., Green, M., et al.: A decreased incidence of post-transplant lymphoproliferative disorder (PTLD) in pediatric liver transplant recipients under primary tacrolimus (FK506) therapy. Program and Abstracts of the 16th Annual Scientific Committee of the American Society for Transplant Physicians, p. 157, Abstract 289, 1997.
12. Cacciarelli, T. V., Reyes, J., Jaffe, R., et al.: Primary tacrolimus (FK 506) therapy and the long-term risk of posttransplant lymphoproliferative disease in pediatric liver transplant recipients. Pediatr. Transplant. *5*:359–364, 2001.
13. Cao, S., Cox, K., Esquivel, C. O., et al.: Posttransplant lymphoproliferative disorders and gastrointestinal manifestations of Epstein-Barr virus infection in children following liver transplantation. Transplantation *66*:851–856, 1998.
14. Cen, H., Breinig, M. C., Atchinson, R. W., et al.: Epstein-Barr virus transmission via the donor-organ in solid-organ transplantation: Polymerase chain reaction and restriction fragment length polymorphism analogue of IR2, IR3, IR4. J. Virol. *65*:976–980, 1991.
15. Chow, J. W., Fine, M. J., Shlaes, D. M., et al.: *Enterobacter* bacteremia: Clinical features and emergence of antibiotic resistance during therapy. Ann. Intern. Med. *115*:585–590, 1991.
16. Cienfugos, J. A., Dominguez, R. M., Tamelchoff, P. J., et al.: Surgical complications in the postoperative period of liver transplantation in children. Transplant. Proc. *16*:1230–1235, 1984.
17. Colonna, J. O., Winston, D. J., Brill, J. E., et al.: Infectious complications in liver transplantation. Arch. Surg. *123*:360–364, 1988.
18. Cox, K. L., Lawrence-Miyasaki, L. S., Garcia-Kennedy, R., et al.: An increased incidence of Epstein-Barr virus infection and lymphoproliferative disorder in young children on FK506 after pediatric liver transplantation. Transplantation *59*:524–529, 1995.
19. Cuervas-Mons, V., Rimola, A., Van Thiel, D. H., et al.: Does previous abdominal surgery alter the outcome of pediatric patients subjected to orthotopic liver transplantation? Gastroenterology *90*:853–857, 1986.
20. Dagan, R., Schwartz, R. H., Insel, R. A., and Menegua, M. A.: Severe diffuse adenovirus 7a pneumonia in a child with combined immunodeficiency: Possible therapeutic effect of human immune serum containing specific neutralizing antibodies. Pediatr. Infect. Dis. J. *3*:246–251, 1984.

21. Dummer, J. S., Hardy, A., Poorsattar, A., and Ho, M.: Early infections in kidney, heart and liver transplant recipients on cyclosporine. Transplantation *36*:259–267, 1983.
22. Dummer, J. S., Siegfried, E., Breinig, M. K., et al.: Infection with human immunodeficiency virus in the Pittsburgh transplant population. Transplantation *47*:134–139, 1989.
23. Fehir, K. M., Decker, T., Samo, T., et al.: Immune globulin (GAMMAGARD) prophylaxis of CMV infections in patients undergoing organ transplantation and allogeneic bone marrow transplantation. Transplant. Proc. *21*:3107–3109, 1989.
24. Fischer, A., Blanche, S., Le Bidois J, et al.: Anti-B-cell monoclonal antibody in the treatment of severe B-cell lymphoproliferative syndrome following bone marrow and solid-organ transplantation. N. Engl. J. Med. *324*:1451–1456, 1991.
25. Gane, E., Saliba, F., Valdecasas, G. J., et al.: Randomized trial of efficacy and safety of oral ganciclovir in prevention of cytomegalovirus disease in liver-transplant recipients. Lancet *350*:1729–1733, 1997.
26. Garrett, T. J., Chadburn, A., Barr, M. L., et al.: Postransplantation lymphoproliferative disorders treated with cyclophosphamide-doxorubicin-vincristine-prednisone chemotherapy. Cancer *72*:2782–2785, 1993.
27. George, D. L., Arnow, P. M., Fox, A. S., et al.: Bacterial infection as a complication of liver transplantation: Epidemiology and risk factors. Rev. Infect. Dis. *13*:387–396, 1991.
28. George, M. J., Snydman, D. R., Werner, B. G., et al.: Use of ganciclovir plus cytomegalovirus immune globulin to treat CMV pneumonia in orthotopic liver transplant recipients. Transplant. Proc. *25*(Suppl. 4):22–24, 1993.
29. Gladdy, R. A., Richardson, S. E., Davies, H. D., and Superina, R. A.: *Candida* infection in pediatric liver transplant recipients. Liver Transplant. Surg. *5*:16–24, 1999.
30. Green, M., and Barbadora, K.: Recovery of ceftazidime-resistant *Klebsiella pneumoniae* from pediatric liver transplant recipients. Pediatr. Transplant. *2*:224–230, 1998.
31. Green, M., Kaufmann, M., Wilson, J., and Reyes, J.: Comparison of intravenous ganciclovir followed by oral acyclovir with intravenous ganciclovir alone for prevention of cytomegalovirus and Epstein-Barr virus disease after liver transplantation in children. Clin. Infect. Dis. *25*:1344–1349, 1997.
32. Green, M., and Michaels, M.: Adenovirus, parvovirus B19 and papillomavirus. *In* Bowden, R. A., Ljungman, P., and Paya, C. (eds.): Transplant Infections. Philadelphia, Lippincott-Raven, 1998, pp. 287–294.
33. Green, M., and Michaels, M.: Infectious complications after solid-organ transplantation. Adv. Pediatr. Infect. Dis. 7:181–204, 1992.
34. Green, M., Michaels, M. G., Webber, S. A., et al.: The management of Epstein-Barr virus associated post-transplant lymphoproliferative disorders in pediatric solid-organ transplant recipients. Pediatr. Transplant. *3*:271–281, 1999.
35. Green, M., Reye, J., and Rowe, D.: New strategies in the prevention and management of Epstein-Barr virus infection and posttransplant lymphoproliferative disease following solid organ transplantation. Curr. Opin. Organ Transplant. *3*:143–147, 1998.
36. Green, M., Tzakis, A., Reyes, J., et al.: Infectious complications of pediatric liver transplantation under FK 506. Transplant. Proc. *23*:3038–3039, 1991.
37. Green, M., Wald, E. R., Tzakis, A., et al.: Aspergillosis of the central nervous system in a pediatric liver transplant recipient and review of the literature. Rev. Infect. Dis. *13*:653–657, 1991.
38. Green, M., Weinfeld, A., Mazariegos, G., and Reyes, J.: Short-course intravenous ganciclovir prophylaxis against cytomegalovirus disease following liver transplantation in children. Pediatr. Transplant. *2*(Suppl. 1):75, 1998.
39. Green, M.: Vancomycin resistant enterococci: Impact and management in pediatrics. Adv. Pediatr. Infect. Dis. *13*:257–277, 1998.
40. Hall, K. A., Copeland, J. G., Zukoski, C. F., et al.: Markers of coccidiomycosis prior to cardiac or renal transplantation and risk of recurrent infection. Transplantation *55*:1422–1425, 1993.
41. Hanto, D., Frizzer, G., Gajl-Peczalska, K., and Simmons, R.: Epstein-Barr virus, immunodeficiency, and B cell lymphoproliferation. Transplantation *39*:461–470, 1985.
42. Hedderwick, S. A., Greenson, J. K., McGaughy, V. R., et al.: Adenovirus cholecystitis in a patient with AIDS. Clin. Infect. Dis. *28*:997–999, 1998.
43. Hiatt, J. R., Ament, M. E., Berquist, M. E., et al.: Pediatric liver transplantation at UCLA. Transplant. Proc. *19*:3282–3288, 1987.
44. Higgins, R., Kusne, S., Reyes, J., et al.: *Mycobacterium* tuberculosis after liver transplantation: Management and guidelines for prevention. Clin. Transplant. *6*:81–90, 1992.
45. Ho, M., and Dummer, J. S.: Risk factors and approaches to infection in transplant recipients. *In* Mandell, G. L., Douglas, R. G. Jr., and Bennett, J. E. (eds.): Principles and Practice of Infectious Diseases. 3rd ed. New York: Churchill Livingstone, 1990.
46. Ho, M., Jaffe, R., Miller, G., et al.: The frequency of Epstein-Barr virus infection and associated lymphoproliferative syndrome after transplantation and its manifestations in children. Transplantation *45*:719–727, 1988.
47. Hofflin, J. M., Potasman, I., Baldwin, J. C., et al.: Infectious complication in heat transplant recipients receiving cyclosporine and corticosteroids. Ann. Intern. Med. *106*:209–216, 1987.
48. Hughes, W. T., Kennedy, W., Dugdale, M., et al.: Prevention of *Pneumocystis carinii* pneumonitis in AIDS patients with weekly dapsone. Lancet *2*:1066, 1990.
49. Hughes, W. T., Rivera, G. K., Schell, M. J., et al.: Successful intermittent chemoprophylaxis for *Pneumocystis carinii* pneumonitis. N. Engl. J. Med. *316*:1627–1632, 1987.
50. Humar, A., Malkan, G., Moussa, G., et al.: Human herpesvirus-6 is associated with cytomegalovirus reactivation in liver transplant recipients. J. Infect. Dis. *181*:1450–1453, 2000.
51. Kapelushnik, J., Or, R., Delukina, A., et al.: Intravenous ribavirin therapy for adenovirus gastroenteritis after bone marrow transplantation. J. Pediatr. Gastroenterol. Nutr. *21*:110–112, 1995.
52. Kenagy, D. N., Schlessinger, Y., Weck, K., et al.: Epstein-Barr virus DNA in peripheral blood leukocytes of patients with post-transplant lymphoproliferative disease. Transplantation *60*:547–554, 1995.
53. Kusne, S., Dummer, J. S., Singh, N., et al.: Infection after liver transplantation: An analysis of 101 consecutive cases. Medicine *67*:132–143, 1988.
54. Leoung, G. S., Feigal, D. W., Montgomery, B., et al.: Aerosolized pentamidine for prophylaxis against *Pneumocystis carinii* pneumonia. N. Engl. J. Med. *323*:769–775, 1990.
55. Lichenstein, I. H., and MacGregor, R. R.: Mycobacterial infections in renal transplant recipients: Report of five cases and review of the literature. Rev. Infect. Dis. *5*:216–226, 1983.
56. Liles, W. C., Cushing, H., Holt, S., et al.: Severe adenovirus nephritis following bone marrow transplantation: Successful treatment with intravenous ribavirin. Bone Marrow Transplant. *14*:663–664, 1993.
57. Malatack, J. J., Gartner, J. C., Urbach, A. H., and Zitelli, B. J.: Orthotopic liver transplantation, Epstein-Barr virus, cyclosporine and lymphoproliferative syndrome: A growing concern. J. Pediatr. *118*:667–675, 1991.
58. Malhorta, K. K., Dash, S. C., Dhawan, I. K., et al.: Tuberculosis and renal transplantation: Observations from an endemic area. Postgrad. Med. J. *62*:359–362, 1986.
59. McDiarmid, S. V., Blumberg, D. A., Remotti, H., et al.: Mycobacterial infections after pediatric liver transplantation: A report of three cases and review of the literature. J. Pediatr. Gastroenterol. Nutr. *20*:425–431, 1995.
60. McDiarmid, S. V., Jordan, S., Lee, G. S., et al.: Prevention and pre-emptive therapy of post-transplant lymphoproliferative disease in pediatric liver recipients. Transplantation *66*:1604–1611, 1998.
61. McGregor, R. S., Zitelli, B. J., Urbach, A. H., et al.: Varicella in pediatric orthotopic liver transplant recipients. Pediatrics *83*:256–261, 1989.
62. Mendez, J. C., Dockrell, D. H., Espy, M. J., et al.: Human beta-herpesvirus interactions in solid-organ transplant recipients. J. Infect. Dis. *183*:179–184, 2001.
63. Michaels, M., Green, M., Wald, E. R., and Starzl, T. E.: Adenovirus infection in pediatric orthotopic liver transplant recipients. J. Infect. Dis. *165*:170–174, 1992.
64. Murphy, G. F., Wood, D. P., McRoberts. J. W., and Henslee-Downey, P. J.: Adenovirus-associated hemorrhagic cystitis treated with intravenous ribavirin. J. Urol. *149*:565–566, 1993.
65. Najarian, J. S., Fryd, D. S., Strand, M., et al.: A single institution, randomized, prospective trial of cyclosporine versus azathioprine-antilymphocyte globulin for immunosuppression in renal allograft recipients. Ann. Surg. *201*:142–157, 1985.
66. Paya, C., Fung, J. J., Nalesnik, M. A., et al.: Epstein-Barr virus-induced posttransplant lymphoproliferative disorders. Transplantation *68*: 1517–1525, 1999.
67. Pohl, C., Green, M., and Wald, E. R.: RSV infection after pediatric liver transplantation. J. Infect. Dis. *165*:166–169, 1992.
68. Quinibi, W., Al-Sibai, M. B., Taher, S., et al.: Mycobacterial infection after renal transplantation: Report of 14 cases and review of the literature. Q. J. Med. *282*:1039–1060, 1990.
69. Ribaud, P., Scieux, C., Freymuth, F., et al.: Successful treatment of adenovirus disease with intravenous cidofovir in an unrelated stem-cell transplant recipient. Clin. Infect. Dis. *28*:690–691, 1999.
70. Riddler, S. A., Breinig, M. C., and McKnight, J. L. C.: Increased levels of circulating Epstein-Barr virus-infected lymphocytes and decreased EBV nuclear antigen antibody responses are associated with the development of posttransplant lymphoproliferative disease in solid-organ transplant recipients. Blood *84*:972–984, 1994.
71. Rollins, N. K., Andrews, W. S., Currino, G., et al.: Infected bile lakes following pediatric liver transplantation: Non-surgical management. Radiology *166*:169–171, 1988.
72. Rowe, D. T., Qu, L., Reyes, J., et al.: Use of quantitative competitive PCR to measure Epstein-Barr virus genome load in peripheral blood of pediatric transplant recipients with lymphoproliferative disorders. J. Clin. Microbiol. *35*:1612–1615, 1997.
73. Saliba, F., Arulnaden, J. L., Gugenheim, J., et al.: CMV hyperimmune globulin prophylaxis after liver transplantation: A prospective randomized controlled study. Transplant. Proc. *21*:2260–2262, 1989.

74. Schroter, G. P. J., Hoelscher, M., Putnam, C. W., et al.: Infections complicating orthotopic liver transplantation. Arch. Surg. *111*:1337–1347, 1976.
75. Shapiro, R. S., Chauvenet, A., McGuire, W., et al.: Treatment of B-cell lymphoproliferative disorders with interferon alpha and intravenous gamma globulin. N. Engl. J. Med. *318*:1334, 1988.
76. Sia, I. G., Wilson, J. A., Groettum, C. M., et al.: Cytomegalovirus (CMV) DNA load predicts relapsing CMV infection after solid organ transplantation. J. Infect. Dis. *181*:717–720, 2000.
77. Singh, N., Dummer, S., Kusne, S., et al.: Infections with cytomegalovirus and other herpesviruses in 121 liver transplant recipients: Transmission by donated organ and the effect of OKT3 antibodies. J. Infect. Dis. *155*:202–206, 1988.
78. Singh, N., and Paterson, D. L.: Mycobacterium tuberculosis infection in solid-organ transplant recipients: Impact and implications for management. Clin. Infect. Dis. *27*:1266–1277, 1998.
79. Smets, F., Bodeus, M., Goubau, P., et al.: Characteristics of Epstein-Barr virus primary infection in pediatric liver transplant recipients. J. Hepatol. *32*:100–104, 2000.
80. Sokal, E. M., Antunes, H., Beguin, C., et al.: Early signs and risk factors for the increased incidence of Epstein-Barr virus-related posttransplant lymphoproliferative diseases in pediatric liver transplant recipients treated with tacrolimus. Transplantation *64*:1438–1442, 1997.
81. Starzl, T. E., Porter, K. A., Iwatsuki, S., et al.: Reversibility of lymphomas and lymphoproliferative lesions developing under cyclosporin-steroid therapy. Lancet *1*:583–587, 1984.
82. Stratta, R. J., Shaefer, M. S., Markin, R. S., et al.: Clinical patterns of cytomegalovirus disease after liver transplantation. Arch. Surg. *124*:1443–1450, 1989.
83. Strernecik, M., Ferrell, S., Asher, N., et al.: Mycobacterial infection after liver transplantation: A report of three cases and review of the literature. Clin. Transplant. *6*:55–61, 1992.
84. The, T. H., van der Ploeg, M., van der Berg, A., et al.: Direct detection of cytomegalovirus in peripheral blood leukocytes: A review of the antigenemia assay and polymerase chain reaction. Transplantation *54*:193–198, 1992.
85. Todo, S., Fung, J. J., Starzl, T. E., et al.: Liver, kidney, and thoracic organ transplantation under FK 506. Ann. Surg. *212*:295–307, 1990.
86. Touraine, J. L., Bosi, E., El Yafi, M. S., et al.: The infectious lymphoproliferative syndrome in transplant recipients under immunosuppressive treatment. Transplant. Proc. *17*:96–98, 1985.
87. Ukah, F. O., Merhave, H., and Kramer, D.: Early outcome of liver transplantation in patients with a history of spontaneous bacterial peritonitis. Transplant. Proc. *25*:1113–1115, 1993.
88. Verma, A., Dhawan, A., Wade, J. J., et al.: *Mycobacterium* tuberculosis infections in pediatric liver transplant recipients. Pediatr. Infect. Dis. J. *19*:625–630, 2000.
89. Winston, D. J., Wirin, D., Shaked, A., and Busuttil, R. W.: Randomized comparison of ganciclovir and high-dose acyclovir for long-term cytomegalovirus prophylaxis in liver transplant recipients. Lancet *246*:69–74, 1995.
90. Wittner, M.: Cryptococcosis. *In* Feigin, R. D., and Cherry, J. D. (eds.): Textbook of Pediatric Infectious Diseases. 2nd ed. Philadelphia, W. B. Saunders, 1987.
91. Wong, S. Y., and Allen, D. M.: Transmission of histoplasmosis via cadaveric renal transplantation: Case report and review of the literature. Clin. Infect. Dis. *14*:232–234, 1992.
92. Wreghitt, T. G., Gray, J. J., Ward, K. N., et al.: Disseminated adenovirus infection after liver transplantation and its possible treatment with ganciclovir. J. Infect. *19*:88–89, 1989.
93. Yoshikawa, T., Ihira, M., Furukawa, H., et al.: Four cases of human herpesvirus 6 variant B infection after pediatric liver transplantation. Transplantation *65*:1266–1269, 1998.
94. Yoshikawa, T., Ihira, M., Suzuki, K., et al.: Human herpesvirus 6 infection after living related liver transplantation. J. Med. Virol. *62*:52–59, 2000.
95. Younes, B. S., McDiarmid, S. V., Hargas, J. H., et al.: The effect of immunosuppression on posttransplant lymphoproliferative disease in pediatric liver transplant patients. Transplantation *70*:94–99, 2000.
96. Zitelli, B. J., Gartner, J. C., Malatach, J. J., et al.: Pediatric liver transplantation: Patient evaluation and selection, infectious complications, and life-style after transplantation. Transplant. Proc. *19*:3309–3316, 1987.

Opportunistic Infections in Kidney Transplantation

GAIL J. DEMMLER

Optimal therapy for end-stage renal disease in children is renal transplantation, which allows most children the best opportunities for normal growth and development and an almost normal lifestyle.[156] However, despite the overall success of renal transplantation, infection remains the major cause of morbidity and mortality in renal transplant recipients.[34,152] A general approach to the renal transplant patient from the perspective of the infectious disease specialist is presented in this chapter. Specific and detailed information regarding the diagnosis and management of each particular pathogen can be found in the respective chapters in the section of this textbook dedicated to infections with specific microorganisms.

Pretransplant Evaluation

The role of the pediatric infectious disease specialist in the care of a renal transplant recipient ideally begins during the pretransplantation period.[114] Before transplantation, the patient should receive a thorough history and physical examination, with a focus on evaluation for evidence of an active infection that may require immediate therapy or, rarely, preclude transplantation (Table 79–1). The history should be comprehensive, yet focus on the details of any history of previous infections that may re-emerge during the post-transplant period, including urinary tract infections (UTIs), mucocutaneous diseases such as herpes simplex, systemic illnesses such as tuberculosis, chronic infections such as hepatitis B or C or human immunodeficiency virus (HIV), and diarrheal diseases. Renal transplant candidates will be undergoing peritoneal or hemodialysis, so a history of previous dialysis catheter–associated infections should be documented, and any current infection should be treated and eliminated before transplantation. Another focus of the history should include an exposure history for travel, especially to areas endemic for organisms such as *Strongyloides stercoralis, Coccidioides immitis, Blastomyces dermatitidis,* or *Histoplasma capsulatum* and for diseases such as malaria and tuberculosis.[59] Other important exposures include blood product transfusions, animal or pet exposure, well water as a source of drinking water, and dietary habits, especially consumption of raw or undercooked eggs or meat or unpasteurized dairy products.[114, 115] In children, a careful history for routine childhood illnesses, including varicella, measles, and rubella, should be documented.[72] Furthermore, the

TABLE 79–1 ■ GUIDELINES FOR PRETRANSPLANT EVALUATION IN PEDIATRIC KIDNEY TRANSPLANT CANDIDATES

History
Past infectious diseases
Routine childhood illnesses
Travel to or residence in areas endemic for fungal or parasitic diseases
Tuberculosis exposure
Animal exposure
Diet preferences and water resources
Vaccinations
Reactions or allergies to anti-microbials
Current or past immunosuppression

Physical
Search for active or latent focus of infection
Nutritional status

Laboratory and Other Testing
PPD
Chest radiograph
Urinalysis and urine culture
Viral serology for CMV, EBV, VZV, erythrovirus, HAV, HBV, HCV, HIV, and others depending on the history
Baseline CMV and EBV DNA PCR or CMV antigenemia if seropositive and post-transplant monitoring is anticipated
Fungal and parasitic serology if travel- or exposure history-positive

Anticipatory Guidance
Update vaccines
Counsel regarding measures to reduce infection risk
Consider antimicrobial prophylaxis if at risk

CMV, cytomegalovirus; EBV, Epstein-Barr virus; HAV, hepatitis A virus; HBV, hepatitis B virus; HCV, hepatitis C virus; HIV, human immunodeficiency virus; PCR, polymerase chain reaction; PPD, purified protein derivative; VZV, varicella-zoster virus.

immunization history of the patient should be documented carefully and updated before transplantation, if needed or indicated. Vaccinations against tetanus, pertussis, and diphtheria; polysaccharide vaccines such as those against pneumococcus and *Haemophilus influenzae* type B; inactivated vaccines against polio and hepatitis A; and recombinant vaccines, such as those for hepatitis B, may be given or updated at any time before transplantation.[21] Meningococcal vaccine may be indicated in special circumstances or at specific ages. The live varicella vaccine is recommended for renal transplant candidates who have not had varicella, and it should be given at least 2 to 4 weeks before transplantation.[167] Measles vaccine should be administered even earlier, preferably months before transplantation. In addition, annual influenza vaccine and a tetanus booster every 10 years are recommended for patients who are renal transplant candidates or recipients. If the child is unable to be fully immunized pretransplant, the routine immunization schedule for the inactivated vaccines may be reinstituted after immunosuppression is decreased, approximately 6 to 12 months after an uncomplicated transplant procedure.[21] Live virus vaccines should be avoided in the post-transplant period in most instances. Close contacts and family members of renal transplant candidates and recipients also should be fully immunized, as well as receive the annual influenza vaccine.[7]

Other important points in the pretransplant evaluation history include allergies or reactions to medications, especially antibiotics, and the use of immunosuppressive agents.

Pretransplant laboratory and diagnostic imaging evaluations for most renal transplant candidates should include a tuberculin skin test, chest radiograph, urine analysis, and urine culture for bacteria. Baseline renal and liver function tests also should be performed. Serologic screening of the transplant recipient's status regarding organisms that may reactivate in the recipient or infect the recipient via the donor organ should be performed; such screening should include tests for cytomegalovirus (CMV), varicella-zoster virus (VZV), Epstein-Barr virus (EBV), erythrovirus, syphilis, toxoplasmosis, hepatitis A, B, and C viruses, and HIV. It may be helpful to save an aliquot of the recipient (and donor) serum in case unusual circumstances occur. Furthermore, in CMV-seropositive transplant candidates, baseline CMV antigenemia or DNA polymerase chain reaction (PCR) may be useful, and in EBV-seropositive candidates, detection of EBV DNA by PCR may be helpful, especially if post-transplant virologic monitoring will be performed. Other laboratory tests or imaging studies may be of use, depending on the patient's exposure history and physical examination.

The pretransplant evaluation also is an opportunity for the infectious disease specialist to counsel the patient and family about measures that may reduce the transplant recipient's risk for development infectious disease complications post-transplant. For example, patients who have an exposure, or even a suspected exposure, to varicella (a.k.a. chickenpox) or zoster (a.k.a. shingles) should contact their physicians immediately to see whether passive immunoprophylaxis with varicella-zoster immune globulin (VZIG) or postexposure antiviral therapy with acyclovir or valacyclovir is indicated. Plans for foreign travel to remote areas should be discussed with the physician as well. The transplant recipient should consume only thoroughly cooked meat and seafood and thoroughly washed fresh fruits and vegetables. In addition, drinking water should be pure. Transplant recipients should avoid, if at all possible, changing cat litter boxes, aquariums, and birdcages and avoid close contact with people who have viral respiratory illnesses. Finally, medical attention should be sought if fever occurs, especially if it is significant or persistent.

Post-transplant Infectious Complications

Infections occurring in the post-transplant period can be grouped into three main time frames: the first month post-transplant (early), the second to the sixth month post-transplant (middle), and the period from 6 months post-transplant onward (late).[130, 145] Although almost any organism or pathogen can infect a transplant recipient at any time, these time periods provide the clinician with a guide to the organisms and disease processes most commonly encountered (Table 79–2).

INFECTIONS OCCURRING DURING THE EARLY POST-TRANSPLANT PERIOD

Infections occurring during the first month after renal transplantation usually are bacterial.[136] Common sites of early infections include the wound, urinary tract, lungs, and indwelling intravascular catheters.[120]

Wound Infections

As with any surgical procedure, wound infections may develop in a renal transplant recipient. They occur in approximately 2 percent of renal transplant recipients and range in severity from a superficial wound infection, easily treated with wound care and antimicrobial therapy, to deep perinephric abscesses that may be difficult to treat and result in transplant nephrectomy.[131, 136] Wound infections

TABLE 79–2 ■ OUTLINE OF A TIMETABLE FOR THE OCCURRENCE OF COMMON INFECTIONS AND USUAL PATHOGENS AFTER KIDNEY TRANSPLANTATION

Early Period
Wound infections
UTI
Bacteremia and sepsis syndrome
Pneumonia
Herpes simplex virus
HBV
Seasonal viruses
Drug reactions

Middle Period
Herpesviruses
- CMV
- EBV
- VZV
- HHV types 6, 7 and 8

Polyomaviruses
- JC
- BK

Papillomaviruses
Adenoviruses
Human erythrovirus
Listeria monocytogenes
Mycobacterium tuberculosis
Atypical mycobacteria
Nocardia
Fungal diseases
Pneumocystis carinii
Parasitic diseases

Late Period
Community-acquired respiratory viruses
UTI
Streptococcus pneumoniae
CMV
EBV
VZV
HBV
HCV
HIV/AIDS

AIDS, acquired immunodeficiency syndrome; CMV, cytomegalovirus; EBV, Epstein-Barr virus; HBV, hepatitis B virus; HCV, hepatitis C virus; HHV, human herpesvirus; HIV, human immunodeficiency virus; UTI, urinary tract infection; VZV, varicella-zoster virus.

are more likely to occur in patients with technical problems associated with the transplant surgery, including urinary leaks, vesicoureteral reflux, wound hematomas, or lymphoceles.[101, 168] Malnutrition during the pretransplant period may impair wound healing and predispose to development of wound infection. Open Penrose drains may increase the likelihood of introducing microorganisms into the wound, whereas closed suction drainage, with a Jackson-Pratt drain, for example, may reduce this risk. In addition, prompt removal of all drains, usually within 5 days in most uncomplicated cases, and prophylaxis with perioperative antibiotics may decrease the incidence of wound infections; such measures are performed routinely in most renal transplant centers. The regimen usually is aimed at both uropathogens and staphylococci. One dose generally is given pretransplant, and the regimen is continued for only 24 hours after transplantation. The diagnosis of a wound infection should be suspected if erythema, warmth, or discharge is present at the wound site or if an unexplained fever develops. Fluid may drain from the wound persistently, or a fluid collection or abscess may be seen on imaging of the deeper operative sites. However, the patient will be receiving immunosuppressive agents, and, therefore, the findings may be unusual or the symptoms blunted. Any fluid or pus obtained should be stained and cultured for bacterial as well as mycobacterial and fungal organisms. Organisms most likely to be identified as causes of wound infection include staphylococci, streptococci, and gram-negative enteric organisms. Unusual, multiply resistant, or nosocomial bacterial pathogens and yeast, most often *Candida albicans,* also may cause wound infections post-transplant. In addition, case reports of wound and perinephric fluid collections infected with *Mycoplasma hominis* have been published.[147] Appropriate antimicrobial therapy, initially broad spectrum and then ultimately tailored to the isolated organism and its susceptibility pattern, should be administered. The duration of appropriate antimicrobial therapy usually is 10 to 14 days or until the wound infection has resolved and the patient has been afebrile for 3 to 5 days. Deep abscesses or unusual organisms may require longer therapy.

Urinary Tract Infections

UTIs are common occurrences after renal transplantation and may affect 35 to 79 percent of renal transplant recipients.[78, 168] They may occur during the early, middle, or late post-transplant period. A UTI that occurs during the early or early-middle post-transplant period often is a severe illness complicated by pyelonephritis, urosepsis, metastatic foci of infection, allograft dysfunction, rejection, and relapse.[103, 132] The risk for developing invasive UTI after renal transplantation appears to be increased in patients with prolonged bladder catheterization (most catheters can be removed during the first few days post-transplant), malnutrition, underlying disorders, renal stones, obstructive uropathy, or a contaminated cadaveric kidney.[114] Surgical complications such as hematoma, reflux or obstruction at the urinary anastomosis, or inability of the bladder to completely empty are associated with UTIs. In addition, young infants, especially if they have vesicoureteral reflux, appear to have a high incidence of complicated UTIs post-transplant.[103] The organisms most commonly isolated from patients with early UTIs include not only the typical gram-negative enteric bacteria but also enterococci, staphylococci, and *Pseudomonas aeruginosa.* Unusual organisms such as *Streptococcus mitis, Serratia marcescens,* and *Corynebacterium urealyticum* also can be found. Antimicrobial therapy should be tailored to the susceptibility pattern of the organism isolated from the urine. Because as many as 30 percent of patients experiencing a UTI during the early post-transplant period have recurrent UTIs, a prolonged 6-week course of antibiotics usually is recommended to reduce the risk of a relapsing kidney infection.[101, 132] Furthermore, antimicrobial prophylaxis may reduce the risk of a UTI developing. For example, trimethoprim-sulfamethoxazole administered for the first 4 months after renal transplantation is effective in preventing most UTIs and can provide prophylaxis against *Pneumocystis carinii* pneumonia and other diseases as well.[48]

Pneumonia

Pneumonia can occur during the first month after renal transplantation and often is associated with prolonged endotracheal intubation. Bacterial pathogens, both gram-positive and gram-negative, acquired from normal oropharyngeal flora, or unusual or multiply resistant organisms, acquired nosocomially, predominate during the early post-transplant period.[115] *Legionella pneumophila,* as well as unusual *Legionella* spp. such as *L. micdadei, L. bozemanii,* and *L. dumoffii*, also may cause pneumonia in transplant recipients.[77, 115] *P. carinii* can cause pneumonia in a transplant recipient during the early post-transplant period, but more often it is associated with disease after the first month post-transplant.[61] Rare or unusual pathogens such as *Rhodococcus equi* may cause pneumonia in these patients.[90] The pneumonia usually is manifested as fever, chills, chest pain, malaise, change in tracheal secretions, cough, dyspnea, tachypnea, change in ventilatory status, rales or rhonchi on auscultation of the lungs, and pulmonary infiltrates on chest radiograph. It may be complicated by pleural effusion, empyema, or pulmonary abscess, and death may occur if the pneumonia is severe and not diagnosed and treated promptly. Treatment with antibiotics effective against the bacterial pathogens isolated from culture of tracheal aspirates, bronchoalveolar lavage fluid, or lung tissue is appropriate.

Bacteremia and Sepsis

Bacteremia and sepsis occurring during the early post-transplant period often are associated with indwelling catheters.[114] The urinary tract, surgical wound, or transplanted or native kidney also may be a source.[96] Both usual and unusual bacterial organisms, as well as yeasts such as *C. albicans,* may be involved. *Listeria monocytogenes* also may cause primary bacteremia or sepsis at any time after kidney transplantation, but the greatest risk occurs during the early period. Complications include meningitis, and as many as 10 percent of these patients die.[102, 141] Renal transplant recipients also are at increased risk for development of bacteremia with *Salmonella* nontyphoidal species.[33, 69, 114] Complications such as urinary tract or graft infection, peritonitis, abscesses, and meningitis can occur, and recurrences are common. Therapy for bacteremia, sepsis, or its complications is tailored toward the susceptibility pattern of the organism isolated from the patient's blood. The duration of therapy for uncomplicated bacteremia usually is 10 to 14 days, but a longer course of treatment may be indicated if abscesses occur or an unusual organism is isolated. Removal of the indwelling catheter may be necessary to clear persistent bacteremia, and abscesses and other foci of infection should be drained.

Other Bacterial Diseases

Pediatric renal transplant recipients also appear to be at increased risk for development of antibiotic-associated colitis caused by *Clostridium difficile.*[161] Infection of a lymphocele with *Pasteurella multocida* has been reported, as has systemic infection with *Bartonella henselae.*[2, 25, 36, 92, 114] A high index of suspicion always must be maintained when evaluating a transplant recipient for infection because the immunosuppression required to maintain the transplanted kidney predisposes the recipient to development of infection with unusual organisms.

Viral Infections

Herpes simplex virus (HSV) is the most common virus encountered during the early post-transplant period, although antiviral prophylaxis significantly reduces the risk of this infection.[38, 39] It occurs less commonly in pediatric (8%) than in adult renal transplant recipients (30%).[114, 115] Most HSV infections encountered post-transplant are due to reactivation of the recipient's strain; however, primary or recurrent infection acquired from the renal allograft may occur, and even primary infection from person-to-person transmission has been documented.[38, 114, 115, 132] Post-transplant HSV infection may be asymptomatic or associated with disease, most commonly oral ulcers in pediatric patients.[56] Genital and perianal ulcers may occur in adolescents and adults. Rarely, HSV may cause disseminated cutaneous lesions or zosteriform eruptions. HSV esophagitis may be manifested as dysphagia, refusal to eat, irritability, and substernal chest pain, and it may complicate oral HSV disease, especially if the oral mucosa has been traumatized by orogastric or nasogastric tubes. Acute, severe hepatitis with hepatic necrosis, often accompanied by hypotension and disseminated intravascular coagulation, also can occur. Tracheobronchitis and pneumonitis may occur as a result of HSV, primarily in patients with pneumonia caused by another pathogen and whose mucosa has been traumatized by endotracheal intubation. It is often severe and life-threatening, even with appropriate supportive care and antiviral therapy.[114] Encephalitis also has been reported in renal transplant recipients.[53] The diagnosis is made by isolation of the virus in cell culture or detection of viral antigen by immunofluorescence or viral DNA by PCR in the end-organ involved. Detection or isolation of HSV in body secretions, however, may represent asymptomatic shedding or disease and should be correlated clinically. Treatment with acyclovir is recommended for those with disease, and HSV-seropositive transplant recipients should receive acyclovir or valacyclovir prophylaxis during the peritransplant period to prevent HSV infection. Most patients receiving ganciclovir, valganciclovir, foscarnet, or cidofovir for CMV prophylaxis also will be protected against HSV.

Seasonal viruses, especially winter respiratory viruses such as respiratory syncytial virus (RSV), influenza viruses, parainfluenza viruses, and adenoviruses; winter diarrhea viruses such as rotavirus; and late summer/early fall viruses such as the enteroviruses can infect the transplant recipient during the early post-transplant period and cause disease. Such infections may be acquired from the family or the community, or they may be nosocomial. The illness associated with these viruses, however, typically is not as severe as the illness seen with the herpes family of viruses or adenoviruses.

Renal transplant recipients who are chronically infected with hepatitis B virus (HBV) may experience liver dysfunction during the early transplant period, but the late post-transplant period, beyond the first year, carries the greatest risk for progression of liver disease to cirrhosis. If a renal transplant recipient acquires HBV soon after transplantation, acute hepatitis can develop, often with death from liver failure.[32, 114]

Noninfectious Causes of Fever

The most common noninfectious cause of fever in the first post-transplant month is allograft rejection.[131] Fever often is the first sign of rejection, especially in children, and rejection should be considered if an infectious source of the fever is not identified. Another common noninfectious cause of fever early after transplantation is antilymphocyte antibody therapy (OKT3). The first two or three doses of OKT3 produce a release of cytokines, which cause fever and chills. In most patients, these symptoms resolve after the third dose. Other noninfectious causes of fever during this period include drug reactions and pulmonary emboli.

INFECTIONS OCCURRING DURING THE MIDDLE POST-TRANSPLANT PERIOD

The cumulative effects of immunosuppression begin to unveil during the period from the second to the sixth month after transplantation. If a significant amount of antirejection therapy is required for multiple episodes of rejection, the effects may be even more pronounced. Such immunosuppression allows classic opportunistic pathogens such as CMV, *P. carinii, Toxoplasma gondii, L. monocytogenes, Aspergillus,* and *Nocardia* to evade immune surveillance and cause disease.[114, 160, 162] Furthermore, reactivation of organisms previously infecting the transplant recipient or the donor allograft may cause disease. These organisms include *Mycobacterium tuberculosis,* HBV, hepatitis C virus (HCV), HIV, *H. capsulatum*, and *C. immitis*. In addition, an occult bacterial focus of infection that was not adequately identified and treated pretransplant may become apparent at this time and cause significant disease.[131]

Herpesviruses

The herpes family of viruses (HSV types 1 and 2, CMV, EBV, VZV, and human herpesvirus [HHV] types 6, 7, and 8) share the biologic properties of latency, reactivation, cell association, and oncogenicity, which renders them the most important group of pathogens that affect renal transplant recipients.[114, 137] Whereas HSV is more important during the early post-transplant period, the other herpes family members are important causes of morbidity and mortality during the middle and late post-transplant periods.[62]

CYTOMEGALOVIRUS. CMV may cause primary infection in a CMV-seronegative transplant recipient through a renal allograft or blood product transfusion from a seropositive donor.[12, 129] Person-to-person transmission also is possible. Recurrent CMV infection develops in seropositive transplant recipients if the recipient's CMV strain becomes reactivated. The renal allograft from a seropositive donor also can be a source of reinfection to the recipient and produce active CMV infection or disease.[24, 57] CMV infection in renal transplant recipients may cause silent or asymptomatic infection; end-organ diseases such as hepatitis, esophagitis, colitis, encephalitis, vasculitis, retinitis; and systematic disease with persistent fever and leukopenia. It has been linked in some studies to allograft dysfunction and nephropathy. CMV also causes depressed cell-mediated immunity and impaired alveolar macrophage function, thus rendering the host more vulnerable to other opportunistic infections such as fungal disease and *P. carinii* pneumonia, and it serves as a cofactor for other viruses such as EBV and HHV-6 and HHV-7.[74, 111, 121, 154] In addition, CMV is associated with acute and chronic rejection and allograft nephropathy, as well as decreased long-term patient survival.[1, 40, 82, 114, 129] Disease caused by CMV can be documented by isolation of CMV from blood or tissue, detection of CMV antigen pp65 in circulating leukocytes, or detection of CMV DNA by PCR or similar assays in blood, bronchoalveolar fluid, or tissue.[16, 17, 117, 118, 129] Isolation of CMV in urine or saliva has little significance, however, and serologic tests should be reserved for pretransplant screening only. Most transplant patients at risk for acquiring CMV disease (i.e., CMV-seropositive recipients or CMV-seronegative recipients who received a renal allograft from a seropositive donor) should be monitored by viral surveillance, usually by testing blood weekly for CMV antigen pp65 or for CMV DNA by PCR.[15, 64] Detection of significant levels of the virus by quantitative or semiquantitative assay usually predicts CMV disease.[155] Preemptive antiviral therapy is generally indicated and results in a decrease or resolution of CMV levels detected in blood.[17, 28, 31, 51, 54, 88] Some patients, however, despite adequate antiviral therapy, will have persistently positive CMV DNA by PCR, which should be interpreted within the clinical context.[16] For example, in some patients who otherwise appear well, the DNA may be fragmented and nonreplicating, whereas in other patients with persistent symptomatology, a strain of CMV resistant to one or more antiviral agents may be the cause. The antiviral agents currently available for the treatment of CMV disease and preemptive therapy for positive CMV markers include ganciclovir, valganciclovir, foscarnet, and cidofovir.[159] For renal transplant patients, 2 to 3 weeks of therapy with ganciclovir usually is adequate for treatment of disease; however, patients with CMV retinitis or repeat episodes of rejection may require maintenance therapy.[70, 104] Preemptive therapy may be continued throughout the period of immunosuppression in patients who are severely immunosuppressed.[54, 64] Foscarnet and cidofovir have significant renal toxicity and should be used with extreme caution in renal transplant recipients. Prophylaxis for CMV disease is indicated in high-risk transplant recipients, and options include intravenous CMV immune globulin, oral and intravenous acyclovir and ganciclovir, and oral valacyclovir and valganciclovir.[19, 46, 51, 85, 104, 140, 146]

EPSTEIN-BARR VIRUS. EBV infection in children who have received a renal transplant may be asymptomatic or may be associated with a variety of different syndromes, including a nonspecific viral syndrome, mononucleosis, post-transplant lymphoproliferative disorder (PTLPD), and lymphoma.[60, 66] Infection and disease may occur after both primary and recurrent EBV infection, but primary infection is more likely to occur and produce PTLPD in children than in adults who have received solid organ transplants.[23, 66] EBV disease may develop as early as 1 month or as long as 5 or more years post-transplant, with the risk accumulating every year of post-transplant survival. Knowledge about post-transplant EBV infection and disease is evolving; as graft survival has improved, with more intense immunosuppressive regimens and other opportunistic infections such as HSV, CMV, and *P. carinii* being managed, EBV has emerged as a formidable obstacle to successful solid organ transplantation in children.[73] The estimated overall risk for development of serious life-threatening EBV-associated illness is at least 4 percent and increases to 10 percent in children who experience a primary infection with EBV after transplantation.[66] Other risk factors for PTLPD in children who have received solid organ transplants include antilymphocyte therapy such as OKT3 for rejection, receipt of tacrolimus rather than cyclosporine for immunosuppression, and CMV donor-recipient mismatch.[35, 71]

Nonspecific viral syndromes and mononucleosis occur earlier during the post-transplant period, whereas lymphoma is more likely to be a manifestation during the late post-transplant period. Uncomplicated post-transplant mononucleosis is characterized by the self-limited illness of fever, pharyngitis, cervical adenopathy, and splenomegaly. The signs and symptoms of PTLPD can be variable but often include persistent fever, weight loss, and generalized adenopathy.[66] The disease frequently is multisystemic and progressive, and involvement of the lungs, gastrointestinal tract, liver, spleen, and brain, and lesions may be detected by computed tomography of the neck, chest, and abdomen.[114] The renal allograft also may be involved and show dysfunction. Lymphoma may be manifested as solid tumors in the renal allograft, lung, liver, spleen, brain, and soft tissues.[60]

Laboratory diagnosis of post-transplant EBV-associated disease is based on detection of EBV DNA in circulating lymphocytes by PCR.[3, 30, 42] Quantitative or semiquantitative assays may show increasing copies of EBV DNA in the circulating lymphocytes of patients who are at risk for PTLPD.[3, 58, 128] If end-organ disease is observed, the diagnosis can be confirmed histopathologically by detection of EBV DNA in tissue by PCR or by in situ hybridization with an EBV-encoded RNA (EBER) probe. The diseases associated with EBV also may be classified in the laboratory as polyclonal or monoclonal. Polyclonal illnesses appear to be more benign than are monoclonal diseases, which often are associated with chromosomal abnormalities and malignant transformation.[114] The virus cannot be cultivated by routine means; when studied by special culture techniques, EBV has been found commonly in the oropharyngeal secretions of seropositive transplant recipients and is not predictive of EBV-associated disease.[114, 128] Similarly, serologic approaches to the diagnosis of EBV infection post-transplant also are nonspecific and difficult to interpret in most patients, unless the recipient clearly has seroconverted during the post-transplant period.

Aggressive or intense treatment of uncomplicated EBV-associated viral syndrome or mononucleosis usually is not necessary because these illnesses appear to be self-limited in most patients. Immunosuppression may be reduced, acyclovir may be administered, and the patient should be monitored carefully. If symptoms in the patient or EBV DNA in the blood persist, PTLPD should be suspected and the diagnosis confirmed. Treatment of established PTLPD is challenging.[55] Mortality rates are high, and the best results appear to occur if the disease is diagnosed and treated early. Preemptive therapy instituted when viral surveillance monitoring detects EBV in circulating lymphocytes before end-organ disease is evident also may be helpful in some patients.[30, 94] Reduction in immunosuppression remains the most widely recommended strategy, but a variety of regimens have been studied as well. Antiviral agents such as acyclovir and ganciclovir appear to reduce EBV replication early in the course of the disease process and may halt the progression of disease in some patients.[115, 159] However, antiviral agents are not effective against latent EBV or cells that have been transformed by the virus. Interferon-α, immune globulin, and anti-CD20 monoclonal antibody preparations such as rituximab have been used with some success in patients with established PTLPD. Experimental protocols evaluating adoptive immunotherapy in transplant recipients also are in progress. In addition, some experts suggest that intense anti-CMV therapy with ganciclovir and CMV hyperimmune globulin may improve survival in certain patients with PTLPD because CMV may serve as a cofactor in progression of disease caused by other members of the herpes family.[1, 18, 111, 144, 154] Treatment of patients with lymphoma includes a reduction in immunosuppression, as well as chemotherapy, radiation therapy, and surgical resection of tumors.

VARICELLA-ZOSTER VIRUS. VZV can cause primary (varicella, a.k.a. chickenpox) or reactivation (zoster, a.k.a. shingles) disease in a renal transplant recipient.[114, 145] Infection with VZV can occur at any time but does so most often during the middle post-transplant period, and it is manifested as fever and painful or pruritic vesicular skin lesions.[104] Hepatitis, encephalitis, and pneumonia also rarely may occur before skin lesions, especially in an immunocompromised host. Varicella occurs more commonly in children and zoster more commonly in adult transplant recipients.[23] In contrast to other herpes family viruses, VZV almost always is transmitted person to person, and rarely, if ever has it been linked to the transplanted allograft.[114] Before routine immunization and antiviral therapy, infection with VZV was a major cause of morbidity and mortality in children receiving solid organ transplants.[23, 44, 132] Untreated primary varicella may continue for several weeks and result in visceral dissemination, pneumonitis, hepatic necrosis, encephalitis, disseminated intravascular coagulation, hemorrhagic skin lesions, and death.[44, 115, 137] Zoster in solid organ transplant recipients may remain localized to a dermatome, but it often will disseminate beyond the dermatomal distribution and produce widespread skin lesions and even visceral dissemination.

The diagnosis of VZV disease often is clinical, but it can be confirmed by isolation of VZV from fresh, vesicular skin lesions or detection of viral antigen by direct immunofluorescence on cells obtained by scraping the base of the skin lesion.[115] Other pathogens, especially HSV, may mimic VZV disease so an accurate viral diagnosis is important. VZV also may be detected by PCR-based DNA detection methods, but these tests are not widely available at this time. Serologic diagnosis of an active VZV infection is difficult. However, routine serologic screening performed in the pretransplant period will identify patients who are seronegative and, therefore, at risk for developing primary infection with VZV.

Treatment of established VZV disease should be instituted as early as possible during the course of the illness because survival is improved if treatment begins before the fifth day of illness.[44] Acyclovir, administered intravenously in high doses (500 mg/m^2 per dose every 8 hours if renal function is normal) for 5 to 10 days or until new lesions have ceased to occur, old lesions have crusted, the fever has resolved, and disease has abated, is recommended for most renal transplant recipients experiencing either primary infection with varicella or zoster with dissemination.[114, 159] Uncomplicated zoster or very mild primary varicella may be treated with oral acyclovir, famciclovir, or valacyclovir, provided that the patient is monitored carefully for clinical response.

Prevention of post-transplant VZV disease can be accomplished by several effective strategies, which should be discussed during the pretransplant evaluation. Transplant recipients who were seronegative for VZV during the pretransplant evaluation should receive varicella vaccine before undergoing transplantation, if possible.[49, 75, 167] Seronegative, unimmunized transplant recipients who are exposed to varicella or zoster during the post-transplant period should receive passive immunoprophylaxis with VZIG. Preemptive therapy with oral acyclovir also is recommended by some experts in this situation because VZIG does not prevent, only attenuates, the postexposure disease process. Finally, acyclovir, valacyclovir, ganciclovir, and valganciclovir administered prophylactically to transplant recipients who are seropositive for HSV or CMV also may provide protection against VZV disease.[85, 114]

HUMAN HERPESVIRUSES. HHV-6, HHV-7, and HHV-8 also infect renal transplant recipients, both by primary infection and by reactivation.[41, 63, 131, 144] Infection with these viruses becomes evident during the middle post-transplant period, but their roles in specific disease processes are unclear.[115, 139, 151] HHV-6 and HHV-7 may act as cofactors in disease progression, especially diseases caused by CMV and EBV.[41, 74, 104, 111, 154] HHV-8 is associated with Kaposi sarcoma post-transplant in severely immunosuppressed adult renal transplant recipients, but it has not been appreciated as a major opportunistic pathogen in pediatric renal transplant recipients to date.[22, 43, 114, 125, 139] HHV-8 may be transmitted through the renal allograft or by blood product transfusion, or it can become reactivated in the recipient post-transplant.[125]

Polyomaviruses and Papillomaviruses

Human polyomaviruses (JC, BK, and SV40) and papillomaviruses (HPV) commonly infect children. They can be detected in the urine of renal transplant recipients and detected serologically, histopathologically, and by PCR in blood, body fluids, and tissue.[4, 37, 47, 50, 105–107, 114, 133] Our knowledge about the roles that these viruses play in the outcome of renal transplant patients, however, is evolving. Adult renal transplant recipients are at increased risk for development of HPV-associated disease such as cervical cancer and anogenital papillomas, whereas pediatric patients may develop numerous disfiguring warts post-transplant, especially if they require severe immunosuppression.[109, 114, 131] Malignant transformation of cutaneous warts caused by high-risk types has been documented.[131] The JC and BK polyomaviruses also appear to have a significant impact on both adult and pediatric renal transplant recipients.[13, 50, 93, 105–107, 126, 133] JC virus causes a rare syndrome called progressive multifocal leukoencephalopathy (PML), and BK virus has been implicated in a variety of syndromes in renal transplant recipients, including ureteral stenosis, hemorrhagic or chronic cystitis, interstitial nephritis with graft failure, allograft nephropathy, and rejection.* Disease associated with these viruses most often occurs during the middle and late post-transplant periods. BK virus may be asymptomatic or cause rising serum creatinine levels, cystitis, tubular necrosis, or allograft rejection. BK virus may be detected in urine by the presence of "decoy cells," which are cells containing intranuclear viral inclusions, or more recently, PCR assays may be used to detect viral DNA. Patients with BK-associated nephropathy may have BK viral DNA detected in their blood or plasma, and renal biopsy may show characteristic viral inclusions. Most recently, viral surveillance in blood or plasma is being studied in renal transplant recipients as a means of predicting the development of BK nephropathy and guide preemptive antiviral and immunosuppressive strategies. Treatment of established BK virus nephropathy includes a reduction in immunosuppression. Cidofovir has activity against BK virus and has been used anecdotally to treat severe disease.[159] Treatment options for PML caused by JC virus, however, are very limited, and most, if not all, patients die of progressive encephalopathy.

Adenoviruses

Adenoviruses may infect pediatric renal transplant recipients at any time, but they are most likely to cause significant disease during the middle post-transplant period. They do not, however, appear to play as important a role in renal transplant outcome as other viruses do, such as the herpes family of viruses, nor are they as prominent in renal transplant recipients as they are in other transplant recipients, such as recipients of liver, lung, bone marrow, or stem cell transplants.[95, 110, 114, 115] Nonetheless, infections with adenoviruses in pediatric renal transplant recipients, when they occur, can be serious and include hemorrhagic cystitis, diarrhea, allograft nephropathy, pneumonia, hepatitis, and disseminated disease with multisystemic involvement.[14, 131, 132, 152, 158, 164] The diagnosis is made by isolation of the virus in respiratory secretions, stool, urine, blood, or tissue. Viral DNA also may be detected by PCR, and characteristic changes may be seen by histopathology in tissue. Treatment of serious adenoviral disease primarily is supportive. Immunosuppression also may be reduced, when possible. Antiviral agents such as ribavirin, ganciclovir, and cidofovir have activity against adenoviruses, but clinical trials documenting efficacy have not been performed.

Human Erythrovirus

Human erythrovirus (human parvovirus B19) has been reported to cause acute and chronic anemia, red cell aplasia, and pancytopenia in renal transplant recipients.[6, 10, 11, 87, 91, 98, 112, 149, 163] Unusual manifestations such as hepatic necrosis also have been reported.[80] Transmission most likely is person to person; however, some reports indicate that the virus may be transmitted in the renal allograft as well.[10, 11] Recent reports suggest that the role that this virus plays in the outcome of renal transplant recipients may be more important than previously recognized, but systemic studies in pediatric patients have not been performed.[10] The diagnosis of acute infection with erythrovirus is supported by seroconversion, detection of specific IgM antibodies in serum, or detection of viral DNA in plasma, blood, body fluids, bone marrow, or tissue. No specific antiviral therapy is available, but anecdotal experience supports a role for intravenous immunoglobulin in some patients.[98]

*See references 13, 26, 37, 65, 67, 106, 113, 122, 124, 131, 133.

Bacterial and Mycobacterial Diseases

Bacteria that commonly produce disease in renal transplant recipients during the middle post-transplant period include *L. monocytogenes,* which often causes sepsis or meningitis.[114, 124] Routine bacterial illnesses that were not identified and properly treated during the pretransplant period also may emerge at this time and cause abscesses, sepsis syndrome, and death.

Mycobacterial disease caused by *M. tuberculosis* may occur at any time after transplantation but occurs most commonly during the middle post-transplant period.[86, 114] *M. tuberculosis* causes disease in approximately 1 percent of renal transplant recipients in the developed continents, such as North America and Europe, and in as many as 15 percent of renal transplant recipients in developing countries with a high prevalence of tuberculosis, such as India.[114, 123, 134, 135] Tuberculosis may develop in renal transplant recipients as a result of both primary and reactivation infection in almost any site, and even transmission from the renal allograft, as well as reactivation in the native kidney, has occurred.[76, 99] *M. tuberculosis* may cause a variety of diseases, including pulmonary infiltrates, cavitary lesions, adenopathy, cutaneous lesions, bone and joint disease, liver or spleen granulomata, and meningitis. Fever is a common occurrence, and miliary or disseminated disease may occur, especially in young children. Because the purified protein derivative (PPD) test is negative in most renal transplant recipients with active tuberculosis, the diagnosis is determined best by detection of acid-fast bacilli in smears from tissue or sputum and by isolation of *M. tuberculosis* in cultures of gastric aspirates, sputum, tracheal secretions, spinal fluid, or tissue.[86, 114] The presence of granulomata in tissue also strongly suggests the diagnosis of tuberculosis. Treatment of tuberculosis in a renal transplant recipient usually includes isoniazid, rifampin, and pyrazinamide for 1 year, although shorter courses may be acceptable in some patients.[83, 114] Other antituberculous drugs may be added to or substituted for this standard regimen, depending on the disease process, the susceptibility pattern of the organism, and potential drug interactions. Because many antituberculosis drugs are excreted by the kidney, doses may need to be adjusted in a renal transplant recipient. Furthermore, because rifampin may interact with cyclosporine, cyclosporine levels should be monitored closely to avoid allograft rejection.[108] If a history of tuberculosis exposure is elicited during the pretransplant evaluation, the transplant candidate should be evaluated for tuberculosis, including having a PPD and chest radiograph.[99, 100, 123] All close contacts should be investigated for evidence of tuberculosis as well. Treatment is recommended if disease is discovered, and prophylaxis with isoniazid is indicated for most patients who have a recently positive PPD on pretransplant evaluation.[83, 114, 115, 135, 166] A transplant recipient who receives an allograft from a donor with a history of tuberculosis or a positive PPD also may be a candidate for prophylaxis with isoniazid post-transplant.[83, 114, 115]

Atypical mycobacteria are ubiquitous nontuberculous mycobacteria that can infect and produce disease in renal transplant recipients. They can cause disease during the middle post-transplant period and are therefore included here. However, most often their effects become evident many years after transplantation, during the late post-transplant period.[29, 100, 114–116] Atypical mycobacteria that have been documented to cause disease in solid organ transplant recipients include *M. kansasii, M. avium–intracellulare, M. fortuitum, M. xenopi, M. haemophilum, M. marinum, M. chelonae, M. abscessus, M. gastri, M. scrofulaceum,* and *M. thermoresistibile.*[114, 115] A high index of suspicion is necessary to detect these elusive pathogens. They should be considered as the cause of disease in patients with persistent cutaneous ulcers, abscesses, adenopathy, pulmonary nodules, wound infections, or bone and joint disease after negative routine bacterial cultures and failure to respond to standard antimicrobial therapy.[131] Disseminated, multisystem disease also can occur. Environmental sources of atypical mycobacteria include contaminated dialysis equipment, soil, and contaminated water in aquariums and pools. The diagnosis is established by isolation of a nontuberculous mycobacterium in fluid or tissue. Granulomata are not observed consistently in tissue, and acid-fast stains may be negative.[131] Treating atypical nontuberculous mycobacteria is difficult, and treatment must be individualized to each patient. Strategies include reduction of immunosuppression and surgical débridement of localized disease. Antimicrobial therapy based on in vitro susceptibility testing of the isolate also should be administered, often for a prolonged period.

Nocardia

Nocardia asteroides is the most common species causing illness in renal transplant recipients; however, other, more unusual *Nocardia* spp., including *N. transvalensis, N. brasiliensis, N. nova, N. otitidis–caviarum,* and *N. farcinica,* also have been shown to cause disease in solid organ transplant recipients.[114, 115, 162] The most common manifestations of nocardial disease in transplant recipients are fever, cough, and pulmonary infiltrates.[162] Pleural effusion, pulmonary nodules, and cavitary lesions also may occur. Cutaneous infection, adenitis, arthritis, meningitis with brain abscesses, and infection of the renal allograft may occur as well. *Nocardia* can be seen on Gram and modified acid-fast stains of sputum, bronchoalveolar lavage fluid, abscess fluid, and tissue. It can be isolated on routine media but may take longer than conventional bacteria to grow. Prolonged treatment with sulfonamides, alone or in combination with trimethoprim, is recommended. Amikacin and other antimicrobials may be added in selected patients with severe disease, provided that renal function is monitored closely.[131] Trimethoprim-sulfamethoxazole prophylaxis for UTI and *P. carinii* also may be effective in preventing disease caused by *Nocardia.*

Fungal Diseases

Fungal infections occur infrequently in renal transplant recipients relative to other solid organ transplant recipients.[114, 115, 131] This lower rate of infection probably is related to technical procedures performed at the time of transplantation and the lower level of immunosuppression required to maintain most renal allografts.[131] However, when they do occur, fungal infections often are serious and life-threatening.[59, 62, 68] Fungal disease in a renal transplant recipient usually is manifested in one of two ways: (1) pulmonary or disseminated disease caused by one of the environment mycoses such as *H. capsulatum* or *C. immitis* and (2) opportunistic infection with fungi that rarely cause disease in a normal host, such as *Candida* spp., *P. carinii, Aspergillus* spp., *Cryptococcus neoformans, Nocardia* spp., and others.[59, 142] Travel to endemic areas increases a transplant recipient's risk for development of histoplasmosis and coccidioidomycosis and may be identified during the pretransplant evaluation. Factors that increase a transplant recipient's risk for acquisition of opportunistic fungal disease include underlying conditions such as diabetes mellitus, repeated episodes of rejection, chronic administration of steroids, prolonged antibiotic use, and CMV infection. Similar to tuberculosis, invasive fungal disease can be a result of primary infection or reactivation infection with secondary dissemination.[131]

P. carinii, currently classified as a fungus, may cause pneumonia in as many as 10 percent of solid organ transplant recipients, most often during the first 6 months post-transplant.[5, 114, 115] It appears to occur more commonly in children than adults and usually causes fever, dyspnea, tachypnea, hypoxemia, and a nonproductive cough.[27, 114] Interstitial pulmonary infiltrates are typical findings, but almost any radiographic picture can be observed, and pneumothorax is a common occurrence in severe disease. The diagnosis can be suspected clinically but is documented best by demonstration of organisms in lung biopsy specimens; bronchoalveolar lavage may provide the diagnosis in some patients. Treatment with high-dose oral or intravenous trimethoprim-sulfamethoxazole for 14 to 21 days is used most often. Intravenous pentamidine may be administered to selected patients, but renal function should be monitored carefully.[131] Corticosteroids may be helpful in treating severe disease if given early in the course. Low-dose oral trimethoprim-sulfamethoxazole provides effective prophylaxis against *P. carinii* pneumonia, as well as UTIs, and usually is administered to renal transplant recipients for at least 6 months post-transplant.[48] Transplant recipients experiencing repeated episodes of rejection, allograft dysfunction, or CMV disease may require a longer period of prophylaxis.[114, 115] Aerosolized pentamidine is an alternative prophylaxis strategy for some patients.[131]

Candida spp., especially *C. albicans,* are the opportunistic fungi most frequently isolated in renal transplant recipients.[114, 115] Other *Candida* spp. isolated include *C. krusei, C. glabrata,* and *C. tropicalis.* Most fungal infections caused by *Candida* spp. occur during the first 2 months post-transplant, usually at the site of indwelling intravascular and urinary catheters.[131] Esophagitis, abscesses, and arthritis also can develop, and endocarditis with metastatic foci can occur if the fungemia persists. Other opportunistic fungi such as *Aspergillus* most often cause sinusitis and pulmonary disease, and lesions in the liver, spleen, and brain are common occurrences.[114, 115, 142] Therefore, a thorough search for metastatic foci always should be undertaken when a primary focus of invasive fungal disease is documented. *C. neoformans* most often causes cutaneous lesions or abscesses and pneumonia with pleural effusion, but meningitis, arthritis, and pyelonephritis also can occur.[114, 115, 138] Exposure to soil or bird droppings provides an epidemiologic clue to the diagnosis. In addition, the Zygomycetes, including *Rhizopus* and *Mucor* spp., can cause disease in solid organ transplant recipients.[142, 143] They most often cause rhinocerebral and pulmonary disease in patients with underlying diabetes mellitus or in those receiving chronic steroid therapy. Cutaneous and soft tissue infections, wound infections, and gastrointestinal disease with perforation also have been described. A variety of unusual fungi such as *Paecilomyces, Fusarium, Bipolaris,* and others have been shown to cause cutaneous infection, usually at the site of indwelling catheters, and *Hansenula anomala* reportedly has caused UTI in a renal transplant recipient.[52, 114, 115]

The endemic dimorphic fungi include *H. capsulatum, C. immitis, B. dermatitidis*, and *Paracoccidioides brasiliensis*. Infection with these organisms can occur anytime after transplantation but usually during the intermediate post-transplant period.[131] These organisms usually are noted in renal transplant recipients who reside in endemic areas. Histoplasmosis is endemic in the central part of the United States and many foreign countries, and nosocomial outbreaks have occurred during hospital construction projects. Fever, chills, and cough are the usual initial signs. Skin lesions, hepatosplenomegaly, and meningitis also can occur. Pancytopenia often is present as well, and the organism frequently is found in the bone marrow of patients with disseminated disease. Coccidioidomycosis is endemic in the southwestern portion of the United States and northern Mexico. It most often is manifested as fever, cough, and pulmonary infiltrates, but extrapulmonary dissemination is common. Blastomycosis is endemic in the southern United States, along the Mississippi and Ohio River valleys, and in the Great Lakes area. It is very uncommon after renal transplantation but most often causes lung and skin lesions. Paracoccidioidomycosis rarely has been reported in renal transplant recipients.[150]

The diagnosis of invasive fungal disease is established best by isolation of the fungus from bone marrow, tissue, or fluid. *C. neoformans* also may be isolated from urine. Fungal serology and tests for cryptococcal antigen may support the diagnosis.[131]

Fungal identification and susceptibility testing now can be performed in reference laboratories and should be used to guide therapy whenever possible. Amphotericin B usually is used to treat invasive fungal disease in transplant recipients, and the deoxycholate, lipid complex, or liposomal forms can be used, provided that renal function is monitored closely.[84] Flucytosine may have additive or synergistic effects against many yeast and fungi. The azole antifungal agents are not nephrotoxic and, thus, are used in renal transplant recipients whenever possible. Many *Candida* spp. are susceptible to fluconazole, and itraconazole and voriconazole may be effective against other fungi such as *Aspergillus*. Itraconazole, however, should be used with caution because it has variable oral absorption and may interact with cyclosporine.[131] Caspofungin also has activity against a variety of opportunistic fungi, including *Aspergillus*. Surgical resection or drainage of abscesses or effusions may be required to treat some forms of invasive disease of the lungs, liver, or spleen. Reduction in immunosuppression, if possible, also may help the host recover from invasive fungal disease.

Parasitic Infections

The parasites most commonly encountered in renal transplant recipients during the intermediate post-transplant period are *T. gondii, S. stercoralis,* and *Trypanosoma cruzi*.[45, 114, 115] These infections most often occur in adults. Children also may be infected with routine parasites such as *Enterobius vermicularis, Ascaris, Giardia,* and others pretransplant. Other parasitic infections that may be found in renal transplant recipients include leishmaniasis, schistosomiasis, and malaria. Renal transplant recipients appear to be at much lower risk than are other solid organ transplant recipients for acquisition of parasitic diseases. *T. gondii* most often occurs as a result of reactivation of latent disease in the donor allograft or recipient.[89] It is encountered most frequently in heart transplant recipients, but any solid organ recipient, including renal, may be affected. Clinical manifestations of infection with *T. gondii* include focal meningoencephalitis, brain abscesses, pneumonia, myocarditis, pericarditis, hepatitis, and retinochoroiditis.[97, 148, 153, 157] The diagnosis may be made by demonstration of the organism in tissue by histopathology, detection of DNA by PCR in body fluids or tissue, or serologically by detection of high titers of IgG and specific IgM antibody to *T. gondii*. Treatment with pyrimethamine, sulfadiazine, and folinic acid usually is recommended; however, some patients also may respond to clindamycin. Routine prophylaxis with trimethoprim-sulfamethoxazole for UTI and *P. carinii* infection may help prevent disease with *T. gondii*. *S. stercoralis* is an important pathogen in adult transplant recipients, but it is rarely, if ever, a significant problem in pediatric patients. Because *S. stercoralis* can be maintained in the human intestinal tract for decades, it can disseminate and cause serious disease in transplant recipients who were infected before transplantation. A complete blood count for eosinophilia should be obtained, and stool and other specimens should be examined for rhabditiform larvae if the pretransplant evaluation revealed travel to endemic areas. Thiabendazole should be given before transplantation if *S. stercoralis* infection has been documented or is suspected. *T. cruzi*, the cause of Chagas disease, rarely has been transmitted by renal transplantation.[45, 81]

INFECTIONS OCCURRING DURING THE LATE POST-TRANSPLANT PERIOD

Infections occurring 6 months or longer after renal transplantation usually are less severe than are those experienced in the earlier periods, especially if the level of immunosuppressive therapy is low and the allograft is functioning well.[130] However, constant vigilance for unusual infections should continue. Chronic rejection or repeated episodes of acute rejection complicated by allograft dysfunction predisposes the patient to more serious opportunistic infections, similar to infections encountered during the first 6 months post-transplant. UTIs that develop during this period, in contrast to UTIs in the early post-transplant period, usually are benign and may be treated with conventional antimicrobial therapy in most instances. Patients also may experience community-acquired infections with respiratory viruses such as influenza virus and RSV, as well as with bacteria such as *Streptococcus pneumoniae*. The only opportunistic infection encountered to any degree during this period is zoster or, rarely, CMV retinitis. The risk for developing PTLPD also persists during this late post-transplant period.

Renal transplant recipients may be chronically infected with HBV or HCV pretransplant. Increased mortality from fulminant hepatitis with hepatic failure may occur during the early pretransplant period, and chronic liver disease, cirrhosis, and liver failure may be seen 10 years or longer after renal transplantation in hepatitis B surface antigen (HBsAg)-positive recipients.[165] All transplant recipients who are not immune to HBV should receive HBV vaccine before transplantation. Most experts agree that renal allografts from HBsAg-positive donors should not be used, but the decision to perform renal transplantation in recipients who are HBsAg-positive is controversial and must be made on an individualized basis. Renal transplant recipients who are infected with HCV pretransplant usually do well during the early post-transplant period, but long-term survival is poorer than in recipients who are not infected with HCV. Not only can chronic liver disease develop, but membranoproliferative glomerulonephritis also has been reported in renal transplant recipients infected with HCV.[20] However, despite these risks, most experts do not consider infection with HCV a contraindication for renal transplantation in patients with end-stage renal disease.[119] Hepatitis G virus also has been detected in the serum of renal transplant recipients, and at least one association with membranous glomerulonephritis has been reported.[8, 9]

HIV may be transmitted by kidney transplantation despite routine screening of donors of blood and organs.[79, 127] The transplant recipient also may become infected with HIV after transplantation.[114, 115] Shortly after transplantation, HIV infection may cause fever and a mononucleosis-like syndrome. Complications of acquired immunodeficiency syndrome may develop during the late transplant period. HIV-infected patients with end-stage renal disease generally are excluded from renal transplantation. However, recent advances in HIV therapy have caused some experts to reconsider this policy on an individual basis.[114, 115]

REFERENCES

1. Acott, P., Lee, S., Bitter-Suermann, H., et al.: Infection concomitant with pediatric renal allograft rejection. Transplantation *62*:689–691, 1996.
2. Ahsan, N., Holman, M., Riley, T., et al.: Peliosis hepatis due to *Bartonella henselae* in transplantation: A hemato-hepato-renal syndrome. Transplantation *65*:1000–1003, 1998.
3. Allen, U., Herbert, D., Pedric, M., et al.: Utility of semiquantitative polymerase chain reaction for Epstein-Barr virus to measure virus load in pediatric organ transplant recipients with and without post-transplant lymphoproliferative disease. Clin. Infect. Dis. *33*:145–150, 2001.
4. Andrews, S. C., Shas, K., Daniel, R., et al.: A serologic investigation of BK virus and JC virus infections in recipients of renal allografts. J. Infect. Dis. *158*:176–181, 1988.
5. Arend, S., Westendrop, R., Kroon, F., et al.: Rejection treatment and cytomegalovirus infection as risk factors for *Pneumocystis carinii* pneumonia in renal transplant recipients. Clin. Infect. Dis. *22*:920–925, 1996.
6. Ashan, N., Holman, M., Gocke, C., et al.: Pure red cell aplasia due to parvovirus B19 infection in solid organ transplantation. Clin. Transplant. *11*:265–270, 1997.
7. Avery, R. K.: Infections and immunizations in organ transplant recipients: A preventive approach. Cleve. Clin. J. Med. *61*:386–392, 1994.
8. Berthoux, P., Dejean, C., Cecillon, S., et al.: High prevalence of hepatitis G (HGV) infection in renal transplantation. Nephrol. Dial. Transplant. *13*:2909–2913, 1998.
9. Berthoux, P., Laurent, B., Cecillon, S., et al.: Membrane proliferative glomerulonephritis and subendothelial deposits (type 1) associated with hepatitis G virus infection. Am. J. Nephrol. *19*:513–518, 1999.
10. Bertoni, E., Rosati, A., Zanazzi, M., et al.: Aplastic anemia due to B19 parvovirus infection in cadaveric renal transplant recipients: An underestimated infectious disease in the immune compromised host. J. Nephrol. *10*:152–156, 1997.
11. Bertoni, E., Rosati, A., Zanazzi, M., et al.: Unusual incidence of aplastic anemia due to B-19 parvovirus infection in renal transplant recipients. Transplant. Proc. *29*:818–819, 1997.
12. Betts, R., Freeman, R., Douglas, R., and Talley, T.: Clinical manifestations of renal allograft derived primary cytomegalovirus infection. Am. J. Dis. Child. *131*:759–763, 1977.
13. Binet, I., Nickeleit, V., Hirsch, H., et al.: Polyomavirus disease under new immunosuppressive drugs: A cause of renal graft dysfunction and graft loss. Transplantation *67*:918–922, 1999.
14. Blohme, L., Nyberg, S., Jeansson, S., and Svalander, C.: Adenovirus infection in a renal transplant patient. Transplant. Proc. *24*:295–296, 1992.
15. Boland, G., deGast, G., Hene, R., et al.: Early detection of active cytomegalovirus (CMV) infection after heart and kidney transplantation by testing for immediate early antigenemia and influence of cellular immunity on the occurrence of CMV infection. J. Clin. Microbiol. *28*:2069–2075, 1990.
16. Boom, R., Sol, C., Schuurman, T., et al.: Human cytomegalovirus DNA in plasma and serum specimens of renal transplant recipients is highly fragmented. J. Clin. Microbiol *40*:4105–4113, 2002.
17. Boom, R., Sol, C., Weel, J., et al.: A highly sensitive assay for the detection and quantitation of human cytomegalovirus DNA in serum and plasma by PCR and electrochemiluminescence. J. Clin. Microbiol. *37*:1489–1497, 2000.
18. Brenig, M., Zitelli, B., Starzl, T., and Ho, M.: Epstein-Barr virus, cytomegalovirus, and other viral infections in children after liver transplantation. J. Infect. Dis. *156*:273–279, 1987.
19. Brennam, D. C., Garlock, K., Singer, G., et al.: Prophylactic oral ganciclovir compared with deferred therapy for control of cytomegalovirus in renal transplant recipients. Transplantation *64*:1843–1846, 1997.
20. Brunkhorst, R., Kliem, V., and Koch, K.: Recurrence of membranoproliferative glomerulonephritis after renal transplantation in a patient with chronic hepatitis C. Nephron *72*:465–467, 1996.
21. Burroughs, M., and Moscona, A.: Immunization of pediatric solid organ transplant candidates and recipients. Clin. Infect. Dis. *30*:857–869, 2000.
22. Cattani, P., Capuano, M., Graffeo, R., et al.: Kaposi's sarcoma associated with previous human herpesvirus 8 infection in kidney transplant recipients. J. Clin. Microbiol. *39*:506–508, 2001.
23. Chavez, B., Gillingham, K., and Mata, A.: Complications by age in primary pediatric renal transplant recipients. Pediatr. Nephrol. *11*:399–403, 1997.
24. Chou, S.: Acquisition of donor strains of cytomegalovirus by renal transplant recipients. N. Engl. J. Med. *314*:1418–1423, 1986.
25. Cline, M., Cummings, O., Goldman, M., et al.: Bacillary angiomatosis in a renal transplant recipient. Transplantation *67*:296–298, 1999.
26. Coleman, D., MacKenzie, E., Gardner, S., et al.: Human polyomavirus (BK) infection and ureteric stenosis in renal allograft recipients. J. Clin. Pathol. *31*:338–347, 1978.
27. Colombo, J., Sammut, P., Langnas, A., and Shaw, B.: The spectrum of *Pneumocystis carinii* infection after liver transplant in children. Transplantation *54*:621–624, 1992.
28. Conti, D., Freed, B., Singh, T., et al.: Preemptive ganciclovir therapy in cytomegalovirus-positive renal transplant recipients. Arch. Surg. *130*:1217–1221, 1995.
29. Costa, J., Meyers, A., Botha, J., et al.: Mycobacterial infections in recipients of kidney allografts. A seventeen-year experience. Acta. Med. Port. *1*:51–57, 1988.
30. Crompton, C., Cheung, C., Conjon, I., et al.: Epstein-Barr virus surveillance after renal transplantation. Transplantation *57*:1182–1189, 1994.
31. Danziger-Isakov, L., and Storch, G.: Prevention and treatment of cytomegalovirus infections in solid organ transplant recipients. Pediatr. Infect. Dis. J. *21*:431–434, 2002.
32. Davis, C., Gretch, D., and Carithers, R.: Hepatitis B and transplantation. Infect. Dis. Clin. North Am. *9*:925–941, 1995.
33. Dhar, J., Al-Khader, A., Al-Sulaiman, M., and Al-Hasami, M.: Non-typhoidal *Salmonella* in renal transplant recipients: A report of twenty cases and review of the literature. Q. J. Med. *78*:235–250, 1991.
34. Dharnidharka, V., and Harmon, W.: Management of pediatric postrenal transplantation infections. Semin. Nephrol. *21*:521–531, 2001.
35. Dharnidharka, V., Ho, P., Stablein, D., et al.: Mycophenolate, tacrolimus, and post-transplant lymphoproliferative disorder: A report of the North American Pediatric Renal Transplant Cooperative Study. Pediatr. Transplant. *6*:396–399, 2002.
36. Dharnidharka, V., Richard, G., Neiberger, R., and Fennell, R.: Cat scratch disease and acute rejection after pediatric renal transplantation. Pediatr. Transplant. *6*:327–331, 2002.
37. Drachenberg, C. B., Beskow, C., Cangno, C., et al.: Human polyomavirus in renal allograft biopsies: Morphological findings and correlation with urine cytology. Hum. Pathol. *30*:970–977, 1999.
38. Dummer, J. S., Armstrong, J., Somers, J., et al.: Transmission of infection with herpes simplex virus by renal transplantation. J. Infect. Dis. *155*:202–206, 1987.
39. Dummer, J. S., Hardy, A., Poorsattar, A., and Ho, M.: Early infections in kidney, heart and liver transplant recipients on cyclosporine. Transplantation *36*:259–267, 1983.
40. Durlik, M., Siennicka, J., Litwinska, B., et al.: Clinical manifestations and diagnosis of cytomegalovirus infection in renal allograft recipients. Transplant. Proc. *33*:1237–1239, 2001.
41. Emery, V. C.: Human herpesviruses 6 and 7 in solid organ transplant recipients. Clin. Infect. Dis. *32*:1357–1360, 2001.
42. Falco, D., Nepomuceno, R., Karm, S., et al.: Identification of Epstein-Barr virus–specific $CD8^+$ T lymphocytes in the circulation of pediatric transplant recipients. Transplantation *74*:501–510, 2002.
43. Fargie, D., Lebbe, C., Marjanovic, Z., et al.: Human herpesvirus-8 and other risk factors for Kaposi's sarcoma in kidney transplant recipients. Transplantation *67*:1236–1242, 1999.
44. Feldhoff, C., Balfour, H., Simmons, R., et al.: Varicella in children with renal transplants. J. Pediatr. *98*:25–31, 1981.
45. Ferraz, A., and Figueiredo, J.: Transmission of Chagas disease through transplanted kidney: Occurrence of the acute form of the disease in two recipients from the same donor. Rev. Inst. Med. Trop. Sao Paulo *35*:461–463, 1993.
46. Flechner, A., Avery, R., Fisher, R., et al.: A randomized prospective controlled trial of oral acyclovir versus oral ganciclovir for cytomegalovirus prophylaxis in high-risk kidney transplant recipients. Transplantation *66*:1682–1688, 1998.
47. Fogazzi, G., Cantu, M., Saglembeni, L.: Decoy cells in the urine due to polyomavirus BK infection easily seen by phase-contrast microscopy. Nephrol. Dial. Transplant. *16*:1496–1498, 2001.
48. Fox, B., Sollinger, H., Belzer, F., et al.: A prospective, randomized, double-blind study of trimethoprim-sulfamethoxazole for prophylaxis of infection in renal transplantation: Clinical efficacy, absorption, trimethoprim-sulfamethoxazole effects on the microflora, and the cost-benefit of prophylaxis. Am. J. Med. *89*:255–274, 1990.
49. Furth, S., and Fivush, B.: Varicella vaccination in pediatric kidney transplant candidates. Pediatr. Transplant. *6*:97–100, 2002.

50. Gardner, S., MacKenzie, E., Smith, C., and Porter, A.: Prospective study of the human polyoma viruses BK and JC and cytomegalovirus in renal transplant recipients. J. Clin. Pathol. *37*:578–586, 1984.
51. Ginevri, F., Losurdo, G., Fontana, I., et al.: Acyclovir plus CMV immunoglobulin prophylaxis and early therapy with ganciclovir are effective and safe in CMV high-risk renal transplant pediatric recipients. Transpl. Int. *11*(Suppl. 1):130–134, 1998.
52. Girardi, M., Glusac, E., and Imaedo, S.: Subcutaneous *Fusarium* foot abscess in a renal transplant patient. Cutis *63*:67–70, 1999.
53. Gomez, E., Melon, S., Aguado, S., et al.: Herpes simplex virus encephalitis in a renal transplant patient: Diagnosis by polymerase chain reaction detection of HSV DNA. Am. J. Kidney Dis. *30*:423–427, 1997.
54. Green, M., and Michaels, M.: Pre-emptive therapy of CMV disease in pediatric transplant recipients. Pediatr. Infect. Dis. *19*:875–877, 2000.
55. Green, M., Michaels, M., Webber, S., et al.: The management of Epstein-Barr virus associated post-transplant lymphoproliferative disorders in pediatric solid-organ transplant recipients. Pediatr. Transplant. *3*:271–281, 1999.
56. Greenberg, M., Friedman, H., Cohen, S., et al.: A comparative study of herpes simplex infections in renal transplant and leukemia patients. J. Infect. Dis. *156*:280–287, 1987.
57. Grundy, J., Super, M., Sweney, P., et al.: Symptomatic cytomegalovirus infection in seropositive kidney recipients: Reinfection with donor virus rather than reactivation of recipient virus. Lancet *2*:132–135, 1988.
58. Gupta, M., Filler, G., Kovesi, T., et al.: Quantitative tissue polymerase chain reaction for Epstein-Barr virus in pediatric solid organ recipients. Am. J. Kidney Dis. *41*:212–219, 2003.
59. Hall, K., Copeland, J., Zuloski, C., et al.: Markers of coccidioidomycosis prior to cardiac or renal transplant and risk of recurrent disease. Transplantation *55*:1422–1425, 1993.
60. Hanto, D., Frizzera, G., Gajl-Peczaiska, K., et al.: Epstein-Barr virus induced B-cell lymphoma after renal transplantation. N. Engl. J. Med. *306*:913–918, 1982.
61. Hardy, A., Wajszczuk, C., Suffredini, F., et al.: *Pneumocystis carinii* pneumonia in renal transplant recipients treated with cyclosporine and steroids. J. Infect. Dis. *149*:143–147, 1984.
62. Harman, W.: Opportunistic infection in children following renal transplantation. J. Pediatr. Nephrol. *5*:118–122, 1991.
63. Herbein, G., Strasswimmer, J., Alteiri, M., et al.: Longitudinal study of human herpesvirus 6 infection in organ transplant recipients. Clin. Infect. Dis. *22*:171–173, 1996.
64. Hibberd, P., Tolkoff-Rubin, N., Conti, D., et al.: Pre-emptive ganciclovir therapy to prevent cytomegalovirus disease in cytomegalovirus antibody–positive renal transplant recipients.: A randomized controlled trial. Ann. Intern. Med. *123*:18–26, 1995.
65. Hirsch, H.: Polyomavirus BK nephropathy: A (re-) emerging complication in renal transplantation. Am. J. Transplant. *2*:25–30, 2002.
66. Ho, M., Jaffe, R., Miller, G., et al.: The frequency of Epstein-Barr virus infection and associated lymphoproliferative syndrome after transplantation and its manifestations in children. Transplantation *45*:719–727, 1988.
67. Howard, D., Smith, S., Butterly, M., et al.: Diagnosis and management of BK polyomavirus interstitial nephritis in renal transplant recipients. Transplantation *68*:1279–1288, 1999.
68. Howard, R., Simmons, R., Najarian, J.: Fungal infections in renal transplant recipients. Ann. Surg. *188*:598–605, 1978.
69. Huang, J., Huang, C., Lai, M., et al.: *Salmonella* infection in renal transplant recipients. Transplant. Proc. *26*:2147–2150, 1994.
70. Humar, A., Gillingham, K., Payne, W., et al.: Association between cytomegalovirus disease and chronic rejection in kidney transplant recipients. Transplantation *68*:1879–1883, 1999.
71. Jamil, B., Nicholls, K., Becker, G., and Walker, R.: Influence of anti-rejection therapy on the timing of cytomegalovirus disease and other infections in renal transplant recipients. Clin. Transplant. *114*:14–18, 2000.
72. Kalman, S., Bakkaloglu, S., Ozkaya, O., et al.: Measles: A rare communicable disease in a child with renal transplantation. Pediatr. Transplant. *6*:432–434, 2002.
73. Karakayali, H., Emiroglu, R., Arslan, G., et al.: Major infectious complications after kidney transplantation. Transplant. Proc. *33*:1816–1827, 2001.
74. Kidd, I., Clark, D., Sabin, C., et al.: Prospective study of human betaherpesviruses following renal transplantation: Association with HHV-7 and CMV co-infection with CMV disease and increased rejection. Transplantation *69*:2400–2404, 2000.
75. Kitai, I., King, S., Gafni, A., et al.: An economic evaluation of varicella vaccine for pediatric liver and kidney transplant recipients. Clin. Infect. Dis. *17*:441–447, 1993.
76. Klemperer, J., Wang, J., Hartman, B., and Stubenbord, W.: *Mycobacterium tuberculosis* infection of a native polycystic kidney following renal transplantation. Transplantation *66*:118–120, 1998.
77. Knirsch, C., Jakob, K., Schoonmaker, D., et al.: An outbreak of *Legionella micdadei* pneumonia in transplant patients: Evaluation, molecular epidemiology and control. Am. J. Med. *108*:290–295, 2000.
78. Krieger, J., Brem, A., and Kaplan, M.: Urinary tract infection in pediatric renal transplantation. Urology *15*:362–369, 1980.
79. Kumar, P., Pearson, J., Martin, D., et al.: Transmission of human immunodeficiency virus by transplantation of a renal allograft with development of the acquired immunodeficiency syndrome. Ann. Intern. Med. *106*:244–245, 1987.
80. Lee, P., Hung, C., Lei, H., et al.: Parvovirus B 19–related acute hepatitis in an immunosuppressed kidney transplant. Nephrol. Dial. Transplant. *15*:1486–1488, 2000.
81. Leiguarda, R., Roncoroni, A., Taratuto, L., et al.: Acute central nervous system infection by *Trypanosoma cruzi* (Chagas disease) in immunosuppressed patients. Neurology *40*:830–831, 1990.
82. Lewis, R., Johnson, P., Golden, D., et al.: The adverse impact of cytomegalovirus infection on clinical outcome in cyclosporine-prednisone treated renal allograft recipients. Transplantation *45*:353–359, 1988.
83. Lichenstein, I., and MacGregor, R.: Mycobacterial infections in renal transplant recipients: Report of five cases and review of the literature. Rev. Infect. Dis. *5*:216–226, 1983.
84. Linden, P., Williams, P., and Chann, K.: Efficacy and safety of amphotericin B lipid complex (ABLC) in solid-organ transplant recipients with invasive fungal infections. Clin. Transplant. *14*:329–339, 2000.
85. Lowance, D., Neumayer, H.-H., Legendre, C., et al.: Valacyclovir for the prevention of cytomegalovirus disease after renal transplantation. N. Engl. J. Med. *340*:1462–1470, 1999.
86. Malhorta, K., Dash, S., Dhawan, I., et al.: Tuberculosis and renal transplantation: Observations from an endemic area. Postgrad. Med. J. *62*:359–362, 1986.
87. Marchand, S., Tchernia, G., Hiesse, C., et al.: Human parvovirus B19 infection in organ transplant recipients. Clin. Transplant. *13*:17–24, 1999.
88. Mas, V., Alvarellos, T., Albano, S., et al.: Utility of cytomegalovirus viral load in renal transplant patients in Argentina. Transplantation *67*:1050, 2000.
89. Mason, J., Ordelheide, K., Grames, G., et al.: Toxoplasmosis in two renal transplant recipients from a single donor. Transplantation *44*:588–591, 1987.
90. Marsh, H., Bowler, I., and Watson, C.: Successful treatment of *Rhodococcus equi* pulmonary infection in a renal transplant recipient. Ann. R. Coll. Surg. Engl. *82*:107–108, 2000.
91. Mathias, R.: Chronic anemia as a complication of parvovirus B 19 infection in a pediatric kidney transplant recipient. Pediatr. Nephrol. *11*:355–357, 1997.
92. Mayo, R., and Lipschultz, D.: An interesting case of failed renal transplant complicated by a lymphocoele infected with *Pasteurella multocida* and a review of the literature. Am. J. Nephrol. *16*:361–366, 1996.
93. McCormick, W., Schochet, S., Sailes, H., and Calverley, J.: Progressive multifocal leukoencephalopathy in renal transplant recipients. Arch. Intern. Med. *136*:829–834, 1976.
94. McDiarmid, S., Jordan, S., Geoffrey, S., et al.: Prevention and preemptive therapy of post-transplant lymphoproliferative disease following solid organ transplantation. Transplantation *68*:1604–1611, 1998.
95. Michaels, M., Green, M., Wald, E. R., and Starzl, T.: Adenovirus infection in pediatric orthotopic liver transplant recipients. J. Infect. Dis. *165*:170–174, 1992.
96. Miemois-Foley, J., Paunio, M., and Lyytikainen, O.: Bacteremia among kidney transplant recipients: A case-control study of risk factors and short-term outcome. Scand. J. Infect. Dis. *32*:69–73, 2000.
97. Mocelin, A., Brandina, P., Gordan, J., et al.: Immunosuppression and circulating *Trypanosoma cruzi* in a kidney transplant recipient. Transplantation *23*:163–164, 1977.
98. Moudgil, A., Snidban, H., Nast, C., et al.: Parvovirus B19 infection–related complications in renal transplant recipients: Treatment with intravenous immune globulin. Transplantation *64*:1847–1850, 1997.
99. Mourad, G., Soulillou, J., Chong, G., et al.: Transmission of *Mycobacterium tuberculosis* with renal allografts. Nephron *41*:82–85, 1985.
100. Mrowka, C., Heintz, B., Reul, J., et al.: Cerebral tuberculoma 11 years after renal transplantation. Am. J. Nephrol. *18*:557–559, 1998.
101. Munoz, P.: Management of urinary tract infections and lymphocele in renal transplant recipients. Clin. Infect. Dis. *33*:(Suppl. 1):53–57, 2001.
102. Mylonakis, E., Hohmann, E., and Calderwood, S.: Central nervous system infection with *Listeria monocytogenes.* 33 years experience at a general hospital and review of 776 episodes from the literature. Medicine (Baltimore) *77*:313–336, 1998.
103. Neuhaus, T., Schwobel, M., Schlumpf, R., et al.: Pyelonephritis and vesiculoureteral reflux after renal transplant in young children. J. Virol. *157*:1400–1403, 1997.
104. Nichols, J., Becker, G., Walker, R.: Influence of anti-rejection therapy on the timing of cytomegalovirus disease and other infections in renal transplant recipients. Clin. Transplant. *14*:14–18, 2000.
105. Nickeleit, V., Hirsch, H., Binet, I., et al.: Polyomavirus infection of renal allograft recipients from latent infection to manifestations of disease. J. Am. Soc. Nephrol. *10*:1080–1089, 1999.
106. Nickeleit, V., Hirsch, H., Zeiler, M., et al.: BK-virus nephropathy in renal transplant–tubular necrosis, MHC-class II expression, and rejection in a puzzling game. Nephrol. Dial. Transplant. *15*:324–332, 2000.

107. Nickeleit, V., Klimkait, T., Binet, I., et al.: Testing for polyomavirus type BK DNA in plasma to identify renal-allograft recipients with viral nephropathy. N. Engl. J. Med. *342*:1309–1315, 2000.
108. Offermann, G., Keller, F., and Molzahn, M.: Low cyclosporin A blood levels and acute graft rejection in a renal transplant recipient during rifampin treatment. Am. J. Nephrol. *5*:385–387, 1985.
109. Ogunbiyi, O., Scholefield, J., Raftery, A., et al.: Prevalence of anal human papillomavirus infection and intraepithelial neoplasia in renal allograft recipients. Br. J. Surg. *81*:365–367, 1994.
110. Ohori, N., Michaels, M., Jaffe, R., et al.: Adenovirus pneumonia in lung transplant recipients. Hum. Pathol. *26*:1073–1079, 1995.
111. Osman, H., Peiris, J., Taylor, C., et al.: Cytomegalovirus disease in renal allograft recipients: Is human herpesvirus 7 a co-factor for disease progression? J. Med. Virol. *48*:295–301, 1996.
112. Pamidi, S., Friedman, K., Kampalath, B., et al.: Human parvovirus B 19 infection presenting as persistent anemia in renal transplant recipients. Transplantation *69*:2666–2669, 2000.
113. Pappo, O., Demetris, A., Raikow, R., et al.: Human polyoma virus infection of renal allografts: Histopathologic diagnosis, clinical significance, and literature review. Mod. Pathol. *9*:105–109, 1996.
114. Patel, R.: Infections in recipients of kidney transplants. Infect. Dis. Clin. North Am. *15*:1–49, 2001.
115. Patel, R., and Paya, C.: Infections in solid-organ transplant recipients. Clin. Microbiol. Rev. *10*:86–124, 1997.
116. Patel, R., Roberts, G., Keating, M., and Paya, C.: Infections due to nontuberculous mycobacteria in kidney, heart and liver transplant recipients. Clin. Infect. Dis. *19*:263–273, 1994.
117. Patel, R., Smith, T. F., Espy, M., et al.: Detection of cytomegalovirus DNA in sera of liver transplant recipients. J. Clin. Microbiol. *32*:1431–1434, 1994.
118. Pellegrin, I., Garrigue, I., and Ekouevi, E.: New molecular assays to predict occurrence of CMV disease in renal transplant recipients. J. Infect. Dis. *182*:36–42, 2000.
119. Pereira, B., Natov, S., Bouthot, B., et al.: Effects of hepatitis C infection and renal transplantation on survival in end-stage renal disease. The New England Organ Bank Hepatitis C Study Group. Kidney Int. *53*:1374–1381, 1998.
120. Peterson, P., Balfour, H., Fryd, D., et al.: Fever in renal transplant recipients: Causes, prognostic significance and changing patterns at the University of Minnesota Hospital. Am. J. Med. *71*:345–351, 1981.
121. Pirsch, J.: Cytomegalovirus infection and posttransplant lymphoproliferative disease in renal transplant recipients: Results of the U.S. multicenter FK506 Kidney Transplant Study Group. Transplantation *68*:1203–1205, 1999.
122. Priftakis, P., Bogdanovic, G., Tyden, G., et al.: Polyomaviruria in renal transplant patients is not correlated to the cold ischemia period or to rejection episodes. J. Clin. Microbiol. *38*:406–407, 2000.
123. Quinibi, W., Al-Sibai, M., Taher, S., et al.: Mycobacterial infection after renal transplant: Report of 14 cases and review of the literature. Q. J. Med. *77*:1039–1060, 1991.
124. Randhawa, P., Finkelstein, S., Scantlebury, V., et al.: Human polyomavirus–associated interstitial nephritis in the allograft kidney. Transplantation *67*:103–109, 1999.
125. Regamey, N., Tamm, M., Wernli, M., et al.: Transmission of human herpesvirus 8 infection from renal-transplant donors to recipients. N. Engl. J. Med. *339*:1358–1363, 1998.
126. Reznick, M., Halleux, J., Urbain, E., et al.: Two cases of progressive multifocal leukoencephalopathy after renal transplantation. Acta Neuropathol. Suppl. *7*:189–191, 1981.
127. Ribot, S., and Eslami, H.: HIV infection in kidney transplant recipients. N. Engl. J. Med. *39*:597–599, 1992.
128. Riddler, S., Brenig, M., and McKnight, J.: Increased levels of circulating Epstein-Barr virus (EBV)-infected lymphocytes and decreased EBV nuclear antigen antibody responses are associated with the development of post transplant lymphoproliferative disease in solid-organ transplant recipients. Blood *3*:972–984, 1994.
129. Robinson, L., Hilinski, J., Graham, F., et al.: Predictors of cytomegalovirus disease among pediatric transplant recipients within one year of renal transplantation. Pediatr. Transplant. *6*:111–118, 2002.
130. Rubin, R.: Infectious disease complications of renal transplantation. Kidney Int. *44*:221–236, 1993.
131. Rubin, R.: Infection in the organ transplant recipient. *In* Rubin, R. H., and Young, L. S. (eds.): Clinical Approach to Infection in the Compromised Host. 3rd ed. New York, Plenum Medical, 1994, pp. 629–705.
132. Rubin, R., Wolfson, J., Cosimi, A., and Tolkoff-Rubin, N.: Infection in the renal transplant recipient. Am. J. Med. *70*:405–411, 1981.
133. Saitoh, K., Sugae, N., Koike, N., et al.: Diagnosis of childhood BK virus cystitis by electron microscopy and PCR. J. Clin. Pathol. *46*:773–775, 1993.
134. Sakhuja, V., Jha, V., Varma, P., et al.: The high incidence of tuberculosis among renal transplant recipients in India. Transplantation *61*:211–215, 1996.
135. Sayiner, A., Ece, T., Duman, S., et al.: Tuberculosis in renal transplant recipients. Transplantation *68*:1268–1271, 1999.
136. Schmaldienst, S., and Horl, W.: Bacterial infection after renal transplantation. Nephron *75*:140–153, 1997.
137. Scroggs, M., Wolfe, J., Bollinger, R., and Sanfilippo, F.: Causes of death in renal transplant recipients. Arch. Pathol. Lab. Med. *111*:983–987, 1987.
138. Shaariah, W., Morad, Z., and Suleiman, A.: Cryptococcosis in renal transplant recipients. Transplant. Proc. *24*:1898–1899, 1992.
139. Sheldon, J., Henry, S., Mourad, M., et al.: Human herpes virus 8 infection in kidney transplant patients in Belgium. Nephrol. Dial. Transplant. *15*:1443–1445, 2000.
140. Shen, G., Alfrey, E., Knoppel, C., et al.: Eradication of cytomegalovirus reactivation disease using high-dose acyclovir and targeted intravenous ganciclovir in kidney and kidney/pancreas transplantation. Transplantation *64*:931–933, 1997.
141. Shorter, G., and Weil, R.: *Listeria monocytogenes* infection after renal transplantation. Arch. Intern. Med. *137*:1395–1399, 1977.
142. Singh, N.: Invasive mycoses in organ transplant recipients: Controversies in prophylaxis and management. J. Antimicrob. Agents Chemother. *45*:749–755, 2000.
143. Singh, N., Gayowski, T., Singh, T., et al.: Invasive gastrointestinal zygomycosis in a liver transplant recipient: Case report and review of zygomycosis in solid-organ transplant recipients. Clin. Infect. Dis. *20*:617–620, 1995.
144. Smith, S., Butterly, D., Alexander, B., and Greenberg, A.: Viral infections after renal transplantation. Am. J. Kidney Dis. *37*:659–676, 2001.
145. Snydman, D. R.: Epidemiology of infections after solid-organ transplantation. Clin. Infect. Dis. *33* (Suppl. 1):5–8, 2001.
146. Snydman, D., Werner, B., Heinze-Lacey, B., et al.: Use of cytomegalovirus immune globulin to prevent cytomegalovirus disease in renal-transplant recipients. N. Engl. J. Med. *317*:1049–1054, 1987.
147. Souweine, B., Mathevon, T., Bret, L., et al.: Successful treatment of infection due to *Mycoplasma hominis* with streptogramins in a renal transplant patient: Case report and review. Clin. Infect. Dis. *26*:1233–1234, 1998.
148. Speirs, G., Hakim, M., and Wreghitt, T.: Relative risk of donor-transmitted *Toxoplasma gondii* infection in heart, liver, and kidney transplant recipients. Clin. Transplant. *2*:257–269, 1988.
149. Sturm, I., Watschinger, B., Geissler, K., et al.: Chronic parvovirus B 19 infection–associated pure red cell anemia in a kidney transplant recipient. Nephrol. Dial. Transplant. *11*:1367–1370, 1996.
150. Sugar, A., Restrepo, A., and Stevens, D.: Paracoccidioidomycosis in the immune suppressed host: Report of a case and review of the literature. Am. Rev. Respir. Dis. *129*:340–342, 1984.
151. Szende, B., Toth, A., Perner, F., et al.: Clinicopathologic aspects of 8 Kaposi's sarcomas among 1009 renal transplant patients: Gen. Diagn. Pathol. *143*:209–213, 1997.
152. Their, M., Holmberg, C., Lautenschlager, I., et al.: Infections in pediatric kidney and liver patients after perioperative hospitalization. Transplantation *69*:1617–1623, 2000.
153. Tolkoff-Rubin, N., and Rubin, R.: Opportunistic fungal and bacterial infections in the renal transplant recipient. J. Am. Soc. Neprhol. *2*(Suppl. 12):264–269, 1992.
154. Tong, C., Bakran, A., Williams, H., et al.: Association of human herpesvirus 7 with cytomegalovirus disease in renal transplant recipients. Transplantation *70*:213–216, 2000.
155. Tong, C., Cuevas, L., Williams, H., and Bakran, A.: Use of laboratory assays to predict cytomegalovirus disease in renal transplant recipients. J. Clin. Microbiol. *36*:2681–2685, 1998.
156. Travis, L., and Kalia, A.: Renal transplantation in children: Experience of 23 years at the Children's Renal Center of the University of Texas Medical Branch at Galveston. J. Tex. Med. *87*:50–56, 1991.
157. Tsanaclis, A., and deMorais, C.: Cerebral toxoplasmosis after renal transplantation. Case Report. Pathol. Res. Proc. *181*:339–343, 1986.
158. Umekawa, T., and Kurita, T.: Acute glomerulonephritis by adenovirus type 11 with and without type 37 after kidney transplantation. Urol. Int. *56*:114–116, 1996.
159. Waugh, S., Pillay, D., Carrington, D., and Carman, W.: Antiviral prophylaxis and treatment (excluding HIV therapy). J. Clin. Microbiol. *25*:241–266, 2002.
160. Weiland, D., Ferguson, R., Peterson, P., et al.: Aspergillosis in 25 renal transplant patients. Ann. Surg. *198*:622–629, 1983.
161. West, M., Pirenne, J., Chavers, B., et al.: *Clostridium difficile* colitis after kidney and kidney-pancreas transplantation. Clin. Transplant. *13*:318–323, 1999.
162. Wilson, J., Turner, H., Kirchner, K., and Chapman, S.: Nocardial infections in renal transplant recipients. Medicine (Baltimore) *68*:38–57, 1989.
163. Wong, T., Chan, P., Leung, C., et al.: Parvovirus B19 infection causing red cell aplasia in renal transplantation on tacrolimus. Am. J. Kidney Dis. *34*:1132–1136, 1999.
164. Yagisawa, T., Takahashi, K., Yamaguchi, Y., et al.: Adenovirus induced nephropathy in kidney transplant recipients. Transplant. Proc. *21*: 2097–2099, 1989.

165. Yagisawa, T., Toma, H., Tanabe, K., et al.: Long-term outcome of renal transplantation in hepatitis B surface antigen–positive patients in cyclosporine era. Am. J. Nephrol. *17*:440–444, 1997.
166. Yildiz, A., Sever, M., Turkman, A., et al.: Tuberculosis after renal transplant: Experience of one Turkish center. Nephrol. Dial. Transplant. *13*:1872–1875, 1998.
167. Zamora, I., Simon, J., DaSilva, M., and Piqueras, A.: Attenuated varicella vaccine in children with renal transplants. Pediatr. Nephrol. *8*:190–192, 1994.
168. Zaontz, M., Hatch, D., and Firlit, C.: Urological complications in pediatric renal transplantation: Management and prevention. J. Urol. *140*:1123–1128, 1988.

CHAPTER 80

Infections Related to Prosthetic or Artificial Devices

RAM YOGEV ■ TINA TAN

The development of biomaterials used in the manufacturing of temporary or permanent implantable prosthetic devices has been one of the greatest advances in modern medicine.[73, 74] These devices have become an integral and important part of the current practice of medicine and have improved greatly the lives and health of countless patients. In the United States, the number and types of permanent prosthetic devices implanted to replace diseased or damaged body parts has increased considerably during the last several decades. An estimated 3 million people or more in the United States currently have some type of long-term biomedical implant.[68, 267, 317] Table 80–1 is a listing of the implantable prosthetic devices in use today.

One of the major medical complications associated with the use of implantable prosthetic devices is infection, which may result in serious tissue destruction and dysfunction of the prosthetic device or in local and systemic consequences that may be life-threatening. In most cases, these infections are very difficult to cure with antimicrobial agents alone and usually require removal of the device as a prerequisite for resolution of the infection.

TABLE 80–1 ■ TEMPORARY OR PERMANENT IMPLANTABLE DEVICES CURRENTLY IN USE

Temporary Devices
Intravascular catheters
Urinary catheters
Endotracheal and tracheostomy tubes
Permanent Devices
Central nervous system shunts
Deep brain stimulators
Peritoneal dialysis catheters
Orthopedic prostheses (artificial hip, knee, and other joints; screws, pins, plates, and rods)
Intracardiac and intravascular prostheses (heart valves, vascular grafts)
Ventricular assist devices
Pacemakers and defibrillators
Ocular prostheses (artificial globes, intraocular lenses, ocular explants)
Implantable pump devices (baclofen, insulin)
Cochlear implant devices
Tissue expander devices

Interaction of the Host with a Prosthetic Device

The prosthetic devices currently in use are composed of a variety of biomaterials, including cobalt-chromium-molybdenum alloy, titanium alloy, and complex polymers such as polytetrafluoroethylene, silicone, and polyethylene, that in general are chosen for their inert, unreactive, and nontoxic qualities. The interplay of both implant and host factors determines the risk of acquiring and the severity of infection. The human body has numerous well-developed defense mechanisms to protect it against possible invasion by various microorganisms. These mechanisms include cellular and humoral immune systems, anatomic barriers, and an elaborate network of cells that phagocytize and destroy invading organisms. The presence of a foreign body may compromise one or more of these defenses and elicit a complex acute or chronic inflammatory response (or both) from the host. Many of these devices breech cutaneous and mucosal barriers, thereby creating a direct route by which bacteria and fungi may invade. In addition, implanted devices may alter the local immunity of the host directly or indirectly.[14, 73, 267, 317, 327]

Shortly after implantation, hydrophobic polymeric materials such as polyethylene, Dacron, polydimethylsiloxane, and polyether urethanes become coated with a layer of host proteins such as plasma and interstitial fluid proteins (fibronectin, albumin, laminin, collagen, immunoglobulin G, fibrinogen) that bind to and are absorbed readily into the surface of the implant.[17, 244, 317] This protein layer (especially fibrinogen) has a major influence on the body's response to and the biocompatibility of the implant. The presence of fibrinogen attracts a large number of phagocytic cells (neutrophils, monocytes/macrophages) to the implant; these cells interact with the implant surface and initiate an acute inflammatory response.[73, 317] Some of these host proteins also serve as a receptor for various colonizing microorganisms. Collagen, laminin, and fibrinogen have been reported to play a role in bacterial adherence,[330] whereas fibronectin has been found to be the major receptor for gram-positive cocci, especially *Staphylococcus aureus*.[262, 321]

Chronic inflammatory responses, also known as foreign body reactions, are seen around many types of biomaterial implants and arise from interactions between the protein-coated surfaces of the implant and host tissues and adhering phagocytic cells such as macrophages and foreign body giant cells. These interactions may result in degradation and damage to the implant from the continuous generation of toxic catabolites and release of inflammatory mediators such as hydrolases, activated complement components, tumor necrosis factor (TNF), interleukins, prostaglandins, coagulation factors, and plasminogen activator by the phagocytic cells.[315, 317, 327]

Interaction of Microorganisms with a Prosthetic Device

Once a prosthetic device is implanted, the surface of the device provides a potential area for bacterial adherence and multiplication. This adherence is a complex process that involves electrostatic attachment of the bacteria to the surface of the implant, bacterial mechanisms that function specifically in attachment, and host-derived substances that coat the prosthetic device and serve as receptors for various bacteria. Bacteria arrive at the surface of the implant by many different routes: they may be inoculated at the time of implantation, the patient may have episodes of transient bacteremia, the device may be exposed by local trauma or infection, or the device may be implanted within an area in which the organism is part of the normal flora.[68, 73]

Adherence of bacteria to the surface of an implant is influenced by numerous different factors, including the material used to make the device, the source of the device material (adherence is greater with synthetic material than with biomaterial), the device surface (irregular more than regular, textured more than smooth, hydrophobic more than hydrophilic), and the shape of the device.[68] Cell surface molecules or structures known as adhesins also play a role in adherence by attaching or binding an organism to specific receptors on implant surfaces; different bacteria use different adhesins to attach to and colonize medical implants. For example, *Staphylococcus epidermidis* uses proteinaceous autolysin and capsular polysaccharide intercellular adhesin for initial adherence to the implant surface and for adherence of bacteria to each other. These bacteria also produce a biofilm that increases cell-to-cell association and allows accumulation of bacteria.[278] *Streptococcus pyogenes* uses lipoteichoic acid as its adhesin, whereas *S. aureus* uses both lipoteichoic acid and host-tissue ligands (e.g., fibronectin, fibrinogen, collagen) for adherence. Binding of *S. aureus* to host-tissue ligands is mediated by genetically defined microbial surface proteins known as microbial surface components recognizing adhesive matrix molecules (MSCRAMM).[69] *Escherichia coli* and other bacteria use fimbriae as an adhesin to mediate binding to receptors on the surfaces of target cells.

Bacteria also can protect themselves from host defenses by synthesizing and excreting numerous complex polysaccharides, known as glycocalyces, that function either as part of the bacterial capsule or as the slime layer. This slime layer is known to play a major role in keeping an organism attached to an implant surface by coalescing with the polysaccharides of other bacteria and with host products to produce a thick, adherent, and somewhat impenetrable biofilm.[328] The biofilm functions by trapping nutrients and protecting the organism from phagocytosis, antimicrobial agents, and competing microflora. It also plays a role in inhibiting the response to chemotactic stimuli, increases both *N*-formyl-methionyl-leucyl-phenylalanine (FMLP)-induced superoxide generation and release of specific granules, and impairs natural killer cell function while also altering the composition of T-lymphocyte cell subpopulations.[116, 159, 328] Therefore, the biofilm aids bacteria in evading host cellular and humoral defense mechanisms and thereby allows the organism to effectively colonize and infect an implanted device.

Substantial progress has been made in our understanding of the pathogenesis, prevention, and treatment of foreign-body infections; this increased knowledge has resulted in a dramatic decrease in the morbidity associated with these infections, as well as subsequent improvement in patient quality of life. In the following sections, we discuss specific device-related infections and the suggested treatment and management of these infections.

Tissue Expanders

The use of soft tissue expansion in reconstructive surgery was reported in the literature first in 1957 and since that time has been used widely for the correction of multiple problems in plastic and reconstructive surgery in the adult and pediatric populations.[9, 15] These expanders consist of an alloplastic prosthesis with a filling port that is implanted into a subcutaneous pocket. The expander is filled with saline through the filling port at various intervals to create adequate expansion of the skin. In children, tissue expansion is used most commonly to provide coverage for skin defects from burns, trauma, hemangiomas, and other congenital deformities.[199]

The most common complication of tissue expansion is infection of the subcutaneous expander pocket, usually with skin organisms introduced during insertion of the expander. Cellulitis of the overlying skin and hematogenous or lymphatic seeding of the expander pocket are seen as well, but occur much less commonly.[9, 108, 147, 199] In several pediatric case series, the infection rate ranged from 3.4 to 11 percent.[108, 199] *S. aureus, S. epidermidis,* and group A streptococci are the microorganisms recovered most commonly from these infections.[108, 147, 198, 199] Less commonly, nontypeable *Haemophilus influenzae,*[199] *Pseudomonas aeruginosa,* and *E. coli* also have been isolated from expander pocket infections.[198]

In cases of subcutaneous pocket infection, treatment consists of removal of the tissue expander, débridement and drainage of the subcutaneous pocket, and administration of intravenous antibiotic therapy tailored to the organism isolated. For cellulitis of the overlying skin of an expander pocket, treatment with intravenous antibiotics but without removal of the tissue expander has been shown to be successful.[9]

The most common empiric antimicrobial therapeutic regimen consists of a first-generation cephalosporin or an extended-spectrum penicillinase-resistant penicillin. Therapy is tailored once identification and antibiotic susceptibility of the organism are determined.

Cochlear Implants

During the last several decades, cochlear implantation has emerged as one of the best methods of providing auditory rehabilitation for the profoundly deaf (congenital or acquired). The goal of this surgery in young children is to provide hearing that is adequate to allow for the development of receptive and expressive language. The surgical technique involves the creation of a C-shaped flap in the postauricular and parietal-occipital scalp skin areas, elevation of the flap, implantation of a multichannel prosthesis, and insertion of an electrode array into the cochlea through openings drilled into the temporal bone.[55, 58, 194]

The most common infectious complications associated with these implants are cellulitis of the overlying skin flap, meningitis, otitis media, and delayed cochlear implant infections leading to extrusion of the implant.* Rates of infection range from 0.3 to 0.5 percent for meningitis, 2 to 3 percent for cellulitis of the skin flap and delayed cochlear implant infections, to 36 percent for otitis media. The reported meningitis has occurred either in association with cerebrospinal fluid (CSF) leakage in persons with a malformed cochlea who undergo cochlear implantation or as a consequence of intracranial spread of a developing middle ear infection along the electrode pathway. Children with cochlear implants may have a higher risk of middle ear infections because of several factors, including the naturally high incidence of acute otitis media (AOM) in this population, the presence of a foreign body in the area of the infection, and the potential for spread of the infection into the cochlea along the electrode pathway. In a study of 50 children who received cochlear implants between 1991 and 1995, researchers found that children prone to otitis media before implantation were at higher risk for development of postimplantation AOM but responded well to routine oral antimicrobial therapy. The overall prevalence and the severity of AOM were not found to be increased in children with cochlear implants.[191]

In cases of cellulitis of the skin flap, intravenous antimicrobial therapy commonly consists of a first-generation cephalosporin or an extended-spectrum penicillinase-resistant penicillin that provides coverage for *S. aureus* and group A streptococci. Empiric antimicrobial therapy for meningitis usually consists of vancomycin and a third-generation cephalosporin that is tailored to the organism isolated. For delayed cochlear implant infection, therapy consists of removal of the implant and administration of intravenous antibiotics.

Ocular Prostheses

This group of prosthetic devices includes artificial globes used primarily for cosmetic purposes, orbital implants, ocular explants, intraocular lenses (IOLs), and contact lenses.

ORBITAL IMPLANTS

Orbital implants are made of hydroxyapatite or porous polyethylene and frequently are used in orbital reconstruction after enucleation or evisceration surgery. Infection of these implants is a rare event, with only a handful of cases reported in the literature.[3, 54, 111, 136, 161, 162, 175, 215] Patients most commonly present with anophthalmic socket pain, discomfort, and irritation while wearing an artificial globe, papillary conjunctivitis of the socket with exudate, and sometimes dehiscence of the overlying conjunctiva.[110, 215] Infection may develop months to years after placement of the implant, and severity ranges from cellulitis to the development of an abscess around the implant itself.

Radiographic studies that can aid in the detection of these types of infection include technetium 99m–labeled leukocyte scintigraphy, which is most useful in detecting early low-grade graft infection,[161] and computed tomography (CT) and magnetic resonance imaging (MRI), which are useful later in the course of the infection to detect the presence of abscesses and tissue structural changes. Gram-positive cocci, primarily *S. aureus* and coagulase-negative staphylococci (CoNS), are the organisms associated most commonly with these infections; however, *H. influenzae, Streptococcus pneumoniae,* alpha-hemolytic streptococci, *Capnocytophaga,* and *Pseudomonas* have been cultured as well.[305, 352, 359]

To cure the infection effectively, treatment involves both removal of the implant and institution of topical and parenteral antibiotic therapy directed against the organism isolated. Empiric therapy directed against gram-positive organisms may be started initially until the results of culture and sensitivity testing are available. The most common empiric regimens include a first-generation cephalosporin, a second-generation cephalosporin, or an extended-spectrum penicillinase-resistant penicillin.

INTRAOCULAR LENSES

Insertion of polymethylmethacrylate (PMMA) IOLs at the time of removal of the cataract is the standard surgical therapy for this disorder. Even though the rate of postoperative infection of IOLs is low (ranging from 0.10% to 0.30%), the infection usually is serious and results in endophthalmitis and permanent loss of vision.[162, 175] The major pathogens associated with this infection are *S. aureus* and *S. epidermidis,* which account for 90 percent of all isolates, although gram-negative bacilli are isolated on occasion.[175] IOL-associated endophthalmitis is a serious infection that is difficult to diagnose and treat.[346] In a few cases, use of topical and systemic antibiotics alone has been successful in eradicating the infection, but in most cases, surgical débridement and systemic antibiotics are required for cure. Empiric therapy for these infections consists of an extended-spectrum penicillinase-resistant penicillin, a second-generation cephalosporin, or in some cases, clindamycin or vancomycin.

CONTACT LENSES

Primarily three different types of contact lenses are available. Hard lenses are made of PMMA, a substance that is impermeable to water and gas. This type of lens is designed to be worn only during waking hours because it limits oxygen flow to the cornea to that which is present in tears. Gas-permeable hard lenses are composed of silicone, cellulose acetate butyrate, or PMMA-silicone copolymers; they allow passage of gas but not fluids through the lens. Hydrophilic or soft lenses are made of a cross-linked hydrogel polymer or copolymer and contain between 38 and 85 percent water by weight; these lenses are permeable to both gas and water and allow the user to wear them continuously. However, for all these types of lenses, infection may result in damage to the corneal epithelium.

The two main infections that occur in association with contact lenses are conjunctivitis and keratitis.[46] The causative bacteria seen most commonly with these infections are *S. aureus,* streptococci, *Pseudomonas* spp. (found in improperly stored cleansing solutions), and fungi. Improper cleaning of soft or hydrophilic lens may cause them to become a source of infection when bacteria penetrate the lens matrix. Treatment usually consists of removal of the lens and application of topical antibiotics. To prevent the development of contact lens–associated infections, users should adhere strictly to the manufacturer's suggested guidelines for wearing and cleaning the lens.

*See references 29, 56–58, 70, 136, 137, 145, 150, 151, 191, 228, 242, 277, 344.

A rare and often devastating infection associated with the use of contact lenses is infection with the fresh-water protozoan *Acanthamoeba*.[54, 135, 215, 307] This organism contaminates the lens when sterility of the cleansing solutions is not maintained; it usually is associated with lens users who prepare their own solutions. This organism is very difficult to eradicate because it is not susceptible to standard antiparasitic agents and it produces a chronic keratitis that can be complicated by corneal perforation and loss of the eye. Corneal transplantation may be necessary in many cases to restore vision.[135, 307]

Left Ventricular Assist Devices

The development and use of mechanical circulatory assist devices has grown very rapidly in the last decade, especially with the shortage of available donor hearts. Such devices have improved considerably the hemodynamic status and quality of life of patients with heart failure who are awaiting cardiac transplantation. Figure 80–1 shows a left ventricular assist device (LVAD), a pneumatically driven pump located outside the heart that draws blood from an inflow cannula in the left ventricular apex and ejects the blood through an outlet into the ascending aorta. Within the pump are several sections of Dacron graft material and two trileaflet porcine valves in the inflow and outflow positions to ensure that blood flow is unidirectional. The pump is encased in titanium and implanted via an extended median sternotomy into the left rectus sheath. A percutaneous driveline connects to an exterior power pack for venting or for pneumatic actuation and exits the body, after passing through a subcutaneous tunnel, in the left lower quadrant. The interior surface of the pump is textured to prevent thrombus formation and encourage the deposition of a biologic pseudo-intimal lining. Once the device is implanted, in most cases it cannot be removed without performing concurrent cardiac transplantation.[132, 165, 203, 205, 241]

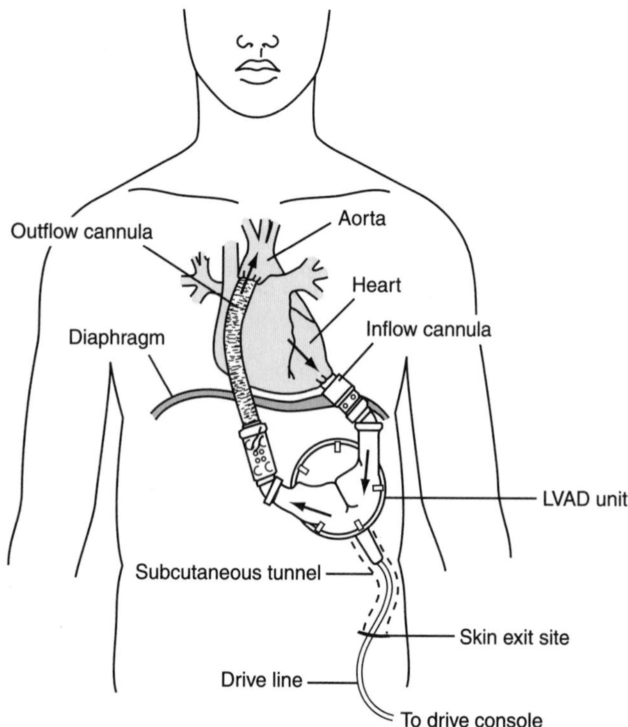

FIGURE 80–1 ■ Left ventricular assist device (LVAD). (Adapted from Fisher, S. A., Trenholme, G. M., Costanzo, M. R., and Piccione, W.: Infectious complications in left ventricular assist device recipients. Clin. Infect. Dis. *24*:18–23, 1997.)

The approach taken by many centers for LVAD infection includes both preventive and interventional steps that are instituted before, during, and after implantation. Preventive strategies are focused on prevention of infections related primarily to the driveline and device pocket through the use of clean implantation techniques and limited traffic in the operating room in which the procedure is being performed. Antibiotic prophylaxis usually is given for 48 hours near the time of LVAD implantation and may include intravenous trimethoprim-sulfamethoxazole, rifampin, and fluconazole with the application of mupirocin ointment to the nares. Additional preventive measures include soaking the surfaces of the LVAD in vancomycin and gentamicin for 30 minutes before placement, irrigating the device pocket with povidone-iodine, and meticulously placing the subcutaneous tunnel in the appropriate position. Postoperative care with sterile and semisterile dressing changes around the driveline is emphasized.[91, 141, 297]

However, despite the preventive measures taken, infection, thromboembolism, and hemorrhage at the time of implantation remain the most common complications associated with the use of mechanical circulatory support devices; of these complications, infection has the most significant impact on morbidity and mortality. Predisposing factors for device-related infection in these patients include contact of blood with the prosthetic surfaces, device-related pockets and cavities, transcutaneous drivelines and power cables, and the duration of mechanical circulatory support. In addition, some evidence indicates that LVAD implantation itself may lead to defects in cellular immunity secondary to an aberrant state of T-cell activation that predisposes LVAD recipients to the development of candidal and other systemic infections.[8] The incidence of infection after LVAD implantation is reported to range between 13 and 80 percent, with most studies documenting an infection rate of 30 to 50 percent.* Most series report that the device pocket and drivelines are the device-related sites that account for most of the infections.

Driveline infections are thought to result from a lack of tissue integration around the driveline that allows the driveline to move and irritate the surrounding tissues, which can result in an exit-site infection and, in some cases, bacteremia. Such infections usually are defined by erythema, drainage, or purulent discharge at the driveline exit site in the presence of a positive culture. Bacteremia developing after implantation of a pump and infections of the pump itself are additional reported complications.[11, 204] In a study of 205 patients who underwent LVAD placement at the Cleveland Clinic, positive blood cultures were noted in 52 percent, driveline-site infections occurred in 22 percent, and pump pocket infections developed in 9.2 percent.[165] Sun and colleagues reported their experience with 95 patients who underwent LVAD insertion.[313] Twenty-six (27%) of these patients experienced device-related infections involving the driveline, device pocket, or blood-contacting surfaces; 15 of the 26 (57.7%) had infections of the driveline site. Persistent bacteremia and progression of infection of the device pocket and driveline can lead to the serious infection of LVAD endocarditis, which mimics prosthetic valve endocarditis, is very difficult to treat, and is associated with a high mortality rate. LVAD endocarditis is defined as positive cultures of the

*See references 11, 91, 100, 141, 204, 206, 250, 291, 313, 348.

LVAD surface in conjunction with clinical signs and symptoms of infection during LVAD support. Manifestations of this condition are varied and range from persistent fever and bacteremia or fungemia to cerebral thromboembolism, LVAD inlet obstruction with hemorrhage, or LVAD outflow graft rupture.[11] In a report by Weyland and associates of 27 patients who underwent LVAD insertion, infections of the driveline developed in 8 (30%) of the 27 recipients, and LVAD endocarditis, defined as positive cultures from the pump chamber, was found in 12 (44%) of the patients; 8 (67%) died of their infection.[348]

Despite a high potential for the development of serious morbidity after LVAD placement, studies have shown that the presence of an infection after LVAD insertion does not seem to have very much influence on eventual cardiac transplantation and post-transplant outcome. During a 5-year period, Argenziano and coworkers compared the effect that infection after LVAD insertion had on mortality, the development of LVAD endocarditis, and eventual heart transplantation.[11] The study found that of 60 patients who underwent LVAD insertion, infection subsequently developed in 29 (48%). The most frequent sites of infection were the blood (27%), LVAD driveline (13%), LVAD surface (13%), and central venous catheter (10%); these sites thus represented 63 percent of all infections.[11] The overall mortality rate, the rate of successful cardiac transplantation, and the rate of infection after transplantation were not influenced by the presence of infection during LVAD support.[11] In another study, Sinha and colleagues reviewed their experience with 86 patients who received LVADs; device-related infections developed in 6, 5 (83%) of which were infections of the pocket. This study also found that the presence of infection during LVAD support did not influence successful cardiac transplantation or patient survival after transplantion.[297]

MICROBIOLOGY OF LEFT VENTRICULAR ASSIST DEVICE INFECTIONS

A variety of organisms have been isolated from LVAD infections. In most series, *S. aureus, S. epidermidis,* and *Enterococcus* spp. are the organisms most commonly isolated from these infections, usually within the first 4 weeks after implantation. Other organisms such as *Enterobacter, P. aeruginosa, Serratia marcescens,* and other gram-negative organisms were isolated more commonly later in the clinical course.[11, 75, 91, 141, 202, 204, 297, 348] Fungal infections (e.g., *Candida albicans*) were reported as well.[75, 141, 202] Investigators suggested that treatment with broad-spectrum antibiotics (common in these patients) rendered them more susceptible to the development of fungal infection.

Management of these infections, especially LVAD endocarditis, presents a major challenge given that the device usually cannot be removed unless simultaneous heart transplantation is performed; moreover, if transplantation is accomplished, multiple issues regarding the immunosuppressed condition of the patient are raised. In most cases, management involves a prolonged course (usually 4 to 6 weeks) of aggressive antimicrobial or antifungal therapy (or both) appropriate for the organism or organisms isolated, with meticulous attention given to skin care around the driveline exit site; débridement, drainage, surgical revision, and irrigation with povidone-iodine of infected wound sites; or, in certain instances, replacement of the LVAD unit or cardiac transplantation before completing antibiotic therapy if a donor heart becomes available and all blood cultures are negative.[91, 141, 204]

Extracorporeal Membrane Oxygenation Circuits

Extracorporeal membrane oxygenation (ECMO) is the method used most commonly for treating severe cardiac and pulmonary failure in neonates and children. Almost 1 percent of all children with open heart surgery will undergo ECMO. In addition to these postcardiotomy patients, a growing number of children receive ECMO for acute decompensation of myocarditis or cardiomyopathy. ECMO also is used to support children after sudden cardiac arrest when conventional closed or open heart massage is unsuccessful. In children, perfusion through the neck venoarterial vessels is the preferred method, but the transsternal approach is used when direct decompression of the distended left ventricle is required. Although the overall survival rate of children managed by ECMO has improved in recent years, it still is only 50 to 70 percent,[18, 342] in contrast to 88 percent in neonates treated for respiratory failure.[7, 260] Multiple cardiac and noncardiac factors are associated with increased morbidity and mortality rates. Patients with a single ventricle or residual cardiac defect after surgery have a less favorable ECMO outcome.[31, 67, 171] Renal dysfunction, multiple organ system failure, initiation of ECMO in the operating room, blood product transfusion, mediastinal bleeding, ECMO circuit problems, and duration of ECMO for longer than 10 days also were predictors of increased mortality.[171, 214] The presence of infection (mostly nosocomial) while being supported by ECMO was associated with increased mortality rates.[176, 214, 263, 364] Of interest, none of the patients who had a positive blood culture in the first 24 hours of ECMO survived.[216]

The same organisms that cause LVAD infections also are associated with ECMO infections.[40, 214] The distribution of these pathogens is similar to their distribution in other patients with infection treated in the intensive care unit, except for an increase in the incidence of *Enterobacter* and *Acinetobacter* infections.[40]

The signs and symptoms of infection often are subtle and nonspecific. Fever develops in only one half of these patients. The value of tachycardia and elevated cardiac output also is limited because these patients frequently are tachycardic with increased cardiac output caused by a systemic inflammatory response (e.g., complement, cytokines such as TNF, interleukin-1 [IL-1], IL-6), which is characteristic of cardiopulmonary bypass procedures.[212] For the same reason, leukocytosis (unless developing acutely) and an elevated erythrocyte sedimentation rate should be interpreted with caution. Consequently, a high index of suspicion with random surveillance of blood and urine cultures and chest radiographs (to rule out pneumonia) is needed to identify these infections.

Most patients undergoing ECMO are treated with multiple broad-spectrum antibiotics. This practice probably is one of the reasons for the increased incidence of multidrug-resistant gram-positive (e.g., *Enterococcus*) and gram-negative bacteria, as well as fungal (e.g., *Candida*) infections. In addition, many of these patients will be colonized with these same bacteria. Therefore, if a deep bronchial suction or urine culture (performed routinely) becomes positive but without supporting evidence of infection (e.g., increased white blood cell [WBC] count, fever), serious effort to distinguish between colonization and infection should be made before initiating an unnecessary change in antimicrobial therapy. If a decision to treat is made, appropriate coverage for both gram-positive and gram-negative organisms should be chosen. If blood, urine, and bronchial cultures remain negative and the patient's condition is not improving or the culture becomes positive for a fungus, antifungal therapy should be added.

Permanent Cardiac Pacemaker and Implantable Cardioverter-Defibrillator Infections

PERMANENT CARDIAC PACEMAKER INFECTIONS

Cardiac pacemakers were developed in the late 1950s, and since that time the field of cardiac pacing has made great strides with regard to the development and design of multiple types of pacemakers and the implantation of millions of devices into both adults and children worldwide. In the United States alone, the number of patients who have permanent pacemakers is estimated at more than 1 million.[83, 337] The two types of permanent pacemaker generators in use include those with transvenous electrodes and those with epicardial electrodes. Both types are implanted in either the chest or the abdominal wall; pacemakers with epicardial electrodes are the ones used most commonly in the pediatric population.[337]

Infection is the most common medical complication of permanent pacemaker implantation, with reported rates ranging from 0.5 percent to as high as 12 percent.[32, 83, 99, 235] However, since the 1980s, the incidence of infection associated with permanent pacemakers has decreased significantly because of improved surgical techniques and better designs of the devices themselves; most series since that time report infection rates no higher than 5.7 percent.[10, 32, 83, 129]

Studies have shown that permanent cardiac pacemaker infections seem to occur more commonly in patients with both local and systemic underlying medical problems, especially diabetes mellitus or an underlying malignancy, or who are undergoing treatment with corticosteroids, anticoagulants, or other types of immunosuppressive therapy.[49, 260] Other well-characterized independent risk factors include surgery related to any part of the pacemaker (especially battery replacement or pacemaker upgrade),[49, 128, 129, 134, 177] the presence of a hematoma after implantation,[42, 49, 131, 170] temporary transvenous pacing,[134, 221] and operative time.[221]

Permanent cardiac pacemaker infections are subdivided into different groups depending on the specific site of involvement and whether they are early infections (<1 to 2 months after implantation) or late infections (>2 months after implantation). The different groups include (1) local inflammation, infection, and the formation of an abscess in the generator pocket or subcutaneous portion of the lead, or in both sites; (2) secondary infection involving either the generator or the electrodes (includes pacemaker endocarditis)[10, 42, 83, 170]; (3) fever plus associated bacteremia, with or without concomitant infective endocarditis, in a patient without any apparent focus of infection[10, 83]; and (4) mediastinitis, pericarditis, bronchopleural cutaneous fistulas, and mixed infections.[83, 235]

The generator pocket and the subcutaneous portions of the leads (transvenous and epicardial) are the most common sites of infection. In a case series of permanent pacemaker infections, Choo and associates reported that generator pocket abscesses were present in 72 percent of the patients and were the only manifestation of infection in almost 40 percent.[49] Pocket infections often are difficult to diagnose and may develop at any time after implantation; however, most tend to develop early. Late infection usually occurs as a consequence of device erosion through the subcutaneous tissue and skin. The infection may remain localized to the pocket or may spread to the adjacent electrodes and lead to the development of bacteremia.[23, 32] Infection of transvenous pacemaker leads may occur in as many as 17 percent of patients who receive permanent pacemakers. These infections often are not apparent initially but have been associated with significant morbidity and mortality. Bluhm reported a 25.3 percent mortality rate in 1734 patients with permanent pacemakers who had retained infected transvenous leads.[32, 120] Infection usually develops along the subcutaneous portion of the leads and, if unrecognized, may progress centrally and result in sustained bacteremia, endocarditis, or both.[32, 120] Infections of the leads tend to occur later than do infections of the pocket, with the median time of occurrence being 7 to 8 months after pacemaker implantation.[32, 33] Endocarditis as a complication of unrecognized infected transvenous leads usually develops an average of 37 months after placement of the pacemaker.[217] Permanent epicardial lead infections generally occur as a complication of infections of the generator pocket, skin erosion, or direct contamination at the time of placement. However, in contrast to infections of the transvenous leads, infections of the epicardial leads usually result in only local symptoms; rarely, they may result in more severe disseminated disease such as pericarditis, mediastinitis, bronchopleural cutaneous fistulas, bacteremia, or sepsis.[23, 235]

Clinical Findings

The diagnosis of pacemaker infection can be difficult to establish because of the nonspecific symptomatology, and months may elapse after the onset of symptoms before diagnosis is made. Symptoms may be confined to a local area or may be more widespread with the development of bacteremia or other systemic effects. Fever (84% to 100%) and chills (75% to 84%) are considered the most common systemic symptoms and are indicators of local infection, especially if they occur after the second postoperative day in association with other signs; however, they may be the only clinical manifestation in more than one third of patients.[42, 170, 213, 217, 222, 349] Early infections are more likely to be accompanied by both local and systemic clinical findings and are manifested more commonly as generator pocket infections, bacteremia, or septicemia[42, 182, 193, 365]; late infections, on the other hand, typically cause vague symptoms that evolve over the course of time and usually are lead-related infections and endocarditis.[49, 166, 170, 333]

Infections of the generator pocket usually cause local swelling, erythema, pain, and drainage (through an incompletely healed incision or fistulous tract) over or adjacent to the generator pocket. Sterile breakdown of the pacemaker pocket develops in an estimated 5 percent of patients with permanent pacemakers, and skin or soft tissue erosion over the electrodes occurs in an additional 2 to 4 percent. Because these complications are associated with a high risk of subsequent development of infections, the presence of any erosion is considered a potential indicator of device-related infection, especially if the erosion occurs later than 24 months after placement of the pacemaker, at which time the infection rate may be as high as 80 percent.[30, 118, 128] Pacemaker-related endocarditis is a relatively rare complication that occurs in 0.05 to 0.5 percent of cases after implantation of a pacemaker. Such endocarditis is associated with a mortality rate of as much as 34 percent in some series.[42, 101, 170] It tends to be a late complication; only 27 to 36 percent of patients are seen within 6 to 12 weeks after the last procedure at the pacemaker implant site, with symptoms developing in most patients a mean of 25 months after the last procedure at the implant site. The diagnosis of pacemaker-related endocarditis is difficult to establish, and usually a delay in making the diagnosis occurs, with a mean interval of 5 to 8 months after the onset of symptoms.[42, 170] Pulmonary symptoms are found in 20 to 45 percent of patients with pacemaker infections and may consist of bronchitis, lung abscess, pneumonia, or pulmonary embolism; these symptoms are seen more commonly in late-onset infection and in patients with intravenous lead–related infection.[42, 170]

A variety of laboratory and imaging studies may be performed to aid in establishing the diagnosis of a pacemaker-related infection. An elevated erythrocyte sedimentation rate is found in 82 to 97 percent of patients, and peripheral leukocytosis is seen in 50 to 66 percent. The presence of a fluid collection around the device as seen on ultrasound is suggestive of device-related infection. Gallium scanning may be performed in an attempt to determine the nature of the fluid (inflammatory versus infectious). Transthoracic echocardiography has emerged as a major tool in diagnosis; studies have shown that this test was able to demonstrate vegetations and other lesions on the electrodes, ventricular endocardium, and tricuspid valve in 90 to 96 percent of patients with pacemaker-related infections.[42, 170, 333]

Microbiology

Staphylococci (*S. aureus* and CoNS) are the most common cause of pacemaker infections, and they account for more than 85 percent of such infections; however, a wide variety of organisms have been isolated.[10, 32, 42, 43, 49, 170, 182, 333] A higher proportion of *S. aureus* is isolated from early infections, whereas CoNS are isolated more commonly from late infections.[32, 65, 182] An increasing number of these organisms are methicillin-resistant. Other gram-positive organisms such as viridans streptococci, streptococci, enterococci, *Listeria,* and *Corynebacteria* have been isolated as well, but each causes less than 1 percent of cases. Gram-negative organisms such as *E. coli, Proteus, Enterobacter cloacae, P. aeruginosa, Klebsiella,* and *S. marcescens* are isolated from 5 to 20 percent of device-related infections. In addition, *Candida, Aspergillus,* and other fungi have been isolated rarely; however, infections with these organisms generally are associated with poor clinical outcomes.[10, 42, 59, 170, 174, 216, 333, 349, 350]

Management and Treatment of Infection

Appropriate therapy for pacemaker-related infections is tailored to the specific clinical situation and depends on several different factors: (1) whether the infection is limited to the generator pocket or subcutaneous electrodes without bacteremia, (2) whether bacteremic pacemaker endocarditis is present with or without involvement of the subcutaneous electrodes, and (3) what organism is involved.

If the infection is limited to the generator pocket or subcutaneous electrodes, optimal treatment consists of both medical and surgical intervention in which all the parts of the infected device are removed. Studies have shown that failure to completely remove all portions of the infected device results not only in failure to cure the infection but also in higher mortality rates.[43, 49, 270, 335] The patient is given parenteral antimicrobial therapy, and an exchange of the pacing system with total removal of the infected device and simultaneous insertion of a new pacemaker at a different site is performed surgically. The infected subcutaneous pocket is drained, débrided, and packed open, and local wound care is instituted. Initial antibiotic therapy should provide coverage for both staphylococci and gram-negative bacteria; therapy is tailored once the organism is identified and antibiotic susceptibility is known. Typical regimens include vancomycin plus an aminoglycoside for a duration of 2 to 4 weeks, or oxacillin or nafcillin plus an aminoglycoside may be used. In certain instances, a new pacemaker cannot be placed at the time of removal of the infected device; in these situations, a period of temporary transvenous pacing is instituted until a new pacemaker can be placed.[182]

The consensus approach to the management of pacemaker endocarditis and bacteremia involves removal of both the generator unit and the electrodes in conjunction with prolonged parenteral antibiotic therapy designed to treat endocarditis (usual duration, 4 to 6 weeks). Mortality rates may be as high as 50 percent for patients in whom total removal of the pacemaker unit is not performed.[10, 42, 43, 170] If the electrodes have been in place for longer than 18 months or large vegetations (>10 mm) are associated with them, extraction of the electrodes by traction may be difficult and risky to perform, so surgical extraction by cardiotomy may be necessary. In patients who require a pacemaker, temporary transvenous pacing may be implemented until a new permanent pacemaker can be placed. Antimicrobial therapy targeted at the causative organism should be administered for a minimum of 2 weeks, and sterility of the blood cultures should be ensured before a new pacemaker generator and electrode are placed. Typical empiric therapy consists of vancomycin plus gentamicin and rifampin; therapy may be tailored once the organism has been identified and its antibiotic susceptibility is known.

INFECTION OF IMPLANTABLE CARDIOVERTER-DEFIBRILLATORS

The first implantable cardioverter-defibrillator (ICD) was placed in 1980, and during the last several decades it has become a successful therapeutic modality for the treatment of patients (both adults and children) with life-threatening ventricular arrhythmias. Older devices required surgical placement of a pulse generator, extrapericardial or epicardial defibrillation patches, and a transvenous rate-sensing electrode. The systems placed today use a rate-sensing lead that is transvenously implanted, a superior vena cava coil electrode, and additional subcutaneous or epicardial electrodes all connected to a pulse generator that is subcutaneously or submuscularly placed and usually is located in a pocket created in the abdominal region.[167, 302, 353]

Infection rates associated with placement of the older devices via thoracotomy or sternotomy ranged from 2 to 11 percent.[303, 322] However, infection rates have decreased substantially with the advent of transvenous non–thoracotomy-placed systems, with rates ranging from 0.8 to 1.5 percent.[112, 239, 298] Most ICD-related infections are clinically apparent within 3 to 6 months after placement, with the generator pocket, subcutaneous patch wound site, epicardial patches, or bacteremia and endocarditis being the most common manifestations. Infection of the generator pocket or subcutaneous patch wound site usually causes local findings of pain, erythema, and fluid collection and drainage from the site. Occasionally, these patients also may be bacteremic or hypotensive. In contrast, infection of the epicardial patches usually results in more systemic symptoms, bacteremia, or pericarditis.[239] The diagnosis of ICD-related infection typically is made on clinical grounds and confirmed by culture of the fluid or drainage around the device.

Microbiology

S. aureus and CoNS are the major pathogens seen with ICD-related infections, and they account for 60 to 80 percent of cases.[178, 239, 282, 303] However, a broad spectrum of other gram-positive, gram-negative, and fungal organisms, including *P. aeruginosa,* corynebacteria, streptococci, *E. coli, Klebsiella, Bacteroides fragilis, Propionibacterium acnes,* atypical mycobacteria, and *Candida* spp., have been isolated from ICD-related infections. Polymicrobial infections may occur in the generator pocket.[178, 239, 282, 298]

Management

To effectively eliminate ICD-related infections, optimal management involves a combination of medical and surgical interventions, especially if the patient is bacteremic or has systemic findings or if the causative organism is *S. aureus*. A regimen of parenteral antibiotics is initiated, and the entire ICD system is removed.[178, 239] The duration of antibiotic therapy varies from 10 days to weeks. In cases in which only the generator pocket is infected, management may consist of the administration of parenteral antibiotics, wound care, and removal of only the generator portion of the device, with implantation of another generator at a different site. For patients whose condition prevents removal of the entire device, treatment of the ICD-related infection includes a prolonged course of parenteral antibiotics, followed by continuous suppressive oral antibiotic therapy.[239, 325]

Prosthetic Joint and Orthopedic Implant Infections

The implantation of prosthetic joints along with the use of other implantable orthopedic devices (e.g., pins, screws, plates, rods, external fixators, Ilizarov apparatus) has improved the quality of life greatly and restored function to patients suffering from debilitating bone and joint disease or injury. Based on conservative estimates, millions of people worldwide have some form of prosthetic joint or other implantable orthopedic device. Of the possible complications associated with implantation, infection is the most serious and occurs in 1 to 5 percent of cases; the resulting consequences include postoperative prosthesis failure, chronic pain, immobility, and, in some cases, loss of the affected limb or, in the worst-case scenario, loss of life.[2, 28, 78, 104, 306] The health care cost in the United States for treating a single prosthetic joint infection is estimated at more than $50,000, with an extrapolated expenditure of more than $100 million per year nationwide.[25, 130, 289, 306]

Prosthetic joints and implantable orthopedic devices may become infected by two major mechanisms: (1) the prosthetic device may be contaminated by microorganisms at the time of implantation either as a result of airborne contamination in the operating room or through direct inoculation at the time of surgery, or (2) the prosthetic device may become infected through hematogenous seeding from bacteremia or by direct contiguous spread from an infection adjacent to the prosthesis. Twenty to 40 percent of prosthetic joint infections arise by hematogenous seeding, with the remainder occurring as a result of airborne or direct inoculation.[1, 37, 185, 186, 196] Infections may remain asymptomatic for years before symptoms become apparent, and usually a long delay occurs between onset of the infection and the appearance of symptoms and confirmation of the diagnosis. The overall rate of prosthetic joint infection has been shown to be highest in the first 6 months postoperatively, with a steady decline after this time. The incidence rate for infection of total-hip and total-knee arthroplasties during the first 2 years postoperatively is reported as 5.9 infections per 1000 joint-years; in contrast, during postoperative years 2 to 10, it is 2.3 infections per 1000 joint-years.[306] The risk of acquiring infection and the incidence of infection depend on the anatomic location of the implanted orthopedic device or prosthetic joint, with hips having the highest risk followed in descending order by the knees, elbows, shoulders, wrists, and ankles.[53, 123, 265, 311] For implantable orthopedic devices, rates of infection range from 2 to 30 percent.[197, 332, 354]

RISK FACTORS

Numerous different factors have been identified as increasing a patient's risk for developing an infection of a prosthetic joint or orthopedic implant. These factors include rheumatoid arthritis, diabetes mellitus, obesity, poor nutritional status, the use of steroids, immunocompromised status, psoriasis, hemophilia, sickle-cell hemoglobinopathy, solid organ transplantation, dialysis-dependent renal failure, joint dislocation, and extremes of age.* In addition, previous surgery at the site of the prosthesis or implant also increases the risk of acquiring an infection. For example, the risk of deep infection in patients undergoing revision of a hip or knee arthroplasty was twofold to eightfold higher in several studies than in patients with primary arthroplasty.[259, 264, 358] The relative risk of development of prosthesis-related infections in patients with poor healing and wound complications increases from 13- to 20-fold after total-knee replacement and from 22- to 52-fold after total-hip replacement.[358]

The implanted metal prosthetic device and the PMMA cement that binds the prosthetic device to adjacent bone also predispose the joint space and the bone to infectious processes, given that both are foreign bodies. In vitro studies have shown that the unpolymerized form of PMMA cement predisposes to infection by inhibiting phagocytic, lymphocytic, and complement functions; the risk of acquiring infection seems to be further enhanced once the cement has polymerized in the body.[252, 253] Cementless prostheses have been designed in an attempt to overcome the problem of infection associated with the PMMA cement. For certain orthopedic implants, the integrity of the skin is compromised chronically, thus providing ready access to organisms from the external environment.

MICROBIOLOGY

More than 65 percent of infections associated with prosthetic joints and implanted orthopedic devices are caused by *S. aureus*, CoNS, beta-hemolytic streptococci, viridans streptococci, and enterococci. Antibiotic resistance in these organisms is increasing, and multiple different strains of staphylococci may be present in a single prosthetic joint infection.[149, 155, 197, 283, 332, 354] Less commonly, aerobic gram-negative bacilli, including *E. coli, Proteus mirabilis, Klebsiella, S. marcescens,* other Enterobacteriaceae, and *P. aeruginosa,* may cause infection. In addition, 4 to 10 percent of infections are caused by anaerobic organisms such as peptostreptococci and *Bacteroides* spp.; polymicrobial infections occur in approximately 12 percent of cases.[149] Infections with fungi, particularly *Candida, Aspergillus,* and *Penicillium* spp., or mycobacteria also have been described.[16, 27, 37, 324] Rarely, a wide spectrum of other organisms, including *Corynebacterium, Propionibacterium,* and *Bacillus* spp., have been reported to cause infection.[37]

*See references 28, 37, 95, 109, 119, 127, 157, 190, 245, 259, 310, 354, 358.

Certain clinic situations may predispose a patient to particular organisms as the cause of infection. Pyogenic skin infections commonly result in staphylococcal and streptococcal infections of prosthetic joints, whereas infections of the teeth and gums are frequent causes of viridans streptococcal and anaerobic infections in prostheses. Genitourinary and gastrointestinal tract procedures or infections frequently are associated with enterococcal and gram-negative bacillary infections of prostheses.[37]

CLINICAL MANIFESTATIONS

The clinical findings and the severity of symptoms seen with prosthetic joint infections are highly variable and determined primarily by three factors: (1) the route of infection—the hematogenous route versus direct inoculation; (2) the virulence of the infecting pathogen—*S. aureus* and, to a lesser extent, beta-hemolytic streptococci and gram-negative bacilli seem to be particularly virulent pathogens capable of producing a fulminant clinical picture, whereas infection with organisms such as CoNS are associated with a more chronic, indolent course; and (3) the nature of the tissue in which the microorganism proliferates—hematomas, seromas, ischemic wounds, and the tissues of diabetic patients and those receiving steroids all enhance the ability of the bacteria to proliferate and spread, thereby promoting the development of a more deep-seated fulminant infection.

The most common initial symptom is joint pain, which occurs in 95 percent of cases. This pain can range from an acute fulminant illness with erythema, severe joint pain, swelling (38%), high fever (43%), and systemic symptoms to, more commonly, a chronic, slowly progressive increasing pain in the joint that may be associated with the formation of a cutaneous draining sinus (32%) but no systemic symptoms.[149] The presence of constant joint pain is more indicative of infection than is the presence of pain occurring only with movement or weight bearing, which is indicative of mechanical loosening and inflammation.[119]

For implantable orthopedic devices, the most common initial symptom of infection is erythema, swelling, pain, or drainage from the area around and adjacent to the implant. Local symptoms also may be associated with fever, especially if the device is extensive or deep seated.

DIAGNOSTIC STUDIES

Laboratory screening tests commonly used to diagnose infection of a prosthetic joint or implanted orthopedic device are the peripheral WBC count, C-reactive protein, and the erythrocyte sedimentation rate. Elevation of one or more of these tests may help support the diagnosis of an infection.[284, 300]

The principal radiologic studies used for detection of an infected prosthetic joint include plain radiographs, arthrograms or sinograms, and radioisotope scans (indium and technetium diphosphate). Abnormalities that may be suggestive of infection and can be seen on plain radiograph include radiolucency at the bone-cement interface, motion and changes in position of the prosthetic components, evidence of osteomyelitis, cement fractures, and periosteal reaction. Intra-articular injection of dye (arthrogram or sinogram—in the presence of a sinus tract) may demonstrate abnormal communications between the joint space and the bone-cement interface. These radiographic abnormalities are present in approximately 50 percent of infected prostheses.[64, 119, 195] Nuclear scans with indium or technetium diphosphate may be used to detect periprosthetic inflammation. Both these scanning techniques are very sensitive but lack specificity. Technetium diphosphate (Tc 99m) shows increased uptake in areas of bone with an enhanced blood supply or increased metabolic activity. Increased uptake normally is seen around uninfected prostheses within the first 6 months after implantation; positive findings after this time are abnormal and reflect inflammation (which could be from a variety of causes) but not specifically infection.[81, 138, 164, 240] Indium 111–labeled leukocyte scanning has been shown to have a specificity of only 50 to 80 percent for knee and hip prosthetic infections.[229, 261] CT and MRI are not used routinely in the evaluation of a patient with a suspected prosthetic implant infection because of the large amount of imaging artifact created by prosthetic devices.[36, 211]

Aspiration of joint fluid for culture and culture of tissue obtained intraoperatively are the optimal ways of making a specific diagnosis of prosthetic joint infection. Joint fluid findings indicative of an infectious process are a high leukocyte count (consisting mainly of polymorphonuclear leukocytes [PMNs]), a high protein content, and a low glucose concentration; however, these changes are not specific for infection and are present in only some patients. The fluid obtained should be cultured for a variety of organisms; Gram stain is positive in 32 percent of cases, and a causative pathogen can be identified in 85 to 98 percent.[82, 237, 301] Intraoperative cultures should include, if possible, any purulent discharge, devitalized bone, and tissue from the bone-cement interface. Histopathologic examination of this tissue usually reveals an infiltration of PMNs consistent with an acute inflammatory reaction but not specific for infection.[121] Gram stain and culture of drainage from an infected orthopedic device should be performed to try to identify a causative organism.

TREATMENT

Successful treatment of a prosthetic joint infection involves extensive surgical débridement of all devitalized bone and tissue, removal of the prosthesis and all associated cement, and prolonged parenteral antibiotic therapy. Microbiologic cure has been found to correlate well with the extent of débridement and the completeness of removal of all residual methylmethacrylate cement.[44] Historically, attempts at simple surgical débridement without removal of the prosthetic device in conjunction with parenteral antibiotic therapy have been successful in only 20 percent of cases, with relapse rates as high as 88 percent by 2 to 4 years after therapy.[93, 286, 351]

Two protocols have been used for the treatment of these infections. A two-stage surgical procedure with prolonged parenteral antibiotic therapy has been shown to be one of the most successful treatment regimens with the best functional results. The first stage involves complete removal of the prosthesis and cement followed by a 6-week regimen of antibiotic therapy empirically chosen to cover the most likely organism and then tailored once identification and antibiotic susceptibility of the organism are available. The second stage involves reimplantation of a new prosthetic device at the end of the antibiotic course. Success rates with this procedure range from 53 to 100 percent.[90, 104, 109, 187, 223] An alternative method of therapy involves a one-stage exchange operation in which the infected prosthetic device and cement are removed, all devitalized tissue and bone are débrided, and a new prosthesis is reimplanted immediately, followed by 6 weeks of parenteral antibiotic therapy. Antibiotic-impregnated (either tobramycin or gentamicin) methylmethacrylate cement is used in these situations, and success rates range from 33 to 80 percent.[39, 45, 84, 127, 208, 266, 326] This procedure is appropriate only for patients whose infections are caused by less virulent microorganisms because of the high failure rates seen when a more virulent organism such as *S. aureus* or a gram-negative bacillus is the cause of the infection.[92]

The Ilizarov method allows simultaneous treatment of infection, bone and joint deformities, bone loss, and shortening of the limb. This device includes proximal and distal circular external rings with wires passing through the bone and soft tissue from one side of the limb to the other. The wires are placed in several planes and orientations to stabilize the bone. The rings are connected with threaded rods and nuts to allow lengthening or shortening of the limb. Although this method is used more often for the treatment of bone nonunion or bone loss with or without infection,[219, 243, 248, 293] David and colleagues used this technique successfully to treat 12 patients who failed total-knee arthroplasty because of infection.[71] Wound infection and chronic osteomyelitis caused by infection of the wire tract occur infrequently and should be treated by débridement of the infected soft tissue and curettage of the infected bone.

Currently, a two-stage prosthetic removal-reimplantation procedure coupled with the incorporation of antibiotic-impregnated cement during reinsertion of the implant, in combination with a 6-week antibiotic regimen, is the mainstay of therapy for infections of prosthetic joints.[105, 223]

For infected implanted orthopedic devices, the success of therapy is based on total removal of the device together with parenteral antibiotic therapy. In cases in which the foreign body cannot be removed, extended parenteral antibiotic therapy should be instituted and continued until the device can be removed. The duration of therapy varies with the severity of the infection and ranges from several weeks to several years.

Central Nervous System Shunts

Infection is a major cause of morbidity in children with CSF shunting procedure. This procedure is performed to divert CSF in symptomatic hydrocephalic patients and is used commonly in patients with anatomic abnormalities (e.g., meningomyelocele and Chiari malformations), in premature newborns with intraventricular hemorrhage or intracranial infections (e.g., congenital cytomegalovirus, congenital toxoplasmosis, bacterial meningitis), and in patients with central nervous system (CNS) tumors or head trauma. Usually, the proximal end of the shunt is placed in the frontal or fourth ventricle and the distal end is inserted into the peritoneal cavity (i.e., ventriculoperitoneal [VP] shunt). Other compartments such as the right atrium (i.e., ventriculoatrial [VA] shunt), the pleural cavity, or the gallbladder can be used to place the distal end. CSF shunts are prone to complications, with a 10-year failure rate of more than 50 percent.[76, 254] The most common complication is mechanical (such as obstruction or overdrainage from siphoning), followed by shunt-related infection. The incidence of shunt-related infection varies considerably, from 0.3 to 40 percent.[50, 61, 85, 168, 285, 331, 360] These infections increase morbidity rates and, in some cases, significantly affect patient outcomes.[207] Recent understanding of some of the factors that contribute to the development of these infections has helped reduce their incidence.[50, 88, 168, 343]

EPIDEMIOLOGY

Almost two thirds of shunt-related infections occur within 1 month after placement of the shunt, and 90 percent of infections are manifested within 6 months.[126, 173, 285] The incidence of shunt-related infections is significantly higher in infants in the first 6 months of life than in older children,[124, 232, 257, 268] and the infection rate is even higher in newborns with intraventricular hemorrhage who undergo shunting in the first week of life.[6] Reasons for the increased incidence of shunt-related infection in very young patients are multifactorial. Several mechanisms that have been suggested include delayed wound healing, higher skin density of bacteria that are more resistant to antibiotics and more adherent to the shunt than in older children, longer duration of hospitalization, surgical technique, and increased exposure to antibiotics just before the shunt is placed.

No significant difference in infection rate is seen in patients with VP or VA shunts,[236, 285, 295] but a lower infection rate was noted in those with lumboperitoneal or cholecystic shunts. An increased risk of development of infection was reported for shunts placed after removal of a previously infected shunt, probably because of incomplete eradication of bacteria.[85, 169, 291] Several other factors, including the underlying cause of the hydrocephalus, the surgeon's experience, the duration of surgery, the number of people in the operating room, and the operative technique (e.g., prophylactic antibiotics, skin preparation, shaveless operation,[143] operative time, open surgery to insert the abdominal catheter versus direct puncture of the abdominal wall with a trocar), have been reported to be associated with an increased incidence of shunt-related infection. Although a trend toward more shunt-related infections has been reported with these factors, it has not been demonstrated consistently.

ETIOLOGY

Staphylococcal species are the most common cause of shunt-related infection, with CoNS (e.g., *S. epidermidis, Staphylococcus capitis, Staphylococcus hominis*) being isolated in 25 to 70 percent of cases[85, 173, 218, 285, 295] (Table 80–2). *S. aureus,* the second most common gram-positive bacterium, is responsible for 10 to 40 percent of cases. Streptococci (e.g., viridans, group B or C, *S. pyogenes, S. pneumoniae,* enterococci) are identified less commonly (3% to 7%). Other gram-positive bacteria such as *Propionibacterium*[320] and *Corynebacterium* (diphtheroids)[12, 117] are isolated as well. The seemingly increased incidence of shunt infection caused by these two groups of bacteria probably is the result of poor culture technique (e.g., failure to use anaerobic culture media, less than 5 to 7 days' incubation period) or misinterpretation of culture results (e.g., culture contamination) leading to underreporting (or both).

Gram-negative bacteria (e.g., *E. coli, Klebsiella, Proteus*) together are the cause of 5 to 25 percent of shunt-related infections.[304] *Pseudomonas* and *Acinetobacter* are reported also, but less commonly. Shunt infections caused by gram-negative bacteria occur more commonly in patients with myelomeningocele and those who had the distal part of their VP shunt inserted into the peritoneal cavity via a percutaneous trocar (i.e., with an inadvertently perforated intestinal tract). Many other etiologic agents, including fungi (e.g., *Candida*,[63, 107, 113] *Histoplasma*,[288] *Cryptococcus*,[148] *Torulopsis*[339]), *Pasteurella multocida*,[180] *Neisseria* spp.,[144, 312] nontuberculous mycobacteria,[47] and others, have been reported less commonly as causing shunt-related infection. With the increase in the number of patients who are immunocompromised for various reasons (e.g., neutropenia, chronic intravenous catheters, prolonged broad-spectrum antibiotic administration, hyperalimentation), the incidence

TABLE 80–2 ■ PATHOGENS CAUSING CEREBROSPINAL FLUID SHUNT INFECTION

Pathogens	Incidence (%)
Gram-Positive Bacteria	
Staphylococcus, coagulase-negative	25–70
e.g., *S. epidermidis*,	
Staphylococcus capitis, Staphylococcus hominis	
Staphylococcus warneri, Staphylococcus lugdunensis	
Staphylococcus haemolyticus	
Staphylococcus aureus	10–40
Streptococci	3–7
e.g., *Streptococcus pyogenes*,	
group B or C streptococci,	
Enterococcus, Streptococcus pneumoniae	
Propionibacterium species	Rare
Corynebacterium species	1–2
Gram-Negative Bacteria	
Escherichia coli	5–25
Klebsiella species	5–10
Proteus species	2–6
Pseudomonas species	2–4
Acinetobacter species	1–3
Other gram-negative bacteria	<1
(e.g., *Neisseria* species, *Haemophilus influenzae, Pasteurella*)	
Fungi	
Candida species	<1%
Histoplasma	
Cryptococcus	
Torulopsis	

of these rare infections will increase. Bacteria that traditionally cause meningitis, such as *H. influenzae,*[269, 309] *S. pneumoniae,*[234] and *Neisseria meningitidis,*[181] were reported as causing shunt-related infection. Whether these cases were isolated shunt infections or an extension of meningitis into the ventricular system (i.e., ventriculitis) is not clear. Therefore, if such bacteria are isolated from a suspected shunt and the patient has a communicating hydrocephalus, lumbar puncture should be performed to rule out meningitis.

PATHOGENESIS

Several observations suggest that most CNS shunt-related infections are caused by inoculation of the organism during surgery or contamination of the device by ward personnel during manipulation.[79, 257, 340] These observations include the facts that common skin flora (e.g., CoNS, *S. aureus*) are the pathogens most frequently encountered, most of the infections occur within the first few weeks after surgery, and irrigation of the system is a risk factor for infection. Another common mechanism (occurring with gram-negative bacterial infections) is retrograde progression of bacteria from the gastrointestinal tract (i.e., bowel perforation)[142, 276] or from the urinary tract (in the case of a ventriculo-ureteral shunt).[103] Other mechanisms by which shunts become infected include (1) hematogenous infection in which a distant site of infection produces bacteremia leading to a shunt infection; this type of infection occurs quite rarely and in most cases represents meningitis with secondary infection of the shunt, such as *S. pneumoniae* or *N. meningitidis* CNS infection in patients with a shunt; and (2) wound or skin infection (e.g., cellulitis, decubitus ulcer) with direct extension from the infection site to the shunt.

The predominant role of CoNS and *S. aureus* in CNS shunt-related infection is the result of their being the major constituents of normal cutaneous flora, especially in young children,[183, 292] and their having the ability to adhere directly to the shunt (e.g., *S. epidermidis*) or to host proteins covering the shunt (e.g., *S. aureus*). In addition, CoNS (and some *S. aureus*) produce large amounts of extracellular slime that completely covers the organism. The clinical relevance of this substance was suggested when excessive production of a "mucoid substance" was found in CoNS isolated from CNS Holter shunts.[21] Other investigators have reported that more than 60 percent of staphylococci isolated from infected shunts produce slime.[72, 87, 122] The slime of *S. epidermidis* is a mixture of teichoic acid and protein.[146] Production of slime also was reported in corynebacterial infection, which may explain the increasing importance of this bacterium in CNS shunt-related infections.[20] The slime facilitates attachment of these organisms to the surface of the shunt and protects the bacteria from the host's immune defenses (i.e., reduces phagocytosis). Once the organisms are attached to the shunt material, they are extremely difficult to remove except by completely replacing the shunt. In addition, antibiotic penetration into the slime is variable and antagonizes the antimicrobial activity of some antibiotics (e.g., vancomycin).[89] The importance of production of slime for the establishment of shunt-related infection caused by CoNS was shown by Younger and colleagues, who found that 88 percent of the CoNS strains isolated from true shunt-related infections produced slime.[361] Moreover, infections caused by nonadherent organisms were significantly more likely to be cured by antibiotics alone (without removal of the colonized shunt) than were infections caused by adherent organisms. Similarly, Diaz-Mitoma and coworkers found that both obstruction of VP shunts and failure to cure the infection with antibiotics alone occurred more frequently when infectious episodes were caused by slime-producing CoNS.[72] Therefore, complete shunt removal should be considered in patients with CoNS or *S. aureus* infection because slime-producing organisms may not be treated effectively when the shunt is in situ.

S. aureus infection is established primarily by the production of adhesin proteins. The most important proteins are fibronectin-binding (finb A and finb B) and fibrinogen-binding (Clf A and Clf B) proteins.[96] The ability to bind to fibronectin is very common in isolated strains of *S. aureus,* and its efficiency depends on the amount of finb A and finb B expressed on the cell surface of the individual isolate. The two fibrinogen-binding proteins attach to different parts of the host ligand, which suggests that they are acting synergistically or allow the bacteria to adhere to the ligand even during unfavorable conditions (e.g., antibodies against one of them).

The immature humoral immune system of young infants is not likely to explain the increased incidence of shunt infection in patients younger than 6 months of age because these infants mount antistaphylococcal antibody responses that are comparable to those of older children.[257] Although levels of immunoglobulins and complement proteins are lower in this young group, levels of these proteins normally are very low in the CSF of older individuals (CSF levels of IgG and IgA are between 0.25% and 0.5% of those in serum). In addition, the types of bacteria causing CNS shunt-related infections are not associated commonly with humoral immunodeficiency states, thus suggesting that humoral protection is less important in CNS shunt-related infections. Little is known about the possible role of reduced tissue immunity in these infections.

The foreign body nature of the shunt apparatus plays an important role in the local host defense defect.[35] Electron-microscopic findings demonstrate irregularities in catheters that allow microorganisms to be buried in the catheter. In addition, the function of neutrophils is suboptimal because phagocytic and bactericidal activities are reduced as a result of the loss of lysosomal contents. Therefore, even when pathogens are phagocytized, they may not be killed and are protected from antibiotics that do not penetrate the cell membrane.

Other mechanisms that may contribute to shunt infection include (1) abnormal CSF flow (not being absorbed by the venous sinuses, thought to be important for prevention of infection in the CNS) and (2) interruption of the blood-brain barrier by the shunt catheter, with the creation of a direct tract between the subcutaneous tissues and the ventricles, resulting in significant compromise in host defenses.[340]

CLINICAL MANIFESTATIONS

The initial signs and symptoms of most patients with shunt-related infection are nonspecific and include mild to moderate fever, malaise, irritability, nausea, vomiting, vague abdominal pain, and headache. With such nonspecific findings, the physician must be careful to differentiate between the possibility of a shunt infection and an intercurrent viral or bacterial infection of the upper respiratory, urinary, or gastrointestinal tract. Examination of the CSF (from a shunt tap) may be of help (see "Diagnosis"). Only a minority of patients have the classic signs and symptoms of CNS inflammation such as stiff neck, bulging fontanelle, change in mental status, cranial nerve palsy, or papilledema. In some patients, the shunt tract may be infected, with evidence of cellulitis or dehiscence (or both) of the surgical wounds. Tenderness, edema, or erythema along the tract itself may be the only sign.

The type of shunt affects the nature of the infection. For example, VP shunt–related infections may cause symptoms and signs confined to the abdominal cavity, such as abdominal pain, tenderness (with or without guarding), intestinal obstruction,[271] or spontaneous bacterial peritonitis.[106] A relatively common complication of VP shunts is an inflammatory peritoneal exudate that may lead to CSF loculation and the subsequent formation of a peritoneal pseudocyst.[86, 273] These pseudocysts often are palpable and can be visualized by ultrasonography or CT. In one third of cases, bacteria are isolated, thus suggesting that infection may play a role in the pathogenesis of pseudocysts. In most cases, however, a high index of suspicion is required because the initial symptoms often are abdominal only, with no signs of shunt malfunction.

A unique complication of patients with ventriculovascular shunts (VA shunt) is the development of immune complex disease such as "shunt nephritis" (a form of acute glomerulonephritis), arthritis, or skin rash. In most of these cases, the infecting organism has been *S. epidermidis*, but other bacteria such as *Corynebacterium* can cause this complication.[34] In the case of shunt nephritis, the patient has fever, edema, malaise, hepatosplenomegaly, hypocomplementemia, anemia, azotemia, hematuria, and proteinuria.[65] Pathologic findings consist of mesangial hypercellularity and granular deposits of immunoglobulins and complement along the glomerular membrane.

DIAGNOSIS

Although shunt-related infections are not common occurrences, the nonspecific signs and symptoms and the insidious onset in many cases render making a diagnosis very difficult. Therefore, any patient with a CNS shunt and fever without an obvious source should be suspected of having a shunt-related infection, especially if the symptoms continue for longer than a week. A higher index of suspicion for shunt-related infection is needed in young patients, in whom fever develops within 3 to 6 months after placement of the shunt. The only definitive diagnostic test is direct observation and culture of the CSF. Tapping the shunt or sampling fluid in direct contact with the shunt should be performed if no signs or symptoms of increased intracranial pressure (ICP) are noted. CT of the head is recommended before the tap is done if such symptoms exist. The shunt tap should be performed with the utmost attention given to sterile technique. The tap should be done by a neurosurgeon or physician who is familiar with the technique and the underlying hardware.

When percutaneous needle aspiration is performed, the area around the shunt reservoir should be scrubbed with antiseptic soap and the surrounding hair shaved (2 inches in each direction). The scalp area should be prepared by repeated application (at least 3 times) of povidone-iodine (Betadine) solution followed by alcohol. A 21- or 23-gauge butterfly needle is placed into the reservoir (or valve if no reservoir is present). Measurement of opening pressure can help in diagnosing a distal malfunction (i.e., increased pressure) or proximal shunt obstruction (i.e., less than expected pressure). CSF sample aliquots then should be allowed to drip into sterile vials. Gentle aspiration of CSF sometimes is performed if no fluid returns spontaneously. If only a few drops of CSF can be obtained, the more important tests, Gram stain and culture, should be performed first. Culturing the shunt wound, blood, or CSF obtained by lumbar puncture (which usually is not communicating with the ventricular fluid) often is unrevealing, misleading, or both. Although bacteremia often is present in patients with VA shunts and may help in diagnosing the etiologic agent, blood cultures generally are negative in patients with all other shunts (e.g., VP or pleural shunts). In addition, CoNS are the most common contaminants of blood cultures, and therefore, interpreting a positive blood culture in these patients would be difficult.

CSF should be tested for glucose concentration, differential cell count, Gram stain, and culture. Protein concentration often is requested, but it is of very limited help in evaluating the presence or absence of an infection because high protein levels are found in many patients with shunt malfunction and no infection. In contrast, normal protein levels have been reported in many patients with shunt-related infections. A low glucose level suggests an infection, but one should confirm that the CSF sample was not diluted before the test was performed. Some physicians use saline to get a better flow of CSF (because of an occluded tube), which may affect the biochemical results. Of importance is to note that in many cases of shunt-related infection, the glucose level is within the normal range. Usually, pleocytosis with a predominance of PMNs is indicative of a shunt-related infection. Although in some cases the finding of a positive CSF culture is interpreted as a shunt-related infection despite a normal WBC count (less than 10 WBCs/mm^3), the absence of clinical symptoms in many of these patients suggests that the positive culture probably represents colonization or contamination. Other cells such as mononuclear cells[173, 304] or eosinophils[323, 334] may predominate during an infection. If eosinophilia is the predominant cellular response, an allergy to the shunt (e.g., silicone[158]) or the materials used for sterilization (e.g., ethylene oxide[255]) or intraventricular administration of antibiotics (e.g., gentamicin,[210] vancomycin[115]) should be considered.

Interpretation of the WBC count should be done cautiously if the red blood cell count is high because the increased number of WBCs can be the result of blood spilling into the CSF without any infection or be part of the inflammatory response to the presence of blood (i.e., chemical ventriculitis). A positive Gram stain with an increased CSF WBC count or reduced glucose level (or both) is helpful in making the diagnosis of shunt infection. A negative Gram stain does not exclude an infection, and one should wait for the culture results. Ventricular fluid always should be cultured anaerobically as well as aerobically. Although most bacteria causing shunt infections grow within 48 to 78 hours, cultures should be held for 7 days (if still negative) for fastidious organisms such as *Propionibacterium*. The possibility of contamination or colonization of the shunt without infection should be considered when the culture is positive but other CSF parameters are normal. If such a scenario occurs and bacteria are growing only from one sample (e.g., a shunt tap) and not from follow-up cultures (i.e., from extraventricular drainage), a shorter course of therapy (see later) may be sufficient.

Blood cultures, a peripheral complete blood count (CBC), and ultrasound of the abdomen (for VP shunts) are of limited value. For example, although 90 percent of patients with VA shunt infection will have a positive blood culture, less than 10 percent of patients with other shunt-related infections will have a positive culture. In addition, in more than one third of patients with shunt-related infection, no elevation in the peripheral WBC count was found. Some investigators suggest that blood or CSF C-reactive protein levels may be helpful in the diagnosis of shunt infection,[340] and in patients with a VA shunt infection, measurement of serum antistaphylococcal antibodies or the C3 and C4 components of the complement cascade may aid in the diagnosis.[22, 280]

TREATMENT

A variety of medical and surgical approaches to treatment of an infected shunt have been suggested. Regimens include (1) the use of antibiotics alone (systemically with or without intraventricular administration) without replacement of the shunt; (2) removal of the infected shunt followed by immediate insertion of a new shunt and the administration of systemic or intraventricular antibiotics, or both; (3) removal of the infected shunt and insertion of an extraventricular device (EVD) to monitor the patient's response to the accompanying antibiotic therapy, with a new shunt inserted only when the ventricular system is sterilized; (4) removal of the infected shunt followed by a stereotactic third ventriculostomy and administration of antibiotics; and (5) externalization of only the distal (e.g., peritoneal) catheter along with administration of systemic or intraventricular antibiotics, or both.

The use of antibiotics alone without surgery was justified by the need to maintain CSF drainage and avoid costly operations and lengthy hospital stay. The low success rate of this approach (33%) and the higher mortality rate associated with it suggest that it should not be used (Table 80–3). Of interest, the failure rate was much higher with infections caused by slime-producing organisms than with infections caused by non–slime-producing bacteria.[72] Only in shunted patients with purulent meningitis caused by *S. pneumoniae*, *N. meningitidis*, or *H. influenzae* did administration of systemic antibiotics alone without removal of the shunt seem to be an acceptable option.[181, 241, 269, 309]

Combining immediate replacement of the infected shunt with a new shunt and antibiotic therapy has a higher rate of success (70%, see Table 80–3) than does the use of antibiotics alone. Nonetheless, it is less effective than is removal

TABLE 80–3 ■ SHUNT INFECTION CURE RATES IN RELATION TO THE THERAPEUTIC APPROACH

Author	Antibiotics Alone*	Antibiotics and Immediate Replacement of the Shunt	Antibiotics and Shunt Removal with an EVD
Schoenbaum[285]	5/30†		25/26
Nelson[226]	10/13		46/46
Salmon[279]		5/10	
Sells[290]	1/8	1/6	9/9
James[154]	3/10		9/10
Venes[329]		6/9	3/3
James[153]	4/11	11/13	16/17
Wald[338]	15/20		
Mates[200]	7/8		
Shurtleff[294]	2/27	6/20	19/19
Morrice[220]	4/14	19/23	14/18
Nicholas[227]			
Frame[98]	8/11	21/27	
Forward[94]	8/15	2/2	13/13
Luthardt[192]	1/17		
O'Brien[231]	11/11	15/19	9/9
Walters[341]	13/92	11/21	44/71
Swayne[316]			19/20
Ronan[274]	3/4	4/7	21/22
Stamos[304]			23/23
Morissette[218]	3/6		3/3
Younger[361]	4/11	42/46	
Total (success rate)	102/308(33%)	143/203(70%)	273/309(88%)

*With and without intraventricular antibiotics.
†Number cured/number treated.
EVD, extraventricular device.

of the infected shunt accompanied by insertion of an EVD and administration of antibiotic therapy (88% success rate, Table 80–3). In addition, lack of the ability to monitor when the ventricular fluid is sterilized results in a longer period of systemic antibiotic therapy (e.g., 4 to 8 weeks), which may lead to an increase in iatrogenic infections and cost. Some surgeons suggest removal of the shunt and delayed replacement (i.e., few days after removal to allow sterilization of the shunt's tract), but this approach is associated with increased morbidity.[94, 341]

For infection that involves only the distal part of the shunt (e.g., pseudocyst, appendicitis,[247] erythema or swelling along the shunt tract, surgical wound infection), externalization of only the distal end of the shunt along with administration of antibiotic therapy is recommended by some neurosurgeons. Potential advantages of this technique include (1) diversion of CSF from an infected area to avoid ascending infection, (2) maintenance of CSF flow to prevent increased ICP, (3) the ability to perform frequent CSF sampling, and (4) the capability of monitoring therapy. The disadvantage is that early infection or colonization of the proximal portion of the shunt may be obscured by the antibiotic treatment and become active after discontinuation of therapy and reinsertion of the distal part.

Internal shunting by a third ventriculostomy (with avoidance of a prosthetic device) was shown to be effective in managing patients with refractory shunt infections who have a noncommunicating hydrocephalus, patent subarachnoid space, and adequate CSF absorption.[94, 160, 218, 226, 295] Shunt independence for extended periods was documented in many patients without myelomeningocele. The success rate is lower in those with myelomeningocele or hemorrhage or after meningitis. Disadvantages of this technique include increased morbidity (e.g., hypothalamic injury, subarachnoid hemorrhage), technical difficulty in younger children, and, if the stereotactic technique is used, cost and availability of the necessary equipment.

The most effective treatment of shunt-related infection is to remove the entire infected shunt and insert an EVD to control ICP and monitor the infection (i.e., provide CSF access). After antibiotic therapy has been successful, a new shunt is replaced. With this approach, treatment success is very high (see Table 80–3), with more rapid clearance of the infection and a shorter duration of therapy. The choice of intravenous antibiotic depends on local patterns of antimicrobial susceptibility and the ability of the antibiotic to penetrate the blood-brain barrier. Because in most places staphylococci are resistant to the semisynthetic penicillins (e.g., nafcillin, oxacillin), vancomycin should be used as initial therapy while awaiting bacteriologic identification and antibiotic sensitivity results. Every effort should be made to discontinue vancomycin as soon as the infecting bacteria are found to be sensitive to the semisynthetic penicillins so that the chance of the bacteria becoming resistant to vancomycin is reduced. In addition, even if in vitro data suggest that the bacteria are highly sensitive to the first-generation cephalosporins (e.g., cephalothin, cefazolin, cephapirin), they should not be used because they penetrate the blood-brain barrier poorly.

To achieve more consistent and efficient eradication of bacteria, the CSF drug level should be at least 10 times higher than the minimal inhibitory concentration (MIC) of the pathogen. Therefore, the dosage of antibiotic or antibiotics and the dosing interval should be maximized (i.e., "meningeal schedule"). If the selected antibiotic does not clear the infection within 2 to 3 days and no improvement occurs in CSF biochemical and WBC parameters (i.e., seemingly no control of the infection), measurement of the ventricular fluid bactericidal titer should be considered. To determine bactericidal titer, 1 mL of CSF (if CSF production is >5 mL/hr) at the expected peak antibiotic level (i.e., 2 to 3 hours after the antibiotic is given parenterally) is diluted serially with culture media to produce dilutions of 1:2, 1:4, 1:8, and 1:16. To these dilutions, an equal amount of medium with 10^5 colonies per milliliter of the offending bacteria is added (the final CSF dilution is 1:4, 1:8, 1:16 and 1:32). After 24 hours of incubation, the tubes are observed for turbidity, which reflects the growth of bacteria. If no turbidity is seen in the 1:8 and 1:16 or higher dilution tubes, the CSF level of the antibiotic probably is sufficient, and continued growth of bacteria from the CSF may be caused by colonization of the EVD or contamination. On the other hand, if turbidity is noted in the tube with less than a 1:8 dilution (i.e., a 1:4 dilution), the CSF level of antibiotic may not be sufficient to combat the infection, and the addition of another antibiotic or change to a different antibiotic is warranted.

In vitro synergy studies can help determine the best drug combination. Rifampin should be considered as one of the drugs in the combination for gram-positive bacteria for three reasons. First, most staphylococci are still sensitive to this antibiotic and their MIC usually is 10-fold lower (i.e., 0.05 μg/mL) than that of other antistaphylococcal drugs (e.g., vancomycin—0.5 μg/mL). Unfortunately, the use of rifampin alone may be followed rapidly by rifampin-resistant variants because they already are present in small numbers in any staphylococcal population. Second, rifampin penetrates CSF well and easily achieves a greater than 10-fold level over the MIC of most staphylococci. Third, rifampin has demonstrated good bactericidal activity even when staphylococci were embedded in slime. In contrast, staphylococcal slime inhibits the antimicrobial activity of vancomycin.[89]

Selection of the initial antibiotic before culture results are known can be based on the patient's clinical and CSF findings. An algorithm for initial antibiotic therapy before CSF culture results are available is presented in Figure 80–2. This algorithm should not be used for neonates or immunocompromised patients with suspected shunt infection because they often have less severe clinical symptoms and CSF response. The decision-making process starts with assessment of the patient's clinical condition. Usually, patients with CNS infection are only mildly symptomatic, whereas patients with *S. aureus* or gram-negative bacterial infection more often are seriously ill.

The next step is evaluation of the Gram stain. If the Gram stain is positive for gram-positive bacteria (e.g., *Staphylococcus*, *Streptococcus*), the drug of choice is vancomycin. If the Gram stain shows gram-negative bacteria, the drug of choice is cefotaxime or ceftriaxone. Treatment with an aminoglycoside is acceptable, but the outcome seems to be less favorable because of poorer penetration into CSF.[304] If the Gram stain is negative, other CSF parameters (e.g., WBC count and glucose) should be examined. If either is abnormal and the patient is not severely sick, vancomycin alone should be started because the chance of a gram-negative infection is very low.[304]

In contrast, if the patient is severely sick, coverage for gram-negative bacteria should be added (i.e., vancomycin and cefotaxime or ceftriaxone). In nontoxic patients with normal CSF parameters and no distal symptoms (e.g., peritonitis, wound or tract infection), antibiotic therapy can be withheld until culture results are known. On the other hand, if distal signs or symptoms exist, therapy is tailored according to the site. In patients with skin involvement, vancomycin is the drug of choice, whereas in febrile patients

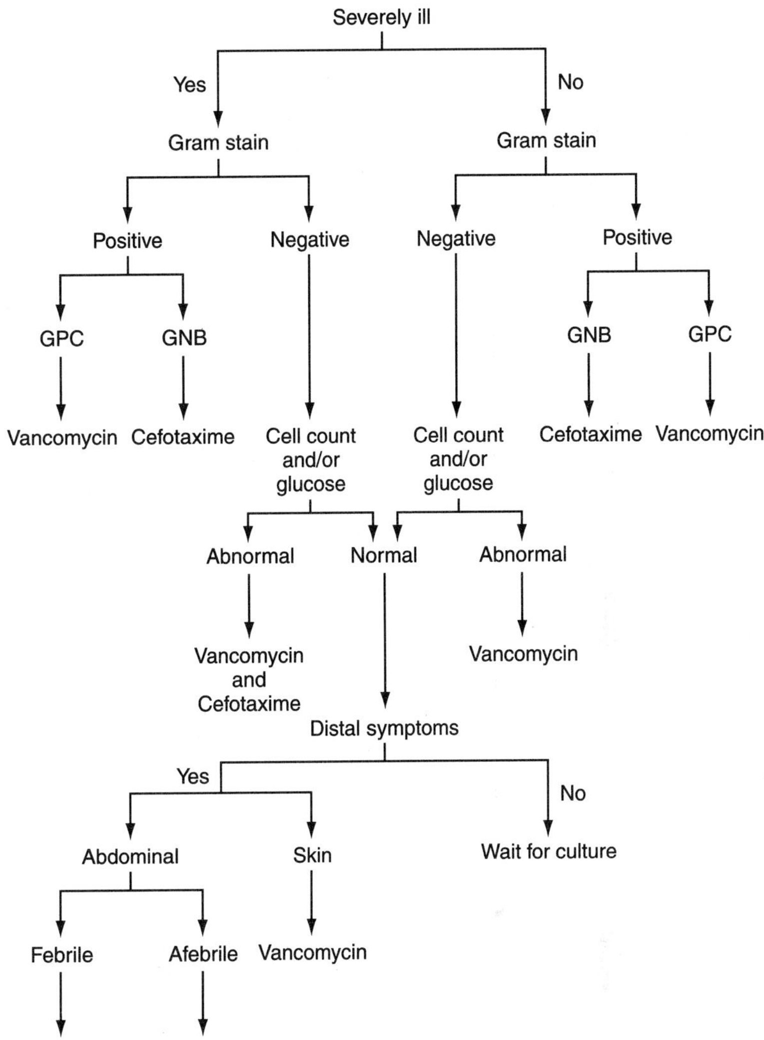

FIGURE 80–2 ■ Algorithm for selection of antibiotic therapy before culture results are known.

with abdominal symptoms, the combination of cefotaxime (or ceftriaxone) and clindamycin (to cover both gram-positive and anaerobic bacteria) is preferred.

Direct instillation of antibiotics into the ventricular system to increase their levels is recommended by some experts. Unfortunately, the suggested doses for intraventricular treatment have been determined empirically on only a small number of patients, and their pharmacokinetics and pharmacodynamics have not been studied well. This therapy is not without hazard, especially when the recommended doses often are much higher than those found to cause neurotoxicity.[19, 272, 345, 347] Pleocytosis and eosinophilia also have occurred in patients receiving intraventricular vancomycin[188] or gentamicin.[210] In addition, preservative-containing preparations should be checked for appropriateness for intraventricular instillation. Limited pharmacokinetic data suggest that clearance of the instilled intraventricular antibiotic is sufficiently slow to allow once-daily administration. If possible, the EVD should be closed for 30 to 60 minutes after the drug is administered. If the EVD cannot be closed and the amount of CSF drainage exceeds 7 to 10 mL/hr, the frequency of intraventricular antibiotic instillation should be increased to twice daily.

Antibiotics commonly recommended for intravenous and intraventricular use according to the etiologic agent are shown in Table 80–4. Because of the potential toxicity of the empirically recommended intraventricular antibiotic doses and the unpredictability of CSF levels, irrigation of the ventricular system with a known concentration of an antibiotic solution is preferred when systemic antibiotics fail to eradicate the bacteria. To achieve irrigation, two EVDs have to be inserted to produce a continuous flow of solution. The concentration of antibiotic in the solution should be equal to the highest safe plasma level when the drug is given intravenously. For example, for treating gram-negative bacteria sensitive to amikacin, amikacin at a dose of 30 to 40 mg/L of saline solution (producing a concentration of 30 to 40 μg/mL) is recommended. Gentamicin at a dose of 10 to 12 mg/L (using a special intrathecal preparation) is an acceptable alternative when the gentamicin MIC for the

TABLE 80–4 ■ RECOMMENDED INTRAVENOUS AND INTRAVENTRICULAR ANTIBIOTIC THERAPY FOR SHUNT INFECTION ACCORDING TO THE ETIOLOGIC AGENT

Etiologic Agent	Antibiotic	Intravenous Dose (mg/kg/day)	Intraventricular Dose (mg/day, 1 Dose)
Bacteria			
Staphylococcus aureus or coagulase-negative			
Methicillin-sensitive	Oxacillin*,†	200 (q8h)	NA
	or		
	Nafcillin*,†	200 (q8h)	50–75
	or		
	Methicillin*,†	200 (8h)	50–100
Methicillin-resistant	Vancomycin†	60 (q8h)	5–10
Streptococcal species	Penicillin*	400,000 u (q6h)	—
or	*or*		
diphtheroids	Ampicillin*	400 (q6h)	10–25
Enterococcus faecalis	Ampicillin*	Doses as above	
	or		
	Penicillin*		NA
	plus		
	Aminoglycoside‡		
Anaerobic bacteria	Metronidazole	30 (q8h)	NA
Escherichia coli, Klebsiella, Proteus, Enterobacter	Cefotaxime	200–300 (q6h)	NA
	or		
	Ceftriaxone	100 (q12h)	NA
	or		
	Amikacin§	22.5 (q8h)	2–8
	or		
	Tobramycin§	7.5 (q8h)	1–4
	or		
	Gentamicin§	7.5 (q8h)	1–4
Pseudomonas spp.	Ceftazidime	200 (q8h)	NA
	or		
	Aminoglycoside		
	plus		
	Broad-spectrum penicillin§		
Fungi			
Candida spp.	Amphotericin B‖	1 (q24h)	0.1–0.25
	AmBisome or Amphotec	5 (q24h)	

*For patients allergic to penicillin, use vancomycin.
†If cerebrospinal fluid levels are not sufficient and the bacteria are sensitive to rifampin, add rifampin, 20 mg/kg/day divided every 12 hours.
‡See doses (for the specific aminoglycoside) for treatment of *E.coli* below.
§The addition of a broad-spectrum penicillin (e.g., piperacillin or ticarcillin, 300 to 400 mg/kg/day divided every 6 hours) may add to the bactericidal activity.
‖If ventricular fluid remains positive after 5 to 7 days of therapy with amphotericin, add flucytosine (150 mg/kg/day divided every 6 hours).
NA, not available.

bacteria is less than 1 μg/mL. The antibiotic solution is administered through one EVD at a rate of 10 mL/hr, and the second EVD is left open to drain the fluid and to remove debris and pus from the ventricles.

When antibiotic therapy is completed, abnormal findings in the CSF such as low glucose or mildly elevated protein or cell counts should not delay reshunting. The duration of treatment is empiric and depends on the etiologic agent, the CSF parameters at initial evaluation, and the time to sterilization. In our institution, we found the following schedule to be successful. If CSF parameters are *normal* but culture yields CoNS only from the operating room (i.e., the initial sample), therapy should be given for only 3 to 4 days. If subsequent cultures also are positive, therapy should continue until negative cultures have been obtained for 7 days. If CSF parameters are *abnormal* in the operating room and culture is positive *only* from that specimen, therapy should continue for 7 days. If subsequent samples show abnormal CSF findings and positive cultures, therapy should be extended until negative cultures have been obtained for 10 days.

A longer duration of antibiotic therapy is recommended with other bacteria (e.g., *S. aureus,* gram-negative bacteria). If culture is positive *only* on samples from the *operating room* and CSF findings are normal, treatment should be given until negative cultures have been obtained for 7 days. In all other situations, therapy should continue until negative cultures have been achieved for 10 days. Reshunting should take place immediately at the end of treatment. No benefit is found in observing the patient for a time without antibiotics for relapse of the infection.[343]

COMPLICATIONS

Shunt infections are associated with increased morbidity and mortality rates. Patients with shunt infection have a threefold increase in shunt-related operations, which contributes to the increased morbidity and cost. In addition, these patients have been shown to have a twofold increase in mortality rate in comparison to patients without shunt infection.[285] Even when the original infection is treated successfully, a secondary infection (or contamination) of the EVD occurred in 5 to 10 percent of cases. To minimize the risk of development of a secondary infection, a sterile closed drainage system should be maintained carefully. Only trained personnel should be allowed to drain CSF samples from the system, and injections into the system should be avoided. Continuous external drainage of CSF also causes loss of electrolytes and fluid. Therefore, routine assessment of serum electrolytes once or twice weekly is recommended, and the total daily amount of drained CSF should be replaced.

PROGNOSIS

Long-term morbidity that occurs after a shunt infection includes seizures, psychomotor retardation, and cognitive deficiency. The intelligence quotient (IQ) scores of children with myelomeningocele who had a shunt-related infection were found to be significantly lower (mean IQ, 72) than the scores in children with shunts but no infection (mean IQ, 95).[207] A trend was observed in which younger children with shunt-related infection had a lower IQ than did older children with shunt infection did, especially if the infection was caused by gram-negative bacteria. With appropriate combined medical and surgical therapy, the mortality rate from shunt infection is low, but any episode of shunt infection appears to increase the probability of another episode developing.

PREVENTION

Preventive measures to reduce the incidence of shunt-related infection include attention to preoperative and intraoperative techniques and the prophylactic use of antibiotics. Bactericidal shampoos (e.g., chlorhexidine) should be used to reduce the bacterial density of the scalp before surgery. Shaving the scalp seems to be a risk factor, so shaveless surgery should be considered.[143] During the operation, only essential personnel should be present, and the skin should be cleaned with a fat solvent, followed by solutions that reduce the number of bacteria (long-acting iodinated compounds) or their ability to adhere to the shunt (bacitracin A).[114] Careful attention should be paid to surgical technique, with contact between the shunt and the skin being avoided. A detailed preoperative protocol developed by Choux and associates has reduced the infection rate from more than 7 percent to less than 1 percent.[50] This protocol emphasized a shorter operating time, less operating room staff and traffic, and fewer manipulations of the shunt. Although Kestle and colleagues were able to reduce the infection rate by using measures similar to those suggested by Choux and coworkers,[168] other studies have failed to show that all the factors emphasized by Choux and associates have a positive effect on the infection rate.[254, 257]

Multiple studies have examined the effect of prophylactic antibiotics for the shunt insertion procedure on reducing the infection rate. Major variations in study design and the number of patients in each study preclude arriving at definitive conclusions. Meta-analyses of well-designed studies suggest that the use of prophylactic antibiotics is associated with a significant reduction in the incidence of infections *if* the baseline rate of shunt infections is greater than 5 to 10 percent.[125, 179] If the infection rate is lower than 5 percent, prophylactic antibiotics are *not* recommended. The choice of antibiotics should be based on the local antibiotic sensitivity pattern of the pathogens commonly causing shunt infections in that area. Preferably, prophylaxis should be started 8 to 12 hours before surgery to allow higher levels of drug to accumulate in skin tissue than would do so if treatment were given just before the operation. The duration of prophylaxis should not exceed 24 to 36 hours. Further studies are needed to identify factors important in the development of shunt-related infections so that better techniques can be developed to further reduce or even eliminate this devastating complication of CNS shunting.

Intracranial Pressure Monitors

ICP monitoring has become an important part of the evaluation, treatment, and management of children with a variety of intracranial pathologic processes,[189] including congenital anomalies (e.g., cranial or craniofacial dysostosis), metabolic diseases (e.g., Reye syndrome), trauma, intraventricular or subarachnoid hemorrhage, intracranial infections (e.g., encephalitis), and other ischemic or hypoxic insults. Several studies have demonstrated the therapeutic and prognostic benefit of ICP monitoring in children with high ICP[97, 156, 184, 319]; nonetheless, this procedure is not without complications such as hematoma, bleeding, leakage of CSF, and infection. ICP monitoring infections include ventriculitis, meningitis, brain abscess, subdural empyema, skin infection, and cranial bone infections.[201, 224, 275, 356]

Several methods are available for monitoring ICP. The intraventricular placement of a catheter with the distal end connected to a pressure transducer is the method used most commonly because of its accuracy and ease of calibration. This procedure also allows drainage of CSF for biochemical or dynamic testing. Disadvantages of ventriculostomy are penetration of the meninges and brain, technical difficulties if the ventricles are small, and a greater risk of developing infection. Other methods used to monitor ICP include a subdural bolt or catheter (only the meninges are penetrated but the brain remains intact), an epidural transducer (the dura remains intact), and a continuous intraparenchymal monitor (i.e., a fiberoptic cable is inserted through the dura into the brain parenchyma, not intraventricularly). Although both the epidural transducer and the intraparenchymal monitor have fewer complications (e.g., infection) than the intraventricular devices do, they are prone to inaccuracies, which limits their use. The choice of the appropriate ICP monitoring method depends on the patient's condition and the risk of the procedure.

EPIDEMIOLOGY

Assessing the true infection rate of ICP monitoring devices is very difficult, mainly because the methods used to define infection (i.e., the inclusion and exclusion criteria) and the use of antibiotics vary widely among reported studies. The incidence of infection ranged from less than 1 percent to 40 percent, but most of the studies reported an incidence of 15 ± 5 percent.* A much higher rate of infection was reported in patients who had devices that penetrated the meninges[14, 140, 201, 224, 275] than in those who had parenchymal monitors.[258]

Multiple factors were suggested as increasing the risk for development of ICP device–related infection (Table 80–5). Patients with intracerebral hemorrhage usually do not have an increased risk of developing infection in comparison to those without such hemorrhage. In contrast, if the bleeding

*See references 14, 51, 52, 60, 140, 163, 201, 209, 224, 230, 233, 246, 258, 275, 287, 299, 308, 336, 355–357.

TABLE 80–5 ■ RISK FACTORS FOR INTRACRANIAL PRESSURE (ICP) MONITORING DEVICE INFECTION

Factors Associated with Increased Risk of Infection
Intraventricular hemorrhage
ICP >20 mm Hg
Open head trauma
Neurosurgical procedure/operation
Dural perforation
Duration of catheterization
Problems with the system
  Disconnections
  Leaks
  Irrigations
  Blockage

Factors Not Associated with Increased Risk of Infection
Head trauma
Intracerebral hemorrhage
Intracranial malignancy
Underlying disease
Drainage of cerebrospinal fluid
Previous ICP monitoring device in the intensive care unit
ICP device dressing changes
ICP device component changes

is intraventricular, the incidence of infection increases dramatically.[201] The rate of infection also is increased in patients with open head trauma in comparison to those with closed head trauma or intracranial malignancy.[145] Neurosurgical operations contributed significantly to the risk of acquiring infection,[201, 314] and the same was noted if the ICP was greater than 20 mm Hg.[201]

Interruption of monitoring system integrity (e.g., in-line stopcocks, number of times that the system was open, blockage of drainage, and irrigation) was identified by several investigators as increasing patients' risk of acquiring infection.[14, 201, 209, 230, 357] The effect of the duration of monitoring on the risk for infection is controversial, especially in patients with ventriculostomy catheters. Although several studies found a correlation between the length of time that the monitoring device was in place and the infection rate,[14, 163, 201, 224, 275, 357] some investigators found no relationship with monitoring duration.[233, 299, 314, 355] The different conclusions probably were the result of differences in the population studied, the type of devices used to measure ICP, the definition of infection, and analysis of the data. As a result of these data, investigators have recommended that the duration of ICP monitoring not be longer than 5 days. If the duration of monitoring must be longer, the monitoring device should be removed and replaced with a new device at a new site.[133, 201]

The need to replace the device at a certain time has been challenged. An analysis of the outcome in 584 patients (receiving 712 ventriculostomy catheters) who had 61 infections showed a steady increase in the daily incidence of infection, with a peak at day 10. The average time to the onset of infection was 6.8 days.[140] In addition, replacing the ventriculostomy catheter before day 5 did not affect the daily rate of infection. The authors concluded that the lowest rate of infection occurred in the first 4 days of monitoring, but that replacement of the catheter by day 5 did not reduce the infection rate, which continued to rise until day 10. The authors recommended that "ICP monitoring (devices) should be removed as quickly as possible," but if "prolonged monitoring is required, there appears to be no benefit from or need for catheter exchange."[140]

Several potential risk factors for ICP monitor–related infection that do not increase the infection rate are shown in Table 80–5.

ETIOLOGY

In general, the microorganisms that cause infections related to ICP monitoring devices are the same as those causing CNS shunt-related infections (see Table 80–2). The major difference is that gram-negative bacteria are isolated more often in ICP monitor–related infection than in CNS shunt-related infections. The more common bacteria include *Enterobacter, Klebsiella, S. marcescens,* and *Acinetobacter.* These bacteria are found in water and cause widespread colonization of hospitalized patients. Colonization of the respiratory tract is an especially common occurrence in patients in the intensive care unit and in those with serious underlying disease. Thus, they are occurring increasingly frequently in ICP monitor–related infections.

CLINICAL MANIFESTATIONS

ICP monitor–related infections often occur in patients with an altered sensorium; therefore, the signs and symptoms of meningeal irritation usually are not present. The clinical diagnosis is complicated further by the fact that these patients often are critically ill and their signs and symptoms are caused by the underlying condition and are not a result of the ICP monitor–related infection. In addition, they may be receiving multiple antibiotics for other sources of infection (e.g., pneumonia, bacteremia, urinary tract infection), both nosocomial and non-nosocomial. Although fever is the most frequent indication of infection, the presence of infections or inflammatory processes at other body sites causes the predictive value of fever to be low. Therefore, providing close follow-up, having a high index of suspicion, and obtaining frequent cultures of CSF when available (e.g., ventriculostomy device) are recommended.

DIAGNOSIS

The predictive value of the peripheral WBC count and differential count is very low, and the only definitive diagnostic tests are the CSF WBC count and culture. CSF biochemistry (i.e., protein and glucose) has a very low predictive value. Although a low level of glucose may be of help in the diagnosis, a normal level does not exclude the possibility of an infection. Most patients with ICP monitor–related infection will have an increased CSF WBC count with a predominance of PMNs. In some cases, with low growth of bacteria, no elevation in CSF WBC counts (less than 10/mm^3) was reported. Most of these cases were caused by CoNS. In such cases, if no other indicators of infection (e.g., clinical symptoms, low glucose) are present, the possibility that the positive cultures represent colonization or contamination should be considered before treatment is initiated.

TREATMENT AND PROPHYLAXIS

The same principles used for the management of CNS shunt infections can be applied to infections associated with ICP monitoring devices. The use of antibiotics alone without removal of the device may be adequate for the treatment of infections associated with devices placed in the subdural or epidural space, unless an abscess or empyema has formed. In the case of ventriculostomy, the infected device should be removed and appropriate antibiotic therapy instituted. Because gram-negative bacteria are almost as common as gram-positive bacteria in causing ICP device–related infections, the initial antibiotic therapy should include both vancomycin and cefotaxime or ceftazidime if the Gram stain is negative. When the etiologic agent is identified, the specific antibiotic or antibiotics can be chosen from Table 80–4. The duration of therapy depends on the etiologic agent and the CSF parameters. In patients with positive CSF culture but minimal CSF pleocytosis, if the CSF culture becomes negative immediately after removal of the catheter, therapy should be given for only 3 or 4 days because the cultures before removal of the catheter reflect colonization and not infection. If subsequent cultures are positive, therapy should continue for 10 days of negative cultures.

Many physicians use prophylactic antibiotics for the duration of ICP monitoring in the hope of preventing infection. Unfortunately, the few studies that have evaluated the utility of antimicrobial agents in preventing such infections did not find any efficacy.[201] Furthermore, Jacobs and Westerband showed that patients who received prophylaxis had statistically significantly higher rates of septic morbidity and pneumonia.[152] Therefore, if prophylactic antibiotics are administered, they should be given for only a short period (i.e., 24 to 36 hours) after placement of the ICP device.

Intrathecal Pump Infusion Devices

The intrathecal pump infusion system currently is used to infuse morphine to treat refractory pain,[238] to deliver baclofen (a gamma-aminobutyric acid agonist), or to treat spasticity of spinal or cerebral origin.[4, 13, 249] In addition, patients with generalized dystonia also benefited from intrathecal baclofen.[5] More than 50,000 patients are being treated with implanted intrathecal pumps for pain or spasticity. Several pump systems are used. The simpler systems consist of an externalized catheter system similar to the Hickman catheter[77] or a subcutaneous reservoir system similar to an intravascular implanted port.[38] The more sophisticated systems include a programmable pump that usually is implanted in an abdominal subcutaneous pocket and connected via a subcutaneous catheter to the subarachnoid space.[24, 38] An optional sideport in some of these implanted pumps allows aspiration of CSF from the subarachnoid space.

Complications of the intrathecal pump system are relatively rare events and include mechanical problems with the catheter such as breaking, kinking, dislodging, or leaking.[318] Skin necrosis also has been reported.[102, 318] The pump itself is very durable and only very rarely causes a mechanical problem. Overdose that may result in coma, respiratory depression, apnea, cardiac conduction abnormalities, hypotension or hypertension, and abnormalities of the pupils was reported as well.[251] Intrathecal baclofen can induce both recurrent and new-onset seizures.[13, 172] In addition, acute withdrawal syndrome was reported when treatment was stopped.[296] Infectious complications included suppuration of the exit site,[41, 80, 139, 256] along the subcutaneous catheter (tunnel infection),[24, 41, 80, 139] or around the pump.[24, 41, 48] Furthermore, more severe infections such as epidural abscess and meningitis also were reported.[26, 41, 62, 66, 80, 225, 281, 362, 363]

EPIDEMIOLOGY

The infection rate of intrathecal pump infusion devices ranges from 0 to 27 percent (median, 4%). Of note, in general the infection rate was lower in studies that included a larger number of patients. A more accurate description of the incidence would be the infection rate per 1000 catheter-days, which ranged from 0 to 2.5. The infection rate was higher in patients with an externalized catheter (0.65 per 1000 catheter-days) than in those who had an implanted system (0.48 per 1000 catheter-days). Most of the infections occurred in the exit site, along the catheter, or in the subcutaneous pocket of the pump, but in as many as 16 percent of cases, the infection involved the epidural space, the meninges, or both.

Infections occur more often within 2 to 4 weeks after insertion of the catheter, which suggests that the initial surgery to place the intrathecal pump system may be a risk factor. Byers and coworkers found that the only risk factor during this surgery associated with infection was a prolonged duration of the procedure (i.e. >100 minutes).[41] Multiple other factors, such as the patient's age, underlying diseases, immune deficiency, other concurrent infections (e.g., pneumonia), previous intrathecal catheter, number of pump refills, intraspinal anesthetics, surgeon's or anesthesiologist's experience with the procedure, and operative complications (e.g., operative loss of blood), were not associated significantly with an increased risk for acquisition of infection.[41] Very thin or malnourished patients may be prone to wound dehiscence, which may increase their vulnerability to infection. In addition, patients with narrowed intervertebral spaces tended to have a longer operation, which puts them at risk for development of infection.

ETIOLOGY

The most common bacteria causing intrathecal device–related infection are from the skin flora. CoNS and *S. aureus* lead the list, but *Streptococcus mitis,*[41] *Streptococcus* group G,[41] *Corynebacterium striatum,*[41] and *Enterococcus faecalis*[101] infections are observed as well. In addition, several studies have reported gram-negative bacteria as the cause of the pump-related infection. Such bacteria include *P. aeruginosa,*[41, 101] *Pseudomonas paucimobilis,*[249] *E. coli,*[80] and *Klebsiella pneumoniae.*[249] One case of *C. albicans* and one case of *Mycobacterium* infection have been reported.[80] A rare case of baclofen vial contamination with the fungus *Wangiella* that caused infection also was reported.[249]

CLINICAL MANIFESTATIONS

Clinical findings depend on the site of the infection. Patients with more severe infections (i.e., epidural abscess, meningitis) may have symptoms of these infections (e.g., fever, irritability, headache, nerve root pain, meningeal signs). In some patients, pain experienced during the injection may be the clue, but in many patients, a high level of awareness for possible infection is important because they will have nonspecific signs and symptoms.

Exit-site and superficial catheter-related infections usually cause local inflammation (e.g., swelling, redness), tenderness, and drainage. The more serious deep tract (tunnel) infections are more difficult to assess. Visible inflammation along the tract or soft fluctuant fluid collection around it may be the only clue. Fever is not always present.

DIAGNOSIS

Performing a complete physical and neurologic examination may be helpful in some cases. A routine CBC is relatively unhelpful because leukocytosis is not always present. MRI may be useful for diagnosing an epidural abscess and evaluating its extent. The only definitive diagnostic tests are

Gram stain and culture of exudate/drainage from the exit site (if available) or an aspirate of the fluid collection along the catheter tract (if tunnel infection is suspected) or the CSF for suspected meningitis. Irrigation of the epidural space with 1 or 2 mL of saline after removal of the pump filter (which should be sent for culture) may help in diagnosing an epidural abscess or empyema.

TREATMENT AND PROPHYLAXIS

If infection has occurred only at the exit site and the superficial catheter tract, local drainage with aggressive cleansing (i.e., topical antibiotics and antiseptics) but without removal of the catheter was suggested.[80] Unfortunately, in some of these patients more severe infections developed (e.g., deep tunnel and epidural abscess). In addition, failure of "catheter-sparing" treatment also was reported.[139, 256] Therefore, removal of the catheter should be considered even for mild infections if they do not respond promptly to therapy. In patients with pocket, epidural, and meningeal infections, the intrathecal pump system should be removed as soon as possible and systemic antibiotic therapy initiated (for selection of drugs and doses, see Table 80–4). Although a few studies have reported clinical improvement (and sometimes cure) of tunnel infection or meningitis with the administration of intravenous antibiotics and retention of the catheter, in many cases the infection recurred when the treatment was stopped.[41, 80] Few reports suggest successful treatment of severe pump infections (including meningitis) without removal of the pump system.[26, 38, 66, 101, 225, 256, 281, 362, 363] In some of these cases, the pathogen was considered to be of low virulence (e.g., CoNS) or colonization. In most of these cases, instillation of antibiotics into the reservoir with cautious flushing of the catheter was combined with systemic antibiotics. The main reason for the intrathecal administration of antibiotics is to increase the level of drug in the CSF. Before antibiotics are added to the baclofen infusion, their compatibility with baclofen should be verified or tested (vancomycin is compatible and can be safely used according to Zed and associates).[362]

No guidelines exist on how to treat severe infections of intrathecal pump systems, but in most cases, removal of the pump system while systemic antibiotics are given and then reimplantation appears to be the treatment of choice. In rare cases in which removal of the pump will be detrimental to the patient, a trial of intrathecal antibiotics may be justified, with close observation to ensure that the patient is not getting worse.

Although many physicians use perioperative (or longer) antibiotics for prophylaxis, their efficacy in preventing infection has not been proved. Therefore, prophylactic antibiotics should not be used but, if given, should not be administered for longer than 24 to 36 hours after the operation.

REFERENCES

1. Ahlberg, A., Carlsson, A. S., and Lindberg, L.: Hematogenous infection in total joint replacement. Clin. Orthop. *137*:69–75, 1978.
2. Ahnfelt, L., Herberts, P., Malchau, H., and Andersson, G. B.: Prognosis of total hip replacement. A Swedish multicenter study of 4,664 revisions. Acta Orthop. Scand. Suppl. *238*:1–26, 1990.
3. Ainbinder, D. J., Haik, B. G., and Tellado, M.: Hydroxyapatite orbital implants abscess: Histological correlation of an infected implant following evisceration. Ophthal. Plast. Reconstruct. Surg. *10*:267–270, 1994.
4. Albright, A. L.: Baclofen in the treatment of cerebral palsy. J. Child Neurol. *11*:77–83, 1996.
5. Albright, A. L., Barry, M. J., and Fasick, P.: Continuous intrathecal baclofen infusion for symptomatic generalized dystonia. Neurosurgery *38*:934–939, 1996.
6. Ammirati, M., and Raimondi, A. J.: Cerebrospinal fluid shunt infections in children. Childs Nerv. Syst. *3*:106–109, 1987.
7. Anderson, H. L., III, Attorri, R. J., Custer, J. R., et al.: Extracorporeal membrane oxygenation for pediatric cardiopulmonary failure. J. Thorac. Cardiovasc. Surg. *99*:1011–1021, 1990.
8. Ankersmit, H. J., Tugulea, S., Spanier, T., et al.: Activation-induced T-cell death and immune dysfunction after implantation of left-ventricular assist device. Lancet *354*:550–555, 1999.
9. Antonyshyn, O., Gruss, J. S., Mackinnon, S. E., and Zuker, R.: Complications of soft tissue expansion. Br. J. Plast. Surg. *41*:239–250, 1988.
10. Arber, N., Pras, E., Copperman, Y., et al.: Pacemaker endocarditis. Report of 44 cases and review of the literature. Medicine (Baltimore) *73*:299–305, 1994.
11. Argenziano, M., Catanese, K. A., Moazami, N., et al.: The influence of infection on survival and successful transplantation in patients with left ventricular assist devices. J. Heart Lung Transplant. *16*:822–831, 1997.
12. Arisoy, E. S., and Demmler, G. J.: *Corynebacterium xerosis* ventriculoperitoneal shunt infection in an infant: Report of a case and review of the literature. Pediatr. Infect. Dis. J. *12*:536–538, 1993.
13. Armstrong, R. W., Steinbok, P., Cochrane, D. D., et al.: Intrathecally administered baclofen for treatment of children with spasticity of cerebral origin. J. Neurosurg. *87*:409–414, 1997.
14. Aucoin, P. J., Kotilainen, H. R., Gantz, N. M., et al.: Intracranial pressure monitors. Epidemiologic study of risk factors and infections. Am. J. Med. *80*:369–376, 1986.
15. Austad, E. D.: Evolution of the concept of tissue expansion. Facial Plast. Surg. *5*:277–279, 1988.
16. Austin, K. S., Testa, N. N., Luntz, R. K., et al.: *Aspergillus* infection of total knee arthroplasty presenting as a popliteal cyst. Case report and review of the literature. J. Arthroplasty 7:311–314, 1992.
17. Baier, R. E., and Dutton, R. C.: Initial events in interactions of blood with a foreign surface. J. Biomed. Mater. Res. *3*:191–206, 1969.
18. Bartlett, R. H., Roloff, D. W., Custer, J. R., et al.: Extracorporeal life support—The University of Michigan experience. J. A. M. A. *283*:904–908, 2000.
19. Bayston, R.: Antibiotic prophylaxis in shunt surgery. Dev. Med. Child Neurol. *17*(Suppl. 35):99–103, 1975.
20. Bayston, R., Compton, C., and Richards, K.: Production of extracellular slime by coryneforms colonizing hydrocephalus shunts. J. Clin. Microbiol. *32*:1705–1709, 1994.
21. Bayston, R., and Penny, S. R.: Excessive production of mucoid substance in *Staphylococcus* SIIA: A possible factor in colonization of Holter shunts. Dev. Med. Child Neurol. *14*(Suppl. 27):25–28, 1972.
22. Bayston, R., and Rodgers, J.: Role of serological tests in the diagnosis of immune complex disease in infection of ventriculoatrial shunts for hydrocephalus. Eur. J. Clin. Microbiol. Infect. Dis. *13*:417–420, 1994.
23. Beeler, B. A.: Infections of permanent transvenous and epicardial pacemakers in adults. Heart Lung *11*:152–156, 1982.
24. Benedetti, C., McDonald, J. S., Lingam, R., and Seitz, M.: Efficacy of a Port-a-Cath epidural system for cancer pain management. Abstract. Anesthesiology *77*(3A):841, 1992.
25. Bengtson, S.: Prosthetic osteomyelitis with special reference to the knee: Risks, treatment and costs. Ann. Med. *25*:523–529, 1993.
26. Bennett, M. I., Tai, Y. M. A., and Symonds, J. M.: Staphylococcal meningitis following Synchromed intrathecal pump implant: A case report. Pain *56*:243–244, 1994.
27. Berbari, E., Hanssen, A., Duffy, M., et al.: Prosthetic joint infection due to *Mycobacterium tuberculosis:* A case series and review of the literature. Am. J. Orthop. *27*:219–227, 1998.
28. Berbari, E. F., Hanssen, A. D., Duffy, M. C., et al.: Risk factors for prosthetic joint infection: Case-control study. Clin. Infect. Dis. *27*:1247–1254, 1998.
29. Berkowitz, R. G., Franz, B. K. H., Shepherd, R. K., et al.: Pneumococcal middle ear infections and cochlear implantation. Ann. Otol. Rhinol. Laryngol. Suppl. *128*:55–56, 1987.
30. Bernstein, A. D., and Parsonnet, V.: Survey of cardiac pacing and defibrillation in the United States in 1993. Am. J. Cardiol. *78*:187–196, 1996.
31. Black, M. D., Coles, J. G., Williams, W. G., et al.: Determinants of success in pediatric cardiac patients undergoing extracorporeal membrane oxygenation. Ann. Thorac. Surg. *60*:133–138, 1995.
32. Bluhm, G.: Pacemaker infections. A clinical study with special reference to prophylactic use of some isoxazolyl penicillins. Acta Med. Scand. (Suppl.) *699*:1–62, 1985.
33. Bluhm, G. L.: Pacemaker infections: A 2-year follow-up of antibiotic prophylaxis. Scand. J. Thorac. Cardiovasc. Surg. *19*:231–235, 1985.
34. Bolton, W. K., Sande, M. A., Normansell, D. E., et al.: Ventriculojugular shunt nephritis with *Corynebacterium bovis.* Am. J. Med. *59*:417–423, 1975.
35. Borges, L. F.: Host defenses. Neurosurg. Clin. North Am. *3*:275–278, 1992.
36. Boutin, R., Brossman, J., Sartoris, D., et al.: Update on imaging or orthopedic infections. Orthop. Clin. North Am. *29*:41–46, 1998.
37. Brause, B. D.: Prosthetic joint infections. Curr. Opin. Rheumatol. *1*:194–198, 1989.
38. Brazenor, G. A.: Long term intrathecal administration of morphine: A comparison of bolus injection via reservoir with continuous infusion by implanted pump. Neurosurgery *21*:484–491, 1987.

39. Buchholz, H. W., Elson, R. A., and Heinert, K.: Antibiotic-loaded acrylic cement: Current concepts. Clin. Orthop. *190*:96–108, 1984.
40. Burket, J. S., Bartlett, R. H., Vander Hyde, K., and Chenoweth, C. E.: Nosocomial infections in adult patients undergoing extracorporeal membrane oxygenation. Clin. Infect. Dis. *28*:828–833, 1999.
41. Byers, K., Axelrod, P., Michael, S., and Rosen, S.: Infections complicating tunneled intraspinal catheter systems used to treat chronic pain. Clin. Infect. Dis. *21*:403–408, 1995.
42. Cacoub, P., Leprince, P., Nataf, P., et al.: Pacemaker infective endocarditis. Am. J. Cardiol. *82*:480–484, 1998.
43. Camus, C., Leport, C., Raffi, F., et al.: Sustained bacteremia in 26 patients with a permanent endocardial pacemaker: Assessment of wire removal. Clin. Infect. Dis. *17*:46–55, 1993.
44. Canner, G. C., Steinberg, M. E., Heppenstall, R. B., and Balderston, R.: The infected hip after total hip arthroplasty. J. Bone Joint Surg. Am. *66*:1393–1399, 1984.
45. Carlsson, A. S., Josefsson, G., and Lindberg, L.: Revision with gentamicin-impregnated cement for deep infection in total hip arthroplasties. J. Bone Joint Surg. Am. *60*:1059–1064, 1978.
46. Chahipa, E., Swarhrick, H. A., Holden, B. A., and Sjostrand, J.: Severe corneal infections associated with contact lens wear. Ophthalmology *94*:17–22, 1987.
47. Chan, K. H., Mann, K. S., and Seto, W. H.: Infection of a shunt by *Mycobacterium fortuitum*: Case report. Neurosurgery *29*:472–474, 1991.
48. Cherry, D. A., Gourlay, G. K., Counsins, M. J., and Gannon, B. J.: A technique for the insertion of an implantable portal system for the long-term epidural administration of opioids in the treatment of cancer pain. Anaesth. Intensive Care *13*:145–152, 1985.
49. Choo, M. H., Holmes, D. R., Gersh, B. J., et al.: Permanent pacemaker infections: Characterization and management. Am. J. Cardiol. *48*:559–564, 1981.
50. Choux, M., Genitori, L., Lang, D., and Lena, G.: Shunt implantation: Reducing the incidence of shunt infection. J. Neurosurg. *77*:875–880, 1992.
51. Clark, W. K., Mulbauer, M. S., Lowrey, R., et al.: Complications of intracranial pressure monitoring in trauma patients. Neurosurgery *25*:20–24, 1988.
52. Cobb, D. K., High, K. P., Sawyer, R. G., et al.: A controlled trial of scheduled replacement of central venous and pulmonary-artery catheters. N. Engl. J. Med. *327*:1062–1067, 1992.
53. Cobb, T. K., and Beckenbaugh, R. D.: Biaxial total wrist arthroplasty. J. Hand Surg. [Am.] *21*:1011–1021, 1996.
54. Cohen, E. J., Buchanan, H. W., Laughrea, P. A., et al.: Diagnosis and management of *Acanthamoeba* keratitis. Am. J. Ophthalmol. *100*:389–395, 1985.
55. Cohen, N. L.: Cochlear implant soft surgery: Fact or fantasy? Otolaryngol. Head Neck Surg. *117*:214–216, 1997.
56. Cohen, N. L., and Hoffman, R. A.: Surgical complications of multichannel cochlear implants in North America. *In* Fraysse, B., and Deguine, O. (eds.): Cochlear Implants: New Perspectives. New York, Karger, 1993, pp. 70–74.
57. Cohen, N. L., and Hoffman, R. A.: Complications of cochlear implant surgery in adults and children. Ann. Otol. Rhinol. Laryngol. *100*:708–711, 1991.
58. Cohen, N. L., Hoffman, R. A., and Stroschein, M.: Medical or surgical complications related to the nucleus multichannel cochlear implant. Ann. Otol. Rhinol. Laryngol. *97*:8–13, 1988.
59. Cohen, T. J., Pons, V. G., Schwartz, J., and Griffin, J. C.: *Candida albicans* pacemaker site infection. Pacing Clin. Electrophysiol. *14*:146–148, 1991.
60. Constantini, S., Cotev, S., Rappaport, Z. H., et al.: Intracranial pressure monitoring after elective intracranial surgery. J. Neurosurg. *69*:540–544, 1988.
61. Cotton, M. F., Hartzenberg, B., Donald, P. R., and Burger, P. J.: Ventriculoperitoneal shunt infections in children: A 6-year study. S. Afr. Med. J. *79*:139–142, 1991.
62. Crawford, M. E., Andersen, H., Augustenborg, G. A., et al.: Pain treatment on outpatient basis utilizing extradural opiates: A Danish multicentre study comprising 105 patients. Pain *16*:41–47, 1983.
63. Cruciani, M., Di Perri, G., Molesini, M., et al.: Use of fluconazole in the treatment of *Candida albicans* hydrocephalus shunt infection. Eur. J. Clin. Microbiol. Infect. Dis. *11*:957–961, 1992.
64. Cuckler, J. M., Star, A. M., Alavi, A., and Noto, R. B.: Diagnosis and management of the infected total joint arthroplasty. Orthop. Clin. North Am. *22*:512–530, 1991.
65. Da Costa, A., Lelievre, H., Kirkorian, G. M., et al.: Role of preaxillary flora in pacemaker infections: A prospective study. Circulation *97*:1791–1795, 1998.
66. Dagi, T. F., Chilton, J., Caputy, A., and Won, D.: Long-term intermittent percutaneous administration of epidural and intrathecal morphine for pain of malignant origin. Am. Surg. *52*:155–158, 1986.
67. Dalton, H. J., Siewers, R. D., Fuhrman, B. P., et al.: Extracorporeal membrane oxygenation for cardiac rescue in children with severe myocardial dysfunction. Crit. Care Med. *21*:1020–1028, 1993.
68. Darouiche, R. O.: Device-associated infections: A macroproblem that starts with microadherence. Clin. Infect. Dis. *33*:1567–1572, 2001.
69. Darouiche, R. O., Landon, G. C., Patti, G. M., et al.: Role of *Staphylococcus aureus* surface adhesions in orthopaedic device infections. J. Med. Microbiol. *46*:75–79, 1997.
70. Daspit, C. P.: Meningitis as a result of cochlear implant: Case report. Otolaryngol. Head Neck Surg. *105*:115–116, 1991.
71. David, R., Shtarker, H., Horesh, Z., et al.: Arthrodesis with the Ilizarov device after failed knee arthroplasty. Orthopedics *24*:33–36, 2001.
72. Diaz-Mitoma, F., Hardin, G. K. M., Hoban, D. J., et al.: Clinical significance of a test for slime production in ventriculoperitoneal shunt infections caused by coagulase-negative staphylococci. J. Infect. Dis. *156*:555–560, 1987.
73. Dickinson, G. M., and Bisno, A. L.: Infections associated with indwelling devices: Concepts of pathogenesis; infections associated with intravascular devices. Antimicrob. Agents Chemother. *33*:597–601, 1989.
74. Dickinson, G. M., and Bisno, A. L.: Infections associated with indwelling devices: Infections related to extravascular devices. Antimicrob. Agents Chemother. *33*:602–607, 1989.
75. Didisheim, P., Olsen, D. B., Farrar, D. J., et al.: Infections and thromboembolism with implantable cardiovascular devices. Trans. Am. Soc. Artif. Intern. Organs *35*:54–70, 1994.
76. Di Rocco, C., Marchese, E., and Velardi, F.: A survey of the first complication of newly implanted CSF shunt devices for the treatment of nontumoral hydrocephalus. Childs Nerv. Syst. *10*:321–325, 1994.
77. Downing, J. E., Busch, E. H., and Stedman, P. M.: Epidural morphine delivered by a percutaneous epidural catheter for outpatient treatment of cancer pain. Anesth. Analg. *67*:1159–1161, 1988.
78. Duggan, J. M., Georgiadis, G. M., and Kleshinski, J. F.: Management of prosthetic joint infections. Infect. Med. *18*:534–541, 2001.
79. Duhaime, A. C., Bonner, K., McGowan, K. L., et al.: Distribution of bacteria in the operating room environment and its relation to ventricular shunt infections: A prospective study. Childs Nerv. Syst. *7*:211–214, 1991.
80. Du Pen, S. L., Peterson, D. G., Williams, A., and Bogosian, A. J.: Infection during chronic epidural catheterization: Diagnosis and treatment. Anesthesiology *73*:905–909, 1990.
81. Duus, B. R., Boeckstyns, M., and Stadeager, C.: The natural course of radionuclide bone scanning in the evaluation of total knee replacement—a 2 year prospective study. Clin. Radiol. *41*:341–343, 1990.
82. Eftehar, N. S.: Wound infection complicating total hip joint arthroplasty. Orthop. Rev. *8*:49–64, 1984.
83. Eggimann, P., and Waldvogel, F.: Pacemaker and defibrillator infections. *In* Waldvogel, F. A., and Bisno, A. L. (eds.): Infections Associated with Indwelling Medical Devices. 3rd ed. Washington, DC, A. S. M. Press, 2000, pp. 247–264.
84. Elson, R.: One-stage exchange in the treatment of the infected total hip arthroplasty. Semin. Arthroplasty *5*:137–141, 1994.
85. Ersahin, Y., McLone, D. G., Storrs, B. B., et al.: Review of 3,017 procedures for the management of hydrocephalus in children. Concepts Pediatr. Neurosurg. *9*:21–33, 1989.
86. Ersahin, Y., Mutluer, S., and Tekeli, G.: Abdominal cerebrospinal fluid pseudocysts. Childs Nerv. Syst. *12*:755–758, 1996.
87. Etienne, J., Charpin, B., Grando, J., et al.: Characterization of clinically significant isolates of *Staphylococcus epidermidis* from patients with cerebrospinal fluid shunt infections. Epidemiol. Infect. *106*:467–475, 1991.
88. Faillace, W. J.: A no-touch technique protocol to diminish cerebrospinal fluid shunt infection. Surg. Neurol. *43*:344–350, 1995.
89. Farber, B. F., Kaplan, M. H., and Clogston, A. G.: *Staphylococcus epidermidis* extracted slime inhibits the antimicrobial action of glycopeptide antibiotics. J. Infect. Dis. *161*:37–40, 1988.
90. Fehring, T. K., Calton, T. F., and Griffin, W. L.: Cementless fixation in 2-stage reimplantation for periprosthetic sepsis. J. Arthroplasty *14*:175–181, 1999.
91. Fischer, S. A., Trenholme, G. M., Costanzo, M. R., and Piccione, W.: Infectious complications in left ventricular assist device recipients. Clin. Infect. Dis. *24*:18–23, 1997.
92. Fitzgerald, R. H., and Jones, D. R.: Hip implant infection. Am. J. Med. *78*(Suppl. 6B):225–228, 1986.
93. Fitzgerald, R. H., Nolan, D. R., Ilstrup, D. M., et al.: Deep wound sepsis following total hip arthroplasty. J. Bone Joint Surg. Am. *59*:847–855, 1977.
94. Forward, K. R., Fewer, H. D., and Stiver, H. G.: Cerebrospinal fluid shunt infections: A review of 35 infections in 32 patients. J. Neurosurg. *59*:389–394, 1983.
95. Foster, M. R., Heppenstall, R. B., Friedenberg, Z. B., and Hozack, W. J.: A prospective assessment of nutritional status and complications in patients with fractures of the hip. J. Orthop. Trauma *4*:49–57, 1990.
96. Foster, T. J., and Hook, M.: Surface protein adhesins of *Staphylococcus aureus*. Trends Microbiol. *6*:484–488, 1998.
97. Fouyas, I. P., Case, A. T. H., Thompson, D., et al.: Use of intracranial pressure monitoring in the management of childhood hydrocephalus and shunt-related problems. Neurosurgery *38*:726–732, 1996.
98. Frame, P. T., and McLaurin, R. L.: Treatment of CSF shunt infections with intrashunt plus oral antibiotic therapy. J. Neurosurg. *60*:354–360, 1984.
99. Frame, R., Brodman, R. F., Furman, S., et al.: Surgical removal of infected transvenous pacemaker leads. Pacing Clin. Electrophysiol. *16*:2343–2348, 1993.

100. Frazier, O. H., Rose, E. A., Macmanus, Q., et al.: Multicenter clinical evaluation of the HeartMate 1000 IP left ventricular assist device. Ann. Thorac. Surg. *53*:1080–1090, 1992.
101. Galloway, A., and Falope, F. Z.: *Pseudomonas aeruginosa* infection in an intrathecal baclofen pump: Successful treatment with adjunct intra-reservoir gentamicin. Spinal Cord *38*:126–128, 2000.
102. Gardner, B.: Intrathecal baclofen—a multicentre clinical comparison of the Medtronics Programmable, Cordis Sector, and constant infusion Infusaid drug delivery systems. Paraplegia *33*:551–554, 1995.
103. Gardner, P., Leipzig, T., and Phillips, P.: Infections of central nervous system shunts. Symposium on infections of the central nervous system. Med. Clin. North Am. *69*:297–314, 1985.
104. Garvin, K. L., and Hanssen, A. D.: Infection after total hip arthroplasty. Past, present, and future. J. Bone Joint Surg. Am. *77*:1576–1588, 1995.
105. Garvin, K. L., Salvati, E. A., and Brause, B. D.: Role of gentamicin-impregnated cement in total joint arthroplasty. J. Bone Joint Surg. Am. *65*:1081–1086, 1988.
106. Gaskill, S. J., and Marlin, A. E.: Spontaneous bacterial peritonitis in patients with ventriculoperitoneal shunts. Pediatr. Neurosurg. *26*:115–119, 1997.
107. Geers, T. A., and Gordon, S. M.: Clinical significance of *Candida* species isolated from cerebrospinal fluid following neurosurgery. Clin. Infect. Dis. *28*:1139–1147, 1999.
108. Gibstein, L. A., Abramson, D. L., Bartlett, R. A., et al.: Tissue expansion in children: A retrospective study of complications. Ann. Plast. Surg. *38*:358–364, 1997.
109. Gillespie, W. J.: Infection in total joint replacement. Infect. Dis. Clin. North Am. *4*:465–484, 1990.
110. Glasgow, B. J., Weinberg, D. A., Shorr, N., and Goldberg, R. A.: Draining cutaneous fistula associated with infections of hydroxyapatite orbital implant. Ophthal. Plast. Reconstr. Surg. *12*:131–135, 1996.
111. Glatt, H. J., Googe, P. B., Powers, T., and Apple, D. J.: Anophthalmic socket pain. Am. J. Ophthalmol. *116*:357–362, 1993.
112. Gold, M. R., Peters, R. W., and Johnson, J. W. Complications associated with pectoral implantation of cardioverter defibrillators. Pacing Clin. Electrophysiol. *20*:208–211, 1997.
113. Gower, D. J., Crone, K., Alexander, E., and Kelly, D. L.: *Candida albicans* shunt infection: Report of two cases. Neurosurgery *19*:111–113, 1986.
114. Gower, D. J., Gower, V. C., Richardson, S. H., and Kelly, D. L.: Reduced bacterial adherence to silicone plastic neurosurgical prosthesis. Pediatr. Neurosci. *12*:127–133, 1985.
115. Grabb, P. A., and Albright, A. I.: Intraventricular vancomycin-induced cerebrospinal fluid eosinophilia: Report of two patients. Neurosurgery *30*:630–635, 1992.
116. Gray, E. D., Peters, G., Verstegen, M., and Regelmann, W. E.: Effect of extracellular slime substance from *Staphylococcus epidermidis* on the human cellular immune response. Lancet *1*:365–367, 1984.
117. Greene, K. A., Clark, R. J., and Zabramski, J. M.: Ventricular CSF shunt infections associated with *Corynebacterium jeikeium*: Report of three cases and review. Clin. Infect. Dis. *16*:139–141, 1993.
118. Griffith, M. J., Mounsey, J. P., Bexton, R. S., and Holden, M. P.: Mechanical, but not infective, pacemaker erosion may be successfully managed by re-implantation of pacemakers. Br. Heart J. *71*:202–205, 1994.
119. Gristina, A. G., and Kolkin, J.: Total joint replacement and sepsis. J. Bone Joint Surg. Am. *65*:128–134, 1993.
120. Grogler, F. M., Frank, G., Greven, G., et al.: Complications of permanent transvenous cardiac pacing. J. Thorac. Cardiovasc. Surg. *69*:895–904, 1975.
121. Gruninger, R. P.: Diagnostic microbiology in bone and joint infections. *In* Gustilo, R. B. (ed.): Orthopaedic Infection: Diagnosis and Treatment. Philadelphia, W. B. Saunders, 1989, pp. 42–51.
122. Guevara, J. A., Zuccaro, G., Trevisan, B. S., and Denoya, C. D.: Bacterial adhesion to cerebrospinal fluid shunts. J. Neurosurg. *67*:438–445, 1987.
123. Gutow, A. P., and Wolfe, S. W.: Infection following total elbow arthroplasty. Hand Clin. *10*:521–529, 1994.
124. Haines, S. J., and Taylor, F.: Prophylactic methicillin for shunt operations: Effects on incidence of shunt malfunction and infection. Childs Brain *9*:10–22, 1982.
125. Haines, S. J., and Walters, B. C.: Antibiotic prophylaxis for cerebrospinal fluid shunts: A metanalysis. Neurosurgery *34*:87–92, 1994.
126. Hanekom, W., and Yogev, R.: Diagnosis and management of CSF shunt infections. Adv. Pediatr. Infect. Dis. *11*:29–54, 1995.
127. Hanssen, A. D., and Rand, J. A.: Evaluation and treatment of infection at the site of a total hip or knee arthroplasty. J. Bone Joint Surg. Am. *80*:910–922, 1998.
128. Harcombe, A. A., Newell, S. A., Ludman, P. F., et al.: Late complications following permanent pacemaker implantation or elective unit replacement. Heart *80*:240–244, 1998.
129. Harjula, A., Jarvinen, A., Virtanen, K. S., and Mattila, S.: Pacemaker infections—treatment with total or partial pacemaker system removal. Thorac. Cardiovasc. Surg. *33*:218–220, 1985.
130. Hebert, C. K., Williams, R. E., Levy, R. S., and Barrack, R. L.: Cost of treating an infected total knee replacement. Clin. Orthop. *331*:140–145, 1996.
131. Heimberger, T. S., and Duma, R. J.: Infections of prosthetic heart valves and cardiac pacemakers. Infect. Dis. Clin. North Am. *3*:221–245, 1989.
132. Helman, D. N., Morales, D. L., Edwards, N. M., et al.: Left ventricular assist device bridge-to-transplant network improves survival after failed cardiotomy. Ann. Thorac. Surg. *68*:1187–1194, 1999.
133. Hickman, K. M., Mayer, B. L., and Muwaswes, M.: Intracranial pressure monitoring: Review of risk factors associated with infection. Heart Lung *19*:84–90, 1990.
134. Hildick-Smith, D. J., Lowe, M. D., Newell, S. A., et al.: Ventricular pacemaker upgrade: Experience, complications and recommendations. Heart *79*:383–387, 1998.
135. Hirst, L. W., Green, W. R., Merz, W., et al.: Management of *Acanthamoeba* keratitis: A case report and a review of the literature. Ophthalmology *91*:1105–1111, 1984.
136. Hoffman, R. A.: Cochlear implant in the child under two years of age: Skull growth, otitis media, and selection. Otolaryngol. Head Neck Surg. *117*:217–219, 1997.
137. Hoffman, R. A., and Cohen, N. L.: Complications of cochlear implant surgery. Ann. Otol. Rhinol. Laryngol. *104*(Suppl. 166):420–422, 1995.
138. Hofmann, A. A., Wyatt, R. W., Daniels, A., et al.: Bone scans after total knee arthroplasty in asymptomatic patients. Cemented versus cementless. Clin. Orthop. *251*:183–188, 1990.
139. Hogan, Q., Haddox, J. D., Abram, S., et al.: Epidural opiates and local anesthetics for the management of cancer pain. Pain *46*:271–279, 1991.
140. Holloway, K. L., Barnes, T., Choi, S., et al.: Ventriculostomy infections: The effect of monitoring duration and catheter exchange in 584 patients. J. Neurosurg. *85*:419–424, 1996.
141. Holman, W. L., Murrah, C. P., Ferguson, E. R., et al.: Infections during extended circulatory support: University of Alabama at Birmingham experience. Ann. Thorac. Surg. *61*:366–371, 1996.
142. Holt, R. J.: Bacteriological studies on colonised ventriculoatrial shunts. Dev. Med. Child Neurol. *12*(Suppl. 22):83–87, 1970.
143. Horgan, M. A., and Piatt, J. H., Jr.: Shaving of the scalp may increase the rate of infection in CSF shunt surgery. Pediatr. Neurosurg. *26*:180–184, 1997.
144. Hornyik, G., and Piatt, J. H., Jr.: Cerebrospinal fluid shunt infection by *Neisseria sicca*. Pediatr. Neurosurg. *21*:189–191, 1994.
145. House, W. F., Luxford, W. M., Courtney, B.: Otitis media in children following cochlear implant. Ear Hear. *6*(Suppl.):24–26, 1985.
146. Hussain, M., Wilcox, M. H., and White, P. J.: The slime of coagulase-negative staphylococci: Biochemistry and relation to adherence. FEMS Microbiol. Rev. *10*:191–207, 1993.
147. Iconomou, T. G., Michelow, B. J., and Zuker, R. M.: Tissue expansion in the pediatric patient. Ann. Plast. Surg. *31*:134–140, 1993.
148. Ingram, C. W., Haywood, H. B., III, Morris, V. M., et al.: Cryptococcal ventricular-peritoneal shunt infection: Clinical and epidemiological evaluation of two closely associated cases. Infect. Control Hosp. Epidemiol. *14*:719–722, 1993.
149. Inman, R. D., Gallegos, K. V., Brause, P. B., et al.: Clinical and microbial features of prosthetic joint infection. Am. J. Med. *77*:47–53, 1984.
150. Ito, J., Fujino, K., Okumura, T., et al.: Surgical difficulties and postoperative problems associated with cochlear implants. Ann. Otol. Rhinol. Laryngol. *104*(Suppl. 166):425–426, 1995.
151. Jackler, R. K., O'Donoghue, G. M., and Schindler, R. A.: Cochlear implantation: Strategies to protect the implanted cochlea from middle ear infection. Ann. Otol. Rhinol. Laryngol. *95*:66–70, 1986.
152. Jacobs, D. G., and Westerband, A.: Antibiotic prophylaxis for intracranial pressure monitors. Natl. Med. Assoc. *90*:417–423, 1998.
153. James, H. E., Walsh, J. W., Wilson, H. D., and Connor, J. D.: Management of CSF shunt infection: A clinical experience. Monogr. Neurol. Sci. *8*:75–77, 1982.
154. James, H. E., Walsh, J. W., Wilson, H. D., et al.: A prospective randomized study of therapy in cerebrospinal fluid shunt infection. Neurosurgery *7*:459–463, 1980.
155. James, P. J., Butcher, I. A., Gardner, E. R., and Hamblen, D. L.: Methicillin-resistant *Staphylococcus epidermidis* in infection in hip arthroplasties. J. Bone Joint Surg. Br. *76*:725–727, 1994.
156. Jenkins, J. G., Glasgow, J. F. T., Black, G. W., et al.: Reye's syndrome: Assessment of ICP monitoring. B. M. J. *294*:337–338, 1987.
157. Jensen, J. E., Jensen, T. G., Smith, T. K., et al.: Nutrition in orthopaedics. J. Bone Joint Surg. Am. *64*:1263–1272, 1982.
158. Jiminez, D. F., Keating, R., and Goodrich, J. T.: Silicone allergy in ventriculoperitoneal shunts. Childs Nerv. Syst. *10*:59–63, 1994.
159. Johnson, G. M., Lee, D. A., Regelmann, W. E., et al.: Interference with granulocyte function by *Staphylococcus epidermidis* slime. Infect. Immun. *54*:13–20, 1986.
160. Jones, R. F. C., Stening, W. A., Kwok, B. C. T., and Sands, T. M.: Third ventriculostomy for shunt infections in children. Neurosurgery *32*:855–859, 1993.
161. Jordan, D. R., Brownstein, S., and Shivinder, S. J.: Abscessed hydroxyapatite orbital implants: A report of two cases. Ophthalmology *103*:1784–1787, 1996.

162. Kaitreider, S. A., and Newman, S. A.: Prevention and management of complications associated with the hydroxyapatite implant. Ophthal. Plast. Reconstr. Surg. *12*:18–31, 1996.
163. Kanter, R. K., Weiner, L. B., Patti, A. M., et al.: Infectious complications and duration of intracranial pressure monitoring. Crit. Care Med. *13*:837–839, 1985.
164. Kantor, S. G., Schneider, R., Insall, J. N., and Becker, M. W.: Radionuclide imaging of asymptomatic versus symptomatic total knee arthroplasties. Clin. Orthop. *260*:118–123, 1990.
165. Kasirajan, V., McCarthy, P. M., Hoercher, K. J., et al.: Clinical experience with long-term use of implantable left ventricular assist devices: Indications, implantation, and outcomes. Semin. Thorac. Cardiovasc. Surg. *12*:229–237, 2000.
166. Kearney, R. A., Eisen, H. J., and Wolf, J. E.: Nonvalvular infections of the cardiovascular system. Ann. Intern. Med. *121*:219–230, 1994.
167. Kennergren, C.: Impact of implant techniques on complications with current implantable cardioverter-defibrillator systems. Am. J. Cardiol. *78*(Suppl. 5A):15–20, 1996.
168. Kestle, J. R. W., Hoffman, H. J., Soloniuk, D., et al.: A concerted effort to prevent shunt infection. Childs Nerv. Syst. *9*:163–165, 1993.
169. Ketoff, J., Klein, R. L., and Maukkassa, K. F.: Ventricular cholecystic shunts in children. J. Pediatr. Surg. *32*:181–183, 1997.
170. Klug, D., Lacroix, D., Savoye, C., et al.: Systemic infection related to endocarditis on pacemaker leads: Clinical presentation and management. Circulation *95*:2098–2107, 1997.
171. Kocis, K. C.: Pediatric cardiac extracorporeal membrane oxygenation: Supporting life or prolonging death? Crit. Care Med. *28*:594–595, 2000.
172. Kofler, M., Kronenberg, M. F., Rifici, C., et al.: Epileptic seizures associated with intrathecal baclofen application. Neurology *44*:25–27, 1994.
173. Kontny, U., Höfling, B., and Gutjahr, P.: CSF shunt infections in children. Infection *21*:89–95, 1993.
174. Kramer, L., Rojas-Corona, R. R., Sheff, D., and Eisenberg, E. S.: Disseminated aspergillosis and pacemaker endocarditis. Pacing Clin. Electrophysiol. *8*:225–229, 1985.
175. Kristinsson, J. K., Sigurdsson, H., Sigfusson, A., et al.: Detection of orbital implant infection with technetium 99m–labeled leukocytes. Ophthal. Plast. Reconstr. Surg. *13*:256–258, 1997.
176. Kulik, T. J., Moler, F. W., Palmisano, J. M., et al.: Outcome-associated factors in pediatric patients treated with extracorporeal membrane oxygenator after cardiac surgery. Circulation *94*(Suppl. II):63–68, 1996.
177. Kusumoto, F. M., and Goldschlager, N.: Cardiac pacing. N. Engl. J. Med. *334*:89–97, 1996.
178. Lai, K. K., and Fontecchio, S. A.: Infections associated with implantable cardioverter-defibrillators placed transvenously and via thoracotomies: Epidemiology, infection control, and management. Clin. Infect. Dis. *27*:265–269, 1998.
179. Langley, J. M., LeBlanc, J. C., Drake, J., and Milner, R.: Efficacy of antimicrobial prophylaxis in placement of cerebrospinal fluid shunts: Meta-analysis. Clin. Infect. Dis. *17*:98–103, 1993.
180. Lee, T., Kerr, R. S., and Adams, C. B.: *Pasteurella multocida*: A rare case of shunt infection. Br. J. Neurosurg. *4*:237–239, 1990.
181. Leggiadro, R. J., Atluru, V. L., and Katz, S. P.: Meningococcal meningitis associated with cerebrospinal fluid shunts. Pediatr. Infect. Dis. J. *3*:489–490, 1984.
182. Lewis, A. B., Hayes, D. L., Holmes, D. R., Jr., et al.: Update on infections involving permanent pacemakers. Characterization and management. J. Thorac. Cardiovasc. Surg. *89*:758–763, 1985.
183. Leyden, J. J., McGinley, K. J., Mills, O. H., and Kligman, A. M.: Age-related changes in the resident bacterial flora of the human face. J. Invest. Dermatol. *65*:379–381, 1975.
184. Lidofsky, S. P., Bass, N. M., Prage, M. C., et al.: Intracranial pressure monitoring and liver transplantation for fulminant hepatic failure. Hepatology *16*:1–4, 1992.
185. Lidwell, O. M., Lowbury, E. J. L., Whyte, W., et al.: Effect of ultraclean air in operating rooms on deep sepsis in the joint after total hip or knee replacement: A randomized study. B. M. J. *250*:99–102, 1982.
186. Lidwell, O. M., Lowbury, E. J. L., Whyte, W., et al.: Airborne contamination of wounds in joint replacement operations: The relationship to sepsis rates. J. Hosp. Infect. *4*:111–131, 1983.
187. Lieberman, J. R., Callaway, G. H., Salvati, E. A., et al.: Treatment of the infected total hip arthroplasty with a two-stage reimplantation protocol. Clin. Orthop. *301*:205–212, 1994.
188. Luer, M. S., and Hatton, J.: Vancomycin administration into the cerebrospinal fluid: A review. Ann. Pharmacother. *27*:912–921, 1993.
189. Luerssen, T. G.: Intracranial pressure: Current status in monitoring and management. Semin. Pediatr. Neurol. *4*:146–153, 1997.
190. Luessenhop, C. P., Higgins, L. D., Brause, B. D., and Ranawat, C. S.: Multiple prosthetic infections after total joint arthroplasty. Risk factor analysis. J. Arthroplasty *11*:862–868, 1996.
191. Luntz, M., Hodges, A. V., Balkany, T., et al.: Otitis media in children with cochlear implants. Laryngoscope *106*:1403–1405, 1995.
192. Luthardt, T.: Bacterial infections in ventriculo-auricular shunt systems. Dev. Med. Child Neurol. *12*(Suppl. 22):105–109, 1970.
193. Lutwick, L. I., Vaghjimal, A., and Connolly, M. W.: Postcardiac surgery infections. Crit. Care Clin. *14*:221–250, 1998.
194. Luxford, W. M., and House, W. F.: House 3M cochlear implant: Surgical considerations. *In* Clark, G. M., and Busby, P. A. (eds.): International Cochlear Implant Symposium and Workshop—Melbourne, 1985. Ann. Otol. Rhinol. Laryngol. *96*(Suppl. 128):12–14, 1987.
195. Lyons, C. W., Berquist, T. H., Lyons, J. C., et al.: Evaluation of radiographic findings in painful hip arthroplasties. Clin. Orthop. *195*:239–251, 1985.
196. Maderazo, E. G., Judson, S., and Pasternak, H.: Late infections of total joint prostheses. A review and recommendations for prevention. Clin. Orthop. *229*:131–142, 1988.
197. Mahan, J., Selgison, D., Henry, S. L., et al.: Factors in pin tract infections. Orthopedics *14*:305–308, 1991.
198. Manders, E. K., Schenden, M. J., Furrey, J. A., et al.: Soft-tissue expansion: Concepts and complications. Plast. Reconstr. Surg. *74*:493–507, 1984.
199. Mason, A. C., Davison, S. P., and Manders, E. K.: Tissue expander infections in children: Look beyond the expander pocket. Ann. Plast. Surg. *43*:539–541, 1999.
200. Mates, S., Glaser, J., and Shapiro, K.: Treatment of cerebrospinal fluid shunt infections with medical therapy alone. Neurosurgery *11*:781–783, 1982.
201. Mayhall, C. G., Archer, N. H., Lamb, V. A., et al.: Ventriculostomy-related infections: A prospective epidemiologic study. N. Engl. J. Med. *310*:553–559, 1984.
202. McBride, L. R., Ruzevich, S. A., Pennington, D. G., et al.: Infectious complications associated with ventricular assist device support. Trans. Am. Soc. Artif. Intern. Organs *33*:201–202, 1994.
203. McCarthy, P. M., Portner, P. M., Oyer, P. E., et al.: Clinical experience with the Novacor ventricular assist system: Bridge-to-transplant and the transition to chronic application. J. Thorac. Cardiovasc. Surg. *102*:578–587, 1991.
204. McCarthy, P. M., Schmitt, S. K., Vargo, R. L., et al.: Implantable LVAD infections: Implications for permanent use of the device. Ann. Thorac. Surg. *61*:359–365, 1996.
205. McCarthy, P. M., Smedira, N. O., Vargo, R. L., et al.: One hundred patients with the HeartMate left ventricular assist device: Evolving concepts and technology. J. Thorac. Cardiovasc. Surg. *115*:904–912, 1998.
206. McCarthy, P. M., Wang, N., and Vargo, R.: Preperitoneal insertion of the HeartMate 1000 IP implantable left ventricular assist device. Ann. Thorac. Surg. *57*:634–638, 1994.
207. McLone, D. G., Czyzewski, D., Raimondi, A. J., and Sommers, R. C.: Central nervous system infections as a limiting factor in the intelligence of children with myelomeningocoele. Pediatrics *70*:338–342, 1982.
208. Miley, G. B., Scheller, A. D. J., and Turner, R. H.: Medical and surgical treatment of the septic hip with one-stage revision arthroplasty. Clin. Orthop. *170*:76–82, 1982.
209. Miller, J. D., Becker, D. P., Ward, J. D., et al.: Significance of intracranial hypertension in severe head injury. J. Neurosurg. *47*:503–516, 1977.
210. Mine, S., Sato, A., Yamaura, A., et al.: Eosinophilia of the cerebrospinal fluid in a case of shunt infection: Case report. Neurosurgery *19*:835–836,1986.
211. Modic, M., Pflanze, W., Feiglin, D., and Belhobek, G.: Magnetic resonance imaging of musculoskeletal infections. Radiol. Clin. North Am. *24*:247–258, 1986.
212. Mojcik, C. F., and Levy, J. H.: Aprotinin and the systemic inflammatory response after cardiopulmonary bypass. Ann. Thorac. Surg. *71*:745–754, 2001.
213. Molina, J. E.: Undertreatment and overtreatment of patients with infected antiarrhythmic implantable devices. Ann. Thorac. Surg. *63*:504–509, 1997.
214. Montgomery, V. L., Strotman, J. M., and Ross, M. P.: Impact of multiple organ system dysfunction and nosocomial infections on survival of children treated with extracorporeal membrane oxygenation after heart surgery. Crit. Care Med. *28*:526–531, 2000.
215. Moore, M. B., McCully, J. P., Luckenback, M., et al.: *Acanthamoeba* keratitis associated with soft contact lenses. Am. J. Ophthalmol. *100*:396–403, 1985.
216. Moorman, J. R., Steinbergen, C., Durack, D. T., et al.: *Aspergillus* infection of a permanent ventricular pacing lead. Pacing Clin. Electrophysiol. 7:361–366, 1984.
217. Morgan, G., Ginks, W., Siddons, H., and Leatham, A.: Septicemia in patients with an endocardial pacemaker. Am. J. Cardiol. *44*:221–224, 1979.
218. Morissette, I., Gourdeau, M., and Francoeur, J.: CSF shunt infections: A fifteen-year experience with emphasis on management and outcome. Can. J. Neurol. Sci. *20*:118–122, 1993.
219. Mornadi, M., Zembo, M. M., and Ciotti, M.: Infected tibial pseudarthrosis: A 2-year follow-up on patients treated by the Ilizarov technique. Orthopedics *12*:497–502, 1989.
220. Morrice, J. J., and Young, D. G.: Bacterial colonisation of Holter valves: A ten-year survey. Dev. Med. Child Neurol. *16*(Suppl. 32):85–90, 1974.
221. Mounsey, J. P., Griffith, M. J., Tynan, M., et al.: Antibiotic prophylaxis in permanent pacemaker implantation: A prospective randomised trial. Br. Heart J. *72*:339–343, 1994.

222. Muers, M. F., Arnold, A. G., and Sleight, P.: Prophylactic antibiotics for cardiac pacemaker implantation: A prospective trial. Br. Heart J. *46*:539–544, 1981.
223. Murray, W. R.: Use of antibiotic-containing bone cement. Clin. Orthop. *190*:89–95, 1984.
224. Narayan, R. K., Kishore, P. R. S., Becker, D. P., et al.: Intracranial pressure: To monitor or not to monitor? A review of our experience with severe head injury. J. Neurosurg. *56*:650–659, 1982.
225. Naveira, F. A., Speight, K. L., and Rauck, R. L., et al.: Meningitis after injection of intrathecal baclofen. Anesth. Analg. *82*:1297–1299, 1996.
226. Nelson, J. D.: Cerebrospinal fluid shunt infections. Pediatr. Infect. Dis. *3*(Suppl.):30–32, 1984.
227. Nicholas, J. L., Kamal, I. M., and Eckstein, H. B.: Immediate shunt replacement in the treatment of bacterial colonisation of Holter valves. Dev. Med. Child Neurol. *12*(Suppl. 22):110–113, 1970.
228. NIH consensus conference. Cochlear implants in adults and children. J. A. M. A. *274*:1955–1961, 1995.
229. Nijhof, M. W., Oyen, W. J., van Kampen, A., et al.: Hip and knee arthroplasty infection. In 111–IgG scintigraphy in 102 cases. Acta Orthop. Scand. *68*:332–336, 1997.
230. North, B., and Reilly, P.: Comparison among three methods of intracranial pressure recording. Neurosurgery *18*:730–732, 1986.
231. O'Brien, M., Parent, A., and Davis, B.: Management of ventricular shunt infections. Childs Brain *5*:304–309, 1979.
232. Odio, C., McCracken, G. H., and Nelson, J. D.: CSF shunt infections in pediatrics. Am. J. Dis. Child. *138*:1103–1108, 1984.
233. Ohrstrom, J. K., Skou, J. K., Ejlertsen, T., Kosteljanetz, M.: Infected ventriculostomy: Bacteriology and treatment. Acta Neurochir. (Wien) *100*:67–69, 1989.
234. O'Keeffe, P. T., and Bayston, R.: Pneumococcal meningitis in a child with a ventriculoperitoneal shunt. J. Infect. *22*:77–79, 1991.
235. Oldershaw, P. J., Sutton, M. G., Ward, D., et al.: Ten-year experience of 359 epicardial pacemaker systems: Complications and results. Clin. Cardiol. *5*:515–519, 1982.
236. Olsen, L., and Frykberg, T.: Complications in the treatment of hydrocephalus in children. Acta Paediatr. Scand. *72*:385–390, 1983.
237. O'Neill, D. A., and Harris, W. H.: Failed total hip replacement: Assessment by plain radiographs, arthrograms and aspiration of the hip joint. J. Bone Joint Surg. Am. *66*:540–546, 1984.
238. Onofrio, B. M., and Yaksh, T. L.: Long-term pain relief produced by intrathecal morphine infusion in 53 patients. J. Neurosurg. *72*:200–204, 1992.
239. O'Nunain, S., Perez, I., Roelke, M., et al.: The treatment of patients with infected implantable cardioverter-defibrillator systems. J. Thorac. Cardiovasc. Surg. *113*:121–129, 1997.
240. Owen, R. J., Harper, W. M., Finlay, D. B., and Belton, I. P.: Isotope bone scans in patients with painful knee replacements: Do they alter management? Br. J. Radiol. *68*:1204–1207, 1995.
241. Oz, M. C., Argenziano, M., Catanese, K. A., et al.: Bridge experience with long-term implantable left ventricular assist devices: Are they an alternative to transplantation? Circulation *95*:1844–1852, 1997.
242. Page, E. L., and Eby, T. L.: Meningitis after cochlear implantation in Mondini malformation. Otolaryngol. Head Neck Surg. *116*:104–106, 1997.
243. Paley, D., Chaludray, M., Pirone, M., et al.: Treatment of malunions and mal-nonunions of the femur and tibia by detailed preoperative planning and the Ilizarov techniques. Orthop. Clin. North Am. *21*:667–679, 1990.
244. Pankowsky, D. A., Ziats, N. P., Topham, N. S., et al.: Morphologic characteristics of absorbed human plasma proteins on vascular grafts and biomaterials. J. Vasc. Surg. *11*:599–606, 1990.
245. Papagelopoulos, P. J., Hay, J. E., Galanis, E., and Morrey, B. F.: Infection around joint replacements in patients who have a renal or liver transplantation. J. Bone Joint Surg. Am. *80*:607–608, 1998.
246. Papo, I., and Caruselli, G.: Long-term intracranial pressure monitoring in comatose patients suffering from head injuries: A critical survey. Acta Neurochir. (Wien) *39*:187–200, 1977.
247. Patrick, D., Marcotte, P., and Garber, G. E.: Acute abdomen in the patient with a ventriculoperitoneal shunt. Can. J. Surg. *33*:37–40, 1990.
248. Pearson, R. L., and Perry, C. R.: The Ilizarov technique in the treatment of infected tibial nonunions. Orthop. Rev. *18*:609–626, 1989.
249. Penn, R. A.: Intrathecal baclofen for spasticity of spinal origin. Seven years of experience. J. Neurosurg. *77*:236–240, 1992.
250. Pennington, D. G., McBride, L. R., Peigh, P. S., et al.: Eight years' experience with bridging to cardiac transplantation. J. Thorac. Cardiovasc. Surg. *107*:472–481, 1994.
251. Perry, H. E., Wright, R. O., Shannon, M. W., et al.: Baclofen overdose: Drug experimentation in a group of adolescents. Pediatrics *101*:1045–1048, 1998.
252. Petty, W.: The effect of methylmethacrylate on bacterial inhibiting properties of normal human serum. Clin. Orthop. *132*:266–277, 1978.
253. Petty, W.: The effect of methylmethacrylate on bacterial phagocytosis and killing by human polymorphonuclear leukocytes. J. Bone Joint Surg. Am. *60*:752–757, 1978.
254. Piatt, J. H.: Cerebrospinal fluid shunt failure: Late is different from early. Pediatr. Neurosurg. *23*:133–136, 1995.
255. Pittman, T., Williams, D., Rathore, M., et al.: The role of ethylene oxide allergy in sterile shunt malfunctions. Br. J. Neurosurg. *8*:41–43, 1994.
256. Plummer, J. L., Cherry, D. A., Cousins, M. J., et al.: Long-term spinal administration of morphine in cancer and non-cancer pain: A retrospective study. Pain *44*:215–220, 1991.
257. Pople, I. K., Bayston, R., and Hayward, R. D.: Infection of cerebrospinal fluid shunts in infants: A study of etiological factors. J. Neurosurg. *77*:29–36, 1992.
258. Pople, I. K., Mulbauer, M. S., Sanford, R. A., et al.: Results and complications of intracranial pressure monitoring in 303 children. Pediatr. Neurosurg. *23*:64–69, 1995.
259. Poss, R., Thornhill, T. S., Ewald, F. C., et al.: Factors influencing the incidence and outcome of infection following total joint arthroplasty. Clin. Orthop. *182*:117–126, 1984.
260. Preventing pacemaker infections. Lancet *1*:537–538, 1986.
261. Pring, D. J., Henderson, R. G., Rivett, A. G., et al.: Autologous granulocyte scanning of painful prosthetic joints. J. Bone Joint Surg. Br. *68*:647–652, 1986.
262. Proctor, R. A.: The staphylococcal fibronectin receptor: Evidence for its importance in invasive infections. Rev. Infect. Dis. *9*(Suppl.):335–340, 1987.
263. Raithel, S. C., Pennington, D. G., Boegner, E., et al.: Extracorporeal membrane oxygenation in children after cardiac surgery. Circulation *86*(Suppl. II):305–310, 1992.
264. Rand, J. A., and Fitzgerald, R. H., Jr.: Diagnosis and management of the infected total knee arthroplasty. Orthop. Clin. North Am. *20*:201–210, 1989.
265. Rand, J. A., Morrey, B. F., and Bryan, R. S.: Management of the infected total joint arthroplasty. Orthop. Clin. North Am. *15*:491–504, 1984.
266. Raut, V. V., Orth, M. S., Orth, M. C., et al.: One stage revision arthroplasty of the hip for deep gram negative infection. Int. Orthop. *20*:12–14, 1996.
267. Reid, G.: Bacterial colonization of prosthetic devices and measures to prevent infection. New Horizons *6*(Suppl. 2):58–63.
268. Renier, D., Lacombe, J., Pierre-Kahn, A., et al.: Factors causing acute shunt infection. Computer analysis of 1174 operations. J. Neurosurg. *61*:1072–1078, 1984.
269. Rennels, M. B., and Wald, E. R.: Treatment of *Haemophilus influenzae* type b meningitis in children with cerebrospinal fluid shunts. J. Pediatr. *97*:424–426, 1980.
270. Rettig, G., Doenecke, P., Sen, L., et al.: Complications with retained transvenous pacemaker electrodes. Am. Heart J. *98*:587–594, 1979.
271. Reynolds, M., Sherman, J. O., and McLone, D. G.: Ventriculoperitoneal shunt infection masquerading as an acute surgical abdomen. J. Pediatr. Surg. *18*:951–954, 1983.
272. Rieder, M. J., Frewen, T. C., DelMaestro, R. F., et al.: The effect of cephalothin prophylaxis on postoperative ventriculoperitoneal shunt infections. Can. Med. Assoc. J. *136*:935–938, 1987.
273. Roitberg, B. Z., Tomita, T., and McLone, D. G.: Abdominal cerebrospinal fluid pseudocyst: A complication of ventriculoperitoneal shunt in children. Pediatr. Neurosurg. *29*:267–273, 1998.
274. Ronan, A., Hogg, G. G., and Klug, G. L.: Cerebrospinal fluid shunt infections in children. Pediatr. Infect. Dis. J. *14*:782–786, 1995.
275. Rosner, M. H., and Becker, D. P.: ICP monitoring: Complications and associated risks factors. Clin. Neurosurg. *23*:494–519, 1976.
276. Rubin, R. C., Ghatak, N. R., and Kisudhipan, P.: Asymptomatic perforated viscus and gram-negative ventriculitis as a complication of valve-regulated ventriculoperitoneal shunts. J. Neurosurg. *37*:616–618, 1972.
277. Rubinstein, J. T., Gantz, F. J., and Parkinson, W. S.: Management of cochlear implant infections. Am. J. Otol. *20*:46–49, 1999.
278. Rupp, M. E., Ulphani, J. S., Fey, P. D., et al.: Characterization of the importance of polysaccharide intercellular/hemagglutinin of *Staphylococcus epidermidis* in the pathogenesis of biomaterial-based infection in a mouse foreign body infection model. Infect. Immun. *67*:2627–2632, 1999.
279. Salmon, J. H.: Adult hydrocephalus: Evaluation of shunt therapy in 80 patients. J. Neurosurg. *37*:423–428, 1972.
280. Samtleben, W., Bauriedel, G., Bosch, T., et al.: Renal complications of infected ventriculoatrial shunts. Artif. Organs *17*:695–701, 1993.
281. Samuel, M., Finnerty, G. T., and Rudge, P.: Intrathecal baclofen pump infection treated by adjuvant intrareservoir antibiotic instillation. J. Neurol. Neurosurg. Psychiatry *57*:1146–1147, 1994.
282. Samuels, L. E., Samuels, F. L., Kaufman, M. S., et al.: Management of infected implantable cardiac defibrillators. Ann. Thorac. Surg. *64*:1702–1706, 1997.
283. Sanderson, P. J.: Infection in orthopaedic implants. J. Hosp. Infect. *18*(Suppl. A):367–375, 1991.
284. Sanzen, L., and Sundberg, M.: Periprosthetic low-grade hip infections. Erythrocyte sedimentation rate and C-reactive protein in 23 cases. Acta Orthop. Scand. *68*:461–465, 1997.
285. Schoenbaum, S. C., Gardner, P., and Shilliot, J.: Infections of cerebrospinal fluid shunts: Epidemiology, clinical manifestations, and therapy. J. Infect. Dis. *131*:543–552, 1975.

286. Schoifet, S. D., and Morrey, B. F.: Treatment of infection after total knee arthroplasty by débridement with retention of the components. J. Bone Joint Surg. Am. *72*:1383–1390, 1990.
287. Schultz, M., Moore, K., and Foote, A. W.: Bacterial ventriculitis and duration of ventriculostomy catheter insertion. J. Neurosci. Nurs. *25*:158–164, 1993.
288. Schwartz, J. G., Tio, F. O., and Fetchick, R. J.: Filamentous *Histoplasma capsulatum* involving a ventriculoatrial shunt. Neurosurgery *18*:487–490, 1986.
289. Sculco, T. P.: The economic impact of infected total joint arthroplasty. Instr. Course Lect. *42*:349–356, 1993.
290. Sells, C. J., Shurtleff, D. B., and Loeser, J. D.: Gram-negative cerebrospinal fluid shunt-associated infections. Pediatrics *59*:614–618, 1977.
291. Selman, W. R., Spetzler, R. F., Wilson, C. B., and Grollmus, J. W.: Percutaneous lumboperitoneal shunt: Review of 130 cases. Neurosurgery *6*:255–257, 1980.
292. Selwyn, S., and Ellis, H.: Skin bacteria and skin disinfection reconsidered. B. M. J. *1*:136–140, 1972.
293. Shtarker, H., David, R., Stolero, J., et al.: Treatment of open tibial fractures with primary suture and Ilizarov fixation. Clin. Orthop. *335*:268–274, 1997.
294. Shurtleff, D. B., Foltz, E. L., Weeks, R. D., and Loeser, J.: Therapy of *Staphylococcus epidermidis:* Infections associated with cerebrospinal fluid shunts. Pediatrics *53*:55–62, 1974.
295. Shurtleff, D. B., Stuntz, J. T., and Hayden, P. W.: Experience with 1201 cerebrospinal fluid shunt procedures. Pediatr. Neurosci. *12*:49–57, 1986.
296. Siegfried, R. N., Jacobson, L., and Chabal, C.: Development of an acute withdrawal syndrome following the cessation of intrathecal baclofen in a patient with spasticity. Anesthesiology *77*:1048–1050, 1992.
297. Sinha, P., Chen, J. M., Flannery, M., et al.: Infections during left ventricular assist device support do not affect posttransplant outcomes. Circulation *102*(Suppl. III):194–199, 2000.
298. Smith, P. N., Vidaillet, H. J., Hayes, J. J., et al.: Infections with nonthoracotomy implantable cardioverter defibrillators: Can these be prevented? Pacing Clin. Electrophysiol. *21*:42–55, 1998.
299. Smith, R. W., and Alksne, J. F.: Infections complicating the use of external ventriculostomy. J. Neurosurg. *44*:567–570, 1976.
300. Spangehl, M., Masri, B., O'Connell, J., and Duncan, C.: Prospective analysis of preoperative and intraoperative investigations for the diagnosis of infection at the sites of 202 revision total hip arthroplasties. J. Bone Joint Surg. Am. *81*:672–683, 1997.
301. Spangehl, M. J., Younger, A. S. E., Masri, B. A., et al.: Diagnosis of infection following total hip arthroplasty. J. Bone Joint Surg. Am. *79*:1578–1588, 1997.
302. Spencer, M., and Bird, G.: Device-related nonintravascular infections. Crit. Care Nurs. Clin. North Am. *7*:685–693, 1995.
303. Spinler, S. A., Nawarskas, J. J., Foote, E. F., et al.: Clinical presentation and analysis of risk factors for infectious complications of implantable cardioverter-defibrillator implantations at a university medical center. Clin. Infect. Dis. *26*:1111–1116, 1998.
304. Stamos, J. K., Kaufman, B. A., and Yogev, R.: Ventriculoperitoneal shunt infections with gram-negative bacteria. Neurosurgery *33*:858–862, 1993.
305. Stark, W. J., Worthen, D. M., Holladay, J. T., et al.: The FDA report on intraocular lenses. Ophthalmology *90*:311–317, 1983.
306. Steckelberg, J. M., and Osmon, D. R.: Prosthetic joint infections. *In* Waldvogel, F. A., and Bisno, A. L. (eds.): Infections Associated with Indwelling Medical Devices. 3rd ed. Washington, DC, A. S. M. Press, 2000, pp. 173–209.
307. Stehr-Green, J., Bailey, T. M., Brandt, F. H., et al.: *Acanthamoeba* keratitis in soft contact lens wearers. J. A. M. A. *258*:57–60, 1987.
308. Stenager, E., Gerner-Smidt, P., and Kock-Jensen, C.: Ventriculostomy-related infections—an epidemiological study. Acta Neurochir. *83*:20–23, 1986.
309. Stern, S., Bayston, R., and Hayward, R. J.: *Haemophilus influenzae* meningitis in the presence of cerebrospinal fluid shunts. Childs Nerv. Syst. *4*:164–166, 1988.
310. Stern, S. H., Insall, J. N., Windsor, R. E., et al.: Total knee arthroplasty in patients with psoriasis. Clin. Orthop. *248*:108–111, 1989.
311. Stewart, M. P. M., and Kelly, I. G.: Total shoulder replacement in rheumatoid disease: 7–13 year followup of 37 joints. J. Bone Joint Surg. Br. *79*:68–72, 1997.
312. Stotka, J. L., Rupp, M. E., Meier, F. A., et al.: Meningitis due to *Neisseria mucosa:* Case report and review. Rev. Infect. Dis. *13*:837–841, 1991.
313. Sun, B. C., Catanese, K. A., Spanier, T. B., et al.: 100 Long-term implantable left ventricular assist devices: The Columbia Presbyterian interim experience. Ann. Thorac. Surg. *68*:688–694, 1999.
314. Sundbärg, G., Kjällquistt, A., Lungberg, N., and Pontén, U.: Complications due to prolonged ventricular fluid pressure recordings in clinical practice. *In* Borck, M., and Dietz, H. (eds.): Intracranial Pressure: Experimental and Clinical Aspects. Berlin, Springer-Verlag, 1972, pp. 348–352.
315. Sutherland, K., Mahoney, J. R., II, Coury, A. J., and Eaton, J. W.: Degradation of biomaterials by phagocyte-derived oxidants. J. Clin. Invest. *92*:2360–2367, 1993.
316. Swayne, R., Rampling, A., and Newsom, S. W. B.: Intraventricular vancomycin for treatment of shunt-associated ventriculitis. J. Antimicrob. Chemother. *19*:249–253, 1987.
317. Tang, L., and Eaton, J. W.: Inflammatory responses to biomaterials. Am. J. Clin. Pathol. *103*:466–471, 1995.
318. Teddy, P., Jamous, A., Gardner, B., et al.: Complications of intrathecal baclofen delivery. Br. J. Neurosurg. *6*:115–118, 1992.
319. Thompson, D. N., Malcolm, G. P., Jones, B. M., et al.: Intracranial pressure in single-suture craniosynostosis. Pediatr. Neurosurg. *22*:235–239, 1995.
320. Thompson, T. P., and Albright, A. L.: *Propionibacterium acnes* infections of cerebrospinal fluid shunts. Childs Nerv. Syst. *14*:378–380, 1998.
321. Toy, P. T. C. Y., Lai, L. W., Drake, T. A., and Sande, M. A.: Effect of fibronectin on adherence of *Staphylococcus aureus* to fibrin thrombi in vitro. Infect. Immun. *48*:83–86, 1985.
322. Trappe, H. J., Pfitzner, P., and Klein, H.: Infections after cardioverter-defibrillator implantation: Observations in 335 patients over 10 years. Br. Heart J. *73*:20–24, 1995.
323. Tung, H., Raffel, C., and McComb, J. G.: Ventricular cerebrospinal fluid eosinophilia in children with ventriculoperitoneal shunts. J. Neurosurg. *75*:541–544, 1991.
324. Tunkel, A. R., Thomas, C. Y., and Wispelwey, B.: *Candida* prosthetic arthritis: Report of a case treated with fluconazole and review of the literature. Am. J. Med. *94*:100–103, 1993.
325. Turkisher, V., Priel, I., and Dan, M.: Successful management of an infected implantable cardioverter defibrillator with oral antibiotics and without removal of the device. Pacing Clin. Electrophysiol. *20*:2268–2270, 1997.
326. Ure, K. J., Amstutz, H. C., Nasser, S., and Schmalzried, T. P.: Direct-exchange arthroplasty for the treatment of infection after total hip replacement. An average ten-year follow-up. J. Bone Joint Surg. Am. *80*:961–968, 1998.
327. Vaudaux, P., Francois, P., Lew, D. P., and Waldvogel, F. A.: Host factors predisposing to and influencing therapy of foreign body infections. *In* Waldvogel, F. A., and Bisno, A. L. (eds.): Infections Associated with Indwelling Medical Devices. 3rd ed. Washington, DC, A. S. M. Press, 2000, pp. 1–26.
328. Vaudaux, P. E., Zulian, G., Huggler, E., and Waldvogel, F. A.: Attachment of *Staphylococcus aureus* to polymethylmethacrylate increases its resistance to phagocytosis in foreign body infection. Infect. Immun. *50*:472–477, 1985.
329. Venes, J. L.: Control of shunt infection: Report of 150 consecutive cases. J. Neurosurg. *45*:311–314, 1976.
330. Vercellotti, G. M., McCarthy, J. D., Lindholm, P., et al.: Extracellular matrix proteins (fibronectin, laminin and type IV collagen) bind and aggregate bacteria. Am. J. Pathol. *120*:13–21, 1985.
331. Vernet, O., Campiche, R., and de Tribolet, N.: Long-term results after ventriculoatrial shunting in children. Childs Nerv. Syst. *9*:253–255, 1993.
332. Vertullo, C. J., Duke, P. F., and Askin, G. N.: Pin-site complications of the halo thoracic brace with routine pin re-tightening. Spine *22*:2514–2516, 1997.
333. Victor, F., DePlace, C., Camus, C., et al.: Pacemaker lead infection: Echocardiographic features, management, and outcome. Heart *81*:82–87, 1999.
334. Vinchon, M., Vallee, L., Prin, L., et al.: Cerebro-spinal fluid eosinophilia in shunt infections. Neuropediatrics *23*:235–240, 1992.
335. Vogt, P. R., Sagdic, K., Lachat, M., et al.: Surgical management of infected permanent transvenous pacemaker systems: Ten year experience. J. Card. Surg. *11*:180–186, 1996.
336. Voldby, B., and Enevoldsen, E. M.: Intracranial pressure changes following aneurysm rupture. Part 1: Clinical and angiopathic correlations. J. Neurosurg. *56*:186–196, 1982.
337. Wade, J. S., and Cobbs, C. G.: Infections in cardiac pacemakers. Curr. Clin. Top. Infect. Dis. *9*:44–61, 1988.
338. Wald, S. L., and McLaurin, R. L.: Cerebrospinal fluid antibiotic levels during treatment of shunt infections. J. Neurosurg. *52*:41–46, 1980.
339. Walter, E. B., Jr., Gingras, J. L., and McKinney, R. E., Jr.: Systemic *Torulopsis glabrata* infection in a neonate. South. Med. J. *83*:837–838, 1990.
340. Walters, B. C.: Cerebrospinal fluid shunt infection. Neurosurg. Clin. North Am. *3*:387–401, 1992.
341. Walters, B. C., Hoffman, H. J., Hendrick, E. B., and Humphreys, R. P.: Cerebrospinal fluid shunt infection: Influences on initial management and subsequent outcome. J. Neurosurg. *60*:1014–1021, 1984.
342. Walters, H. L., III, Hakimi, M., Rice, M. D., et al.: Pediatric cardiac surgical ECMO: Multivariate analysis of risk factors for hospital death. Ann. Thorac. Surg. *60*:329–337, 1995.
343. Wang, K. C., Lee, H. J., Sung, J. N., and Cho, B. K.: Cerebrospinal fluid shunt infection in children: Efficiency of management protocol, rate of persistent shunt colonization, and significance of "off-antibiotics" trial. Childs Nerv. Syst. *15*:38–44, 1999.
344. Wang, R. C., Parisier, S. C., Weiss, M. H., et al.: Cochlear implant flap complications. Ann. Otol. Rhinol. Laryngol. *99*:791–795, 1990.
345. Watanabe, I., Hodges, G. R., Dworzack, D. L., et al.: Neurotoxicity of intrathecal gentamicin: A case report and experimental study. Ann. Neurol. *4*:564–572, 1978.

346. Weber, D. J., Hofman, K. L., Thoft, R. A., and Baker, A. S.: Endophthalmitis following intraocular lens implantation. Rev. Infect. Dis. *8*:12–80, 1986.
347. Weiss, M. H., Kurze, T., and Nulsen, F. E.: Antibiotic neurotoxicity: Laboratory and clinical study. J. Neurosurg. *41*:486–489, 1974.
348. Weyland, M., Hermann, M., Kondruweit, M., et al.: Clinical impact of infections of left ventricular assist device recipients: The importance of site and organism. Transplant. Proc. *29*:3327–3329, 1997.
349. Wilhelm, M. J., Schmid, C., Hammel, D., et al.: Cardiac pacemaker infection: Surgical management with and without extracorporeal circulation. Ann. Thorac. Surg. *64*:1707–1712, 1997.
350. Wilson, H. A., Jr., Downes, T. R., Julian, J. S., et al.: *Candida* endocarditis, a treatable form of pacemaker infection. Chest *103*:283–284, 1993.
351. Wilson, M. G., Kelley, K., and Thornhill, T. S.: Infection as a complication of total knee-replacement arthroplasty. Risk factors and treatment in sixty-seven cases. J. Bone Joint Surg. Am. *72*:878–883, 1990.
352. Wilson, M. W., Wobig, J. L., and Dailey, R. A.: Infection of a porous polyethylene orbital implant with *Capnocytophaga*. Ophthal. Plast. Reconstr. Surg. *14*:398–402, 1998.
353. Wilson, W. R., Greer, G. E., and Grubb, B. P.: Implantable cardioverter-defibrillators in children: A single-institutional experience. Ann. Thorac. Surg. *65*:775–781, 1998.
354. Wimmer, C., Gluch, H., Franzreb, M., and Ogon, M.: Predisposing factors for infection in spine surgery: A survey of 850 spinal procedures. J. Spinal Disord. *11*:124–128, 1998.
355. Winfield, J. A., Rosenthal, P., Kanter, R. K., et al.: Duration of intracranial pressure monitoring does not predict daily risk of infectious complications. Neurosurgery *33*:424–431, 1993.
356. Winn, H. R., Dacey, R. G., and Jane, J. A.: Intracranial subarachnoid pressure recording: Experience with 650 patients. Surg. Neurol. *8*:41–47, 1977.
357. Wyler, A. R., and Kelly, W. A.: Use of antibiotics with external ventriculostomies. J. Neurosurg. *37*:185–187, 1972.
358. Wymenga, A. B., van Horn, J. R., Theeuwes, A., et al.: Perioperative factors associated with septic arthritis after arthroplasty. Prospective multicenter study of 362 knee and 2,651 hip operations. Acta Orthop. Scand. *63*:665–671, 1992.
359. Yeh, L. K., Kao, S. C., Tsai, C. C., et al.: Delayed-onset of *Pseudomonas* infection in a hydroxyapatite orbital implant: A case report. Chung Hua I Hsueh Tsa Chih [Chinese Medical Journal] *62*:832–837, 1999.
360. Yogev, R.: Cerebrospinal fluid shunt infections: A personal view. Pediatr. Infect. Dis. J. *4*:113–118, 1985.
361. Younger, J. J., Christensen, G. D., Bartley, D. L., et al.: Coagulase-negative staphylococci isolated from cerebrospinal fluid shunts: Importance of slime production, species identification, and shunt removal to clinical outcome. J. Infect. Dis. *156*:548–554, 1987.
362. Zed, P. J., Stiver, G., Devonshire, V., et al.: Continuous intrathecal pump infusion of baclofen with antibiotic drugs for treatment of pump-associated meningitis. J. Neurosurg. *92*:347–349, 2000.
363. Zenz, M., Piepenbrock, S., and Tryba, M.: Epidural opiates: Long-term experiences in cancer pain. Klin. Wochenschr. *63*:225–229, 1985.
364. Ziomek, S., Harrell, J. E., Fasules, J. W., et al.: Extracorporeal membrane oxygenation for cardiac failure after congenital heart operation. Ann. Thorac. Surg. *54*:861–868, 1992.
365. Zipes, D. P., and Roberts, D.: Results of the international study of the implantable pacemaker cardioverter-defibrillator. A comparison of epicardial and endocardial lead systems. Circulation *92*:59–65, 1995.

Infections Related to Craniofacial Surgical Procedures

MARC A. MAZADE

Advancements in plastic and reconstructive surgery have created the opportunity for surgeons to offer patients with craniosynostosis, fibrous dysplasia, Crouzon syndrome, Apert syndrome, Treacher Collins syndrome, craniofacial clefts, and other anomalies relief from associated mechanical complications and restoration of a more normal cosmetic appearance. Operative procedures to address these problems involve cranial vault remodeling or reconstruction (or both) or advancement of the midface and maxillary block and, occasionally, correction of malocclusion by repositioning of the mandible. The overall incidence of infection associated with these procedures was 14.7 percent in one study,[9] but it varies greatly and may range from 3 to 45 percent, depending on the number of procedures attempted during a single anesthesia, the duration of surgery, and the structures involved. Bacteria may infect the wound or soft tissue area, may spread by contiguous extension through cortical bone during long periods of contact, or may extend through osteotomies that have disrupted the integrity of the periosteum and cortical bone barriers. Additionally, surgical alteration of the local blood supply to the cranial bones through disruption of medullary channels and removal of the adherent periosteum, as well as the presence of hardware required to secure the bony structures in their new locations, can render infection difficult to treat. Repeated or prolonged hospitalizations for previous surgeries, often for co-morbid conditions such as syndactyly, gastroesophageal reflux, or dysphagia, result in colonization of the skin and sinopulmonary tracts and subsequent postoperative infection with multidrug-resistant bacteria. Attempts to reduce the incidence of infection have made the use of parenteral prophylactic perioperative antibiotic regimens for 2 to 5 days commonplace.

Procedures and Osteotomies

Some familiarity with a few of the more common procedures in craniofacial surgery, beyond basic craniotomy and cranial vault remodeling, is necessary to understand the pathogenesis of associated infectious complications. Although every patient has a unique set of problems, several corrective procedures are used frequently and then modified as specifically needed for each circumstance.

In young children with midfacial retrusion, frontofacial monoblock advancement may be performed.[14] This procedure involves detachment and advancement of the entire facial bony mask, excluding the mandible. Exposure for this procedure commonly requires a large frontal craniotomy, the bone from which may be shaped to complete the repair or used as needed to form a suitable foundation to which the advanced block can be secured. Retraction of the frontal lobes is necessary to provide access to the roof of the orbits, and much of the procedure is performed intracranially. The boundaries of the advancement block are formed by osteotomies performed horizontally along the lower portion of the frontal bone and posteriorly along the roof of the orbits, vertically along the lateral and medial inferior walls and horizontally along the inferior walls of the orbits, and vertically through the zygomatic arches, with subsequent dissection and pterygomaxillary disjunction. Finally, a frontoethmoidal osteotomy divides the posterior portion of the nasal septum to free the monoblock so that it can be advanced and secured in place, perhaps by wiring it anteriorly to a slightly fore-tilted strip of frontal bone and stabilizing it laterally with wired-in strips of calvarial bone grafts to bridge gaps in the zygomatic arches. Bone blocks in the pterygomaxillary area help hold the maxillary portion forward. The temporary dead space created in the anterior cranial fossa after this procedure eventually is obliterated in a growing, developing child, although its persistence is problematic in some.[18] This intracranial procedure is associated with an inherent risk of developing meningitis, which is associated less frequently with the extracranial procedures described later, but it may still occur.[16]

A subcranial Le Forte III osteotomy sometimes is used for the treatment of midface retrusion in children and is preferred in adults.[10, 14] Exposure is provided likewise through a coronal incision, but a craniotomy is not necessary. Neither the orbital roof nor any portion of the frontal bone is advanced with this procedure. Osteotomies are required to free part of the medial, lateral, and inferior walls of the orbit and the nasal bridge, and the remainder of the block is freed by pterygopalatine disjunction and osteotomies of the zygomatic arch and posterior nasal septum. The entire inferior orbital and nasomaxillary unit is brought forward, and interposition grafts, hydroxyapatite and microplates, and wires secure the block in the advanced position. An intraoral stab incision may be required for pterygopalatine disjunction. As in the frontofacial advancement, split calvarial bone grafts bridge the space in the zygomatic arches.

If further advancement of the maxilla is desired, a subsequent Le Forte I osteotomy, which is an isolated maxillary advancement procedure that changes the position of the upper teeth, is performed.[10, 12, 14] This entirely intraoral procedure involves making various buccal sulcus and upper vestibular incisions. The palate and maxillary arch are freed for advancement by transverse osteotomies at the level of the nasal floor, through the nasal septum, and then posteriorly.

Another procedure that may be performed in some cases of Treacher Collins syndrome is the integrale (simultaneous midfacial and mandibular osteotomies).[14] In this complicated procedure requiring a tracheostomy, the midface osteotomies exclude the temporal, lateral walls of the orbits from the advanced block. In addition, C- or inverted V–shaped osteotomies through the mandibular rami with placement of interposition bone grafts and wiring provide advancement of the mandible. Split calvarial bone grafts subsequently reestablish the zygomatic arches. Incidentally, the bone grafts are harvested either by performing a true craniotomy or by removing the outer cortical bone table from the donor site.

More thorough descriptions of these and other operations, such as facial bipartition, are provided in the referenced texts,[10, 14] to which the reader is referred for a better grasp of the inherent risks of bacterial contamination from intraoral, sinus, and skin sources that are specific to each craniofacial procedure. Nonetheless, suffice it to say that the infections encountered usually are caused by bacteria that are resident or pathogenic in the clean-contaminated sites through which incisions and osteotomies are performed and that each additional site that is surgically violated increases the risk of developing infection.

Preoperative Preparation, Intraoperative Irrigation, and Perioperative Antibiotic Therapy

Because wounds created during craniofacial surgery fall between the clean-contaminated and contaminated category,[5, 6] attention to the treatment of dental caries, periodontal disease, and acute sinusitis is prudent before embarking on procedures involving intraoral incisions and trans-sinus osteotomies.[16] Protocols for the administration of perioperative antibiotics and for preoperative preparation of the oral cavity have been developed. Many of these protocols involve intraoral irrigation of the oral cavity with povidone-iodine (Betadine) solutions. Nonetheless, the sinus cavities do not lend themselves to preoperative antiseptic washing. Some surgeons make use of intraoperative antibiotic-containing irrigants to help reduce the incidence of infection. They may be flushed over the intact cranium after subperiosteal exposure and again before skin closure. Others prefer a solution of one part povidone-iodine to four parts saline for intraoperative irrigation.[16] No strong evidence supports any one approach over others for reducing infection.[9]

The choice and duration of perioperative antibiotics vary among surgical centers and their surgical teams. Antibiotic regimens may consist of penicillin; ampicillin-sulbactam; a first-, second-, or third-generation cephalosporin; clindamycin; or any two of these drugs in combination.[5, 6, 8, 9] Erythromycin is used in penicillin-allergic patients in some centers.[1]

Continuation of antibiotics may be necessary for 0 to 5 days postoperatively. The optimal duration is not clear. Higher infection rates have occurred in some centers that tried restricting antibiotics to intraoperative use only.[1] Recent reports from one orthognathic surgical center showed a 10-fold reduction in infection rates with a 5-day antibiotic regimen in comparison to a single-day regimen.[2] Furthermore, isolation of a few infecting organisms that were susceptible in vitro to an antibiotic given 6 hours preoperatively until 48 hours postoperatively suggests that longer durations of treatment with postoperative antibiotics are needed for more heavily contaminated wounds.[5] Some advocates of a shorter duration of treatment with perioperative antibiotics have suggested that longer administration of perioperative antibiotics contributes to infection with gram-negative organisms or may result in infection with more resistant gram-negative bacilli such as *Pseudomonas aeruginosa* or other pathogens such as *Candida albicans*.[6–9]

Nonetheless, although the use of antibiotics indeed does select for these organisms, many single-organism infections occurring after initiation of antibiotics might have been polymicrobial were it not for intraoperative and immediate postoperative treatment. From an infectious disease perspective, continuation of antibiotics beyond the intraoperative period is similar to treatment of an open fracture and not very much like antibiotic prophylaxis in the traditional sense. Perhaps better stated is that the use of intraoperative antibiotics may reduce the inoculum of mucosal flora and that immediate postoperative treatment may kill bacteria that have contaminated other operative sites, including surgically fractured bone.

Epidemiology

Infections that may be encountered include cellulitis and dehiscence of the wound, infection of subgaleal fluid, osteomyelitis, focal soft tissue abscesses, epidural abscesses,[18] and septicemia. In many instances, infection permeates the entire operative field and encompasses any number of these specific entities.[9] Donor bone graft sites may be involved in some instances.

The development of meningitis always is a concern when craniofacial procedures are performed. The occurrence of a cerebrospinal fluid (CSF) leak is a predisposing factor, and meningitis may be manifested years after the procedure in the case of a leak.[16] However, the dura provides a significant barrier to infection when painstaking neurosurgical technique is applied during repair. In fact, no cases of meningitis were identified from a combined report of complications after 567 procedures spanning 6.5 years at Medical City Dallas Hospital and the Division of Plastic Surgery at the University of Pennsylvania, primarily for cranial vault remodeling,[8] nor from an earlier report of 170 transcranial operations spanning 10 years at the South Australian Cranio-Facial Unit in which 53 accidental dural tears occurred and 32 planned dural openings were performed.[7] Nonetheless, meningitis has been documented to occur in association with a frontal abscess with osteomyelitis, subgaleal fluid infection, and contamination of CSF drains.[9]

The Australian group just mentioned documented an average operative time of 10.5 hours for patients in whom a postoperative infection developed, 2.5 hours longer than operations on patients in whom an infection did not develop.[7] However, these observations were confounded by variables such as type of procedure and whether the procedure was a primary or subsequent one. Longer and more complicated monoblock advancement procedures have been associated with infection rates as high as 45 percent,[9] whereas anterior cranial vault remodeling may be associated with infection rates as low as 2.5 percent.[8] In staged or subsequent procedures, the dura encountered during primary craniofacial procedures is manipulated more easily and has better vascularization than does the scarred dura encountered in more complicated and laborious secondary procedures, which are associated with higher rates of infection.[8] Additionally, of note is that craniofacial postoperative infections develop in infants far less frequently than in older children, who develop infections less frequently than do adults.[7, 8] Whether this age difference is a reflection of the types of surgery performed in infants or other microbial or host factors is not clear.

As experience in craniofacial surgery has grown, the reduction in the frequency of infection has been attributed to shortened operative time, attempts to avoid entrance into the contaminated sinus cavities (an easier task in young children, in whom the sinuses are often still poorly developed), and mucosal repair at the end of surgery.[17] The mean time to diagnosis of infection is approximately 10 days.[9]

Microbiology

Organisms causing infection include flora of the skin such as *Staphylococcus aureus, Staphylococcus epidermidis,* beta-hemolytic streptococci, and *Propionibacterium acnes;* resident flora of the oropharynx such as *Bacteroides* spp., *Corynebacterium* spp., various alpha-hemolytic streptococci, *Eikenella corrodens,* and *Haemophilus influenzae* and *parainfluenzae;* and some nosocomial gram-negative bacilli such as *Pseudomonas aeruginosa, Escherichia coli, Klebsiella* spp., and *Acinetobacter calcoaceticus.*[5, 8] Procedures that disrupt the oropharynx and sinus cavities are more apt to be complicated by polymicrobial infections. Procedures that do not violate these spaces are more inclined to be complicated solely by infection with skin flora. The frequency of infection with *Candida* spp. may rival the frequency of infection with more common bacteria.[8, 18]

Evaluation

Postoperative craniofacial surgical infection may be an obvious conclusion if heralded by the development of fever; rapid development of unilateral local soft tissue warmth, tenderness, and erythema; and rapid recurrence of swelling.[4] However, reasons for the delay in diagnosis and definitive treatment of some infections are multifactorial. Postoperative swelling may persist for some time, often improving and worsening in dependent areas according to the patient's sleeping or resting position. Periorbital tissues are particularly prone to fluctuations in swelling. Violaceous discoloration and bruising of the overlying skin may complicate assessment further. In addition, the overall facial appearance of the child may be so altered by the surgical intervention that parents may not recognize subtle signs of infection immediately. In some instances, large distances may separate the child from the craniofacial surgery referral center after discharge from the hospital, and the surgeon must rely on verbal descriptions of the child's postoperative appearance from concerned caregivers. Therefore, patients who live far from the referral center should be educated that prompt local medical evaluation along with a phone call to the craniofacial surgeon at the referral center can assist in early diagnosis, determination of bacteriology by needle aspiration, and initiation of preliminary treatment while traveling back to the referral center. Prescription of oral antibiotics in the hope of preserving the tenuous bone grafts without aspiration may render interpreting subsequent surgical culture results difficult.

Evaluation of extraocular movement may be limited by the age of the child, postoperative swelling, and, frequently, the limited capacity of the patient to comply interactively with the examination. Few operations, however, limit the ability to assess the presence of meningismus. Some patients may exhibit lassitude, lethargy, or increased irritability, subtle signs in children who have limited capacities to communicate.

The wound, which often is a coronal incision, should be examined closely on an ongoing basis. Purulent or seropurulent wound drainage or persistent serous wound drainage usually is indicative of underlying soft tissue and possibly bone infection, although infection may not be limited to the structures located directly beneath an area of wound dehiscence.[4] Drainage at one location along a wound may be the result of inflammatory fluids that originate elsewhere and are following a hydrodynamic gravity flow pattern or an established route to a low-pressure efflux portal at a nonhealing area of the wound, especially when the infection has become well established. Likewise, fluid collections in suborbital areas of the face such as the malar or submalar areas may suggest a local abscess when, in fact, the primary site of infection is cranial.

Laboratory abnormalities may be subtle. Leukocytosis may be present. The erythrocyte sedimentation rate has been shown to peak approximately 5 days after major orthopedic surgery, with a slow and irregular decline for a period of 3 to 9 weeks, but it provides little diagnostic value initially.[3, 11, 15] C-reactive protein (CRP) levels peak within 2 to 3 days but usually normalize within 21 postoperative days.[3, 11, 13, 15] Because an abrupt increase in CRP may be indicative of infection, some orthopedic centers monitor CRP levels after elective procedures to assist in early detection of infection after total-joint replacement and spinal surgery.[11, 15] Similarly, monitoring serial CRP levels is helpful when trying to discriminate between infection and shifting postoperative dependent swelling and in assessing the response to therapy in a craniofacial surgical patient.

Needle aspiration of underlying fluid collections is the best primary means of diagnosing infection, especially if significant residual postoperative swelling has made clinical assessment of a particular area difficult. In most instances, needle aspiration cultures are superior to surface cultures of wound drainage, which often yield coagulase-negative staphylococci of uncertain significance. However, cultures of wound drainage sometimes grow obvious pathogens and may be helpful.

Diagnostic imaging such as computed tomography with contrast or magnetic resonance imaging may identify occult fluid collections, but diagnosing bone infection, especially in the flat bones of the cranium, is difficult with these modalities. Not infrequently, focal enhancement of the meninges in regions where the cranium has been manipulated is noted on postoperative imaging. Corresponding postoperative cerebral gliosis likewise can be difficult to differentiate from cerebritis developing near an area of infection above the dura. Serial weekly or biweekly imaging can provide a means of ongoing evaluation of these abnormalities inasmuch as neurologic manifestations of cerebritis in the frontal lobes may not be elucidated easily.

Treatment

Management of infections complicating craniofacial procedures is primarily surgical. Open débridement, inspection and scraping of contiguous bone, and copious pressurized saline irrigation are essential. The value of adding antibiotics to the irrigant is questionable. Some physicians argue that irrigation with Betadine may devitalize tissues that participate in the healing process and should not be used, whereas others avoid using Betadine irrigation because of concern about systemic iodine absorption.[8] Removal of all hardware provides the best chance for eradicating the infection, but occasionally, as in the case of procedures that involve maxillary distraction devices, removing all the hardware initially is impractical. Nonetheless, distraction pins may dislodge as the integrity of the bone is compromised by infection.

Placement of several drains ensures an opportunity for drainage of what otherwise would remain sequestered focal soft tissue fluid collections. Continuous subgaleal "flow-through" irrigation with saline at a rate of 15 to 30 mL/hr (with or without antibiotic additives) is an adjunctive measure instituted by some surgeons, whereas others question the advisability of performing this approach.[8] Removal of devitalized bone and any bone grafts in the infected surgical bed is an unpopular but necessary part of treatment. Failure to do so may result in multifocal osteomyelitis, possible meningitis or cerebritis, and persistence of chronic infection with potentially multidrug-resistant organisms.

Reluctance by the surgical team to aggressively and widely excise infected bone and remove devitalized bone is understandable because the initial surgery itself involves extensive planning, operative time, and anesthetic risk; in addition, interposition grafts may provide architectural platforms for the advanced structures, and successful treatment of these infections has been reported in some surgical centers in which the initial bony débridement is limited to areas of visibly apparent osteitis.[8] As an advisor, the infectious disease consultant should point out evidence of persistent infection; suggest the possibility of deeper or more serious infection when concern arises; alert the surgical team when a point of failure of medical therapy has been reached; and emphasize that antimicrobial therapy is only an adjuvant to bony débridement and copious intraoperative irrigation, which may improve the outcome and limit the spread of infection.

Recurrent wound dehiscence and continued wound drainage should prompt thorough exploration of the soft tissues and bone for evidence of osteomyelitis or retained hardware, including wires. Advanced infection in devitalized bone cannot be treated effectively in situ, and often entire bone plates must be removed and subsequent cranioplasty performed months later.

For infections that complicate procedures not involving the oropharynx or sinus cavities, an antistaphylococcal antibiotic such as vancomycin, cefazolin, or nafcillin may be an appropriate empiric antibiotic choice pending the results of intraoperative drainage and débridement cultures. A third-generation cephalosporin with or without an aminoglycoside may be considered if the risk of developing infection with a nosocomial pathogen is high because of prolonged hospitalization or persistent tracheal colonization with gram-negative bacilli such as *Pseudomonas*[7] or if infection of the central nervous system threatens. Infections complicating procedures involving the oropharynx or sinuses often are caused by organisms resistant to the perioperative prophylactic antibiotic chosen.[5] Thus, it may be reasonable to consider antibiotic therapy with clindamycin or metronidazole when a cephalosporin has been used or with a second- or third-generation cephalosporin or ampicillin-sulbactam when clindamycin had been used prophylactically. The duration of antibiotic therapy must be individualized to each case. A period of 6 weeks of antibiotics has been suggested for cases in which osteomyelitis is suspected.[16]

REFERENCES

1. Acebal-Bianco, F., Vuylsteke, P. L., Mommaerts, M. Y., and De Clercq, C. A.: Perioperative complications in corrective facial orthopedic surgery: A 5-year retrospective study. J. Oral Maxillofac. Surg. *58*:754–760, 2000.
2. Bentley, K. C., Head, T. W., and Aiello, G. A.: Antibiotic prophylaxis in orthognathic surgery: A 1-day versus 5-day regimen. J. Oral Maxillofac. Surg. *57*:226–230, 1999.
3. Bilgen, O., Atici, T., Durak, K., et al.: C-reactive protein values and erythrocyte sedimentation rates after total hip and total knee arthroplasty. J. Int. Med. Res. *29*:7–12, 2001.
4. Carson, B. S., and Dufresne, C. R.: Surgical complications. *In* Dufresne, C. R., Carson, B. S., and Zinreich, S. J. (eds.): Complex Craniofacial Problems, a Guide to Analysis and Treatment. New York, Churchill Livingstone, 1992, pp. 467–487.
5. Clayman, G. L., Raad, I. I., Hankins, P. D., and Weber, R. S.: Bacteriologic profile of surgical infection after antibiotic prophylaxis. Head Neck *15*:526–531, 1993.
6. Conover, M. A., Kaban, L. B., and Mulliken, J. B.: Antibiotic prophylaxis for major maxillocraniofacial surgery. J. Oral Maxillofac. Surg. *43*:865–870, 1985.
7. David, D. J., and Cooter, R. D.: Craniofacial infection in 10 years of transcranial surgery. Plast. Reconstr. Surg. *80*:213–225, 1987.
8. Fearon, J. A., Yu, J., Bartlett, S. P., et al.: Infections in craniofacial surgery: A combined report of 567 procedures from two centers. Plast. Reconstr. Surg. *100*:862–868, 1997.
9. Israele, V., and Siegel, J. D.: Infectious complications of craniofacial surgery in children. Rev. Infect. Dis. *11*:9–15, 1989.
10. Kawamoto, H. K., Jr., and Cohen, S. R.: Aesthetic Le Forte I, II, and III. *In* Ousterhout, D. K. (ed.): Aesthetic Contouring of the Craniofacial Skeleton. Boston, Little, Brown, 1991, pp. 487–499.
11. Larsson, S., Thelander, U., and Friberg, S.: C-reactive protein (CRP) levels after elective orthopedic surgery. Clin. Orthop. *275*:237–242, 1992.
12. Mason, R. M., and Georgiade, N. G.: Facial osteotomies. *In* Georgiade, N. G., Georgiade, G. S., Riefkohl, R., and Barwick, W. (eds.): Essentials of

Plastic, Maxillofacial, and Reconstructive Surgery. Baltimore, Williams & Wilkins, 1987, pp. 332–340.
13. Rosahl, S. K., Gharabaghi, A., Zink, P. M., and Samii, M.: Monitoring of blood parameters following anterior cervical fusion. J. Neurosurg. *92*(Suppl.):169–174, 2000.
14. Stratoudakis, A. C.: An outline of craniofacial anomalies and principles of their correction. *In* Georgiade, N. G., Georgiade, G. S., Riefkohl, R., and Barwick, W. (eds.): Essentials of Plastic, Maxillofacial, and Reconstructive Surgery. Baltimore, Williams & Wilkins, 1987, pp. 299–331.
15. Thelander, U., and Larsson, S.: Quantitation of C-reactive protein levels and erythrocyte sedimentation rate after spinal surgery. Spine *17*:400–404, 1992.
16. Whitaker, L. A.: Problems and complications in craniofacial surgery. *In* Goldwyn, R. M. (ed.): The Unfavorable Result in Plastic Surgery, Avoidance and Treatment. 2nd ed. Boston, Little, Brown, 1984, pp. 229–250.
17. Whitaker, L. A., Munro, I. R., Salyer, K. E., et al.: Combined report of problems and complications in 793 craniofacial operations. Plast. Reconstr. Surg. *64*:198–203, 1979.
18. Wolfe, S. A.: The monoblock frontofacial advancement: Outcome after retrofrontal epidural abscess. *In* Craniofacial Surgery. Proceedings of the Sixth International Congress of the International Society of Cranio-Facial Surgery. Bologna, Italy, Munduzzi Editore, 1995, pp. 211–213.

Unclassified Infectious Diseases

CHAPTER 82 Kawasaki Disease

STANFORD T. SHULMAN

Kawasaki disease is an acute febrile multisystem vasculitic syndrome of unknown etiology affecting predominantly infants and young children. The diagnosis is based on characteristic clinical features (Table 82–1). Serious complications include coronary arteritis, coronary artery aneurysms and stenoses, coronary thrombosis leading to myocardial infarction, and, rarely, coronary aneurysm rupture.

Synonyms for Kawasaki disease include Kawasaki syndrome and mucocutaneous lymph node syndrome (MCLS, MLNS, or MCLNS). It also has been referred to as lymphomucocutaneous syndrome and similar terms. An earlier term was infantile periarteritis nodosa, a condition that is indistinguishable from fatal Kawasaki disease. The ninth revision of the International Classification of Diseases designates the condition as both Kawasaki disease and mucocutaneous lymph node syndrome (acute) (febrile) (infantile) under rubric 446.1. Before 1983, the National Library of Medicine listed publications of Kawasaki disease under various subject headings, particularly "Lymphatic Diseases." Since 1984, publications have been listed under "Mucocutaneous Lymph Node Syndrome."

Kawasaki disease has become the leading cause of acquired heart disease in children in most developed countries, including the United States and Japan.[340, 341] It has been reported in children of all racial groups and from all continents.

Although the etiology of Kawasaki disease remains unknown, administration of intravenous immunoglobulin (IVIG) and aspirin before the 10th day of illness generally has a dramatic effect on the clinical manifestations and markedly reduces the likelihood of development of coronary abnormalities (see "Treatment").[87, 228, 238, 239, 301, 346]

TABLE 82–1 ■ DIAGNOSTIC CRITERIA FOR KAWASAKI DISEASE

Fever for at least 5 days,* *plus*:
Presence of at least four of the following features:
- Bilateral conjunctival infection
- Polymorphous exanthem
- Changes in the lips and oral cavity (erythema, cracking of lips; oropharyngeal erythema; strawberry tongue)
- Peripheral extremity changes (erythema and swelling of hands and feet; later periungual desquamation, Beau lines)
- Cervical lymphadenopathy (at least 1.5 cm in diameter)

Exclusion of other diseases with similar features

Note: Fever plus three criteria in the presence of coronary abnormalities qualifies.
*In the presence of classic features, experienced clinicians may be able to establish the diagnosis before the fifth day of illness.

History

The illness now bearing his name was recognized first as a clinical entity in 1961 by Dr. Tomisaku Kawasaki, who subsequently became Chairman of the Department of Pediatrics at Tokyo's Japan Red Cross Medical Center. In that year, Kawasaki was the first to identify infants and young children who manifested a distinctive constellation of signs that included prolonged high fever, cervical adenopathy, bilateral conjunctival injection, erythematous rash, desquamation, changes of the mucosa of the upper respiratory tract, and edema and erythema of the extremities. Although the syndrome was impressive, its signs were nonspecific. Tests to rule out other disorders were negative. Thinking that he was observing a distinct clinical syndrome, Kawasaki published a report of his experience with 50 cases of "febrile oculo-oro-cutaneo-acrodesquamatous syndrome with or without acute nonsuppurative cervical lymphadenitis" in 1967.[143, 144, 146] Other Japanese physicians quickly recognized the syndrome after Kawasaki's report was published. Cardiac involvement in this illness was suspected first in 1968, when Yamamoto and Kimura reported an infant with Kawasaki disease who had transient tachycardia with a gallop rhythm, cardiomegaly, and minor electrocardiographic abnormalities.[362] In 1970, the Research Committee of Mucocutaneous Lymph Node Syndrome, sponsored by the Japanese Ministry of Health and Welfare, was organized with Dr. Fumio Kosaki as chairman.[146] The first biennial national epidemiologic survey was performed by this committee in 1970 under the leadership of Dr. I. Shigematsu and was published in 1972.[299] Kawasaki's clinical description of the syndrome has remained the foundation of diagnosis and the basis of clinical and epidemiologic case definitions in use today.

In 1971, physicians at the University of Hawaii, unaware of the Japanese experience, began to recognize patients with an unusual Reiter syndrome–like illness. Before information about Kawasaki disease was published in the English language literature,[146] the illness in Hawaii was recognized as being Kawasaki disease. Information exchanged among Japanese and American investigators led to the 1974 publication of English-language articles by both groups[146, 212–214] and triggered worldwide recognition of cases. In the early 1970s, death from myocardial infarction was reported to occur in approximately 2 percent of cases of Kawasaki disease; recent data reflect much lower mortality rates, less than 0.1 percent.[368] The application of echocardiography in the late 1970s revealed that 20 to 25 percent of patients develop evidence of coronary artery abnormalities.

In the decades before Kawasaki's recognition of the clinical features of the illness, many individual reports of fatal coronary arteritis in children (usually labeled infantile periarteritis nodosa, or IPAN) were published in the pediatric and pathology literature.[36, 47, 225, 267, 273] Clinical details of these cases generally are highly suggestive of Kawasaki disease, and the pathologic features of IPAN are indistinguishable from those of Kawasaki disease, as demonstrated by Landing and Larson in 1977.[170] Almost 100 years before Kawasaki's description, Samuel Gee of St. Bartholomew's Hospital in London reported the case of a 7-year-old boy who at death ("following scarlatinal dropsy") had three coronary aneurysms, each filled with a fresh clot; histologic examination by us is compatible with inactive Kawasaki disease.[91] Japanese investigators recently identified cases of illnesses compatible with Kawasaki disease that occurred in Japan up to three decades before Kawasaki's recognition was made.[145, 298a] In previous decades, patients with Kawasaki disease likely were misdiagnosed with measles, scarlet fever, rubella, or other once-common conditions.[277]

Epidemiology

SOURCES OF EPIDEMIOLOGIC DATA

Epidemiologic data for Kawasaki disease are derived from national surveillance, local passive surveillance, hospital-based case series, and published case reports. As with most notifiable diseases, reporting is incomplete. Passive surveillance data may help to monitor secular trends in occurrence of disease and to identify epidemics but are of little value in estimating the incidence of disease. Outbreak investigations are more sensitive in determining local incidence of disease and enable study of potential risk factors.

The epidemiologic case definitions of Kawasaki disease are strict to exclude from surveillance data other exanthematous conditions that could dilute "true" cases of Kawasaki disease and thereby obscure secular trends in its occurrence. However, the epidemiologic case definitions were not intended for clinical application, a very important point now that effective treatment is available. Less strict application of clinical case criteria is appropriate for the management of patients in view of the potential complications and the recent advances in treatment. Clinicians must be aware that children often present with clinical illnesses that do not fulfill completely the diagnostic criteria for Kawasaki disease but who are nonetheless at risk for development of coronary artery sequelae and, therefore, warrant receiving therapy. These cases generally are considered to be instances of *atypical* or *incomplete* Kawasaki disease.[28, 78, 123, 191, 280] Incomplete presentations of Kawasaki disease are particularly common occurrences in young infants in whom clinical signs often are subtle or fleeting but in whom the highest risk for development of coronary artery abnormalities exists.[276] In the United States, the Centers for Disease Control and Prevention (CDC) case definition usually is used for epidemiologic purposes. The present Japanese epidemiologic case definition has been used since 1984.[368] Both epidemiologic case definitions have been revised, so that earlier data may not be strictly comparable to data collected currently. Nonetheless, the overall number and rate of Kawasaki cases likely have risen over the past decade in Japan[370] and in Britain.[107a] Increased recognition is difficult to separate from true increase in incidence.

GENDER

In virtually all population-based studies in many countries, the ratio of males to females with Kawasaki disease approximates 1.5:1.[340, 341, 363–371] In addition, serious and fatal complications also occur significantly more commonly among males with Kawasaki disease than among females.[232a, 233, 341, 370] Examination of fatal Japanese cases indicated almost three times as many Kawasaki-related fatalities among males compared with females, with a higher ratio in infancy.[233] The basis for the preponderance of Kawasaki disease in males and the even greater predominance of serious coronary artery disease in males with Kawasaki disease is unclear. Of interest is that a male predominance is common to many infectious diseases.

RACE AND ETHNIC BACKGROUND

Because the first cases were recognized in Japanese children and Hawaiians of predominantly Japanese ethnicity, Kawasaki disease initially was presumed to occur most commonly in individuals of Asian background, which more recent data support. Annual incidence rates in Japan are approximately 100 to 112 cases per 100,000 children younger than 5 years of age.[366, 370, 374] In the 15th national survey, incidence rates were 108 in 1997 and 111.7 in 1998.[370] In epidemic years in Japan, however, the annual age-specific incidence rates have reached or exceeded 200 per 100,000 children younger than 5 years of age.[364, 365] Incidence rates in white children in many communities are much lower, approximating 10 per 100,000 children younger than 5 years of age.[53, 306] Surveys in countries with almost exclusively white populations have yielded rates of 5 to 10 cases per 100,000 children younger than 5 years of age.[30, 39, 262, 312] In Washington State, ethnic group–specific incidence rates per 100,000 children younger than 5 years of age were estimated to be 33.3 for Asian Americans, 23.4 for blacks, and 12.7 for whites.[53] Rates of Kawasaki disease for American Indian and Alaska Native children of approximately 4.3 per 100,000 children younger than 5 years of age have been ascertained in the U.S. Indian Health Service.[114a] In Hawaii, with its complex racial-ethnic makeup, Kawasaki disease occurs significantly more often in children of Japanese background. The overall annual incidence in Hawaii is 45 per 100,000 children younger than 5 years of age. The yearly incidence for Japanese and Korean children in Hawaii is 140 cases per 100,000 children and for whites 9 per 100,000, with intermediate rates for those of black, Hispanic, Chinese, Filipino, and Polynesian ancestry.[54] In New Zealand, differences in incidence between white and Polynesian children were not apparent,[92] but in Singapore, an increased occurrence of Kawasaki disease in Chinese compared with Malay children was suggested.[240] A recent report described the epidemiology of Kawasaki disease in Beijing, China, from 1995 to 1999, with the data suggesting that case finding is quite incomplete.[60a] Projecting the Hawaiian data to the entire United States suggests that 3000 to 5000 cases of Kawasaki disease occur annually in the United States. Extrapolation of data from surveys of hospitals in the United States with large children's services leads to estimates of approximately 2500 cases per year in the United States.[340, 341] Recent data from Japan indicate that approximately 6000 Kawasaki patients are diagnosed yearly, with local clusters rather than nationwide outbreaks occurring, as seen in 1979, 1982, and 1985 to 1986.[366]

The higher rates of Kawasaki disease in those of Japanese and some other Asian backgrounds suggest a genetic rather than an environmental basis. This theory is supported by increased rates among third- and fourth-generation immigrants, for example, from Japan to Hawaii. The genetic basis appears rather complex in that no single HLA antigen is common to most cases of Kawasaki disease. Early reports[142, 162, 206] that Kawasaki disease is associated with HLA-Bw 22 (or subtype Bw 54) were not confirmed by subsequent studies in Japan, Hong Kong, or Boston, where HLA-Bw 51 and HLA-B 44 were found more commonly.[41, 163] HLA-Bw 51 also was increased in a series of Israeli patients.[149] A smaller Maryland study suggested that despite an association between Kawasaki disease and HLA-B 44, the A2 B44 Cw5 haplotype was a more specific risk factor for epidemic Kawasaki disease.[130] Studies of HLA class II genes have detected no clear association.[19, 69] To date, no specific HLA marker appears to be a consistent risk factor for Kawasaki disease. Immunoglobulin allotypic markers were studied as possible genetic markers for Kawasaki disease.[307] The kappa chain allotype Km1, which is very common in Asian populations, and the combination of Km1 with Gm heterozygosity were present in significantly greater proportions of white Kawasaki patients than in the control white population. In addition, the haplotype G1m(a),G3m(t) was found significantly more often in Japanese and Japanese-American Kawasaki patients than in race-matched control populations.[307] This study supports a complex genetic basis for susceptibility to Kawasaki disease, but it should be confirmed.

AGE

Kawasaki disease occurs almost exclusively in children. In the United States and Japan, adult cases are quite rare, although numerous reports exist of adults diagnosed by accepted diagnostic criteria.* Many reported adult cases, however, appear to be related more closely to toxic shock syndrome or to drug hypersensitivity reactions than to Kawasaki disease. Kawasaki-like syndromes have been reported in HIV-infected adults, but whether these cases actually represent Kawasaki disease remains unclear.[125a, 266] Perhaps the best-documented adult case was that of a 31-year-old Japanese male (confirmed by Dr. Kawasaki), who later developed bilateral coronary artery aneurysms.[321] Because the signs and symptoms are nonspecific, adults suspected to have Kawasaki disease should be evaluated carefully for infectious, toxic, and other possible causes of illness. The youngest reported case is that of a Japanese girl with onset at 20 days of age.[351a]

Kawasaki disease occurs most commonly in young children: 50 percent are younger than 2 years of age, 80 percent are younger than 5 years of age, and cases are unusual in those older than 12 years of age.[220a, 315] In the United States, the peak age is approximately 18 months, whereas recent data from Japan identify 55 percent younger than 2 years old and the peak age incidence as 9 to 11 months of age.[368, 370] The lower peak age in Japan and perhaps in Hawaii possibly reflects better recognition of Kawasaki disease in infants, in whom Kawasaki disease may be more difficult to diagnose.[33, 123, 276] The age-incidence curve may be helpful in elucidating risk factors for acquiring Kawasaki disease. Such a pattern is compatible with highly transmissible infectious agents, particularly respiratory agents, and also suggests possible transplacental immunity.

A recent report summarized features of 28 Kawasaki patients 8 years of age and older at diagnosis at one Chicago institution.[315] Delays in diagnosis were common occurrences and were related at least partially to the prominence of arthritic and gastrointestinal symptoms in this population.

Japanese mortality data suggest that fatality rates are approximately three times higher in those younger than 1 year old at onset of disease compared with older children and that fatalities occur predominantly in the first several months after onset of Kawasaki disease.[232a, 368] The overall mortality rate in Japan has dropped from the initial report of approximately 2 percent to more recent Japanese estimates of approximately 0.08 percent.[368] Males account for a disproportionate number of deaths in infants and older children.[231, 232a, 233, 368] Long-term mortality rates in a large Japanese Kawasaki disease cohort study are increased over background rates only during the acute stage of illness.[231, 233]

RECURRENT KAWASAKI DISEASE

A recurrence of Kawasaki disease is defined as a new episode of illness meeting Kawasaki disease clinical criteria that begins at least 3 months after the initial episode and after inflammatory markers such as the erythrocyte sedimentation rate have normalized. The frequency of recurrences after first cases of Kawasaki disease in Japan was estimated to be approximately 1.9 percent during a 3-year follow-up period, with approximately 0.07 percent experiencing a third episode.[232] This frequency corresponds to a rate of 5.21 per 1000 person-years for one or more recurrences.[232] With longer follow-up, recurrence rates in Japan may reach 3 percent or more.[370] Recurrences occur most frequently within the first 2 years after the initial episode, especially in males and in children who have their initial episodes before reaching their second birthdays.[232] The frequency of recurrences in Chicago appears to be less than 1 percent, although recurrences have been documented in 2.3 percent of Hawaiian cases followed over the course of a 15-year period (1973 to 1987). The true recurrence rate will be determined only when a specific diagnostic test is available for Kawasaki disease, thus minimizing recognition bias.

FAMILY CASES

Simultaneous or sequential cases of Kawasaki disease in siblings, twin siblings, or other family contacts also have been reported, particularly during epidemics or outbreaks, particularly in Japan.[72, 117, 204, 371] Japanese epidemiologists have documented secondary sibling cases in approximately 1 percent of cases,[370] but such figures are difficult to interpret because the denominator of siblings at risk is not available in most studies. Such data also may be influenced by recognition and reporting biases. Sibling cases are reported to be more common in twins than nontwins. Only two sibling pairs have been recognized in approximately 1000 Chicago patients and none in 400 Los Angeles children.[202]

EPIDEMICS AND OUTBREAKS

Japanese investigators noted large nationwide epidemics of Kawasaki disease in 1979, 1982, and 1985 to 1986, with

*See references 12, 16, 34, 37, 66, 97, 178, 218, 264, 266, 296, 321, 347.

wavelike spread.[365] More localized outbreaks also have been observed. In the United States and elsewhere, community-wide outbreaks have been documented beginning in 1977 to 1978.[22] Investigations of outbreaks provide opportunities to study potential risk and etiologic factors.[22] Clustering of cases within families, schools, or neighborhoods is an unusual occurrence, even during large-scale epidemics. Japanese investigators have associated epidemics with a statistically increased likelihood of second cases in families, fatalities, and recurrent cases, but the implications of these findings are uncertain. A curious note is that since 1986, no Japanese epidemics have been identified, suggesting that the epidemiology of Kawasaki disease may have changed.[368, 374]

GEOGRAPHY

Kawasaki disease has been diagnosed throughout the United States and Japan and from most developed and many developing countries on all continents, including temperate and tropical zones.[30, 39, 41, 290] No striking rural-urban differences have been noted. Elevation, longitude, and latitude have not been implicated, although most reports are from countries with temperate climates. Travel histories of cases are unremarkable, although an anecdotal report of a 7-month-old infant in Australia documents Kawasaki disease onset 17 days after leaving Japan during that country's 1982 epidemic.[312]

In some outbreaks, geographic spread has been noted, for example, in Finland in 1981 to 1982[262] and in the three Japanese epidemics in 1979, 1982, and 1985 to 1986.[230, 363, 365] The 1982 Japanese epidemic[363] started simultaneously in four areas, spreading outward from each, similar to the way that epidemic influenza spreads in Europe and America. In the 1985 to 1986 Japanese epidemic, investigators identified epidemic waves that spread outward from an initial focus in the Tokyo metropolitan area, extending simultaneously northward and southward to involve most of the country within approximately 4 months.[363] A similar but less distinctive pattern of interprefectural progression in waves had been noted in the 1982 Japanese epidemic. Within the northern Tohoku District, for example, Kawasaki disease spread from prefecture to prefecture for a period of approximately 7 months.[363] Korean epidemics were detected 7 and 15 months after the Japanese epidemics of 1979 and 1985 to 1986, respectively.[176, 177, 363]

SEASONALITY

In Japan, Kawasaki disease occurs year-round but is most prevalent in the winter-spring, with peaks occurring usually within the December-to-May period,[367] especially in December and January.[370, 374] In many locales, including various locales within the United States[23, 201, 268, 306] and other countries,[288] outbreaks tend to begin in the winter and continue into the spring. Winter predominance has been observed in at least some Southern Hemisphere countries. That sporadic cases are recognized year-round is somewhat different from the pattern usually observed with highly transmissible respiratory viral diseases that peak in the winter-spring (e.g., measles, rubella, influenza).

COMMUNICABILITY

Little evidence that Kawasaki disease is transmissible from person to person exists. Secondary or co-primary cases in families are documented uncommonly. Often, concomitant nonspecific illnesses are seen in siblings,[286] but likely they are caused by chance. However, several outbreak investigations found a higher rate of antecedent respiratory tract illness in Kawasaki patients compared with matched controls.[22, 351] This incidence is of particular interest in view of the recent finding that immunoglobulin A (IgA) plasma cells infiltrate proximal respiratory tract in fatal cases of Kawasaki disease.[281] History of previous exposure of children with Kawasaki disease to clothes, food, or toys from Japan or elsewhere in Asia and Southeast Asia is a common finding, but the ubiquity of such exposures renders making an interpretation difficult. Japanese family data suggest that sibling cases cluster either on the same day as the index case or 7 days later.[72] Because these results are based on questionnaire data, however, the possibility of ascertainment bias is great; thus, determining whether Japanese familial cases represent co-primary or secondary cases is difficult.

OTHER RISK FACTORS

In addition to linking demographic risk factors to Kawasaki disease, some epidemiologic investigations have linked the disorder to specific exposures that could be related to an etiologic agent. As noted previously, history of more frequent antecedent respiratory illnesses in cases compared with controls was documented two decades ago.[22] Because many viral agents are prevalent in winter-spring when Kawasaki disease is most prevalent, isolation of various viruses from patients and from matched controls is to be expected. Other reported Kawasaki disease associations include exposure to prior carpet cleaning or shampooing, exposure to house dust mites, and residence near bodies of water, particularly septic water.

The association of Kawasaki disease outbreaks with rug or carpet cleaning or shampooing in the houses of patients was observed in some American outbreaks[67, 98, 116, 261, 268, 271] but not in others[52, 196, 222, 268, 274, 275, 342] and also has been associated with non-outbreak cases.[26] In Japan, where carpets are uncommon, Kawasaki disease has been associated with ownership of rugs or tatami mats. In three of the carpet shampoo–associated outbreaks investigated by the CDC, the rug shampooing events clustered significantly in the 2- to 4-week interval before disease onset, with few cases in the 2-week interval immediately preceding disease onset.[268] The significance of the possible shampoo association is doubtful because it has been absent entirely in some well-studied outbreaks.[52, 222] Conceivably, rug shampooing is a marker for aerosolization of a microbial or sensitizing agent present in the carpet, such as mites or microbial agents.

The possibility of a link existing between Kawasaki disease and house dust mites (chiefly *Dermatophagoides farinae* and *Dermatophagoides pteronyssinus*), initially proposed as an allergic hypothesis,[88] gained support when investigators realized that mites and mite antigens are significant components of carpets, rugs, and tatamis. A Japanese group reported *Rickettsia*-like bodies in the digestive systems of mites obtained from the house dust of patients with Kawasaki disease.[104] Other investigators supported the notion that Kawasaki disease might result from an infectious organism in dust mites.[71] However, dust mite counts were not significantly different in the houses of case and control patients,[98, 119] and no evidence was found of specific anti-mite IgE, IgG, or antibodies to *D. pteronyssinus* in patients with Kawasaki disease.[98, 126]

CDC investigators found in a small number of outbreaks that patients with Kawasaki disease lived closer to bodies of water than did control patients.[268, 270, 271] However, other studies, including one in Washington state, did not find proximity to water to be a risk factor.[53]

Etiology

The etiology of Kawasaki disease remains unknown. However, clinical and epidemiologic features strongly suggest that the disease has an infectious cause. A self-limited, generally nonrecurring illness manifested by fever, rash, enanthem, conjunctival infection, and cervical adenitis fits well with an infectious cause. The laboratory features, including an elevated white blood cell count with a "left shift," elevated acute-phase reactants, and pyuria, also suggest infection. Vasculitis with inflammatory cell infiltration (including IgA plasma cells)[281] might be infectious or represent an immune reaction to infection. The epidemiologic features noted previously, including the age distribution, winter-spring seasonality, occurrence of community outbreaks with wavelike geographic spread, and apparent epidemic cycles, are those of a transmissible disease of childhood. The epidemiology of Kawasaki disease resembles that of some other highly transmissible childhood diseases in which only occasional clinically apparent illnesses, perhaps in genetically susceptible children, are detected. It is analogous to poliomyelitis, the relatively uncommon complication of poliovirus infection that occurs in only about 1 of 200 infected children. However, efforts to identify an infectious agent in Kawasaki disease by using conventional bacterial and viral culture and serologic methods, as well as inoculation of primates, mice, and guinea pigs, have failed to yield an infectious cause.[284]

A very attractive hypothesis is that Kawasaki disease is caused by a ubiquitous infectious agent that produces clinically apparent disease only in selected, genetically predisposed individuals, particularly Asians. Its rarity in the first few months of life and in older children and adults suggests an agent to which virtually all adults are immune and from which very young infants are protected by passive maternal antibody. Consistent with this hypothesis is the paucity of evidence of person-to-person spread because most would experience asymptomatic infection and only a very small fraction would develop clinical features of Kawasaki disease.

Numerous microorganisms that have been suggested at one time or another to cause Kawasaki disease include bacteria, leptospires, spirochetes, chlamydia, rickettsia, and viruses. Proposed causative agents that have been investigated with little or no evidence of an etiologic relationship include group A streptococci,[4, 213] *Propionibacterium acnes*,[139, 350] leptospires,[24, 199] *Borrelia* spp.,[40, 199] *Pseudomonas* spp.,[148] *Klebsiella pneumoniae*,[125] *Mycoplasma* spp.,[27, 56, 70, 111, 124, 212, 285, 310] parvovirus,[79, 242, 252] cytomegalovirus,[64, 198] Epstein-Barr virus,[13, 16, 120, 150, 151, 198, 254] varicella-zoster virus,[198] human herpesviruses types 6 and 7,[64, 198, 255] and many other fungi, bacteria, viruses, or vaccines.* Recent chlamydial studies have eliminated this possibility.[105, 298, 316] The hypothesis that Kawasaki disease may be caused by *Rickettsia*-like agents seems very unlikely.†

Yersinia, particularly *Yersinia pseudotuberculosis,* causes a systemic illness resembling Kawasaki disease in selected areas of Japan,[43, 174, 290] but convincing evidence that an etiologic link exists between *Yersinia* and Kawasaki disease is lacking despite use of newer molecular tools.[331]

That Kawasaki disease might be caused by a novel retrovirus was suggested when two groups reported finding reverse transcriptase activity in cultured peripheral blood mononuclear cells from patients with acute Kawasaki disease.[32, 308] Other studies have failed to confirm this finding.[215, 253] Serologic studies for the retroviruses human immunodeficiency virus type 1, human T-cell lymphotrophic virus types I and II, simian immunodeficiency virus, and feline T-cell lymphotrophic virus have been negative,[241, 253, 269, 282] although occasionally Kawasaki disease has been reported in patients with human immunodeficiency virus.[125a, 354]

The hypothesis that Kawasaki disease might be the result of a bacterial superantigenic toxin has been suggested because of possible selective expansion of Vβ_2 and Vβ_8 T-cell receptor families.[1, 2] Superantigens bind to class II major histocompatibility complex molecules on monocytes and B cells and to the T-cell receptor, with resultant activation of large numbers of immunoreactive cells with release of inflammatory cytokines. Superantigens potentially cause expansion of autoreactive T cells.[109, 161] Features of T-cell activation characterize the acute phase of Kawasaki disease. Toxic shock syndrome and Kawasaki disease share the features of fever, rash, conjunctival injection, and convalescent desquamation to some degree, but differences, such as the lack of hypotension in Kawasaki disease and the absence of maculopapular or erythema multiforme–like rashes in toxic shock syndrome, are present.[106, 263] Although one group of investigators reported selective expansion of the Vβ_2 and Vβ_8 T-cell receptor families in acute Kawasaki disease,[1, 2] this finding has not been confirmed by others.[3, 55, 243, 265, 352] Although in one study, 11 of 16 patients with Kawasaki disease were colonized with toxic shock syndrome toxin-1 (TSST-1)–producing staphylococci,[188] comparable *Staphylococcus aureus* colonization rates, including by TSST-1–producing staphylococci, have been found among Kawasaki disease cases and controls in other studies.[188a, 197, 345] Most studies fail to show *any* disturbance of Vβ T-cell receptor expression in Kawasaki disease,[352] calling into question the entire superantigen hypothesis. Recent work indicates that the immune response in Kawasaki disease is oligoclonal (antigen driven, i.e., a response to a conventional antigen) rather than polyclonal (as typically found in superantigen-driven responses).[44, 283]

One suggestion is that Kawasaki disease may be an immunologic response triggered by any of several different microbial agents. Consistent with this hypothesis is documented infection in different individual cases by different microorganisms, failure to detect a single microbiologic or environmental agent after almost three decades of study, and analogies to other multifactorial syndromes, such as aseptic meningitis. However, this hypothesis is difficult to reconcile with the distinctive clinical and laboratory picture of Kawasaki disease and with its epidemiologic features, such as epidemics and wavelike geographic spread.

Efforts to associate Kawasaki disease with exposure to drugs[115] or to such environmental pollutants as toxins, pesticides, chemicals, and heavy metals have failed, although similarities between Kawasaki disease and acrodynia (mercury poisoning) are notable.[15, 257]

Clearly, conventional methodologies have failed to yield the causative agent of Kawasaki disease. Diagnosis is difficult to make, particularly in young infants and in those with incomplete or atypical presentations.[28, 33, 280] A useful diagnostic test probably cannot be developed

*See references 63, 147, 180, 207, 226, 277, 284, 297, 354.

†See references 23, 38, 62, 75, 103, 108, 169, 223, 329, 339, 356.

without the etiologic agent, and more specific therapy and preventative efforts await discovery of the etiologic agent. Researchers hope that utilization of modern molecular biology techniques[279, 283] will lead to significant progress in clarifying the etiology of Kawasaki disease.

Pathology and Pathogenesis

RELATIONSHIP TO INFANTILE PERIARTERITIS NODOSA

Japanese, European, and American investigators quickly recognized the pathologic similarities between IPAN, long known to have a predilection for the coronary arteries, and fatal Kawasaki disease.[5, 20, 21, 170, 175, 334–337] Landing and Larson showed most clearly that IPAN and fatal Kawasaki disease were not distinguishable pathologically.[170, 175] Although some investigators reported that patients with IPAN did not appear to meet case criteria for Kawasaki disease applied retrospectively, this failure likely is to be related to documentation bias and to the young age of many of the patients; infants with Kawasaki disease are less likely to have a classic presentation than are older children.[33, 276] Even when pathologic and clinical criteria are combined, the two diseases appear to be indistinguishable. Adult-type periarteritis nodosa first was described in 1866 by Kussmaul and Maier[168] and differs from IPAN by the presence of hypertension and involvement of small and medium muscular arteries, especially in the lung, kidney, and intestines.[73, 170, 336, 337] The earliest recorded case of possible IPAN may date from 1899.[165] Not until 1959, however, did Munro-Faure[225] delineate a syndrome of infantile necrotizing arteritis with coronary artery involvement, fever, rash, conjunctival and pharyngeal injection, and cervical adenitis. Roberts and Fetterman[273] and others expanded on these observations to define a distinct clinicopathologic syndrome of IPAN.

Coronary artery aneurysms have been detected in patients of all ages since the early 19th century, with a male-to-female ratio of roughly 3:1, including a male preponderance in childhood cases. Childhood death from multiple coronary artery aneurysms was known at least as early as 1871, as reported by Samuel Gee.[91] The cardiac specimen from this case, formalin fixed for more than 130 years in the pathology museum at St. Bartholomew's Hospital, London, recently was sectioned. We found that the coronary arteries showed the characteristic histologic findings of inactive Kawasaki disease and IPAN.[309] Whether these early cases of IPAN or childhood coronary artery aneurysms represented early examples of Kawasaki disease is somewhat speculative; histories usually were scanty.[91, 267] However, clearly, most of these cases greatly resemble (and almost certainly represent) Kawasaki disease.[47 [case 2], 225, 259, 267] From the features of many such early case reports, a reasonably accurate picture of Kawasaki disease as recognized today emerges. In prior decades, cases of Kawasaki disease likely were misdiagnosed as measles, scarlet fever, or other more common conditions.

PATHOLOGIC FEATURES OF KAWASAKI DISEASE

Shortly after Kawasaki provided his original description of what was thought to be a benign mucocutaneous lymph node syndrome,[143] it became evident that cardiac involvement could occur and then that cardiac death could result, generally in the subacute or convalescent stages of illness.[362] Autopsy findings generally reveal a generalized vasculitis that is most severe in the medium-sized arteries, with a marked predilection for the coronary arteries.[9, 10, 74, 170, 235, 336, 337] Small arterioles, larger arteries, capillaries, and veins also are affected to a lesser extent.[10, 73] In more than 80 percent of fatal cases in the acute stage, the immediate cause of death is acute thrombosis of inflamed coronary arteries, with myocardial infarction. In a few early deaths, pancarditis with inflammation of the atrioventricular conduction system apparently causes fatal arrhythmia or intractable congestive heart failure, and a small number of others may be associated with acute coronary rupture. Deaths that occur months to years after the acute episode often are secondary to coronary stenosis with or without thrombosis, with chronic myocardial ischemia or, rarely, rupture of a coronary aneurysm. Aneurysms of other major arteries, including the brachials, renals, and iliacs, also may be present. Although phlebitis may be found, vascular inflammation more typically and more severely affects larger musculoelastic arteries in their extraparenchymal portions. In the acute stage of Kawasaki disease, systemic inflammatory changes are evident in many other organs, including myocardium, pericardium, cardiac valves, cerebrospinal fluid, lung, lymph nodes, pancreas, spleen, and liver, and in larger musculoelastic arteries.[11, 73, 348]

In the early stages of Kawasaki disease vasculitis, edema of endothelial cells with nuclear degeneration with edema and mild adventitial inflammation occur.[9, 74, 235, 334] Initially, inflammatory cells are neutrophils and mononuclear cells, with rapid transition to predominantly mononuclear cells. In larger arteries with vasa vasorum, inflammation occurs in and around these vessels.[9] In more severely involved vessels such as the coronaries, inflammation of the media with edema and necrosis of smooth muscle cells occurs, resulting in a panvasculitis. Fragmentation and destruction of elastin and collagen fibers and splitting of the internal and external elastic laminae occur in severely affected vessels.[9] These changes eventually obscure the various layers of the wall, and structural integrity is lost, resulting in an aneurysm.

One to two months after the onset of the illness, inflammatory cells disappear, and fibrous connective tissue, collagen, and elastic fibers begin to form within the vessel wall. The intima proliferates and thickens. If present, fibrinoid necrosis generally is confined to the area between the thickened intima and the adventitia, probably representing necrotic smooth muscle cells. Over the course of time, the vessel wall may become stenotic or occluded, either by stenosis or by superimposed thrombus. Calcification may occur, and intraluminal thrombus may become organized, remodeled, and recanalized.[9, 235, 292, 325–327] Several groups have investigated the mechanisms of remodeling in Kawasaki disease. Suzuki and colleagues showed by immunohistochemistry that active remodeling continues for at least several years after onset of Kawasaki disease, with luxuriant intimal proliferation and neoangiogenesis.[328] Extensive expression of vascular growth factors, including vascular endothelial growth factor within smooth muscle cells, was evident, particularly in newly formed microvessels in the intima. Gavin and colleagues have shown the prominence of matrix metalloproteinases in this process, particularly within the intima and media.[90]

Few studies of the precise nature of the inflammatory infiltrate in the vessel wall or myocardium have been performed. Terai and colleagues demonstrated helper T cells and monocytes and macrophages in the arterial wall of one patient with fatal acute Kawasaki disease.[343] My group recently demonstrated the presence of many plasma cells of the IgA isotype in the vascular walls of patients who died in the acute stage.[279] Another observation is that the IgA plasma cells are oligoclonal (i.e., appear to be responding in an antigen-driven process)[283] and that they also can be observed in peribronchial, pancreatitic, and renal tissues.[281] A predominance of CD8 cytotoxic and suppressor T cells over CD4 helper T cells in seven of eight acute-stage deaths also was observed in our laboratory by immunohistochemistry.[29]

Other reported findings include renal infarcts and glomerular histologic changes; possible evidence of immune complex deposition,[287] including mesangial deposition of IgM and C3; and multifocal periglomerular infiltration of lymphocytes and IgA plasma cells.[281] Changes have been noted in other arteries, the thymus, and lymph nodes. Tanaka[334] described thymic atrophy (although most patients probably had been treated with steroids) and nondiagnostic lymph node changes. Other reports have described early lymph node biopsies showing multiple foci of necrosis and fibrin thrombi within the microvasculature[96] as well as T-zone hyperplasia, B-zone macrophage infiltration, and immunoblast proliferation.[96, 170, 248] Rowley and colleagues have identified IgA plasma cells not only in vascular and renal tissues but also in pancreatic and peribronchial locations.[281]

Fujiwara and associates[76] found significant atrioventricular conduction system lesions in 5 of 10 autopsy specimens. A strong correlation between electrocardiographic findings, especially P-Q prolongation, and acute inflammation of the atrioventricular conduction system was noted. Severe acute changes were most pronounced at 21 to 31 days after onset. In studies of right ventricular endomyocardial biopsies, Yutani and associates[376, 377] noted some degree of myocarditis and cellular infiltration, ranging from very mild to severe myocardial inflammation, in all 201 specimens from patients with Kawasaki disease.

A histologic and immunochemical study examined the intercostal arteries to compare the nature and developmental processes of lesions with those of the coronary arteries.[203] Although the lesions were similar, they appeared somewhat later in the intercostal arteries. The investigators suggested that a general feature of arterial lesions in Kawasaki disease may be degeneration of medial smooth muscle cells followed by proliferation, in some cases leading to destruction of the medial structure associated with mononuclear cell infiltration, and eventually aneurysm formation, consistent with many earlier observations.

Clinical Manifestations

When manifested completely, Kawasaki disease is a distinctive clinical entity with a predictable course.[50, 143] However, children who do not fulfill the criteria for diagnosis of Kawasaki disease, in fact, may have the illness and are at risk for development of complications, particularly coronary artery disease.[280] (See "Atypical or Incomplete Kawasaki Disease"). The principal clinical diagnostic criteria are presented in Table 82–1. Kawasaki disease should be considered in the differential diagnosis of infants and children with fever for at least 5 days associated with some of the following features: generalized polymorphous erythematous rash, conjunctival injection, characteristic changes of the lips and mouth, bilateral redness and swelling of the hands and feet, and unilateral nonfluctuant cervical lymph node enlargement measuring greater than 1.5 cm. A secure diagnosis, according to accepted clinical criteria (see Table 82–1), is made in patients with fever and at least four of the five clinical criteria and with exclusion of other illnesses that mimic Kawasaki disease. Each of the five clinical features is present in 80 to 90 percent of typical cases, except for cervical lymphadenopathy, which is present in approximately 50 to 75 percent of patients. The most commonly encountered diseases to be excluded are (1) febrile exanthems, presumably viral, including measles; (2) acute streptococcal and staphylococcal infections; and (3) drug hypersensitivity reactions.

Several scoring systems using clinical and laboratory features have been developed, primarily in Japan.[14, 21a, 107, 234] The goal of these systems has been to identify those patients with Kawasaki disease who are at highest risk for having coronary abnormalities and who, thus, would benefit most from IVIG therapy. No such scoring system appears sufficiently sensitive and specific to enable selective therapy (i.e., allowing nontreatment of those predicted to be at low risk for coronary abnormalities). Those patients who are at greatest risk are those younger than 1 year of age; males; those with prolonged or recurrent fever; and those with anemia, hypoalbuminemia, and thrombocytopenia. However, I consider that therapy is indicated for all patients diagnosed within the first 10 days after onset and for those with active inflammation beyond 10 days.

In Kawasaki disease, fever typically is high, spiking, and remittent, with peak temperatures generally exceeding 39.0° C (102° F) and in many cases exceeding 40.0° C (104° F). Unless treated with aspirin or intravenous gamma globulin, fever persists for a mean of 11 days,[112] but it may continue for 3 to 4 weeks, rarely longer. In those treated with 80 to 100 mg/kg/day of aspirin and a single 2 gm/kg dose of IVIG, fever generally resolves within 1 or 2 days.[238]

Vascular injection of the bulbar conjunctivae, much more severe than injection of the palpebral conjunctivae, generally is seen in the first week of illness, usually beginning shortly after fever onset. Generally, no associated exudate nor conjunctival edema or corneal ulceration is present, thus distinguishing the eye findings of Kawasaki disease from purulent conjunctivitis and from Stevens-Johnson syndrome. Mild acute iridocyclitis or anterior uveitis, which may be noted by slit lamp, rapidly resolves and rarely is associated with photophobia or eye pain.[31, 93, 173, 250, 311] Less common ocular findings include superficial punctate keratitis, vitreous opacities, vitreous and chorioretinal inflammation, lateral rectus palsy, periorbital vasculitis, and papilledema.[68, 121, 360]

Changes of the mouth and lips consist of (1) erythema, dryness, fissuring, peeling, cracking, and bleeding of the lips; (2) a "strawberry tongue" indistinguishable from that associated with streptococcal scarlet fever, with erythema and prominent papillae; and (3) diffuse erythema of the oropharyngeal mucosa. Oral ulcerations, pharyngeal exudates, and Koplik spots rarely, if ever, are found in Kawasaki disease.

Extremity changes are among the most distinctive features of Kawasaki disease. The hands and feet become indurated and swollen, with stretched, shiny skin. The palms and soles become erythematous, often with an abrupt change to normal skin at the wrist and ankle. Infants and children frequently refuse to hold objects or to bear weight. In the subacute phase, a distinctive pattern of periungual desquamation of fingers and toes may occur 2 weeks to 2 months after onset of Kawasaki disease. Beau lines, transverse grooves across the nails, may develop and grow out over several months.

The erythematous rash associated with Kawasaki disease may take many forms. Most common is a nonspecific diffuse maculopapular erythematous rash. Occasionally, diffuse scarlatiniform erythroderma or an erythema multiforme–like rash with target lesions develops. Vesicles and bullae are not seen, although very fine pustules occur rarely. Perineal erythema and desquamation are common findings in diapered as well as toilet-trained children in the acute stage of illness. Rashes in Kawasaki disease tend to be most prominent on the trunk but frequently also involve the face and extremities.

Cervical adenopathy is the least common of the principal diagnostic criteria, but sometimes it is the dominant clinical feature.[314] It usually is unilateral and confined to the anterior cervical triangle. To fulfill diagnostic criteria, the enlarged node or mass of nodes is larger than 1.5 cm, is nonfluctuant, usually is not associated with erythema of the overlying skin, and is nontender or only moderately tender. Lymphadenopathy generally is benign and transient. Patients with acute cervical adenitis unresponsive to antibiotic therapy may have Kawasaki disease. Because other Kawasaki features often are present but overlooked, Kawasaki disease should be considered in febrile children with cervical adenitis unresponsive to antibiotics and without an alternate diagnosis.[314]

The associated features of Kawasaki disease reflect its multisystemic nature (Table 82–2). Sterile pyuria reflecting urethritis is found in as many as 75 percent of patients. Meatitis is a common finding. Arthritis in the first week of illness tends to involve multiple joints, including the small interphalangeal joints and large weight-bearing joints. Arthrocentesis during this early phase yields purulent-appearing fluid, with a mean white blood cell count of 125,000 to 300,000/mm^3, normal glucose levels, and negative Gram stain and bacterial cultures.[112, 214] Arthritis developing after the 10th day of illness has a predilection for large weight-bearing joints, especially the knees and ankles, with a somewhat lower synovial fluid white blood cell count.[112, 214] Gastrointestinal complaints occur in approximately one third of acute cases and include nausea, abdominal pain, and some diarrhea. Central nervous system involvement, including aseptic meningitis, occurs in almost one half of patients.[57] Transient unilateral lower motor neuron facial nerve (Bell) palsy occurs rarely,[89] as does sensorineural hearing loss.[323] Obstructive jaundice and acute hydrops of the gallbladder are not uncommon findings, whereas mild to moderate elevations of serum transaminases occur in almost one half of patients. Characteristic extreme irritability is a very common symptom, especially in young infants. Reactivation of inflammation at the site of a previous bacille Calmette-Guérin (BCG) vaccination with acute Kawasaki disease occurs commonly in Japan, where BCG is used widely.[165a]

By far the most important associated feature of Kawasaki disease is cardiac involvement. In addition to the 20 to 25 percent of untreated children who develop coronary artery abnormalities, pericardial effusion, transient myocardiopathy with congestive heart failure, gallop rhythm, nonspecific electrocardiographic changes, and arrhythmia may occur.[131, 134, 136] An imperfect correlation exists between clinically apparent cardiac involvement and echocardiographic evidence of coronary involvement, although in the pre-IVIG era, echocardiographic evidence of mitral regurgitation or pericardial effusion in the acute stage was shown to be predictive of subsequent development of coronary abnormalities.[94]

TABLE 82–2 ■ ASSOCIATED NONCARDIAC FEATURES OF KAWASAKI DISEASE

Arthritis or arthralgia
Aseptic meningitis
Marked irritability
Hydrops of gallbladder
Abdominal pain, diarrhea
Urethritis, meatitis
Hepatic dysfunction, obstructive jaundice
Preceding respiratory illness
Erythema and induration of bacille Calmette-Guérin vaccine site
Peripheral gangrene
Auditory abnormalities
Facial nerve palsy

Clinical Phases of Illness

The clinical course of Kawasaki disease can be divided into acute, subacute, and late or convalescent phases. The acute febrile phase begins with fever, rash, conjunctival injection, strawberry tongue, edema and erythema of the hands and feet, lymphadenitis, and sometimes aseptic meningitis and mild hepatic dysfunction. Evidence of myocarditis, including tachycardia and rarely congestive heart failure or arrhythmias, may develop during this time. Pericardial effusion may be detected by echocardiogram. Without aspirin and IVIG treatment, the acute phase generally lasts for 8 to 30 days (mean, 11 days).[112] After defervescence, the physical findings rapidly disappear, but during this subacute phase, the child may remain irritable and anorectic with decreased activity. Some conjunctival injection may persist. Arthritis may develop in the subacute phase. Desquamation of fingers and toes, typically beginning in the periungual region, and thrombocytosis are very common occurrences in this period. The subacute phase persists until the child returns to his or her normal state of health, approximately 3 to 4 weeks after onset of fever. The time of greatest risk for sudden death from acute coronary artery thrombosis is during the subacute phase and the early convalescent phase. The convalescent phase begins when all clinical signs and symptoms have disappeared and continues until the sedimentation rate returns to normal, usually 6 to 8 weeks after onset.

Atypical or Incomplete Kawasaki Disease

A substantial subset of children present with illnesses that do not completely fulfill diagnostic criteria for Kawasaki disease but that include fever and some features of the disease. This atypical or incomplete Kawasaki disease is associated with risk for development of coronary artery aneurysms[28, 78, 191, 280] but can be very difficult to diagnose. Atypical Kawasaki disease occurs most commonly in young infants, who unfortunately are at greatest risk for coronary disease,[33, 276, 280] and fatalities have occurred. Individual Kawasaki disease manifestations in young infants tend to be milder and more subtle than are those in older children. Kawasaki disease should be considered in the differential diagnosis of prolonged fever in infants because patients are described in whom such fevers are virtually the sole manifestation of Kawasaki disease. Diagnosis usually is based on finding coronary abnormalities by echocardiogram. The existence of these patients emphasizes the need to identify the etiologic agent so that a diagnostic test can be developed. The laboratory profile of atypical cases is similar to that of classic cases. When possible, patients with illnesses suggesting atypical Kawasaki disease should be referred to physicians with considerable experience in making the diagnosis.

Laboratory Findings

A specific diagnostic test for Kawasaki disease is not available and awaits discovery of the etiology of the illness. Thus, the laboratory features of Kawasaki disease are quite nonspecific but nevertheless are characteristic of the illness (Table 82–3). Leukocytosis, especially neutrophilia, with an increased number of immature and mature granulocytes, is a typical finding in the acute stage. White blood cell counts in excess of 30,000/mm^3 occur in approximately 5 percent of patients and in excess of 15,000/mm^3 in about 50 percent. Leukopenia is quite rare. Toxic granulation and Döhle bodies may be seen on peripheral blood smear.[25] Mild to moderate eosinophilia may be present in acute or subacute Kawasaki disease, and eosinophils may infiltrate the coronary microvessels in acute Kawasaki disease.[346a] Anemia may develop, usually with normocytic red blood cell indices, particularly with more prolonged duration of active inflammation. Severe hemolytic anemia requiring transfusions is an unusual occurrence.[46] Curiously, Kawasaki's first patient and only rare subsequent patients have manifested a Coombs-positive hemolytic anemia.[143, 303] Elevation of acute-phase reactants such as the erythrocyte sedimentation rate, C-reactive protein, and α_1-antitrypsin is nearly universal in Kawasaki disease, and these levels usually return to normal by 6 to 10 weeks after illness onset. IVIG therapy leads to elevation of the sedimentation rate and thus is of limited value in following the degree of inflammatory activity in IVIG-treated patients.

A very characteristic feature of the later phases of illness is thrombocytosis, with platelet counts ranging from 500,000 to over 1,000,000/mm^3. Thrombocytosis rarely is present in the first week of illness, usually appears in the second week, and peaks in the third week, with a gradual return to normal by 4 to 8 weeks after onset in uncomplicated cases. The mean peak platelet count is approximately 700,000/mm^3. No differences in ^{65}Cr-labeled autologous platelet survival have been found between cases and controls, and little correlation exists between thrombocytosis and increased platelet aggregation. The latter has been detected in patients with Kawasaki disease from a few days until a year after onset.[361] The rare patients with thrombocytopenia in the acute stage of Kawasaki disease appear to be at increased risk for development of coronary artery disease and myocardial infarction.[244]

Plasma lipids are markedly perturbed in acute Kawasaki disease, with depression of plasma cholesterol, high-density lipoprotein (HDL) cholesterol, and apolipoprotein A-I (apoA-I).[35, 236, 291] Similar changes are reported in other conditions associated with an acute-phase response.[35] Marked appearance of serum amyloid A protein in plasma, associated with HDL-3–like lipoprotein particles, is seen acutely.[35] Cabana and colleagues also showed that total cholesterol, HDL cholesterol, apoA-I, and triglyceride levels normalize over the course of several weeks and that serum amyloid A disappears from plasma. The core composition of HDL normalizes more slowly than do plasma HDL cholesterol and apoA-I levels, suggesting that Kawasaki disease has a profound effect on lipoprotein profile acutely and a more subtle sustained effect on HDL composition.[35]

Mild to moderate elevations in serum transaminases are present in as many as 40 percent of patients and mild hyperbilirubinemia in approximately 10 percent. Hypoalbuminemia appears to indicate more severe and more prolonged acute disease.[107] Urinalysis reveals intermittent mild to moderate sterile pyuria in approximately one third of patients, although suprapubic urine generally does not show pyuria, suggesting urethritis.[58, 213] In those children who undergo lumbar puncture, evidence of aseptic meningitis with a predominance of mononuclear cells, normal glucose, and normal to mildly elevated protein levels is a common finding.[57]

Laboratory tests, even though nonspecific, can provide diagnostic support in patients with clinical features that are suggestive, but not diagnostic, of Kawasaki disease. A moderately to markedly elevated C-reactive protein or erythrocyte sedimentation rate, almost universal in Kawasaki disease, is uncommon in viral exanthems and hypersensitivity reactions. Platelet counts higher than 450,000/mm^3 usually are present in patients evaluated after the seventh day of illness. In cases of atypical Kawasaki disease associated with coronary abnormalities, thrombocytosis and elevated sedimentation rate are very common findings in the acute stage.[191, 280] Clinical experience suggests that Kawasaki disease is very unlikely if platelet counts and acute-phase inflammatory reactants (e.g., erythrocyte sedimentation rate, C-reactive protein, α_1-antitrypsin) are normal after the seventh day of illness.

TABLE 82–3 ■ LABORATORY FEATURES OF KAWASAKI DISEASE

Leukocytosis with neutrophilia
Elevated erythrocyte sedimentation rate
Positive C-reactive protein (and other acute-phase reactants)
Anemia (normochromic, normocytic)
Thrombocytosis
Sterile pyuria
Hypoalbuminemia
Elevated serum transaminases
Blood lipid abnormalities

IMMUNOLOGIC FINDINGS

Studies of children with Kawasaki disease reveal widespread immune perturbations.[305] Some of them presumably reflect responses to antigens involved in the pathogenesis of the disease, and others may represent epiphenomena. Evidence of marked immune activation is present and is reflected by increased levels of a wide variety of cytokines, including tumor necrosis factor–α, interferon-γ, interleukin-1 (IL-1), IL-2, IL-4, IL-6, IL-8, IL-10, and soluble IL-2 receptor.* Increased chemokine and selectin activity in patients with acute Kawasaki disease also have been reported.[332, 358] The most intense immune activation and cytokine production occur during the acute and early subacute phases, the periods of most intense vascular inflammation and of aneurysm formation. A large body of data indicates that the immune perturbations subside as the illness resolves, spontaneously or in response to IVIG therapy,[183] and the benefit of therapy appears to be due to immune modulating effects, although precise details are lacking.[181, 302]

In the acute stage of Kawasaki disease, serum IgG levels are lower than normal for age,[239] whereas in the subacute stage, polyclonal elevation of all immunoglobulin classes generally is found.[189, 193] Serum IgE levels frequently are elevated,[164, 166, 214] with 50 percent of IgE values and 80 percent of IgM values exceeding 2 standard deviations above age-appropriate mean values. The increase in serum immunoglobulins is associated with a very high proportion

*See references 17, 61, 82, 114, 152, 154, 171, 172, 184, 194, 195, 205, 208, 209, 282.

of circulating activated B cells[155] and is reversed by aspirin and IVIG treatment.[183]

Circulating immune complexes can be detected in the subacute and convalescent (but not the acute) stages; they appear not to be related to the development of coronary abnormalities by virtue of their time course of detection[190, 192, 220, 251, 258, 289, 355] and appear to be unaffected by IVIG infusions.[200] Some investigators have detected IgA in the immune complexes.[251] Most IgG circulating immune complexes in Kawasaki disease contain antibodies of the IgG1 and IgG3 subclasses,[60, 192] the Fc portions of which can bind to monocytes and platelets. Immune complexes in Kawasaki disease may aggregate platelets, causing release of vasoactive factors.[192]

Several autoantibodies have been found in Kawasaki disease sera, but antinuclear antibody and rheumatoid factor are very rare findings. Antibodies to type III collagen have been detected,[158] but without clear association with coronary complications. Some acute-phase sera contain IgM antimyosin antibodies directed against epitopes that differ from those reactive with acute rheumatic fever sera, suggesting a possible relationship to myocarditis in Kawasaki disease.[48] Both IgM and IgG antineutrophil cytoplasm antibodies[272, 295, 313] and antimyeloperoxidase antibodies[272] have been reported in Kawasaki disease. IgM or IgG antiendothelial cell antibodies in Kawasaki disease, like those also seen in lupus, graft rejection, and other acute and chronic immune states, have been reported.[185,186] Antiendothelial cell antibodies may injure cells directly or may participate in complement-mediated injury or in antibody-mediated cytotoxic reactions.[129, 182, 185, 186] In one study, antiendothelial cell antibodies were cytotoxic to endothelial cells, even without cytokine prestimulation.[129] Among the endothelial cell antigens of interest are adhesion molecules, E-selectin, and endothelin, all of which may be up-regulated in Kawasaki disease.[81, 153, 224, 247] The precise role of immunologic reactions to endothelial cells in the pathogenesis of Kawasaki disease is unclear. However, the temporal correlation of immune activation, endothelial cell activation,[187, 343] and development of coronary abnormalities, and their suppression by IVIG, are consistent with an immune stimulant that triggers an immune cascade leading to vascular damage through cytokine-induced exposure of endothelial epitopes targeted by destructive autoimmune responses. A body of data has been developed that suggests an important role for vascular endothelial growth factor (VEGF) in the pathogenesis of Kawasaki disease vasculitis.[346b, 374a]

Investigations of the distribution of circulating T cells in the acute and subacute stages of Kawasaki disease have yielded conflicting results that range from no significant change in distribution of CD3, CD4, CD8, and CD19 cells at any stage of illness[44] to significant decreases in circulating CD8[189, 344] or CD4[344] numbers acutely. A recent immunohistochemistry study of eight autopsied acute-stage Kawasaki hearts found activated T cells, a predominance of CD8 cells, and macrophages but no B cells[29]; Terai and associates' study of autopsy results from one child showed predominance of activated CD4 cells and macrophages as well as activated coronary endothelial cells.[343] The presence of activated T cells in peripheral blood in acute Kawasaki disease is controversial.[55]

As discussed in the "Etiology" section, expansion of $V\beta_2$ and $V\beta_8$ T-cell receptor families in acute Kawasaki disease has been reported,[1, 2, 49] but this finding has not been reproduced by others.[3, 197, 216, 243, 265, 345, 352] Such expansion would suggest the possible role of a superantigen in Kawasaki disease or could reflect clonal expansion in certain Vβ families in response to a conventional antigen. However, recent studies demonstrating clonal expansion of CD8 T cells in acute Kawasaki disease support the hypothesis that a conventional antigen, rather than a superantigen, is involved in the pathogenesis,[44] and compelling evidence of an oligoclonal IgA response in the vascular wall strongly supports this finding.[283]

Evidence for activation of polymorphonuclear neutrophils in Kawasaki disease is of interest because these cells, along with monocytes and macrophages, are postulated to mediate endothelial cell damage through production of oxygen radicals.[245, 338, 353] Kawasaki disease also is associated with widespread activation of monocytes and macrophages,[83–85] T lymphocytes,[86, 294, 373] and B lymphocytes.[60] Jejunal mucosal changes similar to delayed-type hypersensitivity in the epithelium and lamina propria have been detected[229] and include decreases in $CD8^+$ cells coupled with increases in $CD4^+$ and $HLA\text{-}DR^+$ cells. Delayed hypersensitivity skin test responsiveness to *Candida*, streptokinase and streptodornase, phytohemagglutinin, and purified protein derivative is suppressed during the acute stage of Kawasaki disease but normalizes within 1 to 2 months.[372] Acute Kawasaki disease is associated with inflammatory reactivation of previous BCG vaccination sites, apparently reflecting both cellular and humoral responses.[165a, 375] Plasma fibronectin levels are reported to be decreased early in illness but to rebound to high levels in the fourth week of illness.[300]

Circulating complement components C3 and C4 are elevated in the first several weeks of illness and then normalize.[110, 190, 200, 255, 300] Nevertheless, complement appears to be activated through the classical pathway,[159] with high plasma C4d levels comparable to those in acute lupus[227] and other complement fragments elevated.[159]

Production of leukotriene B_4 by polymorphonuclear cells is reported to be increased from 13 to 29 days after onset of Kawasaki disease.[102] This powerful endogenous chemoattractant, released by cells at an inflammatory site, may play a role in attracting more inflammatory cells to the site, thus prolonging the period of intense inflammation.[101] Leukotriene E_4 and prostaglandin E_2 also are elevated in Kawasaki disease[80, 179, 210] as are platelet synthesis of thromboxane A_2[113] and plasma levels of thromboxane B_2.

The strongest evidence of the importance of immunologic factors in the pathogenesis of vasculitis in Kawasaki disease is provided by the remarkable beneficial effect, discussed later, of IVIG on the acute febrile illness and the prevention of the development of coronary aneurysms.[228, 238, 239, 248, 301] This observation correlates with the effect of IVIG to reduce B-cell activation, more rapidly normalize T-cell activity, reduce cytokine secretion, and induce disappearance of endothelial cell activation antigens.[181, 187] Potential explanations of the beneficial action of IVIG in Kawasaki disease include the shutting off of endothelial cell activation, down-regulation of immunoglobulin production by a negative feedback mechanism, specific immunoglobulin neutralization of an unknown etiologic agent or toxin, and nonspecific blockade of a receptor for immune complexes or of harmful autoantibodies on the vascular endothelium affecting attachment of platelets or white blood cells.[302]

Treatment in the Acute Stage

INITIAL THERAPY

As soon as Kawasaki disease is diagnosed, patients should undergo a baseline echocardiogram and receive IVIG, 2 g/kg, in a 10- to 12-hour infusion together with high-dose aspirin,

TABLE 82–4 ■ TREATMENT FOR KAWASAKI DISEASE

Acute and Subacute Stages
Intravenous gamma globulin (IVGG), 2 g/kg infusion over 10–12 hours, *plus*:
Aspirin, 80–100 mg/kg/day in four divided doses (until 14th illness day and patient afebrile at least 3–4 days), then 3–5 mg/kg once daily for 6–8 weeks
IVGG may be repeated if fever persists or recurs together with at least one classic sign of Kawasaki disease

Convalescent Stage
No coronary abnormalities: no therapy
Transient coronary abnormalities: aspirin, 3–5 mg/kg once daily at least until resolution of abnormalities
Persistent small to medium coronary aneurysms: aspirin, 3–5 mg/kg once daily
Giant or multiple small coronary aneurysms: aspirin, 3–5 mg/kg once daily, with or without dipyridamole or clopidogrel, with warfarin for most patients
Coronary obstruction: thrombolytic therapy, surgical or interventional procedures

80 to 100 mg/kg/day[50] (Table 82–4). This dosage schedule has been demonstrated to be highly effective in reducing the risk for development of coronary abnormalities.[238] In addition, IVIG and aspirin have been shown to prevent the development of giant coronary artery aneurysms[278] and to have direct benefits on cardiac function.[237] The single-dose schedule is superior to the previously used regimen of 400 mg/kg/day IVIG on each of 4 days with respect to rapidity of defervescence and normalization of acute-phase reactants.[238, 239, 248] The large single-dose infusion generally is well tolerated, even in patients with decreased myocardial function.[238] All patients should be admitted to a hospital to receive IVIG and to be monitored, and a baseline echocardiogram should be obtained. Patients should remain hospitalized until they have been afebrile for at least 24 hours to ensure that they are available for re-treatment if necessary.

Single infusions of IVIG at doses of less than 2 g/kg have not been demonstrated to be effective, despite two pilot trials that studied 1 g/kg dosing.[18, 65] A comprehensive meta-analysis of all Japanese and North American IVIG treatment trials showed that the coronary artery outcome is correlated directly with the total dose of IVIG administered, with 2 g/kg superior to 1.6 g/kg, which is superior to 1.2 and 1 g/kg but is unrelated to the initial aspirin dose used.[346]

Few data are available to guide therapy of patients diagnosed later than 10 days after onset of Kawasaki disease.[196a] Patients who are still febrile or who manifest other signs of active disease may benefit from IVIG and aspirin therapy because it may result in prompt clinical improvement, with subsidence of fever and other signs of inflammation. No evidence exists that this therapy results in lower rates of development of coronary abnormalities, however. Patients beyond the 10th to 12th illness day who have become afebrile and have resolved acute features of Kawasaki disease, however, are unlikely to benefit from IVIG. Such children should be treated instead with aspirin, 3 to 5 mg/kg once daily. Little, if any, evidence suggests a beneficial effect of IVIG in patients who have already developed coronary aneurysms and whose acute manifestations of illness have resolved.[196a]

The aspirin dosage that is studied most thoroughly in the United States is 80 to 100 mg/kg/day, and this dosage should be maintained until approximately the 14th day of illness (when the patient has been afebrile for at least 3 to 4 days), and then reduced to a daily dose of 3 to 5 mg/kg until 2 to 3 months after illness onset in those who have not developed coronary abnormalities. High-dose aspirin is used for its anti-inflammatory activity, whereas the much lower doses inhibit platelet aggregation. Japanese clinicians generally use an intermediate anti-inflammatory dose of 30 to 50 mg/kg/day[167] because of perceived higher rates of untoward effects in Japan. Difficulty in achieving what usually are considered therapeutic anti-inflammatory serum salicylate levels during the acute phase of illness (20 to 25 mg/dL) may complicate aspirin treatment,[122] and selected refractory patients may require salicylate doses in excess of 100 mg/kg/day in order to achieve anti-inflammatory benefit. Koren attributed this phenomenon to impaired absorption and bioavailability and to enhanced salicylate clearance in acute Kawasaki disease.[160] An important note is that with clinical improvement, patients who are receiving very high doses can suddenly increase their salicylate absorption and may become salicylate toxic. Serum salicylate levels should be monitored if symptoms of vomiting, hyperpnea, tinnitus, lethargy, or striking liver function abnormalities develop in children receiving aspirin. One study that randomized patients to salicylate at 80 to 100 mg/kg/day or to 3 to 5 mg/kg/day for initial therapy (with 2 g/kg of IVIG) concluded that whereas no difference in coronary outcome was achieved, a more prompt anti-inflammatory benefit was achieved in the high-dose aspirin group.[217]

Limited data suggest a possible benefit for oral corticosteroids in acute Kawasaki disease, but more data are needed.[51a, 300a] Administration of live parenteral virus vaccines such as varicella and measles-mumps-rubella vaccines should be delayed for 9 to 11 months after treatment with IVIG because the presence of specific antiviral antibody in IVIG may interfere with the immune response to the vaccine.

Rescue Therapy

Most patients with acute Kawasaki disease respond promptly to treatment with IVIG and aspirin, with defervescence and subsidence of inflammatory manifestations being achieved within 48 hours.[50, 238, 301] A subgroup of 5 to 10 percent, however, fail to show significant clinical response or manifest only transient improvement, with recurrent fever and clinical evidence of inflammatory signs. In these patients, increasing the salicylate dose may be beneficial, but administration of a second 2 g/kg dose of IVIG generally is effective in suppressing disease activity.[322] Alternatively, some physicians prefer instead to administer intravenous pulse corticosteroids (30 mg/kg/dose methylprednisolone once daily for 1 to 3 days).[107b, 359] I consider such therapy only for the rare patient with highly refractory acute disease because early Japanese data suggested that steroids may aggravate or predispose the patient to coronary disease.[140] Only one limited comparison between repeat IVIG dosing and corticosteroids has been performed.[107b] A very small number of exceptionally recalcitrant patients have been treated with cytotoxic agents, but the role (if any) of such agents in Kawasaki disease has not been defined.[354a]

Subsequent Management

Patients should be re-evaluated within 2 weeks after hospital discharge and again approximately 6 to 8 weeks after onset of illness because echocardiography at these time points is most likely to detect coronary artery aneurysms should they develop. If baseline and follow-up echocardiograms fail to detect evidence of coronary abnormality, further echocardiograms are unnecessary, although a 1-year follow-up echocardiogram is performed in many centers.[51] Discontinuation of aspirin therapy is standard at 6 to 8 weeks unless evidence of coronary abnormalities exists. To reduce the theoretical (and very low) risk for development of Reye syndrome in patients receiving low-dose aspirin, dipyrimadole or clopidogrel can be substituted for aspirin for a brief time in patients who develop varicella or influenza.

Long-Term Management

The development of coronary artery stenosis that may result in myocardial ischemia and infarction remains the most important long-term clinical problem in patients with Kawasaki disease (see Table 82–4). Patients with medium (6 to 8 mm) and large (more than 8 mm) aneurysms are at substantial risk for later development of stenosis compared with those with small or no aneurysmal changes.[8, 128, 133, 136, 141] Echocardiography and electrocardiography are not sufficiently sensitive to detect stenotic lesions. Exercise and dypyridamole stress thallium-201 myocardial scanning and electron-beam tomography are sensitive noninvasive measures to detect myocardial ischemia,[127, 246, 260] and newer techniques are being developed. Coronary arteriography remains the most definitive method to determine the degree of stenosis and the adequacy of collateral circulation. Intravascular ultrasound is an effective method to evaluate vascular wall morphology during angiography.[317, 324] The indications for and timing of angiography remain controversial, although all patients with evidence of myocardial ischemia or infarction should be studied by angiography to determine the need for intervention.[50] Most experts consider that patients with moderate to severe, single large or multiple coronary aneurysms should have their coronary anatomy defined by angiography at least once after the acute stage of illness to define fully the extent of involvement and to identify potential sites of thrombotic or stenotic complications.[50]

PATIENTS WITH NO EVIDENCE OF CORONARY ARTERY ABNORMALITIES

Patients who have never manifested coronary artery abnormalities have no need for aspirin or other antiplatelet medication beyond 2 to 3 months after onset of illness and no restriction of physical activities in the convalescent stage. Only routine pediatric follow-up beyond 1 year is indicated.[50]

PATIENTS WITH TRANSIENT CORONARY ECTASIA OR ANEURYSMS

Patients with transient coronary artery abnormalities should be treated with aspirin, 3 to 5 mg/kg/day, at least until resolution of abnormalities. Regressed coronary aneurysms (by echocardiography) are not completely normal physiologically.[361a] Such patients should be followed with echocardiographic evaluations every 1 to 2 years and undergo stress testing at least once 3 to 5 years after having Kawasaki disease. Restriction of physical activity is not necessary for patients who have no stress test abnormalities. Angiography is indicated only if electrocardiographic or stress test abnormalities develop.[50]

PATIENTS WITH PERSISTENT SMALL TO MEDIUM SOLITARY CORONARY ANEURYSMS

Patients with solitary small to medium coronary artery aneurysms that persist should be maintained on daily low-dose aspirin with annual echocardiographic follow-up. Stress testing every 1 to 2 years should be performed and the amount of allowable physical activity guided by the results. Angiography should be performed if stenosis is suggested.[50]

PATIENTS WITH GIANT CORONARY ANEURYSMS OR MULTIPLE SMALLER ANEURYSMS

Therapy with aspirin, 3 to 5 mg/kg once daily, with or without dypyridamole, 3 to 4 mg/kg/day in three doses, or clopidogrel, is indicated for children with giant (more than 8 mm in diameter) or multiple coronary aneurysms and should be continued indefinitely.[50] Anticoagulant therapy with warfarin, with the INR maintained at approximately 2.0 to 2.5, should be added in most of these patients because they are at substantial risk for development of coronary thrombosis. All such patients should be under the care of a pediatric cardiologist with experience in managing patients with Kawasaki disease. Cardiac evaluation should be performed every 6 to 12 months with periodic stress testing. Angiography should be performed after the acute stage of disease to define the extent of disease and should be repeated whenever symptoms or stress tests indicate myocardial ischemia. Physical activity should be regulated on the basis of results of the stress test and level of anticoagulation, with participation in strenuous athletics discouraged.[50]

PATIENTS WITH CORONARY OBSTRUCTION

Patients with obstructive lesions or signs of ischemia need to be evaluated promptly for possible intervention. Balloon angioplasty, rotational ablation angioplasty, coronary artery bypass grafting, and even cardiac transplantation all have been employed for patients with Kawasaki disease who also have serious coronary artery pathology.[7, 42, 99, 156] A Japanese national committee has published guidelines for catheter interventional procedures related to stenotic coronary artery lesions.[119a] Arterial bypass grafts have been shown to be superior to venous grafts in patients with Kawasaki disease.[156] Balloon angioplasty procedures have been associated with high rates of restenosis in such patients with coronary stenosis.[7]

Complications

MYOCARDIAL INFARCTION

Myocardial infarction is the most common cause of death in Kawasaki disease. In a cooperative Japanese study of 195 cases, the first myocardial infarction was fatal in 22 percent and asymptomatic in 37 percent.[135] It usually occurred in the first year after onset of disease. Major symptoms were shock, vomiting, and abdominal pain, with chest pain complaints only in children older than 4 years of age. Of those who survived a first attack, 16 percent had a second myocardial infarct.[133, 135] Fatal infarctions tended to involve the left main coronary artery or a combination of the right and left anterior descending coronaries; survivors were most likely to have isolated right coronary involvement.[135] Approximately one half of acute myocardial infarction survivors had one or more complications, including ventricular dysfunction, mitral regurgitation, and arrhythmias. Patients with giant (larger than 8 mm) coronary aneurysms are at greatest risk for developing infarcts. Parents of all children with coronary abnormalities should be instructed to seek emergency medical assistance if chest pain, dyspnea, lethargy, or syncope develops. Prompt fibrinolytic therapy should be attempted at a tertiary care center if acute coronary thrombosis is diagnosed.[132] The degree of reversibility of coronary thrombosis in children with Kawasaki disease may be somewhat less than that in adults with atherosclerotic disease.

OTHER CARDIAC COMPLICATIONS

Other cardiac complications include myocardial fibrosis, valvulitis, and coronary rupture. One review suggested that valvular disease occurs in more than 1 percent of cases, most of which resulted in mitral regurgitation.[6, 157] Patients with well-documented aortic regurgitation also have been observed. One patient with Kawasaki disease developed severe aortic and mitral regurgitation that necessitated two-valve replacement.[95] In one recent study, coronary rupture occurred more commonly among older children who died of Kawasaki disease, whereas myocardial infarction was found more commonly in younger fatal cases.[281]

PERIPHERAL GANGRENE

A rare but very serious complication in the acute febrile stage of Kawasaki disease is severe peripheral ischemia and gangrene of distal extremities.[349] These patients have been young infants up to about 7 months of age with giant coronary aneurysms, and some develop peripheral (especially axillary) arterial aneurysms as well. This complication is virtually unknown in Japan[145] and has been reported primarily in non-Asian children in North America.[349] Possible pathogenic mechanisms of peripheral gangrene include severe arteritis of digital or other small peripheral arteries; arteriospasm of peripheral arteries, perhaps in association with severe vasculitis; thrombosis of inflamed or spastic arteries as a result of stasis and damaged endothelium; thrombosis of a more proximal aneurysm (especially axillary) with embolism distally; rarely, cardiogenic shock; and, most likely, a combination of these factors.[349, 357]

NONVASCULAR COMPLICATIONS

As many as 10 percent of patients with Kawasaki disease develop painful arthritis in the acute stage that may require treatment with a nonsteroidal anti-inflammatory agent. We have had considerable success using naproxen, most often at 10 to 15 mg/kg/day divided in two to three doses for several weeks.

Abdominal pain and diarrhea in the early acute stage usually respond to intravenous hydration and supportive care. Hydrops of the gallbladder presents clinically as right upper quadrant tenderness or mass with or without obstructive jaundice and can be confirmed by ultrasonography. Cholecystectomy is not necessary. Hepatic involvement appears to be entirely self-limited and has not been associated with chronic liver disease.

Rare events that occur in association with Kawasaki disease include hearing loss,[323] facial nerve palsy,[89] pneumonitis, and pulmonary nodules.[70a] Telephone consultation with, or referral to, a center that treats large numbers of patients with Kawasaki disease should be sought by the physician faced with rare or serious complications.

Prognosis

Kawasaki disease normally is an acute and self-limited illness (Table 82–5). However, cardiac abnormalities that develop when the disease is acute may be progressive. Approximately 20 to 25 percent of patients not treated with IVIG develop coronary abnormalities that are detectable by angiography or two-dimensional echocardiography. The risk for development of coronary aneurysms is reduced to approximately 3 percent when IVIG is given in the first 10 days of illness.[238, 239] However, the coronary abnormality rates for young infants treated with IVIG are somewhat higher. Patients with moderate to severe coronary abnormalities are at risk for developing myocardial ischemia, myocardial infarction, and sudden death for at least 5 years after onset of illness.[135, 232a]

Regression of small and medium aneurysms is a common occurrence. Overall, approximately one half of children with coronary aneurysms 4 to 8 weeks after onset demonstrate regression by 2 years, with apparently normal vessels on angiography or echocardiography.[133, 136] Regression of the internal diameter of the vessel to normal may occur by intimal proliferation or by thrombus organization and recanalization. If regression occurs, it does so within 2 years of disease onset.[136] Regressed aneurysmal segments have abnormal functional responses, with decreased ability to dilate in response to exercise or pharmacologic agents.[292, 319] Only a minority of regressed aneurysms progress to stenosis, but tortuosity and coronary thrombosis may occur.[137, 319, 325]

Patients with giant coronary aneurysms are at particular risk for development of significant stenosis with resultant myocardial ischemia.[118, 141] The risk for significant stenosis, usually developing at the inlet or outlet of a moderate to large coronary aneurysm, shows a steady rise over 15 to 20 years of observation.[128, 141, 319, 325] These markedly abnormal vessels are subject to calcification and thrombosis and may lead to myocardial ischemia or infarction. The risk for developing a giant aneurysm also is reduced dramatically by IVIG therapy.[278] In the U.S. Multicenter Kawasaki Disease Study Group experience, only 6 of 800 patients treated with IVIG developed giant aneurysms, but only three developed such changes after IVIG was begun.[45]

TABLE 82–5 ■ CARDIAC ABNORMALITIES IN KAWASAKI DISEASE

Acute Stage
Pericardial effusion
Decreased myocardial function
Mitral regurgitation
Brightness of coronary artery wall on echocardiogram
Enlargement (ectasia) of coronary arteries

Subacute Stage
Coronary aneurysms, irregularity, ectasia
Mitral or aortic regurgitation (rare)
Coronary aneurysm rupture (rare)

Convalescent Stage
Persistent coronary aneurysms
Regressed coronary aneurysms (residual fibrosis)
Coronary artery stenosis
Coronary aneurysm rupture (very rare)

Functional abnormalities of vascular endothelium relaxation have been reported years after onset of Kawasaki disease[59, 219] and warrant further investigation. Newer imaging methods have demonstrated vascular wall changes, sometimes even in patients with no history of abnormalities in the acute phase. The meaning of these findings in those thought to have escaped development of coronary abnormalities with acute Kawasaki disease and their long-term significance are uncertain.

Ten- to 20-year follow-up studies of Kawasaki disease patients have been reported.[128, 141, 318, 325, 326] The arteries most likely to develop stenosis are the right main and left anterior descending. A limited number of postmortem studies of adults with history of diagnosed Kawasaki disease or a compatible clinical illness have been performed. Fatty deposits and advanced changes resembling atherosclerotic disease occasionally have been found,[330] raising the important question of whether Kawasaki disease patients are at increased risk for development of premature or more severe atherosclerosis. Intravascular ultrasound studies show that thickened intima and media and calcification are present in areas of regressed coronary aneurysms.[100, 320]

A survey of Japanese adult cardiologists identified 130 adults with coronary aneurysms detected by angiography to evaluate myocardial infarction or ischemia.[138] Twenty-one of these patients (mean age, 34 years; range, 20 to 63 years) had a history compatible with Kawasaki disease in childhood. These patients had severe coronary disease with myocardial infarction, angina pectoris, mitral regurgitation, arrhythmias, congestive failure, and need for coronary bypass grafting. This study and a similar one in the United States[32a] indicate that the coronary artery sequelae of Kawasaki disease are likely important causes of ischemic heart disease in young adults.

REFERENCES

1. Abe, J., Kotzin, B. L., Jujo, K., et al.: Selective expansion of T cells expressing T-cell receptor variable regions V beta 2 and V beta 8 in Kawasaki disease. Proc. Natl. Acad. Sci. U. S. A. *89*:4066–4070, 1992.
2. Abe, J., Kotzin, B. L., Meissner, C., et al.: Characterization of T cell repertoire changes in acute Kawasaki disease. J. Exp. Med. *177*:791–796, 1993.
3. Abe, J., Takeda, T., Ito, Y., et al.: TCR-Vβ specificity of *Staphylococcus aureus* isolated from acute patients with Kawasaki syndrome. *In* Kato, H. (ed.): Kawasaki Disease. Amsterdam, Elsevier Science, 1995, pp. 127–132.
4. Abe, Y., Nakano, S., Nakahara, T., et al.: Detection of serum antibody by the antimitogen assay against streptococcal erythrogenic toxins: Age distribution in children and the relation to Kawasaki disease. Pediatr. Res. *27*:11–15, 1990.
5. Ahlström, H., Lundström, N. R., Mortensson, W., et al.: Infantile periarteritis nodosa or mucocutaneous lymph node syndrome: A report of four cases and diagnostic considerations. Acta Paediatr. Scand. *66*:193–198, 1977.
6. Akagi, T., Kato, H., Inoue, O., et al.: Valvular heart disease in Kawasaki syndrome: Incidence and natural history. Am. Heart J. *120*:366–372, 1990.
7. Akagi, T., Ogawa, S., Ino, T., et al.: Catheter interventional therapy in Kawasaki disease. J. Pediatr. *137*:181–186, 2000.
8. Akagi, T., Rose, V., Benson, L. N., et al.: Outcome of coronary artery aneurysms after Kawasaki disease. J. Pediatr. *121*:689–694, 1992.
9. Amano, S., Hazama, F., and Hamashima, Y.: Pathology of Kawasaki disease. I. Pathology and morphogenesis of the vascular changes. Jpn. Circ. J. *43*:633–643, 1979.
10. Amano, S., Hazama, F., and Hamashima, Y.: Pathology of Kawasaki disease. II. Distribution and incidence of the vascular lesions. Jpn. Circ. J. *43*:741–748, 1979.
11. Amano, S., Hazama, F., Kubagawa, H., et al.: General pathology of Kawasaki disease. Acta Pathol. Jpn. *30*:681–694, 1980.
12. Anderson, L. J., Morens, D. M., and Hurwitz, E. S.: Kawasaki disease in a young adult. Arch. Intern. Med. *140*:280–281, 1980.
13. Arita, K., Ikuta, K., Nishi, Y., et al.: Heterophile Hanganutziu-Deicher antibodies in sera of patients with Kawasaki diseases. Biken J. *25*:157–162, 1982.
14. Asai, T.: Evaluation method for the degree of seriousness in Kawasaki disease. Acta Paediat. Jpn. *25*:170–175, 1983.
15. Aschner, M., and Aschner, J. L.: Mucocutaneous lymph node syndrome: Is there a relationship to mercury exposure? Am. J. Dis. Child. *143*:1133–1134, 1989.
16. Barbour, A. G., Krueger, G. G., Feorino, P. M., et al.: Kawasaki-like disease in a young adult: Association with primary Epstein-Barr virus infection. J. A. M. A. *241*:397–398, 1979.
17. Barron, K. S., Montalvo, J. F., Joseph, A. K., et al.: Soluble interleukin-2 receptors in children with Kawasaki syndrome. Arthritis Rheum. *33*:1371–1377, 1990.
18. Barron, K. S., Murphy, D. J., Silverman, E. D., et al.: Treatment of Kawasaki syndrome: A comparison of two dosage regimens of intravenously administered globulins. J. Pediatr. *117*:638–644, 1990.
19. Barron, K. S., Silverman, E. D., Gonzales, J. C., et al.: Major histocompatibility complex class II alleles in Kawasaki syndrome: Lack of consistent correlation with disease or cardiac involvement. J. Rheumatol. *19*:1790–1793, 1992.
20. Becker, A. E.: Kawasaki disease. Lancet *1*:864, 1976.
21. Becker, A. E., Beekman, R. P., and van der Hal, A. L.: De infantiele polyarteritis nodosa en de ziekte van Kawasaki ("muco-cutaneous lymph node syndrome"): Twee verschillende ziekten of uitingen van een zelfde ziekteproces? Ned. Tijdschr. Geneeskd. *120*:2147–2151, 1976.

21a. Beiser, A. S., Takahashi, M., Baker, A. L., et al.: A predictive instrument for coronary artery aneurysms in Kawasaki disease. Am. J. Cardiol. *81*:1116–1120, 1998.

22. Bell, D. M., Brink, E. W., Nitzkin, J., et al.: Kawasaki syndrome: Description of two outbreaks in the United States. N. Engl. J. Med. *304*:1568–1575, 1981.
23. Bell, D. M., Morens, D. M., Holman, R. C., et al.: Kawasaki syndrome in the United States. Am. J. Dis. Child. *137*:211–224, 1983.
24. Bergeson, P. S., Serlin, S. P., and Corman, L. I.: Mucocutaneous lymph-node syndrome with a positive Weil-Felix reaction but negative *Leptospira* studies. Lancet *1*:720–721, 1978.
25. Birdi, N., Klassen, T., Quinlan, A., et al.: Role of the toxic neutrophil count in the early diagnosis of Kawasaki disease. J. Rheumatol. *26*:904–908, 1999.
26. Blum-Hoffmann, E., Hoffman, G. F., Wessel, A., et al.: Kawasaki Syndrome: Association mit der Exposition von Teppichshampoo und erfolgreiche Therapie mit Immunoglobulinen in der zweiten Krankheitswoche. Monatsschr. Kinderheilk. *140*:273–276, 1992.
27. Bos, S. E., and Kooi-Voskuyl, M. J. P.: Het mucocutane lymfklier-syndroom, de ziekte van Kawasaki. Ned. Tijdschr. Geneeskd. *122*:1184–1187, 1978.
28. Boven, K., De Fraeff-Meeder, E. R., Spliet, W., et al.: Atypical Kawasaki disease: An often missed diagnosis. Eur. J. Pediatr. *151*:577–580, 1992.
29. Brown, T. J., Crawford, S.E., Cornwall, M. L., et al.: CD8 T lymphocytes and macrophages infiltrate coronary artery aneurysms in acute Kawasaki disease. J. Infect. Dis. *184*:940–943, 2001.
30. Bülow, S. L., Hansen, U. S., Hansen, D., et al.: Kawasaki's sygdom: Forekomst i Danmark i perioden 1981–1990. Ugeskr. Laeger. *156*:4813–4816, 1994.
31. Burke, M. J., and Rennebohm, R. M.: Eye involvement in Kawasaki disease. J. Pediatr. Ophthalmol. Strabismus *18*:7–11, 1981.
32. Burns, J. C., Geha, R. S., Schneeberger, E. E., et al.: Polymerase activity in lymphocyte culture supernatants from patients with Kawasaki disease. Nature *323*:814–816, 1987.

32a. Burns, J. C., Shike, H., Gordon, J. B., et al.: Sequelae of Kawasaki disease in adolescents and young adults. J. Am. Coll. Cardiol. *28*:253–257, 1996.

33. Burns, J. C., Wiggins, J. W., Toews, W. H., et al.: Clinical spectrum of Kawasaki syndrome in infants younger than 6 months of age. J. Pediatr. *109*:759–763, 1986.
34. Butler, D. F., Hough, D. R., Friedman, S. J., et al.: Adult Kawasaki syndrome. Arch. Dermatol. *123*:1356–1361, 1987.
35. Cabana, V. G., Gidding, S. S., Getz, G. S., et al.: Serum amyloid A and high density lipoprotein participate in the acute phase response of Kawasaki disease. Pediatr. Res. *42*:651–655, 1997.
36. Capps, J. A.: Aneurysm of the coronary artery: A report of two cases. Am. J. Med. Sci. *118*:312–318, 1889.
37. Caron, G. A.: Kawasaki disease in an adult. J. A. M. A. *243*:430, 1980.
38. Carter, R. F., Haynes, M. E., and Morton, J.: *Rickettsia*-like bodies and splenitis in Kawasaki disease. Lancet *2*:1254–1255, 1976.
39. Casey, F., Craig, B., Shanks, D., et al.: Kawasaki disease: The Northern Ireland experience. Ir. J. Med. Sci. *162*:397–400, 1993.
40. Centers for Disease Control: Lyme disease. M. M. W. R. Morb. Mortal. Wkly. Rep. *30*:668–672, 1989.
41. Chang, C. C., Hawkins, B. R., Kao, H. K., et al.: Human leukocyte antigens in Southern Chinese with Kawasaki disease. Eur. J. Pediatr. *151*:866, 1992.
42. Checcia, P. A., Pahl, E., Shaddy, R., and Shulman, S. T.: Cardiac transplantation for Kawasaki disease. Pediatrics *100*:695–699, 1997.
43. Chiba, S., Kaneko, K., Hashimoto, N., et al.: *Yersinia pseudotuberculosis* and Kawasaki disease. Pediatr. Infect. Dis. *2*:494, 1983.
44. Choi, I., Chwae, Y., Shim, W., et al.: Clonal expansion of CD8 positive T cells in Kawasaki disease. J. Immunol. *159*:481–486, 1997.

45. Chung, K. J., and U.S. Multicenter Kawasaki Study Group: Incidence and prognosis of giant coronary artery aneurysms in Kawasaki disease. Circulation *80*(Suppl. II):282, 1989.
46. Chusid, M. J., and Tang, T. T.: Fever, diarrhea, anemia, rash, and acrocyanosis in a 2-month-old girl. J. Pediatr. *93*:1052–1057, 1978.
47. Crocker, D. W., Sobin, S., and Thomas, W. C.: Aneurysms of the coronary arteries: Report of three cases in infants and review of the literature. Am. J. Pathol. *33*:819–843, 1957.
48. Cunningham, M. W., Meissner, H. C., Heuser, J. S., et al.: Anti-human cardiac myosin autoantibodies in Kawasaki disease. J. Immunol. *163*:1060–1065, 1999.
49. Curtis, N., Zheng, R., Lamb, J. R., et al.: Evidence for a superantigen-mediated process in Kawasaki disease. Arch. Dis. Child. *72*:308–311, 1995.
50. Dajani, A. S., Taubert, K. A., Gerber, M. A., et al.: Diagnosis and therapy of Kawasaki disease in children. Circulation *87*:1776–1780, 1993.
51. Dajani, A. S., Taubert, K. A., Takahashi, M., et al.: Guidelines for long-term management of patients with Kawasaki disease. Circulation *89*:916–922, 1994.
51a. Dale, R. C., Saleem, M. A., Daw, S., et al.: Treatment of severe complicated Kawasaki disease with oral prednisolone and aspirin. J. Pediatr. *137*:723–726, 2000.
52. Daniels, S. R., Specker, B.: Association of rug shampooing and Kawasaki disease. J. Pediatr. *118*:485–488, 1991.
53. Davis, R. L., Waller, P. L., Mueller, B. A., et al.: Kawasaki syndrome in Washington State: Race-specific incidence rates and residential proximity to water. Arch. Pediatr. Adolesc. Med. *149*:66–69, 1995.
54. Dean, A. G., Melish, M. E., Hicks, R. V., et al.: An epidemic of Kawasaki syndrome in Hawaii. J. Pediatr. *100*:552–557, 1982.
55. DeInocencio, J., and Hirsch, R.: The role of T cells in Kawasaki disease. Crit. Rev. Immunol. *15*:349–357, 1995.
56. Della Porta, G. G., and Alberta, A.: Kawasaki disease in Europe. Lancet *1*:797–798, 1977.
57. Dengler, L. D., Capparelli, E. V., Bastian, J. F., et al.: Cerebrospinal fluid profile in acute Kawasaki disease. Pediatr. Infect. Dis. J. *17*:478–481, 1998.
58. Dennis, M. K., Ayoub, E. M., Graham, T., et al.: Mucocutaneous lymph node syndrome in Florida. J. Fla. Med. Assoc. *64*:21–26, 1977.
59. Dhillon, R., Clarkson, P., Donald, S. E., et al.: Endothelial dysfunction late after Kawasaki disease. Circulation *94*:2103–2106, 1990.
60. Ding, X. T., Yang, X. Q., Li, C. R., et al.: Immunologic abnormalities in children with acute Kawasaki disease. Chin. Med. J. (Engl.) *106*:688–692, 1993.
60a. Du, Z.-D., Zhang, T., Liang, L., et al.: Epidemiologic picture of Kawasaki disease in Beijing from 1995 through 1999. Pediatr. Infect. Dis. J. *21*:103–107, 2002.
61. Eberhard, B. A., Anderson, U., Laxer, R. M., et al.: Evaluation of the cytokine response in Kawasaki disease. Pediatr. Infect. Dis. J. *14*:199–203, 1995.
62. Edlinger, E. A., Benichou, J. J., and Labrune, B.: Positive *Ehrlichia canis* serology in Kawasaki disease. Lancet *1*:1146–1147, 1980.
63. Embil, J. A., McFarlane, E. S., Murphy, D. M., et al.: Adenovirus type 2 isolated from a patient with fatal Kawasaki disease. Can. Med. Assoc. J. *132*:1400, 1985.
64. Enders, G., Biber, M., Meyer, G., et al.: Prevalence of antibodies to human herpesvirus 6 in different age groups, in children with exanthem subitum, other acute exanthematous childhood diseases, Kawasaki syndrome, and acute infections with other herpes viruses and HIV. Infection *18*:12–15, 1990.
65. Engle, M. A., Fatica, N. S., Bussel, J. B., et al.: Clinical trial of single dose intravenous gamma globulin in Kawasaki disease: Preliminary report. Am. J. Dis. Child. *143*:1300–1304, 1989.
66. Everett, E. D.: Mucocutaneous lymph node syndrome (Kawasaki's disease) in adults. J. A. M. A. *242*:542–543, 1979.
67. Fatica, N. S., Ichida, F., Engle, M. A., et al.: Rug shampoo and Kawasaki disease. Pediatrics *84*:231–234, 1989.
68. Felz, M., Patni, A., Brooks, S., et al.: Periorbital vasculitis complicating Kawasaki syndrome in an infant. Pediatrics *101*:6–9, 1998.
69. Fildes, N., Burns, J. C., Newburger, J. W., et al.: The HLA class II region and susceptibility to Kawasaki disease. Tissue Antigens *39*:99–101, 1992.
70. Fowler, R. N., Stevenson, R. E., Burton, O. M., et al.: Mucocutaneous lymph node syndrome in South Carolina. J. South Carolina Med. Assoc. *75*:11–14, 1979.
70a. Freeman, A., Crawford, S. E., Finn, L. S., et al.: Inflammatory pulmonary nodules in Kawasaki disease. (Abstract 1612). Pediatr. Res. *51*:277A, 2002.
71. Fujimoto, T., Kato, H., Ichiose, E., et al.: Immune complex and mite antigen in Kawasaki disease. Lancet *2*:980–981, 1982.
72. Fujita, Y., Nakamura, Y., Sakata, K., et al.: Kawasaki disease in families. Pediatrics *84*:666–669, 1989.
73. Fujiwara, H., Fujiwara, T., Kao, T. C., et al.: Pathology of Kawasaki disease in the healed stage: Relationships between typical and atypical cases of Kawasaki disease. Acta Pathol. Jpn. *36*:857–867, 1986.
74. Fujiwara, H., and Hamashima, Y.: Pathology of the heart in Kawasaki disease. Pediatrics *61*:100–107, 1978.
75. Fujiwara, H., Kao, T. C., Shimizu, J., et al.: Microorganism in the heart in Kawasaki disease. Lancet *2*:620–621, 1983.
76. Fujiwara, H., Kawai, C., and Hamashima, Y.: Clinico-pathologic study of the conduction systems in 10 patients with Kawasaki's disease (mucocutaneous lymph node syndrome). Am. Heart J. *96*:744–750, 1978.
77. Fujiwara, T., Fujiwara, H., and Nakano, H.: Pathological features of coronary arteries in children with Kawasaki disease in which coronary arterial aneurysm was absent at autopsy: Quantitative analysis. Circulation *78*:345–350, 1988.
78. Fukushige, J., Takahashi, N., and Ueda, Y.: Incidence and clinical features of incomplete Kawasaki disease. Acta Paediatr. *83*:1057–1060, 1994.
79. Fukushige, J., Takahashi, N., Ueda K., et al.: Kawasaki disease and parvovirus B19 antibody: Role of immunoglobulin therapy in Kawasaki disease. *In* Kato, H. (ed.): Kawasaki Disease. Amsterdam, Elsevier Science, 1995, pp. 170–173.
80. Fulton, D. R.: Effects of current therapy of Kawasaki disease on eicosanoid metabolism. Am. J. Cardiol. *61*:1323–1327, 1988.
81. Furukawa, S., Imai, K., Matsubara, T., et al.: Increased levels of ICAM-1 in Kawasaki disease. Arthritis Rheum. *35*:672–677, 1992.
82. Furukawa, S., Matsubara, T., Jujoh, K., et al.: Peripheral blood monocyte/macrophages and serum tumor necrosis factor in Kawasaki disease. Clin. Immunol. Immunopathol. *48*:247–251, 1988.
83. Furukawa, S., Matsubara, T., Motohashi, T., et al.: Expression of FcεR2/CD23 on peripheral blood macrophages/monocytes in Kawasaki disease. Clin. Immunol. Immunopathol. *56*:280–286, 1990.
84. Furukawa, S., Matsubara, T., Jujoh, K., et al.: Reduction of peripheral blood macrophages/monocytes in Kawasaki disease by intravenous gamma globulin. Eur. J. Pediatr. *150*:43–47, 1990.
85. Furukawa, S., Matsubara, T., and Yabuta, K.: Mononuclear cell subsets and coronary artery lesions in Kawasaki disease. Arch. Dis. Child. *67*:706–708, 1992.
86. Furumoto, H., Sakano, T., Tanabe, A., et al.: Serum soluble CD8 antigen level is not elevated in mucocutaneous lymph node syndrome (Kawasaki disease) in spite of an increase in serum soluble interleukin 2 receptors. Eur. J. Pediatr. *149*:448–449, 1990.
87. Furusho, K., Kamiya, T., Nakano, H., et al.: High-dose intravenous gamma globulin for Kawasaki disease. Lancet *2*:1055–1058, 1984.
88. Furusho, K., Ohba, T., Soeda, T., et al.: Possible role for mite antigen in Kawasaki disease. Lancet *2*:194–195, 1981.
89. Gallagher, P. G.: Facial nerve paralysis and Kawasaki disease. Rev. Infect. Dis. *12*:403–405, 1990.
90. Gavin, P., Crawford, S., Shulman, S. T., and Rowley, A.H.: Differential expression of matrix metalloproteinases-2 and -9 in coronary aneurysms in acute Kawasaki disease. Submitted.
91. Gee, S. J.: Aneurysms of the coronary arteries in a boy. St. Barth. Hosp. Rep. Lond. *7*:148, 1871.
92. Gentles, T. L., Clarkson, P. M., Trenholme, A. A., et al.: Kawasaki disease in Auckland, 1979–1988. N. Z. Med. J. *103*:389–391, 1990.
93. Germain, B. F., Moroney, J. D., Guggino, G. S., et al.: Anterior uveitis in Kawasaki disease. J. Pediatr. *97*:780–781, 1980.
94. Gidding, S. S., Duffy, C. E., Pajcic, S., et al.: Usefulness of echocardiographic evidence of pericardial effusion and mitral regurgitation in predicting coronary artery aneurysms. Am. J. Cardiol. *60*:76–79, 1987.
95. Gidding, S. S., Shulman, S. T., Ilbawi, M., et al.: Mucocutaneous lymph node syndrome (Kawasaki disease): Delayed aortic and mitral insufficiency secondary to active valvulitis. J. Am. Coll. Cardiol. *7*:894–897, 1986.
96. Giesker, D. W., Krause, P. J., Pastuszak, W. T., et al.: Lymph node biopsy for early diagnosis in Kawasaki disease. Am. J. Surg. Pathol. *6*:493–501, 1982.
97. Glanzer, J. M., Galbraith, W. B., and Jacobs, J. P.: Kawasaki disease in a 28-year-old man. J. A. M. A. *244*:1604–1606, 1980.
98. Glode, M. P., Brogden, R., Joffe, L. S., et al.: Kawasaki syndrome and house dust mite exposure. Pediatr. Infect. Dis. J. *5*:644–648, 1986.
99. Gotteiner, N. L., Mavroudis, C., Backer, C. L., et al.: Coronary artery bypass grafting for Kawasaki disease. Pediatr. Cardiol. *23*:62–67, 2002.
100. Hamada, R., Uehara, R., and Fuyama, Y.: CT detection of coronary calcification in Kawasaki disease. *In* Kato, H. (ed.): Kawasaki Disease. Amsterdam, Elsevier Science, 1995, pp. 598–602.
101. Hamasaki, Y., Ichimaru, T., Koga, H., et al.: Increased in vitro leukotriene B4 production by stimulated polymorphonuclear cells in Kawasaki disease. Acta Paediatr. Jpn. *31*:346–348, 1989.
102. Hamasaki, Y., and Miyazaki, S.: Leukotriene B4 and Kawasaki disease. Acta Paediatr. Jpn. *33*:771–777, 1991.
103. Hamashima, Y., Kishi, K., and Tasaka, K.: *Rickettsia*-like bodies in infantile acute febrile mucocutaneous lymph-node syndrome. Lancet *2*:42, 1973.
104. Hamashima, Y., Tasaka, K., Hoshino, T., et al.: Mite-associated particles in Kawasaki disease. Lancet *2*:266, 1982.
105. Hammerschlag, M., Boman, J., Rowley, A.H.: Failure to demonstrate *Chlamydia pneumoniae* in cardiovascular tissue from children with Kawasaki disease. Pediatr. Infect. Dis J. *20*:76–77, 2001.

106. Hansen, R. C.: Staphylococcal scaled skin syndrome, toxic shock syndrome, and Kawasaki disease. Pediatr. Clin. North Am. *30*:533–544, 1983.
107. Harada, K., Yamaguchi, H., Kato, H., et al.: Indication for IVGG in Kawasaki disease. *In* Takahashi, M., and Taubert, K. A. (eds.): Proceedings of Fourth International Symposium on Kawasaki disease. Dallas, American Heart Association, 1993, pp. 459–462.
107a. Harnden, A., Alves, B., and Sheikh, A.: Rising incidence of Kawasaki disease in England: Analysis of hospital admission data. B. M. J. *324*:1424–1425, 2002.
107b. Hashino, K., Ishii, M., Iemura, M., et al.: Re-treatment for immune globulin–resistant Kawasaki disease: A comparative study of additional immune globulin and steroid pulse therapy. Pediatr. Int. *43*:211–217, 2001.
108. Headings, D. L., and Santosham, M.: Kawasaki disease associated with serologic evidence of Rocky Mountain spotted fever. Johns Hopkins Med. J. *149*:220–221, 1981.
109. Herman, A., Kappler, J. W., Marrack, P., et al.: Superantigens: Mechanism of T cell stimulation and role in immunologic responses. Annu. Rev. Immunol. *9*:745–772, 1991.
110. Herold, B. C., Davis, A. T., Arroyave, C. M., et al.: Cryoprecipitates in Kawasaki syndrome: Association with coronary artery aneurysms. Pediatr. Infect. Dis. J. *7*:255–257, 1988.
111. Hewitt, C. J.: Case of Kawasaki disease. B. M. J. *1*:883–884, 1977.
112. Hicks, R. V., and Melish, M. E.: Kawasaki syndrome: Rheumatic complaints and analysis of salicylate therapy. Arthritis Rheum. *22*:621–622, 1979.
113. Hidaka, T., Nakano, M., Ueta, T., et al.: Increased synthesis of thromboxane A2 by platelets from patients with Kawasaki disease. J. Pediatr. *102*:94–96, 1983.
114. Hirao, J., Hibi, S., Andoh, T., et al.: High levels of circulating IL-4 and IL-10 in Kawasaki disease. Int. Arch. Allergy Immunol. *112*:152–156, 1997.
114a. Holman, R. C., Belay, E. D., Clarke, M. J., et al.: Kawasaki syndrome among American Indian and Alaska Native children, 1980 through 1995. Pediatr. Infect. Dis. J. *18*:451–455, 1999.
115. Hurvitz, H., Branski, D., Gross-Kieselstein, E., et al.: Acetaminophen hypersensitivity resembling Kawasaki disease. Israel J. Med. Sci. *20*:145–147, 1984.
116. Ichida, F., Fatica, N. S., O'Loughlin, J. E., et al.: Epidemiologic aspects of Kawasaki disease in a Manhattan hospital. Pediatrics *84*:235–241, 1989.
117. Imada, Y., Kawasaki, T., and Nakamura, Y.: Cousin cases of Kawasaki disease suggesting person-to-person transmission. Pediatrics *85*:1127, 1990.
118. Inoue, O., Akagi, T., and Kato, H.: Fate of giant coronary artery aneurysms in Kawasaki disease. Circulation *80*(Suppl. II):262, 1989.
119. Ishii, A., Yatani, T., Kato, H., et al.: Mite fauna, housedust, and Kawasaki disease. Lancet *2*:102–103, 1983.
119a. Ishii, M., Ueno, T., Akagi, T., et al.: Guidelines for catheter intervention in coronary artery lesion in Kawasaki disease. Pediatr. Int. *43*:558–562, 2001.
120. Iwanaga, M., Takada, K., Osato, T., et al.: Kawasaki disease and Epstein-Barr virus. Lancet *1*:938–939, 1981.
121. Jacob, J. L., Polomeno, R. C., Chad, Z., et al.: Ocular manifestations of Kawasaki disease (mucocutaneous lymph node syndrome). Can. J. Ophthalmol. *17*:199–202, 1982.
122. Jacobs, J. C.: Salicylate treatment of epidemic Kawasaki disease in New York City. Ther. Drug Monit. *1*:123–130, 1979.
123. Joffe, A., Kabani, A., and Jadavji, T.: Atypical and complicated Kawasaki disease in infants: Do we need criteria? West. J. Med. *162*:322–327, 1995.
124. John, T. J., DeBenedetti, C. D., and Zee, M. L.: Mucocutaneous lymph node syndrome in Arizona. Am. J. Dis. Child. *130*:613–614, 1976.
125. Johnson, D., and Azimi, P.: Kawasaki disease associated with *Klebsiella pneumoniae* bacteremia and parainfluenza type 3 virus infection. Pediatr. Infect. Dis. J. *4*:100, 1985.
125a. Johnson, R. M., Little, J. R., and Storch, G. A.: Kawasaki-like syndromes associated with human immnodeficiency virus infection. Clin. Infect. Dis. *32*:1628–1634, 2001.
126. Jordan, S. C., Platts-Mills, T. A., Mason, W., et al.: Lack of evidence for mite-antigen–mediated pathogenesis in Kawasaki disease. Lancet *1*:931, 1983.
127. Kamiya, T.: How to evaluate myocardial ischemia in Kawasaki disease. *In* Kato, H. (ed.): Kawasaki Disease. Amsterdam, Elsevier Science, 1995, pp. 447–450.
128. Kamiya, T., Suzuki, A., Ono, Y., et al.: Angiographic follow-up study of coronary artery lesion in the cases with a history of Kawasaki disease: With a focus on the follow-up more than 10 years after the onset of the disease. *In* Kato, H. (ed.): Kawasaki Disease. Amsterdam, Elsevier Science, 1995, pp. 569–573.
129. Kaneko, K., Savage, C. O., Pottinger, B. E., et al.: Antiendothelial cell antibodies can be cytotoxic to endothelial cells without cytokine pre-stimulation and correlate with ELISA antibody measurement in Kawasaki disease. Clin. Exp. Immunol. *98*:264–269, 1994.
130. Kaslow, R. A., Bailowitz, A., Lin, F. Y. C., et al.: Association of epidemic Kawasaki syndrome with the HLA-A2, B44, Cw5 antigen combination. Arthritis Rheum. *28*:938–940, 1985.
131. Kato, H.: Natural history of Kawasaki disease. *In* Shiokawa Y. (ed.): Vascular Lesions of Collagen Diseases and Related Conditions. Baltimore, University Park Press, 1977, pp. 281–286.
132. Kato, H.: Intracoronary thrombolytic therapy in Kawasaki disease: Treatment and prevention of acute myocardial infarction. Prog. Clin. Biol. Res. *250*:445–454, 1987.
133. Kato, H.: Long-term consequences of Kawasaki disease: Pediatrics to adults. *In* Kato, H. (ed): Kawasaki Disease. Amsterdam, Elsevier Science, 1995, pp. 557–566.
134. Kato, H., and Ichinose, E.: Cardiovascular involvement in Kawasaki disease. Acta Paediatr. Jpn. *26*:132–145, 1984.
135. Kato, H., Ichinose, E., and Kawasaki, T.: Myocardial infarction in Kawasaki disease. J. Pediatr. *108*:923–928, 1986.
136. Kato, H., Ichinose, E., Yoshioka, F., et al.: Fate of coronary aneurysms in Kawasaki disease: Serial coronary angiography and long-term follow-up study. Am. J. Cardiol. *49*:1758–1766, 1982.
137. Kato, H., Inoue, O., and Akagi, T.: Kawasaki disease: Cardiac problems and management. Pediatr. Rev. *9*:209–217, 1988.
138. Kato, H., Inoue, O., Kawasaki, T., et al.: Adult coronary artery disease probably due to childhood Kawasaki disease. Lancet *340*:1127–1129, 1992.
139. Kato, H., Inoue, O., Koga, Y., et al.: Variant strain of *Propionibacterium acnes*: A clue to the aetiology of Kawasaki disease. Lancet *2*:1383–1387, 1983.
140. Kato, H., Koike, S., and Yokoyama, T.: Kawasaki disease: Effect of treatment of coronary artery involvement. Pediatrics *63*:175–179, 1979.
141. Kato, H., Sugimura, T., Akagi, T., et al.: Long-term consequences of Kawasaki disease. Circulation *94*:1279–1285, 1996.
142. Kato, S., Kimura, M., Tsuji, K., et al.: HLA antigens in Kawasaki disease. Pediatrics *61*:252–255, 1978.
143. Kawasaki, T.: Acute febrile mucocutaneous syndrome with lymphoid involvement with specific desquamation of the fingers and toes in children. Jpn. J. Allerg. *16*:178–222, 1967.
144. Kawasaki, T.: Kawasaki disease. Asian Med. J. *32*:497–506, 1989.
145. Kawasaki, T.: Personal communication, March, 2001.
146. Kawasaki, T., Kosaki, F., Okawa, S., et al.: A new infantile acute febrile mucocutaneous lymph node syndrome (MLNS) prevailing in Japan. Pediatrics *54*:271–276, 1974.
147. Keim, D. E., Keller, E. W., and Hirsch, M. S.: Mucocutaneous lymph-node syndrome and parainfluenza 2 virus infection. Lancet *2*:303, 1977.
148. Keren, G., Barzilay, G., Alpert, G., et al.: Mucocutaneous lymph node syndrome (Kawasaki disease) in Israel. Acta Paediatr. Scand. *72*:455–458, 1983.
149. Keren, G., Danon, Y. L., Orgad, S., et al.: HLA Bw 51 is increased in mucocutaneous lymph node syndrome in Israeli patients. Tissue Antigens *20*:144–146, 1982.
150. Kikuta, H., Mizuno, F., and Osato, T.: Kawasaki disease and an unusual primary infection with Epstein-Barr virus. Pediatrics *73*:413–414, 1984.
151. Kikuta, H., Taguchi, Y., Tomizawa, K., et al.: Epstein-Barr virus genome-positive T lymphocytes in a boy with chronic active EBV infection associated with Kawasaki-like disease. Nature *333*:455–457, 1988.
152. Kim, D. S.: Serum interleukin-6 in Kawasaki disease. Yonsei Med. J. *33*:183–188, 1992.
153. Kim, D. S., and Lee, K. Y.: Serum soluble E-selectin levels in Kawasaki disease. Scand. J. Rheumatol. *23*:283–286, 1995.
154. Kim, D. S., Lee, H. K., Noh, G. W., et al.: Increased serum IL-10 in Kawasaki disease. Yonsei Med. J. *37*:125–130, 1996.
155. Kisimoto, T.: B-cell stimulatory factors (BSFs): Molecular structure, biological function, and regulation of expression. J. Clin. Immunol. *7*:343–355, 1987.
156. Kitamura, S., Kamedo, Y., Sekit, S., et al.: Long-term outcome of myocardial revascularization in Kawasaki disease. J. Thorac. Cardiovasc. Surg. *197*:663–674, 1994.
157. Kitamura, S., Kawashima, Y., Kawachi, K., et al.: Severe mitral regurgitation due to coronary arteritis of mucocutaneous lymph node syndrome. J. Thorac. Cardiovasc. Surg. *80*:629–636, 1980.
158. Kobayashi, S., Wada, N., and Kubo, M.: Antibodies to native type III collagen in the serum of patients with Kawasaki disease. Eur. J. Pediatr. *151*:183–187, 1992.
159. Kohsaka, T., Abe, J., Asahina, T., et al.: Classical pathway complement activation in Kawasaki syndrome. J. Allergy Clin. Immunol. *93*:520–525, 1994.
160. Koren, G., Schaffer, F., Silverman, E. D., et al.: Determinants of low serum salicylates in patients with Kawasaki disease. J. Pediatr. *112*:663–667, 1988.
161. Kotb, M.: Superantigens: A possible link between infection and autoimmunity. *In* Kato, H. (ed.): Kawasaki Disease. Amsterdam, Elsevier Science, 1995, pp. 111–119.
162. Krensky, A. M., Berenberg, W., Shanley, K., et al.: HLA antigens in mucocutaneous lymph node syndrome in New England. Pediatrics *67*:741–744, 1981.

163. Krensky, A. M., Grady, S., Shanley, K. M., et al.: Epidemic and endemic HLA-B and DR associations in mucocutaneous lymph node syndrome. Hum. Immunol. *6*:75–77, 1983.
164. Krous, H. F., Clausen, C. R., and Ray, C. G.: Elevated immunoglobulin E in infantile polyarteritis nodosa. Pediatrics *84*:841–845, 1974.
165. Krzyszkowski, J.: Periarteritis nodosa. Przegl. Post. Nauk. Lek. (Warsaw) *38*:30, 45, 58, 1899.
165a. Kuniyuki, S., and Asada, M.: An ulcerated lesion at the BCG vaccination site during the course of Kawasaki disease. J. Am. Acad. Dermatol. *37*:303–304, 1997.
166. Kusakawa, S., and Heiner, D. C.: Elevated levels of immunoglobulin E in the acute febrile mucocutaneous lymph node syndrome. Pediatr. Res. *10*:108–111, 1976.
167. Kusakawa, S., and Tatara, K.: Efficacies and risks of aspirin in the treatment of Kawasaki disease. Prog. Clin. Biol. Res. *20*:401–413, 1987.
168. Kussmaul, A., and Maier, R.: Über eine bisher nicht beschriebene eigenthümliche Arterienerkrankung (periarteritis nodosa), die mit Morbus Brightii und rapid fortschreitender allgemeiner Muskellahmung einhergeht. Deutsches Arch. F. Klin. Med. *1*:484, 1866.
169. Lambert, H. P., Fisher-Hoch, S. P., and Grover, S. A.: Kawasaki disease and *Coxiella burnetii*. Lancet *2*:844, 1985.
170. Landing, B. H., and Larson, E. J.: Are infantile periarteritis nodosa with coronary artery involvement and fatal mucocutaneous lymph node syndrome the same? Comparison of 20 patients from North America with patients from Hawaii and Japan. Pediatrics *59*:651–662, 1977.
171. Lang, B. A., Silverman, E. D., Laxer, R. M., et al.: Spontaneous tumor necrosis factor production in Kawasaki disease. J. Pediatr. *115*:939–943, 1989.
172. Lang, B. A., Silverman, E. D., Laxer, R. M., et al.: Serum-soluble interleukin-2 receptor levels in Kawasaki disease. J. Pediatr. *116*:592–596, 1990.
173. Lapointe, N., Chad, Z., Lacroix, J., et al.: Kawasaki disease: Association with uveitis in seven patients. Pediatrics *69*:376–379, 1982.
174. Larsen, J. H.: Kawasaki disease: A yersiniosis? J. Infect. Dis. *160*:900, 1989.
175. Larson, E. J.: Comparison of pathology of infantile periarteritis nodosa (IPN) with coronary artery disease in North America with Kawasaki disease (MCLS) in Hawaii and Japan. *In* Japan Medical Research Foundation (ed.): Vascular Lesions of Collagen Diseases and Related Conditions. Tokyo, University of Tokyo Press, 1977, pp. 322–334.
176. Lee, D. B.: Epidemiological survey of Kawasaki syndrome in Korea (1976–1984). J. Cath. Med. Coll. *38*:13–19, 1985.
177. Lee, D. B.: Epidemiologic study of Kawasaki disease in Korea. Prog. Clin. Biol. Res. *250*:55–60, 1987.
178. Lee, T. J., and Vaughan, D.: Mucocutaneous lymph node syndrome in a young adult. Arch. Intern. Med. *139*:104–105, 1979.
179. Lee, T., Furukawa, S., Fukuda, Y., et al.: Plasma prostaglandin E2 level in Kawasaki disease. Prostaglandins Leukotrienes Essential Fatty Acids *31*:53–57, 1988.
180. Lehman, T. J. A., Warren, R., Gietl, D., et al.: Variable expression of *Lactobacillus casei* wall-induced coronary arteritis: An animal model of Kawasaki's disease in selected inbred mouse strains. Clin. Immunol. Immunopathol. *48*:108–118, 1988.
181. Leung, D. Y. M.: Immunomodulation by intravenous immune globulin in Kawasaki disease. J. Allergy Clin. Immunol. *84*:588–594, 1989.
182. Leung, D. Y. M.: The potential role of cytokine-mediated vascular endothelial cell activation in the pathogenesis of Kawasaki disease. Acta Paediatr. Jpn. *33*:739–744, 1991.
183. Leung, D. Y. M., Burns, J. C., Newburger, J. W., et al.: Reversal of lymphocyte activation in vivo in the Kawasaki syndrome by intravenous gammaglobulin. J. Clin. Invest. *79*:468–472, 1987.
184. Leung, D. Y. M., Chu, E. T., Wood, N., et al.: Immunoregulatory T cell abnormalities in mucocutaneous lymph node syndrome. J. Immunol. *130*:2002–2004, 1983.
185. Leung, D. Y. M., Collins, T., LaPierre, L. A., et al.: Immunoglobulin M antibodies present in the acute phase of Kawasaki syndrome lyse cultured vascular endothelial cells stimulated by gamma interferon. J. Clin. Invest. *77*:1428–1435, 1986.
186. Leung, D. Y. M., Geha, R., Newberger, J.: Two monokines, interleukin-1 and tumor necrosis factor, render cultured vascular endothelial cells susceptible to lysis by antibodies circulating during Kawasaki syndrome. J. Exp. Med. *164*:1958–1972, 1986.
187. Leung, D. Y. M., Kurt-Jones, E., Newberger, J. W., et al.: Endothelial cell activation and high interleukin-1 secretion in the pathogenesis of acute Kawasaki disease. Lancet *2*:1298–1302, 1989.
188. Leung, D. Y. M., Meissner, H. C., Fulton, D. R., et al.: Toxic shock syndrome toxin-secreting *Staphylococcus aureus* in Kawasaki syndrome. Lancet *342*:1385–1388, 1993.
188a. Leung, D. Y. M., Meissner, H. C., Shulman, S. T., et al.: Prevalence of superantigen-secreting bacteria in patients with Kawasaki disease. J. Pediatr. *140*:742–746, 2002.
189. Leung, D. Y. M., Seigel, R. L., Grady, S., et al.: Immunoregulatory abnormalities in mucocutaneous lymph node syndrome. Clin. Immunol. Immunopathol. *23*:100–112, 1982.
190. Levinsky, R., and Marshall, W. C.: Circulating immune complexes in mucocutaneous lymph node syndrome. Arch. Dis. Child. *54*:240–245, 1979.
191. Levy, M., and Koren, G.: Atypical Kawasaki disease: Analysis of clinical presentation and diagnostic clues. Pediatr. Infect. Dis. J. *9*:122–126, 1990.
192. Li, C. R., Yang, X. Q., Shen, J., et al.: Immunoglobulin G subclasses in serum and circulating immune complexes in patients with Kawasaki syndrome. Pediatr. Infect. Dis. J. *9*:544–547, 1990.
193. Lin, C. Y., and Hwang, B.: Serial immunologic studies in patients with mucocutaneous lymph node syndrome (Kawasaki disease). Ann. Allergy *59*:291–297, 1987.
194. Lin, C. Y., Lin, C. C., Hwang, B., et al.: Serial changes of serum interleukin-6, interleukin-8, and tumor necrosis factor alpha among patients with Kawasaki disease. J. Pediatr. *121*:924–926, 1992.
195. Lin, C. Y., Lin, C. C., Hwang, B., et al.: Cytokines predict coronary aneurysm formation in Kawasaki disease patients. Eur. J. Pediatr. *152*:309–312, 1993.
196. Lin, F. Y. C., Bailowitz, A., Koslowe, P., et al.: Kawasaki syndrome: A case-control study during an outbreak in Maryland. Am. J. Dis. Child. *139*:277–279, 1985.
196a. Marasini, M., Pongiglione, G., Gazzolo, D., et al.: Late intravenous gamma globulin treatment in infants and children with Kawasaki disease and coronary artery abnormalities. Am. J. Cardiol. *68*:796–797, 1991.
197. Marchette, N. J., Cao, Y., Kihara, S., et al.: Staphylococcal toxic shock syndrome toxin-1, one possible cause of Kawasaki syndrome. *In* Kato, H. (ed.): Kawasaki Disease. Amsterdam, Elsevier Science, 1995, pp. 149–155.
198. Marchette, N. J., Melish, M. E., Hicks, R., et al.: Epstein-Barr virus and other herpes virus infections in Kawasaki syndrome. J. Infect. Dis. *161*:680–684, 1990.
199. Marchette, N. J., Melish, M. E., James, J. F., et al.: Spirochaetal studies in Kawasaki syndrome. Prog. Clin. Biol. Res. *250*:87–99, 1987.
200. Mason, W., Jordan, S., Sakai, R., et al.: Lack of effect of gamma-globulin infusion on circulating immune complexes in patients with Kawasaki syndrome. Pediatr. Infect. Dis. J. *7*:94–99, 1988.
201. Mason, W. H., Schneider, T., Takahashi, M.: The epidemiology and etiology of Kawasaki disease. Cardiol. Young *1*:196–205, 1991.
202. Mason, W. H., and Takahashi, M.: Kawasaki syndrome. Clin. Infect. Dis. *28*:169–185, 1999.
203. Masuda, H., Shozawa, T., Naoe, S., et al.: The intercostal artery in Kawasaki disease: A pathologic study of 17 autopsy cases. Arch. Pathol. Lab. Med. *110*:1136–1142, 1986.
204. Matsubara, T., Furukawa, S., Ino, T., et al.: A sibship with recurrent Kawasaki disease and coronary artery lesion. Acta Paediatr. *83*:1002–1004, 1994.
205. Matsubara, T., Furukawa, S., and Yabuta, K.: Serum levels of tumor necrosis factor, interleukin-2 receptor, and interferon-gamma in Kawasaki disease involved coronary artery lesions. Clin. Immunol. Immunopathol. *56*:29–36, 1990.
206. Matsuda, I., Hattori, S., Nagata, N., et al.: HLA antigens in mucocutaneous lymph node syndrome. Am. J. Dis. Child. *131*:1417–1418, 1977.
207. Matsuno, S., Utagawa, E., and Sugiura, A.: Association of rotavirus infection with Kawasaki syndrome. J. Infect. Dis. *148*:177, 1983.
208. Maury, C. P. J., Salo, E., and Pelkonen, P.: Circulating interleukin-1 beta in patients with Kawasaki disease. N. Engl. J. Med. *312*:1670–1671, 1988.
209. Maury, C. P. J., Salo, E., and Pelkonen, P.: Elevated circulating tumor necrosis factor-alpha in patients with Kawasaki disease. J. Lab. Clin. Med. *113*:651–654.
210. Mayatepek, E., and Lehmann, W. D.: Increased generation of cysteinyl leukotrienes in Kawasaki disease. Arch. Dis. Child. *72*:526–527, 1995.
211. Meissner, H. C., Schlievert, P. M., Shulman, S. T., et al.: A multi-center, controlled, blinded study to evaluate the role of bacterial superantigens in patients with Kawasaki syndrome. Pediatr. Res. *49*:248A, 2001.
212. Melish, M. E., Hicks, R. M., and Larson, E. J.: Mucocutaneous lymph node syndrome (MCLS) in the U.S. Pediatr. Res. *8*:427, 1974.
213. Melish, M. E., Hicks, R. M., and Larson, E. J.: Mucocutaneous lymph node syndrome in the United States. Am. J. Dis. Child. *130*:599–607, 1976.
214. Melish, M. E., Hicks, R. M., and Reddy, V.: Kawasaki syndrome: An update. Hosp. Pract. *17*:99–106, 1982.
215. Melish, M. E., Marchette, N. J., Kaplan, J. C., et al.: Absence of significant RNA-dependent DNA polymerase activity in lymphocytes from patients with Kawasaki syndrome. Nature *337*:288–290, 1989.
216. Melish, M. E., Parsonett, J., Marchette, N. J.: Kawasaki syndrome is not caused by toxic shock syndrome toxin-1 (TSST-1) positive staphylococci. Pediatr. Res. *35*:187A, 1994.
217. Melish, M. E., Takahashi, M., Shulman, S. T., et al.: Comparison of low dose aspirin versus high dose aspirin as an adjunct to IVGG for Kawasaki syndrome. Pediatr. Res. *31*:170A, 1992.
218. Milgrom, H., Palmer, E. L., Slovin, S. F., et al.: Kawasaki disease in a healthy young adult. Ann. Intern. Med. *92*:467–470, 1980.

219. Mitani, Y., Okada, Y., Inoue, M., et al.: Impaired endothelium dependent relaxation of angiographically normal coronary arteries in patients after Kawasaki disease in the long-term follow-up period. *In* Kato, H. (ed.): Kawasaki Disease. Amsterdam, Elsevier Science, 1995, pp. 587–591.
220. Miyata, K., Kawakami, K., Onimaru, T., et al.: Circulating immune complexes and granulocytes chemotaxis in Kawasaki disease. Jpn. Circ. J. *48*:1350–1353, 1984.
220a. Momenah, T., Sanatani, S., Potts, J., et al.: Kawasaki disease in the older child. Pediatrics *102*:e7, 1998.
221. Morens, D. M.: National surveillance of Kawasaki disease. Pediatrics *65*:21–25, 1980.
222. Moren, D. M.: Kawasaki disease and rug shampooing. J. Pediatr. *120*:333–334, 1992.
223. Morens, D. M., and O'Brien, R. J.: Kawasaki disease in the United States. J. Infect. Dis. *137*:91–93, 1978.
224. Morise, T., Takeuchi, Y., Takeda, R., et al.: Increased plasma endothelin levels in Kawasaki disease: A possible marker for Kawasaki disease. Angiology *44*:719–723, 1993.
225. Munro-Faure, H.: Necrotizing arteritis of the coronary vessels in infancy: Case report and review of the literature. Pediatrics *23*:914–926, 1959.
226. Murata, H.: Experimental arteritis on murine with *Candida*: In relation to arteritis in MCLS (author's translation). Kansenshogaku Zasshi *52*:331–337, 1978.
227. Myones, B., Tomita, S., and Shulman, S. T.: Intravenous IgG administration is associated with a decrease in classical pathway activation products in Kawasaki disease. Arthritis Rheum. *34*(Suppl.):S44, 1991.
228. Nagashima, M., Matsushima, M., Matsuoka, H., et al.: High-dose gamma globulin therapy for Kawasaki disease. J. Pediatr. *110*:710–712, 1987.
229. Nagata, S., Yamashiro, Y., Maeda, M., et al.: Immunohistochemical studies on small intestinal mucosa in Kawasaki disease. Pediatr. Res. *33*:557–563, 1993.
230. Nakamura, Y., Yanagawa, H., and Kawasaki, T.: Temporal and geographical clustering of Kawasaki disease in Japan. Prog. Clin. Biol. Res. *250*:19–32, 1987.
231. Nakamura, Y., Yanagawa, H., and Kawasaki, T.: Mortality among children with Kawasaki disease in Japan. N. Engl. J. Med. *326*:1246–1249, 1992.
232. Nakamura, Y., Hirose, K., Yanagawa, H., et al.: Incidence rate of recurrent Kawasaki disease in Japan. Acta Paediatr. *83*:1061–1064, 1994.
232a. Nakamura, Y., Yanagawa, H., Harada, K., et al.: Mortality among persons with a history of Kawasaki disease in Japan: The fifth look. Arch. Pediatr. Adolesc. Med. *156*:162–165, 2002.
233. Nakamura, Y., Yanagawa, H., Kato, H., et al.: Mortality among children with Kawasaki disease: A third look. Acta Paediatr. Jpn. *40*:419–423, 1998.
234. Nakano, H., Ueda, K., Saito, A., et al.: Scoring method for identifying patients with Kawasaki disease at high risk of coronary artery aneurysms. Am. J. Cardiol. *58*:739–742, 1986.
235. Naoe, S., Shibuya, K., Takahashi,M., et al.: Pathological observations concerning the cardiovascular lesions in Kawasaki disease. Cardiol. Young *1*:212–220, 1991.
236. Newburger, J. W., Burns, J. C., Beiser, A. S., et al.: Altered lipid profile after Kawasaki disease. Circulation *85*:625–631, 1991.
237. Newburger, J. W., Sanders, S. P., Burns, J. C., et al.: Left ventricular contractility and function in Kawasaki disease. Circulation *79*:1237–1246, 1989.
238. Newburger, J. W., and the United States Multicenter Kawasaki Study Group: A single infusion of intravenous gamma globulin compared to four daily doses in the treatment of acute Kawasaki syndrome. N. Engl. J. Med. *324*:1633–1639, 1991.
239. Newburger, J. W., Takahashi, M., Burns, J. C., et al.: The treatment of Kawasaki syndrome with intravenous gamma globulin. N. Engl. J. Med. *315*:341–347, 1986.
240. Ng, M. P., Wong, K. Y., Tan, C. L., et al.: Kawasaki disease: The Singapore experience. Ann. Acad. Med. *18*:15–18, 1989.
241. Nigro, G., and Midulla, M.: Retrovirus and Kawasaki disease. Lancet *2*:1045, 1986.
242. Nigro, G., Zerbine, M., Krzystofia, K., et al.: Active or recent par-vovirus B19 infection in children with Kawasaki disease. Lancet *343*:1260–1261, 1994.
243. Nishiyori, A., Sakaguchi, M., Kato, H., et al.: Toxic shock syndrome toxin 1 and Vβ2 expression on T cells in Kawasaki disease. *In* Kato, H. (ed.): Kawasaki Disease. Amsterdam, Elsevier Science, 1995, pp. 139–143.
244. Niwa, K., Aotsuka, M., Karasawa, K., et al.: Thrombocytopenia: A risk factor for acute myocardial infarction during acute Kawasaki disease. Coronary Artery Dis *6*:857–864, 1995.
245. Niwa, Y., and Sohmiya, K.: Enhanced neutrophilic functions in mucocutaneous lymph node syndrome, with special reference to the possible role of increased oxygen intermediate generation in the pathogenesis of coronary thromboarteritis. J. Pediatr. *104*:56–60, 1984.
246. Noto, N., Ayusawa, M., Karasawa, K., et al.: Dobutamine stress echocardiography for detction of coronary artery stenosis in children with Kawasaki disease. J. Am. Coll. Cardiol. *27*:1251–1256, 1996.
247. Ogawa, S., Zhang, J., Yuge, K., et al.: Increased plasma endothelin-1 concentration in Kawasaki disease. J. Cardiovasc. Pharmacol. *22*(Suppl. 8):S364–S366, 1993.
248. Ogino, H., Ogawa, M., Harima, Y., et al.: Clinical evaluation of gammaglobulin preparations for the treatment of Kawasaki disease. Prog. Clin. Biol. Res. *250*:555–556, 1987.
249. Ohga, K., Yamanaha, R., Kinumaki, H., et al.: Kawasaki disease and rug shampoo. Lancet *1*:930, 1983.
250. Ohno, S., Miyajima, T., Higuchi, M., et al.: Ocular manifestations of Kawasaki disease (mucocutaneous lymph node syndrome). Am. J. Ophthalmol. *93*:713–717, 1982.
251. Ohshio, G., Furukawa, F., Khine, M., et al.: High levels of IgA-containing circulating immune complex and secretory IgA in Kawasaki disease. Microbiol. Immunol. *31*:891–898, 1987.
252. Okabe, N., Koboyashi, S., Tatsuzawa, O., et al.: Detection of antibodies to human parvovirus in erythema infectiosum (fifth disease). Arch. Dis. Child. *59*:1016–1019, 1984.
253. Okamoto, T., Kuwabara, H., Shimotohno, K., et al.: Lack of evidence of retroviral involvement in Kawasaki disease. Pediatrics *81*:599, 1988.
254. Okano, M., Hase, N., Sakiyama, Y., et al.: Long-term observation in patients with Kawasaki syndrome and their relation to Epstein-Barr virus infection. Pediatr. Infect. Dis. J. *9*:139–141, 1990.
255. Okano, M., Luka, J., Thiele, G. M., et al.: Human herpesvirus 6 infection and Kawasaki disease. J. Clin. Microbiol. *27*:2379–2380, 1989.
256. Okuni, M., Harada, K., Yamaguchi, H., et al.: Intravenous gamma globulin therapy in Kawasaki disease: Trial of low-dose gamma globulin. Prog. Clin. Biol. Res. *250*:433–439, 1987.
257. Orlowski, J. P., and Mercer, R. D.: Urine mercury levels in Kawasaki disease. Pediatrics *66*:633–636, 1980.
258. Pachman, L. M., Herold, B. C., and Davis, A. T.: Immune complexes in Kawasaki syndrome: A review. Prog. Clin. Biol. Res. *250*:193–207, 1987.
259. Packard, M., and Wechsler, H. F.: Aneurysm of the coronary arteries. Arch. Intern. Med. *43*:1–14, 1929.
260. Pahl, E., Sehgal, R., Chrystof, D., et al.: Feasibility of exercise stress echocardiography for follow-up of children with coronary involvement secondary to Kawasaki disease. Circulation *91*:122–128, 1995.
261. Patriarca, P. A., Rogers, M. F., Morens, D. M., et al.: Kawasaki syndrome: Association with the application of rug shampoo. Lancet *2*:578–580, 1982.
262. Pelkonen, P., and Salo, E.: Epidemiology of Kawasaki disease. Clin. Exp. Rheumatol. *12*(Suppl. 10):S83–S85, 1994.
263. Person, J. R.: Kawasaki disease and staphylococcal exotoxins. Arch. Dermatol. *116*:986, 1980.
264. Phillips, W. G., and Marsden, J. R.: Adult Kawasaki syndrome. Br. J. Dermatol. *129*:330–333, 1993.
265. Pietra, B. A., De Inocencio J., Giannini, E. H., et al.: TCR Vβ family repertoire and T cell activation markers in Kawasaki disease. J. Immunol. *153*:1881–1888, 1994.
266. Porneuf, M., Sotto, A., Barbuat, C., et al.: Kawasaki syndrome in an adult AIDS patient. Int. J. Dermatol. *35*:292–294, 1996.
267. Rae, M. V.: Coronary aneurysms with thrombosis in rheumatic carditis: Unusual occurrence accompanied by hyperleukocytosis in a child. Arch. Pathol. *24*:369–376, 1937.
268. Rauch, A. M.: Kawasaki syndrome: Critical review of U.S. epidemiology. Prog. Clin. Biol. Res. *250*:33–44, 1987.
269. Rauch, A. M., Fultz, P. N., and Kalyanaraman, V. S.: Retrovirus serology and Kawasaki syndrome. Lancet *1*:1431, 1987.
270. Rauch, A. M., Kaplan, S. L., Nihill, M. R., et al.: Kawasaki syndrome clusters in Harris County, Texas, and eastern North Carolina. Am. J. Dis. Child. *142*:441–444, 1988.
271. Rauch, A. M., Glode, M. P., Wiggins, J. W., et al.: Outbreak of Kawasaki syndrome in Denver, Colorado: Association with rug and carpet cleaning. Pediatrics *87*:663–669, 1991.
272. Rider, L. G., Wener, M. H., French, J., et al.: Autoantibody production in Kawasaki syndrome. Clin. Exp. Rheumatol. *11*:445–449, 1993.
273. Roberts, F. B., and Fetterman, G. H.: Polyarteritis nodosa in infancy. J. Pediatr. *63*:519–529, 1963.
274. Rogers, M. F.: Kawasaki syndrome. Am. J. Dis. Child. *140*:191, 1986.
275. Rogers, M. F., Kochel, R. L., Hurwitz, E. S., et al.: Kawasaki syndrome: Is exposure to rug shampoo important? Am. J. Dis. Child. *139*:777–779, 1985.
276. Rosenfeld, E. A., Corydon, K. E., and Shulman, S. T.: Kawasaki disease in infants less than one year of age. J. Pediatr. *126*:524–529, 1995.
277. Rowe, R. D., Rose, V., Wilson, G. J., et al.: Kawasaki disease: A measles cover-up? Can. Med. Assoc. J. *136*:1146, 1987.
278. Rowley, A. H., Duffy, E., and Shulman, S. T.: Prevention of giant aneurysms in Kawasaki disease by intravenous gamma globulin therapy. J. Pediatr. *113*:290–294, 1988.
279. Rowley, A. H., Eckerley, C. A., Jack, H. M., et al.: IgA plasma cells in vascular tissue of patients with Kawasaki syndrome. J. Immunol. *159*:5946–5955, 1997.

280. Rowley, A. H., Gonzalez-Crussi, F., Gidding, S. S., et al.: Incomplete Kawasaki disease with coronary artery involvement. J. Pediatr. *110*:409–413, 1987.
281. Rowley, A. H., Shulman, S. T., Mask, C. A. et al.: IgA plasma cell infiltration in proximal respiratory tract, pancreas, kidney and coronary artery in acute Kawasaki disease. J. Infect. Dis. *182*:1183–1191, 2000.
282. Rowley, A. H., Shulman, S. T., Preble, O. T., et al.: Serum interferon concentrations and retroviral serology in Kawasaki syndrome. Pediatr. Infect. Dis. J. *7*:663–665, 1988.
283. Rowley, A. H., Shulman, S. T., Spike, B. T., et al.: Oligoclonal IgA response in the vascular wall in acute Kawasaki disease. J. Immunol. *166*:1334–1343, 2001.
284. Rowley, A. H., Wolinsky, S. M., Relman, D. A., et al.: Search for highly conserved viral and bacterial nucleic acid sequences corresponding to an etiologic agent of Kawasaki disease. Pediatr. Res. *36*:567–571, 1994.
285. Ruiz, D., and Krober, M. S.: Mucocutaneous lymph node syndrome. J. Oklahoma State Med. Assoc. *70*:351–353, 1977.
286. Russell, A. S., Zaragosa, A. J., and Shea, R.: Mucocutaneous lymph node syndrome in Canada. Can. Med. Assoc. J. *112*:1210–1211, 1975.
287. Salcedo, J. R., Greenberg, L., and Kapur, S.: Renal histology of mucocutaneous lymph node syndrome. Clin. Nephrol. *29*:47–51, 1988.
288. Salo, E.: Kawasaki disease in Finland in 1982–83. Scand. J. Infect. Dis. *25*:497–502, 1993.
289. Salo, E., Kekomaki, R., Pelkonen, P., et al.: Kawasaki disease: Monitoring of circulating immune complexes. Eur. J. Pediatr. *147*:377–380, 1988.
290. Salo, E., Pelkonen, P., and Pettay, O.: Outbreak of Kawasaki syndrome in Finland. Acta Paediatr. Scand. *75*:75–80, 1986.
291. Salo, E., Pesonen, E., and Viikari, J.: Serum cholesterol levels during and after Kawasaki disease. J. Pediatr. *119*:557–561, 1991.
292. Sasaguri, Y., and Kato, H.: Regression of aneurysms in Kawasaki disease: A pathologic study. Pediatrics *100*:225–231, 1982.
293. Sato, K., Ouichi, K., and Taki, M.: *Yersinia pseudotuberculosis* infection in children, resembling Izumi fever and Kawasaki syndrome. Pediatr. Infect. Dis. *2*:123–126, 1983.
294. Sato, N., Sagawa, K., Sasaguri, Y., et al.: Immunopathology and cytokine detection in the skin lesions of patients with Kawasaki disease. J. Pediatr. *122*:198–203, 1993.
295. Savage, C. O. S., Tizard, J., Jayne, D., et al.: Antineutrophil cytoplasm antibodies in Kawasaki disease. Arch. Dis. Child. *64*:360–363, 1989.
296. Saxe, N., Horak, K., and Goldblatt, J.: Mucocutaneous lymph node syndrome in a young adult. S. Afr. Med. J. *68*:1011–1013, 1980.
297. Schnaar, D. A., and Bell, D. M.: Kawasaki syndrome in two cousins with parainfluenza virus infection. Am. J. Dis. Child. *136*:554–555, 1982.
298. Schrag, S. J., Besser, R. E., Olson, C., et al.: Lack of association between Kawasaki syndrome and *Chlamydia pneumoniae* infection: An investigation of a Kawasaki syndrome cluster in San Diego County. Pediatr. Infect. Dis. J. *19*:17–22, 2000.
298a. Shibuya, N., Shibuya, K., Kato, H., et al.: Kawasaki disease before Kawasaki at Tokyo University Hospital. Pediatrics *110*:e17, 2002.
299. Shigematsu, I.: Epidemiology of mucocutaneous lymph node syndrome [Japanese]. Acta Paediatr. Jap. 76:696, 1972.
300. Shimizu, S., Kuratsuji, T., and Ojima, T.: Plasma fibronectin concentrations in mucocutaneous lymph node syndrome. Arch. Dis. Child. *61*:72–74, 1986.
300a. Shinohara, M., Sone, K., Tomomasa, T., et al.: Corticosteroids in the treatment of the acute phase of Kawasaki disease. J. Pediatr. *135*:465–469, 1999.
301. Shulman, S. T.: Management of Kawasaki syndrome: A consensus statement prepared by North American participants of the Third International Kawasaki Disease Symposium: Tokyo, Japan, December, 1988. Pediatr. Infect. Dis. J. *8*:663–667, 1989.
302. Shulman, S. T.: IVGG therapy in Kawasaki disease: Mechanism(s) of action. Clin. Immunol. Immunopathol. *53*:5141–5146, 1989.
303. Shulman, S. T.: Hemolysis in Kawasaki disease [Letter]. Transfusion *31*:572, 1991.
304. Shulman, S. T.: A commentary on disease mechanism. *In* Takahashi, M., and Taubert, K. (eds.): Proceedings of the Fourth International Symposium on Kawasaki Disease. Dallas, American Heart Association, 1993.
305. Shulman, S.T., DeInocencio, J., and Hirsch, R.: Kawasaki disease. Pediatr. Clin. North. Am. *42*:1205–1222, 1995.
306. Shulman, S. T., McAuley, J. B., Pachman, L. M., et al.: Risk of coronary abnormalities due to Kawasaki disease in an urban area with a small Asian population. Am. J. Dis. Child. *141*:420–425, 1987.
307. Shulman, S. T., Melish, M., Inoue, O., et al.: Immunoglobulin allotypic markers in Kawasaki disease. J. Pediatr. *122*:84–86, 1993.
308. Shulman, S. T., and Rowley, A. H.: Does Kawasaki disease have a retroviral etiology? Lancet *2*:545–546, 1986.
309. Shulman, S. T., and Rowley, A. H.: Kawasaki disease before the 1967 description by T. Kawasaki [Abstract 1632]. Pediatr. Res. *47*:277A, 2000.
310. Siegel, C. J., and Wenner, H. A.: The mucocutaneous lymph node syndrome: Description of an affected 21-month-old child in Kansas City. Clin. Pediatr. *15*:1105–1106, 1976.
311. Smith, L. B., Newburger, J. W., and Burns, J. C.: Kawasaki syndrome and the eye. Pediatr. Infect. Dis. J. *8*:116–118, 1989.
312. Smith, P. K., and Goldwater, P. N.: Kawasaki disease in Adelaide: A review. J. Paediatr. Child Health *29*:126–131, 1993.
313. Soppi, E., Salo, E., and Pelkonen, P.: Antibodies against neutrophil cytoplasmic components in Kawasaki disease. A. P. M. I. S. *100*:269–272, 1992.
314. Stamos, J. K., Corydon, K., Donaldson, J. et al.: Lymphadenitis as the dominant manifestation of Kawasaki disease. Pediatrics *93*:525–528, 1994.
315. Stockheim, J. A., Innocentini, N., and Shulman, S. T.: Kawasaki disease in older children and adolescents. J. Pediatr. *137*:250–252, 2000.
316. Strigl, S., Kutlin, A., Roblin, P. M., et al.: Is there an association between Kawasaki disease and *Chlamydia pneumoniae*? J. Infect. Dis. *181*: 2103–2105, 2000.
317. Sugimura, T., Kato, H., Yokoi, H., et al.: Intravascular ultrasound study in Kawasaki disease: Assessment of coronary and systemic arterial pathology and application for coronary intervention. *In* Kato, H. (ed.): Kawasaki Disease. Amsterdam, Elsevier Science, 1995, p. 460.
318. Sugimura, T., Kato, H., Inoue, O., et al.: Long-term consequences of Kawasaki disease: Serial coronary angiography and 10-20 years follow-up study. *In* Kato, H. (ed.): Kawasaki Disease. Amsterdam, Elsevier Science, 1995, pp. 574–579.
319. Sugimura, T., Kato, H., Inoue, O., et al.: Vasodilatory response of the coronary arteries after Kawasaki disease: Evaluation by intracoronary injection of isosorbide dinitrate. Pediatrics *121*:684–688, 1992.
320. Sugimura, T., Kato, H., Inoue, O., et al.: Intravascular ultrasound of coronary arteries in children: Assessment of the wall morphology and the lumen after Kawasaki disease. Circulation *89*:258–265, 1994.
321. Sugiura, K., Sakurai, K., Takamoto, T., et al.: Kawasaki disease in an adult [Japanese]. Intern. Med. *47*:857–860, 1981.
322. Sundel, R., Burns, J. C., Baker, A., et al.: Gamma globulin re-treatment in Kawasaki disease. J. Pediatr. *123*:657–659, 1998.
323. Sundel, R., Newburger, J.W., McGill, T., et al.: Sensorineural hearing loss associated with Kawasaki disease. J. Pediatr. *117*:371–377, 1990.
324. Suzuki, A., Arakaki, Y., Sugiyama, H., et al.: Observation of coronary arterial lesion due to Kawasaki disease by intravascular ultrasound. *In* Kato, H. (ed.): Kawasaki Disease. Amsterdam, Elsevier Science, 1995, pp. 451–459.
325. Suzuki, A., Kamiya, T., Arakaki, Y., et al.: Fate of coronary aneurysms in Kawasaki disease. Am. J. Cardiol. *74*:822–824, 1994.
326. Suzuki, A., Kamiya, T., Ono, Y., et al.: Follow-up study of coronary arterial lesions due to Kawasaki disease. Heart Vessels *3*:159–165, 1987.
327. Suzuki, A., Kamiya, T., Ono, Y., et al.: Functional behavior and morphology of coronary artery wall in Kawasaki disease. J. Am. Coll. Cardiol. *27*:291–296, 1996.
328. Suzuki, A., Miyagawa-Tomita, S., Komatsu, K., et al.: Active remodeling of the coronary arterial lesions in the late phase of Kawasaki disease. Circulation *101*:2935–2941, 2000.
329. Swaby, E. D., Fisher-Hoch, S. P., Lambert, H. P., et al.: Is Kawasaki disease a variant of Q fever? Lancet *2*:146, 1980.
330. Takahashi, K., Naoe, S., Wakayama, M., et al.: Pathologic study of coronary aneurysms in adults who had Kawasaki disease in childhood. *In* Kato, H. (ed.): Kawasaki Disease. Amsterdam, Elsevier Science, 1995, pp. 592–597.
331. Takeda, T., Abe, J., Yoshino, K., et al.: Establishment of a novel superantigen produced by *Yersinia pseudotuberculosis* and its association with systemic Kawasaki disease–like symptoms. *In* Kato, H. (ed.): Kawasaki Disease. Amsterdam, Elsevier Science, 1995, pp. 193–199.
332. Takeshita, S., Dobashi, H., Nakatani, K., et al.: Circulating soluble selectins in Kawasaki disease. Clin. Exp. Immunol. *108*:446–450, 1997.
333. Takeuchi, Y., Suma, K., Shiroma, K., et al.: Coronary artery changes in Kawasaki disease and its surgical treatment by aorto-coronary bypass grafting. Kyobu Geka *31*:356–361, 1978.
334. Tanaka, N.: Kawasaki disease (acute febrile mucocutaneous lymph node syndrome) in Japan: Relationship with infantile periarteritis nodosa. Pathol. Microbiol. *43*:204–218, 1975.
335. Tanaka, N., Naoe, S., and Kawasaki, T.: Pathological study of autopsy cases of MCLS: Relationship with infantile periarteritis nodosa. J. Jpn. Red Cross Center Hosp. *2*:85–94, 1971.
336. Tanaka, N., Sekimoto, K., Fukushima, T., et al.: Pathological study of fatal MCLS cases of Kawasaki disease: Relationship with infantile polyarteritis nodosa. *In* Shiokawa, Y. (ed.): Vascular Lesions of Collagen Diseases and Related Conditions. Baltimore, University Park Press, 1977, p. 44.
337. Tanaka, N., Sekimoto, K., and Naoe, S.: Kawasaki disease: Relationship with infantile periarteritis nodosa. Arch. Pathol. Lab. Med. *100*:81–86, 1976.

338. Tasaka, K., and Hamashima, Y.: Function of phagocytosis and intracellular killing of peripheral neutrophils in Kawasaki disease. Acta Pathol. Jpn. *28*:247–252, 1978.
339. Tasaka, K., Kishi, K., Hirose, S., et al.: *Rickettsia*-like bodies in Kawasaki disease. *In* Shiokawa, Y. (ed.): Vascular Lesions of Collagen Diseases and Related Conditions. Baltimore, University Park Press, 1977, pp. 311–32l.
340. Taubert, K. A., Rowley, A. H., and Shulman, S. T.: Seven-year national survey of Kawasaki disease and acute rheumatic fever. Pediatr. Infect. Dis. J. *13*:704–708, 1994.
341. Taubert, K. A., Rowley, A. H., and Shulman, S. T.: A 10-year (1984–1993) United States hospital survey of Kawasaki disease. *In* Kato, H. (ed.): Kawasaki Disease. Amsterdam, Elsevier Science, 1995, pp. 34–38.
342. Teixeira, O. H. P., and Quinn, A.: Kawasaki syndrome. Am. J. Dis. Child. *140*:190–191, 1986.
343. Terai, M., Kohno, Y., Namba, M., et al.: Class II major histocompatibility antigen expression on coronary arterial endothelium in a patient with Kawasaki disease. Hum. Pathol. *21*:231–234, 1990.
344. Terai, M., Kohno, Y., Niwa, K., et al.: Imbalance among T-cell subsets in patients with coronary arterial aneurysms in Kawasaki disease. Am. J. Cardiol. *60*:555–559, 1987.
345. Terai, M., Miwa, K., Williams, T., et al.: Failure to confirm involvement of staphylococcal toxin in the pathogenesis of Kawasaki disease. *In* Kato, H. (ed.): Kawasaki Disease. Amsterdam, Elsevier Science, 1995, pp. 144–148.
346. Terai, M., and Shulman, S. T.: Prevalence of coronary artery abnormalities in Kawasaki disease is highly dependent on gammaglobulin dose but independent of salicylate dose. J. Pediatr. *131*:888–893, 1997.
346a. Terai, M., Yasukawa, K., Honda, T., et al.: Peripheral blood eosinophilia and eosinophil accumulation in coronary microvessels in acute Kawasaki disease. Pediatr. Infect. Dis. J. *21*:777–780, 2002.
346b. Terai, M., Yasukawa, K., Narumoto, S., et al.: Vascsular endothelial growth factor in acute Kawasaki disease. Am. J. Cardiol. *83*:337–339, 1999.
347. Todd, J. K.: Mucocutaneous lymph node syndrome (Kawasaki disease) in adults. J. A. M. A. *243*:1631, 1980.
348. Tomisawa, M., Onouchi, Z., Goto, M., et al.: Ultrastructure of the myocardium in acute febrile mucocutaneous lymph node syndrome. Jpn. Circ. J. *41*:151–157, 1977.
349. Tomita, S., Chung, K., Mas, M., et al.: Peripheral gangrene associated with Kawasaki disease. Clin. Infect. Dis. *14*:121–126, 1992.
350. Tomita, S., Kato, H., Fujimoto, T., et al.: Cytopathogenic protein in filtrates from cultures of *Propionibacterium acnes* isolated from patients with Kawasaki disease. Br. Med. J. *295*:1229–1232, 1987.
351. Treadwell, T. A., Shahriari, A., Belay, E. D., et al.: Kawasaki syndrome in Colorado [Abstract P1]. Pediatr. Res. *47*(4):559, 2000.
351a. Tsuchida, S., Yamanaka, T., Ysuchida, R., et al.: Epidemiology of infant Kawasaki disease with a report of the youngest neonatal case ever reported in Japan. Acta. Paediatr. *85*:995–997, 1996.
352. Tristani-Fironzi, M., Kamango-Sollo, E. D., Sun, S., et al.: TCR Vβ gene family repertoire and humoral immunity in Kawasaki syndrome. *In* Kato, H. (ed.): Kawasaki Disease. Amsterdam, Elsevier Science, 1995, pp. 200–205.
353. Uchida, N., Asayama, K., Dobashi, K., et al.: Antioxidant enzymes and lipoperoxide in blood in patients with Kawasaki disease: Comparison with the changes in acute infections. Acta Paediatr. Jpn. *32*:242–248, 1990.
354. Viraben, R., and Dupre, A.: Kawasaki disease associated with HIV infection. Lancet *1*:1430–1431, 1987.
354a. Wallace, C. A., French, J. W., Kahn, S. J., et al.: Initial intravenous gamma globulin treatment failure in Kawasaki disease. Pediatrics *105*:e78, 2000.
355. Weindling, A. M., Levinsky, R. J., and Marshall, W. C.: Circulating immune complexes in mucocutaneous lymph node syndrome (Kawasaki disease). Arch. Dis. Child. *54*:241–242, 1979.
356. Weir, W. R., Bouchet, V. A., Mitford, E., et al.: Kawasaki disease in European adult associated with serological response to *Coxiella burnetii*. Lancet *2*:504, 1985.
357. Westphalen, M. A., McGrath, M. A., Kelly, W., et al.: Kawasaki disease with severe peripheral ischemia: Treatment with prostaglandin E1 infusion. J. Pediatr. *112*:431–433, 1988.
358. Wong, M., Silverman, E. D., Fish, E. N.: Evidence for RANTES, MCP-1, and MIP-1β in Kawasaki disease. J. Rheumatol. *24*:1179–1185, 1997.
359. Wright, D. A., Newberger, J. W., Baker, A., et al.: Treatment of immune globulin-resistant Kawasaki disease with pulsed doses of corticosteroids. J. Pediatr. *128*:146–149, 1996.
360. Wurzburger, B. J., and Avner, J. R.: Lateral rectus palsy in Kawasaki disease. Pediatr. Infect. Dis. J. *18*:1029–1030, 1999.
361. Yamada, K., Fukumoto, T., Shinkai, A., et al.: The platelet function in acute febrile mucocutaneous lymph node syndrome and a trial of prevention for thrombosis by antiplatelet agent. Acta Hematol. Jpn. *41*:791–802, 1978.
361a. Yamakawa, R., Ishii, M., Sugimura, T., et al.: Coronary endothelial dysfunction after Kawasaki disease. J. Am. Coll. Cardiol. *31*:1074–1080, 1998.
362. Yamamoto, T., and Kimura, J.: Acute mucocutaneous lymph node syndrome:. A case associated with carditis [Japanese]. Jap. J. Pediatr. *21*:336–339, 1968.
363. Yanagawa, H.: Epidemiology of Kawasaki disease in Japan. Prog. Clin. Biol. Res. *250*:5–17, 1987.
364. Yanagawa, H., Kawasaki, T., and Shigematsu, I.: Nationwide survey on Kawasaki disease in Japan. Pediatrics *80*:58–62, 1987.
365. Yanagawa, H., Nakamura, Y., Kawasaki, T., et al.: Nationwide epidemic of Kawasaki disease in Japan during winter of 1985–86. Lancet *2*:1138–1139, 1986.
366. Yanagawa, H., Nakamura, Y., Ojima, T., et al.: Changes in epidemic pattern of Kawasaki disease in Japan. Pediatr. Infect. Dis. J. *18*:64–66, 1999.
367. Yanagawa, H., Nakamura, Y., Yashiro, M., et al.: A nationwide incidence survey of Kawasaki disease in 1985–1986 in Japan. J. Infect. Dis. *158*:1296–1301, 1988.
368. Yanagawa, H., Nakamura, Y., Yashiro, M., et al.: Results of the nationwide epidemiologic survey of Kawasaki disease in 1995 and 1996 in Japan. Pediatrics *102*:e65, 1998.
369. Yanagawa, H., Nakamura, Y., Yashiro, M., et al.: Update of the epidemiology of Kawasaki disease in Japan: From the 1993–94 nationwide survey. J. Epidemiol. *6*:148–157, 1996.
370. Yanagawa, H., Nakamura, Y., Yashiro, M., et al.: Incidence survey of Kawasaki disease in 1997 and 1998 in Japan. Pediatrics *107*:e33, 2001.
371. Yanagawa, H., Yashiro, M., Nakamura, Y., et al.: Results of 12 nationwide epidemiological incidence surveys of Kawasaki disease in Japan. Arch. Pediatr. Adolesc. Med. *149*:779–783, 1995.
372. Yanase, Y., Takayama, J., Aso, S., et al.: Studies on serum immunoglobulins and delayed skin tests in patients with MCLS. Acta Paediatr. Jpn. *24*:408–409, 1982.
373. Yanase, Y., Tango, T., Okumura, K., et al.: A comparative study of alteration in lymphocyte subsets among varicella, hand-foot-and-mouth disease, scarlet fever, measles, and Kawasaki disease. Microbiol. Immunol. *31*:701–710, 1987.
374. Yashiro, M., Nakamura, Y., Hirose, K., Yanagawa, H.: Surveillance of Kawasaki disease in Japan, 1984–1994. *In* Kato, H. (ed.): Kawasaki Disease. Amsterdam, Elsevier Science, 1995, pp. 15–21.
374a. Yasukawa, K., Terai, M., Shulman, S. T., et al.: Systemic production of vascular endothelial growth factor and fms-like tyrosine kinase-1 receptor in acute Kawasaki disease. Circulation *105*:766–769, 2002.
375. Yokota, S.: Heat shock protein as a predisposing and immunopotentiating factor in Kawasaki disease. Acta Paediatr. Jpn. *33*:756–764, 1991.
376. Yutani, C., Go, S., Kamiya, F., et al.: Cardiac biopsy of Kawasaki disease. Arch. Pathol. Lab. Med. *105*:470–473, 1981.
377. Yutani, C., Okano, K., Kamiya, T., et al.: Histopathological study on right endomyocardial biopsy of Kawasaki disease. Br. Heart J. *43*:589–592, 1980.

CHAPTER 83

Chronic Fatigue Syndrome

LEONARD R. KRILOV

"All cases are unique and very similar to others."
T. S. Eliot. The Cocktail Party, 1949.

Chronic fatigue syndrome (CFS) is an illness complex characterized by a prolonged (6 months or longer) period of constant or intermittent debilitating fatigue in association with multiple, often nonspecific, symptoms that may include new-onset headaches, decreased ability to concentrate, recurrent complaints of sore throat and tender cervical or axillary lymphadenitis, reports of low-grade fever, diffuse muscle or joint pain, postexertional increase in fatigue, and unrefreshing sleep. To date, no specific etiology for this syndrome has been identified, and despite similar arrays of signs and symptoms, patients with CFS likely represent a heterogeneous population. Still, evaluation of groups of patients with this symptom complex has provided information about pathophysiologic changes occurring in patients with CFS, and potentially beneficial, although not curative, approaches to therapy for affected individuals have been developed.

In an attempt to provide a degree of uniformity as a basis for research into the evaluation of such patients, the U.S. Centers for Disease Control and Prevention (CDC) developed a definition of CFS in 1988.[34] These criteria were revised in 1994, with physical signs removed from the definition because they appeared to be unreliably documented in studies, and the required number of symptoms for the diagnosis of CFS decreased from 8 of a list of 11 to 4 of 8 components[28] (Table 83–1). These changes, being less restrictive, might serve to increase the sensitivity of the diagnosis, but they also decrease the specificity. However, these criteria are purely speculative in the absence of any gold standard or definitive diagnostic test for CFS. These 1994 criteria also suggest subdivisions of patients with CFS for research purposes and provide guidelines for nonresearch clinicians as well. Other international groups have generated similar definitions of CFS for evaluating this condition.[50, 73]

TABLE 83–1 ■ CENTERS FOR DISEASE CONTROL AND PREVENTION 1994 WORKSHOP CASE DEFINITION OF CHRONIC FATIGUE SYNDROME

1. Fatigue (persistent or relapsing) that has new or definite onset, is of 6 months or longer duration, and leads to a substantial (>50%) reduction in level of activity,
   Plus:
2. At least four of the following:
   a. Impaired memory or concentration
   b. Sore throat
   c. Tender lymph nodes—cervical or axillary
   d. Myalgias
   e. Arthralgias (multiple joints, without swelling or erythema)
   f. New onset (or in severity) of headaches
   g. Unrefreshing sleep (hypersomnia or insomnia)
   h. Postexertional fatigue lasting longer than 24 hours
   And:
3. The absence of another diagnosis for the individual's signs and symptoms.

Modified from Fukuda, K., Straus, S. E., Hickie, I., et al.: The chronic fatigue syndrome: A comprehensive approach to its definition and study. Ann. Intern. Med. *121*:953–959, 1994.

The primary manifestations of CFS are severe fatigue of greater than 6 months' duration, limiting activity to less than 50 percent of premorbid function in association with multiple other symptoms as outlined in the case definitions of CFS.[28, 34, 50, 73] These symptoms include new or more intense headaches, decreased ability to focus or concentrate, recurrent sore throats, a sensation of tender cervical or axillary lymph nodes, low-grade temperature elevations, myalgias and arthralgias, postexertional fatigue lasting longer than 24 hours, and sleep disturbances (hypersomnia or insomnia). The severity and persistence of these findings vary among individual patients with CSF. Additionally, although not included in the case definitions, many patients report dizziness, especially with changes in position, feeling hot when others are cold or vice versa, chronic costochondritis, and a Raynaud-like phenomenon.

Historical Overview

In all likelihood, CFS is not a new illness. Numerous conditions with features comparable to those of CFS have appeared in the medical literature during the past several centuries.[87] Many of these descriptions attempted to associate an illness characterized by prolonged debilitating fatigue and numerous other symptoms with an infectious agent. These have included chronic brucellosis,[77] chronic enteroviral syndrome,[13, 17, 32] chronic candidiasis,[69] myalgic encephalomyelitis,[2] chronic mononucleosis (Epstein-Barr virus [EBV]),[3, 36, 82, 89] human herpesvirus type 6,[7, 94] human herpesvirus type 7,[22] chronic Lyme disease,[78] and a new retrovirus.[19] Noninfectious conditions described with similarities to CFS include total allergy syndrome, hypoglycemia, neurasthenia, Iceland disease, Royal Free disease, and fibromyalgia rheumatica.[43] In addition to clinical similarity to CFS, all of these conditions, at least at the time they were described, lacked a diagnostic test to confirm a definitive causative agent, and in their acute form, they manifest with fatigue in association with multiple other complaints.

A review of the experience in the mid-1980s associated groups of patients with CFS-like illness to those with chronic EBV infection.[3, 36, 82] These reports described elevated and aberrant patterns of EBV antibody responses in individuals with prolonged fatigue and multiple symptoms consistent with CFS. Acute infectious mononucleosis also, although typically more pronounced, often presents with fatigue, fever, malaise, sore throat, lymphadenitis, and multiple systemic complaints. Subsequent studies, however, revealed that the elevated or pattern of EBV antibody responses in such patients were not consistently different from those seen in others who resolved symptoms of acute EBV infection.[55] Additionally, shedding of EBV in secretions was not increased in these individuals, and no association was found between viral shedding and severity of symptoms.[90] Furthermore, no response to the antiviral drug acyclovir occurred in a group of such patients in a placebo-controlled, double-blind, crossover study, in terms of improvement of clinical symptoms.[83] After these observations were made, the name *chronic fatigue syndrome* was chosen to define this illness,[34] at least until a specific cause or marker for this illness is identified.

Epidemiology

The definitions of CFS allow for attempts to characterize the prevalence and demographic features of this condition. Still, given the vagaries of the symptom complex, possible variations in application of the diagnosis by different health care providers and potential differences within groups of people to seek medical attention for this condition, data reported on these issues may not be a complete representation of the epidemiology of this condition. CFS has been reported in all age groups, including children as young as 5 years of age, and in all ethnic, racial, and socioeconomic groups, but most CFS cases have been reported to occur in middle- to upper-class white women with a median age of 35 to 40 years.[42] Based on a study of physician-diagnosed patients from four cities using the 1988 case definition of CFS,[1] the CDC estimates a minimum prevalence rate of CFS of 2 to 10 cases per 100,000 or higher in adults 18 years of age and older in the United States.[8, 53, 66] Studies from outside the United States have reported similar or higher prevalence rates of CFS in adults.[23, 50]

Although the CDC definition does not include age criteria for the diagnosis of CFS, the prevalence of CFS in the pediatric age range has not been studied well. Some researchers have suggested that the diagnosis of CFS should not be used in children in order to avoid potential delay in making an alternative medical or psychological diagnosis.[65] However, many referral centers have reported groups of pediatric patients, primarily adolescents, with features and clinical course similar to those reported in adults.[5, 10, 24, 44, 52, 76] Furthermore, in these studies, missed or alternative diagnoses were not found despite years of follow-up.

In these pediatric studies, a predominance of females with a median age of 14 years at time of diagnosis was noted. Additionally, these patients are from predominately middle- to upper-class families and, as discussed later, their signs and symptoms at presentation (Table 83–2) and their course of illness are similar to those reported in adults with CFS. CDC studies suggest that the prevalence of CFS in adolescents approaches that reported in adults, but cases in children younger than 12 years of age occur much less commonly.[28] One suggestion is that a shorter duration of symptoms (3 to 4 months versus 6 months) may be appropriate for diagnosing CFS in pediatric patients.[28, 37] Multiple family members with CFS may be seen as well, but to date, evidence that CFS is contagious does not exist.

TABLE 83–2 ■ SYMPTOMS REPORTED BY 58 CHILDREN AND ADOLESCENTS EVALUATED FOR CHRONIC FATIGUE SYNDROME (1989–1994)

Symptom	No. of Patients	Percentage
Fatigue	58	100
Headache	43	74
Sore throat	34	59
Abdominal pain	28	48
Fever	21	36
Impaired cognition	19	33
Myalgia	18	31
Diarrhea	17	29
Adenopathy	17	29
Anorexia	16	28
Nausea/vomiting	15	26
Congestion	13	22
Dizziness	10	17
Arthralgia	10	17
Otitis	6	10
Cough	6	10
Rash	5	9
Sweats	5	9
Chills	4	7
Depression	4	7

From Krilov, L. R., Fisher, M., Friedman, S. B., et al.: Course and outcome of chronic fatigue in children and adolescents. Pediatrics *102*:360–366, 1998.

Etiology and Pathogenesis

INFECTION

As previously noted, an infectious etiology of CFS has not been demonstrated to date, and a single microorganism being the cause of CFS is unlikely. However, an acute infection appears possibly to play a role in precipitating CFS because most (as many as two thirds) patients with CFS relate a sudden onset of their symptoms in association with an acute infection, most often infectious mononucleosis. Lyme disease[51, 78] and an influenza-like illness[35] also have been reported in association with the onset of CFS.

IMMUNOLOGIC DYSFUNCTION

A role for immunologic dysfunction in CFS has been suggested based on numerous studies demonstrating abnormalities in lymphocyte function or cytokine production.[9, 41, 48, 56, 85, 88, 91] However, these findings have not been reproducible in different groups of patients with CSF. Some evidence suggests nonspecific elevation of antibody titers and an increase in allergic symptoms in patients with CSF.[84] However, these findings are mild, and similar immunologic changes may be seen in other conditions, including depression. Individuals with CFS may report an increased frequency and duration of infections compared with their pre-CFS state, but they tend to be mostly routine viral illnesses. Neither unusual or opportunistic infections nor increased risk for developing malignancies has been observed in these individuals. Intravenous immunoglobulin infusions have not demonstrated long-term clinical benefit when administered to patients with CFS and may cause significant adverse reactions.[49, 63, 86]

NEUROLOGIC FEATURES

Many patients with CFS report cognitive impairment that is manifest as decreased ability to concentrate and focus, difficulty processing information, and trouble with word recall. Complaints of headache (new onset or altered pattern) and other neurologic symptoms, such as paresthesias and dysequilibrium, also are reported commonly by CFS patients.

Despite these complaints, physical examination does not reveal abnormal neurologic signs. Formal neuropyschometric testing also may not reveal objective abnormalities to the extent reported by the patient. Whether this discrepancy reflects a problem with testing methodologies or altered perception on the part of the individual is uncertain at this time.[7, 61]

Magnetic resonance imaging studies have been reported to show an increase in cerebral white-matter abnormalities in patients with CFS.[7, 59, 71] Similarly, in many studies, single photon emission computed tomography scanning has demonstrated changes in perfusion in certain areas of the brain in patients with CFS.[15, 26, 72] In other studies, however, abnormalities specific to CFS have not been observed consistently, and methodologic concerns have been raised regarding the interpretation of abnormal findings cited previously.[14, 33] Recently, an abnormality at the base of the fourth ventricle detected on focal computed tomography scan of the base of the brain and responding to neurosurgical intervention has been reported in a group of patients with CFS,[31] but this defect is not seen on routine computed tomography or magnetic resonance imaging scan views, and this observation requires confirmation by other researchers before determining its significance for these patients. At present, imaging of the central nervous system is not indicated routinely in the evaluation of a patient with CFS.

ENDOCRINOLOGIC FACTORS

Subtle defects in the hypothalamic-pituitary-adrenal axis have been described in cohorts of patients with CFS. These abnormalities include decreased free urinary cortisol levels and exaggerated adrenal responsiveness to corticotropin infusion.[21] These changes are quantitatively minor, and mean values are still within normal for age and sex, rendering them unreliable as a diagnostic test for CFS. Similar changes have been described in patients with fibromyalgia and post-traumatic stress disorder.

CARDIOVASCULAR FACTORS

In 1995, investigators at Johns Hopkins Hospital described a cohort of seven adolescents with chronic fatigue and autonomic dysfunction as assessed by tilt-table testing.[70] Furthermore, these patients reported improvement or resolution of symptoms, including fatigue, with treatment of their orthostatic intolerance. Further studies from this group demonstrated some component of orthostatic hypotension in 92 percent of patients with CFS.[6] Studies in groups of adults, in contrast, have had tilt-table test abnormalities noted in only 25 to 40 percent of patients studied.[27, 75] Whether this finding reflects true age-related differences in this phenomenon in patients with CFS is uncertain given potential methodologic differences in the performance of the tests.

The pattern of orthostatic intolerance among adolescents with CFS has been characterized further by Stewart and colleagues and is consistent with the postural orthostatic tachycardia syndrome (POTS).[79–81] Symptoms of POTS may develop after an acute infectious illness or with severe deconditioning and include fatigue, light-headedness, impaired cognition, inappropriate sweating, headache, palpitations, nausea, vomiting, and tremulousness. These authors suggest that CFS may be an extreme expression of POTS in at least some cases.

The importance of these cardiovascular findings in CFS remains unsettled. Subjective components may contribute to defining a tilt-table test as abnormal because subjects are not blinded during these studies. Some healthy individuals also may experience hypotension during these tests. Further studies defining the effect of treatment of POTS on the course of CFS should help to answer this question. In this context, evaluation and therapy of orthostatic changes, especially if dizziness is a significant component of the patient's complaints, may be indicated.

SLEEP PHYSIOLOGY

Sleep disturbances have been described in selected groups of patients with CFS, and some of them may be amenable to therapy.[47, 68] However, no single pattern of sleep abnormality has been reported for these patients, and in our experience, the pattern of hypersomnia or insomnia tends to improve as the patient recovers.

PSYCHOLOGICAL COMPONENTS

Psychological factors have been considered in the etiology and perpetuation of CFS. Adults with CFS have demonstrated a higher frequency of depression and other psychiatric disorders before the onset of their CFS compared with age-matched controls.[1, 46] Certainly, many of the symptoms reported in CFS also are reported commonly in depression. They may include sleep disturbances, loss of energy, difficulty concentrating, changes in appetite, and musculoskeletal complaints. Studies in children and adolescents with CFS also have shown significant psychological features, especially depression and somatization, compared with both healthy controls and those with other chronic illnesses (e.g., juvenile rheumatoid arthritis, cancer, cystic fibrosis).[10, 11, 37, 62, 96] Still, certain features of CFS argue against it being solely a variant of depression. Individuals with CFS do not have the mood-related symptoms reported in those with clinical depression. These mood-related symptoms include negative affect, anhedonia, low self-esteem, or suicidal ideation. Furthermore, patients with CFS and their families have a firm belief that an infectious, immunologic, or other medical cause for their symptoms exists, and the patients desire a return to normal activities.

In considering the possible link between depression or psychological stress and CFS, several possible relationships may exist. Preexisting depression or stress may create a psychological vulnerability that allows for the development of CFS in combination with any of numerous other factors discussed previously. Studies have demonstrated a role for psychological factors predicting the response to mononucleosis and influenza.[35, 39] Similar factors may be involved in the development of CFS. Alternatively, depression may be a physiologic consequence of the central nervous system changes that occur in those who develop CFS, just as decreased concentration and memory occur as part of the syndrome.[37, 96] Furthermore, reactive depression may occur in these patients in response to not being able to participate in their usual activities and to being out of school and separated from friends. Finally, CFS may be, at least in some cases, a manifestation of separation anxiety or school phobia in which secondary gain, as a conversion reaction, is playing a major role. Certainly, at least a subset of adolescents and children with CFS in our experience do not appear eager to return to school or activities, and secondary gain may be playing a role in the perpetuation of their illness.[43]

In summary, each of these potential links between depression or stress and CFS likely plays a role, with the relative contribution of each feature varying for different people. This suggestion is consistent with the overall hypothesis that many different factors appear to contribute to the development and perpetuation of CFS. The relative contribution of these different features may vary from individual to individual and even for the same patient over the course of the illness. The assessment and management of the patient with CFS should attempt to consider these issues and their relative importance for that individual.

Diagnosis, Differential Diagnosis, and Evaluation

The diagnosis of CFS is one of exclusion and requires a comprehensive history. In the pediatric population, this information is obtained best from the patient and parents. Additionally, we request that families bring prior medical records, test results, and pertinent school records in order to facilitate a complete evaluation. This process may be lengthy because the details are complicated, longstanding, and often a source of debate between the patient and parents. The history should focus on the onset of illness, duration and severity of symptoms, prior evaluations (often multiple) as well as medical history before the illness, family history, academic performance, and social history. The physical examination of the individual with suspected CFS almost always is essentially normal despite the multitude of symptoms. Findings of mild pharyngeal erythema and cervical adenopathy commonly are reported. However, finding fever, weight loss, significant adenopathy, or organomegaly should alert the clinician to the possibility of an alternative diagnosis.

DeMeirleir and colleagues reported increased detection of a 37-kd, 2-5A-synthetase binding protein in peripheral blood mononuclear cells from patients with CFS compared with healthy controls.[20] These binding proteins are related to the ribonuclease L antiviral pathway of these cells. This finding requires further confirmation before it can be considered as a potential diagnostic test for CFS. At present, no specific tests for diagnosing CFS exist, and laboratory testing is aimed primarily at eliminating other possible diagnoses. Most patients have undergone multiple laboratory tests before consideration of a diagnosis of CFS, but these tests may be repeated or completed as part of the initial CFS evaluation. Additionally, interpreting previously performed tests may be part of the initial patient assessment. Screening studies may include complete blood count with differential and platelets, erythrocyte sedimentation rate, hepatic and renal function studies, urinalysis, and thyroid function tests. Additional tests that may be indicated based on history and physical examination may include toxicology screening, human immunodeficiency virus serology, antinuclear antibody, rheumatoid factor, tuberculin skin test, and cortisol level. Serologic evaluations for EBV, Lyme disease, and group A streptococcal infection may be requested based on history and physical infection. In most instances, these tests are not indicated; however, they often are obtained before the CFS is suspected, and they need to be appropriately reviewed or repeated as part of the initial evaluation for CFS. Screening radiographic studies may include a chest x-ray or imaging of the paranasal sinuses based on the patient's symptoms.

Elimination of every possible disorder that may cause a patient to experience prolonged fatigue is impossible, but when guided by history, physical examination, and laboratory screening tests as outlined previously, a reliable diagnosis of CFS can be made. Follow-up for periods of 4 to 13 years for pediatric patients diagnosed with CFS have not identified cases of missed or alternative diagnoses for their complaints.[4, 44] In general, the longer the duration and the greater the number of symptoms, the less the need for extensive laboratory evaluations to suggest the diagnosis of CFS. On the other hand, alternative diagnoses should be considered if a single symptom dominates the clinical presentation or if physical examination or laboratory tests reveal significant abnormalities.

Psychosocial assessment is indicated for all children and adolescents presenting for CFS evaluation. The extent of such evaluation may be limited to assessment by primary care personnel or include collaboration with a social worker, psychologist, or psychiatrist based on the individual's needs and the comfort level of the examiner.

Cardiopulmonary and neurologic evaluations may be used in some cases, both to consider possible alternative diagnoses and to assist in assessing factors that may be contributing to the symptoms of CFS.

Management

"One of the essential qualities of the clinician is interest in humanity, for the secret of care of the patient is in caring for the patient."

Dr. Francis Peabody (1926) (Wall plaque, Lobby of the Massachusetts General Hospital)

Management of patients with CFS is aimed at providing a combination of supportive treatment and emotional support.[29] Such an approach is outlined in Table 83–3.

This process can be initiated during the initial evaluation with a discussion of the diagnostic criteria for CFS and a review of previously obtained laboratory tests. The relationship between physical and psychological symptoms can be explained, and the patient and family can be reassured that symptoms are real, even if their symptoms have psychiatric components. Additionally, the patient and family can be

TABLE 83–3 ■ APPROACH TO MANAGEMENT OF CHRONIC FATIGUE SYNDROME IN CHILDREN AND ADOLESCENTS

1. Evaluation and explanation of the diagnosis, including overview of multifactorial components
2. Reassurance that symptoms are real
3. Anticipatory guidance regarding secondary problems, up-and-down course of syndrome, secondary gain
4. Copying skills—modify lifestyle, decrease stress, and have realistic expectations and schedule
5. Cognitive behavioral approaches—gradual increases in activity, an exercise program, attention to sleep patterns, attention to nutrition
6. Psychological support for individual and family
7. Educational issues—return to classes, home tutors, neuropsychiatric testing as indicated
8. Relationship issues—friends and family
9. Follow-up plan—monitor physical symptoms, monitor psychological issues, provide ongoing guidance and reassurance (follow-up visits every 4 to 6 weeks)
10. Minimize: shopping for a doctor; unnecessary testing; family strain; unconventional, unproven, or experimental therapies

Modified from Krilov, L. R., and Fisher, M.: Chronic fatigue syndrome in children and adolescents. Contemp. Pediatr. 19:61–68, 2002.

educated to the fact that most children and adolescents with CFS do well over time[4, 24, 44, 45] and have a better long-term outlook than that described for adults with CFS.[38, 100] Furthermore, emphasizing the frequent ups and downs in symptoms that generally characterize the course of CFS is important in assisting the patient and family in developing coping skills. The latter may include guidance on how to modify lifestyle most appropriately and how to set realistic schedules and goals. Studies from the United Kingdom suggest that formal cognitive behavior therapy[18, 67, 74, 99] or graded exercise programs, or both, may be beneficial for patients with CFS.[30, 97]

Many other therapies have been advocated by different groups for patients with CFS. They may include supplements, such as essential fatty acids,[95] magnesium,[16] liver extract injections,[40] and vitamin and nutritional supplements,[54] as well as pharmacologic treatments, such as steroids,[12, 57, 64] NADH,[92] antidepressants,[60, 93] and growth hormone.[58] Homeopathic therapies, osteopathy, and massage therapy[25] also have been reported to be beneficial in the management of CFS. Most of these approaches have not been studied adequately to allow definitive comment on their potential benefit for a given patient. Still, the clinician should be aware of them to help guide patients who are likely to hear about them from other patients or outside sources, including the Internet.[31, 98, 99]

Prognosis and Future Directions

CFS likely affects heterogeneous groups of patients, and a single etiology or definitive treatment modality most likely will not be uncovered. Nonetheless, studying groups of such patients yields useful information on the pathophysiology of this condition, and useful steps to address and alleviate symptoms for patients have been reported. In addition, the long-term follow-up data demonstrating improvement over time, especially in children and adolescents, without emergence of significant other conditions are encouraging for patients, families, and clinicians caring for such individuals.

REFERENCES

1. Abbey, S. E., and Garfinkel, P. E.: Chronic fatigue syndrome and the psychiatrist. Can. J. Psychiatry *35:*625–633, 1990.
2. Acheson, E. D.: The clinical syndrome variously called benign myalgic encephalomyelitis, Iceland disease and epidemic neuromyasthenia. Am. J. Med. *26:*569–955, 1959.
3. Barnes, D. M.: Mystery disease at Lake Tahoe challenges virologists and clinicians. Science *234:*541–542, 1986.
4. Bell, D. S., Jordan, K., and Robinson, M.: Thirteen-year follow-up of children and adolescents with chronic fatigue syndrome. Pediatrics *107:*994–998, 2001.
5. Bell, K. M., Cookfair, D., Bell, D. S., et al.: Risk factors associated with chronic fatigue syndrome in a cluster of pediatric cases. Rev. Infect. Dis. *13*(Suppl.):S320–S338, 1991.
6. Bou-Holaigah, I., Rowe, P. C., Kan, J., and Calkins, H.: The relationship between neurally mediated hypotension and the chronic fatigue syndrome. J. A. M. A. *274:*961–967, 1995.
7. Buchwald, D., Cheney, P. R., Peterson, D. L., et al.: A chronic illness characterized by fatigue, neurologic and immunologic disorders, and active human herpesvirus type 6 infection. Ann. Intern. Med. *116:*103–113, 1992.
8. Buchwald, D., Umali, P., Umali, J., et al.: Chronic fatigue and the chronic fatigue syndrome: Prevalence in a Pacific Northwest health care system. Ann. Intern. Med. *123:*81–88, 1995.
9. Caligiuri, M., Murray, C., Buchwals, D., et al.: Phenotypic and functional deficiency of natural killer cells of patients with chronic fatigue syndrome. J. Immunol. *139:*3306–3313, 1987.
10. Carter, B. D., Edwards, J. F., Kronenberger, W. G., et al.: Case control study of chronic fatigue in pediatric patients. Pediatrics *95:*179–186, 1995.
11. Carter, B. D., Kronenberger, W. G., Edwards, J. F., et al.: Differential diagnosis of chronic fatigue in children: behavioral and emotional dimensions. Dev. Behav. Pediatr. *17:*16–21, 1996.
12. Cleare, A. J., Heap, E., Malhi, G. S., Wessely S., et al.: Low-dose hydrocortisone in chronic fatigue syndrome: A randomized crossover trial. Lancet *353:*455–458, 1999.
13. Clements, G. B., McGarry, F., Nairn, C., and Galbraith D. N.: Detection of enterovirus-specific RNA in serum: The relationship to chronic fatigue syndrome. J. Med. Virol. *45:*156–161, 1995.
14. Cope, H., and David, A. S.: Neuroimaging in chronic fatigue. J. Neurol. Neurosurg. Psychiatry *60:*471–473, 1996.
15. Costa, D. C., Tannock, C., and Brostoff, J.: Brainstem perfusion is impaired in chronic fatigue syndrome. Q. J. Med. *88:*767–773, 1995.
16. Cox, I. M., Campell, M. J., and Dowson D.: Red blood cell magnesium and chronic fatigue syndrome. Lancet *337:*757–760, 1991.
17. Cunningham, L., Bowles, N. E., Lane, R. J. M., et al.: Persistence of enteroviral RNA in chronic fatigue syndrome is associated with abnormal production of equal amounts of positive and negative strands of enteroviral RNA. J. Gen. Virol. *71:*1399–1402, 1990.
18. Deale, A., Chalder, T., Marks, I., and Wessely, S.: Cognitive behavior therapy for chronic fatigue syndrome: A randomized controlled trial. Am. J. Psychiatry *154:*408–414, 1997.
19. DeFritas, E., Hilliard, B., Cheney, P. R., et al.: Retroviral sequences related to human T-lymphotropic virus type II in patients with chronic fatigue immune dysfunction syndrome. Proc. Natl. Acad. Sci. U. S. A. *88:*2922–2926, 1991.
20. DeMeirleir, K., Bisbal, C., Campine, I., et al.: A 37 kDa 2-5A binding protein as a potential biochemical marker for chronic fatigue syndrome. Am. J. Med. *108:*99–105, 2000.
21. Demitrack, M. A., Dale, J. K., Straus, S. E., et al.: Evidence for impaired activation of the hypothalamic-pituitary-adrenal axis in patients with chronic fatigue syndrome. J. Clin. Endocrinol. Metab. *73:*1224–1234, 1991.
22. DiLuca, D., Zorzenon, M., Mirandola, P., et al.: Human herpesvirus 6 and human herpesvirus 7 in chronic fatigue syndrome. J. Clin. Microbiol. *33:*1660–1661, 1995.
23. Dowsett, E. G., and Colby, J.: Long-term sickness absence due to ME/CFS in UK schools: an epidemiological study with medical and educational implications. J. Chron. Fatigue Synd. *3:*29–42, 1997.
24. Feder, H. M., Dworkin, P. H., and Orkin, C.: Outcome of 48 pediatric patients with chronic fatigue: A clinical experience. Arch. Fam. Med. *3:*1049–1055, 1994.
25. Field, T. M., Sunshine, W., Hernandez-Reif, M., et al.: Massage therapy effects on depression and somatic symptoms in chronic fatigue syndrome. J. Chron. Fatigue Synd. *3:*43–51, 1997.
26. Fischler, B., D'Haenen, H., Cluydts, R., et al.: Comparison of 99m Tc HMPAO SPECT scan between chronic fatigue syndrome, major depression and healthy controls: An exploratory study of clinical correlates of regional cerebral blood flow. Neuropsychobiology *34:*175–183, 1996.
27. Freeman, R., and Komaroff, A. L.: Does the chronic fatigue syndrome involve the autonomic system? Am. J. Med. *102:*357–362, 1997.
28. Fukuda, K., Straus, S. E., Hickie, I., et al.: The chronic fatigue syndrome: A comprehensive approach to its definition and study. Ann. Intern. Med. *121:*953–959, 1994.
29. Fukuda, K., and Gantz, N. M.: Management strategies for chronic fatigue syndrome. Federal Practitioner, July 1995.
30. Fulcher, K. Y., and White, P. D.: Randomised, double-blind, placebo-controlled trial of graded exercise in patients with chronic fatigue syndrome. B. M. J. *314:*1647–1652, 1997.
31. Gantz, N. M., and Coldsmith, E. E.: Chronic fatigue syndrome and fibromyalgia resources on the World Wide Web: A descriptive journey. Clin. Infect. Dis. *32:*938–948, 2001.
32. Gow, J. W., Behan, W. M. H., Simpson, K., et al.: Studies on enterovirus in patients with chronic fatigue syndrome. Clin. Infect. Dis. *18*(Suppl. 1):S126–S129, 1994.
33. Greco, A., Tannock, C., Brostoff, J., and Costa, D. C.: Brain MR in chronic fatigue syndrome. Am. J. Neuroradiol. *18:*1265–1269, 1997.
34. Holmes, G. P., Kaplan, J. E., Gantz, N. M., et al.: Chronic fatigue syndrome: A working case definition. Ann. Intern. Med. *108:*387–389, 1988.
35. Imboden, J. B., Canter, A., and Cluff, L. E.: Convalescence from influenza. Arch. Intern. Med. *108:*115–121, 1961.
36. Jones, J. F., Ray, C. G., Minnich, L. L., et al.: Evidence for Epstein-Barr virus infection in patients with persistent, unexplained illnesses: Elevated anti-early antigen antibodies. Ann. Intern. Med. *102:*1–7, 1985.
37. Joyce, E., Blumentahl, S., and Wessely, S.: Memory, attention, and executive function in chronic fatigue syndrome. J. Neurol. Neurosurg. Psychiatry *60:*495–503, 1996.
38. Joyce, J., Hotopf, M., and Wessely, S.: The prognosis of chronic fatigue and chronic fatigue syndrome: A systematic review. Q. J. Med. *90:*223–233, 1997.
39. Kasl, S. V., Evans, A. S., and Niederman, J. C.: Psychosocial risk factors in the development of infectious mononucleosis. Psychosom. Med. *41:*445–466, 1979.

40. Kaslow, J. E., Rucker, L., and Onishi, R.: Liver extract-folic acid-cyanocobalamin vs. placebo for chronic fatigue syndrome. Arch. Intern Med. *149:*2501–2503, 1989.
41. Klimas, N. G., Salvato, F. R., Morgan, R., and Fletcher, M. A.: Immunologic abnormalities in chronic fatigue syndrome. J. Clin. Microbiol. *28:*1403–1410, 1990.
42. Komaroff, A. L., Fagioli, L. R., Geiger, A. M, et al.: An examination of the working case definition of chronic fatigue syndrome. Am. J. Med. *100:*56–64, 1996.
43. Krilov, L. R.: Chronic fatigue syndrome. Pediatr. Ann. *24:*290–294, 1995.
44. Krilov, L. R., Fisher, M., Friedman, S. B., et al.: Course and outcome of chronic fatigue in children and adolescents. Pediatrics *102:*360–366, 1998.
45. Krilov, L. R., and Fisher, M.: Chronic fatigue syndrome in children and adolescents. Contemp. Pediatr. *19:*61–68, 2002.
46. Kruesi, D., Dale, J., and Straus, S. E.: Psychiatric diagnoses in patients who have chronic fatigue syndrome. J. Clin. Psychiatry *50:*53–56, 1989.
47. Krupp, L. B., Jandorf, L., Coyle, P. K., and Mendelson, W. B.: Sleep disturbance in chronic fatigue syndrome. J. Psychosom. Res. *37:*325–331, 1993.
48. Landay, A. L., Jessop, C., Lennette, E. T., and Levy, J. A.: Chronic fatigue syndrome: Clinical condition associated with immune activation. Lancet *338:*707–721, 1991.
49. Lloyd, A., Hickie, I., Wakefield, D., et al.: A double-blind, placebo-controlled trial of intravenous immunoglobulin therapy in patients with chronic fatigue syndrome. Am. J. Med. *89:*561–568, 1990.
50. Lloyd, A. R., Hickie, I., Boughton, C. R., et al.: Prevalence of chronic fatigue syndrome in an Australian population. Med. J. Aust. *153:*522–528, 1990.
51. MacDonald, K. L., Osterholm, M. T., LeDell, K. H., et al.: A case-controlled study to assess possible triggers and cofactors in chronic fatigue syndrome. Am. J. Med. *100:*548–554, 1996.
52. Marshall, G. S., Gesser, R. M., Yamanishi, K., and Starr, S. E.: Chronic fatigue in children: Clinical features, Epstein-Barr virus and human herpesvirus 6 serology and long term follow-up. Pediatr. Infect. Dis. J. *10:*287–290, 1991.
53. Marshall, G. S.: Report of a workshop on the epidemiology, natural history, and pathogenesis of chronic fatigue syndrome in adolescents. J. Pediatr. *134:*395–405, 1999.
54. Martin, R. W. Y., Ogston, S. A., and Evans, J. R.: Effects of vitamin and mineral supplementations on symptoms associated with chronic fatigue syndrome with coxsackie B antibodies. J. Nutr. Med. *4:*11–23, 1994.
55. Mawle, A. C., Nisenbaum, R., and Dobbins, J. G., et al.: Seroepidemiology of chronic fatigue syndrome: A case-control study. Clin. Infect. Dis. *21:*1386–1389, 1995.
56. Mawle, A. C., Nisenbaum, R., Dobbins, J. G., et al.: Immune responses associated with chronic fatigue syndrome: A case-control study. J. Infect. Dis. *175:*136–141, 1997.
57. McKenzie, R., O'Fallon, A., Dale, J., et al.: Low-dose hydrocortisone for treatment of chronic fatigue syndrome: A randomized controlled trial. J. A. M. A. *280:*1061–1066, 1998.
58. Moorkens, G., Wynants, H., and Abs, R.: Effect of growth hormone treatment in patients with chronic fatigue syndrome. Growth Horm. IGF Res. *8:*131–133, 1998.
59. Natelson, B. H., Cohen, J. M., Brassloff, I., et al.: A controlled study of brain magnetic resonance imaging in patients with the chronic fatigue syndrome. J. Neurol. Sci. *120:*213–217, 1993.
60. Natelson, B. H., Cheu, J., Pareja, J., et al.: Randomized, double-blind, controlled placebo-phase in trial of low dose phenelzine in the chronic fatigue syndrome. Psychopharmacology *124:*226–230, 1996.
61. National Institutes of Allergy Infectious Diseases. CFS. [On-line]. Available: www.niaid.nih.gov./publications/cfs/complete.htm. 1997.
62. Pelcovitz D., Septimus A., Friedman S. B., et al.: Psychosocial correlates of chronic fatigue syndrome in adolescent girls. Dev. Behav. Pediatr. *16:*333–338, 1995.
63. Peterson P. K., Shepard J., Macres M., et al.: A controlled trial of intravenous immunoglobulin G in chronic fatigue syndrome. Am. J. Med. *89:*554–560, 1990.
64. Peterson, P. K., Pheley, A., Schreoppel, J., et al.: A preliminary placebo-controlled crossover trial of fludrocortisone for chronic fatigue syndrome. Arch. Intern. Med. *158:*908–914, 1998.
65. Plioplys, A. V.: Chronic fatigue syndrome should not be diagnosed in children. Pediatrics. *100:*270–271, 1997.
66. Price, P. K., North, C. S., Wessely, S., and Fraser, V. J.: Estimating the prevalence of chronic fatigue syndrome and associated symptoms in the community. Public Health Rep. *107:*514–522, 1992.
67. Prins, J., Bleijenberg, G., Bazelmans, E., et al.: Cognitive behaviour therapy for chronic fatigue syndrome: A multicentre randomized controlled trial. Lancet *357:*841–847, 2001.
68. Regestein, Q. R., and Monk, T. H.: Delayed sleep phase syndrome: a review of its clinical aspects. Am. J. Psychiatry *152:*602–608, 1995.
69. Renfro, L., Feder, H. M., Lane, T. J., et al.: Yeast connection among 100 patients with chronic fatigue. Am. J. Med. *86:*165–168, 1989.
70. Rowe, P. C., Bou-Holaigah, I., Kan, J. S., and Calkins, H.: Is neurally mediated hypotension an unrecognized cause of chronic fatigue? Lancet *345:*623–624, 1995.
71. Schwartz, R. B., Garada, B. M., Komaroff, A. L., et al.: Detection of intracranial abnormalities in patients with chronic fatigue syndrome: Comparison of MR imaging and SPECT. A. J. R. Am. J. Roentgenol. *162:*935–941, 1994.
72. Schwartz, R. B., Komaroff, A. L., Garada, B. M., et al.: SPECT imaging of the brain: Comparison of findings in patients with chronic fatigue syndrome, AIDS dementia complex, and major unipolar depression. A. J. R. Am. J. Roentgenol. *162:*943–951, 1994.
73. Sharpe, M. C.: A report—chronic fatigue syndrome: Guidelines for research. J. R. Soc. Med. *84:*118–121, 1991.
74. Sharpe, M., Hawton, K., Simkin, S., et al.: Cognitive behaviour therapy for the chronic fatigue syndrome: A randomized controlled trial. B. M. J. *312:*22–26, 1996.
75. Sisto, S. A., Tapp, W., Dristal, S., et al.: Vagal tone is reduced during paced breathing in patients with the chronic fatigue syndrome. Clin. Auton. Res. *5:*139–143, 1995.
76. Smith, M. S., Mitchell, J., Corey, L., et al.: Chronic fatigue in adolescents. Pediatrics *88:*195–202, 1991.
77. Spink, W. W.: What is chronic brucellosis? Ann. Intern. Med. *35:*358–374, 1951.
78. Steere, A. C., Taylor, E., McHugh, G. L., and Logigian, E. L.: The overdiagnosis of Lyme disease. J. A. M. A. *269:*1812–1816, 1993.
79. Stewart, J. M., Gewitz, M. H., Weldon, A., and Munoz, J.: Patterns of orthostatic intolerance: The orthostatic tachycardia syndrome and adolescent chronic fatigue. J. Pediatr. *135:*218–225, 1999.
80. Stewart, J. M., Gewitz, M. H., Weldon, A., et al.: Orthostatic intolerance in adolescent chronic fatigue syndrome. Pediatrics *103:*116–121, 1999.
81. Stewart, J. Autonomic nervous system dysfunction in adolescents with postural orthostatic tachycardia syndrome and chronic fatigue syndrome is characterized by attenuated vagal baroreflex and potentiated sympathetic vasomotion. Pediatr. Res. *48:*218–226, 2000.
82. Straus, S. E., Tosato, G., Armstrong, G., et al.: Persisting illness in adults with evidence of Epstein-Barr infection. Ann. Intern Med. *102:*7–16, 1985.
83. Straus, S. E., Dale, D. K., Tobi, M., et al.: Acyclovir treatment of the chronic fatigue syndrome. N. Engl. J. Med. *319:*1692–1698, 1988.
84. Straus, S. E., Dale, J. K., Wright, R., and Metcalfe, D. D.: Allergy and the chronic fatigue syndrome. J. Allergy Clin. Immunol. *81:*791–795, 1988.
85. Straus, S. E., Dale, J. K., Peter, J. B., and Dinarello, C. A.: Circulating lymphokine levels in the chronic fatigue syndrome. J. Infect. Dis. *160:*1085–1086, 1989.
86. Straus, S. E.: Intravenous immunoglobulin treatment for the chronic fatigue syndrome. Am. J. Med. *89:*551–553, 1990.
87. Straus, S. E.: History of chronic fatigue syndrome. Rev. Infect. Dis. *13*(Suppl. 1):S2–S7, 1991.
88. Straus, S. E., Fritz, S., Dale, J. K., et al.: Lymphocyte phenotype and function in the chronic fatigue syndrome. J. Clin. Immunol. *13:*30–40, 1993.
89. Sumaya, C. V.: Serologic and virologic epidemiology of Epstein-Barr virus: Relevance to chronic fatigue syndrome. Rev. Infect. Dis. *13*(Suppl. 1):S19–S25, 1991.
90. Swanink, C. M., Van der Meer, J. W., Vercoulen, J. H., et al.: Epstein-Barr virus (EBV) and the chronic fatigue syndrome: Normal virus load in blood and normal immunologic reactivity in the EBV regression assay. Clin. Infect. Dis. *20:*1390–1392, 1995.
91. Swanink, C. M. A., Vercoulen, J. H. M. M., Galama, J. M. D., et al.: Lymphocyte subsets, apoptosis, and cytokines in patients with chronic fatigue syndrome. J. Infect. Dis. *173:*460–463, 1996.
92. Vollmer-Conna, U., Lloyd, A., Hickie, I., and Wakefield D.: Chronic fatigue syndrome: An immunological perspective. Aust. N. Z. J. Psychiatry *32:*523–527, 1998.
93. Vercoulen, J., Swanink, C. M., Zitman, F. G., et al.: Randomised, double-blind, placebo-controlled study of fluoxetine in chronic fatigue syndrome. Lancet *347:*858–861, 1996.
94. Wakefield, D., Lloyd, A., Dwyer, J., et al.: Human herpesvirus 6 and myalgic encephalomyelitis. Lancet *1:*1059, 1988.
95. Warren, G., McKendrick, M., and Peet, M.: The role of essential fatty acids in chronic fatigue syndrome: A case-controlled study of red-cell membrane essential fatty acids (EFA) and a placebo-controlled treatment study with high-dose of EFA. Acta Neurol. Scand. *99:*112–116, 1999.
96. Weardon, A. J., and Appleby, L.: Research on cognitive complaints and cognitive functioning in patients with chronic fatigue syndrome (CFS): What conclusions can we draw? J. Psychosomatic Res. *41:*197–211, 1996.
97. Wearden, A. J., Morriss, R. K., Mullis, R., et al.: Randomised, double-blind, placebo-controlled treatment trial of fluoxetine and graded exercise for chronic fatigue syndrome. Br. J. Psychiatry *172:*485–492, 1998.
98. Wessely, S.: Chronic fatigue syndrome: Trials and tribulations. J. A. M. A. *286:*1378–1379, 2001.
99. Whiting, P., Bagnall, A. M., Sowden, A. J., et al.: Interventions for the treatment and management of chronic fatigue syndrome, a systematic review. J. A. M. A. *286:*1360–1368, 2001.
100. Wilson, A., Hickie, L., Lloyd, A., et al.: Longitudinal study of outcome of chronic fatigue syndrome. B. M. J. *308:*756–759, 1994.

PART III

Infections with Specific Microorganisms

Bacterial Infections

CHAPTER 84

Nomenclature for Aerobic and Anaerobic Bacteria

DAVID A. BRUCKNER

The following lists represent an update of the current nomenclature, taxonomy, and classification of various microbial agents. Taxonomic methods have evolved from the use of biochemical testing to molecular characterization using 16S or 23S rRNA. Molecular methods have helped to define organism groupings and have led to considerable changes in bacterial nomenclature. The classification process is not complete until molecular and phenotypic descriptions of the studied taxa are provided. The primary purpose of nomenclature is to permit us to know as exactly as possible to what another clinician, microbiologist, epidemiologist, or investigator is referring when describing an organism responsible for infecting individuals or for causing an outbreak. The *International Code of Nomenclature of Bacteria*[18] includes rules on how to name bacteria and use the name. The most comprehensive taxonomic information available for bacteriologic classification can be found in *Bergey's Manual of Determinative Bacteriology,* ninth edition,[7] and in *Bergey's Manual of Systematic Bacteriology,*[6] volumes 1 through 4. Leading journals that contain up-to-date information on nomenclature and new species include the *International Journal of Systematic Bacteriology, Annales de Microbiologie (Institute Pasteur), Current Microbiology, Journal of Clinical Microbiology,* and *Systematic and Applied Microbiology.*

Taxonomic ranks for naming bacterial organisms include kingdom, division, class, order, family, genus, species, and subspecies. All of these ranks have official standing in nomenclature. Ranks below subspecies have no official standing but are used to indicate groups of strains or isolates that can be distinguished by some special characters (Table 84–1). Each taxonomic name should be represented by a nomenclature type. The species is represented by a type strain that is deposited in a recognized culture collection.

Nomenclature priorities for bacteriologic names have dated back to May 1753. Because of difficulties in searching literature and limited available information on described species, approved lists of bacterial names were published in the *International Journal of Systematic Bacteriology* in 1980. Names not included on those lists have lost all standing in nomenclature status.

Historically, bacterial classification has been based on phenotypic characteristics. Multivariate analysis has played a large role in classification since the 1950s. This analysis used biochemical, cultural, and morphologic characteristics and susceptibilities to antibiotics and inorganic compounds to define the degrees of similarities between organisms. More recently, molecular techniques (e.g., DNA hybridization, rRNA-DNA hybridization, gene sequence analysis) have played a major role in determining phylogenetic relationships.

The DNA molecular weight for most bacteria is 1×10^9 to 8×10^9, enough to specify 1500 to 6000 genes. Using nucleic acids, researchers have used numerous parameters to determine taxonomic relationships. These parameters include genome size, mole percent guanine plus cytosine content, DNA relatedness under optimal and supraoptimal conditions for DNA reassociation, and rRNA oligonucleotide sequences. By correlating phenotypic results with DNA homology and rRNA sequence analysis, researchers have been able to select phenotypic tests that can be used more accurately to identify organisms belonging to specific groups.

The following bacterial classification is based on the organism's morphologic and stain characteristics. Organisms included are those that often are associated with pathologic processes or that are medically significant. The current names are those either officially recognized or proposed for recognition and currently used in the literature.[1–19]

TABLE 84–1 ■ BACTERIAL RANKS BELOW SUBSPECIES

Preferred Name	Synonym	When Applied
Biovar features	Biotype	Special biochemical or physiologic
Serovar	Serotype	Distinct antigenic features
Pathovar	Pathotype	Host-specific pathogenic features
Phagovar	Phagotype	Lysis by distinct bacteriophages
Morphovar	Morphotype	Special morphologic features

I. AEROBIC GRAM-POSITIVE COCCI

Characteristics: aerotolerant anaerobes that can occur singly or in pairs, tetrads, chains, or clusters; they can be catalase positive or negative. Organisms positive for coagulase or

clumping factor include *Staphylococcus aureus*, *Staphylococcus intermedius*, *Staphylococcus lugdunensis*, and *Staphylococcus schleiferi* subspecies coagulans.

Current Name	Synonym
CATALASE POSITIVE	
Alloiococcus otitidis	
Kocuria varians	*Micrococcus varians*
Kocuria kristinae	*Micrococcus kristinae*
Kytococcus sedentarius	*Micrococcus sedentarius*
Micrococcus luteus	
Micrococcus lytae	
Staphylococcus aureus spp. *aureus*	
Staphylococcus auricularis	
Staphylococcus capitis spp. *capitis*	
Staphylococcus capitis spp. *ureolyticus*	
Staphylococcus caprae	
Staphylococcus cohnii spp. *cohnii*	
Staphylococcus cohnii spp. *urealyticus*	
Staphylococcus epidermidis	*Staphylococcus albus*
Staphylococcus haemolyticus	
Staphylococcus hominis spp. *hominis*	
Staphylococcus hominis spp. *novobiosepticus*	
Staphylococcus hyicus	
Staphylococcus intermedius	
Staphylococcus lugdunensis	
Staphylococcus pasteuri	
Staphylococcus saccharolyticus	*Peptococcus saccharolyticus*
Staphylococcus saprophyticus spp. *saprophyticus*	*Micrococcus subgroup 3*
Staphylococcus schleiferi spp. *coagulans*	
Staphylococcus schleiferi spp. *schleiferi*	
Staphylococcus simulans	
Staphylococcus warneri	
Staphylococcus xylosus	
Stomatococcus mucilaginosus	
CATALASE NEGATIVE	
Abiotrophia adjacens	*Streptococcus adjacens* Nutritionally variant streptococci
Abiotrophia defectiva	*Streptococcus defectivus* Nutritionally variant streptococci
Abiotrophia elegans	Nutritionally variant streptococci
Aerococcus christensenii	
Aerococcus sanguicola	
Aerococcus urinae	
Aerococcus viridans	
Dolosigranulum pigrum	
Enterococcus avium	*Streptococcus avium* Group D *Enterococcus*
Enterococcus casseliflavus	*Streptococcus casseliflavus*
Enterococcus cecorum	*Streptococcus cecorum*
Enterococcus dispar	
Enterococcus durans	*Streptococcus durans* Group D *Enterococcus*
Enterococcus faecalis	*Streptococcus faecalis* Group D *Enterococcus*
Enterococcus faecium	*Streptococcus faecium* Group D *Enterococcus*
Enterococcus flavescens	
Enterococcus gallinarum	*Streptococcus gallinarum*
Enterococcus hirae	
Enterococcus malodoratus	
Enterococcus mundtii	
Enterococcus pseudoavium	
Enterococcus raffinosus	
Faklamia hominis	
Faklamia ignava	
Faklamia languida	
Faklamia sourekii	
Gemella bergeri	*Gemella bergeriae*
Gemella haemolysans	*Neisseria haemolysans*

Current Name	Synonym
Gemella morbillorum	*Streptococcus morbillorum* *Peptostreptococcus morbillorum*
Gemella sanguis	
Globicatella sanguis	Salt-tolerant viridans streptococci
Helcococcus kunzii	
Ignavigranum ruoffiae	
Lactococcus garviae	*Streptococcus garvieae* Lancefield group N
Lactococcus lactis	
Leuconostoc citreum	
Leuconostoc cremoris	
Leuconostoc dextranicum	
Leuconostoc lactis	
Leuconostoc mesenteroides	
Leuconostoc pseudomesenteroides	
Oenococcus oeni	*Leuconostoc oenos*
Pediococcus acidilactici	
Pediococcus damnosus	
Pediococcus dextrinicus	
Pediococcus equinus	*Streptococcus equinus*
Pediococcus parvulus	
Pediococcus pentosaceus	
Streptococcus acidominimus	
***Streptococcus bovis* group**	Group D streptococci
Streptococcus alatolyticus	
Streptococcus bovis	
Streptococcus equinus	
***Streptococcus milleri* group**	Viridans streptococci
Streptococcus anginosus	
Streptococcus constellatus	
Streptococcus intermedius	
***Streptococcus mitis* group**	Viridans streptococci
Streptococcus mitis	*Streptococcus mitior* *Streptococcus sanguis* II
Streptococcus oralis	
Streptococcus pneumoniae	*Diplococcus pneumoniae*
***Streptococcus mutans* group**	Viridans streptococci
Streptococcus cricetus	
Streptococcus mutans	
Streptococcus rattus	
Streptococcus sobrinus	
***Streptococcus pyogenes* group**	
Streptococcus agalactiae	Group B streptococci
Streptococcus canis	
Streptococcus dysgalactiae spp. *equisimilis*	Group C streptococci *Streptococcus equi* *Streptococcus equi spp. zooepidermidis* *Streptococcus equisimilis* Group G streptococci
Streptococcus iniae	*Streptococcus shiloi*
Streptococcus porcinus	
Streptococcus pyogenes	*Group A streptococci*
***Streptococcus salivarius* group**	Viridans streptococci
Streptococcus salivarius	
Streptococcus thermophilus	
Streptococcus vestibularis	
***Streptococcus sanguis* group**	Viridans streptococci
Streptococcus crista	
Streptococcus gordonii	
Streptococcus parasanguis	
Streptococcus sanguis	
Streptococcus suis	
Tetragenococcus halophilis	*Enterococcus solitarius*
Vaginococcus fluvialis	
Weissella paramesenteroides	*Leuconostoc paramesenteroides*

II. ANAEROBIC GRAM-POSITIVE COCCI

Characteristics: occur singly or in pairs, chains, or clumps

Gemella morbillorum	*Streptococcus morbillorum*
Peptococcus niger	*Micrococcus niger*

Current Name	Synonym
Peptostreptococcus anaerobius	
Peptostreptococcus asaccharolyticus	*Peptococcus asaccharolyticus*
Peptostreptococcus harei	
Peptostreptococcus hydrogenalis	
Peptostreptococcus indolicus	*Peptococcus indolicus*
Peptostreptococcus ivorii	
Peptostreptococcus lacrimalis	
Peptostreptococcus lactolyticus	
Peptostreptococcus magnus	*Peptococcus magnus* *Peptococcus variabilis*
Peptostreptococcus micros	
Peptostreptococcus octavius	
Peptostreptococcus prevotii	*Peptococcus prevotii*
Peptostreptococcus tetradius	*Gaffkya anaerobia*
Peptostreptococcus trisimilis	
Peptostreptococcus vaginalis	
Ruminococcus hansenii	
Ruminococcus productus	

III. AEROBIC GRAM-NEGATIVE COCCI

Characteristics: occur singly or in pairs or clumps; catalase and oxidase positive

Current Name	Synonym
Lautropia mirabilis	*Sarcina mirabilis*
Neisseria canis	
Neisseria cinerea	*Micrococcus cinereus* *Neisseria pharyngis*
Neisseria elongata spp. *elongata*	*Neisseria elongata*
Neisseria elongata spp. *glycolytica*	*Neisseria elongata*
Neisseria elongata spp. *nitroreducens*	*Neisseria elongata* CDC group M-6
Neisseria flavescens	
Neisseria gonorrhoeae	
Neisseria kochii	
Neisseria lactamica	
Neisseria meningitidis	
Neisseria mucosa	
Neisseria parelongata	
Neisseria polysaccharea	
Neisseria sicca	
Neisseria subflava biovar. *flava*	*Neisseria subflava*
Neisseria subflava biovar. *perflava*	*Neisseria subflava*
Neisseria subflava biovar. *subflava*	*Neisseria subflava*
Neisseria weaveri	*Moraxella* species M-5 CDC group M-5

IV. ANAEROBIC GRAM-NEGATIVE COCCI

Characteristics: occur in pairs or clumps

Acidaminococcus fermentans
Megasphaera elsdenii
Veillonella dispar
Veillonella parvula

V. AEROBIC GRAM-POSITIVE BACILLI

Characteristics: rod like; catalase negative or positive; some are acid-fast stain positive, and some have branching; only *Bacillus, Brevibacillus,* and *Brevibacterium* spp. produce spores.

Current Name	Synonym
Actinomadura latina	
Actinomadura madurae	
Actinomadura pelletieri	
Amycolata autotrophica	
Amycolatopsis orientalis	*Nocardia orientalis* *Streptomyces orientalis*
Arthrobacter albus	
Arthrobacter creatinolyticus	
Arthrobacter cumminsii	
Arthrobacter luteolus	
Arthrobacter oxydans	
Arthrobacter woluwensis	
Aureobacterium spp.	*Corynebacterium aquaticum*

Current Name	Synonym
Bacillus anthracis	
Bacillus cereus	
Bacillus circulans	
Bacillus coagulans	
Bacillus licheniformis	
Bacillus megaterium	
Bacillus mycoides	
Bacillus pumilus	
Bacillus sphaericus	
Bacillus subtilis	
Bacillus thuringiensis	
Brevibacillus agri	
Brevibacillus brevis	*Bacillus brevis*
Brevibacillus laterosporus	*Bacillus laterosporus*
	Brevibacterium casei
	CDC coryneform groups B-1 and B-3
Brevibacterium epidermidis	
Brevibacterium mcbrellneri	
Brevibacterium otitidis	
Callatomonas turbata	*Oerskovia turbata*
Cellulomonas hominis	CDC coryneform group A-3
Corynebacterium accolens	
Corynebacterium afermentans spp. *afermentans*	CDC coryneform group ANF-1
Corynebacterium afermentans spp. *lipophilum*	CDC coryneform group ANF-1
Corynebacterium amycolatum	*Corynebacterium xerosis*
	Corynebacterium minutissimum
	Corynebacterium striatum
	CDC coryneform groups F-2 and I-2
Corynebacterium argentoratense	
Corynebacterium auris	CDC coryneform group ANF-1
Corynebacterium confusum	
Corynebacterium coyleae	
Corynebacterium diphtheriae	
Corynebacterium durum	
Corynebacterium falsenii	
Corynebacterium glucuronolyticum	
Corynebacterium imitans	
Corynebacterium jeikeium	*Corynebacterium* group JK
	CDC coryneform group JK
Corynebacterium kroppenstedtii	
Corynebacterium lipophiloflavum	
Corynebacterium macginleyi	CDC coryneform group G-1
Corynebacterium matruchotii	*Bacterionema matruchotii*
Corynebacterium minutissimum	
Corynebacterium mucifaciens	
Corynebacterium pilosum	
Corynebacterium propinquum	CDC coryneform group ANF-3
Corynebacterium pseudodiphtheriticum	*Corynebacterium hofmanii*
Corynebacterium pseudotuberculosis	
Corynebacterium riegellii	
Corynebacterium sanguinis	
Corynebacterium singulare	
Corynebacterium striatum	
Corynebacterium sundsvallense	*Corynebacterium thomssenii*
	Rothia dentocarrosa
Corynebacterium ulcerans	
Corynebacterium urealyticum	*Corynebacterium* group D2
	CDC coryneform group D2
Corynebacterium xerosis	
Curtobacterium spp.	
Dermabacter hominis	CDC fermentative coryneform groups 3 and 5
Dermatophilus congolensis	
Erysipelothrix rhusiopathiae	*Erysipelothrix insidiosa*
Exiguobacterium acetylicum	
Exiguobacterium aurantiacum	*Brevibacterium aurantiacum*
Gardnerella vaginalis	*Haemophilus vaginalis*
	Corynebacterium vaginalis
Gordona aichiensis	*Rhodococcus aichiensis*
	Tsukamura aichiessii
Gordona bronchialis	*Rhodococcus bronchialis*
Gordona rubiopertincta	*Rhodococcus rubiopertincta*
Gordona sputi	*Rhodococcus sputi*
	Rhodococcus chubuensis
Gordona terrae	*Rhodococcus terrae*
Kurthia spp.	

Current Name	Synonym
Listeria bulgaria	
Listeria grayi spp. *grayi*	*Listeria grayi*
Listeria ivanovii spp. *ivanovii*	*Listeria monocytogenes serovar 5*
Listeria ivanovii spp. *londoniensis*	
Listeria monocytogenes	
Microbacterium spp.	CDC coryneform groups A-4 and A-5
Microbacterium arborescens	CDC coryneform group A-4
Microbacterium imperiale	CDC coryneform group A-4
Mycobacterium abscessus	*Mycobacterium chelonae* spp. *abscessus*
Mycobacterium africanum	
Mycobacterium alvei	
Mycobacterium asiaticum	
Mycobacterium aurum	
Mycobacterium avium	
Mycobacterium avium spp. *paratuberculosis*	
Mycobacterium bohemicum	
Mycobacterium bovis	
Mycobacterium branderi	
Mycobacterium brumae	
Mycobacterium celatum	
Mycobacterium chelonae	*Mycobacterium chelonae* spp. *chelonae* *Mycobacterium chelonei*
Mycobacterium chubuense	
Mycobacterium confluentis	
Mycobacterium conspicuum	
Mycobacterium cookii	
Mycobacterium flavescens	
Mycobacterium fortuitum	*Mycobacterium fortuitum* spp. *fortuitum* *Mycobacterium fortuitum* (third complex) sorbitol-positive biovariant *Mycobacterium fortuitum* (third complex) sorbitol-negative biovariant
Mycobacterium gadium	
Mycobacterium gastri	
Mycobacterium genavense	
Mycobacterium gordonae	*Mycobacterium aquae*
Mycobacterium haemophilum	
Mycobacterium hassiacum	
Mycobacterium heckeshornense	
Mycobacterium heidelbergense	
Mycobacterium intracellulare	
Mycobacterium interjectum	
Mycobacterium kansasii	
Mycobacterium kubicae	
Mycobacterium lentiflavum	
Mycobacterium leprae	
Mycobacterium mageritense	
Mycobacterium maichiense	
Mycobacterium malmoense	
Mycobacterium marinum	*Mycobacterium balnei*
Mycobacterium microgenicum	
Mycobacterium microti	
Mycobacterium mucogenicum	*Mycobacterium chelonae*-like organism (MCLO)
Mycobacterium neoaurum	
Mycobacterium nonchromogenicum	
Mycobacterium novocastiense	
Mycobacterium peregrinum	*Mycobacterium fortuitum* biovar. *peregrinum*
Mycobacterium phlei	
Mycobacterium scrofulaceum	
Mycobacterium shimoidei	
Mycobacterium simiae	*Mycobacterium habana*
Mycobacterium smegmatis	
Mycobacterium szulgai	
Mycobacterium terrae	
Mycobacterium thermoresistibile	
Mycobacterium triplex	
Mycobacterium triviale	
Mycobacterium tuberculosis	
Mycobacterium ulcerans	*Mycobacterium buruli*
Mycobacterium vaccae	
Mycobacterium xenopi	
Nocardia asteroides	
Nocardia brasiliensis	
Nocardia brevicatena	
Nocardia farcinica	

Current Name	Synonym
Nocardia nova	
Nocardia otitidiscaviarum	*Nocardia caviae*
Nocardia pseudobrasiliensis	
Nocardia transvalensis	
Nocardiopsis dassonvillei	*Actionmadura dassonvillei*
	Nocardia dassonvillei
Nocardiopsis synnemataformans	
Oerskovia turbata	CDC coryneform groups A-3 and A-4
Oerskovia xanthineolytica	CDC coryneform groups A-1 and A-2
Paenibacillus alvei	*Bacillus alvei*
Paenibacillus macerans	*Bacillus mascerans*
Paenibacillus polymyxa	*Bacillus polymyxa*
Rhodococcus equi	*Corynebacterium equi*
Rothia dentocariosa	*Nocardia dentocariosus*
Streptomyces anulatus	*Streptomyces griseus*
Streptomyces paraguayensis	
Streptomyces somaliensis	
Tropheryma whippelii	
Tsukamurella inchonensis	
Tsukamurella paurometabola	*Gordona aurantiaca*
Tsukamurella pulmonis	
Tsukamurella tyrosinosolvens	
Turicella otitidis	*Rhodococcus aurantiacus*

VI. ANAEROBIC GRAM-POSITIVE BACILLI (NON–SPORE FORMING)

Characteristics: may be long-branching bacilli or pleomorphic coccobacilli

Current Name	Synonym
Actinobaculum schaalii	
Actinobaculum suis	*Actinomyces suis*
Actinomyces europaeus	
Actinomyces georgiae	*Actinomyces* DO8
Actinomyces gerencseriae	*Actinomyces israelii* serotype II
Actinomyces graevenitzii	
Actinomyces israelii	
Actinomyces meyeri	
Actinomyces naeslundii	
Actinomyces neuii spp. *anitratus*	
Actinomyces neuii spp. *neuii*	CDC coryneform group 1
Actinomyces odontolyticus	
Actinomyces radicidentis	
Actinomyces radingae	CDC coryneform group E; APL1
Actinomyces turicensis	CDC coryneform group E; APL10
Actinomyces viscosus	
Arcanobacterium bernardiae	*Actinomyces bernardiae*
	CDC coryneform group 2
Arcanobacterium pyogenes	*Actinomyces pyogenes*
	Corynebacterium pyogenes
Atopobium minutum	*Lactobacillus minutus*
Atopobium parvulum	*Streptococcus parvulus*
	Peptostreptococcus parrulus
Atopobium rimae	*Lactobacillus rimae*
Bifidobacterium adolescentis	
Bifidobacterium angulatum	
Bifidobacterium bifidum	
Bifidobacterium breve	
Bifidobacterium catenulatum	
Bifidobacterium denficolens	
Bifidobacterium dentium	*Bifidobacterium appendicitis*
Bifidobacterium eriksonii	
Bifidobacterium infantis	
Bifidobacterium inopinatum	*Bifidobacterium dentium*
Bifidobacterium longum	
Bifidobacterium pseudocatenulatum	
Collinsella aerofaciens	*Eubacterium aerofaciens*
Cryptobacterium curtum	
Eggerthella lenta	*Eubacterium lentum*
Eubacterium brachy	
Eubacterium combesii	
Eubacterium contortum	
Eubacterium infirmum	
Eubacterium limosum	
Eubacterium minutum	*Eubacterium tardum*
Eubacterium moniliforme	
Eubacterium nitritogenes	

Current Name	Synonym
Eubacterium nodatum	
Eubacterium saburreum	
Eubacterium saphenum	
Eubacterium tenue	
Eubacterium timidum	
Eubacterium yurii spp. *margaretiae*	
Eubacterium yurii spp. *schtitka*	
Eubacterium yurii spp. *yurii*	
Holdemania filiformis	*Eubacterium* S14
Lactobacillus acidophilus	
Lactobacillus brevis	
Lactobacillus casei	
Lactobacillus catenaforme	
Lactobacillus crispatus	
Lactobacillus fermentum	
Lactobacillus gasseri	
Lactobacillus iners	
Lactobacillus jensenii	
Lactobacillus leichmannii	
Lactobacillus oris	
Lactobacillus paracasei spp. paracasei	
Lactobacillus paraplantarum	
Lactobacillus plantarum	
Lactobacillus rhamnosus	*Lactobacillus GG*
Lactobacillus salivarius	
Lactobacillus uli	
Lactobacillus vaginalis	
Mobiluncus curtisii spp. curtisii	
Mobiluncus curtisii spp. holmesii	
Mobiluncus mulieris	
Propionibacterium acnes	
Propionibacterium avidum	
Propionibacterium granulosum	
Propionibacterium lymphophilum	
Propionibacterium propionicus	*Propionibacterium propionicum* *Arachnia propionica* *Actinomyces propionicus*
Pseudoramibactera lactolyticus	*Eubacterium alactolyticum*
Slackia exigua	*Eubacterium exigaum*
Slackia heliotrinireducens	*Peptostreptococcus heliotrinreducens*

VII. ANAEROBIC GRAM-POSITIVE BACILLI (SPORE FORMING)

Characteristics: broad, short bacilli with blunt ends; most organisms readily produce spores except *Clostridium perfringens.*

Current Name	Synonym
Clostridium absonum	
Clostridium argentinense	*Clostridium botulinum* group G *Clostridium subterminale* *Clostridium hastiforme*
Clostridium baratii	*Clostridium barati* *Clostridium paraperfringens* *Clostridium perenne*
Clostridium bifermentans	
Clostridium beijerinckii	
Clostridium botulinum	*Clostridium putrificum*
Clostridium butyricum	*Clostridium pseudotetanicum*
Clostridium cadaveris	
Clostridium carnis	
Clostridium celatum	
Clostridium clostridioforme	*Clostridium clostridiiforme*
Clostridium coccoides	
Clostridium cochlearium	*Clostridium lentoputrescens*
Clostridium cocleatum	
Clostridium difficile	*Clostridium difficilis*
Clostridium fallax	*Clostridium pseudofallax*
Clostridium ghonii	*Clostridium ghoni*
Clostridium glycoficum	
Clostridium haemolyticum	*Clostridium novyi* type D
Clostridium hastiforme	
Clostridium hiranonis	
Clostridium histolyticum	
Clostridium indolis	
Clostridium innocuum	

Current Name	Synonym
Clostridium irregulare	*Clostridium irregularis*
Clostridium leptum	
Clostridium limosum	CDC group P-1
Clostridium malenominatum	
Clostridium novyi	
Clostridium oroticum	*Zymobacterium oroticum*
Clostridium paraputrificum	
Clostridium perfringens	*Clostridium welchii* *Welchia perfringens*
Clostridium piliforme	*Bacillus piliformis*
Clostridium putrefaciens	
Clostridium ramosum	*Eubacterium filamentosum* *Ramibacterium ramosum* *Actinomyces ramosus* *Eubacterium ramosum*
Clostridium septicum	
Clostridium sordellii	
Clostridium sphenoides	
Clostridium sporogenes	Nontoxigenic *Clostridium botulinum*
Clostridium subterminale	
Clostridium symbiosum	*Fusobacterium symbiosum* *Fusobacterium biacutus* *Bacteroides symbiosus*
Clostridium tertium	
Clostridium tetani	
Filifactor villosus	*Clostridium villosum*

VIII. AEROBIC GRAM-NEGATIVE BACILLI: ENTEROBACTERIACEAE

Characteristics: ferment sugars; are oxidase negative; most reduce nitrate to nitrite. Diagnostic laboratories may report *Salmonella* serovars by name (e.g., *Salmonella typhi* or *Salmonella* serovar *typhi*).

Current Name	Synonym
Budvicia aquatica	
Buttiauxella noackiae	CDC enteric group 59
Cedecea davisae	CDC enteric group 15
Cedecea lapagei	
Cedecea neteri	*Cedecea* spp. 4
Cedecea spp. 3	
Cedecea spp. 5	
Citrobacter amalonaticus	*Levinea amalonatica*
Citrobacter braakii	*Citrobacter freundii*
Citrobacter diversus	
Citrobacter farmeri	*Citrobacter amalonaticus* biogroup 1
Citrobacter freundii	*Colobactrum freundii*
Citrobacter gillenii	*Citrobacter* genomospecies 10 *Citrobacter freundii*
Citrobacter koseri	*Citrobacter diversus* *Levinea malonatica*
Citrobacter murliniae	*Citrobacter* genomospecies 11 *Citrobacter freundii*
Citrobacter rodentium	*Citrobacter* genomospecies 9 *Citrobacter freundii*
Citrobacter sedlakii	*Citrobacter* genomospecies 8 *Citrobacter freundii*
Citrobacter werkmanii	*Citrobacter* genomospecies 7 *Citrobacter freundii*
Citrobacter youngae	*Citrobacter* genomospecies 5 *Citrobacter freundii*
Edwardsiella hoshinae	
Edwardsiella tarda	
Enterobacter aerogenes	*Aerobacter aerogenes*
Enterobacter agglomerans group	
Enterobacter amnigenus	
Enterobacter asburiae	CDC enteric group 17
Enterobacter cancerogenus	*Enterobacter taylorae* *Erwinia cancerogena* CDC enteric group 19
Enterobacter cloacae	
Enterobacter gergoviae	
Enterobacter hormaechei	CDC enteric group 75
Enterobacter intermedius	*Enterobacter intermedium*
Enterobacter kobei	
Enterobacter sakazakii	

Current Name	Synonym
Erwinia persicinus	
Escherichia blattae	
Escherichia coli	
Escherichia fergusonii	CDC enteric group 10
Escherichia hermannii	CDC enteric group 11
Escherichia vulneris	CDC enteric group 1
Ewingella americana	CDC enteric group 40
Hafnia alvei	*Enterobacter hafniae*
Klebsiella ornithinolytica	*Klebsiella oxytoca* ornithine positive
Klebsiella oxytoca	
Klebsiella planticola	*Klebsiella travisanii*
Klebsiella pneumoniae spp. *ozaenae*	*Klebsiella ozaenae*
Klebsiella pneumoniae spp. *pneumoniae*	*Klebsiella pneumoniae*
Klebsiella pneumoniae spp. *rhinoscleromatis*	
Kluyvera ascorbata	CDC enteric group 8
Kluyvera cryocrescens	
Kluyvera georgiana	CDC enteric group 36/37
	Kluyvera species group 3
Leclercia adecarboxylata	*Escherichia adecarboxylata*
	CDC enteric group 41
Leminorella grimontii	CDC enteric group 57
Leminorella richardii	
Moellerella wisconsensis	CDC enteric group 46
Morganella morganii spp. *morganii*	*Proteus morganii*
Morganella morganii spp. *sibonii*	*Proteus morganii*
Pantoea agglomerans	*Enterobacter agglomerans*
Pantoea dispersa	
Photorhabdus luminescens	*Xenorhabdus luminescens*
Pragia fontium	
Proteus hauseri	*Proteus vulgaris* biogroup 3
Proteus mirabilis	
Proteus penneri	*Proteus vulgaris* biogroup 1
Proteus vulgaris	*Proteus vulgaris* biogroup 2
Providencia alcalifaciens	*Proteus inconstans*
Providencia heimbachae	
Providencia rettgeri	*Proteus rettgeri*
Providencia rustigianii	*Providencia alcalifaciens* biogroup 3
Providencia stuartii	*Proteus inconstans*
Rahnella aquatilis	
Salmonella bongori	*Salmonella* subgroup 5
Salmonella choleraesuis spp. *arizonae*	*Salmonella* subgroup 3a
Salmonella choleraesuis spp. *choleraesius*	*Salmonella* subgroup 1
Salmonella choleraesuis spp. *diarizonae*	*Salmonella* subgroup 3b
Salmonella choleraesuis spp. *houtenae*	*Salmonella* subgroup 4
Salmonella choleraesuis spp. *indica*	*Salmonella* subgroup 6
Salmonella choleraesuis spp. *salamae*	*Salmonella* subgroup 2
Serratia ficaria	
Serratia fonticola	
Serratia grimesii	*Serratia liquefaciens*
Serratia liquefaciens	*Enterobacter liquefaciens*
Serratia marcescens	
Serratia odorifera	
Serratia plymuthica	
Serratia proteamaculans spp. *proteamaculans*	*Serratia liquefaciens*
Serratia proteamaculans spp. *quinovora*	*Serratia liquefaciens*
Serratia rubidaea	
Shigella boydii	*Shigella* biogroup C
Shigella dysenteriae	*Shigella* biogroup A
Shigella flexneri	*Shigella* biogroup B
Shigella sonnei	*Shigella* biogroup D
Tatumella ptyseos	CDC group EF-9
Trabulsiella guamensis	CDC enteric group 90
Yersinia aldovae	
Yersinia bercovieri	*Yersinia enterocolitica* biogroup 3b
Yersinia enterocolitica	*Pasteurella enterocolitica*
Yersinia frederiksenii	
Yersinia intermedia	
Yersinia kristensenii	
Yersinia mollaretii	*Yersinia enterocolitica* biogroup 3a
Yersinia pestis	*Pasteurella pestis*
Yersinia pseudotuberculosis	*Pasteurella pseudotuberculosis*
Yersinia rohdei	
Yokenella regensburgei	*Koserella trabulsii*
	CDC enteric group 45

IX. AEROBIC GRAM-NEGATIVE BACILLI: NONENTEROBACTERIACEAE; FERMENTATIVE

Characteristics: ferment sugars; are oxidase positive

Current Name	Synonym
Aeromonas allosaccharophila	
Aeromonas bestiarum	
Aeromonas caviae	
Aeromonas enteropelogenes	
Aeromonas hydrophila	*Pseudomonas hydrophila*
Aeromonas jandaei	
Aeromonas media	
Aeromonas salmonicida	
Aeromonas schubertii	
Aeromonas trota	
Aeromonas veronii biotype *sobria*	
Aeromonas veronii biotype *veronii*	
Chromobacterium violaceum	*Bacillus violaceus*
Pasteurella aerogenes	
Pasteurella bettyae	CDC group HB-5
Pasteurella canis	*Pasteurella multocida* biotype 6
Pasteurella dagmatis	*Pasteurella* new species 1 *Pasteurella* "gas"
Pasteurella gallinarum	
Pasteurella haemolytica	
Pasteurella multocida spp. *gallicida*	*Pasteurella septica*
Pasteurella multocida spp. *multocida*	
Pasteurella multocida spp. *septica*	
Pasteurella pneumotropica	
Pasteurella stomatis	
Pasteurella-like	CDC group EF-4
Plesiomonas shigelloides	*Aeromonas shigelloides*
Vibrio alginolyticus	*Vibrio parahaemolyticus* biotype 2
Vibrio carchariae	
Vibrio cholerae	*Vibrio comma*
Vibrio cincinnatiensis	
Vibrio damsela	CDC group EF-5
Vibrio fluvialis	CDC group EF-6
Vibrio furnissii	*Vibrio fluvialis* biogroup 2
Vibrio hollisae	CDC group EF-13 CDC enteric group 42
Vibrio metschnikovii	CDC enteric group 16 *Vibrio cholerae* biovar. proteus
Vibrio mimicus	*Vibrio cholerae* sucrose negative
Vibrio parahaemolyticus	
Vibrio vulnificus	CDC group EF-3 *Beneckea vulnifica*

X. AEROBIC GRAM-NEGATIVE BACILLI: NONENTEROBACTERIACEAE; NONFERMENTATIVE

Characteristics: may or may not oxidize sugars; are catalase positive; are oxidase variable

Current Name	Synonym
Achromobacter piechaudii	*Alcaligenes piechaudii*
Achromobacter xylosoxidans spp. *denitrificans*	*Alcaligenes denitrificans* *Alcaligenes xylosoxidans* spp. *denitrificans* CDC group Vc
Achromobacter xylosoxidans spp. *xylosoxidans*	*Alcaligenes xylosoxidans* *Alcaligenes xylosoxidans* spp. *xylosoxidans* *Alcaligenes denitrificans* spp. *xylosoxidans* *Achromobacter xylosoxidans* CDC groups IIIa and IIIb
Acidovorax delafieldii	*Pseudomonas delafieldii*
Acidovorax facilis	*Pseudomonas facilis*
Acidovorax temperans	*Pseudomonas temperans*
Acinetobacter baumannii	*Acinetobacter anitratus*
Acinetobacter calcoaceticus	*Acinetobacter anitratus* *Acinetobacter calcoaceticus* spp. *calcoaceticus*
Acinetobacter haemolyticus	*Acinetobacter anitratus*
Acinetobacter johnsonii	
Acinetobacter junii	*Acinetobacter anitratus*
Acinetobacter lwoffii	*Acinetobacter calcoaceticus* spp. *lwoffi*
Acinetobacter radioresistens	
Agrobacterium radiobacter	*Agrobacterium tumefaciens* CDC group Vd-3
Alcaligenes faecalis spp. *faecalis*	*Alcaligenes odorans*

Current Name	Synonym
	Pseudomonas odorans
	CDC group VI
Balneatrix alpica	
Bergeyella zoohelcum	*Weeksella zoohelcum*
	CDC group IIj
Brevundimonas diminuta	*Pseudomonas diminuta*
	CDC group Ia
Brevundimonas vesicularis	*Pseudomonas vesicularis*
	Corynebacterium vesiculare
Burkholderia cepacia	*Pseudomonas cepacia*
	Pseudomonas multivorans
	Pseudomonas kingae
	CDC group EO-1
Burkholderia gladioli	*Pseudomonas gladioli*
	Pseudomonas marginata
Burkholderia mallei	*Pseudomonas mallei*
	Actinobacillus mallei
Burkholderia multivorans	*Burkholderia cepacia* genomovar II
Burkholderia pseudomallei	*Pseudomonas pseudomallei*
Burkholderia stabilis	*Burkholderia cepacia* genomovar IV
Burkholderia vietnamiensis	*Burkholderia cepacia* genomovar V
Chryseobacterium gleum	*Flavobacterium gleum*
	CDC group IIb
Chryseobacterium indologenes	*Flavobacterium indologenes*
	CDC group IIb
Chryseobacterium meningosepticum	*Flavobacterium meningosepticum*
	CDC group IIa
Comamonas acidovorans	*Pseudomonas acidovorans*
Comamonas terrigena	CDC group EF-19
Comamonas testosteroni	*Pseudomonas testosteroni*
Empedobacter brevis	*Flavobacterium breve*
Flavobacterium group IIe	CDC group IIe
Flavobacterium group IIh	CDC group IIh
Flavobacterium group IIi	CDC group IIi
Massilia timonae	
Methylobacterium spp.	
Moraxella atlantae	CDC group M-3
Moraxella canis	
Moraxella catarrhalis	*Branhamella catarrhalis*
	Neisseria catarrhalis
Moraxella lacunata	*Moraxella liquefaciens*
Moraxella lincolnii	
Moraxella nonliquefaciens	
Moraxella osloensis	
Myroides odoratum	*Chryseobacterium odoratum*
	Flavobacterium odoratum
	CDC group M-4f
Myroides odoratimimus	
Ochrobactrum anthropi	*Achromobacter* spp. biotypes 1 and 2
	CDC groups Vd-1, Vd-2
Ochrobactrum intermedium	
Oligella ureolytica	CDC group IVe
Oligella urethralis	*Moraxella urethralis*
	CDC group M-4
Pseudomonas aeruginosa	*Pseudomonas pyocyanea*
	Bacterium aeruginosum
Pseudomonas alcaligenes	
Pseudomonas chlororaphis	*Pseudomonas aureofaciens*
Pseudomonas fluorescens	
Pseudomonas luteola	*Chryseomonas luteola*
	CDC group Ve-1
Pseudomonas mendocina	CDC group Vb-2
Pseudomonas oryzihabitans	*Flavimonas oryzihabitans*
	CDC group Ve-2
Pseudomonas pertucinogena	*Bordetella pertussis* rough phase IV
Pseudomonas pseudoalcaligenes	*Pseudomonas alcaligenes* biotype B
Pseudomonas putida	
Pseudomonas stutzeri	CDC group Vb-1
Pseudomonas stutzeri–like	CDC group Vb-3
Psychrobacter immobilis	*Micrococcus cryophilus*
Psychrobacter phenylpyruvicus	*Moraxella phenylpyruvicus*
	CDC group M-2
Ralstonia spp.	CDC group IVc-2
Ralstonia pickettii	*Burkholderia pickettii*
	Pseudomonas pickettii

Current Name	Synonym
	CDC groups Va-1, Va-2, Va-3
	Pseudomonas thomasii
Roseomonas cervicalis	CDC "pink coccoid" group
Roseomonas fauriae	CDC "pink coccoid" group
Roseomonas genomospecies 4	CDC "pink coccoid" group
Roseomonas genomospecies 5	CDC "pink coccoid" group
Roseomonas genomospecies 6	CDC "pink coccoid" group
Roseomonas gilardii	
Shewanella alga	
Shewanella putrefaciens	*Alteromonas putrefaciens*
	Pseudomonas putrefaciens
	CDC groups Ib-1, Ib-2
Sphingobacterium mizutae	*Flavobacterium mizutaii*
Sphingobacterium multivorum	*Flavobacterium multivorum*
	CDC group IIk-2
Sphingobacterium spiritivorum	*Flavobacterium spiritivorum*
	Sphingobacterium versatilis
	CDC group IIk-3
Sphingobacterium thalpophilum	*Flavobacterium thalpophilum*
Sphingobacterium yabuuchiae	
Sphingomonas parapaucimobilis	
Sphingomonas paucimobilis	*Pseudomonas paucimobilis*
	CDC group IIk-1
Sphingomonas sanguis	
Sphingomonas yanoikuyae	
Stenotrophomonas africana	
Stenotrophomonas maltophilia	*Xanthomonas maltophilia*
	Pseudomonas maltophilia
Weeksella virosa	*Flavobacterium genitale*
	CDC group IIf

XI. ANAEROBIC GRAM-NEGATIVE BACILLI

Characteristics: may appear as rods with rounded ends, curved rods, coccobacilli, or slender, spindle-shaped rods with tapered ends. *Dialister* and *Johnsonella* belong to the *Clostridium subphylum*

Current Name	Synonym
Anaerobiospirillum succiniciproducens	
Anaerobiospirillum thomasii	
Anaerorhabdus furcosus	*Bacteroides furcosus*
Bacteroides capillosus	
Bacteroides coagulans	
Bacteroides forsythus	
Bacteroides fragilis group	*True Bacteroides*
Bacteroides caccae	*Bacteroides fragilis* group 3452A
Bacteroides distasonis	
Bacteroides eggerthii	
Bacteroides fragilis	
Bacteroides merdae	*Bacteroides fragilis* T4-1
Bacteroides ovatus	
Bacteroides stercoris	*Bacteroides fragilis* spp. a
Bacteroides thetaiotaomicron	
Bacteroides uniformis	
Bacteroides vulgatus	
Bacteroides putredinis	
Bacteroides pyogenes	*Bacteroides tectus*
Bacteroides splanchnicus	
Bacteroides tectus	*Bacteroides tectum*
Bacteroides ureolyticus	*Bacteroides corrodens*
Bilophila wadsworthia	
Butyrivibrio fibrisolvens	
Catonella morbi	
Centipeda periodontii	
Desulfomonas pigra	
Desulfovibrio desulfuricans	
Dialister pneumosintes	*Bacteroides pneumosintes*
Dichelobacter nodosus	*Bacteroides nodosus*
Fusobacterium alocis	
Fusobacterium gonidiaformans	
Fusobacterium mortiferum	
Fusobacterium naviforme	
Fusobacterium necrogenes	
Fusobacterium necrophorum spp. *funduliforme*	
Fusobacterium necrophorum spp. *necrophorum*	

Current Name	Synonym
Fusobacterium nucleatum spp. *fusiforme*	
Fusobacterium nucleatum spp. *nucleatum*	
Fusobacterium nucleatum spp. *polymorphum*	
Fusobacterium nucleatum spp. *vincentii*	
Fusobacterium periodonticum	
Fusobacterium russii	
Fusobacterium sulci	
Fusobacterium ulcerans	
Fusobacterium varium	*Fusobacterium pseudonecrophorum*
Johnsonella ignava	
Leptotrichia buccalis	
Leptotrichia sanguinegens	
Mitsuokella multacida	*Mitsuokella multiacida*
	Bacteroides multiacidus
Porphyromonas asaccharolytica	*Bacteroides asaccharolyticus*
	Bacteroides melaninogenicus spp. *asaccharolyticus*
Porphyromonas cangingivalis	
Porphyromonas canoris	
Porphyromonas cansulci	
Porphyromonas catoniae	*Oribaculum catoniae*
Porphyromonas circumdentaria	
Porphyromonas crevioricanis	
Porphyromonas endodontalis	*Bacteroides endodontalis*
Porphyromonas gingivalis	*Bacteroides gingivalis*
Porphyromonas gingivicanis	
Porphyromonas levii	*Bacteroides levii*
	Bacteroides melaninogenicus spp. *levii*
Porphyromonas macacae	*Bacteroides macacae*
	Porphyromonas salivosa
Prevotella bivia	*Bacteroides bivius*
Prevotella buccae	*Bacteroides buccae*
	Bacteroides ruminicola spp. *brevis*
	Bacteroides capillus
	Bacteroides pentosaceus
Prevotella buccalis	*Bacteroides buccalis*
Prevotella corporis	*Bacteroides corporis*
Prevotella dentalis	*Mitsuokella dentalis*
	Hallella seregens
Prevotella denticola	*Bacteroides denticola*
Prevotella disiens	*Bacteroides disiens*
Prevotella enoeca	
Prevotella heparinolytica	*Bacteroides heparinolyticus*
Prevotella intermedia	*Bacteroides intermedius*
	Bacteroides melaninogenicus spp. *intermedius*
Prevotella loescheii	*Bacteroides loescheii*
Prevotella melaninogenica	*Bacteroides melaninogenicus*
	Bacteroides melaninogenicus spp. *melaninogenicus*
Prevotella nigrescens	*Prevotella intermedia*
Prevotella oralis	*Bacteroides oralis*
Prevotella oris	*Bacteroides oris*
	Bacteroides ruminicola spp. *brevis*
Prevotella oulorum	*Bacteroides oulorum*
	Prevotella oulora
Prevotella pallens	
Prevotella tannerae	
Prevotella veroralis	*Bacteroides veroralis*
Prevotella zoogleoformans	*Bacteroides zoogleoformans*
Selenomonas artemidis	
Selenomonas dianae	
Selenomonas flueggei	
Selenomonas infelix	
Selenomonas noxia	
Selenomonas sputigena	
Sutterella wadsworthensis	
Tissierella praeacuta	*Bacteroides praeacutus*

XII. AEROBIC GRAM-NEGATIVE FASTIDIOUS COCCOBACILLI

Characteristics: small, curved or straight gram-negative bacilli or coccobacilli; may require CO_2 and enriched media or special conditions for adequate growth

Actinobacillus actinomycetemcomitans	CDC groups HB-3, HB-4
Actinobacillus equuii	
Actinobacillus hominis	

Current Name	Synonym
Actinobacillus lignieresii	
Actinobacillus ureae	*Pasteurella ureae*
Afipia broomeae	
Afipia clevelandensis	
Afipia felis	
Arcobacter butzleri	*Campylobacter butzleri*
Arcobacter cryaerophilus	*Campylobacter cryaerophila*
Bartonella bacilliformis	
Bartonella clarridgieae	
Bartonella elizabethae	*Rochalimaea elizabethae*
Bartonella grahamii	
Bartonella henselae	*Rochalimaea henselae*
Bartonella quintana	*Rochalimaea quintana*
Bartonella vinsonii spp. *arupensis*	*Rochalimaea vinsonii*
Bartonella vinsonii spp. *berkhoffii*	
Bordetella bronchiseptica	CDC group IVa
Bordetella hinzii	
Bordetella holmesii	CDC group NO-2
Bordetella parapertussis	
Bordetella pertussis	
Bordetella trematum	
Brucella abortus	
Brucella canis	
Brucella melitensis	
Brucella suis	
Calymmatobacterium granulomatis	
Campylobacter coli	
Campylobacter concisus	CDC group EF-22
Campylobacter curvus	*Wolinella curva*
Campylobacter fetus spp. *fetus*	*Vibrio fetus*
Campylobacter fetus spp. *venerealis*	
Campylobacter gracilis	*Bacteroides gracilis*
Campylobacter hyointestinalis spp. *hyointestinalis*	
Campylobacter jejuni spp. *doylei*	
Campylobacter jejuni spp. *jejuni*	
Campylobacter lari	*Campylobacter laridis*
Campylobacter mucosalis	
Campylobacter rectus	*Wolinella recta*
Campylobacter showae	
Campylobacter sputorum spp. *paraureolyticus*	
Campylobacter sputorum spp. *sputorum*	
Campylobacter upsaliensis	
Campylobacter ureolyticus	*Bacteroides ureolyticus*
Capnocytophaga canimorsus	CDC group DF-2
Capnocytophaga cynodegmi	CDC group DF-2
Capnocytophaga gingivalis	CDC group DF-1
Capnocytophaga granulosa	
Capnocytophaga haemolytica	
Capnocytophaga ochracea	CDC group DF-1
Capnocytophaga sputigena	CDC group DF-1
Cardiobacterium hominis	CDC group IId
Chlamydia pneumoniae	TWAR
Chlamydia psittaci	
Chlamydia trachomatis	
Chromobacterium violaceum	
Coxiella burnetii	
Dysgonomonas capnocytophagoides	CDC group DF-3
Dysgonomonas gadei	
Ehrlichia species	Human granulocytic ehrlichiosis
Ehrlichia canis	
Ehrlichia chaffeensis	Human monocytic ehrlichiosis
Ehrlichia ewingii	
Ehrlichia sennetsu	
Eikenella corrodens	CDC group HB-1
Francisella philomiragia	*Yersinia philomiragia*
Francisella tularensis biovar. *mediaasiatica*	
Francisella tularensis biovar. *novicida*	*Francisella novicida*
	Pasteurella tularensis
	Bacterium tularense
Francisella tularensis biovar. *palearctica*	*Francisella tularensis* type B
	Bacterium tularense
Francisella tularensis biovar. *tularensis*	*Francisella tularensis* type A
	Pasteurella tularensis
	Bacterium tularense
Haemophilus aphrophilus	CDC group HB-2

Current Name	Synonym
Haemophilus ducreyi	
Haemophilus haemolyticus	
Haemophilus influenzae	*Haemophilus aegyptius*
Haemophilus parahaemolyticus	
Haemophilus parainfluenzae	
Haemophilus paraphrophilus	
Haemophilus segnis	
Helicobacter bilis	
Helicobacter cinaedi	*Campylobacter cinaedi*
Helicobacter bizzozeronii	
Helicobacter canadensis	
Helicobacter canis	
Helicobacter fennelliae	*Campylobacter fennelliae*
Helicobacter heilmannii	*Gastrospirillum hominis*
Helicobacter pullorum	
Helicobacter pylori	*Campylobacter pylori*
Helicobacter rappini	*Flexispira rappini*
Helicobacter westmeadii	
Kingella denitrificans	CDC group TM-1
Kingella kingae	*Moraxella kingae* *Moraxella kingii*
Kingella oralis	
Legionella anisa	
Legionella birminghamensis	
Legionella bozemanii	*Fluoribacter bozemanae*
Legionella cincinnatiensis	
Legionella dumoffii	*Fluoribacter dumoffii*
Legionella feeleii	
Legionella gormanii	
Legionella hackeliae	
Legionella israelensis	
Legionella jordanis	
Legionella lansingensis	
Legionella longbeachae	
Legionella maceachernii	
Legionella micdadei	*Tatlockia micdadei*
Legionella oakridgensis	
Legionella pneumophila	
Legionella sainthelensi	
Legionella tucsonensis	
Legionella wadsworthii	
Orientia tsutsugamushi	*Rickettsia tsutsugamushi*
Rickettsia africae	
Rickettsia akari	
Rickettsia australis	
Rickettsia conorii	
Rickettsia felis	
Rickettsia honei	
Rickettsia japonica	
Rickettsia prowazekii	
Rickettsia rickettsii	
Rickettsia sibirica	
Rickettsia slovaca	
Rickettsia typhi	
Streptobacillus moniliformis	*Haverhillia multiformis*
Suttonella indologenes	*Kingella indologenes*

XIII. MYCOPLASMA (PLEUROPNEUMONIA-LIKE ORGANISMS [PPLO])

Characteristics: small, highly pleomorphic organisms that are difficult to observe with routine stains; require complex medium for growth

Current Name	Synonym
Mycoplasma buccale	
Mycoplasma faucium	
Mycoplasma fermentans	*Mycoplasma incognitus*
Mycoplasma genitalium	
Mycoplasma hominis	
Mycoplasma lipophilum	
Mycoplasma orale	
Mycoplasma penetrans	
Mycoplasma pirum	
Mycoplasma pneumoniae	
Mycoplasma primatum	
Mycoplasma salivarium	

Current Name	Synonym
Mycoplasma spermatophilum	
Ureaplasma parvum	
Ureaplasma urealyticum	T-mycoplasma

XIV. TREPONEMATACEAE (SPIRAL ORGANISMS)

Characteristics: filamentous, spiral organisms that may or may not stain with usual laboratory stains; require complex media or animal host for growth

Current Name	Synonym
Borrelia afzelii	
Borrelia andersonii	
Borrelia anserina	
Borrelia bissettii	
Borrelia burgdorferi	
Borrelia caucasica	
Borrelia crocidurae	
Borrelia duttoni	
Borrelia garinii	
Borrelia hermsii	
Borrelia hispanica	
Borrelia japonica	
Borrelia latyschewii	
Borrelia lonestari	
Borrelia lusitaniae	
Borrelia mazzottii	
Borrelia miyamti	
Borrelia parkeri	
Borrelia persica	
Borrelia recurrentis	
Borrelia tanukii	
Borrelia turdae	
Borrelia turicatae	
Borrelia valaisiana	
Borrelia venezuelensis	
Brachyspira aalborgi	
Brachyspira pilosicoli	*Serpulina pilosicoli*
Leptospira borgpetersenii	
Leptospira inadai	
Leptospira interrogans	
Leptospira interrogans serogroup *autumnalis*	
Leptospira interrogans serogroup *ballum*	
Leptospira interrogans serogroup *bataviae*	
Leptospira interrogans serogroup *canicola*	
Leptospira interrogans serogroup *grippotyphosa*	
Leptospira interrogans serogroup *icterohaemorrhagiae*	
Leptospira interrogans serogroup *pomona*	
Leptospira kirschneri	
Leptospira noguchii	
Leptospira santarosai	
Leptospira weilii	
Spirillum minus	*Spirillum minor*
Treponema amylovorum	
Treponema carateum	
Treponema denticola	
Treponema maltophilum	
Treponema medium	
Treponema minutum	
Treponema pallidum spp. *endemicum*	*Treponema pallidum*
Treponema pallidum spp. *pallidum*	*Treponema pallidum*
Treponema pallidum spp. *pertenue*	*Treponema pertenue*
Treponema pectinovorum	
Treponema phagedenis	
Treponema refringens	
Treponema skoliodontum	
Treponema socranskii	
Treponema vincentii	

REFERENCES

1. Brenner, D. J., O'Connor, S. P., Winkler, H. H., et al.: Proposals to unify the genera *Bartonella* and *Rochalimaea,* with descriptions of *Bartonella quintana* comb. nov., *Bartonella vinsonii* comb. nov., *Bartonella henselae* comb. nov., and *Bartonella elizabethae* comb. nov., and to remove the family Bartonellaceae from the order Rickettsiales. Int. J. Syst. Bacteriol. *43:*777–786, 1993.
2. Brenner, F. W., Villar, R. G., Tauxe, R., et al.: *Salmonella* nomenclature. J. Clin. Microbiol. *38:*2465–2467, 2000.
3. Coykendall, A. L.: Classification and identification of the viridans streptococci. Clin. Microbiol. Rev. *2:*315–328, 1989.
4. Facklam, R.: Newly described, difficult-to-identify, catalase-negative, gram-positive cocci. Clin. Microbiol. Newsletter *23:*1–7, 2001.
5. Farmer, J. J., III, Davis, B. R., Hickman-Brenner, F. W., et al.: Biochemical identification of new species and biogroups of Enterobacteriaceae isolated from clinical specimens. J. Clin. Microbiol. *21:*46–76, 1985.
6. Holt, J. G. (ed.): Bergey's Manual of Systematic Bacteriology. Vol. 1, 1984; Vol. 2, 1986; Vol. 3, 1989; Vol. 4, 1989; Baltimore, Williams & Wilkins.

7. Holt, J. G., Krieg, N. R., Sneath, P. H. A., et al.: Bergey's Manual of Determinative Bacteriology. 9th ed. Baltimore, Williams & Wilkins, 1994.
8. Janda, W. M.: The corynebacteria revisited: New species, identification kits and antimicrobial susceptibility testing. Clin. Microbiol. Newsletter. *21*:175–182, 1999.
9. Kawamura, Y., Hou, X., Sultana, F., et al.: Transfer of *Streptococcus adjacens* and *Streptococcus defectivus* to *Abiotrophia* gen. nov. as *Abiotrophia adjacens* comb. nov. and *Abiotrophia defectiva* comb. nov., respectively. Int. J. Syst. Bacteriol. *45:*798–803, 1995.
10. Kawamura, Y., Hou, X., Sultana, F., et al.: Determination of 16S rRNA sequences of *Streptococcus mitis* and *Streptococcus gordonii* and phylogenetic relationships among members of the genus *Streptococcus*. Int. J. Syst. Bacteriol. *45:*406–408, 1995.
11. McNeil, M. M., and Brown, J. M.: The medically important aerobic actinomycetes: Epidemiology and microbiology. Clin. Microbiol. Rev. *7:*357–417, 1994.
12. Palleroni, N. J., and Bradbury, J. F.: *Stenotrophomonas,* a new bacterial genus for *Xanthomonas maltophilia* (Hugh 1980) Swings et al. 1983. Int. J. Syst. Bacteriol. *43:*606B609, 1993.
13. Ruimy, R., Boiron, P., Boivin, V., et al.: A phylogeny of the genus *Nocardia* deduced from the analysis of small-subunit ribosomal DNA sequences, including transfer of *Nocardia amarae* to the genus *Gordona* as *Gordona amarae* comb. F. E. M. S. Microbiol. Lett. *123:*261–268, 1994.
14. Ruoff, K. L.: Recent taxonomic changes in the genus *Enterococcus.* Eur. J. Clin. Microbiol. Infect. Dis. *9:*75–79, 1990.
15. Shah, H. N., and Collins, M. D.: Proposal for reclassification of *Bacteroides asaccharolyticus, Bacteroides gingivalis,* and *Bacteroides endotalis* in a new genus, *Porphyromonas.* Int. J. Syst. Bacteriol. *38:*128–131, 1988.
16. Shah, H. N., and Collins, M. D.: *Prevotella,* a new genus, to include *Bacteroides melaninogenicus* and related species formerly classified in the genus, *Bacteroides.* Int. J. Syst. Bacteriol. *40:*205–208, 1990.
17. Shinnick, T. M., and Good, R. C.: Mycobacterial taxonomy. Eur. J. Clin. Microbiol. *13:*884–901, 1994.
18. Sneath, P. H. A.: International code of nomenclature of bacteria: Bacteriological Code, 1990 Revision. Am. Soc. Microbiology, 1992.
19. Stackebrandt, E., and Goebel, B. M.: Taxonomic note: A place for DNA-DNA reassociation and 16S rRNA sequence analysis in the present species definition in bacteriology. Int. J. Syst. Bacteriol. *44:*846–849, 1994.

SUBSECTION **1**

GRAM-POSITIVE COCCI

Coagulase-Positive Staphylococcal Infections *(Staphylococcus aureus)*

CARLOS A. SATTLER ■ ARMANDO G. CORREA

Staphylococci are ubiquitous microorganisms that are pathogenic for humans and animals and widely distributed in the environment. They are part of the normal human flora. Coagulase-negative staphylococci *(Staphylococcus epidermidis)* are found universally on the skin and frequently in the nasopharynx, whereas coagulase-positive staphylococci occasionally are carried on the skin, particularly of the face; they rapidly colonize small abrasions and are found in the nose and fingernails of approximately 30 percent of normal adults. Staphylococcal organisms are responsible for an impressive variety of diseases ranging from minor nuisances to major life-threatening and fatal infections. Coagulase-positive staphylococci are the etiologic agents of superficial skin infections, cellulitis, furuncles, wound infections, deep-tissue abscesses, phlebitis, endocarditis, pericarditis, pneumonia, empyema, osteomyelitis, and septic arthritis. Coagulase-negative staphylococci may be responsible for urinary tract infections, bacteremia in newborn and compromised hosts, and infections associated with foreign bodies (particularly cerebrospinal fluid [CSF] shunt devices and cardiac and vascular prostheses) (see Chapter 86).

The Organisms

Staphylococci are nonmotile aerobic or facultatively anaerobic cocci that are cultivated readily in simple microbiologic media. They are spherical organisms ranging from 0.7 to 1.2 μm in diameter and stain gram-positive. In smears of infected tissue, they can be recognized as occurring in pairs and grape-like clusters (Fig. 85–1). Indeed, their appearance prompted their name, from the Greek words *staphylo* (bunch of grapes) and *kokkus* (grain or berry). Staphylococci do not have fastidious growth requirements and multiply well in foodstuffs. They are more resistant to high salt concentrations than most other pathogenic bacteria are; for example, they survive well in ham and salt pork. Staphylococci resist drying and can survive in dust and soil for years. They are tolerant of temperatures to 50° C; this capacity and resistance to drying allow prolonged survival on fomites and clothing.

On blood agar, these organisms form round, convex, shiny opaque colonies 1 to 2 mm in diameter. On this medium, a zone of clear hemolysis surrounding the colony can be recognized for most coagulase-positive strains and some coagulase-negative strains. Production of pigment varies; strains exhibiting a deep yellow or golden pigment generally are coagulase-positive and are known as *Staphylococcus aureus;* those of lesser pathogenicity usually are chalk-white and are known as *S. epidermidis* or *Staphylococcus albus.* Classification by production of pigment is unreliable and has been superseded completely by coagulase determination, which provides a much better basis for general determination of virulence and differentiation of species.

Virulent human staphylococci secrete free coagulase into the broth medium. This free coagulase reacts with coagulase-reacting factor in plasma, with the subsequent conversion of fibrinogen to fibrin and the formation of a fibrin clot. Coagulase also can be evaluated by the use of a test for bound coagulase or clumping factor (Fig. 85–2). This substance is bound to the organism, acts directly on fibrinogen and converts it to fibrin, and is detected by the easily visible clumping or agglutination reaction when a suspension of organisms is incubated with plasma. The bound coagulase test is used

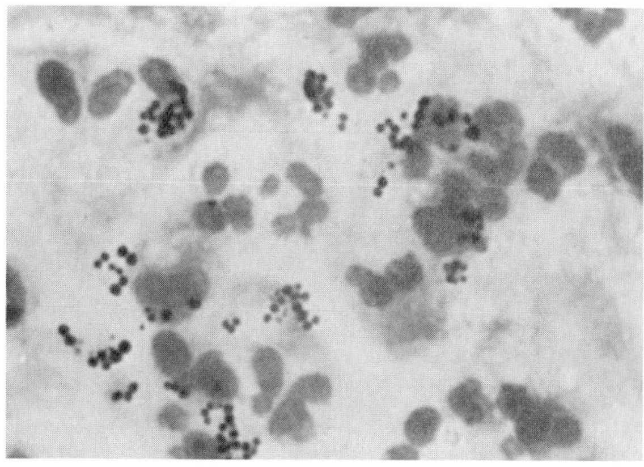

FIGURE 85–1 ■ Staphylococci in pus. The organisms tend to form clusters, are round, and stain purple with Gram stain (positive), similar to bunches of grapes.

most commonly in clinical laboratories. The bound and free forms of coagulase are distinct immunologically but nearly always are present together in virulent organisms. Because fully virulent staphylococci may be nonpigmented, the term *coagulase-positive staphylococcus* is preferred to *S. aureus* and now is considered a synonym.

Identification of Staphylococci

Three species of staphylococci of major clinical importance can be identified by certain characteristics, which are listed in Table 85–1.[255] For routine clinical purposes, carefully performed slide and tube coagulase tests are sufficient to distinguish coagulase-positive staphylococci from coagulase-negative species.

STRUCTURE

Ultrastructural analysis of staphylococci reveals the relatively simple structure typical of prokaryotic cells. The cell wall is composed of inner and outer dense layers apposed to the plasma membrane. Cells divide by binary fission, with a cross-wall composed of three dense layers forming through the center of the cell. The internal structure is relatively simple. Nuclear material is identified as an area of reduced density containing delicate filaments lacking a well-defined nuclear membrane. Membranous structures called mesosomes arise from the plasma membrane and are found variously in contact with the plasma membrane, free in cytoplasm, and in association with nuclear material. The cytoplasm is populated thickly with ribosomes.[293]

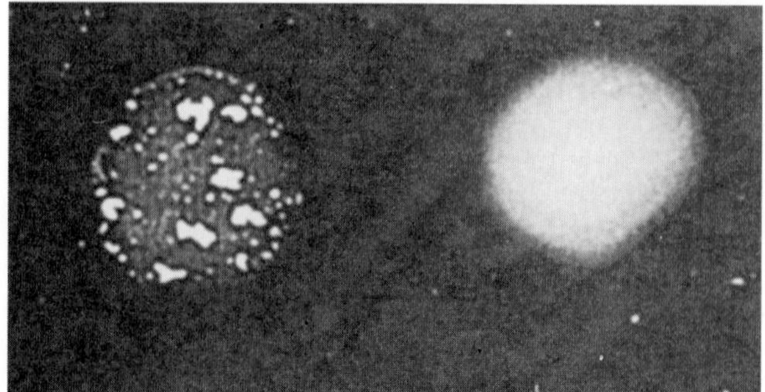

FIGURE 85–2 ■ Bound (slide) coagulase test. A suspension of organisms is mixed with plasma. Immediate clumping (reaction on the *left*) indicates both the presence of bound coagulase and the fact that the organism is coagulase-positive.

TABLE 85–1 ■ IDENTIFICATION OF STAPHYLOCOCCI

Characteristics	*S. aureus*	*S. epidermidis*	*S. saprophyticus*
Coagulase	+	–	–
Acid aerobically from			
Sucrose	+	+	+
Trehalose	+	–	+
Mannitol	+	–	+
Phosphatase	+	+	–
Novobiocin	Sensitive	Sensitive	Resistant

Organisms usually are not encapsulated, but naturally occurring polysaccharide capsules have been demonstrated in human and mouse strains. Four different antigenic types have been identified. In experimental animals, encapsulated organisms appear to have increased virulence. However, most fully virulent staphylococci isolated from severe human infections are not encapsulated. Coagulase-positive staphylococci possess a cell wall with three main components: peptidoglycan, ribitol teichoic acids, and protein A. *S. epidermidis* has a similar cell wall structure, except that the teichoic acids contain glycerol instead of ribitol and protein A is absent. Antibodies to teichoic acids and peptidoglycan are formed in the course of infection. The presence of these antibodies may be useful in the diagnosis of occult infection, particularly osteomyelitis and endocarditis.

Protein A

Staphylococcal protein A, a major component of the cell wall of coagulase-positive staphylococci, has been found to bind to the Fc portion of IgG. This binding is nonimmune. It differs from specific antigen-antibody reactions in that the reaction is nonspecific, although both precipitation and agglutination are observed. Protein A binds the IgG of many mammalian species. This property has rendered protein A a major reagent in many immune assays.

Extracellular Products

Coagulase-positive staphylococci elaborate a wide variety of extracellular toxins, many of which have potent biologic effects in the isolated state on intact animals, tissues, cells, and membranes. These toxins generally are thought to be responsible for the virulence of coagulase-positive staphylococci, and their role in staphylococcal infections in humans has been proved definitively. The important staphylococcal extracellular products include alpha-, beta-, and delta-hemolysins, coagulases, leukocidin, hyaluronidase, staphylokinase, bacteriocins, the epidermolytic toxins, toxic shock syndrome toxin type I (TSST-I), and the enterotoxins.

Hemolysins

Alpha-hemolysin is produced by most coagulase-positive organisms. Because of the impressive hemolytic, dermonecrotic, and lethal properties of the purified toxin, it has received the lion's share of attention given to all the staphylococcal extracellular products. Most, but not all coagulase-positive staphylococci produce alpha-hemolysin. Advances in protein purification have allowed the production of pure toxin; this development, in turn, has led to a better understanding of its properties.

The protein interacts with and damages a variety of cell membranes, releases hemoglobin from erythrocytes of various mammalian and avian species, and is cytotoxic to a number of cell lines in tissue culture. It lyses rabbit and human platelets and disrupts lysosomes. It causes contraction in skeletal and vascular smooth muscle—the latter action perhaps explains its property of causing localized dermal necrosis. Injection of alpha-toxin is lethal to mammals and reptiles, with death occurring within 2 to 5 minutes. Human death has been attributed to preformed alpha-toxin on at least one occasion. In a disaster occurring in Bundaberg, Australia, 12 of 21 children died after receiving diphtheria vaccine that had been contaminated with heavy growth of staphylococci and in which high levels of hemolysin were found.

Anti–alpha-toxin can be demonstrated in normal persons; however, the level of anti–alpha-hemolysin is high in approximately 70 percent of patients with staphylococcal osteomyelitis.[296] In humans and experimental animals, the presence of anti–alpha-hemolysin neither modifies nor prevents staphylococcal infection.

The other hemolytic toxins, beta- and delta-hemolysin, also possess hemolytic and cytotoxic activities, with beta-toxin producing lethal and dermonecrotic effects in addition. Eighty to 100 percent of adults possess antibody to beta-hemolysin.

Despite evidence that these toxins are produced during infection, their role in production of the typical staphylococcal tissue lesion remains unclear.[231] Although these toxins may play important roles in the establishment of infection by interacting with each other and with other biologically active staphylococcal products, this theory has not been proved; infection is not prevented by antitoxin antibody, and virulent staphylococci that lack one or more of these toxins are encountered.[335]

Leukocidin

Even though certain hemolysins are toxic to various leukocytes, the Panton-Valentine leukocidin is the only known extracellular toxin that attacks the leukocyte exclusively.[235] It consists of two protein components that synergistically kill human polymorphonuclear leukocytes and macrophages.[96] Leukocidin injected into rabbits causes a striking fall in levels of circulating and bone marrow leukocytes, followed by marked granulocytosis; these changes occur without death of the rabbits. Leukocidin interacts with the membrane phospholipid and causes depolarization, increased permeability, and cell death. Local secretion of leukocidin might appear to confer an advantage to the staphylococcus by killing leukocytes and thereby preventing phagocytosis and intracellular killing. This proposition remains unproven, however. Levels of antileukocidin rise rapidly in the course of infection,[105, 143] and some evidence indicates that infants and mothers with high levels of antileukocidin antibody are less likely to contract staphylococcal disease in high-risk epidemiologic situations.[22] However, leukocidin is likely to confer only a slight advantage because at least 25 percent of pathogenic staphylococci are leukocidin-negative.

Enzymes

Staphylococci elaborate a variety of enzymes, including hyaluronidase, nuclease, proteases, lipase, catalase, lysozyme, and lactate dehydrogenase, that might play a role in local tissue aggression or the establishment of a nidus of infection.

Other biologically active extracellular products, as yet unidentified, undoubtedly are produced by the staphylococcus. At the time of this writing, no single extracellular product has emerged as the long-sought "virulence factor." The potency and number of these weapons in the armamentarium of the coagulase-positive staphylococcus, in contrast to the small number of extracellular products associated with the much less virulent coagulase-negative staphylococcus, suggest that the synergistic action of these toxins and enzymes may explain the superior ability of coagulase-positive staphylococci to establish infection and cause tissue necrosis.

Several extracellular toxins have been proved to have specific roles in staphylococcal infection or disease: the epidermolytic toxins, TSST-I, and the enterotoxins.

Epidermolytic Toxins

Two biochemically and immunologically distinct exotoxins, epidermolytic toxins A and B (epidermolysins, exfoliatins), can separate adjacent cell layers within the epidermis and cause the various skin manifestations of the staphylococcal scalded skin syndrome. The toxin acts extracellularly and does not induce cell death directly or lysis of the cell membrane or elicit an inflammatory response. It does not damage any organ or cell, except those of the upper epidermis.[80, 179, 184, 207] These low-molecular-weight (approximately 24,000 d) protein exotoxins are elaborated primarily by strains belonging to phage group II (types 3A, 3B, 3C, 55, and 71) but also by nontypeable strains and those belonging to other phage groups.

Toxic Shock Syndrome Toxin Type I

TSST-I was discovered independently in 1981 by two research groups. One group called it low-molecular-weight (approximately 24,000 d) neutral protein staphylococcal enterotoxin F, and the other called it pyrogenic exotoxin C. It was documented to be an excellent marker for staphylococci associated with vaginal toxic shock syndrome (TSS), in which it correctly identified more than 90 percent of strains in blinded testing. In experimental animal models, purified TSST-I can induce the major physiologic changes of TSS: fever, mucous membrane suffusion, renal impairment, hepatic damage, hypocalcemia, lymphocytopenia, and hypotension.[204] TSST-I can be detected in blood, pus, urine, and tissues during human and experimental model TSS.

Enterotoxins

Five antigenically different staphylococcal exotoxins (enterotoxins A to E) that cause emesis in primates have been identified. Most coagulase-positive staphylococci can elaborate at least one enterotoxin given appropriate circumstances. The toxins are heat-stable and resist boiling. Therefore, once sufficient toxin has formed within food, even heating or boiling will not inactivate the toxin. Foods involved in outbreaks of food poisoning frequently have been inoculated by a lesion on the hand of a food handler and then held at temperatures that allow bacterial growth (between 25° and 60° C) for some time before being served. Foods implicated in particular are ham, salads with starch and mayonnaise, salami, poultry, cream sauces, pastries, and dairy products. The mode of action of enterotoxins is not understood completely, but vomiting appears to be induced through action on the central nervous system (CNS). Intravenous injection of purified enterotoxins in laboratory animals causes hypotension, cardiovascular collapse, and death. The significance of these properties of enterotoxins in naturally occurring human infections is unknown, although they may be linked to clinical syndromes, including TSS. Enterotoxin A often is elaborated with TSST-I in menstrual-associated TSS, but it also is elaborated without TSST-I in patients with septicemia in whom TSS does not develop. Staphylococcal enterotoxin B, most often isolated in phage group V organisms, is associated with local infections and pneumonia.[196] Staphylococcal enterotoxin C has been demonstrated by immunohistologic methods to be present in the proximal convoluted tubular cells of the kidneys of 36 percent of patients with sudden infant death syndrome versus 18 percent of controls.[193]

STAPHYLOCOCCAL L-FORMS

L-forms are staphylococcal variants with impaired or absent cell walls. L-forms can be induced in vitro by growing staphylococci in hypertonic media, in the presence of the muralytic enzyme lysostaphin, or with the addition of antibiotics that inhibit the formation of cell walls, such as the penicillin-methicillin group, cycloserine, and vancomycin. These L-forms, or protoplasts, require hypertonic environments for survival, do not accept Gram stain, and are resistant to cell wall–inhibiting antibiotics. Under favorable conditions, L-forms revert to complete bacteria with cell walls. These bacteria, however, differ significantly from the parent strain, with many of them losing such markers as coagulase production, mannitol fermentation, penicillinase elaboration, and phage-typing pattern. Reverted organisms seem to be much less able to colonize and infect experimental animals. Therefore, L-form revertants appear to be considerably deficient in pathogenic potential.

Clinical interest in L-forms has arisen because of concern that antibiotics might induce these forms in vivo. L-forms then might persist in the host in a latent or less virulent phase and revert to a fully virulent state at some time when antibiotics no longer are present. Overt experimental infection with L-forms has been produced with difficulty, with reversion to intact staphylococci being demonstrated in these situations. Identification of L-forms in specimens from human infection or in infected animals treated with antibiotics has been reported exceedingly rarely, despite considerable effort.[324] The presence of latent L-forms remains an attractive hypothesis to explain the well-known tendency of staphylococcal infections to persist and recur. Despite extensive laboratory and clinical investigation, no evidence has demonstrated that L-forms are important causes of bacterial persistence in clinical infections. Extensive searches and special therapy for L-forms rarely are productive.

PHAGE TYPING

Coagulase-positive staphylococci are susceptible to lysis when exposed to bacteriophages. The particular pattern of bacteriophage lysis can be used to identify strains of staphylococci, but bacteriophage typing has been used primarily as an epidemiologic tool for identifying related strains in epidemics. An international system for strain identification by bacteriophage typing has been established, and this method is in widespread use. Another method, serologic typing based on type-specific agglutinogens, is used less frequently. Bacteriophage typing has few clinical correlations and generally is made available through state health departments only for the identification of strains involved in staphylococcal outbreaks. In exceptional cases, it can be used for determining whether a particular infection is a recurrence or a reinfection if organisms from the present and previous infections are available. Staphylococci of phage group 80/81 were widespread during the pandemic of staphylococcal disease in the late 1950s. At present, a wide variety of phage types are involved in staphylococcal disease.

The major clinical correlate of staphylococcal phage typing at present is the association of phage group II strains with various forms of the staphylococcal scalded skin syndrome. The phage group I 29/52 complex is associated with TSS strains, phage group V with enterotoxin B, and phage type 95 with enterotoxin C.[196] In no case is the association absolute; many strains of these phage types are nontoxigenic, and toxigenic strains are prevalent among nontypeable staphylococci and those belonging to other phage groups.

Epidemiology

Coagulase-positive staphylococci are responsible for both sporadic infections and epidemics of varying extent ranging from the intrafamily outbreaks of staphylococcal disease commonly encountered to large and often prolonged hospital-associated outbreaks, such as those emanating from a newborn nursery or a surgical service. Epidemic spread of staphylococci of phage type 80/81 was so widespread in hospitals across North America and the world in the period encompassing the mid-1950s through the early 1960s that it constituted a pandemic. Researchers have suggested that a few "epidemiologically virulent" strains, such as 80/81, are particularly capable of spreading widely and causing disease.

However, just as the factors responsible for the appearance of this staphylococcal pandemic and for other cyclic variations in the prevalence of staphylococcal disease remain unexplained, so do the reasons for its decline. The development of penicillinase-resistant penicillins, the establishment of hospital nosocomial infection surveillance, and the introduction of control measures within hospitals have been cited as being responsible for the decline, as has genetic change within the epidemic strain, but problems remain in accepting any or all of these hypotheses. Because we are largely ignorant of the factors responsible for pandemic spread, we cannot prevent or predict recurrence. However, much has been learned about the modes of spread of staphylococci and various effective measures that can be used to control more limited outbreaks.

Staphylococci may be transmitted by multiple routes, including contact with infected persons, contact with asymptomatic carriers, airborne spread, and contact with contaminated objects. Of these mechanisms, contact with a person who has a staphylococcal lesion appears to be particularly important in the spread of staphylococci. Persons with open draining lesions disseminate organisms into their environment and to others via direct contact. In a hospital, staphylococci may be spread from an infected patient to another on the hands of caretakers, such as physicians or nurses. Hospital personnel with mild or inapparent lesions, such as styes, furuncles, or paronychia, may themselves spread organisms. In family and small community outbreaks, multiple secondary cases frequently can be traced to an individual with a draining lesion. Secondary cases tend to appear for months after the initiating case within these small epidemiologic units.[284]

Staphylococci also may be spread by asymptomatic carriers who have staphylococci in one or more body sites, including the nose, skin, hair, nails, axillae, and perineum. Detailed studies have been performed to delineate factors regulating the carrier state and its establishment and perpetuation, as well as factors responsible for dispersion of organisms from carriers. Asymptomatic carriers may be a source of disease for themselves and others. For example, a wound infection appears to be more likely to develop in a hospitalized patient who becomes a carrier than in a noncarrier. In the past, much attention has been devoted to detecting and attempting to treat nasal carriers of staphylococci; however, studies of nursery outbreaks have indicated that nasal carriage is not as important as is hand transmission in the dispersal of staphylococci.[331] Transmission by hand contact can be minimized by effective handwashing.[106] The problem of hair carriage of staphylococci in operating room personnel has been minimized by using improved head coverings.

Staphylococci are widespread in the environment and can be cultured from clothing, carpets, toiletries (e.g., hairbrushes, razors), and virtually all environmental surfaces. Airborne dissemination of organisms is possible, particularly in operating rooms with poor ventilation and heavy traffic; improved methods of ventilating operating rooms may have reduced the sepsis or colonization rate. Environmental staphylococci may serve as an important reservoir, but direct human-to-human transfer probably is a much more important means of transmission in epidemic situations than is airborne spread or contact with contaminated objects is. Various methods that are used to identify epidemiologic markers in nosocomial outbreaks of staphylococcal infection include phage typing, serotyping, esterase activity, antimicrobial susceptibility patterns, immunoblotting of exported proteins, sodium dodecyl sulfate gel electrophoresis, and toxin production. Molecular typing techniques include plasmid DNA analysis, restriction endonuclease fingerprinting of chromosome DNA, and rapid field-inversion gel electrophoresis. Molecular methods of typing, though often more time-consuming, can offer adjunctive or novel information useful in characterizing strains involved in outbreaks.[211]

The neonatal nursery has been an area of particular concern in the transmission of staphylococci. Until the 1980s, coagulase-positive staphylococci were the major concern. During the pandemic of strain 80/81 disease, outbreaks of serious neonatal disease were commonplace, high colonization rates were found in infants on discharge from the nursery, and in some outbreaks, the subsequent incidence of disease was as high as 50 to 70 percent. Skin disease and infant and maternal mastitis usually appear within 1 to 4 weeks after discharge. Staphylococcal pneumonia, far more common during that period than at present, may not be seen for months after delivery, even though the infecting strain was acquired in a hospital. During the experience with strain 80/81 disease, a particularly high staphylococcal attack rate was seen in the families of colonized infants. The epidemiology of neonatal staphylococcal infections has been reviewed by Baker[19] and Shinefeld.[274]

Various control measures were used successfully to terminate individual outbreaks during this period. Measures to protect the infant from colonization and subsequent development of disease by establishing a barrier at the site of initial colonization included hexachlorophene bathing, application of antibiotic ointment to the umbilicus and circumcision site, and application of an antiseptic dye to the umbilicus. Another approach, deliberate colonization of the umbilicus with an interfering "avirulent" strain, was successful in controlling several epidemics but itself has caused skin disease and, in one case, fatal septicemia.[29, 275] Hexachlorophene bathing became a widespread practice during the period in which nosocomial staphylococcal infections were declining.[106, 245] After approximately a decade of using hexachlorophene, researchers recognized that cutaneous absorption of hexachlorophene could result in potentially toxic hexachlorophene blood levels in infants, particularly premature ones, subjected to repeated daily baths over time. Brain stem abnormalities associated with the use of hexachlorophene have been demonstrated in premature infants. For these reasons, controls were placed on the sale of hexachlorophene, and its routine use was discouraged in 1973. In one neonatal nursery outbreak of methicillin-resistant *S. aureus* (MRSA), the use of 0.3 percent triclosan (Bacti-Stat) was associated with cessation of an outbreak.[341]

Coincident with the widespread discontinuation of hexachlorophene bathing but not necessarily causally related to it, an increased incidence of nursery outbreaks of coagulase-positive staphylococcal disease was reported. Many of these cases have been caused by epidermolytic toxin-producing strains of staphylococci belonging to phage group II. In these outbreaks, limited areas of bullous impetigo developed in most children within 1 to 4 weeks after discharge, with a small number showing the more dramatic manifestations of generalized exfoliative disease. Contemporary epidemics appear to have a much lower incidence of septicemia, pneumonia, and osteomyelitis and less potential for spread to other family members. Personal experience with four such outbreaks in different hospital nurseries has demonstrated that they may arise under various conditions and can be controlled by diverse means.[203]

Patterns of crowding of infants and understaffing contribute to outbreaks. Active clinical and bacteriologic surveillance and cohorting of infants may be effective in reducing outbreaks.[19, 116]

Although nosocomial infection with coagulase-positive staphylococci was not as prevalent in the 1970s and 1980s as in the 1950s, new challenges have become apparent. The frequency of bacteremia related to intravenous catheters and prosthetic devices has increased considerably.[191, 192] Methicillin-resistant staphylococci have become more prevalent in the community and are responsible for widespread nosocomial outbreaks of disease in hospitals.[38, 44, 59, 68, 84, 165, 265, 290, 328] Coagulase-negative staphylococci have become the cause of the nosocomial bacteremia most commonly encountered among neonates in neonatal intensive care services.[84, 93, 98, 99, 118, 136, 151, 221, 268]

Host Defenses

Coagulase-positive staphylococci are ubiquitous in the environment, and approximately 30 percent of the population are carriers. A major defense against staphylococcal infection is intact skin. Minor wounds frequently become colonized and infected and serve as portals to deeper, more significant staphylococcal infection. In some cases, the integumentary infection may be of major importance; in others, minor skin punctures may serve to introduce infection to distant internal sites. Burns, varicella virus and cutaneous herpesvirus infections, primary skin diseases (e.g., atopic eczema), epidermolysis bullosa, and surgical wounds are important portals of entry for staphylococci. In hospitalized patients, intravenous needles and catheters may be sources of staphylococcal infection.[191, 192]

Foreign bodies reduce local resistance to staphylococcal engraftment and are important in the pathogenesis and perpetuation of infection. Noteworthy foreign bodies are CSF shunts, prosthetic cardiac valves, nonabsorbable sutures, vascular prostheses (including arteriovenous shunts for hemodialysis), orthopedic prostheses, nails, and wires.

In neonates, the umbilicus and circumcision sites, which may be colonized within the first few hours of life and from which both local and distant infections may be established, are important portals of entry.

In adults, diabetes mellitus appears to predispose to development of staphylococcal infection, probably for multiple reasons, of which vascular insufficiency is prominent.

Viral respiratory diseases such as measles and influenza predispose to development of pulmonary infection, again predominantly by damaging the integrity of the barrier at the portal of entry. Disruption of the respiratory epithelium and impairment of ciliary motion and other local defenses may allow secondary staphylococcal invasion.

Once the integumental barrier has been breached, the polymorphonuclear leukocyte appears to be the most important line of defense. Successful phagocytosis involves chemotaxis, opsonization, and intracellular killing. The incidence of difficulty with staphylococcal infection is highest in patients with defects in this area of host defense. Granulocytopenia of any origin predisposes to the development of infection, particularly with the host's endogenous bacteria, including staphylococci, *Escherichia coli, Pseudomonas,* and *Klebsiella.*[17]

Patients with disorders in neutrophil chemotaxis are particularly subject to the development of recurrent and severe staphylococcal infections. A heterogeneous group of patients with abnormalities in chemotactic factor generation and with serum inhibitors of white blood cell movement have been described.[279] A disorder in neutrophil movement called the lazy leukocyte syndrome was reported by Miller and associates[214] in 1971. Affected patients have recurrent respiratory infections, gingivitis, and stomatitis. Their leukocytes exhibit normal phagocytosis and intracellular killing but are deficient in both motility toward a chemotactic stimulant and random motility. Despite normal marrow reserves, peripheral neutropenia and depression of neutrophil migration, as measured by the Rebuck skin window, may be noted.

Leukocyte adhesion deficiency is a rare autosomal recessive disorder of leukocytes. Type I deficiency is characterized by recurrent necrotic and indolent infections of soft tissue, delayed healing of wounds, and severely impaired formation of pus despite marked peripheral blood neutrophilia. Staphylococcal or gram-negative enteric bacterial organisms may be cultured from lesions for as long as several weeks in spite of administration of antimicrobial therapy. Persons with leukocyte adhesion deficiency have decreased or absent expression of a family of structurally and functionally related leukocyte surface glycoproteins designated the CD11/CD18 complex. Diminished or absent expression of the CD11/CD18 complex is responsible for failure of the patient's neutrophils to adhere to endothelium and subsequently migrate to specific sites of inflammation.

The diagnosis is made by flow cytometry and measurement of surface CD11/CD18 in stimulated and unstimulated neutrophils by using monoclonal antibodies directed against the CD11/CD18 complex. Treatment of the disorder is largely supportive. Administration of prophylactic antibiotics in an attempt to prevent recurrent infections and HLA-compatible bone marrow transplantation have been used in patients with the severe phenotype.

Patients with Chédiak-Higashi syndrome have recurrent infection in association with neutrophils that are morphologically abnormal, with giant lysosomes present in decreased number. Neutrophils from these patients show depressed chemotaxis, probably because of decreased neutrophil deformability.[314] The lysosomes alter cell motility by compromising the ability of neutrophils to traverse between endothelial cells.

Abnormal neutrophil behavior consisting of diminished phagocytosis and decreased random and directed migration in a patient with recurrent infection has been ascribed to abnormalities of the actin filaments.[37] Treatment involves the administration of prophylactic antibiotics, as well as appropriate antibiotics for specific infections. Ascorbic acid (10 to 20 mg/kg/day) has been shown to rectify the microbicidal effect in some patients.

The disease in another group of patients with profound susceptibility to staphylococcal infection colorfully has been called Job syndrome or, more prosaically, hyper-IgE syndrome. The severe, recurrent staphylococcal infections of the subcutaneous and deep skin tissues are similar to the boils that plagued Job in the Old Testament. These patients characteristically have severe staphylococcal infection with little overt inflammation, a condition suggestive of tuberculous "cold abscesses." Concomitant features of their disease are chronic eczematoid skin disorders, elevated levels of immunoglobulin, extremely elevated IgE levels, eosinophilia, and a generally normal history of infection with other bacteria and viruses. Neutrophils from these patients are adequate in number and show normal phagocytosis and intracellular killing, but they are deficient in migration toward a chemotactic stimulant, as measured by the Boyden chamber assay.[127, 269] The defect in chemotaxis is associated with the production of a chemotactic inhibitor released by mononuclear cells that inhibits normal neutrophil and monocyte chemotaxis. Judicious use of antistaphylococcal antibiotics is the mainstay of management. A small uncontrolled study of interferon-γ and interferon-α demonstrated attenuation of the frequency of infections and a reduction in the severity scores of patients with atopic dermatitis.[248]

Other patients with recurrent severe staphylococcal abscesses and extremely elevated IgE levels have been reported. These patients, whose histories are nearly indistinguishable from those of patients with Job syndrome, probably share the same chemotactic defect.[57] Two of these patients also had partial abnormalities in cell-mediated immunity. These patients have been shown to have extremely high antistaphylococcal-specific IgE, an excess of antistaphylococcal IgM, and deficient *S. aureus* IgA when compared with normal subjects.[76, 269] Researchers have postulated that the high level of antistaphylococcal IgE in serum may create an abnormal local environment surrounding an invading staphylococcus such that mast cell degranulation may be stimulated and polymorphonuclear responses affected adversely.

Once the staphylococcus and the leukocyte are close to one another, opsonization of the bacterium must proceed for phagocytosis to occur. Two systems for opsonization of staphylococci have been described. Serum from normal adults has good opsonic activity when unheated but is generally inactive after heating at 56° C for 1 hour. The heat lability of normal opsonin and the observation of normal or only slightly decreased opsonic activity in unheated sera from patients with agammaglobulinemia[333] indicate that the major opsonin is complement. A few sera, generally from patients convalescing from serious staphylococcal disease, contain heat-stable opsonins, presumably antibody directed at the staphylococcal cell wall components.[172] Therefore, either complement or antibody can provide opsonins for staphylococci; specific antibody is helpful but not required. The clinical correlate to these observations may be found in patients with defective defenses; patients with agammaglobulinemia and defective antibody generally have more severe problems with organisms other than staphylococci, whereas patients with deficiencies in complement components have been reported to have repeated and severe staphylococcal infections.[4, 8, 9, 213, 243]

Once the bacterium has been ingested, intracellular killing proceeds normally. Coagulase-positive staphylococci can survive within polymorphonuclear leukocytes for a considerably longer period than coagulase-negative organisms can. In in vitro studies, after 90 minutes of intracellular residence, 5 percent of coagulase-positive staphylococci remain viable, whereas coagulase-negative strains are killed within 20 minutes.[210] Prolonged intracellular survival may be an important virulence factor separating coagulase-negative from coagulase-positive strains and may provide a mechanism whereby surviving organisms may be carried to distant body sites to establish metastatic foci of infection.

Patients with chronic granulomatous disease of childhood have an inborn error in intraleukocytic killing of catalase-positive bacteria and fungi. These patients have an early onset of recurrent purulent infection of the skin, subcutaneous tissue, lungs, and reticuloendothelial organs, particularly the liver. Persistent purulent lesions with extensive tissue necrosis and granuloma formation are pathologic characteristics.[249] A wide range of catalase-positive organisms, including staphylococci, gram-negative enteric bacteria and anaerobes, mycobacteria, and fungi, are etiologic agents of the multiple infections in these patients. Catalase-negative organisms, notably pneumococci and streptococci, are not a problem to such patients because these organisms cannot break down the hydrogen peroxide produced by their own metabolism within the phagocytic vacuole. Hydrogen peroxide is toxic to the organisms, and buildup of this metabolite causes death.[42, 155]

The leukocytes of patients with this disorder have normal chemotactic and increased phagocytic capacity but cannot generate a normal burst of oxidative metabolic activity.[210] In normal polymorphonuclear leukocytes, this metabolic burst converts oxygen into metabolites that are toxic to bacteria and fungi. Leukocytes from patients with chronic granulomatous disease are deficient in their ability to kill bacteria and reduce oxidative chemicals such as nitroblue tetrazolium dye. The qualitative nitroblue tetrazolium dye reduction test has become a standard diagnostic test for detection of these patients and is as sensitive as are tests that use live bacteria or measure biochemical activity. Although the fundamental enzyme defect has not been elucidated clearly, studies have demonstrated a failure in the activation of nicotinamide adenine dinucleotide phosphate (NADPH) oxidase.[77, 202, 271] Chronic granulomatous disease is caused by mutations involving several genes that encode the components of NADPH oxidase. Approximately 55 percent of these patients have the X-linked variety and an abnormality in gp91phox, the membrane-associated heavy chain of cytochrome b-558. Those who inherit the disease in an autosomal recessive pattern have defects in one of the three cytosolic factors recently identified (p47phox, p22phox, and p67phox). Staphylococci are prominent pathogens in chronic granulomatous disease and produce skin, subcutaneous, and lymph node abscesses; metastatic lung and liver abscesses; and osteomyelitis. The response of these patients to therapy is slow and poor, thus demonstrating the absolute necessity of an intact polymorphonuclear bactericidal system in host defense against staphylococci.

In contrast to the primacy of polymorphonuclear defense against staphylococci, evidence for an important role of specific humoral and cellular immunity in host defense against staphylococci is either lacking or contradictory.

Specific antibody is not required for opsonization of unencapsulated strains of staphylococci. The opsonic activity of serum from patients recovering from staphylococcal endocarditis or other serious disease is greater than that of normal persons.[172, 332] Despite the presence of humoral antibodies to cell wall teichoic acids and to various toxins and enzymes, which are found regularly in those convalescing from serious staphylococcal infection, the patient remains susceptible to recurrence of infection with the same strain of staphylococci. Staphylococcal infections generally occur and progress in the face of some degree of humoral immunity. Specific antibody to one or more staphylococcal components or products does not protect against infection.

Studies of the importance of cell-mediated immunity to the pathogenesis of staphylococcal infection are in their infancy. Evidence from animal studies is fragmentary and not directly applicable to human disease. After induction of delayed hypersensitivity, both increased resistance and increased susceptibility to staphylococcal tissue invasion have been found. Once infection is established, increased tissue destruction may occur in the presence of delayed hypersensitivity.

Clinical evidence from patients with deficient cell-mediated immunity (combined immunodeficiency, thymic aplasia, Nezelof syndrome) suggests that staphylococcal infections are not among the most important pathogens in these patients.

Present evidence, therefore, suggests that intact local skin and mucous membrane barriers are the most important defense against the establishment of staphylococcal infection. Once infection is established, an intact polymorphonuclear response is essential for containment of the infection and clearance of the organisms.

Pathogenesis

Staphylococci cause disease by two mechanisms: direct invasion of tissues with liberation of toxins, which may have effects at sites distant from the focus of infection, and colonization. The hallmark of a staphylococcal lesion is the abscess. Local tissue destruction at the site of inoculation is followed rapidly by hyperemia and a vigorous inflammatory response marked by the accumulation of large numbers of polymorphonuclear leukocytes. Tissue necrosis in the center of the lesion occurs next. At the site of intensive hyperemia surrounding the lesion, a fibrin wall is formed. Liquefaction necrosis occurs centrally; the mature lesion consists of a fibrin wall surrounded by inflamed tissues enclosing a central core of pus consisting of organisms and leukocytes. Live bacteria may persist within these lesions for a considerable period. As pus accumulates, it may drain toward the skin surface or into adjacent tissues, where it forms sinus tracts and secondary abscesses. In the presence of an intact host inflammatory response, this type of reaction may be seen in diverse areas, including the skin and subcutaneous tissues, lymph nodes, joints, renal tissues, liver, parotid glands, muscles, lungs, and long bones.

In addition to local extension, coagulase-positive staphylococci may disseminate hematogenously from this focus of infection, even from abscesses that are trivial in size. Hematogenous dissemination may result in infection of bones, joints, and heart valves. Given the ubiquitous nature of staphylococci, skin and wounds, which are the usual ports of entry, appear to be remarkably resistant to infection. This natural resistance is affected dramatically by the presence of foreign bodies within the wound, such as sutures and bits of soil or gravel. Natural resistance also is affected by the tissue compromise that occurs after ecchymosis or hemorrhage and by vascular insufficiency. Poor personal hygiene likewise predisposes to development of staphylococcal skin infection. Moist, macerated skin is invaded more easily and thus contributes to the increased frequency of staphylococcal skin infection in intertriginous areas and in tropical climates.

Toxigenic staphylococcal disease includes staphylococcal scalded skin syndrome, TSS, and staphylococcal food poisoning. The major manifestations of these diseases are caused by the effects of specific toxins.

Clinical Manifestations

SKIN INFECTIONS

The simplest and most superficial staphylococcal infection is impetigo. Impetigo can be recognized clinically: it generally begins with a slightly tender, erythematous patch or papule, frequently at the site of a minor abrasion, insect bite, or excoriated or macerated area, such as around the nares or mouth.

The erythematous papule may have a transient vesicular stage but rapidly becomes covered with a characteristic dirty-looking, honey-colored crust consisting of dried serous material. Local spread generally is observed, with satellite erythematous papules crusting over and becoming confluent with the parent lesion. Suppuration usually is not seen or occurs late in evolution of the lesion. The lesions of impetigo are moderately painful but frequently are neglected or ignored; several studies have shown that patients wait 2 weeks or longer before seeking medical care. In the United States, staphylococci appear to participate with streptococci in common impetiginous lesions. Previous studies in the United States have indicated that streptococci are found alone in approximately 30 percent of typical impetigo lesions, streptococci and staphylococci occur together in approximately 60 percent, and a pure culture of staphylococci is found in approximately 10 percent.

The epidemiology of impetigo appears to be changing. Impetigo classically was described as a streptococcal or combined staphylococcal and streptococcal disease. Multiple studies now reveal *S. aureus* to be the sole organism in 46 to 64 percent of cases.[23, 26, 69] *S. aureus* may be resistant to erythromycin in as many as 28 percent of cases of impetigo; however, clinical failure rates usually are less than 28 percent. Erythromycin continues to be a useful therapeutic agent, but mupirocin is a reasonable alternative for clinical failures or patients with known erythromycin-resistant strains of *Staphylococcus*.[69, 215] The prevalence of staphylococci has been found to increase with increasing age of the lesion, thus suggesting that the streptococcal infection may be primary, with staphylococci a secondary colonizer or, less frequently, an invader. Moreover, many studies of therapy suggest that penicillin directed against the streptococcus generally is effective, even when penicillin-resistant staphylococci also are present. In some long-neglected lesions, staphylococci may have become the dominant pathogen; for these cases, a course of specific antistaphylococcal therapy may be needed if penicillin has failed.

An etiologic role for *S. aureus* in patients with atopic dermatitis has never been established; however, as many as 93 percent of patients with atopic dermatitis are colonized with this organism.[130] Bacterial colonization has been attributed to hyperkeratosis and dyskeratosis, increased transepidermal loss of water, local immunologic defects inherent to atopic dermatitis, and depressed polymorphonuclear leukocyte chemotaxis. Despite this high rate of colonization, particularly with toxigenic strains,[130] the incidence of severe or systemic infections is relatively low, perhaps because of the enhanced polymorphonuclear leukocyte oxidative metabolism.[131] The degree of colonization increases with the severity of eczema, and lesions that appear to be infected may contain *S. aureus* at rates of 10^7 colony-forming U/cm^2 or greater. Antibacterial treatment without topical steroids reduces the colony count of staphylococci but has little effect on the eczema, which suggests that staphylococci play a secondary rather than a primary role. Oral antibiotic therapy is indicated for pyoderma, superficial pustules, impetiginized lesions, bullous impetigo, and folliculitis. Topical treatment of eczematous areas with class III steroids is associated with decreased bacterial colonization and improved clinical response.[225, 283]

Furuncles or boils are acute circumscribed abscesses of the skin and the immediately underlying subcutaneous tissue. Involvement of only a hair follicle is called folliculitis; involvement of the sweat glands is called hidradenitis. These infections are found commonly in the breasts, axillae, buttocks, thighs, and perineum, with a predilection for moist intertriginous areas. As inflammation progresses, the overlying skin becomes thinned, stretched, and shiny, and exquisite tenderness appears. Usually, no systemic signs occur with small circumscribed abscesses, although even the most minor folliculitis may be followed by bacteremia and dissemination. Larger lesions, called carbuncles, are made of interconnecting abscesses and may be associated with fever and signs of systemic illness.

In newborn infants, the clinical picture may be altered. Multiple abscesses are common findings. They may be associated with little inflammation for some time, but signs of severe systemic illness, septicemia, and shock may develop rapidly in an infant.

Cellulitis is a poorly localized soft tissue infection that occurs with or without a focus of overlying skin infection. Contrary to popular belief, no clues on physical examination lead to a microbiologic diagnosis. Although staphylococcal infections *tend* to be localized, streptococcal infections *tend* to be spreading and diffuse, and *Haemophilus influenzae* type b infections *tend* to have a blue or violaceous hue, none of these observations is of help in evaluating a single patient. Coagulase-positive staphylococcal cellulitis may be extensive and rapidly progressive. Suppuration may occur late or be prevented by early treatment. Careful aspiration of the lesion, together with blood cultures, offers the best approach to determining an etiologic diagnosis. One should remember that cellulitis may be the external manifestation of underlying osteomyelitis, and this diagnosis should be pursued by serial radiographs, bone scans, or magnetic resonance imaging (MRI) during the course of therapy, if clinically indicated.

BREAST ABSCESSES

Coagulase-positive staphylococci are the leading cause of the breast abscesses that occur relatively commonly in newborn infants and nursing mothers.[161, 260]

Infantile breast abscess generally is unilateral, occurs mainly in term infants, particularly girls with physiologic breast enlargement, and is seen primarily within the first 2 weeks of life. Occasionally, patients as old as 8 weeks are found. The most prominent feature is marked erythema and induration of the affected breast. Fever and constitutional signs are absent in most cases, although progressive cellulitis and bacteremia may occur. Surgical drainage nearly always is required, except when spontaneous rupture ensues. Gram stain and culture of pus are important for diagnosis and therapy because gram-negative organisms (particularly *Salmonella* and *E. coli*) also may cause breast abscesses.[47, 260, 286] Because blood culture may be positive (2 of 20 cases in which they were obtained in the series reported by Rudoy and Nelson[260]), parenteral antibiotics should be started after blood is drawn for culture. Adequate surgical drainage appears to be of greatest importance for cure. In some cases, the tissue destruction is sufficiently extensive to cause permanent damage, with a reduction in size and function in adult life.

Maternal mastitis and breast abscess also are of concern to physicians caring for children. Although breast abscesses may occur at any time in girls or women of any age, more than two thirds of cases are seen in nursing mothers at 2 to 8 weeks post partum. Maternal breast abscesses were seen especially frequently during nursery epidemics of staphylococcal infection.[337] Important factors appear to be engorgement of the mammary gland from incomplete emptying of the breast and, in epidemics, colonization of the mother's breast from the infant. In its early stages, mastitis can be recognized as a limited area of tenderness and erythema of the breast, frequently associated with fever. At this stage, culture of breast milk may be misleading because staphylococci can be recovered from the milk of women without infection.[96] Early mastitis is treated best with oral antistaphylococcal antibiotics and frequent and complete emptying of the affected breast. Continued nursing of the affected side has been advocated.[169] When milk secretion is mixed with frank pus, continued lactation may not be wise, and milk should be manually expressed until the infection is under control. Whenever suppuration occurs, incision and drainage are required.

WOUND INFECTIONS

Infection of surgical wounds with coagulase-positive staphylococci has been less of a problem since the mid-1980s, partly because of the improved prophylactic measures used in hospitals. To a large extent, however, the decline appears to be part of a general decrease in the prevalence of nosocomial staphylococcal infection. Nonetheless, surgical wound infections continue to occur, but with reduced frequency, because conditions in wounds are especially favorable to staphylococcal proliferation. Sutures, serum exudation, and tissues with impaired perfusion all promote the growth of staphylococci. Daily careful inspection of wounds, frequent changes of dressings, and early removal of sutures are indicated in the general care of postoperative patients. In the work-up for postoperative fever, nonsurgical clinicians often have a peculiar reluctance to examine the wound. Inspection of the wound and culture and Gram stain of the exudate may be of invaluable assistance in inpatient management.

EYE INFECTIONS

Purulent conjunctivitis may result from coagulase-positive staphylococcal infection. In these cases, Gram stain of the exudate shows polymorphonuclear leukocytes and gram-positive cocci, and staphylococci can be grown in pure culture. The coexistence of coagulase-negative staphylococci and conjunctivitis does not imply causality, except in unusual circumstances. Another common infection, a hordeolum or stye, involves the sebaceous glands or eyelash follicles. When well localized in patients without fever or systemic symptoms, styes may be treated successfully by hot soaks to produce drainage and with antibiotic ophthalmic ointments to prevent secondary conjunctivitis. *S. aureus* colonization of the lids is a common occurrence in atopic patients; however, it does not appear to play a role in chronic allergic conjunctivitis.[309] Whenever associated eyelid cellulitis occurs, systemic antibiotics should be prescribed after culture of the pus. In cases of minor inflammation, oral therapy may suffice, provided that the patient has rapid access to the physician or hospital in the event of extension of the cellulitis.

Staphylococcal cellulitis or skin infection near the eye always should be considered a serious problem because infection may extend into the periorbital tissues and cause orbital cellulitis and, from there, into the cavernous sinus through venous drainage. A diagnosis of cavernous sinus thrombosis cannot always be established in patients with orbital cellulitis, but this complication, as well as ethmoid sinusitis and meningeal extension of infection, is a possible sequela of orbital infection. Cavernous sinus thrombophlebitis is a rapidly progressive disease that continues to be associated with high morbidity (up to 34%[298]) and mortality rates despite the availability of effective antibiotics. Approximately two thirds of cases are caused by *S. aureus,* predominantly from infections occurring on the medial third of the face.[298] It can be recognized by paralysis of cranial nerves III, IV, and VI; proptosis; retinal venous obstruction; and acute visual deterioration, in addition to periorbital swelling and inflammation. Extension to the meninges is a common finding, as are manifestations of systemic septicemia.

In addition to extension from facial infection, orbital cellulitis may arise from dental abscesses, maxillary sinusitis, and in particular, ethmoid sinusitis. Pneumococci are frequent etiologic agents, particularly if the orbital cellulitis arises from sinusitis. In children younger than 5 years of age, *Streptococcus pneumoniae* may occur more frequently such that initial antibiotic therapy must be directed toward treatment of these organisms in addition to coverage for staphylococci. Nasopharyngeal, eye, and skin or pus cultures of facial infection may be valuable, and blood cultures always should be obtained.[246, 316, 327, 337]

EAR, NOSE, AND THROAT INFECTIONS

Staphylococci do not appear to be important pathogens in acute suppurative otitis media,[27, 265] except perhaps in neonates, a group that has been studied inadequately. In a report by Bland,[31] the middle ear pathogens of neonates differed markedly from those of older children. Coagulase-positive staphylococci were prominent offenders and were found in 5 of 18 aspirates but not in the external canal. In the presence of a perforated eardrum, coagulase-positive staphylococci may be secondary invaders but can become serious pathogens, especially for mastoiditis. Little evidence indicates that staphylococci are responsible for pharyngitis. Recovery of staphylococci from throat cultures, of course, occurs commonly in asymptomatic persons. Staphylococci cause other frank suppurative processes of the nasopharynx, including the paranasal sinuses, as well as peritonsillar and retropharyngeal abscesses.

With the publication of several well-documented series of cases,[74, 148, 182] bacterial tracheitis appears to be "an old disease that is becoming prevalent again."[281] Possibly representing superinfection of a larynx and trachea damaged by viral tracheitis, this syndrome is life-threatening, may be rapidly progressive, and holds an intermediate position between epiglottitis and viral tracheobronchitis in most of its clinical manifestations and severity. Severe respiratory difficulty is related to the accumulation of thick purulent secretions in the trachea, as well as marked subglottic edema. It usually is caused by *S. aureus* or *H. influenzae.* The illness begins with hoarseness and inspiratory stridor. High fever and severe respiratory distress develop subsequently. The diagnosis is made by direct laryngoscopy or bronchoscopy showing purulent secretions and subglottic edema. Pneumonia is a frequent association. Administration of antibiotic therapy and provision of an artificial airway by intubation or tracheostomy are required. The illness is severe and may be fatal because of difficulty controlling the airway, septic complications, or both.

Acute suppurative parotitis develops infrequently in children. When present, it occurs in newborns, premature infants, and those with underlying systemic disease. The organism most commonly isolated is *S. aureus,* with *Bacteroides* being the predominant anaerobic organism.[229]

THROMBOPHLEBITIS

Thrombophlebitis and thromboembolism have been a neglected area in pediatrics, although deep vein thrombosis does occur in children, particularly in association with septicemia and trauma.[147] In adults, the bacteremic consequences of infected intravenous catheters and needles are so well recognized that the use of specific prophylactic regimens is common practice. A comprehensive review of infection associated with intravenous therapy demonstrated that coagulase-negative and coagulase-positive staphylococci and the gram-negative organisms *Klebsiella, Enterobacter,* and *Serratia* were isolated from intravenous needles and catheters, whereas *S. aureus* was the leading organism associated with bacteremia. Colonization rates ranged from 4 to 50 percent, with associated sepsis in 0 to 8 percent.[191, 192] Khan and colleagues found that *S. aureus* was the organism most commonly isolated (44%) in a series of 21 pediatric patients with suppurative thrombophlebitis.[163]

In both adults and children, the pediatric scalp vein needle has been associated with a markedly decreased risk of acquiring infection.[65, 66, 241] Major factors in the relative safety of scalp vein needles appear to be lesser trauma to the vein because of a small bore and shorter length, a lesser incidence of local thrombi, and a shorter duration of cannulation because of frequent infiltration. This last aspect may be of major importance, for the rate of positive scalp vein needles equals that of catheters when both are left in place for longer than 102 hours. Only 50 percent of patients with bacteremia associated with intravenous infusions have clinically evident phlebitis in the cannulated vein; therefore, serious bacteremia obviously occurs in the absence of local signs. Based on the considerable experience in adults, reasonable guidelines for prevention of infusion-related sepsis can be formulated:

1. Scalp vein needles or short over-the-needle catheters should be used whenever possible. Longer catheters should be reserved for the critically ill, when a secure line is essential, and should be removed when the danger has passed.
2. The skin should be prepared carefully before insertion of the intravenous needle or catheter. Iodine or iodophor is preferred to alcohol or benzalkonium.
3. Dressings should be changed daily and the puncture site and cannulated vein inspected carefully for signs of inflammation.
4. Whenever possible, intravenous solutions should be mixed in the hospital pharmacy rather than on the ward.
5. The catheter should be removed at the earliest sign of phlebitis or local inflammation, and the catheter tip or intravenous needle should be cultured.
6. The date and time of insertion of the intravenous needle should be recorded on the dressing to ensure removal after 72 hours.[107]

Physicians caring for children have an understandable reluctance to remove a functional intravenous infusion device, but iatrogenic phlebitis frequently is a major setback or life-threatening complication in an already seriously ill child.

When phlebitis, recurrent fever, or persistent fever is encountered in a patient receiving intravenous therapy, the following procedures should be performed:

1. The entire infusion system—bottle, tubing, and needle or cannula—should be removed.
2. The infusion fluid and the needle or cannula tip should be cultured in blood culture media.
3. Pus, if present, should be Gram-stained and cultured.
4. Blood for culture should be obtained from two independent venipunctures.[107]

Infusion-associated bacteremia frequently responds to removal of the infected needle or cannula. In serious illness or if phlebitis is present or pus is seen at removal of the cannula, systemic antibiotic therapy should be initiated empirically. Antibiotic coverage should include drugs effective in the treatment of infection caused by staphylococci and gram-negative enteric organisms, particularly *Klebsiella. Candida* frequently has been the cause of infection associated with total parenteral nutrition.

Particularly severe and frequently lethal suppurative thrombophlebitis has been reported in burned patients who had infected cannulas or intravenous cut-downs. Less than half the diagnoses were made while the patients were alive. In the absence of other foci of infection, the venotomy site should be examined, and, if no pus is encountered, exploratory proximal venotomy should be performed for evidence of suppuration. When suppurative thrombophlebitis is encountered, surgical removal of the infected vein offers the best chance for survival. In this series, most of the responsible organisms were gram-negative, but *S. aureus* was encountered frequently.[285] Suppurative thrombophlebitis should be considered in seriously ill immunocompromised or burned patients, especially when catheter-associated bacteremia fails to respond to removal of the catheter and administration of antibiotic therapy.[163]

Semipermanent indwelling catheters (Hickman, Broviac, Port-A-Cath) now are used widely in children undergoing chemotherapy and long-term hyperalimentation. During the weeks to months that these devices are in place, 20 to 30 percent of sites become infected, and local phlebitis or serious bacteremia may develop. Because these catheters are tunneled subcutaneously for several centimeters from the skin site to entry into a vein, are implanted under strict asepsis, and are designed to form a barrier preventing in-migration of bacteria, they are less prone to infection than are conventional intravascular devices. Because replacement of these devices requires general anesthesia and the sites available for catheter placement are limited, a trial of antibiotic treatment with the catheter in place sometimes may be desirable.[272] In patients who are severely ill with infection or neutropenic, the catheter should be removed immediately and antibiotic therapy administered. For mild to moderately ill patients, blood for culture should be drawn through the catheter as well as at a peripheral site. A trial of antibiotic therapy given through the catheter then may be attempted. This form of therapy may be successful with coagulase-negative staphylococci but has failed to yield satisfactory results when infection is caused by *S. aureus* and *Pseudomonas aeruginosa* or *Candida albicans.*[112] The organisms most commonly recovered are *S. aureus, S. epidermidis,* and gram-negative enterics.[115, 272] Because these organisms are the predominant ones encountered, vancomycin plus an aminoglycoside is the choice for initial empiric therapy.[321]

LYMPHADENITIS

Acute cervical adenitis in both infants[15, 99, 126, 270] and children is frequently of staphylococcal origin. Despite both the widespread clinical assumption that the etiology is overwhelmingly streptococcal and the common clinical practice of prescribing penicillin without obtaining diagnostic cultures, series of infections have shown a prominent[71] or preeminent role of staphylococci.[24, 270] Several investigators have demonstrated the value of needle aspiration of enlarged, inflamed lymph nodes, even in the absence of fluctuation on clinical examination.[24, 71] Culture of lymph node aspirates and provision of antistaphylococcal antibiotics appear to offer the best initial treatment plan for most cases of acute cervical adenitis. Infants with staphylococcal adenitis, particularly in association with nursery epidemics, have been reported with attack rates of 2 and 6 percent in the first few months of life.[15, 73] Although the disease generally has remained limited to the lymph glands, rapid development of staphylococcal pneumonia and bacteremia may occur if patients are untreated or are receiving ineffective therapy with penicillin or ampicillin.[126]

PNEUMONIA

Staphylococcal pneumonia generally is a rapidly progressive process in all age groups. Two main forms are recognized: primary pneumonia caused by direct inoculation through the respiratory tract and secondary or metastatic hematogenous lung infection caused by bacteremic seeding of the lung during the course of endocarditis or septicemia associated with infection at other sites.

Primary staphylococcal pneumonia is chiefly a disease of infancy and early childhood: infants younger than 1 year consistently account for three quarters of cases.* Predisposing factors include cystic fibrosis, chronic lung disease, leukemia, previous antibiotic treatment, preexisting skin infection, and viral respiratory diseases, particularly measles, influenza, and adenovirus infection. In addition, *S. aureus* may be the etiologic organism in nearly a third of malnourished patients with pneumonia. This finding most likely is related to the relative acquired immunodeficiency in this population.[86]

Most patients come to their physician with acute, severe symptoms of fever, lethargy, and significant respiratory distress. The respiratory difficulties consist of tachypnea, grunting, retractions, and cyanosis. Many also have gastrointestinal disturbances, chiefly anorexia, vomiting, and abdominal distention from air swallowing. Occasionally, the distention and gastrointestinal symptoms are so impressive that a primary gastrointestinal etiology is sought. Physical signs on initial examination frequently suggest empyema or pneumothorax. The chest radiograph gives valuable clues to the diagnosis. A characteristic group of radiographic changes, together with a pattern of progression, has been defined.[48]

At very early stages, the chest radiograph may look normal or show only minimal focal segmental or lobar infiltration (Fig. 85–3). In children seen at this stage, rapid progression of radiographic findings within hours occurs commonly. A high proportion of patients either have pleural effusion when first seen or acquire it early in the course of illness. Rebhan and Edwards[254] reported that 59 percent of 329 patients demonstrated effusion on their initial chest radiograph and that subsequent effusion developed in an additional 19 percent. Hendren and Haggerty[122] noted that 71 percent of patients had effusion at some time in the course of the disease. The finding of effusion in most cases has been a common experience. Pneumothorax is another relatively common manifestation of staphylococcal pneumonia; 42 percent of the patients described by Hendren and Haggerty[122] experienced this complication. The sudden development of tension pneumothorax is a particularly severe but relatively frequent clinical event responsible for sudden, severe decompensation. The combination of pneumothorax and empyema—pyopneumonothorax—is highly suggestive of staphylococcal pneumonia.

Pulmonary pneumatoceles generally are seen after the initial stages. They can be recognized as single, though more often multiple, thin-walled, cyst-like, air-filled cavities in the pulmonary parenchyma. Pneumatoceles are thought to result from localized areas of bronchiolar and alveolar necrosis that allow one-way passage of air into the interstitial space. Pneumatocele rupture is one of two mechanisms producing pneumothorax; the other is formation of a bronchopleural fistula caused by localized bronchial wall necrosis. The frequency of pneumatoceles may exceed 85 percent.[122] In most cases, pneumatoceles occur during the

*See references 33, 52, 75, 92, 94, 122, 138, 154, 167, 247, 254, 256, 310.

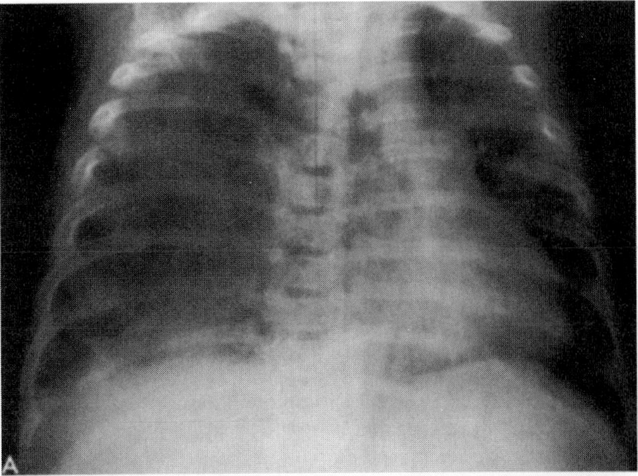

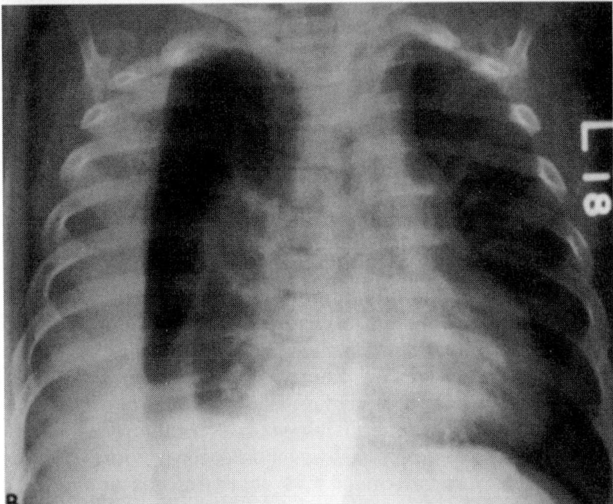

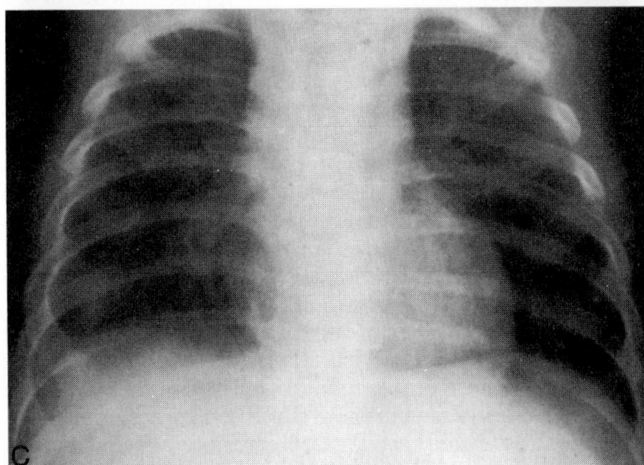

FIGURE 85–3 ■ Staphylococcal pneumonia. *A,* Anteroposterior supine radiograph of an 8-month-old boy acutely ill with fever and respiratory disease of several hours' duration. *B,* A decubitus view of same patient reveals the presence of a right tension pyopneumothorax with a collapsed right lung and shift of the mediastinum to the left. *C,* A follow-up film 5 weeks after intravenous oxacillin therapy for 4 weeks showed marked resolution with minimal residual pleural thickening.

course of infection; a few patients have a pneumatocele at the time of admission.

The diagnosis is established best by isolation of an organism from blood, pleural fluid, or lung tap. The finding of staphylococci in upper respiratory secretions or "sputum" is not sufficient because of their frequent presence in the normal pharynx. A more reliable culture can be obtained by performing deep tracheal suction through an endotracheal tube. For a secure etiologic diagnosis, empyema fluid or lung tap aspirate from an area of infiltration is preferable. Blood cultures frequently are negative in staphylococcal pneumonia. An adequate specimen for culture of the respiratory tract, as well as at least two blood specimens, should be obtained before initiating therapy. In recent years, investigators have recognized that empyema and even pneumatoceles may be seen with gram-negative infection, particularly those caused by *Klebsiella*. To guide the prolonged antibiotic therapy needed for these serious and slowly resolving pneumonias, one should make every attempt to obtain adequate culture specimens from the pleural space or blood before starting antibiotic therapy.

Management of patients with staphylococcal pneumonia requires more than administration of antibiotics. Early consultation with a thoracic surgeon or pediatric surgeon should be obtained and a joint management plan discussed. Having a surgical opinion and expertise available is important for the immediate management of complications such as pneumothorax or bronchopleural fistula. Close observation, preferably in an intensive care unit, is indicated during the acute phase of the disease. Empyema generally is managed best with the implantation of a chest tube for constant drainage. Video-assisted thoracoscopic surgery quickly is becoming an important tool in the management of complicated pneumonia in children.[292] The response to combined drainage and antibiotic therapy usually is slow; fever generally persists beyond 1 week and frequently for at least 2 weeks. High-dose antibiotic therapy should be continued for a minimum of 3 to 4 weeks. The clinical course of patients is such that hospital care usually is required for most of this period.

Despite the severe illness and mortality rate of approximately 10 percent,[122, 254] the long-term prognosis of survivors is excellent. Two large series showed no pulmonary function abnormalities on long-term follow-up.[52, 138] Resolution of pulmonary changes may seem slow, however, because pleural thickening, parenchymal fibrous stranding, and pneumatoceles may persist on chest radiographs for many months.

Large series of patients with staphylococcal pneumonia were compiled from several locations in the United States and Europe from the early 1950s to the mid-1960s, a period when hospital outbreaks of staphylococcal neonatal and wound infections were common events. In some localities, staphylococcal pneumonia again has become a rather rare and sporadic event.[310] In other areas, particularly where staphylococcal infections still are frequent occurrences, primary staphylococcal pneumonia continues to be relatively common. In any case, because this disease is particularly severe and rapidly progressive, the possibility of a staphylococcal etiology should be considered when one is evaluating the condition of any child with fever and respiratory distress.

Secondary metastatic staphylococcal lung infection is being encountered with increasing frequency. In this condition, the lungs are infected hematogenously in patients with widespread focal infections, persistent bacteremia, endocarditis, or some combination thereof.[220] This form of lung infection always is bilateral and multifocal and starts with round, large or small consolidated infiltrates, which represent septic emboli. Pleural effusion and bronchopleural complications frequently develop. Metastatic lung disease has been reported in children and adolescents with severe focal staphylococcal infections, as well as in intravenous drug abusers with right-sided endocarditis. Most reported patients have not been immunocompromised.

BACTEREMIA

Unlike pneumococcal bacteremia in childhood, staphylococcal bacteremia rarely is recognized in the absence of a focus of infection. The focus may be inapparent or exceedingly minor, such as an infected blister or a small furuncle. Bacteremia may occur in the course of a primary infection of the skin or respiratory tract or as a result of intravenous therapy. Frequently, it is not recognized until it has set up a secondary, hematogenously disseminated focus of infection, such as osteomyelitis, septic arthritis, or a deep-tissue infection. Staphylococcal bacteremia should be respected in all circumstances; in some cases it can be an extremely fulminant disease with shock and disseminated intravascular coagulation, and in others, it may persist and recur over a considerable period and be a source of metastatic foci of infection.[82] In every patient with staphylococcal bacteremia, careful consideration should be given to the possibility that endocarditis may have developed so that prolonged parenteral therapy may be given if necessary.

ENDOCARDITIS

During the period in which the incidence of hospital-associated staphylococcal infection and staphylococcal pneumonia has declined, the prevalence of staphylococcal endocarditis in infants, children, and adolescents has increased.[144, 237, 313, 342] For infants and children, this increase has occurred primarily in those with congenital heart disease and is related to the performance of cardiac surgery and cardiac catheterization. In adolescent drug abusers, staphylococcal endocarditis has developed on normal valves in association with intravenous drug injection, and cutaneous abscesses have resulted from "skin popping." The mortality rate from infective endocarditis ranges from 20 to 30 percent.

S. aureus may cause endocarditis in patients with no preexisting heart disease, in those with congenital or rheumatic lesions, and in patients convalescing from cardiac surgery. In four series of pediatric patients with endocarditis, *S. aureus* was responsible for 16 to 45 percent of cases.[34, 144, 227, 299, 313, 342] When patients from the period between 1963 and the early 1990s are analyzed, *S. aureus* was the cause of 35 to 40 percent of all cases.[144, 313] In neonates, the incidence may be more than 50 percent, a finding related to the increased incidence of *S. aureus* bacteremia in this population.[70] A prospective study in France found the risk of development of endocarditis in patients with staphylococcal bacteremia to be 11 percent (4 of 36). Clinical signs were absent in all the children with endocarditis. In this study, the diagnosis was made on the basis of bacteremia and vegetations seen on echocardiograms.[100] Cardiac surgery and cardiac catheterization have been associated with staphylococcal endocarditis more frequently in recent years. Repair of congenital lesions without implantation of prosthetic valves, conduits, or patches is associated with a lower incidence of subsequent endocarditis. Coagulase-positive staphylococcal endocarditis generally occurs within 60 days of surgery. *S. epidermidis* also is an important causative agent in endocarditis complicating heart surgery.

The diagnosis depends on having a high index of suspicion for endocarditis, finding a positive blood culture or serologic evidence of staphylococcal infection, and demonstrating an intracardiac location of disease whenever possible. Patients are likely to be ill. They are febrile and lethargic, and the disease progresses rapidly. Fever and cardiac decompensation are common findings, but the classic changes of endocarditis—anemia, splenomegaly, petechiae, splinter and conjunctival hemorrhages, and Janeway spots—may not be noted initially, in part because the serious symptoms and rapid progression of staphylococcal endocarditis are recognized early, before embolic phenomena or more chronic changes occur. An important note is that a fourth of all patients with endocarditis may have no murmur and a third may have no leukocytosis.[326]

The most important diagnostic signs distinguishing *S. aureus* endocarditis from bacteremia associated with other foci are a new or changing murmur, evidence of vegetations on two-dimensional echocardiograms, and the presence of embolic phenomena.[301] Two-dimensional echocardiography had a sensitivity of 25 to 82 percent in detecting vegetations in three series of pediatric patients with endocarditis.[41, 160, 313] Transesophageal echocardiography has greater sensitivity than the transthoracic approach does. Two studies demonstrated sensitivities of 90 to 100 percent with transesophageal echocardiography versus 50 to 58 percent with the transthoracic approach.[218, 238] The presence of elevated titers of antibodies to teichoic acid[150, 156, 175, 300, 307] and to peptidoglycan[56, 315, 330] has been used to distinguish endocarditis from simple bacteremia, with varying degrees of specificity and sensitivity.

Infective endocarditis has become a frequently recognized infectious complication of illicit drug use. Most patients are male, and their age reflects that of the general population of addicts. The frequency of endocarditis in addicts younger than 20 years has been increasing.[324] In most patients, endocarditis develops on previously normal heart valves. Right-sided endocarditis is particularly prevalent, and patients may have multiple pulmonary abscesses or shifting infiltrates and bacteremia.

Endocardial infection may occur at any time during a period of staphylococcal bacteremia. This fact should be kept in mind, and the need for a prolonged course of antibiotic therapy should be considered in every patient with severe or persistent signs of illness during septicemia. If staphylococcal bacteremia associated with any other focus of infection occurs in a patient with a history of recent cardiac surgery or cardiac catheterization or with any intracardiac foreign body, that patient should be treated as for endocarditis.

Treatment of staphylococcal endocarditis requires a minimum of 4 to 6 weeks of high-dose intravenous antibiotic therapy, preferably with a semisynthetic penicillin (penicillin G, if the organism is sensitive). Antibiotic levels should be quantified to guide therapy and ensure that the peak serum level is at least 8 to 16 times the minimal inhibitory concentration (MIC) for that organism. The aim of this therapy is to eradicate a focus of infection from a relatively avascular area. Response to therapy characteristically is slow, with fever and leukocytosis generally persisting for longer than 1 week. After therapy is discontinued, repeat blood cultures should be performed. If endocarditis occurs in the presence of an intracardiac foreign body, surgical removal may be necessary for bacteriologic cure.

Surgical therapy, such as valve replacement, may be required for patients with severe or progressive cardiac failure.

PURULENT PERICARDITIS

Acute bacterial pericarditis is a rare and extremely serious complication of primary bacterial infection. Associated illness is seen in nearly all patients, respiratory tract infections most frequently, followed by meningitis, osteomyelitis, and skin infections. Coagulase-positive staphylococci are the most common etiologic agents, followed by meningococci, pneumococci, and beta-hemolytic streptococci.

Common initial signs are fever and respiratory distress, including cough, tachypnea, and dyspnea. A considerable proportion of patients have signs of congestive heart failure when seen. Signs of pericardial tamponade are common findings. Pericardial friction rub may or may not be present initially. An electrocardiogram, chest radiograph, and echocardiogram help establish a diagnosis. ST-segment abnormalities are seen most often, but a few patients show decreased voltage. Cardiomegaly with a globular heart shape is noted on chest radiographs in nearly all patients.

Mortality rates have been high (66% in the children reported up to 1967),[103] but they were lower (25%) in a more recent series.[336] The general agreement is that pericardial drainage by pericardiocentesis, pericardiectomy, or both should be performed for both diagnosis and therapy. High-dose antibiotic therapy also must be provided intravenously. Medical treatment without surgical drainage clearly is inferior to combined therapy.[89, 103, 231, 314] Constrictive pericarditis develops in a small minority of patients and requires surgery.[232]

MENINGITIS

S. aureus is an unusual cause of meningitis; it occurs predominantly in patients with CNS abnormalities or in those who have undergone neurosurgical procedures or sustained trauma to the CNS. A review of 40 pediatric patients with *S. aureus* meningitis found that 32 (80%) had an abnormality of the CNS (i.e., recent neurosurgery), 4 (10%) were immunocompromised, and the remaining 4 (10%) had an occult CNS abnormality demonstrated in a subsequent work-up.[104] This study emphasizes the importance of searching for an abnormality of the CNS or an immunologic defect when staphylococcal meningitis is diagnosed.

OSTEOMYELITIS

Osteomyelitis continues to be caused primarily by coagulase-positive staphylococci, although the proportion of infections caused by other organisms, particularly gram-negative enterics, may be increasing.[62, 84, 319] In children, osteomyelitis occurs by two major routes: acute hematogenous dissemination and spread from a contiguous focus of infection.

Acute hematogenous osteomyelitis has different manifestations, depending on the age of the affected patient. These differences are attributable to the differing nature of the vascular bone pattern in (1) infants up to 1 year of age, (2) children between 1 year of age and puberty, and (3) adults after the cessation of bone growth.[306] In infants, membranous bones are affected, as are long bones. Although acute illness with fever has been noted, an infant with osteomyelitis generally has little evidence of systemic toxicity. Local signs usually are absent except for pseudoparalysis or failure to move the affected limb, and multiple bones may be involved. *S. aureus* is the dominant organism, with only a few reports of gram-negative infection, despite the hazard that these organisms generally present in neonates.[166, 180, 329] Antecedent or concomitant infections, particularly of the skin, are common events.

In addition to the benign, poorly localized clinical findings, the distinctive feature of infantile osteomyelitis is a tendency for the development of adjacent septic arthritis, permanent arrest of bone growth, or both. This propensity is due to the fact that infantile bone has vessels that perforate the growth plate, thereby delivering infection to the epiphysis and possibly causing both joint disease and permanent epiphyseal damage.[129, 166, 180]

Hematogenous osteomyelitis in children beyond the neonatal period may occur either as an abrupt illness, with fever and systemic signs of toxicity dominating the clinical picture, or subacutely, with local complaints in the area of the involved bone dominating the clinical picture and normal temperature or low-grade fever. Careful examination of bone, with particular attention given to signs of local tenderness, is mandatory in evaluating children with either type. In children, osteomyelitis most often localizes in the long bones (Fig. 85–4), but osteomyelitis of the pelvis, patella, and small bones of the hands and feet certainly occurs and must be kept in mind because it may be particularly difficult to diagnose.[32, 74]

In childhood, the last ramifications of the nutrient artery to the long bones are the capillary loops located in the metaphysis of the bone just beneath the growth plate. Bacteria localize in the venous lakes below these capillaries and cause thrombosis and retrograde spread of infection. In children older than 1 year, vessels no longer cross the cartilaginous growth plate, and the blood supply to the epiphysis is largely separate from that to the metaphysis. For this reason, metaphyseal infection rarely reaches the joint or the epiphysis, thus explaining why children older than 1 year of age seldom have joint involvement or growth arrest.[306]

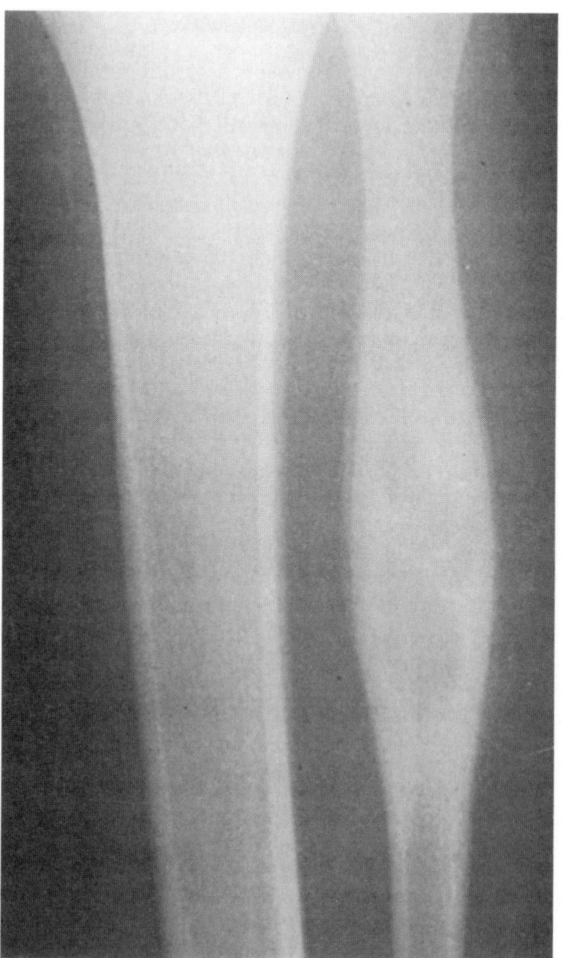

FIGURE 85–4 ■ Chronic staphylococcal osteomyelitis. A well-defined Brodie abscess is present in the fibula of a 7-year-old boy who had a history of several months of pain in the limb without fever. Lytic changes can be seen in the center of the lesion with remodeling of bone and periosteal elevation.

Osteomyelitis does develop in children secondary to open trauma and contiguous infection. Although these cases still are caused predominantly by staphylococci, the range of other possibilities is even wider than in hematogenous osteomyelitis and includes soil and water organisms of generally low pathogenicity, such as *Pseudomonas*. In monitoring patients with contaminated wounds and tissue infections adjacent to bone, one should entertain and diligently investigate the possibility of associated osteomyelitis.

Hematogenous osteomyelitis of long bones is primarily a disease of infants and children. Adults are more likely to have osteomyelitis secondary to infection from a contiguous focus of infection.[319]

Vertebral osteomyelitis is notable for its insidious onset, vague symptoms, and lack of fever or systemic toxicity. It occurs more commonly in adolescents and adults than in the pediatric population. Patients usually report vague back pain present for several weeks. *S. aureus* has been the organism most frequently identified in pediatric patients, but *Salmonella* also has been found with some frequency.[60] In adults, gram-negative enteric organisms may cause disease, particularly when an associated urinary tract infection is present.[289, 319] An increased frequency of vertebral osteomyelitis caused by *Pseudomonas* has been reported in heroin addicts.[289, 335] Cervical osteomyelitis, either as a consequence of hematogenous spread or as a result of direct extension from a contiguous site, may give rise to a prevertebral space infection. Symptoms of such infections include fever, localized pain, and neck stiffness. Symptoms of prevertebral space infections, such as dysphagia, drooling, and shortness of breath, may not be present. Complications can be life-threatening and include cervical spine subluxation or dislocation, mechanical compression of the spinal cord, and vascular compromise from mechanical compression or thrombosis.[28]

Children younger than 5 years of age may initially have diskitis, a usually benign inflammation of the intervertebral disk that may be confused with vertebral osteomyelitis. Because diskitis may be part of the spectrum of vertebral osteomyelitis,[64] careful examination and blood culture should be undertaken when this diagnosis is contemplated, particularly in children older than 5 years of age. Antimicrobial therapy always is indicated in a child with vertebral osteomyelitis.[91b]

The diagnosis of osteomyelitis must be pursued with vigor. Careful examination should reveal marked tenderness over the involved bone; the tender areas may be small and sharply limited. The total white blood cell count frequently is normal and generally of no help in making the diagnosis. The erythrocyte sedimentation rate, though nonspecific, nearly always is elevated. It is of help in monitoring progress of the patient, as well as in making the diagnosis, with the caveat that the erythrocyte sedimentation rate may remain elevated in the first week of treatment. Serum C-reactive protein may be a better monitoring test because it almost always is elevated at initial evaluation and its normalization may follow the clinical course closely.[311] Radionuclide bone scans have been shown to be of value in the early diagnosis of osteomyelitis before the appearance of bone changes on radiographs.[101, 305] Radiographic changes generally are not seen until 10 to 16 days after the onset of infection. MRI is a widely used modality for the diagnosis of musculoskeletal disorders and has the advantage of defining the extent and location of the inflammatory process. Its sensitivity is 97 percent, with specificity ranging from 75 to 92 percent.[198] Blood cultures frequently yield the etiologic agent and should be performed in all cases. Blood culture was positive in 50 and 57 percent of cases of osteomyelitis in children in two series.[32, 74] The sensitivity for retrieval of an organism with combined blood culture and bone aspiration approaches 80 percent.[258]

Bone aspiration or bone biopsy is important for confirmation of osteomyelitis and determination of the etiologic agent. Aspiration is simple and is performed by direct needle puncture into the bone at the point of maximal tenderness or the site of radiographic change. If pus is returned, it is Gram-stained and cultured. The results of Gram staining guide the choice of parenteral antibiotic therapy. If the aspiration does not yield pus, surgical bone biopsy should be performed for culture and drainage. Needle aspiration does not cause significant changes on bone scans and, therefore, should not be postponed for this reason.[49] Because the diagnosis of osteomyelitis mandates a prolonged course of therapy, considerable effort should be expended in the original evaluation to obtain an etiologic diagnosis. Adequate specimens for culture from more than one site give the highest yield.

After the diagnostic efforts, initiation of specific parenteral antibiotic therapy should be based on the results of Gram stain of bone aspirates or biopsy specimens, clinical considerations, or both. Initial coverage should be provided against penicillinase-producing staphylococci. Coverage should be provided for gram-negative enterics in patients with soil-contaminated contiguous wounds or for *Salmonella* in cases of osteomyelitis in children who have hemoglobin S diseases. Fever and local tenderness generally show prompt resolution within 48 hours. Continued hectic fever after therapy is begun requires careful consideration of complete surgical drainage of the involved bone and a meticulous search for other undrained foci of infection.

Therapy for osteomyelitis appears to require a prolonged period and a considerable amount of antibiotic in serum to provide adequate levels in bone. Neither optimum has been defined adequately, and few series reporting "successful" treatment with one or another regimen have had adequate follow-up data. High-dose intravenous antibiotic therapy has been preferred because serum antibiotic levels several times above the MIC of most organisms responsible for osteomyelitis can be achieved reliably. Two retrospective studies provide evidence to support this view. Waldvogel and associates[319] defined intensive therapy as consisting of 4 weeks of high-dose intravenous therapy and found a treatment failure rate of 4 percent for 26 patients receiving this regimen. Chronic infection developed in five of six patients who received less intensive therapy. In children, Dich and colleagues[74] found that chronic or recurrent disease developed in 19 percent of 37 children treated with parenteral therapy for less than 3 weeks, versus only 1 of 48 treated for longer than 3 weeks. Some investigators think that the optimal standard of treatment appears to be parenteral high-dose therapy directed against the organism isolated or empirically against penicillinase-producing staphylococci for a minimum of 4 weeks. After this period, the decision to discontinue therapy should be based on a review of the patient's course, radiographic evidence of healing, and a sedimentation rate that has returned to normal. Oral treatment may be provided after 4 weeks of intravenous therapy for certain patients who are doing well but have persistent elevation of their sedimentation rate. For methicillin-susceptible isolates, dicloxacillin at a dose of 100 mg/kg/24 hr or cephalexin at a dose of 75 mg/kg/day give good serum levels, which should provide adequate bone levels. Clindamycin (30 to 40 mg/kg/day) is an option for patients allergic to or intolerant of β-lactam antibiotics.

Adequate antistaphylococcal serum antibiotic levels exceeding the MIC of the organism can be obtained with high oral doses of certain antibiotics. Providing equivalent oral antibiotic therapy should shorten the duration of hospitalization, but patient tolerance of high doses, patient compliance, and adequate follow-up once a patient has been discharged must be ensured.[45] In many cases, intravenous antibiotics can be provided until the patient has been afebrile for 48 to 72 hours and clearly is improving, at which time oral antibiotics are used to complete the treatment. Good clinical response also occurs with oral treatment after a shorter course of intravenous antibiotic therapy.[239] Management of chronic osteomyelitis continues to be primarily surgical, although antibiotics are a useful adjunct and may be required for prolonged periods.

SEPTIC ARTHRITIS

Staphylococci are frequent etiologic agents of septic arthritis in patients in all age groups, although many other agents also are involved. In neonates, the staphylococcus is the most common etiologic agent.[126, 223, 224] In children 2 months to 4 years of age, *S. aureus* has become the most frequent causative agent, followed by streptococci, pneumococci, and meningococci. *H. influenzae* type b no longer is a common cause of septic arthritis in this age group as a result of the widespread use of the conjugated vaccine against this pathogen. In patients older than 4 years of age, *S. aureus* is predominant among a great variety of other organisms. Sexually active adolescents may have gonococcal arthritis or sterile inflammatory arthritis associated with gonococcal disease. Septic arthritis usually occurs in only one joint, but more than one may be involved, particularly in neonates or in association with neglected and prolonged multifocal bacteremic illness. The large joints—knee, hip, ankle, and elbow—account for 90 percent of infected joints.[36]

In a neonate or young infant, clinical signs of hip involvement may be minimal. Warmth, erythema, and swelling may not be appreciated because of the considerable amount of soft tissue surrounding the joint. Pain on movement and refusal to move the limb may be the only signs. On physical examination, range of movement may appear normal because the strength of the examiner may overcome the resistance of the infant. By the time that signs of joint dislocation become apparent, the damage may be irreparable.[53, 129, 194]

When a diagnosis of septic arthritis has been made by aspiration (joint fluid generally shows >30,000 white blood cells/mm^3, >75% polymorphonuclear leukocytes, glucose two thirds of the serum value, and poor mucin clot), systemic antibiotics should be administered. The choice of antibiotic should be based on Gram stain and a consideration of the probable agents in a child of that age. Antibiotic irrigation of the joint space is unnecessary, except in the case of fungal arthritis, because adequate antibiotic levels can be achieved by systemic therapy.[222] Surgical drainage should be performed immediately if the hip or shoulder joint is involved.

The minimal effective duration of therapy for septic arthritis has not been determined. To continue high-dose, preferably intravenous therapy for 14 to 21 days appears to be prudent in most cases. Hip disease should be treated as osteomyelitis with at least 3 to 4 weeks of therapy. As with osteomyelitis, therapy can be completed with an appropriate oral antibiotic after the patient has been afebrile for at least 48 hours and is improving.

DEEP-TISSUE ABSCESSES

During the course of bacteremia, staphylococci may establish multiple metastatic foci in a wide variety of tissues. Abscesses of the liver, spleen, and pancreas have been reported in association with staphylococcal bacteremia and have been detected at autopsy more often than while patients were alive. Liver abscess has been a rare complication of bacteremia or ascending septic cholangitis. In children, hematogenous spread appears to be most important because patients generally have abscesses in other organs. Liver abscess is seen in children with leukopenia, as in treated leukemia and in white cell dysfunction syndromes (e.g., chronic granulomatous disease).[72, 146] Liver abscess also has been a problem in neonates with bacteremia and after umbilical vein catheterization.[40] Staphylococci and the enteric organisms are encountered most frequently. Drainage along with antibiotic therapy is needed for resolution.[173]

Bacterial muscle abscesses are so common in tropical countries that they form an appreciable proportion of hospital admissions; they are rare in other areas.[133, 273] From sporadic reports in the United States, the clinical behavior appears to be similar in various locales, although muscle abscess is more likely to be misdiagnosed in regions where it is encountered infrequently.[10, 78, 177] Pyomyositis occurs in all groups.[190] The onset is generally subacute, with patients complaining of muscle pain of days' to weeks' duration, followed by fever. Abscesses are found in large striated muscles, particularly the quadriceps. The muscle masses involved, in decreasing order of frequency, are the thigh, buttock, arm, lower part of the leg, groin, chest wall, flank, and shoulder. Two cases of abdominal wall muscle abscesses in children were manifested as acute abdominal pain suggesting peritonitis.[29] These abscesses first appear as firm indurated swellings without significant erythema or heat. Staphylococci are almost the only etiologic agents identified and can be isolated from single or multiple abscesses. Surgical drainage of the mass is diagnostic and therapeutic; large volumes of pus often are recovered. Antistaphylococcal antibiotic therapy should be used as an adjunct. The pathogenesis of the lesion is unexplained, but localization of bacteria within a traumatized or parasitized area has been suggested.

STAPHYLOCOCCAL ENTEROCOLITIS

Enterocolitis caused by staphylococci is an uncommon disease that generally has been described in adult patients given broad-spectrum antibiotics, particularly tetracycline.[121] Diarrhea develops in patients with debilitating diseases, such as cirrhosis, or in those recuperating from gastrointestinal surgery while receiving broad-spectrum antibiotics. Examination of stool shows polymorphonuclear leukocytes in large numbers, with gram-positive cocci as the only or the heavily predominant stool organism. Stool cultures confirm that staphylococci are the primary organism.[152]

Staphylococci should be the predominant organism on both smear and culture in persons with staphylococcal enterocolitis. Staphylococci can be cultured from the stool in smaller numbers from many normal persons. Individuals who merely are colonized never have a predominantly staphylococcal fecal flora.

Staphylococcal enterocolitis has been reported to be severe and occasionally fatal, with deaths caused by overwhelming septicemia or gastrointestinal ulceration. Staphylococci have been recovered from multiple ulcers at all levels of the intestinal tract in fatal cases.[121] In two series of carefully selected patients with staphylococcal enterocolitis, all isolates were found to produce enterotoxin.[119, 152] For this reason, in vivo elaboration of enterotoxin was presumed to be important in the pathogenesis of the diarrhea.

Reports of well-documented staphylococcal enterocolitis are extremely rare in infants and children.[113, 121] Oral and systemic antistaphylococcal antibiotic therapy is indicated whenever a firm diagnosis can be made.

STAPHYLOCOCCAL TOXIN-MEDIATED DISEASES

Staphylococcal Food Poisoning

Within 2 to 6 hours after the ingestion of preformed enterotoxin contaminating various foodstuffs, patients have a sudden onset of recurrent vomiting, which usually ceases by 12 hours after ingestion. Diarrhea also may occur during this period, but fever is not a part of this syndrome.

Staphylococcal Scalded Skin Syndrome

Staphylococcal scalded skin syndrome comprises a spectrum of dermatologic diseases associated with staphylococcal infection. The dermatologic manifestations of the illness differ in degree and extent, but all bear a superficial resemblance to skin lesions secondary to scalding.[195, 207] The skin changes are caused by the action of a soluble exotoxin, the epidermolytic toxin produced by certain strains of staphylococci.[179, 208]

The most severe and generalized form of scalded skin syndrome is an acute, dramatic, bullous desquamation of large areas of skin (Fig. 85–5). It has been known as Ritter disease and pemphigus neonatorum when it occurs in neonates and as toxic epidermal necrolysis or Lyell disease when it occurs in older children and adults. The onset usually is abrupt, with the sudden appearance of diffuse, tender erythroderma. Within 1 to 3 days, a positive Nikolsky sign develops, and flaccid, thin-walled bullae appear. Within hours, the bullae spontaneously rupture, and the superficial epidermis separates in large sheets to reveal widespread areas with a moist red surface. Within 1 to 3 days, these denuded areas dry and the entire body surface undergoes a secondary flaky desquamation. Unless infection or other skin irritation supervenes, the entire skin heals without scarring within 14 days of onset of the process.[186, 187, 207]

The second generalized form of scalded skin syndrome is that of diffuse scarlatiniform erythroderma. Patients with this manifestation also show the abrupt development of diffuse, tender erythroderma, which is indistinguishable from the initial stages of the diffuse epidermolytic form of the disease. The skin appearance also is similar to that of streptococcal scarlet fever, with diffuse erythroderma, sandpaper texture, and increased erythema in skin creases (similar to Pastia lines). Even at the beginning, important clinical differences from streptococcal scarlet fever are evident: the skin is tender to the touch, and no strawberry tongue or palatal exanthem is present. Within 2 to 5 days after the onset of erythroderma, cracks appear about the eyes and mouth; during the next 5 days, the entire skin surface undergoes thick flaky desquamation, which also is identical to the final and healing phase of the most severe form. Therefore, the initial and concluding phases appear to be identical to those of the epidermolytic form, but the intermediate stages of Nikolsky sign formation, flaccid bullae, and extensive epidermal loss do not occur. With both generalized forms of the disease, even experienced physicians may misdiagnose the condition in the early stages as streptococcal scarlet fever. Recognition of the tender or painful skin problem and the early appearance of flaky desquamation lead

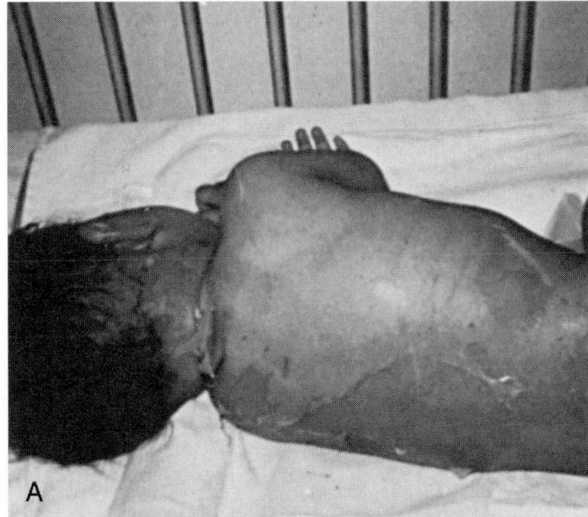

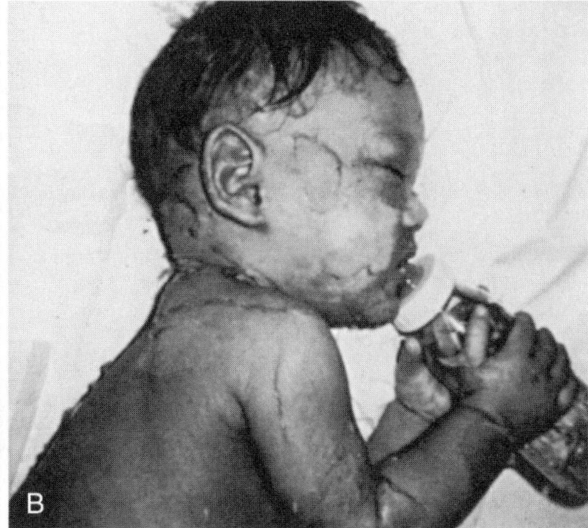

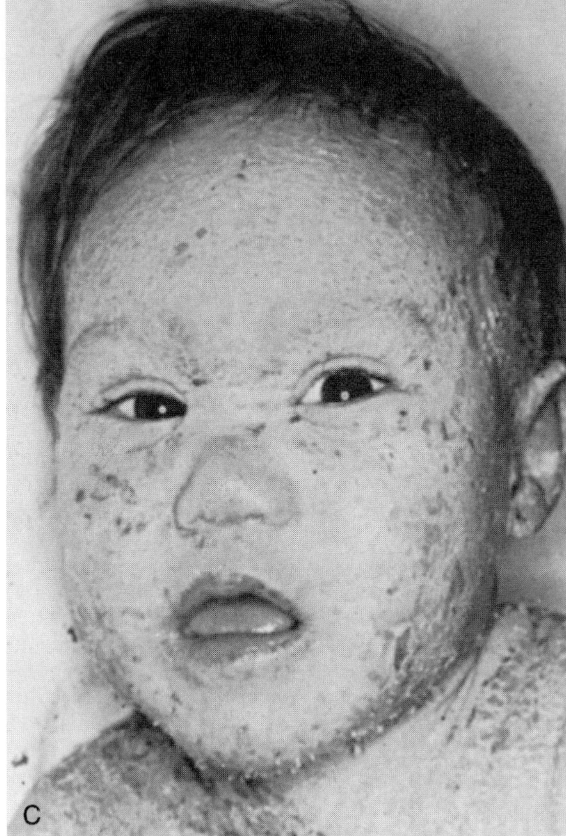

FIGURE 85–5 ■ Staphylococcal scalded skin syndrome with diffuse epidermolytic disease. *A,* Day 2. Extensive undermining of the superficial epidermis results in sloughing of large areas of skin. The skin is diffuse, erythematous, and tender and has a rough texture. Bullae are transient, thin walled, and flaccid and rupture to reveal a moist, red surface. *B,* Day 4. Exfoliated areas dry to a thin, varnish-like finish and then break into large thick flakes. *C,* Day 8. Extensive flaky secondary desquamation occurs in the healing phase, with no scarring.

to a diagnosis of staphylococcal scarlatiniform eruption. Children with either of these two forms of disease generally are febrile and irritable and appear moderately ill. Their skin is tender, and they are uncomfortable when handled or held.

Staphylococci can be isolated from some focus of infection in children with this problem. The focus of infection frequently is distant from the skin, and fluid aspirated from intact bullae repeatedly is found to be sterile. The denuded skin, however, is colonized rapidly. The infected focus usually is minor; conjunctivitis or infected superficial abrasions are encountered most frequently. In neonates, an infected circumcision site is a common finding. On the other hand, the infection itself may be severe and life-threatening; patients with associated endocarditis, septicemia, omphalitis, and severe surgical wound infection have been described.

The two localized forms of scalded skin syndrome are bullous impetigo and bullous varicella, which are truly skin infections. Unlike the two generalized forms, staphylococci are present at the site of the skin manifestations.

Bullous impetigo (Fig. 85–6) is a condition in which single or multiple flaccid bullae arise from normal-appearing skin. Fluid within the bulla may be turbid, cloudy, or frankly purulent. When bullae rupture, their base is moist and erythematous but soon dries to a varnish-like finish. In neonates, lesions of bullous impetigo generally are found around the umbilicus and perineum. If unrecognized and untreated, involvement may be extensive.

Bullous varicella (Fig. 85–7) is an example of viral-bacterial synergism. One to 5 days after onset of the typical lesions of varicella, a sudden change occurs, with the appearance of

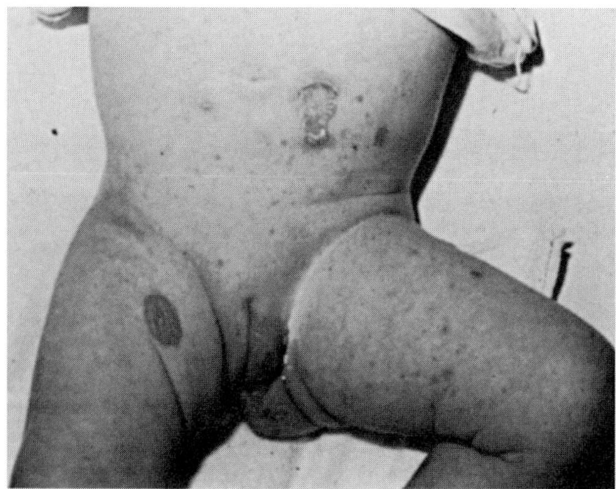

FIGURE 85–6 ■ Staphylococcal scalded skin syndrome with bullous impetigo. In this infant, large flaccid bullae arise from normal-appearing skin. Staphylococci are present within the lesions in bullous impetigo, unlike the situation in the generalized forms.

large flaccid bullae interspersed among the more typical varicella lesions. The bullous lesions usually are multiple and seen in diverse areas of the body; these characteristics create an unusual appearance that generally calls the original diagnosis of varicella into question. Proof of varicella virus infection can be obtained by scraping the base of a vesicle. The Tzanck preparation reveals herpetic giant cells, and varicella virus can be isolated from the typical varicella lesions. Staphylococci can be isolated from the bullous lesions, which have a histologic appearance identical to that of bullous impetigo.[205, 317]

Staphylococci isolated from patients with any of the forms of scalded skin syndrome have the unique property of inducing epidermolysis in newborn mice. This experimental model is indistinguishable clinically, histologically, and ultrastructurally from the most severe form of the disease seen in humans.[179, 212] The mouse model provided a bioassay system that led to the discovery of epidermolytic toxin. The toxin is a low-molecular-weight (26,000 d) protein that causes lysis of the intracellular attachment between cells of the granular layer of the epidermis.[80, 179, 208] The toxin does not cause cell death primarily and does not elicit an inflammatory response. Although the precise site of action is known, the mechanism of action remains elusive. In the generalized forms of staphylococcal scalded skin syndrome, the toxin is released from the site of infection, is disseminated hematogenously, and acts on the granular layers of cells of the superficial epidermis. No evidence of epidermolytic toxin action on other cells of epidermal origin exists. In bullous impetigo and bullous varicella, conditions in which staphylococci are present in the skin, the toxin is produced locally and acts locally.

In the United States, most toxin-producing strains associated with staphylococcal scalded skin syndrome belong to phage group II (phage types 3A, 3B, 3C, 55, and 71), but in Japan, strains of other phage groups appear to be more prevalent. Before the discovery of epidermolytic toxin, some investigators had noted a relationship between phage group II strain type 71, bullous impetigo, and toxic epidermal necrolysis, but until the discovery of epidermolytic toxin, the relationship was not proved nor the mechanism that induces the skin changes elucidated.

Staphylococcal scalded skin syndrome, in all its forms, is primarily a disease of childhood, although it occurs increasingly in adults, generally those with immunosuppression, renal impairment, or both. Adult skin is sensitive to the effects of toxin, and adult protection from staphylococcal scalded skin syndrome appears to be related to some combination of an increased prevalence of preformed antitoxin, metabolic differences, or a greater ability to contain infection.[80, 81] Another form of toxic epidermal necrolysis that is idiopathic or associated with hypersensitivity to drugs is more likely to develop in adults. This form is similar clinically but different histologically and is associated with a higher mortality rate.

The diagnosis may be made on clinical grounds in some patients. However, because the other form of toxic epidermal necrolysis responds to steroids and not to antibiotics, skin biopsy may be necessary in some cases (Fig. 85–8). In staphylococcal toxic epidermal necrolysis, a cleavage plane is seen high in the epidermis, and no significant inflammatory reaction is present. In drug-induced or idiopathic toxic epidermal necrolysis, a cleavage plane is seen either at the level of the dermal-epidermal junction or within the dermis, and intense polymorphonuclear infiltration with extensive epidermal necrosis occurs. An effective diagnostic procedure, simpler even than skin biopsy, is to excise some exfoliated skin

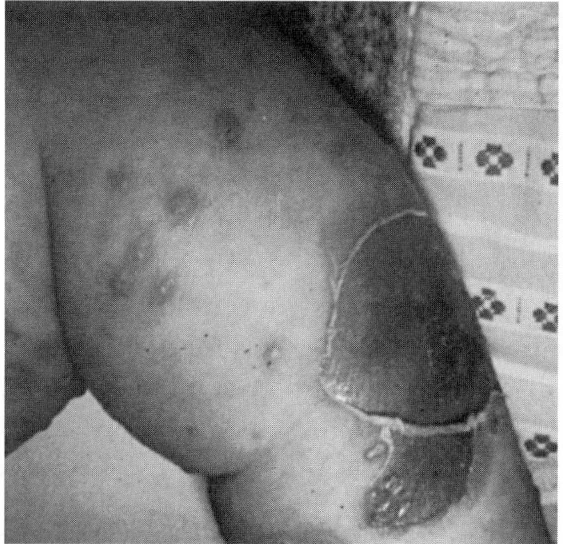

FIGURE 85–7 ■ Staphylococcal scalded skin syndrome with bullous varicella. A large, ruptured bullous lesion is seen among typical smaller varicella vesicles. The bullous lesions appeared 3 days after onset of the varicella rash and represented a distinct superinfection.

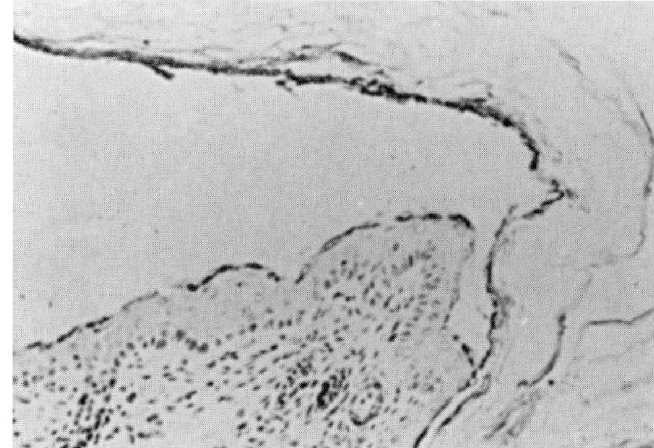

FIGURE 85–8 ■ Staphylococcal scalded skin syndrome. A photomicrograph of a skin biopsy specimen at the margin of a bulla shows the cleavage plane high in the epidermis with no inflammatory reaction or other changes in the epidermis or dermis.

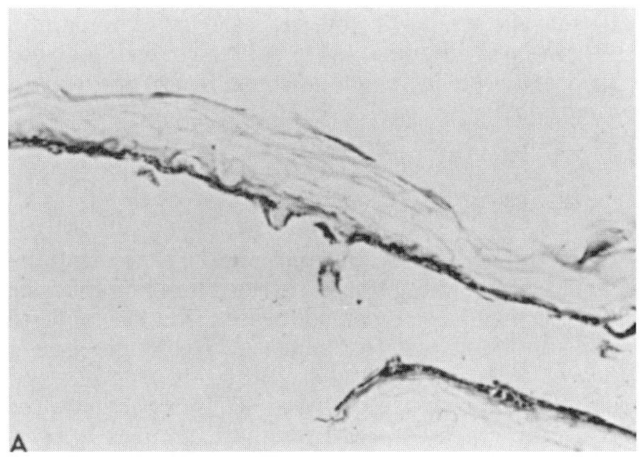

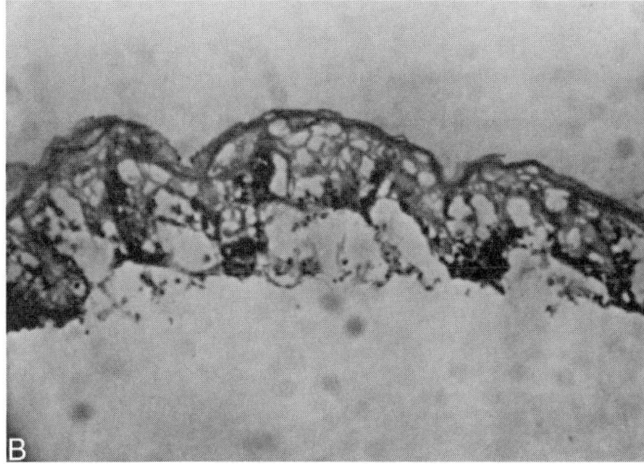

FIGURE 85–9 ■ Differentiation of staphylococcal from idiopathic toxic epidermal necrolysis by sectioning of spontaneously exfoliated skin. *A,* Exfoliated skin from a patient with staphylococcal scalded skin syndrome shows only the stratum corneum and a one-cell layer of the stratum granulosum demonstrating the subcorneal level of the cleavage plane. *B,* Shed skin from a patient with idiopathic nonstaphylococcal toxic epidermal necrolysis shows the entire epidermis involved in a necrotic inflammatory reaction. This process obviously involves deeper layers of skin. (From Honig, P. J., Gaisin, A., and Buck, B. E.: Frozen section differentiation of drug-induced and staphylococcal-induced toxic epidermal necrolysis. J. Pediatr. *92*:504, 1978.)

for frozen and permanent histologic section (Fig. 85–9).[11, 132] In staphylococcal toxic epidermal necrolysis, only the cornified layer is seen, whereas the entire necrotic epidermis can be recognized in the idiopathic or drug-induced form. The diagnosis is confirmed either by isolation of staphylococci and demonstration of toxin production or by histologic study.

Therapy for all the forms of staphylococcal scalded skin syndrome should be directed at eradicating staphylococci from the focus of infection, thereby ending toxin production. Parenteral antibiotics in large doses should be given to patients with extensive skin disease and those with serious infection, whereas oral therapy generally is sufficient for the limited bullous impetigo. Neither topical nor systemic steroids should be used because they have no effect on toxin-mediated skin changes but do enhance infection in the experimental model.[206] A clinical study has confirmed the detrimental effect of steroids.[259] Children with extensively denuded skin should be allowed to rest unclothed on sterile linen and should be handled as little as possible. Topical preparations are without benefit and should not be used because the epidermal damage is self-limited once adequate antibiotics are administered.

Toxic Shock Syndrome

TSS is discussed separately in Chapter 71.

Kawasaki Disease

Kawasaki disease is an acute multisystemic vasculitis of infancy and childhood and is the most common cause of acquired heart disease in Japan and the United States. The diagnosis is made when certain clinical criteria are fulfilled, including high fever, rash, nonexudative conjunctivitis, inflammation of the mucous membranes, erythematous induration of the hands and feet, and cervical lymphadenopathy. An infectious etiology for Kawasaki disease has never been proved. Recent investigations have demonstrated an association of Kawasaki disease with selective expansion of $V_{\beta}2^{+}$ T cells in the peripheral blood, a known consequence of superantigens.[1, 2] This finding was challenged subsequently. Investigators have suggested that Kawasaki disease may be caused by a staphylococcal antigen acting as a superantigen. Lueng and associates[176] recovered *S. aureus* that produced TSST-I in a significantly greater proportion of Kawasaki disease patients than controls and suggested a causal link between TSST-I and Kawasaki disease. In contrast, Melish and associates[209] and Terai and colleagues[297] found no association between *S. aureus* that produces TSST-I and Kawasaki disease. Additional studies are needed to evaluate a potential role for toxin-producing bacteria in Kawasaki disease.

Diagnosis

The diagnosis of significant staphylococcal infections should be pursued with vigor. Collections of pus, whether superficial or deep, should be aspirated or drained surgically for diagnostic and therapeutic purposes. Gram stain and culture should be performed. An aggressive approach to the diagnosis of osteomyelitis by bone aspiration and bone biopsy provides an etiologic security that is helpful during the prolonged treatment phase that necessarily follows. When infection is associated with a foreign body, such as an intravenous catheter or suture, removal and culture of the foreign body help.

At least two blood samples for culture should be obtained before starting therapy for all serious infections. One need not wait for fever spikes or delay therapy to obtain specimens. Blood cultures frequently are negative in serious staphylococcal infection, a fact that demonstrates the need for performing other cultures. Blood cultures are positive in most cases of staphylococcal endocarditis, approximately half the cases of osteomyelitis and septic arthritis, and less than half the cases of pneumonia and deep-tissue abscesses. Measurement of nonspecific indicators of inflammation (e.g., erythrocyte sedimentation rate and C-reactive protein), though of limited value in diagnosis, can be helpful in monitoring the clinical course of infection and response to intervention. Interleukin-6 may be detected in the early phase of infection, before the indicators of inflammation have begun to rise.[280]

Accurate, sensitive serologic methods for making a diagnosis of serious staphylococcal infection would be of great clinical usefulness. An ideal test or battery of tests would detect both bacteremia and invasive nonbacteremic staphylococcal disease but would not be positive in patients with simple superficial infection. This ability would allow a definite etiologic diagnosis in patients with multiple, severe staphylococcal diseases that may not be bacteremic and for which performing direct culture is difficult, such as osteomyelitis, septic arthritis, pneumonia, and liver abscess. Multiple antigens have been used in the search for this ideal test, but at present, none has been sufficiently useful to be made widely available in the clinical laboratory.

Enzyme-linked immunosorbent assay, gel diffusion, and counterimmunoelectrophoresis are useful for detection of antibodies to teichoic acid (a cell wall constituent). These antibodies appear soon after the onset of infection and disappear in late convalescence. More than 90 percent of patients with staphylococcal endocarditis, approximately 70 percent of patients with staphylococcal osteomyelitis, and as many as 50 percent of those with simple uncomplicated bacteremia have detectable antibodies, but they cannot be demonstrated in persons without staphylococcal disease or in those with superficial infection. Antibodies may be detected in nonbacteremic patients with serious invasive disease such as staphylococcal osteomyelitis, septic arthritis, and pneumonia.[150, 156, 157, 307, 308] An IgG response to *S. aureus* collagen-binding protein is present in 60 percent of patients with septic arthritis. Serologic studies, therefore, may be helpful in detecting staphylococcal infection, but the hope that these tests would differentiate reliably between patients with serious infection and those with uncomplicated bacteremia has not been fulfilled. Tests for antibody to alpha-hemolysin have similar limitations.[296] Virtually all adults have detectable antibodies to staphylococcal peptidoglycan. However, with quantitative studies, a threshold level for antibody can be established so that elevated levels can be correlated with recent severe disease.[56, 315, 330] To date, none of these tests are widely available, and we still need serologic tests similar to those used for the diagnosis of streptococcal infection. Evaluation and development of more sensitive and easily performed serologic tests may render diagnosis of staphylococcal infection easier and more secure in the future.

Enterotoxins can be identified by a variety of methods. Immunoassay is used routinely but may lack the sensitivity required to detect levels seen in staphylococcal food poisoning. DNA oligonucleotide probes are highly sensitive, but their clinical utility is limited by the identification of nonexpressed genes.[230]

Treatment

Successful treatment of staphylococcal infection depends on adequate drainage of collections of pus and the rational use of antibiotic therapy. Staphylococcal infections have a particular tendency to persist and recur; for these reasons, prolonged antibiotic therapy usually is required for all but minor infections. Surgical drainage is extremely important and, in some patients with minor superficial abscesses, may be all that is required. For most infections, a period of antibiotic therapy after surgical drainage better ensures that the infection has been contained. Failure to provide surgical drainage is an important reason for persistence or recurrence of organisms. Antibiotics cannot be expected to penetrate into the avascular center of abscess cavities. When abscess cavities are undrained or when antibiotic therapy is discontinued before an area is sterilized, live bacteria may persist and disseminate to cause later recurrence at that site or metastatically.

For moderate to severe staphylococcal infection, the patient should be hospitalized for intravenous therapy, which generally should be given by intermittent infusion. This strategy ensures peak antibiotic levels, which may allow greater penetration into relatively avascular areas. Intramuscular injections rarely are indicated in children because intermittent injections are far more painful than is intravenous administration. A heparin lock may be inserted to provide an intravenous route in an active patient who does not require parenteral fluids.

COAGULASE-POSITIVE STAPHYLOCOCCI

Since the mid-1960s, the vast majority of coagulase-positive staphylococci from most sections of North America and Europe have been penicillinase producers and, therefore, penicillin-resistant. In addition, the distinction formerly drawn between hospital-acquired and community-acquired staphylococci has disappeared. The proportion of penicillin-resistant staphylococci from both sources approaches 90 percent. When coagulase-positive staphylococci are likely to be the cause of infection, treatment with a penicillinase-resistant penicillin or cephalosporin should be initiated before isolation of bacteria and sensitivity testing (Table 85–2). In some locations, methicillin resistance is widespread. Methicillin-resistant organisms cannot be treated adequately with any β-lactam antibiotic, including cephalosporins; vancomycin, therefore, is indicated for MRSA. Vancomycin also is the drug of choice for treating coagulase-negative staphylococci before the return of sensitivity test results. When staphylococci are presumed to be the cause of infection, treating the patient with a penicillinase-resistant antibiotic is mandatory before isolation and adequate sensitivity testing. Coagulase-negative staphylococci also show a high percentage of resistance to penicillin. Remarks about the treatment of coagulase-positive staphylococci apply to treatment of coagulase-negative strains as well.

Penicillin G is the treatment of choice for penicillin-sensitive, non–penicillinase-producing organisms. When properly performed sensitivity tests indicate penicillin sensitivity, therapy should be changed to this antibiotic, which has far greater specific activity than the alternatives do. Conversion from penicillin sensitivity to resistance during the course of infection has not been a clinical problem.

In the far more common situation in which a penicillin-resistant organism is isolated, the semisynthetic penicillinase-resistant penicillins are the drugs of choice for susceptible isolates. Oxacillin and nafcillin are available for parenteral use. Dicloxacillin and cephalexin are the preferred oral agents. Protein binding in vivo affects the amount of antibiotic available for therapy. Penicillin G has the least degree of protein binding, followed by nafcillin, oxacillin, and dicloxacillin. On the other hand, nafcillin, oxacillin, and dicloxacillin show greater specific activity against penicillinase-producing staphylococci than does methicillin. No clinical evidence for the therapeutic superiority of one of these antibiotics over another exists.

For neonates with coagulase-positive staphylococcal infections (Table 85–3), methicillin was considered the drug of choice; it is the antistaphylococcal drug that has been studied most completely.[14, 35, 266] Unfortunately, methicillin no longer is manufactured in the United States, which leaves nafcillin and oxacillin as the only alternatives for this age group.

In all serious staphylococcal infections, some authorities assess serum bactericidal activity against the patient's organism and adjust the dosage and schedule to maintain a peak serum level at least eight times the MIC. The clinician should become familiar with the use of one parenteral and one oral antistaphylococcal penicillin. If clinical response appears to be slow, nothing is to be gained by switching to another antibiotic within this category; instead, microbiologic data should be reviewed and serum antibiotic levels determined.

TABLE 85–2 ■ THERAPY FOR STAPHYLOCOCCAL INFECTION IN INFANTS AND CHILDREN (EXCLUDING NEONATES)

	Oral (Mild–Moderate Infection)		Parenteral (Moderate–Severe Infection)	
	< 40 kg	Children > 40 kg and Adults	< 40 kg	Children > 40 kg and Adults
Penicillins				
Oxacillin			100–200 mg/kg/24 hr in 4–6 doses q4–6hr IV	4–8 g/24 hr in 4–6 doses q4–6hr
Nafcillin			100–200 mg/kg/24 hr in 4–6 doses q4–6hr IV	4–8 g/24 hr in 4–6 doses q4–6hr IV
Cloxacillin	50–100 mg/kg/24 hr in 4 doses	1–2 g/24 hr in 4 doses	—	—
Dicloxacillin	12.5–25 mg/kg/24 hr in 4 doses	1 g/24 hr in 4 doses	—	—
Cephalosporins				
Cephalothin (Keflin)	—	—	100 mg/kg/24 hr in 6 doses q4hr IV	3–12 g/24 hr in 6 doses q4hr IV
Cefazolin (Ancef, Kefzol)	—	—	50–100 mg/kg/24 hr in 3 doses q8hr	2–4 g/24 hr in 3 doses
Cephalexin (Keflex)	25–50 mg/kg/24 hr in 4 doses	1–4 g/24 hr in 4 doses	—	—
Cefadroxil (Duricef, Ultracef)	30 mg/kg/24 hr in 2 doses	1–2 g/24 hr in 2 doses	—	—
Other Agents				
Erythromycin	35–50 mg/kg/24 hr in 4 doses	1–2 g/24 hr in 4 doses	20–30 mg/kg/24 hr q6hr (lactobionate)	10–20 mg/kg/24 hr q6h
Clindamycin	12–30 mg/kg/24 hr in 4 doses	600–1200 mg/24 hr in 3–4 doses	30–40 mg/kg/24 hr q6–8h IV	600–2400 mg/24 hr q6–8h IV
Vancomycin	—	—	40–60 mg/kg/24 hr by continuous IV drip or q6h by drip over 1 hr	1–2 g/24 hr by continuous drip or q6h by drip over 1 hr
Linazolid* (Zyvox)	10 mg/kg/dose q8hr	10 mg/kg/dose q12hr	10 mg/kg/dose q8hr	10 mg/kg/dose q12hr
Quinupristin/dalfopristin (Synercid)	—	—	7.5 mg/kg/dose q8hr	7.5 mg/kg/dose q8hr
Trimethoprim-sulfamethoxazole	8–10 mg/kg/24 hr of TMP in 2 doses	160 mg of TMP q12hr	—	—

*Pediatric dosage not firmly established. The dose for less than 40 kg is recommended for children younger than 11 years.

"Methicillin" Nephropathy

A syndrome consisting of fever, eosinophilia, erythematous rash, proteinuria, and hematuria has been reported in patients receiving methicillin therapy.[18, 262, 340] In a small number of patients with this complication, renal biopsy specimens have provided evidence of interstitial nephritis. Although a hypersensitivity reaction has been postulated to be the cause, the appearance of this complication also was related definitely to the dose of drug and the duration of therapy, and it occurred more commonly in patients receiving more than 200 mg/kg/24 hr for longer than 2 weeks.[88]

This syndrome seems to be rare in children in the United States, even when large doses of methicillin have been used for a prolonged period, and it has been found to be reversible when antibiotic therapy is discontinued.[199, 340] Yow and associates[340] estimate that all the adverse reactions to methicillin occur in less than 1.5 percent of treated children. Although the syndrome of fever, eosinophilia, and interstitial nephritis has been reported most frequently with methicillin therapy, it also is associated with penicillin,[18] ampicillin,[261] nafcillin, and the cephalosporins.[262]

Lesser degrees of toxicity consisting only of proteinuria and microscopic hematuria may be encountered more frequently than is the complete syndrome; hemorrhagic cystitis also has been reported.[39, 266] One approach is to monitor urinalyses two times a week in patients receiving high-dose penicillin or other homologues and discontinue therapy with drugs of this group if definite evidence of nephritis is noted, particularly when associated with fever, rash, and eosinophilia.

Nafcillin and oxacillin have been shown to cause less renal toxicity than does methicillin, probably because they are excreted primarily by the liver rather than the kidneys. They also are the antistaphylococcal drugs of choice for susceptible isolates in patients beyond the newborn period.

Alternative Drugs

Ampicillin has no place in therapy for staphylococcal infections. Less active than penicillin, it also is susceptible to attack by penicillinase. The cephalosporin antibiotics are active against penicillinase-producing staphylococci and cause less irritation of veins with intravenous infusion than do penicillinase-resistant penicillins. A potential disadvantage lies in their broader spectrum of activity, which may promote superinfection with cephalosporin-resistant, gram-negative organisms in a debilitated patient with serious staphylococcal disease. Cephalosporins have been advocated widely for use in patients allergic to penicillin, but because of considerable cross-reactivity, they should be used extremely cautiously, if at all, in patients with a clear history of serious penicillin allergy or anaphylaxis. Among this group of antibiotics, cefazolin is the agent of choice for parenteral use. Serum concentrations of cefazolin are higher, and effective tissue levels appear to be easier to attain. Cephaloridine has been associated with nephrotoxicity. The efficacy of the second- and third-generation cephalosporins against *S. aureus* is reduced. Therefore, these drugs, especially cefotaxime and cefuroxime, should be given in addition

TABLE 85–3 ■ ANTISTAPHYLOCOCCAL THERAPY IN NEONATES WITH MODERATE TO SEVERE INFECTION

	Premature Infants (<2000 g)		Term Infants	
	<1 wk	1–4 wk	<1 wk	1–4 wk
Penicillin IM or IV	50,000–100,000 U/kg/24 hr in 2 doses q12hr	75,000–225,000 U/kg/24 hr in 3 doses q8hr	75,000–150,000 U/kg/24 hr in 3 doses q8hr	100,000–200,000 U/kg/24 hr in 4 doses q6hr
Linezolid IV	Not established	Not established	10 mg/kg/dose q8hr	10 mg/kg/dose q8hr
Oxacillin or nafcillin IV	25–50 mg/kg/dose q12hr	25–50 mg/kg/dose q8hr	25–50 mg/kg/dose q12hr	100–200 mg/kg/24 hr in 4 doses
Vancomycin IV	15 mg/kg/dose q12–24 hr*	15 mg/kg/dose q8–24 hr*	30 mg/kg/24 hr in 2 doses q12hr*	45 mg/kg/24 hr in 3 doses q8hr*

*Administer over a 1-hour period. Monitor serum concentrations during therapy.

to penicillinase-resistant penicillins or a first-generation cephalosporin if *S. aureus* is suspected strongly. With the emergence of community-acquired methicillin-resistant staphylococci (see later), clindamycin and trimethoprim-sulfamethoxazole have become important alternatives in the treatment of mild to moderate staphylococcal infection. Both these drugs are bacteriostatic in their mode of action, but they are not indicated for the initial treatment of life-threatening infections when this organism is suspected.

Two recent additions to the antimicrobial armamentarium against MRSA and other resistant gram-positive organisms are linezolid and quinupristin-dalfopristin. Linezolid, the first of a new family of antimicrobial agents known as oxazolidinones, has demonstrated significant activity against MRSA, vancomycin-resistant enterococci, and penicillin-resistant *S. pneumoniae.* It is available in both oral and intravenous formulations. Quinupristin-dalfopristin is a new injectable streptogramin antibiotic combination that has been found to be effective in the treatment of MRSA and vancomycin-resistant *Enterococcus faecium* infections in patients intolerant of or failing previous therapy. The frequent development of phlebitis with parenteral administration through a peripheral vein mandates the use of central venous access whenever possible. Both these newer agents are very high in cost, so their use should be restricted to specific situations for which other alternatives are not feasible.

METHICILLIN-RESISTANT STAPHYLOCOCCI

The β-lactam resistance of MRSA is caused by the production of a novel penicillin-binding protein (PBP) designated PBP-2′, which unlike the intrinsic set of PBPs (PBP-1 to PBP-4) of *S. aureus,* has remarkably reduced binding affinities to β-lactam antibiotics.[159, 312] Despite the presence of otherwise inhibitory concentrations of β-lactam antibiotics, MRSA can continue to synthesize cell walls solely through the uninhibited activity of PBP-2′.[159, 197] PBP-2′ is encoded by the *mecA* gene, which is carried by a unique mobile genetic element integrated into the *S. aureus* chromosome that is designated "staphylococcal cassette chromosome *mec.*"[128]

MRSA first was described within 1 year of the introduction of penicillinase-resistant penicillins.[142] Initial reports of infection appeared in England in the early 1960s and subsequently were followed by reports from other European countries.[168, 213, 287] In the United States, only sporadic cases were observed initially,[18, 165, 168] and not until 1968 was the first nosocomial outbreak described.[23] Since then, the prevalence of MRSA in the hospital setting has increased steadily.* In a survey of U.S. hospitals performed in 1989, 97 percent reported the presence of MRSA.[38] Risk factors associated with infection or colonization with MRSA were identified and included recent or prolonged hospitalization, exposure to antibiotics, and stay in an intensive care unit.[183] MRSA was thought to be essentially exclusive to the hospital environment.

Nosocomially acquired MRSA appears to be fully virulent, with in vitro characteristics similar to those of methicillin-sensitive staphylococci. It has equivalent virulence in studies of experimental infection in mice, and clinical studies confirm comparable mortality rates.[125, 302] These strains characteristically are multiresistant and usually show little or no sensitivity to cephalosporins, aminoglycosides, erythromycin, clindamycin, and tetracyclines.[6, 325] Strains that appear to be sensitive to cephalosporins by standard disk sensitivity tests are proved resistant in quantitative dilution tests. The clinical efficacy of cephalosporins against methicillin-resistant strains has been poor.[325] Vancomycin is the drug of choice for nosocomially acquired MRSA, alone or together with an aminoglycoside or rifampin. Coagulase-negative staphylococci have a high frequency of methicillin resistance.

Epidemic outbreaks of nosocomially acquired MRSA have been reported. In these outbreaks, researchers have noted that nasopharyngeal colonization with MRSA takes place before infection. A high rate of nasal and hand carriage has been observed in health care workers associated with units that have MRSA outbreaks.[217] The usual approach to outbreaks has been to emphasize handwashing between seeing patients. Strict isolation in a private room generally is advocated, although no scientific information justifies this approach. Single-room isolation usually is impractical in neonatal and pediatric intensive care units, where isolation facilities are in short supply and a single MRSA-colonized patient may occupy a room for months. Strict adherence to universal precautions (body substance isolation) with all moist body fluids and strict handwashing between seeing patients appear to be rational alternatives to "strict isolation."[188] Intranasal application of mupirocin ointment has been found to be capable of eliminating nasal and hand carriage of both colonized patients and hospital staff.[253] Because of its simplicity and reported effectiveness, this measure should be tried in preference to prolonged strict isolation of MRSA-colonized patients. If mupirocin treatment of MRSA-colonized patients is insufficient to curb an outbreak, culturing health care workers and extension of use of mupirocin to colonized health care personnel may be tried. Alternatively, systemic antibiotics may be used. Rifampin has a high degree of activity against MRSA, but the development of resistance remains a problem when this antibiotic is used alone. The combination of novobiocin and rifampin is associated with the development of less resistance than that noted with rifampin alone or when used in combination with

*See references 38, 44, 58, 59, 61, 68, 84, 117, 217, 226, 257, 265, 290, 302, 325, 328.

trimethoprim-sulfamethoxazole.[320] These combinations are not more efficacious in the clearance of MRSA carriage than is the application of mupirocin ointment.

In the 1970s, occasional cases of MRSA infection apparently acquired in the community were observed. However, patients tended to be chronically ill, and many gave a history of nursing home residence, recent admission to acute or chronic health care facilities, previous receipt of antibiotics, or intravenous drug abuse.[178, 201, 264, 291] Hence, in these cases, infections usually were traceable to the hospital setting. By contrast, since the 1980s, cases of apparently true community-acquired MRSA (CA-MRSA) infection in patients without identified risk factors have appeared in the literature. The first reports in children arose from small MRSA outbreak investigations.[55, 120] Subsequently, Rathore and Kline described three patients with deep-seated infections caused by MRSA acquired in the community.[251] In the 1990s, reports of CA-MRSA in patients without known risk factors continued to appear sporadically in the literature. However, most of the infections described occurred in adults.[109, 173, 216] The landmark study describing the changing epidemiology of CA-MRSA in children was published in 1998.[124] Herold and colleagues performed a retrospective review of medical records and compared the rate of *S. aureus* isolation in hospitalized children during two time periods: between 1988 and 1990 and between 1993 and 1995. The prevalence of CA-MRSA in children without identified risk factors was 25.9 times higher in 1993 to 1995 than in 1988 to 1990.[124] After the publication of this article, several reports of CA-MRSA in children without risk factors from different parts of the United States and many regions of the world have appeared.* This explosive increase in reporting that has taken place in the past few years suggests that the problem of CA-MRSA in children without risk factors may be generalizing. Other investigators, however, have not found such an increase, which implies that CA-MRSA in patients without risk factors may be a regional phenomenon.[5, 276, 294, 322]

With regard to the clinical characteristics of CA-MRSA infection in children without risk factors, several reports described a predominance of superficial infections, including subcutaneous abscesses and cellulitis. All 20 patients with CA-MRSA infection described by Bukharie and colleagues had skin or soft tissue infections.[46] Both Frank and colleagues and Herold and associates found a predominance of skin and soft tissue infections in children with CA-MRSA.[97, 124] However, the risk of acquiring severe, life-threatening infection with CA-MRSA was demonstrated in a report describing the deaths of four children ranging in age from 12 months to 13 years.[50] Two patients had necrotizing pneumonia, and septic arthritis and primary sepsis developed in one patient each.

Unlike hospital-acquired MRSA, which generally is multidrug-resistant and frequently only susceptible to vancomycin, CA-MRSA usually is susceptible to most non–β-lactam antibiotics, including clindamycin, gentamicin, trimethoprim-sulfamethoxazole, and tetracycline, in addition to vancomycin. Erythromycin susceptibility is somewhat more variable, with the proportion of susceptible isolates varying from 29 to 80 percent in various studies.[46, 110, 124, 137, 219] An important note is that in vitro as well as some in vivo evidence indicates that in the presence of erythromycin resistance, *S. aureus* could become resistant to clindamycin during therapy with this antibiotic.[77, 200, 234, 323] This phenomenon, inducible macrolide-lincosamide-streptogramin B (MLS_B) resistance, which consists of modification of the target rRNA of *S. aureus,* is mediated by the presence of the resistance-conferring *erm* (erythromycin resistance methylase) gene, which encodes a 23S rRNA methylase.[141, 174] Although 14-membered ring macrolides such as erythromycin are the most potent inducers, lincosamides such as clindamycin also can act as weaker inducers.[174] This ability may have clinical relevance in the setting of infections for which the bacteria are not eliminated quickly and may be exposed to subinhibitory concentrations of clindamycin for any amount of time. Examples include therapy for undrained deep-seated abscesses or treatment of osteoarticular infections. In patients infected with a strain having the inducible MLS_B resistance genotype and expressing the erythromycin-resistant, clindamycin-susceptible phenotype, cases of clindamycin therapeutic failure may appear with increasing frequency in the future as a result of the increasing prevalence of CA-MRSA and the probably increased use of clindamycin in this setting. Therefore, treating patients with infections caused by these particular isolates with an antibiotic other than clindamycin may be prudent, particularly if the infections are severe. For MRSA isolates that are erythromycin-resistant and clindamycin-susceptible, detection of the presence of inducible MLS_B resistance can be performed by the disk approximation method, in which clindamycin- and erythromycin-impregnated disks are set 15 to 20 mm apart over Mueller-Hinton agar containing a standard inoculum of bacteria. After a 24-hour incubation period, if the zone of inhibition around the clindamycin disk is flattened or blunted ("D shaped") on the side facing the erythromycin disk, the isolate is classified as having an inducible MLS_B resistance phenotype.[174]

For severe infections caused by MRSA, the antibiotic of choice is vancomycin. In areas where CA-MRSA has been isolated from children without identified risk factors, severe, life-threatening infections suspected to be caused by *S. aureus* should be treated empirically with both nafcillin and vancomycin because nafcillin is a more active antibiotic than is vancomycin for the treatment of methicillin-susceptible isolates.[12, 95] The addition of gentamicin should be considered for synergistic purposes. Antibiotic therapy can be adjusted subsequently after antibiotic susceptibility testing results are available. In the case of mild or moderate infections, recommendations for empiric therapy include trimethoprim-sulfamethoxazole, clindamycin, linezolid, semisynthetic antistaphylococcal penicillins, or first-generation cephalosporins.

For mild to moderate infections caused by CA-MRSA, empirical treatment may include other antibiotics such as clindamycin, tetracycline, trimethoprim-sulfamethoxazole, or antibiotics recently introduced, such as linezolid or the newer quinolones. Reports of successful treatment of skin and subcutaneous CA-MRSA infection with β-lactam antibiotics suggest that either the infection is cleared by the patient's host defenses or that β-lactam antibiotics are relatively active against these bacterial isolates.[46] Some cases of MRSA actually may be caused by infection with *S. aureus* that lacks the *mecA* gene responsible for true methicillin resistance. The mechanism of resistance in these cases may be hyperproduction of β-lactamase.[149] Frequently in these cases, methicillin resistance is borderline, with MICs of 8 μg/mL or less. Hence, high doses of β-lactam antibiotics may be inhibitory. The clinical significance of these isolates is unknown. In areas where CA-MRSA is a problem, of importance is to consider local antibiotic susceptibility patterns when selecting adequate empiric therapy for infections suspected to be caused by *S. aureus*.

The origin of CA-MRSA is not known. The absence of health care exposure in patients harboring the bacterium, the unique antibiotic susceptibility characteristics of these isolates, and distinctive pulsed-field electrophoresis patterns

*See references 46, 50, 87, 90, 97, 108, 109, 111, 114, 137, 158, 181, 219, 263, 277.

that are different from the patterns of hospital-acquired MRSA isolates for a given institution suggest that the origin may be the community and that these isolates were not merely transferred from the hospital setting.[3, 111] Recently, a new type of staphylococcal cassette chromosome *mec* from two CA-MRSA strains was identified.[189] The unique combination of the gene complex and the much smaller size than the previously identified staphylococcal cassette chromosome *mec* elements of hospital-acquired MRSA also suggests a different origin.[189]

Whether the origin is the hospital or the community, the changing epidemiology of MRSA is remarkably similar to the emergence of penicillin-resistant *S. aureus* that occurred in the 1940s and 1950s.[54] In that period, resistant isolates first appeared in the hospital setting, with only sporadic cases originating in the community. Subsequently, community-acquired penicillinase-producing isolates steadily increased. Currently, penicillin-susceptible isolates are extremely uncommon findings, both in the hospital and in the community. Whether MRSA becomes as widespread as penicillin-resistant *S. aureus* in both the hospital and the community remains to be seen.

Finally, the increasing rate of isolation of MRSA will mandate the use of alternative antibiotics, which in turn may promote the development of additional resistance to other antibiotic classes, the most concerning of which is resistance to glycopeptide antibiotics such as vancomycin. Although vancomycin is the antibiotic of choice for severe MRSA infection, its use must remain monitored and controlled because clinical isolates with decreased susceptibility to this antibiotic, the so-called vancomycin- or glycopeptide-intermediate *S. aureus* (VISA or GISA), already have been reported.[278]

In July 2002, the first documented infection by vancomycin-resistant *S. aureus* in the United States was reported.[51] The isolate, obtained from a catheter exit site of a 40-year-old diabetic patient undergoing chronic dialysis, had high MICs for vancomycin (>128 μg/mL) and oxacillin (>16 μg/mL) but was susceptible to chloramphenicol, linezolid, minocycline, quinupristin-dalfopristin, and trimethoprim-sulfamethoxazole.[51]

Prevention

Staphylococcal infections are so common that virtually everyone has had at least some minor encounters. Skin infections occur more commonly in tropical climates or during warm, humid weather in temperate areas and are likely to arise in moist areas of the body such as the axillae and skin creases. High standards of personal hygiene, careful cleaning, and adequate protection of abrasions and minor lacerations reduce the likelihood of skin infection developing.[295] Early attention to minor infection in these small wounds with careful cleaning and antibiotic ointment may help prevent more serious or invasive infection. We have been impressed repeatedly with the minor nature of the cutaneous source of infection in serious staphylococcal osteomyelitis, pneumonia, and endocarditis.

Person-to-person spread from an overt lesion is a major route for dissemination of infection within families, in hospitals, and in schools. A person with an infected, purulent wound should receive prompt treatment and be excused from school and from such occupations as hospital worker or food handler while the infection is open or draining. At home, special precautions should be taken in care and dressing of the wound. Disposable gauze pads should be used to wash and dry it, and towels and washcloths should not be shared with other members of the family.

NOSOCOMIAL INFECTION

Prevention of transmission of staphylococci within hospitals remains a challenge. Routine environmental cultures and routine culturing of personnel for the identification of asymptomatic carriers have not been found to be effective in identifying problems or pointing the way to solutions. Recognition of an outbreak or cluster of infections on a surgical or medical service is the essential first step in control. Hospital-based infection surveillance systems may detect hospital-acquired infections in some circumstances, but frequently, as with newborns or after simple surgical procedures, the stay in the hospital is short and infection is not apparent until after the patient has been discharged. Unless an easy mechanism for reporting such infections back to hospital infection control personnel is set up and used, a cross-infection problem of considerable size may be present before being recognized. For epidemic outbreaks involving medical or surgical patients, an individualized approach to control must be taken after analyzing the characteristics of the outbreak.[171]

Prevention of MRSA outbreaks is likely to be optimized by strict adherence to handwashing between seeing patients and the faithful performance of universal precautions and isolation of body substances. Studies have shown that MRSA nasal colonization precedes MRSA infection in chronically ill patients.[217] Other studies have demonstrated that nasal application of mupirocin ointment eradicates nasal and hand carriage of MRSA. Therefore, in an outbreak of MRSA, patients at risk should be surveyed for nasal MRSA colonization. Mupirocin should be administered in an attempt to eradicate carriage, in addition to providing appropriate treatment of patients with established infection.[253] If new infections continue to appear, survey and treatment of colonized hospital staff with mupirocin may be effective.

Certain procedures that expose individual patients to a higher risk of acquiring staphylococcal infection include intravenous therapy; cardiac surgical procedures, particularly those involving valve replacement; and CSF shunt placement. Prevention of these infections has been discussed in preceding sections. Simple adherence to accepted surgical principles in the care of wounds and burns is important in the prevention of infection at these sites.

NEONATAL CARE UNITS

Since 1972, numerous outbreaks of staphylococcal disease in nurseries have been reported. In many of these outbreaks, the predominant manifestation has been bullous impetigo. To date, invasive disease appears to be less severe than reported in the outbreaks of the 1950s, and the risk of spread to other family members is lower. An intelligent approach to preventing neonatal infection consists of the following elements:

1. Strict handwashing techniques for all persons handling infants in the nursery, including nursing personnel, physicians, and parents. An effective antistaphylococcal preparation such as chlorhexidine, povidone-iodine, or 0.3 percent triclosan should be used on entering the nursery, and hands should be rewashed between handling babies. Handwashing has been demonstrated to be effective in decreasing the organisms transferred from baby to baby.[281]
2. Absolute prohibition from the nursery of personnel or parents with draining skin lesions.
3. Careful daily examination of infants for pustules, periumbilical or perineal erythema, and bullous lesions, with prompt culture and strict isolation of infected infants. The

circumcision site in boys is particularly likely to become infected.

4. A mechanism for prompt reporting of infection, both major and minor, to the hospital by parents and local pediatricians.

When an outbreak of staphylococcal infections is recognized or when colonization rates are higher than 20 to 30 percent, review of procedures and institution of control measures are indicated. Among the more effective control measures available that can reduce the carrier rate to less than 10 percent are the following:

1. Routine application of a triple-dye mixture to the umbilicus. This method has been shown to be helpful in reducing colonization and terminating an epidemic and has been used widely.[270] Despite the sanctification of this method by time and wide use, the possibility of systemic absorption and toxicity of the dyes has not been evaluated.
2. Routine daily application of antibiotic ointment to the cord and circumcision site.[145, 164] Potential disadvantages with this approach include the possibility of sensitization of some infants to the antibiotic and the potential for altering the microbiologic ecology of the nursery and enhancing the development of antibiotic resistance. The use of bacitracin ointment minimizes both problems. Bacitracin is unlikely to be used systemically in the future. Concern about serious drug allergy and clinically important microbial resistance, therefore, will be eliminated.

All the foregoing approaches reduce colonization of infants by creating a barrier to the establishment of staphylococci at favored sites for colonization.[140] Another approach, which has been effective in controlling epidemics, has been to colonize infants deliberately with a less pathogenic staphylococcus, strain 502A, and thereby prevent the establishment of more pathogenic strains.[275] This technique of bacterial interference is a potential source of iatrogenic disease because 502A has caused episodes of skin infection, serious disease, and death in one case of fatal septicemia.[30, 134]

Procedures of lesser value in dealing with outbreaks of disease are those that reduce the degree of contact of infants within a central nursery by the use of earlier discharge and rooming-in programs and establishment of a strict cohort system so that infants remain with a small group of other babies during their hospital stay. Searching for and treating nasal carriers among nursery personnel are a waste of time and money. Nasal carriers appear to be insignificant factors in the propagation of epidemics and colonization of newborns.

The optimal approach to prevention of nosocomial "late-onset" coagulase-negative staphylococcal sepsis remains unclear. Although a strong association exists between coagulase-negative bacteremia and prolonged venous catheterization and the use of lipid emulsions for hyperalimentation, the benefits of hyperalimentation appear to outweigh the risks. Further investigation is needed to determine safer methods of providing intravenous lipid administration. A preliminary report of a carefully controlled multicenter trial has demonstrated that prophylactic intravenous gamma-globulin therapy administered to infants weighing less than 1500 g in the first week of life, 1 week later, and then every 2 weeks while in intensive care units reduced the incidence of nosocomial bacteremia by approximately a third.[20] Staphylococci, both coagulase-negative and coagulase-positive, were the dominant pathogens in the control group. Another study has demonstrated opsonic activity against coagulase-negative staphylococci in gamma-globulin preparations.[83] Other studies have not found that prophylactic intravenous gamma-globulin therapy confers significant benefit.

In summary, the staphylococcus is a ubiquitous agent and a frequent cause of disease. Prevention of sporadic infections is an issue that affects individual patients. Prevention of nosocomial disease depends on the vigilance of hospital personnel in services as diverse as the operating room, intravenous therapy, and the neonatal nursery in recognizing the potential for infection and developing and maintaining effective control measures.

REFERENCES

1. Abe, J. K., Kotzin, B. L., and Jujo, K.: Selective expansion of T cells expressing T-cell receptor variable regions $V_{\beta}2$ and $V_{\beta}8$ in Kawasaki disease. Proc. Natl. Acad. Sci. U. S. A. *89*:4066–4070, 1992.
2. Abe, J. K., Kotzin, B. L., Meissener, C., et al.: Characterization of T-cell repertoire changes in acute Kawasaki disease. J. Exp. Med. *177*:791–796, 1993.
3. Abi-Hanna, P., Frank, A. L., Quinn, J. P., et al.: Clonal features of community-acquired methicillin-resistant *Staphylococcus aureus* in children. Clin. Infect. Dis. *30*:630–631, 2000.
4. Abramson, N., Alper, C. A., Lachman, P. J., et al.: Deficiency of C3 inactivation in man. J. Immunol. *107*:19–27, 1971.
5. Abudu, L., Blair, I., Fraise, A., and Cheng, K. K.: Methicillin-resistant *Staphylococcus aureus* (MRSA): A community-based prevalence survey. Epidemiol. Infect. *126*:351–356, 2001.
6. Acar, J. F., and Chabbert, Y. A.: Methicillin-resistant staphylococcemia: Bacteriological failure of treatment with cephalosporins. Antimicrob. Agents Chemother. *10*:280–285, 1972.
7. Almquist, E. E.: The changing epidemiology of septic arthritis in children. Clin. Orthop. *68*:96–99, 1970.
8. Alper, C. A., Abramson, N., Johnston, R. B., et al.: Increased susceptibility to infection associated with abnormalities of complement-mediated functions and of the third component of complement (C3). N. Engl. J. Med. *282*:350–354, 1970.
9. Alper, C. A., Colten, R. H., and Rosen, F. S.: Homozygous deficiency of C3 in a patient with repeated infections. Lancet *2*:1179–1181, 1972.
10. Altrocchi, P. H.: Spontaneous bacterial myositis. J. A. M. A. *217*:819–820, 1971.
11. Amon, R. B., and Dimond, R.: Toxic epidermal necrolysis: Rapid differentiation between staphylococcal and drug-induced diseases. Arch. Dermatol. *111*:1433–1437, 1975.
12. Apellaniz, G., Valdes, M., Perez, R., et al.: Comparison of the effectiveness of various antibiotics in the treatment of methicillin-susceptible *Staphylococcus aureus* experimental infective endocarditis. J. Chemother. *3*:91–97, 1991.
13. Arbuthnott, J. P., Kent, K., Lyell, A., et al.: Studies on staphylococcal toxins in relation to toxic epidermal necrolysis (the scalded skin syndrome). Br. J. Dermatol. *86*(Suppl. 8):35–39, 1972.
14. Axline, S. G., Yaffe, S. J., and Simon, H. J.: Clinical pharmacology of antimicrobials in premature infants. II. Ampicillin, methicillin, oxacillin, neomycin and colistin. Pediatrics *39*:97–107, 1967.
15. Ayliffe, G. A. J., Brightwell, K. M., Ball, P. M., et al.: Staphylococcal infection in cervical glands of infants. Lancet *2*:479–484, 1972.
16. Baba, T., Takeuchi, F., Kuroda, M., et al.: Genome and virulence determinants of high virulence community-acquired MRSA. Lancet *359*:1819–1827, 2002.
17. Baehner, R. L.: Neutrophil dysfunction associated with states of chronic and recurrent infection. Pediatr. Clin. North Am. *27*:377–401, 1980.
18. Baehner, R. L., Boxer, L. A., and Davis, J.: The biochemical basis of nitroblue tetrazolium reduction in normal human and chronic granulomatous disease and polymorphonuclear leukocytes. Blood *48*:309–313, 1977.
19. Baker, C. J.: Nosocomial septicemia and meningitis in neonates. Am. J. Med. *70*:698–701, 1981.
20. Baker, C. J., and the Neonatal IVIG Collaborative Study Group: Multicenter trial of intravenous immunoglobulin (IVIG) to prevent preterm infants. Pediatr. Res. *25*:1633, 1989.
21. Baldwin, D. S., Levin, B. B., McCluskey, R. T., et al.: Renal failure and interstitial nephritis due to penicillin and methicillin. N. Engl. J. Med. *279*:1245–1249, 1968.
22. Banffer, J. R.: Anti-leucocidin and mastitis puerperalis. B. M. J. *2*:1224, 1962.
23. Barrett, F. F., McGehee, R. F., and Finland, M.: Methicillin-resistant *Staphylococcus aureus* at Boston City Hospital: Bacteriologic and epidemiologic observations. N. Engl. J. Med. *279*:441–448, 1968.
24. Barton, L. L., and Feigin, R. D.: Childhood cervical lymphadenitis: A reappraisal. J. Pediatr. *84*:846–852, 1974.
25. Barton, L. L., Freidman, A. D., and Portilla, M. G.: Impetigo contagiosa: A comparison of erythromycin and dicloxacillin therapy. Pediatr. Dermatol. *5*:88–91, 1988.
26. Barton, L. L., Freidman, A. D., Sharkey, A. M., et al.: Impetigo contagiosa. III. Comparative efficacy of oral erythromycin and topical mupirocin. Pediatr. Dermatol. *6*:134–138, 1989.

27. Bass, J. W., Cohen, S. H., Corless, J. D., et al.: Ampicillin compared to other antimicrobials in acute otitis media. J. A. M. A. *202*:697–702, 1967.
28. Batista, R. A., Baredes, S., and Krieger, A.: Prevertebral space infections associated with cervical osteomyelitis. Otolaryngol. Head Neck Surg. *108*:160–166, 1993.
29. Beck, W., and Grose, C.: Pyomyositis presenting as acute abdominal pain. Pediatr. Infect. Dis. *3*:445–448, 1984.
30. Blair, E. B., and Tull, A. H.: Multiple infections among newborns resulting from colonization with *Staphylococcus aureus* 502A. Am. J. Clin. Pathol. *52*:42–49, 1969.
31. Bland, R. D.: Otitis media in the first six weeks of life: Diagnosis, bacteriology and management. Pediatrics *49*:187–197, 1972.
32. Blockley, N. J., and Watson, J. T.: Acute osteomyelitis in children. J. Bone Joint Surg. Br. *52*:77–87, 1970.
33. Bloomer, W. E., Giammona, S., Lindskog, C. F., et al.: Staphylococcal pneumonia and empyema in infancy. J. Thorac. Surg. *30*:265–274, 1955.
34. Blumenthal, S., Griffiths, S. P., and Morgan, B. C.: Bacterial endocarditis in children with heart disease. Pediatrics *26*:993–998, 1960.
35. Boe, R. W., Williams, C. P. S., Bennett, J. V., et al.: Serum levels of methicillin and ampicillin in newborn and premature infants in relation to post-natal age. Pediatrics *39*:194–198, 1967.
36. Borella, L., Goobar, J. E., Summitt, R. L., et al.: Septic arthritis in childhood. J. Pediatr. *62*:742–747, 1963.
37. Boxer, L. A., Hedley-Whyte, E. T., and Stossel, T. P.: Neutrophil actin dysfunction and abnormal neutrophil behavior. N. Engl. J. Med. *291*:1093–1099, 1974.
38. Boyce, J. M.: Methicillin-resistant *Staphylococcus aureus*: Detection, epidemiology, and control measures. Infect. Dis. Clin. North Am. *3*:901–913, 1989.
39. Bracis, R., Sandus, C., Kimbrough, R., et al.: Methicillin hemorrhagic cystitis. Presented at the 16th Interscience Conference on Antimicrobial Agents and Chemotherapy, October 1976, Chicago.
40. Brans, Y. W., Aballos, R., and Cassady, G.: Umbilical catheters and hepatic abscesses. Pediatrics *53*:264–268, 1974.
41. Bricker, T., Gutgesell, H. P., Latson, L. A., et al.: Echocardiographic evaluation of endocarditis in children. Pediatr. Cardiol. *3*:350, 1982.
42. Bridges, R. A., Berendes, H., and Good, R. A.: A fatal granulomatous disease of childhood. Am. J. Dis. Child. *97*:387–391, 1959.
43. Brown, J. D., and Wheeler, B.: Pyomyositis: Report of 18 cases in Hawaii. Arch. Intern. Med. *144*:1749–1751, 1984.
44. Brumfitt, W., and Hamilton-Miller, J.: Methicillin-resistant *Staphylococcus aureus*. N. Engl. J. Med. *320*:1188–1196, 1989.
45. Bryson, Y. J., Connor, J. D., Leclerc, M., et al.: Oral dicloxacillin as a mode of therapy of treatment of acute staphylococcal osteomyelitis. Pediatr. Res. *9*:339–345, 1975.
46. Bukharie, H. A., Abdelhadi, M. S., Saeed, I. A., et al.: Emergence of methicillin-resistant *Staphylococcus aureus* as a community pathogen. Diagn. Microbiol. Infect. Dis. *40*:1–4, 2001.
47. Burry, V. F., and Beezley, M.: Infant mastitis due to gram-negative organisms. Am. J. Dis. Child. *124*:736–737, 1972.
48. Campbell, J. A., Gastineau, D. C., and Velias, F.: Roentgen studies in suppurative pneumonia in infants and children. J. A. M. A. *154*:468–472, 1954.
49. Cannale, S. T., Harkness, R. M., Thomas, P. A., et al.: Does aspiration of bones and joints affect results of later bone scanning? J. Pediatr. Orthop. *5*:23–26, 1985.
50. Centers for Disease Control and Prevention: Four pediatric deaths from community-acquired methicillin-resistant *Staphylococcus aureus*—Minnesota and North Dakota, 1997–1999. M. M. W. R. Morb. Mortal. Wkly. Rep. *48*(32):707–710, 1999.
51. Centers for Disease Control and Prevention: *Staphylococcus aureus* resistant to vancomycin—United States, 2002. M. M. W. R. Morb. Mortal. Wkly. Rep. *51*(26):565–567, 2002.
52. Ceruti, E., Contreras, J., and Neira, M.: Staphylococcal pneumonia in childhood. Am. J. Dis. Child. *122*:386–392, 1971.
53. Chacha, P. B.: Suppurative arthritis of the hip joint in infancy. J. Bone Joint Surg. Am. *53*:538–544, 1971.
54. Chambers, H. F.: The changing epidemiology of *Staphylococcus aureus?* Emerg. Infect. Dis. *7*:178–183, 2001.
55. Chartrand, S., Andrews, D., Goering, R., et al.: A community outbreak of serious infections due to methicillin-resistant *Staphylococcus aureus*. Abstract. Presented at the American Society of Microbiology Annual Meeting, 1988, Miami Beach, Florida.
56. Christensson, B., Esperson, F., Hedstrom, S. A., et al.: Solid-phase radioimmunoassay of immunoglobulin G antibodies to *Staphylococcus aureus* peptidoglycan in patients with staphylococcal infections. Acta Pathol. Microbiol. Immunol. Scand. *91*:401–406, 1983.
57. Clark, R. A., Root, R. K., Kimball, H. R., et al.: Defective neutrophil chemotaxis and cellular immunity in a child with recurrent infection. Ann. Intern. Med. *78*:515–519, 1972.
58. Coello, R., Jimenez, J., Garcia, M., et al.: Prospective study of infection, colonization, and carriage of methicillin-resistant *Staphylococcus aureus* in an outbreak affecting 990 patients. Eur. J. Clin. Microbiol. Infect. Dis. *13*:74–81, 1994.
59. Coovadia, Y. M., Bhana, R. H., Johnson, A. P., et al.: Laboratory-confirmed outbreak of rifampicin methicillin-resistant *Staphylococcus aureus* in a newborn nursery. J. Hosp. Infect. *14*:303–312, 1989.
60. Correa, A. G., Edwards, M. S., and Baker, C. J.: Vertebral osteomyelitis in children. Pediatr. Infect. Dis. J. *12*:228–233, 1993.
61. Cox, R. A., Conquest, C., Mallaghan, C., et al.: A major outbreak of methicillin-resistant *Staphylococcus aureus* caused by a new phage-type (EMRSA-16). J. Hosp. Infect. *29*:87–106, 1995.
62. Craigen, M. A., Watters, J., and Hackett, J. S.: The changing epidemiology of osteomyelitis in children. J. Bone Joint Surg. Br. *74*:541–545, 1992.
63. Craven, D. E., Reed, C., Kollisch, N., et al.: A large outbreak of infections caused by a strain of *Staphylococcus aureus* resistant to oxacillin and aminoglycosides. Am. J. Med. *71*:53–58, 1981.
64. Crawford, A. H., Kucharzyk, D. W., Ruda, R., et al.: Diskitis in children. Clin. Orthop. *266*:70–79, 1991.
65. Crenshaw, C. A., Kelly, L., and Turner, R. I.: Prevention of infections at scalp vein sites of needle insertion during intravenous therapy. Am. J. Surg. *124*:43–45, 1972.
66. Crossley, K., and Matson, J. M.: The scalp vein needle: A prospective study of associated complications. J. A. M. A. *220*:985–987, 1972.
67. Curnett, J. P., Kipnes, R. S., and Bevior, B. M.: Defect in pyridine nucleotide–dependent superoxide production by a particulate fraction from the granulocytes of patients with chronic granulomatous disease. N. Engl. J. Med. *293*:628–632, 1975.
68. Dacre, J., Emmerson, A. M., and Jenner, E. A.: Gentamicin methicillin-resistant *Staphylococcus aureus:* Epidemiology and containment of an outbreak. J. Hosp. Infect. *7*:130–136, 1986.
69. Dagan, R., and Bar-David, Y.: Double-blind study comparing erythromycin and mupirocin for treatment of impetigo in children: Implications of a high prevalence of erythromycin-resistant *Staphylococcus aureus* strains. Antimicrob. Agents Chemother. *36*:287–290, 1992.
70. Daher, A. H., and Berkowitz, F. E.: Infective endocarditis in neonates. Clin. Pediatr. (Phila.) *34*:198–206, 1995.
71. Dajani, A. S., Garcia, R. E., and Wolinsky, E.: Etiology of cervical lymphadenitis in children. N. Engl. J. Med. *268*:1329–1333, 1963.
72. Dehner, L. P., and Kissane, J. M.: Pyogenic hepatic abscesses in infancy and childhood. J. Pediatr. *74*:763–773, 1969.
73. Dewar, J., Porter, I. A., and Smylie, H. G.: Staphylococcal infection in cervical glands of infants. Lancet *2*:712–717, 1972.
74. Dich, V. Q., Nelson, J. D., and Haltalin, G.: Osteomyelitis in infants and children: A review of 163 cases. Am. J. Dis. Child. *129*:1273–1278, 1975.
75. Disney, M. E., Wolff, J., and Wood, B. S. B.: Staphylococcal pneumonia in infants. Lancet *1*:767–771, 1956.
76. Dreskin, S. C., Goldsmith, P. K., and Gullin, J. I.: Immunoglobulin E and recurrent infection (Job's) syndrome. J. Clin. Invest. *75*:26–34, 1985.
77. Drinkovic, D., Fuller, E. R., Shore, K. P., et al.: Clindamycin treatment of *Staphylococcus aureus* expressing inducible clindamycin resistance. J. Antimicrob. Chemother. *48*:315–316, 2001.
78. Echeverria, P., and Vaughn, M. C.: Tropical pyomyositis: A diagnostic problem in temperate climates. Am. J. Dis. Child. *129*:856–857, 1975.
79. Edwards, K. M., Dundon, C., and Altemeier, W. A.: Bacterial tracheitis as a complication of viral croup. Pediatr. Infect. Dis. *2*:390–391, 1983.
80. Elias, P. M., Fritsch, P., Dahl, M. V., et al.: Staphylococcal exfoliative toxin: Pathogenesis and subcellular site of action. J. Invest. Dermatol. *65*:501–512, 1975.
81. Elias, P. M., Mittermayer, H., Tappeiner, G., et al.: Staphylococcal toxic epidermal necrolysis (TEN): The expanded mouse model. J. Invest. Dermatol. *63*:467–472, 1974.
82. Esperson, F., Fremodt-Miller, N., Thamdrup Rosendal, V., et al.: *Staphylococcus aureus* bacteremia in children below the age of one year: A review of 407 cases. Acta Pediatr. Scand. *78*:56–61, 1989.
83. Etzioni, A., Obedeanui, S., Blazer, S., et al.: Effect of an intravenous gamma globulin preparation on the opsonophagocytic activity of preterm serum against coagulase-negative staphylococci. Acta Pediatr. Scand. *79*:156–161, 1990.
84. Eykyn, S. J.: Staphylococcal sepsis: The changing pattern of disease and therapy. Lancet *1*:100–103, 1988.
85. Faden, H., and Grossi, M.: Acute osteomyelitis in children: Reassessment of etiologic agents and their clinical characteristics. Am. J. Dis. Child. *145*:65–69, 1991.
86. Fagbule, D. O.: Bacterial pathogens in malnourished children with pneumonia. Trop. Geogr. Med. *45*:294–296, 1993.
87. Feder, H. M., Jr.: Methicillin-resistant *Staphylococcus aureus* infections in 2 pediatric outpatients. Arch. Fam. Med. *9*:560–562, 2000.
88. Feigin, R. D., VanReken, D. E., and Pickering, L. L.: Dosage in methicillin-associated nephropathy. J. Pediatr. *85*:734, 1974.
89. Feldman, W. E.: Bacterial etiologies and mortality of purulent pericarditis in pediatric patients. Am. J. Dis. Child. *133*:641–644, 1979.
90. Fergie, J. E., and Purcell, K.: Community-acquired methicillin-resistant *Staphylococcus aureus* infections in south Texas children. Pediatr. Infect. Dis. J. *20*:860–863, 2000.
91. Fernandez, M., Carrol, C. L., and Baker, C. J.: Discitis and vertebral osteomyelitis in children: An 18-year review. Pediatrics *105*:299–304, 2000.

92. Fisher, J. H., and Swenson, O.: Surgical complications of staphylococcal pneumonia. Pediatrics *20*:835–847, 1957.
93. Fleer, A., Senders, R. C., Visser, M. R., et al.: Septicemia due to coagulase-negative staphylococci in a neonatal intensive care unit: Clinical and bacteriologic features and contaminated parenteral fluids as a source of sepsis. Pediatr. Infect. Dis. *2*:426–431, 1983.
94. Forbes, G. B., and Emerson, G. L.: Staphylococcal pneumonia and empyema. Pediatr. Clin. North Am. *4*:215–230, 1957.
95. Fortun, J., Navas, E., Martinez-Beltran, J., et al.: Short-course therapy for right-side endocarditis due to *Staphylococcus aureus* in drug abusers: Cloxacillin versus glycopeptides in combination with gentamicin. Clin. Infect. Dis. *33*:120–125, 2001.
96. Foster, D., and Harris, R. E.: The incidence of *Staphylococcus pyogenes* in normal human breast milk. J. Obstet. Gynecol. *67*:463–466, 1960.
97. Frank, A. L., Marcinak, J. F., Mangat, P. D., and Schreckenberger, P. C.: Community-acquired and clindamycin-susceptible methicillin-resistant *Staphylococcus aureus* in children. Pediatr. Infect. Dis. J. *18*:993–1000, 1999.
98. Freeman, J., Epstein, M. F., Smith, N. E., et al.: Extra hospital stay and antibiotic usage with nosocomial coagulase negative staphylococcal bacteremia in two neonatal intensive care unit populations. Am. J. Dis. Child. *144*:324–329, 1990.
99. Freeman, J., Goldmann, D. A., Smith, N. E., et al.: Association of intravenous lipid emulsion and coagulase-negative staphylococcal bacteremia in neonatal intensive care units. N. Engl. J. Med. *323*:301–308, 1990.
100. Freidland, I. R., du Pless, J., and Cilliers, A.: Cardiac complications in children with *Staphylococcus aureus* bacteremia. J. Pediatr. *127*:746–748,1995.
101. Gelfand, M. J., and Silberstein, E. G.: Radionuclide imaging use in diagnosis of osteomyelitis in children. J. A. M. A. *237*:245–247, 1977.
102. George, R., Leibrock, L., and Epstein, M.: Long-term analysis of cerebrospinal fluid shunt infections: A 25-year experience. J. Neurosurg. *51*:804–811, 1979.
103. Gersony, W. M., and McCracken, G. H.: Purulent pericarditis in infancy. Pediatrics *40*:224–232, 1967.
104. Givner, L. B., and Kaplan, S. L.: Meningitis due to *Staphylococcus aureus* in children. Clin. Infect. Dis. *16*:766–771, 1993.
105. Gladstone, G. P., and Mudd, S.: The assay of antistaphylococcal leukocidal components in human sera. Br. J. Exp. Pathol. *43*:295–298, 1962.
106. Gluck, L., and Wood, H. F.: Effect of an antiseptic skin care regimen in reducing staphylococcal colonization in newborn infants. N. Engl. J. Med. *265*:1177–1181, 1961.
107. Goldmann, D. A., Maki, D. G., Phame, F. S., et al.: Guidelines for infection control in intravenous therapy. Am. J. Med. *79*:848–850, 1973.
108. Gorak, E. J., Yamada, S. M., and Brown, J. D.: Community-acquired methicillin-resistant *Staphylococcus aureus* in hospitalized adults and children without known risk factors. Clin. Infect. Dis. *29*:797–800, 1999.
109. Gosbell, I. B., Mercer, J. L., Neville, S. A., et al.: Non-multiresistant and multiresistant methicillin-resistant *Staphylococcus aureus* in community-acquired infections. Med. J. Aust. *174*:627–639, 2001.
110. Gottlieb, R. D., Shah, M. K., Perlman, D. C., and Kimmelman, C. P.: Community-acquired methicillin-resistant *Staphylococcus aureus* infections in otolaryngology. Otolaryngol. Head. Neck. Surg. *107*:434–437, 1992.
111. Groom, A. V., Wolsey, D. H., Naimi T. S., et al.: Community acquired methicillin-resistant *Staphylococcus aureus* in a rural American Indian community. J. A. M. A. *286*:1201–1205, 2001.
112. Guggenbichler, J. P., Berchtold, D., Allerberger, F., et al.: In vitro and in vivo effect of antibiotics on catheters colonized by staphylococci. Eur. J. Clin. Microbiol. Infect. Dis. *11*:408–415, 1992.
113. Gutman, L. T., Idriss, Z. H., Gehlbach, S., et al.: Neonatal staphylococcal enterocolitis: Association with indwelling feeding catheters and *S. aureus* colonization. J. Pediatr. *88*:836–839, 1976.
114. Gwynne-Jones, D. P., and Stott, N. S.: Community-acquired methicillin-resistant *Staphylococcus aureus*: A cause of musculoskeletal sepsis in children. J. Pediatr. Orthop. *19*:413–416, 1999.
115. Haffar, A. A., Rench, M. A., Ferry, G. D., et al.: Failure of urokinase to resolve Broviac catheter–related bacteremia in children. J. Pediatr. *104*:256–258, 1984.
116. Haley, R. W., and Bregman, D. A.: The role of understaffing and overcrowding in recurrent outbreaks of staphylococcal infection in a neonatal special care unit. J. Infect. Dis. *145*:875–885, 1982.
117. Haley, R. W., Hightower, A. W., Khabbaz, R. F., et al.: The emergence of methicillin-resistant *Staphylococcus aureus* infections in United States hospitals. Ann. Intern. Med. *97*:297–308, 1982.
118. Hall, S. L.: Coagulase-negative staphylococcal infections in neonates. Pediatr. Infect. Dis. *10*:51–67, 1991.
119. Hallander, H. O., and Korloff, B.: Enterotoxin-producing staphylococci. Acta Pathol. Microbiol. Scand. *71*:359–362, 1967.
120. Hamoudi, A. C., Palmer, R. N., and King, T. L.: Nafcillin resistant *Staphylococcus aureus*: A possible community origin. Infect. Control *4*:153–157, 1983.
121. Hay, P., and McKenzie, P.: Side effects of oxytetracycline therapy. Lancet *1*:945–949, 1954.
122. Hendren, W. H., and Haggerty, R. J.: Staphylococcal pneumonia in infancy and childhood: Analysis of 75 cases. J. A. M. A. *168*:6–16, 1958.
123. Hermansson, G., Bollgren, I., Bugstrom, T., et al.: Coagulase-negative staphylococci as a cause of symptomatic urinary infections in children. J. Pediatr. *84*:807–810, 1974.
124. Herold, B. C., Immergluck, L. C., Maranan, M. C., et al.: Community-acquired methicillin-resistant *Staphylococcus aureus* in children with no identified predisposing risk. J. A. M. A. *279*:593–598, 1998.
125. Hershow, R. C., Khayr, W. F., and Smith, N. L.: A comparison of clinical virulence of nosocomially acquired methicillin-resistant and methicillin-sensitive *Staphylococcus aureus* infections in a university hospital. Infect. Control Hosp. Epidemiol. *13*:587–593, 1992.
126. Hieber, J. P., and Davis, A. T.: Staphylococcal cervical adenitis in young infants. Pediatrics *57*:424–426, 1976.
127. Hill, H. R., and Quie, P. G.: Raised IgE levels and defective neutrophil chemotaxis with eczema and recurrent bacterial infections. Lancet *1*:183–186, 1974.
128. Hiramatsu, K., Katayama, Y., Yuzawa, H., and Ito T.: Molecular genetics of methicillin-resistant *Staphylococcus aureus*. Int. J. Med. Microbiol. *292*:67–74, 2002.
129. Ho, N. K., Low, Y. P., and See, H. F.: Septic arthritis in the newborn: A 17-year clinical experience. Singapore Med. J. *30*:356–358, 1989.
130. Hoeger, P. H., Lens, A. B., and Fournier, J. M.: Staphylococcal skin colonization in children with atopic dermatitis: Prevalence, persistence, and transmission of toxigenic and non-toxigenic strains. J. Infect. Dis. *165*:1064–1068, 1992.
131. Hoeger, P. H., Niggermann, B., and Schoeder, C.: Enhanced basal and stimulated PMN chemiluminescence activity in children with atopic dermatitis: Stimulatory role of colonizing staphylococci? Acta Paediatr. *81*:562–564, 1992.
132. Honig, P. J., Gaisin, A., and Buck, B. E.: Frozen section differentiation of drug-induced and staphylococcal-induced toxic epidermal necrolysis. J. Pediatr. *92*:504, 1978.
133. Horn, C. V., and Master, S.: Pyomyositis tropicans in Uganda. East Afr. Med. J. *45*:563–571, 1968.
134. Houck, P. W., Nelson, J. D., and Kay, J. L.: Fatal septicemia due to *Staphylococcus aureus* 502A. Am. J. Dis. Child. *123*:45–48, 1972.
135. Howie, V. M., Ploussand, J. H., and Lester, R. L.: Otitis media: A clinical and bacteriologic correlation. Pediatrics *45*:29–35, 1970.
136. Huebner, J., Pier, G. B., Maslow, J. N., et al.: Endemic nosocomial transmission of *Staphylococcus epidermidis* bacteremia isolates in a neonatal intensive care unit over 10 years. J. Infect. Dis. *169*:526–531, 1994.
137. Hussain, F. M., Boyle-Vavra, S., Bethel, C. D., and Daum, R. S.: Current trends in community-acquired methicillin-resistant *Staphylococcus aureus* at a tertiary care pediatric facility. Pediatr. Infect. Dis. J. *19*:1163–1166, 2000.
138. Huxtable, K. A., Tucker, A. S., and Wedgwood, R. J.: Staphylococcal pneumonia in childhood. Am. J. Dis. Child. *108*:262–269, 1964.
139. Issekutz, A. C., Lee, K. Y., and Biggar, W. D.: Neutrophil chemotaxis in two patients with recurrent staphylococcal skin infections and hyperimmunoglobulin E. J. Lab. Clin. Med. *92*:640–647, 1978.
140. Jellard, J.: Umbilical cord as a reservoir of infection in a maternity hospital. B. M. J. *1*:925–929, 1957.
141. Jenssen, W. D., Thakker-Varia, S., Dubin, D. T., and Weinstein, M. P.: Prevalence of macrolides-lincosamides-streptogramin B resistance and *erm* gene classes among clinical strains of staphylococci and streptococci. Antimicrob. Agents Chemother. *31*:883–888, 1987.
142. Jevons, M. P.: "Celbenin"-resistant staphylococci. Letter. B. M. J. *1*:124–125, 1961.
143. Johanovsky, J.: Importance of anti-leucocidin and anti-toxin in immunity against staphylococcal infections. Immunotactsforschung *116*:318–320, 1959.
144. Johnson, D. H., Rosenthal, A., and Nadas, A. S.: A forty-year review of bacterial endocarditis in infancy and childhood. Circulation *51*:581–588, 1975.
145. Johnson, J. D., Malachowski, N. C., Vosti, K. L., et al.: A sequential study of various modes of skin and umbilical care and the incidence of staphylococcal colonization and infection in the neonate. Pediatrics *58*:354–361, 1976.
146. Johnston, R. B., and Baehner, R. L.: Chronic granulomatous disease: Correlation between pathogenesis and clinical findings. Pediatrics *48*:730–733, 1971.
147. Jones, D. R. B., and MacIntyre, K.: Venous thromboembolism in infancy and childhood. Arch. Dis. Child. *50*:153–155, 1975.
148. Jones, R., Santos, J. I., and Overall, J. C., Jr.: Bacterial tracheitis. J. A. M. A. *242*:721-726, 1979.
149. Jorgensen, J.: Mechanisms of methicillin resistance in *Staphylococcus aureus* and methods for laboratory detection. Infect. Control Hosp. Epidemiol. *12*:14–19, 1991.
150. Julander, I. G., Grandstrom, M., Hedstrom, S. A., et al.: The role of antibodies against alpha-toxin and teichoic acid in the diagnosis of staphylococcal infections. Infection *11*:77–83, 1983.
151. Kacica, M. A., Horgan, M. J., and Preston, K. E.: Relatedness of coagulase-negative staphylococci causing bacteremia in low-birthweight infants. Infect. Control Hosp. Epidemiol. *15*:658–662, 1994.

152. Kahn, M. Y., and Hall, W. H.: Staphylococcal enterocolitis treatment with oral vancomycin. Ann. Intern. Med. *65*:1–8, 1966.
153. Kallen, P., Nies, K. M., Louie, J. S., et al.: Tropical pyomyositis. Arthritis Rheum. *25*:107–110, 1982.
154. Kanoff, A., Epstein, B., and Kromes, B.: Staphylococcal pneumonia and empyema. Pediatrics *11*:385–391, 1953.
155. Kaplan, E. K., Laxdal, T., and Quie, P. G.: Studies of polymorphonuclear leukocytes from patients with chronic granulomatous disease of childhood: Bactericidal capacity for streptococci. Pediatrics *41*:591–597, 1968.
156. Kaplan, J. E., Palmer, D. L., and Tung, K. S. K.: Teichoic acid antibody and circulating immune complexes in the management of *Staphylococcus aureus* bacteremia. Am. J. Med. *70*:769–774, 1981.
157. Kaplan, S. L., and Feigin, R. D.: Pyogenic liver abscesses in normal children with fever of unknown origin. Pediatrics *58*:614–616, 1976.
158. Karanas, Y. L., Bogdan, M. A., and Chang, J.: Community acquired methicillin-resistant *Staphylococcus aureus* hand infections: Case reports and clinical implications. J. Hand. Surg. [Am.] *25*:760–763, 2000.
159. Katayama, Y., Ito, T., and Hiramatsu, K.: A new class of genetic element, staphylococcus cassette chromosome mec, encodes methicillin resistance in *Staphylococcus aureus*. Antimicrob. Agents Chemother. *44*:1549–1555, 2000.
160. Kavey, R. E., Frank, D. M., Byrum, C. J., et al.: Two-dimensional echocardiographic assessment of infective endocarditis in children. Pediatr. Cardiol. *3*:349, 1982.
161. Keelen, W. C., and Stoltz, C. R.: An unusual epidemic of neonatal mastitis. Am. J. Obstet. Gynecol. *59*:642–647, 1950.
162. Khan, A. J., Evans, H. E., Bombeck, E., et al.: Coagulase-negative staphylococcal bacteriuria: A rarity in infants and children. J. Pediatr. *86*:309–313, 1975.
163. Khan, E. J., Correa, A. G., and Baker, C. J.: Suppurative thrombophlebitis in children: A ten-year experience. Pediatr. Infect. Dis. J. *16*:63–67, 1997.
164. Klainer, L. M., Agrawal, H. S., Mortimer, E. A., et al.: Bacitracin ointment and neonatal staphylococci. Am. J. Dis. Child. *103*:72–76, 1962.
165. Klimek, J. J., Marsik, F. J., Bartlett, R. C., et al.: Clinical, epidemiologic and bacteriologic observations of an outbreak of methicillin-resistant *Staphylococcus aureus* at a large community hospital. Am. J. Med. *61*:340–345, 1976.
166. Knudsen, C. J. M., and Hoffman, E. B.: Neonatal osteomyelitis. J. Bone Joint Surg. Br. *72*:846–851, 1990.
167. Koch, R., Carson, M. J., and Donnell, G.: Staphylococcal pneumonia in children: A review of 83 cases. J. Pediatr. *55*:473–480, 1959.
168. Lacey, R. W.: Genetic basis: Epidemiology and future significance of antibiotic resistance in *Staphylococcus aureus:* A review. J. Clin. Pathol. *26*:899–913, 1973.
169. La Leche League International: The Womanly Art of Breastfeeding. 2nd ed. Franklin Park, 1963.
170. Latham, R. H., Running, K., and Stamm, W. E.: Urinary tract infections in young adult women caused by *Staphylococcus saprophyticus*. J. A. M. A. *250*:3063–3066, 1983.
171. Lavine, D., Hurst, V., Grossman, M., et al.: *Staphylococcus* of a newly recognized bacteriophage type: Report of a hospital outbreak. J. A. M. A. *192*:935–938, 1965.
172. Laxdal, T., Melsner, R. P., Williams, R. G., et al.: Opsonic agglutinating and complement-fixing antibodies in patients with subacute bacterial endocarditis. J. Lab. Clin. Med. *71*:638–653, 1968.
173. Layton, M. C., Hierholzer, W. J., and Patterson, J.: The evolving epidemiology of methicillin-resistant *Staphylococcus aureus* at a university hospital. Infect. Control Hosp. Epidemiol. *16*:12–17, 1995.
174. Leclercq, R., and Courvalin, P.: Bacterial resistance to macrolide, lincosamide, and streptogramin antibiotics by target modification. Antimicrob. Agents Chemother. *35*:1267–1272, 1991.
175. Lee, C. T., and Lewin, E. B.: Teichoic acid serology in various staphylococcal coagulase-positive infections in infants and children. Pediatr. Res. *11*:502–507, 1977.
176. Leung, D. Y., Meissner, H. C., Fulton, D. R., et al.: Toxic shock syndrome toxin–secreting *Staphylococcus aureus* in Kawasaki syndrome. Lancet *342*:1385–1388, 1993.
177. Levin, M. J., Gardner, P., and Waldvogel, F. A.: Tropical pyomyositis: An unusual infection due to *Staphylococcus aureus*. N. Engl. J. Med. *284*:196–198, 1971.
178. Levine, D. P., Cushing, R. D., Jui, J., and Brown, W. J.: Community-acquired methicillin-resistant *Staphylococcus aureus* endocarditis in the Detroit Medical Center. Ann. Intern. Med. *97*:330–338, 1982.
179. Lillibridge, C. B., Melish, M. E., and Glasgow, L. A.: Site of action of exfoliative toxin in the staphylococcal scalded-skin syndrome. Pediatrics *50*:728–738, 1972.
180. Lindblade, B., Ekingren, K., and Aurelius, G.: The prognosis of acute hematogenous osteomyelitis and its complications during early infancy after the advent of antibiotics. Acta Paediatr. Scand. *54*:24–32, 1965.
181. Lindenmayer, J. M., Schoenfeld, S., O'Grady, R., and Carney, J. K.: Methicillin-resistant *Staphylococcus aureus* in a high school wrestling team and the surrounding community. Arch. Intern. Med. *158*:895–899, 1998.
182. Liston, S. L., Gehrz, R. C., Siegel, L. G., et al.: Bacterial tracheitis. Am. J. Dis. Child. *137*:764–767, 1983.
183. Locksley, R. M., Mitchell, L. C., Quinn, T. C., et al.: Multiply antibiotic-resistant *Staphylococcus aureus:* Introduction, transmission, and evolution of nosocomial infection. Ann. Intern. Med. *97*:317–324, 1982.
184. Lowder, J. N., Lazarus, H. M., and Herzig, R. H.: Bacteremias and fungemias in oncologic patients with central venous catheters: Changing spectrum of infection. Arch. Intern. Med. *142*:1456–1459, 1982.
185. Lowenbraun, S., Young, V., and Kenton, D.: Infection from venous scalp vein needles in a susceptible population. J. A. M. A. *212*:451–453, 1970.
186. Lowney, E. D., Baublis, J. V., Kreye, G. M., et al.: The scalded skin syndrome in small children. Arch. Dermatol. *75*:359–369, 1967.
187. Lyell, A.: A review of toxic epidermal necrolysis in Britain. Br. J. Dermatol. *9*:661–669, 1967.
188. Lynch, P., Cummings, M. J., Herriott, M. J., et al.: Implementing and evaluating a system of generic infection control precautions: Body substance isolation. Am. J. Infect. Control *18*:1–12, 1990.
189. Ma, X. X., Ito, T., Tiensasittorn, C., et al.: Novel type of staphylococcal cassette chromosome *mec* identified in community-acquired methicillin-resistant strains. Antimicrob. Agents Chemother. *46*:1147–1152, 2002.
190. Maddox, J. L., Riordan, T. P., and Odom, R. B.: Pyomyositis in a neonate. J. Am. Acad. Dermatol. *10*:391–394, 1984.
191. Maki, D. G.: Nosocomial bacteremia: An epidemiologic overview. Am. J. Med. *70*:719–732, 1981.
192. Maki, D. G., Goldman, D. A., and Rhame, F. S.: Infection control of intravenous therapy. Ann. Intern. Med. *79*:867–889, 1973.
193. Malam, J. E., Carrick, G. F., Telford, D. R., et al.: Staphylococcal toxins and sudden infant death syndrome. J. Clin. Pathol. *45*:716–721, 1992.
194. March, A. W., Riley, L. H., and Robinson, R. A.: Retroperitoneal abscess and septic arthritis of the hip in children. J. Bone Joint Surg. Am. *54*:67–74, 1972.
195. Margileth, A. M.: Scalded skin syndrome: Diagnosis, differential diagnosis and management of 42 children. South. Med. J. *68*:447–452, 1975.
196. Marples, R. R., and Wieneke, A. A.: Enterotoxins and toxic-shock syndrome toxin-1 in non-enteric staphylococcal disease. Epidemiol. Infect. *110*:477–488, 1993.
197. Matthews, P., and Tomasz, A.: Insertional inactivation of the *mec* gene in a transopson mutant of a methicillin-resistant clinical isolate of *Staphylococcus aureus*. Antimicrob. Agents Chemother. *34*:1777–1779, 1990.
198. Mazur, J. M., Ross, G., Cummings, R. J., et al.: Usefulness of magnetic resonance imaging for the diagnosis of acute musculoskeletal infections in children. J. Pediatr. Orthop. *15*:144–147, 1995.
199. McCracken, G.: Commentary. J. Pediatr. *84*:882–883, 1974.
200. McGehee, R. F., Barrett, F. F., and Finland, M.: Resistance of *Staphylococcus aureus* to lincomycin, clindamycin, and erythromycin. Antimicrob. Agents Chemother. *8*:392–397, 1968.
201. McGowan, J. E.: The impact of changing pathogens of serious infections in hospitalized patients. Clin. Infect. Dis. *31*(Suppl.l):124–130, 2000.
202. McPhail, L. C., DeChatelet, L. R., Shirley, P. S., et al.: Deficiency of NADPH oxidase activity in chronic granulomatous disease. J. Pediatr. *90*:213–217, 1977.
203. Melish, M. E.: Bullous varicella: Its association with the staphylococcal scalded skin syndrome. J. Pediatr. *82*:1010–1021, 1973.
204. Melish, M. E., Bertrando, R., and Gluck, L.: Unpublished observations. 1975.
205. Melish, M. E., Frogner, K. S., Hirata, S. A., et al.: Pathogenesis of toxic shock syndrome. Abstract. Pediatr. Res. *19*:301, 1985.
206. Melish, M. E., and Glasgow, L. A.: The staphylococcal scalded skin syndrome: Development of an experimental model. N. Engl. J. Med. *282*:1114–1119, 1970.
207. Melish, M. E., and Glasgow, L. A.: The staphylococcal scalded skin syndrome: The expanded clinical syndrome. J. Pediatr. *78*:959–965, 1971.
208. Melish, M. E., Glasgow, L. A., and Turner, M. E.: The staphylococcal scalded skin syndrome: Isolation and partial characterization of the exfoliative toxin. J. Infect. Dis. *125*:129–140, 1972.
209. Melish, M. E., Parsonett, J., and Marchette, N.: Kawasaki syndrome is not caused by toxic shock syndrome-1 staphylococci. Abstract. Pediatr. Res. *35*:187, 1994.
210. Melley, M. A., Throison, J. B., and Rogus, D. E.: Fate of staphylococci with human leukocytes. J. Exp. Med. *112*:1121–1130, 1974.
211. Meugnier, H., Fernandez, M. P., Bes, M., et al.: rRNA gene restriction patterns as an epidemiological marker in nosocomial outbreaks of *Staphylococcus aureus* infections. Res. Microbiol. *144*:25–33, 1993.
212. Mickenberg, I. D., Root, R. K., and Wolf, S. M.: Leukocyte function in hypergammaglobulinemia. J. Clin. Invest. *49*:1529–1538, 1970.
213. Miller, M. E., and Nilsson, U. R.: A familial deficiency in the phagocytosis enhancing activity of serum related to a dysfunction of the 5th component of complement (C5). N. Engl. J. Med. *282*:354–358, 1970.
214. Miller, M. E., Oski, F. A., and Harris, M. B.: Lazy leukocyte syndrome. Lancet *1*:665–669, 1971.

215. Misko, M. L., Terracina, J. R., and Divin, D. G.: The frequency of erythromycin-resistant *Staphylococcus aureus* in impetiginized dermatoses. Pediatr. Dermatol. *12*:12–15, 1995.
216. Moreno, F., Crisp, C., Jorgensen, J. H., and Patterson, J. E.: Methicillin-resistant *Staphylococcus aureus* as a community organism. Clin. Infect. Dis. *21*:1308–1312, 1995.
217. Muder, R., Brennen, C., Wagener, M. M., et al.: Methicillin-resistant staphylococcal colonization and infection in a long-term care facility. Ann. Intern. Med. *114*:107–112, 1991.
218. Muggae, A., Daniel, W. G., Frank, G., et al.: Echocardiography in infective endocarditis: Reassessment of prognostic implications of vegetation size determined by the transthoracic and transesophageal approach. J. Am. Coll. Cardiol. *14*:631–638, 1989.
219. Naimi, T. S., LeDell, K. H., Boxrud, D. J., et al.: Epidemiology and clonality of community acquired methicillin-resistant *Staphylococcus aureus* in Minnesota, 1996–1998. Clin. Infect. Dis. *33*:990–996, 2001.
220. Naraqi, S., and McDonnell, G.: Hematogenous staphylococcal pneumonia secondary to soft tissue infection. Chest *79*:173–175, 1981.
221. Nataro, J. P., Corcoran, L., Zirin, S., et al.: Prospective analysis of coagulase-negative staphylococcal infection in hospitalized infants. J. Pediatr. *125*:798–804, 1994.
222. Nelson, J. D.: Antibiotic concentrations in septic joint effusion. N. Engl. J. Med. *285*:178–181, 1971.
223. Nelson, J. D.: The bacterial etiology and antibiotic management of septic arthritis in infants and children. Pediatrics *50*:437–441, 1972.
224. Nelson, J. D., and Koontz, W. B.: Septic arthritis in infants and children: A review of 117 cases. Pediatrics *38*:967–971, 1966.
225. Nilsson, E. J., Henning, C. G., and Magnusson, J.: Topical corticosteroids and *Staphylococcus aureus* in atopic dermatitis. J. Am. Acad. Dermatol. *27*:29–34, 1992.
226. Noel, G. J., Kreiswirth, B. N., Edelson, P. J., et al.: Multiple methicillin-resistant *Staphylococcus aureus* strains as a cause for a single outbreak of severe disease in hospitalized neonates. Pediatr. Infect. Dis. J. *11*:184–188, 1992.
227. Normand, J., Bozio, A., Etienne, J., et al.: Changing patterns and prognosis of infective endocarditis in childhood. Eur. Heart J. *16*(Suppl. B):28–31, 1995.
228. Nowel, G. J., and Edelson, P. J.: *Staphylococcus epidermidis* bacteremia in neonates: Further observations and the occurrence of focal infection. Pediatrics *74*:832–837, 1984.
229. Nusem-Horowitz, S., Wolf, M., Coret, A., et al.: Acute suppurative parotitis and parotid abscess in children. Int. J. Pediatr. Otorhinolaryngol. *32*:123–127, 1995.
230. Okoji, C. N., Inglis, B., and Stewart, P. R.: Potential problems in the use of oligonucleotide probes for staphylococcal enterotoxin genes. J. Appl. Bacteriol. *74*:637–644, 1993.
231. Okoroma, E. O., Perry, L. W., and Scott, L. P.: Acute bacterial pericarditis in children: Report of 25 cases. Am. Heart J. *90*:709–713, 1975.
232. O'Toole, R. D., Drew, W. L., and Dahygren, B. J.: An outbreak of methicillin-resistant *Staphylococcus aureus* infection. J. A. M. A. *213*:257–263, 1970.
233. Overturf, G. D., Sherman, M. P., Scheifele, D. W., et al.: Neonatal necrotizing enterocolitis associated with delta toxin-producing methicillin-resistant *Staphylococcus aureus*. Pediatr. Infect. Dis. J. *9*:88–91, 1990.
234. Panagea, S., Perry, J. D., and Gould, F. K.: Should clindamycin be used as treatment of patients with infections caused by erythromycin-resistant staphylococci? J. Antimicrob. Chemother. *44*:581–582, 1999.
235. Panton, P. N., and Valentine, F. C. O.: Staphylococcal toxins. Lancet *1*:506–510, 1932.
236. Parker, M. T., and Hewitt, J. H.: Methicillin resistance in *Staphylococcus aureus*. Lancet *1*:800–804, 1970.
237. Parres, F., Bouza, E., Romero, J., et al.: Infectious endocarditis in children. Pediatr. Cardiol. *11*:77–81, 1990.
238. Pederson, W. R., Walker, M., Olson, J. D., et al.: Value of transesophageal echocardiography as an adjunct to transthoracic echocardiography in the evaluation of native and prosthetic valve endocarditis. Chest *100*:351–356, 1991.
239. Peltola, H., Unkila-Kallio, L., and Kallio, M. J.: Simplified treatment of acute staphylococcal osteomyelitis of childhood. The Finnish study group. Pediatrics *99*:883–884, 1997.
240. Perlman, B. B., and Freedman, L. R.: Experimental endocarditis. III. Natural history of catheter-induced staphylococcal endocarditis following catheter removal. Yale J. Biol. Med. *44*:214–224, 1971.
241. Peter, G., Lloyd-Still, J. D., and Lovejoy, F. H.: Local infection and bacteremia from scalp vein needles and polyethylene catheters in children. J. Pediatr. *80*:78–83, 1972.
242. Peters, G., Locci, R., and Pulverer, G.: Adherence and growth of coagulase-negative staphylococci on the surface of intravenous catheters. J. Infect. Dis. *146*:479–482, 1982.
243. Peterson, P. K., Quie, P. G., Kim, Y., et al.: Recognition of *Staphylococcus aureus* by human phagocytes: Signals and disguises of the bacterial surface. Scand. J. Infect. Dis. *41*(Suppl.):67–78, 1983.
244. Pildes, R. S., Ramamurthy, R. S., and Vidyasagar, D.: Effect of triple dye on staphylococcal colonization of newborn infants. J. Pediatr. *82*:987–990, 1973.
245. Pleuckhahn, V. D.: Hexachlorophene and the control of staphylococcal sepsis in a maternity unit in Geelong, Australia. Pediatrics *51*(Suppl.):368–372, 1973.
246. Price, C. D., Hameroff, S. B., and Richards, R. D.: Cavernous sinus thrombosis and orbital cellulitis. South. Med. J. *64*:1243–1247, 1971.
247. Pryles, C. V.: Staphylococcal pneumonia in infancy and childhood. Pediatrics *21*:609–623, 1958.
248. Pung, Y. H., Vetro, S. W., and Bellanti, J. A.: Use of interferons in atopic (IgE-mediated) diseases. Ann. Allergy *71*:234–238, 1993.
249. Quie, P. G.: Chronic granulomatous disease in childhood. Adv. Pediatr. *16*:287–300, 1969.
250. Raimondi, A. J., Robinson, J. S., and Kuwamura, K.: Complications of ventriculoperitoneal shunting and a critical comparison of the three-piece system and one-piece systems. Childs Brain *3*:321–342, 1977.
251. Rathore, M. B., and Kline, M. W.: Community-acquired methicillin-resistant *Staphylococcus aureus* infections in children. Pediatr. Infect. Dis. J. *8*:645–647, 1989.
252. Raucher, H. S., Hyatt, A. C., Barzilai, A., et al.: Quantitative blood cultures in the evaluation of septicemia in children with Broviac catheters. J. Pediatr. *104*:29–33, 1984.
253. Reagan, D. R., Doebbling, B. N., Pfaller, M. A., et al.: Elimination of coincident *Staphylococcus aureus* nasal and hand carriage with contranasal application of mupirocin calcium ointment. Ann. Intern. Med. *114*:101–106, 1991.
254. Rebhan, A. W., and Edwards, H. E.: Staphylococcal pneumonia: A review of 329 cases. Can. Med. Assoc. J. *82*:513–517, 1960.
255. Recommendation: ICSB Subcommittee on Taxonomy of Staphylococcal Micrococci. Zentralbl. Bakteriol. (Naturwissenschaft) *5*(Suppl.):129–133, 1976.
256. Riley, P. M.: Staphylococcal empyema in infants and children. J. Pediatr. *24*:577–581, 1944.
257. Rosenfeld, C. R., Laptook, A. R., and Jeffrey, J.: Limited effectiveness of triple dye in preventing colonization with methicillin: Resistant *Staphylococcus aureus* in a special care nursery. Pediatr. Infect. Dis. J. *9*:290–291, 1990.
258. Roy, D. R.: Osteomyelitis. Pediatr. Rev. *16*:380–384, 1995.
259. Rudolph, R. I., Schwartz, W., and Leyden, J. J.: Treatment of staphylococcal toxic epidermal necrolysis. Arch. Dermatol. *110*:559–562, 1974.
260. Rudoy, R. C., and Nelson, T. D.: Breast abscess in the neonatal period. Am. J. Dis. Child. *129*:1031–1034, 1975.
261. Ruley, E. J., and Lisi, L. M.: Interstitial nephritis and renal failure due to ampicillin. J. Pediatr. *84*:878–881, 1974.
262. Sanjad, S. A., Hadded, G. G., and Nassar, V. H.: Nephropathy, an underestimated complication of methicillin therapy. J. Pediatr. *84*:873–875, 1974.
263. Santos, F., Mankarious, L. A., and Eavey, R. D.: Methicillin-resistant *Staphylococcus aureus*: Pediatric otitis. Arch. Otolaryngol. Head Neck Surg. *126*:1383–1385, 2000.
264. Saravolatz, L. D., Markowitz, N., Arking, L., et al.: Methicillin-resistant *Staphylococcus aureus*. Epidemiologic observations during a community-acquired outbreak. Ann. Intern. Med. *96*:11–16, 1982.
265. Saravoltz, L. D., Pohlod, D. J., and Arking, L. M.: Community-acquired methicillin-resistant *Staphylococcus aureus* infections: A new source for nosocomial outbreaks. Ann. Intern. Med. *97*:325–329, 1982.
266. Sarff, L. D., and McCracken, G. H.: Methicillin-associated nephropathy or cystitis. J. Pediatr. *90*:1031–1032, 1977.
267. Sarff, L. D., McCracken, G. H., Thomas, M. L., et al.: Clinical pharmacology of methicillin in neonates. J. Pediatr. *90*:1005–1008, 1977.
268. Schmidt, B. K., Kirpalani, H. M., Corey, M., et al.: Coagulase-negative staphylococci as true pathogens in newborn infants: A cohort study. Pediatr. Infect. Dis. *6*:1026–1031, 1987.
269. Schopfer, K., Baerlocker, K., Price, P., et al.: Staphylococcal IgE antibodies, hyperimmunoglobulinemia E and *Staphylococcus aureus* infections. N. Engl. J. Med. *300*:835–838, 1979.
270. Scobie, W.: Acute cervical adenitis in children. Scott. Med. J. *14*:352–355, 1969.
271. Segal, A. W., and Peters, T. J.: Characterization of the enzyme defect in chronic granulomatous disease. Lancet *1*:1363–1365, 1976.
272. Shapiro, E. D., Wald, E. R., Nelson, J. A., et al.: Broviac catheter–related bacteremia in oncology patients. Am. J. Dis. Child. *136*:679–681, 1982.
273. Shepherd, J. J.: Tropical myositis: Is it an entity and what is its cause? Lancet *2*:1240–1242, 1983.
274. Shinefeld, H. R.: Staphylococcal infections. *In* Remington, J., and Klein, J. O. (eds.): Infectious Diseases of the Fetus and Newborn Infant. New York, Harper & Row, 1977.
275. Shinefeld, H. R., Ribble, J. C., Boris, M., et al.: Bacterial interference: Its effect on nursery-acquired infection with *Staphylococcus aureus*. IV. Am. J. Dis. Child. *105*:683–688, 1963.
276a. Shopsin, B., Mathema, B., Martinez, J., et al.: Prevalence of methicillin-resistant and methicillin-susceptible *Staphylococcus aureus* in the community. J. Infect. Dis. *182*:359–362, 2000.

277. Siegel, J. D., Cushion, N. B., Roy, L. C., and Krisher, K. K.: Community-acquired methicillin-resistant *Staphylococcus aureus* infections in children. Abstract No. 597. Presented at the Infectious Diseases Society of America Annual Meeting, 1999, Philadelphia.
278. Smith, T. L., Pearson, M. L., Wilcox, K. R., et al.: Emergence of vancomycin resistance in *Staphylococcus aureus*. Glycopeptide-Intermediate *Staphylococcus aureus* Working Group. N. Engl. J. Med. *340*:493–501, 1999.
279. Snyderman, R., and Pike, M. C.: Disorders of leukocyte chemotaxis. Pediatr. Clin. North Am. *24*:377–393, 1977.
280. Soderquist, B., Sundquist, K., and Vikerfors, T.: Kinetics of serum levels of interleukin-6 in *Staphylococcus aureus* septicemia. Scand. J. Infect. Dis. *24*:607–612, 1992.
281. Sofer, S., Duncan, P., and Cuernick, V.: Bacterial tracheitis: An old disease rediscovered. Clin. Pediatr. (Phila.) *22*:407–411, 1983.
282. Sprunt, K., Redman, W., and Leidy, G.: Antibacterial effectiveness of routine hand washing. Pediatrics *52*:264–271, 1973.
283. Stalder, J. F., Fleury, M., Sourisse, M., et al.: Local steroid therapy and bacterial skin flora in atopic dermatitis. Br. J. Dermatol. *131*:536–540, 1994.
284. Steel, R. W., Ashcraft, E. W., Payton, T. S., et al.: Recurrent staphylococcal infection in a pediatric residential care facility. Am. J. Infect. Control *11*:217–220, 1983.
285. Stein, J. M., and Pruitt, B. A.: Suppurative thrombophlebitis: A lethal iatrogenic disease. N. Engl. J. Med. *282*:1452–1455, 1970.
286. Stether, H., Martin, E., and Plotkin, H.: Neonatal mastitis due to *Escherichia coli*. J. Pediatr. *76*:611–613, 1970.
287. Stewart, G. P., and Holt, R. J.: Evolution of natural resistance to the new penicillins. Br. J. Med. *1*:309–311, 1962.
288. St. Geme, J. W., III, Bell, L. M., Baumgart, S., et al.: Distinguishing sepsis from blood culture contamination in young infants with blood cultures growing coagulase-negative staphylococci. Pediatrics *86*: 157–162, 1990.
289. Stone, D. B., and Bonfigli, M. L.: Pyogenic vertebral osteomyelitis: A diagnostic pitfall for the internist. Arch. Intern. Med. *112*:491–500, 1963.
290. Storch, G., and Rajogopalan, L.: Methicillin-resistant *Staphylococcus aureus* bacteremia in children. Pediatr. Infect. Dis. *5*:59–67, 1986.
291. Strausbaugh, L. J., Jacobson, C., Sewell, D. L., et al.: Methicillin-resistant *Staphylococcus aureus* in extended care facilities: Experiences in a Veterans Affairs nursing home and a review of the literature. Infect. Control. Hosp. Epidemiol. *12*:36–45, 1991.
292. Subramaniam, R., Joseph, V. T., Tan, G. M., et al.: Experience with video-assisted thoracoscopic surgery in the management of complicated pneumonia in children. J. Pediatr. Surg. *36*:316–319, 2001.
293. Suganuma, A.: Fine structure of staphylococci: Electron microscopy in the staphylococci. *In* Cohen, J. O. (ed.): The Staphylococci. New York, Wiley-Interscience, 1972, pp. 21–40.
294. Suntharam, N., Hacek, D., and Peterson, L. R.: Low prevalence of community-acquired methicillin-resistant *Staphylococcus aureus* in adults at a university hospital in the central United States. J. Clin. Microbiol. *39*:1669–1671, 2001.
295. Taplin, D., Lansdell, L., and Allen, A. M.: Prevalence of streptococcal pyoderma in relation to climate and hygiene. Lancet *1*:501–503, 1973.
296. Taylor, A. G., Cook, J., Finclan, W. J., et al.: Serologic tests in the differentiation of staphylococcal and tuberculous bone disease. J. Clin. Pathol. *28*:284–288, 1975.
297. Terai, M., Miwa, K., Williams, T., et al.: The absence of evidence of staphylococcal toxin involvement in the pathogenesis of Kawasaki disease. J. Infect. Dis. *172*:558–561, 1995.
298. Thatai, D., Chandy, L., and Dhar, K. L.: Septic cavernous sinus thrombophlebitis: A review of 35 cases. J. Indian Med. Assoc. *90*:290–292, 1992.
299. Thekekara, A. G., Denham, B., and Duff, D. F.: Eleven-year review of infective endocarditis. Ir. Med. J. *87*:80–82, 1994.
300. Thisyakorn, U. S. A., Shelton, S., Tzou-Yien, L., et al.: Detection of teichoic acid antibodies in children with staphylococcal infections. Pediatr. Infect. Dis. *3*:222–225, 1984.
301. Thompson, R. L.: Staphylococcal infective endocarditis. Mayo Clin. Proc. *57*:106–114, 1982.
302. Thompson, R. L., Cabezudo, I., and Wenzel, R. P.: Epidemiology of nosocomial infections caused by methicillin-resistant *Staphylococcus aureus*. Ann. Intern. Med. *97*:309–317, 1982.
303. Todd, J., and Fishaut, M.: Toxic-shock syndrome associated with phage-group-I staphylococci. Lancet *2*:1116–1118, 1978.
304. Tojo, M., Yamashita, N., Goldmann, D. A., et al.: Isolation and characterization of a capsular polysaccharide adhesion from *Staphylococcus epidermidis*. J. Infect. Dis. *157*:713–722, 1988.
305. Treves, S., Khethy, J., Broker, R. H., et al.: Osteomyelitis: Early scintigraphic detection in children. Pediatrics *57*:173–186, 1976.
306. Trueta, J.: The three types of acute hematogenous osteomyelitis: A clinical and vascular study. J. Bone Joint Surg. Br. *41*:671–680, 1959.
307. Tuazon, C. U.: Teichoic acid antibodies in osteomyelitis and septic arthritis caused by *Staphylococcus aureus*. J. Bone Joint Surg. Am. *64*:762–765, 1982.
308. Tuazon, C. U., and Sheagren, J. M.: Teichoic acid antibodies in the diagnosis of serious infections with *Staphylococcus aureus*. Ann. Intern. Med. *84*:543–546, 1976.
309. Tuft, S. J., Ramakrishnan, M., Seal, D. V., et al.: Role of *Staphylococcus aureus* in chronic allergic conjunctivitis. Ophthalmology *99*:180–184, 1992.
310. Turner, J. A. P.: Staphylococcal pneumonia: A contemporary rarity. Clin. Pediatr. (Phila.) *11*:69–71, 1972.
311. Ukhila-Kallio, L., Kallio, M. J., Eskola, J., et al.: Serum C-reactive protein, erythrocyte sedimentation rate, and white blood cell count in acute hematogenous osteomyelitis of children. Pediatrics *93*:59–62, 1994.
312. Utsui, Y., and Yokota, T.: Role of an altered penicillin-binding protein in methicillin- and cephem-resistant *Staphylococcus aureus*. Antimicrob. Agents Chemother. *28*:397–403, 1985.
313. Van Hare, G. F., Ben-Shachar, G., Liebman, J., et al.: Infective endocarditis in infants and children during the past 10 years: A decade of change. Am. Heart J. *107*:1235–1240, 1984.
314. Van Reken, D., Strauss, A., Hernandez, A., et al.: Infectious pericarditis in children. J. Pediatr. *85*:165–169, 1974.
315. Verbrugh, H. A., Peters, R., Rozenberg-Arska, M., et al.: Antibodies to cell wall peptidoglycan of *Staphylococcus aureus* in patients with serious staphylococcal infections. J. Infect. Dis. *144*:1–9, 1981.
316. Vinnick, L., Cooper, E. B., and Overholt, L. L.: Cavernous sinus thrombosis. Arch. Otolaryngol. *82*:303–306, 1975.
317. Wald, E. R., Levine, M. M., and Togo, Y.: Concomitant varicella and staphylococcal scalded skin syndrome. J. Pediatr. *83*:1011–1019, 1973.
318. Waldman, I. S.: Medical Mycology. Philadelphia, W. B. Saunders, 1974.
319. Waldvogel, F. A., Medoff, G., and Swartz, M. V.: Osteomyelitis: A review of clinical features, therapeutic considerations and unusual aspects. N. Engl. J. Med. *282*:206, 260–266, 316–322, 1970.
320. Walsh, T. J., Standiford, H. C., Reboli, A. C., et al.: Randomized double-blinded trial of rifampin with either novobiocin or trimethoprim-sulfamethoxazole against methicillin-resistant *Staphylococcus aureus* colonization: Prevention of antimicrobial resistance and effect of host factors on outcome. Antimicrob. Agents Chemother. *37*:1334–1342, 1993.
321. Wang, E. E., Prober, C. G., Ford-Jones, L., et al.: The management of central intravenous catheter infections. Pediatr. Infect. Dis. *3*:110–113, 1984.
322. Warshawsky, B., Hussain, Z., Gregson, D. B., et al.: Hospital- and community-based surveillance of methicillin-resistant *Staphylococcus aureus:* Previous hospitalization is the major risk factor. Infect. Control Hosp. Epidemiol. *21*:724–727, 2000.
323. Watanakunakorn, C.: Clindamycin therapy of *Staphylococcus aureus* endocarditis. Clinical relapse and development of resistance to clindamycin, lincomycin, and erythromycin. Am. J. Med. *60*:419–425, 1976.
324. Watanakunakorn, C.: Changing epidemiology of infective endocarditis. Adv. Intern. Med. *22*:21–29, 1977.
325. Watanakunakorn, C.: Treatment of infections due to methicillin-resistant *Staphylococcus aureus*. Ann. Intern. Med. *97*:376–378, 1982.
326. Watanakunakorn, C.: *Staphylococcus aureus* endocarditis at a community teaching hospital, 1980–1991. Arch. Intern. Med. *154*: 2330–2335, 1994.
327. Watters, E. C., Wallar, P. H., Hiles, D. A., et al.: Acute orbital cellulitis. Arch. Ophthalmol. *94*:785–788, 1976.
328. Webster, J., and Faogali, S. L.: Endemic methicillin-resistant *Staphylococcus aureus* in a special care baby unit: A 2-year review. J. Pediatr. Child Health *26*:160–163, 1990.
329. Weissberg, E. D., Smith, A. L., and Smith, D. H.: Clinical features of neonatal osteomyelitis. Pediatrics *53*:505–510, 1974.
330. Wheat, L. J., Wilkinson, B. J., Kohler, R. B., et al.: Antibody response to peptidoglycan during staphylococcal infections. J. Infect. Dis. *147*:16–22, 1983.
331. Williams, C. P. S., and Oliver, T. K. P.: Nursery routines and staphylococcal colonization of the newborn. Pediatrics *44*:640–645, 1969.
332. Williams, R. C., Dossett, J. H., and Quie, P. G.: Comparative studies of immunoglobulin opsonins in osteomyelitis and other established infections. Immunology *17*:249–265, 1969.
333. Williams, R. C., and Quie, P. G.: Opsonic activity of agammaglobulinemic human sera. J. Immunol. *106*:51–55, 1971.
334. Wiseman, G. M.: The hemolysins of *Staphylococcus aureus*. Bacteriol. Rev. *39*:317–344, 1975.
335. Wisseman, G. J., Wood, V. E., and Kroll, L. L.: *Pseudomonas* vertebral osteomyelitis in heroin addicts. J. Bone Joint Surg. Am. *55*:1416–1424, 1973.
336. Wolff, S. M., Dale, D. C., and Clark, R. A.: The Chédiak-Higashi syndrome: Studies of host defense. Ann. Intern. Med. *76*:293–306, 1972.
337. Wysham, D. N., Mulhern, M. E., Navarre, G. C., et al.: Staphylococcal infections in an obstetric unit. II. Epidemic studies of puerperal mastitis. N. Engl. J. Med. *257*:304–308, 1957.
338. Yarrington, C. T.: The prognosis and treatment of cavernous sinus thrombosis: A review of 878 cases in the literature. Ann. Otol. Rhinol. Laryngol. *70*:263–267, 1961.

339. Yogev, R., and Davis, A. T.: Neurosurgical shunt infections: A review. Childs Brain *6*:74–81, 1980.
340. Yow, M. D., Taber, L. H., Barrett, F. F., et al.: A ten-year assessment of methicillin-associated side effects. Pediatrics *58*:329–334, 1976.
341. Zafar, A. B., Butler, R. C., Reese, D. J., et al.: Use of 0.3% triclosan (Bacti-Stat) to eradicate an outbreak of methicillin-resistant *Staphylococcus aureus* in a neonatal nursery. Am. J. Infect. Control *23*:201–208, 1995.
342. Zakrzewski, T., and Keith, J. D.: Bacterial endocarditis in infants and children. J. Pediatr. *67*:1179–1181, 1965.

CHAPTER 86

Coagulase-Negative Staphylococcal Infections

CARINA A. RODRIGUEZ ■ CHRISTIAN C. PATRICK

Coagulase-negative staphylococci increasingly are implicated as causative agents of nosocomial infections and are among the bacteria most frequently isolated in the microbiology laboratory. Their normal habitat includes skin and mucous membranes of humans and animals. This ecologic niche hampers studies on this group of bacteria because they also are frequent contaminants in the clinical microbiology laboratory. Coagulase-negative staphylococci infections occur mainly in immunocompromised patients, particularly those with indwelling medical devices.[155, 174, 197, 243] New epidemiologic and molecular techniques can be useful to identify strain characteristics in nosocomial outbreaks. The pathogenesis of these organisms has advanced, with several possible virulence factors identified. The clinical spectrum of the disease is characterized by a more indolent presentation when compared with other gram-positive cocci. Removal of catheters or prosthetic devices may be necessary for persistent infections. Furthermore, effective therapy can be difficult to achieve because of the high proportion of isolates resistant to antibiotics. This chapter reviews the classification, pathogenesis, diagnosis, clinical manifestations, and treatment of infections caused by these ubiquitous organisms.

Historical Background

Staphylococcus albus was the descriptive term used to define all coagulase-negative staphylococci before 1960. This generic designation was used because so few techniques for species definition existed. Rosenbach in 1884 used the term *S. albus* for coagulase-negative staphylococci to denote the white color imparted by the colony on an agar plate, in contrast to the pathogenic *Staphylococcus aureus,* which had a yellow colony color. Although *S. albus* was considered nonpathogenic at that time, one article published in 1958 described 90 retrospective cases of coagulase-negative staphylococcal infections.[224]

In the 1960s, coagulase-negative staphylococci clearly were identified in association with infections in certain patient populations. Coagulase-negative staphylococci were implicated as the etiologic agent of infections in patients with atrioventricular shunts and peritoneal catheters and in neonatal sepsis.[30, 32, 130, 146, 209]

During the 1960s, *Staphylococcus saprophyticus* was recognized as a singular species and found to be a pathogen in urinary tract infections. Additionally, *Staphylococcus epidermidis* supplanted *S. albus* as a generic term for all coagulase-negative staphylococci other than *S. saprophyticus.* The association of disease with coagulase-negative staphylococci highlighted the need for further specification. Work in the 1970s focused on coagulase-negative staphylococci biotyping (differentiation based on biochemical reactions), and this work continues. Currently, 29 species of coagulase-negative staphylococci are recognized. Now that individual species can be identified, *S. epidermidis* is used as a specific species term and not as a generic term, which has prompted the use of *S. epidermidis sensu stricto* to provide a distinction for a specific species. In this chapter, *S. epidermidis* is synonymous with *S. epidermidis sensu stricto.*

Microbiology

Staphylococci are nonmotile, non–spore-forming, gram-positive bacteria that until recently were classified together with the genera *Stomatococcus* and *Planococcus* in the family Micrococcaceae.[124] Results of DNA-based composition, DNA-rRNA hybridization, and comparative oligonucleotide studies have indicated that staphylococci and micrococci are not closely related.[124] The genus *Staphylococcus* is related most closely to the newly described genus *Macrococcus,* and it has a relatively close relationship to the genera *Bacillus, Salinicoccus, Gamella, Listeria, Planococcus,* and *Brochothrix.*[122] Members of the genus *Staphylococcus* have a low DNA G + C content (30 to 39 mol %), whereas members of the genus *Micrococcus* have a G + C content within the range of 66 to 75 mol percent.[124] Staphylococci can be divided by the ability to produce or not produce coagulase, an extracellular enzyme that promotes the congealing of rabbit plasma. The thermonuclease reaction is particularly useful for rapidly differentiating *S. aureus* (positive) from other staphylococcal species (negative) and is more accurate than are tests based on coagulase production.[100] *S. aureus* also can be differentiated from most coagulase-negative staphylococci by the fermentation of mannitol. Currently, 32 species of staphylococci are recognized, 29 being coagulase-negative staphylococci, and are identified by the following criteria: (1) colony morphology, (2) oxygen requirements, (3) novobiocin resistance, (4) aerobic acid production from carbohydrates, and (5) selected liability to enzymatic activities.[122, 124] Susceptibility to novobiocin is a convenient assay to differentiate *S. saprophyticus* from most coagulase-negative staphylococci from human specimens, including *S. epidermidis. S. saprophyticus,* the uncommon pathogen *Staphylococcus cohnii,* and the rare pathogen *Staphylococcus xylosus* are novobiocin resistant.[182] One should be warned that commercial kits used to identify species of coagulase-negative staphylococci have various degrees of confidence: an identification is made 60 to 95 percent of the time, depending on the species. Most systems are developed to identify especially *S. epidermidis* and *S. saprophyticus* because these are the species clearly associated with clinical diseases.[185] Additionally, DNA-pairing studies have identified intraspecies differences with strains considered to be *S. epidermidis* by biotyping.[258]

Coagulase-negative staphylococci are prototypic gram-positive bacteria. The outermost structure is a cell wall composed primarily of peptidoglycan with teichoic acid molecules and an assortment of interspersed proteins. The teichoic acid has a glycerol backbone, compared with the ribitol of *S. aureus*.[163] Approximately 20 to 30 proteins are located within the cell wall; 15 to 20 of these are surface exposed and thus able to interact with the host.[176]

S. epidermidis and other coagulase-negative staphylococci produce a capsule that appears to be a virulence factor in animal models.[104, 164, 254] However, its presence has been demonstrated in only 9 percent of fresh clinical isolates.[103] A glycocalyx or slime-layer substance is produced by most strains of *S. epidermidis*. This substance is considered a virulence factor that inhibits phagocytosis.[40, 42, 51, 52]

Epidemiology

Epidemiologic studies involving strain delineation of coagulase-negative staphylococci have proved difficult to perform because of the organism's commensal nature on the human body. *S. epidermidis* is the prominent species, accounting for 60 to 90 percent of all staphylococci recovered from humans. The ecologic niches of coagulase-negative staphylococci have allowed a classification, as shown in Table 86–1.

Coagulase-negative staphylococci, except for *S. saprophyticus*, primarily cause nosocomial infections. Antibiotic resistance of coagulase-negative staphylococci is a common occurrence because of selective antibiotic use in the hospital setting. In 1997, the National Nosocomial Infections Surveillance Report noted an 87 percent increase in the rate of oxacillin resistance among coagulase-negative staphylococci isolates from patients in intensive care units when compared with the same period 5 years earlier.[36]

Coagulase-negative staphylococci gain access to the bloodstream primarily by a breakdown of skin or mucocutaneous barriers, by following a prosthetic catheter tract, or through the hub of a central venous catheter. Two studies have addressed the acquisition of *S. epidermidis* as a colonizing organism in low-birth-weight neonates.[46, 91] Both reports described rapid colonization, 75 percent of neonates being colonized by 2 weeks of age, but differed in their findings of increased slime-layer production or antibiotic-resistant organisms with increased colonization time.[46, 91] Although most infants acquire coagulase-negative staphylococci from environmental sources, including hospital personnel, a small percentage are colonized by vertical transmission.[90, 178]

Use of epidemiologic techniques is of paramount importance in coagulase-negative staphylococci infections to identify a strain causing either a common-source outbreak or repeated infections within an individual.[162, 185, 243] Techniques currently available are divided into conventional or molecular and are listed in Table 86–2. Conventional methods are fraught with poor standardization, sensitivity, and specificity. However, a combination of these techniques has been used for strain delineation. With the molecular techniques, plasmid analysis has been used most frequently because of its ease of performance and availability.[93] This latter technique is hampered by the loss or gain of plasmids. Strain typing is a useful adjuvant for determining whether several isolates from one patient or from different patients are the same or different. Typing allows accurate identification of the source, extent, and mechanism of transmission of an outbreak. Antimicrobial susceptibility testing is the method most readily available for typing using a phenotypic characteristic. Multilocus enzyme electrophoresis is another available phenotypic tool. Typing by genotype has proved highly discriminatory and effective for identifying epidemiologically related isolates.[27, 234, 243]

Pathogenesis

Several virulence factors of *S. epidermidis* have been postulated. Most studies have investigated coagulase-negative staphylococci infections involving prosthetic devices.[77] Adherence of organisms to the catheter is the initial step in pathogenesis.[41, 42, 257] Coagulase-negative staphylococci can gain access to the device by either contiguous or bacteremic spread after traversing cutaneous or mucocutaneous barriers. These bacteria may enter the bloodstream through the respiratory tract in mechanically ventilated premature infants

TABLE 86–1 ■ STAPHYLOCOCCI THAT ARE PART OF THE NORMAL FLORA, INCLUDING COMMON SITES OF HABITATION AND PATHOGENIC POTENTIAL

Species	Common Anatomic Site of Habitation	Pathogenic Potential
S. aureus	Nares	Common
S. epidermidis	Nares; axillae; skin of head, arms, and legs	Common
S. saprophyticus	Occasionally from skin	Common
S. haemolyticus	Skin of head, arms, and legs	Uncommon
S. hominis	Axillae; skin of head, arms, and legs	Uncommon
S. lugdunensis	Widely distributed on body	Uncommon
S. simulans	Occasionally from skin	Uncommon
S. cohnii	Occasionally from skin	Uncommon
S. warneri	Occasionally from skin	Uncommon
S. saccharolyticus	Rarely from skin	Uncommon
S. caprae	Occasionally from skin	Rare
S. capitis	Skin of head, face, ears, and arms	Rare
S. auricularis	Ears	Rare
S. schleiferi	? Skin	Rare
S. xylosus	Occasionally from skin	Rare

Modified from Pfaller, M. A., and Herwaldt, L. A.: Laboratory, clinical, and epidemiological aspects of coagulase-negative staphylococci. Clin. Microbiol. Rev. *1*:281–299, 1988.

TABLE 86–2 ■ CURRENT METHODS OF EPIDEMIOLOGIC ANALYSIS OF COAGULASE-NEGATIVE STAPHYLOCOCCI

Conventional	Molecular
Biotyping[95, 170]	Multilocus enzyme electrophoresis[162, 235, 243, 259]
Colony morphology[124]	Plasmid analysis[9, 10, 124, 168, 169, 205, 206, 231, 245]
Antibiograms[8, 92, 93, 124, 129, 141, 151]	Chromosomal analysis[24, 76, 105]
Serology[1, 179, 256]	Polymerase chain reaction amplification[124]
Polypeptide analysis[31, 33, 43, 58, 235]	
Slime-layer production[40, 47]	
Phage typing[39, 50, 171, 222, 229]	
Pyrolysis mass spectrometry[69]	

and through the gastrointestinal tracts of infants with necrotizing enterocolitis. Initial adherence is followed by colonization with formation of multilayered cell clusters, which are embedded in an amorphous extracellular material allowing spread of the infection.[82, 97] Nonspecific electrostatic and hydrophobic interaction is thought to promote initial attachment.[97, 99] Specific binding by adhesins, including a polysaccharide surface antigen, other surface polysaccharides, or proteins[137, 213, 236, 237] can occur with the catheter material or host fibronectin and other proteins.[131, 196, 247]

After coagulase-negative staphylococci are bound, a slime-like substance is extruded, forming a biofilm that covers the organism[41, 257] (Fig. 86–1). Formation of the biofilm occurs in two steps: rapid initial attachment of the bacteria to the surface, followed by a prolonged phase of accumulation that involves cell proliferation and intercellular adhesion. This slime-like layer is not a capsule, and significant progress has been made in defining the molecular mechanisms involved in this process[97] (Table 86–3). The analysis of 213 staphylococcal isolates for production of slime revealed that the expression of the slime-associated antigen appears to be species specific and confined to the *S. epidermidis sensu stricto* isolates. Moreover, these strains produced thicker biofilms when optic density was analyzed.[4] Reports conflict as to the antiphagocytic properties of the slime-like layer,[126, 183, 239] but it does not appear to inhibit *S. epidermidis* from nutrient sources. The slime-like layer also protects the organism from certain antibiotics.[61, 212, 213, 242] The reported effect of the slime on coagulation[34] and the immune system[80, 109] has been challenged.[57] Shiro and associates[214] reported that *S. epidermidis* mutated to delete the production of polysaccharide surface antigen, and slime is avirulent in a rabbit model of endocarditis.

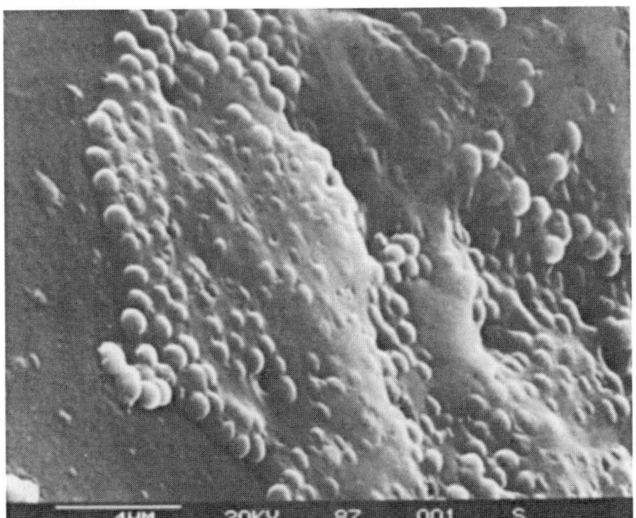

FIGURE 86–1 ■ Scanning electron microscopy of slime-producing coagulase-negative staphylococci. (From Peters, G., Locci, R., and Pulverer, G.: Adherence and growth of coagulase-negative staphylococci on surfaces of intravenous catheters. J. Infect. Dis. *146*:479–482, 1982.)

Numerous exotoxins are produced by coagulase-negative staphylococci: an extracellular metalloprotease with elastase activity; a cysteine protease that degrades human secretory immunoglobulin A, immunoglobulin M, serum albumin, fibrinogen, and fibronectin; and an extracellular serine protease involved in epidermin processing.[97] Two lipases have been postulated to enable skin colonization.[97] Delta toxin, an enteropathogenic toxin, encoded by the *hld* component of the regulatory system *agr*, has been linked to necrotizing enterocolitis in infants.[207]

S. epidermidis also produces bacteriocins called lantibiotics. They may play a role in bacterial interference on skin and mucous membranes, creating an ecological niche for *S. epidermidis*. Epidermin, Pep 5, Epilancin K7, and Epidicin 280 are some of the described *S. epidermidis* bacteriocins.[97]

Surface-exposed proteins have begun to receive attention regarding their role in pathogenesis.[176] Electron microscopy has revealed a fimbria-like protein structure that may play a role in attachment of coagulase-negative staphylococci to foreign materials in the host.[241] A protein-hemagglutinin[74] and surface fibrillar proteins[73] have been associated with attachment to urinary tract epithelium of *S. saprophyticus*. Invasion of this organism has been attributed to a urease.[71, 72]

The peptidoglycan and teichoic acid of *S. epidermidis* stimulates human monocytes to release tumor necrosis factor-α, interleukin-1, and interleukin-6. In addition, extracellular products of *S. epidermidis* interfere with several neutrophil functions.[97]

TABLE 86–3 ■ BIOFILM FORMATION

Mechanisms
Initial Attachment
Physicochemical forces (charge, van der Waals, hydrophobic interactions)
Staphylococcal surface proteins (SSP-1 and SSP-2)
Surface-associated autolysin (AtlE)
Capsular polysaccharide/adhesin (PS/A)
Host-factor binding proteins: fibrinogen-binding protein (Fbe); AtlE*
Adhesin/autolysin (Aas)†
Accumulation Process
Polysaccharide intercellular adhesin (PIA)
Capsular polysaccharide/adhesin (PS/A)
Accumulation-associated protein (AAP)

*AtlE exhibits vitronectin-binding activity.
†Aas binds fibronectin and hemaglutinates sheep erythrocytes
Data from Heilman, C., and Peters, G.: Biology and pathogenesis of *Staphylococcus epidermidis*. *In* Fischetti, V. A., Novick, R. P., Ferretti, J. J., et al. (eds.): Gram-Positive Pathogens. Washington, D.C., ASM Press, 2000, pp. 442–449.

As with other pathogens, low availability of iron in the host has been used by the bacteria as a signal to activate transcription of certain virulence factors. A ferric uptake regulator (Fur)-like protein recently has been identified in *S. epidermidis,*[96] but its role in pathogenesis has not been determined.

Several risk factors for development of coagulase-negative staphylococci infection are caused by changes in host defense. Initial risk factors include a breakdown of the mucocutaneous barrier,[246, 252] immunosuppression,[65, 116, 246, 252] and prior antibiotic therapy.[117, 210] Also, the presence of a prosthetic device, such as an indwelling central venous catheter, cerebrospinal fluid (CSF) shunt, or peritoneal dialysis catheter, can increase the susceptibility to infection.[16, 22, 60, 246, 252]

Opsonophagocytosis is the most important immune defense against coagulase-negative staphylococci.[65, 117, 219, 252] An increased rate of infection has been noted in patients with a dysfunctional opsonophagocytosis system, including neonates[65, 219] and patients receiving continuous ambulatory peritoneal dialysis.[78, 117] Initially, this inhibition of opsonophagocytosis was thought to be caused by the slime layer,[117] but this contention has been questioned.[126]

Clinical Manifestations

Coagulase-negative staphylococci have been implicated in a variety of clinical infections in immunocompetent and immunocompromised patients[123, 174, 198] (Table 86–4). A basic difficulty in interpreting clinical studies of coagulase-negative staphylococci exists because of the different criteria used to define a clinically significant culture.[55] In neonates, immunocompromised patients, and patients with prosthetic implants, repeated isolation of the same phenotypic strain of coagulase-negative staphylococci from blood cultures facilitates interpretation. For catheter-related bacteremia, quantitative cultures from the catheter exhibit a 5- to 10-fold increase in the number of colony-forming units as compared with cultures from a peripheral vessel. The Committee on Infectious Diseases of the American Academy of Pediatrics has suggested the following considerations to distinguish pathogenic, rather than contaminant, coagulase-negative staphylococci: (1) growth within 24 hours, (2) multiple positive blood cultures, (3) symptoms of infection in the patient, (4) presence of an intravascular catheter for 3 days or more, and (5) multidrug resistance of the coagulase-negative staphylococcal strain.[3]

Clinical presentation markedly differs from that of *S. aureus*. In general, infections caused by coagulase-negative staphylococci are more indolent and can present with a subacute or even chronic course.

TABLE 86–4 ■ CLINICALLY IMPORTANT COAGULASE-NEGATIVE STAPHYLOCOCCAL INFECTIONS

Bacteremia
- Neonates
- Leukemia and lymphoma patients
- Bone marrow transplant recipients

Infections in patients with indwelling medical devices
- Central venous catheters
- Cerebrospinal fluid shunts
- Peritoneal dialysis catheter
- Prosthetic values

Other
- Prosthetic joints
- Vascular grafts and prostheses
- Hemodialysis shunt
- Pacemaker
- Scalp electrode

Native valve endocarditis

Urinary tract infections

Miscellaneous
- Endophthalmitis after ocular surgery
- Postoperative wound infections
- Osteomyelitis (sternal wound or hematogenous)
- Toxic shock syndrome

Modified from Patrick, C. C.: Coagulase-negative staphylococci: Pathogens with increasing clinical significance. J. Pediatr. *116*:497–507, 1990.

BACTEREMIA

Coagulase-negative staphylococci, particularly *S. epidermidis*, have become the major nosocomial pathogens in most studies.[55, 144, 192, 228] The analysis of 6,290 nosocomial infections including 110,709 patients from 61 pediatric intensive care units in the United States during 1992 to 1997 showed that bloodstream infections were the most common nosocomial infection; coagulase-negative staphylococcus was the causative agent in 38 percent (717 of 1887) of the cases.[192] This trend has been reported from other centers.[39, 68, 144, 204, 228, 246, 252] These infections occur primarily with the use of indwelling vascular catheters. In febrile immunocompromised pediatric cancer patients, coagulase-negative staphylococci can account for 35 percent of all positive blood culture isolates.[2, 15, 127, 177]

NEONATAL BACTEREMIAS

Coagulase-negative staphylococci are the single most frequent cause of late-onset septicemia among premature infants, especially in low-birth-weight infants.[19, 66, 89, 160, 175] Table 86–5 lists the salient features from six large studies[66, 89, 111, 113, 153, 175] These infections are found predominantly in premature infants with a gestational age of less than 35 weeks. Nosocomial infection risk for low-birth-weight infants can be correlated with an assessment of illness severity score.[79, 81] Premature infants have an immature immune system, particularly in both quantitative and qualitative neutrophil function.[35, 219, 250] The presence of indwelling peripheral or umbilical catheters has been implicated in approximately one half of neonatal coagulase-negative staphylococci bacteremias.[19, 89, 161, 170]

Signs and symptoms of coagulase-negative staphylococci bacteremia are subtle, as are other systemic insults in this patient population. The most common ones are bradycardia and temperature instability, but they are not uniform (see Table 86–5). Skin abscesses have been noted in more than 40 percent of neonates with coagulase-negative staphylococci bacteremia.[175]

Laboratory studies usually are not helpful in identifying patients with coagulase-negative staphylococci bacteremia.[156] Leukocytosis is an inconsistent finding. Reports have conflicted about production of slime, a possible virulence factor, as a marker for infection.[89, 175] One study successfully correlated quantitative blood cultures with specific clinical information to distinguish a true pathogen.[227] Peripheral blood cultures yielding more than 50 colony-forming units per milliliter occurred exclusively in infants with proven septicemia. In contrast, low colony counts were observed in both septicemia and culture contamination. Those patients with low colony counts and septicemia were more likely to

TABLE 86–5 ■ SALIENT ASPECTS OF SIX STUDIES OF COAGULASE-NEGATIVE STAPHYLOCOCCI BACTEREMIA IN NEONATES

	Munson et al., 1982[153] (n = 27)	Fleer et al., 1983[66] (n = 30)	Hall et al., 1987[89] (n = 29)	Patrick et al., 1989[175] (n = 32)	Kacica et al., 1994[111] (n = 47)	Kallman et al., 1997[113] (n = 27)
Patient characteristics						
Mean birth weight (g)	1130	1564	1607	1172	1259	NR
Gestational age	28.9	32.1	31	28.6	29	<30
Central lines (%)	85	NR	34	19	NR	NR
TPN (%)	78	77 (20/26)	NR	91	81	NR
Clinical characteristics						
Apnea or bradycardia (%)	>50	100	62	78	NR	NR
Temperature instability (%)	<50	70	7	22	NR	NR
Tachycardia (%)	>50	100	NR	6	NR	NR
Mortality (%)	0	0 (0/13)	0	0	NR	7.4
Laboratory characteristics						
Slime production, patient isolates (%)	NR	NR	79	54 (6/13)	65	NR
Antibiotic susceptibility	100% S to cephalothin	100% S to cephalothin	83% S to methicillin; 100% S to vancomycin	100% S to vancomycin	48% S oxacillin; 100% S to vancomycin	86% S to methicillin*; 55% S to methicillin†

*Period: 1981–1986.
†Period: 1987–1994.
NR, not reported; R, resistant; S, susceptible; TPN, total parenteral nutrition.

have a central venous line or an abnormal hematologic value (leukocytosis, decreased platelets, or increased immature to total neutrophil ratio).[227]

Two unusual clinical entities merit comment. We have described persistent coagulase-negative staphylococci bacteremia (mean duration of 13 days) despite adequate antibiotic therapy.[175] It occurred in neonates without central venous catheters. No clinical or laboratory evidence was found consistently. Additionally, coagulase-negative staphylococci meningitis has been reported in low-birth-weight neonates with normal CSF profiles.[85] This latter finding has prompted a recommendation that neonates with coagulase-negative staphylococci bacteremia undergo one or more examinations of the CSF to determine the duration of therapy.

Coagulase-negative staphylococci also have been implicated as etiologic agents of necrotizing enterocolitis.[86, 207] At least two studies have shown an association between coagulase-negative staphylococci and necrotizing enterocolitis; one report showed no association.[195] Scheifele and associates[207] have shown that delta toxin, an exoprotein with enteropathic effects, is present in *S. epidermidis*.

Noel and associates[160] have described five cases of right-sided endocarditis in catheterized infants. It can lead to prolonged bacteremia with an associated thrombocytopenia.

LEUKEMIA AND LYMPHOMA

Immunocompromised patients with leukemia, lymphoma, or both are at risk for the development of coagulase-negative staphylococci bacteremia.[2, 15, 70, 127, 186, 187, 211, 246, 252] The occurrence of coagulase-negative staphylococci bacteremia in this patient population is increasing (Table 86–6). The most common portals of entry are the gastrointestinal tract, where chemotherapy causes defects,[246] and the skin, in association with catheter devices. Coagulase-negative staphylococci were the isolates most commonly causing bacteremia in pediatric cancer patients, accounting for 35 percent of all initial isolates.[2, 15, 127, 177] One third of these patients did not have central venous catheters at the time of their bacteremia.[70]

Random amplification of polymorphic DNA analysis and pulsed-field gel electrophoresis of DNA macrorestriction fragments of blood culture coagulase-negative staphylococci isolates obtained from 40 neutropenic hemato-oncologic

TABLE 86–6 ■ CLINICAL CHARACTERISTICS OF COAGULASE-NEGATIVE STAPHYLOCOCCAL BACTEREMIA IN CHILDHOOD CANCER PATIENTS*

	Friedman et al., 1984[70] (n = 150)	Langley & Gold, 1988[127] (n = 100)	Patrick et al., 1989[177] (n = 207)	Aledo et al., 1998[2] (n = 140)	Auletta et al., 1999[15] (n = 102)
Coagulase-negative staphylococci among total bacteremias (%)	12.7	35	35	31.4	35
Patients with central venous catheters (%)	32	53	61	95	95
Mortality (%)	10.5	38	30	<5	19
Patient isolates susceptible to:					
Methicillin (%)	17	38	30	NR	NR
Vancomycin (%)	100	100	100	NR	NR

*Percentages are based on the number of episodes of coagulase-negative staphylococcal sepsis.
NR, not reported.

patients related to 61 episodes of Hickman catheter–related infections allowed the characterization of clonal coagulase-negative staphylococci types that successfully and persistently colonized patients, confirming that the skin flora was the likely source involved in catheter-related infections (CRI) in 75 percent of the patients.[162]

Morbidity from coagulase-negative staphylococci bacteremia is appreciable because of the organism's acquisition of multiple antibiotic resistance, requiring the use of vancomycin or combination antibiotic therapy with potentially toxic effects.[70, 116, 127, 135, 136, 188, 203, 246, 252] We reported no mortality in our study, but two other children's series had 10.5 and 11 percent mortality rates.[70, 127, 177]

HEMATOPOIETIC STEM CELL TRANSPLANTATION

Coagulase-negative staphylococci have become the primary pathogen causing bacteremia in hematopoietic stem cell transplant recipients.[31, 150] These episodes occur most often during periods of agranulocytosis before marrow engraftment[31] and can be fatal.[21] Most of these episodes are a result of the universal use of central venous catheters and the use of broad-spectrum antibiotics. Bacteremia that occurs during the neutropenic phase after hematopoietic stem cell transplantation appears to be associated with early death from invasive fungal infection.[226]

INDWELLING MEDICAL DEVICES

Central Venous Catheters

Infections associated with central venous catheters are caused primarily by coagulase-negative staphylococci, which also can cause infections in peripheral catheters composed of steel or polyethylene.[238] Central venous catheters are of increasing importance in pediatrics for long-term hyperalimentation or administration of medication.[102] Two types of devices are in common use: Broviac and Hickman catheters, which have an external port, and totally implanted vascular access devices.[29, 98, 193] Broviac and Hickman catheters have an exit site where the catheter enters the skin, whereas the totally implanted vascular devices have a subcutaneous tract; all three types have a Dacron cuff that promotes fibrosis, limiting the trafficking of potential pathogens, and an insert site into the major vessel. Thus, infection can occur at the exit site, along the catheter tunnel, or at the catheter vessel insertion site. Totally implanted catheters (e.g., port-A-Cath) have the lowest rates of bacteremia (0 to 0.04 per 100 catheter days), followed by long-term Hickman or Broviac catheters (0.14 per 100 catheter days).[100] Infection at the vessel insertion site can lead to bacteremia or a septic thrombophlebitis, with further complications caused by metastatic spread.[189]

Infectious complications involving central venous catheters have a variable reported frequency of 2.7 to 47 percent[22, 94, 134, 152, 221, 244]; coagulase-negative staphylococci are the pathogen in approximately one half. This variability depends on the definition of a CRI, the type of catheter used, and the presence of hyperalimentation fluid and lipid in the infusion.[139, 213, 215] The use of a guide wire for catheter placement or of a multilumen catheter leads to higher infection rates.[217]

S. epidermidis is the species associated most often with central venous CRIs, identified in approximately 70 percent of coagulase-negative staphylococci central venous CRIs.[22, 94] This prevalence is not unexpected because it is the predominant species colonizing the skin.[125] Other implicated coagulase-negative staphylococci species include *Staphylococcus haemolyticus*, *Staphylococcus warneri*, and *Staphylococcus hominis*.[94]

Diagnosing a true infection caused by *S. epidermidis* versus a contaminated specimen is difficult. Making the diagnosis depends on the patient's clinical status and the isolation of identical isolate strains in repeated cultures. Proper therapy, possibly including removal of a catheter, requires an accurate diagnosis.[190] Additionally, distinction of a central venous catheter–related bacteremia from a bacteremia not associated with a central venous catheter is important. The use of quantitative blood cultures using the DuPont isolator system has shown that catheter-related bacteremias have a 5- to 10-fold difference in bacterial concentration compared with peripheral cultures.[67, 191] Maki and associates[138] have determined that catheter-related bacteremia can be confirmed after removal of the catheter by rolling the distal 5 to 7 cm of the catheter on a culture plate and finding more than 15 colony-forming units.

Therapy for coagulase-negative staphylococci infections involving central venous catheters should include removal of the catheter if the catheter is no longer necessary. Exit-site infections usually can be managed without removing the catheter.[190] Approximately one third of tunnel tract infections can be managed without removing the catheter, but the remaining patients have continued bacteremia or relapse of their bacteremia requiring catheter removal. Catheters should be removed immediately if the patient's clinical status deteriorates.[252] The duration of therapy depends on whether the catheter has been removed and on the patient's underlying immune status.

Central Nervous System Shunts

Central nervous system (CNS) shunts are used commonly to divert or shunt CSF to relieve hydrocephalus.[118] Other prosthetic devices within the CNS have been used to monitor ventricular pressure or to administer chemotherapy.[52] Two types of CNS shunts have been used commonly. The earlier shunts diverted CSF into the right atrium; this technique is used infrequently because of its high complication rate.[149, 165] Ventriculoperitoneal shunts that divert CSF into the peritoneal cavity have been used since the 1960s because of their lower rate of mechanical complications.[118, 154, 165] However, the incidences of infection involving both the ventriculoperitoneal and the ventriculoatrial shunts are comparable.[118, 165, 216] Infection rates are higher in neonates. In both types of CNS shunts, *S. epidermidis* is the principal microorganism implicated, with a 5 to 12 percent infection rate. Coagulase-negative staphylococci account for 60 to 75 percent of all bacterial causes of shunt infections.[118, 158, 216]

The pathogenesis of CSF shunt infections primarily occurs at the insertion site by contamination of the catheter from the patient's skin flora[216] or during subsequent revisions, with a short-term infection rate of 13 percent and a 10-year infection rate of 27 percent.[194] Seventy percent of ventriculoperitoneal shunt infections occur within 2 months of placement of the shunt.[158] The pathogenesis of this infection appears to be similar to the CRI, described in the pathogenesis section. Two other modes of infection involve hematogenous seeding or retrograde migration from the distal end of the shunt.

The diagnosis of CNS shunt infections is difficult to make owing to the differentiation between a true infection and a contaminating organism. The Gram stain of ventricular fluid often is negative, but culture is sensitive. Subtle changes are noted in cerebrospinal and ventricular fluid cell counts or cytochemical findings.[255] Patients with ventriculoatrial shunts often have signs and symptoms compatible with septicemia and the additional complications of glomerulonephritis secondary to immune complexes. In patients with ventriculoperitoneal shunts, because of the distal placement of the catheter into the peritoneum, an intra-abdominal cyst may develop at the distal end of the catheter. Dysfunctions of the shunt secondary to infections often are noted because of signs and symptoms consistent with increased intracranial pressure.

Standard therapy for ventriculoperitoneal shunt infections has been removal of the shunt system and administration of systemic antibiotics.[216, 255] However, this mode of therapy has been challenged, after successful treatment by externalization of the peritoneal end of the ventriculoperitoneal shunt and administration of both intraventricular and systemic antibiotics.[149]

Peritoneal Dialysis Catheters

In 1968, Tenckhoff and Schechter[233] devised a catheter that allowed for peritoneal dialysis with a low infection rate. Infection remains the most common complication of peritoneal dialysis, and *S. epidermidis* is the bacterial pathogen most commonly isolated,[84, 183] representing as many as 50 percent of infecting organisms.[183] The pathogenesis of infections involving the peritoneal dialysis catheter is similar to that of CRIs with infections involving the exit site and along the subcutaneous catheter tunnel, and peritonitis.[183] The prevalence of peritonitis in patients undergoing continuous ambulatory peritoneal dialysis is approximately 60 percent. Signs of peritonitis include fever, abdominal pain, and cloudy peritoneal dialysis, fever being variable. The removal of the catheter usually is not necessary as part of the therapy but may be necessary in refractory cases or when the catheter malfunctions. Antibiotics are administered in the dialysis fluid, and systemic antibiotics also can be used.[63]

Prosthetic Devices

S. epidermidis is the most common cause of prosthetic valve endocarditis, accounting for 25 to 40 percent of all cases.[53, 75, 145, 248, 251] The mortality rate from *S. epidermidis* prosthetic valve endocarditis approaches 70 percent.[5, 54, 115, 145, 146] Commonly, *S. epidermidis* prosthetic valve endocarditis occurs within 60 days after implanting the device and is defined as early prosthetic valve endocarditis. It can occur in the first year after surgery, probably caused by inoculation of the organism at the time of surgery, as noticed by the multiresistant phenotype analysis from these patient isolates.[27] It finally leads to an abscess of the mechanical valve ring. No sign or symptom is consistently diagnostic of prosthetic valve endocarditis, but fever is the most common finding. Classic endocarditis findings as peripheral emboli and multiple positive blood cultures may be lacking in coagulase-negative staphylococci endocarditis. Anemia is the abnormality identified most commonly by laboratory tests. Obtaining blood cultures is imperative in diagnosing prosthetic valve endocarditis. Therapy should include institution of vancomycin and rifampin or an aminoglycoside, with surgical intervention as indicated.[115]

Other Indwelling Medical Devices

Coagulase-negative staphylococci are involved in an expanded spectrum of infections involving indwelling medical devices.[52] They include infections of prosthetic joints,[64, 114] vascular grafts,[17, 56] hemodialysis shunts,[172, 209] and pacemaker pockets.[38, 106, 140, 181] Additionally, osteomyelitis secondary to *S. epidermidis* has been reported to occur after hemodialysis and in neonates after the use of a monitoring scalp electrode.[166]

NATIVE VALVE ENDOCARDITIS

Native valve endocarditis is the only non-nosocomial infection other than *S. saprophyticus* urinary tract infection that is caused by coagulase-negative staphylococci. Coagulase-negative staphylococci are the etiologic agents involved in 22 percent of native valve endocarditis in pediatric patients with previously normal heart valves.[108] These infections usually are subacute and arise from transient bacteremia. Pathogenesis is thought to involve seeding of a previously damaged valve or endocarditis that previously had not been identified.[7, 20]

Staphylococcus lugdunensis has been reported as a cause of severe and destructive endocarditis, with most favorable outcomes occurring in patients who undergo valve replacement.[48] Deep-seated infections associated with bacteremia caused by this organism, including postoperative wound infections, peritonitis, prosthetic infections, osteomyelitis, and septic arthritis, also have been described.[240] Of note is the predominance of sites below the waist, suggesting that its preferential site for colonization may be the perineum.[97] Finally, *S. lugdunensis* may be misidentified as *S. aureus* because it produces clumping factor.[202]

SURGICAL SITE INFECTIONS

Coagulase-negative staphylococci are the second most common cause of postoperative surgical site infections according to recent National Nosocomial Infections Surveillance Report survey data.[36] Most infections probably are caused by the patient's own endogenous skin flora, but outbreaks originating from operating room personnel have been reported.[27]

URINARY TRACT INFECTIONS

S. saprophyticus is the most common coagulase-negative staphylococcus that causes urinary tract infections in both the upper and the lower urinary tracts.[128] These infections predominantly occur in young, healthy, sexually active women,[110, 128, 142] during late summer and fall, with a pattern similar to that of sexually transmitted diseases.[71] Recent sexual intercourse, outdoor swimming, and occupational meat processing have been identified as risk factors.[71] *S. epidermidis* and other coagulase-negative staphylococci rarely cause urinary tract infections but have been noted to produce disease in older adults with urinary tract complications.[87, 132, 159] McDonald and Lohr[147] and Hall and Snitzer[88] have described healthy children with pyelonephritis caused by *S. epidermidis*.

MISCELLANEOUS

Numerous case reports have described *S. epidermidis* as an etiologic agent in a variety of infections. Endophthalmitis secondary to *S. epidermidis* has been reported in patients undergoing ocular surgery or trauma.[18, 28, 184] Postoperative mediastinitis that develops after median sternotomy for open heart surgery can be caused by *S. epidermidis*.[26, 59, 83] Primary osteomyelitis secondary to coagulase-negative staphylococci is a rare occurrence in healthy children.[167]

Staphylococcus caprae[218] and *S. lugdunensis*[202] recently have been linked to bone and joint infections. Of note, coagulase-negative staphylococci have been implicated as a possible cause of toxic shock syndrome.[44]

Treatment

The treatment of coagulase-negative staphylococcal infections,[2] depends on the patient's immunologic status, the presence of an indwelling medical device, and the results of antimicrobial testing. Infections are more difficult to treat when associated with a thrombosed vessel or an intra-atrial thrombus. When an intravascular catheter becomes infected, the presence of vegetation or a thrombus in the heart or great vessels always should be considered.

Many coagulase-negative staphylococci, particularly *S. epidermidis* and *S. haemolyticus*, are resistant to antimicrobial therapy.[11, 13, 39, 49, 62, 79, 210, 225, 249] Methicillin resistance especially is prevalent in nosocomial infections and occurs in approximately 60 percent of cases.[25, 200, 220] Methicillin resistance is more prevalent in patients with prosthetic valve endocarditis.[115] Methicillin-resistant *S. epidermidis* has a high degree of resistance to other antibiotics, such as clindamycin, erythromycin, and gentamicin.[11]

The mechanism of methicillin resistance in coagulase-negative staphylococci is similar to that of *S. aureus* because of the production of an additional non-native penicillin-binding protein (PBP), PBP2a, encoded by the *mecA* gene.[97, 101] PBP2a does not allow the correct binding of β-lactams to the bacterial cell wall. Phenotypic methicillin resistance can be difficult to detect because of the heterogeneous expression of the *mecA* gene by many strains of staphylococci.[101] *S. aureus* breakpoints have been seen to fail to detect many coagulase-negative staphylococci that contained the *mecA* gene involved in staphylococcal resistance. As a consequence, the 1999 National Committee for Clinical Laboratory Standards established new breakpoints for coagulase-negative staphylococci[157] (Table 86–7). In some species other than *S. epidermidis*, the differentiation between *mecA*-negative and *mecA*-positive strains may not be possible to make by susceptibility methods[234] and may falsely designate isolates as oxacillin resistant. Alternative methods for rapid and accurate detection are desirable. A rapid slide agglutination test, performed after induction of the oxacillin-resistant gene, appears to be promising.[101] Testing of coagulase-negative staphylococci using oxacillin screen plate no longer is recommended because of its failure to detect many resistant strains.[234]

Coagulase-negative staphylococci (*S. haemolyticus* and *S. epidermidis*) were the first organisms in which acquired glycopeptide resistance was recognized in 1986.[210] In addition, *S. epidermidis*, *S. haemolyticus*, and *S. hominis* are more likely to be multiresistant to antimicrobial agents than are other coagulase-negative staphylococcal species. A prolonged course of vancomycin is a well-recognized risk factor for the emergence of strains with decreased susceptibility to glycopeptides.[23, 253] Although uncommon occurrences, infections caused by these strains have been described and may become more common. To prevent or delay development of resistance, the Centers for Disease Control and Prevention have published recommendations for the prudent use of vancomycin.[37] Decreased susceptibility occurs more frequently to teicoplanin than to vancomycin. The minimal inhibitory concentrations of teicoplanin usually fall over a wide range, whereas vancomycin minimal inhibitory concentrations tend to remain more stable over a narrower range within the limits of susceptibility.[23] The peptidoglycan of these strains is highly cross-linked, containing additional serine in place of glycine, an alteration that may interfere with glycopeptide binding.[97]

The mechanism for vancomycin-intermediate resistance of *S. aureus* and coagulase-negative staphylococci is unknown. Vancomycin-intermediate *S. aureus* and vancomycin-intermediate coagulase-negative staphylococcal strains have thickened cell walls, as shown by electron microscopy. Vancomycin resistance may be related to an increased ability of these organisms to bind vancomycin at sites other than those to which they normally bind.[97]

For the few isolates that are established to be penicillin susceptible and β-lactamase negative, penicillin is a suitable drug. For organisms that are resistant to penicillin but susceptible to semisynthetic penicillins, nafcillin or oxacillin are the most active antibiotics.[185, 201] A degree of cross-resistance exists between the semisynthetic penicillin-resistant penicillins and cephalosporins.[200] Thus, routine susceptibility testing can indicate that a strain is susceptible to a cephalosporin when in fact it is resistant.[84, 129] As a rule, methicillin resistance can be interpreted as resistance to all β-lactam antibiotics.[107]

Vancomycin is the drug of choice for methicillin-resistant organisms and is recommended for treating severe infections.[3, 120] Coagulase-negative staphylococci can exhibit heteroresistance, defined as a culture population comprising two subpopulations, one susceptible to methicillin and the other resistant.[200, 253] Enhanced detection of this admixture of organisms can be obtained by change in the culture conditions.[148] If these strains are incubated overnight on plates of increasing concentrations of methicillin or vancomycin, a small fraction of the total population will be able to grow at much higher antibiotic concentrations. If these highly resistant subclones are recultured, they may maintain this high

TABLE 86–7 ■ NEW BREAKPOINTS FOR ANTIBIOTIC SUSCEPTIBILITY FOR COAGULASE-NEGATIVE STAPHYLOCOCCI

MICs	Oxacillin Susceptible	Oxacillin Resistant	
CoNS	≤0.25 µg/mL	≥0.5 µg/mL	
S. aureus	≤2 µg/mL	≥4 µg/mL	
Zone Size	**Oxacillin Susceptible**	**Oxacillin Intermediate**	**Oxacillin Resistant**
CoNS	≥18 mm	No intermediate zone	≤17 mm
S. aureus	≥13 mm	11–12 mm	≤10 mm

MICs, minimal inhibitory concentration; CoNS, coagulase-negative staphylococci.
Data from the National Committee for Clinical Laboratory Standards: Performance standards for antimicrobial susceptibility testing. NCCLS approved standard M100-S9. Wayne, PA, National Committee for Clinical Laboratory Standards, 1999.

level of resistance, suggesting a mutant strain. However, in some cases, the highly resistant subclone will revert to methicillin or vancomycin susceptibility when replated, even though it was grown from a single colony. No satisfactory model can explain the mechanism governing heterogeneous resistance. Strains of coagulase-negative staphylococci and *S. aureus* with heterogeneous resistance are stable in the absence of antibiotic selective pressure. These strains may constitute 10 to 15 percent of any coagulase-negative staphylococci or *S. aureus* collection of isolates. In addition, to avoid overlooking these organisms, the clinical microbiology laboratory should attempt to optimize expression of resistance by culturing on salt-containing media at 30° to 35° C.[199] The clinical significance of this heteroresistance in coagulase-negative staphylococci is unknown, but a study of *S. aureus* showed it did not affect outcome.[121]

Several newer antibiotics, including the quinolones and teicoplanin, have shown activity against coagulase-negative staphylococci and could be useful in therapy of multiresistant organisms.[133, 213] Teicoplanin is significantly less active than is vancomycin against coagulase-negative staphylococci, in particular *S. haemolyticus* and, to a lesser extent, *S. epidermidis*. Resistance to these agents also has been observed.[13, 210, 225, 249]

Gentamicin and rifampin are active against coagulase-negative staphylococci, but rapid emergence of resistance has limited their use as single drugs.[39, 143, 201] These two antibiotics have been shown to be synergistic with vancomycin against methicillin-resistant coagulase-negative staphylococci.[135] Additionally, rifampin has been used in neonates with persistent bacteremia to eradicate the organisms.[230] The association of vancomycin and rifampin is the mainstay of the therapy for deep-seated, foreign-body infections. Arditi and Yogev[12] reported a novel antibiotic combination using clindamycin and rifampin. This combination in vitro has allowed rifampin to exert its activity without the development of rifampin resistance.

Excellent in vitro activity of quinupristin-dalfopristin, a streptogramin combination,[14] and linezolid, an oxazolidinone compound that inhibits bacterial growth through inhibition of protein synthesis,[198] has been shown against staphylococcal species tested regardless of the resistance pattern, particularly resistance to methicillin, and these may be therapeutic options for vancomycin-intermediate susceptible isolates.

Prevention

Prevention of coagulase-negative staphylococci infection is difficult because of these organisms' ubiquitous nature as predominant skin commensals. A 3-year analysis by molecular typing of coagulase-negative staphylococci nosocomial infections in a neonatal intensive care unit showed that many of the infections were caused by clonal dissemination and, thus, potentially are preventable by handwashing, reducing the transmission rate from staff to patient or patient to patient.[243] Additionally, proper surgical techniques help minimize these infections associated with installation of indwelling medical devices.

The effort toward developing catheters that are both inert and resistant to bacterial colonization adherence has increased; however, these attempts have been only marginally successful.[119, 173, 180] Catheters with antibiotics or disinfectants impregnated in their surfaces appear promising, but their effect is short-lived.[232]

The use of prophylactic antibiotics during the implantation of an indwelling medical device has not been studied in a controlled manner and appears to promote antibiotic resistance.[8, 9, 45] This idea was challenged in two studies involving cardiovascular surgery patients in whom prophylactic cephalosporins were shown to reduce postoperative wound infections caused by *S. epidermidis*.[112, 223] Prophylaxis with vancomycin during cardiac surgery currently is recommended in hospitals with high incidence of sternal wound infections or prosthetic valve endocarditis caused by resistant coagulase-negative staphylococci.[6] No consensus exists regarding the role of intraoperative antibiotics administered at the time of placement of CSF shunts.[3]

In reference to infection control policies, standard precautions should be used for methicillin-resistant coagulase-negative staphylococci. For vancomycin-intermediate coagulase-negative staphylococci, contact transmission precautions for multidrug-resistant organisms should be used.[3]

Conclusion

Coagulase-negative staphylococci, particularly *S. epidermidis,* are a major source of nosocomial infection in a variety of clinical situations. Most infections occur in patients who are immunosuppressed or have an indwelling medical device. Epidemiologic studies are difficult to perform because of the organisms' commensal existence, but new molecular tools will help to gain insight with regard to the epidemiology of these infections. The pathogenesis of coagulase-negative staphylococci infection is being defined in the context of a CRI. Therapy is difficult to perform because of the usual presence of an indwelling medical device and the multiple antimicrobial resistance of the organisms.

REFERENCES

1. Aasen, J., and Oeding, P.: Antigenic studies on *Staphylococcus epidermidis*. Acta Pathol. Microbiol. Scand. 79:827–834, 1972.
2. Aledo, A., Hellr, G., Ren, L., et al.: Septicemia and septic shock in pediatric patients: 140 Consecutive cases on a pediatric hematology-oncology service. J. Pediatr. Hematol. Oncol. *20*:215–221, 1998.
3. American Academy of Pediatrics: Staphylococcal infections. *In* Pickering, L. K. (ed.): 2000 Red Book: Report of the Committee on Infectious Diseases. 25th ed. Elk Grove Village, IL, American Academy of Pediatrics, 2000, pp. 514–526.
4. Ammendiola, M. G., Di Rosa, R., and Montanaro, L.: Slime production and expression of the slime-associated antigen by staphylococcal clinical isolates. J. Clin. Microbiol. *37*:3235–3238, 1999.
5. Anderson, D. J., Bulkley, B. H., and Hutchins, G. M.: A clinicopathologic study of prosthetic valve endocarditis in 22 patients: Morphologic basis for diagnosis and therapy. Am. Heart J. *94*:325–332, 1977.
6. Anonymous: Antimicrobial prophylaxis in surgery. Med. Lett. Drugs Ther. *39*:97–102, 1997.
7. Archer, G. L.: *Staphylococcus epidermidis* and other coagulase-negative staphylococci. *In* Mandell, G. L., Bennett. J. E., and Dolin, R. (eds.): Principles and Practice of Infectious Diseases. 5th ed. New York, Churchill Livingstone, 2000, pp. 2092–2100.
8. Archer, G.: Antimicrobial susceptibility and selection of resistance among *Staphylococcus epidermidis* isolates recovered from patients with infections of indwelling foreign devices. Antimicrob. Agents Chemother. *14*:353–359, 1987.
9. Archer, G. L., Dietrick, D. R., and Johnston, J. L.: Molecular epidemiology of transmissible gentamicin resistance among coagulase-negative staphylococci in a cardiac surgery unit. J. Infect. Dis. *151*:243–251, 1985.
10. Archer, G. L., Karchmer, A. W., Vishniavsky, N., et al.: Plasmid-pattern analysis for the differentiation of infecting from noninfecting *Staphylococcus epidermidis*. J. Infect. Dis. *149*:913–920, 1984.
11. Archer, G. L., and Climo, M. W.: Antimicrobial susceptibility of coagulase-negative staphylococci. Antimicrob. Agents Chemother. *38*:2231–2237, 1994.
12. Arditi, M., and Yogev, R.: In vitro interaction between rifampin and clindamycin against pathogenic coagulase-negative staphylococci. Antimicrob. Agents Chemother. *33*:245–247, 1989.
13. Arioli, V., and Pallanza, R.: Teicoplanin-resistant coagulase-negative staphylococci. Lancet *1*:39, 1987.

14. Auckenthaler, R., Courvalin, P., Feer, C., et al.: In vitro activity of quinupristin/dalfopristin in comparison with five antibiotics against worldwide clinical isolates of staphylococci. Clin. Microbiol. Infect. *6*:608–612, 2000.
15. Auletta, J., Riordan, M. A., and Nieder, M. L.: Infections in children with cancer: A continued need for the comprehensive physical examination. J. Pediatr. Hematol. Oncol. *21*:501–508, 1999.
16. Baddour, L. M., Smalley, D. L., Kraus, A. P., Jr., et al.: Comparison of microbiologic characteristics of pathogenic and saprophytic coagulase-negative staphylococci from patients on continuous ambulatory peritoneal dialysis. Diagn. Microbiol. Infect. Dis. *5*:197–205, 1986.
17. Bandyk, D. F., Berni, G. A., Thiele, B. L., et al.: Aortofemoral graft infection due to *Staphylococcus epidermidis*. Arch. Surg. *119*:102–108, 1984.
18. Baum, J. L.: Current concepts in ophthalmology: Ocular infections. N. Engl. J. Med. *299*:28–31, 1978.
19. Baumgart, S., Hall, S. E., Campos, J. M., et al.: Sepsis with coagulase-negative staphylococci in critically ill newborns. Am. J. Dis. Child. *137*:461–463, 1983.
20. Belik, J., Finn, G., Rivera, G., et al.: Successful management of bacterial endocarditis of the mitral valve due to *Staphylococcus epidermidis* in an immunocompromised host. Acta. Paediatr. Scand. *69*:731–734, 1980.
21. Bender, J. W., and Hughes, W. T.: Fatal *Staphylococcus epidermidis* sepsis following bone marrow transplantation. Johns Hopkins Med. J. *146*:13–15, 1980.
22. Benezra, D., Kiehn, T. E., Gold, J. W., et al.: Prospective study of infections in indwelling central venous catheters using quantitative blood cultures. Am. J. Med. *85*:495–498, 1988.
23. Biavasco, F., Vignaroli, C., and Varaldo, P. E.: Glycopeptide resistance in coagulase-negative staphylococci. Eur. J. Clin. Microbiol. Infect. Dis. *19*:403–417, 2000.
24. Bialkowska-Hobrzanska, H., Jaskor, D., and Hammerberg, O.: Evaluation of restriction endonuclease fingerprinting of chromosomal DNA and plasmid profile analysis for characterization of multiresistant coagulase-negative staphylococci in bacteremic neonates. J. Clin. Microbiol. *28*:269–275, 1990.
25. Blum, R. A., and Rodvold, K. A.: Recognition and importance of *Staphylococcus epidermidis* infections. Clin. Pharmacol. *6*:464–475, 1987.
26. Bor, D. H., Rose, R. M., and Modlin, J. F.: Mediastinitis after cardiovascular surgery. Rev. Infect. Dis. *5*:885–896, 1983.
27. Boyce, J. M., Potter-Bynoe, G., and Opal, S. M.: A common source outbreak of *Staphylococcus epidermidis* infections among patients undergoing cardiac surgery. J. Infect. Dis. *161*:493–499, 1990.
28. Brinton, G. S., Topping, T. M., and Hyndiuk, R. A.: Posttraumatic endophthalmitis. Arch. Ophthalmol. *102*:547–550, 1984.
29. Broviac, J. W., Cole, J. J., and Scribner, B. H.: A silicone rubber atrial catheter for prolonged parenteral alimentation. Surg. Gynecol. Obstet. *136*:602–606, 1973.
30. Bruce, A. M., Lorber, J., Shedden, W. I. H., et al.: Persistent bacteremia following ventriculo-caval shunt operations for hydrocephalus in infants. Dev. Med. Child. Neurol. *5*:461–470, 1963.
31. Buckner, C. D., Clift, R. A., Sanders, J. E., et al.: Protective environment for bone marrow transplant recipients: A prospective study. Ann. Intern. Med. *89*:893–901, 1978.
32. Buetow, K. C., Klein, S. W., and Lane, R. B.: Septicemia in premature infants. Am. J. Dis. Child. *110*:29–41, 1965.
33. Burnie, J. P., Lee, W., Matthews, R. C., et al.: Immunoblot fingerprinting of coagulase-negative staphylococci. J. Clin. Pathol. *41*:103–110, 1988.
34. Bykowska, K., Ludwicka, A., and Wegrzynowicz, Z.: Anticoagulant properties of extracellular slime substance produced by *Staphylococcus epidermidis*. Thromb. Haemost. *54*:853–856, 1985.
35. Cairo, M. S.: Neonatal neutrophil host defense: Prospects for immunologic enhancement during neonatal sepsis. Am. J. Dis. Child. *143*:40–46, 1989.
36. Centers for Disease Control and Prevention, NNIS System: National Nosocomial Infections Surveillance (NNIS) Report, Data Summary from October 1986–April 1997. Am. J. Infect. Control. *25*:477–487, 1997.
37. Centers for Disease Control and Prevention, Hospital Infection Control Practices Advisory Committee (HICPAC): Recommendations for preventing the spread of vancomycin resistance. M. M. W. R. Morb. Mortal. Wkly. Rep. *44*:1–13, 1995.
38. Choo, M. H., Holmes, D. R., Jr., Gersh, B. J., et al.: Permanent pacemaker infections: Characterization and management. Am. J. Cardiol. *48*:559–564, 1981.
39. Christensen, G. D., Bisno, A. L., and Parisi, J. T., et al.: Nosocomial septicemia due to multiply antibiotic-resistant *Staphylococcus epidermidis*. Ann. Intern. Med. *96*:1–10, 1982.
40. Christensen, G. D., Parisi, J. T., Bisno, A. L., et al.: Characterization of clinically significant strains of coagulase-negative staphylococci. J. Clin. Microbiol. *18*:258–269, 1983.
41. Christensen, G. D., Simpson, W. A., Bisno, A. L., et al.: Adherence of slime-producing strains of *Staphylococcus epidermidis* to smooth surfaces. Infect. Immun. *37*:318–326, 1982.
42. Christensen, G. D., Simpson, W. A., Bisno, A. L., et al.: Experimental foreign body infections in mice challenged with slime-producing *Staphylococcus epidermidis*. Infect. Immun. *40*:407–410, 1983.
43. Clink, J., and Pennington, T. H.: Staphylococcal whole-cell polypeptide analysis: Evaluation as a taxonomic and typing tool. J. Med. Microbiol. *23*:41–44, 1987.
44. Crass, B. A., and Bergdoll, M. S.: Involvement of coagulase-negative staphylococci in toxic shock syndrome. J. Clin. Microbiol. *23*:43–45, 1986.
45. Dandalides, P. C., Rutala, W. A., Thomann, C. A., et al.: Serious postoperative infections caused by coagulase-negative staphylococci: An epidemiological and clinical study. J. Hosp. Infect. *8*:233–241, 1986.
46. D'Angio, C. T., McGowan, K. L., and Baumgart, S.: Surface colonization with coagulase-negative staphylococci in premature neonates. J. Pediatr. *114*:1029–1034, 1989.
47. Davenport, D. S., Massanari, R. M., Pfaller, M. A., et al.: Usefulness of a test for slime production as a marker for clinically significant infections with coagulase-negative staphylococci. J. Infect. Dis. *153*:332–339, 1986.
48. De Hondt, G., Ieven, M., and Vandermersch, C.: Destructive endocarditis caused by *Staphylococcus lugdunensis*: Case report and review of the literature. Acta Clin. Belg. *52*:27–30, 1997.
49. Del Bene, V. E., John, J. F., Jr., Twitty, J. A., et al.: Antistaphylococcal activity of teicoplanin, vancomycin, and other antimicrobial agents: The significance of methicillin resistance. J. Infect. Dis. *154*:349–352, 1986.
50. de Saxe, M. J., Crees-Morris, J. A., Marples, R. R., et al.: Evaluation of current phage-typing systems for coagulase-negative staphylococci. *In* Jeljaszewicz, J. (ed.): Staphylococci and Staphylococcal Infections. Stuttgart, Gustave Fischer Verlag, 1981, pp. 197–204.
51. Dickinson, G. M., and Bisno, A. L.: Infections associated with indwelling devices: Concepts of pathogenesis: Infections associated with intravascular devices. Antimicrob. Agents Chemother. *33*:597–601, 1989.
52. Dickinson, G. M., and Bisno, A. L.: Infections associated with indwelling devices: Infections related to extravascular devices. Antimicrob. Agents Chemother. *33*:602–607, 1989.
53. Dismukes, W. E.: Prosthetic valve endocarditis factors influencing outcome and recommendations for therapy. *In* Bisno, A. L. (ed.): Treatment of Infective Endocarditis. New York, Grune & Stratton, 1981, pp. 167–191.
54. Dismukes, W. E., Karchmer, A. W., Buckley, M. J., et al.: Prosthetic valve endocarditis: Analysis of 38 cases. Circulation *48*:365–377, 1973.
55. Donowitz, L. C., Haley, C. E., Gregory, W. W., et al.: Neonatal intensive care unit bacteremia: Emergence of gram-positive bacteria as major pathogens. Am. J. Infect. Control *15*:141–147, 1987.
56. Dougherty, S. H., and Simmons, R. L.: Infections in bionic man: The pathobiology of infections in prosthetic devices: Parts I and II. Curr. Probl. Surg. *19*:217–319, 1982.
57. Drewry, D. T., Galbraith, L., Wilkinson, B. J., et al.: Staphylococcal slime: A cautionary tale. J. Clin. Microbiol. *28*:1292–1296, 1990.
58. Dryden, M. S., Talsania, H. G., Martin, S., et al.: Evaluation of methods for typing coagulase-negative staphylococci. J. Med. Microbiol. *37*:109–117, 1992.
59. Edwards, M. S., and Baker, C. J.: Median sternotomy wound infections in children. Pediatr. Infect. Dis. J. *2*:105–109, 1987.
60. Etienne, J., Brun, Y., and El Solh, N., et al.: Characterization of clinically significant isolates of *Staphylococcus epidermidis* from patients with endocarditis. J. Clin. Microbiol. *26*:613–617, 1988.
61. Farber, B. F., Kaplan, M. H., and Clogston, A. G.: *Staphylococcus epidermidis* extracted slime inhibits the antimicrobial action of glycopeptide antibiotics. J. Infect. Dis. *161*:27–40, 1990.
62. Fass, R. J., Helsel, V. L., Barnishan, J., et al.: In vitro susceptibilities of four species of coagulase-negative staphylococci. Antimicrob. Agents Chemother. *30*:545–552, 1986.
63. Fine, R. N., Salusky, I. B., Hall, T., et al.: Peritonitis in children undergoing continuous ambulatory peritoneal dialysis. Pediatrics *71*:806–809, 1983.
64. Fitzgerald, R. H., Jr., Nolan, D. R., Ilstrup, D. M., et al.: Deep wound sepsis following total hip arthroplasty. J. Bone Joint Surg. *59*:847–855, 1977.
65. Fleer, A., Gerards, L. J., Aerts, P., et al.: Opsonic defense to *Staphylococcus epidermidis* in the premature neonate. J. Infect. Dis. *152*:930–937, 1985.
66. Fleer, A., Senders, R. C., Visser, M. R., et al.: Septicemia due to coagulase-negative staphylococci in a neonatal intensive care unit: Clinical and bacteriological features and contaminated parenteral fluids as a source of sepsis. Pediatr. Infect. Dis. J. *2*:426–431, 1983.
67. Flynn, P. M., Shenep, J. L., Stokes, D. C., et al.: In situ management of confirmed central venous catheter-related bacteremia. Pediatr. Infect. Dis. J. *6*:729–734, 1987.
68. Freeman, J., Platt, R., Sidebottom, D. G., et al.: Coagulase-negative staphylococcal bacteremia in the changing neonatal intensive care unit population. J. A. M. A. *258*:2548–2552, 1987.
69. Freeman, R., Goodfellow, M., Ward, A. C., et al.: Epidemiological typing of coagulase-negative staphylococci by pyrolysis mass spectrometry. J. Med. Microbiol. *34*:245–248, 1991.

70. Friedman, L. E., Brown, A. E., Miller, D. R., et al.: *Staphylococcus epidermidis* septicemia in children with leukemia and lymphoma. Am. J. Dis. Child. *138*:715–719, 1984.
71. Gatermann, S., Crossley, K. B.: Urinary tract infections. *In* Crossley, K. B., and Archer, G. L. (eds.): The Staphylococci in Human Disease. New York, Churchill Livingstone, 1997, pp. 493–508.
72. Gatermann, S., John, J., and Marre, R.: *Staphylococcus saprophyticus* urease: Characterization and contribution to uropathogenicity in unobstructed urinary tract infections of rats. Infect. Immun. *57*:110–116, 1989.
73. Gatermann, S., Kreft, B., Marre, R., et al.: Identification and characterization of a surface-protein (Ssp) of *Staphylococcus saprophyticus*. Infect. Immun. *60*:1055–1060, 1992.
74. Gatermann, S., Meyer, H. G., and Wanner, G.: *Staphylococcus saprophyticus* hemagglutinin is a 160-kilodalton surface protein. Infect. Immun. *65*:4127–4132, 1992.
75. Gnann, J. W. Jr., and Cobbs, C. G.: Infections of prosthetic valves and intravascular devices. *In* Mandell, G. L., Douglas R. G, Jr., and Bennett J. E (eds.): Principles and Practice of Infectious Diseases. 2nd ed. New York, John Wiley and Sons, 1985, pp. 530–539.
76. Goering, R. V., and Winters, M. A.: Rapid method for epidemiologic evaluation of gram-positive cocci by field inversion gel electrophoresis. J. Clin. Microbiol. *30*:577–580, 1992.
77. Goldman, D. A., and Pier, G. B.: Pathogenesis of infections relapsed to intravascular catheterization. Clin. Microbiol. Rev. *6*:176–192, 1993.
78. Gordon, D. L., Rice, J. L., and Avery, V. M.: Surface phagocytosis and host defense in the peritoneal cavity during continuous ambulatory peritoneal dialysis. Eur. J. Clin. Microbiol. Infect. Dis. *9*:191–197, 1990.
79. Graninger, W., Wenish, C., and Hasenhandl, M.: Treatment of staphylococcal infections. Curr. Opin. Infect. Dis. *8* (Suppl. 1):520–528, 1995.
80. Gray, E. D., Peters, G., Verstegen, M., et al.: Effect of extracellular slime substance from *Staphylococcus epidermidis* on the human cellular immune response. Lancet *1*:365–367, 1984.
81. Gray, J. E., Richardson, D. K., McCormick, M. C., et al.: Coagulase-negative staphylococcal bacteremia among very low birth weight infants: Relation to admission illness severity, resource use, and outcome. Pediatrics *95*:225–230, 1995.
82. Gristina, A. G.: Biomaterial-centered infection: Microbial adhesion versus tissue integration. Science *237*:1588–1595, 1987.
83. Grossi, E. A., Culliford, A. T., and Krieger, K. H., et al.: A survey of 77 major infectious complications of median sternotomy: A review of 7,949 consecutive operative procedures. Ann. Thorac. Surg. *40*:214–223, 1985.
84. Gruer, L. D., Bartlett, R., and Ayliffe, G. A. J.: Species identification and antibiotic sensitivity of coagulase-negative staphylococci from CAPD peritonitis. J. Antimicrob. Chemother. *13*:577–583, 1984.
85. Gruskay, J., Harris, M. C., Costarino, A. T., et al.: Neonatal *Staphylococcus epidermidis* meningitis with unremarkable CSF examination results. Am. J. Dis. Child. *143*:580–582, 1989.
86. Gruskay, J. A., Abbasi, S., Anday, E., et al.: *Staphylococcus epidermidis*-associated enterocolitis. J. Pediatr. *109*:520–524, 1986.
87. Gunn, B. A., and Davis, C. E., Jr.: *Staphylococcus haemolyticus* urinary tract infection in a male patient. J. Clin. Microbiol. *26*:1055–1057, 1988.
88. Hall, D. E., and Snitzer, J. A., III: *Staphylococcus epidermidis* as a cause of urinary tract infections in children. J. Pediatr. *124*:437–438, 1994.
89. Hall, R. T., Hall, S. L., Barnes, W. G., et al.: Characteristics of coagulase-negative staphylococci from infants with bacteremia. Pediatr. Infect. Dis. J. *6*:377–383, 1987.
90. Hall, S. L., Hall, R. T., Barnes, W. G., et al.: Relationship of maternal to neonatal colonization with coagulase-negative staphylococci. Am. J. Perinatol. 7:384–388, 1990.
91. Hall, S. L., Riddell, S. W., Barnes, W. G., et al.: Evaluation of coagulase-negative staphylococcal isolates from serial nasopharyngeal cultures of premature infants. Diagn. Microbiol. Infect. Dis. *13*:17–23, 1990.
92. Hamilton-Miller, J. M. T., and Iliffe, A.: Antimicrobial resistance in coagulase negative staphylococci. J. Med. Microbiol. *19*:217–226, 1985.
93. Hamory, B. H., Parisi, J. T., and Hutton, J. P.: *Staphylococcus epidermidis*: A significant nosocomial pathogen. Am. J. Infect. Control *15*:59–74, 1987.
94. Haslett, T. M., Isenberg, H. D., Hilton, E., et al.: Microbiology of indwelling central intravascular catheters. J. Clin. Microbiol. *26*:696–701, 1988.
95. Hebert, G. A., Cooksey, R. C., Clark, N. C., et al.: Biotyping coagulase-negative staphylococci. J. Clin. Microbiol. *26*:1950–1956, 1988.
96. Heidrich, C., Hantke, K., Bierbaum, G., et al.: Identification and analysis of a gene encoding a Fur-like protein of *Staphylococcus epidermidis*. F. E. M. S. Microbiol. Lett. *140*:253–259, 1996.
97. Heilmann, C., and Peters, G.: Biology and pathogenesis of *Staphylococcus epidermidis*. *In* Fischetti, V. A., Novick, R. P., Ferretti, J. J., et al. (eds.): Gram-Positive Pathogens. Washington, D.C., ASM Press, 2000, pp. 442–449.
98. Hickman, R. O., Buckner, C. D., Clift, R. A., et al.: A modified right atrial catheter for access to the venous system in marrow transplant recipients. Surg. Gynecol. Obstet. *148*:871–875, 1979.
99. Hogt, A. H., Dankert, J., Hulstaert, C. E., et al.: Cell surface characteristics of coagulase-negative staphylococci and their adherence to fluorinated poly (ethyleneprophylene). Infect. Immun. *51*:294–301, 1986.
100. Huebner, J., and Goldman, D. A.: Coagulase negative staphylococci: Role as pathogens. Annu. Rev. Med. *50*:223–236, 2000.
101. Hussain, Z., Stoakes, L., Garrow, S., et al.: Rapid detection of *mecA*-positive and *mecA*-negative coagulase-negative staphylococci by an anti-penicillin binding protein 2a slide latex agglutination test. J. Clin. Microbiol. *38*:2051–2054, 2000.
102. Iannacci, L., and Piomelli, S.: Supportive care for children with cancer: Guidelines of the Children's Cancer Study Group: Use of venous access lines. Am. J. Pediatr. Hematol. Oncol. *6*:277–281, 1984.
103. Ichiman, Y.: Applications of fluorescent antibody for detecting capsular substance in *Staphylococcus epidermidis*. J. Appl. Bacteriol. *56*:311–316, 1984.
104. Ichiman, Y., and Yoshida, K.: The relationship of capsular-type of *Staphylococcus epidermidis* to virulence and induction of resistance in the mouse. J. Appl. Bacteriol. *51*:229–241, 1981.
105. Izard, N. C., Hachler, H., Grehn, M., et al.: Ribotyping of coagulase-negative staphylococci with special emphasis on intraspecific typing of *Staphylococcus epidermidis*. J. Clin. Microbiol. *30*:817–823, 1992.
106. Jara, F. M., Toledo-Pereyra, L., Lewis, J. W., Jr., et al.: The infected pacemaker pocket. J. Thorac. Cardiovasc. Surg. *78*:298–300, 1979.
107. John, J. F., and McNeill, W. F.: Activity of cephalosporins against methicillin-susceptible and methicillin-resistant, coagulase-negative staphylococci: Minimal effect of beta-lactamases. Antimicrob. Agents Chemother. *17*:179–183, 1980.
108. Johnson, C. M., and Rhodes, K. H.: Pediatric endocarditis. Mayo Clin. Proc. *57*:86–94, 1982.
109. Johnson, G. M., Lee, D. A., Regelmann, W. E., et al.: Interference with granulocyte function by *Staphylococcus epidermidis* slime. Infect. Immun. *54*:13–20, 1986.
110. Jordan, P. A., Iravani, A., Richard, G. A., et al.: Urinary tract infection caused by *Staphylococcus saprophyticus*. J. Infect. Dis. *142*:510–515, 1980.
111. Kacica, M. A., Horgan, M. J., Preston, K. E., et al.: Relatedness of coagulase-negative staphylococci causing bacteremia in low-birthweight infants. Infect. Control Hosp. Epidemiol. *15*:658–662, 1994.
112. Kaiser, A. B., Petracek, M. R., Lea, J. W. IV, et al.: Efficacy of cefazolin, cefamandole, and gentamicin as prophylactic agents in cardiac surgery: Results of a prospective, randomized, double-blind trial in 1030 patients. Ann. Surg. *206*:791–797, 1987.
113. Kallman, J., Kihlstrom, E., and Schollin, J.: Increase of staphylococci in neonatal septicaemia: A fourteen-year study. Acta Paediatr. *86*:533–538, 1997.
114. Kamme, C., and Lindberg, L.: Aerobic and anaerobic bacteria in deep infections after total hip arthroplasty: Differential diagnosis between infectious and non-infectious loosening. Clin. Orthop. *154*:201–207, 1981.
115. Karchmer, A. W., Archer, G. L., and Dismukes, W. E.: *Staphylococcus epidermidis* causing prosthetic valve endocarditis: Microbiologic and clinical observations as guides to therapy. Ann. Intern. Med. *98*:447–455, 1983.
116. Karp, J. E., Dick, J. D., Angelopulos, C., et al.: Empiric use of vancomycin during prolonged treatment-induced granulocytopenia: Randomized, double-blind, placebo-controlled clinical trial in patients with acute leukemia. Am. J. Med. *81*:237–242, 1986.
117. Keane, W. F., Comty, C. M., Verbrugh, H. A., et al.: Opsonic deficiency of peritoneal dialysis effluent in continuous ambulatory peritoneal dialysis. Kidney Int. *25*:539–543, 1984.
118. Keucher, T. R., and Mealey, J., Jr.: Long-term results after ventriculoatrial and ventriculoperitoneal shunting for infantile hydrocephalus. J. Neurosurg. *50*:79–186, 1979.
119. Kingston, D., Seal, D., and Hill, I. D.: Self-disinfecting plastics for intravenous catheters and prosthetic inserts. J. Hyg. *96*:185–198, 1986.
120. Kirby, W. M.: Vancomycin therapy in severe staphylococcal infections. Rev. Infect. Dis. *3*(Suppl.):236–239, 1981.
121. Kline, M. W., Mason, E. O., Jr., and Kaplan, S. L.: Outcome of heteroresistant *Staphylococcus aureus* infections in children. J. Infect. Dis. 156:205–208, 1987.
122. Kloos, W. E., Ballard, D. N., George, C. G., et al.: Delimiting the genus *Staphylococcus* through description of *Micrococcus caseolyticus* gen. nov., comb. nov. and the new species *Macrococcus equipercicus* sp. nov., *Macrococcus bovicus* sp. nov., and *Macrococcus carouselicus* sp. nov. Int. J. Syst. Bacteriol. *48*:859–877, 1998.
123. Kloos, W. E., and Bannerman, T. L.: Update of clinical significance of coagulase-negative staphylococci. Clin. Microbiol. Rev. 7:117–140, 1994.
124. Kloos, W. E., and Bannerman, T. L.: *Staphylococcus* and *Micrococcus*. *In* Murray, P. R, Baron, E. J., Pfaller, A., et al. (eds.): Manual of Clinical Microbiology. 7th ed. Washington, D. C., American Society for Microbiology, 1999, pp. 264–282.
125. Kloos, W. E., and Musselwhite, M. S.: Distribution and persistence of *Staphylococcus* and *Micrococcus* species and other aerobic bacteria on human skin. Appl. Microbiol. *30*:381–385, 1975.

126. Kristinsson, K. G., Hastings, J. G., and Spencer, R. C.: The role of extracellular slime in opsonophagocytosis of *Staphylococcus epidermidis*. J. Med. Microbiol. *27*:207–213, 1988.
127. Langley, J., and Gold, R.: Sepsis in febrile neutropenic children with cancer. Pediatr. Infect. Dis. J. *7*:34–37, 1988.
128. Latham, R. H., Running, K., and Stamm, W. E.: Urinary tract infections in young adult women caused by *Staphylococcus saprophyticus*. J. A. M. A. *250*:3063–3066, 1983.
129. Laverdiere, M., Peterson, P. K., and Verhoef, J.: In vitro activity of cephalosporins against methicillin-resistant coagulase-negative staphylococci. J. Infect. Dis. *137*:245–250, 1978.
130. Levison, M. E., and Bush, L. M.: Peritonitis and other intra-abdominal infections. *In* Mandell, G. L., Bennett, J. E., and Dolin. R. (eds.): Principles and Practice of Infectious Diseases. New York, Churchill Livingstone, 2000, pp. 821–856.
131. Lew, D. P.: Physiopathology of foreign body infections. Eur. J. Cancer Clin. Oncol. *25*:1379–1382, 1989.
132. Lewis, J. F., Brake, S. R., Anderson, D. J., et al.: Urinary tract infection due to coagulase-negative *Staphylococcus*. Am. J. Clin. Pathol. *77*:736–739, 1982.
133. Low, D. E., McGeer, A., and Poon, R.: Activities of daptomycin and teicoplanin against *Staphylococcus haemolyticus* and *Staphylococcus epidermidis*, including evaluation of susceptibility testing recommendation. Antimicrob. Agents Chemother. *33*:585–588, 1989.
134. Lowder, J. N., Lazarus, H. M., and Herzig, R. H.: Bacteremias and fungemias in oncologic patients with central venous catheters: Changing spectrum of infection. Arch. Intern. Med. *142*:1456–1459, 1982.
135. Lowy, F. D., Chang, D. S., and Lash, P. R.: Synergy of combinations of vancomycin, gentamicin, and rifampin against methicillin-resistant, coagulase-negative staphylococci. Antimicrob. Agents Chemother. *23*:932–934, 1983.
136. Lowy, F. D., Walsh, J. A., and Mayers, M. M.: Antibiotic activity in-vitro against methicillin-resistant *Staphylococcus epidermidis* and therapy of an experimental infection. Antimicrob. Agents Chemother. *16*:314–321, 1979.
137. Mack, D., Siemssen, N., and Laufs, R.: Parallel induction by glucose of adherence and a polysaccharide antigen specific for plastic-adherent *Staphylococcus epidermidis*: Evidence for functional relation to intracellular adhesion. Infect. Immun. *60*:2048–2057, 1992.
138. Maki, D., Weise, C. E., and Safarin, H. W.: A semi-quantitative culture method for identifying intravenous-catheter-related infection. N. Engl. J. Med. *296*:1305–1309, 1977.
139. Maki, D., Goldman, D., and Rhame, F. S.: Infection control in intravenous therapy. Ann. Intern. Med. *79*:867–887, 1973.
140. Mansour, K. A., Kauten, J. R., and Hatcher, C. R., Jr.: Management of the infected pacemaker: Explanation, sterilization, and reimplantation. Ann. Thorac. Surg. *40*:617–619, 1985.
141. Marples, R. R.: Laboratory assessment in the epidemiology of infections caused by coagulase-negative staphylococci. J. Med. Microbiol. *22*:285–287, 1986.
142. Marrie, T. J., Kwan, C., and Noble, A.: *Staphylococcus saprophyticus* as a cause of urinary tract infections. J. Clin. Microbiol. *16*:427–431, 1982.
143. Marsik, F. J., and Brake, S.: Species identification and susceptibility to 17 antibiotics of coagulase-negative staphylococci isolated from clinical specimens. J. Clin. Microbiol. *15*:640–645, 1982.
144. Martin, M. A., Pfaller, M. A., and Wenzel, R. P.: Coagulase-negative staphylococcal bacteremia: Mortality and hospital stay. Ann. Intern. Med. *110*:9–16, 1989.
145. Masur, H., and Johnson, W. D., Jr.: Prosthetic valve endocarditis. J. Thorac. Cardiovasc. Surg. *80*:31–37, 1980.
146. McCracken, G. H., Jr., and Shinefield, H. R.: Changes in the pattern of neonatal septicemia and meningitis. Am. J. Dis. Child. *112*:33–39, 1966.
147. McDonald, J. A., and Lohr, J. A.: *Staphylococcus epidermidis* pyelonephritis in a previously healthy child. Pediatr. Infect. Dis. J. *13*:1155–1156, 1994.
148. McDougal, L. K., and Thornsberry, C.: New recommendations for disk diffusion antimicrobial susceptibility tests for methicillin-resistant (hetero-resistant) staphylococci. J. Clin. Microbiol. *19*:482–488, 1984.
149. McLaurin, R. L., and Frame, P. T.: Treatment of infections of cerebrospinal fluid shunts. Rev. Infect. Dis. *9*:595–603, 1987.
150. Meyers, J. D.: Infection in bone marrow transplant recipients. Am. J. Med. *81*(Suppl. 1A):27–38, 1986.
151. Mickelsen, P. A., Plorde, J. J., Gordon, K. P., et al.: Instability of antibiotic resistance in a strain of *Staphylococcus epidermidis* isolated from an outbreak of prosthetic valve endocarditis. J. Infect. Dis. *152*:50–58, 1985.
152. Mirro, J., Jr., Rao, B. N., Stokes, D. C., et al.: A prospective study of Hickman/Broviac catheters and implantable ports in pediatric oncology patients. J. Clin. Oncol. 7:214–222, 1989.
153. Munson, D. P., Thompson, T. R., Johnson, D. E., et al.: Coagulase-negative staphylococci septicemia: Experience in a newborn intensive care unit. J. Pediatr. *101*:602–605, 1982.
154. Murtagh, F., and Lehman, R.: Peritoneal shunts in the management of hydrocephalus. J. A. M. A. *202*:1010–1014, 1967.
155. Nafziger, D. A., and Wenzel, R. P.: Coagulase-negative staphylococci: Epidemiology, evaluation, and therapy. Infect. Dis. Clin. North Am. *3*:915–928, 1989.
156. Nataro, J. P., Corcoran, L., Zirin, S., et al.: Prospective analysis of coagulase-negative staphylococcal infections in hospitalized infants. J. Pediatr. *125*:798–804, 1994.
157. National Committee for Clinical Laboratory Standards: Performance standards for antimicrobial susceptibility testing. NCCLS approved standard M100-S9. Wayne, PA, National Committee for Clinical Laboratory Standards, 1999.
158. Nelson, J. D.: Cerebrospinal fluid shunt infections. Pediatr. Infect. Dis. J. *3*(Suppl.):S30–S32, 1984.
159. Nicolle, L. E., Hoban, S. A., and Harding, G. K. M.: Characterization of coagulase-negative staphylococci from urinary tract infections. J. Clin. Microbiol. *17*:267–271, 1983.
160. Noel, G. J., O'Loughlin, J. E., and Edelson, P. J.: Neonatal *Staphylococcus epidermidis* right-sided endocarditis: Description of five catheterized infants. Pediatrics *82*:234–239, 1988.
161. Noel, G. J., and Edelson, P. J.: *Staphylococcus epidermidis* bacteremia in neonates: Further observations and the occurrence of focal infection. Pediatrics *74*:832–837, 1984.
162. Nouwen, J. L., van Belkum, A., de Marie, S., et al.: Clonal expansion of *Staphylococcus epidermidis* strains causing Hickman catheter–related infections in a hemato-oncologic department. J. Clin. Microbiol. *36*:2696–2702, 1998.
163. Oeding, P.: Genus *Staphylococci*. *In* Gergan, T., and Norris, J. R. (eds.): Methods in Microbiology. Vol. 12. New York, Academic Press, 1978, pp. 130–133
164. Ohshima, Y., Schumacher-Perdreau, F., and Peters, G.: Antiphagocytic effect of the capsule of *Staphylococcus simulans*. Infect. Immun. *58*:1350–1354, 1990.
165. Olsen, L., and Frykberg, T.: Complications in the treatment of hydrocephalus in children: A comparison of ventriculoatrial and ventriculoperitoneal shunts in a 20-year material. Acta Paediatr. Scand. *72*:385–390, 1983.
166. Overturf, G. D., and Balfour, G.: Osteomyelitis and sepsis: Severe complications of fetal monitoring. Pediatrics *55*:244–247, 1975.
167. Paley, D., Moseley, C. F., Armstrong, P., et al.: Primary osteomyelitis caused by coagulase-negative staphylococci. J. Pediatr. Orthop. *6*:622–626, 1986.
168. Parisi, J. T.: Coagulase-negative staphylococci and the epidemiological typing of *Staphylococcus epidermidis*. Microbiol. Rev. *49*:126–139, 1985.
169. Parisi, J. T., and Hecht, D. W.: Plasmid profiles in epidemiologic studies of infections by *Staphylococcus epidermidis*. J. Infect. Dis. *141*:637–643, 1980.
170. Parisi, J. T., Lampson, B. C., Hoover, D. L., et al.: Comparison of epidemiologic markers for *Staphylococcus epidermidis*. J. Clin. Microbiol. *24*:56–60, 1986.
171. Parisi, J. T., Talbot, H. W., Jr., and Skahan, J. M.: Development of a phage typing set for *Staphylococcus epidermidis* in the United States. Zentralbl. Bakteriol. [A] *241*:60–67, 1978.
172. Parker, M. A., and Tuazon, C. U.: Cervical osteomyelitis: Infection due to *Staphylococcus epidermidis* in hemodialysis patients. J. A. M. A. *240*:50–51, 1978.
173. Pascual, A., Fleer, A., Westerdaal, N. A. C., et al.: Modulation of adherence of coagulase-negative staphylococci to Teflon catheters in vitro. Eur. J. Clin. Microbiol. *5*:518–522, 1986.
174. Patrick, C. C.: Coagulase-negative staphylococci: Pathogens with increasing clinical significance. J. Pediatr. *116*:497–507, 1990.
175. Patrick, C. C., Kaplan, S. L., Baker, C. J., et al.: Persistent bacteremia due to coagulase-negative staphylococci in low birth weight neonates. Pediatrics *84*:977–985, 1989.
176. Patrick, C. C., Plaunt, M. R., Sweet, S. M., et al.: Defining *Staphylococcus epidermidis* cell wall proteins. J. Clin. Microbiol. *28*:2757–2760, 1990.
177. Patrick, C. C., Shenep, J. L., and Crawford, R.: Coagulase-negative *Staphylococcus* (ConS) bacteremia in a children's cancer hospital [Abstract]. Houston, Tx, Interscience Conference on Antimicrobial Agents and Chemotherapy, Abstract 644, 1989, p. 209.
178. Patrick, C. H., John, J. F., Levkoff, A. H., et al.: Relatedness of strains of methicillin-resistant coagulase-negative *Staphylococcus* colonizing hospital personnel and producing bacteremias in a neonatal intensive care unit. Pediatr. Infect. Dis. J. *11*:935–940, 1992.
179. Pereira, A. T.: Coagulase-negative strains of *Staphylococcus* possessing antigen 51 as agents of urinary tract infection. J. Clin. Pathol. *15*:252–253, 1962.
180. Peters, G., and Pulverer, G.: Pathogenesis and management of *Staphylococcus epidermidis* "plastic" foreign body infections. J. Antimicrob. Chemother. *14*(Suppl. D):67–71, 1984.
181. Peters, G., Saborowski, F., Locci, R., et al.: Investigations on staphylococcal infection of transvenous endocardial pacemaker electrodes. Am. Heart J. *108*:359–365, 1984.
182. Peters, G., von Eiff, C., and Herrmann, M.: The changing pattern of coagulase-negative staphylococci as infectious pathogens. Curr. Opin. Infect. Dis. *8*(Suppl. 1):512–519, 1995.

183. Peterson, P. K., Matzke, G., and Keane, W. F.: Current concepts in the management of peritonitis in patients undergoing continuous ambulatory peritoneal dialysis. Rev. Infect. Dis. *9*:604–612, 1987.
184. Peyman, G. A., Carroll, C. P., and Raichand, M.: Prevention and management of traumatic endophthalmitis. Ophthalmology *87*:320–324, 1980.
185. Pfaller, M. A., and Herwaldt, L. A.: Laboratory, clinical, and epidemiological aspects of coagulase-negative staphylococci. Clin. Microbiol. Rev. *1*:281–299, 1988.
186. Pizzo, P. A., Hathorn, J. W., Hiemenz, J., et al.: A randomized trial comparing ceftazidime alone with combination antibiotic therapy in cancer patients with fever and neutropenia. N. Engl. J. Med. *315*:552–558, 1986.
187. Pizzo, P. A., Ladisch, S., Simon, R. M., et al.: Increasing incidence of gram-positive sepsis in cancer patients. Med. Pediatr. Oncol. *5*:241–244, 1978.
188. Ponce De Leon, S., and Wenzel, R. P.: Hospital-acquired bloodstream infections with *Staphylococcus epidermidis*: Review of 100 cases. Am. J. Med. *77*:639–644, 1984.
189. Power, J., Wing, E. J., Talamo, T. S., et al.: Fatal bacterial endocarditis as a complication of permanent indwelling catheters: Report of two cases. Am. J. Med. *81*:166–168, 1986.
190. Press, O. W., Ramsey, P. G., Larson, E. B., et al.: Hickman catheter infections in patients with malignancies. Medicine (Baltimore) *63*:189–200, 1984.
191. Raucher, H. S., Hyatt, A. C., and Barzilai, A.: Quantitative blood cultures in the evaluation of septicemia in children with Broviac catheters. J. Pediatr. *104*:29–33, 1984.
192. Richards, M. J., Edwards, J. R., Culver, D. H., et al.: Nosocomial infections in pediatric intensive care units in the United States. Pediatrics *103*:e39, 1999.
193. Ross, M. N., Haase, G. M., and Poole, M. A.: Comparison of totally implanted reservoirs with external catheters as venous access devices in pediatric oncologic patients. Surg. Gynecol. Obstet. *167*:141, 1988.
194. Roos, K. L., and Scheld, W. M.: Central nervous system infections. *In* Crossley, K. B., and Archer, G. L. (eds.): The Staphylococci in Human Disease. New York, Churchill Livingstone, 1997, pp. 413–440.
195. Rotbart, H. A., Johnson, Z. T., and Reller, L. B.: Analysis of enteric coagulase-negative staphylococci from neonates with necrotizing enterocolitis. Pediatr. Infect. Dis. J. *8*:140–142, 1989.
196. Rupp, M. E., and Archer, G.: Hemagglutination and adherence to plastic by *Staphylococcus epidermidis*. Infect. Immun. *60*:1055–1060, 1992.
197. Rupp, M. E., and Archer, G. L.: Coagulase-negative staphylococci: Pathogens associated with medical progress. Clin. Infect. Dis. *19*:231–245, 1994.
198. Ryback, M. J., Cappelletty, D. M., Moldovan, T., et al.: Comparative in vitro activities and postantibiotic effects of the oxazolidinone compounds eperezolid (PNU-100592) and linezolid (PNU-100766) versus vancomycin against *Staphylococcus aureus*, coagulase-negative staphylococci, *Enterococcus faecalis*, and *Enterococcus faecium*. Antimicrob. Agents Chemother. *42*:712–724, 1998.
199. Sabath, L. D.: Chemical and physical factors influencing methicillin-resistance of *Staphylococcus aureus* and *Staphylococcus epidermidis*. J. Antimicrob. Chemother. *3*:S47–51, 1977.
200. Sabath, L. D.: Reappraisal of the antistaphylococcal activities of first-generation (narrow-spectrum) and second-generation (expanded-spectrum) cephalosporins. Antimicrob. Agents Chemother. *33*:407–411, 1989.
201. Sabath, L. D., Garner, C., Wilcox, C., et al.: Susceptibility of *Staphylococcus aureus* and *Staphylococcus epidermidis* to 65 antibiotics. Antimicrob. Agents Chemother. *9*:962–969, 1976.
202. Sampathkumar, P., Osmon, D. R., and Cockerill, F. R.: Prosthetic joint infection due to *Staphylococcus lugdunensis*. Mayo Clin. Proc. *75*:511–512, 2000.
203. Sattler, F. R., Foderaro, J. B., and Aber, R. C.: *Staphylococcus epidermidis* bacteremia associated with vascular catheters: An important cause of febrile morbidity in hospitalized patients. Infect. Control *5*:279–283, 1984.
204. Schaberg, D. R., Culver, D. H., and Gaynes, R. P.: Major trends in the microbial etiology of nosocomial infections. Am. J. Med. *91*(Suppl. 3B):72–75, 1991.
205. Schaberg, D. R., and Zervos, M. J.: Intergeneric and interspecies gene exchange in gram-positive cocci. Antimicrob. Agents Chemother. *30*:817–822, 1986.
206. Schaberg, D. R., and Zervos, M.: Plasmid analysis in the study of the epidemiology of nosocomial gram-positive cocci. Rev. Infect. Dis. *8*:705–712, 1986.
207. Scheifele, D. W., Bjornson, G. L., Dyer, R. A., et al.: Delta-like toxin produced by coagulase-negative staphylococci is associated with neonatal necrotizing enterocolitis. Infect. Immun. *55*:2268–2273, 1987.
208. Scheretz, R. J., Falk, R. J., Huffman, K. A., et al.: Infections associated with subclavian Udall catheters. Arch. Intern. Med. *143*:52–56, 1983.
209. Schimke, R. T., Black, P. H., Mark, V. H., et al.: Indolent *Staphylococcus albus* or *aureus* bacteremia after ventriculoatriostomy: Role of foreign body in its initiation and perpetuation. N. Engl. J. Med. *264*:264–270, 1961.
210. Schwalbe, R. S., Stapleton, J. T., and Gilligan, P. H.: Emergence of vancomycin resistance in coagulase-negative staphylococci. N. Engl. J. Med. *316*:927–931, 1987.
211. Shenep, J. L., Hughes, W. T., Robertson, P. K., et al.: Vancomycin, ticarcillin and amikacin compared with ticarcillin-clavulanate and amikacin in the empirical treatment of febrile, neutropenic children with cancer. N. Engl. J. Med. *319*:1053–1058, 1988.
212. Sheth, N. K., Franson, T. R., Rose, H. D., et al.: Colonization of bacteria on polyvinyl chloride and Teflon intravascular catheters in hospitalized patients. J. Clin. Microbiol. *18*:1061–1063, 1983.
213. Sheth, N. K., Franson, T. R., and Sohnle, P. G.: Influence of bacterial adherence to intravascular catheters on in vitro antibiotic susceptibility. Lancet *2*:1266–1268, 1985.
214. Shiro, H., Muller, E., Gutierrez, N., et al.: Transposon mutants or *Staphylococcus epidermidis* deficient in elaboration of capsular polysaccharide/adhesion and slime are avirulent in a rabbit model or endocarditis. J. Infect. Dis. *169*:1042–1049, 1994.
215. Shiro, H., Muller, E., Takeda, S., et al.: Potentiation of *Staphylococcus epidermidis* catheter-related bacteremia by lipid infusions. J. Infect. Dis. *171*:220–224, 1995.
216. Shoenbaum, S. C., Gardner, P., and Shillito, J.: Infections of cerebrospinal fluid shunts: Epidemiology, clinical manifestations, and therapy. J. Infect. Dis. *131*:543–552, 1975.
217. Shulman, R. J., Smith, E. O., Rahman, S., et al.: Single- vs double-lumen central venous catheters in pediatric oncology patients. Am. J. Dis. Child. *142*:893–895, 1988.
218. Shuttleworth, R., Behme, R. J., McNabb, A., et al.: Human isolates of bone and joint infections. J. Clin. Microbiol. *35*:2537–2541, 1997.
219. Schutze, G. E., Hall, M. A., Baker, C. J., et al.: Role of neutrophil receptors in opsonophagocytosis of coagulase-negative staphylococci. Infect. Immun. *59*:2573–2578, 1991.
220. Siebert, W. T., Moreland, N., and Williams, T. W., Jr.: Methicillin-resistant *Staphylococcus epidermidis*. South. Med. J. *71*:1353–1355, 1978.
221. Sitges-Serra, A., Puig, P., and Jaurrieta, E.: Catheter sepsis due to *Staphylococcus epidermidis* during parenteral nutrition. Surg. Gynecol. Obstet. *151*:481–483, 1980.
222. Skahan, J. M., and Parisi, J. T.: Development of a bacteriophage-typing set for *Staphylococcus epidermidis*. J. Clin. Microbiol. *6*:16–18, 1977.
223. Slama, T. G., Sklar, S. J., Misinski, J., et al.: Randomized comparison of cefamandole, cefazolin, and cefuroxime prophylaxis in open-heart surgery. Antimicrob. Agents Chemother. *29*:744–747, 1986.
224. Smith, I. M., Beals, P. D., Kinsbury, K. R., et al.: Observations on *Staphylococcus albus* septicemia in mice and men. Arch. Intern. Med. *102*:375–388, 1958.
225. Smith, J. A., Henry, D. A., Bourgault, A., et al.: Comparison of agar disk diffusion, microdilution broth, and agar dilution for testing antimicrobial susceptibility of coagulase-negative staphylococci. J. Clin. Microbiol. *25*:1741–1746, 1987.
226. Sparrelid, E., Hagglund, H., Remberger, M., et al.: Bacteraemia during aplastic phase after allogeneic bone marrow transplantation is associated with early death from invasive fungal infection. Bone Marrow Transplant. *22*:795–800, 1998.
227. St. Geme, J. W. III, Bell, L. M., Baumgart, S., et al.: Distinguishing sepsis from blood culture contamination in young infants with blood cultures growing coagulase-negative staphylococci. Pediatrics *86*:157–162, 1990.
228. Stillman, R. I., Wenzel, R. P., and Donowitz, L. C.: Emergence of coagulase-negative staphylococci as major nosocomial bloodstream pathogens. Infect. Control *8*:108–112, 1987.
229. Talbot, H. W., Jr., and Parisi, J. T.: Phage typing of *Staphylococcus epidermidis*. J. Clin. Microbiol. *3*:519–523, 1976.
230. Tan, T. Q., Mason, E. O., Jr., Ou, C. N., et al.: Use of intravenous rifampin in neonates with persistent staphylococcal bacteremia. Antimicrob. Agents Chemother. *37*:2401–2406, 1993.
231. Tan, T. Q., Musser, J. M., Shulman, R. J., et al.: Molecular epidemiology of coagulase-negative staphylococcus blood isolated from neonates with persistent bacteremia and children with central venous catheter infections. J. Infect. Dis. *169*:1393–1397, 1994.
232. Tebbs, S. E., and Elliott, T. S. J.: Modification of central venous catheter polymers to prevent in vitro microbial colonization. Eur. J. Clin. Microbiol. Infect. Dis. *13*:111–117, 1994.
233. Tenckhoff, H., and Schechter, H.: A bacteriologically safe peritoneal access device. Trans. Am. Soc. Artif. Intern. Organs *14*:181–187, 1968.
234. Tenover, F. C., Jones, R. N., Swenson, B., et al.: Methods for improved detection of oxacillin resistance in coagulase-negative staphylococci: Results of a multicenter study. J. Clin. Microbiol. *37*:4051–4058, 1999.
235. Thomson-Carter, F. M., and Pennington, T. H.: Characterization of coagulase-negative staphylococci by sodium dodecyl sulfate-polyacrylamide gel electrophoresis and immunoblot analysis. J. Clin. Microbiol. *27*:2199–2203, 1989.
236. Timmermann, C. P., Fleer, A., Besnier, J. M., et al.: Characterization of a proteinaceous adhesion of *Staphylococcus epidermidis* which mediates attachment to polystyrene. Infect. Immun. *59*:4187–4192, 1991.

237. Tojo, M., Yamashita, N., Goldmann, D. A., et al.: Isolation and characterization of a capsular polysaccharide adhesion from *Staphylococcus epidermidis*. J. Infect. Dis. *157*:713–722, 1988.
238. Tully, J. L., Friedland, G. H., Baldini, L. M., et al.: Complications of intravenous therapy with steel needles and small-bore Teflon catheters: A comparative study. Am. J. Med. *70*:702–706, 1981.
239. Van Bronswijk, H., Verbrugh, H. A., Heezius, C. J. M., et al.: Heterogeneity in opsonic requirements of *Staphylococcus epidermidis*: Relative importance of surface hydrophobicity, capsules and slime. Immunology *67*:81–86, 1989.
240. Vandenesch, F., Eykyn, S. J., and Etienne, J. Infections caused by newly-described species of coagulase-negative staphylococci. Rev. Med. Microbiol. *6*:94–100, 1995.
241. Veenstra, G. J., Cremers, F. F. M., van Dijk, H., et al.: Ultrastructural organization and regulation of a biomaterial adhesion of *Staphylococcus epidermidis*. J. Bacteriol. *178*:537–541, 1996.
242. Venditti, M., Santini, C., Serra, P., et al.: Comparative in vitro activities of new fluorinated quinolones and other antibiotics against coagulase-negative *Staphylococcus* blood isolates from neutropenic patients, and relationship between susceptibility and slime production. Antimicrob. Agents Chemother. *33*:209–211, 1989.
243. Villari, P., Sarnataro, C., and Iacuzio, L.: Molecular epidemiology of *Staphylococcus epidermidis* in a neonatal intensive care unit over a three-year period. J. Clin. Microbiol. *38*:1740–1746, 2000.
244. Viscoli, C., Garaventa, A., Boni, L., et al.: Role of Broviac catheters in infections in children with cancer. Pediatr. Infect. Dis. J. *7*:556–560, 1988.
245. Wachsmuth, K.: Molecular epidemiology of bacterial infections: Examples of methodology and investigations of outbreaks. Rev. Infect. Dis. *8*:682–692, 1986.
246. Wade, J. C., Schimpft, S. C., Newman, K. A., et al.: *Staphylococcus epidermidis*: An increasing cause of infection in patients with granulocytopenia. Ann. Intern. Med. *97*:503–508, 1982.
247. Wadstrom, T., and Rozgonyi, F.: Virulence determinants of coagulase-negative staphylococci. *In* Mardh, P. A., and Schleifer, K. H. (eds.): Coagulase-Negative Staphylococci. Stockholm, Almquist and Wiksel International, 1986, pp. 123–130.
248. Watanakunakorn, C.: Prosthetic valve infection endocarditis. Prog. Cardiovasc. Dis. *22*:181–192, 1979.
249. Wilson, A. P. R., O'Hare, M. D., Felmingham, D., et al.: Teicoplanin-resistant coagulase-negative *Staphylococcus*. Lancet *2*:973, 1986.
250. Wilson, C. B.: Immunologic basis for increased susceptibility of the neonate to infection. J. Pediatr. *108*:1–12, 1986.
251. Wilson, W. R., Jaumin, P. M., Danielson, G. K., et al.: Prosthetic valve endocarditis. Ann. Intern. Med. *82*:751–756, 1975.
252. Winston, D. J., Dudnick, D. V., Chapin, M., et al.: Coagulase-negative staphylococcal bacteremia in patients receiving immunosuppressive therapy. Arch. Intern. Med. *143*:32–36, 1983.
253. Wong, S. S., Ho, P. L., Woo, P. C., et al.: Bacteremia caused by staphylococci with inducible vancomycin heteroresistance. Clin. Infect. Dis. *29*:760–767, 1999.
254. Yamada, T., Ichiman, Y., and Yoshida, K.: Possible common biological and immunological properties for detecting encapsulated strains of *Staphylococcus epidermidis*. J. Clin. Microbiol. *26*:2167–2172, 1988.
255. Yogev, R.: Cerebrospinal fluid shunt infections: A personal view. Pediatr. Infect. Dis. J. *4*:113–118, 1985.
256. Yoshida, K., Umeda, A., Ichiman, T., et al.: Cross protection between a strain of *Staphylococcus epidermidis* and eight other species of coagulase-negative staphylococci. Can. J. Microbiol. *34*:913–915, 1988.
257. Younger, J. J., Christensen, G. D., Bartley, D. L., et al.: Coagulase-negative staphylococci isolated from cerebrospinal fluid shunts: Importance of slime production, species identification and shunt removal to clinical outcome. J. Infect. Dis. *156*:548–554, 1987.
258. Zakrzewska-Czerwinska, J., Mordarski, M., Goodfellow, M., et al.: Deoxyribonucleic acid relatedness amongst *Staphylococcus epidermidis* and *Staphylococcus saprophyticus* strains. Zentralbl. Bakteriol. Mikrobiol. Hyg. *269*:179–187, 1988.
259. Zimmerman, R. J., and Kloos, W. E.: Comparative zone electrophoresis of esterases of *Staphylococcus* species isolated from mammalian skin. Can. J. Microbiol. *22*:771–779, 1976.

Group A, Group C, and Group G Beta-Hemolytic Streptococcal Infections

EDWARD L. KAPLAN ■ MICHAEL A. GERBER

Group A Streptococcal Infections

Group A beta-hemolytic streptococci *(Streptococcus pyogenes)* are among the most common pathogenic bacteria isolated from children. They are associated with a wide variety of infections and disease states. Though uniformly sensitive to penicillin and still exquisitely sensitive to many other antibiotics, group A streptococcal infections continue to present formidable clinical and public health problems for pediatricians and other primary care physicians. Although the vast majority of group A streptococcal infections are of short duration and relatively benign, they may be fulminant and life-threatening. The importance of group A streptococcal infections was reinforced at the close of the 20th century by a resurgence of acute rheumatic fever in the United States,[108] as well as the appearance of group A streptococcal toxic shock syndrome with very high morbidity and mortality rates.[146, 147] Additionally, this bacterium is different from other pyrogenic bacteria because of the potential for development of delayed, nonsuppurative sequelae (e.g., acute glomerulonephritis, acute rheumatic fever) after uncomplicated infections.

THE ORGANISM

S. pyogenes (group A streptococcus) is a gram-positive coccus that forms either short or long chains. Group A streptococci produce clear (beta) hemolysis on blood agar, a bacteriologic feature important in their recognition and differentiation from nonhemolytic (gamma) streptococci and from viridans (alpha) streptococci, which cause partial or green hemolysis on sheep blood agar. Although hemolysis is produced on culture plates containing blood from a variety of mammalian species, sheep or horse blood gives the clearest differentiation. Some strains of group A streptococci hemolyze red blood cells slowly or even result in almost greenish hemolysis on the surface of blood agar plates incubated aerobically. These strains can be recognized by their ability to produce clear hemolysis under anaerobic conditions, which is achieved readily by routinely making a short cut or stab into the blood agar at the time of inoculation.[81] Incubation with carbon dioxide or in a candle jar also can be helpful in enhancing beta-hemolysis. Rare strains of group A streptococci are not hemolytic.[75, 83]

More than 130 different types of group A streptococci have been recognized either on the basis of a series of serologically distinct surface proteins, the M proteins, or by sequencing of the *emm* gene, which codes for M protein.[54, 81, 104] The M serotypes of streptococci associated with impetigo and pyoderma are different from those associated with clinical pharyngitis, although a few M types have the capability of producing both kinds of infection.[5] M protein renders group A streptococci resistant to phagocytosis and, therefore, is a major virulence factor for these organisms.

Additional evidence indicates that more M types exist that have not been identified yet; new *emm* sequences are continuing to be described.

The group A streptococcal cell is a complex structure. In rapidly dividing strains (e.g., young cultures, epidemic strains), the cell is covered with a hyaluronic acid capsule that gives the colonies a mucoid or water drop appearance. Protruding from the cell surface and into the hyaluronic capsular layer are microscopic hairlike fimbriae that are responsible for adherence of group A streptococci to epithelial cells. A basic chemical component of these fimbriae is lipoteichoic acid.[11] M protein also is associated with these fimbriae.[57] Other surface proteins of interest are the T and R proteins, the serum opacity factor (SOF) proteins, and proteins that bind nonspecifically to the Fc fragment of gamma-globulins. The function and exact location of these other proteins on the surface of the organism have not been identified precisely. Strains of a particular M type generally are associated with a particular T agglutination pattern.[80] In strains producing serum opacity, the serologically specific SOF protein correlates closely with the M type of the strain. At present, probably more than 30 SOF-positive types of group A streptococci have been recognized; undoubtedly, others have not been identified yet. All these characteristics are useful in epidemiologic studies of streptococcal infections, either in an individual patient or in a community.

In addition to these surface proteins, the carbohydrate moiety responsible for group specificity (e.g., group A carbohydrate) also is found in the cell wall in a position sufficiently superficial to permit reaction with antibody specifically directed toward it. The group A carbohydrate is a polymer of rhamnose units with side chains of *N*-acetylglucosamine, which is responsible for its group (e.g., A) specificity.[112] The structure providing rigidity to the cell wall is another large polymer, a peptidoglycan, that consists of glycan strands cross-linked by peptide bridges. Its role in the pathogenesis of infection is incompletely defined.

Within the cell wall of group A streptococci lies the cell membrane, which is composed mainly of lipoprotein or lipid-protein complexes. This membrane is the outer surface of the osmotically fragile protoplasts, or L-forms, of streptococci. These wall-less forms of group A streptococci are resistant to penicillin.[59]

Intracellular constituents of group A streptococci include, in addition to DNA and RNA, numerous enzymes and hemolysins.[26] Plasmids have been identified that control resistance to certain antibiotics (e.g., erythromycin).[107] Bacteriophages play important roles, including transfer of the determinants of antibiotic resistance and control of pyrogenic exotoxin production in the genetics of group A streptococci.[163, 168]

Group A streptococci produce and release into the surrounding medium a large number of biologically active extracellular products. Some of these products are toxic for human and other mammalian cells. Both streptolysin O (the oxygen-labile hemolysin) and streptolysin S (the oxygen-stable hemolysin) injure cell membranes; these hemolysins not only lyse red blood cells but also damage other eukaryotic cells (including myocardial cells) and membranous subcellular organelles.[14] Streptolysin O is antigenic; streptolysin S is not. The latter hemolysin is bound loosely to the streptococcal cell and is released in a complexed, stable form with a variety of carrier molecules. The pyrogenic exotoxins resemble endotoxin in exhibiting both primary or intrinsic toxicity and secondary toxicity resulting from the development of host hypersensitivity.[99] The outbreak of streptococcal toxic shock syndrome, which became pronounced at the close of the 20th century, was reported to be associated with the reappearance of strains making pyrogenic exotoxin A, but many unanswered questions remain about the precise pathogenesis.[146] Group A streptococci also produce bacteriocins,[148] low-molecular-weight proteins that can kill a variety of other gram-positive bacterial species and, thus, may play a role in promoting infection or even persistence of colonization.

Many of the other extracellular products of group A streptococci are specific enzymes that do not appear to be directly toxic to mammalian or bacterial cells but digest or initiate the breakdown of important biologic substrates. They include the deoxyribonucleases (nucleases A, B, C, and D), the streptokinases (which activate the fibrinolytic or plasmin-plasminogen system), a hyaluronidase, an amylase, a proteinase, an esterase, an NADase (nicotinamide adenine dinucleotidase), and C5a peptidase.

Several of these enzymes are antigenic (e.g., DNase B, streptokinase, hyaluronidase, NADase). Among group A streptococcal surface virulence factors, C5a peptidase plays a major role by inactivating the complement chemotaxin C5a, thereby reducing the early phagocytic response and allowing group A streptococci to become locally established. This extracellular product has been shown to be antigenic in animals and humans.[32]

TRANSMISSION

The mechanism of spread of streptococci from one person to another and from one body site to another varies according to the clinical manifestations of the infection. Epidemiologic studies of patients with streptococcal sore throat indicate that airborne routes of spread (by small-droplet nuclei, dust) and environmental contamination (e.g., contaminated clothing or bedding) play little, if any, role in spread of this kind of group A streptococcal infection.[125] Close personal contact is required for transmission of streptococcal pharyngitis, which occurs apparently by direct projection of large droplets or by physical transfer of respiratory secretions containing the infectious bacteria. Spread within family units, schoolrooms, or other crowded facilities such as military barracks occurs commonly.[47] In addition, residential nursing facilities have proved to be highly susceptible to spread among both staff and patients.

Contaminated food or milk also may result in group A streptococcal infection of the throat and produce a common-source outbreak.[71] Salads containing hard-boiled eggs (e.g., egg salad) appear to be a special problem. Anal carriers have been identified as the source of contagion in several hospital outbreaks of streptococcal wound infections. Some studies have suggested that rectal or anal carriers may be more common than suspected.[100]

The period of greatest contagiousness of streptococcal pharyngitis and scarlet fever is during the acute stage of the illness. Most antibiotic therapy (especially penicillin) rapidly suppresses the growth of group A streptococci and, if continued, most often eradicates them from the upper respiratory tract. A patient can be considered much less contagious after 24 hours of antimicrobial therapy. Most researchers recommend that children can return to school by that time, especially if they are afebrile, with a lessened risk of spread of the organism to close contacts.[143]

Although humans with active, but subclinical infection also may contribute to the spread of group A streptococci, the role of throat "carriers" in the spread of this organism is less important. Most secondary spread occurs during the first 2 weeks after acquisition,[157] but rarely do streptococcal upper respiratory tract carriers spread the organism.[85] In contrast to throat carriage, which may persist for weeks or months, the prolonged presence of group A streptococci in the anterior nares is an unusual finding.

Unlike the upper respiratory tract, where group A streptococci readily can establish infection on an intact epithelial surface, the production of streptococcal impetigo or pyoderma appears to be facilitated by previous disruption of the skin by trauma, insects, or some preexisting skin disorder. Group A streptococci may be found on normal skin for several days to 2 weeks before infection develops,[56] with some other means of access being required. That the source of streptococcal skin infection is the upper respiratory tract does not seem likely. Group A streptococci causing impetigo may be found in the nose or throat, but they usually do not reach this site until several weeks after the establishment of cutaneous infection. One possible source is a skin lesion in another child, with spread occurring by direct contact. Data suggest that spread can occur even by small flies that feed on such lesions.[10] However, the exact role of environmental contamination in the spread of streptococcal impetigo and pyoderma and in secondary infection of wounds, burns, eczema, and other dermatoses is not known. The mechanism of transmission of erysipelas also is poorly understood but may involve spread via the respiratory tract.

Measures to prevent the spread of group A streptococcal infections are variable in their effectiveness. Spread of throat or skin infection within a family unit often occurs before the index case is identified and isolated or treated. In epidemic situations, especially when cases of rheumatic fever or acute nephritis occur, obtaining a culture survey and treating all individuals with positive cultures (mass prophylaxis) may be indicated. Reduction of crowding, especially in sleeping quarters, seems to be an effective long-term method of minimizing the spread of streptococcal sore throat among some populations. In families in which persistence or recurrence of streptococcal infection is a problem, obtaining throat cultures or cultures of the skin lesions of all members (or both) and treating simultaneously of all positive individuals has been successful in eradicating the organism. Some physicians have advocated a role for family pets (dogs) in the transmission of streptococcal infections. However, the available data do not support such transmission as a common occurrence.[16, 37, 166] Control of environmental contamination would be expected to have little or no influence on the spread of group A streptococcal respiratory infection, although it possibly may have an effect in controlling skin or wound infections. Family toothbrushes have been suggested to have a role in the intrafamilial spread of group A streptococci. However, recent guidelines have suggested that to culture family members when invasive group A streptococcal infections have occurred is not always necessary. Because of reported instances in which secondary cases have developed, this guideline remains controversial.[125, 129]

EPIDEMIOLOGY

Group A streptococci have a narrow host range. They are one of the pathogenic bacteria identified almost exclusively in humans and only very rarely are found in other species.[104] In considering the epidemiology of group A streptococcal infections, one must recognize that significant differences exist between throat and skin infections.[158]

Streptococcal impetigo occurs with greatest frequency in preschool children, whereas streptococcal pharyngitis predominantly is a disease of school-age children. Outbreaks of streptococcal respiratory tract infections also have been observed in daycare centers.[142] On average, streptococcal respiratory infections occur at the rate of one every 3 to 5 years during childhood. One comprehensive long-term study suggested that the average child has three documented group A streptococcal infections before reaching the age of 13, but the range was between one and eight incidents per child.[47] Among preschool and early school-age children of certain populations, streptococcal impetigo tends to be a recurrent problem.

The seasonal occurrence and geographic distribution are different for throat and skin infections. Tonsillitis and pharyngitis caused by streptococci occur commonly in temperate and cold climates; streptococcal pyoderma and impetigo appear to occur with greater frequency in hot or tropical climates.[28] Streptococcal sore throat occurs more frequently in the late autumn, winter, and early spring months. In tropical climates, pharyngeal colonization appears to occur more commonly during the rainy season. Streptococcal impetigo is usually a disease of the summer months in temperate climates but may occur with equal frequency year-round in tropical countries. In some tropical climates, group C and G beta-hemolytic streptococci are isolated more frequently from the upper respiratory tract than group A is,[66] which has led some researchers to speculate about a possible etiologic role for group C and G streptococci in the pathogenesis of rheumatic fever.[66]

PATHOGENESIS

No complete explanation is available for the predilection of certain body sites for infection by group A streptococci or for the ability of strains of certain M types to produce pharyngitis or tonsillitis and of others to produce impetigo or pyoderma.

In the establishment of throat infection, a primary requisite is a method of attachment to the epithelial cells of the pharynx. Group A streptococci accomplish such attachment by means of their fimbriae. To initiate an infection, group A streptococci also must compete with the resident pharyngeal flora, notably the alpha-hemolytic or viridans streptococci, which may interfere with the colonization of group A streptococci in the throat,[38] perhaps as a result of the production of a bacteriocin-like substance.[43] However, the relative importance of bacterial interference in preventing colonization of the human upper respiratory tract with group A streptococci is not entirely clear. In fact, the influence of bacteriocin-like substance producers may be minimal in certain situations.[74]

In the production of impetigo, group A streptococci also must vie with other local bacterial flora. Removal of the normal flora increases the time of survival of group A streptococci applied to the skin.[3] Skin lipids, some of which are lethal for group A streptococci in vitro, also may provide a natural barrier against the establishment of streptococcal infection.

Invasion of tissues by group A streptococci may be facilitated by a combination of bacteriologic properties. Damage to leukocytes and to fixed tissue cells may be caused by any of the several toxins produced, and the spread of infection may be aided by specific enzymes that attack hyaluronic acid and fibrin. M protein is antiphagocytic and also contains a moiety that is cytotoxic in the presence of non–type-specific antibody.[13] The protective role of mucosal immunity remains incompletely defined. The hyaluronic acid capsule of group A streptococci may serve as camouflage because it resembles mammalian hyaluronic acid. In addition, several streptococcal substances (streptococcal pyrogenic exotoxins and peptidoglycan) have been shown to have endotoxin-like properties. A role for pyrogenic exotoxins has been postulated in streptococcal toxic shock syndrome and necrotizing fasciitis.[145, 146]

Factors responsible for early host defense against group A streptococci (before the development of antibody) are not understood completely. Type-specific antibody against M protein, which greatly promotes phagocytosis, usually is not detectable until 6 to 8 weeks after the initiation of infection[45]; therefore, its primary role may not be in the limitation or termination of active infection but rather in the prevention of reinfection by the same serologic type. Furthermore, early reports indicate that type-specific immunity may be to specific strains within a given serotype rather than to all strains within a given serotype.[44, 155] The significance of this potentially important observation in the epidemiology of streptococcal infections and in the pathogenesis of nonsuppurative sequelae has not been defined fully. Surface phagocytosis, first by monocytes and later by polymorphonuclear leukocytes, may be the primary mechanism of defense in the early stages of infection.[134] In streptococcal skin infections, an increase in the leukotactic activity of polymorphonuclear leukocytes has been reported.[62]

Approximately 30 minutes after ingestion by a polymorphonuclear leukocyte, the streptococcus may be killed. Occasionally, the reverse occurs because of a phenomenon known as leukotoxicity, which apparently is related to the production of streptolysin S.[118] Degradation of the streptococcus within phagocytes or in tissues is a much slower process, thus suggesting that the human host may not be able to break down the streptococcal cell wall in an efficient manner.[62] This finding appears to be in contrast with the reported engulfment of group A streptococci by respiratory epithelial cells; in this instance, some evidence suggests intracellular survival of the streptococci, which perhaps accounts for the persistence of these organisms in individuals thought to be carriers.[105]

Streptococci can spread to the regional lymph nodes, especially in infections of the pharynx and tonsils.[43] Bacteremia occurs in the absence of underlying systemic disease, such as leukemia or other malignancies,[50, 65] but it is an uncommon occurrence in older children and adults. The reason or reasons for the apparent increase in severe systemic group A streptococcal infections beginning in the 1980s and 1990s and continuing into the 21st century remain incompletely explained. Although certain M types appear to be isolated more commonly from such severe infections, these strains seem to be no different from similar M types causing uncomplicated infections.

The rash and other toxic manifestations of scarlet fever have been attributed to the development of hypersensitivity to the pyrogenic toxins.[113] The toxic manifestations that have been noted in group A streptococcal toxic shock syndrome also may result from a direct influence of the pyrogenic exotoxins on lymphokines such as tumor necrosis factor.[145, 146] In addition, hypersensitivity to other streptococcal products may contribute to the manifestations of streptococcal disease.

Many theories about the pathogenetic mechanisms leading to the development of nonsuppurative complications of streptococcal infection, acute rheumatic fever, and acute glomerulonephritis have been proposed. Most of these hypotheses involve immunologic processes in one way or another.[113, 153] A major impediment toward clarifying the pathogenetic mechanism or mechanisms responsible for the development of nonsuppurative sequelae has been the lack of a suitable animal model for study.

CLINICAL MANIFESTATIONS

Streptococcal pharyngitis or tonsillitis usually is a short-lived clinical illness with a brief incubation period (12 hours to 4 days). It varies greatly in severity, from a subclinical or almost subclinical form, which occurs in 30 to 50 percent of infections, to a very toxic form with high fever, nausea, and vomiting. Extreme toxicity may occur more frequently in epidemic situations, especially food-borne outbreaks, thus suggesting the importance of rapid passage of the infecting organism from person to person in determining the severity of infection. The onset is acute and may be marked by fever, sore throat, headache, or abdominal pain (more common in children). The tonsils and pharynx may appear inflamed or infected but, in the presence of marked edema, may look pale. Exudate is a common finding (50–90%). It usually appears by the second day and typically is discrete and whitish yellow and may become confluent by the following day. Swollen, tender anterior cervical lymph nodes (adenitis) also can be observed in 30 to 60 percent of patients.

The clinical manifestations usually subside spontaneously in 3 to 5 days unless suppurative complications (otitis media, sinusitis, peritonsillar abscess) develop. Patients in whom nonsuppurative sequelae develop usually have a latent period of 1 to 3 weeks during which they seem completely well. After streptococcal infection of the upper respiratory tract, the average latent period for acute glomerulonephritis is 10 days; for acute rheumatic fever, it is 18 days.[158]

An infantile form of streptococcal infection, referred to as streptococcal fever, may take a more prolonged course, with chronic low-grade fever, generalized lymphadenopathy, and a persistent serous nasal discharge; little or no evidence of localized inflammation in the pharyngeal area has been found. The term "streptococcosis," which sometimes has been used to refer specifically to this infantile form, should be used more correctly to indicate the broad spectrum of clinical manifestations that change with age in a manner somewhat analogous to those of tuberculosis.[124]

Scarlet fever is a rare event in infancy, possibly because of placental transfer of maternal antibody to the pyrogenic toxins. A more complete explanation may relate to the necessity for hypersensitization to these exotoxins to develop before this manifestation of streptococcal disease can be expressed.[99] In the mid-20th century, the severe toxic form of scarlet fever was a rare occurrence in most industrialized countries; milder forms of the illness were prevalent. In the late 1980s, reports of an illness characterized by a scarlet fever–like rash but with severe systemic manifestations, including fasciitis, myositis, adult respiratory distress syndrome, and very high mortality rates (up to 30%), became more numerous in the United States.[22, 89]

The characteristic rash is red and finely punctate; it appears initially on the trunk and spreads peripherally to cover almost the entire body in full-blown cases within several hours to several days. A typical feature of the rash is that it fades on pressure and almost always leads to desquamation. Linear red lines may develop in the skin folds of the joints (Pastia lines) or in other areas of the extremities. The strawberry tongue of scarlet fever has a swollen, red, and mottled appearance and eventually peels. A scarlatiniform rash also may occur with streptococcal impetigo and streptococcal wound infections. An enanthema of stippled, bright red or hemorrhagic spots may appear on the soft palate or the anterior pillars of the tonsillar fossae. Exudate and tender cervical nodes may be present as in streptococcal pharyngitis without a rash, but the pharyngeal signs sometimes are minimal.

Streptococcal impetigo may develop a few days to several weeks after deposition of the infecting strain on normal skin; the average latent period is 10 days.[56] In contrast to pharyngitis, this form of group A streptococcal infection frequently is painless, and the patient usually is afebrile. The initial lesion is a superficial vesicle with little surrounding erythema. It rapidly progresses to a pustule and then to a thick, honey-colored crust; this stage may last for a few days to several weeks. Secondary infection with staphylococci is a common development in the pustular and crust stages.[42, 46] Removal of the crusts by trauma or as part of local therapy reveals a moist or purulent undersurface in the earlier stages. The infection does not involve the dermis. On healing, depigmentation may be seen, but rarely does permanent scarring develop. Lesions occur most commonly on the lower extremities but may be seen on other exposed portions of the body such as the upper extremities and the face.

Acute poststreptococcal glomerulonephritis may occur after impetigo or other forms of cutaneous streptococcal infection produced by a nephritogenic strain; curiously, however, rheumatic fever has not been associated with streptococcal skin infections.[160] This concept recently has been challenged by investigators working with populations in which group A streptococcal upper respiratory tract infections are relatively rare events in comparison to streptococcal pyoderma; these populations have very high incidence rates of acute rheumatic fever.[28] At the present time, however, a role for group A streptococcal skin infection in the pathogenesis of rheumatic fever remains unproven. The latent period for acute nephritis is longer after skin infection (3 weeks on average) than after throat infection (10 days on average).[90] The serologic types associated with nephritis after skin infection usually are different from those causing nephritis after throat infection.[158] For example, M-12 has been the classic nephritogenic serotype associated with pharyngitis, whereas serotypes such as M-49, M-55, and M-57 have been associated more frequently with nephritis occurring after skin infection.[158]

Impetigo and more nondescript forms of streptococcal pyoderma may be superimposed on scabies, eczema, other dermatoses, burns, and wounds, which afford a means of access through the cutaneous barrier. Ecthyma is a more deep-seated and chronic form of streptococcal pyoderma found predominantly in tropical climates.[1]

Erysipelas is an unusual type of streptococcal infection that involves the skin and sometimes the adjacent mucous membranes. It is an elevated erythematous lesion that at times exhibits blebs filled with yellowish fluid that may crust over after rupture. The lesion is characterized by a well-demarcated advancing border, more reddened and edematous than the central area, that may fade and become more normal in appearance as the lesion progresses. Erysipelas most often involves the face (especially in children), the extremities, or the body. The lesion may surround a surgical or traumatic wound, an area of dermatosis, or the umbilical stump in a newborn infant. Erysipelas tends not to spread from one body region to another. In erysipelas, the onset is acute and often accompanied by the manifestations of systemic toxicity characteristic of other febrile forms of streptococcal infection. The lesion may last for a few days to several weeks. Relapses are rather common events, with recurrences frequently noted at the same body site.

In addition to causing the infections described earlier, group A streptococci may produce a variety of other clinical findings. Other infections associated with upper respiratory tract infection by these organisms include otitis media, retropharyngeal abscess, sinusitis, mastoiditis, pneumonia, and empyema. Beta-hemolytic streptococci can be recovered from approximately 50 percent of patients with peritonsillar abscess and may act in concert with anaerobic bacteria in the production of this clinical picture.[58] Acute puerperal sepsis, now fortunately a rare occurrence, classically has been associated with group A streptococci. Nursery outbreaks of omphalitis, bacteremia, and meningitis still are reported on occasion.[149] Fatal gangrene,[63] disseminated intravascular coagulopathy,[78] and purpura fulminans[36] may be associated with infection by group A streptococci. These bacteria also are a common cause of perianal cellulitis and vaginitis in children.[4, 100] Subpectoral abscesses and empyema may develop as complications of streptococcal infection of the thumb and index finger as a result of the lymphatic drainage of that part of the hand.[4] Septic complications of varicella, including varicella gangrenosa,[25, 141] osteomyelitis (especially in infants),[67] the hand-foot syndrome,[68] blistering distal dactylitis,[69] necrotizing fasciitis, and toxic shock syndrome, are associated with beta-hemolytic streptococci. Researchers have suggested that streptococcal infections may be responsible for episodes of acute guttate psoriasis.[7]

Streptococcal Upper Respiratory Tract Carrier State

One of the most puzzling aspects of the relationship of group A streptococci and the human host is the streptococcal "carrier" state. Not only does it represent a diagnostic and therapeutic enigma for both the clinician and public health authorities, but the theoretic implications related to the pathogenesis of nonsuppurative sequelae also are intriguing.[85] Data in the literature suggest that group A upper respiratory tract carriers are less dangerous to others because carriers only rarely spread the organism to close contacts. In addition, the risk of developing nonsuppurative sequelae, such as rheumatic fever, appears to be significantly reduced in carriers.[86] The epidemiologic and immunologic reasons for establishment and continuation of the carrier state are not understood.

Much of this confusion has resulted from the definition of the carrier state. In contrast to true infection, in which an organism and evidence of a host immune response are present, group A streptococcal upper respiratory tract carriers may harbor the organism in the upper respiratory tract for prolonged periods without evidence of an immunologic response as measured by a rise in antibody titer to streptococcal antigens.[85]

The explanation for this prolonged persistence of group A streptococci in the upper respiratory tract is unknown. Whether it is due to bacterial or host factors remains unexplained. Recent hypotheses have been proposed to explain persistence of the organism in the upper respiratory tract. Both suggest that internalization of group A streptococci into epithelial cells may explain their ability to continue to survive. Researchers have shown in vitro that stationary-phase organisms are internalized easily by epithelial cells, and others have associated internalization with the presence of fibronectin-binding proteins in specific strains of group A streptococci.[105, 116] Though an attractive explanation because of the inability of penicillin to penetrate the epithelial cell and, therefore, eradicate the organism from the carrier, more data are required to determine the clinical relevance of this phenomenon.

For the clinician, carriers have proved to be particularly problematic.[82, 162] The ability to prospectively identify carriers and separate them from individuals with bona fide upper respiratory tract infection, as well as the reported difficulty in eradicating the organism from the upper respiratory tract of carriers, remains a perplexing and frustrating problem, especially when as many as 5 to 20 percent of children may carry group A streptococci in their upper respiratory tract during the late autumn, winter, and early spring.

Immunologic Response

The large number of somatic constituents and extracellular products of group A streptococci, most of which are antigenic, accounts for the complex nature of the host immune response after group A streptococcal infection. Both humoral and cellular immune responses have been studied, the former more thoroughly than the latter.[161]

Skin and in vitro tests suggest that most adults are hypersensitive to a variety of streptococcal antigenic preparations whereas infants more often are nonreactive. Lymphocyte transformation responses to most streptococcal substances probably are specific in nature and result from previous sensitization. However, some studies indicate that a nonspecific (mitogenic) response may occur with certain extracellular and cellular fractions. Inhibition of leukocyte migration has been demonstrated with fractions of streptococcal culture supernates and with cell membrane and cell wall fractions.[128, 137] Some evidence in humans suggests that the cellular immune response to a streptococcal extracellular antigen is controlled genetically.[137]

Humoral immune responses to numerous somatic components of the group A streptococcal cell have been demonstrated in humans. Of particular interest are antibodies to the group A carbohydrate that are serologically cross-reactive with the glycoprotein of human and bovine heart valves and antibodies to protein components of the group A cell wall or cell membrane that have been reported to be cross-reactive with the sarcolemma of heart muscle.[8]

Antibody to the M protein (type-specific antibody) is of special importance because it is the basis of immunity/protection against reinfection with the same serologic type.[103, 157] Type-specific antibody may be transferred across the placenta from mother to fetus.[170] The development of type-specific antibody can be inhibited partially by prompt penicillin treatment of the streptococcal infection.[40]

Humoral antibodies to specific streptococcal extracellular products can be demonstrated readily by neutralization assays.[20] They have been especially useful in allowing a more precise method of defining streptococcal infection in clinical and epidemiologic studies and in documenting the occurrence of a preceding streptococcal infection in patients with a suspected nonsuppurative complication.

The anti-streptolysin O assay is the streptococcal antibody test used most commonly.[138] Because streptolysin O also is produced by group C and G streptococci, the test is not specific for group A infection. The anti-streptolysin O response can be feeble in patients with streptococcal impetigo or pyoderma[91]; its usefulness for this latter condition is limited. In contrast, the anti-deoxyribonuclease B (anti-DNase B) and the antihyaluronidase responses are reliable after both skin and throat infections.

Another antibody test, the Streptozyme agglutination test, is based on antibody agglutination of erythrocytes coated with a mixture of streptococcal extracellular antigens. It has the theoretic appeal of simplicity, speed, and reaction with numerous streptococcal antigens.[76] Peak titers for an immune response as measured by the Streptozyme test have been demonstrated within the first week or 10 days after the onset of infection,[119] whereas neutralizing antibody titers to streptolysin O (3 to 6 weeks) or anti-DNase B (6 to 8 weeks) do not peak until later. However, because of documented problems of standardization of this reagent (variable results may be obtained with different lots) and because of problems with group specificity, this test should be interpreted with caution.[94, 161] In fact, some studies have indicated problems in interpretation of this test; the World Health Organization has recommended that it not be used.[53]

Antibody titers reported by clinical immunology laboratories may vary. The upper limits of normal are higher for children than for adults, and these values, even for the same age group, are higher in some populations than in others. Interpretation of antibody titers for clinical purposes must take these factors into consideration.[138] Frequently, values given by laboratories for upper limits of normal have been determined on adult sera; these values are often much too low to be used in a pediatric population.

DIAGNOSIS AND DIFFERENTIAL DIAGNOSIS

In patients with acute pharyngitis or tonsillitis, clinicians must rely on a combination of clinical appearance, identification of the organism, and epidemiologic findings to confirm the probability of group A streptococcal infection. The clinical difficulty is compounded because most of the clinical manifestations of streptococcal pharyngitis also can be associated with a variety of other etiologic agents.[18] Moreover, group A streptococci often are found in the throats of normal children and in children whose clinical findings are caused by one of these other agents[159] (see also Chapter 10). Exudative sore throat may be caused by any of several viruses, *Corynebacterium diphtheriae,* gonococci, and groups C and G as well as group A streptococci.[18] The clinical syndrome associated with *Arcanobacterium haemolyticum* can be quite similar and clinically confusing.

Viral pharyngitis may closely mimic streptococcal pharyngitis, which can be ruled out only by the absence of a positive culture for group A streptococci. In children, the white blood cell count may be elevated in viral infection, but a low count indicates that the infection probably is not streptococcal. The C-reactive protein test is only marginally useful in the acute phase of the illness.[97]

Because most streptococcal infections are short-term illnesses and antibody responses can be slow in appearing, streptococcal antibody titers are useful only retrospectively in diagnosing acute group A streptococcal infection. Little reason justifies the use of streptococcal antibody titers in the management of acute pharyngitis. However, in addition to their primary role in supporting the diagnosis of nonsuppurative complications (acute nephritis and acute rheumatic fever), occasionally they may be useful clinically in diagnosing infections that are difficult to culture at the primary site (e.g., streptococcal pneumonia or osteomyelitis) or that have been treated or partially treated with antibiotics. However, the presence of an elevated streptococcal antibody titer does not, by itself, confirm a diagnosis of rheumatic fever.

Numerous clinical schemes have been proposed for differentiating streptococcal from nonstreptococcal pharyngitis, but none of them is entirely satisfactory in making this distinction or in differentiating streptococcal carriers with an intervening nonstreptococcal pharyngitis from those with active streptococcal disease.[84, 159] Clinical manifestations that are most suggestive of a group A streptococcal cause include scarlatiniform rash (which, however, occasionally is associated with staphylococcal, rather than streptococcal, infection), excoriated nares (especially in infants), tender (not merely enlarged) anterior cervical lymph nodes, and a history of close contact with a well-documented case of group A streptococcal infection. The presence of cough, hoarseness, or conjunctivitis renders the diagnosis of streptococcal pharyngitis unlikely. An important note is that exudative pharyngitis in infants usually is nonstreptococcal in etiology.[2] In addition, many clinical scoring systems have been found to be helpful to the clinician in some circumstances, but even they are not entirely reliable.[162]

Cultures may yield invalid results unless specimens are obtained and processed carefully. For cultures of the throat, the affected areas (tonsils and posterior of the pharynx) should be rubbed firmly with a rayon or cotton culture swab. Impetiginous lesions should be cleansed with alcohol and the vesicle punctured or the crust lifted with a sterile needle so that purulent material or the moist base can be touched by the swab.[81] Group A streptococci sometimes can be recovered even from dry crusted lesions if the swab is moistened with culture broth before touching the exposed base of the lesion. Because streptococcal impetigo lesions commonly contain secondarily invading staphylococci, which may overgrow and obscure the colonies of streptococci, cultures should be examined carefully with a hand lens; alternatively, gentian violet or other inhibitors of normal flora may be incorporated into the blood agar plates as an inhibitor of staphylococci.

Presumptive differentiation of group A from other hemolytic streptococci can be achieved by the sensitivity of the former (but relatively few of the latter) to bacitracin but only when tested by a disk designed specifically for this purpose.[81] Definite identification of group A streptococci can be accomplished by several serologic or immunologic techniques—for example, by (1) extraction of the organism by boiling in hydrochloric acid or by several other extraction methods with examination of the resulting extract in a precipitin test, (2) a fluorescent antibody test on isolated colonies or broth cultures, and (3) agglutination of the organisms by group-specific antisera bound to protein A–containing staphylococci.

Numerous rapid techniques for direct identification of group A streptococci from the upper respiratory tract are available commercially. Direct and rapid identification of group A streptococcal antigens from throat swabs (e.g., latex agglutination, enzyme-linked immunosorbent assay, etc.) has become quite popular. The specificity of these tests usually is very good, but published reports indicate that the sensitivity has varied widely.[88, 139] Many guidelines recommend a backup throat culture if a rapid antigen-detection test is negative.[19] These techniques involve extraction of the group-specific carbohydrate from the cell wall of the organism. Available data suggest that the specificity of these tests generally is greater than 90 percent, but the sensitivity has ranged from less than 60 percent to greater than 90 percent.[88]

The advantages of these tests include the ability to identify group A streptococci rapidly and treat the patient while in the physician's office or emergency room. This advantage has appeal, especially in view of data suggesting that in children, the more quickly the patient is treated, the more rapid the clinical response.[127] Studies also have shown that rapid antigen-detection tests can be useful in the detection of group A streptococci in streptococcal pyoderma-like lesions.[95]

Data suggest that the sensitivity of the new tests is improved. This finding has led to the suggestion that a positive rapid antigen-detection test is sufficient proof of group A infection but that a negative rapid antigen-detection test should be confirmed with a conventional throat culture on sheep blood agar. Throat culture remains a "gold standard" for identifying group A streptococci in the upper respiratory tract. Though rarely encountered, false-positive rapid antigen-detection tests also have been documented as a result of cross-reaction with the antigens present in some *Streptococcus milleri* strains.[82] Just as with any other laboratory test, a "learning curve effect" exists with streptococcal rapid antigen-detection tests.[95]

The pharyngeal exudate of infectious mononucleosis tends to be more extensive, thicker, whiter, and more membranous and shaggy than that of streptococcal pharyngitis. The clinical impression usually can be confirmed quickly by the heterophil "spot test" (see Chapter 10).

Generally, making a diagnosis of streptococcal impetigo is safer than making a diagnosis of streptococcal pharyngitis on clinical findings alone. Impetigo in which staphylococci are the primary invader generally is bullous rather than vesicular in type, and on rupture of the vesicle, a crust appears that is paper-thin and white rather than thick and honey colored. Some confusion may result from reports of cultures performed on patients with primary streptococcal impetigo. Staphylococci, often present as secondary invaders, may overgrow the streptococci, which consequently may be missed unless the colonies are well isolated and the bacteriologist has an unusually sharp eye or unless a culture medium inhibitory for staphylococci is used. More recently, a more significant role for pure staphylococcal impetigo has been described.

The vesicles of chickenpox may resemble those of streptococcal impetigo superficially, but they are less transient, are surrounded by a red areola, are more centripetal in distribution (tending to involve the trunk and the proximal portions of the extremities), frequently itch, occur in crops, and often are accompanied by constitutional symptoms. The crusts are not as thick as those of streptococcal impetigo. Worth noting is that the lesions of chickenpox can be infected with streptococci secondarily and that varicella has been identified as an important risk factor for the development of severe and invasive group A streptococcal infection.

PROGNOSIS

Patients with streptococcal sore throat or streptococcal impetigo recover spontaneously. Suppurative complications develop in very few of them, and occasional patients may have a nonsuppurative sequela.

In the general population, the risk of rheumatic fever developing after an untreated bona fide group A streptococcal infection of the upper respiratory tract has been shown to be approximately 3 percent under epidemic conditions but appears to be considerably less (approximately 0.3%) in endemic situations,[140] at least in part because of differences in the definition of infection.[96] Patients who have had one attack of rheumatic fever are at high risk for recurrence of rheumatic fever when reinfected with group A streptococci. Apparently, no risk exists of rheumatic fever developing after streptococcal infection of only the skin; however, this concept has been challenged but not yet substantiated.[28]

The risk of development of acute glomerulonephritis is dependent on whether the infection is caused by a nephritogenic strain. With a nephritogenic strain, the attack rate appears to be approximately 10 to 15 percent, and glomerulonephritis can occur after either a throat or a skin infection.[158]

In contrast to the usual short and often benign course of throat and superficial skin infections, streptococcal cellulitis spreads rapidly both locally and to the regional lymph nodes and bloodstream. In immunosuppressed patients and those with streptococcal infection superimposed on leukemia, lymphoma, or other malignancies, bacteremia may develop, and such patients may have serious life-threatening problems. Patients with puerperal sepsis, neonatal infection, streptococcal toxic shock–like syndrome, or gangrene caused by group A streptococci also have a high mortality rate despite timely initiation and high doses of penicillin therapy.[146]

The prognosis for complete recovery in patients with group A streptococcal toxic shock syndrome and in those with necrotizing fasciitis varies. It has been reported to be greater in adults, especially the elderly, than in the pediatric age group. Early series reported a mortality rate of at least 30 percent in patients with toxic shock syndrome.[147] The mortality with necrotizing fasciitis can be even greater.[145, 146]

TREATMENT

Although group A streptococci are generally susceptible to numerous antibiotics,[35, 51, 111] penicillin remains the drug of choice for treatment, except in patients allergic to it.[19] No group A streptococcal strains have been identified yet that are resistant to penicillin.[106] Although penicillin tolerance has been described in group A streptococci, its clinical significance has not been determined.[98]

However, eradicating group A streptococci from the upper respiratory tract (especially from carriers) with penicillin or other antibiotics sometimes is difficult.[87, 92] This observation has not been explained adequately, but possible reasons include the presence of β-lactamase–producing organisms in the upper respiratory tract, the presence of group A streptococci tolerant to penicillin, and the production of inhibitory substances by certain of the normal upper respiratory tract flora that reduce persistence of the organism. In addition, some evidence suggests that persistence frequently is associated with the upper respiratory tract carrier state.[101]

Erythromycin remains the drug of choice in patients allergic to penicillin. Resistance to erythromycin is relatively rare in many countries (<5%). Recent data from Europe, where macrolides are used widely, show resistance rates in certain countries to be more than 30 percent. In some countries, noticeable increases in macrolide resistance by group A streptococci have been associated with the increased use of macrolides. Although the prevalence of macrolide-resistant group A streptococci generally has been low in North America and of little clinical significance,[70, 167] isolated examples have shown an ability of the organism to become resistant to macrolides.[109] The incidence was high in Japan in the 1960s[48] and also in Finland.[136] No advantages or potential disadvantages have been noted with the use of broad-spectrum antibiotics for group A streptococcal infection.[19] Group A streptococci most frequently are resistant to tetracyclines and sulfonamides. β-Lactamase–resistant antibiotics have been advocated in some studies[23]; a role for β-lactamase production by normal flora in penicillin treatment failures has not been clarified yet.

In the treatment of true streptococcal sore throat, eradication of group A streptococci is necessary to prevent the development of acute rheumatic fever.[30] Current guidelines recommend 10 days of oral penicillin V or erythromycin for penicillin-allergic individuals as being optimal for eradication.[19] Administration of a single intramuscular injection of benzathine penicillin G (1,200,000 U in adults and in children more than 60 lb; 600,000 U in children less than 60 lb) is one method of accomplishing this objective. If a combination of benzathine penicillin and procaine penicillin is used, the total dosage should be based on the amount of benzathine penicillin used.

If oral medication (penicillin or erythromycin) is used, the patient and parent must be impressed with the importance of continuing the medication for a full 10 days. Oral penicillin V (250 mg two to three times a day) is the treatment of choice for children. Because of its taste, many pediatricians prefer amoxicillin. For adolescents, either 250 mg three or four times a day or even 500 mg twice a day has been suggested.[19] In patients with a suspected allergy to penicillin, erythromycin (250 mg four times a day in adults; in children, 40 mg/kg/day in four doses, not to exceed the adult dose) should be used.[41] The exact dose of erythromycin varies with the preparation used (e.g., stearate, estolate, etc.). Other antibiotics that have been used successfully in the treatment of group A beta-hemolytic streptococcal pharyngitis or tonsillitis include clindamycin, amoxicillin or a mixture of amoxicillin with clavulanate acid, and other cephalosporins. Azithromycin and clarithromycin have been used as substitutes for erythromycin.

Because the problem of patient adherence to a 10-day course of oral antibiotics is well recognized, several antibiotics have been approved for short-course therapy (<10 days) for the treatment of group A streptococcal pharyngitis. Such medications include some cephalosporins, as well as one of the newer macrolides. Some published studies show the equivalence of short-course therapy to 10 full days of conventional penicillin V oral therapy. Because of conflicting data, some guidelines still promote caution in using short-course therapy for the treatment of group A streptococcal upper respiratory tract infection.[19]

In patients with strong clinical or epidemiologic evidence of streptococcal infection, the physician may decide to begin therapy before throat culture results are available. If oral therapy is used for initiating treatment, it may be continued or discontinued, depending on the culture report. Alternatively, an intramuscular injection of benzathine penicillin G may be administered at that time if the report is positive. For patients who may not return for a culture report or who may be difficult to contact, one may need to make an immediate clinical judgment whether to prescribe penicillin therapy. In these situations, the use of rapid direct techniques for detection of group A streptococci is advantageous. Because such patients also may be less reliable with respect to completing a course of oral therapy, the use of intramuscular benzathine penicillin G may be preferable in these instances. Even if the decision to treat or not to treat must be made on clinical grounds, throat cultures can be very useful in indicating to the physician the current prevalence and clinical features of streptococcal and nonstreptococcal respiratory illnesses. The use of intramuscular benzathine penicillin G also is advantageous in epidemic situations.

At one time, repeating throat cultures after completion of oral therapy to ensure that group A streptococci had been eradicated was thought to be appropriate. Because studies have shown that many penicillin treatment failures appear to be group A streptococcal upper respiratory tract carriers,[85] in areas where rheumatic fever has not reappeared, guidelines now state that in asymptomatic individuals, routine reculture after administering antibiotic therapy is unnecessary unless unusual epidemiologic circumstances exist, such as a rheumatic individual in the household or epidemic streptococcal disease in the community. Other regimens that have been used for the treatment of patients with persistently positive cultures include clindamycin, a mixture of amoxicillin and clavulanic acid, and rifampin along with either an injection of benzathine penicillin G or 10 days of oral penicillin.[19] In patients with a repeated clinical pattern of treatment failure, determining the serologic group and type of strains recovered may be helpful in ascertaining whether the isolates are the same or different M protein types. Such testing, however, is not done routinely in hospital laboratories, and in these circumstances, contact with a state health department or streptococcal research laboratory will be required. Of importance in "problem" families in which intrafamilial spread occurs is to culture the throats of all members of the family simultaneously and to treat all those who have positive results. The main problem with a persisting carrier state is that it may complicate interpretation of throat cultures obtained at the time of future nonstreptococcal respiratory tract infections.

Researchers have suggested in the literature that rapid treatment of group A streptococcal upper respiratory tract infection tends to promote recurrent streptococcal infections in the future because of suppression of the type-specific antibody response. Some studies, however, have demonstrated no difference in the frequency of recurrence of streptococcal infections whether therapy is started at diagnosis or delayed as long as 48 hours.[60]

In contrast to group A streptococcal pharyngitis or tonsillitis, no authoritative guidelines have been developed for the treatment of streptococcal impetigo.[164] The effectiveness of hygienic measures and local skin care (removal of crusts and use of antibacterial soap) is probably dependent on the thoroughness and perseverance with which they are performed. These measures and the use of local antimicrobial ointments can be sufficient for the management of patients with only a few lesions. However, the use of systemic antibiotics has been associated with rapid clearing of the lesions. Oral or parenteral penicillin or oral erythromycin (in the amounts prescribed for the treatment of streptococcal pharyngitis) should be administered to patients with more severe or persistent infections. In the absence of microbiologic data, many clinicians administer antibiotics that are effective against both streptococci and staphylococci. First-generation cephalosporins and semisynthetic penicillins are also effective. Antibiotic therapy probably does help prevent the spread of streptococcal impetigo in the family.

Whether penicillin or other antibiotic treatment reduces the risk of development of acute nephritis is unclear.[165] One study suggests that penicillin therapy may lower the risk of this complication developing in patients with streptococcal sore throat caused by a nephritogenic strain.[144] However, no definitive proof exists that penicillin therapy reduces the frequency of acute nephritis after the treatment of skin infections. Furthermore, clinical experience indicates that this complication may develop in patients with cutaneous infection caused by a nephritogenic strain of group A streptococci despite adequate penicillin therapy.[90]

Otitis media or cervical adenitis caused by group A streptococci usually responds to regimens prescribed for the treatment of streptococcal sore throat. Patients with peritonsillar abscess require surgical drainage in addition to vigorous parenteral antibiotic therapy. Patients with more serious infections (e.g., mastoiditis, pneumonia, empyema) also should be given intensive systemic therapy. Those with meningitis, arthritis, or osteomyelitis require high-dose intravenous penicillin administered for a relatively long period (see Chapters 38 and 64). Patients with streptococcal toxic shock syndrome and those with necrotizing fasciitis may be treated with parenteral penicillin, but recent evidence suggests that clindamycin, in combination with penicillin, has advantages.[145] In patients allergic to penicillin, clindamycin is an excellent alternative. Because of cross-reactions with penicillin, however, cephalosporins should be used only cautiously in penicillin-allergic patients.

PREVENTION

Antimicrobial agents have been helpful in controlling group A streptococcal infections and their sequelae. However, they do not provide an encompassing solution for this group of diseases, either in industrialized countries or in the developing world, as has been evident from the "resurgence" of rheumatic fever and the appearance of streptococcal toxic shock syndrome in the United States during the 1980s and 1990s. Penicillin's greatest impact has been on the prevention of recurrences of rheumatic fever (see Chapter 35). Prevention of first attacks of rheumatic fever is a problem of greater dimensions because it involves detection, diagnosis, and appropriate treatment in the general population. One cost-effective measure can be achieved by implementing well-conceived secondary prevention programs in defined rheumatic individuals and perhaps by instituting primary prevention programs in school-age children of lower socioeconomic status.

Prevention of spread by isolation, limiting population density, and antibiotic treatment of known cases is discussed in the section on transmission (see earlier). Mass penicillin prophylaxis has been used in epidemics with a well-defined streptococcal etiology,[24] but in actual practice, the epidemic often is subsiding by the time that a large-scale prophylactic effort can be mounted. Intramuscular benzathine penicillin G is very effective for this purpose.[24] The dose is the same as that recommended for treating streptococcal pharyngitis. In populations in which streptococcal infections occur at epidemic or near-epidemic levels over a long period (e.g., certain military populations), repeating the injections of benzathine penicillin at monthly intervals and administering them to all new arrivals may be necessary.

Although guidelines for the management of contacts of patients who have severe streptococcal infections are available and routine surveillance cultures in family members and close contacts are not universally recommended,[125] this matter remains controversial because of documented secondary cases in families.[129] Furthermore, in family studies carried out several decades ago, researchers found that approximately 25 percent of family contacts harbored the organisms in families in which an index case was identified.[47] Because of documented instances in which secondary cases have occurred, some physicians choose to culture close contacts and treat those who are positive for group A streptococci with long-acting benzathine penicillin, long-acting benzathine penicillin plus rifampin, or clindamycin. The effectiveness of such regimens has not been studied; therefore, contacts need to be monitored closely even after being treated.

The question of the possible advantage of performing a tonsillectomy for the prevention of streptococcal infections and their sequelae also has not been settled by well-controlled studies. From the information available, tonsillectomy appears to reduce the frequency of occurrence of clinically apparent streptococcal infections,[122] perhaps rendering it less likely that they receive appropriate treatment.[31] However, one study has indicated that recurrences are more frequent in individuals who have had rheumatic fever and who have large tonsils.[55]

The inability of antibiotics to significantly influence the epidemiology of group A streptococcal infections and their sequelae consistently and favorably is reflected by the concentration of sequelae that recently have occurred in middle-class populations with ready access to medical care.[154] Control measures would be much more effective were a group A streptococcal vaccine available. No entirely satisfactory means of manipulating host defenses to prevent streptococcal infections is available. Several different approaches to streptococcal vaccines are being investigated, including a multivalent type-specific vaccine based on M protein type, a vaccine based on conserved regions of the M protein that are present in all M-protein types, and a third group of candidate vaccines that are based on immunity to extracellular or somatic antigens of the organism not associated with M protein. Early studies in animals have demonstrated immunogenicity in several of these candidate vaccines, and some vaccines based on type-specific immunity have undergone early clinical trials in humans. Though not possible to predict with certainty, the availability of cost-effective group A streptococcal vaccines to the general public does not seem imminent. Large-scale clinical trials in different geographic areas and among different populations ultimately will be required to determine safety and efficacy.

Group C and Group G Streptococcal Infections

THE ORGANISMS

Characterization of beta-hemolytic streptococci by group-specific carbohydrate antigens is complicated by the presence of similar antigens among streptococci that on the basis of biochemical and genetic testing, have been demonstrated to be different species. Organisms that possess either group C or group G Lancefield antigens can be divided into groups based on colony size. Strains that produce small or minute colonies (<0.5 mm in diameter) have been placed in the *Streptococcus anginosus* group (classified as *Streptococcus milleri* by British taxonomists), whereas strains that produce large colonies (≥5 mm in diameter) have been referred to as "true" or "large-colony" group C or group G, depending on the nature of their carbohydrate antigen. However, the taxonomic classification of these streptococci remains unsettled, and undoubtedly more changes will occur before a universally agreed-on scheme is established.[6, 33, 133]

Most group C streptococci are beta-hemolytic on blood agar plates, but all types of hemolysis have been observed. Group C streptococci are aerobic, facultatively anaerobic, coprophilic, and catalase-negative organisms. Rhamnose-*N*-acetylgalactosamine is the group C antigenic determinant in the cell wall. Traditionally, four species possessing this determinant have been differentiated on the basis of their ability to ferment various carbohydrates: *Streptococcus equisimilis, Streptococcus zooepidemicus, Streptococcus equi,* and *Streptococcus dysgalactiae.* However, recent genetic studies have led to the reclassification of group C streptococci into two species—*S. dysgalactiae* and *S. equi*—each with two subspecies. Although most group C streptococci are resistant to bacitracin, at least a third (and in one study as many as 62%) of group C streptococci are bacitracin-sensitive.[6]

S. dysgalactiae subspecies *equisimilis* is the species of group C streptococci that most often colonizes and causes infection in humans. It has been isolated from the nose, throat, and genital tract of asymptomatic children and adults, as well as from the umbilicus of asymptomatic newborns. *S. dysgalactiae* subspecies *equisimilis* produces streptokinase and streptolysin O, and infection may elicit an antibody response to these extracellular antigens similar to that seen with a group A streptococcal infection. Isolation of M protein from strains of *S. dysgalactiae* subspecies *equisimilis* in patients with acute pharyngitis also has been reported.[21] In addition, this organism can cause infection in a variety of domestic animals (e.g., horses, cattle, pigs, chickens). *S. dysgalactiae* subspecies *dysgalactiae* rarely is found in humans but does cause serious mastitis in cows and suppurative polyarthritis in lambs.

S. equi subspecies *zooepidemicus* can cause significant, often epidemic, infections in domestic animals (e.g., horses, cattle, pigs, sheep), but it is an uncommon pathogen in humans. Most human infections have been associated with the consumption of homemade cheese or unpasteurized cow's milk.

S. equi subspecies *equi* rarely is isolated from humans but does cause a serious and highly contagious respiratory disease in horses that is known as strangles.

The vast majority of group G streptococci are beta-hemolytic on blood agar plates. L-Rhamnose is the group G antigenic determinant in the cell wall. Many group G streptococci isolated from infected humans (but not from animals) express an M protein in their cell wall with biologic, immunochemical, and genetic features similar to those of the M protein of group A streptococci.[27, 34] As with group A streptococci, the M protein of group G streptococci is a virulence factor that helps the organism resist phagocytosis. Numerous antigenic variants of M protein are found in group G streptococci, and type-specific opsonic antibodies are produced in response to the M protein of the infecting strain. Recent studies have suggested that human isolates of group G streptococci are sufficiently genetically similar to the human isolates of group C streptococci that are classified as *S. dysgalactiae* subspecies *equisimilis* to also be included in this subspecies.[152]

Several schemes for typing group G streptococci have been based on biochemical properties or bacteriocin typing. Although no association between particular types and infections in humans has been identified, these schemes have been useful in distinguishing human from animal strains and in epidemiologic investigations. T-typing and M-typing schemes similar to those used for group A streptococci also have been devised for group G streptococci. Newer methods such as pulsed-field gel electrophoresis and multilocus enzyme electrophoresis also are being used to type specific strains of group G streptococci.[15] Although most group G streptococci are resistant to bacitracin, various reports have determined that between 8 and 67 percent of group G streptococci are bacitracin-sensitive.[133]

In addition to M protein, human isolates of group G streptococci share other virulence factors with group A streptococci, such as a streptokinase, a hyaluronidase, and a C5a peptidase. Group G streptococci also produce a streptolysin that is antigenically similar to the streptolysin O produced by group A streptococci. Patients with group G streptococcal infections may have a significant increase in anti-streptolysin O titers.

EPIDEMIOLOGY

Group C streptococci are an uncommon cause of human infections but more frequently are pathogenic in animals. Humans infected with this organism often have had some animal contact. Both group C and group G streptococci frequently can be part of the normal human flora of the nasopharynx, skin, and genital tract. Group C streptococci also can be cultured from the umbilicus of asymptomatic newborns, as well as from routine puerperal vaginal cultures. In addition, group G streptococci can be cultured from the gastrointestinal tract. The relatively low virulence of group C and group G streptococci is indicated by the fact that most humans infected with either of these organisms will have some underlying medical disorder (e.g., diabetes mellitus, malignancy, alcohol abuse, immunosuppression).[29, 102]

CLINICAL MANIFESTATIONS

The clinical features of both group C and group G streptococcal pharyngitis are similar to those of group A streptococcal pharyngitis and consist of fever, mild to moderate sore throat, pharyngeal exudate, and cervical adenitis.

Between 1 and 18 percent of asymptomatic people in temperate climates have been reported to harbor group C streptococci in the upper respiratory tract. The proportion of carriers among people living in the tropics is even greater.[66, 120] Such carrier rates render establishing the etiologic role of group C streptococci in acute pharyngitis difficult. Several earlier studies compared the isolation rates of group C streptococci from patients with acute pharyngitis with rates in asymptomatic controls; the results were contradictory.[6, 33] However, several recent investigations have established a strong epidemiologic association between group C streptococci and endemic acute pharyngitis. In two investigations, group C streptococci were isolated significantly more often from college students with acute pharyngitis than from asymptomatic controls.[150, 151] In the other investigation, group C streptococci were isolated significantly more frequently from adults who came to an emergency room with acute pharyngitis (6%) than from asymptomatic controls (1.4%).[115]

In addition to endemic pharyngitis, group C streptococci can cause epidemic food-borne pharyngitis after the ingestion of contaminated products such as unpasteurized cow's milk. Epidemics have been reported from Great Britain, Romania, the United States, and Israel.[6, 33] In one report of a milk-borne epidemic of pharyngitis caused by *S. equi* subspecies *zooepidemicus,* signs of acute glomerulonephritis developed in approximately a third of the patients.[49] This outbreak was related to the consumption of unpasteurized milk from cattle with mastitis. No cases of acute rheumatic fever occurred. Recently, a large outbreak of acute glomerulonephritis in Brazil was attributed to the consumption of unpasteurized cheese containing *S. equi* subspecies *zooepidemicus.*[9] Family outbreaks of group C streptococcal pharyngitis, as well as an outbreak in a residential school for boys, also have been described.

Group C streptococci have been reported as the cause of numerous other uncommon infections, including skin and soft tissue infections, septic arthritis, osteomyelitis, pneumonitis, infective endocarditis, bacteremia and septicemia, meningitis, epiglottitis, pericarditis, urinary tract infections, and sinusitis. These organisms also have been associated with epidemic and nonepidemic cases of puerperal sepsis and endometritis.[79] Recent reports have suggested an association between group C streptococci and reactive arthritis, as well as a toxic shock–like syndrome.[72, 77]

Reports show that 1 to 23 percent of asymptomatic people may carry group G streptococci in their upper respiratory tracts. As with group C streptococci, carrier rates of group G streptococci appear to be even higher in the tropics.[66, 120] Such carrier rates also render establishing the etiologic role of group G streptococci in acute pharyngitis difficult. Several studies have compared the isolation rates of group G streptococci from patients with acute pharyngitis with rates from asymptomatic controls. The results of these studies showed little difference in isolation rates, thus suggesting that group G streptococci may not play an important role in endemic acute pharyngitis. Few of these studies were adequately controlled, prospective investigations, however, and in many, the incidence of group G streptococci in the symptomatic group was so low that it precluded any possibility of demonstrating a statistically significant difference. Support for an etiologic role of group G streptococci in acute pharyngitis comes primarily from anecdotes, small case clusters, and a few large outbreaks, most of which were food-borne. To date, several food-borne outbreaks of group G streptococcal pharyngitis have been reported, all of which occurred in semiclosed populations, including one outbreak at a college cafeteria.[110] In the first reported respiratory outbreak of group G streptococcal pharyngitis in the United States, McCue[114] described 68 cases of acute pharyngitis on a college campus seen during a 9-day period in 1981. The possibility of food-borne spread could not be eliminated completely but seemed unlikely, and airborne droplet transmission appeared to be the most likely mechanism of spread.

Despite evidence supporting the etiologic role of group G streptococci in epidemic pharyngitis, the role of group G streptococci in acute, endemic pharyngitis remains unclear. Previous outbreaks of group G streptococcal pharyngitis had been reported in university-aged or older patients, and all had occurred in semiclosed communities. However, a community-wide respiratory outbreak of group G streptococcal pharyngitis in a pediatric population has been described.[61] During a 6-month period, group G streptococci were isolated from 56 of 222 (25%) consecutive children with acute pharyngitis seen at a private pediatric office. The results of DNA fingerprinting of the group G streptococcal isolates suggested that 75 percent of them were the same strain. The patients with group G streptococcal pharyngitis were comparable to those with group A streptococcal pharyngitis with respect to clinical findings, anti-streptolysin O titer response, and clinical response to antibiotic therapy. However, patients with group G streptococci were significantly older. The findings suggested that antibiotic therapy may have an impact on the clinical course of group G streptococcal pharyngitis. These findings lend support to the theory that group G streptococci may be a more important cause of acute, endemic pharyngitis than was recognized previously.

The actual role of group C and group G streptococci in acute pharyngitis may be underestimated for several reasons. Anaerobic incubation increases the yield of these organisms, but most clinicians do not use anaerobic incubation for throat cultures routinely.[135] Because clinicians generally disregard beta-hemolytic streptococci that are bacitracin-resistant (and most strains of group C and group G streptococci are bacitracin-resistant), many group C and group G streptococci would be missed.

Acute rheumatic fever has not been described as a complication of either group C or group G streptococcal pharyngitis, and even though reports have attempted to link acute glomerulonephritis with group G streptococcal pharyngitis, the evidence is anecdotal and a causal relationship has not been established.[123, 130] Although acute glomerulonephritis has been reported as a complication of group C streptococcal pharyngitis, it is an extremely unusual event.[9, 49, 117] Therefore, the primary reason to identify either group C or group G streptococci as the etiologic agent of acute pharyngitis is to initiate antibiotic therapy that may reduce the clinical impact of the illness. However, no convincing evidence exists as yet from controlled studies of a clinical response to antibiotic therapy in patients with acute pharyngitis and either group C or group G streptococci isolated from the upper respiratory tract.

Group G streptococci also have been reported to be an uncommon cause of puerperal sepsis and occasionally may cause a neonatal infection that clinically is very similar to early-onset group B streptococcal infection. Other infections occasionally caused by group G streptococci include bacteremia, endocarditis, septic arthritis, osteomyelitis, pneumonia, erysipelas and other skin and soft tissue infections, and meningitis.[52, 79] Recently, group G streptococci also have been associated with a toxic shock–like syndrome.[72, 156]

TREATMENT

Penicillin is the antibiotic of choice for treating infections caused by either group C or group G streptococci.[132] Some strains of group C and group G streptococci have been shown to be tolerant to penicillin in laboratory studies, but the clinical significance of this finding is not known.[117, 131] Synergism in producing in vitro killing of group C and group G streptococci has been demonstrated with gentamicin and various β-lactam antibiotics, but no controlled trials have been performed to establish the clinical significance of this finding. Group C and group G streptococci also are susceptible to most β-lactam antibiotics, as well as macrolides, vancomycin, clindamycin, and chloramphenicol. Pharyngitis usually is treated in a similar manner to group A streptococcal upper respiratory infections. More severe infection requires parenteral therapy.

REFERENCES

1. Allan, A. M., Taplin, D., and Twigg, L.: Cutaneous streptococcal infections in Vietnam. Arch. Dermatol. *104*:271–280, 1971.
2. Alpert, J. J., Pickering, M. R., and Warren, R. J.: Failure to isolate streptococci from children under the age of 3 years with exudative tonsillitis. Pediatrics *38*:663–666, 1966.
3. Aly, R., Maibach, H. I., Shinefield, H. R., et al.: Survival of pathogenic microorganisms on human skin. J. Invest. Dermatol. *58*:205–210, 1972.
4. Amren, D. P.: Unusual forms of streptococcal disease. *In* Wannamaker, L. W., and Matsen, J. M. (eds.): Streptococci and Streptococcal Diseases. Recognition, Understanding, and Management. New York, Academic Press, 1972, pp. 545–556.
5. Anthony, B. F., Kaplan, E. L., Wannamaker, L. W., et al.: The dynamics of streptococcal infections in a defined population of children: Serotypes associated with skin and respiratory infections. Am. J. Epidemiol. *104*:652–666, 1976.
6. Arditi, M., Shulman, S. T., Davis, A. T., et al.: Group C beta-hemolytic streptococcal infections in children: Nine pediatric cases and review. Rev. Infect. Dis. *11*:34–45, 1989.
7. Asboe-Hansen, G.: Psoriasis in childhood. *In* Farber, E. M., and Cox, A. J. (eds.): Psoriasis. Proceedings of the International Symposium, Stanford University. Stanford, Stanford University Press, 1971, pp. 53–59.
8. Ayoub, E. M.: Cross-reacting antibodies in the pathogenesis of rheumatic myocardial and valvular disease. *In* Wannamaker, L. W., and Matsen, J. M. (eds.): Streptococci and Streptococcal Diseases: Recognition, Understanding, and Management. New York, Academic Press, 1972, pp. 451–464.
9. Balter, S., Benin, A., Pinto, W. L., et al.: Epidemic nephritis in Nova Serrana, Brazil. Lancet *355*:1776–1780, 2000.
10. Bassett, D. C. J.: Hippelates flies and acute nephritis. Lancet *1*:503, 1967.
11. Beachey, E. H., and Ofek, I.: Epithelial cell binding of group A streptococci by lipoteichoic acid on fimbriae denuded of M protein. J. Exp. Med. *143*:759–771, 1976.
12. Beachey, E. H., Seyer, J. M., Dale, J. B., et al.: Type-specific protective immunity evoked by synthetic peptide of *Streptococcus pyogenes* M protein. Nature *292*:457–459, 1981.
13. Beachey, E. H., and Stollerman, G. H.: Mediation of cytotoxic effects of streptococcal M protein by non–type-specific antibody in human sera. J. Clin. Invest. *52*:2563–2570, 1973.
14. Bernheimer, A. W.: Hemolysins of streptococci: Characterization and effects on biological membranes. *In* Wannamaker, L. W., and Matsen J. M. (eds.): Streptococci and Streptococcal Diseases: Recognition, Understanding, and Management. New York, Academic Press, 1972, pp. 19–31.
15. Bert, F., Branger, C., and Lambert-Zechovsky, N.: Pulsed-field gel electrophoresis is more discriminating than multilocus enzyme electrophoresis and random amplified polymorphic DNA analysis for typing pyogenic streptococci. Curr. Microbiol. *34*:226–229, 1997.
16. Biberstein, E. L., Brown, C., and Smith, T.: Serogroups and biotypes among beta-hemolytic streptococci of canine origin. J. Clin. Microbiol. *11*:558–561, 1980.
17. Bisno, A. L.: Therapeutic strategies for the prevention of rheumatic fever. Ann. Intern. Med. 86:494–496, 1977.
18. Bisno, A. L.: Acute pharyngitis: Etiology and diagnosis. Pediatrics *97*:949–954, 1996.
19. Bisno, A. L., Gerber, M. A., Gwaltney, J. M., Jr., et al.: Group A streptococcal pharyngitis: Diagnosis and management. A practice guideline. Infectious Diseases Society of America. Clin. Infect. Dis. *35*:113–125, 2002.
20. Bisno, A. L., and Stollerman, G. H.: Streptococcal antibodies in the diagnosis of rheumatic fever. *In* Cohen, A. S. (ed.): Laboratory Diagnostic Procedures in the Rheumatic Diseases. Boston, Little, Brown, 1975, pp. 207–263.
21. Bisno, A. L., Collins, C. M., and Turner, J. C.: M protein of group C streptococci isolated from patients with acute pharyngitis. J. Clin. Microbiol. *4*:2511–2515, 1996.
22. Breiman, R. F., David, J. P., Facklam, R. R., et al.: Defining the group A streptococcal toxic shock syndrome: Rationale and consensus definition. J. A. M. A. *269*:390–391, 1993.
23. Brook, I.: The role of beta-lactamase–producing bacteria in the persistence of streptococcal tonsillar infection. Rev. Infect. Dis. *6*:601–607, 1984.
24. Brundage, J. F., Gunzenhauser, J. D., Longfield, J. N., et al.: Epidemiology and control of acute respiratory diseases with emphasis on group A beta-hemolytic streptococcus: A decade of U.S. Army experience. Pediatrics *97*:964–970, 1996.
25. Bullowa, J. G. M., and Wishik, S. M.: Complications of varicella: Their occurrence among 2,534 patients. Am. J. Dis. Child. *49*:923–926, 1935.
26. Calandra, G. B., Whitt, R. S., and Cole, R. M.: Relationship of cellular potential hemolysin in group A streptococci to extracellular streptolysin S. Infect. Immun. *13*:813–817, 1976.
27. Campo, R. E., Schultz, D. R., and Bisno, A. L.: M proteins of group G streptococci: Mechanisms of resistance to phagocytosis. J. Infect. Dis. *171*:601–606, 1995.
28. Carapetis, J. R., Currie, B. J., and Kaplan, E. L.: The epidemiology and prevention of group A streptococcal infections: Acute respiratory tract infections, skin infections and their sequelae at the close of the twentieth century. Clin. Infect. Dis. *28*:205–210, 1999.
29. Carmeli, Y., Schapiro, J. M., Neeman, D., et al.: Streptococcal group C bacteremia: Survey in Israel and analytic review. Arch. Intern. Med. *155*:1170–1176, 1996.
30. Catanzaro, F. J., Rammelkamp, C. H., Jr., and Chamovitz, R.: Prevention of rheumatic fever by treatment of streptococcal infections. II. Factors responsible for failures. N. Engl. J. Med. *259*:51–57, 1958.
31. Chamovitz, R., Rammelkamp, C. H., Jr., Wannamaker, L. W., et al.: The effect of tonsillectomy on the incidence of streptococcal respiratory disease and its complications. Pediatrics *26*:355–367, 1960.
32. Chen, C. C., and Clearly, P. P.: Complete nucleotide sequence of the streptococcal C5a peptidase gene of *Streptococcus pyogenes*. J. Biol. Chem. *265*:3161–3167, 1990.
33. Cimolai, N., Elford, R. W., Bryan, L., et al.: Do the beta-hemolytic non–group A streptococci cause pharyngitis? Rev. Infect. Dis. *10*:587–601, 1988.
34. Collins, C. M., Kimura, A., and Bisno, A. L.: Group G streptococcal M protein exhibits structural features analogous to those of class I M protein of group A streptococci. Infect. Immun. *60*:3689–3696, 1992.
35. Coonan, K. M., and Kaplan, E. L.: In vitro susceptibility of recent North American group A streptococcal isolates to eleven oral antibiotics. Pediatr. Infect. Dis. J. *13*:630–635, 1994.
36. Crawford, S. E., and Riddler, J. G.: Purpura fulminans. Am. J. Dis. Child. *97*:197–201, 1959.
37. Crowder, H. R., Dorn, C. R., and Smith, R. E.: Group A *Streptococcus* in pets and group A streptococcal disease in man. Int. J. Zoonoses *5*:45–54, 1978.
38. Crowe, C. C., Sanders, W. E., Jr., and Longley, S.: Bacterial interference. II. Role of the normal throat flora in prevention of colonization by group A *Streptococcus*. J. Infect. Dis. *128*:527–532, 1973.
39. Cunningham, M. W., and Beachey, E. H.: Peptic digestion of streptococcal M protein. I. Effect of digestion at suboptimal pH upon the biological and immunochemical properties of purified M protein extracts. Infect. Immun. *9*:244–248, 1974.
40. Daikos, G., and Weinstein, L.: Streptococci bacteriostatic antibody in patients treated with penicillin. Proc. Soc. Exp. Biol. Med. *78*:160–163, 1951.
41. Dajani, A. S., Bisno, A. L., Chung, K. J., et al.: Prevention of rheumatic fever: A statement for health professionals by the Committee on Rheumatic Fever, Endocarditis and Kawasaki Disease of the Council on Cardiovascular Disease in the Young, the American Heart Association. Pediatr. Infect. Dis. J. *8*:263–266, 1989.
42. Dajani, A. S., Ferrieri, P., and Wannamaker, L. W.: Endemic superficial pyoderma in children. Arch. Dermatol. *108*:517–522, 1973.
43. Dajani, A. S., Garcia, R. E., and Wolinsky, E.: Etiology of cervical lymphadenitis in children. N. Engl. J. Med. *268*:1329–1333, 1963.
44. De Malmanche, S. A., and Martin, D. R.: Protective immunity to the group A streptococcus may be only strain specific. Med. Microbiol. Immunol. *183*:299–306, 1994.
45. Denny, F. W., Jr., Perry, W. D., and Wannamaker, L. W.: Type-specific streptococcal antibody. J. Clin. Invest. *36*:1092–1100, 1957.
46. Dillon, H. C., Jr.: Impetigo contagiosa: Suppurative and non-suppurative complications. I. Clinical, bacteriologic, and epidemiologic characteristics of impetigo. Am. J. Dis. Child. *115*:530–541, 1968.
47. Dingle, J. H., Badger, G. F., and Jordan, W. S., Jr. (eds.): Illness in the Home. Cleveland, OH, Western Reserve University Press, 1964.

48. Dixon, J. M., and Lipinski, A. E.: Infections with beta-hemolytic streptococcus resistant to lincomycin and erythromycin and observations on zonal-pattern resistance to lincomycin. J. Infect. Dis. *130*:351–356, 1974.
49. Duca, E., Teodorovici, G., Radu, C., et al.: A new nephritogenic streptococcus. J. Hyg. *67*:691–698, 1969.
50. Dudding, B., Humphrey, G. B., and Nesbit, M. E.: Beta-hemolytic streptococcal septicemias in childhood leukemia. Pediatrics *43*:359–364, 1969.
51. Eickhoff, T. C., and Finland, M.: In vitro susceptibility of group A beta hemolytic streptococci to 18 antibiotics. Am. J. Med. Sci. *249*:261–268, 1965.
52. Eriksson, B., Jorup-Ronstrom, C., Karkkonen, K., et al.: Erysipelas: Clinical and bacteriologic spectrum and serological aspects. Clin. Infect. Dis. *23*:1091–1098, 1996.
53. Evaluation of the Streptozyme test for streptococcal antibodies. Bull. World Health Organ. *64*:504, 1986.
54. Facklam, R. F., Martin, D. R., Lovgren, M., et al.: Extension of the Lancefield classification for group A streptococci by addition of 22 new M protein gene sequence types from clinical isolates: *emm* 103 to *emm* 124. Clin. Infect. Dis. *34*:28–38, 2002.
55. Feinstein, A. R., and Levitt, M.: The role of tonsils in predisposing to streptococcal infections and recurrences of rheumatic fever. N. Engl. J. Med. *282*:285–291, 1970.
56. Ferrieri, P., Dajani, A. S., Wannamaker, L. W., et al.: Natural history of impetigo. I. Site sequence of acquisition and familial patterns of spread of cutaneous streptococci. J. Clin. Invest. *51*:2851–2862, 1972.
57. Fischetti, V. A.: Streptococcal M protein: Molecular design and biological behavior. Clin. Microbiol. Rev. *2*:285, 1989.
58. Flodstrom, A., and Hallander, H. O.: Microbiological aspects on peritonsillar abscesses. Scand. J. Infect. Dis. *8*:157–160, 1976.
59. Freimer, E. H.: Studies of L forms and protoplasts of group A streptococci. II. Chemical and immunological properties of the cell membrane. J. Exp. Med. *117*:377–399, 1963.
60. Gerber, M. A., DeMeo, K., Randolph, M. F., et al.: Lack of impact of early antibiotic therapy for streptococcal pharyngitis on recurrence rates. J. Pediatr. *117*:853–858, 1990.
61. Gerber, M. A., Randolph, M. F., Martin, N. J., et al.: Community-wide outbreak of group G streptococcal pharyngitis. Pediatrics *87*:598–603, 1991.
62. Ginsburg, I., and Sela, M. N.: The role of leukocytes and their hydrolases in the persistence, degradation, and transport of bacterial constituents in tissues: Relation to chronic inflammatory processes in staphylococcal, streptococcal, and mycobacterial infections and in chronic periodontal disease. C. R. C. Crit. Rev. Microbiol. *4*:249–322, 1976.
63. Graybill, J. R., Pierson, D. N., and Charache, P.: Tissue antibiotic penetration in streptococcal gangrene. Johns Hopkins Med. J. *133*:45–50, 1973.
64. Greenberg, L. J., Gray, E. D., and Yunis, E. J.: Association of HL-A 5 and immune responsiveness in vitro to streptococcal antigens. J. Exp. Med. *141*:935–943, 1975.
65. Hable, K. A., Horstmeier, C., Wold, A. D., and Washington, J. A., 2nd: Group A β-hemolytic streptococcemia: Bacteriologic and clinical study of 44 cases. Mayo Clin. Proc. *48*:336–339, 1973.
66. Haidan, A., Talay, S. R., Rohde, M., et al.: Pharyngeal carriage of group C and group G streptococci and acute rheumatic fever in an Aboriginal population. Lancet *356*:1167–1169, 2000.
67. Hall, J. E., and Silverstein, E. A.: Acute hematogenous osteomyelitis. Pediatrics *31*:1033–1038, 1963.
68. Haltalin, K. C., and Nelson, J. D.: Hand-foot syndrome due to streptococcal infection. Am. J. Dis. Child. *109*:156–159, 1965.
69. Hays, G. C., and Mullard, J. E.: Blistering distal dactylitis: A clinically recognizable streptococcal infection. Pediatrics *56*:129–131, 1975.
70. Henderson, R. J., Bares, G. J., Rambin, E. D., et al.: Typing and plasmid analysis of clinical isolates of group A beta hemolytic streptococcus with increased resistance to erythromycin. Abstract. Clin. Res. *38*:55, 1990.
71. Hill, H. R., Zimmerman, R. A., Reid, G. V., et al.: Food-borne epidemic of streptococcal pharyngitis at the United States Air Force Academy. N. Engl. J. Med. *280*:917–921, 1969.
72. Hirose, Y., Yagi, K., Honda, H., et al.: Toxic shock–like syndrome caused by non–group A beta-hemolytic streptococci. Arch. Intern. Med. *157*:1891–1894, 1997.
73. Hosein, B., McCarty, M., and Fischetti, V. A.: Amino acid sequence and physicochemical similarities between streptococcal M protein and mammalian tropomyosin. Proc. Natl. Acad. Sci. U. S. A. *76*:3765–3768, 1976.
74. Huskins, W. C., and Kaplan, E. L.: Inhibitory substances produced by *Streptococcus salivarius* and colonization of the upper respiratory tract with group A streptococci. Epidemiol. Infect. *102*:401–412, 1989.
75. James, L., and McFarland, R. B.: An epidemic of pharyngitis due to a nonhemolytic group A *Streptococcus* at Lowry Air Force Base. N. Engl. J. Med. *284*:750–752, 1971.
76. Janeff, J., Janeff, D., Taranta, A., et al.: A screening test for streptococcal antibodies. Lab. Med. *2*:38–40, 1971.
77. Jansen, T. L., Janssen, M., and de Jong, A. J.: Reactive arthritis associated with group C and group G beta-hemolytic streptococci. J. Rheumatol. *25*:1126–1130, 1998.
78. Jewett, J. F.: Coagulopathy syndrome due to streptococci. N. Engl. J. Med. *289*:43–44, 1973.
79. Johnson, C. C., and Tunkel, A. R.: Viridans streptococci and groups C and G streptococci. *In* Mandell, G. L., Bennett, J. E., and Dolin, R. (eds.): Principles and Practice of Infectious Diseases. 5th ed. Philadelphia, Churchill Livingstone, 2000, pp. 2167–2183.
80. Johnson, D. R., and Kaplan, E. L.: A review of the correlation of T-agglutination patterns and M-protein typing and opacity factor production in the identification of group A streptococci. J. Med. Microbiol. *38*:311–315, 1993.
81. Johnson, D. R., and Kaplan, E. (World Health Organization Collaborating Center for Reference and Research on Streptococci; Minneapolis, MN) and Sramek, J., Motlova, J., Bicova, R., et al. (World Health Organization Collaborating Center for Reference and Research on Streptococci; Prague, Czech Republic): Laboratory Diagnosis of Group A Streptococcal Infections: A Laboratory Manual. Geneva, World Health Organization, 1996.
82. Johnson, D. R., and Kaplan, E. L.: False positive rapid antigen detection tests: Reduced specificity in the absence of group A streptococci in the upper respiratory tract. J. Infect. Dis. *183*:1135–1137, 2001.
83. Johnson, D. R., Kaplan, E. L., and Ferrieri, P.: Pharyngitis-associated M-12 group A *Streptococcus* satellite strain: Association with *Neisseria subflava*. Pediatr. Infect. Dis. J. *8*:800–802, 1989.
84. Kaplan, E. L.: Unresolved problems in diagnosis and epidemiology of streptococcal infection. *In* Wannamaker, L. W., and Matsen, J. M. (eds.): Streptococci and Streptococcal Diseases: Recognition, Understanding, and Management. New York, Academic Press, 1972, pp. 557–570.
85. Kaplan, E. L.: The group A streptococcal upper respiratory tract carrier state: An enigma. J. Pediatr. *97*:337–345, 1980.
86. Kaplan, E. L.: Group A streptococcal carriers and contacts: (When) is retreatment necessary? *In* Shulman, S. (ed.): Management of Pharyngitis in an Era of Declining Rheumatic Fever. Columbus, OH, Ross Conference of Pediatric Research, 1984, p. 92.
87. Kaplan, E. L.: Benzathine penicillin G for treatment of group A streptococcal pharyngitis: A reappraisal in 1985. Pediatr. Infect. Dis. *4*:592–596, 1985.
88. Kaplan, E. L.: The rapid identification of group A beta-hemolytic streptococci in the upper respiratory tract: Current status. Pediatr. Clin. North Am. *35*:535–542, 1988.
89. Kaplan, E. L.: Global assessment of rheumatic fever and rheumatic heart disease at the close of the century. Influences and dynamics of populations and pathogens: A failure to realize prevention? T. Duckett Jones Memorial Lecture. Circulation *88*:1964–1972, 1993.
90. Kaplan, E. L., Anthony, B. F., Chapman, S. S., et al.: Epidemic acute glomerulonephritis associated with type 49 streptococcal pyoderma. I. Clinical and laboratory findings. Am. J. Med. *48*:9–27, 1970.
91. Kaplan, E. L., Anthony, B. F., Chapman, S. S., et al.: The influence of the site of infection on the immune response to group A streptococci. J. Clin. Invest. *49*:1405–1414, 1970.
92. Kaplan, E. L., and Johnson, D. R.: Unexplained reduced efficacy of oral penicillin V and intramuscular benzathine penicillin G in the eradication of group A streptococci from children with acute pharyngitis. Pediatrics *108*:1180–1186, 2001.
93. Kaplan, E. L., Johnson, D. R., Nanthapisud, P., et al.: A comparison of group A streptococcal serotypes isolated from the upper respiratory tract in the USA and Thailand: Implications. Bull. World Health Organ. *70*:433–437, 1992.
94. Kaplan, E. L., and Kunde, C.: Quantitative evaluation of variation in composition of the Streptozyme agglutination reagent for detection of antibodies to group A streptococcal extracellular antigens. J. Clin. Microbiol. *14*:678–680, 1981.
95. Kaplan, E. L., Reid, H. F., Johnson, D. R., et al.: Rapid antigen detection in the diagnosis of group A streptococcal pyoderma: Influence of a "learning curve effect" on sensitivity and specificity. Pediatr. Infect. Dis. J. *8*:591–593, 1989.
96. Kaplan, E. L., Top, F. H., Jr., Dudding, B. A., et al.: Diagnosis of streptococcal pharyngitis: Differentiation of active infection from the carrier state in the symptomatic child. J. Infect. Dis. *123*:490–501, 1971.
97. Kaplan, E. L., and Wannamaker, L. W.: C-reactive protein in streptococcal pharyngitis. Pediatrics *60*:28–32, 1977.
98. Kim, K. S.: Clinical perspectives on penicillin tolerance. J. Pediatr. *112*:509–514, 1988.
99. Kim, Y. B., and Watson, D. W., Streptococcal exotoxins: Biological and pathological properties. *In* Wannamaker, L. W., and Matsen, J. M. (eds.): Streptococci and Streptococcal Diseases: Recognition, Understanding, and Management. New York, Academic Press, 1972, pp. 33–50.
100. Kokx, N. P., Comstock, J. A., and Facklam, R. R.: Streptococcal perianal disease in children. Pediatrics *80*:659–663, 1987.
101. Krause, R. M., and Rammelkamp, C. H., Jr.: Studies of the carrier state following infection with group A streptococci. J. Clin. Invest. *41*:575, 1962.

102. Kristensen, B., and Schonheyder, H. C.: A 13-year survey of bacteraemia due to beta-haemolytic streptococci in a Danish county. J. Med. Microbiol. *43*:63–67, 1995.
103. Lancefield, R. C.: Current knowledge of type-specific M antigens of group A streptococci. J. Immunol. *89*:307–313, 1962.
104. Lancefield, R. C.: Group A streptococcal infections in animals: Natural and experimental. *In* Wannamaker, L. W., and Matsen, J. M. (eds.): Streptococci and Streptococcal Diseases: Recognition, Understanding, and Management. New York, Academic Press, 1972, pp. 313–326.
105. LaPenta, D., Rubens, C., Chi, E., and Cleary, P. P.: Group A streptococci efficiently invade human respiratory epithelial cells. Proc. Natl. Acad. Sci. U. S. A. *91*:12115–12119, 1994.
106. Macris, M., Hartman, N., Murray, B., et al.: Studies of the continuing susceptibility to penicillin of group A streptococcal strains isolated over a period spanning eight decades. Pediatr. Infect. Dis. J. *17*:377–381, 1998.
107. Malke, H., Jacob, H. E., and Störl, K.: Characterization of the antibiotic resistance plasmid ERL1 from *Streptococcus pyogenes*. Mol. Gen. Genet. *144*:333–338, 1976.
108. Markowitz, M., and Kaplan, E. L.: Reappearance of rheumatic fever. Adv. Pediatr. *36*:39–66, 1989.
109. Martin, J. M., Green, M., Barbadora, K. A., and Wald, E. R.: Erythromycin-resistant group A streptococci in schoolchildren in Pittsburgh. N. Engl. J. Med. *346*:1200–1206, 2002.
110. Martin, N. J., Kaplan, E. L., Gerber, M. A., et al.: Comparison of epidemic and endemic group G streptococci by restriction enzyme analysis. J. Clin. Microbiol. *28*:1881–1886, 1990.
111. Matsen, J. M., and Coghlan, C. R.: Antibiotic testing and susceptibility patterns of streptococci. *In* Wannamaker, L. W., and Matsen, J. M. (eds.): Streptococci and Streptococcal Diseases: Recognition, Understanding, and Management. New York, Academic Press, 1972, pp. 189–204.
112. McCarty, M.: The streptococcal cell wall. Harvey Lect. *65*:73–96, 1971.
113. McCarty, M.: Theories of pathogenesis of streptococcal complications. *In* Wannamaker, L. W., and Matsen, J. M. (eds.): Streptococci and Streptococcal Diseases: Recognition, Understanding, and Management. New York, Academic Press, 1972, pp. 517–526.
114. McCue, J. D.: Group G streptococcal pharyngitis: Analysis of an outbreak at a college. J. A. M. A. *248*:1333–1336, 1982.
115. Meier, F. A., Centor, R. M., Graham, L., Jr., et al.: Clinical and microbiological evidence for endemic pharyngitis among adults due to group C streptococci. Arch. Intern. Med. *150*:825–829, 1990.
116. Neeman, R., Keller, N., Barzilai, A., et al.: Prevalence of internalization-associated gene, prtF1, among persisting group A streptococcus strains isolated from asymptomatic carriers. Lancet *352*:1974–1977, 1998.
117. Nicholson, M. L., Ferdinand, L., Sampson, J. S., et al.: Analysis of immunoreactivity to a *Streptococcus equi* subsp. *zooepidemicus* M-like protein to confirm an outbreak of poststreptococcal glomerulonephritis, and sequences of M-like proteins from isolates obtained from different host species. J. Clin. Microbiol. *38*:4126–4130, 2000.
118. Ofek, I., Bergner-Rabinowitz, S., and Ginsburg, I.: Oxygen-stable hemolysins of group A streptococci. VII. The relation of the leukotoxic factor to streptolysin S. J. Infect. Dis. *122*:517–522, 1970.
119. Ofek, I., Kaplan, O., Bergner-Rabinowitz, S., et al.: Antibody tests in streptococcal pharyngitis: Streptozyme versus conventional methods. Clin. Pediatr. (Phila.) *12*:341–344, 1973.
120. Ogunbi, O., Lasi, Q., and Lawal, S. F.: An epidemiological study of beta-hemolytic streptococcal infections in a Nigerian (Lagos) urban population. *In* Haverkorn, M. J. (ed.): Streptococcal Disease and the Community. Amsterdam, Excerpta Medica, 1974, pp. 282–284.
121. Pantell, R. H.: Cost-effectiveness of pharyngitis management and prevention of rheumatic fever. Ann. Intern. Med. *86*:497–499, 1977.
122. Paradise, J. L.: Etiology and management of pharyngotonsillitis in children: A current review. Ann. Otol. Rhinol. Laryngol. *155*:51–57, 1992.
123. Poon-King, T., Mohammed, I., Cox, R., et al.: Recurrent epidemic nephritis in South Trinidad. N. Engl. J. Med. *277*:728–733, 1967.
124. Powers, G. F., and Boisvert, P. L.: Tuberculosis and streptococcosis. Yale J. Biol. Med. *15*:517–530, 1943.
125. Prevention of invasive group A streptococcal disease among household contacts of case patients and among postpartum and postsurgical patients: Recommendations of the Centers for Disease Control and Prevention. Clin. Infect. Dis. *35*:950–959, 2002.
126. Rammelkamp, C. H., Jr.: Epidemiology of streptococcal infections. Harvey Lect. *51*:113–142, 1957.
127. Randolph, M. F., Gerber, M. A., DeMeo, K. K., et al.: Effect of antibiotic therapy on the clinical course of streptococcal pharyngitis. J. Pediatr. *106*:870–875, 1985.
128. Read, S. E., Fischetti, V. A., Utermohlen, V., et al.: Cellular reactivity studies to streptococcal antigens: Migration inhibition studies in patients with streptococcal infections and rheumatic fever. J. Clin. Invest. *54*:439–450, 1974.
129. Recco, R., Cortes, H., Zaman, M. M., et al.: Intra-familial transmission of life-threatening group A streptococcal infection. Epidemiol. Infect. *129*:303–306, 2002.
130. Reid, H. F., Bassett, D. C., Poon-King, T., et al.: Group G streptococci in healthy school-children and in patients with glomerulonephritis in Trinidad. J. Hyg. *94*:61–68, 1985.
131. Rolston, K. V., Chandrasekar, P. H., and LeFrock, J. L.: Antimicrobial tolerance in group C and group G streptococci. J. Antimicrob. Chemother. *13*:389–392, 1984.
132. Rolston, K. V., LeFrock, J. L., and Schell, R. F.: Activity of nine antimicrobial agents against Lancefield group C and group G streptococci. Antimicrob. Agents Chemother. *22*:930–932, 1982.
133. Ruoff, K. L., Whiley, R. A., and Beighton, D.: Streptococcus. *In* Murrya, P. R., Baron, E. J., Pfaller, M. A., et al. (eds.): Manual of Clinical Microbiology. 7th ed. Washington, D.C., ASM Press, 1999, pp. 283–296.
134. Sawyer, W. D., Smith, M. R., and Wood, W. B., Jr.: The mechanisms by which macrophages phagocytize encapsulated bacteria in the absence of antibody. J. Exp. Med. *100*:417–424, 1954.
135. Schwartz, R. H., Gerber, M. A., and McCoy, P.: Effect of atmosphere of incubation on the isolation of group A streptococci from throat cultures. J. Lab. Clin. Med. *106*:88–92, 1985.
136. Seppala, H., Nissinen, A., Jarvinen, H., et al.: Resistance to erythromycin in group A streptococci. N. Engl. J. Med. *326*:292–297, 1992.
137. Seravalli, E., and Taranta, A.: Lymphocyte transformation and macrophage migration inhibition by electrofocused and gel-filtered fractions of group A streptococcal filtrate. Cell. Immunol. *14*:366–375, 1974.
138. Shet, A., and Kaplan, E. L.: The clinical use and interpretation of group A streptococcal antibody tests: A practical approach for the pediatrician or primary care physician. Pediatr. Infect. Dis. J. *21*:420–426, 2002.
139. Shulman, S. T.: Streptococcal pharyngitis: Diagnostic considerations. Pediatr. Infect. Dis. J. *13*:567–571, 1994.
140. Siegel, A. C., Johnson, E. E., and Stollerman, G. H.: Controlled studies of streptococcal pharyngitis in a pediatric population. I. Factors related to the attack rate of rheumatic fever. N. Engl. J. Med. *265*:559–566, 1961.
141. Smith, E. W., Garson, A., Jr., Boyleston, J. A., et al.: Varicella gangrenosa due to group A beta-hemolytic *Streptococcus*. Pediatrics *57*:306–310, 1976.
142. Smith, T. D., Wilkinson, V., and Kaplan, E. L.: Group A *Streptococcus*–associated upper respiratory tract infections in a day-care center. Pediatrics *83*:380–384, 1989.
143. Snellman, L. W., Stang, H. J., Stang, J. M., et al.: Duration of positive throat cultures for group A streptococci after initiation of antibiotic therapy. Pediatrics *91*:1166–1170, 1993.
144. Stetson, C. A., Rammelkamp, C. H., Jr., Krause, R. M., et al.: Epidemic acute nephritis: Studies on etiology, natural history and prevention. Medicine (Baltimore) *34*:431–450, 1955.
145. Stevens, D. L.: Streptococcal toxic-shock syndrome: Spectrum of disease, pathogenesis, and new concepts in treatment. Emerg. Infect. Dis. *1*:69–78, 1995.
146. Stevens, D. L.: Life-threatening streptococcal infections: Scarlet fever, necrotizing fasciitis, myositis, bacteremia, and streptococcal toxic shock syndrome. *In* Stevens, D. L., and Kaplan, E. L. (eds.): Streptococcal Infections: Clinical Aspects, Microbiology, and Molecular Pathogenesis. New York, Oxford University Press, 2000, pp. 163–179.
147. Stevens, D. L., Tanner, M. H., Winship, J., et al.: Severe group A streptococcal infections associated with a toxic shock–like syndrome and scarlet fever toxin A. N. Engl. J. Med. *321*:1–7, 1989.
148. Tagg, J. R., Dajani, A. S., Wannamaker, L. W., et al.: Group A streptococcal bacteriocin: Production, purification, and mode of action. J. Exp. Med. *138*:1168–1183, 1973.
149. Tancer, M. L., McManus, J. E., and Bellotti, G.: Group A, type 33, beta-hemolytic streptococcal outbreak on a maternity and newborn service. Am. J. Obstet. Gynecol. *103*:1028–1033, 1969.
150. Turner, J. C., Hayden, G. F., Kiselica, D., et al.: Association of group C beta-hemolytic streptococci with endemic pharyngitis among college students. J. A. M. A. *264*:2644–2647, 1990.
151. Turner, J. C., Hayden, F. G., Lobo, M. C., et al.: Epidemiologic evidence for Lancefield group C beta-hemolytic streptococci as a cause of exudative pharyngitis in college students. J. Clin. Microbiol. *35*:1–4, 1997.
152. Vandamme, P., Pot, B., Falsen, E., et al.: Taxonomic study of Lancefield streptococcal groups C, G, and L (*Streptococcus dysgalactiae*) and proposal of *S. dysgalactiae* subsp. *equisimilis* subsp. *nov*. Int. J. Syst. Bacteriol. *46*:774–781, 1996.
153. Veasy, L. G., and Hill, H. R.: Immunologic and clinical correlations in rheumatic fever and rheumatic heart disease. Pediatr. Infect. Dis. J. *16*:400–407, 1997.
154. Veasy, L. G., Tani, L. Y., and Hill, H. R.: Persistence of acute rheumatic fever in the intermountain area of the United States. J. Pediatr. *124*:9–16, 1994.
155. Villasenor-Sierra, A., McShan, W. M., Salmi, D., et al.: Variable susceptibility to opsonophagocytosis group A *Streptococcus* M-1 strains by human immune sera. J. Infect. Dis. *180*:1921–1928, 1999.
156. Wagner, J. G., Schlievert, P. M., Assimacopoulos, A. P., et al.: Acute group G streptococcal myositis associated with streptococcal toxic shock syndrome: Case report and review. Clin. Infect. Dis. *23*: 1159–1161, 1996.

157. Wannamaker, L. W.: The epidemiology of streptococcal infections. *In* McCarty, M. (ed.): Streptococcal Infections. New York, Columbia University Press, 1954, pp. 157–175.
158. Wannamaker, L. W.: Differences between streptococcal infections of the throat and of the skin. I. N. Engl. J. Med. *282*:23–31, 1970.
159. Wannamaker, L. W.: Perplexity and precision in the diagnosis of streptococcal pharyngitis. Am. J. Dis. Child. *124*:352–358, 1972.
160. Wannamaker, L. W.: The chain that links the heart to the throat. Circulation *48*:9–18, 1973.
161. Wannamaker, L. W.: Immunology of streptococci. *In* Good, R. A., Nahmias, A. J., and O'Reilly, R. J. (eds.): Comprehensive Immunology: Immunology of Human Infection. New York, Plenum, 1981, pp. 47–72.
162. Wannamaker, L. W.: Diagnosis of pharyngitis: Clinical and epidemiologic features. *In* Shulman, S. (ed.): Management of Pharyngitis in an Era of Declining Rheumatic Fever. Columbus, OH, Ross Conference on Pediatric Research, 1984, p. 25.
163. Wannamaker, L. W., Almquist, S., and Skjold, S.: Intergroup phage reactions and transduction between group C and group A streptococci. J. Exp. Med. *137*:1338–1353, 1973.
164. Wannamaker, L. W., and Ferrieri, P.: Streptococcal infections—updated. Dis. Mon. *Oct*:1–40, 1975.
165. Weinstein, L., and Le Frock, J.: Does antimicrobial therapy of streptococcal pharyngitis or pyoderma alter the risk of glomerulonephritis? J. Infect. Dis. *124*:229–231, 1971.
166. Wesley, T. B., Johnson, D. R., Diesch, S. L., et al.: Do beta hemolytic streptococci in the upper respiratory tract (URT) of household dogs constitute a significant zoonotic threat? Abstract. Presented at the Interscience Conference on Antibiotics and Chemotherapy, San Francisco, 1995.
167. Wittler, R. R., Yamada, S. M., Bass, J. W., et al.: Penicillin tolerance and erythromycin resistance of group A beta-hemolytic streptococci in Hawaii and the Philippines. Am. J. Dis. Child. *144*:587–589, 1990.
168. Zabriskie, J. B.: The role of temperate bacteriophage in the production of erythrogenic toxin by group A streptococci. J. Exp. Med. *119*:761–779, 1964.
169. Zaoutis, T., Schneider, B., Steele, M. L., and Klein, J. D.: Antibiotic susceptibility of group C and group G streptococci isolated from patients with invasive infections: Evidence of vancomycin tolerance among group G serotypes. J. Clin. Microbiol. *37*:3380–3383, 1999.
170. Zimmerman, R. A., and Hill, H. R.: Placental transfer of group A type-specific streptococcal antibody. Pediatrics *43*:809–814, 1969.

Group B Streptococcal Infections

JUDITH L. ROWEN ■ CAROL J. BAKER

History

The organism we know as group B *Streptococcus,* or *Streptococcus agalactiae,* was isolated first by Nocard in 1887[232] and for decades was recognized as a cause of bovine mastitis[221] but not human infection. Serologic techniques for differentiating beta-hemolytic streptococci were developed by Lancefield,[181] who also described isolation of group B streptococci from parturient women in 1935.[182] In that same year, Congdon[83] included one fatal puerperal case of group B streptococcal sepsis and pneumonia in a report of streptococcal infections associated with childbirth. The significance of this organism as a human pathogen was reported first by Fry[117] in 1938, who described three cases of fatal puerperal sepsis. Group B streptococcal infections continued to be reported sporadically until the 1960s, when maternal and neonatal infections increasingly were ascribed to this pathogen.[74, 100, 145] In the 1970s, group B *Streptococcus* emerged as the predominant organism causing bacteremia and meningitis in neonates.[18, 35, 115, 149, 242] The incidence of neonatal infection remained stable, with reported attack rates ranging from 0.2 to 5.4 per 1000 live births, until the late 1990s, when maternal intrapartum chemoprophylaxis gained wide acceptance and incidence rates fell.[37, 242, 287, 290] Invasive infection does occur beyond the neonatal period in pregnant women, nonpregnant adults with underlying medical conditions, and the elderly.[104, 150, 235]

Microbiology

ISOLATION AND IDENTIFICATION

Group B streptococci are facultative gram-positive diplococci that grow on a variety of bacteriologic media. Colonies are 3 to 4 mm in diameter, grayish-white, flat, and somewhat mucoid. Colonies are surrounded by a narrow zone of beta-hemolysis that for some strains is detectable only when the colony is lifted from the agar. Nonhemolytic strains account for 1 to 2 percent of isolates and may cause human disease.[18, 273] Differentiation of hemolytic streptococci relies on detection of group-specific antigens within the cell wall. The standard method, as described by Lancefield,[181] requires acid treatment of the bacteria to solubilize the carbohydrate group B antigen, followed by capillary precipitation with hyperimmune rabbit serum. Several newer methods using hyperimmune antisera have been developed, but latex agglutination is used widely because of the commercial availability of test kits, the ease of performing the assay, and the specificity of the results when organisms in pure culture are tested.[298] Other laboratory methods for presumptive identification include testing for resistance to bacitracin or trimethoprim-sulfamethoxazole, hydrolysis of sodium hippurate broth, failure to hydrolyze bile esculin, production of orange pigment when cultured under certain conditions, and CAMP testing. CAMP is an acronym of the names of the authors who first described synergistic hemolysis on sheep blood agar when group B streptococci are grown in the presence of the beta-toxin of *Staphylococcus aureus*.[82]

SEROLOGIC CLASSIFICATION AND ANTIGENIC STRUCTURE

Just as beta-hemolytic streptococci are divided into groups based on cell wall antigens, group B streptococci are divided further into serotypes based on type-specific capsular polysaccharides. The type-specific polysaccharides of group B streptococci (glucose, galactose, glucosamine, and *N*-acetylneuraminic acid) are repeating units of five to seven monosaccharides. All the characterized polysaccharides include an *N*-acetylneuraminic acid (sialic acid) residue, which may be important in the pathogenesis of human infection.[42, 293, 333] Nine such polysaccharides are characterized: Ia, Ib, and II to VIII. Provisional type IX is being considered. A small proportion of strains isolated from infants with systemic infection do not react with hyperimmune sera to the characterized capsular polysaccharides and are called nontypeable. Further differentiation of type Ia strains was based on the presence or absence of a protein antigen known as c, which led to the nomenclature of Ia and Ia/c serotypes. This c protein is present in many other serotypes as well, but it is a rare finding in type III strains.[110] Table 88–1 reviews the major polysaccharide and protein surface antigens of group B streptococci.

EXTRACELLULAR PRODUCTS

Several bacterial products are elaborated by group B streptococci. Type-specific capsular polysaccharide is released from cells, and the amount elaborated has been correlated with virulence.[175, 345] These soluble polysaccharides inhibit opsonophagocytic killing in vitro, thereby providing a mechanism for the documented increase in virulence.[188] Most strains possess C5a-ase, an enzyme of the serine esterase class that inactivates complement component C5a.[143] Because C5a is a potent chemoattractant for neutrophils, this enzyme helps the bacteria evade the host immune system by hindering the accumulation of neutrophils at the site of infection. The beta-hemolysin elaborated by group B streptococci was characterized in 1980, but only recently has its role in virulence been explored through the creation of nonhemolytic and hyperhemolytic mutants.[204, 328] Expression of beta-hemolysin correlates with tissue damage in an in vivo arthritis model and also increases virulence in rats infected via the respiratory route.[231, 256] Other bacterial products of group B streptococci, including CAMP factor, lipoteichoic acid, pigment, hippuricase, neuraminidase, hyaluronidase, and nucleases, have been described, but the contributions of these substances to pathogenesis are not clear.[112, 113, 123, 164, 211, 228, 229, 312]

ANTIMICROBIAL SUSCEPTIBILITY

To date, human isolates of group B streptococci have remained uniformly susceptible to penicillin G. However, approximately 10-fold greater concentrations are required for inhibition and killing of group B streptococci than for group A streptococci. Group B streptococci are also susceptible to other β-lactams,

TABLE 88–1 ■ ANTIGENIC DETERMINANTS OF GROUP B STREPTOCOCCI

Serotypes		Structure/Composition	Comments	Reference
Polysaccharides				
Group B	All	Highly branched; 4 oligosaccharides; probably linked to cell wall peptidoglycan	Antibody not protective	183, 218
Ia	Ia, Ia/c	5-Monosaccharide repeating unit		157
Ib	Ib	5-Monosaccharide repeating unit; identical to Ia except 1–3 instead of 1–4 linkage at the galactose side chain	Homology with oligosaccharides from human milk	157, 255
II	II	7-Monosaccharide repeating unit	2 side chains; sialic acid linked directly to repeating unit	159
III	III	5-Monosaccharide repeating unit	Removal of terminal sialic acid results in a polysaccharide identical to that of type 14 *S. pneumoniae*	114, 158
IV	IV	6-Monosaccharide repeating unit		331
V	V	7-Monosaccharide repeating unit		332
VI	VI	5-Monosaccharide repeating unit; lacks *N*-acetylglucosamine		323
VII	VII	6-Monosaccharide repeating unit		177
VIII	VIII	4-Monosaccharide repeating unit; contains rhamnose		178
Proteins*				
C	Ia/c, Ib, up to 60% of II, many IV, occasional V	Alpha (trypsin-resistant) and beta (trypsin-sensitive) antigens maybe present singly or in combination	Beta binds the Fc portion of human IgA	67, 110, 160, 247
R1, R4	37% of II, 80% of III, occasional IV, many V	5 species known	Found also on groups A and C streptococci; immunologically cross-reactive with X antigen	110, 335
X	Occasional III and IV, many nontypeable strains		Found in 47% of bovine strains	110, 335
V	V	Shares N-terminal sequence homology with alpha c protein		180
Rib	Most invasive strains, including almost all III	Repetitive structure	Not related to alpha c protein; cross-reacts with R28 of group A streptococci	303, 304

*The protein constituents of types VI, VII, and VIII have not yet been evaluated.

cephalosporins, vancomycin, and carbapenems. The prevalence of resistance to the macrolides (erythromycin, clindamycin, clarithromycin) is increasing; previously it was reported in 1 to 3 percent of isolates, but recent studies report resistance to erythromycin in as many as 18 percent of cases and resistance to clindamycin in 7 to 15 percent.[57, 91, 193, 274] Resistance to macrolides is highest in type V strains.[193] Nearly 90 percent of strains are resistant to tetracycline, and resistance to bacitracin, nalidixic acid, trimethoprim-sulfamethoxazole, and metronidazole is uniform.[251] Low-level gentamicin resistance is typical, but when gentamicin is combined with either penicillin G or ampicillin, synergistic killing of group B streptococci occurs in vitro and in vivo.[283, 284, 309]

As many as 5 percent of group B streptococcal isolates have been reported to be tolerant to penicillin.[172] Expression of tolerance requires laboratory conditions that promote a greater than 16-fold discrepancy between minimal inhibitory concentrations and minimal bactericidal concentrations. Tolerant strains are characterized in vitro by delayed penicillin killing, similar rates of killing by penicillin whether growth is exponential or stationary, an additive rather than a synergistic response to the combination of penicillin and gentamicin, and deficient autolysis. The clinical significance, if any, of these laboratory-induced properties remains unknown.[30, 171]

Epidemiology

INCIDENCE

Before the use of maternal intrapartum chemoprophylaxis to prevent early-onset disease became widespread, reported attack rates for group B streptococcal disease in infants ranged from 0.2 to 5.4 per 1000 live births.[33, 242, 329] Early-onset disease (occurring within the first week of life) accounted for approximately 80 percent of cases.[288] Late-onset disease attack rates ranged from 0.3 to 1.8 per 1000 live births.[88, 242] With the advent of maternal intrapartum chemoprophylaxis, the incidence of early-onset disease has fallen 65 percent from 1993 to 1998.[287] Preliminary data from subsequent years suggest that the incidence is continuing to fall, but no change in the incidence of late-onset disease has been noted.[91]

Information relating to infants with onset of group B streptococcal disease beyond 3 months of age is sparse. Several reported infants have had concomitant infection with human immunodeficiency virus (HIV) or have been born before 34 weeks' gestation.[86, 150] Group B streptococcal disease also is a common finding in pregnant women, with clinical manifestations that include urinary tract infection (usually asymptomatic bacteriuria), intra-amniotic infection, postpartum endometritis (often with bacteremia), puerperal sepsis, and, occasionally, meningitis, septic thrombophlebitis, or other serious complications.[27, 107, 241, 290] Attack rates of 2 per 1000 deliveries have been reported.[241] However, nonpregnant adults actually made up most cases (68%) of invasive group B streptococcal disease.[104] In these patients, underlying medical conditions, including diabetes mellitus, malignancy (especially breast cancer), HIV infection, liver disease, stroke and other neurologic disorders, decubitus ulcers, neurogenic bladder, and age 65 years or older, are the rule.[104, 153, 235]

MATERNAL COLONIZATION

Neonatal group B streptococcal infection results from exposure to the organism in the maternal genital tract intrapartum or at delivery.[33] In most cases, the mother is infected asymptomatically or colonized. Maternal colonization rates vary widely and relate to body sites sampled, microbiologic techniques used, and the period of gestation in which cultures are performed.

The site chosen for culture is critical, and sampling of multiple sites improves detection.[27, 32, 87] The distal portion of the vagina more frequently yields group B streptococci than the cervix does.[201, 266] Concomitant sampling of the rectal site results in detection of virtually all carriers. Several investigators have suggested the gastrointestinal tract as the principal reservoir for this organism,[19, 27, 146] and not uncommonly, the rectal site is the only one that yields group B streptococci.[33, 87, 146, 250, 349] The urinary tract is an important site of infection (asymptomatic bacteriuria) because it is a surrogate for a high ($>10^5$ colony-forming units per milliliter) genital inoculum,[226, 342] a marker of increased risk for development of early-onset sepsis in neonates. Bacteriuria mandates therapy during pregnancy.[254]

The manner in which swab specimens from the vagina and rectum are processed also is important in accurately assessing colonization. Allowing women to collect the swabs themselves is acceptable because these specimens are as accurate as ones collected by physicians.[314] Swabs may be placed in transport media at environmental temperatures for as long as 96 hours. Once they reach the laboratory, however, they should be placed in antibiotic-containing broth rather than on solid media because the latter "misses" detection of as many as 50 percent of group B streptococcal carriers.[32, 39] The addition of antibiotics to the broth limits the growth of competing flora and enhances detection.[8, 39, 208] Todd-Hewitt broth with gentamicin and nalidixic acid (selective broth medium)[36] or with colistin (Lim broth)[192] and nalidixic acid is recommended for detection of group B streptococcal colonization.[9, 254] After overnight incubation, the broth is subcultured onto a 5 percent sheep blood agar plate and processed conventionally.

The proximity to delivery also affects the accuracy of predicting colonization at delivery. Ninety-two percent of culture-positive women are identified if lower vaginal and rectal cultures are obtained at a single visit.[92] Furthermore, although rates are similar by trimester, cultures obtained at 35 and 37 weeks' gestation predict colonization at delivery with nearly 95 percent accuracy.[63, 254] Reported colonization rates vary widely, but if the aforementioned methods are used, the overall rate is 25 to 30 percent.[32, 92]

Risk Factors for Colonization during Pregnancy

Much effort has been spent trying to define groups of women at enhanced risk for colonization with group B streptococci. Nonpregnant women have similar colonization rates, suggesting that pregnancy does not affect colonization.[40, 102] Women younger than 20 years of age have higher and multiparous (≥3 pregnancies) women have lower colonization rates.[20, 40, 266, 347, 349] Although group B streptococci are sexually transmissible, the number of sexual partners or the frequency of sexual activity does not influence the status of colonization.[40, 266]

Ethnicity does affect the likelihood of colonization, however. In a survey of 2929 women, 36.7 percent of black women were colonized, a rate significantly greater than the 23.3 percent in women belonging to other ethnic groups.[349] In the same study, Asian women had a significantly lower rate of group B streptococcal colonization (14%) than did any other ethnic group. The multicenter study, conducted by the Vaginal Infections and Prematurity Study Group, evaluated 7742 women at 23 to 26 weeks' gestation and reported that black race, age younger than 20 years, and lower educational level were correlated independently with high group B streptococcal colonization rates.[266]

INFANT COLONIZATION

Acquisition of the organism by infants born to colonized mothers (vertical transmission) occurs in 29 to 72 percent of cases (mean, ≈50%).[6, 20, 33, 85, 92, 242, 296] As with maternal colonization, detection depends on the sites sampled, the culture method, and timing. Acquisition is presumed to occur either by the ascending route through ruptured membranes or from contact with the organism in the genital tract during parturition. Nosocomial transmission occurs uncommonly, but community acquisition occurs frequently.[1, 20, 119, 233] If cultures are obtained immediately after birth, positive results reflect contamination with infected maternal secretions and a high inoculum. Twenty-four to 48 hours is an appropriate age to determine whether the infant has become colonized in the gastrointestinal or respiratory tract after exposure to maternal group B *Streptococcus*. Many sites, including the ear canal, throat, umbilicus, and rectum, have been used for neonatal cultures. Historically, the umbilicus was a reliable site, but routine treatment of the umbilicus with triple dye and other antiseptics diminishes recovery of group B streptococci.[51, 302] Isolation of the organism from the throat or rectum implies replication of organisms at respiratory or gastrointestinal tract sites after the ingestion of infected amniotic fluid or genital secretions. One study determined that sampling the throat and rectum at 24 to 48 hours of age identified all colonized infants.[142]

Factors Influencing Infant Colonization Rates

The single factor most clearly associated with the likelihood of vertical transmission and subsequent neonatal colonization is the number of organisms (inoculum) in the maternal genital tract. Mothers with high numbers of group B streptococcal inocula ($>10^5$ colony-forming units per milliliter) are more likely to transmit the organism to their baby.[13, 20, 146, 161] Vertical transmission is more likely to occur after vaginal delivery than after cesarean section.[142] Prolonged rupture of membranes (>12 hours) also is associated with an increased infant colonization rate.[142] Maternal intrapartum antibiotic therapy substantially diminishes the vertical transmission of group B streptococci.[64, 65, 296, 348] In one study, infant colonization was significantly lower (4% versus 20%) in an obstetric population in which 35 percent of the colonized mothers received intrapartum antibiotics than in another group in which only 17 percent were treated.[142]

Risk Factors for Infant Disease

Vertical transmission is a prerequisite for the development of invasive, early-onset infection.[33, 210, 242] Evidence suggests that approximately 50 percent of late-onset infections also occur after vertical transmission.[88] The degree of colonization or inoculum also increases the likelihood of infant disease; heavily colonized mothers are more likely to have infants with invasive infection, and heavily colonized infants are more likely to have either early- or late-onset disease.[63, 88, 161, 191] Other maternal factors associated with the development of early-onset disease include labor before 37 weeks' gestation, premature rupture of membranes or rupture of membranes more than 18 hours before delivery at any gestation, and intrapartum fever.[18, 63, 88, 115, 242] The association with premature rupture of membranes or premature labor may be a "chicken and egg" phenomenon because colonization with group B streptococci, especially at high inoculum, has been associated with premature rupture of membranes and preterm labor.[5, 144, 209, 213, 265] Other maternal factors associated with an increased attack rate of early-onset infection are black race, age younger than 20 years, history of previous fetal loss, history of urinary tract infection with group B streptococci, and primiparity.[289] Late-onset disease also is associated with young maternal age and black race.[290] Infants who are the product of a multiple pregnancy (e.g., twins, triplets) have been shown to have some enhanced risk for early- and late-onset group B streptococcal disease,[96, 243] but this association has not been demonstrated consistently.[290]

SEROTYPES CAUSING DISEASE

Reports from the 1970s indicated that the group B streptococcal serotypes colonizing pregnant women and neonates were divided fairly evenly among types I, II, and III.[27, 34, 336, 337] However, a new serotype, type V, emerged in the 1990s.[59, 142, 269] In Japan, types VI and VIII are the most common isolates from pregnant women.[179] The representation of serotypes in invasive disease is less balanced, however. When meningitis is present, either as a focus of early-onset disease or as a manifestation of late-onset infection, type III is implicated in most cases (80% to 93%).[34, 337] The distribution of serotypes is relatively balanced when other manifestations of early-onset disease (e.g., bacteremia without a focus or pneumonia) are considered.[34] Type V causes both early- and late-onset infant disease and is the isolate found most commonly in adults with invasive disease, but it appears to lag behind types Ia and III as a cause of infant disease.[59, 269] The least common serotypes causing human disease are types Ib/c, IV, VI, VII, and VIII.

Pathogenesis

For pediatricians, group B streptococcal disease predominantly afflicts neonates, a predilection that results from a unique combination of maternal, bacterial, and host factors. A proposed scheme for the pathogenesis of early-onset infection is outlined in Figure 88–1. First, an organism carried by an asymptomatically colonized mother is transmitted to her neonate. Evidence suggests that this transmission may occur in utero or during parturition. This continuum in time of acquisition is reflected in the time of onset of symptoms; infected neonates often are ill at or within 12 hours of birth (up to 90%), whereas others may not have evidence of disease for a few days.[35, 290] The organism successfully colonizes approximately 50 percent of all infants born to group B streptococcal carriers, yet disease develops in only 1 to 2 percent of these infants.[18, 33, 288] A breach in the delicate interplay of maternal, infant, and bacterial factors allows the organism to invade. Once invasion occurs, a combination of host defenses and therapeutic interventions may halt the progression of disease, or the infant's defenses may fail and the disease may progress and result in tissue damage or death.

MATERNAL FACTORS

The bacterial inoculum in the maternal genital tract determines the likelihood that the organism will be transmitted vertically. Infants born to heavily colonized women are more likely to be colonized themselves and more likely to have

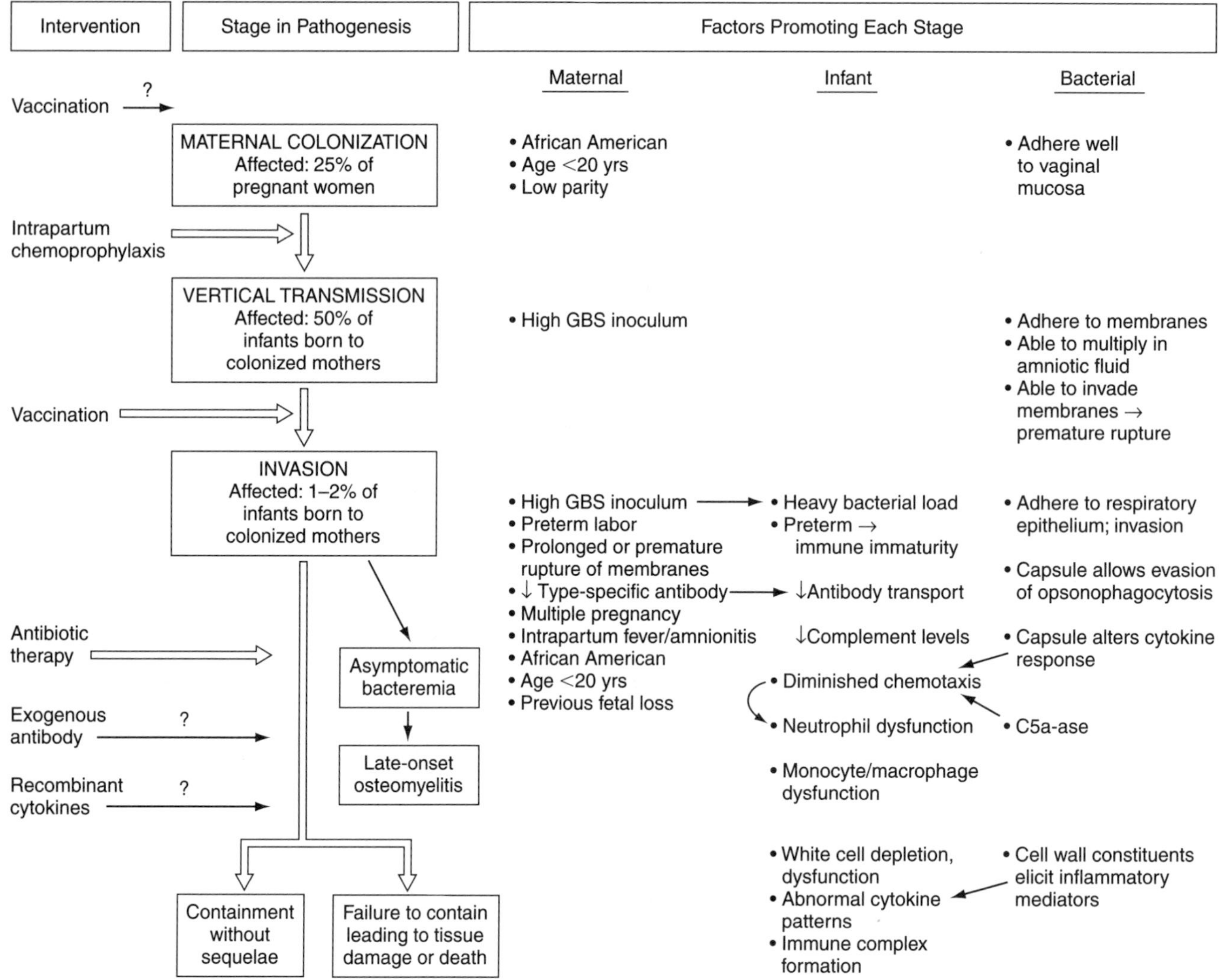

FIGURE 88–1 ■ Proposed scheme for the pathophysiology of group B streptococcal infections in infants.

early-onset disease.[13, 20, 63, 88, 146, 161] Infants delivered prematurely have an increased risk for development of early-onset disease. Heavy maternal colonization may induce preterm delivery,[210, 225, 265] and disease is more likely to develop in the infant in this setting of high bacterial inoculum and immunologic immaturity. Invasive disease also has been reported in neonates delivered by elective cesarean section (intact membranes).[18, 100, 241]

In addition to bacterial inoculum, another critical maternal factor is the concentration of antibody to the serotype-specific polysaccharide capsule of the colonizing strain of group B *Streptococcus* in serum at delivery. Antibody to the type-specific antigen is protective against the homologous serotype in the mouse model; antibody to the group B polysaccharide is not.[183] Baker and associates[38, 43] determined that invasive disease with type III group B streptococci occurred primarily in infants born to women with low concentrations of anti–type III capsular antibody in their sera. Several other investigators also have reported a correlation between low concentrations of antibody to types Ia, Ib, II, and III polysaccharide in maternal delivery sera and the occurrence of early- and late-onset group B streptococcal infant disease.[127, 129] A correlation between antibody concentration and maternal age may explain the epidemiologic association of young maternal age and increased likelihood of neonatal disease.[17] Animal models have demonstrated that antibody directed against the alpha or beta determinants of c protein is protective,[183, 217] but definitive human studies are lacking. Antibody to other protein determinants in some serotypes has been postulated to be partially protective. Titers of antibody to R protein were found to be higher in maternal serum from mothers colonized with R protein–bearing strains whose infants were healthy than from mothers whose infants were ill; such antibodies were protective in a mouse model against some strains.[194, 195]

BACTERIAL FACTORS

To colonize the genital tract or cause disease effectively, the organisms must be able to adhere to host tissue. Group B streptococci adhere well to many types of epithelium, including vaginal epithelium and chorioamnionic membranes.[118, 200, 299, 311] Type III strains adhere more avidly to vaginal cells than do other serotypes in vitro.[62] Furthermore, invasive strains adhere better to epithelial tissue than colonizing strains do.[138] This capacity to adhere to and possibly invade chorioamnionic cells may explain the association of group B streptococcal colonization with preterm labor and premature rupture of membranes.[144] If a breach occurs in the membranes, the bacteria can multiply in amniotic fluid.[139] After transmission and colonization, the capacity of the bacteria to adhere to neonatal epithelial cells may allow them to invade and disseminate. The lung, after aspiration of infected maternal fluids, is a frequent initial site of infection in a newborn with early-onset disease. Group B streptococci can adhere to and invade respiratory epithelial cell lines.[278] In addition, they can invade endothelial cells, which may be a mechanism for some of the pathologic features of disseminated disease.[123] Some researchers have postulated that the bacterial cell wall component lipoteichoic acid confers adherence properties to group B streptococci,[229] but others have suggested other surface proteins.[73, 311]

A well-defined virulence structure of group B streptococci is the capsular polysaccharide. Mouse virulent strains are able to synthesize greater amounts of surface-bound type-specific polysaccharide than are avirulent strains.[345] An unencapsulated mutant, created by inserting a transposon into the gene regulating capsule expression, has significantly less virulence in neonatal rats than does the parent type III strain.[279] As with other encapsulated organisms, the capsule is thought to confer virulence primarily by interfering with opsonophagocytosis. In vitro, the capsule of type III group B streptococci has been shown to prevent the deposition of C3,[206] and the presence of the terminal sialic acid residue on the repeating unit of the polysaccharide is crucial to this interference.[98] Removal of sialic acid residues from the polysaccharide leads to diminished virulence, and a desialylated mutant loses virulence when compared with the parent strain.[334] Furthermore, the presence of this sialic acid moiety prevents activation of the alternative complement pathway, the predominant pathway used by the human host when minimal type-specific antibody is present.[98] In addition, when bacteria grow in the presence of human serum, the quantity of sialic acid increases, thereby potentiating its contribution to virulence.[253] Opsonization may be affected by cell surface components other than capsular sialic acid. C protein also lends relative resistance to opsonization to strains bearing the antigen.[247]

Sialic acid residues on the capsule may interfere with another component of the immune system. In a serum-free system, the desialylated mutant of type III group B streptococci elicited much larger quantities of leukotriene B_4 from macrophages than did the parent strain.[276] Leukotriene B_4 is a potent neutrophil chemoattractant, so this effect may result in diminished influx of effector cells. Similarly, C5a-ase may disable C5a, another host product capable of eliciting neutrophil influx. By enhancing phagocytosis and killing of group B streptococci, C5a also has direct stimulatory effects on neutrophils, so bacterial elaboration of C5a-ase may affect both the accumulation of neutrophils and the efficiency of neutrophil function.[310]

Once invasive infection is established, ongoing replication and digestion of bacteria can instigate host inflammatory responses that may be deleterious. Neonates recovering from group B streptococcal disease have circulating immune complexes for a prolonged period, and immune complexes can contribute to end-organ damage.[317] Additionally, immune complexes containing group B streptococcal components elicit inflammatory mediators such as leukotriene B_4 and interleukin-6 (IL-6). The cytokine response to gram-positive pathogens is not delineated as clearly as that to gram-negative bacteria, partly because of the greater heterogeneity in structure of the latter.[60] Both group B and type III capsular polysaccharides induce the release of IL-6 from monocytes[318]; group B antigen also causes the release of tumor necrosis factor–α (TNF-α).[319] As with other gram-positive pathogens, the cell walls of group B streptococci contain peptidoglycan and lipoteichoic acid. Peptidoglycans from other gram-positive organisms elicit a variety of proinflammatory cytokines such as TNF-α, IL-1, IL-6, and granulocyte colony-stimulating factor.[89, 141, 267] Lipoteichoic acid also induces the release of IL-1β, IL-6, and TNF-α.[58, 168] Group B streptococcal cell wall components likewise exert similar effects. Elaboration of these cytokines has been implicated in the clinical and hemodynamic effects of sepsis.[60] Specifically, blockade of IL-1 activity by administration of an IL-1 receptor antagonist in a piglet model of group B streptococcal sepsis ameliorated systemic hypotension and prolonged survival.[320]

INFANT HOST FACTORS

Neonates have several domains of immune dysfunction that affect their ability to mount a sufficient defense against group B streptococci. Neutrophils are the primary effector cell in host defense against extracellular bacterial pathogens, and neutrophils from neonates have functional abnormalities,[189] including impaired migration to a chemotactic stimulus.[16] The generation of chemotactic activity in neonatal serum in response to group B streptococci is diminished, as is the release of chemotactic factors by neonatal monocytes.[15, 277] Thus, the diminished ability of neutrophils to migrate is amplified by a diminished level of chemotactic stimulation. Phagocytosis and bacterial killing also are impaired when opsonic activity is poor, which is the usual pattern in neonates with sepsis.[189] The neutrophil storage pools of neonates rapidly become depleted during invasive infection, thereby leading to profound neutropenia,[81] an ominous prognostic indicator.[246] These defects in neonatal neutrophils are even more pronounced in infants born prematurely.[189]

Cells of the monocyte/macrophage lineage also may have a role in host defense against group B streptococci, especially in the lungs, where the alveolar macrophage is the first effector cell to encounter pathogens. Defects in the functions of these cells have been described in neonates. Cord blood monocytes have impaired phagocytosis and killing of group B streptococci.[205] In animal models, oxidative metabolism, bacterial uptake, and migration to the site of infection by neonatal macrophages are diminished in response to group B streptococci.[207, 291, 292]

Humoral immunity is compromised in neonates. Both the alternative and classic complement pathways are affected, and premature neonates are impaired more severely.[84, 95] Both pathways are important in the opsonization of group B streptococci.[37] The concentration of type-specific antibody passively acquired from the mother is an important protective factor. Because passive transfer of IgG increases dramatically in the final 8 weeks of pregnancy, premature neonates are again at a disadvantage because they may not receive sufficient amounts of antibodies if they are born before protective levels are transferred.[80]

The pattern of production of cytokines by neonatal immune cells frequently is altered when compared with that of adults. For example, in response to group B streptococci, the level of TNF-α released by neonatal monocytes is increased relative to adults,[319, 338] but levels of IL-8 and leukotriene B_4 are decreased.[277, 285] IL-12 and interferon-γ are associated with improved outcome in an animal model of group B streptococcal infection, but lower quantities of these mediators are released by neonatal mononuclear cells.[163, 202] Cytokine networks are important both in the manifestations of sepsis and in the stimulation of an appropriate immune response, so alterations in expression of cytokines may affect the neonate's response to this pathogen both clinically and immunologically.

Clinical Manifestations

AGE AT ONSET

The paradigm of early- versus late-onset disease in neonates and young infants was described first in 1973 by Baker and associates[35] when they and investigators from Colorado[115] noted the bimodal distribution of group B streptococcal infections. The syndromes of early- and late-onset disease differ in epidemiologic characteristics, pathogenesis, clinical findings, and prognosis. Their major clinical features are detailed in Table 88–2. Early-onset disease occurs in the first week of life, but in most such neonates the disease is recognized at or within 12 hours of birth.[28, 288] Late-onset infection develops in infants between 8 and 90 days of age (median, 27 days; mean, 36 days).[290] Originally, 3 months of age was considered the end of the risk period, but late, late-onset disease, though a rare occurrence, has been reported.[150, 343]

Early-onset disease often, but not universally, occurs in the setting of maternal complications known to increase the risk for development of neonatal sepsis. These complications include labor before 37 weeks' gestation, prolonged rupture of membranes for more than 18 hours, chorioamnionitis, and early postpartum febrile morbidity.[35, 37, 53, 63, 88, 259, 329] The three most frequent clinical findings are bacteremia or septicemia without a focus, pneumonia, and meningitis.[18, 37, 329, 343] The signs are similar for each, and they range from shock and respiratory failure at delivery to asymptomatic infection detected during evaluation of a term neonate because of maternal risk factors known to increase the risk for development of invasive infection.[248, 329] Respiratory signs predominate and include apnea, grunting respirations, tachypnea, and cyanosis.[28, 35] Other signs include lethargy, poor feeding, abdominal distention, pallor, tachycardia, and jaundice. Administration of intrapartum antibiotic prophylaxis to the mother does not alter the findings in infants in whom early-onset disease develops despite prophylaxis; most still become clinically ill in the first 24 hours of life.[71] Fever usually is present in term neonates, but premature infants often are normothermic or hypothermic.[329] The overall case-fatality rate is 6 to 15 percent.[290, 329, 343]

Late-onset disease primarily affects term infants with an unremarkable maternal history and early neonatal course.[35, 88] However, more recent case series suggest that late, late-onset infection develops beyond 3 months of age in a larger number of infants born quite prematurely (<32 weeks' gestation). "Epidemics" of late-onset disease also have occurred in neonatal intensive care units, primarily in preterm neonates infected through nosocomial transmission.[50, 233] Bacteremia without a focus and meningitis are the two most common manifestations of late-onset disease.[115, 343] Osteoarticular infections and cellulitis are additional clinical findings.[29, 94, 343] Whereas early-onset disease most frequently occurs acutely with apnea and hypotension, late-onset disease often is manifested by fever, irritability, and other nonspecific signs.[37] More fulminant, rapidly progressive cases do occur, however.[35] The case-fatality rate ranges from 0 to 6 percent.[290, 343]

BACTEREMIA

Bacteremia without a focus is present in 27 to 87 percent of neonates with early-onset disease.[290, 329, 343] Signs of septicemia, such as respiratory distress and poor perfusion, often are present, especially in prematurely born neonates.[329] Asymptomatic bacteremia also may develop in term infants, and in one series it occurred in 22 percent of cases.[149, 329, 343] These infants probably remained asymptomatic because of early evaluation and institution of empiric therapy.[329] Bacteremia without a focus was noted in 46 percent of late-onset infections reported by Yagupsky and associates.[343] Generally, these infants are mildly ill and have fever and nonspecific signs that should prompt bacteriologic evaluation.

MENINGITIS

Meningitis is documented in 6 to 15 percent of neonates with early-onset disease.[37, 290, 329, 339] As a rule, no signs specifically indicate its presence, thus underscoring the need to evaluate all neonates with presumed early-onset disease for the possibility of meningeal involvement.[329, 340] Early in the course, the cerebrospinal fluid (CSF) white blood cell count may be normal despite isolation of group B streptococci.[79] Respiratory distress is the most frequent clinical finding.[29, 35, 329] Seizures are rarely the initial feature but do occur in as many as 50 percent of affected neonates early in the course of therapy.[35, 79] Postmortem evaluation of infants who die of early-onset group B streptococcal meningitis reveals hemorrhage, prominent basilar involvement, and abundant bacteria with relatively sparse inflammation.[115, 259]

Late-onset meningitis most typically manifests with fever and lethargy, although respiratory distress, coma, and shock also may occur.[35] Classic signs of meningitis, such as a

TABLE 88–2 ■ FEATURES OF GROUP B STREPTOCOCCAL DISEASE IN INFANTS

Feature (References)	Early-Onset Disease	Late-Onset Disease	Late, Late-Onset Disease
Age on onset (37, 290)	<7 days; mean, 8 hr; median, 1 hr	≥7–89 days; mean, 36 days; median, 27 days	≥90 days
Infants affected (35, 96, 290, 329)	Premature neonates, births after maternal obstetric complications	Term infants predominate	Premature neonates <32 wk gestation, immune deficiency
Clinical findings (37)	Acute respiratory distress, apnea and hypotension common	Fever, irritability, nonspecific signs, occasionally fulminant	Fever, irritability nonspecific signs
Manifestations (18, 29, 94, 115, 329, 343)	Septicemia or bacteremia (40%–55%), pneumonia (30%–45%), meningitis (6%–15%)	Bacteremia without a focus (55%), meningitis (35%), osteoarthritis (~5%), cellulitis/adenitis (~2%)	Bacteremia without a focus, focal infections as in late-onset disease
Serotypes isolated (34, 336)	All (Ia, II, III, and V most frequent)	Type III predominates	Type III predominates
Case-fatality ratio (290, 329, 343)	6%–15%	0%–6%	<5%

bulging fontanelle and nuchal rigidity, occur more commonly in neonates with late-onset than early-onset meningitis. Subdural effusions develop in as many as 20 percent of cases, but subdural empyema is a rare occurrence.[18, 35, 109, 214, 282]

Infants who die of late-onset meningitis have purulent leptomeningitis at postmortem examination.[115]

Sequelae occur in 20 to 30 percent of survivors of early- and late-onset meningitis. These sequelae include mental retardation, spastic quadriplegia, cortical blindness, deafness, uncontrolled seizures, hydrocephalus, and speech and language delay.[79, 99, 136, 148, 324] Signs at admission that are correlated with a high likelihood of a poor outcome include hypotension, coma or semicoma, status epilepticus, neutropenia, CSF protein levels greater than 300 mg/dL, and high concentrations of bacterial antigen in CSF.[48, 99, 246]

PNEUMONIA

Respiratory distress is a common initial manifestation in all forms of early-onset group B streptococcal disease.[28, 35, 115, 322, 343] Radiographic findings may include infiltrates suggestive of congenital pneumonia, small pleural effusions, a pattern similar to that of hyaline membrane disease or respiratory distress syndrome, or increased vascular markings as seen in transient tachypnea of the newborn; radiographs also may appear normal despite pulmonary symptoms.[190, 197, 322, 330] In preterm neonates, the findings frequently are identical to those of respiratory distress syndrome, and at autopsy, hyaline membranes containing bacteria and minimal inflammatory infiltrates have been described.[2, 167]

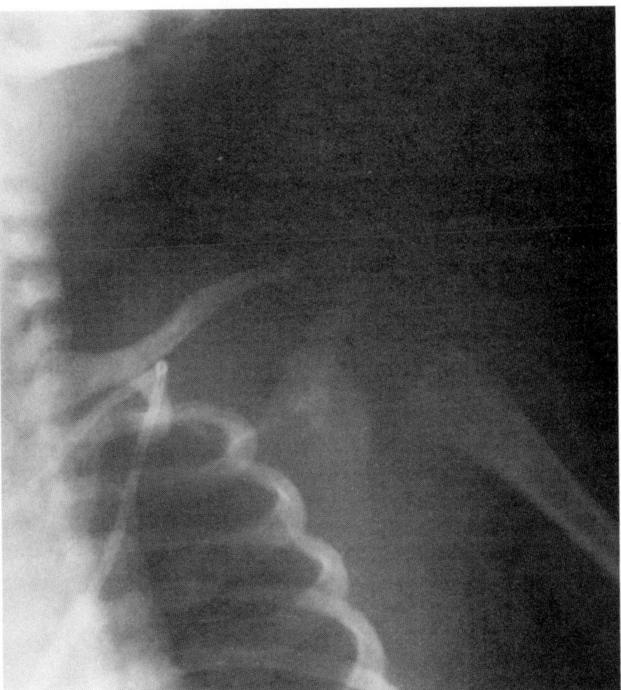

FIGURE 88–2 ■ Radiograph of the left arm of a 26-day-old infant with a 2-day history of diminished movement of that extremity. A well-defined, lytic lesion is present in the proximal end of the humerus. Necrotic material from this area was débrided surgically and grew group B streptococci on culture.

SEPTIC ARTHRITIS AND OSTEOMYELITIS

Osteoarthritis occurs in approximately 5 percent of infants with late-onset infection.[37, 343] Among neonates and young infants with osteomyelitis, group B streptococci have been identified as the causal agent in 5 to 38 percent of cases.[94, 225, 341] The osteoarticular disease usually is more indolent than is the osteomyelitis caused by other etiologic agents in young infants. Decreased motion of the involved extremity and pain with manipulation are common signs. Warmth and redness are uncommon findings but have been described.[94, 261] Systemic signs and symptoms, including fever, are unusual.[14, 23, 94, 212, 215]

The mean age at diagnosis in infants who have septic arthritis without osteomyelitis is 20 days. The clinical picture typically is acute, with a mean of 2 days of abnormal findings before diagnosis.[37] The lower extremities are involved most often, with the hip joint predominating. Concomitant bacteremia occurs in more than 50 percent of cases.[94]

As stated earlier, the osteomyelitis is more indolent, with a mean of 9 days of findings before the diagnosis is made at a mean age of 31 days.[37] The humerus, usually the proximal end, is the bone most frequently involved. The femur is the second most commonly involved bone. Unlike other forms of neonatal osteomyelitis, infection of a single bone is the rule.[94] Blood cultures infrequently are positive, which again contrasts with neonatal osteomyelitis caused by other etiologic agents. However, involvement of the adjacent joint is typical. A lytic lesion often is found on radiographs at admission (Fig. 88–2), thus implying that the process began weeks before. This observation suggests that lytic lesions may be a late phenomenon that develops after seeding of the metaphysis during an episode of asymptomatic, early-onset bacteremia.[37]

CELLULITIS/ADENITIS

In one case series, 2 percent of late-onset group B streptococcal infections were associated with cellulitis/adenitis syndrome.[343] The most frequent sites involved are the face and neck,[29, 137, 244] and the mean age at diagnosis is 5 weeks, with a male preponderance.[29] The typical scenario is one of fever, irritability, poor feeding, and swelling of the affected soft tissue area. Enlarged adjacent lymph nodes become palpable within a few days, the most common site of involvement being the submandibular area. Ipsilateral otitis media was noted in four of five infants with facial or submandibular cellulitis in one case series.[29] Less commonly affected areas reported include the genital or inguinal region (Fig. 88–3), the hand, and the prepatellar bursa.[29, 37, 68, 234, 264] Aspiration of the affected area of cellulitis often yields group B streptococci, and concomitant bacteremia almost always is present.

Nearly every organ has been reported to be a site of group B streptococcal infection in young infants. Table 88–3 lists these reported unusual manifestations of early- and late-onset disease.

LATE, LATE-ONSET INFECTIONS

Late, late-onset infection was reported in 19 percent of cases of late-onset group B streptococcal disease in one case series.[343] Another report of group B streptococcal disease in three HIV-infected children older than 3 months of age supports the recommendation that immunodeficiency be considered in any child infected beyond the usual period of risk.[86] Two of the 18 children reported by Hussain and associates[150] were infected with HIV, and 1 patient had transient hypogammaglobulinemia. The clinical manifestations

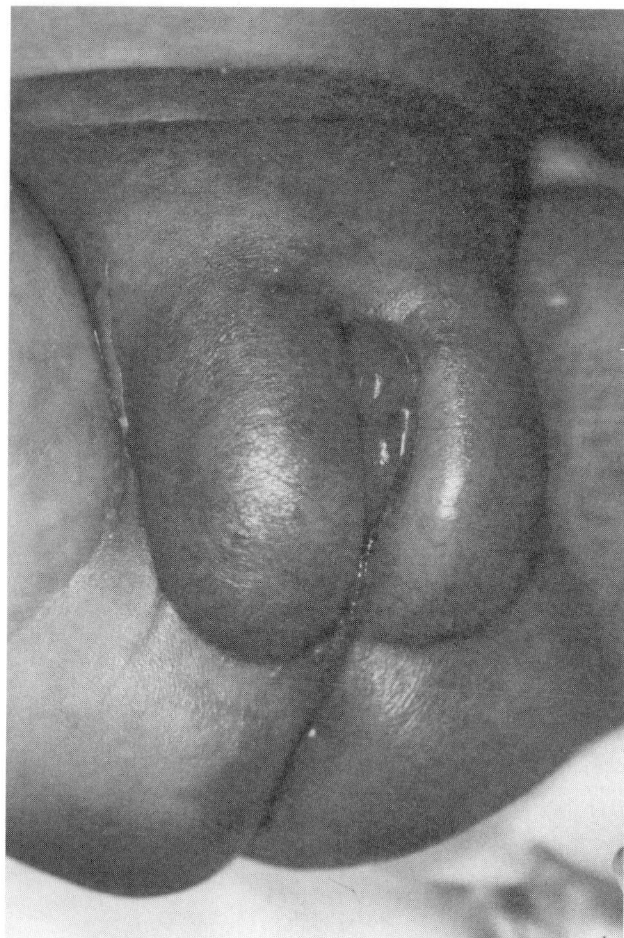

FIGURE 88–3 ■ This 3-month-old female infant who was born after 28 weeks' gestation had fever, lethargy, swelling of the external genitalia, and erythema that extended to the lower part of the abdomen and the thigh. Blood culture grew type Ib/c group B streptococci. (Courtesy of Morven S. Edwards, M.D.)

in these older infants are similar to those in patients with typical late-onset infection; bacteremia without a focus and meningitis are the most common findings.[86, 150] Endocarditis, cellulitis, and central venous catheter infection also have been noted.[107, 150]

RECURRENT INFECTIONS

Second (and sometimes third) episodes of group B streptococcal infection occur in approximately 1 to 2 percent of cases[130] and after early- and late-onset infection. In a case series from Houston, the mean age at recurrence was 44 days, with the mean duration of the interval between the first course of therapy and recurrence being 19 days.[130] Molecular epidemiologic techniques have indicated that most, but not all of these recurrent infections are caused by the strain implicated in the first episode, thus suggesting that persistent mucosal colonization after treatment of the first episode is followed by invasion of the bloodstream. Contaminated breast milk also has been implicated as a source of recurrent infection.[25] No specific risk factors are evident in these infants, but most of them are born prematurely.[130]

TABLE 88–3 ■ UNUSUAL CLINICAL MANIFESTATIONS OF GROUP B STREPTOCOCCAL DISEASE IN INFANTS

Site and Manifestation	Reference
Brain	
Abscess	297
Cerebritis	173
Chronic meningitis	301
Eosinophilic meningitis	222
Subdural empyema	109, 214, 282
Ventriculitis complicating myelomeningocele	101
Eye	
Conjunctivitis	21, 115
Endophthalmitis	55, 131
Ear and Sinus	
Ethmoiditis	149
Otitis media/mastoiditis	29, 103, 282, 294, 313
Cardiovascular/Hematologic	
Asymptomatic bacteremia	149, 263, 271, 305
Acquired protein C deficiency	24
Endocarditis	52, 78, 147, 233, 327
Myocarditis	14
Mycotic aneurysm	3
Pericarditis	135
Respiratory Tract	
Epiglottitis	346
Supraglottitis	196
Tracheitis	241
Pleural empyema	149, 185, 300
Skin and Soft Tissue	
Abscess of cystic hygroma	340
Breast abscess	230, 268
Bursitis	70
Cellulitis/adenitis	12, 29, 108, 137, 149, 244, 245, 280
Dactylitis	116
Fasciitis	125, 262
Impetigo neonatorum	54, 176, 198
Purpura fulminans	152, 199
Omphalitis	56, 154, 321
Rhabdomyolysis	316
Scalp abscess	106, 134
Abdomen	
Adrenal abscess	26, 76, 186, 325
Delayed-onset diaphragmatic hernia	22, 49, 169, 252, 308
Gallbladder distention	249
Infected meconium pseudocyst	126
Peritonitis	75, 77
Urinary Tract	
Renal abscess	325
Urinary tract infection	306, 343

Adapted from Baker, C. J., and Edwards, M. S.: Group B streptococcal infections. *In* Remington, J. S., and Klein, J. O. (eds.): Infectious Diseases of the Fetus and Newborn Infant. 5th ed. Philadelphia, W. B. Saunders, 2001, pp. 1091–1156.

Diagnosis and Differential Diagnosis

LABORATORY STUDIES

The diagnosis of group B streptococcal infection is confirmed by isolation of this pathogen from a normally sterile body site such as blood, CSF, bone aspirate, joint fluid, or soft tissue. Meningitis in early-onset disease is clinically indistinguishable from bacteremia without a focus, and 10 to 38 percent of neonates with meningitis have negative blood culture results,[339] so lumbar puncture is necessary to determine the presence or absence of meningeal involvement.[37] Similarly, group B streptococci grew from CSF cultures in 24 percent of infants with cellulitis/adenitis who underwent lumbar puncture, so lumbar puncture always should be performed in neonates with this finding.[4] Tracheal aspirate cultures that grow group B streptococci indicate neonatal colonization but do not prove pulmonary invasion (pneumonia). Rather, isolation of the organism from blood (or in rare circumstances, lung tissue or the pleural space) is required.

Several methods for detecting group B polysaccharide antigen in body fluid specimens have been developed. The ones used most commonly are countercurrent immunoelectrophoresis, latex particle agglutination, and enzyme immunoassay.[48, 61, 133, 227, 295] The advantage of these methods is their simplicity, rapidity, and ability to detect antigen, even after cultures are rendered sterile by antimicrobial therapy. Their disadvantage is the frequency (up to 10%) of false-positive results, especially when they are used to "screen" asymptomatic infants for sepsis. Their proper use should be limited to the setting of symptomatic infants in whom rapid diagnosis may alter therapy or allow proper tailoring of antibiotic choice—for example, a sick neonate with CSF pleocytosis and previous antibiotic administration. These tests are never useful in infants who appear healthy.

CSF has had detectable group B antigen in 72 to 89 percent of neonates with meningitis; serum is much less likely to be positive. Latex agglutination assays may yield "false positives," and urine specimens should not be tested because they are unreliable.

The finding of gram-positive cocci on Gram stain of a gastric aspirate has been reported in neonates with group B streptococcal sepsis and respiratory distress.[93, 151] However, positive Gram staining also occurs in neonates with noninfectious causes of respiratory distress. Furthermore, some aspirates with gram-positive cocci by Gram stain grow gram-positive organisms other than group B *Streptococcus,* and some aspirates from infants with group B streptococcal bacteremia are gram-negative. Thus, this test has low specificity and is not recommended for routine use.

The white blood cell count of a neonate with proven group B streptococcal sepsis may reflect leukopenia, neutropenia, or leukocytosis.[167, 203, 246, 322] Manroe and associates[203] found the ratio of absolute immature neutrophils to absolute total neutrophils (I:T index) to be the most reliable index for distinguishing respiratory distress caused by group B streptococcal infection from that caused by a noninfectious etiology. Most infected neonates had an elevation greater than 0.20 (91% versus 4% of uninfected infants).

DIFFERENTIAL DIAGNOSIS

The signs and symptoms of early-onset group B streptococcal disease are clinically indistinguishable from neonatal sepsis caused by other bacterial pathogens. The timing may be somewhat different, with group B streptococcal disease appearing earlier and leading to death earlier in fatal cases.[156] The prominence of respiratory signs in early-onset disease has led to confusion with noninfectious causes of respiratory distress such as respiratory distress syndrome, transient tachypnea of the newborn, and persistent fetal circulation.[2, 28, 167, 246, 322] Clinical features that suggest group B streptococcal infection rather than a noninfectious etiology are a history of prolonged rupture of membranes, apnea, and shock in the first 24 hours of life; a 1-minute Apgar score of 5 or less; and rapid progression of pulmonary disease.[2, 28, 322]

The differential diagnosis of late-onset disease depends on the focus of infection. Meningitis in infants of this age also is caused by *Listeria*, *Haemophilus influenzae* type b, *Streptococcus pneumoniae*, *Neisseria meningitidis*, and viruses. If the results of Gram stain analysis of CSF are inconclusive, other potential pathogens should be considered when therapy is selected. The findings of osteomyelitis may be subtle, with refusal to move the arm ascribed to neuromuscular disease or Erb palsy.[23, 94] Careful physical examination usually reveals tenderness over the involved area, and radiographs generally show a lytic defect in the metaphyses.[94] If the organism is isolated from a bone spirate, the diagnosis is definitive. Finally, as seen in Table 88–3, many unusual manifestations of group B streptococcal infection have been described, so this organism should be included in the differential diagnosis of any focal infection occurring in the age group at risk.

Treatment

EMPIRIC TREATMENT

The antimicrobial regimens recommended for the treatment of group B streptococcal infection in infants are summarized in Table 88–4. Penicillin G remains the drug of choice because susceptibility is uniform. In the usual circumstance, however, antimicrobial therapy for group B streptococcal infection is started before culture results are known. Initial empiric therapy for early-onset disease would include ampicillin and gentamicin for the treatment of neonatal pathogens in addition to group B streptococci. Irrespective of gestational age, neonates with suspected meningitis and those whose clinical condition will not permit lumbar puncture should receive high doses of ampicillin (300 mg/kg/day).[10] This combination is more effective than is either ampicillin or penicillin G alone in the killing of most group B streptococcal strains in vitro[283] and in vivo.[309] For suspected late-onset disease, the usual initial therapy includes intravenous ampicillin in combination with cefotaxime or ceftriaxone.[10] If an infant is receiving empiric vancomycin therapy and group B streptococcal meningitis has not been excluded, penicillin G or ampicillin should be added to the regimen because vancomycin is inhibitory in vitro rather than bactericidal and CSF concentrations may not exceed the minimal inhibitory concentration if a high inoculum of group B streptococci is present.[37]

SPECIFIC TREATMENT

Once group B streptococci have been identified in cultures of blood, CSF, or other normally sterile body sites and susceptibility to penicillin has been verified, penicillin G alone should be used to complete therapy. Recommendations concerning the optimal dose and duration have varied, but they should be dictated by the focus and severity of the infection (see Table 88–4). Several issues should be considered when selecting the appropriate dose: (1) the usual minimal bactericidal concentration of penicillin for group B streptococci ranges from 0.04 to 0.8 μg/mL,[37, 170] (2) only 10 to 20 percent of penicillin serum levels reach the CSF, (3) the inoculum of group B streptococci in the CSF of infants with meningitis may reach 10^7 to 10^8 colony-forming units per milliliter,[108] and (4) high doses of penicillin G and ampicillin are safe in neonates.[37] To ensure rapid bacterial killing, especially in infants with meningitis, relatively high doses of penicillin are recommended for both early- and late-onset infections.

TABLE 88–4 ■ TREATMENT OF GROUP B STREPTOCOCCAL INFECTIONS IN INFANTS

Focus of Infection	Antibiotic Dose	Duration
Suspected meningitis (initial empiric therapy)	Ampicillin (300 mg/kg/day) *plus* Gentamicin	Until cerebrospinal fluid sterility or penicillin G susceptibility is documented (minimal inhibitory concentration, 0.6 μg/mL)
Suspected sepsis* (initial empiric therapy)	Ampicillin (100–150 mg/kg/day) *plus* Gentamicin	Until bloodstream sterility is documented
Bacteremia	Penicillin G (200,000 U/kg/day)	10 days
Meningitis	Penicillin G (450,000–500,000 U/kg/day)‡	14 days minimum†
Arthritis	Penicillin G (200,000–300,000 U/kg/day)	2 to 3 weeks
Osteomyelitis	Penicillin G (200,000–300,000 U/kg/day)	3 to 4 weeks
Endocarditis	Penicillin G (200,000–300,000 U/kg/day)	4 weeks

*Assumes that lumbar puncture has been performed and the cerebrospinal fluid has no abnormalities.
†Should be extended to 21 days or longer if ventriculitis, cerebritis, subdural empyema, or other suppurative complications occur.
‡Infants older than 7 days (250,000–450,000 U/kg/day for infants ≤ 7 days).

The infant with meningitis should undergo a second lumbar puncture 24 to 48 hours into therapy to document CSF sterility.[37] Infants with positive CSF cultures should be considered to have ventriculitis with obstruction, severe infection with cerebritis and vasculitis, a very high inoculum, or a penicillin-resistant strain; in this circumstance, appropriate studies should be initiated to determine which of these conditions is present. When CSF sterility and penicillin G susceptibility are verified, penicillin G alone is given for a minimum of 14 days,[10] longer if the course is severe, the infant has ventriculitis, or CSF sterilization is delayed. At the anticipated completion of therapy, contrast-enhanced computed tomography of the head should be performed in complicated cases, including infants who have prolonged fever (>5 days), cerebritis, abscess, subdural empyema, or venous thrombosis. Such complications often correlate with neurologic abnormalities that lead to a poor prognosis for complete central nervous system recovery.[37, 79, 99]

Infants with bacteremia without a focus should receive intravenous therapy for a total of 10 days.[10] A shorter duration has not been documented to be efficacious, and relapses, though rare, have been reported in these circumstances.[72, 90 326] Patients with septic arthritis, osteomyelitis, or endocarditis should be treated for the durations summarized in Table 88–4. Oral therapy has no place in the management of infants with group B streptococcal disease.[10, 37] Alternative agents such as the cephalosporins and vancomycin are active against group B streptococci in vitro,[57, 170] but their efficacy is unknown and they are not recommended in most circumstances.

SUPPORTIVE TREATMENT

The importance of prompt, vigorous, and careful supportive therapy in the successful treatment of infant group B streptococcal infections cannot be overemphasized. Neonates with early-onset disease accompanied by pneumonia should be suspected of having early respiratory failure, and ventilatory support should be initiated before the onset of apnea, septic shock, or frank respiratory failure. Persistent metabolic acidosis and delayed capillary refill should prompt treatment for shock. All patients with signs of impending respiratory or circulatory failure or meningitis should be treated in an intensive care unit. When present, hypoxemia, severe anemia, and acidosis should be corrected, and seizures should be controlled with anticonvulsants. In addition, fluid and electrolyte status should be monitored meticulously. Surfactant should be used as per nursery protocol; improved gas exchange is seen in infected premature neonates who receive surfactant, although the response is slower than in those with respiratory distress syndrome.[140] Finally, if an infant has persistent pulmonary hypertension or if conventional ventilatory therapy has failed, extracorporeal membrane oxygenation may be considered, if available.

ADJUNCTIVE TREATMENT

Adjunctive treatment of life-threatening group B streptococcal disease is aimed at correcting poor host defenses and is being investigated. Such treatment includes intravenous human immunoglobulin, monoclonal antibodies to group B streptococcal polysaccharide antigen, leukocyte transfusion, and growth factors such as granulocyte colony-stimulating factor and granulocyte-monocyte colony-stimulating factor for neutropenia. The efficacy of these agents has not been established definitively, and although they may be used occasionally, they should be considered experimental.

RECURRENT INFECTIONS

In the few infants who experience a recurrence, suppurative foci should be excluded or treated, if present, as should humoral immune deficiency. Immunoglobulin levels should be determined to exclude the latter. Although it may be too early to document humoral immune deficiency unequivocally, total IgG usually is significantly lower than would be expected for age in weeks.[130] Tube dilution susceptibility of isolates from the first and recurrent episodes should be determined to ensure in vitro susceptibility to penicillin. If the reason for the recurrence remains unknown, persistent mucous membrane infection with group B streptococci probably is the source.[37] β-Lactam antibiotics, even when administered by the parenteral route, do not eradicate group B streptococcal colonization reliably.[239] Because rifampin has eradicated mucosal group B streptococcal colonization in a few human cases,[219] this treatment (20 mg/kg/day) may be useful and may be given orally during the last 4 days of parenteral therapy.[130]

Prognosis

The outcome of group B streptococcal disease is related closely to the severity and site of infection at initial evaluation. Improved outcomes after early-onset infection have resulted from greater awareness among pediatricians, thereby allowing earlier intervention, and from improved obstetric management. The latter includes the use of intrapartum antibiotic prophylaxis in women at risk for delivering an infant with early-onset group B streptococcal infection. However, the mortality rate remains substantial at 2 to 8 percent, especially in neonates born at less than 37 weeks' gestation, in whom the mortality rate often exceeds 20 percent.[37, 288] It is hoped that greater implementation of strategies to identify women for chemoprophylaxis will further reduce not only the incidence but also mortality.

Little information is available on the long-term prognosis of survivors of group B streptococcal sepsis without meningitis. In infants with septic shock, the development of periventricular leukomalacia has been reported and associated with neurodevelopmental sequelae. However, the frequency of this association is not known.

For infants with early- or late-onset meningitis, 20 to 30 percent have permanent neurologic sequelae, and 20 percent of these impaired survivors have global mental retardation, cortical blindness, spasticity, or paresis.[79, 99, 136, 148, 324] Whether these rates, which were reported years ago, can be applied to infants currently being treated is unknown. One might hope that improvements in both specific and supportive therapy have diminished the frequency of lasting impairments.

To date, the prognosis for infants with osteoarticular or soft tissue infections with group B streptococci has been excellent.[29, 94] However, omission of early surgical intervention for infections that involve either the hip or shoulder joints might result in epiphyseal injury.

Prevention

The continuing magnitude and severity of group B streptococcal disease and its attendant mortality and morbidity have led to investigations aimed at its prevention. Certainly, decreasing the number of neonates born before 37 weeks' gestation would itself diminish the number of cases. Two general approaches have been proposed: chemoprophylaxis and immunoprophylaxis.

CHEMOPROPHYLAXIS

Three strategies to prevent early-onset group B streptococcal disease through chemoprophylaxis have been evaluated. The first, antenatal treatment of group B streptococcal maternal carriers, temporarily suppresses colonization density but does not eradicate it or interrupt vertical transmission of group B streptococci to neonates.[120, 132] The second, single-dose intramuscular penicillin given to newborns shortly after birth, is controversial.

The two controlled trials evaluating neonatal prophylaxis reached contradictory conclusions.[257, 296] In the first, more than 16,000 newborns received either intramuscular penicillin G or topical tetracycline (prophylaxis for gonococcal ophthalmia neonatorum) within an hour of birth during alternating weeks.[296] In penicillin-treated newborns, the incidence of proven group B streptococcal disease decreased significantly during the first 4 days of life; death rates were similar. In contrast to the experience published elsewhere, few of the neonates with proven group B streptococcal disease whose condition was diagnosed within the first few hours of life had septic shock or severe infection. Furthermore, because no bacterial cultures were obtained before initiation of penicillin therapy, early-onset disease may have occurred but was not documented. In fact, in a second controlled study, blood cultures were obtained before initiation of penicillin therapy, and rates of group B streptococcal bacteremia were similar in the treatment and control groups.[257] In this study of nearly 1200 neonates weighing 2000 g or less at birth, intramuscular penicillin (or no treatment) was given in the first hour of life and continued for 3 days. Penicillin prophylaxis was probably ineffective because almost 90 percent of neonates with early-onset group B streptococcal disease were bacteremic immediately after birth. The results of the second study are supported by numerous observations, thus indicating that early-onset disease often begins in utero.[29, 64, 242, 288, 290]

The third strategy, maternal intrapartum chemoprophylaxis, has been demonstrated to be efficacious in the prevention of vertical transmission of group B streptococci from colonized mothers to their neonates, the development of early-onset disease, and maternal febrile morbidity. Its impact on late-onset disease, if any, has not been documented.

Four controlled trials involving thousands of deliveries have indicated that intrapartum penicillin G or ampicillin given intravenously to group B streptococcal carriers prevents early-onset disease in neonates.[65, 121, 210, 315] The first trial was designed to identify group B streptococcal carriers from vaginal and rectal cultures obtained at 26 to 28 weeks' gestation.[65] Women who were culture-positive and had labor at less than 37 weeks' gestation, rupture of membranes more than 12 hours before delivery, or intrapartum fever (>37.5° C) were randomized to receive intravenous ampicillin during labor or conventional care. Ampicillin reduced the rate of vertical transmission from 51 to 9 percent and the rate of early-onset disease from 6 to 0 percent.[65] This approach—intrapartum chemoprophylaxis for group B streptococcal carriers selected because of one or more risk factors for development of early-onset disease—was recommended in 1992 by the American Academy of Pediatrics.[9] These guidelines provoked controversy,[11, 75] and implementation was problematic.[155]

Consensus recommendations were published[254] and are supported by the Centers for Disease Control and Prevention, the American College of Obstetricians and Gynecologists, and the American Academy of Pediatrics. Key features of these guidelines include a choice of prevention strategies, the use of penicillin G rather than ampicillin as the prophylactic agent, and an empiric algorithm for the management of such infants (Table 88–5). Maternal chemoprophylaxis begins at hospital admission for delivery or at rupture of membranes and consists of intravenous penicillin G (initial dose, 5 million U; subsequent doses, 2.5 million U every 4 hours) until delivery.[315] Penicillin is the preferred drug because it has a narrower spectrum of activity than ampicillin does.

Concern that widespread use of intrapartum ampicillin will result in a greater incidence of ampicillin-resistant neonatal infection has been supported by some case series.[162, 216] Women who are allergic to penicillin are given either intravenous clindamycin (900 mg) every 8 hours or erythromycin (500 mg) every 6 hours until delivery, although neither drug has been evaluated for efficacy and increasing macrolide resistance has led some experts to recommend a first-generation cephalosporin for women with non–immediate-type penicillin allergy.

Criteria for selection of women for chemoprophylaxis is based on either group B streptococcal culture screening at 35 to 37 weeks' gestation or the occurrence of a factor known to significantly increase the risk of development of early-onset disease in the neonate. Risk factors include (1) previous delivery of an infant with documented group B

TABLE 88–5 ■ STRATEGIES TO PREVENT EARLY-ONSET GROUP B STREPTOCOCCAL (GBS) DISEASE BY INTRAPARTUM MATERNAL CHEMOPROPHYLAXIS

Strategy	Antenatal Screening	Selection Criteria	Estimated Proportion of Cases Prevented[254]	Agent/Dose	Optimal Timing
Culture based	Vaginal and rectal cultures at 35–37 wk gestation	All women with (1) previous GBS-infected infant, (2) GBS bacteriuria, or (3) labor at <37 wk *without* culture screening GBS carriers with membrane rupture >18 hr before delivery or intrapartum fever (≥38° C) Other GBS carriers	85%–90%	Penicillin G, 5 million U IV (initial), then 2.5 million U every 4 hr Clindamycin* 900 mg every 8 hr	At admission to ensure ≥2 doses ≥4 hr before delivery
Risk factor based	None	All women with (1) previous GBS-infected infant, (2) GBS bacteriuria, (3) labor at <37 wk, (4) membrane rupture >18 hr before delivery, (5) intrapartum fever (≥38° C)	68%	Same	Same

*If penicillin-allergic, some experts advise cefazolin, 2 g initially and then 1 g every 6 hours if the allergy is not immediate-type.

streptococcal disease, (2) group B streptococcal bacteriuria during pregnancy, (3) labor onset or membrane rupture before 37 weeks' gestation, (4) rupture of membranes more than 18 hours before delivery, and (5) intrapartum fever (≥38.0° C). Women who have the first three risk factors need not be screened because they all should receive chemoprophylaxis. Women who are colonized with group B streptococci but have no risk factors should be given chemoprophylaxis. Such women, delivering at term with no apparent risk factors, account for 30 to 40 percent of cases of early-onset disease.[37, 65, 287] Group B streptococcal carriers who have either intrapartum fever of 38° C or higher or rupture of membranes more than 18 hours before delivery also should receive penicillin G prophylaxis. Women in whom culture screening is negative and who have no identifiable risk factors should be managed routinely (approximately 75% to 80% of obstetric patients).[254]

Although these two strategies have not been compared in clinical trials for safety, efficacy, and cost-effectiveness, each is thought to be cost-beneficial.[7, 224, 275, 344] Since the widespread adoption of chemoprophylaxis, the incidence of early-onset disease has plummeted.[91, 287] Opportunities to prevent early-onset disease still are missed, however, with more protocol omissions occurring when the risk-based strategy is used.[91]

Management of an infant born to a mother given intrapartum penicillin G prophylaxis depends on the clinical findings at birth, gestational age, and the number of doses administered to the mother. If the infant appears healthy, has a gestational age of 35 weeks or more, and has a mother given two or more doses of penicillin G or ampicillin before delivery, neither diagnostic evaluation nor empiric antimicrobial therapy is required. However, to ensure their ongoing stability, such infants are observed in the hospital for as long as 48 hours. Keeping the infant hospitalized through day of life 2 has been challenged because the associated expense affects the cost-benefit ratio of intrapartum prophylaxis.[223] However, an analysis of all live births in the state of Florida for the years 1992 through 1994 demonstrated a 115 percent increase in the rate of readmission for group B streptococcal infection in infants discharged on day of life 1, thus supporting the recommendation to observe infants for 48 hours.[128]

Neonates with signs of sepsis are evaluated and empirically treated for sepsis. Healthy-appearing neonates who are either born at less than 35 weeks' gestation or are born to women given fewer than two doses of penicillin G undergo a limited laboratory evaluation (complete blood count and blood culture) and observation in the hospital for 48 hours without therapy. However, if the subsequent clinical course or the laboratory results suggest infection, therapy is initiated. In the latter circumstance, a full diagnostic evaluation for sepsis should be undertaken before empiric therapy is initiated. The reasons for basing infant management on two or more doses of maternal penicillin before delivery are that (1) amniotic fluid levels of penicillin that will kill group B streptococci are not achieved until at least 3 hours after administration of the first dose[69] and (2) some infants born after administration of only one maternal dose have been shown to be bacteremic.[258]

IMMUNOPROPHYLAXIS

Although effort to implement intrapartum chemoprophylaxis is ongoing, the most promising and potentially lasting method for prevention of early- and late-onset infant infections is immunoprophylaxis. This approach remains investigational, and several reviews have summarized the rationale.[37, 41, 104, 289] It is based on the observation that immunity to group B streptococci correlates with antibody directed against the type-specific capsular polysaccharides of these organisms. These IgG class antibodies, in combination with complement and polymorphonuclear leukocytes, promote opsonization, phagocytosis, and bacterial killing of group B streptococci and protect animals against lethal challenge.[237, 238, 333] Thus, provision of protective levels of type-specific immunity to the infant could be achieved through active immunization of the mother. Baker and associates[47] immunized women at a mean gestation of 31 weeks with purified type III polysaccharide vaccine. Although the immune response was not optimal (54%), placental transport of maternal antibodies (when stimulated) was approximately 70 percent, and in neonates born to women who did respond to vaccination, 75 percent had protective levels of antibodies in their sera at 2 months of age.[47] Other studies immunizing nonpregnant adults with purified capsular polysaccharide vaccines have indicated their safety but also their variable immunogenicity.

Because most pregnant women (estimated at 85% to 90%) have nonprotective levels of these antibodies in their sera at delivery, active immunization of women with improved vaccines has been proposed.[37] Initial results with candidate polysaccharide-protein conjugate vaccines in nonpregnant women suggest their safety and excellent immunogenicity.[44, 45, 166] Animals models have demonstrated antibody transfer to the neonate.[236] However, this method of prevention requires investigation of conjugate vaccines in pregnant women to ensure their safety and immunogenicity, as well as their ability to stimulate type-specific IgG that is transported to the neonate, and a duration of passively acquired antibodies in protective concentrations that extends to the age of 3 months. Furthermore, because maternal immunization is unlikely to be used in the United States, vaccine strategies that avoid their use in pregnancy (i.e., adolescent immunization) should be considered. Finally, vaccination of elderly or nonpregnant adults with defined medical conditions could reduce significantly the disease burden. Because immunoprophylaxis should be the most cost-effective and beneficial prevention strategy for group B streptococcal disease,[224, 254] it should be promoted by physicians, public health officials, parents, pharmaceutical manufacturers, and legislators.

REFERENCES

1. Aber, R. C., Allen, N., Howell, J. T., et al.: Nosocomial transmission of group B streptococci. Pediatrics 58:346–353, 1976.
2. Ablow, R. C., Driscoll, S. G., Effmann, E. L., et al.: A comparison of early-onset group B streptococcal neonatal infection and the respiratory-distress syndrome of the newborn. N. Engl. J. Med. *294*:65–70, 1976.
3. Agarwala, B. N.: Group B streptococcal endocarditis in a neonate. Pediatr. Cardiol. *9*:51–53, 1988.
4. Albanyan, E. A., Baker, C. J.: Is lumbar puncture necessary to exclude meningitis in neonates and young infants: Lessons from group B streptococcus cellulitis-adenitis syndrome. Pediatrics *102*:985–986, 1998.
5. Alger, L. S., Lovchik, J. C., Hebel, J. R., et al.: The association of *Chlamydia trachomatis, Neisseria gonorrhoeae*, and group B streptococci with preterm rupture of the membranes and pregnancy outcome. Am. J. Obstet. Gynecol. *159*:397–404, 1988.
6. Allardice, J. G., Baskett, T. F., Seshia, M. M. K., et al.: Perinatal group B streptococcal colonization and infection. Am. J. Obstet. Gynecol. *142*:617–620, 1982.
7. Allen, U. D., Navas, L., and King, S. M.: Effectiveness of intrapartum penicillin prophylaxis in preventing early-onset group B streptococcal infection: Results of a meta-analysis. Can. Med. Assoc. J. *149:* 1659–1665, 1993.
8. Altaie, S. S., and Dryja, D.: Detection of group B *Streptococcus*: Comparison of solid and liquid culture media with and without antibiotics. Diagn. Microbiol. Infect. Dis. *18*:141–144, 1994.
9. American Academy of Pediatrics: Guidelines for prevention of group B streptococcal infection by chemoprophylaxis. Pediatrics *90*:775–778, 1992.
10. American Academy of Pediatrics: Group B streptococcal infections. *In* Pickering, L. K. (ed.): Red Book: Report of the Committee on Infectious Diseases. 25th ed. Elk Grove Village, IL, 2000, pp. 537–544.
11. American College of Obstetricians and Gynecologists: Group B streptococcal infections in pregnancy: ACOG's recommendations. A. C. O. G. Newsletter *37*:1, 1993.
12. Amoury, R. A., Barth, G. W., Hall, R. T., et al.: Scrotal ecchymosis: Sign of intraperitoneal hemorrhage in the newborn. South. Med. J. *75*:1471–1478, 1982.
13. Ancona, R. J., Ferrieri, P., and Williams, P. P.: Maternal factors that enhance the acquisition of group B streptococci by newborn infants. J. Med. Microbiol. *13*:273–280, 1980.
14. Ancona, R. J., McAuliffe, J., Thompson, T. R., et al.: Group B streptococcal sepsis with osteomyelitis and arthritis. Am. J. Dis. Child. *133*:919–920, 1979.
15. Anderson, D. C., Hughes, B. J., Edwards, M. S., et al.: Impaired chemotaxigenesis by type III group B streptococci in neonatal sera: Relationship to diminished concentration of specific anticapsular antibody and abnormalities of serum complement. Pediatr. Res. *17*:496–502, 1983.
16. Anderson, D. C., Hughes, B. J., and Smith, C. W.: Abnormal mobility of neonatal polymorphonuclear leukocytes. J. Clin. Invest. *59*:810–818, 1981.
17. Anthony, B. F., Concepcion, I. E., Concepcion, N. F., et al.: Relation between maternal age and serum concentration of IgG antibody to type III group B streptococci. J. Infect. Dis. *170*:717–720, 1994.
18. Anthony, B. F., and Okada, D. M.: The emergence of group B streptococci in infections of the newborn infant. Annu. Rev. Med. *28*:355–369, 1977.
19. Anthony, B. F., Okada, D. M., and Hobel, C. J.: Epidemiology of group B *Streptococcus*: Longitudinal observations during pregnancy. J. Infect. Dis. *137*:524–530, 1978.
20. Anthony, B. F., Okada, D. M., and Hobel, C. J.: Epidemiology of the group B *Streptococcus*: Maternal and nosocomial sources for infant acquisitions. J. Pediatr. *95*:431–436, 1979.
21. Armstrong, J. H., Zacarias, F., and Rein, M. F.: Ophthalmia neonatorum: A chart review. Pediatrics *57*:884–892, 1976.
22. Ashcraft, K. W., Holder, T. M., Amoury, R. A., et al.: Diagnosis and treatment of right Bochdalek hernia associated with group B streptococcal pneumonia and sepsis in the neonate. J. Pediatr. Surg. *18*:480–485, 1983.
23. Ashdown, L. R., Hewson, P. H., and Suleman, S. K.: Neonatal osteomyelitis and meningitis caused by group B streptococci. Med. J. Aust. *2*:500–501, 1977.
24. Atalay, S., Imamoglu, A., Ikizler, C., et al.: Mitral valve and left ventricular thrombi in an infant with acquired protein C deficiency. Angiology *46*:87–90, 1995.
25. Atkins, J. T., Heresi, G. P., Coque, T. M., Baker, C. J.: Recurrent group B streptococcal disease in infants: Who should receive rifampin? J. Pediatr. *132*:537–539, 1998.
26. Atkinson, G. O., Jr., Kodroff, M. B., Gay, B. B., et al.: Adrenal abscess in the neonate. Radiology *155*:101–104, 1985.
27. Badri, M. S., Zawaneh, S., Cruz, A. C., et al.: Rectal colonization with group B *Streptococcus*: Relation to vaginal colonization of pregnant women. J. Infect. Dis. *135*:308–312, 1977.
28. Baker, C. J.: Early onset group B streptococcal disease. J. Pediatr. *93*:124–125, 1978.
29. Baker, C. J.: Group B streptococcal cellulitis/adenitis in infants. Am. J. Dis. Child. *136*:631–633, 1982.
30. Baker, C. J.: Antibiotic susceptibility testing in the management of an infant with group B streptococcal meningitis. Pediatr. Infect. Dis. J. *6*:1073–1074, 1987.
31. Baker, C. J.: Immunization to prevent group B streptococcal disease: Victories and vexations. J. Infect. Dis. *161*:917–921, 1990.
32. Baker, C. J.: Inadequacy of rapid immunoassays for intrapartum detection of group B streptococcal carriers. Obstet. Gynecol. *88*:51–55, 1996.
33. Baker, C. J., and Barrett, F. F.: Transmission of group B streptococci among parturient women and their neonates. J. Pediatr. *83*:919–925, 1973.
34. Baker, C. J., and Barrett, F. F.: Group B streptococcal infections in infants: The importance of the various serotypes. J. A. M. A. *230*: 1158–1160, 1974.
35. Baker, C. J., Barrett, F. F., Gordon, R. C., et al.: Suppurative meningitis due to streptococci of Lancefield group B: A study of 33 infants. J. Pediatr. *82*:724–729, 1973.
36. Baker, C. J., Clark, D. J., and Barrett, F. F.: Selective broth medium for isolation of group B streptococci. Appl. Microbiol. *26*:884–885, 1973.
37. Baker, C. J., and Edwards, M. S.: Group B streptococcal infections. *In* Remington, J. S., and Klein, J. O. (eds.): Infectious Diseases of the Fetus & Newborn Infant. 5th ed. Philadelphia, W. B. Saunders, 2001, pp. 1091–1156.
38. Baker, C. J., Edwards, M. S., and Kasper, D. L.: Role of antibody to native type III polysaccharide of group B *Streptococcus* to infant infection. Pediatrics *68*:544–549, 1981.
39. Baker, C. J., Goroff, D. K., Alpert, S. L., et al.: Comparison of bacteriological methods for the isolation of group B *Streptococcus* from vaginal cultures. J. Clin. Microbiol. *4*:46–48, 1976.
40. Baker, C. J., Goroff, D. K., Alpert, S., et al.: Vaginal colonization with group B *Streptococcus*: A study in college women. J. Infect. Dis. *135*:392–397, 1977.
41. Baker, C. J., and Kasper, D. L.: Group B streptococcal vaccines. Rev. Infect. Dis. *7*:458–467, 1985.
42. Baker, C. J., Kasper, D. L., and Davis, C. E.: Immunochemical characterization of the native type III polysaccharide of group B *Streptococcus*. J. Exp. Med. *143*:258–270, 1976.
43. Baker, C. J., Kasper, D. L., Tager, I. B., et al.: Quantitative determination of antibody to capsular polysaccharide in infection with type III strains of group B *Streptococcus*. J. Clin. Med. *59*:810–811, 1977.
44. Baker, C. J. Paoletti, L. C., Rench, M. A., et al.: Use of capsular polysaccharide–tetanus toxoid conjugate for type II group B *Streptococcus* in healthy women. J. Infect. Dis. *182*:1129–1138, 2000.

45. Baker, C. J., Paoletti, L. C., Wessels, M. R., et al.: Safety and immunogenicity of capsular polysaccharide–tetanus toxoid conjugate vaccines for group B streptococcal types Ia and Ib. J. Infect. Dis. *179*:142–150, 1999.
46. Baker, C. J., and Rench, M. A.: Commercial latex agglutination for detection of group B streptococcal antigen in body fluids. J. Pediatr. *102*:393–395, 1983.
47. Baker, C. J., Rench, M. A., Edwards, M. S., et al.: Immunization of pregnant women with a polysaccharide vaccine of group B *Streptococcus*. N. Engl. J. Med. *319*:1180–1185, 1988.
48. Baker, C. J., Webb, B. J., Jackson, C. V., et al.: Countercurrent immunoelectrophoresis in the evaluation of infants with group B streptococcal disease. Pediatrics *65*:1110–1114, 1980.
49. Banagale, R. C., and Watter, J. H.: Delayed right-sided diaphragmatic hernia following group B streptococcal infection: A discussion of its pathogenesis, with a review of the literature. Hum. Pathol. *14*:67–69, 1983.
50. Band, J. D., Clegg, H. W., Haynes, P. S., et al.: Transmission of group B streptococci. Am. J. Dis. Child. *135*:355–358, 1981.
51. Barrett, F. F., Mason, E. O., Jr., and Fleming, D.: The effect of three cord-care regimens on bacterial colonization of normal newborn infants. J. Pediatr. *94*:796–800, 1979.
52. Barton, C. W., Crowley, D. C., Uzardk, K., et al.: A neonatal survivor of group B beta-hemolytic streptococcal endocarditis. Am. J. Perinatol. *1*:214–215, 1984.
53. Becroft, D. M. O., Farmer, K., Mason, G. H., et al.: Perinatal infections by group B β-haemolytic streptococci. Br. J. Obstet. Gynaecol. *83*:960–966, 1976.
54. Belgaumkar, T. K.: Impetigo neonatorum congenita due to group B beta-hemolytic *Streptococcus* infection. J. Pediatr. *86*:982–983, 1975.
55. Berger, B. B.: Endophthalmitis complicating group B streptococcal septicemia. Am. J. Ophthalmol. *92*:681–684, 1981.
56. Bergqvist, G., Hurvall, B., Thal, E., et al.: Neonatal infections caused by group B streptococci. Scand. J. Infect. Dis. *3*:209–212, 1971.
57. Berkowitz, K., Regan, J. A., and Greenberg, E.: Antibiotic resistance patterns of group B streptococci in pregnant women. J. Clin. Microbiol. *28*:5–7, 1990.
58. Bhakdi, S., Klonisch, T., Nuber, P., et al.: Stimulation of monokine production by lipoteichoic acids. Infect. Immun. *59*:4616–4620, 1991.
59. Blumberg, H. M., Stephens, D. S., Modansky, M., et al.: Invasive group B streptococcal disease: The emergence of serotype V. J. Infect. Dis. *173*:365–373, 1996.
60. Bone, R. C.: Gram-positive organisms and sepsis. Arch. Intern. Med. *154*:26–34, 1994.
61. Bortolussi, R., Wort, A. J., and Casey, S.: The latex agglutination test versus counterimmunoelectrophoresis for rapid diagnosis of bacterial meningitis. Can. Med. Assoc. J. *127*:489–493, 1982.
62. Botta, G. A.: Hormonal and type-dependent adhesion of group B streptococci to human vaginal cells. Infect. Immun. *25*:1084–1086, 1979.
63. Boyer, K. M., Gadzala, C. A., Kelly, P. D., et al.: Selective intrapartum chemoprophylaxis of neonatal group B streptococcal early-onset disease. II. Predictive value of prenatal cultures. J. Infect. Dis. *148*:802–809, 1983.
64. Boyer, K. M., Gadzala, C. A., Kelly, P. D., et al.: Selective intrapartum chemoprophylaxis of neonatal group B streptococcal early-onset disease. III. Interruption of mother-to-infant transmission. J. Infect. Dis. *148*:810–816, 1983.
65. Boyer, K. M., and Gotoff, S. P.: Prevention of early-onset neonatal group B streptococcal disease with selective intrapartum chemoprophylaxis. N. Engl. J. Med. *314*:1665–1669, 1986.
66. Boyer, K. M., Kendall, L. S., Papierniak, C. K., et al.: Protective levels of human immunoglobulin G antibody to group B *Streptococcus* type Ib. Infect. Immun. *45*:618–624, 1984.
67. Brady, L. J., Daphtary, U. D., Ayoub, E. M., et al.: Two novel antigens associated with group B streptococci identified by a rapid two-stage radioimmunoassay. J. Infect. Dis. *158*:965–972, 1988.
68. Brady, M. T.: Cellulitis of the penis and scrotum due to group B *Streptococcus*. J. Urol. *137*:736–737, 1987.
69. Bray, R. E., Boe, R. W., and Johnson, W. L.: Transfer of ampicillin into fetus and amniotic fluid from maternal plasma in late pregnancy. Am. J. Obstet. Gynecol. *96*:965–967, 1966.
70. Brian, M. J., O'Ryan, M., and Waagner, D.: Prepatellar bursitis in an infant caused by group B *Streptococcus*. Pediatr. Infect. Dis. J. *11*:502–503, 1992.
71. Bromberger, P., Lawrence, J.M., Braun, D., et al.: The influence of intrapartum antibiotics on the clinical spectrum of early-onset group B streptococcal infection in term infants. Pediatrics *106*:244–250, 2000.
72. Broughton, D. D., Mitchell, W. G., Grossman, M., et al.: Recurrence of group B streptococcal infection. J. Pediatr. *89*:183–185, 1976.
73. Bulgakova, T. N., Grabovskaya, K. B., Roc, M., et al.: The adhesin structures involved in the adherence of group B streptococci to human vaginal cells. Folia Microbiol. (Praha) *31*:394–401, 1986.
74. Butter, M. N. W., and DeMoor, C. E.: *Streptococcus agalactiae* as a cause of meningitis in the newborn, and of bacteremia in adults. Antonie van Leeuwenhoek *33*:439–450, 1967.
75. Callanan, D. O., and Harris, G. G.: Group B streptococcal infection in children with liver disease. Clin. Pediatr. (Phila.) *21*:99–100, 1982.
76. Carty, A., and Stanley, P.: Bilateral adrenal abscesses in a neonate. Pediatr. Radiol. *1*:63–64, 1973.
77. Chadwick, E. G., Shulman, S. T., and Yogev, R.: Peritonitis as a late manifestation of group B streptococcal disease in newborns. Pediatr. Infect. Dis. J. *2*:142–143, 1983.
78. Chattopadhyay, B.: Fatal neonatal meningitis due to group B streptococci. Postgrad. Med. J. *51*:240–243, 1975.
79. Chin, K. C., and Fitzhardinge, P. M.: Sequelae of early-onset group B streptococcal neonatal meningitis. J. Pediatr. *106*:819–822, 1985.
80. Christensen, K. K., Christensen, P., Duc, G., et al.: Correlation between serum antibody-levels against group B streptococci and gestational age in newborns. Eur. J. Pediatr. *142*:86–88, 1984.
81. Christensen, R. D., and Rothstein, G.: Exhaustion of mature marrow neutrophils in neonates with sepsis. J. Pediatr. *96*:316–318, 1980.
82. Christie, R., Atkins, N. E., and Munch-Petersen, E.: A note on a lytic phenomenon shown by group B streptococci. Aust. J. Exp. Biol. Med. Sci. *22*:197–200, 1944.
83. Congdon, P. M.: Streptococcal infection in childbirth and septic abortion. Lancet *2*:1287–1288, 1935.
84. Davis, C. A., Vallota, E. H., and Forristal, J.: Serum complement levels in infancy: Age-related changes. Pediatr. Res. *13*:1043–1046, 1979.
85. Dawodu, A. H., Damole, I. O., and Onile, B. A.: Epidemiology of group B streptococcal carriage among pregnant women and their neonates: An African experience. Trop. Geogr. Med. *35*:145–150, 1983.
86. DiJohn, D., Krasinski, K., and Lawrence, R.: Very late onset of group B streptococcal disease in infants infected with the human immunodeficiency virus. Pediatr. Infect. Dis. J. *9*:925–928, 1990.
87. Dillon, H. C., Jr., Gray, E., Pass, M. A., et al.: Anorectal and vaginal carriage of group B streptococci during pregnancy. J. Infect. Dis. *145*:794–799, 1982.
88. Dillon, H. C., Jr., Khare, S., and Gray, B. M.: Group B streptococcal carriage and disease: A 6-year prospective study. J. Pediatr. *110*:31–36, 1987.
89. Dokter, W. H. A., Dijkstra, A. J., Koopmans, S. B., et al.: G(AnH) MTetra, a naturally occurring 1,6-anhydro muramyl dipeptide, induces granulocyte colony-stimulating factor expression in human monocytes: A molecular analysis. Infect. Immun. *62*:2953–2957, 1994.
90. Dorand, R. D., and Adams, G.: Relapse during penicillin treatment of group B streptococcal meningitis. J. Pediatr. *89*:188–190, 1976.
91. Early-onset group B streptococcal disease—United States, 1998–1999. M. M. W. R. Morb. Mortal. Wkly. Rep. *49*:793–796, 2000.
92. Easmon, C. S. F., Hastings, M. J. G., Neill, J., et al.: Is group B streptococcal screening during pregnancy justified? Br. J. Obstet. Gynaecol. *92*:197–201, 1985.
93. Echeverria, P.: Observations concerning infections with beta-hemolytic streptococci, not group A or D, in neonates. J. Pediatr. *83*:499–500, 1973.
94. Edwards, M. S., Baker, C. J., Wagner, M. L., et al.: An etiologic shift in infantile osteomyelitis: The emergence of the group B *Streptococcus*. J. Pediatr. *93*:578–583, 1978.
95. Edwards, M. S., Buffone, G. J., Fuselier, P. A., et al.: Deficient classical complement pathway activity in newborn sera. Pediatr. Res. *17*:685–688, 1983.
96. Edwards, M. S., Jackson, C. V., and Baker, C. J.: Increased risk of group B streptococcal disease in twins. J. A. M. A. *245*:2044–2046, 1981.
97. Edwards, M. S., Kasper, D. L., and Baker, C. J.: Rapid diagnosis of type III group B streptococcal meningitis by latex particle agglutination. J. Pediatr. *95*:202–205, 1979.
98. Edwards, M. S., Kasper, D. L., Jennings, H. J., et al.: Capsular sialic acid prevents activation of the alternative complement pathway by type III, group B streptococci. J. Immunol. *128*:1278–1283, 1982.
99. Edwards, M. S., Rench, M. A., Haffar, A. A. M., et al.: Long-term sequelae of group B streptococcal meningitis in infants. J. Pediatr. *106*:717–722, 1985.
100. Eickhoff, T. C., Klein, J. O., Daly, A. L., et al.: Neonatal sepsis and other infections due to group B beta-hemolytic streptococci. N. Engl. J. Med. *271*:1221–1228, 1964.
101. Ellenbogen, R. G., Goldmann, D. A., and Winston, K. R.: Group B streptococcal infections of the central nervous system in infants with myelomeningocele. Surg. Neurol. *29*:237–242, 1988.
102. Embil, J. A., Martin, T. R., Hansen, N. H., et al.: Group B beta haemolytic streptococci in the female genital tract: A study of four clinic populations. Br. J. Obstet. Gynaecol. *85*:783–786, 1978.
103. Ermocilla, R., Cassady, G., and Ceballos, R.: Otitis media in the pathogenesis of neonatal meningitis with group B beta-hemolytic *Streptococcus*. Pediatrics *54*:643–644, 1974.
104. Farley, M. M., Harvey, C., Stull, T., et al.: A population-based assessment of invasive disease due to group B *Streptococcus* in nonpregnant adults. N. Engl. J. Med. *328*:1807–1811, 1993.
105. Faro, S.: Group B beta-hemolytic streptococci and puerperal infections. Am. J. Obstet. Gynecol. *139*:686–689, 1981.
106. Feder, H. M., Jr., MacLean, W. C., and Moxon, R.: Scalp abscess secondary to fetal scalp electrode. J. Pediatr. *89*:808–809, 1976.

107. Feder, H. M., Jr., and Pae, K.: Group B streptococcal cellulitis-adenitis in a previously normal child. Pediatr. Infect. Dis. J. *11*:768–769, 1992.
108. Felman, W. E.: Concentrations of bacteria in cerebrospinal fluid of patients with bacterial meningitis. J. Pediatr. *88*:549–552, 1976.
109. Ferguson, L., and Gotoff, S. P.: Subdural empyema in an infant due to group B beta-hemolytic *Streptococcus*. Am. J. Dis. Child. *131*:97, 1977.
110. Ferrieri, P.: Surface-localized protein antigens of group B streptococci. Rev. Infect. Dis. *10*(Suppl):363–366, 1988.
111. Ferrieri, P., Cleary, P. P., and Seeds, A. E.: Epidemiology of group B streptococcal carriage in pregnant women and newborn infants. J. Med. Microbiol. *10*:103–114, 1976.
112. Ferrieri, P., Gray, E. D., and Wannamaker, L. W.: Biochemical and immunological characterization of the extracellular nucleases of group B streptococci. J. Exp. Med. *151*:56–68, 1980.
113. Ferrieri, P., Wannamaker, L. W., and Nelson, J.: Localization and characterization of the hippuricase activity of group B streptococci. Infect. Immun. *7*:747–752, 1973.
114. Fischer, G. W., Lowell, G. H., Crumrine, M. H., et al.: Demonstration of opsonic activity and in vivo protection against group B streptococci type III by *Streptococcus pneumoniae* type 14 antisera. J. Exp. Med. *148*:776–786, 1978.
115. Franciosi, R. A., Knostman, J. D., and Zimmerman, R. A.: Group B streptococcal neonatal and infant infections. J. Pediatr. *82*:707–718, 1973.
116. Frieden, I. J.: Blistering dactylitis caused by group B streptococci. Pediatr. Dermatol. *6*:300–302, 1989.
117. Fry, R. M.: Fatal infections by haemolytic *Streptococcus* group B. Lancet *1*:199–201, 1938.
118. Galask, R. P., Varner, M. W., Petzold, C. R., et al.: Bacterial attachment to the chorioamnionic membranes. Am. J. Obstet. Gynecol. *148*:915–928, 1984.
119. Gardner, S. E., Mason, E. O., Jr., and Yow, M. D.: Community acquisition of group B *Streptococcus* by infants of colonized mothers. Pediatrics *66*:873–875, 1980.
120. Gardner, S. E., Yow, M. D., Leeds, L. J., et al.: Failure of penicillin to eradicate group B streptococcal colonization in the pregnant woman. Am. J. Obstet. Gynecol. *135*:1062–1065, 1979.
121. Garland, S. M., and Fliegner, J. R.: Group B *Streptococcus* and neonatal infections: The case for intrapartum chemoprophylaxis. Aust. N. Z. J. Obstet. Gynaecol. *31*:119–122, 1991.
122. Gibbs, R. S., McDLuffie, R. S., McNabb, et al.: Neonatal group B streptococcal sepsis during 2 years of a universal screening program. Obstet. Gynecol. *84*:496–500, 1994.
123. Gibson, R. L., Lee, M.K., Soderland, C., et al.: Group B streptococci invade endothelial cells: Type III capsular polysaccharide attenuates invasion. Infect. Immun. *61*:478–485, 1993.
124. Gilbert, W. L., Isaacs, D., Burgess, M. A., et al.: Prevention of neonatal group B streptococcal sepsis: Is routine antenatal screening appropriate? Aust. N. Z. J. Obstet. Gynaecol. *35*:120–126, 1995.
125. Goldberg, G. N., Hansen, R. C., and Lynch, P. J.: Necrotizing fasciitis in infancy: Report of three cases and review of the literature. Pediatr. Dermatol. *2*:55–63, 1984.
126. Goldstein, M.: Neonatal fellowship: Group B streptococcal disease of a meconium pseudocyst in a neonate presenting with *E. coli* sepsis. J. Perinatol. *14*:234–236, 1994.
127. Gotoff, S. P., Papierniak, C. K., Klegerman, M. E., et al.: Quantitation of IgG antibody to the type-specific polysaccharide of group B *Streptococcus* type Ib in pregnant women and infected infants. J. Pediatr. *105*:628–630, 1984.
128. Graven, M. A., Cuddeback, J. K., Wyble, L.: Readmission for group B streptococci or *Escherichia coli* infection among full-term, singleton, vaginally delivered neonates after early discharge from Florida hospitals for births from 1992 through 1994. J. Perinatol. *19*:19–25, 1999.
129. Gray, B. M., Pritchard, D. G., and Dillon, H. C., Jr.: Seroepidemiological studies of group B *Streptococcus* type II. J. Infect. Dis. *151*:1073–1080, 1985.
130. Green, P. A., Singh, K. V., Murray, B. E., et al.: Recurrent group B streptococcal infections in infants: Clinical and microbiologic aspects. J. Pediatr. *125*:931–938, 1994.
131. Greene, G. R., Carroll, W. L., Morozumi, P. A., et al.: Endophthalmitis associated with group B streptococcal meningitis in an infant. Am. J. Dis. Child. *133*:752, 1979.
132. Hall, R. T., Barnes, W., Krishnan, L., et al.: Antibiotic treatment of parturient women colonized with group B streptococci. Am. J. Obstet. Gynecol. *124*:630–634, 1976.
133. Hamoudi, A. C., Marcon, M. J., Cannon, H. J., et al.: Comparison of three major antigen detection methods for the diagnosis of group B streptococcal sepsis in neonates. Pediatr. Infect. Dis. J. *2*:432–435, 1983.
134. Handrick, W., Spencker F.-B., and Kunzel, R.: [Scalp infection caused by B-streptococci in a newborn infant following internal cardiotocography.] Zentrabl. Gynakol. *106*:1544–1546, 1984.
135. Harper, I. A.: The importance of group B streptococci as human pathogens in the British Isles. J. Clin. Pathol. *24*:438–441, 1971.
136. Haslam, R. H. A., Allen, J. R., Dorsen, M. M., et al.: The sequelae of group B β-hemolytic streptococcal meningitis in early infancy. Am. J. Dis. Child. *131*:845–849, 1977.
137. Hauger, S. B.: Facial cellulitis: An early indicator of group B streptococcal bacteremia. Pediatrics *67*:376–377, 1981.
138. Helmig, R., Halaburt, J. T., Uldbjerg, N., et al.: Increased cell adherence of group B streptococci from preterm infants with neonatal sepsis. Obstet. Gynecol. *76*:825–828, 1990.
139. Hemming, V. G., Nagarajan, K., Hess, L. W., et al.: Rapid in vitro replication of group B *Streptococcus* in term human amniotic fluid. Gynecol. Obstet. Invest. *19*:124–129, 1985.
140. Herting, E., Gefeller, O., Land, M., et al.: Surfactant treatment of neonates with respiratory failure and group B streptococcal infection. Pediatrics *106*:957–964, 2000.
141. Heumann, D., Barras, C., Severin, A., et al.: Gram-positive cell walls stimulate synthesis of tumor necrosis factor alpha and interleukin-6 by human monocytes. Infect. Immun. *62*:2715–2721, 1994.
142. Hickman, M. E., Rench, M. A., Ferrieri, P., Baker, C.J.: Changing epidemiology of group B streptococcal colonization. Pediatrics *104*:203–209, 1999.
143. Hill, H. R., Bohnsack, J. F., Morris, E. Z., et al.: Group B streptococci inhibit the chemotactic activity of the fifth component of complement. J. Immunol. *141*:3551–3556, 1988.
144. Hillier, S. L., Krohn, M. A., Thwin, S. S., et al.: The association of high-density vaginal colonization by group B *Streptococcus* and preterm birth. Abstracts K189. Presented at the 35th Annual Meeting of the ICAAC, 1995, p. 322.
145. Hood, M., Janney, A., and Dameron, G.: Beta hemolytic *Streptococcus* group B associated with problems of the perinatal period. Am. J. Obstet. Gynecol. *82*:809–818, 1961.
146. Hoogkamp-Korstanje, J. A. A., Gerards, L. J., and Cats, B. P.: Maternal carriage and neonatal acquisition of group B streptococci. J. Infect. Dis. *145*:800–803, 1982.
147. Horigome, H., Ikada, Y., Hirano, T., et al.: Group B streptococcal endocarditis in infancy with a giant vegetation on the pulmonary valve. Eur. J. Pediatr. *153*:140–141, 1994.
148. Horn, K. A., Zimmerman, R. A., Knostman, J. S., et al.: Neurological sequelae of group B streptococcal neonatal infection. Pediatrics *53*:501–504, 1974.
149. Howard, J. B., and McCracken, G. H., Jr.: The spectrum of group B streptococcal infections in infancy. Am. J. Dis. Child. *128*:815–818, 1974.
150. Hussain, S. M., Luedtke, G. S., Baker, C. J., et al.: Invasive group B streptococcal disease in children beyond early infancy. Pediatr. Infect. Dis. J. *14*:278–281, 1995.
151. Ingram, D. L., Pendergrass, E. L., Bromberger, P. I., et al.: Group B streptococcal disease: Its diagnosis with use of antigen detection, Gram's stain, and the presence of apnea, hypotension. Am. J. Dis. Child. *134*:754–758, 1980.
152. Isaacman, S. H., Heroman, W. M., and Lightsey, A. L.: Purpura fulminans following late-onset group B beta-hemolytic streptococcal sepsis. Am. J. Dis. Child. *138*:915–916, 1984.
153. Jackson, L. A., Hilsdon, R., Farley, M. M., et al.: Risk factors for group B streptococcal disease in adults. Ann. Intern. Med. *123*:415–420, 1995.
154. Jacobs, M. R., Koornhof, H. J., and Stein, H.: Group B streptococcal infections in neonates and infants. S. Afr. Med. J. *54*:154–158, 1978.
155. Jafari, H. S., Schuchat, A., Hilsdon, R., et al.: Barriers to prevention of perinatal group B streptococcal disease. Pediatr. Infect. Dis. J. *14*:662–665, 1995.
156. Jeffery, H., Mitchison, R., Wigglesworth, J. S., et al.: Early neonatal bacteraemia. Arch. Dis. Child. *52*:683–686, 1977.
157. Jennings, H. J., Katzenellenbogen, E., Lugowski, C., et al.: Structure of native polysaccharide antigens of type Ia and type Ib group B *Streptococcus*. Biochemistry *22*:1258–1264, 1983.
158. Jennings, H. J., Rosell, K.-G., and Kasper, D. L.: Structural determination and serology of the native polysaccharide antigen of the type III group B *Streptococcus*. Can. J. Biochem. *58*:112–120, 1980.
159. Jennings, H. J., Rosell K.-G., Katzenellenbogen, E., et al.: Structural determination of the capsular polysaccharide antigen of type II group B *Streptococcus*. J. Biol. Chem. *258*:1793–1798, 1983.
160. Jerlström, P. G., Chhatwal, G. S., and Timmis, K. N.: The IgA-binding β antigen of the c protein complex of group B streptococci: Sequence determination of its gene and detection of two binding regions. Mol. Microbiol. *5*:843–849, 1991.
161. Jones, D. E., Kanarek, K. S., and Lim, D. V.: Group B streptococcal colonization patterns in mothers and their infants. J. Clin. Microbiol. *20*:438–440, 1984.
162. Joseph, T. A., Pyati, S. P., and Jacobs, N.: Neonatal early-onset *Escherichia coli* disease. The effect of intrapartum ampicillin. Arch. Pediatr. Adolesc. Med *152*:35–40, 1998.
163. Joyner, J. L., Augustine, N. H, Taylor, K. A., et al.: Effects of group B streptococci on cord and adult mononuclear cell interleukin-12 and interferon-gamma mRNA accumulation and protein secretion. J. Infect. Dis. *182*:974–977, 2000.
164. Jürgens, D., Sterzik, B., and Fehrenbach, F. J.: Unspecific binding of group B streptococcal cocytolysin (CAMP factor) to immunoglobulins and its possible role in pathogenicity. J. Exp. Med. *165*:720–732, 1987.

165. Kasper, D. L., Baker, C. J., Baltimore, R. S., et al.: Immunodeterminant specificity of human immunity to type III group B *Streptococcus*. J. Exp. Med. *149*:327–339, 1979.
166. Kasper, D. L., Paoletti, L. C., Wessels, M. R., et al.: Immune response to type III group B streptococcal polysaccharide–tetanus toxoid conjugate vaccine. J. Clin. Invest. *98*:2308–2314, 1996.
167. Katzenstein, A.-L., Davis, C., and Braude, A.: Pulmonary changes in neonatal sepsis due to group B β-hemolytic *Streptococcus*: Relation to hyaline membrane disease. J. Infect. Dis. *133*:430–435, 1976.
168. Keller, R., Fischer, W., Keist, R., et al.: Macrophage response to bacteria: Induction of marked secretory and cellular activities by lipoteichoic acids. Infect. Immun. *60*:3664–3672, 1992.
169. Kenny, J. D.: Right-sided diaphragmatic hernia of delayed onset in the newborn infant. South. Med. J. *70*:373–375, 1977.
170. Kim, K. S.: Antimicrobial susceptibility of group B streptococci. Antimicrob. Agents Chemother. *35*:83–89, 1985.
171. Kim, K. S.: Clinical perspectives on penicillin tolerance. J. Pediatr. *112*:214–216, 1988.
172. Kim, K. S., and Anthony, B. F.: Penicillin tolerance in group B streptococci isolated from infection neonates. J. Infect. Dis. *144*:411–419, 1981.
173. Kim, K. S., Kaye, K. L., Itabashi, H. H., et al.: Cerebritis due to group B *Streptococcus*. Scand. J. Infect. Dis. *14*:305–308, 1982.
174. Klegerman, M. E., Boyer, K. M., Papierniak, C. K., et al.: Estimation of the protective level of human IgG antibody to the type-specific polysaccharide of group B *Streptococcus* type Ia. J. Infect. Dis. *148*:648–655, 1983.
175. Klegerman, M. E., Boyer, K. M., Papierniak, C. K., et al.: Type-specific capsular antigen is associated with virulence in late-onset group B streptococcal type III disease. Infect. Immun. *44*:124–129, 1984.
176. Kline, A., and O'Donnell, E.: Group B *Streptococcus* as a cause of neonatal bullous skin lesions. Pediatr. Infect. Dis. J. *12*:165–166, 1993.
177. Kogan, G., Brisson, J. R., Kasper, D. L., et al.: Structural elucidation of the novel type VII group B *Streptococcus* capsular polysaccharide by high resolution NMR spectroscopy. Carbohydr. Res. *277*:1–9, 1995.
178. Kogan, G., Uhrin, D., Brisson, J. R., et al.: Structural and immunochemical characterization of the type VIII group B *Streptococcus* capsular polysaccharide. J. Biol. Chem. *271*:8786–8790, 1996.
179. Lachenauer, C. S., Kasper, D. L., Shimada, J., et al.: Serotypes VI and VIII predominate among group B streptococci isolated from pregnant Japanese women. J. Infect. Dis. *179*:1030–1033, 1999.
180. Lachenauer, C. S., Madoff, L. C.: A protective surface protein from type V group B streptococci shares N-terminal sequence homology with the alpha C protein. Infect. Immun. *64*:4255–4260, 1996.
181. Lancefield, R. C.: A serological differentiation of human and other groups of hemolytic streptococci. J. Exp. Med. *57*:571–595, 1933.
182. Lancefield, R. C., and Hare, R.: The serological differentiation of pathogenic and non-pathogenic strains of hemolytic streptococci from parturient women. J. Exp. Med. *61*:335–349, 1935.
183. Lancefield, R. C., McCarty, M., and Everly, W. N.: Multiple mouse-protective antibodies directed against group B streptococci. J. Exp. Med. *142*:165–179, 1975.
184. Larsen, J. W., and Dooley, S. L.: Group B streptococcal infections: An obstetrical viewpoint. Pediatrics *91*:148–149, 1994.
185. LeBovar, Y., Trung, P. H., and Mozziconacci, P.: Neonatal meningitis due to group B streptococci. Ann. Pediatr. *17*:207–213, 1970.
186. Leitner, M., Clarke, T. A., and Feldman, B. H.: Hyperbilirubinemia in association with late onset group B ß-hemolytic streptococcal infection. Pediatrics *63*:686, 1979.
187. Lerner, P. I., Gopalakrishna, K. V., Wolinsky, E., et al.: Group B *Streptococcus (S. agalactiae)* bacteremia in adults: Analysis of 32 cases and review of the literature. Medicine (Baltimore) *56*:457–473, 1977.
188. Levy, N. J., Nicholson-Weller, A., Baker, C. J., et al.: Potentiation of virulence by group B streptococcal polysaccharides. J. Infect. Dis. *149*:851–860, 1984.
189. Lewis, D. B., and Wilson, C. B.: Developmental immunology and role of host defenses in neonatal susceptibility to infection. *In* Remington, J. S., and Klein, J. O. (eds.): Infectious Diseases of the Fetus & Newborn Infant. 4th ed. Philadelphia, W. B. Saunders, 1995, pp. 20–98.
190. Lilien, L. D., Harris, V. J., and Pildes, R. S.: Significance of radiographic findings in early-onset group B streptococcal infection. Pediatrics *60*:360–365, 1977.
191. Lim, D. V., Kanarek, K. S., and Peterson, M. E.: Magnitude of colonization and sepsis by group B streptococci in newborn infants. Curr. Microbiol. *7*:99–101, 1982.
192. Lim, D. V., Morales, W. J., and Walsh, A. F.: Lim group B Strep broth and coagglutination for rapid identification of group B streptococci in preterm pregnant women. J. Clin. Microbiol. *25*:452–453, 1987.
193. Lin, F.Y., Azimi, P.H., Weisman, L.E., et al.: Antibiotic susceptibility profiles for group B streptococci isolated from neonates, 1995–1998. Clin. Infect. Dis. *31*:76–79, 2000.
194. Lindén, V.: Mouse-protective effect of rabbit anti-R-protein antibodies against group B streptococci type II carrying R-protein. Acta Pathol. Microbiol. Immunol. Scand. Sect. B *91*:145–151, 1983.
195. Lindén, V., Christensen, K. K., and Christensen, P.: Correlation between low levels of maternal IgG antibodies to R protein and neonatal septicemia with group B streptococci carrying R protein. Int. Arch. Allergy Appl. Immunol. *71*:168–172, 1983.
196. Lipson, A., Kronick, J. B., Tewfik, L., et al.: Group B streptococcal supraglottitis in a 3-month-old infant. Am. J. Dis. Child. *140*:411–412, 1986.
197. Long, W. A., Lawson, E. E., Harned, H. S., Jr., et al.: Pleural effusion in the first days of life: A prospective study. Am. J. Perinatol. *1*:190–194, 1984.
198. Lopez, J. B., Gross, P., and Boggs, T. R.: Skin lesions in association with β-hemolytic *Streptococcus* group B. Pediatrics *58*:859–860, 1976.
199. Lynn, N. J., Pauly, T. H., and Desai, N. S.: Purpura fulminans in three cases of early-onset neonatal group B streptococcal meningitis. J. Perinatol. *11*:144–146, 1991.
200. Mårdh, P.-A., and Weström, L.: Adherence of bacteria to vaginal epithelial cells. Infect. Immun. *13*:661–666, 1976.
201. MacDonald, S. W., Manuel, F. R., and Embil, J. A.: Localization of group B beta-hemolytic streptococci in the female urogenital tract. Am. J. Obstet. Gynecol. *133*:57–59, 1979.
202. Mancuso, G., Cusumano, V., Genovese, F., et al.: Role of interleukin 12 in experimental neonatal sepsis caused by group B streptococci. Infect. Immun. *65*:3731–3735, 1997.
203. Manroe, B. L., Rosenfeld, C. R., Weinberg, A. G., et al.: The differential leukocyte count in the assessment and outcome of early-onset neonatal group B streptococcal disease. J. Pediatr. *91*:632–637, 1977.
204. Marchlewicz, B. A., and Duncan, J. L.: Properties of a hemolysin produced by group B streptococci. Infect. Immun. *30*:805–813, 1980.
205. Marodi, L., Leijh, P. C. J., and van Furth, R.: Characteristics and functional capacities of human cord blood granulocytes and monocytes. Pediatr. Res. *18*:1127–1131, 1984.
206. Marques, M. B., Kasper, D. L., Pangburn, M. K., et al.: Prevention of C3 deposition by capsular polysaccharide is a virulence mechanism of type III group B streptococci. Infect. Immun. *60*:3986–3993, 1992.
207. Martin, T. R., Rubens, C. E., and Wilson, C. B.: Lung antibacterial defense mechanisms in infant and adult rats: Implications for the pathogenesis of group B streptococcal infections in the neonatal lung. J. Infect. Dis. *157*:91–100, 1988.
208. Mason, E. O., Wong, P., and Barrett, F. F.: Evaluation of four methods for detection of group B streptococcal colonization. J. Clin. Microbiol. *4*:429–431, 1976.
209. Matorras, R., Garcia-Perea, A., Omenaca, F., et al.: Group B *Streptococcus* and premature rupture of membranes and preterm delivery. Gynecol. Obstet. Invest. *27*:14–18, 1989.
210. Matorras, R., Garcia-Perea, A., Omenaca, F., et al.: Intrapartum chemoprophylaxis of early-onset group B streptococcal disease. Eur. J. Obstet. Gynecol. Reprod. Biol. *40*:57–62, 1991.
211. McClean, D.: The capsulation of streptococci and its relation to diffusion factor (hyaluronidase). J. Pathol. Bacteriol. *53*:13–27, 1941.
212. McCook, T. A., Felman, A. H., and Ayoub, E. M.: Streptococcal skeletal infections: Observations in four infants. A. J. R. Am. J. Roentgenol. *130*:465–467, 1978.
213. McDonald, H., Vigneswaran, R., and O'Loughlin, J. A.: Group B streptococcal colonization and preterm labour. Aust. N. Z. J. Obstet. Gynaecol. *29*:291–293, 1989.
214. McReynolds, E. W., and Shane, R.: Diabetes insipidus secondary to group B beta streptococcal meningitis. J. Tenn. Med. Assoc. *67*:117–120, 1974.
215. Memon, I. A., Jacobs, N. M., Yeh, T. F., et al.: Group B streptococcal osteomyelitis and septic arthritis. Am. J. Dis. Child. *133*:921–923, 1979.
216. Mercer, B. M., Carr, T. L., Beazley, D. D., et al.: Antibiotic use in pregnancy and drug-resistant infant sepsis. Am. J. Obstet. Gynecol. *181*: 816–821, 1999.
217. Michel, J. L., Madoff, L. C., Kling, D. E., et al.: Cloned alpha and beta C-protein antigens of group B streptococci elicit protective immunity. Infect. Immun. *59*:2023–2028, 1991.
218. Michon, F., Brisson, J.-R., Dell, A., et al.: Multiantennary group-specific polysaccharide of group B *Streptococcus*. Biochemistry *27*:5341–5351, 1988.
219. Millard, D. D., Bussey, M. E., Shulman, S. T., et al.: Multiple group B streptococcal infections in a premature infant: Eradication of nasal colonization with rifampin. Am. J. Dis. Child. *139*:964–965, 1985.
220. Milligan, T. W., Mattingly, S. J., and Straus, D. C.: Purification and partial characterization of neuraminidase from type III group B streptococci. J. Bacteriol. *144*:164–172, 1980.
221. Minett, F. C., Stableforth, A. W., and Edwards, S. J.: Studies on bovine mastitis. 1. The bacteriology of mastitis. J. Comp. Pathol. *42*:213–231, 1929.
222. Miron, D., Snelling, L. K., Josephson, S. L., et al.: Eosinophilic meningitis in a newborn with group B streptococcal infection. Pediatr. Infect. Dis. J. *12*:966–967, 1993.
223. Mohle-Boetani, J. C., Lieu, T. A., Ray, G. T., Escobar, G., for the Neonatal GBS Prevention Working Group: Preventing neonatal group B streptococcal disease: Cost-effectiveness in a health maintenance organization and the impact of delayed hospital discharge for newborns who received intrapartum antibiotics. Pediatrics *103*:703–710, 1999.

224. Mohle-Boetani, J. C., Schuchat, A., Plikaytis, B. D., et al.: Comparison of prevention strategies for neonatal group B streptococcal infection: A population-based economic analysis. J. A. M. A. *270*:1442–1448, 1993.
225. Mok, P. M., Reilly, B. J., and Ash, J. M.: Osteomyelitis in the neonate. Radiology *145*:677–682, 1982.
226. Moller, M., Thomsen, A. C., Borch, K., et al.: Rupture of fetal membranes and premature delivery associated with group B streptococci in urine of pregnant women. Lancet *2*:69–70, 1984.
227. Morrow, D. L., Kline, J. B., Douglas, S. D., et al.: Rapid detection of group B streptococcal antigen by monoclonal antibody sandwich enzyme assay. J. Clin. Microbiol. *19*:457–459, 1984.
228. Nealon, T. J., and Mattingly, S. J.: Association of elevated levels of cellular lipoteichoic acids of group B streptococci with human neonatal disease. Infect. Immun. *39*:1243–1251, 1983.
229. Nealon, T. J., and Mattingly, S. J.: Role of cellular lipoteichoic acids in mediating adherence of serotype III strains of group B streptococci to human embryonic, fetal, and adult epithelial cells. Infect. Immun. *43*: 523–530, 1984.
230. Nelson, J. D.: Bilateral breast abscess due to group B *Streptococcus*. Am. J. Dis. Child. *130*:567, 1976.
231. Nizet, V., Gibson, R. L., Rubens, C. E.: The role of group B streptococci beta-hemolysin expression in newborn lung injury. Adv. Exp. Med. Biol. *418*:627–630, 1997.
232. Nocard, M.: Sur une mammite contagieuse des vaches laitières. Ann. Inst. Pasteur *1*:109–127, 1887.
233. Noya, F. J. D., Rench, M. A., Metzger, T. G., et al.: Unusual occurrence of an epidemic of type Ib/c group B streptococcal sepsis in a neonatal intensive care unit. J. Infect. Dis. *155*:1135–1144, 1987.
234. Nudelman, R., Bral, M., Sakhai, Y., et al.: Violaceous cellulitis. Pediatrics *70*:157–158, 1982.
235. Opal, S. M., Cross, A., Palmo, M., et al.: Group B streptococcal sepsis in adults and infants: Contrasts and comparisons. Arch. Intern. Med. *148*:641–645, 1988.
236. Paoletti, L. C., Pinel, J., Kennedy, R. C., Kasper, D. L.: Maternal antibody transfer in baboons and mice vaccinated with a group B streptococcal polysaccharide conjugate. J. Infect. Dis. *181*:653–658, 2000.
237. Paoletti, L. C., Wessels, M. R., Michon, R., et al.: Group B *Streptococcus* type II polysaccharide–tetanus toxoid conjugate vaccine. Infect. Immun. *60*:4009–4011, 1992.
238. Paoletti, L. C., Wessels, M. R., Rodewald, A. K., et al.: Neonatal mouse protection against infection with multiple group B streptococcal serotypes by maternal immunization with a tetravalent GBS polysaccharide–tetanus toxoid conjugate vaccine. Infect. Immun. *62*:3236–3243, 1994.
239. Paredes, A. B., Wong, P., and Yow, M. D.: Failure of penicillin to eradicate the carrier state of group B *Streptococcus* in infants. J. Pediatr. *89*:191–193, 1976.
240. Park, J. W.: Bacterial tracheitis caused by *Streptococcus agalactiae*. Pediatr. Infect. Dis. J. *9*:450–451, 1990.
241. Pass, M. A., Gray, B. M., and Dillon, H. C., Jr.: Puerperal and perinatal infections with group B streptococci. Am. J. Obstet. Gynecol. *143*:147–152, 1982.
242. Pass, M. A., Gray, B. M., Khare, S., et al.: Prospective studies of group B streptococcal infections in infants. J. Pediatr. *95*:437–443, 1979.
243. Pass, M. A., Khare, S., and Dillon, H. C.: Twin pregnancies: Incidence of group B streptococcal colonization and disease. J. Pediatr. *97*:635–637, 1980.
244. Patamasucon, P., Siegel, J. D., and McCracken, G. H., Jr.: Streptococcal submandibular cellulitis in young infants. Pediatrics *67*:378–380, 1981.
245. Pathak, A., and Hwu, H.-H.: Group B streptococcal cellulitis. South. Med. J. *78*:67–68, 1985.
246. Payne, N. R., Burke, B. A., Day, D. L., et al.: Correlation of clinical and pathologic findings in early onset neonatal group B streptococcal infection with disease severity and prediction of outcome. Pediatr. Infect. Dis. J. *7*:836–847, 1988.
247. Payne, N. R., and Ferrieri, P.: The relation of the Ib/c protein antigen to the opsonization differences between strains of type II group B streptococci. J. Infect. Dis. *151*:672–681, 1985.
248. Peevy, K. J., and Chalhub, E. G.: Occult group B streptococcal infection: An important cause of intrauterine asphyxia. Am. J. Obstet. Gynecol. *146*:989–990, 1983.
249. Peevy, K. J., and Wiseman, H. J.: Gallbladder distention in septic neonates. Arch. Dis. Child. *57*:75–76, 1982.
250. Persson, K., Bjerre, B., Elfström, L., et al.: Longitudinal study of group B streptococcal carriage during late pregnancy. Scand. J. Infect. Dis. *19*:325–329, 1987.
251. Persson, K. M.-S., and Forsgren, A.: Antimicrobial susceptibility of group B streptococci. Eur. J. Clin. Microbiol. *5*:165–167, 1986.
252. Philipps, A. F., Bierney, J.-P., and Crowe, C. P., Jr.: Neonatal radiology: Acquired diaphragmatic hernia with group B streptococcal pneumonia. J. Perinatol. *15*:160–162, 1995.
253. Platt, M. W., Correa, N., Jr., and Mold, C.: Growth of group B streptococci in human serum leads to increased cell surface sialic acid and decreased activation of the alternative complement pathway. Can. J. Microbiol. *40*:99–105, 1994.
254. Prevention of perinatal group B streptococcal disease: A public health perspective. M. M. W. R. Morb. Mortal. Wkly. Rep. *45*(RR-7):1–24, 1996.
255. Pritchard, D. G., Gray, B. M., and Egan, M. L.: Murine monoclonal antibodies to type Ib polysaccharide of group B streptococci bind to human milk oligosaccharides. Infect. Immun. *60*:1598–1602, 1992.
256. Puliti, M., Nizet, V., von Hunolstein, C., et al.: Severity of group B streptococcal arthritis is correlated with beta-hemolysin expression. J. Infect. Dis. *182*:824–832, 2000.
257. Pyati, S. P., Pildes, R. S., Macobs, N. M., et al.: Penicillin in infants weighing two kilograms or less with early-onset group B streptococcal disease. N. Engl. J. Med. *308*:1383–1389, 1983.
258. Pylipow, M., Gaddis, M., and Kinney, J. S.: Selective intrapartum prophylaxis for group B *Streptococcus* colonization: Management and outcome of newborns. Pediatrics *93*:631–635, 1994.
259. Quirante, J., Ceballos, R., and Cassady, G.: Group B β-hemolytic streptococcal infection in the newborn. Am. J. Dis. Child. *128*:659–665, 1974.
260. Rabalais, G. P., Bronfin, D. R., and Daum, R. S.: Evaluation of a commercially available latex agglutination test for rapid diagnosis of group B streptococcal infection. Pediatr. Infect. Dis. J. *6*:177–181, 1987.
261. Ragnhildstreit, E., and Ose, L.: Neonatal osteomyelitis caused by group B streptococci. Scand. J. Infect. Dis. *8*:219–221, 1976.
262. Ramamurthy, R. S., Srinivasan, G., and Jacobs, N. M.: Necrotizing fasciitis and necrotizing cellulitis due to group B *Streptococcus*. Am. J. Dis. Child. *131*:1169–1170, 1977.
263. Ramsey, P. G., and Zwerdling, R.: Asymptomatic neonatal bacteremia. N. Engl. J. Med. *295*:225, 1977.
264. Rand, T. H.: Group B streptococcal cellulitis in infants: A disease modified by prior antibiotic therapy or hospitalization? Pediatrics *81*:63–65, 1988.
265. Regan, J. A., Chao, S., and James, L. S.: Premature rupture of membranes, preterm delivery, and group B streptococcal colonization of mothers. Am. J. Obstet. Gynecol. *141*:184–186, 1981.
266. Regan, J. A., Klebanoff, M. A., and Nugent, R. P.: The epidemiology of group B streptococcal colonization in pregnancy. Obstet. Gynecol. *77*:604–610, 1991.
267. Reisenfeld-Orn, I., Wolpe, S., Garcia-Bustos, J. F., et al.: Production of interleukin-1 but no tumor necrosis factor by human monocytes stimulated with pneumococcal cell surface components. Infect. Immun. *57*:1890–1893, 1989.
268. Rench, M. A., and Baker, C. J.: Group B streptococcal breast abscess in a mother and mastitis in her infant. Obstet. Gynecol. *73*:875–877, 1989.
269. Rench, M. A., and Baker, C. J.: Neonatal sepsis caused by a new group B streptococcal serotype. J. Pediatr. *122*:638–640, 1993.
270. Rench, M. A., Metzger, T. G., and Baker, C. J.: Detection of group B streptococcal antigen in body fluids by a latex-coupled monoclonal antibody assay. J. Clin. Microbiol. *20*:852–854, 1984.
271. Roberts, K. B.: Persistent group B *Streptococcus* bacteremia without clinical "sepsis" in infants. J. Pediatr. *88*:1059–1060, 1976.
272. Rodewald, A. K., Onderdonk, A. B., Warren, H. B., et al.: Neonatal mouse model of group B streptococcal infection. J. Infect. Dis. *166*:635–639, 1992.
273. Roe, M. H., Todd, J. K., and Favara, B. E.: Non-hemolytic group B streptococcal infections. J. Pediatr. *89*:75–77, 1976.
274. Rolston, K. V. I.: Susceptibility of group B and group G streptococci to newer antimicrobial agents. Eur. J. Clin. Microbiol. *5*:534–536, 1986.
275. Rouse, D. J., Goldenberg, R. L., Cliver, S. P., et al.: Strategies for the prevention of early-onset group B streptococcal sepsis: A decision analysis. Obstet. Gynecol. *83*:483–494, 1994.
276. Rowen, J. L., Smith, C. W., and Edwards, M. S.: Capsule delays elaboration of leukotriene B_4 (LTB_4) by monocytes stimulated with type III group B streptococci (GBS). Abstract. Pediatr. Res. *37*:187, 1995.
277. Rowen, J. L., Smith, C. W., and Edwards, M. S.: Group B streptococci elicit leukotriene B_4 and interleukin-8 from human monocytes: Neonates exhibit a diminished response. J. Infect. Dis. *172*:420–426, 1995.
278. Rubens, C. E., Smith, S., Hulse, M., et al.: Respiratory epithelial cell invasion by group B streptococci. Infect. Immun. *60*:5157–5163, 1992.
279. Rubens, C. E., Wessels, M. R., Heggen, L. M., et al.: Transposon mutagenesis of type III group B *Streptococcus*: Correlation of capsule expression with virulence. Proc. Natl. Acad. Sci. U. S. A. *84*:7208–7212, 1987.
280. Ruiz-Gomez, D., Tarpay, M., and Riley, H. D.: Recurrent group B streptococcal infections: Report of three cases. Scand. J. Infect. Dis. *11*:35–38, 1979.
281. Sánchez, P. J., Siegel, J. D., Cushion, N. B., et al.: Significance of a positive urine group B streptococcal latex agglutination test in neonates. J. Pediatr. *116*:601–606, 1990.
282. Sapir-Ellis, S., Johnson, A., and Austin, T. L.: Group B streptococcal meningitis associated with otitis media. Am. J. Dis. Child. *130*:1003–1004, 1976.
283. Schauf, V., Deveikis, A., Riff, L., et al.: Antibiotic-killing kinetics of group B streptococci. J. Pediatr. *89*:194–198, 1976.
284. Scheld, W. M., Alliegro, G. M., Field, M. R., et al.: Synergy between penicillins and low concentrations of gentamicin in experimental meningitis due to group B streptococci. J. Infect. Dis. *146*:100, 1982.

285. Schibler, K. R., Trautman, M. S., Liechty, K. W., et al.: Diminished transcription of interleukin-8 by monocytes from preterm neonates. J. Leukoc. Biol. *53*:399–403, 1993.
286. Schlievert, P. M., Gocke, J. E., and Deringer, J. R.: Group B streptococcal toxic shock–like syndrome: Report of a case and purification of an associated pyrogenic toxin. Clin. Infect. Dis. *17*:26–31, 1993.
287. Schrag, S. J., Zywicki, S., Farley, M. M., et al.: Group B streptococcal disease in the era of intrapartum antibiotic prophylaxis. N. Engl. J. Med. *342*:15–20, 2000.
288. Schuchat, A.: Group B streptococcal disease in newborns: A global perspective on prevention. Biomed. Pharmacother. *49*:19–25, 1995.
289. Schuchat, A., Deaver-Robinson, K., Plikaytis, B. D., et al.: Multistate case-control study of maternal risk factors for neonatal group B streptococcal disease. Pediatr. Infect. Dis. J. *13*:623–629, 1994.
290. Schuchat, A., Oxtoby, M., Cochi, S., et al.: Population-based risk factors for neonatal group B streptococcal disease: Results of a cohort study in metropolitan Atlanta. J. Infect. Dis. *162*:672–677, 1990.
291. Schuit, K. E., and DeBasio, R.: Kinetics of phagocyte response to group B streptococcal infections in newborn rats. Infect. Immun. *28*:319–324, 1980.
292. Sherman, M. P., and Lehrer, R. I.: Oxidative metabolism of neonatal and adult rabbit lung macrophages stimulated with opsonized group B streptococci. Infect. Immun. *47*:26–30, 1985.
293. Shigeoka, A. O., Rote, N. S., Santos, J. I., et al.: Assessment of the virulence factors of group B streptococci: Correlation with sialic acid content. J. Infect. Dis. *147*:857–863, 1983.
294. Shurin, P. A., Howie, V. M., Pelton, S. I., et al.: Bacterial etiology of otitis media during the first six weeks of life. J. Pediatr. *92*:893–896, 1978.
295. Siegel, J. D., and McCracken, G. H., Jr.: Detection of group B streptococcal antigens in body fluids of neonates. J. Pediatr. *93*:491–492, 1978.
296. Siegel, J. D., McCracken, G. H., Jr., Threlkeld, N., et al.: Single-dose penicillin prophylaxis against neonatal group B streptococcal infections. N. Engl. J. Med. *303*:769–775, 1980.
297. Siegel, J. D., Shannon, K. M., and De Passe, B. M.: Recurrent infection associated with penicillin-tolerant group B streptococci: A report of two cases. J. Pediatr. *99*:920–924, 1981.
298. Slifkin, M., and Pouchet-Melvin, G. R.: Evaluation of three commercially available test products for serogrouping beta-hemolytic streptococci. J. Clin. Microbiol. *11*:249–255, 1980.
299. Sobel, J. D., Myers, P., Levison, M. E., et al.: Comparison of bacterial and fungal adherence to vaginal exfoliated epithelial cells and human vaginal epithelial tissue culture cells. Infect. Immun. *35*:697–701, 1982.
300. Sokal, M. M., Nagaraj, A., Fisher, B. J., et al.: Neonatal empyema caused by group B beta-hemolytic *Streptococcus*. Chest *81*:390–391, 1982.
301. Sokol, D. M., Demmler, G. J., and Baker, C. J.: Unusual presentation of group B streptococcal ventriculitis. Pediatr. Infect. Dis. J. *9*:525–527, 1990.
302. Speck, W. T., Driscol, J. M., Polin, R. A., et al.: Staphylococcal and streptococcal colonization of the newborn infant: Effect of antiseptic cord care. Am. J. Dis. Child. *131*:1005–1008, 1977.
303. Stålhammar-Carlemalm, M., Areschoug, T., Larsson, C., Lindahl, G.: Cross-protection between group A and group B streptococci due to cross-reacting surface proteins. J. Infect. Dis. *182*:142–149, 2000.
304. Stålhammar-Carlemalm, M., Stenberg, L., Lindahl, G.: Protein rib: A novel group B streptococcal cell surface protein that confers protective immunity and is expressed by most strains causing invasive infections. J. Exp. Med. *177*:1593–1603, 1993.
305. Stewardson-Krieger, P. B., and Gotoff, S. P.: Risk factors in early-onset neonatal group B streptococcal infections. Infection *6*:50–53, 1978.
306. St. Laurent-Gagnon, T., and Weber, M. L.: Urinary tract *Streptococcus* group B infection in a 6-week-old infant. J. A. M. A. *140*:1269, 1978.
307. Suara, R. O., Adegbola, R. A., Baker, C. J., et al.: Carriage of group B streptococci in pregnant Gambian mothers and their infants. J. Infect. Dis. *170*:1316–1319, 1994.
308. Suresh, B. R., Rios, A., Brion, L. P., et al.: Delayed onset right-sided diaphragmatic hernia secondary to group B streptococcal infection. Pediatr. Infect. Dis. J. *10*:166–168, 1991.
309. Swingle, H. M., Bucciarfelli, R. L., and Ayoub, E. M.: Synergy between penicillins and low concentrations of gentamicin in the killing of group B streptococci. J. Infect. Dis. *152*:58–66, 1985.
310. Takahashi, S., Nagano, Y., Nagano, N., et al.: Role of C5a-ase in group B streptococcal resistance to opsonophagocytic killing. Infect. Immun. *63*:4764–4769, 1995.
311. Tamura, G. S., Kuypers, J. M., Smith, S., et al.: Adherence of group B streptococci to cultured epithelial cells: Roles of environmental factors and bacterial surface components. Infect. Immun. *62*:2450–2458, 1994.
312. Tapsall, J. W.: Pigment production by Lancefield-group B streptococci (*Streptococcus agalactiae*). J. Med. Microbiol. *21*:75–81, 1986.
313. Tetzlaff, T. R., Ashworth, C., and Nelson, J. D.: Otitis media in children less than 12 weeks of age. Pediatrics *59*:827–832, 1977.
314. Torok, P. G., Dunn, J. R.: Self-collection of antepartum anogenital group B streptococcus cultures. J. Am. Board. Fam. Pract. *13*:107–110, 2000.
315. Tuppurainen, N., and Hallman, M.: Prevention of neonatal group B streptococcal disease: Intrapartum detection and chemoprophylaxis of heavily colonized parturients. Obstet. Gynecol. *73*:583–587, 1989.
316. Turner, M. C., and Naumburg, E. G.: Acute renal failure in the neonate: Two fatal cases due to group B streptococci with rhabdomyolysis. Clin. Pediatr. (Phila.) *25*:189–190, 1987.
317. Vallejo, J. G., Baker, C. J., and Edwards, M. S.: Demonstration of circulating group B streptococcal immune complexes in neonates with meningitis. J. Clin. Microbiol. *32*:2041–2045, 1994.
318. Vallejo, J. G., Baker, C. J., and Edwards, M. S.: Interleukin-6 production by human neonatal monocytes stimulated by type III group B streptococci. J. Infect. Dis. *174*:332–337, 1996.
319. Vallejo, J. G., Baker, C. J., and Edwards, M. S.: The role of bacterial cell wall and capsule in the induction of tumor necrosis factor alpha by type III group B streptococci. Infect. Immun. *64*:5042–5046, 1996.
320. Vallette, J. D., Jr., Goldberg, R. N., Suguihara, C., et al.: Effect of an interleukin-1 receptor antagonist on the hemodynamic manifestations of group B streptococcal sepsis. Pediatr. Res. *38*:704–708, 1995.
321. Van Peenen, P. F., Cannon, R. E., and Seibert, D. J.: Group B beta-hemolytic streptococci causing fatal meningitis. Mil. Med. *130*:65–67, 1965.
322. Vollman, J. H., Smith, W. L., Ballard, E. T., et al.: Early onset group B streptococcal disease: Clinical, roentgenographic, and pathologic features. J. Pediatr. *89*:199–203, 1976.
323. von Hunolstein, C., D'Ascenzi, S., Wagner, B., et al.: Immunochemistry of capsular type polysaccharide and virulence properties of type VI *Streptococcus agalactiae* (group B streptococci). Infect. Immun. *61*:1272–1280, 1993.
324. Wald, E. R., Bergman, I., Taylor, H. G., et al.: Long-term outcome of group B streptococcal meningitis. Pediatrics *77*:217–221, 1986.
325. Walker, K. M., and Coyer, W. F.: Suprarenal abscess due to group B *Streptococcus*. J. Pediatr. *94*:970–971, 1979.
326. Walker, S. H., Santos, A. Q., and Quintero, B. A.: Recurrence of group B III streptococcal meningitis. J. Pediatr. *89*:187–188, 1976.
327. Weinberg, A. G., and Laird, W. P.: Group B streptococcal endocarditis detected by echocardiography. J. Pediatr. *92*:334–336, 1978.
328. Weiser, J. N., and Rubens, C. E.: Transposon mutagenesis of group B *Streptococcus* beta-hemolysin biosynthesis. Infect. Immun. *55*: 2314–2316, 1987.
329. Weisman, L. E., Stoll, B. J., Cruess, D. F., et al.: Early-onset group B streptococcal sepsis: A current assessment. J. Pediatr. *121*:428–433, 1992.
330. Weller, M. H., and Katzenstein, A.: Radiological findings in group B streptococcal sepsis. Radiology *118*:385–387, 1976.
331. Wessels, M. R., Benedí, V.-J., Jennings, H. J., et al.: Isolation and characterization of type IV group B *Streptococcus* capsular polysaccharide. Infect. Immun. *57*:1089–1094, 1989.
332. Wessels, M. R., DiFabio, J. L., Benedí, V-J., et al.: Structural determination and immunochemical characterization of the type V group B *Streptococcus* capsular polysaccharide. J. Biol. Chem. *266*:6714–6719, 1991.
333. Wessels, M. R., Paoletti, L. C., Kasper, D. L., et al.: Immunogenicity in animals of a polysaccharide-protein conjugate vaccine against type III group B *Streptococcus*. J. Clin. Invest. *86*:1428–1433, 1990.
334. Wessels, M. R., Rubens, C. E., Benedí, V.-J., et al.: Definition of a bacterial virulence factor: Sialylation of the group B streptococcal capsule. Proc. Natl. Acad. Sci. U. S. A. *86*:8983–8987, 1989.
335. Wibawan, I. W. T., and Lämmler, C.: Properties of group B streptococci with protein surface antigens X and R. J. Clin. Microbiol. *28*:2834–2836, 1990.
336. Wilkinson, H. W.: Analysis of group B streptococcal types associated with disease in human infants and adults. J. Clin. Microbiol. *7*:176–179, 1978.
337. Wilkinson, H. W., Facklam, R. R., and Wortham, E. C.: Distribution by serological type of group B streptococci isolated from a variety of clinical material over a five-year period (with special reference to neonatal sepsis and meningitis). Infect. Immun. *8*:228–235, 1973.
338. Williams, P. A., Bohnsack, J. F., Augustine, N. H., et al.: Production of tumor necrosis factor by human cells in vitro and in vivo, induced by group B streptococci. J. Pediatr. *123*:292–300, 1993.
339. Wiswell, T. E., Baumgart, S., Gannon, C. M., et al.: No lumbar puncture in the evaluation for early neonatal sepsis: Will meningitis be missed? Pediatrics *95*:803–806, 1995.
340. Wiswell, T. E., and Miller, J. A.: Infections of congenital cervical neck masses associated with bacteremia. J. Pediatr. Surg. *21*:173–174, 1986.
341. Wong, M., Isaacs, D., Howman-Giles, R., et al.: Clinical and diagnostic features of osteomyelitis occurring in the first three months of life. Pediatr. Infect. Dis. J. *14*:1047–1053, 1995.
342. Wood, E. G., and Dillon, H. C., Jr.: A prospective study of group B streptococcal bacteriuria in pregnancy. Am. J. Obstet. Gynecol. *140*:515–520, 1981.
343. Yagupsky, P., Menegus, M. A., and Powell, K. R.: The changing spectrum of group B streptococcal disease in infants: An eleven-year experience in a tertiary care hospital. Pediatr. Infect. Dis. J. *10*:801–808, 1991.

344. Yancy, M. K., and Duff, P.: An analysis of the cost-effectiveness of selected protocols for the prevention of neonatal group B streptococcal infection. Obstet. Gynecol. *83*:367–371, 1994.
345. Yeung, M. K., and Mattingly, S. J.: Biosynthetic capacity for type-specific antigen synthesis determines the virulence of serotype III strains of group B streptococci. Infect. Immun. *44*:217–221, 1984.
346. Young, N., Finn, A., and Powell, C.: Group B streptococcal epiglottitis. Pediatr. Infect. Dis. J. *15*:95–96, 1996.
347. Yow, M. D., Leeds, L. J., Thompson, P. K., et al.: The natural history of group B streptococcal colonization in the pregnant woman and her offspring. I. Colonization studies. Am. J. Obstet. Gynecol. *137*:34–38, 1980.
348. Yow, M. D., Mason, E. O., Leeds, L. J., et al.: Ampicillin prevents intrapartum transmission of group B *Streptococcus*. J. A. M. A. *241*: 1245–1247, 1979.
349. Zaleznik, D. F., Rench, M. A., Hillier, S. L., et al.: Invasive disease due to group B *Streptococcus* in pregnant women and neonates from diverse population groups. Clin. Infect. Dis. *30*:276–281, 2000.

CHAPTER 89

Enterococcal and Viridans Streptococcal Infections

B. KEITH ENGLISH ■ JERRY L. SHENEP

ENTEROCOCCAL INFECTIONS

The enterococci are gram-positive ovoid bacteria that are related closely to the streptococci but now are known to be phylogenetically distinct and make up the genus *Enterococcus*. These organisms are found in the normal bowel flora of humans and many animals and are isolated commonly from environmental sources. Enterococci generally are considered to be of low virulence but have been known to cause human infection for almost a century (reviewed by Murray[134]). These ubiquitous bacteria have become recognized increasingly as important causes of both nosocomial and community-acquired infection in adults[47, 123, 124, 134, 136, 138, 151, 156] and children,* yet the role of *Enterococcus* spp. as a pathogen (or co-pathogen) in certain clinical settings, particularly intra-abdominal and pelvic infections, often remains uncertain.

Enterococci are intrinsically resistant to many antimicrobial agents (including the cephalosporins, oxacillin, clindamycin, and the aminoglycosides). Since the emergence of high-level aminoglycoside resistance in *Enterococcus* spp. more than 30 years ago,[128] increasing percentages of these organisms have acquired clinically significant resistance to β-lactam antibiotics and to vancomycin and other glycopeptides, as well as to aminoglycosides. Infections caused by vancomycin-resistant enterococci (VRE), especially those caused by vancomycin-resistant *Enterococcus faecium* (VREF), are of particular concern because VREF isolates frequently are resistant to all available bactericidal antimicrobial agents.[136, 138] The dramatic increase in nosocomial infections caused by VRE[47, 136, 151] has resulted in failures of antimicrobial therapy[100] and has inspired comparisons with the pre-antibiotic period[3] and even speculation about a "post-antimicrobial era."[33] Concern about additional nosocomial spread of VRE and the potential for transfer of vancomycin-resistant determinants to other pathogens (pneumococci, staphylococci) has led to the development of stringent hospital infection control guidelines designed to interrupt the spread of vancomycin-resistant organisms.[163] Although the impact of VRE infections in children has been less dramatic, increasing numbers of pediatric centers now are reporting infections caused by these organisms.†

*See references 16, 29, 30, 41, 69, 119, 156, 164, 169, 171, 180, 209.
†See references 16, 29, 30, 69, 119, 156, 164, 169, 171, 180, 209.

Microbiology

The genus *Enterococcus* consists of gram-positive cocci that are catalase-negative and occur singly, in pairs, and in short chains. Morphologically, enterococci are indistinguishable from streptococci and traditionally were classified as members of the genus *Streptococcus*. Sherman's early classification scheme[185] divided the streptococci into four groups: pyogenic, viridans, lactic, and enterococcal. By the Lancefield criteria, enterococci were classified as group D streptococci, along with the "nonenterococcal" *Streptococcus bovis* group. However, recent genetic evidence has indicated that the enterococci are sufficiently different from the streptococci to merit the establishment of a separate genus.[53]

Figure 89–1 is a scheme for the differentiation of enterococci from other gram-positive cocci. Catalase-negative gram-positive cocci that have been isolated from human sources include the streptococci, the enterococci, *Lactococcus, Leuconostoc, Pediococcus*, and *Gemella*. Most enterococci produce no (gamma) or partial (alpha) hemolysis on blood agar; differentiation between enterococci and certain alpha-hemolytic or nonhemolytic streptococci and other nonstreptococcal gram-positive cocci may require a series of biochemical tests.[51, 53] Clinical laboratories may identify an organism presumptively on a primary isolation plate as an enterococcus based on colony morphology, Gram stain, and the pyrrolidonyl arylamidase (PYR) test. Most enterococci produce PYR, as do *Streptococcus pyogenes* and nutritionally variant streptococci *(Abiotrophia)*, but not other streptococci. The PYR test is particularly useful for differentiating enterococci from group D streptococci and *Leuconostoc* spp. (see Fig. 89–1). *S. pyogenes* and *Abiotrophia* species are distinguished easily from enterococci by colony morphology, hemolysis, and special growth requirements.

Enterococci are able to hydrolyze esculin in the presence of 40 percent bile salts; of the true streptococci, only group D streptococci (*S. bovis* group) and approximately 5 to 10 percent of viridans streptococci share this characteristic.[53] Enterococci are facultatively anaerobic and grow under harsh conditions that inhibit the growth of streptococci; growth in 6.5 percent sodium chloride at 45°C is a useful confirmatory test. Enterococci produce leucine aminopeptidase, as do streptococci, lactococci, pediococci, and some *Gemella* strains. The presence of group D streptococcal antigen is of limited value because the *S. bovis* group, most

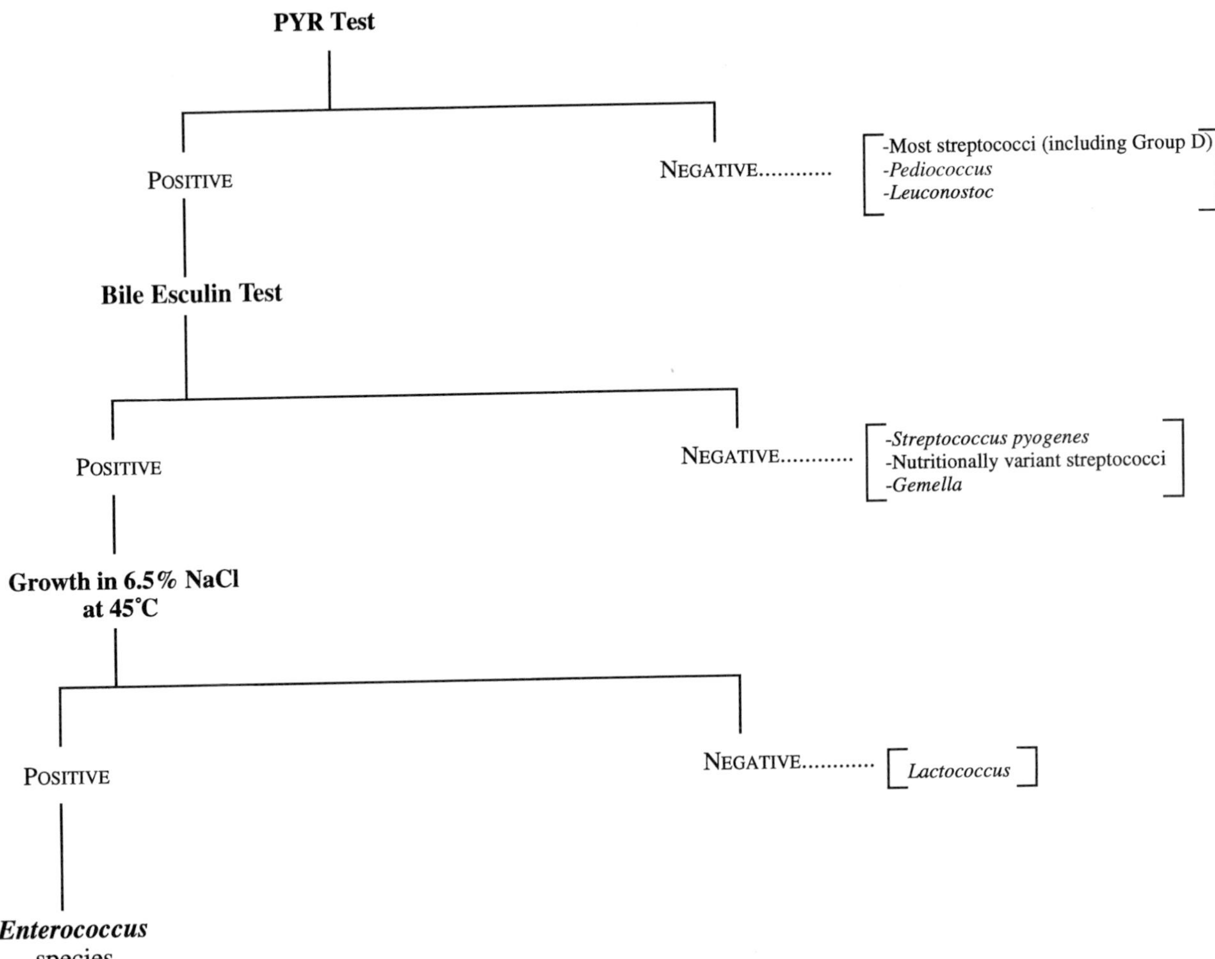

FIGURE 89–1 ■ Differentiation of enterococci from other catalase-negative, gram-positive cocci. PYR, pyrrolidonyl arylamidase.

pediococci, and one half of the clinical *Leuconostoc* isolates share this antigen.[53]

Occasional clinical isolates of *Leuconostoc, Pediococcus,* and *Lactococcus* may be difficult to distinguish from the enterococci. Some strains of *Leuconostoc* and *Pediococcus* may grow in 6.5 percent NaCl at 45° C but they are PYR-negative. Lactococci are PYR-positive, and some isolates will grow in 6.5 percent NaCl; however, most lactococci fail to grow (or grow very slowly) at 45° C. Consequently, definitive confirmation of an organism as an enterococcus may require complete identification to the species level. Molecular techniques promise to provide rapid, reliable identification and speciation of enterococci,[38, 42, 45] but currently they are available only in the research setting.

The genus *Enterococcus* now includes at least 14 "typical" species and three additional "atypical" species (the latter are PYR-negative and grow very slowly in the presence of 6.5% NaCl) (Table 89–1). However, most human clinical isolates are either *Enterococcus faecalis* (60–90%) or *E. faecium* (5–20%), although clusters of human infection caused by *Enterococcus raffinosus*,[24] *Enterococcus casseliflavus*,[143] *Enterococcus avium*,[155] *Enterococcus durans*,[181] and occasional human infections attributable to *Enterococcus gallinarum, Enterococcus mundtii,* and *Enterococcus flavescens* have been reported.[52] Even though *E. faecalis* and *E. faecium* continue to account for most clinical isolates, the percentage of *E. faecium* isolates has been increasing, and relatively more "other" (non-*faecalis*, non-*faecium*) enterococci are being identified by clinical laboratories.[87, 111]

Speciation of enterococci has been useful primarily for epidemiologic purposes, but distinction between the more antibiotic-susceptible *E. faecalis* and the more antibiotic-resistant (see later) *E. faecium* may be helpful in selecting

TABLE 89–1 ■ ENTEROCOCCUS SPECIES

Typical enterococci (PYR +)	*E. faecalis*
	E. faecium
	E. avium
	E. casseliflavus
	E. durans
	E. raffinosus
	E. gallinarum
	E. malodoratus
	E. hirae
	E. mundtii
	E. pseudoavium
	E. dispar
	E. flavescens
	E. sulfureus
Atypical enterococci (PYR −)	E. *cecorum*
	E. *columbae*
	E. *saccharolyticus*

PYR, pyrrolidonyl arylamidase.

optimal therapy for endocarditis and other serious enterococcal infections. A panel of biologic tests can differentiate these two common enterococcal species readily.[53, 93, 134] Most *E. faecalis* isolates (unlike those of *E. faecium*) grow in the presence of 0.04 percent tellurite, reduce tetrazolium to formazan, and produce acid from sorbitol and glycerol.

A variety of molecular techniques, including a modification of pulsed-field gel electrophoresis known as the CHEF (contour-clamped homogeneous electric field electrophoresis) technique[30, 31, 42, 131, 212] and polymerase chain reaction (PCR), are available to assist in the identification of enterococci and determination of the relatedness of enterococcal isolates.[45] These molecular techniques have been particularly valuable in investigations of possible nosocomial transmission of multiresistant enterococci.[30, 31, 42, 45, 53, 131, 153, 172, 212]

Epidemiology

Enterococci are normal flora of the gastrointestinal tract of most humans and have been found in as many as 97 percent of fecal samples from adults in Europe, Asia, and North America (reviewed by Murray[134]). Approximately one half of newborn infants have become colonized with enterococci by 1 week of age.[146] Enterococci are isolated less commonly (<20% of specimens) from other sites, including the vagina, oral cavity, and skin. These organisms also are common inhabitants of the bowel flora of many animals and frequently are present in soil, water, and foods. Enterococci are hardy organisms and may persist for long periods on environmental surfaces, contributing to the potential nosocomial spread of these bacteria.

Human infection by enterococci was reported before the beginning of the 20th century, but the initial patients had infections that uncommonly are associated with enterococci today: enteritis, meningitis, and appendicitis (reviewed by Murray[134]). The ubiquitous presence of enterococci in fecal samples led to the mistaken impression that these organisms caused enteritis and food poisoning. Enterococci are isolated commonly as part of mixed flora in intra-abdominal and pelvic infections, but the contribution of these organisms to the pathogenesis of such infections remains uncertain.[65, 144] However, enterococci were identified as pathogens causing urinary tract infection and endocarditis as early as 1906,[2] with later confirmation made by many studies. Subsequently, enterococci have been documented to cause invasive infection in neonates,[41, 61, 96] patients with malignancies,[69, 70, 130, 184] recipients of bone marrow and solid organ transplants,[7, 91, 94, 154, 175] burn victims,[102] patients with indwelling catheters,[7, 39, 124, 134, 156, 169] and other immunosuppressed or debilitated patients.[21, 124, 134, 156, 169]

In general, enterococcal infections occur less frequently in children (outside the neonatal period) than in adults, and enterococci are less common causes of pediatric (versus adult) urinary tract infection[216] and endocarditis.[193] Much of the published experience with enterococcal infection in children focuses on the neonatal period,[36, 41, 113, 164] and some evidence suggests that late-onset (but not early-onset) neonatal enterococcal infection may be increasing in frequency.[30, 41] Relatively few series of pediatric enterococcal infection have been published.[11, 13, 30, 39, 69, 171]

Enterococci recently have emerged as important nosocomial agents, and they rank as either the second or third most common hospital-acquired pathogens in this country.[47, 82, 123, 151, 176] Evidence of nosocomial spread of enterococci is relatively recent. Initially, all enterococci isolated from hospitalized patients were thought to have originated from the patient's endogenous bowel flora. However, the emergence of multiantibiotic-resistant enterococci prompted the performance of careful epidemiologic studies that documented the nosocomial spread of these organisms.* Many groups have reported that VRE and other enterococci may persist for long periods in the environment and may be spread by either direct patient-to-patient contact via the hands of colonized health care personnel[164] or from contaminated beds or other hospital materials or through contaminated patient equipment, including thermometers.[14, 92, 107]

Of emphasis is that the growing problem of nosocomial infection by VRE is multifactorial; the diversity of isolates found in many hospitals indicates that resistant organisms may be introduced via multiple sources.[30, 46, 62, 132, 137, 169, 184] Consequently, outbreaks of VRE in institutions may be caused by single or multiple clones, although the first recognized outbreak of VRE infection or colonization in a hospital usually is associated with a single clone.[21, 62]

In many reports, separating risk factors for the acquisition of VRE from those for invasive disease caused by these organisms has not been possible, and certain factors probably increase the risk for both VRE colonization and infection. Major risk factors for the acquisition of VRE or for development of infection, or for both, appear to be the severity of underlying illness or immunosuppression; the proximity to patients colonized with VRE (e.g., admission to an intensive care unit [ICU] or a transplant unit); receipt of a bone marrow or solid organ (especially liver) transplant; increasing length of hospital stay; recent cardiothoracic or abdominal surgery; the presence of indwelling central venous or urinary catheters; and previous treatment with vancomycin, broad-spectrum antibiotics (particularly those lacking appreciable anti-enterococcal activity, such as the third-generation cephalosporins), or agents with broad anti-anaerobic activity.† In one recent report, patients with a history of human immunodeficiency virus (HIV) infection also were found to be at higher risk for development of VRE bacteremia.[7] The factors contributing to nosocomial spread of these organisms probably differ from those responsible for the gradual overall increase in resistant strains.[169]

Since the first report of a vancomycin-resistant isolate in 1988,[103] infection and colonization with VRE in the United States have been observed primarily in the ICUs of large teaching hospitals.[136, 138, 151] For example, data reported to the National Nosocomial Infections Surveillance System (NNIS) of the Centers for Disease Control and Prevention (CDC) from January 1989 through March 1993 revealed no vancomycin resistance in hospitals with fewer than 200 beds, a resistance rate of 1.8 percent in hospitals with 200 to 500 beds, and a rate of 3.6 percent in hospitals with more than 500 beds.[151] A 1995 report from the multicenter *Enterococcus* Study Group analyzed 1936 isolates collected from 97 laboratories in 47 states during the last quarter of 1992 and generally confirmed the findings of the NNIS survey.[87] However, infections with VRE are not limited to ICUs. A recent report from the Surveillance and Control of Pathogens of Epidemiologic Importance (SCOPE) group's ongoing surveillance of nosocomial bloodstream infections in 49 U.S. hospitals revealed no overall differences in rates of vancomycin resistance in enterococci isolated from patients located in critical care versus hospital ward settings.[47] Fortunately, VRE infections in children have occurred much less frequently than in adults, and overall

*See references 14, 15, 21, 46, 92, 107, 130, 151, 164, 169, 171, 181, 183, 184.

†See references 14, 21, 43, 44, 62, 75, 107, 130, 163, 171.

rates of vancomycin resistance in enterococci isolated from children's hospitals remain very low. However, increasing numbers of pediatric centers have reported VRE infections.*

In the United States, VRE generally have not been detected in environmental sources or in patients who have not had exposure to hospitals,[136] with rare exceptions.[21] However, the ecology of VRE in Europe differs: VRE have been detected in the feces of nonhospitalized patients and healthy volunteers in several European studies, with rates of VRE colonization as high as 28 percent in adults living in some parts of Belgium (reviewed by Murray[136, 138]). The more widespread occurrence of VRE strains in Europe probably is related to the use of oral glycopeptides such as avoparcin in animal feed and the oral administration of bacterial preparations (possibly contaminated with resistant enterococci) to humans and animals for therapeutic purposes.[136–138]

Initial reports of VRE in the United States were clustered in the northeast region, particularly New York, Maryland, and Pennsylvania,[151] and geographic differences in rates of VRE colonization and infection persist. However, the problem certainly is not limited to one area of the country. Jones and colleagues and the *Enterococcus* Study Group found that all participating laboratories reporting VRE isolates in late 1992 were east of the Mississippi River; most were focused around New York City.[88] However, a follow-up telephone survey in March 1994 revealed that 37 of 75 medical centers not previously reporting VRE subsequently had identified these organisms from one or more clinical specimens, thus expanding the geographic distribution of VRE to include the West Coast (California and Washington), the South (Texas, Florida, and Louisiana), and the North (North Dakota, Michigan, and Wisconsin).[88] Subsequent reports indicate that VRE are found in most parts of the United States and that rates of vancomycin resistance among enterococci isolated from patients in the United States generally are higher than those found in isolates from Canada, western Europe, or Latin America.[111] The reasons for these geographic differences remain uncertain, but the high rates of resistance in the United States may be related to the marked increase in the use of vancomycin in this country during the past 2 decades.[95]

Pathogenesis and Virulence

Enterococci are organisms of low virulence, and their ubiquitous presence in the human gastrointestinal tract probably has contributed to both the spurious association of these organisms with some illnesses (e.g., enteritis) and the failure to recognize other situations in which enterococci are true pathogens (e.g., immunosuppressed and debilitated patients, neonates). When compared with organisms such as *S. pyogenes* and *Staphylococcus aureus,* enterococci are much less virulent in animal models of infection,[83, 123] but they are capable of causing disease at a higher inoculum.

Enterococci rarely cause primary cellulitis or abscesses, although these organisms are isolated frequently as components of polymicrobial wound infections and intra-abdominal and pelvic infections. The contribution of enterococci to the pathogenesis of these polymicrobial infections remains uncertain.[65, 144] In animal models, synergy between enterococci and a variety of other organisms (particularly anaerobes) can be demonstrated, but enterococci injected alone have little propensity to cause either peritonitis or subcutaneous infection.[83, 84, 134, 152] Many clinical trials have concluded that provision of anti-enterococcal therapy generally is not necessary to effect a cure of human intra-abdominal and pelvic infections, even though *Enterococcus* frequently (14–33% of cases) is isolated from primary peritoneal cultures.[65]

Enterococci are an important cause of urinary tract infections in adults (particularly in elderly men, patients with structural abnormalities of the urinary tract, and those with indwelling urinary catheters), but they are associated less frequently with urinary tract infections in children.[5, 216] Enterococci also are important but less frequent (than in adults) causes of bacterial endocarditis in children.[122, 193] Adherence of bacteria to tissue is a necessary first step in the pathogenesis of both urinary tract infection and endocarditis, and evidence suggests that pathogenic enterococci produce factors that mediate adherence to urinary epithelial cells and endocardial tissue (reviewed by Jett and colleagues[83] and Johnson[84]). Enterococcal adhesins include an enterococcal surface protein known as aggregation substance[27, 98] and surface carbohydrates. Lipoteichoic acid, an important adhesin for *S. pyogenes*, does not appear to mediate adherence of enterococci,[190] but it may trigger the host inflammatory response to these organisms.[198]

Nosocomial enterococcal bacteremia in adults frequently is associated with urinary tract and wound infection, but catheter-related bacteremia is of increasing importance. Enterococcal bacteremia without a source occurs relatively more commonly in children,[13, 169] although Bonadio[11] reported that many children with enterococcal bacteremia had an identifiable focus of infection. Enterococcal bacteremia occurs more frequently in patients with severe underlying disease and may be life-threatening. However, the precise contribution of enterococcal bacteremia to morbidity and mortality in severely ill patients remains controversial. Adult ICU patients with enterococcal bacteremia have a very high mortality rate,[67] and some early studies suggested that isolation of *Enterococcus* from the blood merely served to identify a very high-risk group of patients.[134] In several studies, clearance of VRE from the blood was not associated with a reduced mortality rate in this high-risk population. In other studies, spontaneous resolution of VRE bacteremia has been reported, thus suggesting that transient VRE bacteremia or pseudobacteremia (or both) may occur.[204] However, a series of recent studies concluded that effective anti-enterococcal therapy reduces mortality in these patients.[46, 78, 138, 156] Taken together, these findings indicate that at least a subset of high-risk patients with VRE bacteremia are at risk for development of significant morbidity and mortality directly related to the infection.

Clinical Manifestations

Enterococcal infections generally occur less commonly in children than in adults, but *Enterococcus* is a relatively frequent cause of neonatal infections.[41] The types of infections caused by enterococci in children are similar to those in adults,[11, 13, 39, 169] although enterococcal bacteremia may be associated with fewer sequelae in children.[39] In children, as well as in adults, enterococci have become increasingly important nosocomial pathogens.[13, 30, 119, 123, 151] Enterococci are important causes of endocarditis, urinary tract infection, and bacteremia (particularly catheter-related bacteremia) in children, and these organisms are isolated commonly as components of polymicrobial wound, intra-abdominal, and pelvic infections.[11, 13, 124, 134] Meningitis[194] and septic arthritis[162] are rare manifestations of enterococcal infection. Respiratory

*See references 8, 9, 31, 32, 71, 77, 164, 169, 171, 191, 209.

infections caused by enterococci are extremely uncommon, although many neonates with enterococcal infection have pulmonary symptoms.[41]

URINARY TRACT INFECTION

Urinary tract infections are the most common enterococcal infections in adults,[124] and enterococci are important urinary pathogens in children.[40] Most enterococcal urinary tract infections occur in elderly men after undergoing urinary catheterization, instrumentation, or both.[55, 133] Enterococci are infrequent (<5% of isolates) causes of cystitis and pyelonephritis in otherwise healthy children, infants, and neonates[5, 216] and are unusual causes of urinary tract infection in young women.[134] However, some centers are reporting an increasing incidence of both community-acquired and nosocomial urinary tract infection caused by enterococci.[55]

Most enterococcal urinary tract infections in children[5, 40, 108] and adults[55, 123] are nosocomial. Risk factors for development of urinary tract infection by *Enterococcus* include indwelling urinary catheters, instrumentation of the urinary tract, structural abnormalities of the urinary tract, and previous broad-spectrum antimicrobial therapy.[133, 134] The increasing problem of nosocomial enterococcal urinary tract infection[55] is compounded by the growing problem of multi-antibiotic-resistant enterococci.[151]

The genitourinary tract reportedly is the most common entry site leading to enterococcal bacteremia in adults,[67, 99] but it is implicated much less frequently in the etiology of enterococcal bacteremia in children.[11, 13, 39] Christie and colleagues reported that urosepsis was the etiology of 12 percent of episodes of nosocomial enterococcal bacteremia in one children's hospital,[30] but Das and Gray[39] failed to detect any cases of urosepsis in 75 consecutive cases of enterococcal bacteremia in another pediatric hospital during a 3-year period. Other complications of enterococcal urinary tract infection in adults include prostatitis and perinephric abscess.[124]

ENDOCARDITIS

Enterococcal endocarditis was reported first in 1906,[2] and these organisms are important causes of native- and prosthetic-valve endocarditis in children and adults.[1, 122, 167] Either normal or previously damaged valves may be involved. Enterococci cause approximately 5 to 20 percent of cases of native-valve endocarditis in adults (excluding cases in intravenous drug users),[122] approximately 6 to 7 percent of prosthetic-valve endocarditis,[122, 201] and approximately 5 to 10 percent of endocarditis in intravenous drug users.[134] Enterococcal endocarditis in intravenous drug users generally involves the aortic or mitral valves, unlike staphylococcal endocarditis in this setting, which usually involves the tricuspid valve.[134] As with other enterococcal infections, *E. faecalis* causes most cases of endocarditis.

Enterococcal endocarditis primarily is a disease of older men, and the genitourinary tract is the most commonly identified source of the initial bacteremia. Enterococci are relatively less frequent causes of endocarditis in children–less than 5 percent of cases in most series.[85, 86, 192, 193, 199, 218] Typically, enterococcal endocarditis occurs after a subacute course that is clinically indistinguishable from that caused by streptococci.[122] Although the enterococcus is a common neonatal pathogen,[41] reports of neonatal enterococcal endocarditis are extremely rare.[199] The prognosis of enterococcal prosthetic-valve endocarditis is somewhat better than that of native-valve endocarditis caused by these organisms.[1, 167] Aortic-valve involvement is associated with increased morbidity and mortality.[122] Endocarditis rarely complicates nosocomial enterococcal bacteremia.[115, 134, 156]

BACTEREMIA

Enterococcal bacteremia often represents a conundrum. Bacteremia in severely ill hospitalized patients, particularly that caused by VRE, is associated with considerable morbidity and mortality. However, only a portion of that morbidity and mortality can be attributed directly to enterococcal bacteremia per se. Nosocomial enterococcal bacteremia frequently occurs as a component of polymicrobial bacteremia, with 21 to 45 percent of bloodstream isolates of *Enterococcus* being accompanied by one or more other pathogens.[39, 115, 156, 187] As many as one half of cases of catheter-related enterococcal bacteremia are polymicrobial.[119, 156] Many[74, 115] but not all[78, 119] series of patients with enterococcal bacteremia have reported increased mortality rates in patients with polymicrobial bacteremia (including *Enterococcus*) versus isolated enterococcal bacteremia. Mortality in adults with nosocomial enterococcal bacteremia has ranged from 23 to 46 percent,[115, 116, 156] but patients at risk for acquisition of nosocomial enterococcal bacteremia are severely ill and have a poor prognosis independent of the bacteremic event. Hospital-acquired enterococcal infections can be life-threatening,[46, 134, 156] and specific therapy does appear to reduce the mortality rate.[46, 78, 156] Nonetheless, many episodes of enterococcal bacteremia in high-risk patients apparently resolve in the absence of specific therapy.[78, 204] The mortality rate associated with enterococcal bacteremia in children has been lower than that reported in adults in most studies but has ranged from 7.5 percent[39] to 12 percent[13] to 20 percent[11] to 26 percent,[30] depending on the population studied.

In adults, most cases of enterococcal bacteremia are associated with a primary focus, most commonly a urinary tract infection.[69, 101] In contrast, few children with enterococcal bacteremia have urosepsis, and most episodes of enterococcal bacteremia in children have not been associated with any identifiable focus.[13, 169] However, Christie and associates identified a primary focus in 21 of 57 children (37%) with nosocomial enterococcal bacteremia, including 7 patients with urosepsis and 6 with peritonitis.[30] Many children with enterococcal bacteremia do have underlying disease involving the gastrointestinal or respiratory tract.[11, 13] Central venous catheter–related enterococcal bacteremia is a growing problem in both children[11, 13, 30, 39, 41, 156] and adults.[67, 156] In earlier series, infections of vascular catheters were reported to account for only 2 to 14 percent of enterococcal bacteremias (reviewed by Graninger and Ragette[67]), but recent reports have implicated intravascular devices in as many as 22 to 28 percent of these episodes in adults and children.[39, 156]

Most episodes of enterococcal bacteremia do not lead to endocarditis,[115, 134, 156] and endocarditis is particularly uncommon in the setting of nosocomial enterococcal bacteremia. Maki and Agger[115] identified only 1 case of endocarditis in 118 episodes of hospital-acquired enterococcal bacteremia, whereas endocarditis was diagnosed in 12 of 35 patients with community-acquired enterococcal bacteremia.

INTRA-ABDOMINAL INFECTIONS

Most of the published information about the role of *Enterococcus* in intra-abdominal and pelvic infections comes from series of adult patients. Enterococci commonly are isolated as components of polymicrobial infections involving the abdomen or pelvis,[65] and animal models suggest that these organisms can play a synergistic role in the pathogenesis of such infections.[83] However, evidence that the addition of specific anti-enterococcal therapy improves the outcome of human intra-abdominal and pelvic infections, even when enterococci are isolated from peritoneal cultures, is not compelling.[65]

Children with enterococcal bacteremia frequently have underlying conditions related to the gastrointestinal tract.[11, 13, 30] Bonadio reported five cases of enterococcal bacteremia in previously healthy infants with gastroenteritis, six cases associated with bowel obstruction, and one case associated with acute appendicitis without perforation.[11] Boulanger and coworkers[13] identified underlying conditions affecting the gastrointestinal system in 8 of 32 pediatric patients, but they were unable to implicate specifically any of these conditions as the source of the bacteremia. Das and Gray detected underlying chronic gastrointestinal pathology (short-gut syndrome, congenital anomalies of the gastrointestinal tract, ulcerative colitis, chronic liver disease) in fully one third (25 of 75) of pediatric patients with enterococcal bacteremia.[39]

MENINGITIS

Enterococci are rare causes of bacterial meningitis in adults and children. Stevenson and colleagues[194] found only 4 cases of enterococcal meningitis among 493 episodes (0.8%) of bacterial meningitis in adults, and they identified an additional 90 cases in a literature search of the interval 1966 to 1992. These authors reviewed 16 published cases of enterococcal meningitis in children: 11 of these 16 pediatric cases were complications of central nervous system (CNS) trauma or surgery, but 4 children (3 of the 4 were neonates) had primary meningitis.[194] Enterococci are uncommon but well-recognized causes of infection involving cerebrospinal fluid shunts and related devices.[97, 140, 179] Meningitis rarely complicates nosocomial bacteremia in adults[115, 156] but has been reported more frequently in children (particularly neonates) with bacteremia. For example, meningitis developed in 7 percent (4 of 57) of episodes of nosocomial enterococcal bacteremia in children in Cincinnati[30] and in 15 percent (4 of 26) of premature neonates with late-onset enterococcal sepsis in Houston.[41]

Stevenson and associates found that most adults with enterococcal meningitis were immunocompromised (most were receiving steroids) or had a history of CNS trauma or surgery (or both).[194] Enterococcal meningitis has been reported in one adult patient with HIV infection who had completed a course of steroids for presumed *Pneumocystis* pneumonia.[158] Although many children with enterococcal meningitis do have a history of CNS trauma or surgery or are premature infants, most do not have other identifiable predisposing conditions or a history of immunosuppressive therapy.

As with most enterococcal infections, most isolates from cerebrospinal fluid are *E. faecalis,* although meningitis and ventriculoperitoneal shunt infections caused by *E. faecium* have been reported in children.[140, 141]

NEONATAL INFECTIONS

Enterococci are important neonatal pathogens,* and the published experience with neonatal enterococcal infections constitutes much of the pediatric experience with these organisms. Although several large series of neonatal sepsis included few cases of enterococcal infection (reviewed by Klein and Marcy[96]), many centers have reported that *Enterococcus* is a relatively frequent cause of neonatal bacteremia. Siegel and McCracken[189] found that enterococci were second only to group B streptococci as causes of neonatal sepsis at Parkland Hospital in Dallas from 1974 to 1977, with an incidence rate of approximately 1.0 case per 1000 live births. Gladstone and colleagues[61] reported that *Enterococcus* caused 18 of 270 (6.7%) episodes of neonatal sepsis at Yale–New Haven Hospital during the period 1979 to 1988, which ranks fourth in incidence behind group B streptococci (64 cases, 23.7%), *Escherichia coli* (46 cases, 17.0%), and coagulase-negative staphylococci (36 cases, 13.3%). During the 1990s, reports from Houston,[41] Cincinnati,[30] and New York City[119] documented sharp increases in the rate of late-onset neonatal infection with enterococci in both hospitalized high-risk premature neonates and infants[41, 119] and otherwise healthy term newborns with "community-acquired" infextion.[33]

Enterococci cause both early-onset (<7 days of age) and late-onset (>7 days of age) neonatal sepsis. Early-onset disease is indistinguishable from that caused by other neonatal pathogens, but it tends to be less severe.[41] Rates of early-onset disease have remained relatively stable; however, several centers are reporting increasing rates of late-onset infection. Dobson and Baker identified 56 neonates with enterococcal sepsis during a 10-year period at Jefferson Davis Hospital in Houston: 18 of 56 (32%) had early-onset sepsis, 26 of 56 (46%) had late-onset sepsis, and 12 of 56 (21%) had sepsis associated with necrotizing enterocolitis (2 early onset, 10 late onset).[41] In this study, 25 of the 26 infants (96%) with late-onset enterococcal sepsis were premature infants. Christie and colleagues[30] identified 83 cases of enterococcal bacteremia between 1986 and 1992 at Children's Hospital of Cincinnati: 58 of the 83 episodes occurred in neonates. Most cases (57 of 83, 68.7%) were nosocomial, but many (26 of 83, 31.3%) were community acquired. Young infants (<3 months of age) accounted for almost all (24 of 26, 92.3%) of the community-acquired episodes and for many (34 of 57, 59.6%) of the nosocomial infections. Bonadio[11] and Boulanger and colleagues[13] also have reported community-acquired enterococcal bacteremia in young infants.

McNeeley and associates[119] identified 138 episodes of enterococcal bacteremia in a New York City neonatal ICU during a 20-year period and reviewed 100 of the episodes in detail. These authors noted a sharp increase in the rate of enterococcal bacteremia during the second decade (1984 to 1994) of this study and found that most cases occurred in older infants: during this decade, the mean age at onset was 44.7 days (versus 16.1 days during the first decade of the study), and 65 percent (51 of 78) of the episodes occurred after 30 days of age. Most of the infections occurred in neonates with indwelling central venous catheters (77%), and more than one half the patients had evidence of gastrointestinal disease (necrotizing enterocolitis in 33% and abdominal distention in an additional 21%). The overall mortality in this study was 28 percent, although many of the deaths were not attributed to the enterococcal infection. Most (64%) of the episodes of enterococcal bacteremia in this series were polymicrobial.[119]

Nosocomial outbreaks of enterococcal infection, including those caused by VRE, have been reported in several neonatal units in the United States.[30, 36, 113, 164] Indwelling central venous catheters, necrotizing enterocolitis, and intra-abdominal surgery are important predisposing factors for development of nosocomial enterococcal bacteremia in neonates, whereas the genitourinary tract is implicated much less frequently as a source.[30, 119]

Enterococcal bacteremia in neonates and young infants has been associated with diarrhea[11, 41] and with respiratory disease,[11, 41] but a causative role for *Enterococcus* in the pathogenesis of gastroenteritis or pneumonia remains

*See references 11, 13, 36, 41, 61, 96, 113, 119, 164, 189.

undefined. Enterococci rarely cause urinary tract infections in neonates,[11, 30, 41, 119] but nosocomial and community-acquired cases have been reported. Enterococci have been noted to cause a variety of other neonatal infections, including focal skin and soft tissue infections such as scalp abscess,[41] brain abscess,[170] omphalitis,[41] and conjunctivitis.[208]

Most enterococcal infections in neonates are caused by *E. faecalis,* but outbreaks of infection with *E. faecium* have been reported.[36] In the series from Cincinnati reported by Christie and associates and consisting largely of neonates, 82 percent of enterococcal isolates were *E. faecalis* and 14 percent were *E. faecium.*[30] McNeeley and colleagues reported the isolation of *E. faecalis* from 94 of 100 patients and *E. faecium* from 15 of 100 patients in their series (both organisms were isolated from 9 of the patients).[119] Six of the *E. faecium* isolates were resistant to vancomycin, and all six patients with VRE bacteremia died, although only one death appeared to be directly related to the VRE infection.

SEPTIC ARTHRITIS

Enterococci rarely have been reported to cause septic arthritis but can infect native or prosthetic joints. Raymond and colleagues[162] reported a case of enterococcal septic arthritis involving a prosthetic hip and reviewed an additional 18 cases from the literature. Eleven of these 19 episodes involved prosthetic joints (2 hips, 9 knees), and 8 involved native joints; only 1 of the 8 individuals with native-joint arthritis had an underlying abnormality of the joint. In 7 of the 19 episodes, enterococcus was isolated from synovial fluid along with a second organism (3 with coagulase-negative staphylococci, 1 with group B streptococci, 1 with *Pseudomonas,* 1 with *Streptococcus,* and 1 with *Kingella kingae*). Only one pediatric case was identified: a 21-month-old girl with septic arthritis of the wrist whose joint aspirate grew *Enterococcus* spp. and *K. kingae.*[188]

Diagnosis

Enterococcal infections usually are diagnosed by isolation of *Enterococcus* from a culture of blood or another normally sterile site. As discussed earlier, enterococci are ubiquitous inhabitants of the human gastrointestinal tract, and isolation of these organisms from stool or surface cultures is not evidence of invasive infection. Although enterococci are uncommon blood culture contaminants, transient bacteremia or pseudobacteremia (or both) may be caused by these organisms.[78, 204]

More problematic is the interpretation of a positive culture for enterococcus as a component of polymicrobial infections, particularly intra-abdominal and pelvic infections. In this setting, the role of the enterococcus in pathogenesis is uncertain, and therapeutic regimens that do not include anti-enterococcal agents usually suffice to effect a clinical cure.[65] However, rare cases of breakthrough enterococcal bacteremia have been reported with these regimens, and one study found a decreased rate of abdominal surgical wound infections when anti-enterococcal coverage was provided in a prophylactic regimen.[210]

Antimicrobial Susceptibility and Resistance

The increasing importance of *Enterococcus* as a human pathogen, especially in the nosocomial setting,[47, 119, 123, 151] is of particular concern because of the concomitant development of antimicrobial resistance by these organisms. Some enterococci have acquired high-level resistance to all three classes of antimicrobial agents that have been used to treat life-threatening enterococcal infections—β-lactams, aminoglycosides, and glycopeptides. This acquired resistance has occurred in the context of intrinsic (usually lower-level) resistance of enterococci to many antibiotics, and physicians have been confronted with the possibility that invasive disease caused by these organisms might not respond to any antibiotics currently available.

INTRINSIC RESISTANCE

β-Lactam Antibiotics

Relative resistance to β-lactam antibiotics is an intrinsic characteristic of enterococci that occurs even in human populations without previous exposure to antibiotics[125]; such resistance is due to the lower affinity of enterococcal (versus streptococcal) penicillin-binding proteins, especially PBP-5.[124, 213] In general, the penicillin minimal inhibitory concentration (MIC) for most *E. faecalis* isolates (2–8 μg/mL) is at least 10 to 100 times higher than that of most streptococci, and *E. faecium* is even more resistant (MIC of 8–32 μg/mL or higher).[134] Ampicillin is the most active of the β-lactam antibiotics against enterococci, with average MIC values approximately twofold lower than those for penicillin.[124, 134] Nafcillin generally is less active than is penicillin, and methicillin is much less active (MIC >50 μg/mL for *E. faecalis*), as are carbenicillin and ticarcillin. Enterococci exposed to β-lactam antibiotics rapidly become tolerant to the killing effects of these agents.[124, 134] Along with intrinsic resistance to these agents, such tolerance limits the utility of β-lactam monotherapy for the treatment of life-threatening enterococcal infections.

Imipenem has some activity against *E. faecalis* but is much less active against *E. faecium.*[124, 134] None of the cephalosporins currently available has clinically useful activity against the enterococci, and frequent use of broad-spectrum cephalosporins and imipenem has been identified as a risk factor for acquisition of nosocomial enterococcal infection.

Aminoglycosides

Enterococci are intrinsically resistant to all aminoglycosides because of diminished uptake of these drugs. For most *E. faecalis* isolates, the MIC for gentamicin or tobramycin ranges from 8 to 64 μg/mL, and that for streptomycin ranges from 12 to 250 μg/mL.[121, 157, 202] Moellering and colleagues first demonstrated that the addition of a cell wall–active antibiotic results in dramatically increased aminoglycoside uptake by enterococci[127, 221] and that combinations of β-lactam and aminoglycoside antibiotics can lead to synergistic killing of these organisms. All *E. faecium* strains exhibit higher MICs (than *E. faecalis* does) to certain aminoglycosides, including tobramycin, netilmicin, kanamycin, and sisomicin, and these aminoglycosides do not exhibit synergy with β-lactam antibiotics against *E. faecium.*[25, 134]

Other Antibiotics

Under carefully standardized laboratory conditions, enterococci are inhibited by the combination of trimethoprim and sulfamethoxazole (TMP-SMX). However, *Enterococcus* isolates should be considered resistant to TMP-SMX because these organisms are capable of using exogenous folinic acid to evade the antimicrobial action of TMP-SMX.[220] TMP-SMX fails to eradicate enterococci in animal models of infection,[22, 72] and breakthrough enterococcal bacteremia has occurred in patients being treated with TMP-SMX for enterococcal urinary tract infection.[64] Enterococci also are intrinsically resistant to clindamycin, a drug with excellent activity against many other gram-positive cocci. Most enterococci have a clindamycin MIC of 12.5 to 100 µg/mL.[134] As with low-level β-lactam resistance, clindamycin resistance is found in enterococcal isolates from human populations with no previous antibiotic exposure.[125]

ACQUIRED RESISTANCE

Enterococci have acquired resistance to antibiotics by the acquisition of both narrow- and broad-host range plasmids and via the exchange of conjugative transposons (reviewed by Murray[134]). Resistance mediated by broad-host range plasmids is of particular concern because glycopeptide resistance encoded by broad-host range plasmids has been transferred to staphylococci in vitro[147] and theoretically could be transmitted to important human pathogens such as *S. aureus* or *Streptococcus pneumoniae.*

High-Level Resistance to Aminoglycosides

Intrinsic resistance of enterococci to aminoglycosides is caused by poor drug uptake by these organisms and can be overcome effectively both in vitro and in vivo by the addition of cell wall–active antibiotics. In contrast, high-level resistance to aminoglycosides is mediated either by the acquisition of plasmids encoding aminoglycoside-modifying enzymes (affecting all aminoglycosides via several different enzymes) or by ribosomal mutations (streptomycin only). High-level aminoglycoside resistance is of great clinical importance because it eliminates synergism between the affected aminoglycoside or aminoglycosides and β-lactam or glycopeptide antibiotics.[25, 134, 157] All *E. faecium* strains produce a chromosomally encoded aminoglycoside acetyltransferase that eliminates synergistic killing between cell wall–active antibiotics and certain aminoglycosides (including tobramycin, kanamycin, netilmicin, and sisomicin),[25] but it does not result in high-level resistance to these compounds. Consequently, these particular aminoglycosides should not be used to treat infections caused by *E. faecium.*

Enterococci with high-level resistance (MIC usually ≥2000 µg/mL) to streptomycin, kanamycin, and several other aminoglycosides (excluding gentamicin) were identified more than 30 years ago[128] and were widely prevalent in the United States by the mid-1970s.[18] High-level resistance to streptomycin occurs via two mechanisms, ribosomal mutation or enzymatic modification by 6′-adenylyltransferase. Initial reports of high-level resistance to kanamycin were associated with the production of 3′-phosphotransferase.[25, 134]

Horodniceanu and colleagues first reported high-level resistance to gentamicin in *E. faecalis* in 1979,[80] and this resistance was later shown to be mediated by a fusion enzyme containing both 6′-acetyltransferase and 2″-phosphotransferase activity. Expression of this fusion enzyme conferred resistance to all clinically useful aminoglycosides except streptomycin.[104, 105] Enterococci expressing this fusion protein usually have MICs to gentamicin that are 2000 µg/mL or higher. Thus, enterococci expressing this fusion enzyme and the 6′-adenylyltransferase mediating streptomycin resistance (or chromosomally mediated streptomycin resistance) are highly resistant to all available aminoglycosides and generally fail to be killed synergistically by any combination of β-lactam antibiotics and aminoglycosides. Strains of *E. faecalis* resistant to both streptomycin and gentamicin (and thus to all aminoglycosides) were detected first in Houston, Bangkok, and Santiago in 1983.[121, 134] Subsequently, strains of *E. faecalis, E. faecium,* and other enterococci resistant to gentamicin, streptomycin, or both (all) aminoglycosides have become increasingly prevalent[66, 88, 111, 157] (Table 89–2). Although high-level resistance to both streptomycin and gentamicin was described first in *E. faecalis,* it now is at least as common in *E. faecium.*[88] Many medical centers in the United States now report that most enterococcal isolates exhibit high-level resistance to all aminoglycosides.[138]

Several new aminoglycoside-resistant genes were identified in enterococci during the late 1990s (reviewed by Chow[25]). In all, nine different aminoglycoside-modifying enzymes have been characterized, and some enterococci produce three or more enzymes. Strains expressing some of the recently described resistant genes may fail to exhibit synergy between gentamicin and β-lactams despite MICs below those usually associated with high-level resistance. For example, the aph (2″)-Ic gene[28] recently found in clinical isolates of both *E. faecalis* and *E. faecium* results in gentamicin MICs of approximately 256 to 384 µg/mL, lower than the standard screening cutoff for high-level resistance to gentamicin (500 µg/mL). Nonetheless, these organisms are resistant to ampicillin-gentamicin synergism and would not be detected by standard screening methods (see later).

High-Level Resistance to β-Lactams and Production of β-Lactamase

The mechanism of resistance to penicillin, ampicillin, and other β-lactam antibiotics differs among enterococcal species. The high-level β-lactam resistance (ampicillin MIC ≥16 µg/mL) of *E. faecium*[15, 71, 118] and some other non-*faecalis* enterococcal strains[15] has increased considerably during the past decade and is mediated by additional alterations in PBPs, particularly PBP-5.[56, 71, 168] Thus, high-level resistance to ampicillin and other β-lactams in *E. faecium* (and other non-*faecalis* strains) represents an exaggerated form of intrinsic β-lactam resistance. *E. faecalis* isolates also are intrinsically resistant to β-lactams (though less so than *E. faecium*), but little change has occurred in the level of this resistance in recent years. However, some strains of *E. faecalis*[87, 135, 139]—and a single isolate of *E. faecium*[35]—have acquired clinically significant resistance to ampicillin and penicillin via the plasmid-mediated, constitutive production of a β-lactamase enzyme identical to that of *S. aureus.*[222] β-Lactamase–producing strains of *E. faecalis* and *E. faecium* will not be detected by routine susceptibility testing because of a pronounced inoculum effect. Therefore, enzymatic methods such as the nitrocefin test must be used to screen for β-lactamase–producing strains.[93, 135]

Glycopeptide Resistance

VRE were identified first in 1988[103, 205] and rapidly have become a major nosocomial problem. Data collected by the NNIS of the CDC revealed a dramatic increase in the rate of vancomycin resistance in nosocomial isolates of *Enterococcus* during the interval 1989 to 1993.[151] The NNIS survey documented a 26-fold increase in vancomycin resistance among all nosocomial isolates (from 0.3% of enterococcal isolates in 1989 to 7.9% in 1993) and a 34-fold increase in vancomycin resistance among isolates obtained from patients in ICUs (from 0.4% of isolates in 1989 to 13.6% in

TABLE 89–2 ■ ANTIMICROBIAL RESISTANCE PATTERNS OF ENTEROCOCCI

	Gordon et al.[66] (July 1988–April 1989)			Jones et al.[88] (*Enterococcus* Study Group) October 1992–December 1992			Edmond et al.[47] (April 1995–April 1998) (Bloodstream Isolates)			Low et al.[111] (SENTRY Antimicrobial Resistance Surveillance Program) (1997–1999)
	E. faecalis (*n* = 632)	*E. faecium* (*n* = 58)	Total (*n* = 705)	*E. faecalis* (*n* = 1428)	*E. faecium* (*n* = 306)	Total (*n* = 1936)	*E. faecalis* (*n* = 598)	*E. faecium* (*n* = 303)	Total (*n* = 1354)	Total Enterococcal Isolates (*n* = 2303)
Ampicillin resistance (MIC = 16 μg/mL)	0%*	41%†	4%	0.6–0.7%‡	58.7–59.3%	12%	2.7%	81.1%	NA	24%
Streptomycin high-level resistance (MIC >2000 μg/mL)	14%	33%	16%	31.5%	55.7%	36%	NA	NA	NA	40%
Gentamicin high-level resistance (MIC >500 μg/mL)	11%	2%	10%	26.0%	30.8%	27%	NA	NA	NA	31%
Vancomycin resistance (MIC >4 μg/mL)	0.3%	0%	0.3%	2.0%	21.9%	5.6%	3.2%	50.5%	17.7%	17%
Teicoplanin resistance (MIC >4 μg/mL)	0%	0%	0%	0.1%	16%	3.2%	NA	NA	NA	14%

*However, 11 of 632 (1.7%) of *E. faecalis* isolates were β-lactamase producers.
†No β-lactamase-producing strains were identified.
‡Only two β-lactamase-producing isolates were identified.

1993). Rates of vancomycin resistance in enterococci continued to increase during the 1990s (see Table 89–2). By the end of the decade, NNIS reported that approximately one quarter (25.2% in 1999, 24.7% in 2000) of enterococci associated with nosocomial infections in ICU patients in the United States were resistant to vancomycin (www.cdc.gov/ncidod/hip/SURVEILL/NNIS.htm). Vancomycin-resistant strains, particularly those of *E. faecium,* also may exhibit high-level resistance to both β-lactam antibiotics and aminoglycosides, thus rendering treatment of these infections extremely challenging.*

Vancomycin resistance among enterococci is phenotypically and genotypically heterogeneous[4, 62, 137, 138] and may or may not be associated with resistance to other glycopeptides, including teicoplanin. Five major phenotypes of vancomycin resistance (VanA, VanB, VanC, VanD, and VanE) have been characterized. The VanA and VanB phenotypes are most common, and both are transferable. The VanA phenotype is characterized by high-level resistance to vancomycin and teicoplanin, whereas strains with the VanB phenotype exhibit variable levels of resistance to vancomycin but not teicoplanin.[4, 62, 137, 138] The VanC phenotype is limited to *E. gallinarum* and *E. casseliflavus* and is associated with constitutive, low-level, chromosomally mediated (nontransferable) resistance to vancomycin but not teicoplanin.[62, 137, 138, 169] VanD and VanE phenotypes occur uncommonly and are not transferable.

High-level resistance to both vancomycin and teicoplanin (the VanA phenotype) primarily is found in strains of *E. faecium,* whereas most vancomycin-resistant strains of *E. faecalis* express the VanB phenotype and remain susceptible to teicoplanin. Jones and associates and the *Enterococcus* Study Group found that 10 of 11 (91%) vancomycin-resistant strains of *E. faecalis* remained susceptible to teicoplanin (VanB phenotype) whereas 49 of 62 (79%) vancomycin-resistant strains of *E. faecium* were resistant to teicoplanin (VanA phenotype).[88]

The biochemical mechanisms responsible for the major vancomycin-resistant phenotypes are the subject of intense study (reviewed by Murray[138] and Gold[62]). Both VanA and VanB phenotypes are mediated by homologous enzymes that catalyze the formation of an altered, vancomycin-resistant depsipeptide that is incorporated into cell wall peptidoglycan.[4, 138, 169] The *vanA* and *vanB* gene clusters share functional similarities but are regulated quite differently.[62, 138] VanA resistance is transferable by either transposition (e.g., via the transposon Tn1546) or conjugative plasmids. VanB resistance often is encoded by chromosomal DNA but may be transferred by at least two different transposons (Tn1547 and Tn5382).[62, 138] VanC resistance is not transferable.[138, 169] Vancomycin induces the production of enzymes encoded by both the *vanA* and *vanB* gene clusters, whereas teicoplanin induces VanA but not VanB enzymes.[62]

The mechanism of resistance in VanD enterococci is similar to those observed in VanA and VanB strains, and a single isolate of *E. faecalis* has been reported to exhibit a vancomycin-resistant phenotype (VanE) that is very similar to the VanC phenomenon reported in *E. gallinarum* and *E. casseliflavus.*[62]

The peculiar phenomenon of infection caused by vancomycin-dependent enterococci has been described. Fraimow and colleagues[57] reported a urinary tract infection attributable to a strain of *E. faecalis* that would grow only in the presence of vancomycin, and Green and associates[73] reported breakthrough bacteremia with a vancomycin-dependent strain of *E. faecium* occurring during therapy for bacteremia. These organisms are progeny of VanA or VanB enterococci that undergo mutations preventing them from growing in the absence of glycopeptides.

*See references 3, 20, 21, 23, 36, 46, 54, 62, 73, 75, 92, 104, 112, 124, 132, 134, 136, 138, 145, 166, 169, 171.

TESTING FOR ANTIMICROBIAL RESISTANCE IN ENTEROCOCCI

All enterococci isolated from cultures of blood, cerebrospinal fluid, or other normally sterile sites (with the possible exception of urine) should be tested for resistance to β-lactam antibiotics (ampicillin or penicillin, or both, including a test for β-lactamase production), vancomycin, and high levels of aminoglycosides (streptomycin and gentamicin)[53, 163, 169] by using the methodology and interpretative guidelines published by the National Committee for Clinical Laboratory Standards (NCCLS).[142] For multiantibiotic-resistant isolates, testing for susceptibility to alternative agents, including chloramphenicol, ciprofloxacin, erythromycin, novobiocin, quinupristin-dalfopristin, and linezolid, should be considered.[21, 53, 62, 87, 138, 140]

Testing of enterococci for ampicillin (or penicillin) resistance must involve determination of the MIC of these agents and a test for β-lactamase production.[142] Jones and colleagues and the *Enterococcus* Study Group compared three techniques that are used commonly to determine the ampicillin MIC of enterococcal isolates—disk diffusion, broth microdilution, and E-test strips—and found excellent agreement among the three methods.[88] Enterococcal isolates with an MIC of 16 µg/mL or greater to ampicillin or penicillin are considered resistant to these agents.[142] β-Lactamase–producing enterococci cannot be detected by these methods but are identified routinely by performance of the chromogenic nitrocefin assay.[197]

High-level resistance to gentamicin and streptomycin usually may be detected by either agar dilution (high-level resistance to gentamicin, MIC >500 µg/mL; high-level resistance to streptomycin, MIC >2000 µg/mL) or broth microdilution (high-level resistance to gentamicin, MIC >500 µg/mL; high-level resistance to streptomycin, MIC >1000 µg/mL).[142, 195, 197] These isolates also may be identified by disk diffusion with the use of high-content aminoglycoside disks (120-µg gentamicin disk, 300-µg streptomycin disks, ≥10-mm zone = susceptible)[197] or high-range E-test strips.[88, 174] However, the recent identification of novel genes encoding gentamicin resistance in both *E. faecalis* and *E. faecium* has raised concern about continued use of the 500-µg/mL cutoff for detection of high-level resistance to gentamicin (reviewed by Chow[25]). These enterococcal isolates are not killed synergistically by combinations of ampicillin/penicillin and gentamicin, even though gentamicin MICs are 256 to 384 µg/mL. If these isolates become more widely prevalent, modification of the standard screening procedures for high-level aminoglycoside resistance may be required.

Commercially available automated antimicrobial susceptibility testing methods may fail to detect vancomycin resistance in enterococci, particularly the VanB phenotype of moderate resistance,[200] although newer versions of these systems appear to be much more reliable.[60, 206] Routine disk diffusion testing is more dependable but requires an extended incubation time and the use of transmitted light for examination of zone size to be highly accurate.[196, 200] Agar dilution screening using brain-heart infusion agar supplemented with 6 µg/mL vancomycin reliably identifies VRE strains,[142, 197, 211] as does the standard broth microdilution method.[87, 200] E-test glycopeptide strips are a useful alternative to the more cumbersome broth dilution methodology.

Overall reliability of the E-test for detection of vancomycin resistance is very good,[87] although some variability in E-test vancomycin MICs has been noted with reference strains of *E. faecalis*.[200]

Therapy for Enterococcal Infections

Before the emergence of VRE infection as a major nosocomial problem in high-risk patients, the optimal management of serious enterococcal infections (especially endocarditis) was well established. Successful treatment of enterococcal endocarditis required the administration of combination therapy with a cell wall–active agent (usually ampicillin) and an aminoglycoside (gentamicin or streptomycin). Combination therapy also was recommended for other potentially life-threatening enterococcal infections (e.g., sepsis, meningitis) based on the extensive experience with endocarditis. Other enterococcal infections, including urinary tract infections, responded well to monotherapy with a variety of antimicrobials.

In contrast, the optimal therapy for many infections caused by VRE remains uncertain. In the now frequently occurring "worst-case scenario," no reliably bactericidal treatment regimen is available. In addition, the prognosis for patients with VRE infections (including bacteremia) often is related more closely to the underlying disease than to the infection, thus greatly complicating the management of these high-risk patients.

TREATMENT OF INFECTIONS CAUSED BY ANTIBIOTIC-SUSCEPTIBLE ENTEROCOCCI

Any discussion of the treatment of serious enterococcal infection must begin with a review of the large experience in the treatment of enterococcal endocarditis. The difficulty of treating enterococcal endocarditis has been apparent since early reports that penicillin alone failed to cure as many as two thirds of patients with enterococcal endocarditis but was highly effective in the treatment of streptococcal endocarditis (reviewed by Murray[134]). The early failures of penicillin therapy stimulated studies of the in vitro and in vivo effects of β-lactam antibiotics on enterococci; these studies led to the discovery that enterococci were "tolerant" to the killing effects of cell wall–active agents and provided evidence that bactericidal therapy was required to cure bacterial endocarditis reliably.

For more than one half a century, standard therapy for enterococcal endocarditis has included an aminoglycoside plus a cell wall–active agent. Hunter[81] first reported clinical evidence of synergism between penicillin and streptomycin in the treatment of enterococcal endocarditis in 1947, and this synergism subsequently was confirmed for combinations of penicillin or ampicillin and streptomycin or gentamicin both in vitro and in vivo (reviewed by Murray[134]). Moellering and Weinberg[127] first demonstrated that synergy between β-lactams and aminoglycosides was a consequence of increased aminoglycoside uptake by enterococci exposed to cell wall–active agents. Glycopeptides and aminoglycosides also exhibit in vitro and in vivo synergy against "susceptible" (not expressing high-level resistance) strains of enterococci.[79, 122]

The preferred therapy for endocarditis caused by "susceptible" strains of enterococci in both adults[10, 122, 124, 167, 214] and children[37, 193] consists of combination therapy with parenteral ampicillin (or penicillin G) plus parenteral gentamicin (or streptomycin) for a minimal duration of 4 to 6 weeks. Patients with severe penicillin allergy should be treated with vancomycin plus gentamicin or streptomycin. Selected adult patients with a short duration of symptoms and an uncomplicated course may be treated with 4-week regimens[214, 215]; most other patients, including those with mitral-valve involvement, a longer duration of symptoms (especially those with symptoms for >3 months), or prosthetic-valve endocarditis, probably should receive 6-week courses of therapy.[122, 214] Interestingly, several reports indicate that the prognosis of enterococcal prosthetic-valve endocarditis is better than that of native-valve disease, perhaps because of the generally shorter duration of symptoms before diagnosis is made.[122, 167] Many patients with prosthetic-valve endocarditis caused by enterococci can be cured without surgery. Rice and colleagues[167] reported a 69 percent cure rate with medical therapy in patients with enterococcal endocarditis involving prosthetic valves.

The general consensus, based on the experience with enterococcal endocarditis, is that other life-threatening enterococcal infections, including meningitis and septicemia, should be treated with bactericidal regimens.[123, 134, 194] The duration of therapy for uncommon enterococcal infections such as meningitis must be individualized, although 2- to 3-week courses of antibiotics have been reported to cure enterococcal meningitis.[194] The optimal treatment of enterococcal bacteremia, particularly that occurring in the nosocomial setting, remains controversial.

The prognosis for these patients varies widely and often is related more closely to the underlying disease than to the enterococcal infection. In adults, single-drug regimens generally are successful in the treatment of enterococcal bacteremia, thus indicating that bactericidal therapy often is not required.[123, 134]

Considerable clinical experience supports the routine use of single-drug therapy for uncomplicated enterococcal urinary tract infection and for soft tissue infection caused by enterococci. Urinary tract infections by susceptible strains of enterococci generally respond promptly to ampicillin, penicillin, nitrofurantoin, or vancomycin.[123, 133, 134]

TREATMENT OF INFECTIONS CAUSED BY ANTIBIOTIC-RESISTANT ENTEROCOCCI (INCLUDING VANCOMYCIN-RESISTANT ENTEROCOCCI)

Unfortunately, the emergence of enterococci with clinically significant resistance to aminoglycosides, β-lactams, and glycopeptides has complicated greatly the management of endocarditis and other serious infections caused by these organisms. This discussion will focus on the management of endocarditis caused by drug-resistant enterococci because the need to provide bactericidal therapy has been well established in this setting. The general principles probably apply to the management of other life-threatening enterococcal infections (see earlier).

Endocarditis caused by enterococci with high-level resistance to either streptomycin or gentamicin may be treated by substituting the other aminoglycoside in a combination regimen, but isolation of strains with high-level resistance to both aminoglycosides means that no available aminoglycoside will provide synergistic killing in concert with cell wall–active agents.[122, 134] Enterococci resistant to all aminoglycosides have been isolated at an increasing rate from clinical specimens. Jones and colleagues and the *Enterococcus* Study Group[88] found that fully 20 percent of 1936 enterococcal isolates from late 1992 (from 97 participating laboratories in 47 states) exhibited high-level resistance to both gentamicin and streptomycin. Low and associates and the SENTRY Antimicrobial Resistance Surveillance Program[111] reported similar rates of high-level resistance to both gentamicin and streptomycin from 1997 to 1999 (see Table 89–2). No reliably bactericidal regimen is available for the treatment of endocarditis caused by these strains, even if the isolates remain susceptible to other classes of antimicrobials. Based on animal studies, prolonged treatment (8 to 12 weeks or more) with high-dose intravenous ampicillin given by continuous infusion may be tried in this situation (if the isolate is susceptible).[48, 124] Surgical excision of infected valves may be required in such patients.[167] Alternative drugs for treating these infections are needed greatly (see later).

Endocarditis and other serious infections caused by enterococci resistant to β-lactam antibiotics also are increasing in frequency.[71] Endocarditis caused by enterococci (usually *E. faecium*) highly resistant to β-lactams may be treated with vancomycin plus an aminoglycoside (if the strain is susceptible to vancomycin). Endocarditis caused by β-lactamase–producing strains of *E. faecalis* (or, rarely, *E. faecium*) would be expected to respond to ampicillin-sulbactam because this combination is highly effective in animal models.[48] Higher-dose or continuous-infusion ampicillin may be effective in the treatment of endocarditis caused by some strains of enterococci that are "resistant" to ampicillin by current guidelines (MIC ≥16 μg/mL) because sustained plasma concentrations in excess of 100 μg/mL may be achieved with these regimens.[138] However, even high-dose ampicillin therapy probably will fail to cure endocarditis caused by enterococci with ampicillin MICs greater than 64 μg/mL.[17, 62]

Enterococci resistant to vancomycin may remain susceptible to teicoplanin (VanB phenotype). Teicoplanin with or without the addition of an aminoglycoside has been used successfully in the treatment of serious enterococcal infections caused by susceptible isolates,[178] including some cases of endocarditis[160, 178] and meningitis.[109] However, teicoplanin is not available in the United States, treatment of endocarditis with this agent has been associated with both treatment failure and relapse,[160, 178] and high-level teicoplanin resistance may develop even without exposure to the drug.[76] Endocarditis caused by VanB strains of enterococci should be treated with high-dose ampicillin plus gentamicin or streptomycin if resistance to these agents is not present.

Similarly, endocarditis caused by enterococci highly resistant to both vancomycin and teicoplanin (VanA phenotype) but susceptible to β-lactams should be treated with ampicillin plus an aminoglycoside (if high-level resistance to aminoglycosides is not present). Unfortunately, the VanA phenotype is associated primarily with strains of *E. faecium,* which are increasingly resistant to β-lactams.[56, 71, 88] Endocarditis caused by enterococci highly resistant to both glycopeptides and β-lactams is especially difficult to treat. Combinations of ampicillin and vancomycin are not bactericidal against these isolates but may[186] or may not[20] provide additive or synergistic inhibition in vitro. If high-level resistance to aminoglycosides is not present, triple-combination therapy with a β-lactam, a glycopeptide, and an aminoglycoside may achieve bactericidal activity; such combinations are reported to be highly effective in animal models of endocarditis caused by ampicillin- and vancomycin-resistant *E. faecium.*[19] For endocarditis caused by enterococci exhibiting high-level resistance to both gentamicin and streptomycin along with resistance to β-lactams and glycopeptides, no proven effective therapies are available (see later).

Some multiresistant enterococci are susceptible to chloramphenicol, tetracycline, or ciprofloxacin, but these agents are not bactericidal and have not been reported to cure enterococcal endocarditis. Chloramphenicol has been reported to be effective in the treatment of other serious enterococcal infections,[101, 148, 159, 165] but one study found no difference in mortality rates among patients with catheter-related VRE bacteremia who were treated with catheter removal, chloramphenicol, or both.[101] Ciprofloxacin is of limited utility, and increasing numbers of enterococci are resistant to this agent,[88, 177] although newer fluoroquinolones have better in vitro activity against VRE.

Two new classes of antimicrobials with activity against certain VRE isolates, the streptogramins and the oxazolidinones, recently have been developed. Streptogramins are a new class of protein synthesis inhibitor antibiotics and are natural combinations of two chemically unrelated molecules.[110] The first streptogramin antibiotic approved for human use in the United States is a combination of quinupristin and dalfopristin. Quinupristin-dalfopristin is active against most isolates of *E. faecium* (including VREF) but is *not* active against *E. faecalis* at clinically achievable concentrations.[34, 110] Quinupristin-dalfopristin was approved by the Food and Drug Administration (FDA) in September 1999 for the treatment of certain antibiotic-resistant gram-positive infections in adults, including bacteremia caused by VREF. Although time-kill curves indicate that quinupristin-dalfopristin is not reliably bactericidal against strains of *E. faecium,*[34] it may provide bactericidal activity against some multiresistant clinical isolates.[114, 140, 173] Quinupristin-dalfopristin has been reported to effect clinical cures of several serious infections caused by multiresistant *E. faecium,* including ventriculoperitoneal shunt infections in two patients,[140, 203] an infected aortic graft in one patient,[173] and VREF peritonitis in a series of adults.[114] Several studies suggest that treatment with quinupristin-dalfopristin reduces the mortality rate associated with VREF bacteremia in adults[106, 126, 217] and children,[68, 207] and a clinical response to this agent has been reported in approximately 74 to 80 percent of patients with VREF bacteremia.[68, 126, 207, 217]

The lack of a consistent bactericidal effect may limit the utility of this agent in the treatment of endocarditis and other life-threatening infections. Therapy with quinupristin-dalfopristin for 10 weeks was reported to cure one patient with VREF endocarditis, although the bacteremia persisted until the eighth week of therapy.[59] A second patient with VREF endocarditis failed treatment with 2 weeks of quinupristin-dalfopristin monotherapy but was cured by treatment with a combination of quinupristin-dalfopristin, doxycycline, and rifampin.[117] Four other patients with VREF endocarditis failed to respond to quinupristin-dalfopristin.[6, 126]

Quinupristin-dalfopristin therapy generally has been tolerated fairly well in both adults and children, although a high rate of venous phlebitis in recipients has led to a recommendation that the agent be administered through a central venous catheter. Myalgias and arthralgias are commonly reported side effects of this agent.

More than 95 percent of 875 initial patient isolates of VREF were susceptible to quinupristin-dalfopristin in a recent study,[50] but both emergence of resistance to this agent[126, 173] and superinfection with *E. faecalis* and other organisms[26, 217] have been reported during therapy with this drug.

The oxazolidinones are a novel class of synthetic protein synthesis inhibitors that act to inhibit the formation of ribosomal initiation complexes in bacteria.[32] Linezolid, the first oxazolidinone approved for human use, is available in both parenteral and oral formulations (with comparable bioavailability). Linezolid was approved by the FDA in April 2000 for the treatment of selected infections caused by antibiotic-resistant, gram-positive bacteria in adults, including those caused by VRE *(E. faecium* or *E. faecalis).*

Linezolid is active against many antibiotic-resistant, gram-positive pathogens, including methicillin-resistant *S. aureus,* penicillin-resistant *S. pneumoniae,* and vancomycin-resistant isolates of both *E. faecium* and *E. faecalis.*[12, 32, 49, 150] This agent is bacteriostatic against most susceptible organisms, including the enterococci, but it does exhibit bactericidal activity against some strains of pneumococci. Initial studies demonstrated virtually uniform activity of this agent against clinical isolates of enterococci,[12, 49, 150] with 100 percent of 180 strains (representing multiple resistance profiles) inhibited by linezolid concentrations of 1 to 4 μg/mL in one study.[49] Furthermore, initial in vitro studies suggested that the development of resistance would occur very rarely.[89, 223] However, resistance to linezolid has been reported in several patients receiving prolonged courses of therapy with this drug, and it has been associated with clinical failures.[63] In addition, Prystowsky and associates[161] recently reported that the serial passage of VRE strains in doubling dilutions of linezolid in vitro led to the isolation of four linezolid-resistant VRE strains (three *E. faecalis,* one *E. faecium)* with mutations in the 23S rRNA genes.

Linezolid has been reported to effect both bacteriologic and clinical responses in patients with life-threatening VRE infections, including endocarditis,[6, 23] bacteremia,[23, 120, 149] and meningitis,[182, 219] although clinical experience with this agent in these settings is limited. Two patients who responded to linezolid therapy previously had failed therapy with quinupristin-dalfopristin (one with endocarditis[6] and one with persistent VREF bacteremia[120]). Linezolid therapy successfully eradicated bacteremia in three of three patients with endocarditis caused by VREF, although two patients died during therapy (the deaths were not attributed to VRE infection).[6, 23] These initial results are encouraging, but enthusiasm for the use of linezolid to treat serious VRE infection must be tempered by its generally bacteriostatic activity and the potential for increasing resistance to this agent.

Linezolid generally has been tolerated well in both adults and children,[32] with fewer side effects occurring than with quinupristin-dalfopristin. The side effects most frequently reported in patients receiving linezolid have included nausea, diarrhea, and discoloration of the tongue. Although linezolid is a weak competitive inhibitor of monoamine oxidase, no clinical evidence of adverse events caused by this activity of the drug has been reported.[32]

Prevention of Enterococcal Infections

The explosive increase in nosocomial infections caused by VRE and multiantibiotic-resistant enterococci[47, 151] (www.cdc.gov/ncidod/hip/SURVEILL/NNIS.htm) has rendered the prevention of enterococcal infections, particularly those caused by VRE, a public health priority in the United States.[21, 62, 138, 163, 183] In 1995, the Hospital Infection Control Practices Advisory Committee (HICPAC) recommended a series of overlapping strategies designed to prevent development of serious enterococcal infection.[163] These strategies are aimed at simultaneous interruption of the considerable increase in vancomycin resistance in enterococci and prevention of nosocomial infection with these organisms. The implementation of such strategies has been reported to reduce or eliminate the transmission of VRE in health care facilities.[153] However, overall rates of nosocomial infection by VRE continued to increase in the United States from 1995 to 2000 (www.cdc.gov/ncidod/hip/SURVEILL/NNIS.htm), perhaps because the HICPAC guidelines have been followed inconsistently (reviewed by Cetinkaya and colleagues[21]).

REVERSING THE TREND TOWARD VANCOMYCIN AND MULTIPLE-ANTIBIOTIC RESISTANCE IN ENTEROCOCCI

The use of vancomycin* and treatment with broad-spectrum antibiotics, including the third-generation cephalosporins and carbapenems,[46, 58, 70, 132, 136, 144, 166] are risk factors for the development of colonization and infection with VRE.[167] Consequently, the HICPAC and the CDC have recommended that all hospitals, even those at which VRE have not been isolated, should (1) develop a comprehensive antimicrobial utilization plan, (2) oversee surgical prophylaxis, and (3) develop institution-specific guidelines for the proper use of vancomycin.[163]

Efforts to eliminate unnecessary use of vancomycin are of critical importance[163, 183] but may be inadequate unless the use of other classes of antimicrobials is reduced as well (see later). The HICPAC has provided recommendations regarding the acceptable and appropriate use of vancomycin (Table 89–3), as well as recommendations regarding situations in which vancomycin use should be discouraged[163] (Table 89–4).

In addition, effort should be made to reduce the unnecessary use of broad-spectrum antibiotics and certain agents with potent anti-anaerobic activity, particularly in settings with high rates of nosocomial infection (such as ICUs). This effort is necessary because many studies indicate that nonglycopeptide antibiotics also exert selective pressure for VRE strains and that limitation of the use of vancomycin alone will have only a modest effect on reducing VRE colonization and infection (reviewed by Rice[166]). Recent evidence suggests that exposure to agents with broad-spectrum activity (but lacking anti-enterococcal activity), such as the extended-spectrum cephalosporins, may predispose to VRE colonization[44, 166] and that exposure to antimicrobials with potent anti-anaerobic activity (even if they are active against enterococci as well) may promote high-density, prolonged colonization with VRE (by eliminating gut anaerobes that may compete with VRE).[43, 166]

PREVENTING AND CONTROLLING THE SPREAD OF NOSOCOMIAL INFECTION BY VANCOMYCIN-RESISTANT ENTEROCOCCI

The increasing prevalence of *Enterococcus* in nosocomial infections is related to the intrinsic and acquired antimicrobial

TABLE 89–3 ■ SITUATIONS IN WHICH VANCOMYCIN USE IS APPROPRIATE OR ACCEPTABLE

Treatment
Treatment of serious infections caused by β-lactam-resistant, gram-positive microorganisms
Treatment of gram-positive infections in patients with serious allergies to β-lactams
Treatment of antibiotic-associated colitis only when it fails to respond to metronidazole or is severe and potentially life-threatening

Prophylaxis
Endocarditis prophylaxis after certain procedures in high-risk patients according to the American Heart Association guidelines
Prophylaxis for major surgical procedures involving implantation of prosthetic materials or devices (single-dose prophylaxis usually is adequate)

Modified from Recommendations for preventing the spread of vancomycin resistance: Recommendations of the Hospital Infection Control Practices Advisory Committee (HICPAC). M. M. W. R. Recomm. Rep. *44* (RR-12):1–13, 1995.

*See references 14, 58, 75, 90, 107, 130–132, 166, 169, 171, 183, 184.

TABLE 89–4 ■ SITUATIONS IN WHICH VANCOMYCIN USE SHOULD BE DISCOURAGED

Treatment

Empiric therapy for febrile neutropenic patients (unless there is presumptive evidence of an infection caused by gram-positive organisms, such as a Hickman catheter exit-site infection, and the local prevalence of methicillin-resistant *Staphylococcus aureus* strains is substantial)

Treatment of an isolated, single blood culture positive for coagulase-negative *Staphylococcus*

Treatment (chosen for dosing convenience) of infections caused by β-lactam-susceptible, gram-positive microorganisms in patients with renal failure

Continued empiric use of presumed infection in patients whose cultures are negative for β-lactam–resistant gram-positive microorganisms

Primary treatment of antibiotic-associated diarrhea

Eradication of methicillin-resistant *S. aureus* colonization

Prophylaxis

Routine surgical prophylaxis except in a patient with life-threating allergy to β-lactams

Systemic or local prophylaxis for infection of indwelling intravascular catheters

Routine prophylaxis for very low-birth-weight infants

Routine prophylaxis for dialysis patients

Use of vancomycin solution for topical application or irrigation

Selective decontamination of the gastrointestinal tract

Modified from Recommendations for preventing the spread of vancomycin resistance: Recommendations of the Hospital Infection Control Practices Advisory Committee (HICPAC). M. M. W. R. Recomm. Rep. *44* (RR-12):1–13, 1995.

resistance of these organisms, but the factors leading to increased antibiotic resistance in enterococci are not identical to those that predispose to enterococcal colonization or infection, or both. Enterococcal infections increasingly are concentrated in debilitated and immunocompromised patients, including those with malignancies, recipients of bone marrow and solid organ transplants, burn victims, premature neonates, and critically ill patients with indwelling intravascular catheters. Consequently, special attention should be paid to potential outbreaks of VRE infection in hospital wards caring for these high-risk patients.[21]

Efforts to prevent the spread of VRE colonization or infection (or both) probably will be more successful if the VRE isolates are confined to a few patients in a single area of the hospital. Widespread colonization with VRE may precede the identification of infections by these organisms. Therefore, all hospitals should implement active surveillance for VRE and formulate a multidisciplinary plan to prevent nosocomial spread of VRE if such organisms are identified. In hospitals that have not isolated VRE, periodic antimicrobial susceptibility testing should be performed on enterococcal isolates from all sources, particularly from high-risk patient populations such as those in intensive care or transplant units. If VRE are identified, a comprehensive plan to prevent nosocomial spread of these organisms should be instituted immediately. The HICPAC has summarized the essential elements of such a plan.[163] Hospital infection control staff and clinical staff must be notified promptly when VRE are isolated from a clinical sample, and isolation precautions should be implemented immediately to prevent patient-to-patient transmission of VRE. These precautions include gown and glove isolation, vigorous handwashing, dedicated use of noncritical patient items such as thermometers and stethoscopes, and prompt surveillance of any possibly exposed patients for VRE colonization. Additional measures may be necessary in hospitals with endemic VRE or continued VRE transmission despite implementation of the aforementioned measures.[163] Ostrowsky and colleagues[153] reported that an active infection control program that included surveillance cultures and prompt isolation of infected patients successfully reduced the spread of VRE in health care facilities throughout the Sioux land region of Iowa, Nebraska, and South Dakota.

Once VRE become endemic in a hospital unit, achieving complete eradication is very difficult. The duration of VRE colonization in individual patients may be weeks or months,[21, 130] although spontaneous resolution of colonization frequently occurs.[21, 129] Attempts to eradicate colonization in individual patients generally have been unsuccessful.[21, 129] Consequently, the measures recommended by the HICPAC and others are directed at preventing the initial establishment of VRE in hospitals. Implementation of these policies will require the involvement of hospital pharmacy and therapeutics committees, quality assurance programs, and medical staff. Ongoing monitoring of the efficacy of these programs will be required.

REFERENCES

1. Alminrante, B., Tornos, M., Gurgui, M., et al.: Prognosis of enterococcal endocarditis. Rev. Infect. Dis. *13*:1248–1249, 1991.
2. Andrewes, F. W., and Horder, T. J.: A study of the streptococci pathogenic for man. Lancet *2*:708–713, 1906.
3. Armstrong, D., Neu, H., Peterson, L. R., et al.: The prospects of treatment failure in the chemotherapy of infectious diseases in the 1990s. Microb. Drug Resist. *1*:1–4, 1995.
4. Arthur, M., and Courvalin, P.: Genetics and mechanisms of glycopeptide resistance in enterococci. Antimicrob. Agents Chemother. *37*: 1563–1571, 1993.
5. Ashkenazi, S., Even-Tov, S., Samra, Z., et al.: Uropathogens of various childhood populations and their antibiotic susceptibility. Pediatr. Infect. Dis. J. *10*:742–746, 1991.
6. Babcock, H. M., Ritchie, D. J., Christiansen, E., et al.: Successful treatment of vancomycin-resistant *Enterococcus* endocarditis with oral linezolid. Clin. Infect. Dis. *32*:1373–1375, 2001.
7. Bhavnani, S. M., Drake, J. A., Forrest, A., et al.: A nationwide, multicenter, case-control study comparing risk factors, treatment, and outcome for vancomycin-resistant and -susceptible enterococcal bacteremia. Diagn. Microbiol. Infect. Dis. *36*:145–158, 2000.
8. Bingen, E., Lambert-Zechousky, N., Mariane-Kurkdjian, P., et al.: Bacteremia caused by a vancomycin-resistant enterococcus. Pediatr. Infect. Dis. J. *8*:475–476, 1989.
9. Bingen, E. H., Denamur, E., and Lambert-Zechovsky, N. Y.: Evidence for the genetic unrelatedness of nosocomial vancomycin-resistant *Enterococcus faecium* strains in a pediatric hospital. J. Clin. Microbiol. *29*:1888, 1991.
10. Bisno, A. L., Dismukes, W. E., Durack, D. T., et al.: Antimicrobial treatment of infective endocarditis due to viridans streptococci, enterococci, and staphylococci. J. A. M. A. *261*:1471–1477, 1989.
11. Bonadio, W. A.: Group D streptococcal bacteremia in children: Clin. Pediatr. (Phila.) *32*:20–24, 1993.
12. Bostic, G. D., Perri, M. B., Thal, L. A., et al.: Comparative in vitro and bactericidal activity of oxazolidinone antibiotics against multidrug-resistant enterococci. Diagn. Microbiol. Infect. Dis. *30*:109–112, 1998.
13. Boulanger, J. M., Ford-Jones, E. L., and Matlow, A. G.: Enterococcal bacteremia in a pediatric institution: A four year review. Rev. Infect. Dis. *13*:847, 1991.
14. Boyce, J. M., Opal, S. M., and Chow, J. W.: Outbreak of multi-drug resistant *Enterococcus faecium* with transferable vanB class vancomycin resistance. J. Clin. Microbiol. *32*:1148–1153, 1994.
15. Boyce, J. M., Opal, S. M., Potter-Bynoe, G., et al.: Emergence and nosocomial transmission of ampicillin-resistant enterococci. Antimicrob. Agents Chemother. *36*:1032–1039, 1992.
16. Brown, A. E., de Lancastre, H., Henning, K., et al.: Epidemic nosocomial vancomycin-resistant *Enterococcus faecium* (VREF) on a pediatric oncology unit. Paper presented at the 33rd Annual Meeting of the Infectious Diseases Society of America, San Francisco, 1995.
17. Bush, L., Calman, J., Cherney, C. L., et al.: High-level penicillin resistance among isolates of enterococci: Implications for treatment of enterococcal infections. Ann. Intern. Med. *110*:515–520, 1989.
18. Calderwood, S. A., Wennersten, C., and Moellering, R. C., Jr.: Resistance to six aminoglycosidic aminocyclitol antibiotics among enterococci: Prevalence, evolution, and relationship to synergism with penicillin. Antimicrob. Agents Chemother. *12*:401–405, 1977.
19. Caron, F., Pestel, M., Kitzis, M. D., et al.: Comparison of different β-lactam-glycopeptide-gentamicin combinations for and experimental endocarditis caused by highly β-lactam–resistant and highly

glycopeptide-resistant isolate of *Enterococcus faecium*. J. Infect. Dis. *171*:106–112, 1995.
20. Cercenado, E., Eliopoulos, G. M., Wennersten, C. B., et al.: Absence of synergistic activity between ampicillin and vancomycin against highly vancomycin-resistant enterococci. Antimicrob. Agents Chemother. *36*:2201–2203, 1992.
21. Cetinkaya, Y., Falk, P., and Mayhall, C. G.: Vancomycin-resistant enterococci. Clin. Microbiol. Rev. *13*:686–707, 2000.
22. Chenoweth, C. E., Robinson, K. A., and Schaberg, D. R.: Efficacy of ampicillin versus trimethoprim-sulfamethoxazole in a mouse model of lethal enterococcal peritonitis. Antimicrob. Agents Chemother. *34*:1800–1802, 1990.
23. Chien, J. W., Kucia, M. L., and Salata, R. A.: Use of linezolid, an oxazolidinone, in the treatment of multidrug-resistant gram-positive bacterial infections. Clin. Infect. Dis. *30*:146–151, 2000.
24. Chirurgi, V. A., Oster, S. E., Goldberg, A. A., et al.: Ampicillin-resistant *Enterococcus raffinosus* in an acute-care hospital: Case-control study and antimicrobial susceptibilities. J. Clin. Microbiol. *29*:2663–2665, 1991.
25. Chow, J. W.: Aminoglycoside resistance in enterococci. Clin. Infect. Dis. *31*:586–589, 2000.
26. Chow, J. W., Davidson, A., Sanford, E., 3rd, et al.: Superinfection with *Enterococcus faecalis* during quinupristin/dalfopristin therapy. Clin. Infect. Dis. *24*:91–92, 1997.
27. Chow, J. W., Thal, L. A., Perri, M. B., et al.: Plasmid-associated hemolysin and aggregation substance production contributes to virulence in experimental enterococcal endocarditis. Antimicrob. Agents Chemother. *37*:2474–2477, 1993.
28. Chow, J. W., Zervos, M. J., Lerner, S. A., et al.: A novel gentamicin resistance gene in *Enterococcus*. Antimicrob. Agents Chemother. *41*:511–514, 1997.
29. Christenson, J. C., Korgenski, E. K., Jenkins, E., et al.: Detection of vancomycin-resistant enterococci colonization in a children's hospital. Am. J. Infect. Control *26*:569–571, 1998.
30. Christie, C., Hammond, J., Reising, S., et al.: Clinical and molecular epidemiology of enterococcal bacteremia in a pediatric teaching hospital. J. Pediatr. *125*:392–399, 1994.
31. Clark, N. C., Cooksey, R. C., Hill, B. C., et al.: Characterization of glycopeptide-resistant enterococci from U.S. hospitals. Antimicrob. Agents Chemother. *37*:2311–2317, 1993.
32. Clemett, D., and Markham, A.: Linezolid. Drugs *59*:815–827, 2000.
33. Cohen, M.: Epidemiology of drug resistance: Implications for a post-antibiotic era. Science *257*:1050–1055, 1992.
34. Collins, L. A., Malanoski, G. J., Eliopoulos, G. M., et al.: In vitro activity of RP59500, an injectable streptogramin antibiotic, against vancomycin-resistant gram-positive organisms. Antimicrob. Agents Chemother. *37*:598–601, 1993.
35. Coudron, P. E., Markowitz, S. M., and Wong, E. S.: Isolation of a beta-lactamase–producing, aminoglycoside-resistant strain of *Enterococcus faecium*. Antimicrob. Agents Chemother. *36*:1125–1126, 1992.
36. Coudron, P. E., Mayhall, C. G., and Facklam, R. R.: *Streptococcus faecium* outbreak in a neonatal intensive care unit. J. Clin. Microbiol. *20*:1044, 1984.
37. Dajani, A. S.: Infective endocarditis. *In* Kaplan, S. L. (ed.): Current Therapy in Pediatric Infectious Diseases. 3rd ed. St. Louis, Mosby–Year Book, 1993, pp. 129–133.
38. Daly, J. A., Clifton, N. L., and Seskin, K. C.: Use of rapid, nonradioactive DNA probes in culture confirmation tests to detect *Streptococcus agalactiae, Haemophilus influenzae,* and *Enterococcus* spp. from pediatric patients with significant infections. J. Clin. Microbiol. *29*:80, 1991.
39. Das, I., and Gray, J.: Enterococcal bacteremia in children: A review of seventy-five episodes in a pediatric hospital. Pediatr. Infect. Dis. J. *17*:1154–1158, 1998.
40. Davies, H., Jones, E., Sheng, R., et al.: Nosocomial urinary tract infections at a pediatric hospital. Pediatr. Infect. Dis. J. *11*:349–354, 1992.
41. Dobson, S. R. M., and Baker, C. J.: Enterococcal sepsis in neonates: Features by age of onset and occurrence of focal infection. Pediatrics *85*:165, 1990.
42. Donabedian, S., Chow, J. W., Shales, D. M., et al.: DNA hybridization and contour-clamped homogeneous electric field electrophoresis for identification of enterococci to the species level. J. Clin. Microbiol. *33*:141–145, 1995.
43. Donskey, C. J., Chowdhry, T. K., Hecker, M. T., et al.: Effect of antibiotic therapy on the density of vancomycin-resistant enterococci in the stool of colonized patients. N. Engl. J. Med. *343*:1925–1932, 2000.
44. Donskey, C. J., Hanrahan, J. A., Hutton, R. A., et al.: Effect of parenteral antibiotic administration on the establishment of colonization with vancomycin-resistant *Enterococcus faecium* in the mouse gastrointestinal tract. J. Infect. Dis. *181*:1830–1833, 2000.
45. Dutka-Malen, S., Evers, S., and Courvalin, P.: Detection of glycopeptide resistance genotypes and identification to the species level of clinically relevant enterococci by PCR. J. Clin. Microbiol. *33*:24–27, 1995.
46. Edmond, M. B., Ober, J. F., Weinbaum, D. L., et al.: Vancomycin-resistant *Enterococcus faecium* bacteremia: Risk factors for infection. Clin. Infect. Dis. *20*:1126–1133, 1995.
47. Edmond, M. B., Wallace, S. E., McClish, D. K., et al.: Nosocomial bloodstream infections in United States hospitals: A three-year analysis. Clin. Infect. Dis. *29*:239–244, 1999.
48. Eliopoulos, G. M., Thauvin-Eliopoulos, C., and Moellering, R. C., Jr.: Contribution of animal models in the search for effective therapy for endocarditis due to enterococci with high-level resistance to gentamicin. Clin. Infect. Dis. *15*:58–62, 1992.
49. Eliopoulos, G. M., Wennersten, C. B., Gold, H. S., et al.: In vitro activities in new oxazolidinone antimicrobial agents against enterococci. Antimicrob. Agents Chemother. *40*:1745–1747, 1996.
50. Eliopoulos, G. M., Wennersten, C. B., Gold, H. S., et al.: Characterization of vancomycin-resistant *Enterococcus faecium* isolates from the United States and their susceptibility in vitro to dalfopristin-quinupristin. Antimicrob. Agents Chemother. *42*:1088–1092, 1998.
51. Facklam, R., Pigott, N., Franklin, R., et al.: Evaluation of three disk tests for identification of enterococci, leuconostocs, and pediococci. J. Clin. Microbiol. *33*:885–887, 1995.
52. Facklam, R. R., and Collins, M. D.: Identification of *Enterococcus* species isolated from human infections by a conventional test scheme. J. Clin. Microbiol. *27*:731–734, 1989.
53. Facklam, R. R., and Sahm, D. R.: *Enterococcus. In* Murray, P. R., Baron, E. J., Pfaller, M. A., et al. (eds.): Manual of Clinical Microbiology. 6th ed. Washington, D.C., American Society for Microbiology, 1995, pp. 308–314.
54. Fasola, E. L., Moody, J. A., Shanholtzer, C. J., et al.: Bactericidal action of gentamicin against enterococci that are sensitive, or exhibit low- or high-level resistance to gentamicin. Diagn. Microbiol. Infect. Dis. *19*:57–60, 1994.
55. Felmingham, D., Wilson, A. P., Quintant, A. L., et al.: *Enterococcus* species in urinary tract infection. Clin. Infect. Dis. *15*:295–301, 1992.
56. Fontana, R., Amalfitano, G., Rossi, L., et al.: Mechanisms of resistance to growth inhibition and killing by β-lactam antibiotics in enterococci. Clin. Infect. Dis. *15*:486–489, 1992.
57. Fraimow, H. S., Jungkind, D. L., Lander, D. W., et al.: Urinary tract infection with an *Enterococcus faecalis* isolate that requires vancomycin for growth. Ann. Intern. Med. *121*:22–26, 1994.
58. Frieden, T. R., Munsiff, S. S., Low, D. E., et al.: Emergence of vancomycin-resistant enterococci in New York City. Lancet *342*:76–79, 1993.
59. Furlong, W. B., and Rakowski, T. A.: Therapy with RP 59500 (quinupristin/dalfopristin) for prosthetic valve endocarditis due to enterococci with VanA/VanB resistance patterns. Clin. Infect. Dis. *25*:163–164, 1997.
60. Garcia-Garrote, F., Cercenado, E., and Bouza, E.: Evaluation of a new system, VITEK 2, for identification and antimicrobial susceptibility testing of enterococci. J. Clin. Microbiol. *38*:2108–2111, 2000.
61. Gladstone, I. J., Ehrenkranz, R. A., Edberg, S. C., et al.: A ten-year review of neonatal sepsis and comparison with the previous fifty-year experience. Pediatr. Infect. Dis. J. *9*:819–825, 1990.
62. Gold, H.: Vancomycin-resistant enterococci: Mechanisms and clinical observations. Clin. Infect. Dis. *33*:210–219, 2001.
63. Gonzales, R. D., Schreckenberger, P. C., Graham, M. B., et al.: Infections due to vancomycin-resistant *Enterococcus faecium* resistant to linezolid. Lancet *357*:1179, 2001.
64. Goodhard, G. L.: In vivo vs. in vitro susceptibility of *Enterococcus* to trimethoprim-sulfamethoxazole. J. A. M. A. *252*:2748–2749, 1984.
65. Gorbach, S. L.: Intraabdominal infections. Clin. Infect. Dis. *17*:961–967, 1993.
66. Gordon, S., Swenson, J. M., Hill, B. C., et al.: Antimicrobial susceptibility patterns of common and unusual species of enterococci causing infections in the United States: Enterococcal Study Group. J. Clin. Microbiol. *30*:2373–2378, 1992.
67. Graninger, W., and Ragette, R.: Nosocomial bacteremia due to *Enterococcus faecalis* without endocarditis. Clin. Infect. Dis. *15*:49–57, 1992.
68. Gray, J. W., Darbyshire, P. J., Beath, S. V., et al.: Experience with quinupristin/dalfopristin in treating infections with vancomycin-resistant *Enterococcus faecium* in children. Pediatr. Infect. Dis. J. *19*:234–238, 2000.
69. Gray, J. W., and George, R. H.: Experience of vancomycin-resistant enterococci in a children's hospital. J. Hosp. Infect. *45*:11–18, 2000.
70. Gray, J. W., Pedler, S., Kernahan, J., et al.: Enterococcal superinfection in paediatric oncology patients treated with imipenem. Lancet *13*:1487–1488, 1992.
71. Grayson, M. L., Eliopoulos, G. M., Wennersten, C. B., et al.: Increasing resistance to beta-lactam antibiotics among clinical isolates of *Enterococcus faecium*: A 22-year review at one institution. Antimicrob. Agents Chemother. *35*:2180–2184, 1991.
72. Grayson, M. L., Thauvin-Eliopoulos, C., Eliopoulos, G. M., et al.: Failure of trimethoprim-sulfamethoxazole therapy in experimental enterococcal endocarditis. Antimicrob. Agents Chemother. *34*:1792–1794, 1990.
73. Green, M., Shlaes, J. H., Barbadora, K., et al.: Bacteremia due to vancomycin-dependent *Enterococcus faecium*. Clin. Infect. Dis. *20*:712–714, 1995.
74. Gullberg, R. M., Homann, S. R., and Phair, J. P.: Enterococcal bacteremia: Analysis of 75 episodes. Rev. Infect. Dis. *11*:74–85, 1989.
75. Handwerger, S., Raucher, B., Altarac, D., et al.: Nosocomial outbreak due to *Enterococcus faecium* highly resistant to vancomycin, penicillin and gentamicin. Clin. Infect. Dis. *16*:750–755, 1993.

76. Hayden, M. K., Trenholme, G. M., Schultz, J. E., et al.: In vivo development of teicoplanin resistance in a VanB *Enterococcus faecium* isolate. J. Infect. Dis. *167*:1224–1227, 1993.
77. Henning, K. J., Delencastre, H., Eagan, J., et al.: Vancomycin-resistant *Enterococcus faecium* on a pediatric oncology ward: Duration of stool shedding and incidence of clinical infection. Pediatr. Infect. Dis. J. *15*:848–854, 1996.
78. Hoge, C. W., Adams, J., Buchanan, B., et al.: Enterococcal bacteremia: To treat or not to treat, a reappraisal. Rev. Infect. Dis. *13*:600–605, 1991.
79. Hook, E. W. I., Roberts, R. B., and Sande, M. A.: Antimicrobial therapy of experimental endocarditis. Antimicrob. Agents Chemother. *8*:564–570, 1975.
80. Horodniceanu, T., Bougueleret, T., El-Solh, N., et al.: High-level, plasmid-borne resistance to gentamicin in *Streptococcus faecalis* subsp. *zymogenes*. Antimicrob. Agents Chemother. *16*:686–689, 1979.
81. Hunter, T. H.: Use of streptomycin in treatment of bacterial endocarditis. Am. J. Med. *2*:436–442, 1947.
82. Jarvis, W. R., and Martone, W. J.: Predominant pathogens in hospital infections. J. Antimicrob. Chemother. *29*(Suppl. A):19–24, 1992.
83. Jett, B. D., Huycke, M. M., and Gilmore, M. S.: Virulence of enterococci. Clin. Microbiol. Rev. *7*:462–478, 1994.
84. Johnson, A. P.: The pathogenicity of enterococci. J. Antimicrob. Chemother. *33*:1083–1089, 1994.
85. Johnson, D. H., Rosenthal, A., and Nadas, A. S.: Bacterial endocarditis in children under 2 years of age. Am. J. Dis. Child. *129*:183–186, 1975.
86. Johnson, D. H., Rosenthal, A., and Nadas, A. S.: A forty-year review of bacterial endocarditis in infants and children. Circulation *51*:581–588, 1975.
87. Jones, R. N., Erwin, M. E., and Anderson, S. C.: Emerging multiply resistant enterococci among clinical isolates. II. Validation of the e-test to recognize glycopeptide-resistant strains. Diagn. Microbiol. Infect. Dis. *21*:95–100, 1995.
88. Jones, R. N., Sader, H. S., Erwin, M. E., and Anderson, S. C.: Emerging multiply resistant enterococci among clinical isolates. I. Prevalence data from 97 medical center surveillance study in the United States: *Enterococcus* Study Group. Diagn. Microbiol. Infect. Dis. *21*:85–93, 1995.
89. Kaatz, G. W., and Seo, S. M.: In vitro activities of oxazolidinone compounds U100592 and U100766 against *Staphylococcus aureus* and *Staphylococcus epidermidis*. Antimicrob. Agents Chemother. *40*: 799–801, 1996.
90. Kaplan, A. H., Gilligan, P. H., and Facklam, R. R.: Recovery of resistant enterococci during vancomycin prophylaxis. J. Clin. Microbiol. *26*:1216–1218, 1988.
91. Kapur, D., Dorsky, D., Feingold, J. M., et al.: Incidence and outcome of vancomycin-resistant enterococcal bacteremia following autologous peripheral blood stem cell transplantation. Bone Marrow Transplant. *25*:147–152, 2000.
92. Karanfil, L. V., Murphy, M., and Josephson, A.: A cluster of vancomycin-resistant *Enterococcus faecium* in an intensive care unit. Infect. Control Hosp. Epidemiol. *13*:195–200, 1993.
93. Kaufhold, A., and Ferrieri, P.: The microbiologic aspects, including diagnosis, of beta-hemolytic streptococcal and enterococcal infections. Infect. Dis. Clin. North Am. *7*:235–256, 1993.
94. Kirkpatrick, B. D., Harrington, S. M., Smith, D., et al.: An outbreak of vancomycin-dependent *Enterococcus faecium* in a bone marrow transplant unit. Clin. Infect. Dis. *29*:1268–1273, 1999.
95. Kirst, H. A., Thompson, D. G., and Nicas, T. I.: Historical yearly usage of vancomycin. Antimicrob. Agents Chemother. *42*:1303–1304, 1998.
96. Klein, J. O., and Marcy, S. M.: Bacterial sepsis and meningitis. *In* Remington, J. S., and Klein, J. O. (eds.): Infectious Diseases of the Fetus and Newborn Infant. 4th ed. Philadelphia, W. B. Saunders, 1995, pp. 835–890.
97. Koorevaar, C. T., Scherpenzeel, P. G., Neijens, H. J., et al.: Childhood meningitis caused by enterococci and viridans streptococci. Infection *20*:118–121, 1992.
98. Kreft, B., Marre, R., Schramm, U., et al.: Aggregation substance of *Enterococcus faecalis* mediates adhesion to cultured renal tubular cells. Infect. Immun. *60*:25–30, 1992.
99. Krieger, J. N., Kaiser, D. L., and Wenzel, R. P.: Urinary tract etiology of bloodstream infections in hospitalized patients. J. Infect. Dis. *146*:719–723, 1983.
100. Kunin, C.: Resistance to antimicrobial drugs: A worldwide calamity. Ann. Intern. Med. *118*:557–561, 1993.
101. Lautenbach, E., Schuster, M. G., Bilker, W. B., et al.: The role of chloramphenicol in the treatment of bloodstream infection due to vancomycin-resistant *Enterococcus*. Clin. Infect. Dis. *27*:1259–1265, 1998.
102. Law, E. J., Blecher, K., and Still, J. M.: Enterococcal infections as a cause of mortality and morbidity in patients with burns. J. Burn. Care Rehabil. *15*:236–239, 1994.
103. LeClercq, R., Derlot, E., Duval, J., et al.: Plasmid-mediated resistance to vancomycin and teicoplanin in *Enterococcus faecium*. N. Engl. J. Med. *319*:157–161, 1988.
104. LeClercq, R., Dutka-Malen, S., Brisson-Noel, A., et al.: Resistance of enterococci to aminoglycosides and glycopeptides. Clin. Infect. Dis. *15*:495–501, 1992.
105. LeClercq, R., Dutka-Malen, S., Brisson-Noel, A., et al.: Resistance of enterococci to aminoglycosides and glycopeptides. Letter. Clin. Infect. Dis. *16*:331, 1993.
106. Linden, P. K., Pasculle, A. W., McDevitt, D., et al.: Effect of quinupristin/dalfopristin on the outcome of vancomycin-resistant *Enterococcus faecium* bacteraemia: Comparison with a control cohort. J. Antimicrob. Chemother. *39*:145–151, 1997.
107. Livornese, L. L., Jr., Dias, S., Samel, C., et al.: Hospital-acquired infection with vancomycin-resistant *Enterococcus faecium* transmitted by electronic thermometers. Ann. Intern. Med. *117*:112–116, 1992.
108. Lohr, J. A., Donowitz, L. G., and Sadler, J. E., III: Hospital-acquired urinary tract infection. Pediatrics *83*:193–199, 1989.
109. Losonsky, G., Wolf, A., Schwalbe, R., et al.: Successful treatment of meningitis due to multiply resistant *Enterococcus faecium* with a combination of intrathecal teicoplanin and intravenous antimicrobial agents. Clin. Infect. Dis. *19*:163–165, 1994.
110. Low, D. E.: Quinupristin/dalfopristin: Spectrum of activity, pharmacokinetics, and initial clinical experience. Microb. Drug Resist. *1*:223–234, 1995.
111. Low, D. E., Keller, N., Barth, A., et al.: Clinical prevalence, antimicrobial susceptibility, and geographic resistance patterns of enterococci: Results from the SENTRY Antimicrobial Surveillance Program, 1997–1999. Clin. Infect. Dis. *32*(Suppl.):133–145, 2001.
112. Low, D. E., Willey, B. M., and McGeer, A. J.: Multidrug-resistant enterococci: A threat to the surgical patient. Am. J. Surg. *169*(Suppl.):8–12, 1995.
113. Luginbuhl, L. M., Rotbart, H. A., Facklam, R. R., et al.: Neonatal enterococcal sepsis: Case-control study and description of an outbreak. Pediatr. Infect. Dis. J. *6*:1022–1030, 1987.
114. Lynn, W. A., Clutterbuck, E., Want, S., et al.: Treatment of CAPD-peritonitis due to glycopeptide-resistant *Enterococcus faecium* with quinupristin/dalfopristin. Lancet *344*:1025–1026, 1994.
115. Maki, D. G., and Agger, W. A.: Enterococcal bacteremia: Clinical features, the risk of endocarditis, and management. Medicine (Baltimore) *67*:248–269, 1988.
116. Malone, D. A., Wagner, R. A., Myers, J. P., et al.: Enterococcal bacteremia in two large community teaching hospitals. Am. J. Med. *81*:601–606, 1986.
117. Matsumura, S., and Simor, A. E.: Treatment of endocarditis due to vancomycin-resistant *Enterococcus faecium* with quinupristin/dalfopristin, doxycycline, and rifampin: A synergistic drug combination. Clin. Infect. Dis. *27*:1554–1556, 1998.
118. McCarthy, A., Victor, G., Ramotar, K., et al.: Risk factors for acquiring ampicillin-resistant enterococci and clinical outcomes at a Canadian tertiary-care hospital. J. Clin. Microbiol. *32*:2671–2676, 1994.
119. McNeeley, D. F., Saint-Louis, F., and Noel, G. J.: Neonatal enterococcal bacteremia: An increasingly frequent event with potentially untreatable pathogens. Pediatr. Infect. Dis. J. *15*:800–805, 1996.
120. McNeil, S. A., Clark, N. M., Chandrasekar, P. H., et al.: Successful treatment of vancomycin-resistant *Enterococcus faecium* bacteremia with linezolid after failure of treatment with Synercid (quinupristin/dalfopristin). Clin. Infect. Dis. *30*:403–404, 2000.
121. Mederski-Samoraj, B. D., and Murray, B. E.: High-level resistance to gentamicin in clinical isolates of enterococci. J. Infect. Dis. *147*:751–757, 1983.
122. Megran, D. W.: Enterococcal endocarditis. Clin. Infect. Dis. *15*:63–71, 1992.
123. Moellering, R. C., Jr.: Emergence of *Enterococcus* as a significant pathogen. Clin. Infect. Dis. *14*:1173–1176, 1992.
124. Moellering, R. C., Jr.: *Enterococcus* species, *Streptococcus bovis,* and *Leuconostoc* species. *In* Mandell, G. L., Bennett, J. E., and Dolin, R. (eds.): Principles and Practice of Infectious Diseases. 4th ed. New York, Churchill Livingstone, 1995.
125. Moellering, R. C., Jr., and Krogstad, D. J.: Antibiotic resistance in enterococci. *In* Schlessinger, D. (ed.): Microbiology—1979. Washington, D.C., American Society for Microbiology, 1979, pp. 293–298.
126. Moellering, R. C., Jr., Linden, P. K., Reinhardt, J., et al.: The efficacy and safety of quinupristin/dalfopristin for the treatment of infections caused by vancomycin-resistant *Enterococcus faecium:* Synercid Emergency-Use Study Group. J. Antimicrob. Chemother. *44*:251–261, 1999.
127. Moellering, R. C., Jr., and Weinberg, A. N.: Studies on antibiotic synergism against enterococci. II. Effect of various antibiotics on the uptake of C14-labeled streptomycin by enterococci. J. Clin. Invest. *50*:2580–2584, 1971.
128. Moellering, R. C., Jr., Wennersten, C., and Medrek, T.: Prevalence of high-level resistance to aminoglycosides in clinical isolates of enterococci. Antimicrob. Agents Chemother. *1*:335–340, 1970.
129. Mondy, K. E., Shannon, W., and Mundy, L. M.: Evaluation of zinc bacitracin capsules versus placebo for enteric eradication of vancomycin-resistant *Enterococcus faecium*. Clin. Infect. Dis. *33*:473–476, 2001.
130. Montecalvo, M. A., Horowitz, H., and Gedris, C.: Outbreak of vancomycin-, ampicillin-, and aminoglycoside-resistant *Enterococcus faecium* bacteremia in an adult oncology unit. Antimicrob. Agents Chemother. *38*:1363–1367, 1994.

131. Moreno, F., Grota, P., Crisp, C., et al.: Clinical and molecular epidemiology of vancomycin-resistant *Enterococcus faecium* during its emergence in a city in southern Texas. Clin. Infect. Dis. *21*:1234–1237, 1995.
132. Morris, J. G., Jr., Shay, D. K., Hebden, J. N., et al.: Enterococci resistant to multiple antimicrobial agents, including vancomycin. Ann. Intern. Med. *123*:250–259, 1995.
133. Morrison, A. J., Jr., and Wenzel, R. P.: Nosocomial urinary tract infections due to enterococcus: Ten years' experience at a university hospital. Arch. Intern. Med. *146*:1549–1551, 1986.
134. Murray, B. E.: The life and times of the enterococcus. Clin. Microbiol. Rev. *3*:46–65, 1990.
135. Murray, B. E.: Beta-lactamase–producing enterococci. Antimicrob. Agents Chemother. *36*:2355–2359, 1992.
136. Murray, B. E.: Editorial response: What can we do about vancomycin-resistant enterococci. Clin. Infect. Dis. *20*:1134–1136, 1995.
137. Murray, B. E.: Diversity among multidrug-resistant enterococci. Emerg. Infect. Dis. *4*:37–47, 1998.
138. Murray, B. E.: Vancomycin-resistant enterococcal infections. N. Engl. J. Med. *342*:710–721, 2000.
139. Murray, B. E., and Mederski-Samoraj, B.: Transferable beta-lactamase: A new mechanism for in vitro penicillin resistance in *Streptococcus faecalis*. J. Clin. Invest. *72*:1168, 1983.
140. Nachman, S. A., Verma, R., and Egnor, M.: Vancomycin-resistant *Enterococcus faecium* shunt infection in an infant: An antibiotic cure. Microb. Drug Resist. *1*:95–96, 1995.
141. Nagai, K., Yuge, K., Ono, E., et al.: *Enterococcus faecium* meningitis in a child. Pediatr. Infect. Dis. J. *13*:1016–1017, 1994.
142. National Committee for Clinical Laboratory Standards: Performance Standards for Antimicrobial Susceptibility Testing: Eleventh Informational Supplement. NCCLS document M100-S11 [ISBN 1-56238-426-0]. NCCLS, Wayne, PA, 2001, pp. 94–96.
143. Nauschuetz, W. F., Trevino, S. B., Harrison, L. S., et al.: *Enterococcus casseliflavus* as an agent of nosocomial bloodstream infections. Med. Microbiol. Lett. *2*:102–108, 1993.
144. Nichols, R. L., and Muzik, A. C.: Enterococcal infections in surgical patients: The mystery continues. Clin. Infect. Dis. *15*:72–76, 1992.
145. Nicoletti, G., and Stefain, S.: Enterococci: Susceptibility patterns and therapeutic options. Eur. J. Clin. Microbiol. Infect. Dis. *14* (Suppl.):33–37, 1995.
146. Noble, C. J.: Carriage of group D streptococci in the human bowel. J. Clin. Pathol. *31*:1182–1186, 1978.
147. Noble, W. C., Virani, Z., and Cree, R.: Cotransfer of vancomycin and other resistance genes from *Enterococcus faecalis* NCTC12201 to *Staphylococcus aureus*. FEMS Microbiol. Lett. *93*:195–198, 1992.
148. Norris, A. H., Reilly, J. P., Edelstein, P. H., et al.: Chloramphenicol for the treatment of vancomycin-resistant enterococcal infections. Clin. Infect. Dis. *20*:1137–1144, 1995.
149. Noskin, G. A., Siddiqui, F., Stosor, V., et al.: Successful treatment of persistent vancomycin-resistant *Enterococcus faecium* bacteremia with linezolid and gentamicin. Clin. Infect. Dis. *28*:689–690, 1999.
150. Noskin, G. A., Siddiqui, F., Stosor, V., et al.: In vitro activities of linezolid against important gram-positive bacterial pathogens including vancomycin-resistant enterococci. Antimicrob. Agents Chemother. *43*:2059–2062, 1999.
151. Nosocomial enterococci resistant to vancomycin—United States, 1989–1993. M. M. W. R. Morb. Mortal. Wkly. Rep. *42*(30):597–599, 1993.
152. Onderdonk, A. B., Bartlett, J. G., Louie, T. J., et al.: Microbial synergy in experimental intra-abdominal abscess. Infect. Immun. *12*:22–26, 1976.
153. Ostrowsky, B. E., Trick, W. E., Sohn, A. H., et al.: Control of vancomycin-resistant enterococcus in health care facilities in a region. N. Engl. J. Med. *344*:1427–1433, 2001.
154. Patel, R., Allen, S. L., Manahan, J. M., et al.: Natural history of vancomycin-resistant enterococcal colonization in liver and kidney transplant recipients. Liver Transpl. Surg. *7*:27–31, 2001.
155. Patel, R., Keating, M. R., Cockerill, F. R., et al.: Bacteremia due to *Enterococcus avium*. Clin. Infect. Dis. *17*:1006–1011, 1993.
156. Patterson, J. E., Sweeney, A. H., Simms, M., et al.: An analysis of 110 serious enterococcal infections, epidemiology, antibiotic susceptibility, and outcome. Medicine (Baltimore) *74*:191–200, 1995.
157. Patterson, J. E., and Zervos, M. J.: High-level gentamicin resistance in enterococcus: Microbiology, genetic basis, and epidemiology. Rev. Infect. Dis. *12*:644, 1990.
158. Patton, W. N., Bienz, N., Fraknlin, I. M., et al.: Enterococcal meningitis in an HIV positive hemophilic patient. J. Clin. Pathol. *44*:608–609, 1991.
159. Perez Mato, S., Robinson, S., and Begue, R. E.: Vancomycin-resistant *Enterococcus faecium* meningitis successfully treated with chloramphenicol. Pediatr. Infect. Dis. J. *18*:483–484, 1999.
160. Presterl, E., Graninger, W., and Georgopoulos, A.: The efficacy of teicoplanin in the treatment of endocarditis caused by gram-positive bacteria. J. Antimicrob. Chemother. *31*:755–766, 1993.
161. Prystowsky, J., Siddiqui, F., Chosay, J., et al.: Resistance to linezolid: Characterization of mutations in rRNA and comparison of their occurrences in vancomycin-resistant enterococci. Antimicrob. Agents Chemother. *45*:2154–2156, 2001.
162. Raymond, N. J., Henry, J., and Workowski, K. A.: Enterococcal arthritis: Case report and review. Clin. Infect. Dis. *21*:516–522, 1995.
163. Recommendations for preventing the spread of vancomycin resistance: Recommendations of the Hospital Infection Control Practices Advisory Committee (HICPAC). M. M. W. R. Recomm. Rep. *44*(RR-12):1–13, 1995.
164. Rhinehart, E., Smith, N. E., Wennersten, C., et al.: Rapid dissemination of beta-lactamase–producing, aminoglycoside-resistant *Enterococcus faecalis* among patients and staff on an infant-toddler surgical ward. N. Engl. J. Med. *323*:1814–1818, 1990.
165. Ricaurte, J. C., Boucher, H. W., Turett, G. S., et al.: Chloramphenicol treatment for vancomycin-resistant *Enterococcus faecium* bacteremia. Clin. Microbiol. Infect. *7*:17–21, 2001.
166. Rice, L. B.: Emergence of vancomycin-resistant enterococci. Emerg. Infect. Dis. *7*:183–187, 2001.
167. Rice, L. B., Calderwood, S. B., Eliopoulos, G. M., et al.: Enterococcal endocarditis: A comparison of prosthetic and native valve disease. Rev. Infect. Dis. *13*:1–7, 1991.
168. Rice, L. B., Carias, L. L., Hutton-Thomas, R., et al.: Penicillin-binding protein 5 and expression of ampicillin resistance in *Enterococcus faecium*. Antimicrob. Agents Chemother. *45*:1480–1486, 2001.
169. Rice, L. B., and Shlaes, D. M.: Vancomycin resistance in the enterococcus. Pediatr. Clin. North Am. *42*:601–618, 1995.
170. Ries, M., Deeg, K. H., Heininger, U., et al.: Brain abscesses in neonates—report of three cases. Eur. J. Pediatr. *152*:745–746, 1993.
171. Rubin, L. G., Tucci, V., Cercenado, E., et al.: Vancomycin-resistant *Enterococcus faecium* in hospitalized children. Infect. Control Hosp. Epidemiol. *13*:700–705, 1992.
172. Sader, H. S., Pfaller, M. A., Tenover, F. C., et al.: Evaluation and characterization of multiresistant *Enterococcus faecium* from 12 U.S. medical centers. J. Clin. Microbiol. *31*:2840–2842, 1994.
173. Sahgal, V. S., Urban, C., Mariano, N., et al.: Quinupristin/dalfopristin (RP 59500) therapy for vancomycin-resistant *Enterococcus faecium* aortic graft infection: Case report. Microb. Drug Resist. *1*:245–247, 1995.
174. Sanchez, M. L., Barrett, M. S., and Jones, R. N.: The E-test applied to susceptibility tests of gonococci, multiply resistant enterococci, and Enterobacteriaceae producing potent beta-lactamases. Diagn. Microbiol. Infect. Dis. *15*:459–462, 1992.
175. Sastry, V., Brennan, P. J., Levy, M. M., et al.: Vancomycin-resistant enterococci: An emerging pathogen in immunosuppressed transplant recipients. Transplant Proc. *27*:954–955, 1995.
176. Schaberg, D. R., Culver, D. H., and Gaynes, R. P.: Major trends in the microbial etiology of nosocomial infection. Am. J. Med. *91*(Suppl. 3B):72–75, 1991.
177. Schaberg, D. R., Dillon, W. I., Terpenning, M. S., et al.: Increasing resistance of enterococci to ciprofloxacin. Antimicrob. Agents Chemother. *36*:2533–2535, 1992.
178. Schmit, J.: Efficacy of teicoplanin for enterococcal infections: 63 cases and review. Clin. Infect. Dis. *15*:302–306, 1992.
179. Schoenbaum, S. C., Gardner, P., and Shillito, J.: Infections of cerebrospinal fluid shunts: Epidemiology, clinical manifestations, and therapy. J. Infect. Dis. *131*:543–552, 1975.
180. Schuster, F., Graubner, U. B., Schmid, I., et al.: Vancomycin-resistant-enterococci-colonization of 24 patients on a pediatric oncology unit. Klin. Padiatr. *210*:261–263, 1998.
181. Schwartz, M., Slavoski, L., Dash, G., et al.: Nosocomial outbreak of multi-resistant *Enterococcus durans* (VRED): Description of the epidemiology and antimicrobial sensitivity testing. Abstract 68. Paper presented at the 33rd Annual Meeting of the Infectious Diseases Society of America, San Francisco, 1995.
182. Shaikh, Z. H., Peloquin, C. A., and Ericsson, C. D.: Successful treatment of vancomycin-resistant *Enterococcus faecium* meningitis with linezolid: Case report and literature review. Scand. J. Infect. Dis. *33*:375–379, 2001.
183. Shay, D. K., Goldman, D. A., and Jarvis, W. R.: Reducing the spread of antimicrobial-resistant microorganisms: Control of vancomycin-resistant enterococci. Pediatr. Clin. North Am. *42*:703–716, 1995.
184. Shay, D. K., Maloney, S. A., Montecalvo, M., et al.: Epidemiology and mortality risk of vancomycin-resistant enterococcal bloodstream infections. J. Infect. Dis. *172*:993–1000, 1995.
185. Sherman, J. M.: The streptococci. Bacteriol. Rev. *1*:3–97, 1937.
186. Shlaes, D. M., Etter, L., and Gutmann, L.: Synergistic killing of vancomycin-resistant enterococci of classes A, B, and C by combinations of vancomycin, penicillin and gentamicin. Antimicrob. Agents Chemother. *35*:776–779, 1991.
187. Shlaes, D. M., Levy, J., and Wolinsky, E.: Enterococcal bacteremia without endocarditis. Arch. Intern. Med. *141*:578–581, 1981.
188. Shuler, T. E., Riddle, C. D., Jr., and Potts, D. W.: Polymicrobic septic arthritis caused by *Kingella kingae* and *Enterococcus*. Orthopedics *13*:254–256, 1990.
189. Siegel, J. S., and McCracken, G. H., Jr.: Group D streptococcal Infections. J. Pediatr. *93*:542–543, 1978.
190. Simpson, W. A., Courtney, H. S., and Ofek, I.: Interactions of fibronectin with streptococci: The role of fibronectin as a receptor for *Streptococcus pyogenes*. Rev. Infect. Dis. *9*(Suppl.):351–359, 1987.

191. Singh-Naz, N., Sleemi, A., Pikis, A., et al.: Vancomycin-resistant *Enterococcus faecium* colonization in children. J. Clin. Microbiol. *37*: 413–416, 1999.
192. Stanton, B. F., Baltimore, R. S., and Clemens, J. D.: Changing spectrum of infective endocarditis in children. Am. J. Dis. Child *138*:720–725, 1984.
193. Starke, J. R.: Infective endocarditis. *In* Feigin, R. D., and Cherry, J. D. (eds.): Textbook of Pediatric Infectious Diseases. 3rd ed. Philadelphia, W. B. Saunders, 1993, pp. 326–343.
194. Stevenson, K. B., Murray, E. W., and Sarubbi, F. A.: Enterococcal meningitis: Report of four cases and review. Clin. Infect. Dis. *18*: 233–239, 1994.
195. Swenson, J. M., Clark, N. C., Ferraro, M. J., et al.: Development of a standardized screening method for detection of vancomycin-resistant enterococci. J. Clin. Microbiol. *32*:1700–1704, 1994.
196. Swenson, J. M., Ferraro, M. J., Sahm, D. F., et al.: New vancomycin disk diffusion breakpoints for enterococci. The National Committee for Clinical Laboratory Standards Working Group on enterococci. J. Clin. Microbiol. *30*:2525–2528, 1992.
197. Swenson, J. M., Hindler, J. A., and Peterson, L. R.: Special tests for detecting antibacterial resistance. *In* Murray, P. R., Baron, E. J., Pfaller, M. A., et al. (eds.): Manual of Clinical Microbiology. 6th ed. Washington, D.C., American Society for Microbiology, 1995, pp. 1356–1367.
198. Takada, H., Kawabata, Y., Arakaki, R., et al.: Molecular and structural requirements of a lipoteichoic acid from *Enterococcus hirae* ATCC 9790 for cytokine-inducing, antitumor, and antigenic activities. Infect. Immun. *63*:57–65, 1995.
199. Teixeira, O. H., and Francis, C. K.: Enterococcal endocarditis in early infancy. Can. Med. Assoc. J. *127*:612–613, 1982.
200. Tenover, F. C., Swenson, J. M., O'Hara, C. M., et al.: Ability of commercial and reference antimicrobial susceptibility testing methods to detect vancomycin resistance in enterococci. J. Clin. Microbiol. *33*:1524–1527, 1995.
201. Threlkeld, M. G., and Cobbs, C. G.: Infectious disorders of prosthetic valves and intravascular devices. *In* Mandell, G. L., Bennett, J. E., and Dolin, R. (eds.): Principles and Practices of Infectious Diseases. 4th ed. New York, Churchill Livingstone, 1995, pp. 783–793.
202. Tofte, R. W., Solliday, J., and Crossley, K. B.: Susceptibilities of enterococci to twelve antibiotics. Antimicrob. Agents Chemother. *25*:532–533, 1984.
203. Tush, G. M., Huneycutt, S., Phillips, A., et al.: Intraventricular quinupristin/dalfopristin for the treatment of vancomycin-resistant *Enterococcus faecium* shunt infection. Clin. Infect. Dis. *26*:1460–1461, 1998.
204. Urdaneta, M., Hollis, F., and Sperber, S. J.: Vancomycin resistant enterococci in the blood: Do we need to treat? Abstract 65. Paper presented at the 33rd Annual Meeting of the Infectious Diseases Society of America, San Francisco, 1995.
205. Uttley, A. H., Collins, C. H., Naidoo, J., et al.: Vancomycin-resistant enterococci. Letter. Lancet *1*:57–58, 1988.
206. van Den Braak, N., Goessens, W., van Belkum, A., et al.: Accuracy of the VITEK 2 system to detect glycopeptide resistance in enterococci. J. Clin. Microbiol. *39*:351–353, 2001.
207. Verma, A., Dhawan, A., Philpott-Howard, J., et al.: Glycopeptide-resistant *Enterococcus faecium* infections in paediatric liver transplant recipients: Safety and clinical efficacy of quinupristin/dalfopristin. J. Antimicrob. Chemother. *47*:105–108, 2001.
208. Verma, M., Chatwal, J., and Varughese, P.: Neonatal conjunctivitis: A profile. Indian Pediatr. *31*:1357–1361, 1994.
209. von Baum, H., Schehl, J., Geiss, H. K., et al.: Prevalence of vancomycin-resistant enterococci among children with end-stage renal failure: Mid-European Pediatric Peritoneal Dialysis Study Group. Clin. Infect. Dis. *29*:912–916, 1999.
210. Weigelt, J. A., Easley, S. M., Thal, E. R., et al.: Abdominal surgical wound infection is lowered with improved perioperative *Enterococcus* and *Bacteroides* therapy. J. Trauma *34*:579–584, 1993.
211. Willey, B. M., Kreiswirth, B. N., Simor, A. E., et al.: Detection of vancomycin resistance in enterococcus species. J. Clin. Microbiol. *30*:1621–1624, 1992.
212. Willey, B. M., McGeer, A. J., Ostrowski, M. A., et al.: The use of the molecular typing techniques in the epidemiologic investigation of resistant enterococci. Infect. Control Hosp. Epidemiol. *15*:548–556, 1994.
213. Williamson, R., LeBouguenec, C., Gutmann, L., et al.: One or two low affinity penicillin-binding proteins may be responsible for the range of susceptibility of *Enterococcus faecium* to benzylpenicillin. J. Gen. Microbiol. *131*:1933–1940, 1985.
214. Wilson, W. R., Karchmer, A. W., Dajani, A. S., et al.: Antibiotic treatment of adults with infective endocarditis due to streptococci, enterococci, staphylococci, and HACEK microorganisms: American Heart Association. J. A. M. A. *274*:1706–1713, 1995.
215. Wilson, W. R., Wilkowske, C. J., Wright, A. J., et al.: Treatment of streptomycin-susceptible and streptomycin-resistant enterococcal endocarditis. Ann. Intern. Med. *100*:816–823, 1984.
216. Winberg, J., Anderson, H. J., and Bergstrom, T.: Epidemiology of symptomatic urinary tract infection in childhood. Acta Paediatr. Scand. Suppl. *252*:1, 1974.
217. Winston, D. J., Emmanouilides, C., Kroeber, A., et al.: Quinupristin/dalfopristin therapy for infections due to vancomycin-resistant *Enterococcus faecium*. Clin. Infect. Dis. *30*:790–797, 2000.
218. Zakrzewski, T., and Keith, J. D.: Bacterial endocarditis in infants and children. J. Pediatr. *67*:1179–1193, 1965.
219. Zeana, C., Kubin, C. J., Della-Latta, P., et al.: Vancomycin-resistant *Enterococcus faecium* meningitis successfully managed with linezolid: Case report and review of the literature. Clin. Infect. Dis. *33*:477–482, 2001.
220. Zervos, M. J., and Schaberg, D. S.: Reversal of the in vitro susceptibility of enterococci to trimethoprim-sulfamethoxazole by folinic acid. Antimicrob. Agents Chemother. *28*:446–448, 1985.
221. Zimmerman, R. A., Moellering, R. C., Jr., and Weinberg, A. N.: Mechanism of resistance to antibiotic synergism in enterococci. J. Bacteriol. *105*:873–879, 1971.
222. Zscheck, K. K., and Murray, B. E.: Genes involved in the regulation of beta-lactamase production in enterococci and staphylococci. Antimicrob. Agents Chemother. *37*:1966–1970, 1993.
223. Zurenko, G. E., Yagi, B. H., Schaadt, R. D., et al.: In vitro activities of U-100592 and U-100766, novel oxazolidinone antibacterial agents. Antimicrob. Agents Chemother. *40*:839–845, 1996.

VIRIDANS STREPTOCOCCAL INFECTIONS

A group of *Streptococcus* spp. known as viridans, alpha-hemolytic, or oral streptococci are ubiquitously present on the oral mucosa of virtually all humans. These organisms are important pathogens in children and adults alike and cause infections ranging from caries and bacterial endocarditis in immunocompetent hosts to fatal sepsis in neutropenic individuals. Although commonly a cause of infection, viridans streptococci isolated from clinical specimens often are discounted unless endocarditis is suspected. This indifference may reflect both the difficulty that microbiologists have experienced in defining and classifying the members of this group of streptococci and the ensuing challenges in assimilating clinical and microbiologic data.

Each of the terms applied to this group is problematic. Not all members of the alpha-hemolytic streptococci are alpha-hemolytic, some being gamma (non)-hemolytic or even beta-hemolytic. *Streptococcus pneumoniae,* which is beta-hemolytic, is considered to be a separate group. The term *viridans streptococci* is equally problematic because this term is derived from the Latin *viridis,* or green, and refers to the sheen caused by partial hemolysis around alpha-hemolytic colonies on sheep blood agar. The term *oral streptococci* circumvents the problem of outliers in the hemolytic classification schema, but it also is confusing because viridans streptococci are found in sites other than the oral cavity and nonviridans streptococcal species frequently are present in the oral cavity. In accordance with the American Society for Microbiology's most recent efforts in this field,[190] the term *viridans streptococci* will be used here in referring to this diverse group of bacteria in recognition that the member organisms typically, but not invariably, are alpha-hemolytic. Also of emphasis is that viridans does not refer to a species of streptococci but rather to a group of species, erroneous references to *Streptococcus viridans* notwithstanding.[206]

Streptococci have been reclassified on the basis of molecular and genetic studies,[51, 190] which adds to the clinical confusion, at least temporarily. For example, under the new classification system, certain small-colony beta-hemolytic streptococci, including some that are Lancefield group A, now are considered to be viridans streptococci. The

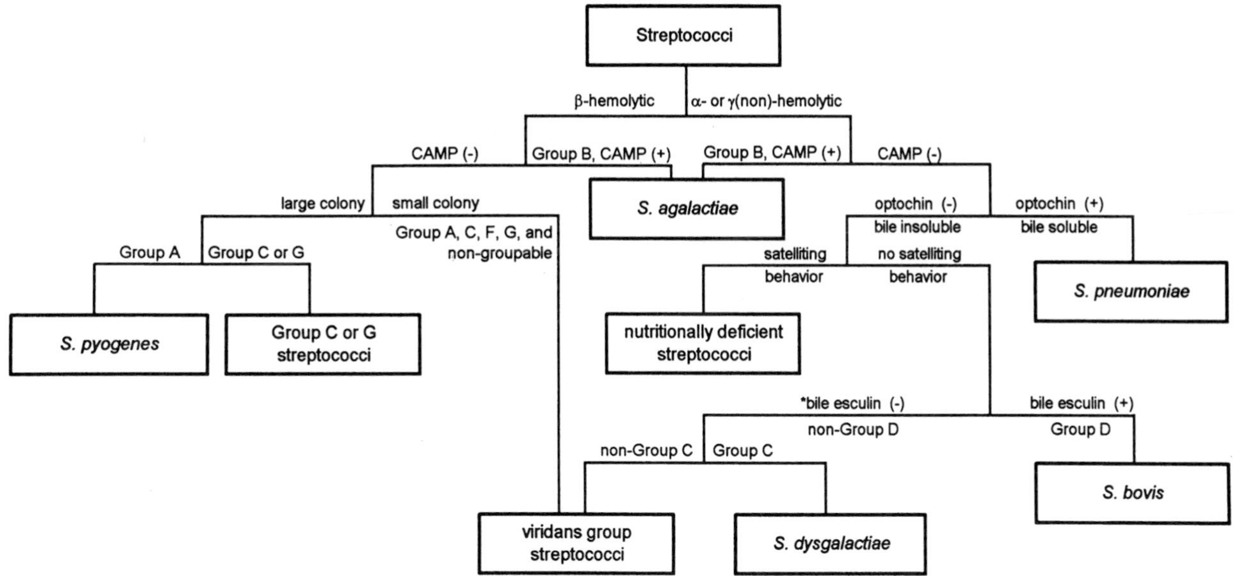

*Occasional viridans streptococcal strains are positive or weakly positive.

FIGURE 89–2 ■ Schema for the identification of clinically important streptococcal species. Viridans group species are, in general, those remaining after identification of other streptococcal species.

hope is that classification based on molecular relatedness eventually will lead to a clearer understanding of the infectious diseases associated with these organisms. One should recognize, however, that the current knowledge of viridans streptococcal infections is based predominantly on observation of the alpha-hemolytic members of the viridans group.

Microbiology

Streptococci are gram-positive, catalase-negative bacteria that are spherical or ovoid and less than 2 mm in diameter. They are facultatively anaerobic and nonmotile and do not produce spores or gas. Some strains require an atmosphere enriched with carbon dioxide (5%). The enterococci (distinguished by their ability to grow in 6.5% sodium chloride) and lactococci (formerly Lancefield group N streptococci) once were considered to be streptococci but now are classified as separate genera.

Figure 89–2 is a schema for classifying the clinically important streptococcal species. Hemolysis of blood agar remains a key tool for classifying streptococci. Strains that are beta-hemolytic are characterized further according to colony size and Lancefield group (a serologic classification system based on cell wall carbohydrate). Group B *Streptococcus agalactiae* strains typically can be identified by beta-hemolysis and a positive CAMP (Christie, Atkins, and Munch-Peterson) test[190]; however, some strains of *S. agalactiae* that are alpha- or gamma-hemolytic also are recognized by a positive CAMP test result.

Large-colony, beta-hemolytic, group A streptococci make up the species *Streptococcus pyogenes.* Other large-colony, beta-hemolytic streptococci occasionally are pathogenic, and most of them are group C or G streptococci. Small-colony, beta-hemolytic streptococci, including groups A, C, G, F, and nongroupable strains, partially constitute the *Streptococcus milleri* group of organisms within the viridans streptococci group. Among the alpha- or gamma-hemolytic streptococci, *S. agalactiae* (group B streptococci) and *S. pneumoniae* generally are identified by a positive CAMP test and Optochin test, respectively. Bile solubility confirms an optochin-susceptible isolate as *S. pneumoniae.*

Nutritionally deficient streptococci are recognized by a requirement for the presence of a second bacterial species (*Staphylococcus aureus* typically is used in testing) to maintain growth on agar. These streptococci generally will grow in blood culture media in the absence of the reduced form of nicotinamide adenine dinucleotide (NADH) produced by a second bacterial species and may demonstrate some growth on agar in the absence of other bacteria. Nutritionally deficient streptococci once were classified as viridans streptococci, but more recent studies have classified these organisms in a new genus: *Abiotrophia adjacens* and *Abiotrophia defectiva.*[115] *Enterococcus* spp. apart, streptococci that are alpha- or gamma-hemolytic possess Lancefield group D antigen, are bile esculin–positive, and may be identified tentatively as *Streptococcus bovis.* Although once included among viridans streptococci, this species now is classified separately from the viridans group.

Strains of one species of group C streptococci, *Streptococcus dysgalactiae,* are alpha- or gamma-hemolytic. These strains also must be distinguished from the viridans group of streptococci. A former streptococcal species included in the viridans group, *Streptococcus morbillorum*, was reclassified as *Gemella morbillorum.*[119] The remaining streptococcal organisms tentatively may be identified as viridans group streptococci. Thus, in practice, viridans streptococci continue to be characterized by the absence of features that distinguish the other major streptococcal pathogens. No characteristics can be used to definitively confirm the identity of viridans streptococci in the standard microbiology laboratory.

Classification of species within the viridans streptococci group also has been problematic. Several schemata have been developed over the years, including those of Carlsson,[37] Coleman and Williams,[47] Facklam,[77] Ruoff and Kunz,[191, 192] and Coykendall.[51] Each of these classification schemata lack reliable markers for member species and thereby result in inconsistent classification of clinical isolates. Consequently, efforts to characterize the clinical features of infections according to individual species of viridans streptococci have had marginal results. Molecular and PCR-based taxonomies have been used to classify viridans streptococci,[4, 51, 160, 189, 250] but these techniques generally are not available in the clinical laboratory. Given the current flux in the taxonomy of these organisms, a simplified, practical approach to classifying viridans streptococci as outlined in Table 89–5 has been advocated.[190] The biochemical tests available in many clinical microbiology laboratories can be used to assign clinical isolates to one of five groups that encompass the 14 clinically important viridans streptococcal species listed in Table 89–5. Rapid molecular and PCR-based tests are available for tentative identification of individual viridans streptococcal species[80, 88, 166, 192]; however, at this time, identification of precise species has little clinical significance except as an epidemiologic tool.

Epidemiology

Viridans streptococci are the predominant microorganisms in the oral flora of humans. These organisms also are found commonly in other areas of the upper respiratory tract, throughout the gastrointestinal tract, and in the female genital tract. Occasionally, viridans streptococci are found as members of the skin flora.

Viridans streptococci begin colonizing neonates shortly after birth. By 1 month of age, virtually all infants are colonized with at least one species of viridans streptococci.[163] The mix of colonizing viridans streptococcal species varies with ontogeny. For example, *Streptococcus mutans,* a species that plays an important role in the development of caries, rarely is found in predentate children but commonly is present after the eruption of teeth.[38, 67, 224] The ecology of other viridans streptococcal species also appears to be affected by the eruption of teeth.[39, 67, 207, 224] In addition to these temporal factors in colonization of infants and children, viridans streptococci have species-specific predilections for certain anatomic areas of the oral cavity and pharynx. For example, *Streptococcus sanguis* is the predominant isolate of the buccal mucosa but rarely is found on the dorsum of the tongue, where *Streptococcus mitis* is the predominant species.[84] Diet also may affect the viridans streptococcal ecology. Consumption of sugar-containing beverages and the low pH that can result from carbohydrate intake, for example, favor colonization with caries-producing *S. mutans.*[95, 222]

Little is known about the transmission of viridans streptococci, but studies of the transmission of *S. mutans* within families indicate that intrafamily transmission commonly occurs.[3, 99, 193] Toothbrushes may be an important vehicle of transmission of viridans streptococci in children.[133] The hands of hospital personnel, especially those with skin disorders such as eczema, also may be a vehicle of transmission of viridans streptococci.[44] In addition, dental records have been suggested as a vehicle in the transmission of viridans streptococci.[52]

Viridans streptococci have an important role in the ecology of the oral flora in that they protect against potentially more invasive pathogens via colonization resistance.[17, 87] This mechanism has been demonstrated by a double-blind study in which patients were treated with either a preparation containing four species of viridans streptococci or a placebo after antibiotic therapy for group A streptococcal pharyngitis. In the treated group, none of 17 patients experienced recurrence of group A streptococcal pharyngitis. In contrast, pharyngitis recurred in 7 (37%) of 19 patients in the placebo group.[182] A second double-blind, placebo-controlled multicenter trial by the same group confirmed the finding of the first study.[183] Viridans streptococci also may have a role in colonization resistance to pathogens such as methicillin-resistant *S. aureus* in the oral cavity of infants[232]; nontypeable *Haemophilus influenzae, S. pneumoniae,* and *Moraxella catarrhalis* at the eustachian tube orifice[223]; and *Neisseria gonorrhoeae* in the female genital tract.[142] In addition to competition for mucosal adherence sites, viridans streptococci produce hydrogen peroxide and bacteriocins that exert a bactericidal effect on certain competing bacteria and may contribute to colonization resistance.[53, 54, 233, 238]

Pathogenesis

Viridans streptococci are organisms of low virulence that usually cause nonpyogenic infection when they do cause infection. They are involved most often in localized infections of the sinuses and oral cavity, including the teeth, in which the tissues are invaded directly by colonizing organisms. Caries is a disease of teeth that develops over a period of years, often in association with *S. mutans* infection.

TABLE 89–5 ■ SIMPLIFIED CLASSIFICATION SCHEMA FOR VIRIDANS STREPTOCOCCI

Group	Species	Hemolysis	Sorbitol	Arginine	Voges-Proskaner	Mannitol	Esculin
S. milleri	*S. anginosus*	α, β, γ	−	+	+	±	±
	S. constellatus					−	
	S. intermedius					±	
S. mutans	*S. mutans*	β, γ, α	+	−	+	+	+
	S. sobrinus						
	S. rattus						
	S. cricetus						
S. salivarius	*S. salivarius*	γ, α	−	−	+	−	+
	S. vestibularis						
S. sanguis	*S. sanguis*	α	−	+	−	−	+
	S. gordonii						+
	S. parasanguis						±
	S. crista						−
S. mitis	*S. mitis**	α	−	−	−	−	−

*Previously included *S. mitis, S. sanguis* II, and *S. oralis.*
Data from Coykendall, A. L.: Classification and identification of the viridans streptococci. Clin. Microbiol. Rev. *2*:315–328, 1989; Ruoff, K. L.: *Streptococcus. In* Murray, P. R., Baron, E. J., Pfaller, M. A., et al. (eds.): Manual of Clinical Microbiology. 6th ed. Washington, D.C., American Society for Microbiology, 1995, pp. 299–307.

Viridans streptococci also have a role in a variety of gingival diseases, possibly including the development of gingival hyperplasia accompanying the chronic administration of phenytoin. In an experimental animal model, phenytoin-induced gingival hyperplasia was enhanced in rats infected with *Streptococcus sobrinus* when compared with uninfected control animals.[155] Occasionally, viridans streptococci, usually *S. milleri* group organisms, cause pyogenic infections, including brain, lung, and abdominal abscesses. An intriguing, but preliminary study suggests that viridans streptococcal–related dental disease is associated with the subsequent development of coronary artery heart disease.[128] Viridans streptococci are among the microorganisms isolated from atherosclerotic plaque, although the role of these microbes in the pathogenesis of atherosclerosis has not been determined.[43] Typically, viridans streptococci cause life-threatening infection only in settings in which the oral mucosa is disrupted and the host's mechanisms of clearance are compromised, such as in patients with neutropenia or cardiac valve disease.

The preponderance of viridans streptococci in the oral flora rather than its virulence accounts for the domination of viridans streptococci in infections originating from the mouth. In a study of 36 children who underwent extraction of normal or abscessed teeth, 11 (30%) had postextraction positive blood cultures.[213] In all 11, viridans streptococci were isolated exclusively. Bacteremia occurred more commonly after removal of diseased teeth (37%), but it also occurred after removal of normal teeth (23%).

A separate study of 58 children undergoing dental extraction included 26 who received penicillin, amoxicillin, or erythromycin prophylaxis because of a risk for development of endocarditis.[50] Only 9 (35%) of the 26 children who received prophylaxis had bacteremia detected as compared with 20 (63%) of 32 children who did not receive prophylaxis ($p < .05$). In this study, viridans streptococci accounted for 37 percent of the blood isolates, strict anaerobes accounted for 26.5 percent, and a variety of organisms accounted for the remainder. The number of colony-forming units per milliliter of blood ranged from 2 to 12. Even within a single colony-forming unit, more than one bacterial species sometimes was found after subculture.

Although these two studies were dissimilar in the diversity of organisms isolated, both indicate that viridans streptococci are the organisms most likely to invade the blood after trauma to the oral cavity. Also reflecting the predominance of these organisms in the oral and salivary flora, bacteremia with viridans streptococci occurs commonly during orthodontic banding[76] and esophageal stricture dilation.[255]

The ability of viridans streptococci to bind to oral mucosa, tooth surfaces, and dental plaque via interaction of specific microbial and host "receptors" accounts for the preferential colonization of the oral cavity by these organisms.[236] This interaction also helps explain the localization of the various viridans streptococcal species to distinct anatomic sites, as well as ontologic factors in colonization. The precise nature of bacterial adherence to the oral mucosa is not defined but appears to involve streptococcal lipoteichoic acid.[104] Through release of modulin protein I/II, viridans streptococci induce the expression of adhesion molecules such as E-selectin and intercellular (ICAM-1) and vascular cell (VCAM-1) adhesion molecules on endothelial cells, promote transendothelial migration of neutrophils in vitro, and induce cytokine release in epithelial (interleukin-6 [IL-6]) and endothelial cells (IL-6 and IL-8).[240, 241] The host's immunologic status also may be an important determinant of adherence and subsequent invasion. For example, immunocompetent individuals produce secretory IgA to *S. mutans*,[11] and such antibody is capable of preventing caries.[149] Viridans streptococci within the biofilm present in dental plaque are 500 or more times resistant to antibiotic treatment than expected by their susceptibility in culture medium, thus suggesting that antibiotic treatment cannot eradicate viridans streptococci from dental plaque, even temporarily.[122]

At the University of Texas M. D. Anderson Cancer Center in Houston, the incidence of viridans streptococcal bacteremia increased extraordinarily between 1972 and 1989, from 1 to 47 cases per 10,000 admissions.[69] An analysis of the risk factors associated with viridans streptococcal bacteremia indicated that prophylactic administration of TMP-SMX or a fluoroquinolone, profound neutropenia, and the administration of antacids or histamine type 2 antagonists each significantly predisposed to the development of bacteremia.[69] Presumably, administration of the implicated antibiotics and antacids favored the overgrowth of viridans streptococci and their proliferation throughout the gastrointestinal tract, which in turn would favor viridans streptococcal bacteremia in an immunocompromised host, especially if the mucosal barrier was disrupted by cytotoxic chemotherapy and the host was neutropenic. Of note, administration of cytarabine (cytosine arabinoside or Ara-C) was not associated with viridans streptococcal sepsis in this study despite being identified as a major risk factor in many other studies.[27, 28, 35, 61, 108, 137, 147, 179]

The ability to adhere to damaged cardiac valves and vegetations is a principal factor in the predominance of viridans streptococcal endocarditis. Strains of viridans streptococci carried by healthy children adhered less well to both buccal and endocardial cells than did disease-producing strains isolated from children with endocarditis.[198, 199] Lipoteichoic acid is thought to help mediate adhesion of viridans streptococci to endocardium, and penicillin prophylaxis may be effective in part because of its reduction of lipoteichoic acid on the bacterial cell surface.[130]

The ability of antibiotics to alter the surface properties of bacteria, even when the bacteria are resistant to the bactericidal action of the drug, may be an important determinant in the effectiveness of prophylactic antibiotics.[130, 204] In the host, fibronectin is an important determinate of viridans streptococcal binding to damaged endothelium. Viridans streptococci do not bind to soluble fibronectin, but a reactive domain becomes available for binding when the fibronectin molecule is immobilized, as is the case in endocarditis.[129] Mutant viridans streptococci that cannot bind to fibronectin were significantly less virulent in an animal model of endocarditis.[129]

The ability of viridans streptococci to induce platelet aggregation also may be involved in the pathogenesis of endocarditis.[81, 134] In viridans streptococci–challenged, anticoagulated rabbits, only microscopic vegetations developed despite fulminant sepsis. In contrast, viridans streptococci–challenged, non-anticoagulated animals tended to have large vegetations and a subacute course.[107] These finding are concordant with those of a separate study in which viridans streptococci–challenged thrombocytopenic rabbits had a greater density of bacteria within vegetations than did nonthrombocytopenic control animals, thus suggesting that platelets limit progression of the disease.[218] Surprisingly, neutropenia appears to have little effect on the susceptibility to endocarditis in animal models but does have a role in containing the infection.[145, 146]

In patients with neutropenic cancer and bone marrow transplants, viridans streptococci cause septic shock and adult respiratory distress syndrome. Viridans streptococci also induce nephritis.[5, 227] In either circumstance, little is known about the mechanisms involved. Viridans streptococci produce no endotoxin, and specific exotoxins have not been identified. Nonetheless, products of these organisms can activate complement[153] and induce the production of tumor necrosis factor–alpha (TNF-α) and TNF-β; IL-1, IL-2, IL-6, and IL-8; interferon-γ1195; and nitric oxide.[18, 72, 141, 159, 208, 210, 221] Strains from patients with sepsis were found to be more active in inducing TNF-β and IL-8 than were colonizing strains from healthy subjects.[211] In a study of two neutropenic patients with fatal viridans streptococcal sepsis, high blood levels of IL-6 were detected, especially late in the course, whereas IL-1 and TNF-α blood levels were not remarkable.[71] Viridans streptococcal lipoteichoic acid is known to induce cytokine and nitric oxide production in vitro,[72, 153] but the clinical significance of these observations is not known.

Clinical Manifestations

The viridans streptococcal species are a diverse group of bacteria, and, consequently, a variety of clinical manifestations are associated with the infections that they cause. Typically, the viridans streptococci cause nonpyogenic infections such as bacteremia and endocarditis, whereas the *S. milleri* group, also referred to as the *Streptococcus intermedius* group, tends to cause invasive pyogenic infections, including bone infections, brain abscesses, appendicitis, and pulmonary and abdominal abscesses.[156]

SEPSIS IN IMMUNOCOMPROMISED HOSTS

For obscure reasons, during the past 2 or 3 decades, the relative incidence of gram-positive bacterial infections, especially viridans streptococcal infection, has increased in immunocompromised hosts. In 1978, viridans streptococci first were perceived as an important cause of sepsis in patients with neutropenic cancer when 29 episodes in adults and children at the National Cancer Institute[169] and 6 episodes in children at M. D. Anderson Cancer Center[103] were reported. Before these reports, the significance of blood isolates of viridans streptococci in this setting generally was not appreciated. No deaths occurred in the original National Cancer Institute series or in a subsequent series from that center,[187] thus suggesting that viridans streptococci produce a benign bacteremia similar to that seen with coagulase-negative staphylococci. In contrast, three of the six children at M. D. Anderson died. Several other centers in Europe and North America have reported fulminant, sometimes fatal, viridans streptococcal sepsis in cancer and transplant patients.* Overall, the death rate associated with viridans streptococcal sepsis has ranged from 0 to 50 percent, with most centers reporting mortality rates of approximately 10 percent. In some centers, viridans streptococci are the most common cause of fatal sepsis.[21, 27, 94] The incidence of viridans streptococcal sepsis appears to be higher in children than in adults.[140, 216]

The oral cavity is the most common portal of entry in immunocompromised hosts. Catheter-related viridans streptococcal bacteremia is an unusual occurrence. However, because administration of antacid is a risk factor,[69] the lower gastrointestinal tract probably is a portal of entry in some patients. Several factors predispose to the development of viridans streptococcal sepsis. Profound neutropenia clearly is a predisposing factor,[27, 69] although viridans streptococcal bacteremia occasionally develops in patients with cancer and absolute neutrophil counts greater than 1000 cells/mL. Mucositis, especially oral mucositis, is a definitive risk factor.[27, 28, 69, 94, 137, 147] Cytarabine appears to be a risk factor even beyond its predisposition to produce clinically evident mucositis.[27, 28, 35, 61, 108, 137, 147, 179] The use of prophylactic TMP-SMX or quinolones also is an important risk factor.[27, 28, 45, 69, 94, 165] The observation that the administration of acyclovir may decrease the incidence of viridans streptococcal bacteremia in transplant patients suggests that herpes simplex virus infection may be a risk factor as well.[180] Allogeneic bone marrow transplantation also has been associated with an increased risk for development of viridans streptococcal sepsis, with a greater than fourfold increase in the mortality rate.[137] An association between development of viridans streptococcal sepsis and menstruation has been noted.[69]

The hallmark clinical feature of viridans streptococcal sepsis in an immunocompromised host is fever, which typically is high, occurs in the presence of neutropenia and mucositis, and frequently lasts for several days after viable organisms are cleared from the blood. Most patients recover uneventfully. However, fulminant septic shock may occur. Shock may appear early, although it often is delayed for 2 or 3 days after the onset of sepsis, and it occurs despite prompt sterilization of blood by effective antibiotics.[216] Adult respiratory distress syndrome frequently occurs in severe cases, usually 2 or 3 days after the initial bacteremia.[10, 69, 106, 225] Focal complications, including pneumonia and meningitis, are uncommon occurrences. Rash and palmar desquamation may be present.[69]

Several studies have implicated *S. mitis* as a more pathogenic species of viridans streptococci with a predilection to cause shock and adult respiratory distress syndrome in patients with cancer,[10, 28, 46, 65, 143, 216, 225] but other studies have not found a clear relationship between clinical features and species.[69] Given the uncertainty in classifying viridans streptococcal species, reported species associations should be viewed cautiously.

NEONATAL SEPSIS, MENINGITIS, AND OTHER INFECTIONS

Viridans streptococci are normal inhabitants of the female genital tract and are a common cause of chorioamnionitis and subsequent abortions.[9] Viridans streptococci also are a frequent cause of neonatal sepsis and meningitis, but this association is not recognized universally.[1, 24, 33, 85, 127, 154, 246] Viridans streptococci ordinarily do not colonize newborns' skin and should not be dismissed as contaminants when isolated from normally sterile sites.[1] In some newborn centers, the incidence of viridans streptococcal bacteremia and meningitis has approached or exceeded that seen with group B streptococci, although viridans streptococcal infections tend to be less severe.[33, 154] *Streptococcus oralis* (*S. mitis*) was found to cause more than one half the cases in one study.[246] The portal of entry of the organism generally is unknown in this setting, but a fetal scalp electrode has been implicated in one case.[86] Unusual manifestations in newborns include pharyngitis and epiglottitis,[30] endocarditis,[144] and conjunctivitis.[120]

ENDOCARDITIS

Viridans streptococci are the most common cause of endocarditis at all ages because of the organism's ability to

*See references 10, 13, 21, 27, 28, 35, 46, 48, 69, 94, 96, 100, 123, 137, 140, 147, 165, 177, 179, 203, 209, 216, 243.

adhere to diseased endocardium and its frequent implication in bacteremia during dental procedures and routine mouth care. Viridans streptococci tend to cause subacute endocarditis; blood cultures may be positive only intermittently. *S. sanguis* and *S. mitis* are the species identified most commonly.[62, 176, 181, 219] Complications of viridans streptococcal endocarditis include septic pulmonary emboli, congestive heart failure, pericarditis, myocardial abscess, meningitis, osteomyelitis, and glomerulonephritis.[121, 176]

PNEUMONIA

Pulmonary infiltrates frequently complicate viridans streptococcal sepsis in neutropenic hosts. In most cases, these infiltrates represent adult respiratory distress syndrome, not primary pneumonia. However, several cases of primary viridans streptococcal pneumonia developing in previously healthy individuals have been reported.[93, 135, 157, 173, 195] In some cases, the diagnosis was supported by multiple blood isolates of viridans streptococci in the absence of endocarditis. The incidence of viridans streptococcal pneumonia may be underestimated significantly because tracheal isolates of viridans streptococci usually are discounted as contaminants. Nonetheless, tracheal isolates probably do represent contamination of the specimen with oral flora in many cases.[184] Given the increasing incidence of viridans streptococcal infection and the escalating prevalence of antibiotic resistance among these organisms, clinicians should consider viridans streptococci as potential causes of pneumonia when they are isolated in the absence of other pathogens.

OSTEOMYELITIS AND SEPTIC ARTHRITIS

Viridans streptococci are unusual causes of osteomyelitis and septic arthritis. Extension of an oral infection into the mandible or maxilla is the most common circumstance in which viridans streptococci cause osteomyelitis,[162] but vertebral osteomyelitis caused by these organisms has been described on several occasions.[2, 34, 57, 188, 234, 244] Infection of the long bones[178] and septic arthritis[14] occur infrequently.

CARIES

Although caries was recognized as an infectious disease in 1890 by workers trained in Robert Koch's laboratory, its infectious nature still is not accepted universally.[8, 12, 66] Evidence that *S. mutans* is the major cause of caries in children and adults alike is substantial,[8, 12, 31, 202, 226, 231, 237] but other viridans streptococci and *Actinomyces* spp. also have cariogenic potential.[202, 237] *S. mutans*, which colonizes the oral cavity only after the eruption of teeth, has a predilection for the dental surfaces, metabolizes sucrose, and produces a strong acid that weakens the mineral matrix of teeth and allows the organisms to penetrate the structure of the teeth.[40, 202] Fluoridation of the water supply has been credited with strengthening tooth enamel, thereby fostering resistance to the harsh acids produced by *S. mutans*.[202] Fluoride has potent antibacterial action against *S. mutans*, particularly at low pH.[40, 239] Thus, our efforts at fluoridation of water supplies may represent, in one form or another, the most widespread and successful use of antibacterial prophylaxis. Topical treatments also provide protection against the cariogenic actions of *S. mutans* and in some circumstances depend on the antibacterial action of fluoride.[102, 228, 235, 253] Short courses of oral antibiotics can reduce colonization with *S. mutans* substantially and may be an important adjunct to the treatment of caries.[215] Specially designed culture systems are available to detect the presence and measure the concentration of *S. mutans* in plaque and thus permit the effects of therapy to be monitored.[31, 245] Because the development of cavities typically requires a few years of infection, opportunity to interrupt the pathogenesis of this disease is ample.[8]

ABSCESSES AND OTHER INFECTIONS

The suppurative infections produced by viridans streptococci typically are caused by the *S. milleri* group: *Streptococcus anginosus, Streptococcus constellatus,* and *S. intermedius*. Because *S. milleri* bacteria inhabit the upper respiratory tract and the gastrointestinal tract and are relatively invasive, these organisms cause sinusitis, otitis media, meningitis, and abdominal abscesses and often are present in brain abscesses.[23, 49, 70, 150, 152, 156, 194] *S. milleri* group organisms may infect the brain via a hematogenous route that originates in the oral cavity or intestinal tract or by direct invasion through the upper respiratory tract. Sepsis in non-neutropenic patients occurs uncommonly, usually in association with an intra-abdominal source.[131, 194] Iatrogenic meningitis from contamination by oral viridans streptococci may complicate lumber puncture or other CNS procedures.[74, 197, 251] Lung abscesses caused by viridans streptococci may result from aspiration of saliva.[112, 173] Empyema and mediastinitis are other reported thoracic infections with viridans streptococci.[19, 112] Viridans streptococci also are found occasionally in liver abscesses[16, 82, 89] and appendicitis.[170]

Diagnosis

Clinically, infections caused by viridans streptococci cannot be distinguished from infections with other gram-positive and gram-negative bacteria. Collection of adequate culture specimens is essential for diagnosis. Viridans streptococcal infections typically are diagnosed by culture of blood or other normally sterile tissues. The organisms may be present in low concentration. A volume of 30 mL of blood has been suggested as the optimal volume for culture in an adult-sized patient.[200] The addition of agents that neutralize the antibacterial effects of fresh blood, such as sodium polyanethole sulfonate, significantly improves the yield of blood cultures.[201] Chemotherapy agents may interfere with the detection of viridans streptococci in blood.[164]

Viridans streptococci normally are not part of the skin flora and ordinarily should not be considered contaminants. Viridans streptococci have been reported to cross-react with *S. pneumoniae* omnisera, potentially leading to false-positive omnisera test results.[106]

Antibiotic Susceptibility

In the past, viridans streptococci have been considered penicillin-sensitive. Today, penicillin-resistant and penicillin-tolerant viridans streptococci are found worldwide as causes of sepsis, endocarditis, meningitis, and other infections, including conjunctivitis of the newborn.[29, 68, 78, 92, 105, 120, 126, 171, 175] Penicillin resistance occurs commonly, particularly in patients receiving long-term penicillin therapy,[7, 25, 161, 214, 217] although even short courses of antibiotics may predispose to colonization with resistant viridans streptococci.[75, 90, 151]

Resistance to cephalosporins also is widespread, with a general pattern of susceptibility being cefotaxime, ceftriaxone more than cefepime, cefuroxime more than ceftazidime, and cephalexin.[59, 136, 167, 247] Previous cephalosporin therapy is a risk factor for cephalosporin resistance, an observation with particular relevance for oncology patients.[116] Resistance to fluoroquinolones, especially ciprofloxacin, is a common finding.[42, 55, 58, 117, 196, 250]

Ominously, viridans streptococci resistant to aminoglycosides,[114] tetracycline,[55, 59, 250] TMP-SMX,[55, 58, 59, 250] clindamycin,[58, 230, 250] erythromycin,[32, 55, 58, 59, 250] other macrolide antibiotics,[6] and vancomycin[205] also have been reported. Overall, vancomycin is the antibiotic with the most reliable activity against viridans streptococci. Teicoplanin also has been used successfully to treat patients with endocarditis caused by viridans streptococci.[248] Antibiotic resistance may develop in all species of viridans streptococci, although *S. mutans* rarely exhibits resistance.[111]

Resistance of viridans streptococci to penicillin appears to involve chromosomally mediated alterations in the organisms' PBPs.[175, 254] Initially, researchers suspected that genes conferring penicillin resistance might have been acquired from *S. pneumoniae*.[64] Subsequent studies, however, indicate that penicillin resistance may have evolved first in *S. mitis* and that *S. pneumoniae* acquired genes mediating penicillin resistance from this and other closely related viridans streptococcal species.[41, 63, 172] Quinolone resistance determinants also are transmitted efficiently between viridans streptococci and *S. pneumoniae*.[110]

The clinical impact of the development of penicillin resistance among viridans streptococci has been far-reaching. The emergence of penicillin-resistant viridans streptococci incidentally may be encouraging the development of vancomycin-resistant enterococci because of the increased use of vancomycin to prevent and treat viridans streptococcal infection in patients with cancer.

Treatment

Empiric antibiotic therapy for viridans streptococci should be based on the local pattern of antibiotic susceptibility among recent clinical isolates. Antimicrobial susceptibility testing of viridans streptococcal isolates is necessary. Limited data indicate that antibiotic susceptibility testing performed with the E-test correlates well with agar dilution susceptibility testing.[185] Although vancomycin-resistant clinical isolates currently are very rare findings, inclusion of vancomycin in susceptibility testing is advisable. For infections other than endocarditis and meningitis, single-antibiotic therapy usually is preferred. An exception is a neutropenic cancer patient because restricting antibiotic therapy to drugs active against gram-positive bacteria exclusively may predispose to the development of gram-negative bacterial infections.[168]

Combination therapy often is advocated for the treatment of viridans streptococcal endocarditis[26, 83, 139, 242] and may be considered for the treatment of meningitis, especially when the infecting organism is tolerant to penicillin.[73] Combinations of penicillins and aminoglycosides or vancomycin and aminoglycosides are used most commonly. Penicillin and vancomycin are thought to increase the uptake of aminoglycosides, thereby leading to synergistic bactericidal activity.[252]

Frequent dosing of antibiotics generally has been recommended; however, viridans streptococci exposed to penicillin or cephalosporin plus aminoglycoside combinations appear to be susceptible to a post-antibiotic effect.[36, 118, 124] Consequently, longer dosing intervals may be satisfactory, but data are currently insufficient to support a recommendation. Viridans streptococcal endocarditis usually is treated for 4 to 6 weeks; the duration of therapy for infections at other sites has not been studied but generally can be guided by site-specific practice and individual clinical response.

In the treatment of endocarditis, penetration of antibiotics into the fibrin vegetation may be impeded markedly. Viridans streptococci produce an exopolysaccharide composed predominantly of dextran, which may limit penetration. Experimental studies indicate that the degree of exopolysaccharide production by viridans streptococcal strains affects the success rate of antimicrobial therapy.[174] In accord with this observation, administration of dextranase to animals with experimental viridans streptococcal endocarditis enhances antibiotic efficacy.[148] In the future, such adjuvant therapies designed to reduce the size or density of valvular vegetations may offer promise for patients not helped by conventional antibiotic therapy for endocarditis.

Another setting in which adjuvant therapy may be considered is viridans streptococcal sepsis in a neutropenic patient who has received cytarabine chemotherapy. One uncontrolled trial suggests that the early addition of high doses of corticosteroids to the antimicrobial therapeutic regimen may reduce the incidence of associated adult respiratory distress syndrome and death.[60] However, data are insufficient to recommend this approach routinely.

Prevention

Attempts to prevent viridans streptococcal infection have focused on three distinct settings: prevention of caries, prevention of endocarditis, and prevention of sepsis in neutropenic cancer patients. Efforts have been successful in the former two settings. However, the emergence of penicillin-resistant viridans streptococci and concern about the possible emergence of vancomycin resistance highlight the need for new approaches to preventing development of infection with these ubiquitous organisms. In developing such methods, investigators should not forget that the resistance to colonization provided by viridans streptococci can protect the host from more virulent pathogens (see "Epidemiology").

The incidence of caries in the United States has been reduced sharply by fluoridation of water supplies, inclusion of fluoride in toothpaste, and modification of diet (e.g., use of sugar substitutes). Fluoride acts as an antibacterial agent while strengthening resistance of the teeth to invasion by bacteria. The use of dental varnishes, gels, and rinses that contain fluoride or other antibacterials such as chlorhexidine or vancomycin may be beneficial in selected cases.[79, 113, 138, 158]

The American Heart Association has led a successful effort to prevent development of endocarditis by systemic antibiotic prophylaxis of patients with known endocardial defects who are undergoing dental procedures. These efforts are aimed especially at preventing development of viridans streptococcal endocarditis, and penicillin is the antibiotic most commonly used. The mechanism or mechanisms by which antibiotic prophylaxis prevents endocarditis are not understood completely. In animals, endocarditis can be prevented by the administration of bacteriostatic antibiotics and by maintaining serum levels of bactericidal antibiotics that are well below the MIC for the colonizing viridans streptococci.[91] Vancomycin has been observed to prevent development of vancomycin-tolerant *S. sanguis* endocarditis in experimentally challenged animals without reducing the incidence or level of bacteremia, thus suggesting that antibiotics may prevent endocarditis by reducing bacterial adherence to endocardium.[20] This hypothesis is supported by a study in which bacteremia, in some cases with antibiotic-resistant organisms, developed in 21 percent of children receiving antibiotic prophylaxis, but endocarditis rarely occurred.[101] However, studies in animals indicate that the probability of preventing endocarditis is correlated with the antibiotic susceptibility of the challenging streptococcal strains.[101]

Prophylaxis should be targeted carefully[229] and administered immediately before initiating dental procedures. Increased numbers of antibiotic-resistant viridans streptococci can be detected within 6 hours of antibiotic treatment, and they persist for 9 days or longer.[125] Experimental studies on the prevention of endocarditis by the administration of antibiotics after challenge with bacterial inocula have yielded inconsistent results,[22, 109, 132] and the clinical utility of this approach is not known. Topical treatment with vancomycin or chlorhexidine has been advocated as an adjuvant to prevent development of endocarditis, but the efficacy of this approach has not been proved.[220, 249]

Viridans streptococcal infections have become a major problem in neutropenic cancer patients and in bone marrow transplant patients in recent years. Because penicillin-resistant viridans streptococci are widespread, some cancer centers include vancomycin in the initial empiric antibiotic regimen for neutropenic patients with unexplained fever.[203] In addition, despite concern about the possibility of inducing vancomycin-resistant bacterial strains, physicians managing bone marrow transplant units are administering intravenous vancomycin prophylactically to high-risk patients in an effort to prevent development of viridans streptococcal sepsis.

A noncontrolled trial of oral vancomycin paste in children receiving cytotoxic chemotherapy suggested efficacy in the prevention of viridans streptococcal infection.[15] However, increased colonization and infection with vancomycin-resistant enterococci are a predictable consequence of increased vancomycin use, which has prompted CDC recommendations to avoid the use of empiric vancomycin therapy when feasible and has led investigators to explore alternatives to the use of empiric or prophylactic vancomycin.

In a comparative trial, penicillin prophylaxis was superior to TMP-SMX prophylaxis in preventing viridans streptococcal infections in cancer patients despite extensive colonization with penicillin-resistant streptococci.[98] In other studies, oral administration of penicillin or roxithromycin, a macrolide antibiotic, also appeared to reduce the incidence of viridans streptococcal infection in cancer patients in comparison to historical controls.[56, 186, 212] In contrast, in a study of prophylactic administration of ampicillin to patients receiving autologous bone marrow transplants, no reduction in the incidence of viridans streptococcal sepsis occurred, whereas the incidence of penicillin resistance increased.[25]

Increased penicillin resistance associated with penicillin prophylaxis has been noted in other prophylactic trials as well.[212] The CDC does not recommend the routine use of penicillin prophylaxis in patients receiving bone marrow transplants.[97] Innovative prophylactic methodologies and carefully designed clinical trials are needed to identify effective prophylactic measures, especially for patient cohorts at high risk.

REFERENCES

1. Adams, J. T., and Faix, R. G.: *Streptococcus mitis* infection in newborns. J. Perinatol. *14*:473–478, 1994.
2. Adeotoye, O., Kupfer, R.: *Streptococcus viridans* vertebral osteomyelitis. J. R. Soc. Med. *92*:306–307, 1999.
3. Alaluusua, S.: Transmission of mutans streptococci. Proc. Finn. Dent. Soc. *87*:443–447, 1991.
4. Alam, S., Brailsford, S. R., Whiley, R. A., et al.: PCR-based methods for genotyping viridans group streptococci. J. Clin. Microbiol. *37*:2772–2776, 1999.
5. Albini, B., Nisengard, R. J., Glurich, I., et al.: *Streptococcus mutans*–induced nephritis in rabbits. Am. J. Pathol. *118*:408–418, 1985.
6. Alcaide, F., Carratala, J., Linares, J., et al.: In vitro activities of eight macrolide antibiotics and RP-59500 (quinupristin-dalfopristin) against viridans group streptococci isolated from blood of neutropenic cancer patients. Antimicrob. Agents Chemother. *40*:2117–2120, 1996.
7. Alvarez, M., Alvarez, M. E., Maiz, L., et al.: Antimicrobial susceptibility profiles of oropharyngeal viridans group streptococci isolates from cystic fibrosis and non–cystic fibrosis patients. Microb. Drug Resist. *4*:123–128, 1998.
8. Anderson, M. H., Molvar, M. P., and Powell, L. V.: Treating dental caries as an infectious disease. Oper. Dent. *16*:21–28, 1991.
9. Ariel, I., and Singer, D. B.: *Streptococcus viridans* infections in midgestation. Pediatr. Pathol. *11*:75–83, 1991.
10. Arning, M., Gehrt, A., Aul, C., et al.: Septicemia due to *Streptococcus mitis* in neutropenic patients with acute leukemia. Blut *61*:364–368, 1990.
11. Arnold, R. R., Mestecky, J., and McGhee, J. R.: Naturally occurring secretory immunoglobulin A antibodies to *Streptococcus mutans* in human colostrum and saliva. Infect. Immun. *14*:355–362, 1976.
12. Asikainen, S., and Alaluusua, S.: Bacteriology of dental infections. Eur. Heart J. *14*(Suppl. K):43–50, 1993.
13. Awada, A., van der Auwera, P., Meunier, F., et al.: Streptococcal and enterococcal bacteremia in patients with cancer. Clin. Infect. Dis. *15*:33–48, 1992.
14. Barbadillo, C., Trujillo, A., Cuende, E., et al.: Septic arthritis due to *Streptococcus viridans*. Clin. Exp. Rheumatol. *8*:520–521, 1990.
15. Barker, G. J., Call, S. K., and Gamis, A. S.: Oral care with vancomycin paste for reduction in incidence of alpha-hemolytic streptococcal sepsis. J. Pediatr. Hematol. Oncol. *17*:151–155, 1995.
16. Bateman, N. T., Eykyn, S. J., and Phillips, I.: Pyogenic liver abscess caused by *Streptococcus milleri*. Lancet *1*:657–659, 1975.
17. Beck, A.: Interference by an alpha-hemolytic *Streptococcus* of beta-hemolytic pathogenic streptococci. Inflammation *3*:463–465, 1979.
18. Benabdelmoumene, S., Dumont, S., Petit, C., et al.: Activation of human monocytes by *Streptococcus mutans* serotype f polysaccharide: Immunoglobulin G Fc receptor expression and tumor necrosis factor and interleukin-1 production. Infect. Immun. *59*:3261–3266, 1991.
19. Berlot, G., Tomasini, A., Cioffi, V., et al.: Fatal *Streptococcus viridans* descending mediastinitis: Case report and review of the literature. Eur. J. Emerg. Med. *4*:111–114, 1997.
20. Bernard, J. P., Francioli, P., and Glauser, M.: Vancomycin prophylaxis of experimental *Streptococcus sanguis:* Inhibition of bacterial adherence rather than bacterial killing. J. Clin. Invest. *68*:1113–1116, 1981.
21. Berner, R., Sauter, S., Duffner, U., et al.: Bacteremic episodes in pediatric oncologic patients, especially caused by the *Streptococcus viridans* group. Klin. Padiatr. *210*:256–260, 1998.
22. Berney, P., and Francioli, P.: Successful prophylaxis of experimental streptococcal endocarditis with single-dose amoxicillin administered after bacterial challenge. J. Infect. Dis. *161*:281–285, 1990.
23. Bertrand, B., Rombaux, P., Eloy, P., et al.: Sinusitis of dental origin. Acta Otorhinolaryngol. Belg. *51*:315–322, 1997.
24. Bignardi, G. E., and Isaacs, D.: Neonatal meningitis due to *Streptococcus mitis*. Rev. Infect. Dis. *11*:86–88, 1989.
25. Bilgrami, S., Feingold, J. M., Dorsky, D., et al.: *Streptococcus viridans* bacteremia following autologous peripheral blood stem cell transplantation. Bone Marrow Transplant. *21*:591–595, 1998.
26. Bisno, A. L., Dismukes, W. E., Durack, D. T., et al.: Antimicrobial treatment of infective endocarditis due to viridans streptococci, enterococci, and staphylococci. J. A. M. A. *261*:1471–1477, 1989.
27. Bochud, P. Y., Calandra, T., and Francioli, P.: Bacteremia due to viridans streptococci in neutropenic patients: A review. Am. J. Med. *97*:256–264, 1994.
28. Bochud, P. Y., Eggiman, P., Calandra, T., et al.: Bacteremia due to viridans *Streptococcus* in neutropenic patients with cancer: Clinical spectrum and risk factors. Clin. Infect. Dis. *18*:25–31, 1994.
29. Boenning, D. A., Nelson, L. P., and Campos, J. M.: Relatively penicillin-resistant *Streptococcus sanguis* endocarditis in an adolescent. Pediatr. Infect. Dis. J. *7*:205–207, 1988.
30. Bos, A. P., Fetter, W. P., Baerts, W., et al.: Streptococcal pharyngitis and epiglottitis in a newborn infant. Eur. J. Pediatr. *151*:874–875, 1992.
31. Bratthall, D.: Mutans streptococci: Dental, oral and global aspects. J. Indian Soc. Pedod. Prev. Dent. *9*:4–12, 1991.
32. Bromberg, K., Orson, J. M., Triedman, R., et al.: Erythromycin-resistant *Streptococcus viridans* in oral flora with prolonged erythromycin therapy. Ann. Intern. Med. *93*:931–932, 1980.
33. Broughton, R. A., Krafka, R., and Baker, C. J.: Non-group D alpha-hemolytic streptococci: New neonatal pathogens. J. Pediatr. *99*:450–454, 1981.
34. Buchman, A. L.: *Streptococcus viridans* osteomyelitis with endocarditis presenting as acute onset lower back pain. J. Emerg. Med. *8*:291–294, 1990.

35. Burden, A. D., Oppenheim, B. A., Crowther, D., et al.: Viridans streptococcal bacteraemia in patients with haematological and solid malignancies. Eur. J. Cancer *27*:409–411, 1991.
36. Buxbaum, A., and Georgopoulos, A.: Postantibiotic effect of ceftriaxone and gentamicin alone and in combination on *Klebsiella pneumoniae, Pseudomonas aeruginosa* and *Streptococcus viridans*. Infection *24*:459–464, 1996.
37. Carlsson, J.: A numerical taxonomic study of human oral streptococci. Odontol. Rev. *19*:137–160, 1968.
38. Caufield, P. W., Cutter, G. R., and Dasanayake, A. P.: Initial acquisition of mutans streptococci by infants: Evidence for a discrete window of infectivity. J. Dent. Res. *72*:37–45, 1993.
39. Caufield, P. W., Dasanayake, A. P., Li, Y., et al.: Natural history of *Streptococcus sanguinis* in the oral cavity of infants: Evidence for a discrete window of infectivity. Infect. Immun. *68*:4018–4023, 2000.
40. Caufield, P. W., and Wannemuehler, Y. M.: In vitro susceptibility of *Streptococcus mutans* 6715 to iodine and sodium fluoride, singly and in combination, at various pH values. Antimicrob. Agents Chemother. *22*:115–119, 1982.
41. Chalkley, L., Schuster, C., Potgieter, E., et al.: Relatedness between *Streptococcus pneumoniae* and viridans streptococci: Transfer of penicillin resistance determinants and immunological similarities of penicillin-binding proteins. F.E.M.S. Microbiol. Lett. *69*:35–42, 1991.
42. Chambers, H. F., Xiang, Q., Liu, Q., et al.: Efficacy of levofloxacin for experimental aortic-valve endocarditis in rabbits infected with viridans group streptococcus or *Staphylococcus aureus*. Antimicrob. Agents Chemother. *43*:2742–2746, 1999.
43. Chiu, B.: Multiple infections in carotid atherosclerotic plaques. Am. Heart J. *138*(Suppl.):534–536, 1999.
44. Church, D. L., and Bryant, H. E.: Investigation of a *Streptococcus viridans* pseudobacteremia epidemic at a university teaching hospital. Infect. Control Hosp. Epidemiol. *10*:416–421, 1989.
45. Classen, D. C., Burke, J. P., Ford, C. D., et al.: *Streptococcus mitis* sepsis in bone marrow transplant patients receiving oral antimicrobial prophylaxis. Am. J. Med. *89*:441–446, 1990.
46. Cohen, J., Donnelly, J. P., Worsley, A. M., et al.: Septicaemia caused by viridans streptococci in neutropenic patients with leukaemia. Lancet *2*:1452–1454, 1983.
47. Coleman, G., and Williams, R. E. A.: Taxonomy of some human viridans streptococci. *In* Wannamaker, L. W., and Matsen, J. M. (eds.): Streptococci and Streptococcal Diseases: Recognition, Understanding, and Management. New York, Academic Press, 1972, pp. 282–299.
48. Collin, B. A., Leather, H. L., Wingard, J. R., et al.: Evolution, incidence, and susceptibility of bacterial bloodstream isolates from 519 bone marrow transplant patients. Clin. Infect. Dis. *33*:947–953, 2001.
49. Corson, M. A., Postlethwaite, K. P., and Seymour, R. A.: Are dental infections a cause of brain abscess? Case report and review of the literature. Oral Dis. *7*:61–65, 2001.
50. Coulter, W. A., Coffey, A., Saunders, I. D., et al.: Bacteremia in children following dental extraction. J. Dent. Res. *69*:1691–1695, 1990.
51. Coykendall, A. L.: Classification and identification of the viridans streptococci. Clin. Microbiol. Rev. *2*:315–328, 1989.
52. Crompton, N., Griffiths, B. M., Wilson, M., et al.: The transfer of bacteria to, and survival on, dental records. Microbios *99*:181–187, 1999.
53. Dajani, A. S., Law, D. J., Bollinger, R. O., et al.: Ultrastructural and biochemical alterations effected by viridin B, a bacterocin of alpha-hemolytic streptococci. Infect. Immun. *14*:776–782, 1976.
54. Dajani, A. S., Tom, M. C., and Law, D. J.: Viridins, bacteriocins of alpha-hemolytic streptococci: Isolation, characterization, and partial purification. Antimicrob. Agents Chemother. *9*:81–88, 1976.
55. de Azavedo, J. C., Trpeski, L., Pong-Porter, S., et al.: In vitro activities of fluoroquinolones against antibiotic-resistant blood culture isolates of viridans group streptococci from across Canada. Antimicrob. Agents Chemother. *43*:2299–2301, 1999.
56. Dekker, A. W., Rozenberg-Arska, M., and Verdonck, L. F.: Prevention of bacteremias caused by alpha-hemolytic streptococci by roxithromycin in patients treated with intensive cytotoxic treatment. Hamatol. Bluttransfusion *33*:551–554, 1990.
57. Demers, C., Tremblay, M., and Lacourciere, Y.: Acute vertebral osteomyelitis complicating *Streptococcus sanguis* endocarditis. Ann. Rheum. Dis. *47*:333–336, 1988.
58. Diekema, D. J., Beach, M. L., and Pfaller, M. A.: Antimicrobial resistance in viridans group streptococci among patients with and without the diagnosis of cancer in the USA, Canada and Latin America. Clin. Microbiol. Infect. *7*:152–157, 2001.
59. Doern, G. V., Ferraro, M. J., Brueggemann, A. B., et al.: Emergence of high rates of antimicrobial resistance among viridans group streptococci in the United States. Antimicrob. Agents Chemother. *40*:891–894, 1996.
60. Dompeling, E. C., Donnelly, J. P., Raemaekers, J. M., et al.: Pre-emptive administration of corticosteroids prevents the development of ARDS associated with *Streptococcus mitis* bacteremia following chemotherapy with high-dose cytarabine. Ann. Hematol. *69*:69–71, 1994.
61. Donnelly, J. P., Dompeling, E. C., Meis, J F., et al.: Bacteremia due to oral viridans streptococci in neutropenic patients with cancer: Cytostatics are a more important risk factor than antibacterial prophylaxis. Clin. Infect. Dis. *20*:469–470, 1995.
62. Douglas, C. W., Heath, J., Hampton, K. K., et al.: Identity of viridans streptococci isolated from cases of infective endocarditis. J. Med. Microbiol. *39*:179–182, 1993.
63. Dowson, C. G., Coffey, T. J., Kell, C., et al.: Evolution of penicillin resistance in *Streptococcus pneumoniae:* The role of *Streptococcus mitis* in the formation of a low-affinity PBP2B in *S. pneumoniae*. Mol. Microbiol. *9*:635–643, 1993.
64. Dowson, C. G., Hutchison, A., Woodford, N., et al.: Penicillin-resistant viridans streptococci have obtained altered penicillin-binding protein genes from penicillin-resistant strains of *Streptococcus pneumoniae*. Proc. Natl. Acad. Sci. U. S. A. *87*:5858–5862, 1990.
65. Dwyer, R., Ringertz, S.: Viridans streptococci in blood cultures. Can we see any patterns of species related to patient category? Review of 229 cases of positive cultures with viridans streptococci. A. P. M. I. S. *105*:972–974, 1997.
66. Edelstein, B. L.: The medical management of dental caries. J. Am. Dent. Assoc. *125*(Suppl.):31–39, 1994.
67. Edwardsson, S., and Mejare, B.: *Streptococcus milleri* (Guthof) and *Streptococcus mutans* in the mouths of infants before and after tooth eruption. Arch. Oral Biol. *23*:811–814, 1978.
68. Elliott, R. H., and Dunbar, J. M.: Antibiotic sensitivity of oral alpha-haemolytic *Streptococcus* from children with congenital or acquired cardiac disease: A prolonged survey. Br. Dent. J. *142*:283–285, 1977.
69. Elting, L. S., Bodey, G. P., and Keefe, B. H.: Septicemia and shock syndrome due to viridans streptococci: A case-control study of predisposing factors. Clin. Infect. Dis. *14*:1201–1207, 1992.
70. Eng, R. H., Mangia, A. J., Smith, S. M., et al.: Meningitis following bacteremia with *Streptococcus sanguis*. N. Y. State J. Med. *89*:625–626, 1989.
71. Engel, A., Kern, P., and Kern, W. V.: Levels of cytokines and cytokine inhibitors in the neutropenic patient with alpha-hemolytic streptococcus shock syndrome. Clin. Infect. Dis. *23*:785–789, 1996.
72. English, B. K., Patrick, C. C., Orlicek, S. L., et al.: Lipoteichoic acid from viridans streptococci induces the production of tumor necrosis factor and nitric oxide by murine macrophages. J. Infect. Dis. *174*:1348–1351, 1996.
73. Entenza, J. M., Caldelari, I., Glauser, M. P., et al.: Importance of genotypic and phenotypic tolerance in the treatment of experimental endocarditis due to *Streptococcus gordonii*. J. Infect. Dis. *175*:70–76, 1997.
74. Enting, R. H., de Gans, J., Blankevoort, J. P., et al.: Meningitis due to viridans streptococci in adults. J. Neurol. *244*:435–438, 1997.
75. Erickson, P. R., and Herzberg, M. C.: Emergence of antibiotic resistant *Streptococcus sanguis* in dental plaque of children after frequent antibiotic therapy. Pediatr. Dent. *21*:181–185, 1999.
76. Erverdi, N., Kadir, T., Ozkan, H., et al.: Investigation of bacteremia after orthodontic banding. Am. J. Orthod. Dentofacial Orthop. *116*:687–690, 1999.
77. Facklam, R. R.: Physiological differentiation of viridans streptococci. J. Clin. Microbiol. *5*:184–201, 1977.
78. Farber, B. F., Eliopoulos, G. M., Ward, J. I., et al.: Multiply resistant viridans streptococci: Susceptibility to beta-lactam antibiotics and comparison of penicillin-binding protein patterns. Antimicrob. Agents Chemother. *24*:702–705, 1983.
79. Fine, J. B., Harper, D S., Gordon, J. M., et al.: Short-term microbiological and clinical effects of subgingival irrigation with an antimicrobial mouthrinse. J. Periodontol. *65*:30–36, 1994.
80. Flynn, C. E., and Ruoff, K. L.: Identification of *"Streptococcus milleri"* group isolates to the species level with a commercially available rapid test system. J. Clin. Microbiol. *33*:2704–2706, 1995.
81. Ford, I., Douglas, C. W., Preston, F. E., et al.: Mechanisms of platelet aggregation by *Streptococcus sanguis,* a causative organism in infective endocarditis. Br. J. Haematol. *84*:95–100, 1993.
82. Ford, J. M., and DuBois, R. E.: Multiloculated hepatic abscess caused by alpha-hemolytic *Streptococcus*. South. Med. J. *77*:514–516, 1984.
83. Francioli, P. B., and Glauser, M. P.: Synergistic activity of ceftriaxone combined with netilmicin administered once daily for treatment of experimental streptococcal endocarditis. Antimicrob. Agents Chemother. *37*:207–212, 1993.
84. Frandsen, E. V., Pedrazzoli, V., and Kilian, M.: Ecology of viridans streptococci in the oral cavity and pharynx. Oral Microbiol. Immunol. *6*:129–133, 1991.
85. Fraser, J. J., Jr., Marks, M. I., and Welch, D. F.: Neonatal sepsis and meningitis due to alpha-hemolytic *Streptococcus*. South. Med. J. *76*:401–402, 1983.
86. Freedman, R. M., and Baltimore, R.: Fatal *Streptococcus viridans* septicemia and meningitis: Relationship to fetal scalp electrode monitoring. J. Perinatol. *10*:272–274, 1990.
87. Fujimori, I., Kikushima, K., Hisamatsu, K., et al.: Interaction between oral alpha-streptococci and group A streptococci in patients with tonsillitis. Ann. Otol. Rhinol. Laryngol. *106*:571–574, 1997.
88. Garnier, F., Gerbaud, G., Courvalin, P., et al.: Identification of clinically relevant viridans group streptococci to the species level by PCR. J. Clin. Microbiol. *35*:2337–2341, 1997.

89. George, S., Wadhera, A., Mersich, K., et al.: Liver abscess due to *Streptococcus sanguis*. Clin. Infect. Dis. *22*:191–192, 1996.
90. Ghaffar, F., Friedland, I. R., Katz, K., et al.: Increased carriage of resistant non-pneumococcal alpha-hemolytic streptococci after antibiotic therapy. J. Pediatr. *135*:618–623, 1999.
91. Glauser, M. P., and Francioli, P.: Successful prophylaxis against experimental streptococcal endocarditis with bacteriostatic antibiotics. J. Infect. Dis. *146*:806–810, 1982.
92. Goldfarb, J., Wormser, G. P., and Glaser, J. H.: Meningitis caused by multiply antibiotic-resistant viridans streptococci. J. Pediatr. *105*: 891–895, 1984.
93. Goolam Mahomed, A., Feldman, C., Smith, C., et al.: Does primary *Streptococcus viridans* pneumonia exist? S. Afr. Med. J. *82*:432–434, 1992.
94. Graber, C. J., de Almeida, K. N., Atkinson, J. C., et al.: Dental health and viridans streptococcal bacteremia in allogeneic hematopoietic stem cell transplant recipients. Bone Marrow Transplant. *27*:537–542, 2001.
95. Grindefjord, M., Dahllof, G., Wikner, S., et al.: Prevalence of mutans streptococci in one-year-old children. Oral Microbiol. Immunol. *6*:280–283, 1991.
96. Groot-Loonen, J. J., van der Noordaa, J., de Kraker, J., et al.: Alpha-hemolytic streptococcal septicemia with severe complications during neutropenia in childhood cancer. Pediatr. Hematol. Oncol. *4*:323–328, 1987.
97. Guidelines for preventing opportunistic infections among hematopoietic stem cell transplant recipients. M. M. W. R. Recomm. Rep. *49*(RR-10):1–125, 2000.
98. Guiot, H. F., van der Meer, J. W., van den Broek, P. J., et al.: Prevention of viridans-group streptococcal septicemia in oncohematologic patients: A controlled comparative study on the effect of penicillin G and cotrimoxazole. Ann. Hematol. *64*:260–265, 1992.
99. Hamada, S., Masuda, N., and Kotani, S.: Isolation and serotyping of *Streptococcus mutans* from teeth and feces of children. J. Clin. Microbiol. *11*:314–318, 1980.
100. Henslee, J., Bostrom, B., Weisdorf, D., et al.: Streptococcal sepsis in bone marrow transplant patients. Lancet *1*:393, 1984.
101. Hess, J., Dankert, J., and Durack, D.: Significance of penicillin tolerance in vivo: Prevention of experimental *Streptococcus sanguis* endocarditis. J. Antimicrob. Chemother. *11*:555–564, 1983.
102. Hirschfeld, Z., Friedman, M., Golomb, G., et al.: New sustained release dosage form of chlorhexidine for dental use: Use for plaque control in partial denture wearers. J. Oral Rehabil. *11*:477–482, 1984.
103. Hoecker, J. L., Pickering, L. K., Groschel, D., et al.: *Streptococcus salivarius* sepsis in children with malignancies. J. Pediatr. *92*:337–338, 1978.
104. Hogg, S. D., and Manning, J. E.: Inhibition of adhesion of viridans streptococci to fibronectin-coated hydroxyapatite beads by lipoteichoic acid. J. Appl. Bacteriol. *65*:483–489, 1988.
105. Holbrook, W. P., Olafsdottir, D., Magnusson, H. B., et al.: Penicillin tolerance among oral streptococci. J. Med. Microbiol. *27*:17–22, 1988.
106. Holmberg, H., Danielsson, D., Hardie, J., et al.: Cross-reactions between alpha-streptococci and Omniserum, a polyvalent pneumococcal serum, demonstrated by direct immunofluorescence, immunoelectroosmophoresis, and latex agglutination. J. Clin. Microbiol. *21*:745–748, 1985.
107. Hook, E. W., III, and Sande, M. A.: Role of the vegetation in experimental *Streptococcus viridans* endocarditis. Infect. Immun. *10*:1433–1438, 1974.
108. Inoue, S., Boyer, D., and Gordon, R.: Interstitial pneumonia and alpha-hemolytic *Streptococcus* sepsis in a child with malignancy who recently received cytosine arabinoside. Pediatr. Infect. Dis. J. *9*:598–600, 1990.
109. James, J., MacFarlane, T. W., McGowan, D. A., et al.: Failure of post-bacteraemia delayed antibiotic prophylaxis of experimental rabbit endocarditis. J. Antimicrob. Chemother. *20*:883–885, 1987.
110. Janoir, C., Podglajen, I., Kitzis, M. D., et al.: In vitro exchange of fluoroquinolone resistance determinants between *Streptococcus pneumoniae* and viridans streptococci and genomic organization of the parE-parC region in *S. mitis*. J. Infect. Dis. *180*:555–558, 1999.
111. Jarvinen, H., Tenovuo, J., and Huovinen, P.: In vitro susceptibility of *Streptococcus mutans* to chlorhexidine and six other antimicrobial agents. Antimicrob. Agents Chemother. *37*:1158–1159, 1993.
112. Jerng, J. S., Hsueh, P. R., Teng, L. J., et al.: Empyema thoracis and lung abscess caused by viridans streptococci. Am. J. Respir. Crit. Care Med. *156*:1508–1514, 1997.
113. Jordan, H. V., and De Paola, P. F.: Effect of a topically applied 3 percent vancomycin gel on *Streptococcus mutans* on different tooth surfaces. J. Dent. Res. *53*:115–120, 1974.
114. Kaufhold, A., and Potgieter, E.: Chromosomally mediated high-level gentamicin resistance in *Streptococcus mitis*. Antimicrob. Agents Chemother. *37*:2740–2742, 1993.
115. Kawamura, Y., Hou, X. G., Sultana, F., et al.: Transfer of *Streptococcus adjacens* and *Streptococcus defectivus* to *Abiotrophia* gen. nov. as *Abiotrophia adiacens* comb. nov. and *Abiotrophia defectiva* comb. nov., respectively. Int. J. Syst. Bacteriol. *45*:798–803, 1995.
116. Kennedy, H. F., Gemmell, C. G., Bagg, J., et al.: Antimicrobial susceptibility of blood culture isolates of viridans streptococci: Relationship to a change in empirical antibiotic therapy in febrile neutropenia. J. Antimicrob. Chemother. *47*:693–696, 2001.
117. Kerr, K. G., Armitage, H. T., and McWhinney, P. H.: Activity of quinolones against viridans group streptococci isolated from blood cultures of patients with haematological malignancy. Support. Care Cancer *7*:28–30, 1999.
118. Kikuchi, K., Enari, T., Minami, S., et al.: Postantibiotic effects and postantibiotic sub-MIC effects of benzylpenicillin on viridans streptococci isolated from patients with infective endocarditis. J. Antimicrob. Chemother. *34*:687–696, 1994.
119. Kilpper-Balz, R., and Schleifer, K.-H.: Transfer of *Streptococcus morbillorum* to the genus *Gemella* as *Gemella haemolysans*. Int. J. Syst. Bacteriol. *38*:442–443, 1988.
120. Kontiainen, S., and Sivonen, A.: Multiply resistant *Streptococcus mitis* isolated from conjunctival exudate of newborns. Eur. J. Clin. Microbiol. *6*:53–55, 1987.
121. Kurland, S., Enghoff, E., Landelius, J., et al.: A 10-year retrospective study of infective endocarditis at a university hospital with special regard to the timing of surgical evaluation in *S. viridans* endocarditis. Scand. J. Infect. Dis. *31*:87–91, 1999.
122. Larsen, T., and Fiehn, N. E.: Resistance of *Streptococcus sanguis* biofilms to antimicrobial agents. A. P. M. I. S. *104*:280–284, 1996.
123. Leblanc, T., Leverger, G., Arlet, G., et al.: Frequency and severity of systemic infections caused by *Streptococcus mitis* and *sanguis* II in neutropenic children. Pathol. Biol. (Paris) *37*:459–464, 1989.
124. Lee, S. Y.: Postantibiotic effects and postantibiotic sub-MIC effects of amoxicillin on *Streptococcus gordonii* and *Streptococcus sanguis*. J. Chemother. *12*:379–384, 2000.
125. Leviner, E., Tzukert, A. A., Benoliel, R., et al.: Development of resistant oral viridans streptococci after administration of prophylactic antibiotics: Time management in the dental treatment of patients susceptible to infective endocarditis. Oral Surg. Oral Med. Oral Pathol. *64*:417–420, 1987.
126. Levy, C. S., Kogulan, P., Gill, V. J., et al.: Endocarditis caused by penicillin-resistant viridans streptococci: 2 cases and controversies in therapy. Clin. Infect. Dis. *33*:577–579, 2001.
127. Lilien, L. D., Wilks, A. K., and Yeh, T. F.: *Streptococcus sanguis* biotype II meningitis in a premature infant. Clin. Pediatr. (Phila.) *21*:465, 1982.
128. Loesche, W. J., Schork, A., Terpenning, M. S., et al.: Assessing the relationship between dental disease and coronary heart disease in elderly U.S. veterans. J. Am. Dent. Assoc. *129*:301–311, 1998.
129. Lowrance, J. H., Baddour, L. M., and Simpson, W. A.: The role of fibronectin binding in the rat model of experimental endocarditis caused by *Streptococcus sanguis*. J. Clin. Invest. *86*:7–13, 1990.
130. Lowy, F. D., Chang, D. S., Neuhaus, E. G., et al.: Effect of penicillin on the adherence of *Streptococcus sanguis* in vitro and in the rabbit model of endocarditis. J. Clin. Invest. *71*:668–675, 1983.
131. Macaluso, A., Simmang, C., and Anthony, T.: *Streptococcus sanguis* bacteremia and colorectal cancer. South. Med. J. *91*:206–207,1998.
132. Malinverni, R., Bille, J., and Glauser, M. P.: Single-dose rifampin prophylaxis for experimental endocarditis induced by high bacterial inocula of viridans streptococci. J. Infect. Dis. *156*:151–157, 1987.
133. Malmberg, E., Birkhed, D., Norvenius, G., et al.: Microorganisms on toothbrushes at day-care centers. Acta Odontol. Scand. *52*:93–98, 1994.
134. Manning, J. E., Hume, E. B., Hunter, N., et al.: An appraisal of the virulence factors associated with streptococcal endocarditis. J. Med. Microbiol. *40*:110–114, 1994.
135. Marrie, T. J.: Bacteremic community-acquired pneumonia due to viridans group streptococci. Clin. Invest. Med. *16*:38–44, 1993.
136. Marron, A., Carratala, J., Alcaide, F., et al.: High rates of resistance to cephalosporins among viridans-group streptococci causing bacteraemia in neutropenic cancer patients. J. Antimicrob. Chemother. *47*:87–91, 2001.
137. Marron, A., Carratala, J., Gonzalez-Barca, E., et al.: Serious complications of bacteremia caused by viridans streptococci in neutropenic patients with cancer. Clin. Infect. Dis. *31*:1126–1130, 2000.
138. Marsh, P. D.: Antimicrobial strategies in the prevention of dental caries. Caries Res. *27*(Suppl. 1):72–76, 1993.
139. Martinez, F., Martin-Luengo, F., Garcia, A., et al.: Treatment with imipenem of experimental endocarditis caused by penicillin-resistant *Streptococcus sanguis*. J. Antimicrob. Chemother. *33*:1201–1207, 1994.
140. Martino, R., Subira, M., Manteiga, R., et al.: Viridans streptococcal bacteremia and viridans streptococcal shock syndrome in neutropenic patients: Comparison between children and adults receiving chemotherapy or undergoing bone marrow transplantation. Clin. Infect. Dis. *20*:476–477, 1995.
141. Matsushita, K., Fujimaki, W., Kato, H., et al.: Immunopathological activities of extracellular products of *Streptococcus mitis,* particularly a superantigenic fraction. Infect. Immun. *63*:785–793, 1995.
142. McBride, M. E., Duncan, W. C., and Knox, J. M.: Bacterial interference of *Neisseria gonorrhoeae* by alpha-haemolytic streptococci. Br. J. Vener. Dis. *56*:235–238, 1980.
143. McWhinney, P. H., Gillespie, S. H., Kibbler, C. C., et al.: *Streptococcus mitis* and ARDS in neutropenic patients. Lancet *337*:429, 1991.
144. Mecrow, I. K., and Ladusans, E. J.: Infective endocarditis in newborn infants with structurally normal hearts. Acta Paediatr. *83*:35–39, 1994.

145. Meddens, M. J., Thompson, J., Eulderink, F., et al.: Role of granulocytes in experimental *Streptococcus sanguis* endocarditis. Infect. Immun. *36*:325–332, 1982.
146. Meddens, M. J., Thompson, J., Mattie, H., et al.: Role of granulocytes in the prevention and therapy of experimental *Streptococcus sanguis* endocarditis in rabbits. Antimicrob. Agents Chemother. *25*:263–267, 1984.
147. Menichetti, F., Del Favero, A., Guerciolini, R., et al.: Viridans streptococci septicemia in cancer patients: A clinical study. Eur. J. Epidemiol. *3*:316–318, 1987.
148. Mghir, A. S., Cremieux, A. C., Jambou, R. , et al.: Dextranase enhances antibiotic efficacy in experimental viridans streptococcal endocarditis. Antimicrob. Agents Chemother. *38*:953–958, 1994.
149. Michalek, S. M., McGhee, J. R., Mestecky, J., et al.: Ingestion of *Streptococcus mutans* induces secretory immunoglobulin A and caries immunity. Science *192*:1238–1240, 1976.
150. Michel, R. S., DeFlora, E., Jefferies, J., et al.: Recurrent meningitis in a child with inner ear dysplasia. Pediatr. Infect. Dis. J. *11*:336–338, 1992.
151. Mogi, A., Nishi, J. I., Yoshinaga, M., et al.: Increased prevalence of penicillin-resistant viridans group streptococci in Japanese children with upper respiratory infection treated by beta-lactam agents and in those with oncohematologic diseases. Pediatr. Infect. Dis. J. *16*: 1140–1144, 1997.
152. Molina, J. M., Leport, C., Bure, A., et al.: Clinical and bacterial features of infections caused by *Streptococcus milleri.* Scand. J. Infect. Dis. *23*:659–666, 1991.
153. Monefeldt, K., Helgeland, K., and Tollefsen, T.: In vitro activation of the classical pathway of complement by a streptococcal lipoteichoic acid. Oral Microbiol. Immunol. *9*:70–76, 1994.
154. Moomjian, A. S., Sokal, M. M., and Vijayan, S.: Pathogenicity of alpha-hemolytic streptococci in the neonate. Am. J. Perinatol. *1*:319–321, 1984.
155. Morisaki, I., Mihara, J., Kato, K., et al.: Phenytoin-induced gingival overgrowth in rats infected with *Streptococcus sobrinus* 6715. Arch Oral Biol. *35*:753–758, 1990.
156. Murray, H. W., Gross, K. C., Masur, H., et al.: Serious infections caused by *Streptococcus milleri.* Am. J. Med. *64*:759–764, 1978.
157. Nascimento-Carvalho, C. M., Brandileone, M. C., Guerra, M. L., et al.: Do viridans streptococci cause pneumonia in children? Pediatr. Infect. Dis. J. *20*:726–728, 2001.
158. Newbrun, E.: Preventing dental caries: Breaking the chain of transmission. J. Am. Dent. Assoc. *123*:55–59, 1992.
159. Orlicek, S. L., Branum, K. C., English, B. K., et al.: Viridans streptococcal isolates from patients with septic shock induce tumor necrosis factor-alpha production by murine macrophages. J. Lab. Clin. Med. *130*:515–519, 1997.
160. Pan, Y. P., Li, Y., and Caufield, P. W.: Phenotypic and genotypic diversity of *Streptococcus sanguis* in infants. Oral Microbiol. Immunol. *16*:235–242, 2001.
161. Parrillo, J. E., Borst, G. C., Mazur, M. H., et al.: Endocarditis due to resistant viridans streptococci during oral penicillin chemoprophylaxis. N. Engl. J. Med. *300*:296–300, 1979.
162. Parrish, L. C., Kretzschmar, D. P., and Swan, R. H.: Osteomyelitis associated with chronic periodontitis: A report of three cases. J. Periodontol. *60*:716–722, 1989.
163. Pearce, C., Bowden, G. H., Evans, M., et al.: Identification of pioneer viridans streptococci in the oral cavity of human neonates. J. Med. Microbiol. *42*:67–72, 1995.
164. Peiris, V., and Oppenheim, B. A.: Antimicrobial activity of cytotoxic drugs may influence isolation of bacteria and fungi from blood cultures. J. Clin. Pathol. *46*:1124–1125, 1993.
165. Persson, L., Vikerfors, T., Sjoberg, L., et al.: Increased incidence of bacteraemia due to viridans streptococci in an unselected population of patients with acute myeloid leukaemia. Scand. J. Infect. Dis. *32*:615–621, 2000.
166. Peterson, E. M., Shigei, J. T., Woolard, A., et al.: Identification of viridans streptococci by three commercial systems. Am. J. Clin. Pathol. *90*:87–91, 1988.
167. Pfaller, M. A., and Jones, R. N.: In vitro evaluation of contemporary beta-lactam drugs tested against viridans group and beta-haemolytic streptococci. Diagn. Microbiol. Infect. Dis. *27*:151–154, 1997.
168. Pizzo, P. A., Ladisch, S., and Ribichaud, K.: Treatment of gram-positive septicemia in cancer patients. Cancer *45*:206–207, 1980.
169. Pizzo, P. A., Ladisch, S., and Witebsky, F. G.: Alpha-hemolytic streptococci: Clinical significance in the cancer patient. Med. Pediatr. Oncol. *4*:367–370, 1978.
170. Poole, P. M., and Wilson, G.: *Streptococcus milleri* in the appendix. J. Clin. Pathol. *30*:937–942, 1977.
171. Potgieter, E., Carmichael, M., Koornhof, H. J., et al.: In vitro antimicrobial susceptibility of *viridans* streptococci isolated from blood cultures. Eur. J. Clin. Microbiol. Infect. Dis. *11*:543–546, 1992.
172. Potgieter, E., and Chalkley, L. J.: Reciprocal transfer of penicillin resistance genes between *Streptococcus pneumoniae, Streptococcus mitior* and *Streptococcus sanguis.* J. Antimicrob. Chemother. *28*:463–465, 1991.
173. Pratter, M. R., and Irwin, R. S.: Viridans streptococcal pulmonary parenchymal infections. J. A. M. A. *243*:2515–2517, 1980.
174. Pulliam, L., Dall, L., Inokuchi, S., et al.: Effects of exopolysaccharide production by viridans streptococci on penicillin therapy of experimental endocarditis. J. Infect. Dis. *151*:153–156, 1985.
175. Quinn, J. P., DiVincenzo, C. A., Lucks, D. A., et al.: Serious infections due to penicillin-resistant strains of viridans streptococci with altered penicillin-binding proteins. J. Infect. Dis. *157*:764–769, 1988.
176. Rapeport, K. B., Giron, J. A., and Rosner, F.: *Streptococcus mitis* endocarditis: Report of 17 cases. Arch. Intern. Med. *146*:2361–2363, 1986.
177. Reed, E., Arneson, M., Vaughan, W., et al.: *Streptococcus viridans* (SV): A significant cause of neutropenic fever (NF) that caused death in some patients not empirically treated for gram-positive (GP) bacteria. Proc. Annu. Meet. Am. Soc. Clin. Oncol. *9*:A1239, 1990.
178. Ribner, B. S., and Freimer, E. H.: Osteomyelitis caused by viridans streptococci. Arch. Intern. Med. *142*:1739, 1982.
179. Richard, P., Amador Del Valle, G., Moreau, P., et al.: Viridans streptococcal bacteraemia in patients with neutropenia. Lancet *345*:1607–1609, 1995.
180. Ringden, O., Heimdahl, A., Lonnqvist, B., et al.: Decreased incidence of viridans streptococcal septicaemia in allogeneic bone marrow transplant recipients after the introduction of acyclovir. Lancet *1*:744, 1984.
181. Roberts, R. B., Krieger, A. G., Schiller, N. L., et al.: Viridans streptococcal endocarditis: The role of various species, including pyridoxal-dependent streptococci. Rev. Infect. Dis. *1*:955–966, 1979.
182. Roos, K., Holm, S. E., Grahn, E., et al.: Alpha-streptococci as supplementary treatment of recurrent streptococcal tonsillitis: A randomized placebo-controlled study. Scand. J. Infect. Dis. *25*:31–35, 1993.
183. Roos, K., Holm, S., Grahn-Hakansson, E., et al.: Recolonization with selected alpha-streptococci for prophylaxis of recurrent streptococcal pharyngotonsillitis—a randomized placebo-controlled multicentre study. Scand. J. Infect. Dis. *28*:459–462, 1996.
184. Rose, H. D.: Viridans streptococcal pneumonia. J. A. M. A. *245*:32, 1981.
185. Rosser, S. J., Alfa, M. J., Hoban, S., et al.: E test versus agar dilution for antimicrobial susceptibility testing of viridans group streptococci. J. Clin. Microbiol. *37*:26–30, 1999.
186. Rozenberg-Arska, M., Dekker, A., Verdonck, L., et al.: Prevention of bacteremia caused by alpha-hemolytic streptococci by roxithromycin (RU-28 965) in granulocytopenic patients receiving ciprofloxacin. Infection *17*:240–244, 1989.
187. Rubin, M., Hathorn, J. W., Marshall, D., et al.: Gram-positive infections and the use of vancomycin in 550 episodes of fever and neutropenia. Ann. Intern. Med. *108*:30–35, 1988.
188. Rubin, M. M., Sanfilippo, R. J., and Sadoff, R. S.: Vertebral osteomyelitis secondary to an oral infection. J. Oral Maxillofac. Surg. *49*:897–900, 1991.
189. Rudney, J D., and Larson, C. J.: Identification of oral mitis group streptococci by arbitrarily primed polymerase chain reaction. Oral Microbiol. Immunol. *14*:33–42, 1999.
190. Ruoff, K. L.: *Streptococcus. In* Murray, P. R., Baron, E. J., Pfaller, M. A., et al. (eds.): Manual of Clinical Microbiology. 6th ed. Washington, D.C., American Society for Microbiology, 1995, pp. 299–307.
191. Ruoff, K. L., and Kunz, L. J.: Identification of viridans streptococci isolated from clinical specimens. J. Clin. Microbiol. *15*:920–925, 1982.
192. Ruoff, K. L., and Kunz, L. J.: Use of the Rapid STREP system for identification of viridans streptococcal species. J. Clin. Microbiol. *18*:1138–1140, 1983.
193. Saarela, M., von Troil-Linden, B., Torkko, H., et al.: Transmission of oral bacterial species between spouses. Oral Microbiol. Immunol. *8*:349–354, 1993.
194. Salavert, M., Gomez, L., Rodriguez-Carballeira, M., et al.: Seven-year review of bacteremia caused by *Streptococcus milleri* and other viridans streptococci. Eur. J. Clin. Microbiol. Infect. Dis. *15*:365–371, 1996.
195. Sarkar, T. K., Murarka, R. S., and Gilardi, G. L.: Primary *Streptococcus viridans* pneumonia. Chest *96*:831–834, 1989.
196. Schmitz, F. J., Fisher, A., Boos, M., et al.: Quinolone-resistance mechanisms and in vitro susceptibility patterns among European isolates of *Streptococcus mitis, Streptococcus sanguis,* and *Streptococcus pneumoniae.* Eur. J. Clin. Microbiol. Infect. Dis. *20*:219–222, 2001.
197. Schneeberger, P. M., Janssen, M., and Voss, A.: Alpha-hemolytic streptococci: A major pathogen of iatrogenic meningitis following lumbar puncture. Case reports and a review of the literature. Infection *24*:29–33, 1996.
198. Schollin, J.: Adherence of alpha-hemolytic streptococci to human endocardial, endothelial and buccal cells. Acta Paediatr. Scand. *77*:705–710, 1988.
199. Schollin, J., and Danielsson, D.: Bacterial adherence to endothelial cells from rat heart, with special regard to alpha-hemolytic streptococci. A. P. M. I. S. *96*:428–432, 1988.
200. Shanson, D. C., Thomas, F., and Wilson, D.: Effect of volume of blood cultured on detection of *Streptococcus viridans* bacteraemia. J. Clin. Pathol. *37*:568–570, 1984.

201. Shanson, D. C., Thomas, F. D., and Johnstone, D.: Improving detection of "viridans *Streptococcus*" bacteraemia by adding sodium polyanethol sulphonate to blood cultures. J. Clin. Pathol. *38*:1346–1348, 1985.
202. Shaw, J. H.: Causes and control of dental caries. N. Engl. J. Med. *317*:996–1004, 1987.
203. Shenep, J. L., Hughes, W. T., Roberson, P. K., et al.: Vancomycin, ticarcillin, and amikacin compared with ticarcillin-clavulanate and amikacin in the empirical treatment of febrile, neutropenic children with cancer. N. Engl. J. Med. *319*:1053–1058, 1988.
204. Shibl, A. M.: Effect of antibiotics on adherence of microorganisms to epithelial cell surfaces. Rev. Infect. Dis. *7*:51–65, 1985.
205. Shlaes, D. M., Marino, J., and Jacobs, M. R.: Infection caused by vancomycin-resistant *Streptococcus sanguis* II. Antimicrob. Agents Chemother. *25*:527–528, 1984.
206. Shulman, S. T.: *Streptococcus viridans*—not! Am. J. Dis. Child. *47*:611, 1993.
207. Smith, D. J., Anderson, J. M., King, W. F., et al.: Oral streptococcal colonization of infants. Oral Microbiol. Immunol. *8*:1–4, 1993.
208. Soell, M., Holveck, F., Scholler, M., et al.: Binding of *Streptococcus mutans* SR protein to human monocytes: Production of tumor necrosis factor, interleukin 1, and interleukin 6. Infect. Immun. *62*:1805–1812, 1994.
209. Sotiropoulos, S. V., Jackson, M. A., Woods, G. M., et al.: Alpha-streptococcal septicemia in leukemic children treated with continuous or large dosage intermittent cytosine arabinoside. Pediatr. Infect. Dis. J. *8*:755–758, 1989.
210. Soto, A., Evans, T. J., and Cohen, J.: Proinflammatory cytokine production by human peripheral blood mononuclear cells stimulated with cell-free supernatants of viridans streptococci. Cytokine *8*:300–304, 1996.
211. Soto, A., McWhinney, P. H., Kibbler, C. C., et al.: Cytokine release and mitogenic activity in the viridans streptococcal shock syndrome. Cytokine *10*:370–376, 1998.
212. Spanik, S., Trupl, J., Kunova, A., et al.: Viridans streptococcal bacteraemia due to penicillin-resistant and penicillin-sensitive streptococci: Analysis of risk factors and outcome in 60 patients from a single cancer centre before and after penicillin is used for prophylaxis. Scand. J. Infect. Dis. *29*:245–249, 1997.
213. Speck, W. T., Spear, S. S., Krongrad, E., et al.: Transient bacteremia in pediatric patients after dental extraction. Am. J. Dis. Child. *130*:406–407, 1976.
214. Sprunt, K., Redman, W., and Leidy, G.: Penicillin-resistant alpha streptococci in pharynx of patients given oral penicillin. Pediatrics *42*:957–968, 1968.
215. Staves, E., and Tinanoff, N.: Decline in salivary *S. mutans* levels in children who have received short-term antibiotic therapy. Pediatr. Dent. *13*:176–178, 1991.
216. Steiner, M., Villablanca, J., Kersey, J., et al.: Viridans streptococcal shock in bone marrow transplantation patients. Am. J. Hematol. *42*:354–358, 1993.
217. Stimmel, H. M., Orchen, J. J., Skaff, D. M., et al.: Penicillin-resistant alpha-hemolytic streptococci in children with heart disease who take penicillin daily. ASDC J. Dent. Child. *48*:29–32, 1981.
218. Sullam, P. M., Frank, U., Yeaman, M. R., et al.: Effect of thrombocytopenia on the early course of streptococcal endocarditis. J. Infect. Dis. *168*:910–914, 1993.
219. Sussman, J. I., Baron, E. J., Tenenbaum, M. J., et al.: Viridans streptococcal endocarditis: Clinical, microbiological, and echocardiographic correlations. J. Infect. Dis. *154*:597–603, 1986.
220. Svinhufvud, L. B., Heimdahl, A., and Nord, C. E.: Effect of topical administration of vancomycin versus chlorhexidine on alpha-hemolytic streptococci in oral cavity. Oral Med. *66*:304–309, 1988.
221. Takada, H., Kawabata, Y., Tamura, M., et al.: Cytokine induction by extracellular products of oral viridans group streptococci. Infect. Immun. *61*:5252–5260, 1993.
222. Takahashi, N., Horiuchi, M., and Yamada, T.: Effects of acidification on growth and glycolysis of *Streptococcus sanguis* and *Streptococcus mutans*. Oral Microbiol. Immunol. *12*:72–76,1997.
223. Tano, K., Olofsson, C., Grahn-Hakansson, E., et al.: In vitro inhibition of S. pneumoniae, nontypable *H. influenzae* and *M. catharralis* by alpha-hemolytic streptococci from healthy children. Int. J. Pediatr. Otorhinolaryngol. *47*:49–56, 1999.
224. Tappuni, A. R., and Challacombe, S. J.: Distribution and isolation frequency of eight streptococcal species in saliva from predentate and dentate children and adults. J. Dent. Res. *72*:31–36, 1993.
225. Tasaka, T., Nagai, M., Sasaki, K., et al.: *Streptococcus mitis* septicemia in leukemia patients: Clinical features and outcome. Intern. Med. *32*:221–224, 1993.
226. Thibodeau, E. A., and O'Sullivan, D. M.: Salivary mutans streptococci and incidence of caries in preschool children. Caries Res. *29*:148–153, 1995.
227. Thorig, L., Daha, M. R., Eulderink, F., et al.: Experimental *Streptococcus sanguis* endocarditis: Immune complexes and renal involvement. Clin. Exp. Immunol. *40*:469–477, 1980.
228. Tinanoff, N.: Review of the antimicrobial action of stannous fluoride. J. Clin. Dent. *2*:22–27, 1990.
229. Tong, D. C., and Rothwell, B. R.: Antibiotic prophylaxis in dentistry: A review and practice recommendations. J. Am. Dent. Assoc. *131*:366–374, 2000.
230. Tuohy, M., and Washington, J. A.: Antimicrobial susceptibility of viridans group streptococci. Diagn. Microbiol. Infect. Dis. *29*:277–280, 1997.
231. Twetman, S., Mattiasson, A., Varela, J. R., et al.: Mutans streptococci in saliva and dental caries in children living in a high and a low fluoride area. Oral Microbiol. Immunol. *5*:169–171, 1990.
232. Uehara, Y., Kikuchi, K., Nakamura, T., et al.: Inhibition of methicillin-resistant *Staphylococcus aureus* colonization of oral cavities in newborns by viridans group streptococci. Clin. Infect. Dis. *32*:1399–1407, 2001.
233. Uehara, Y., Kikuchi, K., Nakamura, T., et al.: H_2O_2 produced by viridans group streptococci may contribute to inhibition of methicillin-resistant *Staphylococcus aureus* colonization of oral cavities in newborns. Clin. Infect. Dis. *32*:1408–1413, 2001.
234. Ullman, R. F., Strampfer, M. J., and Cunha, B. A.: *Streptococcus mutans* vertebral osteomyelitis. Heart Lung *17*:319–321, 1988.
235. Ullsfoss, B. N., Ogaard, B., Arends, J., et al.: Effect of a combined chlorhexidine and NaF mouthrinse: An in vivo human caries model study. Scand. J. Dent. Res. *102*:109–112, 1994.
236. van Houte, J.: Bacterial adherence in the mouth. Rev. Infect. Dis. *5*(Suppl. 4):659–669, 1983.
237. van Houte, J.: Role of micro-organisms in caries etiology. J. Dent. Res. *73*:672–681, 1994.
238. van Loveren, C., Buijs, J. F., en Cate, J. M.: Similarity of bacteriocin activity profiles of mutans streptococci within the family when the children acquire the strains after the age of 5. Caries Res. *34*:481–485, 2000.
239. van Loveren, C., Van de Plassche-Simons, Y. M., De Soet, J. J., et al.: Acidogenesis in relation to fluoride resistance of *Streptococcus mutans*. Oral Microbiol. Immunol. *6*:288–291, 1991.
240. Vernier, A., Diab, M., Soell, M., et al.: Cytokine production by human epithelial and endothelial cells following exposure to oral viridans streptococci involves lectin interactions between bacteria and cell surface receptors. Infect. Immun. *64*:3016–3022, 1996.
241. Vernier-Georgenthum, A., al-Okla, S., Gourieux, B., et al.: Protein I/II of oral viridans streptococci increases expression of adhesion molecules on endothelial cells and promotes transendothelial migration of neutrophils in vitro. Cell. Immunol. *187*:145–150, 1998.
242. Vicente, M. V., Olay, T., and Rodriguez, A.: Experimental endocarditis caused by *Streptococcus sanguis:* Single and combined antibiotic therapy. Antimicrob. Agents Chemother. *20*:10–14, 1981.
243. Watanakunakorn, C., and Pantelakis, J.: Alpha-hemolytic streptococcal bacteremia: A review of 203 episodes during 1980–1991. Scand. J. Infect. Dis. *25*:403–408, 1993.
244. Weber, M., Gubler, J., Fahrer, H., et al.: Spondylodiscitis caused by viridans streptococci: Three cases and a review of the literature. Clin. Rheumatol. *18*:417–421, 1999.
245. Weinberger, S. J., and Wright, G. Z.: A comparison of *S. mutans* clinical assessment methods. Pediatr. Dent. *12*:375–379, 1990.
246. West, P. W., Al-Sawan, R., Foster, H. A., et al.: Speciation of presumptive viridans streptococci from early onset neonatal sepsis. J. Med. Microbiol. *47*:923–928, 1998.
247. Wilcox, M. H., Winstanley, T. G., Douglas, C. W., et al.: Susceptibility of alpha-haemolytic streptococci causing endocarditis to benzylpenicillin and ten cephalosporins. J. Antimicrob. Chemother. *32*:63–69, 1993.
248. Wilson, A. P., and Gaya, H.: Treatment of endocarditis with teicoplanin: A retrospective analysis of 104 cases. J. Antimicrob. Chemother. *38*:507–521, 1996.
249. Wilson, M., Patel, H., and Fletcher, J.: Susceptibility of biofilms of *Streptococcus sanguis* to chlorhexidine gluconate and cetylpyridinium chloride. Oral Microbiol. Immunol. *11*:188–192, 1996.
250. Wisplinghoff, H., Reinert, R. R., Cornely, O., et al.: Molecular relationships and antimicrobial susceptibilities of viridans group streptococci isolated from blood of neutropenic cancer patients. J. Clin. Microbiol. *37*:1876–880, 1999.
251. Yaniv, L. G., and Potasman, I.: Iatrogenic meningitis: An increasing role for resistant viridans streptococci? Case report and review of the last 20 years. Scand. J. Infect. Dis. *32*:693–696, 2000.
252. Yee, Y., Farber, B., and Mates, S.: Mechanism of penicillin-streptomycin synergy for clinical isolates of viridans streptococci. J. Infect. Dis. *154*:531–534, 1986.
253. Zickert, I., Emilson, C. G., Ekblom, K., et al.: Prolonged oral reduction of *Streptococcus mutans* in humans after chlorhexidine disinfection followed by fluoride treatment. Scand. J. Dent. Res. *95*:315–319, 1987.
254. Zito, E. T., and Daneo-Moore, L.: Transformation of *Streptococcus sanguis* to intrinsic penicillin resistance. J. Gen. Microbiol. *134*:1237–1249, 1988.
255. Zuccaro, G., Richter, J. E., Rice, T. W., et al.: Viridans streptococcal bacteremia after esophageal stricture dilation. Gastrointest. Endosc. *48*:568–573, 1998.

CHAPTER 90

Pneumococcal Infections

RONALD DAGAN ■ DAVID GREENBERG ■ MICHAEL R. JACOBS

The pneumococcus *(Streptococcus pneumoniae)* continues to be a leading cause of morbidity and mortality in persons of all ages. Most children experience some form of pneumococcal infection (e.g., otitis media or pneumonia), and sepsis or meningitis develops in some cases. Despite more than a century of research, many of the aspects of pneumococcal disease remain obscure. The continued frequency and severity of pneumococcal diseases, coupled with the knowledge that antimicrobial therapy invariably does not prevent illness or death, and the high and still increasing prevalence of strains of pneumococci resistant to antimicrobial agents serve to underscore the need for better understanding of pneumococcal infections. Currently, attention is concentrated on efforts to prevent these infections by the development and use of appropriate vaccines.

History

Pasteur and Sternberg, working independently in 1880 and 1881, discovered the pneumococcus. Pasteur called the organism *"Microbe septicémique de la salive,"* and Sternberg called it *"Micrococcus pasteri."* Each researcher recovered pneumococci from rabbits injected with human saliva. Friedlander demonstrated pneumococci in tissue from humans with pneumonia in 1882 and, in the following year, found them in most cases of acute pneumonia. Friedlander described both the characteristic capsule and colonial morphologic features of pneumococci and, in 1884, recovered for the first time pneumococci from the blood of patients with pneumonia. During the next few years, pneumococci were found in virtually all types of infection, including meningitis and otitis media. By 1890, researchers had established the pneumococcus as the most common cause of acute pneumonia, and, hence, the term "pneumococcus" emerged. In addition, the pneumococcus became recognized as a principal cause of meningitis and other serious infections.

During the next decade, researchers immunized animals with cell-free filtrates of pneumococci, demonstrated that serum from immune animals could protect against experimental pneumococcal infection, deduced the role of immunity in promoting phagocytosis, and noted agglutination of pneumococci by serum from immune animals. In 1897, Pane treated humans suffering from pneumonia with serum from such animals. By 1900, researchers had laid the foundation for immunotherapy for pneumococcal pneumonia, the only effective treatment until the advent of chemotherapy.

During the next few years, investigators noted that agglutination of pneumococci appeared to depend on the strain isolated. In 1910, Neufeld and Haendel classified pneumococci into several discrete serotypes on the basis of the appearance of capsular swelling, the quellung reaction. Only strains exposed to homologous serum showed capsular swelling. Their work made possible all subsequent epidemiologic investigations of pneumococcal infection, immunotherapy with type-specific serum, and the development of vaccines.

After these discoveries were made, researchers concentrated on several aspects of pneumococcal disease, including identification of additional serotypes and their roles in disease, production and clinical use of antisera, and development of pneumococcal vaccines.

In 1926, the pneumococcus was called *"Diplococcus pneumoniae"* because it usually appears in pairs. In 1974, it was renamed *"Streptococcus pneumoniae"* because it forms long chains when grown in liquid medium. The original classification of pneumococci was limited to types I, II, III, and IV (others). Currently, 90 serotypes have been identified, and certain serotypes have proved to be more virulent than others, with virulence depending, to some extent, on the species of animal infected.

The use of antisera for the treatment of pneumococcal pneumonia proved strikingly effective when type-specific sera were administered. As early as 1913, Cole and associates showed that treatment with antisera lowered fatality rates from 25 to 30 percent to 10.5 percent. In addition to allergic reactions, difficulties associated with this treatment included the necessity of identifying the causative serotype, the need for the earliest possible administration of antisera, and the availability of antisera only to types I, II, and III. White compared the efficacy of early antisera therapy and found that 403 of 1614 (25%) who did not receive any therapy died, 32 of 377 (8.5%) who received therapy within 3 days of onset died, and 24 of 127 (18.9%) who received therapy 4 or more days after onset died. Unfortunately, therapy with antisera had no beneficial effect on other pneumococcal infections such as meningitis and endocarditis. Despite these drawbacks, the use of antisera soon became widespread. The advent of chemotherapy—first sulfa compounds, then penicillin—was followed by a precipitous decline in the use of antisera. Antimicrobial agents killed or inhibited pneumococci, regardless of serotype, and cured patients with previously incurable localized infections.[726]

Coincident with research resulting in the general use of antisera came research into the efficacy of pneumococcal vaccines. Proof of efficacy lagged, and indisputable evidence of protection induced by vaccination was not available until 1945. The ability of pneumococci to cause epidemic pneumococcal pneumonia in young men crowded into army camps or gold mines allowed large-scale trials. Highlights of the development of effective vaccines include the trial of Wright and associates[735] in South Africa beginning in 1911. Using a vaccine made with whole, killed pneumococci, this trial produced inconclusive results. Many trials followed, with some showing trends toward protection. In 1923, Heidelberger and Avery[297] published their classic article in which they stated that protective antibodies were reactive with surface capsular polysaccharides. In 1930, Francis and Tillett[223] showed capsular polysaccharides to be immunogenic for humans. Ekwurzel and colleagues[190] used a vaccine containing such polysaccharides during 1933 to 1937 and showed it to be effective. Smillie and associates used a preparation of serotype 1 polysaccharide to abort a hospital epidemic of pneumonia in State Hospital at Worcester, Massachusetts.[647]

Although many of these studies suggested that specific pneumococcal polysaccharide antigens could confer protection against severe pneumococcal infection, not until 1945, in a trial performed with recruits in the U.S. Army Air Force, were they finally proved by MacLeod and associates[453] to do so. This trial showed vaccination to be strikingly effective in preventing pneumococcal pneumonia caused by serotypes contained in the vaccine, but not in preventing disease caused by other serotypes, thus showing serotype-specific protection.

Regrettably, interest in vaccination waned rapidly with the general availability of penicillin, and manufacturers voluntarily withdrew their vaccines from the market. This unfortunate attitude persisted for the next 2 decades until recognition of the inability of chemotherapy to prevent many deaths from pneumococcal disease.[40] The rapid development and spread of antibiotic resistance among many clinically important strains further emphasized that prevention could be more effective than is treatment for pneumococcal disease. Fortunately, a few farsighted individuals continued to maintain surveillance of the serotypes causing human disease, and their work allowed the reintroduction of pneumococcal vaccines. The current status of vaccines is discussed later in this chapter.

Interested readers should consult both White's *The Biology of Pneumococcus* and Heffron's *Pneumonia, with Special Reference to* Pneumococcus *Lobar Pneumonia,* as well as a comprehensive review by Watson and colleagues, for a complete account of the long and fascinating history of this organism.[296, 722, 726]

The Organism, Host Defense Mechanisms, and Pathogenesis

STRUCTURE OF THE PNEUMOCOCCUS

Pneumococcal cells are surrounded by a trilamellar lipopolysaccharide cytoplasmic membrane that has two electron-dense bands, each 25 to 30 Å wide. A cell wall surrounding the plasma membrane has two bands—an inner 30- to 40-Å-wide band and an outer 60- to 80-Å-wide band. Numerous bridges connect the cell wall and the plasma membrane. The polysaccharide capsule covers the cell wall in encapsulated strains and is seen as a wider, less structured band.[685] A schematic representation of the major structural components and selected cell wall components is shown in Figure 90–1.

CELL WALL STRUCTURE. The predominant structural components of the pneumococcal cell wall are peptidoglycan, teichoic acid (TA), lipoteichoic acid (LTA), and several choline-bound proteins. Choline is a lipid that is an essential growth factor for *S. pneumoniae.*

Peptidoglycan. Peptidoglycan, which accounts for approximately half of the cell wall mass, is a cell wall polymer linked by stem peptides to form a complex, three-dimensional structure.[627] Stem peptides are formed when transpeptidases (also known as penicillin-binding proteins [PBPs]) link pentapeptide chains into linear stem peptides in penicillin-susceptible strains.[627] However, in penicillin-nonsusceptible strains, branched and other variant stem peptides are produced.

Lipoteichoic Acid. LTA also is known as pneumococcal Forssman (F) antigen. The LTA of pneumococci possesses identical repeat and chain structures linked to a cell membrane glycolipid, which anchors LTA to the cell.[214, 215] Phosphocholine is attached to saccharide residues. PspA and other proteins (see later) also are attached to choline residues on LTA.

Teichoic Acid. TA, also known as pneumococcal C-polysaccharide, has a chain structure similar to that of LTA, except that the saccharide differs. TA chains are attached to the cell wall peptidoglycan. Some phosphocholine residues of both LTA and TA are expressed on the cell wall surface, where they are thought to serve three functions[685]: (1) activation of the pneumococcal autolysin (LytA) enzyme, which is responsible for the autolysis of pneumococci; (2) binding of the choline-binding domain of LytA to choline on TA, which may regulate the activity of LytA; and (3) a function associated with transformability (choline-deficient cells lack transformability).

Surface Proteins. Pneumococci have several surface proteins, with the four most important being *pneumococcal*

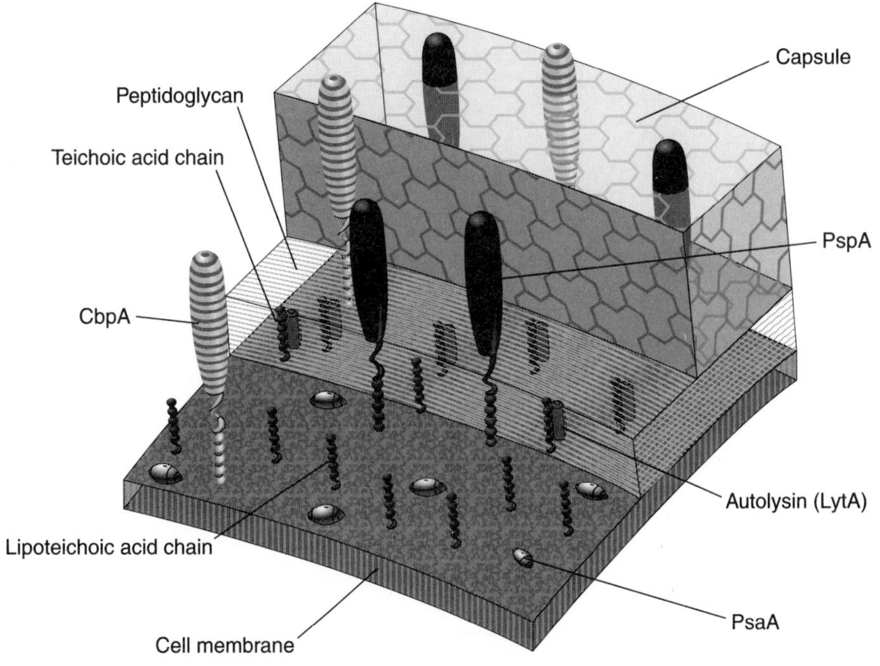

FIGURE 90–1 ■ Schematic three-dimensional representation of the major structural components of the cell membrane, cell wall, and capsule of *Streptococcus pneumoniae.* The locations of selected major virulence factors of the organism are also shown. Chains of lipoteichoic acid are attached to cell membrane glycolipid, whereas surface proteins, such as PspA and CbpA, are in turn attached to the lipoteichoic acid chains via phosphocholine links. Chains of teichoic acid are attached to the peptidoglycan layer via phosphodiester bonds. Autolysin (LytA) is attached to teichoic acid chains via phosphocholine links. PsaA is found on the outer surface of the cell membrane. (Adapted from references 214, 349, 740. Copyright Michael R. Jacobs, used with permission.)

surface protein A (PspA), *pneumococcal surface adhesin A* (PsaA), *choline-binding protein A* (CbpA), and *hyaluronate lyase* (Hyl).

PspA is a cell wall protein with a molecular size of 67 to 99 kd that is bound to TA and LTA by phosphocholine links.[349] This protein extends through the cell wall and capsule to the surface of the organism.[739] PspA exists in various antigenic forms, and epitopes within one PspA molecule can recombine into different types.[91] However, PspA variants usually are sufficiently cross-reactive that immunization with one PspA serotype elicits immunity to other PspA serotypes.

PsaA is a 37-kd surface protein thought to be anchored to the cell membrane and associated with magnesium and zinc transport.[174] It appears to be a lipoprotein and is common to virtually all *S. pneumoniae* isolates.[566] Considerable variation in the amino acid sequences of PsaA from different strains has been detected.[533] The relationship of this protein to other cell wall components has not been determined.[671]

CbpA is a protein similar to PspA and has a mass of 75 kd. It is an adhesin involved in the adherence of pneumococci to cytokine-activated human cells.[591] Several other choline-binding proteins also have been identified.

Hyl is a hyaluronidase that results in breakdown of the hyaluronan and chondroitin sulfate present in the extracellular matrix of human tissues.[349] It is bound to peptidoglycan in the cell wall.

CAPSULE. The capsule of pneumococci consists of polysaccharides that vary in the make-up of monosaccharides, the sequence of monosaccharides in polysaccharides, the linkage of monosaccharides to each other, and the presence of nonsaccharide components.[682] Currently, 90 serotypes consisting of 25 individual serotypes and 65 serotypes grouped into 21 serogroups are known (see the "Microbiology" section later) (Table 90–1). Each serotype has a specific capsular structure, and serotypes within a serogroup often have the same oligosaccharide sequences linked differently.

TABLE 90–1 ■ CAPSULAR SEROTYPES OF *STREPTOCOCCUS PNEUMONIAE*

Serogroup	Danish Serotype	U.S. Serotype	Serogroup	Danish Serotype	U.S. Serotype
	1	1		19F	19
	2	2		20	20
	3	3		21	21
	4	4	Group 22	22A	63
	5	5		22F	22
Group 6	6A	6	Group 23	23A	46
	6B	26		23B	64
Group 7	7A	7		23F	23
	7B	48	Group 24	24A	65
	7C	50		24B	60
	7F	51		24F	24
	8	8	Group 25	25A	NA
Group 9	9A	33		25F	25
	9L	49		27	27
	9N	9	Group 28	28A	79
	9V	68		28F	28
Group 10	10A	34		29	29
	10B	NA		31	31
	10C	NA	Group 32	32A	67
	10F	10		32F	32
Group 11	11A	43	Group 33	33A	40
	11B	76		33B	42
	11C	53		33C	39
	11D	NA		33D	NA
	11F	11		33F	70
Group 12	12A	83		34	41
	12B	NA	Group 35	35A	47, 62
	12F	12		35B	66
	13	13		35C	61
	14	14		35F	35
Group 15	15A	30		36	36
	15B	54		37	37
	15C	77		38	71
	15F	15		39	69
Group 16	16A	NA		40	45
	16F	16	Group 41	41A	74
Group 17	17A	78		41F	38
	17F	17		42	80
Group 18	18A	44		43	75
	18B	55		44	81
	18C	56		45	72
	18F	18		46	73
Group 19	19A	57	Group 47	47A	84
	19B	58		47F	52
	19C	59		48	82

The capsular structure of many serotypes has been determined.[235] Several epidemic clones have been shown to have different serotypes, and extensive genetic changes involving the replacement of entire cassettes of genes related to capsule production are required for capsular switching.[564]

GENETICS AND THE PNEUMOCOCCAL GENOME. The pneumococcal genome has been mapped recently, and 90 to 95 percent of its DNA sequences are known. The genome has been estimated to be 2.0 to 2.1 Mb in size, approximately half that of *Escherichia coli*.[49, 179] The locations of more than 100 genes, including 20 tRNA synthetase and 20 ribosomal protein genes, have been mapped. Genes involved in cell wall synthesis also have been identified.

S. pneumoniae is a naturally transformable bacterium, which means that it is able to take up single-stranded DNA from its environment and incorporate this exogenous DNA into its genome. This process is known as transformational recombination.[487, 656] Recombination is a powerful means of genome evolution and provides a great degree of genome flexibility to this organism. Transformation occurs only at high cell densities (10^5 to 10^8 colony-forming units [cfu]/mL), and a peptide pheromone quorum-sensing signal called activator or competence factor is required.[562] This factor also is termed competence-stimulating peptide.

The genes associated with capsule synthesis also have been characterized for several serotypes. The complete nucleotide sequence of 24 of these genes of several *S. pneumoniae* serotypes has been determined,[33, 234] as has the genetic basis for the structural diversity of capsule polysaccharides within *S. pneumoniae* serogroups.[483, 484] The abundance of transposable elements at the gene locus favors genetic variability of the capsule.[234]

VIRULENCE FACTORS

Animal models of pneumococcal infection have provided considerable insight into the pathogenesis of disease and the association of virulence factors with disease. However, the pneumococcus is primarily a human pathogen, and the host defenses of animal models can vary significantly from those in humans. For example, pneumococci adhere to human but not rabbit polymeric immunoglobulin receptor (pIgR).[746] Additionally, virulence in mice varies considerably with the strain of pneumococcus: pneumococci belonging to serogroups 6, 14, 19, and 23 rarely are virulent in mice, whereas serotypes 1, 2, and 3 usually are virulent.[58, 89, 405] Virulence also may vary according to the mouse strain.[1, 43, 679] Some serotypes can be virulent to one species of animal but not to others. An example is serotype 19F, which rarely is virulent in mice[43] but is highly virulent in guinea pigs.[38] In addition, penicillin resistance appears to be linked to decreased virulence by virtue of the fact that isogenic mutants of a virulent, penicillin-susceptible strain were significantly reduced when transformed into a penicillin-resistant strain with an abnormal *pbp2x* gene.[573] Therefore, many animal models of pneumococcal virulence may not be representative of virulence in humans or representative of all pneumococcal serotypes or antimicrobial-resistant strains.

Although the polysaccharide capsule has been recognized as the major determinant of virulence, relatively little is known about the molecular basis of the pathogenesis of pneumococcal disease. A library of 1786 pneumococcal mutants created by insertion-duplication mutagenesis was analyzed for the ability to survive and replicate in murine models of pneumonia and bacteremia.[411] One hundred eighty-six mutant strains had attenuated virulence; 56 of these strains were genetically characterized, and genomic DNA inserts were sequenced and subjected to database searches. Most of the insertions were in probable operons, but no pathogenicity islands were found. Forty-two novel virulence loci were identified. Five strains showed mutations in genes involved in gene regulation, cation transport, or stress tolerance; the virulence of these strains was shown to be highly attenuated in a murine respiratory tract infection model. Additional experiments also suggest that induction of competence for genetic transformation has a role in virulence.[411] This approach has revealed several previously unrecognized genes required for virulence.

A similar genomic approach was used to look for genes coding for surface-localized proteins that could be targets for protective humoral immunity. By exploiting the whole genome sequence of *S. pneumoniae,* researchers found 130 open-reading frames encoding proteins with secretion motifs or similarity to predicted virulence factors.[733] Mice were immunized with 108 of these proteins, and 6 conferred protection against disseminated pneumococcal infection. Each of the six protective antigens showed broad strain distribution and immunogenicity in human infections. Some of these proteins have been identified as LytB, LytC, and a cell wall–anchored serine protease. Another genomic-based study used a genomic expression library of *S. pneumoniae* screened with convalescent-phase serum for immunoreactive proteins.[749] Six known and 17 unknown pneumococcal proteins were detected. Five of the known proteins were surface-located virulence factors, including PspA and SpsA (CbpA), and 8 of the unknown proteins were putative membrane proteins. The use of these genomic approaches for the identification of novel microbial targets to elicit a protective immune response has been validated, and these new antigens may play a role in the development of improved vaccines against *S. pneumoniae.*

CAPSULE. The capsule is the major determinant of virulence in pneumococci. It prevents phagocytosis by polymorphonuclear leukocytes (PMNs) and macrophages, thereby allowing unrestricted extracellular multiplication of the organism. Because the pneumococcus has 90 antigenically distinct serotypes, production of anticapsular antibody in response to one serotype provides protection only against that serotype or serogroup, whereas nonencapsulated strains are considerably less virulent.[493] The importance of the capsule as a virulence factor is emphasized by the fact that protection from pneumococcal infection can be achieved by capsular-specific antibodies. Despite the large number of additional virulence factors (see the following paragraphs), the capsule remains the single most important determinant of virulence in avoiding host defenses after epithelial barriers have been breached. Other virulence factors are important in breaching host defenses such as epithelial barriers.

NEURAMINIDASES. Neuraminidases are enzymes that cleave terminal sialic acid residues from glycolipids, glycoproteins, and oligosaccharides on eukaryotic cell surfaces; such cleavage may unmask cell surface receptors for pneumococcal adhesins.[533] The neuraminidase NanA has been implicated in the ability of *S. pneumoniae* to colonize and persist in the nasopharynx and the middle ear.[686] A second neuraminidase, NanB, has much weaker activity than NanA does but has optimal activity at pH 5, whereas NanA is most active at pH 7.[533]

PNEUMOLYSIN. Pneumolysin is a 53-kd cytoplasmic protein produced by all pneumococci. It is essential for the initial binding to membrane cholesterol and the interaction leading to subsequent membrane damage.[44] Functions of pneumolysin include the following:

(1) Pore formation in host epithelial cell membranes. Pneumolysin binds to cholesterol in host epithelial cell membranes, where oligomers of pneumolysin molecules assemble to form 35- to 45-nm pores in the cell membrane, which results in lysis of the targeted cell. Pneumolysin is therefore cytotoxic to epithelial cells, and it also slows ciliary beating of bronchial epithelial cells and disrupts the tight junctions between epithelial cells. Pneumolysin also disrupts alveolar epithelial cells and the alveolar-capillary boundary, thereby facilitating entry of pneumococci into the bloodstream and through the blood-brain barrier.[254, 750]

(2) Effects on phagocytic and immune cell function. Pneumolysin attracts neutrophils in the early phases of disease and lymphocytes at a later stage.

(3) Direct activation of the complement system. Expression of pneumolysin by pneumococci reduces serum complement levels and serum opsonic activity.[11]

(4) Promotion of nitric oxide (NO) production by macrophages. NO is produced by an inducible NO synthase (iNOS) during inflammation as an essential element of antimicrobial defense, but it also can contribute to host-induced tissue damage.[87]

SURFACE-LOCATED CHOLINE-BINDING PROTEINS. The virulence of members of the choline-binding protein (Cbp) family and two recently described cell wall hydrolases, LytB and LytC, have been characterized.[265] Cbp-, LytB- and LytC-deficient mutants showed significantly reduced colonization of the nasopharynx. The following proteins of the Cbp family and their virulence mechanisms have been described:

1. *PspA* is a serologically variable protein that has undergone extensive recombination.[311] It is thought to exert its virulence function in systemic infection by interfering with the deposition of complement C3b onto pneumococci or by blocking recruitment of the alternative pathway, thereby reducing the effectiveness of complement receptor–mediated pathways of clearance.[689] PspA recently has been shown to bind to lactoferrin, an iron-sequestering glycoprotein found in mucosal secretions, when the level of free extracellular iron is not sufficient for the growth of pneumococci. This binding is thought to overcome the iron limitation at mucosal surfaces and might represent a potential virulence mechanism for colonization of mucosal surfaces.[285]
2. *CbpA,* or *SpsA,* is a surface protein adhesin that acts as a bridging element between pneumococci and host-cell glycoconjugates on cytokine-activated host cells.[286] This process is thought to be associated with change from nasopharyngeal colonization to invasion of epithelial and endothelial cells.[591] One mechanism by which this process occurs, wherein CbpA binds to the pIgR of human epithelial cells, has been described.[745] The pneumococcus co-opts the transcytosis machinery and gains entry into and across airway epithelial cells. This occurrence is a novel example of a pathogen co-opting the transcytosis machinery to promote translocation across a mucosal barrier.[358]
3. *PsaA* is a surface protein that also is associated with virulence via adhesion to epithelial cells.[565]
4. *Pneumococcal histidine-containing protein A (PhpA)* is a 20-kd protein with putative human complement C3 proteolytic activity. PhpA is a potential candidate for use as a vaccine against systemic pneumococcal disease and otitis media.[746]
5. The *pneumococcal histidine triad (Pht)* proteins PhtA, PhtB, PhtD, and PhtE compose a novel family of homologous surface proteins associated with virulence; they are also potential vaccine candidates.[7] Although antibodies targeting PhtA, PhtB, or PhtD are protective, the function of these proteins remains unknown. The number of histidine and tyrosine residues in these proteins suggests that they may be involved in metal or nucleoside binding.

PHASE VARIATION. Phase variation in the colonial opacity of *S. pneumoniae* has been implicated as a factor in bacterial adherence, colonization, and invasion.[724] On clear media, colonies can appear as opaque or translucent when viewed under magnification with oblique, transmitted light. All strains of *S. pneumoniae* are thought to be capable of phase variation. Opaque colonies are less likely to autolyse, contain less TA but more PspA in their cell walls, and in animal models colonize the nasopharynx poorly but are more virulent when inoculated into sterile sites. Conversely, translucent colonies are more likely to autolyse, contain more TA but less PspA in their cell walls, and colonize the nasopharynx well but are less virulent when inoculated into sterile sites. Translucent colonies become umbilicated as a result of autolysis, whereas opaque colonies remain dome shaped.

PHOSPHORYLCHOLINE ESTERASE. This enzyme has activity that removes phosphorylcholine residues from cell wall TA and LTA.[708] Inactivation of the gene encoding for the enzyme in pneumococcal strains caused a change in colony morphology from translucent (colonizing) to opaque (virulent) and a striking increase in virulence in the intraperitoneal mouse model. Phosphorylcholine esterase, therefore, appears to be a regulatory element involved in the interaction of *S. pneumoniae* with its host.[708]

PNEUMOCOCCAL AUTOLYSIN (LytA). LytA is a 36-kd cell wall protein attached to choline residues on TA and LTA. It is associated with unlinking of cell wall glycan from stem peptides during cell remodeling and division. Autolysin initially was considered to be a significant virulence factor, but more recent work has shown that it plays only a minor role and that immunization with autolysin does not provide protection.[533]

CELL WALL STEM PEPTIDES. The peptidoglycan of gram-positive bacteria triggers the release of cytokine from peripheral blood mononuclear cells.[456] However, 100 to 1000 times more gram-positive peptidoglycan than gram-negative lipopolysaccharide endotoxin is required to release the same amount of cytokine. Simple stem peptides were 10-fold less active than was undigested peptidoglycan in stimulating tumor necrosis factor (TNF). In contrast, complex branched peptides such as tripeptides were at least 100-fold more potent than was the native material. These complex branched peptides represented 2 percent or less of the total material, but their activity in stimulating TNF was almost equal to that of endotoxin.

IRON TRANSPORT. The availability of iron is a major requirement for the growth and survival of many organisms, including S. *pneumoniae.* Two *S. pneumoniae* genetic loci, *pit1* and *pit2,* which encode homologues of ABC iron transporters, are required for iron uptake by this organism.[98] Virulence in mouse models of pulmonary and systemic infection is attenuated moderately with a *pit2*-disrupted strain and attenuated strongly with a *pit1/pit2*-disrupted strain.

IGA PROTEASE. IgA proteases belong to a family of proteins used by a diverse group of bacteria, including *S. pneumoniae,* for colonization and invasion. IgA1 protease allows bacteria to cleave human IgA1 in the hinge region. The exact role of these enzymes in bacterial pathogenesis is understood incompletely, but they are important in bacterial colonization of mucosal membranes in the presence of secretory IgA antibodies by causing local IgA deficiency.[373]

The IgA protease genes of *S. pneumoniae* and *Streptococcus mitis* show extensive polymorphism, which results in enzymes with considerable antigenic diversity.[551]

PHOSPHOGLUCOMUTASE. Phosphoglucomutase is an enzyme that is necessary in one of the early steps in capsular polysaccharide synthesis, and mutants lacking this enzyme do not produce a capsule and are avirulent in immunocompetent, but not immunosuppressed, mice.[289] Other metabolic pathways also are thought to be affected by this enzyme.

FREE OXYGEN RADICALS. Release of free oxygen radicals has been implicated in the pathogenesis of otitis media caused by *S. pneumoniae,* and antibiotic killing of bacteria leads to the release of further free oxygen radicals, which results in tissue damage despite appropriate antibiotic therapy.[669] Reactive oxygen intermediates also mediate brain injury in bacterial meningitis.[36, 445]

NADH OXIDASE. Reduced nicotinamide adenine dinucleotide (NADH) oxidase has been shown to be a virulence factor necessary for *S. pneumoniae* infection. The basis of NADH oxidase as a virulence factor is the conversion of O_2 to H_2O. If O_2 is not reduced fully, it can form superoxide anion (O_2^-) and hydrogen peroxide (H_2O_2), both of which can be toxic to cells.[741]

PYRUVATE OXIDASE. Pyruvate oxidase decarboxylates pyruvate to acetyl phosphate plus H_2O_2 and CO_2 and appears to be associated with regulation of the multiple adhesive properties of pneumococci.[655] A pneumococcal mutant lacking the gene encoding pyruvate kinase showed a greater than 70 percent loss in the ability to attach to all cell types.

PLASMINOGEN BINDING AND PENETRATION OF THE BASEMENT MEMBRANE. Binding of plasminogen plus penetration of the basement membrane is thought to be an essential step in the pathogenesis of bacterial meningitis.[186] Most strains adhere to reconstituted basement membrane, as well as to its purified laminin and collagen IV components, and to bound plasminogen. Penetration of the basement membrane was achieved within 3 to 4 hours in the presence of plasminogen, whereas without plasminogen, no penetration occurred.

HYALURONIDASE. Virtually all pneumococcal strains produce the enzyme hyaluronidase, which is a 107-kd protein. Models used to simulate human meningitis generally use the direct intracerebral route of infection. However, intranasal inoculation would provide a more realistic model, and it recently was achieved by intranasal administration of *S. pneumoniae* with hyaluronidase. This model induced meningitis in 50 percent of inoculated mice, whereas meningitis did not develop in any of the mice inoculated without hyaluronidase. Hyaluronidase was found to facilitate pneumococcal invasion of the bloodstream after colonization of the upper respiratory tract. This murine model mimics important features of human disease, which allows the model to be used to study issues related to the pathophysiology and treatment of pneumococcal meningitis.[748]

PEPTIDOGLYCAN *N*-ACETYLGLUCOSAMINE DEACETYLASE A. The glucosamine and muramic acid residues of the pneumococcal cell wall traditionally are regarded as being *N*-acetylated. However, more than 80 percent of the glucosamine and 10 percent of the muramic acid residues have been shown to be deacetylated, thereby explaining the resistance of peptidoglycan to the hydrolytic action of lysozyme, a muramidase that cleaves the glycan backbone.[707] A gene that encodes for peptidoglycan *N*-acetylglucosamine deacetylase A has been identified. This gene may, therefore, contribute to pneumococcal virulence by providing protection against host lysozyme, which is known to accumulate in high concentrations at sites of infection.

PHAGES. Whereas transformation is recognized as occurring in pneumococci, another mechanism of DNA transfer in pneumococci is transduction of DNA carried by bacteriophages (lysogeny). A high proportion (76% of 791 isolates) of clinical isolates of pneumococci were found to carry multiple copies of LytA, thus indicating the widespread occurrence of lysogeny in pneumococci.[563] The LytA hybridization pattern of a strain has been found to be stable during extensive serial culturing; it is specific for the clonal type of the strain and can be used as a molecular epidemiologic marker.[628] In addition, phage DNA integrated into the pneumococcal genome acts as an integrase to facilitate the introduction of foreign genes into the pneumococcal chromosome.[255]

TOLERANCE. The ability of *S. pneumoniae* to escape lysis and killing by vancomycin and penicillin, a property termed "tolerance," has been described recently.[304] Among 116 clinical isolates of pneumococci, 3 percent and 8 percent were tolerant to vancomycin and penicillin, respectively. Tolerance may contribute to treatment failure, particularly in meningitis, in which bactericidal activity is critical for eradication. A vancomycin- and cephalosporin-tolerant strain of *S. pneumoniae,* the Tupelo strain, has been isolated from the cerebrospinal fluid (CSF) of a patient in whom recrudescence of meningitis developed despite treatment with vancomycin and a third-generation cephalosporin.[469] The defect leading to tolerance in this strain is in the control pathway for triggering of autolysis.

HOST DEFENSE MECHANISMS

Although anticapsular antibody is the most prominent protective mechanism against pneumococcal infection, many host responses to infection occur and many other factors are associated with protection against disease.[493] Pneumococcal infection and disease have been modeled in several animal species. Most are models of sepsis arising from intravenous or intraperitoneal inoculation of bacteria, and only a few were designed to study disease arising from intranasal infection. Chinchillas provide the only animal model of middle ear pneumococcal infection in which the disease can be produced by very small inocula injected into the middle ear or intranasally. This model, developed at the University of Minnesota in 1975, has been used to study pneumococcal pathogenesis at a mucosal site, the immunogenicity and efficacy of pneumococcal capsular polysaccharide vaccine antigens, and the kinetics and efficacy of antimicrobial drugs.[250]

ANTICAPSULAR SERUM IgG ANTIBODY. IgG to the capsular polysaccharide of *S. pneumoniae* is thought to provide the greatest degree of protection against systemic pneumococcal disease, as well as limited protection against colonization. The reference method for measurement of antibody is the opsonophagocytosis assay involving serial dilutions of serum, viable pneumococci, complement, and viable PMNs incubated together for 1 hour.[585] An infant mouse assay system for assessment of protective concentrations of human serum pneumococcal anticapsular antibodies correlated well with opsonophagocytic titer, but not with naturally occurring IgG antibody concentrations or IgG produced in response to nonconjugated polysaccharide vaccines as determined by enzyme-linked immunosorbent assay (ELISA).[353, 498] However, the ELISA method of serotype-specific antibody assay with absorption of cross-reacting antibody to cell wall polysaccharides does correlate well with protection after vaccination with conjugated vaccine, and it is the method used most commonly to predict serotype-specific immunity.[26, 699, 700] The development of a phagocytosis assay based on flow cytometry has not overcome the limitations of the ELISA method and is inferior to the opsonophagocytosis method.[347] Investigation of variable region polymorphisms in IgG that affect protective function has indicated that the capsular polysaccharide antibody repertoire in adults is derived from memory B-cell populations that have switched class and undergone extensive hypermutation.[451] Functionally disparate anticapsular polysaccharide antibodies can arise within individuals both by activation of independent clones and by intraclonal somatic mutation, which illustrates the complexity of assaying and interpreting serum capsular polysaccharide antibody levels.

ANTICAPSULAR IgA ANTIBODY. The role of IgA in the control of invasive mucosal pathogens such as *S. pneumoniae* is understood poorly. Human pneumococcal capsular polysaccharide–specific IgA initiates dose-dependent killing of *S. pneumoniae* in the presence of complement and phagocytes. The majority of specific IgA in serum is of the polymeric form, and the efficiency of killing initiated by this polymeric form exceeds that of monomeric IgA–initiated killing. In the absence of complement, specific IgA induces minimal bacterial adherence, uptake, and killing. Killing of *S. pneumoniae* by resting phagocytes with immune IgA requires complement, predominantly via the C2-independent alternative pathway, which requires factor B, but not calcium. Pneumococcal capsule–specific IgA may have distinct roles in effecting the clearance of pneumococci in the presence or absence of inflammation, and the polymeric form may control pneumococcal infections locally and after the pathogen's entry into the bloodstream by several mechanisms.[343]

PHAGOCYTOSIS AND LEUKOCYTE IgG RECEPTORS. IgG-mediated phagocytosis by PMNs is the main defense against *S. pneumoniae.* Two leukocyte IgG receptors, FcγRIIa and FcγRIIIb, are expressed constitutively on PMNs. Blocking experiments have shown that FcγRIIa is crucial for opsonophagocytosis of serum-opsonized *S. pneumoniae.* In adults, serum-induced phagocytic activity depends mainly on antipneumococcal IgG2 antibodies.[346, 582] However, in infants and young children, the main response to pneumococcal conjugate vaccines is in the IgG1 subclass.[25, 192, 704] Investigators have suggested that IgG1 subclass antibodies are at least as highly functional as is IgG2.[192] Recruitment and function of neutrophils also are important host defenses. In a pneumococcal infection model in immunocompetent and immunodeficient mice intranasally infected with *S. pneumoniae* type 2, immunocompetent BALB/c mice were resistant and immunodeficient CBA/Ca mice were susceptible to infection. BALB/c mice recruited significantly more neutrophils in the lungs, and inflammatory lesions were visible much earlier than were those in CBA/Ca mice.[256]

ANTIBODIES TO SURFACE PROTEINS AND PNEUMOLYSIN. PspA, PsaA, and pneumolysin are common to virtually all pneumococcal isolates. The development of antibodies to PspA, PsaA, and pneumolysin as a result of pneumococcal infection and carriage in young children was determined by measurement of serum antibodies to these proteins by ELISA in children at ages 6, 12, 18, and 24 months and in their mothers. All age groups were shown to produce antibodies to the three proteins, which increased with age and were associated strongly with pneumococcal exposure as a result of carriage or acute otitis media (AOM).[565] IgA to PspA, PsaA, and pneumolysin has been detected by ELISA in the saliva of children aged 6 to 24 months.[640] This finding was associated with pneumococcal carriage and otitis media.

Serum antipneumolysin IgG at the time of hospital admission has been found to be higher in patients with nonbacteremic pneumococcal pneumonia than in patients with bacteremic pneumococcal pneumonia or uninfected control subjects.[497] Serum antipneumolysin IgG levels also rose significantly during convalescence in patients with bacteremic pneumonia, and the levels attained were equal to those observed in nonbacteremic patients. Children aged 6 to 24 months were shown to produce antibodies to pneumolysin, and antibody concentrations increased with age and were associated strongly with pneumococcal exposure, whether by carriage or infection such as AOM.[565] Infants also have been shown to mount a specific antibody response to pneumolysin during AOM.[566]

DEFENSE MECHANISMS OF THE SPLEEN. The spleen is the principal organ that clears pneumococci from the bloodstream.[493] Opsonized particles are removed from the circulation by the liver, but with decreasing opsonization, the spleen increasingly assumes the role of clearance. The slow passage of blood through the spleen and the prolonged contact time with reticuloendothelial cells in the cords of Billmoth and the splenic sinuses allow time for the removal of nonopsonized particles. Overwhelming pneumococcal infection occurs in children and adults whose spleens have been removed or do not function normally. Pneumococcal disease progresses so rapidly in these cases that pneumonia is not detectable clinically or by chest radiographs, although pneumonia is seen at autopsy. The increase in the incidence of pneumococcal bacteremia and meningitis in children with sickle-cell disease is due largely to splenic dysfunction.

VITAMIN A. The association of nasopharyngeal colonization with *S. pneumoniae* and vitamin A supplementation in infants in an area with endemic vitamin A deficiency in South India showed that neonatal vitamin A supplementation delayed the age at which colonization occurs; therefore, it may play a role in lowering morbidity rates associated with pneumococcal disease.[126]

C-REACTIVE PROTEIN. C-reactive protein (CRP) is a normal constituent of human serum that is synthesized by hepatocytes and induced by proinflammatory cytokines. The function of this acute-phase reactant includes activation of complement and enhancement of opsonophagocytosis. CRP binds to phosphorylcholine, a constituent of eukaryotic membranes that also is found on the cell surface of the major bacterial pathogens of the human respiratory tract, including *S. pneumoniae* and *Haemophilus influenzae.* CRP is present in inflamed (0.17 to 42 mg/mL) and uninflamed (<0.05 to 0.88 mg/mL) secretions from the human respiratory tract in sufficient quantities to have an antimicrobial effect. In addition, the CRP gene was expressed in human respiratory epithelial cell cultures. The complement-dependent bactericidal activity of normal nasal airway surface fluid and sputum was abolished when the secretions were pretreated to remove CRP. Human respiratory epithelial cells are capable of CRP expression, and this protein may contribute to bacterial clearance in the human respiratory tract.[266]

PLATELET-ACTIVATING FACTOR RECEPTORS OF AIRWAY EPITHELIAL CELLS. Adherence of pneumococci to cultured human tracheal epithelial cells increased after exposure to acid and decreased after exposure to a specific inhibitor of the receptor for platelet-activating factor.[325] Exposure to acid thus may stimulate the adherence of *S. pneumoniae* to airway epithelial cells via increases in platelet-activating factor receptors. The clinical significance of these findings is not clear.[325]

CYTOKINES. Polymorphonuclear granulocytes, which provide a major defense against *S. pneumoniae* infection, are attracted to and activated by various cytokines, including interleukin-1β (IL-1β), IL-6, TNF-α, IL-8, IL-10, IL-12, interferon-γ, and granulocyte-macrophage colony-stimulating factor.[34] The inflammatory response in bacterial meningitis also is mediated by TNF-α and IL-1, which are produced in the subarachnoid space by cells such as leukocytes, astrocytes, and microglia.[523] Inoculation of pneumococcal cell wall components directly into the CSF of rabbits also results in the induction of an inflammatory response with pleocytosis and increased levels of CSF TNF-α and IL-1.[267] Both TNF-α and IL-1α have been shown to increase mucosal adhesion of pneumococci to tracheal epithelium in a chinchilla trachea whole-organ perfusion model.[687]

RESPIRATORY VIRAL INFECTIONS. The role of respiratory viral infection in predisposing the host to secondary bacterial infection, including pneumonia, empyema, and lung abscess, is well recognized.[432] The lungs of immunocompetent mice infected with influenza A virus on day 1 and *S. pneumoniae* on day 8 demonstrate greater *S. pneumoniae* colony counts, higher neutrophil infiltration, and higher lung levels of IL-1β and TNF-α after exposure to *S. pneumoniae* than do the lungs of control mice not pre-infected with influenza virus.[432]

L-ASCORBIC ACID (VITAMIN C). Degradation of the connective tissue component hyaluronic acid by hyaluronate lysase produced by *S. pneumoniae* is inhibited competitively by L-ascorbic acid (vitamin C).[435] One L-ascorbic acid molecule was found to bind to the active site of the enzyme. The high concentration of L-ascorbic acid in human tissues probably provides a low level of natural resistance to pneumococcal invasion by this mechanism.

LEUKOTRIENES. Leukotrienes are produced by macrophages and are considered important for antibacterial defense in the lung. Leukotrienes comprise a group of highly potent lipid mediators synthesized by the enzyme 5-lipoxygenase. Multidrug resistance protein 1 (mrp1) is a transmembrane protein responsible for the cellular extrusion of leukotrienes from macrophages. In a mouse pneumonia model, mrp1-deficient mice display diminished growth of pneumococci in the lungs and low mortality by a mechanism that involves increased release of leukotriene B_4.[618] Pneumococci also induce the production of leukotrienes in the middle ear, which has been related to up-regulation of two genes that govern the lipoxygenase pathway.[439]

HUMAN ALVEOLAR MACROPHAGE BINDING AND PHAGOLYSOSOMES. Human alveolar macrophages are the major resident phagocytic cells of the lung. After contact with macrophages, bacteria enter phagosomes, which gradually acquire the characteristics of terminal phagolysosomes, with incorporation of lysosome-associated membrane protein. Opsonization with serum containing immunoglobulin resulted in significantly greater binding of pneumococci to macrophages than did opsonization with immunoglobulin-depleted serum.[263] Binding, intracellular localization, and killing of pneumococcus by macrophages each are increased significantly by opsonization with serum containing immunogloblin or complement, or both.

INTRACELLULAR KILLING. Once pneumococci undergo phagocytosis by "professional" phagocytes (leukocytes and macrophages), they are killed.[493] However, researchers have shown that pneumococci can enter and survive inside A549 cells, a human lung alveolar carcinoma (type II pneumocyte) cell line.[670] Not all clinical *S. pneumoniae* isolates were capable of penetrating these cells, and the presence of a polysaccharide capsule also significantly reduced their capacity to penetrate A549 cells. The intracellular activity of various antibiotics against pneumococci in A549 cells showed that in the presence of antibiotics for 18 hours, more than 98 percent of the A549 cells were viable and less than 3 percent of the pneumococci that initially were phagocytosed could be detected intracellularly after exposure to peak serum concentrations of penicillin G, azithromycin, moxifloxacin, trovafloxacin, rifampin, and telithromycin.[461] In the absence of antibiotics, pneumococci were phagocytosed efficiently, but then paradoxically went on to kill all the A549 cells within 18 hours. The clinical significance of these findings is unknown.

COMPLEMENT. The second component of complement (C2) is an important component associated with host defense against encapsulated organisms. Homozygous deficiency of C2 is the deficiency of complement most commonly inherited. Although C2 deficiency can be asymptomatic, patients usually have either autoimmune disease or recurrent pyogenic infection caused by encapsulated bacteria such as *S. pneumoniae, H. influenzae* type b, and *Neisseria meningitidis*. An association between C2 deficiency and IgG subclass deficiency also has been described previously.[35] *S. pneumoniae* challenge of mice deficient in the third component of complement (C3) results in a 2000-fold increase in organism load in the bloodstream in comparison to controls.[117] Binding of pneumococcal CbpA to epithelially produced C3 results in adhesion of pneumococci to type II pulmonary epithelial cells. CbpA-deficient pneumococcal mutants and lysates therefrom fail to bind C3 and demonstrate a moderate decrease in adhesion to type II pulmonary epithelial cells, thus confirming the interaction of CbpA and C3 in adhesion.[649]

POLYMERIC IMMUNOGLOBULIN RECEPTOR. pIgR plays a crucial role in mucosal immunity against microbial infection by transporting polymeric immunoglobulins such as IgA across the mucosal epithelium. Polymeric IgA consists of two IgA molecules joined by a small, polypeptide J-chain. The J-chain shows high affinity for the glycoprotein pIgRs of epithelial cells, which are responsible for externalization of polymeric IgA across cell membranes.[350] However, pIgR also can act as a "Trojan horse" and participate in the pathogenesis of invasive pneumococcal disease as pIgR binds to a major pneumococcal adhesin, CbpA.[745] Expression of pIgR in human nasopharyngeal cells greatly enhances pneumococcal adherence and invasion; this effect is abolished by either insertional knockout of CbpA in pneumococci or antibodies against either pIgR or CbpA.

BASIC FIBROBLAST GROWTH FACTOR. Basic fibroblast growth factor is a neurotrophic factor in the central nervous system that is expressed at high levels in response to seizures or strokes. It also occurs in pneumococcal meningitis, as shown in experimental bacterial meningitis in mice and in children with bacterial meningitis.[319] Patients with meningitis in whom major sequelae or death occurred had much higher levels of CSF basic fibroblast growth factor than did those who survived. In patients with bacterial meningitis who survived, basic fibroblast growth factor decreased significantly in the CSF after 24 to 50 hours of administration of antibiotic therapy. However, its biologic role in the pathophysiology of bacterial meningitis is not known.

GRANULOCYTE COLONY-STIMULATING FACTOR. In a limited study of 22 non-neutropenic adult patients with pneumococcal meningitis, granulocyte colony-stimulating factor (G-CSF), in addition to cefotaxime plus dexamethasone, was administered subcutaneously for 6 days. All patients survived, and in only one patient did a complication develop (bilateral hearing deficit). Improvement of inflammation indices in the CSF was rapid.[169] However, controlled clinical trials are needed. In a rabbit meningitis model, G-CSF increased the percentage of granulocytes in blood but not in CSF and increased CSF TNF-α and IL-1β concentrations.[615] However, G-CSF did not reduce the density of apoptotic neurons in the dentate gyrus of the hippocampus. A second study in a rabbit meningitis model used longer pretreatment with G-CSF and showed more positive results.[522] G-CSF pretreatment attenuated meningeal inflammation and enhanced systemic killing of bacteria. Pretreatment with recombinant human G-CSF in a murine model of pneumococcal pneumonia resulted in improved survival with low, but not high bacterial inocula. Therefore, the benefits of using G-CSF are limited inasmuch as pneumococci already have recruited large numbers of neutrophils in the lungs by this time.[163]

INTRACELLULAR SIGNALING PATHWAYS. Pneumococcal cell walls activate multiple intracellular signaling pathways in microglial brain cells, with induction of an outwardly rectifying K^+ channel; suppression of the constitutively expressed inwardly rectifying K^+ current; and release of TNF-α, IL-6, IL-12, and other inflammatory mediators.[556] The presence of serum strongly facilitated these effects. The mechanisms involved in microglial activation by pneumococcal cell walls were different from those activated by gram-negative lipopolysaccharide.

LACTOFERRIN. Human lactoferrin is an iron-binding glycoprotein that is particularly prominent in exocrine secretions and leukocytes and also is found in serum, especially during inflammation. It is able to sequester iron from microbes and has immunomodulatory functions, including inhibition of both activation of complement and production of cytokines. Binding of human lactoferrin to the surface of *S. pneumoniae* depends entirely on PspA.[280] Prevention of the binding of lactoferrin to pneumococcal PspA could be an important host defense mechanism.

MANNOSE-BINDING LECTIN. Mannose-binding lectin (MBL) is a key mediator of innate host immunity that activates the complement pathway and directly opsonizes some infectious pathogens. Mutations in three codons in the MBL gene have been identified, and individuals homozygous for a mutant genotype have very little or no serum MBL. In a study conducted in the United Kingdom of 229 patients in whom *S. pneumoniae* was isolated from sterile sites, 28 (12%) were homozygous for MBL codon variants versus only 18 of 353 (5%) controls (odds rate of 2.59; 95% confidence interval, 1.39 to 4.83).[597]

PATHOGENESIS OF DISEASE

To cause disease, pneumococci, like other extracellular bacterial pathogens, must adhere to mammalian cells, replicate in situ, be carried to and replicate in parts of the body that normally are free of them, escape phagocytosis, and damage tissue by causing inflammation or producing substances that directly damage cells and, in some cases, invade the bloodstream.[493] As discussed earlier, the vast array of virulence mechanisms available to pneumococci are countered by numerous host defense mechanisms, although some host responses facilitate infection.

Even though colonization with a pneumococcal strain can progress to disease, it usually does not occur, and the development of anticapsular type-specific antibodies occurs within 30 days,[271, 272, 495, 496] at least in older children and adults. If organisms find their way into the eustachian tubes, sinuses, or bronchi, clearance mechanisms, chiefly ciliary action, lead to their rapid removal. After the development of humoral immunity, colonization with a strain may persist for 1 to 12 months, during which time disease may occur in contiguous sites, but the host is protected from invasive disease by circulating type-specific anticapsular IgG. Loss of colonization with a strain is followed, after a variable colonization-free interval, by colonization with a different serotype. Because 90 antigenically distinct serotypes exist, this cycle of colonization accompanied by the development of humoral immunity occurs many times.

Progression of colonization to disease usually requires the combination of two events: first, the acquisition of a serotype to which the host is not immune and, second, a concurrent respiratory viral infection, chronic damage to respiratory epithelium (e.g., smoking or occupational exposure), allergy, or other conditions that result in the development of disease rather than just colonization.[493] Many of these concurrent conditions initiate cytokine activation of the respiratory epithelium, which facilitates increased adhesion of pneumococci to respiratory epithelial cells, as well as invasion of these cells.[432] Mechanisms by which cytokine activation results in these effects include expression of platelet-activating factor and pIgR as discussed earlier. This combination of factors leads to a higher density of colonizing organisms and enables pneumococci to cause infection, including pneumonia, acute exacerbations of chronic bronchitis, sinusitis, otitis media, and mastoiditis, in contiguous respiratory tract sites. Adherence of *S. pneumoniae* to host cells involves an array of surface adhesin molecules such as CbpA, PspA, PspC, Hyl, Ply, PsaA, and both neuraminidases. As discussed earlier, these proteins are involved in interactions with the host complement system (PspA), degradation of hyaluronan of the extracellular matrix (Hyl), lysis of cholesterol-containing membranes (pneumolysin), and binding of metals (divalent cations) such as Mn^{2+} or Zn^{2+} (PsaA) followed by their transport inside the cytoplasm of pneumococci.

Additionally, transepithelial and transendothelial transport of organisms into the bloodstream results in bacteremia, and subsequent transport across other epithelial cells leads to infection of noncontiguous sites such as the leptomeninges, peritoneum, and joint spaces. Such infection occurs in nonimmune hosts by virtue of the fact that pneumococci are able to escape ingestion and killing by host phagocytic cells in the absence of type-specific antibody because the capsule is the major determinant of virulence. *S. pneumoniae* produces few toxins and largely causes disease by its capacity to replicate in host tissues and generate an intense inflammatory response. Cell wall TA and peptidoglycan stimulate the production of cytokines (IL-1, IL-6, IL-8, and TNF) and activate complement by the alternative pathway. The polysaccharide capsule also activates the alternative complement pathway in vitro. Such activation is associated with the release of C5a, a potent attractant for PMNs. The classic complement pathway also is activated by antibody to cell wall polysaccharides in the absence of anticapsular antibody, and an intense inflammatory response fueled by vigorous activation of both the alternative and classical complement pathways accompanies pneumococcal infection of an immunologically naive host.[493] The disease process is largely a result of this inflammation, and its severity is in direct proportion to its intensity. Pneumolysin also is associated with the severity of disease, and injection of pneumolysin into rat lung causes all the histologic findings of pneumonia, whereas immunization of mice with pneumolysin before infection or challenge with pneumolysin knockout pneumococci is associated with a significant reduction in virulence.[47, 207] Numerous other factors contribute to the ability of strains to cause disease and to the severity of disease, as discussed under virulence mechanisms.

Although pneumococci most commonly cause bacteremia, otitis media, pneumonia, and meningitis, they can produce disease in virtually any organ. Before the advent of immunotherapy and chemotherapy, such "unusual" infections were relatively common. Today, they are less so.

Survival of a patient with a pneumococcal disease depends on numerous variables, including the site of infection, the underlying disease, and the patient's age. Before the advent of chemotherapy, pneumococcal meningitis was universally fatal, whereas pneumococcal pneumonia killed approximately 25 percent of patients. Austrian and Gold[40] in 1964 dramatically illustrated the role of age and underlying disease when their survey of mortality associated with bacteremic pneumococcal pneumonia destroyed the complacency produced by the use of antimicrobial agents. The aged and infirm were likely to die despite receiving immediate and appropriate therapy with penicillin. Today, normal children rarely die of pneumococcal disease; thus, the prognosis must be related to the likelihood of permanent sequelae occurring. Pneumococci do not cause necrosis in pulmonary tissue, and survivors rapidly regain normal pulmonary function.[348] Many children recovering from pneumococcal meningitis are found to have neurologic sequelae. Some investigators suggest that the first attack of pneumococcal otitis media in some way predisposes the individual to subsequent attacks of otitis media.[317]

Before the availability of antimicrobial agents, recovery of a patient with pneumococcal pneumonia depended on the development of type-specific antibody. Although serum and white blood cells (WBCs) from nonimmune children kill pneumococci, probably by activation of the alternative complement pathway, they do so slowly. The importance of this pathway is illustrated best by the inability of children with sickle-cell disease to handle pneumococcal infection.[173, 352, 535] These children and others with asplenia may die rapidly despite the administration of prompt, vigorous therapy.[356, 378, 623]

Microbiology

S. pneumoniae is a gram-positive coccus that replicates in pairs and chains in liquid medium. The shape of the individual organism is a lanceolate coccus, usually in pairs with the long axis forming a straight line. Elongated or pointed forms are common.

Pneumococci are cultured readily on blood and chocolate agar media, as well as in suitable liquid culture media for isolation from blood. Isolates are facultative anaerobes, and most strains require atmospheric enrichment with 5 to 10 percent CO_2 for primary isolation[39]; occasional strains are strict anaerobes. Strains can be adapted for growth without CO_2 supplementation by repeated subculture. Detection of nasopharyngeal carriage of pneumococci is a problem because of the presence of other flora; the use of antimicrobial-containing media, such as blood agar supplemented with gentamicin (5 µg/mL), has led to improvements in isolation of pneumococci, particularly resistant strains.[537, 559] However, the sensitivity of current in vitro methods is poor in comparison to the sensitivity of mouse inoculation, although not all serotypes are virulent in mice.[309, 395]

IDENTIFICATION OF PNEUMOCOCCI

Pneumococci usually are identified readily by standard features such as colonial morphology, alpha-hemolysis, negative catalase reaction, optochin susceptibility, bile solubility, and specific reactions with antisera to capsular polysaccharides.[330] *S. pneumoniae* produces an autolytic intracellular enzyme, LytA, that causes the organism to autolyze rapidly when grown on artificial media. Bile salts accelerate this natural autolytic process by combining with the pneumococcal cell and activating its autolysin. Strains with atypical features, such as rounded rather than flat or concentrically ringed colonies, optochin resistance, or lack of capsules, do occur and can result in their misidentification as viridans streptococci. Atypical strains are more likely to be encountered from normal flora sites and with penicillin-resistant strains.

Strains with optochin zones greater than 14 mm can be identified presumptively as pneumococci, whereas strains with 7- to 14-mm zones require confirmation by bile solubility, and strains with no zone usually are not *S. pneumoniae*. However, incubation in carbon dioxide long has been recognized as decreasing the zone size around optochin disks, and incubation in room air generally results in zone sizes increasing if the strain is a pneumococcus or decreasing if the strain is a member of the viridans group of streptococci.[560] Optochin-resistant variants of pneumococci can occur and usually are seen as a subpopulation within the zone of inhibition of an optochin disk, and optochin-resistant mutants can be selected by passage of strains in the presence of optochin.[491] Strains with equivocal optochin zones or atypical colonial morphology can be tested for bile solubility, either directly by placing a drop of bile salt solution (10% sodium deoxycholate) onto colonies and observing for lysis of the colonies or by suspension of organisms in a bile salt solution with a bile salt–free control. Care must be taken in the tube bile solubility test to not obtain false-positive results, which can be caused by the organism suspension being too light or by suspension of organisms in broth rather than saline.[330]

Identification of the capsular polysaccharide serotype or serogroup also is useful in characterizing strains and in confirming the identity of problem strains. This identification is performed by the capsular swelling technique, in which equal volumes of an organism suspension, 0.3 percent methylene blue dye solution, and antiserum are mixed on a glass slide, covered with a cover slip, and read at 1000× magnification by phase-contrast microscopy. Alternatively, organism suspensions can be dried on slides and antiserum and methylene blue dye solution mixed on a cover slip, which then is placed on the slide. The polysaccharide capsule of the pneumococcal organism binds with type-specific antiserum, and organisms can be seen to clump or agglutinate; the resulting change in the refractive index of antibody-coated capsule causes the capsule to appear swollen. Currently, antisera to each serotype or serogroup are available commercially, and factoring antisera to subtype serogroups are available from Statens Serum Institut, Copenhagen, Denmark. The numbering system for the 90 pneumococcal serotypes is shown in Table 90–1.

Currently, 90 serotypes have been identified and are divided into 25 individual serotypes and 21 serogroups in the

Danish classification, which now is used universally.[303] Most serotypes have one antigenic determinant, whereas serogroups have one or more antigenic determinants common to the group and one or more determinants unique to each serotype. Serotypes within a serogroup usually are identified by the serogroup number followed by a letter indicating to which serotype a strain belongs in the Danish system, or they are identified by a unique number in the U.S. system. Except for serogroups 6 and 9, the letters in the Danish system are F for the first subtype, followed by A, B, and so on. Each serogroup contains 2 to 5 related types, and the 21 serogroups include 65 individual subtypes. Serotype numbers 26 and 30 are not in use. Omniserum containing antibodies to all 90 serotypes is available and can be used to confirm the identity of isolates as pneumococci. Because many serotypes or serogroups are included in this reagent, reactions may not always be optimal and usually are stronger in pool or monovalent reagents. Nine antiserum pools classified from A to I, each containing four to seven serotypes or serogroups, also are available and can be used to identify strains in a group of serotypes before individual serotype or serogroup reagents are tested. Other methods of capsular typing, such as latex agglutination, coagglutination, and capillary precipitation, can be used, but these methods are not available commercially.

The ability of a polymerase chain reaction (PCR) method to identify the capsular serotype of pneumococci has been developed on the basis of polymorphisms in two genes common to the different capsule loci.[412] In a limited study, the correct serotype or serogroup was identified in 92 of 93 strains, but this method did not differentiate serotype 6A from 6B strains. This method holds promise as a noncultural method for serotype determination.

DETECTION OF CLONALITY

In addition to phenotypic features, such as serotype and antimicrobial resistance markers, the various DNA fingerprint methods for epidemiologic typing of *S. pneumoniae* that have been used include ribotyping, BOX fingerprinting with the BOX repetitive sequence of *S. pneumoniae* as a DNA probe, PCR fingerprinting with a primer homologous to the enterobacterial repetitive intergenic consensus sequence, pulsed-field gel electrophoresis of large DNA fragments digested by restriction enzymes, and restriction fragment end labeling to detect restriction fragment length polymorphisms of small DNA fragments.[305, 470] The discriminatory power of the individual techniques differed significantly. BOX fingerprinting, pulsed-field gel electrophoresis, and restriction fragment end labeling provided the highest degree of discriminatory power. Ribotyping, BOX fingerprinting, and restriction fragment end labeling were very suitable techniques for computerized data analysis. Pulsed-field gel electrophoresis of large DNA fragments digested by restriction enzymes such as SmaI is the method used most frequently. Descriptions and nomenclature for the 16 major pneumococcal clones that have contributed to the increase in antimicrobial resistance worldwide were published recently.[470]

DIAGNOSIS OF PNEUMOCOCCAL DISEASE

Definitive diagnosis of pneumococcal infection is based on recovery of pneumococci from the site of infection or documentation of pneumococcal bacteremia, whereas presumptive diagnosis is based on detection of pneumococcal cellular components, such as capsular polysaccharide, and on species-specific DNA and RNA sequences from the site of infection or from remote sites such as urine.[330] Definitive diagnosis is confounded in many instances by the need for invasive procedures to obtain specimens (e.g., from the middle ear space) and by nasopharyngeal carriage of pneumococci when sputum is cultured. Pneumococci almost invariably are isolated from CSF in pneumococcal meningitis, even in patients receiving oral antibiotics.[594] However, the diagnosis of pneumococcal pneumonia is more challenging because sputum rarely is available from children and direct lung puncture is performed very infrequently. Detection of pneumococcal bacteremia to prove the diagnosis of pneumococcal pneumonia or other localized infection is valuable, but it does not occur frequently, and the actual prevalence of bacteremic pneumococcal pneumonia in children is not known,[678] although a recent study suggests that it is approximately 17 percent (11/64).[475] Therefore, pediatricians must use other methods to diagnose pneumococcal pneumonia. Signs and symptoms significantly associated with bacteremic pneumococcal pneumonia in children include high temperature (>38.9° C [>102° F]), leukocytosis (>15,000/mm^3), and lobar or segmental consolidation.[678] However, how often these features are associated with nonbacteremic pneumococcal pneumonia is not known.

Direct examination of Gram-stained smears of clinically appropriate material remains the fastest diagnostic method and can be augmented if necessary by direct demonstration of capsular swelling of organisms in the presence of anticapsular antisera. The availability of antigen-detection systems that can be used in urine, serum, CSF, and other specimens, such as capsular antigen detection by counterimmunoelectrophoresis and latex agglutination with polyvalent pneumococcal reagent, generally has not improved patient management because of the low sensitivity and specificity of these methods and the fact that they usually are positive only when a Gram stain also is positive. The concentration of pneumococcal capsular antigen in saliva was evaluated in a recent study by latex agglutination in children with community-acquired pneumonia and in healthy controls. None of the children with pneumonia in this study had a positive blood culture, and pneumococcal capsular antigen was detected in the saliva of 27 percent of children with pneumonia versus 17 percent of controls. More cases (20%) than controls (2%) had a pneumococcal capsular antigen titer of 10 or greater ($p < .01$). Quantitative measurement of pneumococcal capsular antigen in saliva may be valuable in helping make an etiologic diagnosis in children with pneumonia, but its sensitivity is poor and it is confounded by false-positive results caused by pneumococcal carriage.[218]

A newly available, rapid (15 min) immunochromatographic membrane test to detect pneumococcal polysaccharide capsular antigen in urine samples (Binax NOW) has been developed and was evaluated in the diagnosis of bacteremic and nonbacteremic pneumococcal pneumonia. Urine samples were studied in 51 patients with bacteremic and nonbacteremic pneumonia caused by *S. pneumoniae;* the pneumonia was diagnosed by blood culture, and pneumococcal polysaccharide capsular antigen was detected by counterimmunoelectrophoresis in urine samples. Pneumococcal antigen was detected in urine by the immunochromatographic membrane test in 41 of 51 patients with pneumococcal pneumonia (80.4%), including 23 of 28 bacteremic cases (82.1%) and 18 of 23 nonbacteremic cases (78.3%). Antigen also was detected in 7 of 16 patients with a diagnosis of presumptive pneumococcal pneumonia (43.7%) and in 1 of the 16 patients with pneumonia but in whom no pathogen was identified. The specificity of the immunochromatographic membrane test was 97.2 percent, but its sensitivity was only approximately 80 percent, thus limiting its value.[178] Furthermore, the usefulness of this test is questionable because the antigen was detected in urine in 30 of 138 (22%) healthy children with nasopharyngeal carriage of *S. pneumoniae* versus only 3 of 71 (4%) noncarriers ($p < .001$).[284] Thus, the test was shown to be often positive in healthy pneumococcal carriers.

Newer molecular-based methods for the diagnosis of pneumococcal disease include the use of DNA probes to detect pneumolysin, autolysin, and PsaA protein, but considerable practical problems must be overcome before these methods will be clinically applicable.[160] Examples include a commercial method involving real-time PCR for simultaneous detection of *N. meningitidis, H. influenzae,* and *S. pneumoniae* in patients suspected of having meningitis and septicemia. This method is based on detection of the pneumolysin gene for *S. pneumoniae* and uses a single-tube, 5′-nuclease multiplex PCR assay on samples of CSF, plasma, serum, and whole blood. Amplified products are monitored with sequence-specific fluorescent dye–labeled probes. The sensitivity of using clinical samples (CSF, serum, plasma, and whole blood) from culture-confirmed cases of *S. pneumoniae* infection was 91.8 percent. The multiplex assay also was used to test a large number of culture-negative samples, which resulted in the detection of numerous cases of meningococcal, *H. influenzae,* and pneumococcal disease that had not been detected by culture.[128] However, whether these results are true positives or false positives is not known, and in another study, although the sensitivity of PCR amplification of the pneumolysin gene in the serum and CSF of infants and children with culture-proven pneumococcal bacteremia and meningitis was 100 percent, the specificity was poor, with 17 percent of healthy controls being positive.[160] The prevalence of false-positive reactions was highest (33%) in 2-year-old children, the age group with the highest rate of nasopharyngeal carriage of pneumococci. Therefore, although PCR of serum and CSF is a sensitive test for the detection of *S. pneumoniae* in these sites, its high rate of positivity in healthy controls as a result of nasopharyngeal carriage limits its utility in detecting systemic pneumococcal infection.[160]

Another rapid PCR method involving the use of a set of primers that amplify 273 base pairs of the autolysin gene has been developed to identify *S. pneumoniae.* In addition, three sets of primers were designed to amplify a 240–base pair fragment of the PBP-2B gene *(pbp2b)* of penicillin-susceptible *S. pneumoniae* and two common *pbp2b* mutations present in penicillin-resistant *S. pneumoniae* in order to simultaneously identify the penicillin susceptibility of strains. The autolysin gene was identified in all 1062 clinical isolates of *S. pneumoniae* evaluated. In addition, 98.9 percent of 621 penicillin-susceptible isolates were shown to have DNA fragments amplified by the penicillin-susceptible primers, whereas 72.1 percent of 441 penicillin-resistant isolates were detected by the penicillin-resistant *S. pneumoniae* primers.[691] Although further refinement of this method is required, this study has shown that it is possible to identify pneumococci and differentiate penicillin-susceptible from penicillin-resistant *S. pneumoniae* by applying PCR and a combination of primers to detect the susceptible *pbp2b* gene, resistant *pbp2b* gene mutations, and the autolysin gene. In another study, a 208–base pair region of the pneumolysin gene was amplified by PCR in blood specimens from hospitalized children with pneumonia. Whole blood, buffy coat, or plasma samples from 67 children (44%) tested positive by PCR. The sensitivity was 100 percent in 11 culture-confirmed children, and the specificity was 95 percent in control subjects. Age, previous administration of oral antibiotic therapy, and pneumococcal nasopharyngeal colonization did not influence the PCR results, which were more specific than were serologic and urinary antigen testing.[475]

A gene probe for the gene encoding the PsaA protein also has been developed on the basis of PCR assay. PsaA was confirmed to be present in representative strains of all 90 serotypes of *S. pneumoniae.* The specificity of the assay was verified by the lack of signal from analysis of heterologous bacterial species ($n = 30$) and genera ($n = 14$), including viridans group streptococci. The potential of the assay for clinical application was shown by its ability to detect pneumococci in culture-positive nasopharyngeal specimens.[486]

SUSCEPTIBILITY TESTING

Susceptibility testing of pneumococci has been well standardized, and testing can be performed by determination of the minimal inhibitory concentration (MIC) and, for selected agents, by disk diffusion.[333] MICs can be performed by macrodilution or microdilution in cation-supplemented Mueller-Hinton broth enhanced with 5 percent whole defibrinated sheep or horse blood or 5 percent lysed and centrifuged horse blood.[502] If sulfonamides are tested, only the latter supplement should be used to avoid the presence of sulfonamide antagonists. MICs also can be determined by dilution in Mueller-Hinton agar supplemented as just described; agar dilution generally is regarded as the reference method for pneumococci and often is used for developmental work.[330]

Many systems based on frozen or dried microdilution trays are available commercially and used extensively for surveillance testing.[331] As with any system, commercial microdilution panels should be validated and used with appropriate quality controls.

A new method for determination of MICs, the E-test (A. B. Biodisk, Solna, Sweden), is much simpler to use than are the other methods for MIC determination. This method consists of a calibrated antibiotic-impregnated plastic strip that is applied to the surface of an inoculated agar plate. An antibiotic gradient is produced that results in an elliptic zone of inhibition after incubation. The MIC is read at the point where the ellipse of inhibition meets the strip. Evaluation of the E-test has shown that this method generally is reliable, although problems are encountered with some agents because of acidification of the medium during incubation of the plates in CO_2, which is required to ensure the growth of clinical isolates. Agents particularly affected are macrolides and some quinolones.

Disk diffusion also has been standardized well for testing pneumococci against selected agents. Distinction between susceptible and resistant strains is accomplished readily by using the current National Committee for Clinical Laboratory Standards (NCCLS) method involving macrolides, tetracycline, chloramphenicol, trimethoprim-sulfamethoxazole, and clindamycin.[330] For testing penicillin and other β-lactams, disk diffusion is used best as a screening method with 1-μg oxacillin disks that have a susceptible cutoff zone of 20 mm or larger. Strains with zones of 20 mm or larger are fully susceptible to penicillin and other β-lactams. However, strains with zones that are less than 20 mm need to have MICs of penicillin and other appropriate β-lactams determined.[502] Penicillin-susceptible strains with MICs of 0.06 μg/mL usually screen out with resistant strains.

Although interpretative categories for clarifying the significance of MIC values are available, many limitations to the currently available NCCLS pneumococcal breakpoints exist, particularly for agents that can be administered in multiple-dosing regimens and by multiple routes of administration and that are used for infections in different body sites. Breakpoints for parenteral β-lactam agents generally are based on the use of agents in meningitis, whereas those of oral β-lactam agents are based on nonmeningeal infections such as otitis media.[502] Nonmeningeal breakpoints for some parenteral β-lactam agents were introduced in 2002, which to some extent will avoid the use of non–β-lactam agents for serious nonmeningeal pneumococcal infections. These breakpoint changes classify strains previously interpreted as intermediate in sensitivity to penicillin G, cefotaxime, and ceftriaxone as susceptible if the agents are administered parenterally to treat pneumonia and other nonmeningeal infections. Pharmacokinetic and pharmacodynamic parameters have been shown recently to correlate with clinical outcome and offer a more rational approach to predicting antimicrobial efficacy and determining clinically relevant susceptibility breakpoints.[132, 137, 337]

ANTIBIOTIC RESISTANCE

Mechanisms of Antibiotic Resistance

RESISTANCE TO β-LACTAM DRUGS. Widespread resistance to β-lactam and other drug classes has evolved in the most common pathogens, including *S. pneumoniae.* Although pneumococci are naturally transformable organisms, β-lactamase production never has been described in this organism. Instead, a much more complex resistance mechanism has evolved in *S. pneumoniae* that is mediated by sophisticated restructuring of the targets of the β-lactams, the PBPs, and by other newly described mechanisms.[282] The PBP targets in penicillin-resistant strains of *S. pneumoniae* are modified, low–binding affinity versions of the native PBPs. PBP targets may be modified by mutation or by transformation and homologous recombination with DNA from the PBP genes of viridans streptococci. The level of resistance is determined by how many and to what extent targets are modified.[109] Restructuring of PBPs is mediated by stepwise alterations in PBPs. The high-molecular-weight PBPs—types 1A, 2X, and 2B—that usually are detected in *S. pneumoniae* are involved in transpeptidase activity and play an important role in resistance.[283] Alterations in PBP-2B are associated with low-level resistance to penicillin, and alterations in PBP-2X mediate low-level resistance to cephalosporins. The additional alterations in PBP-1A raise penicillin MICs to 1 μg/mL or greater and cefotaxime MICs to 0.5 μg/mL or greater. Genomic comparison between *S. pneumoniae* and commensal *S. mitis* and *Streptococcus oralis* strains has documented the mosaic nature of PBPs between these species, with pneumococci acquiring their altered PBP genes from *S. mitis* and *S. oralis.*[281] Many other mosaic gene clusters not associated with penicillin resistance also have been found.[240] The capacity to produce branched cell wall stem peptides encoded by altered *murM* and *murN* genes, as well as altered PBPs, is required for expression of penicillin resistance in *S. pneumoniae.*[210] The *fibA* and *fibB* genes, which are homologous to the *Staphylococcus aureus femA/B* genes required for expression of methicillin resistance in this organism, encode proteins involved in the formation of interpeptide bridges and also are required for expression of PBP-mediated penicillin resistance.[723] Other mechanisms of β-lactam resistance have been described in laboratory mutants and in a clone of Hungarian pneumococcal strains with notably high levels of β-lactam resistance (penicillin MIC, 16 μg/mL; cefotaxime MIC, 4 μg/mL).[282, 648]

RESISTANCE TO NON–β-LACTAM DRUGS. The molecular and genetic mechanisms of resistance to macrolides, chloramphenicol, tetracycline, fluoroquinolones, and trimethoprim-sulfamethoxazole in *S. pneumoniae* also have been determined. Resistance genes for several agents are carried on a transposon, Tn1545.[131] It confers resistance to three antimicrobial classes—kanamycin (*aphA-3*), macrolide-lincosamide-streptogramin B–type antibiotics (*ermB*), and tetracycline (*tetM*). This transposon has been conjugated and transposed to the chromosome of *Enterococcus faecalis,* oral streptococci, and *Listeria monocytogenes.* The properties of this transposon account for the sudden emergence, rapid dissemination, and stabilization of resistance to multiple antibiotics in *S. pneumoniae* in the absence of plasmids.

Resistance mechanisms include the production of chloramphenicol acetyltransferase, an enzyme capable of catalyzing the conversion of chloramphenicol to nonfunctional derivatives. Chloramphenicol acetyltransferase is encoded by a chloramphenicol acetyltransferase (*cat*) gene identical to the *cat* gene from the *S. aureus* plasmid pC194. Tetracycline resistance occurs through ribosomal protection encoded by the genes *tetM* and *tetO.* The tetM and tetO proteins are thought to cause tetracycline to be released from the ribosome. Resistance to fluoroquinolones primarily involves mutations in the DNA gyrase gene *gyrA* and in the topoisomerase IV genes *parC* and *parE,* as well as an efflux mechanism, which affects some fluoroquinolones. Resistance to trimethoprim is mediated through a single amino acid substitution in the chromosomal dihydrofolate reductase gene of *S. pneumoniae,* which is thought to disrupt the bond with trimethoprim without affecting the action of dihydrofolate reductase. Sulfonamide resistance appears to result from repetitions of one or two amino acids in the chromosomal dihydropteroate synthase.[729]

Two major mechanisms have been described for resistance to erythromycin. Co-resistance to macrolides, clindamycin, and streptogramin B–type antibiotics is a result of modification of the ribosome through methylation of an adenine residue in domain V of the 23S rRNA. Methylation is encoded by a methylase gene, *ermB* (previously called *ermAM*). Resistance only to 14- and 15-membered macrolides (erythromycin, azithromycin, and clarithromycin) but not to 16-membered macrolides (roxithromycin, josamycin, and spiramycin), ketolides, or clindamycin is a result of efflux of the antibiotic from the cell; such resistance is encoded by the gene *mefE* in *S. pneumoniae* and appears to be emerging rapidly as the predominant mechanism of resistance to erythromycin in many countries.[240] Other macrolide resistance mechanisms that have been described recently include mutations in position 2059 of the 23S rRNA and in genes encoding ribosomal protein L4.[667]

VANCOMYCIN TOLERANCE. Although vancomycin resistance has not been described in pneumococci, antibiotic tolerance, the ability of bacteria to survive but not grow in the presence of antibiotics, has been described. It has been shown to be caused by loss of function of the VncS histidine kinase of a two-component gene expression sensor-regulator system in *S. pneumoniae,* which produces tolerance to vancomycin and other classes of antibiotics.[507]

Evolution of Antibiotic Resistance among Pneumococci

Pneumococci initially were susceptible to many antimicrobial agents, but they became resistant with varying degrees of rapidity to many of these agents. The earliest example was the development of resistance to optochin (ethylhydrocupreine) when this agent was used experimentally in mice in the early part of the 20th century. With the introduction of sulfonamides in 1939, pneumococci similarly exhibited an ability to acquire resistance in experimental infections in mice, as well as in a human case of meningitis.[390] Sulfonamide resistance was identified sporadically thereafter, and a trimethoprim-sulfamethoxazole–resistant strain was recognized first in 1972. Trimethoprim-sulfamethoxazole resistance subsequently has become widespread in virtually all serotypes throughout the world, including developing countries, and resistance to this agent is greater than to any other antimicrobial class worldwide.[307] Tetracycline resistance emerged in the 1960s and chloramphenicol resistance in 1970. However, little attention was paid to the development of resistance in this species until 1977, when isolates resistant to several antimicrobial classes, including penicillins, chloramphenicol, tetracyclines, macrolides, clindamycin, and trimethoprim-sulfamethoxazole, were detected in South Africa.[28, 336] Subsequently, multiresistant clones of pneumococci have spread throughout many regions of the world. Noteworthy is that multiresistant clones are confined mostly to serotype 14 and serogroups 6, 9, 19, and 23.[166] Whereas resistance to penicillins occurs in a stepwise fashion and can be overcome by using β-lactams with appropriate pharmacokinetics, resistance to other drug classes usually is absolute, and distinct populations of susceptible and resistant strains are found with agents such as macrolides, clindamycin, tetracyclines, trimethoprim-sulfamethoxazole, and chloramphenicol. Unlike enterococci, resistance to vancomycin has not developed in pneumococci yet, although vancomycin-tolerant strains have been detected.[50, 304]

Cross-resistance among *S. pneumoniae* to macrolides and other classes of antibiotics usually increases with increasing MICs to penicillin[334] (Fig. 90–2). Whereas only 6 percent of penicillin-susceptible pneumococci are resistant to macrolides and 14 percent to trimethoprim-sulfamethoxazole, approximately half of the penicillin-intermediate isolates were resistant to these agents. In the case of penicillin-resistant strains, three quarters were resistant to macrolides, 90 percent to trimethoprim-sulfamethoxazole, and 28 percent to clindamycin. However, this pattern is not the case in all countries, and at least one multiresistant clone resistant to chloramphenicol, tetracycline, erythromycin, clindamycin, and trimethoprim-sulfamethoxazole has remained penicillin-susceptible.[171, 666]

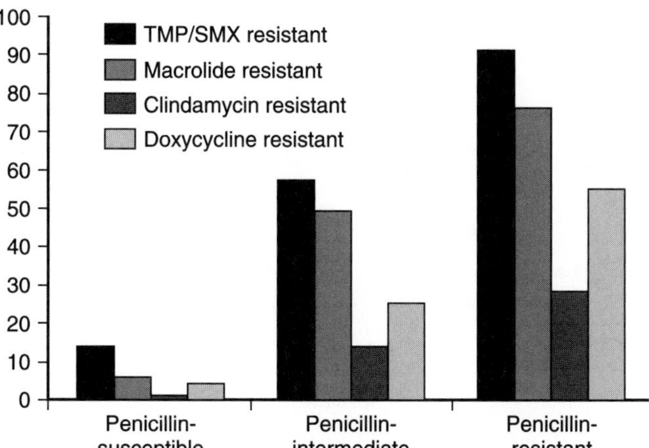

FIGURE 90–2 ■ Pneumococci often are resistant to several drug classes, and cross-resistance to macrolides and other classes of antibiotics increases as minimal inhibitory concentrations of penicillin increase.[334, 641]

Strains of *S. pneumoniae* were exquisitely susceptible to penicillin (MICs of 0.01 to 0.03 μg/mL) when this agent was used clinically first in the 1940s and 1950s, and this MIC range is referred to as the baseline activity of penicillin against *S. pneumoniae*.[330] Evolution of resistance to this class of agents was noted first when a few strains of *S. pneumoniae* were isolated in the 1960s in Australia and New Guinea. These strains had decreased susceptibility to penicillin, with MICs of 0.1 to 0.25 μg/mL, approximately 10-fold higher than the MICs of baseline strains. Strains with penicillin MICs of 2 to 4 μg/mL, approximately 100-fold higher than the baseline strains, were isolated in South Africa in 1977, and subsequently, strains with even higher MICs (16 μg/mL, approximately 1000-fold higher than baseline strains) were described in Hungary.[648] Penicillin MICs of pneumococci are classified conventionally as susceptible if the MICs are 0.06 μg/mL or less, intermediate if the MICs are 0.12 to 1.0 μg/mL, and resistant if the MICs are 2.0 μg/mL or more. This classification is useful mainly in characterizing strains as fully susceptible to β-lactams if susceptible or as having decreased susceptibility if intermediate or resistant. Strains with such decreased susceptibility are better referred to as β-lactam drug challenged because the mechanism of resistance can be overcome if the pharmacokinetics of the β-lactam drug used in serum or at the site of infection exceeds the MIC for 40 to 50 percent of the dosing interval.[133] Similar variations in MIC ranges are seen with all β-lactams, although MIC ranges for many β-lactams are much higher than that for penicillin itself. Agents such as ampicillin, amoxicillin, cefotaxime, and ceftriaxone have MIC ranges similar to that of penicillin, whereas agents such as cefazolin, cefaclor, cefprozil, ceftazidime, and cefixime have much higher MIC ranges. For example, the baseline activity of cefaclor against *S. pneumoniae* is 0.5 to 1 μg/mL, which is approximately a 20- to 30-fold higher concentration than required for penicillin to inhibit the most susceptible strains. Changes in susceptibility over time are illustrated in a study of recent-versus-archived otitis media strains. In this study, the MIC_{90} for cefaclor against archived isolates was 1 μg/mL, whereas the MIC_{90} against recent isolates was greater than 64 μg/mL.[332] A few agents, such as imipenem and meropenem, have slightly lower MIC ranges than penicillin does. Currently, 50 to 60 percent of pneumococci in the United States are penicillin-susceptible, 15 to 20 percent are penicillin-intermediate, and 20 to 30 percent are penicillin-resistant. The proportions of strains in each group vary considerably throughout the world.

Resistance to macrolides in strains of *S. pneumoniae* was noted first in 1964 and was detected sporadically in the United States until it became widespread in the latter half of the 1990s.[307, 321, 390] The baseline activity of macrolides (0.03 μg/mL) and MIC distributions (1000-fold concentration range, 0.03 to >32 μg/mL) against *S. pneumoniae* are somewhat similar to those of penicillin. The MIC distribution of macrolides is trimodal, with strains being exquisitely susceptible (erythromycin MIC, ≤0.03 μg/mL) or highly resistant (erythromycin MIC, ≥32 μg/mL) or demonstrating intermediate resistance (MICs of 1 to 16 μg/mL).[202] These distributions closely correlate with macrolide ribosomal methylase and efflux resistance mechanisms. The prevalence of macrolide resistance and reports of clinical failure resulting from strains with efflux and ribosomal methylase resistance mechanisms continue to increase.* Some authors, however, have argued that isolates with efflux-mediated resistance could be susceptible to the high intracellular

*See references 77, 217, 328, 371, 447, 448, 482, 549, 609, 721.

concentrations that these agents achieve in phagocytic cells and in epithelial lining fluid of the alveoli.[17, 370] However, no clinical or animal data support these arguments for extracellular pathogens such as *S. pneumoniae,* whereas considerable clinical and animal data support the use of current breakpoints.[48, 132, 133, 478] The rising incidence of macrolide-resistant pneumococci was directly proportional to the increasing use of macrolides in various communities and age groups.[236, 321, 549] In a recent report, 18 to 23 percent of pneumococci from the United States were macrolide-resistant[307, 683] as compared with 10 percent from Canada, 11 percent from Latin America, 20 percent from Europe, and 39 percent from the Asia-Pacific region.[307]

Multiple antibiotic–resistant strains have greater selective advantages than do strains resistant to just one antibiotic because the opportunity for positive selection is increased as the number of drug classes to which isolates are resistant increases.[391] Exposure to different classes of antibiotics allows more opportunity for selective advantage to a multiple antibiotic–resistant organism than to a monoresistant strain, which must wait to encounter the one antibiotic to which it is resistant and is likely to be killed by agents of other antibiotic classes. Thus, the increasing prevalence of antibiotic-resistant pneumococci is associated with the increasing prevalence of multidrug-resistant strains.[727] Therefore, one is not surprised that the use of one class of antibiotics (mainly macrolides and trimethoprim-sulfamethoxazole) can be associated with an increase in resistance to other classes of antibiotics (mainly β-lactam drugs).[5, 29, 156, 262] Many authorities now think that antibiotic agents such as the newer macrolides (e.g., clarithromycin and azithromycin) and trimethoprim-sulfamethoxazole are stronger promoters of antibiotic resistance among *S. pneumoniae* than are the β-lactam drugs.[29, 156, 236, 262, 549] Researchers also have suggested that among the β-lactam drugs, cephalosporins are stronger promoters of resistance in *S. pneumoniae* than are the aminopenicillins are.[236, 608]

Although many strains are resistant to tetracyclines and macrolides, they are susceptible to the new tetracycline derivatives, the glycylcyclines, as well as to streptogramins, ketolides, glycopeptides, and rifampin. Many strains are resistant to trimethoprim-sulfamethoxazole worldwide, with more than 40 percent being resistant in the United States. Fluoroquinolones with antipneumococcal activity (e.g., gatifloxacin, levofloxacin, moxifloxacin) are active against most strains of *S. pneumoniae*; however, in several countries where fluoroquinolones have been prescribed widely, clinically relevant levels of resistance have been described.[110, 307, 572] No doubt, antibiotic resistance will continue to evolve and challenge us.

Epidemiology

Pneumococcal infection remains a serious problem at the beginning of the 21st century in both the developed and developing world. It still is a leading cause of death worldwide and a leading cause of morbidity in all countries.

In the United States, since the introduction of *H. influenzae* type b (Hib) vaccination, *S. pneumoniae* has become the leading cause of bacteremia and bacterial meningitis and has remained a major cause of otitis media. This organism causes more deaths than does any other vaccine-preventable organism.[237] The burden of pneumococcal disease in the United States has been estimated to be 125,000 to 500,000 cases of pneumonia, 50,000 cases of bacteremia, 3000 cases of meningitis, and 7 million cases of otitis media, with 40,000 deaths occurring annually.[54, 295, 554] In the developing world, pneumococcal infections are among the leading causes of death in children younger than 2 years of age, with the estimated 1.2 million deaths per year accounting for 9 percent of all deaths.[381]

The only reservoir of *S. pneumoniae* is the human nasopharynx. From there, the organism can (1) enter the bloodstream and cause invasive infections such as sepsis and meningitis and infections in remote foci such as joints, bones, and soft tissues; (2) spread to adjacent mucosal tissues and cause mucosal infections such as otitis media, sinusitis, and pneumonia; and (3) be transmitted by direct contact and through aerosols to other individuals.[141] Acquisition and nasopharyngeal carriage of *S. pneumoniae* are associated with the occurrence of pneumococcal AOM,[197, 413, 446, 744] bacteremia,[270, 419, 442, 463] and pneumonia.[309]

The most common diseases caused by *S. pneumoniae* are related to the upper respiratory tract (mainly otitis media, conjunctivitis, and sinusitis). The least common are invasive infections such as bacteremia and meningitis, whereas pneumonia is of intermediate frequency. Figure 90–3 shows the difference in the order of magnitude of these diseases. The yearly incidence of invasive infections is reported as less than 10 to more than 1000 per 100,000 children younger than 5 years of age in various populations. The incidence of pneumonia usually is reported as a few dozen to a few thousand per 100,000 children younger than 5 years of age. Pneumococci are responsible for 25 to 50 percent of cases of otitis media in children, which translates to more than 10,000 per 100,000 children younger than 5 years of age. Thus, pneumococcal otitis media is roughly up to 1000-fold more common than is invasive pneumococcal infections, and pneumococcal pneumonia is 10- to 100-fold more common than invasive infections.

RISK FACTORS FOR PNEUMOCOCCAL INFECTION

In general, decreased host defenses, especially in humoral immunity, or increased exposure to the organism can be considered the main risk factors for acquiring pneumococcal infection. Risk factors can be divided into various categories, although such division is arbitrary because numerous predisposing conditions can be present.

YOUNG AGE. Young age is perhaps the most important risk factor for acquiring pneumococcal infection because

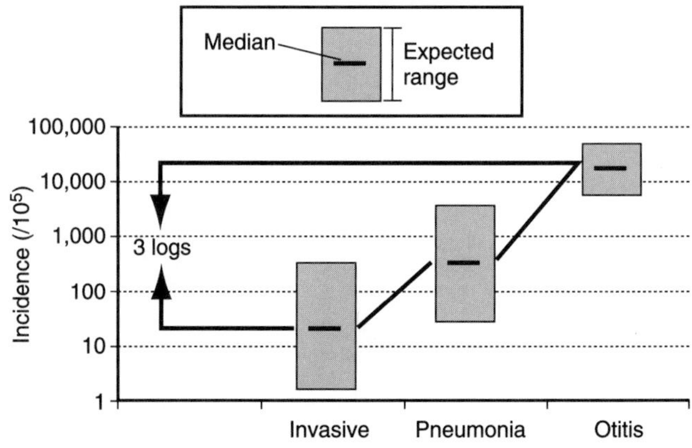

FIGURE 90–3 ■ Relative incidence of pneumococcal invasive infections, pneumonia, and otitis media in children. The figure is based on estimates from global data that have been published or presented at meetings. The *horizontal line* in each box presents the estimated average value and the upper and lower limits of the presumed range.

natural immunity is highly age-dependent. One of the best demonstrations of the relationship between age and immunity to pneumococcal infection was published in 1932 by Sutliff and Finland (Fig. 90–4). Immunity in the first few months of life, derived from maternal antibody passively transferred to the fetus, protects from invasive infection. These antibodies rapidly disappear, and within a few months, the incidence of invasive infection increases. The incidence then starts to decline sharply after the child is 18 months of age, when the child is able to mount an immune response to most pneumococci, coupled with cumulative exposure to the various pneumococcal strains.

ABSENCE OR MALFUNCTION OF THE SPLEEN, INCLUDING HEMOGLOBINOPATHIES. The spleen is the principal organ that clears pneumococci from the bloodstream.[661, 718] Patients in whom the spleen has been removed or does not function normally are at risk for developing overwhelming pneumococcal infection. Children with invasive *S. pneumoniae* from eight children's hospitals in the United States were studied during the period 1993 to 1999. Of 2581 cases, 1 percent were either in children with congenital asplenia or in children who had undergone surgical splenectomy.[619] The mortality rate was high (6/22 [27%]), especially in those with meningitis. Splenic malfunction is considered to be the most important reason for the increased incidence and severity of pneumococcal bacteremia in sickle-cell disease and other sickle hemoglobinopathies (e.g., hemoglobin SC disease or S-β-thalassemia).[532, 534, 619, 742] Although the incidence of pneumococcal infection in children with hemoglobin SC disease is lower than in persons with sickle-cell disease, it is higher than in healthy children.[410, 688] The incidence of overall bacterial sepsis in other hemoglobinopathies (e.g., S-β-thalassemia) is estimated to be intermediate between that for hemoglobin SC and hemoglobin SS disease.[524] The high risk of developing pneumococcal infection in persons with sickle-cell disease is thought to be due to the combination of low levels of circulating antibodies, splenic dysfunction, and complement deficiency, which results in decreased clearance of encapsulated bacteria from the bloodstream.[534, 731] Although the use of prophylactic penicillin has reduced the risk for acquiring pneumococcal disease, children younger than 5 years of age with sickle-cell disease still have increased rates of invasive disease (range, 1230 to 1500/100,000 population).[212, 532, 734, 742]

DEFECTIVE ANTIBODY FORMATION. As reviewed in the "Pathogenesis" and "Prevention" sections of this chapter, defective antibody production against pneumococcal polysaccharides is the rule for most serotypes in those younger than 18 months and may be seen at even older ages for some serotypes. However, at all ages, conditions associated with reduced antibody formation constitute a high risk for acquiring pneumococcal infection in comparison to peers. Such conditions are congenital agammaglobulinemia, acquired common variable hypogammaglobulinemia,[134] selective IgG subclass deficiency,[696] and secondary defective antibody production in diseases such as malignancies and human immunodeficiency virus (HIV) infection. Having HIV infection predisposes individuals to secondary bacterial infection by several mechanisms, but defective antibody production is the most important factor in pneumococcal infection. The ability to produce antipneumococcal capsular antibody is inversely proportional to the peripheral blood CD4 lymphocyte count, especially if it falls below 500/mm^3.[344, 584] *S. pneumoniae* is the most common cause of invasive bacterial infection in HIV-infected children; it accounts for 35 to 50 percent of such episodes, with the relative risk of disease being 3- to 22-fold higher than in children without HIV infection.[21, 62, 201, 224, 454, 481] In one study, the incidence of invasive pneumococcal disease was 6.1 cases per 100 patient-years in HIV-infected children through the age of 7 years.[462]

DEFECTS IN COMPLEMENT. Congenital or acquired deficiencies in C1, C2, and C4 may be associated with increased susceptibility to pneumococcal infection, although cases documenting these associations are rare.[208]

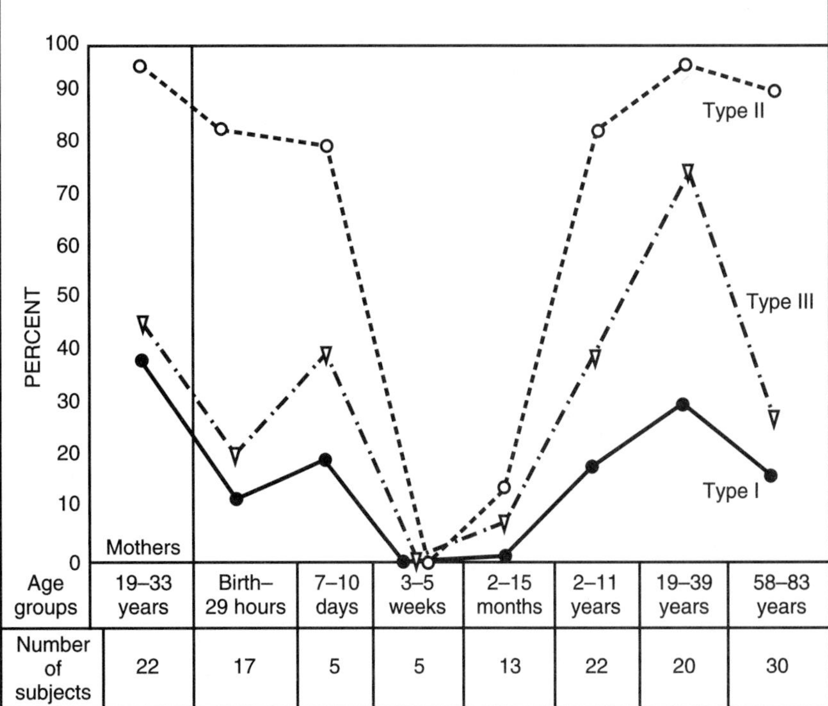

FIGURE 90–4 ■ Percentage of subjects in different age groups whose blood is pneumococcidal.

NEUTROPENIA OR NEUTROPHIL DYSFUNCTION. The primary neutropenias, such as cyclic neutropenia, as well as secondary ones, such as drug-induced neutropenia and aplastic anemia, are associated with an increased incidence of severe pneumococcal infection. In some neutrophil dysfunction states, such as seen in alcoholism, liver cirrhosis, glucocorticoid treatment, and renal insufficiency, an increased incidence of pneumococcal infection is found. However, the incidence is not increased in other granulocyte dysfunction syndromes such as leukocyte adhesion deficiency syndromes[19] and chronic granulomatous disease.[233] In chronic granulomatous disease, although intracellular bacterial killing by polymorphonuclear WBCs is defective, the absence of catalase renders the pneumococcus susceptible to interaction between its endogenous H_2O_2 and myeloperoxidase and the halides present in polymorphonuclear cells.

DIABETES MELLITUS. This condition is associated with a high incidence of pneumococcal infection in adults.[103, 200, 561, 720] However, because diabetes can predispose to pneumococcal infection by several mechanisms, some of which are found only in adults, whether diabetes mellitus in children also is a risk factor for pneumococcal infection is not clear.

CONDITIONS ASSOCIATED WITH DECREASED PULMONARY CLEARANCE. Inflammatory conditions such as asthma, chronic bronchitis, and chronic obstructive lung disease predispose to the development of bacterial infections of the lung, including pneumococcal pneumonia. Both active smoking and passive smoking are associated with chronic lung damage and inflammation and have been shown to be important risk factors for acquiring serious pneumococcal infection.[509] Respiratory viral infections also contribute to decreased pulmonary clearance. However, as described in the "Pathogenesis" and "Prevention" sections of this chapter, viral infections contribute to pneumococcal infection by several additional mechanisms.

CROWDING. Crowding contributes to many factors that increase the risk for acquiring pneumococcal infection, including viral infections, poor hygiene, and increased person-to-person transmission of *S. pneumoniae*. Attendance at daycare centers was the most important risk factor for acquiring invasive pneumococcal infection in children and infants in several studies.[65, 112, 246, 433, 568, 668] In a recent population-based, case-control study, adults aged 18 to 64 years who lived in households that included children attending daycare were at greater risk of acquiring invasive pneumococcal infection.[509] In developed countries, attendance at daycare centers is also the most important risk factor for AOM, including pneumococcal otitis.[500, 596, 694]

NON–BREAST-FEEDING. Breast-feeding may be protective against pneumococcal infection. Human milk has been shown to block the attachment of pneumococci to pharyngeal cells, whereas bovine milk demonstrated only a weak effect.[287] This antibacterial effect could be mediated through several components of the immune system, including secretory IgA, lactoferrin, and lysozyme. Some authors have suggested that breast-feeding protects against otitis media,[23, 97, 184, 694] but others have failed to show this effect.[56] Studies in the United States demonstrated a protective effect of breast-feeding against invasive pneumococcal infections in children in the general population[433] and in Alaskan natives.[246] In Finland, in contrast, no such protective effect was seen.[668]

GENETIC VARIATION IN MANNOSE-BINDING LECTIN. Approximately 5 percent of the population in Europe and North America and an even larger population in many developing countries are homozygous for MBL codon variants. These subjects have more than a 2.5-fold increased risk for acquisition of pneumococcal infection than do those who do not have this variant or are only heterozygous for this variant.[597]

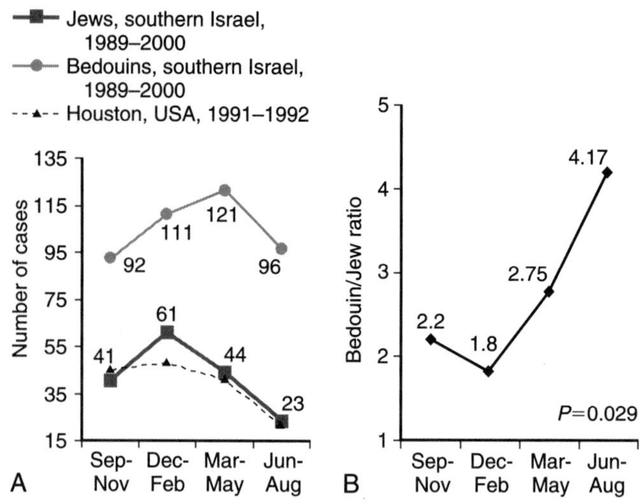

FIGURE 90–5 ■ Seasonality of invasive pneumococcal infection in children from two populations in southern Israel during the years 1989 to 2000 and in Houston during the years 1991 to 1992.[377] *A*, Average number of cases for each season. *B*, Ratio of the average number of cases per season among Bedouin versus Jewish children in southern Israel.

MALE GENDER. Males are affected more often than females in most studies on pneumococcal disease, including studies on pneumococcal bacteremia, pneumonia, meningitis, and otitis media.* The reason for the male preponderance is not understood.

SEASONALITY. The occurrence of pneumococcal infection is related to season. Clustering of invasive infections, pneumonia, and otitis media occurs from September to October through April to May in the Northern Hemisphere (with the opposite picture in the Southern Hemisphere), with peaks usually from December through February.† Variation in the seasonality of carriage of pneumococci also occurs and is lowest in the summer months.[274, 444] This seasonality probably is related, at least in part, to two factors: (1) it parallels the seasonal variations in viral respiratory infections, which play an important role in predisposing to pneumococcal carriage and infection, and (2) the peak pneumococcal infection season coincides with attendance at school and daycare centers, which often excludes the summer months. However, many issues regarding seasonality remain unclear, as exemplified by data from an ongoing surveillance of invasive infections in southern Israel, where two distinct populations live side by side and have two distinct seasonal patterns (Fig. 90–5). In this example, the Jewish population in southern Israel, with a lifestyle equivalent to that of a middle/lower social class Western population, has a seasonality of invasive pneumococcal infection similar to that of developed populations, represented in the figure by children from Houston, Texas.[385] In contrast, the Bedouin population in southern Israel, a population in transition from semi-nomadism to a Western lifestyle and who live in crowded and poorly hygienic

*See references 86, 96, 102, 140, 194, 225, 327, 336, 654, 676.
†See references 92, 140, 194, 228, 269, 270, 272, 361, 377, 383, 488, 659, 703.

conditions with a high birth rate and a disease pattern similar to that in the developing world,[434] does not demonstrate a clear pattern of seasonality. The relative abundance of cases in the spring and summer is speculated to be related to the peak of diarrheal illness in this population.[434] Further understanding of seasonality patterns may contribute to prevention of pneumococcal disease in the future.

NASOPHARYNGEAL CARRIAGE

Because acquisition and carriage of *S. pneumoniae* are associated with infection, that the higher incidence of pneumococcal infection in children than adults is associated with a higher incidence of nasopharyngeal carriage is not surprising. In various parts of the world, the carriage rate is approximately 5 to 10 percent in adults but can reach levels greater than 90 percent under various circumstances in infants and young children. Virtually all individuals carry pneumococci belonging to several serotypes during their lifetime. In a study conducted in the United States,[301] the prevalence of nasopharyngeal carriage in preschool children was 38 to 60 percent versus 29 to 35 percent and 9 to 25 percent in elementary and junior high-school students, respectively. The prevalence in adults with no children at home was 6 percent. In studies in closed populations such as kibbutzim in Israel[81] or a poor and crowded black community in southern Israel,[147] the same differences between children and adults were noted.

Contact with young carriers increases the carriage rate in older children and adults. In the United States, although adults with no children had a carriage rate of 6 percent, the carriage rate increased to 29 percent when children were present at home. Similarly, primary-school children who have siblings younger than 2 years of age carried *S. pneumoniae* more often than did those without young siblings.[449] In a study in Costa Rica, mother-child paired cultures showed an increased prevalence of carriage: from 6 percent at 1 month of age to 39 percent at 12 months of age. At the same time, carriage in mothers increased from 0 to 9.8 percent, thus confirming the influence of infants on adult carriage.[706] In Finland, the increased prevalence of carriage in mothers, fathers, and siblings when the index child grew older resulted in increased rates of pneumococci in the family.[429] In a Swedish study, the observed average duration of carriage was longer in children who had family carriers of the same serotype and, therefore, was suggestive of rapid recirculation in the family.[189]

Acquisition of *S. pneumoniae* may occur during the very first days of life. In infants 2 months of age, the prevalence of carriage ranges from less than 15 percent in some developed countries[22, 79, 158, 270, 429, 444] to greater than 60 percent in developing countries.[125, 226, 268, 464, 480] Colonization peaks toward the second to third year of life.[158, 274, 301] The relationship of age to carriage is not understood, but it depends, at least in part, on the development of specific anticapsular antibodies.[272, 273] In toddlers vaccinated with a pneumococcal conjugate vaccine, nasopharyngeal acquisition of new *S. pneumoniae* serotypes was related inversely to serum levels of specific antipolysaccharide IgG antibodies.[145] In another study, the presence of both circulating IgG and secretory IgA antibodies to the surface pneumococcal protein PsaA was associated with a lower prevalence of nasopharyngeal pneumococcal carriage.[369, 565, 640] The relative role of innate immunity with increasing age is not clear.

Crowding is an important factor that facilitates the spread of *S. pneumoniae*. Therefore, one is not surprised that in the developed world, the nasopharyngeal carriage rate and spread are highest in infants and toddlers attending daycare centers, with levels exceeding 90 percent in some studies,* followed by those living with one sibling or more at home.[22, 158, 449, 555, 702] In addition, the viral infections that are very prevalent in infants and toddlers attending daycare centers enhance *S. pneumoniae* colonization of the nasopharynx.[274, 444, 712] The combination of young age, poor hygienic behavior, and increased incidence of respiratory viral infections renders daycare centers the ideal site for promotion and spread of *S. pneumoniae*. In addition, because of widespread antibiotic use, carriage of antibiotic-resistant *S. pneumoniae* is highest in daycare center attendees.† Daycare centers, thus, are a nucleus of high carriage of *S. pneumoniae*, particularly antibiotic-resistant strains. This nucleus is then responsible for the dissemination of such resistant organisms to other children, mainly to young siblings of daycare center attendees.[143, 158]

The duration of carriage depends on age and serotype and may be related to additional factors such as antibiotic treatment, the immune status of the child, and other unknown factors. Carriage lasts longer in infants and young toddlers than in older children and adults.[146, 189, 272] In a study in Sweden,[189] infants were colonized for an average of 30 days, and after 3 months, 17 percent were carrying the same organism. In a study in the United States in adults, individual serotypes usually persisted for 2 to 4 weeks. The study showed that the first pneumococcal serotype that colonizes infants (usually before 6 months of age) can be detected for as long as 12 months (mean of 4 months).[272]

The relationship between the ability of a specific serotype to colonize the nasopharynx of a child and its ability to cause respiratory or invasive infection is not clear. Some serotypes, such as 6A, 6B, 9V, 14, 18C, 19A, 19F, and 23F, are among the most frequent colonizers in infants and young children in most parts of the world and, thus, often are considered "pediatric" serotypes.[84, 147] Some of these "pediatric" serotypes, such as serotypes 6B and 23F, also are less immunogenic than others, especially in children younger than 2 years, but some can show reduced response even late in childhood. These serotypes are acquired frequently by infants and young children and often are carried for a prolonged period. After the child reaches the age of 2 years, carriage of these "pediatric" serotypes declines rapidly. Although pneumococcal carriage decreases overall with age, the proportion of the "nonpediatric" serotypes increases with age. This phenomenon is demonstrated in Figure 90–6.

In contrast to the "pediatric" serotypes, serotypes such as 1, 5, 7F, and 12 are carried infrequently and are eliminated from the nasopharynx rapidly. However, these serotypes are able to cause disease and even epidemics.[147, 310, 492, 495, 647] The different distribution of serotypes among colonized children, children with invasive infections, and adults with pneumonia is exemplified in Figure 90–7.

Although most colonization occurs without the development of disease, some prospective, longitudinal studies have suggested that most systemic infections develop soon after colonization by a new pneumococcal serotype.[197, 270, 272] Carriers are protected from invasive disease by the development of circulating antibodies. However, such antibodies do not always protect against invasion of contiguous sites, and other studies have shown that a substantial number of pneumococcal otitis media cases occur at any time during nasopharyngeal colonization by a specific serotype.[41, 664]

---

*See references 22, 80, 122, 146, 158, 259, 505, 555, 606, 737.

†See references 70, 146, 158, 172, 259, 372, 570, 606, 607, 665, 698, 737.

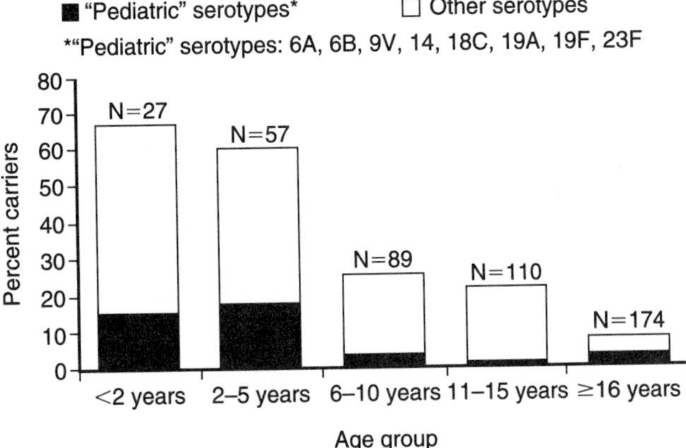

FIGURE 90–6 ■ Nasopharyngeal carriage of *Streptococcus pneumoniae* in a closed African American community living in crowded conditions in southern Israel. (Adapted from Dagan, R., Gradstein, S., Belmaker, I., et al.: An outbreak of *Streptococcus pneumoniae* type 1 in a closed community in southern Israel. Clin. Infect. Dis. *30*:319–321, 2000.)

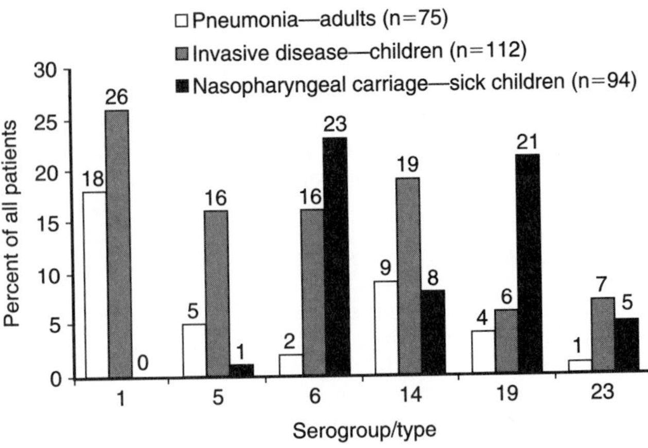

FIGURE 90–7 ■ Distribution of selected serogroups/serotypes in *Streptococcus pneumoniae* isolates from adults with pneumonia, children with invasive infection, and nasopharyngeal specimens from sick children in Kenya. (Adapted from Scott, J. A. G., Hall, A. J., Hannington, A., et al.: Serotype distribution and prevalence of resistance to benzylpenicillin in three representative populations of *Streptococcus pneumoniae* isolates from the coast of Kenya. Clin. Infect. Dis. *27*:1442–1450, 1998.)

The epidemiology of nasopharyngeal carriage of antibiotic-resistant pneumococci is important. The most significant promoter of carriage of antibiotic-resistant *S. pneumoniae* is antibiotic use.* Prolonged carriage of azithromycin-resistant *S. pneumoniae* was observed after a single dose of azithromycin was administered to Australian aboriginals for the treatment of trachoma.[414] Prophylaxis with amoxicillin increased the carriage of penicillin-resistant *S. pneumoniae*.[95] An association between trimethoprim-sufamethoxazole prophylaxis and nasopharyngeal colonization with both trimethoprim-sufamethoxazole– and penicillin-resistant *S. pneumoniae* has been demonstrated.[5, 29, 156]

A series of prospective studies revealed some of the early processes that occur in the nasopharynx during and in the immediate post-treatment period in cases of AOM caused by antibiotic-resistant *S. pneumoniae*.[120, 124, 135, 154, 156] These events can be summarized as follows: (1) most drugs studied had a substantial effect on the nasopharyngeal flora and eradicated or reduced the carriage of pneumococci that were susceptible to the drugs; (2) little, if any effect was seen when the organism had reduced susceptibility to the drugs administered; (3) some drugs, such as azithromycin and trimethoprim-sulfamethoxazole, appeared to promote colonization with resistant *S. pneumoniae;* and (4) β-lactam drugs with higher activity against *S. pneumoniae* in general and against penicillin-nonsusceptible *S. pneumoniae* in particular, such as amoxicillin-clavulanate and cefuroxime-axetil, decreased colonization better than did drugs with poor antipneumococcal activity, such as cefaclor, cefpodoxime, and cefixime.

Even more intriguing than the differential effect of various drugs on carriage of *S. pneumoniae* is the ability of these agents to alter nasopharyngeal colonization. Such alteration occurs by selection of pneumococcal strains that were masked by other organisms or selection of strains that were acquired after initiation of treatment, as was exemplified when children suffering from trachoma received one dose of azithromycin and were monitored for *S. pneumoniae* nasopharyngeal carriage.[414] Before treatment, 68 percent were colonized with *S. pneumoniae,* but only 1 percent had azithromycin-resistant *S. pneumoniae*. Within 2 to 3 weeks after they received treatment, colonization decreased to 29 percent, but 16 percent were colonized with azithromycin-resistant *S. pneumoniae.* Two months later, 78 percent were colonized with *S. pneumoniae* and 27 percent with azithromycin-resistant *S. pneumoniae.* The prevalence of pneumococcal colonization and azithromycin susceptibility returned to pre-exposure values only after 6 months. In another study, cultures obtained shortly after initiation of treatment and immediately after treatment showed that new serotypes, either susceptible or resistant to the treatment drug, appeared in 21, 24, and 31 percent of those treated with azithromycin, amoxicillin-clavulanate, and trimethoprim-sulfamethoxazole, respectively[156] (Fig. 90–8). The proportion of new strains of pneumococci resistant to these drugs was 15, 8, and 27 percent, respectively.

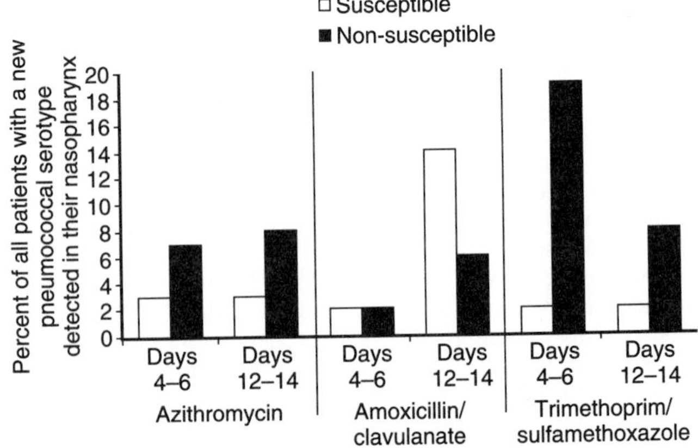

FIGURE 90–8 ■ Nasopharyngeal acquisition of new pneumococcal serotypes during antibiotic treatment of acute otitis media based on susceptibility or resistance to the antimicrobial that was administered. Cultures were obtained 3 to 5 days and 11 to 13 days after initiation of treatment. The regimens were azithromycin, 10 mg/kg as a single dose on day 1, followed by 5 mg/kg once daily for an additional 4 days; amoxicillin-clavulanate, 45/6.6 mg/kg/day in two divided doses for 10 days; and trimethoprim-sulfamethoxazole, 8/40 mg/kg/day in two divided doses for 10 days.[156]

*See references 29, 31, 120, 158, 241, 244, 277, 391, 394, 555, 744.

Prolonged and low-dose antibiotic regimens are suggested to be important contributors to promotion of carriage and spread of antibiotic-resistant *S. pneumoniae.*[123, 277, 308, 450, 616]

One of the serious problems with pneumococcal strains clearly is the emergence of resistance to more than one antibiotic class.[332] This phenomenon explains why the use of one antibiotic may result in carriage of *S. pneumoniae* resistant not only to the antibiotic to which the host was exposed but also to other, unrelated classes of antibiotics. In 1993, approximately one fifth of the pneumococcal strains in Iceland were penicillin-nonsusceptible and 80 percent of them were multidrug-resistant. When the risk for carriage of penicillin-resistant *S. pneumoniae* was investigated, a clear association was found not only with β-lactam use, but also with the use of trimethoprim-sulfamethoxazole and erythromycin.[29] Other authors likewise have shown an association between trimethoprim-sulfamethoxazole use and carriage of penicillin-resistant *S. pneumoniae.*[79, 473]

When a group of children who did not carry trimethoprim-sulfamethoxazole–resistant *S. pneumoniae* were studied longitudinally during therapy for AOM,[156] carriage of trimethoprim-sulfamethoxazole–resistant *S. pneumoniae* was found in 23 percent of patients by day 6 and in 33 percent by day 40. Additionally, penicillin-nonsusceptible *S. pneumoniae* was carried at these times by 26 and 43 percent of children, respectively. This remarkable promotion of colonization with penicillin-resistant strains by trimethoprim-sulfamethoxazole treatment occurred because many strains were resistant to both penicillin and trimethoprim-sulfamethoxazole.

Mass chemoprophylaxis and therapeutic campaigns now are being conducted in different regions against a variety of diseases, which raises concern about the widespread development of resistance. Examples are mass azithromycin treatment campaigns to eradicate trachoma, mass sulfadoxazine-pyrimethamine (Fansidar) treatment (shown to be associated with an increased rate of resistance to trimethoprim-sulfamethoxazole in pneumococci),[204] increasing use of trimethoprim-sulfamethoxazole for prophylaxis of HIV patients, and mass treatment with fluoroquinolones and tetracyclines after exposure to *Bacillus anthracis.*

The dramatic change in nasopharyngeal flora after initiation of antibiotic therapy has two important consequences. First, the phenomenon described earlier predisposes patients to new acquisition of infection with more resistant organisms.[144] Antibiotic treatment not only can increase nasopharyngeal carriage of antibiotic-resistant *S. pneumoniae* but also can induce superinfection of the middle ear with a resistant strain within a few days.[154] Second, the increased prevalence of antibiotic-resistant *S. pneumoniae* in the nasopharynx may increase transmission in crowded conditions such as in extended families and daycare centers.[158, 247, 259, 300, 555, 586, 737] Therefore, the widespread use of antibiotics is likely to be responsible for the increase in antibiotic-resistant *S. pneumoniae,* especially in crowded populations, thus creating a vicious cycle that is difficult, if not impossible, to overcome (Fig. 90–9). The presence of this vicious cycle poses a real challenge to society.

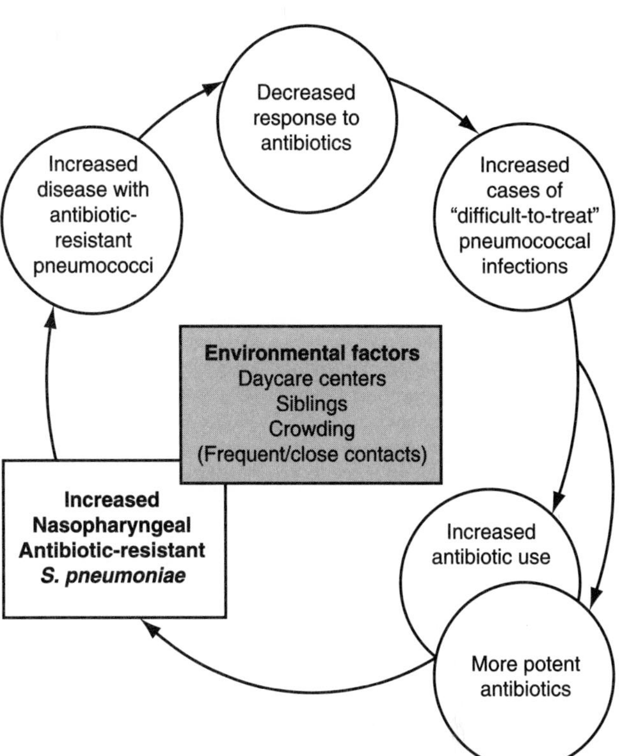

FIGURE 90–9 ■ Chain of events that create a vicious cycle in which antibiotic treatment increases the carriage of antibiotic-resistant pneumococci, which cause more disease with resistant organisms. This situation results in reduced response to antibiotic treatment and an increase in the number of "difficult-to-treat" cases. As a result, the use of antibiotics is increased, especially more potent ones, thus again promoting a further increase in nasopharyngeal carriage of antibiotic-resistant pneumococci.

INVASIVE PNEUMOCOCCAL DISEASE

Although invasive pneumococcal infections occur far less commonly in early childhood than does pneumonia or otitis media, they are an important cause of morbidity and mortality during childhood worldwide. Pneumococci are more common than are Hib and *N. meningitidis* as causes of bacteremia in most countries and rank second after Hib or third after *N. meningitidis* in causing bacterial meningitis. Pneumococci are estimated to be responsible for 25 to 50 percent of cases of bacterial meningitis among children in the United States,[617] Europe,[127] and Africa.[538]

The incidence and severity of invasive pneumococcal disease vary in different populations. Figure 90–10 exemplifies the differences in incidence in various populations by age group. Several important points can be drawn from this figure: (1) an age-dependent pattern exists that is similar in all populations: the highest rate is in infants, the rate decreases rapidly toward the age of 5 years, and then it increases again toward the age of 60 years, with a second peak in persons older than 65; (2) a marked difference exists among various populations in the incidence of invasive infection, and this difference can be up to 100-fold; (3) in general, the incidence in the more industrialized countries is lower than that in less industrialized countries or in less privileged populations, but the U.S. figures seem to be higher than those of other developed populations.

Because invasive pneumococcal infections are detected by blood culture in most cases, variations in the rates of obtaining blood cultures from young children could be responsible, at least in part, for differences in the reported incidence of invasive pneumococcal infection.[203, 293] In contrast to Europe, where most pediatric blood isolates were obtained from hospitalized children, many blood cultures are performed on outpatients in the United States.[293] This difference arises because U.S. practice guidelines recommend blood cultures for children aged 3 to 36 months with high fever and WBC counts of 15,000/mm^3 or greater.[51]

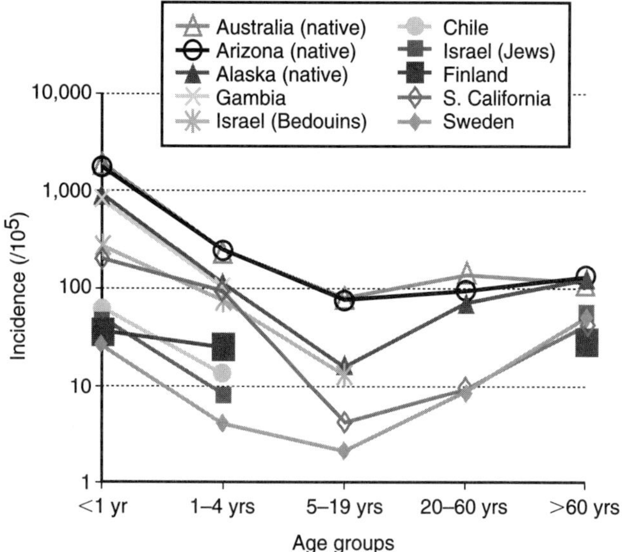

FIGURE 90–10 ■ Age-specific incidence of invasive pneumococcal disease in various populations. Data were obtained from various presentations and publications.

Indeed, several European investigators have noted that the recent rises in reported invasive pneumococcal disease rates might be related to an increasing likelihood of taking blood for culture.[46, 361, 504, 650] Preliminary evidence from Chile also suggests that a considerable proportion of relatively mild invasive infections routinely are unrecognized.[409] This hypothesis can be supported by the fact that the incidence of meningitis is similar in the United States and Europe.[293]

Thus, the incidence of invasive infection in children younger than 5 to 6 years of age in western Europe (e.g., Finland, the United Kingdom, Germany, Switzerland, Denmark, Spain) was fewer than 25 cases per 100,000 population per year in various studies; in Chile, Australia, and New Zealand, it was 25 to 60 per 100,000; and during the same period in the United States, the range was approximately 65 to 75 cases per 100,000.[293] In contrast, the incidence of pneumococcal meningitis in these countries was similar: 3.6 per 100,000 in the United States versus a mean of 4.6 per 100,000 in Europe (range, 2.1–7.0).[293]

Differences in the incidence of invasive pneumococcal infection among populations are not due solely to different blood culture practices because true significant differences can be found within the same country. This difference can be exemplified by comparing the incidence of invasive pneumococcal disease in different ethnic groups in the United States: a higher incidence of invasive pneumococcal disease occurs in African Americans, Alaskan Natives, and specific American Indian populations than in whites (Table 90–2). The incidence of pneumococcal bacteremia and meningitis in Alaskan Native children younger than 5 years of age ranges from 598 cases per 100,000 population in those aged 6 to 11 months to 56 cases per 100,000 population in those aged 36 to 47 months, which is approximately four times that of similarly aged non–Alaskan Native/non–American Indian children.[105] The highest incidence for any ethnic group in the United States is found in Navajo and Apache populations living on reservations in the southwestern United States. The incidence in children aged 1 to 2 years in these populations is 557 to 2396 per 100,000.[129, 513] Among children younger than 5 years, the incidence of invasive pneumococcal disease in African American children in the United States is two to three times higher than that in white children of the same age.[59, 88, 290, 581] In a case-control study of risk factors for the development of invasive disease in young children, the association of race with disease risk was not statistically significant in an analysis that controlled for socioeconomic status.[433] However, other studies have reported persistence of increased risk even when controlling for income.[88, 111, 209, 290, 302] The reasons for the increased incidence in some populations in comparison to others in the United States are unclear.

In other geographic regions, differences among populations also can be observed, again being higher in populations that live in underprivileged conditions, which raises the question of the importance of genetic versus environmental risk factors. In southern Israel, the incidence of pneumococcal invasive infection during the first year of life in Bedouin infants (a population with a lifestyle, birth rate, and general disease incidence similar to that of the developing world) was 270 cases per 100,000 versus 53 per 100,000 in Jewish infants (a population with standards of living comparable to the middle/low social class in the developed world) ($p < .001$).[225] This difference also was found in children aged 1 to 4 years: 75 and 21 cases per 100,000, respectively

TABLE 90–2 ■ INCIDENCE (CASES/100,000 POPULATION) OF INVASIVE PNEUMOCOCCAL DISEASE IN SELECTED U.S. PEDIATRIC POPULATIONS—SELECTED YEARS

Age Group	United States, All Races, 1998[553]	United States, Whites, 1998[553]	United States, African Americans, 1998[553]	Alaska, Natives, 1986–1990[165]	Alaska, Natives, 1986–1997[105]	Navajo American Indians, 1989–1996[513]	Apache American Indians, 1983–1990[129]
0–5 mo	73.4	60.9	163.5	624*	276.8	629*	1820*
6–11 mo	227.8	178.2	542.2	↓	597.7	↓	↓
12–23 mo	184.2	137.2	440.7	↓	453.0	557	↓
24–35 mo	64.7	54.6	116.4	98*	125.2	73*	227*
36–47 mo	26.7	23.9	46.1	↓	56.2	↓	↓
48–59 mo	14.3	9.1	20.6	↓	73.2	↓	↓
5–9 yr	5.7	4.8	9.3	23	—	—	54
10–19 yr	2.9	2.5	4.8	5	—	—	35
All ages	23.2	19.7	49.7	—	—	63	207

*Average of all age groups indicated by arrows.

($p < .001$). In New Zealand, when Maoris, Pacific Islanders, and others were compared, the incidence rates of invasive pneumococcal disease in the first year of life per 100,000 population were 153, 276, and 52, respectively. The respective rates in children younger than 5 years of age were 67, 117, and 36 per 100,000.[709]

Studies on the incidence of invasive pneumococcal infection in developing regions are scanty. In one study in The Gambia, the annual incidence in children younger than 1 and 5 years was 554 and 240 per 100,000, respectively.[518] Another study in The Gambia documented the incidence of invasive pneumococcal infection to be 224, 139, and 82 cases per 100,000 children during the first, second, and third years of life, respectively.[697] *S. pneumoniae* plays a more important role in the acquisition of meningitis in developing countries than in developed countries. Reports from several African countries show that *S. pneumoniae* accounts for 20 to 50 percent of all cases.[538] Data from many other developing populations, especially from countries in Southeast Asia, are lacking but are needed because data from Africa cannot be extrapolated to other developing parts of the world.

The fatality rate of pneumococcal meningitis is higher than that of meningitis caused by other organisms.[538] Mortality rates for invasive pneumococcal infection in developed populations vary between less than 2 percent and 6.6 percent.[140, 167, 276, 477, 581, 709] In contrast, in the developing world, mortality rates for invasive pneumococcal infection, including meningitis, vary from 19 percent in South Africa[320] to as high as 67 percent in Mali and Niger.[536, 538]

Most invasive pneumococcal diseases in children are caused by a limited number of pneumococcal serotypes. However, despite the many studies reporting on serotypes or serogroups published or presented thus far, the data are not yet complete. Data on serotypes are important, especially with regard to the question of coverage of the various conjugate vaccines, as will be discussed in the section on prevention in this chapter. Recently, the extensive literature was summarized by Hausdorff and colleagues in two review articles.[291, 292] The results of their exhaustive review, though showing many gaps in our knowledge, did lead to certain conclusions (Fig. 90–11): (1) in children younger than 5 years of age, the great majority of invasive infections are covered by the 11 serotypes that will be included in future conjugate vaccines (or the cross-reacting serotypes in the same serogroup [serogroups 1, 3, 4, 5, 6, 7, 9, 14, 18, 19, 23]); (2) in some regions, 4 serogroups not present in the 7-valent vaccine (serogroups 1, 3, 5, and 7) are of great importance; (3) in older children and adults (mainly those older than 18 years), the 7-valent vaccine often covers only a minority of cases, whereas the 11-valent vaccine covers a greater percentage; and (4) the 23-valent nonconjugate vaccine provides considerably wider coverage than do the conjugate vaccines, although it may not be immunogenic in infants, young children, or immunocompromised hosts.

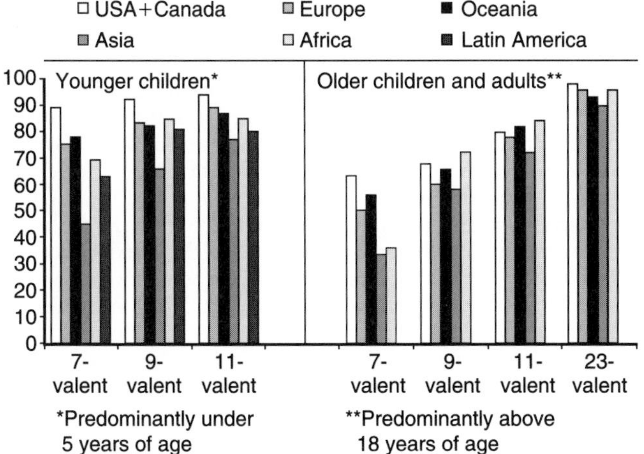

FIGURE 90–11 ■ Coverage of 7-valent, 9-valent, and 11-valent conjugate pneumococcal vaccines and 23-valent nonconjugated pneumococcal polysaccharide vaccine in younger children (predominantly 5 years of age) and older children and adults (predominantly >18 years of age) in various regions of the world.[291, 292]

Many possible reasons can be cited for the diversity of serotype/serogroup distribution in populations, such as differences in living conditions and socioeconomic status and genetic differences among populations. However, Hausdorff and associates suggest that the differences in serotype/serogroup distribution among various geographic regions may be related to differences in the testing and reporting practices of various countries.[293] Some of the serotypes/serogroups may be associated with more severe disease than others. In regions where blood cultures are performed in mildly ill children, such as the United States, the predominance of serogroups such as 6, 9, 14, 18, 19, and 23 can be accentuated, whereas serotypes such as 1, 3, 5, and 7F, which are found in more severe disease, appear to be less important. The importance of having local data on serotype coverage for evaluating disease burden that can be prevented by vaccination always should be considered.

PNEUMONIA

In adults, *S. pneumoniae* is by far the predominant cause of community-acquired bacterial pneumonia. However, this cause is more difficult to assess in children because obtaining bacteriologic specimens such as sputum from infants and young children is difficult. Blood cultures usually are positive in less than 5 percent of the children with any pneumonia and, thus, cannot provide an accurate representation of the pathogens in childhood pneumonia. Nasopharyngeal cultures, as well as antigen detection and PCR, also are difficult to correlate with bacterial pneumonia (see the section on diagnosis). Studies using lung aspirates are helpful, but scant,[710] and most of the recent studies were performed in one developing country (The Gambia). However, data derived from these studies show an important role of *S. pneumoniae* as a causative agent of pneumonia in children.[8, 219–221, 630]

In a recent study conducted in Finland,[711] transthoracic needle aspiration disclosed an etiology in 18 of 26 patients from whom a representative sample specimen was obtained. Of these patients, 10 of 26 (38%) had *S. pneumoniae*–positive lung aspirate cultures, and 1 additional child had a positive blood culture for *S. pneumoniae*. An additional six patients (23%) had a positive PCR test. Thus, in total, 17 of 26 (65%) had at least one test positive for *S. pneumoniae*.

Studies with the newly developed pneumococcal conjugate vaccines in children suggest that the role of *S. pneumoniae* in lower respiratory infections in general and pneumonia in particular may be more important than previously demonstrated. In a study in California,[68] administration of a 7-valent conjugate pneumococcal vaccine reduced cases of clinical pneumonia in children younger than 3.5 years of age by 6.0 percent ($p = .13$) (intention-to-treat analysis). A reduction in the incidence of pneumonia of 8.9 percent ($p = .03$) was found in patients who had clinical features of pneumonia and who had a chest radiograph performed, regardless of the findings. The incidence of pneumonia was reduced by 22.7 percent in cases with a positive finding on the chest radiograph (defined as parenchymal infiltrates, consolidation or effusion [or both], but not perihilar infiltrates only). In South Africa, the administration of three doses of 9-valent conjugate pneumococcal vaccine reduced the incidence of radiologically proven pneumonia by 22.1 percent (p = .049) in children younger than 2 years (Klugman, K., and Madhi, S.: Data presented at the 3rd International Symposium on Pneumococci and Pneumococcal Diseases, Alaska, May 2002). This ability of a pneumococcal vaccine to reduce the incidence of clinical and radiologically documented pneumonia suggests that (1) *S. pneumoniae* is the causative agent in most cases of pneumonia with consolidation in infants and toddlers in the population studied and (2) *S. pneumoniae* is a causative agent in many cases usually considered to be viral. Supportive evidence for the latter suggestion can be derived from a study conducted in Israeli toddlers attending daycare centers.[161] In these toddlers, a 9-valent pneumococcal vaccine reduced the incidence of lower respiratory diseases, including bronchiolitis, cough, and pneumonia, by 16 percent and reduced antibiotic treatment days for these entities by 47 percent. More studies are being undertaken to investigate the potential of pneumococcal conjugate vaccines to reduce the incidence of pneumonia and other lower respiratory tract infections in developing populations (Native Americans and those in The Gambia and the Philippines).

Although pneumonia usually is not a fatal disease in developed countries, it is an important cause of morbidity and hospitalization. Pneumococcal infections are thought to be rare causes of serious lower respiratory tract disease requiring hospitalization in children younger than 6 months.[168] However, *S. pneumoniae* is an important cause of hospitalization for community-acquired pneumonia in older children.[118, 176, 243, 400, 506, 599]

In developing countries, acute respiratory infections in general and pneumonia in particular are the leading causes of morbidity and mortality.[471] The mortality rate from respiratory infections in developing countries is estimated to be 10- to 30-fold higher than that in developed countries.[6, 431] Also estimated is that of the 15 million children younger than 5 years who die annually, approximately 4 million die of pneumonia.[278, 431] When obtained, rates of positive sputum culture for *S. pneumoniae* in developing countries can be as high as 88 percent in children.[61] Using a variety of methods, including antigen detection; cultures from blood, sputum, and pleural and lung aspirates; and antipneumococcal antibody testing, a series of investigations in The Gambia associated *S. pneumoniae* with severe acute lower respiratory tract infections in 20 percent of hospitalized infants and in 61 percent of children aged 1 to 9 years.[220, 221] In another study in The Gambia[219] conducted on ambulatory children younger than 5 years with lower respiratory tract infections, *S. pneumoniae* was associated with 8.6 percent of all cases of clinical acute lower respiratory tract infection, 12.3 percent of episodes of radiologically proven acute lower respiratory tract infection, and 28.0 percent of episodes of lobar pneumonia. Despite the limitations of these diagnostic tests, these results demonstrate the importance of *S. pneumoniae* in severe respiratory infections.

No accurate information exists about the pneumococcal serotypes involved in pneumonia in infants and young children. The only accurate data are for bacteremic pneumococcal pneumonia. In these cases, the serotype distribution is not different from that for other invasive infections. However, the bacteremic cases represent only a minority of pneumococcal pneumonia cases, and one cannot extrapolate these data to nonbacteremic cases. The finding of an impressive reduction in pneumonia after the use of a conjugate pneumococcal vaccine, as reviewed earlier, suggests that most pneumonia cases in the population studied are pneumococcal and caused by serotypes included in the vaccine.

OTITIS MEDIA

Otitis media is the diagnosis that accounts for most office visits in pediatric clinics in the United States. It results in more than 15 million visits per year.[396, 659] In the United States, 10 percent of children have one or more episodes of otitis media by the time that they are 3 months of age, approximately 60 percent by 1 year of age, and more than 80 percent by 3 years of age.[384, 677] More recent statistics show even higher figures: a study involving 2253 infants in the Pittsburgh area showed that 48 percent had one or more episodes of otitis media between 2 and 6 months of age, 79 percent between 2 and 12 months of age, and 91 percent by 24 months of age.[529] Finnish studies in the 1980s showed an incidence of 0.47 to 1.05 episodes per year in infants aged 0 to 12 months.[367, 558, 642] Otitis media often is not perceived as a severe problem in developing countries, but community studies have shown perforation of the tympanic membrane in 0.4 to 6.1 percent and mastoiditis in 0.19 to 0.74 percent of all children.[60] Although serious complications rarely occur, the economic cost of otitis media is estimated at more than $3.5 billion each year in the United States.[239, 659] In one study from the 1990s, the cost of an episode of otitis media in the United States averaged $166.[362] During 1996, approximately 500,000 tympanostomy tubes were placed in children's ears in the United States.[501] AOM also is the leading reason for prescribing antibiotics during childhood.[553]

In a prospective study conducted in southern Israel that examined the burden of AOM on patients and their families,[275] the average number of days of severe crying, temperature higher than 38° C, loss of appetite, and insomnia was 2.9, 7.8, 7.0, and 6.6, respectively. An average of 18.6 days was required for a family to return to normal activity. The number of visits, use of emergency rooms, and care by otolaryngologists averaged 2.6, 0.3, and 0.35 per episode, respectively. The average antibiotic and over- the-counter drug treatment days per episode were 9.1 and 6.6, respectively. Parents lost an average of 1.6 working days, and children lost an average of 3.5 daycare days per episode. The parents thought that during a 1-month follow-up period, an average of 18.6 days were nonroutine days versus only 3.4 such days in controls.

The role of *S. pneumoniae* in otitis media has been studied extensively. During the last decades, many studies with various designs have been performed in many geographic regions. *S. pneumoniae* was the major bacterial cause of otitis media and accounted for 25 to 60 percent of cases.* However, in some recent studies, *H. influenzae* was found more commonly than was *S. pneumoniae* in AOM.[148, 242, 374] *H. influenzae* is a rare finding in first episodes of AOM, but it becomes increasingly common from the third episode onward, whereas *S. pneumoniae* is a common finding in all episodes.[374]

Although the cost of each AOM episode may be relatively low when compared with other infections caused by *S. pneumoniae,* the highest overall cost in all pneumococcal infections is due to otitis media because of the large number of episodes.[436] The estimated cost for meningitis was 11,081 U.S. dollars per case in 1997, for bacteremia it was $2313, and for pneumonia with consolidation it was $1464. In

*See references 69, 74, 149, 170, 182, 193, 249, 335, 351, 374, 382, 452, 494, 588.

contrast, for simple otitis media, the cost was $294 per episode, and for complex otitis media it was $1339 per episode. The cost of tympanostomy tube placement was $2390 per case. The estimated annual cost in the United States was $3 to $5 billion for simple pneumococcal otitis media and approximately $1.3 billion for complex pneumococcal otitis media. In contrast, the annual cost of pneumococcal meningitis was approximately $9 million, that of pneumococcal bacteremia was $35 million, and the annual cost of pneumococcal pneumonia was $113 million.

Antibiotic resistance in *S. pneumoniae* strains causing otitis media is rising sharply, and in some countries, resistance to at least one antibiotic class (in most cases penicillin and other β-lactams) is now the rule, not the exception. Figure 90–12 exemplifies the rapidity of the increase in antibiotic resistance among *S. pneumoniae* isolates from the middle ear fluid of children with AOM in France and Israel in the last decade. A well-established fact is that higher antibiotic resistance rates are found in pneumococci from patients with nonresponsive AOM and recurrent AOM, in whom recent antibiotic treatment is common, as well as in daycare center attendees.[53, 70, 122, 144, 151, 428, 546, 744] In children younger than 18 months, the prevalence of antibiotic-resistant *S. pneumoniae* in AOM is higher than that in older age groups.[53, 70, 146, 335]

Studies of pneumococcal serotypes causing AOM in the last 60 years have demonstrated relatively similar patterns, with the most common serotypes being 6A, 6B, 9V, 14, 19A, 19F, and 23F.[41, 70, 104, 144, 211, 242, 520, 540, 635] (Fig. 90–13). As mentioned in the section on bacteriology, these serotypes also are the most frequent antibiotic-resistant serotypes. Furthermore, the great majority of highly penicillin-resistant and multiply-resistant *S. pneumoniae* belong to five serotypes (6B, 9V, 14, 19F, 23F) and, to a lesser extent, to related serotypes (6A and 19A).[144, 354] This finding is somewhat reassuring with regard to vaccination because the serotypes most frequently associated with resistance are included in the licensed conjugated pneumococcal vaccines, as well as in vaccines being developed. An important note to mention is that because these data were obtained from studies involving middle ear puncture (tympanocentesis or myringotomy) or spontaneously draining ears, the spectrum of cases studied probably could be skewed toward the most severe cases or treatment failures.

As reviewed in the section on prevention, immunization with conjugate pneumococcal vaccine is associated with replacement of vaccine serotypes by other serotypes. Widespread immunization with conjugate vaccine may increase the importance of some nonvaccine serotypes while decreasing that of the serotypes included in the vaccine.

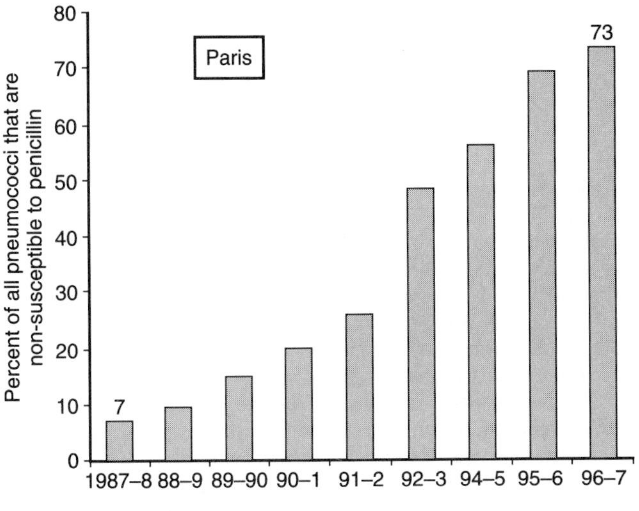

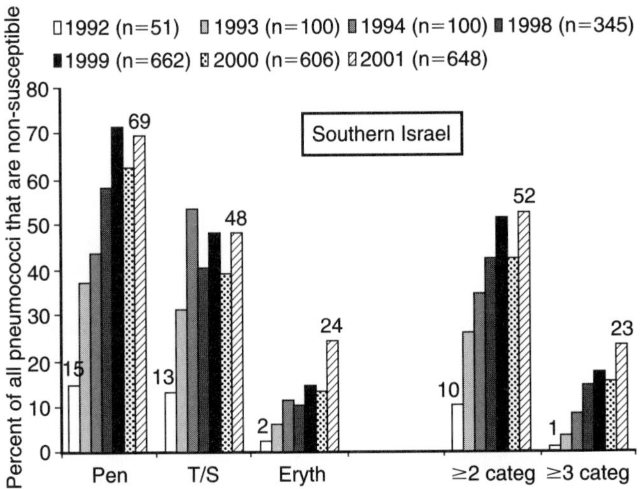

FIGURE 90–12 ■ Rate of increase in antibiotic-nonsusceptible pneumococci isolated from middle ear fluid during acute otitis media episodes in France and Israel during a 10-year period. *Top,* Penicillin-nonsusceptible *Streptococcus pneumoniae* in Paris from 1987 through 1997. A 10-fold increase in resistance to penicillin occurred during this period.[244] *Bottom,* Penicillin-nonsusceptibile *S. pneumoniae* isolated from middle ear fluid during acute otitis media episodes in children in southern Israel from 1992 through 2001.[155] Categ, antibiotic drug category; Eryth, erythromycin; Pen, penicillin; T/S, trimethoprim/sulfamethoxazole. (Data from 1999 to 2001 are unpublished.)

Clinical Syndromes

S. pneumoniae can spread from the nasopharynx, which is its natural niche, to adjacent mucosal surfaces and cause mucosal infections such as AOM, sinusitis, and pneumonia, or it can invade the bloodstream. Infection may spread from the bloodstream to other sites and cause sepsis or meningitis

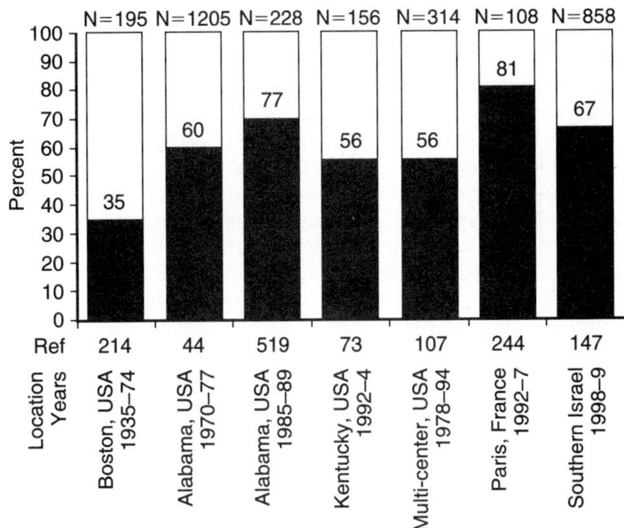

FIGURE 90–13 ■ Relative proportion of serotypes 6A, 6B, 9V, 14, 19A, 19F, and 23F as a group in relation to all other serotypes causing acute otitis media.

or result in focal infection in heart valves, bones, joints, and soft tissues and within the peritoneal cavity. In rare cases such as after penetrating trauma or fracture of the base of the skull, pneumococci can invade the brain directly from the upper respiratory tract. Organisms also can spread through the fallopian tubes to the peritoneal cavity after colonizing the perineum.

The clinical signs and symptoms of patients with pneumococcal infection are diverse. In general, invasive diseases such as bacteremia and meningitis are manifested as fever with temperatures that can exceed 40° C.[45] A peripheral blood leukocyte count of more than 15,000/mm^3 can be found in most patients with bacteremia, and in one study, the average WBC count was 20,000/mm^3, with a range of 16,100 to 24,600/mm^3.[45] In patients with pneumococcal pneumonia, cough and tachypnea are the most common manifestations besides high fever.[672] Pneumococcal pneumonia and other focal infections such as cellulitis, peritonitis, and bone and joint infections often cause similar high temperatures and elevated WBC counts. Other infections such as AOM and sinusitis often have minimal systemic manifestations.

BACTEREMIA. The most common clinical manifestation of invasive pneumococcal disease in children younger than 3 years of age is occult bacteremia, defined as a positive blood culture without a known focus of infection. *S. pneumoniae* has caused an estimated 90 percent of all cases of occult bacteremia since the introduction of Hib conjugated vaccine.[417] Severe complications such as meningitis or sepsis are relatively rare after occult bacteremia—about 6 percent of all cases.[10] The risk for the development of occult bacteremia is age related, with approximately 75 percent of all patients being between 3 and 24 months of age.[338] Signs and symptoms vary among patients with occult bacteremia. In most patients with pneumococcal bacteremia, fever appears within 24 hours of diagnosis. In one study, initial diagnoses at the time of occult bacteremia were AOM in 43 percent of patients, fever without a source in 30 percent, and viral infection in 22 percent.[45] Forty-one (8.7%) patients had complications: persistent bacteremia developed in 4 percent, meningitis in 1.7 percent, pneumonia in 1.7 percent, and cellulitis in 2.5 percent.

Febrile patients with focal infections such as otitis media or upper respiratory tract infection have a lower incidence of bacteremia than do febrile patients without an obvious source of infection (3.3 versus 9.9%, respectively).[467] The height of the fever is associated with a greater risk for development of bacteremia, with temperatures above 40° C being associated with a 25 percent risk.[55] A higher peripheral WBC count (>15,000/mm^3) also is associated with the presence of occult bacteremia.[341, 408] These findings can help in categorizing high- and low-risk patients for the presence of occult bacteremia.

Occult bacteremia resolves spontaneously without complication in most children. However, complications such as meningitis, pneumonia, osteomyelitis, arthritis, cellulitis, and fulminant sepsis develop in approximately 10 percent of patients.[417] The case-fatality rate is usually low and generally less than 1 percent in children without underlying immunologic problems.[366, 581]

Persistent bacteremia and new focal infections were associated with higher temperature (mean of 38.8 versus 37.7° C), greater elevation in WBC count (18,900 versus 14,900/mm^3), age younger than 20 months, and no antibiotic treatment being prescribed during the initial visit.[45]

MENINGITIS. *S. pneumoniae* is either the most frequent or the second most frequent (after *N. meningitidis*) cause of bacterial meningitis in countries where routine vaccination against Hib has been introduced. *S. pneumoniae* most commonly invades the meninges via the bloodstream.[185] However, in rare cases, it can invade the meninges directly, especially after penetrating trauma or fracture of the base of the skull.[617] Patients with underling conditions such as CSF leak, HIV infection, sickle-cell anemia, or asplenia are predisposed to the development of pneumococcal meningitis.[30]

The initial signs and symptoms are variable, and a rapid onset (less than 24 hours of illness) occurs in less than 20 percent of children with pneumococcal meningitis.[83] Patients commonly have the typical signs of meningitis, including fever, nuchal rigidity, irritability or lethargy, and poor feeding. The anterior fontanelle often is bulging. The duration of meningeal signs before admission averages 28 hours but can be as short as 4 hours and as long as 52 hours. Seizures develop in approximately a quarter of patients. Decreased consciousness and septic shock occur in 11 and 16 percent, respectively.[30]

In one study, the mean total CSF WBC count was 1136/mm^3, whereas with Hib disease it was 4612/mm^3 and in *N. meningitis* disease it reached 5476/mm^3.[614] In another study, significantly higher median blood leukocyte counts and lower median CSF protein concentrations, and higher CSF glucose concentrations were found in children with meningitis caused by penicillin-resistant *S. pneumoniae* isolates than in patients with penicillin-susceptible *S. pneumoniae*.[213] However, in a different study, patients with penicillin-susceptible *S. pneumoniae* did not differ from those with penicillin-nonsusceptible *S. pneumoniae* with regard to blood and CSF leukocyte counts and CSF glucose or protein concentrations.[101]

The course of pneumococcal meningitis can be associated with prolonged fever that can last for more than 10 days or with secondary fever higher than 38° C after at least 1 afebrile day after occurrence of the primary fever.[83] This course can be attributed to complications of the primary infection, such as subdural effusion or empyema, but these events are now relatively rare. More commonly, secondary fever is related to intercurrent conditions such as urinary tract infection, otitis media, phlebitis, pneumonia, drug fever, or a nosocomial viral infection.[164] In patients treated with corticosteroids in the first 2 to 4 days, a second spike of fever can be seen after discontinuation of the steroids.[545, 557] The outcome of patients with prolonged or secondary fever is similar to that of other patients with pneumococcal meningitis.[195]

The outcome and long-term complications of pneumococcal meningitis include severe hearing loss (in as many as 46% of patients), seizures, learning or mental difficulties, or paralysis (in as many as 22%).[30] Patients with *S. pneumoniae* meningitis have a higher mortality rate and are at greater risk for development of neurologic sequelae than are patients with *N. meningitidis* or Hib infection.[363, 503] The mortality rate varies from 6.3 to 20 percent.[185, 366, 617] A peripheral WBC count of less than 5000/mm^3 at initial evaluation was recognized as a poor prognostic factor with a high mortality rate.[399] A trend toward a higher mortality rate also was noted if the CSF WBC count was less than 1000/mm^3.[399] A similarly poor outcome can be predicted in patients with pneumococcal meningitis when low CSF glucose concentrations (<1.11 mmol/L)[222] or high CSF protein concentration (>250 mg/dL) are present.[399]

Delayed sterilization of CSF cultures after antimicrobial treatment also has been associated with a poorer outcome.[415]

PNEUMONIA. Pneumococcal pneumonia in its classic form is manifested as an acute illness with rigors, fever with temperatures often exceeding 40°C, general malaise with a productive cough, dyspnea, and chest pain. However, the signs and symptoms may be subtle in young infants. Fever and cough occur in 90 and 70 percent of all patients, respectively.

Lethargy, emesis, rhinorrhea, abdominal pain, and chest pain occur in 10 to 50 percent of patients.[672] Pneumococcal pneumonia can have an atypical and incomplete course, without respiratory symptoms, and in some cases, even an absence of fever or with extrathoracic manifestations. Severe abdominal pain with or without vomiting may be the only initial symptom, especially in left lower lobe pneumonia. Irritation of the meninges in cases of upper lobe pneumonia may elicit meningeal signs without meningitis.

When serologically diagnosed pneumococcal pneumonia was compared with pneumonia caused by respiratory syncytial virus (RSV), the serologically diagnosed pneumococcal pneumonia overlapped with RSV pneumonia. However, pneumococcal pneumonia was associated significantly less often with tachypnea (17 versus 45%, respectively) and a high WBC count (mean of 20,800 versus 12,000/mm^3, respectively), as well as a higher CRP level (mean of 137 versus 28 mg/L, respectively). Alveolar infiltrates were found in 76 versus 15 percent of chest radiographs, respectively.[355] Children with bacteremic pneumococcal pneumonia appeared ill more often than did those with serologically proven pneumococcal pneumonia without bacteremia (79 versus 50%, respectively), and they had typical pneumococcal pneumonia with high fever, leukocytosis, and lobal infiltrates on chest radiographs more often (70 versus 34%, respectively).

Pleural effusion can be found in as many as 40 percent of patients with pneumococcal pneumonia, but only approximately 10 percent have a significant amount of aspiration and only approximately 2 percent have empyema.[437] These patients can have a pleural friction rub, abdominal pain, chest pain, and dullness on percussion. In patients with pleural effusion, fever persists longer than in patients with pneumonia without pleural effusion despite adequate treatment.[672]

In one study conducted in Salt Lake City during the years 1993 to 1999, 153 of 540 (28%) children hospitalized with community-acquired pneumonia had empyema.[106] Pathogenic bacteremia, 26 (41%) cases of which were caused by *S. pneumoniae,* was detected in 64 (42%) of the patients. In nine additional patients, gram-positive cocci were revealed by Gram stain but did not grow in culture. *S. pneumoniae* was the most common pathogen identified in patients with empyema. When compared with patients who had pneumonia only, patients with empyema were more likely to be 3 or more years old, to have had fever for 7 days or longer, to have varicella, and to have received antibiotics and ibuprofen before admission to the hospital.

CRP, the erythrocyte sedimentation rate, and the peripheral blood absolute neutrophil count are significantly higher in pneumococcal pneumonia than in viral pneumonia.[401] Blood culture is positive in no more than 10 percent of patients with pneumococcal pneumonia.[721] Children with bacteremic pneumococcal pneumonia usually have a high temperature and leukocytosis on admission, with peripheral WBC counts exceeding 15,000/mm^3, similar to those without bacteremia.[684] Body temperature, CRP, the erythromycin sedimentation rate, and leukocyte counts are of limited value in differentiating pneumococcal from nonpneumococcal pneumonia in individual patients.

No strict radiologic definition of pneumococcal pneumonia in children is accepted broadly. The classic chest radiographic finding in pneumococcal pneumonia is thought to be an alveolar infiltrate, usually confined to one lobe or a part of it.[521] Such infiltrates are thought to be present in approximately 85 percent of all cases. In studies performing lung aspiration in cases of radiologically proven lobar infiltrates, the proportion of patients in whom *S. pneumoniae* was detected was high.[199, 710, 717] In most instances in which patients with lobar consolidation were studied, the predominant bacterial pathogen was *S. pneumoniae.*[8] In addition, a 63 percent reduction in pneumonia with alveolar infiltrates was demonstrated in a study using this definition when children were vaccinated with a 7-valent pneumococcal conjugated vaccine versus placebo,[68] thus suggesting a major role of *S. pneumoniae* when alveolar infiltrates are present.

In the pre-antibiotic era, the natural course of pneumococcal pneumonia consisted of 7 to 9 days of a stationary phase of symptoms followed by worsening of the systemic signs ("pre-crisis") and subsequently, in those who recovered, defervescence, sweating, polyuria, and a brief febrile attack ("post-crisis").[37, 521] Today, long-term complications are rare developments, and the mortality rate is extremely low—less than 1 percent even in cases of bacteremic pneumonia.[366]

OTITIS MEDIA. *S. pneumoniae* causes 25 to 60 percent of AOM cases.* The bacteriologic outcome of *S. pneumoniae* AOM is less favorable than that caused by other organisms when untreated or treated inappropriately.[386, 494, 519] Also recognized is that commonly used oral antibiotics are not as effective as they were in the past because of increased antibiotic resistance among *S. pneumoniae* isolates.[136, 137, 139]

Some studies have suggested that pneumococcal AOM is more severe than that caused by other pathogens. In addition, a suggestion was made in the 1970s that AOM caused by *S. pneumoniae* was accompanied more frequently by pain and fever than was AOM caused by other pathogens.[316] In addition, on the first day of diagnosis, WBC counts in the middle ear fluid of patients with *S. pneumoniae* AOM were significantly higher than those in the case of AOM caused by other bacterial pathogens.[94] *S. pneumoniae* AOM was associated with significantly higher fever and more redness of the tympanic membrane than was AOM caused by *H. influenzae* or *Moraxella catarrhalis.*[583] The presence of *S. pneumoniae* in the nasopharynx during otitis media was associated with a higher tympanic membrane severity score and higher rates of persistent symptoms on day 5, persistence of tympanic membrane abnormalities on day 28, and recurrence before day 28.[198, 288] Spontaneous remission of the infection occurs less commonly in patients with pneumococcal AOM than in those with other pathogens.[314]

MASTOIDITIS. In the pre-antibiotic era, acute mastoiditis was the most common complication of otitis media and was observed in as many as 20 percent of cases without appropriate treatment. The infectious process may lead to reabsorption of the bony septa of the mastoid air cells and subsequently to the formation of empyema and anatomic loss of the air-cell system.[216] *S. pneumoniae* is the most common cause of acute mastoiditis in children and accounts for 25 to 46 percent of all culture-proven cases.[257, 312] A recent international study suggested that in countries in which otitis media cases are seldom treated with antibiotics, the rate of mastoiditis is greater than in those in which antibiotic treatment of otitis is the rule.[701]

SINUSITIS. The true incidence of pneumococcal sinusitis in children is unknown. It is estimated to be present in 10 percent of all upper respiratory tract infections, but the diagnosis usually is subjective.[714] *S. pneumoniae* is the pathogen most commonly isolated from patients with sinusitis, and it causes 35 to 42 percent of all bacterial cases.[716] The disease can occur at any age, and clinical signs and symptoms depend on the maturation of the different sinuses

*See references 69, 74, 149, 182, 193, 249, 335, 351, 374, 382, 452, 494, 588.

affected. The ethmoid and maxillary sinuses are the sites most commonly involved in children younger than 5 years. Sinusitis is manifested initially as a viral infection, followed by a nasal discharge that frequently is purulent and accompanied by cough. The symptoms are aggravated at night because of postnasal drip from the sinus to the pharynx and larynx. Malodorous breath can be noted, as can vomiting.[324, 359] In cases of sinusitis, isolation of *S. pneumoniae* from the nasal discharge strongly suggests its involvement at the site of infection.

CONJUNCTIVITIS. Bacterial conjunctivitis often is purulent and tends to be bilateral more frequently than is the case with viral conjunctivitis.[713] *S. pneumoniae* causes 12 to 32 percent of all cases of bacterial conjunctivitis.[71, 253, 725]

The syndrome of "conjunctivitis-otitis" was first described in 1982.[78] *H. influenzae* is the most common pathogen and can be isolated in as many as 73 percent of cases from the conjunctiva and the middle ear concomitantly. This rate is higher than that when conjunctivitis is present without AOM.[78]

In a recent study in the United States, the rate of penicillin-nonsusceptible *S. pneumoniae* in isolates taken from children with bacterial conjunctivitis was 28 percent, with most isolates being fully resistant.[71]

BONE AND JOINT INFECTIONS. Septic arthritis caused by S. *pneumoniae* is a relatively rare condition that accounts for 2.2 to 9.7 percent of all cases.[279, 600] Its main initial clinical features are single or multiple swollen, warm, and painful joints. The joints most commonly involved are the knee and the ankle.[326] In one study, the mean duration of symptoms before hospitalization was 2 days, and patients were hospitalized for an average of 11 days. The mean peripheral WBC count was 20,600/mm^3, the erythrocyte sedimentation rate usually was greater than 90 mm/hr, and the CRP concentration generally was higher than 100 mg/L. *S. pneumoniae* can be isolated from synovial fluid or blood in most patients.[600] The outcome is favorable in most cases, unless underlying diseases or sepsis occurs concomitantly.[326]

SOFT TISSUE INFECTIONS. *S. pneumoniae* is an uncommonly recognized etiologic agent of soft tissue infections, but it can cause serious infections of soft tissues, especially in patients with connective tissue diseases such as systemic lupus erythematosus. Other risk factors are HIV infection and corticosteroid treatment. The organism can be isolated from the infected tissue, as well as from blood.[175] *S. pneumoniae* can cause facial cellulitis as well. Periorbital infection can spread and cause infection of the orbit (orbital cellulitis or abscess) manifested as proptosis and ophthalmoplegia, but these sequelae are rare occurrences and usually a complication of purulent sinusitis, or they occur after bacteremia in infants and young children without another apparent source.[631] Most patients are younger than 3 years and previously were healthy. Fever and peripheral WBC counts of more than 15,000/mm^3 can be observed in most patients, and blood cultures frequently are positive. Overall, response to therapy generally is good, and patients usually recover.[258]

PERITONITIS. The term *primary peritonitis* is related to organisms that spread from the blood or via the lymphatic system to the peritoneal cavity and cause infection. Primary peritonitis is a rare condition that accounts for only 17 percent of all cases of peritonitis, and *S. pneumoniae* is the major pathogen in primary peritonitis and is responsible for 38 percent of all cases.[264] Primary pneumococcal peritonitis should be considered in the differential diagnosis of children with an acute abdominal syndrome.[227] This condition can be associated with underlying medical conditions such as nephrotic syndrome, immunocompromised status, or sickle-cell disease.[264] Colonization of the perineum and subsequent spread via the fallopian tube to the peritoneal cavity have been suggested to be an important source in young girls.[643] Indeed, 87 percent of all patients with pneumococcal primary peritonitis are females,[626] in contrast to other invasive infections, for which a male preponderance is observed.[86, 96, 102, 140, 194, 225, 327, 654, 676] Most of the patients are between 4 and 10 years of age.[626] Symptoms include diffuse abdominal pain, fever, vomiting, and diarrhea. Abdominal tenderness can be maximal in the right lower quadrant, which can lead to confusing it with acute appendicitis. In some cases, *S. pneumoniae* can be isolated as the only cause of peritonitis secondary to appendicitis.[299] Cultures should include blood, peritoneal fluid, and a vaginal swab. Some patients need laparotomy or laparoscopy to exclude other pathologies such as appendicitis or a tubo-ovarian abscess.[643] Morbidity and mortality rates can be high when the period without treatment exceeds 1 week, but in most cases, the outcome is favorable when treated adequately.[626]

ENDOCARDITIS. Infection of native valves can lead to distal embolization and heart failure as a result of valve destruction. Cases of *S. pneumoniae* endocarditis, including those caused by penicillin-nonsusceptible strains, were reported with involvement of the aortic and mitral valves.[638] The triad of pneumococcal meningitis, pneumonia, and endocarditis was described first by Osler, but this triad also is known as Austrian syndrome. Today, this entity is an uncommon occurrence because the incidence of *S. pneumoniae* endocarditis has decreased significantly from 10 to 15 percent of all endocarditis cases in the pre-antibiotic era to less than 3 percent today.[329, 488, 674]

PERICARDITIS. In the pre-antibiotic era, *S. pneumoniae* was the pathogen most commonly isolated from purulent pericarditis in children. These infections were common complications of pneumococcal pneumonia. After the introduction of antibiotics, pneumococcal cases decreased from 51 to 9 percent of all pericarditis cases and occurred mainly in adults.[260, 602] Currently, infections of the pericardium are rare findings in children and often are related to underlying medical conditions such as immunodeficiency.[541]

INFECTION IN IMMUNOCOMPROMISED HOSTS. Patients with functional asplenia, including those with hemoglobinopathies, are at high risk for acquisition of invasive pneumococcal infection. In a study of 19 asplenic patients with invasive pneumococcal infection, the clinical findings included fever (86%), shock (27%), petechiae or purpura (27%), disseminated vascular coagulopathy (18%), and respiratory distress (18%). Clinical illness included bacteremia alone (52%), meningitis (26%), bacteremia with otitis/sinusitis (13%), and bacteremia with pneumonia (9%). The mortality rate was 32 percent. No association was noted between antimicrobial resistance and mortality.[619]

HIV-infected children with pneumonia usually have the typical symptoms of fever, shortness of breath, and productive cough associated with pleuritic pain. The chest radiograph shows unilobar or multilobar infiltrates, and peripheral WBC counts often are elevated. A comparison between HIV-infected and non–HIV-infected children with community-acquired pneumonia showed no significant differences between groups with regard to the duration of hospitalization and mortality rates.[455] In contrast, when only patients from the aforementioned groups infected by isolates belonging to the "pediatric serotype group" (see the sections on epidemiology and prevention) were compared, marked differences were observed, such as a higher rate of pneumonia with or without concurrent meningitis in the HIV-infected group and a higher rate of septic shock without focus in the non–HIV-infected group.[455] Recurrence of pneumococcal infection within 6 months from the initial episode is common in patients infected with HIV, particularly children.[245] Most HIV-infected patients recover without significant sequelae, and the clinical course of their systemic infections does not appear to be markedly different from that in healthy children.[345]

Patients with immunodeficiency disorders consisting of antibody and complement deficiencies are at high risk for acquisation of invasive and recurrent pneumococcal infection.[345] Children with nephrotic syndrome have a particularly increased risk for development of pneumococcal peritonitis, mainly during relapse of their renal disease.[206] Other underlying diseases such as hematologic malignancies, diabetes mellitus, and cirrhosis, as well as conditions such as alcoholism, are associated with an increased risk for development of pneumococcal bacteremia and other invasive diseases, mainly in adults.[345]

Children with sickle-cell disease are prone to the development of overwhelming *S. pneumoniae* bacteremia and sepsis, with an incidence of bacteremia in children younger than 3 years of age of 6.1 events per 100 patient-years and a case-fatality rate of 24 percent for *S. pneumoniae* sepsis.[743]

Transplant recipients have long been recognized as being at high risk for the development of invasive pneumococcal disease. Of 42 children who had undergone bone marrow or solid organ transplantation and who became infected with *S. pneumoniae*, 8 (19%) had two or more pneumococcal infections.[620] Solid organ recipients were more likely to have recurrent invasive disease than were recipients of bone marrow transplants. Death occurred in 2 of 42 (5%). Cardiac transplant patients have an incidence of 39 cases of invasive pneumococcal infection per 1000 patients per year,[660] and the highest risk occurs in African American heart transplant recipients who undergo transplantation because of idiopathic dilated cardiomyopathy.

Treatment

Penicillin G is the parenteral drug of choice for disease caused by penicillin-susceptible *S. pneumoniae* strains (defined as those with a penicillin MIC <0.1 µg/mL). The usual doses of penicillin G result in serum concentrations that exceed this level in blood and most other body fluids for an adequate period. Penicillin G is the most common parenteral drug used for the treatment of pneumococcal infection, with doses ranging from 50,000 U/kg/day for minor infections to 300,000 U/kg/day for meningitis. For penicillin-susceptible strains, other parenteral β-lactams such as ampicillin, cefuroxime, cefotaxime, and ceftriaxone provide no advantage over penicillin G, even in serious infections. Macrolides and cephalosporins are an alternative treatment for penicillin-allergic patients if regional data do not show macrolide and cephalosporin resistance. Other agents such as clindamycin, tetracycline, and trimethoprim-sulfamethoxazole are active against *S. pneumoniae,* but resistance to these agents is increasing rapidly in most parts of the world.

In many regions, treatment of penicillin-nonsusceptible *S. pneumoniae* has become a challenge, and reports of treatment failure, especially in patients with invasive multidrug-resistant *S. pneumoniae* infection, have increased.[644] Because isolates of *S. pneumoniae* that are resistant to penicillin frequently are resistant to other drug classes such as cephalosporins (mainly oral), macrolides, and trimethoprim-sulfamethoxazole,[727] the challenge of treatment is becoming complex.

The critical time for treatment of severe pneumococcal infection is during the first few hours after initial evaluation of the patient, before culture results are available and, thus, before knowledge of the presence or susceptibility of the pathogen is obtained. Therefore, the choice of antibiotics must rely on considerations based on the most recent epidemiologic data and the clinical status of the child, as well as the site of infection. Furthermore, because treatment is empiric, the choice of antibiotics must take into account other potential pathogens.

Because treatment of pneumococcal infection is not necessarily similar in each of the clinical entities, specific details are provided for each clinical entity separately.

BACTEREMIA. Results of studies are conflicting with regard to the role of antibiotic treatment of occult pneumococcal bacteremia. In one study, the bacteremia resolved without any need for parenteral antibiotic treatment in 95.7 percent of patients.[12] No significant difference was found between amoxicillin and placebo recipients regarding complications such as meningitis in bacteremic patients, but faster reduction of fever and improvement in clinical appearance were observed in the group treated with amoxicillin.[342] A meta-analysis showed that rates of serious bacterial infection and meningitis did not differ between children who were treated with oral or parenteral antibiotics.[593] In contrast, in another meta-analysis conducted by the same authors, treated patients had fewer serious bacterial infections than did untreated patients (3.3 versus 9.7%), and meningitis developed in only 0.8 percent of the treated group versus 2.7 percent of the untreated group.[595] In one recent study, the rate of persistent pneumococcal bacteremia was significantly higher in patients receiving no therapy for pneumococcal bacteremia than in those receiving either oral or parenteral treatment. A higher prevalence of persistent bacteremia in the orally treated group than in the parenterally treated group also was noted.[45] Thus, in patients suspected of having occult bacteremia, treatment with a β-lactam drug can be initiated, especially if the patient looks toxic or has a high fever. However, if the patient has been immunized with both Hib and pneumococcal conjugate vaccines, does not look toxic, and has no predisposing risk factors such as immunodeficiency, the risk of significant bacteremia resulting in complications is extremely low, and, in this case, withholding treatment is reasonable.[738]

For proven *S. pneumoniae* bacteremia in a previously healthy child who is not critically ill, treatment including oral amoxicillin, amoxicillin-clavulanate, second-generation oral cephalosporins, or parenteral third-generation cephalosporins such as ceftriaxone can be initiated at the usually recommended dosages.[85] In most cases of penicillin-susceptible and penicillin-intermediate *S. pneumoniae* (penicillin MICs ≤1.0 µg/mL), most parenteral and some oral β-lactam antibiotic agents achieve serum concentrations that exceed the MIC of the organism for an adequate period.[393] The exceptions are drugs such as loracarbef, cefaclor, and cefixime, which have little activity against penicillin-nonsusceptible *S. pneumoniae.*

In studies looking at the outcome of children with bacteremia caused by β-lactam–nonsusceptible *S. pneumoniae* (nonsusceptible to penicillin, cefuroxime, or ceftriaxone), no difference in outcome was observed when compared with those with susceptible organisms.[114, 366, 639] However, in critically ill infants and children with invasive *S. pneumoniae* infection, initial antimicrobial therapy should include a third-generation cephalosporin (cefotaxime or ceftriaxone) alone or with vancomycin. Vancomycin should be discontinued as soon as antimicrobial susceptibility test results demonstrate effective alternative agents.[15, 681] For children with severe hypersensitivity to β-lactam antibiotics (i.e., penicillins and cephalosporins), initial management of a potential pneumococcal infection could include clindamycin or vancomycin, in addition to antimicrobial drugs for other potential pathogens, as indicated.

MENINGITIS. Penicillin G, 250,000 to 400,000 U/kg/day, is an excellent treatment regimen for meningitis caused by penicillin-susceptible pneumococci, and ceftriaxone, 100 mg/kg/day, or cefotaxime, 200 to 300 mg/kg/day, are excellent choices for meningitis caused by *S. pneumoniae* susceptible to these drugs.[15] However, treatment failures have been reported in penicillin- and ceftriaxone-nonsusceptible pneumococcal meningitis in patients as well as in animal models.[230, 231] Therefore, because of the increased prevalence of penicillin-, cefotaxime-, and ceftriaxone-resistant *S. pneumoniae,* combination therapy consisting of vancomycin (60 mg/kg/day) and cefotaxime (200 to 300 mg/kg/day) or ceftriaxone (100 mg/kg/day) should be administered initially to all children 1 month of age or older with definite or probable bacterial meningitis. However, vancomycin does not need to be used if compelling evidence indicates that the cause is an organism other than *S. pneumoniae* (e.g., gram-negative diplococci on a CSF smear or during an outbreak of meningococcal disease).[15] Vancomycin should not be given alone because bactericidal concentrations in CSF are difficult to sustain, clinical experience to support its use as monotherapy is minimal, and clinical failure and inadequate CSF drug concentrations have been reported.[9, 705] Therapy should be modified after isolation of the organism and based on the results of susceptibility testing. If the organism is susceptible to the β-lactam agent being used, vancomycin use should be discontinued. Antibiotic treatment in proven pneumococcal meningitis should not be shorter in duration than 10 days, and in complicated cases with a suspected focus, it may need to be provided for an even longer period of time.

When appropriately treated, the clinical manifestations and outcome of meningitis caused by antibiotic-nonsusceptible pneumococci are not significantly different from those caused by antibiotic-susceptible pneumococci.[30, 101, 213, 673]

The combination of ceftriaxone and rifampin in an animal meningitis model had a bactericidal effect in meningitis caused by ceftriaxone-resistant *S. pneumoniae.*[530] The addition of rifampin to vancomycin after 24 to 48 hours of therapy should be considered in the following cases if the isolate is susceptible to rifampin: (1) when the clinical condition has worsened despite therapy with vancomycin and cefotaxime or ceftriaxone, (2) when the subsequent Gram-stained smear or culture of CSF indicates failure to eradicate or substantially reduce the number of organisms, or (3) when the organism has an unusually high cefotaxime or ceftriaxone MIC (>4 μg/mL).[15] Although rifampin resistance is a rare event, rifampin should not be given as monotherapy because resistance may develop during therapy.[681]

Other β-lactam antimicrobial agents that can be used for the treatment of pneumococcal meningitis include meropenem (120 mg/kg/day) and cefepime (150 mg/kg/day).[364, 603, 604]

In patients with severe hypersensitivity to β-lactam antibiotics (i.e., penicillins and cephalosporins), the combination of vancomycin and rifampin should be considered.[231]

Chloramphenicol (75 to 100 mg/kg/day) is an acceptable alternative to β-lactam antibiotics in the case of hypersensitivity to these drugs. However, for unknown reasons, failure occurred in a case of penicillin-nonsusceptible pneumococcal meningitis treated with chloramphenicol.[229] Thus, treatment with chloramphenicol should be reserved for patients with β-lactam hypersensitivity who have pneumococcal meningitis caused by penicillin-susceptible strains.

Much debate has ensued on the role of dexamethasone as adjunctive therapy for pneumococcal meningitis. On the one hand, it might exert a positive effect in decreasing inflammatory reactions, but on the other hand, the same decrease in inflammation may reduce penetration of antibiotic agents into the CSF. A meta-analysis of three randomized, double-blinded, placebo-controlled studies combined with one retrospective study demonstrated a potential benefit of reducing hearing loss and neurologic sequelae after having pneumococcal meningitis.[613] Some studies had suggested a beneficial effect on pneumococcal meningitis when dexamethasone was given for 2 days with or before parenteral antibiotics.[472] Thus, for infants and children 6 weeks of age and older, adjunctive therapy with dexamethasone should be considered after weighing the potential benefits and possible risks. When given in the recommended dosages to children with meningitis treated with dexamethasone, CSF concentrations of vancomycin, ceftriaxone, cefotaxime, and rifampin usually are adequate to treat meningitis caused by most strains of *S. pneumoniae,* but in some parts of the world, the CSF concentration of the drugs might be inadequate because of the high MIC values of ceftriaxone and cefotaxime. Dexamethasone may lead to decreased fever and a misleading impression of clinical improvement, even though CSF sterilization may not have been achieved. In some cases, after discontinuation of the steroids, secondary fever may develop, which also can be misleading and give the impression of a nonresponsive case and lead to use of additional lumbar punctures or other procedures.[195]

Repeat lumbar puncture should be considered after 24 to 48 hours of therapy if the following apply: (1) the organism is not susceptible to penicillin, (2) the results of cefotaxime and ceftriaxone susceptibility testing are not yet available, (3) the patient's condition has not improved or has worsened, or (4) the child has received dexamethasone, which might interfere with the ability to interpret a clinical response, such as the resolution of fever.[15, 195]

PNEUMONIA. *S. pneumoniae* accounts for most cases of bacterial pneumonia in children. Thus, empirical treatment of pneumonia should cover this pathogen, despite the fact that an organism-specific diagnosis is unusual in children with pneumonia. Oral treatment with a β-lactam antibiotic such as amoxicillin, cefuroxime axetil, or amoxicillin-clavulanate is an appropriate option for first-line treatment of ambulatory community-acquired pneumonia in children younger than 5 years of age in most countries.[295]

In most cases of pneumonia caused by penicillin-nonsusceptible *S. pneumoniae,* the outcome is favorable if the penicillin MIC is between 0.1 and 2.0 μg/mL and treatment consists of standard doses of parenteral penicillin G (100,000 to 300,000 U/mg/day), oral amoxicillin or amoxicillin-clavulanate (40 to 50 mg/kg/day), or cefuroxime (30 to 50 mg/kg/day).[295, 672] No difference in outcome was found between patients with community-acquired pneumococcal pneumonia treated with oral amoxicillin-clavulanate and those treated with parenteral ceftriaxone.[592]

For immunocompetent hospitalized patients who are not critically ill on admission, parenteral treatment with β-lactam antibiotics such as cefuroxime, cefotaxime, or ampicillin (with or without β-lactamase inhibitors) is an appropriate option because both *S. pneumoniae* and most other potential organisms are covered.[295]

In adult and pediatric patients with pneumococcal pneumonia treated with standard regimens of parenteral penicillin G or a cephalosporin, the outcome was similar when those infected with penicillin- or cephalosporin-resistant organisms were compared with patients infected with susceptible organisms.[85, 108, 196, 205, 365, 485, 526, 719, 736]

In one retrospective cohort study, adult patients with bacteremic pneumonia caused by isolates that were penicillin-nonsusceptible had a significantly greater risk of dying in the hospital and of having more suppurative complications than did patients with susceptible isolates.[474] However, the mortality rate was not significantly different after adjustment for baseline differences in severity of illness. A population-based active surveillance of pneumococcal disease in the United States found that 12 percent of 5837 cases were fatal.[205] In this study, a higher mortality rate was noted after the fourth hospital day in patients with invasive pneumococcal pneumonia caused by isolates with penicillin MICs of 4 μg/mL or greater. However, potential limitations of this study included absence of data on the severity of illness at initial evaluation, as well as lack of information on the antibiotics used.

Treatment failure and breakthrough meningitis were reported in a patient who was infected by highly resistant *S. pneumoniae* (penicillin MIC of 2 μg/mL, cefuroxime MIC of 2 μg/mL, and cefotaxime MIC >8 μg/mL) treated with cefotaxime and cefuroxime.[100] Because of such cases, some authorities recommend that in critically ill patients with highly resistant *S. pneumoniae*, vancomycin (or in older patients, fluoroquinolones active against *S. pneumoniae)* be added initially to third-generation cephalosporins.[295]

In a series of 32 children with pleural empyema caused by *S. pneumoniae*, those with penicillin-nonsusceptible strains were significantly younger and more frequently were treated previously with antibiotics than were children with penicillin-susceptible strains.[525] However, no significant differences were found between the two groups in the duration of fever and tachypnea, need for surgical treatment, presence of bacteremia, mean duration of therapy, or length of hospital stay.[525] In cases of pleural fluid or empyema in patients infected with highly resistant organisms, vancomycin or rifampin may be added if no clinical response is achieved within 48 to 72 hours.[85]

For β-lactam–allergic patients, macrolides are favored.[364] However, in some areas, macrolide resistance occurs commonly and may lead to treatment failure.[217, 321, 371, 447, 448, 482, 662, 721] Breakthrough pneumococcal bacteremia has been reported during treatment with clarithromycin or azithromycin for community-acquired pneumonia.[371]

Drugs that are not appropriate for treating critically ill patients with pneumococcal pneumonia are the first-generation cephalosporins, ceftazidime, and ticarcillin because most penicillin-resistant *S. pneumoniae* also are resistant to these drugs.[177, 528] Trimethoprim-sulfamethoxazole is not recommended because of the high prevalence of resistance to this drug.[295]

The duration of treatment is related to the clinical findings, clinical response to treatment, and underlying diseases of the patient and generally is 7 to 14 days. For hospitalized patients, 5 to 7 days of parenteral treatment followed by 7 days of oral therapy is recommended,[85, 340] but many clinicians use a shorter course of 7 to 10 days total.

OTITIS MEDIA. Antibiotics are the standard of care for the treatment of AOM in the United States and in many other countries. Although antibiotic therapy is required in only 20 to 30 percent of all cases of AOM, most patients are treated with antibiotics because these cases cannot be identified quickly and easily.[387] As with other infections, the main goal of antibiotic therapy is to eradicate the causative pathogens from the middle ear fluid.[153, 360, 423, 590]

S. pneumoniae is responsible for 30 to 50 percent of all cases of acute bacterial otitis media, and it is the least likely pathogen to resolve without the administration of appropriate antibiotic treatment.[583] After 2 to 7 days, if not treated, approximately 50 percent of all *H. influenzae* organisms are eradicated spontaneously, but less than 20 percent of pneumococci are eradicated spontaneously in AOM.[313] Therefore, *S. pneumoniae* generally is considered the most important organism against which antibiotic treatment should be directed in AOM.

Studies using tympanocentesis before treatment and a second tympanocentesis procedure during treatment to document bacteriologic efficacy ("double-tympanocentesis" bacteriologic outcome studies) have shown that pharmacodynamic models can predict bacteriologic outcome.[133, 150] Studies have shown that the increasing resistance of *S. pneumoniae* to various drugs has increased the complexity of antibiotic treatment of otitis media. In addition to having activity against antibiotic-resistant pneumococci, a drug appropriate for empiric treatment of AOM should be active against the two other main pathogens of otitis media, namely, *H. influenzae* and *M. catarrhalis.* Table 90–3 summarizes the activity of the drugs used commonly against otitis media pathogens, with the pharmacodynamic properties (the relationship between the drug concentration in plasma and at the site of infection) and the MIC of the drug to the infecting organism taken into account. The in vitro activity of oral agents has not always been predictive of their in vivo activity because of incorrect or unavailable interpretative breakpoints, but this deficiency has been rectified for *S. pneumoniae* in the United States since 2000.

Most of the drugs used for the treatment of AOM belong to the β-lactam and macrolide classes; these drugs act against pathogens by a "time-dependent killing" mechanism,[76, 133] which means that an effective dosing regimen for AOM would require that the unbound plasma concentration exceed the MICs of the drug against the causative pathogens for at least 40 to 50 percent of the dosing interval. Although the drug exerts its effect in the middle ear cavity, penetration of the drug into this space is driven by the unbound plasma concentration, which is in equilibrium with the extracellular fluid compartment of tissues and sites such as the middle ear space.

For penicillin-susceptible *S. pneumoniae,* most β-lactam drugs (with the exception of penicillin V and the first-generation oral cephalosporins) reach that goal and are appropriate drugs for otitis media caused by penicillin-susceptible *S. pneumoniae.*

In the case of penicillin-nonsusceptible *S. pneumoniae,* on the other hand, the picture is different. The most active oral β-lactam drugs against penicillin-intermediate isolates are amoxicillin and amoxicillin-clavulanate (clavulanate has no effect on pneumococci, but it is used often to empirically add coverage against β-lactamase–producing organisms). However, most of the oral cephalosporins, with the exception of cefuroxime axetil, cefpodoxime proxetil, and cefprozil, cannot reach the goal of unbound plasma concentrations exceeding the MIC_{90} values for most penicillin-intermediate organisms for 40 to 50 percent of the dosing interval and, thus, are not appropriate for the treatment of AOM in areas where penicillin-intermediate strains occur commonly.[133, 182] For fully penicillin-resistant *S. pneumoniae* strains, of the commonly used β-lactam drugs against AOM, only high-dose amoxicillin (80 to 100 mg/kg/day), amoxicillin-clavulanate (80 to 100 mg/kg/day of the amoxicillin component), and intramuscular ceftriaxone (50 mg/kg/day) reach plasma or middle ear fluid concentrations that are above the MIC values for an appropriate duration. To eradicate *S. pneumoniae* with penicillin MICs of 2.0 μg/mL or more, an amoxicillin or amoxicillin-clavulanate dose of 80 to 100 mg/kg/day (divided into two or three doses) is necessary.[148, 423, 624]

TABLE 90–3 ■ IN VIVO ACTIVITY OF ANTIBIOTIC DRUGS IN COMMON USE FOR THE TREATMENT OF AOM AGAINST THE MAJOR AOM PATHOGENS*

	Antimicrobial Activity					
	Streptococcus pneumoniae†			*Haemophilus influenzae*		
Drug	**Penicillin-Susceptible**	**Penicillin-Intermediate**	**Penicillin-Resistant**	**β-Lactamase–Negative**	**β-Lactamase–Positive**	***Moraxella catarrhalis***
Amoxicillin, 40–50 mg/kg/day	+++	+++	+	++	–	–
Amoxicillin, 80–90 mg/kg/day	+++	+++	+++	+++	–	–
Amoxicillin/clavulanate, 45/6.4 mg/kg/day	+++	++	+	++	++	+++
Amoxicillin/clavulanate, 90/6.4 mg/kg/day	+++	+++	++	+++	+++	+++
Cefuroxime axetil	+++	++	+	++	++	+++
Cefaclor	+++	–	–	+	+	++
Ceftriaxone (50 mg/kg/day)—1 day	+++	++	+	+++	+++	+++
Ceftriaxone (50 mg/kg/day)—3 days	+++	+++	+++	+++	+++	+++
Cefpodoxime proxetil	+++	++	+	+++	+++	+++
Cefprozil	+++	++	+	–	–	++
Cefixime	++	–	–	+++	+++	+++
Cefdinir	+++	+	–	++	+++	+++
Erythromycin/azithromycin/clarithromycin	+++	++‡	–‡	+/–	+/–	++
Clindamycin	+++	++‡	++‡	–	–	–
TMP-SMX	++	–‡	–‡	++	++	++
	S. pneumoniae					
	Macrolide-Susceptible		**Macrolide-Resistant**			
Erythromycin/azithromycin/clarithromycin	+++		–			
Clindamycin	+++		+			
	TMP-SMX–Susceptible		**TMP-SMX–Resistant**			
TMP-SMX	+++		–			

*In vitro activity, pharmacodynamic properties, and if available, the results of bacteriologic outcome studies are taken into account.
†Penicillin-susceptible (MICs ≤0.06 μg/mL), penicillin-intermediate (MICs 0.1–1 μg/mL), penicillin-resistant (MICs ≥2 μg/mL).
+++, Appropriate; ++, may not be appropriate for some strains; +, frequent bacteriologic failures are likely; –, usually associated with bacteriologic failure.
‡When *Streptococcus pneumoniae* is penicillin-nonsusceptible, the prevalence of macrolide, clindamycin, and TMP-SMX resistance among the strains is higher than in penicillin-susceptible ones. This rate can be very high in penicillin-resistant *S. pneumoniae*. (See "Bacteriology").
AOM, acute otitis media; MICs, minimal inhibitory concentrations; TMP-SMX, trimethoprim-sulfamethoxazole.

Among the parenteral cephalosporins, ceftriaxone and cefotaxime have the lowest MICs, but high-level resistance of *S. pneumoniae* to these agents has been reported.[653] Intramuscular ceftriaxone (50 mg/kg/day) given once daily for one to three daily doses is effective for pneumococcal otitis caused by penicillin-susceptible strains. For otitis caused by penicillin-nonsusceptible *S. pneumoniae*, 3 days of treatment may be required.[426, 427]

Resistance to macrolides is significant and affects bacteriologic and clinical outcomes in AOM.[27, 50, 152] All macrolides are efficacious against otitis caused by macrolide-susceptible *S. pneumoniae*. Efficacy was shown for erythromycin,[315] clarythromycin,[313] and azithromycin.[152] However, when the organism is resistant to macrolides, these drugs are not effective because the MIC is too high to be exceeded by the drug concentrations at the site of infection, which has been demonstrated best for azithromycin[149, 152] but can be generalized to other macrolides. In one child, pneumococcal bacteremia and meningitis were reported to have developed during azithromycin therapy for otitis media.[328]

Clindamycin is active against most penicillin-nonsusceptible *S. pneumoniae* strains and may be used to treat pneumococcal AOM that does not respond to β-lactam antibiotics. However, prospective, controlled studies on the bacteriologic and clinical efficacy of clindamycin in the treatment of AOM have not been performed. Furthermore, as described in the section on microbiology, an increasing proportion of *S. pneumoniae* resistant to macrolides also are resistant to clindamycin.

Trimethoprim-sulfamethoxazole no longer is an appropriate choice for empiric treatment of AOM because of the high prevalence of resistance to this drug among *S. pneumoniae* strains in many regions. In the case of AOM caused by *S. pneumoniae* resistant to trimethoprim-sulfamethoxazole, the effect of this drug is no better than that of placebo.[422]

Treatment of nonresponsive AOM (cases refractory to one or more courses of antibiotics) was studied in double-tympanocentesis studies, with bacteriologic outcome as the major end-point.[387] Cefaclor, cefixime, loracarbef, ceftibuten, azithromycin, and trimethoprim-sulfamethoxazole clearly have been shown to be ineffective against nonsusceptible pneumococci and no longer can be recommended for the empiric treatment of nonresponsive AOM.[182] Second-line treatment should be based preferably on middle ear fluid culture results and pathogen susceptibility tests.

For patients with clinically defined treatment failure after receiving 3 to 5 days of initial therapy, suitable second-line agents should be active against penicillin-nonsusceptible pneumococci, as well as β-lactamase–producing *H. influenzae* and *M. catarrhalis*. Three antibiotic drugs fulfill these criteria: amoxicillin-clavulanate, intramuscular ceftriaxone, and, to a lesser extent, cefuroxime axetil.[69, 182, 468] In these cases, amoxicillin-clavulanate should be given at 80 to 100 mg/kg/day of the amoxicillin component. Intramuscular ceftriaxone given for 3 days was found to be superior to a 1-day regimen in cases caused by penicillin-resistant *S. pneumoniae*.[427]

Erythromycin-sulfisoxazole, clarithromycin, and azithromycin may be used as alternatives for penicillin-allergic patients.[424] However, in such cases, tympanocentesis is recommended either before initiation of treatment or after 48 to 72 hours of treatment if no clinical response is observed because the latter drugs have limitations in bacterial coverage.

The recommended duration of treatment usually is 10 days for most antibiotic drug regimens in children younger than 2 years.[388] Recent studies suggest that a shorter treatment course (5 to 7 days) may be adequate, at least for a subgroup of children older than 2 years with uncomplicated otitis.[406, 543, 547] However, data evaluating the bacteriologic outcome and clinical efficacy of shortened antibiotic treatment for AOM are not complete in children younger than 2 years of age, children with severe or complicated AOM, and those with a history of recurrent or chronic otitis media, although such studies are being undertaken. Clinical studies suggest that 5 to 7 days of treatment may not be adequate for these groups of patients.[121, 123, 183, 548] Children attending daycare centers are at particular risk of having a poor response and recurrence if treated for 5 rather than 10 days.[122] Therefore, until the results of more studies are available, shortened antibiotic treatment in AOM cannot be recommended for children younger than 2 years of age, children with severe or complicated AOM, children with chronic or recurrent AOM, and children attending daycare centers.[123, 138]

Prophylactic use of amoxicillin or trimethoprim-sulfamethoxazole at half the therapeutic dose may reduce the number of new episodes significantly in patients with recurrent AOM.* However, this approach may promote carriage of drug-resistant *S. pneumoniae* and lead to development of new infections with resistant organisms.[151] Thus, antibiotic prophylaxis is not recommended except in children with frequently recurrent AOM episodes, defined as three or more documented episodes in 6 months or four or more in 12 months.[425]

SINUSITIS. Although studies on the bacteriology of acute sinusitis are sparse, they suggest that the pathogens causing sinusitis are similar to those causing AOM. Acute bacterial sinusitis usually is a complication of viral rhinosinusitis and occurs in 0.5 to 2 percent of cases. In a study comparing antimicrobial therapy with placebo for the treatment of children with a clinical and radiographic diagnosis of acute bacterial sinusitis, children receiving antimicrobial therapy recovered more quickly and more often than did those receiving placebo.[715] Thus, antimicrobial agents that are effective for the treatment of AOM also are likely to be effective and are recommended for acute sinusitis.[15, 514, 641, 714]

In the selection of appropriate treatment for bacterial sinusitis, physicians should consider the following parameters: (1) the severity of disease: mild (healthy patients with 10 days of persistent anterior and posterior rhinorrhea and fatigue), moderate (patients with 10 days of nasal congestion in whom a low-grade fever developed during the past 3 days, as well as increasing unilateral tenderness over the frontal or maxillary sinuses that becomes aggravated while the patient bends forward), or severe (life-threatening infection); (2) antibiotic use during the 4 to 6 weeks before the onset of infection, which is an important risk factor for the selection of resistant organisms; (3) age younger than 5 years; (4) daycare center attendance; and (5) underlying condition predisposing to invasive infection, such as immunocompromised status.

Amoxicillin is recommended for the initial treatment of children who have uncomplicated acute bacterial sinusitis that is of mild severity, do not attend daycare centers, and have not been treated recently with an antimicrobial.[119] If the patient is allergic to amoxicillin, then cefdinir, cefuroxime axetil, or cefpodoxime can be used (if the allergic reaction was not a type I hypersensitivity reaction). In children with serious allergic reactions, macrolides or clindamycin can be used in an effort to select an antimicrobial of an entirely different class.[119] In patients with disease moderate in severity or those attending daycare, therapy should be initiated with high-dose amoxicillin-clavulanate. Parenteral antibiotic treatment should be considered in patients with severe disease. For patients with mild or moderate disease who are not improving after 72 hours of treatment, therapy should be changed to amoxicillin-clavulanate unless this agent was used initially, in which case treatment options are very limited.[119, 339] In addition, re-evaluation of deteriorating or nonresponsive patients may include computed tomography, fiberoptic endoscopy, or sinus aspiration with culture.[641]

Acute sinusitis should be treated for 7 days after improvement is noted and for at least 10 to 14 days.[514] However, the duration of treatment has not been studied adequately and, therefore, is arbitrary.

CONJUNCTIVITIS. When compared with placebo, topical therapy with polymyxin-bacitracin ointment has been shown to reduce the duration of symptoms by half and to achieve a 2.5-fold increase in the rate of bacteriologic eradication after 8 to 10 days of therapy (31 versus 79%, respectively).[252] Polymyxin B–trimethoprim, applied four times daily for 1 week, also can be an effective broad-spectrum therapy for nonsevere conjunctivitis, although the coverage against gram-positive organisms provided by trimethoprim is less than optimal for some species. Aminoglycoside drops (0.3% gentamicin or 0.3% tobramycin) are inherently less active against gram-positive organisms and have a low therapeutic-toxic ratio as topical agents. Neomycin–polymyxin B–gramicidin drops or neomycin–polymyxin B–bacitracin ointment provides broad-spectrum coverage, but neomycin poses a 10 percent risk of causing hypersensitivity reactions such as contact dermatitis.[713]

Most organisms causing conjunctivitis are susceptible to chloramphenicol.[71, 580] However, significant public and professional concern regarding the use of chloramphenicol eye drops has been raised because of the associated risk of development of bone marrow aplasia.[93, 113]

Increased resistance to polymyxin B–sulfamethoxazole for the treatment of conjunctivitis caused by *S. pneumoniae* in children was reported recently. Topical tetracycline and fluoroquinolones are active against penicillin-resistant *S. pneumoniae* and are considered suitable for the treatment of patients with conjunctivitis that is nonresponsive to the other treatment.[71]

BONE AND JOINT INFECTIONS. In a review of 13 cases of septic arthritis or osteomyelitis caused by penicillin-susceptible *S. pneumoniae*,[4] the drug used most commonly was penicillin, followed by ampicillin. Nafcillin and cefotaxime also were used to treat these patients. In addition, three patients with penicillin-nonsusceptible *S. pneumoniae* were treated for septic arthritis and osteomyelitis with combinations of vancomycin and cefotaxime or ceftriaxone.

Rifampin and clindamycin also were used to treat a patient with septic arthritis of the left hip and osteomyelitis of the proximal end of the femur caused by highly resistant *S. pneumoniae* (penicillin and cefotaxime MICs of 8 μg/mL); this patient also experienced prolonged fever (21 days). The patient had been treated initially with cefotaxime and nafcillin, as well as drainage and irrigation of the infected site.[4]

The duration of treatment with parenteral antibiotics in patients with *S. pneumoniae* bone infection varied from 14 to 196 days and, in those with joint infection, from 12 to 67 days.[4, 52] Parenteral treatment may be followed by oral antibiotic therapy once the patient has improved considerably.

*See references 63, 298, 385, 460, 465, 542, 552, 577, 589, 730.

ENDOCARDITIS. *S. pneumoniae* endocarditis is a rare event and accounts for less than 3 percent of all cases of endocarditis.[329, 490, 674] Cases caused by penicillin-resistant *S. pneumoniae* have been reported exclusively in adults.[638] Treatment is based on a combination of antibiotics and surgery because *S. pneumoniae* endocarditis is associated with rapid destruction of heart valves. Parenteral second- or third-generation cephalosporins are recommended as initial treatment, and the addition of vancomycin is advised in cases of penicillin- or cephalosporin-resistant organisms.[392] Newer fluoroquinolones may serve as an alternative treatment in older patients.[638]

TREATMENT OF PNEUMOCOCCAL INFECTION IN IMMUNOCOMPROMISED HOSTS. Children with underlying conditions such as HIV, nephrotic syndrome, sickle-cell disease, other congenital hemoglobinopathies, or congenital immunoglobulin deficiencies, children receiving immunosuppressive drugs, and children with congenital or acquired asplenia are at increased risk for acquiring *S. pneumoniae* infection in general and for infection caused by drug-resistant organisms in particular.[323, 455, 621, 681] The results of two studies[622, 690] suggested that in HIV-infected adults, the outcome is worse in patients with nonsusceptible *S. pneumoniae* than in those with susceptible *S. pneumoniae*. However, both studies had limitations that preclude arriving at firm conclusions. In regions where penicillin-resistant *S. pneumoniae* occurs commonly, consideration should be given to initiating therapy with vancomycin and cefotaxime or ceftriaxone in critically ill patients until susceptibility results are available; subsequent therapy should be based on these results and the patient's clinical course.

For infants with sickle-cell anemia, oral penicillin prophylaxis against invasive *S. pneumoniae* disease should be initiated as soon as the diagnosis is established, preferably by the time that the infant is 2 months of age. Although the efficacy of antimicrobial prophylaxis has been proved only in patients with sickle-cell anemia, other asplenic children at particularly high risk, such as those with malignant neoplasms or thalassemia, also should receive daily chemoprophylaxis. In general, antimicrobial prophylaxis (in addition to immunization) should be considered strongly for all asplenic children younger than 5 years of age and for at least 1 year after undergoing splenectomy.[14]

The age at which chemoprophylaxis is discontinued often is empiric. Based on a multicenter study, prophylactic penicillin can be discontinued in children with sickle-cell anemia who are receiving regular medical attention and who have not had a severe *S. pneumoniae* infection or surgical splenectomy when they reach at approximately 5 years of age.[14] The appropriate duration of prophylaxis for children with asplenia caused by other conditions is unknown. Some experts continue administering prophylaxis throughout childhood and into adulthood for high-risk patients with asplenia.[14]

For antimicrobial prophylaxis, oral penicillin V (125 mg twice a day for children younger than 5 years and 250 mg twice a day for children 5 years and older) usually is recommended. Some experts recommend amoxicillin (20 mg/kg/day). Breakthrough infections caused by drug-resistant *S. pneumoniae* may occur. Therefore, parents should be aware that all febrile illnesses are potentially serious in immunocompromised children and that immediate medical attention should be sought because the initial signs and symptoms of fulminant bacteremia can be subtle.[14]

In addition to receiving chemoprophylaxis, children 2 years of age and older who are at increased risk of acquiring invasive *S. pneumoniae* infection should be immunized with a pneumococcal conjugate vaccine followed by a 23-valent nonconjugate polysaccharide vaccine 2 months or longer after the last dose of the conjugate vaccine is taken.[553] Indications for immunization are the following: (1) sickle-cell disease; (2) functional or anatomic asplenia; (3) nephrotic syndrome or chronic renal failure; (4) conditions associated with immunosuppression, such as organ or bone marrow transplantation, drug therapy, or cytoreduction therapy (including long-term systemic corticosteroid therapy); (5) HIV infection; and (6) CSF leaks.[15] For details on immunization, see the section on prevention.

MISCELLANEOUS INFECTIONS. Other infections, such as primary peritonitis and orbital cellulitis, should be treated with antibiotic agents that are recommended for bacteremia. Parenteral penicillin, ampicillin and cefotaxime, or ceftriaxone is suitable treatment in most cases, and the addition of vancomycin for drug-resistant *S. pneumoniae* is recommended. Treatment should be adjusted according to susceptibility results.[681]

Prevention

Prevention of pneumococcal infection in all ages is, without doubt, a more effective approach to reducing the burden of pneumococcal disease than is any successful treatment modality. In general, prevention can be divided into nonimmunologic and immunologic strategies (immunoprophylaxis).

NONIMMUNOLOGIC STRATEGIES

This category includes interventions that aim at (1) reducing risk factors that predispose to pneumococcal infection, (2) providing chemical substances (e.g., antibiotics) to abort or prevent pneumococcal colonization or disease, and (3) modifying anatomic abnormalities that predispose to pneumococcal infection.[389]

A factor that is important not only for pneumococcal infection but also for many other serious bacterial infections is the need to improve general health and nutrition worldwide, particularly in developing countries. Many risk factors for acquisition of pneumococcal infection that can be alleviated, include poor living conditions, overcrowding, poor hygiene, malnutrition, and a high prevalence of viral infections, particularly respiratory viruses, measles, and HIV. In the developed world, carriage of pneumococci, especially antibiotic-resistant strains that result in sporadic infections as well as outbreaks, is related to daycare attendance and is proportional to the number of children per group.[112, 122, 155, 158, 433, 568, 668] Therefore, reducing the number of children per group in daycare centers and developing alternative forms of childcare may reduce the rate of pneumococcal morbidity.

Recently, the importance of passive smoking (namely, being in close contact with smokers in the same household) has been highlighted as a risk factor for development of pneumococcal disease.[509] Thus, efforts made to prevent smoking in the home may have an important role in the prevention of pneumococcal infection. Breast-feeding may protect against some infections related to *S. pneumoniae*, such as otitis media.[23, 97, 184, 587, 694] Therefore, breast-feeding should be encouraged, especially in families in which otitis media occurs commonly, although the precise role of prolonged breast-feeding in protecting against pneumococcal infection has not been established.

Antimicrobial chemoprophylaxis is used predominantly for two indications: prevention of recurrent AOM and prevention of pneumococcal sepsis in children with anatomic or functional asplenia. Data now exist to support the common practice of prescribing regular doses of penicillin for children with asplenia or sickle-cell disease.[238] Chemoprophylaxis is used commonly for the prevention of middle ear infections. Controlled clinical trials have compared antimicrobial chemoprophylaxis with placebo, surgery, or historical controls.[73] Various antibiotics were tested (either as ongoing daily prophylaxis or as intermittent treatment during viral infections). Most of the studies, but not all, showed a benefit of chemoprophylaxis over controls, especially for amoxicillin, ampicillin, sulfonamides, and trimethoprim-sulfamethoxazole.* However, those studies were performed before the era of increased antibiotic resistance in *S. pneumoniae*. The dosing schedule recommended for prophylaxis usually is half the daily therapeutic dose given once a day, but the optimal dosing regimen has not been defined.

The potential benefits of otitis media chemoprophylaxis have been weighed against the ability of chemoprophylaxis to alter the nasopharyngeal flora and foster colonization with resistant organisms and thereby compromise the long-term efficacy of the prophylactic drug and contribute to the propagation of resistant organisms throughout the community. As a result, the practice of otitis media chemoprophylaxis has been reduced greatly. In one study,[95] prophylaxis with amoxicillin induced a dramatic increase in the carriage of penicillin-resistant *S. pneumoniae,* as well as increased carriage of other resistant pathogens. The fear of increasing resistance led the Committee on Infectious Diseases of the American Academy of Pediatrics to issue a warning against the widespread use of otitis media prophylaxis and to state in its recent report that "Antimicrobial prophylaxis should be reserved for control of recurrent acute otitis media, defined by 3 or more distinct and well-documented episodes during a period of 6 months or 4 or more episodes during a period of 12 months."[16]

Surgical otitis media prophylaxis by myringotomy and insertion of tympanostomy tubes or adenoidectomy (with or without tonsillectomy) has been recommended for otitis-prone children.[383] Some authorities now prefer this modality to the chemoprophylactic approach because it is not associated with altered flora. However, surgical risks also need to be considered.

A novel approach to prevention of pneumococcal disease is the potential use of oligosaccharides to prevent attachment of organisms, including *S. pneumoniae,* to the respiratory mucosa. Because colonization of the respiratory mucosa can result in local and systemic disease, as well as spread to other individuals, prevention of colonization is a reasonable approach to prevent disease. Human milk oligosaccharides can prevent attachment of *S. pneumoniae* and other organisms to the mucosa of the respiratory tract[18, 747] and have been shown to interfere with the establishment and progression of experimental pneumococcal pneumonia in infant rats.[322] Natural oligosaccharides act as decoys in mucosa (also in saliva, tears, urine, sweat, and breast milk) and bind the carbohydrate-binding proteins of the microbial pathogens and thus prevent mucosal attachment.[389] Despite this promise, a large-scale study examining the efficacy of such an oligosaccharide (3′-sialyllacto-*N*-neoteratose) given intranasally as prophylaxis for AOM and nasopharyngeal carriage of bacteria failed to show any beneficial effect on either outcome.[695]

Other experiments conducted in Finland showed that xylitol (a five-carbon sugar alcohol used extensively as a sweetener in toothpaste, chewing gum, and various foods) inhibited the growth of streptococci, including *S. pneumoniae,* in vitro[397, 398] and prevented the development of otitis media in daycare center attendees when provided as chewing gum, lozenges, or syrup.[692, 693] Whether this approach eventually will develop into a practical strategy to prevent respiratory infections caused by *S. pneumoniae* and other organisms is not clear. Obviously, the concept of reducing nasopharyngeal colonization and thereby the number of episodes of bacterial respiratory infection through competitive inhibition remains "cutting-edge" medicine. Additional new agents, altered doses, or the existing agents or different methods of administration still should be studied.[539]

*See references 63, 298, 385, 460, 465, 542, 552, 577, 589, 730.

IMMUNOPROPHYLAXIS

As discussed in the section on pathogenesis in this chapter, *S. pneumoniae* infections typically are opportunistic infections complicating viral respiratory infection. Recent advances in the development of vaccines against respiratory viruses, especially influenza, RSV, and parainfluenza virus, could therefore reduce the incidence and severity of pneumococcal infection by reducing these preceding viral infections. Some of these vaccines are expected to be licensed and widely used in the next decade. Inactivated influenza vaccines are licensed already and used in children, but routine vaccination has not been supported widely. The expected addition of live attenuated influenza vaccines may herald a new era in the prevention of influenza disease in children.

The reader is referred to the sections on the structure of the pneumococcus, virulence factors, and host defense mechanisms in this chapter for an understanding of the basis for the immune-based strategy of prevention of disease.

Unconjugated Capsular Polysaccharide Vaccines

Efforts to prevent pneumococcal infection by providing specific immunity started more than 100 years ago, as described in the section on history. That both passive immunization (administration of specific antibodies) and active immunization can protect against many pneumococcal infections is well established.

Passively administered serotype-specific antibodies can protect animals and humans against diseases caused by pneumococci. Administration of antisera was associated with improved clinical outcome, including reduced mortality.[107] Human immunoglobulins can prevent experimental pneumococcal bacteremia in mice[115, 598] and otitis media in chinchillas.[634] The finding of low cord blood IgG antibodies, mainly of the IgG1 subset, is predictive of early-onset AOM in infancy.[57, 443, 605] In several clinical studies, bacterial polysaccharide immune globulin (BPIG) obtained by immunizing healthy adults with a 14-valent pneumococcal vaccine (in addition to group C meningococcal and Hib polysaccharide vaccines) decreased the prevalence of AOM[612, 635] and invasive infection[637] in children. High-dose BPIG administered to infant rats resulted in high serum concentrations of serotype-specific IgG against serotype 3 (geometric mean concentrations of 8.2 and 1.4 μg/mL on days 1 and 7, respectively) and, consequently, protection against nasopharyngeal carriage of this serotype.[459]

Immunization with pneumococcal polysaccharide antigens, mainly in adults, has been studied for a long time. First, hexavalent polysaccharide vaccines were introduced in the late 1940s, followed by 14-valent vaccines in the late 1970s and 23-valent vaccines in the early 1980s. The latter, produced by several manufacturers, contains 25 μg of purified, nonconjugated polysaccharide antigens per dose for serotypes 1, 2, 3, 4, 5, 6B, 7F, 8, 9N, 9V, 10A, 11A, 12F, 14, 15B, 17F, 18C, 19A, 19F, 20, 22F, 23F, and 33F. These

23 serotypes account for approximately 90 percent of the serotypes responsible for invasive pneumococcal infection in all age groups in both developed and developing countries.[13, 291, 292, 578, 651] The 23-valent polysaccharide vaccines are tolerated well by healthy children for primary[418, 625] or repeated immunization.[82] However, the presence of preexisting antibodies was associated with an increased incidence of adverse events at the site of infection in adults but less pronounced effects in children.[75, 403, 516]

Generally speaking, these bacterial polysaccharide-based vaccines are poorly immunogenic in infants and toddlers for important disease-causing serotypes, which is to be expected because bacterial capsular polysaccharides induce antibody production primarily by T-cell–independent mechanisms that still are not fully developed in this age group.[574] Polysaccharide-specific IgG concentrations are relatively high in very young infants because they are acquired transplacentally and consist mainly of IgG1. Nasopharyngeal colonization with various serotypes of *S. pneumoniae* results in the natural production of serotype-specific antibodies.[99, 294, 680, 732] The immune response to pneumococcal polysaccharides is serotype-dependent, and some serotypes commonly associated with disease are especially poor immunogens until the child reaches the age of approximately 5 years.[181] Serotypes 6A, 6B, 12, 19A, 19F, and 23F are examples of this phenomenon.[157, 181, 402, 418, 430, 559, 652, 680, 732] As for other species, the IgG subclasses that are produced after exposure to polysaccharide antigens are mainly IgG2 and IgG4.[438] A second dose of polysaccharide vaccine does not provide a booster effect and may even result in a reduced immune response when compared with that following the first dose, which may suggest an antigenic tolerance effect.[75, 703]

Children with certain underlying conditions that predispose to the development of pneumococcal infection respond more poorly to pneumococcal polysaccharide vaccines than do otherwise normal children. Published studies of children with recurrent respiratory tract infections,[191, 306, 610, 611] HIV infection,[32, 248, 544] sickle-cell disease,[64, 703] splenectomy,[3, 571] malignancies,[569] and chronic renal disease[232, 589, 601, 656] all have demonstrated this phenomenon.

In addition to a relatively poor systemic immune response, the polysaccharide vaccines have been shown to induce only minimal mucosal immune responses. Serotype-specific antibodies to pneumococcal serotypes 6A, 14, 18C, and 23F were measured in the sera and middle ear effusions of 14 children who had received a 14-valent pneumococcal capsular polysaccharide vaccine and in controls.[402] Serotype-specific antibody concentrations in middle ear effusions correlated with serum concentrations and generally were higher in pneumococcal vaccine recipients than in control vaccine recipients. IgM class antibodies frequently were seen only in the serum samples, thus suggesting that antibodies diffuse into the middle ear space rather than being synthesized in situ in response to the vaccine. This finding refutes previous theories that local production of antibodies occurs in the middle ear after vaccination.[404, 645, 646]

Limited data exist regarding the efficacy of polysaccharide pneumococcal vaccines in preventing disease in infants and children. A large study conducted in Papua New Guinea on more than 7000 children showed a reduction in mortality rates from acute lower respiratory tract disease.[420, 575, 576] In this study, the effect was dramatic: a 59 percent reduction in mortality rates in all children vaccinated (5 months to 5 years of age) and a 50 percent reduction in children vaccinated before reaching 2 years of age. However, the vaccine did not protect against nonfatal disease. In the United States, researchers have suggested that the polysaccharide vaccines would be 62 percent effective in preventing invasive pneumococcal disease caused by vaccine serotypes in children aged 2 to 5 years.[212] The effectiveness of polysaccharide pneumococcal vaccines in preventing otitis media is not clear. Several studies have shown some reduction in the incidence of otitis media in vaccinated children,[318, 457] but other studies have failed to show this effect.[180, 367, 675] No effect of the use of polysaccharide pneumococcal vaccine on pneumococcal nasopharyngeal carriage could be demonstrated.[147, 157]

The aforementioned data on T-cell–independent polysaccharide pneumococcal vaccines clearly show that the benefit in children was at best marginal and that a need for improved vaccines exists.

Conjugated Capsular Polysaccharide Vaccines

In contrast to the T-cell–independent nature of the immune response that occurs after the administration of bacterial polysaccharides, when these polysaccharides are conjugated to protein, the antibody response changes to a T-cell–dependent one.[42, 187, 368, 579, 636, 658] These conjugate vaccines induce helper T cells to stimulate polysaccharide-specific B cells that not only produce antibodies but also mature into memory cells (Fig. 90–14). Polysaccharide-protein conjugate products characteristically are immunogenic in infancy and result in the production of high concentrations of antibodies. These antibodies have improved functional capacity (determined by avidity and opsonization assays), are long lasting, and induce a brisk and rapid elevation in highly functional antigen-specific antibodies with re-exposure (booster effect).[192]

The development of pneumococcal conjugate vaccines initially used the technology developed for Hib conjugate vaccines. Increasing experience and challenges have led to modifications of that technology, the development of new technologies, and the addition of new protein carriers. Studies were initiated first on monovalent pneumococcal conjugate vaccines. Currently, this technology has brought vaccines with 7 to 11 different conjugated pneumococcal polysaccharide antigens to licensure or phase III trials. Table 90–4 shows the pneumococcal conjugate vaccines that are either licensed in at least one country, are being tested

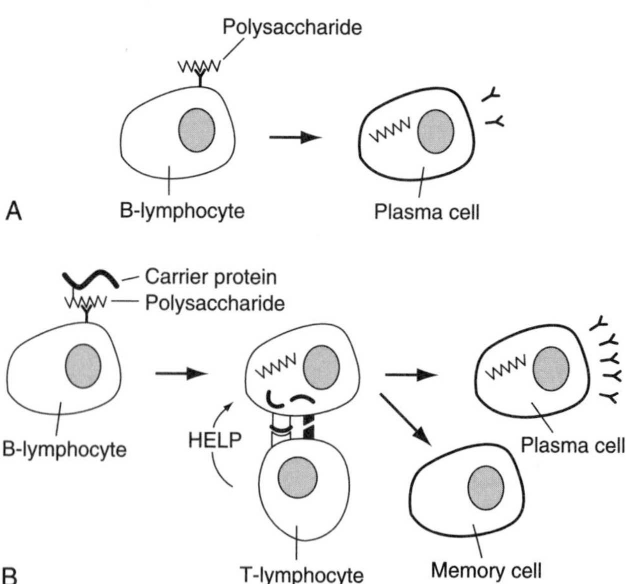

FIGURE 90–14 ■ T-cell–independent *(A)* and T-cell–dependent *(B)* antibody responses to polysaccharide or polysaccharide-protein conjugate antigens. (From Eskola, J., and Anttila, M.: Pneumococcal conjugate vaccines. Pediatr. Infect. Dis. J. *18*:543–551, 1999.)

TABLE 90–4 ■ PNEUMOCOCCAL CONJUGATE VACCINES THAT ARE LICENSED IN AT LEAST ONE COUNTRY, ARE BEING TESTED IN PHASE III, OR ARE IN ADVANCED STAGES OF PHASE II DEVELOPMENT

Vaccine	Valency	Pneumococcal Polysaccharides	Carrier Protein	Manufacturer
PnOMPC7	7-valent	4, 6B, 9V, 14, 18C, 19F, 23F	Meningococcal outer-membrane protein complex	Merck Research Laboratories
PnCRM7	7-valent	4, 6B, 9V, 14, 18C, 19F, 23F	CRM_{197} protein	Wyeth Lederle Vaccine and Pediatrics
PnCRM9	9-valent	1, 4, 5, 6B, 9V, 14, 18C, 19F, 23F	CRM_{197} protein	Wyeth Lederle Vaccine and Pediatrics
PncT/D	11-valent	1, 3, 4, 5, 6B, 7F, 9V, 14, 18C, 19F, 23F	A mixture of tetanus and diphtheria toxoids	Aventis Pasteur
Pn-PD	11-valent	1, 3, 4, 5, 6B, 7F, 9V, 14, 18C, 19F, 23F	*Haemophilus influenzae*—protein D	GlaxoSmithKline

in phase III efficacy studies, or are in advanced phase II (safety and immunology) stages. The rationale for choosing among the 7-, 9-, or 11-valent conjugate vaccines is presented in the section on epidemiology in this chapter.

The main target populations for the development of conjugate pneumococcal vaccines are infants and young children. Conjugate pneumococcal vaccines have been studied in these target populations since the early 1990s. Pneumococcal conjugate vaccines have been found to be safe and well tolerated. The reactions reported usually were local ones, such as pain, redness, and swelling at the injection site. The incidence of fever and irritability was somewhat higher than that reported in studies with the Hib conjugate vaccines or hepatitis B vaccines, perhaps because these vaccines represent 7 to 11 separate monovalent vaccines administered together as opposed to the monovalent Hib conjugate vaccine or hepatitis B vaccine. The 7-valent pneumococcal vaccine conjugated to CRM_{197} protein (PnCRM7) was found to be safe even when administered to low-birth-weight and preterm infants.[633]

All conjugate vaccines tested to date were able to elicit a T-cell–dependent immune response in normal infants and toddlers, namely, priming with immunologic memory and maturation of the functional antibody response, as measured by the predominance of IgG1 subclass antibodies, opsonophagocytic activity assays, and antibody avidity assays.[192, 203] The immunogenicity of one vaccine (PnCRM7) also was studied in various high-risk groups. It was immunogenic in children with sickle-cell disease,[508, 516, 703] HIV infection,[379, 380, 391] and allogeneic bone marrow transplants,[479] as well as in Alaska Natives and American Indians.[476] A 9-valent CRM (PnCRM9) pneumococcal vaccine also was immunogenic in children with sickle-cell disease.[261]

Determining the efficacy of pneumococcal vaccines is complex. Pneumococci cause a range of clinical diseases, and, therefore, several end-points of efficacy trials should be considered. The end-points thought to be of most importance in evaluating pneumococcal vaccines have been (1) prevention of invasive pneumococcal disease as defined by isolation of pneumococci from a normally sterile site (e.g., bacteremia or septicemia, meningitis, osteomyelitis/septic arthritis, and soft tissue infections); (2) prevention of mucosal infections such as otitis media, sinusitis, and nonbacteremic pneumonia; and (3) reduction in nasopharyngeal colonization, which in turn results in a reduction in spread of the organisms (the biologic basis for indirect effects, also known as herd immunity). Because the recent increase in antibiotic resistance among *S. pneumoniae* isolates is associated mainly with a limited number of serotypes, the role of conjugate vaccines in the reduction of disease caused by antibiotic-resistant *S. pneumoniae* may be an important end-point. By the end of the first half of the year 2002, only limited data on the efficacy or effectiveness of these conjugate pneumococcal vaccines were available, and most data were for only one vaccine or its variant (namely, PnCRM7 or PnCRM9). However, these data are promising and will be discussed in this chapter in some detail.

Three efficacy studies with the end-point of a reduction in invasive infections were completed by mid-2002, one with PnCRM7 and one with PnCRM9 vaccine. The first study was a prospective double-blind study of 37,868 healthy infants in northern California, to whom either the PnCRM7 vaccine or a control vaccine was administered at 2, 4, 6, and 12 to 15 months of age.[66] The vaccine was 97.4 percent efficacious (95% confidence interval, 82.7 to 99.9%) against invasive disease caused by the serotypes included in the vaccine in fully vaccinated infants and 93.9 percent efficacious (95% confidence interval, 79.6 to 98.5%) in partially vaccinated infants. No evidence of an increase in invasive disease caused by serotypes that were not included in the vaccine was detected, and thus the overall effect was a reduction in total invasive pneumococcal disease by 89.1 percent (95% confidence interval, 73.7 to 95.8%). This trial was the pivotal efficacy one that led to U.S. licensure of the vaccine by the Food and Drug Administration in February 2000 and subsequent licensure in many other countries. Additional analysis[633] has shown that the vaccine was as effective in the subset of low-birth-weight and premature infants as it was in the full study cohort.

A second large-scale efficacy study with the PnCRM7 vaccine was conducted among American Indian (Navajo and White Mountain Apache) children in the United States. This population has rates of invasive pneumococcal infection that are approximately five times those of the general U.S. population.[129, 513] In a double-blinded, community-randomized study, infants and young children aged 2 months to 2 years received the PnCRM7 vaccine or a control vaccine.[515] A total of 8292 infants from 43 communities were enrolled; of these, 8091 lived in 38 communities that were randomized to the pneumococcal or the control vaccine. During the study period, two cases of invasive pneumococcal infection caused by the serotypes included in the vaccine occurred in the vaccine group versus eight in the control group. After controlling for community randomization, the primary efficacy of the vaccine was 76.8 percent (95% confidence interval, 9.4 to 95.1%), and the intent-to-treat efficacy was 86.4 percent (95% confidence interval, 11 to 96.1%). These results are not statistically different from those of the trial in northern California.

A third efficacy study was conducted with the PnCRM9 vaccine among black infants in South Africa. In a double-blinded, randomized, placebo-controlled study, PnCRM9 was administered at the ages of 6, 10, and 14 weeks according to the World Health Organization Expanded Programme on Immunization. The infants were monitored to 2 years of age, and the study was completed by the end of 2001. By mid-2002, only a preliminary analysis was available. The intent-to-treat analysis showed a reduction of 82.5 percent (95% confidence interval, 39.0 to 96.7%) in invasive infections caused by the serotypes included in the vaccine for children not infected with HIV and a reduction of 65.4 percent (95% confidence interval, 23.8 to 85.7%) in children infected with HIV (Klugman, K., and Madhi, S.: Presented at the 3rd International Symposium on Pneumococci and Pneumococcal Diseases, Alaska, May 2002).

Other important studies on the efficacy of various other vaccines against invasive pneumococcal disease are being conducted or will start shortly in developing and developed countries. The results of these studies should be available before the year 2005 and may enable the licensure of additional conjugate vaccines to prevent invasive pneumococcal disease.

Otitis media is caused by various organisms in addition to *S. pneumoniae* (mainly *H. influenzae* [usually untypeable], *M. catarrhalis,* and less frequently, *Streptococcus pyogenes* and enteric bacteria). Therefore, a positive evaluation of conjugate pneumococcal vaccines must demonstrate not only a reduction in disease caused by the pneumococcal serotypes included in the vaccine but also a parallel increase in episodes caused by other pathogens, especially the pneumococci of serotypes not present in the vaccine. The latter were shown to be isolated with increased frequency from the nasopharynx of children vaccinated with conjugate pneumococcal vaccine (the so-called replacement phenomenon), as will be discussed further in the section.

Pneumococci are found in 25 to 50 percent of cases of AOM occurring in children.[74, 352, 452] The serotypes causing otitis media not always are identical to those causing invasive infection, but the most common serotypes found in otitis media worldwide are included in the 7-, 9-, or 11-valent conjugate vaccines. They include serotypes 3, 6B, 9V, 14, 19F, and 23F.[72, 104, 144, 367] Serotypes 6A and 19A also are important causes of otitis media.[144, 193] These two serotypes are not included in the vaccine, but cross-protection of serotype 6A by antibodies to serotype 6B has been demonstrated.[2, 24, 146, 193, 251, 512, 531] The pneumococcal serotypes included in the various vaccine formulations would account for 50 to 85 percent of all serotypes causing otitis media. Assuming 100 percent efficacy of pneumococcal conjugate vaccines against the serotypes included in the vaccines and no increase in otitis media caused by other pneumococcal serotypes or other pathogens, conjugate pneumococcal vaccines could reduce the incidence of all causes of otitis media by at most 10 to 25 percent. The results of four efficacy/effectiveness studies analyzed by the end of the year 2001 confirmed these expectations.

The northern California study, conducted primarily to determine the efficacy of the PnCRM7 conjugate vaccine against invasive pneumococcal infection,[66] also looked at the reduction in the number of clinic visits for otitis media in 18,927 pneumococcal vaccine recipients and 18,941 control meningococcal vaccine recipients at the ages of 2, 4, 6, and 12 to 15 months. During the 30-month follow-up period, a total of 73,041 visits related to otitis media and 52,789 distinct episodes of otitis media had occurred in the study population. Of those, 5451 subjects had frequent episodes of otitis media (three episodes per 6 months or four episodes per 1 year). The pneumococcal vaccine reduced the number of clinically diagnosed otitis media episodes by 7 percent (95% confidence interval, 4.1 to 7.9%). The effectiveness of the PnCRM7 vaccine against frequent otitis media was 9.3 percent (95% confidence interval, 3.0 to 15.1%) when three episodes in 6 months or four in 12 months were counted, and it was 22.8 percent (95% confidence interval, 6.7 to 36.2%) when a frequency of five episodes in 6 months or six in 12 months were examined. Children who received the pneumococcal conjugate vaccine were 20.1 percent (95% confidence interval, 1.5 to 35.2%) less likely to require placement of a pressure-equalizing tube than were controls. This study was not designed to evaluate the effect of conjugate pneumococcal vaccine on otitis media as a primary outcome, and, therefore, no attempts were made to standardize or validate the clinical diagnoses of otitis media. Hence, the study was able to assess only the effect of PnCRM7 vaccine on otitis media as it is diagnosed and managed in the routine clinical setting. As a result, the authors were not able to examine the efficacy of the vaccine against otitis media caused by pneumococcal serotypes included in the vaccine, except for cultures obtained from spontaneously draining ears. In 23 children, culture of fluid from spontaneously draining ears was positive for pneumococci of the vaccine serotypes, with a 66 percent calculated efficacy against disease caused by serotypes included in the vaccine. However, its efficacy against clinically diagnosed otitis media indicated that the vaccine reduced morbidity attributed to otitis media and medical services used for the management of clinical otitis.

A second study, conducted in Finland, looked at the efficacy of PnCRM7 vaccine against AOM in general and more specifically against otitis media caused by serotypes in the conjugate pneumococcal vaccine under study.[193] A total of 1662 infants were enrolled and randomized in a double-blind manner to receive either the PnCRM7 vaccine or a hepatitis B vaccine at the ages of 2, 4, 6, and 12 months. The clinical diagnosis of AOM was based on predefined criteria, and bacteriologic diagnosis was based on culture of middle ear fluid obtained by myringotomy. The children were monitored through 24 months of age. A total of 2596 episodes of AOM occurred in children who had received three doses of vaccine by the time they reached 6 months of age. The efficacy of the vaccine in reducing cases caused by the serotypes included in the vaccine was 57 percent (95% confidence interval, 46 to 67%). The PnCRM7 vaccine also provided cross-protection against serotypes 6A and 19A. The efficacy of the vaccine in reducing all culture-confirmed pneumococcal infections (including serotypes not included in the vaccine) was 34 percent (95% confidence interval, 24 to 45%). However, the vaccine was not effective against nonvaccine pneumococcal serotypes that are not cross-reactive with the ones included in the vaccine. The vaccine also was ineffective against otitis media caused by *H. influenzae* and *M. catarrhalis,* and a trend toward an increase in the incidence of otitis media among vaccinated children (replacement disease phenomenon) was noted. Thus, the overall high protection provided against the serotypes included in the vaccine was offset partially by an increase in the number of otitis media episodes caused by other serotypes of pneumococci and other pathogens. The overall reduction in the number of episodes of AOM of any cause in the pneumococcal vaccine group was 6 percent (95% confidence interval, –4 to 16%). This difference did not reach statistical significance, but it was within the expected range when all theoretic considerations listed earlier were taken into account, and it also was strikingly similar to the 7 percent reduction in the number of cases of otitis media observed in the California study.[66] In addition, similar to the California study, by the age of 4 to 5 years, the vaccinated subjects had undergone tympanostomy tube placement at a rate that was reduced by 39 percent (95% confidence interval, 4 to 61%) when compared with controls.[527]

A third study was conducted by the same Finish group in parallel with the study just described, but this time with a different 7-valent vaccine (serotypes 4, 6B, 9V, 14, 18C, 19F, and 23F, conjugated to the meningococcal outer-membrane protein complex [OMPC]—PnOMPC7).[375, 376] In this randomized, double-blind, controlled trial, 1666 children were randomized to receive either PnOMPC7 or hepatitis B vaccine at 2, 4, and 6 months of age. At 12 months of age, approximately 22 percent of the PnOMPC7 conjugate vaccine recipients received a nonconjugate 23-valent polysaccharide vaccine as a booster at 12 months, and the others received a fourth dose of PnOMPC7. Follow-up continued through 24 months of age. The methodology was similar to that described earlier for the PnCRM7 conjugate vaccine, including cultures for the diagnosis of otitis media episodes. A total of 2709 otitis media episodes occurred in evaluable children who had completed their three-dose schedule, 360 of which were caused by pneumococci of the serotypes included in the vaccine. The efficacy of the vaccine in reducing the number of cases of otitis media caused by the serotypes included in the vaccine was 56 percent (95% confidence interval, 44 to 66%). In reducing the number of all pneumococcal otitis media episodes, the efficacy was 25 percent (95% confidence interval, 11 to 37%). However, no overall reduction in the number of episodes of otitis media was seen because of an increase in the number of episodes caused by non–vaccine serotype pneumococci and other nonpneumococcal organisms (replacement disease).

The results of the two studies in Finland and the study in northern California are strikingly consistent. They all have shown that (1) the efficacy of the two conjugate vaccines tested thus far in the prevention of otitis media caused by pneumococcal serotypes included in the vaccine was more than 50 percent and that efficacy on the order of magnitude observed for invasive infections (i.e., 90%) cannot be achieved against otitis media, (2) replacement otitis media with pneumococci not included in the vaccine and other organisms such as *H. influenzae* and *M. catarrhalis* occurs and reduces the overall efficacy of the pneumococcal conjugate vaccines against otitis media, and (3) better protection is provided against episodes of more severe otitis media and recurrent otitis media than against simple otitis media. The more severe and recurrent otitis media episodes often are associated with pneumococcal serotypes 6B, 9V, 14, 19F, and 23F, which tend to persist both in the nasopharynx and in the middle ear. These serotypes also tend to be more resistant to antibiotics.[144, 354]

A fourth study was conducted in toddlers attending daycare centers in southern Israel. In this double-blind study, the efficacy of a 9-valent CRM conjugate pneumococcal vaccine (PnCRM9) in reducing nasopharyngeal carriage of *S. pneumoniae* and respiratory infections was compared with that of a control vaccine. This study showed, in conjunction with the extensive reduction in carriage of the serotypes included in the vaccine, especially serotypes 6B, 9V, 14, 19F, and 23F,[142, 146, 161] a 17 percent (95% confidence interval, −0.2 to 33%) reduction in the number of cases of otitis media and a 20 percent (95% confidence interval, 14 to 36%) reduction in antibiotic use for otitis media.[161] These findings support the notion that conjugate pneumococcal vaccines can reduce the morbidity of otitis media, not only by reducing the number of episodes or reducing the severity of otitis media in general but also by selectively reducing otitis media in high-risk groups such as attendees at daycare centers.

Protection against pneumococcal pneumonia by the conjugate pneumococcal vaccines was shown in the PnCRM7 vaccine efficacy trial conducted in northern California.[66, 68] However, pneumococcal pneumonia cases are only infrequently associated with bacteremia, and the PnCRM7 vaccine should provide protection against these invasive episodes to the same degree as all other invasive episodes. Because most cases of pneumonia are nonbacteremic, the great majority remain without a clear bacteriologic diagnosis. In these cases, the role of *S. pneumoniae* can be demonstrated indirectly if the use of a vaccine significantly reduces the occurrence of pneumonia cases. Thus, the conjugate pneumococcal vaccines can be used as surrogates to more accurately estimate the proportion of pneumonia attributable to vaccine serotype pneumococci.

In the northern California study conducted on 37,868 infants given the PnCRM7 vaccine, all clinically diagnosed episodes of pneumonia identified through hospital, outpatient, and emergency records were collected.[68] In total, 3711 clinical episodes of pneumonia that occurred before the children reached the age of 3.5 years were identified; the efficacy of the PnCRM7 vaccine in reducing disease (intent-to-treat analysis) was 6.0 percent (95% confidence interval, 1.5 to 11.0%). Of the 3711 clinical episodes, a chest radiograph was obtained in 2249 episodes, and among these, vaccine efficacy was 8.9 percent (95% confidence interval, 0.9 to 16.3%). Of the 2249 children in whom a chest radiograph was obtained, 737 had a positive chest radiograph (defined as parenchymal infiltrates, consolidation or effusion [or both], but not perihilar infiltrates alone). In these 737 patients, efficacy was 22.7 percent (95% confidence interval, 8.7 to 34.5%). These findings have some limitations because they were not derived from a study in which the primary objective was to evaluate protection against pneumonia. However, the findings suggest two important points: (1) many cases of clinically and radiologically proven pneumonia in children are caused by *S. pneumoniae* by virtue of the fact that vaccination was associated with a marked reduction in not only the "classic" lobar pneumonia usually associated with *S. pneumoniae* but also clinical pneumonia, with negative or minimal findings on the chest radiograph; and (2) the 22.7 percent efficacy observed for pneumonia with radiologically documented findings suggests that at least in the developed world where Hib vaccines are used widely, *S. pneumoniae* causes a high proportion of pneumonia with parenchymal infiltrates.

Similar findings were presented from South Africa in May 2002 (Klugman, K., and Madhi, S.: Presented at the 3rd International Symposium on Pneumococci and Pneumococcal Diseases, Alaska), where the administration of three doses of PnCRM9 at the ages of 6, 10, and 14 weeks reduced the incidence of radiologically proven pneumonia by 22.1 percent (95% confidence interval, 0.1 to 39.5%) in children who were not infected with HIV.

Additional supportive evidence that *S. pneumoniae* may play a more important role in respiratory infections than usually is attributed to this pathogen can be derived from a study in southern Israel among toddlers aged 12 to 35 months who attended daycare centers.[161] In this study, 263 children were randomized to receive either PnCRM9 vaccine or a control vaccine (meningococcus CRM conjugate) in a double-blind fashion. The children were monitored for 5556 child-months. A total of 906 episodes of non–otitis media upper respiratory tract infection were reported for an efficacy estimate of 15 percent (95% confidence interval, 4 to 24%); 596 episodes of lower respiratory tract problems, including bronchiolitis, cough, and pneumonia occurred, and the efficacy of pneumococcal vaccine was 16 percent (95% confidence interval, 2 to 28%). For these two clinical illness categories, children received a total of 3678 days of antibiotics. A reduction of 10 percent in antibiotic days for upper respiratory tract infections was achieved, as was a reduction

TABLE 90–5 ■ STUDIES ON THE EFFECT OF CONJUGATE PNEUMOCOCCAL VACCINE ON CARRIAGE OF *STREPTOCOCCUS PNEUMONIAE* AND ANTIBIOTIC-RESISTANT *S. PNEUMONIAE*

Author	Conjugate Vaccine (Valence)	Site	Age (mo) at Vaccination	Reduction in Serotypes Included in the Vaccine	Reduction in Resistant Pneumococci	Increase in Non-Vaccine Serotypes
Dagan[157]	PnOMPC7	Israel	12–18	Yes	Yes	No
Dagan[159]	PnT; PnD (4-valent)	Israel	2, 4, 6	Yes	Yes	+/–
Obaro[510]	PnCRM5	The Gambia	2, 3, 4	Yes	ND	Yes
Kristinsson[407]	PnT; PnD (8-valent)	Iceland	3, 4, 6	Yes	ND	Yes
Mbelle[466]	PnCRM9	South Africa	1.5, 2.5, 3.5	Yes	Yes	Yes
Edwards[188]	PnCRM9	USA	2, 4, 6, 12	Yes	ND	Yes
Dagan[162]	PnT/D (11-valent)	Israel	2, 4, 6, 12	Yes	Yes	No
Dagan[142,146]	PnCRM9	Israel	12–35	Yes	Yes	Yes
O'Brien[512]	PnCRM7	USA (Native American)	2, 4, 6, 12–15	Yes	ND	Yes
Kilpi[376]	PnCRM7	Finland	2, 4, 6, 12	Yes	ND	ND

PnOMPC, 7-valent pneumococcal vaccine conjugated to the outer-membrane complex of *Neisseria meningitidis* B; PnT, pneumococcal vaccine conjugated to tetanus toxoid; PnD, pneumococcal vaccine conjugated to diphtheria toxoid; PnT/D, pneumococcal vaccine conjugated to a mixture of tetanus and diphtheria toxoid; PnCRM, pneumococcal vaccine conjugated to CRM_{197} protein (PnCRM5, 5-valent; PnCRM7, 7-valent; PnCRM9, 9-valent).

of 47 percent for lower respiratory tract problems in the pneumococcal vaccine group ($p < .001$ versus control children). The incidence of bronchiolitis and pneumonia, often regarded as viral in that age group, was decreased significantly by the administration of this conjugate pneumococcal vaccine, thus suggesting that *S. pneumoniae* plays a role as a pathogen or co-pathogen for these entities.

As stated earlier, control of nasopharyngeal carriage of pneumococci is the key to managing pneumococcal disease and person-to-person spread of *S. pneumoniae.* The nonconjugate pneumococcal vaccines do not have a significant effect on carriage of *S. pneumoniae* in children and adults.[157, 453] In contrast, the conjugate vaccines do have a significant effect on carriage.* Table 90–5 shows the studies conducted and published thus far to document the effect of pneumococcal vaccines on carriage of *S. pneumoniae.* Despite variations in the nature of the conjugate vaccines, populations, and the ages at which the vaccines were administered, a significant reduction in carriage of the serotypes included in the vaccine clearly was observed in all studies. However, in most of the studies, a "replacement" phenomenon occurred: an increase in the carriage of *S. pneumoniae* serotypes not included in the vaccine was observed in conjunction with a decrease in the carriage of serotypes included in the vaccine. Although this replacement phenomenon is remarkable, its clinical significance is not clear. In theory, such a phenomenon could be simply an artifact of "unmasking," in which nonvaccine serotypes are more readily detected in vaccinees than controls because the vaccine serotypes are not present. However, the use of mathematic modeling and testing in controlled vaccine studies strongly suggests that a true "replacement phenomenon" does exist in which non–vaccine-type pneumococci truly are replacing vaccine-type pneumococci.[441] This suggestion is supported by the observation of an increase in the incidence of otitis media caused by organisms not included in the vaccine after vaccination with PnCRM7 and PnOMPC7 in Finland.[193, 375]

The reduction in nasopharyngeal carriage of vaccine serotypes of pneumococci is important because it certainly will reduce the spread of these serotypes. Two studies in different settings clearly have shown the existence of this phenomenon. In one double-blind comparative study conducted in southern Israel, toddlers attending daycare centers were vaccinated with a PnCRM9 vaccine or a control vaccine.[143] In this study, attendees at daycare centers and their younger siblings who stayed home were monitored after vaccination of the daycare attendees. A marked reduction in vaccine-type pneumococcal carriage was seen in the young siblings of those who were vaccinated with the PnCRM9 vaccine when compared with siblings of the controls.[143]

In a second study, Navajo and White Mountain Apache children younger than 2 years of age were randomized according to their community of residence to receive either PnCRM7 or meningococcus C conjugate vaccine. Nasopharyngeal swabs were cultured for *S. pneumoniae* from 598 nonimmunized infants residing in both vaccinated (by PnCRM7 vaccine) and control communities.[511] A 24 percent reduction in carriage of vaccine-associated serotypes was noted in vaccinated infants residing in the PnCRM7 communities versus those living in control vaccine communities. The reduction was found both in infants who lived with a PnCRM7-vaccinated sibling and in those who did not have direct contact with a PnCRM7-vaccinated child. This study demonstrated the indirect protective effect of pneumococcal vaccination on those in the household.

By mid-2001, only one conjugate pneumococcal vaccine had been licensed: the 7-valent pneumococcal CRM vaccine, which has been licensed in more than 30 countries. The vaccine's tradename is Prevnar in the United States and Prevenar in other countries. In the United States, the Advisory Committee on Immunization Practices and the Committee on Infectious Diseases of the American Academy of Pediatrics both have recommended inclusion of PnCRM7 in the routine childhood vaccination schedule.[13, 553] Although the specific wordings of these two recommendations differ slightly in their strength of recommendation for catch-up schedules and high-risk groups, the overall recommendations are as follows: the vaccine should be used for all children aged 2 to 23 months and for children aged 24 to 59 months who are at increased risk for acquiring pneumococcal disease (e.g., children with sickle-cell disease, HIV infection, and other immunocompromising or chronic medical conditions); the vaccine also should be considered for all other children aged 24 to 59 months, with priority given to those aged 24 to 35 months; to children who are of Alaskan Native, American Indian, and African American descent; and to children who attend daycare centers.

*See references 142, 146, 157, 159, 162, 188, 407, 466, 510, 512.

Widespread use of the vaccine in the United States began in the first half of the year 2000. This widespread use has provided additional data on the safety of PnCRM7. Furthermore, preliminary reports from 2001 strongly suggest that the incidence of invasive pneumococcal disease is decreasing sharply in infants and toddlers and even in their household contacts.[67, 632, 728]

Because most antibiotic-resistant *S. pneumoniae* strains belong to only a few serotypes that are included in the conjugate pneumococcal vaccines or are related to these serotypes (see the section on epidemiology and microbiology), vaccines are expected to reduce disease, carriage, and spread of antibiotic-resistant *S. pneumoniae* and may have an impact on the use of antibiotics. Indeed, in all vaccine studies that investigated the effect of conjugate vaccines on nasopharyngeal carriage of antibiotic-resistant *S. pneumoniae,* a reduction in carriage of such strains was observed[142, 157, 159, 162, 466] (Table 90–5). Furthermore, the use of conjugate vaccines reduced the use of antibiotics in two prospective double-blinded studies. In a study conducted in northern California, administration of the PnCRM7 vaccine reduced the use of antibiotics by 5.3 percent in patients given vaccines versus controls; the reduction was 5.0 percent for drugs generally used as first-line agents (such as amoxicillin and ampicillin) and 11.2 percent for those often used as second-line agents (cephalosporins, amoxicillin-clavulanate, and azithromycin) (Black, S., Shinefeld, H.: Presented at the 19th Annual Meeting of the European Society for Pediatric Infectious Diseases, Istanbul, Turkey, April 26 to 28, 2001). In another study performed in toddlers attending daycare centers in southern Israel, the PnCRM9 conjugate vaccine reduced the use of antibiotics in vaccine recipients versus controls by 20 percent,[161] in parallel with the reduction in carriage of antibiotic-resistant *S. pneumoniae* and respiratory diseases. The reduction in both those factors may contribute to reducing antibiotic resistance in the community. However, the overall effect remains to be determined.

Preliminary data from the Centers for Disease Control and Prevention indicate that in the United States, a dramatic reduction in invasive infection caused by pneumococci included in the PnPCV7 vaccine occurred in 2001 in comparison to the years 1999 to 2000. This dramatic reduction was associated with a parallel reduction in invasive infection caused by penicillin-nonsusceptible and macrolide-resistant pneumococci (Whitney, C., and Stephens, D.: Presented at the 3rd International Symposium on Pneumococci and Pneumococcal Diseases, Alaska, May 2002). Longer follow-up is needed to determine whether the reduction will be of long-term duration.

Although invasive infections are the most dramatic part of the pneumococcal disease spectrum, respiratory infections such as otitis media occur far more frequently.[436] In a study investigating current estimates of pneumococcal disease burden, clinical outcome, and vaccine efficacy, researchers estimated that for each annual U.S. birth cohort, routine use of a 7-valent vaccine could prevent 12,000 cases of pneumococcal bacteremia and meningitis, 53,000 cases of pneumococcal pneumonia, and more than 1 million clinical cases of otitis media per year.[436]

Pneumonia has a greater impact globally than does otitis media or even invasive infections do because of the high mortality rate in children in the developing world.[61, 278, 431] However, it is more difficult to study because it does not occur as commonly as does otitis media and bacteriologic documentation rarely is available for this entity in children.

Thus, the protection conferred by the conjugate pneumococcal vaccines with regard to reduction in otitis media, pneumonia, and other mucosal infections, if proven by additional studies, could have an even greater impact on the burden of disease than on prevention of invasive infections.

Potential Future Vaccines and Future Strategies

Studies have been conducted to determine whether immunization of pregnant women with pneumococcal conjugate or nonconjugate vaccines can protect their offspring from pneumococcal diseases during their first few months of life, before they achieve immunity through active vaccination. This suggestion is based on studies that have shown that naturally acquired IgG antibodies readily are transferred transplacentally to the fetus,[20, 116, 130] and clinical studies of maternal immunization with pneumococcal polysaccharide vaccines have resulted in similar observations.[421, 517, 629] In experimental studies, a correlation between higher concentrations of vaccine-specific antibodies at birth and greater response to specific serotypes after subsequent active immunization in the offspring of vaccine recipients has been demonstrated.[416, 440] In one study, administration of a conjugate pneumococcal vaccine to pregnant women[489] resulted not only in efficient transplacental passage of vaccine-induced pneumococcal antibodies (mainly of the IgG1 subtype) but also in prevention of pneumococcal carriage in the offspring of vaccinated mothers. Thus, maternal immunization during pregnancy may prove to be a successful strategy to protect against pneumococcal infection in early infancy, but additional serotypes need to be included in these vaccines.

Adding more polysaccharide capsular antigens to the conjugate pneumococcal vaccines to increase serotype coverage is being investigated. In addition, much effort is being invested in combining the present conjugate pneumococcal vaccine with other childhood vaccines to be given in the same syringe in order to reduce the number of injections needed to immunize infants.

Despite the great potential benefit of the pneumococcal conjugate vaccines, they have two important limitations: inclusion of a limited number of serotypes, which results not only in noncoverage of some other important serotypes causing disease but also in potential replacement disease by serotypes not related to the vaccine, and their high price as a result of complex production and quality control processes.

Many of the proteins mentioned in the section on pathogenesis appear to be suitable antigens for candidate vaccines, and such vaccines that include proteins immunogenic in infants are being developed. The main drawback of protein vaccines is the antigenic variability of many pneumococcal proteins. However, some of the most important proteins considered essential for bacterial virulence have epitopes that are common to many pneumococcal strains. Among these proteins are pneumolysin, PspA, and PsaA.[90] The plasma concentrations of antibodies to these proteins increase with age and are associated strongly with pneumococcal exposure, whether by carriage or infection such as AOM.[565] One suggestion is that antibodies to PsaA may prevent pneumococcal otitis media,[567] but such prevention has not been confirmed. Preliminary studies show that PspA and PsaA given as single antigens or a mixture of antigens are immunogenic and protective in mice and safe and immunogenic in humans.[499] Further studies in humans were expected to begin in 2002. Other candidate protein vaccines are being investigated in animals, but as of mid-2002, they had not yet been administered to humans. An additional novel approach to providing immunization against *S. pneumoniae* infection is to immunize subjects with killed whole-cell *S. pneumoniae* intranasally with an adjuvant. This approach was studied in animal models and showed promising results.[458]

During the next decade, other pneumococcal vaccine prototypes probably will be discovered and developed. Whether they will equal or surpass the beneficial effects of the pneumococcal conjugate vaccines remains to be seen.

REFERENCES

1. Aaberge, I. S., Eng, J., Lermark, G., et al.: Virulence of *Streptococcus pneumoniae* in mice: A standardized method for preparation and frozen storage of the experimental bacterial inoculum. Microb. Pathol. *18*:141–152, 1995.
2. Aaberge, I. S., Lovik, M., Hoogerhout, P., et al.: Pneumococcal type 6B conjugates differ in dependency on adjuvant and booster dose, and induce protection against type 6A as well as type 6. Poster 25. Presented at Pneumococcal Vaccines for the World 1998 Conference, Washington, D.C., 1998, p. 66.
3. Aaberge, I. S., Michaelsen, T. E., and Heier, H. E.: IgG subclass antibody responses to pneumococcal polysaccharide vaccine in splenectomized, otherwise normal, individuals. Scand. J. Immunol. *31*:711–716, 1990.
4. Abbasi, S., Orlicek, S. L., Almohsen, I., et al.: Septic arthritis and osteomyelitis caused by penicillin and cephalosporin-resistant *Streptococcus pneumoniae* in a children's hospital. Pediatr. Infect. Dis. J. *15*:78–83, 1996.
5. Abdel-Haq, N., Abuhammour, W., Asmar, B., et al.: Nasopharyngeal colonization with *Streptococcus pneumoniae* in children receiving trimethoprim-sulfamethoxazole prophylaxis. Pediatr. Infect. Dis. J. *18*:647–649, 1999.
6. Acute respiratory infections in under-fives: 5 million deaths a year. Lancet *2*:699–701, 1985.
7. Adamou, J. E., Heinrichs, J. H., Erwin, A. L., et al.: Identification and characterization of a novel family of pneumococcal proteins that are protective against sepsis. Infect. Immun. *69*:949–958, 2001.
8. Adegbola, R. A., Falade, A. G., Sam, B. E., et al.: The etiology of pneumonia in malnourished and well-nourished Gambian children. Pediatr. Infect. Dis. J. *13*:975–982, 1994.
9. Ahmed, A., Jafri, H., and Lutsar, I.: Pharmacodynamics of vancomycin for the treatment of experimental penicillin- and cephalosporin-resistant pneumococcal meningitis. Antimicrob. Agents Chemother. *43*:876–881, 1999.
10. Alario, A. J., Nelson, E. W., and Shapiro, E. D.: Blood cultures in the management of febrile outpatients late found to have bacteremia. J. Pediatr. *115*:195–199, 1989.
11. Alcantara, R. B., Preheim, L. C., and Gentry-Nielsen, M. J.: Pneumolysin-induced complement depletion during experimental pneumococcal bacteremia. Infect. Immun. *69*:3569–3575, 2001.
12. Alpern, E. R., Alessandrini, E. A., Bell, L. M., et al.: Occult bacteremia from a pediatric emergency department: Current prevalence, time to detection, and outcome. Pediatrics *106*:505–511, 2000.
13. American Academy of Pediatrics. Committee on Infectious Diseases. Policy Statement: Recommendations for the prevention of pneumococcal infections, including the use of pneumococcal conjugate vaccine (Prevnar), pneumococcal polysaccharide vaccine, and antibiotic prophylaxis. Pediatrics *106*:362–366, 2000.
14. American Academy of Pediatrics: *In* Pickering, L. K. (ed.): 2000 Red Book: Report of the Committee on Infectious Diseases. 25th ed. Elk Grove Village, IL, American Academy of Pediatrics, 2000, pp. 66–67.
15. American Academy of Pediatrics: *In* Pickering, L. K. (ed.): 2000 Red Book: Report of the Committee on Infectious Diseases. 25th ed. Elk Grove Village, IL, American Academy of Pediatrics, 2000, pp. 452–460.
16. American Academy of Pediatrics: *In* Pickering, L. K. (ed.): 2000 Red Book: Report of the Committee on Infectious Diseases. 25th ed. Elk Grove Village, IL, American Academy of Pediatrics, 2000, pp. 729–742.
17. Amsden, G. W.: Pneumococcal macrolide resistance—myth or reality? J. Antimicrob. Chemother. *44*:1–6, 1999.
18. Anderson, B., Porras, O., Hanson, L. A., et al.: Inhibition of attachment of *Streptococcus pneumoniae* and *Haemophilus influenzae* by human milk and receptor oligosaccharides. J. Infect. Dis. *153*:232–237, 1986.
19. Anderson, D. C., Schmalstieg, F. C., Finegold, M. J., et al.: The severe and moderate phenotypes of heritable Mac-1, LFA-1 deficiency: Their quantitative definition and relation to leukocyte dysfunction and clinical features. J. Infect. Dis. *152*:668–689, 1985.
20. Anderson, P., Porcelli, S., and Pichichero, M.: Natural maternal and cord serum antibodies to pneumococcal serotypes 6A, 14, 19F and 23F polysaccharides. Pediatr. Infect. Dis. J. *11*:677–679, 1992.
21. Andiman, W. A., Mezger, J., and Shapiro, E.: Invasive bacterial infections in children born to women infected with human immunodeficiency virus type 1. J. Pediatr. *124*:846–852, 1994.
22. Anniansson, G., Alm, B., Andersson, B., et al.: Nasopharyngeal colonization during the first year of life. J. Infect. Dis. *165*(Suppl.):38–42, 1992.
23. Aniansson, G., Alm, B., Andersson, B., et al.: A prospective cohort study on breast-feeding and otitis media in Swedish infants. Pediatr. Infect. Dis. J. *13*:183–188, 1994.
24. Anttila, M., Eklund, C., Eskola, J., and Kayhty, H.: Functional cross-reactivity of antibodies to pneumococcal capsular polysaccharides of serotypes 6A and 6B. Poster 16. Presented at Pneumococcal Vaccines for the World 1998 Conference, Washington, D.C., 1998, p. 66.
25. Anttila, M., Soininen, A., Nieminem, T., et al.: Contribution of serotype specific IgG concentration, subclass ratio, and relative avidity to opsonophagocytic activity against *Streptococcus pneumoniae*. Abstract 58. Presented at Pneumococcal Vaccines for the World 1998 Conference, Washington, D.C., 1998.
26. Anttila, M., Voutilainen, M., Jäntti, V., et al.: Contribution of serotype-specific IgG concentration, IgG subclasses, and relative antibody avidity of opsonophagocytic activity against *Streptococcus pneumoniae*. Clin. Exp. Immunol. *118*:402–407, 1999.
27. Appelbaum, P. C.: Epidemiology and in vitro susceptibility of drug-resistant *Streptococcus pneumoniae*. Pediatr. Infect. Dis. J. *15*:932–934, 1996.
28. Appelbaum, P. C., Bhamjee, A., Scragg, J. N., et al.: *Streptococcus pneumoniae* resistant to penicillin and chloramphenicol. Lancet *2*:995–997, 1977.
29. Arason, V. A., Kristinsson, K. G., Sigurdsson, J. A., et al.: Do antimicrobials increase the carriage rate of penicillin resistant pneumococci in children? Cross sectional prevalence study. B. M. J. *313*:387–391, 1996.
30. Arditi, M., Mason, E. O., Bradley, J. S., et al.: Three-year multicenter surveillance of pneumococcal meningitis in children: Clinical characteristics, and outcome related to penicillin susceptibility and dexamethasone use. Pediatrics *102*:1087–1097, 1998.
31. Arnold, K. E., Leggiadro, R. J., Breiman, R. F., et al.: Risk factors for carriage of drug-resistant *Streptococcus pneumoniae* among children in Memphis, Tennessee. J. Pediatr. *128*:757–764, 1996.
32. Arpadi, S. M., Back, S., O'Brien, J., and Janoff, E. N.: Antibodies to pneumococcal capsular polysaccharides in children with human immuno-deficiency virus infection given polyvalent pneumococcal vaccine. J. Pediatr. *125*:77–79, 1994.
33. Arrecubieta, C., Lopez, R., and Garcia, E.: Molecular characterization of cap3a, a gene from the operon required for the synthesis of the capsule of *Streptococcus pneumoniae* type 3: Sequencing of mutations responsible for the unencapsulated phenotype and localization of the capsular cluster on the pneumococcal chromosome. J. Bacteriol. *176*:6375–6383, 1994.
34. Arva, E., and Andersson, B.: Induction of phagocyte-stimulating and Th1-promoting cytokines by in vitro stimulation of human peripheral blood mononuclear cells with *Streptococcus pneumoniae*. Scand. J. Immunol. *49*:417–423, 1999.
35. Attwood, J. T., Williams, Y., and Feighery, C.: Impaired IgG responses in a child with homozygous C2 deficiency and recurrent pneumococcal septicaemia. Acta Paediatr. *90*:99–101, 2001.
36. Auer, M., Pfister, L. A., Leppert, D., et al.: Effects of clinically used antioxidants in experimental pneumococcal meningitis. J. Infect. Dis. *182*:347–350, 2000.
37. Austrian, R.: Pneumonia in the later years. J. Am. Geriatr. Soc. *29*:481–489, 1981.
38. Austrian, R.: The enduring pneumococcus: Unfinished business and opportunities for the future. *In* Tomasz A. (ed.): *Streptococcus pneumoniae:* Molecular Biology and Mechanisms of Disease. Larchmont, NY, Mary Ann Liebert, Inc., 2000, pp. 3–7.
39. Austrian, R., and Collins, P.: Importance of carbon dioxide in the isolation of pneumococci. J. Bacteriol. *92*:1281–1284, 1966.
40. Austrian, R., and Gold, J.: Pneumococcal bacteremia with a special reference to bacteremic pneumococcal pneumonia. Ann. Intern. Med. *60*:759–776, 1964.
41. Austrian, R., Howie, V. M., and Ploussard, J. H.: The bacteriology of pneumococcal otitis media. Johns Hopkins Med. J. *14*:104–111, 1977.
42. Avery, O. T.: Chemoimmunological studies on conjugated carbohydrate proteins: II. Immunological specificity of synthetic sugar-protein antigens. J. Exp. Med. *50*:533–550, 1929.
43. Azoulay-Dupuis, E., Rieux, V., and Muffat-Joly, M.: Relationship between capsular type, penicillin susceptibility, and virulence of human *Streptococcus pneumoniae* isolates in mice. Antimicrob. Agents Chemother. *44*:1575–1577, 2000.
44. Baba, H., Kawamura, I., Kohda, C., et al.: Essential role of domain 4 of pneumolysin from *Streptococcus pneumoniae* in cytolytic activity as determined by truncated proteins. Biochem. Biophys. Res. Commun. *281*:37–44, 2001.
45. Bachur, R., and Harper, M. B.: Reevaluation of outpatients with *Streptococcus pneumoniae* bacteremia. Pediatrics *105*:502–509, 2000.
46. Baer, M., Vuento, R., and Vesikari, T.: Increase in bacteraemic pneumococcal infections in children. Lancet *345*:661, 1995.
47. Balachandran, P., Hollingshead, S. K., Paton, J. C., and Briles, D. E.: The autolytic enzyme LytA of *Streptococcus pneumoniae* is not responsible for releasing pneumolysin. J. Bacteriol. *183*:3108–3116, 2001.
48. Ball, P.: Therapy for pneumococcal infection at the millennium: Doubts and certainties. Am. J. Med. *107*(Suppl.):77–85, 1999.
49. Baltz, R. H., Norris, F. H., Matsushima, P., et al.: DNA sequence sampling of the *Streptococcus pneumoniae* genome to identify novel targets for antibiotic development. Microb. Drug Resist. *4*:1–9, 1998.

50. Baquero, F., and Loza, E.: Antibiotic resistance of microorganisms involved in ear, nose and throat infections. Pediatr. Infect. Dis. J. *13*(Suppl.):9–14, 1994.
51. Baraff, L. J., Bass, J. W., Fleisher, G. R., et al.: Practice guideline for the management of infants and children 0–36 months of age with fever without source. Pediatrics *92*:1–12, 1993.
52. Bardley, J. S., Kaplan, S. L., Tan, T. Q., et al.: Pediatric pneumococcal bone and joint infections. Pediatrics *102*:1376–1382, 1998.
53. Barry, B., Gehanno, P., Blumen, M., and Boucot, I.: Clinical outcome of acute otitis media caused by pneumococci with decreased susceptibility to penicillin. Scand. J. Infect. Dis. *26*:446–452, 1994.
54. Bartlett, J. G., and Mundy, L. M.: Community-acquired pneumonia. N. Engl. J. Med. *333*:1618, 1995.
55. Bass, J. W., Steele, R. W., Wittler, R. R., et al.: Antimicrobial treatment of occult bacteremia: A multicenter cooperative study. Pediatr. Infect. Dis. J. *12*:466–473, 1993.
56. Bauchner, H., Leventhal, J. M., and Shapiro, E. D.: Studies of breast-feeding and infections: How good is the evidence? J. A. M. A. *256*:887–892, 1996.
57. Becken, E. T., Daly, K. A., Lindgreen, B. R., et al.: Low cord blood pneumococcal antibody concentrations predict more episodes of otitis media. Arch. Otolaryngol. Head Neck Surg. *127*:517–522, 2001.
58. Bedos, J. P., Rolin, O., Bouanchaud, D. H., et al.: Relationship between virulence and resistance to antibiotics in pneumococci. Contribution of experimental data obtained in an animal model. Pathol. Biol. (Paris) *39*:984–990, 1991.
59. Bennett, N. M., Buffington, J., and LaForce, F. M.: Pneumococcal bacteremia in Monroe County, New York. Am. J. Public Health *82*:1513–1516, 1992.
60. Berman, S.: Otitis media in developing countries. Pediatrics *96*:126–131, 1995.
61. Berman, S., and Mcintosh, K.: Selective primary health care: Strategies for control of disease in developing world. Acute respiratory infections. Rev. Infect. Dis. *7*:674–691, 1985.
62. Bernstein, L. J., Krieger, B. Z., Novick, B., et al.: Bacterial infection in the acquired immunodeficiency syndrome of children. Pediatr. Infect. Dis. J. *4*:472–475, 1985.
63. Biedel, C. S.: Modification of recurrent otitis media by short-term sulfonamide therapy. Am. J. Dis. Child. *132*:681–683, 1978.
64. Bjornson, A. B., Falletta, J. M., Verter, J. I., et al.: Serotype-specific immunoglobulin G antibody responses to pneumococcal polysaccharide vaccine in children with sickle cell anemia: Effects of continued penicillin prophylaxis. J. Pediatr. *129*:828–835, 1996.
65. Black, S., Shinefield, H., Elvin, L., and Schwalbe, J.: Pneumococcal epidemiology in childhood in a large HMO population. Abstract 1031. Pediatr. Res. *35*:174, 1994.
66. Black, S., Shinefield, H., Fireman, B., et al.: Efficacy, safety and immunogenicity of heptavalent pneumococcal conjugate vaccine in children. Pediatr. Infect. Dis. J. *19*:187–195, 2000.
67. Black, S., Shinefield, H., Hansen, J., et al.: Post-licensure evaluation of the effectiveness of seven valent pneumococcal conjugate vaccine. Pediatr. Infect. Dis. J. *20*:1105–1107, 2001.
68. Black, S., Shinefield, H., and Ling, S.: Efficacy against pneumonia of heptavalent conjugate pneumococcal vaccine (Wyeth Lederle) in 37,868 infants and children: Expanded data analysis including duration of protection. Presented at the 20th Annual Meeting of the European Society for Paediatric Infectious Diseases (ESPID), Vilnius, Lithuania, 2002, p. 127.
69. Block, S. L.: Causative pathogens, antibiotic resistance and therapeutic considerations in acute otitis media. Pediatr. Infect. Dis. J. *16*:449–456, 1997.
70. Block, S. L., Harrison, C. J., Hedrick, J. A., et al.: Penicillin-resistant *Streptococcus pneumoniae* in acute otitis media: Risk factors, susceptibility patterns and antimicrobial management Pediatr. Infect. Dis. J. *14*:751–759, 1995.
71. Block, S. L., Hedrick, J., Tyler, R., et al.: Increasing bacterial resistance in pediatric acute conjunctivitis (1997–1998). Antimicrob. Agents Chemother. *44*:1650–1654, 2000.
72. Block, S. L., Hedrick, J. A., and Harrison, C. J.: Pneumococcal serotypes from acute otitis media in rural Kentucky. Abstract 1185. Presented at the 39th Interscience Conference on Antimicrobial Agents and Chemotherapy (ICAAC), San Francisco, 1999, p. 677.
73. Bluestone, C. D., and Klein, J. O.: Otitis Media in Infants and Children. 2nd ed. Philadephia, W. B. Saunders, 1995, pp. 188–191.
74. Bluestone, C. D., Stephenson, J. S., and Martin, L. M.: Ten-year review of otitis media pathogens. Pediatr. Infect. Dis. J. *11*(Suppl.):7–11, 1992.
75. Blum, M. D., Dagan, R., Mendelman, P. M., et al.: A comparison of multiple regimens of pneumococcal polysaccharide–meningococcal outer membrane protein complex conjugate vaccine and pneumococcal polysaccharide vaccine in toddlers. Vaccine *18*:2359–2367, 2000.
76. Blumer, J. L.: Implications of pharmacokinetics in making choices for the management of acute otitis media. Pediatr. Infect. Dis. J. *17*:565–570, 1998.
77. Bochud, P. Y., Calandra, T., Moreillon, P., et al.: Breakthrough *Streptococcus pneumoniae* meningitis during clarithromycin therapy for acute otitis media. Eur. J. Clin. Microbiol. Infect. Dis. *20*:136–137, 2001.
78. Bodor, F. F.: Conjunctivitis-otitis syndrome. Pediatrics *69*:695–698, 1982.
79. Bodwell Dunlap, M., and Stimson Harbery, H.: Host influence on upper respiratory flora. N. Engl. J. Med. *255*:640–646, 1956.
80. Bogaert, D., Engelen, M. N., Timmers-Reker, A. J. M., et al.: Pneumococcal carriage in children in the Netherlands: A molecular epidemiological study. J. Clin. Microbiol. *39*:3316–3320, 2001.
81. Borer, A., Meirson, H., Peled, N., et al.: Antibiotic-resistant pneumococci carried by young children do not appear to disseminate to adult members of a closed community. Clin. Infect. Dis. *33*:436–444, 2001.
82. Borgono, J. M., Mclean, A. A., and Vella, P. P.: Vaccination and revaccination with polyvalent pneumococcal polysaccharide vaccines in adults and infants. Proc. Soc. Exp. Biol. Med. *157*:148–154, 1978.
83. Bosu, B. K., and Harper, M. B.: Fever interval before diagnosis, prior antibiotic treatment, and clinical outcome for young children with bacterial meningitis. Clin. Infect. Dis. *32*:556–572, 2001.
84. Box, Q. T., Cleveland, R. T., and Willard, C. Y.: Bacterial flora of the upper respiratory tract. 1. Comparative evaluation by anterior nasal, oropharyngeal, and nasopharyngeal swabs. Am. J. Dis. Child. *102*:293–301, 1961.
85. Bradley, J. S., Kaplan, S. L., Klugman, K. P., and Leggiadro, R. J.: Consensus: Management of infections in children caused by *Streptococcus pneumoniae* with decreased susceptibility to penicillin. Pediatr. Infect. Dis. J. *14*:1037–1041, 1995.
86. Bratton, L., Teele, D. W., and Klein, J. O.: Outcome of unsuspected pneumococcemia in children not initially admitted to the hospital. J. Pediatr. *90*:703–706, 1977.
87. Braun, J. S., Novak, R., Gao, G., et al.: Pneumolysin, a protein toxin of *Streptococcus pneumoniae,* induces nitric oxide production from macrophages. Infect. Immun. *67*:3750–3756, 1999.
88. Breiman, R. F., Spika, J. S., Navarro, V. J., et al.: Pneumococcal bacteremia in Charleston County, South Carolina: A decade later. Arch. Intern. Med. *150*:1401–1405, 1990.
89. Briles, D. E., Crain, M. J., Gray, B. M., et al.: Strong association between capsular type and virulence for mice among human isolates of *Streptococcus pneumoniae.* Infect. Immun. *60*:111–116, 1992.
90. Briles, D. E., Hollingshead, S. K., Nabors, G. S., et al.: The potential for using protein vaccines to protect against otitis media caused by *Streptococcus pneumoniae.* Vaccine *19*(Suppl.):87–95, 2000.
91. Briles, D. E., Tart, R. C., Swiatlo, E., et al.: Pneumococcal diversity: Considerations for new vaccine strategies with emphasis on pneumococcal surface protein A (pspA). Clin. Microbiol. Rev. *11*:645–657, 1998.
92. Brimblecombe, F. S. W., Cruickshank, R., Masters, P. L., et al.: Family studies of respiratory infections. B. M. J. *1*:119–128, 1958.
93. Brodsky, E., Biger, Y., Zeidan, Z., and Schneider, M.: Topical application of chloramphenicol eye ointment followed by fatal bone marrow aplasia. Isr. J. Med. Sci. *25*:54, 1989.
94. Broides, A., Leibovitz, E., Dagan, R., et al.: The cytology of middle ear fluid during acute otitis media. Pediatr. Infect. Dis. J. *21*:57–60, 2002.
95. Brook, I., and Gober, A. E.: Prophylaxis with amoxicillin or sulfisoxazole for otitis media: Effect on the recovery of penicillin-resistant bacteria from children. Clin. Infect. Dis. *22*:143–145, 1996.
96. Broome, C. V., Facklam, R. R., Austrian, R., et al.: Epidemiology of pneumococcal serotypes in the United States, 1978–1979. J. Infect. Dis. *141*:119–123, 1980.
97. Brown, C. E., and Magnuson, B.: On the physics of the infant feeding bottle and middle ear sequela: Ear disease in infants can be associated with bottle feeding. Int. J. Pediatr. Otorhinolaryngol. *54*:13–20, 2000.
98. Brown, J. S., Gilliland, S. M., and Holden, D. W.: A *Streptococcus pneumoniae* pathogenicity island encoding an ABC transporter involved in iron uptake and virulence. Mol. Microbiol. *40*:572–585, 2001.
99. Brussow, H., Baensch, M., and Sidoti, J.: Seroprevalence of immunoglobulin M (IgM) and IgG antibodies to polysaccharides of *Streptococcus pneumoniae* in different age groups of Ecuadorian and German children. J. Clin. Microbiol. *30*:2765–2771, 1992.
100. Buckingham, S. C., Brown, S. P., and Joaquin, V. H.: Breakthrough bacteremia and meningitis during treatment with cephalosporins parenterally for pneumococcal pneumonia. J. Pediatr. *132*:174–176, 1998.
101. Buckingham, S. C., McCullers, J. A., Lujan-Zilbermann, J., et al.: Pneumococcal meningitis in children: Relationship of antibiotic resistance to clinical characteristics and outcomes. Pediatr. Infect. Dis. J. *20*:837–843, 2001.
102. Burke, J. P., Klein, J. O., Gezon, H. M., and Finland, M.: Pneumococcal bacteremia. Review of 111 cases, 1957–1969, with special reference to cases with undetermined focus. Am. J. Dis. Child. *121*:353–359, 1971.
103. Burman, L. A., Norrby, R., and Trollfors, B.: Invasive pneumococcal infections: Incidence, predisposing factors, and prognosis. Rev. Infect. Dis. *7*:133–142, 1985.
104. Butler, J. C., Breiman, R. F., Lipman, H. B., et al.: Serotype distribution of *Streptococcus pneumoniae* infections among pre-school children in the United States, 1978–1994: Implications for a conjugate vaccine. J. Infect. Dis. *171*:885–889, 1995.
105. Butler, J. C., Bulkow, K. R., Parks, D. J., and Parkinson, A. J.: Epidemiology of pneumococcal bacteremia and meningitis during the first 5 years of life in Alaska: Implications for conjugate pneumococcal vaccine

use. Abstract 1058. Presented at the 39th Interscience Conference on Antimicrobial Agents and Chemotherapy (ICAAC), San Francisco, 1999, p. 672.

106. Byington, C. L., Spencer, L. Y., Johnson, T. A., et al.: An epidemiological investigation of a sustained high rate of pediatric parapneumonic empyema: Risk factors and microbiological associations. Clin. Infect. Dis. *34*:434–440, 2002.
107. Casadevall, A., and Scharff, M. D.: Serum therapy revisited: Animal models of infection and development of passive antibody therapy. Antimicrob. Agents Chemother. *38*:1695–1702, 1994.
108. Castillo, E. M., Rickman, L. S., Brodine, S. K., et al.: *Streptococcus pneumoniae:* Bacteremia in an era of penicillin resistance. Am. J. Infect. Control. *28*:239–243, 2000.
109. Chambers, H. F.: Penicillin-binding protein–mediated resistance in pneumococci and staphylococci. J. Infect. Dis. *179*(Suppl. 2):353–359, 1999.
110. Chen, D. K., McGeer, A., de Azavedo, J. C., et al.: Decreased susceptibility of *Streptococcus pneumoniae* to fluoroquinolones in Canada. Canadian Bacterial Surveillance Network. N. Engl. J. Med. *341*:233–239, 1999.
111. Chen, F. M., Breiman, R. D., Farley, M., et al.: Geocoding and linking data from population-based surveillance and the US census to evaluate the impact of median household income on the epidemiology of invasive *Streptococcus pneumoniae* infections. Am. J. Epidemiol. *148*:1212–1218, 1998.
112. Cherian, T., Steinhoff, M. C., Harrison, L. H., et al.: A cluster of invasive pneumococcal disease in young children in child care. J. A. M. A. *271*:695–697, 1994.
113. Chloramphenicol-induced bone-marrow aplasia. N. Engl. J. Med. *277*:1035–1036, 1967.
114. Choi, E. H., and Lee, H. J.: Clinical outcome of invasive infections by penicillin-resistant *Streptococcus pneumoniae* in Korean children. Clin. Infect. Dis. *26*:1346–1354, 1998.
115. Chudwin, D. S.: Prophylaxis and treatment of pneumococcal bacteremia by immune globulin intravenous in a mouse model. Clin. Immunol. Immunopathol. *50*:62–71, 1989.
116. Chudwin, D. S., Wara, D. W., Schiffman, G., et al.: Maternal fetal transfer of pneumococcal capsular polysaccharide antibodies. Am. J. Dis. Child. *139*:378–380, 1985.
117. Circolo, A., Garnier, G., Fukuda, W., et al.: Genetic disruption of the murine complement C3 promoter region generates deficient mice with extrahepatic expression of C3 mRNA. Immunopharmacology *42*:135–149, 1999.
118. Claesson, B. A., Trollfors, B., Brolin, I., et al.: Etiology of community-acquired pneumonia in children based on antibody responses to bacterial and viral antigens. Pediatr. Infect. Dis. J. *8*:856–862, 1989.
119. Clinical practice guideline: Management of sinusitis. Pediatrics *108*:798–808, 2001.
120. Cohen, R., Bingen, E., Varon, E., et al.: Change in nasopharyngeal carriage of *Streptococcus pneumoniae* resulting from antibiotic therapy for acute otitis media in children. Pediatr. Infect. Dis. J. *16*:555–560, 1997.
121. Cohen, R., Levy, C., Boucherat, M., et al.: A multicenter, randomized, double-blind trial of 5 versus 10 days of antibiotic therapy for acute otitis media in young children. J. Pediatr. *133*:634–639, 1998.
122. Cohen, R., Levy, C., Boucherat, M., et al.: Characteristics and outcome of children with acute otitis media attending day care. Abstract 776. Presented at the 39th Interscience Conference on Antimicrobial Agents and Chemotherapy (ICAAC), San Francisco, 1999, p. 666.
123. Cohen, R., Levy, C., Boucherat, M., et al.: Five vs ten days of antibiotic therapy for acute otitis media in young children. Pediatr. Infect. Dis. J. *19*:458–463, 2000.
124. Cohen, R., Navel, M., Grunberg, J., et al.: One dose ceftriaxone vs. ten days of amoxicillin/clavulanate therapy for acute otitis media: Clinical efficacy and change in nasopharyngeal flora. Pediatr. Infect. Dis. J. *18*:403–409, 1999
125. Coles, C. L., Kanungo, R., Rahmathullah, L., et al.: Pneumococcal nasopharyngeal colonization in young south Indian infants. Pediatr. Infect. Dis. J. *20*:289–295, 2001.
126. Coles, C. L., Rahmathullah, L., Kanungo, R., et al.: Vitamin A supplementation at birth delays pneumococcal colonization in south Indian infants. J. Nutr. *131*:255–261, 2001.
127. Connolly, M., and Noah, N.: Surveillance of Bacterial Meningitis in Europe, 1996. London, King's European Meningitis Surveillance Unit, King's College School of Medicine and Dentistry, 1997.
128. Corless, C. E., Guiver, M., Borrow, R., et al.: Simultaneous detection of *Neisseria meningitidis, Haemophilus influenzae,* and *Streptococcus pneumoniae* in suspected cases of meningitis and septicemia using real-time PCR. J. Clin. Microbiol. *39*:1553–1558, 2001.
129. Cortese, M. M., Wolff, M., Almeido-Hill, J., et al.: High incidence rates of invasive pneumococcal disease in the White Mountain Apache population. Arch. Intern. Med. *152*:2277–2282, 1992.
130. Costa Carvalho, B. T., Carneiro-Sampaio, M. M., Sole, D., et al.: Transplacental transmission of serotype specific pneumococcal antibodies in a Brazilian population. Clin. Diagn. Lab. Immunol. *6*:50–54, 1999.
131. Courvalin, P., and Carlier, C.: Transposable multiple antibiotic resistance in *Streptococcus pneumoniae.* Mol. Gen. Genet. *205*:291–297, 1986.
132. Craig, W. A.: Pharmacokinetics/pharmacodynamics parameters; rationale for antibacterial dosing of mice and men. Clin. Infect. Dis. *26*:1–10, 1998.
133. Craig, W. A., and Andes, D.: Pharmacokinetics and pharmacodynamics of antibiotics in otitis media. Pediatr. Infect. Dis. J. *15*:255–259, 1996.
134. Cunningham-Rundles, C.: Clinical and immunologic analyses of 103 patients with common variable immunodeficiency. J. Clin. Immunol. *9*:22–33, 1989.
135. Dabernat, H., Geslin, P., and Megraud, F.: Effects of cefixime or co-amoxiclav treatment on nasopharyngeal carriage of *Streptococcus pneumoniae* and *Haemophilus influenzae* in children with acute otitis media. J. Antimicrob. Chemother. *41*:253–258, 1998.
136. Dagan, R.: Can the choice of antibiotics for acute otitis media be logic? Eur. J. Clin. Microbiol. Infect. Dis. *17*:1–5, 1998.
137. Dagan, R.: Clinical significance of resistant organisms in otitis media. Pediatr. Infect. Dis. J. *19*:378–382, 2000.
138. Dagan, R.: Treatment of acute otitis media—challenges in the era of antibiotic resistance. Vaccine *19*(Suppl.):9–16, 2001.
139. Dagan, R., Abramson, O., Leibovitz, E., et al.: Impaired bacteriologic response to oral cephalosporins in acute otitis media caused by pneumococcus with intermediate resistance to penicillin. Pediatr. Infect. Dis. J. *15*:980–985, 1996.
140. Dagan, R., Engelhard, D., Piccard, E., and Engelhard, D. C.: Epidemiology of invasive childhood pneumococcal infections in Israel. J. A. M. A. *268*:3328–3332, 1992.
141. Dagan, R., and Fraser, D.: Conjugate pneumococcal vaccine and antibiotic-resistant *Streptococcus pneumoniae:* Herd immunity and reduction of otitis morbidity. Pediatr. Infect. Dis. J. *19*(Suppl.):79–88, 2000.
142. Dagan, R., Fraser, D., Janco, J., et al.: Reduction of resistant pneumococcal nasopharyngeal colonization in toddlers attending day care centers after vaccination with a 9-valent CRM_{197} conjugate pneumococcal vaccine (PncCRM9). Abstract O-12. Presented at the 18th Annual Meeting of the European Society for Paediatric Infectious Diseases (ESPID), Noordwije, The Netherlands, 2000, p. 19.
143. Dagan, R., Givon-Lavi, N., Porat, N., et al.: Immunization of toddlers attending day care centers with a 9-valent conjugate pneumococcal vaccine reduces transmission of *Streptococcus pneumoniae* and antibiotic resistant *S. pneumoniae* to their young siblings. Abstract 687. Presented at the 40th Interscience Conference on Antimicrobial Agents and Chemotherapy (ICAAC), Toronto, 2000, p. 244.
144. Dagan, R., Givon-Lavi, N., Shkolnik, L., et al.: Acute otitis media caused by antibiotic-resistant *Streptococcus pneumoniae* in southern Israel: Implication for immunizing with conjugate vaccines. J. Infect. Dis. *181*:1322–1329, 2000.
145. Dagan, R., Givon-Lavi, N., Sikuler-Cohen, M., et al.: Type-specific anti-polysaccharide IgG concentrations correlate with nasopharyngeal acquisition of vaccine serotype pneumococci in toddlers during a 2-year follow-up. Abstract 2040. Presented at the 41st Interscience Conference on Antimicrobial Agents and Chemotherapy (ICAAC), Chicago, 2001, p. 283.
146. Dagan, R., Givon-Lavi, N., Zamir, O., et al.: Reduction of nasopharyngeal carriage of *Streptococcus pneumoniae* after vaccination with a 9-valent pneumococcal conjugate vaccine in toddlers attending day care centers. J. Infect. Dis. *185*:927–936, 2002.
147. Dagan, R., Gradstein, S., Belmaker, I., et al.: An outbreak of *Streptococcus pneumoniae* type 1 in a closed community in southern Israel. Clin. Infect. Dis. *30*:319–321, 2000.
148. Dagan, R., Hoberman, A., Johnson, C., et al.: Bacteriologic and clinical efficacy of high-dose amoxicillin/clavulanate in children with acute otitis media. Pediatr. Infect. Dis. J. *20*:829–837, 2001.
149. Dagan, R., Johnson, C., McLinn, S., et al.: Bacteriologic and clinical efficacy of amoxicillin/clavulanate vs. azithromycin in acute otitis media. Pediatr. Infect. Dis. J. *19*:95–104, 2000.
150. Dagan, R., Klugman, K. P., Craig, W. A., and Baquero, F.: Evidence to support the rationale that bacterial eradication in respiratory tract infection provides guidance for antimicrobial therapy. J. Antimicrob. Chemother. *47*:129–140, 2001.
151. Dagan, R., Leibovitz, E., Cheletz, G., et al.: Antibiotic treatment in acute otitis media promotes superinfection with resistant *Streptococcus pneumoniae* carried before initiation of treatment. J. Infect. Dis. *183*:880–886, 2001.
152. Dagan, R., Leibovitz, E., Fliss, D. M., et al.: Bacteriologic efficacies of oral azithromycin and oral cefaclor in treatment of acute otitis media in infants and young children. Antimicrob. Agents Chemother. *44*:43–50, 2000.
153. Dagan, R., Leibovitz, E., Greenberg, D., et al.: Early eradication of pathogens from middle ear fluid during antibiotic treatment of acute otitis media is associated with improved clinical outcome. Pediatr. Infect. Dis. J. *17*:776–882, 1998.
154. Dagan, R., Leibovitz, E., Greenberg, D., et al.: Dynamics of pneumococcal nasopharyngeal colonization during the first days of antibiotic treatment in pediatric patients. Pediatr. Infect. Dis. J. *17*:880–885, 1998.

155. Dagan, R., Leibovitz, E., Leiberman, A., and Yagupsky, P.: Clinical significance of antibiotic resistance in acute otitis media and implication of antibiotic treatment on carriage and spread of resistant organisms. Pediatr. Infect. Dis. J. *19*(Suppl.):57–65, 2000.
156. Dagan, R., Leibovitz, E., Piglansky, L., and Yagupsky, P.: Effect of antibiotic treatment on pneumococcal nasopharyngeal carriage during and after acute otitis media: Comparison of 3 oral drugs. Abstract 1028. Presented at the 39th Interscience Conference on Antimicrobial Agents and Chemotherapy (ICAAC), San Francisco, 1999, p. 145.
157. Dagan, R., Melamed, R., Muallem, M., et al.: Reduction of nasopharyngeal carriage of pneumococci during the second year of life by a heptavalent conjugate pneumococcal vaccine. J. Infect. Dis. *174*:1271–1278, 1996.
158. Dagan, R., Melamed, R., Muallem, M., et al.: Nasopharyngeal colonization in southern Israel with antibiotic-resistant pneumococci during the first 2 years of life: Relation to serotypes likely to be included in pneumococcal conjugate vaccines. J. Infect. Dis. *174*:1352–1355, 1996.
159. Dagan, R., Muallem, M., Melamed, R., et al.: Reduction of pneumococcal nasopharyngeal carriage in early infancy after immunization with tetravalent pneumococcal vaccines conjugated to either tetanus toxoid or diphtheria toxoid. Pediatr. Infect. Dis. J. *16*:1060–1064, 1997.
160. Dagan, R., Shriker, O., Hazan, I., et al.: Prospective study to determine clinical relevance of detection of pneumococcal DNA in sera of children by PCR. J. Clin. Microbiol. *36*:669–673, 1998.
161. Dagan, R., Sikuler-Cohen, M., Zamir, O., et al.: Effect of a conjugate pneumococcal vaccine on the occurrence of respiratory infections and antibiotic use in day care center attendees. Pediatr. Infect. Dis. J. *20*:951–958, 2001.
162. Dagan, R., Zamir, O., Tirosh, N., et al.: Nasopharyngeal carriage of *Streptococcus pneumoniae* in toddlers vaccinated during infancy with an 11 valent pneumococcal vaccine conjugated to diphtheria and tetanus toxoids. Abstract 47. Presented at the 40th Interscience Conference on Antimicrobial Agents and Chemotherapy (ICAAC), Toronto, 2000, p. 236.
163. Dallaire, F., Ouellet, N., Simard, M., et al.: Efficacy of recombinant human granulocyte colony-stimulating factor in a murine model of pneumococcal pneumonia: Effects of lung inflammation and timing of treatment. J. Infect. Dis. *183*:70–77, 2001.
164. Daoud, A. S., Zaki, M., and al-Saleh, Q. A.: Prolonged and secondary fever in childhood bacterial meningitis. Eur. J. Pediatr. *149*:114–116, 1989.
165. Davidson, M., Parkinson, A. J., Bulkow, L. R., et al.: Epidemiology of invasive pneumococcal disease in Alaska, 1986–1990—ethnic differences and opportunities for prevention. J. Infect. Dis. *170*:368–376, 1994.
166. Davies, T., Goering, R. V., Lovgren, M., et al.: Molecular epidemiological survey of penicillin-resistant *Streptococcus pneumoniae* from Asia, Europe, and North America. Diagn. Microbiol. Infect. Dis. *34*:7–12, 1999.
167. Davis, C. W., and McIntyre, P. B.: Invasive pneumococcal infection in children, 1981–92: A hospital-based study. J. Paediatr. Child Health *31*:317–322, 1995.
168. Davis, H. D., Matlow, A., Petric, M., et al.: Prospective comparative study of viral, bacterial and atypical organisms identified in pneumonia and bronchiolitis in hospitalised Canadian infants. Pediatr. Infect. Dis. J. *15*:371–375, 1996.
169. de Lalla, F., Nicolin, R., and Lazzarini, L.: Safety and efficacy of recombinant granulocyte colony-stimulating factor as an adjunctive therapy for *Streptococcus pneumoniae* meningitis in non-neutropenic adult patients: A pilot study. J. Antimicrob. Chemother. *46*:843–846, 2000.
170. Del Beccaro, M. A., Mendelman, P. M., Inglis, A. F., et al.: Bacteriology of acute otitis media: A new perspective. J. Pediatr. *120*:81–84, 1992.
171. del Castillo, F., Ledesma, F., and García-Perea, A.: Penicillin-susceptible and erythromycin-resistant *Streptococcus pneumoniae* in children with acute mastoiditis. Eur. J. Clin. Microbiol. Infect. Dis. *20*:824–826, 2001.
172. De Lencastre, H. D., Kristinsson, K. G., Brito-Avo, A., et al.: Carriage of respiratory tract pathogens and molecular epidemiology of *Streptococcus pneumoniae* colonization in healthy children attending day care centers in Lisbon, Portugal. Microb. Drug Resist. *5*:19–29, 1999.
173. Dimitrov, N. V., Douwes, F. R., and Bartoletta, B.: Metabolic activity of polymorphonuclear leukocytes in sickle cell anemia. Acta Haematol. *47*:283–291, 1972.
174. Dintilhac, A., Alloing, G., Granadel, C., et al.: Competence and virulence of *Streptococcus pneumoniae*: Adc and PsaA mutants exhibit a requirement for Zn and Mn resulting from inactivation of putative ABC metal permeases. Mol. Microbiol. *25*:727–739, 1997.
175. DiNubile, M. J., Albornoz, M. A., and Stumacher, R. J.: Pneumococcal soft-tissue infections: Possible association with connective tissue diseases. J. Infect. Dis. *163*:897–900, 1991.
176. Djuretic, T., Ryan, M. J., Miller, E., et al.: Hospital admissions in children due to pneumococcal pneumonia in England. J. Infect. *37*:54–58, 1998.
177. Doern, G. V., Brueggemann, A., Holley, H. P., and Rauch, A. M.: Antimicrobial resistance of *Streptococcus pneumoniae* recovered from outpatients in the United States during the winter months of 1994 to 1995: Results of a 30-center national surveillance study. Antimicrob. Agents Chemother. *40*:1208–1213, 1996.
178. Dominguez, J., Gali, N., Blanco, S., et al.: Detection of *Streptococcus pneumoniae* antigen by a rapid immunochromatographic assay in urine samples. Chest *119*:243–249, 2001.
179. Dopazo, J., Mendoza, A., Herrero, J., et al.: Annotated draft genomic sequence from a *Streptococcus pneumoniae* type 19F clinical isolate. Microb. Drug Resist. *7*:99–125, 2001.
180. Douglas, R. M., and Miles, H. B.: Vaccination against *Streptococcus pneumoniae* in childhood: Lack of demonstrable benefit in young Australian children. J. Infect. Dis. *149*:861–869, 1984.
181. Douglas, R. M., Paton, J. C., and Duncan, S. J.: Antibody response to pneumococcal vaccination in children younger than five years of age. J. Infect. Dis. *148*:131–137, 1983.
182. Dowell, S. F., Butler, J. C., Giebink, G. S., et al.: Acute otitis media: Management and surveillance in an era of pneumococcal resistance—a report from the Drug-Resistant *Streptococcus pneumoniae* Therapeutic Working Group. Pediatr. Infect. Dis. J. *18*:1–9, 1999.
183. Dowell, S. F., Marcy, S. M., Philips, W. R., et al.: Otitis media: Principles of judicious use of antimicrobial agents. Pediatrics *101*(Suppl.):165–171, 1998.
184. Duncan, B., Ey, J., Holberg, C. J., et al.: Exclusive breast-feeding for at least 4 months protects against otitis media. Pediatrics *91*:867–872, 1993.
185. Eavery, R. D., Gao, Y., Schuknecht, H. F., and Gonzalez-Fineda, M.: Otologic features of bacterial meningitis of childhood. J. Pediatr. *136*:2025–2029, 1985.
186. Eberhard, T., Kronvall, G., and Ullberg, M.: Surface bound plasmin promotes migration of *Streptococcus pneumoniae* through reconstituted basement membranes. Microb. Pathog. *26*:175–181, 1999.
187. Eby, R.: Pneumococcal conjugate vaccines. Pharm. Biotechnol. *6*:695–718, 1995.
188. Edwards, K. M., Wandling, G., Palmer, P., and Decker, M. D.: Carriage of pneumococci among infants immunized with a 9-valent pneumococcal conjugate vaccine at 2, 4, and 6 months of age. Abstract 34. Presented at the 37th Annual Meeting of the Infectious Diseases Society of America (IDSA), Philadelphia, 1999, p. 28.
189. Ekdahl, K., Ahlinger, I., Hansson, H. B., et al.: Duration of nasopharyngeal carriage of penicillin-resistant *Streptococcus pneumoniae*: Experiences from the South Swedish pneumococcal intervention project. Clin. Infect. Dis. *25*:1113–1117, 1997.
190. Ekwurzel, G. M., Simmons, J. S., Dublin, L. I., et al.: Studies on immunizing substances in pneumococci. VIII. Report on field tests to determine prophylactic value of a pneumococcus antigen. Public Health Rep. *53*:1877–1893, 1938.
191. Epstein, M. M., and Gruskay, F.: Selective deficiency in pneumococcal antibody response in children with recurrent infections. Ann. Allergy Asthma Immunol. *75*:125–131, 1995.
192. Eskola, J., and Anttila, M.: Pneumococcal conjugate vaccines. Pediatr. Infect. Dis. J. *18*:543–551, 1999.
193. Eskola, J., Kilpi, T., Palmu, A., et al.: Efficacy of a pneumococcal conjugate vaccine against acute otitis media. N. Engl. J. Med. *344*:403–409, 2001.
194. Eskola, J., Takala, A. K., Kela, E., et al.: Epidemiology of invasive pneumococcal infections in children in Finland. J A. M. A. *268*:3323–3327, 1992.
195. Esterle, T. M., and Edwards, K. M.: Concerns of secondary fever in *Streptococcus pneumoniae* meningitis in an era of increasing antibiotic resistance. Arch. Pediatr. Adolesc. Med. *150*:552–554, 1996.
196. Ewig, S., Ruiz, M., Torres, A., et al.: Pneumonia acquired in the community through drug-resistant *Streptococcus pneumoniae*. Am. J. Respir. Crit. Care Med. *159*:1835–1842, 1999.
197. Faden, H., Duffy, L., Wasielewski, R., et al.: Relationship between nasopharyngeal colonization and the development of otitis media in children. J. Infect. Dis. *175*:1440–1445, 1997.
198. Faden, H. S., Horomi, M., and Yamanaka, N.: The importance of *Streptococcus pneumoniae:* Colonization on the course of acute otitis media. Pediatric Academic Societies Annual Meeting. Abstract 1393. Pediatr. Res. *49*:244, 2001.
199. Falade, A. G., Mulholland, E. K., Adegbola, R. A., and Greenwood, B. M.: Bacterial isolates from blood and lung aspirate cultures in Gambian children with lobar pneumonia. Ann. Trop. Paediatr. *17*:315–319, 1997.
200. Fang, G. D., Fine, M., Orloff, J., et al.: New and emerging etiologies for community-acquired pneumonia with implications for therapy: A prospective multicenter study of 359 cases. Medicine (Baltimore) *69*:307–316, 1990.
201. Farley, J. J., King, J. C., Jr., Nair, P., et al.: Invasive pneumococcal disease among infected and uninfected children of mothers with human immunodeficiency virus infection. J. Pediatr. *124*:853–858, 1994.
202. Fasola, E. L., Bajaksouzian, S., Appelbaum, P. C., et al.: Variation in erythromycin and clindamycin susceptibilities of *Streptococcus pneumoniae* by four test methods. Antimicrob. Agents Chemother. *41*:129–134, 1997.
203. Fedson, D. S., Musher, D. M., and Eskola, J.: Pneumococcal vaccines. *In* Plotkin, S. A., and Orenstein, W. A. (eds.): Vaccines. 3rd ed. Philadelphia, W. B. Saunders, 1999, pp. 553–607.

204. Feikin, D. R., Dowell, S. F., Nwanyanwu, O. C., et al.: Increased carriage of trimethoprim/sulfamethoxazole-resistant *Streptococcus pneumoniae* in Malawian children after treatment for malaria with sulfadoxine/pyrimethamine. J. Infect. Dis. *181*:1501–1505, 2000.
205. Feikin, D. R., Schuchat, A., Kolczak, M., et al.: Mortality from invasive pneumococcal pneumonia in the era of antibiotic resistance, 1995–1997. Am. J. Public Health *90*:223–229, 2000.
206. Feldhoff, C., Kleine, L., and Bachmann, H.: Peritonitis and infection in children with idiopathic nephrotic syndrome. Klin. Padiatr. *200*:40–44, 1988.
207. Feldman, C., Munro, N. C., Jeffery, P. K., et al.: Pneumolysin induces the salient histologic features of pneumococcal infection in the rat lung in vivo. Am. J. Respir. Cell Mol. Biol. *5*:416–423, 1991.
208. Figueroa, J. E., and Densen, P.: Infectious diseases associated with complement deficiencies. Clin. Microbiol. Rev. *4*:359–395, 1991.
209. Filice, G. A., Van Etta, L. L., Darby, C. P., and Fraser, D. W.: Bacteremia in Charleston Country, South Carolina. Am. J. Epidemiol. *123*:128–136, 1986.
210. Filipe, S. R., and Tomasz, A.: Inhibition of the expression of penicillin resistance in *Streptococcus pneumoniae* by inactivation of cell wall muropeptide branching genes. Proc. Natl. Acad. Sci. U. S. A. *97*:4891–4896, 2000.
211. Finland, M., and Barnes, M.: Changes in occurrence of capsular serotypes of *Streptococcus pneumoniae* at Boston City Hospital during selected years between 1935 and 1974. J. Clin. Microbiol. *5*:154–166, 1977.
212. Fiore, A. E., Levine, O. S., Elliott, J. A., et al.: Effectiveness of pneumococcal polysaccharide vaccine for preschool-age children with chronic disease. Emerg. Infect. Dis. *5*:828–831, 1999.
213. Fiore, A. E., Moroney, J. F., Farley, M. M., et al.: Clinical outcomes of meningitis caused by *Streptococcus pneumoniae* in the era of antibiotic resistance. Clin. Infect. Dis. *30*:71–77, 2000.
214. Fischer, W.: Pneumococcal lipoteichoic and teichoic acid. *In* Tomasz, A. (ed.): *Streptococcus pneumoniae*: Molecular Biology & Mechanisms of Disease. Larchmont, NY, Mary Ann Liebert, Inc., 2000, pp. 155–177.
215. Fischer, W., Markwitz, S., and Labischinski, H.: Small-angle x-ray scattering analysis of pneumococcal lipoteichoic acid phase structure. Eur. J. Biochem. *244*:913–917, 1997.
216. Fliss, D. M., Leiberman, A., and Dagan, R.: Medical sequelae and complications of acute otitis media. Pediatr. Infect. Dis. J. *13*(Suppl.):34–40, 50–54, 1994.
217. Fogarty, C., Goldschmidt, R., and Bush, K.: Bacteremic pneumonia due to multidrug-resistant pneumococci in 3 patients treated unsuccessfully with azithromycin and successfully with levofloxacin. Clin. Infect. Dis. *31*:613–615, 2000.
218. Foo, R. L., Graham, S. M., Suthisarnsuntorn, U., et al.: Detection of pneumococcal capsular antigen in saliva of children with pneumonia. Ann. Trop. Paediatr. *20*:161–163, 2000.
219. Forgie, L. M., Campbell, H., Lloyd-Evans, N., et al.: Etiology of acute lower respiratory tract infections in children in a rural community in The Gambia. Pediatr. Infect. Dis. J. *11*:466–473, 1992.
220. Forgie, L. M., O'Neill, K. P., Lloyd-Evans, N., et al.: Etiology of acute lower respiratory tract infections in Gambian children: I. Acute lower respiratory tract infections in infants presenting at the hospital. Pediatr. Infect. Dis. J. *10*:33–41, 1991.
221. Forgie, L. M., O'Neill, K. P., Lloyd-Evans, N., et al.: Etiology of acute lower respiratory tract infections in Gambian children: II. Acute lower respiratory tract infections in children ages one to nine years presenting at the hospital. Pediatr. Infect. Dis. J. *10*:42–47, 1991.
222. Fortnum, H. M.: Hearing impairment after bacterial meningitis: A review. Arch. Dis. Child. *67*:1128, 1992.
223. Francis, T., Jr., and Tillett, W. S.: Cutaneous reactions in pneumonia. The development of antibodies following the intradermal injection of type-specific polysaccharide. J. Exp. Med. *52*:573–585, 1930.
224. Frankel, R. E., Virata, M., Hardalo, C., et al.: Invasive pneumococcal disease: Clinical features, serotypes, and antimicrobial resistance patterns in cases involving patients with and without human immunodeficiency virus infection. Clin. Infect. Dis. *23*:577–584, 1996.
225. Fraser, D., Givon-Lavi, N., Bilenko, N., and Dagan, R.: A decade (1989–1998) of pediatric invasive pneumococcal disease in two populations residing in one geographic location: Implications for vaccine choice. Clin. Infect. Dis. *33*:421–427, 2001.
226. Fredericksen, B., and Henrichsen, J.: Throat carriage of *Streptococcus pneumoniae* and *Streptococcus pyogenes* among infants and children in Zambia. J. Trop. Pediatr. *34*:114–117, 1988.
227. Freij, B. J., Votteler, T. P., and McCracken, G. H.: Primary peritonitis in previously healthy children. Am. J. Dis. Child. *138*:1058–1061, 1984.
228. Frenck, R. W., Jr., and Glezen, W. P.: Respiratory tract infections in children in day care. Semin. Pediatr. Infect. Dis. *1*:234–244, 1990.
229. Friedland, I. R., and Klugman, K. P.: Failure of chloramphenicol therapy in penicillin-resistant pneumococcal meningitis. Lancet *339*:405–408, 1992.
230. Friedland, I. R., and Klugman, K. P.: Cerebrospinal fluid bactericidal activity against cephalosporin-resistant *Streptococcus pneumoniae* in children with meningitis treated with high-dosage cefotaxime. Antimicrob. Agents Chemother. *41*:1888–1891, 1997.
231. Friedland, I. R., Paris, M., Ehrett, S., et al.: Evaluation of antimicrobial regimens for treatment of experimental penicillin- and cephalosporin-resistant pneumococcal meningitis. Antimicrob. Agents Chemother. *37*:1630–1636, 1993.
232. Fuchshuber, A., Kuhnemund, O., Keuth, B., et al.: Pneumococcal vaccine in children and young adults with chronic renal disease. Nephrol. Dial. Transplant. *11*:468–473, 1996.
233. Gallin, J. I., Buescher, E. S., and Seligmann, B. E.: Recent advances in chronic granulomatous disease. Ann. Intern. Med. *99*:657–674, 1983.
234. Garcia, E., Llull, D., and Lopez, R.: Functional organization of the gene cluster involved in the synthesis of the pneumococcal capsule. Int. Microbiol. *2*:169–176, 1999.
235. Garcia, E., and Lopez, R.: Molecular biology of the capsular genes of *Streptococcus pneumoniae.* FEMS Microbiol. Lett. *149*:1–10, 1997.
236. García-Rey, C., Aguilar, L., Baquero, F., et al.: Importance of local variations in antibiotic consumption and geographical differences of erythromycin and penicillin resistance in *Streptococcus pneumoniae.* J. Clin. Microbiol. *40*:159–164, 2002.
237. Gardner, P., and Schaffner, W.: Immunization of adults. N. Engl. J. Med. *328*:1252, 1993.
238. Gaston, M. H., Verter, J. I., Woods, G., et al.: Prophylaxis with oral penicillin in children with sickle cell anemia: A randomized trial. N. Engl. J. Med. *314*:1593–1599, 1986.
239. Gates, G. A.: Cost-effectiveness considerations in otitis media treatment. Otolaryngol. Head Neck Surg. *14*:525–530, 1996.
240. Gay, K., and Stephens, D. S.: Structure and dissemination of a chromosomal insertion element encoding macrolide efflux in *Streptococcus pneumoniae.* J. Infect. Dis. *184*:56–65, 2001.
241. Gehanno, P., Olivier, C., Boucot, I., et al.: Risk factors for nasopharyngeal carriage of penicillin-resistant *S. pneumoniae*. Abstract 160. Presented at the 15th Annual Meeting of the European Society for Paediatric Infectious Diseases (ESPID), Paris, 1997, p. 80.
242. Gehanno, P., Panaotopoulos, A., Barry, B., et al.: Microbiology of otitis media in the Paris, France, area from 1987 to 1997. Pediatr. Infect. Dis. J. *20*:570–573, 2001.
243. Gendrel, D., Raymond, J., and Moulin, F.: Etiology and response to antibiotic therapy of community-acquired pneumonia in French children. Eur. J. Clin. Microbiol. Infect. Dis. *16*:388–391, 1997.
244. Geslin, P., Buu-Hoi, A., Frémaux, A., and Acar, J. F.: Antimicrobial resistance in *Streptococcus pneumoniae:* An epidemiological survey in France, 1970–1990. Clin. Infect. Dis. *15*:95–98, 1992.
245. Gesner, M., Desiderio, D., Kim, M., and Kaul, A.: *Streptococcus pneumoniae* in human immunodeficiency virus type 1–infected children. Pediatr. Infect. Dis. J. *13*:697–703, 1994.
246. Gessner, B. D., Ussery, X. T., Parkinson, A. J., and Breiman, R. F.: Risk factors for invasive disease caused by *Streptococcus pneumoniae* among Alaska native children younger than two years of age. Pediatr. Infect. Dis. J. *14*:123–128, 1995.
247. Ghaffar, F., Friedland, I. R., and McCracken, G. H., Jr.: Dynamics of nasopharyngeal colonization by *Streptococcus pneumoniae.* Pediatr. Infect. Dis. J. *18*:638–646, 1999.
248. Gibb, D., Spoulou, V., Giacomelli, A., et al.: Antibody responses to *Haemophilus influenzae* type b and *Streptococcus pneumoniae* vaccines in children with human immunodeficiency virus infection. Pediatr. Infect. Dis. J. *14*:129–135, 1995.
249. Giebink, G. S.: The microbiology of otitis media. Pediatr. Infect. Dis. J. *8*(Suppl.):18–20, 1989.
250. Giebink, G. S.: Otitis media: The chinchilla model. Microb. Drug Resist. *5*:57–72, 1999.
251. Giebink, G. S., Meier, J. D., Quartey, M. K., et al.: Immunogenicity and efficacy of *Streptococcus pneumoniae* polysaccharide-protein conjugate vaccines against homologous and heterologous vaccine serotypes in the chinchilla model. J. Infect. Dis. *173*:119–127, 1996.
252. Gigliotti, F., Hendly, J. O., Morgan, J., et al.: Efficacy of topical antibiotic therapy in acute conjunctivitis in children. J. Pediatr. *104*:623–626, 1984.
253. Gigliotti, F., Williams, W. T., Hayden, F. G., et al.: Etiology of acute conjunctivitis in children. J. Pediatr. *98*:531–536, 1981.
254. Gilbert, R. J., Heenan, R. K., Timmins, P. A., et al.: Studies on the structure and mechanism of a bacterial protein toxin by analytical ultracentrifugation and small-angle neutron scattering. J. Mol. Biol. *293*:1145–1160, 1999.
255. Gindreau, E., Lopez, R., and Garcia, P.: Mm1, a temperate bacteriophage of the type 23F Spanish/USA multiresistant epidemic clone of *Streptococcus pneumoniae:* Structural analysis of the site-specific integration system. J. Virol. *74*:7803–7813, 2000.
256. Gingles, N. A., Alexander, J. E., Kadioglu, A., et al.: Role of genetic resistance in invasive pneumococcal infection: Identification and study of susceptibility and resistance in inbred mouse strains. Infect. Immun. *69*:426–434, 2001.
257. Ginsburg, C. M., Rudoy, R., and Nelson, J. D.: Acute mastoiditis in infants and children. Clin. Pediatr. (Phila.) *19*:549–553, 1980.
258. Givner, L. B., Mason, E. O., Jr., Barson, W. J., et al.: Pneumococcal facial cellulitis in children. Pediatrics *106*:E61, 2000.

259. Givon-Lavi, N., Dagan, R., Fraser, D., et al.: Marked differences in pneumococcal carriage and resistance patterns between day care centers located within a small area. Clin. Infect. Dis. *29*:1274–1280, 1999.
260. Go, C., Asnis, D. S., and Saltzman, H.: Pneumococcal pericarditis since 1980. Clin. Infect. Dis. *27*:1338–1340, 1998.
261. Goldblatt, D., Akoto, A. Y., Ashton, L., et al.: Immunogenicity and the generation of immune memory following 9-valent pneumococcal conjugate vaccination in Ghanaian infants with sickle cell disease. Abstract 688. Presented at the 40th Interscience Conference on Antimicrobial Agents and Chemotherapy (ICAAC), Toronto, 2000, p. 245.
262. Goldstein, F. W.: Penicillin-resistant *Streptococcus pneumoniae:* Selection by both β-lactam and non–β-lactam antibiotics. J. Antimicrob. Chemother. *44*:141–144, 1999.
263. Gordon, S. B., Irving, G. R., Lawson, R. A., et al.: Intracellular trafficking and killing of *Streptococcus pneumoniae* by human alveolar macrophages are influenced by opsonins. Infect. Immun. *68*:2286–2293, 2000.
264. Gorensek, M. J., Lebel, M. H., and Nelson, J. D.: Peritonitis in children with nephrotic syndrome. Pediatrics *81*:849–856, 1988.
265. Gosink, K. K., Mann, E. R., Guglielmo, C., et al.: Role of novel choline binding proteins in virulence of *Streptococcus pneumoniae.* Infect. Immun. *68*:5690–5695, 2000.
266. Gould, J. M., and Weiser, J. N.: Expression of C-reactive protein in the human respiratory tract. Infect. Immun. *69*:1747–1754, 2001.
267. Granert, C., Raud, J., Waage, A., et al.: Effects of polysaccharide fucoidin on cerebrospinal fluid interleukin-1 and tumor necrosis factor alpha in pneumococcal meningitis in the rabbit. Infect. Immun. *67*:2071–2074, 1999.
268. Gratten, M., Gratten, H., Poli, A., et al.: Colonisation of *Haemophilus influenzae* and *Streptococcus pneumoniae* in the upper respiratory tract of neonates in Papua New Guinea: Primary acquisition, duration of carriage, and relationship to carriage in mothers. Biol. Neonate *50*:114–120, 1986.
269. Gray, B. M., Converse, G. M., III, and Dillon, H. C., Jr.: Serotypes of *Streptococcus pneumoniae* causing disease. J. Infect. Dis. *140*:979–983, 1979.
270. Gray, B. M., Converse, G. M., III, and Dillon, H. C., Jr.: Epidemiologic studies of *Streptococcus pneumoniae* in infants: Acquisition, carriage and infection during the first 24 months of life. J. Infect. Dis. *142*:923–933, 1980.
271. Gray, B. M., Converse, G. M., III, Huhta, N., et al.: Epidemiologic studies of *Streptococcus pneumoniae* in infants: Antibody response to nasopharyngeal carriage of types 3, 19, and 23. J. Infect. Dis. *144*:312–318, 1981.
272. Gray, B. M., and Dillon, H. C., Jr.: Epidemiological studies of *Streptococcus pneumoniae* in infants: Antibody to types 3, 6, 14, and 23 in the first two years of life. J. Infect. Dis. *158*:948–955, 1988.
273. Gray, B. M., and Dillon, H. C., Jr.: Natural history of pneumococcal infections. Pediatr. Infect. Dis. J. *8*(Suppl.):23–25, 1989.
274. Gray, B. M., Turner, M. E., Dillon, H. C., Jr.: Epidemiologic studies of *Streptococcus pneumoniae* in infants: The effects of season and age on pneumococcal acquisition and carriage in the first 24 months of life. Am. J. Epidemiol. *116*:692–703, 1982.
275. Greenberg, D., Bilenko, N., Fraser, D., et al.: Acute otitis media—burden of diseases on patient and family. Abstract 807. Presented at the 39th Annual Meeting of the Infectious Diseases Society of America (IDSA), San Francisco, 2001, p. 177.
276. Grimpel, E., and Floret, D.: Pneumococcal bacteremia and sepsis in children: A multi-center study in France [French]. Mod. Mol. Infect. *24*:975–981, 1994.
277. Guillemot, D., Carbon, C., Balkau, B., et al.: Low dosage and long treatment duration of beta-lactam: Risk factors for carriage of penicillin-resistant *Streptococccus pneumoniae.* J. A. M. A. *279*:365–370, 1998.
278. Gwatkin, D. R.: How many die? A set of demographic estimates of the annual number of infant and child deaths in the world. Am. J. Public Health *70*:1286–1289, 1980.
279. Hadari, I., Dagan, R., Gedalia, A., et al.: Pneumococcal osteomyelitis. An unusual cluster of cases. Clin. Pediatr. (Phila.) *24*:143–145, 1985.
280. Hakansson, A., Roche, H., Mirza, S., et al.: Characterization of binding of human lactoferrin to pneumococcal surface protein A. Infect. Immun. *69*:3372–3381, 2001.
281. Hakenbeck, R., Balmelle, N., Weber, B., et al.: Mosaic genes and mosaic chromosomes: Intra- and interspecies genomic variation of *Streptococcus pneumoniae.* Infect. Immun. *69*:2477–2486, 2001.
282. Hakenbeck, R., Grebe, T., Zahner, D., et al.: Beta-lactam resistance in *Streptococcus pneumoniae:* Penicillin-binding proteins and non-–penicillin-binding proteins. Mol. Microbiol. *33*:673–678, 1999.
283. Hakenbeck, R., Kaminski, K., Konig, A., et al.: Penicillin-binding proteins in beta-lactam–resistant *Streptococcus pneumoniae.* Microb. Drug Resist. *5*:91–99, 1999.
284. Hamer, D. H., Egas, J., Estrella, B., et al.: Assessment of the Binax NOW *Streptococcus pneumoniae* urinary antigen test in children with nasopharyngeal pneumococcal carriage. Clin. Infect. Dis. *34*:1025–1028, 2002.
285. Hammerschmidt, S., Bethe, G., Remane, P. H., et al.: Identification of pneumococcal surface protein A as a lactoferrin-binding protein of *Streptococcus pneumoniae.* Infect. Immun. *67*:1683–1687, 1999.
286. Hammerschmidt, S., Talay, S. R., Brandtzaeg, P., et al.: SpsA, a novel pneumococcal surface protein with specific binding to secretory immunoglobulin A and secretory component. Mol. Microbiol. *25*:1113–1124, 1997.
287. Hanson, L. A., Ahlstedt, S., Andersson, B., et al.: Protective factors in milk and the development of the immune system. Pediatrics *75*:172–176, 1985.
288. Harabuchi, Y., Kodama, H., and Faden, H.: Outcome of acute otitis media and its relation to clinical features and nasopharyngeal colonization at the time of diagnosis. Acta Otolaryngol. *121*:908–914, 2001.
289. Hardy, G. G., Magee, A. D., Ventura, C. L., et al.: Essential role for cellular phosphoglucomutase in virulence of type 3 *Streptococcus pneumoniae.* Infect. Immun. *69*:2309–2317, 2001.
290. Harrison, L. H., Dwyer, D. M., Billmann, L., et al.: Invasive pneumococcal infection in Baltimore, Md. Arch. Intern. Med. *160*:89–94, 2000.
291. Hausdorff, W. P., Bryant, J., Kloek, C., et al.: The contribution of specific pneumococcal serogroups to different disease manifestations: Implications for conjugate vaccine formulation and use, Part II. Clin. Infect. Dis. *30*:122–140, 2000.
292. Hausdorff, W. P., Bryant, J., Paradiso, P. R., and Siber, G. R.: Which pneumococcal serogroups cause the most invasive disease: Implications for conjugate vaccine formulation and use, Part I. Clin. Infect. Dis. *30*:100–121, 2000.
293. Hausdorff, W. P., Siber, G., and Paradiso, P. R.: Geographical differences in invasive pneumococcal disease rates and serotype frequency in young children. Lancet *357*:950–952, 2001.
294. Hazlewood, M., Nusrat, R., Kumararatne, D. S., et al.: The acquisition of anti-pneumococcal capsular polysaccharide *Haemophilus influenzae* type b and tetanus toxoid antibodies, with age, in the UK. Clin. Exp. Immunol. *93*:157–164, 1993.
295. Heffelfinger, J. D., Dowell, S. F., Jorgensen, J. H., et al.: Management of community-acquired pneumonia in the era of pneumococcal resistance: A report from the Drug-Resistant *Streptococcus pneumoniae* Therapeutic Working Group. Arch. Intern. Med. *160*:1399–1408, 2000.
296. Heffron, R.: Pneumonia with Special Reference to Pneumococcus Lobar Pneumonia. A Commonwealth Fund Book. Cambridge, MA, Harvard University Press, 1939.
297. Heidelberger, M., and Avery, O. T.: The soluble specific substance of pneumococcus. J. Exp. Med. *38*:73, 1923.
298. Heikkinen, T., Ruuskanen, O., Ziegler, T., et al.: Short term use of amoxicillin-clavulanate during upper respiratory tract infection for prevention of acute otitis media. J. Pediatr. *126*:313–316, 1995.
299. Heltberg, O., Korner, B., and Schouenborg, P.: Six cases of acute appendicitis with secondary peritonitis caused by *Streptococcus pneumoniae.* Eur. J. Clin. Microbiol. *3*:141–143, 1984.
300. Henderson, F. W., Gilligan, P. H., Wait, K., and Goff, D. A.: Nasopharyngeal carriage of antibiotic-resistant pneumococci by children in group day care. J. Infect. Dis. *157*:256–263, 1988.
301. Hendley, J. O., Sande, M. A., Stewart, P. M., and Gwaltney, J. M. J.: Spread of *Streptococcus pneumoniae* in families: I. Carriage rates and distribution of types. J. Infect. Dis. *132*:55–61, 1975.
302. Henneberger, P. K., Galaid, E. I., and Marr, J. S.: Descriptive epidemiology of pneumococcal meningitis in New York City. Am. J. Epidemiol. *117*:484–491, 1983.
303. Henrichsen, J.: Six newly recognized types of *Streptococcus pneumoniae.* J. Clin. Microbiol. *33*:2759–2762, 1995.
304. Henriques Normark, B., Novak, R., Ortqvist, A., et al.: Clinical isolates of *Streptococcus pneumoniae* that exhibit tolerance of vancomycin. Clin. Infect. Dis. *32*:552–558, 2001.
305. Hermans, P. W., Sluijter, M., Hoogenboezem, T., et al.: Comparative study of five different DNA fingerprint techniques for molecular typing of *Streptococcus pneumoniae* strains. J. Clin. Microbiol. *33*:1606–1612, 1995.
306. Hidalgo, H., Moore, C., Leiva, L. E., and Sorensen, R. U.: Preimmunization and postimmunization pneumococcal antibody titers in children with recurrent infections. Ann. Allergy Asthma Immunol. *76*:341–346, 1996.
307. Hoban, D. J., Doern, G. V., Fluit, A. C., et al.: Worldwide prevalence of antimicrobial resistance in *Streptococcus pneumoniae, Haemophilus influenzae,* and *Moraxella catarrhalis* in the SENTRY antimicrobial surveillance program, 1997–1999. Clin. Infect. Dis. *32*(Suppl. 2):81–93, 2001.
308. Hoberman, A., Paradise, J. L., and Cohen, R.: Duration of therapy for acute otitis media. Pediatr. Infect. Dis. J. *19*:471–473, 2000.
309. Hodges, R. G., Macleod, C. M., and Berhnard, W. G.: Epidemic pneumococcal pneumonia: III. Pneumococcal carrier studies. Am. J. Hyg. *44*:207–230, 1946.
310. Hoge, C. W., Reichler, M. R., Dominguez, E. A., et al.: An epidemic of pneumococcal disease in an overcrowded, inadequately ventilated jail. N. Engl. J. Med. *331*:643–648, 1994.

311. Hollingshead, S. K., Becker, R., and Briles, D. E.: Diversity of PspA: Mosaic genes and evidence for past recombination in *Streptococcus pneumoniae.* Infect. Immun. *68*:5889–5900, 2000.
312. Hoppe, J. E., Koster, S., Bootz, F., and Niethammer, D.: Acute mastoiditis—relevant once again. Infection *22*:178–182, 1994.
313. Howie, V. M.: Eradication of bacterial pathogens from middle ear infections. Clin. Infect. Dis. *14*(Suppl. 2):209–210, 1992.
314. Howie, V. M., Ploussard, J. H.: The "in vivo sensitivity test"—bacteriology of middle ear exudate. Pediatrics *44*:940–944, 1969.
315. Howie, V. M., and Ploussard, J. H.: Efficacy of fixed combination antibiotics versus separate components in otitis media. Clin. Pediatr. (Phila.) *11*:205–214, 1972.
316. Howie, V. M., Ploussard, J. H., and Lester, R. L., Jr.: Otitis media: A clinical and bacteriological correlation. Pediatrics *45*:29–35, 1970.
317. Howie, V. M., Ploussard, J. H., and Sloyer, J. L., Jr.: The "otitis prone" condition. Am. J. Dis. Child. *129*:676–678, 1975.
318. Howie, V. M., Ploussard, J., Sloyer, J. L., and Hill, J. C.: Use of pneumococcal polysaccharide vaccine in preventing otitis media in infants: Different results between racial groups. Pediatrics *73*:79–81, 1984.
319. Huang, C. C., Liu, C. C., Wang, S. T., et al.: Basic fibroblast growth factor in experimental and clinical bacterial meningitis. Pediatr. Res. *45*:120–127, 1999.
320. Hussey, G., Schaaf, H., Hanslo, D., et al.: Epidemiology of post-neonatal bacterial meningitis in Cape Town children. S. Afr. Med. J. *87*:51–56, 1997.
321. Hyde, T. B., Gay, K., Stephens, D. S., et al.: Macrolide resistance among invasive *Streptococcus pneumoniae* isolates. J. A. M. A. *206*:1857–1862, 2001.
322. Idanpaan-Heikkila, I., Simon, P. M., Zopf, D., et al.: Oligosaccharides interfere with the establishment and progression of experimental pneumococcal pneumonia. J. Infect. Dis. *176*:704–712, 1997.
323. Ilyas, M., Roy, S., Abbasi, S., et al.: Serious infections due to penicillin-resistant *Streptococcus pneumoniae* in two children with nephrotic syndrome. Pediatr. Nephrol. *10*:639–641, 1996.
324. Isaacson, G.: Sinusitis in childhood. Pediatr. Clin. North Am. *43*:1297–1318, 1996.
325. Ishizuka, S., Yamaya, M., Suzuki, T., et al.: Acid exposure stimulates the adherence of *Streptococcus pneumoniae* to cultured human airway epithelial cells. Effects on platelet-activating factor receptor expression. Am. J. Respir. Cell Mol. Biol. *24*:459–468, 2001.
326. Ispahani, P., Weston, V. C., Turner, D. P., and Donald, F. E.: Septic arthritis due to *Streptococcus pneumoniae* in Nottingham, United Kingdom, 1985–1998. Clin. Infect. Dis. *29*:1450–1454, 1999.
327. Istre, G. R., Tarpay, M., Anderson, M., et al.: Invasive disease due to *Streptococcus pneumoniae* in an area with a high rate of relative penicillin resistance. J. Infect. Dis. *156*:732–735, 1987.
328. Jackson, M. A., Burry, V. F., Olson, L. C., and Duthie, S. E.: Breakthrough sepsis in macrolide-resistant pneumococcal infection. Pediatr. Infect. Dis. J. *15*:1049–1050, 1996.
329. Jackson, M. A., and Rutledge, J.: Pneumococcal endocarditis in children. Pediatr. Infect. Dis. *1*:120–122, 1982.
330. Jacobs, M. R.: Treatment and diagnosis of infections caused by drug-resistant *Streptococcus pneumoniae.* Clin. Infect. Dis. *15*:119–127, 1992.
331. Jacobs, M. R.: Emergence of antibiotic resistance in upper and lower respiratory tract infections. Am. J. Manag. Care *5*(Suppl.):651–661, 1999.
332. Jacobs, M. R.: Increasing antibiotic resistance among acute otitis media pathogens and their susceptibility to oral agents based on pharmacodynamic parameters. Pediatr. Infect. Dis. J. *19*(Suppl.):47–56, 2000.
333. Jacobs, M. R., and Appelbaum, P. C.: *Streptococcus pneumoniae:* Activity of newer agents against penicillin-resistant strains. Curr. Infect. Dis. Rep. *1*:13–21, 1999.
334. Jacobs, M. R., Bajaksouzian, S., Zilles, A., et al.: Susceptibilities of *Streptococcus pneumoniae* and *Haemophilus influenzae* to 10 oral antimicrobial agents based on pharmacodynamic parameters: 1997 U.S. surveillance study. Antimicrob. Agents Chemother. *43*:1901–1908, 1999.
335. Jacobs, M. R., Dagan, R., Appelbaum, P. C., and Burch, D.: Prevalence of antimicrobial-resistant pathogens in middle ear fluid: Multinational study of 917 children with acute otitis media. Antimicrob. Agents Chemother. *42*:589–595, 1998.
336. Jacobs, M. R., Koornhof, H. J., Robins-Browne, R. M., et al.: Emergence of multiply resistant pneumococci. N. Engl. J. Med. *299*:735–740, 1978.
337. Jacobs, M. R., and Weinberg, W.: Evidence-based guidelines for treatment of bacterial respiratory tract infections in the era of antibiotic resistance. Manag. Care Interface *14*:68–80, 2001.
338. Jacobs, N. M., Lerdkachornsuk, S., and Metzger, W. I.: Pneumococcal bacteremia in infants and children: A ten-year experience at the Cook County Hospital with special reference to the pneumococcal serotypes isolated. Pediatrics *64*:296–300, 1979.
339. Jacobs, R.: Judicious use of antibiotics for common pediatric respiratory infections. Pediatr. Infect. Dis. J. *19*:938–943, 2000.
340. Jadavji, T., Law, B., Lebel, M. H., et al.: A practical guide for the diagnosis and treatment of pediatric pneumonia. C. M. A. J. *156*(Suppl.):703–711, 1997.
341. Jaffe, D. M., and Fleisher, G. R.: Temperature and total white blood cell count as indicators of bacteremia. Pediatrics *87*:670–674, 1991.
342. Jaffe, D. M., Tanz, R. R., Davis, A. T., et al.: Antibiotic administration to treat possible occult bacteremia in febrile children. N. Engl. J. Med. *317*:1175–1180, 1987.
343. Janoff, E. N., Fasching, C., Orenstein, J. M., et al.: Killing of *Streptococcus pneumoniae* by capsular polysaccharide-specific polymeric IgA, complement, and phagocytes. J. Clin. Invest. *104*:1139–1147, 1999.
344. Janoff, E. N., O'Brien, J., Thompson, P., et al.: *Streptococcus pneumoniae* colonization, bacteremia, and immune response among persons with human immunodeficiency virus infection. J. Infect. Dis. *167*:49–56, 1993.
345. Janoff, E. N., and Rubins, J. B.: Invasive pneumococcal disease in the immunocompromised host. *In* Tomasz, A. (ed.): *Streptococcus pneumoniae—*Molecular Biology and Mechanisms of Disease. Larchmont, NY, Mary Ann Liebert, Inc., 2000, pp. 321–341.
346. Jansen, W. T., Breukels, M. A., Snippe, H., et al.: Fcγ receptor polymorphisms determine the magnitude of in vitro phagocytosis of *Streptococcus pneumoniae* mediated by pneumococcal conjugate sera. J. Infect. Dis. *180*:888–891, 1999.
347. Jansen, W. T., Vakevainen-Anttila, M., Kayhty, H., et al.: Comparison of a classical phagocytosis assay and a flow cytometry assay for assessment of the phagocytic capacity of sera from adults vaccinated with a pneumococcal conjugate vaccine. Clin. Diagn. Lab. Immunol. *8*:245–250, 2001.
348. Jay, S. J., Johanson, W. G., Jr., and Pierce, A. K.: The radiographic resolution of *Streptococcus pneumoniae* pneumonia. N. Engl. J. Med. *293*:798–801, 1975.
349. Jedrzejas, M. J.: Pneumococcal virulence factors: Structure and function. Microbiol. Mol. Biol. Rev. *65*:187–207, 2001.
350. Johansen, F. E., Braathen, R., and Brandtzaeg, P.: Role of J chain in secretory immunoglobulin formation. Scand. J. Immunol. *52*:240–248, 2000.
351. Johnson, C. E., Carlin, S. A., Super, D. M., et al.: Cefixime compared with amoxicillin for treatment of acute otitis media. J. Pediatr. *119*:117–122, 1991.
352. Johnson, R. B., Jr., Newman, S. L., and Struth, A. G.: An abnormality of the alternate pathway of complement activation in sickle-cell disease. N. Engl. J. Med. *288*:803–808, 1973.
353. Johnson, S. E., Rubin, L., Romero-Steiner, S., et al.: Correlation of opsonophagocytosis and passive protection assays using human anticapsular antibodies in an infant mouse model of bacteremia for *Streptococcus pneumoniae.* J. Infect. Dis. *180*:133–140, 1999.
354. Joloba, M. L., Windau, A., Bajaksouzian, S., et al.: Pneumococcal conjugate vaccine serotypes of *Streptococcus pneumoniae* isolates and the antimicrobial susceptibility of such isolates in children with otitis media. Clin. Infect. Dis. *33*:1489–1494, 2001.
355. Juvén, T., Mertsola, J., Toikka, P., et al.: Clinical profile of serologically diagnosed pneumococcal pneumonia. Pediatr. Infect. Dis. J. *20*:1028–1033, 2001.
356. Kabins, S. A., and Lerner, C. C.: Fulminant pneumococcemia and sickle-cell anemia. J. A. M. A. *211*:467–471, 1970.
357. Kadioglu, A., Gingles, N. A., Grattan, K., et al.: Host cellular immune response to pneumococcal lung infection in mice. Infect. Immun. *68*:492–501, 2000.
358. Kaetzel, C. S.: Polymeric Ig receptor: Defender of the fort or Trojan horse? Curr. Biol. *11*:R35–R38, 2001.
359. Kakish, K. S., Mahafza, T., Batieha, A., et al.: Clinical sinusitis in children attending primary care centers. Pediatr. Infect. Dis. J. *19*:1071–1074, 2000.
360. Kaleida, P. H., Casselbrandt, M. L., Rockette, H. E., et al.: Amoxicillin or miringotomy or both for acute otitis media: Results of a randomized clinical trial. Pediatrics *87*:466–474, 1991.
361. Kaltoft, M. S., Zeuthen, N., and Konradsen, H. B.: Epidemiology of invasive pneumococcal infections in children aged 0–6 years in Denmark: A 19-year nationwide surveillance study. Acta Paediatr. Suppl. *435*:3–10, 2000.
362. Kaplan, B., Wandstrat, T. L., and Cunningham, J. R.: Overall cost in the treatment of otitis media. Pediatr. Infect. Dis. J. *16*(Suppl.):9–11, 1997.
363. Kaplan, S. L.: Clinical presentations, diagnosis, and prognostic factors of bacterial meningitis. Infect. Dis. Clin. North Am. *13*:579–594, 1999.
364. Kaplan, S. L., and Mason, E. O.: Management of infections due to antibiotic-resistant *Streptococcus pneumoniae.* Clin. Microbiol. Rev. *11*:628–644, 1998.
365. Kaplan, S. L., Mason, E. O., Jr., Barson, W. J., et al.: Outcome of invasive infections outside the central nervous system caused by *Streptococcus pneumoniae* isolates nonsusceptible to ceftriaxone in children treated with beta-lactam antibiotics. Pediatr. Infect. Dis. J. *20*:392–396, 2001.
366. Kaplan, S. L., Mason, E. O., Wald, E. R., et al.: Six year multicenter surveillance of invasive pneumococcal infections in children. Pediatr. Infect. Dis. J. *21*:141–147, 2002.
367. Karma, P., Pukander, J., and Sipila, M.: Prevention of otitis media in children by pneumococcal vaccination. Am. J. Otolaryngol. *6*:173–184, 1985.

368. Käyhty, H., and Eskola, J.: New vaccines for the prevention of pneumococcal infections. Emerg. Infect. Dis. *2*:289–298, 1996.
369. Käyhty, H., Rapola, S., Simell, B., and Kilpi, T.: Development of serum and salivary antibodies to pneumococcal protein antigens PspA, PsaA and Ply in children. Abstract 018. Presented at the 2nd International Symposium on Pneumococci and Pneumococcal Diseases, Sun City, South Africa, 2000.
370. Kays, M. B., and Denys, G. A.: In vitro activity and pharmacodynamics of azithromycin and clarithromycin against *Streptococcus pneumoniae* based on serum and intrapulmonary pharmacokinetics. Clin. Ther. *23*:413–424, 2001.
371. Kelley, M. A., Weber, D. J., Gilligan, P., et al.: Breakthrough pneumococcal bacteremia in patients being treated with azithromycin and clarithromycin. Clin. Infect. Dis. *31*:1008–1011, 2000.
372. Kellner, J. D., and Ford-Jones, L.: *Streptococcus pneumoniae* carriage in children attending 59 Canadian child care centers. Toronto Child Care Centre Study Group. Arch. Pediatr. Adolesc. Med. *153*:495–502, 1999.
373. Kilian, M., Reinholdt, J., Lomholt, H., et al.: Biological significance of IgA1 proteases in bacterial colonization and pathogenesis: Critical evaluation of experimental evidence. A. P. M. I. S. *104*:321–338, 1996.
374. Kilpi, T., Herva, E., Kaijalainen, T., et al.: Bacteriology of acute otitis media in a cohort of Finnish children followed for the first two years. Pediatr. Infect. Dis. J. *20*:654–662, 2001.
375. Kilpi, T. M., Palmu, A., Leinonen, M., et al.: Efficacy of a seven-valent pneumococcal conjugate vaccine against serotype-specific acute otitis media caused by *Streptococcus pneumoniae*. Abstract 689. Presented at the 40th Interscience Conference on Antimicrobial Agents and Chemotherapy (ICAAC), Toronto, 2000, p. 245.
376. Kilpi, T. M., Palmu, A., Leinonen, M., et al.: Effect of a 7-valent pneumococcal conjugate vaccine on acute otitis media due to vaccine serotypes after boosting with conjugate or polysaccharide vaccines. Abstract G-2036. Presented at the 41st Interscience Conference on Antimicrobial Agents and Chemotherapy (ICAAC), Chicago, 2001, p. 282.
377. Kim, P., Musher, D. M., Glezen, W. P., et al.: Association of invasive pneumococcal disease with season, atmospheric conditions, air pollution, and the isolation of respiratory viruses. Clin. Infect. Dis. *22*:100–106, 1996.
378. King, H., and Schumacker, H. B., Jr.: Splenic studies. I. Susceptibility to infection after splenectomy performed in infancy. Ann. Surg. *136*:239–242, 1952.
379. King, J. C., Vink, P. E., Farley, J. J., et al.: Comparison of the safety and immunogenicity of a pneumococcal conjugate with a licensed polysaccharide vaccine in human immunodeficiency virus and non–human immunodeficiency virus–infected children. Pediatr. Infect. Dis. J. *15*:192–196, 1996.
380. King, J. C., Vink, P. E., Farley, J. J., et al.: Safety and immunogenicity of three doses of a five-valent pneumococcal conjugate vaccine in children younger than two years with and without human immunodeficiency virus infection. Pediatrics *99*:575–580, 1997.
381. Klein, D. L.: Pneumococcal conjugate vaccines: Review and update. Microb. Drug Resist. *1*:49–58, 1995.
382. Klein, J. O.: The microbiology of otitis media. *In* Wiet, R. J., and Coulthard, S. W. (eds).: Proceedings of the Second National Conference on Otitis Media. Columbus, OH, Ross Laboratories, 1979, pp. 43–46.
383. Klein, J. O.: The epidemiology of pneumococcal disease in infants and children. Rev. Infect. Dis. *3*:246–253, 1981.
384. Klein, J. O.: Epidemiology of otitis media. Pediatr. Infect. Dis. J. *8*(Suppl.):9, 1989.
385. Klein, J. O.: Preventing recurrent otitis: What role for antibiotics? Contemp. Pediatr. *11*:44–60, 1994.
386. Klein, J. O.: Otitis media. Clin. Infect. Dis. *19*:823–833, 1994.
387. Klein, J. O.: Clinical implications of antibiotic resistance for the management of acute otitis media. Pediatr. Infect. Dis. J. *17*:1084–1089, 1998.
388. Klein, J. O.: Review of consensus reports on management of acute otitis media. Pediatr. Infect. Dis. J. *18*:1152–1155, 1999.
389. Klein, J. O.: Nonimmune strategies for prevention of otitis media. Pediatr. Infect. Dis. J. *19*(Suppl.):89–92, 2000.
390. Klugman, K. P.: Pneumococcal resistance to antibiotics. Clin. Microbiol. Rev. *3*:171–196, 1990.
391. Klugman, K. P.: Antibiotic selection of multiply resistant pneumococci. Clin. Infect. Dis. *33*:489–491, 2001.
392. Klugman, K. P., and Feldman, C.: Penicillin- and cephalosporin-resistant *Streptococcus pneumoniae*. Drugs *58*:1–4, 1999.
393. Klugman, K. P., Friedland, I. R., and Bradley, J. S.: Bactericidal activity against cephalosporin-resistant *Streptococcus pneumoniae* in cerebrospinal fluid of children with acute bacterial meningitis. Antimicrob. Agents Chemother. *39*:1988–1992, 1995.
394. Klugman, K. P., Koornhof, H. J., and Kuhnle, V.: Clinical and nasopharyngeal isolates of unusual multiply resistant pneumococci. Am. J. Dis. Child. *140*:1186–1190, 1986.
395. Klugman, K. P., Koornhof, H. J., Wasas, A., et al.: Carriage of penicillin-resistant pneumococci. Arch. Dis. Child. *61*:377–381, 1986.
396. Koch, H., and Dennison, N. J.: Office Visits to Pediatricians. Washington, DC, National Ambulatory Medical Care Service, National Center for Health Statistics, 1974.
397. Kontiokari, T., Svanberg, M., Mattila, P., et al.: Quantitative analysis of the effect of xylitol on pneumococcal nasal colonisation in rats. FEMS Microbiol. Lett. *178*:313–317, 1999.
398. Kontiokari, T., Uhari, M., and Koskela, M.: Effect of xylitol on growth of nasopharyngeal bacteria in vitro. Antimicrob. Agents Chemother. *39*:1820–1823, 1995.
399. Kornelisse, R. F., Westerbeek, C. M. L., Spoor, A. B., et al.: Pneumococcal meningitis in children: Prognostic indicators and coutcome. Clin. Infect. Dis. *21*:1390–1397, 1995.
400. Korppi, M., Heiskanen-Kosma, T., and Jalonen, E.: Aetiology of community-acquired pneumonia in children treated in hospital. Eur. J. Pediatr. *152*:24–30, 1993.
401. Korppi, M., Heiskanen-Kosma, T., and Leinonen, M.: White blood cells, C-reactive protein and erythrocyte sedimentation rate in pneumococcal pneumonia in children. Eur. Respir. J. *10*:1125–1129, 1997.
402. Koskela, M.: Antibody response of young children to parenteral vaccination with pneumococcal capsular polysaccharides: A comparison between antibody levels in serum and middle ear effusion. Pediatr. Infect. Dis. J. *5*:431–434, 1986.
403. Koskela, M., Leinonen, M., and Haiva, V. M.: First and second dose antibody responses to pneumococcal polysaccharide vaccine in infants. Pediatr. Infect. Dis. J. *5*:45–50, 1986.
404. Koskela, M., and Luotonen, J.: Recurrent pneumococcal otitis media: Presence of pneumococcal antigens and antibody in middle ear effusion compared with antibody levels in serum. *In* Lim, D. L., Bluestone, C. D., Klein, J. O., et al.: (eds.): Recent Advances in Otitis Media with Effusion. New York, Marcel Decker, 1984, pp. 251–255.
405. Kostyukova, N. N., Volkova, M. O., Ivanova, V. V., et al.: A study of pathogenic factors of *Streptococcus pneumoniae* strains causing meningitis. FEMS Immunol. Med. Microbiol. *10*:133–137, 1995.
406. Kozyrskyj, A. L., Hildes-Ripstein, G. E., Longstaffe, S. E., et al.: Treatment of acute otitis media with a shortened course of antibiotics: A meta-analysis. J. A. M. A. *279*:1736–1742, 1998.
407. Kristinsson, K. G., Sigurdardottir, S. T., Gudnason, T., et al.: Effect of vaccination with octavalent protein conjugated pneumococcal vaccines on pneumococcal carriage in infants. Abstract G-5. Presented at the 37th Interscience Conference on Antimicrobial Agents and Chemotherapy (ICAAC), Toronto, 1997, p. 193.
408. Kuppermann, N., Fleisher, G. R., and Jaffe, D. M.: Predictors of occult pneumococcal bacteremia in young febrile children. Ann. Emerg. Med. *31*:679–687, 1998.
409. Lagos, R., Levine, M. M.: Prospective, population-based surveillance for ambulatory invasive pneumococcal disease in children in Santiago, Chile. Abstract 026. Presented at the Second International Symposium on Pneumococci and Pneumococcal Diseases, Sun City, South Africa, 2000.
410. Lane, P. A., Rogers, Z. R., Woods, G. M., et al.: Fatal pneumococcal septicemia in hemoglobin SC disease. J. Pediatr. *124*:859–862, 1994.
411. Lau, G. W., Haataja, S., Lonetto, M., et al.: A functional genomic analysis of type 3 *Streptococcus pneumoniae* virulence. Mol. Microbiol. *40*:555–571, 2001.
412. Lawrence, E. R., Arias, C. A., Duke, B., et al.: Evaluation of serotype prediction by cpsA-cpsB gene polymorphism in *Streptococcus pneumoniae*. J. Clin. Microbiol. *38*:1319–1323, 2000.
413. Leach, A. J., Boswell, J. B., Asche, V., et al.: Bacterial colonization of the nasopharynx predicts very early onset and persistence of otitis media in Australian Aboriginal infants. Pediatr. Infect. Dis. J. *13*:983–989, 1994.
414. Leach, A. J., Shelby-James, T. M., Mayo, M., et al.: A prospective study of the impact of community-based azithromycin treatment of trachoma on carriage and resistance of *Streptococcus pneumoniae*. Clin. Infect. Dis. *24*:356–362, 1997.
415. Lebel, M. H., and McCracken, G. H., Jr.: Delayed cerebrospinal fluid sterilization and adverse outcome of bacterial meningitis in infants and children. Pediatrics *83*:161–167, 1989.
416. Lee, C. J., Ching, E. D., and Vickers, J. H.: Maternal immunity and antibody response of neonatal mice to pneumococcal type 19F polysaccharide. J. Clin. Microbiol. *29*:1904–1909, 1991.
417. Lee, G. M., and Harper, M. B.: Risk of bacteremia for febrile young children in the post–*Haemophilus influenzae* type b era. Arch. Pediatr. Adolesc. Med. *152*:624–628, 1998.
418. Lee, H. J., Kang, J. H., Henrichsen, J., et al.: Immunogenicity and safety of a 23-valent pneumococcal polysaccharide vaccine in healthy children and in children at increased risk of pneumococcal infection. Vaccine *13*:1533–1538, 1995.
419. Lehmann, D., Gratten, M., and Montgomery, J.: Susceptibility of pneumococcal carriage isolates to penicillin provides a conservative estimate of susceptibility of invasive pneumococci. Pediatr. Infect. Dis. J. *16*:297–305, 1997.
420. Lehmann, D., Marshall, T. F., Riley, I. F., and Alpers, M. P.: Effect of pneumococcal vaccine on morbidity from acute lower respiratory tract infections in Papua New Guinean children. Ann. Trop. Paediatr. *11*:247–257, 1991.
421. Lehmann, D., Pomat, W. S., Combs, B., et al.: Maternal immunization with pneumococcal polysaccharide vaccine in the highlands of Papua New Guinea. Vaccine *20*:1837–1845, 2002.

422. Leiberman, A., Leibovitz, E., and Piglansky, L.: Bacteriologic clinical efficacy of trimethoprim/sulfamethoxazole for the treatment of acute otitis media. Pediatr. Infect. Dis. J. *20*:260–264, 2001.
423. Leibovitz, E., and Dagan, R.: Antibiotic treatment for acute otitis media. Int. J. Antimicrob. Agents *15*:169–177, 2000.
424. Leibovitz, E., and Dagan, R.: Otitis media therapy and drug resistance—Part 1: Management principles. Infect. Med. *18*:212–216, 2001.
425. Leibovitz, E., and Dagan, R.: Otitis media therapy and drug resistance—Part 2: Current concepts and new directions. Infect. Med. *18*:263–270, 2001.
426. Leibovitz, E., Piglansky, L., and Raiz, S.: Bacteriologic efficacy of a three-day intramuscular ceftriaxone regimen in non-responsive acute otitis media. Pediatr. Infect. Dis. J. *17*:1126–1131, 1998.
427. Leibovitz, E., Piglansky, L., Raiz, S., et al.: Bacteriologic and clinical efficacy of one day versus three-day intramuscular ceftriaxone for treatment of non-responsive acute otitis media in children. Pediatr. Infect. Dis. J. *19*:1040–1045, 2000.
428. Leibovitz, E., Raiz, S., Piglansky, L., et al.: Resistance pattern of middle ear fluid isolates in acute otitis media recently treated with antibiotics. Pediatr. Infect. Dis. J. *17*:463–469, 1998.
429. Leino, T., Auranen, K., Jokinen, J., et al.: Pneumococcal carriage in children during their first two years: Important role of family exposure. Pediatr. Infect. Dis. J. *20*:1022–1027, 2001.
430. Leinonen, M., Sakkinen, A., and Kalliokoski, R.: Antibody response to 14-valent pneumococcal capsular polysaccharide vaccine in pre-school age children. Pediatr. Infect. Dis. J. *5*:39–44, 1986.
431. Leowski, J.: Mortality from acute respiratory infections in children under 5 years of age: Global estimates. World Health Stat. Q. *39*:138–144, 1986.
432. LeVine, A. M., Koeningsknecht, V., and Stark, J. M.: Decreased pulmonary clearance of *S. pneumoniae* following influenza A infection in mice. J. Virol. Methods *94*:173–186, 2001.
433. Levine, O. S., Farley, M., Harrison, L. H., et al.: Risk factors for invasive pneumococcal disease in children: A population-based case-control study in North America. Active Bacterial Core Surveillance Team. Pediatrics 103, 1999 *URL:http://www.pediatrics.org/cgi/content/full/3/e28.*
434. Levy, A., Fraser, D., Vardi, H., and Dagan, R.: Hospitalizations for infectious disease in Jewish and Bedouin children in southern Israel. Eur. J. Epidemiol. *14*:179–186, 1998.
435. Li, S., Taylor, K. B., Kelly, S. J., et al.: Vitamin C inhibits the enzymatic activity of *Streptococcus pneumoniae* hyaluronate lyase. J. Biol. Chem. *276*:15125–15130, 2001.
436. Lieu, T. A., Ray, G. T., Black, S. B., et al.: Projected cost-effectiveness of pneumococcal conjugate vaccination of healthy infants and young children. J. A. M. A. *283*:1460–1468, 2000.
437. Light, R. W., Girard, W. M., Jenkinson, S. G., and George, R. B.: Parapneumonic effusions. Am. J. Med. *60*:507–512, 1980.
438. Lim, P. L., and Lau, Y. L.: Occurrence of IGG subclass antibodies to ovalbumin, avidin, and pneumococcal polysaccharide in children. Int. Arch. Allergy Immunol. *104*:137–143, 1994.
439. Lin, J., Vambutas, A., Haruta, A., et al.: Pneumococcus activation of the 5-lipoxygenase pathway and production of glycoproteins in the middle ear of rats. J. Infect. Dis. *179*:1145–1151, 1999.
440. Lin, K. T., and Lee, C. J.: Immune response of neonates to pneumococcal polysaccharide protein conjugate. Immunology *46*:333–342, 1982.
441. Lipsitch, M.: Interpreting results from trials of pneumococcal conjugate vaccines: A statistical test for detecting vaccine-induced increases in carriage of nonvaccine serotypes. Am. J. Epidemiol. *153*:85–92, 2001.
442. Lloyd-Evans, N., O'Dempsey, T. J. D., Baldeh, I., et al.: Nasopharyngeal carriage of pneumococci in Gambian children and in their families. Pediatr. Infect. Dis. J. *15*:866–871, 1996.
443. Lockhart, N. J., Daly, K. A., Lindgren, B. R., et al.: Low cord blood type 14 pneumococcal IgG1 but not IgG2 antibody predicts early infant otitis media. J. Infect. Dis. *181*:1979–1982, 2000.
444. Loda, F. A., Collier, A. M., Glezen, W. P., et al.: Occurrence of *Diplococcus pneumoniae* in the upper respiratory tract of children. J. Pediatr. *87*:1087–1093, 1975.
445. Loeffler, J. M., Ringer, R., Hablutzel, M., et al.: The free radical scavenger alpha-phenyl-tert-butyl nitrone aggravates hippocampal apoptosis and learning deficits in experimental pneumococcal meningitis. J. Infect. Dis. *183*:247–252, 2001.
446. Long, S. S., Henretig, F. M., Teter, M. J., and McGowen, K. L.: Nasopharyngeal flora and acute otitis media. Infect. Immun. *41*:987–991, 1983.
447. Lonks, J., Garau, J., Gomez, L., et al.: Failure of macrolide antibiotic treatment in patients with bacteremia due to erythromycin-resistant *Streptococcus pneumoniae*. Clin. Infect. Dis. *35*:556–564, 2002.
448. Lonks, J. R., and Medeiros, A. A.: High rate of erythromycin and clarithromycin resistance among *Streptococcus pneumoniae* isolates from blood cultures from Providence, R.I. Antimicrob. Agents Chemother. *37*:1742–1745, 1993.
449. López, B., Cima, M. D., and Vázquez, F.: Epidemiological study of *Streptococcus pneumoniae* carriers in healthy primary-school children. Eur. J. Clin. Microbiol. Infect. Dis. *18*:771–776, 1999.
450. Low, D. E., and Scheld, W. M.: Strategies for stemming the tide of antimicrobial resistance. J. A. M. A. *279*:394–395, 1998.
451. Lucas, A. H., Moulton, K. D., Tang, V. R., et al.: Combinatorial library cloning of human antibodies to *Streptococcus pneumoniae* capsular polysaccharides: Variable region primary structures and evidence for somatic mutation of Fab fragments specific for capsular serotypes 6B, 14, and 23F. Infect. Immun. *69*:853–864, 2001.
452. Luotonen, J., Herva, E., Karma, P., et al.: The bacteriology of acute otitis media in children with special reference to *Streptococcus pneumoniae* as studied by bacteriological and antigen detection methods. Scand. J. Infect. Dis. *13*:177–183, 1981.
453. MacLeod, C. M., Hodges, R. G., Heidelberger, M., and Bernhard, W. G.: Prevention of pneumococcal pneumonia by immunization with specific capsular polysaccharides. J. Exp. Med. *82*:445–465, 1945.
454. Madhi, S. A., Petersen, K., Madhi, A., et al.: Increased disease burden and antibiotic resistance of bacteria causing severe community-acquired lower respiratory tract infections in human immunodeficiency virus type 1–infected children. Clin. Infect. Dis. *31*:170–176, 2000.
455. Madhi, S. A., Petersen, K., Madhi, A., et al.: Impact of human immunodeficiency virus type 1 on the disease spectrum of *S. pneumoniae* in South African children. Pediatr. Infect. Dis. J. *19*:1141–1147, 2000.
456. Majcherczyk, P. A., Langen, H., Heumann, D., et al.: Digestion of *Streptococcus pneumoniae* cell walls with its major peptidoglycan hydrolase releases branched stem peptides carrying proinflammatory activity. J. Biol. Chem. *274*:12537–12543, 1999.
457. Mäkela, P. H., Leinonen, M., Pukander, J., and Karma, P.: A study of the pneumococcal vaccine in prevention of clinically acute attacks of recurrent otitis media. Rev. Infect. Dis. *3*(Suppl.):124–132, 1981.
458. Malley, R., Lipsitch, M., Stack, A., et al.: Intranasal immunization with killed unencapsulatd whole cells prevents colonization and invasive disease by capsulated pneumococci. Infect. Immun. *69*:4870–4873, 2001.
459. Malley, R., Stack, A. M., Ferretti, M. L., et al.: Anticapsular polysaccharide antibodies and nasopharyngeal colonization with *Streptococcus pneumoniae* in infant rats. J. Infect. Dis. *178*:878–882, 1998.
460. Mandel, E. M., Casselbrant, M. L., Rockette, H. E., et al.: Efficacy of antimicrobial prophylaxis for recurrent middle ear effusion. Pediatr. Infect. Dis. J. *15*:1074–1082, 1996.
461. Mandell, G. L., and Coleman, E. J.: Activities of antimicrobial agents against intracellular pneumococci. Antimicrob. Agents Chemother. *44*:2561–2563, 2000.
462. Mao, C., Harper, M., McIntosh, K., et al.: Invasive pneumococcal infections in human immunodeficiency virus–infected children. J. Infect. Dis. *173*:870–876, 1996.
463. Mastro, T. D., Ghafoor, A., Nomani, N. K., et al.: Antimicrobial resistance of pneumococci in children with acute lower respiratory tract infection in Pakistan. Lancet *337*:156–159, 1991.
464. Mastro, T. D., Nomani, N. K., Ishaq, Z., et al.: The use of nasopharyngeal isolates of *Streptococcus pneumoniae* and *Haemophilus influenzae* from children in Pakistan for surveillance for antimicrobial resistance. Pediatr. Infect. Dis. J. *12*:824–830, 1993.
465. Maynard, J. E., Fleshman, J. K., and Tschopp, C. F.: Otitis media in Alaskan Eskimo children: Prospective evaluation of chemoprophylaxis. J. A. M. A. *219*:597–599, 1972.
466. Mbelle, N., Huebner, R. E., Wasas, A. D., et al.: Immunogenicity and impact on nasopharyngeal carriage of a nonavalent pneumococcal conjugate vaccine. J. Infect. Dis. *180*:1171–1176, 1999.
467. McCarthy, P. L., Jekel, J. F., Stashwick, C. A., et al.: Further definition of history and observation variables in assessing febrile children. Pediatrics *67*:687–693, 1981.
468. McCracken, G. H., Jr.: Treatment of acute otitis media in an era of increasing microbial resistance. Pediatr. Infect. Dis. J. *17*:576–579, 1998.
469. McCullers, J. A., English, B. K., and Novak, R.: Isolation and characterization of vancomycin-tolerant *Streptococcus pneumoniae* from the cerebrospinal fluid of a patient who developed recrudescent meningitis. J. Infect. Dis. *181*:369–373, 2000.
470. McGee, L., McDougal, L., Zhou, J., et al.: Nomenclature of major antimicrobial-resistant clones of *Streptococcus pneumoniae* defined by the pneumococcal molecular epidemiology network. J. Clin. Microbiol. *39*:2565–2571, 2001.
471. McIntosh, K.: Community-acquired pneumonia. N. Engl. J. Med. *346*:429–437, 2002.
472. McIntyre, P. B., Berkey, C. S., King, S. M., et al.: Dexamethasone as adjunctive therapy in bacterial meningitis. A meta-analysis of randomized clinical trials since 1988. J. A. M. A. *278*:925–931, 1997.
473. Melander, E., Mölstad, S., Persson, K., et al.: Previous antibiotic consumption and other risk factors for carriage of penicillin-resistant *Streptococcus pneumoniae* in children. Eur. J. Clin. Microbiol. Infect. Dis. *17*:834–838, 1998.
474. Metlay, J. P., Hofman, J., Cetron, M. S., et al.: Impact of penicillin susceptibility on medical outcomes for adult patients with bacteremic pneumococcal pneumonia. Clin. Infect. Dis. *30*:520–528, 2000.
475. Michelow, I. C., Lozano, J., Olsen, K., et al.: Diagnosis of *Streptococcus pneumoniae* lower respiratory infection in hospitalized children by

culture, polymerase chain reaction, serological testing, and urinary antigen detection. Clin. Infect. Dis. *34*:E1–E11, 2002.
476. Miernyk, K. M., Parkinson, A. J., Rudolph, K. M., et al.: Immunogenicity of a heptavalent pneumococcal conjugate vaccine in Apache and Navajo Indian, Alaska Native, and non-native American infants aged < 2 years. Clin. Infect. Dis. *31*:34–41, 2000.
477. Miller, E., Waight, P., Efstratiou, A., et al.: Epidemiology of invasive and other pneumococcal disease in children in England and Wales 1996–1998. Acta Paediatr. Suppl. *435*:11–16, 2000.
478. Mitten, M. J., Meulbroek, J., Nukkala, M., et al.: Efficacies of ABT-773, a new ketolide, against experimental bacterial infections. Antimicrob. Agents Chemother. *45*:2585–2593, 2001.
479. Molrine, D., Antin, J., Guinan, E., et al.: Pneumococcal conjugate vaccine (PCV) elicits protective responses in allogeneic bone marrow transplant (BMT) recipients. Abstract G-2035. Presented at the 41st Interscience Conference on Antimicrobial Agents and Chemotherapy (ICAAC), Chicago, 2001, p. 282.
480. Montgomery, J. M., Lehmann, D., Smith, T., et al.: Bacterial colonization of the upper respiratory tract and its association with acute lower respiratory tract infections in Highland children of Papua New Guinea. Rev. Infect. Dis. *23*(Suppl.):1006–1016, 1990.
481. Moore, D., Nelson, M., and Henderson, D.: Pneumococcal vaccination and HIV infection. Int. J. S. T. D. A. I. D. S. *9*:1–7, 1998.
482. Moreno, S., Carcia-Leoni, M. E., Cercenado, E., et al.: Infections caused by erythromycin resistant *Streptococcus pneumoniae*: Incidence, risk factors, and response to therapy in a prospective study. Clin. Infect. Dis. *20*:1195–1200, 1995.
483. Morona, J. K., Miller, D. C., Coffey, T. J., et al.: Molecular and genetic characterization of the capsule biosynthesis locus of *Streptococcus pneumoniae* type 23F. Microbiology *145*:781–789, 1999.
484. Morona, J. K., Morona, R., and Paton, J. C.: Comparative genetics of capsular polysaccharide biosynthesis in *Streptococcus pneumoniae* types belonging to serogroup 19. J. Bacteriol. *181*:5355–5364, 1999.
485. Moroney, J. F., Fiore, A. E., and Harrison, L. H.: Clinical outcomes of bacteremic pneumococcal pneumonia in the era of antibiotic resistance. Clin. Infect. Dis. *33*:797–805, 2001.
486. Morrison, K. E., Lake, D., Crook, J., et al.: Confirmation of psaA in all 90 serotypes of *Streptococcus pneumoniae* by PCR and potential of this assay for identification and diagnosis. J. Clin. Microbiol. *38*:434–437, 2000.
487. Mortier-Barriere, I., Humbert, O., Martin, B., et al.: Control of recombination rate during transformation of *Streptococcus pneumoniae:* An overview. Microb. Drug Resist. *3*:233–242, 1997.
488. Mufson, M. A., Oley, G., and Hughey, D.: Pneumococcal disease in a medium-sized community in the United States. J. A. M. A. *248*:1486–1489, 1982.
489. Munoz, F. M., Englund, J. A., Cheesman, C. C., et al.: Maternal immunization with pneumococcal polysaccharide vaccine in the third trimester of gestation. Vaccine *20*:826–837, 2002.
490. Muñoz, P., Sainz, J., Rodríguez-Creixéms, M., et al.: Austrian syndrome caused by highly penicillin-resistant *Streptococcus pneumoniae.* Clin. Infect. Dis. *29*:1591–1592, 1999.
491. Munoz, R., Fenoll, A., Vicioso, D., et al.: Optochin-resistant variants of *Streptococcus pneumoniae.* Diagn. Microbiol. Infect. Dis. *13*:63–66, 1990.
492. Musher, D. M.: Pneumococcal outbreaks in nursing homes. N. Engl. J. Med. *38*:1915–1916, 1998.
493. Musher, D. M.: *Streptococcus pneumoniae. In* Mandell, G. L., Bennett, J. E., and Dolin, R. (eds.): Principles and Practice of Infectious Disease. 5th ed. Philadelphia, Churchill Livingstone, 2000, pp. 2128–2146.
494. Musher, D., and Dagan, R.: Is the pneumococcus the one and only in acute otitis media? Pediatr. Infect. Dis. J. *19*:399–400, 2000.
495. Musher, D. M., Groover, J. E., Reichler, M. R., et al.: Emergence of antibody to capsular polysaccharides of *Streptococcus pneumoniae* during outbreaks of pneumonia: Association with nasopharyngeal colonization. Clin. Infect. Dis. *24*:441–446, 1997.
496. Musher, D. M., Groover, J. E., Rowland, J. M., et al.: Antibody to capsular polysaccharides of Strepto*coccus pneumoniae:* Prevalence, persistence, and response to revaccination. Clin. Infect. Dis. *17*:66–73, 1993.
497. Musher, D. M., Phan, H. M., and Baughn, R. E.: Protection against bacteremic pneumococcal infection by antibody to pneumolysin. J. Infect. Dis. *183*:827–830, 2001.
498. Musher, D. M., Phan, H. M., Watson, D. A., et al.: Antibody to capsular polysaccharide of *Streptococcus pneumoniae* at the time of hospital admission for pneumococcal pneumonia. J. Infect. Dis. *182*:158–167, 2000.
499. Nabors, G. S., Braun, P. A., Hermann, D. J., et al.: Immunization of healthy adults with a single recombinant pneumococcal surface protein A (PspA) variant stimulates broadly cross-reactive antibodies to heterologous PspA molecules. Vaccine *18*:1743–1754, 2000.
500. Nafstad, P., Hagen, J. A., Oie, L., et al.: Day care centers and respiratory health. Pediatrics *103*:753–758, 1999.
501. National Center for Health Statistics: Ambulatory Surgery in the United States, 1996. Hyattsville, MD, U.S. Department of Health and Human Services, Centers for Disease Control and Prevention, 1998 (advance data from Vital and Health Statistics, No. 300).
502. National Committee for Clinical Laboratory Standards: Performance standards for antimicrobial susceptibility testing. 11th Informational Suppl. Publication M100-S11. Wayne, PA, NCCLS, 2001.
503. Neuman, H. B., and Wald, E. R.: Bacterial meningitis in childhood at the children's hospital of Pittsburg: 1988–1998. Clin. Pediatr. (Phila.) *40*:595–600, 2001.
504. Nielsen, S. V., and Henrichsen, J.: Incidence of invasive pneumococcal disease and distribution of capsular types of pneumococci in Denmark, 1989–1994. Epidemiol. Infect. *117*:411–416, 1996.
505. Nilsson, P., and Laurell, M. H.: Carriage of penicillin-resistant *Streptococcus pneumoniae* by children in day-care centers during an intervention program in Malmo, Sweden. Pediatr. Infect. Dis. J. *20*:1144–1149, 2001.
506. Nohynek, H., Eskola, J., Laine, E., et al.: The causes of hospital-treated acute lower respiratory tract infection in children. Am. J. Dis. Child. *145*:618–622, 1991.
507. Novak, R., Henriques, B., Charpentier, E., et al.: Emergence of vancomycin tolerance in *Streptococcus pneumoniae.* Nature *399*: 590–593, 1999.
508. Nowak-Wegrzyn, A. H., Winkelstein, J. A., Stover, B. M., et al.: Serum opsonic activity for *Streptococcus pneumoniae* types 6B and 14 in infants with sickle cell disease after immunization with pneumococcal protein conjugate vaccine. Pediatric Academic Societies Annual Meeting. Abstract 57. Pediatr. Res. *45*:11, 1999.
509. Nuorti, J. P., Butler, J. C., Farley, M. M., et al.: Cigarette smoking and invasive pneumococcal disease. N. Engl. J. Med. *342*:681–689, 2000.
510. Obaro, S. K., Adegbola, R. A., Banya, W. A., and Greenwood B. M.: Carriage of pneumococci after pneumococcal vaccination. Lancet *348*:272, 1996.
511. O'Brien, K. L., Bronsdon, M. A., Becenti, J., et al.: Ability of a seven valent pneumococcal conjugate vaccine to protect unvaccinated 2 month old infants against nasopharyngeal colonization. Abstract G-2032. Presented at the 41st Interscience Conference on Antimicrobial Agents and Chemotherapy (ICAAC), Chicago, 2001, p. 281.
512. O'Brien, K. L., Bronsdon, M., Carlone, G. M., et al.: Effect of a seven valent pneumococcal conjugate vaccine on nasopharyngeal (NP) carriage among native American infants. Pediatric Academic Societies Annual Meeting. Abstract 1463. Pediatr. Res. *49*:256, 2001.
513. O'Brien, K. L., Croll, J., Parkinson, A. J., et al.: Active laboratory-based surveillance for invasive *Streptococcus pneumoniae* (pneumococcus) among Navajo people in the American southwest, 1989–1996. Abstract 1187. Presented at the 39th Interscience Conference on Antimicrobial Agents and Chemotherapy (ICAAC), San Francisco, 1999, p. 678.
514. O'Brien, K. L., Dowell, S. F., Schwartz, B., et al.: Acute sinusitis: Principle of judicious use of antimicrobial agents. Pediatrics *101*:174–177, 1998.
515. O'Brien, K. L., Moulton, L., Reid, R. R., et al.: Invasive disease efficacy of a 7-valent pneumococcal conjugate vaccine among Navajo and White Mountain Apache Children. Pediatric Academic Societies Annual Meeting. Abstract 1371. Pediatr. Res. *49*:240, 2001.
516. O'Brien, K. L., Swift, A. J., Winkelstein, J. A., et al.: The safety and immunogenicity of heptavalent pneumococcal vaccine conjugated to CRM197 among infants with sickle cell disease. Pediatrics *106*:965–972, 2000.
517. O'Demsey, T. D. J., McArdle, T., Ceesay, S. J., et al.: Immunization with a pneumococcal polysaccharide vaccine during pregnancy. Vaccine *14*:963–970, 1996.
518. O'Dempsey, T. J., McArdle, T. F., Lloyd-Evans, N., et al.: Pneumococcal disease among children in a rural area of west Africa. Pediatr. Infect. Dis. J. *15*:431–437, 1996.
519. Olson, L. C., and Jackson, M. A.: Only the pneumococcus. Pediatr. Infect. Dis. J. *18*:849–850, 1999.
520. Orange, M., and Gray, B. M.: Pneumococcal serotypes causing disease in children in Alabama. Pediatr. Infect. Dis. J. *12*:243–244, 1993.
521. Ort, S., Ryan, R. L., Barden, G., et al.: Pneumococcal pneumonia in hospitalized patients. J. A. M. A. *249*:214–218, 1983.
522. Ostergaard, C., Benfield, T., Gesser, B., et al.: Pretreatment with granulocyte colony-stimulating factor attenuates the inflammatory response but not the bacterial load in cerebrospinal fluid during experimental pneumococcal meningitis in rabbits. Infect. Immun. *67*:3430–3436, 1999.
523. Ostergaard, C., Yieng-Kow, R. V., Benfield, T., et al.: Inhibition of leukocyte entry into the brain by the selectin blocker fucoidin decreases interleukin-1 (IL-1) levels but increases IL-8 levels in cerebrospinal fluid during experimental pneumococcal meningitis in rabbits. Infect. Immun. *68*:3153–3157, 2000.
524. Overturf, G. D.: Infections and immunizations of children with sickle cell disease. Adv. Pediatr. Infect. Dis. *14*:191–218, 1999.
525. Paganini, H., Guiñazú, J. R., Hernándex, C., et al.: Comparative analysis of outcome and clinical features in children with pleural empyema caused by penicillin-nonsusceptible and penicillin-susceptible *Streptococcus pneumoniae.* Int. J. Infect. Dis. *5*:86–88, 2001.

526. Pallares, R., Linares, J., Vadillo, M., et al.: Resistance to penicillin and cephalosporin and mortality from severe pneumococcal pneumonia in Barcelona, Spain. N. Engl. J. Med. *333*:474–480, 1995.
527. Palmu, A. A., Verho, J., Mäkelä, P. H., and Kilpi, T. M.: Long-term efficacy of the seven-valent PncCRM vaccine on otitis media. Presented at the 3rd International Symposium on Pneumococi and Pneumococcal Diseases, Anchorage, Alaska, 2002, p. 72.
528. Pankuch, G. A., Jacobs, M. R., and Appelbaum, P. C.: Susceptibilities of 200 penicillin-susceptible and -resistant pneumococci to piperacillin, piperacillin-tazobactam, ticarcillin, ticarcillin-clavulanate, ampicillin, ampicillin-sulbactam, ceftazidime, and ceftriaxone. Antimicrob. Agents Chemother. *38*:2905–2907, 1994.
529. Paradise, J. L., Rockette, H. E., and Colborn, K.: Otitis media in 2253 Pittsburg-area infants: Prevalence and risk factors during the first two years of life. Pediatrics *99*:318–333, 1997.
530. Paris, M. M., Hickey, S. M., Uscher, M. I., et al.: Effect of dexamethasone on therapy of experimental penicillin- and cephalosporin-resistant pneumococcal meningitis. Antimicrob. Agents Chemother. *38*:1320–1324, 1994.
531. Park, M. K., Sun, Y., Olander, J. V., et al.: The repertoire of human antibodies to the carbohydrate capsule of *Streptococcus pneumoniae* 6B. J. Infect. Dis. *174*:75–82, 1996.
532. Pastor, P., Medley, F., and Murphy, T. V.: Invasive pneumococcal disease in Dallas County, Texas: Results from population-based surveillance in 1995. Clin. Infect. Dis. *26*:590–595, 1998.
533. Paton, J. C., Berry, A. M., and Lock, R. A.: Molecular analysis of putative pneumococcal virulence proteins. Microb. Drug Resist. *3*:1–10, 1997.
534. Pearson, H. A.: Prevention of pneumococcal disease in sickle cell anemia. J. Pediatr. *129*:788–789, 1996.
535. Pearson, H. A., Cornelius, E. A., Schwartz, A. D., et al.: Transfusion-reversible functional asplenia in children with sickle-cell anemia. N. Engl. J. Med. *283*:334–337, 1970.
536. Pécoul, B., Varaine, F., Keita, M., et al.: Long-acting chloramphenicol versus intravenous ampicillin for treatment of bacterial meningitis. Lancet *338*:862–866, 1991.
537. Peled, N., and Yagupsky, P.: Improved detection of *Streptococcus pneumoniae* in middle ear fluid cultures by use of a gentamicin-containing medium. J. Clin. Microbiol. *37*:3415–3416, 1999.
538. Peltola, H.: Burden of meningitis and other severe bacterial infections of children in Africa: Implications for prevention. Clin. Infect. Dis. *32*:64–75, 2001.
539. Pelton, S.: Prevention of acute and recurrent otitis media. Lancet *356*:1370–1371, 2000.
540. Pelton, S. I., and Klein, J. O.: The promise of immunoprophylaxis for prevention of acute otitis media. Pediatr. Infect. Dis. J. *18*:926–935, 1999.
541. Perez Retortillo, J. A., Marco, F., Richard, C., et al.: Pneumococcal pericarditis with cardiac tamponade in a patient with chronic graft-versus-host disease. Bone Marrow Transplant. *21*:299–300, 1998.
542. Perrin, J. M., Charney, E., MacWhinney, J. B., Jr., et al.: Sulfisoxazole as chemoprophylaxis for recurrent otitis media: A double-blind crossover study in pediatric practice. N. Engl. J. Med. *291*:664–667, 1974.
543. Pessey, J. J., Gehanno, P., Thoroddsen, E., et al.: Short course therapy with cefuroxime axetil for acute otitis media: Results of a randomized multicenter comparison with amoxicillin/clavulanate. Pediatr. Infect. Dis. J. *18*:854–859, 1999.
544. Peters, V. B., Diamant, E. P., Hodes, D. S., and Cimino, C. O.: Impaired immunity to pneumococcal polysaccharide antigens in children with human immunodeficiency virus infection immunized with pneumococcal vaccine. Pediatr. Infect. Dis. J. *13*:933–934, 1994.
545. Pichard, E., Gillis, D., Aker, M., and Engelhard, D.: Rebound fever in bacterial meningitis: Role of dexamethasone dosage. Isr. J. Med. Sci. *30*:408–411, 1994.
546. Pichichero, M. E.: Persistent acute otitis media: II. Antimicrobial treatment. Pediatr. Infect. Dis. J. *14*:183–188, 1995.
547. Pichichero, M. E., and Cohen, R.: Shortened course of antibiotic therapy for acute otitis media, sinusitis and tonsillopharyngitis. Pediatr. Infect. Dis. J. *16*:680–695, 1997.
548. Pichichero, M. E., Marscocci, S. M., Murphy, M. L., et al.: A prospective observational study of 5-, 7-, and 10-day antibiotic treatment for acute otitis media. Otolaryngol. Head Neck Surg. *124*:381–387, 2001.
549. Pihlajamäki, M., Kotilainen, P., Kaurila, T., et al.: Macrolide-resistant *Streptococcus pneumoniae* and use of antimicrobial agents. Clin. Infect. Dis. *33*:483–488, 2001.
550. Pomat, W. S., Lehmann, D., Sanders, R. C., et al.: Immunoglobulin G antibody responses to polyvalent pneumococcal vaccine in children in the highlands of Papua New Guinea. Infect. Immun. *62*:1848–1853, 1994.
551. Poulsen, K., Reinholdt, J., Jespersgaard, C., et al.: A comprehensive genetic study of streptococcal immunoglobulin A1 proteases: Evidence for recombination within and between species. Infect. Immun. *66*:181–190, 1998.
552. Prellner, K., Fogle-Hansson, M., Jorgensen, F., et al.: Prevention of recurrent acute otitis media in otitis-prone children by intermittent prophylaxis with penicillin. Acta Otolaryngol. *114*:182–187, 1994.
553. Preventing pneumococcal disease among infants and young children. Recommendations of the Advisory Committee on Immunization Practices (ACIP). M. M. W. R. Recomm. Rep. *49*(RR-9):1–35, 2000.
554. Prevention of pneumococcal disease: Recommendations of the Advisory Committee on Immunization Practices (ACIP). M. M. R. W. Recomm. Rep. *46*(RR-8):1–24, 1997.
555. Principi, N., Marchisio, P., Schito, G. C., and Mannelli, S.: Risk factors for carriage of respiratory pathogens in the nasopharynx of healthy children. Ascanius Project Collaborative Group. Pediatr. Infect. Dis. J. *18*:517–523, 1999.
556. Prinz, M., Kann, O., Draheim, H. J., et al.: Microglial activation by components of gram-positive and -negative bacteria: Distinct and common routes to the induction of ion channels and cytokines. J. Neuropathol. Exp. Neurol. *58*:1078–1089, 1999.
557. Prober, C. G.: The role of steroids in the management of children with bacterial meningitis. Pediatrics *95*:29–31, 1995.
558. Pukander, J., Karma, P., and Sipila, M.: Occurrence and recurrence of acute otitis media among children. Acta Otolaryngol. (Stockh.) *94*:479–486, 1982.
559. Radetsky, M., Istre, G., Johansen, T., et al.: Multiply resistant pneumococcus causing meningitis: Its epidemiology within a day-care centre. Lancet *2*:771–773, 1981.
560. Ragsdale, A., and Sanford, J.: Interfering effect of incubation in carbon dioxide on the identification of pneumococci by optochin discs. Appl. Microbiol. *22*:854–855, 1971.
561. Rahav, G., Toledano, Y., Engelhard, D., et al.: Invasive penumococcal infections: A comparison between adults and children. Medicine (Baltimore) *76*:295–303, 1997.
562. Ramirez, M., Morrison, D. A., and Tomasz, A.: Ubiquitous distribution of the competence related genes coma and comc among isolates of *Streptococcus pneumoniae*. Microb. Drug Resist. *3*:39–52, 1997.
563. Ramirez, M., Severina, E., and Tomasz, A.: A high incidence of prophage carriage among natural isolates of *Streptococcus pneumoniae*. J. Bacteriol. *181*:3618–3625, 1999.
564. Ramirez, M., and Tomasz, A.: Acquisition of new capsular genes among clinical isolates of antibiotic-resistant *Streptococcus pneumoniae*. Microb. Drug Resist. *5*:241–246, 1999.
565. Rapola, S., Jäntti, V., Haikala, R., et al.: Natural development of antibodies to pneumococcal surface protein A, pneumococcal surface adhesin A, and pneumolysin in relation to pneumococcal carriage and acute otitis media. J. Infect. Dis. *182*:1146–1152, 2000.
566. Rapola, S., Kilpi, T., Lahdenkari, M., et al.: Antibody response to the pneumococcal proteins pneumococcal surface adhesin A and pneumolysin in children with acute otitis media. Pediatr. Infect. Dis. J. *20*:482–487, 2001.
567. Rapola, S., Kilpi, T., Lahdenkari, M., et al.: Do antibodies to pneumococcal surface adhesin A prevent pneumococcal involvement in acute otitis media? J. Infect. Dis. *184*:577–581, 2001.
568. Rauch, A. M., O'Ryan, M., Van, R., and Pickering, L. K.: Invasive disease due to multiply resistant *Streptococcus pneumoniae* in a Houston, Tex, day-care center. Am. J. Dis. Child. *144*:923–927, 1990.
569. Rautonen, J., Siimes, M. A., Lundstrom, U., et al.: Vaccination of children during treatment for leukemia. Acta Paediatr. *75*:579–585, 1986.
570. Reichler, M. R., Allphin, A. A., Breiman, R. F., et al.: The spread of multiply resistant *Streptococcus pneumoniae* at a day care center in Ohio. J. Infect. Dis. *166*:1146–1153, 1992.
571. Reinert, R. R., Kaufhold, A., Kuhnemund, O., and Lutticken, R.: Serum antibody responses to vaccination with 23-valent pneumococcal vaccine in splenectomized patients. Int. J. Med. Microbiol. Virol. Parasitol. Infect. Dis. *281*:481–490, 1994.
572. Resistance of *Streptococcus pneumoniae* to fluoroquinolones—United States, 1995–1999. M. M. W. R. Morb. Mortal. Wkly. Rep. *50*(30):800–804, 2001.
573. Rieux, V., Carbon, C., and Azoulay-Dupuis, E.: Complex relationship between acquisition of β-lactam resistance and loss of virulence in *Streptococcus pneumoniae*. J. Infect. Dis. *184*:66–72, 2001.
574. Rijkers, G. T., Sanders, E. A. M., Breukels, M. A., and Zegers, B. J. M.: Responsiveness of infants to capsular polysaccharides: Implications for vaccine development. Rev. Med. Microbiol. *7*:3–12, 1996.
575. Riley, I. D., Lehmann, D., Alpers, M. P., et al.: Pneumococcal vaccine prevents death from acute lower-respiratory-tract infections in Papua New Guinean children. Lancet *2*:877–881, 1986.
576. Riley, I. D., Lehmann, D., and Alpers, M. P.: Pneumococcal vaccine trials in Papua New Guinea: Relationships between epidemiology of pneumococcal infection and efficacy of vaccine. Rev. Infect. Dis. *13*(Suppl.):535–541, 1991.
577. Roark, R., and Berman, S.: Continuous twice daily or once daily amoxicillin prophylaxis compared with placebo for children with recurrent acute otitis media. Pediatr. Infect. Dis. J. *16*:376–381, 1997.
578. Robbins, J. B., Austrian, R., Lee, C. J., et al.: Considerations for formulating the second-generation pneumococcal capsular polysaccharide

vaccine with emphasis on the cross-reactive types within groups. J. Infect. Dis. *148*:1136–1159, 1983.
579. Robbins, J. B., and Schneerson, R.: Polysaccharide-protein conjugates: A new generation of vaccines. J. Infect. Dis. *161*:821–832, 1990.
580. Robert, P. Y., and Adenis, J. P.: Comparative review of topical ophthalmic antibacterial preparations. Drugs *61*:175–185, 2001.
581. Robinson, K. A., Baughman, W., Rothrock, S. G., et al.: Epidemiology of invasive *Streptococcus pneumoniae* infections in the United States, 1995–1998. Opportunities for prevention in the conjugate vaccine era. J. A. M. A. *285*:1729–1735, 2001.
582. Rodriguez, M. E., van der Pol, W. L., Sanders, L. A., et al.: Crucial role of FcγRIIa (CD32) in assessment of functional anti–*Streptococcus pneumoniae* antibody activity in human sera. J. Infect. Dis. *179*:423–433, 1999.
583. Rodriguez, W. J., and Schwartz, R. H.: *Streptococcus pneumoniae* causes otitis media with higher fever and more redness of tympanic membrane than *Haemophilus influenzae* or *Moraxella catarrhalis*. Pediatr. Infect. Dis. J. *18*:942–944, 1999.
584. Rodriguez-Barradas, M. C., Musher, D. M., Lahart, C., et al.: Antibody to capsular polysaccharides of *Streptococcus pneumoniae* after vaccination of human immuno-deficiency virus–infected subjects with 23-valent pneumococcal vaccine. J. Infect. Dis. *165*:553–556, 1992.
585. Romero-Steiner, S., Libutti, D., Pais, L. B., et al.: Standardization of an opsonophagocytic assay for the measurement of functional antibody activity against *Streptococcus pneumoniae* using differentiated HL-60 cells. Clin. Diagn. Lab. Immunol. *4*:415–422, 1997.
586. Rosén, C., Christensen, P., Hovelius, B., and Prellner, K.: A longitudinal study of the nasopharyngeal carriage of pneumococci as related to pneumococcal vaccination in children attending day-care centers. Acta Otolaryngol. (Stockh.) *98*:524–532, 1984.
587. Rosen, I. A., Hakansson, A., and Aniansson, G.: Antibodies to pneumococcal polysaccharides in human milk: Lack of relationship to colonization and acute otitis media. Pediatr. Infect. Dis. J. *15*:498–507, 1996.
588. Rosenblüt, A., Santolaya, M. E., González, P., et al.: Bacterial and viral etiology of acute otitis media in Chilean children. Pediatr. Infect. Dis. J. *20*:501–507, 2001.
589. Rosenfeld, R. M.: What to expect from medical treatment of otitis media. Pediatr. Infect. Dis. J. *14*:731–738, 1995.
590. Rosenfeld, R. M., Vertrees, J. E., Carr, J., et al.: Clinical efficacy of antimicrobial drugs for acute otitis media: Metaanalysis of 5400 children from thirty-three randomized trials. J. Pediatr. *124*:355–367, 1994.
591. Rosenow, C., Ryan, P., Weiser, J. N., et al.: Contribution of novel choline-binding proteins to adherence, colonization and immunogenicity of *Streptococcus pneumoniae*. Mol. Microbiol. *25*:819–829, 1997.
592. Roson, B., Carratala, J., Tubau, F., et al.: Usefulness of betalactam therapy for community-acquired pneumonia in the era of drug-resistant *Streptococcus pneumoniae:* A randomized study of amoxicillin-clavulanate and ceftriaxone. Microb. Drug Resist. *7*:85–96, 2001.
593. Rothrock, S. G., Green, S. M., Harper, M. B., et al.: Parenteral vs oral antibiotics in the prevention of serious bacterial infections in children with *Streptococcus pneumoniae* occult bacteremia: A meta-analysis. Acad. Emerg. Med. *5*:599–606, 1998.
594. Rothrock, S. G., Green, S. M., Wren, J., et al.: Pediatric bacterial meningitis: Is prior antibiotic therapy associated with an altered clinical presentation? Ann. Emerg. Med. *21*:146–152, 1992.
595. Rothrock, S. G., Harper, M. B., Green, S. M., et al.: Do oral antibiotics prevent meningitis and serious bacterial infections in children with *Streptococcus pneumoniae* occult bacteremia? A meta-analysis. Pediatrics *99*:438–444, 1997.
596. Rovers, M. M., Zielhuis, G. A., Ingels, K., et al.: Day-care and otitis media in young children: A critical overview. Eur. J. Pediatr. *158*:1–6, 1999.
597. Roy, S., Knox, K., Segal, S., et al.: MBL genotype and risk of invasive pneumococcal disease: A case-control study. Lancet *359*:1569–1573, 2002.
598. Rubin, L. G., Mardy, G. V., Pais, L., and Carlone, G.: Human anticapsular concentration required for protection against experimental pneumococcal bacteremia. Abstract G47. Presented at the 35th Interscience Conference on Antimicrobial Agents and Chemotherapy (ICAAC), San Francisco, 1995, p. 166.
599. Ruuskanen, O., Nohynek, H., Ziegler, T., et al.: Pneumonia in childhood: Etiology and response to antimicrobial therapy. Eur. J. Clin. Microbiol. Infect. Dis. *11*:217–223, 1992.
600. Ryan, M. J., Kavanagh, R., Wall, P. G., and Hazleman, B. L.: Bacterial joint infections in England and Wales: Analysis of bacterial isolates over a four year period. Br. J. Rheumatol. *36*:370–373, 1997.
601. Rytel, M. W., Dailey, M. P., Schiffman, G., et al.: Pneumococcal vaccine immunization of patients with renal impairment. Proc. Soc. Exp. Biol. Med. *182*:468–473, 1986.
602. Saenz, R. E., Sanders, C. V., Aldridge, K. E., and Patel, M. M.: Purulent pericarditis with associated cardiac tamponade caused by a *Streptococcus pneumoniae* strain highly resistant to penicillin, cefotaxime, and ceftriaxone. Clin. Infect. Dis. *26*:762–763, 1998.
603. Saez-Llorens, X., Castano, E., Garcia, R., et al.: Prospective randomized comparison of cefepime and cefotaxime for treatment of bacterial meningitis in infants and children. Antimicrob. Agents Chemother. *39*:937–940, 1995.
604. Saez-Llorens, X., and McCracken, G. H.: Antimicrobial and anti-inflammatory treatment of bacterial meningitis. Infect. Dis. Clin. North Am. *13*:619–636, 1999.
605. Salazar, J. C., Daly, K. A., Giebink, G. S., et al.: Low cord blood pneumococcal immunoglobulin G (IgG) antibodies predict early onset acute otitis media in infancy. Am. J. Epidemiol. *145*:1048–1056, 1997.
606. Sá-Leão, R., Tomasz, A., Santos Sanches, I., et al.: Carriage of internationally spread clones of *Streptococcus pneumoniae* with unusual drug resistance patterns in children attending day care centers in Lisbon, Portugal. J. Infect. Dis. *182*:1153–1160, 2000.
607. Sá-Leão, R., Tomasz, A., Santos Sanches, I., et al.: Genetic diversity and clonal patterns among antibiotic-susceptible and -resistant *Streptococcus pneumoniae* colonizing children: Day care centers as autonomous epidemiological units. J. Clin. Microbiol. *38*:4137–4144, 2000.
608. Samore, M. H., Magill, M. K., Alder, S. C., et al.: High rates of multiple antibiotic resistance in *Streptococcus pneumoniae* from healthy children living in isolated rural communities: Association with cephalosporin use and intrafamilial transmission. Pediatrics *108*:856–865, 2001.
609. Sanchez, C., Armengol, R., Lite, J., et al.: Penicillin-resistant pneumococci and community-acquired pneumonia. Lancet *339*:988, 1992.
610. Sanders, L. A., Rijkers, G. T., Kuis, W., et al.: Defective antipneumococcal polysaccharide antibody response in children with recurrent respiratory tract infections. J. Allergy Clin. Immunol. *91*:110–119, 1993.
611. Sanders, L. A., Rijkers, G. T., Tenbergen Meekes, A. M., et al.: Immunoglobulin isotype-specific antibody responses to pneumococcal polysaccharide vaccine in patients with recurrent bacterial respiratory tract infections. Pediatr. Res. *37*:812–819, 1995.
612. Santosham, M., Reid, G., and Almeido-Hill, J.: Efficacy of bacterial polysaccharide immune globulin for prevention of bacteremia pneumococcal infections in Apache children. Abstract 1055. Pediatr. Res. *31*:178, 1992.
613. Schaad, U. B., Kaplan, S. L., and McCracken, G. H.: Steroid therapy for bacterial meningitis. Clin. Infect. Dis. *20*:685–690, 1995.
614. Schaad, U. B., Krucko, J., and Pfenninger, J.: An extended experience with cefuroxime therapy of childhood bacterial meningitis. Pediatr. Infect. Dis. *3*:410–416, 1984.
615. Schmidt, H., Stuertz, K., Bruck, W., et al.: Intravenous granulocyte colony-stimulating factor increases the release of tumour necrosis factor and interleukin-1 beta into the cerebrospinal fluid, but does not inhibit the growth of *Streptococcus pneumoniae* in experimental meningitis. Scand. J. Immunol. *49*:481–486, 1999.
616. Schrag, S. J., Peña, C., Fernández, J., et al.: Effect of short-course, high-dose amoxicillin therapy on resistant pneumococcal carriage. J. A. M. A. *286*:49–56, 2001.
617. Schuchat, A., Robinson, K., Wenger, J. D., et al.: Bacterial meningitis in the United States in 1995. Active Surveillance Team. N. Engl. J. Med. *337*:970–976, 1997.
618. Schultz, M. J., Wijnholds, J., Peppelenbosch, M. P., et al.: Mice lacking the multidrug resistance protein 1 are resistant to *Streptococcus pneumoniae*–induced pneumonia. J. Immunol. *166*:4059–4064, 2001.
619. Schutze, G., Mason, E. O., Barson, W., et al.: Invasive pneumococcal infections in children with asplenia. Pediatr. Infect. Dis. J. *21*:278–282, 2002.
620. Schutze, G. E., Mason, E. O., Wald, E. R., et al.: Pneumococcal infections in children after transplantation. Clin. Infect. Dis. *33*:16–21, 2001.
621. Scott, J. A. G., Hall, A. J., Hannington, A., et al.: Serotype distribution and prevalence of resistance to benzylpenicillin in three representative populations of *Streptococcus pneumoniae* isolates from the coast of Kenya. Clin. Infect. Dis. *27*:1442–1450, 1998.
622. Scott, J. A. G., Hall, A. J., Muyodi, C., et al.: Aetiology, outcome, and risk factors for mortality among adults with acute pneumonia in Kenya. Lancet *355*:1225–1230, 2000.
623. Seeler, R. A., Metzger, W., and Mufson, M. A.: *Diplococcus pneumoniae* infections in children with sickle cell anemia. Am. J. Dis. Child. *123*:8–10, 1972.
624. Seikel, K., Shelton, S., and McCracken, G. H.: Middle ear fluid concentrations of amoxicillin after large dosages in children with acute otitis media. Pediatr. Infect. Dis. J. *17*:969–970, 1998.
625. Sell, S. H., Wright, P. F., and Vaughn, W. K.: Clinical studies of pneumococcal vaccines in infants: I. Reactogenicity and immunogenicity of two polyvalent polysaccharide vaccines. Rev. Infect. Dis. *3*(Suppl.):97–107, 1981.
626. Sen, S., Lalitha, M. K., Fenn, A. S., and Mammen, K. E.: Primary peritonitis in children. Ann. Trop. Paediatr. *3*:53–56, 1983.
627. Severin, A., Severina, E., and Tomasz, A.: Abnormal physiological properties and altered cell wall composition in *Streptococcus pneumoniae* grown in the presence of clavulanic acid. Antimicrob. Agents Chemother. *41*:504–510, 1997.
628. Severina, E., Ramirez, M., and Tomasz, A.: Prophage carriage as a molecular epidemiological marker in *Streptococcus pneumoniae*. J. Clin. Microbiol. *37*:3308–3315, 1999.

629. Shahid, N. S., Steinhoff, M. C., Hoque, S. S., et al.: Serum, breast milk, and infant antibody after maternal immunization with pneumococcal vaccine. Lancet *346*:1252–1257, 1995.
630. Shann, F.: Etiology of severe pneumonia in children in developing countries. Pediatr. Infect. Dis. J. *5*:247–252, 1986.
631. Shapiro, E. D., Wald, E. R., and Brozanski, B. A.: Periorbital cellulitis and paranasal sinusitis: A reappraisal. Pediatr. Infect. Dis. J. *1*:91–94, 1982.
632. Shinefield, H., Black, S., Elvin, L., et al.: Impact of the introduction of pneumococcal conjugate vaccine on the epidemiology of invasive disease in children less than five years of age within Northern California Kaiser Permanente (NCKP). Presented at the 20th Annual Meeting of the European Society for Paediatric Infectious Disease, Vilnius, Lithuania, 2002, p. 127.
633. Shinefield, H., Black, S., Ray, P., et al.: Efficacy, immunogenicity and safety of heptavalent pneumococcal conjugate vaccine in low birth weight and preterm infants. Pediatr. Infect. Dis. J. *21*:182–186, 2002.
634. Shurin, P. A., Giebink, G. S., Wegman, D. G., et al.: Prevention of pneumococcal otitis media in chinchillas with human bacterial polysaccharide immune globulin. J. Clin. Microbiol. *26*:755–759, 1988.
635. Shurin, P. A., Rehmus, J. M., Johnson, C. E., et al.: Bacterial polysaccharide immune globulin for prophylaxis of acute otitis media in high-risk children. J. Pediatr. *123*:801–810, 1993.
636. Siber, G. R.: Pneumococcal disease: Prospects for a new generation of vaccines. Science *265*:1385–1387, 1994.
637. Siber, G. R., Thompson, C., Raymond Reid, G., et al.: Evaluation of bacterial polysaccharide immune globulin for the treatment or prevention of *Haemophilus influenzae* type b and pneumococcal disease. J. Infect. Dis. *165*(Suppl.):129–133, 1992.
638. Siegel, M., and Timpone, J.: Penicillin-resistant *Streptococcus pneumoniae* endocarditis: A case report and review. Clin. Infect. Dis. *32*:972–974, 2001.
639. Silverstein, M., Bachur, R., and Harper, M. B.: Clinical implications of penicillin and ceftriaxone resistance among children with pneumococcal bacteremia. Pediatr. Infect. Dis. J. *18*:35–41, 1999.
640. Simell, B., Korkeila, M., Pursiainen, H., et al.: Pneumococcal carriage and otitis media induce salivary antibodies to pneumococcal surface adhesin A, pneumolysin, and pneumococcal surface protein A in children. J. Infect. Dis. *183*:887–896, 2001.
641. Sinus and Allergy Health Partnership: Antimicrobial treatment guidelines for acute bacterial rhinosinusitis. Otolaryngol. Head Neck Surg. *123*:5–31, 2000.
642. Sipila, M., Pukander, J., Karma, P.: Incidence of acute otitis media up to the age of 1 1/2 years in urban infants. Acta Otolaryngol. (Stockh.) *104*:138–145, 1987.
643. Sirotnak, A. P., Eppes, S. C., and Klein, J. D.: Tuboovarian abscess and peritonitis caused by *Streptococcus pneumoniae* serotype 1 in young girls. Clin. Infect. Dis. *22*:993–996, 1996.
644. Sloas, M. M., Barrett, F. F., Chesney, P. J., et al.: Cephalosporin treatment failure in penicillin- and cephalosporin-resistant *Streptococcus pneumoniae* meningitis. Pediatr. Infect. Dis. J. *11*:662–666, 1992.
645. Sloyer, J. K., Jr., Howie, V. M., Ploussard, J. H., et al.: The immune response to acute otitis media in children. I. Serotypes isolated and serum and middle ear fluid antibody in pneumococcal otitis media. Infect. Immun. *9*:1028–1032, 1974.
646. Sloyer, J. L., Jr., Ploussard, J. H., and Howie, V. M.: Efficacy of pneumococcal polysaccharide vaccine in preventing acute otitis media in infants in Huntsville, Alabama. Rev. Infect. Dis. *3*(Suppl.):119–123, 1981.
647. Smillie, W. G., Warnock, G. H., and White, H. J.: A study of a type 1 pneumococcus epidemic at the state hospital at Worcester, Mass. Am. J. Public Health *28*:293–302, 1938.
648. Smith, A. M., and Klugman, K. P.: Non–penicillin-binding protein mediated high-level penicillin and cephalosporin resistance in a Hungarian clone of *Streptococcus pneumoniae.* Microb. Drug Resist. *6*:105–110, 2000.
649. Smith, B. L., and Hostetter, M. K.: C3 as substrate for adhesion of *Streptococcus pneumoniae.* J. Infect. Dis. *182*:497–508, 2000.
650. Smith, M. D., Stuart, J. R., Andrews, N. J., et al.: Invasive pneumococcal infection in south and west England. Epidemiol. Infect. *120*:117–123, 1998.
651. Sniadack, D. H., Schwartz, B., Lipman, H., et al.: Potential interventions for the prevention of childhood pneumonia: Geographic and temporal differences in serotype and serogroup distribution of sterile site pneumococcal isolates from children—implications for vaccine strategies. Pediatr. Infect. Dis. J. *14*:503–510, 1995.
652. Soininen, A., Lahdenkari, M., Kilpi, T., et al.: Antibody response to pneumococcal capsular polysaccharides in children with acute otitis media. Pediatr. Infect. Dis. J. *21*:186–192, 2002.
653. Spangler, S. K., Jacobs, M. R., Pankuch, G. A., and Appelbaum, P. C.: Susceptibility of 170 penicillin-susceptible and penicillin-resistant pneumococci to six oral cephalosporins, four quinolones, desacetylcefotaxime, Ro 23-9424 and RP 67829. J. Antimicrob. Chemother. *31*:273–280, 1993.
654. Spanjaard, L., van der Ende, A., Rumke, H., et al.: Epidemiology of meningitis and bacteraemia due to *Streptococcus pneumonia* in the Netherlands. Acta Paediatr. Suppl. *435*:22–26, 2000.
655. Spellerberg, B., Cundell, D. R., Sandros, J., et al.: Pyruvate oxidase, as a determinant of virulence in *Streptococcus pneumoniae.* Mol. Microbiol. *19*:803–813, 1996.
656. Spika, J. S., Halsey, N. A., Le, C. T., et al.: Decline of vaccine-induced antipneumococcal antibody in children with nephrotic syndrome. Am. J. Kidney Dis. *7*:466–470, 1986.
657. Steffen, S. E., and Bryant, F. R.: Purification and characterization of the RecA protein from *Streptococcus pneumoniae.* Arch. Biochem. Biophys. *382*:303–309, 2000.
658. Stein, K. E.: Thymus-independent and thymus-dependent responses to polysaccharide antigens. J. Infect. Dis. *165*(Suppl.):49–52, 1992.
659. Stool, S. E., and Field, M. J.: The impact of otitis media. Pediatr. Infect. Dis. J. *8*(Suppl.):11–14, 1989.
660. Strovall, S. H., Ainley, K. A., Mason, E. O., et al.: Invasive pneumococcal infections in pediatric cardiac transplant patients. Pediatr. Infect. Dis. J. *20*:946–950, 2001.
661. Styrt, B.: Infection associated with asplenia: Risks, mechanisms, and prevention. Am. J. Med. *88*:33N–42N, 1990.
662. Sutcliffe, J., Tait-Kamradt, A., and Wondrack, L.: *Streptococcus pneumoniae* and *Streptococcus pyogenes* resistant to macrolides but sensitive to clindamycin: A common resistance pattern mediated by an efflux system. Antimicrob. Agents Chemother. *40*:1817–1824, 1996.
663. Syriopoulou, V., Daikos, G. L., Soulis, K., et al.: Epidemiology of invasive childhood pneumococcal infections in Greece. Acta Paediatr. Suppl. *435*:30–34, 2000.
664. Syrjänen, R., Herva, E., Leino, T., et al.: Length of nasopharyngeal carriage of pneumococci before pneumococcal acute otitis media. FinOM Study Group, National Public Health Institute. Presented at the 19th Annual Meeting of the European Society for Paediatric Infectious Diseases (ESPID), Istanbul, Turkey, 2001, p. 6.
665. Syrogiannopoulos, G. A., Grivea, I. N., Beratis, N. G., et al.: Resistance patterns of *Streptococcus pneumoniae* from carriers attending day-care centers in southwestern Greece. Clin. Infect. Dis. *25*:188–194, 1997.
666. Syrogiannopoulos, G. A., Ronchetti, F., Dagan, R., et al.: Mediterranean clone of penicillin-susceptible, multidrug-resistant serotype 6B *Streptococcus pneumoniae* in Greece, Italy and Israel. Int. J. Antimicrob. Agents *16*:219–224, 2000.
667. Tait-Kamradt, A., Davies, T., Appelbaum, P. C., et al.: Two new mechanisms of macrolide resistance in clinical strains of *Streptococcus pneumoniae* from Eastern Europe and North America. Antimicrob. Agents Chemother. *44*:3395–3401, 2000.
668. Takala, A. K., Jero, J., Kela, E., et al.: Risk factors for primary invasive pneumococcal disease among children in Finland. J. A. M. A. *273*:859–864, 1995.
669. Takoudes, T. G., and Haddad, J., Jr.: Free radical production by antibiotic-killed bacteria in the guinea pig middle ear. Laryngoscope *111*:283–289, 2001.
670. Talbot, U. M., Paton, A. W., and Paton, J. C.: Uptake of *Streptococcus pneumoniae* by respiratory epithelial cells. Infect. Immun. *64*:3772–3777, 1996.
671. Talkington, D. F., Brown, B. G., Tharpe, J. A., et al.: Protection of mice against fatal pneumococcal challenge by immunization with pneumococcal surface adhesin a (PsaA). Microb. Pathog. *21*:17–22, 1996.
672. Tan, T. Q., Mason, E. O., Barson, W. J., et al.: Clinical characteristic and outcome of children with pneumonia attributable to penicillin-susceptible and penicillin-nonsusceptible *Streptococcus pneumoniae.* Pediatrics *102*:1369–1375, 1998.
673. Tan, T. Q., Schutze, G. E., Mason, E. O., and Kaplan, S. L.: Antibiotic therapy and acute outcome of meningitis due to *Streptococcus pneumoniae* considered intermediately susceptible to broad-spectrum cephalosporins. Antimicrob. Agents Chemother. *38*:918–923, 1994.
674. Taylor, S., and Sanders, C.: Unusual manifestations of invasive pneumococcal infections. Am. J. Med. *107*(Suppl.):12–27, 1999.
675. Teele, D. W., and Klein, J. O.: Use of pneumococcal vaccine for prevention of recurrent acute otitis media in infants in Boston. Rev. Infect. Dis. *3*(Suppl.):113–118, 1981.
676. Teele, D. W., Klein, J. O., and Rosner, B. A.: Epidemiology of otitis media in children. Ann. Otol. Rhinol. Laryngol. *89*(Suppl. 68):5–6, 1980.
677. Teele, D. W., Klein, J. O., and Rosner, B. A.: Epidemiology of otitis media during the first seven years of life in children in greater Boston: A prospective, cohort study. J. Infect. Dis. *160*:83–94, 1989.
678. Teele, D. W., Pelton, S. I., Grant, M. J., et al.: Bacteremia in febrile children under 2 years of age: Results of cultures of blood of 600 consecutive febrile children seen in a "walk-in" clinic. J. Pediatr. *87*:227–230, 1975.
679. Teitelbaum, R., Lifshitz, S., Ling, E., et al.: Vulnerability to *Streptococcus pneumoniae* infection: Difference between microbial strains and genetically determined host reponse in adult mice. Abstract 983. Presented at the 41st Interscience Conference on Antimicrobial Agents and Chemotherapy, Chicago, 2001, p. 52.
680. Temple, K., Greenwood, B., Inskip, H., et al.: Antibody response to pneumococcal capsular polysaccharide vaccine in African children. Pediatr. Infect. Dis. J. *10*:386–390, 1991.

681. Therapy for children with invasive pneumococcal infections. American Academy of Pediatrics Committee on Infectious Diseases. Pediatrics *99*:289–299, 1997.
682. Thijssen, M. J., Bijkerk, M. H., Kamerling, J. P., et al.: Synthesis of four spacer-containing 'tetrasaccharides' that represent four possible repeating units of the capsular polysaccharide of *Streptococcus pneumoniae* type 6B. Carbohydr. Res. *306*:111–125, 1998.
683. Thornsberry, C., Sahm, D. F., Kelly, L. J., et al.: Regional trends in antimicrobial resistance among clinical isolates of *Streptococcus pneumoniae, Haemophilus influenzae,* and *Moraxella catarrhalis* in the United States: Results from the TRUST Surveillance Program, 1999–2000. Clin. Infect. Dis. *34*(Suppl.):4–16, 2002.
684. Toikka, P., Virkki, R., Mertsola, J., et al.: Bacteremic pneumococcal pneumonia in children. Clin. Infect. Dis. *29*:568–572, 1999.
685. Tomasz, A.: *Streptococcus pneumoniae:* Functional anatomy. *In* Tomasz, A. (ed.): *Streptococcus pneumoniae:* Molecular Biology and Mechanisms of Disease. Larchmont, NY, Mary Ann Liebert, Inc., 2000, pp. 9–21.
686. Tong, H. H., Blue, L. E., James, M. A., et al.: Evaluation of the virulence of a *Streptococcus pneumoniae* neuraminidase-deficient mutant in nasopharyngeal colonization and development of otitis media in the chinchilla model. Infect. Immun. *68*:921–924, 2000.
687. Tong, H. H., Fisher, L. M., Kosunick, G. M., et al.: Effect of tumor necrosis factor alpha and interleukin 1-alpha on the adherence of *Streptococcus pneumoniae* to chinchilla tracheal epithelium. Acta. Otolaryngol. *119*:78–82, 1999.
688. Toppley, J. M., Cupidore, L., Vaidya, S., et al.: Pneumococcal and other infections in children with sickle cell–hemoglobin C (SC) disease. J. Pediatr. *101*:176–179, 1982.
689. Tu, A. H., Fulgham, R. L., McCrory, M. A., et al.: Pneumococcal surface protein A inhibits complement activation by *Streptococcus pneumoniae.* Infect. Immun. *67*:4720–4724, 1999.
690. Turett, G. S., Blum, S., Fazal, B. A., et al.: Penicillin resistance and other predictors of mortality in pneumococcal bacteremia in a population with high human immunodeficiency virus seroprevalence. Clin. Infect. Dis. *29*:321–327, 1999.
691. Ubukata, K., Asahi, Y., Yamane, A., et al.: Combinational detection of autolysin and penicillin-binding protein 2B genes *of Streptococcus pneumoniae* by PCR. J. Clin. Microbiol. *34*:592–596, 1996.
692. Uhari, M., Kontiokari, T., and Kiemela, M.: A novel use of xylitol sugar in preventing acute otitis media. Pediatrics *102*:879–884, 1998.
693. Uhari, M., Kontiokari, T., Koskela, M., and Niemela, M.: Xylitol chewing gum in prevention of acute otitis media: Double-blind randomized trial. B. M. J. *313*:1180–1184, 1996.
694. Uhari, M., Mantysaari, K., and Niemela, M.: A meta-analytic review of the risk factors for acute otitis media. Clin. Infect. Dis. *22*:1079–1083, 1996.
695. Ukkonen, P., Varis, K., Jernsfors, M., et al.: Treatment of acute otitis media with an antiadhesive oligosaccharide: A randomized, double-blind, placebo-controlled trial. Lancet *356*:1398–1402, 2000.
696. Umetsu, D. T., Ambrosino, D. M., Quinti, I., et al.: Recurrent sinopulmonary infection and impaired antibody response to bacterial capsular polysaccharide antigen in children with selective IgG subclass deficiency. N. Engl. J. Med. *313*:1247–1251, 1985.
697. Usen, S., Adegbola, R., Mulholland, K., et al.: Epidemiology of invasive pneumococcal disease in the Western Region, The Gambia. Pediatr. Infect. Dis. J. *17*:23–28, 1998.
698. Ussery, X. T., Gessner, B. D., Lipman, H., et al.: Risk factors for nasopharyngeal carriage of resistant *Streptococcus pneumoniae* and detection of a multiply resistant clone among children living in the Yukon-Kuskokwin Delta Region of Alaska. Pediatr. Infect. Dis. J. *15*:986–992, 1996.
699. Väkeväinen, M., Eklund, C., Eskola, J., and Käyhty, H.: Cross-reactivity of antibodies to pneumococcal capsular polysaccharides of seropypes 6A and 6B evoked by different pneumococcal conjugate vaccines. J. Infect. Dis. *184*:789–793, 2001.
700. Väkeväinen, M., Jansen, W., Saeland, E., et al.: Are the opsonic activities of antibodies in infant sera measured by different pneumococcal phagocytic assays comparable? Clin. Diagn. Lab. Immunol. *8*:363–369, 2001.
701. Van Zuijlen, D. A., Schilder, A. G. M., Van Balen, F. A. M., and Hoes, A. W.: National differences in incidence of acute mastoiditis: Relationship to prescribing patterns of antibiotics for acute otitis media? Pediatr. Infect. Dis. J. *20*:140–144, 2001.
702. Varon, E., Levy, C., De La Rocque, F., et al.: Impact of antimicrobial therapy on nasopharyngeal carriage of *Streptococcus pneumoniae, Haemophilus influenzae,* and *Branhamella catarrhalis* in children with respiratory tract infections. Clin. Infect. Dis. *31*:477–481, 2000.
703. Vernacchio, L., Neurfeld, E. J., MacDonald, K., et al.: Combined schedule of 7-valent pneumococcal conjugate vaccine followed by 23-valent pneumococcal vaccine in children and young adults with sickle cell disease. J. Pediatr. *133*:275–278, 1998.
704. Vidarsson, G., Sugurdardottir, S., Gudnason, T., et al.: Isotypes and opsonophagocytosis of pneumococcus type 6B antibodies elicited in infants and adults by an experimental pneumococcus type 6B–tetanus toxoid vaccine. Infect. Immun. *66*:2866–2870, 1998.
705. Viladrich, P. F., Gudiol, F., Linares, J., et al.: Evaluation of vancomycin for therapy of adult pneumococcal meningitis. Antimicrob. Agents Chemother. *35*:2467–2472, 1991.
706. Vives, M., Garcia, M. E., Saenz, P., et al.: Nasopharyngeal colonization in Costa Rican children during the first year of life. Pediatr. Infect. Dis. J. *16*:852–858, 1997.
707. Vollmer, W., and Tomasz, A.: The pgdA gene encodes for a peptidoglycan *N*-acetylglucosamine deacetylase in *Streptococcus pneumoniae.* J. Biol. Chem. *275*:20496–20501, 2000.
708. Vollmer, W., and Tomasz, A.: Identification of the teichoic acid phosphorylcholine esterase in *Streptococcus pneumoniae.* Mol. Microbiol. *39*:1610–1622, 2001.
709. Voss, L., Lennon, D., Okesene-Gafa, K., et al.: Invasive pneumococcal disease in a pediatric population, Auckland, New Zealand. Pediatr. Infect. Dis. J. *13*:873–878, 1994.
710. Vuori-Holopainen, E., and Peltola, H.: Reappraisal of lung tap: Review of an old method for better etiologic diagnosis of childhood pneumonia. Clin. Infect. Dis. *32*:715–726, 2001.
711. Vuori-Holopainen, E., Salo, E., Saxén, H., et al.: Etiological diagnosis of childhood pneumonia by use of transthoracic needle aspiration and modern microbiological methods. Clin. Infect. Dis. *34*:583–590, 2002.
712. Wadowsky, R. M., Mietzner, S. M., Skoner, D. P., et al.: Effect of experimental influenza A virus infection on isolation of *Streptococcus pneumoniae* and other aerobic bacteria from the oropharynges of allergic and nonallergic adult subjets. Infect. Immun. *63*:1153–1157, 1995.
713. Wald, E. R.: Conjunctivitis in infants and children. Pediatr. Infect. Dis. J. *16*(Suppl.):17–20, 1997.
714. Wald, E. R.: Diagnosis and management of sinusitis in children. Semin. Pediatr. Infect. Dis. *9*:4–11, 1998.
715. Wald, E. R., Chiponis, D., and Ledesma-Medina, J.: Comparative effectiveness of amoxicillin and amoxicillin–clavulanate potassium in acute paranasal sinus infections in children: A double-blind, placebo-controlled trial. Pediatrics *77*:795–800, 1986.
716. Wald, E. R., Milmoe, G. J., Bowen, A., et al.: Acute maxillary sinusitis in children. N. Engl. J. Med. *304*:749–754, 1981.
717. Wall, R. A., Corrah, P. T., Mabey, D. C. W., and Greenwood, B. M.: The etiology of lobar pneumonia in The Gambia. Bull. World Health Organ. *64*:553–558, 1986.
718. Wara, D. W.: Host defense against *Streptococcus pneumoniae:* The role of the spleen. Rev. Infect. Dis. *3*:299–309, 1981.
719. Watanabe, H., Sato, S., Kawakami, K., et al.: A comparative clinical study of pneumonia by penicillin-resistant and -sensitive *Streptococcus pneumoniae* in a community hospital. Respirology *5*:59–64, 2000.
720. Watanakunakorn, C., and Bailey, T. A.: Adult bacteremic pneumococcal pneumonia in a community teaching hospital, 1992–1996. A detailed analysis of 108 cases. Arch. Intern. Med. *157*:1965–1971, 1997.
721. Waterer, G. W., Jennings, S. G., and Wunderink, R. G.: The impact of blood cultures on antibiotic therapy in pneumococcal pneumonia. Chest *116*:1278–1281, 1999.
722. Watson, D. A., Musher, D. M., and Jacobson, J. W.: A brief history of the pneumococcus in biomedical research: A panoply of discovery. Clin. Infect. Dis. *17*:913–924, 1993.
723. Weber, B., Ehlert, K., Diehl, A., et al.: The fib locus in *Streptococcus pneumoniae* is required for peptidoglycan crosslinking and PBP-mediated beta-lactam resistance. FEMS Microbiol. Lett. *188*:81–85, 2000.
724. Weiser, J. N.: Phase variation in colony opacity by *Streptococcus pneumoniae.* Microb. Drug Resist. *4*:129–135, 1998.
725. Weiss, A., Brinser, J. H., and Nazar-Stewart, V.: Acute conjunctivitis in childhood. J. Pediatr. *122*:10–14, 1993.
726. White, B.: The Biology of Pneumococcus. Cambridge, MA, Commonwealth Fund, Harvard University Press, 1938.
727. Whitney, C. G., Farley, M. M., Hadler, J., et al.: Increasing prevalence of multidrug-resistant *Streptococcus pneumoniae* in the United States. N. Engl. J. Med. *343*:1917–1924, 2000.
728. Whitney, C. G., Farley, M. M., Hadler, J., et al.: Decline in invasive pneumococcal disease in the US in 2000: An effect on pneumococcal conjugate vaccine? Abstract G-2041. Presented at the 41st Interscience Conference on Antimicrobial Agents and Chemotherapy (ICAAC), Chicago, 2001, p. 284.
729. Widdowson, C. A., and Klugman, K.: Molecular mechanisms of resistance to commonly used non-betalactam drugs in *Streptococcus pneumoniae.* Semin. Respir. Infect. *14*:255–268, 1999.
730. Williams, R. L., Chalmers, T. C., Stange, D. C., et al.: Use of antibiotics in preventing recurrent acute otitis media and in treating otitis media with effusion. A meta-analytic attempt to resolve the brouhaha. J. A. M. A. *370*:1344–1351, 1993.
731. Winkelstein, J. A., and Drachman, R. H.: Deficiency of pneumococcal serum opsonizing activity in sickle cell disease. N. Engl. J. Med. *279*:459–466, 1968.
732. Witt, C. S., Pomat, W., Lehmann, D., and Alpers, M. P.: Antibodies to pneumococcal polysaccharides in pneumonia and response to pneumococcal vaccination in young children in Papua New Guinea. Clin. Exp. Immunol. *83*:219–224, 1991.
733. Wizemann, T. M., Heinrichs, J. H., Adamou, J. E., et al.: Use of a whole genome approach to identify vaccine molecules affording protection

against *Streptococcus pneumoniae* infection. Infect. Immun. *69*:1593–1598, 2001.

734. Wong, W. Y., Overturf, G. D., and Powars, D. R.: Infection caused by *Streptococcus pneumoniae* in children with sickle cell disease: Epidemiology, immunologic mechanisms, prophylaxis, and vaccination. Clin. Infect. Dis. *14*:1124–1136, 1992.
735. Wright, A. E., Morgan, W. P., Colebrook, L., et al.: Observations on prophylactic inoculation against pneumococcus infections, and on the results which have been achieved by it. Lancet *1*:87–95, 1914.
736. Wu, T.-T., Hsueh, P.-R., Lee, L.-N., et al.: Pneumonia caused by penicillin-nonsusceptible *Streptococcus pneumoniae:* Clinical characteristics, prognostic factors, and outcomes. J. Formos. Med. Assoc. *99*:18–23, 2000.
737. Yagupsky, P., Porat, N., Fraser, D., et al.: Acquisition, carriage and transmission of pneumococci with decreased antibiotic susceptibility in young children attending a day care facility in southern Israel. J. Infect. Dis. *177*:1003–1012, 1998.
738. Yamamoto, L. G.: Revising the decision analysis for febrile children at risk for occult bacteremia in a future era of widespread pneumococcal immunization. Clin. Pediatr. (Phila.) *40*:583–594, 2001.
739. Yother, J., Leopold, K., White, J., et al.: Generation and properties of a *Streptococcus pneumoniae* mutant which does not require choline or analogs for growth. J. Bacteriol. *180*:2093–2101, 1998.
740. Yother, J., and White, J. M.: Novel surface attachment mechanism of the *Streptococcus pneumoniae* protein PspA. J. Bacteriol. *176*:2976–2985, 1994.
741. Yu, J., Bryant, A. P., Marra, A., et al.: Characterization of the *Streptococcus pneumoniae* NADH oxidase that is required for infection. Microbiology *147*:431–438, 2001.
742. Zangwill, K. M., Vadheim, C. M., Vannier, A. M., et al.: Epidemiology of invasive pneumococcal disease in Southern California: Implications for the design and conduct of a pneumcoccal conjugate vaccine efficacy trial. J. Infect. Dis. *174*:752–759, 1996.
743. Zarkowsky, H. S., Gallagher, D., Gill, F. M., et al.: Bacteremia in sickle hemoglobinopathies. J. Pediatr. *109*:579–585, 1986.
744. Zenni, M. K., Cheatham, S. H., Thompson, J. M., et al.: *Streptococcus pneumoniae* colonization in the young child: Association with otitis media and resistance to penicillin. J. Pediatr. *127*:533–537, 1995.
745. Zhang, J. R., Mostov, K. E., Lamm, M. E., et al.: The polymeric immunoglobulin receptor translocates pneumococci across human nasopharyngeal epithelial cells. Cell *102*:827–837, 2000.
746. Zhang, Y., Masi, A. W., Barniak, V., et al.: Recombinant PhpA protein, a unique histidine motif–containing protein from *Streptococcus pneumoniae,* protects mice against intranasal pneumococcal challenge. Infect. Immun. *69*:3827–3836, 2001.
747. Zopf, D., and Roth, S.: Oligosaccharide anti-infective agents. Lancet *347*:1017–1021, 1996.
748. Zwijnenburg, P. J., van der Poll, T., Florquin, S., et al.: Experimental pneumococcal meningitis in mice: A model of intranasal infection. J. Infect. Dis. *183*:1143–1146, 2001.
749. Zysk, G., Bongaerts, R. J., ten Thoren, E., et al.: Detection of 23 immunogenic pneumococcal proteins using convalescent-phase serum. Infect. Immun. *68*:3740–3743, 2000.
750. Zysk, G., Schneider-Wald, B. K., Hwang, J. H., et al.: Pneumolysin is the main inducer of cytotoxicity to brain microvascular endothelial cells caused by *Streptococcus pneumoniae.* Infect. Immun. *69*:845–852, 2001.

Miscellaneous Gram-Positive Cocci

THOMAS G. BOYCE ■ RANDALL G. FISHER ■ WILLIAM C. GRUBER

This chapter discusses relatively uncommon gram-positive cocci that are of importance because of their unusual antimicrobial sensitivities and their increasing recognition as pathogens in hospitalized patients. The reader is referred to a recent review of these organisms for more details.[14]

Leuconostoc Species

BACTERIOLOGY

Leuconostoc spp. are facultatively anaerobic gram-positive cocci that usually appear in pairs or chains. They are catalase-negative, Vogues-Proskauer test–positive, and leucine aminopeptidase–positive. In addition, colonies often are alpha-hemolytic on blood agar and also may react with group D streptococcal antiserum. These properties are shared by viridans streptococci, with which *Leuconostoc* spp. often are confused.[16] They also may resemble enterococci, except that they are pyrrolidone carboxylyl peptidase–-negative. Differences include the production of gas from glucose and high-level resistance to vancomycin.

EPIDEMIOLOGY

Leuconostoc spp. commonly are found on plants, especially sugar cane and leafy vegetables. They also are found in dairy products and wine.[37] They are used in the food industry as starter cultures in food production.[26, 47] Though not a part of the normal human flora,[3] *Leuconostoc* occasionally is recovered from vaginal swabs in healthy individuals.[40] Studies also have shown colonization of mucosal surfaces in some hospitalized individuals.[22] Case reports of pediatric infection began to appear in the 1980s.[10, 23, 25, 52]

PATHOPHYSIOLOGY

Leuconostoc spp. rarely are pathogenic. Underlying disease states or immune compromise, gastrointestinal tract disease (especially short-gut syndrome), previous or current antibiotic therapy, venous or gastrointestinal tract access devices, recent invasive procedures, and infancy are thought to be risk factors.[12, 13, 22, 37] Frequently, *Leuconostoc* organisms are isolated as part of a polymicrobial infection after a patient has been treated with vancomycin.[14] Of the first 21 cases reported in the English literature, 12 were in children, 10 of whom were younger than 1 year of age. Documented portals of entry include central lines[3, 23] and gastrostomy tubes.[25] Contaminated enteral formula also has been implicated.[6, 25, 33] Occasional sporadic cases without a known risk factor have been reported,[10, 22] which underscores the pathogenic potential of *Leuconostoc* infection.

CLINICAL MANIFESTATIONS

Bacteremia, by far the most common clinical manifestation of *Leuconostoc* infection, is heralded by fever and usually leukocytosis in patients with the risk factors outlined earlier. Gastrointestinal disturbances, especially diarrhea, are common occurrences.[3] Infants are prone to emesis. *Leuconostoc* bacteremia in association with cough and chest radiograph findings consistent with pneumonia was reported in a child with acquired immunodeficiency syndrome (AIDS).[37] *Leuconostoc citreum* has been isolated from the lung tissue of a 33-year-old patient with AIDS who also had *Pneumocystis carinii* pneumonia.[19] Small necrotic cavities scattered through both lungs were associated with gram-positive cocci in tissue. Patients with dental infections,[52] peritonitis, osteomyelitis,[31] and meningitis[10, 17] also have been described. Meningitis has been reported in an otherwise healthy 16-year-old patient and in a neonate with fatal infection despite high cerebrospinal fluid bactericidal antibiotic titers.[10, 17] A nosocomial cluster of five cases of urinary tract infection caused by *Leuconstoc pseudomesenteroides* has been reported,[5] as has a cluster of three cases of *Leuconostoc* septicemia in critically ill postsurgical patients.[43]

DIAGNOSIS

Cultures are usually positive within 24 to 48 hours, but *Leuconostoc* spp. are somewhat fastidious. Identification of vancomycin-resistant *Streptococcus* should raise suspicion of *Leuconostoc* infection and prompt additional biochemical studies,[37] including evaluation for the production of gas in deMan Rogosa Sharpe (MRS) broth, failure to hydrolyze arginine, and delayed esculin hydrolysis.

TREATMENT

Treatment with relatively high doses of penicillin or ampicillin frequently is successful in eradicating infection. When possible, access devices should be removed. *Leuconostoc* spp. are most sensitive to the primitive β-lactam antibiotics, especially penicillin and ampicillin, although penicillin tolerance is common.[25, 49] They also frequently are sensitive to erythromycin, cephalothin, and the aminoglycosides. *Leuconostoc* spp. have variable resistance to clindamycin and trimethoprim-sulfamethoxazole. Resistance increases with later generations of cephalosporins.[22, 49] *Leuconostoc* spp. are intrinsically vancomycin-resistant because their pentapeptide cell wall precursors end in D-Ala-lactate rather than the usual D-Ala-alanine.[21] Vancomycin cannot bind the lactate. This mode of resistance is the same as that possessed by vancomycin-resistant enterococci. However, whereas resistance in enterococci is plasmid derived and transferable, in *Leuconostoc* spp. it is chromosomally mediated, constitutional, and not transferable.

Pediococcus Species

BACTERIOLOGY

Pediococci also are intrinsically vancomycin-resistant, facultatively anaerobic, gram-positive cocci. They appear most characteristically in tetrads on Gram stain, although they may appear in pairs or clusters.[20] The genus name *Pediococcus* is derived from the Greek word *pedium*, which means "plane." The name, therefore, suggests that they are a genus of cocci that grow in a single plane. It is a misnomer, however, because pediococci are the only lactic acid bacteria that divide into two planes.[18] They are catalase- and oxidase-negative. They do not reduce nitrates, and no gas is produced in MRS broth.[45] *Leuconostoc* spp. are pyrrolidone carboxylyl peptidase–negative.[15] Most isolates react with Lancefield group D streptococcal antibodies.[45] They are leucine aminopeptidase–positive, which distinguishes them from *Leuconostoc* spp.[15] They produce white, opaque, nonhemolytic colonies on sheep blood agar.

Pediococci produce powerful bacteriocins, which are substances that kill other bacteria. The bacteriocins of pediococci are particularly active against other gram-positive organisms[9] but also are active against *Clostridium botulinum* spores,[34] some gram-negative organisms,[46] and *Listeria monocytogenes*.

EPIDEMIOLOGY

Like *Leuconostoc* and other lactic acid bacteria, pediococci are found on plants, in dairy products, and in alcohol-containing beverages, for which certain species are associated with spoilage.[50] They also are used in the formation of silage[45] and as starter cultures for some meat products. Pediococci are not thought to be part of the normal flora, but they have been isolated from saliva and stool on rare occasion.[41] Though formerly thought to be nonpathogenic, pediococci now are considered rare opportunistic pathogens with minimal virulence.

PATHOPHYSIOLOGY

Pediococci rarely are pathogenic. Many cases of blood isolates occur in patients without symptoms of infection or in polymicrobial cultures in which the significance of the isolate cannot be assessed adequately.[30] One case of a patient with a clinical picture of septic shock in whom the only organism recovered was *Pediococcus pentosaceus* has been reported.[11] Risk factors for development of bacteremia, with or without symptoms, appear to be the extremes of age, recent abdominal surgery or tube feeding, broad-spectrum antimicrobial therapy, and the presence of severe underlying disease states.[30] However, because the overall number of reported cases is small, the relative risk of these factors is uncertain.

CLINICAL MANIFESTATIONS AND DIAGNOSIS

Most patients are either asymptomatic or have fever as the only symptom. Six of the first 12 reported patients with *Pediococcus* bacteremia had concomitant pneumonia. Fifty-six percent of adult patients were either receiving tube feedings or had undergone abdominal surgery within 30 days of isolation of the organism.[30] The three reported pediatric cases were in infants, and all had underlying gastrointestinal tract anomalies. A 16-day-old infant had congenital jejunoileal atresia and had undergone surgical repair just 8 days before evaluation for illness.[30] Her acute illness was characterized by emesis and a 200-g weight loss, but she was afebrile at initial examination. The second patient was a 64-day-old boy with gastroschisis who had undergone two abdominal surgical procedures.[1] His fever reached 101.5°F, and his peripheral white blood cell count was 38,000 with a significant left shift. The third patient was a 3-month-old girl who had undergone surgical repair of gastroschisis on the first day of life.[2] Lethargy, direct hyperbilirubinemia, and a cerebrospinal fluid pleocytosis were the initial manifestations of illness. Blood cultures grew *Pediococcus* spp., and the spinal fluid (obtained after initiation of antibiotics) was sterile. She responded to a 21-day course of ampicillin and gentamicin.

Isolation of pediococci in localized infections, especially from abdominal sites, occurs commonly but is virtually always part of a polymicrobial process. The relative importance of pediococci in these sites is difficult to assess. Recently, a case of *Pediococcus* bacteremic pneumonia was reported in a previously healthy pregnant woman.[42] Among 31 cases of *Pediococcus* infection submitted to the Centers for Disease Control and Prevention laboratory, 17 were from blood culture isolates (including 2 reported cases of endocarditis), and 4 strains were associated with urinary tract infections. Other sources included catheter tips, wounds, peritoneal fluid, cerebrospinal fluid, lung, and bone.[14]

The diagnosis of infection with pediococci is made by identifying vancomycin-resistant, gram-positive cocci in the characteristic tetrads. Many pediococci initially are misidentified as *Streptococcus equinus*, *Streptococcus constellatus*, or group D *Streptococcus*, not *Enterococcus*. The reported cases of pediococcal infection, therefore, may represent only a fraction of the total number of infections.

TREATMENT

Pediococci generally are susceptible to penicillin, ampicillin, imipenem, clindamycin, and first- and second-generation cephalosporins. Although both imipenem and penicillin are highly active against pediococci, they do not appear to be bactericidal. Pediococci are moderately resistant to the quinolones, tetracycline,[50] and trimethoprim-sulfamethoxazole.[39] Pediococci, like *Leuconostoc*, are intrinsically resistant to vancomycin. Resistance is not plasmid mediated, nor can it be transferred to other bacteria.[50] Sensitivity to ticarcillin and cefotaxime, when measured by agar dilution, is poor despite large zones of inhibition on disk susceptibility testing.[50] Occasionally, inducible resistance to erythromycin occurs, although most isolates remain sensitive. Aminoglycoside sensitivity is variable.

Aerococcus Species

BACTERIOLOGY

The genus *Aerococcus* contains two species, *viridans* and *urinae*. Until recently, *viridans* was considered the only species, and in earlier papers, *A. urinae* was referred to as an *Aerococcus*-like organism, or ALO.[8] Aerococci are catalase-negative, nonmotile, gram-positive cocci that preferentially appear in tetrads but sometimes in pairs or clusters. These relatively slow-growing organisms produce small, well-delineated, translucent, and alpha-hemolytic colonies on blood agar.[7] They also are weakly bile esculin–positive and pyrrolidone carboxylyl peptidase–negative. They ferment mannose and mannitol.[38] Like enterococci, most aerococci will grow in 6.5 percent salt.[29]

EPIDEMIOLOGY

Aerococci are distributed throughout the world and are contaminants of air and dust.[24] They also have been found on meat, on raw vegetables, and in small numbers on human skin.[4] In hospitals, aerococci have been cultured from all areas, including operating suites and delivery rooms.[27] They also are found in salt water, where they cause a fatal disease in lobsters.[35]

Disease in humans is an uncommon occurrence, and the organism usually is recovered from the bloodstream in patients with infective endocarditis. Most patients are elderly, but infections in infants and neonates also have been reported.[32, 35] Rapidly fatal bacteremia has been described in patients with profound neutropenia.[28]

PATHOPHYSIOLOGY

In most circumstances, aerococci are saprophytic. The exact conditions that favor infection have not been elucidated clearly. Some cases of *A. urinae* infection have occurred after genitourinary tract surgery. One case of septic arthritis developed after an elective abortion.[51] Immunocompromised patients are at higher risk, but infections in otherwise well persons have been described.[38] One report of meningitis in newborns found adherence of aerococci to inflammatory cells and suggested a role of as-yet-undefined adhesion factors.[32] Work in laboratory animals also has shown that a protease isolated from *A. viridans* cleaves the hemagglutinin of influenza virus and potentiates both viral replication and disease in mice.[44]

CLINICAL MANIFESTATIONS

Most cases of *A. viridans* bacteremia have been found in association with signs and symptoms of subacute infective endocarditis, although septic emboli and cardiac failure have not been described. *A. urinae* causes urinary tract infection with dysuria and frequency, usually in the absence of fever.[7] *Aerococcus* infection in childhood is an uncommon occurrence. One case of bacteremia in a 1-month-old has been reported.[35] The patient had a 2-day history of loose stool, irritability, and drowsiness and on physical examination was noted to have mottled skin, circumoral cyanosis, and agitation. Cerebrospinal fluid and urine were normal, but blood cultures grew a pure growth of *A. viridans*. No predisposing factors were identified.

Nathavitharana and associates[32] reported three cases of meningitis caused by *A. viridans*: a 7-month-old girl with jerking movements of the extremities, irritability, and a bulging fontanelle; a 5-month-old girl with fever, decreased appetite, and generalized convulsions; and a 24-month-old girl whose illness was manifested as fever, vomiting, and the neurologic signs of truncal ataxia, flaccidity, and hypoactive deep-tendon reflexes. All three patients had elevated cerebrospinal fluid white blood cell counts with 55 to 93 percent segmented forms. Remarkably, all these patients had a history of prolonged illness (1 week to 2 months) before being seen by a physician, in contrast to patients with other causes of bacterial meningitis. No risk factors for development of infection were identified in any of these patients, who were thought to have normal immune function.

Swanson and colleagues[48] reported a case of penicillin-resistant *A. viridans* bacteremia in an 11-month-old girl receiving prophylactic penicillin for sickle-cell disease. The patient responded clinically to a 10-day course of therapy with cephalosporins.

Bone and joint infections and wound or other localized infections are exceedingly rare occurrences and not distinguishable from similar syndromes caused by more common organisms.

DIAGNOSIS

Careful observation of both appearance on Gram stain and growth in culture is key to making the diagnosis of aerococcal infection. On Gram stain, aerococci resemble staphylococci, and on blood agar, they resemble viridans group streptococci. One series revealed that 1 percent of 719 cultures called streptococci were actually aerococci[36]; another study reclassified 3 percent of 168 cultures.[4] In their propensity to tetrad formation, they mimic pediococci. However, all aerococci are vancomycin-sensitive. In their bile esculin hydrolysis and growth in 6.5 percent salt, they resemble enterococci; unlike enterococci, however, aerococci are pyrrolidone carboxylyl peptidase–negative and do not form chains.

TREATMENT

Aerococci generally are sensitive to penicillin, ampicillin, the cephalosporins, chloramphenicol, and the macrolides. They usually are intermediately susceptible or resistant to sulfonamides and aminoglycosides.[4, 24] One report suggests that *A. viridans* and *A. urinae* have distinct antibiograms[29]; specifically, *A. urinae* is more sensitive to penicillin and resistant to sulfonamides, whereas *A. viridans* is more resistant to penicillin and sensitive to the sulfonamides.[4] Individual case reports do not confirm these in vitro observations, and no large clinical trials of antimicrobial susceptibility have been performed.

REFERENCES

1. Atkins, J. T., Tillman, J., Tan, T. Q., et al.: *Pediococcus pentosaceus* catheter-associated infection in an infant with gastroschisis. Pediatr. Infect. Dis. J. *13*:75–76, 1994.
2. Barton, L. L., Rider, E. D., and Coen, R. W.: Bacteremic infection with *Pediococcus:* Vancomycin-resistant opportunist. Pediatrics *107*:775–776, 2001.
3. Bernaldo de Quiros, J. C., Munoz, P., Cercenado, E., et al.: *Leuconostoc* species as a cause of bacteremia: Two case reports and a literature review. Eur. J. Clin. Microbiol. Infect. Dis. *10*:505–509, 1991.
4. Buu-Hoi, A., Branger, C., and Acar, J. F.: Vancomycin-resistant streptococci or *Leuconostoc* sp. Antimicrob. Agents Chemother. *28*:458–460, 1985.
5. Cappelli, E. A., Barros, R. R., Camello, T. C., et al.: *Leuconostoc pseudomesenteroides* as a cause of nosocomial urinary tract infections. J. Clin. Microbiol. *37*:4124–4126, 1999.
6. Carapetis, J., Bishop, S., Davis, J., et al.: *Leuconostoc* sepsis in association with continuous enteral feeding: Two case reports and a review. Pediatr. Infect. Dis. J. *13*:816–823, 1994.
7. Christensen, J. J., Gutschik, E., Friis-Moller, A., et al.: Urosepticemia and fatal endocarditis caused by aerococcus-like organisms. Scand. J. Infect. Dis. *23*:717–721, 1991.
8. Christensen, J. J., Vibits, H., Ursing, J., et al.: *Aerococcus*-like organism, a newly recognized potential urinary tract pathogen. J. Clin. Microbiol. *29*:1049–1053, 1991.
9. Cintas, L. M., Rodriguez, J. M., Fernandez, M. F., et al.: Isolation and characterization of pediocin L50, a new bacteriocin from *Pediococcus acidilactici* with a broad inhibitory spectrum. Appl. Environ. Microbiol. *61*:2643–2648, 1995.
10. Coovadia, Y. M., Solwa, Z., and van den Ende, J.: Meningitis caused by vancomycin-resistant *Leuconostoc* sp. J. Clin. Microbiol. *25*:1784–1785, 1987.
11. Corcoran, G. D., Gibbons, N., and Mulvihill, T. E.: Septicaemia caused by *Pediococcus pentosaceus:* A new opportunistic pathogen. J. Infect. *23*:179–182, 1991.
12. Dhodapkar, K. M., and Henry, N. K.: *Leuconostoc* bacteremia in an infant with short-gut syndrome: Case report and literature review. Mayo Clin. Proc. *71*:1171–1174, 1996.
13. Espinoza, R., Kusne, S., Pasculle, A. W., et al.: *Leuconostoc* bacteremia after liver transplantation: Another cause of vancomycin resistant gram-positive infection. Clin. Transplant. *11*:322–324, 1997.
14. Facklam, R., and Elliott, J. A.: Identification, classification, and clinical relevance of catalase-negative, gram-positive cocci, excluding the streptococci and enterococci. Clin. Microbiol. Rev. *8*:479–495, 1995.
15. Facklam, R., Hollis, D., and Collins, M. D.: Identification of gram-positive coccal and coccobacillary vancomycin-resistant bacteria. J. Clin. Microbiol. *27*:724–730, 1989.
16. Facklam, R., Pigott, N., Franklin, R., et al.: Evaluation of three disk tests for identification of enterococci, leuconostocs, and pediococci. J. Clin. Microbiol. *33*:885–887, 1995.
17. Friedland, I. R., Snipelisky, M., and Khoosal, M.: Meningitis in a neonate caused by *Leuconostoc* sp. J. Clin. Microbiol. *28*:2125–2126, 1990.
18. Garvie, E. I.: Genus *Pediococcus. In* Butler, J. P. (ed.): Bergey's Manual of Systematic Bacteriology. Vol. II. Baltimore, Williams & Wilkins, 1986, pp. 1075–1079.
19. Giacometti, A., Ranaldi, R., Siquini, F. M., et al.: *Leuconostoc citreum* isolated from lung in AIDS patient. Lancet *342*:622, 1993.
20. Green, M., Barbadora, K., and Michaels, M.: Recovery of vancomycin-resistant gram-positive cocci from pediatric liver transplant recipients. J. Clin. Microbiol. *29*:2503–2506, 1991.
21. Handwerger, S., Horowitz, H., Coburn, K., et al.: Infection due to *Leuconostoc* species: Six cases and review. Rev. Infect. Dis. *12*:602–610, 1990.
22. Handwerger, S., Pucci, M. J., Volk, K. J., et al.: Vancomycin-resistant *Leuconostoc mesenteroides* and *Lactobacillus casei* synthesize cytoplasmic peptidoglycan precursors that terminate in lactate. J. Bacteriol. *176*:260–264, 1994.
23. Hardy, S., Ruoff, K. L., Catlin, E. A., et al.: Catheter-associated infection with a vancomycin-resistant gram-positive coccus of the *Leuconostoc* sp. Pediatr. Infect. Dis. J. *7*:519–520, 1988.
24. Heilesen, A. M.: Septicaemia due to *Aerococcus urinae.* Scand. J. Infect. Dis. *26*:759–760, 1994.
25. Isenberg, H. D., Vellozzi, E. M., Shapiro, J., et al.: Clinical laboratory challenges in the recognition of *Leuconostoc* spp. J. Clin. Microbiol. *26*:479–483, 1988.
26. Jeppesen, V. F., and Huss, H. H.: Characteristics and antagonistic activity of lactic acid bacteria isolated from chilled fish products. Int. J. Food Microbiol. *18*:305–320, 1993.
27. Kerbaugh, M. A., and Evans, J. B.: *Aerococcus viridans* in the hospital environment. Appl. Microbiol. *16*:519–523, 1968.
28. Kern, W., and Vanek, E.: *Aerococcus* bacteremia associated with granulocytopenia. Eur. J. Clin. Microbiol. *6*:670–673, 1987.
29. Kristensen, B., and Nielsen, G.: Endocarditis caused by *Aerococcus urinae,* a newly recognized pathogen. Eur. J. Clin. Microbiol. Infect. Dis. *14*:49–51, 1995.
30. Mastro, T. D., Spika, J. S., Lozano, P., et al.: Vancomycin-resistant *Pediococcus acidilactici:* Nine cases of bacteremia. J. Infect. Dis. *161*:956–960, 1990.
31. Mulford, J. S., and Mills, J.: Osteomyelitis caused by *Leuconostoc* species. Aust. N. Z. J. Surg. *69*:541–542, 1999.
32. Nathavitharana, K. A., Arseculeratne, S. N., Aponso, H. A., et al.: Acute meningitis in early childhood caused by *Aerococcus viridans.* B. M. J. *286*:1248, 1983.
33. Noriega, F. R., Kotloff, K. L., Martin, M. A., et al.: Nosocomial bacteremia caused by *Enterobacter sakazakii* and *Leuconostoc mesenteroides* resulting from extrinsic contamination of infant formula. Pediatr. Infect. Dis. J. *9*:447–449, 1990.
34. Okereke, A., and Montville, T. J.: Bacteriocin-mediated inhibition of *Clostridium botulinum* spores by lactic acid bacteria at refrigeration and abuse temperatures. Appl. Environ. Microbiol. *57*:3423–3428, 1991.
35. Park, J. W., and Grossman, O.: *Aerococcus viridans* infection. Case report and review. Clin. Pediatr. (Phila.) *29*:525–526, 1990.
36. Parker, M. T., and Ball, L. C.: Streptococci and aerococci associated with systemic infection in man. J. Med. Microbiol. *9*:275–302, 1976.
37. Peters, V. B., Bottone, E. J., Barzilai, A., et al.: *Leuconostoc* species bacteremia in a child with acquired immunodeficiency syndrome. Clin. Pediatr. (Phila.) *31*:699–701, 1992.
38. Pien, F. D., Wilson, W. R., Kunz, K., et al.: *Aerococcus viridans* endocarditis. Mayo Clin. Proc. *59*:47–48, 1984.
39. Riebel, W. J., and Washington, J. A.: Clinical and microbiologic characteristics of pediococci. J. Clin. Microbiol. *28*:1348–1355, 1990.
40. Rogosa, M., and Sharpe, M. E.: Species differentiation of human vaginal lactobacilli. J. Gen. Microbiol. *23*:197, 1960.
41. Ruoff, K. L., Kuritzkes, D. R., Wolfson, J. S., et al.: Vancomycin-resistant gram-positive bacteria isolated from human sources. J. Clin. Microbiol. *26*:2064–2068, 1988.
42. Sarma, P. S., and Mohanty, S.: *Pediococcus acidilactici* pneumonitis and bacteremia in a pregnant woman. J. Clin. Microbiol. *36*:2392–2393, 1998.
43. Scano, F., Rossi, L., Cattelan, A., et al.: *Leuconostoc* species: A case-cluster hospital infection. Scand. J. Infect. Dis. *31*:371–373, 1999.
44. Scheiblauer, H., Reinacher, M., Tashiro, M., et al.: Interactions between bacteria and influenza A virus in the development of influenza pneumonia. J. Infect. Dis. *166*:783–791, 1992.
45. Sire, J. M., Donnio, P. Y., Mesnard, R., et al.: Septicemia and hepatic abscess caused by *Pediococcus acidilactici.* Eur. J. Clin. Microbiol. Infect. Dis. *11*:623–625, 1992.
46. Skytta, E., Haikara, A., and Mattila-Sandholm, T.: Production and characterization of antibacterial compounds produced by *Pediococcus damnosus* and *Pediococcus pentosaceus.* J. Appl. Bacteriol. *74*:134–142, 1993.
47. Stiles, M. E.: Bacteriocins produced by *Leuconostoc* species. J. Dairy Sci. *77*:2718–2724, 1994.

48. Swanson, H., Cutts, E., and Lepow, M.: Penicillin-resistant *Aerococcus viridans* bacteremia in a child receiving prophylaxis for sickle-cell disease. Clin. Infect. Dis. *22*:387–388, 1996.
49. Swenson, J. M., Facklam, R. R., and Thornsberry, C.: Antimicrobial susceptibility of vancomycin-resistant *Leuconostoc, Pediococcus,* and Lactobacillus species. Antimicrob. Agents Chemother. *34*:543–549, 1990.
50. Tankovic, J., Leclercq, R., and Duval, J.: Antimicrobial susceptibility of *Pediococcus* spp. and genetic basis of macrolide resistance in *Pediococcus acidilactici* HM3020. Antimicrob. Agents Chemother. *37*:789–792, 1993.
51. Taylor, P. W., and Trueblood, M. C.: Septic arthritis due to *Aerococcus viridans*. J. Rheumatol. *12*:1004–1005, 1985.
52. Wenocur, H. S., Smith, M. A., Vellozzi, E. M., et al.: Odontogenic infection secondary to *Leuconostoc* species. J. Clin. Microbiol. *26*:1893–1894, 1988.

SUBSECTION **2**

GRAM-NEGATIVE COCCI

Moraxella catarrhalis

BARBARA W. STECHENBERG

Once thought to be an unimportant commensal organism in the human respiratory tract, *Moraxella catarrhalis* now is recognized as an important pathogen in respiratory tract diseases, particularly otitis, sinusitis, and lower tract disease. The initial paper by Ghon and Pfeiffer[21] published in 1902 described gram-negative cocci in sputum referred to as *Micrococcus catarrhalis*. Since then, the organism has undergone several changes in nomenclature, first to *Neisseria catarrhalis* because of its resemblance to other *Neisseria* organisms. In 1970, in recognition of the contributions of Sarah Branham, the name was changed to *Branhamella catarrhalis*.[8] More recently, that this organism should be a member of the genus *Moraxella* has become clear; thus, the name was changed to *M. catarrhalis*. With the transition in nomenclature, the last 2 decades have seen a parallel rebirth of this organism as a mucosal pathogen.

Microbiology

M. catarrhalis is a gram-negative diplococcus that is morphologically indistinguishable from *Neisseria*. It has a tendency to resist decolorizing.[1] The organism is kidney shaped, with the flat sides abutting each other. The size varies, but it may be larger than meningococcus or gonococcus. However, the resemblance on sputum Gram stain or conjunctival smear to gonococcus can be striking and clinically confusing.

The organism grows well on blood or chocolate agar and forms small, opaque, grayish colonies that are circular and nonhemolytic. They have poor adhesion to the agar surface, on which they act like hockey pucks when pushed over the surface of the agar plate.[13] The use of selective media such as modified Thayer-Martin or TV broth (Mueller-Hinton broth supplemented with trimethoprim and vancomycin) increases the likelihood of recovering *M. catarrhalis* from the complex flora of the mucosal surfaces.

Isolates of *M. catarrhalis* cannot utilize maltose, glucose, lactose, or sucrose as carbohydrate sources. *M. catarrhalis* is oxidase-positive and produces deoxyribonuclease. Hydrolysis of DNA and tributyrin are valuable differentiating tests. Several rapid tests such as butyrate hydrolysis, Tween 80 hydrolysis, and selective DNase agar have been described.[45, 51] Fatty-acid analysis also has been used to identify atypical strains.

The surface of *M. catarrhalis* is composed of outer-membrane proteins, lipo-oligosaccharide, and pili. The organism does not appear to have a capsule, and the role of the pili is not defined well. Initial attempts to isolate outer-membrane proteins by detergent fractionation of cell envelopes were unsuccessful. By using a technique involving the collection of outer-membrane vesicles, which are released into the culture media, and then examination by sodium dodecyl sulfate–polyacrylamide gel electrophoresis (SDS-PAGE), Bartos and Murphy[4] identified eight proteins designated outer-membrane proteins A through H. The outer-membrane protein patterns of strains from diverse geographic and clinical sources were strikingly homogeneous.

Preliminary studies of the lipo-oligosaccharide of *M. catarrhalis* show that it is more antigenically conserved than are those of other gram-negative bacteria, thus rendering it a reasonable candidate for vaccine studies.[35, 48]

Restriction endonuclease analysis has been used as an epidemiologic tool to distinguish strains of *M. catarrhalis*. Patterson and associates[38] used the technique to evaluate a nosocomial outbreak and to demonstrate the lack of association of other strains. Dickinson and coworkers[12] used a similar technique to study isolates from children with otitis media.

Pathogenesis

The ability of *M. catarrhalis* to produce disease, particularly in sequestered areas such as the ear and lung, indicates that this organism possesses virulence mechanisms that allow it not only to grow in these anatomic sites but also to produce pathologic effects. The presence of endotoxin in the *M. catarrhalis* outer membrane undoubtedly is important for its pathogenic potential, especially in situations in which inflammation plays a major role. Very little is known about the mechanisms involved in colonization and disease production.

A body of literature concerning the immune response to *M. catarrhalis* and the antigenic composition of this organism is accumulating rapidly.[9, 10, 30] Goldblatt and associates[22] demonstrated that children younger than 4 years possess IgG1 and IgG2, which recognize an 82-kDA outer-membrane protein exclusively, but that older children mount an IgG3 response to a broad range of outer-membrane proteins. Faden and colleagues[19] developed a technique to measure opsonic antibody with the use of outer-membrane, antigen-coated beads. Convalescent sera opsonized homologous, antigen-coated sera significantly more often than acute sera did.

Unhanand and coworkers[47] used a murine model to study the pulmonary clearance of *M. catarrhalis* from infected lungs. They investigated 10 strains and found marked variability in clearance rates and recruitment of phagocytic cells. With this model, Maciver and associates[32] actively immunized animals with the outer-membrane vesicles of *M. catarrhalis* and passively immunized animals with rabbit antiserum raised against these vesicles. Both experiments resulted in enhanced pulmonary clearance of both homologous and heterologous strains. The same model has been used to evaluate the role of a large, antigenically conserved protein of *M. catarrhalis* in pulmonary clearance, as well as the role of outer-membrane protein B in the defense mechanisms of the lung.[26] The contribution of these proteins, as well as of lipo-oligosaccharide in host defenses, continues to unfold.

Epidemiology

M. catarrhalis is a normal inhabitant of the upper respiratory tract and is recovered exclusively from humans. The rate of colonization is highest in the early years and then declines steadily to less than 5 percent in adult life.[49] Prevalence studies report that as many as 50 percent of children are colonized with *M. catarrhalis*.[28, 33] Faden and associates[18] monitored a large cohort of children from birth to 2 years of age. Sixty-six percent became colonized by 1 year of age and 77.5 percent by 2 years of age. Nasopharyngeal colonization was increased during visits for otitis media in comparison to well-child visits. Otitis-prone children were colonized by 6 months of age. Restriction endonuclease analysis showed marked heterogeneity, with children acquiring and eliminating numerous different strains over time.[16]

Numerous studies have documented the increased prevalence of *M. catarrhalis* as a pathogen in otitis media.[28, 50] Shurin and colleagues[43] noted that isolation of *M. catarrhalis* from middle ear exudates increased from 6.4 percent between 1979 and 1980 to 26.5 percent between 1980 and 1982. A similar increase in *M. catarrhalis* as a pathogen in sinusitis has been reported.[52]

Once colonization of the oropharynx occurs, colonization of the tracheobronchial tree may follow, but usually only if other risk factors are operative. In adults, these risk factors include previous cardiorespiratory disease, smoking, corticosteroids, immunosuppressive agents, malignancy, and intercurrent viral illnesses.[24, 51] In children, many of the cases of pneumonia are associated with a preceding viral illness, prematurity, underlying lung disease, IgG deficiency, or other risk factors.

Nosocomial transmission has been well documented by DNA restriction endonuclease analysis.[11, 38] In pediatric intensive care units, endotracheal intubation and frequent suctioning have been identified as risk factors for the development of pneumonia and bacterial tracheitis.[11, 17]

Other interesting associations need to be investigated further. Seddon and associates[42] noted that colonization with *M. catarrhalis* occurred more commonly in asthmatic than in normal children. Whether the organism might be a trigger or pathogen in these children remains to be seen. Gottfarb and Brauner[23] found a high carriage rate of *M. catarrhalis* in children with severe persistent cough.

Infection with *M. catarrhalis* has a seasonality in both adults and children.[24, 43, 50] Infection is much more likely to occur in the winter-spring months.

Clinical Manifestations and Diagnosis

Otitis media caused by *M. catarrhalis* is indistinguishable clinically from otitis caused by other pathogens such as *Streptococcus pneumoniae* and *Haemophilus influenzae*. *M. catarrhalis* may be isolated as a single agent or in combination with other organisms. In one study, children with *M. catarrhalis* were less likely to have a serum C-reactive protein level greater than 1.0 mg/dL than were children with either of the other two major pathogens.[50]

Because tympanocentesis usually is not performed in routine cases, the exact etiology of an episode of acute otitis media generally is not known. One study found that *Moraxella* was an unusual organism as a single agent in children whose acute otitis media had been treated recently.[25] Nonetheless, in a study of persistent otitis, Pichichero and Pichichero[39] demonstrated *Moraxella* in 7 percent of specimens. The spontaneous resolution rate of *M. catarrhalis* may be high,[2] and this fact should be considered when therapy is planned.

The clinical manifestations of acute sinusitis caused by *M. catarrhalis* are similar to those of other organisms; therefore, the choice of antibiotic should be made with consideration of this organism as a potential pathogen.

Lower respiratory tract disease caused by *M. catarrhalis* may have a broad clinical spectrum; however, because sputum samples often are not available in children, many cases documented in the literature have been severe. Berg and Bartley[5] described five premature infants, all younger than 6 months, in whom precipitous clinical deterioration developed after 2 to 4 days of a prodrome consisting of cough, tachypnea, and intercostal retractions. They all required assisted ventilation, which is common in young infants with severe pneumonia.[5, 11, 16] Some cases of *M. catarrhalis* pneumonia have been associated with bacteremia.

Underlying conditions such as leukemia, acquired immunodeficiency syndrome, and trauma have been reported to predispose a patient to development of infection with *M. catarrhalis*.[33, 53] An association with immunoglobulin deficiency has been demonstrated in some patients with disease caused by this organism.[9] In adults, *M. catarrhalis* pneumonia occurs more commonly in patients with human immunodeficiency virus infection, malignancy, or chronic lung problems.[22, 51] The role of this organism in less severe manifestations probably is limited.[29]

Bacterial tracheitis caused by *M. catarrhalis* has been reported in both immunocompromised hosts and hosts with normal immune systems.[17]

M. catarrhalis also has caused a wide variety of other infections. Urethritis caused by this organism can be mistaken for infection with *Neisseria gonorrhoeae*.[44] Several cases of conjunctivitis have been reported; when present in the newborn period, *M. catarrhalis* can mimic the ophthalmia neonatorum of *N. gonorrhoeae*.[46] The relationship of neonatal infections to maternal vaginal carriage of *Moraxella* has not been established.[37]

More severe infections with *M. catarrhalis* include meningitis and bacteremia, so this organism should be considered in appropriate circumstances, especially in immunocompromised children.

Children with *M. catarrhalis* bacteremia may have many different manifestations. Some patients have petechial or purpuric rashes, rendering the clinical picture indistinguishable from that of meningococcemia. Others have been neutropenic and have required mechanical ventilation.[6] Baron and Shapiro[3] reported two cases of unsuspected bacteremia in children with nonspecific symptoms. Their presentations were similar to those of children with occult pneumococcal bacteremia. An immunocompetent child with *M. catarrhalis* bacteremia and preseptal cellulitis has been reported.[41]

Meningitis can occur from hematogenous spread of *M. catarrhalis* from the nasopharynx or as a consequence of ventriculoperitoneal shunt placement or surgery. Rarely, suppurative arthritis has been seen in children and adults.[27, 34] Endocarditis is a rare occurrence, as is peritonitis.

Treatment

In the past, *M. catarrhalis* was susceptible to all β-lactam antibiotics. In the late 1970s, however, β-lactamase–producing strains of *M. catarrhalis* were isolated in Europe. In the United States, a parallel increase in the frequency of isolation of β-lactamase–producing *M. catarrhalis* has been noted, so it is not unusual for a laboratory to report that more than 90 percent of strains are β-lactamase producers.

The β-lactamases BRO-1, BRO-2, and BRO-3 are of chromosomal origin. Laboratory detection of β-lactamase activity depends on the assay used; the chromogenic cephalosporin nitrocefin usually is recommended.[15] The β-lactamase inhibitors clavulanic acid, sulbactam, and tazobactam are active against the enzymes produced by *Moraxella*. Most β-lactamase–positive isolates will respond to achievable concentrations of β-lactam/β-lactamase inhibitor antimicrobial combinations, cephalosporins, and cephamycins.[14, 20] Because of the high prevalence of β-lactamase–producing strains, many laboratories choose not to do any such testing.

Among the oral cephalosporins active against β-lactamase–positive strains of *Moraxella*, the minimal inhibitory concentration increases twofold to fourfold in the presence of β-lactamase BRO-1 but not β-lactamase BRO-2; cefixime is more active than are the older cephalosporins.[36] Resistance to tetracycline (by the nontransferable Tet B determinant) and erythromycin has been reported, but such resistance is a rare finding.[7, 40]

In vitro, *M. catarrhalis* usually is susceptible to ampicillin-sulbactam, amoxicillin-clavulanate, erythromycin, azithromycin, clarithromycin, trimethoprim-sulfamethoxazole, aztreonam, tetracyclines, chloramphenicol, fluoroquinolones (e.g., ciprofloxacin), aminoglycosides, and second- or third-generation cephalosporins such as cefprozil, cefpodoxime, cefixime, cefdinir, and loracarbef.[31] *M. catarrhalis* also is susceptible to cefuroxime and cefaclor, although the latter may be less active. The *Moraxella* organism is resistant to clindamycin, vancomycin, and oxacillin.

Prevention

Prevention of nosocomial *M. catarrhalis* infection is dependent on sound practices of infection control, especially with regard to pulmonary toilet. Prevention of other infections with this organism has not been attempted, except for the use of prophylactic antibiotics for recurrent otitis media.

REFERENCES

1. Ainsworth, S. M., Nagy, S. B., Morgan, L. A., et al.: Interpretation of gram-stained sputa containing *Moraxella (Branhamella) catarrhalis.* Clin. Microbiol. *28*:2559–2560, 1990.
2. Barnett, E. D., and Klein, J. O.: The problem of resistant bacteria for the management of acute otitis media. Pediatr. Clin. North Am. *42*:509–518, 1995.
3. Baron, J., and Shapiro, E. D.: Unsuspected bacteremia caused by *Branhamella catarrhalis.* Pediatr. Infect. Dis. J. *4*:100–101, 1985.
4. Bartos, L. C., and Murphy, T. F.: Comparison of the outer membrane proteins of 50 strains of *Branhamella catarrhalis.* J. Infect. Dis. *158*:761–765, 1988.
5. Berg, R. A., and Bartley, D. L.: Pneumonia associated with *Branhamella catarrhalis* in infants. Pediatr. Infect. Dis. J. *6*:569–573, 1987.
6. Bonadio, W. A.: *Branhamella catarrhalis* bacteremia in children. Pediatr. Infect. Dis. J. *7*:738–739, 1988.
7. Brown, B. A., Wallace, R. J., Flanagan, C. W., et al.: Tetracycline and erythromycin resistance among clinical isolates of *Branhamella catarrhalis.* Antimicrob. Agents Chemother. *33*:1631–1633, 1989.
8. Catlin, B. W.: Transfer of the organism named *Neisseria catarrhalis* to *Branhamella* gen. nov. Int. J. Syst. Bacteriol. *20*:155–159, 1970.
9. Catlin, B. W.: *Branhamella catarrhalis*: An organism gaining respect as a pathogen. Clin. Microbiol. Rev. *3*:293–320, 1990.
10. Chapman, A. J., Musher, D. M., Jonsson, S., et al.: Development of bactericidal antibody during *Branhamella catarrhalis* infection. J. Infect. Dis. *151*:878–882, 1985.
11. Cook, P. P., Heent, D. W., and Syndman, D. R.: Nosocomial *Branhamella catarrhalis* in a pediatric intensive care unit: Risk factors for disease. J. Hosp. Infect. *13*:299–307, 1989.
12. Dickinson, D. P., Loos, B. G., Dryja, D. M., et al.: Restriction fragment mapping of *Branhamella catarrhalis:* A new tool for studying the epidemiology of this middle ear pathogen. J. Infect. Dis. *158*:208, 1988.
13. Doern, G. V.: *Branhamella catarrhalis*: Phenotypic characteristics. Am. J. Med. *88*:335–355, 1990.
14. Doern, G. V., and Jones, R. N.: Antimicrobial susceptibility testing of *Haemophilus influenzae, Branhamella catarrhalis* and *Neisseria gonorrhoeae.* Antimicrob. Agents Chemother. *32*:1747–1753, 1988.
15. Doern, G. V., and Tubert, A. T.: Detection of β-lactamase activity among clinical isolates of *Branhamella catarrhalis* with six different β-lactamase assays. J. Clin. Microbiol. *25*:1380–1383, 1987.
16. Dyson, C., Poonyth, H. O., Watkinson, et al.: Life threatening *Branhamella catarrhalis* pneumonia in young infants. J. Infect. *21*:305–307, 1990.
17. Ernst, T. N., and Philp, M.: Bacterial tracheitis caused by *Branhamella catarrhalis.* Pediatr. Infect. Dis. J. *6*:574, 1987.
18. Faden, H., Harabuchi, Y., Hong, J. J., et al.: Epidemiology of *Moraxella catarrhalis* in children during the first 2 years of life: Relationship to otitis media. J. Infect. Dis. *169*:1312–1317, 1994.
19. Faden, H., Hong, J. J., and Pahade, N.: Immune response to *Moraxella catarrhalis* in children with otitis media: Opsonophagocytosis with antigen-coated latex beads. Ann. Otol. Rhinol. Laryngol. *103*:522–524, 1994.
20. Fung, C.-P., Yeo, S.-F., and Livermore, D. M.: Susceptibility of *Moraxella catarrhalis* isolates to β-lactam antibiotics in relation to β-lactamase pattern. J. Antimicrob. Chemother. *33*:215–222, 1994.
21. Ghon, A., and Pfeiffer, H.: Der *Mikvococcus catarrhalis* (R. Pfeiffer) als krankheitserreger. Z. Klin. Med. *44*:263–281, 1902.
22. Goldblatt, D., Turner, M. W., and Levinsky, R. J.: *Branhamella catarrhalis*: Antigenic determinants and the development of the IgG subclass response in childhood. J. Infect. Dis. *162*:1128–1135, 1990.
23. Gottfarb, P., and Brauner, A.: Children with persistent cough: Outcome with treatment and role of *Moraxella catarrhalis?* Scand. J. Infect. Dis. *26*:545–551, 1994.
24. Hager, H., Verghese, A., Alvarez, S., et al.: *Branhamella catarrhalis* respiratory infections. Rev. Infect. Dis. *9*:1140–1149, 1987.
25. Harrison, C. J., Marks, J. I., and Welch, D. F.: Microbiology of recently treated acute otitis media compared with previously untreated acute otitis media. Pediatr. Infect. Dis. J. *4*:641–646, 1985.
26. Helminen, M. E., Maciver, I., Paris, M., et al.: A mutation affecting expression of a major outer protein of *Moraxella catarrhalis* alters resistance and survival in vivo. J. Infect. Dis. *168*:1194–1201, 1993.
27. Izraeli, S., Flasterstein, B., Shamir, R., et al.: *Branhamella catarrhalis* as a cause of suppurative arthritis. Pediatr. Infect. Dis. J. *8*:256–257, 1989.
28. Klein, J. O.: Otitis media. Clin. Infect. Dis. *19*:823–833, 1994.
29. Korppi, M., Katila, M. L., Jaaskelainen, J., et al.: Role of *Moraxella (Branhamella) catarrhalis* as a respiratory pathogen in children. Acta Paediatr. *81*:993–996, 1992.
30. Leinonen, M., Luotonen, J., Herva, E., et al.: Preliminary serologic evidence for a pathogenic role of *Branhamella catarrhalis.* J. Infect. Dis. *144*:570–574, 1981.
31. Lemmen, S. W., Anding, K., Engels, I., et al.: Bactericidal activity of clarithromycin and cefaclor against *Streptococcus pneumoniae* and *Moraxella catarrhalis* in healthy volunteers. J. Antimicrob. Chemother. *33*:673–674, 1994.

32. Maciver, I., Unhanand, M., McCracken, G. H., et al.: Effect of immunization on pulmonary clearance of *Moraxella catarrhalis* in animal model. J. Infect. Dis. *168*:469–472, 1993.
33. Marchant, C. D.: Spectrum of disease due to *Branhamella catarrhalis* in children with particular reference to acute otitis media. Am. J. Med. *88*(Suppl. 5A):155–195, 1990.
34. Melendez, P. R., and Johnson, R. H.: Bacteremia and septic arthritis caused by *Moraxella catarrhalis*. Rev. Infect. Dis. *13*:428–429, 1991.
35. Murphy, T. F.: The surface of *Branhamella catarrhalis*: A systematic approach to the surface antigens of an emerging pathogen. Pediatr. Infect. Dis. J. *8*:575–577, 1989.
36. Nash, D. R., Flanagan, C., Steele, L. C., et al.: Comparison of the activity of cefixime and activities of other oral antibiotics against adult clinical isolates of *Moraxella (Branhamella) catarrhalis* containing BRO-1 and BRO-2 and *Haemophilus influenzae*. Antimicrob. Agents Chemother. *35*:192–194, 1991.
37. Ohlsson, A., and Bailey, T.: Neonatal pneumonia caused by *Branhamella catarrhalis*. Scand. J. Infect. Dis. *17*:225–228, 1985.
38. Patterson, J. E., Patterson, T. F., Farrel, P., et al.: Evaluation of restriction endonuclease analysis as an epidemiologic typing system for *Branhamella catarrhalis*. J. Clin. Microbiol. *27*:994–946, 1989.
39. Pichichero, M. E., and Pichichero, C. L.: Persistent acute otitis media. I. Causative organisms. Pediatr. Infect. Dis. J. *14*:178–183, 1995.
40. Roberts, M. C., Pang, Y., Spencer, R. C., et al.: Tetracycline resistance in *Moraxella (Branhamella) catarrhalis*: Demonstration of two clonal outbreaks by using pulsed-field gel electrophoresis. Antimicrob. Agents Chemother. *35*:2453–2455, 1991.
41. Rotta, A. T., and Asmar, B. I.: *Moraxella catarrhalis* bacteremia and preseptal cellulitis. South. Med. J. *87*:541–542, 1994.
42. Seddon, P. C., Sunderland, D., O'Halloran, S. M., et al.: *Branhamella catarrhalis* colonization in preschool asthmatics. Pediatr. Pulmonol. *13*:133–135, 1992.
43. Shurin, P. A., Marchant, C. D., Kim, C. H., et al.: Emergence of beta-lactamase–producing strains of *Branhamella catarrhalis* as important agents of otitis media. Pediatr. Infect. Dis. J. *2*:34–38, 1983.
44. Smith, G.: *Branhamella catarrhalis* infection imitating gonorrhea in a man. N. Engl. J. Med. *326*:1277, 1987.
45. Speeleveld, E., Fossepre, J. M., Gordts, B., Van Landuyt, H. W.: Comparison of three rapid methods, tributyrin, 4-methylumbelliferyl butyrate, and indoxyl acetate, for rapid identification of *Moraxella catarrhalis*. J. Clin. Microbiol. *32*:1362–1363, 1994.
46. Stull, T. L., and Stanford, E. J.: Pseudogonococcal ophthalmia neonatorum caused by *Branhamella catarrhalis*. Pediatr. Infect. Dis. J. *5*:104–105, 1986.
47. Unhanand, M., Maciver, I., Ramilo, O., et al.: Pulmonary clearance of *Moraxella catarrhalis* in an animal model. J. Infect. Dis. *165*:644–650, 1992.
48. Vaneechoutte, M., Verschraegen, G., Claeys, G., et al.: Serologic typing of *Branhamella catarrhalis* strains on the basis of lipopolysaccharide antigens. J. Clin. Microbiol. *28*:182–187, 1990.
49. Vaneechoutte, M., Verschraegen, G., Claeys, G., et al.: Respiratory tract carrier rates of *Moraxella Branhamella catarrhalis* in adults and children and interpretation of the isolation of *Moraxella catarrhalis* from sputum. J. Clin. Microbiol. *28*:2674–2680, 1990.
50. Van Hare, G. F., Shurin, P. A., Marchant, C. D., et al.: Acute otitis media caused by *Branhamella catarrhalis*: Biology and therapy. Rev. Infect. Dis. *9*:16–27, 1987.
51. Verghese, A., and Berk, S. L.: *Moraxella (Branhamella) catarrhalis*. Infect. Dis. Clin. North Am. *5*:523–538, 1991.
52. Wald, E. R., Reilly, J. S., Casselbrant, M., et al.: Treatment of acute maxillary sinusitis in childhood: A comparative study of amoxicillin and cefaclor. J. Pediatr. *104*:297–302, 1984.
53. Wong, V. K., and Ross, L. A.: *Branhamella catarrhalis* septicemia in an infant with AIDS. Scand. J. Infect. Dis. *20*:559–560, 1988.

CHAPTER 93 Meningococcal Disease

MARSHA S. ANDERSON ■ MARY P. GLODÉ ■ ARNOLD L. SMITH

Epidemic meningococcal meningitis was described first by Gaspard Vieusseux in Geneva in the spring of 1805. In a monograph titled "The Disease Which Raged During the Spring of 1805," he wrote

> It commences suddenly with prostration of strength, often extreme: the face is distorted, the pulse feeble. There appears a violent pain in the head, especially over the forehead; then there comes pain of the heart or vomiting of greenish material, stiffness of the spine, and in infants, convulsions. In cases which were fatal, loss of consciousness occurred. The course of the disease is very rapid, termination by death or by cure. In most of the patients who died in 24 hours or a little after, the body is covered with purple spots at the moment of death or very little time afterward.[171]

Today, meningococcus continues to be a cause of endemic and epidemic disease. In the United States, approximately 3000 cases occur each year, and 95 to 97 percent of them are sporadic.[141, 181] However, epidemics in Brazil in the early 1970s and in Finland in 1975 serve as a reminder of the potential virulence of this organism. In São Paulo, Brazil, during the epidemic period, invasive meningococcal disease developed in almost 1 in every 300 inhabitants during a 1-year period.[33]

The reader is referred to several excellent reviews of meningococcal disease that have been published recently.[79, 83, 121, 142, 143]

Microbiology

The family Neisseriaceae contains five genera: *Neisseria, Kingella, Eikenella, Simonsiella,* and *Alysiella*. In addition, it includes three Centers for Disease Control and Prevention (CDC) groups that commonly are found as normal mouth flora in dogs: CDC groups EF-4a, EF-4b, and M-5. Previously, the family contained the genera *Acinetobacter, Moraxella,* and *Psychrobacter;* however, they have not been included in the most recent classification.[92]

The *Neisseria* genus was named for Dr. Albert Neisser, who described the organism of gonorrhea in 1879. The genus *Neisseria* contains 16 species; the ones of human origin are *Neisseria gonorrhoeae, Neisseria meningitidis, Neisseria sicca, Neisseria lactamica, Neisseria subflava, Neisseria flavescens, Neisseria mucosa, Neisseria cinerea, Neisseria polysacchreae,* and *Neisseria elongata.*[92]

N. meningitidis is a gram-negative coccus, usually less than 1 μm in diameter. It classically occurs in pairs with adjacent sides flattened, similar to kidney beans. Occasionally, the organism divides in two planes at right angles to one another, which results in the formation of tetrads. The organisms are nonmotile and aerobic (but facultatively anaerobic), produce catalase and oxidase, and may be encapsulated. *N. meningitidis* oxidizes glucose and maltose to acid, thereby distinguishing it from *N. gonorrhoeae,* which oxidizes only glucose. However, certain rare strains of *N. meningitidis* that fail to produce acid from either glucose or maltose have been reported. Fresh isolates have complex nutritional requirements and grow best on chocolate or blood agar. Incubation in a humidified 10 percent carbon dioxide environment is not essential, but enhances growth. Morphologically, the colonies are bluish-gray in appearance and will produce beta-hemolysis after 48 to 72 hours of incubation on 5 percent horse blood agar.[19]

N. meningitidis can be transformed by DNA originating in other species of *Neisseria*. This process is facilitated by the recognition of specific nucleotide sequences in *Neisseria* DNA by the outer membrane.[92] Thus, when a *Neisseria* spp. cohabiting the nasopharynx with *N. meningitidis* dies and releases its DNA, the co-resident meningococcus can take up DNA and incorporate it into its genome. Although this sequence of events rarely occurs, if the new DNA confers a selective advantage to the recipient meningococcus, the trait encoded by the incoming DNA may be retained. This mechanism is the means by which sulfonamide and penicillin G resistance has arisen in *N. meningitidis*.[93] Many commensal *Neisseria* strains that also inhabit the nasopharynx are relatively resistant to penicillin G. DNA fragments from *N. lactamica* and *N. polysacchareae* encoding penicillin resistance are found in penicillin-resistant *N. meningitidis*.[145] Transformation of new DNA into *N. meningitidis* also can introduce genes that modify the structure of the bacterium. Serotyping of group A, B, and C meningococci has provided valuable macro-epidemiologic information.[49] As immunity to one capsular polysaccharide develops in a population, the organism clearly is capable of acquiring DNA encoding for an alternative capsule. Serogroup B to C switching has been observed in a population[161] and a contact of a case.[172] Genes whose products aid the bacterium in surviving in the host or are involved in housekeeping functions also appear to undergo horizontal gene transfer from commensal *Neisseria* to *N. meningitidis*.[91] This phenomenon probably is responsible for the occasional report of commensal *Neisseria* causing meningitis.[5] In one case, the strain was a virulent meningococcus that acquired a gene for polysaccharide synthesis from sucrose; this additional property led it to being identified as *N. subflava* rather than *N. meningitidis*.

In addition to the transformation route for varying the antigenic phenotype, meningococci also have an intrinsic mechanism for varying the number of surface antigens. This process, called *phase variation,* is caused by repetitive (microsatellite) tracts in the coding sequence. When the bacterial chromosome is replicated at the time of cell division, the number of these repeats is not precisely synthesized. Thus, the new bacterial chromosome may contain a gene with a different number of the repeats. Because 30 or more tetrameric repeats often are present, a variable gain or loss of 1 or more repeats can turn the gene on or off. Researchers have estimated that at least 65 genes in *N. meningitidis*, including *porA,* are subject to this on/off mechanism.[44, 165] Capsule synthesis is switched on and off by this mechanism. This ability portends against a successful vaccine for serogroup B meningococci.

Like other gram-negative bacteria, the outer and inner cell membranes of *Neisseria* are phospholipid bilayers. These membranes sandwich a layer of peptidoglycan. Lipo-oligosaccharide (LOS), which is similar to the lipopolysaccharide in gram-negative enteric bacteria, is associated with the outer leaflet of the outer cell membrane. Outer-membrane proteins that function as porins are an integral part of the outer membrane. Some of these outer-membrane proteins are opacity proteins and facilitate adherence and invasion.[111] Outside the outer membrane, meningococci possess a polysaccharide capsule that protects the organism from phagocytosis.

Meningococci also have pili, which seem to be important in some phases of adherence to host cells, colonization, and invasion. The genes that code for pili also can be turned on and off, so at times the organism may not express pili. This mechanism may help meningococci detach and allow the organism to be transmitted to another site or another host.[64] Antigenic variation in pili by a cassette mechanism permits the bacterium to escape the host's immune system.[58] In addition, both outer-membrane proteins and LOS display antigenic variation by the repetitive tetrameric mechanism.

For epidemiologic purposes, meningococci are divided into serogroups, serotypes, and subtypes. Differences in capsular polysaccharides, outer-membrane proteins, and LOS constitute the basis for these classifications. The capsular polysaccharides are antigenic and the basis for serogroup designation. Thirteen serogroups currently are recognized: A, B, C, D, H, I, K, L, X, Y, Z, W135, and 29E.[3] Serogroups A, B, and C are the most common causes of invasive disease worldwide. Table 93–1 lists the chemical composition of the capsule from the serogroups most commonly associated with meningococcal disease.[9, 74]

Serotyping of organisms is based on antigenic differences in outer-membrane proteins called porins. Porins are protein channels in the outer membrane that permit nutrients and certain antibiotics to diffuse into the periplasmic space. A single locus encodes porin B, but two mutually exclusive alleles have antigenic differences. All meningococci have either antigenic class 2 or class 3 porin B. These differences permit serotyping. Differentiation of subtypes is based on antigenic differences in porin A. This highly variable antigen is called a class 1 outer-membrane protein, and more than 20 serotypes and 16 subtypes have been identified. Antigenic specificity is achieved by the generation of monoclonal antibodies to the major protein (primarily class 2 or 3), LOS, and the class 1 protein. The designation B:2a:P1.1:L3,7 indicates that the serogroup B strain is an "a" subtype of class 2 proteins, is a "one" of class 1 protein, and possesses two LOS antigens: 3 and 7.[56]

Type 2 protein antigen is isolated from more than 50 percent of cases in the United States and Canada and is an antigenic determinant in group B and C strains. These protein antigens not only are important as epidemiologic markers but also can induce protective bactericidal antibodies.[50]

Epidemiology

The incidence of meningococcal disease varies significantly by geographic location. Endemic disease, which occurs in developed countries such as the United States and Europe, has an incidence of 0.9 to 3.0 cases per 100,000 population per year.[119, 126, 141, 159] In developing countries, the rate is approximately 10 times higher (10 to 25 per 100,000 inhabitants per year).[59] The highest rate of meningococcal disease is found in a multicountry belt across sub-Saharan Africa, which has been termed the *meningitis belt.* Serogroup A

TABLE 93–1 ■ CHEMICAL STRUCTURE OF GROUP-SPECIFIC POLYSACCHARIDE CAPSULE OF MENINGOCOCCI

Group	Chemical Composition of Capsule
A	2-Acetamido-2-deoxy-D-mannopyranosyl phosphate
B	α-2,8-*N*-acetylneuraminic acid
C	α-2,9-*O*-acetylneuraminic acid
D	Composition not known
X	2-Acetimido-2-deoxy-D-glucopyranosyl phosphate
Y	4-*O*-α-D-glucopyranosyl-*N*-acetylneuraminic acid
Z	Composition not known
29E	3-Deoxy-D-manno-octulosonic acid
W135	4-*O*-α-D-galactopyranosyl-*N*-acetylneuraminic acid

meningococcal disease is prevalent there and occurs in epidemics, during which the incidence of meningococcal disease is as high as 1000 per 100,000 inhabitants (1%). Spread of clonal strains of group A meningococcus may be a factor in Africa's unusually high rate of epidemic disease. Clonal strains can migrate transcontinentally and cause epidemics; one example is the clonal group A meningococcus electrophoretic type III-1 (ET III-1), which caused epidemics in China, Nepal, Saudi Arabia, Chad, and Kenya in the 1980s.[107, 126]

International outbreaks of *N. meningitidis* infection occurred in 1987 and 2000 and were associated with Muslims making the annual pilgrimage to Mecca. The disease spread to persons of all nationalities represented, some of whom returned home before becoming ill.[107, 131] In some cases, close contacts of travelers were infected. Several cases in U.S. citizens were attributed to the outbreaks. The 1987 outbreak was linked to serogroup A, whereas the 2000 outbreak was caused by serogroup W135.[100, 105, 131]

Serogroups A, B, and C account for more than 90 percent of meningococcal disease worldwide. Currently in the United States, Serogoups B, C, and Y each account for approximately one third of cases.[159] Serogroup A, which causes periodic epidemics in developing countries, is responsible for only occasional cases of meningococcal disease in the United States. Serogroup B usually causes sporadic disease but occasionally is associated with outbreaks.[149] Serogroup C, though also a cause of sporadic disease, has been associated with numerous outbreaks in the United States, Canada, and Europe.[70] School-related outbreaks of serogroup C meningococcal disease also have been reported.[108, 183] The incidence of serogroup C disease has increased in the United States during the last few years, with many outbreaks being caused by a clone identified as ET-24.[142] Disease caused by serogroup W135 occurs infrequently and, like serogroup Y, has been associated with meningococcal pneumonia.[142, 173]

Meningococcal disease in the United States peaks during the months November through March,[140, 142] with the highest attack rate occurring in February and the lowest attack rate in September. In Africa, epidemic disease develops during the dry season and decreases once the rainy season starts.[127] Males and females are affected equally.

The risk of contracting meningococcal disease is related inversely to age, with the highest rates of disease seen in children younger than 1 year.[159] As many as 49 percent of cases occur in children younger than 2 years.[72] However, in epidemics, an age shift occurs, with older children, adolescents, and young adults more often affected.[149] A progressive increase in the development of protective antibodies against meningococci takes place between the ages of 2 and 12 years. Neonates usually are protected by passive IgG transfer in utero if the mother has antimeningococcal antibody. In general, the development of bactericidal antibodies to meningococci increases in children at a rate of approximately 5 percent per year.[55]

The precise epidemiology of meningococcal disease was defined elegantly in a series of observations in New Jersey military recruits. An inverse correlation was noted between the age-related incidence of meningococcal disease in the United States and the prevalence of serum bactericidal activity against three pathogenic strains of *N. meningitidis*.[55] The investigators prospectively studied all incoming recruits to Fort Dix and demonstrated that recruits who lacked bactericidal activity against case strains had a 38 percent attack rate if they were exposed and acquired a meningococcal strain.[55] Usually, nasopharyngeal carriage was an immunizing process. Carriage induced the formation of protective antibodies against homologous strains, but it also produced cross-reacting antibodies to heterologous strains of pathogenic meningococci. Antibody production typically was seen within 2 weeks of the acquisition of carriage.[55, 56]

In addition to nasopharyngeal carriage, other processes may contribute to meningococcal antibody formation. Certain strains of cross-reacting bacteria such as *Escherichia coli* and *Bacillus* produce capsular polysaccharides that are immunologically identical to the capsules of meningococci serogroups A, B, and C, and are thus a potential immunizing source against invasive meningococcal disease in the general population.[56, 77, 169]

Nasopharyngeal carriage of *N. meningitidis* is lowest in infants and children and highest in adolescents and young adults. One study reported that 2.4 percent of asymptomatic infants and children had a positive nasopharyngeal culture for *N. meningitidis* during a nonepidemic period.[94] A study of 1500 Norwegians found that the carriage rate was 32.7 percent in persons 20 to 24 years of age and 10 percent in those older than 25.[22] Other investigators have shown that approximately 20 percent of children harbor meningococcal species in their nasopharynx, but most of these isolates are atypical, nontypeable strains that ferment lactose in addition to glucose and maltose.[56]

Nasopharyngeal meningococcal carriage in household contacts of persons with documented meningococcal disease is approximately 10 percent.[94, 117, 137] Several studies have shown that the carriage rate increases if infants or children are in the home.[77, 117] In one outbreak of serogroup C meningococcal disease, carriage rates were 37.8 percent in households in which an infant had the disease, 17.5 percent in households in which a child had the disease, and 6.9 percent in households in which an adult had the disease.[77]

Nasopharyngeal carriage is a common occurrence after household contact with an index case, and colonization can persist for weeks to months. Without chemoprophylaxis, as many as 35 percent of contacts become colonized by the eighth week. The median duration of carriage is 9 months.[94] However, in nearly 40 percent of individuals, it may exceed 16 months.[57] An association between smoking and an increased rate of meningococcal carriage has been demonstrated.[153, 157] In addition, passive smoke has been implicated in increasing the risk for acquisition of meningococcal disease in children younger than 5 years by 7.5 times that of the general population.

The factors responsible for converting nasopharyngeal colonization to invasive disease have not been established firmly. Many people in whom invasive disease subsequently develops are colonized shortly before the illness begins. Probably, these individuals lack bactericidal antibody, and for some reason, protective antibody does not develop with acquisition of the pathogenic strain. Other risk factors associated with invasive disease include young age, crowding (new military recruits, college freshmen in dormitories),[18, 101] lower socioeconomic class,[142] concurrent upper respiratory infection,[106, 182] specific immune deficiencies (properdin or terminal complement),[45] functional or anatomic asplenia,[48] and active or passive smoking.[47, 153]

Speculation regarding the role of other upper respiratory pathogens in meningococcal disease has prompted several observations. The peak incidence of meningococcal infection has been noted to mirror the peaks of such agents as influenza and *Mycoplasma*. Several studies have shown an association between colonization or infection with respiratory viruses or *Mycoplasma* and an increased risk for development of meningococcal disease.[21, 68, 106, 147] Simultaneous outbreaks of meningococcal and influenza or echovirus infections have been documented.[89, 182] In addition, one study suggested that the incidence of meningococcal disease and the resultant morbidity and mortality increased in the 5 weeks after the occurrence of influenza-like syndromes.[106] One postulation is that viral pathogens may temporarily affect the immune response and facilitate meningococcal disease. Another possibility is that viral infection disrupts the normal respiratory epithelium and thereby increases the likelihood that colonizing meningococci might become invasive.[106] Having had a preceding viral respiratory disease is not a prerequisite for the establishment of meningococcal carriage or disease. However, its occurrence may increase the risk for development of invasive meningococcal disease.

Individuals with late complement component deficiencies (C5, C6, C7, C8, or C9) and properdin pathway deficiencies are at risk for acquiring meningococcal disease.[45] These defects usually are inherited, and there may be a history of meningococcal disease or repeated meningococcal infections in other members of the family. Acquired complement deficiencies associated with diseases such as systemic lupus erythematosus, nephrotic syndrome, and chronic liver disease also are thought to increase the risk for development of meningococcal disease.[85] A Russian study found the incidence of complement deficiency in first episodes of meningococcal disease to be approximately 1 percent.[129] In Italy, the prevalence of complement deficiency in patients with meningococcal meningitis was 17 percent.[31] The decision regarding whom to screen for complement deficiency should be based partly on the prevalence of meningococcal disease in a given country. In countries where the incidence of meningococcal disease is high, complement deficiency is less likely to be found. In countries such as the United States, where the incidence is relatively low, complement screening may be justified.

The chance of finding a complement or alternative pathway (properdin) deficiency substantially increases in patients with recurrent meningococcal disease or uncommon serogroups. Complement or properdin deficiency in a patient with infection by an unusual serogroup was found to range in frequency from 31 to 50 percent.[46, 114] Therefore, screening all individuals who have unusual serogroups is reasonable. CH_{50}, a test that generally is available, will screen for the combined activity of C1 through C9. If a complement deficiency is found, the individual should receive meningococcal vaccine. In addition, family members who are found to be complement deficient also should receive vaccine.

Some investigators have shown that although persons with complement deficiency are more at risk for acquisition of meningococcal disease, the disease that they get often is mild. Meningococcal infection activates the complement system, and the LOS present in the bacterial outer membrane probably is responsible for the activation. In fatal cases, intense activation has continued until the time of death.[16] The case-fatality rate in complement-deficient individuals is approximately 3 percent.[144] Complement-deficient individuals are thought to be unable to maintain the high-level complement pathway activation and, therefore, have less severe disease.

Properdin deficiency, which impairs activation of the alternative complement pathway, is X-linked and has been associated with fulminant meningococcal disease.[34, 46] The case-fatality rate in one kindred was 75 percent for persons with meningococcal disease.[11] Screening of individuals with exceptionally fulminant disease or individuals who have a family history of meningococcal infection should be considered. AP50 will screen for properdin deficiency in the alternative complement pathway. If a deficiency is documented, those individuals and their family members could receive the quadrivalent meningococcal vaccine to prevent the development of disease by at least some serogroups of meningococcus.

Pathology and Pathogenesis

The mechanisms by which meningococci invade humans are understood only partially. We do know that encapsulated, typeable meningococci are virulent, whereas nonencapsulated strains are relatively nonpathogenic. Even among encapsulated strains, differences in virulence between case and carrier strains of *N. meningitidis* have been demonstrated in an animal model.[67] The presence of a polysaccharide capsule enhances susceptibility to invasiveness by resisting opsonization and subsequent phagocytosis.

The human nasopharynx is the only natural reservoir of *N. meningitidis*.[155] Once pathogenic meningococci have colonized the respiratory tract of susceptible persons, either they become invasive or antibody develops to the organism and confers immunity. Meningococci adhere to nonciliated, columnar epithelial cells in the nasopharynx via pili. Binding induces endocytosis of the organism into the epithelial cell, and the bacteria may penetrate the epithelial barrier via phagocytotic vacuoles.[154] If antibody is insufficient and invasion occurs, the individual may become bacteremic. Occasionally, unsuspected meningococcal bacteremia has been detected on blood culture and spontaneously cleared on a follow-up culture without administration of antibiotics.[158] However, in most cases, clearing does not occur, and the individual becomes progressively sicker. Bacteria in the blood may seed the meninges and cause meningitis.

Meningococci are gram-negative organisms, and LOS is a major component of the bacterial cell membrane. Meningococci release blebs, which have an outer membrane laden with LOS, from their surfaces. LOS is a potent endotoxin, and concentrations of LOS correlate with the severity of disease.[14–16] LOS induces the release of a host of inflammatory and anti-inflammatory mediators—tumor necrosis factor–α (TNF-α), interferon-γ, interleukin-1 (IL-1), IL-6, IL-8, IL-10, and IL-1 receptor antagonist—concentrations of which also are correlated with the severity of disease.[53, 86, 166, 167, 175] TNF-α down-regulates thrombomodulin expression on endothelial cells, thereby leading to decreased activity of proteins S and C.[27, 112] Like TNF-α, many of the mediators directly or indirectly contribute to the development of a procoagulant state that results in the formation of microthrombi characteristically found in the skin, digits and extremities, and organs.

Cytokines play an important role in development of the shock frequently seen in meningococcemia. Release of cytokines induces activation of neutrophils and up-regulation of adhesion molecules, which may promote endothelial damage and capillary leak.[41] Vasodilation also may occur secondary to increased production of nitric oxide by endothelial cells.[104] Compensatory vasoconstriction of splanchnic, skin, and renal vessels subsequently may not be sufficient to maintain adequate blood pressure. Endotoxin-related or cytokine-mediated cardiac dysfunction also may contribute to the development of heart failure and hypotension.[120] Profound capillary leak in the pulmonary bed may lead to the development of acute respiratory distress syndrome.

The disseminated intravascular coagulation (DIC) commonly seen in meningococcemia also is thought to be a consequence of activation of the coagulation system by endotoxin.[139] Experimental animal work has suggested a synergistic effect of meningococcal endotoxin and material egested from leukocytes containing meningococci in the initiation of DIC.[36]

The pathologic lesions seen in fulminant meningococcal disease are similar to those that the generalized Shwartzman reaction induces in rabbits by endotoxin. The pathogenesis of tissue injury in meningococcal disease is mediated through the effects of endotoxin. Davis and Arnold[32] investigated the relative potency of meningococcal endotoxins in comparison to *E. coli* and *Salmonella typhimurium* endotoxin. Meningococcal and enteric endotoxins were equally potent in mouse lethality assays and in their ability to induce a generalized Shwartzman reaction. However, meningococcal endotoxins were 5- to 10-fold more potent in eliciting the dermal Shwartzman reaction. The authors postulated that the greater skin potency of endotoxin preparations from meningococci may explain the prominence of purpuric skin lesions in patients with meningococcemia. In addition, circulating concentrations of endotoxin in those with meningococcemia may be 50 to 100 times that of other gram-negative infections.[130]

Shortly after receiving bactericidal antibiotics, some patients undergo marked clinical deterioration, including hypotension and occasionally death. Rapid liberation of endotoxin (and the resultant stimulation of cytokine release) from lysing organisms probably is the cause of this phenomenon.[98] Variations in the amount of endotoxin liberated by a given isolate may occur. In one study, strains from individuals with invasive disease released higher amounts of endotoxin than did isolates from carriers.[97]

A pathology study of 200 fatal meningococcal infections published by Hardman[62] illustrates the ability of the meningococcus to affect virtually any organ, either directly or indirectly. Approximately 40 percent of the patients had meningococcemia and meningitis. Except for adults with meningitis, the average survival time for all cases was 72 hours or less. The major organ systems involved at autopsy in these 200 cases were the heart, central nervous system, skin, mucous and serous membranes, and adrenals.

Myocarditis occurred in 78 percent of cases (the histology of this lesion is discussed separately; see the section "Pericarditis and Myocarditis"). In patients with myocarditis, pulmonary edema also was noted, and pleural effusions were found in 30 percent. Acute myocarditis was thought to be the primary factor responsible for the fatal outcome.

Cutaneous hemorrhage occurred in 69 percent of the fatal infections and ranged from isolated petechiae to diffuse purpura. The extent or location of hemorrhage did not correlate with infection caused by any particular serotype of *N. meningitidis*. Hemorrhage frequently was associated with acute vasculitis and with fibrin deposition in arterioles, capillaries, and glomeruli.

Acute meningitis was noted at autopsy in 68 percent of the infections. Acute inflammatory cells were present in the leptomeninges and perivascular spaces; vasculitis of small meningeal veins also was noted. Encephalitis was seen primarily in adult patients in whom meningitis developed without meningococcemia. Brain abscesses were found in two patients. In almost one half the patients with acute meningococcemia, *N. meningitidis* was isolated from otherwise normal cerebrospinal fluid (CSF).

Adrenal hemorrhage and necrosis occurred in 48 percent of autopsy cases. Diffuse adrenal hemorrhage was seen in approximately 50 percent of adult cases and in more than 80 percent of pediatric cases. Adrenal vasculitis and acute inflammation were not detected. In this study, some patients had a typical Waterhouse-Friderichsen syndrome (purpura and circulatory collapse) but had normal adrenals on gross and microscopic examinations. Hardman[62] postulated that circulatory failure was caused by endotoxic shock rather than adrenal insufficiency.

Focal areas of inflammation and petechial hemorrhage were seen in many other tissues, including the synovium, skeletal muscle, and the tracheobronchial tree.

An association was found between the pathologic findings and the infecting serogroup of *N. meningitidis*. Serogroup A infections were associated most frequently with encephalitis; serogroup B and C infections were associated with necrotizing myocarditis.

Clinical Manifestations

The spectrum of disease caused by *N. meningitidis* ranges from asymptomatic transient bacteremia, which clears spontaneously, to fulminant sepsis resulting in death only a few hours after the first symptoms occur.[158]

MENINGOCOCCEMIA/MENINGITIS

Serious or invasive disease usually is manifested in one of two ways: meningococcemia or meningitis (either with or without meningococcemia).

The signs and symptoms of meningococcemia are variable. Early in the course, evidence of an upper respiratory infection, including coryza, pharyngitis, tonsillitis, and laryngitis, may be present. Patients generally are febrile, with complaints of headache, lethargy, and vomiting. Severe myalgia with muscle tenderness and joint pain also may be the initial complaint.[11, 37] The typical patient with meningococcemia has a short history of upper respiratory symptoms, fever, and a hemorrhagic rash. Signs of severe circulatory collapse often develop. Purpura and shock frequently occur within hours of the onset of symptoms.

The skin manifestations of meningococcemia range from a diffuse mottling to extensive purpuric lesions (Figs. 93–1 and 93–2). Unfortunately, some variation in the type of rash

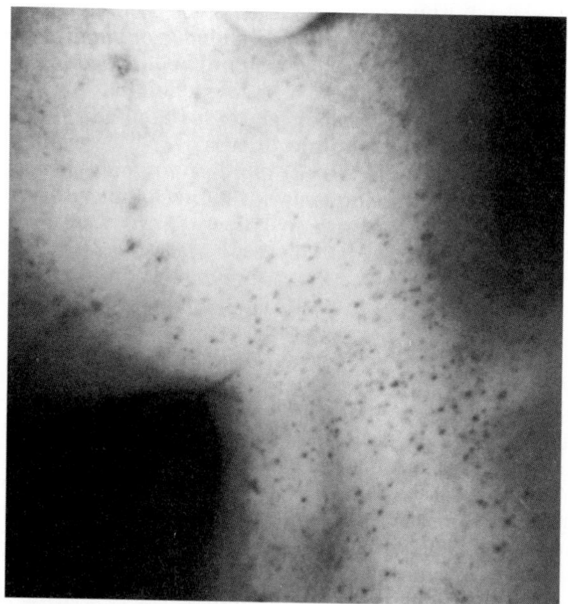

FIGURE 93–1 ■ Petechial lesions are seen on the face and neck of a young child with meningococcemia.

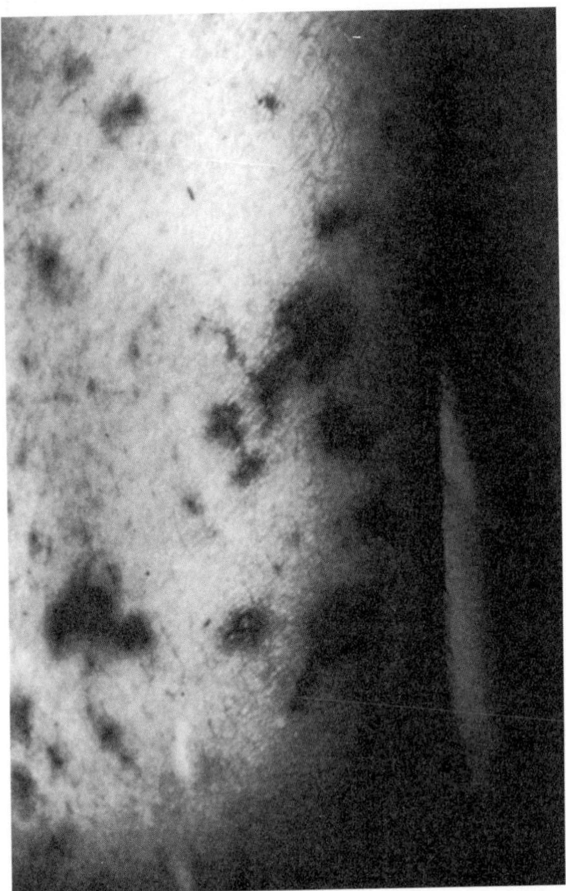

FIGURE 93–2 ■ Extensive purpuric lesions occurring in a child with overwhelming meningococcemia and disseminated intravascular coagulation.

is seen. Petechiae are present in 50 to 60 percent of patients.[78] However, 7 percent have fewer than 12 petechiae, and 1 to 2 percent have no rash at all.[95] One prospective multicenter study found that 13 percent of children had only a maculopapular rash and the classic hemorrhagic rash did not develop,[95] thus rendering differentiation from a viral exanthem particularly difficult to make. A pink macular rash resembling early varicella is another variant sometimes seen in children; these lesions often are tender. They may occur in crops, as petechiae do, and are seen most frequently on the trunk and extremities.[37, 66]

The finding of petechiae or purpura in a febrile child should increase the index of suspicion for meningococcemia or other serious disease (e.g., infectious, neoplastic, immunologic). Acral distribution of a rash is particularly worrisome for meningococcemia or another infectious vasculitic process. A study of 129 febrile patients with petechiae found that 20.2 percent had invasive bacterial disease.[170] Ten percent of the total group had infections caused by *N. meningitidis*. Therefore, obtaining blood cultures for all febrile patients with petechiae seems reasonable. Lumbar puncture should be performed if clinically indicated or if the blood culture is ultimately positive. Antibiotic therapy in these patients should include coverage for meningococcus.

Purpura is a feature of fulminant cases and does not arise from the petechiae but is a separate and distinct lesion.[78] Pathologically, it consists of microvascular dermal thrombosis and hemorrhage, sometimes progressing to frank necrosis. Purpura is noted in 16 to 24 percent of patients.[132, 140, 180] Acquired protein S and C deficiencies have been described in some patients with purpura fulminans.[132, 133] One study showed a mortality rate of 50 percent in patients in whom purpura developed. Progressive purpura was accompanied by declining protein C levels, and the level of protein C was related inversely to the clinical severity of the disease.[132]

Patients with meningitis often are febrile, with headache, vomiting, irritability, stiff neck, and sometimes seizures. The patient may have a history of lethargy or may be obtunded. The same prodromal symptoms that are seen in meningococcemia often are present. Infants initially may be febrile and irritable, with increased sleeping and poor feeding. In neonates, physical findings of meningismus, such as the Kernig and Brudzinski signs, frequently are absent. The anterior fontanelle, if open, may be full and tense.

The most common neurologic complications of meningitis are hydrocephalus, cranial nerve palsies (especially hearing loss), subdural effusion or empyema, cerebral edema, cortical vein thrombosis, and cerebral infarction. Neurologic sequelae occur much more commonly in patients with meningitis, but complications such as cerebral infarction also can be seen in children with meningococcemia and shock.[118]

Cerebral edema and cranial nerve palsies may be present at the initial evaluation or may develop shortly thereafter. Sixth nerve and third nerve palsies are suggestive of increased intracranial pressure and impending herniation, respectively. The development of either of these signs indicates an urgent intracranial process.[118] Hearing loss occurs in 5 to 10 percent of patients with meningitis. Auditory testing should be performed on all patients with meningitis after recovery.

Subdural effusions or empyemas should be considered in patients with fever persisting after 8 days of therapy (in the absence of a sterile repeat CSF culture), vomiting, or the development of signs of increased intracranial pressure after the initial few days of treatment. Drainage is recommended only if the effusions are infected (empyemas) or are large enough to produce either focal neurologic signs or increased intracranial pressure.[118]

Vascular thrombosis or cerebral infarction, or both, can be caused by arterial or venous thrombosis. Venous thrombosis occurs more often and generally is not seen before the second week; hemorrhagic infarction of the brain then may occur. Cerebral infarction also may be seen in patients without arterial or venous thrombosis who are in shock with prolonged hypotension and cerebral ischemia. Cerebral infarction in these individuals is an early event.

Hydrocephalus occurs most frequently in young children and those with a delayed diagnosis or severe disease. It tends to develop 3 to 4 weeks after the onset of illness. Inflammation with deposition of collagen and proliferation of fibroblasts in the meninges produces an obstruction to the flow of the CSF. A progressive increase in head circumference should alert the clinician to the possibility of hydrocephalus.[118] Imaging (computed tomography, magnetic resonance imaging) studies are diagnostic.

Neonatal meningococcemia and meningitis are uncommon occurrences but have been reported. In one report, a 2-week-old infant died after a brief febrile illness with both CSF and blood cultures positive for meningococcus. Maternal endocervical colonization was documented. In addition, the mother's pharyngeal culture grew *N. meningitidis*.[75] If endocervical colonization by *N. meningitidis* is found prenatally, treatment with antibiotics probably should be initiated in an attempt to eradicate colonization before delivery, or intrapartum antibiotics should be administered. Ceftriaxone would seem to be a reasonable choice. Rifampin and ciprofloxacin are not advocated for use during pregnancy.

CHRONIC MENINGOCOCCEMIA

Chronic meningococcemia, first described in 1902, is defined as meningococcal septicemia without meningeal symptoms in which fever has persisted for at least a week before initiation of any antibiotic therapy.[39, 116] Table 93–2 presents the differential diagnosis of chronic meningococcemia. Benoit[7] reviewed 148 cases of chronic meningococcemia in the United States in 1963; patients ranged in age from 3 months to 62 years. The major symptoms included fever and chills (present in 100% of patients), skin rash (93.2%), arthralgias (70.3%), and headache (61.5%). The patients generally were not toxic and were in good health before becoming infected. The mean duration of illness before diagnosis was 6 to 8 weeks (range, 1 to 40 weeks). Symptoms tended to be intermittent; the rash often appeared in association with fever and then disappeared over the course of the next several days. Bacteremia also may be intermittent. In the Benoit study, the average patient had five blood cultures before meningococci were isolated. However, after a blood culture yielded the organism, most subsequent cultures were positive. Some investigators report that the organism often is isolated in the first blood culture of children.[87] The arthralgias also tended to be intermittent in nature.

In Benoit's series,[7] localizing complications developed in almost 40 percent of patients with chronic meningococcemia. The meninges were the most common site of localization; meningitis developed in 15.5 percent of patients. Other localized infections included carditis, nephritis, epididymitis, conjunctivitis, iritis, and retinitis. In only one instance was an organism recovered from the joint. The average duration of meningococcemia in patients with complications was 10.2 weeks, as opposed to 4 to 8 weeks in patients without any localization.

The diagnosis is established by identifying the organism in blood cultures. Antibiotic therapy results in prompt defervescence and dramatic recovery.

The pathophysiologic mechanisms permitting chronic meningococcemia remain unclear. No evidence indicates that the organisms are less virulent than are other meningococci; therefore, a defect in host immunity has been suggested. A hypersensitivity basis for this disease has been postulated, and one theory is that the skin changes and arthritis may be secondary to antigen-antibody complexes.[116] In contrast to acute meningococcemia, bacteria almost never are found by biopsy or culture of skin lesions in patients with chronic meningococcemia, and the histologic type is distinct from that seen in skin lesions of patients with acute meningococcemia.[7, 62, 116]

TABLE 93–2 ■ DIFFERENTIAL DIAGNOSIS OF CHRONIC MENINGOCOCCEMIA

Acute rheumatic fever
Subacute bacterial endocarditis
Henoch-Schönlein purpura
Malaria
Typhoid
Miliary tuberculosis
Gonococcemia
Erythema multiforme
Erythema nodosum
Secondary syphilis
Rat-bite fever
Rocky Mountain spotted fever
Typhus
Collagen vascular disease
Neoplastic processes

MENINGOCOCCAL PNEUMONIA

Meningococcal pneumonia occurs in conjunction with meningococcemia or meningitis in 8 to 15 percent of cases.[80] However, the meningococcus also can play a role as a primary respiratory pathogen.

Primary meningococcal pneumonia, once considered a rare disease, now is recognized as the most common form of meningococcal disease in certain military recruit populations and has been reported to cause 4.5 percent of all bacterial pneumonias in a general hospital population.[80, 90]

Patients with preceding viral pneumonias are at risk for development of meningococcal pneumonia; more than 100 cases of meningococcal pneumonia occurred during the influenza pandemic of 1918 and 1919. In addition to disease in military recruits, nosocomial acquisition of meningococcal pneumonia in hospitalized patients has been reported.[25]

Making a diagnosis of meningococcal pneumonia is difficult because isolation of the organism from sputum does not distinguish a meningococcal carrier from an individual with meningococcal pneumonia. In addition, routine sputum cultures do not include media selective for the meningococcus. Blood cultures are positive in only 15 percent.[80]

Koppes and associates[80] reported on 68 cases of meningococcal pneumonia; diagnostic criteria included (1) a compatible clinical syndrome, (2) a radiograph demonstrating infiltrates or effusion, (3) transtracheal aspirate culture yielding the organism and a consistent Gram stain, and (4) isolation of *N. meningitidis* from pleural fluid or blood. All 68 meningococcal pneumonia cases were group Y; during the same period, 10 cases of meningococcemia and 6 cases of meningitis caused by group Y occurred. The high ratio of pneumonia to meningitis in this study suggested that group Y organisms may be more likely than other serogroups to cause pneumonia, and this observation has been substantiated by other investigators.[134, 142] Pneumonia caused by group B or C meningococci has been reported, usually in association with meningococcemia or meningitis.[179]

Primary meningococcal pneumonia usually is associated with a gradual onset of symptoms and history of an antecedent upper respiratory infection. Rales and fever are found in most patients, and 80 percent have pharyngitis. The radiograph often shows involvement of the lower lobes with patchy alveolar infiltrates. More than one lobe is involved in 40 percent of patients. Twenty-five percent have pleural effusions. Petechiae, purpura, or shock was not present in any of the patients with pneumonia reported by Koppes and colleagues.[80]

The pathogenesis of this disease is thought to be pulmonary infection via inhalation of droplets. The epidemiologic importance of meningococcal pneumonia was emphasized in a report from the CDC discussing nosocomial transmission of group Y *N. meningitidis* in oncology patients.[25] The index case had meningococcal pneumonia, and meningococcal bacteremia developed in one other patient in an adjacent room; in three additional patients, group Y *N. meningitidis* was isolated from nasopharyngeal cultures. Airborne dissemination seemed to be the mode of transmission. Respiratory isolation of a patient with suspected meningococcal pneumonia is indicated.

Penicillin therapy for penicillin-sensitive meningococcal pneumonia results in a prompt clinical response. Ninety-three percent of the patients reported by Koppes and colleagues[80] were afebrile after receiving 3 days of therapy. Third-generation cephalosporins such as ceftriaxone and cefotaxime may be the current drugs of choice pending definitive identification.

OTHER MENINGOCOCCAL SYNDROMES

Conjunctivitis

Primary meningococcal conjunctivitis is clinically indistinguishable from acute bacterial conjunctivitis caused by other organisms. Usually, it occurs in children as the acute onset of unilateral purulent conjunctivitis.[6] It has been reported in individuals from 2 days of age to adulthood.[100] Gram stain of the purulent material typically shows gram-negative diplococci that sometimes may be confused with gonococcal conjunctivitis. Barquet and colleagues[6] showed that 44 percent of the isolates were serogroup B meningococci.

Complications of primary meningococcal conjunctivitis reported by Barquet and associates[6] included sepsis or meningitis in approximately 18 percent. The symptoms of systemic meningococcal disease occurred 3 to 96 hours after the onset of conjunctivitis (mean, 41 hours). Patients treated with only topical therapy at the time that they were evaluated initially for conjunctivitis were 19 times more likely to contract systemic disease eventually than were patients treated with systemic therapy ($p = .001$). Ocular complications occurred in 15.5 percent of patients and included corneal ulcers (10.7%), keratitis, hemorrhage, and iritis.

Pharyngitis

Making a diagnosis of meningococcal pharyngitis is difficult because, like group A beta-hemolytic streptococci, isolation of meningococcus from the pharynx does not establish that this organism is the etiologic agent. In fact, most individuals who harbor meningococci in their nasopharynx are asymptomatic carriers. However, Banks[4] noted overt nasopharyngitis in one third of patients with meningococcal sepsis or meningitis. Pizzi,[128] in describing a severe epidemic of meningococcal meningitis, noted that individuals with a sore throat often had a pure culture of meningococci. Olcen and associates[117] performed cultures on the family members of 21 consecutive patients with meningococcal disease and found that 61 percent of the family members with a sore throat or other upper respiratory symptoms were meningococcal carriers versus 14 percent of asymptomatic family members.

On occasion, individuals with symptomatic pharyngitis have cultures performed and the laboratory reports growth of *N. meningitidis*. If the patient is febrile, we recommend obtaining a blood culture and administering systemic antibiotic therapy. If the blood culture is negative, the patient should be treated with an antibiotic that will eradicate the meningococcus (see "Chemoprophylaxis"). If the patient is afebrile and asymptomatic, we recommend eradication of the organism with one of the antibiotics recommended for chemoprophylaxis.

Arthritis

Meningococcal arthritis occurs primarily in adults. The overall incidence, as a complication of bacteremia, is approximately 2 to 14 percent.[60, 180] Two forms of meningococcal arthritis exist. The first form is seen within the first few days of treatment and is characterized by severe arthralgia and few objective signs of joint inflammation. The pathogenesis of this arthritis is suggested to be an inflammatory response to viable organisms that have seeded the synovium during the initial bacteremia. The second, more common form appears to be a hypersensitivity phenomenon. It is usually noted 3 to 7 days after the recognition of meningococcemia, often at a time when the patient appears to be improving from the meningitis or sepsis. The knee, wrist, elbow, and ankle joints are involved most commonly.[60]

In both forms, the arthritis usually is monoarticular or oligoarticular with an effusion, minimal pain, erythema, and limitation of motion. Organisms very seldom are cultured from the effusion; joint fluid culture yields meningococci in less than 10 percent of cases. The exception is a child with suppurative arthritis on initial evaluation. In one study, 8 percent of patients with meningococcal infections had arthritis; 75 percent were culture-positive when samples were taken before the patients received antibiotics.[179, 180]

Synovial fluid leukocyte counts vary widely, but counts greater than 100,000/mm^3 occur in the early form.[125] The mean leukocyte count in synovial fluid was 33,000 to 43,000 cells/mm^3 in a study performed by Greenwood and Whittle.[58] The appearance of arthritis often is accompanied by a rise in temperature; in 7 of 47 patients with arthritis, a characteristic skin lesion appeared at the same time.[62] These lesions began as skin hyperpigmentation but progressed to vesiculation and ulceration; biopsies showed vasculitis. Additional evidence of concurrent vasculitis is suggested by reports of episcleritis and mild proteinuria developing simultaneously with arthritis.[58]

On histologic examination, the synovium is infiltrated with mononuclear cells that contain IgM, C3, and meningococcal antigen,[58] findings strongly suggestive of an immune complex–mediated disease. No specific therapy is indicated, and the arthritis resolves spontaneously. Controversy exists regarding the role of intermittent closed drainage of the joint space.[12] Permanent joint deformity is uncommon in this disease and occurs in approximately 10 percent of cases.[146] Edwards and Baker[40] reported allergic complications of meningococcal disease in 10 percent of 86 children monitored prospectively. More than 83 percent of the 86 cases that they studied were serogroup B, although late-onset arthritis and vasculitis also have been reported with serogroup A and C disease.

Permanent joint damage is an unusual finding that occurs in approximately 1.5 percent of patients with arthritis. Potential sequelae include ankylosis, decreased range of motion, and bone necrosis.[85]

Pericarditis and Myocarditis

Pericarditis as a complication of meningococcal disease occurs in 3 to 5 percent of cases, although one series reported a 19 percent incidence in 32 patients with meningococcal meningitis.[38, 109] It generally occurs in patients with meningococcemia but has been reported as an isolated event without septicemia or meningitis.[65]

Pericarditis is presumed to be a late complication of meningococcal disease because clinical symptoms such as fever, dyspnea, and substernal chest pain (or even cardiac tamponade) usually do not appear until the fourth to seventh day of illness. However, several investigators have noted early evidence of pericarditis based on the electrocardiographic or radiographic data of patients examined at the time of hospital admission.

Because most symptomatic pericardial effusions develop late in the course of the illness, are serous in nature, and are sterile, the pathophysiologic mechanism is presumed to be a hypersensitivity reaction. Uncontrolled studies have reported successful use of steroids in the treatment of this complication.[103] However, one report documented pericarditis and the development of tamponade in a patient receiving steroids.[123]

The clinical course of meningococcal pericarditis usually is benign, but pericardial compression requiring pericardiocentesis can occur.[123] Early relapses also have been reported, but they were self-limited. The development of constrictive pericarditis requiring pericardectomy likewise has been reported.[123, 148, 174]

Myocarditis was noted at autopsy in 78 percent of patients with fatal meningococcal disease.[62] It was seen most often in adults but was more severe in children. Rosenblatt and colleagues[140] found myocarditis at autopsy in 10 of 12 children with fatal meningococcal infection. On pathologic examination, these children had collections of inflammatory cells in the myocardial interstitium and focal extravasation of erythrocytes with acute vasculitis. Abscesses and endocarditis were not seen. Inflammation occasionally may involve the atrioventricular node and has been reported as a cause of sudden death in a patient recovering from meningococcal meningitis.[138]

MISCELLANEOUS MENINGOCOCCAL INFECTIONS

Several unusual syndromes, including primary meningococcal pericarditis,[170] mesenteric adenitis,[81] peritonitis,[81] and genitourinary infections, have been reported.[43]

Laboratory Findings and Diagnosis

Wong and colleagues[180] reviewed 100 meningococcal infections in children seen at their institution between 1985 and 1988. Leukopenia (white blood cell count $<5000/mm^3$) was present in 21 percent, and thrombocytopenia was noted in 14 percent. Fifty-five patients had meningitis. Eleven percent of those with culture-positive meningitis had no CSF abnormalities on chemistry panels or examination.

Hyponatremia is seen in some patients with meningitis. Inappropriate secretion of antidiuretic hormone is the mechanism. In one study of 43 children with meningococcal meningitis, this syndrome developed in 7 percent.[42]

Other laboratory abnormalities observed in patients with sepsis or shock include abnormal coagulation panels (DIC), acidosis, and abnormal liver function studies.

The gold standard for diagnosis is based on recovering the organism from blood, CSF, or petechiae. Blood culture alone is positive approximately 50 percent of the time in patients who have not received antibiotics.[180] Rapid diagnosis often can be made by Gram stain of CSF in patients with meningitis. Characteristic gram-negative diplococci are seen. Caution should be exercised in relying solely on the Gram stain and initiating broad therapy until the organism is identified by culture. Over-decolorized gram-positive cocci of *Streptococcus pneumoniae* on occasion have been confused with meningococci on Gram stain.

In patients who have skin lesions, a rapid presumptive diagnosis of meningococcemia frequently can be made by needle aspiration and Gram stain of a skin lesion. Needle aspiration yields gram-negative diplococci on a Gram-stained specimen in approximately 50 percent of patients with acute meningococcal infection.[168] Culturing the aspirate obtained further increases the yield. Correlation of the Gram stain with the clinical findings is important because disseminated gonococcal infections also may cause skin lesions that yield gram-negative diplococci on Gram stain.

Counterimmunoelectrophoresis and latex agglutination have been used to detect circulating antigen in the serum, CSF, and urine of patients with meningococcal disease.[177] These tests are of particular benefit in cases of partially treated meningococcal meningitis, in which culture and Gram stain may be negative. Cross-reactions with certain *E. coli* or *Bacillus* strains may occur. Fecal contamination is more likely to occur with bag collection of the urine specimen, which may have important clinical significance in a neonate with meningitis because *E. coli* strains possessing the K1 capsular antigen are a common cause of neonatal meningitis. These K1 *E. coli* strains have a capsule that is immunochemically identical to the meningococcus group B capsule, and thus the use of meningococcus group B antisera as a reagent also detects *E. coli* K1 antigen in body fluids.[96]

Polymerase chain reaction (PCR), one of the newer tests for detection of *N. meningitidis*, may be very helpful diagnostically in patients who have partially treated meningococcemia or meningitis. Once antibiotics have been given, the chance that a blood culture will be positive decreases to less than 5 percent.[20] One study showed the sensitivity and specificity of PCR for *N. meningitidis* to be 91 percent in CSF specimens. Treatment with antibiotics before performing the test did not decrease the test's sensitivity or specificity.[113] The use of this test in confirming meningococcal infection in patients pretreated with antibiotics may be valuable in subsequent patient management, follow-up, and prompt institution of chemoprophylaxis in contacts. One report from the United Kingdom describes the use of a multiplex PCR assay for the simultaneous detection of *N. meningitidis, Haemophilus influenzae*, and *S. pneumoniae* from clinical samples of CSF and whole blood. Corless and coworkers found that the sensitivity for detection of the three organisms ranged from 88.4 to 91.8 percent with 100 percent specificity.[29] Commercially available assays such as this one would greatly facilitate etiologic diagnosis in children with sepsis or meningitis. Currently, meningococcal PCR is in use in the United Kingdom but is available in the United States only as a research test.

Mortality and Prognosis

The overall mortality of invasive meningococcal disease in the United States is 7 to 19 percent,[70, 115, 141, 156] and numerous scoring systems have been devised in an attempt to predict prognosis in these patients. These scoring systems were reviewed in an article by Kirsch and colleagues.[79] Stiehm and Damrosch[156] originally developed a meningococcal prognostic scoring system based on five features that indicated a grave prognosis: (1) the presence of petechiae for less than 12 hours before admission, (2) the presence of hypotension, (3) the absence of meningitis, (4) a peripheral white blood cell count less than $10,000/mm^3$, and (5) an erythrocyte sedimentation rate less than 10 mm/hr. Patients who had three or more of these features had a mortality rate of 90 percent, whereas the mortality rate for patients with two or fewer of these criteria was 9 percent.

The Glasgow Meningococcal Septicaemia Prognostic Score is another validated scoring system developed to assess patients clinically and facilitate admission of the most severely ill children to intensive care units.[150, 162] This scoring system, which evaluates seven key items (hypotension, difference in skin and core temperature, coma, acute deterioration, absence of meningismus, progressive purpura, and base deficit), has been used by many researchers to define criteria for entry into clinical trials.

In a review of 100 cases of meningococcal disease at the Los Angeles Children's Hospital in California, five features were identified that were correlated with a poor prognosis: shock or seizures on initial evaluation, hypothermia, total white blood cell count less than $5000/mm^3$, platelet count less than $100,000/mm^3$, and the development of purpura fulminans. The overall mortality rate in this series was 10 percent.[180]

Most prognostic scoring systems and clinical reviews agree that purpura fulminans and shock are uniformly poor prognostic signs. Individuals with only meningitis have a lower case-fatality rate than do those with bacteremia or an isolate from another source (2% versus 12%).[141] Presumably, this difference is a function of the virulence of the organism, the ability of the immune system to contain the infection, or both. Case-fatality rates also differ by serogroup and are higher in W135 disease (21%) than in serogroup C (14%), Y (9%), or B (6%).[141]

Evidence suggests that the existence of a genetic component of host cytokine production may be associated with the severity of disease. Westendorp and coauthors[176] reported that families with low TNF production or high IL-10 production have an increased risk for having fatal outcomes with meningococcal disease. Recently, investigators have been studying variants of proinflammatory host genes (TNF-α, IL-1) to determine whether polymorphisms in them might be linked to the severity of disease. Read and colleagues found that homozygosity of certain alleles at the IL-1 locus increased the risk for death in individuals with meningococcal disease and suggested that the IL-1 genotype may be associated with fatal outcomes.[136]

Treatment

Therapy for meningococcal disease has evolved during the last century. In the early 1900s, treatment consisted of the administration of intravenous and intrathecal horse serum and drainage of the CSF. The mortality rate associated with this therapy was 26 percent.[66] The use of sulfonamides lowered the death rate to 5 to 10 percent.[61] With the emergence of sulfa-resistant strains, penicillin was added to the regimen and still is used for treating susceptible meningococcal infections. Uniformly penicillin-susceptible isolates of meningococci are no longer the rule, however. Relatively resistant strains have been reported in the United States, Spain, the United Kingdom, Greece, Switzerland, Romania, Belgium, South Africa, Canada, and Croatia.[13, 71, 124, 160, 182] Isolates that are absolutely resistant to penicillin (minimal inhibitory concentration >1.0 μg/mL) have been documented from Spain and the United Kingdom.[124, 160] Genotypic and phenotypic studies of resistant isolates from Spain revealed that the strains were genetically diverse and did not arise from a single clone.[184] In addition, Mendelman and colleagues[99] demonstrated that these strains have a penicillin-binding protein (PBP3) with reduced penicillin-binding capacity when compared with sensitive strains. These strains appear to have arisen by the acquisition of segments of genes (by transformation) from naturally resistant commensal *Neisseria*, *N. flavescens*, and *N. lactamica*.[152] The gene encoding PBP2, *penA* in commensal *Neisseria*, encodes for a protein that has less avidity for penicillin G. Transformation of *N. meningitidis* with *penA* from these strains leads to a slight decrease in penicillin G susceptibility; repeated transformation will yield a penicillin-resistant strain.

In 1988, penicillin-resistant meningococci also were reported from South Africa and the United Kingdom; these strains had acquired a gonococcal plasmid encoding for the production of β-lactamase.[160]

Prompt institution of antibiotic therapy for suspected meningococcal infection may be lifesaving. If possible, blood should be drawn for culture before the administration of antibiotics, but collection of specimens should not delay such administration. A lumbar puncture can be performed in stable patients, but the procedure should not delay administration of antibiotics. CSF obtained after the initiation of antibiotic therapy may be sterile, but pleocytosis will be apparent. Patients who are unstable or have significant coagulopathy should have the lumbar puncture deferred. The clinical manifestation of *N. meningitidis* meningitis may be similar to that of meningitis caused by *S. pneumoniae* or *H. influenzae*. Therefore, empiric antibiotic therapy should take into consideration the most likely pathogens. In children older than 1 month with meningitis, vancomycin plus cefotaxime (or vancomycin and ceftriaxone) is an appropriate regimen until a definitive diagnosis is made. Similarly, empiric therapy for children younger than 1 month includes ampicillin and cefotaxime, with consideration given to the addition of vancomycin.[143]

For penicillin-susceptible meningococcemia or meningitis, intravenous penicillin G, 250,000–300,000 U/kg/day given in divided doses every 4 hours for 7 days, is effective. The third-generation cephalosporins ceftriaxone (100 mg/kg/day intravenously in two divided doses) and cefotaxime (200 mg/kg/day intravenously in four divided doses) also are effective. Cefotaxime or ceftriaxone is recommended for travelers from Spain, Italy, and parts of Africa because of reports of penicillin resistance in these areas.[102]

In confirmed cases of meningococcal disease, comparisons of penicillin G with ceftriaxone have shown ceftriaxone to be as efficacious. Necrotic skin lesions were seen more commonly in the penicillin group, but complication and mortality rates were equivalent otherwise.[164] Meningococcal disease has been treated successfully with ceftriaxone given intravenously in both once-a-day (80 to 100 mg/kg/day) and twice-a-day (100 mg/kg/day in two divided doses) dosing regimens.[164] Chloramphenicol is an alternative choice for penicillin-allergic patients. Currently, routine susceptibility testing of the isolate is not recommended. However, in selected patients not responding as expected, susceptibility testing may be warranted. With all cases of meningococcal disease, eradicating colonization of the index case is important (see "Chemoprophylaxis").

The administration of steroids is controversial. For patients with Waterhouse-Friderichsen syndrome, treatment with steroids is indicated. However, treatment of meningococcal meningitis with steroids has been debated in the literature for years. Proponents of steroids point to the *H. influenzae* type b meningitis studies, in which treatment with steroids decreased hearing loss. The thought is that steroids, through anti-inflammatory effects, will decrease the number of polymorphonuclear neutrophils, macrophages, and cytokines in the central nervous system and thus decrease central nervous system immune-mediated damage and hearing loss. Opponents of the use of steroids argue that no conclusive studies have shown steroids to be of benefit in treating meningococcal meningitis and that risks include gastrointestinal ulceration, decreased penetration of antibiotics into the central nervous system (because of decreased meningeal inflammation), and steroid-induced psychosis. If steroids are used, using them early (preferably close to the time that the first dose of antibiotic is administered) seems prudent. However, antibiotics never should be withheld while waiting for steroids to be given.

EXPERIMENTAL/ADJUNCTIVE THERAPIES

Many adjunctive and experimental therapies have been tried or are being evaluated. Anti-endotoxin therapies and protein C concentrate infusions are the most recent

TABLE 93–3 ■ RECENT STUDIES OF ALTERNATIVE THERAPIES FOR SEVERE MENINGOCOCCEMIA OR SEPSIS SYNDROME

Year	Study	Authors	Randomized/ Placebo Controlled	Eligible Patients	Patients (*N*)	Results
1997	Protein C	Smith, O. P., White, B., Vaughan, D., et al.[151]	No/No	3 mo–27 yr, severe meningococcemia with septic shock and purpura fulminans	12	0 Deaths, 2 patients with amputations. Favorable results when compared with historical mortality rate of 50% in patients with shock
1999	HA-1A	Derkx, B., Wittes, J., and McCloskey, R.[35]	Yes/Yes	3 mo–18 yr, petechiae or purpura, hypotension, toxicity, or end-organ dysfunction	269	No statistically significant reduction in 28-day mortality demonstrated. Mortality rate of HA-1A, 18%; placebo group, 28% (p = .11)
2000	rBPI	Levin, M. A., Quint, P. A., Goldstein, B., et al.[88]	Yes/Yes	2 wk–18 yr, petechiae or purpura and severe disease	393*	No statistically significant reduction in mortality (7.4% for rBPI, 9.9% for placebo). Treatment group had fewer amputations, trend toward improved outcomes
2001	Protein C	Bernard, G. R., Vincent, J. L., Laterre, P. F., et al.[8]	Yes/Yes	Severe sepsis (any organism, known or suspected) with organ dysfunction†	1690	Significant reduction in mortality (30.8% for placebo vs. 24.7% for the treatment group); increased risk of bleeding in the treatment group

*Fifty-seven patients died before receiving drug or placebo (after randomization) and were not included in this analysis.
†This study enrolled adults with severe clinical sepsis (meningococcemia was not a criterion for entrance).

additions (Table 93–3). Two anti-endotoxin therapies have been evaluated in clinical trials: HA-1A and recombinant bactericidal/permeability increasing protein (rBPI). HA-1A, a human monoclonal antibody to endotoxin, was evaluated in a randomized, double-blind, placebo-controlled trial in 269 patients with severe meningococcemia. Although the 28-day mortality rate in the treatment group was 18 percent versus 28 percent in the placebo group, it was not statistically significant (p = .11).[35] BPI is a naturally occurring protein in neutrophil azurophilic granules. It binds to and neutralizes the effects of endotoxin. Administration of rBPI was studied in 393 children with presumed meningococcal disease. No difference was found in mortality rates (7.4% for rBPI versus 9.9% for placebo). A trend toward reduction of amputations occurred in the treatment group that approached statistical significance (p = .067).[88]

Recombinant protein C concentrate infusions have been studied in adults in a large randomized, placebo-controlled trial of 1690 patients with severe sepsis. A reduction in the mortality rate was demonstrated, but the treatment group had an increased risk of bleeding.[8] No large clinical trials have been performed in children with meningococcal disease. However, Smith and coworkers[151] compared 12 children with severe meningococcemia and purpura fulminans treated with protein C concentrate with historical controls. No deaths occurred in the treated patients, versus a 50 percent rate in historical controls. A large, randomized clinical trial is needed to evaluate this therapy for safety and efficacy.

Additional supportive measures such as prophylactic low-dose heparin occasionally are used.[178] Many investigators have studied the effect of heparin on survival and DIC in patients with meningococcemia, and no consistent beneficial effect on these parameters has been noted. Serious side effects directly attributed to heparin therapy have been reported rarely, particularly if the dose of heparin used is that required to maintain normal blood coagulability rather than hypocoagulability.[51] The difficulty in adjusting the dose in small infants may lead to heparin intoxication. A retrospective chart review of 24 patients with purpura fulminans showed less necrosis of the digits and extremities in patients treated with heparin, but the results were not statistically significant.[82]

Numerous other experimental therapies have been attempted in patients with fulminant meningococcemia. Anecdotal reports or small case series describe the use of tissue plasminogen activator,[2, 110] antithrombin III infusion,[24] topical nitroglycerin,[69, 103] plasmapheresis,[23] and extracorporeal membrane oxygenation.[84] Continuous caudal block has been used to restore lower extremity perfusion.[163] Evidence is insufficient to argue that any of these therapies has a significant impact on outcomes in meningococcal disease. Larger, multicenter studies are needed to evaluate their efficacy.

CHEMOPROPHYLAXIS

The ability of *N. meningitidis* to spread from person to person and cause epidemic disease has been recognized since the 1800s. The secondary attack rate in households with an index case is approximately 1000 times the attack rate in the general population.[3, 153] Household crowding and young age are factors that increase the secondary attack rate. The mode of transmission is direct contact with respiratory droplets or secretions. For these reasons, chemoprophylaxis is recommended for household contacts of an index case and for young daycare center contacts. Persons who have had significant contact with the oral secretions of an index case also should be considered for prophylaxis. Several epidemiologic studies have suggested that casual acquaintances (such as school-age classmates) were not at increased risk, although numerous authors have reported secondary cases in this population.[73, 76] Prophylaxis is indicated for health care workers who have had intimate exposure to nasopharyngeal secretions (e.g., mouth-to-mouth resuscitation).[52] The period of communicability of the index patient is not well established. Most public health authorities recommend that persons in contact with the patient for as long as 7 days before the onset of illness be considered for prophylaxis. Prophylaxis should be instituted as soon as possible after identification of the index case. Waiting for laboratory confirmation of a case is not necessary if the clinical picture is most consistent with meningococcal infection. Nasopharyngeal cultures are not recommended because many nonpathogenic *Neisseria* spp. may colonize the nasopharynx.

Index patients should receive chemoprophylaxis before discharge unless they have been treated with ceftriaxone (or cefotaxime). Abramson and Spika[1] reported that 4 of 14 (29%) patients with meningococcal infection treated with intravenous penicillin were culture-positive from the respiratory tract 1 week after completion of therapy.

Secondary cases originally were defined as those occurring more than 24 but less than 31 days after onset of disease in the index case. With this definition, approximately 50 percent of secondary cases will occur in the first 7 days after identification of the index case. Initiating prophylaxis as soon as possible is essential and should be based on the clinical findings in the index case (e.g., fulminant meningococcemia) or on laboratory culture data if the disease is manifested as bacterial meningitis, septic arthritis, or other such conditions.

The original drug used for chemoprophylaxis was sulfadiazine. However, a large percentage of strains now are resistant to sulfa, and rifampin currently is the drug of choice for chemoprophylaxis. Table 93–4 lists four antibiotics that are highly effective in eradicating meningococcus from the nasopharynx. Rifampin generally is well tolerated but has many side effects, including orange urine and sweat, orange staining of contact lenses, and stimulation of liver microsomal enzymes leading to a reduction in levels of other concurrent medications (e.g., oral contraceptives, anticoagulants, digoxin, phenytoin). The development of resistant strains rarely has been reported.[28] Ciprofloxacin, ceftriaxone, and rifampin have been evaluated in a randomized, comparative study.[30] All three drugs were highly effective in eradicating meningococcal carriage. Ceftriaxone probably is the drug of choice for a pregnant contact and may be indicated for children because a single intramuscular injection may result in greater compliance than four doses of rifampin. Ciprofloxacin is contraindicated in individuals younger than 18 years of age because of evidence of cartilage damage in juvenile beagles. Azithromycin was studied in a randomized, controlled trial comparing 500 mg of azithromycin given once orally with rifampin, 600 mg twice daily orally for 2 days. Carriage was eradicated in 56 of 60 (93%) colonized adults treated with azithromycin versus 95% of the 59 colonized adults treated with rifampin.[54]

As mentioned in the section on meningococcal vaccines, the development of secondary disease also can be prevented by immunization of contacts. We recommend administering both immunization and chemoprophylaxis whenever possible (with the realization that no protection against group B meningococci currently is provided by immunization).

The single most important element of chemoprophylaxis is education of contacts regarding the need for immediate medical attention if signs or symptoms of a febrile illness develop. No prophylactic strategy is 100 percent effective, and ill contacts should be evaluated with a high suspicion for meningococcal disease.

TABLE 93–4 ■ CHEMOPROPHYLAXIS REGIMENS FOR ERADICATION OF *NEISSERIA MENINGITIDIS*

Drug	Age	Dose/Duration
Rifampin*	Children ≤1 mo	5 mg/kg/dose bid orally for 2 days (4 doses)
	Children >1 mo	10 mg/kg/dose bid orally for 2 days (4 doses)
	Adults	600 mg bid orally for 2 days (4 doses)
Ceftriaxone	Children ≤15 yr	125 mg IM, single dose
	Children >15 yr	250 mg IM, single dose
	Adults	250 mg IM, single dose
Ciprofloxacin†	Children	Not recommended
	Adults	500 mg orally, single dose
Azithromycin‡	Adults	500 mg orally, single dose (only studied in adults)

*Rifampin is not recommended for pregnant women (teratogenicity in laboratory animals). The reliability of oral contraceptives may be affected by rifampin therapy; therefore, alternative contraceptive measures should be used during and for the month after rifampin administration.
†Ciprofloxacin is not recommended in children, pregnant women, or lactating women. Ciproflaxacin can be used in children if no acceptable alternative is available.
‡Azithromycin is not currently listed in the Centers for Disease Control and Prevention recommendations for prophylaxis.

Meningococcal Vaccines

POLYSACCHARIDE VACCINES

Primary prevention of meningococcal disease is essential or several reasons. The initial manifestation of the disease may be fulminant, with no opportunity for antibiotics to influence the course of the disease. Antibiotic-resistant strains now are recognized, and chemoprophylaxis of contacts is a cumbersome and often ineffective public health measure. Mass immunization offers the opportunity to prevent both endemic and epidemic disease worldwide.

The primary approach to the development of meningococcal vaccines has been to purify capsular polysaccharides from the cell surface of the organism. These polysaccharides can be well defined chemically and physically, and isolation of the capsular polysaccharide from other components of the cell wall to produce a product that is free of contaminating endotoxin and cell surface proteins has been possible.

Early clinical studies of a bivalent vaccine consisting of meningococcal A and C polysaccharides demonstrated that the vaccine was safe and effective in adults and older children. Subsequently, a quadrivalent vaccine composed of groups A, C, W135, and Y was licensed and is used routinely by the U.S. military; it is recommended for travelers visiting countries with a high incidence of meningococcal disease. The tetravalent vaccine also is used in individuals with functional or anatomic asplenia and in persons with complement or properdin deficiencies.

Meningococcal vaccines have been effective in the control of epidemic disease.[122] In addition, a meningococcal A/C polysaccharide vaccine was effective in preventing secondary cases of meningococcal disease in household contacts.[60] In this study, vaccination was given to household contacts on the day after admission of the index case. Nine cases of confirmed or probable meningococcal disease occurred in the control group vaccinated with tetanus toxoid, but only 1 case of possible meningococcal infection in the 520 contacts who received meningococcal vaccine. Approximately 50 percent of secondary cases may appear 5 or more days after meningococcal disease is diagnosed in the index case. Immunization of contacts may be useful as a supplement to chemoprophylaxis of contacts.

Recently, public health authorities have focused on a change in the epidemiology of meningococcal disease in the United States consisting of an increase in incidence rates in young adults. Numerous studies have identified an increased risk of acquisition of invasive disease in college freshmen living in dormitories.[17, 63, 101] Although routine immunization of all college freshmen living in dorms may not be cost-effective, the Advisory Committee on Immunization Practices and the American Academy of Pediatrics both have published recommendations that health care providers, colleges, and public health authorities should inform entering freshmen students of the availability of the quadrivalent meningococcal vaccine.[36, 101]

POLYSACCHARIDE/PROTEIN CONJUGATE VACCINES

Two major problems remain with meningococcal vaccines. The pure polysaccharide vaccines are not immunogenic or protective in young children, and an effective and immunogenic group B vaccine is not available yet. To overcome the lack of adequate immunogenicity of plain polysaccharide vaccines in infants, protein-polysaccharide conjugate vaccines have been developed. A group A/C conjugate meningococcal vaccine has been licensed in Great Britain and has been effective in controlling group C meningococcal disease.[135] Clinical trials of the safety and immunogenicity of these conjugate vaccines currently are under way in the United States.

Development of an immunogenic group B meningococcal vaccine has been problematic because the polysaccharide capsule of group B meningococci is not immunogenic in animals or humans. Teleologic explanations for this lack of immunogenicity have led to numerous interesting hypotheses. The chemical composition of the group B capsule is a polymer of two to eight neuraminic acids. In 1983, Finnish investigators reported that horse antiserum to group B meningococci reacted with glycoproteins isolated from human and rat brains.[46a] Furthermore, binding was higher in human fetal brain than in postnatal brain, a finding consistent with the fact that the fetal brain contains more polysialosyl glycopeptides than the postnatal brain does. Based on this experimental evidence, the authors recommended caution in development of a vaccine because of concern for induction of cross-reacting antibodies against neuronal tissue.

Several different strategies have been used in the development of a meningococcal group B vaccine. A serotype protein vaccine was constructed with membrane vesicles from a serotype 2b strain and noncovalent complexing of this protein with the group B capsular polysaccharide. This vaccine induced bactericidal antibody but did not induce antibodies against the polysaccharide capsule as measured by an enzyme-linked immunosorbent assay. A similar vaccine was studied in 171,800 students in Norway, and the calculated rate of protection was 57.2 percent.[10] The authors concluded that the effect was insufficient to justify a public vaccination program. A similar vaccine was given to 2.4 million children 3 months to 6 years of age in São Paulo. A case-control study showed that the estimated vaccine efficacy for children 48 months of age and older was 74 percent.[33] The vaccine was much less effective in younger children. Another approach has been to develop a protein-polysaccharide conjugate vaccine with the capsular polysaccharide of *E. coli* K92, an organism with a capsular polysaccharide that cross-reacts with that of both group B and group C meningococci. This vaccine induces antibody in animals and will be tested in humans.

A better understanding of the pathophysiologic mechanism of meningococcal disease may lead to more detailed knowledge of the bacterial structures critical for antigenicity and immunogenicity in humans. Development of a safe and effective vaccine that can induce protection against all encapsulated meningococci in all age groups is the ultimate goal.

REFERENCES

1. Abramson, J. S., and Spika, J. S.: Persistence of *Neisseria meningitidis* in the upper respiratory tract after intravenous antibiotic therapy for systemic meningococcal disease. J. Infect. Dis. *151*:370–371, 1985.
2. Aiuto, L., Barone, S., Cohen, P., et al.: Recombinant tissue plasminogen activator restores perfusion in meningococcal purpura fulminans. Crit. Care Med. *25*:1590–1593, 1997.
3. Analysis of endemic meningococcal disease by serogroup and evaluation of chemoprophylaxis. J. Infect. Dis. *134*:201–204, 1976.
4. Banks, H.: Meningococcosis: A protean disease. Lancet *2*:635–640, 1948.
5. Baraldes, M., Domingo, P., Barrio, J., et al.: Meningitis due to *Neisseria subflava*: Case report and review. Clin. Infect. Dis. *30*:615–617, 2000.
6. Barquet, N., Gasser, I., Domingo, P., et al.: Primary meningococcal conjunctivitis: Report of 21 patients and review. Rev. Infect. Dis. *12*:838–847, 1990.
7. Benoit, F.: Chronic meningococcemia. Medicine (Baltimore) *35*:103, 1963.
8. Bernard, G., Vincent, J., Laterre, P., et al.: Efficacy and safety of recombinant human activated protein C for severe sepsis. N. Engl. J. Med. *344*:699–709, 2001.
9. Bhattacharjee, A. K., and Jennings, H. J.: Characterization of 3-deoxy-D-manno-octulosonic acid as a component of the capsular polysaccharide antigen from *Neisseria meningitidis* serogroup 29-e. Biochem. Biophys. Res. Commun. *61*:489–493, 1974.
10. Bjune, G., Hoiby, E. A., Gronnesby, J. K., et al.: Effect of outer membrane vesicle vaccine against group B meningococcal disease in Norway. Lancet *338*:1093–1096, 1991.
11. Boger, W.: Fulminating meningococcemia. N. Engl. J. Med. *231*:385–387, 1944.
12. Boger, W.: Purulent meningococcal arthritis. Am. J. Med. Sci. *208*:708–717, 1944.
13. Boras, A., Bozinovic, D., Tenover, F., and Popovic, T.: First report of *Neisseria meningitidis* intermediately resistant to penicillin in Croatia. J. Clin. Microbiol. *39*:823, 2001.
14. Brandtzaeg, P., Halstensen, A., Kierulf, P., et al.: Molecular mechanisms in the compartmentalized inflammatory response presenting as meningococcal meningitis or septic shock. Microb. Pathog. *13*:423–432, 1992.
15. Brandtzaeg, P., Kierulf, P., Gaustad, P., et al.: Plasma endotoxin as a predictor of multiple organ failure and death in systemic meningococcal disease. J. Infect. Dis. *159*:195–294, 1989.
16. Brandtzaeg, P., Mollnes, T. E., and Kierulf, P.: Complement activation and endotoxin levels in systemic meningococcal disease. J. Infect. Dis. *160*:58–65, 1989.
17. Bruce, M., Rosenstein, N., Capparella, J., et al.: Meningococcal disease in college students. Abstract. Paper presented at the 39th Annual Meeting of the Infectious Diseases Society of America, 1999, Philadelphia.
18. Brundage, J., and Zollinger, W.: Evolution of Meningococcal Disease Epidemiology in the U.S. Army. Vol. 1. Boca Raton, FL, CRC Press, 1987, pp. 5–23.
19. Buchanan, R., and Gibbons, N. (eds.): Bergey's Manual of Determinative Bacteriology. Baltimore, Williams & Wilkins, 1974, p. 427.
20. Cartwright, K., Reilly, S., White, D., and Stuart, J.: Early treatment with parenteral penicillin in meningococcal disease. B. M. J. *305*:143–147, 1992.

21. Cartwright, K. A., Jones, D. M., Smith, A. J., et al.: Influenza A and meningococcal disease. Lancet *338*:554–557, 1991.
22. Caugant, D. A., Hoiby, E. A., Magnus, P., et al.: Asymptomatic carriage of *Neisseria meningitidis* in a randomly sampled population. J. Clin. Microbiol. *32*:323–330, 1994.
23. Churchwell, K., McManus, M., Kent, P., et al.: Intensive blood and plasma exchange for treatment of coagulopathy in meningococcemia. J. Clin. Apheresis *10*:171–177, 1995.
24. Cobroft, R., and Henderson, A.: Meningococcal purpura fulminans treated with antithrombin III concentrate: What is the optimal replacement therapy? Aust. N. Z. J. Med. *24*:575–576, 1994.
25. Cohen, M. S., Steere, A. C., Baltimore, R., et al.: Possible nosocomial transmission of group Y *Neisseria meningitidis* among oncology patients. Ann. Intern. Med. *91*:7–12, 1979.
26. Committee on Infectious Disease: Meningococcal disease prevention and control strategies for practice-based physicians (addendum: recommendations for college students). Pediatrics *106*:1500–1504, 2000.
27. Conway, E., and Rosenberg, R.: Tumor necrosis factor suppresses transcription of the thrombomodulin gene in endothelial cells. Mol. Cell. Biol. *8*:5588–5592, 1988.
28. Cooper, E. R., Ellison, R. T., Smith, G. S., et al.: Rifampin-resistant meningococcal disease in a contact patient given prophylactic rifampin. J. Pediatr. *108*:93–96, 1986.
29. Corless, C., Guiver, M., Borrow, R., et al.: Simultaneous detection of *Neisseria meningitidis, Haemophilus influenzae,* and *Streptococcus pneumoniae* in suspected cases of meningitis and septicemia using real-time PCR. J. Clin. Microbiol. *39*:1553–1558, 2001.
30. Cuevas, L. E., Kazembe, P., Mughogho, G. K., et al.: Eradication of nasopharyngeal carriage of *Neisseria meningitidis* in children and adults in rural Africa: A comparison of ciprofloxacin and rifampicin. J. Infect. Dis. *171*:728–731, 1995.
31. D'Amelio, R., Agostoni, A., Biselli, R., et al.: Complement deficiency and antibody profile in survivors of meningococcal meningitis due to common serogroups in Italy. Scand. J. Immunol. *35*:589–595, 1992.
32. Davis, C. E., and Arnold, K.: Role of meningococcal endotoxin in meningococcal purpura. J. Exp. Med. *140*:159–171, 1974.
33. de Morales, J. C., Perkins, B. A., Camargo, M. C., et al.: Protective efficacy of a serogroup B meningococcal vaccine in Sao Paulo, Brazil [published erratum appears in Lancet 1992 Dec 19–26; *340*(8834–8835):1554]. Lancet *340*:1074–1078, 1992.
34. Densen, P., Weiler, J. M., Griffiss, J. M., and Hoffmann, L. G.: Familial properdin deficiency and fatal meningococcemia. Correction of the bactericidal defect by vaccination. N. Engl. J. Med. *316*:922–926, 1987.
35. Derkx, B., Wittes, J., and McCloskey, R: Randomized, placebo-controlled trial of HA-1A, a human monoclonal antibody to endotoxin in children with meningococcal septic shock. Clin. Infect. Dis. *28*:770–777, 1999.
36. DeVoe, I. W., and Gilka, F. Disseminated intravascular coagulation in rabbits: Synergistic activity of meningococcal endotoxin and materials egested from leucocytes containing meningococci. J. Med. Microbiol. *9*:451–458, 1976.
37. Dickson, R., McKinnon, N., Magner, D., et al.: Meningococcal infection. Lancet *2*:631–634, 1941.
38. Dixon, L. M., and Sanford, H. S.: Meningococcal pericarditis in the antibiotic era. Milit. Med. *136*:433–438, 1971.
39. Dock, W.: Intermittent fever of seven months duration due to meningococcemia. J. A. M. A. *83*:399–400, 1924.
40. Edwards, M. S., and Baker, C. J.: Complications and sequelae of meningococcal infections in children. J. Pediatr. *99*:540–545, 1981.
41. Eley, B., and Levin, M.: Septic shock with special reference to meningococcal disease. Curr. Opin. Infect. Dis. *7*:345–350, 1994.
42. Ellsworth, J., Marks, M. I., and Vose, A.: Meningococcal meningitis in children. C. M. A. J. *120*:155–158, 1979.
43. Faur, Y., Weisburd, M., and Wilson, M.: Isolation of *Neisseria meningitidis* from the genito-urinary tract and. J. Clin. Microbiol. *2*:178–182, 1975.
44. Feavers, I. M.: ABC of meningococcal diversity. Nature *404*:451–452, 2000.
45. Figueroa, J. E., and Densen, P.: Infectious diseases associated with complement deficiencies. Clin. Microbiol. Rev. *4*:359–395, 1991.
46. Fijen, C. A., Kuijper, E. J., Hannema, A. J., et al.: Complement deficiencies in patients over ten years old with meningococcal disease due to uncommon serogroups. Lancet *2*:585–588, 1989.
46a. Finne, J., Leinonen, M., and Makela, P. H.: Antigenic similarities between brain components and bacteria causing meningitis. Implications for vaccine development and pathogenesis. Lancet *2*(8346):355–357, 1983.
47. Fisher, M., Hedberg, K., Cardosi, P., et al.: Tobacco smoke as a risk factor for meningococcal disease. Pediatr. Infect. Dis. J. *10*:979–983, 1997.
48. Francke, E., and Neu, H.: Postsplenectomy infection. Surg. Clin. North Am. *61*:135–155, 1981.
49. Frasch, C., Zollinger, W., Poolman, J.: Serotype antigens of *Neisseria meningitidis* and a proposed scheme for design of serotypes. Rev. Infect. Dis. *7*:504–510, 1985.
50. Frasch, C. E.: Role of protein serotype antigens in protection against disease due to *Neisseria meningitidis*. J. Infect. Dis. *136*(Suppl.):84–90, 1977.
51. Gerard, P., Moriau, M., Bachy, A., et al.: Meningococcal purpura: Report of 19 patients treated with heparin. J. Pediatr. *82*:780–786, 1973.
52. Gilmore, A., Stuart, J., and Andrews, N.: Risk of secondary meningococcal disease in health-care workers. Lancet *356*:1654–1655, 2000.
53. Girardin, E., Grau, G. E., Dayer, J. M., et al.: Tumor necrosis factor and interleukin-1 in the serum of children with severe infectious purpura. N. Engl. J. Med. *319*:397–400, 1988.
54. Girgis, N., Sultan, Y., Frenck, R., Jr., et al.: Azithromycin compared with rifampin for eradication of nasopharyngeal colonization by *Neisseria meningitidis*. Pediatr. Infect. Dis. J. *17*:816–819, 1998.
55. Goldschneider, I., Gotschlich, E. C., and Artenstein, M. S.: Human immunity to the meningococcus. I. The role of humoral antibodies. J. Exp. Med. *129*:1307–1326, 1969.
56. Goldschneider, I., Gotschlich, E. C., and Artenstein, M. S.: Human immunity to the meningococcus. II. Development of natural immunity. J. Exp. Med. *129*:1327–1348, 1969.
57. Greenfield, S., Sheehe, P. R., and Feldman, H. A.: Meningococcal carriage in a population of "normal" families. J. Infect. Dis. *123*:67–73, 1971.
58. Greenwood, B., and Whittle, H.: The pathogenesis of meningococcal arthritis. In Dumonde, D., Path, M. (eds.): Infection and Immunology in Rheumatic Diseases. Philadelphia, J. B. Lippincott, 1976, pp. 119–127.
59. Greenwood, B. M., Bradley, A. K., and Wall, R. A.: Meningococcal disease and season in sub-Saharan Africa. Lancet *2*:829–830, 1985.
60. Greenwood, B. M., Hassan-King, M., and Whittle, H. C.: Prevention of secondary cases of meningococcal disease in household contacts by vaccination. B. M. J. *1*:1317–1319, 1978.
61. Haggerty, R., and Zaia, M.: Acute bacterial meningitis. Adv. Pediatr. *13*:129–173, 1964.
62. Hardman, J.: Fatal meningococcal infections: The changing pathologic picture in the '60s. Milit. Med. *133*:951–964, 1968.
63. Harrison, L., Dwyer, D., Maples, C., and Billmann, L.: Risk of meningococcal infection in college students. J. A. M. A. *281*:1906–1910, 1999.
64. Hart, C., and Rogers, T.: Meningococcal disease. J. Med. Microbiol. *39*:3–25, 1993.
65. Herman, R., and Rubin, H.: Meningococcal pericarditis without meningitis presenting as tamponade. N. Engl. J. Med. *290*:143–144, 1974.
66. Herrick, W.: Extrameningeal meningococcus infections. Arch. Intern. Med. *23*:409–418, 1919.
67. Holbein, B. E.: Differences in virulence for mice between disease and carrier strains of *Neisseria meningitidis*. Can. J. Microbiol. *27*:738–741, 1981.
68. Hubert, B., Watier, L., Garnerin, P., and Richardson, S.: Meningococcal disease and influenza-like syndrome: A new approach to an old question. J. Infect. Dis. *166*:542–545, 1992.
69. Irazuzta, J., and McManus, M. L.: Use of topically applied nitroglycerin in the treatment of purpura fulminans. J. Pediatr. *117*:993–995, 1990.
70. Jackson, L. A., Schuchat, A., Reeves, M. W., and Wenger, J. D.: Serogroup C meningococcal outbreaks in the United States: An emerging threat. J. A. M. A. *273*:383–389, 1995.
71. Jackson, L. A., Tenover, F. C., Baker, C., et al.: Prevalence of *Neisseria meningitidis* relatively resistant to penicillin in the United States, 1991. Meningococcal Disease Study Group. J. Infect. Dis. *169*:438–441, 1994.
72. Jackson, L. A., Wenger, J. D.: Laboratory-based surveillance for meningococcal disease in selected areas, United States, 1989–1991. Mor. Mortal. Wkly. Rep. C. D. C. Surveill. Summ. *42*:21–30, 1993.
73. Jacobson, J. A., Camargos, P. A., Ferreira, J. T., and McCormick, J. B.: The risk of meningitis among classroom contacts during an epidemic of meningococcal disease. Am. J. Epidemiol. *104*:552–555, 1976.
74. Jennings, H. J., Bhattacharjee, A. K., Bundle, D. R., et al.: Structures of the capsular polysaccharides of *Neisseria meningitidis* as determined by ^{13}C-nuclear magnetic resonance spectroscopy. J. Infect. Dis. *136*(Suppl.):78–83, 1977.
75. Jones, R. N., Slepack, J., and Eades, A.: Fatal neonatal meningococcal meningitis. Association with maternal cervical-vaginal colonization. J. A. M. A. *236*:2652–2653, 1976.
76. Kaiser, A., Hennekens, C., Saslaw, M., et al.: Seroepidemiology and chemoprophylaxis of disease due to sulfonamide-resistant *Neisseria meningitidis* in a civilian population. J. Infect. Dis. *130*:217–224, 1974.
77. Kaspar, D., Winkelhake, J., and Zollinger, W.: Immunochemical similarity between polysaccharide antigens of *Escherichia coli* 07:K1(L):NM and group B *Neisseria meningitidis*. J. Immunol. *110*:262–268, 1973.
78. Kaufman, B., Levy, H., Zaleznak, B., et al.: Statistical analysis of 242 cases of meningococcus meningitis. Pediatrics *38*:705–716, 1951.
79. Kirsch, E., Barton, P., Kitchen, L., and Giroir, B.: Pathophysiology, treatment and outcome of meningococcemia: A review and recent experience. Pediatr. Infect. Dis. J. *15*:967–979, 1996.
80. Koppes, G., Ellenbogen, E., and Gebhart, R.: Group Y meningococcal disease in United States Air Force recruits. Am. J. Med. *62*:661–666, 1977.
81. Kunkel, M. J., Brown, L. G., Bauta, H., Iannini, P. B.: Meningococcal mesenteric adenitis and peritonitis in a child. Pediatr. Infect. Dis. J. *3*:327–328, 1984.
82. Kuppermann, N., Inkelis, S., and Saladino, R.: The role of heparin in the prevention of extremity and digit necrosis in meningococcal purpura fulminans. Pediatr. Infect. Dis. J. *13*:867–873, 1994.

83. Leake, J., Perkins, B. A.: Meningococcal disease: Challenges in prevention and management. Infect. Med. *17*:364–377, 2000.
84. Leclerc, F., Martinot, A., Cremer, R., et al.: ECMO for refractory cardiorespiratory failure due to meningococcal disease. Lancet *349*:1397–1398, 1997.
85. Lehman, T. J., Bernstein, B., Hanson, V., et al.: Meningococcal infection complicating systemic lupus erythematosus. J. Pediatr. *99*:94–96, 1981.
86. Lehmann, A., Halstensen, A., Sornes, S., et al.: High levels of interleukin-10 during the initial phase of fulminant meningococcal septic shock. J. Infect. Dis. *171*:229–232, 1995.
87. Leibel, R., Fangman, J., and Ostrovsky, M.: Chronic meningococcemia in childhood. Am. J. Dis. Child. *127*:94–98, 1974.
88. Levin, M., Quint, P., Goldstein, B., et al.: Recombinant bactericidal/permeability-increasing protein (rBPI) as adjunctive treatment for children with severe meningococcal sepsis: A randomized trial. Lancet *356*:961–967, 2000.
89. Levitt, L. P., Bond, J. O., Hall, I. E., Jr., et al.: Meningococcal and ECHO-9 meningitis. Report of an outbreak. Neurology *20*:45–51, 1970.
90. Lewis, J., Arnold, C., Alexander, J.: Meningococcal pneumonia. Am. J. Clin. Pathol. *59*:388–390, 1973.
91. Linz, B., Schenker, M., Zhu, P., and Achtman, M.: Frequent interspecific genetic exchange between commensal neisseriae and *Neisseria meningitidis*. Mol. Microbiol. *36*:1049–1058, 2000.
92. Maiden, M. C.: Population genetics of a transformable bacterium: The influence of horizontal genetic exchange on the biology of *Neisseria meningitidis*. F. E. M. S. Microbiol. Lett. *112*:243–250, 1993.
93. Maiden, M. C.: Horizontal genetic exchange, evolution, and spread of antibiotic resistance in bacteria. Clin. Infect. Dis. 27(Suppl. 1):12–20, 1998.
94. Marks, M. I., Frasch, C. E., and Shapera, R. M.: Meningococcal colonization and infection in children and their household contacts. Am. J. Epidemiol. *109*:563–571, 1979.
95. Marzouk, O., Thomson, A., Sills, J., et al.: Features and outcome in meningococcal disease presenting with maculopapular rash. Arch. Dis. Child. *66*:485–487, 1991.
96. McCracken, G., Sarff, L., Glode, M., et al.: Relation between *E. coli* K1 capsular polysaccharide antigen and clinical outcome in neonatal meningitis. Lancet *2*:246–250, 1974.
97. Mellado, M., Rodriguez-Contreras, R., Fernandez-Crehuet, M., et al.: Endotoxin liberation by strains of *N. meningitidis* isolated from patients and healthy carriers. Epidemiol. Infect. *106*:289–295, 1991.
98. Mellado, M., Rodriguez-Contreras, R., Mariscal, A., et al.: Effect of penicillin and chloramphenicol on the growth and endotoxin release by *N. meningitidis*. Epidemiol. Infect. *106*:283–288, 1991.
99. Mendelman, P., Campos, J., Chaffin, D., et al.: Relative penicillin G resistance in *Neisseria meningitidis* and reduced affinity of penicillin-binding protein 3. Antimicrob. Agents Chemother. *32*:706–709, 1988.
100. Meningococcal disease among travelers returning from Saudi Arabia. M. M. W. R. Morb. Mortal. Wkly. Rep. 36:559, 1987.
101. Meningococcal disease and college students. Recommendations of the Advisory Committee on Immunization Practices (ACIP). M. M. W. R. Morb. Mortal. Wkly. Rep. *49*(RR-7):13–20, 2000.
102. Meningococcal infections. In Pickering, L. (ed.): Red Book 2000. Report of the Committee on Infectious Diseases. Elk Grove Village, IL, American Academy of Pediatrics, 2000, pp. 396–401.
103. Meyer, M., Irazuzta, J., and Tozibikian, H.: Topical nitroglycerin and pain in purpura fulminans. J. Pediatr. *134*:639–641, 1999.
104. Moncada, S., and Higgs, E.: Endogenous nitric oxide: Physiology, pathology and clinical relevance. Eur. J. Clin. Invest. *21*:361–374, 1991.
105. Moore, P. S., Harrison, L. H., Telzak, E. E., et al.: Group A meningococcal carriage in travelers returning from Saudi Arabia. J. A. M. A. *260*:2686–2689, 1988.
106. Moore, P. S., Hierholzer, J., DeWitt, W., et al.: Respiratory viruses and mycoplasma as cofactors for epidemic group A meningococcal meningitis. J. A. M. A. *264*:1271–1275, 1990.
107. Moore, P. S., Reeves, M. W., Schwartz, B., et al.: Intercontinental spread of an epidemic group A *Neisseria meningitidis* strain. Lancet *2*:260–263, 1989.
108. Morrow, H. W., Slaten, D. D., Reingold, A. L., et al.: Risk factors associated with a school-related outbreak of serogroup C meningococcal disease. Pediatr. Infect. Dis. J. *9*:394–398, 1990.
109. Morse, J., Oretsky, M., and Hudson, J.: Pericarditis as a complication of meningococcal meningitis. Ann. Intern. Med. *74*:212–217, 1971.
110. Nadel, S., De Munter, C., Britto, J., et al.: Recombinant tissue plasminogen activator restores perfusion in meningococcal purpura fulminans. Crit. Care Med. *26*:971–972, 1998.
111. Nassif, X., and So, M.: Interaction of pathogenic neisseriae with nonphagocytic cells. Clin. Microbiol. Rev. *8*:376–388, 1995.
112. Nawroth, P., and Stern, D.: Modulation of endothelial cell hemostatic properties by tumor necrosis factor. J. Exp. Med. *320*:1165–1172, 1986.
113. Ni, H., Knight, A., Cartwright, K., et al.: Polymerase chain reaction for diagnosis of meningococcal meningitis. Lancet *340*:1432–1434, 1993.
114. Nielsen, H. E., Koch, C., Magnussen, P., and Lind, I.: Complement deficiencies in selected groups of patients with meningococcal disease. Scand. J. Infect. Dis. *21*:389–396, 1989.
115. Niklasson, P., Lundbergh, P., and Strandell, T.: Prognostic factors in meningococcal disease. Scand. J. Infect. Dis. *3*:17–25, 1971.
116. Ognibene, A., and Dito, W.: Chronic meningococcemia. Arch. Intern. Med. *114*:29–32, 1964.
117. Olcen, P., Kjellander, J., Danielsson, D., and Lindquist, B. L.: Epidemiology of *Neisseria meningitidis;* prevalence and symptoms from the upper respiratory tract in family members to patients with meningococcal disease. Scand. J. Infect. Dis. *13*:105–109, 1981.
118. Oppenheimer, E., and Rosman, N.: Bacterial meningitis in childhood: Neurologic complications and their management. Pediatr. Neurol. *287*:285–298, 1976.
119. Outbreaks of group B meningococcal disease—Florida, 1995 and 1997. M. M. W. R. Morb. Mortal. Wkly. Rep. *47*:833–837, 1998.
120. Parillo, J.: Pathogenic mechanisms of septic shock. N. Engl. J. Med. *328*:307–343, 1993.
121. Pastor, P., Medley, F. B., and Murphy, T. V.: Meningococcal disease in Dallas County, Texas: Results of a six-year population-based study. Pediatr. Infect. Dis. J. *19*:324–328, 2000.
122. Peltola, H., Makela, H., Kayhty, H., et al.: Clinical efficacy of meningococcus group A capsular polysaccharide vaccine in children three months to five years of age. N. Engl. J. Med. *297*:686–691, 1977.
123. Penny, J., Grace, W., and Kennedy, R.: Meningococcal pericarditis. Am. J. Cardiol. *18*:281–285, 1966.
124. Perez-Trallero, E., Aldamiz-Echeverria, L., and Perez-Yarza, E. G.: Meningococci with increased resistance to penicillin. Lancet *335*:1096, 1990.
125. Pinals, R., and Ropes, M.: Meningococcal arthritis. Arthritis Rheum. *7*:241–258, 1964.
126. Pinner, R. W., Gellin, B. G., Bibb, W. F., et al.: Meningococcal disease in the United States—1986. Meningococcal Disease Study Group. J. Infect. Dis. *164*:368–374, 1991.
127. Pinner, R. W., Onyango, F., Perkins, B. A., et al.: Epidemic meningococcal disease in Nairobi, Kenya, 1989. The Kenya/Centers for Disease Control (CDC) Meningitis Study Group. J. Infect. Dis. *166*:359–364, 1992.
128. Pizzi, M.: A severe epidemic of meningococcus meningitis in Chile, 1941–42. Am. J. Public Health *34*:231–238, 1944.
129. Platonov, A., Beloborodov, V., and Vershinina, I.: Meningococcal disease in patients with late complement deficiency: Studies in the U.S.S.R. Medicine (Baltimore) *72*:374–392, 1993.
130. Poolman, J., van der Ley, P., and Tommassen, J.: Surface Structures and Secreted Products of Meningococci. Chichester, England, Wiley, 1995, pp. 21–34.
131. Popovic, T., Sacchi, C. T., Reeves, M. W., et al.: *Neisseria meningitidis* serogroup W135 isolates associated with the ET-37 complex. Emerg. Infect. Dis. *6*:428–429, 2000.
132. Powars, D., Larsen, R., Johnson, J., et al.: Epidemic meningococcemia and purpura fulminans with induced protein C deficiency. Clin. Infect. Dis. *17*:254–261, 1993.
133. Powars, D., Rogers, Z., Patch, M., et al.: Purpura fulminans in meningococcemia: Association with acquired deficiencies of proteins C and S. N. Engl. J. Med. *317*:571–572, 1987.
134. Racoosin, J., Whitney, C., Conover, C., and Diaz, P.: Serogroup Y meningococcal disease in Chicago, 1991–1997. J. A. M. A. *280*: 2094–2098, 1998.
135. Ramsay, M., Andrews, N., Kaczmarski, E., and Miller, E.: Efficacy of meningococcal serogroup C conjugate vaccine in teenagers and toddlers in England. Lancet *357*:195–196, 2001.
136. Read, R., Camp, N., Di Giovine, F., et al.: An interleukin-1 genotype is associated with fatal outcome of meningococcal disease. J. Infect. Dis. *182*:1557, 2000.
137. Riedo, F. X., Plikaytis, B. D., and Broome, C. V.: Epidemiology and prevention of meningococcal disease. Pediatr. Infect. Dis. J. *14*:643–657, 1995.
138. Robboy, S.: Atrioventricular node inflammation: Mechanism of sudden death in protracted meningococcemia. N. Engl. J. Med. *286*:1091–1093, 1972.
139. Rodriguez-Erdmann, F.: Intravascular activation of the clotting system with phospholipids. Blood *26*:541–553, 1965.
140. Rosenblatt, J., Ray, C., and Enquist, R. W.: Meningococcal infections in children: Observations on prognosis and therapy. Personal communication, 1978.
141. Rosenstein, N. E., and Perkins, B. A.: Update on *Haemophilus influenzae* serotype b and meningococcal vaccines. Pediatr. Clin. North Am. *47*: 337–352, 2000.
142. Rosenstein, N. E., Perkins, B. A., and Stephens, D. S.: The changing epidemiology of meningococcal disease in the United States, 1992–1996. J. Infect. Dis. *180*:1894–1901, 1999.
143. Rosenstein, N. E., Perkins, B. A., Stephens, D. S., et al.: Meningococcal disease. N. Engl. J. Med. *344*:1378–1388, 2001.
144. Ross, S. C., Densen, P.: Complement deficiency states and infection: Epidemiology, pathogenesis and consequences of neisserial and other infections in an immune deficiency. Medicine (Baltimore) *63*:243–273, 1984.
145. Saez-Nieto, J., Lujan, R., Berron, S., et al.: Epidemiology and molecular basis of penicillin-resistant *Neisseria meningitidis* in Spain: A 5-year history (1985–1989). Clin. Infect. Dis. *14*:394–402, 1992.

146. Scheim, A.: Articular manifestations of meningococcic infections. Arch. Intern. Med. *62*:963–978, 1938.
147. Scholten, R. J., Bijlmer, H. A., Tobi, H., et al.: Upper respiratory tract infection, heterologous immunisation and meningococcal disease. J. Med. Microbiol. *48*:943–946, 1999.
148. Scott, L., Knox, D., Perry, L., et al.: Meningococcal pericarditis. Am. J. Cardiol. *29*:104–108, 1972.
149. Serogroup B meningococcal disease—Oregon, 1994. M. M. W. R. Morb. Mortal. Wkly. Rep. *44*:121–124, 1995.
150. Sinclair, J., Skeoch, C., and Hallworth, D.: Prognosis of meningococcal septicaemia. Lancet *3*:38, 1987.
151. Smith, O., White, B., Vaughn, D., et al.: Use of protein-C concentrate, heparin, and haemodiafiltration in meningococcus-induced purpura fulminans. Lancet *350*:1590–1593, 1997.
152. Spratt, B., Zhang, Q., Jones, D., et al.: Recruitment of a penicillin-binding protein gene from *Neisseria flavescens* during the emergence of penicillin-resistant *Neisseria meningitidis*. Proc. Natl. Acad. Sci. U. S. A. *86*:315–328, 1989.
153. Stanwell-Smith, R. E., Stuart, J. M., Hughes, A. O., et al.: Smoking, the environment and meningococcal disease: A case control study. Epidemiol. Infect. *112*:315–328, 1994.
154. Stephens, D., and Farley, M.: Pathogenic events during infection of the human nasopharynx with *Neisseria meningitidis* and *Haemophilus influenzae*. Rev. Infect. Dis. *12*:22–23, 1991.
155. Stephens, D., Hoffman, L., and McGee, Z.: Interaction of *Neisseria meningitidis* with human nasopharyngeal mucosa: Attachment and entry into columnar epithelial cells. J. Infect. Dis. *148*:369–376, 1983.
156. Stiehm, E., and Damrosch, D.: Factors in the prognosis of meningococcal infection. J. Pediatr. *68*:457–467, 1966.
157. Stuart, J. M., Cartwright, K. A., Robinson, P. M., and Noah, N. D.: Effect of smoking on meningococcal carriage. Lancet *2*:723–725, 1989.
158. Sullivan, T., and La Scolea, L.: *Neisseria meningitidis* bacteremia in children: Quantitation of bacteremia and spontaneous clinical recovery without antibiotic therapy. Pediatrics *80*:63–73, 1987.
159. Summary of notifiable disease, U.S. 1999. M. M. W. R. Morb. Mortal. Wkly. Rep. *48*:1–105, 2001.
160. Sutcliffe, E. M., Jones, D. M., el-Sheikh, S., and Percival, A.: Penicillin-insensitive meningococci in the UK. Lancet *1*:657–658, 1988.
161. Swartley, J., Marfin, A., Edupuganti, S., et al.: Capsule switching of *Neisseria meningitidis*. Proc. Natl. Acad. Sci. U. S. A. *94*:271–276, 1997.
162. Thompson, A., Sills, J., and Hart, C.: Validation of the Glasgow meningococcal septicacemia prognostic score: A 10-year retrospective survey. Crit. Care Med. *19*:26–30, 1991.
163. Tobias, J., Haun, S., Helfaer, M., et al.: Use of continuous caudal block to relieve lower extremity ischemia caused by vasculitis in a child with meningococcemia. J. Pediatr. *115*:1019–1021, 1989.
164. Tuncer, A., Gar, I., Ertem, U., et al.: Once daily ceftriaxone for meningococcemia and meningococcal meningitis. Pediatr. Infect. Dis. J. *7*:711–713, 1988.
165. van de Ende, A., Hopman, C., and Dankert, J.: Multiple mechanism of phase variation of PorA in *Neisseria meningitidis*. Infect. Immun. *68*:6685–6690, 2000.
166. van Deuren, M., ven-Jongekrijg, J., Demacker, P., et al.: Differential expression of proinflammatory cytokines and their inhibitors during the course of meningococcal infections. J. Infect. Dis. *169*:157–161, 1994.
167. van Deuren, M., van der ven-Jongekrijg, J., Bartelink, A., et al.: Correlation between proinflammatory cytokines and anti-inflammatory mediators and the severity of disease in meningococcal infections. J. Infect. Dis. *172*:632–638, 1995.
168. van Deuren, M., van Dijke, B., Koopman, R. J., et al.: Rapid diagnosis of acute meningococcal infections by needle aspiration or biopsy of skin lesions. B. M. J. *306*:1229–1232, 1993.
169. Vann, W. F., Liu, T. Y., and Robbins, J. B.: *Bacillus pumilus* polysaccharide cross-reactive with meningococcal group A polysaccharide. Infect. Immun. *13*:1654–1662, 1976.
170. Van Nguyen, Z., Nguyen, E., and Weiner, L.: Incidence of invasive bacterial disease in children with fever and petechiae. Pediatrics *74*:77–80, 1984.
171. Vieusseux, G.: Memoire sur la maladie qui a regre a Geneve au printemps de 1805. J. Med. Chir. Pharm. *11*:163, 1806.
172. Vogel, U., Claus, H., Frosch, M.: Rapid serogroup switching in *Neisseria meningitidis*. N. Engl. J. Med. *342*:219–220, 2000.
173. Weightman, N. C., and Johnstone, D. J.: Three cases of pneumonia due to *Neisseria meningitidis,* including serogroup W135. Eur. J. Clin. Microbiol. Infect. Dis. *18*:456–458, 1999.
174. Weis, E., and Silber, E.: Acute constrictive pericarditis. J. Pediatr. *58*:548–553, 1961.
175. Westendorp, R. G., Langermans, J. A., de Bel, C. E., et al.: Release of tumor necrosis factor: An innate host characteristic that may contribute to the outcome of meningococcal disease. J. Infect. Dis. *171*:1057–1060, 1995.
176. Westendorp, R. G., Langermans, J. A., Huizinga, T. W., et al.: Genetic influence on cytokine production and fatal meningococcal disease. Lancet *349*:170–173, 1997.
177. Whittle, H., Tugwell, P., Egler, L., et al.: Rapid bacteriologic diagnosis of pyogenic meningitis by latex agglutination. Lancet *2*:619–621, 1974.
178. Wilson, F., and Morse, S.: Therapy of acute meningococcal infections: Early volume expansion and prophylactic low dose heparin. Am. J. Med. Sci. *264*:445–455, 1972.
179. Wolf, R., and Birbara, C.: Meningococcal infections at an army training center. Am. J. Med. *44*:243–255, 1968.
180. Wong, V., Hitchcock, W., and Mason, W.: Meningococcal infections in children: A review of 100 cases. Pediatr. Infect. Dis. J. *8*:224–227, 1989.
181. Woods, C., Rosenstein, N., and Perkins, B.: *Neisseria meningitidis* outbreaks in the United States, 1994–1997. Abstract. Paper presented the 38th Annual Meeting of the Infectious Diseases Society of America, 1998, Denver.
182. Young, L., LaForce, F., Head, J., et al.: A simultaneous outbreak of meningococcal and influenza infections. N. Engl. J. Med. *287*:5–9, 1972.
183. Zangwill, K. M., Schuchat, A., Riedo, F. X., et al.: School-based clusters of meningococcal disease in the United States: Descriptive epidemiology and a case-control analysis. J. A. M. A. *277*:389–395, 1997.
184. Zhang, Q., Jones, D., Saez-Nieto, J., et al.: Genetic diversity of penicillin-binding protein 2 genes of penicillin-resistant strains of *Neisseria meningitidis* revealed by fingerprinting of amplified DNA. Antimicrob. Agents Chemother. *34*:1523–1528, 1990.

CHAPTER 94 Gonococcal Infections

CHARLES R. WOODS

Gonorrhea, the foremost manifestation of human disease caused by *Neisseria gonorrhoeae* (the gonococcus), is one of the oldest known human diseases. Hippocrates called the disease "strangury" in the fifth and fourth centuries BC. Galen coined the name gonorrhea, meaning "flow of semen," in the second century AD. The association of the disease with sexual activity was recognized early, and sexual abstinence plus washing of the eyes of newborns was prescribed by Greco-Roman physicians for treatment of the disease. Gonorrhea also has been known as "clap" since the late 1300s. The origin of this term is unclear but may have derived from the Les Clapier district of Paris, where prostitutes were housed during the Middle Ages.[166, 208]

After syphilis appeared in Europe in the late 15th century, the two diseases were thought to represent different manifestations of the same infection, and they often coexisted then as today. The description by Neisser of *N. gonorrhoeae* in stained smears of urethral and other exudates in 1879 and culture of the organism by Leistikow and Löffler in 1882 provided the foundation for modern understanding of the clinical spectrum of gonococcal diseases. The advent of safe and effective antimicrobial agents, first sulfonamides in 1936 and then penicillin in 1943, was the next major advance in combating gonorrhea.[166, 208] Further understanding of the clinical aspects of the disease was facilitated by the development of Thayer-Martin medium in 1962.[292] Modern knowledge of the molecular pathogenesis of *N. gonorrhoeae* infection began in 1963 with the observation by Kellogg and colleagues that gonococcal strains with differences in colony morphology also varied in virulence.[168]

The potential reproductive sequelae of gonococcal infections, the ever-growing resistance to antimicrobial agents, and disproportionate case burdens in public clinics continue to cast *N. gonorrhoeae* infection as a major public health problem.[54, 193, 248] The ultimate hope of many current investigations is the development of an effective vaccine.[69, 279]

In infants, the gonococcus causes primarily ophthalmia neonatorum. Wound infections, including scalp abscess (often associated with fetal monitoring), funisitis, and vaginitis may occur. Infection can disseminate from any colonized or infected skin or mucous membrane site and may result in sepsis, meningitis, septic arthritis, or endocarditis. In prepubertal children, gonococcal infection usually involves the genital tract and almost always is transmitted sexually. Vaginitis is the most common manifestation. Extension to the upper genital tract in girls can occur but is a very uncommon finding. Urethritis can develop in boys but rarely does so. Anorectal and tonsillopharyngeal infections also can occur in prepubertal children.

In adolescents, as in adults, the most common clinical manifestations are urethritis, endocervicitis, and salpingitis in females and urethritis in males. Epididymitis, bartholinitis, pelvic inflammatory disease (PID), and perihepatitis can occur as a result of extension from primary genital infections. Rectal and pharyngeal infections and disseminated disease, which may include reactive or septic arthritis, also are seen. Additional information on gonococcal infections is provided in Chapter 49.

Epidemiology of Gonococcal Infection

An estimated 1 million new cases of gonococcal infection occur yearly in the United States, only about one third of which are reported. Adolescents 15 to 19 years old currently have the highest reported incidence of infection (Fig. 94–1). Gonococcal infections are second only to *Chlamydia* infections in incidence among reportable diseases for 15- to 24-year-olds in the United States.[57] The cost of treatment of gonococcal infections was estimated at $1 billion in 1994.[155] Gonococcal infections are relatively rare occurrences in Canada and much of western Europe but remain common in developing countries.[146] Rates of gonorrhea increased in the Baltic countries of Europe in the early 1990s and in young persons in England and Wales in the mid-1990s.[295]

After World War II, reported cases of gonorrhea in the United States declined from 204 per 100,000 in 1950 to 129 per 100,000 in 1958. The 1960s and early 1970s, in association with changing sexual mores, saw yearly increases until a peak of 472 reported cases per 100,000 was reached in 1975. This increase occurred in all age groups. Most age- and sex-specific rates of gonorrhea subsequently declined such that the national rate reached a nadir of 122 per 100,000 in 1997, which was near the *Healthy People 2000* national goal of 100 cases per 100,000. In 1999, the overall population rate was 132.7 per 100,000, with nearly equal rates in males and females. This change may reflect a new trend of increasing rates or improved case finding or recognition. Case fatalities for gonococcal infections rarely occur, with approximately four deaths per year (caused by gonococcal sepsis) reported in the United States from 1989 to 1998.[55, 57, 193, 248]

Rates of gonococcal infection are higher in female children and adolescents than in males (see Fig. 94–1). In young adulthood, rates in males begin to exceed those of females in most populations. Rates in African American adolescents of both genders greatly exceed those of white adolescents, and this trend continues into adulthood.[57] Low socioeconomic

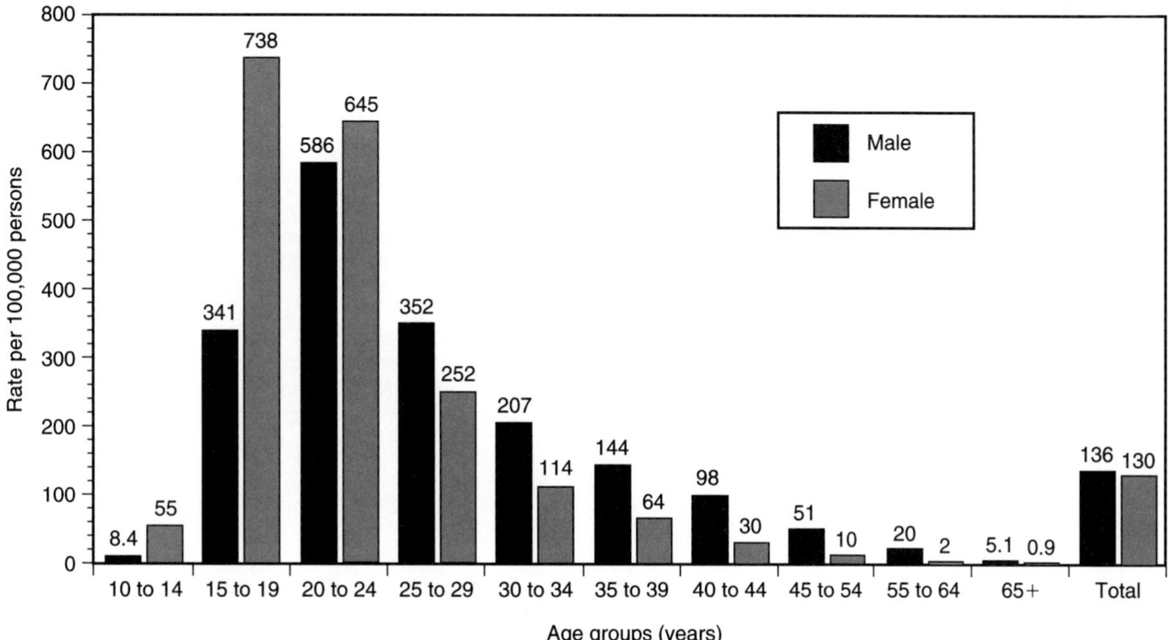

FIGURE 94–1 ■ Rates of gonococcal infection by age and gender in the United States in 1999. (Based on data from Centers for Disease Control and Prevention: Sexually transmitted diseases surveillance 1999 supplement: Gonococcal isolate surveillance project [GISP] annual report—1999. Atlanta, U.S. Department of Health and Human Services, Public Health Service, October 2000.)

status, early onset of sexual activity, unmarried marital status, and past gonococcal infections are risk factors for acquiring gonococcal infection, as are prostitution and illicit drug use.[15, 36] The prevalence of gonococcal infection in adolescents attending private clinics probably is lower than that in those seeking care in publicly funded settings.[21] For women, the use of hormonal contraceptives may increase the risk of acquiring infection, whereas the use of spermicides or diaphragms appear to be at least partially protective.[190, 191]

Homosexual and bisexual males have lower rates of gonococcal infection than in past years, but they still may have higher rates than exclusively heterosexual persons do.[176] Among human immunodeficiency virus (HIV)-infected persons included in the Adult/Adolescent Spectrum of HIV Disease Project in the United States from 1991 to 1998, 9.5 cases occurred per 1000 person-years. An increasing trend was noted over the study period in men who have sex with men, whereas a decline occurred in those with heterosexual contact as their HIV exposure risk.[98]

Gonococcal rates exceed 200 per 100,000 in most southeastern states and are less than 100 per 100,000 in most northeastern and western states.[57] Areas with higher rates of adult disease also have higher numbers of pediatric cases,[95, 115] a finding that reflects the adult origin of virtually all pediatric cases.

Rates of gonorrhea are based primarily on detection of symptomatic infection. Asymptomatic chronic infection in adults is well documented and may account for 5 percent of cases.[146] Such persons can transmit the infection. Some untreated cases will resolve over time. Data also indicate that asymptomatic infection occurs in children, including prepubertal children.[3, 108, 140, 152]

Humans are the only reservoir of *N. gonorrhoeae.* Exudate and secretions from infected mucosal surfaces allow transmission during the intimate contact of sexual acts, parturition, and, rarely, household exposure. The incubation period usually is 2 to 7 days. No evidence of airborne transmission of gonococci exists; contact with viable microbes is required for transmission. Gonococci survive on surfaces outside the human body only for short periods of time (probably minutes). Although organisms can be cultured from environmental sources (e.g., toilet seats) for up to 3 hours after artificial inoculation in large numbers, viable gonococci have not been recovered from random samplings in public restrooms.[117]

Gonococcal conjunctivitis can be acquired nonvenereally,[183] vulvovaginitis potentially could be acquired when a child sleeps in the same bed with an infected family member,[117] and sharing of bath towels and other similar objects has been suspected as the cause of epidemics in prepubescent girls living together.[279] However, nonsexual transmission rarely occurs and never should be presumed without extensive investigation of the social setting of the infected child.[217]

The risk of a male acquiring urethral infection after a single episode of vaginal intercourse with an infected female is estimated to be 20 percent. With four exposures, the risk increases to 60 to 80 percent. The prevalence of infection in females named as sexual contacts of males with gonococcal urethritis has been reported to be 50 to 90 percent.[143, 149]

Microbiology

Neisseria spp. are aerobic, gram-negative, nonmotile, non–spore-forming cocci that occur in pairs (diplococci) with adjacent sides flattened. They have the typical gram-negative microbial outer membrane overlying a thin peptidoglycan layer and cytoplasmic membrane. The species lacks a true polysaccharide capsule but produces a surface polyphosphate that provides a hydrophilic, negatively charged surface.[220] In Gram stains of clinical specimens, the microbes frequently are observed within phagocytes.[274]

Gonococci are able to use glucose, lactate, and pyruvate as carbon sources but cannot use other carbohydrates, which is the basis for the carbohydrate utilization tests used for speciation of *Neisseria* (Table 94–1). Catalase and cytochrome oxidase are produced by the gonococcus, as in most *Neisseria* spp., but gonococci do not produce appreciable amounts of superoxide dismutase. Growth is optimal in a 5 percent CO_2 atmosphere at 35 to 37° C and a pH of 6.5 to 7.5. Gonococci do not survive below pH 6.0, grow poorly below 30° C, and do not survive above 40° C.

Neisseria spp. require enriched media, including free iron, to support their growth. Multiple colony types are evident when a single isolate is grown on clear agar. Small convex glistening colonies are piliated, whereas larger, flatter colonies are nonpiliated. In vitro passage usually results in loss of pili. Under low-power microscopy, some colonies appear opaque or granular, and others are transparent. The former represent colonies in which most cells express one or more opacity-associated proteins (Opa), whereas in the latter colonies, most cells do not express these proteins.[34, 39, 168, 281, 288, 289, 300]

CULTURE FROM CLINICAL SPECIMENS

The organisms usually are cultured on chocolate blood agar in an atmosphere enriched by carbon dioxide. If the clinical

TABLE 94–1 ■ BIOCHEMICAL CHARACTERISTICS DIFFERENTIATING SPECIES OF THE GENUS *NEISSERIA*

	N. gonorrhoeae	*N. meningitidis*	*N. sicca*	*N. subflava*	*N. flavescens*	*N. mucosa*	*N. lactamica*
Acid from							
Glucose	+	+	+	+	–	+	+
Maltose	–	+	+	+	–	+	–
Sucrose	–	–	+	±	–	+	–
Lactose	–	–	–	–	–	–	+
Polysaccharide Produced from 5% sucrose	0	0	+	±	+	+	0
Reduction of							
Nitrate	–	–	–	–	–	+	–
Nitrite	–	±	+	+	+	+	+
Pigment	–	–	±	+	+	+	–
Extra CO_2 for growth	+	+	–	–	–	–	–

specimen has been obtained from a highly contaminated site (e.g., rectum, cervix), a selective medium containing nystatin, vancomycin, trimethoprim, and colistin (e.g., modified Thayer-Martin medium) to suppress contaminating flora allows the growth of most *Neisseria* spp. One must remember that a few strains of gonococci are inhibited by vancomycin (see later).[34, 205] Chocolate agar without antimicrobial agents is preferred if the culture is from a usually sterile area such as blood, cerebrospinal fluid (CSF), synovial fluid, or a skin lesion. Gonococcal colonies usually are evident on agar plates within 24 to 48 hours after inoculation. Frequent propagation is necessary to maintain isolates because viability is lost rapidly after 48 hours of growth.

Because gonococci cannot tolerate drying, clinical specimens must be plated as soon as possible onto appropriate media. Transport bottles that contain medium and a CO_2-enriched atmosphere should be used if definitive processing of the specimen must be delayed. Transport bottles should be maintained upright to preserve the CO_2 atmosphere.

In addition to sugar fermentation patterns (see Table 94–1) and oxidase positivity, other biochemical reactions also can be used to differentiate between *Neisseria* spp. or confirm that an isolate is *N. gonorrhoeae.*[61] Enzyme substrate tests that identify the presence or absence of 1-hydroxy-prolylaminopeptidase, gamma-glutamyl aminotransferase, and beta-galactosidase enzymes are available as an adjunctive means of confirmation.[84] Gonococci possess only the former. These reactions alone will not distinguish *N. gonorrhoeae* from several commensal *Neisseria* spp. Antigen-detection–based tests, including fluorescent antibody staining, also can be used to confirm the identity of an isolate as *N. gonorrhoeae.*[169] Tests based on detection of gonococcal nucleic acid sequences, which are being used increasingly for diagnostic purposes, also can be used to confirm the identify of gonococcal isolates from cultures (see "Diagnostic Testing" and "Medicolegal Issues" later).

GENETIC CHARACTERISTICS

Gonococci have a circular chromosome of 2219 kb, which is about one half the size of the *Escherichia coli* genome.[93] Piliated gonococcal cells (the natural in vivo state) are competent for genetic transformation by exogenous DNA at all stages of growth.[24] Only homologous DNA is taken into the cell.[100] Gonococci are highly autolytic and release DNA in a biologically active form. Thus, different strains are readily able to exchange genetic material. Such exchange can lead to further genetic and phenotypic diversity, which helps maintain the species in its human hosts and facilitates transfer of chromosomal antibiotic resistance genes.[262]

A 36-kb conjugal plasmid is present in many gonococci. It efficiently mobilizes its own transfer and other non–self-mobilizable plasmids (e.g., the 4.5- and 7.5-kb penicillinase plasmids), but not chromosomal genes.[23, 251] Extrachromosomal, nonplasmid DNA circles recently have been identified in wild-type gonococcal isolates. They may play a role in gene recombination, amplification of chromosomal genes, and transformation.[17]

Gonococci possess multiple restriction endonucleases and their corresponding DNA methylases.[287] No bacteriophages for *N. gonorrhoeae* are known, and no drug resistance transposon systems have been identified.[279] The species is relatively nonmutagenic and lacks photoreactivation and error-prone repair systems.[45]

The entire *N. gonorrhoeae* strain FA1090 is being sequenced. A macrorestriction map with the positions of many genetic markers has been available since 1991.[93, 231]

STRAIN TYPING

The ability to differentiate one strain from another permits investigation of the epidemiology of transmission of gonorrhea and assessment of virulence factors. Numerous methods have been applied to gonococci.

Auxotyping classifies strains according to their ability to grow or not grow in the absence of 11 specific compounds, including amino acids (e.g., arginine, proline), purines, and pyrimidines (e.g., hypoxanthine, uracil), and other nutrients (e.g., thiamine). Approximately 20 auxotype phenotypes are recognized. Genetic studies have shown that multiple mutations in the same biochemical pathway can lead to the same phenotype, such that a single auxotype can represent many genotypes.[269] Auxotypes are stable in vitro, however, and organisms cultured from sexual partners are of a similar auxotype.[48, 52] The auxotype of greatest epidemiologic importance is designated arginine-, hypoxanthine-, and uracil-negative (AHU^-). Such strains are unable to grow in the absence of these compounds. AHU^- strains typically are more resistant to killing by normal human serum, are more likely to cause asymptomatic infections in males, and are found more frequently in patients with disseminated infection.[102] AHU^- strains often are vancomycin-susceptible.[205]

Numerous serotyping schemes have been attempted,[62] but the best and most widely available serologic technique is based on antigenic heterogeneity of the porin protein (formerly called protein I) contained in the outer membrane of the gonococcus.[10, 160, 172, 260, 261] Two immunochemically distinct serogroups, PorA and PorB, exist and can be subdivided into serovars by using sets of monoclonal antibodies. Serovars remain stable in vitro and are designated IA-x or IB-x, where *x* is the numeral of the serovar. At least 26 IA and 31 IB serotypes have been identified.[58] Serotyping can be combined with auxotyping to further discriminate among gonococcal strains.[148, 236] Limitations of auxotype-serovar classification include restricted supplies of reagents and batch-to-batch variation in monoclonal antibodies. In addition, common serovars may have such significant genetic diversity that this typing method may not provide sufficient discrimination for some epidemiologic evaluations.

Antimicrobial susceptibility patterns (antibiograms) have been used in the past as an adjunctive tool, but the usefulness of this method for long-term epidemiologic studies has been compromised by the ability of gonococci to transfer genetic elements for antibiotic resistance between strains.[279]

Genotyping methods have been applied to *N. gonorrhoeae* in the past 2 decades. Simple restriction endonuclease methods with rare-cutting enzymes[107, 235] have been supplanted by polymerase chain reaction (PCR)-based methods and pulsed-field gel electrophoresis (PFGE). Arbitrarily primed PCR (AP-PCR) has been used, but the reproducibility of this method can be problematic.[44, 188] PFGE and Opa typing, which involves PCR primers that are able to generate DNA bands from each of the 11 *opa* genes, followed by restriction enzyme digestion, each appear able to produce higher discrimination among gonococcal isolates than does serotyping combined with AP-PCR.[188]

Sequencing of the *por* gene also appears to be highly discriminatory between strains,[74] and PCR amplification of the *por* gene with restriction enzyme digestion provides discrimination similar to combined auxotyping-serotyping.[97] Repetitive-element sequence–based PCR (rep-PCR), which uses longer primers than does AP-PCR and is a more reproducible method, correlates well with PFGE for analysis of gonococcal strains.[236] Rep-PCR is a rapid method that can be performed directly on colonies without having to purify microbial DNA, which is required with most other genotyping methods.[309]

Pathogenesis

A continuously expanding body of literature describes the pathogenesis of *N. gonorrhoeae*. Gonococci are able to survive in the urethra in the face of hydrodynamic forces that tend to wash other microbes away and persist there despite close proximity and even attachment to the hoards of neutrophils that respond to their presence. These observations suggest an ability to adhere to mucosal epithelia and evade the host's acute innate immune response. Individuals also can have repeated infections by the same gonococcal strain, thus suggesting that the organism can thwart established local immune responses, probably through frequent antigenic variation. The tissue damage that occurs in the fallopian tubes during salpingitis implies one or more directly toxic moieties or factors that can trigger a deleterious host response.[109, 279] Much progress has been made in understanding the mechanisms that account for these properties.

Clinical studies largely have focused on the adaptation of organisms to specific anatomic areas (rectum, blood, endocervix, etc.) in older adolescents and adults. However, this information probably holds true for most infections in infants and children. Recent insight into the molecular pathogenesis of gonococcal infection has been derived from in vitro molecular studies involving cell lines and fallopian tube organ cultures and experimental infections in human males.[69, 195, 196, 244] Currently, no adequate animal models of gonococcal infection exist.

After adherence to host epithelial cells, some gonococcal microbes are able to invade, replicate intracellularly inside phagosomes/vacuoles, and exit the basal (but not lateral) surface of the cell via exocytosis[196, 202, 215] (Fig. 94–2). Adjacent nonepithelial cells are sloughed, probably because of the toxicity of lipo-oligosaccharide (LOS) and peptidoglycans.[124] Mucosal cell damage and submucosal invasion are followed by an influx of neutrophils, with submucosal microabscess formation and exudation of purulent materials into the lumen of the infected organ.[307]

The initial steps in pathogenesis may result from the synergistic effects of pili, Opa proteins, and porin proteins.[18, 126] Close interactions of *N. gonorrhoeae* with mucosal cells, erythrocytes, spermatozoa, and polymorphonuclear cells are well described. Species specificity is demonstrated by greater adherence of gonococci to human cells than to nonhuman cells. The best-characterized microbial factors and host responses that appear to play important roles in pathogenesis are discussed in the following sections.

VIRULENCE FACTORS

Characteristics of *N. gonorrhoeae* strains that appear to have a role in virulence include (1) pili, (2) opacity proteins, (3) porin protein, (4) the ability to survive in low iron environments, (5) IgA protease, (6) LOS, (7) cell wall peptidoglycan, and (8) reduction modifiable protein (Rmp). Many other gonococcal gene products and molecular systems have been identified, and further elucidation of the roles of many of them in virulence probably is forthcoming.

THE PRESENCE OF PILI. Gonococci predominately are piliated in vivo and express type IV pili. Pili essentially cover the whole surface of the cell and are arranged in individual fibrils or fibrillar aggregates. Pili consist primarily of polymers of an 18-kd subunit now denoted as PilE. A single pilus is approximately 6 nm in diameter and up to several micrometers in length.[202] Each may contain thousands of PilE subunits.[41] The PilC protein is present in lower numbers in the pilus but appears to be the key pilus adhesin. PilC interaction with CD46 molecules, which are present on most human cells and serve as receptors for C3b, C4b, and measles and other viruses, appears to be a key step in the initiation of microbial adherence to host cells.[42, 165, 170, 255, 257]

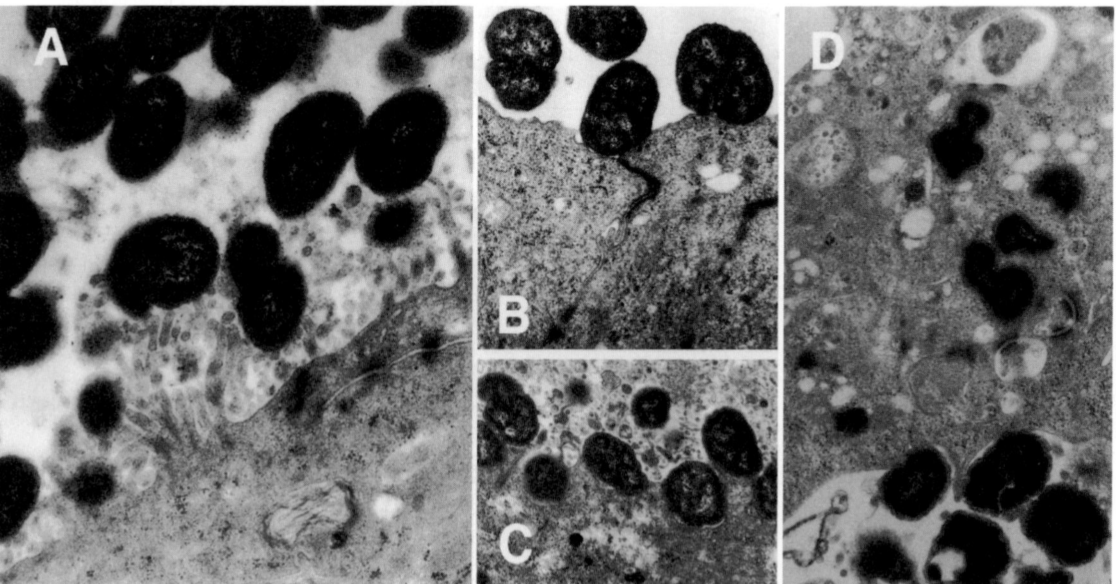

FIGURE 94–2 ■ Electron micrographs of *Neisseria gonorrhoeae* strain MS11 interactions with polarized T84 human epithelial cell monolayers. At early stages of infection, the microbes adhere to the apical plasma membrane as microcolonies. Adherent bacteria are surrounded by a matrix of microvilli *(A)*. Bacteria subsequently disperse from the microcolony and adhere as a monolayer in which bacterial and host-cell membranes are tightly apposed *(B* and *C)*. The region of contact between the bacteria and the host-cell membrane enlarges *(C)*, with subsequent internalization of the microbes *(D)*. Bacteria then traverse the host cell and exit via the basolateral membrane *(D)*. (Photographs by Magdalene So, with permission, from the *Annual Review of Cell and Developmental Biology,* Volume 16. © 2000 by Annual Reviews. www.AnnualReviews.org.)

Binding of pili to a host-cell membrane induces at least two responses in the host cell: Ca^{2+} release from intracellular stores[164] and cytoskeletal rearrangements with the formation of cortical plaques that represent an accumulation of actin, ezrin, and other phosphotyrosine-containing proteins.[199, 200] The latter results in elongation of the microvilli that embrace the microbe. Plaque formation appears to be induced by retraction of the attached pilus, and retraction is dependent on another pilus protein designated PilT.[201]

Gonococcal pili undergo both phase variation (switching from piliated to nonpiliated states) and high-frequency antigenic variation.[41] These variations occur during natural infection and in vitro passage.[264] Pili have a common N-terminal domain, semivariable domains in the midportion, and two hypervariable regions in the carboxyl terminus of the pilin protein subunit.[280] Relatively invariant regions occur between the variable domains. The pilin protein consists of 159 to 160 amino acids. A disulfide bridge is formed by cysteine residues at amino acids 121 and 151.

The genetic mechanism of pilus antigenic variation has been studied extensively. The chromosome contains either one or two complete pilin genes. The expressed gene contains an intact promoter region, a ribosome binding site, and a seven–amino acid signal sequence in addition to the pilin sequence. Scattered around the chromosome are six to eight loci that contain varying portions of the pilin sequence without the promoter region or the 5′ end of the structural gene. Some loci may contain many incomplete pilin sequences arranged head-to-tail that differ slightly from one another. Movement of these sequences into the active expression site through nonreciprocal combination events results in antigenic variation of the pilus protein. If recombination leads to a faulty pilin subunit product that cannot be processed into a mature pilus, the progeny of that organism become nonpiliated (phase variation). Subsequent recombination events can allow reversion back to the piliated phase.[132, 203, 204, 219, 263, 280, 290]

In addition to promoting adhesion to epithelial cells, pili also provide a twitching motility, are involved in DNA transformation, and may play a role in resistance to ingestion by phagocytic cells.[202]

OPACITY-ASSOCIATED PROTEINS. Opa proteins also influence adherence of the gonococcus to host cells. The isolation of particular Opa protein phenotypes from different anatomic sites or at different times during the menstrual cycle has suggested that these proteins contribute to the ability of the organism to succeed in a given niche. Opa proteins (formerly designated protein II) are a set of as many as 12 related proteins that are variably present in gonococcal outer membranes. Opa proteins are 24 to 28 kd in size and confer increased opacity on colonies of organisms by promoting adherence of the organisms to one another. A given strain has the capacity to make at least 10 different Opa proteins but appears to express no more than 5 at the same time. Some cells express no Opa proteins. Like pili, Opa proteins undergo both antigenic and phase variation. Both types of variation can occur within a single colony, such that sector variations in opacity can be seen.[26, 279, 288, 289]

Each *opa* gene is present as a complete gene with its own promoter and is transcribed at all times. Phase variation in expression occurs at the translational level. Each gene has a varying number of pentameric CTCTT repeat units adjacent to the ATG start codon. When the number of repeats is divisible by three, the transcribed mRNA is translationally in frame and the Opa protein is expressed. The number of pentameric repeats is subject to high-frequency variation. Antigenic variation results from recombinations between the two hypervariable regions in each of the *opa* genes.[73, 283–285] Two classes of host-cell receptors for Opa proteins have been identified. Heparan sulfate–proteoglycan (HSPG) receptors are present on epithelial cells and interact with one particular Opa protein variant (Opa_{50}). HSPG binding can stimulate the lipid hydrolysis enzymes phosphatidylcholine-specific phospholipase C and acid sphingomyelinase and thereby lead to clathrin-independent endocytosis. HSPG-Opa binding also can lead to interactions with serum factors such as vitronectin and fibronectin, which then mediate endocytosis via host-cell integrin receptors. The CD66 family is present on epithelial cells and neutrophils, recognizes many different Opa proteins, and mediates nonopsonic phagocytosis, which is distinct from antibody- and complement-mediated phagocytosis.[89, 90, 122, 177, 202, 297]

PORIN PROTEIN. Formerly designated protein I, porin protein is the most common gonococcal outer-membrane protein. Porin is 34 to 36 kd, is exposed on the surface, exists as a trimer in the membrane, and is physically proximate to LOS and Rmp.[27, 141] The trimer forms an anion-specific pore in the bacterial membrane that allows the entry of small, water-soluble molecules.[310] The *por* locus has two alleles that encode chemically and immunologically distinct classes of porin protein—PorA and PorB—that are similar to porin proteins in other gram-negative bacteria. A given strain expresses only PorA or PorB, and many antigenic variants of both exist (thereby forming the basis for serotyping).[47, 172]

The porin trimer appears to translocate into the host-cell membrane and is able to disrupt neutrophil degranulation, the oxidative burst, and phagosome maturation,[133, 189, 209] in addition to induction of apoptosis in epithelial cells and neutrophils in vitro.[212] Exposure to gonococcal porin protein induces the typical structural and biochemical changes seen in apoptotic cells.[211] Porin translocation permits rapid Ca^{2+} influx into the host cell from the external environment.[212] Porin proteins also may play a role in endocytosis mediated by the binding of HSPG and Opa protein[18] and down-regulation of complement by binding with C4b-binding protein.[237]

THE ABILITY TO UTILIZE IRON. Iron is an essential nutrient for *N. gonorrhoeae,* and in host tissues, iron is sequestered in hemin compounds as ferritin or is bound to lactoferrin or transferrin. The species does not produce any siderophores but relies on an iron-repressible system that scavenges iron from transferrin, lactoferrin, and hemoglobin. This system is composed of numerous proteins, some of which serve as receptors for the aforementioned iron-bearing ligands.[25, 64, 79, 302] The ability to use iron from transferrin is a general property of pathogenic *Neisseria* spp. Transferrin- and lactoferrin-binding proteins are required for gonococci to cause experimental urethritis.[78]

IgA PROTEASE. All gonococci (and meningococci, but not nonpathogenic *Neisseria*) make a protease that cleaves both serum and secretory IgA1 (but not IgA2) at the hinge region with the release of Fab and Fc fragments. This protease may help the organism evade host IgA at the mucosal surface, especially early in secondary infections when preexisting antibodies may be present. However, mutant strains without the IgA protease have limited ability to grow inside epithelial cells. The protease appears to cleave a host-cell intracellular protein (LAMP1) that is involved in phagosome compartmentalization.[185] IgA1 protease is not required for gonococci to cause experimental urethritis,[159] thus suggesting that its intraphagosome function may be more important in pathogenesis.

LIPO-OLIGOSACCHARIDE. Gonococci express LOS complexes of 3 to 7 kd on their cell surface. LOS consists of a lipid A moiety and a core polysaccharide composed of ketodeoxyoctanoic acid, heptose, glucose, galactose, glucosamine, galactosamine, or any combination of these constituents.[128] The lack of a long polymeric sugar attached to the core distinguishes LOS from the lipopolysaccharides of other gram-negative bacteria. The core sugar antigens of LOS are subject to intrastrain and interstrain variation, and a single strain may express as many as six variants of LOS.[92, 127] Numerous genes are involved in LOS synthesis; these genes undergo high-frequency phase variation similar to *opa* genes.[121] LOS terminal sugars mimic the structure of certain human glycosphingolipids.[128]

Gonococci with predominately short LOS appear to be more sensitive to killing by human serum but also more able to invade eukaryotic cells. Strains with longer LOS are more serum-resistant but noninvasive.[298] Longer LOS moieties are sialylated readily with host neuraminic acid by a bacterial sialyltransferase that appears to shield both LOS and porin molecules from antibody binding, thus providing protection from complement-mediated killing in serum.[32, 303]

Because strains of *N. gonorrhoeae* isolated from blood are serum-resistant, this property may be important for invasion of the host. In addition, patients with defects in the complement cascade are susceptible to recurrent episodes of gonococcemia, which suggests that the bactericidal qualities of serum are important. Therefore, LOS should be considered a virulence factor. Evidence suggests that LOS from serum-sensitive strains can activate the classical complement pathway and may do so in the absence of antibody.[266]

CELL WALL PEPTIDOGLYCAN. Gonococci shed membrane fragments with peptidoglycan into their environment during exponential growth. Peptidoglycan monomers have numerous biologic properties, including activation of complement and modulation of mononuclear cell proliferation. These fragments also damage fallopian tube mucosa in organ culture, thus suggesting a pathogenic role for the compounds in invasive disease.[124, 196]

REDUCTION MODIFIABLE PROTEIN. Rmp (formerly designated protein III) is an antigenically conserved, 30- to 31-kD protein that is present in all pathogenic *Neisseria*. Rmp is located proximate to LOS and porin in the outer membrane. Antibodies that bind to Rmp epitopes block the bactericidal effect of the complement-fixing IgM antibodies that recognize LOS. Women with preexisting anti-Rmp antibodies appear to be more susceptible to the development of infection than are those without such antibodies.[246, 247, 279]

CHARACTERISTICS OF STRAINS CAUSING DISSEMINATED DISEASE

The increased virulence of some strains is suggested by observations such as those of a microepidemic of gonorrhea involving one asymptomatically infected male and eight female contacts.[136] Seven of the women were infected symptomatically, and four experienced disseminated infection. Clinical data repeatedly have shown that most infected women have asymptomatic infection and dissemination occurs relatively rarely.

Strains of *N. gonorrhoeae* obtained from adult patients with disseminated disease usually are less susceptible to the bactericidal activity of sera[35, 71, 244, 245, 268] (see discussion of LOS earlier). These strains have an atypical growth pattern on agar[206] that reflects the absence of Opa protein expression, which suggests that the genetic variation described provides rapid adaptation to different niches and probably helps organisms elude the host response.[22] Nutritional requirements usually include arginine, uracil, and hypoxanthine (AHU⁻), substances not required for the growth of other strains.[171] A high degree of sensitivity to penicillin has been characteristic of most strains from patients with disseminated disease.[306] Many also are susceptible to vancomycin, which may prevent their detection in selective media but not in the usual media used for blood culture.

HOST RESPONSE

The adult response to local and systemic infection with *N. gonorrhoeae* has been investigated extensively, but no such studies have been performed on infected children. Gonococcal infections usually are characterized by intense inflammation that involves neutrophilic and mononuclear granulocytes. The vast majority of gonococcal cells ingested by neutrophils are killed.[49] Gonococci are susceptible to the oxidative products produced by neutrophils but also can be killed efficiently by nonoxidative products such as cathepsin G.[267]

An intact complement system is essential for successful eradication of the organism. Persons with inherited or acquired complement deficiencies may be predisposed to disseminated gonococcal infection, as is the case with meningococcal infections. Appproximately 13 percent of patients with disseminated disease have complement deficiencies.[104, 221]

Adherence of gonococci in vitro induces the activation of nuclear factor κB and activator protein 1, which leads to upregulation of mRNA for and release of a number of cytokines and chemokines: macrophage colony-stimulating factor, tumor necrosis factor–α (TNF-α), tumor growth factor–β, monocyte chemoattractant protein 1, and inteleukin-1β (IL-1β), IL-6, and IL-8.[216] Intra-urethral challenge leads to increased levels of IL-8, IL-6, and TNF-α in urine before the onset of symptoms and in plasma at the onset of symptoms.[238]

Multiple episodes of gonorrhea may occur in a single individual in a short time, even by the same strain. The antigenic diversity and ease of altering the antigenicity of both pili and opacity proteins undoubtedly contribute to the insufficiency of the host response in preventing reinfection.

Circulating humoral antibody to the infecting strain is measured by an assay of bactericidal antibody and is present in most persons who have prolonged mucosal colonization with *N. gonorrhoeae*.[153, 167] In addition, women in whom PID develops usually produce bactericidal antibody during the infection. IgA- and IgG-blocking antibodies against some gonococcal antigens appear to block killing of the bacteria mediated by otherwise bactericidal IgG and IgM antibodies (see Rmp information earlier).[244] Serum antibody responses are greater in patients with invasive disease (e.g., bacteremia, salpingitis).

Secretory IgA antibody is present in the urethral exudate of men with gonorrhea and in the genital secretions of women with gonorrhea.[222] The development of local IgA antibody occurs more rapidly and is more transient than is development of the serum bactericidal response. The microbial IgA1 protease is not required for infection but may play a role in reinfection.

A cellular immune response to gonococcal antigens in patients with uncomplicated gonorrhea has been demonstrated in vitro.[180] The significance of this response in the control or prevention of infection is unknown.

Perinatal Gonococcal Infections

Since the 1970s, health clinics have encouraged the routine screening of sexually active women for gonorrhea. Such screening is especially important during pregnancy, and rates of gonorrhea in pregnant women range from rare to approximately 10 percent. Adolescent girls have an even higher prevalence of gonorrhea than that of older women of child-bearing age do (see Fig. 94–1), and this prevalence probably translates into higher rates of gonorrhea in pregnant adolescents. Rates of gonococcal infection in neonates reflect the frequency of infection in pregnant women. Recognition of gonorrhea early in pregnancy identifies a population at risk that should be monitored sequentially for reinfection throughout pregnancy.[161]

The spectrum of infection with *N. gonorrhoeae* appears to be similar in pregnant and nonpregnant women. Most women are asymptomatic. Pharyngeal infection seems to occur more commonly during pregnancy, perhaps reflecting altered sexual practices. One study reported that 39 percent of patients with *N. gonorrhoeae* at any site had concurrent involvement of the pharynx and that 30 percent had pharyngeal infection as the sole manifestation.[77] In adolescent girls, pregnancy and menstruation are associated with disseminated disease.[142]

Gonorrheal infection puts both the mother and infant at risk for the development of other forms of gonococcal disease. Pregnant women have an increased risk of developing gonococcal septic arthritis, and most such cases occur during the third trimester or in the immediate postpartum period.[37, 142] Although the incidence of gonococcal arthritis is low, many cases have occurred in pregnant adolescents.

Gonococcal PID and acute salpingitis also may complicate the pregnancy of an infected woman.[116] These complications usually occur during the first trimester and have been associated with a high rate of fetal loss. An increased incidence of postpartum fever in women with untreated gonorrhea also has been noted. A new mother with complications of peripartum gonorrhea may have difficulty providing care for her child.[157]

Maternal gonococcal infection has been associated with abnormalities in labor and delivery that may affect the infant adversely. Prolonged rupture of membranes, premature delivery, chorioamnionitis, funisitis, and a clinical diagnosis of sepsis occur frequently in infants with *N. gonorrhoeae* detected in the gastric aspirate during delivery.[7, 101, 135, 252]

Hazards to the fetus that are posed by maternal gonorrhea include septic abortion, perinatal death, prematurity, perinatal distress, and premature rupture of membranes. Table 94–2 tabulates the proportions in six studies of infants born to infected mothers who experienced these problems. A controlled study in an area of high prevalence of gonorrhea found that maternal infection with *N. gonorrhoeae* was associated significantly with preterm birth and that 14 percent of preterm births in this population were attributable to gonococcal infection.[103]

GONOCOCCAL OPHTHALMIA NEONATORUM

Epidemiology

Researchers have recognized for centuries that ophthalmia neonatorum occurs in infants born to women with a vaginal discharge. Recommendations for flushing the eyes of a newborn commonly were given before the 20th century.[198] In the late 1800s, Neisser helped establish the relationship between the gonococcus and neonatal ophthalmia.

By 1881, Dr. Carl Sigmund Franz Credé had recognized that asymptomatic disease in the mother was a potential source of infection.[83] Gonorrhea was highly prevalent in Europe, and Credé described an increased incidence in patients from lower socioeconomic backgrounds. Mechanical cleansing of the birth canal failed to protect the infant from gonococcal ophthalmia neonatorum (GON), which was occurring in approximately 10 percent of newborns in major cities. The infection was the cause of a large proportion of admissions to schools for the blind.[16] Credé described the technique of instillation of 2 percent silver nitrate ($AgNO_3$) into the infant's conjunctival sac, which remains one method for recommended preventive procedures today.

By 1930, most states in the United States required that all newborns receive $AgNO_3$ prophylaxis (i.e., the Credé procedure). At present, prophylaxis of some form is required by most states. GON decreased as a cause of admission to schools for the blind in the United States, from an average of 24 percent from 1906 to 1911 to 0.5 percent from 1951 to 1955.

The worldwide decline in adult gonorrhea in the 1950s probably contributed to the decreased recognition of disease in newborns during that period. The incidence of GON rose in the 1960s and 1970s along with the increased incidence of gonorrhea in the general population and was very high in some developing nations.[177] In Los Angeles, California, the rate rose from 9 per 100,000 live births in 1957 to 1958 to 56 per 100,000 live births in 1962 to 1963. In a New York hospital between 1970 and 1973, a rate of 145 per 100,000 births was reported, and in a hospital in North Carolina during 1969 and 1970, a rate of 265 per 100,000 live births was proved by culture.[278] In the late 1970s and 1980s, GON again subsided in developed countries, but it has remained a major problem in underdeveloped nations.

Factors associated with higher rates of GON include lower socioeconomic class of the mother. An increased incidence of GON in infants of unwed mothers and mothers who have not had prenatal care also may exist.[275] Previous treatment of gonorrhea during pregnancy likewise is associated with an increased incidence of GON.[161]

TABLE 94–2 ■ OUTCOME OF PREGNANCY IN MOTHERS WHO WERE INFECTED WITH *NEISSERIA GONORRHOEAE* AT DELIVERY

Outcome	Charles et al[63a] (N = 14)*	Sarrel and Pruett[261a] (N = 37)	Israel et al.[157] (N =39)	Amstey and Steadman[7] (N = 222)*	Edwards et al.[101] (N = 19)*	Handsfield and Holmes[136] (N = 12)*	Totals
Normal or term infant	—	13 (35%)	30 (77%)	142 (64%)	7 (37%)	—	192/317 (61%)
Aborted	—	13 (35%)	1 (2%)	24 (11%)	—	—	38/298 (13%)
Perinatal death	—	3 (8%)	1 (2%)	15 (8%)	2 (11%)	—	21/317 (7%)
Premature	—	6 (17%)	5 (13%)	49 (22%)	8 (42%)	8 (67%)	76/329 (23%)
Perinatal distress	—	—	2 (5%)	—	2 (10%)	—	4/58 (7%)
Premature rupture of membranes	6 (43%)	8 (21%)	—	52 (26%)	12 (63%)	9 (75%)	87/304 (29%)

*Data were provided in which the outcomes of pregnancies of mothers not infected with *N. gonorrhoeae* were shown to be significantly more favorable.

The incidence of prematurity in infants with GON often is reported to be higher. Whether it is due to an adverse effect of gonorrhea on the pregnancy or because GON may be recognized more readily in premature infants has not been established. Premature rupture of membranes appears to increase the risk of GON occurring.

Prevention

At present, prophylaxis for GON continues to be accomplished mainly through the local instillation of either 1 percent $AgNO_3$ or one of several antimicrobial agents. In the United States, prophylaxis for GON is recommended for all infants immediately after birth and is required by law in most states. Currently, prophylaxis regimens using a 1 percent solution of $AgNO_3$, 1 percent tetracycline ointment, or 0.5 percent erythromycin ophthalmic ointment are considered equally effective. Each is available in single-dose units, which are preferred over multidose tubes. One unit should be instilled into the eyes of every neonate as soon as possible after delivery and definitely within 1 hour after birth. Povidone-iodine 2.5 percent solution also may be effective, but more studies are needed before it is recommended for routine use.[5] Bacitracin does not appear to be an effective agent for prevention of GON.[123]

The efficacy of tetracycline and erythromycin in the prevention of tetracycline-resistant and penicillinase-producing *N. gonorrhoeae* ophthalmia (such strains are often tetracycline-resistant as well) is unknown. Both probably are effective because of the high concentration of drug in these preparations. Studies of these agents for prevention of *C. trachomatis* ophthalmia have been conflicting. Povidone-iodine may be more effective in preventing *C. trachomatis* ophthalmia than is topical $AgNO_3$ or erythromycin. None of these agents prevents chlamydial colonization of the nasopharynx. Some Western countries with low rates of gonococcal and chlamydial infection do not recommend routine ophthalmic prophylaxis.[5, 131]

Numerous studies have compared the efficacy of $AgNO_3$ and no prophylaxis or another agent in the prevention of GON, and these studies have been reviewed elsewhere.[65, 223, 253] Until the late 1900s, most studies of the efficacy of $AgNO_3$ were not randomized and did not document rates of perinatal gonococcal exposure in the infants studied. Such studies involving large numbers of infants consistently have shown lower rates of GON in treated groups than in untreated controls. Observations of a decreased frequency of blindness from GON in the population during the last half century, even during periods of increased rates of gonorrhea in women of child-bearing age, further support the benefits of $AgNO_3$ prophylaxis.

In a randomized trial reported in 1988 of Kenyan infants born to mothers with gonorrhea, rates of GON were 42 percent in the control group, 7 percent in the 1 percent $AgNO_3$ group (83% reduction), and 3 percent in the 1 percent tetracycline group (93% reduction). The two treatment arms were not statistically different.[179] In a randomized trial in the United States involving infants born to women without gonococcal infection, infants treated with 1 percent $AgNO_3$ had a 39 percent lower rate (statistically significant) of conjunctivitis of any type in the first 2 months of life than did infants receiving no prophylaxis. Infants treated with 0.5 percent erythromycin ointment in this trial had a 31 percent reduction in comparison to control infants, but this result was not statistically significant.[19]

The major advantages to the use of $AgNO_3$ for prophylaxis are the lack of allergic potential, the absence of development of bacterial resistance to the compound, and very low cost. Two newborn nursery–based outbreaks of erythromycin-resistant staphylococcal conjunctivitis have been associated with the use of erythromycin eye ointment as ocular prophylaxis, but the outbreaks remitted when $AgNO_3$ was substituted. Disadvantages include the problem of conjunctival irritation along with the development of exudate in numerous babies and the fact that it is not effective treatment if infection already is established when drops are instilled into the eye. A solution of $AgNO_3$ that becomes concentrated may cause ophthalmic injury, but this problem largely has been alleviated by dispensing each dose in ampules, which prevents evaporation.

Failure of $AgNO_3$ prophylaxis (as well as other agents for prevention of GON) does occur. If gonococcal infection of the eye has begun before birth, $AgNO_3$ is not expected to prevent further progression. The increased risk of development of infection that has been observed in association with premature rupture of membranes could be predicted because of the exposure to infection before actual delivery. In some cases of premature rupture of membranes, active GON can be present at the time of birth. Improper administration of $AgNO_3$, such that the solution does not reach the conjunctival sac or irrigation is performed too quickly after instillation, and inadvertent omission of prophylaxis also can lead to apparent failure.

In spite of these problems, the use of 1 percent $AgNO_3$ remains a widely accepted, carefully evaluated, and safe form of GON prophylaxis. The occasional failure of $AgNO_3$ prophylaxis emphasizes that it is preferable to prevent GON through identification and treatment of pregnant women.

INFANTS BORN TO MOTHERS WITH GONOCOCCAL INFECTION. Because of the potential for failure of topical regimens to prevent GON when infection already is established and the increased risk for such failure to occur in infants born to mothers with known gonococcal infection, these infants should be treated with a single parenteral dose of a third-generation cephalosporin (see "Treatment" later).

Clinical Features

The newborn eye is subject to colonization with numerous bacterial organisms that cause infections that are usually clinically mild, nonprogressive, and characterized by conjunctival discharge. The bacteria most commonly associated with conjunctival discharge are *Haemophilus influenzae, Streptococcus pneumoniae, Staphylococcus aureus, Neisseria cinerea, Klebsiella pneumoniae,* enterococci, and *C. trachomatis.*[96, 175] Viral causes include herpes simplex virus and adenoviruses. In contrast, infection of the eye of a newborn with *N. gonorrhoeae* results in disease of a severity that, though frequently mild, can be rapidly destructive and lead to scarring and blindness. The chemical conjunctivitis that can result from $AgNO_3$ prophylaxis typically starts within 6 to 24 hours after administration and disappears within 24 to 48 hours.

Colonization during delivery is followed by an incubation period of 2 to 5 and usually less than 3 days, but cases occasionally may be recognized for 2 to 3 weeks after delivery.[114] A discharge typically develops that initially is watery but usually becomes thick and mucopurulent within a short time and may contain blood. The disease generally is bilateral. Early findings include prominent edema of the conjunctivae and lids, followed by edema and later ulceration of the cornea or spread to wider areas in severe cases. Rapid arrest of the disease is essential because the degree of corneal involvement determines whether vision will be preserved. Some cases are self-limited and have a benign outcome, and occasional cases of asymptomatic GON have been discovered during routine screening.[234] Perforation of the globe and panophthalmitis can result from extensive local disease. The conjunctivae may serve as a portal of entry for gonococcal septicemia, arthritis, or other manifestations of invasive disease, but such events are uncommon occurrences.

A presumptive diagnosis may be made by demonstrating typical gram-negative diplococci by Gram stain of conjunctival exudate. Because other organisms also may cause exudative infection of the conjunctivae, laboratory confirmation of the diagnosis of GON depends on culture of *N. gonorrhoeae.* In addition, a thorough physical examination and a blood culture should be performed to evaluate the infant for the presence of other distant foci of gonococcal disease or for systemic disease.

Invasive disease rarely occurs in patients with GON. Evaluation of CSF probably is unnecessary in an infant who otherwise appears to be well (see the later section "Systemic Disease in the Neonate"). Obtaining a blood culture before the administration of any antimicrobial agents (other than topically) probably is the best approach. Neonates with blood cultures that become positive for *N. gonorrhoeae* should undergo CSF evaluation for evidence of meningitis.

GONOCOCCAL SCALP ABSCESS AND OTHER LOCAL INFECTIONS

Gonococcal infections of scalp wounds that occur after fetal monitoring have been observed quite frequently.[86] The lesions may produce extensive local inflammatory disease and necrosis and can be a focus for disseminated infection. A scalp wound in a neonate should be cultured for gonococci as well as other likely pathogens, which include *Staphylococcus* spp., group B streptococci, *H. influenzae,* and gram-negative enteric flora. Herpes simplex also may be present in areas of injury to the scalp of newborns. Overall, approximately 1 in 200 births that are monitored with fetal scalp electrodes has been complicated by infection at the monitoring site.[233]

Neonatal gonococcal vulvovaginitis, proctitis, rhinitis, funisitis, and urethritis have been described but are infrequent findings.[131] Gonococcal colonization of the oropharynx or gastric fluid, or both, occurs relatively frequently in perinatally exposed infants, however. Pharyngeal colonization is present in as many as 35 percent of neonates who have GON.[112] A summary of selected studies on the incidence of neonatal gonococcal colonization and disease in exposed infants is presented in Table 94–3.

SYSTEMIC DISEASE IN THE NEONATE

Disseminated disease occurs in 1 percent or less of infants perinatally exposed to gonococcal infection[12] (see Table 94–3). Septic arthritis is the most common form of disseminated gonococcal infection in neonates. Gonococcal arthritis of the newborn was described extensively between 1900 and 1930 by Cooperman[75, 76] and Wehrbein,[301] and recent case reports suggest that the disease remains similar. Clinical findings usually become evident when the infant is 1 to 4 weeks of age. Although a few infants with gonococcal arthritis will have evidence of GON or other sites of mucosal or skin infection at the time of onset of arthritis, most do not.

The signs and symptoms of gonococcal septic arthritis are similar to those of joint infection caused by other microbes in the neonatal period, including a predominance of polyarticular involvement. Infection most frequently involves the ankles, knees, wrists, and hands.[75] The hip may be infected with minimal signs other than pseudoparesis. Involvement of a joint may include suppurative arthritis, inflammatory disease of the periarticular structures, and tenosynovitis of a joint. Leukocytosis usually occurs, and most infants have a positive culture and compatible Gram stain from the synovial fluid of the involved joint.[119]

In a hospital-associated outbreak of gonococcal polyarthritis that occurred in 1927, infections of the joint developed in 53 of 67 infected infants (79%). Other studies of outbreaks have indicated that perhaps 15 percent of children with gonorrhea acquire gonococcal arthritis. These rates probably are considerably higher than the estimated 1 to 3 percent incidence in adults and suggest an increased risk of dissemination in infants and children. For example, case reports have described gonococcal arthritis in both mother and newborn infant.[125] Prompt drainage of septic hips, along with initiation of antimicrobial therapy, is necessary because of the risk of development of aseptic necrosis of the femoral head. Long-term dysfunction from gonococcal infection of other joints is an uncommon occurrence.[76, 131, 145, 173]

Although gonococcal sepsis can develop in neonates with or without associated septic arthritis, the bacteremic phase of spread to the joints from the initial sites of infection generally is clinically silent. Premature infants seem to be more at risk for development of sepsis with bacteremia than do term infants. Meningitis has been documented but appears to be an exceedingly rare manifestation of neonatal gonococcal infection.[31, 131, 135] In the newborn period, the gastric aspirate may be cultured to determine contamination from a maternal source.

Gonococcal Disease beyond the Neonatal Period

LOWER GENITAL TRACT INFECTION IN PREPUBERTAL GIRLS

Excluding the neonatal period, gonococcal vaginitis or vulvovaginitis is the most common form of gonorrhea in

TABLE 94–3 ■ INCIDENCE OF NEONATAL GONOCOCCAL DISEASE IN EXPOSED INFANTS

Site of Neonatal Infection	Rate of Positive Cultures	Population	Reference
Conjunctiva	0–10%	Exposed infants who had $AgNO_3$ ocular prophylaxis	Edwards et al.,[101] Allen and Barrere,[4] Armstrong et al.,[10a] Laga et al.,[177]
	2–48%	Exposed infants who had no ocular prophylaxis	Rothenberg,[253] Fransen et al.,[112] Laga et al.,[177]
Orogastric fluid	26–40%	Infants of infected mothers	Handsfield et al.,[135] Edwards et al.,[101]
Oropharynx	35%	Infants with gonococcal ophthalmia	Laga et al.[177]
Disseminated disease as a proportion of all neonatal gonorrhea	0–1% (rare)	Reported series of neonatal gonococcal disease	Folland et al.,[110] Tomeh and Wilfert,[292a] Wald et al.,[299] Edwards et al.,[101] Fransen et al.[112]

prepubertal girls. In contrast to postpubertal females, the anestrogenic vaginal mucosa of prepubertal girls creates an alkaline environment that is colonized and infected more readily with *N. gonorrhoeae.* Infection of the endocervix, urethra, paraurethral and Bartholin glands, and upper genital tract occurs only rarely. Gonococcal vaginitis in prepubertal girls almost always is symptomatic, with vulvar erythema and a profuse vaginal discharge. The girl may complain of dysuria, urinary frequency, vulvar discomfort, or pain while walking.[213, 268, 271] Asymptomatic cases may occur but appear to be uncommon.

Symptoms and signs should resolve promptly within a few days after treatment is initiated, but acute manifestations may persist for several weeks if the child is not treated. The natural course of disease is for the inflammation to subside and the discharge to become scant and seropurulent. Infection may resolve spontaneously but occasionally may persist until the girl reaches puberty.

Prepubertal vulvovaginitis can be caused by numerous irritative and infectious agents, including pinworms, foreign bodies, group A streptococci, *Neisseria meningitidis, Neisseria sicca,* and *Branhamella catarrhalis* (see also Chapter 49). Vulvovaginitis can mimic urinary tract infection, and pyuria can be seen on urinalysis with gonococcal and other etiologies of vulvovaginitis.[113, 187]

Although ascending infection seldom occurs, it may result in salpingitis or peritonitis. One study found that 10 percent of girls with gonorrhea had signs compatible with peritonitis, including fever, diffuse abdominal pain, leukocytosis, and decreased bowel sounds.[43] Salpingitis and periappendicitis may cause findings similar to those of appendicitis. Therefore, perineal examination for vaginal irritation or discharge is important before performing abdominal surgery in young girls.[11]

In children with gonorrheal infection of the genitourinary tract, concomitant anorectal and tonsillopharyngeal colonization occurs commonly.[218]

LOWER GENITAL TRACT INFECTION IN POSTMENARCHEAL FEMALES

Gonococcal infections in adolescent girls are similar to those in adults. The endocervix is the primary site of urogenital infection, although the external genitalia, urethra, vulvar mucosa, and vestibular glands also may be infected. Symptoms of acute infection usually begin 3 to 5 days after exposure, with development of a profuse, purulent vaginal discharge. The vulvar tissues are inflamed, with resultant pruritus and a burning sensation. Urethritis often is present initially and can lead to dysuria with urinary frequency and urgency. Urethral discharge can be seen but is much less prominent than in males. A purulent discharge from the vestibular and paraurethral glands also may be noted.

The endocervical mucosa is edematous, inflamed, and often friable. A profuse yellow-green discharge is present and detaches easily from the surface. The zone of endocervical ectopy that normally is present in as many as 50 percent of adolescents may appear bright red, does not bleed easily when touched with swabs, and should not be mistaken for cervicitis. Ectopy that appears swollen and friable suggests cervicitis. Nabothian inclusion cysts (transparent and grayish) also are normal findings.

Infection of the Bartholin (major vestibular) gland or paraurethral (Skene) gland ducts may develop during acute gonorrhea. Bartholin gland abscesses appear as large, circumscribed, painful swellings of the dorsal aspect of the labium minus (see Fig. 49–12). They occur in 5 percent of females with endocervical gonorrhea.[241] Paraurethral duct abscesses (see Fig. 49–11) appear as small painful swellings in the urethrovaginal septum and may cause dysuria. Rupture into the urethra can create a urethral diverticulum. Bartholin gland or paraurethral duct abscesses should be incised and drained, but small asymptomatic nodules do not require drainage.

If untreated, the acute symptoms of gonococcal infection generally subside in 8 to 10 weeks. Persisting acute symptoms are more likely to represent reinfection than chronic infection. Chronic urethritis, thickening of the vestibular glands and paraurethral ducts, and chronic cervicitis can occur. A secondary nonspecific vaginitis can develop as a result of irritation of the mucosa from persisting profuse endocervical discharge.

Mucopurulent cervicitis can be caused by *N. gonorrhoeae, C. trachomatis, Gardnerella vaginalis, Mycoplasma hominis, Ureaplasma urealyticum,* and group B streptococci. The overlap in clinical manifestations of infections caused by these microbes and the frequency of infection by two or more simultaneously prevent diagnosis by clinical findings alone.

Adolescents may be unaware of their infection, especially if they have a preexisting profuse discharge as a result of nonspecific vaginitis or trichomoniasis. Early recognition and treatment of lower genital tract gonococcal infection may prevent extension to and complications of upper genital tract infection. Therefore, sexually active adolescent females should be examined for gonococcal infection as part of their routine health care.[140, 258]

A review of reported complications in 1232 cases of gonococcal vaginitis in the pre-antibiotic era revealed that 35 percent had urethritis, 19 percent had proctitis, and 6 percent had peritonitis.[20]

UPPER GENITAL TRACT INFECTION IN POSTMENARCHEAL FEMALES

PID will develop in 10 to 17 percent of females with endocervical gonococcal infection. Conditions encompassed by the term PID include endometritis, parametritis, salpingitis (see Fig. 49–24), oophoritis, tubo-ovarian abscess, and pelvic peritonitis. PID can be caused by a variety of bacteria. Anaerobes, including *Bacteroides, Peptococcus,* and *Peptostreptococcus* spp., are the organisms most commonly recovered. *N. gonorrhoeae* is present in 25 to 50 percent of cases, similar to the proportion of cases from which *C. trachomatis* is recovered. Coliform organisms, *G. vaginalis, M. hominis, U. urealyticum,* and various streptococcal species also may be involved. PID develops when these organisms are able to ascend into the uterus, fallopian tubes, and beyond from the lower genital tract. Multiple species may be involved in a single episode. Gonococcal PID often occurs during or just after menses.[105, 142] Identification of the specific microbial cause or causes of PID is complicated by the difficulty of obtaining fallopian tube specimens before initiating therapy.

Common findings in PID include an acute onset of lower abdominal pain with tenderness, fever, tenderness on lateral motion of the cervix, adnexal tenderness that generally is bilateral, and adnexal fullness. Vaginal discharge, urinary symptoms, and irregular vaginal bleeding usually are variably present. In moderate to severe cases, abdominal pain frequently is bilateral, exacerbated with movement, and continuous. Nausea, vomiting, marked abdominal tenderness, an abdomen that appears tense, and fever exceeding 39°C may be present. Such patients often appear ill and may have tachycardia consistent with the height of fever.[265] Leukocytosis and elevated erythrocyte sedimentation rates are common findings. Alternatively, PID may be clinically silent or cause only mild pain without discernible tenderness, vaginal discharge, or leukocytosis. Such mild cases can go unrecognized by patients and physicians.

Making the diagnosis of PID may be difficult, and the differential diagnosis includes numerous other lower abdominal conditions, such as appendicitis, ectopic pregnancy, cholecystitis, mesenteric adenitis, pyelonephritis, and septic abortion. Sonography and pregnancy testing may be helpful in diagnostic decision making. No single symptom, sign, or laboratory finding is sensitive and specific for the diagnosis of PID. Combinations of findings can improve the sensitivity but do so at the expense of reduced specificity, and vice versa.

Initiation of empiric therapy for PID should be considered if the minimal criteria of lower abdominal tenderness, adnexal tenderness, and cervical motion tenderness all are present and no other cause for these findings is readily apparent. More elaborate evaluation may be needed in some cases because incorrect diagnosis and management might lead to unnecessary morbidity. Additional criteria that support the diagnosis of PID include an oral temperature higher than 38.3° C (101° F), an abnormal cervical or vaginal discharge, elevated erythrocyte sedimentation rate, elevated C-reactive protein level, and laboratory documentation of cervical infection with *N. gonorrhoeae* or *C. trachomatis*. Some cases may require pursuit of definitive criteria for diagnosing PID, which include histopathologic evidence of endometritis on endometrial biopsy, transvaginal or abdominal ultrasonography or other imaging studies that show thickened fluid-filled fallopian tubes with or without free pelvic fluid or a tubo-ovarian abscess, and laparoscopic abnormalities consistent with PID.[56, 158]

The outcome for fertility probably is improved with prompt and vigorous therapy. In the past, physicians have recommended that all adolescents suspected of having PID be hospitalized for therapy. More recently, inpatient observation and treatment have been recommended when a surgical emergency (e.g., ectopic pregnancy or appendicitis) cannot be excluded; when compliance with or tolerance of an outpatient treatment regimen and follow-up within 72 hours cannot be ensured; when the illness appears to be severe (e.g., pelvic or tubo-ovarian abscess, overt peritonitis); or when the patient is immunocompromised, is pregnant, or has failed to respond to outpatient therapy.[5] All courses of therapy should include treatment that is appropriate for *C. trachomatis* and other causes of PID, in addition to *N. gonorrhoeae*.

Complications of PID include tubo-ovarian abscess, perihepatitis (Fitz-Hugh–Curtis syndrome), future ectopic pregnancy, and infertility. Perihepatitis is characterized by right upper quadrant abdominal pain that may radiate to the shoulder. Nausea, fever, and other symptoms and signs of PID may be present as well. Leukocytosis occurs commonly, and liver enzymes are elevated in some cases. The differential diagnosis of perihepatitis includes pleuritis, cholelithiasis, subphrenic abscess, and perforated ulcers.[186]

An estimated 15 percent of women may be sterile after having a single episode of PID and 50 percent after three infections. Because of scarring and fibrosis in the fallopian tube, patency is compromised and fertility is jeopardized.[50, 106] PID in adolescents is particularly likely to result in infertility and ectopic pregnancy, and PID is the single most common cause of infertility in young women.[40, 210] Between 1970 and 1980, the rate of ectopic pregnancies per 1000 live births increased from 4.8 to 14.5, and between 1975 and 1981, the rate of hospitalization of females 15 to 19 years of age for salpingitis was 4 per 100,000.[299] These increases correlated with rising rates of gonococcal infection in the affected populations. Data from several studies of gonococcal disease in adolescents are presented in Table 94–4.

Risk factors for development of PID include young age at the time of acquisition of gonococcal disease or other sexually transmitted diseases (STDs), a history of previous PID, multiple sexual partners, and the use of an intrauterine device (IUD) for contraception. The immature cervix may be at particular risk for progression to upper tract disease.[273] Disseminated gonococcal infection may accompany asymptomatic infection of an IUD,[72] and the rate of acute PID in those who use IUDs may be increased.

GENITAL TRACT INFECTION IN MALES

Urethritis is the primary manifestation of gonococcal infection in males of all ages beyond the neonatal period. Even in young boys, the disease usually is symptomatic and resembles gonococcal urethritis in men.[82, 116] Dysuria, purulent discharge, or both develop 2 to 7 days after exposure. Patients usually are afebrile. Purulence typically is greater than with nongonococcal urethritis, but symptoms often are mild enough that patients may delay seeking medical care for weeks. Associated inguinal adenopathy occurs rarely.

At least 5 percent of cases of gonococcal urethritis in males are asymptomatic, and asymptomatic infection can occur at all ages. Asymptomatic pyuria is a manifestation with which the pediatrician should be familiar.[87] It may be the only finding in some cases and should raise suspicion of gonococcal or chlamydial infection in boys who may have been sexually abused or in sexually active adolescent males.

Gonococcal urethritis in prepubertal boys is a less frequent event than is vaginitis in girls because of gender differences in rates of sexual abuse. In children with gonorrheal infection of the genitourinary tract, concomitant anorectal and tonsillopharyngeal colonization occurs commonly.[218]

Males with asymptomatic infection are a major reservoir for transmission to their sexual partners.[87, 110] Untreated male urethral infection may persist as long as 6 months.

TABLE 94–4 ■ PREVALENCE OF GONORRHEA AND OTHER SEXUALLY TRANSMITTED DISEASES IN CLINICS FOR ADOLESCENTS

Reference	Location	Total Clinic Population Studied	Gonorrhea (%)	*Chlamydia* Infection (%)	Other
Shafer et al., 1984[266]	California	366	15	4	*Trichomonas* infection
Golden et al., 1984[119a]	New York	186	10	10	Syphilis *Trichomonas* infection
Demetriou et al., 1984[92a]	Oklahoma	839	14	—	
Mulcahy and Lacey, 1987[210a]	Leeds	210	14	16	*Trichomonas* infection
Jamison et al., 1995[158a]	Colorado	632	7	—	Human papillomavirus infection

Complications of gonococcal infection in males now occur much less frequently than in the pre-antibiotic era. Epididymitis is the most common complication. Unilateral swelling, pain, and erythema in the posterior aspect of the scrotum are the usual features. Fever may occur. If untreated, the infection may progress to involve the ipsilateral testis. Hydrocele may result from secretion of fluid into the potential space of the tunica vaginalis. Epididymitis can lead to testicular infarction, abscess, infertility, prostatitis, paraurethral abscesses, and penile lymphangitis, but these local complications are rare occurrences. Perihepatitis in males has been described but occurs extremely infrequently.[174]

DISSEMINATED DISEASE

Dissemination requires bacteremic spread from local infection of the mucous membranes of the genital tract, rectum, pharynx, or conjunctiva to other remote sites. The risk of dissemination in children after mucosal infection appears to be higher than the 1 to 3 percent rate in adults. In adults, dissemination seems to be more common with asymptomatic infections, many of which are caused by AHU$^-$ gonococcal strains (see "Pathogenesis" earlier).[171] Deficits in the complement system have been associated with disseminated disease in adults, but the frequency of such deficiencies in children is unknown.

As in neonates, gonococcal arthritis is the most common form of disseminated disease in older children, adolescents, and adults. The ankles, knees, wrists, and hands are involved most frequently. The clinical findings are not distinctive from those of other microbial causes of septic arthritis. Polyarticular involvement occurs less commonly than in neonates, but it does occur.[80] Gram stain and synovial fluid cultures often are negative. Therefore, empiric coverage for *N. gonorrhoeae* must be considered when septic arthritis develops in a sexually active adolescent or a child who may have been sexually abused.

Typically, the patient has a single, most severely affected joint, and myositis and tenosynovitis may be prominent findings. Gonococcal arthritis in older children and adolescents resembles that of adults and may be accompanied by cutaneous lesions (see later).[4] Osteomyelitis rarely occurs but has been reported in all age groups, usually in association with septic arthritis.[9]

Treatment of gonococcal arthritis depends on prompt recognition of the disease. Cultures of all mucous membranes (nasopharyngeal, rectal, vaginal or endocervical, conjunctival), blood culture, and aspiration of the involved joint should be performed. The local signs of gonococcal arthritis may not respond to antibiotic therapy for several days. Serial needle aspiration rather than open drainage usually is sufficient for relief of pain and recovery without sequelae (the hip may be an exception).

Gonococcemia usually is clinically silent but can cause a syndrome of migratory polyarthralgia, fever, and rash that precedes the onset of arthritis by several days to a week. The symptomatic course generally is only mild to moderate in severity. Blood cultures often are negative by the time that care is sought. Gonococcemia-related symptoms may resolve after several days, even without treatment. Rare cases can resemble meningococcemia with purpura and fulminant sepsis with disseminated intravascular coagulopathy, and some of these cases will be fatal.[227]

The skin lesions associated with gonococcemia usually are pustules on an erythematous base (Fig. 94–3), but petechiae, papules, and hemorrhagic bullae can occur. The development of skin lesions in conjunction with septic arthritis also has been called the arthritis-dermatitis syndrome. The lesions usually arise on the extremities and are fewer than 20 in number. Low-grade fever is most common, but high fever with shaking chills may occur. Tenosynovitis is present in a fourth of these patients. Leukocytosis, pyuria, and elevated liver enzyme test results may be seen. The resultant septic joints usually become clinically apparent during the second week after the onset of disseminated infection.

ANORECTAL GONORRHEA

Gonococcal anorectal infection (proctitis) frequently is asymptomatic but can be associated with pruritus, tenesmus, purulent discharge, or rectal bleeding. Rectal infection can occur as a result of rectal intercourse or inoculation

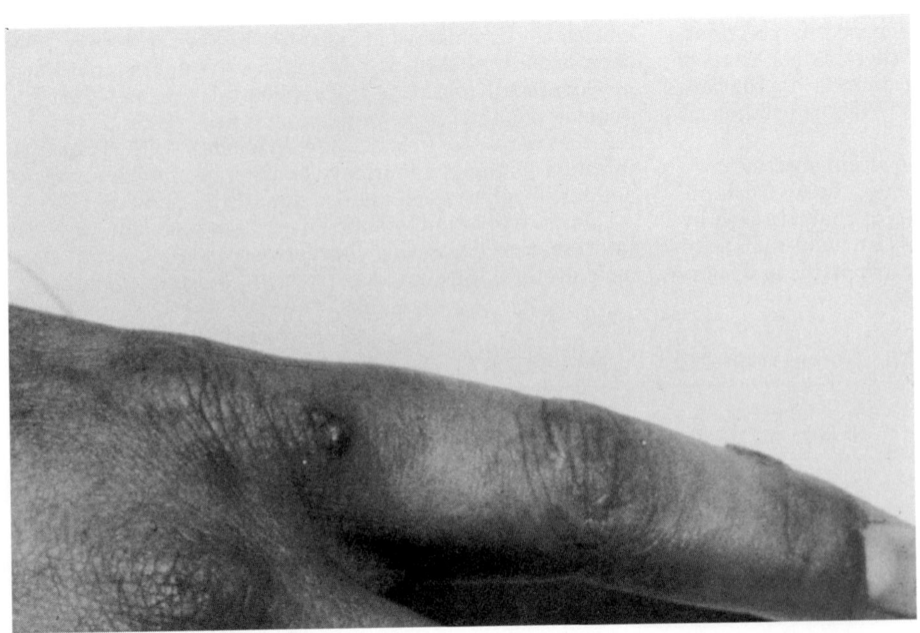

FIGURE 94–3 ■ Skin lesion typical of the arthritis-dermatitis syndrome of disseminated gonococcal infection: necrotic pustule with an erythematous halo. (Courtesy of Daniel P. Krowchuk, M.D.)

TABLE 94–5 ■ SEXUALLY TRANSMITTED DISEASES IN PREPUBERTAL CHILDREN EVALUATED FOR SUSPECTED SEXUAL ABUSE

Reference	No. of Children Evaluated	Number (%) Who Had Diagnosis of:				
		Gonorrhea	Chlamydiosis	*Syphilis*	Trichomoniasis	*Condylomata Acuminata*
Wald et al., 1980[299]	189	28 (14.8%)	ND	ND	ND	ND
Rimsza and Niggemann, 1982[249]	285	21 (7.4%)	ND	0	ND	ND
White et al., 1983[304]	409	46 (10%)	ND	6 (5.5%)	4 (18%)	3 (5.6%)
Ingram et al., 1984[153]	50	10 (20%)	3 (6%)	ND	2 (4%)	ND
DeJong, 1986[91]	532	25 (4.7%)	ND	1 (0.2%)	ND	3 (0.6%)
Ingram et al., 1992[152]	1469	41 (2.8%)	17 (1.2%)	1 (0.1%)	3 (2%)	28 (2%)
Siegal et al., 1995[271]	855*	12 (1.4%)	11 (1.3%)	0	4 (0.5%)	ND
Muram et al., 1996[213]	865	12 (1.4%)	ND	ND	ND	ND

*These children also were evaluated for HIV infection, and all were found to be uninfected.
ND, no data.

from vaginal secretions. Approximately 40 percent of females with genital gonococcal infection have positive anorectal cultures. Rectal infection is an unusual finding in males in the absence of rectal intercourse.[282]

PHARYNGEAL GONORRHEA

Pharyngeal gonococcal infection in all age groups beyond the neonatal period is acquired by orogenital contact. Pharyngeal gonorrhea may be asymptomatic without evidence of inflammation or may cause an exudative tonsillopharyngitis that can mimic group A streptococcal or viral infection. Cervical adenopathy also may be present in some cases. In sexually abused children, the pharynx may be the only site of infection. It may be the only culture-positive site in some cases of disseminated gonococcal infection, and pharyngeal infection possibly is a factor predisposing to dissemination. Pharyngeal infection usually resolves spontaneously within 10 to 12 weeks but should be treated when recognized.

Throat cultures for *N. gonorrhoeae* should be considered in sexually active adolescents with pharyngitis, asymptomatic orogenital contacts of infected persons, patients with disseminated disease in whom other sites of initial infection are not readily apparent, and children who have been sexually abused.

Current treatment regimens for genital gonococcal infection are effective in eradicating gonococcal infection from the pharynx. Routine throat cultures for screening all sexually active adolescents are not cost-effective, but throat culture may be considered for those who give a history of frequent orogenital sexual activity.*

CONJUNCTIVITIS BEYOND INFANCY

Gonococcal ophthalmia sometimes is seen in children and adults. Direct inoculation of the eye can occur as a result of fomite transmission from infected persons. Clinical findings typically include a profuse purulent discharge, chemosis, eyelid edema, keratitis, and fever. The initial ocular discharge may be watery before turning purulent. The acute phase may mimic orbital cellulitis. Untreated infection, as with neonates, can lead to corneal opacification, ulceration, and rupture of the globe with resultant visual loss. Some cases may be minimally symptomatic, with a minimal inflammatory response and spontaneous resolution.[183, 187, 234]

*See references 1, 38, 63, 81, 91, 129, 147, 218, 225, 272, 304, 307.

OTHER FORMS OF GONOCOCCAL DISEASE

Gonococcal meningitis is a rare condition but may occur with or without associated signs of gonococcemia or septic arthritis. Pyomyositis of the biceps and soft tissue abscesses remote from the genital area have been reported. A gonococcal abscess arising in an area of blunt trauma to a hand, with associated endocervical infection, recently has been described in an adolescent.[120] Ventriculoperitoneal shunt–associated infection, endocarditis, and myocarditis caused by *N. gonorrhoeae* have been reported in adults and can be expected to occur occasionally in children and adolescents.[142] The pediatric experience with gonococcal infection of these types is minimal.

Gonococcal Infection and Sexual Abuse of Children

When gonococcal infection or any other STD is identified in a prepubertal child or in adolescents who are not sexually active within their peer groups, sexual abuse must be considered to have occurred unless proved otherwise.[5] Sexual abuse has been reported in approximately 10 percent of all self-reporting populations of girls during childhood in numerous studies, and rates in boys are approximately 3 percent.[13, 256] Approximately 1 percent of children appear to experience serious forms of sexual abuse yearly.[6]

STDs occur in 3 to 20 percent of sexually abused children.[91, 152, 153, 213, 249, 271, 299, 304] Table 94–5 summarizes the STD diagnoses from eight studies involving children who had been evaluated for suspected sexual abuse. Gonorrhea was the STD most frequently recognized in abused children when gonococcal infection was highly prevalent in the general population. As a result of improved control of gonorrhea in the 1980s, fewer pediatric cases are being recognized in the United States. Nonetheless, girls who are exposed to an infected male appear to have a high rate of acquired disease. In an outbreak in an orphanage, 53 of 95 abused girls were found to have contracted infection.[2]

Although only a minority of children who have experienced sexual abuse subsequently contract an STD, the diagnosis of an STD is a very important indication that the child has been in an abusive setting, and an STD may be the sole finding on physical examination.[150] For this reason, the examination should be thorough, and genital, rectal, and pharyngeal cultures should be obtained. Vaginal cultures are satisfactory in prepubertal girls. Only after puberty should endocervical cultures be obtained. Blood should be drawn for culture if the physician has reason to consider disseminated disease. Other sites (conjunctivae, joint fluid) should be cultured if clinically indicated. Cultures should be handled in a manner that will ensure legal acceptance if needed (see later).

All children with gonococcal infections (including neonates) should be evaluated for other STDs, including *C. trachomatis,* syphilis, hepatitis B virus, and HIV.[5, 130, 258]

Observations that most children evaluated for sexual abuse do not have gonococcal infection or other STDs and that the vast majority of prepubertal girls with gonococcal infection have clinical signs of vulvovaginitis[213, 268, 270, 271] have led to suggestions that selective criteria be used to determine which children who are being examined for potential sexual abuse need to be evaluated for the presence of gonococcal infection and other STDs.[151, 271] These criteria are the known presence of any STD in the child, a sibling, another household member, a close associate of the child, or the apparent perpetrator or when the history or physical findings suggest that oral, genital, or rectal contact has occurred.[151] Recent studies have shown that the use of these criteria is highly unlikely to miss any children with gonococcal or chlamydial infection while decreasing the number of potentially sexually abused children who must undergo culture.[151, 154]

The following general issues should be noted:

1. Many institutions have a service that is particularly skilled in interviewing and examining children suspected of having experienced sexual abuse. This group, if available, should be involved in the work-up from the initial contact.[224]
2. If the child is symptomatic, all available and appropriate cultures and examinations should be completed before the child receives therapy.
3. All culture and examination samples must be labeled thoroughly and clearly. Timely delivery to the appropriate laboratory must be ensured, by personal delivery if necessary. The clinician should have a policy regarding the identification of specimens and should establish a chain of custody such that the results can be supported in court procedures when issues of the child's safety are being considered.
4. Testing for gonorrhea in infants and children should be performed with only standard culture systems of isolation (see "Diagnostic Testing" later).
5. If sexual abuse is confirmed or suspected by the social history, physical findings, or laboratory results, the child should not leave the clinic until the child's safety has been ensured. Safety issues usually are assessed by the department of social services or ensured by hospitalization of the child pending further investigation. The Child Abuse Reporting Law mandates reporting suspected and confirmed cases to the social service of the county in which the child resides.
6. Most children who have been the victims of sexual abuse will not have specific physical findings to confirm the diagnosis. Oral sexual contact is a common form of abuse, as are fondling and external genital contact, all of which may not result in apparent injury.
7. If the child has gonorrhea, other members of the family may be infected as well. In particular, other female children are especially likely to be infected and should be examined.[108, 115]
8. Internal pelvic examinations are indicated very rarely. Exceptions are the presence of a foreign body or major trauma. If an internal examination of a prepubertal girl is requested, it should be performed by an experienced examiner.
9. Children often have compelling reasons to deny abuse and fail to disclose sexual abuse, even to skillful diagnostic interviewers.[182] Denial is not compelling disproof of abuse.
10. Sexual abuse of children usually is a chronic and recurring condition. Consequently, if the child remains unprotected, repeated episodes are very likely to occur. If the perpetrator has an STD, the child may have recurrent episodes of that STD.[181]
11. Asymptomatic gonococcal infections occur commonly.[28, 108, 140] Strong consideration should be given to obtaining material for culture in the absence of symptoms, especially for adolescents and high-risk children as identified earlier.

Diagnostic Testing

Isolation of *N. gonorrhoeae* in culture remains the standard for diagnosis of gonococcal infection, but nonculture DNA-based tests have become widely used in recent years. Only culture should be used for rectal or pharyngeal specimens. Serologic tests based on complement fixation, latex agglutination, enzyme-linked immunoabsorbance, and other techniques have been developed, but the sensitivities of these methods are about 70 percent, which limits their use primarily to studies of immune response and pathogenesis.[144, 146, 259]

A diagnosis of *N. gonorrhoeae* infection at any site should prompt evaluation for the presence of other common STDs, if not already done[258] (see also Chapter 49).

CULTURE

In adults, culture of clinical specimens is 80 to 95 percent sensitive when promptly inoculated and incubated. Cultures of adult male urethral specimens, blood, and other normally sterile body sites tend to have sensitivities in the higher range.[146] Because false-positive cultures are not thought to occur, specificity and positive predictive values are 100 percent. Culture probably has similar sensitivity in adolescents and children. Vaginal specimens are adequate for diagnosis in prepubertal girls, so obtaining endocervical specimens is unnecessary.

The use of selective media such as modified Thayer-Martin is required for culture of endocervical, rectal, and pharyngeal specimens. Selective or nonselective media (chocolate agar) can be used for male urethral cultures, with equal sensitivity. Plating of specimens on both types of media may improve the sensitivity, but the incremental yield is small and probably not cost-effective for routine practice.[29, 85, 242]

In sexually mature females with endocervical gonococcal infection, the urethra, Bartholin gland ducts, and Skene gland ducts usually also are infected. Cultures from these sites may improve the overall yield/sensitivity, in part by avoiding the sampling errors that can occur with any single culture, but again, the incremental yield is small enough to render obtaining such cultures unnecessary in routine clinical settings. Culture of the rectum and pharynx in females can be considered optional except when evaluating for sexual abuse.[29, 163]

In males, sites to be cultured depend on the sexual orientation and the anatomic sites exposed. In men who have sex with men, rectal infection is almost as frequent as is urethritis, and pharyngeal infections occur in approximately 5 percent.[33, 146, 197]

GRAM-STAINED SMEARS

The presence of gram-negative diplococci on Gram staining of clinical specimens generally cannot be relied on to make a diagnosis of gonococcal infection. Nonpathogenic *Neisseria* spp. and *N. meningitidis* are morphologically indistinguishable from gonococci, although the former rarely are cell associated. The exception may be symptomatic gonococcal urethritis in males, in which a positive Gram stain has sensitivity of 90 to 95 percent. The specificity of a negative Gram stain appears to be at least 95 percent for specimens from the male urethra, endocervix, and rectum.[146, 254]

NONCULTURE DIAGNOSTICS

Nonculture diagnostic tests have become widely used in the United States for rapid diagnosis of gonococcal (and chlamydial) infection. Many of these tests now offer the advantage of using urine samples rather than the more invasive swabs and also permit evaluation for *C. trachomatis* with the same specimen. Numerous gonococcal antigen-detection tests have been developed, but they have been supplanted largely by nucleic acid detection methods. Culture remains the definitive test for medicolegal purposes (see the next section). In addition, because of ever-increasing resistance to the available antimicrobial agents, monitoring of gonococcal susceptibility by culture is necessary at the local level.

Nonamplified DNA-DNA hybridization probe tests (e.g., Gen-Probe Pace 2) have been the nonculture tests most frequently used in the United States in recent years. These tests are based on a single-stranded DNA probe complementary to gonococcal rRNA. Sensitivity is 89 to 97 percent with a specificity of 99 percent.[134, 146, 184, 226]

Several amplified nucleic acid detection tests also have been developed, and a few are in use. These tests are as sensitive as is culture, appear to have a specificity of at least 99 percent, and can be used to evaluate first-void urine specimens, which permits screening for gonococcal infection in males and females when genital examination is impractical. Currently available assays include the ligase chain reaction (LCR) assay, a standard PCR-based assay (Amplicor CT/NG), and strand displacement amplification coupled with a fluorescent energy measurement process (BDProbeTec ET System).[67, 230, 277, 294, 296]

MEDICOLEGAL ISSUES

N. meningitidis and other members of the Neisseriaceae family are morphologically and often biochemically similar to *N. gonorrhoeae* and may be isolated from sites such as the vagina, blood, and nasopharynx.[94, 99, 305] Accurate identification of *Neisseria* organisms from any pediatric specimen is essential because misidentification of nongonococcal species as *N. gonorrhoeae* may lead to very serious social consequences for children and their families by precipitating concern regarding sexual abuse. Culture remains the medicolegal standard because of the possibility of false-positive results with nonculture methods. Nonculture methods consistently identify more clinical specimens as positive than standard cultures do,[296] and determining whether such results indicate greater sensitivity, increased false positivity, or a combination of both has been difficult.

For medicolegal purposes, the Centers for Disease Control and Prevention (CDC) has defined three levels of diagnosis based on clinical and laboratory findings. They are more stringent than are the case definitions used for public health surveillance. A *suggestive diagnosis* is defined by presence of mucopurulent endocervical or urethral exudate and sexual exposure to a person with gonococcal infection. A *presumptive diagnosis* requires two of three criteria: typical gram-negative *intracellular* diplococci on a Gram stain of urethral exudate from males or endocervical secretions; growth of apparent *N. gonorrhoeae* from such specimens on culture medium, defined as typical colonial morphology, positive oxidase reaction, and typical gram-negative morphology; and detection of *N. gonorrhoeae* by a nonculture laboratory test. A *definitive diagnosis* requires isolation of *N. gonorrhoeae* from clinical specimens by culture, as in the second criterion for a presumptive diagnosis, and confirmation of identity by biochemical, enzymatic, serologic, or nucleic acid testing.[61]

COLLECTION OF CLINICAL SPECIMENS

Urethral exudate from males may be obtained by passing small swabs or bacteriologic loops 2 to 4 cm into the urethra.[137] Endocervical specimens are obtained by speculum examination with swabs inserted 1 to 2 cm into the external os after the cervix has been cleansed of external exudate and vaginal secretions. The swab should be rotated gently for as long as 10 seconds.[250] Self-obtained vaginal swabs also provide adequate specimens for nonculture methods such as LCR.[276] This technique has been studied in adolescents. Vaginal specimens collected with tampons also can be used with nonculture methods.[291]

In persons with symptomatic anorectal infection, rectal specimens should be obtained by anoscopic means, which increases the sensitivity. In asymptomatic persons, rectal specimens can be procured by blindly inserting a swab 2 to 3 cm into the anal canal and applying lateral pressure to avoid entering into any fecal mass. Swabs that are grossly contaminated with fecal matter should be discarded.[88, 308]

When urine specimens can be used for nonculture methods, the first 15 to 30 mL of voided urine should be collected.[192, 214] The posterior of the pharynx, the tonsillar areas, and the faucial pillars should be swabbed to obtain adequate specimens for the diagnosis of pharyngeal infection.[146]

Antimicrobial Susceptibility

Sulfanilamide was introduced in 1936 and represented a major improvement over previous therapies that included local genital irrigation with solutions of silver nitrate or potassium permanganate.[229] Widespread resistance to sulfanilamide had occurred by 1944. As successive agents have become available, multidrug-resistant strains are being seen with increasing frequency in many parts of the world. Ongoing analysis of gonococcal isolates for antibiotic susceptibility to the available antimicrobial agents remains essential for the maintenance of effective empiric therapeutic regimens.

In the 1940s, virtually all gonococcal isolates were highly susceptible to penicillin. Despite a gradual increase in the mean minimal inhibitory concentration (MIC) to penicillin from the mid-1950s through the mid-1970s, almost all strains had penicillin MICs of less than 0.5 μg/mL. This low-level resistance is mediated by alterations at a genetic locus called *penA* that result in modification of its product, penicillin-binding protein 2 (PBP-2). Two other loci designated *mtr,* which encodes an efflux pump that reduces concentrations of multiple antibiotics, and *penB,* which is an allele of *por,* the gene of the porin protein, also mediate low-level resistance to penicillins. *PenB* encodes a porin with a mutation that decreases permeability to hydrophilic antibiotics.[118]

In 1976, strains of *N. gonorrhoeae* were discovered that had acquired plasmid-conferring resistance to penicillin through the production of penicillinase (a TEM-1 β-lactamase). These strains were found in many parts of the Far East and London, and in the Far East they constituted approximately 30 percent of the isolates in some cities. The strains caused the expected spectrum of clinical disease, and treatment with penicillin was not effective. Penicillinase-producing gonococci contain one of two closely related 5.3- or 7.2-kb plasmids (Pc^r) that carry a Tn2 transposon system. This plasmid appears to have been acquired from *Haemophilus ducreyi*.[8, 46, 66, 232] In 1983, an outbreak of chromosomally mediated, penicillin-resistant (MICs of 2 to 4 µg/mL), non–penicillinase-producing gonococci was reported from North Carolina.[109] Such strains have been seen subsequently in other areas of the country.

Resistance to tetracycline antibiotics emerged in the 1980s and subsequently increased. Three chromosomal loci designated *mtr, penB,* and *tet* mediate low-level resistance. High-level resistance to tetracycline is conferred by *tetM,* which resides on a 38-kb plasmid (Tc^r) that is a derivative of the 36-kb conjugal plasmid. *tetM* produces a cytoplasmic protein that protects ribosomes from tetracycline. Tc^r gonococci can transfer this plasmid as well as Pc^r efficiently to other gonococcal strains.[207, 279]

Spectinomycin resistance was described first in 1987 in U.S. military personnel in Korea. This agent had been introduced as the drug of choice there in 1981 because of high rates of penicillin resistance. Treatment failures actually began to occur in 1983. Resistance is chromosomally mediated and results in alteration of the ribosomal target site of the drug.[30, 46] The widespread use of spectinomycin was associated with a decline in the rate of penicillin resistance.[30]

Ciprofloxacin and other fluoroquinolone antibiotics became widely available for the treatment of gonococcal infection in the 1980s. Resistance to these agents has been noted since the early 1990s and has increased in prevalence in some areas of Southeast Asia to levels that have required discontinuation of their use as first-line agents.[111] In Hawaii in 1999, 9.5 percent of isolates were resistant to ciprofloxacin, but resistance elsewhere in the United States remained low at 0.2 percent.[58, 59] Fluoroquinolones no longer are recommended for initial treatment of gonococcal infection in Hawaii. Low-level resistance to fluoroquinolones is associated with mutations in the DNA gyrase gene *gyrA,* and high-level resistance has been linked to mutations in the topoisomerase gene *parC.*[156]

In 1986, the CDC initiated the Gonococcal Isolate Surveillance Project to monitor the antimicrobial sensitivities of *N. gonorrhoeae* in STD clinics in 21 cities in the United States.[53] This system was expanded to 26 sites in the 1990s.[58] In 1989, 13 percent of the *N. gonorrhoeae* isolates evaluated were resistant to penicillin, tetracycline, or both.[54] In 1999, such strains accounted for 28 percent of all isolates.[58] Among isolates resistant or intermediately resistant to ciprofloxacin in the United States in 1999, 37 percent also were penicillinase producing and 44 percent were resistant to tetracycline.[59]

Many gonococcal strains in some parts of the world also are resistant to streptomycin and rifampin.[220] Recently, strains resistant to azithromycin and erythromycin have been identified in the United States.[59]

Treatment

Because of ever-changing gonococcal susceptibility patterns and variations in susceptibility in different international regions, practitioners should remain alert for modifications of treatment guidelines for their respective geographic locations. Based on the current prevalence of penicillin resistance in *N. gonorrhoeae* strains in the United States, extended-spectrum, parenterally administered cephalosporins are recommended as initial therapy in children. These cephalosporins or quinolone antibiotics are recommended for adults. Ordinarily, quinolones are not recommended for use in persons younger than 18 years of age, but they may be considered in selected circumstances when the potential benefits of therapy appear to outweigh the potential risks. Increasing resistance to tetracycline antibiotics currently precludes the use of these agents as empiric therapy. Resistance to spectinomycin remains rare in the United States, and this compound still is an effective alternative in most cases when other agents cannot be used.[5]

In adults with an uncomplicated gonococcal infection of any site, 99 percent of cases are cured by ceftriaxone. As a general rule, children treated with ceftriaxone do not require follow-up cultures, but if other treatment regimens are used, follow-up cultures may be indicated. Experience in adults, including pregnant women,[239] suggests that oral cefixime may be considered for uncomplicated gonococcal infections in children, provided that follow-up is ensured. Cefixime has an antimicrobial spectrum similar to that of ceftriaxone, but in adults, the 400-mg oral dose does not provide as high or as sustained a bactericidal concentration as that provided by 125-mg parenteral dose of ceftriaxone. Nonetheless, clinical trials have shown cure rates of 97 percent in adults with uncomplicated gonococcal infection treated with cefixime. Other cephalosporins that are safe and highly effective against uncomplicated gonococcal infection in adults, and probably in children as well, include cefotaxime, ceftizoxime, cefotetan, and cefoxitin.

Ciprofloxacin and ofloxacin are the quinolones most widely used for gonococcal infection. Cure rates for uncomplicated gonococcal infection with both agents exceed 98 percent in adults. Other quinolones that also may be effective against gonococcal infection are enoxacin, lomefloxacin, and norfloxacin.

The following recommendations for treatment of childhood gonorrhea in the United States are based on the 1998 guidelines from the CDC[56] and the 2000 Report of the Committee on Infectious Diseases of the American Academy of Pediatrics.[5] Pediatric patients encompass children from birth through adolescence. Children who are postpubertal or who weigh more than 45.4 kg (100 lb) should be treated with dosage regimens as defined for adults. The recommended regimens generally have not been studied in populations of prepubertal children with either uncomplicated or complicated gonococcal infection, but they are likely to be highly effective in most cases, as they are for older adolescents and adults.

PRESUMPTIVE TREATMENT OF CONCURRENT *C. TRACHOMATIS* INFECTION

Persons with gonococcal infection, including children, are at high risk for acquiring concurrent chlamydial infection. In adolescents, treatment of gonococcal cervicitis with drug regimens that are effective against gonococci but not *Chlamydia* has been associated with a high incidence of residual salpingitis in females and urethritis in males because of the ongoing presence of *C. trachomatis.*[228, 240, 243, 265] Therefore, treatment recommendations for gonococcal infections beyond the neonatal period include agents active against both organisms. Penicillin, amoxicillin, ceftriaxone, or spectinomycin alone will fail to eradicate *Chlamydia.* Trimethoprim-sulfamethoxazole, tetracycline, doxycycline, azithromycin, and erythromycin are effective in vitro and in many clinical forms of *Chlamydia* disease.

TREATMENT OF INFANTS BORN TO MOTHERS WITH GONOCOCCAL INFECTION

Infants born to mothers with untreated gonorrhea are at high risk of acquiring infection (e.g., ophthalmia, disseminated gonococcal infection); consequently, even without overt signs of infection, such infants should be treated with a single injection of ceftriaxone (25 to 50 mg/kg intravenously or intramuscularly, not to exceed 125 mg). Ceftriaxone should be given cautiously to hyperbilirubinemic infants, especially premature ones. A single dose of cefotaxime (100 mg/kg intravenously or intramuscularly) is an acceptable alternative. Topical prophylaxis for neonatal ophthalmia is not adequate therapy for documented infections of the eye or other sites.

TREATMENT OF NEONATES WITH GONOCOCCAL INFECTION

Neonates with clinical evidence suggestive of gonococcal infection at any site (including the eye) should be evaluated for disseminated disease. The evaluation should include a thorough physical examination, especially of the joints. Exudate from the eyes or other sites of apparent local infection should be sent for Gram stain and culture on appropriate media. Blood should be cultured as well. CSF culture should be performed in infants who have fever or who are not otherwise well. CSF culture also should be performed if the clinical findings could be compatible with other bacterial causes of sepsis or meningitis in the neonate or in infants with a known positive blood culture for *N. gonorrhoeae*. Some experts suggest that a CSF culture be performed in all neonates with potential gonococcal infection of any type.

The presence of typical gram-negative diplococci in Gram-stained specimens is sufficient justification to begin treatment of GON or gonococcal infection in other sites. The absence of gram-negative diplococci in Gram-stained specimens is not sufficient to abrogate presumptive treatment of GON in a neonate with conjunctival exudate. Tests for concomitant *C. trachomatis* infection, HIV infection, and congenital syphilis should be performed in infants with gonococcal infection at any site. The mother and her partners should be evaluated for gonococcal infection (and other STDs) and treated according to the recommendations for gonococcal infection in adolescents and adults (see the next section).

Infants with GON can be treated with a single dose of ceftriaxone (25 to 50 mg/kg intravenously or intramuscularly, not to exceed 125 mg).[178] This regimen also may be used for infants with other sites of nondisseminated gonococcal infection, including the rectum, pharynx, vagina, and urethra.[113] A single dose of cefotaxime (100 mg/kg given intravenously or intramuscularly) is an alternative treatment of GON. Some experts prefer to continue parenteral therapy with one of these agents until blood cultures (with or without CSF cultures) have been negative for 48 to 72 hours. Infants with GON also should receive eye irrigation with saline solution immediately on recognition and at frequent intervals until the discharge is eliminated. Topical antimicrobial agents alone are inadequate and are unnecessary when the recommended systemic antibiotics are given.

Simultaneous infection with *C. trachomatis* has been reported and should be considered a potential explanation for neonates who do not respond satisfactorily to the recommended treatment.

DISSEMINATED GONOCOCCAL INFECTION OR SCALP ABSCESS. The recommended therapy for gonococcal arthritis, scalp abscess, and sepsis is ceftriaxone (25 to 50 mg/kg intravenously or intramuscularly given once a day) for 7 days or cefotaxime (50 mg/kg/day given intravenously or intramuscularly in two divided doses) for 7 days. Cefotaxime is preferred for infants with hyperbilirubinemia. If meningitis is present, treatment should be continued for 10 to 14 days with consideration of use of higher daily doses of these agents.

TREATMENT OF GONOCOCCAL INFECTIONS BEYOND THE NEONATAL PERIOD

Treatment recommendations based on weight for uncomplicated and complicated gonococcal infection are outlined in Table 94–6. Treatment recommendations for adolescents are the same as those for adults. For treatment recommendations for PID, see Tables 49–7 and 49–8. All treatment regimens include agents active against *C. trachomatis* in addition to *N. gonorrhoeae*.

CHILDREN ALLERGIC TO CEPHALOSPORINS. Selection of alternative antibiotic therapy in persons with a history of a reaction to a cephalosporin must be guided by the severity of the reaction and the availability of suitable alternative regimens.[60] For those with uncomplicated gonococcal infection who are unable to take cephalosporins and who also are too young to receive a quinolone, spectinomycin (40 mg/kg given intramuscularly, with a maximal dose of 2 g) can be used. If spectinomycin is not available readily, the use of other agents such as ciprofloxacin may be considered. Doxycycline is an option for children 8 years of age or older if the gonococcal isolate is known to be susceptible. Doxycycline may be considered for the treatment of susceptible isolates in children younger than 8 years of age if necessary (no suitable alternatives). Azithromycin also may be an option in some circumstances (see later).

UNCOMPLICATED PHARYNGEAL GONORRHEA. Gonococcal infection of the pharynx is more difficult to eradicate than is infection of urogenital and anorectal sites. Chlamydial infection of the pharynx is an unusual occurrence, but genital co-infection may be present. A single dose of ceftriaxone (125 mg, intramuscularly) is the preferred treatment of uncomplicated pharyngeal gonococcal infection. For those unable to tolerate ceftriaxone, single doses of ciprofloxacin or ofloxacin (as in Table 94–6) may be used. Trimethoprim-sulfamethoxazole given orally once daily for 5 days may be effective as well. Spectinomycin is unreliable against *N. gonorrhoeae* in the pharynx; it eradicates the organism in only approximately 50 percent of cases. If spectinomycin is required because of allergies or contraindications to the other recommended treatments, pharyngeal culture should be performed 3 to 5 days after completion of therapy to verify eradication of the infection.

INFECTION WITH HUMAN IMMUNODEFICIENCY VIRUS. Children and adolescents infected with HIV who acquire a gonococcal infection should receive the same treatment as persons without HIV infection.

CONCURRENT SYPHILIS INFECTION. A single dose of ceftriaxone is not adequate for the treatment of syphilis. Longer courses of therapy are required (see Chapter 150). *Treponema pallidum* is not susceptible to fluoroquinolones or spectinomycin.

PREGNANCY. Pregnant women should not be treated with quinolone or tetracycline agents. Those unable to take one of the recommended cephalosporin regimens can be treated with spectinomycin. Azithromycin may be considered if the recommended cephalosporins or spectinomycin cannot be used.

TABLE 94–6 ■ TREATMENT OF GONOCOCCAL INFECTIONS IN CHILDREN BEYOND THE NEWBORN PERIOD AND ADOLESCENTS[*][†]

Disease Category	Prepubertal Children Who Weigh <100 lb (45 kg)	Adolescents and Postpubertal Childen Who Weigh >100 lb (45 kg)
Uncomplicated gonococcal infections[‡]		
Vulvovaginitis, endocervicitis, urethritis, proctitis, or pharyngitis[§]	Ceftriaxone, 125 mg IM in a single dose or Spectinomycin,[§] 40 mg/kg (maximum, 2 g) IM in a single dose plus[†] Erythromycin, 50 mg/kg/day (maximum, 2 g/day) in 4 divided doses for 7 days or Azithromycin, 20 mg/kg (maximum, 1 g) in a single dose	Ceftriaxone, 125 mg IM in a single dose[‖] or Cefixime,[¶] 400 mg orally in a single dose[‖] or Ciprofloxacin,[**] 500 mg orally in a single dose[‖] or Ofloxacin,[**] 400 mg orally in a single dose plus[†] Doxycycline,[††] 100 mg orally twice a day for 7 days or Azithromycin, 1 g orally in a single dose
Conjunctivitis[‡‡]	Ceftriaxone, 50 mg/kg (maximum, 1 g) IM in a single dose	Ceftriaxone, 1 g IM in a single dose
Pelvic inflammatory disease		See Chapter 49, Tables 49–7 and 49–8
Disseminated gonococcal infection[§§][‖‖]		
Arthritis, sepsis, arthritis-dermatitis syndrome	Ceftriaxone, 50 mg/kg/day (maximum, 1 g/day) IV or IM once a day for 7 days[¶¶]	Ceftriaxone, 1 g IV or IM given once a day for 7 days[¶¶] or Cefotaxime, 1 g IV every 8 hr for 7 days[¶¶]
Meningitis or endocarditis	Ceftriaxone, 50 mg/kg/day (maximum, 2 g/day) IV or IM given every 12 hr; for meningitis, the duration is 10–14 days; for endocarditis, at least 28 days	Ceftriaxone, 1–2 g IV every 12 hr; for meningitis, the duration is 10–14 days; for endocarditis, at least 28 days

[*]See text for a discussion of the treatment options for patients with allergies to the recommended regimens.
[†]In addition to the recommended treatment of gonococcal infection, therapy for *Chlamydia trachomatis* is recommended because of the common occurrence of co-infections with these microbes.
[‡]Hospitalization should be considered for persons who are unlikely to receive the prescribed treatment because of personal or parent/guardian failure to adhere to the regimen or those whose infection has not responded to outpatient therapy.
[§]Spectinomycin is not recommended for the treatment of pharyngeal infection. In persons who cannot take a cephalosporin or a fluoroquinolone, a 5-day oral regimen of trimethoprim-sulfamethoxazole may be given. If spectinomycin must be used for pharyngeal infection, follow-up cultures should be performed.
[‖]Alternative regimens for uncomplicated infection include spectinomycin (2 g IM in a single dose), ceftizoxime, cefotaxime, cefotetan, and cefoxitin. Spectinomycin is not recommended for pharyngitis.
[¶]Experience in adults suggests that cefixime can be considered for use in children for uncomplicated gonococcal infection, but few data are available to confirm its effectiveness for gonococcal infection in children.
[**]Fluoroquinolones are contraindicated for women who are pregnant or nursing and usually for persons younger than 18 years (see text).
[††]Doxcycline is not recommended for routine use in children younger than 8 years.
[‡‡]Eyes should be lavaged with saline initially and at regular intervals until secretions no longer continue to accumulate.
[§§]Hospitalization is required. For older children and adolescents, parenteral therapy can be discontinued 24 to 48 hours after improvement occurs and the 7-day course completed with an appropriate oral antimicrobial such as cefixime (400 mg orally twice a day), ciprofloxacin (500 mg orally twice a day), or ofloxacin (400 orally twice a day). Both ciprofloxacin and ofloxacin are contraindicated for women who are pregnant and nursing and usually for persons younger than 18 years (see text).
[‖‖]Persons with disseminated gonococcal infection also should receive one of the age-appropriate regimens listed in this table for treatment of possible *C. trachomatis* co-infection as part of treatment in persons with uncomplicated gonococcal infection.
[¶¶]Some experts advise a 10- to 14-day course of therapy for gonococcal sepsis or septic arthritis.
IM, intramuscularly; IV, intravenously.
Based on recommendations put forth by Centers for Disease Control and Prevention: 1998 Guidelines for treatment of sexually transmitted diseases. M. M. W. R. Recomm. Rep. *47* (RR-1):1–116, 1998; and American Academy of Pediatrics: Gonococcal infections. *In* Pickering, L.K. (ed.): 2000 Red Book: Report of the Committee on Infectious Diseases. 25th ed. Elk Grove Village, IL, American Academy of Pediatrics, 2000, pp. 254–260.

Azithromycin (2 g, orally) is effective against uncomplicated gonococcal infection in adolescents and adults, but it is expensive and associated with gastrointestinal distress too frequently to be recommended for routine treatment of gonorrhea. Patients should be observed for at least 30 minutes after the ingestion of a 2 g-dose of azithromycin to monitor tolerance of the medication.[60] An oral dose of 1 g of azithromycin cures approximately 93 percent of uncomplicated gonococcal infections in adults. Though better tolerated, this dose is not sufficiently effective for routine use. Nonetheless, azithromycin may be useful in circumstances in which patients are unable to take standard regimens because of allergies, pregnancy, or concerns of age-related toxicity (e.g., dental staining with tetracyclines, cartilage concerns with quinolones) or when no other alternatives are available. A single dose of 20 mg/kg (maximum, 1 g) is recommended for the treatment of chlamydial infection in children, but no dose recommendations for azithromycin are available for the treatment of gonococcal infection in children.[5]

Follow-up

The recommended regimens have such high cure rates that routine repeat testing for cure no longer is recommended.[56, 68] Obtaining follow-up cultures may be prudent if atypical therapies are used or if compliance is uncertain. Treatment failures can occur, and cultures should be repeated when symptoms persist after treatment. Gonococcal isolates recovered in the setting of treatment failure should be tested for susceptibility to multiple antimicrobial agents. Apparent treatment failure also may be the result of reinfection.

Prevention and Control of Gonococcal Infections

All gonococcal infections must be reported to public health officials. Effort should be made to evaluate, counsel, and treat all sexual partners who were exposed to the index case within 2 weeks before the onset of symptoms or diagnosis in the index case. The exposure period may be extended to 1 month before diagnosis in patients identified with asymptomatic infection.[139, 146] When patients with gonococcal infection are hospitalized, including infants with ophthalmia neonatorum,[5] standard precautions are recommended.

Condoms provide a high degree of protection against the acquisition and transmission of genital infection.[162, 293] Other barrier contraceptive measures and topical spermicidal and bactericidal agents likewise can reduce the likelihood of acquiring gonococcal (and chlamydial) infection.[14, 51, 194, 286] Postexposure prophylactic antibiotics also reduce the risk of developing infection but are unlikely to be cost-effective.[138]

PREVENTION OF NEONATAL INFECTION

Pregnant adolescents should have an endocervical culture for *N. gonorrhoeae* as part of their initial prenatal care visit. A second culture late in the third trimester should be performed for those at high risk of exposure during pregnancy. For infected pregnant women, fluoroquinolone or tetracycline antibiotics should not be used because of potential fetal toxicity.[5]

PREVENTION OF GONOCOCCAL OPHTHALMIA NEONATORUM

See the earlier sections on GON.

VACCINE DEVELOPMENT

Research into the development of vaccines for gonococcal infection is ongoing. Two factors render it a difficult problem: the rapid antigenic variation in gonococcal surface proteins and the reality that natural genital infection does not induce a sufficient immune response to prevent later reinfection by the same strain. The development of a gonococcal vaccine shares the difficulties of similar efforts that are under way to produce vaccines effective against serogroup B strains of *N. meningitidis*. Combinations of recombinant antigens from multiple porin or Opa proteins probably hold the most hope.[70]

Acknowledgment

The author would like to acknowledge the contribution of Dr. Laura Gutman to this edition through her authorship of this chapter in previous editions.

REFERENCES

1. Abbott, S. L.: Gonococcal tonsillitis-pharyngitis in a 5-year-old girl. Pediatrics *52*:287–289, 1973.
2. Ahmed, H. J., Ilardi, I., Antognoli, A., et al.: An epidemic of *Neisseria gonorrhoeae* in a Somali orphanage. Int. J. STD AIDS *3*:52–53, 1992.
3. Alexander, W. J., Griffith, H., Housch, J. G., et al.: Infections in sexual contacts and associates of children with gonorrhea. Sex. Transm. Dis. *11*:156–158, 1984.
4. Allen, J. H., and Barrere, L. E.: Prophylaxis of gonorrhea ophthalmia of the newborn. J. A. M. A. *141*:522–525, 1949.
5. American Academy of Pediatrics: Gonococcal infections. *In* Pickering, L. K. (ed.): 2000 Red Book: Report of the Committee on Infectious Diseases. 25th ed. Elk Grove Village, IL, American Academy of Pediatrics, 2000, pp. 254–260.
6. American Academy of Pediatrics Committee on Child Abuse and Neglect: Guidelines for the evaluation of sexual abuse of children. Pediatrics *87*:254–260, 1991.
7. Amstey, M. S., and Steadman, K. T.: Asymptomatic gonorrhea and pregnancy. J. Am. Vener. Dis. Assoc. *3*:14–16, 1976.
8. Anderson, B., Albritton, W. L., Biddle, J., and Johnson, S. R.: Common b-lactamase–specifying plasmid in *Haemophilus ducreyi* and *Neisseria gonorrhoeae*. Antimicrob. Agents Chemother. *25*:296–297, 1984.
9. Angevine, C. D., Hall, C. B., and Jacox, R. F.: A case of gonococcal osteomyelitis: A complication of gonococcal arthritis. Am. J. Dis. Child. *130*:1013–1014, 1976.
10. Apicella, M. A.: Serogrouping of *Neisseria gonorrhoeae:* Identification of four immunologically distinct acidic polysaccharides. J. Infect. Dis. *134*:377–383, 1976.
10a. Armstrong, J. H., Zacarias, F., and Rein, M. F.: Ophthalmia neonatorum: A chart review. Pediatrics *57*:884–892, 1976.
11. Auman, G. L., and Waldenberg, L. M.: Gonococcal periappendicitis and salpingitis in a prepubertal girl. Pediatrics *58*:287–288, 1976.
12. Babl, F. E., Ram, S., Barnett, E. D., et al.: Neonatal gonococcal arthritis after negative prenatal screening and despite conjunctival prophylaxis. Pediatr. Infect. Dis. J. *19*:346–349, 2000.
13. Badgley, R. F., et al.: Sexual Offenses against Children. Ottawa, Canada, Minister of Supply and Services, 1984.
14. Barlow D.: The condom and gonorrhea. Lancet *2*:811, 1977.
15. Barnes, R. C., and Holmes K. K.: Epidemiology of gonorrhea: Current perspectives. Epidemiol. Rev. *6*:1, 1984.
16. Barsam, P. C.: Specific prophylaxis of gonorrheal ophthalmia neonatorum: A review. N. Engl. J. Med. *274*:731–734, 1966.
17. Barten, R., and Meyer, T. F.: DNA circle formation in *Neisseria gonorrhoeae:* A possible intermediate in diverse genomic recombination processes. Mol. Gen. Genet. *264*:691–701, 2001.
18. Bauer, F. J., Rudel, T., Stein, M., and Meyer, T. F.: Mutagenesis of the *Neisseria gonorrhoeae* porin reduces invasion in epithelial cells and enhances phagocyte responsiveness. Mol. Microbiol. *31*:903–913, 1999.
19. Bell, T. A., Grayston, J. T., Krohn, M. A., et al.: Randomized trial of silver nitrate, erythromycin, and no eye prophylaxis for the prevention of conjunctivitis among newborns not at risk for gonococcal ophthalmitis. Pediatrics *92*:755–760, 1993.
20. Benson, R. A., and Weinstock, E.: Gonorrheal vaginitis in children: A review of the literature. Am. J. Dis. Child. *59*:1083–1096, 1940.
21. Best, D., Ford, C. A., and Miller, W. C.: Prevalence of *Chlamydia trachomatis and Neisseria gonorrhoeae* infection in pediatric private practice. Pediatrics *108*:e103, 2001.
22. Birji, M., and Everson, J. J.: Comparative virulence of opacity variance of *Neisseria gonorrhoeae* strain P9. Infect. Immun. *31*:965–970, 1981.
23. Biswas, G. D., Blackman, E. Y., and Sparling, P. F.: High-frequency conjugal transfer of a gonococcal penicillinase plasmid. J. Bacteriol. *143*:1318–1324, 1980.
24. Biswas, G. D., Sox, T., Blackman, E., and Sparling, P. F.: Factors affecting genetic transformation of *Neisseria gonorrhoeae*. J. Bacteriol. *129*:983–992, 1977.
25. Biswas, G. D., and Sparling, P. F.: Characterization of *lbpA,* the structural gene for a lactoferrin receptor in *Neisseria gonorrhoeae.* Infect. Immun. *63*:2958–2967, 1995.
26. Black, W. J., Schwalbe, R. S., Nachamkin, I., and Cannon, J. G.: Characterization of *Neisseria gonorrhoeae* protein II phase variation by use of monoclonal antibodies. Infect. Immun. *45*:453–457, 1984.
27. Blake, M. S., and Gotschlich, E. C.: Purification and partial characterization of the major outer membrane protein of *Neisseria gonorrhoeae.* Infect. Immun. *36*:277–283, 1982.
28. Bogaerts, J., Lepage, P., DeClercq, A., et al.: Etiology and outcome of acute pelvic inflammatory disease. J. Infect. Dis. *158*:510–517, 1988.
29. Bonin P., Tanino, T. T., and Handsfield, H. H.: Isolation of *Neisseria gonorrhoeae* on selective and nonselective media in a sexually transmitted disease clinic. J. Clin. Microbiol. *92*:218–220, 1984.
30. Boslego, J. W., Tramont, E. C., Takafuji, E. T., et al.: Effect of spectinomycin use on the prevalence of spectinomycin-resistant and of penicillinase-producing *Neisseria gonorrhoeae.* N. Engl. J. Med. *317*: 272–278, 1987.
31. Bradford, W. L., and Kelley, H. W.: Gonococcic meningitis in a newborn infant. Am. J. Dis. Child *46*:543–549, 1933.
32. Bramley, J., Demarco de Hormaeche, R., Constantinidou, C., et al.: A serum-sensitive, sialyltransferase-deficient mutant of *Neisseria gonorrhoeae* defective in conversion to serum resistance by CMP-NANA or blood cell extracts. Microb. Pathog. *18*:187–195, 1995.

33. Bro-Jorgensen, A., and Jensen T.: Gonococcal pharyngeal infections: Report of 110 cases. Br. J. Vener. Dis. *49*:491, 1973.
34. Bronson, J. E., Holmberg, I., Nygren, B., et al.: Vancomycin-sensitive strains of *Neisseria gonorrhoeae:* A problem for the diagnostic laboratory. Pont. J. Vener. Dis. *49*:452–453, 1973.
35. Brooks, F., Israel, K. S., and Petersen, B. H.: Bactericidal and opsonic activity against *Neisseria gonorrhoeae* in sera from patients with disseminated gonococcal infection. J. Infect. Dis. *134*:450–462, 1976.
36. Brooks, G. F., Darrow, W. W., and Day, J. A.: Repeated gonorrhea: An analysis of importance and risk factors. J. Infect. Dis. *137*:161–169, 1978.
37. Brown, D.: Gonococcal arthritis in pregnancy. South. Med. J. *66*:693–695, 1973.
38. Brown, R. T., Lossick, J. G., Mosure, D. J., et al.: Pharyngeal gonorrhea screening in adolescents: Is it necessary? Pediatrics *84*:623–625, 1989.
39. Brown, W. J., and Kraus, S. T.: Gonococcal colony types. J. A. M. A. *228*:862–863, 1974.
40. Brunham, R. C., Binns, B., Guijon, F., et al.: Etiology and outcome of acute pelvic inflammatory disease. J. Infect. Dis. *158*:510–517, 1988.
41. Buchanan T. M.: Antigenic heterogeneity of gonococcal pili. J. Exp. Med. *151*:1470, 1975.
42. Buchanan T. M.: Attachment role of gonococcal pili: Optimum conditions and quantitation of adherence of isolated pili to human cells in vitro. J. Clin. Invest. *61*:931, 1978.
43. Burry, V. F.: Gonococcal vulvovaginitis and possible peritonitis in prepubertal girls. Am. J. Dis. Child. *121*:536–537, 1971.
44. Camarena, J. J.: DNA amplification fingerprinting for subtyping *Neisseria gonorrhoeae* strains. Sex. Transm. Dis. *22*:128–136, 1995.
45. Campbell, L. A., and Yashin, R. E.: Mutagenesis of *Neisseria gonorrhoeae:* Absence or error-prone repair. J. Bacteriol. *106*:288–293, 1984.
46. Cannon, J. G., and Sparling, P. F.: The genetics of the gonococcus. Annu. Rev. Microbiol. *38*:111–133, 1984.
47. Carbonetti, N. H., Simnad, V. I., Seifert, H. S., et al.: Genetics of protein I of *Neisseria gonorrhoeae:* Construction of hybrid porins. Proc. Natl. Acad. Sci. U. S. A. *85*:6841–6845, 1988.
48. Carifo, K., and Catlin, B. W.: *Neisseria gonorrhoeae* autotyping: Differentiation of clinical isolates based on growth responses on chemically defined media. Appl. Microbiol. *26*:223–230, 1973.
49. Casey, S. G., Shafer, W. M., and Spitznagel, J. K.: *Neisseria gonorrhoeae* survive intraleukocytic oxygen-independent antimicrobial capacities of anaerobic and aerobic granulocytes in the presence of pyocin lethal for extracellular gonococci. Infect. Immun. *52*:384–389, 1986.
50. Cates, W.: Sexually transmitted organisms and infertility: The proof of the pudding. Sex. Transm. Dis. *11*:113–116, 1984.
51. Cates, W. Jr., Weisner, P. J., and Curran, J. W..: Sex and spermicides: Preventing unintended pregnancy and infection. J. A. M. A. *248*:1636–1637, 1982.
52. Catlin, B. W.: Nutritional profiles of *Neisseria gonorrhoeae, Neisseria meningitidis*, and *Neisseria lactamica* in chemically defined media and the use of growth requirements for gonococcal typing. J. Infect. Dis. *128*: 178–194, 1973.
53. Centers for Disease Control and Prevention: Sentinel surveillance system for antimicrobial resistance in clinical isolates of *Neisseria gonorrhoeae*. M. M. W. R. Morb. Mortal. Wkly. Rep. *36*(35):585–586, 591–593, 1987.
54. Centers for Disease Control and Prevention: Plasmid-mediated antimicrobial resistance in *Neisseria gonorrhoeae*—United States, 1988 and 1989. M. M. W. R. Morb. Mortal. Wkly. Rep. *39*(17):284–293, 1990.
55. Centers for Disease Control and Prevention: Special focus: Surveillance for sexually transmitted diseases. M. M. W. R. CDC Surveill. Summ. *42*(3):1–39, 1993.
56. Centers for Disease Control and Prevention: 1998 Guidelines for treatment of sexually transmitted diseases. M. M. W. R. Recomm. Rep. *47*(RR-1):1–116, 1998.
57. Centers for Disease Control and Prevention: Summary of notifiable diseases, United States, 1999. M. M. W. R. Morb. Mortal. Wkly. Rep. *48* (53):1–101, 1999 [published April 6, 2001].
58. Centers for Disease Control and Prevention: Sexually transmitted diseases surveillance 1999 supplement: Gonococcal isolate surveillance project (GISP) annual report—1999. Atlanta, U.S. Department of Health and Human Services, Public Health Service, October 2000. *http://www.cdc.gov/nchstp/dstd/Stats_Trends/99GISP/gisp99.pdf.*
59. Centers for Disease Control and Prevention: Fluoroquinolone-resistance in *Neisseria gonorrhoeae,* Hawaii, 1999, and decreased susceptibility to azithromycin in *N. gonorrhoeae,* Missouri, 1999. M. M. W. R. Morb. Mortal. Wkly. Rep. *49*(37):833–837, 2000.
60. Centers for Disease Control and Prevention: Alternatives to spectinomycin for the treatment of *Neisseria gonorrhoeae. http://www.cdc.gov/std/specshortage.htm*
61. Centers for Disease Control and Prevention: *N. gonorrhoeae. http://www.cdc.gov.ncidod/dastlr/gcdir/*NeIdent/Ngon.html.
62. Centers for Disease Control and Prevention: *N. gonorrhoeae* serotyping. *http://www.cdc.gov.ncidod/dastlr/gcdir/serotyp.htm.*
63. Chacko, M. R., Phillips, S., and Jacobson, M. S.: Screening for pharyngeal gonorrhea in the urban teenager. Pediatrics *70*:620–623, 1982.

63a. Charles, A. G., Cohen, S., Kass, M. B., et al.: Asymptomatic gonorrhea in prenatal patients. Am. J. Obstet. Gynecol. *108*:595–599, 1970.

64. Chen, C. J., Sparling, P. F., Lewis, L. A., et al.: Identification and purification of a hemoglobin-binding outer membrane protein from *Neisseria gonorrhoeae.* Infect. Immun. *64*:5008–5014, 1996.
65. Chen J.-Y.: Prophylaxis of ophthalmia neonatorum: Comparison of silver nitrate, tetracycline, erythromycin, and no prophylaxis. Pediatr. Infect. Dis. *11*:1026–1030, 1992.
66. Chen, S.-T., and Clowes, R. C.: Nucleotide sequence comparisons of plasmids pHD131, pJBl, pFA3, and pFA7 and p-lactamase expression in *Escherichia coli, Haemophilus influenzae*, and *Neisseria gonorrhoeae.* J. Bacteriol. *169*:3124–3130, 1987.
67. Ching, S., Lee, H., Hook, E. W., 3rd, et al.: Ligase chain reaction for detection of *Neisseria gonorrhoeae* in urogenital swabs. J. Clin. Microbiol. *33*:3111–3114, 1995.
68. Christian, C. W., Pinto-Martin, J. A., and McGowan, K. L.: The management of prepubertal children with gonorrhea. Clin. Pediatr. *34*:415–418, 1995.
69. Cohen, M. S., and Cannon, J. G.: Human experimentation with *Neisseria gonorrhoeae:* Progress and goals. J. Infect. Dis. *179*(Suppl. 2):375–379, 1999.
70. Cohen, M. S., Cannon, J. C., Jerse, A. E., et al.: Human experimentation with *Neisseria gonorrhoeae:* Rationale, methods, and implications for the biology of infection and vaccine development. J. Infect. Dis. *169*:532–537, 1994.
71. Cohen, M. S., and Sparling, P. F.: Mucosal infection with *Neisseria gonorrhoeae.* J. Clin. Invest. *89*:1699–1707, 1992.
72. Colin, M. J., and Weissmann, G.: Disseminated gonococcal infection and tenosynovitis from an asymptomatically infected intrauterine contraceptive device. N. Engl. J. Med. *294*:598–599, 1976.
73. Connell, T. D., Black, W. J., Kawula, T. H., et al.: Recombination among protein II genes of *Neisseria gonorrhoeae* generates new coding sequences and increases structural variability in the protein II family. Mol. Microbiol. *2*:227–236, 1988.
74. Cooke, S. J., de la Paz, H., Poh., C. L., et al.: Variation within serovars of *Neisseria gonorrhoeae* detected by structural analysis of outer-membrane protein PIB and by pulsed-field gel electrophoresis. Microbiology *143*:1415–1422, 1997.
75. Cooperman, M. B.: *Gonococcus* arthritis in infancy: A clinical study of forty-four cases. Am. J. Dis. Child. *33*:932–948, 1927.
76. Cooperman, M. B.: End results of gonorrheal arthritis: A review of seventy cases. Am. J. Surg. *5*:241–251, 1928.
77. Corman, L. C., Levison, M. E., Knight, R., et al.: The high frequency of pharyngeal gonococcal infection in a prenatal clinic population. J. A. M. A. *230*:568–570, 1974.
78. Cornelissen, C. N., Kelley, M., Hobbs, M. M., et al.: The transferring receptor expressed by gonococcal strain FA 1090 is required for the experimental infection of human male volunteers. Mol. Microbiol. *27*:611–616, 1998.
79. Cornelissen, C., and Sparling, P. F.: Iron piracy: Acquisition of transferrin-bound iron by bacterial pathogens. Mol. Microbiol. *14*:843–850, 1994.
80. Coulter, K.: Migratory polyarthritis in a nine-year-old girl. Pediatr. Infect. Dis. J. *9*:856–857, 1990.
81. Cramolini, G. M., and Litt, I. F.: The pharynx as the only positive culture site in an adolescent with disseminated gonorrhea. J. Pediatr. *100*:644–646, 1982.
82. Crawford, G., Knapp, J. S., Hale, J., et al.: Asymptomatic gonorrhea in men caused by gonococci with unique nutritional requirements. Science *196*:1352, 1977.
83. Credé, C. S. F.: Reports from the obstetrical clinic in Leipzig: Prevention of eye inflammation in the newborn. Am. J. Dis. Child. *121*:3–4, 1971.
84. D'Amato, R. F., Eriquez, L. A., Tomfohrde, K. M., and Singerman, E.: Rapid identification of *Neisseria gonorrhoeae* and *Neisseria meningitidis* by using enzymatic profiles. J. Clin. Microbiol. *7*:77–81, 1978.
85. Danielsson, D., and Johannisson, G.: Culture diagnosis of gonorrhea. A comparison of the yield with selective and non-selective gonococcal culture media inoculated in the clinic and after treatment of specimens. Acta Derm. Venereol. *53*:75–80, 1973.
86. D'Auria, A., Tan, L., Kreitzer, M., et al.: Gonococcal scalp-wound infection. M. M. W. R. *24*:115–116, 1975.
87. Dawar, S., and Hellerstein, S.: Gonorrhea as a cause of asymptomatic pyuria in adolescent boys. J. Pediatr. *81*:357–358, 1972.
88. Deheragoda, P.: Diagnosis of rectal gonorrhea by blind anorectal swabs compared with direct vision swabs taken via a proctoscope. Br. J. Vener. Dis. 53:311, 1977.
89. Dehio, C., Gray-Owen, S. D., and Meyer, T. F.: The role of neisserial opa proteins in interactions with host cells. Trends Microbiol. *6*:489–495, 1998.
90. Dehio, M., Gomez-Duarte, O. G., Dehio, C., and Meyer, T. F.: Vitronectin-dependent invasion of epithelial cells by *Neisseria gonorrhoeae* involves alpha (v) integrin receptors. F. E. B. S. Lett. *424*:84–88, 1998.
91. DeJong, A. R.: Sexually transmitted diseases in sexually abused children. Sex. Transm. Dis. *13*:123–126, 1986.
92. Demarco de Hormaeche, R., Jessop, H., and Senior, K.: Gonococcal variants selected by growth in vivo or in vitro have antigenically different LPS. Microb. Pathog. *4*:289–297, 1988.

92a. Demetriou, E., Sackett, R., Welch, D. F., et al.: Evaluation of an enzyme immunoassay for detection of *Neisseria gonorrhoea* in an adolescent population. J. A. M. A. *252*:247–250, 1984.

93. Dempsey, J. F., Litaker, W., Madhure, T. L., et al.: Physical map of the chromosome of *Neisseria gonorrhoeae* FA1090 with locations of genetic markers. J. Bacteriol. *173*:5476–5486, 1991.

94. Denison, M. R., Perlman, S., and Anderson, R. D.: Misidentification of *Neisseria* species in a neonate with conjunctivitis. Pediatrics *81*:877–888, 1988.

95. Desenclos, J.-C. A., Garrity, D., and Wroten, J.: Pediatric gonococcal infection, Florida, 1984 to 1988. Am. J. Public Health *82*:426–428, 1992.

96. Di Bartolomeo, S., Mirta, D. H., Janer, M., et al.: Incidence of *Chlamydia trachomatis* and other potential pathogens in neonatal conjunctivitis. Int. J. Infect. Dis. *5*:139–143, 2001.

97. Dice, L. R.: Measure of the amounts of ecological association between species. Ecology *26*:297–302, 1945.

98. Do, A. N., Hanson, D. L., Dworkin, M. S., et al.: Risk factors for and trends in gonorrhea incidence among persons infected with HIV in the United States. A. I. D. S. *15*:1149–1155, 2001.

99. Dossett, J. H., Appelbaum, P. C., Knapp, J. S., et al.: Proctitis associated with *Neisseria cinerea* misidentified as *Neisseria gonorrhoeae* in a child. J. Clin. Microbiol. *21*:575–577, 1985.

100. Dougherty, T. J., Asmus, A., and Tomasz, A.: Specificity of DNA uptake in genetic transformation of gonococci. Biochem. Biophys. Res. Commun. *86*:97–104, 1979.

101. Edwards, L. E., Barrada, M. I., Hamann, A. A., et al.: Gonorrhea in pregnancy. Am. J. Obstet. Gynecol. *132*:637–641, 1978.

102. Eisenstein, B. I., Lee, T. J., and Sparling, P. F.: Penicillin sensitivity and serum resistance are independent attributes of strains of *Neisseria gonorrhoeae* causing disseminated gonococcal infection. Infect. Immun. *15*:834–841, 1977.

103. Elliott, B., Brunham, R. C., Laga, M., et al.: Maternal gonococcal infection as a preventable risk factor for low birth weight. J. Infect. Dis. *161*:531–536, 1990.

104. Ellison, R. T., III, Curd, J. G., Kholer, P. F., et al.: Underlying complement deficiency in patients with disseminated gonococcal infection. Sex. Transm. Dis. *14*:201–204, 1987.

105. Eschenbach, D. A.: Acute pelvic inflammatory disease: Etiology, risk factors, and pathogenesis. Clin. Obstet. Gynecol. *19*:147–169, 1976.

106. Eschenbach, D. A., Buchanan, T. M., Pollock, H. M., et al.: Polymicrobial etiology of acute pelvic inflammatory disease. N. Engl. J. Med. *293*:166–171, 1975.

107. Falk, E. S., Danielsson, D., Bjornvatn, B., et al.: Genomic fingerprinting in the epidemiology of gonorrhoea. Acta Derm. Venereol. *65*:2235–2239, 1985.

108. Farrell, M. K., Billimire, M. E., Shamroy, J. A., et al.: Prepubertal gonorrhea: A multidisciplinary approach. Pediatrics *67*:151–153, 1981.

109. Faruki, H., Kohmescher, R. N., McKinney, W. P., and Sparling, P. F.: A community-based outbreak of infection with penicillin-resistant *Neisseria gonorrhoeae* not producing penicillinase (chromosomally medicated resistance). N. Engl. J. Med. *313*:607–611, 1985.

110. Folland, D. S., Burke, R. E., Hinman, A. R., et al.: Gonorrhea in preadolescent children: An inquiry into source of infection and mode of transmission. Pediatrics *60*:153–156, 1977.

111. Forsyth, A., Moyes, A., and Young, H.: Increased ciprofloxacin resistance in gonococci isolated in Scotland. Lancet *356*:1984–1985, 2000.

112. Fransen, L., Nsanze, H., Klaus, V., et al.: Ophthalmia neonatorum in Nairobi, Kenya: The roles of *Neisseria gonorrhoeae* and *Chlamydia trachomatis*. J. Infect. Dis. *153*:862–869, 1986.

113. Frewen, T. C., and Bannatyne R. M.: Gonococcal vulvovaginitis in prepubertal girls. Clin. Pediatr. (Phila.) *18*:491–493, 1979.

114. Friendly, D. S.: Gonococcal conjunctivitis of the newborn. Clin. Prac. Child. Hosp. *25*:1–9, 1969.

115. Geidinghagen, D. H., Hoff, G. L., and Biery, R. M.: Gonorrhea in children: Epidemiologic unit analysis. Pediatr. Infect. Dis. J. *11*:973–974, 1992.

116. Genadry, R. R., Thompson, B. H., and Niebyl, J. R.: Gonococcal salpingitis in pregnancy. Am. J. Obstet. Gynecol. *126*:512–513, 1976.

117. Gilbaugh, J. H., and Fuchs, P. C.: The gonococcus and the toilet seat. N. Engl. J. Med. *301*:91–93, 1979.

118. Gill, M. J., Simjee, S., Al-Hattawi, K., et al.: Gonococcal resistance to β-lactams and tetracycline involves mutation in loop 3 of the porin encoded at the penB locus. Antimicrob. Agents Chemother. *42*: 2799–2803, 1998.

119. Glaser, S., Boxerbaum, B., and Kennell, J. H.: Gonococcal arthritis in the newborn: Report of a case and review of the literature. Am. J. Dis. Child. *112*:135–138, 1966.

119a. Golden, N., Hammerschlag, M., Hewkoff, S., et al.: Prevalence of *Chlamydia trachomatis* cervical infections in female adolescents. Am. J. Dis. Child. *138*:562–564, 1984.

120. Gomperts, B. N., and White, L. K.: Gonococcal hand abscess. Pediatr. Infect. Dis. J. *19*:671–672, 2000.

121. Gotschlich, E. C.: Genetic locus for the biosynthesis of the variable portion of *Neisseria gonorrhoeae* lipooligosaccharide. J. Exp. Med. *180*:2181–2190, 1994.

122. Grassme, H., Gulbins, E., Brenner, B., et al.: Acidic sphingomyelinase medicates entry of *N. gonorrhoeae* into nonphagocytic cells. Cell *91*:605–615, 1997.

123. Greenberg, M., and Vandow, J. E.: Ophthalmia neonatorum: Evaluation of different methods of prophylaxis in New York City. Am. J. Public Health *51*:836–845, 1961.

124. Gregg, C. R., Melly, M. A., Hellerqvist, C. G., et al.: Toxic activity of purified lipopolysaccharide as *N. gonorrhoeae* for human fallopian tube mucosa. J. Infect. Dis. *143*:432–439, 1983.

125. Gregory, J. E., Chisom, J. L., and Meadows, A. T.: Gonococcal arthritis in an infant. Br. J. Vener. Dis. *48*:306–307, 1972.

126. Griffiss, J. M., Lammel, C. J., Wang, J., et al.: *Neisseria gonorrhoeae* coordinately uses Pili and Opa to activate HEC-1–B cell microvilli, which causes engulfment of the gonococci. Infect. Immun. *67*:3469–3480, 1999.

127. Griffiss, J. M., O'Brien, J. P., Yamasaki, R., et al.: Physical heterogeneity of neisserial lipooligosaccharides reflects oligosaccharides that differ in apparent molecular weight, chemical composition, and antigenic expression. Infect. Immun. *55*:1792–1800, 1987.

128. Griffiss, J. M., Schneider, H., Mandrell, R. E., et al.: Lipooligosaccharides: The principal glycolipids of the neisserial outer membrane. Rev. Infect. Dis. *10*(Suppl. 2):287–295, 1988.

129. Groothuis, J. R., Bischoff, M. C., and Jauregui, L. E.: Pharyngeal gonorrhea in young children. Pediatr. Infect. Dis. J. *2*:99–101, 1983.

130. Gutman, L. T., Herman-Giddens, M. E., and McKinney, R. E., Jr.: Pediatric acquired immunodeficiency syndrome: Barriers to recognizing the role of child sexual abuse. Am. J. Dis. Child. *147*:775–780, 1993.

131. Gutman, L. T., and Holmes, K. K.: Gonococcal infections. *In* Remington, J. S., and Klein, J. O. (eds.): Infectious Diseases of the Fetus and Newborn Infant. 3rd ed. Philadelphia, W. B. Saunders, 1990.

132. Haas, R., Schwartz, H., and Meyer, T. F.: Release of soluble pilin antigen coupled with gene conversion in *Neisseria gonorrhoeae*. Proc. Natl. Acad. Sci. U. S. A. *84*:9079–9083, 1987.

133. Haines, K. A., Reibman, J., Tang, X. Y., et al.: Effects of protein I of *Neisseria gonorrhoeae* on neutrophil activation: Generation of diacylglycerol from phosphatidylcholine via a specific phospholipase C is associated with exocytosis. J. Cell Biol. *114*:433–442, 1991.

134. Hale, Y. M., Melton, M. E., Lewis, J. S. and Willis, D. E.: Evaluation of the PACE 2 *Neisseria gonorrhoeae* assay by three public health laboratories. J. Clin. Microbiol. *31*:451–453, 1993.

135. Handsfield, H. H., Hodson, W. A., and Holmes, K. K.: Neonatal gonococcal infection. 1. Orogastric contamination with *Neisseria gonorrhoeae*. J. A. M. A. *225*:697–701, 1973.

136. Handsfield, H. H., and Holmes, K. K.: Microepidemic of virulent gonococcal infection. J. Am. Vener. Dis. Assoc. *1*:20–22, 1974.

137. Handsfield, H. H., Lipman, T. O., Harnisch, J. P., et al.: Asymptomatic gonorrhea in men: Diagnosis, natural course, prevalence and significance. N. Engl. J. Med. *290*:117–123, 1974.

138. Harrison, W. O., Hooper, R. R., Weisner, P. J., et al.: A trial of minocycline given after exposure to prevent gonorrhea. N. Engl. J. Med. *300*:1074–1078, 1979.

139. Hart, G.: Epidemiologic treatment for syphilis and gonorrhea. Sex. Transm. Dis. *7*:149, 1980.

140. Hein, K., Marks, A., and Cohen, M. I.: Asymptomatic gonorrhea: Prevalence in a population of urban adolescents. J. Pediatr. *90*:634–635, 1977.

141. Hitchcock, P. J.: Analyses of gonococcal lipopolysaccharide in whole cell lysates by sodium dodecyl sulfate–polyacrylamide gel electrophoresis: Stable association of lipopolysaccharide with the major outer membrane protein (protein 1) of *Neisseria gonorrhoeae*. Infect. Immun. *46*:202, 1984.

142. Holmes, K. K., Counts, G. W., and Beaty, H. N.: Disseminated gonococcal infection. Ann. Intern. Med. *74*:979–993, 1971.

143. Holmes, K. K., Johnson, D. W., and Trostle, H. J.: An estimate of the risk of men acquiring gonorrhea by sexual contact with infected females. Am. J. Epidemiol. *91*:170–174, 1970.

144. Holmes, K. K., et al.: Is serology useful in gonorrhea? A critical analysis of factors influencing serodiagnosis. *In* Brook, G. F., et al.: (eds.): Immunobiology of *Neisseria gonorrboeae*. American Society for Microbiology, 1978, p. 370.

145. Holt L. E.: Gonococcus infections in children with especial reference to their prevalence in institutions and means of prevention. N. Y. Med. J. *81*:521–527, 1905.

146. Hook, E. W., and Handsfield, H. H.: Gonococcal infections in the adult. *In* Holmes, K. K., Mårdh, P. A., Sparling, P. F., et al.: (eds.): Sexually Transmitted Diseases. 3rd ed. New York, McGraw-Hill, 1999.

147. Hook, E. W., Holmes, K. K.: Gonococcal infections. Ann. Intern. Med. *102*:229–243, 1985.

148. Hook, E. W., 3rd, Judson, F. N., Handsfield, H. H., et al.: Auxotype/serovar diversity and antimicrobial resistance of *Neisseria gonorrhoeae* in two mid-sized American cities. Sex. Transm. Dis. *14*:141–146, 1987.

149. Hooper, R. R., Reynolds, G. H., Jones, O. G., et al.: Cohort study of venereal disease: I. The risk of gonorrhea transmission from infected women to men. Am. J. Epidemiol. *108*:136–144, 1978.

150. Ingram, D. L.: The gonococcus and the toilet seat revisited. Pediatr. Infect. Dis. *8*:191, 1989.

151. Ingram, D. L., Everett, V. D., Flick, L. A. R., et al.: Vaginal gonococcal cultures in sexual abuse evaluations: Evaluation of selective criteria for preteenaged girls. Pediatrics *99*:e8, 1997.
152. Ingram, D. L., Everett, V. D., Lyna, P. R., et al.: Epidemiology of adult sexually transmitted disease agents in children being evaluated for sexual abuse. Pediatr. Infect. Dis. J. *11*:945–950, 1992.
153. Ingram, D. L., Runyan, D. K., Collins, A. D., et al.: Vaginal *Chlamydia trachomatis* infection in children with sexual contact. Pediatr. Infect. Dis. *3*:97–99, 1984.
154. Ingram, D. M., Miller, W. C., Schoenbach, V. J., et al.: Risk assessment for gonococcal and chlamydial infections in young children undergoing evaluation for sexual abuse. Pediatrics *107*:e73, 2001.
155. Institute of Medicine: The Hidden Epidemic: Confronting Sexually Transmitted Diseases. Washington, D.C., National Academy Press, 1997.
156. Ison, C. A., Woodford, P. J., Madders, H., and Claydon, E.: Drift in susceptibility of *Neisseria gonorrhoeae* to ciprofloxacin and emergence of therapeutic failure. Antimicrob. Agents Chemother. *42*:2919–2922, 1998.
157. Israel, K. S., Rissing, K. B., and Brooks, G. F.: Neonatal and childhood gonococcal infections. Clin. Obstet. Gynecol. *18*:143–151, 1975.
158. Jacobson, L., and Westrom, L.: Objectivized diagnosis of acute pelvic inflammatory disease. Am. J. Obstet. Gynecol. *105*:1088–1098, 1969.
158a. Jamison, J. H., Kaplan, D. W., Hamman, R., et al.: Spectrum of genital human papillomavirus infection in a female adolescent population. Sex. Transm. Dis. *22*:236, 1995.
159. Johannsen, D. B., Johnston, D. M., Koymen, H. O., et al.: A *Neisseria gonorrhoeae* immunoglobulin A1 protease mutant is infectious in the human challenge model of urethral infection. Infect. Immun. *67*: 3009–3013, 1999.
160. Johnston, K. H., Holmes, K. K., and Gotschlich, E. C.: The serological classification of *Neisseria gonorrhoeae.* 1. Isolation of the outer membrane complex responsible for serotypic specificity. J. Exp. Med. *143*:741–758, 1976.
161. Jones, D. E. D., Brame, R. G., and Jones, C. P.: Gonorrhea in obstetric patients. J. Am. Vener. Dis. Assoc. *2*:30–32, 1976.
162. Judson, F. N., and Maltz, A. B.: A rational basis for the epidemiologic treatment of gonorrhea in a clinic for sexually transmitted diseases. Sex. Transm. Dis. *5*:89, 1978.
163. Judson, F. N., and Werness, B. A.: Combining cervical and anal-canal specimens for gonorrhea on a single culture plate. J. Clin. Microbiol. *12*:216, 1980.
164. Kallstrom, H., Islam, M. S., Berggren, P. O., and Jonsson, A. B.: Cell signaling by the type IV pili of pathogenic *Neisseria.* J. Biol. Chem. *273*:21777–21782, 1998.
165. Kallstrom, H., Liszewski, M. K., Atkinson, J. P., and Jonsson A. B.: Membrane cofactor protein (MCP or CD46) is a cellular pilus receptor for pathogenic *Neisseria.* Mol. Microbiol. *25*:639–647, 1997.
166. Kampmeier, R. H.: Identification of the gonococcus by Albert Neisser. Sex. Transm. Dis. 5:71, 1978.
167. Kasper, D. L., Rice, P. A., and McCormack, W. M.: Bactericidal antibody in genital infections due to *Neisseria gonorrhoeae.* J. Infect. Dis. *135*:243–251, 1977.
168. Kellogg, D.S., et al.: *Neisseria gonorrhoeae*: 1. Virulence genetically linked to clonal variation. J. Bacteriol. *85*:1274, 1963.
169. Kellogg, J. A., and Orwig, L. K.: Comparison of Gonogen, Gono Gen II and Micro Trak Direct Fluorescent-Antibody Test with carbohydrate fermentation for confirmation of culture isolates of *Neisseria gonorrhoeae.* J. Clin. Microbiol. *33*:474–476, 1995.
170. Koomey, M.: Implications of molecular contacts and signaling initiated by *Neisseria gonorrhoeae.* Curr. Opin. Microbiol. *4*:53–57, 2001.
171. Knapp, J. S., and Holmes, K. K.: Disseminated gonococcal infections caused by *Neisseria gonorrhoeae* with unique nutritional requirements. J. Infect. Dis. *132*:204–208, 1975.
172. Knapp, J. S., Tam, M. R., Nowinski, R. C., et al.: Serological classification of *Neisseria gonorrhoeae* with use of monoclonal antibodies to gonococcal outer membrane protein I. J. Infect. Dis. *150*:44–48, 1984.
173. Kohen, D. P.: Neonatal gonococcal arthritis: Three cases and review of the literature. Pediatrics *53*:436–440, 1974.
174. Krieger, J. N.: Prostatitis, epididymitis, and orchitis. *In* Mandell, G. L., Douglas, R. G., and Bennett, J. E. (eds.): Principles and Practice of Infectious Disease. Churchill Livingstone, 1985, pp. 745–748.
175. Krohn, M. A., Hillier, S. L., Bell, J. A., et al.: The bacterial etiology of conjunctivitis in early infancy. Am. J. Epidemiol. *138*:326–332, 1993.
176. Lafferty, W., Hughes, J. P., and Handsfield, H. H.: Sexually transmitted disease in men who have sex with men: Acquisition of gonorrhea and nongonococcal urethritis by fellatio and implications for STD/HIV prevention. Sex. Transm. Dis. *24*:272–278, 1997.
177. Laga, M., Meheus, A., and Piot, P.: Epidemiology and control of gonococcal ophthalmia neonatorum. Bull. World Health Organ. *67*:471–477, 1989.
178. Laga, M., Naamara, W., Brunham, R. C., et al.: Single-dose therapy of gonococcal ophthalmia neonatorum with ceftriaxone. N. Engl. J. Med. *315*:1382–1385, 1986.
179. Laga, M., Plummer, F. A., Piot, P., et al.: Prophylaxis of gonococcal and chlamydial ophthalmia neonatorum. N. Engl. J. Med. *318*:653–657, 1988.
180. Landolfo, P. J., Marrie, T. J., Nelson, N. A., and Ronald, A. R.: Cell-mediated immune response in gonococcal infection. Can. J. Microbiol. *27*:76–80, 1981.
181. Laras, L., Craighill, M., Woods, E. R., et al.: Epidemiologic observations of adolescents with *Neisseria gonorrhoeae* genital infections treated at a children's hospital. Adolesc. Pediatr. Gynecol. *7*:9–12, 1994.
182. Lawson, L., and Chaffin, M.: False negatives in sexual abuse disclosure interviews. J. Interpersonal Violence *7*:532–542, 1992.
183. Lewis, L. S., Glauser, T. A., and Joffe, M. D.: Gonococcal conjunctivitis in prepubertal children. Am. J. Dis. Child. *144*:546–548, 1990.
184. Limberger, R. J., Biega, R., Evancoe, A., et al.: Evaluation of culture and the Gen-Probe PACE 2 assay for detection of *Neisseria gonorrhoeae* and *Chlamydia trachomatis* in endocervical specimens transported to a state health laboratory. J. Clin. Microbiol. *30*:1162–1166, 1992.
185. Lin, L., Ayala, P., Larson, J., et al.: The *Neisseria* type 2 Iga1 protease cleaves LAMP1 and promotes survival of bacteria within epithelial cells. Mol. Microbiol. *24*:1083–1094, 1997.
186. Litt, I. F., and Cohen, M. I.: Perihepatitis associated with salpingitis in adolescents. J. A. M. A. *240*:1253, 1978.
187. Litt, I. F., Edberg, S. C., and Finberg, L.: Gonorrhea in children and adolescents: A current review. J. Pediatr. *85*:595–607, 1974.
188. Looveren, M. V., Ison, C. A., Ieven, M., et al.: Evaluation of the discriminatory power of typing methods for *Neisseria gonorrhoeae.* J. Clin. Microbiol. *37*:2183–2188, 1999.
189. Lorenzen, D. R., Gunther, D., Pandit, J., et al.: *Neisseria gonorrhoeae* porin modifies the oxidative burst of human professional phagocytes. Infect. Immun. *68*:6215–6222, 2000.
190. Louv, W. C., Austin H., Alexander, W., et al.: A clinical trial of nonoxynol-9 for preventing gonococcal and chlamydial infections. J. Infect. Dis. *158*:518–523, 1988.
191. Louv, W. C., Austin, H., Perlman, J., and Alexander, W. J.: Oral contraceptive use and the risk of chlamydial and gonococcal infection. Am. J. Obstet. Gynecol. *160*:396–402, 1989.
192. Luciano, A. A., and Grubin, L.: Gonorrhea screening: Comparison of three techniques. J. A. M. A. *243*:680–681, 1980.
193. Mascola, L., Albritton, W. L., Cates, W., et al.: Gonorrhea in American teenagers, 1960–1981. Pediatr. Infect. Dis. J. *2*:302–303, 1983.
194. McCormack, W. M., and Reynolds, G. H.: Effect of menstrual cycle and method of contraception on recovery of *Neisseria gonorrhoeae.* J. A. M. A. *247*:1292–1294, 1982.
195. McGee, Z. A., Johnson, A. P., and Taylor-Robinson, D.: Pathogenic mechanisms of *Neisseria gonorrhoeae:* Observations on damage to human fallopian tubes in organ culture by gonococci of colony type I or type 4. J. Infect. Dis. *143*:413–422, 1981.
196. McGee, Z. A., Stephens, D. S., Hoffman, L. H., et al.: Mechanisms of mucosal invasion by pathogenic *Neisseria.* Rev. Infect. Dis. *5*(Suppl. 4):708, 1983.
197. McMillan, A., and Young, H.: Gonorrhea in the homosexual man: Frequency of infection by culture site. Sex. Transm. Dis. *5*:146, 1978.
198. Mellin, G. W.: Ophthalmia neonatorum: Yesterday, today, tomorrow. Sight-Saver Rev. *31*:102–113, 1961.
199. Merz, A. J., Enns, C. A., and So, M.: Type IV pili of pathogenic *Neisseriae* elicit cortical plaque formation in epithelial cells. Mol. Microbiol. *32*:1316–1332, 1999.
200. Merz, A. J., and So, M.: Attachment of piliated, Opa⁻ and Opc⁻ gonococci and meningococci to epithelial cells elicits cortical actin rearrangements and clustering of tyrosine-phosphorylated proteins. Infect. Immun. *65*:4341–4349, 1997.
201. Merz, A. J., So, M., and Sheetz, M. P.: Pilus retraction powers bacterial twitching motility. Nature *407*:98–102, 2000.
202. Merz, A. J., and So, M.: Interactions of pathogenic *Neisseriae* with epithelial cell membranes. Annu. Rev. Cell Dev. Biol. *16*:423–457, 2000.
203. Meyer, T. F., Billyard, E., Haas, R., et al.: Pilus genes of *Neisseria gonorrhoeae:* Chromosomal organization and DNA sequence. Proc. Natl. Acad. Sci. U. S. A. *81*:6110–6114, 1984.
204. Meyer, T. F., Mlawer, N., and So, M.: Pilus expression in *Neisseria gonorrhoeae* involves chromosomal rearrangement. Cell *30*:45–52, 1982.
205. Mirrett, S., Reller, L. B., and Knapp, J. S.: *Neisseria gonorrhoeae* strains inhibited by vancomycin in selective media and correlation with auxotype. J. Clin. Microbiol. *14*:94–99, 1981.
206. Morello, J. A., Lerner, S. A., and Bohnhoff, M.: Characteristics of atypical *Neisseria gonorrhoeae* from disseminated and localized infections. Infect. Immunol. *13*:1510–1516, 1976.
207. Morse, S. A., Johnson, S. R., Biddle, J. W., and Roberts, M. C.: High-level tetracycline resistance in *Neisseria gonorrhoeae* is result of acquisition of streptococcal term determinant. Antimicrob. Agents Chemother. *30*:664–670, 1986.
208. Morton, R. S. (ed): Gonorrhoea. Vol. 9. *In* Major Problems in Dermatology. Philadelphia, W. B. Saunders, 1977.
209. Mosleh, I. M., Huber, L. A., Steinlein, P., et al.: *Neisseria gonorrhoeae* porin modulates phagosome maturation. J. Biol. Chem. *273*:35332–35338, 1998.
210. Mueller, B. A., Luz-Jimenez, M., Daling, J. R., et al.: Risk factors for tubal infertility. Sex. Transm. Dis. *19*:28–34, 1992.

210a. Mulcahy, F. M., and Lacey, C. J. N.: Sexually transmitted infections in adolescent girls. Genitourin. Med. *63*:119–121, 1987.
211. Muller, A., Gunther, D., Brinkmann, V., et al.: Targeting of the pro-apoptotic VDAC-like porin (PorB) of *Neisseria gonorrhoeae* to mitochondria of infected cells. E. M. B. O. J. *19*:5332–5343, 2000.
212. Muller, A., Gunther, D., Dux, F., et al.: Neisserial porin (PorB) causes rapid calcium influx in target cells and induces apoptosis by the activation of cysteine proteases. E. M. B. O. J. *18*:339–352, 1999.
213. Muram, D., Speck, P. M, and Dockter, M.: Child sexual abuse examination: Is there a need for routine screening for *N. gonorrhoeae?* J. Pediatr. Adolesc. Gynecol. *9*:79–80, 1996.
214. Murray, E. S. Bentan, M. J., Coppola, S. R., et al.: New options for diagnosis and control of gonorrheal urethritis in males using uncentrifuged first voided urine (FVU) as a specimen for culture. Am. J. Public Health *69*:596–598, 1979.
215. Naumann, M., Rudel, T., and Meyer, T. F.: Host cell interactions and signaling with *Neisseria gonorrhoeae.* Curr. Opin. Microbiol. *2*:62–70, 1999.
216. Naumann, M., Wessler, S., Bartsch, C., et al.: *Neisseria gonorrhoeae* epithelial cell interaction leads to the activation of the transcription factors nuclear factor kB and activator protein 1 and the induction of inflammatory cytokines. J. Exp. Med. *186*:247–258, 1997.
217. Neinstein, L. S., Goldenring, J., and Carpenter, S.: Nonsexual transmission of sexually transmitted diseases: An infrequent occurrence. Pediatrics *74*:67–76, 1984.
218. Nelson, J. D., Mohs, E., Dajani, A. S., et al.: Gonorrhea in preschool- and school-age children: Report of the Prepubertal Gonorrhea Cooperative Study Group. J. A. M. A. *236*:1359–1364, 1976.
219. Nicolson, I. J., Perry, A. C., Virji, M., et al.: Localization of antibody-binding sites by sequence analysis of cloned pilin genes from *Neisseria gonorrhoeae.* J. Gen. Microbiol. *133*:825–833, 1987.
220. Noegel, A., and Gotschlich, E. C.: Isolation of a high molecular weight polyphosphate from *Neisseria gonorrhoeae.* J. Exp. Med. *157*:2049-2060, 1983.
221. O'Brien J. P., Goldenberg, D. L., and Rice, P. A.: Disseminated gonococcal infection: A prospective analysis of 49 patients and a review of pathophysiology and immune mechanisms. Medicine (Baltimore) *2*:395–406, 1983.
222. O'Reilly, R. J., Lee, L., and Welch, B. G.: Secretory IgA antibody responses to *Neisseria gonorrhoeae* in the genital secretions of infected females. J. Infect. Dis. *133*:113–125, 1976.
223. Oriel, J. D.: Ophthalmia neonatorum: Relative efficacy of current prophylactic practices and treatment. J. Antimicrob. Chemother. *14*: 209–220, 1984.
224. Orr, D. P., and Preitto, S. V.: Emergency management of sexually abused children: The role of the pediatric resident. Am. J. Dis. Child. *133*:628–631, 1979.
225. Osborne, N. G., and Grubin, L.: Colonization of the pharynx with *Neisseria gonorrhoeae.* Sex. Transm. Dis. *6*:253–256, 1979.
226. Panke, E. S., Yang, L. I., Leist, P. A., et al.: Comparison of Gen-Probe DNA probe test and culture for the detection of *N. gonorrhoeae* in endocervical specimens. J. Clin. Microbiol. *29*:883–888, 1991.
227. Pasquariello, C. A., Plotkin, S. A., Rice, R. J., et al.: Fatal gonococcal septicemia. Pediatr. Infect. Dis. *4*:204–206, 1985.
228. Patamasucon, P., Rettig, P. J., and Nelson, J. D.: Cefuroxime therapy of gonorrhea and co-infection with *Chlamydia trachomatis* in children. Pediatrics *68*:534–538, 1981.
229. Pelouze, P. S.: Gonorrhea in the Male and Female. Philadelphia, W. B. Saunders, 1941.
230. Peralta, L., Durako, S. J., Ma, Y., et al.: Correlation between urine and cervical specimens for the detection of cervical *Chlamydia trachomatis* and *Neisseria gonorrhoeae* using ligase chain reaction in a cohort of HIV infected and uninfected adolescents. J. Adol. Health *29*(Suppl.):87–92, 2001.
231. Perrin, A., Nassif, X., and Tinsley, C.: Identification of regions of the chromosome of *Neisseria meningitidis* and *Neisseria gonorrhoeae* which are specific to the pathogenic *Neisseria* species. Infect. Immun. *67*:6119–6129, 1999.
232. Phillips, L.: P-lactamase–producing penicillin-resistant gonococcus. Lancet *2*:656, 1976.
233. Plavidal, F. J., and Werch, A.: Fetal scalp abscess secondary to intrauterine monitoring. Am. J. Obstet. Gynecol. *125*:65–68, 1976.
234. Podgore, J. K., and Holmes, K. K.: Ocular gonococcal infection with minimal or no inflammatory response. J. A. M. A. *246*:242–243, 1981.
235. Poh, C. L., Khng, H. P., Lim, C. K., and Loh, G. K.: Molecular typing of *Neisseria gonorrhoeae* by restriction fragment length polymorphisms. Genitourin. Med. *68*:106–110, 1992.
236. Poh, C. L., Ramachandran, V., and Tapsall, J.: Genetic diversity of *Neisseria gonorrhoeae* IB-2 and IB-6 isolates revealed by whole-cell repetitive element sequence-based PCR. J. Clin. Microbiol. *34*:292–295, 1996.
237. Ram, S., Gulati, S., McQuillen, D. P., et al.: Interactions between *Neisseria gonorrhoeae* and C4b-binding protein: A molecular basis for gonococcal serum resistance. Abstract. Mol. Immunol. *36*:297, 1999.
238. Ramsey, K. H., Schneider, H., Cross, A. S., et al.: Inflammatory cytokines produced in response to experimental human gonorrhea. J. Infect. Dis. *172*:186–191, 1995.
239. Ramus, R. M., Sheffield, J. S., Mayfield, J. A., and Wendel, G. D.: A randomized trial that compared oral cefixime and intramuscular ceftriaxone for the treatment of gonorrhea in pregnancy. Am. J. Obstet. Gynecol. *185*:629–632, 2001.
240. Rawstrom, S. A., Hammerschlag, M. R., Gullans, C., et al.: Ceftriaxone treatment of penicillinase-producing *Neisseria gonorrhoeae* infections in children. Pediatr. Infect. Dis. *8*:445–448, 1989.
241. Rees E.: Gonococcal bartholinitis. Br. J. Vener. Dis. *43*:150–156, 1967.
242. Reichart, C. A., Rupkey, L. M., Brady, W. E., and Hook, E. W., 3rd: Comparison of GC-Lect and modified Thayer-Martin media for isolation of *Neisseria gonorrhoeae.* J. Clin. Microbiol. *27*:808–811, 1989.
243. Rettig, P. J., and Nelson, J. D.: Genital tract infection with *Chlamydia trachomatis* in prepubertal children. J. Pediatr. *99*:206–210, 1981.
244. Rice, P. A., and Kasper, D. L.: Characterization of serum resistance of *Neisseria gonorrhoeae* that disseminate: Roles of blocking antibody in gonococcal outer membrane protein. J. Clin. Invest. *70*:157–167, 1982.
245. Rice, P. A., McCormack, W. M., and Kasper, D. L.: Natural serum bactericidal activity against *N. gonorrhoeae* isolates from disseminated, locally invasive, and uncomplicated disease. J. Immunol. *124*:2105–2109, 1980.
246. Rice, P. A., McQuillen, D. P., Gulati, S., et al.: Serum resistance of *Neisseria gonorrhoeae.* Does it thwart the inflammatory response and facilitate the transmission of infection? Ann. N. Y. Acad. Sci. *730*:7–14, 1994.
247. Rice, P. A., Vayo, H. E., Tam, M. R., and Blake, M. S.: Immunoglobulin G antibodies directed against protein III block killing of serum-resistant *Neisseria gonorrhoeae* by immune serum. J. Exp. Med. *164*:1735–1748, 1986.
248. Rice, R. J., Aral, S. O., Blount, J. H., et al.: Gonorrhea in the United States 1975–1989: Is the giant only sleeping? Sex. Transm. Dis. *14*:83–87, 1987.
249. Rimsza, M. E., and Niggemann, E. H.: Medical evaluation of sexually abused children: A review of 311 cases. Pediatrics *69*:8–14, 1982.
250. Ris, H. W., and Dodge, R. W.: Gonorrhea in adolescent girls in a closed population: Prevalence, diagnosis and treatment. Am. J. Dis. Child. *123*:185, 1972.
251. Roberts, M., and Falkow, S.: Conjugal transfer of R plasmids in *Neisseria gonorrhoeae.* Nature *266*:630–631, 1977.
252. Rothbard, M. J., Gregory, T., and Salerno, L. J.: Intrapartum gonococcal amnionitis. Am. J. Obstet. Gynecol. *121*:565–566, 1975.
253. Rothenberg, R.: Ophthalmia neonatorum due to *Neisseria gonorrhoeae:* Prevention and treatment. Sex. Transm. Dis. *6*(Suppl. 2):187–191, 1979.
254. Rothenberg, R. B., Simon, R., Chipperfield, E., and Catterall, R. D.: Efficacy of selected diagnostic tests for sexually transmitted diseases. J. A. M. A. *235*:49–51, 1976.
255. Rudel, T., Scheurerpflug, I., and Meyer, T. F.: *Neisseria* PilC protein identified as type-4 pilus tip-located adhesin. Nature *373*:357–359, 1995.
256. Russell, D. E. H.: The incidence and prevalence of intrafamilial and extrafamilial sexual abuse of female children. Child Abuse Negl. *7*:133–142, 1983.
257. Rytkönen, A., Johansson, L., Asp, V. et al.: Soluble pilin of *Neisseria gonorrhoeae* interacts with human target cells and tissue. Infect. Immun. *69*:6419–6426, 2001.
258. Sanders, J. M., Brookman, R. R., Brown, R. C., et al.: Committee on Adolescence: Role of the pediatrician in management of sexually transmitted diseases in children and adolescents. Pediatrics *79*:454–456, 1987.
259. Sandstrom, E., and Danielsson, D.: A Survey of gonococcal serology. *In* Danielsson, D, et al.: (eds.): Genital Infections and Their Complications. Stockholm, Almqvist & Wiksell, 1975, p. 253.
260. Sandström, E. G., and Danielsson, D.: Serology of *Neisseria gonorrhoeae:* Classification by coagglutination. Acta Pathol. Microbiol. Scand. *88*:27–38, 1980.
261. Sandström, E. G., Knapp, J. S., and Buchanan, T. M.: Serology of *Neisseria gonorrhoeae:* W-antigen serogrouping by coagglutination and protein I serotyping by enzyme-linked immunosorbent assay both detect protein I antigens. Infect. Immun. *35*:229–239, 1982.
261a. Sarrel, P. M., and Pruett, K. A.: Symptomatic gonorrhea during pregnancy. Obstet. Gynecol. *32*:670–673, 1968.
262. Sarubbi, F. A., Jr., and Sparling, P. F.: Transfer of antibiotic resistance in mixed cultures of *Neisseria gonorrhoeae.* J. Infect. Dis. *130*:660–663, 1974.
263. Segal, E., Hagblom, P., Seifert, H. S., and So, M.: Antigenic variation of gonococcal pilus involves assembly of separated silent gene segments. Proc. Natl. Acad. Sci. U. S. A. *83*:2177–2181, 1986.
264. Seifert, H. S., Wright, C. J., Jerse, A. E., et al.: Multiple gonococcal pilin antigenic variants are produced during experimental human infections. J. Clin. Invest. *93*:2744–2749, 1994.
265. Shafer, M.-A. B., Irwin, C. E., and Sweet, R. L.: Acute salpingitis in the adolescent female. J. Pediatr. *100*:339–350, 1982.
266. Shafer, W. M., Joiner, K., Guymon, L. F., et al.: Serum sensitivity of *Neisseria gonorrhoeae:* The role of lipopolysaccharide. J. Infect. Dis. *149*:175–183, 1984.
267. Shafer, W., Onunka, V. C., and Martin, L. E.: Antigonococcal activity of human neutrophil cathepsin G. Infect. Immun. *54*:184–188, 1986.

268. Shapiro, R. A., Schubert, C. J., and Siegel, R. M.: *Neisseria gonorrhea* infections in girls younger than 12 years of age evaluated for vaginitis. Pediatrics *104*:e72, 1999.

269. Shinners, E. N., and Catlin, B. W.: Arginine and pyrimidine biosynthetic defects in *Neisseria gonorrhoeae* strains isolated from patients. J. Bacteriol. *151*:295–302, 1982.

270. Sicoli, R. A., Losek, J. D., Hudlett, J. M., et al.: Indications for *Neisseria gonorrhoeae* cultures in children with suspected sexual abuse. Arch. Pediatr. Adolesc. Med. *149*:86–89, 1995.

271. Siegel, R. M., Schubert, C. J., Myers, P. A., and Shapiro, R. A.: The prevalence of sexually transmitted diseases in children and adolescents evaluated for sexual abuse in Cincinnati: Rationale for limited STD testing in prepubertal girls. Pediatrics *96*:1090–1094, 1995.

272. Silber, T. J., and Controni, G.: Clinical spectrum of pharyngeal gonorrhea in children and adolescents: A report of sixteen patients. J. Adolesc. Health Care *4*:51–54, 1983.

273. Singer, A.: The uterine cervix from adolescence to the menopause. Br. J. Obstet. Gynaecol. *82*:81–99, 1975.

274. Smith, A. L.: Principles of Microbiology. 10th ed. St. Louis, Mirror/Mosby, 1985.

275. Smith, J. A.: Ophthalmia neonatorum in Glasgow. Scott. Med. J. *14*:272–279, 1969.

276. Smith, K., Harrington, K., Wingood, G., et al.: Self-obtained vaginal swabs for diagnosis of treatable sexually transmitted diseases in adolescent girls. Arch. Pediatr. Adolesc. Med. *155*:676–679, 2001.

277. Smith, K. R., Ching, S., Lee, H., et al.: Evaluation of ligase chain reaction for use with urine for identification of *Neisseria gonorrhoeae* in females attending a sexually transmitted disease clinic. J. Clin. Microbiol. *33*:455–457, 1995.

278. Snowe, R. J., and Wilfert, C. M.: Epidemic reappearance of gonococcal ophthalmia neonatorum. Pediatrics *57*:110–114, 1973.

279. Sparling, P. F.: Biology of *Neisseria gonorrhoeae*. *In* Holmes, K. K., Mårdh, P. A., Sparling, P. F., et al.: (eds.): Sexually Transmitted Diseases. 3rd ed. New York, McGraw-Hill, 1999.

280. Sparling, P. F., Cannon, J. G., and So, M.: Phase and antigenic variation of pili and outer membrane protein II of *Neisseria gonorrhoeae*. J. Infect. Dis. *153*:196–201, 1986.

281. Sparling, P. F., and Yobs, A. R.: Colonial morphology of *Neisseria gonorrhoeae* isolated from males and females. J. Bacteriol. *93*:513, 1967.

282. Speck, W. T., and Lawsky, A. R.: Symptomatic anorectal gonorrhea in an adolescent female. Am. J. Dis. Child. *122*:438–439, 1971.

283. Stern, A., Brown, M., Nickel, P., and Meyer, T. F.: Opacity genes in *Neisseria gonorrhoeae:* Control of phase and antigenic variation. Cell *47*:61–71, 1986.

284. Stern, A., and Meyer, T. F.: Common mechanism controlling phase and antigenic variation in pathogenic *Neisseria*. Mol. Microbiol. *1*:5–12, 1987.

285. Stern, A., Nickel, P., Meyer, T. F., and So, M.: Opacity determinants of *Neisseria gonorrhoeae*: Gene expression and chromosomal linkage to the gonococcal pilus gene. Cell *37*:447–456, 1984.

286. Stone, K. M., Grimes, D. A., and Magder, L. S.: Personal protection against sexually transmitted diseases. Am. J. Obstet. Gynecol. *155*:180–188, 1986.

287. Sullivan, K. M., et al.: Characterization of DNA restriction and modification activities in *Neisseria* species. F. E. M. S. Microbiol. Lett. *44*:389, 1987.

288. Swanson, J.: Studies on gonococcus infection: XIV. Cell wall protein differences among color/opacity colony variants of *Neisseria gonorrhoeae*. Infect. Immun. 21:292, 1978.

289. Swanson J.: Colony opacity and protein II compositions of gonococci. Infect. Immun. *37*:359, 1982.

290. Swanson, J., Robbins, K., Barrera, O., and Koomey, J. M.: Gene conversion variations generate structurally distinct pilin polypeptides in *Neisseria gonorrhoeae*. J. Exp. Med. *165*:1016–1025, 1987.

291. Tabrizi, S. N., Paterson, B. A., Fairley, C. K., et al.: Comparison of tampon and urine as self-administered methods of specimen collection in the detection of *Chlamydia trachomatis, Neisseria gonorrhoeae* and *Trichomonas vaginalis* in women. Int. J. STD AIDS *9*:347–349, 1998.

292. Thayer, J. D., and Martin, J. E.: Selective medium for the cultivation of *N. gonorrhoeae* and *N. meningitidis*. Public Health Rep. *79*:49, 1964.

292a. Tomeh, M. O., and Wilfert, C. M.: Venereal diseases of infants and children at Duke University Medical Center. N. C. Med. J. *34*:109–113, 1973.

293. Upchurch, D. M., Brady, W. E., Reichart, C. A., Hook, E. W. III: Behavioral contributions to acquisition and transmission of *Neisseria gonorrhoeae*. J. Infect. Dis. *161*:938–941, 1990.

294. Van Der Pol, B., Ferrero, D., Barrington, L. B., et al.: Multicenter evaluation of the BDProbe Tec ET system for detection of *Chlamydia trachomatis* and *Neisseria gonorrhoeae* in urine specimens, female endocervical swabs, and male urethral swabs. J. Clin. Microbiol. *39*:1008–1016, 2001.

295. Van Duynhoven, Y. T. H. P.: The epidemiology of *Neisseria gonorrhoeae* in Europe. Microbes Infect. *1*:455–464, 1999.

296. Van Dyck, E., Ieven, M., Pattyn, S., et al.: Detection of *Chlamydia trachomatis* and *Neisseria gonorrhoeae* by enzyme immunoassay, culture, and three nucleic acid amplification tests. J. Clin. Microbiol. *39*:1751–1756, 2001.

297. Van Putten, J. P., Duensing, T. D., and Cole, R. L.: Entry of opaA+ gonococci into Hep-2 cells requires concerted action of glycosaminoglycans, fibronectin and integrin receptors. Mol. Microbiol. *29*:369–379, 1998.

298. Van Putten, J. P. M., and Robertson, B. D.: Molecular mechanisms and implications for infection of lipopolysaccharide variation in *Neisseria*. Mol. Microbiol. *16*:847–853, 1995.

299. Wald, E. R., Woodward, C. L., Marston, G., et al.: Gonorrheal disease among children in a university hospital. Sex. Transm. Dis. *7*:41–43, 1980.

300. Walstad, D. L., Guymon, L. F., and Sparling, P. F.: Altered outer membrane protein in different colonial types of *Neisseria gonorrhoeae*. J. Bacteriol. *129*:1623–1627, 1977.

301. Wehrbein, H. L.: Gonococcus arthritis: A study of six hundred cases. Surg. Gynecol. Obstet. *49*:105–113, 1929.

302. West, S. E. H., and Sparling, P. F.: Response of *Neisseria gonorrhoeae* to iron limitation: Alterations in expression of membrane proteins without apparent siderophore production. Infect. Immun. *47*:388–394, 1985.

303. Wetzler, L. M., Barry, K., Blake, M. S., et al.: Gonococcal lipooligosaccharide sialylation prevents complement-dependent killing by immune sera. Infect. Immun. *60*:39–43, 1992.

304. White, S. T., Loda, F. A., Ingram, D. L., et al.: Sexually transmitted diseases in sexually abused children. Pediatrics *72*:16–21, 1983.

305. Whittington, W. L., Rice, R. J., Biddle, J. W., et al.: Incorrect identification of *Neisseria gonorrhoeae* from infants and children. Pediatr. Infect. Dis. *7*:3–10, 1988.

306. Wiesner, P. J., Handsfield, H. H., and Holmes, K. K.: Low antibiotic resistance of gonococci causing systemic infection. N. Engl. J. Med. *288*:1221–1222, 1973.

307. Wiesner, P. J., Tronca, E., Bonin, P., et al.: Clinical spectrum of pharyngeal gonococcal infection. N. Engl. J. Med. *288*:181, 1973.

308. William, D. C., Felman, Y. M., and Riccardi, N. B.: The utility of anoscopy in the rapid diagnosis of symptomatic anorectal gonorrhea in men. Sex. Trans. Dis. *8*:16–17, 1981.

309. Woods, C. R., Versalovic, J., Koeuth, T., and Lupski, J. R.: Whole cell rep-PCR allows rapid assessment of clonal relationships of bacterial isolates. J. Clin. Microbiol. *31*:1927–1931, 1993.

310. Young, J. D.-E., Blake, M., Mauro, A., and Cohn, Z. A.: Properties of the major outer membrane protein from *Neisseria gonorrhoeae* incorporated into model lipid membranes. Proc. Natl. Acad. Sci. U. S. A. *80*:3831–3835, 1983.

GRAM-POSITIVE BACILLI

CHAPTER 95 Diphtheria

RALPH D. FEIGIN ■ BARBARA W. STECHENBERG ■ PAULA HERTEL

Diphtheria is an acute infectious disease caused by *Corynebacterium diphtheriae* or, less commonly, *Corynebacterium ulcerans. Corynebacterium pseudotuberculosis* infection may cause a diphtheria-like disease in humans, but it is seen primarily in sheep and goats and is not discussed further. Generalized or localized symptoms appear after the production and elaboration of a toxin that is an extracellular protein metabolite of toxinogenic strains of the causative organism. Nontoxigenic strains also cause disease, but it is usually less severe.

Before the discovery of antitoxin at the turn of the 20th century, the "strangling angel of children," as diphtheria once was called, was a significant cause of mortality in children and adults.[89] Apparent reference to diphtheria can be traced to as early as the fourth century BC. It was recognized as a specific entity in 1821 by Pierre Brettoneau, who suggested that the disease was caused by a germ and could be transmitted from person to person. In 1883, the causative agent was identified by Klebs in stained smears from diphtheritic membranes; a year later, Löffler grew the organism on artificial media and showed that in guinea pigs it caused a fatal infection closely resembling human disease.

The toxin was purified in 1889 by Roux and Yersin, who found that toxin alone could cause the disease. Shortly thereafter, Behring and Kitasato discovered antitoxins when they immunized animals with toxins rather than bacteria. The use of antitoxin to treat children with diphtheria at the turn of the 20th century resulted in one of the largest decreases in mortality by a therapeutic intervention. In Germany alone, an estimated 45,000 lives were saved each year.[46]

Etiology

Corynebacteria (Klebs-Löffler bacilli) are irregularly staining, gram-positive, nonmotile, nonsporulating, pleomorphic bacilli.[38] The club-shaped appearance of the bacillus is not a true morphologic feature but results from attempting to grow the bacillus on media that are nutritionally inadequate (Löffler media). The organism can be recovered most readily on media containing selective inhibitors that retard the growth of other microorganisms; a sheep blood agar–based medium containing fosfomycin (for selectivity) and Tindale medium (tellurite medium with cystine) are ideal.[31, 32] *C. ulcerans* and *C. diphtheriae* will grow on supplement-free blood agar, chocolate agar, and other standard media as well.[31] Colonies of *C. diphtheriae* (with the exception of the lipophilic, gray *intermedius*) and *C. ulcerans* appear grayish-white on Löffler medium. On tellurite medium, three diphtheria colony types can be distinguished: *mitis, gravis,* and *intermedius. Mitis* colonies are smooth, black, and convex; they do not ferment starch or glycogen and are hemolytic. *Gravis* colonies are gray, radially striate, and semirough; ferment starch and glycogen; and usually are not hemolytic. *Intermedius* colonies are small and smooth and have a black center; they do not ferment starch or glycogen and are not hemolytic. *C. ulcerans* colonies resemble *gravis* on Tindale medium but differ in that they are hemolytic. Like *gravis,* they ferment starch and glycogen. All diphtheria biotypes and *C. ulcerans* are characterized by cystinase activity and absence of pyrazinamidase activity. *C. ulcerans* may be distinguished from *C. diphtheriae* by its urease activity and ability to liquefy gelatin. Biotype *belfanti*, which does not occur in a toxigenic form, may be distinguished from the three potentially toxigenic diphtheria biotypes by its inability to reduce nitrate on Tindale medium and from *C. ulcerans* by its lack of production of urease.[31] Ribotyping and pulsed-field gel electrophoresis, both of which involve restriction digestion of genomic bacterial DNA followed by gel electrophoresis and Southern blotting, permit more specific typing within each diphtheria biotype and aid in the epidemiologic study of outbreaks.[28, 77]

C. diphtheriae biotypes *intermedius, gravis*, and *mitis* and *C. ulcerans* all have been observed in a toxigenic form. *Intermedius* was the biotype isolated most commonly in the United States between 1971 and 1981. Furthermore, of the strains isolated, *intermedius* was found to be toxigenic more often than was either *mitis* or *gravis.*[23] In the United Kingdom between 1993 and 1998 and similarly in other parts of Europe, the biovar *gravis* has represented the vast majority of nontoxigenic isolates, followed by *mitis* and, finally, *belfanti.*[32] In a surveillance study in a Northern Plains Native American Community in the United States in 1996, of four nontoxigenic isolates obtained, two were of biotype *mitis* and two were *gravis.*[43] The toxigenic isolates originating from various countries in Asia, Africa, and the Middle East that were reported to a U.K. diphtheria reference laboratory between 1993 and 1998 were, with the exception of one *intermedius* isolate, all of biotype *mitis* or *gravis.*[32] Similar findings were reported in the study conducted in the United States described previously.[43] A significant overall increase in the proportion of nontoxigenic isolates has been observed in Europe and Australia in recent years.[41] The reason for this increase is not clear, but one hypothesis is that increased immunity to toxigenic strains secondary to immunization has altered this statistic.

No functional or significant differences have been detected in the exotoxins elaborated by the three strains of *C. diphtheriae* or by *C. ulcerans.* Only strains that are lysogenic for beta-prophage or a closely related phage carrying the gene for toxin production produce diphtheria toxin. One or more *tox* gene sequences may exist in the bacterial genome, and the most highly toxigenic strains contain three or more copies.[63] Phage multiplication is not a necessary prerequisite for the production of toxin. The capacity to synthesize toxin depends on both genetic and nutritional factors. Toxin-producing cells apparently are those in which spontaneous induction of the prophage to the phage occurs.[37] The most important factor controlling the yield of toxin is the concentration of inorganic iron in the culture medium.[26] Growth of *C. diphtheriae* in iron-deficient media prolongs the duration of induction lysis and is associated with a high yield of toxin. High concentrations of iron inhibit the production of toxin. Production of toxin also can be increased by the use of ultraviolet radiation. Conversion to a toxigenic strain occurs in nature, as has been demonstrated by restriction enzyme studies of carriers of both toxigenic and nontoxigenic strains in Manchester, England.

The ability of a strain of *C. diphtheriae* to elaborate toxin can be demonstrated by using one of several methods. Necrosis of tissue in guinea pigs has been replaced by the widely used Elek or modified Elek test, which is based on gel diffusion of toxin from organisms inoculated onto agar adjacent to antitoxin-containing disks.[32, 34] The latter test depends on the demonstration of a precipitin band between the toxin and antitoxin. Polymerase chain reaction (PCR) has been used to detect toxigenicity.[76] PCR may produce false-positive results, however, if an isolate's genome contains a partial or nonfunctional toxin gene sequence, and this test is thus of limited value in terms of determining toxigenicity unless used in conjunction with a functional assay. An increasing number of cases of nontoxigenic diphtheria that are positive by PCR have been reported from Ukraine and Russia.[42, 66]

Diphtheria toxin is lethal to humans in an amount of approximately 130 μg/kg body weight. Cytoplasmic internalization of as little as one molecule of toxin has been shown to cause cell death.[10] Both toxigenic and nontoxigenic strains of *C. diphtheriae* can cause disease, but only strains that produce toxin cause disease with symptoms of myocarditis and neuritis.

Epidemiology

C. diphtheriae infection is acquired by contact with either a carrier or a person with the disease. The bacteria may be transmitted via droplets during coughing, sneezing, or talking. Some reports suggest that skin carriers of *C. diphtheriae* are more infectious than are either nose or throat carriers and that skin carriers may serve as potential reservoirs for the initiation of epidemic spread.[11, 52] In areas in which skin infections are endemic, levels of natural immunization may be high.[20] This phenomenon is illustrated particularly well in a survey of tetanus and diphtheria immunity in a rural Kenyan community, in which age was not found to be predictive of immunity and no correlation was found between levels of antibody for tetanus and diphtheria.[61] Person-to-person transmission of *C. ulcerans* is not known to occur, although *C. ulcerans* was isolated from the siblings of two patients reported in the United Kingdom between 1995 and 1997.[17] Data at this time are insufficient to draw conclusions. Cases of respiratory diphtheria caused by *C. diphtheriae* and by *C. ulcerans* have been documented in association with contaminated unpasteurized milk taken from cows with infected teats.[18, 44, 87] *C. diphtheriae* has been isolated from horses, dogs, and other domestic animals, and *C. ulcerans* has been reported to infect ground squirrels in the United States, although transmission to humans has not been reported.[51, 75] Fomites and dust may serve as vehicles for transmission of *C. diphtheriae*, but this mode is comparatively unimportant.

Diphtheria is distributed worldwide and remains endemic in many developing countries, including Turkey, Bangladesh, and areas of Africa, Asia, and South America. The incidence of diphtheria declined markedly after the extensive use of diphtheria toxoid after World War II. From 1970 through 1976, the average number of cases of diphtheria reported annually in the United States was 248.[67] From 1980 to 1995, only 41 cases of diphtheria, 70 percent of which were in patients older than 15 years of age and inadequately immunized, were reported in the United States.[13, 69, 78] Four of these cases were fatal and involved unimmunized children. Maintenance of immunity in adults requires a booster vaccination every 10 years. The Centers for Disease Control and Prevention estimated in the mid-1990s that less than 50 percent of adults in the United States had received their 10-year booster and that 40 to 50 percent of adults were susceptible to diphtheria.[67, 78] In addition, the toxoid vaccine does not provide any protection against nontoxigenic strains.

The incidence peaks during the cooler autumn and winter months. However, several epidemics, primarily in the southern part of the United States, have occurred in late summer and fall and corresponded to a high prevalence of *C. diphtheriae* skin infections. Between the years 1971 and 1981, the incidence of diphtheria was highest in the western region of the United States. Also noteworthy is that a 100-fold greater incidence of diphtheria occurs in Native Americans than in the general population.[23] This difference may not reflect a race difference so much as socioeconomic factors.

Evidence that diphtheria is diagnosed more frequently in chronic alcoholics and the indigent than in the general population is significant. In a 1993 to 1994 outbreak in St. Petersburg, Russia, 69 percent of a total of 42 deaths occurred in individuals classified as chronic alcoholics.[80] Between 1972 and 1982, three outbreaks occurred in the indigent alcoholic population living in Seattle's Skid Road.[50] Cutaneous infections accounted for 86 percent of the 1100 total cases. The first outbreak was caused by a single toxigenic *intermedius* biotype clone, whereas the other two involved nontoxigenic *mitis* and *gravis* strains. The incidence was highest in winter and spring.

Native Americans also represent a disproportionate number of diphtheria cases, the reasons for which are unclear, but apparently, infection is endemic in some closely knit communities. During 1974 and 1975, 27 percent of Native Americans in the Skid Road population were affected, compared with 5 percent of the white population. A surveillance study conducted in 1996 in a Northern Plains American Indian community was initiated after *C. diphtheriae* was isolated from the skin of a resident of the community. The woman was a chronic alcoholic admitted to the hospital for detoxification and treatment of severe necrotizing leg ulcers, from which a toxigenic *mitis* biotype was isolated. In the following 4 months, 11 positive cultures were obtained from the community: 6 pharyngeal isolates from patients with pharyngitis, 1 ear isolate from a patient with suppurative otitis media, and 4 positive throat swabs from asymptomatic household contacts of the index cases. Of the 11 total isolates, 6 were biotype *mitis* and 5 were *gravis*; 9 were toxigenic or weakly so. The two nontoxigenic isolates were biotype *gravis*. Ribotyping indicated that the isolates were related closely to each other genetically and to strains obtained from past cases from the same area; they were different from organisms obtained from other parts of the United States and from the former Soviet Union, where an ongoing epidemic was occurring at the time.[88]

A similar study was conducted in a Koorie (Aborigine) community in Victoria, Australia, in 1994 after three cases of nontoxigenic *C. diphtheriae* endocarditis were diagnosed in the community. Of 359 asymptomatic (with the exception of 4 people who had chronic skin ulcers swabbed) contacts of the index cases who were screened, 12 produced positive cultures for nontoxigenic *C. diphtheriae*. Five of them were of the same biovar *gravis* clone as were the three index cases.[53]

A major epidemic began in 1990 in the new independent states of the former Soviet Union and spread throughout the area. Between 1990 and 1997, approximately 150,000 cases of diphtheria were reported, with approximately 4000 fatalities.[49, 77] The epidemic was attributed to decreasing immunization rates and immunity in adults and children and to movement of large numbers of people during the collapse of the USSR. Apparently, multiple foci of infection existed across the continent. For example, most of the epidemic isolates from Ukraine and Russia were biotype *gravis*, but further molecular characterization of the *tox* genes from these areas revealed distinct epidemic strains were in each location.[54] Superimposed over the steady increase in the number of cases from 1990 through 1994, a seasonal variation typical of the Northern Hemisphere also was observed, with a significant peak in the number of diagnoses in October and November and a trough from April to July.[49] A mass immunization program was initiated in Russia in 1993, with a resultant 10 percent drop in the number of new cases reported between 1994 and 1995 (versus twofold to threefold increases in the number of cases each year for the preceding 3 years).[41] The World Health Organization also held training workshops and assembled laboratory kits to assist in the proper diagnosis of diphtheria. Making the diagnosis was difficult, if not impossible, in many countries affected by the epidemic as a result of a lack of supplies, expertise, or both because occurrence of the disease had been rare before the epidemic. As cases also began to appear in Europe with increasing frequency during this period, the European Working Group on Diphtheria (ELWGD) and reference laboratories were assembled to assist in an effort to increase routine screening for diphtheria. The ELWGD since has expanded and currently includes 20 participating countries, including representatives in both western and eastern Europe, the United States, Australia, and Southeast Asia.[33]

Pathogenesis and Pathology

Diphtheria is initiated by entry of *C. diphtheriae* into the nose or mouth, where the bacilli remain localized on the mucosal surfaces of the upper respiratory tract. Occasionally, the ocular or genital mucous membranes serve as the site of localization. The bacilli are unable to invade intact skin but may infect preexisting skin lesions. After a 2- to 4-day period of incubation, lysogenized strains may elaborate toxin.

Diphtheria toxin is secreted as a single polypeptide with a molecular weight of 60,525. The toxin initially is absorbed onto the target cell membrane and then undergoes receptor-mediated endocytosis with subsequent release into the cytoplasm. The toxin is composed of two subunits. The larger B subunit is involved in receptor binding, whereas the A subunit is enzymatically active. The A subunit catalyzes linkage of the adenosine diphosphate (ADP)–ribosyl group of nicotinamide adenine dinucleotide to protein synthesis elongation factor 2 (ADP-ribosylation), which inactivates elongation factor 2 and thereby inhibits protein synthesis. ADP-ribosylation also is the mechanism of action of other toxins, including cholera and pertussis. Diphtheria toxin also has been shown to mediate DNA fragmentation and cytolysis by a mechanism independent of the inhibition of protein synthesis and similar to that of tumor necrosis factor.[22]

Toxin-mediated tissue necrosis is most marked in the vicinity of colonization. A local inflammatory response follows and, coupled with the necrotic tissue, produces a patchy exudate that initially can be removed. As production of toxin increases, the area of infection widens and deepens, and a fibrinous exudate develops. A tough adherent membrane results from coagulation of the exudates and varies from gray to black, depending on the amount of blood that it contains. In addition to fibrin, the membrane contains inflammatory cells, red blood cells, patches of organisms, and superficial epithelial cells. Because the latter are an integral part of the membrane, attempts to remove the membrane are followed by bleeding. Edema of the soft tissues beneath the membrane may be marked. The edematous tissue and the diphtheritic membrane may encroach on the airway. The membrane sloughs spontaneously during the recovery period, although sloughing also can occur during the acute phase of the illness and lead to aspiration. Occasionally, secondary bacterial infection (classically caused by *Streptococcus pyogenes*) develops. Respiratory embarrassment or suffocation may occur with involvement of the larynx or tracheobronchial tree, and bronchopneumonia may develop if exudate enters the small airways and alveoli. Infection of these sites is an uncommon occurrence, however. Infection of the esophagus and stomach has been reported, with pseudomembranous lesions indistinguishable from those found in the respiratory tract.[56]

Toxin produced at the site of infection is distributed throughout the body via the bloodstream and the lymphatics. This distribution occurs most readily when the pharynx and tonsils are covered by a diphtheritic membrane. Any organ or tissue can be damaged as a result of diphtheria toxin, but lesions of the heart, nervous system, and kidneys are particularly prominent. Clinical manifestations appear after a variable latent period ranging, for example, from 10 to 14 days for myocarditis and from 3 to 7 weeks for manifestations in the nervous system such as peripheral neuritis. Antitoxin can neutralize circulating toxin or toxin that is absorbed onto cells but is ineffective once cells have been penetrated. Thus, early treatment is essential to limit tissue damage.

The most prominent pathologic findings are necrosis and toxic hyaline degeneration of various organs and tissues. In the heart, edema, congestion, mononuclear cell infiltration, and fatty accumulation in muscle fibers and the conducting system may be observed.[72] Burch and associates[21] demonstrated mitochondrial damage with depletion of glycogen and accumulation of lipid droplets in the damaged myofibrils. Toxin may be observed within the myocardial cells with fluorescent antibody staining.[48] If the patient survives, muscle regeneration and interstitial fibrosis can be seen. A toxic neuritis with fatty degeneration of paranodal myelin can be noted early in the disease course; segmental demyelination occurs later.[8] Liver necrosis may develop, possibly associated with hypoglycemia. Adrenal hemorrhage and acute tubular necrosis of the kidney can also occur.

Clinical Manifestations

The signs and symptoms of diphtheria depend on the site of infection, the immunization status of the host, and whether toxin has been distributed to the systemic circulation.

The incubation period ranges from 1 to 6 days. Diphtheria can be classified clinically on the basis of the anatomic location of the initial infection and the diphtheritic membrane (nasal, tonsillar, pharyngeal, laryngeal or laryngotracheal, gastroesophageal, conjunctival, skin, and genital). More than one anatomic site may be involved simultaneously.

Nasal diphtheria initially resembles a common cold and is characterized by mild rhinorrhea and a paucity of systemic symptoms. Gradually, the nasal discharge becomes serosanguineous and then mucopurulent, and it excoriates the nares and upper lip. A foul odor may be noticed, and careful inspection reveals a white membrane on the nasal septum. Absorption of toxin usually is slow and, when coupled with the lack of systemic symptoms, frequently delays accurate diagnosis. The nasal form of the disease occurs most often in infants.

Tonsillar and pharyngeal diphtherias begin as an insidious, but more severe form of the disease. Anorexia, malaise, low-grade fever, and pharyngitis are noted initially. Within 1 or 2 days, a membrane appears that varies in extent, depending on the immune status of the host. In some partially immune persons, a membrane may not develop. The white or gray adherent membrane may cover the tonsils and pharyngeal walls and extend into the uvula and soft palate or down into the larynx and trachea. Attempts to remove the membrane are followed by bleeding. Cervical lymphadenitis is variable. In some cases, it is associated with edema of the soft tissues of the neck and may be so severe that it gives the appearance of a "bull neck." In a 1970 epidemic, "erasure" edema of the neck was noted in patients with pharyngeal diphtheria.[65] Patients with erasure edema did not have a classic bull neck appearance, but the edema was characterized by obliteration of the sternocleidomastoid muscle border, the mandible, and the median border of the clavicle. The edema was brawny, pitting, warm to the touch, and tender to palpation. Erasure edema was noted in 29 percent of immunized patients and 30 percent of nonimmunized or inadequately immunized persons. It occurred most commonly in children older than 6 years of age and generally was associated with infection by the *gravis* or *intermedius* strain of *C. diphtheriae.*

The course of pharyngeal diphtheria depends on the degree of elaboration of the toxin and the extent of the membrane. In severe cases, respiratory and circulatory collapse may occur. The pulse rate is increased disproportionately to body temperature, which generally remains normal or slightly elevated. The palate may be paralyzed. This paralysis may be unilateral or bilateral and associated with difficulty swallowing and regurgitating.[29] Stupor, coma, and death may occur within a week to 10 days. In less severe cases, recovery may be slow and may be complicated by the development of myocarditis or neuritis. In mild cases, the membrane sloughs off in 7 to 10 days, and recovery is uneventful.

Laryngeal diphtheria generally reflects a downward extension of the membrane from the pharynx. Occasionally, only the larynx is involved, and in these patients toxicity is less prominent. The clinical findings are indistinguishable from other types of infectious croup. Noisy breathing, progressive stridor, hoarseness, and a dry cough may be noted. Suprasternal, subcostal, and supraclavicular retractions reflect severe laryngeal obstruction, which may be fatal unless alleviated. Occasionally, in a mild case, an acute and fatal obstruction may occur because of a partially detached piece of membrane that occludes the airway. In severe cases of laryngeal diphtheria, the membrane may extend downward and invade the entire tracheobronchial tree. Rarely, laryngeal diphtheria is primary and does not reflect an extension of disease from the pharynx. In these cases, toxicity and signs of toxemia generally are less prominent. Two cases of isolated diphtheritic tracheitis have been reported in the literature.[12, 85]

Cutaneous disease, unlike pharyngeal disease, is a more common occurrence in warmer climates and often is caused by nontoxigenic strains. In some countries with tropical and subtropical climates, such as Uganda, Tanzania, Sri Lanka, and Samoa, *C. diphtheriae* has been isolated from as many as 60 percent of skin lesions in children.[52] Cutaneous diphtheria is more contagious than is respiratory diphtheria, and this form of the disease may be an important source of person-to-person transmission of diphtheritic organisms and outbreaks in indigenous populations in which overcrowding and poor hygiene are important risk factors.[11, 20, 52] The skin lesions begin as vesicles or pustules that progress to typical ulcers with sharply defined borders, membranous bases, and surrounding erythema and edema. They may be covered with a dark pseudomembrane. The lesions occur most commonly on the legs, feet, and hands. For the first 1 to 2 weeks, the lesions are painful. Spontaneous healing generally takes 6 to 12 weeks, but lesions have been reported to persist for up to a year.[52]

Conjunctival, aural, and vulvovaginal diphtheria also may occur. Conjunctival lesions usually are limited to the palpebral conjunctiva, which appears red, edematous, and membranous. Rarely, conjunctival lesions have been associated with corneal erosion.[82] Aural diphtheria is characterized by the development of otitis externa with a persistent purulent and frequently foul-smelling discharge.

Clinical syndromes other than typical diphtheria have been associated with isolation of the organism and include meningitis, endocarditis, osteomyelitis, and hepatitis. In most cases, these syndromes have occurred in patients with underlying problems such as structural or valvular heart disease or intravenous drug use or in people from poor socioeconomic backgrounds.[27, 87]

Several cases of septic arthritis caused by nontoxigenic *C. diphtheriae* have been described.[1, 47, 87] A 27-month-old child had septic arthritis of the hip and skin lesions on the lower extremities, which were the presumed portal of entry for the organism.[1] This child had received four doses of diphtheria and tetanus toxoids and pertussis vaccine, but because the *C. diphtheriae* strain was nontoxigenic, immunization with toxoid would not provide protection. In this case, the organism was sensitive to penicillin, cefuroxime, cephalothin, and clindamycin but was resistant to oxacillin, an antistaphylococcal antibiotic often used for the treatment of septic arthritis when the causative organism cannot be identified. A similar, earlier case was described in an immunocompetent, fully vaccinated 2-year-old child who had skin lesions from which *C. diphtheriae* was isolated. The skin lesions also were assumed to be the portal of entry for the organism; pan-sensitive *C. diphtheriae* were isolated from both the skin and articular aspirate.[47] In New South Wales, Australia, within a 12-month period, four cases of septic arthritis complicating endocarditis caused by the nontoxigenic *gravis* variety of *C. diphtheriae* were reported, in addition to three cases of endocarditis caused by the same strain but without septic arthritis.[87] One case was in a 12-year-old boy who died, five of the patients were in their 20s, and the seventh patient was 49 years old. Three of the patients had underlying cardiac abnormalities, and one used intravenous drugs. This same clone was isolated from three patients in a Koorie (Aborigine) community in Victoria, Australia, who were afflicted with endocarditis and from five asymptomatic contacts.[53] Two of the patients, one of whom had a history of alcohol abuse, were members of the same family. The third patient also had a septic sternoclavicular joint from which the same organism was isolated. A case of nontoxigenic *C. diphtheriae* sepsis complicated by the presence of splenic and hepatic abscesses was reported in British Columbia, Canada; this patient had a history of chronic lymphocytic leukemia.[55]

Complications secondary to elaborated diphtheria toxin may affect any system, but myocarditis and involvement of the nervous system are most characteristic. Myocarditis may occur after both mild and severe cases of diphtheria. Generally, it develops in patients in whom administration of antitoxin is delayed. Myocarditis most commonly appears in the second week of the disease, but it can appear as early as the first or as late as the sixth week of illness. Tachycardia, a muffled first heart sound, murmurs, and arrhythmias such as atrioventricular dissociation indicate myocardial involvement. Echocardiography may show left ventricular dysfunction.[3, 45, 62] Although some cases may result in cardiac failure, most myocardial complications are temporary.

Neurologic complications appear after a variable latent period, are predominantly bilateral, are motor rather than sensory, and usually resolve completely. Paralysis of the soft palate is a most common occurrence and generally appears in the third week. It is manifested by a nasal quality in the voice, nasal regurgitation, and difficulty swallowing. Ocular paralysis usually occurs around the fifth week of illness and is characterized by blurring of vision and difficulty with accommodation. Internal strabismus also may be noted. Paralysis of the diaphragm, peripheral neuropathy involving the limbs, and loss of deep tendon reflexes likewise are reported as complications of diphtheria. When they occur and an elevated cerebrospinal fluid protein also is documented, the syndrome is indistinguishable clinically from Guillain-Barré syndrome.

Rarely, 2 or 3 weeks after the onset of illness, involvement of the vasomotor centers results in hypotension and cardiac failure. Gastritis, hepatitis, nephritis, and hemolytic-uremic syndrome also have been reported as complications of diphtheria.[84]

Information on the effects, if any, of diphtheria on the fetus during pregnancy was not available until fairly recently. El Seed and associates[35] reported a case of pharyngeal diphtheria in a pregnant woman that occurred during the first trimester of pregnancy. Apart from vaginal bleeding, no complications of pregnancy were noted. Severe diphtheritic toxemia in the mother was characterized by quadriparesis, from which she fully recovered. A physically normal female infant was delivered at term. In this single case, severe diphtheritic toxemia during pregnancy was not associated with any teratogenic effect in the fetus and did not impair intrauterine fetal growth.

Diagnosis

The diagnosis of diphtheria should be based initially on clinical findings because any delay in therapy poses a serious risk to the patient.

Accurate diagnosis depends on isolation of the organism. Examination of direct smears of diphtheritic lesions remains an important, though often inaccurate, supplement to clinical examination. Identification by fluorescent antibody technique may be reliable, but only in the hands of highly experienced personnel. Counterimmunoelectrophoresis has been shown to have high validity and predictivity.[74] However, because of the nature of the disease, waiting for laboratory confirmation is not practical.

Material obtained from beneath the membrane, where organisms are most highly concentrated, or a portion of the membrane itself should be obtained for culture.[5, 25] *C. diphtheriae* is relatively resistant to drying. The use of a non-nutritive, moisture-reducing transport medium helps prevent the overgrowth of other microorganisms. The laboratory should be notified about the possibility of diphtheria so that appropriate culture media are inoculated. A Löffler slant, a tellurite plate, and a blood agar plate should be inoculated.

Diphtheria bacilli that are recovered should be tested for toxigenicity. An immunodiffusion assay, the Elek test, is used most commonly.[34] A modified Elek assay that consists of placement of an antitoxin-impregnated disk onto an agar plate has been described.[31] The disk then is surrounded by inoculates of the clinical specimen and positive controls. When compared with the conventional Elek assay, in the modified test, which uses "spot" inoculations of numerous colonies directly from the primary plate, results reportedly are available more rapidly (16 to 24 hours), with fewer false-positive and false-negative results. Toxin neutralization in Vero cells (in vitro) is considered the gold standard procedure. In vivo testing in guinea pigs or the rabbit neutralization test, which formerly was the most widely used method of determining toxigenicity, now rarely is used. Rapid testing for diphtheria toxin by PCR specific for the "A" or "B" portion of the toxin gene is sensitive and has produced positive results in specimens stored for as long as 12 months before performance of the assay.[7, 58, 59, 73, 76] The immune status of patients can be determined by toxin neutralization in Vero cells.[71] This method still is used frequently but is difficult to standardize because it uses cultured cells and also relies heavily on individual interpretation of results. Enzyme-linked immunosorbent assay (ELISA) is a more rapid and quite sensitive method, but it detects some nonspecific antibodies; thus, when antitoxin levels are in the low range, the assay may generate falsely elevated results.[68] Finally, a delayed fluorescence immune assay (DELFIA) method was developed by Aggerbeck and colleagues in 1996 and has been reported to have good sensitivity, specificity, and reproducibility.[2, 16] Levels of diphtheria antitoxin of 0.01 IU/mL or higher generally are accepted as protective. A skin-testing method, the Schick test, also has been used to assess immunity.

The Schick test was used previously to determine the immune status of the patient. It is not helpful in early diagnosis because it cannot be read for several days, and currently it is not widely used. In the Schick test, a measured amount of purified diphtheria toxin (0.1 mL) is injected intracutaneously. A hypersensitivity reaction indicates an inadequate presence of antitoxin. A toxoid control also is injected, in the opposite arm, to help distinguish between a reaction to toxin and a reaction to other antigens in the toxin preparation.

Other laboratory studies are of little diagnostic value. The white blood cell count may be normal or elevated. Rarely, anemia develops as a result of rapid hemolysis of red blood cells. Examination of cerebrospinal fluid may reveal a minimal elevation of protein and, rarely, a mild pleocytosis in patients with diphtheritic neuritis. Hypoglycemia, glucosuria, or both may occur and reflect hepatic toxicity. An elevation in blood urea nitrogen may develop in patients with acute tubular necrosis. An electrocardiogram should be obtained and may reveal ST-segment and T-wave changes or arrhythmias indicative of myocarditis.

Differential Diagnosis

Mild forms of nasal diphtheria in a partially immunized host may resemble the common cold. When the nasal discharge is more serosanguineous or purulent, nasal diphtheria must be distinguished from a foreign body in the nose, sinusitis, adenoiditis, or the snuffles of congenital syphilis. Careful examination of the nose with a nasal speculum, sinus radiographs, and appropriate serologic tests for syphilis are helpful in excluding these disorders.

Tonsillar or pharyngeal diphtheria must be differentiated from streptococcal pharyngitis. Generally, streptococcal pharyngitis is associated with more severe pain on swallowing, higher temperature, and a relatively nonadherent membrane limited to the tonsils. In some patients, pharyngeal diphtheria and streptococcal pharyngitis coexist.

Tonsillar and pharyngeal diphtheria also must be differentiated from infectious mononucleosis (lymphadenopathy and splenomegaly are common findings, atypical lymphocytes are generally present, and heterophile antibody may be present), nonbacterial membranous tonsillitis (the white blood cell count generally is low, throat cultures reveal normal flora, and the course is unaffected by antibiotics), primary herpetic tonsillitis (the presence of gingivitis, stomatitis, and discrete lesions of the tongue and palate may be helpful), Vincent angina (may be indistinguishable), and thrush (constitutional symptoms are absent, and lesions are present on the buccal mucosa and tongue). Tonsillar and pharyngeal diphtheria also must be differentiated from blood dyscrasias such as agranulocytosis and leukemia (a complete blood count and bone marrow study are helpful), post-tonsillectomy faucial membranes (membranes are stationary and do not spread), and oropharyngeal involvement by toxoplasmosis, *Arcanobacterium,* cytomegalovirus, tularemia, and salmonellosis (associated signs and symptoms and appropriate cultures and serologic tests may be diagnostic).[39]

Laryngeal diphtheria must be differentiated from spasmodic or nonspasmodic croup, acute epiglottitis, laryngotracheobronchitis, aspirated foreign bodies, peripharyngeal and retropharyngeal abscesses, and laryngeal papillomas, hemangiomas, or lymphangiomas. A careful history, followed by careful visualization in the hospital under controlled conditions, aids in making a correct diagnosis.

Prevention

Diphtheria is prevented on a community-wide basis most effectively by active immunization. The preferred immunizing agent for children younger than 6 years of age is diphtheria toxoid given in combination with tetanus toxoid and pertussis antigen.[30] Primary immunization is carried out conveniently and effectively by giving diphtheria and tetanus toxoids and pertussis vaccine at 2, 4, and 6 months of age, with booster doses given at 12 to 18 months and again between 4 and 6 years of age. Booster doses with adult-type diphtheria and tetanus toxoids adsorbed (Td) should be given at 10-year intervals to all immunized persons. Td contains no more than 2 Lf (limes flocculating) diphtheria toxoid per dose, as compared with the 7 to 25 Lf in the pediatric diphtheria and tetanus toxoids and pertussis vaccine adsorbed preparations. Primary immunization of children older than 7 years of age may be performed with Td. Two doses are given intramuscularly at least 4 weeks apart, with a booster dose provided 1 year later. Children and adults who are severely immunocompromised or undergoing chronic hemodialysis should use the standard immunization schedule, although response may be suboptimal.[36, 40, 60]

Most local and systemic reactions to the diphtheria and tetanus toxoids and pertussis vaccine, including fever, have been related to the pertussis component.[9, 24] Administration of tetanus and diphtheria toxoids is not followed by the high incidence of reactions associated with the use of pediatric diphtheria and tetanus toxoids and pertussis vaccine. For this reason, tetanus and diphtheria toxoids may be administered safely without obtaining an earlier skin test. At least one study showed that 7.5 Lf toxoid can be given safely to adults without a higher risk of reactions occurring.[14] Primary immunization against diphtheria for infants with progressive neurologic disorders, as well as completion of the primary immunization series in patients who have experienced an untoward reaction to an earlier diphtheria and tetanus toxoids and pertussis vaccine injection, may be performed with diphtheria and tetanus toxoids with adjuvant rather than diphtheria and tetanus toxoids and pertussis vaccine.[4]

A recent report of 97 preterm infants who received diphtheria and tetanus toxoids and acellular pertussis vaccine (DTaP) (94 of these infants also received *Haemophilus influenzae* type b [Hib] vaccine) showed that although most infants tolerated the vaccination without side effects, a subgroup of very-low-birth-weight infants (mean of 873 g) had either recurrence or an increase in the number of apneic and bradycardic episodes in the 48 hours after receiving vaccination. The apneic and bradycardic episodes were present before immunization in every case.[83]

Booster doses of tetanus and diphtheria toxoids should be given at 10-year intervals to all immunized persons. Levels of diphtheria antitoxin of 0.01 IU/mL or higher generally are accepted as protective.

Diphtheria immunization is not always followed by complete protection.[64] Immunization is directed against the phage-mediated toxin, not against infection. Therefore, fully immunized persons may be carriers or may have disease caused by nontoxigenic strains. An investigation conducted during an epidemic in Texas showed no statistical difference in the risk of diphtheria infection developing in those with full, lapsed, inadequate, or no previous diphtheria immunization; however, a 30-fold increased risk of development of symptomatic diphtheria in those with no immunization and an 11.5-fold increase in those with inadequate immunization was noted.[70] The most important health problem in the United States today is inadequate immunization of the population. Immunization rates in adults are poorer than those in infants and children because of failure to maintain adequate immunity through appropriate booster immunization. A 70 to 80 percent immunization level is thought to be required to prevent epidemic spread.[23]

Prevention of diphtheria also depends on management of the contacts of known cases of diphtheria and carriers of the organism and on isolation of patients to minimize the spread of disease. Individuals at risk of contracting the disease from the index case include those who have had close respiratory or physical contact or prolonged close proximity with the infected person, including members of the case's household.[17] Specifically, family members who share body towels and cups or eating utensils, share a bed or a bedroom with more than two people, or take a bath less than once a week have a significantly greater risk of contracting the disease from the infected patient. A history of eczema in the contact also has been associated with a significantly increased risk of contracting diphtheria from the index case.[79] The patient is infectious until diphtheria bacilli no longer can be cultured from the site of infection. Two or three consecutive negative cultures at least 24 hours apart are required, and antibiotic therapy must be complete for 24 hours before the patient is released from isolation. If obtaining cultures is not possible, isolation may be ended after the completion of 14 days of appropriate antibiotic treatment.[6]

Cultures should be taken from the nose and throat of all close contacts, who should be kept under surveillance for 7 days (as an outpatient is acceptable).[5] Regardless of their immunization status, they should be treated with a single intramuscular dose of benzathine penicillin G, 600,000 U for those weighing less than 30 kg and 1.2 million U for those weighing greater than 30 kg, or a 7-day course of erythromycin, 40 to 50 mg/kg/day (maximum, 2 g/day) divided into four doses.[5] The immune status of each contact should be determined; individuals for whom the status is inadequate, including those who have had the primary series but more than 5 years has elapsed since their last booster dose, should receive an injection of diphtheria toxoid. In addition, patients with diphtheria should be immunized during convalescence because infection may not confer immunity.[6] Asymptomatic carriers who previously were not immunized against diphtheria should have cultures taken, receive diphtheria toxoid and penicillin or erythromycin (as described earlier), and be seen daily by a physician. Asymptomatic contacts who are found to carry a toxigenic strain should be subjected to the same isolation and treatment measures as the index case.[6] If daily surveillance is not possible, benzathine penicillin is preferred over erythromycin for treatment because failure to adhere to an oral drug regimen need not be of concern. If a contact is experiencing symptoms when seen, treatment of diphtheria is indicated. Of importance is to initiate prophylactic therapy in contacts who have not been immunized, before the results of culture are received. Management of carriers is described in the next section. Contacts whose occupations involve close contact with unimmunized children or food handling (especially milk) should refrain from working until cultures are confirmed to be negative.[6]

Treatment

Treatment of diphtheria is predicated on neutralization of free toxin and eradication of *C. diphtheriae* or *C. ulcerans* by the use of antibiotics. Disease caused by *C. ulcerans* should be treated in the same manner as that caused by *C. diphtheriae*.[3, 81] The decision to administer equine antitoxin should be based on the site and size of the membrane, the degree of toxicity, and the duration of illness.[15]

Antitoxin must be administered as early as possible by the intravenous route and in a dosage sufficient to neutralize all free toxin. A single dose is used to avoid the risk of sensitization developing from repeated doses of horse serum. Tests for sensitivity to horse serum must be performed before antitoxin is administered. For this purpose, 0.02 mL of a 1:1000 dilution of antitoxin in saline can be given intracutaneously. Positive (histamine) and negative (isotonic saline) controls should be applied similarly. A positive reaction consists of a wheal at least 3 mm larger than the negative control with surrounding erythema at the site of injection within 15 to 20 minutes and necessitates desensitization. The histamine control must be positive if test results are to be considered valid. As an alternative, the test may be performed with a drop of serum diluted 1:100 and applied to the site of a superficial scratch, prick, or puncture on the volar aspect of the forearm. Controls should be applied and results interpreted as described for intracutaneous administration.[5]

If a patient has been shown to be sensitive to horse serum, the serum should be provided in a slowly increasing dosage given at 15-minute intervals. Several regimens have been used. One recommended regimen is as follows[5]:

0.1 mL of a 1:1000 dilution intravenously
0.3 mL of a 1:1000 dilution intravenously
0.6 mL of a 1:1000 dilution intravenously
0.1 mL of a 1:100 dilution intravenously
0.3 mL of a 1:100 dilution intravenously
0.6 mL of a 1:100 dilution intravenously
0.1 mL of a 1:10 dilution intravenously
0.3 mL of a 1:10 dilution intravenously
0.6 mL of a 1:10 dilution intravenously
0.1 mL undiluted intravenously
0.3 mL undiluted intravenously
0.6 mL undiluted intravenously
1.0 mL undiluted intravenously

The intravenous route for desensitization is considered safest because it offers good control, but protocols involving the intradermal, subcutaneous, and intramuscular routes also have been used frequently.[5]

If no reaction has occurred, the remaining material is given by slow intravenous infusion. Intravenous administration results in more rapid excretion of antitoxin into saliva, thereby rendering it atoxic and preventing further absorption of toxin in the oropharynx, but it does not result in more rapid systemic elimination of antitoxin than does intramuscular administration.[86] Reactions should be treated with aqueous epinephrine (1:1000) provided intravenously.

The antitoxin dosage is empiric. Pharyngeal or laryngeal disease of 48 hours' duration or less should be treated with 20,000 to 40,000 U, nasopharyngeal disease with 40,000 to 60,000 U, and severe pharyngeal or laryngeal diphtheria with 80,000 to 120,000 U. The last dose also should be given to patients with mixed clinical symptoms, as well as to those with brawny edema or disease of longer than 48 hours' duration. The value of antitoxin in the treatment of cutaneous disease is a matter of debate, but some experts recommend 20,000 to 40,000 U because toxic effects have been reported.[5]

Antibiotics are not a substitute for treatment with antitoxin. Still, penicillin and erythromycin are effective against most strains of *C. diphtheriae* and should be provided. Penicillin and erythromycin also are effective in eradicating group A hemolytic streptococci, which may complicate as many as 30 percent of cases of diphtheria. Treatment consists of a 14-day course of penicillin or erythromycin. Penicillin may be given as aqueous penicillin G, 100,000 to 150,000 U/kg/day in four divided doses intravenously or as procaine penicillin 25,000 to 50,000 U/kg/day (maximum of 1.2 million U) in two divided doses intramuscularly. Patients who are sensitive to penicillin should be given erythromycin in a daily dosage of 40 to 50 mg/kg (maximum of 2 g/day) in four divided doses for 14 days. When the patient is able to tolerate oral medications, erythromycin or penicillin V, 125 to 150 mg four times daily orally, may be used in place of the intravenous antibiotics.[5] Follow-up cultures should be obtained at least 2 weeks after antibiotic therapy is complete; if they are positive, an additional 10 days of erythromycin should be given.[5] Some erythromycin resistance has been observed, but it is uncommon and its epidemiologic significance is not known.[5, 6] Penicillin is recommended as first-line treatment in Vietnam based on sensitivity data.[57] Amoxicillin, rifampin, and clindamycin provided in appropriate dosages also may be effective. Lincomycin and tetracycline have proved to be less effective, and cephalexin, oxacillin, and colistin have been shown to be ineffective against *C. diphtheriae*. The end-point of therapy is two to three consecutive negative cultures at least 24 hours apart. In addition to receiving antibiotic therapy, patients with diphtheria should be immunized during convalescence because infection may not confer immunity.[5]

The carrier state has been effectively treated with a single intramuscular dose of benzathine penicillin G (600,000 U for children weighing less than 30 kg or 1.2 million U for persons weighing 30 kg or more) or oral erythromycin

(40 to 50 mg/kg/day for children and 1 g/day for adults) for 7 to 10 days.[5] Carriers should have repeat pharyngeal cultures performed a minimum of 2 weeks after antibiotic therapy is complete; if the repeat cultures are positive, carriers should receive an additional course of antibiotics.

SUPPORTIVE TREATMENT

Bed rest is extremely important and should be required for 2 to 3 weeks. Serial electrocardiograms should be obtained two or three times each week for 4 to 6 weeks to detect myocarditis as early as possible. Absolute bed rest must be enforced if myocarditis is detected because sudden death has been precipitated by excessive activity. A patient with myocarditis may undergo digitalization if congestive heart failure develops. However, digitalization for arrhythmias caused by diphtheria may be contraindicated. In severe disease, prednisone, 1.0 to 1.5 mg/kg/day for 2 weeks, has been shown to lessen the incidence of myocarditis.

Hydration should be maintained and a high-calorie liquid or soft diet provided. Secretions should be suctioned as needed to prevent aspiration. Palatal and pharyngeal paralysis increases the risk of aspiration occurring, so gavage via a polyethylene tube is indicated in these patients.

The quality of the voice and the gag reflex should be checked regularly for assessment of progression of the disease. Laryngeal diphtheria may require relief of obstruction with a tracheostomy. This procedure should be performed before the patient has become exhausted.

Adequate immunity does not develop in at least one half of the patients who recover from diphtheria, and they remain subject to reinfection. Therefore, immunization is indicated after recovery of the patient.

Prognosis

Many factors affect the prognosis in cases of diphtheria, the most important being the immunization status of the host. Both morbidity and mortality rates are increased significantly in patients who are unimmunized or inadequately immunized. The rapidity with which medical care is sought and the diagnosis of diphtheria suggested has a great impact on outcome. If specific treatment is provided on the first day of disease, the mortality rate may be reduced to less than 1 percent; delay in providing treatment until day 4 may be associated with a 20-fold increase in the mortality rate.

The virulence of the infecting organism and the location of infection are important prognostic factors. Infection with a nontoxigenic *C. diphtheriae* strain may cause disease but does not lead to myocarditis, neuritis, and other toxin-related phenomena. Toxigenic disease may vary from mild to severe. In cases of mild diphtheria, membrane sloughing and full recovery generally occur within 7 days. Disease caused by toxigenic *gravis* strains tends to be more severe and carries a poorer prognosis. Although diphtheria may affect the skin, nasopharynx, and other mucous membranes, involvement of the larynx heralds a more complicated course. Laryngeal diphtheria increases the risk of development of airway obstruction and promotes systemic absorption of the toxin. These patients require close monitoring of respiratory function and for involvement of other organ systems. Laryngeal diphtheria is more likely to be fatal in infants.

Few laboratory parameters indicate the severity of diphtheria. However, the development of amegakaryocytic thrombocytopenia and leukocytosis with counts of greater than 25,000 cells/mm^3 has been associated with a poor outcome.

The prognosis in the patient with diphtheria remains guarded until recovery is complete. At any time during the course of the illness, complications such as laryngeal obstruction, shock, and ventricular fibrillation may occur suddenly and unexpectedly. In patients with myocardial involvement, permanent damage to the heart, specifically fibrosis, may occur and lead to later complications. In addition, potentially severe neurologic manifestations such as phrenic nerve paralysis may appear late in the course of the disease.

Persistence of *C. diphtheriae* may be noted in the nasopharynx of 5 to 10 percent of convalescing patients. Recovery from diphtheria is followed by immunity that is demonstrable for at least a year after illness in 50 percent of patients. Second attacks are rare events; nonetheless, immunization should be performed after recovery.

Before the use of antitoxin and the availability of antibiotics, the mortality rate from diphtheria was 30 to 50 percent. Death was most common in children younger than 4 years of age and was the result of suffocation. At present, the worldwide mortality rate is between 5 and 10 percent, with no clear association with age.

REFERENCES

1. Afghani, B., and Stutman, H. R.: Bacterial arthritis caused by *Corynebacterium diphtheriae*. Pediatr. Infect. Dis. J. *12*:881–882, 1993.
2. Aggerbeck, H., Norgaard-Pedersen, B., and Heron, I.: Simultaneous quantitation of diphtheria and tetanus antibodies by double antigen, time-resolved fluorescence immunoassay. J. Immunol. Methods *190*: 171–183, 1996.
3. Ahmad, N., Gainsborough, N., and Paul, J.: An unusual case of diphtheria and its complications. Hosp. Med. *61*:436–437, 2000.
4. American Academy of Pediatrics: Report of the Committee on Infectious Diseases. 22nd ed. Elk Grove Village, IL, American Academy of Pediatrics, 1991, pp. 195–199.
5. American Academy of Pediatrics: Diphtheria. *In* Pickering, L. K., Peter, G., Baker, L., et al. (eds.): 2000 Red Book: Report of the Committee on Infectious Diseases. 25th ed. Elk Grove Village, IL, American Academy of Pediatrics, 2000, pp. 230–234.
6. American Public Health Association: Diphtheria. *In* Chin, J. (ed.): Control of Communicable Diseases Manual. Washington, D.C., American Public Health Association, 2000, pp. 165–170.
7. Aravina-Roman, M., Bowman, R., and O'Neill, G.: Polymerase chain reaction for the detection of toxigenic *Corynebacterium diphtheriae*. Pathology *27*:71–73, 1995.
8. Baba, M., Gilliatt, R. W., Harding, A. E., Reiners, K.: Demyelination following diphtheria toxin in the presence of axonal atrophy. J. Neurol. Sci. *64*:199–211, 1984.
9. Baraff, L. J., Manclark, C. R., Cherry, J. D., et al.: Analyses of adverse reactions to diphtheria and tetanus toxoids and pertussis vaccine by vaccine lot, endotoxin content, pertussis vaccine potency and percentage of mouse weight gain. Pediatr. Infect. Dis. J. *8*:502–507, 1989.
10. Battistini, A., Curatola, A. M., Gallinare, P., et al.: Inhibition of protein synthesis by diphtheria toxin induces a peculiar pattern of synthesized protein species. Exp. Cell Res. *176*:174–179, 1988.
11. Belsey, M. A., Sinclair, M., Roder, M. R., et al.: *Corynebacterium diphtheriae* skin infections in Alabama and Louisiana: A factor in the epidemiology of diphtheria. N. Engl. J. Med. *280*:135–141, 1969.
12. Berner, R., Leititis, J. U., Furste, H. O., Brandis, M.: Bacterial tracheitis caused by *Corynebacterium diphtheriae*. Eur. J. Pediatr. *156*:207–208, 1997.
13. Bisgard, K. M., Hardy, I. R. B., Popovic, T., et al.: Respiratory diphtheria in the United States, 1980 through 1995. Am. J. Public Health *88*: 787–791, 1998.
14. Bjorkholm, B., Granstrom, M., Wahl, M., et al.: Adverse reactions and immunogenicity in adults to regular and increased dosage of diphtheria vaccine. Eur. J. Clin. Microbiol. *6*:637–640, 1987.
15. Bjorkholm, B., Olling, S., Larsson, P., et al.: An outbreak of diphtheria among Swedish alcoholics. Infection *15*:354–358, 1987.
16. Bonin, E., Tiru, M., Hallander, H., Bredberg-Raden, U.: Evaluation of single- and dual antigen delayed fluorescence immunoassay in comparison to an ELISA and the in vivo toxin neutralisation test for detection of diphtheria toxin antibodies. J. Immunol. Methods *230*:131–140, 1999.
17. Bonnet, J. M., and Begg, N. T.: Control of diphtheria: Guidance for consultants in communicable disease control. Commun. Dis. Public Health *2*:242–249, 1999.

18. Bostock, A. D., Gilbert, F. R., Lewis, D., Smith, D. C.: *Corynebacterium ulcerans* infection associated with untreated milk. J. Infect. *9*:286–288, 1984.
19. Bowler, C. J., Mandal, B. K., Schlecht, B., et al.: Diphtheria: The continuing hazard. Arch. Dis. Child. *63*:194–195, 1988.
20. Bray, J. P., Burt, E. G., Potter, E. J., et al.: Epidemic diphtheria and skin infections in Trinidad. J. Infect. Dis. *126*:34–40, 1972.
21. Burch, G. E., Sun, S. C., Sohal, R. S., et al.: Diphtheritic myocarditis: A histochemical and electron microscopic study. Am. J. Cardiol. *21*:261–268, 1968.
22. Chang, M. P., Bramhall, J., Graves, S., et al.: Internucleosomal DNA cleavage precedes diphtheria toxin–induced cytolysis: Evidence that cell lysis is not a simple consequence of translation inhibition. J. Biol. Chem. *264*:15261–15267, 1989.
23. Chen, R. T., Broome, C. V., Weinstein, R. A., et al.: Diphtheria in the United States, 1971–1981. Am. J. Public Health *75*:1393–1397, 1985.
24. Cherry, J. D., Baraff, L. J., and Hewlett, E.: The past, present, and future of pertussis: The role of adults in epidemiology and future control. West. J. Med. *150*:319–328, 1989.
25. Clarridge, J. E., Popovic, T., and Inzana, T. J.: Diphtheria and other corynebacterial and coryneform infections. *In* Hausler, W. J., and Sussman, M. (eds.): Topley and Wilson's Microbiology and Microbial Infections. Vol. 3. New York, Oxford University Press, 1998, pp. 347–371.
26. Collier, R. J., and Kandel, J.: Structure and activity of diphtheria toxin. I. Thiol-dependent dissociation of a fraction of toxin into enzymatically active and inactive fragments. J. Biol. Chem. *246*:1496–1503, 1971.
27. Davidson, S., Rotem, Y., Bogkowski, B., Rubinstein, E.: *Corynebacterium diphtheriae* endocarditis. Am. J. Med. Sci. *271*:351–353, 1976.
28. DeZoysa, A., Efstratiou, A., George, R. C., et al.: Molecular epidemiology of *Corynebacterium diphtheriae* from northwestern Russia and surrounding countries studied by using ribotyping and pulsed-field gel electrophoresis. J. Clin. Microbiol. *33*:1080–1083, 1995.
29. Dietze, W. E., and Sudderth, J. F.: Post-diphtheria polyneuritis: Three case reports. Laryngoscope *82*:765–770, 1972.
30. Diphtheria, tetanus and pertussis: Guidelines for vaccine prophylaxis and other preventive measures. M. M. W. R. Morb. Mortal. Wkly. Rep. *30*:392–407, 1981.
31. Efstratiou, A., Engler, K., Mazurova, I. K., et al.: Current approaches to the laboratory diagnosis of diphtheria. J. Infect. Dis. *181*(Suppl. 1):138–145, 2000.
32. Efstratiou, A., and George, R. C.: Laboratory guidelines for the diagnosis of infections caused by *Corynebacterium diphtheriae* and *C. ulcerans*. Commun. Dis. Public Health *2*:250–257, 1999.
33. Efstratiou, A., and Roure, C.: The European Laboratory Working Group on Diphtheria: A global microbiologic network. J. Infect. Dis. *181*(Suppl. 1):146–151, 2000.
34. Elek, S. D.: The plate virulence test for diphtheria. J. Clin. Pathol. *2*:250–258, 1949.
35. El Seed, A. M., Dafalla, A. A., and Abboud, O. I.: Fetal immune response following maternal diphtheria during pregnancy. Ann. Trop. Paediatr. *1*:217–219, 1981.
36. Enke, B. U., Bokenkamp, A., Offner, G., et al.: Response to diphtheria and tetanus booster vaccination in pediatric renal transplant recipients. Transplantation *64*:237–241, 1997.
37. Freeman, V. J.: Studies on virulence of bacteriophage-infected strains of *Corynebacterium diphtheriae*. J. Bacteriol. *61*:675–688, 1951.
38. Funke, G., and Bernard, K.: Coryneform gram-positive rods. *In* Murray, P. R., Baron, E. J., Pfaller, M. A., et al. (eds.): Manual of Clinical Microbiology, 7th ed. Washington, D.C., ASM Press, 1999, pp. 319–340.
39. Gaston, D. A., and Zurowski, S. M.: *Arcanobacterium haemolyticum* pharyngitis and exanthem. Arch. Dermatol. *132*:61–64, 1996.
40. Ghio, L., Pedrazzi, C., Assael, B. M., et al.: Immunity to diphtheria and tetanus in a young population on a dialysis regimen or with a renal transplant. J. Pediatr. *130*:987–989, 1997.
41. Gilbert, L.: Infections with *Corynebacterium diphtheriae*—changing epidemiology and clinical manifestations. Commun. Dis. Intell. *21*:161–164, 1997.
42. Gluskevich, T. G., and Zherebko, G.: Study of the role of non-toxigenic *C. diphtheriae* strains on the aetiology of diphtheria in the Ukraine. Abstract. *In* Programme and Abstracts of the Fifth International Meeting of the European Laboratory Working Group on Diphtheria (Halkidiki, Greece, June 1998). London, Public Health Laboratory Service, 1998, p. 32.
43. Golaz, A., Lance-Parker, S., Welty, T., et al.: Epidemiology of diphtheria in South Dakota. S. D. J. Med. *53*:281–285, 2000.
44. Goldie, W., and Maddock, E. C. G.: A milk-borne outbreak of diphtheria. Lancet *1*:285–286, 1943.
45. Groundstroem, K. W. E., Molnar, G., and Lumio, J.: Echocardiographic follow-up of diphtheric myocarditis. Cardiology *87*:79–81, 1996.
46. Grundbacher, F. J.: Behring's discovery of diphtheria and tetanus antitoxins. Immunol. Today *13*:188–190, 1992.
47. Guran, P., Mollaret, H., Chatelain, R., et al.: Septic arthritis due to a nontoxigenic diphtheria bacillus.] [French.] Arch. Fr. Pediat. *36*:926–929, 1979.
48. Hadfield, T., McEvoy, P., Polotsky, Y., et al.: The pathology of diphtheria. J. Infect. Dis. *181*(Suppl. 1):116–120, 2000.
49. Hardy, I. R. B., Dittmann, S., and Sutter, R. W.: Current situation and control strategies for resurgence of diphtheria in newly independent states of the former Soviet Union. Lancet *347*:1739–1744, 1996.
50. Harnisch, J. P., Tronca, E., Nolan, C. M., et al.: Diphtheria among alcoholic urban adults: A decade of experience in Seattle. Ann. Intern. Med. *111*:71–82, 1989.
51. Hart, R. J. C.: *Corynebacterium ulcerans* in humans and cattle in North Devon. J. Hyg. Camb. *92*:161–164, 1984.
52. Hofler, W.: Cutaneous diphtheria. Int. J. Dermatol. *30*:845–847, 1991.
53. Hogg, G. G., Strachan, J. E., Huayi, L., et al.: Non-toxigenic *Corynebacterium diphtheriae* biovar *gravis:* Evidence for an invasive clone in a south-eastern Australian community. Med. J. Aust. *164*:72–75, 1996.
54. Holmes, R.: Biology and molecular epidemiology of diphtheria toxin and the *tox* gene. J. Infect. Dis. *181*(Suppl. 1):156–167, 2000.
55. Isaac-Renton, J. L., Boyko, W. J., Chan, R., Crichton, E.: *Corynebacterium diphtheriae* septicemia. Am. J. Clin. Pathol. *75*:631–634, 1981.
56. Jennis, F., and Bale, P. M.: Fatal respiratory and gastric diphtheria in an adult. Med. J. Aust. *2*:760–762, 1966.
57. Kneen, R., Pham, N. G., Solomon, T., et al.: Penicillin vs. erythromycin in the treatment of diphtheria. Clin. Infect. Dis. *27*:845–850, 1998.
58. Kobaidze, K., Popovic, T., Nakao, H., Quick, L.: Direct polymerase chain reaction for detection of toxigenic *Corynebacterium diphtheriae* strains from the Republic of Georgia after prolonged storage. J. Infect. Dis. *181*(Suppl. 1):152–155, 2000.
59. Komiya, T., Shibata, N., Ito, M., et al.: Retrospective diagnosis of diphtheria by detection of the *C. diphtheriae tox* gene in a formaldehyde-fixed throat swab using PCR and sequencing analysis. J. Clin. Microbiol. *38*:2400–2402, 2000.
60. Kreft, B., Klouche, M., Kreft, R., et al: Low efficiency of active immunization against diphtheria in chronic hemodialysis patients. Kidney Int. *52*:212–216, 1997.
61. Kurtzhals, J. A. L., Kjeldsen, K., Hey, A. S., et al.: Immunity to tetanus and diphtheria in rural Africa. Am. J. Trop. Med. Hyg. *56*:576–579, 1997.
62. Loukoushkina, E. F., Bobko, P. V., Kolbasova, E. V., et al.: The clinical picture and diagnosis of diphtheritic carditis in children. Eur. J. Pediatr. *157*:528–533, 1998.
63. Lubran, M. M.: Bacterial toxins. Ann. Clin. Lab. Sci. *18*:58–71, 1988.
64. McCloskey, R. V.: Diphtheria antitoxin titers in hospital workers after a single dose of adult-type diphtheria tetanus toxoid. Am. J. Med. Sci. *258*:209–213, 1969.
65. McCloskey, R. V., Eller, J. J., Green, M., et al.: The 1970 epidemic of diphtheria in San Antonio. Ann. Intern. Med. *75*:495–503, 1971.
66. Mazurova, I. K., et al. Characterization of non-toxigenic *tox* bearing *Corynebacterium diphtheriae* in the waning Russian epidemic. Abstract. *In* Programme and Abstracts of the Fifth International Meeting of the European Laboratory Working Group on Diphtheria (Halkidiki, Greece, June 1998). London, Public Health Laboratory Service, 1998, p. 33.
67. Medical News and Perspectives: Diphtheria in Russia: A reminder of risk. J. A. M. A. *273*:1245, 1995.
68. Melville-Smith, M., and Balfour, A.: Estimation of *Corynebacterium diphtheriae* antitoxin in human sera: A comparison of an enzyme-linked immunosorbent assay with the toxin neutralisation test. J. Med. Microbiol. *25*:279–283, 1988.
69. Miller, L. W., Older, J. J., Drake, J., et al.: Diphtheria immunization: Effect upon carriers and the control of outbreaks. Am. J. Dis. Child. *123*:197–199, 1972.
70. Mirchamsy, H., Hamedi, H., Fatch, G., et al.: Oral immunization against diphtheria and tetanus infections by fluid diphtheria and tetanus toxoids. Vaccine *12*:1167–1172, 1994.
71. Miyamura, K., Nishio, S., Ito, A., et al.: Micro cell culture method for determination of diphtheria toxin and antitoxin titres using VERO cells. I. Studies on factors affecting the toxin and antitoxin titration. J. Biol. Stand. *2*:189–201, 1974.
72. Morales, A. R., Vichitbandha, P., Chandruang, P., et al.: Pathological features of cardiac conduction disturbances in diphtheric myocarditis. Arch. Pathol. *91*:1–7, 1971.
73. Nakao, H., and Popovic, T. Development of a direct PCR assay for detection of the *diphtheria* toxin gene. J. Clin. Microbiol. *35*:1651–1655, 1997.
74. Natu, M., Borole, D., Shaikh, N., et al.: Comparative assessment of laboratory procedures: Diphtheria. Indian J. Pathol. Microbiol. *29*:31–35, 1986.
75. Olson, M. E., Goemans, I., Bolingbroke, D., Lundberg, S.: Gangrenous dermatitis caused by *Corynebacterium ulcerans* in Richardson ground squirrels. J. Am. Vet. Med. Assoc. *193*:367–368, 1988.
76. Pallen, M. J., Hay, A. J., Puckey, L. H., et al.: Polymerase chain reaction for screening clinical isolates of corynebacteria for the production of diphtheria toxin. J. Clin. Pathol. *47*:353–356, 1994.
77. Popovic, T., Mazurova, I., Efstratiou, A., et al.: Molecular epidemiology of diphtheria. J. Infect. Dis. *181*(Suppl. 1):168–177, 2000.

78. Popovic, T., Wharton, M., Wenger, J. D., et al.: Are we ready for diphtheria? A report from the Diphtheria Diagnostic Workshop, Atlanta, 11 and 12 July 1994. J. Infect. Dis. *171*:765–767, 1995.
79. Quick, M. L., Sutter, R. W., Kobaidze, K., et al.: Risk factors for diphtheria: A prospective case-control study in the Republic of Georgia, 1995–1996. J. Infect. Dis. *181*(Suppl. 1):121–129, 2000.
80. Rakhmanova, A. G., Lumio, J., Groundstroem, K., et al.: Diphtheria outbreak in St. Petersburg: Clinical characteristics of 1860 adult patients. Scand. J. Infect. Dis. *28*:37–40, 1996.
81. Respiratory diphtheria caused by *Corynebacterium ulcerans*—Terre Haute, Indiana, 1996. M. M. W. R. Morb. Mortal. Wkly. Rep. *46*:330–332, 1997.
82. Rysselaere, M., and Vanneste, L.: Diphtheria of the eye. Bull. Soc. Belge Ophtalmol. *201*:89–92, 1982.
83. Sanchez, P. J., Laptook, A. R., Fisher, L., et al.: Apnea after immunization of preterm infants. J. Pediatr. *130*:746–52, 1997.
84. Sheth, K. J., and Sarff, L. D.: Hemolytic uremic syndrome associated with *Corynebacterium diphtheria* infection. Int. J. Pediatr. Nephrol. *7*:17–20, 1986.
85. Suresh, G. K., Dhawan, A., and Kohli, V.: Tracheal diphtheria mimicking bacterial tracheitis. Pediatr. Infect. Dis. J. *11*:502, 1992.
86. Tasman, A., Minkenhof, J. E., Vink, H. H., et al.: Importance of intravenous injection of diphtheria antiserum. Lancet *1*:1299–1304, 1958.
87. Tiley, S. M., Kociuba, K. R., Heron, L. G., et al.: Infective endocarditis due to nontoxigenic *Corynebacterium diphtheriae*: Report of seven cases and review. Clin. Infect. Dis. *16*:271–275, 1993.
88. Toxigenic *Corynebacterium diphtheriae*—Northern Plains Indian Community, August–October 1996. M. M. W. R. Morb. Mortal. Wkly. Rep. *46*:506–510, 1997.
89. Wilson, G. S.: The necessity for a safe milk-supply. Lancet *2*:829–832, 1933.

ADDITIONAL READING

Barksdale, L.: *Corynebacterium diphtheriae* and its relatives. Bacteriol. Rev. *34*:378–422, 1970.
Pappenheimer, A. M., Jr.: Diphtheria toxin. *In* Ajl, S. J., Kadis, S., and Montie, T. C. (eds.): Microbial Toxins. Vol. 11B. New York, Academic Press, 1973.
Wood, W. B., Jr.: From Miasmas to Molecules. New York, Columbia University Press, 1961.
Zamiri, I.: *Corynebacterium*. *In* Collee, V. G., Fraser A. G., Marmion, B. P., and Simmons, A. (eds.): Mackie and McCartney Practical Medical Microbiology. 14th ed. New York, Churchill Livingstone, 1996, pp. 299–307.

Anthrax

MORVEN S. EDWARDS

Anthrax is a toxigenic disease of herbivores for which humans are an incidental host. The term *anthrax*, derived from the Greek *anthrakos*, or coal, refers to the black eschar characteristic of cutaneous anthrax. The three human forms of anthrax are cutaneous, which accounts for 95 percent of infections in the United States; inhalational; and gastrointestinal, which has not been reported in the United States. Each may occur in children,[16, 21, 32, 38] and any form may be complicated by the development of meningitis.

Historical Aspects

Anthrax has been recognized since antiquity. The earliest recorded reference to a disease believed to be anthrax is a description in *Exodus* of a plague that caused the death of all of the Egyptians' cattle.[5] Hippocrates described carbuncles, which are thought to represent the cutaneous form of anthrax. In the early 17th century, an anthrax pandemic referred to as the "Black Bane" caused 60,000 human deaths in Europe.[5] By the 18th century, several excellent descriptions of the clinical disease in humans had appeared.

Bacillus anthracis occupies a unique position in the history of infectious diseases. The organism was seen microscopically first by Delafond in 1838. It was isolated and cultivated in 1877 by Robert Koch, who demonstrated its proliferation in vivo, thus establishing a model for the causation of infectious disease. In 1881, both Louis Pasteur and W. S. Greenfield[35] demonstrated the protective value of a live vaccine of anthrax bacilli (attenuated by heating) in animal immunization studies. These initial demonstrations of the efficacy of a bacterial vaccine provided the basis for the prevention of infectious diseases by immunization.

During World War I, *B. anthracis* was manufactured as a biologic warfare agent, and it has continued to be a focus of biologic warfare research programs. The facts that anthrax can be transmitted by the respiratory route, that inhalational anthrax is usually a fatal infection, and that *B. anthracis* spores are stable in the environment all raise concern that anthrax could be used as a biologic terrorist agent.[26] The accidental release of anthrax spores from a military research facility in Sverdlovsk in the former Soviet Union in 1979 resulted in at least 68 deaths from inhalational anthrax.[23] One estimate is that the aerosolized release of 100 kg of anthrax spores upwind of the Washington, D.C., area would result in between 130,000 and 3 million deaths.[18]

In October and November 2001, 22 cases of inhalational and cutaneous anthrax in the United States were identified. A single anthrax strain was implicated. The apparent source of the anthrax was five letters sent through the U.S. Postal Service. This outbreak has had a substantial impact on the health care system and has revealed the potential impact of a bioterrorism event on society.[4]

Bacteriology

B. anthracis is an aerobic, nonmotile, spore-forming rod in the family Bacillaceae. Optimal growth occurs at 36°C in nonselective media. Colonies are gray-white, rough, and flat and may have comma-shaped projections resulting from the outgrowth of chains of bacilli from the edges of the colony, which gives it a "Medusa head" appearance. Individual colonies are 4 to 5 mm in diameter, with a ground-glass appearance, and exhibit tenacity or a "beaten egg white" appearance when lifted with an inoculating loop.[11] A three-layered capsule, which is associated with virulence and production of toxin, may be delineated by electron microscopy.[13] Encapsulation occurs with growth on enriched media. Gram stain of clinical material reveals large, square-ended, gram-positive rods that occur singly or in short chains without a visible capsule. The equatorial or paracentral spores are not visible in smears fixed promptly after collection. After 24 to 48 hours of aerobic incubation, strands of rods are arranged in "boxcar" or "bamboo" fashion, and sporulation occurs. Small numbers of bacteria are pathogenic for mice, guinea pigs, and rabbits, and death usually occurs 2 to 5 days after inoculation. Currently, no method exists for serologically classifying strains of *B. anthracis*.

Transmission and Epidemiology

Domestic herbivores—cattle, sheep, horses, goats, and swine—are the most important agricultural sources of anthrax, but all domestic and many wild animals may serve as hosts. Animals are infected by the ingestion of spores from infected pastures. Spores germinate in vivo, and death, associated with massive septicemia, usually occurs in 1 or 2 days. Anthrax is endemic in areas where an animal-soil-animal cycle is established because the spores can survive indefinitely in a dry environment. Uncultivated soil with a pH greater than 6.0 and ambient temperature greater than 15.5° C provide an environment favorable for the persistence of spores.[37]

Direct contact with contaminated animal meat or carcasses or with contaminated animal products such as hides, hair, wool, bone meal, and animal feed can transmit anthrax spores to humans.[8] Commercially processed products such as shaving brushes and saddle blankets have been implicated as sources of infection. Cutaneous anthrax may be transmitted through the deposition of spores or bacilli into abrasions or cuts in the skin by nonbiting insects such as houseflies.[22] Rubbing with contaminated fingers or possibly an insect vector may lead to cutaneous involvement of the eyelids.[41] Tying the umbilicus with a dirty thread may have provided a portal of entry for a neonate with *B. anthracis* sepsis.[25] Although discharge from cutaneous lesions theoretically is infectious, no confirmed cases of person-to-person transmission have been reported. Blood-sucking insects, including mosquitoes and stable flies, may be vectors of the disease.[36, 37]

Inhalational anthrax, or woolsorters' disease, results from the inhalation of spores. The estimated infectious dose required to cause inhalational anthrax in humans is 8000 to 50,000 spores.[26] One case of inhalational anthrax in the United States occurred in a weaver whose imported yarn was contaminated with *B. anthracis*.[6] Gastrointestinal anthrax is caused by the ingestion of contaminated meat. Children of industrial workers have acquired infection, presumably from contaminated clothing.[5] A newborn was reported to have contracted anthrax meningitis from his mother, who was septicemic at the time of delivery.[14]

An estimated 2000 to 20,000 human cases of anthrax occur yearly.[15] Regions of high prevalence include South and Central America, southern and eastern Europe, Asia, Africa, the Caribbean, and the Middle East. The incidence probably correlates with the enzootic status of the disease in the livestock in these countries. Familial clustering has been associated with exposure to diseased animals.[1, 27] In endemic areas, children frequently contract cutaneous anthrax from direct contact with animals.[25] More than 50 percent of 448 patients with cutaneous anthrax reported from the Gambia were younger than 15 years of age, and 11 percent were younger than 2 years.[13] Both sexes are equally affected.

In the United States, epizootics of anthrax occur in the lower Mississippi valley and in parts of California, Texas, Missouri, Nebraska, and South Dakota[39]; sporadic cases have been reported from almost every state. The incidence of human anthrax in this country has decreased significantly since the early 1900s, when more than 100 cases were reported annually. Cutaneous infections are reported sporadically.[17] Cases often are associated with exposure to contaminated animal products in commercial preparations, but exposure to indigenous animal anthrax does occur in the United States.[33] Two members of a farmer's family ate hamburgers made from an anthrax-infected steer in Minnesota in 2000. The family members received antibiotic prophylaxis and anthrax vaccine and remained well.[17] In children, a history of exposure may be difficult to elicit. For example, the only known source in an 11-year-old child with a cutaneous lesion was proximity to a bone meal factory, which he passed on the way to school.[19]

The recent outbreak of anthrax in the United States in 2001 was a bioterrorism event in which dissemination of spores of a single anthrax strain apparently was accomplished by letters processed by the U.S. Postal Service. Cases were identified in four states and in Washington, D.C. Inhalational anthrax is a rare occupational disease in the United States, and the diagnosis should be considered suggestive of a bioterrorism event.[4]

Pathogenesis and Pathology

Three virulence factors have been described for *B. anthracis*: edema toxin, lethal toxin, and a poly-D-glutamic acid capsule. One plasmid regulates production of the toxins, and another regulates capsule production. Toxemia is the critical factor in determining morbidity. Three endotoxin components, protective antigen (PA), lethal factor (LF), and edema factor (EF), combine to form two binary toxins. Edema toxin consists of EF, which is a calmodulin-dependent adenylate cyclase,[20] and PA, which is the receptor-binding component mediating entry of the toxin into the host cell. Edema toxin induces an increase in intracellular cyclic adenosine monophosphate levels and is responsible for the massive edema that occurs in cutaneous anthrax. Lethal toxin consists of LF, a zinc metalloprotease that inactivates mitogen-activated protein kinase in vitro,[12] and PA. Lethal toxin stimulates production of the proinflammatory cytokines tumor necrosis factor–α and interleukin-1β, which contribute to causing death in overwhelming infection. The capsule inhibits phagocytosis, and each of the toxins inhibits priming of neutrophils by lipopolysaccharide, thereby modulating the inflammatory response.[40]

Infection is initiated when anthrax endospores reach a primary site and low-level germination occurs. Endospores germinate when they are phagocytosed by macrophages. Macrophages containing bacilli migrate to the regional lymph nodes.[10] Interstitial edema, lymphatic dilatation, and thrombosis and necrosis of blood vessels are characteristic microscopic features of cutaneous anthrax lesions. Erythrocytes extravasate freely into the interstitial fluid. Few neutrophils or other inflammatory cells are present unless the lesion is infected secondarily. Hemorrhagic lymphadenitis involving regional lymph nodes occurs in all forms of anthrax. In pulmonary anthrax, spores entering the alveoli are carried through lymphatic channels to the hilar lymph nodes, where germination occurs. The massive hemorrhagic mediastinal lymphadenitis that follows can cause blockage of lymphatic drainage routes and may be causally related to the pulmonary edema and respiratory distress observed clinically.[38] Primary focal hemorrhagic necrotizing pneumonia may be observed at the pulmonary portal of entry.[2] Edema and small necrotic ulcers of the mucosa of the gastrointestinal tract are characteristic autopsy findings in intestinal anthrax. Dissemination to the central nervous system may occur by hematogenous or lymphatic routes. Hemorrhage involving the meninges and intense arteritis are uniform findings in patients who die of anthrax meningitis, but pathologic changes in brain tissue have not been observed.

Clinical Manifestations

CUTANEOUS ANTHRAX

The lesions of cutaneous anthrax occur mainly on exposed areas of the body. In one report, the distribution in young children was 52 percent of lesions on the head and neck, 28 percent on the trunk, and 20 percent on the extremities, whereas in older children, the distribution was 70 percent, 16 percent, and 14 percent, respectively.[16] Endospores are introduced through abraded or injured skin. Lesions usually are single and associated with regional adenitis. After an incubation period of 2 to 5 days, a small, nontender, but frequently pruritic papule develops at the site of inoculation. The lesion progresses to a serous or serosanguineous vesicle with surrounding nonpitting edema within 36 hours. Satellite vesicles, sometimes referred to as a "pearly wreath,"[41] may be seen on occasion. The lesion undergoes central necrosis, with a black eschar left behind[29] (Fig. 96–1). The term *malignant edema* is used to describe severe lesions, particularly those involving the head and neck, that may be associated with systemic toxicity and occlusion of the airway. Small children may appear acutely ill with a temperature of 39° C to 40° C and leukocytosis with counts of 20,000 to 30,000 cells/mm^3.[31] Approximately 5 percent of patients are bacteremic. With appropriate therapy, the edema usually resolves within 2 to 3 days, but the central lesion continues its evolution unaffected. The eschar is usually 1 to 3 cm in diameter, with sharply defined margins seen 1 week to 10 days after onset. Separation of the eschar may take several weeks, and healing occurs with variable central scarring.[19]

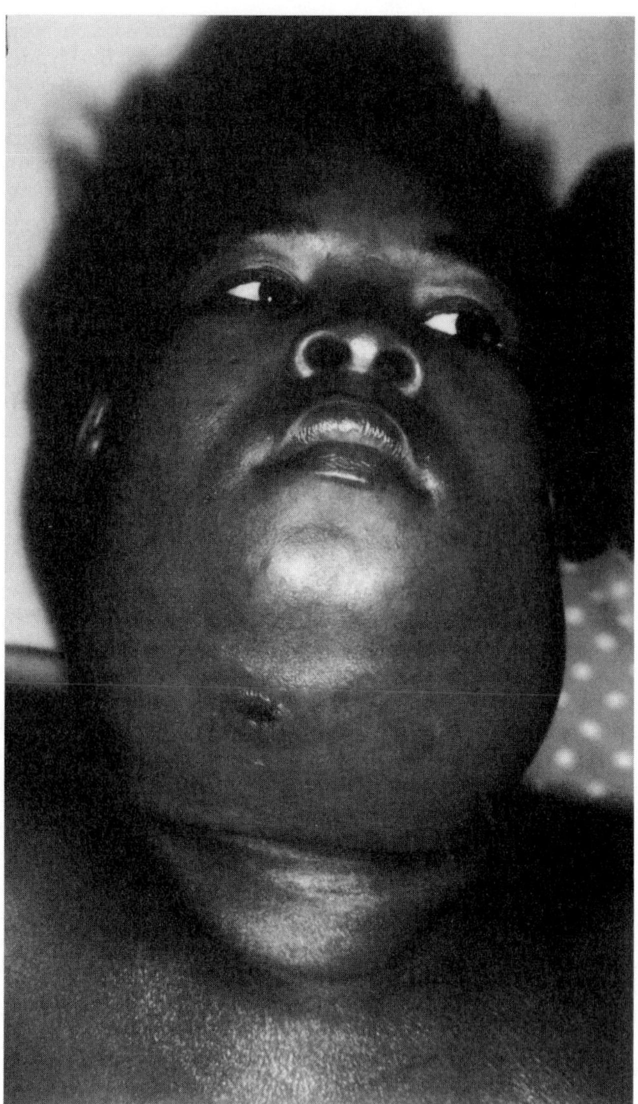

FIGURE 96–1 ■ Cutaneous anthrax with associated massive submental edema. The lesion is located at the site of a small, initially trivial laceration that served as the portal of entry for the anthrax endospores. The patient received ampicillin and recovered completely. (Courtesy of M. Thomas Casey, M.D.)

INHALATIONAL ANTHRAX

Inhalational anthrax is a biphasic illness. Symptoms in the initial stage—malaise, low-grade fever, myalgia, and nonproductive cough—are nonspecific and resemble those of a viral upper respiratory illness or bronchitis. After several days, dyspnea and stridor initiate onset of the second stage, which usually terminates fatally within 24 hours. Chest radiographs show a widened mediastinum with smooth borders and evidence of hemorrhagic mediastinitis and pleural effusions.[38] The pleural effusions often are large and usually contain bloody fluid. Pulmonary infiltrates usually are the result of superimposed bacterial infection. In the recent cases from the United States, computed tomographic scans of the chest showed the characteristic findings of hemorrhagic mediastinal and hilar lymph nodes and mediastinal edema, as well as pleural effusions.[4]

GASTROINTESTINAL ANTHRAX

After an incubation period of 2 to 5 days following the ingestion of contaminated meat, symptoms of diffuse abdominal pain with rebound tenderness and fever develop. Vomiting of blood-tinged or coffee ground–like material and melena are common symptoms and are secondary to ulceration of the intestinal mucosa.[24] The pain decreases, and massive ascites develop 24 to 48 hours after the onset of symptoms. Abdominal radiographs at this time show edematous loops of bowel and decreased air. If the abdomen is explored, findings include enlarged, erythematous mesenteric lymph nodes and straw-colored to purulent ascitic fluid in which organisms are readily visible.[3] Death usually occurs in association with significant blood loss, fluid and electrolyte imbalances, and subsequent shock. If the patient survives the acute illness, the edema and melena subside in 10 to 14 days.

Involvement of the oral cavity, the oropharynx, or both with anthrax lesions has been reported in association with the ingestion of contaminated water-buffalo meat.[28] Initial symptoms include neck swelling caused by edema and enlargement of the cervical lymph nodes, dysphagia, and respiratory difficulty. Lesions on the tonsils or posterior of the pharynx progress from an area of edema to a pseudomembrane-covered ulcer over a 1- to 2-week period. The oropharyngeal form of anthrax, though uncommon, has a more favorable prognosis than does the classic gastrointestinal disease.

MENINGITIS

The primary focus in anthrax meningitis usually is the skin, although involvement of the lungs or intestines has been described. In one report of 70 patients ranging in age from newborn to 71 years, no primary focus could be found in 12 percent of patients.[14] Young and middle-aged males are affected most frequently as a result of occupational exposure. The onset of meningitis is sudden. In addition to meningeal signs, clinical features include nausea and vomiting, myalgia, chills, dizziness, and occasionally, a petechial rash. Progressive neurologic deterioration with delirium, convulsions, and coma usually occurs in 2 to 4 days. Although less than 5 percent of patients survive the acute illness, survival without apparent neurologic sequelae has been reported in at least three children, two of whom had cutaneous lesions at the time of diagnosis.[30, 32, 34]

Examination of cerebrospinal fluid (CSF) reveals (1) gross or microscopic hemorrhage, (2) leukocytosis consisting predominantly of polymorphonuclear leukocytes, (3) elevated protein, and (4) depressed glucose levels. Gram-positive rods can be seen easily on smears of CSF. Peripheral leukocytosis is a common finding, and the white blood cell count may be as high as 60,000 to 80,000 cells/mm^3. Blood cultures yield the organism in 70 percent and CSF cultures in virtually 100 percent of patients.[14]

Diagnosis and Differential Diagnosis

B. anthracis may be demonstrated by direct smear and cultured from vesicular fluid or exudate from cutaneous lesions and from pleural fluid, blood, and CSF in systemic infections. Definitive diagnosis requires specialized testing through public health reference laboratories. Direct fluorescent antibody or polymerase chain reaction and serologic tests to detect capsule and cell wall antigens are available through these laboratories. The ELISA to detect immunoglobulin G to *B. anthracis* protective antigen is highly sensitive, has good specificity, and yields a positive result as early as 10 days after the onset of symptoms.[4, 15]

The lesion of cutaneous anthrax must be differentiated from ecthyma gangrenosum and from ulcerative skin lesions with regional lymphadenopathy, including rat-bite fever, ulceroglandular tularemia, plague, glanders, rickettsialpox, cowpox, and orf. Staphylococcal lymphangitis may be distinguished from anthrax by the discharge of purulent material and by the inflammatory response observed microscopically. The first stage of inhalational anthrax and the clinical features of the intestinal form are nonspecific, so a history of exposure is extremely important for establishing the diagnosis. The mediastinal widening that occurs early in the course of inhalational anthrax can cause confusion with that seen in acute bacterial mediastinitis and in fibrous mediastinitis caused by *Histoplasma capsulatum*.[10] Gastrointestinal anthrax must be differentiated from other causes of abdominal catastrophe and, if bleeding is present, from duodenal ulcer, typhoid, and intestinal tularemia. Anthrax causes a hemorrhagic meningitis, which must be differentiated from subarachnoid hemorrhage.[14]

Treatment

Penicillin historically has been the treatment of choice. However, naturally resistant strains occur, and penicillin or tetracycline resistance can be induced. Empiric treatment for inhalational anthrax should be initiated with ciprofloxacin, 10 to 15 mg/kg every 12 hours (not to exceed 1 g/day) intravenously, and for cutaneous infection if (1) signs of systemic toxicity are present, (2) lesions are located on the head and neck, and (3) extensive edema is present.[31] Ciprofloxacin in the same dose may be given by the oral route for less severe cutaneous anthrax. Doxycycline is an alternative antimicrobial. The dosage is 100 mg every 12 hours (children older than 8 years and heavier than 45 kg); 2.2 mg/kg every 12 hours (children older than 8 years and weighing 45 kg or less); and 2.2 mg/kg every 12 hours (children 8 years of age or younger). One or two additional antimicrobials should be administered intravenously with either ciprofloxacin or doxycycline as initial therapy until susceptibility testing is available for treatment of inhalational, gastrointestinal, or severe cutaneous anthrax and anthrax meningitis. Other agents with in vitro activity include rifampin, clindamycin, vancomycin, imipenem, penicillin, ampicillin, clarithromycin, and chloramphenicol. If the organism is determined to be susceptible to penicillin, penicillin may be administered at a dosage of 300,000 to 400,000 U/kg/day intravenously or 50,000 U/kg/day orally. Therapy should be continued for 60 days.

Supportive therapy includes attention to details of fluid and electrolyte balances, endotracheal intubation if indicated to maintain a patent airway, and local care for cutaneous lesions. Systemic steroids may reduce the severity of infections in patients with massive edema[31] or meningitis.[32] A specific anthrax antitoxin is not available.

Prognosis

Before the introduction of penicillin, cutaneous anthrax was fatal in approximately 20 percent of patients. With effective treatment, the mortality rate has been reduced to less than 1 percent. Cutaneous anthrax of the eyelid may be complicated by ectropion of the upper lid and corneal scarring with blindness.[41] Immunity probably is lifelong in most patients. Although second attacks of cutaneous anthrax have been recorded, they have not been confirmed serologically and usually are mild.[9, 16] Fatality rates are high for all forms of systemic anthrax and range from 50 to 100 percent for gastrointestinal anthrax to virtually 100 percent for inhalational anthrax, but children who survive these infections have no apparent sequelae.

Prevention

The only human anthrax vaccine licensed in the United States is anthrax vaccine adsorbed (AVA) (BioThrax, BioPort Corporation), which is prepared from a cell-free filtrate of *B. anthracis* that contains no dead or live bacteria.[26] It is an aluminum hydroxide–precipitated preparation of protective antigen from an attenuated, nonencapsulated anthrax strain. Routine vaccination is indicated for individuals engaged in work involving the production of quantities or concentrations of *B. anthracis* in culture and in activities involving a high potential for aerosol production. The primary immunization series consists of three subcutaneous injections at 0, 2, and 4 weeks and three booster vaccinations at 6, 12, and 18 months. To maintain immunity, an annual booster dose is recommended.[26] Administration of antibiotic in combination with vaccination optimizes prevention of the disease after known exposure to anthrax spores. In the event of a biologic anthrax attack, children exposed to spores should receive ciprofloxacin as postexposure prophylaxis for 60 days. Doxycycline is an alternative antimicrobial for prophylaxis. If penicillin sensitivity is established, prophylactic therapy can be changed to ampicillin, 40 mg/kg divided into three doses taken every 8 hours (children weighing less than 20 kg) or 500 mg orally every 8 hours (children weighing

20 kg or more). Although no data in children are available, the vaccine probably would be safe and effective.[18]

Worldwide, anthrax is controlled through livestock immunization programs. Procedures to prevent the spread of anthrax in animals include disposal of contaminated carcasses by burning and annual vaccination of livestock in known enzootic areas. All suspected or proven cases of anthrax should be reported to public health officials. Hospitalized patients should be kept under isolation until the lesions are bacteriologically sterile. Contaminated dressings and clothing must be burned or sterilized, and the patient's room must be disinfected to destroy spores.

REFERENCES

1. Abdenour, D., Larouze, B., Dalichaouche, M., et al.: Familial occurrence of anthrax in eastern Algeria. J. Infect. Dis. *155*:1083, 1987.
2. Abramova, F. A., Grinberg, L. M., Yampolskaya, O. V., et al.: Pathology of inhalational anthrax in 42 cases from the Sverdlovsk outbreak of 1979. Proc. Natl. Acad. Sci. U. S. A. *90*:2291, 1993.
3. Alizad, A., Ayoub, E. M., and Makki, N.: Intestinal anthrax in a two-year-old child. Pediatr. Infect. Dis. J. *14*:394, 1995.
4. Bartlett, J. G., Inglesby, T. V., Jr., and Borio, L.: Management of anthrax. Clin. Infect. Dis. *35*:851, 2002.
5. Brachman, P. S.: Anthrax. Ann. N. Y. Acad. Sci. *174*:577, 1970.
6. Brachman, P. S.: Inhalation anthrax. Ann. N. Y. Acad. Sci. *353*:83, 1980.
7. Bradaric, N., and Punda-Polic, V.: Cutaneous anthrax due to penicillin-resistant *Bacillus anthracis* transmitted by an insect bite. Lancet *340*:306, 1992.
8. Christie, A. B.: Anthrax. Practitioner *191*:588, 1963.
9. Christie, A. B.: The clinical aspects of anthrax. Postgrad. Med. J. *49*:565, 1973.
10. Dixon, T. C., Meselson, M., Guillemin, J., et al.: Anthrax. N. Engl. J. Med. *341*:815, 1999.
11. Doyle, R. J., Keller, K. F., and Ezzell, J. W.: *Bacillus. In* Lennette, E. H., Balows, A., Hauser, W. J., Jr., et al. (eds.): Manual of Clinical Microbiology, 4th ed. Washington, DC, American Society for Microbiology, 1985, pp.211–215.
12. Duesbery, N. S., Webb, C. P., Leppla, S. H., et al.: Proteolytic inactivation of MAP-kinase-kinase by anthrax lethal factor. Science *280*:734, 1998.
13. Gerhardt, P.: Cytology of *Bacillus anthracis*. Fed. Proc. *26*:1504, 1967.
14. Haight, T. H.: Anthrax meningitis: Review of literature and report of two cases with autopsies. Am. J. Med. Sci. *224*:57, 1952.
15. Harrison, L. H., and Ezzell, J. W., Veterinary Laboratory Investigation Center, et al.: Evaluation of serologic tests for diagnosis of anthrax after an outbreak of cutaneous anthrax in Paraguay. J. Infect. Dis. *160*:706, 1989.
16. Heyworth, B., Ropp, M. E., Voos, U. G., et al.: Anthrax in the Gambia: An epidemiological study. B. M. J. *4*:79, 1975.
17. Human ingestion of *Bacillus anthracis*–contaminated meat—Minnesota, August 2000. M. M. W. R. Morb. Mortal. Wkly. Rep. *49*:813, 2000.
18. Inglsby, T. V., Henderson, D. A., Bartlett, J. G., et al.: Anthrax as a biological weapon. Medical and public health management. J. A. M. A. *281*:1735, 1999.
19. Lamb, R.: Anthrax. B. M. J. *1*:157, 1973.
20. Leppla, S. H.: *Bacillus anthracis* calmodulin dependent adenylate cyclase: Chemical and enzymatic properties and interactions with eucaryotic cells. Adv. Cyclic Nucleotide Protein Phosphorylation Res. *17*:189, 1984.
21. Manios, S., and Kavaliotis, I.: Anthrax in children: A long forgotten, potentially fatal infection. Scand. J. Infect. Dis. *11*:203, 1979.
22. McKendrick, D. R. A.: Anthrax and its transmission to humans. Cent. Afr. J. Med. *26*:126, 1980.
23. Meselson, M., Guillemin, J., Hugh-Jones, M., et al.: The Sverdlovsk anthrax outbreak of 1979. Science *266*:1202, 1994.
24. Nalin, D. R., Sultana, B., Sahunja, R., et al.: Survival of a patient with intestinal anthrax. Am. J. Med. *62*:130, 1977.
25. Özkaya, E., Kirimi, E., Berktas, M., et al.: *Bacillus anthracis* sepsis in a newborn. Pediatr. Infect. Dis. J. *19*:487, 2000.
26. Recommendations of the Advisory Committee on Immunization Practices (ACIP). Use of anthrax vaccine in the United States. M. M. W. R. Morb. Mortal. Wkly. Rep. *49*(RR-15):1, 2000.
27. Seboxa, T., and Goldhagen, J.: Anthrax in Ethiopia. Trop. Geogr. Med.*41*: 108, 1989.
28. Sirisanthana, T., Navachareon, N., Tharavichitkul, P., et al.: Outbreak of oral-pharyngeal anthrax: An unusual manifestation of human infection with *Bacillus anthracis*. Am. J. Med. Hyg. *33*:144, 1984.
29. Smego, R. A., Jr., Gebrian, B., and Desmangels, G.: Cutaneous manifestations of anthrax in rural Haiti. Clin. Infect. Dis. *26*:97, 1998.
30. Tabatabaie, P., and Syadati, A.: *Bacillus anthracis* as a cause of bacterial meningitis. Pediatr. Infect. Dis. J. *12*:1035, 1993.
31. Tahernia, A. C.: Treatment of anthrax in children. Arch. Dis. Child. *42*:181, 1967.
32. Tahernia, A. C., and Hashemi, G.: Survival in anthrax meningitis. Pediatrics *50*:329, 1972.
33. Taylor, J. P., Dimmitt, D. C., Ezzell, J. W., et al.: Indigenous human cutaneous anthrax in Texas. South. Med. J. *86*:1, 1993.
34. Tengio, F. U.: Anthrax meningitis: Report of two cases. East Afr. Med. J. *50*:337, 1973.
35. Tigertt, W. D.: Anthrax. William Smith Greenfield, M.D., F.R.C.P., Professor Superintendent, The Brown Animal Sanatory Institution (1878–1881). Concerning the priority due to him for the production of the first vaccine against anthrax. J. Hyg. Camb. *85*:415, 1980.
36. Turell, M. J., and Knudson, G. B.: Mechanical transmission of *Bacillus anthracis* by stable flies *(Stomoxys calcitrans)* and mosquitoes *(Aedes aegypti* and *Aedes taeniorhynchus)*. Infect. Immun. *55*:1859, 1987.
37. Van Ness, G. B.: Ecology of anthrax. Science *172*:1303, 1971.
38. Vessal, K., Yeganehdoust, J., Dutz, W., et al.: Radiological changes in inhalation anthrax: A report of radiological and pathological correlation in two cases. Clin. Radiol. *26*:471, 1975.
39. Wolff, A. H., and Heimann, H.: Industrial anthrax in the United States. Am. J. Hyg. *53*:80, 1951.
40. Wright, G. G., and Mandell, G. L.: Anthrax toxin blocks priming of neutrophils by lipopolysaccharide and by muramyl dipeptide. J. Exp. Med. *164*:1700, 1986.
41. Yorston, D., and Foster, A.: Cutaneous anthrax leading to corneal scarring from cicatricial ectropion. Br. J. Ophthalmol. *73*:809, 1989.

CHAPTER 97 *Bacillus cereus*

THOMAS G. CLEARY

Recognition of *Bacillus cereus* pathogenicity was delayed until clarification of the taxonomy of the genus *Bacillus* in the early 1950s. Multiple early reports of food poisoning and other infections, including gastroenteritis, bacteremia-septicemia, cellulitis, ear and eye infections, endocarditis, and urinary tract infection, that were attributed to *Bacillus subtilis* or to other *Bacillus* spp. probably were caused by *B. cereus.*[83] *B. cereus* can give rise to two distinct forms of food-borne disease related to different toxins, the emetic and the diarrheal syndromes, as well as occasionally to localized and systemic disease.[35, 51]

The diarrheal syndrome was recognized first by Hauge[41] in 1955 after four clinically similar outbreaks in Norway occurred. This common form of disease was related to a great variety of foods, such as meat and vegetable soup, poultry, pudding, sauce, pasta, cake, and milk. In 1974, Mortimer and McCann[64] described a vomiting syndrome associated with the consumption of fried rice in Chinese restaurants. Despite widespread recognition in Europe, *B. cereus* outbreaks have been reported infrequently in the United States. The first documented outbreak in the United States occurred in 1970.[61]

Bacteriology

Members of the genus *Bacillus* are aerobic or facultative anaerobic, gram-positive or gram-variable, spore-forming rods. They are distributed widely in the environment because of the high resistance of their endospores to extreme conditions, including heat, cold, desiccation, salinity, and radiation.[27, 72] Based on the high variability in guanine and cytosine content, from 32 to 69 percent, the debate ensues regarding the classification of *Bacillus* spp.[88]

B. cereus belongs to the group of gram-positive rods that produce central or terminal ellipsoid or cylindric spores that do not distend the sporangia.[88] Studies of DNA-DNA hybridization and 16S and 23S rRNA sequencing, as well as enzyme electrophoretic patterns, have shown a close relationship among *B. cereus, Bacillus anthracis, Bacillus mycoides,* and *Bacillus thuringiensis*; these organisms are so closely related that they all may be considered variants of *B. cereus*. Differentiation, particularly between *B. cereus* and the insect pathogen *B. thuringiensis,* sometimes is difficult to make in the diagnostic laboratory. Polymerase chain reaction technology has been used for the identification of species.[15]

B. cereus is a flagellated, motile, gram-positive rod, typically 1.0 to 1.2 μm in diameter by 3.0 to 5.0 μm in length. The organism sporulates freely on many media under well-aerated conditions, but vegetative cells also can grow anaerobically. It is able to metabolize glucose, fructose, and sucrose but not pentose and other sugar alcohols. It produces acid from glucose but not from arabinose, xylose, or mannitol. Starch hydrolysis and catalase production are similar to those of the other members of the genus. The presence of lipid globules or protoplasts is a characteristic that it shares with *Bacillus megaterium*.[52] Colonies on blood agar are large, flat, granular, and slightly green tinged. *B. cereus* is differentiated from *B. anthracis* by motility, hemolysis, lack of lysis by gamma-phage, penicillin resistance, and absence of a capsule in *B. cereus*.[27] However, morphologic differentiation may be difficult with nonmotile *B. cereus* strains and *B. anthracis* strains that are occasionally weakly hemolytic.

Growth and multiplication of vegetative cells occur in a temperature range of 10° C to 50° C, with an optimum of 28° C to 35° C. Some strains responsible for milk spoilage can grow at temperatures as low as 5° C,[52, 72] but few strains are able to produce toxin at temperatures below 7° C.[72] Variations in toxin levels found in certain foods also can be related to pH levels, sugar content, the presence of other lactic acid bacteria, and aeration.[77, 78]

Serologic differentiation of *Bacillus* spp. is hampered by cross-reactive antigens and autoagglutination of spores caused by hydrophobic surface properties. Serologic typing based on the flagellar (H) antigen can be used during an outbreak to distinguish between strains and to determine the similarity of isolates obtained from humans with the strains isolated from suspect foods.[27] The serotype scheme is based on 42 H antisera raised against prototype strains. A common flagellar antigenic epitope has been suggested. Detection of the flagellar antigen by enzyme-linked immunosorbent assay is perhaps more sensitive than is detection by the agglutination method.[65] In addition to serology and biotyping (based on biochemical typing), plasmid analysis and phage typing have proved useful epidemiologically.[2, 52, 75, 92] Techniques such as pyrolysis mass spectrometry and gas liquid chromatography of whole-cell fatty acids are showing promise.[27]

Diagnosis of the rare extraintestinal infection is made by isolation from normally sterile sites (blood or tissue) after overnight incubation on nutrient or blood agar; clinical specimens from normally nonsterile sites (feces, vomitus) and food or environmental samples require selective techniques. Polymyxin B is used as a selective agent, and the lecithinase reaction of the organism on egg yolk and its inability to catabolize mannitol permit presumptive identification with a variety of media: mannitol–egg yolk–polymyxin B, Kim and Goepfert medium, and polymyxin B–pyruvate–egg yolk–mannitol with bromothymol blue or bromocresol purple.[27]

Epidemiology

B. cereus in the spore and vegetative form is a ubiquitous organism found in soil, water, vegetation, and food products, especially cereals, dairy products, dried foods, spices, meat products, and vegetables.[52]

The emetic syndrome typically is associated with cooked rice, usually fried, from Chinese restaurants.[64] Saving portions of boiled rice at room temperature overnight until required for frying once was a common practice. Refrigerating boiled rice makes the grains stick together and, hence, less convenient for frying.[79] The spores of *B. cereus* survive cooking and are capable of germination and outgrowth.[36, 38] The optimal temperature for growth in boiled rice is between 30° C and 37° C, although growth does occur during storage at 15° C to 43° C.[36] Most samples of uncooked rice contain multiple serotypes of *B. cereus,* and little difference occurs in the growth rate of the various serotypes in boiled rice at 22° C, but spores of serotype 1 strains are more resistant to heating at 95° C, which probably is the reason that this serotype usually is implicated in outbreaks.[66]

Starchy dried foods other than rice, including pulse and cereals, frequently are contaminated.[14] Tortillas can be contaminated with the water used in preparation and from the hands of producers.[18] A specific food has been incriminated in 49 of 58 recent outbreaks in the United States. Chinese food accounted for 50 percent of them, followed by Mexican food, beef, fruits, and vegetables.[7] Other foods implicated, particularly in the enterotoxin syndrome, included beef stew,[26] turkey loaf,[34] barbecued pork,[55] macaroni and cheese,[44] and potatoes.[48] Among the factors thought to contribute to the outbreaks, the most frequent were improper storage or holding temperature (94%), contaminated equipment (53%), inadequate cooking (32%), and poor personal hygiene (24%).[7, 8]

Studies in three different populations in South Africa and London, including school-age children, found the organism in 18 to 43 percent of fecal samples.[87] The organism, thus, can be part of the normal intestinal flora. *B. cereus* does not persist in the intestine after ingestion.[33] Outbreaks of *B. cereus* have been recognized widely in Europe but rarely in the United States. In the Netherlands, *B. cereus* reportedly was the cause of 22.4 percent of food-borne disease outbreaks of known bacterial cause. Similarly, in Finland, it accounted for 11.9 percent of outbreaks. However, in most places, *B. cereus* is incriminated in 0.9 to 7 percent of outbreaks of food-related disease and 0.7 to 3 percent of cases.[52] In the United States, 10 outbreaks of *B. cereus* gastroenteritis affecting 133 persons were reported to the Centers for Disease Control and Prevention (CDC) between 1966 and 1975. Seven of the outbreaks were of the diarrheal syndrome, and three were of the emetic type.[79] For the period 1973 to 1987, 58 of 2841 (2%) food-borne disease outbreaks of known etiology and 1123 of the 124,994 (1%) total cases related to them were attributed to *B. cereus*.[7] The susceptibility of children to this pathogen is evident from the report of an outbreak involving two daycare centers,[50] as well as other reports that included neonates, children, and adolescents.[30, 43, 47, 67, 71, 84, 95] Only a small fraction of outbreaks are reported to the CDC; small outbreaks of mild, brief illness are less likely to be reported. It is thought that 10^5 to 10^8 organisms per gram need to be ingested to cause the emetic syndrome and 10^5 to 10^7 cells or spores (total dose) ingested to cause the enterotoxin syndrome.[39]

For infections not related to food, groups at risk include neonates,[30, 67] immunocompromised hosts,[4, 19, 29, 38, 43, 47, 75, 81] intravenous drug abusers,[22, 81] and patients with intravascular devices or artificial prostheses.[4, 5, 29, 30, 75, 76]

Pathogenesis

B. cereus produces an enormous range of extracellular metabolites, including peptides with antibiotic properties (biocerin, cerein, thiocillins), β-lactamases, hydrolases, nuclease, urease, and proteases.[83] Two different groups of toxins, known as diarrheal enterotoxins and emetic toxin, are responsible for the clinical syndromes of food poisoning.[59, 89] Some strains may be able to produce both toxins based on the evidence that culture filtrates derived from strains isolated from emetic poisoning occasionally are able to produce a positive rabbit ileal loop assay.[72]

Biologic activities of diarrheal enterotoxins can be demonstrated in multiple different assay systems. Three enterotoxins are produced. Purification plus isolation of multiple toxic fractions with some, but not all, of these activities has caused confusion.[27, 82] Evaluation of the toxic activity of whole-cell suspension, cell-free culture filtrates, and the purified enterotoxin complex classically has included the rabbit ileal loop fluid accumulation assay, vascular permeability in rabbit skin, dermonecrosis and intestinonecrosis, mouse lethality, cytotoxicity, and hemolysis.[11, 17, 54, 80, 85, 90] Toxin assays initially were difficult to interpret because different strains and different growth media and conditions of isolation produce various degrees of activity.[37] In general, good correlation exists between rabbit ileal loop activity and the vascular permeability assay. Complete characterization of the three diarrheal enterotoxins is not available.[57]

The emetic toxin cereulide is a heat-stable (126° C for 90 minutes) ring-shaped dodecadepsipeptide with a molecular weight of 1.2 kDA[60]; it is stable between pH 2 and 11 and protease-resistant. Unlike the diarrheal toxins, it is preformed in foods, so the presence of living organisms at the time of ingestion is not necessary to cause symptoms.[35, 83] Rice culture filtrates derived from emetic syndrome–associated strains cause cytoplasmic vacuolation and swollen mitochondria in HEp-2 cells, characteristics suggestive of uncoupling of oxidative phosphorylation.[69] Emetic activity occurs through the serotonin 5-HT_3 receptor and stimulation of the vagus afferent nerve.[1]

Among the multiple other substances with relevant activity, two groups are associated with local infection.[85, 86] Cereolysin, or hemolysin I, is a thiol-activated cytolysin. Phospholipase C– or lecithinase-like substances, including a sphingomyelinase and two hydrolases with preference for phosphatidylcholine and phosphatidylinositol, also exist. These enzymes induce the release of lysosomal enzymes from neutrophils that probably are involved in tissue damage, especially in wound and ocular infections.[27, 97]

Clinical Manifestations

FOOD POISONING

DIARRHEAL SYNDROME. The enterotoxins preformed in food or produced in vivo in the intestine after the ingestion of bacilli cause profuse, watery, nonbloody diarrhea accompanied by abdominal pain and cramps, nausea, and on a few occasions, vomiting or low-grade fever.[3, 26, 34, 48, 52, 56, 74] The typical incubation period is 8 to 16 hours, and the clinical characteristics resemble the food poisoning of *Clostridium perfringens*. The interval between ingestion and the onset of symptoms reflects the time required for production of toxin in the gut. The symptoms resolve within approximately 12 to 24 hours but occasionally can last 2 days to 2 weeks.[34] The diarrhea (3 to 10 bowel movements per day) rarely leads to dehydration in healthy individuals. In the elderly, bloody stools can occur.[34] The most prevalent flagellar H serotypes are 1, 2, 6, 8, 10, 12, and 19. Serotyping is available at research laboratories.[14, 26, 55, 87]

EMETIC SYNDROME. The usual illness is characterized by a rapid onset (within 1 to 5 hours after the ingestion of contaminated food) of nausea, vomiting, and malaise, occasionally followed by diarrhea hours later.[64] Infrequently, the diarrhea is reported to last several days.[93] The short incubation reflects the ingestion of preformed emetic toxin.

EXTRAINTESTINAL INFECTIONS

EYE INFECTION. Keratitis, conjunctivitis, endophthalmitis, and panophthalmitis can be produced by *B. cereus*. Endophthalmitis that develops after the occurrence of penetrating wounds is caused by this organism in 27 to 46 percent of cases.[24, 91] A history of soil contamination or the presence of a metal foreign body should raise clinical suspicion. Less frequently, corneal ulcers and surgical procedures are predisposing factors.[42, 91] Exogenous endophthalmitis usually progresses rapidly, with deterioration of vision in less than 48 hours. Severe pain is accompanied by chemosis, periorbital swelling, proptosis, and pus in the anterior chamber. The classic lesion is a corneal ring abscess, similar to that produced by *Pseudomonas* and *Proteus* spp. Endogenous cases may have subretinal exudation, retinal hemorrhage, and perivasculitis. Associated systemic symptoms are not unusual manifestations.[22] The outcome is poor, with almost one half of patients left with visual acuity no better than simple light perception.[91] Many patients require enucleation. Endogenous ophthalmitis is associated with the use of illicit intravenous drugs or transfusion of contaminated blood products and subsequent bacteremic seeding of one eye.[22, 75, 81, 91]

The pathogenesis of *B. cereus* on ocular tissue has been linked to the lecithinase activity of phospholipase C. A toxin fraction, hemolysin BL, that is formed by three separate components produces similar destruction of retinal tissue in vitro and in animal experiments.[9] Its relationship with the diarrheal enterotoxin is not clear.[11]

WOUND AND SOFT TISSUE INFECTIONS. Wound infections of variable severity related to trauma, burns, or postsurgical complications occasionally are reported.[84–86, 95] Because *Bacillus* is a common environmental contaminant, proof of the relevance of a *B. cereus* isolate is clearer if the organism is obtained from deep tissue in heavy pure growth. Severe infections in persons involved in motor vehicle accidents can be complicated by necrotizing fasciitis and require extensive débridement.[95] Superficial, benignly infected wounds are common findings in the tropics.[28] Immunosuppressed patients may contract a severe gas gangrene–like infection[60] requiring amputation[40] or a less severe primary cutaneous infection manifested by vesicles, pustules, or cellulitis.[43]

MUSCULOSKELETAL INFECTIONS. Cases of chronic osteomyelitis occur rarely and result from accidental or surgical trauma. Radical débridement and antibiotic treatment are required.[75] Because *B. cereus* can be found as a co-pathogen with other more frequent pathogenic bacteria, resolution of symptoms is delayed until eradication of the organism.[71] Acute osteomyelitis may occur in drug abusers.[75, 81]

BACTEREMIA AND SEPTICEMIA. Bacteremia occurs with indwelling catheters and other foreign bodies, contaminated intravenous drugs (e.g., heroin), and blood products, particularly platelets.[16, 29, 98] Immunosuppression and impaired neutrophil killing, such as occur in those with neutropenia secondary to malignancy or chemotherapy and in neonates with immaturity of the immune system, are major contributors to morbidity in systemic *B. cereus* infection.[4, 17, 45, 67, 68] Disseminated intravascular coagulation, multiorgan failure, and a fulminant course may occur in neonates and compromised hosts. Endocarditis is an infrequent complication of bacteremia that usually occurs in intravenous drug abusers or individuals with a chronic intravascular device.[75, 81] Vegetations can form over mechanical prosthetic valves or pacemaker wires, requiring their replacement.[75, 76] Morbidity and mortality rates are high in patients with valvular heart disease. Fatal serosanguineous pericarditis in a patient undergoing hemodialysis has been reported.[31]

PNEUMONIA. Primary pulmonary disease rarely has been recorded. The manifestation can be subacute and consist of cough, fever, dyspnea, chest pain, and hemoptysis, with progression to necrotizing pneumonia, cavitation, and empyema. Pleural fluid may appear serosanguineous or sanguinopurulent.[12, 45] Underlying predisposing conditions include leukemia, alcohol abuse, chronic hepatitis, and steroid use.[12, 29, 45, 75] Multiorgan disease in premature neonates with necrotizing pneumonia usually is fatal.[49] Blood culture is positive in 75 percent of cases, followed by pleural fluid and sputum culture in 40 to 60 percent.[12] The pleural space may become contaminated with *B. cereus* by mishandling of the thoracic drainage system in patients with other causes of pleuritis.[46]

INFECTION OF THE CENTRAL NERVOUS SYSTEM. Intracranial shunts and penetrating surgical or traumatic cranial wounds expose the central nervous system to environmental *B. cereus*.[30, 73] Spinal anesthesia[29] was associated with *Bacillus* infection in the past. Contamination in the operating room through the linen is a potential source.[5, 6] Premature neonates are susceptible to meningeal seeding by dissemination of intravascular infection related to catheters.[67] As in patients with other serious infections, those who are immunosuppressed are at higher risk.[45] The cerebrospinal fluid in *B. cereus* meningitis is purulent, with white blood cell counts of more than $1000/mm^3$, a predominance of polymorphonuclear leukocytes, and moderate increments in protein content. Gram stain is positive in 70 percent of cases. Multiple brain abscesses may result from hematogenous spread in patients with leukemia.[45, 47] Sequelae include hydrocephalus and brain damage. Often, the infection is fatal unless caused by a contaminated spinal anesthetic, in which case the course is usually more benign.

LIVER FAILURE. Fulminant hepatitis and rhabdomyolysis have been associated with the emetic toxin. The toxin inhibits hepatic mitochondrial fatty-acid oxidation. Liver changes include fatty infiltrates and midzonal necrosis.[58]

PSEUDOINFECTIONS. Pseudoepidemics with *B. cereus* are a challenge for the clinical microbiologist.[62] Because these spore formers are so hardy, they are common laboratory contaminants. *Bacillus* spp. isolated from clinical specimens usually should be considered a contaminant, although their pathogenic potential is well known.[23, 29, 45, 68, 75, 81, 85, 86] Pseudoinfections have been associated with contaminated blood culture media, syringes, blood culture analyzers, and fiberoptic bronchoscopes.[23] Colonization of umbilical cord stumps and eye surfaces by contaminated diapers may cause pseudo-outbreaks in nurseries.[96]

Complications

Death rarely ever results from the food-poisoning syndromes. Rapidly spreading wound infections may require amputation of extremities,[38] and ocular infections can lead to loss of vision with or without enucleation.[42, 91, 97] The risk of death in patients with septicemia, endocarditis, and meningitis is related to the underlying condition and severity of the disease.[4, 43, 63, 67, 76]

Diagnosis

The laboratory finding of *B. cereus* in a foodstuff without quantitative cultures and without epidemiologic data is insufficient to establish its role in an outbreak.[93] In practice, appropriate specimens often are either unavailable or submitted long after the incident, thereby rendering their microbiologic significance questionable. During analysis of foods not involved in food-borne illness, the bacteria may be found in counts of 10^1 to 10^6 organisms per gram.[13, 14, 18, 36, 66, 77] Diagnosis of the diarrheal form of *B. cereus* food poisoning is supported by the isolation of 10^5 or more organisms per gram from epidemiologically incriminated food.[63, 79] The levels of *B. cereus* found in the implicated foods usually are in the range of 5×10^5 to 9.5×10^8 colony-forming units per gram. With the exception of milk, the products rarely appear to be spoiled in spite of the bacteria's high density. Isolation of more than 10^5 organisms per gram in feces during an acute attack provides supportive evidence for the presumed diagnosis and confirms the association if the same serotype is isolated from incriminated food.

The organisms that produce emetic toxin are present in concentrations of 1.0×10^3 to 5.0×10^{10} colony-forming units per gram. Reheating may decrease or eliminate the organisms and leave the toxin intact but render isolation of the organism difficult to accomplish.[27, 93]

Commercial immunoassay kits (reversed passive latex agglutination test, enzyme-linked immunosorbent assay, and microslide immunodiffusion assay) are available for the detection of *B. cereus* diarrheal toxin. The kits may detect a variety of proteins, however.[10, 25] Experimental techniques based on the detection of genes for phospholipase C and sphingomyelinase by polymerase chain reaction have been developed for the identification of *B. cereus* in food products.[70]

The relevance of clinical isolates in extraintestinal syndromes can be assessed by the degree of growth (heavy versus scanty), the number of occasions that growth was obtained, the source of the material cultured, and predisposing or underlying conditions.[86] For suspected endophthalmitis, both aqueous and vitreous samples should be obtained if possible before the initiation of antibiotics.[24]

Treatment

During a mild, self-limited attack of food poisoning, patients require only supportive therapy.[79] Usually, oral fluid and electrolyte replacement is adequate[34] (Table 97–1).

TABLE 97–1 ■ MANAGEMENT AND COMPLICATIONS ASSOCIATED WITH *BACILLUS CEREUS* INFECTIONS

Condition	Management	Complications
Food poisoning	Supportive measures; hydration	Usually none; liver failure rarely reported
Ocular	Systemic, topical, intravitreal antibiotics: vancomycin or clindamycin ± aminoglycosides; surgical: early vitrectomy	Severe decreased visual acuity, blindness, enucleation
Septicemia	Removal of IV device, foreign body; IV antibiotics (according to sensitivity); vancomycin	Localization of infection: endophthalmitis, endocarditis, meningitis; death
Pneumonia/pleuritis	IV antibiotics; drainage of pleural space; resection of necrotic tissue	Death
Meningitis	IV antibiotics; removal of infected intracranial shunts or cerebrospinal fluid reservoirs	Hydrocephalus, brain damage, death
Wound/subcutaneous infection	IV antibiotics; surgical débridement	Amputation, death

No antibiotic therapy is required, except in cases of nongastrointestinal infection. The production of three different β-lactamases by most of the organisms renders penicillin derivatives, including third-generation cephalosporins, ineffective against *B. cereus*. Most strains are susceptible to chloramphenicol, vancomycin, clindamycin, aminoglycosides, erythromycin, tetracycline, imipenem, and ciprofloxacin.[4, 20, 85, 86, 94] Definitive antibiotic therapy should be based on the antibiogram susceptibility, but initial empiric therapy with clindamycin or vancomycin, with or without an aminoglycoside, is appropriate, pending susceptibility data.[4, 12, 23, 47, 71, 95] Ciprofloxacin has been reported to be useful in the treatment of recurrent pneumonia and bacteremia[32] and may have advantages in the penetration of respiratory and eye secretions,[53] but other options for children younger than 18 years of age are preferred.

Immediate empiric coverage for *B. cereus* is indicated for endophthalmitis in groups at risk. Selection of the antibiotic and the appropriate means of administration are matters of controversy.[24] Clindamycin and an aminoglycoside[97] or vancomycin[91] are the best options. Together with antibiotics administered parenterally, topical and periocular antibiotics are considered adjunctive therapy. In cases of penetrating trauma, early vitrectomy and intravitreal antibiotics (vancomycin in combination with amikacin) should be considered.[24, 91]

Surgical débridement of necrotic tissue, drainage of closed-space infections, and prompt removal of foreign bodies and indwelling catheters are important aspects of successful therapy.[12, 21, 71] Some bacteremic patients may be cured by removal of the intravenous catheter only.[75]

Prevention and Control

Low-level contamination in food products is difficult to avoid, but proper food handling should diminish the proliferation of bacilli.[72] Practical precautions for handling cereals and rice include not preparing large quantities at a single time and maintaining the food at a hot temperature (>63° C) or cooling it quickly. The food must not be stored under warm conditions, especially in the range of 15° C to 50° C.[14, 36]

REFERENCES

1. Agata, N., Ohta, M., Mori, M., Isobe, M.: A novel dodecadepsipeptide, cereulide, is an emetic toxin of *Bacillus cereus*. FEMS Microbiol. Lett. *129*:17–20, 1995.
2. Ahmed, R., Sankar-Mistry, P., Jackson, S., et al.: *Bacillus cereus* phage typing as an epidemiological tool in outbreaks of food poisoning. J. Clin. Microbiol. *33*:636–640, 1995.
3. Baddour, L. M., Gala, S. M., Griffin, R., et al.: A hospital cafeteria-related food-borne outbreak due to *Bacillus cereus*: Unique features. Infect. Control 7:462–465, 1986.
4. Banerjee, C., Bustamante, C. I., Wharton, R., et al.: *Bacillus* infections in patients with cancer. Arch. Intern. Med. *148*:1769–1774, 1988.
5. Barrie, D., Wilson, J. A., Hoffman, P. N., et al.: *Bacillus cereus* meningitis in two neurosurgical patients: An investigation into the source of the organism. J. Infect. *25*:291–297, 1992.
6. Barrie, D., Hoffman, P. N., Wilson, J. A., et al.: Contamination of hospital linen by *Bacillus cereus*. Epidemiol. Infect. *113*:297–306, 1994.
7. Bean, N. H., and Griffin, P. M.: Foodborne disease outbreaks in the United States, 1973–1987: Pathogens, vehicles and trends. J. Food Prot. *53*:804–817, 1990.
8. Bean, N. H., Griffin, P. M., Goulding, J. S., Ivey, C. B.: Foodborne disease outbreaks, 5-year summary, 1983–1987. Mor. Mortal. Wkly. Rep. C. D. C. Surveill. Summ. *39*:15–55, 1990.
9. Beecher, D. J., Pulido, J. S., Barney, N. P., et al.: Extracellular virulence factors in *Bacillus cereus* endophthalmitis: Methods and implication of involvement of hemolysin BL. Infect. Immun. *63*:632–639, 1995.
10. Beecher, D. J., and Wong, A. C.: Identification and analysis of the antigens detected by two commercial *Bacillus cereus* diarrheal enterotoxin immunoassay kits. Appl. Environ. Microbiol. *60*:4614–4616, 1994.
11. Beecher, D. J., and Wong, A. C.: Improved purification and characterization of hemolysin BL, a hemolytic dermonecrotic vascular permeability factor from *Bacillus cereus*. Infect. Immun. *62*:980–986, 1994.
12. Bekemeyer, W. B., and Zimmerman, G. A.: Life threatening complications associated with *Bacillus cereus* pneumonia. Am. Rev. Respir. Dis. *131*:466–469, 1985.
13. Beuchat, L. R., Ma-Lin, C. F., and Carpenter, J. A.: Growth of *Bacillus cereus* in media containing plant seed materials and ingredients used in Chinese cookery. J. Appl. Bacteriol. *48*:397–407, 1980.
14. Blakey, L. J., and Priest, F. G.: The occurrence of *Bacillus cereus* in some dried foods including pulses and cereals. J. Appl. Bacteriol. *48*:397–407, 1980.
15. Brousseau, R., Saint-Onge, A., Prefontaine, G., et al.: Arbitrary primer polymerase chain reaction, a powerful method to identify *Bacillus thuringiensis* serovars and strains. Appl. Environ. Microbiol. *59*:114–119, 1993.
16. Bryce, E. A., Smith, J. A., Tweeddale, M., et al.: Dissemination of *Bacillus cereus* in an intensive care unit. Infect. Control Hosp. Epidemiol. *14*:459–462, 1993.
17. Burdon, A. L., Davis, J. S., and Wende, R. D.: Experimental infection of mice with *Bacillus cereus*: Studies of pathogenesis and pathologic changes. J. Infect. Dis. *117*:307–316, 1967.
18. Capparelli, E., and Mata, L.: Microflora of maize prepared as tortillas. Appl. Microbiol. *29*:802–806, 1975.
19. Christenson, J. C., Byington, C., Korgenski, E. K., et al: *Bacillus cereus* infections among oncology patients at a children's hospital. Am. J. Infect. Control. *27*:543–546, 1999.
20. Conrod, J. D., Leadley, P. J., and Eickhoff, T. C.: Antibiotic susceptibility of *Bacillus* species. J. Infect. Dis. *123*:102–105, 1971.
21. Cotton, D. J., Gill, V. J., Marshal, D. J., et al.: Clinical features and therapeutic interventions in 17 cases of *Bacillus* bacteremia in an immunosuppressed patient population. J. Clin. Microbiol. *25*:672–674, 1987.
22. Cowan, C. L., Jr., Madden, W. M., Hatem, G. F., et al.: Endogenous *Bacillus cereus* panophthalmitis. Ann. Ophthalmol. *19*:65–68, 1987.
23. Cunha, B. A.: Pseudomeningitis: Another nosocomial headache. Infect. Control Hosp. Epidemiol. *9*:391–393, 1988.
24. David, D. B., Kirkby, G. R., and Noble, B. A.: *Bacillus cereus* endophthalmitis. Br. J. Ophthalmol. *78*:577–580, 1994.
25. Day, T. L., Tatani, S. R., Notermans, S., et al.: A comparison of ELISA and RPLA for detection of *Bacillus cereus* diarrhoeal enterotoxin. J. Appl. Bacteriol. *77*:9–13, 1994.

26. DeBuono, B. A., Brondum, J., Kramer, J. M., et al.: Plasmid, serotypic and enterotoxin analysis of *Bacillus cereus* in an outbreak setting. J. Clin. Microbiol. *26*:1571–1574, 1988.
27. Drobniewski, F. A.: *Bacillus cereus* and related species. Clin. Microbiol. Rev. *6*:324–338, 1993.
28. Dryden, M. S., and Kramer, J. M.: Toxigenic *Bacillus cereus* as a cause of wound infections in the tropics. J. Infect. *15*:207–212, 1987.
29. Farrar, W. E., Jr.: Serious infections due to "non-pathogenic" organisms of the genus *Bacillus*. Am. J. Med. *34*:134–141, 1963.
30. Feder, H. M., Garibaldi, R. A., Nurse, B. A., et al.: *Bacillus* species isolates from cerebrospinal fluid in patients without shunts. Pediatrics *82*:909–913, 1988.
31. Fricchione, L. F., Sepkowitz, D. V., Gradon, J. D., et al.: Pericarditis due to *Bacillus cereus* in an intravenous drug user. Rev. Infect. Dis. *13*:774, 1991.
32. Gascoigne, A. D., Richards, J., Gould, K., et al.: Successful treatment of *Bacillus cereus* infection with ciprofloxacin. Thorax *46*:220–221, 1991.
33. Ghosh, A. C.: Prevalence of *Bacillus cereus* in the faeces of healthy adults. J. Hyg. *80*:233–236, 1978.
34. Giannella, R. A., and Brasile, L.: A hospital food-borne outbreak of diarrhea caused by *Bacillus cereus*: Clinical, epidemiologic, and microbiologic studies. J. Infect. Dis. *139*:366–370, 1979.
35. Gilbert, R. J., and Kramer, J. M.: *Bacillus cereus* enterotoxins: Present status. Biochem. Soc. Trans. *12*:198–200, 1984.
36. Gilbert, R. J., Stringer, M. F., and Peace, T. C.: The survival and growth of *Bacillus cereus* in boiled and fried rice in relation to outbreaks of food poisoning. J. Hyg. *73*:433–444, 1974.
37. Glatz, B. A., and Goepfert, J. M.: Defined conditions for synthesis of *Bacillus cereus* enterotoxin by fermenter-grown cultures. Appl. Environ. Microbiol. *32*:400–404, 1976.
38. Gonzalez, I., Lopez, M., Mazas, M., et al.: The effect of recovery conditions on the apparent heat resistance of *Bacillus cereus* spores. J. Appl. Bacteriol. *78*:548–554, 1995.
39. Granum, P. E., and Lund, T.: *Bacillus cereus* and its food poisoning toxins. FEMS Microbiol. Lett. *157*:223–228, 1997.
40. Groschell, D., Burgess, M. A., and Bodey, G. P.: Gas gangrene–like infection with *Bacillus cereus* in a lymphoma patient. Cancer *37*:988–992, 1976.
41. Hauge, S.: Food poisoning caused by aerobic spore-forming bacilli. J. Appl. Bacteriol. *18*:591–595, 1955.
42. Hemadi, R., Zaltas, M., Paton, B., et al.: Bacillus-induced endophthalmitis: New series of 10 cases and review of the literature. Br. J. Ophthalmol. *74*:26–29, 1990.
43. Henrickson, K. J., Shenep, J. L., Flynn, P. M., et al.: Primary cutaneous *Bacillus cereus* infection in neutropenic children. Lancet *1*:601–603, 1989.
44. Holmes, J. R., Plunkett, T., Pate, P., et al.: Emetic food poisoning caused by *Bacillus cereus*. Arch. Intern. Med. *141*:766–767, 1981.
45. Ihde, D. C., and Armstrong, D.: Clinical spectrum of infection due to *Bacillus* species. Am. J. Med. *55*:839–846, 1973.
46. Jacobs, J. A., and Stobberingh, E. E.: Infection due to a contaminated thoracic drainage system. J. Hosp. Infect. *24*:23–28, 1993.
47. Jenson, H. B., Levy, S. R., Duncan, C., et al.: Treatment of multiple brain abscesses caused by *Bacillus cereus*. Pediatr. Infect. Dis. J. *8*:795–798, 1989.
48. Jephcott, A. E., Barton, B. W., Gilbert, R. J., et al.: An unusual outbreak of food poisoning associated with meals-on-wheels. Lancet *2*:129–130, 1977.
49. Jevon, G. P., Dunne, W. M., Hicks, M. J., et al.: *Bacillus cereus* pneumonia in premature neonates: A report of two cases. Pediatr. Infect. Dis. J. *12*:251–253, 1993.
50. Khodr, M., Hill, S., Perkins, L., et al.: *Bacillus cereus* food poisoning associated with fried rice at two child day care centers: Virginia, 1993. M. M. W. R. Morb. Mortal. Wkly. Rep. *43*:177–178, 1994.
51. Kotiranta, A., Lounatmaa, K., and Haapasalo, M.: Epidemiology and pathogenesis of *Bacillus cereus* infections. Microbes Infect. *2*:189–198, 2000.
52. Kramer, J. M., and Gilbert, R. J.: *Bacillus cereus* and other *Bacillus* species. *In* Doyle, M. P. (ed.): Foodborne Bacterial Pathogens. 1st ed. New York, Marcel Dekker, 1989, pp. 21–70.
53. Lesk, M. R., Ammann, H., Marcil, G., et al.: The penetration of oral ciprofloxacin into the aqueous humor, vitreous and subretinal fluid of humans. Am. J. Ophthalmol. *115*:623–628, 1993.
54. Lettau, L. A., Benjamin, D., Cantrell, H. F., et al.: *Bacillus* species pseudomeningitis. Infect. Control Hosp. Epidemiol. *9*:394–398, 1988.
55. Luby, S., Jones, J., Dowda, H., et al.: A large outbreak of gastroenteritis caused by diarrheal toxin–producing *Bacillus cereus*. J. Infect. Dis. *167*:1452–1455, 1993.
56. Lund, B. M.: Foodborne disease due to *Bacillus* and *Clostridium* species. Lancet *336*:982–987, 1990.
57. Lund, T., and Granum, P. E.: Characterisation of a non-haemolytic enterotoxin complex from *Bacillus cereus* after a foodborne outbreak. FEMS Microbiol. Lett. *141*:151–156, 1996.
58. Mahler, H., Pasi, A., Kramer, J. M., et al.: Fulminant liver failure in association with the emetic toxin of *Bacillus cereus*. N. Engl. J. Med. *336*:1142–1148, 1997.
59. Melling, J., Capel, B. J., Turnbul, P. C., et al.: Identification of a novel enterotoxigenic activity associated with *Bacillus cereus*. J. Clin. Pathol. *29*:938–940, 1976.
60. Meredith, F. T., Fowler, V. G., Gautier, M., et al.: *Bacillus cereus* necrotizing cellulitis mimicking clostridial myonecrosis: Case report and review of the literature. Scand. J. Infect. Dis. *29*:528–529, 1997.
61. Midura, T., Gerber, M., Wood, R., et al.: Outbreak of food poisoning caused by *Bacillus cereus*. Public Health Rep. *85*:45–48, 1970.
62. Morrell, R. M., Jr., and Wasilauskas, B. L.: Tracking laboratory contamination by using a *Bacillus cereus* pseudoepidemic as an example. J. Clin. Microbiol. *30*:1469–1473, 1992.
63. Morris, J. G., Jr.: *Bacillus cereus* food poisoning. Arch. Intern. Med. *141*:711, 1981.
64. Mortimer, P. R., and McCann, G.: Food poisoning episodes associated with *Bacillus cereus* in fried rice. Lancet *1*:1043–1045, 1974.
65. Murakami, T., Hiraoka, K., Mikami, T., et al.: Detection of *Bacillus cereus* flagellar antigen by enzyme-linked immunosorbent assay (ELISA). Microbiol. Immunol. *35*:223–234, 1991.
66. Parry, J. M., and Gilbert, R. J.: Studies on the heat resistance of *Bacillus cereus* spores and growth of the organism in boiled rice. J. Hyg. *84*:77–82, 1980.
67. Patrick, C. C., Langston, C., and Baker, C. J.: *Bacillus* species infections in neonates. Rev. Infect. Dis. *111*:612–615, 1989.
68. Richard, V., Van der Auwera, P., Snoeck, R., et al.: Nosocomial bacteremia caused by *Bacillus* species. Eur. J. Clin. Microbiol. Infect. Dis. *7*:783–785, 1988.
69. Sakurai, N., Koike, K. A., Irie, Y., et al.: The rice culture filtrate of *Bacillus cereus* isolated from emetic-type food poisoning causes mitochondrial swelling in a HEp-2 cell. Microbiol. Immunol. *38*:337–340, 1994.
70. Schraft, H., and Griffiths, M. W.: Specific oligonucleotide primers for detection of lecithinase-positive *Bacillus* spp. by PCR. Appl. Environ. Microbiol. *61*:98–102, 1995.
71. Schricker, M. E., Thompson, G. H., and Schreiber, J. R.: Osteomyelitis due to *Bacillus cereus* in an adolescent: Case report and review. Clin. Infect. Dis. *18*:863–867, 1994.
72. Schultz, F. J., and Smith, J. L.: *Bacillus*: Recent advances in *Bacillus cereus* food poisoning research. *In* Hui, Y. H., Gorham, J. R., and Murrel, K. D. (eds.): Foodborne Disease Handbook. New York, Marcel Dekker, 1994, pp. 29–62.
73. Siegman-Igra, Y., Lavochkin, J., Schwartz, D., et al.: Meningitis and bacteremia due to *Bacillus cereus*: A case report and a review of *Bacillus* infections. Isr. J. Med. Sci. *19*:546–551, 1983.
74. Slaten, D. D., Oropeza, R. I., and Werner, S. B.: An outbreak of *Bacillus cereus* food poisoning: Are caterers supervised sufficiently? Public Health Rep. *107*:477–480, 1992.
75. Sliman, R., Rehm, S., and Shlaes, D. M.: Serious infections caused by *Bacillus* species. Medicine (Baltimore) *66*:218–223, 1987.
76. Steen, M. K., Bruno-Murtha, L. A., Chaux, G., et al.: *Bacillus cereus* endocarditis: Report of a case and review. Clin. Infect. Dis. *14*:945–946, 1992.
77. Sutherland, A. D.: Toxin production by *Bacillus cereus* in dairy products. J. Dairy Res. *60*:569–574, 1993.
78. Sutherland, A. D., and Limond, A. M.: Influence of pH and sugars on the growth and production of diarrhoeagenic toxin by *Bacillus cereus*. J. Dairy Res. *60*:575–580, 1993.
79. Terranova, W., and Blake, P. A.: *Bacillus cereus* food poisoning. N. Engl. J. Med. *298*:143–144, 1978.
80. Thompson, N. E., Ketterhagen, M. J., Bergdoll, M. S., et al.: Isolation and some properties of an enterotoxin produced by *Bacillus cereus*. Infect. Immun. *43*:887–894, 1984.
81. Tuazon, C. U., Murray, H. W., Levy, C., et al.: Serious infections from *Bacillus* sp. J. A. M. A. *241*:1137–1140, 1979.
82. Turnbull, P. C.: Studies on the production of enterotoxins by *Bacillus cereus*. J. Clin. Pathol. *29*:941–948, 1976.
83. Turnbull, P. C.: *Bacillus cereus* toxins. Pharmacol. Ther. *13*:453–505, 1981.
84. Turnbull, P. C., French, T. A., and Dowsett, E. G.: Severe systemic and pyogenic infections with *Bacillus cereus*. B. M. J. *1*:1628–1629, 1977.
85. Turnbull, P. C., Jorgensen, K., Kramer, J. M., et al.: Severe clinical conditions associated with *Bacillus cereus* and the apparent involvement of exotoxins. J. Clin. Pathol. *32*:289–293, 1979.
86. Turnbull, P. C., and Kramer, J. M.: Non-gastrointestinal *Bacillus cereus* infections: An analysis of exotoxin production by strains isolated over a two year period. J. Clin. Pathol. *36*:1091–1096, 1983.
87. Turnbull, P. C., and Kramer, J. M.: Intestinal carriage of *Bacillus cereus*: Faecal isolation studies in three population groups. J. Hyg. *95*:629–638, 1985.
88. Turnbull, P. C., and Kramer, J. M.: *Bacillus*. *In* Murray, P. R., Baron, E. J., and Pfaller, M. A. (eds.): Manual of Clinical Microbiology. 6th ed. Washington, D.C., American Society for Microbiology, 1995, pp. 349–356.
89. Turnbull, P. C., Kramer, J. M., Jorgensen, K., et al.: Properties and production characteristics of vomiting, diarrheal and necrotizing toxins of *Bacillus cereus*. Am. J. Clin. Nutr. *32*:219–228, 1979.
90. Turnbull, P. C., Nottingham, J. F., and Ghosh, A. C.: A severe necrotic enterotoxin produced by certain food, food poisoning and other clinical isolates of *Bacillus cereus*. Br. J. Exp. Pathol. *58*:273–280, 1977.

91. Vahey, J. B., and Flynn, H. W., Jr.: Results in the management of *Bacillus* endophthalmitis. Ophthalmol. Surg. *22*:681–686, 1991.
92. Vaisanen, O. M., Mwaisumo, N. J., and Salkinoja-Salonen, M. S.: Differentiation of dairy strains of the *Bacillus cereus* group by phage typing, minimum growth temperature, and fatty acid analysis. J. Appl. Bacteriol. *70*:315–324, 1991.
93. Vandeloski, J., and Gensheimer, K. F.: *Bacillus cereus:* Maine. M. M. W. R. Morb. Mortal. Wkly. Rep. *35*:408–410, 1986.
94. Weber, D. J., Saviteer, S. M., Rutala, W. A., et al.: In vitro susceptibility of *Bacillus* spp to selected antimicrobial agents. Antimicrob. Agents Chemother. *32*:642–645, 1988.
95. Wong, M. T., and Dolan, M. J.: Significant infections due to *Bacillus* species following abrasions associated with motor vehicle–related trauma. Clin. Infect. Dis. *15*:855–857, 1992.
96. Young, E. J., Wallace, R. J., Ericsson, C. D., et al.: Panophthalmitis due to *Bacillus cereus*. Arch. Intern. Med. *140*:559–560, 1980.
97. Youngs, E. R., Roberts, C., Kramer, J. M., et al.: Dissemination of *Bacillus cereus* in a maternity unit. J. Infect. *10*:228–232, 1985.
98. Zaza, S., Tokars, J. I., Yomtovian, R., et al.: Bacterial contamination of platelets at a university hospital: Increased identification due to intensified surveillance. Infect. Control Hosp. Epidemiol. *15*:82–87, 1994.

Arcanobacterium haemolyticum

JAMES D. CHERRY ■ ALAN M. SHAPIRO

Arcanobacterium haemolyticum is a pleomorphic gram-positive coryneform rod that causes pharyngitis and exanthem in children and young adults.[13, 31, 35, 39]

History

This diphtheroid was first noted by MacLean and colleagues[35] in association with exudative pharyngitis in American servicemen in the South Pacific during World War II. The organism originally was named *Corynebacterium haemolyticum* but was reclassified in 1986 as *A. haemolyticum* on the basis of phenetic, peptidoglycan, fatty acid, menaquinone, and DNA data.[11–13] The association between infection with *A. haemolyticum* and pharyngitis was observed repeatedly over the years, but a cause-and-effect relationship between the organism and illness has been established only relatively recently.[8, 34, 39]

The Organism

MICROBIOLOGY[13, 15, 20, 54, 57]

A. haemolyticum is a gram-positive to gram-variable pleomorphic rod. Its laboratory characteristics are presented in Table 98–1. The organism grows best at 37° C on a blood- or serum-enriched medium with the addition of 5 percent carbon dioxide. Alternatively, it grows well anaerobically. On rabbit or human blood agar, colonies are pinpoint (0.5 mm) at 24 hours; they increase to 1 to 1.5 mm after 48 hours. At this time, a unique black opaque dot is noted in the center of the colony, and this dot remains on the agar when the colony is scraped away.

At 24 hours, a 1-mm zone of hemolysis develops around colonies grown on human or rabbit blood agar. The hemolytic zone increases to 3 to 5 mm by 48 hours. Both growth and red cell hemolysis are minimal on horse and sheep blood agar. Because throat cultures usually are performed on sheep blood agar plates, the hemolytic activity of *A. haemolyticum* may be missed.

Colonies of *A. haemolyticum* can be of either the smooth or rough biotypes on horse blood agar.[10] These biotypes also differ in their hemolysis and biochemical properties. Smooth colonies predominate in wound infections and frequently utilize sucrose and trehalose, are beta-hemolytic, and lack β-glucuronidase. Rough colonies are found almost exclusively in the respiratory tract and do not utilize sucrose and trehalose, are nonhemolytic, and are β-glucuronidase–positive.

A. haemolyticum resembles *Actinomyces pyogenes* (formerly *Corynebacterium pyogenes*), a common cause of bovine mastitis and a rare cause of skin ulcers in children.[28] These organisms can be differentiated by several means. *A. pyogenes* is able to hydrolyze gelatin and ferment xylose. In addition, *A. haemolyticum* has a positive reverse CAMP (Christie, Atkins, and Munch-Petersen) test in that it inhibits the beta-hemolysis of *Staphylococcus aureus*, whereas *A. pyogenes* shows slight enhancement of beta-hemolysis.[19] *A. haemolyticum*'s poor growth on tellurite medium and lack of catalase help distinguish it from *Corynebacterium diphtheriae*, which also causes pharyngitis.[24, 30, 31]

TOXIN PRODUCTION

A. haemolyticum liberates three toxins: phospholipase D (PLD), a hemolysin, and neuraminidase.[13] PLD is a

TABLE 98–1 ■ IDENTIFICATION CHARACTERISTICS OF *ARCANOBACTERIUM HAEMOLYTICUM*

Test or Characteristic	Finding
Catalase	Negative
Beta-hemolysis	Positive (a narrow zone of slight hemolysis after 48 hr on sheep blood)
Nitrate reduction	Negative
Pigment production	White or gray
Urease	Negative
Gelatin hydrolysis	Negative
Motility	Negative
Esculin hydrolysis	Negative
Carbohydrate utilization	
Glucose	Positive
Maltose	Positive
Sucrose	Positive (requires rabbit serum for growth in peptone water)
Mannitol	Negative
Xylose	Negative

Data from Collins, M. D., and Cummins, C. S.: Genus *Corynebacterium*. *In* Sneath, P. H. A., Main, N. S., Sharpe, M. E., et al. (eds.): Bergey's Manual of Systemic Bacteriology. Vol. 2. Baltimore, Williams & Wilkins, 1986, pp. 266–276.

dermonecrotic toxin that after intradermal inoculation in rabbits and guinea pigs causes local hemorrhagic necrosis; injection of PLD also is lethal in rabbits.[46] The PLD gene of *A. haemolyticum* has a high degree of homology to that of *Corynebacterium pseudotuberculosis*.[14, 37] PLD has been shown to be involved in the virulence of *C. pseudotuberculosis*; PLD mutants are less pathogenic in experimental infections in goats.[36] The PLD of *C. pseudotuberculosis* is similar biochemically and shares some biologic activity with the PLD that is found in brown recluse spider venom and that plays a role in the venom's toxicity.[5, 31] *A. haemolyticum* carries a gene similar to the gene encoding the erythrogenic toxin of *Streptococcus pyogenes*.[13]

ANTIMICROBIAL SUSCEPTIBILITY

Almost all *A. haemolyticum* strains are highly susceptible to erythromycin (minimal inhibitory concentration <0.06 µg/mL). However, erythromycin is not bactericidal.[7, 35, 54] Carlson and colleagues[9] reported an *A. haemolyticum* isolate from a diabetic foot ulcer that was exceptionally resistant to macrolides, clindamycin, tetracycline, and ofloxacin. Waagner[54] noted that of 100 pharyngeal isolates, all were inhibited by concentrations of 0.25 µg/mL or less of penicillin G and by 1.0 µg/mL of penicillin V.[54] However, tolerance to penicillin has been observed.[35, 44] In one study, the minimal bactericidal concentration–minimal inhibitory concentration ratio varied from 1:1 to 1:8.[35] In addition to being sensitive to penicillin and erythromycin, *A. haemolyticum* also is sensitive to other β-lactams, clindamycin, chloramphenicol, azithromycin, vancomycin, ciprofloxacin, tetracyclines, and rifampin; most strains are resistant to sulfonamides and trimethoprim-sulfamethoxazole.[7, 9, 54]

A vancomycin-resistant *A. haemolyticum* isolated from stool during an outbreak of vancomycin-resistant enterococci has been described. It contained the *vanA* gene primarily found in *Enterococcus faecium*.[47]

Epidemiology

Although similar organisms are common causes of infection in animals, humans appear to be the primary host of *A. haemolyticum*.[48, 54] The organism is isolated primarily from throat specimens in patients with pharyngitis,[35, 39, 54] although it also may be a commensal of human skin.[34] It likewise may be a commensal in the throat but often is overlooked because laboratories frequently do not differentiate diphtheroids, which are considered "normal flora." In addition, because *A. haemolyticum* often is found in polymicrobial respiratory infections with classic respiratory pathogens, including *S. pyogenes*, it sometimes is missed when these more classic pathogens are identified.[31]

Although no definitive data are available, spread from person to person is assumed to be from the throat discharge of an infected person to the throat of a susceptible host. Transmission could occur directly or indirectly by fomites. Secondary cases in families indicate that spread is from person to person rather than from an environmental source.[18, 39]

In an 8-year study, the organism was found to be isolated from throat specimens in each year, with isolation rates varying from 0.2 to 0.7 percent.[39] The peak age for contracting illness caused by *A. haemolyticum* is during the second decade of life; in contrast, the peak age for developing pharyngitis caused by *S. pyogenes* is during the first decade of life.[18, 35, 39] In two studies, illnesses occurred more commonly in females than in males.[18, 39] In a review of *A. haemolyticum* systemic and deep-seated infections, a preponderance of males over females was found in adolescents with no risk factors for development of invasive disease.[52] No seasonal prevalence has been reported.

TABLE 98–2 ■ SIGNS AND SYMPTOMS IN CHILDREN, ADOLESCENTS, AND YOUNG ADULTS WITH *ARCANOBACTERIUM HAEMOLYTICUM* INFECTION

	Frequency (%)
Symptoms	
Sore throat	100
Rash	40–70
Pruritus	50
Fever	40–75
Hoarseness	60
Cough (nonproductive)	40–60
Vomiting	30
Signs	
Pharyngitis or tonsillitis	100
Exudative	50–70
Palatal petechiae	30
Glossitis	25
Cervical lymphadenitis	40–75
Rash	40–70
Scarlatiniform	50
Urticarial	5
Maculopapular	25

Data from references 18, 27, 35, 39, 54.

Pathogenesis and Pathology

Few data are available regarding pathogenesis and pathology. The dermonecrotic toxin probably plays a role in pharyngitis. Skin biopsy specimens were taken from the exanthem in two patients, and both showed only a mild lymphohistiocytic perivascular infiltrate.[39] Cultures of both samples were negative, and no IgG, IgA, or IgM deposition was noted. These findings suggest that the rash may be toxin-mediated, like the rash in group A streptococcal infections.

A. haemolyticum has been found to persist intracellularly,[45] which might account for failure of penicillin treatment in some cases.

In one study, 5 of 42 patients were found to have apparent dual infections with Epstein-Barr virus and *A. haemolyticum*.[35] The authors of this study suggested that immune suppression by the virus contributes to a more marked effect of the bacterial infection in the throat.

With regard to the immune response to *A. haemolyticum*, paired acute and convalescent sera showed the development of a humoral response to four distinct cell wall–associated proteins on Western blot analysis in 7 of 8 patients with culture-confirmed infection.[42]

Clinical Manifestations

PHARYNGITIS

Pharyngitis* is the most common finding in *A. haemolyticum* infection. Signs and symptoms associated with pharyngitis are presented in Table 98–2. The illness is

*See references 2, 8, 18, 21, 23, 24, 27, 34, 35, 39, 41, 43, 49–51, 54.

indistinguishable from that caused by group A streptococci; frequently, it resembles Epstein-Barr virus infectious mononucleosis. Several patients with typical infectious mononucleosis had laboratory evidence of infection with both Epstein-Barr virus and *A. haemolyticum*.[22, 23, 35] Peritonsillar abscess caused by *A. haemolyticum* has been reported on several occasions.[3, 30, 32, 38] The most common exanthem is scarlatiniform, which has an onset 1 to 4 days after the beginning of pharyngeal symptoms. The rash is most prominent on the extensor surfaces of the arms and legs (see Fig. 67–19). Circumoral pallor, which is seen with group A streptococcal scarlet fever, does not seem to occur with *A. haemolyticum* infection. The rash may progress to involve the chest and back; it usually spares the palms, soles, and face, and it rarely involves the abdomen and buttocks.

The rash frequently is pruritic and may be urticarial. Erythema multiforme has been described.[2] Recently, Gaston and Zurowski[21] reported a 20-year-old man who had, in addition to pharyngitis, a rash involving mainly his hands and feet. His feet were swollen, and on the soles were erythematous macules, petechiae, and vesicles. His palms were tender, and 2- to 4-mm erythematous macular lesions that contained small central vesicles were present.

The duration of the exanthem has not been described adequately in the literature. In one study, exanthem was noted to persist for longer than 2 days in 69 percent of patients.[39]

On occasion, *A. haemolyticum* infection has been manifested as a grayish-white pharyngeal pseudomembrane that has been confused with diphtheria.[2, 24, 26, 30] *C. diphtheriae* and *A. haemolyticum* are diphtheroids that cannot be distinguished on Gram stain but can be differentiated by their biochemical properties.

SKIN INFECTIONS

In the initial report of infections with *A. haemolyticum* in 1946, MacLean and associates[35] noted both pharyngitis in U.S. servicemen and skin infections in the native populations of the South Pacific Islands. Cutaneous infections have been observed mainly in tropical countries.[54] The most common manifestations are ulcerative lesions that resemble ecthyma. Cellulitis, wound infections, and paronychia all have been noted.[6, 17, 18, 29, 38, 40, 54, 58] In wound infections, mixed infections with *A. haemolyticum* and other organisms are common findings.

OTHER MANIFESTATIONS

Isolated instances of septicemia, brain abscess, meningitis, meningoencephalitis, orbital cellulitis, endocarditis, osteomyelitis, deep soft tissue infections, pleural empyema, cavitary pneumonia, and sinusitis have been attributed to *A. haemolyticum* infection.* Most of these serious infections occurred in adults and frequently were associated with underlying conditions such as diabetes, a malignancy, or intravenous drug use. In a 1998 review of systemic and deep-seated infections caused by *A. haemolyticum*, Skov and associates[52] identified two groups of patients. The first group was composed of middle-aged to elderly adults who were immunocompromised or had other known risk factors for development of serious infectious disease. The second group consisted of preteens to young adults with no known risk factors except for one individual receiving steroid treatment for Epstein-Barr virus infection.

*See references 1, 4, 16, 19, 22, 23, 25, 33, 52, 54–56, 59.

DIFFERENTIAL DIAGNOSIS

Pharyngitis caused by *A. haemolyticum* must be differentiated from all other causes of pharyngitis (see Chapter 10). Of particular importance is distinguishing *A. haemolyticum* pharyngitis from *S. pyogenes* pharyngitis. Such differentiation can be achieved with certainty only by specific culture. In *A. haemolyticum* infection, the rapid group A streptococcal antigen tests will be negative, as will the usual group A streptococcal culture. These negative tests in specimens from adolescents should suggest strongly the possibility of *A. haemolyticum* pharyngitis.

When exanthem occurs, the confusion with illness caused by *S. pyogenes* is more pronounced. In many cases, the rash in patients infected with *A. haemolyticum* is scarlatiniform. However, the lack of typical circumoral pallor and a tendency for more discrete lesions in *A. haemolyticum* infection occasionally may help in making the clinical diagnosis.

Other common causes of pharyngitis and exanthem in adolescents and young adults are *Mycoplasma pneumoniae* and Epstein-Barr virus infections. As noted by Mackenzie and colleagues,[34] *A. haemolyticum* and Epstein-Barr virus coinfections are not uncommon occurrences. Concurrent *M. pneumoniae* pneumonia and *A. haemolyticum* empyema and bacteremia have been reported in a previously healthy 20-year-old man.[53]

Cutaneous infections, including subacute ulcerations, wound infections, cellulitis, and paronychia caused by *A. haemolyticum*, must be differentiated from those caused by other organisms such as staphylococci and streptococci.

Specific Diagnosis

A specific diagnosis is made by culturing *A. haemolyticum* from the pharynx, a skin lesion, or a sterile body site in invasive infections. Culturing is done best with rabbit or human blood agar and the addition of 5 percent carbon dioxide.[13, 15, 54, 57] An important note is that horse or sheep blood agar, which generally is used for culture of *S. pyogenes*, is not satisfactory for the growth and identification of *A. haemolyticum*. Using biochemical identification systems such as the API (RAPID) Coryne strip (API bioMérieux, La-Balme-les-Grottes, France) or the Biolog system (Biolog, Hazelwood, CA) can help differentiate *A. haemolyticum* from other coryneform bacteria. The Biolog system can make the identification in 4 hours.[20]

Treatment

A. haemolyticum is highly sensitive to numerous antibiotics.[7, 10, 35, 43, 54] Although no specific treatment studies have been performed, the experience in several large studies suggests that both penicillin and erythromycin are effective.[7, 27, 35, 39] Clinical failure with penicillin has been noted.[2, 45, 54] Therefore, erythromycin has been suggested for first-line therapy for certain indications such as *A. haemolyticum* tonsillitis.[9] Carlson and coworkers[9] suggest using either a broad-spectrum β-lactam antibiotic or clindamycin or macrolides for serious systemic *A. haemolyticum* infection, although these authors do acknowledge that macrolides do not provide anaerobic coverage. An alternative approach would be to use high-dose penicillin plus an aminoglycoside.[52, 54]

Prognosis

The prognosis in cases of *A. haemolyticum* pharyngitis is good, even in untreated patients. However, invasive disease can be fatal, and peritonsillar abscess requires prompt surgical intervention and appropriate antimicrobial therapy.

REFERENCES

1. Altmann, G., and Bogokovsky, B.: Brain abscess due to *Corynebacterium haemolyticum*. Lancet *1*:338–339, 1973.
2. Banck, G., and Nyman, M.: Tonsillitis and rash associated with *Corynebacterium haemolyticum*. J. Infect. Dis. *154*:1037–1040, 1986.
3. Barnham, M., and Bradwell, R. A.: Acute peritonsillar abscess caused by *Arcanobacterium haemolyticum*. J. Laryngol. Otol. *106*:1000–1001, 1992.
4. Ben-Yaacob, D., Waron, M., Boldur, I., et al.: Septicemia due to *Corynebacterium haemolyticum*. Isr J. Med. Sci. *20*:431–433, 1984.
5. Bernheimer, A. W., Campbell, B. J., and Forrester, L. J.: Comparative toxinology of *Loxosceles reclusa* and *Corynebacterium pseudotuberculosis*. Science *228*:590–591, 1985.
6. Bowness, P., Bower, M., Montgomery, J., et al.: The bacteriology of skin sores in Goroka children. Papua New Guinea Med. J. *27*:83–87, 1984.
7. Carlson, P., Kontiainen, S., and Renkonen, O. V.: Antimicrobial susceptibility of *Arcanobacterium haemolyticum*. Antimicrob. Agents Chemother. *38*:142–143, 1994.
8. Carlson, P., Kontianinen, S., Renkonen, O. V., et al.: *Arcanobacterium haemolyticum* and streptococcal pharyngitis in army conscripts. Scand. J. Infect. Dis. *27*:17–18, 1995.
9. Carlson, P., Korpela J., Walder M., et al.: Antimicrobial susceptibilities and biotypes of *Arcanobacterium haemolyticum* blood isolates. Eur. J. Clin. Microbiol. Infect. Dis. *18*:915–917, 1999.
10. Carlson, P., Lounatmaa, K., and Kontiainen, S.: Biotypes of *Arcanobacterium haemolyticum*. J. Clin. Microbiol. *32*:1654–1657, 1994.
11. Collins, M. D., and Cummins, C. S.: Genus *Corynebacterium*. *In* Sneath, P. H. A., Mair, N. S., Sharpe, M. E., et al. (eds.): Bergey's Manual of Systemic Bacteriology. Vol. 2. Baltimore, Williams & Wilkins, 1986, pp. 266–276.
12. Collins, M. D., Jones, D., and Schofield, G. M.: Reclassification of *Corynebacterium haemolyticum* (MacLean, Liebow and Rosenberg) in the genus *Arcanobacterium* gen. nov. as *Arcanobacterium haemolyticum* nom. rev., comb. nov. J. Gen. Microbiol. *128*:1279–1281, 1982.
13. Coyle, M. B., and Lipsky, B. A.: Coryneform bacteria in infectious diseases: Clinical and laboratory aspects. Clin. Microbiol. Rev. *3*:227–246, 1990.
14. Cuevas, W. A., and Songer, J. G.: *Arcanobacterium haemolyticum* phospholipase D is genetically and functionally similar to *Corynebacterium pseudotuberculosis* phospholipase D. Infect. Immun. *61*:4310–4316, 1993.
15. Cummings, L. A., Wu, W. K., Larson, A. M., et al.: Effects of media, atmosphere, and incubation time on colonial morphology of *Arcanobacterium haemolyticum*. J. Clin. Microbiol. *31*:3223–3226, 1993.
16. Dobinsky, S., Noesselt, T., Rucker, A, et al.: Three cases of *Arcanobacterium haemolyticum* associated with abscess formation and cellulitis. Eur. J. Clin. Microbiol. Infect. Dis. *18*:804–806, 1999.
17. Esteban, J., Zapardiel, J., and Soriano, F.: Two cases of soft-tissue infection caused by *Arcanobacterium haemolyticum*. Clin. Infect. Dis. *18*:835–836, 1994.
18. Fell, H. W. K., Nagington, J., Naylor, G. R. E., et al.: *Corynebacterium haemolyticum* infections in Cambridgeshire. J. Hyg. Camb. *79*:269–275, 1977.
19. Ford, J. G., Yeatts, R. P., and Givner, L. B.: Orbital cellulitis, subperiosteal abscess, sinusitis, and septicemia caused by *Arcanobacterium haemolyticum*. Am. J. Ophthalmol. *120*:261–262, 1995
20. Funke, G., von Graevenitz, A., Clarridge, J. E., 3rd., et al.: Clinical microbiology of coryneform bacteria. Clin. Microbiol. Rev. *10*:125–159, 1997.
21. Gaston, D. A., and Zurowski, S. M.: *Arcanobacterium haemolyticum* pharyngitis and exanthem. Arch. Dermatol. *132*:61–64, 1996.
22. Givner, L. B., McGehee, D., Taber, L. H., et al.: Sinusitis, orbital cellulitis and polymicrobial bacteremia in a patient with primary Epstein-Barr virus infection. Pediatr. Infect. Dis. J. *3*:254–256, 1984.
23. Goudswaard, J., van de Merwe, D. W., van der Sluys, P., et al.: *Corynebacterium haemolyticum* septicemia in a girl with mononucleosis infectiosa. Scand. J. Infect. Dis. *20*:339–340, 1988.
24. Green, S. L., and LaPeter, K. S.: Pseudodiphtheritic membranous pharyngitis caused by *Corynebacterium haemolyticum*. J. A. M. A. *245*:2330–2331, 1981.
25. Jobanputra, R. S., and Swain, C. P.: Septicaemia due to *Corynebacterum haemolyticum*. J. Clin. Pathol. *28*:798–800, 1975.
26. Kain, K. C., Noble, M. A., Barteluk, R. L., et al.: *Arcanobacterium hemolyticum* infection: Confused with scarlet fever and diphtheria. J. Emerg. Med. 9:33–35, 1991.
27. Karpathios, T., Drakonaki, S., Zervoudaki, A., et al.: *Arcanobacterium haemolyticum* in children with presumed streptococcal pharyngotonsillitis or scarlet fever. J. Pediatr. *121*:735–737, 1992.
28. Kotrajaras, R. P., Buddhavudhikral, S., Sukroongreung, S., et al.: Endemic leg ulcers caused by *Corynebacterium pyogenes* in Thailand. Int. J. Dermatol. *21*:407–409, 1982.
29. Kotrajaras, R., and Tagami, H.: *Corynebacterium pyogenes:* Its pathogenic mechanism in epidemic leg ulcers in Thailand. Int. J. Dermatol. *26*:45–50, 1987.
30. Kovatch, A. L., Schuit, K. E., and Michaels, R. H.: *Corynebacterium haemolyticum* peritonsillar abscess mimicking diphtheria. J. A. M. A. *249*:1757–1758, 1983.
31. Linder, R.: *Rhodococcus equi* and *Arcanobacterium haemolyticum*: Two "coryneform" bacteria increasingly recognized as agents of human infection. Emerg. Infect. Dis. *3*:145–153, 1997.
32. Lipsky, B. A., Goldberger, A. C., Tompkins, L. S., et al.: Infections caused by nondiphtheria corynebacteria. Rev. Infect. Dis. *4*:1220–1235, 1982.
33. Locksley, R. M.: The lowly diphtheroid: Nondiphtheria corynebacterial infections in humans. West. J. Med. *137*:45–52, 1982.
34. Mackenzie, A., Fuite, L. A., Chan, F. T. H., et al.: Incidence and pathogenicity of *Arcanobacterium haemolyticum* during a 2-year study in Ottawa. Clin. Infect. Dis. *21*:177–181, 1995.
35. MacLean, P. D., Liebow, A. A., and Rosenberg, A. A.: A hemolytic corynebacterium resembling *Corynebacterium ovis* and *Corynebacterium pyogenes* in man. J. Infect. Dis. *79*:69–90, 1946.
36. McNamara P. J., Bradley G. A., and Songer J. G.: Targeted mutagenesis of the phospholipase D gene results in decreased virulence of *Corynebacterium pseudotuberculosis*. Mol. Microbiol. *12*:921–930, 1994.
37. McNamara, P. J., Cuevas, W. A., and Songer, J. G.: Toxic phospholipases D of *Corynebacterium pseudotuberculosis, C. ulcerans* and *Arcanobacterium haemolyticum:* Cloning and sequence homology. Gene *156*:113–118, 1995.
38. Miller, R. A., and Brancato, F.: Peritonsillar abscess associated with *Corynebacterium haemolyticum*. West. J. Med. *140*:449–451, 1984.
39. Miller, R. A., Brancato, F., and Holmes, K. K.: *Corynebacterium haemolyticum* as a cause of pharyngitis and scarlatiniform rash in young adults. Ann. Intern. Med. *105*:867–872, 1986.
40. Montgomery, J.: The aerobic bacteriology of infected skin lesions in children of the Eastern Highlands Province. Papua New Guinea Med. J. *28*:93–103, 1985.
41. Moreno, M. M., Valle, V. A., and Aguillar, A. L.: Pharyngitis caused by *Arcanobacterium haemolyticum*. An. Esp. Pediatr. *30*:209–210, 1989.
42. Nyman, M., Alugupalli, K. R., Stromberg, S., et al.: Antibody response to *Arcanobacterium haemolyticum* infection in humans. J. Infect. Dis. *175*:1515–1518, 1997.
43. Nyman, M., and Banck, G.: The clinical picture in throat infections caused by *Corynebacterium haemolyticum*. Hygiea Swedish Med. Assoc. 109–110, 1984.
44. Nyman, M., Banck, G., and Thore, M.: Penicillin tolerance in *Arcanobacterium haemolyticum*. J. Infect. Dis. *161*:261–265, 1990.
45. Osterlund, A.: Are penicillin treatment failures in *Arcanobacterium haemolyticum* pharyngotonsillitis caused by intracellularly residing bacteria? Scand. J. Infect. Dis. *27*:131–134, 1995.
46. Patocka, F., Mara, M., Soucek, A., et al.: Observations on the biological properties of atypical haemolytic corynebacteria isolated from man as compared with *Corynebacterium haemolyticum*, *Corynebacterium pyogenes bovis* and *Corynebacterium ovis*. J. Hyg. Epidemiol. Microbiol. Imunol. *6*:1–12, 1962.
47. Power, E. G., Abdulla, Y. H., Talsania, H. G., et al.: *vanA* genes in vancomycin-resistant clinical isolates of *Oerskovia turbata* and *Arcanobacterium (Corynebacterium) haemolyticum*. J. Antimicrob. Chemother. *36*:595–606, 1995.
48. Roberts, R. J.: Isolation of *Corynebacterium haemolyticum* from a case of ovine pneumonia. Vet. Rec. *84*:490, 1969.
49. Robinson, B. E., and Murray, D. L.: *Corynebacterium haemolyticum* and pharyngitis. Ann. Intern. Med. *106*:778–779, 1987.
50. Ryan, W. J.: Throat infection and rash associated with an unusual corynebacterium. Lancet *2*:1345–1347, 1972.
51. Selander, B., and Ljungh, A.: *Corynebacterium haemolyticum* as a cause of nonstreptococcal pharyngitis. J. Infect. Dis. *154*:1041, 1986.
52. Skov, R. L., Sanden, A. K., Danchell, V. H., et al.: Systemic and deep-seated infections caused by *Arcanobacterium haemolyticum*. Eur. J. Clin. Microbiol. Infect. Dis. *17*:578–582, 1998.
53. Stacey, A., and Bradlow, A.: *Arcanobacterium haemolyticum* and *Mycoplasma pneumoniae* co-infection. J. Infect. *38*:41–42, 1999.
54. Waagner, D. C.: *Arcanobacterium haemolyticum*: Biology of the organism and diseases in man. Pediatr. Infect. Dis. J. *10*:933–939, 1991.
55. Waller, K. S., and Wood, B. P.: Cavitary pneumonia due to *Arcanobacterium hemolyticum*. Am. J. Dis. Child. *145*:209–210, 1991.
56. Washington, J. A., Martin, W. J., and Spiekerman, R. E.: Brain abscess with *Corynebacterium haemolyticum*: Report of a case. Am. J. Clin. Pathol. *56*:212–215, 1971.
57. Wat, L. L., Fleming, C. A., Hodge, D. S., et al.: Selective medium for isolation of *Arcanobacterium haemolyticum* and *Streptococcus pyogenes*. Eur. J. Clin. Microbiol. Infect. Dis. *10*:443–446, 1991.
58. Wickremesinghe, R. S. B.: *Corynebacterium haemolyticum* infections in Sri Lanka. J. Hyg. Camb. *87*:271–277, 1981.
59. Worthington, M. G., Daly, B. D. T., and Smith, F. E.: *Corynebacterium haemolyticum* endocarditis on a native valve. South. Med. J. *78*: 1261–1262, 1985.

CHAPTER 99 Erysipelothrix rhusiopathiae

RANDALL G. FISHER ■ WILLIAM C. GRUBER ■ THOMAS G. BOYCE

Erysipelothrix rhusiopathiae (insidiosa) first was identified definitively by Rosenbach[26] in 1884 as a cause of the cutaneous disease erysipeloid. Although most commonly associated with localized skin infection in humans, this organism has been associated with sepsis,[10, 24, 31] chronic skin eruption,[8, 13] and endocarditis.[2, 10, 18, 19, 25, 31]

Bacteriology

E. rhusiopathiae is a slender, pleomorphic, gram-positive, unencapsulated rod that produces 0.1-mm bluish colonies on blood agar. Some strains produce alpha-hemolysis in 48 to 72 hours. Gelatin inoculated by stab inconsistently forms the "test tube brush" appearance diagnostic of this organism.[10] *Erysipelothrix* is differentiated from morphologically similar *Listeria monocytogenes* and diphtheroids by the absence of motility and catalase production and the presence of hydrogen sulfide production in triple sugar iron medium.[10, 31]

Epidemiology

First isolated from mice in 1880 by Koch, *Erysipelothrix* is a common commensal of wild and domestic mammals, birds, and fish.[10, 31] The *Erysipelothrix* organism may lead a saprophytic existence in soil. First identified by Loeffler in 1882 as the causative agent of swine erysipelas, it remains an important epidemic cause of disease in these animals, with losses in excess of $25 million annually.[10] Sheep, rabbits, cattle, turkeys, and rats are subject to infection with this organism. *Erysipelothrix* has been recovered from wild moose and domestic emus.[4, 17] *E. rhusiopathiae* survives salting and smoking procedures. Pieces of meat may contain the organism for 170 days after pickling, but exposure to moist heat for 15 minutes at 55° C[30] will kill most strains.[10] Not surprisingly, fish handlers, meat processors, poultry workers, veterinarians, abattoir workers, and food handlers are at risk for exposure to *Erysipelothrix*.[22] Isolates of the same serotype may demonstrate genetic diversity, so serotyping may not be completely reliable as an epidemiologic tool for tracking outbreaks.[5]

Pathophysiology

Human infection is largely accidental and results from contamination of skin abrasions during handling of infected material. Males are infected more commonly than are females, perhaps because of increased exposure. The presence of an antiphagocytic capsule may be a virulence factor for *E. rhusiopathiae*.[28] In vitro study shows that encapsulated strains are poorly phagocytized by macrophages unless immune serum is provided; furthermore, ingested bacteria are able to replicate within the macrophage. The ability to survive and replicate within macrophages probably is due to failure of the encapsulated strains to induce an oxidative burst.[27] Disease usually is self-limited and most often involves the hands. Biopsy of skin lesions shows a marked inflammatory response. The difficulty in obtaining bacteriologic confirmation has been attributed to the organism's location in the deep part of the pars reticularis of the corium.[6]

Clinical Manifestations

Human disease typically manifests as a mild, localized cutaneous eruption; a more severe, generalized cutaneous form; or a septicemia often associated with endocarditis. Localized cutaneous infection, the erysipeloid of Rosenbach,[26] is the most common manifestation of *Erysipelothrix* disease.[22] After a 1- to 4-day incubation period, an acute localized lesion appears at the site of an abrasion contaminated with *E. rhusiopathiae*–colonized material. Slowly progressive, purplish-red, painful induration is a typical finding. Absence of suppuration and involution without desquamation help distinguish this lesion from streptococcal or staphylococcal infection. Occasionally, the skin may show sharply circumscribed bluish-red lesions, similar to the cutaneous manifestations in swine.[10, 31] Fever and other constitutional symptoms are uncommon findings and occur in less than 10 percent of cases unless bacteremia supervenes.[8, 22] Untreated infection usually is self-limited, with an average duration of 3 weeks. Lymphangitis and adenitis occur in 10 percent of cases, and in 20 percent, progression of disease extends from lesions on the hand to the wrist and forearm.[14] A 7-week-old infant with localized *E. rhusiopathiae* infection of the knee and no known source of exposure has been reported,[16] and a 6-year-old girl with *Erysipelothrix* pyopneumothorax has been described.[23]

Cutaneous eruptions rarely may occur in areas distant from the site of inoculation[15] and appear as violaceous lesions with advancing pink borders. Bullous vesiculation has been described.[8] In 1921, Prausnitz[24] reported the first case of apparent septicemia in childhood when the organism was isolated from the blood of a 10-year-old boy.

E. rhusiopathiae rarely is associated with the bite of a domestic dog or cat.[1] In one prospective study of infected domesticated animal bite wounds, two patients who had cat bite wounds infected with *E. rhusiopathiae* were identified.[29] Cultures were processed carefully and performed in reference laboratories.

An uncommon, but important complication of *Erysipelothrix* infection is endocarditis. Presumed or proven endocarditis accounts for 90 percent of serious *E. rhusiopathiae* infections.[9] Patients with congenital heart disease or heart valve damage secondary to acute rheumatic fever are at greatest risk for developing endocarditis. However, previously normal heart valves can be infected,[10, 18] and valvular and myocardial abscesses have been described.[21] Unlike diphtheroid endocarditis, *E. rhusiopathiae* endocarditis usually does not involve prosthetic valves, and unlike endocarditis caused by *Bacillus* spp., it is not associated with intravenous drug abuse.[9] In a review of 1989 cases of endocarditis from 13 series,[2] *Erysipelothrix* was documented in two patients. *Erysipelothrix* endocarditis commonly involved the aortic valve. The overall mortality in reported cases is 38 percent. Curiously, no history or physical evidence of cutaneous lesions is found in as many as 50 percent of cases of endocarditis, and a history of exposure to contaminated material often is lacking. Although immunocompromised individuals[19] may be at increased risk, serious infection also occurs in otherwise normal hosts,[3, 10, 18] particularly in association with occupational exposure.

Diagnosis

For localized disease, the diagnosis depends largely on the clinical appearance of the lesion in conjunction with an appropriate history of exposure. Attempts to culture the organism from material collected by swab or by aspiration of a local lesion almost always are unsuccessful, presumably because of the bacteria's location deep within the skin.[6, 31] However, biopsy samples of affected skin cultured in broth generally will yield the offending bacteria. Amplification and detection of *Erysipelothrix* DNA by polymerase chain reaction show promise in animal models of infection.[17] *Erysipelothrix* is isolated commonly from the blood of patients with septicemia or endocarditis and can be found in affected heart valves at autopsy or at the time of valve replacement.[8] A high index of suspicion is important for making the diagnosis of endocarditis. The organism has been misidentified as a viridans group streptococcus because of its pleomorphic coccoid appearance, alpha-hemolysis, and catalase-negative character. Abbreviated identification schemata that do not include testing for hydrogen sulfide production sometimes lead to misidentification as lactobacilli or enterococci.[7]

Treatment

E. rhusiopathiae is exquisitely sensitive to penicillin. Localized disease usually can be treated with oral medication, but high parenteral doses occasionally are necessary, particularly for disseminated disease.[10] Treatment of *E. rhusiopathiae* endocarditis is similar to treatment of endocarditis caused by viridans streptococci. At least 12 million U of penicillin administered for 4 weeks has been curative in adult patients, but many patients have been treated for 6 weeks or longer. Concomitant administration of an aminoglycoside has been used in some cases. *Erysipelothrix* is resistant to vancomycin.[12] Prompt microbiologic differentiation of *E. rhusiopathiae* from other gram-positive organisms is important in guiding antimicrobial selection because vancomycin often is used as empiric therapy for endocarditis. Hyperimmune serum, which at one time was advocated for therapy, is of little value. The risk of acquiring disease is minimized by protecting persons exposed to potentially contaminated material.

REFERENCES

1. Abedini, S., and Lester, A.: [*Erysipelothrix rhusiopathiae* bacteremia after dog bite.] [Danish.] Ugeskr. Laeger *159*:4400–4401, 1997.
2. Ben-Chetrit, E., Muiad, N., and Levo, Y.: Infective endocarditis caused by uncommon bacteria. Scand. J. Infect. Dis. *15*:179–183, 1983.
3. Callon, R. A. J., and Brady, P. G.: Toothpick perforation of the sigmoid colon: An unusual case associated with *Erysipelothrix rhusiopathiae* septicemia. Gastrointest. Endosc. *36*:141–143, 1990.
4. Campbell, G. D., Addison, E. M., Barker, I. K., et al.: *Erysipelothrix rhusiopathiae*, serotype 17, septicemia in moose (*Alces alces*) from Algonquin Park, Ontario. J. Wildl. Dis. *30*:436–438, 1994.
5. Chooromoney, K. N., Hampson, D. J., Eamens, G. J., et al.: Analysis of *Erysipelothrix rhusiopathiae* and *Erysipelothrix tonsillarum* by multilocus enzyme electrophoresis. J. Clin. Microbiol. *32*:371–376, 1994.
6. Dhttman, G.: Schweinrotlauf und Erysipeloid. Beitr. Klin. Chir. *123*:461–470, 1921.
7. Dunbar, S. A., and Clarridge, J. E., 3rd: Potential errors in recognition of *Erysipelothrix rhusiopathiae*. J. Clin. Microbiol. *38*:1302–1304, 2000.
8. Ehrlich, J. C.: *Erysipelothrix rhusiopathiae* infection in man. Arch. Intern. Med. *78*:565–577, 1944.
9. Gorby, G. L., and Peacock, J. E. J.: *Erysipelothrix rhusiopathiae* endocarditis: Microbiologic, epidemiologic, and clinical features of an occupational disease. Rev. Infect. Dis. *10*:317–325, 1988.
10. Grieco, M. H., and Sheldon, C.: *Erysipelothrix rhusiopathiae*. Ann. N. Y. Acad. Sci. *174*:523–532, 1970.
11. Griffiths, G. L., and Buller, N.: *Erysipelothrix rhusiopathiae* infection in semi-intensively farmed emus. Aust. Vet. J. *68*:121–122, 1991.
12. Johnson, A. P., Uttley, A. H., Woodford, N., et al.: Resistance to vancomycin and teicoplanin: An emerging clinical problem. Clin. Microbiol. Rev. *3*:280–291, 1990.
13. Klauder, J. V.: Erysipeloid as an occupational disease. J. A. M. A. *111*:1345–1348, 1938.
14. Klauder, J. V.: *Erysipelothrix rhusiopathiae* infection in swine and in human beings. Arch. Dermatol. Syph. *50*:151–159, 1944.
15. Kramer, M. R., Gombert, M. E., Corrado, M. L., et al.: *Erysipelothrix rhusiopathiae* endocarditis. South. Med. J. *75*:892, 1982.
16. Lacroix, J., Delage, G., and Mitchell, G.: Erysipeloid in an infant. J. Pediatr. *99*:745–746, 1981.
17. Makino, S., Okada, Y., Maruyama, T., et al.: Direct and rapid detection of *Erysipelothrix rhusiopathiae* DNA in animals by PCR. J. Clin. Microbiol. *32*:1526–1531, 1994.
18. Morris, C. A., Schwabacher, H., Lynch, P. G., et al.: Two fatal cases of septicaemia due to *Erysipelothrix insidiosa*. J. Clin. Pathol. *18*:614–617, 1965.
19. Muirhead, N., and Reid, T. M. S.: *Erysipelothrix rhusiopathiae* endocarditis. J. Infect. *2*:83–85, 1980.
20. Mutalib, A., Keirs, R., and Austin, F.: Erysipelas in quail and suspected erysipeloid in processing plant employees. Avian Dis. *39*:191–193, 1995.
21. Nandish, S., and Khardori, N.: Valvular and myocardial abscesses due to *Erysipelothrix rhusiopathiae*. Clin. Infect. Dis. *29*:1351–1352, 1999.
22. Nelson, E.: Five hundred cases of erysipeloid. Rocky Mountain Med. J. *52*:40–42, 1955.
23. Panhotra, B. R., Agarwal, K. C., Kumar, L., et al.: *Erysipelothrix rhusiopathiae* infection in a child: A case report with review of literature. Indian Pediatr. *16*:547–549, 1979.
24. Prausnitz, C.: Bakteriologische Untersuchung über Schweinrotlauf beim Menschen. Zentralbl. Bakteriol. Mikrobiol. Hyg. *85*:362, 1921.
25. Reboli, A. C., and Farrar, W. E.: *Erysipelothrix rhusiopathiae*: An occupational pathogen. Clin. Microbiol. Rev. 2:354–359, 1989.
26. Rosenbach, F. J.: Experimentelle morphologische und klinische Studie über die (krankheitserregenden) Mikroorganismen des Schweinrotlaufs, des Erysipeloids und der ma use Sepsis. Z. Hyg. Infektionskrankheit *63*:343–371, 1909.
27. Shimoji, Y., Yokomizo, Y., Sekizaki, T., et al.: Presence of a capsule in *Erysipelothrix rhusiopathiae* and its relationship to virulence for mice. Infect. Immun. *62*:2806–2810, 1994.
28. Shimoji, Y., Yokomizo, Y., and Mori, Y.: Intracellular survival and replication of *Erysipelothrix rhusiopathiae* within murine macrophages: Failure of induction of the oxidative burst of macrophages. Infect. Immun. *64*:1789–1793, 1996.
29. Talan, D. A., Citron, D. M., Abrahamian, F. M., et al.: Bacteriologic analysis of infected dog and cat bites. Emergency Medicine Animal Bite Infection Study Group. N. Engl. J. Med. *340*:85–92, 1999.
30. Watarai, M., Sawada, T., Nakagomi, M., et al.: Comparison of etiological and immunological characteristics of two attenuated *Erysipelothrix rhusiopathiae* strains of serotypes 1a and 2. J. Vet. Med. Sci. *55*:595–600, 1993.
31. Woodbine, M.: *Erysipelothrix rhusiopathiae:* Bacteriology and chemotherapy. Bacteriol. Rev. *14*:161–178, 1947.

Listeriosis

ROBERT BORTOLUSSI ■ TIMOTHY MAILMAN

Murray and associates[105] first isolated *Listeria monocytogenes* in 1926 while investigating an epidemic of perinatal infection with monocytosis in laboratory rabbits. The first reported human disease caused by *Listeria* was published 3 years later,[111] and neonatal infection was described in 1936.[22] Since then, the organism has been isolated with increasing frequency from the elderly, pregnant women, immunocompromised individuals, and neonates. A large body of information has accumulated, and several comprehensive reviews have been published.[16, 45, 128] More recently, food-borne outbreaks of *Listeria* gastroenteritis have refocused attention on the organism.[124]

The Organism

Listeria is a regular, short, facultatively anaerobic, non-spore-forming, gram-positive rod that is motile and forms bluish-gray colonies on nutrient agar. The genus is thought to be named in honor of Lord Lister, the father of antiseptic technique. Of the six *Listeria* spp. *(Listeria monocytogenes, Listeria innocua, Listeria grayi, Listeria welshimeri, Listeria seeligeri,* and *Listeria ivanovii),* only *L. monocytogenes* and *L. ivanovii* have been reported to infect humans.[59, 85] Various features of *L. monocytogenes* have been used to separate it from nonpathogenic *Listeria* spp. and other gram-positive rods.[131] The following four characteristics are used commonly for such differentiation: (1) *Listeria* exhibits a characteristic tumbling motility at 25° C (77° F), with reduced motility at 37° C (98.6° F); (2) it grows with a narrow zone of beta-hemolysis (nonhemolytic strains exist but rarely appear in clinical material) and exhibits a rectangular area of increased hemolysis when streaked on blood agar in proximity to *Staphylococcus aureus* (Christie, Atkins, Munch-Peterson [CAMP] test); (3) it is catalase-positive; and (4) it ferments α-methyl-D-mannoside and L-rhamnose but not D-xylose. *Listeria* organisms tolerate low temperatures, high salt concentrations, and high pH, which allows replication in soil, water, sewage, manure, animal feed, and more importantly, refrigerated foods. Cold enrichment procedures have been used to improve the isolation rate from clinical material, but generally they are not recommended.[12, 45, 128]

After the early work of Paterson,[113] Seeliger and Finger[132] performed an extensive serologic characterization of *L. monocytogenes*. At least 17 serotypes have been identified on the basis of somatic and flagellar antigens, but 3 (1/2a, 1/2b, 4b) account for the vast majority of clinical isolates and also are the serotypes most commonly found in food.[97, 114]

Transmission

The factors involved in transmission are not fully characterized. Early recognition of the disease in animals led to the suggestion that listeriosis was mainly a zoonosis. Although direct transmission has been reported in high-risk occupational groups such as veterinarians and farm workers, most infections in North America occur in urban areas with no epidemiologic explanation.[21, 104] An outbreak described by Schlech and colleagues[125] involving the consumption of cabbage contaminated with *Listeria* from animal manure provided the initial evidence that food-borne transmission can occur. Since then, numerous outbreaks have been linked to food-borne listeriosis.* Most incidents have been associated with the consumption of contaminated dairy products.[45, 86] However, pâté, pork tongue in jelly, ready-cooked chicken, and hot dogs also have been implicated.[66, 69, 98, 129] The mean incubation period for food-borne listeriosis is approximately 3 weeks. Nosocomial spread has been reported in several nursery outbreaks.[40, 50, 81, 127]

Epidemiology

L. monocytogenes colonizes humans and a variety of mammals worldwide.[131] In the United States, approximately 1 to 5 percent of the population carry the organism in their feces.[77] It is a growing concern to the food industry because contamination of unpasteurized dairy products, smoked fish, and meat processing environments is being recognized increasingly.[124] Nonetheless, listeriosis remains an uncommon infection. In the United States, estimates of its incidence range from 0.4 to 0.7 case per 100,000 population.[138] Listeriosis reported in the United States has a nonuniform age distribution, with most cases occurring in pregnant women, their newborns, and the elderly (Fig. 100–1). Although cases can occur in otherwise healthy subjects,[128, 148] immunocompromised persons with hematologic malignancies (particularly those receiving fludarabine), organ transplant recipients,[104, 110, 135] and the population positive for the human immunodeficiency virus are at significantly increased risk. Other host factors associated with listeriosis include diabetes mellitus, renal failure requiring dialysis, hemochromatosis, and cirrhosis. Several major North American and European outbreaks of food-borne listeriosis have been described.[45, 66, 98, 128] Perinatal attack rates during such outbreaks reach as high as 1.3 percent of all deliveries.[125] Molecular techniques involving multilocus enzyme electrophoresis and gene restriction fragment length polymorphism have been used successfully to track epidemic and sporadic strains found in food from index patients' refrigerators.[66, 114, 120] Rapid polymerase chain reaction (PCR)-based DNA fingerprinting techniques such as PCR ribotyping and arbitrarily primed PCR are being used increasingly to define strains.[4, 92, 107]

Pathogenesis and Pathology

The gross and microscopic findings in listeriosis are well documented. Although multiple granulomata are characteristic of disseminated disease, the basic pathologic change of suppurative inflammation is nonspecific.[75] Examination of the placenta of infants with early-onset infection reveals macroabscesses, funisitis, and villitis in most cases.[140]

L. monocytogenes is a facultative intracellular pathogen that has been used extensively to study cell-mediated immunity

*See references 6, 45, 66, 69, 86, 98, 124, 129, 145, 146.

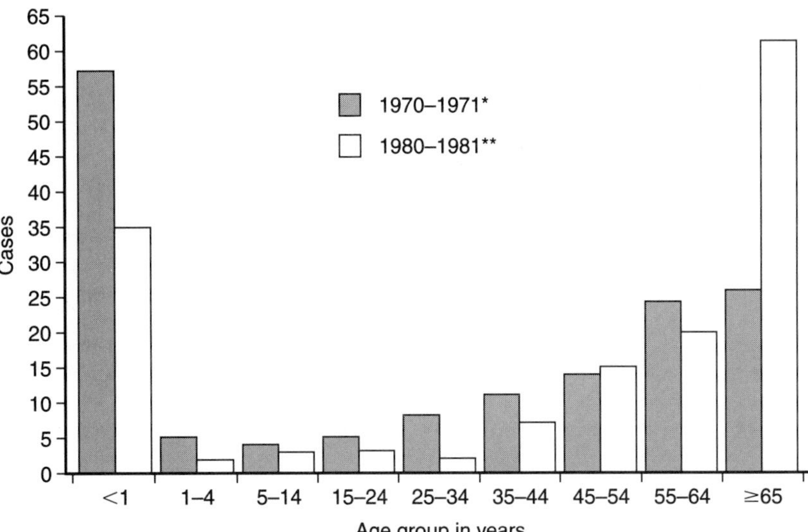

FIGURE 100–1 ■ Human listeriosis cases by age group for the United States, 1970–1971 and 1980–1981. (From Albritton, W. L., Cochi, S. L., and Feeley, J. C.: Overview of neonatal listeriosis. Clin. Invest. Med. 7:311–314, 1984.)

and the biochemical and pharmacologic abnormalities associated with infection.[7, 13, 64, 78, 93, 96, 137, 151] Resident macrophages in the liver and spleen provide an environment for intracellular growth; however, nonprofessional phagocytic cells (hepatocytes, enterocytes, and fibroblasts) also permit intracellular proliferation.[27, 43, 56, 70, 79, 117] Numerous virulence factors and their genes have been defined,[57, 115] and their roles in the stages of pathogenesis (internalization, vacuole escape, intracellular proliferation, and intercellular spread) are the focus of active research. The cycle begins with adhesion to a eukaryotic cell and subsequent internalization, which is mediated, in part, by proteins known as internalins.[18] Once inside the host cell, *Listeria* uses a hemolysin to escape into the cytoplasm.[116] The hemolysin secreted by *L. monocytogenes*, termed listerolysin O (LLO), has been purified and its gene, *hly*, sequenced.[26, 115] It is a pore-forming protein (antigenically similar to the streptolysin O produced by group A streptococci) that causes lysis of host-cell vacuoles with the subsequent release of *Listeria* into the host cytoplasm. Monoclonal antibody to LLO provides resistance to *Listeria* infection in a murine model of infection.[17, 32, 33] Once in the cytoplasm, *Listeria* uses the ActA protein to promote actin polymerization, which is responsible for their intracellular movement. The intracellular cycle is complete after replication and escape from the host cell.[71, 146]

For many years, resistance to *L. monocytogenes* and other facultative intracellular bacteria has been attributed almost exclusively to a repertoire of T cells and a host of induced cytokines.[53, 93, 99, 152] Recently, renewed recognition of the role of phagocytic cells has emerged.[31, 88]

Peak immunity to *Listeria* in adults is expressed after 5 to 6 days of infection, a time that coincides with the maximal T-cell response.[15, 76, 99, 133] Cytokines such as granulocyte colony-stimulating factor, tumor necrosis factor, and interleukin-6 (IL-6), IL-10, IL-12, IL-15, and IL-18 are induced and mediate clearance of *Listeria*.*

In newborn animals, susceptibility to *L. monocytogenes* appears to be associated with delayed activation of T cells and natural killer (NK) cells.[14, 36, 90] Components of the immune system are not competent early in life. In particular, antigen-presenting cell and T-cell interaction[91] and T-cell receptor and NK cell activity are immature in animal models.[36, 91] Similar processes appear to operate in humans.[65] Suppression of NK cells by cord blood cells also is possible.[30] Synthesis of interferon-γ, interferon-α, and IL-2, all of which modulate the immune response and macrophage activation, is deficient in newborns.[42, 133] However, newborn animals can be protected against *L. monocytogenes* infection by pretreatment with interferon or inducers of interferon.[16, 20, 24]

In older children and young adults, *Listeria* infection is a rare occurrence; however, underlying diseases or medications that interfere with cell-mediated immunity may increase susceptibility.[130] Cyclosporine, which blocks production of cytokine, is associated with increased susceptibility.[62]

Factors involved in mucosal colonization and invasion have been understood poorly.[112] Recently, researchers have shown that internalin, a surface-expressed protein on *L. monocytogenes,* mediates invasion of human enterocytes and crossing of the intestinal barrier.[54, 82] The intestinal mucosa is a depot for *L. monocytogenes*–specific effector $CD8^+$ T cells, which accumulate during and after infection.[63] Systemic spread of the organism after intestinal invasion is the usual mode of infection in nonperinatal infection.[70]

Clinical Manifestations

Although a variety of clinical manifestations are described in *L. monocytogenes* infection, the vast majority of pediatric infections occur in the first months of life. The initial clinical features are similar to those of the more prevalent group B streptococcal infection.[8] The serotype distribution of *L. monocytogenes* appears to depend on the age at onset. Serotypes 1a and 1b occur more commonly in the early-onset form of disease (<7 days of age), and serotype 4b occurs in the late-onset form (>7 days of age).[3]

The early-onset form of neonatal listeriosis usually is diagnosed within the first 24 hours of life, and affected infants have respiratory distress or pneumonia, septicemia, and, occasionally, meningitis[2, 3, 39, 86, 139, 148] (Table 100–1). Mothers of these infants frequently have an influenza-like

*See references 28, 29, 73, 80, 87, 108, 109, 144, 149, 152, 154.

TABLE 100–1 ■ FEATURES OF EARLY- AND LATE-ONSET NEONATAL LISTERIOSIS*

	Early Onset[2, 3, 39, 86, 140]	Late-Onset[3, 41, 74, 89, 128, 148]
Age at onset (median in days)	<0.1 (<0.1–1.3)	28 (7–140)
Birth weight (median in grams)	2250 (1800–2540)	3100 (3000–3150)
Percentage of isolates from		
Cerebrospinal fluid	5 (2–7)	63 (30–87)
Blood and cerebrospinal fluid	10 (6–26)	25 (13–4)
Blood alone	74 (45–88)	12 (0–30)
Other only†	5 (0–24)	0
Newborn and maternal	72 (54–93)	4 (0–8)
Percent mortality	38 (22–63)	3 (0–10)
Percentage with obstetric complications	63 (38–87)	3 (0–7)

*This table shows the median values and ranges of results from various publications.
†Sources other than blood and cerebrospinal fluid included cutaneous, gastric, throat, urine, and rectal sources.

illness with fever, malaise, headache, gastrointestinal symptoms, or pharyngitis in the few days preceding delivery.[60, 86, 118] During labor, maternal fever and green- or brown-stained amniotic fluid may be seen.[2, 83, 84] More severely affected infants are infected in utero, are born prematurely, and often are critically ill at birth. Widespread microabscesses and macroabscesses may occur and are demonstrable externally as discrete roseolar or pustular lesions on the skin and pharynx. The rash has been termed *granulomatosis infantisepticum* (Fig. 100–2). Depression at birth, respiratory distress, apnea, lethargy, and fever are common initial features, but diarrhea, conjunctivitis, and myocarditis all have been described.[84] The respiratory symptoms may mimic those of respiratory distress syndrome. Patchy bronchopneumonic infiltrates, probably caused by aspiration of infected amniotic fluid, may be seen on chest radiographs. In addition, intrauterine infection may result in spontaneous abortion or stillbirth.[60] However, colonized asymptomatic neonates[83] have been reported, as have colonized household contacts.[126]

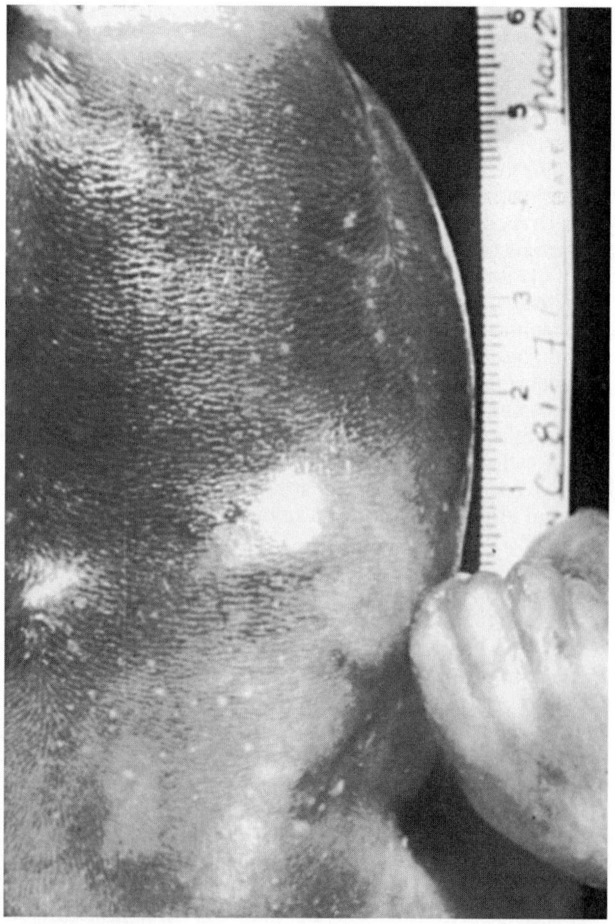

FIGURE 100–2 ■ Typical pustular rash on abdomen of stillborn infant with listeriosis. Note the small pale granuloma measuring 1 to 3 mm and the dark erythema surrounding these lesions.

The late-onset form of neonatal listeriosis occurs less commonly than does the early-onset form and usually affects term infants, who appear healthy until the onset of meningitis or, less commonly, septicemia 1 to 8 weeks after birth.[3, 41, 60, 74, 127] Enterocolitis caused by *L. monocytogenes* has been seen.[81] Clinical manifestations in late-onset meningitis may be quite subtle and include fever, irritability, lethargy, and poor feeding.[74, 127] Cerebrospinal fluid (CSF) findings are variable. Although pleocytosis usually is significant, not all infections will have a polymorphonuclear cell predominance. The maternal history in these cases usually is negative. An outbreak of neonatal listeriosis associated with mineral oil reported by Schuchat and associates[127] provides insight into the pathophysiology of the late-onset form of disease. During the outbreak, babies were bathed after birth with mineral oil, which was applied liberally over the entire body, including the face. A strain identical to one causing the infection was isolated from a mineral oil container in the delivery room. Despite intensive investigation, no other source of infection was identified. The incubation period before the development of symptoms was 5 days, whereas the median age at first positive culture for infants was 7 days. The initial symptoms and signs in infants were those of the late-onset form of infection: fever and meningitis. Seven of 10 infants had a positive CSF culture.

Immunocompromised patients can have a variety of clinical findings, most commonly meningitis or septicemia.[68] Although patients receiving immunosuppressive therapy have a high incidence of infection, their clinical features are similar to those of non-immunosuppressed patients with *Listeria* infection.[130] Rhombencephalitis, brain abscess, arthritis, osteomyelitis, endocarditis, endophthalmitis, liver abscess, and peritonitis also have been reported in nonpediatric patients.* Rarely, invasive listeriosis has been seen in children who are otherwise well.[94, 97, 128, 148] Increasingly, *Listeria* is being recognized as a cause of febrile gastroenteritis.

*See references 1, 5, 19, 23, 35, 44, 52, 89, 94, 106, 135.

Diagnosis

Appropriate specimens for staining and culture vary with the clinical syndrome, but investigation of the usual sources, such as blood, CSF, amniotic fluid, and genital tract secretions, is most productive. Because prompt recognition is essential, examination of Gram-stained material (ear, meconium, and placenta) from newborns is recommended in suspected early-onset sepsis.[83] Pathologic specimens (e.g., biopsy material, placental or fetal tissue) may reveal the characteristic Gram stain morphology and pathologic features, such as microabscesses and granulomata. Selective culture media such as PALCAM (polymixin B-acriflavine-lithium chloride-ceftazidime-esculin-mannitol agar) or modified Oxford agar may be helpful for isolation from contaminated material such as stool or vaginal secretions.[95, 114] Laboratories undertaking primary isolation must be aware of the similarities between *L. monocytogenes* and frequently discarded "commensals."[97]

After 48 hours' incubation at 37°C on 5 percent sheep blood agar, colonies are gray with a narrow zone of beta-hemolysis. The Gram stain appearance of short rods has been confused with lancet-shaped pneumococci. Traditionally, identification is based on morphology; tumbling motility; beta-hemolysis; positive catalase, esculin, and CAMP tests; and the carbohydrate utilization pattern. Commercial kits are available for the rapid identification of *Listeria* from culture. These kits include DNA probes, latex agglutination, and enzyme immunoassay methods.

Despite extensive attempts to develop serologic techniques for the diagnosis of listeriosis, none has proved satisfactory, and few centers attempt serodiagnosis.[10, 61] At present, a confirmed diagnosis requires isolation of the organism.

Histologic diagnosis from pathologic material should be attempted if the organism is not cultured. Specific fluorescent antibody staining,[25] nucleic acid hybridization,[136] and PCR[4, 67] generally are not available in the routine diagnostic laboratory, but they do offer the potential for development in the future, especially in patients pretreated with antibiotics and for rapid food surveillance.

Treatment

Prompt administration of antibiotic therapy is required in most cases of listeriosis for the prevention of death or severe sequelae. Fortunately, antibiotic resistance in *L. monocytogenes* strains is low.[150] The bactericidal activity of the antibiotics commonly used is influenced in vitro by such factors as inoculum size, type of medium, and the definition of end-points.[37, 89] Similar to a few other bacteria, *L. monocytogenes* demonstrates tolerance to some antibiotics in vitro; the minimal bactericidal concentration is more than fourfold the minimal inhibitory concentration.[37, 102] Thus, the antibiotics commonly recommended for treatment—ampicillin, penicillin, erythromycin, and tetracycline—are only bacteriostatic at concentrations usually achieved in blood.[37, 46, 47, 142, 147] Relapse of *L. monocytogenes* infection after apparent therapeutic success has been documented in immunocompromised patients, thus suggesting that bactericidal regimens may be needed in such patients.[122]

Other antibiotics have been considered for possible therapy. Some studies have shown trimethoprim-sulfamethoxazole and rifampin to be effective in eradicating *Listeria* in vivo.[55, 58, 100, 123] These drugs appear to be bactericidal and have been used successfully in a few cases of human listeriosis.[51, 135] Rifampin and trimethoprim-sulfamethoxazole offer a theoretic advantage over other drugs because of their better intracellular penetration. Many newer antibiotics, such as the quinolones, macrolides, and imipenem, have only moderate activity in vitro against *Listeria*. Most quinolone and macrolide antibiotics are bacteriostatic only, and in vivo studies with these agents are not promising.[101, 121] In addition, *L. monocytogenes* is resistant to cephalosporin antibiotics.[37] Vancomycin has been used in a few penicillin- and sulfa-allergic patients with some success, but experience with this drug is limited.[119]

Combinations of antibiotics for therapy and in vitro testing also have shown varying results. Ampicillin plus gentamicin has a synergistic effect on most *Listeria* strains.[34, 100, 103, 141] Partial synergy appears to occur with combinations of ampicillin or vancomycin and rifampin, but combinations of penicillin G and rifampin have shown activity ranging from synergy to antagonism.[100] In an in vivo model of *L. monocytogenes* encephalitis, the combinations ampicillin/gentamicin and co-trimoxazole/rifampin were highly active against intracerebral bacteria.[11] Although controversy exists, antagonism also appears to occur between a number of other antibiotic combinations (erythromycin and penicillins, erythromycin and aminoglycosides, penicillins and chloramphenicol, and penicillins and tetracycline).[37, 46, 100] On the basis of results of in vitro susceptibility testing and in vivo models, ampicillin plus gentamicin has proved to be the most reliable synergistic combination and remains the recommended initial therapy for patients suspected of having listeriosis. Trimethoprim-sulfamethoxazole may be considered for use in non-perinatal listeriosis, particularly in the presence of penicillin allergy, but it cannot be recommended for use in perinatal infections because of the concern of bilirubin toxicity with sulfonamides. The use of rifampin alone or in combination requires further study. The duration of therapy depends on the clinical syndrome, the presence of underlying disease, and the response to treatment. In newborns, 2 weeks of antibiotic therapy usually appears to be adequate.

Some animal studies raise new possibilities for the treatment of listeriosis. Nanoparticle-bound ampicillin can be transported into the intracellular space and has been found to be significantly more effective than is free ampicillin in eradicating *Listeria* in an animal model.[153] Liposomal encapsulation also results in marked enhancement of the therapeutic activity of ampicillin.[9]

Prognosis

Precise morbidity and mortality data for *L. monocytogenes* infection are not available. Maternal listeriosis may result in abortion or stillbirth. Fetal mortality rates probably are high with gestational listeriosis, although the relative risk of intrauterine death is not known. Convincing evidence that *L. monocytogenes* is associated with repeated abortions is lacking.[49]

Among reported cases of early-onset sepsis, the recent mortality rate in North America is approximately 40 percent[2, 39] (see Table 100–1). Most survivors appear to be normal.[38, 39, 139] Sequelae are related to the associated complications of prematurity, pneumonia, and sepsis; hydrocephalus and cerebral palsy also have been reported.[38, 72] Early treatment of maternal disease would appear to affect fetal and neonatal outcome favorably.[39, 72]

Late-onset *Listeria* meningitis has a mortality rate of less than 10 percent. The outcome after *Listeria* meningitis may be more favorable than that associated with other types of bacterial meningitis.[74, 148] Major sequelae are hydrocephalus and mental retardation. Beyond the newborn period, the outcome of listeriosis depends on the nature of any underlying disease and the availability of intensive medical care.

Prevention

The sporadic nature of the disease in North America emphasized the need for collaborative investigation and reporting of infections by physicians and veterinarians to public health authorities.[12, 45] In the early 1990s, epidemiologists in the United States and Canada endorsed making listeriosis a notifiable disease.[114, 138] Since then, the important role of food in the transmission of sporadic cases has been linked firmly.[128] Aggressive investigation of cases and close inspection and testing of food and food-handling facilities in the United States have been under way since the early 1990s.[92, 138] By tracking strains of *L. monocytogenes* from patients' refrigerators to retail sources, specific foods have been identified. Strict adherence to regulations for pasteurization of raw milk is important to inactivate the organism and prevent listeriosis.[143] However, contamination of food can occur during the preparation and processing of pasteurized milk products and ready-to-eat meat or poultry products. Recommendations for persons at high risk, such as pregnant women and immunocompromised patients, include avoiding soft cheeses and delicatessen meats and reheating leftover foods or ready-to-eat foods (e.g., hot dogs).[114, 138] Preventive strategies involving inspection of food and facilities and dissemination of recommendations and educational materials appear to have reduced the incidence of listeriosis in the developed nations.[4, 48, 138]

During a *Listeria* outbreak, prompt investigation and treatment of pregnant women with a febrile "influenza-like" illness have been advocated.[12, 72] The attack rate for late-onset disease in colonized infants is not known, and no data demonstrate that treatment of colonized infants can either eradicate asymptomatic carriage or prevent infection.

Careful attention to the handling of infected infants in a neonatal unit in an attempt to prevent transmission is of the utmost importance for preventing nosocomial infection.[40, 127]

REFERENCES

1. Ackermann, G., Schoen, H., Schaumann, R., et al.: Rapidly growing tumor-like brain lesion. Infection *29*:278–279, 2001.
2. Ahlfors, C. E., Goetzman, B. W., Halsted, C. C., et al.: Neonatal listeriosis. Am. J. Dis. Child. *131*:405–408, 1977.
3. Albritton, W. L., Wiggins, G. L., and Feeley, J. C.: Neonatal listeriosis: Distribution of serotypes in relation to age at onset of disease. J. Pediatr. *88*:481–483, 1976.
4. Allmann, M., Hofelein, C., Koppel, E., et al.: Polymerase chain reaction (PCR) for detection of pathogenic microorganisms in bacteriological monitoring of dairy products. Res. Microbiol. *146*:85–97, 1995.
5. Armstrong, R. W., and Fung, P. C.: Brainstem encephalitis (rhombencephalitis) due to *Listeria monocytogenes*: Case report and review. Clin. Infect. Dis. *16*:689–702, 1993.
6. Ashton, F. E., Ewan, E. P., and Farber, J. M.: Evidence for *Listeria* transmission by food. Can. Dis. Wkly. Rep. *15*:216–220, 1988.
7. Azri, S., and Renton, K. W.: Depression of murine hepatic mixed function oxidase during infection with *Listeria monocytogenes*. J. Pharmacol. Exp. Ther. *243*:1089–1094, 1987.
8. Baker, C. J., and Barrett, F. F.: Group B streptococcal infections in infants: The importance of serotypes. J. A. M. A. *230*:1158–1160, 1974.
9. Bakker-Woundenberg, I. A. J. M., Lokerse, A. F., Vink-van den Berg, J. C., et al.: Liposome-encapsulated ampicillin against *Listeria monocytogenes* in vivo and in vitro. Infection *16*(Suppl. 2):165–170, 1988.
10. Berche, P., Reich, K. A., Bonnichon, M., et al.: Detection of anti-listerolysin O for serodiagnosis of human listeriosis. Lancet *335*:624–627, 1990.
11. Blanot, S., Boumaila, C., and Berche, P.: Intracerebral activity of antibiotics against *Listeria monocytogenes* during experimental rhombencephalitis. J. Antimicrob. Chemother. *44*:565–568, 1999.
12. Bortolussi, R.: An ongoing problem: Perinatal infection due to *Listeria monocytogenes*, an old pathogen reborn. J. Clin. Invest. Med. *7*:213–215, 1984.
13. Bortolussi, R.: Neonatal listeriosis: Where do we go from here? Pediatr. Infect. Dis. *4*:228–229, 1985.
14. Bortolussi, R., Campbell, N., and Krause, V.: Dynamics of *Listeria monocytogenes* type 4b infection in pregnant and infant rats. J. Clin. Invest. Med. *7*:273–279, 1984.
15. Bortolussi, R., Issekutz, T., Burbridge, S., et al.: Neonatal host defense mechanisms against *Listeria monocytogenes* infection: The role of lipopolysaccharides and interferons. Pediatr. Res. *25*:311–315, 1989.
16. Bortolussi, R., McGregor, D. D., Kongshavn, P. A. L., et al.: Host defense mechanisms to perinatal and neonatal *Listeria monocytogenes* infection. Surv. Synth. Pathol. Res. *3*:311–332, 1984.
17. Bouwer, H. G. A., Gibbins, B. L., Jones, S., et al.: Antilisterial immunity includes specificity to listeriolysin O (LLO) and non–LLO-derived determinants. Infect. Immun. *62*:1039–1045, 1994.
18. Braun, L., Dramsi, S., Dehoux, H., et al.: InlB: An invasion protein of *Listeria monocytogenes* with a novel type of surface association. Mol. Microbiol. *25*:285–294, 1997.
19. Braun, T. I., Travis, D., Dee, R. R., et al.: Liver abscess due to *Listeria monocytogenes*: Case report and review. Clin. Infect. Dis. *17*:267–269, 1993.
20. Buchmeier, N. A., and Schreiber, R. D.: Immunology: Requirement of endogenous interferon-γ production for resolution of *Listeria monocytogenes* infection. Proc. Natl. Acad. Sci. U. S. A. *82*:7404–7408, 1985.
21. Buchner, L. H., and Schneirson, S. S.: Clinical and laboratory aspects of *Listeria monocytogenes* infections. Am. J. Med. *45*:904–921, 1968.
22. Burn, C. G.: Clinical and pathological features of an infection caused by a new pathogen of the genus *Listerella*. Am. J. Pathol. *12*:341–348, 1936.
23. Carvajal, A., and Frederiksen, W.: Fatal endocarditis due to *Listeria monocytogenes*. Rev. Infect. Dis. *10*:616–623, 1988.
24. Chen, Y., Nakane, A., and Minagawa, T.: Recombinant murine gamma interferon induces enhanced resistance to *Listeria monocytogenes* infection in neonatal mice. Infect. Immun. *57*:2345–2349, 1989.
25. Cherry, W. B., and Moody, M. D.: Fluorescent antibody techniques in diagnostic microbiology. Bacteriol. Rev. *29*:222–250, 1965.
26. Cossart, P.: The listeriolysin O gene: A chromosomal locus crucial for the virulence of *Listeria monocytogenes*. Infection *16*(Suppl. 2):157–159, 1988.
27. Cowart, R. E., Lashmet, J., McIntosh, M. E., et al.: Adherence of a virulent strain of *Listeria monocytogenes* to the surface of a hepatocarcinoma cell line via lectin-substrate interaction. Arch. Microbiol. *153*:282–286, 1990.
28. Deckert, M., Soltek, S., Geginat, G., et al.: Endogenous interleukin-10 is required for prevention of a hyperinflammatory intracerebral immune response in *Listeria monocytogenes* meningoencephalitis. Infect. Immun. *69*:4561–4571, 2001.
29. Desiderio, J. V., Kiener, P. A., Lin, P.-F., et al.: Protection of mice against *Listeria monocytogenes* infection by recombinant human tumor necrosis factor alpha. Infect. Immun. *57*:1615–1617, 1989.
30. Dominquez, E., Madrigal, J. A., Layrisse, Z., and Cohen, S. B.: Fetal natural killer cell function is suppressed. Immunology *94*:109–114, 1998.
31. Drevets, D. A.: Dissemination of *Listeria monocytogenes* by infected phagocytes. Infect. Immun. *67*:3512–3517, 1999.
32. Edelson, B. T., Cossart, P., Unanue, E. R.: Cutting edge: Paradigm revisited: Antibody provides resistance to *Listeria* infection. J. Immunol. *163*:4087–4090, 1999.
33. Edelson, B. T., and Unanue, E. R.: Intracellular antibody neutralizes *Listeria* growth. Immunity *14*:503–512, 2001.
34. Edmiston, C. E., and Gordon, R. C.: Evaluation of gentamicin and penicillin as a synergistic combination in experimental murine listeriosis. Antimicrob. Agents Chemother. *16*:862–863, 1979.
35. Ellis, L. C., Gitelis, S., and Huber, J. F.: Joint infections due to *Listeria monocytogenes:* Case report and review. Clin. Infect. Dis. *20*:1548–1550, 1995.
36. Emoto, M., Miyamoto, M., Emoto, Y., et al.: A critical role of T-cell receptor gamma/delta cells in antibacterial protection in mice early in life. Hepatology *33*:887–893, 2001.
37. Espaze, E. P., and Reynaud, A. E.: Antibiotic susceptibilities of *Listeria:* In vitro studies. Infection *16*(Suppl. 2):160–164, 1988.
38. Evans, J. R., Allen, A. C., Bortolussi, R., et al.: Follow-up study of survivors of fetal and early-onset neonatal listeriosis. J. Clin. Invest. Med. *7*:329–334, 1984.
39. Evans, J. R., Allen, A. C., Stinson, D. A., et al.: Perinatal listeriosis: Report of an outbreak. Pediatr. Infect. Dis. *4*:237–241, 1985.
40. Facinelli, B., Varaldo, P. E., Casolari, C., et al.: Cross-infection with *Listeria monocytogenes* confirmed by DNA fingerprinting. Lancet *2*:1247–1248, 1988.
41. Filice, A. G., Cantrell, H. F., Smith, A. B., et al.: *Listeria monocytogenes* infection in neonates: Investigation of an epidemic. J. Infect. Dis. *138*:17–23, 1978.
42. Frenkel, L., and Bryson, Y. J.: Ontogeny of phytohemagglutinin-induced gamma interferon by leukocytes of healthy infants and children: Evidence for decreased production in infants younger than 2 months of age. J. Pediatr. *111*:97–100, 1987.
43. Gaillard, J.-L., Berche, P., Mounier, J., et al.: In vitro model of penetration and intracellular growth of *Listeria monocytogenes* in the human enterocyte-like cell line caco-2. Infect. Immun. *55*:2822–2829, 1987.

44. Gallagher, P. G., Amedia, C. A., and Watankunakom, C.: *L. monocytogenes* endocarditis in a patient on chronic hemodialysis, successfully treated with vancomycin and gentamicin. Infection *14*:125, 1986.
45. Gellin, B. G.: Listeriosis. J. A. M. A. *261*:1313–1319, 1989.
46. Gordon, R. C., Barrett, F. F., and Clark, D. J.: Influence of several antibiotics, singly and in combination, on the growth of *Listeria monocytogenes*. J. Pediatr. *80*:667–670, 1972.
47. Gordon, R. C., Barrett, F. F., and Yow, M. D.: Ampicillin treatment of listeriosis. J. Pediatr. *77*:1067–1070, 1970.
48. Goulet, V., de-Valk, H., Pierre, O., et al.: Effect of prevention measures on incidence of *human* listeriosis, France, 1987–1997. Emerg. Infect. Dis. *7*:983–989, 2001.
49. Gray, M. L., Seeliger, H. P. R., and Potel, J.: Perinatal infections due to *Listeria monocytogenes:* Do these affect subsequent pregnancies? Clin. Pediatr. (Phila.) *2*:614–623, 1963.
50. Green, H. T., and Macaulay, M. B.: Hospital outbreak of *Listeria monocytogenes* septicemia: A problem of cross infection? Lancet *2*:1039–1040, 1978.
51. Gunther, G., and Philipson, A.: Oral trimethoprim as follow-up treatment of meningitis caused by *Listeria monocytogenes*. Rev. Infect. Dis. *10*:53, 1988.
52. Harris, J. O., Marquez, J., Swerdloff, M. A., et al.: *Listeria* brain abscess in the acquired immunodeficiency syndrome. Arch. Neurol. *46*:250, 1989.
53. Hauf, N., Goebel, W., Serfling, E., et al.: *Listeria monocytogenes* infection enhances transcription factor NF-κB in $P388D_1$ macrophage-like cells. Infect. Immun. *62*:2740–2747, 1994.
54. Havell, E. A., Beretich, G. R., Jr., and Carter, P. B.: The mucosal phase of *Listeria* infection. Immunology *201*:164–177, 1999.
55. Hawkins, A. E., Bortolussi, R., and Issekutz, A. C.: In vitro and in vivo activity of various antibiotics against *Listeria monocytogenes* type 4b. Clin. Invest. Med. *7*:335–341, 1984.
56. Hess, C. B., Niesel, D. W., Cho, Y. J., et al.: Bacterial invasion of fibroblasts induces interferon production. J. Immunol. *138*:3949–3953, 1987.
57. Hess, J., Gentschev, I., Szalay, G., et al.: *Listeria monocytogenes* p60 supports host cell invasion by an in vivo survival of attenuated *Salmonella typhimurium*. Infect. Immun. *63*:2047–2053, 1995.
58. Hof, H., and Waldenmeier, G.: Therapy of experimental listeriosis: An evaluation of different antibiotics. Infection *16*(Suppl. 2):171–174, 1988.
59. Holt, J. G., Krieg, N. R., Sneath, P. H. A., et al. (eds.): *In* Bergey's Manual of Determinative Bacteriology. Baltimore, Williams & Wilkins, 1994, pp. 566–567.
60. Hood, M.: Listeriosis as an infection of pregnancy manifested in the newborn. Pediatrics *27*:390–396, 1961.
61. Hudak, A. P., Lee, S. H., Issekutz, A. C., et al.: Comparison of three serological methods—enzyme-linked immunosorbent assay, complement fixation, and microagglutination—in diagnosis of human perinatal *Listeria monocytogenes* infection. Clin. Invest. Med. *7*:349–354, 1984.
62. Hügin, A. W., Cerny, A., Wrann, M., et al.: Effect of cyclosporin A on immunity to *Listeria monocytogenes*. Infect. Immun. *52*:12–17, 1986.
63. Huleatt, J. W., Pilip, I., Kerksiek, K., and Pamer, E. G.: Intestinal and splenic T cell responses to enteric *Listeria monocytogenes* infection: Distinct repertoires of responding CD8 T lymphocytes. J. Immunol. *166*: 4065–4073, 2001.
64. Inoue, S., Itagaki, S., and Amano, F.: Intracellular killing of *Listeria monocytogenes* in the J774.1 macrophage-like cell line and the lipopolysaccharide (LPS)-resistant mutant LPS1916 cell line defective in the generation of reactive oxygen intermediates after LPS treatment. Infect. Immun. *63*:1876–1886, 1995.
65. Issekutz, T., Evans, J., and Bortolussi, R.: The immune response of human neonates to *Listeria monocytogenes* infection. Clin. Invest. Med. *7*:281–286, 1984.
66. Jacquet, C., Catimel, B., Brosch, R., et al.: Investigations related to the epidemic strain involved in the French listeriosis outbreak in 1992. Appl. Environ. Microbiol. *61*:2242–2246, 1995.
67. Jaton, K., Sahli, R., and Bille, J.: Development of polymerase chain reaction assays for detection of *Listeria monocytogenes* in clinical cerebrospinal fluid samples. J. Clin. Microbiol. *30*:1931–1936, 1992.
68. Jurado, R. L., Farley, M. M., Pereira, E., et al.: Increased risk of meningitis and bacteremia due to *Listeria monocytogenes* in patients with human immunodeficiency virus infection. Clin. Infect. Dis. *17*:224–227, 1993.
69. Kaczmarski, E. B., and Jones, D. M.: Listeriosis and ready-cooked chicken. Lancet *1*:549, 1989.
70. Karunasagar, I., Senghaas, B., Krohne, G., et al.: Ultrastructural study of *Listeria monocytogenes* entry into cultured human colonic epithelial cells. Infect. Immun. *62*:3554–3558, 1994.
71. Kathariou, S., Rocourt, J., Hof, H., et al.: Levels of *Listeria monocytogenes* hemolysin are not directly proportional to virulence in experimental infections of mice. Infect. Immun. *56*:534–536, 1988.
72. Katz, V. L., and Weinstein, L.: Antepartum treatment of *Listeria monocytogenes* septicemia. South. Med. J. *75*:1353–1354, 1982.
73. Kayashima, S., Tsuru, S., Hata, N., et al.: Therapeutic effect of granulocyte colony-stimulating factor (G-CSF) on the protection against *Listeria* infection in SCID mice. Immunology *80*:471–476, 1993.
74. Kessler, S. L., and Dajani, A. S.: *Listeria* meningitis in infants and children. Pediatr. Infect. Dis. J. *9*:61–62, 1990.
75. Klatt, E. C., Pavlova, Z., Teberg, A. J., et al.: Epidemic perinatal listeriosis at autopsy. Hum. Pathol. *17*:1278–1281, 1986.
76. Kohl, S., West, M. S., and Loo, L. S.: Defects in interleukin-2 stimulation of neonatal natural killer cytotoxicity to herpes simplex virus–infected cells. J. Pediatr. *112*:976–981, 1988.
77. Koneman, E. W., Allen, S., Janda, W. M., et al. (eds.): Color Atlas and Textbook of Diagnostic Microbiology. 5th ed. Philadelphia, Lippincott-Raven, 1997, pp. 664–667.
78. Kongshaven, P. A. A., and Skamene, E.: The role of natural resistance in protection of the murine host from listeriosis. Clin. Invest. Med. *7*:253–257, 1984.
79. Kuhn, M., and Goebel, W.: Identification of an extracellular protein of *Listeria monocytogenes* possibly involved in intracellular uptake by mammalian cells. Infect. Immun. *57*:55–61, 1989.
80. Langermans, J. A. M., Mayanski, D. M., Nibbering, P. H., et al.: Effect of IFN-γ and endogenous TNF on the histopathological changes in the liver of *Listeria monocytogenes*–infected mice. Immunology *81*:192–197, 1994.
81. Larsson, S., Cederberg, A., Ivarsson, S., et al.: *Listeria monocytogenes* causing hospital acquired enterocolitis and meningitis in newborn infants. B. M. J. *2*:473–474, 1978.
82. Lecuit, M., Vandormael-Pournin, S., Lefort, J., et al.: A transgenic model for *listeriosis:* Role of internalin in crossing the intestinal barrier. Science *292*:1722–1725, 2001.
83. Lennon, D., Lewis, B., Mantell, C., et al.: Epidemic perinatal listeriosis. Pediatr. Infect. Dis. *3*:30–34, 1984.
84. LeSouef, P. N., and Walters, B. N. J.: Neonatal listeriosis. Med. J. Aust. *2*:188–191, 1981.
85. Lessing, M. P., Curtis, G. D., and Bowler, I. C.: *Listeria ivanovii* infection. J. Infect. *29*:230–231, 1994.
86. Linnan, M. J., Mascola, L., Lou, X. D., et al.: Epidemic listeriosis associated with Mexican-style cheese. N. Engl. J. Med. *319*:823–828, 1988.
87. Liu, A., Simpson, R. J., and Cheers, C.: Role of interleukin-6 in T-cell activation during primary and secondary infection with *Listeria monocytogenes*. Infect. Immun. *63*:2790–2792, 1995.
88. Lopez, S., Marco, A. J., Prats, N., and Czuprynski, C. J.: Critical role of neutrophils in eliminating *Listeria monocytogenes* from the central nervous system during experimental murine listeriosis. Infect. Immun. *68*:4789–4791, 2000.
89. Louthrenoo, W., and Schumacher, H. R.: *Listeria monocytogenes* osteomyelitis complicating leukemia: Report and literature review of *Listeria* osteoarticular infections. J. Rheumatol. *17*:107–110, 1990.
90. Lu, C. Y.: The delayed ontogenesis of 1a-positive macrophages: Implications for host defense and self-tolerance in the neonate. Clin. Invest. Med. *7*:263–267, 1984.
91. Lu, C. Y., and Unanue, E. R.: Ontogeny of murine macrophages: Functions related to antigen presentation. Infect. Immun. *36*:169–175, 1982.
92. MacGowan, A. P., O'Donaghue, K., Nicholls, S., et al.: Typing of *Listeria* spp. by random amplified polymorphic DNA (RAPD) analysis. J. Med. Microbiol. *38*:322–327, 1993.
93. Mackaness, G. B.: The immunological basis of acquired cellular resistance. J. Exp. Med. *120*:105–119, 1964.
94. Massarotti, E. M., and Dinerman, H.: Septic arthritis due to *Listeria monocytogenes:* Report and review of the literature. J. Rheumatol. *17*:111–113, 1990.
95. McBride, M. E., and Girard, K. F.: Procedure for the selective isolation of *Listeria monocytogenes*. J. Lab. Clin. Med. *55*:153–157, 1960.
96. McCallum, R. E., and Sword, C. P.: Mechanisms of pathogenesis in *Listeria monocytogenes* infection. V. Early imbalance in host energy metabolism during experimental listeriosis. Infect. Immun. *5*:863–871, 1972.
97. McLauchlin, J.: Distribution of serovars of *Listeria monocytogenes* isolated from different categories of patients with listeriosis. Eur. J. Clin. Microbiol. Infect. Dis. *9*:210–213, 1990.
98. McLauchlin, J., Hall, S. M., Velani, S. K., et al.: Human listeriosis and pat J: A possible association. B. M. J. *303*:773–775, 1991.
99. Mercado, R., Vijh, S., Allen, S. E., et al.: Early programming of T cell populations responding to bacterial infection. J. Immunol. *165*: 6833–6839, 2000.
100. Meyer, R. D., and Liu, S.: Determination of the effect of antimicrobics in combination against *Listeria monocytogenes*. Diagn. Microbiol. Infect. Dis. *6*:199–206, 1986.
101. Michelet, C., Leib, S. L., Bentue-Ferrer, D., and Tauber, M. G.: Comparative efficacies of antibiotics in a rat model of meningoencephalitis due to *Listeria monocytogenes*. Antimicrob. Agents Chemother. *43*:1651–1656, 1999.
102. Moellering, R. C., Medoff, G., Leech, I., et al.: Antibiotic synergism against *Listeria monocytogenes*. Antimicrob. Agents Chemother. *1*:30–34, 1972.
103. Mohan, K., Gordon, R. C., Beaman, T. C., et al.: Synergism of penicillin and gentamicin against *Listeria monocytogenes* in ex vivo hemodialysis culture. J. Infect. Dis. *135*:51–54, 1977.
104. Moore, R. M., and Zehmer, R. B.: Listeriosis in the United States, 1971. J. Infect. Dis. *127*:610–611, 1973.
105. Murray, E. G. D., Webb, R. A., and Swann, M. B. R.: A disease of rabbits characterized by large mononuclear leucocytosis, caused by a hitherto

undescribed bacillus *Bacterium monocytogenes* (n. sp.). J. Pathol. Bacteriol. *29*:407–439, 1926.
106. Myers, J. P., Peterson, G., and Rashid, A.: Peritonitis due to *Listeria monocytogenes* complicating continuous ambulatory peritoneal dialysis. J. Infect. Dis. *148*:1130, 1983.
107. Nadon, C. A., Woodward, D. L., Young, C., et al.: Correlations between molecular subtyping and serotyping of *Listeria monocytogenes*. J. Clin. Microbiol. *39*:2704–2707, 2001.
108. Nakane, A., Okamoto, M., Asano, M., et al.: An anti-CD3 monoclonal antibody protects mice against a lethal infection with *Listeria monocytogenes* through induction of endogenous cytokines. Infect. Immun. *61*:2786–2793, 1993.
109. Neighbors, M., Xu, X., and Barrat, F. J.: A critical role for interleukin 18 in primary and memory effector responses to *Listeria monocytogenes* that extends beyond its effects on interferon gamma production. J. Exp. Med. *194*:343–354, 2001.
110. Nieman, R. E., and Lorber, B.: Listeriosis in adults: A changing pattern: Report of eight cases and review of the literature, 1968–1978. Rev. Infect. Dis. *2*:207–227, 1980.
111. Nyfeldt, A.: Etiologie de la mononucleose infectieuse. Compt. Rend. Soc. Biol. *101*:590–591, 1929.
112. Okamoto, M., Nakane, A., and Minagawa, T.: Host resistance to an intragastric infection with *Listeria monocytogenes* in mice depends on cellular immunity and intestinal bacterial flora. Infect. Immun. *62*:3080–3085, 1994.
113. Paterson, J. S.: The antigenic structure of organisms of the genus *Listerella*. J. Pathol. Bacteriol. *51*:427–436, 1940.
114. Pinner, R. W., Schuchat, A., Swaminathan, B., et al.: Role of foods in sporadic listeriosis. II. Microbiologic and epidemiologic investigation. J. A. M. A. *267*:2046–2050, 1992.
115. Portnoy, D. A., Chakraborty, T., Goebel, W., et al.: Molecular determinants of *Listeria monocytogenes* pathogenesis. Infect. Immun. *60*:1263–1267, 1992.
116. Portnoy, D. A., Jacks, P. S., and Hinrichs, D. J.: Role of hemolysin for the intracellular growth of *Listeria monocytogenes*. J. Exp. Med. *167*:1459–1471, 1988.
117. Rakhmilevich, A. L.: Evidence for a significant role of $CD4^+$ T cells in adoptive immunity to *Listeria monocytogenes* in the liver. Immunology *82*:249–254, 1994.
118. Ray, C. G., and Wedgewood, R. J.: Neonatal listeriosis. Pediatrics *34*:378–392, 1964.
119. Renoult, E., Chabot, F., Aymard, B., et al.: Treatment of *Listeria* bacteremia with vancomycin. Rev. Infect. Dis. *13*:181–182, 1991.
120. Riedo, F. X., Pinner, R. W., de Lourdes Tosca, M., et al.: A point-source foodborne listeriosis outbreak: Documented incubation period and possible mild illness. J. Infect. Dis. *170*:693–696, 1994.
121. Rolston, K. V. I., and Bodey, G. P.: Activity of new antimicrobial agents against *Listeria monocytogenes*. Eur. J. Clin. Microbiol. *6*:686–688, 1987.
122. Sauders, B. D., Wiedmann, M., and Desjardins, M.: Recurrent *Listeria monocytogenes* infection: Relapse or reinfection with a unique strain confirmed by molecular subtyping. Clin. Infect. Dis. *33*:257–259, 2001.
123. Scheld, W. M.: Evaluation of rifampin and other antibiotics against *Listeria monocytogenes* in vitro and in vivo. Rev. Infect. Dis. *5*(Suppl. 3): 593–599, 1983.
124. Schlech, W. F.: Foodborne listeriosis. Clin. Infect. Dis. *31*:770–775, 2000.
125. Schlech, W. F., Lavigne, P. M., Bortolussi, R. A., et al.: Epidemic listeriosis: Evidence for transmission by food. N. Engl. J. Med. *308*:203–206, 1983.
126. Schuchat, A.: Gastrointestinal carriage of *Listeria monocytogenes* in household contacts of patients with listeriosis. J. Infect. Dis. *167*:1261–1262, 1993.
127. Schuchat, A., Lizano, C., Broome, C. V., et al.: Outbreak of neonatal listeriosis associated with mineral oil. Pediatr. Infect. Dis. J. *10*:183–189, 1991.
128. Schuchat, A., Swaminathan, B., and Broome, C. V.: Epidemiology of human listeriosis. Clin. Microbiol. Rev. *4*:169–183, 1991.
129. Schwartz, B., Broome, C. V., Brown, G. R., et al.: Association of sporadic listeriosis with consumption of uncooked hot dogs and undercooked chicken. Lancet *2*:779–782, 1988.
130. Skogberg, K., Syrjanen, J., Jahkota, M., et al.: Clinical presentation and outcome of listeriosis in patients with and without immunosuppressive therapy. Clin. Infect. Dis. *14*:815–821, 1992.
131. Seeliger, H. P. R.: Listeriosis. New York, S. Karger, 1961.
132. Seeliger, H. P. R., and Finger, H.: Analytical serology of *Listeria*. *In* Kwapinski, J. B. G. (ed.): Analytical Serology of Microorganisms. New York, John Wiley & Sons, 1969, pp. 549–608.
133. Serushago, B., MacDonald, C., Lee, S. H. S., et al.: Interferon-γ detection in cultures of newborn cells exposed to *Listeria monocytogenes*. J. Interferon Cytokine Res. *15*:633–635, 1995.
134. Spitzer, P. G., and Hammer, S. M.: Treatment of *Listeria monocytogenes* infection with trimethoprim-sulfamethoxazole: Case report and review of the literature. Rev. Infect. Dis. *8*:427, 1986.
135. Stamm, A. M., Dismukes, W. E., Simmons, B. P., et al.: Listeriosis in renal transplant recipients: Report of an outbreak and review of 102 cases. Rev. Infect. Dis. *4*:665–682, 1982.
136. Steinman, C. R.: Specific detection and semiquantitation of microorganisms in tissue by nucleic acid hybridization. I. Characterization of the method and application to model systems. J. Lab. Clin. Med. *86*:164–174, 1975.
137. Sword, C. P.: Mechanisms of pathogenesis in *Listeria monocytogenes* infection. I. The influence of iron. J. Bacteriol. *92*:536–542, 1966.
138. Tappero, J. W., Schuchat, A., Deaver, K. A., et al.: Reduction in the incidence of human listeriosis in the United States: Effectiveness of prevention efforts? J. A. M. A. *273*:1118–1122, 1995.
139. Teberg, A. J., Yonekura, M. L., Salminen, C., et al.: Clinical manifestations of epidemic neonatal listeriosis. Pediatr. Infect. Dis. J. *6*:817–820, 1987.
140. Topalovski, M., Yang, S. S., and Boonpasat, Y.: Listeriosis of the placenta: Clinicopathologic study of seven cases. Am. J. Obstet. Gynecol. *169*:616–620, 1993.
141. Traub, W. H.: Perinatal listeriosis. Chemotherapy *27*:423–431, 1981.
142. Tsai, Y. H., Hirth, R. S., and Leitner, F.: A murine model for listerial meningitis and meningoencephalomyelitis: Therapeutic evaluation of drugs in mice. Chemotherapy *26*:196–206, 1980.
143. Update—listeriosis and pasteurized milk. M. M. W. R. Morb. Mortal. Wkly. Rep. *37*:764–765, 1988.
144. van Furth, R., van Zwet, T. L., Buisman, A. M., et al.: Anti–tumor necrosis factor antibodies inhibit the influx of granulocytes and monocytes into an inflammatory exudate and enhance the growth of *Listeria monocytogenes* in various organs. J. Infect. Dis. *170*:234–237, 1994.
145. Varughese, P. V., and Carter, A. O.: Human listeriosis in Canada. Can. Dis. Wkly. Rep. *15*:213–215, 1988.
146. Vazquez-Boland, J., Kuhn, M., Berche, P., et al.: *Listeria* pathogenesis and molecular virulence determinants. Clin. Microbiol. Rev. *14*:584–640, 2001.
147. Vischer, W. A., and Rominger, C.: Rifampicin against experimental listeriosis in the mouse. Chemotherapy *24*:104–111, 1978.
148. Visintine, A. M., Oleske, J. M., and Nahmias, A. J.: *Listeria monocytogenes* infection in infants and children. Am. J. Dis. Child. *131*:393–397, 1977.
149. Wagner, R. D., Maroushek, N. M., Brown, J. F., et al.: Treatment with anti–interleukin-10 monoclonal antibody enhances early resistance to but impairs complete clearance of *Listeria monocytogenes* infection in mice. Infect. Immun. *62*:2345–2353, 1994.
150. Walsh, D., Duffy, G., Seridan, J. J., et al.: Antibiotic resistance among *Listeria monocytogenes,* in retail foods. J. Appl. Microbiol. *90*:517–522, 2001.
151. Wilder, M. S., and Sword, C. P.: Mechanisms of pathogenesis in *Listeria monocytogenes* infection. II. Characterization of listeriosis in the CD-1 mouse and survey of biochemical lesions. J. Bacteriol. *93*:531–542, 1967.
152. Yajima, T., Nishimura, H., and Ishimitsu, R.: Overexpression of IL-15 in vivo increases antigen-driven memory CD8 T cells following a microbe exposure. J. Immunol. *168*:1198–1203, 2002.
153. Youssef, M., Fattal, E., Alonso, M.-J., et al.: Effectiveness of nanoparticle-bound ampicillin in the treatment of *Listeria monocytogenes* infection in athymic nude mice. Antimicrob. Agents Chemother. *32*:1204–1207, 1988.
154. Zhan, Y., and Cheers, C.: Differential induction of macrophage-derived cytokines by live and dead intracellular bacteria in vitro. Infect. Immun. *63*:720–723, 1995.

Tuberculosis

JEFFREY R. STARKE ■ KIMBERLY C. SMITH

Tuberculosis still ranks as one of the three most important infectious diseases in the world in terms of morbidity and mortality. Recognizable in skeletons from the Stone Age and in mummified corpses from the Egyptian Old Kingdom, tuberculosis became more widespread in western Europe after the plague years of the Middle Ages and the epidemic during the era of urbanization and industrialization in the 18th and 19th centuries.[144] At that time, scrofula affected more than half the young inhabitants of workhouses and orphanages.

As similar social trends developed outside Europe, tuberculosis followed. In the eastern cities of the United States (Boston, New York, and Philadelphia), the mortality rate from tuberculosis was about 400 per 100,000 population. With improving socioeconomic conditions, the mortality rate fell to 200 per 100,000 around 1900 and to 26 per 100,000 by 1950. Stress in all its forms—famine, war, rationing, long working hours, child labor, population displacement, crowded living and working conditions—favors the spread of tuberculosis in human beings, whereas years of peace and plenty favor its rapid decline.[143, 415] The decrease in the Western world in the incidence of tuberculosis was accentuated by the discovery, development, and widespread use of antituberculosis drugs beginning in the late 1940s.

Another important factor leading to the decline of tuberculosis in Western countries was the recognition in the 1920s of the importance of bovine tuberculosis and its successful eradication as a public health problem in the United States by gradual slaughter of infected cattle and almost universal pasteurization of milk.

Tuberculosis was recognized as a clinical entity in the early 19th century by Schönlein, who first used the term *tuberculosis* in 1830, and by Laennec in Paris, among others. Credit for extensively detailed descriptions of the primary focus goes to Anton Ghon (1866–1936), professor of pathology in Prague. In 1882, Koch identified *Mycobacterium tuberculosis.* The special diagnostic tools essential to understanding the disease in children were provided by Escherich, who in 1898 set up the first diagnostic radiography for children; by von Pirquet, Mantoux, Mandel, and Moro, who developed tuberculin testing between 1907 and 1910; and by Meunier and DeLille, who in 1898 taught the usefulness of gastric lavage in children. Revealing, long-term studies on the natural history of tuberculosis in children and on chemotherapy and prevention came principally from Scandinavia (Wallgren, Ustvedt, Holm, Hyge) and the United States (Brailey, Hardy, Lincoln, Hsu, Ferrebee).

Terminology—Exposure, Infection, Disease[15]

The pathophysiology of tuberculosis is complicated, and the delay between acquisition of infection and manifestation of disease renders certain pathophysiologic events less distinct. This chapter will consider three major stages of tuberculosis: exposure, infection, and disease.[502]

Exposure means that the child has had significant contact with an adult or adolescent with infectious pulmonary tuberculosis. The contact investigation—examining individuals close to a person suspected of having tuberculosis by performing a tuberculin skin test, chest radiograph, and physical examination—is the most important activity in a community to prevent cases of tuberculosis in children.[52, 218] The most frequent setting for exposure of a child is the household, but it can occur in a school, daycare center, or other closed setting.[211] In this stage, the tuberculin skin test is negative, the chest radiograph is normal, and the child lacks signs or symptoms of disease. Some exposed children may have inhaled droplet nuclei infected with *M. tuberculosis* and have early infection, but the clinician cannot know it because it takes up to 3 months for delayed hypersensitivity to tuberculin—a positive skin test—to develop. Children younger than 5 years of age who are in the exposure stage should be treated to prevent the rapid development of disseminated or meningeal tuberculosis, which can occur before the skin test becomes reactive.[152, 314, 342, 377]

Infection occurs when the individual inhales droplet nuclei containing *M. tuberculosis,* which becomes established intracellularly within the lung and associated lymphoid tissue. The hallmark of latent tuberculosis infection is a reactive tuberculin skin test. In this stage, the child has no signs or symptoms and the chest radiograph is either normal or reveals only granuloma or calcifications in the lung parenchyma or regional lymph nodes, or in both tissues. In developed countries, virtually all children with tuberculosis infection should receive treatment, usually with isoniazid, to prevent the development of disease in the near or distant future.

Disease occurs when signs or symptoms or radiographic manifestations caused by *M. tuberculosis* become apparent. The word *tuberculosis* refers to disease. Not all infected individuals have the same risk of contracting disease. An immunocompetent adult with untreated tuberculosis infection has approximately a 5 to 10 percent *lifetime* risk of developing disease; half the risk exists in the first 2 to 3 years after infection occurs. Adults with tuberculosis infection who then become infected with human immunodeficiency virus (HIV) have a 5 to 10 percent *annual* risk of developing tuberculosis disease.[458] Historical studies have shown that disease, often serious, life-threatening forms, will develop in as many as 40 percent of immunocompetent infants with untreated tuberculosis infection within 1 to 2 years.

Epidemiology

INCIDENCE AND PREVALENCE

Between 20 and 45 percent of the world's population (about 2 billion people) are infected with *M. tuberculosis,* and more than 90 percent of new cases occur in the developing world, where resources are very limited.[516] According to the World Health Organization (WHO), in 1997 only 32 percent of the world's population lived in areas where effective tuberculosis control programs were fully operational.[373] In 1998, the WHO estimated that 8 million new cases and 2 million deaths from tuberculosis occurred worldwide.[416, 576] Approximately

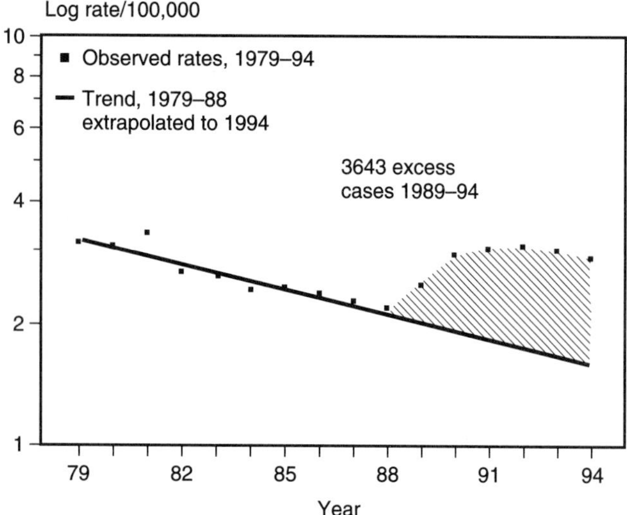

FIGURE 101–1 ■ Observed and expected tuberculosis cases in children younger than 15 years in the United States, 1979 to 1994.

40 percent of new cases and about 5 percent of deaths were predicted to occur in children younger than 15 years.[276] The inability to control tuberculosis despite the availability of effective, relatively inexpensive therapy is one of the greatest medical failures of our time.[199, 489, 501]

Between 1953, when reporting began, and 1985, the number of annually reported tuberculosis cases in the United States fell by 74 percent from 84,304 to 22,201.[92, 426] In 1985, the overall case rate was approximately 10 per 100,000 population. At that time, the incidence curve flattened out, and for the first time since 1953, case numbers and rates increased to a peak of 26,673 cases in 1992. Between 1985 and 1992 in the United States the total tuberculosis case numbers rose 20 percent.[73] During that same time, the number of pediatric tuberculosis cases rose 40 percent[245, 548] (Fig. 101–1). Most experts cite four probable causes for the increases: (1) the co-epidemic of HIV infection; (2) increasing rates of tuberculosis in foreign-born individuals in the United States; (3) increased transmission among adults in congregate settings, including jails and prisons, nursing homes, homeless shelters, HIV treatment facilities, hospitals, and, rarely, schools[35, 38, 53, 344, 397]; and (4) a decline in the public health infrastructure in many areas of the country.[66, 110, 417, 503] After several years of intense and expensive effort, the number of tuberculosis cases in the United States declined again. In 2000, a total of 16,377 tuberculosis cases (5.8 cases per 100,000 population) were reported in the United States, a 7 percent decrease from 1999 and 39 percent decrease from 1992.[94] Rates have decreased in the United States through the end of the decade in all groups except immigrants from high-risk countries. However, the annual cost of tuberculosis in the United States still approaches $1 billion.[65] An estimated 4 to 6 percent of the U.S. population, or about 15 million people, are infected with *M. tuberculosis*. This group represents a large reservoir from which cases of tuberculosis disease will emerge in the future if these individuals are not treated.

The resurgence of tuberculosis in the United States between 1985 and 1992 was associated with the emergence of multidrug-resistant tuberculosis (MDR-TB), strains that are resistant to at least isoniazid and rifampin and may be resistant to other antituberculosis medications as well. MDR-TB is difficult and expensive to treat, and the mortality rates may be as high as 50 percent in complicated cases.[183, 236] Since 1993, the incidence of resistance to isoniazid has remained stable, and the incidence of MDR-TB has decreased. In 2000, 8 percent of isolates were resistant to at least isoniazid, and 1 percent were resistant to at least isoniazid and rifampin (MDR-TB) in the United States.[94]

MDR-TB has become an important problem in many areas of the world.[151] Global surveys conducted between 1996 and 1998 in 58 geographic areas showed a median prevalence of MDR-TB of 1 percent, but in some regions the rates were alarming: 14 percent in Estonia, 10 percent in the Henan Province in China, and 9 percent in Latvia and parts of Russia.[161] In adults, drug resistance in *M. tuberculosis* usually is secondary, the resistance emerging during therapy because treatment is inadequate or interrupted.[169] In children, drug resistance usually is primary in that the child is infected with a strain that already has become resistant.[374, 445, 447, 529] Rates of drug resistance in children tend to mirror those in adults in the same population.[509–511] Rates of drug resistance may be higher in developing countries because of difficulty in completing therapy, inadequate supply of medications, and use of over-the-counter cough medications that often contain isoniazid or rifampin.

Since treatment became available in the late 1940s, tuberculosis has been concentrated in certain high-risk groups in the United States[93] (Table 101–1). Tuberculosis occurs most commonly in areas with ethnically diverse populations, including large urban areas, coastal states, and states bordering Mexico[83, 91, 95] (Fig. 101–2). Tuberculosis disproportionately effects ethnic and minority populations in the United States. In 2000, the Centers for Disease Control and Prevention (CDC) reported the highest overall *number* of cases in blacks, 5161 cases, but the case *rate* was highest among Asians, with 32.9 cases per 100,000 population.[94, 375] Among non-Hispanic whites the case rate was 1.9 (22% of all cases), for Asian/Pacific Islanders the rate was 32.9 (21%), among blacks the rate was 15.2 (32%), among Hispanics the rate was 10.8 (23%), and in Native American/Alaskan natives the rate was 11.4 (1%).

During the 1990s, immigration from a high-prevalence country was the single largest risk factor for tuberculosis, with rates among foreign-born persons four to six times higher than those for U.S.-born persons. In 2001, the CDC reported that almost 50 percent of all cases occurred in foreign-born individuals. Tuberculosis is endemic in most

TABLE 101–1 ■ HIGH-RISK GROUPS FOR TUBERCULOSIS INFECTION AND DISEASE

Groups at High Risk of Exposure or Infection
Close contacts of person with TB
Foreign-born persons from high-risk countries
  (Asia, Africa, Latin America, Russia, Eastern Europe)
Residents and employees of high-risk congregate settings
  (correctional institutions, nursing homes, homeless shelters, hospitals serving high-risk populations, drug treatment centers)
Medically underserved, low-income populations
High-risk racial or ethnic minority populations
Injection-drug users
Children exposed to adults in high-risk categories

Groups at Higher Risk for Disease Once Infected
Immunosuppressed patients, including HIV-infected
Recent TB infection (within past 2 yr)
Persons with certain medical conditions
  (diabetes mellitus, silicosis, cancer, end-stage renal disease, gastrectomy, body weight ≤90% of ideal)
Injection-drug users
History of inadequately treated TB
Children ≤4 yr old, especially infants

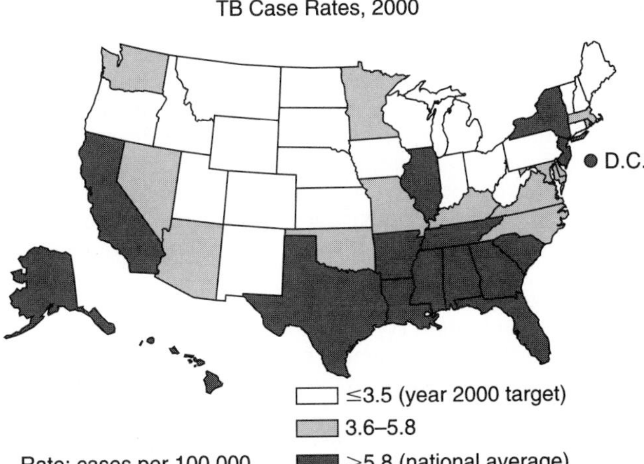

FIGURE 101–2 ■ Tuberculosis case rates by state, 2000. (From Centers for Disease Control and Prevention: Surveillance reports: Reported TB in the United States, 2000. Mor. Mortal. Wkly. Rep. C. D. C. Surveill. Summ. 2001.)

developing countries, and between 30 and 50 percent of recent immigrants to the United States have latent tuberculosis infection on entry into the country.[526] During the immigration process, adults are screened for tuberculosis disease with a chest radiograph, but skin testing to detect tuberculosis infection is not required. Children younger than 15 years receive neither a chest radiograph nor a tuberculin skin test.[455] Among children in the United States, being born in a country with a high rate of tuberculosis is the most important risk factor for having tuberculosis infection. Foreign-born adopted children also are at risk for having tuberculosis infection and disease.[168, 289, 434] People who enter the United States illegally may be unable or afraid to seek medical treatment, even when they are ill. Studies have shown that in most immigrants in whom tuberculosis develops, it does so within 5 years of immigration, thus indicating that many cases could be prevented if appropriate screening and treatment programs were conducted.

Other important risk factors for tuberculosis in adults include lower socioeconomic status, migrant work,[85] HIV infection, drug use, homelessness, travel to high-prevalence countries, history of incarceration, and occupations with exposure to high-risk populations (see Table 101–1). Children from high-risk population groups or children who have contact with adults in these groups may be at increased risk for developing tuberculosis infection.

Age has an important influence on tuberculosis case rates. During 2000, 6 percent of cases in the United States occurred in children younger than 15 years, 10 percent in persons 15 to 24 years old, 34 percent in persons 25 to 44 years old, 28 percent in persons 45 to 64 years old, and 22 percent in persons older than 64 years.[94] The highest case rates among children are in those younger than 5 years. Children 5 to 14 years of age—the so-called favored age—have a consistently lower case rate than does any other segment of the population. In early childhood, the incidence is not significantly different in girls and boys, although adolescent girls generally experience higher rates of disease than adolescent boys do.[59]

The age at which tuberculosis disease initially develops varies among ethnic groups. White persons develop tuberculosis more commonly as older adults, whereas African Americans and Hispanics have a higher incidence of disease as young adults or children (Fig. 101–3). Many of the risk factors for acquisition of tuberculosis, such as HIV infection, drug use, history of incarceration, and recent immigration, are more common in young adults in their twenties, thirties, and forties, a time when contact with children is more likely. Other factors may influence the peak age distribution of tuberculosis among different groups, including recent immigration, socioeconomic status, high-risk behavior, and possibly genetic susceptibility.

Inherited susceptibility to tuberculosis may contribute to differences among various ethnic groups. Laboratory animals as well as humans have been shown to differ in genetic susceptibility to tuberculosis.[321, 461] In the United States, highly urbanized immigrants, such as Jews from European ghettos, fared much better than their rural Irish and African counterparts did, presumably because generations of exposure to tuberculosis in previous European epidemics had selected in favor of more resistant individuals.[409] As the disease spread to other continents, previously unexposed populations may have been more susceptible to tuberculosis and experienced higher rates of disease.

In most U.S. locales that have had recent increases in tuberculosis, the demographic groups with the greatest tuberculosis morbidity also have large numbers of HIV-infected persons.[104, 210, 365] The HIV epidemic has had a profound effect on the epidemiology of tuberculosis in children by two mechanisms[441]: (1) most important, HIV-infected adults with tuberculosis may transmit *M. tuberculosis* to children in their environment, and tuberculosis disease will develop in some of them, and (2) children with HIV infection are at increased risk of progressing from asymptomatic tuberculosis infection to disease.[275, 320] Several studies have demonstrated increased rates of childhood tuberculosis associated with increased rates of disease among HIV-infected adults in the community.[198, 252] Tuberculosis probably is underdiagnosed in HIV-infected children, especially in the developing world, because of the similarity of its clinical manifestations with other opportunistic pulmonary diseases and the difficulty of confirming the diagnosis with the skin test or culture. All children with suspected tuberculosis disease should have HIV serotesting because the two infections are linked epidemiologically and many experts prolong treatment in HIV-infected children with tuberculosis.[193, 573]

The site of manifestation of tuberculosis disease differs between adults and children. Although pulmonary disease is most common for all ages, extrapulmonary tuberculosis occurs more often in children. Because HIV co-infection increases the risk for development of extrapulmonary disease, rates have increased in adults during the past 15 years. Generally, 25 percent of pediatric cases are extrapulmonary, with 75 percent being pulmonary. In 1985, before widespread HIV infection occurred, 85 percent of adults had

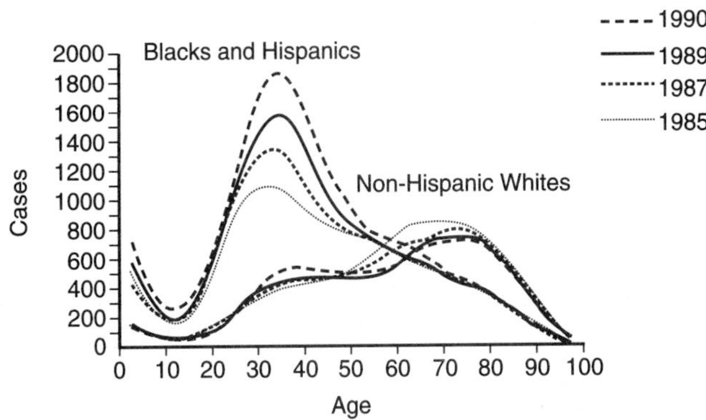

FIGURE 101–3 ■ Tuberculosis cases in Hispanics and blacks versus non-Hispanic whites in the United States, 1985 to 1990.

pulmonary disease and 15 percent had extrapulmonary disease. With the spread of HIV infection, these numbers have shifted, and in 2000, the CDC reported that 80 percent of all new cases, including adults and children, were pulmonary and 20 percent were extrapulmonary.[94] Comparing the site of extrapulmonary disease in children and adults in 1985, before the acquired immunodeficiency syndrome (AIDS) epidemic, shows some important differences. First, approximately 70 percent of extrapulmonary tuberculosis in children involved the lymph nodes, as opposed to 25 percent in adults (Fig. 101–4). Second, tuberculous meningitis accounted for 13 percent of extrapulmonary disease in children versus 4 percent in adults. Genitourinary involvement occurred in 16 percent of adults, but it was a rare finding in children. Although the proportion of extrapulmonary cases in adults has increased as a result of the HIV/AIDS epidemic, extrapulmonary disease still occurs more commonly in children.

For many decades, clinicians have noted a seasonal occurrence of tuberculosis in children, strikingly higher from January to June in the Northern Hemisphere.[212] Closer contact among family members indoors during inclement weather and more frequent coughing produced by winter and spring respiratory infections may be determining factors in this pattern.

TRANSMISSION

Transmission of tuberculosis is from one human to another, usually via infected droplets of mucus that become airborne when an individual coughs, sneezes, or laughs.[103] The droplets dry and become droplet nuclei, which may remain suspended in air for hours. Only particles less than 10 μm in diameter are small enough to reach the alveoli.[428] Transmission sometimes occurs by direct contact with infected discharges (sputum, saliva, urine, or drainage from an open sinus or abscess); it occasionally occurs by means of heavily contaminated fomites, such as shoes, gastric lavage tubes, bronchoscopes, or syringes prepared by someone with positive sputum.[206] Rare cases of tuberculosis transmitted via a lung transplant have been reported.[349, 424] Dogs may be a source of infection for children because dogs are susceptible to the human type of tubercle bacillus.[422]

The collective experience of many clinicians is that children usually are infected by an adult or adolescent in the immediate household, most often a parent, grandparent, older sibling, boarder, or household employee.[37] Casual extrafamilial contact is the source of infection much less often, but physicians, babysitters, schoolteachers, music teachers, school bus drivers, parishioners, nurses, gardeners, and candy store keepers have been implicated in individual cases and in hundreds of mini-epidemics.[21, 57, 147, 297, 302, 568] Attention has been drawn to the prevalence of active tuberculosis among residents of nursing homes for the elderly. Children visiting their grandparents have contracted tuberculosis in this setting. Within the household of an infectious adult, infants and toddlers almost always become infected. Also at high risk are older children and teenagers who wait on the ailing adult, whereas children between 6 and 12 years of age often escape infection. Adults with pulmonary disease who are receiving regular, appropriate chemotherapy probably rarely infect children; much more dangerous are those with chronic tuberculous disease that is unrecognized, inadequately treated, or in relapse because of the development of resistance.

Wallgren[564] was the first to point out that children with tuberculosis rarely, if ever, infect other children. Many children with the disease have tuberculin-negative siblings and parents. Children with tuberculosis often have been cared for by their families or in hospitals and institutions without infecting their contacts. When transmission of *M. tuberculosis* has been documented in children's hospitals, it almost invariably has come from an adult with undiagnosed pulmonary tuberculosis.[22, 176, 257, 258, 358, 569] Adults accompanying a child with suspected tuberculosis disease should be screened as soon as possible for pulmonary tuberculosis.[60, 106, 259, 260, 500] In tuberculous children, tubercle bacilli in endobronchial secretions are relatively sparse, and cough is not characteristic of endothoracic tuberculosis or miliary disease. When young children cough, they lack the tussive force of adults. Specimens collected by bronchoalveolar lavage or early-morning gastric aspiration from children with clinically suspected tuberculosis seldom if ever have acid-fast bacilli seen on smears. Only about 40 percent eventually will grow *M. tuberculosis* by culture.[492, 505] Young infants with congenital tuberculosis or advanced, postnatally acquired pulmonary disease are more likely to have smear- or culture-positive specimens (80%) than older children are.[343, 549] Therefore, specimens and secretions from infants, children with cavitary lesions, and intubated patients should be handled as potentially infectious.[334] Most pre-adolescent children with tuberculosis, however, are not contagious and do not require isolation. Tuberculosis in adolescents may be more typical of adult-type reactivation disease, including the presence of cavitary lesions with smear- and culture-positive sputum. Children or adolescents who have symptomatic pulmonary tuberculosis with features of adult-type tuberculosis should be treated as

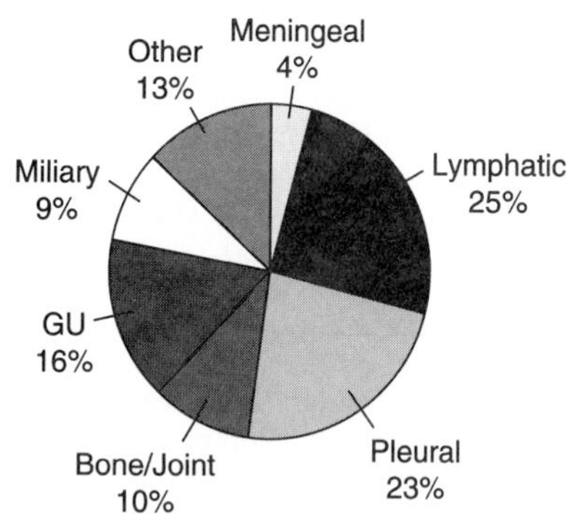

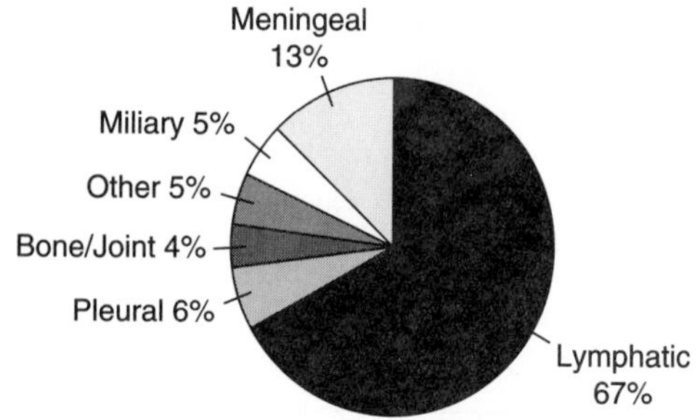

FIGURE 101–4 ■ Extrapulmonary disease by site in adults and children in the United States. (From the Centers for Disease Control and Prevention.)

potentially contagious until mycobacterial smears and cultures are negative.[74, 117, 164]

Children nonetheless play an extremely important role in the transmission of tuberculosis, not so much because they are likely to contaminate their immediate environment, but rather because they may harbor a partially healed infection that lies dormant, only to reactivate as infectious pulmonary tuberculosis many years later under the social, emotional, and physiologic stresses arising during adolescence, pregnancy, or old age. Thus, children infected with *M. tuberculosis* constitute a long-lasting reservoir of tuberculosis in the population.

The risk of infection in child contacts of adults receiving antituberculosis chemotherapy often is a matter of practical concern. Several studies reveal that most contacts are infected by the index case before the diagnosis is made and treatment is initiated. Although it is not possible to carry out a definitive clinical study, evidence indicates that patients receiving effective chemotherapy rarely transmit *M. tuberculosis*. Nonetheless, to avoid exposing children to adults with positive sputum smears or positive cultures and to assume that adults positive by smear or culture remain infectious for at least several weeks after the start of therapy seem prudent.

Mycobacteriology

The genus *Mycobacterium,* closely related by its cell wall antigens to the genera *Corynebacterium* and *Nocardia,* presently is classified in the order Actinomycetales and the family Mycobacteriaceae.[27] Mycobacteria are nonmotile, non–spore-forming, pleomorphic, weakly gram-positive rods 1 to 5 μm long, typically slender and slightly "bent." Some appear beaded, and some are clumped. In general, species pathogenic for humans are more acid-fast, have more exacting nutritional requirements, grow more slowly, form less pigment, and are more sensitive to chemotherapeutic agents than are the saprophytic species.

The cell wall constituents of mycobacteria determine their most striking biologic properties. The cell walls contain 20 to 60 percent lipids by dry weight, largely bound to proteins and carbohydrates. These organisms are more resistant than are most others to light, alkali, acid, and the bactericidal action of antibodies. Their growth is slow, with a generation time of 14 to 24 hours, perhaps because of the slow metabolic exchange through the waxy "capsule." Their hydrophobic properties render them difficult to study.

Acid-fastness, that is, the capacity to form stable mycolate complexes with certain aryl methane dyes (specifically, carbolfuchsin, crystal violet, auramine, and rhodamine, which then are not removed readily even by rinsing with 95 percent ethanol plus hydrochloric acid), is the hallmark of mycobacteria.[27] The cells appear red when stained with fuchsin (as with the Ziehl-Neelsen or Kinyoun stains), appear purple with crystal violet, or exhibit yellow-green fluorescence under ultraviolet light (when stained with auramine and rhodamine, as in Truant stain). Truant stain, in experienced hands, is considered the best stain for specimens expected to contain small numbers of organisms.

Identification of mycobacteria depends on their staining properties and on their biochemical and metabolic characteristics. Mycobacteria are obligate aerobes. On the whole, their growth requirements are simple. *M. tuberculosis* can grow in "classic" media, whose essential ingredients are egg yolk and glycerin (Löwenstein-Jensen, Petragnani, Dorset); often, a dye such as malachite green to inhibit contaminants; and sometimes, potatoes, charcoal, and so on, which probably neutralize growth inhibitors. They also can grow in simple synthetic media, frequently with an admixture of asparagine, glutamate, or amino acid mixtures (Middlebrook 7H9, Tween-albumin). Once grown, they can be replated on media also containing antituberculosis drugs to determine drug susceptibility patterns. Isolation on solid media often takes 3 to 6 weeks, followed by another 2 to 4 weeks for drug susceptibility results. Improvements in laboratory methods have permitted more rapid culture, identification, and drug susceptibility testing of mycobacteria, such as by an automatic radiometric method known as the BACTEC (Becton Dickinson, Towson, MD) method, in which a decontaminated, concentrated specimen is inoculated into a bottle of medium containing carbon 14–labeled palmitic acid as the substrate.[469] As mycobacteria metabolize the carbon 14 palmitic acid, carbon dioxide 14 accumulates in the head space of the bottle, where radioactivity can be measured. Unfortunately, cross-contamination of bottles has been reported and has resulted in false-positive cultures.[145] The addition of appropriate dilutions of antituberculosis drugs permits an evaluation of drug susceptibility. The time for identification and drug susceptibility testing can be reduced to 1 to 3 weeks, depending on the size of the inoculum.

Bacteriophage typing to determine the relatedness of isolates has advanced slowly. Progress is being made, however, in standardization of techniques, and phage typing already is of use in strain identification for epidemiologic purposes. However, a newer technique, restriction fragment length polymorphism analysis of mycobacterial DNA, has become a powerful tool for determining strain relatedness in both outbreaks and routine epidemiology of tuberculosis in a community.[8, 474]

Resistance and Immunity

Natural resistance to tuberculosis infection varies greatly among animal species; humans, guinea pigs, and rabbits are highly susceptible. However, Lurie[321] experimentally bred resistant rabbits and showed that although the virulent tubercle bacilli disseminated just as well in the resistant rabbits, multiplication within tissues was inhibited. Thus, the differences between resistant and susceptible rabbits appeared to lie in the ability of the former to produce an effective immune response, and this ability seemed to be controlled genetically.

Additional evidence that genetic factors influence susceptibility comes from data involving twins. Kallmann and Reisner[255] noted that when one homozygous twin suffered from tuberculosis, the other twin had a higher chance of being affected than was the case with heterozygous twins. Gender affects resistance, and females appear to be especially susceptible during adolescence. The negative nitrogen and calcium balance that can arise during adolescence may account in part for susceptibility at this age.[250]

Likewise, young age appears to predispose to tuberculosis.[443, 549] However, it is impossible to be sure that the apparent susceptibility is not due to a larger dose of bacteria because of more intimate contact between very young children and their infectors. Although diabetes mellitus affects the resistance of adults, whether it affects that of children is not clear. Many viral infections depress tuberculin reactivity, but only measles and perhaps influenza have been incriminated in lowering resistance to tuberculosis.[39, 64, 204, 506, 585] Unfortunately, natural resistance is ill defined and poorly understood.

Marfan noted in 1886 that acquired resistance to tuberculosis does occur. He commented on the infrequency of pulmonary tuberculosis in later life in people who contract scrofula, provided that the scrofula heals before adolescence (the Marfan law). As in other infections characterized by intracellular parasitism *(Brucella, Listeria, Salmonella),* macrophages become altered conspicuously through the action of an intermediate product (lymphokine) released when antigen interacts with sensitive lymphoid cells. Synchronously with the appearance of hypersensitivity, macrophages develop the ability to ingest and kill enormous numbers of organisms. The spread of tuberculosis in experimental animals and in people in whom tuberculin hypersensitivity has been suppressed with steroids accidentally or intentionally suggests that tuberculin hypersensitivity indeed is a desirable accompaniment of tuberculosis infection.

Cell-mediated immunity is regarded as most important in host defense against *M. tuberculosis.*[123] The T-cell–mediated immune response involves a variety of cell subsets that are involved in numerous functions, including protection, delayed hypersensitivity, cytolysis, and establishment of memory immunity.[388] The functions also involve an array of cytokines, several of which direct cells of the monocyte/macrophage axis to contain and destroy the invading bacilli.[17, 521] The exact role of individual cytokines is not yet clear, but an emerging concept is that much of the clinical response to the presence of *M. tuberculosis* is determined by the balance of the cellular-cytokine response, which to some degree is under genetic influence.[388]

Pathogenesis

PORTAL OF ENTRY

The tubercle bacillus usually is inhaled. The observations of Riley[428] suggest that a single tubercle bacillus can initiate infection. Ghon, Kuedlich, and their associates (Table 101–2) reported that the primary focus found in 2114 autopsies on children was the lung in 95.93 percent of cases. Especially significant is that their study was done at a time when bovine tuberculosis, which might have produced many primary gastrointestinal foci, was much more common than it is today. Ingestion probably accounts for a small percentage of primary pulmonary foci and for some gastrointestinal foci, particularly in infants who have consumed milk containing bovine tubercle bacilli. Contamination of a superficial skin or mucous membrane lesion, such as an abrasion of the sole of the foot or the elbow, an insect bite, ritual circumcision, or infection of the vulva, may lead to infection. Infection by inoculation with a sputum-contaminated syringe has been reported in more recent years.[206] True congenital infection, though rare, may occur as a result of either lymphohematogenous spread in the mother during pregnancy or smoldering endometritis.[551]

TABLE 101–2 ■ PORTAL OF ENTRY OF TUBERCLE BACILLI

Respiratory (%)		Nonrespiratory (%)	
Lung	95.93*	Bowel	1.14
Tonsils	0.09	Skin	0.14
Nose	0.09	Eye	0.05
Middle ear	0.09	Parotid	0.05
Total†	96.20	Total	1.38

*Of 2114 autopsies on children.
†Undetermined, 2.4%.
Data from Ghon, A., and Kuedlich, H.: Die Eintrittspforten der Infektion. *In* Engel, S., and Pirquet, C. (eds.): Handbuch der Kindertuberkulose. Stuttgart, Germany, Georg Thieme Verlag, 1930.

INCUBATION PERIOD

The incubation period from the time that the tubercle bacillus enters the body until cutaneous sensitivity develops has been found to be 3 weeks to 3 months. With both bacille Calmette-Guérin (BCG) and experimental infections, the incubation period is shorter when the inoculum is large, and clinical experience suggests that the same is true in humans. Debré, for example, noted long ago that tuberculosis acquired by an infant from its mother was likely to be much more severe than an infection acquired from a visitor to the home. Animal experiments support this concept. The end of the incubation period coincides with the onset of tuberculin hypersensitivity and may be accompanied by a period lasting from 1 to 3 weeks that Wallgren called fever of onset or fever of invasion. At this time, the tissue reaction intensifies throughout the primary complex and may permit the complex to be visible on x-ray films.

THE "TIMETABLE" OF TUBERCULOSIS

Wallgren's tremendous experience with tuberculous children in institutions permitted him to recognize and describe the usual early course and timing of the initial infection and each of its best-known complications.[567] His timetable concept is an extremely useful one for clinicians because it permits a realistic prognosis, an understanding of what complications to look for and when, and a more productive approach to finding the infectious source case (Fig. 101–5).

Symptomatic, massive lymphohematogenous spread (i.e., miliary or acute meningeal tuberculosis) is seen in only 0.5 to 3 percent of infected children. When it does occur, the usual onset is 2 to 6 months after initial infection. Endobronchial tuberculosis, possibly with segmental pulmonary lesions, develops slightly later on average. The metastatic lesions of bones and joints, which can be expected in 5 percent of untreated infected children, usually do not appear until about 1 year after infection at the earliest.[193] Renal lesions come later still, 5 to 25 years after initial infection. The relationship between the anatomic site of tuberculosis and the median age of onset in children is shown in Table 101–3. The interval between the initial infection and the appearance of chronic pulmonary tuberculosis is extremely variable but can be months to decades, depending mainly on the age of the child at the time of infection. In adolescents, the interval is likely to be short, but in infants, much longer.

In summary, the first 5 years after initial tuberculosis infection in childhood, especially the first year, is the time when complications usually occur. Later in life, during times of stress, a previously silent or arrested lesion may reactivate and become dangerous to the patient as well as highly infectious to others.

Clinical Forms of Tuberculosis in Children

ENDOTHORACIC

Asymptomatic Tuberculosis Infection

Asymptomatic (or latent) infection can be defined as infection associated with tuberculin hypersensitivity and a positive tuberculin test but with no striking clinical or radiographic manifestations. Computed tomography may reveal enlarged lymph nodes in the chest, even though the plain radiograph is normal.[129] Occasionally, low-grade fever is found at the onset, usually by chance. If the child has been in recent contact with a person who has contagious

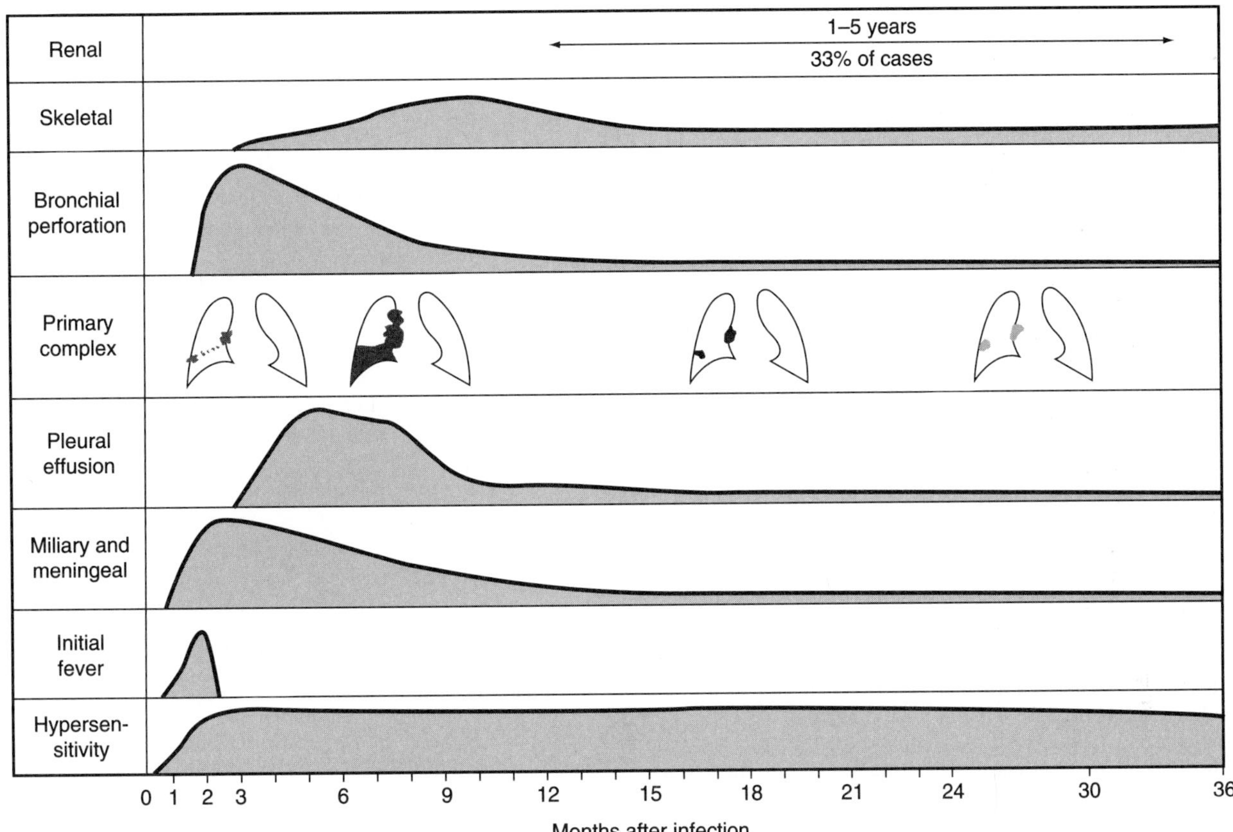

FIGURE 101–5 ■ The timetable of tuberculosis.

tuberculosis and the tuberculin test is positive, disease should be ruled out immediately with a chest radiograph and a thorough physical examination. Asymptomatic tuberculosis infection occurs more frequently in children of elementary school age than in adolescents or infants. Some 40 to 50 percent of infections in infants younger than 1 year and 80 to 95 percent in older children can be expected to cause no specific recognizable symptom or radiographic findings.[396] Gastric washings in these patients, even when performed with great care, yield a very low percentage of positive results.

A clinician making a diagnosis of tuberculosis infection in a child must assume, however, that the patient might be in the earliest stage of infection and at risk for the development of symptomatic disease in the near future. A careful history and investigation of contacts should be undertaken immediately for determination, if possible, of the date of exposure. Chemotherapy must be started and the patient closely monitored not only to detect any toxic effect of chemotherapy and monitor adherence with treatment but also to be sure that disease does not develop.

TABLE 101–3 ■ MEDIAN AGE OF CHILDREN* WITH TUBERCULOSIS BY PREDOMINANT SITE OF INVOLVEMENT, UNITED STATES, 1988

Site	No. of Cases (%)	Median Age (yr)
Pulmonary	1213 (77.5)	6
Lymphatic	209 (13.3)	5
Pleural	49 (3.1)	16
Meningeal	29 (1.9)	2
Bone/joint	19 (1.2)	8
Other	15 (1.0)	12
Miliary	14 (0.9)	1
Genitourinary	13 (0.8)	16
Peritoneal	4 (0.3)	13
Not stated	1 (0.1)	—
Total	1566 (100.0)	6

*Younger than 20 years.

The Endothoracic Primary Complex and Its Complications

The primary complex, described by Ghon,[177] includes three elements: the primary focus, lymphangitis, and regional lymphadenitis. This complex holds true for every primary infection, regardless of the portal of entry. Ghon noted that at least 70 percent of primary pulmonary foci are subpleural. Thus, pleurisy is almost a regular feature of the primary complex.

Evolution of the primary pulmonary focus begins with an acute inflammatory reaction around tubercle bacilli inhaled into an alveolus, with the localized alveolar consolidation varying from the size of a pea to the size of a walnut. Macrophages appear within hours in the inflammatory exudate and change into clusters of epithelioid cells to form tubercles. In turn, these tubercles may resolve and disappear, or central caseation consisting of incomplete cell autolysis may develop. The caseous lesion contains large numbers of multiplying tubercle bacilli that spread rapidly from the primary focus via the regional lymphatic vessels to the regional lymph nodes, with areas of inflammation being set up along the way that later may caseate and calcify.[407]

The primary pulmonary focus has been studied carefully by numerous investigators (Table 101–4). Plotting their locations on a normal chest radiograph creates a pattern

TABLE 101–4 ■ LOCATION OF THE PRIMARY PULMONARY FOCUS

	No. of Patients	%
Right upper lobe	138	27
Right middle lobe	40	7
Right lower lobe	107	20
Left upper lobe	122	24
Left lower lobe	104	20
Total	511	98

Data from Ghon, A., and Kuedlich, H.: Die Eintrittspforten der Infektion. *In* Engel, S., and Pirquet, C. (eds.): Handbuch der Kindertuberkulose. Stuttgart, Germany, Georg Thieme Verlag, 1930.

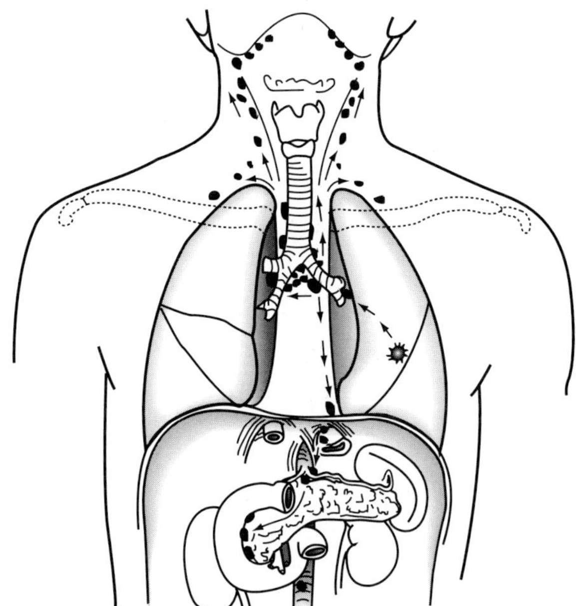

FIGURE 101–6 ■ Schematic composite drawing illustrating wide lymphogenic spread of the tuberculosis infection from a primary pulmonary focus in the base of the left upper lobe. The infection extended cephalad to the submandibular nodes in the head and caudad as far as the pancreatic nodes in the abdomen. (From Caffey, J.: Pediatric X-Ray Diagnosis. 7th ed. Chicago, Year Book, 1978.)

resembling the scatter of birdshot on a paper target. Thus, all parts of the lung apparently are at equal risk of being seeded. The thought that the primary focus has a predilection for the lower fields of the lung probably arises from the fact that the lung is pyramid shaped, with more basilar than apical lung tissue.

Many investigators concur that 70 to 85 percent of primary infections are initiated by one focus.[177, 396, 523] In a study of 170 cases, Ghon[177] found two foci in 15 percent, three in 7 percent, four in 3 percent, and five in 2 percent. Multiple lung foci can result, though rarely, from the ingestion and inhalation of tubercle bacilli. This pattern of disease was shown clearly in the results of pathologic studies on the 71 infants who died in the "Lübeck disaster" of the 1930s, an incident in which 251 newborn infants mistakenly had been given live tubercle bacilli by mouth instead of BCG vaccine. Fifteen of the infants were found to have primary lung lesions at autopsy, and all 251 had primary intestinal lesions.

Although the lymphadenitis cannot be detected clinically and rarely is apparent even on radiographs, the hallmark of initial tuberculosis infection is the relatively large size and importance of the adenitis as opposed to the relatively insignificant size of the initial focus in the lung, skin, or elsewhere. The development of tuberculin hypersensitivity within 3 to 12 weeks after initial acquisition of infection enhances the cellular reaction throughout the primary complex, but with a particularly prominent effect on the primary focus and the regional lymph nodes. At this time, the infection may spread along nearby lymphatic chains to involve more distant nodes. The lymphatic drainage of the lungs is outlined in Table 101–5; it occurs predominantly from left to right. One is not surprised, therefore, that the nodes in the right upper paratracheal area appear to be the ones most often affected. Many primary lesions are subpleural, and the lymphatic drainage of the apical pleura is to the cervical nodes. Moreover, the paratracheal chains have communications with both the deep cervical nodes and the abdominal nodes, as shown in Figure 101–6. Among 54 patients with the primary lesion in the right upper lobe, Blacklock found that 14 had involvement of the deep cervical nodes on the same side and 3 had involvement of the abdominal nodes.

TABLE 101–5 ■ LYMPHATIC DRAINAGE OF THE LUNG

Right upper lobe	→	Right paratracheal chain
Right middle lobe	→	Right and left paratracheal nodes
Right lower lobe	→	Subcarinal nodes
Left upper lobe	→	Left paratracheal nodes
Left lower lobe	→	Left paratracheal nodes
Lingula	→	Subcarinal nodes
Subcarinal nodes	→	Right paratracheal nodes

Based on data of Rouviere, quoted by Courtice, F. C., and Simmonds, W. J.: Physiological significance of lymph drainage of the serous cavities and lungs. Physio. Rev. *34*:419–442, 1954.

Bronchial obstruction as a result of enlargement of the peribronchial lymph nodes was reported by Ghon[177] and others. It was not until the 1920s that Wallgren[565] and others elucidated the role of these large nodes in producing the radiographic shadows variously called epituberculosis, collapse-consolidation, and segmental lesions that so often are seen in cases of childhood tuberculosis.[177, 305, 456, 565] At the end of the incubation period, as tuberculin sensitivity develops, the hilar lymph nodes enlarge greatly, and in many cases, caseous foci appear within them. Acid-fast studies of smears and sections have confirmed that this caseum has few tubercle bacilli. As the nodes enlarge, they frequently impinge on the neighboring regional bronchus and compress it and cause diffuse inflammation of its wall, even to the point of obstructing the lumen.[305, 453, 454, 496] Daly and colleagues,[120] in their study of endobronchial tuberculosis in children at Bellevue, found this mechanism to be the cause of obstruction in half their patients. Other mechanisms of obstruction include damage to the bronchial cartilage leading to gradual (or rarely, abrupt) perforation of the bronchus and the formation of plugs of semiliquid toothpaste-like caseum that partially or completely occludes the bronchus. In some cases, endobronchial granulomatous tissue forms around the stoma of the fistula and obstructs the lumen.

Three immediate results of bronchial obstruction are possible.[305]

The first is sudden death by asphyxia, fortunately an extremely rare event.[291]

The second is obstructive hyperaeration (also called obstructive emphysema) of a lobar segment, a lobe, or even

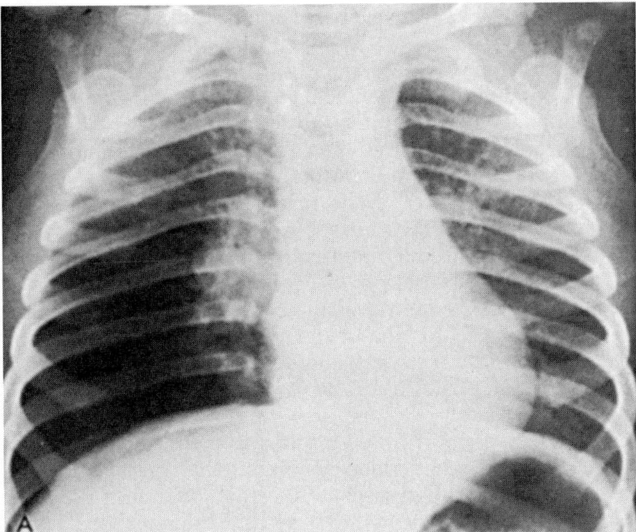

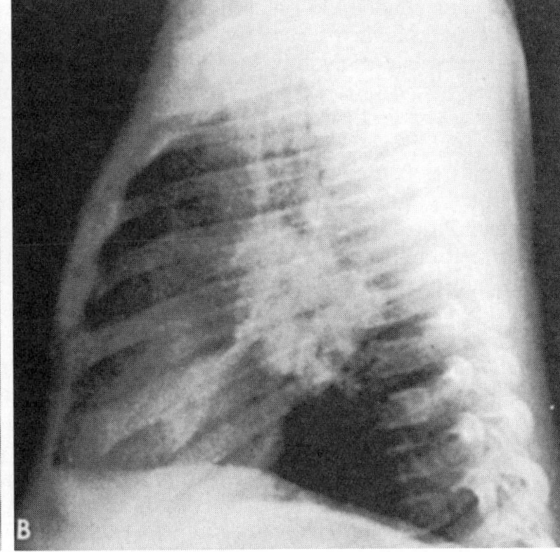

FIGURE 101–7 ■ X-ray film of an 8-month-old girl with obstructive hyperaeration of the right lower lobe as a result of tuberculosis. *A,* Note the hyperlucent right lower lobe and shift of the heart and mediastinum away from the ball valve obstruction to the left. *B,* Note the large hilar lymph nodes, which are compressing the right lower lobe bronchi. Tuberculosis should be considered in patients with hyperaeration of unknown etiology.

an entire lung.[335] This result is unusual (in Walker's series,[561] it occurred in 7 of 538 children with primary tuberculosis of the lungs, whereas half had segmental lesions). When it does occur, it usually affects children younger than 2 years, and it may be accompanied by wheezing. Physical examination generally is of little help; radiographs, best taken on expiration, show hyperaeration, which usually is not accompanied by mediastinal displacement, probably because of fixation by the tuberculous mediastinal nodes (Fig. 101–7). Aspiration of a foreign body always must be considered in the differential diagnosis. The obstruction ultimately resolves by itself; however, corticosteroids may be added to the chemotherapeutic regimen to hasten recovery.[367, 368, 538] Surgical removal of the obstructing nodes has been successful but rarely is performed.[126]

The third possible result of bronchial obstruction is the appearance of a segmental lesion, fan shaped on a radiograph, representing mainly atelectasis, and almost always involving the very segment occupied by the primary pulmonary focus[287, 360] (Fig. 101–8). Actually, the radiographic opacity results from a combination of several elements: the primary pulmonary focus, the caseous material from an eroded bronchus, the inflammatory response elicited by the caseum, and atelectasis. In some instances, acute secondary infection plays a role. Children with secondary bacterial pneumonia often initially have high fever, cough, and rales; the signs and symptoms respond to conventional antibiotics, but the chest radiographic findings usually do not clear because of the underlying tuberculosis. The relative roles of these various elements often cannot be assessed; sometimes

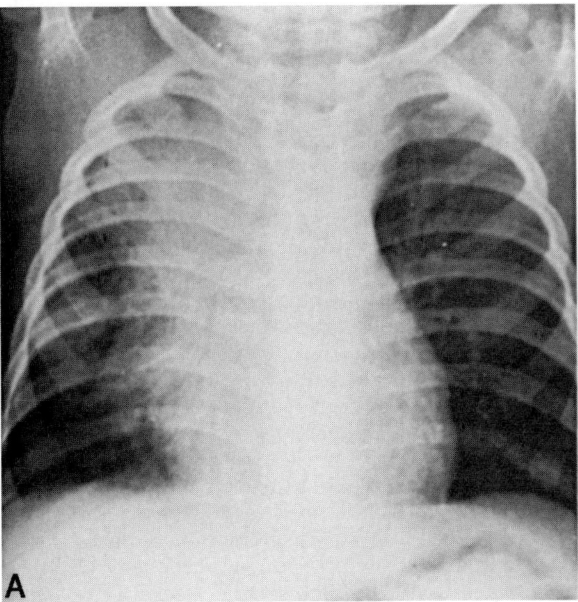

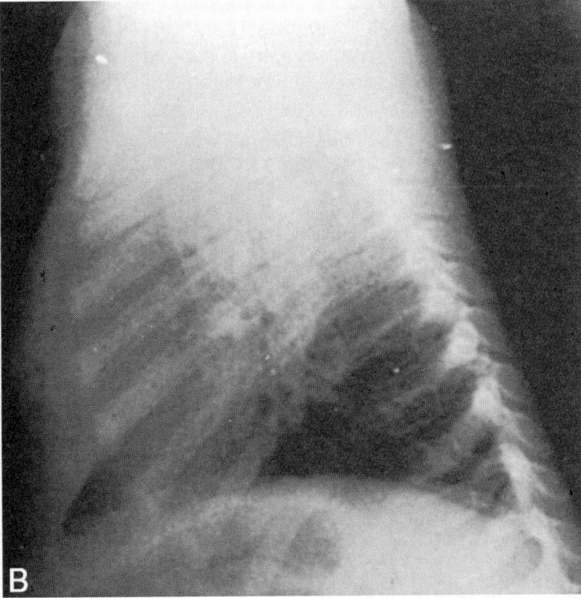

FIGURE 101–8 ■ *A* and *B,* Roentgenograms of an 8-month-old boy with primary tuberculosis infection. The posteroanterior film shows collapse-consolidation of the right upper lobe, hilar and paratracheal adenopathy, and pleural reaction. Note the narrowed right bronchi.

atelectasis is conspicuous, and at other times consolidation is the salient pathologic process, with the volume of the segment undiminished or even increased (hence the descriptive term *collapse-consolidation lesion,* preferred by some clinicians to the less accurate term *atelectasis*).

The percentage of infected children in whom segmental lesions develop has been estimated by several investigators. All agree that the younger the child, the more commonly that collapse-consolidation lesions occur (Table 101–6). The segmental lesion is likely to form during the first 3 to 6 months after acquisition of infection (50 of 65 in Payne's series).[396] Multiple segmental lesions can occur simultaneously (18 of 160 children in Payne's experience). When multiple lesions develop, the segmental lesions usually form in one lung, but occasionally, the lobes or segments of both lungs are affected. Sometimes, segmental lesions and obstructive hyperaeration occur simultaneously. The physical signs and symptoms of segmental lesions—cough, rales, localized wheezing, egophony—are surprisingly meager but are more common in infants because of the smaller size of their airways.

Although segmental lesions and hyperaeration are the most common findings produced by enlarging thoracic lymph nodes, others occur. Enlarged peritracheal nodes may cause stridor and respiratory distress. Subcarinal nodes may impinge on the esophagus and cause difficulty swallowing, followed occasionally by the formation of an esophageal diverticulum, or the nodes may rupture directly into the esophagus and produce a bronchoesophageal fistula. Enlarged lymph nodes may compress the subclavian vein and produce edema of the hand and arm, or they may erode major blood vessels, including the aorta. They also may rupture into the mediastinum and point in the left, or more often the right, supraclavicular fossa. Compression of the left recurrent laryngeal nerve has been reported. Compression of the left phrenic nerve leads to paralysis of the left leaf of the diaphragm in an estimated 0.1 to 0.3 percent of tuberculous children. Rupture into the pericardial sac will be described later.

The late results of bronchial obstruction include the following possibilities: (1) complete re-expansion of the lung and resolution of the radiographic findings; (2) disappearance of the segmental lesion, with residual calcification of the primary focus or the regional lymph nodes; or (3) scarring and progressive contraction of the lobe or segment, usually associated with bronchiectasis.[305] Permanent anatomic sequelae result from segmental lesions in approximately 60 percent of all cases, even though the abnormality usually is not apparent on plain radiographs. Cylindric (rarely saccular) bronchiectasis, sometimes stenoses, and elongation or shortening can be demonstrated on bronchography. Fortunately, most of these abnormalities are asymptomatic in the upper lobes. However, secondary infection may occur in the middle and lower lobes and cause the middle lobe syndrome.[63] Occasionally, the chronic vascularity that accompanies bronchiectasis leads to poor oxygen saturation during exercise and to restricted body growth. In addition, bronchogenic carcinoma may arise years later in the old scarred lesions remaining in the bronchus.

Calcification of the primary complex, when it appears, always results from caseation. In calcified caseum, as in bone, the predominant calcium salt is tribasic calcium phosphate. Calcification of caseous lesions occurs much more readily in children than in adults, probably because children's calcium and phosphorus plasma levels are higher. In the infants who were victims of the Lübeck disaster, autopsy showed calcification to be present as early as 58 days after the onset of massive infection. Payne,[396] in a study of calcification in 299 children from Newcastle-on-Tyne, reported calcification visible on the chest radiographs of 1 child within 6 months of infection, 38 within 12 months, 104 within 18 months, 165 within 24 months, 252 within 3 years, and 299 within 4 years.

Calcium usually is deposited as fine particles and creates a stippled effect (Fig. 101–9), but it may be deposited in large, even enormous masses.[396] Calcification may persist without much change, or it may start resorbing within 5 years and eventually disappear completely. Occasionally, it progresses to ossification with the formation of true bone and functional bone marrow. Calcification, if visible at all on radiographs, most often involves the regional lymph nodes.[58] Sometimes, however, the primary pulmonary focus or the entire primary complex, including the lymphangitis, calcifies (Fig. 101–10).

Calcification took place in 75 to 80 percent of the 525 children with pulmonary tuberculosis monitored by Payne.[396] Currently, extensive calcification occurs uncommonly in the Western world, probably because tuberculous lesions treated early with isoniazid rarely caseate and caseation is a prerequisite for calcification.

Pleural Effusion

Pleural effusion can be localized or generalized, unilateral or bilateral.[303] Localized pleural effusion so frequently accompanies the primary pulmonary focus that it is practically a component of the primary complex. All tuberculous serous effusions probably originate in the discharge of bacilli into the cavity from an adjacent lesion—in the case of the pleura, from a subpleural pulmonary focus or from subpleural caseous lymph nodes. The breakthrough may be small and the pleuritis localized and asymptomatic, or it may occur in the form of a generalized effusion, usually 3 to 6 months after infection occurs (Fig. 101–11). In 75 percent of Wallgren's cases,[565] later calcification of the pulmonary focus or regional lymph nodes proved the effusion to be on the same side as the original primary focus. Seemingly without logical explanation are the following clinical observations: tuberculous pleural effusion is rare in children younger than 2 years and uncommon in children younger than 5 years (perhaps because sensitivity to tuberculin is lower in the very young), is more common in boys than in girls, almost never is associated with a segmental lesion, and rarely is associated with miliary tuberculosis.

The onset of pleurisy usually is abrupt and resembles bacterial pneumonia, with fever, chest pain, shortness of breath, and, on physical examination, dullness to percussion and diminished breath sounds. Fever may be high and, in untreated cases, last for several weeks. Occasionally, it is difficult to differentiate an effusion from an extensive pneumonic lesion; lateral decubitus radiographic views are helpful in confirming the presence of pleural fluid.

TABLE 101–6 ■ PERCENTAGE OF TUBERCULIN CONVERTERS AND AGE AT WHICH SEGMENTAL LESIONS (SL) DEVELOP

Age at Infection (yr)	Converters with SL		Total Converters (No.)
	No.	*%*	
0–1	77	43	180
1–5	35	24	147
6–10	31	25	121
11–15	16	16	97
Total	159	29	545

After Payne, M., quoted by Miller, F. J. W., Seale, R. M. E., and Taylor, M. D.: Tuberculosis in Children. Boston, Little, Brown, 1963.

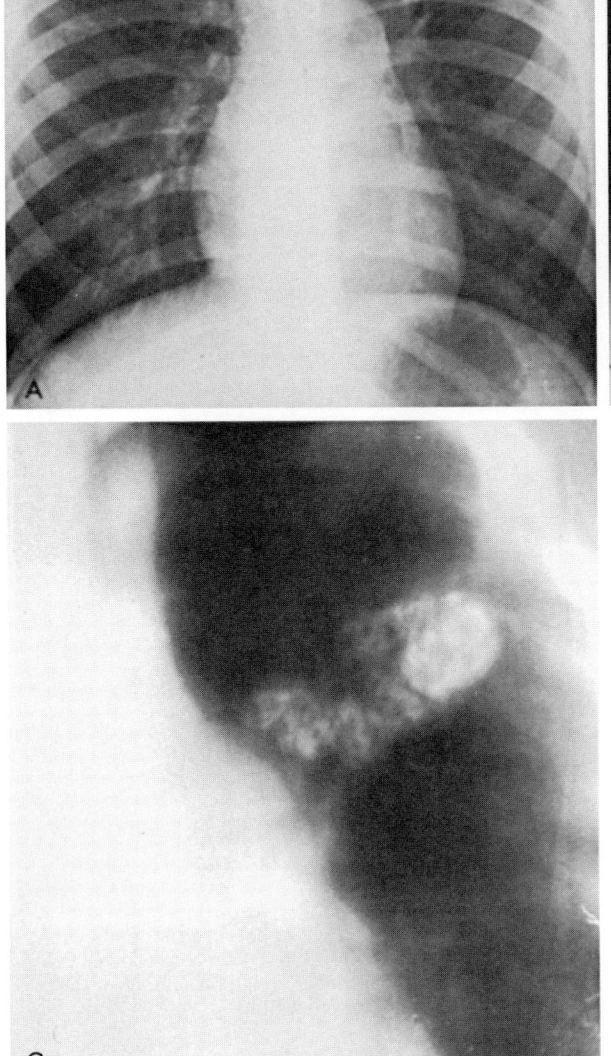

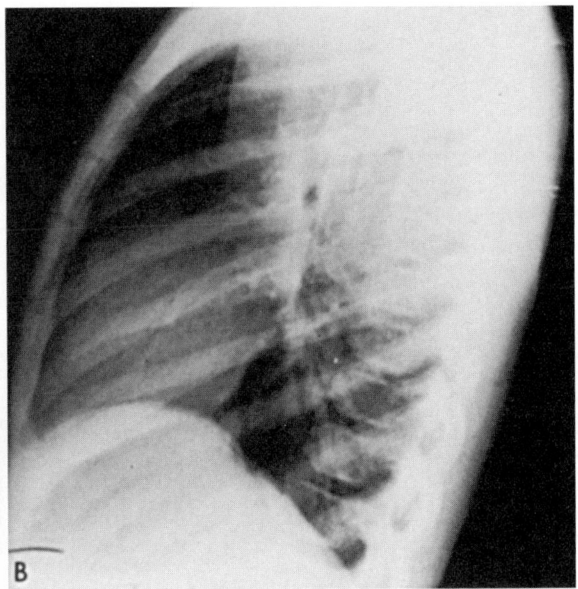

FIGURE 101–9 ■ Film of a 7-year-old boy with a calcified left upper lobe, primary complex. *A,* Posteroanterior film of the chest. *B,* Lateral film of the chest. Note the fine granular calcific pattern, which clearly is seen on the tomogram *(C).*

Thoracentesis is, of course, the essential diagnostic procedure. The puncture should be made in the area shown on the radiograph to have the greatest fluid accumulation. No more than 30 mL of pleural fluid should be withdrawn; otherwise, the protein loss from this usually protein-rich fluid may be considerable. The fluid generally is greenish-yellow, occasionally blood tinged, with a specific gravity of 1.012 to 1.022, a high protein content, and often a low glucose level (<30 mg/dL), and it has several hundred white cells per cubic millimeter with a predominance of neutrophils or lymphocytes, depending on the age of the effusion. The cells in tuberculous pleural effusion are predominantly T lymphocytes, which are present in higher proportion than in blood.[158, 468] Tubercle bacilli generally are present in such small numbers that results from direct smears and cultures are apt to be disappointing; smears almost always are negative, and pleural fluid cultures are positive in less than 30 percent of cases. Pleural punch biopsy is a useful diagnostic procedure because both the finding of typical tubercles on histologic study and culture of the tiny "plug" from the trocar are much more likely to establish the diagnosis than is culture of pleural fluid.[299, 316]

The prognosis for children with tuberculous effusion always has been relatively good when compared with that for other overt forms of tuberculosis, even in the days before chemotherapy.[307, 316] Permanent impairment of pulmonary function is surprisingly uncommon after pleural effusion.[167] The development of scoliosis is a remote possibility and should be guarded against while the patient recovers.

Progressive Pulmonary Tuberculosis

In this serious complication of the primary complex, the primary pulmonary focus, instead of resolving or calcifying, enlarges steadily and develops a large caseous center. This center then liquefies and empties into an adjacent

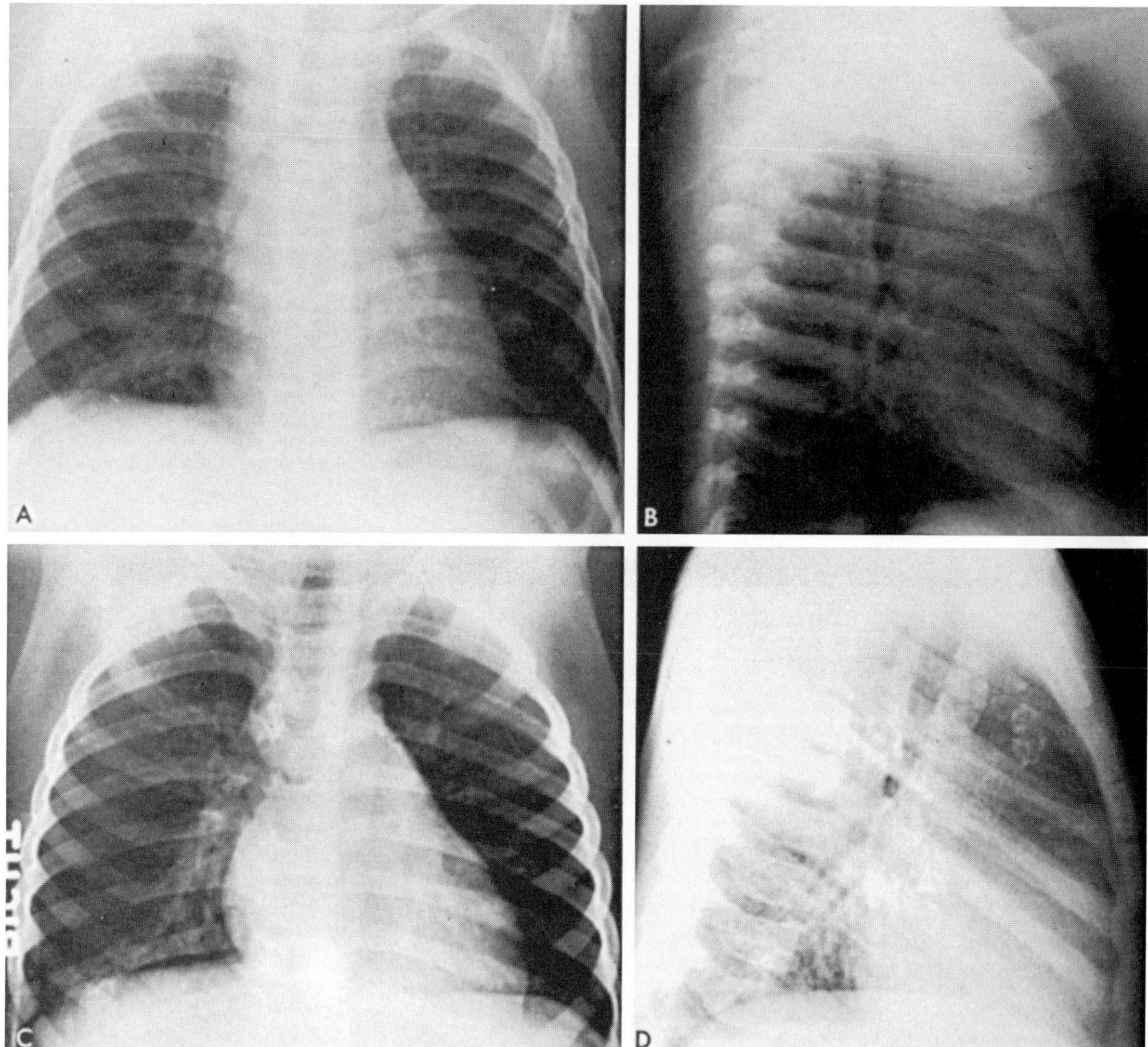

FIGURE 101–10 ■ *A* and *B*, Roentgenograms of a 7-month-old girl with mild fullness of the right upper mediastinum and a hazy infiltrate in the right lower lobe. A skin test for tuberculosis was positive. She was treated for tuberculosis and clinically improved. *C*, The same patient 3.5 years later has a calcified primary complex in the right upper and lower lobes over the diaphragm. *D*, The anterior location of the upper lobe complex is seen clearly on the lateral chest film.

bronchus to create a "primary cavity"[528] (Fig. 101–12); the liquefaction is associated with particularly large numbers of tubercle bacilli. The tubercle bacilli further disseminate to other parts of the lobe and to the entire lung, where other foci of infection form. On rare occasion, an enlarging primary focus ruptures into the pleural cavity and creates a pneumothorax, bronchopleural fistula, or caseous pyopneumothorax or into the pericardial sac or the mediastinum.

Whereas clinical symptoms often are minimal when the primary focus is uncomplicated, a progressive lesion often is accompanied by more severe fever, cough, malaise, and weight loss, as well as classic signs of cavitation such as egophony.[444] Before chemotherapy, the inability to contain the primary focus was associated with a grave outlook: 25 to 65 percent of patients thus affected died. Now, with appropriate treatment, the prognosis is good.

It may be difficult to distinguish between progressive pulmonary tuberculosis and a simple tuberculous focus with a superimposed acute bacterial pneumonia caused by *Staphylococcus, Klebsiella,* or anaerobes. Antimicrobial agents effective against these pathogens may be indicated, in addition to appropriate antituberculosis drugs. Sometimes, especially during convalescence from pulmonary parenchymal lesions, bullous lesions appear and persist for several months. They seem to be associated, in children as in adults, either with "tears" in damaged alveolar walls or with the emptying of caseum out of cavities.[335]

Chronic Pulmonary Tuberculosis

Chronic pulmonary tuberculosis, sometimes referred to as adult or reactivation tuberculosis, is the type of disease seen in pulmonary tissue sensitized and immunized by an earlier tuberculosis infection. For many years, ongoing debate centered around whether the lesions of chronic pulmonary tuberculosis, more localized than those of the initial tuberculous lesion and less likely to spread to lymph nodes and the bloodstream, were due to "endogenous reinfection." Evidence has accumulated during subsequent decades that endogenous reinfection is the usual event.[507] However, reinfection with a different strain of *M. tuberculosis* has been documented and may be more common in areas where tuberculosis is quite prevalent.[475]

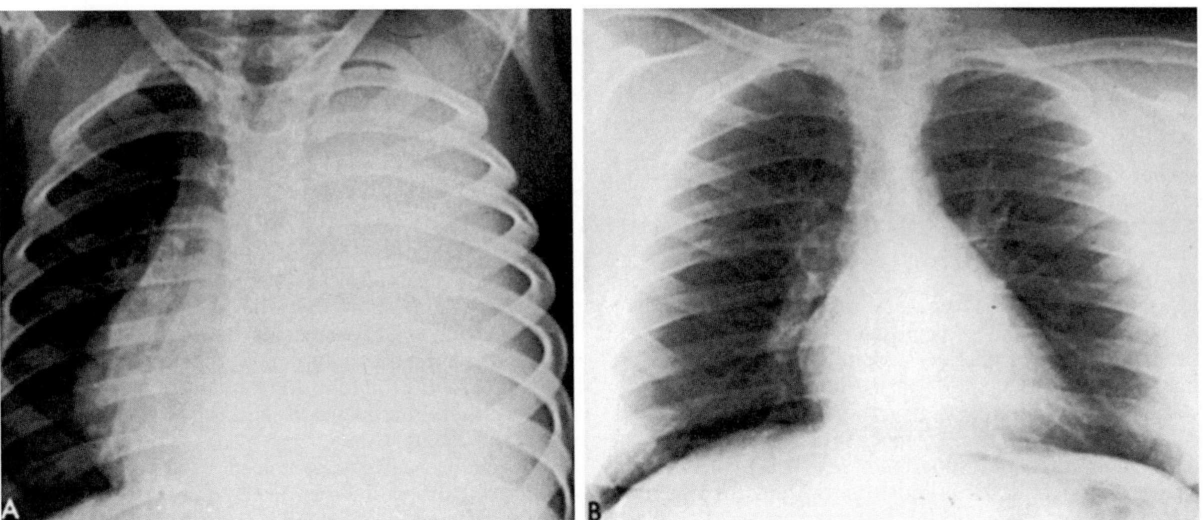

FIGURE 101–11 ■ Roentgenograms of a 5-year-old boy with massive left pleural effusion caused by tuberculosis. *A,* Posteroanterior film of the chest. *B,* The same patient 6 years later with a normal chest film and no physical complaint.

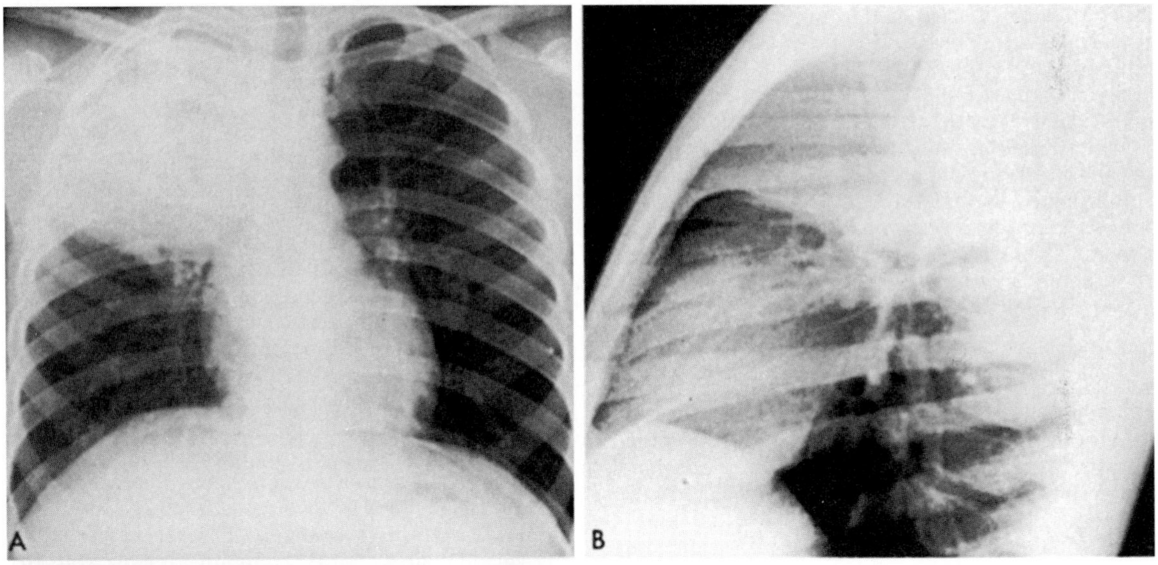

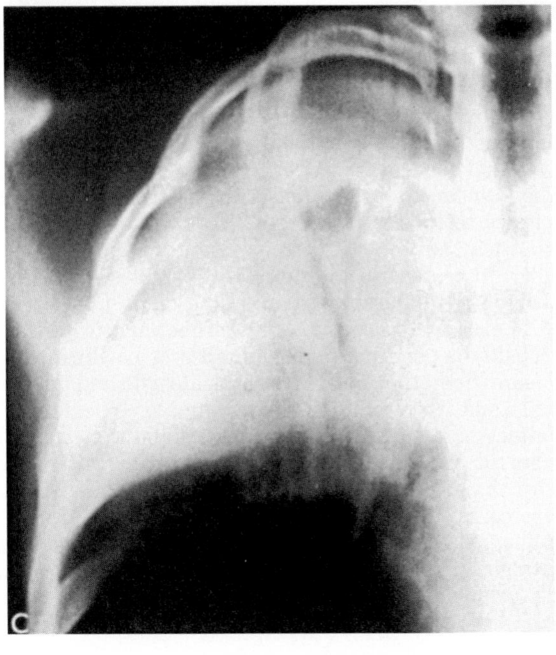

FIGURE 101–12 ■ Tuberculosis in a 9-year-old boy with an expanding right upper lobe consolidation. *A,* Posteroanterior film of the chest. *B,* Lateral film of the chest. *C,* A tomogram shows an air bronchogram and a cystic cavitary lesion.

Careful long-term studies of children have revealed a continuum of involvement in many cases: first the primary focus, followed within a few years in some patients by infraclavicular small round foci in the lung apices that often were calcified (Assmann foci, Simon foci) and thought to result from hematogenous spread at the time of initial infection. Later, these foci disappear spontaneously or remain visible as tiny calcifications or as larger "round foci," which may, if untreated, progress to the typical lesions of chronic pulmonary tuberculosis.

Even before the discovery of antituberculosis drugs, chronic pulmonary tuberculosis was a rare occurence in children (6–7% in the Lincoln and colleagues' series[304] of closely monitored patients at Bellevue Hospital). It appears more frequently in children in the lower socioeconomic strata of society and more frequently in girls than boys. Chronic pulmonary tuberculosis rarely develops in children who survive with a healed, untreated tuberculosis infection acquired before 2 years of age, but it is much more frequent in children who acquire their initial infection after 7 years of age and particularly if they become infected close to the onset of puberty. In the latter case, the "adult" type of lesion often develops in the very lobe where the primary lesion occurred. In this situation, progressive pulmonary tuberculosis cannot be differentiated from chronic pulmonary tuberculosis. Now, with effective treatment, such differentiation is unimportant.[200]

Cough, fever of unknown origin, chest pain, hemoptysis, and supraclavicular adenitis are the most common clinical manifestations. Essential diagnostic procedures are the tuberculin skin test and appropriate chest radiographs, often including such special procedures as tomograms or lordotic views. An intense search for tubercle bacilli must be made in sputum, gastric washings, and, if necessary, secretions obtained by bronchoscopy.

Myocardial and Pericardial Tuberculosis

Tubercles often are found in the heart in miliary tuberculosis, and although it is exceedingly rare, myocardial caseation has been described, usually secondary to direct spread from mediastinal glands and accompanied by paroxysmal tachycardia or arrhythmias.[566]

Tuberculous pericarditis, though more common than is symptomatic tuberculous myocarditis, occurred in only 0.4 percent of 2500 children monitored by Lincoln and Sewell[307] at Bellevue and in 4 percent of 200 children in Boyd's series.[56] It occurs more commonly in males than in females. In most cases, tuberculous pericarditis probably arises by direct invasion or by lymphatic drainage from caseous lymph nodes in the subcarinal area or from nodes close to the ductus arteriosus, with resulting exudation of hemorrhagic fluid and the development of granulation tissue on both the parietal and visceral surfaces of the pericardium.[429] Pericardial fluid may be serofibrinous or hemorrhagic; tubercle bacilli rarely are found on smears.[226] Sometimes, extensive fibrosis leads to obliteration of the pericardial sac, with the development, usually years later, of constrictive pericarditis.

The initial symptoms generally are nonspecific: low-grade fever, poor appetite, failure to gain weight, and, rarely, chest pain. On examination, a pericardial friction rub may be heard, or if a large effusion already is present, distant heart sounds, tachycardia, and a narrow pulse pressure may suggest the diagnosis. The diagnosis then is confirmed by radiography, echocardiography, electrocardiography, tuberculin skin test, and aspiration of fluid for culture. Before the advent of chemotherapy, approximately half the patients succumbed. Now, with appropriate drugs and possibly corticosteroids to diminish the size of the effusion[515] and also occasional partial pericardiectomy, the outlook is excellent.

Lymphohematogenous Spread

Tubercle bacilli from the lymphadenitis of the primary complex are disseminated during the incubation period in all cases of tuberculosis infection. The results of liver biopsy of young asymptomatic tuberculin converters (indicating recent infection) show that the liver always is involved.[105] Tubercle bacilli can reach deep, distant organs via the bloodstream or lymphatic channels. Autopsies on individuals who have died soon after development of initial infection show that bacilli often are deposited in the liver, spleen, skin, and apical pulmonary tissue.

The clinical picture produced by lymphohematogenous spread probably is determined by host susceptibility at the time of spread and by the quantity of tubercle bacilli released.[553] Three clinical forms can be recognized:

1. The lymphohematogenous spread may be occult, in which case it usually remains so, or it may be occult initially with metastatic, extrapulmonary lesions appearing months or years later (for example, renal tuberculosis).[422]
2. So-called protracted hematogenous tuberculosis, rarely seen today, is characterized by high, spiking fever, marked leukocytosis, hepatomegaly and splenomegaly, and general glandular enlargement, sometimes with repeated evidence of metastatic seeding in the choroid, kidneys, and skin. Calcifications may appear subsequently, often in large numbers, in the pulmonary apices (Simon foci) and in the spleen, thus attesting to the earlier dissemination of tubercle bacilli via blood. The tuberculin skin test usually is strongly positive. Bone marrow biopsy may confirm the clinical impression, but treatment often must be started on a presumptive basis. Although this type of tuberculosis in past years often ended tragically in tuberculous meningitis, today, it is completely treatable if diagnosed in time.
3. The third form of lymphohematogenous spread, analogous to sepsis with pyogenic bacteria, is miliary tuberculosis.[228] It usually arises from discharge of a caseous focus, often a lymph node, into a blood vessel such as a pulmonary vein; it may be self-propagating, with repeated discharge arising at various sites. Most common during the first 2 to 6 months after infection in infancy, it can arise even in adults who have apparently well-healed, calcified lesions.[271, 452, 579]

Miliary disease provides a striking illustration of the difference in susceptibility of tissue to tubercle bacilli; tubercles tend to be larger and more numerous in the lung, spleen, liver, and bone marrow than in the heart, pancreas, and brain. The number of fixed intravascular phagocytes, as well as the relative tortuosity of the smaller blood vessels themselves, must play an important role in determining tissue susceptibility. In acute caseating miliary tuberculosis, the lesions are likely to be numerous and sometimes almost coalescent.

The clinical picture of miliary tuberculosis varies greatly, probably depending on the number of bacilli in the bloodstream. Sometimes, the patient is afebrile and appears to be well, and the condition is diagnosed by chance during contact investigation of another individual with infectious tuberculosis. The onset can be insidious, often occurring after the patient has had another precipitating infection. In rare cases, the onset is abrupt. Drowsiness, loss of weight and appetite, persistent fever, weakness, rapid breathing with a rustling sound on auscultation of the lungs, occasionally cyanosis, and almost always a palpable spleen are the clinical manifestations that lead the clinician to obtain a chest radiograph.

Usually within no more than 3 weeks after the onset of symptoms, tubercles, sometimes tiny and at times large, can be seen evenly distributed throughout both lung fields[387]; in the early stages, they often are detected best on a lateral view of the retrocardiac space (Fig. 101–13). The incidence of choroidal tubercles varies greatly; it has been reported variously as 13 and 87 percent. Recurrent pneumothorax, subcutaneous emphysema, pneumomediastinum, and pleural effusion are less serious, but well-recognized complications of miliary tuberculosis. Second attacks have been reported.[579] Cutaneous lesions, including painful nodules, papulonecrotic tuberculids, and purpuric lesions, may appear in crops.[266]

The diagnosis usually is established by means of the clinical picture and a chest radiograph; sometimes it is confirmed by a liver or skin biopsy; by culturing *M. tuberculosis* from the gastric aspirate, urine, or bone marrow[105, 203]; or by fiberoptic bronchoscopy and transbronchial biopsy.[67] Treatment usually is very successful.

EXTRATHORACIC SPREAD

Central Nervous System Tuberculosis[499]

Tubercle bacilli are distributed by the bloodstream into all parts of the central nervous system during lymphohematogenous spread.[306] Surprisingly, they do not multiply as well in nervous tissue as in other areas such as the lung. Thus, central nervous system tuberculosis, though an early manifestation of infection, usually does not appear simultaneously with miliary spread, but days later. The tubercle bacilli can affect the central nervous system in various ways[547, 560] and produce tuberculous meningitis,[232, 519] serous meningitis,[301, 547] tuberculoma,[380, 547] or tuberculous brain abscess, or it can affect mainly the spinal cord and cause spinal tuberculous leptomeningitis.[539]

Tuberculous meningitis arises from caseous foci, often very small ones, situated in the brain or meninges.[423] In time, the caseous foci discharge tubercle bacilli directly into the subarachnoid space. The thick, gelatinous exudate lies in the meshes of the pia-arachnoid in the brain, where it infiltrates the walls of meningeal arteries and veins and produces inflammation, caseation, and obstruction; the exudate can extend along small vessels into the cortex, where it causes occlusion and produces infarcts. This same exudate interferes with normal flow of cerebrospinal fluid in and out of the ventricular system and with absorption of the fluid by the pacchionian bodies. The predilection of the exudate for the base of the brain accounts for the frequent involvement of the third, sixth, and seventh nerves and the optic chiasm. The combination of vascular lesions producing infarcts,[298] interference with cerebrospinal fluid flow resulting in hydrocephalus, and direct cranial nerve involvement, especially of the eye, causes the devastating damage that all too often results from tuberculous meningitis.

Tuberculous meningitis has been estimated to develop in 1 of every 300 untreated infections.[241] Practically never seen in infants younger than 4 months, it is most common in children younger than 6 years, usually appears within 2 to 6 months after initial infection, and accompanies miliary tuberculosis in about 50 percent of cases. Tuberculosis should be suspected as the cause of meningitis that is accompanied by cranial nerve involvement, hydrocephalus, or evidence of inflammation at the base of the brain.

The onset of tuberculous meningitis usually is gradual and occurs over a period of approximately 3 weeks; in some cases it seems to be precipitated by a viral infection, a fall, or a blow on the head. Occasionally, the onset is abrupt and marked by a convulsion. A convenient approach is for the clinician to divide the course into three stages.[232] The first stage is characterized by personality change, irritability, anorexia, listlessness, and some fever. After 1 or 2 weeks, the disease passes into the second stage, when signs of increased intracranial pressure and cerebral damage appear: drowsiness, stiff neck,

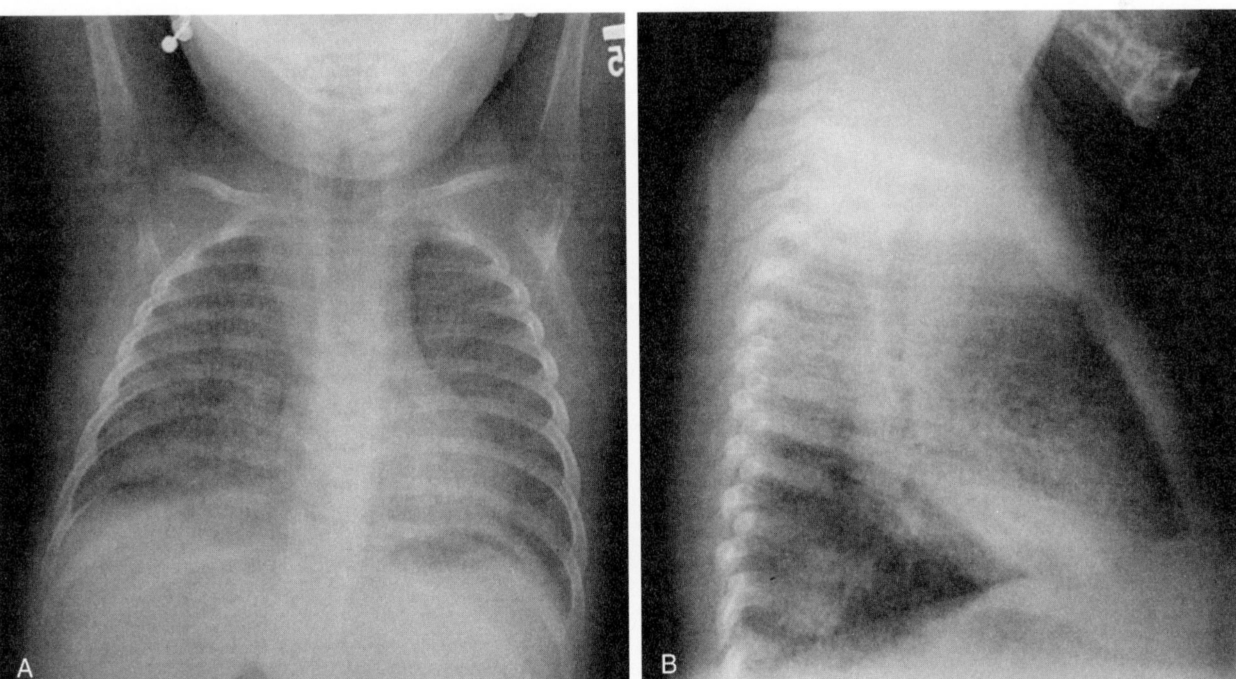

FIGURE 101–13 ■ Miliary tuberculosis in an infant. The numerous tubercles can be seen on both the posteroanterior *(A)* and lateral *(B)* views.

cranial nerve palsies, inequality of the pupils, vomiting, tache cérébrale, absence of the abdominal reflexes, and convulsions that may be tonic or clonic, focal, or generalized. The third stage is characterized by coma, irregular pulse and respirations, and rising fever. Occasionally, papilledema is noted.

Aids in diagnosis are a history of contact with an adult who has tuberculosis (however, the family history of tuberculosis often is "negative" because the incubation period of meningitis is short and the contagious adult has not been discovered yet[133]); a tuberculin skin test (positive in only 50% of cases); positive tuberculin skin tests in siblings; a chest radiograph, which often reveals pulmonary disease; and changes and the characteristic findings from spinal fluid. However, ventricular cerebrospinal fluid may be relatively normal because it is obtained proximal to the site of inflammation. The lumbar spinal fluid usually is clear and under substantially increased pressure. It will contain 50 to 500 white blood cells/mm^3, with polymorphonuclear leukocytes predominant early and lymphocytes predominant later. The spinal fluid glucose level may be at the lower limits of normal if the patient is examined early in the second stage, and it falls by 5 mg or so each day; by the third stage it usually is very low. The protein content may be normal at the time of the first spinal tap, but it rises steadily to very high concentrations, at which time a pellicle will develop on the fluid on standing. Tubercle bacilli may be found in the pellicle but are scarce at best. Only approximately 50 percent of cases of tuberculous meningitis in children can be confirmed by spinal fluid culture. Gastric washings should be cultured, not only to confirm the diagnosis in retrospect but also to permit drug susceptibility testing of the organisms.[580]

Computed tomography or magnetic resonance imaging[192, 383] is recommended for the evaluation of all patients with tuberculous meningitis. Both permit recognition and follow-up of tuberculomas,[546, 578] infarction, or vasculitis, and hydrocephalus that might require shunting.[116, 247, 514]

Profound abnormalities in the electrolyte pattern of intracellular and extracellular fluid and spinal fluid have been reported in patients with tuberculous meningitis.[410] These abnormalities consist mainly of low sodium and chloride levels, with low or normal plasma potassium levels, accompanied by high sodium levels in red cells and skeletal muscle.[201] High levels of antidiuretic hormone (syndrome of "inappropriate" antidiuretic hormone secretion) may cause hypotonic expansion of the extracellular fluid. Because intense vomiting and dehydration usually accompany tuberculous meningitis, the electrolyte disturbances usually include severe hypochloremia. Salt wasting in the urine occurs in rare cases. Determination of the spinal fluid chloride concentration is useless because it merely reflects the plasma level.

A good prognosis depends on immediate treatment without awaiting epidemiologic and bacteriologic confirmation of the diagnosis.[227] Before chemotherapy was used, every case of true tuberculous meningitis was fatal within 3 to 4 weeks, whereas today, appropriate treatment during the first stage allows survival in nearly every case, although the patient's intelligence may never return to its previous level. When initiated during the second stage, treatment results in survival in 75 percent or more of patients. If patients in coma when treatment is begun, they rarely recover unscathed. Very young age and the occurrence of convulsions generally are poor prognostic factors. Hydrocephalus, usually of the communicating type, occurs frequently (38% in one series) and is largely responsible for poor outcomes. Relieving the hydrocephalus surgically appears to improve the sensorium, vision, and neurologic deficit. Studies support the early use of ventriculoperitoneal shunting in patients severely ill at the time of admission.[288, 390] Infarcts caused by vasculitis also can leave catastrophic residua. The role of corticosteroids in the treatment of intracranial tuberculosis is discussed later in this chapter.

The long-term sequelae of tuberculous meningitis are numerous and include blindness, deafness, intracranial calcification, diabetes insipidus, obesity, paraplegia, and mental retardation.[317]

Serous tuberculous meningitis is uncommon (13% of 500 cases in the experience of Udani and associates[547]). Apparently, it develops when a tuberculous focus close to the subarachnoid space causes a lymphocytic reaction in the subarachnoid space without the actual presence of tubercle bacilli.[583] In the days before the advent of chemotherapy, "serous" meningitis was differentiated readily from "true" tuberculous meningitis because the former was the only nonfatal form of tuberculous meningitis. Today, such differentiation is no longer possible because treatment is begun immediately, so true tuberculous meningitis does not develop.

Tuberculoma is manifested clinically as a brain tumor.[24, 125, 135] As many as 30 percent of brain tumors are tuberculomas, depending on the incidence of tuberculosis in the particular population under study (in India, for instance). Tuberculomas occur most often in children younger than 10 years of age and often are located at the base of the brain around the cerebellum.[563] In contrast, tuberculomas in adults more often are supratentorial. Headache, convulsions, fever, and other symptoms and signs usually associated with brain abscess or tumor also characterize tuberculoma. Only careful evaluation, including inquiry about exposure to tuberculosis, a tuberculin skin test, chest radiography, and computed tomography, will permit recognition of these cases in time to begin appropriate chemotherapy before neurosurgical intervention is needed. A fairly recently recognized phenomenon is a symptomatic intracranial tuberculoma appearing and enlarging during treatment of meningeal, miliary, and even pulmonary tuberculosis.[5, 296, 414, 466, 533] This phenomenon appears to be mediated immunologically; it usually responds to corticosteroids and does not necessitate a change in antituberculosis chemotherapy. In addition, some small children with severe pulmonary or disseminated tuberculosis have one or several tuberculomas but a normal spinal fluid evaluation.[133, 243] Computed tomography or magnetic resonance imaging of the head should be performed whenever neurologic signs or symptoms accompany tuberculosis.

Tuberculous brain abscess is a rarely reported form of central nervous system tuberculosis that tends to occur at an older age than tuberculoma does.[283, 574] Pathologically, the lesion lacks the giant-cell and granulomatous reaction associated with tuberculoma. Focal neurologic signs occur commonly. Computed tomography and magnetic resonance imaging, if used routinely in cases of tuberculous meningitis, may permit more frequent recognition of this type of abscess, which requires surgical intervention as well as chemotherapy. Intramedullary tuberculoma of the spinal cord is exceedingly rare.[248, 323] It can be manifested as recurrent abdominal pain.[46, 380]

Spinal tuberculous leptomeningitis occurs more often in older children and adults than in infants[318]; in Udani and coworkers' series[547] of 500 cases, only 2 percent fell into this last age group. Protein levels in the spinal fluid are elevated substantially, and sometimes partial or total block may be noted on myelography. Exudate may completely surround the spinal cord.

Cutaneous Tuberculosis

The manifestations of cutaneous tuberculosis can be classified in children according to a modification of the earlier classifications designed for adults[281]: (1) lesions produced by inoculation from an exogenous source[403, 457] in a previously uninfected child, in a previously infected child, or after inoculation with BCG vaccine; (2) lesions resulting from hematogenous dissemination[266]; (3) lesions arising from an endogenous source; and (4) erythema nodosum. A newer classification has been proposed and perhaps is more useful for adults than for children.[45]

Skin lesions associated with the primary complex may be caused by direct inoculation of tubercle bacilli into a traumatized area, such as a lesion on the sole of a child's bare foot, a mosquito bite on the face, an abraded elbow, or the foreskin at the time of ritual circumcision. The initial skin focus usually is a small, painless nodule, sometimes with tiny satellite lesions that soon turn into indolent ulcers without surrounding inflammation. The most striking feature is regional lymphadenitis, which often is what convinces the patient to see a physician. Fever and systemic reactions generally are minimal; low-grade pyogenic infection and cat-scratch fever (*Bartonella* infection) always must be considered in the differential diagnosis. A strongly positive tuberculin skin test usually is obtained. Needle aspiration and culture may differentiate disease caused by *M. tuberculosis* from that caused by environmental mycobacteria.

Scrofuloderma indicates tuberculosis of the skin overlying a caseous lymph node (most often in the cervical area) that has ruptured to the outside and left either a shallow ulcer or a deep sinus, sometimes surrounded by a cluster of nodules. In the past, scrofuloderma was a frequent manifestation of tuberculosis in children and usually left extensive scars. Today, it is a rare occurence because the diagnosis generally is made before node rupture. Chemotherapy often forestalls the need for surgical excision.

Manifestations that result from hematogenous dissemination are papulonecrotic tuberculids and tuberculosis verrucosa cutis. Papulonecrotic tuberculids[472] are miliary tubercles in the skin that usually appear as tiny papules with "apple-jelly" centers, most often on the trunk, thighs, and face. They frequently are similar to papular urticaria or early varicella lesions, or they may be confused with the skin lesions of Letterer-Siwe disease. Skin biopsy provides a reliable diagnosis. Lupus vulgaris is a rare form of chronic, indolent tuberculosis, usually on the face, that often seems to evolve from tuberculids, very rarely at the site of BCG inoculation.

Tuberculosis verrucosa cutis is a condition characterized by large (several centimeters in diameter) papulonecrotic tuberculids. The lesions usually appear on the arms, legs, or buttocks, suggesting that trauma may play some part in their causation. Fungal infection is the main consideration in the differential diagnosis.

Erythema nodosum formerly was a common manifestation of hypersensitivity to tuberculin. It occurs mostly in young teenage girls. Usually beginning with fever and systemic toxicity soon after initial infection, erythema nodosum is characterized by large, deep, painful, indurated nodules on the shins and sometimes on the thighs, elbows, and forearms. The nodules gradually change from light pink to a bruise-like color. Erythema nodosum is not specific for tuberculosis but also occurs with streptococcal and meningococcal infections, histoplasmosis, coccidioidomycosis, sarcoidosis, drug sensitivity reactions, and perhaps cat-scratch disease. Tuberculin hypersensitivity is pronounced in children with tuberculosis underlying erythema nodosum, and tuberculin skin testing should be performed with caution. These patients may or may not have associated tuberculous lesions, but some clinicians believe that these patients have a greater chance of suffering complications. Skin biopsy reveals only nonspecific changes regardless of cause and, therefore, is useless in diagnosis. Both fever and nodules clear within 2 or 3 weeks.

Skeletal Tuberculosis

Bone and joint tuberculosis can be expected in 1 to 5 percent of children whose initial infection with tubercle bacilli is untreated. Usually, the tubercle bacilli are disseminated to skeletal structures during lymphohematogenous spread of the initial infection.[31] The disease becomes symptomatic during the first 1 to 3 years after infection. Each of the most frequently involved bones and joints has a characteristic "incubation period" (e.g., 1 month for dactylitis but about 30 months for tuberculosis of the hip). In very young children, blood flow through growing bone is intense; consequently, they suffer from skeletal tuberculosis more often than older children do. The lesion usually starts as an area of endarteritis in the metaphysis of the long bone, where the blood supply is particularly abundant; lesions can be single or multiple.[412, 464] Bone infection can be initiated by two other mechanisms, particularly in the vertebrae: (1) direct extension via the lymphatics from a caseous paravertebral lymph node[68] and (2) direct local hematogenous or lymphatic extension from a neighboring bone. As bone is destroyed progressively by pressure necrosis and cold abscess formation, a nearby joint may become involved.[413, 550, 562]

The bones most often affected are the vertebrae.[386] In one study of 1074 patients with the disease, 440 had involvement of the vertebrae; 89, the knee; 81, the hip; and 51, the elbow.[543] The upper extremities and non–weight-bearing bones, such as the skull, clavicle, and mandible, rarely are involved.[202, 205] Often a history of trauma is present and may play some part in activating an underlying lesion or may serve simply to draw attention to the process.

Tuberculous spondylitis, or tuberculosis of the vertebrae, frequently affects the thoracic vertebrae, particularly the 12th one.[207, 209] In one series of 64 cases of spinal tuberculosis in children, the lesions were in the thoracic area in 24 children, in the lumbar area in 19, and in both areas in 13. Cervical involvement is a rare finding.[222] Most often, 2 vertebrae are involved, but sometimes 3, 4, or even as many as 11 (usually contiguous, but at times with "skips") are affected. The body of the vertebra is affected far more often than is the spinous processes or the arch.

The progression of tuberculous spondylitis, as seen on radiographs, is from slight narrowing of the disk space with only minimal disk involvement and slight collapse and "wedging" of the vertebral body; to marked narrowing of the disk space with collapse, wedging of the bodies, and resulting angulation of the spine (gibbus); to extensive destruction of the bodies with severe kyphosis (Pott disease).

Paravertebral abscess (Pott abscess), retropharyngeal abscess, psoas abscess, and neurologic lesions are serious complications to be expected in 10 to 30 percent of cases of spondylitis. Neurologic complications most often arise from cervical and lumbar vertebral lesions and consist of various degrees of neuroplegia, paraplegia, or even quadriplegia. The complications are caused by inflammation of the spinal cord secondary to a neighboring cold abscess, by caseum or granuloma in the extradural space, or by spinal vessel thrombosis.

The signs and symptoms of spondylitis include "night cries" and restless sleep, a low-grade daily fever, and a peculiar position (such as torticollis with cervical lesions) or gait. Findings on physical examination may include marked "guarding" because of dorsal muscle spasm, pain when the back is "pounded," a deformity (such as gibbus), or reflex changes (including clonus). Occasionally, the presence of referred chest pain leads to discovery of a paravertebral abscess on the chest radiograph. With chemotherapy and, when necessary, surgery, the outlook for both eventual clinical healing and neural recovery is in the range of 80 to 90 percent, although patients may not gain their full expected height.

Tuberculosis of the knee can be divided into several clinical types[208]: (1) effusion into the joint without bone erosion and with little restriction of motion, (2) thickening and fibrosis of the synovial membrane without bone erosion but often with considerable restriction of motion, (3) synovial disease and a bone focus but an intact joint space, and (4) synovial disease with diminished range of motion.[40, 562] Some degree of pain, stiffness, and limping, usually intermittent in milder cases, first calls attention to the problem.

Tuberculosis of the hip, in some series of patients more common than tuberculosis of the knee, should be considered in the differential diagnosis when a child refuses to walk or a limp develops. Nowadays, when the disease still is limited at the time of discovery to the acetabulum or to the head of the femur and no intra-articular disease is present, good mobility of the joint usually can be preserved.

Tuberculous dactylitis (spina ventosa)[197] is the most common form of skeletal tuberculosis in infants. Endarteritis is followed by swelling (often painless), and cystic bone lesions are seen on radiographs. A cold abscess may form and drain spontaneously. The prognosis for recovery without deformity is surprisingly good and was so even before chemotherapy was available.

Tuberculous arthritis is a rare finding in children.[119] Usually monarticular, it involves primarily the weight-bearing joints and only exceptionally the joints of the upper extremities.[40] Bacterial cultures and histologic examination of the synovium establish the diagnosis.[562]

The diagnosis of skeletal tuberculosis should be considered immediately in any child who is known to have been infected with tubercle bacilli and in whom a bone or joint lesion develops and in any child with a persistent, not otherwise explained bone or joint lesion.[557] The differential diagnosis must include low-grade infections caused by *Staphylococcus, Haemophilus influenzae, Salmonella,* and *Brucella;* fungal infections; rheumatoid arthritis; malignant disease of bone; eosinophilic granuloma (particularly with skull or pelvic lesions); and osteochondrosis resulting from aseptic necrosis of bone (particularly Legg-Calvé-Perthes disease and tuberculosis of the hip).

Children with bone and joint tuberculosis usually react strongly to tuberculin. Although the number of tubercle bacilli in an active bone lesion is much lower than in a lung lesion, the organisms almost invariably can be recovered on culture, and a great effort to do so should be made by means of aspiration or open biopsy.[191]

Treatment of skeletal tuberculosis includes both chemotherapeutic and orthopedic interventions, the former by far the more important. Orthopedic procedures can be used for several purposes: (1) diagnosis, (2) evacuation of caseum and necrotic bone, (3) immobilization of a joint, and (4) reconstruction or strengthening of damaged bone. Since the advent of chemotherapy, any indicated surgical procedure can be performed without fear of subsequent sinus formation. However, the trend has been toward reliance on drug therapy with increasingly conservative surgical management. Controlled trials of treatment undertaken in different parts of the world by the Medical Research Council Working Party on Tuberculosis of the Spine and others have demonstrated the remarkable effectiveness of ambulatory treatment with different regimens of chemotherapy in children and adults,[234, 339–341] including short-course chemotherapy.[195]

Tuberculosis of the Superficial Lymph Nodes (Scrofula)

Striking enlargement of the superficial regional lymph nodes is an integral component of the primary tuberculous complex. The tonsillar and submandibular nodes are involved most often and probably represent extension from the paratracheal lymph nodes (and not from a primary lesion in the tonsil, as once was thought); occasionally, these nodes are involved when the primary lesion occurs in the mucous membranes of the mouth, a rare event. Enlarged supraclavicular nodes may accompany a primary pulmonary lesion in the upper lung fields. Enlarged axillary and epitrochlear nodes can result from a primary skin lesion of the elbow or hand, often a small, rather insignificant-looking area that has, however, been present for some time. Preauricular adenitis suggests a focus on the scalp or forehead or in the lacrimal sac, sometimes attributed to an insect bite. With inguinal adenitis, careful examination of the sole of the foot may reveal a small ulcer, often at the base of the toes.

When the superficial lymph nodes are involved early in the course of infection—the normal event—the enlargement usually is painless and the node or nodes rubbery and discrete. Low-grade fever generally is present, sometimes unnoticed by the parents. Occasionally, acute respiratory infections seem to precipitate or aggravate superficial tuberculous lymphadenitis, and the patient has high fever, some local pain, and perilymphadenitis. Rarely, the patient is seen first with a fluctuant mass, and the overlying skin is shiny and erythematous.[121]

The diagnosis usually is not obvious, so it is wise in all cases of superficial cervical and supraclavicular lymphadenitis to perform a throat culture, radiography of the chest, and a Mantoux tuberculin test. If the node is fluctuant, it should be aspirated and cultured for mycobacteria as well as pyogenic bacteria.[292] In preauricular, axillary, and inguinal adenitis, a possible primary skin lesion should be sought diligently. If a lesion is found, a biopsy should be performed, in addition to a tuberculin skin test, chest radiography, and a careful history.

Currently, in addition to pyogenic infection, cat-scratch disease, tularemia, malignant tumors, sarcoid, and mycobacteria other than *M. tuberculosis* also must be considered as a possible cause.[30, 286] If the adenitis is due to infection with *M. tuberculosis,* the induration from a Mantoux tuberculin skin test usually is greater than 15 mm, whereas mycobacteria other than *M. tuberculosis* produce a less intense reaction. The key to distinguishing tuberculosis from infection by another mycobacterium generally is epidemiologic—has the child been exposed to tuberculosis?

Because infection with pyogenic bacteria often enhances mycobacterial adenitis, a frequently wise approach is to institute therapy with a conventional antibacterial agent while awaiting the results of skin test, chest radiography, and cultures. If the adenitis persists and evidence of mycobacterial infection is elicited, antituberculosis drug therapy should be initiated and surgical excision seriously considered.[286, 453] Surgical excision currently is the treatment of choice for adenitis caused by mycobacteria other than *M. tuberculosis.* In the case of lymphadenitis caused by *M. tuberculosis*, the response to antituberculosis drugs is likely to be good. On the other hand, the adenitis is more likely to extend down into the mediastinum and be difficult to remove. Under these circumstances, surgical excision probably is unwise, whereas a few weeks of corticosteroid and antituberculosis therapy may be very effective.[71, 244, 286]

Superficial tuberculous lymphadenitis sometimes occurs early in the course of lymphohematogenous spread, in which case it often is manifested as "general glandular enlargement" accompanied by swinging fever, malaise, and weight loss. The tuberculin test almost always is positive in immunocompetent patients and should be included in the investigation of every patient with general glandular enlargement.

Finally, tuberculous adenitis, either localized or generalized, can occur in adolescents or young adults who were infected months or even years earlier, whose infection has been quiescent, and in whom the appearance of lymphadenitis heralds reactivation of the tuberculosis infection.[285]

Ocular Tuberculosis

Ocular tuberculosis is an uncommon finding in children.[132] When it does occur, the conjunctiva and the cornea are the areas most often involved.

The conjunctiva can serve as the initial portal of entry for tubercle bacilli, especially after trauma. Unilateral lacrimation and reddening may lead to the discovery of yellowish-gray nodules, usually on the palpebral conjunctiva. Preauricular adenitis appears early; the submandibular and cervical nodes also may enlarge. A tuberculin skin test and biopsy with culture can be performed to confirm the diagnosis.

Phlyctenular conjunctivitis probably is one of the hypersensitivity phenomena of childhood tuberculosis. Tubercle bacilli have, on rare occasion, been isolated from the small, grayish, jelly-like nodules usually clustered on the limbus and surrounded by dilated conjunctival vessels. Pain and photophobia are intense, and the lesions may recur in crops for weeks and affect one or both eyes. In the differential diagnosis, foreign body, herpes simplex virus conjunctivitis, vernal conjunctivitis, and trachoma should be considered. Tuberculin sensitivity is apt to be pronounced, and 1 tuberculin unit of purified protein derivative (PPD) should be used in the initial tuberculin skin test. Fortunately, hydrocortisone drops are effective in controlling both a strong local reaction to the diagnostic tuberculin test and the discomfort from the underlying disease. The prognosis for complete recovery is excellent, provided that the phlyctenules do not ulcerate and leave corneal scars. Systemic chemotherapy should be started immediately after the diagnostic procedures are completed.

Although tuberculosis of the ciliary body and iris has been reported rarely in children, tubercles of the choroid often have been found in patients with miliary tuberculosis (up to 70% of patients in some series) and occasionally in children with a seemingly uncomplicated infection.[361, 384] Frequently multiple, the tubercles heal slowly with deposition of retinal pigment; residual scarring apparently can be prevented with steroid therapy. Tuberculous uveitis and tuberculosis manifested as an orbital mass are rare clinical entities.[467]

Tuberculosis of the Middle Ear

Tuberculosis of the middle ear is a relatively rare manifestation of the disease.[159, 319, 322, 364, 439] It occurs as a primary focus in the area of the eustachian tube (because of reflux up the tube) in neonates who have aspirated infected amniotic fluid or in older infants who have ingested tuberculous material. It can occur as a metastatic lesion in older children who have a primary focus elsewhere. If it is a primary focus, regional lymphadenitis involves the preauricular lymph node or the anterior cervical chain, and facial paralysis occurs frequently. The primary focus always is unilateral. Otorrhea is common and painless but may become foul smelling because of bacterial contamination with enteric organisms. Older patients may complain of tinnitus and "funny noises." The eardrum often is damaged extensively. A large central perforation or several perforations are characteristic findings. A tuberculin skin test, biopsy, and careful cultures for tubercle bacilli are essential. Once greatly feared for the almost inevitable loss of hearing and the frequent occurrence of tuberculous meningitis, tuberculous otitis media now heals well with appropriate chemotherapy.[364]

Gastrointestinal and Abdominal Tuberculosis

Tuberculosis of the mouth occured more commonly in the days of bovine tuberculosis than it does today; at that time, scrofula often represented a primary complex in the mouth or tonsils, with associated submandibular or cervical lymphadenitis.[348] A primary focus in the mouth generally consists of a painless ulcer or mass of granulation tissue around a tooth socket or in the gingivolabial sulcus, with enlarged submental or submandibular nodes. Primary tuberculosis of the tonsils begins as a painless swelling of one tonsil, sometimes with an ulcer or yellowish node and, of course, enlargement of the regional lymph nodes. If tubercles found on histologic examination of a tonsil removed at tonsillectomy are unaccompanied by lymphadenitis, the lesion is considered a metastatic rather than a primary lesion. Tuberculosis of the esophagus occurs rarely, if ever, in children; sometimes, dysphagia is produced by a mass of mediastinal nodes, which may rupture into the lumen and later heal, possibly leaving an esophageal diverticulum.

Abdominal tuberculosis may occur after the ingestion of tubercle bacilli or as a part of generalized lymphohematogenous spread, but tuberculous enteritis always has been uncommon.[47, 432, 524, 527] When tubercle bacilli penetrate the gut wall, they usually do so via the Peyer patches or the appendix, where they give rise to local ulcers followed by mesenteric lymphadenitis and sometimes peritonitis.[19] Occasionally, especially in older children, tuberculous enteritis accompanies extensive pulmonary cavitation. Symptoms and signs include vague abdominal pain, intussusception, blood in the stool, and sinus formation after a seemingly routine appendectomy.

The spleen is seeded during the initial lymphohematogenous spread. Only rarely are the tubercles numerous and large enough to undergo caseation and calcify.[277] The reticuloendothelial system of the liver is involved also. Symptoms are rare occurrences except in miliary tuberculosis, in which the liver may be enlarged markedly, or in congenital tuberculosis, in which both the liver and spleen usually are enlarged.[325]

Mesenteric lymphadenitis can arise as part of an intra-abdominal primary complex or by extension from tuberculous thoracic or pelvic lymph nodes; often asymptomatic, it may be discovered later when calcified. It can cause ascites and dilatation of the superficial abdominal veins, but the symptom most frequently attributed to mesenteric lymphadenitis is colicky abdominal pain after exercise, probably because adhesions are stretched.

Tuberculous peritonitis can be a result of direct extension from a primary intestinal focus, adjacent mesenteric lymph nodes, or tuberculous salpingitis.[100, 131, 175] It may be "plastic" or accompanied by a serous effusion. On palpation, a mass of lymph nodes often can be felt, and the abdomen may have a characteristic "doughy" feeling. Paracentesis should be performed with care because the intestine may be immobilized by adhesions. Even with a large effusion, absorption usually occurs within a month. Malignancy must, of course, be considered strongly in the differential diagnosis, and biopsy may be necessary even if the tuberculin skin test is positive. Laparoscopy frequently is useful, as is fine-needle aspiration[311] and ultrasonography.[256] The ascitic-blood glucose ratio of the aspirated peritoneal fluid can be helpful in differentiating tuberculous peritonitis from ascites of other causes.[577]

Renal Tuberculosis

Renal tuberculosis is a late and uncommon complication of pulmonary disease; it rarely occurs less than 4 or 5 years after primary infection and is, therefore, likely to be diagnosed during adolescence.[154, 476] However, tubercle bacilli can be recovered from the urine in many cases of miliary tuberculosis and some cases of pulmonary tuberculosis in young children. Hematogenous dissemination can give rise to tubercles in the glomeruli, with resultant caseating and sloughing, but tiny lesions, which then discharge tubercle bacilli into the tubules. Occasionally, an encapsulated caseous mass develops in the zone between the renal pyramid and cortex; it may calcify in situ or discharge into the pelvis of the kidney and form a cavity quite analogous to a pulmonary cavity. Infection can be unilateral or bilateral and can spread downward to involve the bladder. Frequently, dysuria, hematuria, and "sterile" pyuria are the initial findings in the urine; they may occur grossly but often not until late in the course of a disease that causes strikingly few symptoms. Appropriate examination and culture of single early-morning urine specimens rarely fail to reveal tubercle bacilli. Intensive chemotherapy renders surgical intervention a rare necessity.[476] One should remember that urine from patients with renal tuberculosis is highly infectious and that such children should be isolated until their urine is sterile.

Dialysis and Renal Transplant-Associated Tuberculosis

Infections are a common cause of morbidity and mortality in patients with end-stage renal disease. Depressed cellular immunity, as manifested by cutaneous anergy, delayed homograft rejection, and a depressed lymphocyte count, has been demonstrated in uremic patients, whereas cell-mediated immunity appears to recover in stable patients treated by long-term hemodialysis. Thus, it is not surprising that tuberculosis occurs more frequently in patients maintained on dialysis than in the general population and that when it does become active, it does so before or early in the course of dialysis. Extrapulmonary involvement (mediastinal, meningeal, pleural, osseous, and renal) and miliary tuberculosis appear relatively frequently in this group. In these patients, fever of unknown origin should lead to suspicion of active tuberculosis.[18, 269] Tuberculosis also can originate in the transplanted organ.[556]

Genital Tuberculosis

Tuberculosis of the genital tract is an uncommon finding in both sexes before puberty.[476] It usually arises as a metastatic lesion during lymphohematogenous spread and occasionally by direct extension from an adjacent lesion of bone, gut, or the urinary tract. Genital tuberculosis is a particular hazard for adolescent girls with tuberculosis infection. Frequently, other forms of tuberculosis associated with initial infection, such as a pleural effusion, also are present. The fallopian tubes are involved in 90 to 100 percent of cases, the endometrium in 50 percent, the ovaries in 20 to 30 percent, and the cervix in 2 to 4 percent.[448] With tubal involvement, peritoneal tuberculosis occurs frequently.

Lower abdominal pain and amenorrhea usually prompt the patient to seek medical care. A lower abdominal mass, free peritoneal fluid, and constitutional symptoms may or may not be present. Chemotherapy is effective, but infertility remains a potential sequela of the disease.

Tuberculosis of the external genitalia has been seen as a manifestation of child abuse.

Genital tuberculosis can occur in males as primary tuberculosis of the penis after ritual circumcision; many such instances were reported in the past.[212] Massive inguinal lymphadenopathy in a circumcised infant should arouse suspicion of a possible tuberculous etiology. Epididymitis or epididymo-orchitis can occur in early childhood.[186] These disorders are characterized by nodular, painless swelling of the scrotum and a dragging pain in the groin and have a gradual onset rather than the acute onset that results after trauma, torsion of the testis, mumps orchitis, or epididymitis associated with bacterial infection.

Inoculation Tuberculosis

More than 200 cases of syringe-transmitted tuberculosis have been described in the world literature.[206] It has become more common since the widespread use of injectable penicillin and routine childhood immunization and usually has occurred as a result of contamination of the syringe or the solution by an individual with infectious sputum. If the recipient has not been infected previously, the lesion in the muscle or subcutaneous tissue will be the primary focus, and the regional lymph nodes will enlarge, caseate, and under favorable circumstances, calcify. However, at least 10 infants thus infected have died as a result of generalized tuberculosis, and in others, bone tuberculosis has developed. If the recipient already is tuberculin-positive, a tuberculous abscess will form without regional lymphadenitis. In this case, an injection abscess must be differentiated from a deep tuberculous abscess arising in the stage of hematogenous dissemination.

Perinatal Tuberculosis (Congenital and Postnatal)

Transmission of *M. tuberculosis* from mother to infant via the placenta or amniotic fluid has been reported in approximately 300 patients.[72] Infection of the placenta has been demonstrated, and tubercle bacilli have been grown from the tissues of stillborn infants and from living infants within a few days of birth. Perinatal tuberculosis can be acquired by the infant via one of several routes:

1. By transplacental spread via the umbilical vein from a mother with primary hematogenous tuberculosis occurring during pregnancy (i.e., true congenital tuberculosis). The liver is enlarged, enlarged lymph nodes may be present at the porta hepatis, and evidence of widespread miliary disease may be seen in the infant (i.e., the infant may have a primary liver complex or primary lung complexes).

2. By in utero aspiration of amniotic fluid infected from endometritis in the mother or from the placenta. This route of infection also constitutes true congenital tuberculosis. In both these situations, clinical onset of signs and symptoms is apt to be rapid (by 2 to 3 weeks of age) and include failure to thrive, fever, respiratory distress, and hepatosplenomegaly.

3. By ingestion of infected amniotic fluid or secretions during delivery. This mechanism would seem to be less well

documented than the first two routes, but it certainly is a possibility.

4. By inhalation of tubercle bacilli at or soon after birth from the mother, other relatives, or attendants with infectious pulmonary tuberculosis. This route is the most common mode of transmission to newborns.

5. By ingestion of infected breast milk or cow's milk.

One cannot always be sure of the type of infection in a particular neonate; only clear-cut evidence of a primary complex in the liver establishes a definite diagnosis of congenital tuberculosis. However, the presence of early forms of tuberculosis (such as pleural, miliary, or meningeal) in the mother during pregnancy or the puerperium also is strong evidence of true congenital tuberculosis in the infant.

Routes 4 and 5 are really "postnatally" acquired tuberculosis and need, for epidemiologic purposes, to be distinguished from routes 1, 2, and 3. Neonates with these types of tuberculosis usually lack striking clinical features until they are 1 or 2 months of age.

The diagnosis of perinatal tuberculosis is apt to be difficult and often delayed.[295] Disease in the mother often is overlooked; the mother may have pleural effusion, fever of unknown origin, cough, endometritis, and other symptoms without the tuberculous etiology being recognized. The early symptoms and signs in the neonate likewise are overlooked frequently and may be similar to those caused by other congenital infections. Once the diagnosis is suspected, treatment should be started immediately, and diagnostic procedures should be carried out rapidly and aggressively.

The clinical manifestations vary, probably depending on the size of the infecting dose of bacilli and the site and size of the caseous lesions.[336, 370] In many of the reported cases, tuberculosis disease was discovered only at autopsy.[225] Symptoms usually appeared during the second week of life and included loss of appetite and failure to gain weight, fever, nasal or ear discharge, cough, bronchopneumonia, jaundice, hepatomegaly, and splenomegaly occurring later.[72] Wasting has been noted frequently and, in one case, clearly was shown to be caused by hypoadrenocorticism.[359]

Because the tuberculin skin test very rarely is positive in infants, demonstration of tubercle bacilli in gastric washings, middle ear fluid, lymph node biopsy, lung biopsy, skin biopsy, bone marrow aspirate, endotracheal aspirate, or lung biopsy is essential.[194] Examination of the placenta for organisms or characteristic histopathologic changes can be extremely helpful and should be done when tuberculosis is diagnosed in the mother around the time of delivery. Successful treatment of congenital tuberculosis has been reported by several investigators, although clinical response may be very slow and extensive calcification of the lungs, liver, spleen, and muscles may result.[261, 264, 370, 483, 495]

Tuberculosis in Adolescents

Tuberculosis in adolescents has become relatively more important as the incidence of infection in childhood has lessened.[29, 369, 481] Logically, it should be considered in two ways: first, tuberculosis acquired as an initial infection during the adolescent years, and second, tuberculosis infection acquired in early life and reactivated during adolescence.[372] In actual practice, it is often difficult or impossible to separate the two, and most clinical reports and studies do not.

Tuberculosis in adolescents may occur exactly as it does in young children, or a classic primary complex may progress rapidly to chronic pulmonary tuberculosis while the hilar lymph node involvement characteristic of childhood tuberculosis remains present. The Medical Research Council in 1963 published a report on 504 cases of tuberculosis in adolescents, including 316 cases of pulmonary tuberculosis, 44 cases of pleural effusion, 44 with hilar lymph node enlargement, 6 cases of miliary and 5 of meningeal tuberculosis, 13 with bone and joint disease, and 8 with genitourinary tuberculosis. In their series of cases of primary tuberculosis in adults, Stead[507] included 11 adolescents, 2 with simple primary tuberculosis, 5 with pleurisy and effusion, and 1 with progressive pulmonary tuberculosis.

From the extensive clinical experience of Lincoln and Sewell[307] and others, several observations emerge. Tuberculosis infection in early infancy rarely leads to pulmonary tuberculosis in adolescence, perhaps because it has several years in which to heal, whereas tuberculosis infection acquired after 7 years of age and, in particular, acquired after 10 years of age is prone to progress. When *M. tuberculosis* is acquired during adolescence, chronic pulmonary tuberculosis may develop within 1 to 3 years. Moreover, the risk of pulmonary tuberculosis is two to six times greater for adolescent girls than for adolescent boys. In both sexes, the adolescent growth spurt is the time of greatest risk. The work of Johnston[250] suggests that at least in girls, the depressant effect of puberty on calcium and nitrogen retention may be correlated with the failure of tuberculosis infection to heal.

Tuberculosis and Pregnancy

In the era before chemotherapy, whether pregnancy and tuberculosis affected each other adversely was an ongoing controversy. Since the advent of chemotherapy, however, the prognosis has improved greatly.[166] The main problems now are serious unrecognized tuberculosis in a pregnant woman, sometimes with a fatal outcome, or serious unrecognized disease in her infant. Another problem is whether pregnancy influences the risk of progression of tuberculosis infection to disease; the data are conflicting in this regard. Tuberculin skin testing probably is valid during pregnancy; chest radiographs (with shielding) should be obtained for all tuberculin-positive pregnant patients. Therapy, when indicated, can safely include isoniazid, which crosses the placenta but apparently without ill effects, rifampin, and ethambutol. The safety of pyrazinamide in pregnancy has not been established, but a growing number of experts recommend it because anecdotal data have not shown it to be harmful to the mother or fetus. Streptomycin, because of fetal ototoxicity, is not recommended.[490]

Should a mother receiving antituberculosis therapy breast-feed?[491] It is probably safe for her to do so because the drugs, though found in milk, are present only in small amounts.

Tuberculosis and Human Immunodeficiency Virus Infection

In adults infected with both HIV and *M. tuberculosis,* the rate of progression from asymptomatic infection to disease is increased greatly.[442] The clinical manifestations of tuberculosis in HIV-infected adults are typical when the $CD4^+$ cell count is higher than 500/mm^3. As the $CD4^+$ cell count falls, manifestations become "atypical." Extrapulmonary foci occur in as many as 60 percent of profoundly immunocompromised patients.[25] Pulmonary cavities are rare findings; lower lobe infiltrates or nodules often accompanied by thoracic adenopathy are common occurrences, especially if the patient's tuberculosis infection is recent. Of course, many patients have a nonreactive tuberculin skin test. Sputum is less likely to be produced or to contain visible acid-fast organisms on stained smears; more invasive procedures such as bronchoscopy often are required to isolate *M. tuberculosis* and to rule out other causes of opportunistic lung disease. Malabsorption of antituberculosis drugs in HIV-infected patients can lead to prolonged symptoms and disease.[400]

When tuberculosis develops in HIV-infected children, the clinical features tend to be fairly typical of childhood tuberculosis in immunocompetent children, although the disease often progresses more rapidly and the clinical manifestations are more severe.[54, 97, 270, 362, 535] An increased tendency for extrapulmonary disease may be noted. Making the diagnosis can be very difficult; a diligent search for an infectious adult in the child's environment may yield the best clues to the correct diagnosis.[274]

Diagnosis

HOW CHILDREN WITH TUBERCULOSIS ARE DISCOVERED

In the developing world, the only way that children with tuberculosis disease are discovered is when they have a profound illness that is consistent with one manifestation of tuberculosis. Having an ill adult contact is an obvious clue to the correct diagnosis. The only available laboratory test usually is an acid-fast smear of sputum, which the child rarely produces. In many regions, chest radiography is not available. To aid in diagnosis, a variety of scoring systems based on available tests, clinical signs and symptoms, and known exposures have been devised.[347, 571] However, no single clinical scoring system has been validated, and the sensitivity and specificity of these systems can be very low and lead to both overdiagnosis and underdiagnosis of tuberculosis.[268, 347]

In industrial countries, children with tuberculosis usually are discovered in one of two ways.[141, 272, 443] Obviously, one way is consideration of tuberculosis as the cause of a symptomatic illness.[436] Discovering an adult contact with infectious tuberculosis is an invaluable aid to diagnosis; the "yield" from a contact investigation usually is higher than that from cultures from the child.[36] Culture from the infectious adult case may yield the only drug susceptibility results for the child because cultures from children with tuberculosis frequently are negative. The second way is discovery of a child with pulmonary tuberculosis during the contact investigation of an adult with tuberculosis.[330, 356, 493, 517] Typically, the affected child has few or no symptoms, but investigation reveals a positive tuberculin skin test and an abnormal chest radiograph. In some areas of the United States, as many as 50 percent of children with pulmonary tuberculosis are discovered in this manner, before significant symptoms have begun. It is rare to find tuberculosis disease in a U.S.-born child as the result of a community- or school-based tuberculin skin testing program, although foreign-born children with tuberculosis may be found in this manner.[142]

TUBERCULIN SENSITIVITY AND THE SKIN TEST

Sensitization to tuberculin is induced by infection with living tubercle bacilli. Specific tuberculin sensitivity to either *M. tuberculosis* or other mycobacteria can be transferred in humans by injection of lymphocytes from sensitized donors and also by injection of certain purified mycobacterial protein antigens.

The time of appearance of sensitivity in animals after infection with tubercle bacilli depends on the number of tubercle bacilli in the infective dose and on the virulence—that is, the rate of multiplication of the organisms—and likely such also is the case in humans.[26] For all practical purposes in humans, tuberculin reactivity seems to appear in 3 to 6 weeks, rarely a few days earlier, and occasionally as long as 3 months after initial infection.

The tuberculin sensitivity reaction has been studied best in the skin, although it can be elicited in any tissue of a sensitive subject (conjunctiva, lung, meninges, kidney, and so on) after injection of tuberculoprotein. At first, an inflammatory reaction appears at the site of injection, with predominance of segmented neutrophils, followed by immigration of macrophages and T lymphocytes, until the entire area of induration consists of mononuclear cells.

The size of the induration depends on the amount of tuberculoprotein injected and the availability of sensitized T lymphocytes in sufficient number. Multiple tuberculin skin tests given simultaneously result in smaller individual reactions, probably because of a finite number of sensitized cells in the body. Corticosteroids,[55, 324, 449] adrenocorticotropic hormone, nitrogen mustard, irradiation, and viral infections such as measles, influenza, and mumps diminish tuberculin reactivity, perhaps simply by inducing lymphopenia.[506] The size of the induration seems to depend on at least two additional factors: the local behavior of the skin (the disappearance time for wheals of normal saline solution, the so-called Aldrich-McClure test, is accelerated during fever, pregnancy, cachexia, and extreme malnutrition) and the number of actively multiplying tubercle bacilli in the body, which can be demonstrated in animals and probably in humans as well. That still other factors must be involved is clear because 10 to 20 percent of immunocompetent patients with proven tuberculosis are tuberculin-negative during initial disease, with tuberculin sensitivity often regained during treatment.[405] Decreased T-lymphocyte blastogenesis has been demonstrated in some cases, and inhibition by B lymphocytes may play a role.

Temporary desensitization to tuberculin occurs most strikingly during measles and has been studied carefully. Full reactivity diminished during the incubation period and returned within approximately 1 month after appearance of the exanthem.[204] Influenza and administration of influenza and measles vaccines tend to depress sensitivity but rarely suppress it entirely.[64, 585] Whether other viral diseases and vaccines regularly are less active in this regard and what the important factors may be are not known.[39] If a temporary desensitizing effect occurs in bacterial infections such as scarlet fever, it probably depends on factors such as hyperthermia and dehydration.

Sensitization to tuberculin as a result of infection with *M. tuberculosis* tends to persist undiminished for life.[153, 196, 219] The likelihood of tuberculin sensitivity disappearing seems to be greater when the lesion is negligible. That low degrees of sensitivity to *M. tuberculosis* are induced by mycobacteria other than *M. tuberculosis* also is clear. Previous receipt of BCG vaccine can cause increased reactivity to tuberculin, but the association is weaker than many clinicians suspect.[10, 78, 315, 363, 460] Less than 50 percent of infants given BCG vaccination have a reactive tuberculin skin test at 9 to 12 months of age, and the great majority will have a nonreactive skin test by the time they are 5 years of age. Older children and adults who receive BCG vaccination have a reactive skin test and keep it longer, but by 10 to 15 years after vaccination, most individuals have lost tuberculin skin test reactivity.[112, 346] Repeated administration of BCG vaccine can maintain tuberculin reactivity.[233] Repeated tuberculin skin tests in a person sensitized previously by BCG vaccination, infection with *M. tuberculosis,* or probably infection by an environmental mycobacterium may increase the reaction to subsequent tuberculin skin tests (called the booster phenomenon).[42, 171, 459, 536]

The antigens currently used in tuberculin testing are crude extracts consisting of a mixture of many antigens, some species-specific, some shared among many species. Standardized, isolated, purified mycobacterial antigens are needed badly in clinical practice. The major antigen used in tuberculin testing is PPD, obtained from filtrates of heat-killed tubercle bacilli. Batch 49608, prepared by Dr. Florence Seibert in 1939, was designated by the WHO as the international standard tuberculin, the only one to be called PPD-S. All other PPD preparations are referred to simply as PPD or as PPD-T. However, each batch now must be stabilized with Tween 80 at 5 ppm to minimize adherence to glass and plastic and must be identified by manufacturer and lot number.

A tuberculin unit is the activity contained in a specified weight of PPD-S. The standard test dose, 5 tuberculin units, refers to the equivalence in biologic activity, determined in the guinea pig, of a commercial PPD preparation with that contained in 5 tuberculin units of PPD-S. Products labeled 1 tuberculin unit and 250 tuberculin units are calculated dilutions based on 5 tuberculin units. However, it long has been recognized that the potency of PPD doses varies from batch to batch.

The Mantoux test is the reference test. A graduated syringe and a 26- or 27-gauge needle are used for injection of 0.1 mL of PPD into the most superficial layer of the epidermis of the forearm, which raises an immediate wheal (Fig. 101–14). Under optimal circumstances, the needle should not be withdrawn for a few seconds to minimize leakage. The reference test uses a dose of 5 tuberculin units. One tuberculin unit very rarely should be used, for example, if extreme hypersensitivity is suspected, as when a tuberculous eye lesion or erythema nodosum is present. The reading should be made at 48 to 72 hours, with the forearm slightly flexed. Any induration (not erythema) should be measured, preferably with calipers, and the diameter at right angles to the axis of administration recorded in millimeters. Use of the words "negative" and "positive" should be avoided because interpretation can change as more epidemiologic information becomes known. The previous widespread use of multiple-puncture tests led to the practice of allowing parents to interpret the results and report them to the clinician. This practice assumes parental knowledge of and adherence to a broad range of motivational behavior and skills. No study has demonstrated that parents can read positive skin tests accurately, but that they may not correctly interpret or report positive results has been well documented.[101, 102, 188, 217] Two recent studies have demonstrated that pediatric care providers tend to under-read Mantoux tuberculin skin tests.[77, 265]

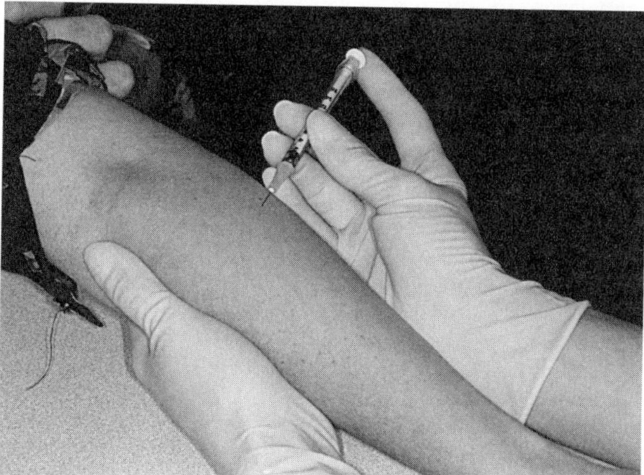

FIGURE 101–14 ■ A useful technique for performing a Mantoux tuberculin skin test on a child. The needle is applied perpendicular to the long axis of the arm to attain better control.

Variability in Mantoux test reading has been shown to be great by several studies.[33] Such variability can be minimized only by ongoing training of both testers and readers and by concentrating the responsibility of testing and reading to a small number of trained individuals.

The importance of the tuberculin test cannot be overemphasized as the main criterion for diagnosing tuberculosis infection in an individual child. Only rarely is the tuberculin test negative in an infected child, usually as a result of anergy from overwhelming infection, from viral infection, from HIV infection, from the use of immunosuppressive drugs, or because of factors not yet understood.[513] Anergy in tuberculosis can be selective for tuberculin; "control" skin tests may be positive but the Mantoux test negative in a child with tuberculosis disease.[504]

Several changes in recommendations for interpretation of the Mantoux test, which has a sensitivity and specificity of only approximately 95 percent, have been made.[223] When a test with these characteristics is applied to a population with a 90 percent prevalence of tuberculosis infection, the positive predictive value of the skin test is 99 percent, an excellent result. However, if the same test is applied to a population with only a 1 percent prevalence of infection, the positive predictive value drops to 15 percent; 85 percent of the "positive" results are false positives created by biologic variability, nonspecific reactions, and infection with environmental mycobacteria. Because the skin test is the only test to detect tuberculosis infection, true positives cannot be distinguished from false-positive results by further testing. These false-positive results lead to unnecessary treatment, cost, and anxiety for the patient, family, and clinician. In short, the low sensitivity and specificity of the tuberculin skin test render the test undesirable for use in persons from low-prevalence groups. The trend in the United States is to reduce or eliminate routine testing of low-risk children but target children with specific risk factors for one-time or periodic tuberculosis skin testing.[12, 89, 357]

Several recently published studies have shown that a questionnaire can be used in the United States to identify children with significant risk factors for tuberculosis infection, who then can receive a tuberculin skin test.[172, 313, 389, 435] Factors that consistently correlate with having a positive tuberculin skin test include contact with a case of tuberculosis, having other family members with a positive tuberculin skin test, and foreign birth in or extensive travel to a high-prevalence country.[451]

The CDC and the American Academy of Pediatrics (AAP) have recommended varying the size of induration considered positive in various groups, according to their risk factors (Table 101–7), in an attempt to minimize the incidence of false-negative results in children most likely to have rapid progression of asymptomatic tuberculosis infection to disease and the false-positive results in persons with no known risk factors for tuberculosis. In general in the United States, previous receipt of BCG vaccine should not influence interpretation of the initial tuberculin skin test of a child.[249]

TABLE 101–7 ■ AMOUNT OF INDURATION IN REACTION TO A MANTOUX TUBERCULIN SKIN TEST CONSIDERED POSITIVE (INDICATING PROBABLE INFECTION WITH *MYCOBACTERIUM TUBERCULOSIS*)

Reaction Size	Risk Factors
≥5 mm	Contact with infectious cases Abnormal chest radiograph HIV infection or other immunocompromise
≥10 mm	Birth or previous residence in a high-prevalence country Residence in long-term care or corrections facility Certain medical risk factors: diabetes mellitus, silicosis, renal disease Occupation in health care field, exposure to patients with tuberculosis Member of a local high-risk group Close contact with a high-risk adult (except health care workers) Age <4 yr
≥15 mm	No risk factors

DIAGNOSTIC MYCOBACTERIOLOGY IN CHILDREN[438]

The demonstration of acid-fast bacilli in stained smears of sputum is presumptive evidence of pulmonary tuberculosis in most patients. However, in children, tubercle bacilli usually are relatively few in number, and sputum cannot be obtained from children younger than approximately 10 years. Gastric washings, which often are used in lieu of sputum, can be contaminated with acid-fast organisms from the mouth. However, fluorescence microscopy of gastric washings has been found useful, particularly in a setting where malnutrition and tuberculin-negative tuberculosis are rampant.[293] Tubercle bacilli in cerebrospinal fluid, pleural fluid, lymph node aspirate, and urine are sparse; thus, only rarely are direct-stained smears for tubercle bacilli of any use in pediatric practice. Cultures for tubercle bacilli are of great importance, not only to confirm the diagnosis but increasingly to permit testing for drug susceptibility. If culture and drug susceptibility data are available from the associated adult case and the child has classic features of tuberculosis (positive skin test, consistent abnormal chest radiograph), obtaining cultures from the child adds little to management.

Painstaking collection of specimens is essential for diagnosing children because fewer organisms usually are present than in adults. Gastric lavage should be performed in the very early morning, when the patient has had nothing to eat or drink for 8 hours and before the patient has a chance to wake up and start swallowing saliva, which could dilute the bronchial secretions that were brought up during the night and made their way into the stomach. Inhalation of superheated nebulized saline before gastric lavage has been reported to increase the bacteriologic yield.[178] The stomach contents should be aspirated first. Then, no more than 50 to 75 mL of sterile distilled water (not saline) should be injected through the stomach tube and the aspirate added to the first collection. The gastric acidity (poorly tolerated by tubercle bacilli) should be neutralized immediately. Concentration and culture should be performed as soon as possible after collection. However, even with optimal, in-hospital collection of three early-morning gastric aspirate samples, *M. tuberculosis* can be isolated from only 30 to 40 percent of children and 70 percent of infants with pulmonary tuberculosis.[69, 504, 549] The yield from random outpatient gastric aspirate samples usually is low.

Bronchial secretions obtained by stimulating cough with an aerosol solution can be used in older children.[76] The aerosol is heated in a nebulizer at 46 to 52° C (114.8 to 125.6° F) and administered to the patient for 15 to 30 minutes. This method gives good results and may be superior to gastric lavage both in yield of positive cultures and in patient acceptance.[76, 465] The bronchial aspirate obtained at bronchoscopy often is thick, and the laboratory will process it with a mucolytic agent such as *N*-acetyl-L-cysteine. In most studies, the yield of *M. tuberculosis* from bronchoscopy specimens has been lower than from properly obtained gastric aspirates.[1, 96]

Cerebrospinal fluid, pleural fluid, and synovial fluid (as much fluid as possible should be collected) usually are centrifuged and the sediment used for stained smear and culture. An overnight urine specimen should be obtained in the early morning and taken immediately to the laboratory for processing because the organisms tolerate the low pH of urine poorly. Lymph node aspirates and bits of biopsy tissue can be inoculated directly into a fluid medium such as Middlebrook 7H9.

Staining and examination of smears, as well as inoculation of special media, incubation in a carbon dioxide environment, strain differentiation based on many cultural characteristics, and drug susceptibility testing, all require equipment, skills, and experience beyond those available in the usual clinic or hospital laboratory. Thus, most laboratories depend on regional or reference laboratories for procedures beyond their scope.

Despite an enormous amount of research and thousands of publications on the subject, the only definite way to diagnose active tuberculosis is by demonstration of tubercle bacilli in tissues or secretions. No single species-specific antigen of *M. tuberculosis* ever has been identified. The search for quick, simple, inexpensive, specific, sensitive immunologic and chemical detection techniques is ongoing.

NUCLEIC ACID AMPLIFICATION

The main form of nucleic acid amplification studied in children with tuberculosis is polymerase chain reaction (PCR), which uses specific DNA sequences as markers for microorganisms.[155, 329] Various PCR techniques, most using the mycobacterial insertion element IS6110 as the DNA marker for *M. tuberculosis* complex organisms,[14, 80] have a sensitivity and specificity of more than 90 percent in comparison to sputum culture for detecting pulmonary tuberculosis in adults. However, test performance varies even among reference laboratories.[378, 450] The test is relatively expensive, calls for fairly sophisticated equipment, and requires scrupulous technique to avoid cross-contamination of specimens. In the United States, it is approved for use only on acid-fast stain–positive specimens.

Evaluation of PCR in childhood tuberculosis has been limited. When compared with a clinical diagnosis of pulmonary tuberculosis in children, the sensitivity of PCR has varied from 25 to 83 percent and specificity has varied from 80 to 100 percent.[130, 395, 406, 478] PCR of gastric aspirates may be positive in a recently infected child even when the chest radiograph is normal, thus demonstrating the occasional arbitrariness of the distinction between tuberculosis infection and disease in children. PCR may have a useful but limited role in evaluating children for tuberculosis. A negative PCR never eliminates tuberculosis as a diagnostic possibility, and a positive result does not confirm it. The major use of PCR will be in evaluating children with significant pulmonary disease when the diagnosis is not established readily by clinical or epidemiologic grounds. PCR may be particularly helpful in evaluating immunocompromised children with pulmonary disease, especially those with HIV infection, although published reports of its performance in such children are lacking. PCR also may aid in confirming the diagnosis of extrapulmonary tuberculosis, but only a few reports have been published.[184, 328, 351]

SEROLOGY AND ANTIGEN DETECTION

Despite hundreds of studies published during the past century, serology has found little place in the routine diagnosis of tuberculosis in adults or children.[122] Some studies have used enzyme-linked immunosorbent assay to detect antibodies to whole bacterial cells or to various purified or complex antigens of *M. tuberculosis* in children.[122, 253, 254] In general, both the sensitivity and specificity of the various tests have been unacceptably low.[43, 229] Tests using the mycobacterial antigen A60 have shown both good[128] and bad[545] results in children. No available serodiagnostic test for tuberculosis is adequate under various clinical conditions to be useful for children.

Mycobacterial antigen detection has been evaluated in clinical samples from adults but rarely from children.[433] Most of these techniques require technically advanced equipment (such as high-pressure liquid chromatography apparatus) and expertise that are not available where tuberculosis in children is common.

Treatment

MANAGEMENT OF TUBERCULOUS CHILDREN

Treatment of cavitary tuberculosis in adults is one of the most scientifically accurate areas in all of medicine and one of the finest examples of international professional cooperation in all of history. Because tubercle bacilli in adult patients with tuberculosis can be seen and cultured, their numbers quantified, and the size of the cavities that they produce measured and because there are so many cases of tuberculosis in the world, researchers have been able to ask precise questions about treatment and to design prospective cooperative studies that yield accurate answers about the effect of individual drugs, multiple drug regimens, drug dosage, duration of chemotherapy, rest, and surgical procedures on the course of the disease. Although chemotherapy without doubt has been extremely effective in treating childhood tuberculosis, recommendations for treatment historically have been based to a great extent on analogy with adults, on "custom," and on "experience" because in children the tubercle bacilli are fewer in number and not readily accessible and the lesions are not as easy to evaluate as cavities. However, during the past 2 decades, a large number of treatment trials for children have been reported, which has led to dramatic changes in the therapeutic approach to childhood tuberculosis.

As recently as the early 1980s, the recommended treatment duration for children with tuberculosis disease was 12 to 18 months. Although these regimens are effective when used properly, actual failure rates are high because of poor adherence over the long period of treatment. Newer regimens often are called "short-course" chemotherapy because treatment durations as short as 6 months are routinely successful. However, the key to the new approach is not the short duration but the intensive initial therapy with three or more antituberculosis drugs.

Antituberculosis Drugs (Tables 101–8 and 101–9)

Isoniazid (INH) is the mainstay of therapy for tuberculosis in children. Cheap, highly effective in preventing the multiplication of tubercle bacilli, of low molecular weight and, therefore, readily diffusible to all tissues in the body,[136] and

TABLE 101–8 ■ COMMONLY USED DRUGS FOR THE TREATMENT OF TUBERCULOSIS IN CHILDREN

Drug	Dosage Forms	Daily Dose (mg/kg/day)	Twice-Weekly Dose (mg/kg/dose)	Maximal Daily Dose
Ethambutol	Tablets: 100 mg 400 mg	15–25	50	2.5 g
Isoniazid*†	Scored tablets: 100 mg 300 mg Syrup‡: 10 mg/mL	10–15†	20–30	Daily, 300 mg Twice weekly: 900 mg
Pyrazinamide	Scored tablets: 500 mg	20–40	50	2 g
Rifampin*	Capsules: 150 mg 300 mg Syrup: Formulated in syrup from capsules	10–20	10–20	Daily, 600 mg Twice weekly: 900 mg
Streptomycin (IM administration)	Vials: 1 g 4 g	20–40	20–40	

*Rifamate is a capsule containing 150 mg of isoniazid and 300 mg of rifampin. Two capsules provide the usual adult (>50 kg body weight) daily doses of each drug.

†When isoniazid is used in combination with rifampin, the incidence of hepatotoxicity increases if the isoniazid dose exceeds 10 mg/kg/day.

‡Most experts advise against the use of isoniazid syrup because of instability and a high rate of gastrointestinal adverse reaction (diarrhea, cramps).

TABLE 101–9 ■ DRUGS FOR TREATMENT OF DRUG-RESISTANT TUBERCULOSIS IN CHILDREN

Drugs	Dosage Forms	Daily Dosage (mg/kg/day)	Maximum Daily Dose
Capreomycin	Vials: 1 g	15–30 (IM)	1 g
Ciprofloxacin	Tablets: 250 mg 500 mg 750 mg	Adults: 500–1500 mg in 2 divided doses	1.5 g
Clofazimine	Capsules: 50 mg 100 mg	50–100 mg/day	200 mg
Cycloserine	Capsules: 250 mg	10–20	1 g
Ethionamide	Tablets: 250 mg	15–20 given in 2 or 3 divided doses	1 g
Kanamycin	Vials: 75 mg/2 mL 500 mg/2 mL 1 g/3 mL	15–30 (IM)	1 g
Levofloxacin	Tablets: 250 mg 500 mg 750 mg	Adults: 500–750 mg total/day	750 mg
Para-aminosalicylic acid	Packets: 4 g	200–300 given in 2 to 4 divided doses	12 g

relatively nontoxic to children, INH is one of the most nearly perfect drugs in the pediatrician's armamentarium. It can be administered orally or intramuscularly. When INH is taken orally, high plasma, sputum, and spinal fluid levels are reached within a few hours and persist for at least 6 to 8 hours.[290, 385] Because of the slow multiplication of *M. tuberculosis,* the total daily dose can be given at one time. The usual level necessary to inhibit multiplication of tubercle bacilli is 0.02 to 0.05 μg/mL.

Human variation in the acetylation rate of INH to an inactive compound is known to be determined genetically.[333] Rapid acetylation occurs more frequently in black people and Asians than in whites. Although a simple method, specifically the use of a urine sample, now is available for classifying patients as slow or rapid inactivators of INH, the normal way of coping with the problem in children has been to give a sufficiently large dose of INH to ensure an adequate level even in rapid inactivators.[332, 555]

The principal toxic effects of INH are peripheral neuritis and hepatitis. Peripheral neuritis resulting from competitive inhibition of pyridoxine utilization is a rare event in North American children because both milk and meat are the main dietary sources of pyridoxine.[49] In some well-nourished children, serum pyridoxine concentrations are depressed by INH, but clinical signs are not apparent.[399] In the case of most children, therefore, the use of supplementary pyridoxine is not necessary. However, in teenagers whose diets may be inadequate, in children from ethnic groups with low milk and meat intake, and in breast-fed babies, pyridoxine supplementation (25 to 50 mg/day) is important. Peripheral neuritis, when it does occur, usually is manifested by "pins and needles" sensations in the hands and feet.

Hepatotoxicity from INH, rare in children, increases in frequency with age.[34, 79, 279, 309, 366, 382, 411, 494, 508] Its cause is unclear.[280] Rapid acetylators are no more susceptible than are slow acetylators.[156, 332] Simultaneous use of alcohol, phenytoin, piperazine, and especially rifampin (RIF) seems to increase the likelihood of hepatotoxicity occurring.[79, 284] Monitoring of aspartate aminotransferase and alanine aminotransferase sometimes reveals transient increases during treatment with INH, but the levels usually return spontaneously to normal without interruption of treatment. Liver enzyme abnormalities in adolescents receiving INH are rather common occurrences and usually disappear spontaneously, but severe hepatitis can occur.[173, 310, 391, 484, 552]

The possible occurrence of hepatitis raises the question of routine monitoring of liver enzyme levels once a month in all children receiving INH. The advantage of doing so has to be weighed not only against the expense but particularly against the difficulty of ensuring regular monthly visits if the patient and parents know that every clinic visit entails a venipuncture. Most experts prefer to substitute routine questions about appetite and well-being, determination of weight, and a check of the appearance of the sclera and the size of the liver.[70] Patients should be counseled to stop taking INH and contact the clinician immediately if significant nausea, vomiting, abdominal pain, or jaundice occurs during the use of INH.

Allergic manifestations of INH hypersensitivity are extraordinarily rare. Convulsions have been reported after doses of 100 mg/kg or more as in suicide attempts.[337, 376, 392, 463]

The usual dosage in children is 10 to 20 mg/kg/day, to a maximum of 300 mg/day. INH is available in tablets of 100 and 300 mg. The original liquid preparation of INH in syrup was abandoned when investigators found that the drug was unstable in sucrose. A syrup of INH in sorbitol (10 mg/mL) is now on the market and appears to be satisfactory; however, it is unstable at 37° C (98.6° F) and should be kept cool. Significant gastrointestinal intolerance (nausea, diarrhea) develops in many children while taking the INH suspension. If tablets are used, they are crushed easily in a dessert spoon, to which then is added in the same spoon a vehicle such as applesauce, mashed banana, thawed undiluted frozen orange juice, or another palatable medium. The crushed tablets must never be added to the nursing bottle or offered in milk or water because they will be ingested only partially. If INH is given concurrently with RIF, the dose should not exceed 10 mg/kg/day.[382] If the intramuscular form is used, for example, in a child with meningitis who is vomiting, the daily dose is the same as the daily oral dose but usually is divided and given every 8 to 12 hours. INH can interact with several other drugs, particularly theophylline, and the dosage of each may need to be modified in a patient taking several drugs.[23] INH also can increase serum phenytoin levels by blocking its metabolism in the liver, thereby leading to toxicity.[350]

RIF is a semisynthetic drug derived from *Streptomyces mediterranei*. Active against a wide variety of both intracellular and extracellular organisms, it is more effective against mycobacteria than is any other drug except INH. Most clinical isolates are susceptible to 5 μg/mL or less. The drug is absorbed readily from the gastrointestinal tract in the fasting state; peak serum levels of 6 to 10 μg/mL are achieved within 2 hours, and the drug is distributed widely in body fluids and tissues, including spinal fluid.[134] Excretion is mainly via the biliary tract; however, effective levels are achieved in the kidneys and urine. In many patients receiving RIF treatment, tears, saliva, urine, and stool turn orange as the result of a harmless metabolite, but patients always must be warned in advance. Drawbacks include (1) the relatively high cost of treatment; (2) the rare occurrence of explosive hypersensitivity reactions with hemolytic anemia, which, however, usually accompany intermittent (separated by weeks or months) rather than daily RIF therapy; (3) the occasional occurrence of leukopenia or thrombocytopenia while the patient is taking daily RIF[180]; (4) the fact that RIF can render birth control pills inactive when both are used (an alternative method of birth control must be used); and finally—most serious of all for children—(5) a "therapeutic orphan" clause in the United States for children younger than 5 years, which also means that no formulation is commercially available for young children. However, RIF easily can be made into a suspension for use in children.

RIF should be used alone only when treating tuberculosis infection with an INH-resistant organism. If one uses INH, 20 mg/kg, and RIF, 15 to 20 mg/kg, the incidence of hepatotoxicity is appreciable. Therefore, when using the two together, one would be wise to approximate INH, 10 mg/kg, and RIF, 15 to 20 mg/kg. Rifamate is a capsule containing both INH (150 mg) and RIF (300 mg). Two capsules supply the usual adult (more than 50 kg) daily dose of each drug. Rifamate may be appropriate for older children and adolescents.[3] Rifater contains INH, RIF, and pyrazinamide (PZA) together in one pill in varying concentrations. Rifapentine is a new rifamycin with a very long half-life. Pharmacokinetic studies have been performed in adolescents, but no data on its effectiveness in adolescents or children have been published.[331]

PZA contributes to the killing of *M. tuberculosis*, particularly at a low pH such as within macrophages.[437] The exact mechanism of action of PZA is a subject of controversy. PZA has no effect on extracellular tubercle bacilli in vitro but clearly contributes to the killing of intracellular bacilli. Primary resistance is very rare, except that *Mycobacterium bovis* is resistant. The drug diffuses readily into all areas, including spinal fluid.[157] The usual adult daily dose is 30 to 40 mg/kg. The adult dose is tolerated well by children, results in high cerebrospinal fluid concentrations, and clearly is effective in therapy trials for tuberculosis in children.[137, 430, 440, 497] PZA appears to exert its maximal effect during the first 2 months of therapy. Hepatotoxicity can occur at high doses but rarely does at the usual dose. PZA routinely causes an increase in serum uric acid concentration by inhibiting its excretion through the kidneys. Toxic reactions in adults include flushing, cutaneous hypersensitivity, arthralgia, and overt gout; however, the considerable experience with this drug in children in Latin American countries, Hong Kong, and the United States has revealed few problems. It plays a major role in intensive, short-course treatment regimens.[181, 497]

Ethambutol (EMB) has been used for many years as a companion drug for INH in adults. The usual oral dose is 15 mg/kg/day. At this dose, the drug primarily is bacteriostatic, its major role being to prevent the emergence of resistance to other drugs. However, at doses of 25 mg/kg/day or 50 mg/kg given twice a week, EMB has some bactericidal action.[115, 174] Unfortunately, at these higher doses, optic neuritis or red-green color blindness has occurred in some adults. Regular visual field and color chart testing should detect these reversible effects early. Although the incidence of ophthalmologic toxicity in children is extremely low, if it occurs at all, EMB is not recommended for routine use in young children, in whom visual field and color discrimination tests are difficult and inaccurate. However, it is used frequently and safely in children with life-threatening forms of tuberculosis or drug-resistant tuberculosis.

Ethionamide is a very effective and well-tolerated drug in children at a dose of 15 to 20 mg/kg/day divided into two or three doses given after meals. Children rarely complain about its sulfurous taste, which is repulsive to adults. Related to INH, it likewise diffuses readily into spinal fluid.[138, 139, 224] Ethionamide is used in cases of drug-resistant tuberculosis. Unfortunately, no convenient pediatric dosage form is available.

Streptomycin (STM) is used in conjunction with INH and RIF in life-threatening forms of tuberculosis. It is bactericidal and tolerated well in children in the usual dose of 20 to 40 mg/kg/day intramuscularly up to 1 g. Usually, STM can be discontinued within 1 to 3 months if clinical improvement is definite, whereas the other two or three drugs are continued by mouth.

Para-aminosalicylic acid, either the sodium or the potassium salt, formerly was part of the standard treatment of tuberculosis. However, it is a purely bacteriostatic drug that has been superseded by more powerful drugs (RIF, PZA). It is used only for the treatment of drug-resistant tuberculosis.

Other antituberculosis drugs that may be needed for patients whose mycobacteria are resistant to INH or RIF are the aminoglycosides kanamycin, amikacin, and capreomycin, each of which has a spectrum of activity that differs from that of STM with respect to individual mycobacterial strains. Cycloserine and viomycin are other drugs sometimes used in patients with multidrug resistance. Clofazimine[242] and rifabutin (related to RIF) are newer drugs that have antimycobacterial activity but have been used mainly in children who have AIDS and are suffering from *Mycobacterium avium–intracellulare* infection. Clofazimine also is used for infection with *Mycobacterium leprae*.

Several of the fluoroquinolones, especially levofloxacin and ciprofloxacin, have significant antituberculosis activity,[267, 355] but they cannot be used routinely in children because of the possible destruction of growing cartilage seen in animal models.[541] However, the dire consequences of drug-resistant tuberculosis lead many experts to use them successfully in children with MDR-TB disease.[230]

Microbiologic Basis for Treatment[498]

Laboratory observations of *M. tuberculosis* and the results of clinical therapy trials have led to a hypothesis concerning the actions of various drugs and drug combinations.[149, 189, 352, 353] The tubercle bacillus can be killed only during replication, which occurs in organisms that are active metabolically. In one model, bacilli in a host exist in different populations (Table 101–10). They are active metabolically and replicate freely where oxygen tension is high and the pH is neutral or alkaline. Environmental conditions for growth are best within cavities, and such conditions can lead to a large bacterial population. Adults with reactivation-type pulmonary tuberculosis usually have all three populations of tubercle bacilli. Children with pulmonary tuberculosis and

TABLE 101–10 ■ IN VIVO LOCATION OF *MYCOBACTERIUM TUBERCULOSIS:* A MODEL

	Population Size	Metabolism and Replication	pH	Most Effective Drugs
Cavity	10^7–10^9	Active and rapid	Neutral or alkaline	INH, RIF, STM
Closed caseous lesions	10^5–10^7	Slow and intermittent	Neutral	RIF, INH
Within macrophages	10^4–10^6	Very slow	Acid	PZA, RIF, INH

INH, isoniazid; PZA, pyrazinamide; RIF, rifampin, STM, streptomycin.

patients of all ages with only extrapulmonary tuberculosis are infected with a much smaller number of tubercle bacilli because the cavitary population is not present.

Naturally occurring drug-resistant mutant organisms occur within large populations of tubercle bacilli even before chemotherapy is started.[190] All known genetic loci for drug resistance in *M. tuberculosis* are located on the chromosome; no plasmid-mediated resistance is known. The rate of resistance within populations of organisms is related to the rate of mutations at these loci.[11, 343, 522, 525, 530, 581, 582] Although a large population of bacilli as a whole may be considered drug-susceptible, a subpopulation of drug-resistant organisms occurs at a fairly predictable rate. The mean frequency of these drug-resistant mutants is about 10^{-6} but varies among drugs: STM, 10^{-5}; INH, 10^{-6}; and RIF, 10^{-7}.[124] A cavity containing 10^9 tubercle bacilli has thousands of single drug–resistant mutant organisms, whereas a closed caseous lesion contains few, if any, resistant mutants.

The two microbiologic properties of population size and drug resistance mutation explain why single antituberculosis drugs cannot cure cavitary tuberculosis. In the mid-1940s, STM alone was given to adults with cavitary pulmonary tuberculosis.[338] Within 3 months, 80 percent of patients had significant numbers of STM-resistant organisms. This phenomenon has been observed for every antituberculosis drug subsequently developed. However, the natural occurrence of resistance to one drug is independent of resistance to any other drug because the resistance loci are not linked. The chance of having even one organism "naturally" resistant to two drugs is on the order of 10^{-11} to 10^{-13}. Populations of this size in patients are extremely rare, and mutants naturally resistant to two drugs are nonexistent.

The population size of tubercle bacilli within a patient determines the appropriate therapy. For patients with large bacterial populations (adults with cavities or extensive infiltrates), many single drug–resistant mutants are present, and at least two antituberculosis drugs must be used. Conversely, for patients with tuberculosis infection but no disease, the bacterial population is small (about 10^3 to 10^4 organisms), drug-resistant mutants are rare, and a single drug can be used. Children with pulmonary tuberculosis and patients of all ages with extrapulmonary tuberculosis have medium-sized populations in which drug-resistant mutants may or may not be present. In general, these patients should be treated with at least two drugs.

Some antituberculosis drugs, such as INH, RIF, and STM, are bactericidal against *M. tuberculosis.* Other drugs, including ethionamide, para-aminosalicylic acid, and low-dose EMB, are bacteriostatic. The earliest treatment regimens for tuberculosis combined the killing action of a bactericidal drug with a bacteriostatic drug that would suppress replication of drug-resistant mutant organisms. A small number of organisms survived despite chemotherapy, and 18 to 24 months of treatment was necessary to permit host defenses to eliminate persisting organisms. Despite the prolonged treatment period, relapse rates were 5 to 15 percent, mostly a result of poor adherence to treatment.

The availability of RIF and the rediscovery of PZA in the early 1970s effected radical change in antituberculosis chemotherapy. These two drugs have the most potent sterilizing action, the ability to kill tubercle bacilli within lesions as quickly as possible.[246] The addition of RIF to INH for the treatment of pulmonary tuberculosis leads to cure rates approaching 100 percent with only 9 months of treatment.[146, 246] The further addition of PZA shortens the necessary treatment duration to only 6 months.

Treatment of the Stages of Tuberculosis

EXPOSURE

Children exposed to potentially infectious adults with pulmonary tuberculosis should begin treatment, usually with INH only, if the child is younger than 5 years of age or has other risk factors for the rapid development of tuberculosis disease, such as immunocompromise of some kind. Failure to do so may result in the development of severe tuberculosis disease even before the tuberculin skin test becomes reactive; the "incubation period" of disease may be shorter than that for the skin test. The child is treated for a minimum of 3 months after contact with the infectious case is broken (by physical separation or by effective treatment of the case). After 3 months, the tuberculin skin test is repeated. If the second test is positive, infection is documented and INH should be continued for a total duration of 9 months; if the second skin test is negative, treatment can be stopped. If the exposure was to a person with an INH-resistant but RIF-susceptible isolate, RIF is the recommended treatment.

Two special circumstances of exposure deserve attention. A difficult situation arises when exposed children are anergic because of HIV infection. These children are particularly vulnerable to rapid progression of tuberculosis, and it will not be possible to determine whether infection has occurred. In general, these children should be treated as though they have tuberculosis infection.

The second situation is potential exposure of a newborn to a mother (or other adult) with a positive tuberculin skin test or, rarely, a nursery worker with contagious tuberculosis.[300, 512] Management is based on further evaluation of the mother:

1. *The mother has a normal chest radiograph.* No separation of the infant and mother is required. Although the mother should receive treatment of tuberculosis infection and other household members should be evaluated for tuberculosis infection or disease, the infant needs no further work-up or treatment unless a case of disease is found.

2. *The mother has an abnormal chest radiograph.* The mother and child should be separated until the mother has been evaluated thoroughly. If the radiograph, history, physical examination, and analysis of sputum reveal no evidence of pulmonary tuberculosis in the mother, a reasonable assumption is that the infant is at low risk of acquiring

infection. The radiographic abnormality is due to another cause or a quiescent focus of previous tuberculosis infection. However, if the mother remains untreated, contagious tuberculosis may develop later, and the infant will be exposed. Both the mother and infant should receive appropriate follow-up care, but the infant does not need treatment. If the radiograph and clinical history are suggestive of pulmonary tuberculosis, the child and mother should remain separated until both have begun appropriate chemotherapy. The infant should be evaluated for congenital tuberculosis. The placenta should be examined. If the mother has no risk factors for drug-resistant tuberculosis, the infant should receive INH and close follow-up care. The infant should have a tuberculin skin test at 3 or 4 months after the mother is judged to no longer be contagious; evaluation of the infant at this time follows the guidelines for other exposure of children. If no infection is documented at this time, it would be prudent to repeat the tuberculin skin test in 6 to 12 months. If the mother has tuberculosis caused by a multidrug-resistant isolate of *M. tuberculosis* or she has poor adherence to therapy, the child should remain separated from her until she is no longer contagious or the infant can be given BCG vaccine and be kept separated until the vaccine "takes" (marked by a reactive tuberculin skin test).

INFECTION

The recommendation for treatment of asymptomatic tuberculin-positive individuals is based on data from several well-controlled studies; it applies particularly to children and adolescents who are at high risk for the development of overt disease but at very low risk for development of the main toxic manifestation of INH therapy, which is hepatitis.[59, 140, 165, 371, 382, 486] The large, carefully controlled U.S. Public Health Study of 1955, followed by others both in this country and abroad, demonstrated the favorable effect of 12 months of INH on the incidence of complications as a result of both lymphohematogenous and pulmonary spread.[221] The younger the tuberculin reactor, the greater the benefit.[114]

The American Thoracic Society, CDC, and AAP[13, 16] recommend that INH treatment of tuberculosis infection be given to the following groups:

1. Household members and other close associates of potentially infectious tuberculosis cases. All contacts of any age with a Mantoux tuberculin skin test reading of 5 mm or greater and without a documented history of reaction in the past should be considered recently infected and receive therapy.
2. Newly infected people regardless of age who have had a tuberculin skin test conversion within the past 2 years.
3. People with HIV infection or at risk for development of HIV infection who have a reaction of 5 mm or greater to a Mantoux test.
4. People of any age with past tuberculosis who received inadequate treatment.
5. People of any age with a significant tuberculin reaction and an abnormal but stable chest radiograph.
6. People with significant tuberculin reactions who have special clinical situations, including silicosis, diabetes mellitus, prolonged corticosteroid therapy, immunosuppressive therapy, hematologic malignancy, and end-stage renal disease.
7. All children and adolescents with a "positive" tuberculin skin test.

The question arises regarding how long the protective effect can be expected to last. Comstock and associates,[111] in their final report on INH prophylaxis in Alaska, demonstrated the protective effect of 1 year of chemoprophylaxis to be 19 years at least. Hsu[220] reported on 2494 patients monitored for up to 30 years and showed that adequate drug prophylaxis prevented reactivation of tuberculosis infection during adolescence and into young adulthood. It seems reasonable to hope that the decreased risk of active tuberculosis after INH prophylaxis may in fact be lifelong in individuals infected with INH-susceptible tubercle bacilli. Failure of INH after exposure to INH-resistant *M. tuberculosis* has been documented. No controlled study of an alternative regimen has been reported. RIF alone is recommended and widely used, although failures have been reported.[312]

The dosage of INH to be used has had little study. Most investigators have used a regimen based on 4 to 8 mg/kg of body weight per day, usually taken all at once, for a period of 6 to 12 months. A dose of 5 mg/kg/day was found satisfactory in one study.[113] Most clinicians prescribe a dose of 10 to 15 mg/kg/day to a total of 300 mg/day for treatment of infection to be sure of achieving therapeutic levels even in patients who inactivate the drug rapidly by acetylation.

The duration of INH treatment initially was set arbitrarily at 12 months.[235] A large trial comparing regimens of daily INH taken for 12, 24, and 52 weeks with placebo for their ability to prevent tuberculosis disease was conducted on adults in Eastern Europe with old fibrotic lesions caused by tuberculosis. Therapy for 1 year was most effective, especially if the patients were adherent. However, therapy for 24 weeks afforded a fairly high level of protection. A subsequent analysis concluded that the 24-week duration of preventive therapy was more cost-effective for adults than was the 52-week duration.[485] Subsequently, many health departments have accepted 6 months of INH preventive therapy as their standard regimen for adults. However, the cost-effectiveness analysis does not apply to children. A recent review of all published studies concluded that the effectiveness of INH therapy increased up to 9 months' duration, but no additional benefit was achieved with a longer duration.[16] A duration of 9 months is recommended for children and adults by the AAP and CDC.[16] INH is taken daily under self-supervision or can be taken twice weekly under directly observed therapy. When the child is infected with an INH-resistant but RIF-susceptible strain of *M. tuberculosis,* RIF should be substituted for INH and given for 6 months' duration. If the infecting strain is resistant to both INH and RIF, usually two other drugs are used; an expert in tuberculosis should be consulted in this situation.

DISEASE IN ADULTS

A shorter duration of antituberculosis chemotherapy is desirable for several reasons: (1) it may be significantly less expensive than traditional therapy; (2) the patient is exposed to potentially toxic drugs for shorter periods of time; (3) more time and resources can be allotted to ensure adherence with treatment; and (4) if a patient absconds from treatment, a greater likelihood will exist that bacteriologic cure already has been achieved as a result of the early and rapid sterilizing activity of the newer regimens.[4]

A 9-month regimen of INH and RIF cures more than 98 percent of cases of drug-susceptible pulmonary tuberculosis in adults.[146, 473] Both drugs are given daily for the first 2 weeks to 2 months and then can be given daily or twice weekly under directly observed therapy for the remaining 7 to 8 months with equivalent results and rates of adverse reactions. When given twice weekly, the RIF dose is the same as the daily dose, but the INH dose is increased to 900 mg in adults. Twice-weekly administration is supported by pharmacologic and animal model data determining the area-under-the-curve characteristics for these antituberculosis drugs.[4] Unfortunately, durations of therapy with only INH and RIF for less than 9 months are unacceptable because failure and relapse rates exceed 10 percent.

When three or more antituberculosis drugs are used initially, treatment durations of 6 months are routinely successful.[107] Regimens using INH, RIF, PZA, and STM during the initial phase (2 months), followed by INH and RIF in the continuation phase (4 months), routinely yield cure rates greater than 98 percent and relapse rates below 4 percent.[20, 62, 470] If PZA is excluded from the initial phase, the rate of bacteriologic failure rises to 7 to 10 percent.[213] However, exclusion of STM does not affect cure or relapse rates appreciably.[213, 487] Use of PZA beyond the first 2 months of therapy does not add any benefit.[214] Regimens of 4 months' total duration have unacceptably high relapse rates of 10 percent or greater. On the basis of all reported studies, the American Thoracic Society and CDC currently recommend for the treatment of pulmonary tuberculosis in adults a 6-month regimen using INH, RIF, and PZA for 2 months, followed by 4 months of daily or twice-weekly doses of INH and RIF.[13] EMB is added to the initial regimen if the risk of INH resistance is high (greater than 4% incidence in the community or the patient already has been treated for tuberculosis).

CHEMOTHERAPY FOR CHILDREN

Clinical trials of antituberculosis drugs in children are difficult to perform, mostly because of the difficulty in obtaining positive cultures at diagnosis or relapse and the need for very long-term follow-up.[497] Historically, recommendations for treating children with tuberculosis have been extrapolated from clinical trials of adults with pulmonary tuberculosis.[480] However, during the past 2 decades, a large number of clinical trials involving only children have been reported. In 1983, Abernathy and colleagues[2] reported successful treatment of 50 children with tuberculosis in Arkansas with INH and RIF daily for 1 month, then twice weekly for 8 months. The success rate virtually was 100 percent. Most pulmonary infiltrates cleared by the end of therapy, but hilar adenopathy usually was still present radiographically and then gradually cleared over a period of 2 to 3 years. Patients with only hilar adenopathy can be treated successfully with INH and RIF for 6 months.[239, 419]

Several major studies of 6-month therapy in children with at least three drugs in the initial phase have been reported.* The most commonly used regimen was 6 months of INH and RIF supplemented during the first 2 months with PZA. The overall success rate has been greater than 98 percent and the incidence of clinically significant adverse reactions less than 2 percent. Regimens not using STM were as successful as those that included it. Using twice-weekly medications (under directly observed therapy) during the continuation phase was as effective and safe as was daily administration. Three studies used twice-weekly therapy throughout the treatment regimen with excellent success.[282, 534, 554] The 6-month, three-drug regimen is successful, tolerated well, and less expensive.[542] It also effects a cure faster, so the likelihood of successful treatment is greater if the child becomes nonadherent later in therapy.

*See references 7, 8, 20, 48, 231, 282, 401, 505, 534, 540, 554.

EXTRAPULMONARY TUBERCULOSIS

Controlled treatment trials for various forms of extrapulmonary tuberculosis are rare. In most reports, extrapulmonary cases have been combined with pulmonary cases and often are not analyzed separately. Several of the 6-month, three-drug trials in children included extrapulmonary cases.[48, 282] Most non–life-threatening forms of extrapulmonary tuberculosis respond well to a 9-month course of INH and RIF[148, 150] or to a 6-month regimen including INH, RIF, and PZA.[237] One exception may be bone and joint tuberculosis, which may have a high failure rate when 6-month chemotherapy is used, especially if surgical intervention has not occurred.[148]

Tuberculous meningitis usually is not included in trials of extrapulmonary tuberculosis therapy because of its serious nature and low incidence. Treatment with INH and RIF for 12 months generally is effective.[558] In the 1950s, Lorber[318] treated children with tuberculous meningitis for only 6 months with good results. A more recent study from Thailand showed that a 6-month regimen that included PZA for serious tuberculous meningitis led to fewer deaths and better outcomes than did longer regimens that did not contain PZA.[240] Most children are treated initially with four drugs (INH, RIF, PZA, and ethionamide or STM). Treatment with PZA and the fourth drug is stopped after 2 months, and INH and RIF are continued for a total of 6 to 9 months.[139]

DRUG-RESISTANT TUBERCULOSIS IN CHILDREN

The incidence of drug-resistant tuberculosis is increasing in the United States and the world because of poor adherence by the patient, the availability of some antituberculosis drugs in noncontrolled over-the-counter formulations, and poor management by physicians.[50, 170, 326, 379] In the United States, approximately 10 percent of *M. tuberculosis* isolates are resistant to at least one drug.[51, 82, 84] Initial drug resistance rates of up to 80 percent have been noted in adults with pulmonary tuberculosis in some countries,[327] and rates of 20 to 30 percent are common findings. Resistance is most common to STM and INH and still is relatively rare to RIF.[127, 215, 354, 584] Certain epidemiologic factors—disease in an Asian or Hispanic immigrant to the United States, homelessness in some communities, and history of previous antituberculosis therapy—correlate with drug resistance in adult patients.[6, 27, 28, 394] Patterns of drug resistance in children tend to mirror those found in adult patients in the population.[81, 427, 446, 462, 488, 509, 511] Outbreaks of drug-resistant tuberculosis in children occurring at schools have been reported.[81, 425] Individual cases also have been recognized. The key to determining drug resistance in childhood tuberculosis usually comes from the drug susceptibility results of the infectious adult contact case's isolate.

Therapy for drug-resistant tuberculosis is successful only when at least two bactericidal drugs are given to which the infecting strain of *M. tuberculosis* is susceptible.[183, 393, 447, 510, 531] If only one effective drug is given, secondary resistance will develop. When INH resistance is considered a possibility on the basis of epidemiologic risk factors or the identification of an INH-resistant source case isolate, an additional drug—usually EMB or STM—should be given initially to the child until the exact susceptibility pattern is determined and a more specific regimen can be designed.[522] Exact treatment regimens must be tailored to the specific pattern of drug resistance. The duration of therapy usually is extended to at least 9 to 12 months if either INH or RIF can be used and to at least 18 to 24 months if resistance to both drugs is present.[236] Occasionally, surgical resection of a diseased lung or lobe is required.[238, 408] An expert in tuberculosis always should be involved in the management of children with drug-resistant tuberculosis infection or disease.

ADHERENCE AND DIRECTLY OBSERVED THERAPY

Nonadherence with drug treatment by patients is a major problem in tuberculosis control because of the long-term nature of its treatment.[345, 518, 559] As treatment regimens become shorter in duration, adherence assumes an even greater importance.[44] *Suspected* cases of tuberculosis must be reported to the local health department so that it can perform the necessary contact investigations and assist both patients and health care providers in overcoming barriers to adherence. To comply, the patient and family must know what is expected of them through verbal and written instructions in the patient's first language. An assessment of potential nonadherence should be made at the beginning of therapy.[32] Missed appointments should be brought quickly to the attention of the responsible public health officials, who may be able to use incentives/enablers, behavior modification, or, rarely, confinement to ensure adherence. The success of twice-weekly therapy, especially after a period of daily administration of medications, allows directly observed therapy to be given by a health care professional in cases of proven or suspected nonadherence.[99, 237] Most experts think that twice-weekly medication should be administered only under the direct observation of a health care worker.[278, 570] Direct observation means that a health care worker or other nonrelated third party (e.g., teacher, school nurse, social worker) is physically present while the patient ingests the medication. As many as 50 percent of patients taking long-term antituberculosis medications will have significant nonadherence, and its occurrence is not predictable by the physician. In most communities in the United States and an increasing number of other nations, directly observed therapy is the standard of care for all patients with tuberculosis disease.[98, 160, 575]

SUMMARY OF TREATMENT RECOMMENDATIONS

1. A regimen of INH and RIF for 6 months, supplemented with PZA during the first 2 months, is standard therapy for children with drug-susceptible intrathoracic tuberculosis in the United States and Canada.
2. An alternative regimen is INH and RIF for 9 months. The disadvantages of this regimen include a longer duration, the potential for increased drug resistance occurring during therapy, and less effectiveness if the patient absconds from treatment. This regimen should be used only if PZA cannot be tolerated.
3. After an initial 2 weeks to 2 months of daily drug administration, drugs can be given twice weekly under directly observed therapy with excellent effectiveness.[404] With patients for whom social or other restraints prevent reliable daily self-administration even during the initial phase of therapy, drugs can be given two or three times per week from the beginning under directly observed therapy.
4. In most cases, extrapulmonary tuberculosis can be treated with the same regimens as used for pulmonary tuberculosis, although data for tuberculous meningitis and bone or joint disease are relatively lacking.
5. In cases of possible initial INH resistance, EMB or STM should be added to the initial phase of all regimens until drug susceptibilities are known.[85]
6. Optimal therapy for tuberculosis in children with HIV infection has not been established. Most HIV-infected adults with tuberculosis respond well to antituberculosis drugs but may require longer durations of treatment.[251, 520] Immunosuppressed children with tuberculosis, including those with HIV infection, should be treated with at least three drugs initially, and treatment should be continued for a minimum of 9 months. HIV testing is recommended for all infants and children with tuberculosis disease.
7. Tuberculosis disease occurring during pregnancy should be treated with a 9-month regimen of INH and RIF supplemented during the initial phase with EMB (STM should not be used). The use of PZA in pregnant patients is controversial, though probably safe.

CORTICOSTEROIDS

Corticosteroids have a place in the treatment of patients with tuberculosis. They should never be used except under cover of effective antituberculosis drugs. Corticosteroids would be expected to be beneficial in situations in which the host inflammatory reaction is contributing to tissue damage or is impairing function.

Corticosteroids often are a useful addition to antituberculosis drugs if suppression of inflammatory reaction is desired, such as in the following situations[479]:

1. In patients with tuberculous meningitis in whom increased intracranial pressure is present. The major actions are to reduce vasculitis, inflammation, and, ultimately, intracranial pressure. Not only is reduction of pressure per se desirable, but lowering the pressure also probably favors the circulation of chemotherapeutic drugs through the brain and meninges.[163, 179] One study demonstrated lower rates of mortality and long-term neurologic sequelae in patients with tuberculous meningitis treated with corticosteroids than in non–steroid-treated control patients.[179]
2. In patients with acute pericardial effusion in whom tamponade is occurring. Relief of symptoms takes place within hours.[429, 515]
3. In patients with pleural effusion, a shift of the mediastinum, and acute respiratory embarrassment.[294, 482] The long-term course probably is the same with or without steroids, but symptomatic improvement usually is dramatic.
4. In patients with miliary tuberculosis if the inflammatory reaction is so severe that it produces alveolocapillary block with cyanosis.
5. In patients with enlarged mediastinal lymph nodes that are causing (1) respiratory difficulty or (2) a severe collapse-consolidation lesion, particularly in the middle or lower lobes, where bronchiectasis is likely to be a troublesome sequela.[367, 368] Under either of these circumstances, a course of corticosteroids is warranted, with the realization that it will be more successful in a younger infection because inflammation characterizes the early stages of tuberculosis. If caseation already is advanced, steroids will be of little benefit.

The dosage of corticosteroids should be in the anti-inflammatory range, that is, prednisone, 1 to 2 mg/kg/day for 4 to 6 weeks with gradual withdrawal. Some experts prefer dexamethasone, but no comparative trials have been published.

ACTIVITY

Activity need not be restricted in children with tuberculosis, except when a particular complication is inevitable (shortness of breath in pleural effusion, immobilization for a vertebral lesion). During the early months of treatment, patients probably should avoid competitive sports, excessive study, fatigue, and sunburn.

ISOLATION

Isolation should be maintained for children with cavitary lesions, productive cough with acid-fast stain–positive sputum, draining sinuses, or renal tuberculosis until their secretions are negative on smear and preferably on culture. Young children are practically noninfectious because they rarely cough and because their bronchial secretions contain few bacilli when compared with those of adults with tuberculosis. Guidelines issued by the CDC state that most children with typical tuberculosis do not require isolation in the hospital.[88] Children with possible pulmonary tuberculosis should be treated as potentially infectious if they have a cavity or extensive upper lobe infiltrate, if they have a productive cough (especially if the sputum is acid-fast smear–positive), or during high-risk procedures such as bronchoscopy.

FOLLOW-UP

Follow-up of children treated with antituberculosis drugs has become somewhat more streamlined in recent years. While receiving chemotherapy, the patient should be seen monthly, both to encourage regular intake of the prescribed drugs and to check, by a few simple questions (concerning appetite, well-being) and a few observations (weight gain; appearance of the skin and sclerae; palpation of the liver, spleen, and lymph nodes), that the disease is not spreading and that toxic effects of the drugs are not appearing.[572] Repeat chest radiographs should be obtained 1 to 2 months after the onset of chemotherapy to ascertain the maximal extent of disease before chemotherapy takes effect; thereafter, radiographs rarely are necessary.[273] Chemotherapy has been so successful that follow-up beyond its termination is not necessary, except for children with serious disease, such as tuberculous meningitis, or those with extensive residual chest radiographic findings at the end of chemotherapy.

CASE REPORTING

Every case of definite or suspected tuberculosis, by law,[87] must be reported immediately by telephone to the health authority[182] to ensure (1) prompt contact investigation[218] and (2) free antituberculosis drugs, which are available for diagnosed cases and for intimate contacts in almost every state of the United States and in many countries.

Prevention

Prevention of tuberculosis can be subdivided logically to consider the following circumstances:

1. Protection against exposure to the disease.
2. Use of antituberculosis drugs in tuberculin-negative individuals at high risk for infection.
3. Immunization of tuberculin-negative individuals.

Protection against exposure to disease is the ideal form of prevention. It presupposes thorough pre-employment and ongoing case-finding programs among all who come in contact with children, including daycare center and school personnel, Sunday school personnel, music and art teachers, hospital nurses, babysitters, household servants, food handlers, beauticians, and barbers. Numerous epidemics, mini-epidemics, and mass exposures in newborn nurseries have been traced to such infected individuals.

IMMUNIZATION

Immunization against tuberculosis theoretically would be a tremendous boon to humanity, but in practice, it has been fraught with very great difficulty. Various strains of mycobacteria and diverse nonliving immunogenic fractions have been studied. The impossibility of standardizing vaccines in the early days, the lack of any clinically useful test reflecting the immune status of the individual, and the relatively slow course of the disease have handicapped epidemiologic studies considerably. Furthermore, the very lack of adequate scientific data has intensified national and individual emotional responses to the point where rational approaches to data gathering and interpretation are often impossible. Although the use of tuberculosis vaccines for control of tuberculosis has waned in recent years in industrialized countries because of the falling incidence of the disease, new interest in them has cropped up because of their beneficial effect in certain types of malignancy. New insights into their mode of action may prove fruitful in the long run in understanding immunity to tuberculosis, as well as to neoplasia, and might lead to a greatly improved and clinically useful vaccine.

BCG was developed at the Institut Pasteur in Paris by Calmette and Guérin, who, starting in 1908, made 231 passages of a strain of *M. bovis* on a beef bile medium, thereby producing marked attenuation. Injected into laboratory animals, this strain was shown to increase resistance to challenge with virulent *M. tuberculosis*. In 1921, it first was administered orally to newborn infants and since then has been given to more than 4 billion people.

BCG vaccine attempts to replace the potentially dangerous primary infection with *M. tuberculosis* with an innocuous primary infection with the bacillus of Calmette and Guérin, thus activating host-cell–mediated immunity with minimal chance of causing progressive disease so that an infection with *M. tuberculosis* will be of the "reinfection" type.[308]

Strain variation and lack of standardization are basic problems in evaluating the results of immunization.[187, 532] BCG was maintained for many years by serial passage at the Institut Pasteur and distributed to hundreds of laboratories all over the world. Not until 1966 did the WHO Expert Committee on Biological Standardization adopt formal requirements for the maintenance of frozen "seed lots" to minimize the inevitable mutations that have produced BCG vaccines with widely varying characteristics. Routine quality control measures carried out by the production laboratory include an identity test, a test for contamination, a safety test in guinea pigs, estimate of the total bacillary mass, viability, and a test of heat stability. Periodic assessment of the allergenic capacity in humans is part of quality control testing. The WHO, through its International Reference Preparation for BCG Vaccine and through quality control testing on request carried out in its several cooperating laboratories, has helped decrease the gross variations in BCG vaccine found until quite recent years.

Vaccination techniques and dosages are quite variable. Intradermal injection is the most precise technique. Multiple-puncture techniques are popular because they are easy, but reported results consistently are inferior to those obtained with intradermal injection. Oral vaccination, the original method of administration, largely has been abandoned because of poor results. The actual dose of BCG at present usually is approximately 10^6 culturable particles. Because in animals large doses produce better resistance to challenge than small ones do, the largest convenient dose is used. However, in neonates, who have a higher incidence of untoward reactions, the customary approach is to halve the dose generally used in older infants and children to prevent local complications.

The usual local reaction to intradermal BCG vaccine is the development of a papule at the site of vaccination, and this papule reaches its maximal diameter (10 to 20 mm) in the sixth week. A small crust that may form on the papule detaches at about this time, with only a small ulcer remaining that may discharge a surprising amount of pus. Most ulcers are healed by the 10th week. A small scar is visible in almost all BCG-vaccinated individuals. Enlargement of the regional lymph nodes occurs regularly and is painless, sometimes ending in calcification. Abscess formation with breakdown is rare, but it occurs more often in infants.

Untoward reactions to BCG rarely have been a problem.[544] Fatalities caused by progressive disease have been reported in no more than 40 vaccine recipients (of an estimated 3+ million), usually (but not always) children with well-documented immunodeficiency.[75, 162, 185, 398, 402] No return of the attenuated strain to virulence has ever been noted. In countries where BCG is used routinely for immunization of neonates, osteomyelitis has been diagnosed in some 5 per 100,000 neonates. It usually becomes manifested when the child is between 5 and 33 months of age, when a tender swelling is noted near a joint; bone destruction is well localized and responds to conservative treatment. On the whole, BCG is one of the safest vaccines in use.

In many countries where BCG is given routinely, the incidence of HIV infection in adults and children is high.[61, 431] Reports of local and systemic complications from BCG vaccine in HIV-infected people are increasing, but the true magnitude of the interaction is not known yet.[41, 216, 381, 418] In most cases, BCG complications occur shortly after vaccination, but in one man with AIDS, adenitis as a result of BCG occurred 30 years after inoculation.[421] Routine treatment of patients with previous BCG vaccination who subsequently become immunocompromised is not recommended, but the clinician should be aware of previous BCG vaccination if signs or symptoms of mycobacterial infection occur.

The susceptibility of BCG to INH occasionally comes into question (1) if a rather severe reaction with an indolent draining ulcer, a draining lymph node, or osteomyelitis develops in a BCG vaccinee or (2) when simultaneous use of INH prophylaxis and BCG vaccine appears desirable (e.g., in the neonate of a mother with active tuberculosis). *M. bovis* and the various strains known as BCG *are* susceptible to approximately the same concentration of INH as is *M. tuberculosis.* Despite the effectiveness of INH, BCG organisms apparently do multiply sufficiently, when a large immunizing dose is given, to induce tuberculin sensitivity and, presumably, cell-mediated immunity. Canetti and his group in the 1950s developed an INH-resistant strain of BCG for immunization, but it proved to be excessively attenuated and its use was abandoned.

The effectiveness of revaccination has never been evaluated scientifically and is not recommended.

The efficacy of BCG vaccines in humans has been evaluated in several large, well-controlled studies (Table 101–11). Three of these trials showed excellent protection, two showed mediocre protection, and two showed little or no effect of BCG. Another study, not tabulated because its numbers are relatively small, is the "experiment of nature" reported by Hyge in 1957. Hyge observed an epidemic of tuberculosis in a school for girls, where 105 girls initially were tuberculin-negative, 130 were tuberculin-positive, and 133 were BCG-immunized. In this group, the total incidence of tuberculosis was 23 times as high in the tuberculin-negative as in the BCG-immunized girls. Explanations for these differences in outcomes among trials must be sought in (1) the quality and characteristics of the BCG vaccine used in the particular trial, (2) the possible immunizing effect (in Georgia and Alabama) of infections with other mycobacteria,[477] (3) the possibly greater effectiveness of BCG vaccine in areas of high tuberculosis prevalence, and (4) methodologic variations among the trials.

The most recent large study of BCG effectiveness is the Chingleput Study, started in 1968 in Chingleput District near Madras, South India, an area where sensitization with environmental mycobacteria is prevalent. People of all ages were vaccinated with one of two BCG vaccines or a placebo; only the incidence of adult-type pulmonary tuberculosis in the three groups was compared (i.e., not the forms usually found in children). Over the ensuing years, no difference in incidence was noted among the three groups. This disturbing result has been the subject of several WHO investigations because BCG is one of the vaccines recommended for all children in the Expanded Program of Immunization sponsored by the WHO itself.[420] Another study of neonatal vaccination with BCG in England reported very favorable results with BCG.[118]

A group at the Harvard School of Public Health reviewed all published studies of BCG efficacy in a meta-analysis.[109] Most published trials were not analyzed because of serious flaws in their experimental design or reporting. Among all trials and case-control studies included, the average protection

TABLE 101–11 ■ SUMMARY OF SEVEN LARGE CONTROLLED TRIALS OF BACILLUS CALMETTE-GUÉRIN (BCG) IMMUNIZATION AGAINST TUBERCULOSIS

Trial	Investigators	Intake Period	Vaccine Laboratory	Duration of Observation (yr)	% Protection from BCG
North America: Native Americans	Stein and Aronson, 1953	1935–1938	Phipps	9–11	80
Chicago: Infants	Rosenthal et al., 1961	1937–1948	Tice	12–23	75
Britain: Schoolchildren	Medical Research Council, 1971	1950–1952	Copenhagen	15	78
South India: Rural population	Frimodt-Moller et al., 1964	1950–1955	Madras	2.5–7	60/31*
Puerto Rico: Children	Palmer et al., 1958	1949–1951	New York State	5.5–7.5	31
Georgia, Alabama: Population	Comstock and Palmer, 1966	1950	Tice	14	14
Georgia: Schoolchildren	Comstock and Webster, 1969	1947	Tice	20	0

*The initial estimate of efficacy was 60 percent. Subsequently, when follow-up was extended to 9 to 14 years, the efficacy figure declined to 31 percent.

Adapted from Sutherland, quoted by Eickhoff, T. C.: The current status of BCG immunization against tuberculosis. Annu. Rev. Med. *28*:411–423, 1977.

against tuberculosis disease by various BCG preparations was 50 percent. The protective levels were higher for disease in children, particularly for meningitis and tuberculosis-associated death.[108] However, ascertainment bias and lack of standardized case definitions render the results of these analyses very difficult to interpret. The BCG vaccines prevent many cases of tuberculosis in children, but the effect is quite variable. That BCG vaccines are not an instrument of tuberculosis control also has become apparent because they do not prevent infection with *M. tuberculosis,* their protective effect is short lived, and vaccinating infants does little to prevent future cases of contagious tuberculosis among adults in a community.

The role of BCG vaccine in the United States today is very limited. The Advisory Committee on Immunization Practices of the U.S. Public Health Service and the Advisory Council for the Elimination of Tuberculosis recommend BCG only for tuberculin-negative infants and children in the United States who (1) are at high risk for intimate and prolonged exposure to persistently untreated or ineffectively treated adults with infectious pulmonary tuberculosis, cannot be removed from the source of infection, and cannot be placed on long-term preventive therapy or (2) continuously are exposed to people with tuberculosis resistant to INH and RIF.[90] A few observers, however, are more inclined toward the use of BCG in neonates who are at any risk of exposure to tuberculosis whatsoever.[262, 263, 471, 537]

Contraindications to the use of BCG for prevention of tuberculosis include congenital immunodeficiency, known HIV infection (in the United States; the WHO recommends giving BCG to asymptomatic HIV-infected infants who reside in areas with high tuberculosis rates), leukemia, lymphoma, and generalized malignancy, as well as treatment with corticosteroids, alkylating agents, antimetabolites, and radiation.

SELECTED READINGS

Brailey, M. E.: Tuberculosis in White and Negro Children. II. The Epidemiologic Aspects of the Harriet Lane Study. Cambridge, MA, Harvard University Press, 1958.

Dubos, R., and Dubos, J.: The White Plague: Tuberculosis, Man and Society. Boston, Little, Brown, 1952. Reissued by Rutgers University Press, 1987.

Friedman, L. N. (ed.): Tuberculosis: Current Concepts and Treatment. Boca Raton, FL, CRC Press, 1999.

Grange, J. M.: Mycobacteria and Human Disease. London, Edward Arnold, 1988.

Hardy, J. B.: Tuberculosis in White and Negro Children. I. The Roentgenologic Aspects of the Harriet Lane Study. Cambridge, MA, Harvard University Press, 1958.

Kubica, G. P., and Wayne, L. G.: The Mycobacteria. Parts A and B. New York, Marcel Dekker, 1984.

Lincoln, E. M., and Sewell, E. M.: Tuberculosis in Children. New York, McGraw-Hill, 1963.

Miller, F. J. W.: Tuberculosis in Children. New York, Churchill Livingstone, 1981.

Miller, F. J. W., Seal, R. M. E., and Taylor, M. D.: Tuberculosis in Children. Boston, Little, Brown, 1963.

Reichman, L. B., and Hershfield, E. S. (eds.): Tuberculosis: A Comprehensive International Approach. New York, Marcel Dekker, 1999.

Seminars in Pediatric Infectious Disease. Vol. 10, No. 4, 1993 (entire volume devoted to tuberculosis in children).

REFERENCES

1. Abadco, D., and Steiner, P.: Gastric lavage is better than bronchoalveolar lavage for isolation of *Mycobacterium tuberculosis* in childhood pulmonary tuberculosis. Pediatr. Infect. Dis. J. *11*:735–738, 1992.
2. Abernathy, R. S., Dutt, A. K., Stead, W. W., et al.: Short-course chemotherapy for tuberculosis in children. Pediatrics *72*:801–806, 1983.
3. Acocella, G.: The use of fixed dose combinations in antituberculous chemotherapy: Rationale for their application in daily, intermittent and pediatric regimes. Bull. Int. Union Tuberc. Lung Dis. *65*:77–83, 1990.
4. Acocella, G., and Angel, S. H.: Short-course chemotherapy of pulmonary tuberculosis: A new approach to drug dosages in the initial intensive phase. Am. Rev. Respir. Dis. *134*:1283–1286, 1986.
5. Afghani, B., and Lieberman, J. M.: Paradoxical enlargement or development of intracranial tuberculomas during therapy: Case report and review. Clin. Infect. Dis. *19*:1092–1099, 1994.
6. Aitken, M. L., Sparks, R., Anderson, K., et al.: Predictors of drug resistant diseases: *Mycobacterium tuberculosis.* Am. Rev. Respir. Dis. *130*:831–833, 1984.
7. Albisua, I., Artigao, F. B., Del Castillo, F., et al.: Twenty years of pulmonary tuberculosis in children: What has changed? Pediatr. Infect. Dis. J. *21*:91–97, 2002.
8. Al-Dossary, F. S., Ong, L. T., Correa, A. G., and Starke, J. R.: Treatment of childhood tuberculosis with a six month directly observed regimen of only two weeks of daily therapy. Pediatr. Infect. Dis. J. *21*:91–97, 2002.
9. Alland, D., Kolkut, G. E., Moss, A., et al.: Transmission of tuberculosis in New York City: An analysis by DNA fingerprinting and conventional epidemiologic methods. N. Engl. J. Med. *330*:1710–1716, 1994.
10. Almeida, L. M. D., Barbieri, M. A., Da Paixao, A. C., et al.: Use of purified protein derivative to assess the risk of infection in children in close contact with adults with tuberculosis in a population with high Calmette-Guérin bacillus coverage. Pediatr. Infect. Dis. J. *20*:1061–1065, 2001.
11. Altamirano, M., Marostenmaki, J., Wong, A., et al.: Mutations in the catalase-peroxidase gene from isoniazid-resistant *Mycobacterium tuberculosis* isolates. J. Infect. Dis. *169*:1162–1165, 1994.
12. American Thoracic Society: Control of tuberculosis in the United States. Am. Rev. Respir. Dis. *146*:1623–1633, 1993.
13. American Thoracic Society: Treatment of tuberculosis and tuberculosis infection in adults and children. Am. J. Respir. Crit. Care Med. *144*:1359–1374, 1994.
14. American Thoracic Society: Rapid diagnostic tests for tuberculosis: What is the appropriate use? Am. J. Respir. Crit. Care Med. *15*:1804–1814, 1997.
15. American Thoracic Society: Diagnostic standards and classification of tuberculosis in adults and children. Am. J. Respir. Crit. Care Med. *161*:1376–1395, 2000.
16. American Thoracic Society and Centers for Disease Control and Prevention: Targeted tuberculin testing and treatment of latent tuberculosis infection. Am. J. Respir. Crit. Care Med. *161*(Suppl.):221–247, 2000.
17. Anderson, P., Munk, M. E., Pollock, J. M., and Doherty, T. M.: Specific immune-based diagnosis of tuberculosis. Lancet *356*:1099–1104, 2000.
18. Andrew, O. T., Schoenfeld, R. Y., Hopewell, P. C., et al.: Tuberculosis in patients with end-stage renal disease. Am. J. Med. *68*:59–65, 1980.
19. Andronikou, S., Welman, C. J., and Kader, E.: The CT features of abdominal tuberculosis in children. Pediatr. Radiol. *32*:75–81, 2002.
20. Aquinas, S. M.: Short-course therapy for tuberculosis. Drugs *24*:118–132, 1982.
21. Askew, G. L., Finelli, L., Hutton, M., et al.: *Mycobacterium tuberculosis* transmission from a pediatrician to patient. Pediatrics *100*:19–23, 1997.
22. Aznar, J., Safi, H., Romero, J., et al.: Nosocomial transmission of tuberculosis infection in pediatrics wards. Pediatr. Infect. Dis. J. *14*:44–48, 1995.
23. Baciewicz, A. M., and Self, T. H.: Isoniazid interactions. South. Med. J. *78*:714–718, 1985.
24. Bagga, A., Kalra, V., and Ghai, O. P.: Intracranial tuberculoma evaluation and treatment. Clin. Pediatr. (Phila.) *27*:487–490, 1988.
25. Barber, T. W., Craven, D. E., and McCabe, W. R.: Bacteremia due to *Mycobacterium tuberculosis* in patients with human immunodeficiency virus infection: A report of 9 cases and a review of the literature. Medicine (Baltimore) *69*:375–383, 1990.
26. Barclay, W. R.: Does a positive tuberculin test indicate the presence of live tubercle bacilli? J. A. M. A. *232*:755, 1975.
27. Barksdale, L., and Kim, K. S.: *Mycobacterium.* Bacteriol. Rev. *41*:217–372, 1977.
28. Barnes, P. F.: The influence of epidemiologic factors on drug resistance rates in tuberculosis. Am. Rev. Respir. Dis. *136*:325–328, 1987.
29. Barry, M. A., Shirley, L., Grady, M. T., et al.: Tuberculosis infection in urban adolescents: Results of a school-based testing program. Am. J. Public Health *80*:439–441, 1990.
30. Barton, L. L., and Feigin, R. D.: Childhood cervical lymphadenitis: A reappraisal. J. Pediatr. *84*:846–852, 1974.
31. Bavadekan, A. V.: Osteoarticular tuberculosis in children. Prog. Pediatr. Surg. *15*:131–151, 1982.
32. Bayer, R., and Wilkinson, D.: Directly observed therapy for tuberculosis: History of an idea. Lancet *345*:1545–1548, 1995.
33. Bearman, J. E., Kleinman, H., Glyer, V. V., et al.: Study of variability in tuberculin skin reading. Am. Rev. Respir. Dis. *90*:913–919, 1964.
34. Beaudry, P. H., Brickman, H. F., and Wise, M. B.: Liver enzyme disturbances during isoniazid chemoprophylaxis in children. Am. Rev. Respir. Dis. *110*:581–584, 1974.
35. Beck-Sague, C., Dooley, S. W., Hutton, M. D., et al.: Hospital outbreak of multidrug-resistant *Mycobacterium tuberculosis* infections: Factors in transmission to staff and HIV-infected patients. J. A. M. A. *268*: 1280–1286, 1992.

36. Behr, M. A., Hopewell, P. C., Paz, E. A., et al.: Predictive value of contact investigation for identifying recent transmission of *Mycobacterium tuberculosis*. Am. J. Respir. Crit. Care Med. *158*:465–469, 1998.
37. Behr, M. A., Warren, S. A., Salamon, H., et al.: Transmission of *Mycobacterium tuberculosis* from patients smear negative for acid-fast bacilli. Lancet *353*:444–449, 1999.
38. Bellin, E. Y., Fletcher, D. D., and Safyer, S. M.: Association of tuberculosis infection with increased time in or admission to the New York City jail system. J. A. M. A. *269*:2228–2231, 1993.
39. Belsey, M. A.: Tuberculosis and varicella infections in children. Am. J. Dis. Child. *113*:444–448, 1967.
40. Berney, S., Goldstein, M., and Bishko, F.: Clinical and diagnostic features of tuberculous arthritis. Am. J. Med. *53*:36–42, 1972.
41. Besnard, M., Sauvion, S., Offredo, C., et al.: Bacillus Calmette-Guérin infection after vaccination of human immunodeficiency virus–infected children. Pediatr. Infect. Dis. J. *12*:993–997, 1993.
42. Besser, R. E., Pakiz, B., Schulte, J., et al.: Risk factors for positive Mantoux tuberculin skin tests in children in San Diego, California: Evidence for boosting and possible food borne transmission. Pediatrics *108*:305–310, 2001.
43. Beyazova, U., Rota, S., Ceuheroglu, C., et al.: Humoral immune response in infants after BCG vaccination. Tubercle Lung Dis. *76*:248–253, 1995.
44. Beyers, N., Gie, R., Schaaf, H., et al.: Delay in the diagnosis, notification and initiation of treatment and compliance in children with tuberculosis. Tubercle Lung Dis. *75*:260–265, 1994.
45. Beyt, B. E., Jr., Ortbals, D. W., Santa Cruz, D. J., et al.: Cutaneous mycobacteriosis: Analysis of 34 cases with a new classification of the disease. Medicine (Baltimore) *60*:96–109, 1980.
46. Bhagwati, S. N.: Spinal intramedullary tuberculoma in children. Childs Brain *5*:568, 1979.
47. Bhansali, S. K.: Abdominal tuberculosis: Experience with 300 cases. Am. J. Gastroenterol. *67*:324–337, 1977.
48. Biddulph, J.: Short-course chemotherapy for childhood tuberculosis. Pediatr. Infect. Dis. J. *9*:794–801, 1990.
49. Biehl, J. P., and Vilter, R. W.: Effects of isoniazid on pyridoxine metabolism. J. A. M. A. *156*:1549–1552, 1954.
50. Bifani, P. J., Plikaytis, B. B., Kapur V., et al.: Origin and interstate spread of a New York City multidrug-resistant *Mycobacterium tuberculosis* clone family. J. A. M. A. *275*:452–457, 1996.
51. Bloch, A., Cauthen, G., Onorato, I., et al.: Nationwide survey of drug-resistant tuberculosis in the United States. J. A. M. A. *271*:665–671, 1994.
52. Bloch, A. B., and Snider, D. E., Jr.: How much tuberculosis in children must we accept? Am. J. Public Health *76*:14–15, 1986.
53. Blumberg, H. M., Watkins, D. L., Berschling, J. D., et al.: Preventing the nosocomial transmission of tuberculosis. Ann. Intern. Med. *122*:658–663, 1995.
54. Blusse van Oud-Alblas, H. J., van Vliet, M. E., Kimpen, J. L., et al.: Human immunodeficiency virus infection in children hospitalized with tuberculosis. Ann. Trop. Paediatr. *22*:115–123, 2002.
55. Bovornkitti, S., Kangsdal, P., Sathirapat, P., et al.: Reversion and reconversion rate of tuberculin skin test reactions in correlation with the use of prednisone. Dis. Chest *38*:51–55, 1960.
56. Boyd, G. L.: Tuberculosis pericarditis in children. Am. J. Dis. Child. *86*:293–300, 1953.
57. Braden, C. R.: Infectiousness of a university student with laryngeal and cavitary tuberculosis. Investigative Team. Clin. Infect. Dis. *21*:565–570, 1995.
58. Brailey, M. E.: Observations on the development of intrathoracic calcification in tuberculin-positive infants. Bull. Johns Hopkins Hosp. *61*:258–271, 1937.
59. Brailey, M. E.: Tuberculosis in White and Negro Children. II. The Epidemiologic Aspects of the Harriet Lane Study. Cambridge, MA, Harvard University Press, 1958.
60. Bratcher, D. F., Stover, B. H., Lane, N. E., et al.: Compliance with national recommendations for tuberculosis screening and immunization of health care workers in a children's hospital. Infect. Control Hosp. Epidemiol. *21*:338–340, 2000.
61. Braun, M. M., Byers, R. H., Heyward, W. L., et al.: Acquired immunodeficiency syndrome and extrapulmonary tuberculosis in the United States. Arch. Intern. Med. *150*:1913–1916, 1990.
62. British Thoracic Society: A controlled trial of 6 months' therapy in pulmonary tuberculosis. Final report: Results during the 36 months after the end of chemotherapy and beyond. Br. J. Dis. Chest *78*:330–336, 1984.
63. Brock, R. C.: Post-tuberculous bronchostenosis and bronchiectasis of the middle lobe. Thorax *5*:5–39, 1950.
64. Brody, J. A., and McAlister, R.: Depression of tuberculin sensitivity following measles vaccination. Am. Rev. Respir. Dis. *90*:607–611, 1964.
65. Brown, E. R., Miller, B., Taylor, W. R., et al.: Health-care expenditures for tuberculosis in the United States. Arch. Intern. Med. *155*:1595–1600, 1995.
66. Brudney, K., and Dobkin, J.: Resurgent tuberculosis in New York City: Human immunodeficiency virus, homelessness and the decline of tuberculosis control programs. Am. Rev. Respir. Dis. *144*:745–749, 1991.
67. Burk, J. R., Viroslav, J., and Bynum, L. J.: Miliary tuberculosis diagnosed by fiberoptic bronchoscopy and transbronchial biopsy. Tubercle *59*:107–109, 1978.
68. Burke, H. E.: Pathogenesis of Pott's disease. Trans. Am. Clin. Climatol. Assoc. *59*:122–137, 1948.
69. Burroughs, M., Beitel, A., Kawamura A., et al.: Clinical presentation of tuberculosis in culture-positive children. Pediatr. Infect. Dis. J. *18*: 440–446, 1999.
70. Byrd, R. B., Horn, B. R., Solomon, D. A., et al.: Toxic effects of isoniazid in tuberculous chemoprophylaxis: Role of biochemical monitoring in 1,000 patients. J. A. M. A. *241*:1239–1241, 1979.
71. Campbell, I. A., and Dyson, A. J.: Lymph node tuberculosis: A comparison of various methods of treatment. Tubercle *58*:171–179, 1977.
72. Cantwell, M., Shehab, Z., Costello, A., et al.: Brief report: Congenital tuberculosis. N. Engl. J. Med. *330*:1051–1054, 1994.
73. Cantwell, M., Snider, D. E., Jr., Cauthen, G., et al.: Epidemiology of tuberculosis in the United States, 1985 through 1992. J. A. M. A. *272*:535–539, 1994.
74. Cardona, M., Bek, M. D., Mills, K., et al.: Transmission of tuberculosis from a seven-year-old child in a Sydney school. J. Paediatr. Child Health *35*:375–378, 1999.
75. Carlgren, L. E., Hansson, C. G., Henricsson, L., et al.: Fatal BCG infection in an infant with congenital lymphocytopenic agammaglobulinemia. Acta Paediatr. Scand. *55*:636–644, 1966.
76. Carr, D. T., Karlson, A. G., and Stilwell, G. G.: A comparison of cultures of induced sputum and gastric washings in the diagnosis of tuberculosis. Mayo Clin. Proc. *42*:23–25, 1967.
77. Carter, E. R., and Lee, C. M.: Interpretation of the tuberculin skin test reaction by pediatric providers. Pediatr. Infect. Dis. J. *21*:200–203, 2002.
78. Carvalho, A. C., Kritski, A. L., and De Reimer K.: Tuberculin skin testing among BCG-vaccinated children who are household contacts. Int. J. Tuberc. Lung Dis. *5*:297, 2001.
79. Casteels-Van Daele, M., Igodt-Ameye, L., Corbeel, L., et al.: Hepatotoxicity of rifampin and isoniazid in children. J. Pediatr. *86*:739–741, 1975.
80. Cave, M., Eisenach, K., McDermott, P., et al.: IS6110: Conservation of sequence in the *Mycobacterium tuberculosis* complex and its utilization in DNA fingerprinting. Mol. Cell. Probes *5*:73–80, 1991.
81. Centers for Disease Control and Prevention: Interstate outbreak of drug-resistant tuberculosis involving children—California, Montana, Nevada, Utah. M. M. W. R. Morb. Mortal. Wkly. Rep. *32*(39):516–518, 1983.
82. Centers for Disease Control and Prevention: Primary resistance to antituberculosis drugs—United States. M. M. W. R. Morb. Mortal. Wkly. Rep. *32*(40):521–523, 1983.
83. Centers for Disease Control and Prevention: A strategic plan for the elimination of tuberculosis from the United States. M. M. W. R. Morb. Mortal. Wkly. Rep. *38*(16):269–272, 1989.
84. Centers for Disease Control and Prevention: National action plan to combat multidrug-resistant tuberculosis. M. M. W. R. Recomm. Rep. *41*(RR-11):5–48, 1992.
85. Centers for Disease Control and Prevention: Prevention and control of tuberculosis in migrant farm workers. Recommendations of the Advisory Council for the Elimination of Tuberculosis. M. M. W. R. Recomm. Rep. *41*(RR-10):1–15, 1992.
86. Centers for Disease Control and Prevention: Initial therapy for tuberculosis in the era of multidrug resistance. M. M. W. R. Recomm. Rep. *42*(RR-7):1–8, 1993.
87. Centers for Disease Control and Prevention: Tuberculosis control laws—United States, 1993. M. M. W. R. Recomm. Rep. *42*(RR-15):1–28, 1993.
88. Centers for Disease Control and Prevention: Guidelines for preventing the transmission of *Mycobacterium tuberculosis* in health-care facilities, 1994. M. M. W. R. Recomm. Rep. *43*(RR-13):1–133, 1994.
89. Centers for Disease Control and Prevention: Screening for tuberculosis and tuberculosis infection in high-risk populations. Recommendations of the Advisory Council for the Elimination of Tuberculosis. M. M. W. R. Recomm. Rep. *44*(RR-11):19–34, 1995.
90. Centers for Disease Control and Prevention: The role of BCG vaccine in the prevention and control of tuberculosis in the United States: A joint statement by the Advisory Council for the Elimination of Tuberculosis and the Advisory Committee on Immunization Practices. M. M. W. R. Recomm. Rep. *45*(RR-4):1–18, 1996.
91. Centers for Disease Control and Prevention: Reported Tuberculosis in the United States, 1998. M. M. W. R. Morb. Mortal. Wkly. Rep. 48:16, 999.
92. Centers for Disease Control and Prevention: Tuberculosis elimination revisited: Obstacles, opportunities, and a renewed commitment. Advisory Council for the Elimination of Tuberculosis (ACET) M. M. W. R. Recomm. Rep. *48*(RR-9):1–13, 1999.
93. Centers for Disease Control and Prevention: Core Curriculum on Tuberculosis: What a Clinician Should Know. 4th ed. Atlanta, U. S. Department of Health and Human Services, 2000.
94. Centers for Disease Control and Prevention: Surveillance reports: Reported TB in the United States, 2000. Mor. Mortal. Wkly. Rep. C. D. C. Surveill. Summ. 2001.
95. Centers for Disease Control and Prevention: Preventing and controlling tuberculosis along the U.S.-Mexican border. M. M. W. R. Recomm. Rep. *50*(RR-1):1–27, 2001.

96. Chan, S., Abadco, D., and Steiner, P.: Role of flexible fiberoptic bronchoscopy in the diagnosis of childhood endobronchial tuberculosis. Pediatr. Infect. Dis. J. *13*:506–509, 1994.
97. Chan, S. P., Birnbaum, J., and Rao, M.: Clinical manifestation and outcome of tuberculosis in children with acquired immunodeficiency syndrome. Pediatr. Infect. Dis. J. *15*:443–447, 1996.
98. Chaulk, C. P., Moore-Rice, K., Rizzo, R., et al.: Eleven years of community-based directly observed therapy for tuberculosis. J. A. M. A. *274*: 945–951, 1995.
99. Chaulk, C. P., and Kazandijian, V. A.: Directly observed therapy for treatment completion of pulmonary tuberculosis. Consensus statement of the Public Health Tuberculosis Guidelines Panel. J. A. M. A. *279*: 943–948, 1998.
100. Chavalittamvong, B., and Talalak, P.: Tuberculous peritonitis in children. Prog. Pediatr. Surg. *15*:161–167, 1982.
101. Cheng, T. L., Miller, E. B., Ottolini, M., et al.: Tuberculosis testing. Physician attitudes and practices. Arch. Pediatr. Adolesc. Med. *150*:682–685, 1996.
102. Cheng, T. L., Ottolin, M., Getson, P., et al.: Poor validity of parent reading of skin test induration in a high risk population. Pediatr. Infect. Dis. J. *15*:90–91, 1996.
103. Chin, D. P., Crane, C. M., Diul, M. Y., et al.: Spread of *Mycobacterium tuberculosis* in a community implementing recommended elements of tuberculosis control. J. A. M. A. *283*:2968–2974, 2000.
104. Chintu, C., Bhat, G., Luo, C., et al.: Seroprevalence of human immunodeficiency virus type 1 infection in Zambian children with tuberculosis. Pediatr. Infect. Dis. J. *12*:499–504, 1993.
105. Choremis, C., Vlachos, J., Vlachou, C. A., et al.: Needle biopsy of the liver in various forms of childhood tuberculosis. J. Pediatr. *62*:203–207, 1963.
106. Christie, C. D. C., Contaniou, P., Marx, M. L., et al.: Low risk for tuberculosis in a regional pediatric hospital: Nine-year study of community rates and the mandatory employee tuberculin skin test program. Infect. Control Hosp. Epidemiol. *19*:168–174, 1998.
107. Cohn, D. L., Catlin, B. J., Peterson, K. C., et al.: A 62-dose, 6-month therapy for pulmonary and extrapulmonary tuberculosis. Ann. Intern. Med. *112*:407–415, 1990.
108. Colditz, G., Berkey, C. S., Mosteller, F., et al.: The efficacy of bacillus Calmette-Guérin vaccination of newborns and infants in the prevention of tuberculosis: Meta-analysis of the published literature. Pediatrics *96*:29–35, 1995.
109. Colditz, G., Brewer, T., Berkey, C., et al.: Efficacy of BCG vaccine in the prevention of tuberculosis: Meta-analysis of the published literature. J. A. M. A. *271*:698–702, 1994.
110. Comstock, G. W.: Variability of tuberculosis trends in a time of resurgence. Clin. Infect. Dis. *19*:1015–1022, 1994.
111. Comstock, G. W., Baum, C., and Snider, D. E., Jr.: Isoniazid prophylaxis among Alaskan Eskimos: Final report of the Bethel isoniazid studies. Am. Rev. Respir. Dis. *119*:827–830, 1979.
112. Comstock, G. W., Edwards, L. B., and Nabangxang, H.: Tuberculin sensitivity eight to fifteen years after BCG vaccination. Am. Rev. Respir. Dis. *103*:572–575, 1971.
113. Comstock, G. W., Hammes, L. M., and Pio, A.: Isoniazid prophylaxis in Alaskan boarding schools: Comparison of two doses. Am. Rev. Respir. Dis. *100*:773–779, 1969.
114. Comstock, G. W., Livesay, V. T., and Woolpert, S. F.: Prognosis of a positive tuberculin reaction in childhood and adolescence. Am. J. Epidemiol. *99*:131–138, 1974.
115. Crowle, A. J., Sbarbaro, J. A., Judson, F. N., et al.: The effect of ethambutol on tubercle bacilli within cultured human macrophages. Am. Rev. Respir. Dis. *132*:742–745, 1985.
116. Curless, R. G., and Mitchell, C. D.: Central nervous system tuberculosis in children. Pediatr. Neurol. *7*:270–274, 1991.
117. Curtis, A., Ridzon, R., Vogel, R., et al.: Extensive transmission of *Mycobacterium tuberculosis* from a child. N. Engl. J. Med. *341*: 1491–1495, 1999.
118. Curtis, H. M., Bamford, F. N., and Leck, I.: Incidence of childhood tuberculosis after neonatal BCG vaccination. Lancet *1*:145–148, 1984.
119. Dall, L., Long, L., and Stanford, J.: Poncet's disease: Tuberculosis rheumatism. Rev. Infect. Dis. *11*:105–107, 1989.
120. Daly, J. F., Brown, D. S., Lincoln, E. M., et al.: Endobronchial tuberculosis in children. Dis. Chest *22*:380–398, 1952.
121. Dandapat, M. C., Mishra, B. M., Dash, S. P., et al.: Peripheral lymph node tuberculosis: Review of 80 cases. Br. J. Surg. *77*:911–912, 1990.
122. Daniel, T., and Debanne, S.: The serodiagnosis of tuberculosis and other mycobacterial diseases by enzyme-linked immunosorbent assay. Am. Rev. Respir. Dis. *135*:1137–1151, 1987.
123. Dannenberg, A. M., Jr.: Delayed-type hypersensitivity and cell-mediated immunity in the pathogenesis of tuberculosis. Immunol. Today *12*:228–234, 1991.
124. David, H. L.: Probability distribution of the drug-resistant mutants in unselected populations of *Mycobacterium tuberculosis*. Appl. Microbiol. *20*:810–814, 1970.
125. De Angelis, L. M.: Intracranial tuberculoma: Case report and review of the literature. Neurology *31*:1133–1136, 1981.
126. de Blic, J., Azevedo, I., Burren, C., et al.: The value of flexible bronchoscopy in childhood pulmonary tuberculosis. Chest *100*:188–192, 1991.
127. Debré, R., Noufflard, H., Brissaud, H. E., et al.: Infection of children by strains of tubercle bacilli initially resistant to streptomycin or to isoniazid. Am. Rev. Respir. Dis. *80*:326–331, 1959.
128. Delacourt, C., Gobin, J., Gaillard, J., et al.: Value of ELISA using antigen 60 for the diagnosis of tuberculosis in children. Chest *104*:393–398, 1993.
129. Delacourt, C., Mani, T. M., Bonnerot, V., et al.: Computed tomography with normal chest radiograph in tuberculous infection. Arch. Dis. Child. *69*:430–432, 1993.
130. Delacourt, C., Poveda, J. D., Churean, C., et al.: Use of polymerase chain reaction for improved diagnosis of tuberculosis in children. J. Pediatr. *126*:703–709, 1995.
131. Dineen, P., Homan, W. P., and Grafe, W. R.: Tuberculous peritonitis: 43 years' experience in diagnosis and treatment. Ann. Surg. *184*:717–722, 1976.
132. Dinning, W. J., and Mauston, S.: Cutaneous and ocular tuberculosis: A review. J. R. Soc. Med. *78*:576–581, 1985.
133. Doerr, C. A., Starke, J. R., and Ong, L. T.: Clinical and public health aspects of tuberculous meningitis in children. J. Pediatr. 127:27–33, 1995.
134. D'Oliveira, J. J. G.: Cerebrospinal fluid concentrations of rifampin in meningeal tuberculosis. Am. Rev. Respir. Dis. *106*:432–437, 1972.
135. Domingo, Z., and Peter, J. C.: Intracranial tuberculomas: An assessment of a therapeutic 4-drug trial in 35 children. Pediatr. Neurosci. *15*:161–167, 1989.
136. Donald, P. R., Gent, W. L., Seifart, H., et al.: Cerebrospinal fluid isoniazid concentrations in children with tuberculous meningitis: The influence of dosage and acetylation status. Pediatrics *89*:247–250, 1992.
137. Donald, P. R., and Seifart, H.: Cerebrospinal fluid pyrazinamide concentrations in children with tuberculous meningitis. Pediatr. Infect. Dis. J. 7:469–471, 1988.
138. Donald, P. R., and Seifart, H. I.: Cerebrospinal fluid concentrations of ethionamide in children with tuberculous meningitis. J. Pediatr. *115*:483–486, 1989.
139. Donald, P. R., Schoeman, J. F., VanZyl, L. E., et al.: Intensive short-course chemotherapy in the management of tuberculous meningitis. Int. J. Tuberc. Lung Dis. *2*:704–711, 1998.
140. Dormer, B. A., Harrison, I., Swart, J. A., et al.: Prophylactic isoniazid protection of infants in a tuberculosis hospital. Lancet *2*:902–903, 1959.
141. Driver, C., Luallen, J., Good, W., et al.: Tuberculosis in children younger than five years old: New York City. Pediatr. Infect. Dis. J. *14*:117–121, 1995.
142. Driver, C. R., Valway, S. E., Cantwell, M. E., et al.: Tuberculin skin test screening of school children in the United States. Pediatrics *98*:97–102, 1996.
143. Drucker, E., Alcabes, P., Bosworth, W., et al.: Childhood tuberculosis in the Bronx, New York. Lancet *343*:1482–1485, 1994.
144. Dubos, R., and Dubos, J.: The White Plague: Tuberculosis, Man and Society. New Brunswick, NJ, Rutgers University Press, 1987.
145. Dunlap, N. E., Harris, R. H., Benjamin, W. H., Jr., et al.: Laboratory contamination of *Mycobacterium tuberculosis* cultures. Am. J. Respir. Crit. Care Med. *152*:1702–1704, 1995.
146. Dutt, A. K., Jones, L., and Stead, W. W.: Short-course chemotherapy for tuberculosis with largely twice-weekly isoniazid-rifampin. Chest *75*:441–447, 1979.
147. Dutt, A. K., Mehta, J. B., Whitaker, B. J., et al.: Outbreak of tuberculosis in a church. Chest *107*:447–452, 1995.
148. Dutt, A. K., Moers, D., and Stead, W. W.: Short-course chemotherapy for extrapulmonary tuberculosis. Ann. Intern. Med. *107*:7–12, 1986.
149. Dutt, A. K., and Stead, W. W.: Present chemotherapy for tuberculosis. J. Infect. Dis. *146*:698–704, 1982.
150. Dutt, A. K., and Stead, W. W.: Tuberculous pleural effusion: 6-month therapy with isoniazid and rifampin. Am. Rev. Respir. Dis. *145*: 1429–1432, 1992.
151. Dye, C., Espinal, M. A., Watt, C. J., et al.: Worldwide incidence of multidrug resistant tuberculosis. J. Infect. Dis. *185*:1197–1202, 2002.
152. Eamranond, P., and Jaramillo, E.: Tuberculosis in children: Reassessing the need for improved diagnosis in global control strategies. Int J. Tuberc. Lung Dis. *5*:594–603, 2001.
153. Edwards, L. B., and Hardy, J. B.: Relation of the degree of sensitivity to tuberculin to the persistence of sensitivity and to prognosis in young children. Bull. Johns Hopkins Hosp. *78*:13–20, 1946.
154. Ehrlich, R. M., and Lattimer, J.: Urogenital tuberculosis in children. J. Urol. *105*:461–465, 1971.
155. Eisenach, K. D., Sifford, M. D., Cave, M. D., et al.: Detection of *Mycobacterium tuberculosis* in sputum samples using a polymerase chain reaction. Am. Rev. Respir. Dis. *144*:1160–1163, 1991.
156. Ellard, G. A.: Hepatic toxicity of isoniazid among rapid and slow acetylators of the drug. Am. Rev. Respir. Dis. *118*:628–629, 1978.
157. Ellard, G. A., Humphries, M. J., Gabriel, M., et al.: Penetration of pyrazinamide into the cerebrospinal fluid in tuberculous meningitis. B. M. J. *294*:284–285, 1987.

158. Ellner, J. J.: Pleural fluid and peripheral blood lymphocyte function in tuberculosis. Ann. Intern. Med. *89*:932–933, 1978.
159. Emmett, J. R., Fischer, N. D., and Biggers, W. P.: Tuberculous mastoiditis. Laryngoscope *87*:1157–1163, 1977.
160. Enarson, D. A.: The International Union Against Tuberculosis and Lung Disease model national tuberculosis programs. Tubercle Lung Dis. *76*:95–99, 1995.
161. Espinal, M. A., Laszlo, A., Simonsen, L., et al.: Global trends in resistance to antituberculosis drugs. N. Engl. J. Med. *344*:1294–1303, 2001.
162. Esterly, J. R., Sturner, W. Q., Esterly, N. B., et al.: Disseminated BCG in twin boys with presumed chronic granulomatous disease of childhood. Pediatrics *48*:141–144, 1977.
163. Excobar, J. A., Belsey, M. A., Dueñas, A., et al.: Mortality from tuberculous meningitis reduced by steroid therapy. Pediatrics *56*:1050–1055, 1975.
164. Fennelly, K. P., and Nardell, E. A.: The relative efficacy of respirators and room ventilation in preventing occupational tuberculosis. Infect. Control Hosp. Epidemiol. *19*:754–759, 1998.
165. Ferrebee, S. H.: Controlled chemoprophylaxis trials in tuberculosis: A general review. Adv. Tuberc. Res. *17*:28–106, 1969.
166. Figueroa-Damian, R., and Arredondo-Garcia, J. L.: Neonatal outcome of children born to women with tuberculosis. Arch. Med. Res. *32*:66–69, 2001.
167. Filler, J., and Porter, M.: Physiologic studies of the sequelae of tuberculous pleural effusion in children treated with antimicrobial drugs and prednisone. Am. Rev. Respir. Dis. *88*:181–188, 1963.
168. Francis J., Reed, A., Yohannes, F., et al.: Screening for tuberculosis among orphans in a developing country. Am. J. Prev. Med. *22*:117–119, 2002.
169. Frieden, T. R., Fujiwara, P. I., Washko, R. M., et al.: Tuberculosis in New York City: Turning the tide. N. Engl. J. Med. *333*:229–233, 1995.
170. Frieden, T. R., Sterling, T., Pablos-Mendez, A., et al.: The emergence of drug-resistant tuberculosis in New York City. N. Engl. J. Med. *328*:521–526, 1993.
171. Friedland, I. R.: The booster effect with repeat tuberculin testing in children and its relationship to BCG vaccination. S. Afr. Med. *77*:387–389, 1990.
172. Froehlich, H., Ackerson, L. M., and Morozumi, P. A.: Targeted testing of children for tuberculosis: Validation of a risk assessment questionnaire. Pediatrics *107*:e54, 2001.
173. Gal, A. A., and Klatt, E. C.: Fatal isoniazid hepatitis in a child. Pediatr. Infect. Dis. J. *5*:490–491, 1986.
174. Gangadharam, P. R. J., Pratt, P. F., Perumal, U. K., et al.: The effects of exposure time, drug concentration, and temperature on the activity of ethambutol versus *Mycobacterium tuberculosis*. Am. Rev. Respir. Dis. *141*:1478–1482, 1990.
175. Gaur, S., Kesarwala, H., and Frenkel, L. D.: Tuberculous peritonitis in an adolescent female. Pediatr. Infect. Dis. J. *18*:859–862, 1987.
176. George, R. H., Gully, P. R., Gill, O. N., et al.: An outbreak of tuberculosis in a children's hospital. J. Hosp. Infect. *8*:129–142, 1986.
177. Ghon, A.: The Primary Lung Focus of Tuberculosis in Children. London, J. A. Churchill, 1916.
178. Giammona, S. T., and Zelkowitz, P. S.: The use of superheated nebulized saline and gastric lavage to obtain bacterial cultures in primary pulmonary tuberculosis in children. Am. J. Dis. Child. *117*:198–200, 1969.
179. Girgis, N. I., Fariz, Z., Kilpatrick, M. E., et al.: Dexamethasone adjunctive treatment for tuberculous meningitis. Pediatr. Infect. Dis. J. *10*: 179–182, 1991.
180. Girling, D. J: Adverse reactions to rifampicin in antituberculosis regimens. J. Antimicrob. Chemother. *3*:115, 1977.
181. Girling, D. J.: Role of pyrazinamide in primary chemotherapy for pulmonary tuberculosis. Tubercle *65*:1–4, 1984.
182. Glassroth, J., Bailey, W. C., Hopewell, P. C., et al.: Why tuberculosis is not prevented. Am. Rev. Respir. Dis. *141*:1236–1240, 1990.
183. Goble, M., Iseman, M. D., Madsen, L. A., et al.: Treatment of 171 patients with pulmonary tuberculosis resistant to isoniazid and rifampin. N. Engl. J. Med. *328*:527–532, 1993.
184. Gomez, L. P., Morris, S. L., and Panduro, A.: Rapid and efficient detection of extra-pulmonary *Mycobacterium tuberculosis* by PCR analysis. Int. J. Tuberc. Lung Dis. *4*:361–370, 2000.
185. Gonzalez, B., Moreno, S., Burdach, R., et al.: Clinical presentation of bacillus Calmette-Guérin infections in patients with immunodeficiency syndromes. Pediatr. Infect. Dis. J. *8*:201–206, 1989.
186. Gorse, G. J., and Belshe, R. B.: Male genital tuberculosis: A review of the literature with instructive case reports. Rev. Infect. Dis. *7*:511–524, 1985.
187. Grange, J. M., Gibson, J., Osborn, T. W., et al.: What is BCG? Tubercle *64*:129–139, 1983.
188. Graziani, A. L., and MacGregor, R. R.: Self-reading of tuberculin testing vs. physician reading. Infect. Dis. Clin. Pract. *4*:72–74, 1995.
189. Grosset, J.: Bacteriologic basis for short-course chemotherapy for tuberculosis. Clin. Chest Med. *1*:231–241, 1980.
190. Grosset, J. H.: Present status of chemotherapy for tuberculosis. Rev. Infect. Dis. *11*(Suppl. 2):342–347, 1989.
191. Grosskopf, I., David, A., Charach, G., et al.: Bone and joint tuberculosis: A 10-year review. Isr. J. Med. Sci. *30*:278–283, 1994.
192. Gupta, R., Gupta, S., Dingh, D., et al.: MR imaging and angiography in tuberculous meningitis. Neuroradiology *36*:87–92, 1994.
193. Gutman, L., Moye, J., Zimmer, B., et al.: Tuberculosis in human immunodeficiency virus–exposed or –infected United States children. Pediatr. Infect. Dis. J. *13*:963–968, 1994.
194. Hageman, J., Shulman, S., Schreiber, M., et al.: Congenital tuberculosis: Critical reappraisal of clinical findings and diagnostic procedures. Pediatrics *66*:980–984, 1980.
195. Hannachi, J., Martin, M., Boulabal, F., et al.: Comparison of three daily short-course regimens in osteoarticular tuberculosis in Algiers. Bull. Int. Union Tuberc. *57*:46–47, 1982.
196. Hardy, J. B.: Persistence of hypersensitivity to old tuberculin following primary tuberculosis in childhood: A long-term study. Am. J. Public Health *36*:1417–1426, 1946.
197. Hardy, J. B., and Hartmann, J. R.: Tuberculous dactylitis in childhood. J. Pediatr. *30*:146–156, 1947.
198. Harries, A. D.: Tuberculosis and human immunodeficiency virus infection in developing countries. Lancet *335*:387–390, 1990.
199. Harries, A. D., Hargreaves, N. J., Graham, S., et al.: Childhood tuberculosis in Malawi: Nationwide case-finding and treatment outcomes. Int. J. Tuberc. Lung Dis. *6*:424–431, 2002.
200. Harris, V. J., Dida, F., Lander, S. S., et al.: Cavitary tuberculosis in children. J. Pediatr. *90*:660–661, 1977.
201. Harrison, H. E., Finberg, L., and Fleischman, E.: Disturbances of ionic equilibrium of intracellular and extracellular electrolytes in patients with tuberculous meningitis. J. Clin. Invest. *31*:300–308, 1952.
202. Haygood, T., and Williamson, S.: Radiographic findings of extremity tuberculosis in childhood: Back to the future? Radiographics *14*:561–570, 1994.
203. Heinle, E. W., Jr., Jensen, N. N., and Westerman, M. P.: Diagnostic usefulness of marrow biopsy in disseminated tuberculosis. Am. Rev. Respir. Dis. *91*:701–705, 1965.
204. Helms, S., and Helms, P.: Tuberculin sensitivity during measles. Acta Tuberc. Scand. *35*:166–171, 1956.
205. Heney, C., Baise, T., and Cohen, M. A.: Tuberculosis of the mandible: A case report. Pediatr. Infect. Dis. J. *7*:74–76, 1988.
206. Heycock, J. B., and Noble, T. C.: Four cases of syringe-transmitted tuberculosis. Tubercle *42*:25–27, 1961.
207. Hodgson, A. R., Wong, W., and Yau, A. C. M. A.: X-ray Appearances of Tuberculosis of the Spine. Springfield, IL, Charles C Thomas, 1969.
208. Hoffman, E. B., Allin, J., Campbell, J. A., and Leisegang, F. M.: Tuberculosis of the knee. Clin. Orthop. *398*:100–106, 2002.
209. Hoffman, E. B., Crosier, J. H., and Cremin, B. J.: Imaging in children with spinal tuberculosis. J. Bone Joint Surg. Br. *75*:233–239, 1993.
210. Hoffman, N. D., Kelly, C., and Futterman, D.: Tuberculosis infection in human immunodeficiency virus–positive adolescents and young adults: A New York City cohort. Pediatrics *97*:198–203, 1996.
211. Hoge, C., Fisher, L., Donnell, D., et al.: Risk factors for transmission of *Mycobacterium tuberculosis* in a primary school outbreak: Lack of racial difference in susceptibility to infection. Am. J. Epidemiol. *139*:520–530, 1994.
212. Holt, L. E.: Tuberculosis acquired through ritual circumcision. J. A. M. A. *61*:99–102, 1913.
213. Hong Kong Chest Service/British Medical Research Council Fifth Collaborative Study: Controlled clinical trial of five 6-month regimens of chemotherapy for pulmonary tuberculosis. Am. Rev. Respir. Dis. *136*:1339–1342, 1987.
214. Hong Kong Chest Service/British Medical Research Council: Controlled trial of 2, 4 and 6 months of pyrazinamide in 6-month, three times weekly regimens for smear positive pulmonary tuberculosis, including an assessment of a combined preparation of isoniazid, rifampin and pyrazinamide: Results at 30 months. Am. Rev. Respir. Dis. *143*:700–706, 1991.
215. Honore, N., and Cole, S.: Streptomycin resistance in mycobacteria. Antimicrob. Agents Chemother. *38*:238–241, 1994.
216. Houde, C., and Dery, P.: *Mycobacterium bovis* sepsis in an infant with human immunodeficiency virus infection. Pediatr. Infect. Dis. J. *7*:810, 1988.
217. Howard, T. P., and Soloman, D. A.: Reading the tuberculin skin test: Who, when and how? Arch. Intern. Med. *148*:2457–2459, 1988.
218. Hsu, K. H. K.: Contact investigation: A practical approach to tuberculosis eradication. Am. J. Public Health *53*:1761–1769, 1963.
219. Hsu, K. H. K.: Tuberculin reaction in children treated with isoniazid. Am. J. Dis. Child. *137*:1090–1092, 1983.
220. Hsu, K. H. K.: Thirty years after isoniazid: Its impact on tuberculosis in children and adolescents. J. A. M. A. *251*:1283–1285, 1984.
221. Hsu, K. H. K., and Starke, J. R.: Diagnosis and treatment of tuberculous infection. Semin. Pediatr. Infect. Dis. *4*:283–290, 1993.
222. Hsu, L. C. S., and Leong, J. C. Y.: Tuberculosis of the lower cervical spine (C2 to C7). A report on 40 cases. J. Bone Joint Surg. Br. *66*:1–5, 1984.
223. Huebner, R. E., Schein, M. F., and Bass, J. B.: The tuberculin skin test. Clin. Infect. Dis. *17*:968–975, 1993.
224. Hughes, I. E., Smith, H., and Kane, P. O.: Ethionamide: Its passage into the cerebrospinal fluid in man. Lancet *1*:616–617, 1962.

225. Hughesdon, M. R.: Congenital tuberculosis. Arch. Dis. Child. *21*:121–138, 1946.
226. Hugo-Hamman, C. T., Scher, H., and DeMoor, M. M. A.: Tuberculous pericarditis in children: A review of 44 cases. Pediatr. Infect. Dis. J. *13*:13–18, 1994.
227. Humphries, M. J., Teoh, R., Lau, J., et al.: Factors of prognostic significance in Chinese children with tuberculous meningitis. Tubercle *71*:161–168, 1990.
228. Hussey, G., Chisholm, T., and Kibel, M.: Miliary tuberculosis in children: A review of 94 cases. Pediatr. Infect. Dis. J. *10*:832–836, 1991.
229. Hussey, G., Kibel, M., and Dempster, W.: The serodiagnosis of tuberculosis in children: An evaluation of an ELISA test using IgG antibodies to *M. tuberculosis*, strain H37RV. Ann. Trop. Paediatr. *11*:113–118, 1991.
230. Hussey, G., Kibel, M., and Parker, N.: Ciprofloxacin treatment of multiply drug-resistant extrapulmonary tuberculosis in a child. Pediatr. Infect. Dis. J. *11*:408–409, 1992.
231. Ibanez, S., and Ross, G.: Quimioterapia abreviada de 6 meses en tuberculosis pulmonar infantil. Rev. Chil. Pediatr. *51*:249–252, 1980.
232. Idriss, Z. H., Sinno, A., and Kronfol, N. M.: Tuberculous meningitis in childhood: Forty-three cases. Am. J. Dis. Child. *130*:364–367, 1976.
233. Ildirim, I., Hacimustafaoglu, M., and Ediz, B.: Correlation of tuberculin induration with the number of bacillus Calmette-Guérin vaccines. Pediatr. Infect. Dis. J. *14*:1060–1063, 1995.
234. Ingalhalikar, V. T., Deostale, D. A., and Abhyankar, V. K.: Nonimmobilization of surgically treated tuberculosis of spine in children. Prog. Pediatr. Surg. *15*:153–157, 1982.
235. International Union Against Tuberculosis Committee on Prophylaxis: Efficacy of various durations of isoniazid preventive therapy for tuberculosis: Five years of follow-up in the IUAT trial. Bull. World Health Organ. *60*:555–564, 1982.
236. Iseman, M. D.: Treatment of multidrug-resistant tuberculosis. N. Engl. J. Med. *329*:784–791, 1993.
237. Iseman, M. D., Cohn, D. L., and Sbarbaro, J. A.: Directly observed treatment of tuberculosis: We can't afford not to try it. N. Engl. J. Med. *328*:576–578, 1993.
238. Iseman, M. D., Madsen, L., Goble, M., et al.: Surgical intervention in the treatment of pulmonary disease caused by drug-resistant *Mycobacterium tuberculosis*. Am. Rev. Respir. Dis. *141*:623–625, 1990.
239. Jacobs, R. F., and Abernathy, R. S.: The treatment of tuberculosis in children. Pediatr. Infect. Dis. *4*:513–517, 1985.
240. Jacobs, R. F., Sunakorn, P., Chotpitayasunonah, T., et al.: Intensive short course chemotherapy for tuberculous meningitis. Pediatr. Infect. Dis. J. *11*:194–198, 1992.
241. Jaffe, I. P.: Tuberculous meningitis in childhood. Lancet *1*:738, 1982.
242. Jagannath, C., Reddy, M. V., Kailasam, S., et al.: Chemotherapeutic activity of clofazimine and its analogues against *Mycobacterium tuberculosis*. Am. J. Respir. Crit. Care Med. *151*:1083–1086, 1995.
243. Janner, D., Kirk, S., and McLeary, M.: Cerebral tuberculosis without neurologic signs and with normal cerebrospinal fluid. Pediatr. Infect. Dis. J. *19*:763–764, 2000.
244. Jawahar, M. S., Sivasubramanian, S., Vijayan, V. K., et al.: Short course chemotherapy for tuberculous lymphadenitis in children. B. M. J. *301*:359–362, 1990.
245. Jereb, J., Kelly, G., and Porterfield, D.: The epidemiology of tuberculosis in children. Semin. Pediatr. Infect. Dis. *4*:220–231, 1993.
246. Jindani, A., Aber, V. R., Edwards, E. A., et al.: The early bactericidal activity of drugs in patients with pulmonary tuberculosis. Am. Rev. Respir. Dis. *121*:939–949, 1980.
247. Jinkins, J. R.: Computed tomography of intracranial tuberculosis. Neuroradiology *33*:126–135, 1991.
248. John, J. F., and Douglas, R. G.: Tuberculous arachnoiditis. J. Pediatr. *86*:235–237, 1975.
249. Johnson, H., Lee, B., Doherty, E., et al.: Tuberculin sensitivity and the BCG scar in tuberculosis contacts. Tubercle Lung Dis. *76*:122–125, 1995.
250. Johnston, J. A.: Nutritional Studies in Adolescent Girls and Their Relation to Tuberculosis. Springfield, IL, Charles C Thomas, 1953.
251. Jones, B. E., Otaya, M., Antoniskis, D., et al.: A prospective evaluation of antituberculosis therapy in patients with human immunodeficiency virus infection. Am. J. Respir. Crit. Care Med. *150*:1499–1502, 1994.
252. Jones, D., Malecki, J., Bigler, W., et al.: Pediatric tuberculosis and human immunodeficiency virus infection in Palm Beach County, Florida. Am. J. Dis. Child. *146*:1166–1170, 1992.
253. Kalish, S. B., Radiu, R. C., Phair, J. P., et al.: Use of an enzyme-linked immunosorbent assay technique in the differential diagnosis of active pulmonary tuberculosis in humans. J. Infect. Dis. *147*:523–530, 1983.
254. Kalish, S. B., Rodin, R. C., Levitz, D., et al.: Enzyme-linked immunosorbent assay method for IgG antibody to purified protein derivative in cerebrospinal fluid of patients with tuberculous meningitis. Ann. Intern. Med. *99*:630–633, 1983.
255. Kallmann, I. J., and Reisner, D.: Twin studies on the genetic factors in tuberculosis. Am. Rev. Tuberc. *47*:549, 1943.
256. Kedar, R. P., Shah, P. P., Shivde, R. S., et al.: Sonographic findings in gastrointestinal and peritoneal tuberculosis. Clin. Radiol. *49*:24–29, 1994.
257. Kellerman, S. E., Saiman, L., San Gabriel, P., et al.: Observational study of the use of infection control interventions for *Mycobacterium tuberculosis* in pediatric facilities. Pediatr. Infect. Dis. J. *20*:566–570, 2001.
258. Kellerman, S., Saiman, L., Soto-Irizarry, M., et al.: Costs associated with tuberculosis control programs at hospitals caring for children. Pediatr. Infect. Dis. J. *18*:604–608, 1999.
259. Kellerman, S. E., Simonds, D., Banerjee, S., et al.: APIC and CDC survey of *Mycobacterium tuberculosis* isolation and control practices in hospitals caring for children. Part I: Patient and family isolation policies and procedures. Am. J. Infect. Control *26*:478–482, 1998.
260. Kellerman, S. E., Simonds, D., Banergee, S., et al.: APIC and CDC survey of *Mycobacterium tuberculosis* isolation and control practices in hospitals caring for children. Part 2: Environmental and administrative controls. Am. J. Infect. Control *26*:483–487, 1998.
261. Kendig, E. L., Jr.: Tuberculosis in the very young: Report of three cases of infants less than one month of age. Am. Rev. Tuberc. *70*:161–165, 1954.
262. Kendig, E. L., Jr.: Prognosis of infants born of tuberculous mothers. Pediatrics *26*:97–100, 1960.
263. Kendig, E. L., Jr.: The place of BCG vaccine in the management of infants born of tuberculous mothers. N. Engl. J. Med. *281*:520–523, 1969.
264. Kendig, E. L., Jr., and Rodgers, W. L.: Tuberculosis in the neonatal period. Am. Rev. Tuberc. Pulm. Dis. *77*:418–422, 1958.
265. Kendig, E. L., Kirkpatrick, B. V., Carter, W. H., et al.: Under reading of the tuberculin skin test reaction. Chest *113*:1175–1177, 1998.
266. Kennedy, C., and Knowles, G. K.: Miliary tuberculosis presenting with skin lesions. B. M. J. *3*:356, 1975.
267. Kennedy, N., Fox, R., Kisyombe, G. M., et al.: Early bactericidal and sterilizing activities of ciprofloxacin in pulmonary tuberculosis. Am. Rev. Respir. Dis. *148*:1547–1551, 1993.
268. Khan, E. A., and Starke, J. R.: Diagnosis of tuberculosis in children: Increased need for better methods. Emerg. Infect. Dis. *1*:115–123, 1995.
269. Khan, M. A., Chandrasekaran, B., and Needle, M.: Tuberculosis in chronic renal failure. Letter. Arch. Intern. Med. *141*:1554, 1981.
270. Khouri, Y., Mastrucci, M., Hutto, C., et al.: *Mycobacterium tuberculosis* in children with human immunodeficiency virus type 1 infection. Pediatr. Infect. Dis. J. *11*:950–955, 1992.
271. Kim, J. H., Langston, A. A., and Gallis, H. A.: Miliary tuberculosis: Epidemiology, clinical manifestations, diagnosis and outcome. Rev. Infect. Dis. *12*:583–590, 1990.
272. Kimerling, M. E., Vaughn, E. S., and Dunlap, N. E.: Childhood tuberculosis in Alabama: Epidemiology of disease and indicators of program effectiveness, 1983 to 1993. Pediatr. Infect. Dis. J. *14*:678–684, 1995.
273. Kisembo, H. N., Kawooya, M. G., Zirembozi, G., and Okwera, A.: Serial chest radiographs in the management of children with a clinical suspicion of pulmonary tuberculosis. J. Trop. Pediatr. *47*:276–283,2001.
274. Kiwanuka J., Graham, S. M., Coulter, J. B., et al.: Diagnosis of pulmonary tuberculosis in children in an HIV-endemic area, Malawi. Ann. Trop. Paediatr. *21*:5–14, 2001.
275. Klausner, J. D., Ryder, R. W., Baende, E., et al.: *Mycobacterium tuberculosis* in household contacts of human immunodeficiency virus type 1–seropositive patients with active pulmonary tuberculosis in Kinshasa, Zaire. J. Infect. Dis. *168*:106–111, 1993.
276. Kochi, A.: The global tuberculosis situation and the new control strategy of the World Health Organization. Tubercle *72*:1–6, 1991.
277. Kohli, V., Kumar, L., and Kataria, S.: Multiple hepatosplenic tuberculous abscesses in an eight-year-old boy. Pediatr. Infect. Dis. J. *15*:178–179, 1996.
278. Kohn, M. R., Arden, M. R., Vasilakis, J., et al.: Directly observed preventive therapy: Turning the tide against tuberculosis. Arch. Pediatr. Adolesc. Med. *150*:727–729, 1996.
279. Kopanoff, D. E., Snider, D. E., and Caras, G. J.: Isoniazid-related hepatitis: A United States Public Health Service Cooperative Surveillance Study. Am. Rev. Respir. Dis. *117*:991–1001, 1978.
280. Kumar, A., Misra, P. K., Mehotra, R., et al.: Hepatotoxicity of rifampin and isoniazid: Is it all drug-induced hepatitis? Am. Rev. Respir. Dis. *143*:1350–1352, 1991.
281. Kumar, B., Rai, R., Kaur, I., et al.: Childhood cutaneous tuberculosis: A study over 25 years from northern India. Int. J. Dermatol. *40*:26–32, 2001.
282. Kumar, L., Dhand, R., Singhi, P. D., et al.: A randomized trial of fully intermittent vs. daily followed by intermittent short-course chemotherapy for childhood tuberculosis. Pediatr. Infect. Dis. J. *9*:802–806, 1990.
283. Kumar R., Pandery, C. K., Bose, N., and Sahay S.: Tuberculosis brain abscess: Clinical presentation, pathophysiology and treatment (in children). Childs Nerv. Syst. *18*:118–123, 2002.
284. Kutt, H., Brennan, R., Dehejia, H., et al.: Diphenylhydantoin intoxication: A complication of isoniazid therapy. Am. Rev. Respir. Dis. *101*:377–384, 1970.
285. Lai, K. K., Stottmeier, K. D., Sherman, I. H., et al.: Mycobacterial cervical lymphadenopathy: Relation of etiologic agents to age. J. A. M. A. *251*:1286–1288, 1984.
286. Lake, A. M., and Oski, F. A.: Peripheral lymphadenopathy in childhood: Ten-year experience with excisional biopsy. Am. J. Dis. Child. *132*:357–359, 1978.

287. Lamont, A., Cremin, B., and Pettenet, B.: Radiologic patterns of pulmonary tuberculosis in the pediatric age group. Pediatr. Radiol. *16*:2–7, 1986.
288. Lamprecht, D., Schoeman, J., Donald, P., and Hartzenberg, H.: Ventriculoperitoneal shunting in childhood tuberculosis meningitis. Br. J. Neurosurg. *15*:119–125, 2001.
289. Lange, W. R., Warnock-Eckhart, E., and Bean, M. E.: *Mycobacterium tuberculosis* infection in foreign born adoptees. Pediatr. Infect. Dis. J. *8*:625–629, 1989.
290. Lanier, V. S., Russell, W. F., Jr., Heaton, A., et al.: Concentrations of active isoniazid in serum and cerebrospinal fluid of patients with tuberculosis treated with isoniazid. Pediatrics *21*:910–915, 1958.
291. Larmola, E.: Two cases of sudden death in infants recovering from primary tuberculosis. Acta Tuberc. Scand. *21*(Suppl.):67, 1949.
292. Lau, S. K., Kwan, S., Lee, J., et al.: Source of tubercle bacilli in cervical lymph nodes: A prospective study. J. Laryngol. Otol. *105*:558–561, 1991.
293. Laven, G. T.: Diagnosis of tuberculosis in children using fluorescence microscopic examination of gastric washings. Am. Rev. Respir. Dis. *115*:743–749, 1977.
294. Lee, C., Wang, W., Lan, R., et al.: Corticosteroids in the treatment of tuberculous pleurisy: A double-blind, placebo-controlled randomized study. Chest *94*:1256–1259, 1988.
295. Lee, L. H., Le Vea, C. M., and Graman, P. S.: Congenital tuberculosis in a neonatal intensive care unit: Case report, epidemiologic investigation and management of exposures. Clin. Infect. Dis. *27*:474–477, 1998.
296. Lees, A., Macleod, A., and Marshall, J.: Cerebral tuberculoma developing during treatment of tuberculous meningitis. Lancet *1*:1208–1211, 1980.
297. Leggiadro, R. J., Collery, B., and Dowdy, S.: Outbreak of tuberculosis in a family day care home. Pediatr. Infect. Dis. J. *8*:52–54, 1989.
298. Leiguarda, R., Berthier, M., Starkstein, S., et al.: Ischemic infarction in 25 children with tuberculous meningitis. Stroke *19*:200–204, 1988.
299. Levine, H., Metzger, W., Lacera, S., et al.: Diagnosis of tuberculous pleurisy by culture of pleural biopsy specimen. Arch. Intern. Med. *126*:269–271, 1970.
300. Light, I. J., Saidleman, M., and Sutherland, J. M.: Management of newborns after nursery exposure to tuberculosis. Am. Rev. Respir. Dis. *109*:415–419, 1974.
301. Lincoln, E. M.: Tuberculous meningitis in children: With special reference to serous meningitis. Am. Rev. Tuberc. *56*:75–94, 95–109, 1947.
302. Lincoln, E. M.: Epidemics of tuberculosis. Adv. Tuberc. Res. *14*:159–197, 1965.
303. Lincoln, E. M., Davies, P. A., and Bovornkitti, S.: Tuberculous pleurisy with effusion in children. Am. Rev. Tuberc. *77*:271–289, 1958.
304. Lincoln, E. M., Gilbert, L., and Morales, S. M.: Chronic pulmonary tuberculosis in individuals with known previous primary tuberculosis. Dis. Chest *38*:473–482, 1960.
305. Lincoln, E. M., Harris, L. C., Bovornkitti, S., et al.: Endobronchial tuberculosis in children. Am. Rev. Tuberc. Pulm. Dis. *77*:39–61, 1958.
306. Lincoln, E. M., Sabato, V. R., and Davies, P. A.: Tuberculous meningitis in children. J. Pediatr. *57*:807–823, 1960.
307. Lincoln, E. M., and Sewell, E. M.: Tuberculosis in Children. New York, McGraw-Hill, 1963.
308. Lindgren, I.: Pathology of tuberculous infection in BCG-vaccinated humans. Adv. Tuberc. Res. *14*:203–231, 1965.
309. Linna, O., and Uhari, M.: Hepatotoxicity of rifampicin and isoniazid in children treated for tuberculosis. Eur. J. Pediatr. *134*:227–229, 1980.
310. Litt, I. F., Cohen, M. I., and McNamara, H.: Isoniazid hepatitis in adolescents. J. Pediatr. *89*:133–135, 1976.
311. Liu, K. W., Chan, Y. L., Tseng, R., et al.: Childhood abdominal tuberculosis: The role of echo-guided fine-needle aspiration in its management. Surg. Endosc. *8*:326–328, 1994.
312. Livengood, J. R., Sigler, T. G., Foster, L. R., et al.: Isoniazid-resistant tuberculosis: A community outbreak and report of a rifampin prophylaxis failure. J. A. M. A. *253*:2847–2849, 1985.
313. Lobato, M., and Hopewell, P.C.: *Mycobacterium tuberculosis* infection after travel to or contact with visitors from countries with high prevalence of tuberculosis. Am. J. Respir. Crit. Care Med. *158*:1871–1875, 1998.
314. Lobato, M. N., Mohle-Boetani, J. C., and Royce, S. E.: Missed opportunities for preventing tuberculosis among children younger than five years of age. Pediatrics *106*:e75, 2000.
315. Lockman, S., Tappero, J. W., Kenyon, T. A., et al.: Tuberculin reactivity in a pediatric population with high BCG vaccination coverage. Int. J. Tuberc. Lung Dis. *3*:23–30, 1999.
316. Loddenkemper, R.: Prospective individual comparison of blind needle biopsy and of thoroscopy in the diagnosis and differential diagnosis of tuberculous pleurisy. Scand. J. Respir. Dis. *102*(Suppl.):196–198, 1978.
317. Lorber, J.: Intracranial calcification following tuberculous meningitis in children. Am. Rev. Tuberc. Pulm. Dis. *78*:38–61, 1958.
318. Lorber, J.: Isoniazid and streptomycin in tuberculous meningitis. Lancet *1*:1140–1142, 1964.
319. Lucente, F. E., Tobias, G. W., Parisier, S. C., et al.: Tuberculous otitis media. Laryngoscope *88*:1107–1116, 1978.
320. Luo, C., Chintu, C., Bhat, G., et al.: Human immunodeficiency virus type-1 infection in Zambian children with tuberculosis: Changing seroprevalence and evaluation of a thiacetazone-free regimen. Tubercle Lung Dis. *75*:110–115, 1994.
321. Lurie, M. B.: Resistance to Tuberculosis: Experimental Studies in Native and Acquired Defense Mechanisms. Cambridge, MA, Harvard University Press, 1964.
322. MacAdam, A. M., and Rubio, T.: Tuberculous otomastoiditis in children. Am. J. Dis. Child. *131*:152–156, 1977.
323. MacDonnell, A. H., Baird, R. W., and Bronze, M. S.: Intramedullary tuberculomas of the spinal cord: Case report and review. Rev. Infect. Dis. *12*:432–439, 1990.
324. MacGregor, R. R., Sheagren, J. N., Lipsett, M. B., et al.: Alternate-day prednisone therapy: Evaluation of delayed hypersensitivity response, control of disease and steroid side effects. N. Engl. J. Med. *280*:1427–1431, 1969.
325. Maharaj, B., Leary, W. P., and Pudifin, D. J.: A prospective study of hepatic tuberculosis in 41 black patients. Q. J. Med. *242*:517–522, 1987.
326. Mahmoudi, A., and Iseman, M.: Pitfalls in the care of patients with tuberculosis: Common errors and their association with the acquisition of drug resistance. J. A. M. A. *270*:65–68, 1993.
327. Manalo, F., Tan, F., Sbarbaro, J. A., et al.: Community-based short-course treatment of pulmonary tuberculosis in a developing nation: Initial report of an eight-month, largely intermittent, regimen in a population with a high prevalence of drug resistance. Am. Rev. Respir. Dis. *142*:1301–1305, 1990.
328. Mancao, M. Y., Nolte, F. S., Nahmias, A. J., et al.: Use of polymerase chain reaction for diagnosis of tuberculous meningitis. Pediatr. Infect. Dis. J. *13*:154–155, 1994.
329. Manjunath, N., Shankar, P., Rajan, L., et al.: Evaluation of a polymerase chain reaction for the diagnosis of tuberculosis. Tubercle *72*:21–27, 1991.
330. Marks, S. M., Taylor, Z., Qualls, N. L., et al.: Outcomes of contact investigations of infectious tuberculosis patients. Am. J. Respir. Crit. Care Med. *162*:2033–2038, 2000.
331. Marshall, J. D., Abdel-Rahman, S., Johnson, K., et al.: Rifapentine pharmacokinetics in adolescents. Pediatr. Infect. Dis. J. *18*:882–888, 1999.
332. Martinez-Roig, A., Cami, J., Llorens-Terol, J., et al.: Acetylation phenotype and hepatotoxicity in the treatment of tuberculosis in children. Pediatrics *77*:912–915, 1986.
333. Mason, E., and Russell, D. W.: Isoniazid acetylation rates (phenotypes) of patients being treated for tuberculosis. Bull. World Health Organ. *45*:617–624, 1971.
334. Matlow, A. G., Harrison, A., Monteath, A., et al.: Nosocomial transmission of tuberculosis (TB) associated with a case of an infant with peritoneal TB. Infect. Control Hosp. Epidemiol. *21*:222–223, 2000.
335. Matsaniotis, N., Kattanis, C., Economou-Mavrou, C., et al.: Bullous emphysema in childhood tuberculosis. J. Pediatr. *71*:703–708, 1967.
336. McCray, M. K., and Esterly, M. B.: Cutaneous eruptions in congenital tuberculosis. Arch. Dermatol. *117*:460–464, 1981.
337. McKenzie, S. A., McNab, A. J., and Katz, G.: Neonatal pyridoxine responsive convulsions due to isoniazid therapy. Arch. Dis. Child. *51*:567–568, 1976.
338. Medical Research Council Investigation: Streptomycin treatment of pulmonary tuberculosis. B. M. J. *2*:769–782, 1948.
339. Medical Research Council Working Party on Tuberculosis of the Spine: Five-year assessment of controlled trials of inpatient and outpatient treatment and of plaster-of-paris jackets for tuberculosis of the spine in children on standard chemotherapy: Studies in Masan and Pusan, Korea. J. Bone Joint Surg. Br. *58*:399–411, 1976.
340. Medical Research Council Working Party on Tuberculosis of the Spine: Five-year assessment of controlled trials of ambulatory treatment, débridement and anterior spinal fusion in the management of tuberculosis of the spine; studies in Bulawayo (Rhodesia) and in Hong Kong. J. Bone Joint Surg. Br. *60*:163–177, 1978.
341. Medical Research Council Working Party on Tuberculosis of the Spine: Twelfth report: Controlled trial of short-course regimens of chemotherapy in the ambulatory treatment of spinal tuberculosis. J. Bone Joint Surg. Br. *75*:240–248, 1993.
342. Mehta, J. B., and Bentley, S.: Prevention of tuberculosis in children: Missed opportunities. Am. J. Prev. Med. *8*:283–286, 1992.
343. Meier, A., Kirschner, P., Bange, F., et al.: Genetic alterations in streptomycin-resistant *Mycobacterium tuberculosis:* Mapping of mutations conferring resistance. Antimicrob. Agents Chemother. *38*:228–233, 1994.
344. Menzies, R., Fanning, A., Yuan, L., et al.: Tuberculosis among health-care workers. N. Engl. J. Med. *332*:92–98, 1995.
345. Menzies, R., Rocher, I., and Vissandjee, B.: Factors associated with compliance in treatment of tuberculosis. Tubercle Lung Dis. *74*:32–37, 1993.
346. Menzies, R., and Vissandjee, B.: Effect of bacille Calmette-Guérin vaccination on tuberculin reactivity. Am. Rev. Respir. Dis. *141*:621–625, 1992.
347. Migliori, G. B., Borghesi, A., Rossanigo, P., et al.: Proposal of an improved score method for the diagnosis of pulmonary tuberculosis in childhood in developing countries. Tubercle Lung Dis. *73*:145–149, 1992.
348. Miller, F. J. W., Seale, R. M. E., and Taylor, M. D.: Tuberculosis in Children. Boston, MA, Little, Brown, 1963, p. 214.

349. Miller, R. A., Lanza, L. A., Kline, J. N., et al.: *Mycobacterium tuberculosis* in lung transplant recipients. Am. J. Respir. Crit. Care Med. *152*:374–376, 1995.
350. Miller, R. R., Porter, J., and Greenblatt, D. J.: Clinical importance of the interaction of phenytoin and isoniazid: A report from the Boston Collaborative Drug Surveillance Program. Chest *75*:356–358, 1979.
351. Miorner, H., Sjobring, U., Nayak, P., et al.: Diagnosis of tuberculous meningitis: A comparative analysis of 3 immunoassays, an immune complex assay and the polymerase chain reaction. Tubercle Lung Dis. *76*:381–386, 1995.
352. Mitchison, D. A.: Basic mechanisms of chemotherapy. Chest *76*(Suppl.):771–781, 1979.
353. Mitchison, D. A.: The action of anti-tuberculous drugs in short-course chemotherapy. Tubercle *66*:219–225, 1985.
354. Mitchison, D. A., and Nunn, A. J.: Influence of initial drug resistance on the response to short-course chemotherapy of pulmonary tuberculosis. Am. Rev. Respir. Dis. *133*:423–428, 1986.
355. Mohanty, K. C., and Dhamgaye, T. M.: Controlled trial of ciprofloxacin in short-term chemotherapy for pulmonary tuberculosis. Chest *104*:1194–1198, 1993.
356. Mohle-Boetani, J. C., and Flood, J.: Contact investigations and the continued commitment to control tuberculosis. J. A. M. A. *287*:1040–1041, 2002.
357. Mohle-Boetani, J. C., Miller, B., Halpern, M., et al.: School-based screening for tuberculous infection: A cost benefit analysis. J. A. M. A. *274*:613–619, 1995.
358. Moore, M., Schulte, J., Valway, S., et al.: Evaluation of transmission of *Mycobacterium tuberculosis* in a pediatric setting. J. Pediatr. *133*:108–112, 1998.
359. Morens, D. M., Baublis, J. V., and Heidelberger, K. P.: Congenital tuberculosis and associated hypoadrenocorticism. South. Med. J. *72*:160–161, 165, 1979.
360. Morrison, J. B.: Natural history of segmental lesions in primary pulmonary tuberculosis. Arch. Dis. Child. *48*:90–98, 1973.
361. Morse, M. L., Karr, D. J., and Menddman, P. M.: Ocular tuberculosis in a five-month-old. Pediatr. Infect. Dis. J. *7*:514–516, 1988.
362. Moss, W. J., Dedyo, T., Suarez, M., et al.: Tuberculosis in children infected with human immunodeficiency virus: A report of five cases. Pediatr. Infect. Dis. J. *11*:114–120, 1992.
363. Mudido, P. M., Guwratudde, D., Nakakeeto, M. K., et al.: The effect of bacilli Calmette-Guérin vaccination at birth on tuberculin skin test reactivity in Ugandan children. Int. J. Tuberc. Lung Dis. *3*:891–895, 1999.
364. Mumtaz, M. A., Schwartz, R. H., Grundfast, K. M., et al.: Tuberculosis of the middle ear and mastoid. Pediatr. Infect. Dis. *2*:234–236, 1983.
365. Murray, J. F.: Cursed duet: HIV infection and tuberculosis. Respiration *57*:210–220, 1990.
366. Nakajo, M. M., Rao, M., and Steiner, P.: Incidence of hepatotoxicity in children receiving isoniazid chemoprophylaxis. Pediatr. Infect. Dis. J. *8*:649–650, 1989.
367. Nemir, R. L., Cardona, J., Lacoius, A., et al.: Prednisone therapy as an adjunct in the treatment of lymph node–bronchial tuberculosis in childhood: A double-blind study. Am. Rev. Respir. Dis. *88*:189–198, 1963.
368. Nemir, R. L., Cardona, J., Vaziri, F., et al.: Prednisone as an adjunct in the chemotherapy of lymph node–bronchial tuberculosis in childhood: A double-blind study. II. Further term observation. Am. Rev. Respir. Dis. *95*:402–410, 1967.
369. Nemir, R. L., and Krasinski, K.: Tuberculosis in children and adolescents in the 1980's. Pediatr. Infect. Dis. J. *7*:375–379, 1988.
370. Nemir, R. L., and O'Hare, D.: Congenital tuberculosis. Am. J. Dis. Child. *139*:284–287, 1985.
371. Nemir, R. L., and O'Hare, D.: Tuberculosis in children 10 years of age and younger: Three decades of experience during the chemotherapeutic era. Pediatrics *88*:236–241, 1991.
372. Nemir, R. L., and Teichner, A.: Management of tuberculin reactors in children and adolescents previously vaccinated with BCG. Pediatr. Infect. Dis. *2*:446–451, 1983.
373. Netto, E. M., Dye, C., and Raviglione, M. C.: Progress in global tuberculosis control 1995–1996, with emphasis on 22 high-incidence countries. Global Monitoring and Surveillance Project. Int. J. Tuberc. Lung Dis. *3*:310–320, 1999.
374. Nivin, B., Nicholas, P., Gayer M., et al.: A continuing outbreak of multidrug-resistant tuberculosis, with transmission in a hospital nursery. Clin. Infect. Dis. *26*:303–307, 1998.
375. Nolan, C. M., and Elarth, A. M.: Tuberculosis in a cohort of Southeast Asian refugees. Am. Rev. Respir. Dis. *137*:805–809, 1988.
376. Nolan, C. M., Elarth, A. M., and Barr, H. W.: Intentional isoniazid overdose in young Southeast Asian refugee women. Chest *93*:803–806, 1988.
377. Nolan, R., Jr.: Childhood tuberculosis in North Carolina: A study of the opportunities for intervention in the transmission of tuberculosis in children. Am. J. Public Health *76*:26–30, 1986.
378. Noordhoek, G., Kolk, A., Bjune, G., et al.: Sensitivity and specificity of PCR for detection of *Mycobacterium tuberculosis:* A blind comparison study among seven laboratories. J. Clin. Microbiol. *32*:277–284, 1994.
379. Nunn, P., and Felten, M.: Surveillance of resistance to antituberculosis drugs in developing countries. Tubercle Lung Dis. *75*:163–167, 1994.
380. Obaegbulam, S. C.: Spinal extraosseous extradural tuberculoma. Tubercle *58*:97, 1977.
381. O'Brien, K., Ruff, A., Louis, M., et al.: Bacillus Calmette-Guérin complications in children born to HIV-1-infected women with a review of the literature. Pediatrics *95*:414–418, 1995.
382. O'Brien, R. J., Long, M. W., Cross, F. S., et al.: Hepatotoxicity from isoniazid and rifampin among children treated for tuberculosis. Pediatrics *72*:491–499, 1983.
383. Offenbacher, H., Fazekas, F., Schmidt. R., et al.: MRI in tuberculous meningoencephalitis: Report of four cases and review of the neuroimaging literature. J. Neurol. *238*:340–344, 1991.
384. Olazabal, F.: Choroidal tubercles: A neglected sign. J. A. M. A. *200*:104–107, 1967.
385. Olson, W. A., Pruitt, A. W., and Dayton, P. G.: Plasma concentration of isoniazid in children with tuberculous infections. Pediatrics *67*:876–878, 1981.
386. Omari, B., Robertson, J. M., Nelson, R. J., et al.: Pott's disease: A resurgent challenge to the thoracic surgeon. Chest *95*:145–150, 1989. (See also follow-up letters, Chest *96*:955–956, 1989.)
387. Optican, R. J., Ost, A., and Ravin, C. E.: High-resolution computed tomography in the diagnosis of miliary tuberculosis. Chest *102*:941–943, 1992.
388. Orme, I. M., Andersen, P., and Boom, W. H.: T cell response to *Mycobacterium tuberculosis.* J. Infect. Dis. *167*:1481–1497, 1993.
389. Ozuah, P. O., Ozuah, T. P., Stein, R. E. K., et al.: Evaluation of a risk assessment questionnaire used to target tuberculin skin testing in children. J. A. M. A. *285*:451–453, 2001.
390. Palur, R., Rajohekhar, V., Chandy, M. J., et al.: Shunt surgery for hydrocephalus in tuberculous meningitis: A long-term follow-up study. J. Neurosurg. *74*:64–69, 1991.
391. Paluschi, V. J., O'Hare, D., and Lawrence, R. M.: Hepatotoxicity and transaminase measurement during isoniazid chemoprophylaxis in children. Pediatr. Infect. Dis. J. *14*:144–148, 1995.
392. Parish, R. E., and Brownstein, D.: Emergency department management of children with acute isoniazid poisoning. Pediatr. Emerg. Care *2*:88–90, 1986.
393. Park, M. M., Davis, A. L., Schluger, N. W., et al.: Outcome of MDR-TB patients, 1983–1993: Prolonged survival with appropriate therapy. Am. J. Respir. Crit. Care Med. *153*:317–324, 1996.
394. Passannante, M., Gallagher, C., and Reichman, L.: Preventive therapy for contacts of multidrug-resistant tuberculosis: A Delphi study. Chest *106*:431–434, 1994.
395. Pastrana, D. G., Torronteras, R., Caro, P., et al.: Comparison of Amplicor, in-house polymerase chain reactions and conventional culture for the diagnosis of tuberculosis in children. Clin. Infect. Dis. *32*:17–22, 2001.
396. Payne, M., quoted by Miller, F. J. W., Seale, R. M. E., and Taylor, M. D.: Tuberculosis in Children. Boston, MA, Little, Brown, 1963.
397. Pearson, M. L., Jereb, J. A., Frieden, T. R., et al.: Nosocomial transmission of multidrug-resistant *Mycobacterium tuberculosis:* A risk to patients and healthcare workers. Ann. Intern. Med. *117*:191–196, 1992.
398. Pederson, F. K., Schiotz, P. O., Valerius, N. H., et al.: Fatal BCG infection in an immunocompetent girl. Acta Paediatr. Scand. *67*:19–23, 1978.
399. Pellock, J. M., Howell, J., Kendig, E. L., Jr., et al.: Pyridoxine deficiency in children treated with isoniazid. Chest *87*:658–661, 1985.
400. Peloquin, C. A., MacPhee, A. A., and Berning, S. E.: Malabsorption of antimycobacterial medications. N. Engl. J. Med. *329*:1122–1123, 1993.
401. Pelosi, F., Budani, H., Rubenstein, C., et al.: Isoniazid, rifampin and pyrazinamide in the treatment of childhood tuberculosis with duration adjusted to clinical status. Abstract. Am. Rev. Respir. Dis. *131*(Suppl.): 229, 1985.
402. Peltola, H., Salmi, I., Vahvanen, V., et al.: BCG vaccination as a cause of osteomyelitis and subcutaneous abscess. Arch. Dis. Child. *59*:157–161, 1984.
403. Pereira, C. A., Webber, B., and Orson, J. M.: Primary tuberculous complex of the skin. J. A. M. A. *235*:942, 1976.
404. Perry, S., and Starke, J. R.: Adherence to prescribed treatment and public health aspects of tuberculosis in children. Semin. Pediatr. Infect. Dis. *4*:291–298, 1993.
405. Pesanti, E.: The negative tuberculin skin test: Tuberculin, HIV and anergy panels. Am. J. Respir. Crit. Care Med. *149*:1699–1709, 1994.
406. Pierre, C., Olivier, C., Lecossier, D., et al.: Diagnosis of primary tuberculosis in children by amplification and detection of mycobacterial DNA. Am. Rev. Respir. Dis. *147*:420–424, 1993.
407. Pineda, P., Leung, A., Muller, N., et al.: Intrathoracic pediatric tuberculosis: A report of 202 cases. Tubercle Lung Dis. *74*:261–266, 1993.
408. Pomerantz, M., Madsen, L., Goble, M., et al.: Surgical management of resistant mycobacterial tuberculosis and other mycobacterial pulmonary infections. Ann. Thorac. Surg. *52*:1108–1112, 1991.
409. Pospelov, L. E., Matrakshin, A. G., Chernousova, L. N., et al.: Association of various genetic markers with tuberculosis and other lung disease in Tuvinian children. Tubercle Lung Dis. *77*:77–80, 1996.
410. Rao, P. T., Chitra, D. R., and Krishniah, H. G.: A study of the early clinical signs and biochemical values of cerebro-spinal fluid in the course of tuberculous meningitis during treatment and other factors influencing the prognosis. Indian J. Pediatr. *26*:178–186, 1959.

411. Rapp, R. S., Campbell, R. W., Howell, J. C., et al.: Isoniazid hepatotoxicity in children. Am. Rev. Respir. Dis. *118*:794–796, 1978.
412. Rasool, M. N.: Osseous manifestations of tuberculosis in children. J. Pediatr. Orthop. *21*:749–755, 2001.
413. Rasool, M., Govender, S., and Naidoo, K.: Cystic tuberculosis of bone in children. J. Bone Joint Surg. Br. *76*:113–117, 1994.
414. Ravenscroft, A., Schoeman, J. F., and Donald, P. R.: Tuberculous granulomas in childhood tuberculous meningitis: Radiologic features and course. J. Trop. Pediatr. *47*:5–12, 2001.
415. Raviglione, M. C., Rieder, H. L., Styblo, K., et al.: Tuberculosis trends in Eastern Europe and the former USSR. Tubercle Lung Dis. *75*:400–416, 1994.
416. Raviglione, M. C., Snider, D., Jr., and Kochi, A.: Global epidemiology of tuberculosis: Morbidity and mortality of a worldwide epidemic. J. A. M. A. *273*:220–226, 1995.
417. Reichler, M. R., Reves, R., Bur, S., et al.: Evaluation of investigations conducted to detect and prevent transmission of tuberculosis. J. A. M. A. *287*:991–995, 2002.
418. Reichman, L. B.: Why hasn't BCG proved dangerous in HIV-infected patients? J. A. M. A. *261*:3246, 1989.
419. Reis, F. J., Bedran, M. B., Mowra, J. A., et al.: Six-month isoniazid-rifampin treatment for pulmonary tuberculosis in children. Am. Rev. Respir. Dis. *142*:996–999, 1990.
420. Report of a WHO Study Group: BCG vaccination policies. WHO Technical Report Series No. 652, 1980–1981.
421. Reynes, J., Perez, C., Lamaury, I., et al.: Bacille Calmette-Guérin adenitis 30 years after immunization in a patient with AIDS. J. Infect. Dis. *160*:727, 1989.
422. Rich, A. R.: The Pathogenesis of Tuberculosis. 2nd ed. Springfield, IL, Charles C Thomas, 1951.
423. Rich, A. R., and McCordock, H. A.: The pathogenesis of tuberculous meningitis. Bull. Johns Hopkins Hosp. *52*:5–35, 1933.
424. Ridgeway, A. L., Warner, G. S., Phillips. P., et al.: Transmission of *Mycobacterium tuberculosis* to recipients of single lung transplants from the same donor. Am. J. Respir. Crit. Care Med. *153*:1166–1168, 1996.
425. Ridzon, R., Kent, J. H., Valway, S., et al.: Outbreak of drug-resistant tuberculosis with secondary-generation transmission in a high school in California. J. Pediatr. *131*:863–868, 1997.
426. Rieder, H. L., Cauthen, G. M., Comstock, G. W., et al.: Epidemiology of tuberculosis in the United States. Epidemiol. Rev. *11*:79–98, 1989.
427. Riley, L. W., Arathoon, E., and Loverde, V. D.: The epidemiologic patterns of drug-resistant *Mycobacterium tuberculosis* infections: A community-based study. Am. Rev. Respir. Dis. *139*:1282–1285, 1989.
428. Riley, R. L.: Airborne transmission. *In* Johnson, J. E. (ed.): Rational Therapy and Control of Tuberculosis. Gainesville, University of Florida Press, 1970.
429. Rooney, J. J., Crocco, J. A., and Lyons, H. A.: Tuberculous pericarditis. Ann. Intern. Med. *72*:73–78, 1970.
430. Roy, V., Tekur, U., and Chopra, K.: Pharmacokinetics of pyrazinamide in children suffering from pulmonary tuberculosis. Int. J. Tuberc. Lung Dis. *3*:133–137, 1999.
431. Ryder, R. W., Oxtoby, M. J., Mvula, M., et al.: Safety and immunogenicity of bacille Calmette-Guérin, diphtheria-tetanus-pertussis, and oral polio vaccines in newborn children in Zaire infected with human immunodeficiency virus type 1. J. Pediatr. *122*:697–702, 1993.
432. Saczek, K. B., Schaaf, H. S., Vors, M., et al.: Diagnostic dilemmas in abdominal tuberculosis in children. Pediatr. Surg. Int. *17*:111–115, 2001.
433. Sada, E., Aguilar, D., Torres, M., et al.: Detection of lipoarabinomannan as a diagnostic test for tuberculosis. J. Clin. Microbiol. *30*:2415–2418, 1992.
434. Saiman, L., Aronson, J., Zhou, J., et al.: Prevalence of infectious diseases among internationally adopted children. Pediatrics *108*:608–612, 2001.
435. Saiman, L., San Gabriel, P., Schultz, J., et al.: Risk factors for latent tuberculosis infection among children in New York City. Pediatrics *107*:999–1003, 2001.
436. Salazar, G. E., Schmitz, T. L., Cama, R., et al.: Pulmonary tuberculosis in a developing country. Pediatrics *108*:448–453, 2001.
437. Salfinger, M., Crowle, A. J., and Reller, L. B.: Pyrazinamide and pyrazinoic acid activity against tubercle bacilli in cultured human macrophages and in the BACTEC system. J. Infect. Dis. *162*:201–207, 1990.
438. Salfinger, M., and Pfyfler, G. E.: The new diagnostic mycobacteriology laboratory. Eur. J. Clin. Microbiol. *13*:961–979, 1994.
439. Saltzman, S. J., and Feigin, R. D.: Tuberculous otitis media and mastoiditis. J. Pediatr. *79*:1004–1006, 1971.
440. Sanchez-Albisua, I., Vidal, M. L., Joya-Verde, G., et al.: Tolerance of pyrazinamide in short course chemotherapy for pulmonary tuberculosis in children. Pediatr. Infect. Dis. J. *16*:760–763, 1997.
441. Sassan-Morokro, M., DeCock, K. M., Ackah, A., et al.: Tuberculosis and HIV infection in children in Abidjon, Cote d'Ivoire. Trans. R. Soc. Trop. Med. Hyg. *88*:178–181, 1994.
442. Sathe, S. S., and Reichman, L. B.: Mycobacterial disease in patients infected with human immunodeficiency virus. Clin. Chest Med. *10*:445–463, 1989.
443. Schaaf, H. S., Beyers, N., Gie, R. P., et al.: Respiratory tuberculosis in childhood: The diagnostic value of clinical features and special investigations. Pediatr. Infect. Dis. J. *14*:189–194, 1995.
444. Schaaf, H. S., Gie, R. P., Beyers, N., et al. Tuberculosis in infants less than 3 months of age. Arch. Dis. Child. *69*:371–374, 1993.
445. Schaaf, H. S., Gie, R. P., Beyers, N., et al.: Primary drug-resistant tuberculosis in children. Int. J. Tuberc. Lung Dis. *4*:1–7, 2000.
446. Schaaf, H. S., Gie, R. P., Beyers N., et al.: Primary drug-resistant tuberculosis. Pediatr. Infect. Dis. J. *19*:695–699, 2000.
447. Schaaf, H. S., Gie, R. P., Kennedy, M., et al.: Evaluation of young children in contact with adult multi-drug resistant pulmonary tuberculosis: A 30-month follow-up. Pediatrics *109*:765–771, 2002.
448. Schaefer, G.: Tuberculosis in Obstetrics and Gynecology. Boston, MA, Little, Brown, 1956.
449. Schick, B., and Dolgin, J.: The influence of prednisone on the Mantoux reaction in children. Pediatrics *31*:856–859, 1963.
450. Schluger, N., Kinney, D., Harkin, T., et al.: Clinical utility of the polymerase chain reaction in the diagnosis of infections due to *Mycobacterium tuberculosis*. Chest *105*:1116–1121, 1994.
451. Scholten, J. W., Fujiwara, P. I., and Frieden, T. R.: Prevalence and factors associated with tuberculosis infection among new school entrants, New York City, 1991–1993. Int. J. Tuberc. Lung Dis. *3*:31–41, 1999.
452. Schuit, K. E.: Miliary tuberculosis in children. Am. J. Dis. Child. *133*:583–585, 1979.
453. Schuit, K. E., and Powell, D. A.: Mycobacterial lymphadenitis in childhood. Am. J. Dis. Child. *132*:675–677, 1978.
454. Schwartz, P.: Lymph node tuberculosis: A decisive factor in pulmonary pathology. Arch. Pediatr. *74*:159–177, 201–218, 1957.
455. Schwartzman, K., and Menzies, D.: Tuberculosis screening of immigrants to low-prevalence countries. Am. J. Respir. Crit. Care Med. *161*:780–789, 2000.
456. Seal, R. M. E., and Thomas, S. M. E.: Endobronchial tuberculosis in children. Lancet *2*:995–996, 1956.
457. Sehgal, V. N., and Wagh, S. A.: Cutaneous tuberculosis. Int. J. Dermatol. *29*:237–252, 1990.
458. Selwyn, P., Hartel, D., Lewis, V., et al.: A prospective study of the risk of tuberculosis among intravenous drug users with human immunodeficiency virus infection. N. Engl. J. Med. *320*:545–550, 1989.
459. Sepulveda, R. L., Burr, C., Ferrer, X., et al.: Booster effect of tuberculosis testing in healthy 6-year-old school children vaccinated with bacille Calmette-Guérin at birth in Santiago, Chile. Pediatr. Infect. Dis. J. *7*:578–582, 1988.
460. Sepulveda, R. L., Heiba, I. M., King, A., et al.: Evaluation of tuberculin reactivity in BCG-immunized siblings. Am. J. Respir. Crit. Care Med. *149*:620–624, 1994.
461. Sepulveda, R. L., Heiba, I. M., Navarrete, C., et al.: Tuberculin reactivity after newborn BCG immunization in mono- and dizygotic twins. Tubercle Lung Dis. *75*:138–143, 1994.
462. Shafer, R., Small, P., Larkin, C., et al.: Temporal trends and transmission patterns during the emergence of multidrug-resistant tuberculosis in New York City: A molecular epidemiologic assessment. J. Infect. Dis. *171*:170–176, 1995.
463. Shah, B. R., Santucci, K., Sinert, R., et al.: Acute isoniazid neurotoxicity in an urban hospital. Pediatrics *95*:700–704, 1995.
464. Shannon, F. B., Moore, M., Houkom, J. A., et al.: Multifocal cystic tuberculosis of bone. J. Bone Joint Surg. Am. *72*:1089–1092, 1990.
465. Shata, A. M. A., Coulter, J. B. S., Parry, C. M., et al.: Sputum induction for the diagnosis of tuberculosis. Arch. Dis. Child. *74*:535–537, 1996.
466. Shepard, W. E., Field, M. L., James, D. H., et al.: Transient appearance of intracranial tuberculomas during treatment of tuberculous meningitis. Pediatr. Infect. Dis. J. *5*:599–601, 1986.
467. Sheridan, P. H., Edman, J. B., and Starr, S. E.: Tuberculosis presenting as an orbital mass. Pediatrics *67*:874–875, 1981.
468. Shimokata, K., Kawachi, H., Kishumoto, H., et al.: Local cellular immunity in tuberculous pleurisy. Am. Rev. Respir. Dis. *126*:822–824, 1982.
469. Siddiqi, S. H., Hwangbo, C. C., Silcox, V., et al.: Rapid radiometric methods to detect and differentiate *Mycobacterium tuberculosis/M. bovis* from other mycobacterial species. Am. Rev. Respir. Dis. *130*:634–640, 1984.
470. Singapore Tuberculosis Service/British Medical Research Council: Five-year follow-up of a clinical trial of three 6-month regimens of chemotherapy given intermittently in the continuation phase in the treatment of pulmonary tuberculosis. Am. Rev. Respir. Dis. *137*: 1147–1150, 1988.
471. Sirinavin, S., Chotpitayasunondh, T., Suwanjutha, S., et al.: Efficacy of neonatal bacillus Calmette-Guérin vaccination against tuberculosis. Pediatr. Infect. Dis. J. *10*:359–365, 1991.
472. Sloan, J. B.: Papulonecrotic tuberculid in a 9-year-old American girl: Case report and review of the literature. Pediatr. Dermatol. *7*:191–195, 1990.
473. Slutkin, G., Schecter, G. F., and Hopewell, P. C.: The results of 9-month isoniazid-rifampin therapy for pulmonary tuberculosis under program conditions in San Francisco. Am. Rev. Respir. Dis. *138*:1622–1624, 1988.
474. Small, P., Hopewell, P., Singh, S., et al.: The epidemiology of tuberculosis in San Francisco: A population-based study using conventional and molecular methods. N. Engl. J. Med. *330*:1703–1709, 1994.

475. Small, P. M., Shafer, R. W., Hopewell, P. C., et al.: Exogenous reinfection with multidrug-resistant *Mycobacterium tuberculosis* in patients with advanced HIV infection. N. Engl. J. Med. *328*:1137–1144, 1993.
476. Smith, A. M., and Lattimer, J. K.: Genitourinary tract involvement in children with tuberculosis. N. Y. State J. Med. *73*:2325–2328, 1973.
477. Smith, D., Reeser, P., and Musa, S.: Does infection with environmental mycobacteria suppress the protective response to subsequent vaccination with BCG? Tubercle *66*:17–23, 1985.
478. Smith, K. C., Starke, J. R., Eisenach, K., et al.: Detection of *Mycobacterium tuberculosis* in clinical specimens from children using a polymerase chain reaction. Pediatrics *97*:155–160, 1996.
479. Smith, M. H. D.: The role of adrenal steroids in the treatment of tuberculosis. Pediatrics *22*:774–776, 1958.
480. Smith, M. H. D.: What about short course and intermittent chemotherapy for tuberculosis in children? Pediatr. Infect. Dis. *1*:298–303, 1982.
481. Smith, M. H. D.: Tuberculosis in children and adolescents. Clin. Chest Med. *10*:381–395, 1989.
482. Smith, M. H. D., and Matsaniotis, N.: Treatment of tuberculous pleural effusions with particular reference to adrenal corticosteroids. Pediatrics *22*:1074–1087, 1959.
483. Snider, D. E., Jr., and Block, A. B.: Congenital tuberculosis. Tubercle *65*:81–82, 1984.
484. Snider, D. E., Jr., and Caras, G. J.: Isoniazid-associated hepatitis deaths: A review of available information. Am. Rev. Respir. Dis. *145*:494–497, 1992.
485. Snider, D. E., Jr., Caras, G. J., and Kaplan, J. P.: Preventive therapy with isoniazid: Cost-effectiveness of different durations of therapy. J. A. M. A. *255*:1579–1583, 1986.
486. Snider, D. E., Jr., and Farer, L. S.: Preventive therapy for tuberculous infection: An intervention in need of improvement. Am. Rev. Respir. Dis. *130*:35–356, 1984.
487. Snider, D. E., Graczyk, J., Bek, E., et al.: Supervised six-month treatment of newly diagnosed pulmonary tuberculosis using isoniazid, rifampin, and pyrazinamide with and without streptomycin. Am. Rev. Respir. Dis. *130*:1091–1094, 1984.
488. Snider, D. E., Jr., Kelly, G. D., Cauthen, G. M., et al.: Infection and disease among contacts of tuberculosis cases with drug-resistant and drug-susceptible bacilli. Am. Rev. Respir. Dis. *132*:125–128, 1985.
489. Snider, D. E., Jr., and LaMontagne, J.: The neglected global tuberculosis problem: A report of the 1992 World Congress on Tuberculosis. J. Infect. Dis. *169*:1189–1196, 1994.
490. Snider, D. E., Jr., Layde, P. M., Johnson, M. W., et al.: Treatment of tuberculosis during pregnancy. Am. Rev. Respir. Dis. *122*:65–79, 1980.
491. Snider, D. E., Jr., and Powell, K. E.: Should women taking antituberculosis drugs breastfeed? Arch. Intern. Med. *144*:589–590, 1984.
492. Somu, N., Swaminathan, S., Paramisivan, C. N., et al.: Value of bronchoalveolar lavage and gastric lavage in the diagnosis of pulmonary tuberculosis in children. Tuberc. Lung. Dis. *76*:295–299, 1995.
493. Soren, K., Saiman, L., Irigoyen, M., et al.: Evaluation of household contacts of children with positive tuberculin skin tests. Pediatr. Infect. Dis. J. *18*:949–955, 1999.
494. Spyridis, P., Sinaniotis, C., Papadea, I., et al.: Isoniazid liver injury during chemoprophylaxis in children. Arch. Dis. Child. *54*:65–67, 1979.
495. Stallworth, J. R., Brasfield, D. M., and Tiller, R. E.: Congenital miliary tuberculosis proved by open lung biopsy specimen and successfully treated. Am. J. Dis. Child. *134*:320–321, 1980.
496. Stansberry, S. D.: Tuberculosis in infants and children. J. Thorac. Imaging *5*:17–27, 1990.
497. Starke, J. R.: Multidrug therapy for tuberculosis in children. Pediatr. Infect. Dis. J. *9*:785–793, 1990.
498. Starke, J. R.: Current chemotherapy for tuberculosis in children. Infect. Dis. Clin. North Am. *6*:215–238, 1992.
499. Starke, J. R.: Tuberculosis of the central nervous system in children. Semin. Pediatr. Neurol. *6*:318–331, 1999.
500. Starke, J. R.: Transmission of *Mycobacterium tuberculosis* to and from children and adolescents. Semin. Pediatr. Infect. Dis. *12*:115–123, 2001.
501. Starke, J. R.: Childhood tuberculosis: Ending the neglect. Int. J. Tuberc. Lung Dis. *6*:373–374, 2002.
502. Starke, J. R., and Correa, A. G.: Management of mycobacterial infection and disease in children. Pediatr. Infect. Dis. J. *14*:455–470, 1995.
503. Starke, J. R., Jacobs, R., and Jereb, J.: Resurgence of tuberculosis in children. J. Pediatr. *120*:839–855, 1992.
504. Starke, J. R., and Taylor-Watts, K. T.: Tuberculosis in the pediatric population of Houston, Texas. Pediatrics *84*:28–35, 1989.
505. Starke, J. R., and Taylor-Watts, K. T.: Six-month chemotherapy of intrathoracic tuberculosis in children. Abstract. Am. Rev. Respir. Dis. *139*(Suppl.):314, 1989.
506. Starr, S., and Berkovich, S.: Effects of measles, gammaglobulin-modified measles and vaccine measles on the tuberculin test. N. Engl. J. Med. *270*:386–391, 1964.
507. Stead, W. W.: Pathogenesis of a first episode of chronic pulmonary tuberculosis in man: Recrudescence of residuals of the primary infection or exogenous reinfection? Am. Rev. Respir. Dis. *95*:729–745, 1967.
508. Stein, M. T., and Liang, D.: Clinical hepatotoxicity of isoniazid in children. Pediatrics *64*:499–505, 1979.
509. Steiner, M., Steiner, P., and Schmidt, H.: Primary drug-resistant tuberculosis in children: A continuing study of the incidence of disease caused by primarily drug-resistant organisms in children observed between the years 1965 and 1968 at the Kings County Medical Center of Brooklyn. Am. Rev. Respir. Dis. *102*:75–82, 1970.
510. Steiner, P., and Rao, M.: Drug-resistant tuberculosis in children. Semin. Pediatr. Infect. Dis. *4*:275–282, 1993.
511. Steiner, P., Rao, M., and Mitchell, M.: Primary drug-resistant tuberculosis in children: Correlation of drug-susceptibility patterns of matched patient and source-case strains of *Mycobacterium tuberculosis*. Am. J. Dis. Child. *139*:780–782, 1985.
512. Steiner, P., Rao, M., Victoria, M. S., et al.: Miliary tuberculosis in two infants after nursery exposure: Epidemiologic, clinical, and laboratory findings. Am. Rev. Respir. Dis. *113*:267–271, 1976.
513. Steiner, P., Rao, M., Victoria, M. S., et al.: Persistently negative tuberculin reactions: Their presence among children culture positive for *Mycobacterium tuberculosis*. Am. J. Dis. Child. *134*:747–750, 1980.
514. Stevens, D. L., and Everett, E. D.: Sequential computerized axial tomography in tuberculous meningitis. J. A. M. A. *239*:642, 1978.
515. Strang, J. I. G., Kakaza, H. H. S., Gibson, D. G., et al.: Controlled trial of prednisolone as adjunct in treatment of tuberculous constrictive pericarditis in Transkei. Lancet *2*:1418–1422, 1987.
516. Sudre, P., Dam, G. T., and Kochi, A.: Tuberculosis: A global overview of the situation today. Bull. World Health Organ. *70*:149–159, 1992.
517. Sullama, P. M., Slutkin, G., and Hopewell, P. C.: The benefits of evaluating close associates of child tuberculin reactors from a high prevalence group. Am. J. Public Health *76*:1109–1111, 1986.
518. Sumartojo, E.: When tuberculosis treatment fails: A social behavior account of patient adherence. Am. Rev. Respir. Dis. *147*:1311–1320, 1993.
519. Sumaya, C. V., Simek, M., and Smith, M. H. D.: Tuberculous meningitis in children during the isoniazid era. J. Pediatr. *87*:43–49, 1975.
520. Sunderam, G., McDonald, R. J., Maniatis, T., et al.: Tuberculosis as a manifestation of the acquired immunodeficiency syndrome (AIDS). J. A. M. A. *256*:362–366, 1986.
521. Swaminathan, S., Gong, J., Zhang, M., et al.: Cytokine production in children with tuberculous infection and disease. Clin. Infect. Dis. *28*:1290–1293, 1999.
522. Swanson, D. S., and Starke, J. R.: Drug-resistant tuberculosis in pediatrics. Pediatr. Clin. North Am. *42*:553–581, 1995.
523. Sweany, H. C.: Studies on the pathogenesis of primary tuberculous infection. Am. Rev. Tuberc. *27*:559–588, 1933.
524. Tabrisky, J., Lindstrom, R. R., Peters, R., et al.: Tuberculous enteritis. Am. J. Gastroenterol. *63*:49–57, 1975.
525. Takiff, H., Salazar, L., Guerrero, C., et al.: Cloning and nucleotide sequence of *Mycobacterium tuberculosis gyrA* and *gryB* genes and detection of quinoline resistance mutations. Antimicrob. Agents Chemother. *38*:773–780, 1994.
526. Talbot, E. A., Moore, M., McCray, E., and Binkin, N. J.: Tuberculosis among foreign-born persons in the United States, 1993–1998. J. A. M. A. *284*:2894–2900, 2000.
527. Talwar, B. S., Talwar, R., Chowdhary, B., and Prasad, P.: Abdominal tuberculosis in children: An Indian experience. J. Trop. Pediatr. *46*:368–370, 2000.
528. Teeratkulpisarn, J., Lumbigagnon, P., Pairojkul, S., et al.: Cavitary tuberculosis in a young infant. Pediatr. Infect. Dis. J. *13*:545–546, 1994.
529. Teixeira, L., Perkins, M. D., Johnson, J. L., et al.: Infection and disease among household contacts of patients with multi-drug resistant tuberculosis. Int. J. Tuberc. Lung Dis. *5*:321–328, 2001.
530. Telenti, A., Imboden, P., Marchesi, F., et al.: Detection of rifampin-resistance mutations in *Mycobacterium tuberculosis*. Lancet *341*:647–650, 1993.
531. Telzak, E. E., Sepkowitz, K., Alpert, P., et al.: Multidrug-resistant tuberculosis in patients without HIV infection. N. Engl. J. Med. *333*:907–911, 1995.
532. tenDam, H. G.: Research on BCG vaccination. Adv. Tuberc. Res. *21*:79–106, 1984.
533. Teoh, R., Humphries, M. J., and Sister Gabriel O'Mahony: Symptomatic intracranial tuberculoma developing during treatment of tuberculosis: Report of 10 patients and review of the literature. Q. J. Med. *63*:449–460, 1987.
534. Te Water Naude, J. M., Donald, P. R., Hussey, G. D., et al.: Twice weekly vs. daily chemotherapy for childhood tuberculosis. Pediatr. Infect. Dis. J. *19*:405–410, 2000.
535. Thomas, P., Bornschlegel, K., Singh, T. P., et al.: Tuberculosis in human immunodeficiency virus–infected and human immunodeficiency virus–exposed children in New York City. Pediatr. Infect. Dis. J. *19*:700–706, 2000.
536. Thompson, W. J., Glassroth, J. L., Snider, D. E., Jr., et al.: The booster phenomenon in serial tuberculin testing. Am. Rev. Respir. Dis. *119*:587–597, 1979.
537. Tidjani, O., Amedome, A., and tenDam, H. G.: Protective effect of BCG vaccination of the newborn against childhood tuberculosis in an African community. Tubercle *67*:269–281, 1986.
538. Toppet, M., Malfroot, A., Derde, M. P., et al.: Corticosteroids in primary tuberculosis with bronchial obstruction. Arch. Dis. Child. *65*:1222–1226, 1990.

539. Traub, M., Colchester, A. C., Kingsley, D. P., et al.: Tuberculosis of the central nervous system. Q. J. Med. *53*:81–100, 1984.
540. Tsakalidis, D., Pratsidou, P., Hitoglou-Makedou, A., et al.: Intensive short course chemotherapy for treatment of Greek children with tuberculosis. Pediatr. Infect. Dis. J. *11*:1036–1042, 1992.
541. Tsukamura, M.: In vitro antituberculosis activity of a new antibacterial substance ofloxacin (DL8280). Am. Rev. Respir. Dis. *131*:348–351, 1985.
542. Tuberculosis in Children: Guidelines for diagnosis, prevention and treatment (Statement of the Scientific Committee of the International Union Against Tuberculosis and Lung Diseases). Bull. Int. Union Tuberc. Lung Dis. *66*:61–67, 1991.
543. Tuli, S. M.: Tuberculosis of the Spine. New Delhi, Amerind Publishing, 1975.
544. Turnbull, F. M., McIntyre, P. B., Achat, H. M., et al.: National study of adverse reactions after vaccination with bacilli Calmette-Guérin. Clin. Infect. Dis. *34*:447–453, 2002.
545. Turneer, M., VanNerom, E., Nyabenda, J., et al.: Determination of humoral immunoglobulins M and G directed against mycobacterial antigen 60 failed to diagnose primary tuberculosis and mycobacterial adenitis in children. Am. J. Respir. Crit. Care Med. *150*:1508–1512, 1994.
546. Tyler, B., Bennett, H., and Kim, J.: Intracranial tuberculomas in a child: Computed tomographic scan diagnosis and nonsurgical management. Pediatrics *71*:952–954, 1983.
547. Udani, P. M., Parekh, U. C., and Dastur, D. K.: Neurological and related syndromes in CNS tuberculosis: Clinical features and pathogenesis. J. Neurol. Sci. *14*:341–357, 1971.
548. Ussery, X. T., Valway, S. E., McKenna, M., et al.: Epidemiology of tuberculosis among children in the United States. Pediatr. Infect. Dis. J. *15*:697–704, 1996.
549. Vallejo, J., Ong, L., and Starke, J.: Clinical features, diagnosis and reatment of tuberculosis in infants. Pediatrics *94*:1–7, 1994.
550. Vallejo, J., Ong, L. T., and Starke, J. R.: Tuberculous osteomyelitis of the long bones in children. Pediatr. Infect. Dis. J. *14*:542–546, 1995.
551. Vallejo, J. G., and Starke, J. R.: Tuberculosis and pregnancy. Clin. Chest Med. *13*:693–707, 1992.
552. Vanderhoof, J. A., and Ament, M. E.: Fatal hepatic necrosis due to isoniazid chemoprophylaxis in a 15-year-old girl. J. Pediatr. *88*:867–868, 1976.
553. Van Zwanenberg, D.: Influence of the number of bacilli on the development of tuberculous disease in children. Am. Rev. Respir. Dis. *82*:31–44, 1960.
554. Varudkar, B. L.: Short-course chemotherapy for tuberculosis in children. Indian J. Pediatr. *52*:593–597, 1985.
555. Venkataraman, P., Menon, N. K., Nair, N. G. B., et al.: Classification of subjects as slow or rapid inactivators of isoniazid based on the ratio of urinary excretion of acetylisoniazid to isoniazid. Tubercle *53*:84–91, 1972.
556. Verma, A., Dhawan, A., Wade, J. J., et al.: *Mycobacterium tuberculosis* infection in pediatric liver transplant recipients. Pediatr. Infect. Dis. J. *19*:625–630, 2000.
557. Versfeld, G. A., and Soloman, A.: A diagnostic approach to tuberculosis of bones and joints. J. Bone Joint Surg. Br. *64*:446–449, 1982.
558. Visudhiphan, P., and Chiemchanya, S.: Tuberculous meningitis in children: Treatment with isoniazid and rifampin for twelve months. J. Pediatr. *114*:875–879, 1989.
559. Volmink, J., Matchaba, P., and Garner, P.: Directly observed therapy and treatment adherence. Lancet *355*:1345–1350, 2000.
560. Waeker, N. J., Jr., and Connor, J. D.: Central nervous system tuberculosis in children: A review of 30 cases. Pediatr. Infect. Dis. J. *9*:539–543, 1990.
561. Walker, C. H. M.: Pulmonary primary tuberculosis in childhood. Lancet *1*:218–224, 1955.
562. Wallace, K., and Cohen, A. S.: Tuberculous arthritis: Report of two cases with review of biopsy and synovial fluid findings. Am. J. Med. *61*:277–282, 1976.
563. Wallace, R. C., Burton, E. M., Barrett, F. F., et al.: Intracranial tuberculosis in children: CT appearance and clinical outcome. Pediatr. Radiol. *21*:241–246, 1991.
564. Wallgren, A.: On contagiousness of childhood tuberculosis. Acta Paediatr. *22*:229–234, 1937.
565. Wallgren, A.: Pulmonary Tuberculosis in Adults and Children. New York, Thomas Nelson & Sons, 1939.
566. Wallgren, A.: Tuberculous heart disease. Acta Med. Scand. *196*(Suppl.): 132–144, 1947.
567. Wallgren, A.: The time-table of tuberculosis. Tubercle *29*:245–251, 1948.
568. Washko, R., Robinson, E., Fehrs, L. J., et al.: Tuberculosis transmission in a high school choir. J. Sch. Health *68*:256–259, 1998.
569. Weinstein, J., Barrett, C., Baltimore, R., et al.: Nosocomial transmission of tuberculosis from a hospital visitor on a pediatrics ward. Pediatr. Infect. Dis. J. *14*:232–234, 1995.
570. Weis, S., Slocum, P., Blais, F., et al.: The effects of directly observed therapy on the rates of drug resistance and relapse in tuberculosis. N. Engl. J. Med. *330*:1179–1184, 1994.
571. Weismuller, M. M., Graham, S. M., Claessens, N. J. M., et al.: Diagnosis of childhood tuberculosis in Malawi: An audit of hospital practice. Int. J. Tuberc. Lung Dis. *6*:432–438, 2002.
572. Werhane, M. J., Snukst-Torbeck, G., and Schraufnagel, D. E.: The tuberculosis clinic. Chest *96*:815–818, 1989.
573. Whalen, C., Horsburgh, C., Hom, D., et al.: Accelerated course of human immunodeficiency virus infection after tuberculosis. Am. J. Respir. Crit. Care Med. *151*:129–135, 1995.
574. Whitener, D. R.: Tuberculous brain abscess. Arch. Neurol. *35*:148–155, 1978.
575. World Health Organization: Treatment of Tuberculosis: Guidelines for National Programmes. 2nd ed. Geneva, WHO/TB/97.220, 1997.
576. World Health Organization: The World Health Report 1999. Making a Difference. Geneva, World Health Organization, 1999.
577. Wilkins, E. G. L.: Tuberculous peritonitis: Diagnostic value of the ascitic/blood glucose value. Tubercle *65*:47–52, 1984.
578. Witrak, B. J., and Ellis, G. T.: Intracranial tuberculosis: Manifestations on computerized tomography. South. Med. J. *78*:386–392, 1985.
579. Wright, F. W., and Hamilton, W. S.: Miliary tuberculosis twice. Br. J. Dis. Chest *68*:210–212, 1974.
580. Zarabi, M., Sane, S., and Girdany, B. R.: Chest roentgenogram in the early diagnosis of tuberculous meningitis in children. Am. J. Dis. Child. *121*:389–392, 1971.
581. Zhang, Y.: Genetic basis of isoniazid resistance of *Mycobacterium tuberculosis*. Rev. Microbiol. *144*:143–150, 1993.
582. Zhang, Y., Heym, B., Allen, B., et al.: Catalase-peroxidase gene and isoniazid resistance of *Mycobacterium tuberculosis*. Nature *358*:591–593, 1992.
583. Zinneman, H. H., and Hall, W. H.: Transient tuberculous meningitis. Am. Rev. Respir. Dis. *114*:1185–1188, 1976.
584. Zitrin, C. M., and Lincoln, E. M.: Initial tuberculous infection due to drug-resistant organisms: With a review of the world literature on initial infection due to isoniazid-resistant tubercle bacilli. J. Pediatr. *58*:219–223, 1961.
585. Zweiman, B., Pappano, J. E., Jr., and Hildrath, E. A.: Effect of influenza vaccine administration on tuberculin skin sensitivity. Dis. Chest. *52*:46–49, 1967.

CHAPTER 102 Other Mycobacteria

J. THOMAS CROSS, JR. ■ RICHARD F. JACOBS

The definition of mycobacteria other than tubercle bacilli is quite confusing. Ernest Runyon, in his address to the International Conference on Atypical Mycobacteria, probably defined them best: "Tubercle bacilli include *Mycobacterium tuberculosis, Mycobacterium bovis*, and *Mycobacterium africanum*. Together with *Mycobacterium microti* (not pathogenic for humans), these organisms constitute the tubercle bacillus complex."[130] Any mycobacterium not listed in this group is considered to be in the "other" grouping. Mycobacteria other than those causing tuberculosis and leprosy were not recognized as causes of disease in humans until the 1950s.[159] The incidence of disease caused by these organisms remained fairly stable until the acquired immunodeficiency syndrome (AIDS) epidemic began in the 1980s. The most common forms of the disease are chronic pulmonary disease resembling tuberculosis (occurring mainly in adults), cervical adenopathy in children, skin and soft tissue infection, and disseminated disease in immunocompromised persons.[115] In the mid-1980s, the incidence of infections with atypical mycobacteria increased markedly, probably because of the increased number of immunocompromised patients (e.g., because of AIDS, organ transplantation) and the significant improvement in microbiologic methods for cultivating these organisms in the last 30 or so years.[180, 185]

Epidemiology

The atypical mycobacteria are ubiquitous in nature. They are found in soil, animals, milk,[42] and food. Of importance in some hospital-acquired infections or infections in immunocompromised hosts is the presence of the organisms in common tap water.[16, 57, 105, 151] Exposure to environments (especially soil) colonized by these organisms seems to be important for acquisition of disease in children. Organisms commonly found in soil include *Mycobacterium scrofulaceum, Mycobacterium flavescens, Mycobacterium avium–intracellulare* (MAI), *Mycobacterium gastri, Mycobacterium terrae, Mycobacterium fortuitum,* and *Mycobacterium chelonae*. Water is an important source for all of the previously named organisms and also for *Mycobacterium kansasii, Mycobacterium marinum, Mycobacterium gordonae*, and *Mycobacterium xenopi*. In contrast, humans are the only known reservoirs for *M. tuberculosis*. In a survey from the Centers for Disease Control and Prevention (CDC), 35 percent of mycobacteria isolated in laboratories were nontuberculous.[52] MAI accounted for 66 percent of the nontuberculous isolates, followed by *M. fortuitum* (19%), *M. kansasii* (9%), and *M. scrofulaceum* (6%). These data were collected in 1980 before the present AIDS epidemic and before the rapid increase in the number and types of immunocompromised patients; therefore, current rates probably are much higher.

Geography also appears to have some bearing on the prevalence of these infections. The southeastern part of the United States has much higher rates in children than does the Northeast or the Northwest. *M. avium* complex (MAC) was seen most commonly along the coastal borders of the United States and in the states bordering Canada. The highest rates were seen in Hawaii (10.9 cases per 100,000 population), Connecticut (8.9 cases per 100,000 population), and Florida (8.4 cases per 100,000 population). High rates, however, also were seen in Kansas and the desert Southwest, thus demonstrating the widespread nature of this organism in causing disease. In contrast, *M. kansasii* was seen most commonly in the midwestern part of the United States and almost never was seen in the Southeast.[52] States with rates of *M. kansasii* higher than 0.75 case per 100,000 included Missouri, Illinois, Kentucky, Indiana, Kansas, Nebraska, Louisiana, Texas, Arizona, and Florida. North Carolina, a state with one of the highest rates of MAC (>4.8 cases per 100,000 population), had very few cases of *M. kansasii* (0.00 to 0.25 cases per 100,000 population). *M. marinum* frequently was isolated from coastal areas, whereas *M. xenopi* was scattered across the United States, with 50 percent of case being found in just three states (Connecticut, Wisconsin, and California). For all the nontuberculous species, males and rural residents also had a much higher incidence of infection.[136] Extrapolation of these rates to determine disease patterns is not without problems, however. The number of mycobacterial isolates could be skewed easily by the presence of multiple isolates from a single patient, or it may just represent colonization. Nonetheless, these rates can help predict which species of nontuberculous mycobacteria are most likely to be encountered in a particular geographic region while the physician awaits final identification and sensitivity testing on an isolated nontuberculous organism.

The site of isolation from the human source can be helpful in determining the type of mycobacteria that may be involved in the disease process. *M. avium* and *M. intracellulare* are responsible for lymphadenitis, particularly in children. These two organisms also are responsible for pulmonary disease and disseminated disease to bones and occasionally to the meninges. *M. kansasii* is associated most commonly with infections of pulmonary origin and disseminated lesions in adults; rarely, it is associated with adenitis and skin granuloma in children. *M. scrofulaceum* also causes lymphadenitis in children, and *M. marinum* is responsible for skin granuloma and ulcers after exposure to certain salt-water beaches, swimming pools, and tropical fish tanks. The rapid growers (*M. fortuitum* and *M. chelonae*) rarely are responsible for pulmonary and disseminated disease in adults and children.

A familial immune defect predisposing to disseminated atypical mycobacterial infection in childhood has been reported.[93] The six children studied had disseminated infection with atypical mycobacteria and no obvious evidence of immunodeficiency. Clinical and immunologic features seem to indicate that these children acquire infections similar to Lsh/Ity/Bcg-susceptible mice. Ongoing studies to determine the defect may provide insight into the mechanisms by which certain children are susceptible to mycobacterial infections whereas in others exposed to the same environmental factors, disseminated disease does not develop.

Microbiology

Runyon and Timpe in their monumental work on atypical mycobacteria suggested a useful classification system based on three characteristics of the organisms: production of pigment, rate of growth, and colonial characteristics.[128, 129, 159] The four groups are group I—photochromogens, which produce bright yellow to red pigment in the presence of light; group II—scotochromogens, which produce yellow to orange pigment in the dark; group III—nonphotochromogens, which are nonpigment producers; and group IV—rapid growers, which generally grow in less than a week. Kubica published an updated version of Runyon's classification in 1978, and it was useful for many years.[86] Subsequently, a more "simplified" classification based on the growth rates of the organisms alone was proposed.[180]

The atypical mycobacteria still are differentiated by most clinical laboratories on the basis of various morphologic, physiologic, and biochemical characteristics (Tables 102–1 and 102–2). The difficulty with identifying many of these organisms is their slow growth rates with standard techniques. Beginning sensitivity testing as soon as an organism is cultivated and thought to be the pathogen responsible is useful because several months may be required for proper identification and susceptibility testing. Serologic tests can be helpful in identifying some of the organisms.[35, 87, 128, 162, 167, 180, 181, 185] However, in clinical medicine, they rarely are of value for diagnosis in individual patients. A study using humoral immunoglobulins against mycobacterial antigens failed to diagnose tuberculosis or nontuberculous adenitis in children.[163]

Blood cultures for mycobacteria are best performed with the Isolator lysis-centrifugation system (Wampole Laboratories, Cranbury, NJ) or the radiometric BACTEC 13A blood culture bottle (Becton-Dickinson Diagnostic Instrument Systems, Cockeysville, MD).[1, 78, 79] Blood collected in

TABLE 102–1 ■ CHARACTERISTICS OF SLOW-GROWING PATHOGENIC MYCOBACTERIA

Organism	Growth Present (° C)			Growth Rate (Days)	Niacin	Nitrate Reduction	Pigment Dark	Pigment Light	Growth in 5% NaCl
	25	*37*	*45*						
Mycobacterium tuberculosis	–	+	–	12–28	+	+	–	–	–
Mycobacterium bovis	–	+	–	21–40	–	–	–	–	–
Photochromogens, Runyon group I									
Mycobacterium kansasii	+	+	–	10–21	–	+	–	+	–
Mycobacterium marinum	+	±	–	7–14	–	–	–	+	–
Scotochromogens, Runyon group II									
Mycobacterium scrofulaceum	+	+	–	10–28	–	–	+	+	–
Mycobacterium szulgai	+	+	–	12–28	–	+	+	+	–
Mycobacterium gordonae	+	+	–	10–28	–	–	+	+	–
Nonchromogens, Runyon group III									
Mycobacterium avium	+	+	+	10–21	–	–	–	–	–
Mycobacterium intracellulare	+	+	–	10–21	–	–	–	–	–
Mycobacterium ulcerans	–	–	–	28–60	–	–	–	–	?
Mycobacterium xenopi	–	+	–	14–28	–	–	–	–	–

ethylenediaminetetraacetic acid or coagulated blood is not acceptable. Body fluids such as cerebrospinal fluid, pleural fluid, and peritoneal fluid can be inoculated directly into BACTEC or Septi-Chek (Becton-Dickinson) broth, particularly if only small volumes are available. Gene probes became commercially available in the late 1980s. They involve DNA probes complementary to species-specific sequences of rRNA for the identification of *M. tuberculosis*, MAC, *M. gordonae*, and *M. kansasii* (AccuProbe; Gen-Probe, San Diego, CA).[54]

Polymerase chain reaction (PCR) assay has been evaluated for the routine detection of *M. tuberculosis* in the clinical laboratory and compared with fluorochrome smear and culture. Two large studies compared PCR with the standard technique and found that the sensitivity of PCR assay was 84 percent in both studies.[28, 49] In another study, a multiplex PCR assay for immediate identification of various *Mycobacterium* spp. was shown to be 97.9 percent sensitive and 96.9 percent specific.[84] The PCR testing offered by commercial laboratories at present is not approved by the Food and Drug Administration for in vitro diagnosis. The sensitivity and specificity of this test vary widely among laboratories.[113]

Manifestations of Nontuberculous Mycobacterial Infection in Children

LYMPHADENITIS

Lymphadenitis is the most common manifestation of atypical mycobacterial infection in children. It also can occur rarely in adults.[37, 91, 98] All nodes in the cervical chain can be affected, but the nodes of the submandibular region appear to be the ones most commonly involved.[39] The parotid gland also can be affected.[32] The differential diagnosis frequently centers on deciding whether a malignant process versus a nonmalignant process is present. Nonmalignant processes to consider include mononucleosis, bacterial adenitis, cat-scratch disease, toxoplasmosis, and *M. tuberculosis* infection. Most mycobacterial cases of lymphadenitis are caused by the nontuberculous organisms. However, the clinician must also consider the possibility of *M. tuberculosis*.[30] No clinical features help the clinician discern between nontuberculous mycobacterial infection and tuberculosis. The use of histopathology has been postulated to help differentiate between atypical and tuberculous infections.[119] In this retrospective study, the finding of ill-defined (nonpalisading) granulomas, irregular or serpiginous granulomas, a predominantly nonspecific granulomatous response, predominantly sarcoid-like granulomas, or lack of significant caseation was seen more commonly with nontuberculous lymphadenitis. Additionally, nontuberculous infections had neutrophils predominantly in the center of the necrosis, whereas in tuberculous infections, neutrophils were scattered throughout the specimen. A prospective study investigating these findings has not been published to date, and other authors have not noted similar patterns.[11]

In a Canadian study, the rate of atypical mycobacteria as a cause of lymphadenitis was 1.21 cases per 100,000 children, whereas the rate for tuberculosis was 0.3 case per 100,000 children.[141] Authors from San Diego report a marked increase in the number of infections in children.[120] Other authors around the world have reported a markedly increased incidence of infection with these organisms in immunocompetent children.[51] In one study, the incidence increased from 1 case between 1987 and 1990 to 85 cases between 1991 and 1993.[90] In a large study compiled by Lincoln and Gilbert involving 243 children, more than 50 percent were younger than 3 years of age and 80 percent were younger than 5 years.[97] In contrast, one study showed that the mean age had increased to 5.2 years.[177]

TABLE 102–2 ■ CHARACTERISTICS OF RAPID MYCOBACTERIAL GROWERS

Runyon Group IV	Optimum Temperature	Growth Rate	Niacin	Nitrate Reduction	Growth in 5% NaCl
Mycobacterium fortuitum	37° C	3–7 days	–	+	+
Mycobacterium abscessus	37° C	3–7 days	–	–	+
Mycobacterium chelonae	37° C	3–7 days	–	–	–

Most patients have no systemic symptoms and normal chest radiographs; other laboratory studies generally are not helpful. The mean duration of swelling is approximately 6 weeks. Historically, the cervical nodes are most commonly affected in children, although a recent study from Greece reports submandibular prominence.[104]

Infections are caused mainly by MAI and *M. scrofulaceum*. A large prospective study spanning 32 years from 1958 to 1990 showed that MAC has become the predominant etiologic agent and has surpassed *M. scrofulaceum* from earlier in the study.[183] Case reports involving *M. fortuitum* also have been published.[126] Lymphadenitis caused by *M. haemophilum* is being diagnosed in immunocompetent children in increasing numbers.[7, 133] Samra and colleagues demonstrated that the BACTEC radiometric system or MB Redox broth (Heipha Diagnostika Biotest, Hiedelberg, Germany) is superior to Löwenstein-Jensen (Heipha Diagnostika Biotest) media for isolation of *M. haemophilum.* This organism is thought to have been underdiagnosed previously because of the widespread use of Löwenstein-Jensen media. *Mycobacterium malmoense* also has been described as an etiologic agent of cervical lymphadenitis in children.[161] Haas and associates have described *Mycobacterium heidelbergense*, a new agent of mycobacterial lymphadenitis in children.[60]

The usefulness of mycobacterial antigens in skin testing for the diagnosis of atypical mycobacterial infection versus tuberculous lymphadenitis is controversial. The use of purified protein derivative type B (PPD-B; *M. intracellulare*), PPD-Y (*M. kansasii*), PPD-G (*M. scrofulaceum*), and PPD-T (*M. tuberculosis*) was compared to discern whether children with active lymphadenitis caused by the atypical mycobacteria could be distinguished from those with tuberculosis.[72] Patients with confirmed nontuberculous adenitis were six times more likely to have greater than 10-mm induration to PPD-B than were children with negative culture or biopsy results. In all groups except those with confirmed *M. tuberculosis*, responses to PPD-T were significantly smaller than those to the nontuberculous mycobacterial antigens. The results of the study seem to indicate that the use of nontuberculous mycobacterial antigens could be helpful in diagnosing mycobacterial cervical adenopathy. However, the specificity for nontuberculous organisms is unknown.

Needle aspiration of an affected node can be a valuable diagnostic tool. Cultures for bacterial and mycobacterial etiologies should be performed, and recovery rates in children with cervical lymphadenitis range from 60 to 88 percent.[9, 14, 77, 187] The aspirate should be inoculated onto aerobic and anaerobic media, as well as Sabouraud agar and mycobacterial media (Löwenstein-Jensen slants or Middlebrook media). Use of the BACTEC system can be very helpful; mycobacteria can be isolated as early as 12 to 17 days after inoculation.[146]

Recently, preoperative diagnosis of *M. avium* lymphadenitis was accomplished with the use of PCR of gastric aspirates in two children.[59] Further studies are needed to conclude whether it could be a noninvasive method of diagnosing this infection.

The best treatment of atypical mycobacteria–caused lymphadenitis is complete excision of the involved lymph node.[166] Incision and drainage without excision result in a high rate of secondary drainage, and subsequent excision of the remaining tissue is required for cure.[4, 132, 139] Small uncontrolled trials have attempted to use antimicrobials alone for lymphadenitis caused by nontuberculous mycobacteria.[99] Preliminary results have been successful, but use of toxic agents for prolonged periods of time was required. Controlled trials have not been published.

ACQUIRED IMMUNODEFICIENCY SYNDROME AND ATYPICAL MYCOBACTERIA

Surveys have noted an increasing rate of nontuberculous infection in children with AIDS.[71] Approximately 6 percent of adults and 4 percent of children with AIDS reported to the CDC had disseminated MAC infection as their AIDS-defining disease.[20] Autopsy studies show that MAC infection is present in 20 to 50 percent of adult human immunodeficiency virus (HIV)-infected patients.[124, 176, 179] In a retrospective study from 1990 to 1996 in New York City, 26 percent of children had evidence of MAC infection at the time of their deaths.[75] MAC infection was thought to be the cause of death in 13 percent of the 54 children with HIV infection, and the mean age at death was 7.8 years. However, in two autopsy studies of opportunistic infection in HIV-infected children in Latin America and Argentina, only 2.7 and 3.4 percent, respectively, had evidence of disseminated disease.[41, 122] In these studies, 62 percent (Argentina) and 72 percent (Latin America) of the children studied were younger than 1 year of age. These data indicate that MAI infection is seen less commonly in younger children with HIV.

In the CDC study, MAC was the nontuberculous mycobacterium most commonly isolated. *M. kansasii* and *M. scrofulaceum* were found in one case each. In adult studies, the incidence of infection with *M. kansasii* and *M. scrofulaceum* also is quite low.[38, 70] More than 70 percent of the children with MAC and AIDS had evidence of disseminated disease. Almost all had CD4 counts less than 100 cells/mm^3. Clinical findings included failure to maintain growth curves, anorexia, fever, abdominal pain, and anemia. The median age at diagnosis was 46 months, with a median of 9 months elapsing between the onset of symptoms and positive cultures. Once nontuberculous mycobacterial infection was diagnosed in these patients, they survived less than 10 months. Blood cultures have 90 to 95 percent sensitivity in detecting disseminated MAC infection in adult patients with AIDS.[63]

MAI has been shown to infect the esophagus, stomach, and intestine of pediatric patients with AIDS.[76] Patients with extensive MAI infection of the small and large intestines have severe, persistent diarrhea.

Mycobacterium genavense has been shown to cause infection in children with HIV infection.[112] The children were febrile and had abdominal cramps and diarrhea. CD4 lymphocyte counts were less than 400/mm^3. The organism was found in numerous stool samples and lymph node specimens. Multiple-drug regimens that include amikacin, ethambutol, rifampin, and clarithromycin may be useful in treating this infection.

For treatment of MAC infection in HIV-infected children, combination therapy is recommended.[6] Clarithromycin (15 mg/kg/day divided into two oral doses, maximum of 500 mg) and ethambutol (15 to 20 mg/kg/day in a single dose, maximum of 1600 mg) should be included. Additionally, the use of rifabutin (5 to 10 mg/kg/day once daily, maximum of 300 mg), ciprofloxacin (20 to 30 mg/kg/day intravenously or orally once daily, maximum of 1.5 g), or azithromycin (10 mg/kg once daily) can be considered. Because of their liquid form, clarithromycin and azithromycin have become available therapy for many infections in pediatric patients, including otitis media, pharyngitis, and skin infections.[82] The use of granulocyte colony-stimulating factor as an adjunct to antimicrobial therapy for disseminated MAC infection has been reported,[116] but additional data are needed to determine the usefulness of this agent.

For secondary prevention of recurrent disease, lifelong prophylaxis with clarithromycin is recommended (15 mg/kg/day in two divided doses, maximum of 500 mg), in combination with at least one of the following: ethambutol (15 to 20 mg/kg/day once daily), rifabutin (5 mg/kg/day once daily, maximum of 300 mg), or ciprofloxacin (20 to 30 mg/kg/day in two divided doses, maximum of 1.5 g).

The use of rifabutin or azithromycin (5 mg/kg/day once daily, maximum of 250 mg, or 20 mg/kg once weekly) for prophylaxis has been recommended based on adult studies in an attempt to delay and prevent MAC bacteremia in adults with CD4 cell counts less than 100 cells/mm^3. The U.S. Public Health Service and the Infectious Disease Society of America have published guidelines for the prevention of opportunistic infections, including disseminated MAC.[164] These guidelines incorporate age-specific CD4 counts at which prophylaxis should be used: children 6 years or older, less than 50 cells/μL; children 2 to 6 years old, less than 75 cells/μL; children 1 to 2 years old, less than 500 cells/μL; and children younger than 12 months, less than 750 cells/μL. Azithromycin (20 mg/kg once weekly) appears to be effective. A phase I/II study of prophylactic rifabutin for prevention of disseminated MAC infection in children demonstrated a side effect of bilateral, stellate, corneal deposits without associated uveitis in 6 of 25 children.[143]

The emergence of resistance is a concern with the MAC prophylactic regimens in patients with AIDS. In some trials, 9 percent of adults receiving azithromycin prophylaxis and 5 percent of adults receiving clarithromycin prophylaxis had breakthrough MAC bacteremia. Of these cases, 11 and 58 percent of the azithromycin and clarithromycin breakthrough isolates, respectively, were macrolide-resistant.[5, 62]

PULMONARY INFECTIONS

Reviews from the late 1970s showed that pulmonary disease caused by atypical mycobacteria usually was caused by *M. kansasii* and MAC.[26, 53, 127] MAC infection most commonly occurred during the sixth decade, whereas *M. kansasii* infection occurred in individuals a decade younger. Men were affected most commonly, in ratios as high as 4 to 1. Chronic obstructive pulmonary disease as noted by radiographic findings was found in 50 to 60 percent of patients with atypical mycobacterial pulmonary infections. Bullous lung disease was seen in 24 to 39 percent. The lobar distribution and severity of disease were similar for atypical mycobacterial agents and *M. tuberculosis,* with one exception: *M. kansasii* was much more prone to produce unilateral disease, which occurred nearly 60 percent of the time as compared with 35 percent of the time in MAC or *M. tuberculosis* infection. Typically, disease begins in the posterior portions of the upper lobes. Progression to cavitary disease occurred in 87 percent of patients with *M. tuberculosis* and MAC infections and in 96 percent of patients with *M. kansasii* infection. Rare case reports of mediastinal mass lesions in children caused by nontuberculous mycobacteria have been published.[47]

Hilar and mediastinal adenopathy was an uncommon finding, particularly with MAC (4%) and *M. kansasii* (0.5%). Pleural effusions were rare findings and occurred in 6 percent of patients with MAC and 4 percent with *M. kansasii.* Treatment at that time generally involved three to four courses of drug therapy, including regimens of isonicotinic acid hydrazide, *p*-aminosalicylic acid, streptomycin, and rifampin. The American Thoracic Society recommends a four-drug regimen for MAC pulmonary infection in adults: isoniazid (300 mg), rifampin (600 mg), ethambutol (25 mg/kg for 2 months, then 15 mg/kg), and streptomycin (0.5 to 1.0 g five times each week for 8 to 12 weeks, then 0.5 to 1.0 g two or three times each week for 3 months, as tolerated).[171] Drugs are administered for 18 to 24 months, with a minimum of 12 months of culture negativity required while receiving therapy. A previous clinical investigation revealed success rates between 25 and 80 percent, and the best response rate was noted with a three-drug regimen of ethambutol, ethionamide, and cycloserine.[44] Resectional surgery appeared to have poor outcomes. For *M. kansasii* pulmonary infection, the American Thoracic Society recommendations include isoniazid (300 mg/day), ethambutol (15 mg/kg/day), and rifampin (600 mg/day) for 18 months in adults.

Patients with cystic fibrosis have been noted to have an increased incidence of infection with nontuberculous mycobacteria. Prevalence rates of 2 to 20 percent have been reported.[3, 65, 66, 81] A study from France involving children aged 1 to 18 years indicated that mycobacterial species were isolated from 6.6 percent of routine sputum samples and that 1.9 percent had documented mycobacterial lung infection.[46] Mycobacterial infections are seen more commonly in older patients with cystic fibrosis. Frequent intravenous antibiotic use is a possible risk factor for colonization with nontuberculous mycobacteria.[160] Organisms most commonly found are MAC, *M. kansasii, M. fortuitum,* and *M. chelonae.* Bacterial contamination, particularly with *Pseudomonas aeruginosa,* of the acid-fast bacilli cultures from cystic fibrosis patients has been a major problem that has rendered isolation of mycobacteria more difficult.[144] Another confounding problem is the difficulty in differentiating infection from colonization in cystic fibrosis patients.[81] The American Thoracic Society recommends radiographic changes, isolation of multiple colonies of the same species, and the absence of other potential pathogens as criteria for the diagnosis of pathogenic infection with nontuberculous mycobacteria.[2] Discernment is even more difficult in the setting of the chronic lung disease seen in cystic fibrosis patients. Kilby and associates[81] suggest that repeated isolation of nontuberculous mycobacteria associated with pulmonary cavities or infiltrates that do not improve with aggressive standard antibacterial treatment could indicate active mycobacterial disease in patients with cystic fibrosis.

M. xenopi has been described in adults as a cause of infection of the pulmonary tract.[142] The mean age at infection was 62 years, and it occurred in a mainly Canadian population. Eighty-six percent of the patients had underlying pulmonary pathology, including chronic obstructive pulmonary disease, previous pulmonary tuberculosis, carcinoma of the lung, sarcoidosis, and cystic fibrosis. Additionally, a case was reported of a 7-year-old boy with leukemia in whom pneumonia with *M. xenopi* developed and was successfully treated with 2 years of therapy that included ethambutol and clarithromycin.[92]

Mycobacterium simiae has been isolated in adults with underlying pulmonary abnormalities.[10, 85] *M. simiae* is the most drug-resistant of all the nontuberculous mycobacteria. Some isolates are resistant even to all drugs tested.

Mycobacterium szulgai has been described in several case series as a cause of lung disease.[103, 174] Disease occurred in elderly white men and resembled chronic tuberculosis. Therapeutic regimens effective against *M. avium* appeared to provide good clinical outcomes.

SKIN INFECTIONS

Mycobacterium marinum

M. marinum is photochromogenic and was identified as a pathogen in fish in 1926 by Aronson.[97] The skin lesions usually result from light trauma (abrasions) in swimming pools or other bodies of water when the surfaces of the pool are colonized by *M. marinum*.[34, 109] Fish tanks also have been implicated and generally involve a finger.[156] Most cases occur in children between the ages of 10 and 16 years. The most common sites are the elbows, knees, and ankles. Cooler superficial portions of the body are affected most frequently. Other exposed body areas can be involved, depending on what part of the body has made contact with the surface containing the mycobacterium (e.g., the nose in divers).[110] Regional spread of lesions has been reported.[148]

The incubation period from exposure to formation of a small indurated area that ulcerates generally is 3 weeks. The lesion then crusts and forms a granuloma with a small crater. The lesions usually are painless and resolve in several months; occasionally, they can last longer. Unlike in other mycobacterial diseases, regional nodes are not involved.

Infection with this organism usually is benign. A main consequence, however, is that patients with *M. marinum* infection frequently will have conversion of their PPD-T test to positive.[97] The natural reservoir for *M. marinum*, which requires a cool incubator (32° C), is in fish and other cold-blooded animals. Generally, only small numbers of organisms may be isolated in some granulomas.

Treatment of *M. marinum* has been successful with rifampin and ethambutol,[165, 184] and one report showed good results with rifampin alone.[40] An accompanying editorial, however, cautioned against the use of rifampin alone and recommended using rifampin with ethambutol.[17] The duration of therapy, according to the literature, varies from several weeks to 18 months. In general, response to therapy is rapid, and treatment should be continued for 4 to 6 weeks after clinical resolution.[40]

Mycobacterium ulcerans

In 1948, MacCallum[102] reported the first cases of disease caused by *Mycobacterium ulcerans*. Most cases since then have occurred in remote, tropical, or subtropical areas of the world, including parts of Africa and Australia.[101, 125] In a 1-year period, 23 cases of Buruli ulcer caused by *M. ulcerans* occurred in Lambarene (Gabon).[19] Cases also have been reported in Mexico.[97] The natural reservoir for *M. ulcerans* is unknown, although one report suggests the spines of a tall prickly grass known as *Echinocloa pyrimidalis*.[149] The lesions caused by *M. ulcerans* occur mainly on the cooler superficial portions of the body. Patients harboring this organism are in otherwise good health without underlying immunodeficiency.[27] Scraping of the skin by thorns or pieces of wood has been implicated as the route of inoculation in many of the cases. The organism is very fastidious, with growth seen only between 30° C and 35° C.

The incubation period for this painless infection also is approximately 3 weeks. Regional lymphadenitis rarely occurs with this organism. The infection has three distinct stages, and knowledge of them can be helpful in making the diagnosis and providing treatment. The disease begins as a hard, mobile nodule. It frequently is associated with pruritus and in Zaire is termed *mputa matadi* (the itching stone). This stage is known as the pre-ulcerative stage.

In some patients, the infection resolves on its own, but in others, it progresses to the ulcerative stage. In contrast to *M. marinum,* in which the lesions are relatively short lived and do not progress past the ulcerative stage, the lesions of *M. ulcerans* usually last 6 to 9 months and can frequently progress and lead to deformities of limbs that may require amputation.[97] The organisms can be isolated in large numbers from the periphery of ulcers adjacent to normal tissue, which again contrasts with infection by *M. marinum*, in which very few organisms are found in the lesions.

The infection generally involves subcutaneous adipose tissue and leads to areas of fat necrosis, which then proceeds to overlying necrosis of the adjacent skin. The lesions can become enormous, sometimes involving a complete limb. Even though numerous organisms are seen in the progressing edge of the infection, little evidence of a cellular immune response is apparent. Additionally, anergy to skin reagents prepared from *M. ulcerans* (burulin) frequently is noted at this stage.[150] Finally, the next stage, called the reactive phase, is reached. Cellular infiltrates with granuloma formation occur in the lesion. The number of organisms in the lesion decreases dramatically, and a positive skin test reaction develops to the burulin. Infection with *M. ulcerans* also can cause conversion of a patient's PPD response to positive; however, conversion is seen in only approximately 50 percent of cases.[27] Finally, healing may take place, but with fibrosis left in its wake.

Treatment of *M. ulcerans* infection is anecdotal at best. Treatment choices are based on the stage of infection. Lesions in the pre-ulcerative stage are best treated with excision and primary closure.[56] Successful therapy in the anergic progressive stage is considered the most difficult and involves appropriate antimycobacterial therapy for the infection. Success has been reported with both isonicotinic acid hydrazide and streptomycin or diaminodiphenylsulfone and oxytetracycline combinations,[27] as well as sulfamethoxazole, rifampin, minocycline,[147] and clofazimine.[101] In the final stage, healing should be promoted with as little deformity or loss of function as possible, the use of skin grafting and splinting, and excision of fibrous tissue.[56, 125] Disseminated infection in an immunocompetent child along with the development of multifocal osteomyelitis has been described.[67] See also Chapter 103.

Other Mycobacteria in Skin Disease

M. haemophilum has produced painful subcutaneous nodules in immunocompromised patients, particularly those with renal transplants.[36, 182] In addition, *M. haemophilum* has produced disseminated disease, including bacteremia, osteomyelitis, and pulmonary disease, in immunocompromised patients.[154] *M. chelonae* has been found to be a cause of disseminated cutaneous infection.[169] Steroid use is the predisposing factor for infection with this organism. *M. fortuitum* has been implicated in cutaneous lesions in a child involved in a motor scooter accident, with the subsequent development of lesions at the site of knee lacerations; regional adenopathy of the inguinal nodes also developed.[140] *M. fortuitum-chelonae* complex has been responsible for superficial skin abscesses in children.[13] *M. fortuitum* in adult studies also has been implicated in severe infections in immunocompromised hosts; these infections usually are rapidly disseminating, with high mortality.[182] *M. avium* has been isolated from an eyelid abscess with drainage.[138] Treatment of cutaneous disease caused by these organisms is difficult at best. Four- or five-drug therapy has been tried, but with poor results.

Organisms Seen in Children

Specific organisms and treatment guidelines are discussed in the following sections. Table 102–3 provides a quick guide to some of the more commonly used antimycobacterial agents.

MYCOBACTERIUM AVIUM–INTRACELLULARE COMPLEX

MAC consists of *M. avium* and *M. intracellulare.* These organisms are slow-growing, obligate aerobes that require

TABLE 102–3 ■ ANTIMYCOBACTERIAL AGENTS*

Drug	Dosage	Form
Amikacin (A)	15–20 mg/kg/day divided q8h	IV or IM
Azithromycin (Z)	500 mg bid (adults/adolescents); 10–12 mg/kg/day (children)	PO
Cefoxitin (X)	80–160 mg/kg/day divided q4–6h	IV or IM
Ciprofloxacin (C)	20–30 mg/kg/day divided q12h (adults only in U.S.)	PO or IV
Clarithromycin (CL)	15–30 mg/kg/day divided q12h	PO
Clofazimine (CLO)	1–2 mg/kg/day	PO
Doxycycline (D)	2–4 mg/kg/day divided q12h (older than 8 yr)	PO, IV
Ethambutol (ETB)	15–25 mg/kg/day	PO
Ethionamide (ETH)	10–20 mg/kg/day divided q12h	PO
Isoniazid (I)	10–14 mg/kg/day	PO
Pyrazinamide (PZA)	15–30 mg/kg/day	PO
Rifabutin (RIB)	5–10 mg/kg/day; maximum of 300 mg/day (adults)*	PO
Rifampin (RIF)	10–20 mg/kg/day divided q12–24h	PO or IV
Streptomycin (S)	20–30 mg/kg/day	IM

Infections

Disseminated MAC: HIV infected: CL (or Z) + ETB (± RIB)
Disseminated MAC: HIV-negative, immunocompromised: RIF + ETB + INH + S or A
Mycobacterium kansasii: RIF + ETB + I
Mycobacterium marinum: ETB + RIF, or D or TMP-SMX
Mycobacterium chelonae: A ± CLO or CL alone
Mycobacterium fortuitum: A + X + probenicid or A + C + sulfonamide
Mycobacterium abscessus: CL alone or A alone

*Not approved for use in children.
MAC, *M. avium* complex; TMP-SMX, trimethoprim-sulfamethoxazole.
Data based on references 58, 71, 94, 95, 131, 165, 171, 173, 182, 184.

2 to 6 weeks for colony formation on solid media. Colonies usually are smooth but may be rough and can be transparent or opaque. These organisms will grow on routine bacterial media, but growth is achieved best on selective mycobacterial media such as Löwenstein-Jensen medium or Middlebrook 7K10 and 7K11 agar. Nucleic acid hybridization probes using target sequences of ribosomal RNA are available commercially for rapid identification of clinical isolates.[96, 111] MAC infection is diagnosed most commonly by culture of blood or bone marrow.

In a study of 56 isolates from pediatric patients involving sequence analysis of the ribosomal internal transcribed spacer, Hazra and colleagues showed that the closely related Mav-B and Mav-A sequevars caused the vast majority of disease.[64] Patients from geographically diverse areas of the United States (Boston, Miami, and Los Angeles) had isolates with closely related patterns. The finding of related strains causing disease in epidemiologically unrelated patients is most consistent with two hypotheses: a similar subset of *M. avium* strains is more virulent and, therefore, more likely to cause disease in humans, and pathogenic strains are more prevalent in the environment.

M. avium was recognized in 1890 as the causative agent of disease in chickens.[182] *M. intracellulare* was designated in 1967 and at the time was difficult to distinguish routinely from *M. avium*—thus the name *M. avium-intracellulare*. Today, with the use of DNA probes, most seroagglutination types have been discerned between the two groups. *M. avium* is the most common nontuberculous mycobacterium causing disease in humans, but isolates from environmental sources are more likely to be *M. intracellulare*. Both these organisms can be found in birds, soil, dust, and fresh or salt water. Infections caused by MAC strains isolated from adult patients with AIDS could be identified as either serotype 4 or 8, in contrast to patients without AIDS, in whom no predominant serotype has been identified.[80, 186] Nearly all isolates of MAC from patients with AIDS have been identified as *M. avium;* in patients without AIDS, the rate of *M. avium* falls to approximately 55 percent and that of *M. intracellulare* to 32 to 40 percent.[58, 186]

Lung disease has been the major manifestation of MAC infection in nonimmunocompromised adults. Most investigators thought that MAC infection occurred mainly in patients with deficient immunity or underlying lung disease. Later reports, however, seemed to indicate that normal adult hosts are at risk for development of infection with MAC and that rates are increasing.[74, 121] Case reports involving children are lacking in detail because they usually appear within discussions of adult patients.[123]

Pediatric case reports of disseminated disease caused by MAI/MAC have appeared in the literature. Children have had ulcerative lesions of their colon[33]; mesenteric disease with abscess formation[138]; hematogenous spread to the liver, spleen, kidneys, and adrenal cortex; epididymis[145]; bone lesions[168]; and skin lesions. Disseminated osteomyelitis rarely is caused by nontuberculous mycobacteria, but if it occurs, *M. intracellulare* most commonly is isolated.[25, 83] Septic arthritis also has been reported in association with osteomyelitis.[50] Immunocompromised patients with disseminated MAI infection historically require multiple-drug therapy, including a combination of isoniazid, ethambutol, clofazimine, and rifabutin.[94] However, some reports indicate that disseminated disease in HIV-infected patients may respond to only two agents, as mentioned earlier in the AIDS section. The addition of other agents may be necessary because of the high incidence of resistant organisms. A preliminary report showed that interferon-γ may be effective when combined with conventional therapy in some patients who are refractory to standard chemotherapy alone.[69]

Bacterial peritonitis is a common occurrence in patients regularly undergoing ambulatory peritoneal dialysis for chronic renal failure. Reports of nontuberculous mycobacteria causing peritonitis have been noted.[61, 117, 178] In cases involving nontuberculous mycobacteria with foreign bodies, such as Tenckhoff catheters, the development of infected sinus tracts is frequent. Additionally, antituberculous drug regimens in these cases generally are unsuccessful. Although the mycobacteria were sensitive to the agents used, the patients continued to have sinus tract drainage without improvement, even after removal of the foreign body.

MYCOBACTERIUM SCROFULACEUM

M. scrofulaceum has many characteristics similar to those of *M. avium* and *M. intracellulare* and can be found in soil, water, and dairy products. This organism is associated most commonly with lymphadenitis in children 1 to 5 years of age and rarely causes other manifestations in humans. Skin and bone lesions have been reported in two children chronically infected with *M. scrofulaceum* for as long as 10 years.[43, 175] Few data are available on chemotherapeutic agents for treatment of infection with this organism. Based on susceptibility patterns, three or more drugs may be necessary for treatment of serious disease. Lymphadenitis can be cured with complete excision of the lymph node.

MYCOBACTERIUM KANSASII

Of the photochromogens, *M. kansasii* is the one most commonly isolated in humans. In contrast to MAI and

M. scrofulaceum, *M. kansasii* rarely is isolated in soil but has been cultured from water[8] and milk.[22, 23] Chronic pulmonary infection is the most common manifestation of this disease and is seen mainly in adults, particularly those with AIDS. Pulmonary disease occurs infrequently in children. Some children have a course similar to that of adults, with underlying pulmonary disease caused by previous tuberculosis or chronic pulmonary disease.[12, 108] In contrast, other children have acute symptoms of classic bacterial pneumonia with an abrupt onset of fever and sputum production, as well as lung consolidation on physical examination and radiographs.[12, 21] Pleural effusions also can occur. In contrast to some of the other nontuberculous organisms, *M. kansasii* is sensitive to most of the antituberculous drugs, particularly rifampin. Thus, treatment of infections with this organism is accomplished easily. Most authorities recommend the use of three drugs, including rifampin, isoniazid, and ethambutol. The treatment course usually requires a minimum of 12 months, with therapy for as long as 24 months needed in some patients. Patients with AIDS and *M. kansasii* infection have responded to this three-drug regimen, but the total duration of therapy is unknown at this time. In children with AIDS, the diagnosis of *M. kansasii* infection is rare, and the clinical response to therapy has been poor.[71] Cases have been reported in other immunocompromised children, including a 7-month-old boy from Texas with disseminated *M. kansasii* infection and numerous organisms found in his spleen at autopsy.[107] *M. kansasii* also has been reported to cause meningitis; the patients died despite the use of antimycobacterial therapy.[73, 135]

MYCOBACTERIUM MALMOENSE

Buchholz and coworkers reviewed infections with *M. malmoense* in the United States from 1993 to 1995.[18] Only 1 of 73 patients was younger than 10 years of age. This patient had cervical lymphadenitis and was cured with surgical excision alone. This organism, which frequently is overlooked on standard Löwenstein-Jensen egg medium, grows at between 25° C and 37° C. The organism is slow growing, and it may require 8 to 12 weeks for colonies to become visible on solid media. The BACTEC system was shown to be superior in isolating *M. malmoense* in one study of children with lymphadenitis.[68] Bone marrow involvement also was described in a patient with chronic granulocytic leukemia.[45] The aforementioned study by Buchholz and colleagues demonstrated that prolonged combination therapy with isoniazid, rifampin, ethambutol, and pyrazinamide after surgical excision was effective in some cases.

MYCOBACTERIUM CHELONAE AND *MYCOBACTERIUM FORTUITUM*

M. chelonae is the most important rapidly growing pathogenic mycobacterium, but its taxonomy is quite confusing.[55] Since Grange's presentation in 1981, the organism's taxonomy has continued to be in flux. The *M. chelonae* group consists of *M. chelonae* (formerly *M. chelonae* subsp. *chelonae*), *Mycobacterium abscessus* (formerly *M. chelonae* subsp. *abscessus*), and a third biovariant known as *M. chelonae*–like organisms.[89] The *M. fortuitum* group consists of *M. fortuitum*, *Mycobacterium peregrinum*, and a third unnamed biovariant.[89] *M. fortuitum* is associated closely with *M. chelonae*. The two groups can be differentiated on the biochemical basis of nitrate reduction and iron uptake. Wallace and associates[169] have provided the largest series of patients with skin, soft tissue, and bone involvement with *M. chelonae*. Steroid use seemed to be the factor associated most commonly with the development of disease.

M. fortuitum and *M. chelonae* have been implicated in sternal wound infections and endocarditis and have occurred in outbreak-type settings.[88, 131, 157] Patients responded to surgical débridement and amikacin with cefoxitin. A case series from Hong Kong reported successful treatment of *M. fortuitum* sternotomy infections with the use of single-daily-dose ofloxacin as monotherapy in three patients.[188] Adult renal transplant patients also have been described with skin and subcutaneous tissue involvement caused by *M. chelonae*.[31] *M. chelonae* likewise has been described as an etiologic agent for otitis media, probably from contamination of ear, nose, and throat instruments with colonized water sources.[100]

M. abscessus, as stated earlier, is related closely to *M. chelonae* and should be designated as a separate species.[89] Manifestations of infection with this organism usually are related to pulmonary, cutaneous, or disseminated infections.[172] Clarithromycin may be effective for *M. chelonae* infection.[173] Maxson and associates[106] reported on a case of osteomyelitis caused by *M. abscessus* that was controlled with long-term clarithromycin monotherapy.

Mycobacterium smegmatis, which resembles *M. fortuitum* except for the absence of a positive 3-day arylsulfatase test result, is a rapid grower that is responsible for skin and soft tissue infections.[170] A case of disseminated infection has been reported in a child with inherited interferon-γ receptor deficiency.[118]

Mycobacterium septicum is a newly described, rapidly growing species associated with catheter-related bacteremia.[137] It resembles *M. fortuitum* and *Mycobacterium senegalense*.

Other Sites of Infection

Carpal tunnel syndrome in adults has been reported as being caused by *M. szulgai*, an uncommon scotochromogenic mycobacterium.[153] Effective treatment included débridement, ethambutol, and rifampin. Other infections in humans include choroiditis,[29] panniculitis,[134] genitourinary tract infection,[15, 158] and synovitis.[155] Ear infections with nontuberculous mycobacteria also have been reported, as has mastoiditis.[48, 114, 152,] Recently, infection of Broviac catheters in pediatric leukemic patients and hemodialysis catheters has been described.[24, 92] In all cases, removal of the catheter was required for resolution of the infection.

With the continued proliferation of immunocompromised patients because of AIDS, as well as new treatment modalities that induce an immunocompromised state (organ transplantation, new immunosuppressive drugs, etc.), the atypical mycobacteria probably will continue to remain important pathogens. With newer isolation techniques and new technology such as DNA probes, our ability to diagnose these infections and our understanding of the pathogenesis of the infections that these organisms produce should improve, as should our ability to treat these infections.

REFERENCES

1. Agy, M. B., Wassis, C. K., Plorde, J. J., et al.: Evaluation of four mycobacterial blood culture media: BACTEC 13A, Isolator/BACTEC 12B, Isolator/Middlebrook Agar and a biphasic medium. Diagn. Microbiol. Infect. Dis. *12*:303–308, 1989.
2. Ahn, C. H., McLarty, J. W., Ahn, S. S., et al.: Diagnostic criteria for pulmonary disease caused by *Mycobacterium kansasii* and *Mycobacterium intracellulare*. Am. Rev. Respir. Dis. *125*:388–391, 1982.

3. Aitken, M. L., Burke, W., McDonald, G., et al.: Nontuberculous mycobacterial disease in adult cystic fibrosis patients. Chest *103*:1096–1099, 1993.
4. Altman, R. P., and Margileth, A. M.: Cervical lymphadenopathy from atypical mycobacteria: Diagnosis and surgical treatment. J. Pediatr. Surg. *10*:419–422, 1975.
5. Alvarez-Elcoro, S., and Enzler, M.J.: The macrolides: Erythromycin, clarithromycin, and azithromycin. Mayo Clin. Proc. *74*:613–634, 1999.
6. Antiretroviral therapy and medical management of pediatric HIV infection and 1997 USPHS/IDSA report on the prevention of opportunistic infections in persons infected with human immunodeficiency virus. Pediatrics. *102*(4 Pt 2):999–1085, 1998.
7. Armstrong, K. L., James, R. W., Dawson, D. J., et al.: *Mycobacterium haemophilum* causing perihilar or cervical lymphadenitis in healthy children. J. Pediatr. *121*:202–205, 1992.
8. Bailey, R. K., Wyles, S., Dingley, M., et al.: The isolation of high catalase *Mycobacterium kansasii* from tap water. Am. Rev. Respir. Dis. *101*:430, 1970.
9. Barton, L. L., and Feigin, R. D.: Childhood cervical lymphadenitis: A reappraisal. J. Pediatr. *84*:846–852, 1974.
10. Bell, R. C., Higuchi, J. H., Donovan, W. N., et al.: *Mycobacterium simiae:* Clinical features and follow-up of twenty-four patients. Am. Rev. Respir. Dis. *127*:35–38, 1983.
11. Benjamin, D. R.: Granulomatous lymphadenitis in children. Arch. Pathol. Lab. Med. *111*:750–753, 1987.
12. Bialkin, G., Pollak, A., and Weil, A. J.: Pulmonary infection with *Mycobacterium kansasii.* Am. J. Dis. Child. *101*:739, 1961.
13. Blacklock, Z. M., and Dawson, D. J.: Atypical mycobacteria causing non-pulmonary disease in Queensland. Pathology *11*:283–287, 1979.
14. Brook, I.: Aerobic and anaerobic bacteriology of cervical adenitis in children. Clin. Pediatr. (Phila.) *19*:693–696, 1980.
15. Brooker, W. J., and Aufderheide, A. C.: Genitourinary tract infections due to atypical mycobacteria. J. Urol. *124*:242–244, 1980.
16. Brooks, R. W., Parker, B. C., Gruft, H., et al.: Epidemiology of infection by nontuberculous mycobacteria. Am. Rev. Respir. Dis. *130*:630–633, 1984.
17. Brown J. W., III, and Sanders, C. V.: *Mycobacterium marinum* infections: A problem of recognition, not therapy? Arch. Intern. Med. *147*:817–818, 1987.
18. Buchholz, U. T., McNeil, M. M., Keyes, L. E., and Good, R. C.: *Mycobacterium malmoense* infections in the United States, January 1993 through June 1995. Clin. Infect. Dis. *27*:551–558, 1998.
19. Burchard, G. D., and Bierther, M.: Buruli ulcer: Clinical pathological study of 23 patients in Lambarene, Gabon. Trop. Med. Parasitol. *37*:1–8, 1986.
20. Centers for Disease Control and Prevention: HIV/AIDS surveillance report. *Feb*:1–23, 1993.
21. Chapman, J. S.: Varieties of tuberculosis in children. Minn. Med. *42*:1773, 1959.
22. Chapman, J. S., Bernard, J. S., and Speight, M.: Isolation of mycobacteria from raw milk. Am. Rev. Respir. Dis. *91*:351, 1965.
23. Chapman, J. S., and Speight, M.: Isolation of atypical mycobacteria from pasteurized milk. Am. Rev. Respir. Dis. *98*:1052, 1968.
24. Chawla, P.G., and Nevins, T.E.: Management of hemodialysis catheter related bacteremia: A 10 year experience. Pediatr. Nephrol. *14*:198–202, 2000.
25. Chicoine, L., La Pointe, N., Simoneau, R., et al.: "Anonymous" mycobacterial infection causing disseminated osteomyelitis and skin lesions. Can. Med. Assoc. J. *98*:1059, 1968.
26. Christensen, E. E., Dietz, G. W., Ahn, C. H., et al.: Initial roentgenographic manifestations of pulmonary *Mycobacterium tuberculosis, M. kansasii,* and *M. intracellulare* infections. Chest *80*:132–136, 1981.
27. Clancy, J. K., Dodge, O. G., Lunn, H. F., et al.: Mycobacterial skin ulcers in Uganda. Lancet *2*:951–954, 1961.
28. Clarridge, J., Shawar, R., Shinnick, T., et al.: Large-scale use of polymerase chain reaction for detection of *Mycobacterium tuberculosis* in a routine mycobacteriology laboratory. J. Clin. Microbiol. *31*:2049–2056, 1993.
29. Clever, V. G.: Choroidal involvement with *Mycobacterium intracellulare.* Ann. Ophthalmol. *12*:1409–1411, 1980.
30. Colville, A.: Retrospective review of culture-positive mycobacterial lymphadenitis cases in children in Nottingham, 1979–1990. Eur. J. Clin. Microbiol. Infect. Dis. *12*:192–195, 1993.
31. Cooper, J. F., Lichtenstein, M. J., Graham, B. S., et al.: *Mycobacterium chelonae:* A cause of nodular skin lesions with a proclivity for renal transplant recipients. Am. J. Med. *86*:173–177, 1989.
32. Currarino, G., Votteler, T. H., and Weinberg, A.: Atypical mycobacterial infection of intraparotid lymph nodes: Clinical and sialographic observations. Pediatr. Radiol. *6*:10–12, 1977.
33. Cuttino, J. T., and McCabe, A. M.: Pure granulomatous nocardiosis: A new fungus disease distinguished by intracellular parasitism. Am. J. Pathol. *25*:1, 1949.
34. Dailloux, M., Morlot, M., and Sirbat, C.: Etude des facteurs intervenant sur la presence des mycobacteries atypiques dans l'eau d'une piscine. Rev. Epidemiol. Sante Publique *28*:299–306, 1980.
35. Davidson, P. T.: Introduction (international conference on atypical mycobacteria). Rev. Infect. Dis. *3*:816–818, 1981.
36. Davis, B. R., Brumbach, M. T., Sanders, W. J., et al.: Skin lesions caused by *Mycobacterium haemophilum.* Ann. Intern. Med. *97*:723–724, 1982.
37. Deepe, G. S., Jr., Capparell, R., and Coonrod, J. D.: Atypical mycobacterial lymphadenitis in an adult. Chest *78*:882–883, 1980.
38. Delabie, J., DeWolfe-Peeters, C., Bobbaers, H., et al.: Immunophenotypic analysis of histocytes involved in AIDS-associated *Mycobacterium scrofulaceum* infection: Similarities with lepromatous lepra. Clin. Exp. Immunol. *85*:214–218, 1991.
39. Dhooge, I., Dhooge, C., De-Baets, F, et al.: Diagnostic and therapeutic management of atypical mycobacterial infections in children. Eur. Arch. Otorhinolaryngol. *250*:387–391, 1993.
40. Donta, S. T., Smith, P. W., Levitz, R. E., et al.: Therapy of *Mycobacterium marinum* infections. Arch. Intern. Med. *146*:902–904, 1986.
41. Drut, R., Anderson, V., Greco, M. A., et al.: Opportunistic infections in pediatric HIV infection: A study of 74 autopsy cases from Latin America. Pediatr. Pathol. Lab. Med. *17*:569–576, 1997.
42. Dunn, B. L., and Hodgson, D. J.: Atypical mycobacteria in milk. J. Appl. Bacteriol. *52*:373–376, 1982.
43. Dustin, P., Demol, P., Derks-Jacobovitz, D., et al.: Generalized fatal chronic infection by *Mycobacterium scrofulaceum* with severe amyloidosis in a child. Pathol. Res. Pract. *168*:237–248, 1980.
44. Dutt, A. K., and Stead, W. W.: Long-term results of medical treatment in *Mycobacterium intracellulare* infection. Am. J. Med. *67*:449–453, 1979.
45. Engervall, P., Bjorkholm, M., Petrini, B., et al.: Disseminated *Mycobacterium malmoense* infection in a patient with chronic granulocytic leukaemia. J. Intern. Med. *234*:231–233, 1993.
46. Fauroux, B., Delaisi, B., Clement, A., et al.: Mycobacterial lung disease in cystic fibrosis: A prospective study. Pediatr. Infect. Dis. J. *16*:354–358, 1997.
47. Fergie, J. E., Milligan, T. W., Henderson, B. M., and Stafford, W. W.: Intrathoracic *Mycobacterium avium* complex infection in immunocompetent children: Case report and review. Clin. Infect. Dis. *24*:250–253, 1997.
48. Flint, D., Mahadevan, M., Gunn, R., and Brown, S.: Nontuberculous mycobacterial otomastoiditis in children: Four cases and a literature review. Int. J. Pediatr. Otorhinolaryngol. *51*:121–127, 1999.
49. Forbes, B., and Hicks, K.: Direct detection of *Mycobacterium tuberculosis* in respiratory specimens in a clinical laboratory by polymerase chain reaction. J. Clin. Microbiol. *31*:1688–1694, 1993.
50. Frosch, M., Roth, J., Ullrich, K., and Harms, E: Successful treatment of *Mycobacterium avium* osteomyelitis and arthritis in a non-immunocompromised child. Scand. J. Infect. Dis. *32*:3328–3329, 2000.
51. Gill, M. J., Fanning, E. A., and Chomyc, S.: Childhood lymphadenitis in a harsh northern climate due to atypical mycobacteria. Scand. J. Infect. Dis. *19*:77–83, 1987.
52. Good, R. C., and Snider, D. E., Jr.: Isolation of nontuberculous mycobacteria in the United States, 1980. J. Infect. Dis. *146*:829–833, 1982.
53. Gorse, G. J., Fairshter, R. D., Friedly, G., et al.: Nontuberculous mycobacterial disease: Experience in a southern California hospital. Arch. Intern. Med. *143*:225–228, 1983.
54. Goto, M., Oka, S., Okuzumi, K., et al.: Evaluation of acridinium ester-labeled DNA probes for identification of *Mycobacterium tuberculosis* and *Mycobacterium avium–Mycobacterium intracellulare* complex in culture. J. Clin. Microbiol. *29*:2473–2476, 1991.
55. Grange, J. M.: *Mycobacterium chelonae.* Tubercle *62*:273–276, 1981.
56. Grange, J. M.: Mycobacteria and the skin. Int. J. Dermatol. *21*:497–503, 1982.
57. Gruft, H., Falkinham, J. O., III, and Parker, B. C.: Recent experience in the epidemiology of disease caused by atypical mycobacteria. Rev. Infect. Dis. *3*:990–996, 1981.
58. Guthertz, L. S., Damsker, B., Bottone, E. J., et al.: *Mycobacterium avium* and *Mycobacterium intracellulare* infections in patients with and without AIDS. J. Infect. Dis. *160*:1037–1041, 1989.
59. Haas, W. H., Amthor, B., Engelmann, G., et al.: Preoperative diagnosis of *Mycobacterium avium* lymphadenitis in two immunocompetent children by polymerase chain reaction of gastric aspirates. Pediatr. Infect. Dis. J. *17*:1016–1020, 1998.
60. Haas, W. H., Butler, W. R., Kirshner, P., et al.: A new agent of mycobacterial lymphadenitis in children: *Mycobacterium heidelbergense* sp. nov. J. Clin. Microbiol. *35*:3203–3209, 1997.
61. Hakim, A., Hisam, N., and Reuman, P. D.: Environmental mycobacterial peritonitis complicating peritoneal dialysis: Three cases and review. Clin. Infect. Dis. *16*:426–431, 1993.
62. Havlir, D. V., Dube, M. P., Sattler, F. R., et al.: Prophylaxis against disseminated *Mycobacterium avium* complex with weekly azithromycin, daily rifabutin, or both. N. Engl. J. Med. *335*:392–398, 1996.
63. Havlir, D., Kemper, C. A., and Deresinski, S. C.: Reproducibility of lysis-centrifugation cultures for quantification of *Mycobacterium avium* complex bacteremia. J. Clin. Microbiol. *31*:1794–1798, 1993.
64. Hazra, R., Lee, S. H., Maslow, J. N., and Husson R. N.: Related strains of *Mycobacterium avium* cause disease in children with AIDS and in children with lymphadenitis. J. Infect. Dis. *181*:1298–1303, 2000.

65. Hjelt, K., Hojlyng, N., Howitz, P., et al.: The role of mycobacteria other than tuberculosis (MOTT) in patients with cystic fibrosis. Scand. J. Infect. Dis. *26*:569–576, 1994.
66. Hjelte, L., Petrini, B., Kallenius, G., et al.: Prospective study of mycobacterial infections in patients with cystic fibrosis. Thorax *45*:397–400, 1990.
67. Hofer, M., Hirschel, B., Kirschner, P., et al.: Brief report: Disseminated osteomyelitis from *Mycobacterium ulcerans* after a snakebite. N. Engl. J. Med. *328*:1007–1009, 1993.
68. Hoffner, S. E., Henriques, B., Petrini, B., et al.: *Mycobacterium malmoense*: An easily missed pathogen. J. Clin. Microbiol. *29*:2673–2674, 1991.
69. Holland, S. M., Eisenstein, E. M., Kuhns, D. B., et al.: Treatment of refractory disseminated nontuberculous mycobacterial infection with interferon gamma. N. Engl. J. Med. *330*:1348–1355, 1994.
70. Horsburgh, C. R., and Selik, R. M.: The epidemiology of disseminated nontuberculous mycobacterial infection in the acquired immunodeficiency syndrome (AIDS). Am. Rev. Respir. Dis. *139*:4–7, 1989.
71. Hoyt, L., Oleske, J., Holland, B., et al.: Nontuberculous mycobacteria in children with acquired immunodeficiency syndrome. Pediatr. Infect. Dis. J. *11*:354–360, 1992.
72. Huebner, R. E., Schein, M. F., Cauthen, G. M., et al.: Usefulness of skin testing with mycobacterial antigens in children with cervical lymphadenopathy. Pediatr. Infect. Dis. J. *11*:450–456, 1992.
73. Huempfner, H. R., Kingsolver, W. R., and Deuschle, K. W.: Tuberculous meningitis caused by both *Mycobacterium tuberculosis* and atypical mycobacteria. Am. Rev. Respir. Dis. *94*:612, 1966.
74. Iseman, M. D.: *Mycobacterium avium* complex and the normal host: The other side of the coin. N. Engl. J. Med. *321*:896–897, 1989.
75. Johann-Liang, R., Cervia, J. S., and Noel, G. J.: Characteristics of human immunodeficiency virus–infected children at the time of death: An experience in the 1990s. Pediatr. Infect. Dis. J. *16*:1145–1150, 1997.
76. Kahn, E.: Gastrointestinal manifestations in pediatric AIDS. Pediatr. Pathol. Lab. Med. *17*:171–208, 1997.
77. Kent, D. C.: Tuberculous lymphadenitis: Not a localized disease process. Am. J. Med. Sci. *254*:866–873, 1967.
78. Kiehn, T. E., and Cammarata, R.: Laboratory diagnosis of mycobacterial infections in patients with acquired immunodeficiency syndrome. J. Clin. Microbiol. *24*:708–711, 1986.
79. Kiehn, T. E., and Cammarata, R.: Comparative recoveries of *Mycobacterium avium–M. intracellulare* from isolator lysis-centrifugation and BACTEC 13A blood culture systems. J. Clin. Microbiol. *26*:760–761, 1988.
80. Kiehn, T. E., Edwards, F. F., Brannon, P., et al.: Infections caused by *Mycobacterium avium* complex in immunocompromised patients: Diagnosis by blood culture and fecal examination, antimicrobial susceptibility tests, and morphological and seroagglutination characteristics. J. Clin. Microbiol. *21*:168–173, 1985.
81. Kilby, J., Gilligan, P., Yankaskas J., et al.: Nontuberculous mycobacteria in adult patients with cystic fibrosis. Chest *102*:70–75, 1992.
82. Klein, J. O.: Clarithromycin: Where do we go from here? Pediatr. Infect. Dis. J. *12*(Suppl.):148–151, 1993.
83. Koenig, M. G., Collins, R. D., and Heyssel, R. M.: Disseminated mycobacteriosis caused by Battey-type mycobacteria. Ann. Intern. Med. *64*:145, 1966.
84. Kox, L. F. F., Jansen, H. M., Kuijper, S., and Kolk, A. H. J.: Multiplex PCR assay for immediate identification of the infecting species in patients with mycobacterial disease. J. Clin. Microbiol. *35*:1492–1498, 1997.
85. Krasnow, I., and Gross, W.: *Mycobacterium simiae* infection in the United States. Am. Rev. Respir. Dis. *111*:357–360, 1975.
86. Kubica, G. P.: Current nomenclature of the mycobacteria. Bull. Int. Union Tuberc. *53*:192, 1978.
87. Kubica, G. P., and Wayne, L. G.: The Mycobacteria: A Sourcebook, Part A. New York, Marcel Dekker, 1984, pp. 38–41.
88. Kuritsky, J. N., Bullen, M. G., Broome, C. V., et al.: Sternal wound infections and endocarditis due to organisms of the *Mycobacterium fortuitum* complex. Ann. Intern. Med. *98*:938–939, 1983.
89. Kusunoki, S., and Ezaki, T.: Proposal of *Mycobacterium peregrinum* sp. nov., nom. rev., and elevation of *Mycobacterium chelonae* subsp. *abscessus* (Kubica et al.) to species status: *Mycobacterium abscessus* comb. nov. Int. J. Syst. Bacteriol. *42*:240–245, 1992.
90. Kuth, G., Lamprecht, J., and Haase, G.: Cervical lymphadenitis due to mycobacteria other than tuberculosis: An emerging problem in children? J. Otorhinolaryngol. *57*:36–38, 1995.
91. Lai, K. K., Stottmeier, K. D., Sherman, I. H., et al.: Mycobacterial cervical lymphadenopathy: Relation of etiologic agents to age. J. A. M. A. *251*:1286–1288, 1984.
92. Levendoglu-Tugal, O., Munoz, J., Brudnicki, A., et al.: Infections due to nontuberculous mycobacteria in children with leukemia. Clin. Infect. Dis. *27*:1227–1230, 1998.
93. Levin, M., Newport, M. J., D'Souza, S., et al.: Familial disseminated atypical mycobacterial infection in childhood: A human mycobacterial susceptibility gene? Lancet *345*:79–83, 1995.
94. Levin, R. H., and Bolinger, A. M.: Treatment of nontuberculous mycobacterial infections in pediatric patients. Clin. Pharm. *7*:545–551, 1988.
95. Lewis, L. L.: Nontuberculous mycobacterial infections. In Pizzo P. A., and Wilfert, C. M., (eds.): Pediatric AIDS: The Challenge of HIV Infection in Infants, Children, and Adolescents. 2nd ed. Baltimore, Williams & Wilkins, 1994, pp. 308–320.
96. Lim, S. D., Lopez, J., Ford, E., et al.: Genotypic identification of pathogenic *Mycobacteria* species by using a nonradioactive oligonucleotide probe. J. Clin. Microbiol. *29*:1276–1278, 1991.
97. Lincoln, E. M., and Gilbert, L. A.: Disease in children due to mycobacteria other than *Mycobacterium tuberculosis*. Am. Rev. Respir. Dis. *105*:683–714, 1972.
98. Lindberg, M. C., and Thomas, G. G.: Lymphadenitis due to atypical mycobacteria. Ala. Med. *59*:19–21, 1989.
99. Losurdo, G., Castagnola, E., Cristina, E., et al.: Cervical lymphadenitis caused by nontuberculous mycobacteria in immunocompetent children: Clinical and therapeutic experience. Head Neck *20*:245–249, 1998.
100. Lowry, P. W., Jarvis, W. R., Oberle, A. D., et al.: *Mycobacterium chelonae* causing otitis media in an ear-nose-and-throat practice. N. Engl. J. Med. *319*:978–982, 1988.
101. Lunn, H. F., and Rees, R. J. W.: Treatment of mycobacterial skin ulcers in Uganda with a riminophenazine derivative (B663). Lancet *1*:246, 1964.
102. MacCallum, P.: A new mycobacterial infection in man. I. Clinical aspects. J. Pathol. Bacteriol. *60*:93, 1948.
103. Maloney, J. M., Gregg, C. R., Stephens, D. S., et al.: Infections caused by *Mycobacterium szulgai* in humans. Rev. Infect. Dis. *9*:1120–1126, 1987.
104. Maltezou, H. C., Spyridis, P., and Kafetzis, D. A.: Nontuberculous mycobacterial lymphadenitis in children. Pediatr. Infect. Dis. J. *18*:968–970, 1999.
105. Mankiewicz, E., and Majdaniw, O.: Atypical mycobacteria in tapwater. Can. J. Public Health *73*:358–360, 1982.
106. Maxson, S., Schutze, G. E., and Jacobs, R. F.: *Mycobacterium abscessus* osteomyelitis: Treatment with clarithromycin. Infect. Dis. Clin. Pract. *3*:203–206, 1994.
107. McCracken, G. H., Jr., and Reynolds, R. C.: Primary lymphopenic immunologic deficiency: Disseminated *Mycobacterium kansasii* infection. Am. J. Dis. Child. *120*:143, 1970.
108. Merckx, J. J., Soule, E. H., and Karlson, A. G.: The histopathology of lesions caused by infection with unclassified acid-fast bacteria in man. Am. J. Clin. Pathol. *41*:244, 1964.
109. Mollohan, C. S., and Romer, M. S.: Public health significance of swimming pool granuloma. Am. J. Public Health *51*:883, 1961.
110. Morgan, J. K., and Blowers, R.: Swimming pool granuloma in Britain. Lancet *1*:1034, 1964.
111. Musial, C. E., Tice, L. S., Stockman, L., et al.: Identification of mycobacteria from culture by using the Gen-Probe rapid diagnostic system for *Mycobacterium avium* complex and *Mycobacterium tuberculosis* complex. J. Clin. Microbiol. *26*:2120–2123, 1988.
112. Nadal, D., Caduff, R., Kraft, R., et al.: Invasive infection with *Mycobacterium genavense* in three children with the acquired immunodeficiency syndrome. Eur. J. Clin. Microbiol. Infect. Dis. *12*:37–43, 1993.
113. Noordhoek, G. T., Kolk, A. H. J., Bjune, G., et al.: Sensitivity and specificity of PCR for detection of *Mycobacterium tuberculosis*: A blind comparison study among seven laboratories. J. Clin. Microbiol. *32*:277–284, 1994.
114. Nylen, O., Alestig, K., Fasth, A., et al.: Infections of the ear with nontuberculous mycobacteria in three children. Pediatr. Infect. Dis. J. *13*:653–656, 1994.
115. O'Brien, R. J.: The epidemiology of nontuberculous mycobacterial disease. Clin. Chest Med. *10*:407–418, 1989.
116. Peacock, K. H., Lewis, L., and Lavoie, S.: Erosive mediastinal lymphadenitis associated with *Mycobacterium avium* infection in a pediatric acquired immunodeficiency syndrome patient. Pediatr. Infect. Dis. J. *19*:576–578, 2000.
117. Perlino, C. A.: *Mycobacterium avium* complex: An unusual cause of peritonitis in patients undergoing continuous ambulatory peritoneal dialysis. Clin. Infect. Dis. *17*:1083–1084, 1993.
118. Pierre-Audigier, C., Jouanguy, E., Lamhamedi, S., et al.: Fatal disseminated *Mycobacterium smegmatis* infection in a child with inherited interferon γ receptor deficiency. Clin. Infect. Dis. *24*:982–984, 1997.
119. Pinder, S. E., and Colville, A.: Mycobacterial cervical lymphadenitis in children: Can histological assessment help differentiate infections caused by non-tuberculous mycobacteria from *Mycobacteria tuberculosis*? Histopathology *22*:59–64, 1993.
120. Pransky, S. M., Reismann, B. K., Kearns, D. B., et al.: Cervicofacial mycobacterial adenitis in children: Endemic to San Diego? Laryngoscope *100*:920–925, 1990.
121. Prince, D. S., Peterson, D. D., Steiner, R. M., et al.: Infection with *Mycobacterium avium* complex in patients without predisposing conditions. N. Engl. J. Med. *321*:863–868, 1989.
122. Quijano, G., Siminovich, M., and Drut, R.: Histopathologic findings in the lymphoid and reticuloendothelial system in pediatric HIV infection: A postmortem study. Pediatr. Pathol. Lab. Med. *17*:845–856, 1997.
123. Reich, J. M., and Johnson, R. E.: *Mycobacterium avium* complex pulmonary disease: Incidence, presentation, and response to therapy in a community setting. Am. Rev. Respir. Dis. *143*:1381–1385, 1991.

124. Reichert, C. M., O'Leary, T. J., Levens, D. L., et al.: Autopsy pathology in the acquired immune deficiency syndrome. Am. J. Pathol. *112*:357–382, 1983.
125. Reid, I. S.: *Mycobacterium ulcerans* infection: A report of 13 cases at the Port Moresby General Hospital, Papua Med. J. Aust. *1*:427, 1967.
126. Rivron, M. J., Hughes, E. A., Sibert, J. R., et al.: Cervical lymphadenitis in childhood due to mycobacteria of the fortuitum group. Arch. Dis. Child. *54*:312–313, 1979.
127. Rosenzweig, D. Y.: Pulmonary mycobacterial infections due to *Mycobacterium intracellulare-avium* complex: Clinical features and course in 100 consecutive cases. Chest *75*:115–119, 1979.
128. Runyon, E. H.: Anonymous mycobacteria in pulmonary disease. Med. Clin. North Am. *43*:273–290, 1959.
129. Runyon, E. H.: Pathogenic mycobacteria. Adv. Tuberc. Res. *14*:235–287, 1965.
130. Runyon, E. H.: Mycobacteria: An overview. Rev. Infect. Dis. *3*:819–821, 1981.
131. Safranek, T. J., Jarvis, W. R., Carson, L. A., et al.: *Mycobacterium chelonae* wound infections after plastic surgery employing contaminated gentian violet skin-marking solution. N. Engl. J. Med. *317*:197–201, 1987.
132. Salyer, K. E., Votteler, T. P., and Dorman, G. W.: Surgical management of cervical adenitis due to atypical mycobacteria in children. J. A. M. A. *204*:1037–1040, 1968.
133. Samra, Z., Kaufmann, L, Zeharia, A., et al.: Optimal detection and identification of *Mycobacterium haemophilum* in specimens from pediatric patients with cervical lymphadenopathy. J. Clin. Microbiol. *37*:832–834, 1999.
134. Sanderson, T. L., Moskowitz, L., Hensley, G. T., et al.: Disseminated *Mycobacterium avium-intracellulare* infection appearing as a panniculitis. Arch. Pathol. Lab. Med. *106*:112–114, 1982.
135. Sanford, J. P., and Barnett, J. A.: Atypical mycobacterial organisms as encountered in a general hospital and its clinics. *In* Chapman, J. S. (ed.): The Anonymous Mycobacteria in Human Disease. Springfield, IL, Charles C Thomas, 1960, p. 98.
136. Schaefer, W. B.: Incidence of the serotypes of *Mycobacterium avium* and atypical mycobacteria in human and animal diseases. Am. Rev. Respir. Dis. *97*:18–23, 1968.
137. Schinsky, M. F., McNeil, M. M., Whitney, A. M., et al.: *Mycobacterium septicum* sp. nov., a new rapidly growing species associated with catheter-related bacteraemia. Int. J. Syst. Evolution. Microbiol. *2*:575–581, 2000.
138. Schonell, M. E., Crofton, J. W., Stuart, A. E., et al.: Disseminated infection with *Mycobacterium avium*. I. Clinical features, treatment and pathology. Tubercle *49*:12, 1968.
139. Schuit, K. E., and Powell, D. A.: Mycobacterial lymphadenitis in childhood. Am. J. Dis. Child. *132*:675–677, 1978.
140. Shocket, E., Drosd, R. E., and Tate, C. F., Jr.: Granuloma of the skin due to *Mycobacterium fortuitum*. South. Med. J. *57*:1352, 1964.
141. Sigalet, D., Lees, G., and Fanning, A.: Atypical tuberculosis in the pediatric patient: Implications for the pediatric surgeon. J. Pediatr. Surg. *27*:1381–1384, 1992.
142. Simor, A. E., Salit, I. E., and Vellend, H.: The role of *Mycobacterium xenopi* in human disease. Am. Rev. Respir. Dis. *129*:435–438, 1984.
143. Smith, J. A., Mueller, B. U., Nussenblatt, R. B., and Whitcup, S. M.: Corneal endothelial deposits in children positive for human immunodeficiency virus receiving rifabutin prophylaxis for *Mycobacterium avium* complex bacteremia. Am. J. Ophthalmol. *127*:164–169, 1999.
144. Smith, M. J., Efthimiou, J., Hodson, M. E., et al.: Mycobacterial isolations in young adults with cystic fibrosis. Thorax *39*:369–375, 1984.
145. Snijder, J.: Morphological aspect of atypical mycobacterioses. *In* Selected Papers. Vol. 10. Royal Netherlands Tuberculosis Association, The Hague, 1967, p. 99.
146. Sommers, H. M., and Good, R. C.: Mycobacterium. *In* Lennette, E. H., Balows, A., Hausler, W. J., Jr., et al. (eds.): Manual of Clinical Microbiology. 4th ed. American Society for Microbiology, 1985, pp. 216–240.
147. Song, M., Vincke, G., Vanachter, H., et al.: Treatment of cutaneous infection due to *Mycobacterium ulcerans*. Dermatologica *171*:197–199, 1985.
148. Speight, E. L., and Williams, H. C.: Fish tank granuloma in a 14-month-old girl. Pediatr. Dermatol. *14*:209–212, 1997.
149. Stanford, J. L., and Paul, R. C.: A preliminary report on some studies of environmental mycobacteria. Ann. Soc. Belg. Med. Trop. *53*:321, 1973.
150. Stanford, J. L., Revill, W. D. L., Gunthorpe, W. J., et al.: The production and preliminary investigation of burulin, a new skin test reagent for *Mycobacterium ulcerans* infection. J. Hyg (Camb.) *74*:7, 1975.
151. Steadham, J. E.: High catalase strains of *Mycobacterium kansasii* isolated from water in Texas. J. Clin. Microbiol. *11*:496–498, 1980.
152. Stewart, M. G., Troendle-Atkins, J., Starke, J. R., et al.: Nontuberculous mycobacterial mastoiditis. Arch. Otolaryngol. Head Neck Surg. *121*:225–228, 1995.
153. Stratton, C. W., Phelps, D. B., and Reller, L. B.: Tuberculoid tenosynovitis and carpal tunnel syndrome caused by *Mycobacterium szulgai*. Am. J. Med. *65*:349–351, 1978.
154. Straus, W. L., Ostroff, S. M., Jernigan, D. B., et al.: Clinical and epidemiologic characteristics of *Mycobacterium haemophilum*, an emerging pathogen in immunocompromised patients. Ann. Intern. Med. *120*:118–125, 1994.
155. Sutker, W. L., Lankford, L. L., and Tompsett, R.: Granulomatous synovitis: The role of atypical mycobacteria. Rev. Infect. Dis. *1*:729–735, 1979.
156. Swift, S., and Cohen, H.: Granulomas of the skin due to *Mycobacterium balnei* after abrasions from a fish tank. N. Engl. J. Med. *267*:1244, 1962.
157. Syed, A. U., Hussain, R., Bhat, A. N., et al.: Mediastinitis due to *Mycobacterium fortuitum* infection following Fontan operation in a child. Scand. Cardiovasc. J. *31*:311–313, 1997.
158. Thomas, E., Hillman, B. J., and Stanisic, T.: Urinary tract infection with atypical mycobacteria. J. Urol. *124*:748–750, 1980.
159. Timpe, A., and Runyon, E. H.: Relationship of "atypical" acid-fast bacilli to human disease: Preliminary report. J. Lab. Clin. Med. *44*:202–209, 1954.
160. Torrens, J. K., Dawkins, P., Conway, S. P., and Moya, E.: Non-tuberculous mycobacteria in cystic fibrosis. Thorax *53*:182–185, 1998.
161. Tortoli, E., Piersimoni, C., Bartoloni, A., et al.: *Mycobacterium malmoense* in Italy: The modern Norman invasion? Eur. J. Epidemiol. *13*:341–346, 1997.
162. Tsukamura, M.: A review of the methods of identification and differentiation of mycobacteria. Rev. Infect. Dis. *3*:841–861, 1981.
163. Turneer, M., Van-Nerom, E., Nyabenda, J., et al.: Determination of humoral immunoglobulins M and G directed against mycobacterial antigen 60 failed to diagnose primary tuberculosis and mycobacterial adenitis in children. Am. J. Respir. Crit. Care Med. *150*:1508–1512, 1994.
164. 1999 USPHS/IDSA guidelines for the prevention of opportunistic infections in persons infected with human immunodeficiency virus. U.S. Public Health Service (USPHS) and Infectious Diseases Society of America (IDSA). M. M. W. R. Morb. Mortal. Wkly. Rep. *48*(RR-10):1–59, 61–66, 1999.
165. Van Dyke, J. J., and Lake, K. B.: Chemotherapy for aquarium granuloma. J. A. M. A. *233*:1380–1381, 1975.
166. Venkatesh, V., Everson, N. W., and Johnstone, J. M.: Atypical mycobacterial lymphadenopathy in children: Is it underdiagnosed? J. R. Coll. Surg. Edinburgh *39*:301–303, 1994.
167. Vestal, A. L.: Procedures for the Isolation and Identification of Mycobacteria. CDC Publication No. 76–8230. Washington, D.C., Department of Health, Education and Welfare, 1975.
168. Vollini, F., Cotton, R., and Lester, W.: Disseminated infection caused by Battey type mycobacteria. Am. J. Clin. Pathol. *43*:39, 1965.
169. Wallace, R. J., Brown B. A., and Onyi, G. O.: Skin, soft tissue, and bone infections due to *Mycobacterium chelonae*: Importance of prior corticosteroid therapy, frequency of disseminated infections, and resistance to oral antimicrobials other than clarithromycin. J. Infect. Dis. *166*:405–412, 1992.
170. Wallace, R. J., Nash, D. R., Tsukamura, M., et al.: Human disease due to *Mycobacterium smegmatis*. J. Infect. Dis. *158*:52, 1988.
171. Wallace, R. J., Jr., O'Brien, R., Glassroth, J., et al.: Diagnosis and treatment of disease caused by nontuberculous mycobacteria. Am. Rev. Respir. Dis. *142*:940–953, 1990.
172. Wallace, R. J., Swenson, J. M., Silcox, V. A., et al.: Spectrum of disease due to rapidly growing mycobacteria. Rev. Infect. Dis. *5*:657–679, 1983.
173. Wallace, R. J., Tanner, D., Brennan, P. J., et al.: Clinical trial of clarithromycin for cutaneous (disseminated) infection due to *Mycobacterium chelonae*. Ann. Intern. Med. *119*:482–486, 1993.
174. Wayne, L. G., and Sramek, H. A.: Agents of newly recognized or infrequently encountered mycobacterial diseases. Clin. Microbiol. Rev. *5*:1–25, 1992.
175. Weed, L. A., Karlson, A. G., Ivins, J. C., et al.: Recurring migratory chronic osteomyelitis associated with saprophytic acid-fast bacilli: Report of a case of 10 years' duration apparently cured by surgery. Proc. Staff Meeting Mayo Clin. *31*:238, 1956.
176. Welch, K., Finkbeiner, W., Apers, C. E., et al.: Autopsy findings in the acquired immune deficiency syndrome. J. A. M. A. *252*:1152–1159, 1984.
177. White, M. P., Bangash, H., Goel, K. M., et al.: Non-tuberculous mycobacterial lymphadenitis. Arch. Dis. Child. *61*:368–371, 1986.
178. White, R., Abreo, K., Flanagan, R., et al.: Nontuberculous mycobacterial infections in continuous ambulatory peritoneal dialysis patients. Am. J. Kidney Dis. *22*:581–587, 1993.
179. Wilkes, M. S., Fortin, A. H., Felix, J. C., et al.: Value of necropsy in acquired immunodeficiency syndrome. Lancet *2*:85–88, 1988.
180. Wolinsky, E.: Nontuberculous mycobacteria and associated diseases. Am. Rev. Respir. Dis. *119*:107–159, 1979.
181. Wolinsky, E.: Mycobacteria: Significance of speciation and sensitivity tests. *In* Lorian, V. (ed.): Significance of Medical Microbiology in the Care of Patients. Baltimore, Williams & Wilkins, 1982, pp. 103–110.
182. Wolinsky, E.: Mycobacterial diseases other than tuberculosis. Clin. Infect. Dis. *15*:1–10, 1992.
183. Wolinsky, E.: Mycobacterial lymphadenitis in children: A prospective study of 105 nontuberculous cases with long-term follow-up. Clin. Infect. Dis. *20*:954–963, 1995.

184. Wolinsky, E., Gomez, F., and Zimpfer, F.: Sporotrichoid *Mycobacterium marinum* infection treated with rifampin-ethambutol. Am. Rev. Respir. Dis. *105*:964–967, 1972.
185. Woods, G. L., and Washington, J. A., II: Mycobacteria other than *Mycobacterium tuberculosis*: Review of microbiologic and clinical aspects. Rev. Infect. Dis. *9*:275–294, 1987.
186. Yakrus, M. A., and Good, R. C.: Geographic distribution frequency and specimen source of *Mycobacterium avium* complex serotypes isolated from patients with acquired immunodeficiency syndrome. J. Clin. Microbiol. *28*:926–929, 1990.
187. Yamauchi, T., Ferrieri, P., and Anthony, B. F.: The aetiology of acute cervical adenitis in children: Serological and bacteriological studies. J. Med. Microbiol. *13*:37–43, 1980.
188. Yew, W. W., Kwan, S. Y. L., Ma, W. K., et al.: Single daily-dose ofloxacin monotherapy for *Mycobacterium fortuitum* sternotomy infection. Chest *96*:1150–1152, 1989.

CHAPTER 103

Leprosy and Buruli Ulcer: The Major Cutaneous Mycobacterioses

WAYNE M. MEYERS

Mycobacterial infections in humans date to at least the 10th millenium BC. Bartels[7] in 1907 detected convincing evidence of tuberculosis in a Neolithic skeleton found near Heidelberg, Germany, and Ruffer[191] in 1910 noted Pott disease in an Egyptian priest from approximately 1000 BC. The origins of mycobacterial infections in humans are unknown, but most authorities speculate that domestication of animals in the Neolithic era promoted the transmission of mutants of *Mycobacterium tuberculosis* from livestock to humans. The origins of leprosy and Buruli ulcer and their respective etiologic agents are understood less well but may involve interplay among environmental mycobacteria, animals, and humans. After tuberculosis, leprosy and Buruli ulcer are, respectively, the second and third most common mycobacterial infections in humans. Furthermore, leprosy and Buruli ulcer are the two most common cutaneous mycobacterioses.

Tuberculosis and many other cutaneous mycobacterial infections are discussed in Chapters 101 and 141. This chapter is devoted to an extended coverage of the two cutaneous mycobacterioses that are of greatest medical importance: leprosy and Buruli ulcer.

Leprosy

Leprosy is a chronic infectious disease caused by *Mycobacterium leprae* that principally affects the cooler parts of the body, especially the skin, upper respiratory tract, testes, eyes, and superficial segments of peripheral nerves. The geographic origin of this infection is unknown, but nearly every part of the world has been affected at some time. The World Health Organization (WHO) reported that in 1999, approximately 800,000 patients were being treated for active leprosy and that also in 1999, 738,000 new patients were reported.[246] Many authorities consider that the total global prevalence of patients with active leprosy is 1.5 to 2 million and that several more million suffer serious sequelae. In the Middle Ages, leprosy occurred commonly in Europe and may have been transported to the Western Hemisphere by Portuguese and Spanish explorations beginning in the 15th century and later by slaves from Africa. At least two foci in the United States, however, were established in the 19th century by specific immigrations: Asian people brought leprosy to the Hawaiian Islands and started an epidemic in the highly susceptible Hawaiians,[155] and Scandinavians introduced leprosy into the northern midwest region of the United States.[127]

The stigmas suffered by patients with leprosy frequently are severe and, in Western cultures, are attributable at least partially to a misunderstanding of what is called leprosy in the Old Testament.[16] Other cultures not influenced by Judaic laws and traditions, however, have similar or more severe attitudes toward leprosy patients. For example, the Chinese literature indicates that as early as the eighth century BC, patients with symptoms now recognized as those were stigmatized.[207] Because of enduring irrational attitudes based on the premise that relevant Old Testament references are to the same single disease now called leprosy, a brief explanation of "Old Testament leprosy" follows.

The Hebrew word *tsara'ath* was rendered *lepra* when the Old Testament was translated into Greek in the third and second centuries BC. In preparing the Latin Vulgate version in AD 405, Jerome used the word *lepra* directly from the Greek. In the first English translation from the Vulgate in 1384, Wycliffe translated *lepra* as *leprosy*, perhaps because leprosy, then common in Europe and Great Britain, seemed to portray an image of an unholy and loathsome human condition. In the original text, *tsara'ath* was not a specific disease but probably a group of diseases, the identities of which are obscure, and the word more generally referred to ceremonial uncleanness. Old Testament *tsara'ath*, as described, for example, in Leviticus 13 and 14, had none of the distinctive clinical features of leprosy. Thus, no rationale exists for attitudes toward leprosy that are based on Old Testament *tsara'ath*. Continuing effort must be made to minimize the stigma peculiarly associated with leprosy. To help achieve this goal, the Fifth International Leprosy Congress in 1948 adopted a resolution to abandon the word leper for leprosy patient.[120] Hansen disease is preferred by some physicians as a synonym for leprosy. Because of the stigma of leprosy, the physician must consider carefully the social implications of a diagnosis of leprosy, especially in children.

THE ORGANISM

M. leprae is a species in the order Actinomycetales and the family Mycobacteriaceae. This bacillus was seen first by Hansen in 1873 in Bergen, Norway, in lepromas from Norwegian patients, and this organism was the first reported bacterium causing chronic disease in humans.

M. leprae is an acid-fast bacillus (AFB) 0.3 to 0.5 μm wide by 4 to 7 μm long. The acid-fastness of *M. leprae* is weaker than that of other mycobacteria, but as in other mycobacteria, the acid-fastness is related to mycolic acid in the cell wall.[6] Viable, undamaged *M. leprae* organisms stain solidly, but degenerating bacilli first stain irregularly, then become granular, and eventually lose acid-fastness completely. The persistence of bacillary carcasses can be verified by silver staining techniques.[231] Staining quality, therefore, provides a rapid method for determining the effectiveness of therapy. In vitro cultivation of *M. leprae* frequently is claimed, but all claims have been refuted or are as yet unsubstantiated.[110, 187] Because *M. leprae* still cannot be cultivated, identification depends on criteria other than those used routinely for cultivable mycobacteria. Current criteria for *M. leprae* are the following: (1) it does not grow on routine laboratory media, (2) it infects the footpads of mice in a characteristic manner,[203] (3) acid-fastness is extractable with pyridine,[32] (4) the organism invades nerves of the host, (5) suspensions of dead bacilli produce a characteristic pattern of reactions when injected into the skin of patients (lepromin reaction) with the various clinical forms of leprosy, (6) it produces the species-specific antigen phenolic glycolipid-1 (PGL-1),[61] and (7) it demonstrates species-specific DNA sequences.[248]

Electron micrographs of *M. leprae* reveal a cell wall 15 to 20 nm thick around a cytoplasmic membrane that gives rise to mesosomes extending into the cytoplasm. *M. leprae* divides by transverse fission. Its cell walls contain arabinogalactan, mycolates, peptidoglycan, and protein.[132]

The genome of *M. leprae* is small (3,268,203 base pairs) in comparison to that of *M. tuberculosis* (approximately 4.4 million base pairs).[27] Gene deletion and decay have markedly limited the metabolic activities of *M. leprae* and may contribute significantly to failure to cultivate the organism and to its long generation time in the mouse footpad (14 days). In suitable hosts, the generation time of *M. leprae* has been speculated to be considerably shorter than 14 days.[81] For example, very young infants may have highly bacilliferous leprosy.[18, 69] Localization of infections to the cooler parts of the body,[13] selective growth in the footpads of immunologically intact mice and in the ears of hamsters, and the high susceptibility of the armadillo (central body temperature of 32° C to 35° C [89.6° F to 95° F]) to disseminated infections all suggest that the optimal temperature for growth of *M. leprae* is below 37° C (98.6° F).[136]

TRANSMISSION

The modes of transmission of *M. leprae* in nature have not been established. The frequency in children of a single early lesion in skin that usually is covered by clothing argues against the development of such lesions at the site of contact with *M. leprae*.[8] For many years, skin-to-skin contact between the patient and healthy subjects was considered the most important means of transmission, and this concept cannot be abandoned readily[119]; however, it has been challenged in recent years. Intact skin of heavily infected patients discharges small numbers of *M. leprae*, but ulcers in the skin may be a source of large numbers of bacilli. Thus, skin-to-skin contact and fomites containing *M. leprae* could be sources of infection. That the nasal mucosa of lepromatous patients harbors massive numbers of *M. leprae* has been known since Hansen's original discovery, and studies suggest that the respiratory passages could be a source of infecting bacilli.[40] *M. leprae* may bind to nasal mucosal cells by first binding fibronectin and attaching to fibronectin receptors on mucosal cells.[23] *M. leprae* organisms ejected in nose blowing remain viable under ambient conditions for as long as 1 week,[37] and disseminated leprosy develops in immunosuppressed mice after the inhalation of aerosol that contains *M. leprae*.[181] Breast tissue and milk from lepromatous patients contain *M. leprae*, and infants may acquire infection from this source.[169]

Placental transmission of leprosy has been a subject of conjecture for some time, but evidence is growing for a significant influence of leprosy on fetal development and for intrauterine infection of the fetus. In a study of 116 pregnant leprosy patients in Ethiopia, the placentas were small, birth weights were low, and growth rates of the infants were retarded.[45] Mean birth weights of infants of lepromatous and healthy control mothers were 2558 and 3280 g, respectively. Estrogen excretion levels at 32 to 40 weeks' gestation are reduced in leprosy patients, which suggests fetoplacental dysfunction.[47] IgA and IgM antibodies for *M. leprae* are present in the cord blood of 30 to 50 percent of babies delivered by mothers with lepromatous leprosy.[133] Evidence is strong for synthesis of fetal antibodies to *M. leprae* or antigens thereof. On occasion, *M. leprae* has been demonstrated in placentas and cord blood.[89, 224] *M. leprae*–specific IgA and IgM levels rose in infants of lepromatous mothers during the 3- to 24-month period after birth,[134] and two such infants had clinical leprosy at 9 and 17 months of age.[46] Leprosy in young infants may be a common occurrence in areas of high endemicity. In a report combining cases on file in the Leprosy Registry at the Armed Forces Institute of Pathology, cases cited in the literature, and personal observations by experienced leprologists, a total of at least 49 leprosy patients younger than 1 year of age were identified.[18] In only half of these infants did the mother have leprosy or a history of leprosy. The youngest infant was 2½ months old at diagnosis. The fact that many of the mothers never had clinical leprosy suggests that they had an evanescent *M. leprae* bacteremia during gestation. A substantial bacteremia is a common finding in multibacillary disease[44] and is detectable in as many as 15 percent of paucibacillary patients.[111]

The discoveries of a naturally acquired leprosy-like disease in recently captured wild armadillos in Louisiana,[234] chimpanzees,[43, 73] a mangabey monkey from West Africa,[147] and a cynomolgus macaque from the Philippines[225] provide reason to consider that leprosy is a zoonosis.[138, 233] Reports of naturally acquired leprosy in armadillos range from 3 to 53 percent in the southern region of the United States.[99, 218, 219] In all these species, the histopathologic changes resemble those in leprosy in humans, and the bacilli that cause the infection cannot be distinguished from *M. leprae*.[13, 139, 146] Leprosy has been transmitted successfully from the mangabey monkey to other mangabey, rhesus, and African green monkeys.[100, 250]

Some authorities suggest that insects may ingest *M. leprae* during a blood meal from lepromatous patients and harbor viable bacteria, but the natural transmission of leprosy by insects remains unproved and is disregarded widely.

EPIDEMIOLOGY

Highest prevalences are found in tropical Africa, South America, and Southeast Asia. Approximately 73 percent of all patients live in Southeast Asia (65% in India), 12 percent in Africa, and 8 percent in the Americas. Based on limited whole-population surveys in endemic areas, the total number of active patients may exceed the number reported by the WHO by a significant margin. The stigma of the disease and inefficiency in health care delivery systems contribute to this disparity in statistics.[118] In 1995, approximately 6000 patients with a history of leprosy resided in the United States,[91] with 101 new patients (L. Pfeifer, personal communication, Hansen's Disease Center, Baton Rouge, LA) reported in 1998, down from an annual high in recent times of 361 in 1985. Most of these patients are immigrants, but a few indigenous patients regularly come from Hawaii, Louisiana, and Texas. No instances of secondary transmission from imported cases within the United States have been reported; thus, immigrants with leprosy present no known public health risk to the population of the United States. The same probably is true for other nonendemic countries that receive many immigrants from endemic areas.

Hansen's discovery of the leprosy bacillus developed from his conviction that leprosy was a specific contagious disease. This conviction was based on clinical and anatomic findings but, more important, on epidemiologic observations. In 1871 and 1872, he studied 69 families in western Norway in which several members had leprosy. The prevailing concept of that era was that leprosy was hereditary, but from data gathered on these families, Hansen showed that patients always had contact with another leprosy patient. Members of the same families with no such contacts were free of leprosy.[78] Hansen thus reasoned, after his pioneering observation of the leprosy bacillus in 1873, that the spread of leprosy depended on dissemination of this etiologic agent in a susceptible population.

The leprosy epidemic in Nauru in the central Pacific demonstrates how rapidly leprosy can spread in a leprosy-naive population.[74] Leprosy was introduced into this small island in 1912, and by 1924, one third of the 2500 inhabitants had leprosy.

The prevailing concept has been that an individual becomes infected only after experiencing repeated exposure. This concept now is doubted, and a single exposure may be sufficient in optimal conditions. However, in any patient-contact situation, the number of viable *M. leprae* being shed by the patient and the degree of susceptibility of the contact both may vary. Thus, long periods of association may be necessary before optimal conditions for infection exist.

Lymphocyte transformation studies show that occupational contacts of leprosy patients in Ethiopia have the highest rate of sensitization (58%) to *M. leprae*, followed closely by household contacts (47%). Noncontacts living in endemic areas have a lower rate of sensitization, but approximately 29 percent of the population still is sensitized.[70]

Geographic, ethnic, and socioeconomic factors may contribute to the spread of leprosy by affecting the number of untreated or ineffectively treated bacillary-positive patients and the opportunities for exposure. The percentage of patients who harbor large numbers of bacilli—generally, those with lepromatous leprosy—is related to ethnic background. In some Asian populations, for example, 50 percent or more of those with leprosy have lepromatous leprosy; in Africans, this figure is 5 to 10 percent. Socioeconomic factors are difficult to assess, and their relationship to the prevalence or clinical severity of leprosy is unknown. Nutritional status may or may not be important. The Nauru leprosy epidemic, indolent from 1912 through 1920, became rampant after a devastating epidemic of influenza (30% mortality) left a debilitated population with marked dietary deficiencies. During the next 4 years, the annual incidence of leprosy rose from 4 to 346, but the role played by malnutrition is obscure.[74] Ryrie[192] in Malaya noted that during the Japanese occupation, the severity of leprosy worsened, which he attributed to a combination of malnutrition and psychic trauma. Skinsnes and Higa[208] drew similar conclusions from a study of mortality in leprosaria in China during World War II. Nonetheless, convincing evidence that the prevalence of leprosy is unusually high in chronically malnourished populations is lacking.

Improvements in housing and other living conditions may play a role in the declining prevalence of leprosy. No other factor satisfactorily explains the virtual disappearance of leprosy from northern Europe after the Middle Ages and from Scandinavia in the 20th century, long before any effective chemotherapy was available. If the disease is airborne, the construction of dwellings that provide less confined sleeping quarters in this era could have contributed in a major way to the disappearance of leprosy in northern Europe and Scandinavia. Consistent with this concept is the inadequate housing that prevails in all geographic areas in which leprosy is a common finding today.

The presumed increased susceptibility of children is difficult to establish and may depend more on exposure to contagious patients and genetic predisposition than on other factors. The proportion of children among all detected patients is 20 to 30 percent.[62, 162] Of the 615 known patients who became infected in Louisiana between 1855 and 1970, 5 percent had disease onset at 0 to 9 years of age, and 19 percent were in the 10- to 19-year-old age group.[54] Lara,[116] in a study of 2000 children who lived in a leprosarium in the Philippines in an era when effective chemotherapy was not available, noted that leprosy developed in 470 (23%). Of these 470 patients, 254 were monitored closely, and in approximately 75 percent, the lesions healed spontaneously. Thus, active, persistent disease developed in approximately 6 percent of the children who were heavily exposed to leprosy. In most populations studied, only 5 to 10 percent of individuals are susceptible to leprosy.

In adults, leprosy occurs more commonly in men than in women (2:1 to 3:1); in children, the sex ratio is approximately 1:1.

Genetic factors may influence the susceptibility of an individual to leprosy.[205] If one twin has leprosy, the chance that leprosy will develop in a monozygotic twin is 60 to 85 percent versus a 15 to 25 percent risk for dizygotic twins.[79] Certain human leukocyte antigens (HLA-DR) appear to be associated with specific forms of leprosy. In Suriname, HLA-DR3 is a frequent occurrence in mixed populations with tuberculoid leprosy and rare in lepromatous patients; however, in Indians with tuberculoid leprosy, HLA-DR2 predominates.[228] DR antigens may influence the presentation of antigens of *M. leprae* to T cells and may thus affect the immune response to leprosy.[164]

In Texas and Louisiana, the ratios of autochthonous to imported leprosy patients are the highest in the continental United States. Indigenous leprosy is highly prevalent in armadillos in only those two states,[14, 209, 233, 234] and contact with such wild infected armadillos probably transmits leprosy to humans.[122, 240] No cases of transmission of leprosy to humans from naturally infected mangabey monkeys or chimpanzees have been reported, but this potential exists.[73, 140]

PATHOGENESIS AND PATHOLOGY

M. leprae causes disease by its ability to survive and multiply in macrophages (Fig. 103–1). If macrophages of the host digest the bacilli early, disease is not detectable, or the patient has only minimal lesions. If the macrophages are

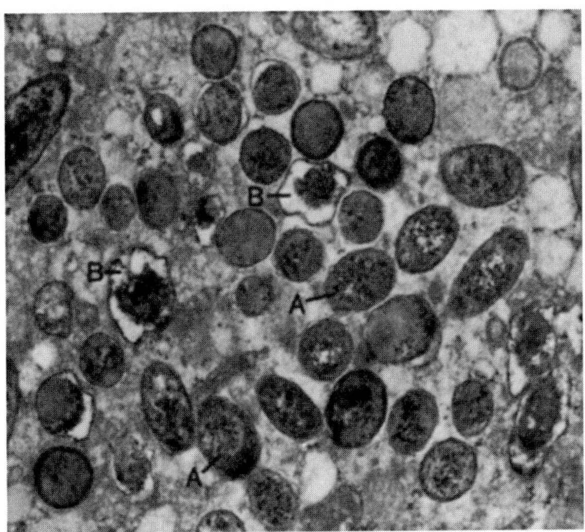

FIGURE 103–1 ■ Electron micrograph of a portion of a globus of *Mycobacterium leprae* within a histiocyte in a leproma in the skin. Cross sections of both well-preserved *(A)* and degenerated *(B)* bacilli are presented (×45,000). (Courtesy of Dr. S. C. Chang.)

totally incapable of destroying the organisms, a widely disseminated lepromatous leprosy will follow. Survival of *M. leprae* in macrophages depends on the immune response of the patient; hence, a knowledge of immunity to *M. leprae* is necessary background for understanding the mechanism of pathologic changes in leprosy.

Immunity

The ability of an individual to resist *M. leprae* is assessed readily by the induration provoked by an intradermal injection of a suspension of killed *M. leprae* prepared from lepromatous tissue. Lepromatous nodules of patients were the traditional source, but now infected tissue from armadillos commonly is used.[141] The reagent is known as lepromin and the response as the lepromin reaction. This reaction, first studied by Hayashi and later evaluated by Mitsuda,[149] has two components: an early response at 48 hours (Fernandez reaction) and a late response at 3 to 4 weeks (Mitsuda reaction). The Mitsuda reaction is the most consistent and is used by clinicians as an aid in classification of the clinical forms of leprosy. Mitsuda reactions are strongly positive (more than 5 mm in diameter) in tuberculoid patients, weak or negative (0 to 2 mm) in lepromatous patients, and intermediate (3 to 5 mm) in borderline patients. The reactions are a direct measure of delayed hypersensitivity or cell-mediated immunity (CMI) to *M. leprae* antigens; hence, lepromatous patients are anergic to *M. leprae*. The lepromin reaction has no value in diagnosis because a high percentage of any population is Mitsuda-positive. Even in children without leprosy, the Mitsuda reaction is positive in 20 percent of those younger than 5 years and in two thirds of those 7 to 9 years of age.[76] Modifications of the lepromin reaction with the use of concentrated lepromin show that macrophages at the test site in lepromatous patients cannot clear *M. leprae* from the skin whereas in tuberculoid patients, the bacilli are destroyed efficiently.[31]

Nonspecific factors participate in host defense against *M. leprae*. Complement, for example, promotes phagocytosis of leprosy bacilli.[197] After phagocytosis, phagolysosomal fusion and intracellular killing occur, perhaps by oxygen-independent mechanisms.

Although the precise mechanisms of specific immunity remain elusive, abundant experimental evidence indicates that in a lepromatous patient, CMI to *M. leprae* is suppressed markedly. Skin test reactions to many antigens often are depressed, but they are depressed most consistently and most severely to *M. leprae*.[19] The degree of suppression is gradually less pronounced in clinical forms of disease that are progressively nearer tuberculoid leprosy.

A continuous decrease occurs in the sensitivity of peripheral blood lymphocytes to *M. leprae* that proceeds from tuberculoid to lepromatous patients.[158] Many investigators consider that the defect in CMI to *M. leprae* is in T-lymphocyte function or in the interaction of T lymphocytes with macrophages. Total numbers of circulating T lymphocytes are decreased in lepromatous patients,[48] but no consistent alteration occurs in the percent distribution of circulating T-cell subsets, particularly in the helper-suppressor (T_H1-T_H2) cell ratio.[178] T-lymphocyte subsets in leprosy lesions in the skin, however, show marked differences in T_H1-T_H2 distributions in the different forms of leprosy.[152, 153, 177] In tuberculoid lesions, T_H1 cells are plentiful and distributed within the granulomas, whereas T_H2 cells are in the mantle of the granuloma. In lepromatous lesions, T_H1 and T_H2 cells are admixed among the macrophages. Suppressor activity is generated by lepromin in vitro in peripheral leukocytes from lepromatous patients, but not in cells from tuberculoid patients.[131] This suppressor activity also may be induced by the unique phenolic glycolipid (PGL-1) of *M. leprae*,[86, 130] but it is unrelated to the type of leprosy.[175] PGL-1 abounds in the tissues of lepromatous patients. Secondary immunosuppression in advanced lepromatous leprosy may result from blockade of thymus-dependent areas of lymph nodes by *M. leprae*–laden macrophages.[221] Specific suppressor T-cell activity in immunosuppression in leprosy remains controversial.[105]

Macrophages of lepromatous patients are thought to have the capacity to kill, digest, and clear *M. leprae* if they are activated.[85] Patients with lepromatous leprosy, however, fail to produce interleukin-2 (IL-2), but IL-2 restores the proliferation of lymphocytes in response to specific antigens.[80] There is also defective interferon-γ (IFN-γ) production by lymphocytes from lepromatous patients on stimulation by *M. leprae* antigens.[161] IL-2–bearing lymphocytes are reduced markedly in lepromatous infiltrations in tissues.[151] Thus, suppressor T cells may influence IL-2 production in situ and reduce the proliferation of specifically sensitized T cells to release IFN-γ, with the result that macrophages are not activated. The injection of IFN-γ into the skin of lepromatous patients causes a local influx of $CD4^+$ T cells along with the formation of epithelioid and giant cells and a reduction in bacillary load.[104] IL-2 and IFN-γ, when available in quantity, may thus prove to be important immunotherapeutic agents for lepromatous leprosy. Therapy with these cytokines, however, induces the secretion of tumor necrosis factor-α (TNF-α). The activity of this toxic molecule may be inhibited by thalidomide or pentoxifylline.[103, 216]

Immunoglobulin production (IgG, IgA, and IgM) usually is elevated only slightly in tuberculoid patients but is elevated markedly in lepromatous patients.[21] Circulating antibody to mycobacterial antigens correspondingly increases.[159] The total number of B lymphocytes is increased in the blood of lepromatous patients.[59]

The role of immunologic processes in damage to nerves in leprosy is unknown. Some observations suggest that antineural antibodies in the sera of many patients, especially those with lepromatous disease, are related to such damage.[167] TNF-α is associated with macrophage infiltration of peripheral nerves in reversal reactions.[113]

Histopathology

Biopsy specimens from well-defined lesions of leprosy should be taken from the active border and fixed in buffered

10 percent formalin or other suitable fixative. The Fite-Faraco staining method is used because the Ziehl-Neelsen stain does not demonstrate *M. leprae* optimally in tissue sections. DNA probes specific for *M. leprae* are available and are useful in identifying leprosy bacilli in tissue or nasal secretions.[40, 248] Specimens for DNA studies should be preserved in 70 percent ethyl alcohol.[55] A histopathologic diagnosis of leprosy must not be made unless the evidence is convincing. The pathologist must avoid making ambiguous evaluations such as "consistent with leprosy."

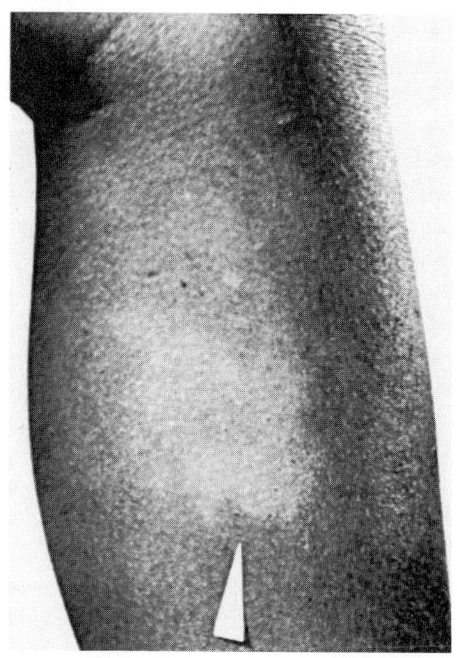

FIGURE 103–2 ■ Hypopigmented macule of indeterminate leprosy on the calf of a Filipino (Armed Forces Institute of Pathology [AFIP] 74-9029-1).

INDETERMINATE LEPROSY

In indeterminate leprosy (Fig. 103–2), the immune potential of the patient is not portrayed clearly in the cellular reaction. Only a mild chronic inflammation with small infiltrations of lymphocytes or histiocytes along neurovascular channels and sometimes around appendages occurs (Fig. 103–3). If leprosy is suspected, all nerves in the dermis and subcutaneous tissue in numerous sections of the biopsy specimen must be searched for AFB, even if no inflammatory changes within the nerves are present (see Fig. 103–3). Sometimes AFB appear only in the arrector pili muscles or subepidermal zone.[183] A histopathologic diagnosis of leprosy cannot be made unreservedly in indeterminate leprosy without demonstrating AFB. Molecular biologic studies are rarely helpful in diagnosing indeterminate leprosy.

TUBERCULOID LEPROSY

Patients with tuberculoid (TT) leprosy (Fig. 103–4) have a high level of CMI to *M. leprae*, which is reflected in the cellular reaction. Granulomas composed of epithelioid cells, Langhans giant cells, and lymphocytes are present in the dermis or subcutaneous tissue (Fig. 103–5*A*). Frequently, upper dermal granulomas invade the lower layers of the epidermis (see Fig. 103–5*B*). Damage to nerves is a

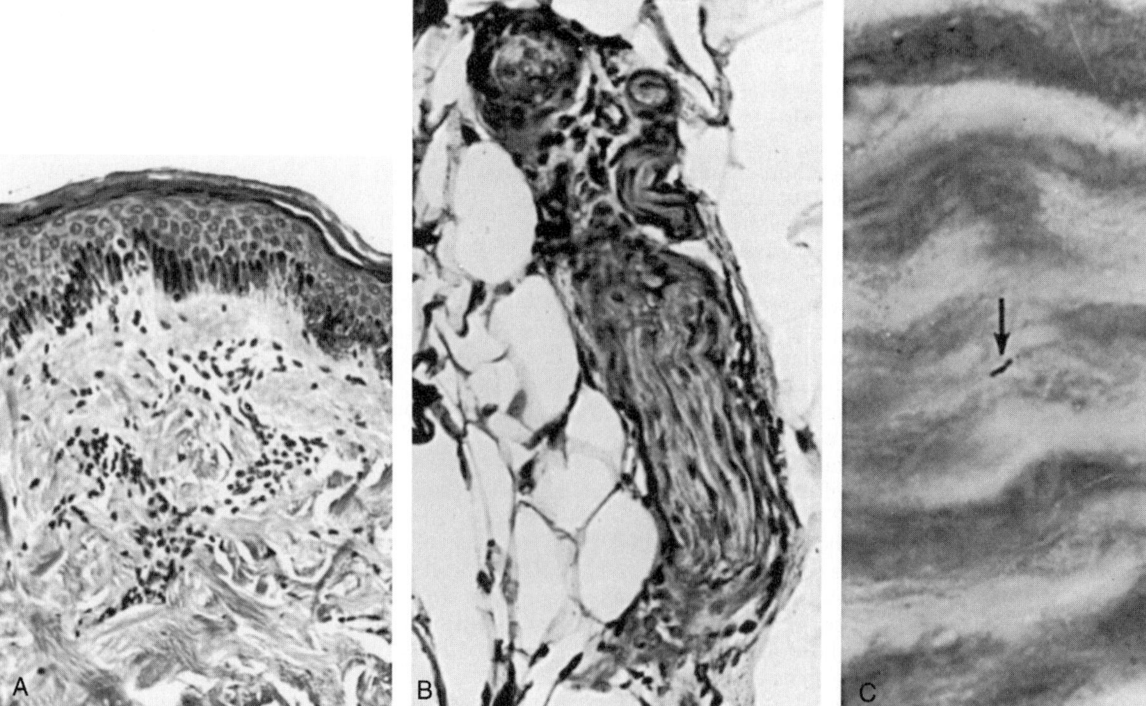

FIGURE 103–3 ■ *A,* Indeterminate leprosy showing mild infiltrations of lymphocytes and histiocytes along neurovascular channels (hematoxylin and eosin, × 20) (AFIP 75-2627). *B,* Nerve in subcutaneous tissue of the same section as in *A.* Only a few lymphocytes are seen around this intact nerve (hematoxylin and eosin, ×195) (AFIP 75-2626). *C,* The nerve shown in *B* contained a few acid-fast bacilli *(arrow)* (Fite-Faraco, ×1890) (AFIP 72-12469).

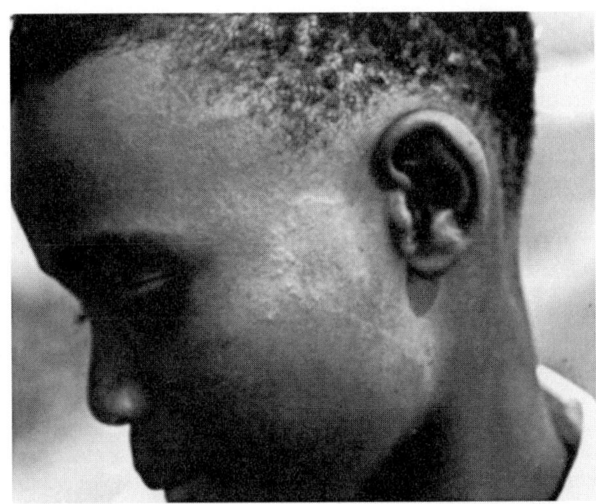

FIGURE 103–4 ■ Tuberculoid leprosy in a 12-year-old Zairian boy. This lesion was the only one, and it has a well-defined papulated border with central healing (AFIP 75-15598).

distinctive feature—in old advanced lesions, all cutaneous nerves may be damaged beyond recognition (see Fig. 103–5*C*). Schwann cells are increased in number in early lesions, and the nerves are invaded by mononuclear cells. Bacilli are a rare finding, and often many sections must be searched for a single bacillus to be found. The bacilli usually are within remnants of dermal nerves but sometimes are located just beneath the epidermis.

When major nerve trunks are involved, they contain typical tuberculoid infiltrates that eventually may replace the entire nerve. Occasionally, caseous "abscesses" are present in large nerves, but they are a rare occurrence in children.

BORDERLINE LEPROSY

Borderline leprosy represents a broad spectrum of clinical (Fig. 103–6) and histopathologic variations (see Table 103–1). In the borderline-tuberculoid (BT) variety, strong CMI still is evident by the large numbers of epithelioid cells and lymphocytes. The nerves usually are damaged less and are

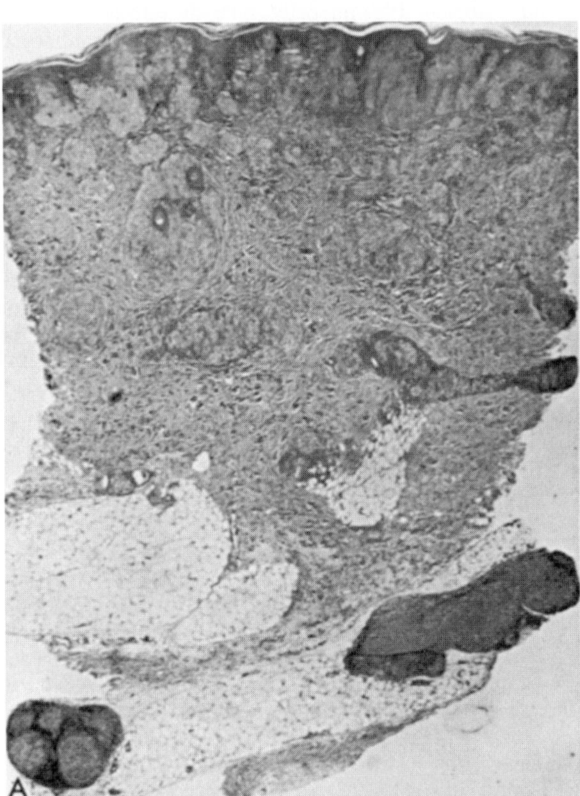

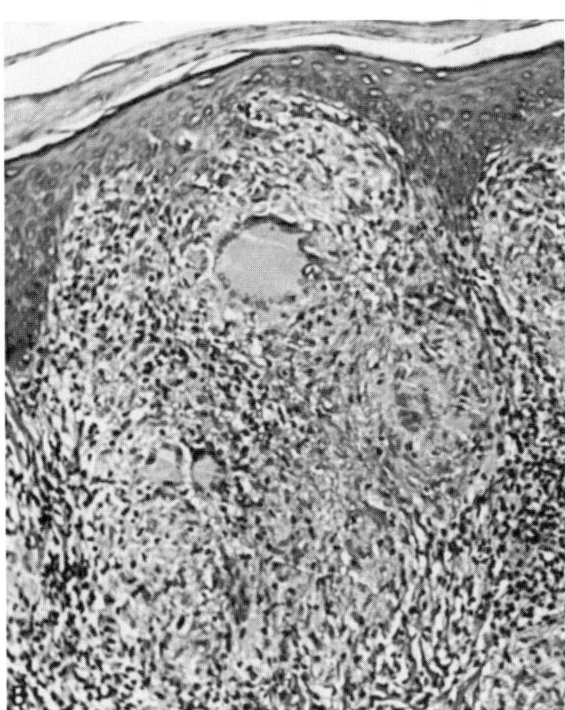

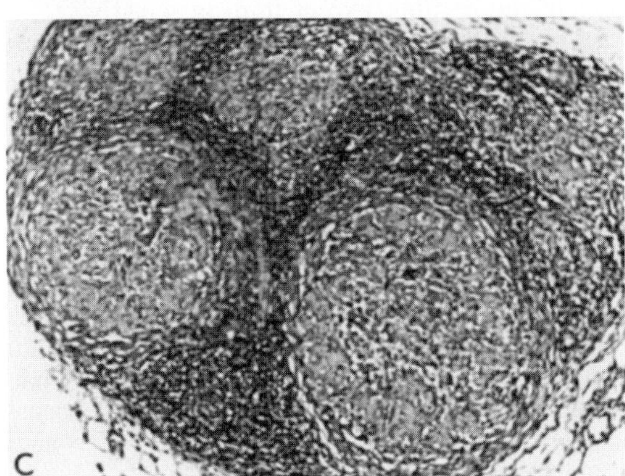

FIGURE 103–5 ■ *A,* Tuberculoid leprosy with a dense granulomatous infiltration in the middle and upper dermis and in and around nerves in the subcutaneous tissue (hematoxylin and eosin, × 9) (AFIP 72-12492). *B,* Same section as in *A.* The granulomas are composed of epithelioid cells, Langhans giant cells, and lymphocytes and are invading the epidermis (hematoxylin and eosin, × 115) (AFIP 72-12465). *C,* High magnification of a nerve in the subcutaneous tissue seen in *A.* Nerves are nearly completely replaced by granulomas. Rare bacilli were in the remaining remnants of nerves (hematoxylin and eosin, ×130) (AFIP 72-12463).

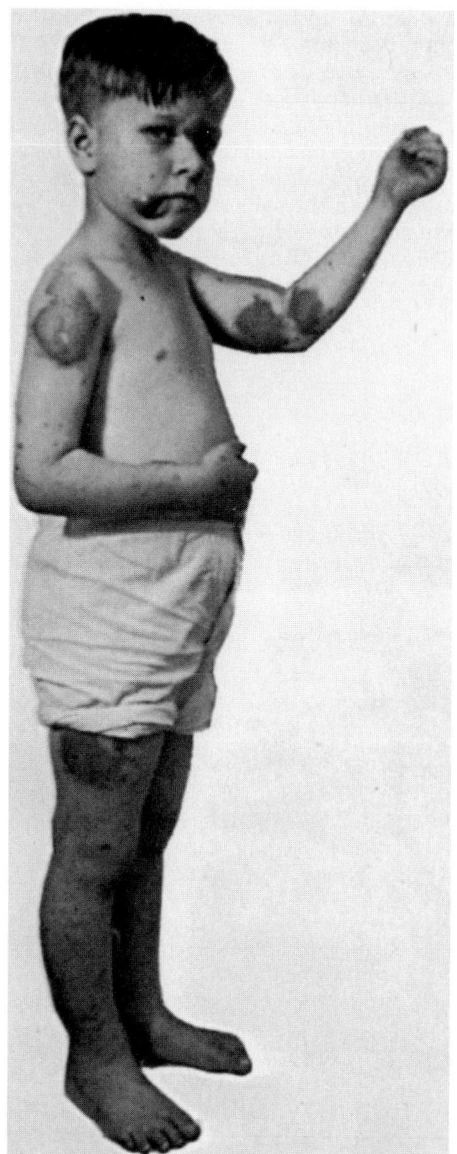

FIGURE 103–6 ■ Borderline lepromatous leprosy in a 6-year-old boy. Many small papular lesions and a few larger erythematous plaques undergoing reversal reaction can be noted(AFIP 77-9195[A]-1).

identifiable more readily than in TT leprosy. Usually, *M. leprae* organisms are found easily in the Schwann cells of nerves (Fig. 103–7) or in the subepidermal zone. In midborderline (BB) leprosy, the epithelioid cells are not surrounded by large numbers of lymphocytes, and Langhans giant cells are not common findings. The subepidermal area is free of infiltrating cells and nerves are not damaged severely, but the perineurium often is laminated by invading epithelioid cells. Some histopathologists do not recognize BB leprosy as an entity because the features usually suggest that the lesion is either on the BT or the borderline-lepromatous (BL) side of the spectrum of the disease.[98] BL lesions reveal a low level of CMI. The granulomas are composed mostly of macrophages but contain irregularly distributed lymphocytes. A few nests of epithelioid cells are present in the granulomas. The perineurium of the nerves is infiltrated with cellular exudates. Nerves are easily identified and contain many bacilli.

LEPROMATOUS LEPROSY

Prelepromatous lesions show only a mild proliferation of macrophages around vessels, nerves, and appendages. AFB are few and often difficult to demonstrate.

Anergy to *M. leprae* becomes apparent early in the lepromatous lesion (Fig. 103–8), with the bacilli-laden macrophage (Virchow cell or lepra cell) being the predominant inflammatory cell. In early lesions, they tend to accumulate around vessels, nerves, and appendages, but they eventually replace the entire dermis in a fully developed leproma (Fig. 103–9*A*). The infected macrophages are supported by a delicate stroma and supplied by a rich network of capillaries. As the macrophages age, they become vacuolated (foamy), largely because of their lipid content. In developing lesions, the intracellular bacilli are arranged in small bundles (see Fig. 103–9*B*); in advanced lesions, dense masses of bacilli called *globi* may replace nearly the entire cytoplasm of the macrophage. Infiltrating cells do not invade the epidermis but leave a narrow subepidermal clear zone. Many bacilli are found in the dermal nerves and frequently in endothelial cells and the walls of blood vessels,[157] the arrectores pilorum muscles, and the epithelial cells of hair follicles. Plasma cells vary in numbers and probably reflect B-lymphocyte hyperactivity.[59] Few lymphocytes are in a lepromatous lesion. Large nerve trunks may show typical lepromatous infiltrations.

Occasionally in patients with lepromatous (LL) leprosy, elevated firm nodules form in the skin, especially in relapsing disease. Because of the characteristic histologic pattern of these lesions, in which the histiocytes resemble fibrocytes, this form is called histoid leprosy.[232]

LL leprosy is disseminated widely, and lepromatous infiltrations frequently are found in the upper respiratory tract as far down as the larynx and in the eyes and testes. In adults, the testes frequently are infiltrated, with subsequent development of sterility and gynecomastia, but these complications are rare findings in children.

Lymph nodes often are infiltrated by bacilli-laden macrophages, especially in the medulla and paracortical areas (Figs. 103–10 and 103–11).

CLINICAL MANIFESTATIONS

The incubation period varies (usually 2 to 5 years), and no prodromal manifestations are well established. Some experienced clinicians working in areas of high prevalence recognize early signs of nerve involvement (localized paresthesia, itching, or numbness) before any visible lesions develop.

After the incubation period, lesions of varying description appear. The nature of the lesions depends on the immune response of the patient to *M. leprae*. Thus far, no strain variations of the bacillus, except in drug sensitivity, have been detected.[247] Most clinicians today follow the classification scheme outlined by Ridley and Jopling,[184] and Table 103–1 summarizes their criteria. Classification is important because it aids in establishing the prognosis and treatment program for the patient.

Virtually all patients with leprosy have peripheral neuropathy if cutaneous sensory changes are included, and approximately 25 percent have significant deformity. In experimental studies, the pathogenesis of peripheral neuritis in leprosy involves bacillation of the endothelial cells of epineural and perineural blood vessels and lymphatics.[198, 199] Surface proteins of *M. leprae* may bind the bacillus to Schwann cells via lamimin.[176, 206] Detailed discussions of peripheral neuropathy in leprosy may be consulted for further coverage of this important topic.[193]

TABLE 103–1 ■ CRITERIA FOR CLASSIFICATION OF LEPROSY

Group	Clinical Features	Histologic Features	Lepromin Reaction (Mitsuda)	Bacillary Density
Tuberculoid (TT)	A single or few anesthetic macules or plaques Borders well defined Peripheral nerve involvement common	Epithelioid-lymphocyte granulomas, with or without giant cells, in skin and nerves No subepidermal clear zone Bacilli in nerves, but rare	Strongly positive	Rare
Borderline-tuberculoid (BT)	Lesions similar to those of TT but more numerous Borders of lesions less distinct Satellite lesions sometimes present around larger lesions Peripheral nerve involvement common	Granulomas similar to those in TT Nerves are infiltrated Bacilli frequently found in nerves	Positive	Scanty
Borderline (BB)	More lesions than in BT Borders more vague Satellite lesions often seen Peripheral nerve involvement common	Epithelioid cells and histiocytic infiltrations focalized by lymphocytes Nerves show increased cellularity Bacilli readily found in nerves	Negative or weakly positive	Moderate
Borderline-lepromatous (BL)	Lesions are numerous and similar to those of BB Some nerve damage	Histiocytic infiltrations show a tendency to evolve toward both epithelioid cells and foamy cells Lymphocytes present Nerves have less cellular infiltration Bacilli plentiful in nerves	Negative	Heavy
Lepromatous (LL)	Multiple, nonanesthetic, macular or papular, symmetrically distributed lesions No neural lesions until late Late complications of madarosis, leonine facies, testicular damage, etc.	Foamy histiocytes containing large numbers of bacilli Few or no lymphocytes Subepidermal clear zone Numerous bacilli in nerves and perineurium without significant intraneural cellular infiltration	Negative	Very heavy
Indeterminate (I)	Vaguely defined hypopigmented or erythematous macule	Often indistinguishable from "mild nonspecific dermatitis" Lymphocytes and histiocytes around skin appendages and nerves	Weakly positive or negative	Negative or scanty

Ocular complications in leprosy are well known. Therefore, all patients with leprosy should be evaluated by an ophthalmologist at diagnosis and periodically re-evaluated, especially during any reactional episodes.

Indeterminate Leprosy

An indeterminate lesion is the first manifestation in most patients, and it may heal spontaneously, remain unchanged for months or years, or gradually progress toward TT or LL leprosy. Patients with indeterminate leprosy have a single or a few macules in the skin (see Fig. 103–2). The macule is defined poorly and mildly hypopigmented in deeper pigmented skin and slightly erythematous in lighter skin. Skin

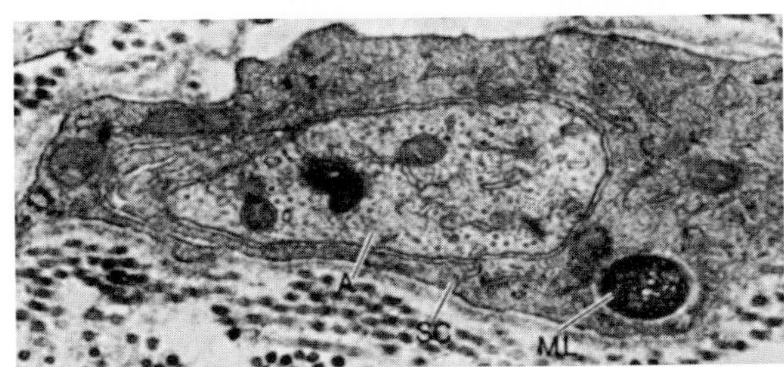

FIGURE 103–7 ■ Electron micrograph of a portion of a damaged dermal nerve in borderline leprosy. A nonmyelinated axon (A) is surrounded by a Schwann cell (SC) that contains a single *Mycobacterium leprae* bacillus (ML) (×60,000). (Courtesy of Dr. S. C. Chang.)

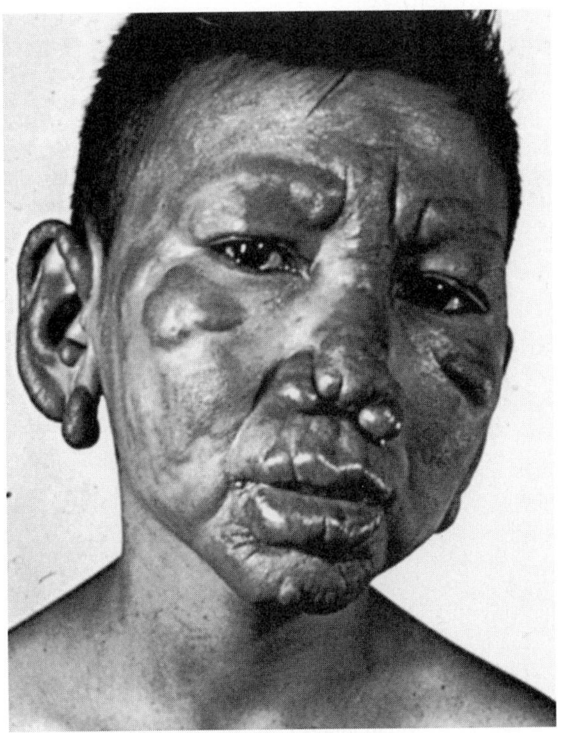

FIGURE 103–8 ■ Advanced lepromatous leprosy in an adolescent Filipino boy. Note the loss of eyebrows and thickening of the ears (AFIP 77-9359-2).

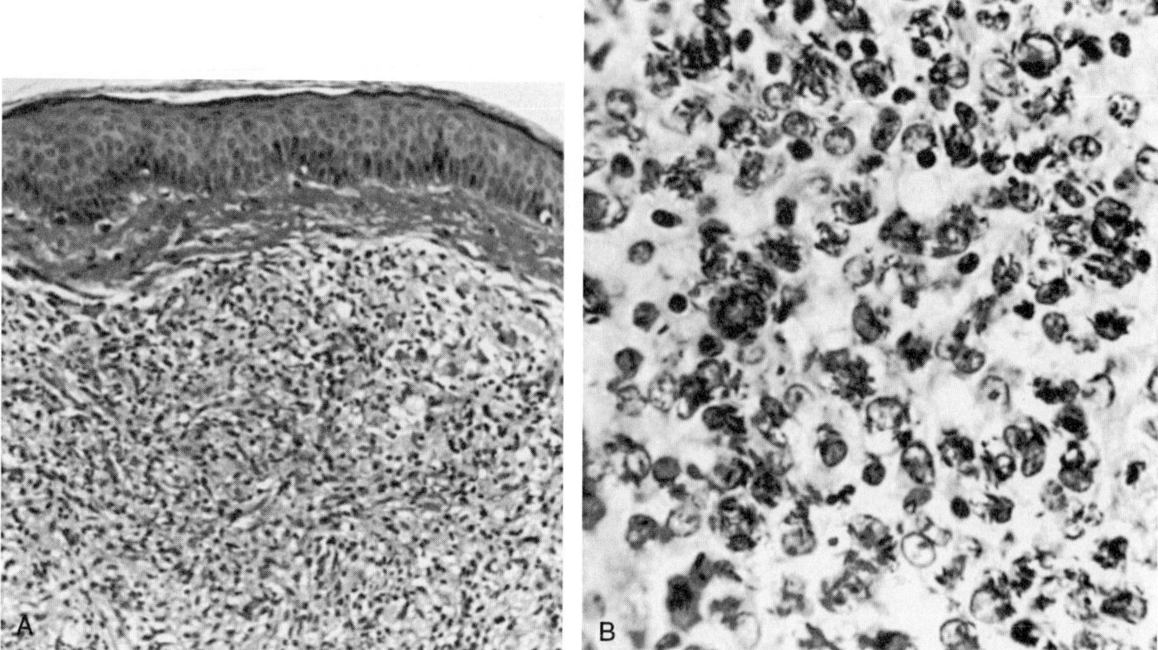

FIGURE 103–9 ■ *A,* Advanced lepromatous leprosy showing replacement of dermis by foamy histiocytes (lepra cells) and a thin subepidermal clear zone (hematoxylin and eosin, ×208) (AFIP 65-1653). *B,* Higher magnification showing clumps of *Mycobacterium leprae* in histiocytes in a leproma in the skin (Fite-Faraco, ×657) (AFIP 56-19549).

texture, sensation, and sweating within early macules are normal or only slightly altered. No damage occurs to peripheral nerves, and skin smears from the lesions rarely contain bacilli. The diagnosis can be made only by finding AFB in histopathologic sections.

Tuberculoid Leprosy

Patients with TT leprosy have a single or several asymmetrically distributed hypopigmented skin lesions (see Fig. 103–4). Tuberculoid lesions arise de novo or evolve from indeterminate macules. The lesion may be macular or infiltrated, but the borders always are sharply demarcated from the surrounding normal skin and frequently are finely papulated. Lesions range in size from less than 1 cm to those that cover entire regions such as the thigh or buttock. Many TT lesions heal spontaneously. In large, active lesions, the centers often are healed and repigmented, though somewhat atrophic.

In TT lesions, sensory loss with impaired sweating and eventual loss of hair occur. On the face, because of its rich innervation, the detection of hypoesthesia in early lesions requires discriminating tests. Conversely, clinicians may mistakenly diagnose leprosy in areas of the body that normally are hypoesthetic (e.g., over the elbows or knees).

Involvement of peripheral nerves commonly occurs in TT leprosy (Fig. 103–12), and cutaneous nerves often can be palpated adjacent to or within lesions. The regional nerve trunks most commonly enlarged are the ulnar from the olecranon groove to the midarm, the lateral popliteal just distal to the head of the fibula, and the posterior tibial in the

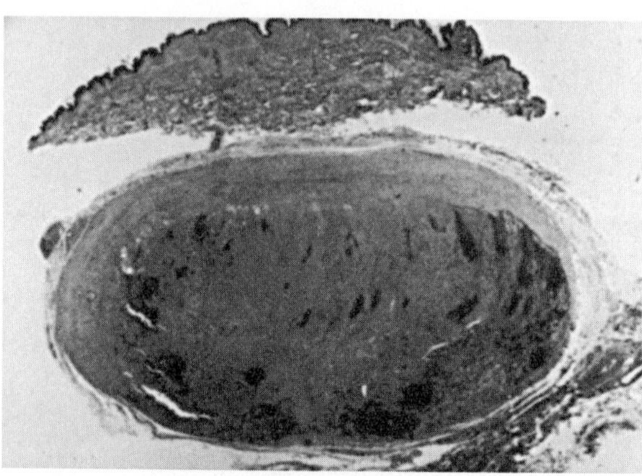

FIGURE 103–10 ■ Lymph node in the subcutaneous tissue of the forearm of a patient with lepromatous leprosy. Lepra cells have nearly completely replaced the lymphoid tissue (dark-staining areas) (hematoxylin and eosin, ×11) (AFIP 72-12502).

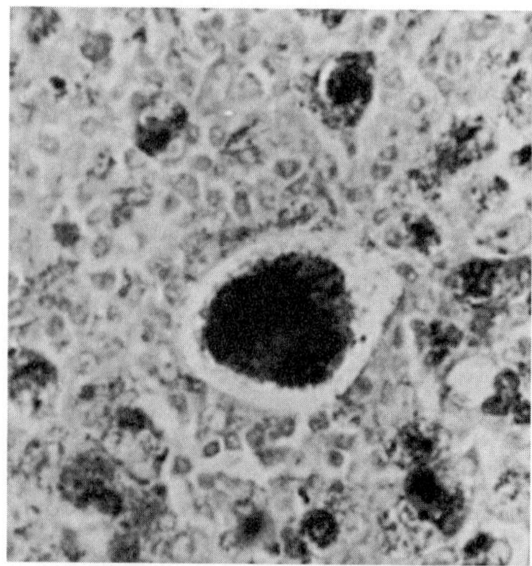

FIGURE 103–11 ■ High magnification of the lymph node in Figure 103–10 demonstrating globi of *Mycobacterium leprae* in histiocytes (Fite-Faraco, ×645) (AFIP 72-12509).

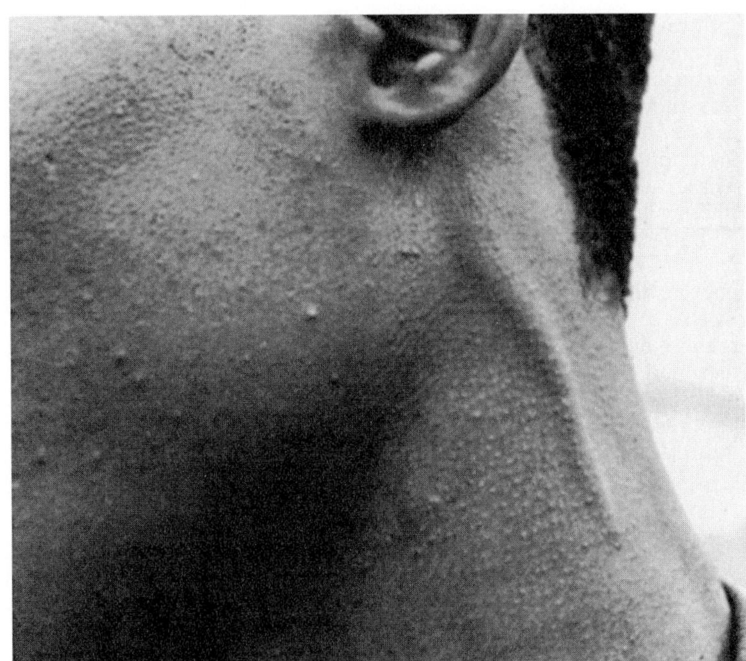

FIGURE 103–12 ■ Enlargement of the great auricular nerve in an adolescent Zairian boy. A large macule of tuberculoid leprosy in the area of the angle of the mandible is now nearly inactive and barely visible (AFIP 77-9359-5).

medial aspect of the ankle. Enlarged or tender nerves anywhere should alert the clinician to the possibility of leprosy. Any readily palpable cutaneous nerve probably is enlarged, but evaluating the size of the nerve trunk requires experience because of the wide range in normal size.

Borderline Leprosy

Borderline leprosy, sometimes called dimorphous or intermediate leprosy, has features of both the LL and the TT forms and represents a continuous spectrum of disease ranging from near-tuberculoid to near-lepromatous. It is an unstable form of leprosy and may evolve gradually toward TT leprosy by undergoing reversal reactions or be downgraded toward LL leprosy. Table 103–1 describes the three major subgroups of borderline leprosy: borderline-tuberculoid (BT), borderline (BB), and borderline-lepromatous (BL).

In BT leprosy, the number of lesions usually is greater than that in TT leprosy, and the borders of each lesion, macule, or plaque are defined less sharply than in TT leprosy. Often, small satellite lesions occur around larger macules or plaques. In BL leprosy, widespread nodular infiltrations or plaques of varying size occur (see Fig. 103–6).

Damage to nerves and the resulting deformity develop early and often are widespread. Pain in nerves or neurotropic changes (e.g., sensory changes that lead to damaged hands or feet or a muscular weakness such as footdrop) frequently bring the patient to the physician. Severe damage to nerves is infrequent in early childhood but can be disastrous. Prevention of this complication is an important goal of leprosy detection programs and of treatment of every leprosy patient.

Lepromatous Leprosy

In LL leprosy, the bacilli multiply freely and the disease disseminates widely, often before striking cutaneous manifestations occur, in contrast to the strict localization of lesions in TT leprosy. LL leprosy may evolve from indeterminate or BB leprosy or may be the first recognizable form. In its earliest form, LL leprosy is manifested as "juvenile leprosy," a clinical entity delineated from observations on large numbers of children in homes for children of patients with leprosy in India.[156] This form, also called *prelepromatous leprosy*, is difficult to detect and frequently goes unrecognized until a more advanced stage develops. Skin texture may be altered slightly, but the vague macules with indistinct borders are detected only under appropriate lighting, preferably daylight. No changes occur in sensation or sweating in the macules, and frequently AFB are not detectable in smears from skin. Histopathologic sections may reveal a few bacilli to confirm the diagnosis; however, if leprosy is suspected, the patient should be monitored until an explanation for the mild skin changes is found. If leprosy is present and not detected and treated, advanced forms of LL leprosy will develop in many of these patients (Fig. 103–13).

The hypopigmented or slightly erythematous macules of early LL leprosy, like those of juvenile leprosy, are missed easily because they are also vague and have slight, if any, sensory changes. These macules usually are small but gradually may coalesce and cover large areas of skin, even nearly the entire body. Making a clinical diagnosis then is difficult, and over the course of a few years, advanced LL leprosy develops. If skin smears or biopsy specimens are taken in the macular stage, making the diagnosis almost always is ensured. If the disease is not diagnosed and treated in the macular stage,

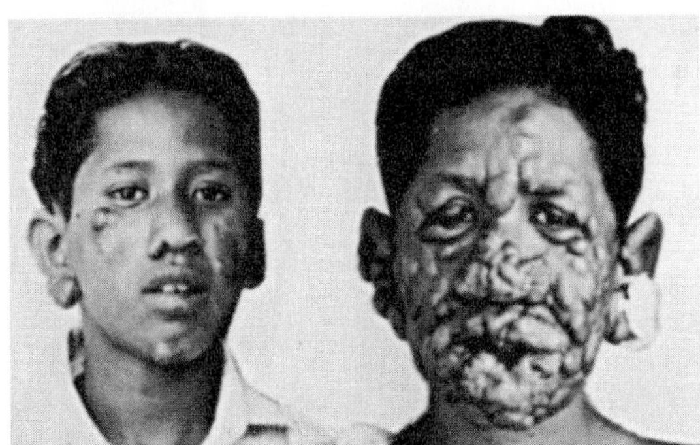

FIGURE 103–13 ■ Progression of lepromatous leprosy in a Hawaiian boy. The photograph on the *left* was taken in 1931, when the patient was 13 years old, and the photograph on the *right* was taken 2 years later. No effective chemotherapy was available in that era (AFIP 75-2479[A]-2).

infiltration of the skin will increase gradually, and nodules may develop. The skin is infiltrated most heavily in the cooler portions of the body, notably the ears (pinnae) and face. By this time, nerves usually are enlarged, and early signs of sensory loss in the hands and feet are present. The eyebrows are thinned and eventually lost, beginning at the lateral edges. These advanced changes of LL leprosy are not common findings in young children but are well known (Fig. 103–14).

Patients of Latin American ancestry, especially those from Mexico and Costa Rica, may contract the highly anergic diffuse form of LL leprosy called *Lucio leprosy*. The disease is so diffuse that often it is not recognized until the patient begins to have sensory changes in the hands and feet, and the eyebrows and other body hair begin to disappear. In advanced forms of Lucio leprosy, a marked obstructive vasculitis in the skin, with the production of dermal infarcts and irregular ulcers, occurs *(Lucio phenomenon)*.[117]

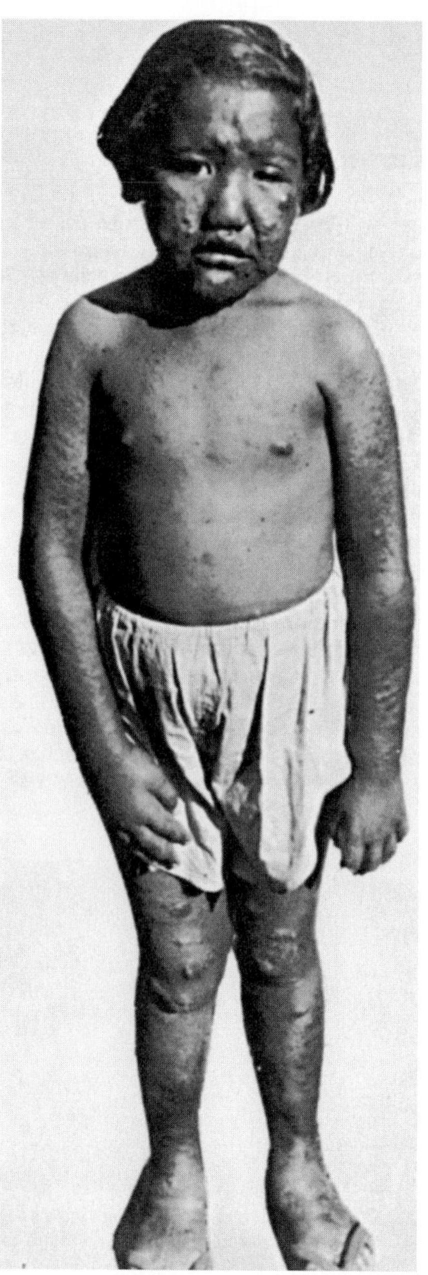

FIGURE 103–14 ■ Advanced lepromatous leprosy in a 6-year-old Hawaiian girl. Diffuse infiltration of the skin and many nodules are apparent (AFIP 75-15806-A).

Lucio leprosy has been reported in children as young as 7 years of age.[196]

Neuritic Leprosy

Rarely, leprosy involves one or more major nerve trunks unaccompanied by cutaneous lesions. These patients have anesthesia, paresis, or wasting of muscles in the affected area. Nerve trunks frequently are painful, enlarged, and tender. Leprosy must be suspected in patients with any peripheral neuritis that has these features. Chronic neuritis with pain and enlargement and tenderness of peripheral nerves often persist for years after the patient has completed chemotherapy for leprosy.[83]

REACTIONS

The course of leprosy, treated or nontreated, often is interrupted by acute episodes called reactions, which fall into two general categories: reversal reactions (or type 1) and erythema nodosum leprosum (ENL) (or type 2).

Reversal Reactions

Reversal reactions complicate borderline leprosy and represent delayed hypersensitivity reactions with an upgrading of CMI toward TT leprosy. Lesions become erythematous and edematous, and neuritis is a common occurrence (Fig. 103–15). Patients who are lepromin-positive and have IgM antibodies to PGL-1 are most at risk for reversal reactions.[185] Proliferation of sensitized T lymphocytes initiates reversal reactions, releasing lymphokines that amplify the inflammatory response, calling in and activating macrophages.[188] Immunohistopathologic evidence has shown that effective chemotherapy for both paucibacillary and multibacillary patients may activate CMI and provoke clinical or subclinical reversal reactions. For example, expression of HLA-DR is increased, which may enhance IFN-γ production by lymphocytes in granulomas.[35] It is

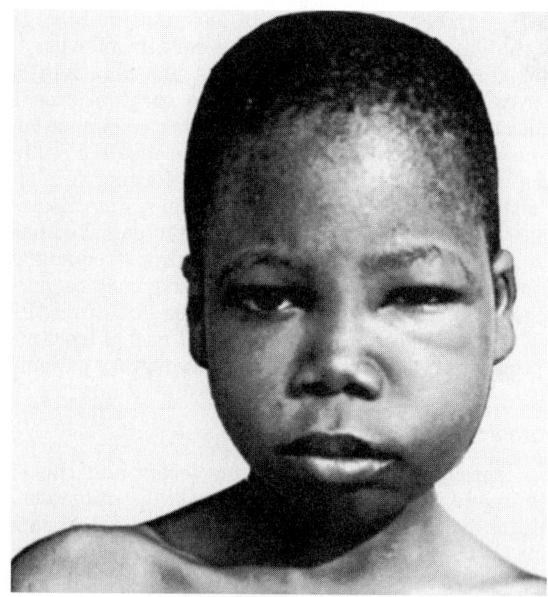

FIGURE 103–15 ■ Reversal reaction in an 8-year-old Zairian boy with borderline-tuberculoid leprosy. The left side of his face is swollen, and mild palsy is present from the facial nerve damage. The patient responded rapidly to steroid therapy (AFIP 77-9359[A]-1).

expressed histopathologically by edema accompanied by an increase in the number of lymphocytes, often with epithelioid cells and giant cells. In severe reactions, necrosis within the granulomas may occur. An increase in levels of TNF-α occurring during reactions may partially explain this necrosis.[200] Patients undergoing such reactions must be observed closely so that sensory loss and deformities are minimized. By repeated reversal reactions, borderline leprosy, even cases close to LL disease, may be upgraded gradually to TT leprosy, often with disastrous peripheral neuropathy.

Differentiating reversal reactions from relapsing lesions frequently is difficult and requires careful correlation of clinical and histopathologic findings. This correlation is becoming increasingly important in endemic areas where shorter-term chemotherapeutic regimens of fixed duration are used.[57, 135] The following criteria for differentiating relapses and reversal reactions are suggested: a *relapse* involves an increased number of lesions, positive skin smears for AFB (for BB and BL patients), tissue reaction inconsistent with a reversal reaction, and a favorable response to chemotherapy; a *reversal reaction,* on the other hand, involves an exacerbation of existing lesions, skin smears negative for AFB, tissue reaction consistent with a reversal reaction, and a rapid response to anti-inflammatory drugs.

Erythema Nodosum Leprosum

Formerly, ENL developed in approximately 50 percent of LL patients after they had undergone a few months of chemotherapy; however, with the addition of clofazimine to the standard therapeutic regimen, the frequency is much reduced. Tender subcutaneous nodules that become erythematous (Fig. 103–16) develop rapidly; the nodules often are accompanied by fever and occasionally by synovitis and iridocyclitis. ENL resembles the Arthus reaction and is thought to result from immune complex formation.[63] Immune complexes may form within lesions by the local release of antigens of *M. leprae* and could modulate the development of T-cell populations in situ. For example, numbers of helper T lymphocytes are increased in lesions of ENL.[150] Serum TNF-α is elevated in ENL.[195, 200] In the nodule, an infiltration of neutrophils and sometimes an intense vasculitis may occur. Ulceration of the skin frequently accompanies severe ENL. Glomerulonephritis sometimes complicates ENL; secondary amyloidosis is a late sequela of repeated reactions and may be a consequence of the neutrophilic leukocytosis.[126] Although neutrophilic infiltration is considered by many physicians to be the hallmark of the tissue reaction, tissue from an occasional patient with clinically typical ENL does not show neutrophils. In such patients, demonstration of serum amyloid A and C-reactive protein may aid in establishing the diagnosis of ENL.[87]

DIAGNOSIS AND DIFFERENTIAL DIAGNOSIS

The cardinal signs of leprosy are hypoesthetic lesions of the skin, enlarged peripheral nerve or nerves, and AFB in skin smears. In the absence of another clear explanation, any one of these signs strongly suggests leprosy.

An experienced observer can make a clinical diagnosis in most patients, except those with early leprosy, with a high degree of accuracy. Histopathologic evaluation, however, is recommended strongly for accurate classification and documentation.

Patients with leprosy may be found in almost any geographic area. An awareness of this fact will minimize missed and delayed diagnoses, especially in areas of low prevalence. In the United States, the usual delay in making the diagnosis after the patient's first visit to a physician for symptoms related to leprosy is approximately 1.5 to 2 years. This delay often significantly worsens the prognosis.

The history is important. Contact with patients with leprosy or residence in an endemic area raises suspicion of leprosy in a patient with a chronic lesion of the skin. Sensory loss or unexplained damage to hands or feet suggests damage to nerve trunks. Sometimes, a footdrop or clawhand will bring the patient to a physician. Occasionally, LL patients will consult an otolaryngologist first because of a chronic stuffy nose.

The clinician must evaluate sensory changes in a lesion by using the precautions already mentioned. The modalities usually tested are light touch with the use of a few fibers of cotton or calibrated nylon threads and heat-cold discrimination with the use of warm and cold water in test tubes. Much patience and repeated testing often are necessary in evaluating young children. Spontaneous sweating can be observed directly, or induced sweating can be evaluated.[125] Hair may be completely preserved in early lesions but lost in advanced lesions.

The main nerve trunks must be palpated for tenderness and enlargement. Skin in the area of discrete lesions also must be palpated gently to detect enlargement of cutaneous nerves. In the world population, leprosy is the most common cause of peripheral neuropathy and thus must be considered in any patient with peripheral neuropathy.[193]

Obtaining and examining smears for AFB is an important diagnostic procedure and should be controlled carefully by

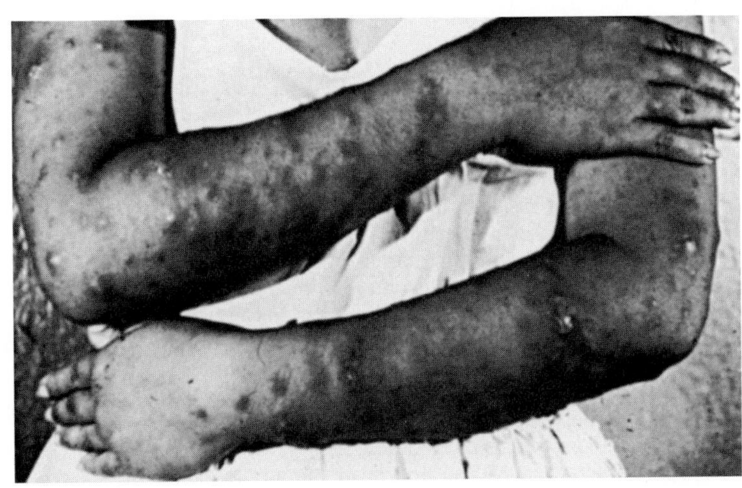

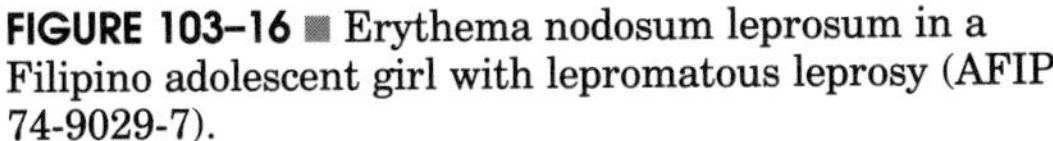

FIGURE 103–16 ■ Erythema nodosum leprosum in a Filipino adolescent girl with lepromatous leprosy (AFIP 74-9029-7).

experienced laboratories. Briefly, smears are made from the edge of discrete macules or plaques, nodules, ear lobes, and the nasal mucosa. Skin smears are made by squeezing and holding a fold of skin between the thumb and forefinger to avoid getting blood in the smear and by making a short, shallow slit in the skin with a razor blade or scalpel. The instrument then is turned at a right angle to the slit, and the edges of the incision are scraped. The cells and fluid thus obtained are spread on a slide, heat-fixed, and stained by the Ziehl-Neelsen method.[230] Evaluation of smears should not be done by researchers unfamiliar with their interpretation. An occasional AFB may, for example, be a harmless contaminant in the staining reagents.

The lepromin reaction is useless for the diagnosis of leprosy. The currently available skin tests with soluble *M. leprae* antigens are unreliable.[77] Enzyme-linked immunosorbent assays and gelatin particle agglutination tests for antibodies to the PGL-1 of *M. leprae* are available.[24, 72, 90] Although specificity for *M. leprae* is high, these tests detect antibodies to PGL-1 in only approximately 50 percent of paucibacillary patients. Other serologic tests for antibodies to *M. leprae*–specific epitopes on protein moieties of the bacillus are being evaluated.[168] PGL-1 antigen is detectable in the serum and urine of most multibacillary patients.[163, 251]

Reliance on DNA probes and polymerase chain reaction (PCR) technology may prove useful in the diagnosis of leprosy in tissue sections, skin smears, and nasal smears.[40, 215, 248] Because these methods can detect a single leprosy bacillus, interpretation of results, particularly in highly endemic areas, is difficult. Careful clinicopathologic correlation is essential when basing diagnosis on DNA findings.[226]

The differential diagnosis of leprosy in children is an extensive subject and can be discussed only briefly here. Superficial mycoses and postinflammatory changes commonly are confused with early leprosy. Changes in pigmentation may be caused, for instance, by scars, birthmarks, and actinic dermatitis. In areas where dermal filariasis is endemic, vague macules in a black-skinned patient may appear identical to the early macules of leprosy.[17, 128, 137] Among the many infiltrated lesions of the skin that can resemble leprosy are leishmaniasis, lymphoma, granuloma annulare, granuloma multiforme (Mkar disease), lupus erythematosus, psoriasis, pityriasis rosea, sarcoidosis, and neurofibromatosis. Peripheral neuropathies that may simulate leprosy are those seen in Morvan disease, syringomyelia, lead intoxication, diabetes mellitus, primary amyloidosis of nerves, and familial hypertrophic neuropathy.

Cardiolipin antibody assays of sera from patients with advanced LL leprosy frequently give false-positive reactions for syphilis.

PROGNOSIS

Without chemotherapy, the prognosis in all patients except those with limited and self-healing disease potentially is poor. Patients with borderline or advanced TT leprosy frequently become mutilated because of damage to nerves. Borderline patients can downgrade toward LL leprosy. In patients with LL leprosy, the disease is progressive and can cause death from laryngeal obstruction. Secondary amyloidosis is a frequent late sequela. Blindness may result from lagophthalmic keratitis or repeated episodes of iridocyclitis. General debility and deformity eventually prevent gainful employment in many patients.

With adequate specific chemotherapy and control of reactions, the prognosis is good in nearly all patients. If therapy is started early, the prognosis usually is excellent, and deformity and mutilation are prevented. Even after successful chemotherapy, however, some patients continue to suffer significant neuritis and loss of peripheral nerve function. Sometimes this "silent neuropathy" goes unnoticed by both the patient and the physician.[39, 227] Appropriate early attention to anesthetic hands and feet and restoration of function by reconstructive surgery can prevent most mutilation.

The lepromin test is a valuable prognostic tool because it measures the CMI potential of the host to infection by *M. leprae*.[97] Patients with early macular lesions who are lepromin-negative have a poorer prognosis than that for patients who are lepromin-positive if treatment cannot be administered. Histopathologic evaluation made before instituting chemotherapy is important for determining the prognosis and, if available, should not be neglected.

TREATMENT

Once a diagnosis of leprosy is established, chemotherapy must be initiated and appropriate measures instituted for preventing or correcting deformity in patients with neurotropic changes.[26, 58, 115] The three chemotherapeutic agents most commonly used are dapsone, clofazimine, and rifampin. Although the WHO recommends only clinical findings for assessment of the therapeutic response in field programs, clinicians may wish to use additional evaluations. The effectiveness of chemotherapy is assessed readily in patients with LL or near-LL leprosy by the staining quality of *M. leprae* in skin smears. Obtaining skin smears is recommended every 6 months to 1 year until the smears are negative. The response to chemotherapy in TT patients and most borderline patients is determined by the clinical response and by histopathologic evaluation. Viability of *M. leprae* in tissues is assessed in unusual cases in the mouse footpad.

Combined chemotherapy is increasingly being accepted for all forms of active leprosy. Although experimental data are limited,[204] the growing body of clinical data indicates that multidrug therapy has replaced monotherapy.[41, 118] In fact, monotherapy with any chemotherapeutic agent no longer is advised. The regimens recommended currently for multidrug therapy are given later, after a brief discussion of the most used individual drugs.

Dapsone

In 1941, Faget and associates at Carville, Louisiana, introduced the sulfones as the first chemotherapeutic agents regularly effective for leprosy and thereby revolutionized the care of leprosy patients.[51] The sulfone in common use is diaminodiphenylsulfone, or dapsone, available in the United States as Avlosulfon. Dapsone is an antimetabolite for *M. leprae* and is a bacteriostatic agent. The drug usually is given orally at 6 to 10 mg/kg body weight per week, divided into equal daily doses. The effect of dapsone on the bacilli is slow; 3 to 6 months of treatment is necessary to render bacilli from LL patients noninfectious for the mouse footpad. Sulfone-resistant strains of *M. leprae* are being detected with increasing frequency,[236, 237] and monotherapy with dapsone is not recommended.

Dapsone usually is well tolerated but may provoke one or more of the following side reactions: dermatitis, anemia, hepatitis, or psychosis.

Clofazimine

Clofazimine (Lamprene) is a bacteriostatic riminophenazine dye that has both anti–*M. leprae* and anti-inflammatory activities, which render it a useful drug for the treatment of patients who are prone to ENL reactions.[52] The mechanism of bacteriostasis may involve enhancement of oxygen-dependent killing of *M. leprae* and binding to bacterial DNA. The adult dose of clofazimine ranges from 50 to 300 daily, and some authorities recommend 1 mg/kg/day for children. The lower dosages are used for maintenance therapy once a good clinical response has been achieved, and the higher dosages may be needed to control ENL. The major side reactions to clofazimine are hyperpigmentation of skin and enteritis. Enteritis is experienced only at the higher dosages generally used for ENL. The hyperpigmentation subsides with the clinical improvement in leprosy, and both hyperpigmentation and enteritis resolve after drug withdrawal. Although two instances of clofazimine-resistant *M. leprae* infection have been reported, the validity of these observations is uncertain.[106, 235] For some time, clofazimine has been considered safe in pregnancy, but one report describes three neonatal deaths in 15 observed pregnancies.[53] Association of the drug with the deaths was not established. Monotherapy with clofazimine is not recommended.

Rifampin

Rifampin is an antibiotic that inhibits bacterial DNA-dependent RNA polymerase and is rapidly bactericidal for *M. leprae*. A single large dose can render a highly positive LL patient noninfectious within 1 week. Dosages of 15 to 20 mg/kg/day have been given to children (maximal dose, 600 mg/day). Optimal doses for children with leprosy have not been reported. Adult doses range from 300 to 600 mg daily.[244] Many side reactions to rifampin have been described, and the relevant literature must be consulted.[20] Rifampin-resistant leprosy has been reported,[92, 249] so monotherapy with rifampin is not recommended.

Multidrug Therapy

Because of drug-resistant *M. leprae*, combined drug regimens are mandatory for the treatment of all forms of leprosy.[49, 204, 236, 237] The first large-scale multidrug therapy for leprosy was initiated in Malta in 1972. Rifampin, dapsone, prothionamide, and isoniazid were used. Evaluation of the patients approximately 20 years later revealed a single relapse; however, presumed "persisting" *M. leprae* organisms were detected.[60, 102]

Combined drug therapy minimizes drug-resistant strains of *M. leprae* and may eliminate some "persisting" organisms. Persisting *M. leprae* are viable bacilli that can be isolated in small numbers from patients who are clinically responding well to therapy. These persisting *M. leprae* bacilli are sensitive to the drug in question when tested in the mouse footpad and may account for relapses when treatment is discontinued. Persisting *M. leprae* organisms have been detected after as many as 5 years of rifampin, 6 years of clofazimine, and 22 years of dapsone therapy.

In 1982, a WHO study group recommended the multidrug therapy regimens described hereafter.[245] Patients were divided into paucibacillary and multibacillary groups. Paucibacillary patients (usually indeterminate, TT, and BT) were defined originally as those with negative skin smears at all sites or those who have fewer than four lesions and no clinical peripheral neuritis. Subsequently, for field programs, paucibacillary patients are classified only as those who have fewer than four lesions, without reference to skin smear evaluation. All other patients are multibacillary.

The multidrug therapy regimens were designed primarily for field programs, and they use, for example, pulsed supervised monthly rather than daily rifampin.[10] Multidrug therapy is well tolerated, and compliance in large-scale control programs has been satisfactory. The efficacy of multidrug therapy has been promising[238]: in two surveys involving approximately 112,000 multibacillary patients monitored for as long as 9 years after therapy, the cumulative risk of relapse was 0.77 percent. Anecdotal descriptions of certain groups of highly bacilliferous patients with relapse rates of up to 20 percent and recurrences developing 5 years or more after therapy have been reported.[94] These and other results suggest that therapeutic regimens for multibacillary patients should be given for longer than 2 years. In most reports, relapse rates in paucibacillary patients exceed those in multibacillary patients. In my experience in evaluating histopathologic specimens, many patients classified clinically as paucibacillary were, in fact, multibacillary. The potential for relapse after multidrug therapy regimens must await long-term, large-scale follow-up results.[93] Peripheral neuropathy sometimes persists after completion of these therapeutic regimens.[83] The trend in 2001 was to reduce the duration of treatment and change the therapeutic regimens—even to the extreme of a single-dose regimen composed of rifampin, ofloxacin, and minocycline for single-lesion therapy. Many of these innovations are interwoven into the WHO Elimination of Leprosy Program and have provoked critical concern by some authorities.[56, 210]

REGIMEN FOR PAUCIBACILLARY PATIENTS (INDETERMINATE, TUBERCULOID, AND BORDERLINE-TUBERCULOID)

In adults, rifampin, 600 mg once a month, plus dapsone, 100 mg daily, is given for 6 months, and treatment then is stopped. After the conclusion of multidrug therapy, the patient should be seen every 3 to 6 months. All apparent relapses require histopathologic examination for establishing whether the lesions represent relapses or reversal reactions. Relapsing patients must be treated again. The aforementioned multidrug therapy is not used alone in patients with concurrent tuberculosis.

REGIMEN FOR MULTIBACILLARY PATIENTS (LEPROMATOUS, BORDERLINE-LEPROMATOUS, AND BORDERLINE)

In adults, rifampin, 600 mg monthly, dapsone, 100 mg daily, and clofazimine, 50 mg daily, are given. If patient compliance is questionable, the rifampin and 300 mg of clofazimine should be given monthly under supervision, in addition to the 50 mg daily. These drugs must be given for 2 years. For patients in whom the hyperpigmentation caused by clofazimine is unacceptable, daily doses of 250 to 375 mg of prothionamide or ethionamide may be substituted for clofazimine.

DOSAGES OF MULTIDRUG THERAPY FOR CHILDREN

Pediatric dosages of multidrug therapy are given in Table 103–2.[101]

RECOMMENDATIONS FOR THE UNITED STATES

The Hansen's Disease Center, Baton Rouge, Louisiana, recommends the following variations of the WHO's recommended multidrug therapy regimens for adult patients in the United States:

- *Paucibacillary disease*: dapsone, 100 mg daily, plus rifampin, 600 mg daily, for 1 year.
- *Multibacillary disease*: dapsone, 100 mg daily, plus

TABLE 103–2 ■ DOSAGE OF MULTIDRUG THERAPY FOR CHILDREN

Weight (kg)	Percentage of Adult Dose
Under 15	25
15–30	50
30–45	75
Over 45	100

From Jopling, W. H.: Handbook of Leprosy. London, William Heinemann, 1984.

rifampin, 600 mg daily, and clofazimine, 50 mg daily, for 2 years. Minocycline, 100 mg daily, is substituted for clofazimine in patients who will not take clofazimine.

OTHER DRUGS UNDER INVESTIGATION

Other potential antileprosy drugs that are undergoing advanced clinical evaluation and may gain general use include fluoroquinolones (pefloxacin and ofloxacin), the macrolide clarithromycin, and the tetracycline minocycline.[64, 66, 75, 96]

Treatment of Reactions

Patients undergoing a reaction should be observed daily in the early stages and hospitalized if the symptoms are severe. Formerly, specific therapy was stopped or the dosage reduced during reactions, but these measures no longer are recommended.[245] Damage to eyes and neurotropic changes may ensue rapidly without immediate attention. Nerve tenderness and function must be assessed frequently during reactions. Acute inflammation of isolated lesions without damage to nerves is likely to be of little consequence except for cosmetic considerations, but the patient should be monitored closely.

REVERSAL (TYPE 1) REACTION

Patients with painful, tender nerves must receive immediate care, usually in the hospital. Analgesics are given, and the affected area is put at rest. Large daily doses of corticosteroids are started and tapered to a minimal effective dose until the reaction subsides. Conversion to alternate-day steroid regimens may be attempted when long-term treatment is necessary. Some clinicians use clofazimine for chronic reversal reactions, but it is not recommended for the initial treatment of reactions with acute neuritis. Clofazimine probably is consistently efficacious only for ENL.[88]

ERYTHEMA NODOSUM LEPROSUM (TYPE 2) REACTION

Mild ENL is treated with analgesics; more severe ENL is treated with thalidomide or corticosteroids. Pediatric doses of thalidomide in ENL have not been established, but the initial adult dose is 100 mg four times daily followed by a minimal effective dose, usually 100 mg daily. The teratogenic action of thalidomide demands that appropriate measures be taken in the treatment of fertile females. For the rare patient who does not respond to thalidomide or in fertile females, corticosteroids or clofazimine is used. Corticosteroids, if used, are administered in the usual dosage schedules, beginning with large doses and tapering to a minimal effective level. Some clinicians use an alternate-day regimen when long-term steroid therapy is necessary, thus minimizing the well-known side effects. A few studies suggest that pentoxifylline or pentoxifylline plus clofazimine is effective for ENL.[160, 216, 239]

Clofazimine is effective in most patients with ENL and does not have the disadvantages of thalidomide or corticosteroids. The anti-inflammatory action of clofazimine is not manifested until after 4 to 6 weeks of continuous use. The dosage must be adjusted to the minimal effective level.

Iridocyclitis requires emergency measures. Local corticosteroids must be added to systemic anti-inflammatory regimens and ophthalmologic consultation obtained.

PREVENTION

Precise recommendations for the prevention of leprosy in individuals have not been formulated. Control programs today are based on the general principles that (1) the number of contagious patients is reduced by chemotherapy and (2) the surveillance of contacts will detect early leprosy. To accomplish these goals, appropriate education of the public and medical personnel and population surveys in areas of higher prevalence must be implemented. In endemic areas, improved housing probably is a highly important preventive measure by reducing close contact of patients with healthy individuals.

The most important obstacles to improving control of leprosy include persistence of *M. leprae* in treated patients, the cost and toxicity of antileprotic medications, the long term of therapeutic regimens, patient compliance, and the social stigma of leprosy.[180]

For the eradication of leprosy, zoonotic sources of *M. leprae* must be taken into account.[140]

Chemoprophylaxis

Chemoprophylaxis with dapsone for close contacts has limited usefulness but is not recommended for large populations.[38] This recommendation is based on the probability that long-term use would be irregular and dapsone-resistant *M. leprae* may develop.[244]

Vaccination, Immunoprophylaxis, and Immunotherapy

The WHO initiated an Immunology of Leprosy Program (IMMLEP) in 1974 with two primary goals: (1) development of a vaccine against leprosy and (2) development of reagents for detecting subclinical leprosy. Achievement of both goals could diminish profoundly the incidence of leprosy. *M. leprae*, or specific antigens thereof, for the IMMLEP studies were obtained from experimentally infected armadillos. Vaccines composed of heat-killed whole *M. leprae* alone or in combination with live bacille Calmette-Guérin (BCG) have been found to be safe and induce delayed-type hypersensitivity to *M. leprae* in a high percentage of lepromin-negative individuals. Several other vaccines based on cultivable mycobacteria (*Mycobacterium vaccae, Mycobacterium "w,"* and the Indian Cancer Research Centre [ICRC] bacillus) induce similar responses.[11, 107, 212] Field trials of these vaccines for the immunoprophylaxis of leprosy are in progress; however, because of the chronicity and low prevalence of the disease, meaningful evaluation of their efficacy will require extended follow-up observations.[12] Because infection-induced immunity is not observed regularly in leprosy, a reasonable doubt exists that vaccines containing only *M. leprae* will be protective. Hence, combined vaccines of killed *M. leprae* and live BCG have been studied. Such vaccines convert lepromin-negative contacts of leprosy patients to positive reactors[30] and upgrade LL patients toward the tuberculoid region of the disease spectrum.[142] Vaccines based on cell wall fractions of *M. leprae* are being studied.[65] The WHO does not recommend BCG vaccination for the prevention of leprosy.[9] This decision was based on the highly variable results of extensive studies in Burma, Papua

New Guinea, and Uganda.[245] Another trial in India involving 270,000 individuals confirmed that over a 12½ year follow-up, BCG vaccination was only appproximately 25 percent effective against leprosy.[217]

Initial evaluations of a large-scale immunoprophylaxis trial of heat-killed *M. leprae* plus BCG vaccine in humans in Venezuela showed no better protection than did BCG alone 5 years after vaccination.[33] A randomized trial of a single BCG vaccination, repeated BCG, or BCG plus killed *M. leprae* involving 121,020 individuals in Malawi gave the following results over a 5- to 9-year follow-up: a single BCG vaccination afforded 50 percent protection against leprosy, a second BCG vaccination added appreciably to this protection, but the addition of killed *M. leprae* to BCG did not enhance protection against leprosy.[108]

LEPROSY AND ACQUIRED IMMUNODEFICIENCY SYNDROME

Because *M. tuberculosis, Mycobacterium avium–intracellulare*, and *Mycobacterium kansasii* are frequent opportunistic pathogens in patients with the acquired immunodeficiency syndrome (AIDS), observations on AIDS in patients with leprosy are of interest. In one study in Zambia, antibodies to HIV were found in 33 percent of new leprosy patients versus 7 percent of controls.[129] Perhaps the positivity of some of these patients with leprosy can be explained by cross-reactivity between antibodies to HIV-1 and the lipoarabinomannan of *M. leprae*.[109] In other populations in Africa, HIV infection constituted an overall risk factor of 2.2 for leprosy, with 4 to 23 percent of cases of multibacillary leprosy attributable to HIV co-infection.[15] Other prospective studies show that HIV infection may not be a risk factor for acquisition of leprosy in some populations.[112, 201] Only a few detailed clinicopathologic reports on individuals co-infected with *M. leprae* and HIV exist.[95, 114, 154] In these patients, no consistent deleterious effect of HIV infection on the clinical or pathologic findings of leprosy occurred. These observations are supported by a study of the parameters of CMI in co-infected patients in Brazil.[194] In these patients with borderline leprosy, the quality of the granulomas in the infiltrations of leprosy were not altered significantly despite low $CD4^+$ T-cell counts. The incidence of reversal reactions (type 1) and neuritis is increased in multibacillary patients co-infected with HIV.[22] Perhaps, as previously suggested,[121] the observations in patients co-infected with HIV and *M. leprae* will lead to some revisions of the immunopathogenesis of leprosy.

Buruli Ulcer

Mycobacterium ulcerans causes indolent, necrotizing cutaneous ulcers that are known classically as Buruli ulcers. Other names for these lesions include Bairnsdale or Searle ulcer in Australia and Kumusi ulcer in Papua New Guinea. Buruli ulcer, however, seems most appropriate because Clancey and colleagues were the first to name the disease, after the site of the first large epidemic, which was located in Buruli County, Uganda.[25] Furthermore, Cook in Uganda described lesions that fit Buruli ulcer as early as 1897.[34] Today, researchers recognize that many infections with *M. ulcerans* are not manifested as ulcers, and, thus, *M. ulcerans* infection is a technically more appropriate name for the disease. A few infections have been acquired by North American travelers to endemic countries,[29, 202] and patients with Buruli ulcers frequently come to European medical centers for treatment.[4]

THE ORGANISM

MacCallum and associates in 1948 in Australia were the first to isolate the etiologic agent in culture.[123] *M. ulcerans* is strongly acid-fast, with an optimal growth temperature of 30° C to 32° C on routine mycobacteriologic media such as Löwenstein-Jensen medium. The organism is a slow grower, and several months may be required to achieve isolation in primary culture. Microaerophilic conditions promote the growth of *M. ulcerans,* and the organism is strikingly sensitive to temperatures of 37° C or higher.[143, 166] This temperature sensitivity often reduces rates of cultivation of the etiologic agent in laboratories remote from endemic areas.

M. ulcerans is the only mycobacterium known to elaborate a necrotizing and immunosuppressive toxin.[170, 179] This toxin is a polyketide called mycolactone.[67, 68] Although mycolactone is viewed as the dominant virulence factor of *M. ulcerans*, other factors may participate (e.g., phospholipases).[71] The phenolic mycosides of *M. ulcerans* and *Mycobacterium marinum* are identical, and sequences for the 16S rRNA gene differ by only 1 base pair.[36, 186] Specific insertion sequences for *M. ulcerans* have been characterized and are available for identification of the organism by PCR.[214] Variations in the 3′ end of the 16S rRNA sequence are related to geographic origin and are used to divide the organism into African, American, Asian, and Australian strains.[174]

TRANSMISSION AND EPIDEMIOLOGY

Endemic foci of *M. ulcerans* infections usually occur in rural settings near permanent wetlands in warm countries, especially in terrain subject to seasonal flooding. Reports of patients with Buruli ulcers have come from at least 27 countries, principally in the tropics. A few patients live in nontropical climates such as China,[50] Japan,[220] and southern Australia.[229] Today, the largest numbers of reported patients live in West Africa (Benin, Burkina Faso, Côte d'Ivoire, Ghana, Guinea, Liberia, and Nigeria).[172] In these countries, the disease is re-emerging rapidly, with an estimated total annual incidence exceeding 7000 patients. Other countries in which the disease is well known to be endemic include Malaysia, Indonesia, Papua New Guinea, Peru, Suriname, French Guiana, Cameroon, Equatorial Guinea, Gabon, Angola, Democratic Republic of Congo, and Uganda.[84, 135] Observers attribute this re-emergence to environmental factors such as deforestation, artificial topographic alterations (dams and irrigation systems), and increasing populations engaged in basic manual agriculture in wetlands.[145]

Individuals of all ages are affected, but the highest frequencies are in children 15 years of age or younger—usually approximately 75 percent of all cases.[124] The sexes are affected equally, and a racial predilection is unknown. Anecdotal observations of children in families of multiple parentage suggest a possible genetic predisposition. Seasonal variations in incidence occur in some foci.[82, 182] Approximately 80 percent of the lesions are on the limbs, with highest frequencies involving the lower extremities.

Although Buruli ulcer long has been associated with riverine environments, repeated long-term studies on a large variety of flora, fauna, water, and mud samples have failed to reveal *M. ulcerans* in nature by culture.[5, 171] With the development of molecular biologic techniques for the identification of *M. ulcerans*, the organism was detected in the environment in Australia by PCR.[189, 190, 213] With the increased understanding of this fastidious organism now available, researchers expect that successful culture of *M. ulcerans* from nature will be achieved soon.[172]

Although the ultimate source of *M. ulcerans* remains obscure, the organism has been discovered in aquatic insects such as water bugs, firefly larvae, and beetles obtained from stagnant water in endemic areas of West Africa.[172, 173] Some physicians speculate that *M. ulcerans* is a saprophytic or commensal organism that thrives in the mud, flora, or fauna of the cool microaerophilic environment of the bottom of stagnant water, well protected from the lethal ultraviolet radiation that prevails in the tropics. Koalas and possums in Australia acquire infections in the wild that are typical of Buruli ulcer.[148, 172]

Buruli ulcer rarely, if ever, is contagious. The distribution of patients, even in highly endemic foci, is random, thus suggesting that each patient is exposed to environmental sources, such as swamps where villagers work their gardens and obtain water for domestic use and especially where children play.

The mode or modes of transmission to humans have not yet been delineated completely; however, the most plausible route is by trauma at sites of skin recently contaminated by *M. ulcerans*.[144] Many patients give a history of specific antecedent penetrating trauma at the site of their initial lesion (e.g., wounds from a gunshot or land mine, thrown stones, or even hypodermic injection) (see Fig. 103–17). The organism may be spread by aerosol from the surface of ponds or be carried by fomites or insects to skin surfaces. Insects may introduce *M. ulcerans* into the skin, but this means of transmission has not been proved. Although proposed by some authorities, transmission by nasorespiratory passage with a subsequent bacteremia appears unlikely.

PATHOGENESIS AND PATHOLOGY

The pathologic features of early *M. ulcerans* infection are determined primarily by two properties of the etiologic agent: optimal growth at 30° C to 33° C and elaboration of a toxin. The temperature requirement tends to favor the development of lesions in skin, and the toxin destroys tissues and suppresses immune responses. The spectrum of clinical and histopathologic forms of infection suggests that some patients have innate resistance or resistance develops soon after infection, whereas others acquire resistance late or, occasionally, never.

A skin test with burulin, a purified sonicate of *M. ulcerans*, reveals that most patients do not have delayed-type hypersensitivity to *M. ulcerans* early in the infection but mount a cellular response as healing begins.[211] Very few studies have investigated the immunology of Buruli ulcer. *M. ulcerans* profoundly suppresses both B and T lymphocytes in vitro.[170] Mycolactone, a toxin of *M. ulcerans*, is thought to prevent sensitization of T lymphocytes to mycobacterial antigens and to inhibit production of TNF by monocytes and IL-2 by T lymphocytes.[67, 68, 165] These activities partly explain the immunologic unresponsiveness and reduced inflammatory reaction at the site of the lesion.

Based on the current understanding of the natural history of *M. ulcerans* infection, pathogenesis may proceed as follows: After inoculation of the etiologic agent deep into the skin or subcutaneous tissue, a latent phase occurs during which the mycobacterium proliferates slightly, possibly initially intracellularly, and begins to elaborate small amounts of toxin that causes necrosis, especially of fatty tissue. This necrosis provides a microaerophilic environment and perhaps nutrients favorable for the accelerated growth of *M. ulcerans* and elaboration of increased amounts of toxin. During this necrotic phase, no significant cellular response occurs.[28, 29, 42] In some patients, at this stage a subcutaneous nodule begins to develop with clusters of *M. ulcerans* in the center surrounded by a zone of necrosis. In highly resistant patients, this lesion may self-heal, perhaps without ulceration, or form a small, sharply delineated ulcer. In others, the skin is undermined by the necrosis and eventually breaks down into larger ulcers with widely undermined skin. In the least resistant individuals, a nodule never develops and the necrosis spreads rapidly and widely to cover large body surface areas, but ulceration, if it takes place at all, is a late event. Eventually, the necrotic stage ceases in most patients, either because the toxin is neutralized or because production is interrupted. At this time, a granulomatous stage begins to develop, followed by healing and scarring.

Microscopically, the active ulcer shows extensive coagulation necrosis of the subcutaneous tissue down to and often including the fascia. The deep layers of necrosis reveal masses of AFB, often with mineralization and extensive vasculitis. Marked edema is present, and fat cells enlarge and die, with only their cellular ghost outlines remaining.

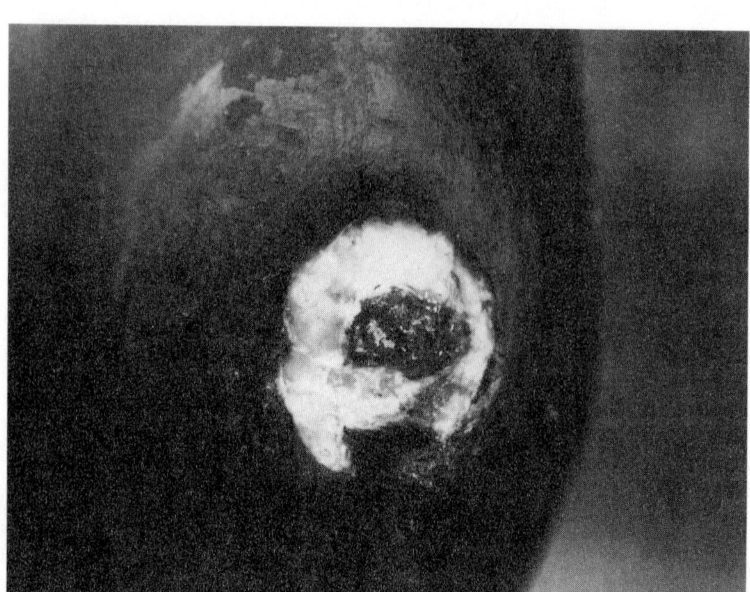

FIGURE 103–17 ■ *Mycobacterium ulcerans* infection in the deltoid area of a 12-year-old Angolan boy. This pristine ulcer developed 3 months after a hypodermic injection at this site. The ulcer is undermined with a necrotic base, along with induration of the adjacent skin (AFIP 76-11034-5).

The dermis and surrounding tissue seldom contain AFB. Lesions sometimes provoke a reactive (contiguous) osteitis that leads to necrosis of cortical bone and osteomyelitis. Metastatic lesions may develop in skin and bone from bacteremia and produce skin lesions distant from the original lesion and frequently focal or multifocal osteomyelitis. Regional lymph nodes may show massive necrosis and contain large numbers of AFB, especially in the capsule. Visceral organs are not known to be involved, but no necropsies of patients who died of disseminated disease have been reported.

CLINICAL MANIFESTATIONS

Incubation and Forms of Lesions

In one study of specific trauma related to lesions, the incubation period ranged from 2 weeks to 3 years, with a mean of 3 months.[144] The following are the various forms of lesions of *M. ulcerans* infection according to the WHO designations[241, 242]:

PAPULE. The papular stage has been described only in patients from Australia. These papules are painless and elevated and measure up to 1 cm in diameter.

NODULE. Nodules are primarily subcutaneous and firm, measure approximately 2 cm in diameter, and are painless, though often pruritic. The overlying skin may be discolored. This stage is the initial one in most Africans, and in the Kikongo language the disease is called "mputa matadi" because the nodule is a "rock-hard lesion."

PLAQUE. Plaques are firm, elevated, painless, well-defined lesions more than 2 cm in largest dimension. Their borders are irregular. This stage often is the one in which physicians initially see the patient, but the lesion may or may not arise from a nodule. The skin over the lesion is reddened or discolored. These lesions may ulcerate in the late stages.

EDEMATOUS FORM. Most edematous lesions do not begin in the nodular stage but spread directly from the initial nidus of infection. Spread often is rapid and wide and covers, for example, entire limbs or major portions of the trunk. This type of lesion is characterized by diffuse nonpitting swelling and vague margins. Lesions are firm and frequently painful, with color changes and scaling on the skin surface.

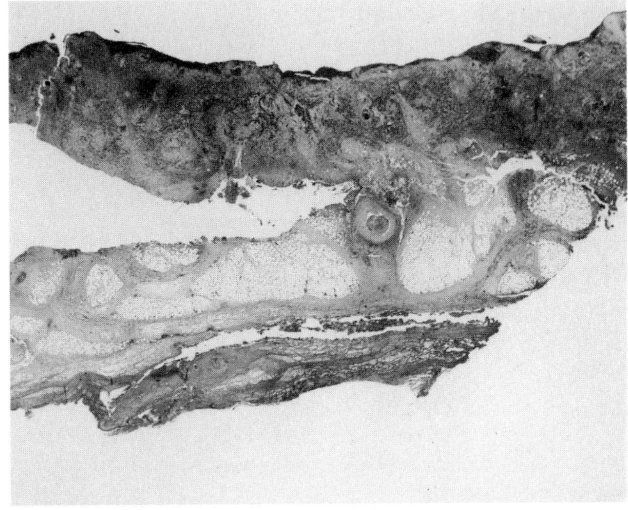

FIGURE 103–19 ■ Histopathologic section of the undermined edge of the ulcer in Figure 103–18. Note the coagulation necrosis of the entire panniculus and fascia, as well as vasculitis and thrombosis of a blood vessel (hematoxylin and eosin, ×7.5) (AFIP 95-5277).

ULCERATIVE FORMS. Classically, when fully developed, pristine ulcers have undermined edges surrounded by a zone of induration and often desquamation of the epidermis (Figs. 103–18 to 103–20). In the base of the ulcerated area, a whitish necrotic slough and sometimes eschar develop. An oily exudate frequently oozes from the dependent area (Fig. 103–21). Old ulcers tend to begin healing in the uppermost part while activity continues in the dependent portion. Collections of fluid in this area probably continue to support the growth of *M. ulcerans,* which sustains progression of the lesion.

The ulcerative forms are divided into *major* and *minor* ulcers. Both forms tend to self-heal. A major ulcer is large

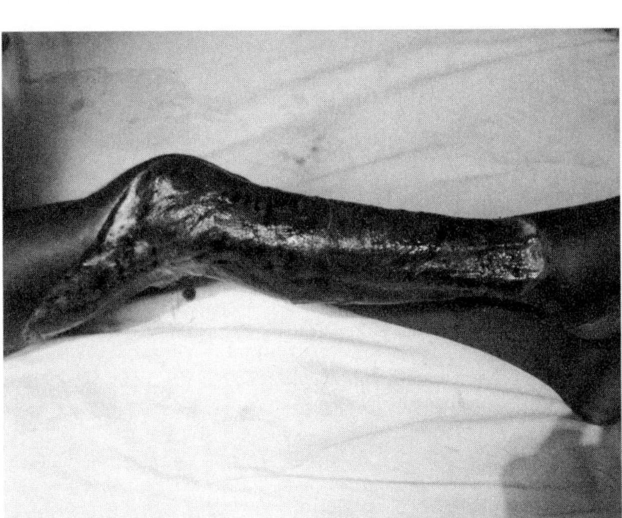

FIGURE 103–18 ■ A lesion of *Mycobacterium ulcerans* infection often involves large areas of the extremities. The lesion in this 9-year-old boy from Togo followed penetrating trauma and has been partially excised, but the disease remains active on the thigh.

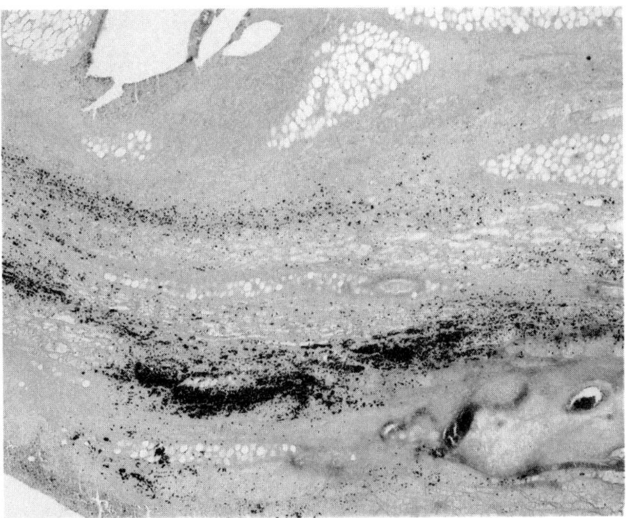

FIGURE 103–20 ■ Ziehl-Neelsen staining of the necrotic panniculus and fascia of a parallel section of Figure 103–19 reveals massive invasion by *Mycobacterium ulcerans* organisms (black clumps) (×30) (AFIP 95-5281).

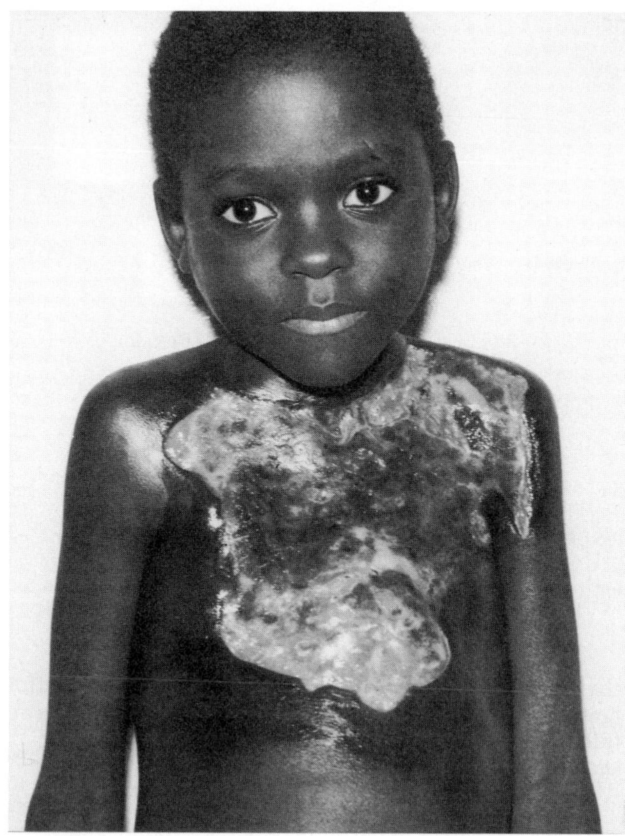

FIGURE 103–21 ■ Ulcerative lesion of *Mycobacterium ulcerans* infection in a girl. The center is scarring, but active disease is present at the edges, especially in dependent areas. Adequate treatment will require wide excision (AFIP 74-4472). (Photo by D. H. Connor.)

and chronic. Minor ulcers are small (1 to 2 cm in diameter), are sharply delineated, and heal early. Both ulcerative forms begin as subcutaneous nodules.

Bone Involvement

Reactive osteitis occasionally develops from destruction of the overlying skin and soft tissue. Bone becomes devitalized and necrotic, with the development of sequestra (Figs. 103–22 and 103–23).

M. ulcerans–specific osteomyelitis develops in approximately 10 percent of all patients. Most likely it is a result of metastatic spread of *M. ulcerans* from a distant, earlier cutaneous lesion (Fig. 103–24). The overlying skin ordinarily is intact, but swelling and inflammation occur over the site of bone involvement. If the condition goes untreated, a draining fistula usually develops. Osteomyelitis often results in amputation.

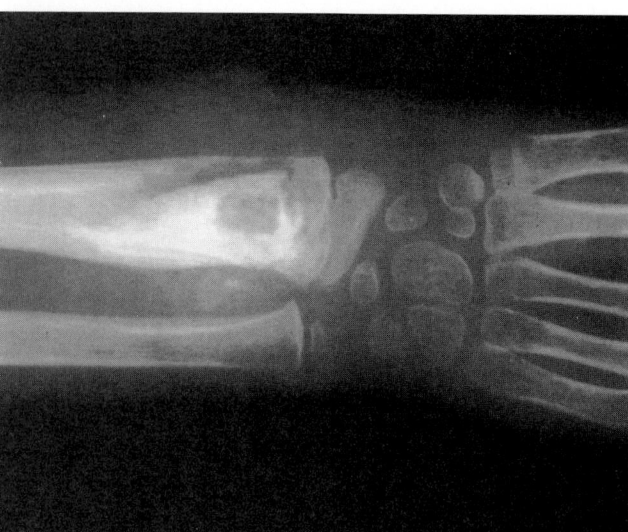

FIGURE 103–23 ■ Radiographic changes in bone underlying the lesion in Figure 103–22. Contiguous reactive osteitis and necrosis of the cortex of the distal end of the radius are present, along with early sequestration and osteomyelitis.

Complications

Infection may traverse the deep fascia and damage, for example, tendons, nerves, joints, genitalia, and periorbital tissues, with subsequent enucleation of the eye required. Healing leads to fibrosis and scarring. The scar may form keloids and often causes major contraction deformities, especially in lesions that cross joints (Fig. 103–25). Squamous

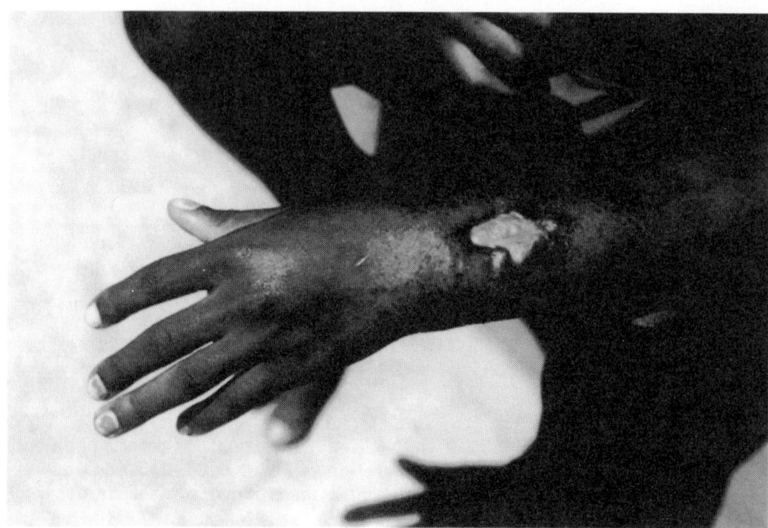

FIGURE 103–22 ■ Congolese boy with *Mycobacterium ulcerans* infection on his forearm. The deep tissues have been invaded, with the development of reactive osteitis. See Figure 103–23.

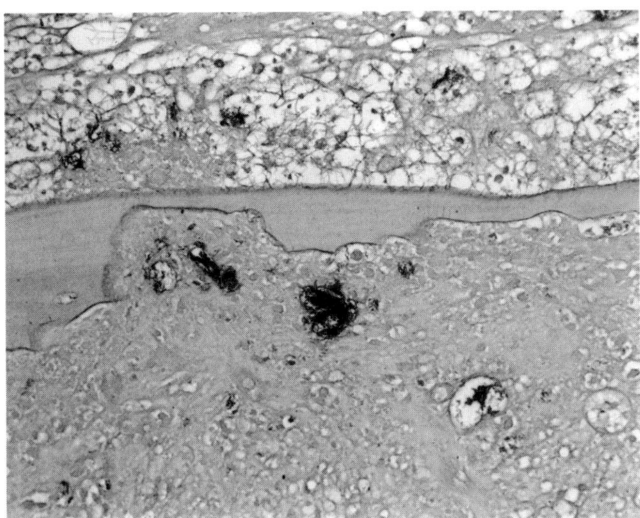

FIGURE 103–24 ■ Ziehl-Neelsen–stained section showing metastatic osteomyelitis of the tibia in a 5-year-old boy in Benin. The lesion developed after *Mycobacterium ulcerans* infection of the contralateral leg. Note the necrosis of marrow and erosion of a trabecula in the vicinity of clusters of *M. ulcerans* (black clumps) (×150).

cell carcinoma may develop in healed lesions, especially those that are nonpigmented. Skin grafting will prevent most of these complications.

Most disease-related deaths result from septicemia, gas gangrene, or tetanus.

DIAGNOSIS AND DIFFERENTIAL DIAGNOSIS

To an experienced observer, an accurate clinical diagnosis often can be made.[242, 243] In the ulcerated forms, a Ziehl-Neelsen stain of exudate from the undermined edge obtained with a cotton swab will reveal clusters of extracellular AFB. The same material, obtained by swab after decontamination, may be used for culture on Löwenstein-Jensen or other suitable mycobacterial media. The incubation temperature must be 30° C to 32° C. If culture cannot be performed locally, transport media may be inoculated with material from the cotton swab and maintained at 4° C while in transport to a specialized laboratory. The transport medium is composed of Middlebrook 7H9 broth supplemented with polymyxin B, amphotericin B, nalidixic acid, trimethoprim, azlocillin, and 0.5 percent agar. Molecular biologic analysis techniques consisting of PCR for the identification of *M. ulcerans* are available.[213] Tissue for histopathologic analysis should be obtained from the edge of the ulcer and must include all levels, including the fascia. Fixation in 4 percent buffered formalin is adequate.

The following are a few of the differential diagnostic possibilities:

- Papules—insect bites, verruca vulgaris, pityriasis, granuloma annulare
- Nodules—lipoma, sebaceous cyst, onchocerciasis, furuncle
- Plaques—leprosy, mycosis, necrobiosis, psoriasis
- Edema—bacterial cellulitis, actinomycosis, elephantiasis, pyomyositis
- Ulcers—tropical phagedenic ulcer, noma, stasis ulcer, leishmaniasis

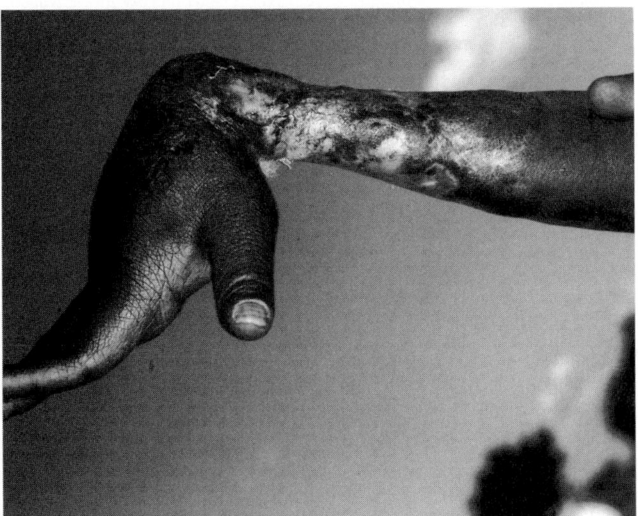

FIGURE 103–25 ■ Untreated but healed *Mycobacterium ulcerans* infection in a child. The circumferential constricting scar has caused a contraction deformity, subluxation of the wrist, and lymphedema of the hand (AFIP 65-2982). (Photo by D. H. Connor.)

PROGNOSIS

Without treatment, Buruli ulcer often leads to deforming depressed scars, contraction deformities, or amputation. The stigma of the deformities and the socioeconomic burden of the disease often are marked.[3] With early appropriate treatment, including excision and grafting, the prognosis usually is excellent. However, metastatic lesions and local recurrences occurs frequently enough to warrant vigilant follow-up.[1]

TREATMENT

In an attempt to minimize the danger of *M. ulcerans* bacteremia, antibiotics should be given before any surgical procedure is undertaken for active disease. Although treatment is not standardized, many surgeons prescribe clarithromycin and rifampin and have patients continue antibiotic therapy for several weeks after surgery.

Papules and pre-ulcerative nodules seldom are diagnosed, even in endemic areas; however, wide excision and primary closure usually are curative.[223]

Plaques and edematous forms are excised widely down to fascia or through the fascia if it is necrotic. Muscle usually is not damaged, but if so, the excision is extended into muscle. The lateral extent of excision often is difficult to determine. By careful palpation, the physician can establish an approximate limit of the disease. Exploratory incisions and blunt dissection may help determine the limit of induration and necrosis.

Very small ulcers can be excised and closed primarily, as for nodules. Large ulcers are excised widely. Again, the required extent of surgery may be determined by exploratory lateral excision and blunt dissection.

Split-skin autografting of surgical defects usually is performed after a bed of granulation tissue has formed. Postoperative care, including physiotherapy, should be designed to prevent contractures.

Bone lesions should be referred to specialists.

Heat therapy without surgical excision has been successful for appropriate lesions but must be applied assiduously with all necessary controls.[143]

PREVENTION

In an endemic tropical rural setting where children usually are scantily attired, prevention of contamination of the skin from environmental sources is virtually impossible. Wearing trousers seems to prevent development of infection.[124] Protected water supplies in villages would reduce exposure somewhat; however, such protective measures usually are futile in rural areas of developing countries.

Vaccination with BCG has a moderate protective effect against *M. ulcerans* infections for 6 to 12 months.[222] Studies are under way to determine whether repeated BCG vaccination may render the population more immune to *M. ulcerans* infection, as was found for leprosy.[108] Other vaccines based on virulence factors of *M. ulcerans* (e.g., the toxin) are being studied.

HUMAN IMMUNODEFICIENCY VIRUS AND BURULI ULCER

Because Buruli ulcer primarily is a disease of children in rural areas, very few patients have been reported with both Buruli ulcer and HIV infection. The few relevant reports available, however, indicate that HIV infection does not alter the course of treated Buruli ulcer disease.[2]

REFERENCES

1. Aguiar, J., and Steunou, C.: Les ulcères de Buruli en zone rurale au Bénin: Pris en charge de 635 cas. Med. Trop. (Mars.) *57*:83–90, 1997.
2. Allen, S.: Buruli ulcer and HIV infection. Int. J. Dermatol. *31*:744–745, 1992.
3. Asiedu, K., and Etuaful, S.: Socioeconomic implications of Buruli ulcer in Ghana; a three-year review. Am. J. Trop. Med. Hyg. *59*:1015–1022, 1998.
4. Bär, W., Rüsch-Gerdes, S., Richter, E., et al.: *Mycobacterium ulcerans* infection in a child from Angola: Diagnosis by direct detection and culture. Trop. Med. Int. Health *3*:189–196, 1998.
5. Barker, D. J. P., Clancey, J. K., and Rao, S. K.: Mycobacteria on vegetation in Uganda. East Afr. Med. J. *49*:667–671, 1972.
6. Barksdale, L., and Kim, K. S.: Mycobacterium. Bacteriol. Rev. *41*:217–372, 1977.
7. Bartels, P.: Tuberculose in der Jüngeren Steinzeit. Arch. Anthropol. *6*:243–255, 1907.
8. Bechelli, L. M., Gallego Garbajosa, P. G., Gyi, M. M., et al.: Site of early skin lesions in children with leprosy. Bull. World Health Organ. *48*:107–111, 1973.
9. Bechelli, L. M., Gallego Garbajosa, P. G., Gyi, M. M., et al.: BCG vaccination of children against leprosy: Seven-year findings of the controlled WHO trial in Burma. Bull. World Health Organ. *48*:323–334, 1973.
10. Becx-Bleuminck, M.: Operational aspects of multidrug therapy. Int. J. Lepr. *57*:540–551, 1989.
11. Bhatki, W. S., Chulawala, R. G., Bapat, C. V., et al.: Reversal reaction in lepromatous patients induced by a vaccine containing killed ICRC bacilli—A report of five cases. Int. J. Lepr. *51*:466–472, 1983.
12. Bhutani, L. K., Nath, I., Mehra, N. K., et al.: Grand round: Leprosy. Lancet *345*:697–703, 1995.
13. Binford, C. H., Meyers, W. M., and Walsh, G. P.: Leprosy: State of the art. J. A. M. A. *247*:2283–2292, 1982.
14. Binford, C. H., Meyers, W. M., Walsh, G. P., et al.: Naturally acquired leprosy-like disease in the nine-banded armadillo *(Dasypus novemcinctus)*: Histopathologic and microbiologic studies of tissues. J. Reticuloendothel. Soc. *22*:377–388, 1977.
15. Borgdorff, M. W., van den Broek, J., Chum, H. J., et al.: HIV-1 infection as a risk factor for leprosy; a case-control study in Tanzania. Int. J. Lepr. *61*:556–562, 1993.
16. Brody, S. N.: The Disease of the Soul. Leprosy in Medieval Literature. Ithaca, N.Y., Cornell University Press, 1974.
17. Browne, S. G.: Onchocercal depigmentation. Trans. R. Soc. Trop. Med. Hyg. *54*:325–334, 1960.
18. Brubaker, M. L., Meyers, W. M., and Bourland, J.: Leprosy in children one year of age and under. Int. J. Lepr. *53*:517–523, 1985.
19. Bullock, W. E.: Studies of the immune mechanism in leprosy. N. Engl. J. Med. *278*:298–304, 1968.
20. Bullock, W. E.: Rifampin in the treatment of leprosy. Rev. Infect. Dis. *5*(Suppl. 3):606–613, 1983.
21. Bullock, W. E., Ho, M. F., and Chen, M. J.: Studies of immune mechanisms in leprosy. II. Quantitative relationships of IgG, IgA, and IgM immunoglobulins. J. Lab. Clin. Med. *75*:863–870, 1970.
22. Bwire, R., and Kawuma, H. J. S.: Type 1 reactions in leprosy, neuritis and steroid therapy: The impact of the human immunodeficiency virus. Trans. R. Soc. Trop. Med. Hyg. *88*:315–316, 1994.
23. Byrd, S. R., Gelber, R., and Bermudez, L. E.: Roles of soluble fibronectin and β_1 integrin receptors in the binding of *Mycobacterium leprae* to nasal epithelial cells. Clin. Immunol. Immunopathol. *69*:266–271, 1993.
24. Cho, S. N., Chatterjee, D., and Brennan, P. J.: A simplified serological test for leprosy based on a 3,6-di-*O*-methylglucose–containing synthetic antigen. Am. J. Trop. Med. Hyg. *35*:167–172, 1986.
25. Clancey, J. K., Dodge, O. G., Lunn, H. F., et al.: Mycobacterial skin ulcers in Uganda. Lancet *2*:951–954, 1961.
26. Cochrane, R. G., and Davey, T.F. (eds.): Leprosy in Theory and Practice. 2nd ed. Bristol, England, John Wright & Sons, 1964.
27. Cole, S. T., Elglmeier, K., Parkhill, J., et al.: Massive gene decay in the leprosy bacillus. Nature *409*:1007–1011, 2001.
28. Connor, D. H., and Lunn, F.: Buruli ulceration: A clinicopathologic study of 38 Ugandans with *Mycobacterium ulcerans* infection. Arch. Pathol. *81*:183–189, 1966.
29. Connor, D. H., Meyers, W. M., and Krieg, R. E.: Infection by *Mycobacterium ulcerans*. *In* Binford, C. H., and Connor, D.H. (eds.): Pathology of Tropical and Extraordinary Diseases. An Atlas. Vol. 1. Washington, D.C., Armed Forces Institute of Pathology, 1976, pp. 226–235.
30. Convit, J., Aranzazu, N., Ulrich, M., et al.: Immunotherapy with a mixture of *Mycobacterium leprae* and BCG in different forms of leprosy and in Mitsuda-negative contacts. Int. J. Lepr. *50*:415–424, 1982.
31. Convit, J., Avila, J. L., Goihman, M., et al.: A test for the determination of competency in clearing bacilli in leprosy patients. Bull. World Health Organ. *46*:821–826, 1972.
32. Convit, J., and Pinardi, M. E.: A simple method for the differentiation of *Mycobacterium leprae* from other mycobacteria through routine staining technics. Int. J. Lepr. *40*:130–132, 1972.
33. Convit, J., Sampson, C., Zuniga, M., et al.: Immunoprophylactic trial with combined *Mycobacterium leprae*/BCG vaccine against leprosy: Preliminary results. Lancet *339*:446–450, 1992.
34. Cook, A.: Mengo Hospital Notes. Kampala, Uganda, Makerere Medical School Library, 1897. (Cited in B. M. J. *2*:37–379, 1970.)
35. Cree, I. A., Coghill, G., Subedi, A. M. C., et al.: Effects of treatment on the histopathology of leprosy. J. Clin. Pathol. *48*:304–307, 1995.
36. Daffe, M., Varnerot, A., and Levy-Frebault, V. V.: The phenolic mycoside of *Mycobacterium ulcerans*: Structure and taxonomic implications. J. Gen. Microbiol. *138*:131–137, 1992.
37. Davey, T. F., and Rees, R. J. W.: The nasal discharge in leprosy: Clinical and bacteriological aspects. Lepr. Rev. *45*:121–134, 1974.
38. Dayal, R., and Bharadwaj, V. P.: Prevention and early detection of leprosy in children. J. Trop. Pediatr. *41*:132–138, 1995.
39. de Rijk, A. J., Gabre, S., Byass, P., et al.: Field evaluation of WHO—MDT of fixed duration, at ALERT, Ethiopia: The AMFES project—II. Reaction and neuritis during and after MDT in PB and MB leprosy patients. Lepr. Rev. *65*:320–332, 1994.
40. de Wit, M. Y. L., Douglas, J. T., McFadden, J., et al.: Polymerase chain reaction for detection of *Mycobacterium leprae* in nasal swab specimens. J. Clin. Microbiol. *31*:502–506, 1993.
41. Dietrich, M., Gaus, W., Kern, P., et al.: An international randomized study with long-term follow-up of single versus combination chemotherapy of multibacillary leprosy. Antimicrob. Agents Chemother. *38*:2249–2257, 1994.
42. Dodge, O. G.: Mycobacterial skin ulcers in Uganda: Histopathological and experimental aspects. J. Pathol. Bacteriol. *88*:167–174, 1964.
43. Donham, K. J., and Leininger, J. R.: Spontaneous leprosy-like disease in a chimpanzee. J. Infect. Dis. *136*:132–136, 1977.
44. Drutz, D. J., Chen, T. S. N., and Lu, W. H.: The continuous bacteremia of lepromatous leprosy. N. Engl. J. Med. *287*:159–164, 1972.
45. Duncan, M. E.: Babies of mothers with leprosy have small placentae, low birth weights and grow slowly. Br. J. Obstet. Gynaecol. *87*:471–479, 1980.
46. Duncan, M. E., Melsom, R., Pearson, J. M. H., et al.: A clinical and immunological study of four babies of mothers with lepromatous leprosy, two of whom developed leprosy in infancy. Int. J. Lepr. *51*:7–17, 1983.
47. Duncan, M. E., and Oakey, R. E.: Estrogen excretion in pregnant women with leprosy: Evidence of diminished fetoplacental function. Obstet. Gynecol. *60*:82–86, 1982.
48. Dwyer, J. M., Bullock, W. E., and Fields, J. P.: Disturbances of the blood; T:B lymphocyte ratio in lepromatous leprosy. N. Engl. J. Med. *288*:1036–1039, 1973.
49. Ellard, G. A.: Rationale of the multidrug regimens recommended by a World Health Organization Study Group on Chemotherapy of Leprosy for Control Programs. Int. J. Lepr. *52*:395–401, 1984.
50. Faber, W. R., Pereira Arias-Bouda, L. M., Zeegelaar, J. E., et al.: First reported case of *Mycobacterium ulcerans* infection in a patient from China. Trans. R. Soc. Trop. Med. Hyg. *94*:277–279, 2000.
51. Faget, G. H., Pogge, R. C., Johansen, F. A., et al.: The Promin treatment of leprosy: A progress report. Public Health Rep. *58*:1729–1741, 1943.
52. Fajardo, T. T., Abalos, R. M., dela Cruz, E. C., et al.: Clofazimine therapy for lepromatous leprosy: A historical perspective. Int. J. Dermatol. *38*: 70–74, 1999.
53. Farb, H., West, D. P., and Pedvis-Leftick, A.: Clofazimine in pregnancy complicated by leprosy. Obstet. Gynecol. *59*:122–123, 1982.

54. Feldman, R. A., and Sturdivant, M.: Leprosy in Louisiana 1855–1970. An epidemiologic study of long-term trends. Am. J. Epidemiol. *102*:303–310, 1975.
55. Fiallo, P., Williams, D. L., Chan, G. P., et al.: Effects of fixation on polymerase chain reaction detection of *Mycobacterium leprae*. J. Clin. Microbiol. *30*:3095–3098, 1992.
56. Fine, P. E. M., and Warndorff, D. K.: Leprosy by the year 2000—What is being eliminated? Lepr. Rev. *68*:201–202, 1997.
57. Flaguel, B., Wallach, D., Vignon-Pennamen, M., et al.: Late onset of reversal reaction in borderline leprosy. J. Am. Acad. Dermatol. *20*:857–860, 1989.
58. Fritschi, E. P.: Reconstructive Surgery in Leprosy. Bristol, England, John Wright & Sons, 1971.
59. Gajl-Peczalska, K. J., Lim, S. D., Jacobson, R. R., et al.: B lymphocytes in lepromatous leprosy. N. Engl. J. Med. *288*:1033–1035, 1973.
60. Gatt, P.: The Malta experience. 1972–1992: 20 years after starting the eradication project in Malta. Int. J. Lepr. *61*:304, 1993.
61. Gaylord, H., and Brennan, P. J.: Leprosy and the leprosy bacillus: Recent developments in characterization of antigens and immunology of the disease. Annu. Rev. Microbiol. *41*:645–675, 1987.
62. Gehr, E.: Leprosy in childhood. Doc. Med. Geog. Trop. *9*:101–124, 1957.
63. Gelber, R. H., Drutz, D. J., Epstein, W. V., et al.: Clinical correlates of C1q-precipitating substances in the sera of patients with leprosy. Am. J. Trop. Med. Hyg. *23*:471–475, 1974.
64. Gelber, R. H., Fukuda, K., Byrd, S., et al.: A clinical trial of minocycline in lepromatous leprosy. B. M. J. *304*:91–92, 1992.
65. Gelber, R. H., Mehra, V., Bloom, B., et al.: Vaccination with pure *Mycobacterium leprae* proteins inhibits *M. leprae* multiplication in mouse footpads. Infect. Immun. *62*:4250–4255, 1994.
66. Gelber, R. H., Murray, L. P., Siu, P., et al.: Efficacy of minocycline in single dose and at 100 mg twice daily for lepromatous leprosy. Int. J. Lepr. *62*:568–573, 1994.
67. George, K. M., Barker, L. P., Welty, D. M., et al.: Partial purification and characterization of biological effects of a lipid toxin produced by *Mycobacterium ulcerans*. Infect. Immun. *66*:587–593, 1998.
68. George, K. M., Chatterjee, D., Gunawardana, G., et al.: Mycolactone: A polyketide toxin from *Mycobacterium ulcerans* required for virulence. Science *283*:854–857, 1999.
69. Girdhar, B. K., Girdhar, A., Ramu, G., et al.: Borderline leprosy (BL) in an infant: Report of a case and a brief review. Lepr. India *55*:333–337, 1983.
70. Godal, R.: Growing points in leprosy research. (3) Immunological detection of sub-clinical infection in leprosy. Lepr. Rev. *45*:22–30, 1974.
71. Gomez, A., Mve-Obiang, A., Vray, B., et al.: Detection of phospholipase C (PLC) in nontuberculous mycobacteria and its possible role in hemolytic activity. J. Clin. Microbiol. *39*:1396–1401, 2001.
72. Gonzalez-Abreu, E., Mora, N., Perez, M., et al.: Serodiagnosis of leprosy in patients' contacts by enzyme-linked immunosorbent assay. Lepr. Rev. *61*:145–150, 1990.
73. Gormus, B. J., Xu, K., Alford, P. L., et al.: A serologic study of naturally-acquired leprosy in chimpanzees. Int. J. Lepr. *59*:450–457, 1991.
74. Grant, A. M. B.: Leprosy at Nauru since 1928. Int. J. Lepr. *2*:305–310, 1934.
75. Grosset, J. H.: Progress in the chemotherapy of leprosy. Int. J. Lepr. *62*:268–277, 1994.
76. Guinto, R. S., Doull, J. A., and Mabalay, E. B.: The Mitsuda reaction in persons with and without household exposure to leprosy. Int. J. Lepr. *23*:135–138, 1955.
77. Gupte, M. D., Anantharaman, D. S., Nagaraju, B., et al.: Experiences with *Mycobacterium leprae* soluble antigens in a leprosy endemic population. Lepr. Rev. *61*:132–144, 1990.
78. Harboe, M.: The work and concepts of Armauer Hansen: How do they stand today? Ethiop. Med. J. *21*:123–126, 1983.
79. Harboe, M.: The immunology of leprosy. *In* Hastings, R. C. (ed.): Leprosy (Medicine in the Tropics Series). Edinburgh, Churchill Livingstone, 1985, pp. 53–87.
80. Haregewoin, A. T., Godal, T., Mustafa, A. S., et al.: T-cell conditioned media reverse T-cell unresponsiveness in lepromatous leprosy. Nature *303*:342–344, 1983.
81. Hastings, R. C., Morales, M. J.: Observations, calculations, and speculations on the growth and death of *M. leprae* in vivo. Int. J. Lepr. *50*:579–582, 1982.
82. Hayman, J.: Clinical features of *Mycobacterium ulcerans* infection. Aust. J. Dermatol. *26*:67–73, 1985.
83. Hiltaharjee, A., Croft, R., Alam, R., et al.: Chronic neurotrophic pain in treated leprosy. Lancet *356*:1080–1081, 2000.
84. Horsburg, C. R., Jr., and Meyers, W. M.: Buruli ulcer. *In* Horsburgh, C. R., Jr., and Nelson, A. M. (eds.): Pathology of Emerging Infections. Washington, D.C., American Society for Microbiology, 1997, pp. 119–134.
85. Horwitz, M. A., Levis, W. R., and Cohn, Z. A.: Defective production of monocyte-activating cytokines in lepromatous leprosy. J. Exp. Med. *159*:666–678, 1984.
86. Hunter, S. W., Fujiwara, T., and Brennan, P. J.: Structure and antigenicity of the major specific glycolipid antigen of *Mycobacterium leprae*. J. Biol. Chem. *257*:15072–15078, 1982.
87. Hussain, R., Lucas, S. B., Kifayet, A., et al.: Clinical and histological discrepancies in diagnosis of ENL reactions classified by assessment of acute phase proteins SAA and CRP. Int. J. Lepr. *63*:222–230, 1995.
88. Imkamp, F. M. J. H.: Clofazimine (Lamprene or B663) in lepra reactions. Lepr. Rev. *52*:135–140, 1981.
89. Inaba, T.: Ueber die Histopathologischen und Bakteriologischen Untersuchungen der Plazenta bei Leprosen. La Lepro. *9*(Suppl. III), 1938.
90. Izumi, S., Fujiwara, T., Ikeda, M., et al.: Novel gelatin particle agglutination test for serodiagnosis of leprosy in the field. J. Clin. Microbiol. *28*:525–529, 1990.
91. Jacobson, R. R.: Carville and Hansen's disease control: Past, present and future. Int. J. Lepr. *63*:272–273, 1995.
92. Jacobson, R. R., and Hastings, R. C.: Rifampin-resistant leprosy. Lancet *2*:1304–1305, 1976.
93. Jakeman, P.: Risk of relapse in multibacillary leprosy. Lancet *345*:4–5, 1995.
94. Jamet, P., Ji, B., and the Marchoux Chemotherapy Study Group: Relapse after long-term follow up of multibacillary patients treated by WHO multidrug regimen. Int. J. Lepr. *63*:195–201, 1995.
95. Janssen, F., Wallach, D., Khuong, M. A., et al.: Association de maladie de Hansen et d'infection par le virus de l'immunodéficience humaine. Deux observations. Presse Med. *17*:1652–1653, 1988.
96. Ji, B., Jamet, P., Perani, E. G., et al.: Powerful bactericidal activities of clarithromycin and minocycline against *Mycobacterium leprae* in lepromatous leprosy. J. Infect. Dis. *168*:188–190, 1993.
97. Job, C. K.: The Kellersberger Memorial Lecture, 1983. The lepromin test and its role in the management of leprosy. Ethiop. Med. J. *21*:233–242, 1983.
98. Job, C. K., and Chacko, C. J. G.: A simplified 6 group classification of leprosy. Lepr. India *54*:26–32, 1982.
99. Job, C. K., Harris, E. B., Allen, J. L., et al.: A random survey of leprosy in wild nine-banded armadillos in Louisiana. Int. J. Lepr. *54*:453–457, 1986.
100. Johnstone, P. A. S., Meyers, W. M., Binford, C. H., et al.: Recent advances in the development of nonhuman primates as animal models for leprosy. Scand. J. Lab. Anim. Sci. *16*(Suppl. 1):102–105, 1989.
101. Jopling, W. H.: Handbook of Leprosy. London, William Heinemann, 1984.
102. Jopling, W. H., Ridley, M. J., Bonnici, E., et al.: A followup investigation of the Malta project. Lepr. Rev. *55*:247–253, 1984.
103. Kaplan, G.: Recent advances in cytokine therapy of leprosy. J. Infect. Dis. *167*(Supp):18–22, 1993.
104. Kaplan, G., Mathur, N. K., Job, C. K., et al.: Effect of multiple interferon-γ injections on the disposal of *Mycobacterium leprae*. Proc. Natl. Acad. Sci. U. S. A. *86*:8073–8077, 1989.
105. Kaplan, G., Sampaio, E. P., Walsh, G. P., et al.: Influence of *Mycobacterium leprae* and its soluble products on the cutaneous responsiveness of leprosy patients to antigen and recombinant interleukin 2. Proc. Natl. Acad. Sci. U. S. A. *86*:6269–6273, 1989.
106. Kar, H. K., Bhatia, V. N., and Harikrishnan, S.: Combined clofazimine- and dapsone-resistant leprosy: A case report. Int. J. Lepr. *54*:389–391, 1986.
107. Kar, H. K., Sharma, A. K., Misra, R. S., et al.: Reversal reaction in multibacillary leprosy patients following MDT with and without immunotherapy with a candidate for an antileprosy vaccine, *Mycobacterium w*. Lepr. Rev. *64*:219–226, 1993.
108. Karonga Prevention Trial Group: Randomised controlled trial of single BCG, repeated BCG, or combined BCG and killed *Mycobacterium leprae* vaccine for prevention of leprosy and tuberculosis in Malawi. Lancet *348*:17–24, 1996.
109. Kashala, O., Marlink, R., Ilunga, M., et al.: Infection with human immunodeficiency virus type 1 (HIV-1) and human T cell lymphotropic viruses among leprosy patients and contacts: Correlation between HIV-1 cross-reactivity and antibodies to lipoarabinomannan. J. Infect. Dis. *169*:296–304, 1994.
110. Kato, L.: Leprosy associated mycobacteria: Implications. Acta Leprol. *7*:1–6, 1989.
111. Kaur, I., Kaur, S., Sharma, V. K., et al.: Bacillaemia and *Mycobacterium leprae* cell wall antigen in paucibacillary leprosy. Indian J. Lepr. *65*:283–288, 1993.
112. Kawuma, H. J. S., Bwire, R., and Adatu-Engwau, F.: Leprosy and infection with the human immunodeficiency virus in Uganda; a case-control study. Int. J. Lepr. *62*:521–526, 1994.
113. Khanolkar Young, S., Rayment, N., Brickell, P. M., et al.: Tumour necrosis factor-alpha (TNF-α) synthesis is associated with the skin and peripheral nerve pathology of leprosy reversal reactions. Clin. Exp. Immunol. *99*:196–202, 1995.
114. Lamfers, E. J., Bastiaans, A. H., Mravunac, M., et al.: Leprosy in the acquired immunodeficiency syndrome. Ann. Intern. Med. *107*:111–112, 1987.
115. Languillon, J., and Carayon, A.: Précis de Léprologie. Paris, Masson, 1969.
116. Lara, C. B.: Leprosy in children. General considerations: Initial and early changes. Philipp. J. Lepr. *1*:22–57, 1966.

117. Latapi, F., and Zamora, A. C.: The "spotted" leprosy of Lucio: An introduction to its clinical and histological study. Int. J. Lepr. *16*:421–429, 1948.
118. Lechat, M. F.: Global evaluation of the introduction of multidrug therapy. Leprosy Epidemiology Bulletin No. 4. Brussels, Belgium, World Health Organization Collaborating Center for the Epidemiology of Leprosy, January 1990.
119. Leiker, D. L.: On the mode of transmission of *Mycobacterium leprae*. Lepr. Rev. *48*:9–16, 1977.
120. Leprosy News and Notes: Fifth International Leprosy Congress—1948. The words "leper" and "leprosy." Int. J. Lepr. *16*:243, 1948.
121. Lucas, S. B.: Human immunodeficiency virus and leprosy. Lepr. Rev. *64*:97–103, 1993.
122. Lumpkin, L. R., III, Cox, F., and Wolf, J. E., Jr.: Leprosy in five armadillo handlers. J. Am. Acad. Dermatol. *9*:899–903, 1983.
123. MacCallum, P., Tolhurst, J. C., Buckle, G., and Sissons, H. A.: A new mycobacterial infection in man. J. Pathol. Bacteriol. *60*:93–122, 1948.
124. Marston, B. J., Diallo, M. O., Horsburgh, C. R., Jr., et al.: Emergence of Buruli ulcer disease in the Daloa region of Côte d'Ivoire. Am. J. Trop. Med. Hyg. *52*:219–224, 1995.
125. Mathur, N. K., Pasricha, J. S., Pal, D., et al.: Comparison of cutaneous autonomic and somatic nervous functions in the lesions of leprosy. Int. J. Lepr. *39*:146–150, 1971.
126. McAdam, K. P. W. J., Anders, R. F., Smith, S. R., et al.: Association of amyloidosis with erythema nodosum leprosum reactions and recurrent neutrophil leucocytosis in leprosy. Lancet *2*:572–576, 1975.
127. McCoy, W.: History of leprosy in the United States. Am. J. Trop. Med. *18*:19–34, 1938.
128. McDougall, A. C., and Waudby, H.: Dermal microfilariasis and leprosy. Lepr. Rev. *48*:161–168, 1977.
129. Meeran, K.: Prevalence of HIV infection among patients with leprosy and tuberculosis in rural Zambia. B. M. J. *298*:364–365, 1989.
130. Mehra, V., Brennan, P. J., Rada, E., et al.: Lymphocyte suppression in leprosy induced by unique *M. leprae* glycolipid. Nature *308*:194–196, 1984.
131. Mehra, V., Mason, L. H., Rothman, W., et al.: Delineation of a human T-cell subset responsible for lepromin-induced suppression in leprosy patients. J. Immunol. *125*:1183–1188, 1980.
132. Melancon-Kaplan, J., Hunter, S. W., McNeil, M., et al.: Immunologic 0significance of *Mycobacterium leprae* cell walls. Proc. Natl. Acad. Sci. U. S. A. *85*:1917–1921, 1988.
133. Melsom, R., Harboe, M., and Duncan, M. E.: IgA, IgM and IgG anti-*M. leprae* antibodies in babies of leprosy mothers during the first two years of life. Clin. Exp. Immunol. *49*:532–542, 1982.
134. Melsom, R., Harboe, M., Duncan, M. E., et al.: IgA and IgM antibodies against *Mycobacterium leprae* in cord sera and in patients with leprosy: An indication of intrauterine infection in leprosy. Scand. J. Immunol. *14*:343–352, 1981.
135. Meyers, W. M.: Mycobacterial infections of the skin. *In* Doerr, W., and Seifert, G. (eds.): Tropical Pathology. 2nd ed. Berlin, Springer-Verlag, 1995, pp. 291–377.
136. Meyers, W. M., Binford, C. H., Walsh, G. P., et al.: Animal models of leprosy. *In* Leive, L., and Schlessinger, D. (eds.): Microbiology—1984. Washington, D.C., American Society for Microbiology, 1984, pp. 307–311.
137. Meyers, W. M., Connor, D. H., Harman, L. E., et al.: Human streptocerciasis: A clinico-pathologic study of 40 Africans (Zairians), including identification of the adult filaria. Am. J. Trop. Med. Hyg. *21*:528–545, 1972.
138. Meyers, W. M., Gormus, B. J., and Walsh, G. P.: Nonhuman sources of leprosy. Int. J. Lepr. *60*:477–481, 1992.
139. Meyers, W. M., Gormus, B. J., and Walsh, G. P.: Experimental leprosy. *In* Hastings, R. C. (ed.): Leprosy. 2nd ed (Medicine in the Tropics Series). Edinburgh, Churchill Livingstone, 1994, pp. 385–408.
140. Meyers, W. M., Gormus, B. J., Walsh, G. P., et al.: Naturally acquired and experimental leprosy in nonhuman primates. Am. J. Trop. Med. Hyg. *44*(Suppl.):24–27, 1991.
141. Meyers, W. M., Kvernes, S., and Binford, C. H.: Comparison of reactions to human and armadillo lepromins in leprosy. Int. J. Lepr. *43*:218–225, 1975.
142. Meyers, W. M., McDougall, A. C., Fleury, R. H., et al.: Histologic responses in sixty multibacillary leprosy patients inoculated with *Mycobacterium leprae* and live BCG. Int. J. Lepr. *56*:302–309, 1988.
143. Meyers, W. M., Shelly, W. M., and Connor, D. H.: Heat treatment of *Mycobacterium ulcerans* infections without surgical excision. Am. J. Trop. Med. Hyg. *23*:924–929, 1974.
144. Meyers, W. M., Shelly, W. M., Connor, D. H., et al.: *Mycobacterium ulcerans* infections developing at the sites of trauma to skin. Am. J. Trop. Med. Hyg. *23*:919–923, 1974.
145. Meyers, W. M., Tignokpa, N., Priuli, G. B., et al.: *Mycobacterium ulcerans* infection (Buruli ulcer): First reported patients from Togo. Br. J. Dermatol. *134*:1116–1121, 1996.
146. Meyers, W. M., Walsh, G. P., Brown, H. L., et al.: Naturally acquired leprosy-like disease in the nine-banded armadillo *(Dasypus novemcinctus)*: Reactions in leprosy patients to lepromins prepared from naturally infected armadillos. J. Reticuloendothel. Soc. *22*:369–375, 1977.
147. Meyers, W. M., Walsh, G. P., Brown, H. L., et al.: Leprosy in a mangabey monkey: Naturally acquired infection. Int. J. Lepr. *53*:1–14, 1985.
148. Mitchell, P. J., Jerrett, I. V., and Slee, K. J.: Skin ulcers caused by *Mycobacterium ulcerans* in koalas near Bairnsdale, Australia. Pathology *16*:256–260, 1984.
149. Mitsuda, K.: On the value of a skin reaction to a suspension of leprous nodules. Hifuka Hinyoka Zasshi (Jpn. J. Dermatol. Urol.) *19*:697–708, 1919. In Japanese. English translation in Int. J. Lepr. *21*:347–358, 1953.
150. Modlin, R. L., Gebhard, J. F., Taylor, C. R., et al.: In situ characterization of T-lymphocyte subsets in the reactional states of leprosy. Clin. Exp. Immunol. *53*:17–24, 1983.
151. Modlin, R. L., Hoffman, F. M., Horowitz, D. A., et al.: In situ identification of cells in human leprosy granulomas with monoclonal antibodies to interleukin-2 and its receptor. J. Immunol. *132*:3085–3090, 1984.
152. Modlin, R. L., Hoffman, F. M., Taylor, C. R., et al.: T lymphocyte subsets in the skin lesions of patients with leprosy. J. Am. Acad. Dermatol. *8*:182–189, 1983.
153. Modlin, R. L., Melancon-Kaplan, J., Young, S. M. M., et al.: Learning from lesions: Patterns of tissue inflammation in leprosy. Proc. Natl. Acad. Sci. U. S. A. *85*:1213–1217, 1988.
154. Moran, C. A., Nelson, A. M., Tuur, S. M., et al.: Leprosy in five human immunodeficiency virus–infected patients. Mod. Pathol. *8*:662–664, 1995.
155. Mourit, A. A. M.: The Path of the Destroyer. A History of Leprosy in the Hawaiian Islands. Honolulu, Honolulu Star-Bulletin, 1916.
156. Muir, E.: Juvenile leprosy. Int. J. Lepr. *4*:45–48, 1936.
157. Mukherjee, A., Meyers, W. M.: Endothelial cell bacillation in lepromatous leprosy: A case report. Lepr. Rev. *58*:419–424, 1987.
158. Myrvang, B., Godal, T., Ridley, D. S., et al.: Immune responsiveness to *Mycobacterium leprae* and other mycobacterial antigens throughout the clinical and histopathological spectrum of leprosy. Clin. Exp. Immunol. *14*:541–553, 1973.
159. Navalkar, R. G., Norlin, M., and Ouchterlony, O.: Characterization of leprosy sera with various mycobacterial antigens using double diffusion-in-gel analysis. Int. Arch. Allergy *28*:250–260, 1965.
160. Nery, J. A. C., Perissé, A. R. S., Sales, A. M., et al.: The use of pentoxifylline in the treatment of type 2 reactional episodes in leprosy. Indian J. Lepr. *72*:457–467, 2000.
161. Nogueira, N., Kaplan, G., Levy, E., et al.: Defective γ-interferon production in leprosy. Reversal with antigen and interleukin-2. J. Exp. Med. *158*:2165–2170, 1983.
162. Noussitou, F. M.: Leprosy in Children. Geneva, World Health Organization, 1976.
163. Olcen, P., Harboe, M., Warndorff, T., et al.: Antigens of *M. leprae* and anti-*M. leprae* antibodies in the urine of leprosy patients. Lepr. Rev. *54*:203–216, 1983.
164. Ottenhoff, T. H. M.: State of the Art Lectures: Immunology of leprosy: Lessons from and for leprosy. Int. J. Lepr. *62*:108–121, 1994.
165. Pahlaven, A., Wright, D. J. M., Andrews, C., et al.: The inhibitory action of *Mycobacterium ulcerans* soluble factor on monocyte/T cell cytokine production and NFκB function. J. Immunol. *163*:3928–3935, 1999.
166. Palomino, J. C., Obiang, A. M., Realini, L., et al.: Effect of oxygen on *Mycobacterium ulcerans* growth in the BACTEC system. J. Clin. Microbiol. *36*:3420–3422, 1998.
167. Park, J. Y., Cho, S. N., Youn, J. K., et al.: Detection of antibodies to human nerve antigens in sera from leprosy patients by ELISA. Clin. Exp. Immunol. *87*:368–372, 1992.
168. Parkash, O. M., Chaturvedi, V., Girdhar, B. K., et al.: A study on performance of two serological assays for diagnosis of leprosy patients. Lepr. Rev. *66*:26–30, 1995.
169. Pedley, J. C.: The presence of *M. leprae* in human milk. Lepr. Rev. *38*:239–242, 1967.
170. Pimsler, M., Sponsler, T. A., and Meyers, W. M.: Immunosuppressive properties of the soluble toxin from *Mycobacterium ulcerans*. J. Infect. Dis. *157*:577–580, 1988.
171. Portaels, F.: Contribution a l'étude des mycobactéries de l'environment au Bas-Zaire. Ann. Soc. Belge Med. Trop. *53*:373–387, 1973.
172. Portaels, F., Chemlal, K., Elsen, P., et al.: *Mycobacterium ulcerans* in wild animals. Rev. Sci. Tech. Off. Int. Epiz. *20*:252–264, 2001.
173. Portaels, F., Elsen, P., Guimaraes-Peres, A., et al.: Insects in the transmission of *Mycobacterium ulcerans* infection (Buruli ulcer). Lancet *353*:986, 1999.
174. Portaels, F., Fonteyne, P. A., De Beenhouwer, H., et al.: Variability of 3′ end of 16S rRNA sequence of *Mycobacterium ulcerans* is related to geographic origin of isolates. J. Clin. Microbiol. *34*:962–965, 1996.
175. Prasad, H. K., Mishra, R. S., and Nath, I.: Phenolic glycolipid-I of *Mycobacterium leprae* induces general suppression of in vitro concanavalin A responses unrelated to leprosy type. J. Exp. Med. *165*:239–244, 1987.
176. Rambukkana, A., Yamada, H., Zanazzi, G., et al.: Role of α-dystroglycan as a Schwann cell receptor for *M. leprae*. Science *282*:2076–2079, 1998.
177. Rangdaeng, S., Scollard, D. M., Suriyanon, V., et al.: Studies of human leprosy lesions in situ using suction-induced blisters. 1. Cellular components of new, uncomplicated lesions. Int. J. Lepr. *57*:492–498, 1989.

178. Rea, T. H., Bakke, A. C., Parker, J. W., et al.: Peripheral blood T lymphocyte subsets in leprosy. Int. J. Lepr. *52*:311–317, 1984.
179. Read, R. G., Heggie, C. M., Meyers, W. M., et al.: Cytotoxic activity of *Mycobacterium ulcerans*. Infect. Immun. *9*:1114–1122, 1974.
180. Recommendations of the International Task Force for Disease Eradication. M. M. W. R. Recomm. Rep. *42*(RR-16):1–38, 1993.
181. Rees, R. J. W., and McDougall, A. C.: Airborne infection with *Mycobacterium leprae* in mice. J. Med. Microbiol. *10*:63–68, 1977.
182. Revill, W. D. L., and Barker, D. J. P.: Seasonal distribution of mycobacterial skin ulcers. Br. J. Prev. Soc. Med. *26*:23–27, 1972.
183. Ridley, D. S.: Skin Biopsy in Leprosy. 2nd ed. Basel, Geigy, 1985.
184. Ridley, D. S., and Jopling, W. H.: Classification of leprosy according to immunity. A five-group system. Int. J. Lepr. *34*:255–273, 1966.
185. Roche, P. W., Theuvenet, W. L., and Britton, W. J.: Risk factors for type-1 reactions in borderline leprosy patients. Lancet *338*:654–657, 1991.
186. Rogall, T. J., Wolters, J., Flohr, T., et al.: Towards a phylogeny and definition of species at the molecular level within the genus *Mycobacterium*. Int. J. Syst. Bacteriol. *40*:323–330, 1990.
187. Rojas-Espinosa, O., and Løvik, M.: *Mycobacterium leprae* and *Mycobacterium lepraemurium* in domestic and wild animals. Rev. Sci. Tech. Off. Int. Epiz. *20*:219–251, 2001.
188. Rook, G. A. W.: The immunology of leprosy. Tubercle *64*:297–312, 1983.
189. Ross, B. C., Johnson, P. D. R., Oppedisano, F., et al.: Detection of *Mycobacterium ulcerans* in environmental samples during an outbreak of ulcerative disease. Appl. Environ. Microbiol. *63*:4135–4138, 1997.
190. Ross, B. C., Marino, L., Oppedisano, F., et al.: Development of a PCR assay for rapid diagnosis of *Mycobacterium ulcerans* infection. J. Clin. Microbiol. *35*:1696–1700, 1997.
191. Ruffer, M. A.: Pott'sche Krankeit an Einer Ägyptischen Mumie aus der Zeit der 21 Dynastie (um 1000 v. Chr.). Zur Historischen Biol. d. Krankheitserreger. Vol. 3. Topelmann, Giessen, 1910, pp. 9–16.
192. Ryrie, G. A.: Some impressions of Sungei Buloh Leper Hospital under Japanese occupation. Lepr. Rev. *18*:10–17, 1947.
193. Sabin, T. D., Swift, T. R., and Jacobson, R. R.: Leprosy. *In* Dyck, P. J., Thomas, P. K., Griffin, I. W., et al. (eds.): Peripheral Neuropathy. Vol. 2. Philadelphia, W. B. Saunders, 1993, pp. 1354–1379.
194. Sampaio, E. P., Caneshi, J. R. T., Nery, J. A. C., et al.: Cellular immune response to *Mycobacterium leprae* infection in human immunodeficiency virus–infected individuals. Infect. Immun. *63*:1848–1854, 1995.
195. Sarno, E. N., Grau, G. E., Vieira, L. M. M., et al.: Serum levels of tumor necrosis factor-alpha and interleukin-1B during leprosy reactional states. Clin. Exp. Immunol. *84*:103–108, 1991.
196. Saul, A., and Novales, J.: La lèpre de Lucio-Latapi et le phénomène de Lucio. Acta Leprol. *92*:115–132, 1983.
197. Schlesinger, L. S., and Horwitz, M. A.: Complement receptors and complement component C3 mediate phagocytosis of *Mycobacterium tuberculosis* and *Mycobacterium leprae*. Int. J. Lepr. *58*:200–201, 1990.
198. Scollard, D. M.: Endothelial cells and the pathogenesis of lepromatous neuritis: Insights from the armadillo model. Microbes Infect. 2:1835–1843, 2000.
199. Scollard, D. M., McCormick, G., and Allen, J. L.: Localization of *Mycobacterium leprae* to endothelial cells of epineural and perineural blood vessels and lymphatics. Am. J. Pathol. *154*:1611–1620, 1999.
200. Sehgal, V. N., Bhattacharya, S. N., Chattopadhya, D., et al.: Tumor necrosis factor: Status in reactions in leprosy before and after treatment. Int. J. Dermatol. *32*:436–439, 1993.
201. Sekar, B., Jayasheela, M., Chattopadhya, D., et al.: Prevalence of HIV infection and high-risk characteristics among leprosy patients of South India: A case-control study. Int. J. Lepr. *62*:527–531, 1994.
202. Semret, M., Koromihis, G., MacLean, J. D., et al.: *Mycobacterium ulcerans* infection (Buruli ulcer): First reported case in a traveler. Am. J. Trop. Med. Hyg. *61*:689–693, 1999.
203. Shepard, C. C.: The experimental disease that follows the injection of human leprosy bacilli into foot pads of mice. J. Exp. Med. *112*:445–454, 1960.
204. Shepard, C. C.: Combinations involving dapsone, rifampin, clofazimine, and ethionamide in the treatment of *M. leprae* infections in mice. Int. J. Lepr. *44*:135–139, 1976.
205. Shields, E. D., Russell, D. A., Pericak-Vance, M. A.: Genetic epidemiology of the susceptibility to leprosy. J. Clin. Invest. *79*:1139–1143, 1987.
206. Shimoji, Y., Ng, V., Matsumura, K., et al.: A 21-kDa surface protein of *Mycobacterium leprae* binds peripheral nerve laminin-2 and mediates Schwann cell invasion. Proc. Natl. Acad. Sci. U. S. A. *96*:9857–9862, 1999.
207. Skinsnes, O. K.: Leprosy in society. II. The pattern of concept and reaction to leprosy in Oriental antiquity. Lepr. Rev. *35*:106–122, 1964.
208. Skinsnes, O. K., and Higa, L. H.: The role of protein malnutrition in the pathogenesis of ulcerative "lazarine" leprosy. Int. J. Lepr. *44*:346–358, 1976.
209. Smith, J. H., Folse, D. S., Long, E. G., et al.: Leprosy in wild armadillos *(Dasypus novemcinctus)* of the Texas Gulf Coast: Epidemiology and mycobacteriology. J. Reticuloendothel. Soc. *34*:75–88, 1983.
210. Smith, W. C. S.: We need to know what is happening to the incidence of leprosy. Lepr. Rev. *68*:195–200, 1997.
211. Stanford, J. L.: Immunologically important constituents of mycobacteria: Antigens. *In* Ratledge, C., and Stanford, J. L. (eds.): Biology of the Mycobacteria. New York, Academic, 1983, p. 113.
212. Stanford, J. L., Rook, G. A. W., Bahr, G. M., et al.: *Mycobacterium vaccae* in immunoprophylaxis and immunotherapy of leprosy and tuberculosis. Vaccine *8*:525–530, 1990.
213. Stinear, T. P., Jenkin, G. S., Davies, J. K., et al.: *Mycobacterium ulcerans* in the environment from an endemic region in South Eastern Australia with sequence-capture PCR. Appl. Environ. Microbiol. *66*:3206–3213, 2000.
214. Stinear, T. P., Ross, B. C., Davies, J. K., et al.: Identification and characterization of IS2404 and IS2606: Two distinct repeated sequences for detection of *Mycobacterium ulcerans* by PCR. J. Clin. Microbiol. *37*:1018–1023, 1999.
215. Sung, K. J., Kim, S. B., Choi, J. H., et al.: Detection of *Mycobacterium leprae* DNA in formalin-fixed, paraffin-embedded samples from multibacillary and paucibacillary leprosy patients by polymerase chain reaction. Int. J. Dermatol. *32*:710–713, 1993.
216. Talhari, S., Orsi, A. N., Talhari, A. C., et al.: Pentoxifylline may be useful in the treatment of type 2 leprosy reactions. Lepr. Rev. *66*:261–263, 1995.
217. Tripathy, S. R.: BCG trial in leprosy. Indian J. Lepr. *56*:686–687, 1984.
218. Truman, R. W., Job, C. K., and Hastings, R. C.: Antibodies to the phenolic glycolipid-1 antigen for epidemiologic investigations of enzootic leprosy in armadillos (*Dasypus novemcinctus*). Lepr. Rev. *61*:19–24, 1990.
219. Truman, R. W., Kumaresan, J. A., McDonough, C. M., et al.: Seasonal and spatial trends in the detectability of leprosy in wild armadillos. Epidemiol. Infect. *106*:549–560, 1991.
220. Tsukamura, M., Kaneda, K., Imaeda, T., et al.: A taxonomic study on a *Mycobacterium* which caused skin ulcer in a Japanese girl and resembled *Mycobacterium ulcerans*. Kekkaku *64*:1–7, 1989.
221. Turk, J. L.: Cell-mediated immunological processes in leprosy. Lepr. Rev. *41*:207–222, 1970.
222. Uganda Buruli Group: BCG vaccination against *Mycobacterium ulcerans* infection (Buruli ulcer). Lancet *1*:111–115, 1969.
223. Uganda Buruli Group: Clinical features and treatment of pre-ulcerative Buruli lesions (*Mycobacterium ulcerans* infection). B. M. J. *2*:390–393, 1970.
224. Valla, M. C.: Lèpre et grossesse. Lyon, France, Thèse de Médecine, 1976.
225. Valverde, C. R., Canfield, D., Tovara, R., et al.: Spontaneous leprosy in a wild-caught cynomolgus macaque. Int. J. Lepr. *66*:140–148, 1998.
226. van Beers, S. M., Izumi, S., Madjid, B., et al.: An epidemiological study of leprosy infection by serology and polymerase chain reaction. Int. J. Lepr. *62*:1–9, 1994.
227. Van Brakel, W. H., and Khawas, I. B.: Silent neuropathy in leprosy: An epidemiological description. Lepr. Rev. *65*:350–360, 1994.
228. VanEden, W., DeVries, R. R. P., Deamaro, J., et al.: HLA-DR associated genetic control of the type of leprosy in a population from Surinam. Hum. Immunol. *4*:343–350, 1982.
229. Veitch, M. G. K., Johnson, P. D. R., Flood, P. E., et al.: A large localized outbreak of *Mycobacterium ulcerans* infection on a temperate southern Australian island. Epidemiol. Infect. *119*:313–318, 1997.
230. Vettom, L., Pritze, S.: Reliability of skin smear results: Experiences with quality control of skin smears in different routine services in leprosy control programmes. Lepr. Rev. *60*:187–196, 1989.
231. Wabitsch, K. R., and Meyers, W. M.: Histopathologic observations on the persistence of *Mycobacterium leprae* in the skin of multibacillary leprosy patients under chemotherapy. Lepr. Rev. *59*:341–346, 1988.
232. Wade, H. W.: The histoid variety of lepromatous leprosy. Int. J. Lepr. *31*:129–142, 1963.
233. Walsh, G. P., Meyers, W. M., Binford, C. H., et al.: Leprosy as a zoonosis: An update. Acta Leprol. *6*:51–60, 1988.
234. Walsh, G. P., Storrs, E. E., Meyers, W. M., et al.: Naturally acquired leprosy-like disease in the nine-banded armadillo *(Dasypus novemcinctus)*: Recent epizootiologic findings. J. Reticuloendothel. Soc. *22*:363–367, 1977.
235. Warndorff Van Diepen, T.: Clofazimine-resistant leprosy, a case report. Int. J. Lepr. *50*:139–142, 1982.
236. Waters, M. F. R.: The diagnosis and management of dapsone-resistant leprosy. Lepr. Rev. *48*:95–105, 1977.
237. Waters, M. F. R.: The treatment of leprosy. Tubercle *64*:221–232, 1983.
238. Waters, M. F. R.: Relapse following various types of multidrug therapy in multibacillary leprosy. Lepr. Rev. *66*:1–9, 1995.
239. Welsh, O., Gomez, M., Mancias, C., et al.: A new therapeutic approach to type II leprosy reaction. Int. J. Dermatol. *38*:931–933, 1999.
240. West, B. C., Todd, J. R., Lary, C. H., et al.: Leprosy in six isolated residents of northern Louisiana. Time-clustered cases in an essentially non-endemic area. Arch. Intern. Med. *148*:1987–1992, 1988.
241. World Health Organization: *In* Asiedu, K., Scherpbier, R., and Raviglione, M. (eds.): Buruli Ulcer: *Mycobacterium ulcerans* Infection. WHO/CDS/CPE/GBUI/2000.1, 2000.
242. World Health Organization: *In* Buntine, J., and Croft, K. (eds.): The Management of *Mycobacterium ulcerans* Disease (Buruli Ulcer). WHO/CDS/CPE/GBUI/2001.2, 2001.

243. World Health Organization: *In* Portaels, F., Johnson, P. D. R., and Meyers, W. M. (eds): Diagnosis of *Mycobacterium ulcerans* Disease (Buruli Ulcer). WHO/CDS/CPE/GBUI/2001.3, 2001.
244. World Health Organization Expert Committee on Leprosy: World Health Organ. Tech. Rep. Ser. No. 607, 1977.
245. World Health Organization: Chemotherapy of leprosy for control programmes. World Health Organ. Tech. Rep. Ser. No. 675, 1982.
246. World Health Organization Wkly. Epidemiol. Rec. No. 28, July 14, 2000.
247. Williams, D. L., Gillis, T. P.: A study of relatedness of *Mycobacterium leprae* isolates using restriction fragment length polymorphism analysis. Acta Leprol. 7(Suppl. 1):226–230, 1989.
248. Williams, D. L., Gillis, T. P., Booth, R. J., et al.: The use of a specific DNA probe and polymerase chain reaction for the detection of *Mycobacterium leprae*. J. Infect. Dis. *162*:193–200, 1990.
249. Williams, D. L., Waguespack, C., Eisenach, K., et al.: Characterization of rifampin resistance in pathogenic mycobacteria. Antimicrob. Agents Chemother. *38*:2380–2386, 1994.
250. Wolf, R. H., Gormus, B. J., Martin, L. N., et al.: Experimental leprosy in three species of monkeys. Science *227*:529–531, 1985.
251. Young, D. B., Harnisch, J. P., Knight, J., et al.: Detection of phenolic glycolipid-1 in sera from patients with lepromatous leprosy. J. Infect. Dis. *152*:1078–1080, 1985.

CHAPTER 104 Nocardia

TONI DARVILLE ■ RICHARD F. JACOBS

Nocardia spp. are obligate aerobic bacilli that exist throughout the world as soil and dust saprophytes. These organisms are non–spore-forming, thin, branching, gram-positive, partially acid-fast, filamentous bacteria. Humans become infected with *Nocardia* by two primary routes: inhalation of contaminated airborne dust particles or traumatic implantation of the bacterium into subcutaneous tissue. Pulmonary disease caused by *Nocardia asteroides* is the form of nocardiosis recognized most commonly in the United States. The pulmonary event may be subclinical or transient, or it may provoke an acute or chronic process mimicking staphylococcal or fungal pneumonia, tuberculosis, or carcinoma. Hematogenous dissemination may occur, especially in immunocompromised hosts. The central nervous system (CNS) is the most common site of dissemination, with involvement manifested most often as a brain abscess. Cutaneous nocardiosis may be acute, subacute, or chronic. This form of disease is seen predominantly in immunocompetent hosts, with *Nocardia brasiliensis* being the agent identified most frequently.

In 1888, Nocard noted an aerobic actinomycete in bovine farcy, a chronic wasting disease in cattle characterized by pulmonary abscesses and draining cutaneous sinus tracts. Eppinger first described human disease in 1890. The earliest pediatric case was documented in 1895 in a boy with pulmonary and subcutaneous infection.[4]

The Organism

Nocardia spp. are included among the aerobic actinomycetes. They are gram-positive bacteria that are more filamentous and branched and grow more slowly than do other aerobic and facultatively anaerobic bacteria. They commonly produce a fungus-like mycelium that fragments or breaks up into rod-shaped and short coccoid forms. *Nocardia* spp. grow well aerobically on a variety of simple media (e.g., blood agar, brain-heart infusion agar); adding carbon dioxide (10%) promotes more rapid growth. They are inhibited by antibiotics and antifungal agents, so media containing such agents do not support the growth of *Nocardia*. Because of their growth on commonly used fungal media (e.g., Sabouraud dextrose agar), as well as on some mycobacterial media (e.g., Löwenstein-Jensen medium), many *Nocardia* samples may be misdirected to the mycology or mycobacteriology section of clinical laboratories for identification. *N. asteroides* complex is the predominant pathogenic species (consisting of the species *N. asteroides sensu stricto*, *Nocardia farcinica*, and *Nocardia nova*) and accounts for more than 90 percent of cases of nocardiosis. Other pathogenic species include *N. brasiliensis, Nocardia otitidiscavarium (caviae),* and *Nocardia transvaliensis.* Microscopic and colonial morphology, various biochemical tests, and thin-layer chromatography are among the current laboratory methods used for speciation.

Nocardia spp. grow in temperatures of 25° C to 45° C; growth at higher temperatures may be used for differentiation. In pure culture, small, chalky white, heaped, wrinkled, or verrucose colonies appear in 3 to 5 days. Mature colonies usually are light orange and have a velvety appearance caused by the production of rudimentary aerial mycelia. They have the odor of a musty basement or freshly turned soil. Of note is that detection of colonies from clinical specimens such as respiratory secretions may require 2 to 4 weeks. In mixed culture, rapidly growing bacteria may obscure small *Nocardia* colonies. Use of modified Thayer-Martin medium may enhance recovery.[28]

Gram stain of a portion of a colony shows delicate, branching filaments no more than 1 μm in diameter. The delicate filaments may fragment and produce bacillary or coccoid forms. Many *Nocardia* spp. are partially acid-fast (i.e., when compared with *Mycobacterium* spp., they retain fuchsin less tenaciously). A modified Ziehl-Neelsen or Kinyoun stain that decolorizes with 1 percent sulfuric acid instead of the more active acid alcohol is best for demonstrating acid-fast *Nocardia* in clinical specimens. Acid-fastness is characteristic of nocardiae in tissue or primary colonial isolates but is lost quickly on subculture; not all pathogenic strains of *Nocardia* are acid-fast.[5] *N. asteroides* often survives the *N*-acetylcysteine digestion procedure (without sodium hydroxide) that is performed on sputum or bronchial washings, and yet some positive sputum specimens may be rendered falsely negative.[27] Thus, cultures of sputum and bronchial washings for isolation of *Nocardia* should be performed both before and after the digestion procedure.

Epidemiology, Transmission, and Pathogenesis

Nocardia spp. occasionally can be skin contaminants or respiratory tract saprophytes.[15, 32, 38] Bronchial obstruction or decreased bronchociliary clearance predisposes to colonization.[32] Most infections occur in the lungs, presumably via inhalation, with dissemination to the CNS occurring in as many as one third of affected patients. Although nocardiosis occurs in immunocompetent persons, as many as 70 percent of patients are immunosuppressed by medications or underlying disease.[17] The typical patient has compromised cellular immunity (steroids, organ transplantation, cytotoxic chemotherapy, acquired immunodeficiency syndrome [AIDS]). Communicability from human to human has not been a problem. The incidence of nocardiosis in the United States has been estimated to be approximately 1000 new cases per year.[12]

Systemic nocardiosis usually is caused by the bacterium *N. asteroides*. Pulmonary and systemic infection with *N. otitidiscavarium (caviae)* has been documented in both normal and immunocompromised hosts.[9, 12] *N. farcinica* has been reported as a human pathogen in the United States.[35, 44] In a series of 200 cases of *Nocardia* infection presented by Wallace and associates,[44] the isolates designated *N. farcinica* were from patients with severe illness, 56 percent of whom had disseminated infections. *N. farcinica* isolates were characterized by resistance to third-generation cephalosporins.

Traumatic implantation of aerobic actinomycetes into deep subcutaneous tissue may result in an indolent condition called actinomycotic mycetoma (to distinguish it from the eumycotic mycetomas caused by true fungi). Actinomycotic mycetomas usually involve the lower extremities and usually are caused by *Actinomadura madurae,* a non–acid-fast aerobic actinomycete. "Madura foot" is a chronic infection of deep subcutaneous tissue and bone. Mycetomas, the cause of which may be *N. brasiliensis*, have been described in Mexican and South American field workers. This *Nocardia* sp. also has been documented as an opportunistic pathogen prevalent in Florida, with a predilection for diabetics.[36]

In addition to the classic mycetoma, traumatic introduction of *Nocardia* spp. from soil may result in wound infections that occur after a more acute or subacute course. Post-traumatic endophthalmitis[14] and post-sternotomy mediastinitis[39, 45] have been described. The organism can be introduced into the skin by tick[25] and other insect bites[29] or by a cat scratch[33] and result in cellulitis, pustules, or pyoderma; these conditions occasionally disseminate in immunocompromised persons.[20, 21]

Nocardiosis was once considered a rare disease in humans; however, it is being recognized more and more frequently.[26] It has been diagnosed in persons ranging from 4 weeks to 82 years of age, and except in cases of localized cellulitis, almost all patients have one or more severe underlying diseases (e.g., lupus erythematosus, asthma, glomerulonephritis, ulcerative colitis, bronchiectasis, tuberculosis, rheumatoid arthritis, sarcoidosis). Patients with lymphoreticular neoplasms and transplant recipients seem to be particularly at risk. In addition, the risk of acquiring infection is increased in those with chronic pulmonary disease and in any patient who is receiving long-term corticosteroid treatment. Severe infection with this catalase-positive organism may develop in children with chronic granulomatous disease.[18] Although Nocardia is not a surveillance organism for AIDS, patients with AIDS may contract nocardiosis.[19]

The immune response to *Nocardia* is multifaceted.[2] Neutrophils are mobilized to the site of infection and are the predominant cell type found in lesions. However, neutrophils only inhibit the organisms and limit the spread of infection until an adequate cell-mediated immune response develops or until effective antimicrobial agents are administered. Immune T cells are vital in clearing *Nocardia* from the lung and preventing dissemination; thus, that many predisposing conditions for nocardiosis involve inadequate cell-mediated immunity is not surprising. Activated macrophages induce cytotoxic T cells effective against *N. asteroides. Nocardia* may survive inside neutrophils and macrophages by inhibiting phagosome-lysosome fusion and by the production of catalase and superoxide dismutase, which inactivate the myeloperoxidase system. *Nocardia* organisms exhibit a differential ability to evade phagosome-lysosome fusion that depends on their state of growth, possibly related to specific cell wall mycolic acids detected only in log-phase cells.[3] Differential cell wall characteristics also may influence the ability of nocardiae to exhibit specific organ tropism (e.g., the brain).[6] Antibody may play a role in host defense through enhancement of macrophage activities. Thus, although antecedent conditions of nocardiosis frequently involve dysfunctional cellular immunity, other preconditions include neutrophil and immunoglobulin disorders.

Pathology

The lesions of nocardiosis are suppurative, whether in the lung or in subcutaneous tissue, and they involve primarily proliferation of neutrophils rather than formation of granulomas. Pulmonary nocardiosis in immunocompetent patients often resembles pulmonary actinomycosis in that it results in a chronic localized pneumonia that often abuts the pleura.[17] Indolent progressive fibrosis resembling fibronodular tuberculosis may occur. Nocardiosis is more aggressive in immunocompromised patients and is manifested as multifocal necrotizing pneumonia with confluent abscess formation. *Nocardia* spp. tend to invade the pleura and chest wall, with tissue planes disregarded in the process. Little evidence of encapsulation is characteristic of all organs invaded and probably accounts for the ready dissemination of organisms from the initial pulmonary focus.

N. asteroides organisms appear as delicate, beaded, branching filaments in tissue stained with Gram stain or modified acid-fast stain (Fig. 104–1). *Nocardia* spp. are not visible in hematoxylin and eosin preparations or in sections stained with periodic acid–Schiff for fungi. Methenamine silver preparations sometimes detect tissue organisms; overstaining with silver enhances visualization.

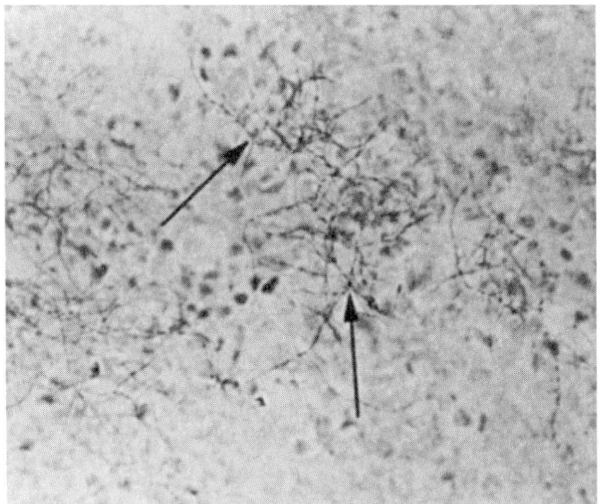

FIGURE 104–1 ■ Appearance of *Nocardia asteroides* and *Nocardia brasiliensis (arrows)* in a properly decolorized acid-fast smear. Organisms appear as fragmented bacilli with stain concentrated in a beaded fashion along portions of the filaments (×160).

Clinical Manifestations and Diagnosis

The most common manifestation of nocardiosis in the United States is pulmonary disease in a patient with underlying immunosuppression.[12, 30, 32] Infection may remain localized to the lung or may disseminate hematogenously to the CNS and skin and, more rarely, to almost any organ in the body. In high-risk patients, the diagnosis should be suspected when CNS manifestations, particularly signs of a brain tumor or abscess or soft tissue swelling or abscess, develop in conjunction with a current or recent subacute or chronic pulmonary infection.

Although sulfonamides are the most effective drugs for treatment of nocardiosis, invasive infections have been described in immunocompromised persons receiving oral trimethoprim-sulfamethoxazole (TMP-SMX) as prophylaxis for *Pneumocystis carinii* pneumonia[43] and in patients with chronic granulomatous disease who are receiving TMP-SMX prophylaxis.[37]

Clinical manifestations are not specific and include anorexia, weight loss, productive cough, pleural pain, dyspnea, and, occasionally, hemoptysis.[12] Untreated pulmonary nocardiosis usually runs a chronic course, much like tuberculosis, but it also may clear spontaneously and obscure the source of subsequent metastatic infection. The diverse clinical and radiographic manifestations, including acute bronchopneumonia, lobar pneumonia or necrotizing pneumonia with single or multiple abscesses, and pleural empyema, may mimic more common pulmonary infections such as mycobacterial, staphylococcal, and fungal pneumonia. Normal hosts or patients with only slightly impaired host defenses may have only mild respiratory tract symptoms of several months' duration.[13]

The CNS is the most common secondary site of infection, and such infection occurs in as many as one third of patients. Most experts recommend performing routine cranial computed tomography for patients with pulmonary nocardiosis, even when they are asymptomatic because of the frequency of involvement of the CNS. Brain abscesses are the most common manifestation; meningitis is reported less frequently, often (in 43% of cases) associated with an abscess.[8]

Other clinical manifestations reported include tracheitis, peritonitis, iliopsoas abscess, hematogenous endophthalmitis, endocarditis, mediastinitis, septic arthritis, and osteomyelitis.[12] Traumatic inoculation may result in localized disease manifested as cellulitis, subcutaneous abscess, or a lymphocutaneous syndrome in which one or more cutaneous nodules are associated with regional adenopathy or suppurative lymphadenitis.[24] *Nocardia* spp. may cause cervicofacial disease and cervical adenitis in children.[23] Bacteremic nocardiosis is reported rarely and usually is associated with endovascular foreign bodies in patients receiving chronic steroid therapy.[22]

In a recent retrospective review of cases of pediatric nocardiosis admitted to Arkansas Children's Hospital, 5 children with nocardiosis were identified from more than 100,000 admissions in a 10-year period. Four of the five patients had received a transplant within the previous year. Three of these patients had pulmonary disease caused by *N. asteroides*, and one transplant recipient had skin involvement with *N. brasiliensis* at a central venous line site. One immunocompetent 5-year-old boy contracted CNS infection caused by *N. asteroides* 2 months after incurring a penetrating brain injury.[16]

The diagnosis of nocardiosis is established in one third of cases by sputum analysis and culture. Although *Nocardia* spp. at times can be respiratory saprophytes, withholding therapy from immunocompromised persons when cultures repeatedly are positive is difficult. Bronchoalveolar lavage or lung biopsy may be required to establish the diagnosis. The demonstration of tissue invasion confirms active infection. Humoral methods used to diagnose nocardiosis generally lack specificity because of the high degree of serologic cross-reactivity that occurs among *Nocardia* spp. and between *Mycobacterium* and *Streptomyces* spp.[7] However, an enzyme immunoassay using a 55-kDA protein that has apparent specificity for *N. asteroides* is encouraging.[1, 7] Further work is required before a serologic test for nocardiosis is commercially available.

Treatment and Prognosis

Sulfonamides are the most effective and best-studied drugs for the treatment of nocardiosis.[34, 37, 42] Sulfisoxazole (150 mg/kg/day every 4 to 6 hours) therapy for 3 to 6 months is standard. Therapy for 6 to 12 months is indicated for those patients with invasive infections or for immunocompromised patients. More recently, TMP-SMX, the only available intravenous sulfonamide formulation in the United States, has been used successfully at doses of 15 mg/kg/day of TMP and 75 mg/kg/day of SMX, either parenterally or orally.[37, 40, 42] The toxicity of the combination exceeds that of sulfonamides alone, especially in patients receiving myelosuppressive therapy. Sulfonamides used alone remain the treatment of choice for nocardiosis.

The use of drugs other than sulfonamides always must be supported by susceptibility testing. Disk diffusion testing is practical for most antibiotics,[43] so alternative therapies can be selected when sulfonamides fail or cannot be given because of patient intolerance or allergy. Clinical experience with minocycline and amikacin is encouraging. Amoxicillin–clavulanic acid holds promise as an alternative oral β-lactam antibiotic for treating infections with *N. brasiliensis,* commonly a β-lactamase producer.[41] Therapy for *N. farcinica* infection is problematic because isolates often demonstrate high-level resistance to cephalosporins, ampicillin, aminoglycosides other than amikacin, and erythromycin but usually are susceptible to amikacin, ciprofloxacin, imipenem, and sulfamethoxazole.[44] Sulfonamides (with or without trimethoprim) are the therapy of choice for *N. farcinica*. Because *N. farcinica* shows resistance to multiple antimicrobials, clinical isolates identified initially as *Nocardia* should be evaluated further in a reference laboratory if necessary. The oxazolidinone linezolid is the first antimicrobial shown to be active in vitro against all *Nocardia* spp. and may be a therapeutic option in some patients as clinical efficacy is evaluated.[10]

Combinations of amikacin and imipenem with cefotaxime and TMP-SMX display synergy for destroying most *Nocardia* strains, although the value of and need for combined therapy remain unsettled issues. The variable and chronic course of nocardiosis precludes determining sharp therapeutic end-points. Metastatic lesions can appear during or after an otherwise effective course of sulfonamide therapy with maintenance of the recommended 100- to 150-μg/mL level in serum or plasma. Because the tendency for relapse or the late appearance of metastatic disease is a concern, therapy often is continued for many months. Patients with AIDS probably should be treated indefinitely. Surgical drainage of abscesses is important because metastatic abscesses can appear in the face of adequate therapy until surgical drainage is achieved.[15] Brain abscesses may respond to antimicrobial treatment without surgery.

Despite specific therapy, the mortality rate is 25 to 40 percent.[31, 32] Most reported cases involving dissemination to the CNS have been fatal. Factors associated with increased mortality rates in one reported patient series were treatment with corticosteroids or antineoplastic agents, underlying Cushing disease, disseminated disease involving two or more noncontiguous organs or the CNS, and the presence of symptoms for less than 3 weeks before initial evaluation.[31]

REFERENCES

1. Angeles, A. M., and Sugar, A. M.: Rapid diagnosis of nocardiosis with an enzyme immunoassay. J. Infect. Dis. *155*:292–296, 1987.
2. Beaman, B. L., and Beaman, L.: *Nocardia* species: Host-parasite relationships. Clin. Microbiol. Rev. *7*:213–264, 1994.
3. Beaman, B. L., and Moring, S. E.: Relationship among cell wall composition, state of growth, and virulence of *Nocardia asteroides* GUH-2. Infect. Immun. *56*:557–563, 1988.
4. Beckmeyer, W. J.: Nocardiosis: Report of a successfully treated case of cutaneous granuloma. Pediatrics *23*:33–39, 1959.
5. Berd, D.: Laboratory identification of clinically important aerobic actinomycetes. Appl. Microbiol. *25*:665–681, 1973.
6. Black, C. M., Paliescheskey, M., Beaman, B. L., et al.: Acidification of phagosome in murine macrophages: Blockage by *Nocardia asteroides*. J. Infect. Dis. *154*:952–958, 1986.
7. Boiron, P., and Stynen, D.: Immunodiagnosis of nocardiosis. Gene *115*:219–222, 1992.
8. Bross, J. E., and Gordon, G.: Nocardial meningitis case reports and review. Rev. Infect. Dis. *3*:160–165, 1991.
9. Brown, R. A., Janda, W. M., and Hellermen, D. V.: Pulmonary *Nocardia caviae* infection. Clin. Microbiol. Newsl. *4*:65–66, 1982.
10. Brown-Elliott, B. A., Ward, S. C., Crist, C. J., et al.: In vitro activities of linezolid against multiple *Nocardia* species. Antimicrob. Agents Chemother. *45*:1295–1297, 2001.
11. Causey, W. A.: *Nocardia caviae*: A report of 13 new isolations with clinical correlation. Appl. Microbiol. *28*:193–198, 1974.
12. Curry, W. A.: Human nocardiosis: A clinical review with selected case reports. Arch. Intern. Med. *140*:818–826, 1980.
13. Feigin, D. S.: Nocardiosis of the lung: Chest radiographic findings in 21 cases. Radiology *159*:9–14, 1986.
14. Ferry, A. P., Font, R. L., Weinberg, R. S., et al.: Nocardial endophthalmitis: Report of two cases studied histopathologically. Br. J. Ophthalmol. *72*:55–61, 1988.
15. Frazier, A. R., Rosenow, E. C., III, and Roberts, G. D.: Nocardiosis: A review of 25 cases occurring during 24 months. Mayo Clin. Proc. *50*:657–663, 1975.
16. Harik, N. K., Jacobs, R. F., and Darville, T.: Nocardiosis in children: Five cases. J. Invest. Med. 49:108, 2001.
17. Heffner, J. E.: Pleuropulmonary manifestations of actinomycosis and nocardiosis. Semin. Respir. Infect. *3*:352–361, 1988.
18. Idriss, Z. H., Cunningham, R. J., and Wilfert, C. M.: Nocardiosis in children. Pediatrics *55*:479–484, 1975.
19. Javalry, K., Horowitz, H. W., and Wormser, G. P.: Nocardiosis in patients with human immunodeficiency virus infection: Report of 2 cases and review of the literature. Medicine (Baltimore) *71*:128–138, 1980.
20. Kahn, F. W., Gornick, C. C., and Tofte, R. W.: Primary cutaneous *Nocardia asteroides* infection with dissemination. Am. J. Med. *70*:859–863, 1981.
21. Kalb, R. E., Kaplan, M. H., and Grosman, M. E.: Cutaneous nocardiosis. J. Am. Acad. Dermatol. *13*:125–133, 1985.
22. Kontoyiannis, D. P., Ruoff, K., Hooper, D. C.: *Nocardia* bacteremia: Report of 4 cases and review of the literature. Medicine (Baltimore) *77*:255–267, 1998.
23. Lampe, R. M., Baker, C. J., Septimus, E. J., et al.: Cervicofacial nocardiosis in children. J. Pediatr. *99*:593–595, 1981.
24. Law, B. L., and Marks, M. I.: Pediatric nocardiosis. Pediatrics *70*:560–564, 1982.
25. Leggiadro, R. J., and Miller, R. B.: Cutaneous nocardiosis presenting as a tick-borne infection. Pediatr. Infect. Dis. J. *6*:421–422, 1987.
26. Murray, J. F., Finegold, S. M., Froman, S., et al.: The changing spectrum of nocardiosis. Am. Rev. Respir. Dis. *83*:315–330, 1961.
27. Murray, P. R., Neeren, R. L., and Niles, A. C.: Effect of decontamination procedures on recovery of *Nocardia* spp. J. Clin. Microbiol. *25*:2010–2011, 1987.
28. Murray, P. R., Niles, A. C., and Heeren, R. L.: Modified Thayer-Martin medium for recovery of *Nocardia* species from contaminated specimens. J. Clin. Microbiol. *26*:1219–1220, 1988.
29. O'Conner, P. T., and Dire, D. J.: Cutaneous nocardiosis associated with insect bites. Cutis *50*:301–302, 1992.
30. Palmer, D. L., Harvey, R. L., and Wheeler, J. K.: Diagnostic and therapeutic considerations in *Nocardia asteroides* infection. Medicine (Baltimore) *53*:391–401, 1974.
31. Present, C. A., Wiernik, P. H., and Serpick, A. A.: Factors affecting survival in nocardiosis. Am. Rev. Respir. Dis. *108*:1444–1451, 1973.
32. Rosett, W., and Hodges, G. R.: Recent experiences with nocardial infections. Am. J. Med. Sci. *276*:279–285, 1978.
33. Sachs, M. K.: Lymphocutaneous *Nocardia brasiliensis* infection acquired from a cat scratch: Case report and review. Clin. Infect. Dis. *15*:710–711, 1992.
34. Schiff, T. A., McNeil, M. M., and Brown, J. M.: Cutaneous *Nocardia farcinica* infection in a nonimmunocompromised patient: Case report and review. Clin. Infect. Dis. *16*:756–760, 1993.
35. Shetty, A. K., Arvin, A. M., Gutierrez, K. M.: *Nocardia farcinica* pneumonia in chronic granulomatous disease. Pediatrics 104:961–964, 1999.
36. Smego, R. A., Jr., and Gallis, H. A.: The clinical spectrum of *Nocardia brasiliensis* infection in the United States. Rev. Infect. Dis. *6*:164–180, 1984.
37. Smego, R. A., Jr., Moeller, M. G., and Gallis, H. A.: Trimethoprim-sulfamethoxazole therapy for *Nocardia* infections. Arch. Intern. Med. *143*:711–718, 1983.
38. Stropnik, Z.: Isolation of *Nocardia asteroides* from human skin. Sabouraudia *4*:41–44, 1965.
39. Thaler, F., Gotainer, B., Teodori, G., et al.: Mediastinitis due to *Nocardia asteroides* after cardiac transplantation. Intensive Care Med. *18*:127–128, 1992.
40. van Burik, J.-A., Hackman, R. C., Nadeem, S. Q., et al.: Nocardiosis after bone marrow transplantation: A retrospective study. Clin. Infect. Dis. *22*:1154–1160, 1997.
41. Wallace, R. J., Nash, D. R., Johnson, W. K., et al.: β-Lactam resistance in *Nocardia brasiliensis* is mediated by β-lactamase and reversed in the presence of clavulanic acid. J. Infect. Dis. *156*:959–966, 1987.
42. Wallace, R. J., Septimus, E. J., Williams, T. W., et al.: Use of trimethoprim-sulfamethoxazole for treatment of infections due to *Nocardia*. Rev. Infect. Dis. *4*:315–325, 1982.
43. Wallace, R. J., and Steele, L. C.: Susceptibility testing on *Nocardia asteroides* for the clinical laboratory. Diagn. Microbiol. Infect. Dis. *9*:155–166, 1988.
44. Wallace, R. J., Jr., Tsukamura, M., Brown, B. A., et al.: Cefotaxime-resistant *Nocardia asteroides* strains are isolates of the controversial species *Nocardia farcinica*. J. Clin. Microbiol. *28*:2726–2732, 1990.
45. Yew, W. W., Wong, P. C., Kwan, S. Y. L., et al.: Two cases of *Nocardia asteroides* sternotomy infection treated with ofloxacin and a review of other active antimicrobial agents. J. Infect. Dis. *23*:297–302, 1991.

CHAPTER 105 Miscellaneous Gram-Positive Bacilli

THOMAS G. BOYCE ■ WILLIAM C. GRUBER ■ RANDALL G. FISHER

The gram-positive rods encompass a vast number of species. They are widespread in the environment and are part of the normal flora of animals and humans. This chapter focuses on gram-positive bacilli that are encountered uncommonly as pathogens in healthy persons. Many of these organisms, however, show increasing prominence as causes of disease in immunocompromised patients.[8] Bacteria from the following genera are discussed: *Corynebacterium* (other than *Corynebacterium diphtheriae*) and *Rhodococcus*.

Corynebacterium

This genus comprises a large number of organisms possessing little pathogenic potential, with some notable exceptions.

The most infamous member of this genus, *C. diphtheriae* (see Chapter 95), is a cause of a potentially lethal pharyngeal infection with systemic manifestations. *Corynebacterium jeikeium* (formerly *Corynebacterium* group JK) can be a major nosocomial agent of bacteremia and endocarditis; other species commonly are associated with infections in animals and rarely cause invasive infection in humans.[60, 84] For an exhaustive consideration of coryneform bacteria, the reader is referred to a review by Funke and colleagues.[36]

BACTERIOLOGY

Corynebacterium spp. derive their name from their club-like shape. Because of their resemblance to *C. diphtheriae,* they are included in the heterogeneous group of diphtheroids. Snapping division produces the angular and palisade arrangement of cells responsible for their characteristic gram-positive, "Chinese letters" microscopic appearance.[17] Organisms are facultatively anaerobic or aerobic and do not produce spores. They are nonmotile and catalase-positive and contain mycolic acid in their cell walls. Clinically relevant species include *C. diphtheriae, C. jeikeium, Corynebacterium pseudotuberculosis, Corynebacterium xerosis, Corynebacterium amycolatum, Corynebacterium pseudodiphtheriticum, Corynebacterium minutissimum, Corynebacterium striatum, Corynebacterium ulcerans,* and *Corynebacterium urealyticum.* Species can be differentiated according to biochemical tests and fermentation of sugars.[17, 36, 82]

EPIDEMIOLOGY

Corynebacterium spp. can be part of the normal skin and upper respiratory tract flora and commonly colonize hospitalized patients. Nosocomial acquisition of *C. jeikeium* has been characterized most completely, and as many as 35 percent of hospitalized patients may be colonized with *C. jeikeium.* The organism may be isolated at the time of admission,[37] with the skin, groin, and rectum being common sites of recovery. Wounds and suppurative sites quickly become colonized.[37] Hospital personnel caring for oncology patients have higher rates of hand colonization with pathogenic *Corynebacterium* than those found in nurses caring for dermatology patients.[48] Not surprisingly, transmission from patient to patient can occur in the hospital environment, and selective antibiotic pressure has been shown to augment colonization with *Corynebacterium.*[59, 66, 108] Outbreaks of bacteremic infection have been reported in hematology wards,[78, 93] and DNA restriction fragment analysis and hybridization techniques have been used to document spread.[59, 75]

PATHOPHYSIOLOGY

Corynebacterium spp., particularly *C. jeikeium,* possess lipophilic properties that may account for their ability to proliferate on skin that has a higher lipid content; organisms have been isolated from sebum-filled eccrine gland biopsy specimens in an adolescent with malignancy.[52] Breach of skin integrity clearly is an important risk factor for development of local infection and bacteremia with *Corynebacterium,* and plastic intravascular catheters increase the risk of developing infection.[80] Certain isolates of *C. pseudotuberculosis* and *C. ulcerans* can express diphtheria-like toxins,[107] which may confer virulence.

Some *Corynebacterium* spp., notably *C. jeikeium* and *C. urealyticum,* commonly show resistance to penicillins, cephalosporins, aminoglycosides, erythromycin, and tetracycline.[25, 37, 60, 66, 70, 82, 91] Strains with a significant DNA relationship to the *C. jeikeium*–type strain demonstrate penicillin resistance.[81] Resistant organisms have been noted to have significantly thickened cell walls in comparison to susceptible strains, but the functional importance of this feature is unknown.[10]

CLINICAL MANIFESTATIONS

Systemic infections with *Corynebacterium* generally are not clinically distinguishable from serious infections caused by other pathogens. Immunocompromised patients are at the highest risk for development of disease caused by *Corynebacterium,*[44, 83] but infections in neonates and immunocompromised older children also have been described.[9, 25, 55] Risk factors include male gender, neutropenia, broad-spectrum antibiotic exposure, and prolonged hospital stay.[78, 93] Catalase production may be responsible for the rare infection with non-JK *Corynebacterium* spp. found in children with chronic granulomatous disease.[55] *Corynebacterium* spp. are responsible for approximately 9 percent of early-onset and 4 percent of cases of late-onset prosthetic valve endocarditis.[106]

C. jeikeium is a pathogen of particular concern. In 1976, this agent first was described as a cause of serious infection in four patients, including an 11-year-old boy with a ventriculoatrial shunt.[44] Immunocompromised patients, particularly those with leukemia, are vulnerable to bacteremia. These high-risk subjects may have a local inflammatory lesion at the site of infection or a disseminated, hemorrhagic, or necrotic papular exanthem. *C. jeikeium* has been recovered from disseminated lesions in a 14-year-old boy with leukemia.[52] A literature review of 83 neutropenic patients (nearly all adults) with *C. jeikeium* sepsis found the following risk factors for development of infection: presence of a central venous catheter, male gender, profound and prolonged neutropenia, and exposure to multiple antibiotics. Skin lesions were reported in 48 percent and pulmonary infiltrates in 36 percent of patients. The overall case-fatality rate was 34 percent but was reduced to 5 percent in patients after recovery from neutropenia.[101]

Infections with *C. jeikeium* also have been reported after trauma, ventriculoperitoneal shunting procedures,[2, 56] orthopedic procedures,[16] bone marrow aspiration,[25] and placement of a central venous catheter.[25] *C. jeikeium* now is recognized to be one of the most common causes of prosthetic valve endocarditis in adults.[70] Curiously, the cutaneous findings of bacteremia so commonly observed in cancer patients generally are absent in patients with endocarditis.[22]

Although primarily a pathogen in farm animals, *C. pseudotuberculosis* can cause localized suppurative granulomatous lymphadenitis in humans[60]; almost all cases are associated with animal contact, particularly with sheep and goats.[38] The clinical findings and histology may mimic the much more common cat-scratch disease, and Gram stain and culture are required to differentiate the two entities.[68] Most cases have been reported from Australia.[74]

C. xerosis has been reported as a rare cause of endocarditis, arthritis, and ventriculoperitoneal shunt infection.[4, 11] Most persons with endocarditis have a prosthetic heart valve.[29, 62] Recently, Funke and associates demonstrated by chemical testing and molecular genetic investigation that many isolates tentatively identified as *C. xerosis* actually are *C. amycolatum.*[35] *C. amycolatum* is much more likely than is *C. xerosis* to be multidrug-resistant.[36] A case of fatal sepsis caused by *C. amycolatum* in a premature newborn has been reported.[9]

C. pseudodiphtheriticum, a commensal of the oropharynx, can cause pneumonia, bronchitis, or tracheitis.[1, 18, 21] Lung disease usually occurs in the setting of underlying cardiopulmonary pathology or immunocompromise.[42] Its onset typically is acute, but fever may be noticeably absent.[63] At least 18 cases of *C. pseudodiphtheriticum* endocarditis, including 3 infections in children with congenital heart disease, have been reported.[69] Infection of allograft material is a common finding; native heart valves may be involved but usually in the context of preexisting lesions or intravenous drug abuse. Three cases of exudative pharyngitis with a pseudomembrane mimicking diphtheria, one in a 4-year-old girl from Arkansas, have been reported to be caused by *C. pseudodiphtheriticum*.[51]

C. minutissimum traditionally has been regarded as the cause of the mild cutaneous disease erythrasma, which is characterized by scaly, pruritic, red-brown patches usually occurring in the axilla or groin. Although *C. minutissimum* may play a role, erythrasma probably is a polymicrobial process.[36] *C. minutissimum* is recognized as a rare nosocomial infectious complication of malignancy and dialysis and has been implicated in a case of pyelonephritis in an 8-month-old child with posterior urethral valves.[20]

C. striatum has been recovered from purulent sputum of hospitalized patients and from infected central venous catheter sites.[103] It has been reported as a cause of fatal pulmonary infection and endocarditis.[59, 65, 84] *C. striatum* was responsible for a nosocomial outbreak in 14 patients during a 12-month period in a surgical intensive care unit. Endotracheal intubation for longer than 24 hours was the only risk factor found to predispose to acquisition of infection.[13] *C. striatum* also has been reported as a cause of meningitis and ventriculoperitoneal shunt infection.[49, 104]

C. ulcerans derives its name from its association with ulcerative pharyngitis. Although it is more commonly a pathogen of nonhuman primates,[73] infection can occur in humans after contact with animals or consumption of contaminated raw milk.[7, 23] Toxigenic strains of *C. ulcerans* can produce a syndrome indistinguishable from that caused by toxigenic *C. diphtheriae*.[79, 100]

C. urealyticum (formerly *Corynebacterium* group D2) is a cause of alkaline-encrusted cystitis and pyelitis, primarily in the elderly.[31, 91] It is associated less commonly with infection at other sites and with bacteremia.[90] An 8-year-old boy with chemotherapy-induced neutropenia and a necrotic soft tissue infection of the scrotum caused by *C. urealyticum* has been reported.[85]

DIAGNOSIS

The diagnosis of *Corynebacterium* infection is based on isolation of the organism from clinical material. This organism is commonly accompanied by other pathogens. Similar to *Mycobacterium* and *Nocardia* spp., *Corynebacterium* organisms have mycolic acid in their cell wall. However, the chains are shorter, and the organisms are not acid-fast. *Corynebacterium* may be difficult to distinguish from some *Rhodococcus* spp.[17] Colonies of *C. jeikeium* may demonstrate a metallic sheen when grown on agar.[44] Most *Corynebacterium* spp. can be differentiated quickly from each other by sugar fermentation, hydrolysis of urea, and reduction of nitrate.[99] Selective media containing kanamycin or trimethoprim-sulfamethoxazole have been useful in the recovery of multidrug-resistant strains of *Corynebacterium*.[43] Erythrasma usually is diagnosed by the typical coral-red fluorescence under Wood lamp examination.

TREATMENT

Empiric therapy must account for the frequency of infection with *C. jeikeium*, which often is resistant to multiple antibiotics but susceptible to vancomycin.[36] In some series of immunocompromised patients, this organism was the *Corynebacterium* sp. most commonly encountered.[92, 105] Hence, vancomycin is recommended for empiric treatment of suspected *Corynebacterium* infection until susceptibility data are known. Treatment can be changed to a penicillin or cephalosporin, if appropriate. Two-drug therapy generally is recommended for treatment of *Corynebacterium* endocarditis; for gentamicin-susceptible strains, penicillin-gentamicin combinations have been shown to be synergistic, regardless of whether the strains are susceptible to penicillin.[70] Rarely, resistance to vancomycin is encountered. A woman with prosthetic valve endocarditis caused by a vancomycin-resistant *Corynebacterium* sp. was treated successfully with imipenem and ciprofloxacin.[6] Removal of infectious sources such as central nervous system shunts and central venous catheters may be required for cure. Scrupulous attention to skin hygiene may reduce colonization of hospital personnel and the incidence of patient-to-patient transmission of pathogenic strains.[27, 78] Management of toxigenic *C. ulcerans* infection is identical to that for infection caused by toxigenic *C. diphtheriae*, including the use of antitoxin.[100] Erythrasma usually responds to treatment with a macrolide.

Rhodococcus

The genus *Rhodococcus* contains at least 15 species, of which *Rhodococcus equi* is the most clinically relevant to humans. This organism derives its name from its role as a cause of pyogranulomatous pneumonia in young horses.[76] It has assumed a prominent role as a cause of human pulmonary disease in immunocompromised patients, particularly those with human immunodeficiency virus infection.[30, 45, 87] For a comprehensive discussion of this organism, readers are referred to a review by Cornish and Washington.[19]

BACTERIOLOGY

R. equi is a catalase-positive, urease-positive, oxidase-negative, gram-positive rod. The organism assumes a more coccoid morphology in solid media and a more bacillary form in liquid media. Its cell wall contains mycolic acid, which renders it acid-fast when grown on Löwenstein-Jensen medium and stained with Kinyoun stain.[39]

EPIDEMIOLOGY

R. equi is a soil organism, and its growth is enriched by the manure of herbivores. Despite the common occurrence of this pathogen as a cause of veterinary infections, exposure to animals does not appear to be necessary for acquisition of human infection[76]; most reported human patients have not had exposure to a farm or animals.[45] Hospital outbreaks of infection associated with patient-to-patient transmission have not been reported. However, in a retrospective analysis of 24 cases of *R. equi* infection, 6 patients had shared a hospital room with a patient with *R. equi* pneumonia, thus raising the possibility that nosocomial transmission occurs.[5]

PATHOPHYSIOLOGY

The prominence of pulmonary infection suggests that the respiratory tract is a common portal of entry. After gaining access to the lower respiratory tract, organisms are taken up by alveolar macrophages; Mac-1 macrophage receptors and complement are required for binding.[46] The appearance of pyogranulomatous lesions is consistent with the role of *R. equi* as an intracellular parasite containing mycolic acid, a possible virulence factor in the cell wall.[40, 77] Surface 15- and 17-kDA antigens expressed by an 85-kb plasmid appear to confer virulence in mice and foals,[94] and virulent strains seem to have an increased capacity for intracellular survival in macrophages.[47] Most *R. equi* isolates from patients with acquired immunodeficiency syndrome (AIDS) express either the 15- to 17-kDA antigens or a 20-kDA antigen that appears to confer intermediate virulence. However, most isolates from patients without AIDS express none of these antigens.[95] Other factors may play a role in promoting *Rhodococcus* disease in humans.[96] Death of parasitized macrophages may release enzymes that further contribute to tissue damage. $CD4^+$ lymphocytes are essential for pulmonary clearance of *R. equi* in a mouse model,[54] which may help explain the high risk of infection associated with cellular immunodeficiency.

CLINICAL MANIFESTATIONS

Infection typically results in a subacute pneumonia that develops over a period of several weeks. Symptoms such as cough and fever commonly occur, but progression of disease may be relatively silent. Although most infections currently occur in patients with AIDS, malignancy and transplantation also pose a risk. Pulmonary infection in children with leukemia has been described.[3, 67] Infection may be accompanied by other pathogens, particularly in patients with AIDS.

Pulmonary infection often is pleural based and associated with cavitation.[45] Empyema may occur as a complication. Lung tissue demonstrating malacoplakia, an unusual-appearing granulomatous inflammation with aggregates of histiocytes that contain concentrically layered basophilic inclusions, should raise suspicion of the presence of *R. equi* infection.[15, 41, 86]

Extrapulmonary disease is seen at diagnosis in 7 percent of patients with pneumonia.[102] Manifestations of infection include otitis/mastoiditits,[3, 50, 61] abscess,[32] osteomyelitis,[12, 33, 72] meningitis,[24, 88] pericarditis,[58] lymphadenitis,[58] and endophthalmitis.[28] The organism has been grown from a biopsy specimen of a granulomatous skin lesion in an immunocompetent 7-year-old girl.[64] *R. equi* also has been reported as a cause of peritonitis in patients undergoing chronic peritoneal dialysis.[14, 97]

DIAGNOSIS

The diagnosis relies on isolation of *Rhodococcus* from clinical material. Although sputum specimens may be positive, bronchoalveolar lavage or lung biopsy may be required. The physician should be alert to the possible coexistence of *R. equi* with other pathogens. In the laboratory, confusion of this organism with *Corynebacterium*, acid-fast organisms, and other gram-positive coccobacilli has been shown to delay diagnosis.[26] Positive findings on Gram stain and Kinyoun stain should be interpreted in the context of clinical information.[87] Organisms appear salmon-pink when grown on blood agar and orange on Löwenstein-Jensen medium.[8] Differentiating from acid-fast bacteria on smears sometimes can be difficult. Combined use of a siderophore detection medium, ethylene glycol degradation, and β-galactosidase activity may help differentiate *Rhodococcus* from *Nocardia* and rapid-growing mycobacteria.[34] DNA restriction fragment analysis and ribotyping show promise in aiding in the identification and tracking of *Rhodococcus* spp.[57]

TREATMENT

Clinical isolates commonly are resistant to penicillins and cephalosporins. Even if the organisms are susceptible in vitro, β-lactam antibiotics should be avoided because of the rapid development of resistance.[53] Erythromycin, clindamycin, rifampin, aminoglycosides, vancomycin, fluoroquinolones, and imipenem are active against *R. equi*.[71] Synergy has been demonstrated with various combinations of these agents. Including rifampin or erythromycin in a two-drug combination has been recommended because of penetrance in macrophages.[8, 89] Combinations of antibiotics that included vancomycin were found to be most effective in clearing infection in a mouse model.[71]

Cure rates in adults with lung infection are approximately 60 percent when antibiotic therapy alone is used but may reach 75 percent when antibiotic therapy is combined with surgical resection of infected pulmonary tissue.[45] However, surgery has not been shown to increase survival rates.[5] Pediatric patients generally have fared better than have adults, but most reported cases in children have been in non-AIDS patients.[8] Relapse occurs commonly, but the optimal duration of therapy to prevent relapse is unknown. For patients with AIDS, some authors recommend a minimum of 2 months of therapy followed by long-term suppressive therapy.[53] Relapse has been reported to occur at extrapulmonary sites in 13 percent of immunocompromised patients,[102] often without reappearance of pulmonary disease. Treatment of *R. equi* peritonitis in patients receiving peritoneal dialysis has been reported to be successful with intraperitoneal imipenem or vancomycin for 14 days.[14, 98] Removal of the peritoneal dialysis catheter may be required for cure.

REFERENCES

1. Ahmed, K., Kawakami, K., Watanabe, K., et al.: *Corynebacterium pseudodiphtheriticum*: A respiratory tract pathogen. Clin. Infect. Dis. *20*:41–46, 1995.
2. Allen, K. D., and Green, H. T.: Infections due to a 'Group JK' corynebacterium. J. Infect. *13*:41–44, 1986.
3. Allen, V. D., Niec, A., Kerem, E., et al.: *Rhodococcus equi* pneumonia in a child with leukemia. Pediatr. Infect. Dis. J. *8*:656–658, 1989.
4. Arisoy, E. S., Demmler, G. J., and Dunne, W. M., Jr.: *Corynebacterium xerosis* ventriculoperitoneal shunt infection in an infant: Report of a case and review of the literature. Pediatr. Infect. Dis. J. *12*:536–538, 1993.
5. Arlotti, M., Zoboli, G., Moscatelli, G. L., et al.: *Rhodococcus equi* infection in HIV-positive subjects: A retrospective analysis of 24 cases. Scand. J. Infect. Dis. *28*:463–467, 1996.
6. Barnass, S., Holland, K., and Tabaqchali, S.: Vancomycin-resistant *Corynebacterium* species causing prosthetic valve endocarditis successfully treated with imipenem and ciprofloxacin. J. Infect. *22*:161–169, 1991.
7. Barrett, N. J.: Communicable disease associated with milk and dairy products in England and Wales: 1983–1984. J. Infect. *12*:265–272, 1986.
8. Berkowitz, F. E.: The gram-positive bacilli: A review of the microbiology, clinical aspects, and antimicrobial susceptibilities of a heterogeneous group of bacteria. Pediatr. Infect. Dis. J. *13*:1126–1138, 1994.
9. Berner, R., Pelz, K., Wilhelm, C., et al.: Fatal sepsis caused by *Corynebacterium amycolatum* in a premature infant. J. Clin. Microbiol. *35*:1011–1012, 1997.
10. Blom, J., and Heltberg, O.: The ultrastructure of antibiotic-susceptible and multi-resistant strains of group JK diphtheroid rods isolated from clinical specimens. Acta Pathol. Microbiol. Immunol. Scand. [B] *94*:301–308, 1986.

11. Booth, L. V., Richards, R. H., and Chandran, D. R.: Septic arthritis caused by *Corynebacterium xerosis* following vascular surgery. Rev. Infect. Dis. *13*:548–549, 1991.
12. Bouchou, K., Cathebras, P., Dumollard, J. M., et al.: Chronic osteitis due to *Rhodococcus equi* in an immunocompetent patient. Letter. Clin. Infect. Dis. *20*:718–720, 1995.
13. Brandenburg, A. H., van Belkum, A., van Pelt, C., et al.: Patient-to-patient spread of a single strain of *Corynebacterium striatum* causing infections in a surgical intensive care unit. J. Clin. Microbiol. *34*:2089–2094, 1996.
14. Brown, E., and Hendler, E.: *Rhodococcus* peritonitis in a patient treated with peritoneal dialysis. Am. J. Kidney Dis. *14*:417–418, 1989.
15. Byard, R. W., Thorner, P. S., Edwards, V., et al.: Pulmonary malacoplakia in a child. Pediatr. Pathol. *10*:417–424, 1990.
16. Claeys, G., Vershchraegen, G., DeSmet, L., et al.: *Corynebacterium* JK (Johnson-Kay strain) infection of a Küntscher-nailed tibial fracture. Clin. Orthop. *202*:227–229, 1986.
17. Collins, M. D., and Cummins, C. S.: *Corynebacterium. In* Bergey's Manual of Systematic Bacteriology. Vol. 2. Baltimore, Williams & Wilkins, 1986, pp. 1266–1276.
18. Colt, H. G., Morris, J. F., Marston, B. J., et al.: Necrotizing tracheitis caused by *Corynebacterium pseudodiphtheriticum*: Unique case and review. Rev. Infect. Dis. *13*:73–76, 1991.
19. Cornish, N., and Washington, J. A.: *Rhodococcus equi* infections: Clinical features and laboratory diagnosis. Curr. Clin. Top. Infect. Dis. *19*:198–215, 1999.
20. Craig, J., Grigor, W., Doyle, B., et al.: Pyelonephritis caused by *Corynebacterium minutissimum*. Pediatr. Infect. Dis. J. *13*:1151–1152, 1994.
21. Craig, T. J., Maguire, F. E., and Wallace, M. R.: Tracheobronchitis due to *Corynebacterium pseudodiphtheriticum*. South. Med. J. *84*:504–506, 1991.
22. Dan, M., Somer, I., Knobel, B., et al.: Cutaneous manifestations of infection with *Corynebacterium* group JK. Rev. Infect. Dis. *10*:1204–1207, 1988.
23. de Carpentier, J. P., Flanagan, P. M., Singh, I. P., et al.: Nasopharyngeal *Corynebacterium ulcerans:* A different diphtheria. J. Laryngol. Otol. *106*:824–826, 1992.
24. DeMarais, P. L., and Kocka, F. E.: *Rhodococcus* meningitis in an immunocompetent host. Clin. Infect. Dis. *20*:167–169, 1995.
25. Dietrich, M. C., Watson, D. C. and Kumar, M. L.: *Corynebacterium* group JK infections in children. Pediatr. Infect. Dis. J. *8*:233–236, 1989.
26. Doig, C., Gill, M. J., and Church, D. L.: *Rhodococcus equi*—an easily missed opportunistic pathogen. Scand. J. Infect. Dis. *23*:1–6, 1991.
27. Eagan, J. A., Blevins, A., and Armstrong, D.: Prevention of skin colonization and subsequent bacteremia with CDC-JK organisms in patients with cancer. Cancer Pract. *1*:325–328, 1993.
28. Ebersole, L. L., and Paturzo, J. L.: Endophthalmitis caused by *Rhodococcus equi* Prescott serotype 4. J. Clin. Microbiol. *26*:1221–1222, 1988.
29. Eliakim, R., Silkoff, P., Lugassy, G., et al.: *Corynebacterium xerosis* endocarditis. Arch. Intern. Med. 143:1995, 1983.
30. Emmons, W., Reichwein, B., and Winslow, D. L.: *Rhodococcus equi* infection in the patient with AIDS: Literature review and report of an unusual case. Rev. Infect. Dis. *13*:91–96, 1991.
31. Estorc, J. J., de La Coussaye, J. E., Viel, E. J., et al.: Teicoplanin treatment of alkaline encrusted cystitis due to *Corynebacterium* group D2. Eur. J. Med. *1*:183–184, 1992.
32. Fierer, J., Wolf, P., Seed, L., et al.: Non-pulmonary *Rhodococcus equi* infections in patients with acquired immune deficiency syndrome (AIDS). J. Clin. Pathol. *40*:556–558, 1987.
33. Fischer, L., Sterneck, M., Albrecht, H., et al.: Vertebral osteomyelitis due to *Rhodococcus equi* in a liver transplant recipient. Clin. Infect. Dis. *26*:749–752, 1998.
34. Fiss, E., and Brooks, G. F.: Use of a siderophore detection medium, ethylene glycol degradation, and beta-galactosidase activity in the early presumptive differentiation of *Nocardia, Rhodococcus, Streptomyces,* and rapidly growing *Mycobacterium* species. J. Clin. Microbiol. *29*:1533–1535, 1991.
35. Funke, G., Lawson, P. A., Bernard, K. A., et al.: Most *Corynebacterium xerosis* strains identified in the routine clinical laboratory correspond to *Corynebacterium amycolatum*. J. Clin. Microbiol. *34*:1124–1128, 1996.
36. Funke, G., von Graevenitz, A., Clarridge, J. E., 3rd, et al.: Clinical microbiology of coryneform bacteria. Clin. Microbiol. Rev. *10*:125–159, 1997.
37. Gill, V. J., Manning, C., Lamson, M., et al.: Antibiotic-resistant group JK bacteria in hospitals. J. Clin. Microbiol. *13*:472–477, 1981.
38. Goldberger, A. C., Lipsky, B. A., and Plorde, J. J.: Suppurative granulomatous lymphadenitis caused by *Corynebacterium ovis* (pseudotuberculosis). Am. J. Clin. Pathol. *76*:486–490, 1981.
39. Goodfellow, M.: *Rhodococcus. In* Bergey's Manual of Systematic Bacteriology. Vol. 4. Baltimore, Williams & Wilkins, 1989.
40. Gotoh, K., Mitsuyama, M., Imaizumi, S., et al.: Mycolic acid–containing glycolipid as a possible virulence factor of *Rhodococcus equi* for mice. Microbiol. Immunol. *35*:175–185, 1991.
41. Guerrero, M. F., Ramos, J. M., Renedo, G., et al.: Pulmonary malacoplakia associated with *Rhodococcus equi* infection in patients with AIDS: Case report and review. Clin. Infect. Dis. *28*:1334–1336, 1999.
42. Gutierrez-Rodero, F., Ortiz de la Tabla, V., Martinez, C., et al.: *Corynebacterium pseudodiphtheriticum*: An easily missed respiratory pathogen in HIV-infected patients. Diagn. Microbiol. Infect. Dis. *33*:209–216, 1999.
43. Hamilton, D. J., Ulness, B. K., Baugher, L. K., et al.: Comparison of a novel trimethoprim-sulfamethoxazole–containing medium (XT80) with kanamycin agar for isolation of antibiotic-resistant organisms from stool and rectal cultures of marrow transplant patients. J. Clin. Microbiol. *25*:1886–1890, 1987.
44. Hande, K. R., Witebsky, F. G., Brown, M. S., et al.: Sepsis with a new species of *Corynebacterium*. Ann. Intern. Med. *85*:423–426, 1976.
45. Harvey, R. L., and Sunstrum, J. C.: *Rhodococcus equi* infection in patients with and without human immunodeficiency virus infection. Rev. Infect. Dis. *13*:139–145, 1991.
46. Hondalus, M. K., Diamond, M. S., Rosenthal, L. A., et al.: The intracellular bacterium *Rhodococcus equi* requires Mac-1 to bind to mammalian cells. Infect. Immun. *61*:2919–2929, 1993.
47. Hondalus, M. K., and Mosser, D. M.: Survival and replication of *Rhodococcus equi* in macrophages. Infect. Immun. *62*:4167–4175, 1994.
48. Horn, W. A., Larson, E. L., McGinley, K. J., et al.: Microbial flora on the hands of health care personnel: Differences in composition and antibacterial resistance. Infect. Control Hosp. Epidemiol. *9*:189–193, 1988.
49. Hoy, C. M., Kerr, K., and Livingston, J. H.: Cerebrospinal fluid-shunt infection due to *Corynebacterium striatum*. Letter. Clin. Infect. Dis. *25*:1486–1487, 1997.
50. Ibarra, R., and Jinkins, J. R.: Severe otitis and mastoiditis due to *Rhodococcus equi* in a patient with AIDS. Case report. Neuroradiology *41*:699–701, 1999.
51. Izurieta, H. S., Strebel, P. M., Youngblood, T., et al.: Exudative pharyngitis possibly due to *Corynebacterium pseudodiphtheriticum,* a new challenge in the differential diagnosis of diphtheria. Emerg. Infect. Dis. *3*:65–68, 1997.
52. Jerdan, M. S., Shapiro, R. S., Smith, N. B., et al.: Cutaneous manifestations of *Corynebacterium* group JK sepsis. J. Am. Acad. Dermatol. *16*:444–447, 1987.
53. Johnson, D. H., and Cunha, B. A.: *Rhodococcus equi* pneumonia. Semin. Respir. Infect. *12*:57–60, 1997.
54. Kanaly, S. T., Hines, S. A., and Palmer, G. H.: Failure of pulmonary clearance of *Rhodococcus equi* infection in $CD4^+$ T-lymphocyte–deficient transgenic mice. Infect. Immun. *61*:4929–4932, 1993.
55. Kaplan, A., and Israel, F.: *Corynebacterium aquaticum* infection in a patient with chronic granulomatous disease. Am. J. Med. Sci. *296*:57–58, 1988.
56. Keren, G., Geva, T., Bogokovsky, B., et al.: *Corynebacterium* group JK pathogen in cerebrospinal fluid shunt infection. Report of two cases. J. Neurosurg. *68*:648–650, 1988.
57. Lasker, B. A., Brown, J. M., and McNeil, M. M.: Identification and epidemiological typing of clinical and environmental isolates of the genus *Rhodococcus* with use of a digoxigenin-labeled rDNA gene probe. Clin. Infect. Dis. *15*:223–233, 1992.
58. Lee-Chiong, T., Sadigh, M., Simms, M., et al.: Case reports: Pericarditis and lymphadenitis due to *Rhodococcus equi*. Am. J. Med. Sci. *310*:31–33, 1995.
59. Leonard, R. B., Nowowiejski, D. J., Warren, J. J., et al.: Molecular evidence of person-to-person transmission of a pigmented strain of *Corynebacterium striatum* in intensive care units. J. Clin. Microbiol. *32*:164–169, 1994.
60. Lipsky, B. A., Goldberger, A. C., Tompkins, L. S., et al.: Infections caused by nondiphtheria corynebacteria. Rev. Infect. Dis. *4*:1220–1235, 1982.
61. Lopes Cardoso, F. L., Machado, E. S., Souza, M. J., et al.: *Rhodococcus equi* mastoiditis in a patient with AIDS. Clin. Infect. Dis. *22*:713, 1996.
62. Lortholary, O., Buu-Hoi, A., Fagon, J. Y., et al.: Mediastinitis due to multiple resistant *Corynebacterium xerosis*. Clin. Infect. Dis. *16*:172, 1993.
63. Manzella, J. P., Kellogg, J. A., and Parsey, K. S.: *Corynebacterium pseudodiphtheriticum*: A respiratory tract pathogen in adults. Clin. Infect. Dis. *20*:37–40, 1995.
64. Martin, T., Hogan, D. J., Murphy, F., et al.: *Rhodococcus* infection of the skin with lymphadenitis in a nonimmunocompromised girl. J. Am. Acad. Dermatol. *24*:328–332, 1991.
65. Martinez-Martinez, L., Suarez, A. I., Ortega, M. C., et al.: Fatal pulmonary infection caused by *Corynebacterium striatum*. Clin. Infect. Dis. *19*:806–807, 1994.
66. McGowan, J. E., Jr.: JK coryneforms: A continuing problem for hospital infection control. J. Hosp. Infect. *11*(Suppl. A):358–366, 1988.
67. McGowan, K. L., and Mangano, M. F.: Infections with *Rhodococcus equi* in children. Diagn. Microbiol. Infect. Dis. *14*:347–352, 1991.
68. Mills, A. E., Mitchell, R. D., and Lim, E. K.: *Corynebacterium pseudotuberculosis* is a cause of human necrotising granulomatous lymphadenitis. Pathology *29*:231–233, 1997.
69. Morris, A., and Guild, I.: Endocarditis due to *Corynebacterium pseudodiphtheriticum*: Five case reports, review, and antibiotic susceptibilities of nine strains. Rev. Infect. Dis. *13*:887–892, 1991.
70. Murray, B. E., Karchmer, A. W., and Moellering, R. C., Jr.: Diphtheroid prosthetic valve endocarditis. A study of clinical features and infecting organisms. Am. J. Med. *69*:838–848, 1980.

71. Nordmann, P., Kerestedjian, J. J., and Ronco, E.: Therapy of *Rhodococcus equi* disseminated infections in nude mice. Antimicrob. Agents Chemother. *36*:1244–1248, 1992.
72. Novak, R. M., Polisky, E. L., Janda, W. M., et al.: Osteomyelitis caused by *Rhodococcus equi* in a renal transplant recipient. Infection *16*:186–188, 1988.
73. Panaitescu, M., Maximescu, P., Michel, J., et al.: Respiratory pathogens in non-human primates with special reference to *Corynebacterium ulcerans*. Lab. Anim. *11*:155–157, 1977.
74. Peel, M. M., Palmer, G. G., Stacpoole, A. M., et al.: Human lymphadenitis due to *Corynebacterium pseudotuberculosis:* Report of ten cases from Australia and review. Clin. Infect. Dis. *24*:185–191, 1997.
75. Pitcher, D., Johnson, A., Allerberger, F., et al.: An investigation of nosocomial infection with Cory*nebacterium jeikeium* in surgical patients using a ribosomal RNA gene probe. Eur. J. Clin. Microbiol. Infect. Dis. *9*:643–648, 1990.
76. Prescott, J. F.: *Rhodococcus equi*: An animal and human pathogen. Clin. Microbiol. Rev. *4*:20–34, 1991.
77. Prescott, J. F., Johnson, J. A., and Markham, R. J.: Experimental studies on the pathogenesis of *Corynebacterium equi* infection in foals. Can. J. Comp. Med. *44*:280–288, 1980.
78. Quinn, J. P., Arnow, P. M., Weil, D., et al.: Outbreak of JK diphtheroid infections associated with environmental contamination. J. Clin. Microbiol. *19*:668–671, 1984.
79. Respiratory diphtheria caused by *Corynebacterium ulcerans*—Terre Haute, Indiana, 1996. M. M. W. R. Morb. Mortal. Wkly. Rep. *46*:330–332, 1997.
80. Riebel, W., Frantz, N., Adelstein, D., et al.: *Corynebacterium* JK: A cause of nosocomial device-related infection. Rev. Infect. Dis. *8*:42–49, 1986.
81. Riegel, P., de Briel, D., Prevost, G., et al.: Genomic diversity among *Corynebacterium jeikeium* strains and comparison with biochemical characteristics and antimicrobial susceptibilities. J. Clin. Microbiol. *32*:1860–1865, 1994.
82. Riley, P. S., Hollis, D. G., Utter, G. B., et al.: Characterization and identification of 95 diphtheroid (group JK) cultures isolated from clinical specimens. J. Clin. Microbiol. *9*:418–424, 1979.
83. Rozdzinski, E., Kern, W., Schmeiser, T., et al.: *Corynebacterium jeikeium* bacteremia at a tertiary care center. Infection *19*:201–204, 1991.
84. Rufael, D. W., and Cohn, S. E.: Native valve endocarditis due to *Corynebacterium striatum:* Case report and review. Clin. Infect. Dis. *19*:1054–1061, 1994.
85. Saavedra, J., Rodriguez, J. N., Fernandez-Jurado, A., et al.: A necrotic soft-tissue lesion due to *Corynebacterium urealyticum* in a neutropenic child. Clin. Infect. Dis. *22*:851–852, 1996.
86. Scannell, K. A., Portoni, E. J., Finkle, H. I., et al.: Pulmonary malacoplakia and *Rhodococcus equi* infection in a patient with AIDS. Chest *97*:1000–1001, 1990.
87. Scott, M. A., Graham, B. S., Verrall, R., et al.: *Rhodococcus equi*—an increasingly recognized opportunistic pathogen. Report of 12 cases and review of 65 cases in the literature. Am. J. Clin. Pathol. *103*:649–655, 1995.
88. Scotton, P. G., Tonon, E., Giobbia, M., et al.: *Rhodococcus equi* nosocomial meningitis cured by levofloxacin and shunt removal. Clin. Infect. Dis. *30*:223–224, 2000.
89. Sirera, G., Romeu, J., Clotet, B., et al.: Relapsing systemic infection due to *Rhodococcus equi* in a drug abuser seropositive for human immunodeficiency virus. Rev. Infect. Dis. *13*:509–510, 1991.
90. Soriano, F., Ponte, C., Ruiz, P., et al.: Non–urinary tract infections caused by multiply antibiotic-resistant *Corynebacterium urealyticum.* Clin. Infect. Dis. *17*:890–891, 1993.
91. Soriano, F., Ponte, C., Santamaria, M., et al.: *Corynebacterium* group D2 as a cause of alkaline-encrusted cystitis: Report of four cases and characterization of the organisms. J. Clin. Microbiol. *21*:788–792, 1985.
92. Soriano, F., Zapardiel, J., and Nieto, E.: Antimicrobial susceptibilities of *Corynebacterium* species and other non–spore-forming gram-positive bacilli to 18 antimicrobial agents. Antimicrob. Agents Chemother. *39*:208–214, 1995.
93. Stamm, W. E., Tompkins, L. S., Wagner, K. F., et al.: Infection due to *Corynebacterium* species in marrow transplant patients. Ann. Intern. Med. *91*:167–173, 1979.
94. Takai, S., Iie, M., Watanabe, Y., et al.: Virulence-associated 15- to 17-kilodalton antigens in *Rhodococcus equi*: Temperature-dependent expression and location of the antigens. Infect. Immun. *60*:2995–2997, 1992.
95. Takai, S., Imai, Y., Fukunaga, N., et al.: Identification of virulence-associated antigens and plasmids in *Rhodococcus equi* from patients with AIDS. J. Infect. Dis. *172*:1306–1311, 1995.
96. Tan, C., Prescott, J. F., Patterson, M. C., et al.: Molecular characterization of a lipid-modified virulence-associated protein of *Rhodococcus equi* and its potential in protective immunity. Can. J. Vet. Res. *59*:51–59, 1995.
97. Tang, S., Lo, C. Y., Lo, W. K., et al.: *Rhodococcus* peritonitis in continuous ambulatory peritoneal dialysis. Nephrol. Dial. Transplant. *11*:201–202, 1996.
98. Tang, S., Lo, C. Y., Lo, W. K., et al.: Optimal treatment regimen for CAPD peritonitis caused by *Rhodococcus* species. Letter. Nephrol. Dial. Transplant. *12*:1080–1081, 1997.
99. Thompson, J. S., Gates-Davis, D. R., and Yong, D. C.: Rapid microbiochemical identification of *Corynebacterium diphtheriae* and other medically important corynebacteria. J. Clin. Microbiol. *18*:926–929, 1983.
100. Three cases of toxigenic *Corynebacterium ulcerans* infection. Commun. Dis. Rep. C. D. R. Wkly. *10*:49, 52, 2000.
101. van der Lelie, H., Leverstein-Van Hall, M., Mertens, M., et al.: *Corynebacterium* CDC group JK *(Corynebacterium jeikeium)* sepsis in haematological patients: A report of three cases and a systematic literature review. Scand. J. Infect. Dis. *27*:581–584, 1995.
102. Verville, T. D., Huycke, M. M., Greenfield, R. A., et al.: *Rhodococcus equi* infections of humans. 12 cases and a review of the literature. Medicine (Baltimore) *73*:119–132, 1994.
103. Watkins, D. A., Chahine, A., Creger, R. J., et al.: *Corynebacterium striatum*: A diphtheroid with pathogenic potential. Clin. Infect. Dis. *17*:21–25, 1993.
104. Weiss, K., Labbe, A. C., and Laverdiere, M.: *Corynebacterium striatum* meningitis: Case report and review of an increasingly important *Corynebacterium* species. Clin. Infect. Dis. *23*:1246–1248, 1996.
105. Williams, D. Y., Selepak, S. T., and Gill, V. J.: Identification of clinical isolates of nondiphtherial *Corynebacterium* species and their antibiotic susceptibility patterns. Diagn. Microbiol. Infect. Dis. *17*: 23–28, 1993.
106. Wilson, W. R., Danielson, G. K., Giuliani, E. R., et al.: Prosthetic valve endocarditis. Mayo Clin. Proc. *57*:155–161, 1982.
107. Wong, T. P., and Groman, N.: Production of diphtheria toxin by selected isolates of *Corynebacterium ulcerans* and *Corynebacterium pseudotuberculosis*. Infect. Immun. *43*:1114–1116, 1984.
108. Young, V. M., Meyers, W. F., Moody, M. R., et al.: The emergence of coryneform bacteria as a cause of nosocomial infections in compromised hosts. Am. J. Med. *70*:646–650, 1981.

SUBSECTION **4**

ENTEROBACTERIA

CHAPTER 106 *Citrobacter*

THOMAS G. BOYCE ■ WILLIAM C. GRUBER ■ RANDALL G. FISHER

Citrobacter, a genus of enteric gram-negative rods closely related to *Salmonella*, has been associated increasingly with human disease. *Citrobacter* strains are found infrequently as normal inhabitants of the intestinal tract of humans and animals,[30, 63] but they have been associated with urinary tract infection,[5, 15, 30, 36, 39, 40] osteomyelitis,[39] diarrhea,[11, 21, 66] and invasive disease in immunocompromised hosts.[28, 30, 39, 40] As detailed in a recent review by Doran, *Citrobacter* is associated frequently with sepsis, meningitis, and brain abscess in neonates.[10]

Bacteriology

In 1931, Werkman and Gillen[63] proposed the generic term *Citrobacter* for citrate-positive coli-aerogenes intermediates isolated from stool. This genus now includes 11 species, the most commonly identified of which are *Citrobacter freundii, Citrobacter koseri (formerly Citrobacter diversus),* and *Citrobacter amalonaticus.*[6] *Citrobacter* spp. are straight, facultatively anaerobic bacilli possessing peritrichous flagella that confer motility. In addition to utilization of citrate, these organisms hydrolyze urea and ferment glucose, with the production of gas.[55] They grow on ordinary media as gray, opaque, round colonies producing a strong, fetid odor. Unlike *Salmonella, Citrobacter* grows in the presence of potassium cyanide. Indole-negative strains that produce hydrogen sulfide are classified as *C. freundii*. Indole-positive, hydrogen sulfide–negative strains are differentiated by their ability to ferment malonate; *C. koseri* ferments malonate, whereas *C. amalonaticus* does not.[1] Antigenic schemata have been developed to classify the O somatic antigens of *Citrobacter*[16, 20, 66]; these antigens show cross-reactivity with the O antigens of other members of the family Enterobacteriaceae.

Epidemiology

Meningitis caused by *Citrobacter* was reported first in 1960 with two cases of *C. freundii* infection.[25] In the decade from 1970 to 1979, 69 cases of *Citrobacter* meningitis were reported,[17] and 4 percent of neonatal meningitis cases reported in the First Neonatal Meningitis Cooperative Study Group were caused by *Citrobacter.*[44] *C. koseri* is the species usually isolated from patients with meningitis; central nervous system infection occurs less commonly with *C. freundii.*[10, 17] Most of the cases in the United States are reported from southern states; biotype d or serotypes O2 and O1[17] are the isolates of *C. koseri* most commonly encountered.

Most cases of neonatal meningitis caused by this organism have been sporadic. The source of sporadic cases usually is unknown, but nine cases clearly have been documented to be vertically transmitted from mother to infant.[10] In addition, several well-documented nosocomial outbreaks of infection have been reported.[12, 15, 16, 38, 48, 50, 66] The source usually is the gastrointestinal tract or the hands of nursery staff. One cluster was associated with contaminated formula.[60] Once *Citrobacter* is introduced into a neonatal nursery, colonization may exceed 79 percent.[16] Parry and associates[48] described a nursery outbreak in which 11 of 128 infants were colonized with *C. koseri* over the course of an observation period of 3 months; meningitis developed in 2 of the colonized infants. Additional colonization of neonates appeared to be eliminated by removal of a nurse with persistent hand carriage of the organism.

In another outbreak,[66] introduction of *C. koseri* into the nursery was linked to an infant admitted with meningitis. Thirty-one percent of infants in the nursery subsequent to the admission of the index case were found to be colonized with *C. koseri* of the same serotype and biotype. Meningitis developed in a second infant with the organism during the observation period of this study. Umbilical colonization of infants in this cluster occurred more commonly than did rectal colonization, but rectal colonization was more persistent and lasted as long as 4 months. Two nurses were found to have hand colonization with the organism, and reintroduction of these bacteria into the nursery was linked to a pregnant nurse who at delivery had perineal cultures yielding the epidemic strain. She was implicated in the colonization of her own infant, as well as three other neonates. Corresponding culture data from a reference hospital revealed an overall neonatal *Citrobacter* colonization rate of 1 to 10 percent during a 5-year period, with no invasive disease.

Although *Citrobacter* increasingly has been isolated from debilitated adult patients,[64] particularly as a urinary tract,[30, 39, 40] soft tissue,[18, 39, 40] and bone[40] pathogen, *Citrobacter* infection in children older than 2 months is an unusual occurrence. In older children, *Citrobacter* spp. are more likely to cause opportunistic infection in an immunocompromised host or, occasionally, urinary tract infection. One study demonstrated *Citrobacter* to be responsible for 37 (1.4%) urinary tract infections in children during a 3-year period.[13] One quarter of the infections were nosocomially acquired, and one third occurred in children with urinary tract abnormalities.

Pathophysiology

Citrobacter infrequently colonizes the intestinal tract and perineum of humans.[30] Vertical transmission of strains shown to be identical by DNA typing demonstrates that newborns can acquire colonization at the time of passage through the birth canal of a colonized mother.[26, 47] Onset of disease beyond the first week of life commonly is related to colonization of the infant in the nursery. As with other types of gram-negative neonatal meningitis, infection of the central nervous system results from bacteremic seeding of the meninges in a colonized infant. The basis for the particular invasiveness of *Citrobacter* in neonates and its propensity to cause multiple brain abscesses is largely unexplained. *Citrobacter* spp. possess the ability to invade, transcytose, and multiply within human brain microvascular endothelial cells in vitro.[2] Many strains of *C. koseri* appear to be able to produce brain pathology in the mouse, but the degree of damage appears to be related to the virulence of the strain and the age of the mouse.[35, 56] Differences in strains related to the presence of an outer-membrane protein with a molecular weight of 32,000 have been associated with differences in brain histopathology in one infant rat model of *C. koseri* meningitis.[34] Strains isolated from the cerebrospinal fluid (CSF) of infants with meningitis more commonly possess this outer-membrane protein than do strains isolated from other body sites.[35]

In an immunocompromised patient, broad use of antimicrobial agents may produce selective pressure leading to increased colonization with *Citrobacter*. Increased bacterial density combined with a blunted immune response may result in invasive disease. Some strains of *C. freundii* have been shown to produce Shiga toxins (verotoxins) nearly identical to those produced by enterohemorrhagic strains of *Escherichia coli*.[53] At least one outbreak of gastroenteritis and the hemolytic-uremic syndrome caused by Shiga toxin–producing *C. freundii* has been reported.[61]

Clinical Manifestations

Citrobacter, like other neonatal pathogens, can cause early- as well as late-onset infection. In a review of 74 cases of neonatal meningitis caused by these bacteria,[17] the mean age at onset reported for early disease was 7 days; 85 percent of patients were included in this group, whereas 15 percent of cases occurred in infants older than 3 weeks. Twenty-three (31%) of the 74 patients were younger than 36 weeks' gestational age at birth, which suggests that preterm infants have an increased risk for acquiring *Citrobacter* infection. Prematurity is an even more common finding (71%) in cases proved to be vertically acquired.[10]

The clinical signs and symptoms are those typical of neonatal sepsis. Fever, lethargy, poor feeding, vomiting, irritability, bulging fontanelle, seizures, and jaundice are common initial features. Umbilical infection and surgical manipulation of colonized umbilical stumps occasionally have preceded development of bacteremia and meningitis.[48] The white blood cell count may show leukocytosis or leukopenia. Findings in the CSF are consistent with most types of neonatal bacterial meningitis and usually consist of increased polymorphonuclear cells, elevated protein, and depressed glucose levels; gram-negative rods may be seen on smear. Of *Citrobacter* meningitis cases in which the results of blood cultures are reported, 80 percent document concurrent bacteremia.[10]

Citrobacter is a particularly devastating cause of neonatal meningitis. The most common *Citrobacter* spp. causing neonatal meningitis is *C. koseri*, which accounts for more than 80 percent of cases.[10] Central nervous system infection with this organism produces multiple brain abscesses with unusually high frequency.[17, 23, 31, 35, 37] In extensive reviews by Graham and Band[17] and by Doran,[10] 75 percent of *Citrobacter* meningitis cases resulted in intracerebral abscesses. By comparison, the incidence of abscess formation in non-*Citrobacter* gram-negative meningitis is reported to be as low as 10 percent.[17] The case-fatality rate for *Citrobacter* meningitis is approximately 30 percent, and at least 75 percent of surviving infants have neurologic sequelae such as mental retardation, hemiparesis, seizures, and developmental delay.[10] The presence of a brain abscess appears to contribute significantly to morbidity and mortality.[9, 16, 17] For unknown reasons, intracerebral abscesses appear to be less likely to develop in neonates with vertically acquired *Citrobacter* meningitis.[10] Rarely, *Citrobacter* infection in the neonatal period may lead to focal infection not involving the central nervous system. A case of septic arthritis and osteomyelitis of the shoulder in a 3-week-old infant has been reported.[27]

In adults, *Citrobacter* is isolated most commonly from the urinary tract.[30, 39, 40] In earlier studies, 5 to 12 percent of bacterial isolates from urinary tract infections in adult patients were *Citrobacter* spp.[11, 65] More recently, in a health maintenance organization, *Citrobacter* spp. accounted for only 0.8 percent of 4342 isolates from women with acute uncomplicated cystitis.[22] *Citrobacter* also is an uncommon cause of urinary tract infection in children.[13] Sputum is the second most common clinical specimen to yield *Citrobacter* in adults.[30] Lung abscess,[14] pneumonia,[39, 40] bronchitis,[28] and septic arthritis[39] also have been reported. *Citrobacter* is an occasional cause of bacteremia in hospitalized patients and accounts for approximately 0.5 percent of blood culture isolates.[49, 54] In one series, all 45 patients had at least one underlying disease, with malignancies (particularly intra-abdominal tumors) and hepatobiliary stones being the most frequent coexisting conditions.[54] Polymicrobial bacteremia occurred in one third of patients. The case-fatality rate was 18 percent.

Gastrointestinal disease occasionally has been attributed to *Citrobacter*, but frequent isolation of this agent from normal stool often renders this diagnosis equivocal. This genus was implicated first in an outbreak of mild gastroenteritis by Barnes and Cherry[4] in 1946, and an outbreak of watery diarrhea in a Virginia infant care unit included two infants in whom isolates of enterotoxin-liberating *Citrobacter* were obtained from stool.[21] Some studies have found a higher incidence of *Citrobacter* isolation from the stool of patients with enterocolitis syndrome than from the stool of control patients.[66] Shiga toxin (verotoxin)-producing *C. freundii* isolated from organically grown parsley was associated with an outbreak of diarrhea and hemolytic-uremic syndrome in a daycare setting.[61] *C. freundii* was found to be a cause of appendicitis in a healthy adult,[39] peritonitis in adults with liver disease or pancreatitis,[39] neutropenic colitis after chemotherapy for breast cancer,[8] and meningitis in adults as a complication of neurosurgery.[59] Bone and soft tissue infections also can occur[7, 57]; in one adult series, 3 percent of *Citrobacter* pathogens were isolated from joints or bone.[39]

Diagnosis

The biochemical characteristics of *C. koseri* include a lack of production of hydrogen sulfide on triple sugar iron agar, a negative Voges-Proskauer reaction, utilization of citrate, motility, production of indole, decarboxylation of ornithine but not lysine, and production of acid from adonitol.[1] Identification of this organism as a pathogen in a nursery setting should heighten suspicion of its possible role in subsequent neonatal infections. *C. freundii* is indole-negative and hydrogen sulfide–positive, which differentiates it from *C. koseri*. *C. amalonaticus* differs from *C. koseri* in the former organism's inability to ferment malonate. *C. freundii* and *C. amalonaticus* account for a significant proportion of disease caused by *Citrobacter* in immunocompromised persons and should be suspected particularly in this group of patients.[28]

Infants with invasive *Citrobacter* disease have clinical characteristics similar to those of infants with sepsis and meningitis of other cause. Such infants should undergo a thorough evaluation, including blood and urine culture, as well as CSF studies. Brain imaging studies should be performed once the diagnosis is established. Computed tomography is the test most commonly used, although ultrasonography often is more feasible for an unstable neonate and may be nearly as sensitive in detecting abscesses.[37, 45, 67] Serial imaging studies should be performed because abscesses may develop during the first few weeks of illness. In cases in which CSF cultures are negative because of previous administration of antimicrobial therapy, surgical aspiration of abscesses sometimes will enable identification of the organism.

Treatment

Most *C. koseri* organisms are resistant to ampicillin (97% in one series[39]) and sensitive to aminoglycosides and third-generation cephalosporins.[10] However, a 4-year experience with neonatal septicemia caused by *C. koseri* has been described in which all of 13 isolates were resistant to gentamicin but susceptible to third-generation cephalosporins.[12] The resistance patterns of *C. freundii* were reported in a national surveillance study of nosocomial bloodstream infections.[49] Of the 23 *C. freundii* isolates tested, resistance to piperacillin, piperacillin-tazobactam, ceftriaxone, and ceftazidime was a common finding (39% to 48%). Isolates generally were susceptible to the aminoglycosides and ciprofloxacin (91% to 96%), and all *C. freundii* isolates tested were susceptible to cefepime and imipenem.

Some *Citrobacter* isolates contain chromosomally mediated group I β-lactamases. These bacteria possess a gene that, when triggered by exposure to cephalosporins or by spontaneous mutation, produces a cephalosporinase capable of inactivating cephalosporins.[29] Clinically, it is manifested as treatment failure and emergence of drug resistance to various cephalosporins despite initial susceptibility.[41] In one study, the presence of group I β-lactamases was much more common with *C. freundii* (9 of 22 isolates) than with *C. koseri* (0 of 7 isolates).[29] Resistance was associated with previous receipt of an extended-spectrum β-lactam antibiotic. Cefepime appears to be more resistant to hydrolysis by these inducible β-lactamases,[52] although a highly cefepime-resistant strain was described recently.[3]

Treatment of *Citrobacter* meningitis often requires a multidisciplinary effort involving neurosurgeons as well as pediatricians. Although cerebral abscesses usually are aspirated or drained surgically, some patients are treated with antibiotics alone, and neither approach has been demonstrated to be clearly superior. When abscesses are inaccessible or small and not progressive, conservative management may be considered.[10] Ventriculostomy plus craniectomy with open drainage of abscesses has been required in some children to effect bacteriologic cure, and shunt placement for hydrocephalus often is required.

In general, antibiotic therapy for gram-negative neonatal meningitis has proved disappointing[42, 43] (see Chapter 77). No evidence exists to support one combination of antibiotics over another for the treatment of *Citrobacter* meningitis. However, usually a third- or fourth-generation cephalosporin in combination with an aminoglycoside is used initially.[10] Chloramphenicol,[9, 16, 24] imipenem-cilastatin,[11, 24] and trimethoprim-sulfamethoxazole[19] also have been used successfully.

Poor meningeal penetration of aminoglycosides, in addition to the presence of intracranial abscesses, renders the use of antibiotic therapy for *Citrobacter* meningitis especially difficult. The ability of this organism to persist in the brain is demonstrated by its recovery 4 years after neonatal infection.[11] Cranial computed tomography generally is used for evaluation of complications such as hydrocephalus and multicystic encephalomalacia (Fig. 106–1). Administration of antibiotics intrathecally or directly into abscess cavities has been tried but has not been shown convincingly to be of benefit.[19, 20, 23, 33, 38, 46, 51, 58, 62] In a randomized controlled trial, intrathecal administration of gentamicin for the treatment of neonates with gram-negative meningitis was associated with a poorer outcome.[44]

Neonates with gram-negative meningitis should undergo repeat lumbar puncture approximately 72 hours after beginning therapy to document sterilization of the CSF. The duration of therapy with intravenous antibiotics generally is a minimum of 21 days for gram-negative neonatal meningitis. For cases complicated by intracranial abscesses, prolonged

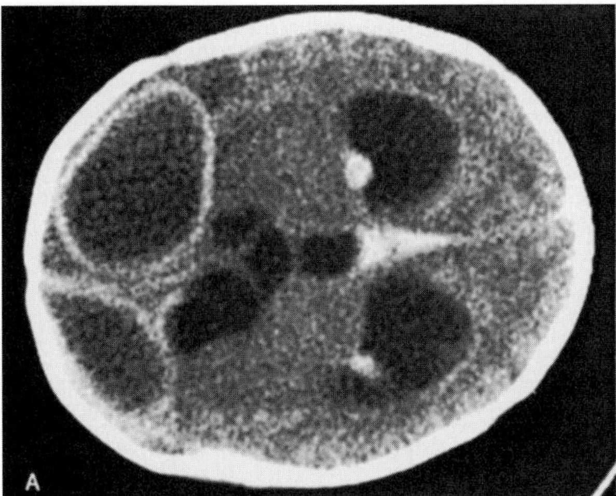

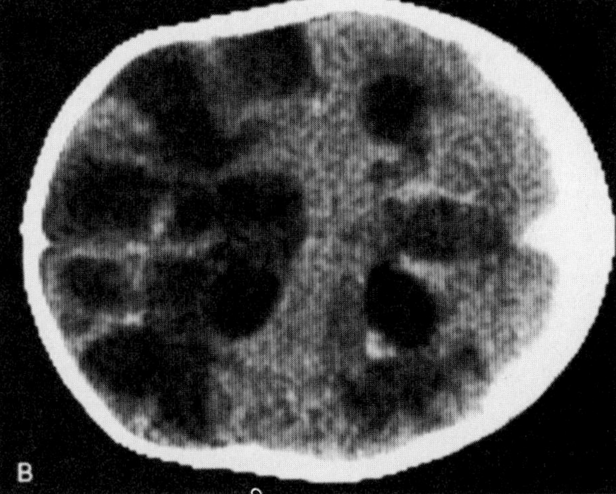

FIGURE 106–1 ■ Computed tomogram demonstrating progressive abscess formation and encephalomalacia in an infant at 3 weeks of age *(A)* and 6 weeks of age *(B)*, despite bacteriologic "cure" of *Citrobacter* meningitis.

therapy is indicated (usually 4 to 6 weeks after sterilization of CSF).[10, 32]

Scrupulous attention to implementation of preventive infection control practices has been recommended to stem nursery outbreaks.[16, 48, 66] These prophylactic measures include skin and umbilical cord care, elimination of crowding with isolation of infected infants and carriers, and good handwashing practices. Exclusion of colonized personnel and temporary closing of the nursery have been followed by a reduction in neonatal *C. koseri* colonization. Although cohorting of colonized infants is a reasonable practice, multiple sources of introduction of *Citrobacter* may limit the efficacy of this approach in some outbreaks.[15]

Treatment of *Citrobacter* infection beyond the neonatal period requires the choice of an appropriate antibiotic, along with drainage of abscesses and appropriate débridement of wounds. Therapy should be guided by antimicrobial susceptibility testing. The outcome depends largely on the preceding debility of the host and the location of the infection. Significant mortality is associated with septicemia or pulmonary disease in immunocompromised persons.[28, 30, 39, 40, 54]

REFERENCES

1. Altmann, G., Sechter, I., Cahan, D., et al.: *Citrobacter diversus* isolated from clinical material. J. Clin. Microbiol. *3*:390–392, 1976.
2. Badger, J. L., Stins, M. F., and Kim, K. S.: *Citrobacter freundii* invades and replicates in human brain microvascular endothelial cells. Infect. Immun. *67*:4208–4215, 1999.
3. Barnaud, G., Labia, R., Raskine, L., et al.: Extension of resistance to cefepime and cefpirome associated to a six amino acid deletion in the H-10 helix of the cephalosporinase of an *Enterobacter cloacae* clinical isolate. FEMS Microbiol. Lett. *195*:185–190, 2001.
4. Barnes, L. A., and Cherry, C. B.: A group of paracolon organisms having apparent pathogenicity. Am. J. Public Health *36*:481–483, 1946.
5. Barton, L. L., and Walentik, C.: *Citrobacter diversus* urinary tract infection. Am. J. Dis. Child. *136*:467–468, 1982.
6. Brenner, D. J., O'Hara, C. M., Grimont, P. A., et al.: Biochemical identification of *Citrobacter* species defined by DNA hybridization and description of *Citrobacter gillenii* sp. nov. (formerly *Citrobacter* genomospecies 10) and *Citrobacter murliniae* sp. nov. (formerly *Citrobacter* genomospecies 11). J. Clin. Microbiol. *37*:2619–2624, 1999.
7. Bruehl, C. L., and Listernick, R.: *Citrobacter freundii* septic arthritis. J. Paediatr. Child. Health. *28*:402–403, 1992.
8. Clemons, M. J., Valle, J. W., Harris, M., et al.: *Citrobacter freundii* and fatal neutropenic enterocolitis following adjuvant chemotherapy for breast cancer. Clin. Oncol. (R. Coll. Radiol.) *9*:172–175, 1997.
9. Curless, R. G.: Neonatal intracranial abscess: Two cases caused by *Citrobacter* and a literature review. Ann. Neurol. *8*:269–272, 1980.
10. Doran, T. I.: The role of *Citrobacter* in clinical disease of children: Review. Clin. Infect. Dis. *28*:384–394, 1999.
11. Eppes, S. C., Woods, C. R., Mayer, A. S., et al.: Recurring ventriculitis due to *Citrobacter diversus:* Clinical and bacteriologic analysis. Clin. Infect. Dis. *17*:437–440, 1993.
12. Giacoia, G. P., and West, K.: Sepsis with *Citrobacter diversus* in sick newborns. Am. J. Perinatol. *6*:49–54, 1989.
13. Gill, M. A., and Schutze, G. E.: *Citrobacter* urinary tract infections in children. Pediatr. Infect. Dis. J. *18*:889–892, 1999.
14. Gilman, R. M., Irwin, R. S., and Garrity, F. L.: Community-acquired *Citrobacter diversus* infections. Respir. Care *25*:66–71, 1980.
15. Goering, R. V., Ehrenkranz, N. J., Sanders, C. C., et al.: Long term epidemiological analysis of *Citrobacter diversus* in a neonatal intensive care unit. Pediatr. Infect. Dis. J. *11*:99–104, 1992.
16. Graham, D. R., Anderson, R. L., Ariel, F. E., et al.: Epidemic nosocomial meningitis due to *Citrobacter diversus* in neonates. J. Infect. Dis. *144*:203–209, 1981.
17. Graham, D. R., and Band, J. D.: *Citrobacter diversus* brain abscess and meningitis in neonates. J. A. M. A. *245*:1923–1925, 1981.
18. Grant, M. D., Horowitz, H. I., and Lorian, V.: Gangrenous ulcer and septicemia due to *Citrobacter*. N. Engl. J. Med. *280*:1286–1287, 1969.
19. Greene, G. R., Heitlinger, L., and Madden, J. D.: *Citrobacter* ventriculitis in a neonate responsive to trimethoprim-sulfamethoxazole. Clin. Pediatr. (Phila.) *22*:515–517, 1983.
20. Gross, R. J., Rowe, B., and Easton, J. A.: Neonatal meningitis caused by *Citrobacter koseri*. J. Clin. Pathol. *26*:138–139, 1973.
21. Guerrant, R. L., Dickens, M. D., Wenzel, R. P., et al.: Toxigenic bacterial diarrhea: Nursery outbreak involving multiple bacterial strains. J. Pediatr. *89*:885–891, 1976.
22. Gupta, K., Scholes, D., and Stamm, W. E.: Increasing prevalence of antimicrobial resistance among uropathogens causing acute uncomplicated cystitis in women. JAMA. *281*:736–738, 1999.
23. Gwynn, C. M., and George, R. H.: Neonatal *Citrobacter* meningitis. Arch. Dis. Child. *48*:455–458, 1973.
24. Haimi-Cohen, Y., Amir, J., Weinstock, A., et al.: The use of imipenem-cilastatin in neonatal meningitis caused by *Citrobacter diversus*. Acta Paediatr. *82*:530–532, 1993.
25. Harris, D., and Cone, T. E., Jr.: *Escherichia freundii* meningitis: Report of two cases. J. Pediatr. *56*:774–777, 1960.
26. Harvey, B. S., Koeuth, T., Versalovic, J., et al.: Vertical transmission of *Citrobacter diversus* documented by DNA fingerprinting. Infect. Control Hosp. Epidemiol. *16*:564–569, 1995.
27. Hayani, K. C.: *Citrobacter koseri* osteomyelitis in an infant. Acta Paediatr. Jpn. *39*:390–391, 1997.
28. Hodges, G. R., Degener, C. E., and Barnes, W. G.: Clinical significance of *Citrobacter* isolates. Am. J. Clin. Pathol. *70*:37–40, 1978.
29. Jacobson, K. L., Cohen, S. H., Inciardi, J. F., et al.: The relationship between antecedent antibiotic use and resistance to extended-spectrum cephalosporins in group I beta-lactamase–producing organisms. Clin. Infect. Dis. *21*:1107–1113, 1995.
30. Jones, S. R., Ragsdale, A. R., Kutscher, E., et al.: Clinical and bacteriologic observations on a recently recognized species of Enterobacteriaceae, *Citrobacter diversus*. J. Infect. Dis. *128*:563–565, 1973.
31. Kaplan, A. M., Itabashi, H. H., Yoshimori, R., et al.: Cerebral abscesses complicating neonatal *Citrobacter freundii* meningitis. West. J. Med. *127*:418–422, 1977.
32. Kline, M. W., and Kaplan, S. L.: *Citrobacter diversus* and neonatal brain abscess. Pediatr. Neurol. *3*:178–180, 1987.
33. Kline, M. W.: *Citrobacter* meningitis and brain abscess in infancy: Epidemiology, pathogenesis, and treatment. J. Pediatr. *113*:430–434, 1988.
34. Kline, M. W., Kaplan, S. L., Hawkins, E. P., et al.: Pathogenesis of brain abscess formation in an infant rat model of *Citrobacter diversus* bacteremia and meningitis. J. Infect. Dis. *157*:106–112, 1988.
35. Kline, M. W., Mason, E. O., Jr., and Kaplan, S. L.: Characterization of *Citrobacter diversus* strains causing neonatal meningitis. J. Infect. Dis. *157*:101–105, 1988.
36. Lesseva, M. I., and Hadjiski, O. G.: Analysis of bacteriuria in patients with burns. Burns *21*:3–6, 1995.
37. Levine, R. S., Rosenberg, H. K., Zimmerman, R. A., et al.: Complications of *Citrobacter* neonatal meningitis: Assessment by real-time cranial sonography correlated with CT. A. J. N. R. Am. J. Neuroradiol. *4*:668–671, 1983.
38. Lin, F. C., Devoe, W. F., Morrison, C., et al.: Outbreak of neonatal *Citrobacter diversus* meningitis in a suburban hospital. Pediatr. Infect. Dis. J. *6*:50–55, 1987.
39. Lipsky, B. A., Hook, E. W., 3rd, Smith, A. A., et al.: *Citrobacter* infections in humans: Experience at the Seattle Veterans Administration Medical Center and a review of the literature. Rev. Infect. Dis. *2*:746–760, 1980.
40. Madrazo, A., Geiger, J., and Lauter, C. B.: *Citrobacter diversus* at Grace Hospital, Detroit, Michigan. Am. J. Med. Sci. *270*:497–501, 1975.
41. Marshall, W. F., and Blair, J. E.: The cephalosporins. Mayo Clin. Proc. *74*:187–195, 1999.
42. McCracken, G. H., Jr., and Mize, S. G.: A controlled study of intrathecal antibiotic therapy in gram-negative enteric meningitis of infancy. Report of the Neonatal Meningitis Cooperative Study Group. J. Pediatr. *89*:66–72, 1976.
43. McCracken, G. H., Jr., Mize, S. G., and Threlkeld, N.: Intraventricular gentamicin therapy in gram-negative bacillary meningitis of infancy. Report of the Second Neonatal Meningitis Cooperative Study Group. Lancet *1*:787–791, 1980.
44. McCracken, G. H., Jr.: New developments in the management of children with bacterial meningitis. Pediatr. Infect. Dis. *3*(Suppl.):32–34, 1984.
45. Meier, A., Chusid, M. J., and Sty, J. R.: Neonatal *Citrobacter* meningitis: Neurosonographic observations. J. Ultrasound Med. *17*:399–401, 1998.
46. Morgan, M. G., Stuart, C., Leanord, A. T., et al.: *Citrobacter diversus* brain abscess: Case reports and molecular epidemiology. J. Med. Microbiol. *36*:273–278, 1992.
47. Papasian, C. J., Kinney, J., Coffman, S., et al.: Transmission of *Citrobacter koseri* from mother to infant documented by ribotyping and pulsed-field gel electrophoresis. Diagn. Microbiol. Infect. Dis. *26*:63–67, 1996.
48. Parry, M. F., Hutchinson, J. H., Brown, N. A., et al.: Gram-negative sepsis in neonates: A nursery outbreak due to hand carriage of *Citrobacter diversus*. Pediatrics. *65*:1105–1109, 1980.
49. Pfaller, M. A., Jones, R. N., Marshall, S. A., et al.: Inducible amp C beta-lactamase producing gram-negative bacilli from blood stream infections: Frequency, antimicrobial susceptibility, and molecular epidemiology in a national surveillance program (SCOPE). Diagn. Microbiol. Infect. Dis. *28*:211–219, 1997.
50. Ribeiro, C. D., Davis, P., and Jones, D. M.: *Citrobacter koseri* meningitis in a special care baby unit. J. Clin. Pathol. *29*:1094–1096, 1976.
51. Rose, S. J.: Neonatal meningitis due to *Citrobacter koseri*. J. Perinat. Med. *7*:273–275, 1979.

52. Sanders, W. E., Jr., Tenney, J. H., and Kessler, R. E.: Efficacy of cefepime in the treatment of infections due to multiply resistant *Enterobacter* species. Clin. Infect. Dis. *23*:454–461, 1996.
53. Schmidt, H., Montag, M., Bockemuhl, J., et al.: Shiga-like toxin II–related cytotoxins in *Citrobacter freundii* strains from humans and beef samples. Infect. Immun. *61*:534–543, 1993.
54. Shih, C. C., Chen, Y. C., Chang, S. C., et al.: Bacteremia due to *Citrobacter* species: Significance of primary intraabdominal infection. Clin. Infect. Dis. *23*:543–549, 1996.
55. Smith, R. F., Dayton, S. L., and Chipps, D. D.: Recognition of *Citrobacter diversus* in the clinical laboratory. Appl. Microbiol. *25*:157–158, 1973.
56. Soriano, A. L., Russell, R. G., Johnson, D., et al.: Pathophysiology of *Citrobacter diversus* neonatal meningitis: Comparative studies in an infant mouse model. Infect. Immun. *59*:1352–1358, 1991.
57. Stricker, T., Frohlich, S., and Nadal, D.: Osteomyelitis and septic arthritis due to *Citrobacter freundii* and *Haemophilus influenzae* type b. J. Paediatr. Child. Health *34*:90–91, 1998.
58. Tamborlane, W. V. F., and Soto, E. V.: Experience and reason—briefly recorded. *Citrobacter diversus* meningitis: A case report. Pediatrics *55*:739–741, 1975.
59. Tang, L. M., Chen, S. T., and Lui, T. N.: *Citrobacter* meningitis in adults. Clin. Neurol. Neurosurg. *96*:52–57, 1994.
60. Thurm, V., and Gericke, B.: Identification of infant food as a vehicle in a nosocomial outbreak of *Citrobacter freundii:* Epidemiological subtyping by allozyme, whole-cell protein and antibiotic resistance. J. Appl. Bacteriol. *76*:553–558, 1994.
61. Tschape, H., Prager, R., Streckel, W., et al.: Verotoxinogenic *Citrobacter freundii* associated with severe gastroenteritis and cases of haemolytic uraemic syndrome in a nursery school: Green butter as the infection source. Epidemiol. Infect. *114*:441–450, 1995.
62. Vogel, L. C., Ferguson, L., and Gotoff, S. P.: *Citrobacter* infections of the central nervous system in early infancy. J. Pediatr. *93*:86–88, 1978.
63. Werkman, C. H., and Gillen, G. F.: Bacteria producing trimethylene glycol. J. Bacteriol. *23*:167–182, 1932.
64. Werthamer, S., and Weiner, M.: Subacute bacterial endocarditis due to *Flavobacterium meningosepticum.* Am. J. Clin. Pathol. *57*:410–412, 1972.
65. Wientzen, R. L., McCracken, G. H., Jr., Petruska, M. L., et al.: Localization and therapy of urinary tract infections of childhood. Pediatrics *63*:467–474, 1979.
66. Williams, W. W., Mariano, J., Spurrier, M., et al.: Nosocomial meningitis due to *Citrobacter diversus* in neonates: New aspects of the epidemiology. J. Infect. Dis. *150*:229–235, 1984.
67. Wilson, D. A., Nguyen, D. L., and Marshall, K.: Sonography of brain abscesses complicating *Citrobacter* neonatal meningitis. Am. J. Perinatol. *5*:37–39, 1988.

Enterobacter

THOMAS G. BOYCE ■ WILLIAM C. GRUBER ■ RANDALL G. FISHER

Enterobacter is a genus of Enterobacteriaceae that is an increasingly frequent cause of nosocomial pediatric infection. *Enterobacter* can cause infection of postsurgical wounds, meningitis, and infection of the gastrointestinal, urinary, and respiratory tracts. The development of resistance to antibiotics commonly used for the treatment of infection is an increasingly common occurrence. For a more detailed overview of *Enterobacter* spp., the reader is referred to a review by Sanders and Sanders.[80]

Bacteriology

Enterobacter spp. are named for their enteric recovery as gram-negative bacteria.[79] They are found frequently in soil, water, and sewage. These organisms are facultatively anaerobic and motile by peritrichous flagella. They yield positive results on the malonate, citrate, and Voges-Proskauer tests. Taxonomic studies have led to several classifications of species contained in this genus. With the reclassification of *Enterobacter agglomerans* as *Pantoea agglomerans* (see Chapter 118), *Enterobacter cloacae, Enterobacter aerogenes,* and *Enterobacter sakazakii* are the species recovered most commonly from clinical material.[5, 14, 21, 26, 34, 46, 96, 97] Additional species in the *Enterobacter* genus that rarely are recovered from human infections include *Enterobacter amnigenus, Enterobacter asburiae, Enterobacter gergoviae, Enterobacter intermedium,* and *Enterobacter cancerogenus* (formerly *Enterobacter hormaechei), Enterobacter dissolvens, Enterobacter nimipressuralis,* and *Enterobacter hormaechei.*[1, 37, 69]

Epidemiology

Enterobacter is encountered most often as a hospital-acquired pathogen in patients with chronic illness.[5, 14, 21, 26, 46, 96, 97] A recent surveillance study at 50 American medical centers demonstrated *Enterobacter* to be the eighth most common cause of nosocomial bloodstream infections; it accounted for 230 (5%) of 4725 isolates,[73] 71 percent of which were *Enterobacter cloacae*, 23 percent were *Enterobacter aerogenes*, and 6 percent were other species of *Enterobacter*. *Enterobacter* infections are particularly common occurrences in intensive care units. In a Centers for Disease Control and Prevention survey, *Enterobacter* was one of the five pathogens most commonly encountered in intensive care units, and it was responsible for 8.6 percent of reported infections.[46] In one pediatric hospital, *Enterobacter* spp. (primarily *E. cloacae*) were the most common cause of enteric bacteremia and accounted for 14 percent of all bacteremic episodes during a 3-year period.[5] Multiple outbreaks caused by *Enterobacter* have been described in neonatal intensive care nurseries.* In some series, as many as a third of *Enterobacter* bacteremias are polymicrobial, which is a more frequent finding than with other gram-negative bacteremias.[16, 34]

The most frequently cited risk factor for acquisition of *Enterobacter* infection is recent treatment with antibiotics, particularly third-generation cephalosporins.[3–5, 13, 17, 20, 34, 47, 94] Other risk factors include prolonged hospital stay, especially in an intensive care unit; the presence of serious underlying illness (such as burns, malignancy, and diabetes); prematurity in a neonate; immunosuppression; and the presence of a foreign device.[80]

Vertical spread of *Enterobacter* from mother to infant may occur at the time of birth.[32] Environmental sources implicated in outbreaks of infection have included intravenous fluids,[29, 59, 60, 88, 95] chronic hand dermatitis of a care provider,[9] contaminated infant formula,[11, 22, 68] blood gas machines,[2, 51] and rectal thermometers.[91]

Ribotyping, pulsed-field electrophoresis, and restriction fragment polymorphism analysis of DNA from clinical

*See references 6, 31, 44, 51, 57, 72, 82, 91, 92, 99.

isolates have been useful in discriminating possible sources of contamination and patient-to-patient transfer of individual strains.[12, 21, 22, 40, 43, 52, 80] Plasmid profiles often are of little value because many strains of *Enterobacter* possess few, if any, plasmids.[80] Most cases are not associated with an outbreak, and an endogenous origin of infection is a more common means of acquisition than is the patient's environment,[73] which explains why recent antimicrobial use by the patient is such a strong predictor of infection.

Pathophysiology

Newborn infants often are colonized by *Enterobacter* in the gastrointestinal tract soon after birth,[10] and acquisition of hospital strains by immunocompromised newborn infants occurs commonly.[10, 33] *Enterobacter* then may contaminate the compromised respiratory tract. The oropharynx commonly is colonized by *Enterobacter* by the time the infant is 1 month of age; colonization rates generally are lower in breast-fed infants.[8] Newborns with gastrointestinal abnormalities requiring prolonged parenteral nutrition have higher rates of colonization with *Enterobacter* and a higher incidence of sepsis.[74] Enteric organisms are recovered less commonly from the oropharynx of healthy older children and adults, but increased colonization is noted during illness (see also Chapter 109).

The ability of *Enterobacter* spp. to develop inducible resistance to penicillins and cephalosporins increases their pathogenic potential. All species of *Enterobacter* possess a chromosomally encoded class C (Bush group I) β-lactamase, which usually is produced in small amounts.[80] This enzyme has a high affinity for third-generation cephalosporins but a low maximal hydrolysis rate.[63] Consequently, the β-lactamase mediates resistance to these antibiotics only when it is produced in large quantities.[55] Resistance emerges after a mutation in the *ampD* gene, which normally prevents high-level expression of this β-lactamase. Such mutants are considered "stably de-repressed." The addition of a β-lactamase inhibitor (such as clavulanic acid) does not increase the activity of β-lactam antibiotics against *Enterobacter*. In fact, the addition of a β-lactamase inhibitor may actually decrease activity against the organism by inducing the class C β-lactamase.[93] Resistance can develop during therapy (usually with a cephalosporin) in an isolate that initially is demonstrated to be susceptible,[45, 80] and such resistance can be detected as early as 24 hours after the initiation of therapy, or it may be delayed 2 to 3 weeks.[20] More recently, resistant strains of *Enterobacter* that produce plasmid-mediated extended-spectrum β-lactamases also have been isolated.[75]

In one study, gram-negative fecal aerobic flora was eradicated completely after 24 hours of administration of ceftriaxone therapy, only to be replaced within 10 days (mean of 6.7 days) by *Pseudomonas aeruginosa*, *Enterobacter,* and *Citrobacter* organisms resistant to all β-lactam antibiotics.[41] Though uncommon, the combination of reduced outer-membrane permeability and high-level production of β-lactamase renders some clinical isolates of *Enterobacter* resistant to carbapenems (imipenem and meropenem) and fourth-generation cephalosporins (cefepime).[15, 24, 53, 54, 63, 90]

Other than the presence of endotoxin, factors responsible for the virulence of *Enterobacter* spp. are not well defined.[49] In vitro, an *Escherichia coli* enterotoxigenic plasmid can be transferred and expressed in *Enterobacter*, thus indicating the potential for transfer of virulence factors to *Enterobacter* from other species.[102] Shiga toxin–producing *E. cloacae* has been isolated from the stool of a 5-month-old girl with the hemolytic-uremic syndrome.[70] However, *E. coli* OR:H9, which also produced Shiga toxin, was isolated from the child's stool as well, thus rendering the cause of the child's symptoms unclear. Like other organisms associated with central venous catheter infections, *Enterobacter* may adhere irreversibly to catheter material and promote colonization and infection.[71] Certain ribotypes have been encountered more commonly as community or bloodstream isolates, a finding indicative of the presence of as yet undefined factors affecting virulence.[98] The propensity of *E. sakazakii* to produce neonatal meningitis complicated by abscesses and cerebral infarction is unexplained.[11, 22, 100]

Clinical Manifestations

Infection caused by *Enterobacter* commonly is indistinguishable from illness caused by other enteric pathogens. Sources of infection include central venous catheters and the urinary and biliary tracts.[5, 7, 34, 46, 56] *Enterobacter* commonly colonizes respiratory tract secretions in intubated patients, and it is implicated increasingly as a cause of nosocomial pneumonia.[46] It is also one of the most common causes of pneumonia that develops after lung transplantation.[58] Neonatal infection deserves special mention because of the prominence of *E. sakazakii* as a cause of devastating meningitis.

Similar to *Citrobacter koseri* (formerly *Citrobacter diversus*) (see Chapter 106), *E. sakazakii* causes neonatal meningitis complicated by cerebral abscess or infarction.[11, 22, 48, 100, 101] Poor feeding, irritability, jaundice, a full anterior fontanelle, and fever or hypothermia are initial features that are shared with other gram-negative causes of bacterial meningitis. However, the mortality rate reaches 50 percent, and almost all survivors suffer severe neurologic complications.[100] This severe morbidity is consistent with the development of multiple cystic lesions of the brain in 50 percent of surviving neonates. Serial computed tomography commonly reveals the evolution of lesions most consistent with initial cerebral infarction rather than primary abscess formation.[35, 100] Cystic lesions that occur subsequently may be purulent abscesses from which the organism can be cultured, or they may be sterile fluid collections.[18] *Enterobacter* spp. also may be associated with necrotizing enterocolitis in the newborn; they were the third most common isolate recovered from peritonitis exudates in a series of patients with necrotizing enterocolitis.[67]

In older immunocompromised children, development of bacteremia complicated by sepsis is a significant risk. Central venous catheterization and gastrointestinal tract pathology appear to pose a greater risk for bacteremia than does development of infection of the urinary tract.[5, 21, 34, 56] Bacteremia is accompanied by shock in close to one third of patients, but disseminated intravascular coagulation occurs in less than 5 percent of patients.[13, 16, 34] Seeding of metastatic foci occurs relatively uncommonly. Overall case-fatality rates with bacteremia vary but usually are approximately 30 percent.[80] Factors associated with a poor prognosis include age younger than 18 months, inadequacy of antimicrobial chemotherapy, septic shock, the type of underlying disease, the presence of pulmonary infection, thrombocytopenia, and a requirement for intensive care.[13, 16, 34] Absence of fever during the course of infection may be a particularly ominous sign; indeed, four of five afebrile subjects died in one series.[13]

Some *Enterobacter* spp. recovered from children with diarrhea have been reported to produce enterotoxin,[19] although a causative role in enteritis has not been established. Other manifestations of *Enterobacter* infection include endophthalmitis,[65, 66] endometritis,[38] wound infections,[34] diskitis,[76, 85] endocarditis,[89] and osteomyelitis.[25, 86] *Enterobacter* also has caused syndromes classically associated with other agents, such as gas gangrene,[30] childhood purpura fulminans,[42] ecthyma gangrenosum,[77] and necrotizing fasciitis.[50]

Diagnosis

The diagnosis of *Enterobacter* infection relies primarily on isolation of the organism in culture from clinical material. The ability to detect pathogens directly in tissue with biotinylated probes offers promise for making a rapid diagnosis.[61] Motility, ornithine decarboxylase production, and the absence of deoxyribonuclease help distinguish the genus from *Klebsiella* and *Serratia*. Patterns of sugar fermentation and decarboxylase production also differentiate the species. Ribotyping is a highly discriminatory and reproducible method for typing *E. cloacae*, the most common cause of infection.[36] Other useful molecular techniques include restriction endonuclease analysis of chromosomal DNA, pulsed-field gel electrophoresis, random amplification of polymorphic DNA, and amplification of short interspersed repetitive sequences.[80] Most often, molecular typing methods are used in concert with biotyping, serotyping, or bacteriocin typing.

Treatment

Treatment of *Enterobacter* infection is made problematic by resistance to cephalosporins. Antibiotic resistance may be present at the time of initial isolation or may develop during therapy.[21, 45] This problem is compounded by the common observation of resistance to extended-spectrum penicillins and, to a lesser extent, aminoglycosides. The risk for development of resistance to cephalosporins, piperacillin, and aminoglycosides has been reported to be higher at a tertiary care center than at a primary care hospital.[28] Previous administration of third-generation cephalosporins increases the risk of multiresistant *Enterobacter* isolates being found in an initial, positive blood culture.[5, 20] However, hospitalized newborns may acquire multiresistant strains quickly, even though they themselves have not been treated with cephalosporins.[10] In turn, isolation of multiresistant *Enterobacter* in blood culture is associated with a higher case-fatality rate than is isolation of a more sensitive *Enterobacter* strain.[20, 83] Though less common, resistance to imipenem has been reported.[27, 53, 87] Cefepime, a fourth-generation cephalosporin, generally maintains activity against *Enterobacter* spp. that possess class C β-lactamase,[81] although minimal inhibitory concentrations may be somewhat higher.[63] Emergence of cefepime resistance during therapy has been described in a liver transplant recipient with a hepatic abscess caused by *E. aerogenes*.[54] The accompanying editorial cautions against the use of cefepime in patients who have high-density infections (e.g., poorly draining liver abscess) caused by ceftazidime-resistant strains of *Enterobacter*.[63]

In a recent nationwide survey of nosocomial bloodstream infections, rates of *Enterobacter* resistance to third-generation cephalosporins (ceftazidime, ceftriaxone) and broad-spectrum semisynthetic penicillins (piperacillin), with or without a β-lactamase inhibitor (tazobactam), were high and ranged from 35 to 50 percent.[73] Notably, cefepime and imipenem inhibited 97 to 100 percent of isolates. Susceptibility to aminoglycosides and fluoroquinolones ranged from 92 to 98 percent, and 85 to 96 percent of isolates were susceptible to trimethoprim-sulfamethoxazole. Because resistance patterns may vary with geographic location, local susceptibility data should be used to guide initial therapy.

Some investigators recommend initial combination therapy that includes an aminoglycoside plus either cefepime or a carbapenem (imipenem or meropenem) until the results of susceptibility testing are available. The addition of an aminoglycoside does not prevent the development of resistance to extended-spectrum cephalosporins.[20] When organisms are susceptible, extended-spectrum penicillins are preferable to cephalosporins because of the lower likelihood that resistance will develop during or subsequent to therapy.[20] In strains resistant to gentamicin and tobramycin, amikacin may be a suitable alternative. Good responses to therapy and return of gentamicin susceptibility in hospital *Enterobacter* strains have occurred after routine substitution of amikacin for gentamicin.[78, 84] Trimethoprim-sulfamethoxazole alone (or combined with an aminoglycoside) and quinolones appear to be good alternatives for the treatment of *Enterobacter* infections, including meningitis.[5, 23, 39, 64, 101]

Enterobacter meningitis creates special concerns. As is common with other forms of neonatal enteric meningitis, even susceptible organisms often persist in cerebrospinal fluid for 5 days or longer.[48] Cephalosporin monotherapy appears to be less effective than is combination therapy with an aminoglycoside. Trimethoprim-sulfamethoxazole also has been used successfully.[101] Intrathecal administration of antibiotics does not appear to be of benefit, however.[62] The physician should anticipate the potential development of cerebral abscesses, infarctions, and cysts in newborn infants with *E. sakazakii* infection. The use of serial computed tomography should be considered, and a neurosurgeon should be sought for drainage of abscesses and management of fluid accumulation.

REFERENCES

1. Abbott, S. L., and Janda, J. M.: *Enterobacter cancerogenus ("Enterobacter taylorae")* infections associated with severe trauma or crush injuries. Am. J. Clin. Pathol. *107*:359–361, 1997.
2. Acolet, D., Ahmet, Z., Houang, E., et al.: *Enterobacter cloacae* in a neonatal intensive care unit: Account of an outbreak and its relationship to use of third generation cephalosporins. J. Hosp. Infect. *28*:273–286, 1994.
3. al Ansari, N., McNamara, E. B., Cunney, R. J., et al.: Experience with *Enterobacter* bacteraemia in a Dublin teaching hospital. J. Hosp. Infect. *27*:69–72, 1994.
4. Anderson, E. L., and Hieber, J. P.: An outbreak of gentamicin-resistant *Enterobacter cloacae* infections in a pediatric intensive care unit. Infect. Control *4*:148–152, 1983.
5. Andresen, J., Asmar, B. I., and Dajani, A. S.: Increasing *Enterobacter* bacteremia in pediatric patients. Pediatr. Infect. Dis. J. *13*:787–792, 1994.
6. Archibald, L. K., Ramos, M., Arduino, M. J., et al.: *Enterobacter cloacae* and *Pseudomonas aeruginosa* polymicrobial bloodstream infections traced to extrinsic contamination of a dextrose multidose vial. J. Pediatr. *133*:640–644, 1998.
7. Ashkenazi, S., Even-Tov, S., Samra, Z., et al.: Uropathogens of various childhood populations and their antibiotic susceptibility. Pediatr. Infect. Dis. J. *10*:742–746, 1991.
8. Baltimore, R. S., Duncan, R. L., Shapiro, E. D., et al.: Epidemiology of pharyngeal colonization of infants with aerobic gram-negative rod bacteria. J. Clin. Microbiol. *27*:91–95, 1989.
9. Beck-Sague, C. M., Chong, W. H., Roy, C., et al.: Outbreak of surgical wound infections associated with total hip arthroplasty. Infect. Control Hosp. Epidemiol. *13*:526–534, 1992.
10. Berkowitz, F. E., and Metchock, B.: Third-generation cephalosporin-resistant gram-negative bacilli in the feces of hospitalized children. Pediatr. Infect. Dis. J. *14*:97–100, 1995.
11. Biering, G., Karlsson, S., Clark, N. C., et al.: Three cases of neonatal meningitis caused by *Enterobacter sakazakii* in powdered milk. J. Clin. Microbiol. *27*:2054–2056, 1989.

12. Bingen, E., Denamur, E., Lambert-Zechovsky, N., et al.: Rapid genotyping shows the absence of cross-contamination in *Enterobacter cloacae* nosocomial infections. J. Hosp. Infect. *21*:95–101, 1992.
13. Bodey, G. P., Elting, L. S., and Rodriguez, S.: Bacteremia caused by *Enterobacter:* 15 years of experience in a cancer hospital. Rev. Infect. Dis. *13*:550–558, 1991.
14. Bonadio, W. A., Margolis, D., and Tovar, M.: *Enterobacter cloacae* bacteremia in children: A review of 30 cases in 12 years. Clin. Pediatr. (Phila.) *30*:310–313, 1991.
15. Bornet, C., Davin-Regli, A., Bosi, C., et al.: Imipenem resistance of *Enterobacter aerogenes* mediated by outer membrane permeability. J. Clin. Microbiol. *38*:1048–1052, 2000.
16. Bouza, E., Garcia de la Torre, M., Erice, A., et al.: *Enterobacter* bacteremia: An analysis of 50 episodes. Arch. Intern. Med. *145*:1024–1027, 1985.
17. Burchard, K. W., Barrall, D. T., Reed, M., et al.: *Enterobacter* bacteremia in surgical patients. Surgery *100*:857–862, 1986.
18. Burdette, J. H., and Santos, C.: *Enterobacter sakazakii* brain abscess in the neonate: The importance of neuroradiologic imaging. Pediatr. Radiol. *30*:33–34, 2000.
19. Chatterjee, B. D., Thawani, G., and Sanyal, S. N.: Etiology of acute childhood diarrhea in Calcutta. Trop. Gastroenterol. *10*:158–166, 1989.
20. Chow, J. W., Fine, M. J., Shlaes, D. M., et al.: *Enterobacter* bacteremia: Clinical features and emergence of antibiotic resistance during therapy. Ann. Intern. Med. *115*:585–590, 1991.
21. Chow, J. W., Yu, V. L., and Shlaes, D. M.: Epidemiologic perspectives on *Enterobacter* for the infection control professional. Am. J. Infect. Control *22*:195–201, 1994.
22. Clark, N. C., Hill, B. C., O'Hara, C. M., et al.: Epidemiologic typing of *Enterobacter sakazakii* in two neonatal nosocomial outbreaks. Diagn. Microbiol. Infect. Dis. *13*:467–472, 1990.
23. D'Antuono, V. S., and Brown, I.: Successful treatment of *Enterobacter* meningitis with ciprofloxacin. Clin. Infect. Dis. *26*:206–207, 1998.
24. De Gheldre, Y., Maes, N., Rost, F., et al.: Molecular epidemiology of an outbreak of multidrug-resistant *Enterobacter aerogenes* infections and in vivo emergence of imipenem resistance. J. Clin. Microbiol. *35*:152–160, 1997.
25. Dubey, L., Krasinski, K., and Hernanz-Schulman, M.: Osteomyelitis secondary to trauma or infected contiguous soft tissue. Pediatr. Infect. Dis. J. 7:26–34, 1988.
26. Ehni, W. F., Reller, L. B., and Ellison, R. T., 3rd: Bacteremia in granulocytopenic patients in a tertiary-care general hospital. Rev. Infect. Dis. *13*:613–619, 1991.
27. Ehrhardt, A. F., Sanders, C. C., Thomson, K. S., et al.: Emergence of resistance to imipenem in *Enterobacter* isolates masquerading as *Klebsiella pneumoniae* during therapy with imipenem/cilastatin. Clin. Infect. Dis. *17*:120–122, 1993.
28. Ellner, P. D., Fink, D. J., Neu, H. C., et al.: Epidemiologic factors affecting antimicrobial resistance of common bacterial isolates. J. Clin. Microbiol. *25*:1668–1674, 1987.
29. *Enterobacter cloacae* bloodstream infections associated with contaminated prefilled saline syringes—California, November 1998. M. M. W. R. Morb. Mortal. Wkly. Rep. *47*:959–960, 1998.
30. Fata, F., Chittivelu, S., Tessler, S., et al.: Gas gangrene of the arm due to *Enterobacter cloacae* in a neutropenic patient. South. Med. J. *89*:1095–1096, 1996.
31. Fok, T. F., Lee, C. H., Wong, E. M., et al.: Risk factors for *Enterobacter* septicemia in a neonatal unit: Case-control study. Clin. Infect. Dis. *27*:1204–1209, 1998.
32. Fryklund, B., Tullus, K., Berglund, B., et al.: Importance of the environment and the faecal flora of infants, nursing staff and parents as sources of gram-negative bacteria colonizing newborns in three neonatal wards. Infection *20*:253–257, 1992.
33. Fryklund, B., Tullus, K., and Burman, L. G.: Epidemiology of enteric bacteria in neonatal units—influence of procedures and patient variables. J. Hosp. Infect. *18*:15–21, 1991.
34. Gallagher, P. G.: *Enterobacter* bacteremia in pediatric patients. Rev. Infect. Dis. *12*:808–812, 1990.
35. Gallagher, P. G., and Ball, W. S.: Cerebral infarctions due to CNS infection with *Enterobacter sakazakii*. Pediatr. Radiol. *21*:135–136, 1991.
36. Garaizar, J., Kaufmann, M. E., and Pitt, T. L.: Comparison of ribotyping with conventional methods for the type identification of *Enterobacter cloacae*. J. Clin. Microbiol. *29*:1303–1307, 1991.
37. Gaston, M. A.: *Enterobacter:* An emerging nosocomial pathogen. J. Hosp. Infect. *11*:197–208, 1988.
38. Gibbs, R. S., Blanco, J. D., and Bernstein, S.: Role of aerobic gram-negative bacilli in endometritis after cesarean section. Rev Infect. Dis. *7(Suppl.* 4):690–695, 1985.
39. Goepp, J. G., Lee, C. K., Anderson, T., et al.: Use of ciprofloxacin in an infant with ventriculitis. J. Pediatr. *121*:303–305, 1992.
40. Grattard, F., Pozzetto, B., Berthelot, P., et al.: Arbitrarily primed PCR, ribotyping, and plasmid pattern analysis applied to investigation of a nosocomial outbreak due to *Enterobacter cloacae* in a neonatal intensive care unit. J. Clin. Microbiol. *32*:596–602, 1994.
41. Guggenbichler, J. P., Kofler, J., and Allerberger, F.: The influence of third-generation cephalosporins on the aerobic intestinal flora. Infection *13*(Suppl.):137–139, 1985.
42. Gurses, N., and Ozkan, A.: Neonatal and childhood purpura fulminans: Review of seven cases. Cutis *41*:361–363, 1988.
43. Haertl, R., and Bandlow, G.: Molecular typing of *Enterobacter cloacae* by pulsed-field gel electrophoresis of genomic restriction fragments. J. Hosp. Infect. *25*:109–116, 1993.
44. Harbarth, S., Sudre, P., Dharan, S., et al.: Outbreak of *Enterobacter cloacae* related to understaffing, overcrowding, and poor hygiene practices. Infect. Control Hosp. Epidemiol. *20*:598–603, 1999.
45. Heusser, M. F., Patterson, J. E., Kuritza, A. P., et al.: Emergence of resistance to multiple beta-lactams in *Enterobacter cloacae* during treatment for neonatal meningitis with cefotaxime. Pediatr. Infect. Dis. J. *9*:509–512, 1990.
46. Jarvis, W. R., and Martone, W. J.: Predominant pathogens in hospital infections. J. Antimicrob. Chemother. *29*(Suppl. A):19–24, 1992.
47. Johnson, M. P., and Ramphal, R.: Beta-lactam–resistant *Enterobacter* bacteremia in febrile neutropenic patients receiving monotherapy. J. Infect. Dis. *162*:981–983, 1990.
48. Kaplan, S. L., and Patrick, C. C.: Cefotaxime and aminoglycoside treatment of meningitis caused by gram-negative enteric organisms. Pediatr. Infect. Dis. J. *9*:810–814, 1990.
49. Keller, R., Pedroso, M. Z., Ritchmann, R., et al: Occurrence of virulence-associated properties in *Enterobacter cloacae.* Infect. Immun. *66*:645–649, 1998.
50. Kronish, J. W., and McLeish, W. M.: Eyelid necrosis and periorbital necrotizing fasciitis: Report of a case and review of the literature. Ophthalmology *98*:92–98, 1991.
51. Lacey, S. L., and Want, S. V.: An outbreak of *Enterobacter cloacae* associated with contamination of a blood gas machine. J. Infect. *30*:223–226, 1995.
52. Lambert-Zechovsky, N., Bingen, E., Denamur, E., et al.: Molecular analysis provides evidence for the endogenous origin of bacteremia and meningitis due to *Enterobacter cloacae* in an infant. Clin. Infect. Dis. *15*:30–32, 1992.
53. Lee, E. H., Nicolas, M. H., Kitzis, M. D., et al.: Association of two resistance mechanisms in a clinical isolate of *Enterobacter cloacae* with high-level resistance to imipenem. Antimicrob. Agents Chemother. *35*:1093–1098, 1991.
54. Limaye, A. P., Gautom, R. K., Black, D., et al.: Rapid emergence of resistance to cefepime during treatment. Clin. Infect. Dis. 25:339–340, 1997.
55. Lindberg, F., and Normark, S.: Contribution of chromosomal beta-lactamases to beta-lactam resistance in enterobacteria. Rev. Infect. Dis. *8*(Suppl. 3):292–304, 1986.
56. Lohr, J. A., Donowitz, L. G., and Sadler, J. E., 3rd: Hospital-acquired urinary tract infection. Pediatrics *83*:193–199, 1989.
57. Loiwal, V., Kumar, A., Gupta, P., et al.: *Enterobacter aerogenes* outbreak in a neonatal intensive care unit. Pediatr. Int. *41*:157–161, 1999.
58. Low, D. E., Kaiser, L. R., Haydock, D. A., et al.: The donor lung: Infectious and pathologic factors affecting outcome in lung transplantation. J. Thorac. Cardiovasc. Surg. *106*:614–621, 1993.
59. Maki, D. G., Rhame, F. S., Mackel, D. C., et al.: Nationwide epidemic of septicemia caused by contaminated intravenous products. I. Epidemiologic and clinical features. Am. J. Med. *60*:471–485, 1976.
60. Matsaniotis, N. S., Syriopoulou, V. P., Theodoridou, M. C., et al.: *Enterobacter* sepsis in infants and children due to contaminated intravenous fluids. Infect. Control *5*:471–477, 1984.
61. Matsuhisa, A., Saito, Y., Sakamoto, Y., et al.: Detection of bacteria in phagocyte-smears from septicemia-suspected blood by in situ hybridization using biotinylated probes. Microbiol. Immunol. *38*:511–517, 1994.
62. McCracken, G. H., Jr., and Mize, S. G.: A controlled study of intrathecal antibiotic therapy in gram-negative enteric meningitis of infancy: Report of the neonatal meningitis cooperative study group. J. Pediatr. *89*:66–72, 1976.
63. Medeiros, A. A.: Relapsing infection due to *Enterobacter* species: Lessons of heterogeneity. Clin. Infect. Dis. *25*:341–342, 1997.
64. Meis, J. F., Groot-Loonen, J., and Hoogkamp-Korstanje, J. A.: A brain abscess due to multiply-resistant *Enterobacter cloacae* successfully treated with meropenem. Clin. Infect. Dis. *20*:1567, 1995.
65. Milewski, S. A., and Klevjer-Anderson, P.: Endophthalmitis caused by *Enterobacter cloacae.* Ann. Ophthalmol. *25*:309–311, 1993.
66. Mirza, G. E., Karakucuk, S., Doganay, M., et al.: Postoperative endophthalmitis caused by an *Enterobacter* species. J. Hosp. Infect. *26*:167–172, 1994.
67. Mollitt, D. L., Tepas, J. J., 3rd, and Talbert, J. L.: The microbiology of neonatal peritonitis. Arch. Surg. *123*:176–179, 1988.
68. Noriega, F. R., Kotloff, K. L., Martin, M. A., et al.: Nosocomial bacteremia caused by *Enterobacter sakazakii* and *Leuconostoc mesenteroides* resulting from extrinsic contamination of infant formula. Pediatr. Infect. Dis. J. *9*:447–449, 1990.
69. O'Hara, C. M., Steigerwalt, A. G., Hill, B. C., et al.: *Enterobacter hormaechei*, a new species of the family Enterobacteriaceae formerly known as enteric group 75. J. Clin. Microbiol. *27*:2046–2049, 1989.

70. Paton, A. W., and Paton, J. C.: *Enterobacter cloacae* producing a Shiga-like toxin II–related cytotoxin associated with a case of hemolytic-uremic syndrome. J. Clin. Microbiol. 34:463–465, 1996.
71. Penner, J., Allerberger, F., Dierich, M. P., et al.: In vitro experiments on catheter-related infections due to gram-negative rods. Chemotherapy *39*:336–354, 1993.
72. Peters, S. M., Bryan, J., and Cole, M. F.: Enterobacterial repetitive intergenic consensus polymerase chain reaction typing of isolates of *Enterobacter cloacae* from an outbreak of infection in a neonatal intensive care unit. Am. J. Infect. Control *28*:123–129, 2000.
73. Pfaller, M. A., Jones, R. N., Marshall, S. A., et al.: Inducible amp C beta-lactamase producing gram-negative bacilli from blood stream infections: Frequency, antimicrobial susceptibility, and molecular epidemiology in a national surveillance program (SCOPE). Diagn. Microbiol. Infect. Dis. *28*:211–219, 1997.
74. Pierro, A., van Saene, H. K., Jones, M. O., et al.: Clinical impact of abnormal gut flora in infants receiving parenteral nutrition. Ann. Surg. *227*:547–552, 1998.
75. Pitout, J. D., Thomson, K. S., Hanson, N. D., et al.: Plasmid-mediated resistance to expanded-spectrum cephalosporins among *Enterobacter aerogenes* strains. Antimicrob. Agents Chemother. *42*:596–600, 1998.
76. Porter, P., and Wray, C. C.: *Enterobacter agglomerans* spondylodiscitis: A possible, unrecognized complication of tetracycline therapy. Spine *25*:1287–1289, 2000.
77. Rajan, R. K.: Spontaneous bacterial peritonitis with ecthyma gangrenosum due to *Escherichia coli*. J. Clin. Gastroenterol. *4*:145–148, 1982.
78. Raz, R., Sharir, R., Shmilowitz, L., et al.: The elimination of gentamicin-resistant gram-negative bacteria in a newborn intensive care unit. Infection *15*:32–34, 1987.
79. Richard, C.: *Enterobacter*. *In* Butler, J. P. (ed.): Bergey's Manual of Systematic Bacteriology. Vol. 1. Baltimore, Williams & Wilkins, 1984, pp. 465–467.
80. Sanders, W. E., Jr., and Sanders, C. C.: *Enterobacter* spp.: Pathogens poised to flourish at the turn of the century. Clin. Microbiol. Rev. *10*:220–241, 1997.
81. Sanders, W. E., Jr., Tenney, J. H., and Kessler, R. E.: Efficacy of cefepime in the treatment of infections due to multiple resistant *Enterobacter* species. Clin. Infect. Dis. *23*:454–461, 1996.
82. Shi, Z. Y., Liu, P. Y., Lau, Y. J., et al.: Epidemiological typing of isolates from an outbreak of infection with multidrug-resistant *Enterobacter cloacae* by repetitive extragenic palindromic unit b1-primed PCR and pulsed-field gel electrophoresis. J. Clin. Microbiol. *34*:2784–2790, 1996.
83. Shlaes, D. M.: The clinical relevance of *Enterobacter* infections. Clin. Ther. *15*:21–28, 1993.
84. Shulman, S. T., and Yogev, R.: Treatment of pediatric infections with amikacin as first-line aminoglycoside. Am. J. Med. *79*:43–50, 1985.
85. Solans, R., Simeon, P., Cuenca, R., et al.: Infectious discitis caused by *Enterobacter cloacae*. Ann. Rheum. Dis. *51*:906–907, 1992.
86. Syrogiannopoulos, G. A., McCracken, G. H., Jr., and Nelson, J. D.: Osteoarticular infections in children with sickle cell disease. Pediatrics *78*:1090–1096, 1986.
87. Thomson, K. S., Sanders, C. C., and Chmel, H.: Imipenem resistance in *Enterobacter*. Eur. J. Clin. Microbiol. Infect. Dis. *12*:610–613, 1993.
88. Tresoldi, A. T., Padoveze, M. D., Trabasso, P., et al.: *Enterobacter cloacae* sepsis outbreak in a newborn unit caused by contaminated total parenteral nutrition solution. Am. J. Infect. Control *28*:258–261, 2000.
89. Tunkel, A. R., Fisch, M. J., Schlein, A., et al.: *Enterobacter* endocarditis. Scand. J. Infect. Dis. *24*:233–240, 1992.
90. Tzouvelekis, L. S., Tzelepi, E., Kaufmann, M. E., et al.: Consecutive mutations leading to the emergence in vivo of imipenem resistance in a clinical strain of *Enterobacter aerogenes*. J. Med. Microbiol. *40*:403–407, 1994.
91. van den Berg, R. W., Claahsen, H. L., Niessen, M., et al.: *Enterobacter cloacae* outbreak in the NICU related to disinfected thermometers. J. Hosp. Infect. *45*:29–34, 2000.
92. van Nierop, W. H., Duse, A. G., Stewart, R. G., et al.: Molecular epidemiology of an outbreak of *Enterobacter cloacae* in the neonatal intensive care unit of a provincial hospital in Gauteng, South Africa. J. Clin. Microbiol. *36*:3085–3087, 1998.
93. Varaldo, P. E., Biavasco, F., Mannelli, S., et al.: Distribution and antibiotic susceptibility of extraintestinal clinical isolates of *Klebsiella, Enterobacter* and *Serratia* species. Eur. J. Clin. Microbiol. Infect. Dis. *7*:495–500, 1988.
94. Walder, M., Haeggman, S., Tullus, K., et al.: A hospital outbreak of high-level beta-lactam–resistant *Enterobacter* spp.: Association more with ampicillin and cephalosporin therapy than with nosocomial transmission. Scand. J. Infect. Dis. *28*:293–296, 1996.
95. Wang, S. A., Tokars, J. I., Bianchine, P. J., et al: *Enterobacter cloacae* bloodstream infections traced to contaminated human albumin. Clin. Infect. Dis. *30*:35–40, 2000.
96. Watanakunakorn, C., and Weber, J.: *Enterobacter* bacteremia: A review of 58 episodes. Scand. J. Infect. Dis. *21*:1–8, 1989.
97. Weischer, M., and Kolmos, H. J.: Retrospective 6-year study of *Enterobacter* bacteraemia in a Danish university hospital. J. Hosp. Infect. *20*:15–24, 1992.
98. Weischer, M., and Kolmos, H. J.: Ribotyping of selected isolates of *Enterobacter cloacae* and clinical data related to biotype, phage type, O-serotype, and ribotype. A. P. M. I. S. *101*:879–886, 1993.
99. Wenger, P. N., Tokars, J. I., Brennan, P., et al.: An outbreak of *Enterobacter hormaechei* infection and colonization in an intensive care nursery. Clin. Infect. Dis. *24*:1243–1244, 1997.
100. Willis, J., and Robinson, J. E.: *Enterobacter sakazakii* meningitis in neonates. Pediatr. Infect. Dis. J. *7*:196–199, 1988.
101. Wolff, M. A., Young, C. L., and Ramphal, R.: Antibiotic therapy for *Enterobacter* meningitis: A retrospective review of 13 episodes and review of the literature. Clin. Infect. Dis. *16*:772–777, 1993.
102. Yamamoto, T., Honda, T., Miwatani, T., et al.: A virulence plasmid in *Escherichia coli* enterotoxigenic for humans: Intergenetic transfer and expression. J. Infect. Dis. *150*:688–698, 1984.

CHAPTER 108 Diarrhea- and Dysentery-Causing *Escherichia coli*

SHELDON L. KAPLAN ■ GERALD T. KEUSCH

The concept that certain *Escherichia coli* strains are enteric pathogens is not new. With information derived from the limited techniques available 75 years ago, Adam[4] postulated the existence of a group of *E. coli* "dyspepsia" bacteria responsible for neonatal and infantile diarrhea. Bray determined that many, but not all, isolates from cholera infantum were agglutinated with antiserum prepared from a strain isolated from a child with typical cholera infantum, whereas *E. coli* organisms from other sources were not.[18] Somewhat later, the initial isolate used by Bray to develop the antiserum was serotyped by the Kauffman scheme as O111:B4, one of the now classic groups of enteropathogenic *E. coli* (EPEC) (Table 108–1). The first outbreak of infantile gastroenteritis associated with a specific *E. coli* strain in the United States occurred in 1947 and was caused by an O111:B4 strain.[70]

Causative Organisms

During the past 45 years, a restricted number of *E. coli* bearing certain of the approximately 180 known somatic O antigens

TABLE 108–1 ■ SEROLOGIC SPECIFICITIES OF DIARRHEOGENIC *ESCHERICHIA COLI*

Classic Enteropathogenic	Enterotoxigenic	Enteroinvasive	Enterohemorrhagic	Enteroaggregative
O44 : H34	O6 : H —, 12, 16, 40	O28 : H —	O26 : H11	Nontypable
O55 : H6, 7, 32	O8 : H —, 42	O29 : H —	O103 : H2	Rough
O86 : H2, 34	O25 : H —, 42	O32 : H —	O104 : H21	O3 : H2
O111 : H2, 7, 12	O27 : H7	O42 : H —	O128 : H2	O6 : H1
O114 : H2	O29 : H21	O112 : H —	O145 : H —	O11 : H16
O119 : H6	O63 : H —, 12	O121 : H —	O157 : H—, 7	O15 : H21
O124 : H?	O78: H11, 12	O124 : H —	Many others	O44 : H18
O125 : H21	O117 : H4	O136 : H —		O77 : H18
O126 : H2, 5	O128 : H21	O143 : H —		O89 : H—
O127 : H4, 6, 21	O153 : H45	O144 : H —		O92 : H23
O128 : H2	O159 : H4, 21	O152 : H —		O111 : H21
O142 : H6, 34	Others	Others		O125 : H30
O158 : H23				O126 : H10, 27
				O127 : H2
				O128 : H8, 35
				O146 : H39
				O148 : H28

of the genus have been shown to be associated with intestinal infection (see Table 108–1). The association of serotype and virulence is even more striking when the combination of O and the 60 or so H (flagellar) antigens is used.[45] Only a small percentage of the approximately 10,000 O:H serotypes possible are known to be enteric pathogens. Five well-defined groups of *E. coli* have been characterized on the basis of clinical, biochemical, and molecular/genetic criteria and accepted by most workers in the field: (1) enterotoxigenic *E. coli* (ETEC), which produces one or both types of secretory enterotoxins known as LT (heat-labile toxin) and ST (heat-stable toxin); (2) EPEC, defined by its pattern of adherence to tissue culture cells and ability to polymerize cellular actin and produce a characteristic alteration in the microvillus membrane termed the *attaching and effacing* (A/E) lesion; (3) enterohemorrhagic *E. coli* (EHEC), which produces cytotoxins (Stx) related to Shiga toxin (also termed *Shiga-like toxins* [SLTs] or *verotoxins*) and may cause bloody diarrhea, hemorrhagic colitis, and hemolytic-uremic syndrome (HUS) or thrombotic thrombocytopenic purpura (TTP); (4) enteroinvasive *E. coli* (EIEC), which is capable of invading intestinal epithelial cells and causing a dysenteric illness; and (5) enteroaggregative *E. coli* (EAggEC), which adheres in vitro to HEp-2 cells in a characteristic autoaggregative manner and is associated with persistent diarrhea in infants.[75] A sixth category of diarrheogenic *E. coli* that has been accepted by several investigators is diffusely adherent *E. coli,* which has a diffuse adherence pattern when incubated with cultured epithelial cells and elaborates an alpha-hemolysin and cytotoxic necrotizing factor 1 that appear to be involved in the pathogenesis of the diarrhea that it causes.[27, 93, 96]

As described later, the virulence of diarrheogenic *E. coli* is polygenic and determined by genes encoding colonization factors, such as adhesins, invasins, toxins, and factors that alter the cellular cytoskeleton.

Transmission and Epidemiology

Diarrhea-causing *E. coli* strains are worldwide in distribution. The route of infection is, in the last analysis, fecal-oral; however, several additional factors may be interposed between the two orifices, including transmission by person-to-person contact; transmission via water, milk, or food; and even the intercession of flies or other insects as intermediate vectors. Unfortunately, few epidemiologic investigations are germane to the question of transmission.

ENTEROTOXIGENIC *ESCHERICHIA COLI*

Spurred by the remarkable progress in understanding the role of a protein enterotoxin in the pathogenesis of cholera and careful, thorough studies of ETEC diarrhea in animals, Sack and colleagues[122] provided the first evidence of ETEC diarrhea in humans. Numerous studies since then involving both pediatric and adult populations have established that ETEC accounts for approximately 20 to 30 percent of diarrhea episodes in the developing world and is the most common bacterial pathogen in visitors to these countries (traveler's diarrhea). ETEC remains the most common pathogen in U.S. travelers to Mexico and travelers returning to The Netherlands.[3, 17, 131] It is encountered less frequently in technically advanced nations such as the United States, except in certain populations living in more primitive conditions, such as Native Americans on reservations.[104, 123] In one multicenter U.S. study, ETEC accounted for 1.4 percent (2/147) of acute nondysenteric diarrhea in children treated as outpatients.[21] In Swiss children admitted to hospitals for acute diarrhea, 7 of 166 (4.2%) had ETEC isolated from stool cultures.[42]

Among children in developing countries, ETEC often causes two to three episodes of diarrhea per year and may be responsible for more than 25 percent of diarrheal episodes in such children.[15] Estimates indicate that ETEC causes approximately 380,000 annual deaths in children younger than 5 years worldwide.[142] ETEC is acquired by ingesting contaminated water or food, and as many as 10^8 bacteria may be required for clinical illness.[38] The incubation period is 14 to 50 hours.[92] A domestic U.S. outbreak of diarrhea at Crater Lake National Park in Oregon was traced to ETEC organisms in the water supply.[120] The few environmental surveillance studies that have been performed indicate that ETEC can be found in both water[122] and food. ETEC was detected in numerous food samples in the United States, including cheese, hamburger, sausage, and seafood.[86, 124] This finding suggests that a variety of foodstuffs may be capable of supporting growth and facilitating transmission of ETEC. Because large numbers of organisms are required for experimental infection, transmission probably would require multiplication of the inoculum, and food is a good vehicle for such multiplication.

ENTEROPATHOGENIC *ESCHERICHIA COLI*

Neter and associates[102] initially used the term *EPEC* to denote a limited group of *E. coli* serotypes associated with nursery outbreaks of diarrheal disease to separate it from other *E. coli* serogroups causing urinary tract infection, septicemia, peritonitis, or meningitis. However, in recent years, specific virulence markers of EPEC have been discovered that are independent of serotype. More specifically, serotype is associated with, but does not define the virulence of an isolate. In addition, the epidemiology of EPEC has changed, and the original classic serotypes no longer are found primarily in neonatal nursery outbreaks, which in the past provided an epidemiologic clue for the diagnosis of EPEC infection; rather, they are associated more commonly with sporadic or endemic diarrhea during the first year of life,[146] although they may cause nonspecific watery diarrhea in adults as well.[130]

The impossibility of diagnosing EPEC infections by serotyping methods alone has made it difficult to conduct good studies of EPEC epidemiology in the United States. EPEC is an important enteric pathogen in children in developing countries. However, establishing the prevalence of these infections is difficult without the use of sophisticated methods of investigation. In developing countries, the association between EPEC and diarrhea in children is strongest in infants younger than 6 months.[30, 50] Rates of EPEC infection in young children may be even higher than those of rotavirus infection.[30, 50, 118] Breast-feeding offers some level of protection against EPEC because of the presence in breast milk of both immune factors and oligosaccharides that inhibit adherence of EPEC to epithelial cells.[31] In industrialized countries such as the United States, EPEC generally is not considered to be a cause of childhood diarrhea as frequently as in the past, although EPEC still is identified in this setting.[35] In an outpatient setting in the United States, 2 of 147 cases of nondysenteric acute diarrhea were caused by EPEC.[21] In 166 Swiss children admitted to hospitals with diarrhea, 13 (7.8%) had EPEC isolated from stool cultures.[42]

ENTEROHEMORRHAGIC *ESCHERICHIA COLI*

Since its discovery in 1977, EHEC has been identified as an important and increasingly common human pathogen. These organisms are commensals in cattle, and one is not surprised that large outbreaks of human infection have been associated with the ingestion of undercooked hamburger, especially from fast-food restaurants. In meat-processing plants where bulk ground beef is prepared for the fast-food industry, meat from one contaminated carcass can contaminate and distribute the organisms to a huge number of beef patties. Careful prospective epidemiologic surveillance in Minnesota has revealed an increase in the incidence of EHEC from 0.5 to 2.0 per 100,000 children younger than 18 years during the period 1979 to 1988,[81] similar to the incidence of EHEC determined in the state of Washington in the late 1980s, 2.1 per 100,000. Very young children are not a target group for EHEC. Rather, severe and complicated illness occurs most often in children 2 to 10 years of age or in the elderly. Ground beef is identified as the most common source of EHEC infection. However, several other food sources of transmission, including unpasteurized apple cider, mayonnaise, milk, dry fermented sausage, lettuce, and water, have been documented, and both person-to-person and cattle-to-person routes have been implicated. Many of these unusual modes of transmission also are linked with cattle, such as poorly washed apples dropped in cow pastures and used to make cider or surface water supplies in proximity to areas where cattle graze.

The epidemiology of EHEC-associated HUS is of current interest because these episodes account for most cases of acute renal failure in children in the United States and approximately 250 deaths per year. Although cases of Shiga toxin–producing *Shigella dysenteriae* type 1 were associated with HUS in the mid-1970s in Bangladesh, this organism rarely is encountered in the United States. The etiology of most cases of HUS in the United States was unexplained until Stx-producing EHEC was identified. Strong epidemiologic evidence associates EHEC with HUS. In one series of patients from Canada, 60 percent of patients with HUS had either neutralizable free Stx or Stx-producing *E. coli* in their stool, and 75 percent had serum antibody against Stx.[112] Cases in the United States have been associated almost exclusively with EHEC serotype O157:H7. However, this finding may be due primarily to the fact that it is the only Stx-producing *E. coli* for which clinical microbiology laboratories test. During a large outbreak of *E. coli* O157:H7 infection associated with fast-food restaurant hamburgers on the West Coast of the United States in 1993, of the 732 affected individuals identified, 195 were admitted to the hospital, HUS developed in 55 (7.5%), and 4 died.[53] Investigation of this outbreak demonstrated that small numbers of bacteria (in the range of a few hundred) constituted an infectious dose. Among 93 cases reported in Washington State in 1987, HUS or TTP developed in 11 (12%), for an approximate incidence of 0.23 per 100,000.[110] The highest incidence of HUS occurs in children younger than 5 years, in whom the age-specific incidence ranged from 2.6 to 5.8 per 100,000 in Minnesota,[81] Washington,[110] and Oregon.[119] In the 2000 FoodNet Annual Report, *E. coli* O157:H7 accounted for 2 cases per 100,000, and more than 40 percent of those with confirmed infection were hospitalized.[24] In the multicenter study of mild acute diarrhea in outpatients in the United States, 5 of 147 (3.4%) cases were caused by EHEC,[21] a frequency very similar to that in Swiss children hospitalized for community-acquired diarrhea.[42] The incidence of HUS in Argentina, 21.7 per 100,000, is four to eight times higher and primarily is due to non-O157:H7 Stx-producing EHEC serotypes.[77] In fact, more than 100 non-O157:H7 serotypes have been associated with hemorrhagic colitis or HUS in Canada. Many of these serotypes have been implicated in both sporadic and outbreak disease in the United States[16] (e.g., an outbreak caused by O104:H21 acquired from contaminated milk[91]).

HUS is seasonal in the United States and Canada (most common during the summer months), although no specific seasonal risk factor or factors for infection with Stx-producing *E. coli* are known. Other epidemiologic data suggest that poor children are at lower risk for the development of HUS, perhaps because they already have immunity to EHEC or Stx toxins through early contact with the organisms in their environment.[28] Researchers also have suggested that the risk of acquiring HUS is increased in patients treated with the antimicrobial agent trimethoprim-sulfamethoxazole (TMP-SMX) (relative risk, 3.1; confidence limits, 0.6 to 9.8) or other antibiotics, including β-lactam agents.[73, 155] A similar association between the use of antibiotics and HUS caused by *S. dysenteriae* type 1 has been suggested.[19] However, these studies did not use a randomized placebo-controlled design, and the association may reflect selection bias because both the use of antibiotics and systemic complications are associated with more severe disease. Other studies have found no association.[110] In vitro data suggest that subinhibitory concentrations of TMP-SMX and other antibiotics may increase Stx expression,[66] perhaps related to enhanced release of toxin from damaged organisms.[8] The relevance of these observations is, however, uncertain. The prolonged use of antimotility agents is reported to be associated with more serious systemic complications of EHEC infection.[25, 26]

In the United Kingdom and the United States, HUS and TTP are associated predominantly with Stx2-producing *E. coli* O157:H7.[81, 111] In Buenos Aires, Argentina, which has the highest reported incidence of HUS in the world, non-O157:H7 Stx2-producing strains are isolated most commonly.[77] Similarly, in Australia, other serotypes, especially O111, have been associated with major outbreaks and significant levels of HUS.[22]

ENTEROINVASIVE *ESCHERICHIA COLI*

As with EPEC, few studies have been performed on the epidemiology of EIEC. The outbreak that led to the definition of EIEC occurred in 1971, when bloody diarrhea was traced to the consumption of French Camembert cheese contaminated with *E. coli* O124.[80] Small outbreaks or sporadic cases involving a limited number of serotypes have been reported from numerous countries, including the United States, France, Japan, and Brazil.[80, 107, 138, 148, 150] Prospective studies in Thailand using cDNA probes for EIEC invasion genes indicate that as many as 5 percent of sporadic diarrheal episodes and 10 percent of bloody diarrhea cases may be caused by EIEC strains. The epidemiology of the cases is complicated by the fact that in contrast to the initial descriptions of EIEC-associated disease, most EIEC infections are probably neither dysenteric nor characterized by bloody diarrhea but, rather, remain a mildly febrile watery diarrhea. In this sense, EIEC infection resembles *Shigella sonnei* infection more than it does the more virulent *S. dysenteriae* or *Shigella flexneri* infection. Because these manifestations are also similar to ETEC diarrhea, the role of EIEC would be overlooked without the use of routine screening for EIEC virulence traits, which is not practical at present.

Multiplication to high numbers may be important for transmission of EIEC because infection with 10^8 bacteria has been demonstrated to be necessary for experimental dysentery in human volunteers.[38] In this regard, EIEC appears to differ epidemiologically from *Shigella* spp., for which 10^4 or fewer organisms are sufficient to cause disease. This finding also suggests that EIEC is likely to be food-borne. In food, EIEC can multiply to a sufficient inoculum and is unlikely to be transmitted by direct contact, which is consistent with the finding in a food-borne outbreak caused by a nontypeable EIEC that secondary person-to-person transmission, so commonly observed in *Shigella* infection, did not occur in EIEC infection.[138]

ENTEROAGGREGATIVE *ESCHERICHIA COLI*

EAggEC first was recognized by its ability to aggregate in a "stacked-brick" appearance on epithelial cells in tissue culture. EaggEC does not secrete ST or LT enterotoxins. Epidemiologic evidence, human volunteer studies, and animal models all associate organisms that demonstrate this property with diarrheal disease.[12, 84] The full epidemiology of these strains is not known yet because it remains difficult to establish EAggEC as the cause of disease, in large part because the major means of detection has been to observe pattern of adherence of isolates to HEp-2 cells.[83] DNA-based methods are available and involve the use of a gene probe to a segment of DNA associated with the EAggEC phenotype but probably distinct from the gene mediating this property itself. Moreover, depending on the location from which the isolates were obtained, *E. coli* showing aggregative phenotypes in tissue culture does not hybridize with this probe and is polymerase chain reaction (PCR)-negative with the primers currently available. Even so, EAggEC is considered a leading cause of persistent diarrhea in children in developing countries.[27, 52] In prospective cohort studies in India, EPEC strains were isolated more frequently from patients with acute diarrhea, whereas EAggEC strains were isolated more frequently from patients with diarrhea persisting for more than 14 days.[62] Patients with EAggEC had a mean duration of diarrhea of 17.0 ± 14.4 days, significantly longer than that of other pathogens isolated in this setting. EAggEC, however, often is found in any appropriately studied population, and asymptomatic excretion rates can be as high as 28 percent,[97] thus rendering epidemiologic studies of EAggEC even more difficult to interpret.[144]

Clinical Manifestations

Diarrhea-causing *E. coli* may be responsible for a variety of clinical syndromes because virtually all known mechanisms of diarrhea, including secretory toxins, cytotoxic toxins, invasion, and pathogenic adherence, are present in *E. coli*. The clinical manifestations are largely a function of the pathogenic mechanisms used by the different classes of *E. coli*, as determined by their complement of virulence genes (Table 108–2). Thus, invasive strains (e.g., EIEC) produce inflammatory diarrhea with fever, abdominal pain, nausea, vomiting, and leukocytes and blood in the stool.

TABLE 108–2 ■ RELATIONSHIP OF *ESCHERICHIA COLI* VIRULENCE GENES TO CLINICAL PATTERNS OF DIARRHEA

Pathogen Group*	Virulence Genes†									Clinical Disease
	EAF	*A/E*	*LA*	*AA*	*LT/ST*	*CFA*	*Invasion Plasmid*	*Stx*	*ShET-2*	
ETEC	–	–	–	–	+	+	–	–	–	Watery
EPEC	+	+	+	–	–	–	–	–	–	Watery
EHEC	–	+	–	–	–	–	–	+	–	Bloody (hemorrhagic colitis)
EIEC	–	–	–	–	–	–	+	–	+	Bloody (dysentery)
EAggEC	–	–	–	+	+‡	–	–	–	–	Watery (persistent)

*ETEC, enterotoxigenic *E. coli*; EPEC, enteropathogenic *E. coli*; EHEC, enterohemorrhagic *E. coli*; EIEC, enteroinvasive *E. coli*; EAggEC, enteroaggregative *E. coli*.
†EAF, EPEC adherence factor; A/E, attaching and effacing changes; LA, localized adherence pattern; AA, autoaggregative attaching pattern; LT/ST, heat-labile and heat-stable toxins; CFA, colonization factor antigens; invasion,chromosomal and plasmid factors mediating cell invasion; Stx, shiga family cytotoxins; ShET-2, plasmid-encoded *Shigella* enterotoxin-2, highly homologous to the plasmid-encoded EIEC toxin.
‡Enteroaggregative stable toxin (EAST) is a member of the ST family.

TABLE 108–3 ■ AGE-RELATED PATTERNS OF *ESCHERICHIA COLI* DIARRHEA

Pathogen Classification	Age at Highest Risk	Characteristics of Diarrhea		
		Bloody	*Watery*	*Inflammatory*
EAggEC	<6 mo	–	+++	–
EPEC	<1 yr	–	+++	–
ETEC	>1 yr	–	+++	–
EIEC	>2 yr	++	+	+++
EHEC	2–10 yr	+++	+	–

EAggEC, enteroaggregative *E. coli*; EHEC, enterohemorrhagic *E. coli*; EIEC, enteroinvasive *E. coli*; EPEC, enteropathogenic *E. coli*; ETEC, enterotoxigenic *E. coli*.

Noninvasive, cytotoxin-producing EHEC strains cause a frankly bloody diarrhea associated with leukocytosis but without pus cells in stool or fever. Secretory LT- or ST-producing organisms cause less fever but result in brisk, watery diarrhea with the potential for significant dehydration. Adherent EPEC and EAggEC strains also cause noninflammatory and otherwise nonspecific watery diarrhea.

The age-specific predilections of the various *E. coli* pathogens are presented in Table 108–3. E. *coli* diarrhea in the first year of life generally is caused by EPEC or EAggEC, although ETEC also can be responsible. The clinical manifestations are all similar and do not have any characteristic features, unless a dysentery-like illness or hemorrhagic colitis is noted.

ENTEROTOXIGENIC *ESCHERICHIA COLI*

ETEC causes watery, nonmucoid, nonbloody diarrhea in infants, older children, and adults and is a common cause of traveler's diarrhea. The onset of diarrhea is abrupt, with an incubation period of 14 to 50 hours. Stool frequency varies from a few to more than 10 per day, and a striking absence of leukocytes is noted when the diarrheal stool is examined by light microscopy. These patients may or may not be vomiting, but they are commonly febrile (38 to 40° C), except in the case of adults with traveler's diarrhea. In older children, ETEC disease cannot be distinguished clinically from the multiple other causes of acute nonspecific watery diarrhea. The illness is usually self-limited to 3 to 5 days but occasionally lasts beyond a week. Severely dehydrating illness that resembles clinical cholera can occur but is not common. Variability in the clinical picture may be due to age differences and preexisting immunity, but it can be attributed to differences in the infecting inoculum as well. DuPont and colleagues[38] produced mild diarrhea (three watery stools per day for 2 to 3 days) when 10^8 bacteria were fed to adult volunteers, whereas 10^{10} organisms caused more pronounced diarrhea (more than five stools per day for 4 to 5 days), with mucus but no blood observed in some subjects. A number of subjects also had abdominal cramping, but no tenesmus was present, and all remained afebrile. This clinical picture is typical of traveler's diarrhea in adults.[87] Although the illness is usually self-limited, the diarrhea can result in severe dehydration necessitating aggressive fluid therapy.

ENTEROPATHOGENIC *ESCHERICHIA COLI*

Much of the published data on the clinical aspects of infection with EPEC are historical and based solely on serotype diagnosis. In recent years, there has been a paucity of cases of EPEC infection documented by contemporary criteria, especially in developed countries. In the United States and other developed countries, EPEC is a cause of sporadic diarrhea. EPEC infection primarily is a disease of acute diarrhea in young children, especially those younger than 2 years.[96] In the Swiss study conducted with modern diagnostic methods, the mean age of the 13 hospitalized children with EPEC diarrhea was 1.4 years (range, 0.5 to 3.0 years).[42] Fever was low-grade, and vomiting occurred in 69 percent. Volume depletion was considered moderate in five and severe in two children. Although nursery outbreaks are no longer common, severe illness still can develop in infants infected with EPEC,[62] with high mortality rates ranging from 25 to 70 percent, depending on the study.[35] In contrast, limited investigations using an experimental EPEC infection model in adult volunteers show that mild watery diarrhea occurs 3 to 16 hours after inoculation and generally lasts less than 2 days. Diarrhea occasionally was copious and in some cases was associated with abdominal cramps, nausea, vomiting, malaise, and fever.[36] This clinical picture is consistent with disease caused by outbreaks of EPEC in adults and traveler's diarrhea caused by EPEC. EPEC also has been implicated in chronic diarrhea in the United States and elsewhere, with serious nutritional consequences that may require total parenteral nutrition and hospital stays as long as 120 days.[121] In prospective studies of EPEC diarrhea in young infants in Brazil[50] and Ethiopia,[145] fever, vomiting, and dehydration all were observed commonly. The clinical significance of chronic diarrhea may be increased by the underlying malnutrition of infants in developing countries. In many settings, especially where effective oral rehydration programs are in place, chronic diarrhea and associated malnutrition are now more important causes of diarrheal deaths than acute diarrhea and dehydration are.[14]

These manifestations of EPEC infection are distinct from the classic epidemic nursery outbreaks of cholera infantum of the past. In this setting, the first signs and symptoms may be mild and nonspecific but commonly are followed by vomiting and diarrhea of increasing severity. Stools contain neither mucus nor blood, and the volume tends to fluctuate over the course of a period of weeks. Plain abdominal radiographs show only nonspecific dilation of small bowel loops, although severe ileus not attributable to hypokalemia develops in many patients. During periods of profuse watery diarrhea, infants may lose as much as 15 percent of body weight, thereby leading to profound electrolyte disturbances and severe dehydration along with central nervous system manifestations such as irritability, hypertonicity, convulsions, and coma. Fluid requirements seldom drop below 300 mL/kg/day and increase to 500 mL/kg/day during relapses. Circulatory collapse can occur and recur despite adequate replacement of fluids and achievement of electrolyte balance. In an earlier epidemic in Virginia, Belnap and O'Donnell[10] described fatal infections caused by *E. coli* O111:B4 occurring after 3 weeks of illness and associated with renal failure, coma, and signs of disseminated intravascular coagulation, but blood cultures typically remained negative. The fatality rate was age-dependent; although the overall mortality was 16 percent, the rate in neonates was 40 percent. This study and others have noted that breast-fed infants are relatively protected against infection by these organisms.

ENTEROHEMORRHAGIC *ESCHERICHIA COLI*

As early as 1971, a distinctive clinical diarrheal syndrome was recognized that was characterized by bloody diarrhea in addition to cramping and colonic inflammatory changes, usually right sided.[116] In 1983, this illness was associated with an otherwise rare *E. coli* serotype, O157:H7, and a characteristic syndrome, hemorrhagic colitis, was defined.[117] The organisms causing this syndrome, grouped together as EHEC, initially were identified in 1977 because of their ability to produce cytotoxins. EHEC now has been shown to cause a wide spectrum of diseases that may be confined to the gastrointestinal tract or, in a sizable proportion (typically between 5 and 10%), can become systemic. After an incubation period of 3 to 4 days (range, 1 to 8 days), the local gastrointestinal illness usually begins with nonbloody diarrhea that can progress to bloody diarrhea after 1 or 2 days. Hemorrhagic colitis accounts for approximately 90 percent of the clinical manifestations of *E. coli* O157:H7 infection. Further progression may occur over the course of the next day or two and result in the passage of frank blood, the pathognomonic clinical feature of hemorrhagic colitis. Associated manifestations include vomiting in approximately 50 percent of patients and abdominal pain. Fever may occur but typically is low-grade. This clinical picture may be confused with other conditions such as appendicitis, intussusception, inflammatory bowel disease, ischemic colitis, and diverticulitis. The difficulty in making the diagnosis can lead to inappropriate drug therapy or even surgery.[54, 60] In 90 percent of patients, the hemorrhagic colitis resolves. A serious complication is the development of HUS or TTP.[54] HUS is characterized by the triad of acute renal failure, thrombocytopenia, and hemolytic anemia and develops in approximately 10 percent of infected children younger than 10 years.[96] The acute mortality rate is approximately 5 percent, and renal failure will eventually develop in many more patients during the next several decades. TTP and HUS have the same clinical features, but TTP generally occurs in older adults and is associated with prominent neurologic findings, including behavioral changes, altered consciousness or coma, and seizures, as well as fever.[57]

A prospective study in Canada identified *E. coli* O157:H7 in 15 percent of 125 patients with grossly bloody diarrhea over the course of a 6-month period.[112] The age range was 15 months to 73 years; however, almost half patients were younger than 10 years. The illness was similar to that described earlier, with a mean duration of 7.8 days, but it was significantly longer in children (9.1 ± 2 days) than adults (6.6 ± 1.1 days). Sigmoidoscopy findings were abnormal in seven of eight adults examined, with hyperemic mucosa in six and superficial ulcerations in one. Biopsy samples showed mild mucosal inflammation in four of five patients. In another study, the findings on colonoscopy in 10 patients with hemorrhagic colitis caused by *E. coli* O157:H7 included severe inflammation (predominantly right sided), marked edema, easy hemorrhage, and the frequent appearance of longitudinal ulcer-like lesions.[134] Because both local and systemic manifestations in EHEC infection are caused, at least partially, by Stx, the presence of these same toxins in the intestinal lumen in patients with non-O157:H7 infection puts them at risk for hemorrhagic colitis and HUS. No comparative data are available to assess the relative risk in O157:H7 and non-O157:H7 EHEC infection.

ENTEROINVASIVE *ESCHERICHIA COLI*

Naturally acquired EIEC infection causes a mild to moderately severe dysentery syndrome consisting of fever, malaise, diarrhea, tenesmus, and abdominal cramping.[38, 150] Watery diarrhea usually occurs at the onset of the illness and progresses to mucoid diarrhea with streaks of blood or microscopic hematochezia, but rarely to the classic small-volume, grossly bloody, dysenteric stool seen with *Shigella* infection. Of 204 cases reported in one study, grossly bloody stool occurred in only 4.[50] In two of these patients, sigmoidoscopy revealed superficial ulcerations in one and hyperemia alone in the second. As in *Shigella* infection, however, the stool is loaded with inflammatory cells, indicative of the invasive nature of the organism. Vomiting and dehydration can occur, the latter generally being mild. Fever of 38 to 39.5° C is a typical symptom that occurs early in association with malaise, myalgia, and headache and lasts for 2 to 3 days. In most instances, the diarrhea ceases in a week or less but, in a few patients, may continue for 2 weeks or more. In adult volunteers with experimentally induced EIEC disease, febrile illness developed approximately 11 hours (range, 8 to 24 hours) after ingestion of the inoculum.[38] Chills, myalgia, headache, and profuse diarrhea or abdominal cramps and tenesmus rapidly followed. In 2 of 13 subjects, this picture was associated with systemic toxicity and transient hypotension consistent with bacteremia, even though blood cultures were negative for all patients. Clinical dysentery with bloody stools occurred in several subjects, and reddened, friable mucosa with multiple bleeding points was seen by sigmoidoscopy. Clinical illness was controlled quickly with parenteral ampicillin therapy.

ENTEROAGGREGATIVE *ESCHERICHIA COLI*

Few studies have described the clinical features of EAggEC infection. However, EAggEC is associated with watery diarrhea, which may progress to persistent diarrhea and last 14 days or longer,[12, 97] and it has been associated with some cases of persistent diarrhea in human immunodeficiency virus–positive patients.[85] Fever and vomiting are typically absent. EAggEC has been associated with bloody diarrhea in some studies,[39] although this manifestation does not appear to be typical. The clinical findings in these patients may be aggravated by secondary lactase deficiency and progressive nutritional deterioration. In at least two studies, experimental inoculation of clinical EAggEC isolates into adult volunteers has resulted in clinical manifestations that included diarrhea, abdominal cramps, and borborygmi in some, but not all volunteers, even with doses as large as 10^{10} bacteria.

Pathogenesis

ENTEROTOXIGENIC *ESCHERICHIA COLI*

Spurred by the remarkable progress in understanding the pathogenesis of human cholera after the discovery of cholera enterotoxin and based on precedents from veterinary medicine for similar toxins in watery *E. coli* diarrhea in animals, Sack and colleagues[122] provided the first evidence that *E. coli* diarrhea in humans also could be related to secretory enterotoxins. ETEC makes ST, LT, or both toxins. Studies of ST have revealed that they are of two major types: STa (sometimes called ST-I or STh, for human ST), of importance in human infections, and STb (sometimes called ST-II or STp, for porcine ST), of importance in veterinary infections. STa is a small peptide (approximately 2 kd) without a subunit structure; contains three disulfide bonds, which accounts for its heat stability; is methanol-soluble; and causes gut fluid secretion in suckling mice. ST is made as a larger precursor molecule that is modified post-translationally and by extracellular processing.[114, 139] STa, which causes intestinal fluid and electrolyte secretion, has an immediate and reversible onset of action; it produces increased levels of intracellular cyclic guanosine monophosphate (cGMP) by activation of guanylate cyclase,[48, 88, 132] although other pathways, including protein kinase C, may participate in the guanylate cyclase response.[29, 153] The major STa receptor is a membrane-spanning enzyme (guanylate cyclase C).[96] The in vivo suckling mouse model for fluid secretion has been the standard assay for STa. However, other quantitative methods are now available and include quantitating the activation of particulate guanylate cyclase in tissue culture of intestinal cell lines, radioimmunoassay, and enzyme-linked immunosorbent assay (ELISA). STa also is 50 percent homologous with an endogenous mammalian ligand, guanylin, that binds to and activates guanylate cyclase C.[32] Guanylin is present in intestinal epithelial cells and is thought to play a role in regulating fluid and electrolyte secretion in the intestine. As described in greater detail later, EAggEC also makes an enterotoxin (known as EAST-1) that has significant homology with STa.

The second ST, STb, described in 1970,[90] is methanol-insoluble and inactive in the suckling mouse model, but it does cause intestinal fluid secretion in weaned pigs. Host susceptibility to STb may be related to the sensitivity of STb to protease because the administration of trypsin inhibitors can render mice susceptible to the effects of STb.[126] Like STa, STb is made as a large precursor molecule that is processed and secreted from the bacterium as a 5.2-kd, mature 48–amino acid protein containing two disulfide bonds.[74] No homology exists between STa and STb, and the two toxins are not cross-neutralizable. STb does not lead to alterations in sodium or chloride flux but instead probably affects bicarbonate excretion. STb also may open a receptor-operated calcium channel in the plasma membrane. Although STb-producing strains have been isolated from humans with diarrhea,[78, 108] whether they may be responsible for human disease is not clear.

The LT family of toxins includes LTI, which is similar structurally and functionally to cholera toxin, with approximately 80 percent homology at the amino acid level. Furthermore, a type II protein secretion pathway that is highly homologous to the secretion pathway for cholera toxin by *Vibrio cholerae* is required for secretion of LT by ETEC.[142] LTI can be subdivided into LThI and LTpI, which are antigenic variants of human and porcine origin.[58] These toxins are composed of one A subunit enzyme that activates adenylate cyclase and five B subunit monomers that form a multivalent pentameric structure responsible for receptor recognition and binding to susceptible cells. LTI binds to G_{M1} ganglioside, like cholera toxin, as well as to a glycoprotein receptor present on the intestinal brush border membrane.[96] LT and cholera toxin share the identical adenosine diphosphate–ribosyl transferase enzymatic activity for the same target. Both covalently transfer the adenosine diphosphate–ribosyl moiety from nicotinamide adenine dinucleotide to the guanosine 5′-triphosphate–binding regulatory component of the adenylate cyclase enzyme complex. This transfer leads to permanent activation of the cyclase enzyme and continuous production of cyclic adenosine monophosphate (cAMP). In turn, high levels of cAMP activate chloride secretory mechanisms in crypt cells by supraphoshorylation of chloride channels, which stimulates secretion of Cl^- from secretory crypt cells and inhibits NaCl absorptive mechanisms in villus cells.[96] For these reasons, diarrhea caused by LT^+ *E. coli* is similar pathophysiologically to that associated with cholera. The combination of increased chloride secretion and diminished sodium absorption leads to the accumulation of large amounts of isotonic fluid in the gut lumen that is in excess of the intestinal absorptive capacity and thus results in watery diarrhea. Other mechanisms of action leading to diarrhea by LT have been proposed. Otherwise similar LTs but not neutralized with antisera raised to cholera toxins are designated LTII, but they do not appear to be involved in human disease.

After the discovery of *E. coli* enterotoxins in animal strains, veterinarians who were studying *E. coli* infections (colibacillosis) in newborn piglets quickly realized that production of enterotoxins by ETEC, though necessary, was not sufficient to explain its virulence. As early as 1967, Smith and Halls[136] observed a marked proliferation of *E. coli* in the proximal part of the small bowel of animals with spontaneous colibacillosis. Strains isolated from infected animals, when fed to newborn piglets, also heavily colonized the proximal portion of the gut and caused diarrhea, whereas isolates from healthy animals failed to do either. Smith and Halls suggested that virulent colibacillosis strains of *E. coli* adhered to the intestinal mucosa and evaded clearance mechanisms of the gut, with subsequent multiplication to very high numbers. Additional studies soon confirmed this process for porcine pathogens and further suggested that a surface antigen, K-88, was responsible for adhesion.[76, 135] This finding was consistent with the already known properties of K-88, a fimbrial protein mediating hemagglutination in the presence of mannose (termed mannose-resistant hemagglutination), which distinguished it from the type 1 pili that result in mannose-sensitive hemagglutination.[135]

Because the two properties, toxin and adhesin, were controlled by plasmid genes, Smith and Linggood[137] could create mutants expressing none, one, or both proteins by inserting or removing the two plasmids independently. They showed convincingly that K-88 was the adherence (colonization) factor and that a noncolonizing toxigenic organism was virtually avirulent when fed to intact animals (Table 108–4). Both factors were, in fact, required for full virulence, unless the intestine first was ligated to prevent clearance of nonadhering toxigenic strains.

Adherence of human ETEC to intestinal epithelial cells is also due to the presence of microbial surface antigens that intimately interact with as yet unknown constituents on the gut cell surface (Fig. 108–1). The adherence antigens of these strains, known as colonization factor antigens (CFAs), are different from those present on animal strains (K-88, K-99, and others), thus establishing the basis for specificity of the host range. The best characterized and most frequently encountered adhesins from human strains are CFA I and CFA II.[43, 44] The latter actually is composed of three distinct antigens designated coli-surface–associated antigens 1 to 3 (cs1 to cs3). CFA I and CFA II, except for cs3, are synthesized as long, slender fimbriae on the bacterial surface (Fig. 108–2). In contrast, cs3 (and a few other adhesins) are nonfimbriate in nature. Whereas fimbriate CFAs mediate mannose-resistant hemagglutination of human and bovine

TABLE 108–4 ■ CONVERSION OF AVIRULENT *ESCHERICHIA COLI* O9:H19 INTO AN ENTEROVIRULENT STRAIN BY INSERTION OF PLASMIDS MEDIATING K-88 ADHESIN AND ENTEROTOXIN PRODUCTION

Plasmid Present		Colonization ($\log_{10}$/g)		Clinical Response
K-88	*Enterotoxin*	*Jejunum*	*Colon*	*No. with Diarrhea/Total*
No	No	5.3	8.4	0/8
Yes	No	8.3	9.7	3/11 (mild)
No	Yes	4.4	6.9	0/6
Yes	Yes	9.5	9.5	12/16

Data from Smith, H. W., and Linggood, M. A. : Observations on the pathogenic properties of the K 88, Hly and Ent plasmids of *Escherichia coli* with particular reference to porcine diarrhea. J. Med. Microbiol. *4*:467–485, 1971.

erythrocytes, which aids in their detection, nonfimbriate antigens may not be detectable as hemagglutinins. However, these proteins all impart high surface hydrophobicity to the organisms, which allows hydrophobic interactions to overcome the repulsive electrostatic charges of the epithelial cell.[46] Other CFAs include CFA III and IV, the latter being composed of a family of antigens: cs4, cs5, and cs6.[71]

CFA genes are present on plasmids. Of particular interest and possible epidemiologic importance is the observation that the genes for CFA I and II are usually on plasmids containing ST genes or sometimes ST and LT genes. This association of colonization and ST genes may explain why ST appears to be the more frequently encountered of the two *E. coli* enterotoxins. These plasmids also are found primarily in a limited number of serotypes of ETEC from patients (Table 108–5), presumably because they are stable in the genetic environment of these strains. Such organisms have been called reservoir serotypes because they are responsible for most endemic ETEC disease.[45] LT-only ETEC strains generally do not produce CFA I or II, may be of diverse serotype, and readily lose the *ent* (enterotoxin) gene in vitro.

Further work has extended these observations to many other strains virulent for humans[4, 19] and has established a consistent principle: noninvasive diarrhea-causing ETEC strains require at least two virulence attributes, including (1) adhesins to permit colonization of the intestine, presumably leading to (2) production of enterotoxins, which actually cause secretion of water and electrolytes and lead to diarrhea.

ENTEROPATHOGENIC *ESCHERICHIA COLI*

True virulence attributes now are used to define and detect EPEC. Among these attributes is the ability to adhere to HEp-2 cells in a characteristic localized adherence (LA)

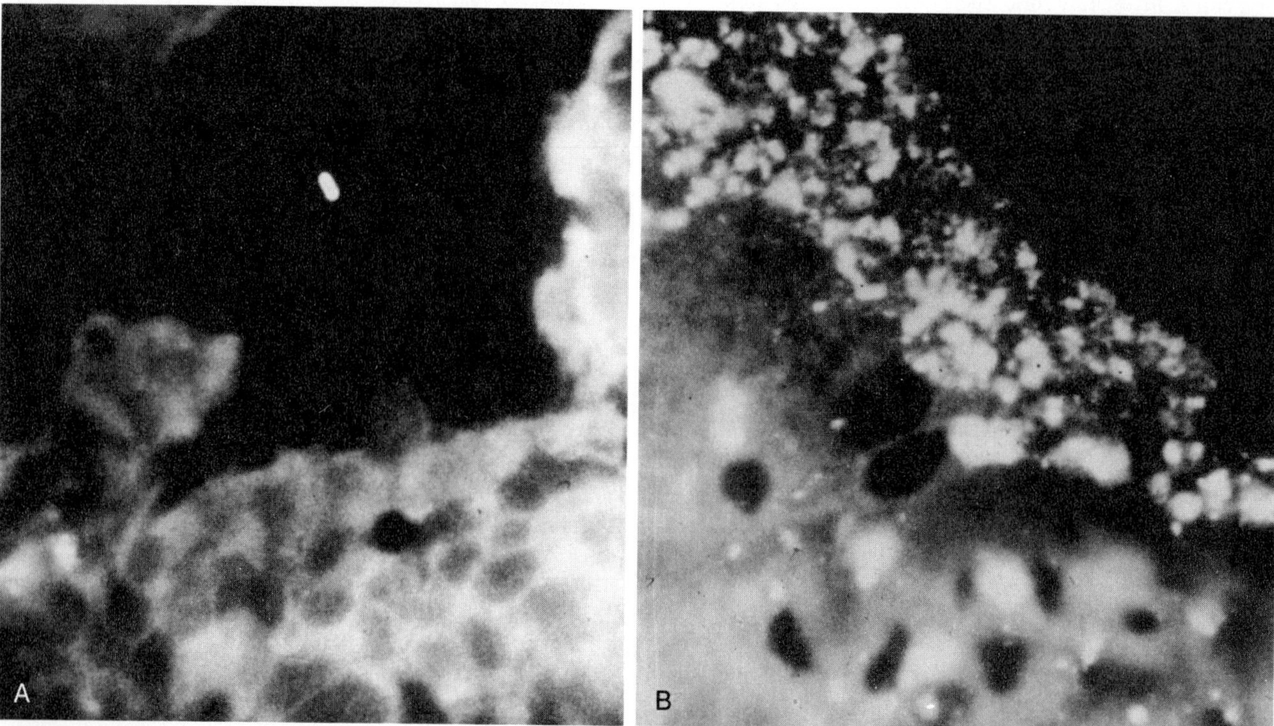

FIGURE 108–1 ■ *A,* Laboratory-passaged avirulent *Escherichia coli* H10407 in infant rabbit intestine. No adherent, colonizing bacteria are seen. *B,* Fresh, virulent H10407 organisms at the same time interval in infant rabbit intestine are closely adherent to the brush border (indirect immunofluorescent stained section, ×1000). (Courtesy of Drs. Dolores and Doyle Evans, Department of Microbiology, Baylor College of Medicine.)

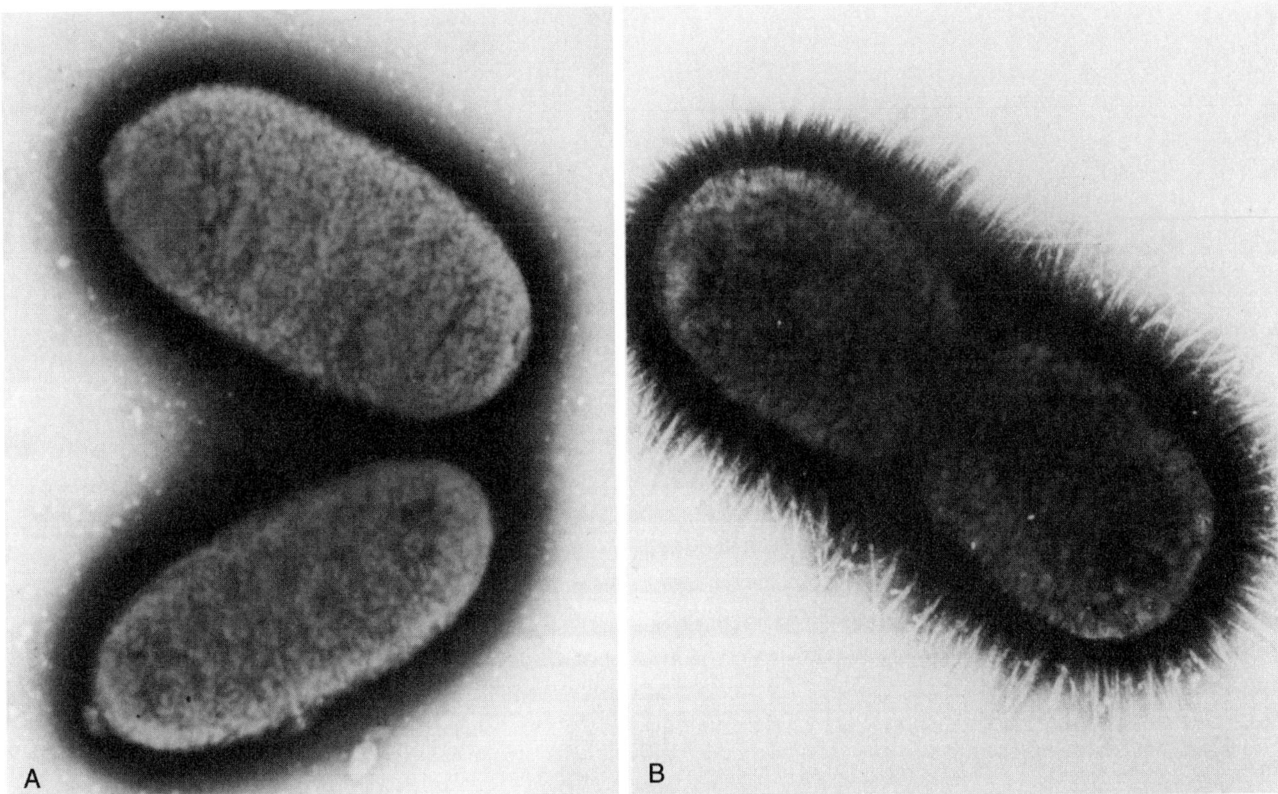

FIGURE 108–2 ■ *A,* Electron micrograph of negatively stained cells of avirulent *Escherichia coli* H10407. Note the bald appearance of the outer surface of the organism. *B,* Similar view of virulent, fresh *E. coli* H10407. Note the hairy surface of the organism as a result of colonization factor (×20,000). (Courtesy of Drs. Dolores and Doyle Evans, Department of Microbiology, Baylor College of Medicine.)

pattern, in which the bacteria grow as a microcolony on one region of the HEp-2 cell membrane[35] (Fig. 108–3). Demonstration of the LA phenotype in tissue culture cells or hybridization with an EPEC adherence factor (EAF) DNA probe is sufficient for the putative identification of EPEC.[63] EPEC causes actin polymerization of target cells at sites of attachment, a virulence property readily detected in tissue culture (e.g., HEp-2 cells) by a fluorescent actin-staining test (FAST).[70] In this procedure, HEp-2 cells are infected with the organism and subsequently exposed to a fluorescein-labeled mushroom toxin specific for filamentous polymerized actin. Under the microscope, the brightly fluorescing actin beneath the organism easily is seen outlining the microbe (Fig. 108–4).

EPEC infection results in villus atrophy that frequently is accompanied by crypt hypertrophy. Bacteria can be found attached intimately to epithelial cells, and the microvilli disappear (or become effaced), the so-called A/E lesion. Pathogenesis is considered to involve three distinct stages.[35] Localized adherence of EPEC to epithelial cells appears to be the first event, and it is mediated initially by the plasmid-encoded EAF.[35] Other plasmid-associated fimbriae subsequently were identified and termed *bundle-forming pili* for their characteristic bundled appearance on electron microscopy.[49] Although bundle-forming pili are essential for localized adherence, they are not sufficient, and other gene products clearly are involved.[35] The second step is the intimate attachment of EPEC to intestinal epithelial cells. During this process, epithelial cell microvilli disappear directly below the attached bacteria and appear to elongate adjacent to the organisms. To make the resulting cuplike pedestal that defines the A/E lesion (Fig. 108–5), epithelial cells must reorganize the various cytoskeletal elements, including actin, the light chain of myosin, α-actinin, talin,

TABLE 108–5 ■ CORRELATION OF PRODUCTION OF TOXIN AND COLONIZATION FACTOR WITH VIRULENCE IN HUMAN *ESCHERICHIA COLI*

Strain Studied	Virulence*	Toxin†	Colonization	Colonization Factor Antigen Production‡
H10407 passaged	No	Yes	No	No
H10407 fresh	Yes	Yes	Yes	Yes
H10407 revertant	No	Yes	No	No

*Experimental diarrhea in animal models.
†Small bowel fluid secretion response to cell-free toxins.
‡Electron-microscopic visualization of colonization factor.
Data from Evans, D. G., Silver, R. P., Evans, D. J. Jr., et al.: Plasmid-controlled colonization factor associated with virulence in *Escherichia coli* enterotoxigenic for humans. Infect. Immun. *12*:656–667, 1975.

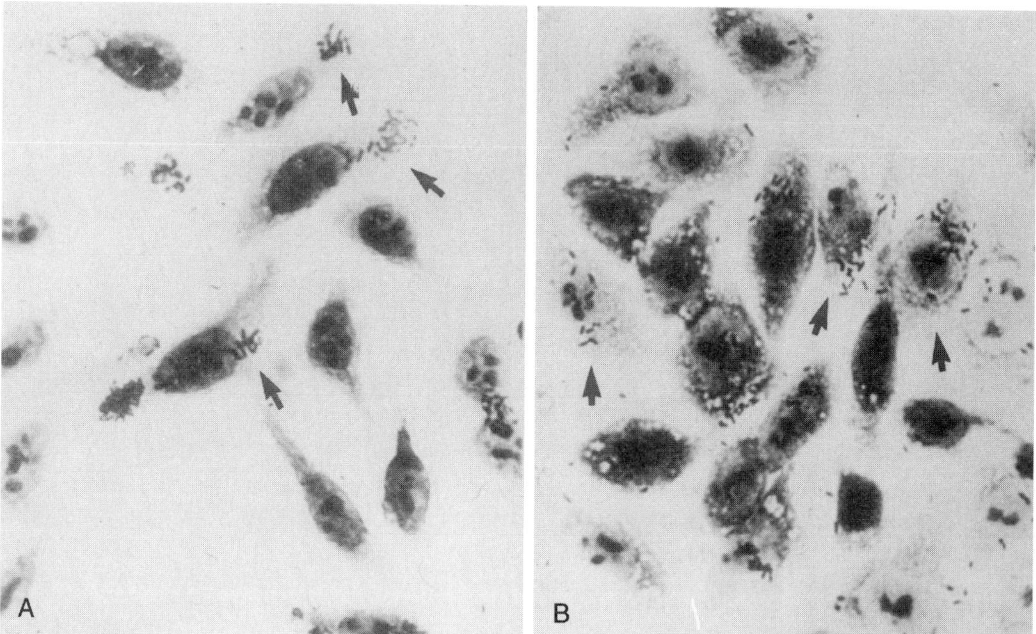

FIGURE 108–3 ■ Patterns of adherence of *Escherichia coli* to HEp-2 cells in tissue culture. Typical enteropathogenic *E. coli* associates with HEp-2 cells in the pattern shown in *A,* termed localized adherence (LA). The *arrows* point to cells where growing microcolonies of bacteria are attached to focal areas of the cell membrane. Other *E. coli* organisms isolated from patients with diarrhea adhere over the entire HEp-2 cell membrane, as shown in the cells identified with *arrows* in *B.* This pattern of interaction is termed diffuse adherence (DA). Whereas the LA phenotype has been associated definitively with the capacity to induce diarrhea in experimental models, no convincing evidence of virulence in DA strains has been obtained to date.

and ezrin.[35] One gene required for these physiologic events to proceed, *eaeA,* is situated in a 35-kb region of the chromosome termed the *locus of enterocyte effacement.*[64] The *eaeA* gene product is a 94-kd outer-membrane protein named *intimin* that has five antigenically distinct subtypes mediating attachment to different regions of the intestine. The receptor for intimin is of bacterial origin and is designated the translocated intimin receptor (Tir).[51] A highly homologous *eaeA* gene has been identified in EHEC strains as well and is associated with A/E lesions. The homology between *eaeA* and the *inv* (invasin) gene product of *Yersinia* strains, which recognizes membrane proteins of the integrin family and results in cell invasion, suggests that *eaeA* also may bind to cell integrins. Although EPEC has been reported to be invasive in vitro, it is not invasive to the same degree as EIEC or *Shigella,* and the relevance of this invasiveness to pathogenesis is not known. A second gene in

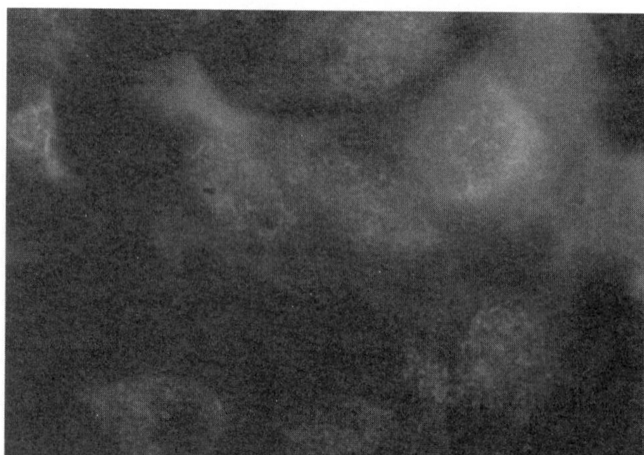

FIGURE 108–4 ■ Some *Escherichia coli* strains have the capacity to attach to the eukaryotic cell membrane and induce polymerization of actin beneath the membrane. This property may be demonstrated by the fluorescent actin staining test, in which polymerized F-actin is detected by a fluorescein-tagged mushroom toxin specific for this form of actin. In this figure, the bacteria are attached to HEp-2 cells, and the induced actin polymerization revealed by the fluorescent reagent highlights the organisms, which are seen as bright rods on the infected cells.

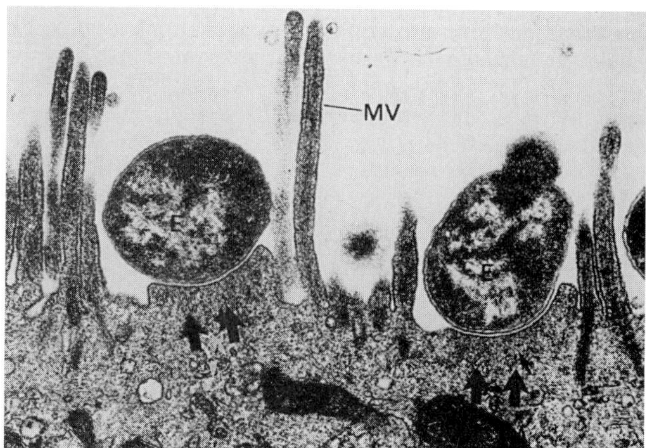

FIGURE 108–5 ■ High-power electron micrograph of intestinal epithelium infected by classic enteropathogenic *Escherichia coli* strains (E), with occasional intact microvilli (MV) and pedestal formation indicated by *double arrows.* This figure shows not only the structural alterations and loss of the brush border but also the close apposition of the organisms to the epithelial cells. (Courtesy of Ralph A. Gianella, Department of Medicine, University of Cincinnati School of Medicine.)

the locus of the enterocyte effacement region, *eaeB,* encodes a 33-kd secreted protein essential for the development of A/E lesions. EPEC alters epithelial cell signal transduction pathways, particularly the protein kinase/phosphatase pathways, and causes an elevation in intracellular calcium levels.[35] The locus of enterocyte effacement also contains genes encoding a type III secretion system and other secreted proteins essential for virulence.

Despite detailed knowledge of the interaction of EPEC with epithelial cells in vitro, how EPEC causes diarrhea in vivo is not clear. Loss of microvilli has been suggested to result in malabsorption. However, sometimes the diarrhea begins 3 hours after oral delivery of EPEC in volunteers, thus suggesting initiation of a secretory process.[35]

Other *E. coli* strains adhere to HEp-2 cells with a second pattern of interaction called diffuse adherence (DA), in which the organisms attach over the entire cell surface rather than at just a localized region (see Fig. 108–3). The pathogenic significance of these DA strains is still unclear,[141] and because DA strains are not usually classic EPEC serotypes, they are not considered further in this chapter.

ENTEROHEMORRHAGIC *ESCHERICHIA COLI*

Although O157:H7 is the prototypic EHEC isolated from patients with typical hemorrhagic colitis,[116] approximately 100 other serotypes also cause this clinical syndrome.[53, 65] Some of them may, in some settings, be more prevalent (e.g., O26:H11, formerly included in the classic EPEC serotypes but now reclassified as EHEC because of its ability to produce high levels of Stx toxins).[76] EHEC strains are typically LT/ST- and EAF-negative and, therefore, distinct from ETEC and EPEC, but like the latter, many but not all polymerize actin, are FAST-positive, possess a 60-Md plasmid encoding a fimbrial adhesin involved in attachment to epithelial cell lines, contain a homologue of the *eae* gene, and cause the A/E lesion.[147] EHEC also produces large amounts of bacteriophage-encoded Stx,[11] which may account for many of the clinical manifestations of hemorrhagic colitis.

Stx toxins were discovered by Konowalchuk and associates,[72] who reported finding cytotoxic activity in culture filtrates of certain strains of *E. coli* isolated from patients with diarrhea. The activity was heat-labile, could not be neutralized by antisera to LT, and was toxic to Vero cells. It therefore was designated verotoxin, and the strains producing it were called verotoxigenic *E. coli*. A few years later, O'Brien and Holmes[105] observed that verotoxins were neutralized by antisera to Stx from *Shigella,* and they were renamed *SLTs*. These toxins now more correctly are designated Stx. They constitute a family of proteins that share the identical enzymatic action and target cell binding specificity. In addition to the originally described *E. coli* Stx1 (originally named *SLT-1),* the existence of a second related toxin not neutralized by Shiga antibody soon became apparent and now is known as Stx2.[105] Subsequently, at least two other members of the Stx2 family have been described: Stx2c, from human patients with diarrhea, and STx2e, from swine with a characteristic toxin-mediated illness, edema disease.[79]

In contrast to Stx of *S. dysenteriae* type 1, encoded by chromosomal genes, and LT and ST, carried by plasmids, Stx toxins in *E. coli* are encoded by genes present on temperate bacteriophages. The *stx1* gene differs from the *Shigella stx* gene encoding Stx by three nucleotide changes that result in a single conservative amino acid substitution in the A subunit: threonine to serine.[57] The *stx2* genes are organized in an operon like those of the *stx* and *stx1* genes but share approximately 56 to 58 percent nucleotide and amino acid homology with the *stx* and *stx1* A and B subunit genes.[61] All three toxins are composed of a single A subunit and five noncovalently linked B subunits responsible for toxin binding to globotrioacyl ceramide (Gb_3) and related glycolipids on host cells.[37] All Stx toxins have an identical mechanism of action, cleavage of the *N*-glycosidic bond in a specific adenosine of the 28S rRNA in the 60S ribosomal subunit.[40] This single cleavage event results in irreversible cessation of protein synthesis and ultimately leads to cell death. Intestinal villus cells are susceptible to the action of toxin and may be defective in the absorption of sodium as a result, thereby possibly contributing to the diarrhea. Evidence suggests that Stx induces local inflammatory cytokine production, with potential effects on epithelial cell and mucosal integrity. Furthermore, the host's inflammatory response actually may stimulate the production of Stx because in vitro, both H_2O_2 and neutrophils augment production of Stx.[152]

Epidemiologic evidence strongly links Stx-producing strains to hemorrhagic colitis and, in addition, to the associated systemic complications of HUS and TTP.[53, 67, 117] The mechanisms underlying HUS and TTP are not certain but appear to be due to the effects of toxin on vascular endothelial cells, possibly in concert with lipopolysaccharide and a variety of cytokines, which initiates events resulting in endothelial cell injury and platelet thrombi and, subsequently, the characteristic thrombotic microangiopathy.[28, 68, 106] Other possible initiation factors include abnormal von Willebrand factor, but whether this abnormality is a cause or a consequence of disease is not known.[89] Stx1 has been shown to decrease production of prostacyclins; however, the role of this event in the pathogenesis of HUS remains uncertain.[68]

Other factors that may play a role in the pathogenesis of disease caused by *E. coli* O157:H7 include a colonization factor, intimin, encoded by the *eae* gene. The genes encoding intimin, Tir, the type III secretion system, and secreted proteins reside on a 35-kb pathogenicity island called the LEE (locus of enterocyte effacement), which may be more critical for EPEC than EHEC for virulence.[37] A 60-Md plasmid that contains genes encoding an enterohemolysin commonly is found in O157:H7 strains, but its role in production of disease is unclear.

ENTEROINVASIVE *ESCHERICHIA COLI*

In 1967, Trabulsi and coworkers[148] in Brazil and Sakazaki and associates[125] in Japan described the isolation of certain *E. coli* serotypes from patients with a disease resembling bacillary dysentery but with negative cultures for *Shigella*. These isolates possessed a critical virulence hallmark associated with *Shigella,* namely, the ability to invade intestinal and other epithelial cells[107] (Fig. 108–6). Hence, they have been called EIEC, and a limited number of serotypes, distinct from the EPEC O groups but often cross-reactive with *Shigella* O antigens, have been found to possess this property (see Table 108–1). The genetic and molecular basis of invasion by *Shigella* has been well defined during the past decade, and the same plasmid and chromosomal genes encoding invasion properties and mechanisms appear to be present in EIEC as well.[59, 76, 113, 126] The invasive process for EIEC is thought to be the same as that for *Shigella* spp. It has been well characterized and involves four main steps: (1) initial entry into cells, (2) intracellular multiplication, (3) intracellular and intercellular spread, and (4) host-cell killing. The process is complex and involves multiple genes on both the invasion plasmid and the chromosome.[1]

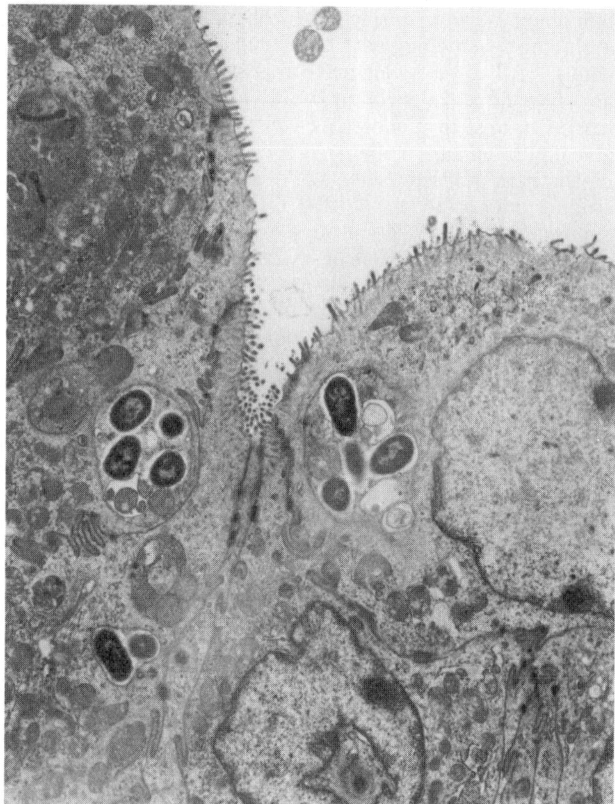

FIGURE 108–6 ■ Electron micrograph of enteroinvasive *Escherichia coli* infection of intestinal mucosa. The intracellular location of the bacteria clearly is seen within membrane-bound vesicles in two adjacent infected cells. The pathogenesis of enteroinvasive *E. coli* infection involves the invasion of intestinal cells and local cell-to-cell spread, as shown here, by a mechanism identical to that of *Shigella* species. (Courtesy of Saul Tzipori, D.V.M., Department of Comparative Medicine, Tufts University School of Veterinary Medicine.)

EIEC produces toxins reported to be structurally distinct from the Stx of *S. dysenteriae* type 1 and the Stx1 and Stx2 of EHEC.[47] Nonetheless, studies suggest that EIEC toxins possess many properties in common with the Shiga family of toxins, including the ability to cause fluid secretion in animal models.[47] EIEC may contain a plasmid-borne gene that encodes a 63-kd protein; a mutation in this gene substantially decreases the enterotoxic activity of the parent strain.[98]

ENTEROAGGREGATIVE *ESCHERICHIA COLI*

When the HEp-2 cell adherence assay was applied to the study of *E. coli* isolated from infants with diarrhea and performed in a specified manner, a third pattern of adherence called aggregative (or autoaggregative) was observed.[95, 99] In contrast to LA or DA, in which organisms are found almost exclusively in association with cells, aggregative strains autoagglutinate in a typical "stacked-brick" pattern on the edges of HEp-2 cells, as well as between them. Because LA and DA strains sometimes have been called enteroadherent *E. coli* (EAEC), the term *EAggEC* has been suggested to refer specifically to the autoaggregative isolates. EAggEC now is defined as *E. coli* that adheres to HEp-2 cells in an aggregative pattern and does not secrete heat-labile or heat-stable enterotoxins.[52] Adherence of EAggEC is mediated by at least two fimbriae (aggregative adherence fimbriae I and II), although many strains lack these fimbriae.[27] Dispersin, a novel 10-kd colonization factor encoded by the *aap* gene, is carried by most EAggEC strains and participates in the formation of a surface coat that acts to disperse bacteria.[133]

Serotypes of EAggEC isolates are often nontypeable or rough and, when typeable, are distinct from those of other diarrhea-causing *E. coli* (see Table 108–1). They are negative with probes for other *E. coli* virulence factors; however, they possess a 60- to 65-Md plasmid that can transfer the aggregative phenotype to rough *E. coli* K-12. EAggEC produces a novel low-molecular-weight ST (EAST, for enteroaggregative stable toxin), which like classic ST, increases cGMP within target cells.[127] However, in contrast to ST, EAST appears to be inactive in the well-known infant mouse test, and EAST^{+} strains fail to hybridize with ST probes. EAST-1 is a 38–amino acid protein with four cysteine residues. The role of EAST in EAggEC pathogenesis is unknown, and it has been found in several different types of enteric *E. coli* that do not have an aggregative phenotype. EAggEC also elaborates another toxin, plasmid-encoded toxin (Pet), that causes cytotoxicity in explanted colonic tissue.[133]

The in vivo significance of the EAggEC phenotype is indicated by the ability of the organisms to cause diarrhea in the gnotobiotic pig model, in which they are found in association with the villus tip in the characteristic aggregative fashion (S. Tzipori, personal communication) (Fig. 108–7). Cytotoxic effects have been noted on necropsy specimens from patients who died of EAggEC persistent diarrhea, as well as in intestinal cell tissue cultures.[96] Markers of inflammation were detected in stool samples of travelers with diarrhea from whom EAggEC was isolated, consistent with studies in children.[52] Experimental infections in human adult volunteers with four different EAggEC strains resulted in symptomatic disease in three of five individuals infected with one of these strains, whereas the other three strains failed to elicit diarrhea.[94] No single putative virulence factor predicted clinical response to these isolates. EAggEC has been isolated frequently from infants with persistent diarrhea, and a specific association is suggested. EAggEC strains have been

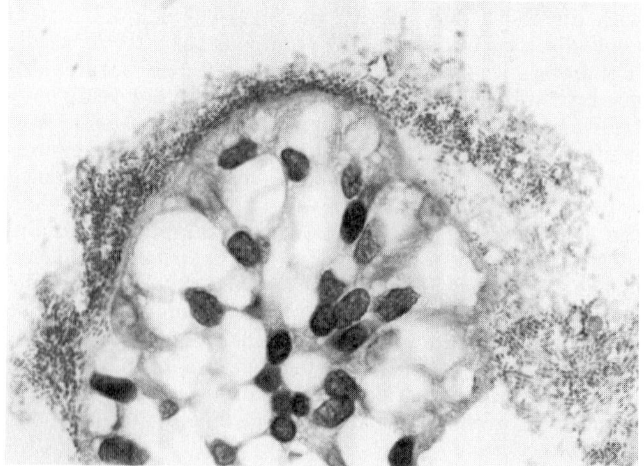

FIGURE 108–7 ■ Enteroaggregative *Escherichia coli* (EAggEC) infection of the gnotobiotic pig intestine. This photomicrograph shows the characteristic "stacked-brick" appearance of the aggregative organisms over the surface of the intestinal epithelium in vivo in the same manner described for EAggEC adherence to HE-2 cells in tissue culture. (Courtesy of Saul Tzipori, D.V.M., Department of Comparative Medicine, Tufts University School of Veterinary Medicine.)

shown to cause a destructive lesion with shortening of the villi, hemorrhagic necrosis of the villus tips, a mild inflammatory response with edema, and mononuclear infiltration when injected into rabbit loops.[97] Widespread use of a DNA probe for the aggregative phenotype[9] has demonstrated that not all phenotypically aggregative strains are probe-positive. A specific probe that will hybridize with all EAggEC strains has yet to be defined but will facilitate the study of these organisms in the future.

Diagnosis and Differential Diagnosis

Specialized laboratory tests are required to identify enterovirulent *E. coli.* Most diagnostic microbiology laboratories do not perform these studies routinely; hence, pathogenic *E. coli* will be called either normal flora or an EPEC strain, depending on whether they agglutinate with commercially available EPEC typing sera. Serotyping *E. coli* isolates from diarrhea patients still has some value because clinical isolates of ETEC, EPEC, EHEC, and EIEC usually are restricted to a limited number of serogroups distinctive for each. Unfortunately, except for EPEC and a few EHEC serotypes, the antisera needed are not available commercially. Many virulence factors have been identified that as discussed earlier, define different groups of *E. coli* enteric pathogens. A consensus definition has been developed that requires that to be considered a typical EPEC, an isolate must produce an A/E lesion, be Shiga toxin–negative, and possess the EAF plasmid.[96] Atypical EPEC strains lack the EAF plasmid and are related more closely to Shiga toxin–producing *E. coli.* Currently, in industrialized countries, atypical EPEC strains predominate.[149] Although these factors can be detected in the laboratory by gene probe or PCR, by ELISA, or in some instances by phenotyping a physiologic assay (e.g., cell culture), for the next several years at least, specific identification will not be available to clinicians except in unusual circumstances.

Because of the potential of EHEC infection to cause systemic microangiopathic complications, specific diagnosis is of clinical importance. For culture techniques, the earlier in the course of illness that a stool specimen is obtained, the more likely that *E. coli* O157:H7 will be recovered (recovery is achieved in most cases if specimens are obtained within 1 to 2 days of the onset of diarrhea versus a 33% rate as disease progresses). Currently, the laboratory can use sorbitol-MacConkey agar to screen colonies for sorbitol fermentation or the methylumbelliferylglucuronide test for the production of β-glucuronidase because *E. coli* O157:H7 is almost uniquely sorbitol- and glucuronidase-negative. However, these techniques are only 50 to 60 percent sensitive in detecting these organisms. Furthermore, some sorbitol-fermenting O157:H7 isolates, as well as a large number of other sorbitol-fermenting EHEC, are capable of causing severe illness and HUS that are missed by sorbitol-MacConkey agar.

ELISAs for O157 lipopolysaccharide and other outer-membrane proteins have been developed, but the former is specific for just one serotype and is not very sensitive, and the value of outer-membrane protein markers for non-O157:H7 EHEC has not been established. Detecting Shiga toxin in stool specimens is currently the recommended approach for the most sensitive means of identifying EHEC, either directly or after overnight broth enrichment.[69] These tests are more sensitive than culture techniques and are not dependent on serotype. Commercial enzyme immunoassays for Stx have been approved by the Food and Drug Administration for either confirmation of isolates as producers of toxin or rapid direct diagnosis based on detecting the presence of Stx1 or Stx2 in stool. At present, early diagnosis of EHEC may be of major epidemiologic importance. It also can serve to alert clinicians to the potential of systemic microangiopathy and, when improved therapeutic measures become available, to signal early initiation of therapy, which should improve the outcome measurably. Despite the detection of Shiga toxin by these rapid assays, isolation of the organism remains critical for serotyping and other epidemiologic purposes.

Diagnosis of ETEC would require identifying the LT or ST genes in an isolate or, after isolation and growth in vitro, detecting their products by ELISA. PCR techniques are available that allow direct detection of LT or ST genes from stool without the need for performing culture.[21] A retrospective diagnosis can be made by detecting a rise in antitoxin antibody, especially for LT. ELISA for CFA antigens of ETEC also could be useful. EPEC can be detected reliably by DNA probes for the 60-Md EAF adherence plasmid or by tissue culture assay for the LA pattern or the FAST$^{\pm}$ phenotype. The only way to confirm EAggEC at present is by tissue culture assay for the aggregative adherence phenotype. DNA probes are available for an aggregative adherence-associated DNA sequence, but a significant proportion of clinical isolates from all regions of the world are probe-negative. EIEC strains are, in general, responsible for only a fraction of diarrheal illnesses. Detection relies primarily on identification of invasion genes or gene products that share these virulence factors, as for *Shigella.*[20] Tissue culture also can be used to demonstrate the invasive capacity of these strains. Although some other enterovirulent *E. coli* can invade mammalian cells to a limited extent, no overlap exists with the invasive capacity of EIEC.

In sum, this is a sorry state that is amenable to change as more sophisticated methods become available, but only if sufficient priority is given to rapid diagnosis to decrease the cost involved. Diagnosis is important to avoid the danger of administering inappropriate therapy and to increase the likelihood that necessary therapy will be started early in the course of the illness. Other identifiable agents that should be treated differently may cause similar illnesses; such agents include human rotavirus strains in children younger than 2 years; *V. cholerae, Vibrio parahaemolyticus,* or related marine vibrios; *Salmonella* and *Shigella* spp.; *Campylobacter* spp., especially in adolescents in the United States; and *Yersinia enterocolitica*. Rotavirus can be diagnosed readily by commercially available ELISAs. Although an endemic focus of cholera exists in the United States along the Louisiana/Texas Gulf Coast, only a few indigenous cases occur, probably because the risk factor, ingestion of raw shellfish, is limited and a large inoculum is required. The same is true of infection with *V. parahaemolyticus. Salmonella* and *Shigella* both cause an exudative stool similar to that caused by EIEC, with many polymorphonuclear leukocytes visible, and this simple test can be of diagnostic significance, especially when routine stool culture for *Salmonella* and *Shigella* is negative. *Campylobacter* is the leading cause of food-borne diarrhea in the United States, and the highest age-specific incidence occurs in infants (approximately 14 cases/100,000 person-years).[5] The laboratory must use special selective media cultured at 42° C under 10 percent carbon dioxide to isolate these organisms. *Y. enterocolitica* infection is a rare occurrence in the United States but can masquerade as ETEC because both organisms initially are likely to be considered a normal stool coliform to be discarded by the laboratory. Unlike ETEC, however, *Y. enterocolitica* does not require special tests to demonstrate its virulence attributes; rather, a high index of suspicion and additional classic diagnostic microbiologic testing will suffice.

Prognosis

EPEC, EAggEC, and ETEC do not cause systemic infections or complications except those resulting from dehydration or the consequences of nutritional depletion. Thus, the prognosis is related directly to the availability and adequacy of fluid therapy. When this need is dealt with correctly in an otherwise healthy and well-nourished patient, the principal complication is the rare instance of monosaccharide intolerance. In infants or young children in developing countries with protein-energy malnutrition, however, chronic diarrhea and progressive worsening of nutritional status commonly are observed, sometimes terminating fatally. When food is withheld from either well- or poorly nourished youngsters, hypoglycemia may occur and produce seizures, coma, or even death. Rarely, loss of water in excess of salt causes hypertonic dehydration, with serum sodium concentrations above 160 mEq/L, a situation that may cause seizures, coma, and death as well.

EAggEC has been associated with persistent diarrhea lasting longer 14 days in young infants and children, which may result in part from feeding lactose-containing diets to those with secondary lactase deficiency. Persistent diarrhea, however, leads to nutritional deterioration, may be difficult to control, and may culminate in death from sepsis or other infections. Inflammatory diarrhea caused by EIEC also results in nutritional deterioration, with significant protein losses occurring via the gut.

EHEC is associated significantly with HUS and, especially in adults, TTP. As many as 10 percent of patients may die early in the course of the systemic phase of either HUS or TTP. Although the renal failure of HUS is generally reversible with good management of fluid and electrolytes and the use of dialysis as needed, permanent damage to the kidneys is, contrary to earlier more optimistic assessments, likely to occur in 50 percent or more patients over the course of 1 or 2 decades, and many of them will require permanent dialysis or transplantation in the future. The prognosis in TTP is related directly to initiation of plasmapheresis, which has been documented to reduce mortality rates significantly. No such benefit has been noted in HUS.

Treatment

In all age groups, the principal treatment of the intestinal manifestations of *E. coli* enteric infection is replacement of fluids and electrolytes; with maintenance of fluid balance, the disease is self-limited to a week or less in most patients and lasts no more than 2 weeks in nearly all. The earlier that fluid replacement therapy is begun, the better the prognosis, particularly when one considers that clinical signs of dehydration do not develop until a 5 percent loss of body weight occurs and that sustained loss of more than 10 percent of body weight is incompatible with survival. This percentage does not allow much margin of safety and mandates close attention to fluid balance.

When shock is present (usually with altered consciousness and an absent or thready pulse) or oral rehydration is not successful because of persistent vomiting, patients must be rehydrated by intravenous infusion of an electrolyte solution such as lactated Ringer solution. For patients in shock, a volume of 30 mL/kg body weight should be given over the course of 1 hour, followed by an additional 40 mL/kg body weight in the next 2 hours. When dehydration is less severe, initial replacement of losses usually can be accomplished by oral rehydration. Patients not in shock, who may have normal findings on physical examination or may manifest poor skin turgor, tachycardia, postural hypotension, and oliguria (along with irritability and a sunken fontanelle in the very young), should receive 50 to 120 mL/kg of fluid, depending on the severity of dehydration, as rapidly as they can be encouraged to drink over a period of 4 hours. Pulse, blood pressure, urine volume, skin turgor, general appearance, and thirst are monitored as indicators of response. Adults may need as much as a liter an hour to establish rehydration, and they, as well as youngsters, may tire of drinking and fail to keep up with requirements. Thus, several prerequisites must be ensured for oral therapy: (1) the patient not be in shock, (2) the patient be fully conscious, (3) the patient be able to drink (vomiting, particularly common in youngsters, is not an absolute contraindication, for frequent small oral feedings are usually largely retained; once the metabolic abnormality begins to reverse toward normal, vomiting ceases), (4) bowel sounds be present, and (5) renal function be normal. Current recommendations in the United States and Europe suggest the use of hypotonic fluid containing 30 to 60 mEq of sodium per liter. In the developing world, where cholera is a common occurrence, the World Health Organization recommends that a solution containing 90 mEq of sodium be used for all cases of diarrhea because of the large sodium losses that occur in cholera and the desire to avoid the need to choose among formulations because of difficulty in making an etiologic diagnosis. Current studies to evaluate a new solution with a reduced sodium and glucose content are under way, and the results are likely to influence future recommendations.

Although rehydration therapy is the cornerstone of management, antibiotic therapy should be considered in some cases. In most *E. coli*–associated diarrheal illnesses, the disease is mild and of relatively short duration, and therefore, no specific antimicrobial therapy is required. Studies to address this issue have found the effects of antibiotics beneficial in some circumstances. For example, in traveler's diarrhea secondary to ETEC, antibiotic therapy can shorten the duration of illness and decrease its severity.[41, 100] Prophylactic antibiotic therapy, however, probably carries more risk than benefit and generally is not recommended. When antibiotics are used, TMP-SMX therapy presently is recommended for children with traveler's diarrhea caused by susceptible isolates; fluoroquinolones are the drugs of choice for adults when chemoprophylaxis is indicated.[115] Antimotility agents such as loperamide generally are not needed but should be used cautiously if prescribed, with great attention paid to dosage, especially in very young patients.[143] Dysentery is a contraindication to the use of antimotility agents, which may be a risk factor for the development of ileus and abdominal distention. Current Food and Drug Administration recommendations preclude giving 4-fluoroquinolones to infants and children younger than 17 years because the possibility of cartilage damage has been raised by animal toxicology studies, although no convincing evidence has shown that it is an actual risk in humans.

Children in developing countries with ETEC diarrhea also may benefit from receiving antibiotic therapy.[103] Resistance of ETEC to TMP-SMX was noted in U.S. troops in Saudi Arabia, where 44 percent of isolates were resistant.[109] EIEC infection theoretically would benefit even more from antibiotic therapy, given its pathogenic similarity to shigellosis and the known benefits of the early use of antibiotics. However, no controlled studies have validated this benefit for EIEC. In experimentally induced disease, DuPont and colleagues[38] reported that parenteral ampicillin, 2 g/24 hr for 3 days, produced a bacteriologic cure and rapid clinical response with defervescence and improvement of diarrhea in adults. TMP-SMX and ampicillin are the current drugs of choice, unless resistance is a problem.

A novel treatment approach was reported by DiCesare and associates,[34] who evaluated SP-303, a plant-derived product with antisecretory properties, in a randomized placebo-controlled study of acute diarrhea in 184 U.S. travelers to Mexico and Jamaica. SP-303 shortened the duration of traveler's diarrhea by 21 percent; ETEC was the etiologic agent of traveler's diarrhea in 19 percent of the subjects. Human breast milk contains oligosaccharides that can partially bind to ETEC and presumably block attachment to intestinal epithelial cells.[82] However, bovine hyperimmune milk from cows immunized against ETEC and EPEC is not effective treatment or prophylaxis for ETEC or EPEC diarrhea.[23, 140]

Epidemic EPEC infection, especially in the newborn, appears to be affected favorably by antibiotic therapy.[101] The potential for this pathogen to cause prolonged disease and a history of high rates of mortality in neonates suggest the need for antibiotic trials in this age group. Based on limited data, either TMP-SMX or oral nonabsorbable antibiotics such as gentamicin or colistin usually are recommended, although antibiotic resistance occurs very commonly and may alter the choice of antibiotics based on local susceptibility patterns.[8, 151]

Antibiotic treatment of EHEC is still controversial but generally is not recommended. The important question of whether antibiotics increase the likelihood of HUS or TTP remains controversial and unanswered.[6, 13, 25] Large, probably multicenter, double-blind, placebo-controlled studies will be needed to address this problem. The efficacy of a synthetic verotoxin receptor to prevent HUS in children with hemorrhagic colitis caused by *E. coli* O157:H7 is as yet unproved.[7] It is hoped that identification of the complete sequence of *E. coli* O157:H7 will allow greater understanding of the pathogenesis of hemorrhagic colitis and HUS and perhaps innovative approaches to treatment and prevention.[56]

Persistent diarrhea caused by EAggEC appears to be as much a nutritional problem as a specific infection treatable with antibiotics. By the time that the prolonged symptoms are noted, however, antibiotics may have been tried already, with little impact on the diarrhea, and the problem now is the effect of damage to the brush border of the gut cell. Nutritional management, focused first on reduction and possibly removal of lactose and then on elemental diets per os or parenterally if necessary in the event of continuing illness, remains the therapeutic strategy of choice.

Immunocompromised hosts, especially children with acquired immunodeficiency syndrome, may require prolonged antibiotic therapy for protracted or recrudescent diarrhea, even when it is caused by bacteria that normally produce only self-limited disease. Malnourished children and children with other serious underlying illness also fit this category. In these patients, systemic invasion may develop along with associated complications, including shock and renal failure. In addition, prolonged carrier states are common findings, with frequent relapses requiring chronic antibiotic therapy for suppression of relapse.

Practically speaking, in most instances of *E. coli* diarrhea, the clinician is left to make therapeutic decisions without knowing the etiologic agent responsible. For reasons already outlined, routine diagnostic microbiology laboratories cannot distinguish pathogenic from nonpathogenic *E. coli,* with the exception of classic EPEC serotypes and O157:H7 EHEC. No system of national referral laboratories is available for identification of sporadic isolates, and even when an outbreak is investigated by local or national public health laboratories, several days or more likely weeks will be required. Clinical decisions regarding the administration of antibiotic therapy, therefore, are made on purely clinical grounds with criteria such as the history, duration, and severity of the illness; the age and immunologic competence of the patient; and the nature of the diarrheal stool (for example, watery, inflammatory, bloody, or dysenteric). Empiric antimicrobial therapy is more justifiable for immunocompromised hosts, for patients with prolonged or severe illness or a history of relevant risk factors (specific food ingestion, travel, exposure to known contacts, etc.), and for cases of inflammatory or dysenteric illness.

Prevention

The nature of protective immunity still is not well understood, and no vaccines are available for clinical use. Of interest, however, is the modest protective effect against ETEC diarrhea observed in the first few months after an immunization trial in Bangladesh with a killed whole-cell cholera vaccine plus cholera toxin B subunit, which has homology with the *E. coli* LT B subunit. This result is encouraging because experimentally, antitoxin can prevent symptoms of disease caused by ETEC. Although ST alone does not stimulate an immune response, coupling to a protein carrier induces a protective response to challenge with ST or ST-producing ETEC in experimental animals. Synthetic ST, modified to be biologically inactive, also has been coupled to LT B subunit epitopes by genetic fusion or chemical coupling of the two peptides and used as an experimental vaccine to stimulate antibody to both toxins.

Other approaches to ETEC vaccines follow the tactics being used for cholera as well. For example, the use of CFAs as vaccine antigens is analogous to exploitation of the TcpA adherence pilus antigen in *V. cholerae.* Unfortunately, protection afforded by ETEC CFAs in experimental models is specific, and multiple CFAs are now known, thus suggesting the need for a multicomponent vaccine. The observation that some of these antigens (CFA I, II, and IV) appear to predominate in nature may limit the number of CFA antigens needed for an effective vaccine. An oral formalin-inactivated whole-cell ETEC plus recombinant cholera toxin B subunit vaccine has been shown to be immunogenic and safe in infants and children.[128, 129] The efficacy of this vaccine is being investigated in Egypt. Other studies have shown that in adults, antibodies develop to the recombinant ETEC colonization factor cs6 and LT when they are delivered together transcutaneously in a patch.[55] Unfortunately, most ST-only isolates of ETEC do not express fimbriate colonization factors and would be unaffected by a CFA-based vaccine.

Vaccine development for other enterovirulent *E. coli* strains lags behind that for ETEC. The identification of virulence molecules, such as EAF, the *eae* genes that encode the ability to cause A/E lesions in the brush border, the invasive genes of EIEC, and the Stx of EHEC, suggests that the future development of vaccines for these other classes of diarrhea-causing *E. coli* now can proceed with clearly defined target antigens available. Experimental data in rabbits suggest that either parenteral immunization with recombinant Stx1 B subunit or oral administration of a live cholera vaccine expressing recombinant Stx1 B subunit can induce protective immune responses.[2] Antibody raised to a flagellin-like 30-kd outer-membrane protein of EAggEC encoded by the 60-Md plasmid blocks enteroaggregative adherence to HEp-2 cells in vitro and thus could be a potential in vivo immunization strategy.[33]

Epidemic nursery outbreaks of diarrhea in newborn infants can be controlled by the application of antiquated but still perfectly valid principles of preventive medicine. Prompt diagnosis and treatment and scrupulous attention to details of handwashing and environmental sanitation to eliminate person-to-person transmission are still effective, whereas prophylactic antimicrobials have no role to play. Outbreaks in neonatal nurseries can be contained by epidemiologic control measures such as cohorting, by screening staff for carriage, and if necessary, by closing the unit until it is decontaminated. In contrast, preventing sporadic *E. coli* diarrhea is difficult. In communities with obvious deficits in water supply and feces disposal, correction of these problems will lead to a diminished incidence of diarrheal diseases in general. For the diarrhea of travelers, several studies indicate that prophylactic antibiotics can protect adult travelers, at least for a limited time. However, they provide no magic bullet to eliminate the problem, and the risk of selection of resistant organisms and drug side effects limits the use of antibiotic prophylaxis to short-term travelers with business or diplomatic missions that would be hindered significantly by an episode of diarrhea. The use of tetracyclines is not recommended for children younger than 8 years because of deposition in teeth and bones, and no studies of TMP-SMX have been conducted in children. Some evidence has been presented for the efficacy of bismuth compounds, such as bismuth subsalicylate, for the prevention of ETEC diarrhea in adults. However, the concern for bismuth toxicity with prolonged use in young children would render it a problematic solution for pediatric *E. coli* diarrhea and its prevention.

REFERENCES

1. Acheson, D. W. K., and Keusch, G. T.: *Shigella* and enteroinvasive *Escherichia coli*. *In* Blaser, M. J., Smith, P. D., Ravdin J. I., et al. (eds.): Infections of the Gastrointestinal Tract. New York, Raven Press, 1995, pp. 763–784.
2. Acheson, D. W. K., Levine, M. M., Kaper, J. B., et al.: Protective immunity to Shiga-like toxin I following oral immunization with Shiga-like toxin I B-subunit–producing *Vibrio cholerae* CVD 103-HgR. Infect. Immun. *64*:355–357, 1996.
3. Adachi, J. A., Ericsson, C. D., Jiang, Z.-D., et al.: Natural history of enteroaggregative and enterotoxigenic *Escherichia coli* infection among US travelers to Guadalajara, Mexico. J. Infect. Dis. *185*:1681–1683, 2002.
4. Adam, A.: Biology of colon bacillus in dyspepsia, and its relation to pathogenesis and to intoxication. J. Kinderheilk. *101*:295–314, 1923.
5. Alkruse, S. F., Stern, N. J., Fields, P. I., and Swerdlow, D. L.: *Campylobacter jejuni*—an emerging foodborne pathogen. Emerg. Infect. Dis. *5*:28–35, 1999.
6. Al-Qarawi, S., Fontaine, R. E., and Al-Qahtani, M.-S.: An outbreak of hemolytic uremic syndrome associated with antibiotic treatment of hospital inpatients for dysentery. Emerg. Infect. Dis. *1*:138–140, 1995.
7. Armstrong, G. D., Rowe, P. C., Goodyer, P. et al.: A phase I study of chemically synthesized verotoxin (Shiga-like toxin) Pk-trisaccharide receptors attached to Chromosorb for preventing hemolytic-uremic syndrome. J. Infect. Dis. *171*:1042–1045, 1995.
8. Ashkenazi, S., and Cleary, T. G.: Antibiotic treatment of bacterial gastroenteritis. Pediatr. Infect. Dis. J. *10*:140–148, 1991.
9. Baudry, B., Savarino, S. J., Vial, P., et al.: A sensitive and specific DNA probe to identify enteroaggregative *Escherichia coli*, a recently discovered diarrheal pathogen. J. Infect. Dis. *161*:1249–1251, 1990.
10. Belnap, W. D., and O'Donnell, J. J.: Epidemic gastroenteritis due to *Escherichia coli* O-111: A review of the literature with the epidemiology, bacteriology, and clinical findings of a large outbreak. J. Pediatr. *47*:178–193, 1955.
11. Bettelheim, K. A., Brown, J. E., Lolekha, S., et al.: Serotypes of *Escherichia coli* that hybridized with DNA probes for genes encoding Shiga-like toxin I, Shiga-like toxin II, and serogroup 0157 enterohemorrhagic *E. coli* fimbriae isolated from adults with diarrhea in Thailand. J. Clin. Microbiol. *28*:293–295, 1990.
12. Bhan, M. K., Raj, P., Levine, M. M., et al.: Enteroaggregative *Escherichia coli* associated with persistent diarrhea in a cohort of rural children in India. J. Infect. Dis. *159*:1061–1064, 1989.
13. Bin Saeed, A. A. A., El Bushra, E., and al-Hamdan, N. A.: Does treatment of bloody diarrhea due to *Shigella dysenteriae* type 1 with ampicillin precipitate hemolytic uremic syndrome? Emerg. Infect. Dis. *1*:134–137, 1995.
14. Black, R. E.: Persistent diarrhea in children of developing countries. Pediatr. Infect. Dis. *12*:751–761, 1993.
15. Black, R. E., Brown, K. H., Becker, S., et al.: Longitudinal studies of infectious diseases and physical growth of children in rural Bangladesh. II. Incidence of diarrhea and association with known pathogens. Am. J. Epidemiol. *115*:315–324, 1982.
16. Bokete, T. N., O'Callahan, C. M., Clausen, C. R., et al.: Shiga-like toxin–producing *Escherichia coli* in Seattle children: A prospective study. Gastroenterology *105*:1724–1731, 1993.
17. Bouckenooghe, A. R., Jiang, Z.-D., De La Cabada, F. J., et al.: Enterotoxigenic *Escherichia coli* as cause of diarrhea among Mexican adults and US travelers to Mexico. J. Travel Med. *9*:137–140, 2002.
18. Bray, J. S. B.: Bray's discovery of pathogenic *Esch. coli* as a cause of infantile gastroenteritis. Arch. Dis. Child. *48*:923–926, 1973.
19. Butler, T., Islam, M. R., Azad, M. A. K., et al.: Risk factors for development of hemolytic uremic syndrome during shigellosis. J. Pediatr. *110*:894–897, 1987.
20. Caeiro, J.-P., Estrada-Garcia, T., Jiang, Z.-D., et al.: Improved detection of enteroinvasive *Escherichia coli* among patients with travelers' diarrhea, by use of the polymerase chain reaction technique. J. Infect. Dis. *180*:2053–2055, 1999.
21. Caeiro, J. P. Mathewson, J. J., Smith, M.A., et al.: Etiology of outpatient pediatric nondysenteric diarrhea: A multicenter study in the United States. Pediatr. Infect. Dis. J. *18*:94–97, 1999.
22. Cameron, A. S., Beers, M. Y., Walker, C. C., et al.: Community outbreak of hemolytic uremic syndrome attributable to *Escherichia coli* O111:NMC South Australia, 1995. M. M. W. R. Morb. Mortal. Wkly. Rep. *44*:550–558, 1995.
23. Casswell, T. H., Sarker, S. A., Faraque, S. M., et al.: Treatment of enterotoxigenic and enteropathogenic *Escherichia coli*–induced diarrhea in children with bovine immunoglobulin milk concentrated from hyperimmunized cows: A double-blind, placebo-controlled, clinical trial. Scand. J. Gastroenterol. *35*:711–718, 2000.
24. Centers for Disease Control and Prevention: FoodNet Annual Reports—2000. http://www.cdc.gov/foodnet/annuals.htm.
25. Cimolai, N., Carter, J. E., Morrison, B. J., et al.: Risk factors for the progression of *Escherichia coli* O157:H7 enteritis to hemolytic-uremic syndrome. J. Pediatr. *116*:589–592, 1990.
26. Cimolai, N., Morrison, B. J., and Carter, J. E.: Risk factors for the central nervous system manifestations of gastroenteritis-associated hemolytic-uremic syndrome. Pediatrics *90*:616–621, 1992.
27. Clarke, S. C.: Diarrhoeagenic *Escherichia coli*—an emerging problem? Diagn. Microbiol. Infect. Dis. *41*:93–98, 2001.
28. Cleary, T. G., and Lopez, E. L.: The Shiga-like toxin producing *Escherichia coli* and hemolytic uremic syndrome. Pediatr. Infect. Dis. J. *8*:720–724, 1989.
29. Crane, J. K., Weehner, M. S., Bolen, E. J., et al.: Regulation of intestinal guanylate cyclase by the heat stable enterotoxin of *Escherichia coli* (STa) and protein kinase C. Infect. Immun. *60*:5004–5012, 1992.
30. Cravioto, A., Reyes, R., Ortega, R., et al.: Prospective study of diarrhoeal disease in a cohort of rural Mexican children: Incidence and isolated pathogens during the first two years of life. Epidemiol. Infect. *101*:123–134, 1988.
31. Cravioto, A., Tello, A., Villagan, H., et al.: Inhibition of localized adhesion of enteropathogenic *Escherichia coli* to HEp-2 cells by immunoglobulin and oligosaccharide fractions of human colostrum and breast milk. J. Infect. Dis. *163*:1247–1255, 1991.
32. Currie, M. G., Fok, K. F., Kato, J. et al.: Guanylin: An endogenous activator of intestinal guanylate cyclase. Proc. Natl. Acad. Sci. U. S. A. *89*:947–951, 1992.
33. Debroy, C., Yearly, J., Wilson, R. C. A., et al.: Antibodies raised against the outer membrane protein interrupt adherence of enteroaggregative *Escherichia coli*. Infect. Immun. *63*:2873–2879, 1995.
34. DiCesare, D., DuPont, H. L., Mathewson, J. J., et al.: A double blind, randomized, placebo-controlled study of SP-303 (Provir) in the symptomatic treatment of acute diarrhea among travelers to Jamaica and Mexico. Am. J. Gastroenterol. *97*:2585–2588, 2002.
35. Donnenberg, M. S.: Enteropathogenic *Escherichia coli*. *In* Blaser, M. J., Smith, P. D., Ravdin J. I., et al. (eds.): Infections of the Gastrointestinal Tract. New York, Raven Press, 1995, pp. 709–726.
36. Donnenberg, M. S., Tacket, C. O., James, S. P., et al.: The role of the *eaeA* gene in experimental enteropathogenic *Escherichia coli* infection. J. Clin. Invest. *92*:1412–1417, 1993.
37. Donnenberg, M. S., and Whittam, T. S.: Pathogenesis and evolution of virulence in enteropathogenic and enterohemorrhagic *Escherichia coli*. J. Clin. Invest. *107*:539–548, 2001.
38. DuPont, H. L., Formal, S. B., Hornick, R. B., et al.: Pathogenesis of *Escherichia coli* diarrhea. N. Engl. J. Med. *285*:1–9, 1971.
39. Embaye, H., Hart, C. A., Getty, B., et al.: Effects of enteropathogenic *Escherichia coli* on microvillar membrane proteins during organ culture of rabbit intestinal mucosa. Gut *33*:1184–1189, 1992.
40. Endo, Y., Tsurugi, K., Yutsudo, T., et al.: Site of action of a Verotoxin (VT2) from *Escherichia coli* O157:H7 and of Shiga toxin on eukaryotic ribosomes: RNA N-glycosidase activity of the toxin. Eur. J. Biochem. *171*:45–50, 1988.
41. Ericsson, C. P., DuPont, H. L., Mathewson, J., et al.: Treatment of traveler's diarrhea with sulfamethoxazole and trimethoprim and loperamide. J. A. M. A. *263*:257–261, 1990.
42. Essers, B., Burnens, A. P., Lanfranchini, F. M., et al.: Acute community-acquired diarrhea requiring hospital admission in Swiss children. Clin. Infect. Dis. *31*:192–196, 2000.

43. Evans, D. G., Evans, D. J., Jr., and DuPont, H. L.: Virulence factors of enterotoxigenic *Escherichia coli*. J. Infect. Dis. *136*(Suppl.):118–123, 1977.
44. Evans, D. G., Silver, R. P., Evans, D. J., Jr., et al.: Plasmid-controlled colonization factor associated with virulence in *Escherichia coli* enterotoxigenic for humans. Infect. Immun. *12*:656–667, 1975.
45. Evans, D. J., Jr., and Evans, D. G.: Classification of pathogenic *Escherichia coli* according to serotype and the production of virulence factors, with special reference to colonization-factor antigens. Rev. Infect. Dis. *5*(Suppl.):692–701, 1983.
46. Faris, A., Wadstrom, T., and Freer, J. H.: Hydrophobic adsorptive and hemagglutinating properties of *Escherichia coli* possessing colonization factor antigens (CFA/I or C FA/II), type 1 pili, or other pili. Curr. Microbiol. *5*:67–72, 1981.
47. Fasano, A., Kay, B., Russell, R. G., et al.: Enterotoxin and cytotoxin production by enteroinvasive *Escherichia coli*. Infect. Immun. *58*:3717–3723, 1990.
48. Giannella, R. A., Luttrell, M., and Thompson, M.: Binding of *Escherichia coli* heat-stable enterotoxin to receptors on rat intestinal cells. Am. J. Physiol. *243*:G36–G41, 1983.
49. Giron, J. A., Ho, A. S. Y., and Schoolnik, G. K.: An indelible bundle-forming pilus of enteropathogenic *Escherichia coli*. Science *254*:710–713, 1991.
50. Gomes, T. A. T., Rassi, V., Macdonald, K. L., et al.: Enteropathogens associated with acute diarrheal disease in urban infants in Sao Paulo, Brazil. J. Infect. Dis. *164*:331–337, 1991.
51. Goosney, D. L., Knoechel, D. G., and Finlay, B. B.: Enterpathogenic *E. coli, Salmonella,* and *Shigella*: Masters of host cell cytoskeletal exploitation. Emerg. Infect. Dis. *5*:216–223, 1999.
52. Greenberg, D. E., Jiang, Z.-D., Steffen, R., et al.: Markers of inflammation in bacterial diarrhea among travelers with a focus on enteroaggregative *Escherichia coli* pathogenicity. J. Infect. Dis. *185*:944–949, 2002.
53. Griffin, P. M.: *Escherichia coli* O157:H7 and other enterohemorrhagic *Escherichia coli*. *In* Blaser, M. J., Smith, P. D., Ravdin J. I., et al. (eds.): Infections of the Gastrointestinal Tract. New York, Raven Press, 1995, pp. 739–761.
54. Griffin, P. M., and Tauxe, R. V.: The epidemiology of infections caused by *Escherichia coli* O157:H7, other enterohemorrhagic *E. coli* and the associated hemolytic uremic syndrome. Epidemiol. Rev. *13*:60–98, 1991.
55. Güerena-Burgueno, F., Hall, E. R., Taylor, D. N., et al.: Safety and immunologenicity of a prolonged enterotoxigenic *Escherichia coli* vaccine administered transcutaneously. Infect. Immun. *70*:1874–1880, 2002.
56. Hayashi, T., Makino, K., Ohnishi, M., et al.: Complete genome sequence of enterohemorrhagic *Escherichia coli* O157:H7 and genomic comparison with a laboratory strain K-12. DNA Res. *8*:11–22, 2001.
57. Hofmann, S. L.: Southwestern internal medicine conference: Shiga-like toxin in hemolytic-uremic syndrome and thrombotic thrombocytopenic purpura. Am. J. Med. Sci. *306*:398–406, 1993.
58. Honda, T., Tsuji, T., Takeda, Y., et al.: Immunological non-identity of heat-labile enterotoxins from human and porcine enterotoxigenic *Escherichia coli*. Infect. Immun. *33*:677–682, 1981.
59. Hromockyj, A. E., and Maurelli, A. T.: Identification of an *Escherichia coli* gene homologous to virR, a regulator of *Shigella* virulence. J. Bacteriol. *171*:2879–2881, 1989.
60. Hunt, C. M., Harvey, J. A., Youngs, E. R., et al.: Clinical and pathological variability of infection by enterohaemorrhagic (verocytotoxin producing) *Escherichia coli*. J. Clin. Pathol. *43*:847–852, 1989.
61. Jackson, M. P., Newland, J. W., Holmes, R. K., et al.: Nucleotide sequence analysis of the structural gene for Shiga-like toxin I by bacteriophage 933J from *Escherichia coli*. Microbiol. Pathog. *2*:147–153, 1987.
62. Jacobs, S. I., Holzel, A., Wolman, B., et al.: Outbreak of infantile gastroenteritis caused by *Escherichia coli* O114. Arch. Dis. Child. *45*:656–663, 1970.
63. Jerse, A. E., Martin, W. C., Galen, J. E., et al.: Oligonucleotide probe for detection of the enteropathogenic *Escherichia coli* (EPEC) adherence factor of localized adherent EPEC. J. Clin. Microbiol. *28*:2842–2844, 1990.
64. Kaper, J. B.: Molecular genetics of attaching and effacing *E. coli*. *In* Karmali, M. A., and Goglio, A. G. (eds.): Recent Advances in Verocytotoxin-Producing *Escherichia coli* Infections. Amsterdam, Elsevier, 1994, pp. 223–231.
65. Kaper, J. B.: Enterohemorrhagic *Escherichia coli*. Curr. Opin. Microbiol. *1*:103–108, 1998.
66. Karch, H.: Growth of *Escherichia coli* in the presence of trimethoprim/sulfamethoxazole facilitates detection of Shiga like toxin producing strains by colony blot assay. F. E. M. S. Microbiol. Lett. *35*:141–145, 1986.
67. Karmali, M. A., Petric, M., Lim, C., et al.: The association between idiopathic hemolytic uremic syndrome and infection by Verotoxin-producing *Escherichia coli*. J. Infect. Dis. *151*:775–782, 1985.
68. Kavi, J., and Wise, R.: Causes of the haemolytic uraemic syndrome. B. M. J. *298*:65–66, 1989.
69. Kehl, S. C.: Role of the laboratory in the diagnosis of enterohemorrhagic *Escherichia coli* infections. J. Clin. Microbiol. *40*:2711–2715, 2002.
70. Knutton, S., Baldwin, T., Williams, P. H., et al.: Actin accumulation at sites of bacterial adhesion to tissue culture cells: Basis of a new diagnostic test for enteropathogenic and enterohemorrhagic *Escherichia coli*. Infect. Immun. *57*:1290–1298, 1989.
71. Knutton, S., McConnell, M. M., Rowe, B., et al.: Adhesion and ultrastructural properties of human enterotoxigenic *Escherichia coli* producing colonization factor antigens III and IV. Infect. Immun. *57*:3364–3371, 1989.
72. Konowalchuk, J., Speirs, J. I., and Stavric, S.: Vero response to a cytotoxin of *Escherichia coli*. Infect. Immun. *18*:775–779, 1977.
73. Kovacs, M. J., Roddy, J., Gregoire, S., et al.: Thrombotic thrombocytopenic purpura following hemorrhagic colitis due to *Escherichia coli* O157:H7. Am. J. Med. *88*:177–179, 1990.
74. Kupersztoch, Y. M., Tachias, K., Moonman, C. R., et al.: Secretion of methanol-insoluble heat-stable enterotoxin (STb): Energy and secA dependent conversion of pre-STb to an intermediate indistinguishable from the extracellular toxin. J. Bacteriol. *172*:2427–2432, 1990.
75. Levine, M. M.: *Escherichia coli* infections. N. Engl. J. Med. *313*:445–447, 1985.
76. Levine, M. M., Xu, J. G., Kaper, J. B., et al.: A DNA probe to identify enterohemorrhagic *Escherichia coli* of O157:H7 and other serotypes that cause hemorrhagic colitis and hemolytic uremic syndrome. J. Infect. Dis. *156*:175–182, 1987.
77. Lopez, E. L., Diaz, M., Grinstein, S., et al.: Hemolytic uremic syndrome and diarrhea in Argentine children: The role of Shiga-like toxins. J. Infect. Dis. *160*:469–475, 1989.
78. Lortie, L. A. Dubreuil, J. D., and Harel, J.: Characterization of *Escherichia coli* strains producing heat-stable enterotoxin b (STb) isolated from humans with diarrhea. J. Clin. Microbiol. *29*:656–659, 1991.
79. MacLeod, D. L., and Gyles, C. L.: Purification and characterization of an *Escherichia coli* Shiga-like toxin II variant. Infect. Immun. *58*:1232–1239, 1990.
80. Marier, R., Wells, J. G., Swanson, R. C., et al.: An outbreak of enteropathogenic *Escherichia coli* foodborne disease traced to imported French cheese. Lancet *2*:1376–1378, 1973.
81. Martin, D. L., MacDonald, K. L., White, K. E., et al.: The epidemiology and clinical aspects of the hemolytic uremic syndrome in Minnesota. N. Engl. J. Med. *323*:1161–1167, 1990.
82. Martin-Sosa, S., Martín, M.-J., and Hueso, P.: The sialylated fraction of milk oligosaccharides in partially responsible for binding to enterotoxigenic and uropathogenic *Escherichia coli* human strains. J. Nutr. *132*:3067–3072, 2002.
83. Mathewson, J. J., and Cravioto, A.: HEp-2 cell adherence as an assay for virulence among diarrheagenic *Escherichia coli*. J. Infect. Dis. *159*:1057–1060, 1989.
84. Mathewson, J. J., Johnson, P. C., DuPont, H. L., et al.: Pathogenicity of enteroadherent *Escherichia coli* in adult volunteers. J. Infect. Dis. *154*:524–527, 1986.
85. Mayer, H. B., Acheson, D. W. K., and Wanke, C. A.: Enteroaggregative *Escherichia coli* are a potential cause of persistent diarrhea in adult HIV patients in the United States. Abstract. Presented at the 31st US-Japan Cholera and Related Diarrheal Disease Conference, 1995.
86. Mehlman, I. J., Fishbein, M., Gorbach, S. L., et al.: Pathogenicity of *Escherichia coli* recovered from food. J. Assoc. Anal. Chem. *59*:67–80, 1976.
87. Merson, M. H., Morris, G. K., Sack, D. A., et al.: Travelers' diarrhea in Mexico: A prospective study of physicians and family members attending a congress. N. Engl. J. Med. *294*:1299–1305, 1976.
88. Mezoff, A. G., Giannella, R. A., Eade, M. N., et al.: *Escherichia coli* enterotoxin (STa) binds to receptors, stimulates guanyl cyclase and impairs absorption in rat colon. Gastroenterology *102*:816–822, 1992.
89. Moake, J. L.: Haemolytic-uraemic syndrome: Basic science. Lancet *343*:393–397, 1994.
90. Moon, H. W., and Whipp, S. C.: Development of resistance with age by swine intestine to effects of enteropathogenic *Escherichia coli*. J. Infect. Dis. *122*:220–223, 1970.
91. Moore, K., Damrow, T., and Jankowski, S.: Outbreak of acute gastroenteritis attributable to *Escherichia coli* serotype O104:H21—Helena, Montana, 1994. M. M. W. R. Morb. Mortal. Wkly. Rep. *44*:501–503, 1995.
92. Nalin, D. R., McLaughlin, J. C., Rahaman, M., et al.: Enteropathogenic *Escherichia coli* and idiopathic diarrhoea in Bangladesh. Lancet *2*:1116–1119, 1975.
93. Nataro, J. P.: Enteroaggregative and diffusely adherent *Escherichia coli*. *In* Blaser, M. J., Smith, P. D., Ravdin J. I., et al. (eds.): Infections of the Gastrointestinal Tract. New York, Raven Press, 1995, pp. 727–737.
94. Nataro, J. P., Deng, Y., Cookson, S., et al.: Heterogeneity of enteroaggregative *Escherichia coli* virulence demonstrated in volunteers. J. Infect. Dis. *171*:465–468, 1995.
95. Nataro, J. P., Deng, Y., Maneval, D. R., et al.: Aggregative adherence fimbriae I of enteroaggregative *Escherichia coli* mediate adherence to HEp-2 cells and hemagglutination of human erythrocytes. Infect. Immun. *60*:2297–2304, 1992.

96. Nataro, J. P., and Kaper, J. B.: Diarrheagenic *Escherichia coli*. Clin. Microbiol. Rev. *11*:142–201, 1998.
97. Nataro, J. P., Kaper, J. B., Robins-Browne, R., et al.: Patterns of adherence of diarrheagenic *Escherichia coli* to HEp-2 cells. J. Pediatr. Infect. Dis. *6*:829–831, 1987.
98. Nataro, J. P., Seriwatana, J., Fasano, A., et al.: Identification and cloning of a novel plasmid-encoded enterotoxin of enteroinvasive *Escherichia coli* and *Shigella* strains. Infect. Immun. *63*:4721–4728, 1995.
99. Nataro, J. P., Yikang, D. Giron, J. A., et al.: Aggregative adherence fimbria I expression in enteroaggregative *Escherichia coli* requires two unlinked plasmid regions. Infect. Immun. *61*:1126–1131, 1993.
100. National Institutes of Health Consensus Development Conference: Travelers' diarrhea. Rev. Infect. Dis. *8*(Suppl. 2):109–233, 1986.
101. Nelson, J. D.: Duration of neomycin therapy for enteropathogenic *Escherichia coli* diarrheal disease: A comparative study of 113 cases. Pediatrics *48*:248–258, 1971.
102. Neter, E., Krons, R. F., and Trussel, R. E.: Association of *Escherichia coli* serotype O111 with two hospital outbreaks of epidemic diarrhea of the newborn infant in New York State during 1947. Pediatrics *12*:377–383, 1953.
103. Oberhelman, R. A., de la Cabada, F. J., Garibay, E. V., et al.: Efficacy of trimethoprim-sulfamethoxazole in treatment of acute diarrhea in a Mexican pediatric population. J. Pediatr. *110*:960–965, 1987.
104. Oberhelman, R. A., Laborde, D., Mera, R., et al.: Colonization with enteroadherent, enterotoxigenic and enterohemorrhagic *Escherichia coli* among day-care center attendees in New Orleans, Louisiana. Pediatr. Infect. Dis. J. *17*:1159–1162, 1998.
105. O'Brien, A. D., and Holmes, R. K.: Shiga and Shiga-like toxins. Microbiol. Rev. *51*:206–220, 1987.
106. Obrig, T. G., Vecchio, P. H. D., Brown, E. J., et al.: Direct cytotoxic action of Shiga toxin on human vascular endothelial cells. Infect. Immun. *56*:2373–2378, 1988.
107. Ogawa, H., Nakamura, A., and Sakazaki, R.: Pathogenic properties of "enteropathogenic" *Escherichia coli* from diarrheal children and adults. Jpn. J. Med. Sci. Biol. *21*:333–349, 1968.
108. Okamoto, K., Fujii, Y., Akashi, N., et al.: Identification and characterization of heat-stable enterotoxin-II producing *Escherichia coli* from patients with diarrhea. Microbiol. Immunol. *37*:411–414, 1993.
109. Oldfield, E. C., III, Wallace, M. R., Hyams, K. C., et al.: Endemic infectious diseases of the Middle East. Rev. Infect. Dis. *13*(Suppl.):199–217, 1991.
110. Ostroff, S. M., Kobayashi, J. M., and Lewis, J. H.: Infections with *Escherichia coli* O157:H7 in Washington State: The first year of statewide disease surveillance. J. A. M. A. *262*:355–359, 1989.
111. Ostroff, S. M., Tarr, P. I., Neill, M. A., et al.: Toxin genotypes and plasmid profiles as determinants of systemic sequelae in *Escherichia coli* O157:H7 infections. J. Infect. Dis. *160*:994–998, 1989.
112. Pai, C. H., Gordon, R., Sims, H. V., et al.: Sporadic cases of hemorrhagic colitis associated with *Escherichia coli* O157:H7: Clinical, epidemiologic and bacteriologic features. Ann. Intern. Med. *101*:738–742, 1984.
113. Pal, T., Formal, S. B., and Hale, T. L.: Characterization of virulence marker antigen of *Shigella* spp. and enteroinvasive *Escherichia coli*. J. Clin. Microbiol. *27*:561–563, 1989.
114. Rasheed, J. K., Buzman-Verduzco, L. M., and Kupersztoch, Y. M.: Two precursors of the heat-stable enterotoxin of *Escherichia coli*: Evidence of extracellular processing. Mol. Microbiol. *4*:265–273, 1990.
115. Rendi-Wagner, P., and Kollaritsch, H.: Drug prophylaxis for travelers' diarrhea. Clin. Infect. Dis. *34*:628–633, 2002.
116. Riley, L. W.: The epidemiologic, clinical, and microbiological features of hemorrhagic colitis. Annu. Rev. Microbiol. *41*:383–407, 1987.
117. Riley, L. W., Remis, R. S., Helgerson, S. D., et al.: Hemorrhagic colitis associated with a rare *E. coli* serotype. N. Engl. J. Med. *308*:681–685, 1983.
118. Robins-Browne, R., Still, C. S., Miliotis, M. D., et al.: Summer diarrhoea in African infants and children. Arch. Dis. Child. *55*:923–928, 1980.
119. Rogers, M. F., Rutherford, G. W., Alexander, S. R., et al.: A population-based study of hemolytic uremic syndrome in Oregon, 1979–1982. Am. J. Epidemiol. *123*:137–142, 1986.
120. Rosenberg, M. L., Koplan, J. P., Wachsmuth, I. K., et al.: Epidemic diarrhea at Crater Lake from enterotoxigenic *Escherichia coli*: A large waterborne outbreak. Ann. Intern. Med. *86*:714–718, 1977.
121. Rothbaum, R., McAdams, A. J., Ginnella, R., et al.: A clinicopathological study of enterocyte-adherent *Escherichia coli*: A cause of protracted diarrhea in infants. Gastroenterology *83*:441–454, 1982.
122. Sack, R. B., Gorbach, S. L., Banwell, J. G., et al.: Enterotoxigenic *Escherichia coli* isolated from patients with severe cholera-like disease. J. Infect. Dis. *123*:378–385, 1971.
123. Sack, R. B., Hirschhorn, N., Brownlee, I., et al.: Enterotoxigenic *Escherichia coli*–associated diarrheal disease in Apache children. N. Engl. J. Med. *292*:1041–1045, 1975.
124. Sack, R. B., Sack, D. A., Mehlman, I. J., et al.: Enterotoxigenic *Escherichia coli* isolated from food. J. Infect. Dis. *135*:313–317, 1977.
125. Sakazaki, R., Tamura, L., and Saito, M.: Enteropathogenic *Escherichia coli* associated with diarrhea in children and adults. Jpn. J. Med. Sci. Biol. *20*:387–399, 1967.
126. Sansonetti, P. J.: Genetic and molecular basis of epithelial cell invasion by *Shigella* species. Rev. Infect. Dis. *13*(Suppl.):285–292, 1991.
127. Savarino, S., Fasano, A., Watson, J., et al.: Enteroaggregative *Escherichia coli* heat stable enterotoxin 1 represents another subfamily of *E. coli* heat-stable toxin. Proc. Natl. Acad. Sci. U. S. A. *90*:3093–3097, 1993.
128. Savarino, S. J., Hall, E. R., Bassily, S., et al.: Oral, inactivated, whole cell enterotoxigenic *Escherichia coli* plus cholera toxin B subunit vaccine: Results of the initial evaluation in children. J. Infect. Dis. *179*:107–114, 1999.
129. Savarino, S. J., Hall, E. R., Bassily, S., et al.: Introductory evaluation of an oral, killed whole cell enterotoxigenic *Escherichia coli* plus cholera toxin B subunit vaccine in Egyptian infants. Pediatr. Infect. Dis. J. *21*:322–330, 2002.
130. Schroeder, S. A., Caldwell, J. R., Vernon, T. M., et al.: A water borne outbreak of gastroenteritis in adults associated with *Escherichia coli*. Lancet *1*:737–740, 1968.
131. Schultsz, C., Ende, J., Cobelens, F., et al.: Diarrheagenic *Escherichia coli* and acute and persistent diarrhea in returned travelers. J. Clin. Microbiol. *38*:3550–3554, 2000.
132. Schulz, S., Green, C. K., Yuen, P. S. T., et al.: Guanyl cyclase is a heat-stable enterotoxin receptor. Cell *63*:941–948, 1990.
133. Sheikh, J., Czeczulin, J. R., Harrington, S., et al.: A novel dispersin protein in enteroaggregative *Escherichia coli*. J. Clin. Invest. *110*:1329–1337, 2002.
134. Shigeno, T., Akamatsu, T., Fujimori, K., et al.: The clinical significance of colonoscopy in hemorrhagic colitis due to enterohemorrhagic *Escherichia coli* O157:H7 infection. Endoscopy *34*:311–314, 2002.
135. Smith, H. W.: Neonatal *Escherichia coli* infections in domestic mammals: Transmissibility of pathogenic characteristics. *In* Knight, K., and Elliot, J. (eds.): Acute Diarrhea in Childhood. New York, Elsevier, 1976, pp. 45–64.
136. Smith, H. W., and Halls, S.: Observations by the ligated intestinal segment and oral inoculation methods on *Escherichia coli* infections in pigs, calves, lambs, and rabbits. J. Pathol. Bacteriol. *93*:499–529, 1967.
137. Smith, H. W., and Linggood, M. A.: Observations on the pathogenic properties of the K 88, Hly and Ent plasmids of *Escherichia coli* with particular reference to porcine diarrhea. J. Med. Microbiol. *4*:467–485, 1971.
138. Snyder, J. D., Wells, J. G., Yashuk, J., et al.: Outbreak of invasive *Escherichia coli* gastroenteritis on a cruise ship. Am. J. Trop. Med. Hyg. *33*:281–284, 1984.
139. So, M., and McCarthy, B. J.: Nucleotide sequence of the bacterial transposon TN1981 encoding a heat-stable enterotoxin (ST) and its identification in enterotoxigenic *Escherichia coli* strains. Proc. Natl. Acad. Sci. U. S. A. *77*:4011–4015, 1980.
140. Tacket, C. O., Losonsky, G., Livio, S., et al.: Lack of prophylactic efficacy of an enteric-coated bovine hyperimmune milk product against enterotoxigenic *Escherichia coli* challenge administered during a standard meal. J. Infect. Dis. 180:2056–2059, 1999.
141. Tacket, C. O., Moseley, S. L., Kay, B., et al.: Challenge studies in volunteers using *Escherichia coli* strains with diffuse adherence to HEp-2 cells. J. Infect. Dis. *162*:550–552, 1990.
142. Tauschek, M., Gorrell, R. J., Strugnell, R. A., and Robins-Browne, R. M.: Identification of a protein secretory pathway for the secretion of heat-labile enterotoxin by an enterotoxigenic strain of *Escherichia coli*. Proc. Natl. Acad. Sci. U. S. A. *99*:7066–7071, 2002.
143. Taylor, D. N., Sanchez, J. L., Candler, W., et al.: Treatment of travelers' diarrhea: Ciprofloxacin plus loperamide compared with ciprofloxacin alone: A placebo-controlled, randomized trial. Ann. Intern. Med. *114*:731–734, 1991.
144. Thea, D. T., St. Louis, M. E., Atido, U., et al.: A prospective study of diarrhea and HIV-1 infection among 429 Zairian infants. N. Engl. J. Med. *329*:1696–1702, 1993.
145. Thorén, A., Stintzing, G., Tufvesson, B., et al.: Aetiology and clinical features of severe infantile diarrhoea in Addis Ababa, Ethiopia. J. Trop. Pediatr. *28*:127–131, 1982.
146. Toledo, M. R. F., Alvariza, M. C. B., Murahovschi, J., et al.: Enteropathogenic *Escherichia coli* serotypes and endemic diarrhea in infants. Infect. Immun. *39*:586–589, 1983.
147. Toth I., Cohen, M. L., Rumschlag, H. S., et al.: Influence of the 60 megadalton plasmid on adherence of *Escherichia coli* O157:H7 and genetic derivatives. Infect. Immun. *58*:1223–1231, 1990.
148. Trabulsi, L. R., Fernandes, M. R., and Zuliani, M. E.: Novas bacterias patogenicas para o intestino do homen. Rev. Inst. Med. Trop. Sao Paulo *9*:31–39, 1967.
149. Trabulsi, L. R., Keller, R., and Gomes, T. A. T.: Typical and atypical enteropathogenic *Escherichia coli*. Emerg. Infect. Dis. *8*:508–513, 2002.
150. Tulloch, E. F., Ryan, K. J., Formal, S. B., et al.: Invasive enteropathic *Escherichia coli* dysentery: An outbreak in 28 adults. Ann. Intern. Med. *79*:13–17, 1973.
151. Vila, J., Vargas, M., Casals, C., et al.: Antimicrobial resistance of diarrheagenic *Escherichia coli* isolated from children under the age of 5 years from Ifakara, Tanzania. Antimicrob. Agents Chemother. *43*:3022–3024, 1999.

152. Wagner, P. L., Acheson, D. W., and Waldor, M. K.: Human neutrophils and their products induce Shiga toxin production by enterohemorrhagic *Escherichia coli*. Infect Immun 69:1934–1937, 2001.
153. Weikel, C. S., Spann, C. L., Chambers, C. P., et al.: Phorbol esters enhance the cyclic GMP response of T84 cells to the heat-stable enterotoxin of *Escherichia coli* (STa). Infect. Immun. *58*:1402–1407, 1990.
154. Whip, S. C.: Protease degradation of *Escherichia coli* heat-stable, mouse-negative, pig-positive enterotoxin. Infect. Immun. *55*:2057–2060, 1987.
155. Wong, C. S., Jelacic, S., Habeeb, R. L., et al.: The risk of the hemolytic uremic syndrome after antibiotic treatment of *Escherichia coli* O157:H7 infections. N. Engl. J. Med. *342*:1930–1936, 2000.

CHAPTER 109 *Klebsiella*

WILLIAM C. GRUBER ■ RANDALL G. FISHER ■ THOMAS G. BOYCE

Klebsiella is a genus of Enterobacteriaceae that is a frequent cause of nosocomial pediatric infection. Classically described by Friedländer[34] as a cause of pneumonia, *Klebsiella* can cause infections of the urinary tract, lung, and central venous catheters in the high-risk newborn and the immunocompromised older child.[17]

Bacteriology

Klebsiella organisms were named for Edwin Klebs, the noted German bacteriologist.[78] Distinguishing features of *Klebsiella* spp. include the absence of motility and the presence of a polysaccharide capsule that gives rise to large mucoid colonies on solid media. The organisms are oxidase-negative and citrate-positive; they ferment inositol and hydrolyze urea but do not produce ornithine decarboxylase or hydrogen sulfide. Acetoin and 2,3-butanediol predominate over acidic end-products during sugar fermentation (positive result on the Voges-Proskauer test). Microbiologists commonly agree on the existence of four species of *Klebsiella*: *Klebsiella pneumoniae* (the most common human pathogen), *Klebsiella oxytoca* (a less common human pathogen), *Klebsiella terrigena,* and *Klebsiella planticola.* Until recently, *K. planticola* was recovered almost exclusively from soil and aquatic environments; reports suggest that this organism may be a relatively common neonatal pathogen in some parts of the world.[84, 102] *K. planticola* may express virulence factors similar to those of *K. pneumoniae.*[85] Organisms are defined serologically by their capsular polysaccharide (K antigens) and lipopolysaccharide (O antigens). Significant cross-reactivity exists between the capsule of some pneumococci (e.g., 19F) and *Klebsiella*.[62] The reader is referred to a review by Podschun and Ullmann[86] for a detailed description of *Klebsiella* spp.

Epidemiology

Friedländer[34] proposed that *K. pneumoniae* was the most common cause of community pneumonia, an observation that was refuted by Fraenkel's[32] observations on pneumococcal pneumonia. *K. pneumoniae* accounts for less than 10 percent of hospitalized cases of pneumonia in adults.[19] *Klebsiella* spp. occur primarily as opportunistic nosocomial pathogens of the urinary tract, respiratory tract, biliary tract, and bloodstream. In one survey performed by the Centers for Disease Control and Prevention, the nosocomial *K. pneumoniae* infection rate was 16.7 infections per 10,000 patients discharged.[48] Hand carriage generally is regarded as the common mode of transmission.[37] Environmental sources of *Klebsiella* spp. have included contaminated blood pressure monitoring equipment,[89] ventilator traps,[37] dialysate,[58] ultrasonography coupling gel,[35] dextrose solution,[60] and hand disinfectant.[92] The emergence of plasmid-mediated β-lactamase resistance can be responsible for the rapid spread of resistant organisms to susceptible patients in intensive care settings.[10, 12] Outbreaks may be complex; patient-to-patient transmission of epidemic strains containing different plasmids may be interspersed with sporadic, nonepidemic *Klebsiella* infections.[12] *Klebsiella* spp. are second only to *Escherichia coli* as causes of sepsis[36]; the highest rates of infection are reported from larger hospitals affiliated with medical schools.

Klebsiella spp. commonly are highlighted as pathogens of debilitated adults and alcoholics,[54] but by 1985, nearly 50 percent of reported *Klebsiella* outbreaks were in neonatal intensive care units.[48] Newborn outbreaks continue to occur frequently worldwide.[2, 7, 22, 28, 44, 81, 91] Most such outbreaks have been associated with *K. pneumoniae* infection, but scattered nursery outbreaks of *K. oxytoca* infection also have been reported.[6, 101] A high percentage of infants in intensive care settings may become colonized with hospital strains of *Klebsiella*.[41] Infecting organisms have been isolated from care providers and from mothers of colonized infants.[22] One report described a newborn outbreak associated with infestation of a neonatal unit by cockroaches colonized with infecting *Klebsiella* strains.[23] *Klebsiella* may spread from newborn units to adult units; interhospital and international transmissions of resistant strains have been described.[21, 28, 96] Ribotyping, pulsed-field gel electrophoresis, and DNA amplification techniques have proved valuable in characterizing *Klebsiella* strains associated with outbreaks.[63, 98] Different ribotypes that share plasmids conferring antibiotic resistance can be responsible for pediatric infections in a particular institution.[12] Strains expressing extended-spectrum β-lactamases may become endemic and may present a complex and diverse pattern of enzyme production with resistance to β-lactamase inhibitors.[29, 31]

Pathophysiology

Pneumonias caused by *Klebsiella* most commonly arise from colonization of the upper respiratory tract, followed by aspiration of organisms to the lower respiratory tract. Some degree of gram-negative oropharyngeal colonization is a normal finding in newborns. The oropharynx of nearly one third of healthy newborns is colonized by gram-negative rods, including *Klebsiella*, by 1 month of age; colonization rates generally are lower in breast-fed infants.[9] Antibiotic pressure in high-risk newborns and older children has been observed to promote overgrowth of *Klebsiella*.[11, 95]

Enteric organisms are recovered less frequently from the oropharynx of healthy older children and adults; oral colonization with gram-negative rods is increased during illness,[50] after postoperative viral infections,[51, 88] and in debilitated adults.[65] Increased adherence of gram-negative rods to oropharyngeal cells contributes to increased colonization.[51] Elastase made by polymorphonuclear cells contributes to such colonization by reducing the fibronectin coating of sugar receptors.[25] The capsule plays an initial role in epithelial cell interactions but is not required for an adhesin interaction with the cell surface.[30] Adherence properties may be affected by plasmid content[27] and may be transferred between *E. coli* and *K. pneumoniae*.[47]

In animal models of sepsis, capsular polysaccharide (K antigens) is a virulence factor; monoclonal antibodies to the K antigens reduce severity of illness in mice.[61] In a mouse model of urinary tract infection, the K antigens appear to be more important in infection than is the lipopolysaccharide (O antigens), and clinical strains deficient in lipopolysaccharide retain virulence by resistance of the capsule to complement.[3, 18] In one series of adult human subjects, capsular type K2 was associated commonly with asymptomatic bacteriuria and cystitis but not pyelonephritis; the presence of type 1 fimbriae bore a closer relationship to upper urinary tract infection.[83] Neutrophils play an important role in clearance of *Klebsiella,* and phagocytosis is augmented by leukotrienes.[66]

Clinical Manifestations

Klebsiella infection shows little clinical distinction from diseases produced by other enteric pathogens. The organism generally occurs less commonly than does group B *Streptococcus* or *E. coli* as a cause of "early-onset" or "late-onset" newborn infection.[38, 69] However, investigators from Spain[44] reported a 7-year interval during which *K. pneumoniae* was the most common cause of newborn bacteremia. Risk factors for acquisition of neonatal *Klebsiella* infection include prematurity, presence of indwelling catheters, previous antibiotic treatment, and parenteral nutrition.[91] Newborn infection is characterized by typical features of pneumonia, sepsis, and meningitis.[69] *Klebsiella* spp. have been isolated commonly from blood and peritoneal fluid in outbreaks of necrotizing enterocolitis.[39, 72] Less common manifestations in infants include toxic epidermal necrolysis,[42, 80] conjunctivitis,[59] parotitis,[20] retropharyngeal abscess,[24] subdural hematoma,[75] psoas abscess,[4] and renal abscess.[100]

Klebsiella is an unusual cause of infection in the otherwise healthy older child. The classic Friedländer pneumonia of the debilitated adult[34] is a rare occurrence in children. The identification of pulmonary infection should suggest the possibility of underlying immunodeficiency or significant malnutrition.[46, 52] If pneumonia caused by *Klebsiella* does occur, progression to lung abscesses should be anticipated.

Lung abscesses may develop within days to weeks after *Klebsiella* infection. Formation of an abscess occurs more commonly during *Klebsiella* pulmonary infection than during any other community-acquired infection.[19] A rare but devastating outcome is massive pulmonary gangrene—the rapid total destruction of part of the lung presumed to be caused by vascular compromise. This complication is heralded by radiographs showing small cavities that later coalesce into a large cavity with an intracavitary mass of necrotic lung.[74, 77] Researchers have speculated that *Klebsiella* lung infection is accompanied by coincident anaerobic infection that contributes to or is primarily responsible for the pathologic process.[19]

Catheterization of the urinary tract can be associated with urinary tract *Klebsiella* infection, but bacteremia is an uncommon complication in the immunocompetent child.[26, 64] Approximately 10 percent of nosocomial urinary tract infections observed in infants after surgery are caused by *Klebsiella*.[26] Focal renal infection progressing to a renal abscess has been described.[57] *K. pneumoniae* bacteremia has been associated with lesions of the gastrointestinal tract, presence of an indwelling central venous catheter, and neutropenia. Curiously, patients with short-bowel syndrome seem to be at greater risk than are patients with inflammatory bowel disease or malignant disease for acquisition of catheter-associated *Klebsiella* or *Enterobacter* bacteremia. *K. pneumoniae* was a constituent of polymicrobial bacteremia in 15 such patients (26%).[14] Mortality rates have ranged from 5 to 20 percent; higher death rates occur in children infected with an aminoglycoside-resistant strain.[13, 48] Pneumonia, shock, and disseminated intravascular coagulation are poor prognostic factors in children with underlying malignant disease. Rare clinical presentations include multifocal osteomyelitis[55] and endophthalmitis.[67] Solid organ pediatric transplant recipients may have high rates of acquisition of drug-resistant *Klebsiella*.[90] *Klebsiella* spp. have been described as frequently occurring pathogens in children and adults with sickle-cell disease in West Africa.[1]

Diagnosis

Klebsiella spp. characteristically grow as large mucoid colonies on MacConkey agar. Citrate-containing media can be used to facilitate isolation of *Klebsiella* strains because these organisms can use citrate as a sole carbon source.[78] Serotyping with specific antisera usually is determined by countercurrent immunoelectrophoresis or a Quellung test.[8] In situ hybridization techniques have been used to identify *Klebsiella* in phagocytes from blood specimens,[68] and restriction enzyme analysis and ribotyping of clinical isolates have been used to characterize nosocomial spread of antibiotic-resistant strains.[12, 40] However, conventional, commonly used microbiologic methods may misidentify some *Klebsiella* spp., particularly *K. planticola* and *K. terrigena*.[73] Rarely, blood cultures have required longer than 72 hours of incubation for radiometric detection of *Klebsiella*.[70]

Treatment

Empiric antimicrobial therapy should be guided by an understanding of antimicrobial susceptibilities of *Klebsiella* in the hospital. Therapy with a cephalosporin plus an aminoglycoside (rather than a cephalosporin alone) has been associated with a more favorable outcome in patients with cancer who are infected with susceptible strains.[13] However, antimicrobial therapy for *Klebsiella* infections is made problematic by the resistance to penicillins and cephalosporins conferred by extended-spectrum β-lactamases (ESBLs).[10, 12, 15, 43] *Klebsiella* with ESBL are widely distributed, and regional differences in susceptibility occur.[53] Outer-membrane protein changes and porin deficiencies of some strains can augment resistance to third-generation cephalosporins.[5, 93] Suboptimal clinical outcomes occur when extended-spectrum cephalosporins are used to treat serious infections caused by ESBL-producing *Klebsiella* spp.[79a] Carbapenems (imipenem or meropenem) should be considered the agents of choice and included in the antibiotic regimen for treatment of infections caused by ESBL-producing *Klebsiella* spp. Some investigators have reported significant correlation between production of ESBL and ciprofloxacin resistance.[79, 97] Plasmid-mediated resistance to aminoglycosides also occurs commonly.[6, 22, 36, 76] Antibiotic pressure is important in increasing the risk for acquiring resistant isolates.[87] In some nursery outbreaks, switching from gentamicin to amikacin has been associated with return of the gentamicin susceptibility of *Klebsiella* isolates.[6, 45] Imipenem or the combination of piperacillin and tazobactam may demonstrate good antimicrobial activity against multiply resistant organisms.[49, 82, 87] However, the combination of β-lactamase and porin deficiency has been associated with resistance to imipenem,[16] and hyperproduction of some β-lactamases can limit the effectiveness of β-lactam–β-lactamase inhibitor combinations.[33] Experience with use of ciprofloxacin in young children is limited because of observations of irreversible cartilage injury in laboratory animals after administration of this quinolone. However, successful treatment of a multidrug-resistant *K. pneumoniae* has been reported in a preterm infant without observable short-term adverse effects.[56] Strict adherence to infection control policies that promote restricted antibiotic use, cohorting, and handwashing may help to prevent the spread of resistant *Klebsiella* strains.[6, 22, 41, 71, 94]

REFERENCES

1. Aken'Ova, Y. A., Bakare, R. A., Okunade, M. A., and Olaniyi, J.: Bacterial causes of acute osteomyelitis in sickle cell anaemia: Changing infection profile. West Afr. J. Med. *14*:255–258, 1995.
2. Akindele, J. A., and Gbadegesin, R. A.: Outbreak of neonatal *Klebsiella* septicaemia at the University College Hospital, Ibadan, Nigeria: Appraisal of predisposing factors and preventive measures. Trop. Geogr. Med. *46*:151–153, 1994.
3. Alvarez, D., Merino, S., Tomas, J. M., et al.: Capsular polysaccharide is a major complement resistance factor in lipopolysaccharide O side chain–deficient *Klebsiella pneumoniae* clinical isolates. Infect. Immun. *68*:953–955, 2000.
4. Andreou, A., Karasavvidou, A., Papadopoulou, F., et al.: Iliopsoas abscess in a neonate. Am. J. Perinatol. *14*:519–521, 1997.
5. Ardanuy, C., Linares, J., Dominguez, M. A., et al.: Outer membrane profiles of clonally related *Klebsiella pneumoniae* isolates from clinical samples and activities of cephalosporins and carbapenems. Antimicrob. Agents Chemother. *42*:1636–1640, 1998.
6. Aronsson, B., Eriksson, M., Herin, P., et al.: Gentamicin-resistant *Klebsiella* spp. and *Escherichia coli* in a neonatal intensive care unit. Scand. J. Infect. Dis. *23*:195–199, 1991.
7. Arredondo-Garcia, J. L., Diaz-Ramos, R., Solorzano-Santos, F., et al.: Neonatal septicaemia due to *K. pneumoniae:* Septicaemia due to *Klebsiella pneumoniae* in newborn infants: Nosocomial outbreak in an intensive care unit. Rev. Latinoam. Microbiol. *34*:11–16, 1992.
8. Ayling-Smith, B., and Pitt, T. L.: State of the art in typing: *Klebsiella* spp. J. Hosp. Infect. *16*:287–295, 1990.
9. Baltimore, R. S., Duncan, R. L., Shapiro, E. D., et al.: Epidemiology of pharyngeal colonization of infants with aerobic gram-negative rod bacteria. J. Clin. Microbiol. *27*:91–95, 1989.
10. Bauernfeind, A., Rosenthal, E., Eberlein, E., et al.: Spread *of Klebsiella pneumoniae* producing SHV-5 beta-lactamase among hospitalized patients. Infection *21*:18–22, 1993.
11. Bennet, R., Eriksson, M., Nord, C. E., et al.: Fecal bacterial microflora of newborn infants during intensive care management and treatment with five antibiotic regimens. Pediatr. Infect. Dis. *5*:533–539, 1986.
12. Bingen, E. H., Desjardins, P., Arlet, G., et al.: Molecular epidemiology of plasmid spread among extended broad-spectrum beta-lactamase–producing *Klebsiella pneumoniae* isolates in a pediatric hospital. J. Clin. Microbiol. *31*:179–184, 1993.
13. Bodey, G. P., Elting, L. S., Rodriquez, S., et al.: *Klebsiella* bacteremia: A 10-year review in a cancer institution. Cancer *64*:2368–2376, 1989.
14. Bonadio, W. A.: *Klebsiella pneumoniae* bacteremia in children: Fifty-seven cases in 10 years. Am. J. Dis. Child. *143*:1061–1063, 1989.
15. Bradford, P. A., Cherubin C. E., Idemyor, V., et al.: Multiply resistant *Klebsiella pneumoniae* strains from two Chicago hospitals: Identification of the extended-spectrum TEM-12 and TEM-10 ceftazidime-hydrolyzing beta-lactamases in a single isolate. Antimicrob. Agents Chemother. *38*:761–766, 1994.
16. Bradford, P. A., Urban, C., Mariano, N., et al.: Imipenem resistance in *Klebsiella pneumoniae* is associated with the combination of ACT-1, a plasmid-mediated AmpC beta-lactamase, and the foss of an outer membrane protein. Antimicrob. Agents Chemother. *41*:563–569, 1997.
17. Brown, R. B., Cipriani, D., Schulte, M., et al.: Community-acquired bacteremias from tunneled central intravenous lines: Results from studies of a single vendor. Am. J. Infect. Control *22*:149–151, 1994.
18. Camprubi, S., Merino, S., Benedi, V. J., et al.: The role of the O-antigen lipopolysaccharide and capsule on an experimental *Klebsiella pneumoniae* infection of the rat urinary tract. FEMS Microbiol. Lett. *111*:9–13, 1993.
19. Carpenter, J. L.: *Klebsiella* pulmonary infections: Occurrence at one medical center and review. Rev. Infect. Dis. *12*:672–682, 1990.
20. Coban, A., Ince, Z., Ucsel, R., et al.: Neonatal suppurative parotitis: A vanishing disease? Eur. J. Pediatr. *152*:1004–1005, 1993.
21. Cookson, B., Johnson, A. P., Azadian, B., et al.: International inter- and intrahospital patient spread of a multiple antibiotic-resistant strain of *Klebsiella pneumoniae*. J. Infect. Dis. *171*:511–513, 1995.
22. Coovadia, Y. M., Johnson, A. P., Bhana, R. H., et al.: Multiresistant *Klebsiella pneumoniae* in a neonatal nursery: The importance of maintenance of infection control policies and procedures in the prevention of outbreaks. J. Hosp. Infect. *22*:197–205, 1992.
23. Cotton M. F., Wasserman, E., Pieper, C. H., et al.: Invasive disease due to extended spectrum beta-lactamase–producing *Klebsiella pneumoniae* in a neonatal unit: The possible role of cockroaches. J. Hosp. Infect. *44*:13–17, 2000.
24. Coulthard, M., and Isaacs, D.: Retropharyngeal abscess. Arch. Dis. Child. *66*:1227–1230, 1991.
25. Dal Nogare, A. R., Toews, G. B., and Pierce, A. K.: Increased salivary elastase precedes gram-negative bacillary colonization in postoperative patients. Am. Rev. Respir. Dis. *135*:671–675, 1987.
26. Davies, H. D., Jones, E. L., Sheng, R. Y., et al.: Nosocomial urinary tract infections at a pediatric hospital. Pediatr. Infect. Dis. *11*:349–354, 1992.
27. Denoya, C. D., Trevisan, A. R., and Zorzopulos, J.: Adherence of multiresistant strains of *Klebsiella pneumoniae* to cerebrospinal fluid shunts: Correlation with plasmid content. J. Med. Microbiol. *21*:225–231, 1986.
28. Eisen, D., Russell, E. G., Tymms, M., et al.: Random amplified polymorphic DNA and plasmid analyses used in investigation of an outbreak of multiresistant *Klebsiella pneumoniae*. J. Clin. Microbiol. *33*:713–717, 1995.
29. Essack, S. Y., Hall, L. M., Pillay, D. G., et al.: Complexity and diversity of *Klebsiella pneumoniae* strains with extended-spectrum beta-lactamases isolated in 1994 and 1996 at a teaching hospital in Durban, South Africa. Antimicrob. Agents Chemother. *45*:88–95, 2001.
30. Favre-Bonte, S., Joy, B., and Forestier, C.: Consequences of reduction of *Klebsiella pneumoniae* capsule expression on interactions of this bacterium with epithelial cells. Infect. Immun. *67*:554–561, 1999.
31. Fiett, J., Palucha, A., Miaczynska, B., et al.: A novel complex mutant beta-lactamase, TEM-68, identified in a *Klebsiella pneumoniae* isolate from an outbreak of extended-spectrum beta-lactamase–producing klebsiellae. Antimicrob. Agents Chemother. *44*:1499–1505, 2000.
32. Fraenkel, A.: Bakteriologische Mitteilungen. Leitsch. F. Klin. Med. *10*:401–411, 1886.
33. French, G. L., Shannon, K. P., and Simmons, N.: Hospital outbreak of *Klebsiella pneumoniae* resistant to broad-spectrum cephalosporins and beta-lactam–beta-lactamase inhibitor combinations by hyperproduction of SHV-5 beta-lactamase. J. Clin. Microbiol. *34*:358–363, 1996.
34. Friedländer, C.: Über die Schizomyceten bei der acuten fibrosen Pneumonie. Arch. Pathol. Anat. Physiol. Klin. Med. *87*:319–324, 1882.
35. Gaillot, O., Maruejouls, C., Abachin, E., et al.: Nosocomial outbreak of *Klebsiella pneumoniae* producing SHV-5 extended-spectrum beta-lactamase, originating from a contaminated ultrasonography coupling gel. J. Clin. Microbiol. *36*:1357–1360, 1998.
36. Garcia de la Torre, M., Romero-Vivas, J., Martinez-Beltran, J., et al.: *Klebsiella* bacteremia: An analysis of 100 episodes. Rev. Infect. Dis. *7*:143–150, 1985.
37. Gorman, L. J., Sanai, L., Notman, A. W., et al.: Cross infection in an intensive care unit by *Klebsiella pneumoniae* from ventilator condensate. J. Hosp. Infect. *23*:27–34, 1993.
38. Grauel, E. L., Halle, E., Bollmann, R., et al.: Neonatal septicaemia: Incidence, etiology and outcome: A 6-year analysis. Acta Paediatr. Scand. *360*(Suppl.):113–119, 1989.
39. Gregersen, N., Van Nierop, W., Von Gottberg, A., et al.: *Klebsiella pneumoniae* with extended spectrum beta-lactamase activity associated with a necrotizing enterocolitis outbreak. Pediatr. Infect. Dis. J. *18*:963–967, 1999.
40. Haertl, R., and Bandlow, G.: Use of small fragment restriction endonuclease analysis (SF-REA) for epidemiological fingerprinting of *Klebsiella oxytoca*. Int. J. Med. Microbiol. Virol. Parasitol. Infect. Dis. *280*:312–318, 1994.
41. Hambraeus, A., Lagerqvist-Widh, A., Zettersten, U., et al.: Spread of *Klebsiella* in a neonatal ward. Scand. J. Infect. Dis. *23*:189–194, 1991.
42. Hawk, R. J., Storer, J. S., and Daum, R. S.: Toxic epidermal necrolysis in a 6-week-old infant. Pediatr. Dermatol. *2*:197–200, 1985.
43. Heritage, J., Hawkey, P. M., Todd, N., et al.: Transposition of the gene encoding a TEM-12 extended-spectrum beta-lactamase. Antimicrob. Agents Chemother. *36*:1981–1986, 1992.

44. Hervas, J. A., Alomar, A., Salva, F., et al.: Neonatal sepsis and meningitis in Mallorca, Spain, 1977–1991. Clin. Infect. Dis. *16*:719–724, 1993.
45. Hesseling, P. B., Mouton, W. L., Henning, P. A., et al.: A prospective study of long-term use of amikacin in a paediatrics department: Indications, administration, side-effects, bacterial isolates and resistance. S. Afr. Med. J. *78*:192–195, 1990.
46. Hughes, W. T.: Pneumonia in the immunocompromised child. Semin. Respir. Infect. *2*:177–183, 1987.
47. Jallat, C., Darfeuille-Michaud, A, Girardeau, J. P., et al.: Self-transmissible R plasmids encoding CS31A among human *Escherichia coli* strains isolated from diarrheal stools. Infect. Immun. *62*:2865–2873, 1994.
48. Jarvis, W. R., Munn, V. P., Highsmith, A. K., et al.: The epidemiology of nosocomial infections caused by *Klebsiella pneumoniae*. Infect. Control *6*:68–74, 1985.
49. Jett, B. D., Ritchie, D. J., Reichley, R., et al.: In vitro activities of various beta-lactam antimicrobial agents against clinical isolates of *Escherichia coli* and *Klebsiella* spp. resistant to oxyimino cephalosporins. Antimicrob. Agents Chemother. *39*:1187–1190, 1995.
50. Johanson, W. G., Pierce, A. K., and Sanford, J. P.: Changing bacterial flora of hospitalized patients. N. Engl. J. Med. *281*:1137–1140, 1969.
51. Johanson, W. G., Higuchi, J. H., Chaudhuri, T. R., et al.: Bacterial adherence to epithelial cells in bacillary colonization of the respiratory tract. Am. Rev. Respir. Dis. *121*:55–63, 1980.
52. Johnson, A. W., Osinusi, K., Aderele, W. I., et al.: Bacterial aetiology of acute lower respiratory infections in pre-school Nigerian children and comparative predictive features of bacteraemic and non-bacteraemic illnesses. J. Trop. Pediatr. *39*:97–106, 1993.
53. Jones, R. N., Jenkins, S. G., Hoban, D. J., et al.: In vitro efficacy of six cephalosporins tested against Enterobacteriaceae isolated at 38 North American medical centers participating in the SENTRY Antimicrobial Surveillance Program, 1997–1998. Int. J. Antimicrob. Agents *15*:111–118, 2000.
54. Jong, G. M., Hsiue, T. R., Chen, C. R., et al.: Rapidly fatal outcome of bacteremic *Klebsiella pneumoniae* pneumonia in alcoholics. Chest *107*:214–217, 1995.
55. Kishan, J., Mir, N. A., Elzouki, A. Y., et al.: Radiological case of the month: *Klebsiella* multifocal osteomyelitis. Am. J. Dis. Child. *142*:687–688, 1988.
56. Khaneja, M., Naprawa, J., Kumar, A., et al.: Successful treatment of late-onset infection due to resistant *Klebsiella pneumoniae* in an extremely low birth weight infant using ciprofloxacin. J. Perinatol. *19*:311–314, 1999.
57. Klar, A., Hurvitz, H., Berkun, Y., et al.: Focal bacterial nephritis (lobar nephronia) in children. J. Pediatr. *128*:850–853,1996.
58. Kolmos, H. J: *Klebsiella pneumoniae* in a nephrological department. J. Hosp. Infect. *5*:253–259, 1984.
59. Krohn, M. A., Hillier, S. L., Bell, T. A., et al.: The bacterial etiology of conjunctivitis in early infancy: Eye Prophylaxis Study Group. Am. J. Epidemiol. *138*:326–332, 1993.
60. Lalitha, M. K., Kenneth, J., Jana, A. K., et al.: Identification of an IV-dextrose solution as the source of an outbreak of *Klebsiella pneumoniae* sepsis in a newborn nursery. J. Hosp. Infect. *43*:70–73, 1999.
61. Lang, A. B., Bruderer, U., Senyk, G., et al.: Human monoclonal antibodies specific for capsular polysaccharides of *Klebsiella* recognize clusters of multiple serotypes. J. Immunol. *146*:3160–3164, 1991.
62. Lee, C. J.: Bacterial capsular polysaccharides: Biochemistry, immunity and vaccine. Mol. Immunol. *24*:1005–1019, 1987.
63. Lhopital, S., Bonacorsi, S., Meis, D., et al.: Molecular markers for differentiation of multiresistant *Klebsiella pneumoniae* isolates in a pediatric hospital. Infect. Control Hosp. Epidemiol. *18*:743–748, 1997.
64. Lohr, J. A., Donowitz, L. G., and Sadler, J. E.: Hospital-acquired urinary tract infection. Pediatrics *83*:193–199, 1989.
65. Mackowiak, P. A., Martin, R. M., Jones, S. R., et al.: Pharyngeal colonization by gram-negative bacilli in aspiration-prone persons. Arch. Intern. Med. *138*:1224–1227, 1978.
66. Mancuso, P., Nana-Sinkam, P., and Peters-Golden, M.: Leukotriene B_4 augments neutrophil phagocytosis of *Klebsiella pneumoniae*. Infect. Immun. *69*:2011–2016, 2001.
67. Margo, C. E., Mames, R. N., and Guy, J. R.: Endogenous *Klebsiella* endophthalmitis: Report of two cases and review of the literature. Ophthalmology *101*:1298–1301, 1994.
68. Matsuhisa, A., Saito, Y., Sakamoto, Y., et al.: Detection of bacteria in phagocyte-smears from septicemia-suspected blood by in situ hybridization using biotinylated probes. Microbiol. Immunol. *38*:511–517, 1994.
69. McCracken, G. H. J., Mize, S. G., and Threlkeld, N.: Intraventricular gentamicin therapy in gram-negative bacillary meningitis of infancy: Report of the Second National Meningitis Cooperative Study Group. Lancet *1*:787–791, 1980.
70. Meadow, W. L., and Schwartz, I. K.: Time course of radiometric detection of positive blood cultures in childhood. Pediatr. Infect. Dis. *5*:333–336, 1986.
71. Meyer, K. S., Urban, C., Eagan, J. A., et al.: Nosocomial outbreak of *Klebsiella* infection resistant to late-generation cephalosporins [see comments]. Ann. Intern. Med. *119*:353–358, 1993.
72. Mollitt, D. L., Tepas, J. J., and Talbert, J. L.: The microbiology of neonatal peritonitis. Arch. Surg. *123*:176–179, 1988.
73. Monnet, D., Freney, J., Brun, Y., et al.: Difficulties in identifying *Klebsiella* strains of clinical origin. Int. J. Med. Microbiol. *274*:456–464, 1991.
74. Moon, W. K., Im, J. G., Yeon, K. M., et al.: Complications of *Klebsiella* pneumonia: CT evaluation. J. Comput. Assist. Tomogr. *19*:176–181, 1995.
75. Ng, P. C., Fok, T. F., Lee, C. H., et al.: Massive subdural haematoma: An unusual complication of septicaemia in preterm very low birthweight infants. J. Pediatr. Child Health. *34*:296–298, 1998.
76. Nathoo, K. J., Mason, P. R., Gwanzura, L., et al.: Severe *Klebsiella* infection as a cause of mortality in neonates in Harare, Zimbabwe: Evidence from postmortem blood cultures. Pediatr. Infect. Dis. *12*:840–844, 1993.
77. O'Reilly, G. V., Dee, P. M., and Otteni, G. V.: Gangrene of the lung: Successful medical management of three patients. Diagn. Radiol. *126*:575–579, 1978.
78. Orskov, I.: *Klebsiella. In* Krieg, N. R., and Holt, J. G. (eds.): Bergey's Manual of Systematic Bacteriology. Vol. 1. Baltimore, Williams & Wilkins, 1984, pp. 461–465.
79. Paterson, D. L., Mulazimoglu, L., Casellas, J. M., et al. Epidemiology of ciprofloxacin resistance and its relationship to extended-spectrum beta-lactamase production in *Klebsiella pneumoniae* isolates causing bacteremia. Clin. Infect. Dis. *30*:473–478, 2000.
79a. Paterson, D. L., Ko, W.-C., Von Gottberg, A., et al.: Outcome of cephalosporin treatment for serious infections due to apparently susceptible organisms producing extended-spectrum β-lactamases: Implications for the clinical microbiology laboratory. J. Clin. Microbiol. *39*:2206–2212, 2001.
80. Picard, E., Gillis, D., Klapholz, L., et al.: Toxic epidermal necrolysis associated with *Klebsiella pneumoniae* sepsis. Pediatr. Dermatol. *11*:331–334, 1994.
81. Pierce, J. R., Merenstein, G. B., and Stocker, J. T.: Immediate postmortem cultures in an intensive care nursery. Pediatr. Infect. Dis. *3*:510–513, 1984.
82. Pillay, T., Pillay, D. G., Adhikari, M., et al.: Piperacillin/tazobactam in the treatment of *Klebsiella pneumoniae* infections in neonates. Am. J. Perinatol. *15*:47–51, 1998.
83. Podschun, R., Sievers, D., Fischer, A., et al.: Serotypes, hemagglutinins, siderophore synthesis, and serum resistance of *Klebsiella* isolates causing human urinary tract infections. J. Infect. Dis. *168*:1415–1421, 1993.
84. Podschun, R., Acktun, H., and Okpara, J.: Isolation of *Klebsiella planticola* from newborns in a neonatal ward. J. Clin. Microbiol. *36*:2331–2332, 1998.
85. Podschun, R., Fischer, A., and Ullman, U.: Expression of putative virulence factors by clinical isolates of *Klebsiella planticola*. J. Med. Microbiol. *49*:115–119, 2000.
86. Podschun, R., and Ullmann, U.: *Klebsiella* spp. as nosocomial pathogens: Epidemiology, taxonomy, typing methods, and pathogenicity factors. Clin. Microbiol. Rev. *11*:589–603, 1998.
87. Quinn, J. P.: Clinical significance of extended-spectrum beta-lactamases. Eur. J. Clin. Microbiol. Infect. Dis. *13*(Suppl. 1):S39–S42, 1994.
88. Ramirez-Ronda, C. H., Fuxench-Lopez, Z., and Nevarez, M.: Increased pharyngeal bacterial colonization during viral illness. Arch. Intern. Med. *141*:1599–1603, 1981.
89. Ransjo, U., Good, Z., Jalakas, K., et al.: An outbreak of *Klebsiella oxytoca* septicemias associated with the use of invasive blood pressure monitoring equipment. Acta Anaesthesiol. Scand. *36*:289–291, 1992.
90. Rebuck, J. A., Olsen, K. M., Fey, P. D., et al.: Characterization of an outbreak due to extended-spectrum beta-lactamase–producing *Klebsiella pneumoniae* in a pediatric intensive care unit transplant population. Clin. Infect. Dis. *31*:1368–1372, 2000.
91. Reish, O., Ashkenazi, S., Naor, N., et al.: An outbreak of multiresistant *Klebsiella* in a neonatal intensive care unit. J. Hosp. Infect. *25*:287–291, 1993.
92. Reiss, I., Borkhardt, A., Fussle, R., et al.: Disinfectant contaminated with *Klebsiella oxytoca* as a source of sepsis in babies. Lancet *356*:310, 2000.
93. Rice, L. B., Carias, L. L., Hujer, A. M., et al.: High-level expression of chromosomally encoded SHV-1 beta-lactamase and an outer membrane protein change confer resistance to ceftazidime and piperacillin-tazobactam in a clinical isolate of *Klebsiella pneumoniae*. Antimicrob. Agents Chemother. *44*:362–367, 2000.
94. Royle, J., Halasz, S., Eagles, G., et al.: Outbreak of extended spectrum beta lactamase producing *Klebsiella pneumoniae* in a neonatal unit. Arch. Dis. Child. Fetal Neonatal Ed. *80*:F64–F68, 1999.
95. Sakata, H., Fujita, K., and Yoshioka, H.: The effect of antimicrobial agents on fecal flora of children. Antimicrob. Agents Chemother. *29*:225–229, 1986.

96. Saurina, G., Quale, J. M., Manikal, V. M., et al.: Antimicrobial resistance in Enterobacteriaceae in Brooklyn, NY: Epidemiology and relation to antibiotic usage patterns. J. Antimicrob. Chemother. *45*:895–898, 2000.
97. Schumacher, H., Scheibel, J., and Moller, J. K.: Cross-resistance patterns among clinical isolates of *Klebsiella pneumoniae* with decreased susceptibility to cefuroxime. J. Antimicrob. Chemother. *46*:215–221, 2000.
98. Sechi, L. A., Spanu, T., Sanguinetti, M., et al.: Molecular analysis of *Klebsiella pneumoniae* strains isolated in pediatric wards by ribotyping, pulsed field gel electrophoresis and antimicrobial susceptibilities. New Microbiol. *24*:35–45, 2001.
99. Shannon, K., Fung, K., Stapleton, P., et al.: A hospital outbreak of extended-spectrum beta-lactamase–producing *Klebsiella pneumoniae* investigated by RAPD typing and analysis of the genetics and mechanisms of resistance. J. Hosp. Infect. *39*:291–300, 1998.
100. Sood, S. K., Mulvihill, D., and Daum, R. S.: Intrarenal abscess caused by *Klebsiella pneumoniae* in a neonate: Modern management and diagnosis. Am. J. Perinatol. *6*:367–370, 1989.
101. Tullus, K., Ayling-Smith, B., Kuhn, I., et al.: Nationwide spread of *Klebsiella oxytoca* K55 in Swedish neonatal special care wards. A. P. M. I. S. *100*:1008–1014, 1992.
102. Westbrook, G. L., O'Hara, C. M., Roman, S. B., et al.: Incidence and identification of *Klebsiella planticola* in clinical isolates with emphasis on newborns. J. Clin. Microbiol. *38*:1495–1497, 2000.

CHAPTER 110 *Morganella morganii*

WILLIAM C. GRUBER ■ RANDALL G. FISHER ■ THOMAS G. BOYCE

Like *Proteus* and *Providencia* spp., *Morganella morganii* has emerged as an important nosocomial pathogen, most often in association with urinary tract or wound infection. Although most descriptions of infection are in adult populations, infections in children do occur.

Bacteriology

M. morganii (formerly *Proteus morganii*) is a motile gram-negative bacillus commonly found in the feces of humans, other mammals, and reptiles.[23] The organism was elevated to genus rank because of genetic differences from *Proteus,* with which it is otherwise biologically similar.[6] Most strains do not ferment lactose. *M. morganii, Proteus,* and *Providencia* are distinguished from other members of Enterobacteriaceae by their ability to deaminate phenylalanine and lysine. Organisms are indole-positive and ornithine decarboxylase–positive. Like *Proteus* and *Providencia, M. morganii* produces urease, but this enzyme is unrelated genetically and serologically to those of the other two genera.[16, 23] Unlike *Proteus, M. morganii* does not demonstrate swarming activity on 1.5 percent agar.[23] (This organism liquefies gelatin and does not produce hydrogen sulfide.) For detailed discussion of taxonomy and characterization of *Morganella morganii,* the reader is referred to the review by O'Hara and coworkers.[22]

EPIDEMIOLOGY

Like *Proteus* and *Providencia* spp., *Morganella* organisms are found commonly in soil, sewage, and manure. Like *Proteus mirabilis, M. morganii* commonly invades the instrument-fitted urinary tract and surgical wounds; adults in inpatient surgical units have the greatest risk for acquiring colonization and infection.[1] The institutionalized elderly also have frequent infection with these organisms. Urinary tract colonization with *Morganella* accompanying groin skin colonization in elderly persons may account for the greater frequency of urinary tract infections in this population.[12] *M. morganii* accounted for nearly 10 percent of 145 consecutive complicated, multidrug-resistant urinary tract infections.[9] *Escherichia coli* and *P. mirabilis* account for most urinary tract infections in childhood, but *M. morganii* has been implicated in some cases of cystitis and pyelonephritis. In contrast with well-described nursery epidemics of *P. mirabilis* infection,[3, 8] no *M. morganii* neonatal outbreaks have been described, and infections of the central nervous system are rare occurrences in newborns.[11, 31] Ribotyping is a sensitive method for molecular characterization of isolates that may aid in analysis of outbreaks.[25]

Pathophysiology

Factors that predispose the urinary tract to invasion by *P. mirabilis* and *Providencia* spp. also may favor *M. morganii* colonization and infection. These organisms split urea, forming ammonium hydroxide and increasing local pH, which results in toxicity to renal cells and potentiation of urolithiasis.[5, 21] The ability of *P. mirabilis* to regenerate more rapidly in urine with faster generation at alkaline pH, compared with *M. morganii,* may provide a selective advantage for *P. mirabilis* in establishing itself as a urinary tract pathogen.[30]

Clinical Manifestations

Urinary tract infection with *M. morganii* often is associated with an elevated urinary pH. Urolithiasis can occur, although perhaps less frequently than during infection with *P. mirabilis.*[4] *M. morganii* has been recovered from less than 10 percent of adult bacteremic episodes, but mortality rates have exceeded 20 percent.[1] Other reported complications identified in immunocompromised or instrument-fitted patients include meningitis,[14, 19] arthritis,[18, 29] empyema,[15] peritonitis,[15] and skin infection.[2] *M. morganii* has been recovered alone or in combination with other organisms from surgical wounds[9] and soft tissue abscesses in children.[7] Perinatal bacterial sepsis and brain abscess have been described.[26–28, 31]

Diagnosis

M. morganii produces a reddish-brown pigment when cultured on nutrient media supplemented with 5 percent tryptophan.[23] Production of urease and deamination of tryptophan help distinguish this bacterium from other organisms. Unlike the closely related *Proteus* and *Providencia* spp., *M. morganii* generally ferments only glucose and mannose and does not produce a red color on lysine iron agar.[23] *M. morganii* may be missed or mistaken for other organisms in the common circumstance of polymicrobial infection in the catheterized patient. In one series, *M. morganii* was actually among the most common bacteriuric species in patients with long-term catheterization but was commonly missed by reference laboratories.[10] The clinical laboratory should be directed to look for this organism, particularly in circumstances of nosocomial urinary tract infection and sepsis.

Treatment

Effective treatment of local infections or septicemia relies on appropriate choice of an antibiotic, often including an aminoglycoside, in combination with surgical débridement and drainage of abscesses as necessary. Variability in antimicrobial susceptibility can be wide among *M. morganii* and the related *Proteus* and *Providencia* strains, emphasizing the importance of identification of species and susceptibility testing.[24] Complex combinations of aminoglycoside resistance that differ by hospital and geographic region can occur.[20] Fortunately, most urinary tract infections respond to ampicillin or third-generation cephalosporins, but failure to clear bacteria should alert the physician to the possibility of urolithiasis or structural abnormality[4]; removal of stones or surgical correction of anatomic defects is often required for cure. Aztreonam has shown effectiveness in therapy for as many as 98 percent of multidrug-resistant strains.[9]

REFERENCES

1. Adler, J. L., Burke, J. P., Martin, D. F., et al.: *Proteus* infection in a general hospital. II. Some clinical and epidemiological characteristics. Ann. Intern. Med. *75*:531–536, 1971.
2. Bagel, J., and Grossman, M. E.: Hemorrhagic bullae associated with *Morganella morganii* septicemia. J. Am. Acad. Dermatol. *12*:575–576, 1985.
3. Becker, A. H.: Infection due to *Proteus mirabilis* in a newborn nursery. Am. J. Dis. Child. *104*:355–359, 1962.
4. Bensman, A., Roubach, L., Allouch, G., et al.: Urolithiasis in children: Presenting signs, etiology, bacteriology and localisation. Acta Paediatr. Scand. *72*:879–883, 1983.
5. Braude, A. I., and Siemienski, J.: Role of bacterial urease in experimental pyelonephritis. J. Bacteriol. *80*:171–179 1960.
6. Brenner, D. J., Farmer, J. J., III, Fanning, G. R., et al.: Deoxyribonucleic acid relatedness of *Proteus* and *Providencia* species. Int. J. Syst. Bacteriol. *28*:269–282, 1978.
7. Brook, I., and Martin, W. J.: Aerobic and anaerobic bacteriology of perirectal abscess in children. Pediatrics *66*:282–284, 1980.
8. Burke, J. P., Ingall, D., Klein, J. O., et al.: *Proteus mirabilis* infections in a hospital nursery traced to a human carrier. N. Engl. J. Med. *284*:115–121, 1971.
9. Cox, C. E.: Aztreonam therapy for complicated urinary tract infections caused by multidrug-resistant bacteria. Rev. Infect. Dis. 7(Suppl. 4):S767–S77l, 1985.
10. Damron, D. J., Warren, J. W., Chippendale, G. R., et al.: Do clinical microbiology laboratories report complete bacteriology in urine from patients with long-term urinary catheters? J. Clin. Microbiol. *24*:400–404, 1986.
11. Darby, C. P., and Hill, O.: *Proteus morganii* meningitis treated with trimethoprim-sulfamethoxazole (co-trimoxazole). Clin. Pediatr. *14*:669–672, 1975.
12. Ehrenkranz, N. J., Alfonso, B. C., Eckert, D. G., et al.: Proteeae species bacteriuria accompanying Proteeae species groin skin carriage in geriatric outpatients. J. Clin. Microbiol. *27*:1988–1991, 1989.
13. Haddad, J. J., Inglesby, T. V. J., and Addonizio, L.: Head and neck infections in pediatric cardiac transplant patients. Ear Nose Throat J. *74*:422–425, 1995.
14. Isaacs, R. D., and Ellis-Pegler, R. B.: Successful treatment of *Morganella morganii* meningitis with pefloxacin mesylate. J. Antimicrob. Chemother. *20*:769–770, 1987.
15. Isobe, H., Motomura, K., Kotou, K., et al.: Spontaneous bacterial empyema and peritonitis caused by *Morganella morganii*. J. Clin. Gastroenterol. *18*:87–88, 1994.
16. Jones, B. D., and Mobley, H. L.: Genetic and biochemical diversity of ureases of *Proteus, Providencia,* and *Morganella* species isolated from urinary tract infection. Infect. Immun. *55*:2198–2203, 1987.
17. Kaslow, R. A., Lindsey, J. O., Bison, A. L., et al.: Nosocomial infection with highly resistant *Proteus rettgeri:* Report of an epidemic. Am. J. Epidemiol. *104*:278–286, 1976.
18. Katz, L. M., Lewis, R. J., and Borenstein, D. G.: Successful joint arthroplasty following *Proteus morganii (Morganella morganii)* septic arthritis: A four-year study. Arthritis Rheum. *30*:583–585, 1987.
19. Mastroianni, A., Coronado, O., and Chiodo, F.: *Morganella morganii* meningitis in a patient with AIDS. J. Infect. *29*:356–357, 1994.
20. Miller, G. H., Sabatelli, F. J., Hare, R. S., et al.: The most frequent aminoglycoside resistance mechanisms—changes with time and geographic area: A reflection of aminoglycoside usage patterns? Aminoglycoside Resistance Study Groups. Clin. Infect. Dis. *24*:S46–S62, 1997.
21. Musher, D. M., Griffith, D. P., Yawn, D., et al.: Role of urease in pyelonephritis resulting from urinary tract infection with *Proteus.* J. Infect. Dis. *131*:177–181, 1975.
22. O'Hara, C. M., Brenner, F. W., and Miller, J. M.: Classification, identification, and clinical significance of *Proteus, Providencia,* and *Morganella.* Clin. Microbiol. Rev. *13*:534–546, 2000.
23. Penner, J. L.: *Morganella. In* Krieg, N. R., and Holt, J. G. (eds.): Bergey's Manual of Systematic Bacteriology. Vol. 1. Baltimore, Williams & Wilkins, 1984, pp. 497–498.
24. Piccolomini, R., Cellini, L., Allocati, N., et al.: Comparative in vitro activities of 13 antimicrobial agents against *Morganella-Proteus-Providencia* group bacteria from urinary tract infections. Antimicrob. Agents Chemother. *31*:1644–1647, 1987.
25. Pignato, S., Giammanco, G. M., Grimont, F., et al: Molecular characterization of the genera *Proteus, Morganella,* and *Providencia* by ribotyping. J. Clin. Microbiol. *37*:2840–2847, 1999.
26. Ranu, S. S., Valencia, G. B., and Piecuch, S.: Fatal early onset infection in an extremely low birth weight infant due to *Morganella morganii*. J. Perinatol. *19*:533–535, 1999.
27. Rowen, J. L., and Lopez, S. M.: *Morganella morganii* early onset sepsis. Pediatr. Infect. Dis. J. *17*:1176–1177, 1998.
28. Salen, P. N., and Eppes, S.: *Morganella morganii:* A newly reported rare cause of neonatal sepsis. Acad. Emerg. Med. *4*:711–714, 1997.
29. Schonwetter, R. S., and Orson, F. M.: Chronic *Morganella morganii* arthritis in an elderly patient. J Clin. Microbiol. *26*:1414–1415, 1988.
30. Senior, B. W.: *Proteus morganii* is less frequently associated with urinary tract infections than *Proteus mirabilis:* An explanation. J. Med. Microbiol. *16*:317–322, 1983.
31. Verboon-Maciolek, M., Vandertop, W. P., Peters, A. C., et al.: Neonatal brain abscess caused by *Morganella morganii*. Clin. Infect. Dis. *20*:471, 1995.

Proteus

WILLIAM C. GRUBER ■ RANDALL G. FISHER ■ THOMAS G. BOYCE

Proteus spp. are pathogens that are increasingly associated with pediatric illness. Neonatal meningitis and pediatric urinary tract infections are the most common childhood settings in which these organisms are isolated, but infections of other organ systems have been described.

Bacteriology

Proteus spp. are motile, gram-negative bacilli that do not ferment lactose and are distinguished from other members of Enterobacteriaceae by their ability to deaminate phenylalanine and lysine. Rapid and abundant production of urease further differentiates *Proteus* from *Providencia*.[25] *Proteus vulgaris* and *Proteus mirabilis* tend to form a thin, spreading growth (swarm) on the surface of moist agar media, often overgrowing other bacterial isolates. They also produce hydrogen sulfide and liquefy gelatin. *P. mirabilis* is distinguished from other *Proteus* spp. (e.g., *P. vulgaris)* by its inability to produce indole from tryptophan. Disparate DNA content and anomalous biochemical and serologic reactions have caused *Proteus morganii* to be renamed *Morganella morganii* (see Chapter 110),[25] and both terms for this organism appear in the clinical literature. For detailed discussion of taxonomy and characterization of *Proteus* spp., the reader is referred to the review by O'Hara and coworkers.[35]

Epidemiology

Proteus spp. are found commonly in soil, sewage, and manure. Although they are normal inhabitants of the colon and perineum, their numbers can be increased in persons receiving antibiotic therapy.[22]

First reported by Buisine and Henninot in 1949,[10] neonatal meningitis caused by *P. mirabilis* accounts for approximately 4 percent of all neonatal meningitis cases.[32] Nursery outbreaks have been attributed to contaminated equipment and human carriers. Vertical transmission from mother to infant has been confirmed by DNA fingerprinting and ribotyping methods.[8] In Becker's series[5] of patients with *P. mirabilis* neonatal meningitis, all affected infants came from the same nursery and all were exposed to mist from an apparatus that yielded *P. mirabilis*. The importance of hand carriage was well documented by Burke and associates[11]; newborn umbilical colonization and invasive disease were linked to a single nurse from whom *P. mirabilis* was cultured from hands, rectum, and vagina. Ribotyping is a sensitive method for molecular characterization of isolates that may aid in analysis of outbreaks.[38]

Proteus infection after the first few months of life most commonly involves the urinary tract. Although *Escherichia coli* accounts for most urinary tract infections in childhood, *Proteus* spp. commonly are implicated in reported series of cystitis and pyelonephritis[7, 17, 23, 49]; *P. mirabilis* is the most common species of *Proteus* isolated. *P. mirabilis* has been cultured more frequently from the urethra of uncircumcised than of circumcised male infants and has replaced *E. coli* as the most prevalent pathogen in one consecutive series of male patients presenting with initial urinary tract infection.[23, 50]

Proteus urinary tract infection is one of the most common presenting signs of urolithiasis in childhood,[15] and *P. mirabilis* supplants *E. coli* as the major urinary tract pathogen in children susceptible to formation of renal stones.[7] Diagnosis of more than 50 percent of pediatric urolithiasis cases is based on preceding urinary tract infection, and *Proteus* is responsible for as many as 65 percent of these infections.[7] Isolation of this organism as a pathogen on urine culture should alert the physician to the possible presence of a urinary tract stone.

Pathophysiology

Most cases of central nervous system infection caused by *Proteus* occur in neonates and are thought to arise by bacteremic spread of the organism to the brain or meninges. Contiguous spread to the brain from localized infections is reported occasionally.[31] As is the case with *Citrobacter* meningitis, a propensity for formation of central nervous system abscesses remains unexplained. Rabbit models of *P. mirabilis* meningitis have shown that in vivo concentrations of gentamicin necessary to produce bacterial killing are 10 to 30 times higher than those predicted from in vitro susceptibility testing.[48] Reduced aminoglycoside effect may be secondary to depressed cerebrospinal fluid pH associated with *P. mirabilis* infection.[48] Whatever the mechanism, lack of effective antimicrobial activity in the ventricles accounts in part for the persistence of organisms at these sites.

Numerous factors may predispose the urinary tract to invasion by *Proteus*. *Proteus* splits urea, forming ammonium hydroxide and increasing local pH, which results in toxicity to renal cells and potentiation of urolithiasis.[9, 34] The ability of *P. mirabilis* to regenerate more rapidly in urine with faster generation at alkaline pH, compared with *M. morganii (P. morganii)*, may provide a selective advantage for *P. mirabilis* in establishing itself as a urinary tract pathogen.[42] Biochemically complex struvite ($MgNH_4PO_4$) stones provide a refuge for *Proteus* organisms and form a barrier to effective antimicrobial therapy.[7] Struvite stone formation is a major cause of urinary bacterial persistence in adult women without azotemia,[47] and a similar case probably can be made for the pediatric patient with urolithiasis. *P. mirabilis* ureases demonstrated lower affinities for substrate but hydrolyzed urea 6 to 25 times faster than did enzymes from other species, which may explain the frequent association of this species with the formation of stones.[19] Organisms have been shown to be taken up by human renal epithelium, by an actin-independent mechanism.[12] Pili may enhance the virulence of *Proteus* in pyelonephritis by increasing adherence of organisms to the renal pelvis.[44] Flagella have been implicated in the spread of this organism in the urinary tract[36]; the ability to invade host urothelial cells is coupled closely with the ability of *P. mirabilis* to differentiate into hyperflagellated, filamentous swarm cells capable of rapid spread on the surface of moist agar media.[2] The role of fimbriae as a factor predisposing to ascending infection is less clear.[4, 30] Swarming behavior might inherently assist ascending colonization of the urinary tract, as demonstrated in a mouse model of infection.[3] A putative gene regulator for swarming behavior (RsbA) may act to identify environmental conditions that favor swarming.[6] The reader is referred to the review by Rozalski and colleagues[40] for a more in-depth review of *Proteus* virulence factors.

Clinical Manifestations

P. mirabilis can produce a broad spectrum of signs and symptoms in association with neonatal infection. Most patients present with typical signs and symptoms of early-onset neonatal sepsis, including nonspecific lethargy, fever, and poor feeding; manifestations of sepsis may include septic arthritis and osteomyelitis. A minority of patients present after the first week of life. Meningitis may occur with either early- or late-onset disease. Brain abscesses associated with subtle clinical abnormalities rarely develop for weeks to months before presentation.[13] *Proteus* brain abscesses are associated with a high degree of mortality, frequent complications, and increased risk of development of neurologic deficits in survivors.[20, 27, 45] Hydrocephalus is a particularly frequent complication and should be anticipated. Destruction of the brain may progress to porencephaly or compartmentalization of ventricles and often requires surgical intervention.[20] Computed tomography is useful, especially for diagnosing and then following the progression of cerebral complications.[45]

Urinary tract infection with these bacteria involves predominantly involves younger patients and often is associated with an elevated urinary pH; clinical findings and urine abnormalities often are less striking than in patients with *E. coli* urinary tract infections.[23] As many as 30 percent of patients demonstrate recurrent infection during the 12 months after initial treatment.[23] Indwelling urinary catheters increase the risk for acquiring *Proteus* colonization and infection. Long-term indwelling urinary catheters may become blocked by encrustations of aggregated struvite crystals; prolonged colonization with urease-producing *P. mirabilis* is associated with this complication.[26]

Proteus spp. often are implicated as agents of septicemia in adult patients and cause approximately 8 percent of gram-negative bacteremias in this group.[16, 24] In 60 percent of *Proteus* bacteremic episodes in adults, the urinary tract has been determined to be the source[16]; no anatomic source is identified in 20 percent of cases of *Proteus* bacteremia. The species responsible for most cases of *Proteus* bacteremia are *P. mirabilis* and, less commonly, *P. vulgaris*. The overall incidence of gram-negative enteric bacteremia in the pediatric age group is lower than that in adults; 5 percent of such cases are caused by *Proteus*.[16] As in adults, the genitourinary tract is the source most commonly identified.[16] Mortality rates average less than 40 percent and depend strongly on the severity of underlying disease in the host.[16, 24]

Osteomyelitis,[21, 37, 48] pneumonia,[16, 24, 39] mastoiditis,[31] and wound infections[24] also occur. A recent survey of 41 otogenic brain abscesses in pediatric and adult patients implicated *Proteus* as a major pathogen.[43] Pediatric osteomyelitis secondary to contiguous infection of traumatized soft tissue often is polymicrobial, and *Proteus* has been implicated as a copathogen in at least 10 percent of such cases.[37] Sickle-cell anemia is a risk factor.[1, 21]

Diagnosis

Proteus is suspected readily because of its ability to swarm on the surface of moist agar. A selective medium developed for the isolation of Proteeae relies on the ability of all members to produce a dark brown pigment in medium containing DL-tryptophan.[18] Production of urease, lack of indole production from tryptophan, and a positive result with ornithine decarboxylase testing distinguish *P. mirabilis* from *Providencia* and other *Proteus* spp.[25]

Treatment

Treatment of meningitis caused by *Proteus* should conform to standard regimens recommended for gram-negative meningitis. However, *P. mirabilis* usually is sensitive to ampicillin, and administration of this drug alone or combined with an aminoglycoside often is suitable therapy once the identity and susceptibilities of the infecting organism are known.[41] A third-generation cephalosporin often is an alternative, but resistant extended-spectrum β-lactamase–producing strains and β-lactamase inhibitor–resistant strains have been described in pediatric populations.[14, 28] Consecutive lumbar punctures should be performed for *Proteus* meningitis until cerebrospinal fluid cultures are sterile. A minimum of 2 weeks of antibiotic therapy is recommended after bacteriologic cure. Ventricular aspiration or drainage of abscesses may be required to direct therapy on the basis of persistence of organisms at these sites. Open drainage of abscesses often is necessary, but resolution of abscess formation with antibiotic therapy alone has been reported.[46] Intraventricular antibiotics are not of proven benefit in terms of mortality or morbidity but have been used to clear ventricular colonization. A 15-year-old boy with *Proteus* mastoiditis and meningitis was treated successfully with intravenous trimethoprim-sulfamethoxazole.[31]

Effective treatment of local infections or septicemia relies on appropriate choice of antibiotics, often including an aminoglycoside, combined with surgical débridement and drainage of abscesses as necessary. Aminoglycoside resistance patterns are complex and may differ by hospital and geographic region.[33] Most urinary tract infections caused by *P. mirabilis* respond to ampicillin, but some organisms have been shown to acquire a plasmid-mediated β-lactamase.[29] Failure to clear bacteria should alert the physician to the possibility of the presence of urolithiasis or of a structural abnormality; removal of stones or surgical correction of anatomic defects often is required for cure.

REFERENCES

1. Aken'Ova, Y. A., Bakare, R. A., Okunade, M. A., and Olaniyi, J.: Bacterial causes of acute osteomyelitis in sickle cell anaemia: Changing infection profile. West Afr. J. Med. *14*:255–258, 1995.
2. Allison, C., Coleman, N., Jones P. L., et al.: Ability of *Proteus mirabilis* to invade human urothelial cells is coupled to motility and swarming differentiation. Infect. Immun. *60*:4740–4746, 1992.
3. Allison, C., Emody, L., Coleman, N., et al.: The role of swarm cell differentiation and multicellular migration in the uropathogenicity of *Proteus mirabilis*. J. Infect. Dis. *169*:1155–1158, 1994.
4. Bahrani, F. K., Massad, G., Lockatell, C. V., et al.: Construction of an MR/P fimbrial mutant of *Proteus mirabilis:* Role in virulence in a mouse model of ascending urinary tract infection. Infect. Immun. *62*:3363–3371, 1994.
5. Becker, A. H.: Infection due to *Proteus mirabilis* in a newborn nursery. Am. J. Dis. Child. *104*:355–359, 1962.
6. Belas, R., Schneider, R., and Melch, M.: Characterization of *Proteus mirabilis* precocious swarming mutants: Identification of rsbA, encoding a regulator of swarming behavior. J. Bacteriol. *180*:6126–6139, 1998.
7. Bensman, A., Roubach, L., Allouch, G., et al.: Urolithiasis in children: Presenting signs, etiology, bacteriology and localisation. Acta Paediatr. Scand. *72*:879–883, 1983.
8. Bingen, E., Boissinot, C., Desjardins, P., et al.: Arbitrarily primed polymerase chain reaction provides rapid differentiation of *Proteus mirabilis* isolates from a pediatric hospital. J. Clin. Microbiol. *31*:1055–1059, 1993.
9. Braude, A. I., and Siemienski, J.: Role of bacterial urease in experimental pyelonephritis. J. Bacteriol. *80*:171–179, 1960.
10. Buisine, A., and Henninot, E.: Les meningites a *Proteus* chez l'enfant. Ann. Biol. Clin. 7:448, 1949.

11. Burke, J. P., Ingall, D., Klein, J. O., et al.: *Proteus mirabilis* infections in a hospital nursery traced to a human carrier. N. Engl. J. Med. *284*:115–121, 1971.
12. Chippendale, G. R., Warren, J. W., Trifillis, A. L., and Mobley, H. L.: Internalization of *Proteus mirabilis* by human renal epithelial cells. Infect. Immun. *62*:3115–3121, 1994.
13. Darby, C. P., Conner, E., and Kyong, C. U.: *Proteus mirabilis* brain abscess in a neonate. Dev. Med. Child Neurol. *20*:366–375, 1978.
14. de Champs, C., Bonnet, R., Sirot, D., et al: Clinical relevance of *Proteus mirabilis* in hospital patients: A two year survey. J. Antimicrob. Chemother. *45*:537–539, 2000.
15. Diamond, D. A.: Clinical patterns of paediatric urolithiasis. Br. J. Urol. *68*:195–198, 1991.
16. duPont, H. L., and Spink, W. H.: Infections due to gram-negative organisms: An analysis of 860 patients with bacteremia at the University of Minnesota Medical Center, 1958–1966. Medicine (Baltimore) *48*:307–329, 1969.
17. Ginsburg, C. M., and McCracken, G. H., Jr.: Urinary tract infections in young infants. Pediatrics *69*:409–412, 1982.
18. Hawkey, P. M., McCormick, A., and Simpson, R. A.: Selective and differential medium for the primary isolation of members of the Proteeae. J. Clin. Microbiol. *23*:600–603, 1986.
19. Jones, B. D., and Mobley, H. L.: Genetic and biochemical diversity of ureases of *Proteus, Providencia,* and *Morganella* species isolated from urinary tract infection. Infect. Immun. *55*:2198–2203, 1987.
20. Kalsbeck, J. E., DeSousa, A. L., Kleiman, M. B., et al.: Compartmentalization of the cerebral ventricles as a sequela of neonatal meningitis. J. Neurosurg. *52*:547–552, 1980.
21. Kanfaoui, A., Graide, D., Petein, M., et al.: *Proteus mirabilis* osteomyelitis of the ribs in a girl with sickle cell anaemia. Eur. J. Pediatr. *158*:767, 1999.
22. Kaslow, R. A., Lindsey, J. O., Bison, A. L., et al.: Nosocomial infection with highly resistant *Proteus rettgeri:* Report of an epidemic. Am. J. Epidemiol. *104*:278–286, 1976.
23. Khan, A. J., Ubriani, R. S., Bombach, E., et al.: Initial urinary tract infection caused by *Proteus mirabilis* in infancy and childhood. J. Pediatr. *93*:791–793, 1978.
24. Kreger, B. E., Craven, D. E., Carling, P. C., et al.: Gram-negative bacteremia. III. Reassessment of etiology, epidemiology and ecology in 612 patients. Am. J. Med. *68*:332–343, 1980.
25. Krieg, N. R., and Holt, J. G. (eds.): Bergey's Manual of Systematic Bacteriology. Baltimore, Williams & Wilkins, 1984, pp. 491–494.
26. Kunin, C. M.: Blockage of urinary catheters: Role of microorganisms and constituents of the urine on formation of encrustations. J. Clin. Epidemiol. *42*:835–842, 1989.
27. Levy, H. L., and Ingall, D.: Meningitis in neonates due to *Proteus mirabilis*. Am. J. Dis. Child. *114*:320–324, 1967.
28. Luzzaro, F., Perilli, M., Amicosante, G., et al.: Properties of multidrug-resistant, ESBL-producing *Proteus mirabilis* isolates and possible role of beta-lactam/beta-lactamase inhibitor combinations. Int. J. Antimicrob. Agents *17*:131–135, 2001.
29. Mariotte, S., Nordmann, P., and Nicolas, M. H.: Extended-spectrum beta-lactamase in *Proteus mirabilis*. J. Antimicrob. Chemother. *33*:925–935, 1994.
30. Massad, G., Lockatell, C. V., Johnson, D. E., et al.: *Proteus mirabilis* fimbriae: Construction of an isogenic pmfA mutant and analysis of virulence in a CBA mouse model of ascending urinary tract infection. Infect. Immun. *62*:536–542, 1994.
31. McConville, J. H., and Manzella, J. P.: Parenteral trimethoprim/sulfamethoxazole for gram-negative bacillary meningitis. Am. J. Med. Sci. *287*:43–45, 1984.
32. McCracken, G. H., Jr.: New developments in the management of children with bacterial meningitis. Pediatr. Infect. Dis. *3*:S32–S34, 1984.
33. Miller, G. H., Sabatelli, F. J., Hare, R. S., et al.: The most frequent aminoglycoside resistance mechanisms—changes with time and geographic area: A reflection of aminoglycoside usage patterns? Aminoglycoside Resistance Study Groups. Clin. Infect. Dis. *24*:S46–S62, 1997.
34. Musher, D. M., Griffith, D. P., Yawn, D., et al.: Role of urease in pyelonephritis resulting from urinary tract infection with *Proteus*. J. Infect. Dis. *131*:177–181, 1975.
35. O'Hara, C. M., Brenner, F. W., and Miller, J. M.: Classification, identification, and clinical significance of *Proteus, Providencia,* and *Morganella*. Clin. Microbiol. Rev. *13*:534–546, 2000.
36. Pazin, G. J., and Braude, A. I.: Immobilizing antibodies in urine. 2. Prevention of ascending spread of *Proteus mirabilis*. Invest. Virol. *122*:129–133, 1974.
37. Pichichero, M. E., and Friesen, H. A.: Polymicrobial osteomyelitis: Report of three cases and review of the literature. Rev. Infect. Dis. *4*: 86–96, 1982.
38. Pignato, S., Giammanco, G. M., Grimont, F., et al.: Molecular characterization of the genera *Proteus, Morganella,* and *Providencia* by ribotyping. J. Clin. Microbiol. *37*:2840–2847, 1999.
39. Pine, J. R., and Hollman, J. L.: Elevated pleural fluid pH in *Proteus mirabilis* empyema. Chest *84*:109–111, 1983.
40. Rozalski, A., Sidorczyk, Z., and Kotelko, K.: Potential virulence factors of *Proteus* bacilli. Microbiol. Mol. Biol. Rev. *61*:65–89, 1997.
41. Scherzer, A. L., Kaye, D., and Shinefield, H. R.: *Proteus mirabilis* meningitis: Report of two cases treated with ampicillin. J. Pediatr. *68*:731–740, 1966.
42. Senior, B. W.: *Proteus morganii* is less frequently associated with urinary tract infections than *Proteus mirabilis:* An explanation. J. Med. Microbiol. *16*:317–322, 1983.
43. Sennaroglu, L., and Sozeri, B.: Otogenic brain abscess: Review of 41 cases. Otolaryngol. Head Neck Surg. *123*:751–755, 2000.
44. Silverblatt, F. J.: Host-parasite interaction in the rat renal pelvis: A possible role for pili in the pathogenesis of pyelonephritis. J. Exp. Med. *140*:1696–1711, 1974.
45. Smith, M. L., and Mellor, D.: *Proteus mirabilis* meningitis and cerebral abscess in the newborn period. Arch. Dis. Child. *55*:308–310, 1980.
46. Spirer, Z., Jurgenson, U., Lazewnick, R., et al.: Complete recovery from an apparent brain abscess treated without neurosurgery: The importance of early CT scanning. Clin. Pediatr. *21*:106–109, 1982.
47. Stamey, T. A.: Pathogenesis and Treatment of Urinary Tract Infections. Baltimore, Williams & Wilkins, 1980.
48. Strausbaugh, L. J., and Sande, M. A.: Factors influencing the therapy of experimental *Proteus mirabilis* meningitis in rabbits. J. Infect. Dis. *137*:251–260, 1978.
49. Wientzen, R. L., McCracken, G. H., Jr., Petruska, M. L., et al.: Localization and therapy of urinary tract infections of childhood. Pediatrics *63*:467–473, 1979.
50. Wiswell, T. E., Miller, G. M., Gelston, H. M., et al.: Effect of circumcision status on periurethral bacterial flora during the first year of life. J. Pediatr. *113*:442–446, 1988.

CHAPTER 112 *Providencia*

WILLIAM C. GRUBER ■ RANDALL G. FISHER ■ THOMAS G. BOYCE

The genus *Providencia,* named after the city of Providence, Rhode Island, comprises pathogens most commonly associated with urinary tract infections. *Providencia* spp. are encountered most often as pathogens in hospitals or chronic care facilities and can be responsible for outbreaks of multidrug-resistant infection.[26]

Bacteriology

Providencia organisms are motile gram-negative bacilli that do not ferment lactose and are distinguished from other members of the family Enterobacteriaceae by their ability to deaminate phenylalanine and lysine.[8, 23] The genus distinguishes "urease-negative" organisms *Providencia rettgeri, Providencia stuartii, Providencia alcalifaciens, Providencia rustigianii,* and *Providencia heimbachae* from the otherwise biochemically similar "urease-positive" *Proteus* spp.[15, 23] Urease is produced by most strains of *P. rettgeri* and by 15 percent or fewer strains of *P. stuartii.*[23] *Providencia* also differs from the other Proteeae genera in its ability to produce acid from inositol. Strains are differentiated further by reactivity with straight-chain hydroxy alcohols.[23] For detailed discussion of taxonomy and characterization of *Providencia* spp., the reader is referred to the review by O'Hara and coworkers.[21]

Epidemiology

Providencia organisms are recovered infrequently from stool in healthy human subjects but frequently colonize indwelling or condom urinary catheters, particularly in persons receiving antibiotic therapy.[5, 10, 16, 26, 27] *Providencia* spp. have been recognized as pathogens for more than 50 years[7]; *P. rettgeri* and *P. stuartii* are the species most commonly implicated in urinary tract infection.[10, 12, 13, 18, 27] Multiple biotypes of *P. stuartii* have been identified in hospital outbreaks, indicating the probability of multiple sources of colonization.[2] Ribotyping is a sensitive method for molecular characterization of isolates that may aid in analysis of outbreaks.[25]

Pathophysiology

P. stuartii does not appear to have greater access to the urinary tract compared with other bacteria; in patients who are catheterized for long periods of time, the incidence of bacteriuria caused by this organism is equivalent to those caused by other uropathogens.[26] Rather, *P. stuartii* manifests an extraordinary ability to persist within the catheterized urinary tract.[27] Bacteriuria may take weeks to months to clear. A mannose-resistant, *Klebsiella*-like hemagglutinin may play an important role in the persistence of *P. stuartii* and its adherence to urinary tract catheters.[20]

Despite the similarities between *Proteus mirabilis* (the major pathogen responsible for urolithiasis in children)[4] and urease-producing *Providencia* spp., the latter organisms rarely are associated with formation of stones. *P. stuartii* occasionally produces urease with a higher affinity for substrate, but *P. mirabilis* ureases hydrolyze urea 6 to 25 times faster.[14] Restriction enzyme analysis of genes coding for the respective enzymes shows significant divergence.[14] These differences may explain the more frequent association of *P. mirabilis* with formation of stones.

Some strains of *P. alcalifaciens* have been isolated more commonly in children with diarrhea, and enteropathogenicity has been demonstrated in HEp-2 cells and a rabbit model.[1, 2] In children with diarrhea, *P. alcalifaciens* often is associated with other enteric pathogens, so its role in pathogenesis remains unclear.[3]

Clinical Manifestations

Although *Escherichia coli* and *Proteus* spp. account for most urinary tract infections in childhood, *Providencia* spp. have been reported as a cause of infection in children with spinal injury and long-term urinary tract catheterization.[17, 18] Most infections, however, have been described in the elderly or adult spinal injury patient who requires urinary tract catheterization for a long period of time.[26] Clinical findings are typical of those associated with urinary tract infection. In the rare setting of bacteremia, vascular collapse may occur.[17]

Diagnosis

Providencia should be suspected when indole-positive, urease-negative, gram-negative rods, which oxidatively deaminate tryptophan, are isolated in culture. Because chronically catheterized patients may be colonized with multiple organisms, *Providencia* spp. frequently are overlooked or misidentified.[7] Therefore, clinical laboratories should be encouraged to identify all bacterial colonies in chronically catheterized individuals in whom infection is suspected. Identification is particularly important because of the marked differences in susceptibility of uropathogens.[24]

Treatment

Empirical therapy should be guided by antimicrobial susceptibility testing of the patient's isolate and a knowledge of susceptibilities of previously identified *Providencia* within the care facility. Removal of urinary tract catheters speeds eradication of these pathogens. Strains of *P. stuartii* and *P. rettgeri* commonly are resistant to many antibiotics. Since the 1970s, multidrug resistance has emerged[22]; many strains are resistant to sulfonamides, trimethoprim, nitrofurantoin, nalidixic acid, penicillins, cephalosporins, and aminoglycosides; some singular strains are resistant to most antibiotics in common use.[24] Much of the observed resistance appears to be plasmid based[11]; quinolones and aztreonam have shown some promise in the treatment of such cases.[6, 9] Complex combinations of aminoglycoside resistance that differ by hospital and geographic region can occur.[19] Organisms that are resistant to gentamicin and tobramycin may remain susceptible to amikacin.

REFERENCES

1. Albert, M. J., Ansaruzzaman, M., Bhuiyan, N. A., et al.: Characteristics of invasion of HEp-2 cells by *Providencia alcalifaciens*. J. Med. Microbiol. *42*:186–190, 1995.
2. Albert, M. J., Alam, K., Ansaruzzaman, M., et al.: Pathogenesis of *Providencia alcalifaciens*-induced diarrhea. Infect. Immun. *60*:5017–5024, 1992.
3. Albert, M. J., Faruque, A. S., and Mahalanabis, D.: Association of *Providencia alcalifaciens* with diarrhea in children. J. Clin. Microbiol. *36*:1433–1435, 1998.
4. Bensman, A., Roubach, L., Allouch, G., et al.: Urolithiasis in children: Presenting signs, etiology, bacteriology and localisation. Acta Paediatr. Scand. *72*:879–883, 1983.
5. Breitenbucher, R. B.: Bacterial changes in the urine samples of patients with long-term indwelling catheters. Arch. Intern. Med. *144*:1585–1588, 1984.
6. Cox, C. E.: Aztreonam therapy for complicated urinary tract infections caused by multidrug-resistant bacteria. Rev. Infect. Dis. 7(Suppl. 4):S767–S771, 1985.
7. Damron, D. J., Warren, J. W., Chippendale, G. R., et al.: Do clinical microbiology laboratories report complete bacteriology in urine from patients with long-term urinary catheters? J. Clin. Microbiol. *24*:400–404, 1986.
8. Ewing, W. H., Tanner, K. E., and Dennard, D. A.: The Providence Group: An intermediate group of enteric bacteria. J. Infect. Dis. *94*:134–140, 1954.
9. Fang, G. D., Brennen, C., Wagener, M., et al.: Use of ciprofloxacin versus use of aminoglycosides for therapy of complicated urinary tract infection: Prospective, randomized clinical and pharmacokinetic study. Antimicrob. Agents Chemother. *35*:1849–1855, 1991.
10. Fierer, J., and Ekstrom, M.: An outbreak of *Providencia stuartii* urinary tract infections: Patients with condom catheters are a reservoir of the bacteria. J. A. M. A. *245*:1553–1555, 1981.
11. Hawkey, P. M.: *Providencia stuartii:* A review of a multiply antibiotic-resistant bacterium. J. Antimicrob. Chemother. *13*:209–226, 1984.
12. Hawkey, P. M., Penner, J. L., Potten, M. R., et al.: Prospective survey of fecal, urinary tract, and environmental colonization by *Providencia stuartii* in two geriatric wards. J. Clin. Microbiol. *16*:422–426, 1982.
13. Hollick, G. E., Nolte, F. S., Calnan, B. J., et al.: Characterization of endemic *Providencia stuartii* isolates from patients with urinary devices. Eur. J. Clin. Microbiol. *3*:521–525, 1984.

14. Jones, B. D., and Mobley, H. L.: Genetic and biochemical diversity of ureases of *Proteus, Providencia,* and *Morganella* species isolated from urinary tract infection. Infect. Immun. *55*:2198–2203, 1987.
15. Jones, B. D., and Mobley, H. L.: *Proteus mirabilis* urease: Genetic organization, regulation, and expression of structural genes. J. Bacteriol. *170*:3342–3349, 1988.
16. Kaslow, R. A., Lindsey, J. O., Bison, A. L., et al.: Nosocomial infection with highly resistant *Proteus rettgeri:* Report of an epidemic. Am. J. Epidemiol. *104*:278–286, 1976.
17. Keren, G., and Tyrrel, D. L.: Gram-negative septicemia caused by *Providencia stuartii.* Int. J. Pediatr. Nephrol. *8*:91–94, 1987.
18. McHale, P. J., Walker, F., Scully, B., et al.: *Providencia stuartii* infections: A review of 117 cases over an eight-year period. J. Hosp. Infect. *2*:155–165, 1981.
19. Miller, G. H., Sabatelli, F. J., Hare, R. S., et al.: The most frequent aminoglycoside resistance mechanisms—changes with time and geographic area: A reflection of aminoglycoside usage patterns? Aminoglycoside Resistance Study Groups. Clin. Infect. Dis. *24*:S46–S62, 1997.
20. Mobley, H. L., Chippendale, G. R., Tenney, J. H., et al.: MR/K hemagglutination of *Providencia stuartii* correlates with adherence to catheters and with persistence in catheter-associated bacteriuria. J. Infect. Dis. *157*:264–271, 1988.
21. O'Hara, C. M., Brenner, F. W., and Miller, J. M.: Classification, identification, and clinical significance of *Proteus, Providencia,* and *Morganella.* Clin. Microbiol. Rev. *13*:534–546, 2000.
22. Overturf, G. D., Wilkins, J., and Ressler, R.: Emergence of resistant *P. stuartii* to multiple antibiotics: Specification and biochemical characterization of *Providencia.* J. Infect. Dis. *129*:353–357, 1974.
23. Penner, J. L.: *Providencia. In* Krieg, N. R., and Holt, J. G. (eds.): Bergey's Manual of Systematic Bacteriology. Vol. 1. Baltimore, Williams & Wilkins, 1984, pp. 494–496.
24. Piccolomini, R., Cellini, L., Allocati, N., et al.: Comparative in vitro activities of 13 antimicrobial agents against *Morganella-Proteus-Providencia* group bacteria from urinary tract infections. Antimicrob. Agents Chemother. *31*:1644–1647, 1987.
25. Pignato, S., Giammanco, G. M., Grimont, F., et al.: Molecular characterization of the genera *Proteus, Morganella,* and *Providencia* by ribotyping. J. Clin. Microbiol. *37*:2840–2847, 1999.
26. Warren, J. W.: *Providencia stuartii:* A common cause of antibiotic-resistant bacteriuria in patients with long-term indwelling catheters. Rev. Infect. Dis. *8*:61–67, 1986.
27. Warren, J. W., Tenney, J. H., Hoopes, J. M., et al.: A prospective microbiologic study of bacteriuria in patients with chronic indwelling urethral catheters. J. Infect. Dis. *146*:719–723, 1982.

CHAPTER 113 *Shigella*

THOMAS G. CLEARY

Historical Background

The term *dysentery* classically has been used to describe the frequent, painful passage of stools containing blood and mucus. The syndrome has been recognized since the time of Hippocrates. The differentiation of dysentery into bacillary and amebic forms followed the recognition by Shiga in 1898 that one form of dysentery was associated with a bacterium in the stools of affected individuals; their sera also were found to agglutinate the bacillus. In recognition of his achievement, the genus was named after Shiga. An estimated 164.7 million cases of shigellosis occur annually, with 1.1 million deaths, 61 percent of which involve children younger than 5 years.[114]

The most important subsequent advance has been the recognition of the molecular basis of *Shigella* virulence. Forty years ago, researchers demonstrated that shigellae invade the corneal epithelium of guinea pigs and cause keratoconjunctivitis (Sereny test). Subsequently, Formal and colleagues[72] showed that *Shigella flexneri* invades the intestinal epithelium. Since 1980, Sansonetti, Maurelli, and other investigators[193, 194, 197] have identified multiple plasmid and chromosomal virulence genes and their associated protein products. The 120- to 140-megadalton virulence plasmid is absolutely necessary (but not sufficient) for a strain to cause disease; chromosomal genes also are necessary for full virulence. *Shigella*-like enteroinvasive *Escherichia coli* have the same or closely related genes and produce a similar clinical syndrome.

The Organism

Shigellae are small, nonencapsulated gram-negative rods that are members of the family Enterobacteriaceae. Technically, they are *E. coli,* but for reasons of tradition and clinical usefulness, the designation as a separate genus has been preserved. The shigellae do not ferment lactose or do so slowly and are nonmotile (lack the H [flagellar] antigen). They lack urease and do not produce hydrogen sulfide on triple sugar iron media or gas during metabolism of carbohydrate.[64] The somatic antigen (or O antigen) side chains that determine serotype and serogroup are attached as multiple repeating units to the lipid A core and core oligosaccharides shared with other members of Enterobacteriaceae. Envelope or K antigens that are heat labile also have been described, although their clinical relevance is uncertain.

SEROGROUP CLASSIFICATION

Four serogroups, or species, of *Shigella* are defined on the basis of serologic similarities and biochemical reactions. Group A (*Shigella dysenteriae*), the mannitol nonfermenters, includes 13 serotypes having O antigens that do not cross-react immunologically. Two additional provisional serovars, types 14 and 15, also are pathogenic.[10] Serogroup D (*Shigella sonnei*), the ornithine decarboxylase–positive, slow lactose fermenters, share the same lipopolysaccharide. *Shigella* strains that ferment mannitol (unlike *S. dysenteriae*) but do not decarboxylate ornithine or ferment lactose (unlike *S. sonnei*) are classified as serogroups B and C; of these, the strains that express lipopolysaccharides that are related to each other immunologically are group B (*Shigella flexneri*), whereas those whose O antigens are unrelated to each other or to other shigellae are group C (*Shigella boydii*). Multiple serotypes of *S. flexneri* (1a, 1b, 2a, 2b, 3a, 3b, 4a, 4b, 5a, 5b, 6, X variant, and Y variant) and of *S. boydii* (18 serotypes) exist.

Epidemiology

Because shigellae are spread through a fecal-oral route, they are especially prevalent where hygiene is poor. The organisms can be cultured from around toilets in homes where shigellae have caused disease. Toilet paper does not prevent contamination of fingers. Thus, handwashing and wearing gloves are mandatory procedures for those caring for patients with bacillary dysentery. Shigellae are transmitted easily from person to person because the inoculum size required to cause disease is as few as 10 organisms in the case of *S. dysenteriae* serotype 1[61] and a few hundred organisms in the cases of *S. sonnei* and *S. flexneri*.[58] Patients who lack the acid barrier provided by a normally functioning stomach because of prior gastrectomy or use of antacid are at increased risk of acquiring infection. Shigellae survive for as long as 30 days in foods such as milk, whole eggs, oysters, shrimp, and flour.[141] Epidemics usually are associated with exposure to contaminated water or food,[219] although as might be predicted from the inoculum size, outbreaks related to swimming also occur.[131] Houseflies can be colonized with shigellae in their guts without illness and pass shigellae in their feces. Feces adherent to their legs can lead to contamination of food. Flies have been implicated in epidemics of shigellosis, particularly where the fly population is large. *Shigella* infection shows seasonal variation. In North America, relatively few cases occur in the winter, whereas in tropical regions, the peak is during the rainy season. Thus, shigellae are worldwide and thrive where susceptible individuals are grouped together (including institutions for the retarded or mentally ill, prisoner-of-war camps, Indian reservations, the military, daycare centers, and the developing world).[108, 171, 208] Spread within family groups is a typical occurrence.

The species of *Shigella* causing most infections vary according to regions. In the developed countries, *S. sonnei* is the most common species, followed by *S. flexneri* (approximately 70% *S. sonnei* and 25% *S. flexneri*); however, in the developing world, this pattern is reversed, and occasional outbreaks of *S. dysenteriae* serotype 1 occur. The pattern of infection associated with the developing world was seen in the United States early in the 20th century.

Humans and other primates can be infected with shigellae, and an age-related risk of acquiring symptomatic shigellosis exists. Unlike *Salmonella* spp., which cause disease most frequently in the first few months of life, shigellae infrequently cause illness in the first 6 months of life. The peak incidence occurs between 1 and 4 years of age, with fewer cases occurring between 5 and 9 years of age. Adults account for a minority of cases, although young mothers are at risk, presumably because they care for susceptible infants and because they traditionally handle fecal material more regularly than men do. Women may thus be exposed to larger inocula that overcome partial immunity.

Pathogenesis

INVASIVENESS AND TOXIN PRODUCTION

The ability to invade mammalian cells is the most important virulence trait of *Shigella* spp.[75, 119, 123, 154, 165] Invasion of M cells overlying Peyer patches may be the earliest event. Uptake of organisms by macrophages under the M cells induces production of cytokines and recruitment of polymorphonuclear leukocytes. Apoptosis is induced in macrophages after ingestion of *Shigella;* these events are accompanied by release of interleukin (IL)-1, IL-1β, and IL-18, which in turn triggers other inflammatory events.[196, 223, 224] Polymorphonuclear leukocytes enter the gut lumen by moving between epithelial cells. The gaps between epithelial cells may be the portal of entry of bacteria into the epithelium. After penetration of intestinal epithelial cells, shigellae are located in vacuoles derived from the cytoplasmic membrane of the mucosal cells. The bacteria lyse these vacuoles, move intracellularly, multiply, kill the epithelial cells, and infect adjacent cells. Cell death is followed by formation of ulcerations and microabscesses in the colon. Unlike *Salmonella* infection, *Shigella* infection rarely spreads beyond the lamina propria, so bacteremia and metastatic infections are uncommon events.

The genetic basis of virulence has been studied extensively. Invasiveness is the result primarily of genes on a large 120- to 140-megadalton (200- to 220-kb) virulence plasmid.[82, 83, 89, 193–195, 197] The invasive plasmid antigen (ipa) region includes genes for four polypeptides needed for invasion; these genes are *ipaA, ipaB, ipaC,* and *ipaD*. The proteins produced by these loci are recognized by the humoral immune system. The product of the *ipaB* locus is essential for induction of apoptosis in macrophages.[225] The *mxi-spa* region of the virulence plasmid is necessary for orientation of the *ipa*-encoded proteins into the outer membrane of the bacteria. The *virG* gene encodes a protein that causes intracellular and intercellular spread of shigellae after invasion of epithelial cells. The *virF* gene regulates a locus (*virB*) that is responsible for positive regulation of the *ipa* genes.[185] Although less important, chromosomal loci also regulate virulence.[168] Lipopolysaccharides probably play a role in resistance to nonspecific host defense mechanisms that are encountered during invasion of tissue. Smooth colonies express the complete complex of lipopolysaccharide O side chains required for full virulence, that is, ability to invade epithelial cells, to multiply within them, and to resist phagocytosis.[78, 166] Rough colonial variants that lack complete lipopolysaccharides do not penetrate epithelial cells efficiently and are avirulent. Chromosomal loci regulate expression of the virulence plasmid. The keratoconjunctivitis provocation (*kcpA*) gene is a positive regulator of the *virG* virulence plasmid gene that determines ability to spread within and between cells. The chromosomal *virR* gene is a temperature regulator that represses expression of *ipa* genes at 30° C but not at 37° C.

Some strains of *Shigella* produce toxins that injure mammalian cells. A chromosomal locus in *S. dysenteriae* serotype 1 encodes a protein synthesis–inhibiting exotoxin (Shiga toxin) that is clearly a major virulence factor in this serotype (and in the enterohemorrhagic *E. coli* serotypes that have the same or closely related genes).[24, 203] This toxin is composed of a single copy of an A subunit (32,000 daltons) that is linked to five copies of B subunits (7790 daltons).[163] The B subunits bind to a glycolipid cell receptor, globotriaosylceramide, followed by internalization. The A subunit cleaves an adenine residue from the eukaryotic 28S ribosomal subunit. The resulting block in elongation factor 1–dependent binding of aminoacyl tRNA to the ribosome causes cell death through inhibition of protein synthesis.[163] Shiga toxin once was considered to be a neurotoxin because its administration to mice or rabbits caused paralysis and death[38, 46, 93]; it now is thought to target primarily the vascular endothelium. It causes fluid accumulation in rabbit ileal loops,[66, 109] probably related to reduced fluid uptake by damaged villus cells.

The severity of *S. dysenteriae* serotype 1 infection relative to other *Shigella* serotypes is thought to be caused by production of Shiga toxin. Enterohemorrhagic *E. coli* serotypes, such as *E. coli* O157:H7, produce an identical (Shiga toxin 1) or similar (Shiga toxin 2) toxin and, like *S. dysenteriae* serotype 1, cause bloody diarrhea and hemolytic-uremic syndrome. Enteroinvasive *E. coli* serotypes do not produce these toxins.[52] *Shigella* serotypes other than *S. dysenteriae* serotype 1 produce little or no Shiga toxin, although other exotoxins are made.[24]

S. flexneri 2a strains make an enterotoxin referred to as ShET1. All *S. flexneri* 2a strains produce this enterotoxin, whereas only 3.3 percent of other *Shigella* serotypes and no enteroinvasive *E. coli* serotypes possess the gene for this toxin.[160] Genes of an additional toxin, designated *Shigella* enterotoxin, or Sen, have been found in 75 percent of enteroinvasive *E. coli* serotypes and 83 percent of *Shigella* strains.[151] These enterotoxins may be the cause of the watery diarrhea often seen early in the course of shigellosis.

IMMUNE RESPONSE

Serum IgG, IgM, and IgA responses occur to both the lipopolysaccharide and invasion plasmid antigens of shigellae.[162] Secretory IgA specific to both of these sets of antigens occurs in both human milk and feces.[51] Many investigators consider that protection is primarily serotype specific. The level of IgG antibodies to lipopolysaccharide present in an individual before infection appears to determine whether symptomatic shigellosis develops.[55] No clear proof currently exists about the role of antibodies to the invasion plasmid virulence proteins or to the toxins. Cell-mediated immunity against shigellae may also play a role in resolution of infection. Production of NK cell–mediated interferon-γ may be essential to defense from shigella.[218] Antibody-dependent cellular cytotoxicity against shigellae has been demonstrated.

The levels of cytokines tumor necrosis factor (TNF)-α, IL-1β, IL-1RA, IL-6, IL-8, and granulocyte-monocyte colony-stimulating factor (GM-CSF) in stool correlate with the severity of shigellosis. In contrast to other cytokines, interferon-γ and its receptor[179] are depressed early and rise during recovery. Fecal concentrations of TNF-α, IL-1β, IL-1RA, IL-6, IL-8, and GM-CSF are significantly higher in patients with *S. dysenteriae* serotype 1 than in those with *S. flexneri* infection.[182] Elevated TNF-α and IL-6 levels in stool and serum have been associated with complications during infection with *S. dysenteriae* serotype 1.[86] Infiltration of polymorphonuclear leukocytes and lymphocytes into the intestine is controlled by these cytokines. Epithelial cell production of IL-8[192] and a low IL-1RA/IL-1 ratio[12] are responsible for the severe inflammation. T lymphocytes with both suppressor-cytotoxic and helper-inducer phenotypes are recruited into the epithelium and lamina propria during infection with *Shigella*, related in part to the induction of HLA-DR expression in the rectal mucosa.[181] Peripheral blood lymphocytes of infected individuals respond to shigella antigens in vitro with production of interferon-γ and IL-10.[191]

Pathology

The main morphologic changes of shigellosis (superficial ulcerations, focal hemorrhages, mucosal edema, erythema, and friability) occur in the colon where the organisms invade.[98, 204] The rectosigmoid and distal segments of the colon typically are involved more severely than is the proximal colon. The epithelial cell damage may cause development of a pseudomembrane composed of thick, fibropurulent exudate tightly adherent to the necrotic ulcerated colonic mucosa. Pseudopolyposis also has been reported.[43] On microscopic examination, damage to epithelial cells, ulcerations, goblet cell depletion, and intense polymorphonuclear and mononuclear infiltration with crypt abscesses occur. Rectal mucosa shows increased numbers of $CD8^+$ and $\gamma\delta^+$ T cells.[95] Vessels in the lamina propria are congested or thrombosed. Perforation of the colon usually does not occur as part of the colitis.[22] Histologic changes in general are more severe and persistent[96] with *S. dysenteriae* than with *S. flexneri*.[9] Evidence of inflammation and proinflammatory cytokines persists for at least a month after clinical resolution.[180]

Clinical Manifestations

The incubation period may be as short as 12 hours or as long as a few days (if a low number of organisms are ingested). Onset of high fever, toxicity, and crampy abdominal pain is sudden. During the first 48 hours, high-volume watery diarrhea may occur (small-bowel phase of disease); subsequently, small-volume, bloody, and mucous diarrhea develops in association with urgency and tenesmus (large-bowel disease). In some cases, the watery diarrhea persists for several days, without subsequent development of dysentery. Other children present with bloody or mucous diarrhea.

Physical examination shows fever, signs of toxicity, tenderness over the lower abdominal quadrants, and hyperactive bowel sounds. Signs of dehydration may be present. Rectal examination reveals severe tenderness. Rectal prolapse may be present, particularly when diarrhea is associated with malnutrition.

The course without therapy typically lasts 7 to 10 days. Protein-losing enteropathy occurs during shigellosis; this enteropathy is severe with *S. dysenteriae* serotype 1.[31] In addition, anorexia related to fever and abdominal pain further contributes to malnutrition; anorexia is a particular problem in *S. dysenteriae* type 1 infection.[178] These facts may explain partly the hypoproteinemia and adverse effect on growth of severe shigellosis. Malnutrition is associated with a more severe course of shigellosis. Fever may not develop, even when severe dysentery is present. Chronic infection may last for months, despite appropriate antibiotic therapy. It may cause further deterioration of the nutritional status, which together with other complications (such as ileus, bacteremia, and pneumonia) is associated with overall increased mortality from shigellosis.

Although the organism usually is excreted for only a few days or weeks (range, 1 to 30 days), carriage for many months is well documented.[53, 124] Although the illness usually is acute, a chronic carrier state can occur in the malnourished individual. Surprisingly, asymptomatic infection of toddlers living in an endemic area is common; for example, most *Shigella* infections in Mexican children who were cultured each week from birth were not associated with illness.[80]

EXTRAINTESTINAL MANIFESTATIONS AND COMPLICATIONS

Seizures have been reported in 10 to 45 percent of hospitalized children with culture-proven shigellosis.[17, 20, 23, 57, 70] In outpatient settings, the frequency of seizures is very low. Those children who develop neurologic complaints may have lethargy, severe headache, disorientation, hallucinations, or self-limited convulsions lasting less than 15 minutes.[15, 18, 20, 147] Seizures are most likely to occur in the very young, those with a high peak body temperature, and those with a family history of convulsive disorders.[17, 115] Seizures can be focal, although usually they are generalized. When symptoms related to the nervous system occur, they are likely to do so early in the illness, often even preceding development of diarrhea. Death rarely has been described[91]; most children recover completely with no residual neurologic deficits.[18] In contrast, in Bangladesh, where seizures in shigellosis typically are associated with factors known to alter consciousness (e.g., hypoglycemia, hyponatremia, fever), mortality rates are high.[112] The pathogenesis of neurologic signs and symptoms during episodes of shigellosis is unclear. Hypoglycemia and electrolyte abnormalities are found in a few patients.[18] Direct invasion of the central nervous system during *Shigella* bacteremia is a very rare occurrence.[220] Simple febrile seizures might explain convulsions in a few children with dysentery, but some children who have seizures during episodes of shigellosis do not experience seizures during other febrile infections and are outside the age range usually associated with febrile seizures.[18] Shiga toxin formerly was thought to cause the neurologic symptoms because it was considered to be a neurotoxin. However, data now clearly demonstrate that Shiga toxin is not responsible.[16]

Severe toxic encephalopathy has been described. This syndrome (ekiri), as originally described in Japan, was characterized by dysentery with hyperpyrexia, convulsions, sensory disturbances, and rapid progression to death.[186] The children died with cerebral edema early in the course of disease (6 to 48 hours after onset). Mild hyponatremia has been a common finding.[77] The children with ekiri did not have sepsis, disseminated intravascular coagulation, hemolytic-uremic syndrome, or severe dehydration. This toxic encephalopathy is a rare event. Whether this syndrome is part of a continuum of central nervous system dysfunctions with seizures and other encephalopathic symptoms or has a completely different pathogenesis is not clear.

Hemolytic-uremic syndrome (microangiopathic hemolytic anemia, thrombocytopenia, and acute renal failure) or isolated hemolysis has been reported, mainly after infections with *S. dysenteriae* serotype 1 and rarely after infection with *S. flexneri*.[176] Vascular endothelial cell damage by Shiga toxin is considered to be the initial event, although endotoxin absorbed from the gut also may play a role.[113]

Ileus that progresses to toxic megacolon with distended loops and eventual intestinal perforation[21] is seen mainly with *S. dysenteriae* serotype 1 infection.

Septicemia in shigellosis is a rare occurrence, except in malnourished children, young infants, and those with *S. dysenteriae* serotype 1 infections.[85, 137, 199] The mortality rate is at least twice as high in dysentery-associated sepsis as in shigellosis uncomplicated by bacteremia. The serogroup-related mortality risk in shigellemia has been reported to be 85 percent for *S. dysenteriae,* 43 percent for *S. flexneri,* and 25 percent for *S. sonnei* infection; bacteremia rarely is reported for *S. boydii*.[135] In Bangladesh, *Shigella* bacteremia was found in 4 percent of patients.[209] When bacteremia occurs with dysentery, it is as likely to be caused by other enteric bacteria as by the *Shigella* itself. The occurrence of *Klebsiella, E. coli,* and other enteric pathogens in blood cultures of children with shigellosis presumably reflects the loss of the barrier function of the intestinal mucosa that occurs during severe colitis.[153] *Shigella* bacteremia may be complicated by disseminated intravascular coagulation and multiorgan failure. Bronchopneumonia may develop in septicemic children,[5] but its pathogenesis is unclear. Children who die with shigellosis often have pneumonia at autopsy.[43]

Other extraintestinal infections rarely are caused by *Shigella*. Vaginitis with a bloody discharge (sometimes lasting for months in the absence of specific therapy) may occur, usually without concurrent or recent diarrhea.[56, 149] *Shigella* cystitis, not always associated with diarrhea, has been described, usually in girls.[23] Conjunctivitis, keratitis, corneal ulcers, and iritis are other uncommon manifestations of shigellosis that usually are assumed to occur after autoinoculation.[23, 212] Reactive arthritis or Reiter syndrome (arthritis, urethritis, conjunctivitis) may develop after episodes of shigellosis,[44] especially in adults who are HLA-B27 positive; reactive arthritis is an uncommon occurrence in children. Hepatitis with mildly abnormal liver function test results has been described.[207] Myocarditis manifested clinically by hypotension despite fluid replacement, arrhythmia, heart block, or decreased voltage on electrocardiography and pathologically by interstitial lymphocytic infiltrates and focal necrosis has been described.[184]

SHIGELLOSIS IN THE NEONATAL PERIOD

Bacillary dysentery is a rare occurrence in newborns.[25, 63, 68, 84, 120] More than one half of the reported neonatal cases occurred during the first 3 days of life, consistent with fecal-oral transmission during delivery,[79, 157] usually from a symptomatic mother. Although the neonate with shigellosis usually has only low-grade fever with diarrhea of variable severity,[6, 117, 144] both septicemia[122, 177] and chronic diarrhea are more common occurrences than in older children. Intestinal perforation has been reported in neonatal shigellosis.[206] Diarrhea more often is nonbloody in infants; fever also occurs less commonly than in older children.[94] Data on age-related mortality caused by shigellosis in developing countries suggest that the mortality rate of the neonate is more than twice as high as that of older children.

SHIGELLOSIS IN ACQUIRED IMMUNODEFICIENCY SYNDROME

Unlike the usual short self-limited course of shigellosis, *Shigella* infection in patients also infected with human immunodeficiency virus may be chronic and relapsing, despite appropriate antibiotic treatment,[202] or it may be complicated by bacteremia.[26]

Laboratory Findings

The fecal leukocyte examination is helpful in evaluating the patient with febrile diarrhea. Direct microscopic examination of fecal mucus stained with methylene blue shows many polymorphonuclear leukocytes in patients with colitis, including most patients with shigellosis.[88] The blood leukocyte count in patients with shigellosis often is within normal limits, although leukopenia or leukocytosis may occur.[13] The differential of the blood leukocyte count typically shows an increased percentage of band forms (a shift to the left). Approximately one third of children with shigellosis have more bands than segmented neutrophils in their peripheral blood smear. A leukemoid reaction, with a peripheral leukocyte count greater than 50,000/mm^3, has been reported, mainly with infections due to *S. dysenteriae* serotype 1.[42] A leukemoid reaction has been reported in as many as 10 percent of the patients infected with the Shiga bacillus. When examination of cerebrospinal fluid is performed in children with neurologic symptoms, normal results usually are obtained, although some patients have a mild lymphocytic pleocytosis. Likewise, when electroencephalography is performed, the results usually are within normal limits.[18]

Diagnosis

Bacillary dysentery usually is suspected in children who present with bloody diarrhea, high fever, and generalized toxicity. However, approximately one half of the children do not develop bloody diarrhea during the course of their disease. This fact is especially relevant in developed countries, where most of the infections are caused by *S. sonnei*.

Thus, the presence of only watery diarrhea does not exclude the possibility of shigellosis in an ill patient with high fever.

ISOLATION TECHNIQUES

Proof of the diagnosis of suspected bacillary dysentery often is problematic. Definite diagnosis of *Shigella* infection depends on isolation of the organism from stool specimens or rectal swabs. However, the bacteria may not survive in fecal specimens during transit; furthermore, special selective media are necessary for isolation. Recovery of shigellae is easier early in the course of the disease than later because the number of viable organisms in stools decreases significantly during late stages of the disease. Even in adult volunteer studies, when appropriate stool cultures were obtained daily, cultures still failed to isolate shigellae in approximately 20 percent of those who had ingested the organism and developed diarrhea.

Several measures increase the likelihood of isolating the *Shigella*. Specimens should be processed without delay. If a specimen cannot be processed immediately, a transport medium, such as buffered glycerol saline, should be used. More than one stool culture or rectal swab should be obtained and inoculated promptly onto at least two different culture media. Specimens should be plated lightly onto MacConkey, xylose-lysine-deoxycholate, or eosin–methylene blue agar, whereas a heavier plating is necessary for the more inhibitory *Shigella-Salmonella* medium.[146, 211] After overnight incubation at 37° C, lactose-negative colonies are transferred to triple sugar iron and lysine iron agar slants and incubated again overnight. Slants showing characteristic reactions of alkaline red slants, acid butt, and production of gas are tested biochemically for presumptive identification and then serologically for definitive identification. Because many of the O antigens of *Shigella* and those of *E. coli* have antigenic similarities, serologic techniques cannot be used as the sole determinant in identifying *Shigella* strains.

OTHER DIAGNOSTIC METHODS

Because presumptive identification of *Shigella* takes at least 48 hours and definite identification about 72 hours, attempts to develop rapid diagnostic methods are being made, especially because institution of early treatment is important in shigellosis. Latex agglutination assays that detect *Shigella* antigens now are available commercially. They usually are employed for identification of colonies suspected of being shigellae or for testing enrichment broth cultures.[142] The assays detect the four *Shigella* serogroups and are based on color reactions. These assays are not used for direct identification of shigellae in stool specimens.

Identification of shigellae by specific DNA probes with use of either restriction fragments or synthetic oligonucleotides[158] based on detecting virulence genes located on the 120- to 140-megadalton plasmid has been described. Because the invasion plasmids of shigellae, like other plasmids, may be lost spontaneously, a DNA probe derived from *S. flexneri ipaH* gene, a multicopy element that is found both on the chromosome and on the invasion plasmid of shigellae, has been developed and found to be more sensitive than are probes used previously.[215] The use of these probes is not practical for clinical settings. Use of the polymerase chain reaction (PCR) in vitro amplification of nucleic acids, to detect shigellae directly from stool specimens, has been reported.[73] PCR can detect as few as 10 colony-forming units of *S. flexneri* in stool specimens, whereas the sensitivities of DNA probe hybridization (with no amplification) and standard biochemical methods are 10^3 and 10^6 colony-forming units, respectively. PCR for *ipaH* genes is more sensitive than is culture; 28 percent of patients with dysentery with a positive PCR assay result are culture negative.[74, 99]

Serologic studies are not helpful in establishing the diagnosis of shigellosis in the individual patient; humoral antibodies develop after clinical recovery. Serologic studies, however, may be helpful in epidemiologic studies to define spread of the disease in a population.[23]

Sigmoidoscopy and barium enema study are not necessary unless they are indicated to rule out other conditions. When these procedures are performed in patients with a possibility of having shigellosis, caution is necessary because of the diffuse acute colitis.

Differential Diagnosis

Colitis of any etiology manifesting with acute-onset bloody diarrhea with fever and abdominal cramps can mimic shigellosis. Etiologic agents to be considered include *Campylobacter* spp., *Salmonella* spp., *Clostridium difficile, Yersinia enterocolitica, Shigella* spp., *Vibrio parahaemolyticus,* enteroinvasive *E. coli,* enterohemorrhagic *E. coli* (such as serotype O157:H7), *Balantidium coli,* and *Entamoeba histolytica.* The initial presentation of inflammatory bowel disease can mimic shigellosis.

Etiologic diagnosis of the acute colitis syndrome on the basis of clinical presentation is difficult to make, although some data suggest a specific causative agent. In developed countries, *Campylobacter* is the most common cause of acute infectious colitis. Shigellosis should be suspected when evidence exists of person-to-person spread and when convulsions or other neurologic symptoms develop. In the first few months of life, *Salmonella* is the most common infectious cause of bloody diarrhea and *Shigella* is very rare. A history of previous antibiotic treatment is suggestive of diarrhea related to *C. difficile,* and previous consumption of seafood suggests *V. parahaemolyticus*. *Yersinia* infections are found mainly in the cooler regions of Europe and North America; the disease may mimic acute appendicitis because of the right lower quadrant pain associated with mesenteric lymphadenitis. Enterohemorrhagic *E. coli* infection often causes bloody diarrhea with little or no fever, in contrast to shigellosis, in which high fever is a typical event. Negative stool cultures for the mentioned bacterial pathogens may suggest infection by enteroinvasive *E. coli.* Amebiasis causes a colitis similar to that caused by *Shigella,*[205] although it is of slower onset, with a lower degree of fever; the findings on fecal leukocyte examination are negative. The involvement of the colon with amebiasis is less diffuse than in shigellosis; areas of normal mucosa are found between ulcerations. A prolonged course with negative cultures should raise concern about the possible presence of either ulcerative colitis or Crohn disease. When watery diarrhea is present, the list of possible etiologic agents is even longer, although many of the agents causing watery diarrhea are associated with little or no fever and thus are not confused with those causing shigellosis. Diagnosis usually cannot be made by clinical presentation alone and depends on culture results or other specific laboratory assays.

Treatment

FLUID ADMINISTRATION

Dehydration is less a problem with shigellosis than with rotavirus or toxigenic *E. coli* infection. However, some children with shigellosis, particularly young infants, have dehydration during the course of the disease. The high-volume watery diarrhea seen early in the course of the disease may cause excess losses of fluids and electrolytes; likewise, in patients with severe colitis, the systemic toxicity and vomiting may cause anorexia that interferes with intake of fluid.

Assessment of the hydration status of the patient on admission is mandatory, with early institution of appropriate fluid and electrolyte therapy needed. The World Health Organization's oral rehydration therapy with glucose-electrolyte solutions is usually effective.[150] This solution contains 90 mEq/L of sodium, 20 mEq/L of potassium, 80 mEq/L of chloride, 30 mEq/L of bicarbonate or citrate, and 20 g/L of glucose. Oral rehydration therapy should be given with additional water containing no electrolytes to prevent hypernatremia; this therapy is particularly important in children too young to express their need for additional free water. In infants, two parts of oral rehydration solution should be followed by one part of water without electrolytes. Administration of intravenous fluid therapy is necessary in children who are comatose, have an ileus, or are in shock when they are first seen. Early (12 to 24 hours after oral fluids are begun) reinstitution of breast milk or other food is mandatory.

ANTIBIOTIC THERAPY

Children who are suffering from dysentery always should be treated with antimicrobials. Antibiotic therapy for milder illness is controversial. Treatment with an agent to which the *Shigella* is susceptible results in rapid improvement. Shedding of the organisms in stools stops within 1 to 2 days, so that intrafamilial spread may be decreased. Although use of antibiotics may favor emergence of resistant organisms, most authorities recommend that antibiotics be started when shigellosis first is suspected clinically, before culture confirmation of the infection is obtained. Therapy should be stopped or changed on the basis of culture results (e.g., another pathogen or a resistant *Shigella* is isolated) and clinical response.

The choice of antimicrobial agent is complicated by the increasing frequency of plasmid-mediated antibiotic resistance.[65, 69, 190] Organisms resistant to ampicillin, trimethoprim-sulfamethoxazole, tetracycline, and chloramphenicol have been reported from the Middle East,[1, 7, 11, 19, 66, 87, 104, 221] Africa,[1, 35, 45, 106, 136, 152] South America,[126, 151, 159, 175] Europe,[24, 47, 100, 107, 116, 133, 216] Eurasia,[22, 167, 222] Asia,[3, 8, 33, 110, 125, 127, 129, 132] and the South Pacific. Multiresistant strains also are found commonly in some parts of the United States. Multiresistant *Shigella* spp. are particularly likely to emerge in individuals who are exposed to multiple antibiotics[210] (e.g., patients with acquired immunodeficiency syndrome) and those who recently have traveled to areas with known resistance. Likewise, children in daycare centers are at risk of acquiring resistant organisms because the frequent use of antibiotics for otitis media may favor selection and emergence of resistant enteric organisms and because crowding and poor hygiene facilitate transmission.[37]

In general, shigellae are susceptible in vitro to ceftriaxone, cefotaxime, cefixime, nalidixic acid, and quinolones both in the United States and elsewhere. However, prevalent serotypes and resistance patterns vary from year to year in a given locale. Typically, rates of resistance are related to the severity of disease caused by a given serotype. The more likely an organism is to cause severe disease, the more likely that resistant strains will emerge. Thus, *S. dysenteriae* serotype 1 is more likely to be multiply resistant than is *S. flexneri; S. flexneri* is more likely to be resistant than is *S. sonnei*. Thus, *S. dysenteriae* serotype 1 often is resistant even to drugs still effective against other shigellae. For example, in Africa[35, 106] and Asia,[27, 29, 50, 132, 148] Shiga bacilli resistant to nalidixic acid and ciprofloxacin have been reported. Nalidixic acid–resistant *S. flexneri* also have been recognized occasionally.[49] Thus, local resistance patterns, history of travel to an area of frequent resistance,[210] and severity of illness should determine treatment.

Given the frequent occurrence of resistant organisms, optimal empirical therapy in children with dysentery should be a third-generation cephalosporin or nalidixic acid. When susceptibility data are known, a third-generation cephalosporin (ceftriaxone, 50 mg/kg/day parenterally as one daily dose for 5 days [maximum, 1.5 g/dose]; cefixime, 8 mg/kg/day orally as one daily dose for 5 days [maximum, 400 mg/day]), trimethoprim-sulfamethoxazole (10/50 mg/kg/day given orally or parenterally divided every 12 hours for 5 days [maximum, 160/600]), or nalidixic acid (55 mg/kg/day given orally divided every 6 hours for 5 days) may be used in children; although less well studied, ampicillin-sulbactam and pivmecillinam also have been shown to be effective in children. An oral fluoroquinolone (ciprofloxacin, norfloxacin) appears to be optimal for adults.[14, 32, 90, 121, 134, 173, 188] Limited data suggest that not all of these agents are equally effective, even when in vitro data suggest susceptibility. In children, oral cefixime appears to be superior to ampicillin-sulbactam.[90] Adults do not respond well to usual doses of cefixime.[189] Norfloxacin is clinically superior to nalidixic acid in both children and adults with shigellosis.[32, 183] Ampicillin, tetracycline, and chloramphenicol are used infrequently now for shigellosis.

Use of the quinolones has been a problem in children. Nalidixic acid therapy is effective treatment,[187] although plasmid-mediated resistance to nalidixic acid of *S. dysenteriae* serotype 1 strains in Bangladesh[27, 29, 148] has emerged and spread rapidly. Various other quinolones have been effective in adult patients with shigellosis, but they are not approved for use in children younger than 17 years of age because of potential damage to the cartilage of epiphyseal plates.[183] However, nalidixic acid does not cause arthropathy or limit growth when it is used for a short time.[161] As resistance continues to increase, situations are likely to occur in which a quinolone is the only option for treatment of a child with severe shigellosis. Limited data for children suggest that norfloxacin at a dose of 10 to 15 mg/kg/day or ciprofloxacin at a dose of 10 mg/kg every 12 hours (maximum, 500 mg/dose) for 5 days is effective therapy.[130, 188] In adults, short-course therapy (1 or 2 days) with ciprofloxacin has been effective for treatment of infections caused by *Shigella* spp. other than *S. dysenteriae,* for which a 10-dose, 5-day regimen is superior.[30]

Because the patterns of antibiotic resistance of shigellae change, susceptibility testing should be performed on all clinical isolates, and the treatment should be changed accordingly. The recommended duration of antibiotic therapy for shigellosis usually is 5 days. However, studies in adults and children have shown that short-course treatment is nearly as effective as are multiple doses in terms of symptomatic improvement,[76, 134] although eradication of the organism from stools is less likely to occur with a single-dose regimen.[101] Because a major goal of antibiotic therapy is to reduce person-to-person transmission, multiple doses are preferred.

After initiation of therapy, a resistant organism can be suspected in the event of persistence of fever, grossly bloody stools, or unchanged frequency of stools by day 3 of therapy.[97] Persistent presence of large numbers of fecal leukocytes (>50 per high-power field) and erythrocytes (>5 per high-power field) at day 5 also suggests resistance.

These findings are important because both morbidity and mortality rates are higher when the organism is not susceptible to the initial drug of choice.[104] Protein-losing enteropathy is a more likely occurrence with resistant *Shigella* if an inadequate agent has been used.[31]

ADJUNCTIVE THERAPY

As with other forms of infectious colitis, antimotility agents should be avoided. Antimotility drugs, such as diphenoxylate (Lomotil), prolong the duration of fever, diarrhea, and excretion of the organism.[60] Intestinal motility and the constant fluid flow have been speculated as actually being important host defense factors for rapid clearing of the organism and recovery from the infection.

A high-protein diet given during convalescence may be important, particularly in settings in which malnutrition, growth retardation, and hypoproteinemia are major complications of shigellosis.[102, 103, 139] Vitamin A (200,000 IU) has been found to speed resolution of illness in a population in which vitamin A deficiency is a common occurrence.[92]

Prognosis

Most patients recover eventually with or without specific antimicrobial therapy, although illness may be prolonged and severe if it is not treated.[41] The mortality rate in developed countries is less than 1 percent, and life-threatening complications are rare occurrences. With appropriate antibiotic therapy, defervescence usually occurs within 24 hours, and the diarrhea decreases dramatically in 2 or 3 days. If left untreated, the disease usually lasts a week or more. In developing countries, childhood shigellosis is associated with significant morbidity and mortality (10% to 30%),[28] particularly if it is caused by *S. dysenteriae* serotype 1. Children with malnutrition are particularly likely to have a complicated course.[48] Shigellosis in malnourished children often causes a vicious circle of further impaired nutrition, and repeated infections that may be associated with impaired growth. Young infants and children whose course is complicated by bacteremia also are at increased risk of dying.[164]

Prevention

In developed countries where person-to-person transmission of shigellae is the major mode of infection, personal hygiene measures are most important.[111] Special attention should be given in daycare centers, which sometimes play a central role in community-wide outbreaks of shigellosis.[143] The close contact among children too young to control their excretions renders this setting ideal for fecal-oral spread of the organism. Moreover, children attending daycare centers frequently transmit infection to their families. Handwashing after defecation and before meals is important and helpful in preventing spread.[111] Daycare personnel who prepare food should avoid diaper-changing duties. Sick children should be excluded from the daycare center or cohorted, and mothers should be educated as to the possibility of being infected by their children and use of the necessary precautions. Proper cooking of potentially infected food, appropriate refrigeration, and exclusion of persons with diarrhea from handling food are important precautions. Education of staff members in proper hygiene is essential to infection control.[170]

Patients with diarrhea in institutional and hospital settings should be isolated for prevention of outbreaks. Aggressive investigation and early initiation of appropriate antibiotic therapy in cases of bacillary dysentery are important measures in reducing excretion of virulent shigellae and stopping spread of the disease. Use of antibiotics for prophylaxis is not recommended, however.

In developing countries, a safe water supply and appropriate sanitation systems are important measures for reducing the risk of shigellosis. Chlorination of drinking water is important. Water stored in vessels that permit hand dipping has been defined as a risk factor.[213] Food prepared by street vendors also has been recognized as a risk factor. Prolonged breast feeding is the best practical strategy for prevention of shigellosis (and most other enteric infections) in infants in most of the developing world.[4, 54, 138] Educational efforts to promote breast feeding in these areas are key to child survival. Human milk contains specific secretory IgA antibodies against both *Shigella* lipopolysaccharides and virulence plasmid–coded antigens.[51] Lactoferrin and other nonspecific (nonantibody) factors in human milk, the effect of human milk on the type of intestinal flora, and the supply of an uncontaminated food source all may contribute to the protective effect of breast feeding against diarrheal disease.

Epidemiologic data suggest that prior infection with shigellae confers resistance to subsequent illness caused by organisms of the same serotype. Serotype-specific (lipopolysaccharide-based) vaccines have been made.[71, 72] Although early studies showed that immunization by the parenteral route with killed vaccines was not effective, interest in this approach continues. Several oral, live organism–based *Shigella* vaccines have been studied. Avirulent mutants of *S. flexneri* that lack the ability to invade the intestinal mucosa are safe and effective in monkeys. However, multiple doses of large numbers of organisms were required to protect humans. Attenuated vaccines prepared from streptomycin-dependent mutant strains were effective but somewhat unstable.[140] Genetically attenuated *S. flexneri* strains conferred protection but caused diarrhea when fed to some volunteers. No effective, licensed vaccine against shigellosis is available.[128]

REFERENCES

1. Adeleye, I. A.: Conjugal transferability of multiple antibiotic resistance in three genera of Enterobacteriaceae in Nigeria. J. Diarrhoeal Dis. Res. *10*:93–96, 1992.
2. Admoni, O., Yagupsky, P., Golan, A., et al.: Epidemiological, clinical and microbiological features of shigellosis among hospitalized children in northern Israel. Scand. J. Infect. Dis. *27*:139–144, 1995.
3. Agarwal, S. K., Tewari, M., and Banerjee, G.: A study on transferable R-plasmids among *Shigella* species at Lucknow. J. Commun. Dis. *29*:351–354, 1997.
4. Ahmed, F., Clemens, J. D., Rao, M. R., et al.: Community-based evaluation of the effect of breast feeding on the risk of microbiologically confirmed or clinically presumptive shigellosis in Bangladeshi children. Pediatrics *90*:406–411, 1992.
5. Alam, A. N., Chowdhurg, A. A. K. M., Kabir, I. A. K. M., et al.: Association of pneumonia with under-nutrition and shigellosis. Indian Pediatr. *21*:609–613, 1984.
6. Aldrich, J. A., Flowers, R. P., and Hall, F. K.: *S. sonnei* septicemia in a neonate: A case report. J. Am. Osteopath. Assoc. *79*:93–98, 1979.
7. al-Eissa, Y., al-Zamil, F., al-Kharashi, M., et al.: The relative importance of *Shigella* in the aetiology of childhood gastroenteritis in Saudi Arabia. Scand. J. Infect. Dis. *24*:347–351, 1992.
8. Aleksic, S., Katz, A., Aleksic, V., et al.: Antibiotic resistance of *Shigella* strains isolated in the Federal Republic of Germany 1989–1990. Int. J. Med. Microbiol. Virol. Parasitol. Infect. Dis. *279*:484–493, 1993.
9. Anand, B. S., Malhotra, V., Bhattacharya, S. K., et al.: Rectal histology in acute bacillary dysentery. Gastroenterology *90*:654–660, 1986.
10. Ansaruzzaman, M., Kibriya, A. K. M. G., Rahman, A., et al.: Detection of provisional serovars of *S. dysenteriae* and designation as *S. dysenteriae* serotypes 14 and 15. J. Clin. Microbiol. *33*:1423–1425, 1995.
11. Araj, G. F., Uwaydah, M. M., and Alami, S. Y.: Antimicrobial susceptibility patterns of bacterial isolates at the American University Medical Center in Lebanon. Diagn. Microbiol. Infect. Dis. *20*:151–158, 1994.

12. Arondel, J., Singer, M., Matsukawa, A., et al.: Increased interleukin-1 (IL-1) and imbalance between IL-1 and IL-1 receptor antagonist during acute inflammation in experimental shigellosis. Infect. Immun. *67*:6056–6066, 1999.
13. Ashkenazi, S., Amir, J., Dinari, T., et al.: The differential leukocyte count in acute gastroenteritis: An aid to early diagnosis. Clin. Pediatr. *22*:356–358, 1983.
14. Ashkenazi, S., Amir, J., Waisman, Y., et al.: A randomized double-blind study comparing cefixime and TMP/SMX in the treatment of childhood shigellosis. J. Pediatr. *123*:817–821, 1993.
15. Ashkenazi, S., Bellah, G., and Cleary, T. G.: Hallucinations as an initial manifestation of childhood shigellosis. J. Pediatr. *114*:95–97, 1989.
16. Ashkenazi, S., Cleary, K. R., Pickering, L. K., et al.: The association of Shiga toxin and other cytotoxins with the neurologic manifestations of shigellosis. J. Infect. Dis. *161*:961–965, 1990.
17. Ashkenazi, S., Dinari, G., Weitz, R., et al.: Convulsions in shigellosis: Evaluation of possible risk factors. Am. J. Dis. Child. *137*:985–987, 1983.
18. Ashkenazi, S., Dinari, G., Zevulunov, A., et al.: Convulsions in childhood shigellosis: Clinical and laboratory features in 153 children. Am. J. Dis. Child. *141*:208–210, 1987.
19. Ashkenazi, S., May-Zahav, M., Sulkes, J., et al.: Increasing antimicrobial resistance of *Shigella* isolates in Israel during the period 1984 to 1992. Antimicrob. Agents Chemother. *39*:819–823, 1995.
20. Avital, A., Maayan, C., and Goitein, K. J.: Incidence of convulsions and encephalopathy in childhood *Shigella* infections. Clin. Pediatr. *21*:645–648, 1982.
21. Aysev, A. D., and Guriz, H.: Drug resistance of *Shigella* strains isolated in Ankara, Turkey, 1993–1996. Scand. J. Infect. Dis. *30*:351–353, 1998.
22. Azad, M. A., Islam, M., and Butler, T.: Colonic perforation of *S. dysenteriae* 1 infection. Pediatr. Infect. Dis. *5*:103–104, 1986.
23. Barrett-Connor, E., and Connor, J. D.: Extraintestinal manifestations of shigellosis. Am. J. Gastroenterol. *53*:234–245, 1970.
24. Bartlett, A. V., III, Prado, D., Cleary, T. G., et al.: Production of Shiga toxin and other cytotoxins by serogroups of *Shigella*. J. Infect. Dis. *154*:996–1002, 1986.
25. Barton, L. L., and Pickering, L. K.: Shigellosis in the first week of life. Pediatrics *52*:437–438, 1973.
26. Baskin, D. H., Lax, J. D., and Barenberg, D.: *Shigella* bacteremia in patients with the acquired immunodeficiency syndrome. Am. J. Gastroenterol. *82*:338–341, 1986.
27. Bennish, M., Eusof, A., and Kay, B.: Multiresistant *Shigella* infections in Bangladesh. Lancet *2*:441, 1985.
28. Bennish, M. L., Harris, J. R., Wojtyniak, B. J., et al.: Death in shigellosis: Incidence and risk factors in hospitalized patients. J. Infect. Dis. *161*:500–506, 1990.
29. Bennish, M. L., Salam, M. A., Hossain, M. A., et al.: Antimicrobial resistance of *Shigella* isolates in Bangladesh, 1983–1990: Increasing frequency of strains multiply resistant to ampicillin, trimethoprim-sulfamethoxazole, and nalidixic acid. Clin. Infect. Dis. *14*:1055–1060, 1992.
30. Bennish, M. L., Salam, M. A., Khan, W. A., et al.: Treatment of shigellosis. III. Comparison of one- or two-dose ciprofloxacin with standard 5-day therapy. Ann. Intern. Med. *117*:727–734, 1992.
31. Bennish, M. L., Salam, M. A., and Wahed, M. A.: Enteric protein loss during shigellosis. Am. J. Gastroenterol. *88*:53–57, 1993.
32. Bhattacharya, K., Bhattacharya, M. K., Dutta, D., et al.: Double-blind, randomized clinical trial for safety and efficacy of norfloxacin for shigellosis in children. Acta Paediatr. *86*:319–320, 1997.
33. Bhattacharya, M. K., Bhattacharya, S. K., Paul, M., et al.: Shigellosis in Calcutta during 1990–1992: Antibiotic susceptibility pattern and clinical features. J. Diarrhoeal Dis. Res. *12*:121–124, 1994.
34. Boehme, C., Rodriguez, G., Illesca, V., et al.: Shigellosis in children of the IX region of Chile: Clinical and epidemiologic aspects and antibiotic sensitivity. Rev. Med. Chile *120*:1261–1266, 1992.
35. Bogaerts, J., Verhaegen, J., Munyabikali, J. P., et al.: Antimicrobial resistance and serotypes of *Shigella* isolates in Kigali, Rwanda (1983 to 1993): Increasing frequency of multiple resistance. Diagn. Microbiol. Infect. Dis. *28*:165–171, 1997.
36. Bratoeva, M. P., John, J. F., and Barg, N. L.: Molecular epidemiology of trimethoprim-resistant *Shigella boydii* serotype 2 strains from Bulgaria. J. Clin. Microbiol. *30*:1428–1431, 1992.
37. Brian, M. J., Van, R., Townsend, I., et al.: Evaluation of the molecular epidemiology of an outbreak of multiply resistant *Shigella sonnei* in a day-care center by using pulsed-field gel electrophoresis and plasmid DNA analysis. J. Clin. Microbiol. *31*:2152–1256, 1993.
38. Bridgwater, F. A. J., Morgan, R. S., Rowson, K. E. K., et al.: The neurotoxin of *Shigella shigae:* Morphological and functional lesions produced in the central nervous system of rabbits. Br. J. Exp. Pathol. *36*:447, 1955.
39. Brown, J. E., Griffin, D. E., Rothman, S. W., et al.: Purification and biological characterization of Shiga toxin from *Shigella dysenteriae* 1. Infect. Immun. *36*:996–1005, 1982.
40. Brown, J. E., Rothman, S. W., and Doctor, B. P.: Inhibition of protein synthesis in intact HeLa cells by *Shigella dysenteriae* 1 toxin. Infect. Immun. *29*:98–107, 1980.
41. Burry, V. F., Thurn, A. N., and Co, T. G.: Shigellosis: An analysis of 239 cases in a pediatric population. Mo. Med. *65*:671–674, 1968.
42. Butler, T. C., Islam, M. R., and Bardhan, P. K.: The leukemoid reaction in shigellosis. *In* Rahaman, M. M., Greenough, W. B., Novak, N. R., et al. (eds.): Shigellosis: A Continuing Global Problem. Bangladesh, International Centre for Diarrhoeal Disease Research, 1983, p. 154.
43. Butler, T., Dunn, D., Dahms, B., et al.: Causes of death and the histopathologic findings in fatal shigellosis. Pediatr. Infect. Dis. J. *8*:767–772, 1989.
44. Calin, A., and Fries, J. F.: An "experimental" epidemic of Reiter's syndrome revisited: Follow-up evidence on genetic and environmental factors. Ann. Intern. Med. *84*:564–566, 1976.
45. Casalino, M., Nicoletti, M., Salvia, A., et al.: Characterization of endemic *Shigella flexneri* strains in Somalia: Antimicrobial resistance, plasmid profiles, and serotype correlation. J. Clin. Microbiol. *32*:1179–1183, 1994.
46. Cavanagh, J. B., Howard, J. G., and Whitby, J. L.: The neurotoxin of *Shigella shigae:* A comparative study of the effects produced in various laboratory animals. Br. J. Exp. Pathol. *37*:272–276, 1956.
47. Cheasty, T., Skinner, J. A., Rowe, B., and Threlfall, E. J.: Increasing incidence of antibiotic resistance in shigellas from humans in England and Wales: Recommendations for therapy. Microb. Drug. Resist. *4*:57–60, 1998.
48. Chopra, M., Wilkinson, D., and Stirling, S.: Epidemic *Shigella dysentery* in children in northern KwaZulu-Natal. S. Afr. Med. J. *87*:48–51, 1997.
49. Chu, Y. W., Houang, E. T., Lyon, D. J., et al.: Antimicrobial resistance in *Shigella flexneri* and *Shigella sonnei* in Hong Kong, 1986 to 1995. Antimicrob. Agents. Chemother. *42*:440–443, 1998.
50. Chunder, N., Bhattacharya, S. K., Biswas, D., et al.: Isolation of a fluoroquinolone resistant *Shigella dysenteriae* 1 strain from Calcutta. Indian J. Med. Res. *106*:494–496, 1997.
51. Cleary, T. G., Winsor, D. K., Reich, D., et al.: Human milk immunoglobulin A antibodies to *Shigella* virulence determinants. Infect. Immun. *57*:1675–1679, 1989.
52. Cleary, T. G., and Murray, B. E.: Lack of Shiga-like cytotoxin production by enteroinvasive *E. coli*. J. Clin. Microbiol. *26*:2177–2179, 1988.
53. Clemens, D., Ellis, C. J., and Allan, R. N.: Persistent shigellosis. Gut *29*:1277–1278, 1988.
54. Clemens, J. S., Stanton, B., Stohl, B., et al.: Breast-feeding as a determinant of severity of shigellosis. Am. J. Epidemiol. *123*:710–720, 1986.
55. Cohen, D., Green, M. S., Block, C., et al.: Serum antibodies to lipopolysaccharide and natural immunity to shigellosis in an Israeli military population. J. Infect. Dis. *157*:1068–1071, 1988.
56. Davis, T. C.: Chronic vulvovaginitis in children due to *S. flexneri*. Pediatrics *56*:41–44, 1975.
57. Donald, W. D., Winkler, C. H., Jr., and Bargeron, L. M., Jr.: The occurrence of convulsions in children with *Shigella* gastroenteritis. J. Pediatr. *48*:323–327, 1956.
58. DuPont, H. L., Hornick, R. B., Dawkins, A. T., et al.: The response of man to virulent *Shigella flexneri* 2a. J. Infect. Dis. *119*:296–299, 1969.
59. DuPont, H. L., Hornick, R. B., Snyder, M. J., et al.: Immunity in shigellosis. II. Protection induced by oral live vaccine or primary infection. J. Infect. Dis. *125*:12–16, 1972.
60. DuPont, H. L., and Hornick, R. B.: Adverse effect of Lomotil therapy in shigellosis. J. A. M. A. *226*:1525–1528, 1973.
61. DuPont, H. L., Levine, M. M., Hornick, R. B., et al.: Inoculum size in shigellosis and implications for expected mode of transmission. J. Infect. Dis. *159*:1126–1128, 1989.
62. Eidlitz-Marcus, T., Cohen, Y. H., Nussinovitch, M., et al.: Comparative efficacy of two- and five-day courses of ceftriaxone for treatment of severe shigellosis in children. J. Pediatr. *123*:822–824, 1993.
63. Emanuel, B., and Sherman, J. O.: Shigellosis in a neonate. Clin. Pediatr. *14*:725–726, 1975.
64. Ewing, W. H.: Edwards and Ewing's Identification of Enterobacteriaceae. 4th ed. New York, Elsevier Science, 1986.
65. Farrar, W. E., Eidson, M., Guerry, P., et al.: Interbacterial transfer of R-factor in the human intestine: In vitro acquisition of R-factor mediated kanamycin resistance by a multi-resistant strain of *S. sonnei*. J. Infect. Dis. *126*:27–33, 1972.
66. Fernandez, A., Sninsky, C. A., O'Brien, A. D., et al.: Purified *Shigella* enterotoxin does not alter intestinal motility. Infect. Immun. *43*:477–481, 1984.
67. Finkelman, Y., Yagupsky, P., Fraser, D., et al.: Epidemiology of *Shigella* infections in two ethnic groups in a geographic region in southern Israel. Eur. J. Clin. Microbiol. Infect. Dis. *13*:367–373, 1994.
68. Floyd, T., Higgins, A. R., and Kader, M. A.: Studies in shigellosis. V. The relationship of age to the incidence of *Shigella* infections in Egyptian children, with special reference to shigellosis in the newborn and infant in the first six months of life. Am. J. Trop. Med. Hyg. *5*:119–130, 1956.
69. Fontaine, O.: Antibiotics in the management of shigellosis in children: What role for the quinolones? Rev. Infect. Dis. *11*:S1145–S1150, 1989.
70. Forbes, G.: Neurologic complications of systemic disease. Postgrad. Med. *15*:157, 1954.
71. Formal, S. B., Hale, T. L., and Kapfer, C.: *Shigella* vaccines. Rev. Infect. Dis. *11*:S547–S551, 1989.

72. Formal, S. B., Kent, T. H., Austin, S., et al.: Fluorescent-antibody and histological studies of vaccinated control monkeys challenged with *Shigella flexneri*. J. Bacteriol. *91*:2368–2376, 1966.
73. Frankel, G., Riley, L., Giron, J. A., et al.: Detection of *Shigella* in feces using DNA amplification. J. Infect. Dis. *161*:1252–1256, 1990.
74. Gaudio, P. A., Sethabutr, O., Echeverria, P., and Hoge, C. W.: Utility of a polymerase chain reaction diagnostic system in a study of the epidemiology of shigellosis among dysentery patients, family contacts, and well controls living in a shigellosis-endemic area. J. Infect. Dis. *176*:1013–1018, 1997.
75. Gemski, P., Jr., Takeuchi, A., Washington, O., et al.: Shigellosis due to *Shigella dysenteriae*. 1. Relative importance of mucosal invasion versus toxin production in pathogenesis. J. Infect. Dis. *126*:523–530, 1972.
76. Gilman, R. H., Spira, W., Rabbani, H., et al.: Single dose ampicillin therapy for severe shigellosis in Bangladesh. J. Infect. Dis. *143*:164–169, 1981.
77. Goren, A., Freier, S., and Passwell, J. H.: Lethal toxic encephalopathy due to childhood shigellosis in a developed country. Pediatrics *89*:1189–1193, 1992.
78. Gots, R. E., Formal, S. B., and Gianella, R. A.: Indomethacin inhibition of *Salmonella typhimurium, Shigella flexneri,* and cholera-mediated rabbit ileal secretion. J. Infect. Dis. *130*:280–284, 1974.
79. Greenberg, M., Frant, S., and Shapiro, R.: Bacillary dysentery acquired at birth. J. Pediatr. *17*:363–366, 1940.
80. Guerrero, L., Calva, J. J., Morrow, A. L., et al.: Asymptomatic *Shigella* infections in a cohort of Mexican children younger than two years of age. Pediatr. Infect. Dis. J. *13*:597–602, 1994.
81. Haider, K., Huq, M. I., Samadi, A. R., et al.: Plasmid characterization of *Shigella* spp. isolated from children with shigellosis and asymptomatic excretors. J. Antimicrob. Chemother. *16*:691–698, 1985.
82. Hale, T. L., Oaks, E. V., and Formal, S. B.: Identification and characterization of virulence-associated, plasmid-coded proteins of *Shigella* spp. and enteroinvasive *E. coli*. Infect. Immun. *50*:620–623, 1985.
83. Hale, T. L., Sansonetti, P., Schad, P. A., et al.: Characterization of virulence plasmids and plasmid-mediated outer membrane proteins in *Shigella flexneri, Shigella sonnei* and *Escherichia coli*. Infect. Immun. *40*:340–350, 1983.
84. Haltalin, K. C.: Neonatal shigellosis. Am. J. Dis. Child. *114*:603–611, 1967.
85. Haltalin, K. C., and Nelson, J. D.: Coliform septicemia complicating shigellosis in children. J. A. M. A. *192*:441–443, 1965.
86. Harenda de Silva, D. G., Mendis, L. N., Sheron, N., et al.: Concentrations of IL-6 and TNF in serum and stools of children with *S. dysenteriae* 1 infection. Gut *34*:194–198, 1993.
87. Harnett, N.: High-level resistance to trimethoprim, cotrimoxazole and other antimicrobial agents among clinical isolates of *Shigella* species in Ontario, Canada: An update. Epidemiol. Infect. *109*:463–472, 1992.
88. Harris, J. C., DuPont, H. L., and Hornick, R. B.: Fecal leukocytes in diarrheal illness. Ann. Intern. Med. *76*:697–703, 1972.
89. Harris, J. R., Wachsmuth, I. K., Davis, B. R., et al.: High molecular weight plasmid correlates with *Escherichia coli* enteroinvasiveness. Infect. Immun. *37*:1295–1298, 1982.
90. Helvaci, M., Bektaslar, D., Ozkaya, B., et al.: Comparative efficacy of cefixime and ampicillin-sulbactam in shigellosis in children. Acta Paediatr. Jpn. *40*:131–134, 1998.
91. Hoefnagel, D.: Fulminating, rapidly fatal shigellosis in children. N. Engl. J. Med. *258*:1256–1257, 1958.
92. Hossain, S., Biswas, R., Kabir, I., et al.: Single dose vitamin A treatment in acute shigellosis in Bangladesh children: Randomised double blind controlled trial. BMJ *316*:422–426, 1998.
93. Howard, J. G.: Observations on the intoxication produced in mice and rabbits by the neurotoxin of *Shigella shigae*. Br. J. Exp. Pathol. *36*:439–443, 1955.
94. Huskins, W. C., Griffiths, J. K., Faruque, A. S. G., et al.: Shigellosis in neonates and young infants. J. Pediatr. *125*:14–22, 1994.
95. Islam, D., and Christensson, B.: Disease-dependent changes in T-cell populations in patients with shigellosis. A. P. M. I. S. *108*:251–260, 2000.
96. Islam, D., Veress, B., Bardhan, P. K., et al.: Quantitative assessment of IgG and IgA subclass producing cells in rectal mucosa during shigellosis. J. Clin. Pathol. *50*:513–520, 1997.
97. Islam, M. R., Alam, A. N., Hussain, M. S., et al.: Effect of antimicrobial (nalidixic acid) therapy in shigellosis and predictive values of outcome variables in patients susceptible or resistant to it. J. Trop. Med. Hyg. *98*:121–125, 1995.
98. Islam, M. M., Azad, A. K., Bardhan, P. K., et al.: Pathology of shigellosis and its complications. Histopathology *24*:65–71, 1994.
99. Islam, M. S., Hossain, M. S., Hasan, M. K., et al.: Detection of *Shigellae* from stools of dysentery patients by culture and polymerase chain reaction techniques. J. Diarrhoeal Dis. Res. *16*:248–251, 1998.
100. Jensen, G., Wandall, D. A., Gaarslev, K., et al.: Antibiotic resistance in *Shigella* and *Salmonella* in a region of Lithuania. Eur. J. Clin. Microbiol. Infect. Dis. *15*:872–876, 1996.
101. Kabir, I., Butler, T., and Khanam, A.: Comparative efficacies of single intravenous doses of ceftriaxone and ampicillin for shigellosis in a placebo-controlled trial. Antimicrob. Agents Chemother. *29*:645–648, 1986.
102. Kabir, I., Butler, T., Underwood, L. E., et al.: Effects of a protein rich diet during convalescence from shigellosis on catch up growth, serum proteins, and insulin like growth factor I. Pediatr. Res. *32*:689–692, 1992.
103. Kabir, I., Rahman, M. M., Haider, R., et al.: Increased height gain of children fed a high-protein diet during convalescence from shigellosis: A six-month follow-up study. J. Nutr. *128*:1688–1691, 1998.
104. Kagalwalla, A. F., Khan, S. N., Kagalwalla, Y. A., et al.: Childhood shigellosis in Saudi Arabia. Pediatr. Infect. Dis. J. *11*:215–219, 1992.
105. Kariuki, S., Gilks, C., Brindle, R., et al.: Antimicrobial susceptibility and presence of extrachromosomal deoxyribonucleic acid in *Salmonella* and *Shigella* isolates from patients with AIDS. East Afr. Med. J. *71*:292–296, 1994.
106. Kariuki, S., Muthotho, N., Kimari, J., et al.: Molecular typing of multi-drug resistant *Shigella dysenteriae* type 1 by plasmid analysis and pulsed-field gel electrophoresis. Trans. R. Soc. Trop. Med. Hyg. *90*:712–714, 1996.
107. Kaminski, N., Bogomolski, V., and Stalnikowicz, R.: Acute bacterial diarrhoea in the emergency room: Therapeutic implications of stool culture results. J. Accid. Emerg. Med. *11*:168–171, 1994.
108. Keusch, G. T., and Bennish, M. L.: Shigellosis: Recent progress, persisting problems and research issues. Pediatr. Infect. Dis. J. *8*:713–719, 1989.
109. Keusch, G. T., and Jacewicz, M.: The pathogenesis of *Shigella* diarrhea. V. Relationship of Shiga enterotoxin, neurotoxin, and cytotoxin. J. Infect. Dis. *131*:S33, 1975.
110. Khalil, K., Khan, S. R., Mazhar, K., et al.: Occurrence and susceptibility to antibiotics of *Shigella* species in stools of hospitalized children with bloody diarrhea in Pakistan. Am. J. Trop. Med. Hyg. *58*:800–803, 1998.
111. Khan, M. U.: Interruption of shigellosis by handwashing. Trans. R. Soc. Trop. Med. Hyg. *76*:164–165, 1982.
112. Khan, W. A., Dhar, U., Salam, M. A., et al.: Central nervous system manifestations of childhood shigellosis: Prevalence, risk factors, and outcome. Pediatrics *103*:E18, 1999.
113. Koster, F., Levin, J., Walker, L., et al.: Hemolytic-uremic syndrome after shigellosis: Relation to endotoxemia and circulating immune complexes. N. Engl. J. Med. *298*:927–933, 1978.
114. Kotloff, K. L., Noriega, F. R., Samandari, T., et al.: *Shigella flexneri* 2a strain CVD 1207, with specific deletions in *virG, sen, set,* and *guaBA,* is highly attenuated in humans. Infect. Immun. *68*:1034–1039, 2000.
115. Kowlessar, M., and Forbes, G. B.: The febrile convulsion in shigellosis. N. Engl. J. Med. *258*:520–523, 1958.
116. Kozlova, N. S.: Plasmids of antibiotic-resistant strains of *Shigella* isolated in Leningrad and Leningrad region. Antibiot. Khimioter. *38*:9–14, 1993.
117. Kraybill, E. N., and Controni, G.: Septicemia and enterocolitis due to *S. sonnei* in a newborn infant. Pediatrics *42*:529–531, 1968.
118. LaBrec, E. H., and Formal, S. B.: Experimental *Shigella* infections. IV. Fluorescent antibody studies of an infection in guinea pigs. J. Immunol. *87*:562–572, 1961.
119. LaBrec, E. H., Schneider, H., Magnani, T. J., et al.: Epithelial cell penetration as an essential step in the pathogenesis of bacillary dysentery. J. Bacteriol. *88*:1503–1518, 1964.
120. Landsberger, M.: Bacillary dysentery in a newborn infant. Arch. Pediatr. *59*:330–332, 1942.
121. Leibovitz, E., Janco, J., Piglansky, L., et al.: Oral ciprofloxacin vs. intramuscular ceftriaxone as empiric treatment of acute invasive diarrhea in children. Pediatr. Infect. Dis. J. *19*:1060–1067, 2000.
122. Levin, S. E.: *Shigella* septicemia in the newborn infant. J. Pediatr. *71*:917–918, 1967.
123. Levine, M. M., DuPont, H. L., Formal, S. B., et al.: Pathogenesis of *Shigella dysenteriae* 1 (Shiga) dysentery. J. Infect. Dis. *127*:261–270, 1973.
124. Levine, M. M., DuPont, H. L., Khodabandebou, M., et al.: Long-term *Shigella*-carrier state. N. Engl. J. Med. *288*:1169–1171, 1973.
125. Lim, Y. S., and Tay, L.: Serotype distribution and antimicrobial resistance of *Shigella* isolates in Singapore. J. Diarrhoeal Dis. Res. *9*:328–331, 1991.
126. Lima, A. A., Lima, N. L., Pinho, M. C., et al.: High frequency of strains multiply resistant to ampicillin, trimethoprim-sulfamethoxazole, streptomycin, chloramphenicol, and tetracycline isolated from patients with shigellosis in northeastern Brazil during the period 1988 to 1993. Antimicrob. Agents Chemother. *39*:256–259, 1995.
127. Lin, S. R., and Chang, S. F.: Drug resistance and plasmid profile of shigellae in Taiwan. Epidemiol. Infect. *108*:87–97, 1992.
128. Lindberg, A. A., and Pal, T.: Strategies for development of potential candidate *Shigella* vaccines. Vaccine *11*:168–179, 1993.
129. Ling, J. M., Shaw, P. C., Kam, K. M., et al.: Molecular studies of plasmids of multiply-resistant *Shigella* spp. in Hong Kong. Epidemiol. Infect. *110*:437–446, 1993.
130. Lolekha, S., Vibulbandhitkit, S., and Poonyarit, P.: Response to antimicrobial therapy for shigellosis in Thailand. Rev. Infect. Dis. *13*:S342–S346, 1991.
131. Makintubee, S., Mallonee, J., and Istre, G. R.: Shigellosis outbreak associated with swimming. Am. J. Public Health *77*:166–168, 1987.

132. Mamun, K. Z., Tabassum, S., Hussain, M. A., and Shears, P.: Antimicrobial susceptibility of *Shigella* from a rural community in Bangladesh. Ann. Trop. Med. Parasitol. *91*:643–647, 1997.
133. Maraki, S., Georgiladakis, A., Christidou, A., et al.: Antimicrobial susceptibilities and beta-lactamase production of *Shigella* isolates in Crete, Greece, during the period 1991–1995. A. P. M. I. S. *106*:879–883, 1998.
134. Martin, J. M., Pitetti, R., Maffei, F., et al.: Treatment of shigellosis with cefixime: Two days vs. five days. Pediatr. Infect. Dis. J. *19*:522–526, 2000.
135. Martin, T., Habbick, B. F., and Nyssen, J.: Shigellosis with bacteremia: A report of two cases and a review of the literature. Pediatr. Infect. Dis. *2*:21–26, 1983.
136. Mason, P. R., Nathoo, K. J., Wellington, M., et al.: Antimicrobial susceptibilities of *Shigella dysenteriae* type 1 isolated in Zimbabwe: Implications for the management of dysentery. Cent. Afr. J. Med. *41*:132–137, 1995.
137. Mata, L. G.: The Children of Santa Maria Cauque: A Prospective Field Study of Health and Growth. Cambridge, MIT Press, 1978.
138. Mata, L. J., Urrutia, J. J., Garcia, B., et al.: *Shigella* infections in breast fed Guatemalan Indian neonates. Am. J. Dis. Child. *117*:142–146, 1969.
139. Mazumder, R. N., Hoque, S. S., Ashraf, H., et al.: Early feeding of an energy dense diet during acute shigellosis enhances growth in malnourished children. J. Nutr. *127*:51–54, 1997.
140. Mel, D. M., Terzin, A. L., and Vuksic, L.: Studies on vaccination against bacillary dysentery. 3. Effective oral immunization against *Shigella flexneri* 2a in a field trial. Bull. World Health Organ. *32*:647–655, 1965.
141. Merson, M. H., Goldmann, D. A., Boyer, K. M., et al.: An outbreak of *Shigella sonnei* gastroenteritis on Colorado River raft trips. Am. J. Epidemiol. *100*:186–196, 1974.
142. Metzler, J., and Nachamkin, I.: Evaluation of latex agglutination test for the detection of *Salmonella* and *Shigella* spp. by using broth enrichment. J. Clin. Microbiol. *26*:2501–2504, 1988.
143. Mohle-Boetani, J. C., Stapleton, M., Finger, R., et al.: Community-wide shigellosis: Control of an outbreak and risk factors in child day care centers. Am. J. Public Health *85*:812–816, 1995.
144. Moore, E. E.: *Shigella sonnei* septicemia in a neonate. Br. Med. J. *1*:22–23, 1974.
145. Morgan, D. R., DuPont, H. L., Wood, L. V., et al.: Cytotoxicity of leukocytes from normal and *Shigella*-susceptible (opium-treated) guinea pigs against virulent *Shigella sonnei*. Infect. Immun. *46*:22–24, 1984.
146. Morris, G. K., Koehler, J. A., Gangarosa, E. J., et al.: Comparison of media for direct isolation and transport of shigellae from fecal specimens. Appl. Microbiol. *19*:434–437, 1970.
147. Mulligan, K., Nelson, S., Friedman, H. S., et al.: Shigellosis-associated encephalopathy. Pediatr. Infect. Dis. J. *11*:889–890, 1992.
148. Munshi, M. H., Sack, D. A., Haider, K., et al.: Plasmid-mediated resistance to nalidixic acid in *Shigella dysenteriae* type 1. Lancet *2*:419–421, 1987.
149. Murphy, T. V., and Nelson, J. D.: *Shigella* vaginitis: Report on 38 patients and review of the literature. Pediatrics *63*:511–516, 1979.
150. Nalin, D. R., and Cash, R. A.: Oral or nasogastric maintenance of cholera and other severe diarrhea in children. J. Pediatr. *78*:355–358, 1971.
151. Nataro, J. P., Seriwatana, J., Fasano, A., et al.: Identification and cloning of a novel plasmid encoded enterotoxin of enteroinvasive *E. coli* and *Shigella* strains. Infect. Immun. *63*:4721–4728, 1995.
152. Navia, M. M., Capitano, L., Ruiz, J., et al.: Typing and characterization of mechanisms of resistance of *Shigella* spp. isolated from feces of children under 5 years of age from Ifakara, Tanzania. J. Clin. Microbiol. *37*:3113–3117, 1999.
153. Neglia, T. G., Marr, T. J., and Davis, A. T.: *Shigella* dysentery with secondary *Klebsiella* sepsis. J. Pediatr. *63*:253–254, 1976.
154. Neill, R. J., Gemski, P., Formal, S. B., et al.: Deletion of Shiga toxin gene in a chlorate-resistant derivative of *Shigella dysenteriae* type 1 that retains virulence. J. Infect. Dis. *158*:737–741, 1988.
155. Nelson, J. D., and Haltalin, K. C.: Comparative efficacy of cephalexin and ampicillin for shigellosis and other types of acute diarrhea in infants and children. Antimicrob. Agents Chemother. 7:415–420, 1975.
156. Nelson, J. D., Kusmiesz, H., and Jackson, L. H.: Comparison of trimethoprim/sulfamethoxazole and ampicillin for shigellosis in ambulatory patients. J. Pediatr. *89*:491–493, 1976.
157. Neter, E.: *S. sonnei* infection at term and its transfer to the newborn. Obstet. Gynecol. *17*:517–519, 1961.
158. Newland, J. W., and Neill, R. J.: DNA probes for Shiga-like toxins I and II and for toxin-converting bacteriophages. J. Clin. Microbiol. *26*:1292–1297, 1988.
159. Notario, R., Morales, E., Carmelengo, E., et al.: Enteropathogenic microorganisms in children with acute diarrhea in 2 hospitals of Rosario, Argentina. Medicina (B Aires) *53*:289–299, 1993.
160. Noriega, F. R., Liao, F. M., Formal, S. B., et al.: Prevalence of *Shigella* enterotoxin 1 among *Shigella* clinical isolates of diverse serotypes. J. Infect. Dis. *172*:1408–1410, 1995.
161. Nuutinen, M., Turtinen, J., and Uhari, M.: Growth and joint symptoms in children treated with nalidixic acid. Pediatr. Infect. Dis. J. *13*:798–800, 1994.
162. Oaks, E. V., Hale, T. L., and Formal, S. B.: Serum immune response to *Shigella* protein antigens in rhesus monkeys and humans infected with *Shigella* spp. Infect. Immun. *53*:57–63, 1986.
163. O'Brien, A. D., and Holmes, R. K.: Shiga and Shiga-like toxins. Microbiol. Rev. *51*:206–220, 1987.
164. O'Connor, H. J., and O'Callaghan, U.: Fatal *S. sonnei* septicemia in an adult complemented by marrow aplasia and intestinal perforation. J. Infect. *3*:277–279, 1981.
165. Ogawa, H.: Experimental approach in studies on pathogenesis of bacillary dysentery: With special reference to the invasion of bacilli into intestinal mucosa. Acta Pathol. Jpn. *20*:261–277, 1970.
166. Okamura, N., Nagai, T., and Nakaya, R., et al.: HeLa cell invasiveness and O antigen of *Shigella flexneri* as separate and prerequisite attributes of virulence to evoke keratoconjunctivitis in guinea pigs. Infect. Immun. *39*:505–513, 1983.
167. Ozturk, M. K., Caksen, H., and Sumerkan, B.: Convulsions in childhood shigellosis and antimicrobial resistance patterns of shigella isolates. Turk. J. Pediatr. *38*:183–188, 1996.
168. Pal, T., Newland, J. W., Tall, B. D., et al.: Intracellular spread of *Shigella flexneri* associated with the *kcpA* locus and a 140-kilodalton protein. Infect. Immun. *57*:477–486, 1989.
169. Patton, C., Gangarosa, E. J., Weissman, J., et al.: Diagnostic value of indirect hemagglutination in the seroepidemiology of *Shigella* infections. J. Clin. Microbiol. *3*:143–148, 1976.
170. Pickering, L. K., Bartlett, A. V., and Woodward, W. E.: Acute infectious diarrhea among children in day care: Epidemiology and control. Rev. Infect. Dis. *8*:539–547, 1986.
171. Pickering, L. K., and Woodward, W. E.: Diarrhea in day care centers. Pediatr. Infect. Dis. *1*:47–52, 1982.
172. Prado, D., Cleary, T. G., Pickering, L. K., et al.: The relation between production of cytotoxin and clinical features in shigellosis. J. Infect. Dis. *154*:149–155, 1986.
173. Prado, D., Lopez, E., Liu, H., et al.: Ceftibuten and TMP/SMX for treatment of *Shigella* and enteroinvasive *E. coli* disease. Pediatr. Infect. Dis. J. *11*:644–647, 1992.
174. Prado, D., Liu, H., Valasquez, T., et al.: Comparative efficacy of pivmecillinam and cotrimoxazole in acute shigellosis in children. Scand. J. Infect. Dis. *25*:713–719, 1993.
175. Prado, V., Pidal, P., Arellano, C., et al: Antimicrobial multiresistance of *Shigella* sp strains in a semirural community of northern Santiago. Rev. Med. Chile *126*:1464–1471, 1998.
176. Rahaman, M. M., Jamiul Alam, A. K. M., Islam, M. R., et al.: Shiga bacillus dysentery associated with marked leukocytosis and erythrocyte fragmentation. Johns Hopkins Med. J. *136*:65–70, 1975.
177. Raderman, J. W., Stoller, K. P., and Pomerance, J. J.: Bloodstream invasion with *S. sonnei* in an asymptomatic newborn infant. Pediatr. Infect. Dis. *5*:379–380, 1986.
178. Rahman, M. M., Kabir, I., Mahalanabis, D., et al.: Decreased food intake in children with severe dysentery due to *S. dysenteriae* 1 infection. Eur. J. Clin. Nutr. *46*:833–838, 1992.
179. Raqib, R., Ljungdahl, A., Lindberg, A. A., et al.: Local entrapment of interferon gamma in the recovery from *Shigella dysenteriae* type 1 infection. Gut *38*:328–336, 1996.
180. Raqib, R., Lindberg, A. A., Wretlind, B., et al.: Persistence of local cytokine production in shigellosis in acute and convalescent stages. Infect. Immun. *63*:289–296, 1995.
181. Raqib, R., Reinholt, F. P., Bardhan, P. K., et al.: Immunopathological patterns in the rectal mucosa of patients with shigellosis: Expression of HLA-DR antigens and T lymphocyte subsets. A. P. M. I. S. *102*:371–380, 1994.
182. Raqib, R., Wretlind, B., Andersson, J., et al.: Cytokine secretion in acute shigellosis is correlated to disease activity and directed more to stool than to plasma. J. Infect. Dis. *171*:376–384, 1995.
183. Rogerie, F., Ott, D., Vandepitte, J., et al.: Comparisons of norfloxacin and nalidixic acid for treatment of dysentery caused by *S. dysenteriae* type 1 in adults. Antimicrob. Agents Chemother. *29*:883–886, 1986.
184. Rubenstein, J. S., Noah, Z. L., Zales, V. R., et al.: Acute myocarditis associated with *S. sonnei* gastroenteritis. J. Pediatr. *122*:82–84, 1993.
185. Sakai, T., Sasakawa, C., Makino, S., et al.: DNA sequence and product analysis of the *virF* locus responsible for Congo red binding and cell invasion in *Shigella flexneri* 2a. Infect. Immun. *54*:395–402, 1986.
186. Sakamoto, A., and Kamo, S.: Clinical, statistical observations on Ekiri and bacillary dysentery: A study of 785 cases. Ann. Paediatr. *186*:1–18, 1956.
187. Salam, M. A., and Bennish, M. L.: Therapy of shigellosis. 1. Randomized, double-blind trial of nalidixic acid in childhood shigellosis. Pediatrics *113*:901–907, 1988.
188. Salam, M. A., Dhar, U., Khan, W. A., and Bennish, M. L.: Randomised comparison of ciprofloxacin suspension and pivmecillinam for childhood shigellosis. Lancet *352*:522–527, 1998.
189. Salam, M. A., Seas, C., Khan, W. A., et al.: Treatment of shigellosis. IV. Cefixime is ineffective in shigellosis in adults. Ann. Intern. Med. *123*:505–508, 1995.
190. Salzman, T. C., Scher, C. D., and Moss, R.: Shigellae with transferable drug resistance: Outbreak in a nursery for premature infants. J. Pediatr. *71*:21–26, 1967.
191. Samandari, T., Kotloff, K. L., Losonsky, G. A., et al: Production of IFN-gamma and IL-10 to *Shigella* invasins by mononuclear cells from volunteers orally inoculated with a Shiga toxin–deleted *Shigella dysenteriae* type 1 strain. J. Immunol. *164*:2221–2232, 2000.

192. Sansonetti, P. J., Arondel, J., Huerre, M., et al.: Interleukin-8 controls bacterial transepithelial translocation at the cost of epithelial destruction in experimental shigellosis. Infect. Immun. *67*:1471–1480, 1999.
193. Sansonetti, P. J., Hale, T. L., Dammin, G. I., et al.: Alterations in the pathogenicity of *Escherichia coli* K-12 after transfer of plasmids and chromosomal genes from *Shigella flexneri*. Infect. Immun. *39*:1392–1402, 1983.
194. Sansonetti, P. J., Kopecko, D. J., and Formal, S. B.: *Shigella sonnei* plasmids: Evidence that a large plasmid is necessary for virulence. Infect. Immun. *34*:75–83, 1981.
195. Sansonetti, P. J., Kopecko, D. J., and Formal, S. B.: Involvement of a plasmid in the invasive ability of *Shigella flexneri*. Infect. Immun. *35*:852–860, 1982.
196. Sansonetti, P. J., Phalipon, A., Arondel, J., et al.: Caspase-1 activation of IL-1beta and IL-18 are essential for *Shigella flexneri*-induced inflammation. Immunity *12*:581–590, 2000.
197. Sasakawa, C., Kamata, K., Sakai, T., et al.: Molecular alteration of the 140-megadalton plasmid associated with the loss of virulence and Congo red binding activity in *Shigella flexneri*. Infect. Immun. *51*:470–475, 1986.
198. Schaad, U. B., Salam, M. A., Aujard, Y., et al.: Use of fluoroquinolones in pediatrics: Consensus report of an International Society of Chemotherapy commission. Pediatr. Infect. Dis. J. *14*:1–9, 1995.
199. Scragg, J. N., Rubidge, C. J., and Appelbaum, P. C.: *Shigella* infection in African and Indian children with special reference to *Shigella* septicemia. J. Pediatr. *93*:796–797, 1978.
200. Sereny, B.: Experimental *Shigella* keratoconjunctivitis. Acta Microbiol. Acad. Sci. Hung. *2*:293–296, 1955.
201. Sharp, T. W., Thornton, S. A., Wallace, M. R., et al.: Diarrheal disease among military personnel during Operation Restore Hope, Somalia, 1992–1993. Am. J. Trop. Med. Hyg. *52*:188–193, 1995.
202. Simor, A. E., Poon, R., and Borczyk, A.: Chronic *Shigella flexneri* infection preceding development of acquired immunodeficiency syndrome. J. Clin. Microbiol. *27*:353–355, 1989.
203. Smith, H. R., Scotland, S. M., Chart, H., et al.: Vero cytotoxin production and presence of VT genes in strains of *Escherichia coli* and *Shigella*. FEMS Microbiol. Lett. *42*:173, 1987.
204. Speelman, P., Kabir, I., and Islam, M.: Distribution and spread of colonic lesions in shigellosis: A colonoscopic study. J. Infect. Dis. *150*:899–903, 1984.
205. Speelman, P., McGlaughlin, R., Kabir, I., et al.: Differential clinical features and stool findings in shigellosis and amoebic dysentery. Trans. R. Soc. Trop. Med. Hyg. *81*:549–551, 1987.
206. Starke, J. R., and Baker, C. J.: Neonatal shigellosis with bowel perforation. Pediatr. Infect. Dis. *4*:405–407, 1985.
207. Stern, M. S., and Gitnick, G. L.: *Shigella* hepatitis. J. A. M. A. *235*:2628, 1976.
208. Stoll, B. J., Glass, R. I., Huq, M. I., et al.: Surveillance of patients attending a diarrhoeal disease hospital in Bangladesh. Br. Med. J. *285*:1185–1188, 1982.
209. Struelens, M. J., Patte, D., Kabir, I., et al.: *Shigella* septicemia: Prevalence, presentation, risk factors, and outcome. J. Infect. Dis. *152*:784–790, 1985.
210. Tauxe, R. V., Puhr, N. D., Wells, J. G., et al.: Antimicrobial resistance of *Shigella* isolates in the USA: The importance of international travelers. J. Infect. Dis. *162*:1107–1111, 1990.
211. Taylor, W. I., and Harris, B.: Isolation of shigellae. II. Comparison of plating media and enrichment broths. Am. J. Clin. Pathol. *44*:471–475, 1965.
212. Tobias, J. D., Starke, J. R., and Tosi, M. F.: *Shigella* keratitis: A report of two cases and a review of the literature. Pediatr. Infect. Dis. *6*:79–81, 1987.
213. Tuttle, J., Ries, A. A., Chimba, R. M., et al.: Antimicrobial resistant epidemic *S. dysenteriae* type 1 in Zambia: Modes of transmission. J. Infect. Dis. *171*:371–375, 1995.
214. Varsano, I., Eidlitz-Marcus, T., Nussinovitch, M., et al.: Comparative efficacy of ceftriaxone and ampicillin for treatment of severe shigellosis in children. J. Pediatr. *118*:627–632, 1991.
215. Venkatesan, M. M., Buysse, J. M., and Kopecko, D. J.: Use of *Shigella flexneri ipaC* and *ipaH* gene sequences for the general identification of *Shigella* spp. and enteroinvasive *Escherichia coli*. J. Clin. Microbiol. *27*:2687–2691, 1989.
216. Vila, J., Gascon, J., Abdalla, S., et al.: Antimicrobial resistance of *Shigella* isolates causing traveler's diarrhea. Antimicrob. Agents Chemother. *38*:2668–2670, 1994.
217. Watanabe, H., Nakamura, A., and Timmis, K.: Small virulence plasmid of *Shigella dysenteriae* 1 strain W30864 encodes a 41,000-dalton protein involved in formation of specific lipopolysaccharide side chains of serotype 1 isolates. Infect. Immun. *46*:55–63, 1984.
218. Way, S. S., Borczuk, A. C., Dominitz, R., and Goldberg, M. B.: An essential role for gamma interferon in innate resistance to *Shigella flexneri* infection. Infect. Immun. *66*:1342–1348, 1998.
219. Weissman, J. B., Williams, S. V., Hinman, A. R., et al.: Foodborne shigellosis at a country fair. Am. J. Epidemiol. *100*:178–185, 1974.
220. Whitfield, C., and Humphries, J. M.: Meningitis and septicemia due to shigellae in a newborn infant. J. Pediatr. *70*:805–806, 1967.
221. Yolken, R. H., Ojeh, C., Khatri, I. A., et al.: Intestinal mucins inhibit rotavirus replication in an oligosaccharide-dependent manner. J. Infect. Dis. *169*:1002–1006, 1994.
222. Yurdakok, K., Sahin, N., Ozmert, E., and Berkman, E.: *Shigella* gastroenteritis: Clinical and epidemiological aspects, and antibiotic susceptibility. Acta Paediatr. Jpn. *39*:681–684, 1997.
223. Zychlinsky, A., Fitting, C., Cavaillon, J. M., et al.: IL-1 is released by murine macrophages during apoptosis induced by *S. flexneri*. J. Clin. Invest. *94*:1328–1332, 1994.
224. Zychlinsky, A., Perdomo, J. J., and Sansonetti, P. J.: Molecular and cellular mechanisms of tissue invasion by *S. flexneri*. Ann. N. Y. Acad. Sci. *730*:197–208, 1994.
225. Zychlinsky, A., Kenny, B., Menard, R., et al.: *IpaB* mediates macrophage apoptosis induced by *S. flexneri*. Mol. Microbiol. *11*:619–627, 1994.

Serratia

WILLIAM C. GRUBER ■ RANDALL G. FISHER ■ THOMAS G. BOYCE

Like other members of Enterobacteriaceae, the genus *Serratia* contains species increasingly associated with opportunistic infection in the compromised host. One of the oldest bacterial organisms to be named,[98] *Serratia marcescens* is the chief species associated with disease in humans and has been associated with infection of the urinary tract, the respiratory tract, local wounds, and central venous catheters. Illness may be complicated by bacteremia and meningitis. Treatment of infection may be made exceptionally difficult because of frequent resistance of these organisms to penicillins, cephalosporins, and aminoglycosides.

Bacteriology

S. marcescens can produce a red pigment resembling blood on contaminated foodstuffs. As early as the sixth century, the "miraculous" appearance of blood on food provoked both superstition and scientific investigation. Troops were goaded into battle and religious beliefs gained support because of the fortuitous growth of the saprophyte in bread.[98] In 1819, *S. marcescens* was named by Bizio, who correctly interpreted the discoloration of cornmeal to be caused by a living organism.[65] The genus name honors the Italian physicist Serrafino Serrati, who Bizio thought had been slighted in favor of Robert Fulton as inventor of the steamboat; *marcescens* was drawn from the Latin word meaning "to decay."

We now recognize the genus *Serratia* as straight, motile, catalase-positive, gram-negative rods. Colonies are opaque, iridescent, and white, pink, or red on solid agar. Organisms are Voges-Proskauer test–positive.[45] The genus may be distinguished from other enterobacteria (genera) by its use of caprylate or L-fucose as a sole carbon source and its hydrolysis of gelatin.[45, 93] Clinically relevant strains include *S. marcescens, Serratia liquefaciens, Serratia odorifera, Serratia ficara,* and *Serratia plymuthica.*[17, 34] For a detailed discussion of properties of *S. marcescens*, the reader is referred to the review by Hejazi and Falkiner.[46]

Epidemiology

S. marcescens was thought to be nonpathogenic in earlier times and was used as a biologic marker of transmission as early as 1906. In that year, N. H. Gordon, commissioned to study the atmospheric hygiene of the British House of Commons, gargled a liquid culture of *S. marcescens* and then quoted Shakespeare to an audience of agar plates in the otherwise empty House.[40, 98] The organism subsequently was recovered from the plates, documenting the possibility of aerosol transmission of bacteria. (Gordon reported no ill effects.) The importance of *S. marcescens* as a biologic marker for hand-to-hand bacterial transmission, ascension of bacteria in the urinary tract in catheterized patients, and bacteremia after dental extraction is reviewed in detail by Yu.[98] Most remarkably, in investigations in 1950 and 1952 to judge the threat of biologic warfare to the United States, the Navy released *S. marcescens* into the Pacific, where it became aerosolized and drifted as far as 80 meters inland.[6] Although an epidemic of infection with *S. marcescens* in a San Francisco hospital coincided with this event, subsequent serotype and biotype analyses cast doubt on any relationship to the Navy experiments.[33] Rather, the early San Francisco hospital experience heralded the increased frequency of nosocomial infections that would be observed in subsequent years.[98]

Sporadic nosocomial outbreaks of infection were reported first in the 1950s and 1960s.[62, 77, 96] Early outbreaks in a pediatric ward and neonatal nursery were attributed to contaminated intravenous solution and caps of bottles containing saline used to moisten umbilical cords.[62] As reviewed by Yu,[98] environmental sources before 1979 included disinfectants, water from ultrasonic nebulizers, respirators, arterial pressure monitors, and fiberoptic bronchoscopes. Environmental sources since have included suction traps,[70] intra-aortic pressure transducers,[11, 94] contaminated handwashing brushes,[5] illicit intravenous drug paraphernalia,[26] contaminated urologic instruments,[31] colonized disinfectants or soaps,[32, 60, 63] contaminated infant parenteral nutrition fluid,[35] contaminated whole blood or blood products,[39, 78] and inadequately sterilized breast milk pumps.[42] However, hand-to-hand transmission appears to be the primary mechanism of nosocomial spread. In one dramatic outbreak, spread of an organism with the same serotype, phage type, and antimicrobial sensitivity pattern was documented among four geographically separated teaching hospitals in the same region[83]; spread probably was caused by passive carriage of *S. marcescens* on the hands of rotating personnel. That an increase in nosocomially acquired S. *marcescens* infection was becoming a worldwide concern was apparent by 1979.[17] Outbreaks in neonatology units and pediatric wards have been widespread, persistent, and associated with high morbidity and mortality rates.[5, 14, 70, 90] At the peak of one epidemic of invasive *S. marcescens* disease in a neonatal nursery, more than 90 percent of infants were colonized with the epidemic strain.[30] Increased rates of colonization have been associated with nearly 10-fold increases in rates of *S. marcescens* bacteremia and meningitis.[100] Outbreaks of multidrug-resistant strains have been especially troublesome in surgical subspecialty wards, and an outbreak has been reported in a bone marrow transplantation unit.[18, 53]

Biotyping may be successful in characterizing isolates, which then can be traced in the hospital environment.[44, 89] Ribotyping or identification of a unique biochemical characteristic has proved useful for demonstrating cross-contamination across hematology, gastroenterology, and neonatology units in a pediatric hospital.[12, 36] Use of typing methods may be particularly important because drug-resistant and drug-susceptible isolates of *Serratia* may cocirculate.[24] Banding differences from pulsed-field gel electrophoresis of DNA digests are relatively restricted in number from outbreak strains; increases in banding patterns may reflect genetic drift over time.[8] Such DNA techniques have aided in making decisions about cohorting and closure of neonatal units and have been used to demonstrate cross-contamination of wards.[48, 68] DNA amplification techniques offer promise for characterizing isolates in future outbreaks and defining antimicrobial susceptibility.[47, 60, 86]

Pathophysiology

Pathologic findings in sepsis are similar to those in infections due to other gram-negative enteric bacilli. Postmortem examination of the lungs of patients with radiologic findings in *S. marcescens* pneumonia reveals a focal necrotizing pneumonia in most instances and hemorrhagic manifestations in some.[10]

Several properties may enhance virulence of *Serratia* in human infection. The 56-kd protease of *S. marcescens* appears to possess properties of a virulence factor. It enhances vascular permeability through activation of the Hageman factor–kallikrein–kinin pathway in vivo.[61] The protease also has the capacity to degrade host proteins important in humoral immune response, such as immunoglobulins and fibronectin,[69] and inactivates the chemotactic effect of C5a.[73] *Serratia* hemolysin may increase indirectly vascular permeability, local edema, and accumulation of granulocytes. Clinical strains appear to possess increased adherence properties in comparison to environmental isolates.[9] Compared with some enteric organisms, *Serratia* adheres better to bladder epithelial cells, which may facilitate urinary tract infection.[28]

Both cell-mediated immunity and humoral immunity may be important factors in protection from *Serratia* infection and illness. In a murine model of immunization against *S. marcescens,* only the transfer of both antiserum and spleen cells from vaccinated mice increased bacterial clearance from the liver and survival after infection.[57]

Resistance of *S. marcescens* to aminoglycosides generally is plasmid mediated. Resistance to aminoglycosides may be conferred by one of several genes producing acetylating, phosphorylating, or adenylating enzymes.[1, 2, 18, 49, 66] Risk of acquiring infection with aminoglycoside resistance increases with exposure to these agents.[41, 99] However, in some patients, repeated hospitalizations have shown greater importance than use of aminoglycoside as a risk factor for development of infection with resistant strains.[7] High levels of resistance to penicillins and cephalosporins are mediated by one or more plasmids. Cephalosporin resistance also may be derived chromosomally (see also Chapter 107).[24, 37, 64, 76] Chromosomally mediated β-lactam resistance may be inducible in the presence of high levels of penicillin, particularly when plasmid-derived β-lactamase is blocked by clavulanic acid.[19] Transposable plasmid elements may seem in part responsible for the rapid spread of multiple-drug resistance.[79, 80, 85] Plasmids conferring multiple-drug resistance are transferable from *S. marcescens* to *Klebsiella* and may be responsible for sequential nosocomial outbreaks of different genera sharing common drug resistance patterns.[92]

Clinical Manifestations

First described in a patient with bronchiectasis as a cause of "blood-tinged" sputum colored by the organism,[97] *S. marcescens* commonly is associated with urinary tract, respiratory tract, central venous catheter, and bacteremic infections.[2] Other species, including *S. liquefaciens, S. ficara, S. odorifera,* and *S. plymuthica,* are less common causes of disease.[13, 22, 29, 34, 87]

Chromogenic *S. marcescens* was responsible for the historically interesting and reportedly benign "red diaper syndrome," which persisted for 7 months in the infant of a genetics professor.[95] However, in at least one series, the organism has been identified as one of the top five causes of neonatal sepsis[43] and now is recognized as a major pathogen of the compromised newborn. Disease in newborn intensive care units commonly is associated with high rates of underlying respiratory illness.[71] Other preexisting risk factors include necrotizing enterocolitis, intravenous catheters, and cardiac disease. Clinical illness shares features in common with other neonatal enteric pathogens; apnea, hypotension, and respiratory distress are frequent occurrences. Pneumonia with empyema has been reported.[52] Meningitis may occur as a complication, and antibiotic resistance may emerge during therapy for bacteremia or localized infection.[20] Significant brain injury caused by ventriculitis, brain abscesses, or porencephalic cysts is observed in most infants with meningitis.[20, 58]

In older children and adults, *Serratia* spp. are isolated most frequently from the urinary tract.[2, 83] Instrumentation, catheterization, and clustering of susceptibles are important risk factors.[7, 21, 49, 81, 84] By the 1970s, increased frequencies of serious infection, such as endocarditis, were noted in intravenous drug abusers.[26] In some series of respiratory and urinary tract infections, *S. marcescens* was observed to be associated more commonly than any other enteric pathogen with the complication of bacteremia.[51, 56] As is true of other causes of gram-negative sepsis, *Serratia* sepsis characterized by shock, pneumonia, or hemorrhage confers a substantially poorer prognosis.[15, 82] However, the risk for development of these complications in patients with cancer was observed by Saito and associates[82] to be somewhat lower than that of their previous experience with other pathogens, such as *Escherichia coli* and *Pseudomonas aeruginosa.* When predictive factors of mortality were sought in 385 subjects with nosocomial bacteremia, *S. marcescens* was not an independent predictor of death.[67] Other infections caused by *Serratia* include soft tissue infections, abscesses, endophthalmitis (including a case occurring after septicemia in an infant),[3, 4] osteomyelitis and arthritis,[91] and peritonitis in dialysis patients.[25]

Diagnosis

The diagnosis of *Serratia* infection relies primarily on isolation of organisms from clinical material. Nonspecific laboratory tests occasionally may be misleading. For example, *Serratia* meningitis in the neonate may be accompanied by a normal cerebrospinal fluid white blood cell count or only a modest cerebrospinal fluid pleocytosis.[20] Although *S. marcescens* is famous historically because of its chromogenic potential, most strains are nonpigmented. Hydrolysis of gelatin distinguishes *S. marcescens* from *Klebsiella* and *Enterobacter* in the clinical microbiology laboratory. The presence of ornithine decarboxylase and fermentation of sorbitol but not arabinose help to differentiate *S. marcescens* further from other *Serratia* spp.[45] Biotyping,[44] DNA and RNA detection techniques,[60] and antimicrobial susceptibilities[89] can be used to characterize strains.

Treatment

Empirical decisions about antibiotic treatment of *Serratia* infection should rely on knowledge of hospital flora. Therapy should be tailored once susceptibilities are known. In the newborn, meningitis and its complications should be suspected, and interventions should be guided by imaging of the central nervous system. Imaging techniques may be useful in guiding needle aspiration of abscesses.[72] Recommended antibiotic therapy for neonatal meningitis is a cephalosporin and an aminoglycoside for susceptible strains. Still, mortality rates remain high (>45%), even with appropriate antibiotic management.[20]

In older children and adults, reported response rates for bacteremic infection have been 75 percent for patients who received appropriate antibiotics, 22 percent for those who received inappropriate antibiotics, and 29 percent for those who received no antibiotics.[82] Patients who continue to have positive blood culture results while receiving appropriate antibiotic therapy have a poor prognosis. Inclusion of a penicillin or cephalosporin for susceptible strains should be considered. In Saito's review[82] of 118 patients with *Serratia* bacteremia, patients who received only an aminoglycoside had the poorest response rate among those who received appropriate therapy; those who received a cephalosporin, alone or in combination, fared better. *Serratia* generally have proved to be susceptible to third-generation cephalosporins in recent surveys of hospitals from North America.[50] However, the physician needs to be wary of potential resistance to cephalosporins and penicillins caused by the production of extended-spectrum β-lactamases. *Serratia* spp. are among the genera most likely to hyperproduce AmpC β-lactamase, leading to resistance to the extended-spectrum cephalosporins. The carbopenems imipenem and meropenem are among the antibiotics of choice for *Serratia* spp. resistant to ceftazidime or those producing extended-spectrum β-lactamases. An extended-spectrum metallo–β-lactamase mediating resistance to imipenem has been described.[75]

Amikacin historically has been effective in the treatment of gentamicin-resistant strains.[27, 59] As recently as 1985, amikacin was recommended as a first-line antibiotic for treatment of pediatric nosocomial infection when *Serratia* or other enterics with resistance potential were suspected.[88] However, since the 1980s, outbreaks of *S. marcescens* infections caused by amikacin-resistant strains have been reported.[74] Quinolones have been used with some success for treatment of organisms resistant to other agents,[38] but resistance to these drugs also has been identified.[55]

Cohorting and attempts to remove environmental sources of infection have been successful in ending epidemics but typically require several months.[23] Rarely, neonatal intensive care units have been closed to admissions to halt epidemics.[16, 70]

REFERENCES

1. Acar, J. F., Witchitz, J. L., Goldstein, F., et al.: Susceptibility of aminoglycoside-resistant gram-negative bacilli to amikacin: Delineation of individual resistance patterns. J. Infect. Dis. *134*(Suppl.):S280–S285, 1976.
2. Acar, J. F.: *Serratia marcescens* infections. Infect. Control 7:273–278, 1986.
3. al Hazzaa, S. A., Tabbara, K. F., and Gammon, J. A.: Pink hypopyon: A sign of *Serratia marcescens* endophthalmitis. Br. J. Ophthalmol. *76*:764–765, 1992.

4. Alvarez, R., Adan, A., Martinez, J. A., et al.: Haematogenous *Serratia marcescens* endophthalmitis in an HIV-infected intravenous drug addict. Infection *18*:29–30, 1990.
5. Anagnostakis, D., Fitsialos, J., Koutsia, C., et al.: A nursery outbreak of *Serratia marcescens* infection: Evidence of a single source of contamination. Am. J. Dis. Child. *135*:413–414, 1981.
6. Anonymous: Biologic testing involving human subjects by the Department of Defense, 1977: Hearings before the Subcommittee on Health and Science Research of the United States Senate. Washington, D.C., Government Printing Office, 1977.
7. Arroyo, J. C., Milligan, W. L., Postic, B., et al.: Clinical, epidemiologic and microbiologic features of a persistent outbreak of amikacin-resistant *Serratia marcescens*. Infect. Control *2*:367–372, 1981.
8. Aucken, H. M., Boquete, T., Kaufmann, M. E., and Pitt, T. L.: Interpretation of band differences to distinguish strains of *Serratia marcescens* by pulsed-field gel electrophoresis of XbaI DNA digests. Epidemiol. Infect. *125*:63–70, 2000.
9. Aucken, H. M., and Pitt, T. L.: Antibiotic resistance and putative virulence factors of *Serratia marcescens* with respect to O and K serotypes. J. Med. Microbiol. *47*:1105–1113, 1998.
10. Balikian, J. P., Herman, P. G., and Godleski, J. J.: *Serratia* pneumonia. Radiology *137*:309–311, 1980.
11. Beck-Sague, C. M., and Jarvis, W. R.: Epidemic bloodstream infections associated with pressure transducers: A persistent problem. Infect. Control Hosp. Epidemiol. *10*:54–59, 1989.
12. Bingen, E. H., Mariani-Kurkdjian, P., Lambert-Zechovsky, N. Y., et al.: Ribotyping provides efficient differentiation of nosocomial *Serratia marcescens* isolates in a pediatric hospital. J. Clin. Microbiol. *30*:2088–2091, 1992.
13. Bollet, C., Grimont, P., Gainnier, M., et al.: Fatal pneumonia due to *Serratia proteamaculans* subsp. *quinovora*. J. Clin. Microbiol. *31*:444–445, 1993.
14. Bollmann, R., Halle, E., Sokolowska-Kohler, W., et al.: Nosocomial infections due to *Serratia marcescens:* Clinical findings, antibiotic susceptibility patterns and fine typing. Infection *17*:294–300, 1989.
15. Bouza, E., Garcia de la Torre, M., Erice, A., et al.: *Serratia* bacteremia. Diagn. Microbiol. Infect. Dis. *7*:237–247, 1987.
16. Braver, D. J., Hauser, G. J., Berns, L., et al.: Control of a *Serratia marcescens* outbreak in a maternity hospital. J. Hosp. Infect. *10*:129–137, 1987.
17. Brooks, H. J., Chambers, T. J., and Tabaqchali, S.: The increasing isolation of *Serratia* species from clinical specimens. J. Hyg. *82*:31–40, 1979.
18. Bullock, D. W., Bidwell, J. L., Reeves, D. S., et al.: Outbreaks of hospital infection in southwest England caused by gentamicin-resistant *Serratia marcescens*. J. Hosp. Infect. *3*:263–273, 1982.
19. Bush, K., Flamm, R. K., Ohringer, S., et al.: Effect of clavulanic acid on activity of beta-lactam antibiotics in *Serratia marcescens* isolates producing both a TEM beta-lactamase and a chromosomal cephalosporinase. Antimicrob. Agents Chemother. *35*:2203–2208, 1991.
20. Campbell, J. R., Diacovo, T., and Baker, C. J.: *Serratia marcescens* meningitis in neonates. Pediatr. Infect. Dis. J. *11*:881–886, 1992.
21. Cann, K. J., Johnstone, D., and Skene, A. I.: An outbreak of *Serratia marcescens* infection following urodynamic studies. J. Hosp. Infect. *9*:291–293, 1987.
22. Chmel, H.: *Serratia odorifera* biogroup 1 causing an invasive human infection. J. Clin. Microbiol. *26*:1244–1245, 1988.
23. Christensen, G. D., Korones, S. B., Reed, L., et al.: Epidemic *Serratia marcescens* in a neonatal intensive care unit: Importance of the gastrointestinal tract as a reservoir. Infect. Control *3*:127–133, 1982.
24. Coleman, D., Falkiner, F. R., Carr, M. E., et al.: Simultaneous outbreaks of infection due to *Serratia marcescens* in a general hospital. J. Hosp. Infect. *5*:270–282, 1984.
25. Connacher, A. A., Old, D. C., Phillips, G., et al.: Recurrent peritonitis caused by *Serratia marcescens* in a diabetic patient receiving continuous ambulatory peritoneal dialysis. J. Hosp. Infect. *11*:155–160, 1988.
26. Cooper, R., and Mills, J.: *Serratia* endocarditis: A follow-up report. Arch. Intern. Med. *140*:199–202, 1980.
27. Craven, P. C., Jorgensen, J. H., Kaspar, R. L., et al.: Amikacin therapy of patients with multiply antibiotic-resistant *Serratia marcescens* infections: Development of increasing resistance during therapy. Am. J. Med. *62*:902–910, 1977.
28. Daifuku, R., and Stamm, W. E.: Bacterial adherence to bladder uroepithelial cells in catheter-associated urinary tract infection. N. Engl. J. Med. *314*:1208–1213, 1986.
29. Darbas, H., Jean-Pierre, H., and Paillisson, J.: Case report and review of septicemia due to *Serratia ficaria*. J. Clin. Microbiol. *32*:2285–2288, 1994.
30. Duggan, T. G., Leng, R. A., Hancock, B. M., et al.: *Serratia marcescens* in a newborn unit: Microbiological features. Pathology *16*:189–191, 1984.
31. Echols, R. M., Palmer, D. L., King, R. M., et al.: Multidrug-resistant *Serratia marcescens* bacteriuria related to urologic instrumentation. South. Med. J. *77*:173–177, 1984.
32. Ehrenkranz, N. J., Bolyard, E. A., Wiener, M., et al.: Antibiotic-sensitive *Serratia marcescens* infections complicating cardiopulmonary operations: Contaminated disinfectant as a reservoir. Lancet *2*:1289–1292, 1980.
33. Farmer, J. I., Davis, B. R., and Grimont, P. A. D.: Source of American *Serratia*. Lancet *2*:459–460, 1977.
34. Fitzgerald, P., Drew, J. H., and Kruszelnicki, I.: *Serratia:* A problem in a neonatal nursery. Aust. Paediatr. J. *20*:205–207, 1984.
35. Frean, J. A., Arntzen, L., Rosekilly, I., et al.: Investigation of contaminated parenteral nutrition fluids associated with an outbreak of *Serratia odorifera* septicaemia. J. Hosp. Infect. *27*:263–273, 1994.
36. Geiseler, P. J., Harris, B., and Andersen, B. R.: Nosocomial outbreak of nitrate-negative *Serratia marcescens* infections. J. Clin. Microbiol. *15*:728–730, 1982.
37. Gianneli, D., Tzelepi, E., Tzouvelekis, L. S., et al.: Dissemination of cephalosporin-resistant *Serratia marcescens* strains producing a plasmidic SHV type beta-lactamase in Greek hospitals. Eur. J. Clin. Microbiol. Infect. Dis. *13*:764–767, 1994.
38. Goldstein, E. J., Alpert, M. L., Najem, A., et al.: Norfloxacin in the treatment of complicated and uncomplicated urinary tract infections: A comparative multicenter trial. Am. J. Med. *82*:65–69, 1987.
39. Gong, J., Hogman, C. F., Hambraeus, A., et al.: Transfusion-associated *Serratia marcescens* infection: Studies of the mechanism of action. Transfusion *33*:802–808, 1993.
40. Gordon, W. H.: Report on an investigation of the ventilation of the debating chamber of the House of Commons. Parliamentary Command Paper, 1906, p. 3035.
41. Graham, D. R., Clegg, H. W. D., Anderson, R. L., et al.: Gentamicin treatment associated with later nosocomial gentamicin-resistant *Serratia marcescens* infections. Infect. Control *2*:31–37, 1981.
42. Gransden, W. R., Webster, M., French, G. L., et al.: An outbreak of *Serratia marcescens* transmitted by contaminated breast pumps in a special care baby unit. J. Hosp. Infect. *7*:149–154, 1986.
43. Grauel, E. L., Halle, E., Bollmann, R., et al.: Neonatal septicaemia: Incidence, etiology and outcome: A 6-year analysis. Acta Paediatr. Scand. *360*(Suppl.):113–119, 1989.
44. Grimont, P. A., and Grimont, F.: Biotyping of *Serratia marcescens* and its use in epidemiological studies. J. Clin. Microbiol *8*:73–83, 1978.
45. Grimont, P. A. D., and Grimont, F.: *Serratia. In* Krieg, N. R., and Holt, J. G. (eds.): Bergey's Manual of Systematic Bacteriology. Vol. 1. Baltimore, Williams & Wilkins, 1984, pp. 476–484.
46. Hejazi, A., and Falkiner, F. R.: *Serratia marcescens*. J. Med. Microbiol. *46*:903–912, 1997.
47. Hejazi, A., Keane, C. T., and Falkiner, F. R.: The use of RAPD-PCR as a typing method for *Serratia marcescens*. J. Med. Microbiol. *46*:913–919, 1997.
48. Hoyen, C., Rice, L., Conte, S., et al: Use of real time pulsed field gel electrophoresis to guide interventions during a nursery outbreak of *Serratia marcescens* infection. Pediatr. Infect. Dis. J. *18*:357–360, 1999.
49. John, J. F. J., and McNeill, W. F.: Characteristics of *Serratia marcescens* containing a plasmid coding for gentamicin resistance in nosocomial infections. J. Infect. Dis. *143*:810–817, 1981.
50. Jones, R. N., Jenkins, S. G., Hoban, D. J., et al.: In vitro efficacy of six cephalosporins tested against Enterobacteriaceae isolated at 38 North American medical centres participating in the SENTRY Antimicrobial Surveillance Program, 1997–1998. Int. J. Antimicrob. Agents *15*:111–118, 2000.
51. Karnad, A., Alvarez, S., and Berk, S. L.: Pneumonia caused by gram-negative bacilli. Am. J. Med. *79*:61–67, 1985.
52. Khan, E. A., Wafelman, L. S., Garcia-Prats, J. A., and Taber, L. H.: *Serratia marcescens* pneumonia, empyema and pneumatocele in a preterm neonate. Pediatr. Infect. Dis. J. *16*:1003–1005, 1997.
53. Knowles, S., Herra, C., Devitt, E., et al.: An outbreak of multiply resistant *Serratia marcescens:* The importance of persistent carriage. Bone Marrow Transplant. *25*:873–877, 2000.
54. Konig, W., Faltin, Y., Scheffer, J., et al.: Role of cell-bound hemolysin as a pathogenicity factor for *Serratia* infections. Infect. Immun. *55*: 2554–2561, 1987.
55. Korner, R. J., Nicol, A., Reeves, D. S., et al.: Ciprofloxacin-resistant *Serratia marcescens* endocarditis as a complication of non-Hodgkin's lymphoma. J. Infect. *29*:73–76, 1994.
56. Krieger, J. N., Kaiser, D. L., and Wenzel, R. P.: Urinary tract etiology of bloodstream infections in hospitalized patients. J. Infect. Dis. *148*:57–62, 1983.
57. Kumagai, Y., Okada, K., and Sawae, Y.: The effect of humoral and cell-mediated immunity in resistance to systemic *Serratia* infection. J. Med. Microbiol. *36*:245–249, 1992.
58. Lam, A. H., Berry, A., deSilva, M., et al.: Intracranial *Serratia* infection in preterm newborn infants. Am. J. Neuroradiol. *5*:447–451, 1984.
59. Leonard, J. M., McGee, Z. A., and Alford, R. H.: Gentamicin-resistant bacillary infection: Clinical features and amikacin therapy. Arch. Intern. Med. *138*:201–205, 1978.
60. Liu, P. Y., Lau, Y. J., Hu, B. S., et al.: Use of PCR to study epidemiology of *Serratia marcescens* isolates in nosocomial infection. J. Clin. Microbiol. *32*:1935–1938, 1994.
61. Matsumoto, K., Yamamoto, T., Kamata, R., et al.: Pathogenesis of serratial infection: Activation of the Hageman factor–prekallikrein cascade by serratial protease. J. Biochem. *96*:739–749, 1984.
62. McCormack, R. C., and Kunin, C. M.: Control of a single source nursery epidemic due to *Serratia marcescens*. Pediatrics *37*:750–755, 1966.

63. McNaughton, M., Mazinke, N., and Thomas, E.: Newborn conjunctivitis associated with triclosan 0.5 percent antiseptic intrinsically contaminated with *Serratia marcescens*. Can. J. Infect. Control *10*:7–8, 1995.
64. Medeiros, A. A., and O'Brien, T. F.: Contributions of R factors to the antibiotic resistance of hospital isolates of *Serratia*. Antimicrob. Agents Chemother. *8*:30–35, 1968.
65. Merlino, C. P.: Bartolomeo Bizio's letter to the most eminent priest, Angelo Bellani, concerning the phenomenon of the red-colored polenta. J. Bacteriol. *9*:527–543, 1924.
66. Meyer, R. D.: Patterns and mechanisms of emergence of resistance to amikacin. J. Infect. Dis. *136*:449–452, 1977.
67. Miller, P. J., and Wenzel, R. P.: Etiologic organisms as independent predictors of death and morbidity associated with bloodstream infections. J. Infect. Dis. *156*:471–477, 1987.
68. Miranda, G., Kelly, C., Solorzano, F., et al.: Use of pulsed-field gel electrophoresis typing to study an outbreak of infection due to *Serratia marcescens* in a neonatal intensive care unit. J. Clin. Microbiol. *34*:3138–3141, 1996.
69. Molla, A., Matsumoto, K., Oyamada, I., et al.: Degradation of protease inhibitors, immunoglobulins, and other serum proteins by *Serratia* protease and its toxicity to fibroblast in culture. Infect. Immun. *53*:522–529, 1986.
70. Montanaro, D., Grasso, G. M., Annino, I., et al.: Epidemiological and bacteriological investigation of *Serratia marcescens* epidemic in a nursery and in a neonatal intensive care unit. J. Hyg. *93*:67–78, 1984.
71. Newport, M. T., John, J. F., Michel, Y. M., et al.: Endemic *Serratia marcescens* infection in a neonatal intensive care nursery associated with gastrointestinal colonization. Pediatr. Infect. Dis. *4*:160–167, 1985.
72. Obana, W. G., Cogen, P. H., Callen, P. W., et al.: Ultrasound-guided aspiration of a neonatal brain abscess. Childs Nerv. Sys. *7*:272–273, discussion 274, 1991.
73. Oda, T., Kojima, Y., Akaike, T., et al.: Inactivation of chemotactic activity of C5a by the serratial 56-kilodalton protease. Infect. Immun. *58*:1269–1272, 1990.
74. Okuda, T., Endo, N., Osada, Y., et al.: Outbreak of nosocomial urinary tract infections caused by *Serratia marcescens*. J. Clin. Microbiol. *20*:691–695, 1984.
75. Osano, E., Arakawa, Y., Wacharotayankun, R., et al.: Molecular characterization of an enterobacterial metallo beta-lactamase found in a clinical isolate of *Serratia marcescens* that shows imipenem resistance. Antimicrob. Agents Chemother. *38*:71–78, 1994.
76. Pagani, L., Luzzaro, F., Ronza, P., et al.: Outbreak of extended-spectrum beta-lactamase–producing *Serratia marcescens* in an intensive care unit. FEMS Immunol. Med. Microbiol. *10*:39–46, 1994.
77. Rabinowitz, K., and Schiffrin, R.: A ward contamination by *Serratia marcescens*. Acta Med. Orient. *11*:181–184, 1952.
78. Roth, V. R., Arduino, M. J., Nobiletti, J., et al.: Transfusion-related sepsis due to *Serratia liquefaciens* in the United States. Transfusion *40*:931–935, 2000.
79. Rubens, C. E., McNeill, W. F., and Farrar, W. E. J.: Evolution of multiple-antibiotic-resistance plasmids mediated by transposable plasmid deoxyribonucleic acid sequences. J. Bacteriol. *140*:713–719, 1979.
80. Rubens, C. E., Farrar, W. E. J., McGee, Z. A., et al.: Evolution of a plasmid mediating resistance to multiple antimicrobial agents during a prolonged epidemic of nosocomial infections. J. Infect. Dis. *143*:170–181, 1981.
81. Rutala, W. A., Kennedy, V. A., Loflin, H. B., et al.: *Serratia marcescens* nosocomial infections of the urinary tract associated with urine measuring containers and urinometers. Am. J. Med. *70*:659–663, 1981.
82. Saito, H., Elting, L., Bodey, G. P., et al.: *Serratia* bacteremia: Review of 118 cases. Rev. Infect. Dis. *11*:912–920, 1989.
83. Schaberg, D. R., Alford, R. H., Anderson, R., et al.: An outbreak of nosocomial infection due to multiply resistant *Serratia marcescens:* Evidence of interhospital spread. J. Infect. Dis. *134*:181–188, 1976.
84. Schaberg, D. R., Haley, R. W., Highsmith, A. K., et al.: Nosocomial bacteriuria: A prospective study of case clustering and antimicrobial resistance. Ann. Intern. Med. *93*:420–424, 1980.
85. Schaberg, D. R., Rubens, C. E., Alford, R. H., et al.: Evolution of antimicrobial resistance and nosocomial infection: Lessons from the Vanderbilt experience. Am. J. Med. *70*:445–448, 1981.
86. Senda, K., Arakawa, Y., Ichiyama, S., et al.: PCR detection of metallo-beta-lactamase gene (blaIMP) in gram-negative rods resistant to broad-spectrum beta-lactams. J. Clin. Microbiol. *34*:2909–2913, 1996.
87. Serruys-Schoutens, E., Rost, F., and Depre, G.: A nosocomial epidemic of *Serratia liquefaciens* urinary tract infection after cystometry. Eur. J. Clin. Microbiol. *3*:316–317, 1984.
88. Shulman, S. T., and Yogev, R.: Treatment of pediatric infections with amikacin as first-line aminoglycoside. Am. J. Med. *79*:43–50, 1985.
89. Sifuentes-Osornio, J., Ruiz-Palacios, G. M., and Groschel, D. H.: Analysis of epidemiologic markers of nosocomial *Serratia marcescens* isolates with special reference to the Grimont biotyping system. J. Clin. Microbiol. *23*:230–234, 1986.
90. Stamm, W. E., Kolff, C. A., Dones, E. M., et al.: A nursery outbreak caused by *Serratia* marcescens: Scalp-vein needles as a portal of entry. J. Pediatr. *89*:96–99, 1976.
91. Svensson, O., Parment, P. A., and Blomgren, G.: Orthopaedic infections by *Serratia marcescens:* A report of seven cases. Scand. J. Infect. Dis. *19*:69–75, 1987.
92. Thomas, F. E., Jackson, R. T., Melly, A., et al.: Sequential hospitalwide outbreaks of resistant *Serratia* and *Klebsiella* infections. Arch. Intern. Med. *137*:581–584, 1977.
93. Verrall, R.: *Serratia marcescens*. Infect. Control *4*:469–471, 1983.
94. Villarino, M. E., Jarvis, W. R., O'Hara, C., et al.: Epidemic of *Serratia marcescens* bacteremia in a cardiac intensive care unit. J. Clin. Microbiol. *27*:2433–2436, 1989.
95. Waisman, H. A., and Stone, W. H.: The presence of *Serratia marcescens* as the predominating organism in the intestinal tract of the newborn: The occurrence of the "red diaper syndrome." Pediatrics *21*:8–12, 1958.
96. Wheat, R. P., Zuckerman, A., and Rantz, L. A.: Infection due to chromobacteria: Report of eleven cases. Arch. Intern. Med. *88*:461–466, 1951.
97. Woodward, H. M. M., and Clarke, K. B.: A case of infection in man by the *Bacterium prodigiosum*. Lancet *1*:314–315, 1913.
98. Yu, V. L.: *Serratia marcescens:* Historical perspective and clinical review. N. Engl. J. Med. *300*:887–893, 1979.
99. Yu, V. L., Oakes, C. A., Axnick, K. J., et al.: Patient factors contributing to the emergence of gentamicin-resistant *Serratia marcescens*. Am. J. Med. *66*:468–472, 1979.
100. Zaidi, M., Sifuentes, J., Bobadilla, M., et al.: Epidemic of *Serratia marcescens* bacteremia and meningitis in a neonatal unit in Mexico City. Infect. Control Hosp. Epidemiol. *10*:14–20, 1989.

Salmonella

THOMAS G. CLEARY

Microbiology

The classification of *Salmonella* is confusing because multiple nomenclature systems are used (Table 115–1). In this chapter, we use the current designation of the Centers for Disease Control and Prevention (CDC) rather than either the complete name or the traditional clinical shorthand that referred to each of the 2463 serovars of *Salmonella* as though they were separate species. In hospital laboratories, *S.* ser. Choleraesuis and *S.* ser. Typhi are distinguished biochemically from other *Salmonella* spp. Serogroup, based on O (somatic) antigen, also usually is determined on initial isolation, and organisms that are not *S.* ser. Typhi or *S.* ser. Choleraesuis are reported as *Salmonella* serogroup A, B, C1, D1, and so on. Common *Salmonella* spp. and their serogroups are shown in Table 115–2. *Salmonella* serotype is defined by the serogroup antigens, the flagellar (H) antigens, and the virulence (Vi) antigen. H antigens can be either phase 1 (nonspecific) or phase 2 (specific). The Vi antigen, a heat-labile polysaccharide found on *S.* ser. Typhi,

TABLE 115–1 ■ EXAMPLES OF CURRENT *SALMONELLA* NOMENCLATURE

CDC Designation	Complete Name	Previous Designation
S. ser Typhi	*S. enterica* * subsp. *enterica* ser. Typhi	*S. typhi*
S. ser. Enteritidis	*S. enterica* subsp. *enterica* ser. Enteritidis	*S. enteritidis*
S. IIIa 18:z_4,z_{23}: -	*S. enterica* subsp. *arizonae* ser. 18:z_4,z_{23}: -	*Arizona hinshawii* ser. 7a, 7b:1,2,5: -
S. ser. Marina	*S. enterica* subsp. *houtenae* ser. Marina	*S. marina*

**S. choleraesuis* and *S. enteritidis* also are designations commonly used for the species.

S. ser. Dublin, and *S.* ser. Paratyphi C, may block agglutination caused by antibodies to O antigen. Serotyping generally is done in state or county public health department laboratories. Although serotyping is an important epidemiologic tool for defining outbreaks, it is much more useful when an unusual type is disease associated. When a common serotype is associated with an outbreak (e.g., *S.* ser. Typhimurium), biochemical phenotype, antibiogram, plasmid characterization,[197] bacteriophage typing,[26, 83] outer-membrane protein analysis, pulsed-field gel electrophoresis, and randomly amplified polymorphic DNA may help determine whether a single-strain common-source outbreak is in progress.

Six subgroups of *Salmonella* have been proposed on the basis of DNA relatedness. Most serotypes, including almost all of the serotypes important in human and animal disease, belong to subgroup I. *Arizona* now is considered part of the genus *Salmonella*.

Salmonellae are motile (due to peritrichous flagellae), nonencapsulated, gram-negative bacilli of the Enterobacteriaceae family. Most ferment glucose, maltose, and mannitol but do not use lactose or sucrose. All pathogenic *Salmonella* other than *S.* ser. Typhi produce gas. *Salmonella* spp. are facultative anaerobes. Blood agar or chocolate agar supports their growth when they are present as the sole organisms in blood, cerebrospinal fluid, or joint fluid. For specimens containing mixed flora (e.g., stool), selective media such as *Salmonella-Shigella* (SS agar) or bismuth sulfate agar must be used.

TABLE 115–2 ■ *SALMONELLA* SPECIES INCLUDED IN MAJOR SEROGROUPS

Serogroup*	Representative Serotypes
A	*S.* ser Paratyphi A
B	*S.* ser Paratyphi B
	S. ser Saint-Paul
	S. ser Agona
	S. ser Derby
	S. ser Typhimurium
	S. ser Heidelberg
C1	*S.* ser Paratyphi C
	S. ser Choleraesuis
	S. ser Montevideo
	S. ser Infantis
C2	*S.* ser Newport
C3	*S.* ser Santiago
D1	*S.* ser Typhi
	S. ser Enteritidis
	S. ser Dublin
D2	*S.* ser Strasbourg
E1	*S.* ser Anatum
E2	*S.* ser Newington
E3	*S.* ser Illinois

*Human infections with organisms in serogroups E4, F, G1, G2, H, and I and the O antigens not given sergroup designation (O17 through O67) are relatively uncommon.

Epidemiology

NONTYPHOIDAL *SALMONELLA*

PUBLIC HEALTH ISSUES. In most of the world, the prevalence of *Salmonella* varies according to the water supply, waste disposal, food preparation practices, and climate. However, the incidence of nontyphoidal salmonellosis in the United States has been increasing steadily despite good public health measures. During the last 40 years, a greater than sixfold increase in reported nontyphoidal *Salmonella* infection in the United States has occurred; 40,000 to 50,000 cases are reported each year. This figure reflects industrial-scale food production and distribution,[36] misuse of antimicrobial agents (in both humans and animals) that alter the gastrointestinal flora and thereby increase host susceptibility to *Salmonella,* and probably an increasing number of immunocompromised persons in the population.

THE SIGNIFICANCE OF ANIMAL RESERVOIRS. Unlike *Shigella* spp., which infect only primates, nontyphoidal *Salmonella* spp. infect a variety of animals (including poultry, livestock, and pets). Thus, animals and animal products (including meat and dairy products), water, and infected humans can be the source of infection. Spread of resistant organisms from food animals to humans has been shown.[164] *Salmonella* spp. have been isolated from up to 50 percent of poultry,[28] 16 percent of pork, 5 percent of beef, and 40 percent of frozen egg products in retail stores. Undercooked eggs (e.g., in Caesar salad, egg-dipped bread, homemade eggnog) may be contaminated by organisms on the shell surface or transovarially directly through the egg yolk. Grade A shell eggs have been implicated in more than 80 percent of recent outbreaks.[163] Even in the absence of recognized outbreaks, eggs probably are important vehicles of infection; foods containing eggs that have been undercooked are more likely to have been consumed during the 3 days before illness in sporadic cases than in control cases.[110]

The risk of outbreaks occurring was demonstrated when milk contaminated with *S.* ser. Typhimurium was distributed in Chicago, Illinois. Reports estimated that more than 150,000 became ill, with more than 16,000 culture-confirmed cases, 2777 persons hospitalized, and 14 fatalities.[23] Ice cream, cream cakes, and mayonnaise commonly have been incriminated as the source of infections. Fruits and vegetables rarely are vehicles.[38]

Some serotypes are associated with particular reservoirs. For example, *S.* ser. Dublin is associated with dairy cattle and thus frequently is found in those who drink raw milk.[233] *S.* ser. Choleraesuis is associated with pigs. Infection with *S.* ser. Marina is associated with contact with pet iguanas. *Salmonella* group F, *S.* ser. Typhimurium, *S.* ser. Muenchen, and *S.* ser. Java infections have been traced to pet turtles. Reptiles, including rattlesnakes, are important *S.* IIIa 18:z_4,z_{23}:- *(Arizona hinshawii)* reservoirs.

HUMANS AS A RESERVOIR. After infection, nontyphoidal *Salmonella* spp. are excreted in feces for a median of 5 weeks. Children younger than 5 years of age may excrete the organisms for 20 weeks after having an illness, but older children and adults usually excrete *Salmonella* less than 8 weeks. *S.* ser. Typhi may be excreted chronically, particularly in the presence of gallbladder disease. Food handlers who are excreting *Salmonella* spp. represent an important risk group.

BACTERIAL CHARACTERISTICS FAVORING SURVIVAL. *Salmonella* spp. are hardy. They survive refrigeration and sometimes heating; they may remain viable at ambient or reduced temperatures for weeks. When contaminated foods are cooked for less than 12 minutes at temperatures below 150° F (65.5° C), salmonellae may remain viable. *Salmonella* spp. are killed by heating to 130° F (54.4° C) for 1 hour or 140° F (60° C) for 15 minutes. Salmonellae survive for hours on the hands of slaughterhouse workers.[182] They have been found to survive in flour for nearly a year. *S.* ser. Tennessee has been reported to remain viable for 2 to 8 days on glass, stainless steel, enameled surfaces, rubber mattress, linen, and a rubber tabletop.[247] Nosocomial infections have been related to contaminated medical equipment (e.g., endoscopes) and diagnostic or pharmacologic preparations, particularly those of animal origin (e.g., pituitary extracts, bile salts, pancreatic extracts, pepsin, vitamins).

THE RELATIONSHIP OF AGE TO RISK OF DISEASE. The highest incidence rates occur in children younger than 5 years of age, especially those younger than 1 year, and in individuals older than 70 years of age.

Nursery outbreaks often can be traced to an infected mother,[1, 2, 18, 134] with subsequent spread through health care personnel.[215, 248] The mother of the index case can be symptomatic[78, 151, 205] or asymptomatic,[248] recovering from recent infection,[2, 173, 219] or a chronic carrier.[212] Low-birth-weight infants appear to be at higher risk than do full-term infants for acquiring *Salmonella* infection.[21, 215, 248] The source of infection occasionally is contaminated food but more often fomites (delivery room resuscitators,[206] rectal thermometers,[121, 154] suction devices,[130] water baths for heating formula,[197] soap dispensers,[162] scales,[6, 22, 248] tables,[248] air-conditioning filters,[248] and plumbing[158]). Nursery outbreaks often are extraordinarily difficult to stop. They have been reported to last several months[154, 178, 248] to several years.[78, 158, 229] Contamination sometimes can become so widespread that other areas of the hospital also experience cases.[152, 217] Nursery outbreaks occur far more commonly with *Salmonella* than with other bacterial enteropathogens. Such outbreaks sometimes are caused by multiresistant *Salmonella*.[134]

SEASONALITY. *Salmonella* infection occurs in warm months, when there are more food-borne outbreaks related to contaminated food, contaminated hands of food handlers, or contaminated fomites.

INOCULUM SIZE REQUIRED TO CAUSE DISEASE. The estimated inoculum size required to cause symptomatic disease in healthy adult volunteers is 10^5 to 10^{10} organisms,[25] but the number of organisms required to cause symptoms in infants and children probably is much lower. In contrast, large inocula are not required for *Shigella* infection, which occurs in adult volunteers exposed to as few as 10 organisms. In some outbreaks, very small inocula of *Salmonella* appear to have caused disease. Large inocula (e.g., 10^9) may cause severe symptoms, even in healthy children.[232] The incubation period usually is shorter than 6 to 72 hours but depends on inoculum size, bacterial virulence, and host immunocompetence. Communicability parallels the duration of fecal excretion; nontyphoidal *Salmonella* may be carried for several months. The probability of salmonellosis is increased when a member of the household is infected. Infants especially may be susceptible to acquiring *Salmonella* infection directly or indirectly from ill family members. In a retrospective review of 187 infants younger than 1 year of age with *Salmonella* gastroenteritis, 39 percent had at least one family contact with diarrhea, and 71 percent of the contacts had stool cultures positive for *Salmonella*.[249] *Salmonella* spp. rarely have been isolated during studies of gastroenteritis in day-care centers, perhaps suggesting that larger inocula are required to cause illness in toddlers and older children.[44, 140, 184]

ANTIBIOTIC SELECTION PRESSURE. Since the mid 1960s, *Salmonella* spp. have become increasingly resistant to ampicillin, chloramphenicol, and trimethoprim-sulfamethoxazole (TMP-SMX). Multiresistant strains have included *S.* ser. Typhimurium, which is the most common serotype in Europe and the United States, and *S.* ser. Heidelberg, *S.* ser. Agona, *S.* ser. Muenchen, *S.* ser. Enteritidis, and *S.* ser. Hadar. Antibiotic resistance usually is transferable between organisms through plasmids that carry genes encoding resistance factors.[95] Previous exposure to antibiotics is significantly more common in individuals who develop both antibiotic-resistant and antibiotic-susceptible salmonellosis. Patients who are infected with antibiotic-resistant strains are more likely to be hospitalized, to be very young, to be black, and to have been exposed recently to antibiotic agents.[135] Previous use of antimicrobial agents for treatment of other illnesses is a significant risk factor for acquiring multiresistant *Salmonella* infection.[145, 198] Perhaps the most important factor is the overuse and misuse of antibiotics in animals raised for food.[47, 115, 116, 139, 226] Subtherapeutic concentrations of antibiotics used to enhance growth and to prevent infection promote intestinal colonization by antibiotic-resistant bacteria, including *Salmonella;* these organisms may be found in feces and may contaminate meat at the time of slaughter. Plasmid analysis and antibiotic susceptibility patterns have linked *Salmonella* outbreaks to specific farms and slaughterhouses.[115, 116, 164]

SALMONELLA SER. TYPHI

An estimated 12.5 million cases occur annually in the world, with an incidence of 365 cases per 100,000 persons. *S.* ser. Typhi is the most common *Salmonella* isolate in many developing countries; the incidence in these countries is estimated at 10 to 540 cases per 100,000 persons. In developed countries, the annual incidence is 0.2 to 3.7 cases per 100,000 persons in western Europe, the United States, and Japan and 4.3 to 14.5 cases per 100,000 persons in southern Europe.[67] In the United States, approximately 1700 total cases were reported (1.0 case per 100,000 persons) in 1955. In 1988, approximately 400 total cases were reported (0.018 case per 100,000 persons). Approximately 28 percent of infections occurred in individuals 19 years of age or younger. It frequently is stated that the highest incidence is between 5 and 12 years; however, recent data from India challenge this view and suggest that children younger than 5 years of age are infected commonly if blood cultures are obtained routinely during febrile episodes.[221] In the United States, persons traveling to developing countries are a high-risk group; 62 to 81 percent of infections are related to foreign travel, especially to Mexico, India, the Philippines, Pakistan, El Salvador, and Haiti. Of these areas, the Indian subcontinent has the highest incidence of typhoid among travelers.[5, 37, 67, 159, 210]

THE RESERVOIR. Humans are the reservoir for *S.* ser. Typhi; infection implies direct or indirect contact with an infected person. Animal products transmit *S.* ser. Typhi if they are contaminated by infected humans during processing. The most common mode of transmission is food or water contaminated by human feces. Water-borne typhoid fever epidemics are especially important. Congenital transmission can occur from a bacteremic mother to her fetus transplacentally or at the time of delivery through the fecal-oral route.

THE RELEVANCE OF INOCULUM SIZE TO DISEASE. As with nontyphoidal *Salmonella*, more than 10^5 organisms are required to cause clinical illness in adults.[118]

ANTIBIOTIC RESISTANCE. The worldwide frequency of antibiotic-resistant *S.* ser. Typhi has been increasing since the 1960s[223] but remains much lower than that of nontyphoidal *Salmonella*. Extensive protracted outbreaks have been reported throughout Asia, the Middle East, and Central and South America. Epidemic enteric fever in Mexico caused by chloramphenicol-resistant strains lasted for 2 years in the early 1970s.[242] These outbreaks may have been related to widespread availability and inappropriate use of antimicrobial agents (especially chloramphenicol) as over-the-counter drugs in these areas.

Pathophysiology

Host susceptibility is understood most easily in terms of specific events in pathogenesis. Tables 115–3 and 115–4 show the relevance of specific host and bacterial virulence factors in salmonellosis. The outcome of *Salmonella* ingestion depends on both the bacteria and the host.

Various *Salmonella* strains can (1) adhere to, invade, and multiply in intestinal epithelium; (2) produce cholera toxin–like enterotoxin that increases cyclic adenosine monophosphate levels within intestinal crypt cells, causing a net efflux of electrolytes and water into the intestinal lumen; (3) be taken up by M cells overlying Peyer patches of the distal ileum and proximal colon; (4) survive in macrophages of Peyer patches, mesenteric lymph nodes, and the extraintestinal reticuloendothelial system; and (5) survive in the bloodstream.[76, 77, 86] Specific genes (on virulence plasmids and in *Salmonella* pathogenicity islands on the chromosome) encode virulence factors necessary for each step in these processes. Pathologic findings include hypertrophy and hyperplasia of the intestinal and mesenteric lymphoid tissues, liver, and spleen in *S.* ser. Typhi infection. In contrast, *S.* ser. Typhimurium and other nontyphoidal serotypes cause diffuse colitis, mucosal edema, and crypt abscesses as the major pathologic abnormalities.[28, 55] Some of these virulence genes are shared by all *Salmonella*, whereas others are serotype specific. Differences in invasiveness of various serotypes exist. For example, *S.* ser. Typhi, *S.* ser. Choleraesuis, *S.* ser. Heidelberg,[120, 156] and *S.* ser. Dublin[233] are more likely to enter the blood and to seed distant sites. Virulence plasmids have been identified in *S.* ser. Typhi, *S.* ser. Typhimurium, and *S.* ser. Dublin.[19]

Nursery *Salmonella* outbreaks have demonstrated dramatically the variability in severity of illness related to strain or serotype. For example, in nursery outbreaks of *S.* ser. Oranienburg[229] and *S.* ser. Newport,[134] grossly bloody stools were found in 76 to 90 percent of infected infants, with 10 to 11 percent febrile and only 9 to 11 percent asymptomatic. Watery, green, nonbloody diarrhea has been a common occurrence with *S.* ser. Typhimurium,[2] *S.* ser. Virchow,[202] and *S.* ser. Nienstedten.[217] A high frequency of asymptomatic infections has been seen during nursery outbreaks with *S.* ser. Heidelberg (38% asymptomatic),[21] *S.* ser. Virchow (42% asymptomatic),[202] and *S.* ser. Tennessee (100% asymptomatic).[248]

Because of the broad host range, which genes are required for disease in humans compared with animals remains unclear. For example, *S.* ser Typhimurium has genes that allow it to cause a nondiarrheal typhoidal illness

TABLE 115–3 ■ SUSCEPTIBILITY TO *SALMONELLA* SPECIES INFECTION

Patient Group at Risk	Mechanism
Newborn	Achlorhydria, rapid gastric emptying Poorly developed cell-mediated immunity Complement deficiency Immunoglobulin deficiency in premature infants
Sickle-cell anemia	Reticuloendothelial system overload during hemolysis Functional asplenia Tissue infarcts Defective opsonization
Neutropenia (congenital or acquired)	Polymorphonuclear neutrophils needed for killing
Chronic granulomatous disease	Defective killing by polymorphonuclear neutrophils
AIDS	Low CD4 ? Effects of malnutrition on cell-mediated immunity Survival of organisms in macrophages (PhoP/PhoQ, spvA–D, R)
Organ transplantation, immunosuppression	Defective cell-mediated immunity
Gastrectomy	Loss of stomach acid barrier
Malaria	Reticuloendothelial overload during hemolysis Abnormal complement levels Abnormal macrophage function
Bartonellosis	Reticuloendothelial overload during hemolysis
Schistosomiasis	*Salmonella* sequestered in schistosomes protected from host defenses and antibiotics

TABLE 115–4 ■ PATHOPHYSIOLOGIC BASIS OF SELECTED CLINICAL FEATURES OF SALMONELLOSIS

Disease Manifestation	Mechanisms and Bacterial Genes
Bloody diarrhea	*sip* A–D mediated invasion (SPI-1) and interleukin-8 mediated inflammation
Watery diarrhea	*stn* enterotoxin (cholera-like toxin) *SopB* (SPI-5)-mediated intestinal inflammation and fluid secretion Serotypes that include transepithelial polymorphonuclear leukocyte migration (e.g., *S.* ser. Typhimurium) are more likely to cause diarrhea than are those that do not (e.g., *S.* ser. Typhi)
Bacteremia	*viaB* (Vi synthesis) capsular antigen interferes with C3 binding (*S.* ser. Typhi, *S.* ser. Dublin, *S.* ser. Paratyphi C) *rck* resistance to serum complement (virulence plasmid encoded) *rfb* encodes lipopolysaccharide synthesis; lipopolysaccharide contributes to persistence of bacteremia
Relapses, prolonged fever, failure of certain antibiotics	Survival in macrophages (SPI-2 encoded *sseABC* and *spiC*, SPI-3 encoded *mgtCB*, SPI-4 encoded cytotoxin and virulence plasmid genes *spvRABCD*)

in mice; but in humans, it typically causes symptoms related primarily to intestinal involvement. Researchers estimate that more than 200 genes determine *S.* ser. Typhimurium virulence in mice. The clinical variability in host range and disease manifestations is due to the fact that *Salmonella* vary in their possession and expression of virulence genes.[150]

Genes relevant to the intestinal phase of illness are encoded primarily in *Salmonella* pathogenicity island 1 (SPI-1). The *invA–H* chromosomal genes are necessary for adherence to and invasion of intestinal mucosal cells[76]; most of the genes described so far appear to be involved in secretion or transport of virulence proteins.[99, 241] Genes related to the *Shigella* invasion plasmid antigens (*ipaA–D*) have been described in *Salmonella* spp.[126, 127]; these *Salmonella* genes (*sipA–D*) encode the proteins that interact with host cells to cause bacterial uptake and intracellular movement.

The role of host cells in the invasion process is complex. After *S.* ser. Typhimurium comes in contact with epithelial cells, activation of epidermal growth factor receptor occurs, which then activates a kinase that turns on phospholipase A_2 so that arachidonic acid is generated. Arachidonic acid is converted to leukotriene D_4, which opens calcium channels and causes membrane ruffling, cytoskeletal changes, and uptake of bacteria.[76] Nonphagocytic cells, including epithelial cells, are adapted poorly for killing of internalized bacteria. Not only do *Salmonella* spp. survive in vacuoles within epithelial cells, but they also can replicate actively.[77] *S.* ser. Typhi survives better in human than in mouse macrophages, whereas Typhimurium survives better in mouse macrophages.[31, 216] Several sets of genes appear to allow *Salmonella* to survive within the hostile environment of macrophages. The PhoP/PhoQ system, the *spvA–D* and *spvR* plasmid loci, and genes in SPI-2, SPI-3, and SPI-4 seem to be key to this process.[101, 102] The presence of virulence plasmids appears to be more common in blood isolates of *S.* ser. Typhimurium than in fecal isolates (76% vs. 42%).[75] However, *S.* ser. Typhi and *S.* ser. Paratyphi A do not contain virulence plasmids and yet are invasive.

The development of diarrhea depends on host and pathogen factors. An influx of polymorphonuclear leukocytes into the mucosa must occur for diarrhea to develop.[245] Neutropenic animals fail to develop fluid secretion when they are infected with *Salmonella*[246]; infiltration of leukocytes is thought to trigger production of prostaglandin because fluid secretion can be blocked by indomethacin.[87] A cholera toxin–like enterotoxin is made by approximately two thirds of *Salmonella* strains, including *S.* ser. Typhimurium and *S.* ser. Typhi.[123]

For most nontyphoidal *Salmonella,* infection does not extend beyond the lamina propria and the local lymphatics. In contrast, *S.* ser. Typhi, *S.* ser. Dublin, and *S.* ser. Choleraesuis rapidly invade the bloodstream with relatively little intestinal involvement. Some virulence genes confer a survival advantage to the organisms if they get into the extraintestinal milieu. Vi capsular antigen present in *S.* ser. Typhi, *S.* ser. Dublin, and *S.* ser. Paratyphi C interferes with C3 binding. Mutations in lipopolysaccharide genes decrease invasiveness of *S.* ser. Typhi and *S.* ser. Choleraesuis but not of *S.* ser. Typhimurium.[77, 166] *S.* ser. Dublin, *S.* ser. Typhimurium, and *S.* ser. Enteritidis have virulence genes that confer resistance to complement by preventing the formation and insertion of the C5b–9 membrane attack complex. Patients with sickle-cell anemia have complement defects and defects in opsonization of *S.* ser. Typhimurium.[107] Newborns also have complement deficiencies that may explain their high frequency of *Salmonella* infection and their susceptibility to bacteremic complications seldom seen in normal hosts.

Multiple host defense strategies have evolved to deal with these virulence factors; host susceptibility often can be related directly to defects in these defense mechanisms. The host tries to kill ingested organisms in the stomach, to inhibit their growth in the gut, to limit their spread beyond the intestine, and to clear them by immune mechanisms.

At a pH of 2.0, most *Salmonella* spp. are killed rapidly.[84] When gastric pH is raised by oral administration of antacid, susceptibility increases.[85, 118, 198] Slow gastric emptying also is protective. *Salmonella* ingested in water passes through the stomach more rapidly than when the same inoculum is ingested in food. Rapid transit through the small bowel decreases the contact time of organisms with the mucosa. Therefore, patients with decreased intestinal motility caused by medication or anatomic factors have increased severity and complications and may have a prolonged carrier state. Prior antimicrobial exposure increases the risk of incurring infection with both antimicrobial-susceptible and antimicrobial-resistant strains of *Salmonella.*[181] The normal flora may compete for substrates, lower the local pH by production of short-chain fatty acids, and produce antibacterial substances such as colicins. Some patients with gastroenteritis have progression or exacerbation of symptoms when antibiotics are given.[201]

Salmonella are able to survive in macrophages but not in polymorphonuclear leukocytes. Thus, patients with neutropenia (e.g., congenital, related to chemotherapy) or neutrophil dysfunction (e.g., chronic granulomatous disease) are at high risk for development of disseminated infection. Patients who have been bacteremic with a nontyphoidal *Salmonella* are at increased risk for having a relapse if leukopenia is present.[80]

Cell-mediated immunity generally is thought to be more important than humoral immunity in clearance of *Salmonella.* T-cell activation of macrophages is necessary to kill intracellular *Salmonella.*[147] Oral immunization with an attenuated typhoid vaccine primes lymphocytes to produce cytokines typical of a T_H1 response (high interferon-γ/low interleukin-4) to the flagellar antigen.[230] Healthy individuals vaccinated with either oral or parenteral typhoid vaccines develop antibody-dependent cellular cytotoxicity mediated by IgA, IgG, or both.[53] However, studies of serum and secretory antibodies to O and H antigens have not demonstrated protection; relapses of typhoid fever have occurred despite high antibody titers. Immunity may be short-lived. In a study of 14 individuals (17 to 28 years of age) with acute typhoid fever, cell-mediated immunity persisted for 16 weeks; intestinal secretory IgA persisted for 48 weeks; and IgG, IgM, and anti-O and anti-H agglutinins persisted for 2 years, 16 weeks, 16 weeks, and 36 weeks, respectively.[214]

Impaired cell-mediated immunity probably explains the high frequency of bacteremia with nontyphoidal *Salmonella* in children with human immunodeficiency virus infection.[207] Cell-mediated immunity also is defective in malnutrition, and this fact further contributes to the susceptibility of persons with malnutrition,[222] including human immunodeficiency virus–infected patients. Defective cell-mediated immunity can be congenital or acquired (tumors,[104] collagen vascular disease, organ transplantation,[69] chemotherapy, glucocorticosteroids).[193] Inherited deficiency in the interleukin-12/interferon-γ pathway results in susceptibility to recurrent *Salmonella* and *Mycobacterium* infections. Defects have been described in which patients have mutations in interleukin-12, interleukin-12 receptor, or interferon-γ receptor. Both complete and partial deficiency syndromes have been described.[9, 10, 125] An increased risk of acquiring disease exists in settings in which reticuloendothelial function or cell-mediated immunity is impaired[169, 225] or immature.[172] For example, hemolytic anemias are thought to cause reticuloendothelial overload. Children with sickle-cell anemia commonly become bacteremic and develop osteomyelitis.[149, 228, 252, 256] Sickle-C and S-Thal also sometimes develop osteomyelitis.[46]

Malaria predisposes to salmonellosis by multiple mechanisms.[144] During the rainy season, when malaria is most common, 50 percent of blood cultures taken from West African children younger than 5 years of age with pneumonia are positive for *Salmonella* or coliform species.[176]

Schistosomiasis predisposes to *Salmonella* infections and prolonged bacteremia[199]; reticuloendothelial cell killing of *Salmonella* is impaired, and *Salmonella* colonizes the schistosomes. Pili on *Salmonella* adhere to the surface of *Schistosoma mansoni* and *Schistosoma haematobium*.[142] In Gabonese children with bacteremic nontyphoidal *Salmonella*, rectal biopsy specimens show the eggs of *Schistosoma intercalatum* in 90 percent of cases.[82]

Although the bulk of the evidence suggests that humoral immunity is less important, data demonstrate that preterm neonates who are infected with *S.* ser. Typhimurium may have a lower risk of complications (e.g., intestinal perforation, meningitis, endophthalmitis, sepsis, pyelitis) if they are given intravenous immune globulin plus cefoperazone than do control subjects given cefoperazone alone (16% vs. 82%); mortality also is decreased (12% vs. 41%).[94]

Clinical Manifestations

Salmonella may cause acute or chronic asymptomatic infection. Symptomatic infections include acute gastroenteritis, bacteremia with or without local suppuration, and enteric fever. Specific serotypes are associated more commonly with certain clinical syndromes. *S.* ser. Typhimurium, the most common isolate in the United States, causes acute intestinal infection, sometimes without symptoms. *S.* ser. Choleraesuis almost always is isolated only from the blood. *S.* ser. Typhi and *S.* ser. Paratyphi A, B, and C cause enteric fever.

ACUTE ASYMPTOMATIC INFECTION

Asymptomatic infections usually are identified by stool cultures obtained during epidemiologic investigations. A study of Mexican infants showed that 74 percent of nontyphoidal *Salmonella* infections were asymptomatic.[52]

ACUTE GASTROENTERITIS

The most common clinical illness caused by *Salmonella* is gastroenteritis. Nausea, vomiting, and crampy abdominal pain begin 6 to 72 hours (median, 24 hours) after ingestion of contaminated food or water. The abdominal pain may be severe enough to suggest appendicitis. Diarrhea usually is moderate in volume and, depending on the serotype, may contain blood. Headaches, malaise, myalgias, and fevers are common findings. These symptoms usually resolve in approximately a week without antibiotic therapy; symptoms may persist in the very young and those with underlying diseases. In neonates, loose, green, mucous stools or, less often, bloody diarrhea is seen; fever is a common occurrence with *Salmonella* gastroenteritis during the first months of life.[120] Reactive arthritis develops in some adults after otherwise uncomplicated *Salmonella* gastroenteritis; this complication rarely occurs in children.

BACTEREMIA WITH OR WITHOUT METASTATIC FOCAL INFECTION

Some *Salmonella* serotypes (e.g., *S.* ser. Typhi; *S.* ser. Choleraesuis; *S.* ser. Paratyphi A, B, and C; *S.* ser. Heidelberg; *S.* ser. Typhimurium; *S.* ser. Enteritidis; *S.* ser. Saint-Paul; *S.* ser. Newport; *S.* ser. Panama; *S.* ser. Dublin) have a propensity to invade the bloodstream; others (e.g., *S.* ser. Tennessee, *S.* ser. Weltevreden[251]) rarely seem to cause bacteremia. Fever, chills, diaphoresis, myalgias, anorexia, and weight loss may last for days or weeks. Stool cultures may be negative; diarrhea may not precede the fever. A child sometimes can have afebrile diarrhea and yet be bacteremic for several days.[128] The true frequency of bacteremia is uncertain. Depending on the patient's age, geographic location, and nature of the study (prospective versus retrospective), 2 to 45 percent of infections are bacteremic.[54, 120, 156, 172, 222, 236, 251, 253] Bacteremia probably occurs more commonly in the newborn (in some studies as high as 30% to 50%) than in the older child,[120] although not all studies have reached this conclusion.[156] The true risk of bacteremia in the first year of life is likely to be in the 2 to 6 percent range.[54, 236] Hemolytic anemia, especially sickle-cell anemia, is associated with a high risk of development of *Salmonella* bacteremia. Persistent or recurrent bacteremia occurs in patients with acquired immunodeficiency syndrome (AIDS), schistosomiasis, and intravascular focal infection. Adults who become bacteremic with *Salmonella* are more likely to do so without a preceding gastroenteritis and to have a high mortality rate, presumably because they so often are immunocompromised.[106] Children more typically are relatively immunocompetent; most often they develop bacteremia associated with diarrhea and have a much better prognosis.[136, 156] Even children with neoplastic disease may have a relatively benign course when they are bacteremic with *Salmonella* spp.[175]

Focal suppurative infections may occur almost anywhere; the most common sites are bones (particularly in sickle-cell anemia)[26, 228, 252] and the central nervous system.[29, 63, 131, 143, 200] The risk for development of focal infections during bacteremia is higher (36%) in those with underlying conditions than in previously healthy children (2.5%).[255] Meningitis has a high morbidity, with acute hydrocephalus, seizures, ventriculitis, abscesses, subdural empyema, and cerebral infarction. Long-term neurologic sequelae include mental retardation, hemiparesis, chronic hydrocephalus, epilepsy, visual impairment, and athetosis.[46] Neurologic sequelae are particularly common in those who have prolonged fever (>10 days) while receiving antibiotic therapy.[119] Mortality from meningitis has been as high as 40 to 60 percent in the past, even with appropriate treatment; recent data suggest that mortality is now much lower. Relapses even after prolonged therapy occur commonly (reflecting the intracellular localization of *Salmonella* and the difficulty of achieving adequate intracellular levels of antibiotics). Fifty to 75 percent of nontyphoidal *Salmonella* meningitis occurs in the first 4 months of life.[46] The serotypes causing meningitis, including *S.* ser. Typhimurium, *S.* ser. Heidelberg, *S.* ser. Enteritidis, *S.* ser. Saint-Paul, *S.* ser. Havana, *S.* ser. Oranienburg, *S.* ser. Newport, and *S.* ser. Panama,[46, 249] are serotypes commonly associated with bacteremia. In infants, complications include pneumonia,[21] osteomyelitis,[60, 133, 252] septic arthritis,[21, 215] pericarditis,[105, 155] pyelitis,[231] peritonitis,[2] otitis media,[2] mastitis,[171] cholecystitis,[103] endophthalmitis,[51] cutaneous abscesses,[190] and infected cephalhematoma.[60] In adults and occasionally in older children, femoral and distal aorta (mycotic aneurysms),[46] heart valves,[46] scrotum,[239] testicles,[46] prostate,[213] ovaries,[46] and fallopian tubes[213] also may be infected.

Hemolytic-uremic syndrome associated with *S.* ser. Typhimurium[64, 153] and *S.* ser. Typhi[20] has been reported. Because the cytotoxins produced by various *Salmonella* strains are distinct immunologically from Shiga toxin produced by *Shigella dysenteriae* 1 and the Shiga toxins produced by enterohemorrhagic *Escherichia coli,*[14] the association of hemolytic-uremic syndrome with salmonellosis may represent undiagnosed dual infection with toxin-producing organisms.

ENTERIC FEVER

Enteric fever usually is caused by *S.* ser. Typhi and, less often, other invasive *Salmonella,* including *S.* ser. Paratyphi and *S.* ser. Choleraesuis. In contrast to sepsis caused by other gram-negative bacilli, the onset of symptoms in enteric fever is insidious.[118] After an incubation period of 10 to 14 days (range, 6 to 21 days), which generally is related to the inoculum size, fever, malaise, anorexia, and abdominal pain develop during a 2- to 3-day period. The incubation period tends to be somewhat shorter with paratyphoid fever. The temperature rises in small increments, usually reaching 40° C to 40.5° C by the end of the first week of illness. The temperature does not return to normal but rather rises to higher peaks each afternoon, with higher nadirs each subsequent morning during the first week. Eventually, the fever is unremittent; spikes in temperature occur without any return to normal.

Constipation occurs in approximately 50 percent of cases, whereas diarrhea occurs in approximately 30 percent of patients. When diarrhea develops, it usually does so after the patient has been febrile for several days; it is small volume, resembles pea soup, and contains erythrocytes but usually is not grossly bloody. Fecal leukocytes are present in nearly all patients with diarrhea.[204] Diarrhea occurs more commonly with paratyphoid than with typhoid fever.[238] Vomiting is mild and not sustained.

A dull, continuous frontal headache begins during the first 2 days of fever; headache is present in approximately 75 percent of patients. Confusion or delirium occurs more commonly than does a normal mental status in adults. Children commonly complain of headache; they often are drowsy, irritable, or delirious.[59] Mild arthralgia involving multiple joints and vague, poorly localized back pain occur in nearly 60 percent of patients.

Physical examination during the first week may show a relative bradycardia for the degree of fever. The patient has a dull, expressionless, toxic facies; coated tongue, a musty "damp hay–like" odor, and a tender, doughy abdomen with slight guarding also are present. On occasion, a child may have a cough; it tends to be minimal and unimpressive. The skin is dry with little sweating. Meningismus may occur early in the illness.

During the second week, rose spots may appear on the abdomen or chest and less often on the back, upper arms, and thighs. They typically begin between days 7 and 10 as crops of 10 to 15 lesions, each measuring 2 to 4 mm. More lesions may occur in paratyphoid. They are blanching, erythematous, slightly raised lesions that last approximately 3 days. Rose spots occur in a minority of patients and are difficult to recognize in dark-skinned individuals. New crops of rose spots may continue for 1 to 2 weeks.

The spleen becomes palpable, soft, and tender by early in the second week of illness. Respiratory symptoms may progress, and epistaxis occasionally may occur. If left untreated, enteric fever has a prolonged course, with continuous high temperature of 39.5° C to 40.5° C for as long as 4 weeks, followed by a gradual return to normal beginning during the third or fourth week. A rapid drop in temperature late in illness suggests intestinal hemorrhage or perforation[24]; such a drop in temperature typically is followed by a rise a few hours later as peritonitis develops. Intestinal hemorrhage and intestinal perforation[24, 33, 88] may occur in the second to fourth week in as many as 3 percent of patients with typhoid fever.[33] Late in the course of untreated typhoid, the mental status changes to a "coma vigil," in which the patient lies with open eyes, mutters, and is oblivious to the surroundings.

Most complications develop during the second or third week of illness. Complications include acalculous cholecystitis,[250] hepatitis,[192] osteomyelitis,[179] arthritis,[179] parotitis, myocarditis, pneumonia, meningitis, pyelonephritis, and orchitis.[138] Suppurative lymphadenitis,[168] tonsillitis,[124, 213] infected prosthetic heart valves,[11] and pancreatitis[209] rarely occur. Patients who have thalassemia or glucose-6-phosphate dehydrogenase deficiency may have hemolysis during typhoid fever.[238] The relapse rate is 5 to 20 percent, even when appropriate therapy has been given. Relapses typically are milder than the initial illness.

In some geographic areas, such as Indonesia, where an exceptionally virulent *S.* ser. Typhi is endemic, toxemia, delirium, obtundation, coma, and shock sometimes occur.[118, 138] Some serotypes in Indonesia (e.g., H1-j) appear to be less virulent than others, suggesting that properties of the flagellar antigen may be important to virulence.[100]

Typhoid fever is variable in its clinical course; patients commonly lack some of the features. Variations on the classic theme include a completely afebrile course occurring in debilitated patients, a high spiking fever from the first day (particularly in children), a focal presentation (e.g., pneumonia, nephritis), and a severe course during relapses. Infants are said to be at higher risk for development of massive hepatomegaly, thrombocytopenia, and other complications.[191] The mortality rate is high in the neonatal period.[194] Infants and toddlers often have a nondescript febrile illness misinterpreted as a "viral syndrome." In children younger than 2 years of age, the fever may last for as little as 1 to 5 days, despite the presence of *S.* ser. Typhi or *S.* ser. Paratyphi in the blood; low-grade fever (temperature of 38.3° C to 38.8° C) and cough may be the only findings in such children.[73] Prolonged hypothermia during convalescence occurs in some children.

Both typhoid and nontyphoidal *Salmonella* infections during pregnancy increase the risk of aborting the fetus.[162, 227] Spontaneous abortion or premature labor usually can be prevented by early treatment.[220] Transmission of *S.* ser. Typhi rarely occurs in utero.[40] Typically, premature delivery occurs during the second to fourth week of untreated maternal typhoid fever.[98] In the pre-antibiotic era, 40 percent of women with typhoid delivered prematurely; the remainder carried to term, although only 17 percent of infants survived.[58] If infection occurs late in gestation and is treated appropriately, the infant may survive.

ASYMPTOMATIC CHRONIC CARRIER STATE

Chronic carriers excrete *Salmonella* in stools for longer than 1 year after having gastroenteritis-enterocolitis or enteric fever. Approximately 1 to 4 percent of patients who recover from enteric fever caused by *S.* ser. Typhi chronically excrete the organism[160]; less than 1 percent of patients with nontyphoidal *Salmonella* excrete for such a prolonged period.[30, 39] Nontyphoidal infection is associated with excretion for a mean of 5 weeks, although children younger than

5 years of age,[30] females, the elderly, and patients with biliary tract disease are more likely to become carriers. The biliary tract is infected in almost all chronic carriers of *S.* ser. Typhi. As many as 10^6 organisms per gram of feces may be excreted.[160] The significance of chronic excretion is that such patients serve as a source of infection to their contacts. Chronic carriers represent an epidemiologically important reservoir of *S.* ser. Typhi; they often are the source of typhoid fever outbreaks. In the United States, although typhoid fever is generally imported, as many as 30 percent of infections result from exposure to previously diagnosed or newly diagnosed chronic carriers.[210]

Patients who have a history of *S. haematobium* or tuberculous infections of the urinary tract may develop chronic urinary carriage after a bout of typhoid fever.[70, 199] Other predisposing conditions include hydronephrosis, strictures, and kidney stones.

Diagnosis

The symptoms in *Salmonella* gastroenteritis overlap sufficiently with those seen in other diarrheal illnesses that laboratory studies generally are required to prove the diagnosis. Young children with diarrhea may develop dehydration and electrolyte abnormalities. The fecal leukocyte examination is positive for polymorphonuclear leukocytes in 36 to 82 percent of nontyphoidal cases,[108, 185] but this finding is nonspecific. On the rare occasions when proctoscopy has been done, typical findings have included mucosal edema, hyperemia, friability, and hemorrhages.[55] Definitive diagnosis can be made only by isolation of the organism. In patients with gastroenteritis, cultures of stool or rectal swabs are positive in most infected individuals. Stool culture is preferable to swab culture, particularly for evaluation of long-term carriers. Overnight enrichment in selenite broth increases the yield from stool cultures. The optimal agar for isolation of the organism (SS, Hektoen, MacConkey, xylose-lysine-deoxycholate, xylose-lysine-tergitol 4 agar, brilliant green agar, or modified semisolid Rappaport-Vassiliadis medium [MSRV]) is open to debate. MSRV has a high yield but cannot be used for isolating *S.* ser. Typhi or nonmotile strains and has a lower specificity than does SS agar.[208]

Salmonella usually can be isolated readily from blood by use of conventional media if the patient is bacteremic. In patients with extraintestinal focal nontyphoidal infection, specimens from the affected areas may have positive Gram stains and grow the organism.

Enteric fever should be suspected on the basis of the setting and clinical course. Laboratory abnormalities are common but nonspecific occurrences. A normocytic, normochromic anemia and leukopenia or neutropenia, perhaps caused by hemophagocytosis in the bone marrow, often are present.[148] Clotting abnormalities consistent with disseminated intravascular coagulation (e.g., thrombocytopenia, hypofibrinogenemia) may occur[32] but usually are transient and not associated with clinically significant bleeding. In enteric fever, electrolyte values usually are normal, but increases in alkaline phosphatase, serum lactate dehydrogenase, serum aspartate aminotransferase, and serum cholesterol are frequent occurrences. A transient proteinuria sometimes occurs during the first week of enteric fever. Cultures from multiple sites should be submitted for suspected enteric fever; culture of bone marrow has the highest yield,[112, 114, 240] particularly if the patient has had antibiotic pretreatment. During the first week of typhoid fever, approximately 90 percent of patients have positive blood and bone marrow cultures but negative stool and urine cultures. During subsequent weeks, the yield of blood and bone marrow cultures decreases as the yield of stool and urine cultures increases. Culture of duodenal fluid obtained by string capsules can be as sensitive as is culture of bone marrow aspirates.[17, 114, 240] One study found that in those children able to tolerate the string test, culture was positive in 85 percent (compared with blood test, positive in 62%).[12] The overall frequency of positive cultures during the course of typhoid is blood (40–54%), urine (7–10%), stool (approximately 35%), bone marrow (80–90%), rose spots (approximately 65%), and duodenal string test culture (58–85%).[89, 114]

The Widal test measures antibodies against the O and H antigens of *S.* ser. Typhi. Although many patients with enteric fever may have a fourfold rise in the titer of paired sera during the second week of illness, both false-negative and false-positive test results occur. Those with acute or chronic liver disease as well as patients infected with other gram-negative enteric bacilli may develop cross-reacting antibodies. Recipients of the typhoid vaccine show positive Widal test results, which can be misleading. These titers may be more useful in children with typhoid who are living in a nonendemic area, such as the United States. Although those who have a negative titer early in infection tend to keep a negative titer, most develop titers of 1:80 or more.[48] Interpretation of Widal test results is aided by information about seropositivity in the population to which the patient belongs.[45, 237]

A variety of diagnostic kits, including serologic tests such as passive hemagglutination, passive bacterial agglutination, latex particle agglutination slide tests, counterimmunoelectrophoresis, radioimmunoassay, and enzyme-linked immunosorbent assay with use of monoclonal antibodies, have been developed.[122] Molecular techniques used primarily in epidemiologic studies include DNA hybridization studies, phage typing, chromosome analysis, and plasmid analysis. Other methods based on early detection of *Salmonella* in feces have been described and shown to have good sensitivity and specificity[7, 81, 161] but have not been used widely.

Differential Diagnosis

Salmonella gastroenteritis cannot be distinguished clinically from other infectious causes of acute diarrhea reliably, although history and epidemiology sometimes may suggest an etiologic agent. Bloody diarrhea with mucus can be caused by *Salmonella, Shigella,* enteroinvasive *Escherichia coli,* enterohemorrhagic *E. coli, Campylobacter* spp., *Yersinia enterocolitica, Clostridium difficile, Trichuris trichiura,* and *Entamoeba histolytica*. Watery diarrhea may be caused by rotavirus or other viral enteropathogens or, less commonly, enterotoxin-producing bacterial pathogens. When abdominal pain and tenderness are severe, appendicitis, perforated viscus, and mesenteric adenitis are in the differential diagnosis.

Enteric fever can mimic other infections of the reticuloendothelial system, including Epstein-Barr virus infection, disseminated histoplasmosis, tuberculosis, ehrlichiosis, brucellosis, leptospirosis, tularemia, plague, malaria, systemic *Bartonella henselae* infection, and typhus. Noninfectious illnesses with prolonged fever that sometimes can be confused with typhoid include juvenile rheumatoid arthritis and other collagen vascular diseases, Kawasaki syndrome, and lymphomas. An early diagnosis often is difficult to make because the findings are nonspecific. Findings that are particularly helpful in discriminating typhoid fever from other prolonged febrile illnesses include severe cough and chest pain (more typical of lobar pneumonia), diarrhea with grossly obvious blood (more typical of dysentery), acute onset of chills (more typical of malaria), and marked lower abdominal pain early in the febrile illness (more typical of bacillary dysentery, *Y. enterocolitica* infection, and salpingitis).

Treatment

For those children with salmonellosis for whom antibiotic treatment is appropriate, the interpretation of antimicrobial susceptibility studies is important. Drugs such as aminoglycosides, polymyxins, tetracyclines, and first- and second-generation cephalosporins (e.g., cephalothin, cefazolin, cefuroxime, cefamandole) have a poor clinical track record, despite apparent in vitro susceptibility. The drugs that typically are useful in treatment of children with *Salmonella* infections are shown in Table 115–5. The emergence of *S.* ser. Typhimurium DT104 in the United States has led to a dramatic increase in multiresistant (ampicillin, chloramphenicol, streptomycin, sulfonamides, tetracycline) organisms.[93] However, most nontyphoidal *Salmonella* in the United States still are sensitive to ampicillin, chloramphenicol, amoxicillin–clavulanic acid, and TMP-SMX; ceftriaxone resistance, although described, is rare.[111]

GASTROENTERITIS

As with all forms of gastroenteritis, fluid and electrolyte replacement and maintenance are the first order of business. For most patients, oral rehydration is all that is necessary to treat *Salmonella* gastroenteritis. The general thought is that *Salmonella* gastroenteritis should not be treated with antibiotics because these agents do not shorten the course of illness. Multiple agents,[13] including ampicillin, amoxicillin,[129, 170, 183] neomycin,[15, 183] chloramphenicol,[146] TMP-SMX,[129, 211] azithromycin,[42] cefixime,[42] ceftriaxone,[43] and ciprofloxacin, have been shown to be ineffective.[211] Antibiotics prolong excretion of *Salmonella*.[13, 15, 61, 129, 170, 183] However, *Salmonella* serotypes typically have been grouped together for these treatment studies as though they were all the same organism. Given the variability in expression of virulence genes, whether treatment may be useful for some serotypes that possess particular virulence traits remains an open question.

Exceptions to the generalization that *Salmonella* gastroenteritis should not be treated include children at high risk for developing complications, including those with underlying diseases or receiving therapies that impair host defenses. Examples of children who probably ought to be given antibiotics are infants in the first 3 months of life; those ill with AIDS or malignant diseases; and children with hemolytic anemias, particularly sickle-cell anemia. Treatment of these patients is debatable; the data from neonates suggest that antibiotics make little difference in the course.[2, 68, 129, 196, 229] However, because the risk of development of bacteremia is high, antibiotics likely will continue to be used in such settings. Because bacteremia occurs in a relatively small fraction of infections, determining whether treatment of gastroenteritis prevents bacteremia is impossible without conducting a massive study. Because whether treatment is indicated is debatable, also debatable is how long it should be done when elected. Probably no more than 5 days of antibiotics are indicated, barring complications. Although antibiotic resistance is an increasingly important problem, those who require antibiotic therapy for *Salmonella* gastroenteritis not thought to be life-threatening usually should be given ampicillin or amoxicillin, pending susceptibility testing.

TABLE 115–5 ■ ANTIBIOTICS COMMONLY USEFUL IN THE TREATMENT OF *SALMONELLA* INFECTIONS

Drug	Dose
Ampicillin	200 mg/kg/day in 4 doses PO, IM, or IV
TMP-SMX	10 mg/kg/day TMP, 50 mg/kg/day SMX in 2 doses PO or IV
Cefotaxime	150–200 mg/kg/day in 3 doses IM or IV
Ceftriaxone	100 mg/kg/day in 1 or 2 doses IM or IV
Chloramphenicol	75 mg/kg/day in 4 doses PO

TMP-SMX, trimethoprim-sulfamethoxazole.

EXTRAINTESTINAL INFECTIONS

Any child who appears to be toxic enough that bacteremia is suspected also should be started on antibiotic treatment until blood cultures exclude the diagnosis. For children with bacteremic nontyphoidal *Salmonella* and focal extraintestinal complications, a third-generation cephalosporin (e.g., ceftriaxone, cefotaxime) or chloramphenicol is an appropriate choice. If the patient appears to have a life-threatening infection, ampicillin should be used only if evidence exists that the pathogen is not ampicillin resistant. Children at high risk of having recurrence of bacteremia (those with congenital or acquired immunodeficiencies, such as AIDS) may require a third-generation cephalosporin or a fluoroquinolone to achieve cure; frequent recurrences of life-threatening infection sometimes necessitate use of lifelong maintenance therapy.[49, 117]

Meningitis should be treated with a third-generation cephalosporin because these agents have good penetration into cerebrospinal fluid; ampicillin and chloramphenicol use has been associated with higher relapse rates and lower cure rates than have third-generation cephalosporins.[131] Meningitis must be treated for at least 4 weeks; approximately three fourths of those who have relapses have been treated for 3 weeks or less.[46]

A bactericidal agent, such as ampicillin or a third-generation cephalosporin, is preferred for treatment of endovascular infections (e.g., endocarditis, mycotic aneurysm).

For extraintestinal infections, the duration of antibiotic treatment is usually 10 to 14 days in children with bacteremia, 4 to 6 weeks in those with acute osteomyelitis, and 4 weeks in those with meningitis. Collections of pus should be drained. Schistosomiasis, when present, must be treated to achieve resolution of the coincident *Salmonella* infection.

TYPHOID FEVER

The response to treatment with antibiotics is relatively slow. Fever may persist for many days, even after bacteremia has resolved. The emergence and spread of multidrug-resistant *S.* ser. Typhi (MDRST) since 1989 has caused a shift in empirical therapy from chloramphenicol, TMP-SMX, or ampicillin to a fluoroquinolone in adults and a third-generation cephalosporin, such as ceftriaxone, in children. MDRST is particularly common in the Indian subcontinent, Southeast Asia, and Africa; strains resistant to ciprofloxacin are being recognized increasingly.[203]

In the United States, MDRST is less of a problem than it is elsewhere; most strains are sensitive to ampicillin and chloramphenicol.[210] Recent data suggest that *S.* ser. Typhi is still sensitive consistently to ceftriaxone and ciprofloxacin, although nalidixic acid–resistant isolates are becoming more common in those who have traveled to the Indian subcontinent.[5] Such strains respond poorly to fluoroquinolones and may require several courses of treatment.[244] When the patient has a history of recent travel to an area with MDRST or of contact with a person returning from such an area, the choice of empirical treatment should take this information into account. Third-generation cephalosporins are effective against *S.* ser. Typhi strains resistant to ampicillin, chloramphenicol, and TMP-SMX[71, 122, 131, 157, 165, 180, 224, 235] and are appropriate for children with suspected or proven MDRST. Some studies suggest that cefoperazone may have advantages in typhoid fever over chloramphenicol treatment (more rapid sterilization and defervescence),[180] perhaps related to its biliary excretion.[57] Data suggest that TMP-SMX may not be as effective as is ampicillin or chloramphenicol in typhoid fever.[90] Aztreonam also is less effective than is chloramphenicol for strains susceptible to both agents.[96]

Although 2 weeks of antibiotic treatment usually is given, data suggest that shorter courses with some drugs may be adequate. A short course of ceftriaxone (once daily for 3 to 5 days) is as effective and safe as a 2- to 3-week course of chloramphenicol in adults and, on the basis of relatively small numbers, probably also in children.[3, 165] A 5-day course of ceftriaxone (50 to 70 mg/kg/day as a single dose) was associated with a significantly more rapid defervescence (average, 3.9 days until afebrile) than was oral cefixime (7.5 mg/kg/dose twice daily for 14 days) or intramuscular aztreonam (50 to 70 mg/kg/dose every 8 hours for 7 days); relapse rates were similar (approximately 5%).[92]

Concerns about toxicity of fluoroquinolones in children have limited their use to situations in which infection is caused by an organism proved to be resistant to all of the usual antibiotics but sensitive to a fluoroquinolone. Ciprofloxacin (500 mg twice daily for 10 days in adults) causes defervescence in an average of 4.2 days with infrequent relapses, even with MDRST.[8] Children with MDRST who have been treated with ciprofloxacin (10 mg/kg/day) became afebrile in 3.3 days, and 94 percent achieved clinical cure, with no relapses or carriers detected on follow-up.[65] Ofloxacin (20 mg/kg twice daily for 10 days) is associated with more rapid defervescence than is TMP-SMX.[218] Ofloxacin is associated with more rapid defervescence and better cure rates than is cefixime.[35] Very short courses of ofloxacin (2 or 3 days) may be followed by relapse, especially if the organism is resistant to nalidixic acid.[174]

Other agents have been described that may occasionally be useful. Furazolidone (7.5 mg/kg/day) is nearly as effective as is chloramphenicol in strains susceptible to both drugs (86% vs. 90% cure).[66] Despite low serum levels, azithromycin appears to be equivalent to chloramphenicol or ciprofloxacin; the high intracellular concentration in macrophages (>100 times serum levels) of azithromycin presumably accounts for its efficacy.[34, 91] When MDRST is nalidixic acid resistant, azithromycin is more effective than is ofloxacin.[41]

A variety of nonantimicrobial measures should be considered as part of the management of *S.* ser. Typhi infections. Dexamethasone, although potentially increasing the relapse rate,[50] is indicated for patients with severe typhoid fever presenting with delirium, stupor, shock, or coma; the dose is 3 mg/kg initially and then eight doses of 1 mg/kg every 6 hours for 48 hours. This therapy lowers mortality from 35 to 55 percent to 10 percent.[113, 189] Antipyretics were thought at one time to be dangerous in typhoid fever[62]; whether this is correct is doubtful on the basis of recent experience.[176]

Intestinal hemorrhage or perforation during enteric fever generally is considered to be an indication for surgical intervention.[24, 33, 88, 141] Resection of 10 cm of intestine proximal and distal to the perforation appears to improve outcome compared with other surgical approaches.[16] Antibiotic coverage should be broadened to include anaerobes and gram-negative enterics when perforation occurs.[24]

CHRONIC CARRIERS

In general, patients who are not food handlers should probably not be cultured or given special treatment after having a bout of gastroenteritis caused by a nontyphoidal *Salmonella*. On the other hand, carriers of *S.* ser. Typhi should be decolonized to decrease the risk to close contacts. Those who have a normal gallbladder can be treated with high-dose intravenous ampicillin, oral ampicillin, or amoxicillin combined with probenecid for 6 weeks or, when a multiresistant organism is present, with a fluoroquinolone, such as norfloxacin[97] or ciprofloxacin.[74] Chronic carriers who cannot be decolonized are treated with cholecystectomy if cholelithiasis or cholecystitis is present; such patients should receive ampicillin intravenously for 7 to 10 days before and 30 days after cholecystectomy.

Prevention

PUBLIC HEALTH MEASURES

Recognition of an increased frequency of human infections with an unusual serotype should be followed by an epidemiologic investigation aimed at detecting the source and vehicle. Intervention to stop such outbreaks then can be attempted. Judicious use of antibiotics in dairy and livestock animals,[115] careful food processing and storage, and proper preparation of foods are helpful in decreasing transmission of infection. Appropriate sewage disposal, assurance of a safe water supply, prevention of sale of pet turtles, inspection of cosmetics for contamination, and adequate cleaning of medical equipment are important public health strategies. Families with small children should be informed of the risks associated with pet reptiles and encouraged to avoid such unnecessary risks.

PERSONAL HYGIENIC MEASURES

Person-to-person spread can be decreased by giving attention to handwashing after defecation or diaper changing, frequent handwashing during preparation of foods that might be contaminated (e.g., meat), and exclusion of infected individuals from food-handling tasks.

INFECTION CONTROL

Hospitalized children with *Salmonella* gastroenteritis should be isolated (enteric precautions) until stool cultures are negative. Children with extraintestinal infections should be isolated until stool studies exclude intestinal infection or colonization.

NURSERY OUTBREAKS

Neonatal *Salmonella* infection outbreaks should be investigated to determine the source. Cultures of fomites sometimes reveal a removable focus. Neonates and the staff caring for them should be cohorted during outbreaks, with use of enteric precautions in dealing with those infants who are excreting the organism. Surveillance cultures should be done on feces of not only sick infants but also well babies to cohort more appropriately. With current early postpartum discharge policies, reporting *Salmonella* infections in infants is important in detecting outbreaks. Isolation and cohorting can be effective in controlling such outbreaks.[196]

BREAST FEEDING

In the developing world, breast feeding is key because human milk contains secretory IgA and other factors that protect infants from *Salmonella* spp.[27, 72, 79, 186, 187]

VACCINATION

Several vaccines have been developed for typhoid fever.[137] Vaccination of children is indicated when the risk for development of typhoid fever is high (e.g., living with a chronic carrier or in an endemic area) but probably is underused[234] (e.g., Latin America, Asia, Africa).[37] Two vaccines are available: (1) an oral live attenuated Ty21a vaccine (Vivotif Berna, Swiss Serum and Vaccine Institute) and (2) a parenteral purified Vi capsular polysaccharide vaccine (Typhim Vi, Pasteur Mérieux).[132, 188] Neither of these vaccines has been compared with the others in a controlled trial.

The Ty21a vaccine has been evaluated in both liquid and capsule forms. Ty21a oral vaccine is well tolerated; abdominal pain, nausea, vomiting, and rashes occur rarely. A randomized, placebo-controlled trial of more than 32,000 schoolchildren 6 to 7 years of age demonstrated that three doses of a liquid vaccine preparation given during a 1-week period, preceded by a 1-g tablet of sodium bicarbonate to neutralize gastric acid, had a 3-year protective efficacy of 96 percent.[243] However, children younger than 2 years of age fail to develop either humoral or cellular immunity.[137, 167] Randomized, placebo-controlled studies of a gelatin capsule formulation containing sodium bicarbonate and an enteric-coated capsule without bicarbonate given at three doses in 1 week or three doses during a 21-day interval were performed in children older than 6 years.[137] The enteric-coated capsule formulation given at three doses in 1 week had an efficacy of 65 percent during a 5-year period; this efficacy was not improved by giving the doses every 21 days. Sodium bicarbonate lowers efficacy. The liquid formulation appears to be more protective than is the enteric-coated capsule; efficacy persisted during a 5-year follow-up.[137] The form licensed in the United States is an enteric-coated capsule preparation meant to be given in four separate doses on alternate days taken 1 hour before meals. Revaccination with the entire four-dose series is recommended every 5 years in high-risk settings. Because the Ty21a oral vaccine is a live attenuated *Salmonella*, it should not be used in immunocompromised hosts or in those taking antibiotics at the time of vaccination.[37] The antimalarial mefloquine inhibits growth of the attenuated organism, and thus vaccination should be delayed for 24 hours after its use.

Several large field trials suggest that the Vi capsular vaccine as a single 25-µg dose has an efficacy of 55 and 75 percent in adults and children older than 5 years of age, respectively.[4, 188] Although fever, malaise, local pain, and tenderness occur with this vaccine, it has two major advantages over the Ty21a oral vaccines: it does not require refrigeration, and only a single dose is required for protection. It has the advantage of being safer than the whole-cell vaccine and may be used in children as young as 2 years of age.

A new Vi–*Pseudomonas aeruginosa* exotoxin A conjugate vaccine has shown good efficacy (>90%) with minimal toxicity in 2- to 5-year-old children.[254] This vaccine is not yet commercially available.

Prognosis

Salmonella gastroenteritis usually is a self-limited disease in the normal host, although chronic diarrhea sometimes develops after an acute episode. Extraintestinal focal infections with nontyphoidal *Salmonella* are difficult to cure, particularly if they involve the meninges or occur in compromised hosts. *Salmonella* spp. meningitis may relapse if the course of treatment is too short. Likewise, bacteremia, as well as focal infection, recurs after treatment in severely compromised hosts, particularly those with AIDS. Relapse after typhoid fever has long been recognized as a risk.

REFERENCES

1. Abramson, H.: Infections with *S. typhimurium* in the newborn. Am. J. Dis. Child. *74*:576–586, 1947.
2. Abroms, I. F., Cochran, W. D., Holmes, L. B., et al.: A *Salmonella newport* outbreak in a premature nursery with a one-year follow-up. Pediatrics *37*:616–623, 1966.
3. Acharya, G., Butler, T., Ho, M., et al.: Treatment of typhoid fever: Randomized trial of a three-day course of ceftriaxone versus a fourteen-day course of chloramphenicol. Am. J. Trop. Med. Hyg. *52*:162–165, 1995.
4. Acharya, I. L., Lowe, C. U., Thapa, R., et al.: Prevention of typhoid fever in Nepal with the Vi capsular polysaccharide of *Salmonella typhi*. N. Engl. J. Med. *317*:1101–1104, 1987.
5. Acker, M. L., Puhr, N. D., Tauxe, R. V., and Mintz, E. D.: Laboratory-based surveillance of *Salmonella* serotype Typhi infections in the United States: Antimicrobial resistance on the rise. J. A. M. A. *283*:2668–2673, 2000.
6. Adler, J. L., Anderson, R. L., Boring, J. R., et al.: A protracted hospital-associated outbreak of salmonellosis due to a multiple antibiotic–resistant strain of *S. indiana*. J. Pediatr. *77*:970–975, 1970.
7. Aguirre, P. M., Cacho, J. B., Folgueira, L., et al.: Rapid fluorescence method for screening *Salmonella* spp. from enteric differential agars. J. Clin. Microbiol. *28*:148–149, 1990.
8. Alam, M. N., Haq, S. A., Das, K. K., et al.: Efficacy of ciprofloxacin in enteric fever: Comparison of treatment duration in sensitive and multidrug resistant *Salmonella*. Am. J. Trop. Med. Hyg. *53*:306–311, 1995.
9. Altare, F., Durandy, A., Lammas, D., et al.: Impairment of mycobacterial immunity in human interleukin-12 receptor deficiency. Science *280*:1432–1438, 1998.
10. Altare, F., Lammas, D., Revy, P., et al.: Inherited interleukin 12 deficiency in a child with Bacille Calmette-Guérin and *Salmonella enteritidis* disseminated infection. J. Clin. Invest. *102*:2035–2040, 1998.
11. Alvarez-Elcoro, S., Soto-Ramirez, L., and Mateos-Mora, M.: *Salmonella* bacteremia in patients with prosthetic heart valves. Am. J. Med. *77*:61–66, 1984.
12. Antony, T. J., Patwari, A. K., Anand, V. K., et al.: Duodenal string test in typhoid fever. Indian Pediatr. *30*:643–647, 1993.
13. Aserkoff, B., and Bennett, J. V.: Effect of antibiotic therapy in acute salmonellosis on the fecal excretion of salmonellae. N. Engl. J. Med. *281*:636–640, 1969.
14. Ashkenazi, S., Cleary, T. G., Murray, B. E., et al.: Quantitative analysis and partial characterization of cytotoxin production by *Salmonella* strains. Infect. Immun. *56*:3089–3094, 1988.
15. Association for Study of Infectious Diseases: Effect of neomycin in non-invasive *Salmonella* infections of the gastrointestinal tract. Lancet *2*: 1159–1161, 1970.
16. Athie, C. G., Guizar, C. B., Alcantara, A. V., et al.: Twenty-five years of experience in the surgical treatment of perforation of the ileum caused by *Salmonella typhi* at the General Hospital of Mexico City, Mexico. Surgery *123*:632–636, 1998.
17. Avendano, A., Herrera, P., Horwitz, I., et al.: Duodenal string cultures: Practicality and sensitivity for diagnosing enteric fever in children. J. Infect. Dis. *153*:359–362, 1986.
18. Baine, W. B., Gangarosa, E. J., Bennett, J. V., et al.: Institutional salmonellosis. J. Infect. Dis. *128*:357–360, 1973.
19. Baird, G. D., Manning, E. J., and Jones, P. W.: Evidence for related virulence sequences in plasmids of *Salmonella dublin* and *Salmonella typhimurium*. J. Gen. Microbiol. *131*:1815–1823, 1985.

20. Baker, N. M., Mills, A. E., Rachman, I., et al.: Hemolytic uraemic syndrome in typhoid fever. Br. Med. J. *2*:84–87, 1974.
21. Bannerman, C. H.: *S. heidelberg* enteritis: An outbreak in the neonatal unit of Harare Central Hospital. Cent. Afr. J. Med. *31*:1–4, 1985.
22. Bate, J. G., and James, U.: *Salmonella typhimurium* infection dust-borne in a children's ward. Lancet *2*:713, 1958.
23. Bean, N. H., Griffin, P. M., Goulding, J. S., et al.: Foodborne disease outbreaks, 5-year summary, 1983–1987. M. M. W. R. *39*(SS-1):15–57, 1990.
24. Bitar, R., and Tarpley, J.: Intestinal perforation in typhoid fever: A historical and state-of-the-art review. Rev. Infect. Dis. *7*:257–270, 1985.
25. Blaser, M. J., and Newman, L. S.: A review of human salmonellosis. I. Infective dose. Rev. Infect. Dis. *4*:1096–1106, 1982.
26. Borecka, J., Hocmannova, M., and van Leeuwen, W. J.: Nosocomial infection of nurslings caused by multiple drug-resistant strain of *S. typhimurium*. Utilization of a new typing method based on lysogeny of strains. Zentralbl. Bakteriol. 1 Abt. Orig. A *2336*:262, 1976.
27. Borgnolo, G., Barbone, F., Scornavacca, G., et al.: A case-control study of *Salmonella* gastrointestinal infection in Italian children. Acta Paediatr. *85*:804–808, 1996.
28. Boyd, J. F.: Pathology of the alimentary tract of *S. typhimurium* food poisoning. Gut *26*:935–944, 1985.
29. Bryan, J. P., Rocha, H., and Scheld, W. M.: Problems in salmonellosis: Rationale for clinical trials with newer β-lactam agents and quinolones. Rev. Infect. Dis. *8*:189–207, 1986.
30. Buchawald, D. S., and Blaser, M. J.: A review of human salmonellosis. II. Duration of excretion following infection with non-typhi *Salmonella*. Rev. Infect. Dis. *6*:345–356, 1984.
31. Buckmeier, N. A., and Heffron, F.: Intracellular survival of wild type *Salmonella typhimurium* and macrophage sensitive mutants in diverse populations of macrophages. Infect. Immun. *57*:1–7, 1989.
32. Butler, T., Bell, W. R., Levin, J., et al.: Typhoid fever: Studies of blood coagulation, bacteremia, and endotoxemia. Arch. Intern. Med. *138*:407–410, 1978.
33. Butler, T., Knight, J., Nath, S. K., et al.: Typhoid fever complicated by intestinal perforation: A persisting fatal disease requiring surgical management. Rev. Infect. Dis. *7*:244–256, 1985.
34. Butler, T., Sridhar, C. B., Daga, M. K., et al.: Treatment of typhoid fever with azithromycin versus chloramphenicol in a randomized multicenter trial in India. J. Antimicrob. Chemother. *44*:243–250, 1999.
35. Cao, X. T., Kneen, R., Nguyen, T. A., et al.: A comparative study of ofloxacin and cefixime for treatment of typhoid fever in children. The Dong Nai Pediatric Center Typhoid Study Group. Pediatr. Infect. Dis. J. *18*:245–248, 1999.
36. Centers for Disease Control: Multistate outbreak of *Salmonella poona* infections: United States and Canada. M. M. W. R. *40*:549, 1991.
37. Centers for Disease Control: Typhoid immunization: Recommendations of the Immunization Practices Advisory Committee (ACIP). M. M. W. R. *39*:1–5, 1990.
38. Centers for Disease Control: Update: *Salmonella enteritidis* infections and grade A shell eggs: United States 1989. M. M. W. R. *37*:490, 1989.
39. Challapalli, M., Cherubin, C., and Cunningham, D. G.: Lack of chronic carriage of *Salmonella typhimurium*. Pediatr. Infect. Dis. J. *8*:531–540, 1989.
40. Chin, K. C., Simmons, E. J., and Tarlow, M. J.: Neonatal typhoid fever. Arch. Dis. Child. *61*:1228–1230, 1986.
41. Chinh, N. T., Parry, C. M., Ly, N. T., et al.: A randomized controlled comparison of azithromycin and ofloxacin for treatment of multidrug-resistant or nalidixic acid–resistant enteric fever. Antimicrob. Agents Chemother. *44*:1855–1859, 2000.
42. Chiu, C. H., Lin, T. Y., and Ou, J. T.: A clinical trial comparing oral azithromycin, cefixime and no antibiotics in the treatment of acute uncomplicated *Salmonella* enteritis in children. J. Paediatr. Child Health *35*:372–374, 1999.
43. Chiu, C. H., Lin, T. Y., and Ou, J. T.: A pilot study of seven days of ceftriaxone therapy for children with *Salmonella* enterocolitis. Chang Gung. Yi Xue Za Zhi *20*:115–121, 1997.
44. Chorba, T. L., Meriwether, R. A., Jenkins, B. R., et al.: Control of a non-foodborne outbreak of salmonellosis: Day care in isolation. Am. J. Public Health *77*:979–981, 1987.
45. Chow, C. B., Wang, P. S., Cheung, M. W., et al.: Diagnostic value of the Widal test in childhood typhoid fever. Pediatr. Infect. Dis. J. *6*:914–917, 1987.
46. Cohen, J. I., Bartlett, J. A., and Corey, G. R.: Extra-intestinal manifestations of *Salmonella* infections. Medicine (Baltimore) *66*:349–388, 1987.
47. Cohen, M. L., and Tauxe, R. V.: Drug-resistant *Salmonella* in the United States: An epidemiologic perspective. Science *234*:964–969, 1986.
48. Colon, A. R., Gross, D. R., and Tamer, M. A.: Typhoid fever in children. Pediatrics *56*:606–609, 1975.
49. Connolly, M. J., Snow, M. N., and Ingham, H. R.: Ciprofloxacin treatment of recurrent *Salmonella* septicemia in a patient with acquired immune deficiency syndrome. J. Antimicrob. Chemother. *18*:647–648, 1986.
50. Cooles, P.: Adjuvant steroids and relapse of typhoid fever. J. Trop. Med. Hyg. *89*:229–231, 1986.
51. Corman, L. I., Poirier, R. H., Littlefield, C. A., et al.: Endophthalmitis due to *S. enteritidis*. J. Pediatr. *95*:1001–1002, 1979.
52. Cravioto, A., Reyes, R. E., Trujillo, F., et al.: Risk of diarrhea during the first year of life associated with initial and subsequent colonization by specific enteropathogens. Am. J. Epidemiol. *131*:886–904, 1990.
53. D'Amelio, R., Tagliabue, A., Nencioni, L., et al.: Comparative analysis of immunological responses to oral (Ty21a) and parenteral (TAB) typhoid vaccines. Infect. Immun. *56*:2731–2735, 1988.
54. Davis, R. C.: *Salmonella* sepsis in infancy. Am. J. Dis. Child. *135*:1096–1099, 1981.
55. Day, D. W., Mandal, B. K., and Morson, B. C.: The rectal biopsy appearances in *Salmonella* colitis. Histopathology *2*:117–131, 1978.
56. de Jong, R., Altare, F., Haagen, I. A., et al.: Severe mycobacterial and *Salmonella* infections in interleukin-12 receptor–deficient patients. Science *280*:1435–1438, 1998.
57. Demmerich, B., Lode, H., Borner, K., et al.: Biliary excretion and pharmacokinetics of cefoperazone in humans. J. Antimicrob. Chemother. *12*:27–37, 1983.
58. Diddle, A. W., and Stephens, R. L.: Typhoid fever in pregnancy. Am. J. Obstet. Gynecol. *38*:300–305, 1939.
59. Dietrich, H. F.: Typhoid fever in children. J. Pediatr. *10*:191–201, 1937.
60. Diwan, N., and Sharma, K. B.: Isolation of *S. typhimurium* from cephalohematoma and osteomyelitis. Indian J. Med. Res. *67*:27–29, 1978.
61. Dixon, J. M. S.: Effect of antibiotic treatment on duration of excretion of *S. typhimurium* by children. Br. Med. J. *2*:1343–1345, 1965.
62. Dowdle, E.: The reaction of patients with typhoid fever to the administration of aspirin. S. Afr. Med. J. *May 19*:474–477, 1956.
63. Dunn, D. W., McAllister, J., and Craft, J. C.: Brain abscess and empyema caused by *Salmonella*. Pediatr. Infect. Dis. *3*:54–57, 1984.
64. Dutta, P., Bhattacharya, S. K., Dutta, D., et al.: Hemolytic uremic syndrome following *Salmonella typhimurium* enteritis. Indian J. Pediatr. *56*:409–410, 1989.
65. Dutta, P., Rasaily, R., Saha, M. R., et al.: Ciprofloxacin for treatment of severe typhoid fever in children. Antimicrob. Agents Chemother. *37*:1197–1199, 1993.
66. Dutta, P., Rasaily, R., Saha, M. R., et al.: Randomized clinical trial of furazolidone for typhoid fever in children. Scand. J. Gastroenterol. *28*:168–172, 1993.
67. Edelman, R., and Levine, M. M.: Summary of an international workshop on typhoid fever. Rev. Infect. Dis. *8*:329–349, 1986.
68. Edgar, W. M., and Lacey, B. W.: Infection with *S. heidelberg*: An outbreak presumably not foodborne. Lancet *1*:161, 1963.
69. Ejlertsen, T., and Aunsholt, N. A.: *Salmonella* bacteremia in renal transplant recipients. Scand. J. Infect. Dis. *21*:241–244, 1989.
70. Farid, Z., Bassily, S., Kent, D. C., et al.: Chronic urinary *Salmonella* carriers with intermittent bacteremia. J. Trop. Med. Hyg. *73*:153–157, 1970.
71. Farid, Z., Girgis, N., and Abu El Ella, A.: Successful treatment of typhoid fever in children with parenteral ceftriaxone. Scand. J. Infect. Dis. *19*: 467–468, 1987.
72. Feachem, R. G., and Koblinsky, M. A.: Interventions for the control of diarrhoeal diseases among young children: Promotion of breastfeeding. Bull World Health Organ. *62*:271, 1984.
73. Ferreccio, C., Levine, M. M., Manterola, A., et al.: Benign bacteremia caused by *S. typhi* and *paratyphi* in children younger than 2 years. J. Pediatr. *104*:899–901, 1984.
74. Ferreccio, C., Morris, J. G., and Valdivieso, C., et al.: Efficacy of ciprofloxacin in the treatment of chronic typhoid carriers. J. Infect. Dis. *157*:1235–1239, 1988.
75. Fierer, J., Krause, M., Tauxe, R., et al.: *Salmonella typhimurium* bacteremia: Association with the virulence plasmid. J. Infect. Dis. *166*:639–642, 1992.
76. Finlay, B. B.: Molecular and cellular mechanisms of *Salmonella* pathogenesis. Curr. Top. Microbiol. Immunol. *192*:163–185, 1994.
77. Finlay, B. B., and Falkow, S.: Comparison of the invasion strategies used by *S. choleraesuis*, *S. flexneri*, and *Y. enterocolitica* to enter cultured animal cells. Biochimie *70*:1089–1099, 1988.
78. Foley, A. R.: An outbreak of paratyphoid B fever in a nursery of a small hospital. Can. J. Public Health *38*:73, 1947.
79. France, G. L., Marmer, D. J., and Steele, R. W.: Breast-feeding and *Salmonella* infection. Am. J. Dis. Child. *134*:147–152, 1980.
80. Galofre, J., Moreno, A., Mensa, J., et al.: Analysis of factors influencing the outcome and development of septic metastasis or relapse in *Salmonella* bacteremia. Clin. Infect. Dis. *18*:873–878, 1994.
81. Geers, T. A., and Backes, B. A.: Evaluation of two rapid methods to screen pathogens from stool specimens. Am. J. Clin. Pathol. *91*:327–330, 1989.
82. Gendrel, D., Kombila, M., Beaudoin-Leblevec, G., et al.: Nontyphoidal salmonellal septicemia in Gabonese children infected with *Schistosoma intercalatum*. Clin. Infect. Dis. *18*:103–105, 1994.
83. Gershman, M.: Single phage typing set for differentiating *Salmonella*. J. Clin. Microbiol. *5*:302–314, 1977.
84. Giannella, R. A., Broitman, S. A., and Zamcheck, N.: Influence of gastric acidity on bacterial and parasitic enteric infections: A perspective. Ann. Intern. Med. *78*:271–276, 1973.
85. Giannella, R. A., Broitman, S. A., and Zamcheck, N.: *Salmonella* enteritis. I. Role of reduced gastric secretion in pathogenesis. Dig. Dis. *16*: 1000–1006, 1971.
86. Giannella, R. A., Formal, S. B., Dammin, G. J., et al.: Pathogenesis of salmonellosis: Studies of fluid secretion, mucosal invasion, and morphologic reaction in the rabbit ileum. J. Clin. Invest. *52*:441–453, 1973.
87. Giannella, R. A., Gots, R. E., Charney, A. N., et al.: Pathogenesis of *Salmonella*-mediated intestinal fluid secretion: Activation of adenylate

cyclase and inhibition by indomethacin. Gastroenterology *69*:1238–1245, 1975.

88. Gibney, E. J.: Typhoid perforation. Br. J. Surg. *76*:887–889, 1989.
89. Gilman, R. H., Terminel, M., and Levine, M. M.: Relative efficacy of blood, urine, rectal swab, bone marrow, and rose spot cultures for recovery of *S. typhi* in typhoid fever. Lancet *1*:1211–1213, 1975.
90. Gilman, R. H., Terminel, M., Levine, M. M., et al.: Comparison of trimethoprim/sulfamethoxazole and amoxicillin in therapy of chloramphenicol-resistant and chloramphenicol-sensitive typhoid fever. J. Infect. Dis. *132*:630–636, 1975.
91. Girgis, N. I., Butler, T., Frenck, R. W., et al.: Azithromycin versus ciprofloxacin for treatment of uncomplicated typhoid in a randomized trial in Egypt that included patients with multidrug resistance. Antimicrob. Agents. Chemother. *43*:1441–1444, 1999.
92. Girgis, N. I., Sultan, Y., Hammad, O., et al.: Comparison of the efficacy, safety and cost of cefixime, ceftriaxone and aztreonam in the treatment of multidrug resistant *S. typhi* septicemia in children. Pediatr. Infect. Dis. J. *14*:603–605, 1995.
93. Glynn, M. K., Bopp, C., Dewitt, W., et al.: Emergence of multidrug-resistant *Salmonella enterica* serotype typhimurium DT104 infections in the United States. N. Engl. J. Med. *338*:1333–1338, 1998.
94. Gokalp, A. S., Toksoy, H. B., Turkay, S., et al.: Intravenous immunoglobulin in the treatment of *Salmonella typhimurium* infections in preterm neonates. Clin. Pediatr. *33*:349–352, 1994.
95. Goldstein, F. W., Chumpitaz, J. C., Guevara, J. M., et al.: Plasmid-mediated resistance to multiple antibiotics in *Salmonella typhi.* J. Infect. Dis. *153*:261–266, 1986.
96. Gotuzzo, E., Echevarria, J., Carrillo, C., et al.: Randomized comparison of aztreonam and chloramphenicol in treatment of typhoid fever. Antimicrob. Agents Chemother. *38*:558–562, 1994.
97. Gotuzzo, E., Guerra, J. G., Benavente, L., et al.: Use of norfloxacin to treat chronic typhoid carriers. J. Infect. Dis. *157*:1221–1225, 1988.
98. Griffith, J. P. C., and Ostheimer, M.: Typhoid fever in children. Am. J. Med. Sci. *124*:868–888, 1902.
99. Groisman, E. A., and Ochman, G.: Cognate gene clusters govern invasion of host epithelial cells by *S. typhimurium* and *Shigella flexneri.* EMBO J. *12*:3779–3787, 1993.
100. Grossman, D. A., Witham, N., Burr, D. H., et al.: Flagellar serotypes of *S. typhi* in Indonesia: Relationships among motility, invasiveness, and clinical illness. J. Infect. Dis. *171*:212–216, 1995.
101. Gulig, P. A., and Curtiss, R.: Plasmid-associated virulence of *Salmonella typhimurium.* Infect. Immun. *55*:2891–2900, 1987.
102. Gulig, P. A., Danbara, H., Guiney, D. G., et al.: Molecular analysis of *spv* virulence genes of the *Salmonella* virulence plasmids. Mol. Microbiol. *7*:825–830, 1993.
103. Guthrie, K. J., and Montgomery, G. I.: Infections with *Bacterium enteritidis* in infancy with the triad of enteritis, cholecystitis and meningitis. J. Pathol. Bacteriol. *49*:393, 1939.
104. Hadfield, T. L., Monson, M. H., and Wachsmoth, I. K.: An outbreak of antibiotic-resistant *Salmonella enteritidis* in Liberia, West Africa. J. Infect. Dis. *151*:790–795, 1985.
105. Haggman, D. L., Rehm, S. J., Moodie, D. S., et al.: Non-typhoidal *Salmonella* pericarditis: A case report and review of the literature. Pediatr. Infect. Dis. J. *5*:259–264, 1986.
106. Han, T., Sokal, J. E., and Neter, E.: Salmonellosis in disseminated malignant diseases: A seven-year review (1959–1963). N. Engl. J. Med. *276*:1045, 1967.
107. Hand, W. L., and King, N. L.: Serum opsonization of *Salmonella* in sickle cell anemia. Am. J. Med. *64*:388–395, 1978.
108. Harris, J. C., DuPont, H. L., and Hornick, R. B.: Fecal leukocytes in diarrheal illness. Ann. Intern. Med. *76*:697–700, 1972.
109. Hearne, S. E., Whigham, T. E., and Brady, C. E.: Pancreatitis and typhoid fever. Am. J. Med. *86*:471–473, 1989.
110. Hedberg, C. W., David, M. J., White, K. E., et al.: Role of egg consumption in sporadic *Salmonella enteritidis* and *Salmonella typhimurium* infections in Minnesota. J. Infect. Dis. *167*:107–111, 1993.
111. Herikstat, H., Hayes, P., Hogan, J., et al.: Ceftriaxone-resistant *Salmonella* in the United States. Pediatr. Infect. Dis. J. *16*:904–905, 1997.
112. Hoffman, S. L., Edman, D. C., Punjabi, N. H., et al.: Bone marrow aspirate culture superior to streptokinase clot culture and 8 ml 1:10 blood-to-broth ratio blood culture for diagnosis of typhoid fever. Am. J. Trop. Med. Hyg. *35*:836–839, 1986.
113. Hoffman, S. L., Punjabi, N. H., Kumala, S., et al.: Reduction of mortality in chloramphenicol-treated severe typhoid fever by high dose dexamethasone. N. Engl. J. Med. *310*:82–88, 1984.
114. Hoffman, S. L., Punjabi, N. H., Rockhill, R. C., et al.: Duodenal string-capsule culture compared with bone marrow, blood, and rectal swab cultures for diagnosing typhoid and paratyphoid fever. J. Infect. Dis. *149*:157–161, 1984.
115. Holmberg, S. D.: Drug-resistant *Salmonella* species from animals fed antimicrobics. Infect. Dis. Newslett. *5*:25, 1986.
116. Holmberg, S. D., Osterholm, M. T., Senger, K. A., et al.: Drug-resistant *Salmonella* from animals fed antimicrobials. N. Engl. J. Med. *311*:617–622, 1984.
117. Hoppe, J. E., Dopfer, R., Huber, S., et al.: Eradication of *Salmonella dublin* in an immunodeficient child by combined use of ceftriaxone and ciprofloxacin after failure of either agent alone. Infection *17*:399–400, 1989.
118. Hornick, R. B., Griesman, S. E., Woodward, T. E., et al.: Typhoid fever. Pathogenesis and immunologic control. Parts I and II. N. Engl. J. Med. *283*:686–691, 739–746, 1970.
119. Huang, L. T., Ko, S. F., and Lui, C. C.: *Salmonella* meningitis: Clinical experience of third-generation cephalosporin. Acta Paediatr. *86*:1056–1058, 1997.
120. Hyams, J. S., Durbin, W. A., Grand, R. J., et al.: *Salmonella* bacteremia in the first year of life. J. Pediatr. *96*:57–59, 1980.
121. Im, S. W. K., Chow, K., and Chau, P. Y.: Rectal thermometer–mediated cross-infection with *S. wadsworth* in a pediatric ward. J. Hosp. Infect. *2*:171–174, 1981.
122. Isomaki, O., Vuento, R., and Granfors, K.: Serological diagnosis of *Salmonella* infections by enzyme immunoassay. Lancet *1*:1411–1414, 1989.
123. Jiwa, S. F.: Probing for enterotoxigenicity among the salmonellae: An evaluation of biological assays. J. Clin. Microbiol. *14*:463–472, 1981.
124. Johnson, P. C., and Sabbaj, J.: Typhoid tonsillitis. J. A. M. A. *244*:362, 1980.
125. Jouanguy, E., Doffinger, R., Dupuis, S., et al.: IL-12 and IFN-γ in host defense against mycobacteria and salmonella in mice and men. Curr. Opin. Immunol. *11*:346–351, 1999.
126. Kaniga, K., Trollinger, D., and Galan, J. E.: Identification of two targets of the type III protein secretion system encoded by the *inv* and *spa* loci of *Salmonella typhimurium* that have homology to the *Shigella* IpaD and IpaA proteins. J. Bacteriol. *177*:7078–7085, 1995.
127. Kaniga, K., Tucker, S., Trollinger, D., et al.: Homologs of the *Shigella* IpaB and IpaC invasins are required for *Salmonella typhimurium* entry into cultured epithelial cells. J. Bacteriol. *177*:3965–3971, 1995.
128. Katz, B. Z., and Shapiro, E. D.: Predictors of persistently positive blood cultures in children with "occult" *Salmonella* bacteremia. Pediatr. Infect. Dis. *5*:713–714, 1986.
129. Kazemi, M., Bumpert, T. G., and Marks, M. I.: A controlled trial comparing trimethoprim/sulfamethoxazole, ampicillin, and no therapy in the treatment of *Salmonella* gastroenteritis in children. J. Pediatr. *83*:646–650, 1973.
130. Khan, M. A., Abdur-Rab, M., Israr, N., et al.: Transmission of *S. worthington* by oropharyngeal suction in hospital neonatal unit. Pediatr. Infect. Dis. J. *10*:668–672, 1991.
131. Kinsella, T. R., Yoger, R., Shulman, S. T., et al.: Treatment of *Salmonella* meningitis and brain abscess with the new cephalosporins: Two case reports and a review of the literature. Pediatr. Infect. Dis. J. *6*:476–480, 1987.
132. Klugman, K. P., Gilbertson, I. T., Koornhof, H. J., et al.: Protective activity of Vi capsular polysaccharide vaccine against typhoid fever. Lancet *2*:1165–1169, 1987.
133. Konzert, W.: *Salmonella* osteomyelitis in reference to *S. typhimurium* epidemics in a newborn infant ward. Wien. Klin. Wochenschr. *81*:713–716, 1969.
134. Lamb, V. A., Mayhall, C. G., Spadora, A. C., et al.: Outbreak of *Salmonella typhimurium* gastroenteritis due to an imported strain resistant to ampicillin, chloramphenicol and trimethoprim/sulfamethoxazole in a nursery. J. Clin. Microbiol. *20*:1076–1079, 1984.
135. Lee, L. A., Puhr, N. D., Maloney, E. K., et al.: Increase in antimicrobial-resistant *Salmonella* infections in the US, 1989–1990. J. Infect. Dis. *170*:128–134, 1994.
136. Lee, S. C., Yang, P. H., Shieh, W. B., et al.: Bacteremia due to non-typhi *Salmonella*: Analysis of 64 cases and review. Clin. Infect. Dis. *19*:693–696, 1994.
137. Levine, M. M., Taylor, D. N., and Ferereccio, C.: Typhoid vaccines come of age. Pediatr. Infect. Dis. J. *8*:374–381, 1989.
138. Levine, M. M.: Typhoid fever and enteric fever. *In* Kass, E., and Platt, R. (eds.): Current Therapy in Infectious Diseases. Toronto, B. C. Decker, 1986.
139. Levy, S. B.: Man, animals, and antibiotic resistance. Pediatr. Infect. Dis. *4*:3–5, 1985.
140. Lieb, S., Gunn, R. A., and Taylor, D. N.: Salmonellosis in a day care center. J. Pediatr. *100*:1004, 1982.
141. Lizarralde, E.: Typhoid perforation of the ileum in children. J. Pediatr. Surg. *16*:1012–1016, 1981.
142. LoVerde, P. T., Amento, C., and Higashi, G. I.: Parasite-parasite interaction of *Salmonella typhimurium* and *Schistosoma.* J. Infect. Dis. *141*:177–185, 1980.
143. Low, L. C., Lam, B. C., Wong, W. T., et al.: *Salmonella meningitis* in infancy. Aust. Paediatr. J. *20*:225–228, 1984.
144. Mabey, D. C., Brown, A., and Greenwood, B. M.: *Plasmodium falciparum* malaria and *Salmonella* infections in Gambian children. J. Infect. Dis. *155*:1319, 1987.
145. MacDonald, K. L., Cohen, M. L., Hargrett-Bean, N. T., et al.: Changes in antimicrobial resistance of *Salmonella* isolated from humans in the United States. J. A. M. A. *258*:1496–1499, 1987.
146. MacDonald, W. B., Friday, F., and McEacharn, M.: The effect of chloramphenicol in *Salmonella enteritis* in infancy. Arch. Dis. Child. *29*:238, 1954.
147. Mackaness, G. B., Blander, R. V., and Collins, F. M.: Host-parasite relations in mouse typhoid. J. Exp. Med. *124*:573–583, 1966.
148. Mallouh, A. A., and Sadi, A. R.: White blood cells and bone marrow in typhoid fever. Pediatr. Infect. Dis. J. *6*:527–529, 1987.

149. Mallouh, A. A., and Salamah, M. M.: Pattern of bacterial infections in homozygous sickle cell disease. Am. J. Dis. Child. *139*:820–826, 1985.
150. Marcus, S. L., Brumell, J. H., Pfeifer, C. G., and Brett Finlay, B.: Salmonella pathogenicity islands: Big virulence in small packages. Microbes Infect. *2*:145–156, 2000.
151. Martyn-Jones, D. M., and Pantin, G. C.: Neonatal diarrhea due to *S. paratyphi*. Br. J. Clin. Pathol. *9*:128, 1956.
152. Marzetti, G., Laurenti, F., deCaro, M., et al.: *Salmonella münchen* infections in newborns and small infants. Clin. Pediatr. (Phila.) *12*:93–97, 1973.
153. Maudgil, A., Bhan, M. K., and Khoshoo, V.: Hemolytic uremic syndrome associated with *Salmonella typhimurium*. Indian Pediatr. *24*:608–609, 1987.
154. McAllister, T. A., Roud, J. A., and Marshall, A., et al.: Outbreak of *Salmonella eimsbuettel* in newborn infants spread by rectal thermometers. Lancet *1*:1262–1264, 1986.
155. McKinlay, B.: Infectious diarrhea of the newborn caused by an unclassified species of *Salmonella*. Am. J. Dis. Child. *54*:1252, 1937.
156. Meadow, W. L., Schneider, H., and Beem, M.: *Salmonella enteritidis* bacteremia in childhood. J. Infect. Dis. *152*:185–189, 1985.
157. Meloni, T., Marinaro, A. M., Desole, M. G., et al.: Ceftriaxone treatment of *Salmonella* enteric fever. Pediatr. Infect. Dis. J. *7*:734–735, 1986.
158. Mendis, N. M. P., de la Motte, P. U., Gunatillaka, P. D. P., et al.: Protracted infection with *S. bareilly* in a maternity hospital. J. Trop. Med. Hyg. *79*:142–150, 1976.
159. Mermin, J. H., Townes, J. M., Gerber, M., et al.: Typhoid fever in the United States, 1985–1994: Changing risks of international travel and increasing antimicrobial resistance. Arch. Intern. Med. *158*:633–638, 1998.
160. Merselis, J. G., Kaye, D., Connolly, C. S., et al.: Quantitative bacteriology of the typhoid carrier state. Am. J. Trop. Med. Hyg. *13*:425, 1964.
161. Metzler, J., and Nachamkin, I.: Evaluation of a latex agglutination test for the detection of *Salmonella* and *Shigella* spp. by using broth enrichment. J. Clin. Microbiol. *26*:2501–2504, 1988.
162. Michel, J., Malpuach, G., Godeneche, P., et al.: Clinical and bacterological study of a salmonellosis epidemic in a hospital *(Salmonella oranienburg)*. Pediatrie *25*:13–19, 1970.
163. Mishu, B., Koehler, J., Lee, L. A., et al.: Outbreaks of *Salmonella enteritidis* infections in the US, 1985–1991. J. Infect. Dis. *169*:547–552, 1994.
164. Molbak, K., Baggesen, D. L., Aarestrup, F. M., et al.: An outbreak of multidrug-resistant, quinolone-resistant *Salmonella enterica* serotype Typhimurium DT104. N. Engl. J. Med. *34*:1420–1425, 1999.
165. Moosa, A., and Rubidge, C. J.: Once daily ceftriaxone vs. chloramphenicol for treatment of typhoid fever in children. Pediatr. Infect. Dis. J. *8*: 696–699, 1989.
166. Mroczenski-Wildey, M. J., Di, F. J., and Cabello, F. C.: Invasion and lyssi of HeLa cell monolayers by *S. typhi*: The role of lipopolysaccharide. Microb. Pathog. *6*:143–152, 1989.
167. Murphy, J. R., Grez, L., Schlesinger, L., et al.: Immunogenicity of *S. typhi* Ty21a vaccine for young children. Infect. Immun. *59*:4291–4293, 1991.
168. Naqvi, S. H., Thobani, S., Moazam, F., et al.: Generalized suppurative lymphadenitis with typhoidal salmonellosis. Pediatr. Infect. Dis. J. *7*:882–883, 1988.
169. Nelson, J. D., and McCracken, G. H.: What next? J. Pediatr. Infect. Dis. *16*:10–16, 1990.
170. Nelson, J. D., Kusmiesz, H., Jackson, L. H., et al.: Treatment of *Salmonella* gastroenteritis with ampicillin, amoxicillin, or placebo. Pediatrics *65*:1125–1130, 1980.
171. Nelson, J. D.: Suppurative mastitis in infants. Am. J. Dis. Child. *125*:458–459, 1973.
172. Nelson, S. J., and Granoff, D.: *Salmonella* gastroenteritis in the first three months of life. Clin. Pediatr. *21*:709–712, 1982.
173. Neter, E.: Observation on the transmission of salmonellosis in man. Am. J. Public Health *40*:929, 1950.
174. Nguyen, T. C., Solomon, T., Mai, X. T., et al.: Short courses of ofloxacin for the treatment of enteric fever. Trans. R. Soc. Trop. Med. Hyg. *91*:347–349, 1997.
175. Novak, R., and Feldman, S.: Salmonellosis in children with cancer. Am. J. Dis. Child. *133*:298–300, 1979.
176. Noyola, D. E., Fernandez, M., and Kaplan, S. L.: Reevaluation of antipyretics in children with enteric fever. Pediatr. Infect. Dis. J. *17*:691–695, 1998.
177. Olsvik, O., Sorum, H., Birkness, K., et al.: Plasmid characterization of *Salmonella typhimurium* transmitted from animals to humans. J. Clin. Microbiol. *22*:336–338, 1985.
178. Omland, T., and Gardborg, O.: *Salmonella enteritidis* infections in infancy with special reference to a small nosocomial epidemic. Acta Paediatr. Belg. *49*:583–590, 1960.
179. Ortiz-Neu, C., Marr, J. S., Cherubin, C. E., et al.: Bone and joint infections due to *Salmonella*. J. Infect. Dis. *138*:820–828, 1978.
180. Pape, J. W., Gerdes, H., Oriol, L., et al.: Typhoid fever: Successful therapy with cefoperazone. J. Infect. Dis. *153*:272–276, 1986.
181. Pavia, A. T., Shipman, L. D., Wells, J. G., et al.: Epidemiologic evidence that prior antimicrobial exposure decreases resistance to infection by antimicrobial-sensitive *Salmonella*. J. Infect. Dis. *161*:255–260, 1990.
182. Pether, J. V., and Gilbert, R. J.: The survival of salmonellas on finger-tips and transfer of the organisms to foods. J. Hyg. (Lond.) *69*:673–681, 1971.
183. Pettersson, T., Klemola, E., and Wager, O.: Treatment of acute cases of *Salmonella* infection and *Salmonella* carriers with ampicillin and neomycin. Acta Med. Scand. *175*:185, 1964.
184. Pickering, L. K.: Bacterial and parasitic enteropathogens in day care. Semin. Pediatr. Infect. Dis. *1*:263, 1990.
185. Pickering, L. K., DuPont, H. L., Olarte, J., et al.: Fecal leukocytes in enteric infections. Am. J. Clin. Pathol. *68*:562–565, 1977.
186. Pickering, L. K., Kohl, S., and Cleary, T. G.: Humoral factors in breast milk that protect against diarrhea. *In* Jensen, R. G., and Neville, M. C. (eds.): Human Lactation. New York, Plenum, 1985, p. 63.
187. Pickering, L. K., and Ruiz-Palacios, G.: Antibodies in milk directed against specific enteropathogens. *In* Hamosh, A., and Goldman, A. S. (eds.): Human Lactation 2. New York, Plenum, 1986, p. 499.
188. Plotkin, S. A., and Bouveret-Le Cam, N.: A new typhoid vaccine composed of the Vi capsular polysaccharide. Arch. Intern. Med. *155*:2293–2299, 1995.
189. Punjabi, N. H., Hoffman, S. L., Edman, D. C., et al.: Treatment of severe typhoid fever in children with high dose dexamethasone. Pediatr. Infect. Dis. J. *7*:598–600, 1988.
190. Puri, V., Thirupuram, S., Khalil, A., et al.: Nosocomial *S. typhimurium* epidemic in a neonatal special care unit. Indian Pediatr. *17*:233–239, 1980.
191. Rajajee, S., Anandi, T. B., Subha, S., et al.: Patterns of resistant *S. typhi* infection in infants. J. Trop. Pediatr. *41*:52–54, 1995.
192. Ramachandran, S., Godfrey, J. J., and Perera, M. V.: Typhoid hepatitis. J. A. M. A. *230*:236–240, 1974.
193. Ramos, J. M., Garcia-Corbeira, P., Aguado, J. M., et al.: Clinical significance of primary vs. secondary bacteremia due to nontyphoid *Salmonella* in patients without AIDS. Clin. Infect. Dis. *19*:777–780, 1994.
194. Reed, R. P., and Klugman, K. P.: Neonatal typhoid fever. Pediatr. Infect. Dis. J. *13*:774–777, 1994.
195. Rejnmark, L., Stoustrup, O., Christensen, I., and Hansen, A.: Impact of infecting dose on severity of disease in an outbreak of food-borne *Salmonella enteritidis*. Scand. J. Infect. Dis *29*:37–40, 1997.
196. Rice, P. A., Craven, P. C., and Wells, J. G.: *Salmonella heidelberg* enteritis and bacteremia: An epidemic on two pediatric wards. Am. J. Med. *60*:509–516, 1976.
197. Riley, L. W., and Cohen, M. L.: Plasmid profiles and *Salmonella* epidemiology. Lancet *1*:573, 1982.
198. Riley, L. W., Cohen, M. L., Seals, J. E., et al.: Importance of host factors in human salmonellosis caused by multi-resistant strains of *Salmonella*. J. Infect. Dis. *149*:878–883, 1984.
199. Rocha, H., Kirk, J. W., and Hearey, C. D.: Prolonged *Salmonella* bacteremia in patients with *Schistosoma mansoni* infection. Arch. Intern. Med. *128*:254–257, 1971.
200. Rodriguez, R. E., Valero, V., and Watanakunakorn, C.: *Salmonella* focal intracranial infections: Review of the world literature (1884–1984) and report of an unusual case. Rev. Infect. Dis. *8*:31–41, 1986.
201. Rosenthal, S. L.: Exacerbation of *Salmonella* enteritis due to ampicillin. N. Engl. J. Med. *280*:147–148, 1969.
202. Rowe, B., Giles, C., and Brown, G. L.: Outbreak of gastroenteritis due to *S. virchow* in a maternity hospital. Br. Med. J. *3*:561–564, 1969.
203. Rowe, B., Ward, L. R., and Threlfall, E. J.: Multidrug-resistant *Salmonella typhi*: A worldwide epidemic. Clin. Infect. Dis. *24*(Suppl. 1): S106–S109, 1997.
204. Roy, S. K., Speelman, P., Butler, T., et al.: Diarrhea associated with typhoid fever. J. Infect. Dis. *151*:1138–1143, 1985.
205. Rubinstein, A. D., Feemster, R. F., and Smith, H. M.: Salmonellosis as a public health problem in wartime. Am. J. Public Health *34*:841, 1944.
206. Rubinstein, A. D., and Fowler, R. N.: Salmonellosis of the newborn with transmission by delivery room resuscitators. Am. J. Public Health *45*:1109, 1955.
207. Ruiz-Contreras, J., Ramos, J. T., Hernandez-Sampelayo, T., et al.: Sepsis in children with HIV infection: The Madrid HIV Pediatric Infection Collaborative Study Group. Pediatr. Infect Dis. J. *14*:522–526, 1995.
208. Ruiz-Gomez, J., Lorente Salinas, I., Perez Salmeron, J., et al.: Evaluation of methods for isolation of *Salmonella* species using modified Rappaport-Vassiliadis medium and *Salmonella-Shigella* agar. Eur. J. Clin. Microbiol. Infect. Dis. *17*:791–793, 1998.
209. Russell, I. J., Forgacs, P., and Geraci, J. E.: Pancreatitis complicating typhoid fever. J. A. M. A. *235*:753–754, 1976.
210. Ryan, C. A., Hargrett-Bean, N. T., and Blake, P. A.: *Salmonella typhi* infections in the United States, 1975–1984: Increasing role of foreign travel. Rev. Infect. Dis. *11*:1–8, 1989.
211. Sanchez, C., Garcia Restoy, E., Garau, J., et al.: Ciprofloxacin and TMP/SMX versus placebo in acute uncomplicated *Salmonella* enteritis: A double-blind trial. J. Infect. Dis. *168*:1304–1307, 1993.
212. Sanders, D. Y., Sinal, S. H., and Morrison, L.: Chronic salmonellosis in infancy. Clin. Pediatr. (Phila.) *13*:640–643, 1974.
213. Saphra, I., and Winter, J. W.: Clinical manifestations of salmonellosis in man: An evaluation of 7779 human infections identified at the New York *Salmonella* Center. N. Engl. J. Med. *256*:1128, 1957.
214. Sarasombath, S., Banchuin, N., Sukosol, T., et al.: Systemic and intestinal immunities after natural typhoid infection. J. Clin. Microbiol. *25*:1088–1093, 1987.
215. Sasidharan, C. K., Rajagopal, K. C., Jayaram, C. K., et al.: *S. typhimurium* epidemic in newborn nursery. Indian J. Pediatr. *50*:599–605, 1983.

216. Schwan, W. R., Huang, X., Hu, L., and Kopecko, D. J.: Differential bacterial survival, replication and apoptosis-inducing ability of *Salmonella* serovars within human and murine macrophages. Infect. Immun. *68*:1005–1013, 2000.
217. Seals, J. E., Parrott, P. L., McGowan, J. E., et al.: Nursery salmonellosis: Delayed recognition due to unusually long incubation period. Infect. Control *4*:205–208, 1983.
218. Secmeer, G., Kanra, G., Figen, G., et al.: Ofloxacin versus co-trimoxazole in the treatment of typhoid fever in children. Acta Paediatr. Jpn. *39*:218–221, 1997.
219. Seligman, E.: Mass invasion of salmonellae in a babies ward. Ann. Paediatr. *172*:406, 1949.
220. Seoud, M., Saade, G., Uwaydah, M., et al.: Typhoid fever in pregnancy. Obstet. Gynecol. *71*:711–714, 1988.
221. Sinha, A., Sazawal, S., Kumar, R., et al.: Typhoid fever in children aged less than 5 years. Lancet *354*:734–737, 1999.
222. Sirinavin, S., Jayanetra, P., Lolekha, S., et al.: Predictors for extraintestinal infection in *Salmonella* enteritis in Thailand. Pediatr. Infect. Dis. J. *7*:44–48, 1988.
223. Smith, S. M., Palumbo, P. E., and Edelson, P. J.: *Salmonella* strains resistant to multiple antibiotics: Therapeutic implications. Pediatr. Infect. Dis. *3*:455–460, 1984.
224. Soe, G. B., and Overturf, G. D.: Treatment of typhoid fever and other systemic salmonellosis with cefotaxime, ceftriaxone, cefoperazone, and other newer cephalosporins. Rev. Infect. Dis. *9*:719–736, 1987.
225. Sperber, S. J., and Schleupner, C. J.: Salmonellosis during infection with human immunodeficiency virus. Rev. Infect. Dis. *9*:925–934, 1987.
226. Spika, J. S., Waterman, S. H., Soo Hoo, G. W., et al.: Chloramphenicol-resistant *Salmonella newport* traced through hamburger to dairy farms. N. Engl. J. Med. *316*:565–570, 1987.
227. Stuart, B. M., and Pullen, R. L.: Typhoid: Clinical analysis of 360 cases. Arch. Intern. Med. *78*:629, 1946.
228. Syrogiannopoulos, G. A., McCracken, G. H., and Nelson, J. D.: Osteoarticular infections in children with sickle cell disease. Pediatrics *78*:1090–1096, 1986.
229. Szanton, V. L.: Epidemic salmonellosis: A 30-month study of 80 cases of *S. oranienburg* infection. Pediatrics *20*:794–808, 1957.
230. Sztein, M. B., Wasserman, S. S., Tacket, C. O., et al.: Cytokine production patterns and lymphoproliferative responses in volunteers orally immunized with attenuated vaccine strains of *S. typhi*. J. Infect. Dis. *170*:1508–1517, 1994.
231. Szmuness, W., Sikorska, J., Szymanek, E., et al.: The microbiological and epidemiological properties of infections caused by *S. enteritidis*. J. Hyg. (Lond.) *64*:9–21, 1966.
232. Taylor, D. N., Bopp, C., Birkness, K., et al.: An outbreak of salmonellosis associated with a fatality in a healthy child: A large dose and severe illness. Am. J. Epidemiol. *119*:907–912, 1984.
233. Taylor, D. N., Beid, J. M., Munro, J. S., et al.: *Salmonella dublin* infections in the United States, 1979–1980. J. Infect. Dis. *146*:322–327, 1982.
234. Taylor, D. N., Levine, M. M., Kuppens, L., and Ivanoff, B.: Why are typhoid vaccines not recommended for epidemic typhoid fever? J. Infect. Dis. *180*:2089–2090, 1999.
235. Ti, T. Y., Monteiro, E. H., Lam, S., et al.: Ceftriaxone therapy in bacteremic typhoid fever. Antimicrob. Agents Chemother. *28*:540–543, 1985.
236. Torrey, S., Fleisher, G., and Jaffe, D.: Incidence of *Salmonella* bacteremia in infants with *Salmonella* gastroenteritis. J. Pediatr. *108*:718–721, 1986.
237. Tsang, R. S., Chau, P. Y., Lam, S. K., et al.: Antibody response to the lipopolysaccharide and protein antigens of *Salmonella typhi* during typhoid infection. Clin. Exp. Immunol. *46*:508–514, 1981.
238. Thisyakorn, U., Mansuwan, P., and Taylor, D. N.: Typhoid and paratyphoid fever in 192 hospitalized children in Thailand. Am. J. Dis. Child. *141*:862–865, 1987.
239. Uwyyed, K., and Uromen, A.: Scrotal abscess with bacteremia caused by *Salmonella* group D after ritual circumcision. Pediatr. Infect. Dis. J. *9*:65–66, 1990.
240. Vallenas, C., Hernandez, H., Kay, B., et al.: Efficacy of bone marrow, blood, stool, and duodenal contents cultures for bacteriologic confirmation of typhoid fever in children. Pediatr. Infect. Dis. *4*:496–498, 1985.
241. Van Gijsegem, F., Genin, S., and Boucher, C.: Conservation of secretion pathways for pathogenicity determinants of plant and animal bacteria. Trends Microbiol. *1*:175–180, 1993.
242. Vazquez, V., Calderon, E., and Rodriguez, R. S.: Chloramphenicol-resistant strains of *Salmonella typhi*. N. Engl. J. Med. *286*:1220, 1972.
243. Wahdan, M. H., Serie, C., and Cerisier, Y.: A controlled field trial of live *Salmonella typhi* strain Ty21a oral vaccine against typhoid: Three-year results. J. Infect. Dis. *145*:292–295, 1982.
244. Wain, J. Hoa, N. T., Ching, N. T., et al.: Quinolone-resistant *Salmonella typhi* in Viet Nam: Molecular basis of resistance and clinical response to treatment. Clin. Infect. Dis *25*:1404–1410, 1997.
245. Wallis, T. S., Starkey, W. G., Stephen, J., et al.: The nature and role of mucosal damage in relation to *Salmonella typhimurium* induced fluid secretion in the rabbit ileum. J. Med. Microbiol. *22*:39–49, 1986.
246. Wallis, T. S., Hawker, R. J., Candy, D. C., et al.: Quantification of the leucocyte influx into rabbit ileal loops induced by strains of *S. typhimurium* of different virulence. J. Med. Microbiol. *30*:149–156, 1989.
247. Watt, J., and Carlton, E.: Studies of the acute diarrheal diseases. XVI. An outbreak of *S. typhimurium* infection among newborn premature infants. Public Health Rep. *60*(pt I):734–810, 1945.
248. Watt, J., Wegman, M. E., Brown, O. W., et al.: Salmonellosis in a premature nursery unaccompanied by diarrheal diseases. Pediatrics *22*:689–705, 1958.
249. Wilson, R., Feldman, R. A., Davis, J., et al.: Salmonellosis in infants: The importance of intrafamilial transmission. Pediatrics *69*:436–438, 1982.
250. Winkler, A. P., and Gleich, S.: Acute acalculous cholecystitis caused by *Salmonella typhi* in an 11-year-old. Pediatr. Infect. Dis. *7*:125–128, 1988.
251. Wittler, R. R., and Bass, J. W.: Non-typhoidal *Salmonella* enteric infections and bacteremia. Pediatr. Infect. Dis. J. *8*:364–367, 1989.
252. Wright, J., Thomas, P., and Serjeant, G. R.: Septicemia caused by *Salmonella* infection: An overlooked complication of sickle cell disease. J. Pediatr. *130*:394–399, 1997.
253. Yamamoto, L. G., and Ashton, M. J.: *Salmonella* infections in infants in Hawaii. Pediatr. Infect. Dis. J. *7*:48–52, 1988.
254. Ying, F., Lin, C., Ho, V. A., et al.: The efficacy of a *Salmonella typhi* Vi conjugate vaccine in two-to-five year old children. N. Engl. J. Med. *344*:1263–1269, 2001.
255. Zaidi, E., Bachur, R., and Harper, M.: Non-typhi *Salmonella* bacteremia in children. Pediatr. Infect. Dis. J. *18*:1073–1077, 1999.
256. Zarkovsky, H. S., Gallagher, D., and Gill, F. M.: Bacteremia in sickle hemoglobinopathies. J. Pediatr. *109*:579–585, 1986.

CHAPTER 116 Plague (*Yersinia pestis*)

MARIA D. GOLDSTEIN

History

Yersinia pestis has been responsible for the most devastating epidemics in human history. Possibly the first mention of plague dates back to 1320 BC, in I Samuel, Chapters 5 and 6. The next recorded outbreak was in AD 542 during Justinian's reign, when an estimated 100 million people died.[45] This epidemic was followed by a quiescent period lasting until 1346, when plague appeared during the siege of the city of Kaffa in the Crimea. The epidemic quickly spread through most of Europe, becoming known as the black death. One third of the population of Europe died in its aftermath. Between the 14th and 20th centuries, plague remained endemic in most of Europe and Russia, with resultant frequent outbreaks.[40]

In 1894, Yersin and Kitasato, working independently, first described the bacillus responsible for plague.[44] At about that same time, the role played by rats and fleas in the spread of the disease became known. In 1900, plague was introduced to San Francisco by rats aboard ships docking there. The disease spread to ground squirrels and then to other wild animals of the American Southwest.[43] In 1943, effective antibiotics against *Y. pestis* became available.[40] Thanks to these advances, plague is a rare occurrence today in the United States. However, plague continues to be endemic in many parts of the world, leading to recent outbreaks in Madagascar, Peru, and India. Although antibiotics have been effective in the treatment and prophylaxis of plague, resistance is being noted increasingly.[16] Furthermore, the potential of aerosolized *Y. pestis* as a biologic weapon is being scrutinized, leading to renewed interest in the understanding and study of this organism.[26]

Bacteriology

Y. pestis belongs in the family Enterobacteriaceae. It is a small, pleomorphic, nonmotile, gram-negative bacillus. With Wayson, Giemsa, and Gram stains, the bacillus takes on bipolar or safety-pin morphologic features.[14]

Y. pestis grows at temperatures ranging from 0° C to 40° C (32° F to 104° F); the optimal temperature is 28° C (82.4° F). On first isolation at 35° C (95° F) on 5 percent blood agar, the colonies are pinpoint in size, growing to 1 to 2 mm after 2 days. They are nonhemolytic on 5 percent sheep blood agar.

Depending on the clinical nature of the disease, blood cultures, sputum samples, or aspirates of enlarged nodes should be examined for typical bacilli. The isolated bacilli can be identified by the following criteria. *Y. pestis* is nonmotile at 37° C and 22° C (98.6° F and 71.6° F). The organism usually is negative for urea hydrolysis but may be positive in freshly isolated strains. The organism is positive for esculin, ß-galactosidase, catalase, and methyl red. The oxidase, indole, and Voges-Proskauer reactions are negative. It ferments glucose, maltose, salicin, xylose, arabinose, dextrin, trehalose, and mannitol. It does not produce acid from lactose, sucrose, rhamnose, melibiose, adonitol, cellobiose, sorbose, or dulcitol. It does not use citrate, and it does not grow in potassium cyanide. *Y. pestis* is negative for lysine, ornithine decarboxylase, and arginine dihydrolase.[41, 50]

Positive cultures show pinpoint colonies within 24 to 48 hours after inoculation. However, laboratories that are fully automated or semiautomated may not detect *Y. pestis*. Nonautomated laboratories may require as long as 6 days to identify the organism. Because of lack of standarized susceptibility testing procedures, isolates should be sent to a reference laboratory for susceptibility testing.[26]

Y. pestis strains vary in their degree of virulence. The following determinants of virulence are chromosomally mediated: (1) an antiphagocytic capsular material known as fraction 1, (2) the endogenous purine synthesis that allows the organism to grow within macrophages, and (3) the ability to absorb iron from the medium. Several plasmids have been implicated in the development of other virulence factors. A plasmid of 9-kb pairs contains the determinant of secretory protein that kills other bacterial strains. A plasmid of 72-kb pairs that all pathogenic *Y. pestis* strains contain confers the requirement for environmental calcium to be present for the organism to grow at 37° C (98.6° F). When grown under this condition, *Y. pestis* produces V and W antigens that are necessary for virulence.[21] Toxins have been produced by all fully virulent strains. Both an exotoxin and an endotoxin have been found to contribute to the lethal effects of plague.[50]

Transmission

HOST

Historically, epidemics of plague usually were transmitted by the fleas of infected rats. This form of spread is more likely to occur in urban, rat-infested, and crowded dwellings and may result in epidemics. In the United States, plague is transmitted sporadically to humans after contact with an enzootic sylvatic focus.[28] Infected wild rodents perpetuate the plague bacillus in a given ecosystem by virtue of their ability to withstand an inoculum of *Y. pestis* many times larger than that necessary to cause disease in humans or domestic animals. After becoming inoculated, the wild rodent may become bacteremic and infect the fleas that feed on it; these in turn transmit the plague bacillus to another rodent. Hibernating animals are especially resistant to clinical infection. Animals inoculated before going into hibernation may survive through the winter and not succumb until after they come out of their burrows, thus reintroducing the bacillus in the new season.[23] Carnivores are relatively resistant to infection but contribute to the spread of the organism by transporting infected fleas from one area to another.[28]

The role of domestic animals in bridging the gap between sylvatic plague and human infection has been studied extensively.[38, 44, 48] Cats and dogs are susceptible to both natural and experimental plague. Epizootics in cats have been observed in conjunction with plague epidemics in humans.[44] Experimentally infected cats develop severe systemic illness, with bacteremia and abscess formation at the site of the inoculum. Between 1977 and 1998, 23 cases of feline-associated human plague infection were reported.[19] Five of these cases were fatal; two of them presented with primary pneumonic plague, and one with septicemic plague. Many of these cases were misdiagnosed at presentation, leading to delays in treatment and, in some cases, fatalities. This diagnosis should be entertained especially in the western states of Arizona, California, Colorado, and New Mexico. No seasonal variation in the occurrence of cat-associated illness was noted.[19]

A total of 10 other cases reported in the literature of feline transmission of plague to humans involved four veterinarians.[15] Dogs also are susceptible, but their disease is milder.[48] Swine are resistant to plague, the only evidence of subclinical infection being the presence of antibodies to the fraction 1 antigen of *Y. pestis*. Domestic animals, by virtue of their intimate contact with both wildlife and humans, may be responsible for some cases of human plague. This danger is accentuated by a dearth of symptoms in some animals.[38]

VECTOR

Plague is transmitted to humans by the bite of an infected flea, the skinning and evisceration of infected animals,[29] or the inhalation of infected droplets from a case of pneumonic plague.[32] Infrequent portals of entry include the conjunctiva[38] and the pharynx.[37, 46]

The efficiency of the flea as a vector for human disease depends on the likelihood that the infected flea will feed on a person and that the flea will regurgitate the bacillus into the victim's bloodstream in the process of feeding.[28] Flea species vary in both of these attributes. Wild rodent fleas, for example, are reluctant to feed on humans and do it only under duress (e.g., when the natural host dies). Fleas of domestic animals are more likely to bite humans.

The Oriental rat flea, *Xenopsylla cheopis*, is the most efficient transmitter of plague because of its willingness to bite people and its propensity for regurgitating large numbers of bacilli in the process.[28] When the Oriental rat flea ingests infected blood, the actions of a coagulase produced by *Y. pestis* and a trypsin-like enzyme present in the flea's stomach result in the formation of an infected clot that blocks the flea's proventriculus. In obstructing the flea's intestinal tract, the clot allows further replication of bacteria. When the flea tries to feed again, it regurgitates large numbers of plague bacilli. The formation and dissolution of the fibrin clot are temperature dependent. At temperatures above 27° C (80.6° F), a fibrinolytic enzyme is activated that dissolves the clot and allows the flea to dispose of the bacillus. One postulation is that this temperature-dependent phenomenon is responsible for the observed cyclic nature of urban plague epidemics, which tend to subside with the advent of hot weather.[5]

In contrast, fleas in which the intestinal tracts do not become blocked contribute to the endemicity of plague by harboring the organism and transmitting it in sublethal doses.[10] Sylvatic plague depends on the rodent flea as the vector. This flea, although not as efficient as the rat flea in transmitting the bacillus, may itself become a reservoir of *Y. pestis* by surviving for 12 to 15 months after the original host dies. In the new season, it reintroduces the plague bacillus into the new rodent population.[44] The observation that *Y. pestis* can survive in the soil during interepizootics suggests another mechanism of transmission of plague.[22]

Epidemiology

The plague bacillus exists in enzootic cycles involving wild animals or domestic rats. In urban plague, the course of events usually is initiated by the introduction of the plague bacillus from an enzootic focus into a susceptible rat population. With humans and rats living in proximity, an epizootic in rats then may be followed by an epidemic in people.[44] The epidemic may subside with the advent of hot, humid weather[5] or the obliteration of the rat population.[44] Such epidemics rarely occur today but have been described in the former South Vietnam[3, 30] and most recently in India.[11] In 1992, 1582 cases of human plague were reported to the World Health Organization from nine countries, including Brazil, Madagascar, Myanmar (formerly Burma), Tanzania, Vietnam, and the United States.[52]

In the United States today, people become infected most frequently by direct contact with a sylvatic reservoir of infection. Sporadic human cases usually result from working or hunting in a plague-infested area[28] and increasingly from living near foci of infection as suburban spread encroaches on the natural habitats of rodents.[12] In recent years, domestic animals, especially cats, have been responsible for a significant proportion of human cases.

Sylvatic plague epizootics occur in the summer seasons. Most cases of rural plague occur between April and September. The rare occurrence of human plague in the winter months usually is associated with hunting and direct exposure to infected tissues.[9, 29]

The continental United States has a large enzootic focus that includes 130 counties in 15 western states. Surveillance for plague in rodents during the 1990s has identified infected animals farther east than ever before reported. The plague bacillus has now been isolated in wild rodents in eastern Montana, western Nebraska, western North Dakota, and eastern Texas.[12] Between 1925 and 1965, the number of reported cases in the United States averaged between two and three per year.[6, 7] During the 1970s, 105 cases were reported.[29] The number of cases reported in 1980 through 1982 showed a similar increasing trend.[7] Between 1970 and 1979, 53 percent of cases were in females, in contrast to the period 1926 to 1969, when only 27 percent were in females. Approximately 60 percent of cases occur in persons younger than 20 years.[29] However, of 10 confirmed cases reported in the United States in 1993, the age distribution was 22 to 96 years. Five of the patients were older than 65 years.[12] Native Americans living on reservations in the states of Arizona, New Mexico, and Utah are at increased risk. In the period 1970 to 1979, 35 percent of cases in these three states occurred in Native Americans.[7, 29] Many of the patients were infected within 1 mile of their residence and almost all within their state of residence.[24] Seven of the 10 patients described in 1993 were exposed in their home sites, and one, a veterinarian, was exposed at work.[12] On occasion, plague has been acquired by a traveler in an endemic area who then traveled during the incubation period to a plague-free region of the country. This set of circumstances shows why all physicians need to be aware of the presenting symptoms and signs of plague and to obtain an accurate travel history.[31]

Pathogenesis and Pathology

The portal of entry of the plague bacillus determines, to some extent, the form the disease will take. By far the most common portal of entry is the skin when it is bitten by an infected flea. Broken skin may provide access for direct inoculation while infected animals are being handled. After overcoming the skin barrier, the organisms move through the lymphatics to the regional lymph nodes, where they elicit an inflammatory response. The infection may be localized at this site, with subsequent formation of antibody and recovery. This clinical form is known as pestis minor. The bacillus commonly is disseminated through the bloodstream. Distant organ involvement may include the liver, spleen, kidneys, lungs, and meninges. Disseminated intravascular coagulation is a common finding in fatal cases. Coagulation defects, including thrombocytopenia and elevated fibrin split products,[3] as well as fibrin deposits in the glomeruli,[18, 44] may be present. Bacteremia is not synonymous with severe disease and occurs commonly in relatively mild cases.[44]

The major determinant of severity seems to be the presence of high levels of endotoxin. The toxin of *Y. pestis* has the biologic properties of typical endotoxin. When injected into experimental animals, it can cause the clinical symptoms and signs and pathologic changes characteristic of endotoxic shock and death. The quantity of endotoxin necessary to kill is estimated to be comparable to that present in a lethal dose of live bacteria.[1, 51] The murine toxin of *Y. pestis* has a direct inhibitory effect in vitro on the respiration of heart mitochondria of rats and mice, whereas it has little or no effect on the mitochondria of rabbits, chimpanzees, dogs, and monkeys. The differing sensitivities in vitro correlate with the susceptibilities in vivo of these species to *Y. pestis* infection.[47]

Achieving high levels of toxin depends on the ability of the bacillus to replicate in the infected host. Resistance to phagocytosis had been assumed to be related to virulence. More recent experimental evidence has shown that virulent *Y. pestis* organisms are phagocytosed but, in contrast with avirulent ones, are not killed. They continue to replicate freely in macrophages, allowing the accumulation of endotoxin.[27, 47]

When the lung is the portal of entry, the disease usually is more fulminant. After being inhaled, bacilli replicate freely in the alveolar spaces. Severe pneumonia, endotoxemia, and septicemia ensue and, if untreated, cause death. In fatal cases, the thoracic lymph nodes show infarction, necrosis, and liquefaction, with pus formation. Edema and inflammation of the surrounding tissue are common findings.[44] The mucosa of trachea and bronchi is covered by bloody, frothy exudate. Submucosal hemorrhages and areas of necrosis may surround the trachea. The pleural surfaces contain hemorrhagic lesions and fibrinous adhesions. The lung parenchyma may be consolidated or show signs of acute edema.[44] The predominant histologic feature is an alveolar exudate consisting of histiocytes and polymorphonuclear leukocytes.[18]

Other organs also are involved. The kidneys may appear grossly hemorrhagic and contain areas of necrosis. Microscopic examination reveals leukocytic infiltrates of congested veins and capillaries. Glomeruli with fibrin thrombi frequently are found in patients with disseminated intravascular coagulation.[18] Biopsy of purpuric skin lesions reveals subepithelial hemorrhages and fibrin deposit in the capillaries. These changes are indistinguishable from those seen in a generalized Shwartzman reaction.[3]

Clinical Manifestations

The incubation period of *Y. pestis* generally is 3 to 4 days but may be as short as a few hours or as long as 10 days. The onset of illness usually is abrupt, beginning with fever, malaise, weakness, and headache.[44, 45] Fever is high, frequently accompanied by shaking chills.[38] The appearance of a visible and palpable bubo may be preceded by pain and tenderness at that site.[45]

On physical examination, the patient is "toxic," apprehensive, and tachycardic. The inoculation site in the skin may not be evident or may be marked by a carbuncle. In bubonic plague, typical large, fixed, edematous, and exquisitely tender nodes are present at one anatomic site.[30] In decreasing order of frequency, the areas of nodal involvement are the groin (including femoral and inguinal nodes), axilla, and neck.[44] Any lymph node may suppurate, sometimes presenting an atypical picture (e.g., if intra-abdominal nodes are involved, an acute abdominal emergency may be suspected).[45] Septicemia as an initial presentation of *Y. pestis* infection is not rare.[24] Twenty-five percent of the patients presented without adenopathy in the 71 confirmed cases of plague in New Mexico from 1980 to 1984. All patients with septicemic presentation had fever and chills, and most had tachycardia, tachypnea, and relative hypotension. Seventy-two percent had gastrointestinal symptoms. Plague pneumonia was twice as likely to occur among septicemic as among bubonic plague patients. Septicemic patients were significantly older and more likely to die than were patients with a bubonic presentation. Although septicemic plague occurred more often in older patients, those younger than 30 years of age with septicemic presentation were more likely to die.[24]

As a result of its nonspecific presentation, septicemic plague is difficult to diagnose early. Of 27 patients with plague admitted to Indian Medical Center in Gallup, New Mexico, between 1965 and 1989, 5 presented with a nonspecific febrile syndrome with upper respiratory symptoms. They were prescribed penicillin. Three of the five patients died. Another five patients presented with a nonspecific febrile syndrome associated with chills, myalgias, and anorexia. These patients were not treated initially with antibiotics, and three of the five died.[15] The index of suspicion must be high, therefore, because early diagnosis is imperative for avoiding a high mortality rate. Persons presenting with what appears to be community-acquired, gram-negative sepsis and who reside in or have a history of recent travel to endemic areas of plague must be evaluated for and treated with antibiotics effective against *Y. pestis*.[36]

Gastrointestinal symptoms occur in patients with plague, especially those with septicemic plague.[23] Between 1980 and 1984, more than half of the 71 patients with plague in New Mexico presented with gastrointestinal symptoms that sometimes preceded the appearance of the buboes in the bubonic cases. Common symptoms are abdominal pain, nausea, vomiting, and diarrhea. These symptoms are thought to be a general response of the body to gram-negative septicemia. On occasion, hepatosplenomegaly and mesenteric or retroperitoneal lymphadenopathy have masqueraded as an acute abdomen.[25, 31]

Neurologic manifestations caused by the effects of toxin on the brain are common findings. The patient with plague may suffer from insomnia, delirium, stupor, weakness, staggering gait, vertigo, disorders of speech, and loss of memory.[35] *Y. pestis* meningitis is relatively rare, but it does occur. Children younger than 15 years of age seem to be more susceptible, and septicemic patients are four times more likely to develop it than are patients with bubonic plague. It often manifests itself while the patient is well into a course of antibiotic therapy for bubonic or septicemic plague.[2] When intravascular coagulation supervenes, renal involvement may be manifested by acute cortical or tubular necrosis. Hepatic involvement may be evidenced by mildly elevated liver enzymes.[44] Hantavirus pulmonary syndrome may mimic septicemic or pneumonic plague; furthermore, they both share similar geographic distribution, and, therefore, patients for whom this diagnosis is contemplated should be treated with antibiotics to cover the possibility of plague.[42]

Primary pneumonic plague has identical constitutional symptoms but follows a fulminant course with a more pronounced pulmonary component. Within 20 to 24 hours after the onset of the illness, tachypnea, dyspnea, and cough productive of bloody mucopurulent sputum supervene. If early and effective treatment is not instituted, the patient usually dies.[44]

Differential Diagnosis

Because of the rarity of plague today, the diagnosis often is delayed or missed. Bubonic plague may be confused with other diseases affecting the skin and lymph nodes. The diagnosis of staphylococcal or streptococcal adenitis can be established easily by culture. Lymphogranuloma venereum is more indolent, has milder systemic symptoms, and is associated with anogenital ulcer. Syphilitic adenitis usually is nontender. With cat-scratch disease and *Pasteurella multocida* infections, the constitutional symptoms are few, and the patient typically has a history of animal exposure. Tularemia has a more gradual onset.[44] In their later stages, the ulcerated skin lesions of plague may resemble anthrax.[30]

Diagnosis

The most important factor in the prompt diagnosis of plague is a high index of suspicion. Suspicion should trigger immediate notification to the local or state health department. The state reference laboratory can arrange for rapid diagnostic tests.

Bacterial staining of lymph node material by Gram, Wayson, or Wright stain often shows the typical bipolar plague organisms. In the septicemic form of the disease, similar bacterial staining of venous blood frequently permits visualization of the plague bacillus.[33] Fluorescent antibody staining of direct smears and tissues may provide a rapid, presumptive diagnosis of plague.[26] More recent rapid tests, such as enzyme-linked immunosorbent assay F1 antigen detection and polymerase chain reaction, have shown promise in the laboratory or in outbreaks, but they are not widely available.[13]

Treatment

Therapeutic decisions cannot await culture results. All patients suspected of having plague should receive prompt antimicrobial therapy after appropriate blood and tissue have been obtained for cultures, fluorescent antibody staining, and serologic testing.

The sulfonamides and streptomycin proved effective when they were introduced first in the 1940s. Resistant strains to one or the other of these antibiotics soon appeared.[4, 46] Despite the paucity of published trials in humans on antibiotic effectiveness, other than streptomycin and tetracycline, the Working Group on Civilian Biodefense Consensus Statement[26] recommends gentamicin as an effective alternative to streptomycin for patients needing parenteral antibiotics. Gentamicin has been used frequently in the last 10 years and has shown comparable outcomes to streptomycin in one case series (Lucy Boulanger, M.D., Indian Health Service). In vitro and in vivo studies in mice corroborate its effectiveness against *Y. pestis* infections.[50]

For acutely ill patients thought to have plague infection, streptomycin and gentamicin are the drugs of choice. If available, streptomycin is given intramuscularly in the dosage of 20 to 30 mg/kg/day in two divided doses.[35] Gentamicin is administered at 7.5 mg/kg/day to children and 3 to 5 mg/kg/day to adults in three divided doses, intravenously or intramuscularly. Antibiotic susceptibility testing should be carried out because *Y. pestis* plasmid-mediated multiple antibiotic resistance has been described.[20]

When plague meningitis develops, chloramphenicol, 50 to 100 mg/kg/day (after administration of an initial dose of 25 mg/kg) intravenously in four divided doses, is the treatment of choice. The duration of therapy is determined by the length and severity of the illness. Treatment is continued for at least 7 days in patients with uncomplicated disease.[11]

Patients older than 8 years of age who do not require hospitalization receive tetracycline at a dose of 25 to 50 mg/kg/day every 4 to 6 hours up to a total daily dose of 1 g in children and 2 g in adults. When outpatient treatment is given, the patient should be observed closely for the first 3 days to ensure resolution of the disease.[11] Sulfonamides may be used for prophylaxis in pediatric patients as an alternative to the tetracycline class of antibiotics.[26]

Prognosis

In outbreaks of untreated plague, the mortality rate has ranged between 40 and 70 percent. Pneumonic plague almost invariably is fatal without treatment. With prompt specific antimicrobial therapy, the overall mortality rate for plague has dropped to 5 percent.[32] Complications during convalescence include polyarthritis, small lung abscesses, delayed suppuration of buboes,[30] and meningitis. *Staphylococcus aureus* and *Pseudomonas* spp. may superinfect involved lymph nodes.[45] Immunity usually ensues after clinical or asymptomatic infection, but natural reinfection rarely has been observed.[45]

Prevention and Control

Hygienic measures and eradication of rats from areas of human habitations have all but eliminated epidemics of urban plague. When epizootics occur in wild rodents, control measures must be directed against rodents and fleas. Vector control can be achieved by the use of insecticides in fields and housing areas. In plague-endemic areas, the public must be instructed to avoid burrows, not to handle sick or dead rodents, to deflea household pets, and to eliminate trash near living areas.[8] The immune status of domestic animals can be used as a surveillance tool to ascertain the presence of *Y. pestis* in the community. Dogs, cats, and swine develop antibodies to the fraction 1 antigen of *Y. pestis*.[38, 48]

Patients with plague should be isolated with respiratory precautions until they are bacteriologically sterile. Contacts of patients with pneumonic plague receive chemoprophylaxis with tetracycline at 25 to 50 mg/kg/day up to 2 g in adults and up to 1 g in children 8 years and older. Younger children receive trimethoprim-sulfamethoxazole at 40 mg/kg/day (sulfamethoxazole) in two equal doses orally.[26] The 6-day quarantine period for international travel for contacts of patients with plague does not guarantee the clearance of the bacillus from asymptomatic pharyngeal carriers.[4] Public and professional education in endemic zones is of paramount importance for ensuring prompt reporting of human and animal cases.

Plague vaccines had been used since the late 19th century for individuals at high risk for occupational exposure. They are no longer being manufactured in the United States. Research in this area is continuing.[26]

REFERENCES

1. Albizo, J. M., and Surgalla, M. J.: Isolation and characterization of *Pasteurella pestis* endotoxin. Infect. Immun. *2*:229–236, 1970.
2. Becker, T. M., Poland, J. D., Quan, T. J., et al.: Plague meningitis: A retrospective analysis of cases reported in the United States, 1970–1979. West. J. Med. *147*:554–557, 1987.
3. Butler, T.: A clinical study of bubonic plague. Am. J. Med. *53*:268–276, 1972.
4. Cantey, J. R.: Plague in Vietnam. Arch. Intern. Med. *133*:280–283, 1974.
5. Cavanaugh, D. C.: Specific effect of temperature upon transmission of the plague bacillus by the Oriental rat flea, *Xenopsylla cheopis*. Am. J. Trop. Med. Hyg. *20*:264–273, 1971.
6. Centers for Disease Control and Prevention: Plague: United States, 1976. M. M. W. R. *28*:159, 1977.
7. Centers for Disease Control and Prevention: Plague in the United States, 1982. M. M. W. R. *32*:19SS–24SS, 1983.
8. Centers for Disease Control and Prevention: Plague: Human plague in the United States, 1983. M. M. W. R. *32*:329–330, 1983.
9. Centers for Disease Control and Prevention: Plague: Winter plague Colorado, Washington, Texas, 1983–1984. M. M. W. R. *33*:145–148, 1984.
10. Centers for Disease Control and Prevention: Plague vaccine. M. M. W. R. *31*:301–303, 1982.
11. Centers for Disease Control and Prevention: Plague Treatment Guidelines. Bacteriologic Zoonoses Branch, Division of Vector-Borne Infectious Diseases, Fort Collins, CO, 80522.
12. Centers for Disease Control and Prevention: Human plague: United States, 1993–1994. M. M. W. R. *43*:242–246, 1994.
13. Chanteau, S., Rahalison, L., Ratsitorahina, M., et al.: Early diagnosis of bubonic plague using F1 antigen capture ELISA assay and rapid immunogold dipstick. Int. J. Med. Microbiol. *290*:279–283, 2000.
14. Chen, T. H., and Elberg, S. S.: *Yersinia, Pasteurella,* and *Francisella. In* Braude, A. I., Davis, C. E., and Fierer, J. (eds.): Medical Microbiology and Infectious Diseases. Philadelphia, W. B. Saunders, 1981, pp. 393–399.
15. Crook, D., and Tempest, B.: Plague: A review of 27 cases. Arch. Intern. Med. *152*:1253–1256, 1992.
16. Dennis, D. T., and Hughes, J. M.: Multidrug resistance in plague. N. Engl. J. Med. *337*:702–704, 1997.
17. Eidson, M., Tierney, L., Rollag, O. J., et al.: Feline plague in New Mexico: Risk factors and transmission to humans. Am. J. Public Health *78*:1333–1335, 1988.
18. Finegold, M. J.: Pathogenesis of plague. Am. J. Med. *45*:549–555, 1968.
19. Gage, K. L., Dennis, D. T., Orloski, K .A., et al.: Cases of cat-associated human plague in the western US, 1977–1998. Clin. Infect. Dis. *30*:893–900, 2000.

20. Galimand, M., Guiyoule, A., Berbaud, G., et al.: Multidrug resistance in *Yersinia pestis* mediated by transferable plasmid. N. Engl. J. Med. *337*:677–680, 1997.
21. Ganem, D. E.: Plasmids and pestilence: Biological and clinical aspects of bubonic plague. West. J. Med. *144*:447–451, 1986.
22. Goldenberg, M. I., and Kartman, L.: Role of soil in the ecology of *Pasteurella pestis*. Bacteriol. Proc. *66*:54–57, 1966.
23. Hull, H. F., Montes, J. M., and Mann, J. M.: Plague masquerading as gastrointestinal illness. West. J. Med. *145*:485–487, 1986.
24. Hull, H. F., Montes, J. M., and Mann, J. M.: Septicemic plague in New Mexico. J. Infect. Dis. *155*:113–118, 1987.
25. Humphrey, M., McGiuney, R., Perkins, C., et al.: *Yersinia pestis:* A case of mistaken identity. Pediatr. Infect. Dis. J. *7*:365–366, 1988.
26. Inglesby, T. V., Dennis, D. T., Henderson, D. A., et al.: Plague as a biological weapon. J. A. M. A. *283*:2281–2290, 2000.
27. Janssen, W. A., and Surgalla, M. J.: Plague bacillus: Survival within host phagocytes. Science *163*:950–952, 1969.
28. Kartman, L., Goldenberg, M. I., and Hubbert, W. T.: Recent observations on the epidemiology of plague in the United States. Am. J. Public Health *56*:1554–1569, 1966.
29. Kaufmann, A. F., Boyce, J. M., and Martone, W. J.: Trends in human plague in the United States. J. Infect. Dis. *141*:522–524, 1980.
30. Legters, L. J., Cottingham, A. J., and Hunter, D. H.: Clinical and epidemiologic notes on a defined outbreak of plague in Vietnam. Am. J. Trop. Med. Hyg. *19*:639–652, 1970.
31. Leopold, J. C.: Septicemic plague in a 14-month old. Pediatr. Infect. Dis. J. *5*:108–110, 1986.
32. Maegraith, B. G.: Plague. *In* Adams, A. R., and Maegraith, B. G. (eds.): Clinical Tropical Diseases. Oxford, Blackwell Scientific, 1970, pp. 325–336.
33. Mann, J. M., Hull, H. F., Schmid, G. P., et al.: Plague and the peripheral smear. J. A. M. A. *251*:953, 1984.
34. Mann, J. M., Martone, W. J., Boyce, J. M., et al.: Endemic human plague in New Mexico: Risk factors associated with infection. J. Infect. Dis. *140*:397–401, 1979.
35. Mann, J. M., Schaudler, L., and Cushing, A.: Pediatric plague. Pediatrics *69*:762–767, 1982.
36. Mann, J. M., Schmid, G. P., Stoesz, P. A., et al.: Peripatetic plague. J. A. M. A. *247*:47–48, 1982.
37. Marshall, J. D., Guy, D. V., and Gibson, F. L.: Asymptomatic pharyngeal plague infection in Vietnam. Am. J. Trop. Med. Hyg. *16*:175–177, 1967.
38. Marshall, J. D., Harrison, D. N., Murr, J. A., et al.: The role of domestic animals in the epidemiology of plague. III. Experimental infection in swine. J. Infect. Dis. *125*:556–559, 1972.
39. Martin, A. R., Hurtado, F. P., Plessak, R. A., et al.: Plague meningitis. Pediatrics *40*:610–616, 1967.
40. McNeill, W. H. (ed.): Plagues and People. Garden City, NY, Anchor Press of Doubleday, 1976.
41. Mollaret, H. H., and Thal, E.: *Yersinia*. *In* Buchanan, R. E., and Gibbons, N. E. (eds.): Bergey's Manual of Determinative Bacteriology. 8th ed. Baltimore, Williams & Wilkins, 1974, pp. 330–332.
42. Peters, C. J., Simpson, G. L., and Levy, H.: Spectrum of hantavirus infection. Annu. Rev. Med. *50*:531–545, 1999.
43. Plague, Historical Notes. Can. Med. Assoc. J. *119*:10, 1978.
44. Pollitzer, R.: Plague. W. H. O. Monogr. No. 22. Geneva, 1954.
45. Reed, W. P., Palmer, D. L., Williams, R. C., et al.: Bubonic plague in the southwestern United States. Medicine (Baltimore) *49*:465–486, 1970.
46. Reiley, C. G., and Kates, E. D.: The clinical spectrum of plague in Vietnam. Arch. Intern. Med. *126*:990–994, 1970.
47. Rust, J. H., Jr., Cavanaugh, D. C., Kadis, S., et al.: Plague toxin: Its effect in vitro and in vivo. Science *142*:408–409, 1963.
48. Rust, J. H., Cavanaugh, D. C., O'Shita, R., et al.: The role of domestic animals in the epidemiology of plague. I. Experimental infection of dogs and cats. J. Infect. Dis. *124*:522–526, 1971.
49. Smith, M. D., Vinh, D. X., Nguyen, T. T. et al.: In vitro antimicrobial susceptibilities of strains of *Yersinia pestis*. Antimicrob. Agents Chemother *39*:2153–2154, 1995.
50. Sonnenwirth, A. C.: *Yersinia*. *In* Lennette, E. H., Spaulding, E. H., and Trauant, J. P. (eds.): Manual of Clinical Microbiology. 2nd ed. Washington, D. C., American Society for Microbiology, 1974, pp. 222–229.
51. Walker, R. V., Bomes, M. G., and Thiggins, E. D.: Composition of and physiopathology produced by plague endotoxins. Nature *209*:1246, 1966.
52. World Health Organization: Weekly Epidemiological Record *69*:5–12, 1994.

CHAPTER 117 Other *Yersinia* Species

CHARLES R. WOODS

Yersinia are gram-negative, coccobacillary organisms that are primarily zoonotic. The genus is a member of the family Enterobacteriaceae and consists of 11 species, 3 of which are clearly human pathogens[64]: *Yersinia pestis, Yersinia pseudotuberculosis* (both formerly included in the genus *Pasteurella*), and *Yersinia enterocolitica. Y. pestis,* the causative agent of plague, is found in rodents and insect vectors and is discussed in Chapter 116. *Y. enterocolitica* and *Y. pseudotuberculosis* are responsible for a variety of syndromes, some of which originally were called pseudotuberculosis. Infections caused by these enteropathogenic *Yersinia* are now collectively called yersiniosis, which is the focus of this chapter. Molecular phylogenetic analysis suggests that *Y. pestis* evolved from *Y. pseudotuberculosis* sometime between 1500 and 20,000 years ago.[3]

During the past 3 decades, *Y. enterocolitica* has been recognized as an important human pathogen worldwide and is a common cause of gastroenteritis in some pediatric populations of the industrialized world.[1, 43, 51, 105] It also has drawn attention because of its immunologic or postinfectious manifestations, which include reactive arthritis and erythema nodosum.[43] *Y. pseudotuberculosis,* although widespread in nature, is a much less common cause of human disease.[64] In Japan, it has been associated with clinical illness that at times has resembled Kawasaki disease.

Historical Aspects

In 1883, Malassez and Vignal[117] described a bacterium that produced a disease they named pseudotuberculosis. When injected into guinea pigs, the organism produced tuberculosis-like lesions. It grew at 4° C and multiplied better at 22° C than at 37° C. This observation was confirmed in 1910 by Albrecht,[10] who labeled the disease enteritis follicularis suppurativa. The first case of mesenteric adenitis, the most common syndrome produced by *Y. pseudotuberculosis,* was reported in 1913 by Saisawa.[157] A second instance of disease that indicated its capacity to produce death (bacteremia and multiple hepatic abscesses) was recorded in 1949 by Hassig and colleagues.[70] Masshoff[119] was the first to recover the organism from a culture of mesenteric lymph nodes of a patient with the clinical picture of acute appendicitis. Masshoff and Dolle[120] subsequently described the histologic picture produced by *Y. pseudotuberculosis*. In 1954, Knapp and Masshoff[95] first reported the clinical features of infection produced by this organism. Only 14 cases of this infection had been described up to that time.[50]

The existence of a species of *Yersinia* other than that causing pseudotuberculosis was suggested in 1933 by Gilbert,[57] who reported an unusual infection in animals. Schleifstein and Coleman[158, 159] examined numerous organisms that were isolated between 1933 and 1957 from stool cultures of human cases of diarrhea from which *Salmonella* and *Shigella* could not be recovered and that resembled the infections in animals reported by Gilbert. They identified an organism that had not been described previously and named it *Bacterium enterocoliticum*. In 1964, it was named *Y. enterocolitica* by Frederiksen.[54]

The genus is named for A. J. Yersin, the French bacteriologist who first isolated the plague bacillus.[169] During the past 40 years, an extensive literature detailing the microbiology, pathology, epidemiology, molecular pathogenesis, and clinical features of disease caused by *Y. pseudotuberculosis* and *Y. enterocolitica* has been developed.[*]

Microbiology

Yersinia organisms are relatively large (0.5 to 1.0 by 1 to 2 μm or larger), gram-negative, ovoid or rod-shaped. Both *Y. enterocolitica* and *Y. pseudotuberculosis* are motile at 22° C to 25° C but not at 37° C. Like other members of Enterobacteriaceae, *Yersinia* organisms are facultative anaerobes and grow well on ordinary media. On Gram staining, *Y. pseudotuberculosis* appears as a large coccobacillus. Staining with methylene blue and carbol fuchsin discloses a bipolar (safety pin) morphology of most but not all strains. *Y. enterocolitica* is somewhat smaller and shows little if any bipolarity.[166, 169]

Yersinia organisms may be confused with coliforms such as *Escherichia coli, Morganella, Proteus, Shigella, Salmonella,* and *Providencia* or with *Y. pestis, Brucella,* and *Achromobacter,* unless careful biochemical and physiologic studies are conducted. *Yersinia* reduce nitrates and are oxidase negative, catalase positive, urease positive, and citrate negative. They ferment glucose, maltose, mannitol, glycerol, xylose, and fructose, producing acid but no gas with each sugar. *Yersinia* organisms usually do not ferment lactose but produce α-D-galactosidase. They do not ferment dulcitol, inositol, raffinose, or rhamnose. On lysine-iron agar slants, *Yersinia* organisms produce an alkaline slant with an acid butt. They do not produce hydrogen sulfide. The Voges-Proskauer reaction is negative at 37° C but may be positive at 25° C for some strains of *Y. enterocolitica*. All strains of *Y. pseudotuberculosis* and most strains of *Y. enterocolitica* isolated in Europe are indole negative. Most strains of *Y. enterocolitica* found in the United States have been indole positive.[46, 61, 80, 132, 136, 166, 169]

Although these two species of *Yersinia* share many properties, they are distinguishable on the basis of several biochemical activities, antigenic structure, and sensitivity to various *Yersinia* phages.[154] *Y. enterocolitica* produces an acid slant and acid butt on triple sugar iron agar caused by fermentation of sucrose, whereas *Y. pseudotuberculosis* produces an alkaline slant and an acid butt. *Y. enterocolitica* elaborates ornithine decarboxylase and ferments sucrose and amygdalin. *Y. pseudotuberculosis* does none of these, but it ferments adonitol, which *Y. enterocolitica* does not.[80, 169]

Commercially available tests used to identify Enterobacteriaceae in clinical laboratories may not contain the biochemical reactions needed to identify specific *Yersinia* spp. Traditional macroscale biochemical testing may be required to distinguish *Y. enterocolitica* and *Y. pseudotuberculosis* from nonpathogenic *Yersinia* spp.[109]

*See references 13, 21–23, 40, 43, 48, 50, 72, 73, 78, 83, 92–95, 105, 113, 126, 153, 166, 168, 169, 172, 183.

TYPING OF *YERSINIA* STRAINS

Biotyping and serotyping have been the predominant methods used to characterize strains of *Y. enterocolitica*. At least 54 to 60 serotypes of *Y. enterocolitica* exist on the basis of variability of somatic O antigens, but only 11 typically are associated with human disease.[21, 22, 51, 64, 180] Six biotypes of *Y. enterocolitica,* designated 1A, 1B, and 2 to 5, have been defined on the basis of differences in the following: lipase activity; salicin acid production; esculin hydrolysis; indole production; ornithine decarboxylase; Voges-Proskauer test; pyrazinamide activity; nitrate reduction; and fermentations of xylose, trehalose, sorbose, and inositol.[21, 31, 178]

Only a few serotype:biotype combinations are regarded as human pathogens: O:8, O:4, O:13a,13b, O:18, O:20, and O:21 (biotype 1B); O:9 and O:5,27 (biotype 2); O:1,2,3 and O:5,27 (biotype 3); O:3 (biotype 4); and O:2,3 (biotype 5).[184] These pathogenic strains, which carry *Yersinia* virulence plasmids (pYV), generally have negative test results for pyrazinamidase activity, esculin hydrolysis, and salicin fermentation. Nonpathogenic strains, generally of biotype 1A, have positive test results for each of them.[38, 49, 88] Data suggest that some biotype 1A strains that lack pYV and other *Yersinia* virulence factors also may cause gastroenteritis.[63]

Strains of *Y. enterocolitica* can be typed genetically by repetitive element-based (interrepeat) polymerase chain reaction (PCR), arbitrarily primed PCR,[133] pulsed-field gel electrophoresis,[127] and ribotyping.[110] These methods allow distinction between strains within biotypes and serotypes and may be useful for outbreak and other epidemiologic investigations.

At least 11 antigenic groups of *Y. pseudotuberculosis* exist on the basis of variation of somatic O antigens. They have been labeled 1a, 1b, 2a, 2b, 2c, 3, 4a, 4b, 5a, 5b, and 6.[75, 82, 116] Type 2 is related antigenically to *Salmonella* group B and type 4 to *Salmonella* groups D and H.[61] *Y. pseudotuberculosis* strains also can be typed by arbitrarily primed PCR.[116]

Epidemiology

Although most of the early reports of yersiniosis caused by *Y. pseudotuberculosis* and *Y. enterocolitica* emanated from northern Europe, these microbes have been identified with increasing frequency in all parts of the world,[12] with the possible exception of South America. During 1996 to 1998, the rate of food-borne disease caused by yersiniosis microbes in five areas of the United States was 1 per 100,000 population.[32]

YERSINIA ENTEROCOLITICA

Y. enterocolitica is distributed worldwide but is isolated most frequently in cooler climates.[125] Whether such geographic differences reflect differences in reservoirs or culinary practices that may enhance the risk of acquisition of this organism or rather represent differences in surveillance for the disease and use of more sensitive culturing techniques in these areas is unclear.[43] Increased frequency of infections during fall and winter months has been reported from Europe[175] and the United States,[1] but no seasonality is evident among outbreaks of disease where more than three cases of *Y. enterocolitica* disease have been identified.[43]

Geographic differences in serotype distribution and frequency also exist. Sporadic infections caused by serotypes O:3 and O:9 are common occurrences in Europe,[8, 76] but outbreaks rarely have occurred.[43] In North America, multiple serotypes have been responsible for sporadic disease,[17, 20, 31, 60, 161, 164] but more recently serotype O:3 has become predominant.[31, 47, 105] Five outbreaks in the United States have been caused by serotype O:8 and two in Canada by serotypes O:5 and O:5,27.[43] Disease caused by serotype O:8 has been reported in Europe.[76]

The true incidence and prevalence of *Y. enterocolitica* infection are not known.[43] The reported proportional frequency of isolation of *Y. enterocolitica* from stool cultures from patients with diarrhea has ranged from 0 to 3.2 percent in series from Europe, the United States, and New Zealand (Table 117–1).[45, 51, 76, 105, 118, 123, 161] Symptomatic infection occurs more commonly in children. Most series demonstrate a slight male predominance of approximately 1.3:1.[47, 51, 118, 178]

Animals and water sources are the primary environmental reservoirs for *Y. enterocolitica,* but the biotypes and serotypes of the strains found in them usually differ from those causing human disease.[31, 43, 161] Blood transfusions also may be a source of *Y. enterocolitica* infection.[33]

Animal Reservoirs

Y. enterocolitica strains have been isolated from a wide variety of mammals (dogs, pigs, sheep, rabbits, guinea pigs, cows, horses, chinchillas, monkeys), frogs, fish, flies, fleas, snails, crabs, and oysters. Birds do not appear to be a major reservoir for *Y. enterocolitica*, although avian isolates have been reported.[43, 80, 113]

Pigs appear to be an important reservoir for the human pathogenic serotypes O:3 and O:9 in Europe and Japan and serotype O:3 in North America and South Africa.[43, 105, 143] The biochemical and phage typing profiles of isolates from pigs are similar to those of strains commonly responsible for human infections.[183] *Y. enterocolitica* has been isolated from the tongue, tonsils, and cecal contents of swine and from pork, ham, and butchershop cutting boards.[43, 61] Pig farmers in Finland were 3 times and 2.4 times as likely to have seropositivity to serotypes O:3 and O:9, respectively, than were berry farmers.[160]

Wild rodents captured in areas of Japan where human infections caused by *Y. enterocolitica* serotype O:8 had occurred were shown to harbor isolates of the same serotype.[41] Two distinct serotype O:8 strains, defined by restriction enzyme analysis of the virulence plasmids, were isolated from both humans and rodents. This finding suggests that rodents are a potential source of sporadic human infection in Japan.

Apparent transmission to humans from dogs and cats also has been reported. A fecal-oral or oral-oral route has been postulated but not confirmed. Little evidence supports airborne or insect vector-borne transmission.[43]

Foods and Water

In Belgium, the country with the highest numbers of cases of yersiniosis in the world, ingestion of raw pork is a common occurrence. A case-control study demonstrated that infection with serotypes O:3 and O:9 was highly associated with ingestion of raw pork during the 2 weeks preceding the illness.[175] Laboratory surveillance that began in 1967 showed yearly increases in cases through 1986. After a media campaign to dissuade people from eating raw or undercooked pork or pork products and to educate consumers regarding good hygiene practices during food preparation, the number of isolations of *Y. enterocolitica* decreased from a high of 1469 in 1986 to 707 in 1996.[184] Changes in techniques for slaughtering also may have contributed to this decline. Preparation of chitterlings in the household was a risk factor for *Y. enterocolitica* infection among children in Michigan.[1]

Ingestion of water contaminated with serotype O:8 has led to sporadic cases and outbreaks.[43] Bean sprouts that had been immersed in contaminated water were the source of an outbreak in Pennsylvania in 1982. Ingestion of tofu (bean curd) packed in untreated spring water that was subsequently found to be contaminated with *Y. enterocolitica* caused 44 cases of symptomatic infection in Washington State in 1981 and 1982.[174] Serotypes commonly found in water samples rarely are isolated from humans with symptomatic disease, however.[31]

Contaminated milk has been implicated as the source of several large outbreaks of *Y. enterocolitica* infection.[18, 43, 180] Whipped cream and ice cream may harbor the organism. Contamination of milk products after pasteurization has been documented. *Y. enterocolitica* has been found in raw milk samples from cows and goats. Samples of beef, lamb, poultry, oysters, and a variety of vegetables also have been found to be contaminated with *Y. enterocolitica*.[29, 43, 61]

Serotypes O:3, O:4,33, O:5,27, O:7,8, O:8, O:10, O:13, and O:16 cause most human disease in North America but rarely are isolated in surveillance of water or food samples. Serotype O:8 strains have been cultured from cattle, milk, and water samples[132]; serotype O:4,33 strains have been isolated from pigs and cattle; and serotype O:4,32 strains have been found in cheese, ham, sausage, raw beef, and one pancake specimen.[31, 161, 180]

TABLE 117–1 ■ PERCENTAGE OF STOOL CULTURES YIELDING *YERSINIA ENTEROCOLITICA*

Country	Years	Population	Total Cultures	Percentage *Y. enterocolitica*
Canada[118]	1977–1978	Symptomatic children	6364	2.8
The Netherlands[76]	1982–1984	Enteritis patients <40 years	827	2.9
Italy[123]	1981–1985	Children with diarrhea	2500	1.4*
New Zealand[51]	1988–1993	Patients with gastroenteritis	231,128	0.6
United States (Detroit, MI)[45]	May–November 1977	Children with diarrhea	1262	0
United States (New York State)[161]	1976–1980	Survey of cultures from a state laboratory, six hospitals, and several daycare centers	2487	0.9†
United States‡ (7 cities)[105]	November 1989–January 1990	All stool cultures submitted to seven hospitals	4841	0.8

*Yearly percentages during the 5 years ranged from 0 to 4.4 percent.
†This increased to 4.0 percent of 3035 isolates when cultures from an outbreak and other screenings were included.
‡Includes Detroit, MI.

Incubation, Carriage, and Transmission in Humans

The incubation period of *Y. enterocolitica* enterocolitis ranges from 1 to 14 days.[43, 105] The minimal infective dose of *Y. enterocolitica* is not known. Ingestion of 3.5×10^9 organisms by a volunteer resulted in diarrhea in less than a day, but such large inocula are unlikely to be encountered clinically. The duration of excretion of the organism after infection in children ranges from 14 to 97 days (mean, 42 days).[118] The impact, if any, of antibiotic treatment on the duration of carriage is not known.

Transmission to household members occurs uncommonly, even among young children, who are at higher risk for development of symptomatic disease.[18, 118, 174] Six percent of household contacts developed disease in one outbreak,[174] but several large outbreaks with no secondary household cases have been reported.[43]

Yersinia enterocolitica and Blood Transfusion–Related Sepsis

Sporadic cases of *Y. enterocolitica* sepsis related to contamination of transfusions of red blood cells have been recognized since 1987 and have occurred in the United States, Europe, and Australia.[33] *Y. enterocolitica* is the most common cause of transfusion-related sepsis.[87] Among 20 cases from the United States, chills occurred in 16, fever in 14, hypotension in 13, and disseminated intravascular coagulation in 7.[39] Death attributable to *Y. enterocolitica* infection occurred in 12, one half of which occurred within 25 hours of receipt of the contaminated transfusion. Among the 20 donors, 13 had had gastrointestinal symptoms within the month before blood donation, and 16 had titers equal to or greater than 1:128 (considered positive).

In many cases of transfusion-related sepsis, the contaminated red blood cell units had been stored for 25 days or more.[71] After experimental inoculation of small numbers of *Y. enterocolitica* into packed cells kept at 4° C, the organisms continue to replicate, reaching concentrations of 100 colony-forming units (CFU)/mL in 7 days and 10^6 CFU/mL in 21 days. High levels of endotoxin can result from such replication and have been documented in samples from red blood cell units that led to transfusion-related sepsis.[39]

Human Outbreaks

Outbreaks of *Y. enterocolitica* disease have involved communities, families (with interfamily spread), hospitals, and schools. The sources of the organism have been various foods and animals, especially dogs. A review of these outbreaks suggests that infection may be more common than has been recognized. Yersiniosis also resembles disease caused by *Salmonella* and *Shigella* in many respects, including the environmental sources of the organisms, the clinical syndromes, and the occurrence of asymptomatic infection.

OUTBREAKS IN SCHOOLS AND COMMUNITIES. A community outbreak caused by a serotype O:8 strain occurred in New York State in 1976.[18] At least 222 children and employees had a yersiniosis-like illness during a 10-week period. Illness was associated with drinking chocolate milk purchased in school cafeterias. The milk apparently was contaminated after pasteurization during hand mixing with chocolate syrup. Transmission of infection from ill children to household contacts was not observed. School-related outbreaks also have occurred in Japan.[14, 197]

In the summer of 1982, an estimated several thousand persons in several southern states who consumed milk from a single dairy developed yersiniosis. A total of 172 culture-positive infections were confirmed, many as a result of hospitalization for illness. Seventeen patients underwent appendectomy; 24 others suffered extraintestinal spread of infection. The strain involved was designated serotype O:13a,13b.[180] An outbreak associated with consumption of pasteurized milk in Vermont and New Hampshire in 1995 probably resulted from contamination after pasteurization with a serotype O:8 strain, possibly from rinsing bottles with untreated well water.[4]

FAMILY EPIDEMICS. Twenty-one persons were involved in an outbreak of yersiniosis involving four families in North Carolina that had an unusually high attack rate.[65] Eighteen were children who ranged in age from 3 to 13 years; 16 of the 21 had diarrhea and fever, and 5 were asymptomatic. *Y. enterocolitica* was recovered from the spleen of the youngest child at autopsy. The diagnosis was established serologically in the others. A dog that had given birth to puppies that had died of a diarrheal illness a week before the families became ill appeared to be the source of the infection.

NOSOCOMIAL OUTBREAKS. A young child who was hospitalized in Finland with acute gastroenteritis was the source case of infection in a housekeeping worker and four nurses who cared for her.[177] The infecting strain was serotype O:9. Another hospital outbreak involved nine patients in Canada.[146] It was caused by a serotype O:5 strain. Person-to-person contact was considered the likely mode of transmission.

Prevention of Disease

During outbreaks, efforts should be made to identify both environmental sources and vehicles of transmission.[43] A single environmental source can harbor multiple serotypes of *Y. enterocolitica,* such that resulting outbreaks may be polyclonal in nature.[174] Enteric precautions should be used for hospitalized patients with diarrhea caused by *Y. enterocolitica* (as with other causes of gastroenteritis).[43] At the population level, decreased consumption of raw or undercooked pork products potentially can reduce the incidence of infection.[175, 184]

YERSINIA PSEUDOTUBERCULOSIS

Y. pseudotuberculosis may infect individuals of all ages, but at least 75 percent of patients with clinically apparent disease are children younger than 15 years of age.[82, 154] Infection in young infants has been reported.[82, 190] Of 130 cases diagnosed in Great Britain from 1959 to 1970, boys were involved three times more frequently than were girls.[113] Infections occur more commonly during the cold months of the year.[82, 154] The seasonal winter peak of human infection produced by *Y. pseudotuberculosis* is similar to that seen in wild and domesticated animals.[92, 93, 154]

The attack rates for children living in rural and urban areas appear to be the same.[154] *Y. pseudotuberculosis* occasionally has been recovered from healthy persons. Exposure to the organism appears to be an uncommon occurrence; antibody to *Y. pseudotuberculosis* was detected in only 1 of 2000 sera from individuals with no history of yersiniosis.[54]

Y. pseudotuberculosis is distributed worldwide in a large variety of animals and birds, but infection is an uncommon occurrence.[58] Guinea pigs, rodents, and rabbits are infected most often [113] and may suffer a plague-like illness.[58, 80] Lesions in guinea pigs may be confused easily with those caused by *Y. pestis*. Rats and other rodents also may have plague-like disease caused by *Y. pseudotuberculosis*. Infection has been reported in a variety of domestic animals (cattle, sheep, goats, cats, dogs, hamsters), commercially raised fur bearers (chinchillas, mink, coypu), and other wild or captive animals (rabbits, raccoons, foxes, deer, beavers, monkeys, puma, kangaroos). *Y. pseudotuberculosis* has been found in more than 50 species of birds,[69, 89, 113] and epizootics have occurred among turkeys, ducks, pigeons, and doves and in aviaries of canaries and finches.[113, 154] Strains obtained from animals and birds in the United States are predominantly of serotypes 1a, 1b, and 3.[113]

The incubation period for human disease may be as short as 41 hours or as long as 20 days.[82] The organism can survive in fresh tap water for 46 days at room temperature and for 8 months at 4° C. It can survive at 4° C in meat for up to 145 days and in milk and bread for 2 to 3 weeks.[113]

A family outbreak of mesenteric adenitis caused by *Y. pseudotuberculosis* that involved four siblings aged 7 to 14 years has been reported.[145] A pet dog was shown to have rising antibody titers at the time the children were ill.

Three outbreaks in Japan have been described.[82] Eating sandwiches prepared by a single bakery at an athletic event was the primary risk factor for 67 cases that occurred in a 3-week period. Two additional outbreaks occurred in small villages where the only risk factor appeared to be drinking unchlorinated well water or mountain stream water. Samples of the water sources yielded isolates of the same serotypes causing disease. Two or more serotypes were present in each village outbreak. Children were much more likely to have clinical disease than were adults.

Pathology

The diseases produced by *Y. enterocolitica* and *Y. pseudotuberculosis* are similar and share the histopathologic theme of involvement of the lymphoid tissues of the intestinal mucosa and mesentery.

YERSINIA ENTEROCOLITICA

Y. enterocolitica infection predominantly affects the gastrointestinal tract. The most severe clinical symptoms correlate with an acute terminal ileitis. The mucosal surface of the ileum and other involved sites may be inflamed diffusely. Ulcerations may occur throughout the gastrointestinal tract and may be small and superficial or extend to the muscularis propria. Mucosal and submucosal hyperplasia of the Peyer patches occurs with scattered micbroabscess formation.

Ulcers occur primarily over the sites of lymphoid tissue within the mucosa, which accounts for their more longitudinal appearance in the small intestine and an oval or punctate appearance in the stomach and colon. Ulcerations are characterized by necrosis of the epithelial layer. In the colon, the necrosis also may extend through the superficial third of the crypts. Large colonic ulcerations covered by pseudomembranes or mucoid debris are seen occasionally. Ulcerations may progress to perforation, with subsequent peritonitis or gastrointestinal hemorrhage in severe cases.[26, 59, 182, 183]

The inflammatory response in the mucosa consists mainly of neutrophils and mononuclear cells. Lymphocytes and plasma cells also may be seen. Giant cells are not seen, although a granulomatous appearance can be imparted by the presence of plump epithelioid histiocytes.[59, 182, 183] Numerous colonies of gram-negative bacteria often can be seen beneath the mucosal ulcerations and within the microabscesses that occur in the lymphoid tissues.[59]

The appendix usually appears normal on gross inspection, but small focal ulcerations frequently are present.[6] Large areas of necrosis are found occasionally, and acute, suppurative appendicitis has been reported.[26, 86, 118] Periappendicular inflammation may result from a true appendicitis or an adjacent terminal ileitis.[183]

Mesenteric adenitis, the hallmark of infection caused by *Y. pseudotuberculosis,* also is a common feature of enterocolitis caused by *Y. enterocolitica*. The lymph nodes usually show numerous large pyroninophilic cells and mitotic figures in the cortical area and marginal sinuses. Small collections of leukocytes in the germinal centers are seen in some cases and suggest formation of microabscesses. In severe cases, extensive areas of necrosis circumscribed by a neutrophilic infiltrate may be seen. The sinusoids can become filled with neutrophils and mononuclear cells. The germinal centers often appear reactive.

The histopathologic appearance of the mesenteric adenitis of infection caused by *Y. enterocolitica* can resemble the adenitides caused by cat-scratch disease *(Bartonella henselae),* toxoplasmosis, infectious mononucleosis, and *Y. pseudotuberculosis*.[6, 183, 191] The necrotizing epithelioid granulomata that may be present in the mesenteric adenitis caused by *Y. pseudotuberculosis* have not been described in infection caused by *Y. enterocolitica*.

YERSINIA PSEUDOTUBERCULOSIS

Numerous reports* collectively have described the pathology of infection caused by *Y. pseudotuberculosis*. Grossly enlarged, soft, and inflamed mesenteric lymph nodes are the predominant finding on laparotomy. They frequently are located at the ileocecal angle. Punctate hemorrhages and small, yellow microabscesses may be present on the surfaces of the nodes at the height of infection. The appendix usually appears normal, but the terminal ileum and cecum occasionally appear inflamed. A necrotic purulent mass sometimes is seen in the mesentery.

Histopathologic findings in the mesenteric lymph nodes include enlarged follicles and small abscesses; hyperplasia of reticulum cells; necrosis of the nodes with infiltrates of neutrophilic leukocytes and plasma cells; and, in some instances, punctate hemorrhages. Scattered clusters of neutrophils may be seen within the sinusoids and germinal centers without formation of abscess or necrosis. Atypical mononuclear cells, some of which may be mitotic, may be present in the sinusoids. When necrosis is absent, large numbers of eosinophilic leukocytes occasionally are seen surrounding reticulogranulocytic infiltrates in the nodes. Giant cells can occur and may cause the histologic picture to be confused with that of tuberculosis.

The mesenteric adenitis produced by *Y. pseudotuberculosis* appears to progress through histopathologic stages akin to those of other pyogenic infections that can lead to formation of abscesses.[46, 66] Reticulogranulocytic infiltration is followed by formation of an abscess, with subsequent organization and clearing of the abscess. The inflammatory process of *Y. pseudotuberculosis* appears to remain confined to the lymph nodes without rupture through the nodal capsule.

Focal mucosal ulcerations may be seen in the ileum and are more likely to be found at the site of Peyer patches. Aggregates of neutrophilic leukocytes similar to those in

*See references 46, 50, 52, 78, 93, 112, 119, 120, 126, 145, 189.

mesenteric nodes may be seen in germinal centers within mucosal lymphoid tissue. Fibrinoid material may be a prominent feature at these sites. Small areas of necrosis surrounded by reticulum cells and leukocytes also may be present in the submucosal follicles.[52, 93, 119, 189] Ulcerated lymphoid follicles in the intestinal wall are connected to the regional lymph nodes by a lymphangitis. This anatomic situation is analogous to the primary complex of tuberculosis.

Despite a clinical picture of acute appendicitis as the presenting feature of infection by *Y. pseudotuberculosis,* the appendix typically is grossly and microscopically normal. Inflammatory changes, when present, usually are in the form of a periappendicitis. Phlegmonous appendicitis can result from infection caused by *Y. pseudotuberculosis* but is rare.[46, 75]

Pathogenesis

The pathogenesis of infection by the two enteropathogenic *Yersinia* has been studied extensively. After ingestion and successful transit to the small intestine, these *Yersinia* are able to penetrate into the lamina propria primarily by passing through the cytoplasm of M cells that reside on the mucosal surface of Peyer patches. The bacteria are internalized in membrane-bound vacuoles in which they survive but do not replicate. After reaching the lamina propria, the microbes multiply as extracellular microcolonies in lymph follicles and Peyer patches. Neutrophils and macrophages infiltrate these sites in response to the infection, ultimately creating microabscesses, but *Y. enterocolitica* is able to resist phagocytosis and intracellular killing by neutrophils and macrophages. *Yersinia* also inhibit production of tumor necrosis factor-α and interferon-γ and induce apoptosis in host macrophages. The microbes then disseminate to the mesenteric lymph nodes, apparently through lymphatic vessels. Infection usually is contained at this point, although abscesses often develop within the nodes.

Systemic spread occurs occasionally, more commonly with infection by serotype O:8 strains. Control of infection caused by *Y. enterocolitica* is the result of T-cell responses that lead to restriction of bacterial growth in infected organs through stimulation of production of *Yersinia*-specific antibody by B cells and cytokine-mediated activation of macrophages that ultimately overcomes the antiphagocyte strategies of *Yersinia*. Productions of tumor necrosis factor-α and interferon-γ appear to be essential parts of the host response to *Yersinia* infections. Once successfully phagocytosed, *Yersinia* generally do not survive.[40–42, 134]

Only a few of the many serotypes of *Yersinia* are capable of infecting humans. Numerous virulence factors have been

TABLE 117–2 ■ KNOWN AND PUTATIVE *YERSINIA* VIRULENCE FACTORS*

Stage of Pathogenesis	Determinant	Genomic Origin†	Function	Conditions of Expression
Gastric transit	Urease	Chromosome	Aids survival of gastric acidity	
Mucosal invasion	Invasin (inv)	Chromosome	Attachment, invasion via β_1 integrins; broad host/cell range	28° C
	Attachment invasion locus (Ail)	Chromosome	Attachment, lesser invasion factor; more host specific than invasin; serum resistance	37° C
	Yersinia adhesin A (YadA)	Plasmid	Attachment, invasion; reduces opsonization by C3b by binding complement factor H; ?role in resistance to antibacterial polypeptides (e.g., bactericidal permeability-increasing protein)	37° C and *any* calcium concentration
Disruption of phagocyte function	Effector proteins (act on host cells)	Plasmid		37° C and low calcium concentration
	YopH		Tyrosine phosphorylase that prevents phagocytosis by macrophages by preventing assembly of focal adhesion structures of phagocytes	
	YopE		Phagocytosis resistance via induction of host cell actin filament rearrangements	
	YopJ/P		Cysteine protease that inhibits mitogen-activated protein kinase and nuclear factor κB signaling via interruption of post-translational covalent additions of ubiquitin-like molecules to these enzymes; this prevents production of cytokines (TNF-α), inhibits the host immune response, and triggers apoptosis of macrophages	
	YpkA/YopO		Serine kinase, causes rounding up of cells, specific target unknown	
	YopT		Disruption of actin filaments	
	YopM		Role unclear; inhibits thrombin-induced platelet activation in vitro but is delivered intracellularly during infection	
	Host cell membrane attachment, pore insertion proteins	Plasmid		37° C and low calcium concentration
	YopB and YopD		Pore formation in host cell membrane to allow translocation of effector proteins into the host cell; ?suppression of IL-8 secretion by epithelial cells	

Continued

TABLE 117–2 ■ KNOWN AND PUTATIVE *YERSINIA* VIRULENCE FACTORS*—cont'd

Stage of Pathogenesis	Determinant	Genomic Origin†	Function	Conditions of Expression
	YopQ (YopK)		Controls translocation via modulating the size of the puttative YopB, YopD pore in the host cell membrane	
	YopN		Involved in control of translocation, perhaps stabilizing contact between the bacterium and host cell membranes	
	LcrV		Assists extrusion of Yops B and D to the host cell membrane; homologue of the *Y. pestis* V antigen; antibodies against V antigen appear to be protective at the serotype level	
	Yop secretion apparatus (Ysc) (28 proteins in total)	Plasmid		37° C and low calcium concentration
	YscD, YscR, YscU, and LcrD/YscV (6 proteins in total)		Form a complex that spans the inner bacterial membrane (?gated pore/channel)	
	YscC secretin		Forms a pore in the outer bacterial membrane that may connect with the inner membrane pore	
	YscN		ATPase that energizes Yop transfer across the membranes	
	LcrQ (in *Y. pseudotuberculosis*), YscM1 and YscM2 (in *Y. enterocolitica*)		Negative *yop* gene regulators that when secreted decrease in concentration in the bacterium, allowing *yop* expression	
	Cytosolic chaperones (Syc) (6 proteins in total)	Plasmid	Secretion/translocation pilots or antidegradation roles for effector proteins	37° C and low calcium concentration
Colonization of Peyer patches and lymph nodes	*Yersinia* phospholipase A	Plasmid	?Serum resistance, ?inhibition of phagocytosis	37° C and low calcium concentration
Iron metabolism	Yersiniabactin	Chromosome (high pathogenicity island)	Siderophore	37° C, iron starvation
Diarrhea	*Yersinia* heat-stable enterotoxin (Yst)	Chromosome	Fluid secretion in intestine; precise role in pathogenesis of disease in humans is unclear	28° C (in vitro)
?Systemic invasion	O antigen	Chromosome	Component of lipopolysaccharide; complement/serum resistance?	

*The pathogenesis/virulence roles of several gene products encoded on the *Yersinia* virulence plasmid pYV have yet to be determined, and additional functions may be identified for other gene products. Additional chromosomally encoded virulence factors are suspected, with investigations ongoing in multiple laboratories.

†Plasmid refers to the *Yersinia* virulence plasmid pYV.

Lcr, low calcium response; Yop, *Yersinia* outer-membrane protein (although not all such designated proteins reside in the outer membrane).

Data in the table are compiled from references 21, 40, 62, 73, 99, 106, 134, 151, 163, 196.

identified among these "pathogenic" strains (Table 117–2). Most of them are encoded on the *Yersinia* virulence plasmid pYV. At least eight chromosomal loci that encode novel *Yersinia* virulence factors have been found by tagged mutagenesis studies.[62] Much of this knowledge has been gained through mouse and rabbit models of human infection and observations of interactions of *Yersinia* with in vitro cell culture models.[25, 41, 73, 114, 141]

The distinctions in pathogenesis between the two enteropathogenic *Yersinia* and *Y. pestis* appear to be caused in part by the presence in *Y. pestis* of (1) two additional plasmids that encode a plasmin activator and a mouse exotoxin and (2) a hemin storage locus on its chromosome. These additional factors may enable *Y. pestis* to survive in and transmit between fleas and rodents. Such transmission does not occur with the enteropathogenic *Yersinia*.[151]

MUCOSAL INVASION

Two outer-membrane proteins encoded by chromosomal genes permit entry into a variety of mammalian cell types in vitro and are likely to be responsible for the ability of *Yersinia* to invade into and through the intestinal mucosal epithelium. They have been named invasin and the attachment invasin locus protein (Ail). All isolates of *Y. enterocolitica* that are virulent in humans contain DNA sequences that encode for invasin and Ail. Nonpathogenic strains do not contain the genetic code for Ail, but most contain invasin genes that cannot be expressed because of chromosomal rearrangements. These proteins appear unique to the genus *Yersinia*.[83, 122, 138]

Invasin attaches to receptors in the β_1 integrin family and induces an actin-mediated endocytosis of the microbe. It binds β_1 integrins with approximately 100-fold higher affinity than do natural ligands such as fibronectin. Such high-affinity binding triggers endocytosis-like internalization that involves clathrin.[42] Invasin is expressed maximally at ambient temperatures when the organism is in stationary phase. *Y. enterocolitica* microbes living in the environment probably exist in a stationary phase–like state and, thus, may be primed maximally for invasion of the host after ingestion. Invasin expression also can remain elevated at 37° C when the pH is 5.5, and such conditions are encountered during passage through the intestinal tract. Ail is expressed maximally at 37° C, functions both as an adhesin and an invasion factor, and plays a role in the resistance of *Y. enterocolitica* to the bactericidal activity of human serum.[83, 84, 138]

Flagellum-dependent motility appears to be required for invasin-mediated invasion of cells by *Y. enterocolitica.*[195]

THE VIRULENCE PLASMID

Pathogenic strains of *Y. enterocolitica* harbor a plasmid that consists of approximately 70 kb (denoted pYV) and encodes the low calcium response (LCR) system of *Yersinia,* which involves a complex response to environmental conditions of 37° C and calcium concentrations of less than 2.5 mM, both of which describe the intracellular compartment of mammalian cells.[40, 163] Plasmid-encoded factors are required for survival and extracellular multiplication after reaching the Peyer patches. Plasmid-cured derivatives are ingested rapidly and killed by neutrophils in the Peyer patches, whereas wild-type strains are able to proliferate and spread through the lamina propria to adjacent villi. Plasmid-encoded factors are not required for *Y. enterocolitica* to penetrate the intestinal mucosa.[73]

The *Y. enterocolitica* pYV contains approximately 70 genes, of which approximately 53 have protein products with known or putative functions. (Many of them are listed among the virulence factors in Table 117–2.) pYV encodes *Yersinia* adhesin A and a system of six effector proteins that are delivered into host cells (primarily phagocytic granulocytes) through a complex mechanism of regulatory proteins, secretion chaperones, and proteins that act as secretion channels or pores in the bacterial and host cell membranes. The effector proteins and several others involving pore formation are designated Yops (*Yersinia* outer-membrane proteins), although most of them now are known not to reside in the outer membrane. The secretion system is of the type III class, which denotes secretion of bacterial proteins only in response to contact with a mammalian cell. Similar type III secretion systems are found in *Salmonella* and *Shigella.*[40, 163]

The complete pYV nucleotide sequences of *Y. enterocolitica* serogroups O:8 (designated pYVe8081) and O:9 (pYVe227) and *Y. pestis* (pCD1) are known. Most of the pYV sequence of *Y. pseudotuberculosis* YPIII (piB1) also is known. In DNA cross-hybridization studies, the pYVs of *Y. enterocolitica* serogroups O:9, O:3, and O:5 show 90 percent nucleotide identity with one another, 75 percent identity with the pYV of serogroup O:8, and 55 percent identity with the pYV of *Y. pestis* and *Y. pseudotuberculosis*. Despite the nucleotide divergence between the pYVs of the three *Yersinia* spp., the overall structures and most of the genes are highly similar among them. The *Yersinia* LCR plasmids are nonconjugative.[40, 163]

YERSINIA ADHESIN A

Yersinia adhesin A (YadA) is a multifunctional virulence factor of *Y. enterocolitica*. YadA is approximately 50 kD and probably forms tetrameric fibrillae on the microbial surface. Its gene resides on the pYV plasmid and is transcribed at 37° C independently of the calcium concentration. YadA binds to extracellular matrix proteins, such as collagen, and mediates adhesion to cells. It may play a role in translocation of Yop effector proteins into eukaryotic cells. YadA also inhibits the terminal complement attack complex, reduces opsonization by C3b through binding of complement factor H, and contributes to the ability of *Y. enterocolitica* to resist killing by antimicrobial polypeptides of human granulocytes. YadA knockout mutants are far less virulent in mice than is the parent wild-type strain.[40, 73, 187]

A MOLECULAR MODEL OF *YERSINIA* PATHOGENESIS

Pathogenic strains of *Y. enterocolitica* require calcium concentrations equivalent to those of serum and extracellular fluids in humans for growth at body temperature. Plasmid proteins, however, are synthesized maximally at 37° C under conditions of low calcium concentrations, such as those found intracellularly. These regulatory effects of environmental calcium concentrations permit free growth of *Yersinia* during extracellular life and production of factors that inhibit phagocytosis by macrophages and neutrophils when *Yersinia* pass through the intracellular compartment during mucosal invasion or come into contact with these granulocytes.[40, 41, 73]

A model of how pathogenic *Yersinia* living in cold (28° C or less) environmental reservoirs are able to establish infection in the mammalian host can now be described at the molecular level (see Table 117–2). The microbes living in the environment express invasin, which renders them ready to attach and invade the intestinal mucosa after ingestion. Expression of invasin continues at body temperature during gastric passage to the intestines. Survival of gastric acidity is assisted by a urease-producing system. During intracellular passage through M cells in the small intestine, pYV genes are likely to be activated (conditions of low calcium, 37° C). YadA can be produced at body temperature and may assist in mucosal invasion. Transcytosis from the intestinal lumen to the lamina propria appears to occur by a clathrin-mediated process that probably is a normal function of the host cell, once internalization is triggered. Ail also is synthesized after ingestion and probably promotes attachment to migrating cells in the lamina propria that may facilitate extracellular spread of the microbes to regional lymph nodes and perhaps the liver and spleen. To survive this journey, *Yersinia* must evade phagocytosis by macrophages and neutrophils. YadA can inhibit complement opsonization, reducing the likelihood of phagocytosis. Once contact between the microbe and a host granulocyte occurs, the previously activated type III secretion system encoded by the pYV comes into play. A plugged outer-membrane pore in the bacterium is opened (involving functions of pYV products LcrQ/YscM1-YscM2, YscC secretin, and YscN), and a contiguous pore is inserted into the granulocyte cell membrane (involving Yops B, D, Q, and N and LcrV). Effector proteins (Yops E, H, J/P, O, M, and T) then are translocated into the granulocyte cytoplasm, disrupting its abilities to ingest the bacterium and produce cytokines and triggering apoptotic cell death.

IRON METABOLISM AND VIRULENCE

Iron is an essential growth factor for most bacteria, many of which release siderophores (high-affinity chelators) that bind ferric iron and are then taken up again through receptors by the microbe. *Y. enterocolitica* serotype O:8 and other biotype 1B strains synthesize a chromosomally encoded siderophore, designated yersiniabactin, that sits on the outer membrane of the bacterium. The presence of this siderophore decreases the concentration of environmental iron required for optimal growth and probably accounts for the increased virulence observed for serotype O:8 strains.[43, 73] The gene encoding

TABLE 117–3 ■ CLINICAL FEATURES OF *YERSINIA ENTEROCOLITICA* INFECTION IN CHILDREN

	Sweden[16] 1967–1973	Finland[115] 1974–1978	Canada[47] 1972	Canada[118] 1977–1978	United States[105] 1989–1990	United States[128] 1988–1991	Combined Totals
Number	31	35	40	57	37*	48	248
Age ≤5 years	28	26	19	NS†	≥28	NS	≥101/142 (≥71%)
Fever (>38° C)	15	6	36	39	35	44	175/248 (71%)
Diarrhea	31	26	32	56	37	45	227/248 (92%)
Grossly bloody	2	NS	7	NS	14	22	45/156 (29%)
Abdominal pain	4	6	20	31/48	NS	NS	61/154 (40%)
Vomiting	NS	12	12	22	18	23	87/217 (40%)
Rash‡	NS	2	2	NS	NS	NS	4/75 (5%)
Appendectomy	0	0	4	1	0	0	5/200 (2%)
Serotype O:3	31	NS	34	57	34	NS	156/165 (94%)

*All were black children; seven different cities, 3-month period.
†More than half of these children were younger than 2 years.
‡Maculopapular rash or urticaria.
NS, not specified.

yersiniabactin and those required for its biosynthesis, transport, and regulation compose the core of what is termed a high-pathogenicity island because of the high lethality for mice that its presence confers.[144]

Serotypes O:8, O:4, O:13, O:18, O:20, and O:21 (all biotype 1B and historically considered "American" strains) are highly lethal to mice after intraperitoneal injection and are able to evoke a keratoconjunctivitis after inoculation into the conjunctival sac of guinea pigs (the positive Sereny test result). Oral infection in mice predominantly produces the features of mesenteric adenitis and systemic infection rather than simple gastroenteritis, which is characteristic of human infection by American strains. The "European" serotypes, O:3, O:9, and O:5,27, yield a negative Sereny test result and cause mild diarrhea but not death in mice. The European serotypes of *Y. enterocolitica* do not produce yersiniabactin but are able to use siderophores synthesized by other organisms.[41, 73, 122]

Deferoxamine, a *Streptomyces*-derived siderophore used clinically to treat iron overload states, can be used by *Y. enterocolitica* strains as a source of iron. The increased availability of ferric iron that exists in iron overload states such as hemochromatosis and diseases such as thalassemia that require frequent red blood cell transfusions also facilitates survival and growth of *Y. enterocolitica*. Thus, iron overloading and deferoxamine are independent risk factors for development of systemic disease after intestinal infection with *Y. enterocolitica*.[43]

ENTEROTOXIN PRODUCTION

All enteropathogenic strains of *Y. enterocolitica* produce a heat-stable enterotoxin that closely resembles the heat-stable toxin of *E. coli*. Both enterotoxins induce increases in levels of cyclic guanylic acid levels in intestinal epithelial cells. The *Y. enterocolitica* enterotoxin is not plasmid encoded, and its presence does not correlate with the expression of other virulence phenotypes.[58] Because the enterotoxin is not produced in vitro at temperatures exceeding 30° C, production in the gastrointestinal tract and thus a causative role in diarrhea were thought to be unlikely.[43] However, observations in the young rabbit oral infection model have shown that enterotoxin-negative mutants did not induce diarrhea and that the wild-type strain did. This finding suggests that the enterotoxin may, indeed, play a role in causing the diarrhea frequently associated with *Y. enterocolitica* infection in children.[73, 137]

GASTRIC ACIDITY AS A PROTECTIVE HOST FACTOR

Although *Y. enterocolitica* is able to grow under conditions at pH 5.0 to 9.0, optimal growth occurs at pH 7.0 to 8.0. Gastric acidity, thus, may play a protective role against some *Yersinia* inocula, although pathogenic *Yersinia* produce a urease enzyme that facilitates survival. Therefore, therapeutic agents or clinical conditions that result in reduced gastric acidity may predispose patients to development of infection. *Y. enterocolitica* bacteremia has been reported after gastrectomy.[43, 99]

Clinical Manifestations

Clinical disease caused by *Y. enterocolitica* occurs far more frequently than that caused by *Y. pseudotuberculosis*.[51, 107, 108] Historically, diarrheal illness has been considered the hallmark of *Y. enterocolitica* and the pseudoappendicular syndrome of mesenteric adenitis indicative of *Y. pseudotuberculosis*. However, each species can cause enterocolitis and mesenteric adenitis. Various other clinical infections and postinfection syndromes also are caused by these microbes. In series of patients presenting with acute abdominal pain suggestive of appendicitis, the incidence of serologic evidence of *Yersinia* infection has ranged from 7 to 31 percent.[15]

YERSINIA ENTEROCOLITICA

The clinical features of the disease caused by *Y. enterocolitica*, primarily an acute enteritis, have been described by many investigators.* The clinical manifestations depend to a degree on the age and physiologic condition of the host.[43, 118, 145] Enterocolitis is the most common presentation and occurs most often in young children. The pseudoappendicular syndrome, which results primarily from mesenteric adenitis and mimics acute appendicitis, occurs more commonly in older children and young adults.[18, 43, 77, 86, 131, 150] Asymptomatic infection can occur, but the relative frequency compared with symptomatic disease is unknown. The predominant clinical features of *Y. enterocolitica* infection in children are summarized in Table 117–3.

*See references 16, 35, 43, 47, 68, 98, 104, 105, 114, 115, 118, 146, 150, 178.

Enterocolitis

Y. enterocolitica enterocolitis is characterized by diarrhea and abdominal pain. The diarrhea usually persists for 7 to 14 days.[105, 118, 183] A range of 1 to 46 days of diarrhea has been reported.[97] As many as 10 percent of cases may persist for 30 days or more,[118] and chronic diarrhea persisting for several months has been described.[47]

During the first week of symptoms, patients commonly have 3 to 10 stools per day, with a gradual decrease in frequency thereafter. Stools typically are greenish, exhibit variable consistency (usually watery or mucoid), and are not remarkably malodorous. Gross blood is noted in approximately 25 to 50 percent of patients. Vomiting occurs in 40 percent of cases. Nausea is a common occurrence. The abdominal pain can be colicky, diffuse, or localized to the right lower quadrant or epigastrium. Fever occurs commonly and usually is of low grade but may exceed 40° C; it usually resolves within a week.[1, 115]

Most cases are self-limited, but some children require hospitalization. Among 60 children hospitalized in Michigan between 1990 and 1997, the mean number of hospital days required was 4 (range, 1 to 17 days).[1]

Fecal leukocytes are present commonly but not universally. The peripheral white blood cell count may range from 5600 to more than 30,000/mm^3. Most are greater than 15,000/mm^3. Band forms often exceed 15 percent of the total. Infants frequently exhibit an immature-to-total neutrophil ratio greater than 0.5.[1, 105, 115] An absolute monocytosis may be seen in two thirds of patients.[101] Culture-negative cerebrospinal fluid pleocytosis can occur.[1]

Radiologic examination by upper gastrointestinal barium studies in 24 adult patients with severe diarrhea caused by *Y. enterocolitica* showed abnormalities of the terminal ileum in 21 cases.[182] Diffuse thickening of the mucosal folds was seen in 16 and nodular filling defects in 11. The radiographic appearance suggested the presence of one or more ulcerations of the terminal ileum in 11 patients. Dilation of the terminal ileum was noted in 12 patients, and extrinsic compression, presumably from enlarged lymph nodes, was present in 4. In some instances, the findings were suggestive of the terminal ileitis of Crohn disease. Follow-up studies performed 2 months after acute illness showed decreased but persistent thickening of mucosal folds in 8 patients. Barium enema studies were performed in 15 patients and showed no striking abnormalities other than mucosal ulcerations, which were seen best on air-contrast studies.[183]

Mesenteric lymphadenopathy can be seen on computed tomographic scans[181] (Fig. 117–1). Among 13 adults who had colonoscopy or sigmoidoscopy for severe diarrhea caused by *Y. enterocolitica,* abnormalities were seen in 8; the mucosa appeared diffusely swollen, erythematous, and friable in 6, and 2 had only small, 1- to 2-mm aphthoid ulcerations. Serial procedures showed both macroscopic and microscopic healing of ulcers within 4 to 5 weeks.[182] Aphthoid ulcerations may be seen throughout the colon[181] (Fig. 117–2).

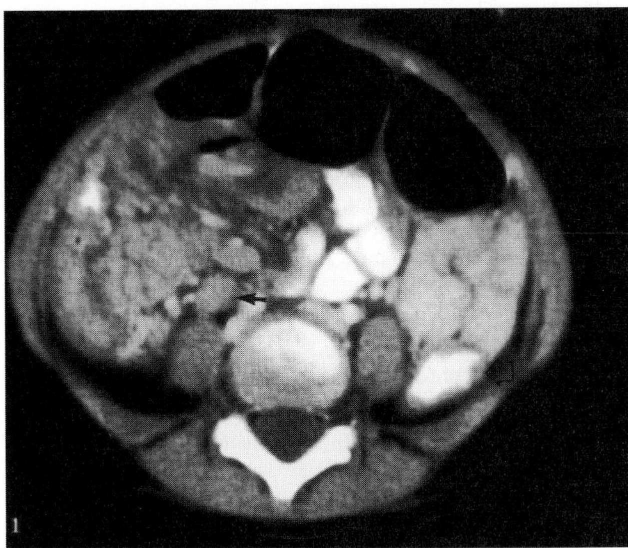

FIGURE 117–1 ■ Mesenteric lymphadenopathy *(solid arrow)* and thickened bowel wall *(open arrow)* seen on computed tomographic imaging of a toddler with a 1-week history of severe abdominal pain, fever, vomiting, and nonbloody diarrhea. Stool culture on cefsoludin-irgasan-novobiocin agar yielded growth of *Y. enterocolitica,* serotype O:8. (From Tuohy, A. M., O'Gorman, M., Byington, C., et al.: *Yersinia* enterocolitis mimicking Crohn's disease in a toddler. Pediatrics *104*[issue 3]:e36, 1999.)

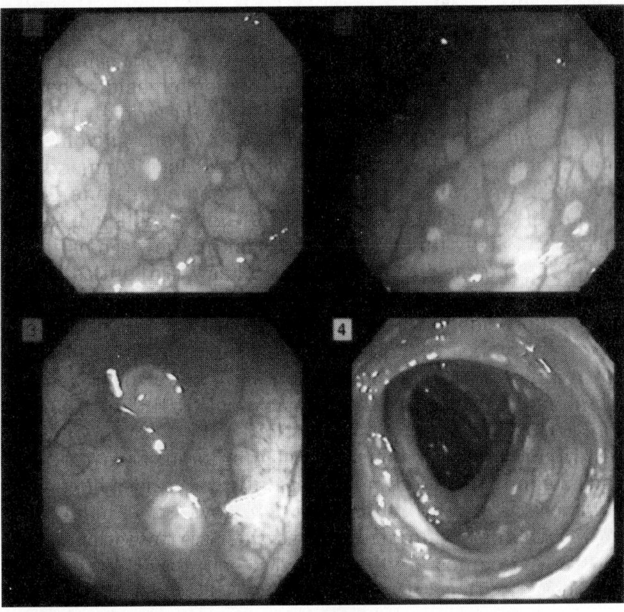

FIGURE 117–2 ■ Mutiple mucosal aphthoid ulcerations, 2- to 3-mm in size, as seen during colonoscopy in the child described in Figure 117–1. (From Tuohy, A. M., O'Gorman, M., Byington, C., et al.: *Yersinia* enterocolitis mimicking Crohn's disease in a toddler. Pediatrics *104*[issue 3]:e36, 1999.)

Pseudoappendicitis–Mesenteric Adenitis

The syndrome of pseudoappendicitis, characterized in most cases by a normal appendix and an intense suppurative mesenteric adenitis, has attracted considerable attention since it was reported first in 1953.[119, 120] The first recognized cases were caused by *Y. pseudotuberculosis,* but most cases reported in recent years have been caused by *Y. enterocolitica.*[27, 85, 104]

Fever, abdominal pain, right lower quadrant tenderness, and leukocytosis are the primary features of *Y. enterocolitica*-induced pseudoappendicular syndrome.[43, 86] Some patients also have features of enterocolitis (nausea, vomiting, and diarrhea). The clinical presentation often is highly suggestive of acute appendicitis, such that laparotomy is required. Among a series of 581 patients in Scandinavia who underwent laparotomy for suspected appendicitis, 3.8 percent of cultures of stool or operative specimens yielded *Y. enterocolitica.*[131] Another 284 patients with similar symptoms were observed, and 5.6 percent of stool cultures from these cases yielded *Y. enterocolitica*. In a similar Scandinavian series of 205 patients who underwent appendectomy, 22 subsequently were diagnosed by serology as having *Y. enterocolitica* infection.[86] The findings on laparotomy usually are mesenteric lymphadenitis, terminal ileitis, and a normal or slightly inflamed appendix.[18, 43, 86, 131]

A study of 40 cases of granulomatous appendicitis found evidence suggesting infection caused by *Y. enterocolitica* in 4, *Y. pseudotuberculosis* in 4, and both in 2 specimens by PCR analysis.[103] Two patients in the series subsequently were diagnosed as having Crohn disease, but causation cannot be inferred.

Asymptomatic Infection

In an unknown number of cases, infection by *Y. enterocolitica* is entirely asymptomatic. In a study of the distribution of antibodies to *Y. enterocolitica* in sera collected for various purposes in Ontario, Canada, from 4209 persons who had no evidence of infection by this organism, specific antibody was present in 199 (serotype O:3 in 158 and serotype O:9 in 41).[178]

Other Presentations of Acute Infection

Bacteremia can occur[30, 36, 43, 124] and may result in spread of infection to virtually any body site. Such events occur uncommonly and are seen more often in adults than in children. In childhood, bacteremia occurs more commonly in infants than in older children.[1] The risk for development of bacteremia during gastroenteritis in infants younger than 3 months may be as high as 30 percent.[128] Bacteremias may be transient and asymptomatic or lead to septic shock and death. Septic cases tend to occur among patients with underlying illnesses and are associated with mortality rates of 34 to 50 percent.[43]

Y. enterocolitica may cause focal infections in many extraintestinal sites, even in the absence of detectable bacteremia. Pharyngitis has been reported and occurs primarily in adults. Cervical adenopathy may be associated with *Y. enterocolitica* pharyngitis, and gastrointestinal symptoms may be absent.[43] One adult with pharyngitis died of associated septic shock.[152] Conjunctivitis and panophthalmitis caused by *Y. enterocolitica* have been described. Parinaud oculoglandular syndrome,[37] inguinal adenopathy,[190] and suppurative lymphadenitis[179] have been reported.

Cellulitis, soft tissue abscesses, and wound infections have been reported. Cellulitis may have associated vesiculobullous lesions. An erysipelas-like rash, maculopapular rash, and urticaria have also been described in association with infection caused by *Y. enterocolitica*.[16, 27, 43, 67, 161, 174, 193]

Pancreatitis, cholecystitis, diverticulitis, and intestinal perforation have been described.[108, 142] Peritonitis also can occur but is extremely rare,[147] especially considering the frequency of mesenteric adenitis. Pneumatosis intestinalis has been reported in an infant.[1] Pneumonia, pleural empyema, lung abscess, hepatic and splenic abscesses, urinary tract infection, and renal abscess also have been reported.[43] Glomerulonephritis that usually is transient has been reported.[44, 55] Cases of meningitis, osteomyelitis, septic arthritis, pyomyositis (including psoas muscle abscess), endocarditis, mycotic aneurysm, and intravenous catheter–related infection caused by *Y. enterocolitica* have been described.[11, 28, 43, 74, 167, 169] Thrombocytopenia[60] and hemolytic anemia[96] have occurred in association with infection caused by *Y. enterocolitica*.

Underlying Conditions That Predispose to Bacteremia

Y. enterocolitica bacteremias that occur in patients beyond early infancy most often occur in those with chronic illnesses or iron overload states. Thalassemias are such conditions that occur most commonly in children.[35, 53, 91] Among 144 Italian children with thalassemia who were receiving deferoxamine therapy and frequent blood transfusions, 14 developed infection caused by *Y. enterocolitica* during a 12-month period.[35] Septicemia occurred in 5 of the 14 and was preceded by enterocolitis or mesenteric adenitis in each case. All 14 recovered after receiving 2 weeks of therapy with intravenous trimethoprim-sulfamethoxazole. A similar proportion of children with thalassemias observed in two centers in Canada between 1979 and 1994 also developed invasive disease caused by *Y. enterocolitica*.[5] Bacteremia can be associated temporally with blood transfusions in such patients, suggesting that transfusions may be the source of infection or predispose to development of infection in some cases.[108]

Hemochromatosis, cirrhosis, and other liver diseases may facilitate *Y. enterocolitica* bacteremia, also on the basis of excess availability of serum iron. Deferoxamine therapy itself is a risk factor for development of sepsis caused by *Y. enterocolitica* because of the ability of the microbe to extract iron from this compound. Immunosuppressive therapies, diabetes mellitus, and malnutrition also may predispose to development of *Y. enterocolitica* bacteremia.[43]

Postinfectious Syndromes

A reactive arthritis may occur 1 to 14 (usually 4 to 10) days after the cessation of acute illness.* Most such events occur in adults with a slight female predominance, but 8 of 74 cases in one series from Sweden were in children 11 to 20 years of age (5 males, 3 females).[194] In a series from the Netherlands, 10 percent of children with yersiniosis, most of whom were 7 years of age or older, developed arthritis.[77] The knees, ankles, and wrists are affected most commonly, and in approximately 50 percent of cases, only one or two joints are involved. Hands, fingers, toes, shoulders, hips, and elbows also may be involved. Pain usually is severe, and the arthritis is additive and usually not migratory. The inflammatory process is self-limited and may persist for 2 months or longer in two thirds of cases, with one third persisting for 4 months or longer.

Erythema nodosum also occurs as a postinfectious manifestation and is a more common occurrence in adults than in children. It can occur alone or in association with arthritis.[77] Tendinitis, myositis, myocarditis, urethritis, uveitis, and conjunctivitis also can occur in association with arthritis. Many but not all patients who develop these postinfectious reactions are HLA-B27 positive.[1] Some patients manifest the full Reiter syndrome.[77, 97, 155, 165] Acute glomerulonephritis has been linked to infection with serotype O:3 strains in one series of adults.[55]

The erythrocyte sedimentation rate exceeds 60 mm/hr in approximately 50 percent of cases. Joint effusions usually are inflammatory, but cell counts and differentials are variable and occasionally mimic septic arthritis. Immune complexes have been found in joint fluid. Nonsteroidal anti-inflammatory agents and corticosteroids, both intra-articular and systemically administered, have been used for symptomatic relief for this process.[149]

Yersinia antigens but not intact bacteria have been found in synovial tissue obtained several weeks to months after onset of reactive arthritis. *Y. enterocolitica* is able to survive within in vitro cultures of human synovial cells for as long as 6 weeks, with resultant deposition of residual antigen

*See references 6, 7, 9, 12, 74, 77, 150, 176, 182, 194.

aggregates within the cells.[81] Synovial fluid–derived T cells from patients with *Y. enterocolitica*–induced reactive arthritis have been demonstrated to respond to several *Y. enterocolitica* antigens: heat shock protein 60, urease beta subunit, ribosomal L2 protein, and a region of the plasmid-encoded tyrosine phosphatase YopH that is highly homologous to the catalytic domain of eukaryotic protein tyrosine phosphatases.[102, 121, 140] Epitopes on *Yersinia*-produced proteins may be able to trigger cross-reactive immunologic recognition of host proteins that leads to chronic inflammation in susceptible persons.[85]

Antibodies against *Y. enterocolitica* have been detected in patients with disorders of the thyroid, including Graves disease, thyroid adenoma, and Hashimoto thyroiditis.[162] Antibodies induced in mice by two low-molecular-weight, outer-membrane proteins cross-react with the thyrotropin receptor.[111] These observations may reflect autoantibodies that cross-react with *Yersinia* epitopes rather than a causal link between yersiniosis and thyroid disease.[43, 148]

Brachial plexus neuropathy and transverse myelitis, each occurring after the resolution of gastrointestinal symptoms caused by *Y. enterocolitica*, have been described in one patient.[170]

Various chronic ailments have been described among a group of 160 Scandinavian patients observed for 4 to 14 years after having acute yersiniosis.[156] They included persistent joint complaints, ankylosing spondylitis (in HLA-B27–positive patients), iridocyclitis, chronic hepatitis, chronic abdominal pain, rheumatoid arthritis, chronic nephritis, thyroid disease, and neurologic ailments. Observed deaths among these patients exceeded the expected number. These findings require confirmation before causal links can be considered, however.

YERSINIA PSEUDOTUBERCULOSIS

The pseudoappendicular syndrome that results from mesenteric adenitis is the primary disease produced by *Y. pseudotuberculosis*.* The chief complaint is abdominal pain, either diffuse or localized to the right lower quadrant. Fever of varying degrees (38° C to 40° C) almost always is present. Tenderness over the McBurney point usually is present. All of these symptoms are highly suggestive of acute appendicitis. Diarrhea may occur but often is absent. Mild leukocytosis occurs, but white blood cell counts usually are less than 20,000/mm^3. The clinical course almost always is benign, with recovery usually beginning approximately the fifth day of illness. On laparotomy, the appendix is normal in most cases but occasionally appears inflamed or suppurative. The mesenteric lymph nodes are enlarged and may appear necrotic.

Efforts have been made to distinguish the pseudoappendicular syndrome caused by *Y. pseudotuberculosis* from that caused by *Y. enterocolitica*.[23, 61] *Y. pseudotuberculosis* adenitis is less likely to have associated enterocolitis and may have a shorter febrile course, but no clear distinction can be made on clinical grounds alone.

A fulminant typhoidal or septicemic form of infection caused by *Y. pseudotuberculosis* can occur but appears to affect primarily older adults with debilitating conditions, such as diabetes or liver disease. This syndrome often is fatal.[93, 154] Isolated cervical adenitis and terminal ileitis have been described.[189] Subacute and recurrent disease can occur.[112] Hepatic abscess,[70] erythema nodosum,[154] and nonsuppurative arthritis[34] also have been reported in association with infection caused by *Y. pseudotuberculosis*.

Y. pseudotuberculosis and Kawasaki Disease–like Illness

In Korea and Japan, *Y. pseudotuberculosis* strains have been responsible for a clinical syndrome that can mimic Kawasaki disease.[34] This manifestation of disease occurs primarily in outbreaks and has also been described as scarlet fever like.[135] A transient (2 to 3 days) erythematous maculopapular rash, strawberry tongue, conjunctivitis, and desquamation can occur, generally in association with gastrointestinal symptoms and fever. Erythema nodosum, lymphadenopathy, uveitis, and coronary aneurysms have occurred in some of these cases, as has acute interstitial nephritis that can lead to transient renal failure.[2, 100, 135] Among a series of 33 patients (median age, 5 years) with such presentations, 20 had elevated antibody titers against *Y. pseudotuberculosis*–derived mitogen, which can function as a superantigen.[2] As in Kawasaki disease, $V_\beta 3$ T lymphocytes were increased in many of these patients compared with healthy control subjects.

Differential Diagnosis

The differential diagnosis of *Yersinia* enterocolitis includes both viral and other bacterial causes of acute gastroenteritis. When the symptoms of mesenteric adenitis are predominant and severe, appendicitis and other causes of an acute abdomen must be considered. The acute terminal ileitis caused by *Yersinia* infections also can be similar to the gastrointestinal manifestations of Crohn disease, ulcerative colitis, cat-scratch disease, anisakiasis, amebiasis, actinomycosis, typhoid fever, and lymphoma.[59, 77, 135, 183, 189]

Cases of infection caused by *Y. enterocolitica* with concomitant recovery of *Salmonella, Campylobacter,* and rotavirus antigen in stool specimens have been observed.[1]

Diagnosis

The most effective approach to the diagnosis of yersiniosis is isolation of the organism from the stool of patients with enteritis caused by *Y. enterocolitica* or from the infected mesenteric lymph nodes of those infected by *Y. pseudotuberculosis*. *Y. enterocolitica* occasionally can be recovered from involved mesenteric lymph nodes or the distal ileum.[43] Cultures of feces from individuals with acute suppurative mesenteric adenitis usually fail to grow either organism.

Isolating *Yersinia* from extraintestinal specimens such as lymph nodes and blood is not difficult because they grow on ordinary media (e.g., blood agar) and on several selective and differential media employed for enteric bacteria. Isolating from fecal specimens is more difficult, however, because *Yersinia* multiply more slowly than do other enteric bacteria at 37° C and have no characteristic colony morphology. Selective media have been developed, but many clinical laboratories culture stool specimens for *Yersinia* spp. only on request because of the costs of these media and the relatively low frequency of occurrences of these pathogens in the community.

Yersinia grow well on MacConkey agar but are much smaller than are other enteric bacteria after standard incubation at 37° C. Cefsulodin-irgasan-novobiocin agar plates have been designed specifically for the isolation of *Yersinia* spp. from stool specimens. After incubation for 48 hours,

---

*See references 19, 46, 50, 52, 61, 75, 79, 92, 93, 112, 135, 153, 154, 185, 189.

Yersinia colonies appear dark pink with translucent borders and occasionally are surrounded by a zone of precipitated bile. Cefsulodin-irgasan-novobiocin agar inhibits the growth of most other bacteria, except for *Citrobacter* spp. (positive citrate reactions of which allow their distinction). If a dedicated medium for *Yersinia* isolation is not used, MacConkey agar can be examined after 24 hours at 35° C to 37° C for small colorless colonies that become much larger after an additional 24 hours of incubation at room temperature. Most *Y. enterocolitica* strains are lactose negative.[64] *Yersinia* can be differentiated readily from *Salmonella* because the latter are motile at 37° C, urease negative, citrate positive, and lysine positive. Most *Salmonella* strains also produce gas during fermentation and produce hydrogen sulfide. *Shigella* are urease negative and lack motility at room temperature.[169]

Yersinia spp. grow faster at 37° C than at room temperature. However, growth occurs readily at 22° C to 28° C, and these lower temperatures are recommended for primary isolation.[64] Because of the ability of *Yersinia* to grow at even colder temperatures, specimens can be inoculated into phosphate-buffered saline, refrigerated at 4° C to 6° C, and subcultured periodically (up to 4 weeks) if the routine plates that were inoculated with the specimen remain negative. Such "cold enrichment" greatly enhances the isolation rate of *Yersinia* spp. and may be the most reliable method for isolating these organisms from fecal specimens. However, many of the *Yersinia* isolates recovered by cold enrichment represent either *Y. enterocolitica* serotypes that usually are not associated with human disease or other *Yersinia* spp. that have roles that remain unclear.

Pathologic or virulent *Yersinia* strains can be distinguished in most instances from nonpathogenic strains by three biochemical tests that are associated with absence of the virulence plasmid. The virulent strains lack pyrazinamidase activity, do not ferment salicin, and do not hydrolyze esculin. On Congo red–magnesium oxalate agar during incubation at 36° C, fresh pathologic isolates (but not those that have been subcultured serially) grow as small red colonies, demonstrating the virulence plasmid–determined properties of Congo red dye uptake and calcium-dependent growth.[49]

SEROLOGY

Serology can be performed with microtiter techniques and is most reliable for serotypes O:3 and O:9 of *Y. enterocolitica*.[24, 183] Antibody to the infecting serotype usually is absent at the onset of disease. Peak titers usually are reached 3 to 4 weeks after onset of clinical illness and fall during the next 3 to 5 months. Low postconvalescent titers may persist for months.[183] Microhemagglutination, complement fixation, and enzyme immunoassays are available in a few commercial laboratories.[64]

Agglutinin titers of 1:128 or higher for *Y. enterocolitica* in previously normal healthy individuals are suggestive of infection.[24] Titers of 1:200 or higher were present within 3 weeks of onset of illness in 62 of 65 Canadian children who suffered infection with serotype O:3.[118] Fourfold rises in titer rarely were seen. Negative or minimal titers (1:32 or lower) do not rule out yersiniosis in infants or immunosuppressed patients. Serologic responses occur more commonly and are of higher titer among patients with extraintestinal systemic infection. Prozone reactions may occur at dilutions of 1:32 or lower. Marked cross-agglutination occurs between *Y. enterocolitica* serotype O:9 and *Brucella abortus, Morganella morganii,* and *Salmonella*.[24]

Antibodies to *Y. pseudotuberculosis* often are detectable at the onset of clinical signs of infection and may be highest during the acute phase of illness.[75]

MOLECULAR TECHNIQUES

PCR assays have been developed for *Y. enterocolitica* and *Y. pseudotuberculosis* with use of primers that allow assessment of 16S rRNA sequences as well as of specific plasmid- and chromosome-encoded genes.[34, 103, 129, 130, 186, 188] PCR techniques have been used to identify *Yersinia* organisms in blood, tissue, water, and food samples.

Treatment

Most patients with yersiniosis do not require treatment because the disease usually is self-limited. Seriously ill patients generally have responded to treatment with chloramphenicol, gentamicin, or tetracyclines, but clinical success has not been uniform. Of these agents, tetracyclines have been the traditional agent of choice.[61, 183] However, *Y. enterocolitica* isolates resistant to the tetracyclines have been reported in recent years. Two percent of a sample of *Y. enterocolitica* isolates from Canada in 1992 were resistant to tetracycline,[139] and 10 percent of a sample of *Y. enterocolitica* isolates from the Netherlands from 1982 to 1991 were resistant to doxycycline.[171]

More than 99 percent of 1060 isolates of *Y. enterocolitica* collected in Canada in the years 1972 to 1976, 1980, 1985, and 1990 were susceptible in vitro to piperacillin, cefotaxime, aztreonam, gentamicin, tobramycin, amikacin, trimethoprim-sulfamethoxazole, chloramphenicol, and ciprofloxacin. No evidence of decreasing susceptibility to any of these agents was found across the periods that were sampled. These results were mirrored by a study of 335 isolates obtained in the Netherlands from 1982 to 1991. All of these isolates were susceptible to ceftazidime, cefepime, imipenem, trimethoprim-sulfamethoxazole, ciprofloxacin, and ofloxacin. Aminoglycosides were effective against more than 99 percent, chloramphenicol against 94 percent, and cefuroxime against 90 percent. Seven multidrug-resistant isolates were present among the isolates from Canada, but none was found among those from the Netherlands.[139, 171]

The vast majority of *Y. enterocolitica* isolates, regardless of serotype, are resistant to ampicillin, ticarcillin, and first-generation cephalosporins. Most of them also are resistant to amoxicillin–clavulanic acid. Azithromycin was active in vitro against 50 percent of the 335 isolates in the Netherlands, but almost all isolates were resistant to erythromycin and clarithromycin.[139, 171]

The decreasing effectiveness of tetracyclines in vitro raises the question of whether these agents should be the first choice for treatment of infection caused by *Y. enterocolitica*. A retrospective review of 43 cases (with patient ages ranging from 3 to 89 years) treated for *Y. enterocolitica* septicemia in France between 1985 and 1991 showed that third-generation cephalosporins were effective in 85 percent of cases in which they were used, although aminoglycosides or fluoroquinolones usually were administered concurrently.[56] Fluoroquinolones alone or in combination with other agents cured all 15 patients. Seven children with bacteremia and diarrhea in Michigan responded well to cefotaxime.[1]

In a double-blind, placebo-controlled trial of trimethoprim-sulfamethoxazole for treatment of children with gastroenteritis caused by *Y. enterocolitica,* the clinical course of illness was not shortened.[136] The children had been ill for a mean of 12 days before treatment was begun, however.

Systemic infections, extraintestinal focal infections, and enterocolitis in compromised hosts should be treated with antibiotics.[43] The in vitro susceptibilities and limited clinical data suggest that children with such infections should be treated with a third-generation cephalosporin, an aminoglycoside, or both. Trimethoprim-sulfamethoxazole also may be used.[35, 77] Fluoroquinolones probably would be effective, but they are not approved for use in children.

Even less clinical and in vitro susceptibility data are available for *Y. pseudotuberculosis*. These infections probably can be managed identically to *Y. enterocolitica* infections. All isolates of *Y. enterocolitica* and *Y. pseudotuberculosis* should be examined for susceptibility to a variety of antibacterial drugs.

Other *Yersinia* Species

Eight other "nonpestis" *Yersinia* spp. (*Yersinia frederiksenii, Yersinia intermedia, Yersinia kristensenii, Yersinia aldovae, Yersinia bercovieri, Yersinia mollaretii, Yersinia rohdei,* and *Yersinia ruckeri*) occasionally have been isolated from clinical specimens, but their roles as human pathogens remain unclear.[64, 161, 172] Each except *Y. aldovae* has been isolated from humans worldwide, including persons with gastrointestinal disorders.[172] These microbes also can be found in fresh-water sources, sewage, dogs, pigs, cattle, wild mammals, birds, reptiles, fish, and some foods, especially milk and meat products. These organisms are similar biochemically to one another and have been termed atypical *Y. enterocolitica.*[43] None contains the *Yersinia* virulence plasmid pYV.[122] Some contain other large plasmids distinct from pYV, carriage of which may be associated with the ability to cause diarrhea in humans.[137, 172] A heat-stable enterotoxin has been found in isolates of *Y. bercovieri.*[173] These *Yersinia* spp. can grow at 4° C and on cefsulodin-irgasan-novobiocin agar and can multiply in refrigerated foods. Use of cold enrichment techniques may enhance recovery of these organisms. Their isolation from clinical specimens should neither be disregarded nor deemed causative of clinical disease without careful epidemiologic considerations.[64]

REFERENCES

1. Abdel-Haq, N. M., Asmar, B. I., Abuhammour, W. M., and Brown, W. J.: *Yersinia enterocolitica* infection in children. Pediatr. Infect. Dis. J. *19*:954–958, 2000.
2. Abe, J., Onimaru, M., Matsumoto, S., et al.: Clinical role for a superantigen in *Yersinia pseudotuberculosis* infection. J. Clin. Invest. *99*:1823–1830, 1997.
3. Achtman, M., Zurth, K., Morelli, G., et al.: *Yersinia pestis*, the cause of plague, is a recently emerged clone of *Yersinia pseudotuberculosis*. Proc. Natl. Acad. Sci. U. S. A. *96*:14043–14048, 1999.
4. Ackers, M. L., Schoenfeld, S., Markman, J., et al.: An outbreak of *Yersinia enterocolitica* O:8 infections associated with pasteurized milk. J. Infect. Dis. *181*:1834–1837, 2000.
5. Adamkiewicz, T. V., Berkovitch, M., Krishman, C., et al.: Infection due to *Yersinia enterocolitica* in a series of patients with β-thalassemia: Incidence and predisposing factors. Clin. Infect. Dis. *27*:1362–1366, 1998.
6. Ahlqvist, J., Ahvonen, P., Räsänen, J. A., et al.: Enteric infection with *Yersinia enterocolitica*: Large pyroninophilic cell reaction in mesenteric lymph nodes associated with early production of specific antibodies. Acta Pathol. Microbiol. Scand. *79A*:109–122, 1971.
7. Aho, K., Ahvonen, P., Lassus, A., et al.: HL-A 27 in reactive arthritis: A study of *Yersinia* arthritis and Reiter's disease. Arthritis Rheum. *17*:521–526, 1974.
8. Ahvonen P.: Human yersiniosis in Finland. 1. Bacteriology and serology. Ann. Clin. Res. *4*:30–38, 1972.
9. Ahvonen, P., Sievers, K., and Aho, K.: Arthritis associated with *Yersinia enterocolitica* infection. Acta Rheumatol. Scand. *15*:232–253, 1969.
10. Albrecht, H.: Zur Aetiologie der Enteritis follicularis suppurativa. Wien. Klin. Wochenschr. *23*:991, 1910.
11. alMohsen, I., Luedtke, G., and English, B. K.: Invasive infections caused by *Yersinia enterocolitica* in infants. Pediatr. Infect. Dis. J. *16*:253–255, 1997.
12. Anonymous: Worldwide spread of infection with *Yersinia enterocolitica*. WHO Chron. *30*:494–496, 1976.
13. Arvastson, B., Damgaard, K., and Winblad, S.: Clinical symptoms of infection with *Yersinia enterocolitica*. Scand. J. Infect. Dis. *3*:37–40, 1971.
14. Asakawa, Y., Akahane, S., Kheata, N., et al.: Two community outbreaks of human infection with *Yersinia enterocolitica*. J. Hyg. (Camb.) *71*:715–723, 1973.
15. Attwood, S. E., Healy, K., Caffarkey, M. T., et al.: *Yersinia* infection and abdominal pain. Lancet *1*:529–533, 1987.
16. Bergstrand, C. G., and Winblad, S.: Clinical manifestations of infection with *Yersinia enterocolitica* in children. Acta Paediatr. Scand. *63*:875–877, 1974.
17. Bissett, M. L.: *Yersinia enterocolitica* isolates from humans in California, 1968–1975. J. Clin. Microbiol. *4*:137–144, 1976.
18. Black, R. E., Jackson, R. J., Tsai, T., et al.: Epidemic *Yersinia enterocolitica* infection due to contaminated chocolate milk. N. Engl. J. Med. *298*:76–79, 1978.
19. Blattner, R. J.: Acute mesenteric lymphadenitis. J. Pediatr. *74*:479–481, 1969.
20. Bottone, E. J.: Current trends of *Yersinia enterocolitica* isolates in the New York City area. J. Clin. Microbiol. *17*:63–67, 1983.
21. Bottone, E. J.: *Yersinia enterocolitica*: Overview and epidemiologic correlates. Microbes Infect. *1*:323–333, 1999.
22. Bottone, E. J.: *Yersinia enterocolitica*: A panoramic view of a charismatic microorganism. Crit. Rev. Microbiol. *5*:211–241, 1977.
23. Bottone, E. J., Chester, B., Malowany, M. S., et al.: Unusual *Yersinia enterocolitica* isolates not associated with mesenteric lymphadenitis. Appl. Microbiol. *27*:858–861, 1974.
24. Bottone, E. J., and Sheehan, D. J.: *Yersinia enterocolitica*: Guidelines for serologic diagnosis of human infections. Rev. Infect. Dis. *5*:898–906, 1983.
25. Bovallius, A., and Nilsson, G.: Ingestion and survival of *Y. pseudotuberculosis* in HeLa cells. Can. J. Microbiol. *21*:1997–2007, 1975.
26. Bradford, W., Noce, P., and Gutman, L.: Pathologic features of enteric infection with *Yersinia enterocolitica*. Arch. Pathol. *98*:17–22, 1974.
27. Braunstein, H., Tucker, E. B., and Gibson, B. C.: Mesenteric lymphadenitis due to *Yersinia enterocolitica*: Report of a case. Am. J. Clin. Pathol. *55*:506–510, 1971.
28. Brennessel, D. J., Robbins, H., and Hindman, S.: Pyomyositis caused by *Yersinia enterocolitica*. J. Clin. Microbiol. *20*:293–294, 1984.
29. Brocklehurst, T. E., Zaman-Wong, C. H., and Lund, B. M.: A note on the microbiology of retail packs of prepared salad vegetables. J. Appl. Bacteriol. *63*:409–415, 1987.
30. Caplan, L. M.: *Yersinia enterocolitica* septicemia. Am. J. Clin. Pathol. *69*:189, 1978.
31. Caprioli, T., Drapeau, A. J., and Kasatiya, S.: *Yersinia enterocolitica*: Serotypes and biotypes isolated from humans and the environment in Quebec, Canada. J. Clin. Microbiol. *8*:7–11, 1978.
32. Centers for Disease Control and Prevention: Incidence of food-borne illnesses: Preliminary data from the Food-borne Diseases Active Surveillance Network (FoodNet)—United States, 1998. M. M. W. R. Morb. Mortal. Wkly. Rep. *48*:189–194, 1999.
33. Centers for Disease Control: *Yersinia enterocolitica* bacteremia and endotoxin shock associated with red blood cell transfusions—United States, 1991. M. M. W. R. Morb. Mortal. Wkly. Rep. *40*:176–178, 1991.
34. Cheong, H. I., Park, H. W., Koo, J. W., et al.: Diagnosis of *Yersinia* pseudotuberculosis infection by polymerase chain reaction. Pediatr. Infect. Dis. J. *15*:596–599, 1996.
35. Cherchi, G. B., Pacifico, L., Cossellu, S., et al.: Prospective study of *Yersinia enterocolitica* infection in thalassemic patients. Pediatr. Infect. Dis. J. *14*:579–584, 1995.
36. Chessum, B., Frengley, J. D., Fleck, D. G., et al.: Case of septicemia due to *Yersinia enterocolitica*. B. M. J. *3*:466, 1971.
37. Chin, G. N., and Noble, R. C.: Ocular involvement in *Yersinia enterocolitica* infections presenting as Parinaud's oculoglandular syndrome. Am. J. Ophthalmol. *83*:19–23, 1977.
38. Cimolai, N., Trombley, C., and Blair, G.: Implications of *Yersinia enterocolitica* biotyping. Arch. Dis. Child. *70*:19–21, 1994.
39. Cookson, S. T., Arduino, M. J., Aguero, S. M., et al.: *Yersinia enterocolitica*-contaminated red blood cells (RBCs): An emerging threat to blood safety. Abstract J99. Abstracts of the 36th Interscience Conference on Antimicrobial Agents and Chemotherapy, New Orleans, LA, American Society for Microbiology, 1996, p. 237.
40. Cornelis, G. R., Boland, A., Boyd, A. P., et al.: The virulence plasmid of *Yersinia,* an antihost genome. Microbiol. Mol. Biol. Rev. *62*:1315–1352, 1998.
41. Cornelis, G., Laroche, Y., Balligand, G., et al.: *Yersinia enterocolitica*, a primary model for bacterial invasiveness. Rev. Infect. Dis. *9*:64–86, 1987.
42. Cossart, P.: Subversion of the mammalian cell cytoskeleton by invasive bacteria. J. Clin. Invest. *100*(Suppl.):S33–S37, 1997.

43. Cover, T. L., and Aber, R. C.: *Yersinia enterocolitica*. N. Engl. J. Med. *321*:16–24, 1989.
44. Cusack, D., Martin, P., Schinittger, T., et al.: I.g.A. Nephropathy in association with *Yersinia enterocolitica*. Irish J. Med. Sci. *152*:311–312, 1983.
45. Dajani, A., and Maurer, M.: Is *Yersinia enterocolitica* gastroenteritis a Canadian disease? J. Pediatr. *97*:165–166, 1980.
46. Daniels, J. J. H.: Enteric infections with *Pasteurella pseudotuberculosis:* An acute abdominal syndrome. J. Int. Coll. Surg. *38*:397–411, 1962.
47. Delorme, J., Laverdiere, M., Martineau, B., et al.: Yersiniosis in children. Can. Med. Assoc. J. *110*:281–284, 1974.
48. Fällman, M., Persson, C., and Wolf-Watz, H.: *Yersinia* proteins that target host cell signaling pathways. J. Clin. Invest. *100*(Suppl.):S15–S18, 1997.
49. Farmer, J. J., III, Carter, G. P., Miller, V. L., et al.: Pyrazinamidase, CR-MOX agar, salicin fermentation–esculin hydrolysis, and D-xylose fermentation for identifying pathogenic serotypes of *Yersinia enterocolitica*. J. Clin. Microbiol. *30*:2589–2594, 1992.
50. Feldman, W. H., and Karlson, A. G.: Pseudotuberculosis. *In* Hull, T. (ed.): Diseases Transmitted from Animals to Man. 5th ed. Springfield, IL, Charles C Thomas, 1963.
51. Fenwick, S. G., and McCarthy, M. D.: *Yersinia enterocolitica* is a common cause of gastroenteritis in Auckland. N. Z. Med. J. *108*:269–271, 1995.
52. Finlayson, N. B., and Fagundes, B.: *Pasteurella pseudotuberculosis* infection: Three cases in the United States. Am. J. Clin. Pathol. *55*:24–29, 1971.
53. Fontani, C., Valeri M., and Pifferesi, M.: *Yersinia enterocolitica* septicemia in a girl with thalassemia major. Pediatr. Med. Clin. *10*:657–658, 1988.
54. Frederiksen, W.: Human pseudotuberculosis in Denmark. Symp. Series Immunobiol. Stand. *9*:137, 1968.
55. Friedberg, M., Denneberg, T., Brun, C., et al.: Glomerulonephritis in infections with *Yersinia enterocolitica* O-serotype 3. Acta Med. Scand. *209*:103–110, 1981.
56. Gayraud, M., Scavizzi, M. R., Mollaret, H. H., et al.: Antibiotic treatment of *Yersinia enterocolitica* septicemia: A retrospective review of 43 cases. Clin. Infect. Dis. *17*:405–410, 1993.
57. Gilbert, R.: Interesting cases and unusual specimens. Annual Report of the Division of Laboratory Research. Albany, New York, New York State Department of Health, 1933, p. 57.
58. Gillespie, J. H., and Timoney, J. F.: Hagan and Bruner's Infectious Diseases of Domestic Animals. 7th ed. Ithaca, Comstock, 1981, pp. 96–97.
59. Gleason, T. H., and Patterson, S. D.: The pathology of *Yersinia enterocolitica* ileocolitis. Am. J. Surg. Pathol. *6*:347–355, 1982.
60. Glud, T. K., and Laursen, B.: *Yersinia enterocolitica* infection complicated by severe thrombocytopenia resistant to high-dose intravenous immunoglobulin. Acta Med. Scand. *217*:233–234, 1985.
61. Goodwin, C. S.: *Yersinia* infections including mesenteric adenitis, and gastrointestinal tuberculosis. *In* Goodwin, C. S. (ed.): Microbes and Infection of the Gut. Melbourne, Blackwell Scientific, 1984, pp. 241–251.
62. Gort, A. S., and Miller, V. L.: Identification and characterization of *Yersinia enterocolitica* genes induced during systemic infection. Infect. Immun. *68*:6635–6642, 2000.
63. Grant, T., Bennett-Wood, V., and Robins-Browne, R. M.: Characterization of the interaction between *Yersinia enterocolitica* biotype 1A and phagocytes and epithelial cells in vitro. Infect. Immun. *67*:4307–4375, 1999.
64. Gray, L. D.: *Escherichia, Salmonella, Shigella,* and *Yersinia*. *In* Murray, P. R. (ed.): Manual of Clinical Microbiology. 6th ed. Washington, D. C., ASM Press, 1995, pp. 450–456.
65. Gutman, L. T., Ottesen, E. A., Quan, T. J., et al.: An inter-familial outbreak of *Yersinia enterocolitica* enteritis. N. Engl. J. Med. *288*:1372–1377, 1973.
66. Haenselt, V.: Zur Kenntnis der abscedierenden reticulocytaren Lymphadenitis (Masshoff). Arzt. Wochenschr. *12*:509, 1957.
67. Hagan, A. G., Lassen, J., and Berge, L. N.: Erysipelas-like disease caused by *Yersinia enterocolitica*. Scand. J. Infect. Dis. *6*:101–102, 1974.
68. Hallstrom, K., Sairanen, E., and Ohela, K.: A pilot clinical study of yersinioses in South-Eastern Finland. Acta Med. Scand. *191*:485–491, 1972.
69. Hamasaki, S., Hayashidani, H., Keneko, K., et al.: A survey for *Yersinia pseudotuberculosis* in migratory birds in coastal Japan. J. Wildl. Dis. *25*:401–403, 1989.
70. Hassig, A., Karrer, J., and Pusterla, F.: Über Pseudotuberculoses beim Menschen. Schweiz. Med. Wochenschr. *79*:791, 1949.
71. Hastings, J. G. M., Batta, K., Gourevitch, D., et al.: Fatal transfusion reaction due to *Yersinia enterocolitica*. J. Hosp. Infect. *27*:75–79, 1993.
72. Hayashidani, H., Ohtomo, Y., Toyokawa, Y., et al.: Potential sources of sporadic human infection with *Yersinia enterocolitica* serovar O:8 in Aomori Prefecture, Japan. J. Clin. Microbiol. *33*:1253–1257, 1995.
73. Heesemann, J., Gaede, K., and Autenrieth, I. B.: Experimental *Yersinia enterocolitica* infection in rodents: A model for human yersiniosis. A. P. M. I. S. *101*:417–429, 1993.
74. Hewstone, A. S., and Davidson, G. P.: *Yersinia enterocolitica* septicaemia with arthritis in a thalassaemic child. Med. J. Aust. *1*:1035–1038, 1972.
75. Hnatko, S. I., and Rodin, A. E.: *Pasteurella pseudotuberculosis* infection in man. Can. Med. Assoc. J. *88*:1108–1112, 1963.
76. Hoogkamp-Korstanje, J. A. A., De Koning, J., and Samsom, J. P.: Incidence of human infection with *Yersinia enterocolitica* serotypes O3, O8, and O9 and the use of indirect immunofluorescence in diagnosis. J. Infect. Dis. *153*:138–141, 1986.
77. Hoogkamp-Korstanje, J. A. A., and Stolk-Engelaar, V. M. M.: *Yersinia enterocolitica* infection in children. Pediatr. Infect. Dis. J. *14*:771–775, 1995.
78. Horstebrock, R.: Zur Frage der "abscedierenden, retikulocytaren Lymphadenitis (Masshoff)." Zentralbl. Allg. Pathol. *91*:221, 1954.
79. Hubbert, W. T., Petenyi, C. W., Glasgow, L. A., et al.: *Yersinia* tuberculosis infection in the United States: Septicemia, appendicitis, and mesenteric lymphadenitis. Am. J. Trop. Med. Hyg. *20*:679–684, 1971.
80. Hubbert, W. T.: Yersiniosis in mammals and birds in the United States: Case reports and review. Am. J. Trop. Med. Hyg. *21*:458–463, 1972.
81. Huppertz, H., and Heesemann, J.: Experimental *Yersinia* infection of human synovial cells: Persistence of live bacteria and generation of bacterial antigen deposits including "ghosts," nucleic acid–free bacterial rods. Infect. Immun. *64*:1484–1487, 1996.
82. Inoue, H., Nakashima, H., Ishida, T., et al.: Three outbreaks of *Yersinia pseudotuberculosis* infections. Zentralbl. Bakteriol. Mikrobiol. Hyg. *186*:504–511, 1988.
83. Isberg, R. R.: Mammalian cell adhesion functions and cellular penetration of enteropathogenic *Yersinia* species. Mol. Microbiol. *3*:1449–1453, 1989.
84. Isberg, R. R., Voorhis, D. L., and Falkow, S.: Identification of invasin: A protein that allows enteric bacteria to penetrate cultured mammalian cells. Cell *50*:769–778, 1987.
85. Jansson, E., Wallgren, G. R., and Ahvonen, P.: *Yersinia enterocolitica* as a cause of acute mesenteric lymphadenitis. Acta Paediatr. Scand. *57*:448–450, 1968.
86. Jepsen, O. B., Korner, B., Lauritsen, K. B., et al.: *Yersinia enterocolitica* infection in patients with acute surgical abdominal disease: A prospective study. Scand. J. Infect. Dis. *8*:189–194, 1976.
87. Jones, B. L., and Hanson, M. F.: Prevention of transfusion of *Yersinia enterocolitica*. J. Hosp. Infect. *28*:236–238, 1994.
88. Kandolo, K., and Wauters, G.: Pyrazinamidase activity in *Yersinia enterocolitica* and related organisms. J. Clin. Microbiol. *21*:980–982, 1985.
89. Kato, Y., Ito, K., Kubo, Y., et al.: Occurrence of *Yersinia enterocolitica* in wild-living birds. Appl. Environ. Microbiol. *49*:198–200, 1985.
90. Kay, B. A., Wachsmuth, K., Gemski, P., et al.: Virulence and phenotypic characterization of *Yersinia enterocolitica* isolated from humans in the United States. J. Clin. Microbiol. *17*:128–138, 1983.
91. Kelly, D. A., Price, E., Jani, B., et al.: *Yersinia* enterocolitis vs. iron overload. J. Pediatr. Gastroenterol. Nutr. *6*:643–645, 1987.
92. Knapp, W.: *Pasteurella pseudotuberculosis* als erreger einer mesenterialen Lymphadenitis beim Menschen. Zentralbl. Bakteriol. *161*:422–424, 1954.
93. Knapp, W.: Mesenteric adenitis due to *Pasteurella pseudotuberculosis* in young people. N. Engl. J. Med. *259*:776–778, 1958.
94. Knapp, W., and Steuter, W.: Untersuchungen über den Nachweis komplementbindender und agglutinierender Antikorper gegen *Pasteurella pseudotuberculosis* in Sera infizierter und immunisierter Menschen and Tiere. Z. Immunitatsforsch. Exp. Ther. *113*:370–374, 1956.
95. Knapp, W., and Masshoff, W.: Zur Ätiologie der abszedierenden retikulozytaren Lymphadenitis: Einer praktisch wichtigen, vielfach unter dem Bilde einer akuten Appendizitis verlaufenden Erkrankung. Dtsch. Med. Wochenschr. *79*:1266–1271, 1954.
96. von Knorring, J., and Petterson, T.: Haemolytic anaemia complicating *Yersinia enterocolitica* infection: Report of a case. Scand. J. Haematol. *9*:149, 1972.
97. Kobayashi, S., Ogasawara, M., Maeda, K., et al.: Antibodies against *Yersinia enterocolitica* in patients with Reiter's syndrome. J. Lab. Clin. Med. *105*:380–389, 1985.
98. Kohl, S., Jacobson, J. A., and Nahmias, A.: *Yersinia enterocolitica* infections in children. J. Pediatr. *89*:77–79, 1976.
99. Koning-Ward, T. F., and Robins-Browne, R. M.: Analysis of the urease gene complex of members of the genus *Yersinia*. Gene *182*:225–228, 1996.
100. Koo, J. W., Park, S. N., Choi, S. M., et al.: Acute renal failure associated *with Yersinia pseudotuberculosis* infection in children. Pediatr. Nephrol. *10*:582–586, 1996.
101. Krogstad, P., Mendelman, P. M., Miller, V. L., et al.: Clinical and microbiologic characteristics of cutaneous infection with *Yersinia enterocolitica*. J. Infect. Dis. *165*:740–743, 1992.
102. Lahesmaa, R., Soderberg, C., Bliska, J., et al.: Pathogen antigen- and superantigen-reactive synovial fluid T cells in reactive arthritis. J. Infect. Dis. *172*:1290–1297, 1995.
103. Lamps, L. W., Madhusudhan, K. T., Greenson, J. K., et al.: The role of *Yersinia enterocolitica* and *Yersinia pseudotuberculosis* in granulomatous appendicitis: A histologic and molecular study. Am. J. Surg. Pathol. *25*:508–515, 2001.
104. Larsen, J. H.: Human yersiniose. Ugeskr. Laeger *134*:431, 1972.
105. Lee, L. A., Taylor, J., Carter, G. P., et al.: *Yersinia enterocolitica* O:3: An emerging cause of pediatric gastroenteritis in the United States. J. Infect. Dis. *163*:660–663, 1991.
106. Lee, V. T., and Schneewind, O.: Type III secretion machines and the pathogenesis of enteric infections caused by *Yersinia* and *Salmonella* spp. Immunol. Rev. *168*:241–255, 1999.
107. Leino, R., and Kalliomaki, J. L.: Yersiniosis as an internal disease. Ann. Intern. Med. *81*:458–461, 1974.

108. Leino, R., Granfars, K., Havia, T., et al.: Yersiniosis as a gastrointestinal disease. Scand. J. Infect. Dis. *19*:63–68, 1987.
109. Linde, H.-J., Neubauer, H., Meyer, H., et al.: Identification of *Yersinia* species by the Vitek GNI Card. J. Clin. Microbiol. *37*:211–214, 1999.
110. Lobato, M. J., Landeras, E., González-Hevia, M. A., and Mendoza, M. C.: Genetic heterogeneity of clinical strains of *Yersinia enterocolitica* traced by ribotyping and relationships between ribotypes, serotypes, and biotypes. J. Clin. Microbiol. *36*:3297–3302, 1998.
111. Luo, G., Seetharamaiah, G. S., Niesel, D. W., et al.: Purification and characterization of *Yersinia enterocolitica* envelope proteins which induce antibodies that react with human thyrotropin receptor. J. Immunol. *152*:2555–2561, 1994.
112. Mair, N. S., Mair, H. J., Stirk, E. M., et al.: Three cases of acute mesenteric lymphadenitis due to *Pasteurella pseudotuberculosis*. J. Clin. Pathol. *13*:432–439, 1960.
113. Mair, N. S.: Yersiniosis (infections due to *Yersinia pseudotuberculosis* and *Yersinia enterocolitica*). *In* Hubbert, W. T., McCollough, W. F., and Schnurrenberger, P. R. (eds.): Diseases Transmitted from Animals to Man. 6th ed. Springfield, IL, Charles C Thomas, 1975, pp. 174–185.
114. Maki, M., Gronroos, P., and Vesikari, T.: In vitro invasiveness of *Yersinia enterocolitica* isolated from children with diarrhea. J. Infect. Dis. *138*:677–680, 1978.
115. Maki, M., Vesikari, T., Rantala, I., et al.: Yersiniosis in children. Arch. Dis. Child. *55*:861–865, 1980.
116. Makino, S., Okada, Y., Maruyama, T., et al.: PCR-based random amplified polymorphic DNA fingerprinting of *Yersinia pseudotuberculosis* and its practical applications. J. Clin. Microbiol. *32*:65–69, 1994.
117. Malassez, L., and Vignal, W.: Tuberculos zoologique (forme ou aspect ou tuberculose sans bacillus). Arch. Physiol. Norm. Pathol. *53*:2, 1883.
118. Marks, M. I., Pai, C. H., Lafleur, L., et al.: *Yersinia enterocolitica* gastroenteritis: A prospective study of clinical, bacteriologic, and epidemiologic features. J. Pediatr. *96*:26–31, 1980.
119. Masshoff, W.: Eine neuartige Form der mesenterialen Lymphadenitis. Dtsch. Med. Wochenschr. *78*:532–535, 1953.
120. Masshoff, W., and Dolle, W.: Über eine besondere Form der sog. mesenterialen Lymphadenopathie: "Die abscedierende reticulocytare Lymphadenitis." Virchows Arch. Pathol. Anat. *323*:664–684, 1953.
121. Mertz, A. K. H., Ugrinovic, S., Lauster, R., et al.: Characterization of the synovial T cell response to various recombinant *Yersinia* antigens in *Yersinia enterocolitica*–triggered reactive arthritis. Arthritis Rheum. *41*:315–326, 1998.
122. Miller, V. L., Farmer, J. J., III, Hill, W. E., et al.: The ail locus is found uniquely in *Yersinia enterocolitica* serotypes commonly associated with disease. Infect. Immun. *57*:121–131, 1989.
123. Mingrone M. G., Fantasia M., Figura N., et al.: Characteristics of *Yersinia enterocolitica* isolated from children with diarrhea in Italy. J. Clin. Microbiol. *25*:1301–1304, 1987.
124. Mollaret, H.-H., et al.: Les septicemies humaines—"*Yersinia enterocolitica*": Propos de dix-sept cas recents. Presse Med. *19*:345, 1971.
125. Mollaret, H. H., Bercovier, H., and Alonso, J. M.: Summary of the data received at the WHO Reference Center for *Yersinia enterocolitica*. Contrib. Microbiol. Immunol. *5*:174–184, 1979.
126. Mollaret, H.-H.: Un domaine pathologique nouveau. Ann. Biol. Clin. *30*:1–5, 1972.
127. Najdenski, H., Iteman, I., and Carniel, E.: Efficient subtyping of pathogenic *Yersinia enterocolitica* strains by pulsed-field gel electrophoresis. J. Clin. Microbiol. *32*:2913–2920, 1994.
128. Naqvi, S. H., Swierkosz, E. M., Gerard, J., and Mills, J. R.: Presentation of *Yersinia enterocolitica* enteritis in children. Pediatr. Infect. Dis. J. *12*:386–389, 1993.
129. Neubauer, H., Hensel, A., Aleksic, S., and Meyer, H.: Evaluation of a *Yersinia* adhesion gene (yadA) specific PCR for the identification of enteropathogenic *Yersinia enterocolitica*. Int. J. Food Microbiol. *57*:225–227, 2000.
130. Neubauer, H., Hensel, A., Aleksic, S., and Meyer, H.: Identification of *Yersinia enterocolitica* within the genus *Yersinia*. Syst. Appl. Microbiol. *23*:58–62, 2000.
131. Nilehn, B., and Sjostrom, B.: Studies on *Yersinia enterocolitica*: Occurrence in various groups of acute abdominal disease. Acta Pathol. Microbiol. Scand. *71*:612–628, 1967.
132. Nilehn, B.: Studies on *Yersinia enterocolitica*: With special reference to bacterial diagnosis and occurrence in human enteric disease. Acta Pathol. Microbiol. Scand. *206*(Suppl.):1–48, 1969.
133. Odinot, P. T., Meis, J. F. G. M., Van Den Hurk, P. J. J. C., et al.: PCR-based characterization of *Yersinia enterocolitica*: Comparison with biotyping and serotyping. Epidemiol. Infect. *115*:269–277, 1995.
134. Orth, K., Xu, Z., Mudgett, M. B., et al.: Disruption of signaling by *Yersinia* effector YopJ, a ubiquitin-like protein protease. Science *290*:1594–1597, 2000.
135. Paff, J. R., Triplett, D. A., and Saari, T. N.: Clinical and laboratory aspects of *Yersinia pseudotuberculosis* infection with a report of two cases. Am. J. Clin. Pathol. *66*:101–110, 1976.
136. Pai, C. H., Gillis, F., Tuomanen, E., et al.: Placebo-controlled double-blind evaluation of trimethoprim-sulfamethoxazole treatment of *Yersinia enterocolitica* gastroenteritis. J. Pediatr. *104*:308–311, 1984.
137. Pai, C. H., and Mors, V.: Production of enterotoxin by *Yersinia enterocolitica*. Infect. Immun. *19*:908–911, 1978.
138. Pepe, J. C., Badger, J. L., and Miller, V. L.: Growth phase and low pH affect the thermal regulation of the *Yersinia enterocolitica inv* gene. Mol. Microbiol. *11*:123–125, 1994.
139. Preston, M. A., Brown, S., Borczyk, A. A., et al.: Antimicrobial susceptibility of pathogenic *Yersinia enterocolitica* isolated in Canada from 1972–1990. Antimicrob. Agents Chemother. *38*:2121–2124, 1994.
140. Probst, P., Hermann, E., Hermann-Meyer zum Buschenfelde, K., et al.: Identification of the *Yersinia enterocolitica* urease B subunit as a target antigen for human synovial T lymphocytes in reactive arthritis. Infect. Immun. *61*:4507–4509, 1993.
141. Quan, T. J., Meek, J. L., Tsuchiya, K. R., et al.: Experimental pathogenicity of recent North American isolates of *Yersinia enterocolitica*. J. Infect. Dis. *129*:341–344, 1974.
142. Rabinovitz, M., Stremple, T. H., Granforo, K., et al.: *Yersinia enterocolitica* infections complicated by intestinal perforation. Arch. Intern. Med. *147*:1062–1063, 1987.
143. Rabson, A. R., and Koornhof, H. J.: *Yersinia enterocolitica* infections in South Africa. S. Afr. Med. J. *46*:798–803, 1972.
144. Rakin, A., Noelting, S., Schubert, S., and Heesemann, J.: Common and specific characteristics of the high-pathogenicity island of *Yersinia enterocolitica*. Infect. Immun. *67*:5265–5274, 1999.
145. Randall, K. J., and Mair, N. S.: Family outbreak of *Pasteurella pseudotuberculosis* infection. Lancet *1*:1042–1043, 1962.
146. Ratman, S., Mercer, E., Picco, B., et al.: A nosocomial outbreak due to *Yersinia enterocolitica* serotype O:5, biotype 1. J. Infect. Dis. *145*: 242–247, 1982.
147. Reed, R. P., Robins-Browne, R. M., and Williams, M. L.: *Yersinia enterocolitica* peritonitis. Clin. Infect. Dis. *25*:1468–1469, 1997.
148. Resetkova, E., Notenboom, R., Arreaza, G., et al.: Seroreactivity to bacterial antigens is not a unique phenomenon in patients with autoimmune thyroid diseases in Canada. Thyroid *4*:269–274, 1994.
149. Rodnan, G. P., Schumacher, H. R., and Zvaifler, N. J.: Primer on the Rheumatic Diseases. 8th ed. Atlanta, Arthritis Foundation, 1983, pp. 93–94.
150. Rodriguez, W. J., Controni, G., Cohen, G. J., et al.: *Yersinia enterocolitica* in children. J. A. M. A. *242*:1978–1980, 1979.
151. Roggenkamp, A., Geiger, A. M., Leitritz, L., et al.: Passive immunity to infection with *Yersinia* spp. mediated by anti-recombinant V antigen is dependent on polymorphism of V antigen. Infect. Immun. *65*:446–451, 1997.
152. Rose, E. B., Camp, C. J., and Antes, E. J.: Family outbreak of fatal *Yersinia enterocolitica* pharyngitis. Am. J. Med. *82*:636–637, 1987.
153. Ryser, R. J., and Hornick, R. B.: A review of "new" bacterial strains causing diarrhea. *In* Remington, J. S., and Swartz, M. N. (eds.): Clinical Topics in Infectious Diseases. New York, McGraw-Hill, 1981, pp. 184–210.
154. Saari, T. N., and Tripplet, D. A.: *Yersinia pseudotuberculosis* mesenteric adenitis. J. Pediatr. *85*:656–659, 1974.
155. Saari, M., Make, M., Paivonsal, T., et al.: Acute anterior uveitis and conjunctivitis following *Yersinia* infection in children. Int. Ophthalmol. Med. *9*:237–241, 1986.
156. Saebo, A., and Lassen, J.: *Yersinia enterocolitica*: An inducer of chronic inflammation. Int. J. Tissue Reac. *16*:51–57, 1994.
157. Saisawa, K.: Über die Pseudotuberkulose beim Menschen. Zeitschr. Hyg. *73*:353, 1913.
158. Schleifstein, J., and Coleman, M. B.: An identified microorganism resembling *B. ligneri* and *Past. pseudotuberculosis* and pathogenic for man. N. Y. State J. Med. *39*:1749, 1939.
159. Schleifstein, J., and Coleman, M. B.: *Bacterium enterocoliticum*. Annual Report, Division of Laboratories and Research. Albany, New York, New York State Department of Health, 1943, p. 56.
160. Seuri, M., and Granfors, K.: Antibodies against *Yersinia* among farmers and slaughterhouse workers. Scand. J. Work Environ. Health *18*:128–132, 1992.
161. Shayegani, M., DeForge, L., McGlynn, D. M., et al.: Characteristics of *Yersinia enterocolitica* and related species isolated from human and environmental sources. J. Clin. Microbiol. *14*:304–312, 1981.
162. Shenkman, L., and Bottone, E. J.: Antibodies to *Yersinia enterocolitica* in thyroid disease. Ann. Intern. Med. *85*:735–739, 1976.
163. Snellings, N. J., Popek, M., and Lindler, L.E.: Complete DNA sequence of *Yersinia enterocolitica* serotype O:8 low-calcium-response plasmid reveals a new virulence plasmid–associated replicon. Infect. Immun. *69*:4627–4638, 2001.
164. Snyder, J. D., Christenson, E., and Feldman, R. A.: Human *Yersinia enterocolitica* infections in Wisconsin: Clinical, laboratory and epidemiologic features. Am. J. Med. *72*:768–774, 1982.
165. Solem, J., and Lassen, J.: Reiter's disease following *Yersinia enterocolitica* infection. Scand. J. Infect. Dis. *3*:83, 1971.

166. Sonnenwirth, A. C.: *Yersinia*. *In* Lennett, E. H., Spaulding, E. H., and Truant, J. P. (eds.): Manual of Clinical Microbiology. 2nd ed. Washington, D.C., American Society of Microbiology, 1954, pp. 222–229.
167. Sonnenwirth, A. C.: *Yersinia enterocolitica* as an etiologic agent in meningitis. Bact. Proc. Abstr. M. *128*:87, 1969.
168. Sonnenwirth, A. C.: *Yersinia enterocolitica*. N. Engl. J. Med. *283*:1468, 1970.
169. Sonnenwirth, A. C.: Isolation and characterization of *Yersinia enterocolitica*. Mt. Sinai. J. Med. *43*:736–745, 1976.
170. Sotaniemi, K. A.: Neurologic complications associated with yersiniosis. Neurology *33*:95–97, 1983.
171. Stolk-Engelaar, V. M. M., Meis, J. F. G. M., Mulder, J. A., et al.: In-vitro antimicrobial susceptibility of *Yersinia enterocolitica* isolates from stools of patients in The Netherlands from 1982–1991. J. Antimicrob. Chemother. *36*:839–843, 1995.
172. Sulakvelidze, A.: Yersiniae other than *Y. enterocolitica, Y. pseudotuberculosis,* and *Y. pestis*: The ignored species. Microbes Infect. *2*:497–513, 2000.
173. Sulakvelidze, A., Kreger, A., Joseph, A., et al.: Production of enterotoxin by *Yersinia bercovieri,* a recently identified *Yersinia enterocolitica*-like species. Infect. Immun. *67*:968–971, 1999.
174. Tackett, C. O., Ballard, J., Harris, N., et al.: An outbreak of *Yersinia enterocolitica* infections caused by contaminated tofu (soybean curd). Am. J. Epidemiol. *121*:705–711, 1985.
175. Tauxe, R. V., Vandepitta, J., Mautero, G., et al.: *Yersinia enterocolitica* infections and pork: The missing link. Lancet *1*:1129–1133, 1987.
176. Thomas, A. F., Solomon, L., and Rabson, A.: Polyarthritis associated with *Yersinia enterocolitica* infection. S. Afr. Med. J. *49*:18–20, 1975.
177. Toivanen, P., Toivanen, A., Olkkonen, L., et al.: Hospital outbreak of *Yersinia enterocolitica* infection. Lancet *1*:801–803, 1973.
178. Toma, S.: Survey on the incidence of *Yersinia enterocolitica* in the province of Ontario. Can. J. Public Health *64*:477–487, 1973.
179. Toshniwal, R., Kocka, F. E., and Kallick, C. A.: Suppurative lymphadenitis with *Yersinia enterocolitica*. Eur. J. Clin. Microbiol. *4*:587–588, 1985.
180. Toma, S., Wauters, G., McClure, H. M., et al.: O:13a, 13b, a new pathogenic serotype of *Yersinia enterocolitica*. J. Clin. Microbiol. *20*:843–845, 1984.
181. Tuohy, A. M. O'Gorman, M., Byington, C., et al.: *Yersinia* enterocolitis mimicking Crohn's disease in a toddler. Pediatrics *104*:e36, 1999.
182. Vantrappen, G., Ponette, E., Geboes, K., et al.: *Yersinia* enteritis and enterocolitis: Gastroenterological aspects. Gastroenterology *72*:220–227, 1977.
183. Vantrappen, G., Geboes, K., and Ponette, E.: *Yersinia* enteritis. Med. Clin. North Am. *66*:639–653, 1982.
184. Verhaegen, J., Charlier, J., Lemmens, P., et al.: Surveillance of human *Yersinia enterocolitica* infections in Belgium: 1967–1996. Clin. Infect. Dis. *27*:59–64, 1998.
185. Vilinskas, J., Tilton, R. C., and Kriz, J. J.: A new clinical entity: Human infection with *Yersinia* presenting as an acute abdomen. Am. J. Surg. 7:568, 1971.
186. Vishnubhatla, A., Fung, D. Y., Oberst, R. D., et al.: Rapid 5′ nuclease (TaqMan) assay for detection of virulent strains of *Yersinia enterocolitica*. Appl. Environ. Microbiol. *66*:4131–4135, 2000.
187. Visser, L. G., Hiemstra, P. S., Van Den Barselaar, M. T., et al.: Role of YadA in resistance to killing of *Yersinia enterocolitica* by antimicrobial polypeptides of human granulocytes. Infect. Immun. *64*:1653–1658, 1996.
188. Waage, A. S., Vardund, T., Lund, V., and Kapperud, G.: Detection of low numbers of pathogenic *Yersinia enterocolitica* in environmental water and sewage samples by nested polymerase chain reaction. J. Appl. Microbiol. *87*:814–821, 1999.
189. Weber, J., Finlayson, N. B., and Mark, J. B. D.: Mesenteric lymphadenitis and terminal ileitis due to *Yersinia pseudotuberculosis*. N. Engl. J. Med. *283*:172–174, 1970.
190. Wilson, H. D., McCormick, J. S., and Feely, J. C.: *Yersinia enterocolitica* infection in a 4-month-old infant associated with infection in household dogs. J. Pediatr. *89*:767–769, 1976.
191. Winblad, S., Nilehn, B., and Jonsson, M.: Two further cases, bacteriologically verified, of human infection with "*Pasteurella X*" (syn. *Yersinia enterocolitica*). Acta Pathol. Microbiol. Scand. *67*:537–541, 1966.
192. Winblad, S., Nilehn, B., and Sternby, N. H.: *Yersinia enterocolitica (Pasteurella X)* in human enteric infections. B. M. J. *2*:1363–1366, 1966.
193. Winblad, S.: Erythema nodosum associated with infection with *Yersinia enterocolitica*. Scand. J. Infect. Dis. *1*:11–16, 1969.
194. Winblad, S.: Arthritis associated with *Yersinia enterocolitica* infections. Scand. J. Infect. Dis. *7*:191–195, 1975.
195. Young, G. M., Badger, J. L., and Miller, V. L.: Motility is required to initiate host cell invasion by *Yersinia enterocolitica.* Infect. Immun. *68*:4323–4326, 2000.
196. Zhang, L., Radziejewska-Lebrecht, J., Krajewska-Pietrasik, D., et al.: Molecular and chemical characterization of the lipopolysaccharide O-antigen and its role in the virulence of *Yersinia enterocolitica* serotype O:8. Mol. Microbiol. *23*:63–76, 1997.
197. Zen-Yoji, H., Maruyama, T., Sakai, S., et al.: An outbreak of enteritis due to *Yersinia enterocolitica* occurring at a junior high school. Jpn. J. Microbiol. *17*:220–222, 1973.

CHAPTER 118 Miscellaneous Enterobacteria

THOMAS G. BOYCE ■ RANDALL G. FISHER ■ WILLIAM C. GRUBER

This chapter focuses on three less commonly isolated organisms of the family Enterobacteriaceae, *Edwardsiella tarda, Hafnia alvei,* and *Pantoea agglomerans.* Each of these organisms, although uncommon, can cause significant disease in certain clinical circumstances.[43]

Edwardsiella tarda

BACTERIOLOGY

E. tarda is a non-lactose-fermenting, gram-negative bacillus that is indole positive and produces hydrogen sulfide. It ferments only glucose and maltose. The species name *tarda* reflects its biochemical inactivity. It usually is lysine and ornithine decarboxylase positive.[19] The organism resembles *Salmonella* both biochemically and clinically.[31] *Salmonella,* however, usually ferments annitol, sorbitol, and rhamnose. *Edwardsiella*'s innate resistance to colistin also distinguishes it from *Salmonella.*[45]

E. tarda grows well on usual differential media in the laboratory and produces smooth, glistening, semitranslucent colonies.

EPIDEMIOLOGY

E. tarda is an organism associated with fresh water and marine life and has been isolated from turtles, fish, pelicans, alligators, seals, and toads.[31] It also is found in snakes and lizards. Case reports of human disease have implicated ornamental fish,[66] pet turtles,[46] snakes,[55] and catfish[6, 13, 27] as sources of infection.

Patients with chronic liver disease, chronic ethanol abuse, steroid therapy, and hemoglobinopathy are particularly susceptible to infection with *E. tarda.*[31] Any condition associated with iron overload also is a potential risk factor.

Infection with *E. tarda* is global but more common in tropical and subtropical climates, particularly Southeast Asia, Africa, and Latin America.[32] The elderly and the very young seem to be at increased risk for development of severe illness.[9] Asymptomatic carrier states have been well documented,[51] but no true epidemic has been reported, and person-to-person transmission has not been established directly.[17]

PATHOPHYSIOLOGY

Invasiveness of the organism in both HeLa and HEp-2 cells,[52] siderophore production, elaboration of a cell-associated hemolysin,[28] and resistance to complement-mediated lysis may contribute to virulence, although no clear associations have been made.[30] Hemolytic activity requires the presence of two genes, *ethA* and *ethB*. The *ethA* gene codes for the hemolysin, whereas the *ethB* gene codes for an activation/secretion protein, which is necessary for activation of the hemolysin. Transcription of the *ethB* gene is regulated by iron, which may explain the association between iron overload states and severe infection with *E. tarda*.[28] Hemolysin activity appears to be necessary for both cell entry and cytotoxicity to occur.[63]

CLINICAL MANIFESTATIONS

Infections with *E. tarda* can be divided broadly into two types, intestinal and extraintestinal. Gastrointestinal infection usually causes self-limited enteritis, with intermittent watery diarrhea and low-grade fever.[34] Nausea and vomiting usually are not seen. On occasion, enterocolitis or a dysentery-like illness is noted.[39] Because most laboratories do not specifically culture stool specimens for *Edwardsiella,* most cases are unrecognized.

Wound infection is the most common extraintestinal infection. Most of the wounds are caused by fish fins or snakes; wounds sustained in automobile accidents also have been implicated.[31] Cellulitis or abscesses may be produced. Coinfection with other organisms, particularly *Aeromonas hydrophila,* is a common occurrence.[27, 61]

Septicemia with *E. tarda* is a rare but serious infection that carries a mortality rate of approximately 45 percent. Most patients with septicemia have underlying conditions, such as liver disease, iron overload, and immune suppression. Septicemia occasionally occurs after a mild diarrheal illness.[13] Infants without other risk factors have been described.[67] Septicemia presents with high fever, shock, and often disseminated intravascular coagulation. Meningitis also has been reported.[50, 59] Death sometimes occurs despite administration of appropriate antimicrobial therapy.

Other syndromes associated with infection with *E. tarda* include an enteric fever–like illness,[13] multiple liver abscesses,[75] osteomyelitis,[55] septic arthritis,[6] cellulitis,[22] myonecrosis,[61] necrotizing fasciitis,[42] endocarditis,[47] uterine pyomyoma,[73] tubo-ovarian abscess,[53] and peritonitis.[13] Patients with sickle-cell disorders may be predisposed to development of bone infection with *E. tarda,* as they are with *Salmonella*.[59, 72] Interestingly, all reported cases are in patients with SC hemoglobinopathy rather than homozygous sickle-cell disease.

DIAGNOSIS AND TREATMENT

Diagnosis rests on identification of *E. tarda* in culture. The major pitfall is mistaking it for *Salmonella*.

E. tarda is sensitive in vitro to most antibiotics used routinely in the treatment of gram-negative infections, including β-lactams, cephalosporins, aminoglycosides, and fluoroquinolones.[12] It is sensitive also to chloramphenicol. Resistance has been demonstrated to polymyxin B, colistin, and occasionally penicillin.[12, 13] The organism almost universally elaborates a β-lactamase, but no resistance to β-lactams other than penicillin has been reported.[12]

Gastrointestinal disease usually does not require treatment. Severe disease, such as septicemia or meningitis, probably should be treated with the combination of a β-lactam and an aminoglycoside,[31] even though synergy has not been demonstrated.

Hafnia alvei

BACTERIOLOGY

H. alvei is a facultatively anaerobic, gram-negative bacillus, formerly referred to as *Enterobacter hafnia*.[60] This indole-negative, catalase-positive, and oxidase-negative organism is positive for both lysine and ornithine decarboxylases. It is motile at lower temperatures but may be immotile at 35° C and above. *H. alvei* ferments mannitol, maltose, and sucrose. It grows well on blood or MacConkey agar as a nonlactose fermenter, producing gray-white, slightly elevated, glistening colonies.[18]

EPIDEMIOLOGY

H. alvei has been found in soil, dairy products, sewage, and the feces of humans and animals. Some question exists as to whether it is part of the endogenous microflora of the gut[56] or whether an asymptomatic "carrier" state exists. One study from Japan cultured *H. alvei* from as many as 13 percent of healthy subjects[41]; however, other epidemiologic surveys have shown the incidence to be less than 2 percent.[57]

Long regarded as a nonpathogen, *H. alvei* now clearly has been associated with enteritis and rarely has been isolated in pure culture from other sites, including blood, cerebrospinal fluid, peritoneal fluid, and urine. Infection appears to be opportunistic.

PATHOPHYSIOLOGY

The pathophysiology of *H. alvei* has been investigated most thoroughly with regard to its production of gastrointestinal symptoms.[2] Albert and associates[3] showed that although *H. alvei* elaborated neither enterotoxins nor a Shiga-like toxin and was not invasive in HeLa cell assays or by Sereny test, it did produce diarrhea in experimental animals whether it was given parenterally or by mouth. Sections of intestines from infected animals showed lesions indistinguishable from those caused by enteropathogenic *Escherichia coli*. In contrast to most strains of *H. alvei,* diarrheogenic strains possess the *eaeA* gene. This gene appears to be necessary but not sufficient for formation of the characteristic attaching-effacing lesions in the intestinal brush border.[29, 58] Janda and colleagues[33] have presented data suggesting that diarrheogenic *H. alvei* isolates actually are either unusual biotypes of *E. coli* or a new species in the genus *Escherichia*.

CLINICAL MANIFESTATIONS

Cases of diarrhea caused by *H. alvei* have been reported primarily in children.[2, 3] Most patients with gastroenteritis secondary to *H. alvei* report 6 to 12 episodes of watery diarrhea per day, low-grade or no fever, and nausea with or without vomiting. Mucus sometimes is found in stools, but blood is not.[56, 71] In most patients, symptoms last for a few days, but symptoms persist for more than a week in some patients.[56] One patient with a reactive arthritis from *H. alvei* enteritis has been described.[48]

Extraintestinal *H. alvei* infection usually occurs in hospitalized patients. In the largest series reported, the organism was isolated from 80 samples collected from 61 patients; 57 (93%) of patients had underlying illnesses, most commonly malignant neoplasms.[26] Nearly one half of isolates were from the respiratory tract. Other sites included blood, skin, wounds, urine, and intra-abdominal abscesses. In 60 samples (75%), other organisms were cultured concomitantly.

One 20-day-old premature baby with necrotizing enterocolitis grew *H. alvei* from blood and stool.[23] Yeager and associates[74] reported four cases of pneumatosis intestinalis in patients after undergoing bone marrow transplantation, and one of the four grew *H. alvei* in pure culture from blood. An 8-year-old boy with acquired immunodeficiency syndrome had recurrent episodes of *H. alvei* bacteremia.[14] Both episodes were associated with fever and diarrhea; the second episode also was associated with pneumonia and pleural effusion, the cause of which is unclear. A well-documented case of pneumonia in a 54-year-old woman with acquired immunodeficiency syndrome in whom the pleural fluid grew a pure culture of *H. alvei* has been reported.[20]

Wound abscess caused by *H. alvei* has been reported.[1] A 2-year-old liver transplant recipient developed hepatic abscess and bacteremia with *H. alvei* and *Enterococcus faecalis*.[7] One case of meningitis in a 1-year-old infant without known predisposing risk factors has been reported.[44] An interesting case of a woman with rheumatoid arthritis who contracted endophthalmitis with *H. alvei* in mixed culture has been described; the woman used snake powder as a food seasoning.[11] Two case reports of persistent bacteremia with this organism, alone and in mixed cultures, are found in the older literature. One of these patients was a previously well 13-year-old girl.[25]

DIAGNOSIS AND TREATMENT

Diagnosis is made by isolation of the organism from stools or from normally sterile body fluids.

Gunthard and Pennekamp[26] have reported the susceptibility results of 80 *H. alvei* isolates recovered from 61 patients during a 2½-year period. All isolates tested were susceptible to ciprofloxacin. Isolates also generally were susceptible to tobramycin (99%), imipenem (99%), piperacillin (92%), trimethoprim-sulfamethoxazole (90%), ceftriaxone (88%), and ceftazidime (88%). Nearly all isolates were resistant to ampicillin and to amoxicillin–clavulanic acid. *H. alvei* is constitutively cephalothin resistant.[71] One report describes an inducible β-lactamase that rendered the isolate ceftazidime resistant.[64]

Treatment probably is not necessary for most cases of gastroenteritis. Treatment of invasive infection should be based on susceptibility testing; initiation of empirical therapy with a third-generation cephalosporin and an aminoglycoside is reasonable pending results.

Pantoea agglomerans

First identified as a plant pathogen and named after Erwin Smith in 1917, the genus *Erwinia* has an extended domain as an infectious microbe, including production of disease in humans.[10, 62, 68] A member of this group of organisms, *P. agglomerans (Enterobacter agglomerans, Erwinia herbicola)* has been established as a cause of conjunctivitis,[10] central nervous system infections,[10, 69] urinary tract infections,[62, 68] pneumonia,[4] and nosocomial infections secondary to contaminated intravenous fluids.[24, 37]

BACTERIOLOGY

Species definition within *Erwinia* has been controversial and confusing. One suggestion is that the anaerogenic clinically relevant *Erwinia* of the *herbicola-lathryi* group be renamed *E. agglomerans* or *P. agglomerans*.[19, 35, 70] In clinical microbiology, both of these terms tend to be used interchangeably. This species consists of facultatively anaerobic, fermentative, hydrogen sulfide–negative, gram-negative rods; they do not possess oxidase, phenylalanine deaminase, proteinase, or arginine dehydrolase.[19] None possesses decarboxylates ornithine.[35] They are motile, have peritrichous flagella, and produce a yellow pigment. Strains grow well at 37° C (98.6° F) on standard agar. When colonies are viewed microscopically after growth for 18 to 20 hours, characteristic biconvex spindle-shaped bodies and bacterial aggregates often can be seen.[10, 68] Almost all strains isolated from clinical specimens and grown on agar slants show characteristic elongated, spheroid aggregates,[68] called symplasmata by Cruickshank,[15] who first described them.

EPIDEMIOLOGY

Microorganisms of the genus *Erwinia* long have been recognized as phytopathogens producing dry necrosis, wilts, and soft rots in plants, and they have been associated more recently with disease in trout and leafhoppers.[62, 68] *P. agglomerans (E. herbicola)* was isolated in humans first from stool specimens of patients with typhoid fever in the 1920s and given the name *Bacterium typhi flavum* because of the organism's alleged capacity to be transformed into *Salmonella typhi* in subculture. Identification of saprophytic human strains followed, and the biochemical and cultural identity of *B. typhi flavum* with the *E. herbicola-lathryi* group finally was established.[19]

The first reports of *P. agglomerans* as a human pathogen appeared in the 1960s. Subsequently, a nationwide outbreak of infection caused by this organism was traced to contaminated liners from caps of parenteral solution bottles.[36, 37] The importance of this organism as a nosocomial cause of bacteremia is emphasized by the 17 percent mortality rate in patients receiving an infusion with the contaminated intravenous fluid.[36] A trend toward an increased mortality rate occurred in infected individuals younger than 20 years. Lipid-based medications support rapid bacterial growth at room temperature and, in the absence of strict aseptic handling, have been implicated in nosocomial *P. agglomerans* bloodstream infections.[8] *Pantoea* outbreaks have also been traced to contaminated blood products; prolonged storage of packed red blood cells at 4° C provides conditions that allow these organisms to grow and subsequently to produce high concentrations of endotoxin.[5] Cotton used to filter heroin has been implicated as a source of infection ("cotton fever") in intravenous drug users.[21]

Outbreaks in pediatric hospitals caused by contaminated intravenous solutions also have been described.[40] At least one retrospective review of *Erwinia* organisms isolated from clinical specimens suggested a predisposition to infection in the pediatric age group[10]; however, other studies have noted no preference based on season, sex, age, or residence in hospitals.[68]

PATHOPHYSIOLOGY

The true incidence of clinical infection caused by *P. agglomerans* is difficult to ascertain because of the common association of this microbe with other organisms when it is obtained from clinical specimens. Nonetheless, accumulation of case reports in which this organism is isolated in pure culture from infected material leaves little doubt that *P. agglomerans* can be a human pathogen, apart from its role as a nosocomial contaminant. This organism has little inherent invasiveness. Evidence for animal pathogenicity of *Erwinia* strains isolated from plants and humans is limited; intraperitoneal injection of 10^{13} washed organisms into mice or guinea pigs does not cause symptoms, whereas inoculation of 10^{25} organisms leads to death within 36 hours.[15]

Most strains appear to act as saprophytes in humans,[68] but the organism has been isolated from purulent wounds of the extremities acquired through lacerations or thorn pricks, which suggests agricultural injury as a possible mode of infection.[68] Most serious infections have occurred in individuals with a breach of host defenses (e.g., immunocompromised individuals or patients who received contaminated intravenous fluid).

CLINICAL MANIFESTATIONS

P. agglomerans bacteremia often is associated with fever, shaking chills, and systemic toxicity characteristic of gram-negative sepsis. However, these symptoms frequently have been misinterpreted in hospitalized patients who unknowingly were administered contaminated intravenous fluids.[37]

Eye and skin infections caused by *P. agglomerans* are particularly prominent. Bottone and Schneierson[10] included six cases of conjunctivitis, five of which occurred in infants from whom this organism was isolated. However, only two of the isolates were in pure culture, and a description of the clinical course of these children was not included in the report. *Erwinia* endophthalmitis has been associated with penetration of the eye by a foreign body in a 14-year-old boy.[49] Skin infection in association with a casted fracture has been described in an elderly patient,[68] and wound infections from which this organism was isolated have been described subsequently, most often in association with agricultural injury.[68] Four isolates were obtained in mixed cultures from skin lesions of children younger than 5 years of age, but their possible role in those infections was not confirmed.[10] *P. agglomerans* was the only organism isolated from six consecutive blood cultures in a 9-year-old boy with osteomyelitis.[38] A 13-year-old boy developed septic arthritis caused by *P. agglomerans* 1 month after sustaining an injury from a plant thorn to his knee.[16] A case of *P. agglomerans* spondylodiskitis has been reported.[54]

Primary lung disease caused by these bacteria is an extremely uncommon occurrence and has been reported in an adult with chronic bronchitis.[4] This organism is a very rare cause of meningitis. A contaminated incubator has been implicated in two cases of neonatal central nervous system infection,[65] and a cisternal tap revealed the presence of *P. agglomerans* in an unrelated case in a newborn whose clinical course was not described.[10] A 57-year-old man with tetralogy of Fallot and cyanosis had a brain abscess in which *P. agglomerans* organisms grew in pure culture.[69] Presenting manifestations included headaches, seizures, and left-sided weakness, which occurred during a 2-week period before admission. The patient recovered after drainage of the abscess and gentamicin therapy.

DIAGNOSIS

Identifying this organism often is difficult; in March 1972, as part of a quality control program, *P. agglomerans* was sent as an unknown organism to 250 U.S. hospitals and was identified incorrectly 45 percent of the time.[37] Even when fully identified in isolates from human sources, *P. agglomerans* often is considered a contaminant or saprophyte. The organisms have been identified mistakenly as *Citrobacter, E. coli, Flavobacterium,* and *Klebsiella*. In addition to routine microbiologic studies, identification of yellow-pigmented colonies and observation of the characteristic spindle-shaped bodies and symplasmata can aid in this differentiation. Symplasmata (elongated, spheroid aggregates) are seen best in the condensation water of slant cultures.[68] Spindle-shaped bodies termed Wetzsteinformen by German authors are observed best on standard agar with a low-power microscope lens.[68]

TREATMENT

Most localized infections respond to treatment that includes an aminoglycoside. Persistent localized infection with this organism should prompt a search for an organic foreign body, given the organism's tendency to live as a saprophyte or as a pathogen in vegetable material. In addition to appropriate antimicrobial therapy, treatment of bacteremia should include removal of any potentially contaminated intravenous access. The physician should be alert to the possibility of a common source of infection in nosocomial outbreaks.[37] In view of the rarity of bacteremia caused by *P. agglomerans,* single sporadic cases should be investigated, and clusters of two or more cases should lead to immediate inquiry into possible sources of contamination. Formal surveillance programs have been the key to early recognition and abortion of epidemics.[37]

REFERENCES

1. Agustin, E. T. and Cunha, B. A.: Buttock abscess due to *Hafnia alvei*. Letter. Clin. Infect. Dis. *20*:1426, 1995.
2. Albert, M. J., Alam, K., Islam, M., et al.: *Hafnia alvei,* a probable cause of diarrhea in humans. Infect. Immun. *59*:1507–1513, 1991.
3. Albert, M. J., Faruque, S. M., Ansaruzzaman, M., et al.: Sharing of virulence-associated properties at the phenotypic and genetic levels between enteropathogenic *Escherichia coli* and *Hafnia alvei*. J. Med. Microbiol. *37*:310–314, 1992.
4. Al-Damluji, S., Dickinson, C. M., and Beck, A.: *Enterobacter agglomerans:* A new cause of primary pneumonia. Thorax *37*:865–866, 1982.
5. Arduino, M. J., Bland, L. A., Tipple, M. A., et al.: Growth and endotoxin production of *Yersinia enterocolitica* and *Enterobacter agglomerans* in packed erythrocytes. J. Clin. Microbiol. *27*:1483–1485, 1989.
6. Ashford, R. U., Sargeant, P. D., and Lum, G. D.: Septic arthritis of the knee caused by *Edwardsiella tarda* after a catfish puncture wound. Med. J. Aust. *168*:443–444, 1998.
7. Barry, J. W., Dominguez, E. A., Boken, D. J., et al.: *Hafnia alvei* infection after liver transplantation. Clin. Infect. Dis. *24*:1263–1264, 1997.
8. Bennett, S. N., McNeil, M. M., Bland, L. A., et al.: Postoperative infections traced to contamination of an intravenous anesthetic, propofol. N. Engl. J. Med. *333*:147–154, 1995.
9. Bockemuhl, J., Pan-Urai, R., and Burkhardt, F.: *Edwardsiella tarda* associated with human disease. Pathol. Microbiol. *37*:393–401, 1971.
10. Bottone, E., and Schneierson, S. S.: *Erwinia* species: An emerging human pathogen. Am. J. Clin. Pathol. *57*:400–405, 1972.

11. Caravalho, J., Jr., McMillan, V. M., Ellis, R. B., et al.: Endogenous endophthalmitis due to *Salmonella arizonae* and *Hafnia alvei*. South. Med. J. *83*:325–327, 1990.
12. Clark, R. B., Lister, P. D., and Janda, J. M.: In vitro susceptibilities of *Edwardsiella tarda* to 22 antibiotics and antibiotic–beta-lactamase–inhibitor agents. Diagn. Microbiol. Infect. Dis. *14*:173–175, 1991.
13. Clarridge, J. E., Musher, D. M., Fainstein, V., et al.: Extraintestinal human infection caused by *Edwardsiella tarda*. J. Clin. Microbiol. *11*:511–514, 1980.
14. Conte, M., Castagnola, E., Venzano, P., et al.: Bacteremia caused by *Hafnia alvei* in a human immunodeficiency virus–infected child. Letter. Pediatr. Infect. Dis. J. *15*:182–183, 1996.
15. Cruickshank, J. C.: A study of the so-called bacterium *Typhi flavum*. J. Hyg. *35*:354–371, 1935.
16. De Champs, C., Le Seaux, S., Dubost, J. J., et al.: Isolation of *Pantoea agglomerans* in two cases of septic monoarthritis after plant thorn and wood sliver injuries. J. Clin. Microbiol. *38*:460–461, 2000.
17. Desenclos, J. C., Conti, L., Junejo, S., et al.: A cluster of *Edwardsiella tarda* infection in a day-care center in Florida. J. Infect. Dis. *162*:782, 1990.
18. Englund, G. W.: Persistent septicemia due to *Hafnia alvei*. Report of a case. Am. J. Clin. Pathol. *51*:717–719, 1969.
19. Ewing, W. H., and Fife, M. A.: *Enterobacter agglomerans* (Beijerinck) comb. nov. (the *herbicola-lathryi* bacteria). Int. J. Syst. Bacteriol. *22*:4–11, 1972.
20. Fazal, B. A., Justman, J. E., Turett, G. S., et al.: Community-acquired *Hafnia alvei* infection. Clin. Infect. Dis. *24*:527–528, 1997.
21. Ferguson, R., Feeney, C., and Chirurgi, V. A.: *Enterobacter agglomerans*–associated cotton fever. Arch. Intern. Med. *153*:2381–2382, 1993.
22. Fournier, S., Pialoux, G., Feuillie, V., et al.: *Edwardsiella tarda* septicemia with cellulitis in a patient with AIDS. Letter. Eur. J. Clin. Microbiol. Infect. Dis. *16*:551–553, 1997.
23. Ginsberg, H. G., and Goldsmith, J. P.: *Hafnia alvei* septicemia in an infant with necrotizing enterocolitis. J. Perinatol. *8*:122–123, 1988.
24. Goncalves, C. R., Vaz, T. M., Leite, D., et al.: Molecular epidemiology of a nosocomial outbreak due to *Enterobacter cloacae* and *Enterobacter agglomerans* in Campinas, Sao Paulo, Brazil. Rev. Inst. Med. Trop. Sao Paulo *42*:1–7, 2000.
25. Grajupa, L. A., Mukhopadhyay, D., and Grossman, B. J.: Chronic polymicrobial bacteremia. Clin. Pediatr. *14*:280–283, 1975.
26. Gunthard, H., and Pennekamp, A.: Clinical significance of extraintestinal *Hafnia alvei* isolates from 61 patients and review of the literature. Clin. Infect. Dis. *22*:1040–1045, 1996.
27. Hargreaves, J. E., and Lucey, D. R.: Life-threatening *Edwardsiella tarda* soft-tissue infection associated with catfish puncture wound. J. Infect. Dis. *162*:1416–1417, 1990.
28. Hirono, I., Tange, N., and Aoki, T.: Iron-regulated haemolysin gene from *Edwardsiella tarda*. Mol. Microbiol. *24*:851–856, 1997.
29. Ismaili, A., Bourke, B., de Azavedo, J. C., et al.: Heterogeneity in phenotypic and genotypic characteristics among strains of *Hafnia alvei*. J. Clin. Microbiol. *34*:2973–2979, 1996.
30. Janda, J. M., Abbott, S. L., Kroske-Bystrom, S., et al.: Pathogenic properties of *Edwardsiella* species. J. Clin. Microbiol. *29*:1997–2001, 1991.
31. Janda, J. M., and Abbott, S. L.: Infections associated with the genus *Edwardsiella:* The role of *Edwardsiella tarda* in human disease. Clin. Infect. Dis. *17*:742–748, 1993.
32. Janda, J. M., and Abbott, S. L.: Unusual food-borne pathogens. *Listeria monocytogenes, Aeromonas, Plesiomonas,* and *Edwardsiella* species. Clin. Lab. Med. *19*:553–582, 1999.
33. Janda, J. M., Abbott, S. L., and Albert, M. J.: Prototypal diarrheagenic strains of *Hafnia alvei* are actually members of the genus *Escherichia*. J. Clin. Microbiol. *37*:2399–2401, 1999.
34. Kourany, M., Vasquez, M. A., and Saenz, R.: Edwardsiellosis in man and animals in Panama: Clinical and epidemiological characteristics. Am. J. Trop. Med. Hyg. *26*:1183–1190, 1977.
35. Lindh, E., Kjaeldgaard, P., Frederiksen, W., et al.: Phenotypical properties of *Enterobacter agglomerans (Pantoea agglomerans)* from human, animal and plant sources. A. P. M. I. S. *99*:347–352, 1991.
36. Maki, D. G., and Martin, W. T.: Nationwide epidemic of septicemia caused by contaminated infusion products. IV. Growth of microbial pathogens in fluids for intravenous infusions. J. Infect. Dis. *131*:267–272, 1975.
37. Maki, D. G., Rhame, F. S., Mackel, D. C., et al.: Nationwide epidemic of septicemia caused by contaminated intravenous products. I. Epidemiologic and clinical features. Am. J. Med. *60*:471–485, 1976.
38. Marklein, G., Waschkowski, G., and Reichertz, C.: Septicaemia caused by Erwinia herbicola in an 8-year-old boy [in German (author's transl)]. Klin. Padiatr. *193*:394–397, 1981.
39. Marsh, P. K., and Gorbach, S. L.: Invasive enterocolitis caused by *Edwardsiella tarda*. Gastroenterology *82*:336–338, 1982.
40. Matsaniotis, N. S., Syriopoulou, V. P., Theodoridou, M. C., et al.: *Enterobacter* sepsis in infants and children due to contaminated intravenous fluids. Infect. Control *5*:471–477, 1984.
41. Matsumoto, H.: Studies on the *Hafnia* isolated from normal human. Jpn. J. Microbiol. *7*:105–114, 1963.
42. Matsushima, S., Yajima, S., Taguchi, T., et al.: A fulminating case of *Edwardsiella tarda* septicemia with necrotizing fasciitis [in Japanese]. Kansenshogaku Zasshi *70*:631–636, 1996.
43. Mayer, K. H., and Zinner, S. H.: Bacterial pathogens of increasing significance in hospital-acquired infections. Rev. Infect. Dis. *7*(Suppl 3):S371–S379, 1985.
44. Mojtabaee, A., and Siadati, A.: *Enterobacter hafnia* meningitis. J. Pediatr. *93*:1062–1063, 1978.
45. Muyembe, T., Vandepitte, J., and Desmyter, J.: Natural colistin resistance in *Edwardsiella tarda*. Antimicrob. Agents Chemother. *4*:521–524, 1973.
46. Nagel, P., Serritella, A., and Layden, T. J.: *Edwardsiella tarda* gastroenteritis associated with a pet turtle. Gastroenterology *82*:1436–1437, 1982.
47. Nettles, R. E., and Sexton, D. J.: Successful treatment of *Edwardsiella tarda* prosthetic valve endocarditis in a patient with AIDS. Clin. Infect. Dis. *25*:918–919, 1997.
48. Newmark, J. J., Hobbs, W. N., and Wilson, B. E.: Reactive arthritis associated with *Hafnia alvei* enteritis. Arthritis Rheum. *37*:960, 1994.
49. Oesterle, C. S., Kronenberg, H. A., and Peyman, G. A.: Endophthalmitis caused by an *Erwinia* species. Arch. Ophthalmol. *95*:824–825, 1977.
50. Okubadejo, O. A., and Alausa, K. O.: Neonatal meningitis caused by *Edwardsiella tarda*. Br. Med. J. *3*:357–358, 1968.
51. Onogawa, T., Terayama, T., Zen-yoji, H., et al.: Distribution of *Edwardsiella tarda* and hydrogen sulfide–producing *Escherichia coli* in healthy persons [in Japanese]. Kansenshogaku Zasshi *50*:10–17, 1976.
52. Phillips, A. D., Trabulsi, L. R., Dougan, G., et al.: *Edwardsiella tarda* induces plasma membrane ruffles on infection of HEp-2 cells. FEMS Microbiol. Lett. *161*:317–323, 1998.
53. Pien, F. D., and Jackson, M. T.: Tuboovarian abscess caused by *Edwardsiella tarda*. Am. J. Obstet. Gynecol. *173*:964–965, 1995.
54. Porter, P., and Wray, C. C.: *Enterobacter agglomerans* spondylodiscitis: A possible, unrecognized complication of tetracycline therapy. Spine *25*:1287–1289, 2000.
55. Rao, K. R., Shah, J., Rajashekaraiah, K. R., et al.: *Edwardsiella tarda* osteomyelitis in a patient with SC hemoglobinopathy. South. Med. J. *74*:288–292, 1981.
56. Reina, J., Hervas, J., and Borrell, N.: Acute gastroenteritis caused by *Hafnia alvei* in children. Clin. Infect. Dis. *16*:443, 1993.
57. Ridell, J., Siitonen, A., Paulin, L., et al.: *Hafnia alvei* in stool specimens from patients with diarrhea and healthy controls. J. Clin. Microbiol. *32*:2335–2337, 1994.
58. Ridell, J., Siitonen, A., Paulin, L., et al.: Characterization of *Hafnia alvei* by biochemical tests, random amplified polymorphic DNA PCR, and partial sequencing of 16S rRNA gene. J. Clin. Microbiol. *33*:2372–2376, 1995.
59. Sachs, J. M., Pacin, M., and Counts, G. W.: Sickle hemoglobinopathy and *Edwardsiella tarda* meningitis. Am. J. Dis. Child. *128*:387–388, 1974.
60. Sakazaki, R.: Genus IX. *Hafnia. In* Krieg, N. R., and Holt, J. G. (eds.): Bergey's Manual of Systematic Bacteriology. Vol. 1. Baltimore, Williams & Wilkins, 1984, pp. 484–486.
61. Slaven, E. M., Lopez, F. A., Hart, S. M., et al.: Myonecrosis caused by *Edwardsiella tarda:* A case report and case series of extraintestinal *E. tarda* infections. Clin. Infect. Dis. *32*:1430–1433, 2001.
62. Starr, M. P., and Chatterjee, A. K.: The genus *Erwinia:* Enterobacteria pathogenic to plants and animals. Annu. Rev. Microbiol. *26*:389–426, 1972.
63. Strauss, E. J., Ghori, N., and Falkow, S.: An *Edwardsiella tarda* strain containing a mutation in a gene with homology to shlB and hpmB is defective for entry into epithelial cells in culture. Infect. Immun. *65*:3924–3932, 1997.
64. Thomson, K. S., Sanders, C. C., and Washington, J. A., 2nd: Ceftazidime resistance in *Hafnia alvei*. Antimicrob. Agents Chemother. *37*:1375–1376, 1993.
65. Urmenyi, A. M. C., and Franklin, A. W.: Neonatal death from pigmented coliform infection. Lancet *1*:313–315, 1961.
66. Vandepitte, J., Lemmens, P., and de Swert, L.: Human edwardsiellosis traced to ornamental fish. J. Clin. Microbiol. *17*:165–167, 1983.
67. Vohra, K., Torrijos, E., Jhaveri, R., et al.: Neonatal sepsis and meningitis caused by *Edwardsiella tarda*. Pediatr. Infect. Dis. J. *7*:814–815, 1988.
68. von Graevenitz, A.: *Erwinia* species isolates. Ann. N. Y. Acad. Sci. *174*:436–443, 1970.
69. Wechsler, A., Bottone, E., Lasser, R., et al.: Brain abscess caused by an *Erwinia* species. Report of a case and review of the literature. Am. J. Med. *51*:680–684, 1971.
70. Werkman, C. H., and Gillen, G. F.: Bacteria producing trimethylene glycol. J. Bacteriol. *23*:167–182, 1932.
71. Westblom, T. U., and Milligan, T. W.: Acute bacterial gastroenteritis caused by *Hafnia alvei*. Clin. Infect. Dis. *14*:1271–1272, 1992.
72. Wilson, J. P., Waterer, R. R., Wofford, J. D., Jr., et al.: Serious infections with *Edwardsiella tarda*. A case report and review of the literature. Arch. Intern. Med. *149*:208–210, 1989.

73. Yang, C. H., and Wang, C. K.: *Edwardsiella tarda* bacteraemia—complicated by acute pancreatitis and pyomyoma. J. Infect. *38*:124–126, 1999.
74. Yeager, A. M., Kanof, M. E., Kramer, S. S., et al.: Pneumatosis intestinalis in children after allogeneic bone marrow transplantation. Pediatr. Radiol. *17*:18–22, 1987.
75. Zighelboim, J., Williams, T. W., Jr., Bradshaw, M. W., et al.: Successful medical management of a patient with multiple hepatic abscesses due to *Edwardsiella tarda*. Clin. Infect. Dis. *14*:117–120, 1992.

CHAPTER 119 *Aeromonas*

RALPH D. FEIGIN

Aeromonas spp. were recognized for their role in disease first by Sanarelli in 1891. His findings associated aeromonads with bacteremic "red leg" disease in frogs.[123] Studies by Hill and associates in 1954 further linked the first human disease, acute fulminating metastatic myositis, with *Aeromonas* infection.[18] In general, *Aeromonas* have been considered opportunistic pathogens for humans; however, these organisms have been identified with increasing frequency as primary pathogens in the normal individual as well as in the compromised host.

Aeromonas organisms are found as normal flora in nonfecal sewage and are isolated from tap water, canals, streams, and rivers. Aeromonads are pathogens for cold-blooded animals (fish, amphibians, and reptiles).

Epidemiology

Ewing and associates[37] and other investigators have isolated *Aeromonas* from tap water and from the water or sediments of rivers, especially during periods when the water temperature was relatively warm.[64, 88, 129] Hazen and colleagues[52] recovered *Aeromonas hydrophila* from 135 of 147 natural water sources in 30 states of the United States and reported that its density was higher in flowing (lotic) than in calm (lentic) water systems and lower in fresh-water systems than in saline; however, *Aeromonas* could not be recovered from waters in which the saline content approached that of sea water or from extremely polluted waters. Leclerc and Buttiaux[74] found *Aeromonas* in 30 percent of more than 9000 samples of drinking water in France. *Aeromonas* also have been recovered from hospital water supplies.[88, 105, 106] More recently, *A. hydrophila* has been isolated from bottled water, prompting the development of regulations in Canada to prevent contamination of bottled water by this organism.[144]

Aeromonas survives readily on surfaces such as bench tops and moistened paper towels. Slotnick[133] recovered *Aeromonas* from a moistened paper towel that had been allowed to dry 24 hours after its application. When the towel was placed in a humidified closed environment, the period was extended to 2 weeks.

A. hydrophila may be found in the mouths of fish, alligators, turtles, tadpoles, and frogs.[55] It also has been found in the feces of guinea pigs and laboratory mice.[33] Ticks are another source of *Aeromonas*. Unusual sources of *Aeromonas* infection include contamination of home or hospital hemodialysis equipment,[61, 111] tornado-associated wound contamination,[41] and contamination of blood or blood products.[108, 112] San Joaquin and colleagues[121] noted that *Aeromonas* organisms also have been found in ornamental aquaria belonging to patients with *Aeromonas*-associated gastroenteritis; however, they found that isolates from the aquaria differed in susceptibility testing from the gastrointestinal isolates, and, thus, the aquaria probably were not the sources of infection.

Aeromonas have been isolated from a large proportion of ready-to-eat salads.[84] Thirty-five percent of *Aeromonas* salad isolates were *A. hydrophila* or *Aeromonas sobria*. All isolates tested in this study had at least one marker of enteropathogenicity, including hemolysin and cytotoxin production. Nonetheless, few if any cases of diarrhea have been associated with ingestion of these salads in the immunocompetent host.

In 1988, California made infection by *Aeromonas* a reportable condition, thereby permitting the first population-based study of the epidemiology of infection caused by this organism. The overall incidence rate for *Aeromonas* isolation was 10.6 cases per 1 million population. The gastrointestinal tract was the most common site of infection (81% of cases), followed by wounds (9%). Five (2%) of 219 patients with *Aeromonas* infection died; all had serious underlying medical conditions.[68]

Etiologic Agent

Aeromonas organisms are motile, asporogenous gram-negative rods that contain a single polar flagellum. The organisms are oxidase and catalase positive and produce acid or gas during carbohydrate fermentation. They can grow between 0° C and 41° C. Growth may occur within a pH range of 5.5 to 9. Lipase, gelatinase, DNase, and other exoenzymes are formed by these organisms.[36, 128, 141]

Aeromonads grow well on blood agar; most strains produce a large zone of beta-hemolysis on this medium, although nonhemolytic strains exist. *Aeromonas* colonies on blood agar have a ground-glass appearance and a fruity odor.[145] Aeromonads also grow on MacConkey, eosin–methylene blue, *Salmonella-Shigella*, and triple sugar iron media.

The sensitivity and specificity of various media for detection of *Aeromonas* spp. in fecal specimens have been evaluated.[96, 116, 140] Isolation is achieved readily on any of the following: pril-xylose-ampicillin agar, xylose-sodium, deoxycholate citrate agar, alkaline peptonic water, inositol–brilliant green bile salts agar, trypticase soy broth with ampicillin, and dextrin-fuchsin-sulfite agar.[140] The colonies appear almost colorless on these media, with the exception of growth on dextrin-fuchsin-sulfite agar, on which they appear dark red.

Mishva and associates[91] evaluated five selective agars. Of these, sheep blood agar with 30 mg ampicillin/L (ASBA 30) permitted the greatest number of *Aeromonas* colonies to grow while also inhibiting the competing fecal flora. They recommend that ASBA 30 be used with DNase–toluidine blue agar (DNTA) to detect the ampicillin-susceptible strains and the nonhemolytic strains. The combination of ASBA 30–DNTA allowed detection of 98 percent of all isolates.

Strains of motile *Aeromonas* isolates can be identified to species level by use of the following tests: production of esculin, formation of gas from glucose, production of acetoin, production of acid from mannitol and arabinase, decarboxylation of lysine and ornithine, dehydrolation of arginine, and pyrazinamide hydrolysis in a semisolid medium.[143] *Aeromonas caviae* and *A. hydrophila* hydrolyze pyrazinamide, whereas all strains of *A. sobria* show no production of pyrazinamide. This absence of pyrazinamidase is a convenient phenotype marker for *A. sobria*.

Detection of *Aeromonas* by use of strain-specific fluorescent antibody has been described.[140] The technique is not satisfactory; only a small percentage of isolates react with prepared antisera, which suggests the presence of numerous serogroups. For typing of *Aeromonas* strains, restriction endonuclease analysis of whole-cell DNA appears to be valuable.[73]

Until recently, *Aeromonas* was considered a member of the Vibrionaceae family, which included the genera of *Vibrio* and *Plesiomonas*. However, molecular genetic techniques have identified that these three genera are not related evolutionarily, and aeromonads in fact represent a family of their own.[28] *Aeromonas* have long been viewed as belonging to one of two major groups on the basis of their ability to grow at different temperatures. Mesophiles were those strains that grew at 35° C to 37° C, and psychrophilic strains were more prevalent at lower temperatures (22° C to 28° C). These two groups could be distinguished not only by optimal growth conditions but also by elaboration of pigmentation on tyrosine agar and production of indole.

Although the strains of psychrophilic *Aeromonas* spp. have remained stable, the isolation of various strains of mesophilic species has multiplied greatly. Several classifications within the genus are in use. The genus previously has been classified as follows: *Aeromonas hydrophila* (including biovars *hydrophila* and *anaerogenes*), *A. sobria*, and *Aeromonas salmonicida*. Schubert[127] classified *Aeromonas* into *Aeromonas hydrophila* (subspecies *hydrophila, anaerogenes,* and *proteolytica*); *Aeromonas punctata* (subspecies *punctata* and *caviae*); and *A. salmonicida, Aeromonas achromogenes,* and *Aeromonas masoucida*. *A. hydrophila* is the proposed type species. *Aeromonas proteolytica* and *A. salmonicida* have not been isolated from humans.

In addition, numerous new species, including *Aeromonas media* (similar to *A. salmonicida*),[5] *Aeromonas veronii*,[54] *Aeromonas schubertii*,[17, 53] *Aeromonas jandaei*,[15] *Aeromonas trota*,[16] *Aeromonas allosaccharophila*,[82] *Aeromonas encheleia*,[35] *Aeromonas bestiarum*,[4] *Aeromonas popoffii*,[58] and *Aeromonas eucrenophila*,[128] have been described. Other isolates include *Aeromonas enteropelogenes* and *Aeromonas ichthiosmia*, which appear to be similar to previously identified species.[27] Of the species isolated currently, *A. hydrophila, A. caviae,* and *A. veronii* have been associated most often with human infections.[59]

Aeromonas is confused most frequently with Enterobacteriaceae. The oxidase test always should be performed to aid in differentiation; *Aeromonas* organisms generally are oxidase positive, whereas Enterobacteriaceae organisms are oxidase negative. McGrath and associates[86] described oxidase-variable strains of *A. hydrophila*. These strains are oxidase positive when grown on nonselective media but oxidase negative when grown on differential or gram-negative media. Organic acid end-products of lactose fermentation can inhibit the oxidase reaction. Paik[102] also has shown that a platinum wire loop should be used for oxidase testing; use of an iron-containing loop can cause false-positive oxidase results.

Aeromonas is susceptible to ceftriaxone (8 μg/mL), chloramphenicol (2 to 4 μg/mL), gentamicin (0.5 to 2 μg/mL), streptomycin (16 μg/mL), and trimethoprim-sulfamethoxazole (<0.5/9.5 μg/mL).[37, 38, 100, 113, 140] Reinhardt and George[114] determined that the most active on a weight basis were ciprofloxacin, enoxacin, and norfloxacin; nalidixic acid and trimethoprim-sulfamethoxazole also possessed good activity. Neither sulfamethoxazole nor trimethoprim alone was active. In addition, they did not note appreciable differences in susceptibility among species or in susceptibility between fecal versus nonenteric isolates. In contrast, Motyl and colleagues[95] noted higher levels of resistance to various antibiotics among *A. hydrophila* strains compared with *A. sobria* or *A. caviae* as judged by minimal inhibitory concentration. Susceptibility to cephalothin may serve as a useful criterion in the identification of *A. sobria*.[95, 122] *Aeromonas* organisms consistently are resistant to penicillin, ampicillin, carbenicillin, cephalothin, erythromycin, clindamycin, and vancomycin. Sawai and associates[126] demonstrated that resistance to β-lactam antibiotics is caused by the production of a species-specific chromosome-mediated β-lactamase. It is not R plasmid mediated. In 1980, McNicol and coworkers[87] reported the recovery of *Aeromonas* isolates from the Chesapeake Bay that were resistant to tetracycline and polymyxin B. They also noted that 57 percent of isolates from Bangladesh had a multiple streptomycin-chloramphenicol-tetracycline resistance phenotype that correlated with the presence of a larger plasmid.

Pathogenesis

A. hydrophila produces numerous extracellular toxins and enzymes. Alpha- and beta-hemolysins may be significant virulence factors in the pathogenesis of *A. hydrophila* infection. Most clinical isolates are beta-hemolytic, and hemolysis is a common feature of infection caused by *Aeromonas*.

Alpha-hemolysin is released from cells during a stationary growth phase. Alpha-hemolysin has a molecular weight of 50,000[78, 80] to 65,000[80] and is stable at room temperature between pH 3.5 and pH 9.5. It is heat labile. Alpha-hemolysin is cytotoxic to HeLa cells and human embryonic lung fibroblasts.[139] When injected into rabbit skin, it causes dermonecrosis. Intraperitoneal injection of alpha-hemolysin is lethal for rabbits and mice.

Beta-hemolysin has a molecular weight of 49,000 to 53,000 and is released near the end of the logarithmic phase of growth of the *Aeromonas* organism. It is heat labile and resists destruction by trypsin and pronase.[80] It causes dermonecrosis of rabbit skin and is lethal for rabbits, rats, and mice. It is cytotoxic to HeLa cells and to human diploid lung fibroblasts.[138]

Both alpha- and beta-hemolysin in high concentrations produce hemorrhagic enteritis in a rabbit ileal loop; however, neither hemolysin is clearly established as a virulence factor in diarrheal disease.[79] Antibodies to either hemolysin neutralize both toxins.

In 1975, Sanyal and associates[124] demonstrated that the enterotoxins from *A. hydrophila* were enterotoxigenic. Subsequently, enterotoxigenic *A. hydrophila* has been isolated from humans,[14, 46–49, 64, 142] water sources, fish, and pigs.[11, 100] *Aeromonas* enterotoxin has a molecular weight of 15,000 to 20,000 and is heat labile.

Aeromonas also produces a heat-stable enterotoxin, proteinase A and B, endopeptidase, staphylolytic enzyme, fibrinolysin, and leukocidin.[78] The precise relationship of these toxins and enzymes to the pathogenesis of human infection is not clear.

Strains of *Aeromonas* produce proteases, DNase, lecithinase, and elastase.[1] These extracellular enzymes may have pathologic significance. *Aeromonas* strains that possess hemolytic and cytotoxic capabilities and that are characterized as HG1/BD-2 type strains have been related strongly to patients with diarrheal disease.[71]

Antihemolysin and agglutinating and precipitating antibodies to *A. hydrophila* have been detected in patients with systemic *Aeromonas* infections but not in those with superficial infections. Increases in the antihemolysin titer to as high as 1:1280 and in the agglutinin titer to 1:640 have been noted.[19]

Burke and colleagues[13] found that many strains associated with diarrhea were able to hemagglutinate cells from human, horse, rat, and guinea pig; 68 percent of these strains displayed fucose-resistant hemagglutination. They suggested that these properties may contribute to virulence.

Ketover and associates[65] showed that normal serum promotes phagocytosis and intracellular killing of *Aeromonas* by normal white blood cells. In contrast, sera from two patients with fatal *Aeromonas* infections failed to do so. One patient had a rise in the serum opsonic antibody titer from less than 1:5 in the acute stage of disease to 1:5120 in the convalescent stage. These studies suggest that a specific opsonizing antibody that is present in normal serum and normal bactericidal activity of neutrophils are required to prevent invasive *A. hydrophila* infections.

Of interest is the lack of clear correlation between known virulence properties and enteropathogenicity in humans. Morgan and coworkers[92] challenged 57 volunteers with five strains of *A. hydrophila* known to produce cytotoxin, hemolysin, enterotoxin, lysine decarboxylase, acetylmethylcarbinol, and DNase. All strains produced purulent hemorrhagic fluid accumulation in rabbit ileal loops, but they induced diarrhea in only 2 of 57 human volunteers. Similarly, Kindschuh and colleagues[67] found that most *A. hydrophila* strains produce a cytotoxin and that no correlation exists between the production of cytotoxin and gastroenteritis. In addition, Mégraud[89] noted that only 11 of 44 strains isolated from the feces of children with diarrhea yielded virulence factors, such as cytotoxin, hemolysin, and hemagglutinin. Most recently, investigators have researched the role of enhanced virulence with serial passages of some *A. caviae* diarrheal strains in mice.[70]

The flexible type IV pili of *Aeromonas* are the predominant pili expressed on fecal isolates of diarrhea-associated species of *Aeromonas*. They represent a family of type IV pili that have been designated Bfp for bundle-forming pili. Kirov and associates[69] have presented compelling evidence to support the concept that Bfp pili are important intestinal colonization factors.

Kuijper and colleagues[72] also found that correlation between cytotoxigenic strains and the presence of diarrhea was not significant and that the development of diarrhea was associated strongly with host factors such as age.

Serogroup analysis may be helpful in establishing which *Aeromonas* isolates can cause human disease. Serogroups O:11, O:34, and O:16 predominate as causes of clinical infection.[60]

Clinical Manifestations

Aeromonas has been implicated as a cause of septicemia, gastroenteritis, peritonitis, skin and wound infections, osteomyelitis, septic arthritis, ocular infections, myositis, urinary tract infections, pneumonia, meningitis, and hemolytic-uremic syndrome in children. Most of these manifestations of infection have been noted in both normal and compromised hosts.[10, 39]

Sepsis caused by *Aeromonas* has been reported in children.* Because *Aeromonas* infection is not a reportable disease, the total number of afflicted children is not known. Although septicemia caused by *Aeromonas* has occurred in normal children, most of those affected have had a disorder known to impair the normal host response to infection or a disorder in which the intact skin as a barrier to infection has been destroyed. *Aeromonas* has been noted in children with leukemia (particularly those with neutropenia), aplastic anemia, cirrhosis, hemoglobinopathies, malnutrition, burns, and renal failure. The clinical manifestations of septicemia are similar to those noted in other gram-negative enteric bloodstream infections with high fever and shock. During the course of septicemia in some of these patients, ecthyma gangrenosum also has been noted. The reported case-fatality rate of 50 percent despite antibiotic therapy presumably is related to the severity of the underlying disorders and not to an unusual virulence of the organism. The propensity for infection in the compromised host suggests, in fact, that *Aeromonas* organisms are of low virulence for the human host. Bacteremia with *A. sobria* and *A. punctata* also has been described.[61, 112, 132]

Meningitis caused by *Aeromonas* also has been reported in children.[40, 41, 146] In one reported review of 20 years' experience with gram-negative bacillary meningitis, *Aeromonas* spp. accounted for 2 percent of the cases.[139] The course was fulminant, and the patients died despite having received antibiotic therapy. All of these children could be considered immunocompromised as a result of sickle-cell anemia (a 23-month-old child) or age (neonates).

Gastrointestinal infections caused by *Aeromonas* have been reported with greater frequency within the pediatric population. *A. hydrophila, A. sobria, A. caviae,* and *A. punctata* have been recovered from stool specimens of patients with gastroenteritis.[14, 23, 42, 61, 94] In 1961, Martinez-Silva and colleagues[83] described an epidemic of enteritis in a newborn nursery affecting nine infants (eight as newborns and one 7-day-old baby). *Aeromonas* was found in the stools of six of these infants. One newborn infant died, the only patient with a pure growth of *Aeromonas* in a stool specimen. In 1964, Rosner[119] reported severe gastroenteritis in a child with growth of *A. hydrophila* from four stool cultures. In 1991, one study reported 224 cases of *Aeromonas* gastroenteritis in Iowa during a period from January to June.[110] Aeromonads have been detected worldwide as the sole pathogen causing diarrhea in 2 to 20 percent of affected children and only 0 to 2 percent of children without diarrhea.[24, 32, 47, 137]

In an attempt to assess the role of *Aeromonas* in diarrheal disease, numerous investigators have evaluated the fecal carriage rate of the organism.[51] Freij[41] described a study performed by other investigators who recovered *Aeromonas* from 0 of 300 adults and from 31 of 4426 (0.7%) children younger than 2 years of age. Pitarangsi and coworkers[107] reported carrier rates of between 16 and 27 percent in various districts in Thailand and noted the same frequency of *A. hydrophila* in stools of Thais with and without

*See references 12, 26, 30, 50, 57, 65, 98, 103, 118, 125, 144–147.

diarrhea. In contrast, *A. hydrophila* was recovered from the stools of American Peace Corps volunteers more frequently when they had diarrhea than when their stool frequency was normal. Only three *Aeromonas* isolates were reported from 1685 rectal swab cultures obtained from 1217 children hospitalized for gastroenteritis in Manitoba, Canada. Bhat and colleagues[8] recovered *Aeromonas* from 7 of 133 patients with acute diarrhea in a valley in India and found both *Aeromonas* and *Plesiomonas shigelloides* in the well water commonly used by these individuals.

Gracey and associates[48, 49] described a prospective study in Australia of 1156 children with diarrhea and an equal number of age- and sex-matched control subjects. Enterotoxigenic *Aeromonas* organisms were isolated from 10.2 percent of children with diarrhea compared with 0.6 percent of children who were well. *Aeromonas* was the only potential pathogen recovered in 6.5 percent of children with diarrhea. Cases of *Aeromonas* infection peaked during the summer months. The mean duration of diarrhea was 15.3 days, and 33 percent of the children required hospitalization. These investigators described three clinical syndromes of *Aeromonas* gastroenteritis: (1) watery diarrhea, vomiting, and low-grade fever in 41 percent; (2) diarrhea with blood and mucus in 22 percent; and (3) prolonged diarrhea of more than 2 weeks' duration in 37 percent.

Many investigators[2, 22, 97, 99, 120] have attempted to describe gastrointestinal infections caused by *Aeromonas*. A 15-year study of the rate of *Aeromonas* spp. in gastroenteritis in hospitalized children was performed by Gluskin and associates.[44] One hundred forty-six strains of *Aeromonas* spp. were isolated from 32,810 fecal specimens from 13,820 hospitalized patients. These isolates constituted 4 percent of all pathogenic bacterial strains cultured. Most of the cases of diarrhea (94%) occurred in children younger than 3 years of age. The peak incidence occurred in those between 2 and 6 months of age. Bloody diarrhea occurred in 7 percent of children. Several investigators[2, 120] have detected a larger number of cases of *Aeromonas*-associated diarrhea in the summer months than in other months, whereas Challapali and colleagues[22] found no seasonal patterns of *Aeromonas* isolation. The greatest number of cases occurred in children younger than 12 months to 3 years of age.

Symptoms included diarrhea, bloody stools, vomiting, abdominal cramps, mild dehydration, and fever. *Aeromonas*-associated diarrhea resembled other types of bacterial diarrhea, except that fecal leukocytes were absent in children with *Aeromonas*-associated diarrhea; in contrast, fecal leukocytes were found in 60 percent of children with other types of bacterial enteritis.[22] A cholera-like illness caused by enterotoxigenic *A. sobria* has been described.[23] Gastroenteritis caused by *A. sobria* and *A. hydrophila* tended to be acute, whereas diarrhea associated with *A. caviae* frequently was chronic, lasting 4 to 6 weeks in untreated patients.

Interestingly, San Joaquin and Pickett[120] described three patients with *A. caviae* diarrhea who originally presented with failure to thrive presumed to be secondary to formula intolerance. These patients' diarrhea improved after administration of trimethoprim-sulfamethoxazole. Moyer[97] noted that although *A. caviae* is considered nonpathogenic, five pediatric patients with otitis media who were treated with penicillin or ampicillin subsequently developed diarrhea in which *A. caviae* was the only potential enteric pathogen. The prior therapy with antibiotics to which *Aeromonas* spp. are known to be resistant probably contributed to colonization of the gastrointestinal tract with *A. caviae* and subsequent development of diarrhea. These four patients also were treated successfully with trimethoprim-sulfamethoxazole.

Outbreaks of diarrhea associated with *Aeromonas* in day-care centers have been described.[32] *A. caviae, A. hydrophila,* and *A. sobria* were the strains recovered most commonly.

Complications of *Aeromonas* intestinal infection included gram-negative bacteremia, intussusception, internal hernia strangulation, hemolytic-uremic syndrome,[10, 115] and failure to thrive. Peritonitis has been reported in a 5-year-old patient with a ruptured appendix.[57] No additional clinical information about this patient was provided.

A. hydrophila has been recovered from the skin or from wound infections of children.* Most of these patients have been normal hosts; three had leukemia. In 40 percent of these cases, *Aeromonas* was not recovered from the lesion in pure culture. The lower extremity was involved in 75 percent of these cases. Exposure to water was noted in 40 percent of these cases; alligator bite, snakebites, stepping on glass, and burns were other presumed predisposing factors. Clinical manifestations included cellulitis, hemorrhagic blebs, and purulent diarrhea with fever and leukocytosis. Secondary bacteremia and osteomyelitis have been reported.[9]

I have recovered *Aeromonas* from skin lesions that have been the result of tick bites. In each of these cases, a circumscribed area of purple discoloration has surrounded the bite, and nonpurulent drainage from the center of the lesion yielded the organism. These patients sought medical attention because the local lesion had persisted or had increased in size during a period of 1 to 2 weeks. *A. schubertii* also has been isolated from traumatic wound infections.[17]

Ecthyma gangrenosum caused by *Aeromonas hydrophila* has been described in several children with leukemia.[65, 98, 130] I have seen ecthyma gangrenosum in several children with *Aeromonas* septicemia who have had malignant or hepatobiliary disease.

Lopez and associates[81] described an 8-year-old child with acute myelogenous leukemia with bacteremia and osteomyelitis; *Aeromonas* grew from a bone aspirate of this patient. Blatz[9] reported finding osteomyelitis and *Aeromonas* bacteremia in a previously healthy 16-year-old patient; a bone aspirate was not attempted. Septic arthritis caused by *A. hydrophila* also has been described in a child with leukemia; the organism was recovered from the second metacarpophalangeal joint at autopsy.[30]

Aeromonas has been recovered from the conjunctiva of a previously healthy 7-year-old boy whose eye had been penetrated by a safety pin and from the anterior chamber of an 8-year-old boy who developed endophthalmitis after receiving a corneal laceration from a fishhook.[26, 134] *A. sobria* endophthalmitis has been described in a 14-year-old patient after a penetrating eye injury occurred in which a cormorant pecked the patient's eye.[75]

Although numerous cases of *Aeromonas* urinary tract infections have been reported in adults, only two cases have been reported in children. McCracken and Barkley[85] reported the recovery of *A. hydrophila* in pure culture from the urine of a 5-month-old boy with diarrhea. Bartolomé and colleagues[7] described a case of urinary tract infection associated with diarrhea in a male neonate with bilateral ureterohydronephrosis and bladder involvement from posterior urethral valves.

Myositis caused by *Aeromonas* also has been described in children. A 9-year-old girl and a 16-year-old boy both required amputation of their legs as a result of *Aeromonas* myositis.[31, 135] Necrosis of muscle was noted in both cases, and gas was seen on the radiographs before amputation in the 9-year-old girl. Fatal myofascial necrosis also has been

*See references 7, 9, 31, 39, 57, 65, 85, 98, 104, 118, 130, 136, 140.

reported in a patient with a history of aplastic anemia.[45] *A. hydrophila* also have been isolated from abscesses caused by snakebites.[62]

Aeromonas organisms have been recovered from the throat and sputum of two children with pneumonia. In one of those patients, both *A. hydrophila* and *Streptococcus pneumoniae* were obtained from sputum of a patient who had been hospitalized after a near-drowning accident.

A. hydrophila has been isolated from lung abscess at autopsy of a 16-year-old girl with *A. hydrophila* septicemia and leukemia.[30]

Diagnosis and Differential Diagnosis

Aeromonas should be considered a possible cause of infection in children with any of the disorders previously noted. It always should be included as a possible cause of gastroenteritis, bacteremia, and skin infection in the compromised host.

In general, *Aeromonas* organisms are recognized only when they grow from body fluids or tissues that normally are sterile. The best methods for isolation of *Aeromonas* have been described (see "Etiologic Agent").

A. hydrophila in food can be detected by an enzyme-linked immunosorbent assay.[90] These organisms also have been identified in environmental samples by use of 16S rDNA–targeted oligonucleotide primers.[34] Many sophisticated techniques, including rRNA sequencing, DNA-DNA reassociation techniques, and polymerase chain reaction, have been used to continue to identify and differentiate *Aeromonas* spp.[29, 59, 66]

Treatment and Prognosis

Infection with *Aeromonas* occurs infrequently; controlled studies to permit recommendation of one antibiotic in preference to all others are not available. Penicillin-hydrolyzing β-lactamases have been detected in most strains of *Aeromonas*, rendering those strains resistant to ampicillin.[93] Piperacillin shows variable activity against *Aeromonas* spp., whereas the ticarcillin-clavulanate combination generally is active. In vitro, *Aeromonas* generally is susceptible to chloramphenicol, aminoglycosides, trimethoprim-sulfamethoxazole, aztreonam, quinolones, and the third-generation cephalosporins.[63] In my experience, chloramphenicol or third-generation cephalosporins have proved efficacious. A drug to which the organism is sensitive should be provided (usually intravenously). The duration of administration depends on the site of infection and the clinical response to therapy. The occurrence of *Aeromonas* infections predominantly in the compromised host accounts for the high case-fatality rate despite administration of an antibiotic agent to which the organism is susceptible.

REFERENCES

1. Agarwal, R. K., Kapoor, K. N., and Kumar, A.: Virulence factors of Aeromonads—an emerging food borne pathogen problem. J. Commun. Dis. *30*:71–78, 1998.
2. Agger, W. A., McCormick, J. D., and Gurwith, M. J.: Clinical and microbial features of *Aeromonas hydrophila*–associated diarrhea. J. Clin. Microbiol. *21*:909–913, 1985.
3. Albert, M. J., Ansaruzzaman, M., Talukder, K. A., et al.: Prevalence of enterotoxin genes in *Aeromonas* spp. isolated from children with diarrhea, healthy controls, and the environment. J. Clin. Microbiol. *38*:3785–3790, 2000.
4. Ali, A., Carnahan, A. M., Altwegg, M., et al.: *Aeromonas bestiarum* sp. nov. (formerly genomospecies DNA group 2 *A. hydrophilia*), a new species isolated from non-human sources. J. Clin. Microbiol. *5*:156–165, 1996.
5. Allen, D. A., Austin, B., and Colwell, R. R.: *Aeromonas media*, a new species isolated from river water. Int. J. Syst. Bacteriol. *33*:599, 1983.
6. Asao, T., Kozaki, S., Kato, K., et al.: Purification and characterization of an *Aeromonas hydrophila* hemolysin. J. Clin. Microbiol. *24*:228–232, 1986.
7. Bartolomé, R. M., Andreu, A., Xercavins, M., et al.: Urinary tract infection by *Aeromonas hydrophila* in a neonate. Infection *17*:172–173, 1989.
8. Bhat, P., Shanthakumari, S., and Rajan, D.: The characterization and significance of *Plesiomonas shigelloides* and *Aeromonas hydrophila* isolated from an epidemic of diarrhoea. Indian J. Med. Res. *62*:1051–1060, 1974.
9. Blatz, D. J.: Open fracture of the tibia and fibula complicated by infection with *Aeromonas hydrophila:* A case report. J. Bone Joint Surg. Am. *61*:790–791, 1979.
10. Bogdanovic, R., Cobeljic, M., Markovic, M., et al.: Haemolytic-uraemic syndrome associated with *Aeromonas hydrophila* enterocolitis. Pediatr. Nephrol. *5*:293–295, 1991.
11. Boulanger, Y., Lallier, R., and Cousineau, G.: Isolation of enterotoxigenic *Aeromonas* from fish. Can. J. Microbiol. *23*:1161–1164, 1977.
12. Bulger, R. J., and Sherris, J. C.: The clinical significance of *Aeromonas hydrophila*: Report of two cases. Arch. Intern. Med. *118*:562–564, 1966.
13. Burke, V., Cooper, M., and Robinson, J.: Haemagglutination patterns of *Aeromonas* spp. related to species and source of strains. Aust. J. Exp. Biol. Med. Sci. *64*:563–570, 1986.
14. Burke, V., Gracey, M., Robinson, J., et al.: The microbiology of childhood gastroenteritis: *Aeromonas* species and other infective agents. J. Infect. Dis. *148*:68–74, 1983.
15. Carnahan, A., Fanning, G. R., and Joseph, S. W.: *Aeromonas jandaei* (formerly genospecies DNA group 9 *A. sobria*), new sucrose-negative species isolated from clinical specimens. J. Clin. Microbiol. *29*:560–564, 1991.
16. Carnahan, A. M., Chakraborty, T., Fanning, G. R., et al.: *Aeromonas trota* sp. nov., an ampicillin-susceptible species isolated from clinical specimens. J. Clin. Microbiol. *29*:1206–1210, 1991.
17. Carnahan, A. M., Marii, M. A., Fanning, G. R., et al.: Characterization of *Aeromonas schubertii* strains recently isolated from traumatic wound infections. J. Clin. Microbiol. *27*:1826–1830, 1989.
18. Caselitz, F. H.: How the *Aeromonas* story started in medical microbiology. Med. Microbiol. Lett. *5*:46–54, 1996.
19. Caselitz, F. H., Freitag, V., and Jannasch, G.: Demonstration of specific antibodies in sera of patients with infections caused by *Aeromonas hydrophila*. Zentralbl. Bakteriol. Mikrobiol. Hyg. A *233*:347–354, 1975.
20. Chakraborty, T., Huhle, B., Bergbauer, H., and Goebel, W.: Cloning, expression, and mapping of the *Aeromonas hydrophila* aerolysin gene determinant in *Escherichia coli* K-12. J. Bacteriol. *167*:368–374, 1986.
21. Chakraborty, T., Montenegro, M. A., Sanyal, S. C., et al.: Cloning of enterotoxin gene from *Aeromonas hydrophila* provides conclusive evidence of production of a cytotonic enterotoxin. Infect. Immun. *46*: 435–441, 1984.
22. Challapali, M., Tess, B. R., Cunningham, D. G., et al.: *Aeromonas*-associated diarrhea in children. Pediatr. Infect. Dis. *7*:693–698, 1988.
23. Champsaur, H., Andremont, A., Mathieu, D., et al.: Cholera-like illness due to *Aeromonas sobria*. J. Infect. Dis. *145*:248–254, 1982.
24. Chopra, A. K., and Houston, C. W.: Enterotoxins in *Aeromonas*-associated gastroenteritis. Microbes Infect. *1*:1129–1137, 1999.
25. Chopra, A. K., Houston, C. W., Peterson J. W., and Jin, G. F.: Cloning, expression, and sequence analysis of a cytolytic enterotoxin gene from *Aeromonas hydrophila*. Can. J. Microbiol. *39*:513–523, 1993.
26. Cohen, K. L., Holyk, P. R., McCarthy, L. R., et al.: *Aeromonas hydrophila* and *Plesiomonas shigelloides* endophthalmitis. Am. J. Ophthalmol. *96*:403–404, 1983.
27. Collins, M. D., Martinez-Murcia, A. J., and Cai, J.: *Aeromonas enteropelogenes* and *Aeromonas ichthiosmia* are identical to *Aeromonas trota* and *Aeromonas veronii*, respectively, as revealed by small-subunit rRNA sequence analysis. Int. J. Syst. Bacteriol. *43*:855–856, 1993.
28. Colwell, R. R., MacDonell, M. T., and DeLey, J.: Proposal to recognize the family Aeromonadaceae fam. nov. Int. J. Syst. Bacteriol. *36*:473–477, 1986.
29. Davin-Regli, A., Bollet, C., Chamorey, E., et al.: A cluster of cases of infections due to *Aeromonas hydrophila* revealed by combined RAPD and ERIC-PCR. J. Med. Microbiol. *47*:499–504, 1998.
30. Dean, H. M., and Post, R. M.: Fatal infection with *Aeromonas hydrophila* in a patient with acute myelogenous leukemia. Ann. Intern. Med. *66*:1177–1179, 1967.
31. Deepe, G. S., and Coonrod, J. D.: Fulminant wound infection with *Aeromonas hydrophila*. South. Med. J. *73*:1546–1547, 1980.
32. de la Morena, M. L., Van, R., Singh, K., et al.: Diarrhea associated with *Aeromonas* species in children in day care centers. J. Infect. Dis. *168*:215–218, 1993.
33. Dobrescu, L.: Enterotoxigenic *Aeromonas hydrophila* from a case of piglet diarrhea. Zentralbl. Veterinarmed. B *25*:713–718, 1978.
34. Dorsch, M., Ashbolt, N. J., Cox, P. T., et al.: Rapid identification of *Aeromonas* species using 16S rDNA targeted oligonucleotide primers: A molecular approach based on screening of environmental isolates. J. Appl. Bacteriol. *77*:722–726, 1994.

35. Esteve, C., Gutierrez, M. C., and Ventosa, A.: *Aeromonas encheleia* sp. nov., isolated from European eels. Int. J. Syst. Bacteriol. *45*:462–466, 1995.
36. Ewing, W. H., and Hugh, R.: *Aeromonas*. *In* Lennette, E. H., Spaulding, E. H., and Truant, J. P. (eds.): Manual of Clinical Microbiology. 2nd ed. Washington, D.C., American Society for Microbiology, 1974, pp. 230–237.
37. Ewing, W. H., Hugh, R., and Johnson, J. G.: Studies on the *Aeromonas* Group. Public Health Service, Communicable Disease Center, 1961, pp. 1–8.
38. Fainstein, V., Weaver, S., and Bodey, G. P.: In vitro susceptibilities of *Aeromonas hydrophila* against new antibiotics. Antimicrob. Agents Chemother. *22*:513–514, 1982.
39. Fraire, A. E.: *Aeromonas hydrophila* infection. J. A. M. A. *239*:192, 1978.
40. Freij, B. J.: *Aeromonas:* Biology of the organism and diseases in children. Pediatr. Infect. Dis. *3*:164–175, 1984.
41. Freij, B. J.: Human disease other than gastroenteritis caused by *Aeromonas* and *Plesiomonas*. *Aeromonas* Symposium, Manchester, England, September 5–6, 1986, pp. 19–20.
42. Fritsche, D., Dahn, R., and Hoffmann, G.: *Aeromonas punctata* subsp. *caviae* as the causative agent of acute gastroenteritis. Zentralbl. Bakteriol. Mikrobiol. Hyg. A *233*:232–235, 1975.
43. Gilbert, D. N., Sanford, J. P., Kutscher, E., et al.: Microbiologic study of wound infections in tornado casualties. Arch. Environ. Health *26*:125–130, 1973.
44. Gluskin, I., Batash, D., Shoseyov, D., et al.: A 15-year study of the role of *Aeromonas* spp. in gastroenteritis in hospitalised children. J. Med. Microbiol. *37*:315–318, 1992.
45. Gonzalez-Barca, E., Ardanuy, C., Carratala, J., et al.: Fatal myofascial necrosis due to imipenem-resistant *Aeromonas hydrophila*. Scand. J. Infect. Dis. *29*:91–92, 1997.
46. Goodwin, C. S., Harper, W. E. S., Steward, J. K., et al.: Enterotoxigenic *Aeromonas hydrophila* and diarrhoea in adults. Med. J. Aust. *1*:25–26, 1983.
47. Gracey, M.: Gastroenteritis in Australian children—studies on the aetiology of acute diarrhea. Ann. Trop. Pediatr. *8*:68–75, 1988.
48. Gracey, M., Burke, V., and Robinson, J.: *Aeromonas*-associated gastroenteritis. Lancet *2*:1304–1306, 1982.
49. Gracey, M., Burke, V., Rockhill, R. C., et al.: *Aeromonas* species as enteric pathogens. Lancet *1*:223–224, 1982.
50. Gupta, P., Ramachandran, V. G., and Seth, A.: Early onset neonatal septicemia caused by *Aeromonas hydrophilia*. Indian Pediatr. *33*:703–704, 1996.
51. Gurwith, M. J., and Williams, T. W.: Gastroenteritis in children: A two-year review in Manitoba. I. Etiology. J. Infect. Dis. *136*:239–247, 1977.
52. Hazen, T. E., Fliermans, C. B., and Hirsch, R. P.: Prevalence and distribution of *Aeromonas hydrophila* in the United States. Appl. Environ. Microbiol. *36*:731–738, 1978.
53. Hickman-Brenner, F. W., Fanning, G. R., Arduino, M. J., et al.: *Aeromonas schubertii*, a new mannitol-negative species found in human clinical specimens. J. Clin. Microbiol. *26*:1561–1564, 1988.
54. Hickman-Brenner, F. W., MacDonald, K. L., Steigerwalt, A. G., et al.: *Aeromonas veronii*, a new ornithine decarboxylase–positive species that may cause diarrhea. J. Clin. Microbiol. *25*:900–906, 1987.
55. Hird, D. W., Diesch, S. L., McKinnel, R. G., et al.: *Aeromonas hydrophila* in wild-caught frogs and tadpoles *(Rana pipiens)* in Minnesota. Lab. Anim. Sci. *31*:166–169, 1981.
56. Howard, S. P., and Buckley, J. T.: Molecular cloning and expression in *Escherichia coli* of the structural gene for the hemolytic toxin aerolysin from *Aeromonas hydrophila*. Mol. Gen. Genet. *204*:289–295, 1986.
57. Hunter, W. F., and Atkinson, H. M.: Infection due to *Aeromonas hydrophila*. Med. J. Aust. *1*:565, 1968.
58. Huys, G., Kampfer P., Altwegg, M., et al.: *Aeromonas popoffii* sp. nov., a mesophilic bacterium isolated from drinking water, production plants, and reservoirs. Int. J. Syst. Bacteriol. *47*:1165–1171, 1997.
59. Janda, J. M., and Abbott S. L.: Evolving concepts regarding the genus *Aeromonas:* An expanding panorama of species, disease presentations, and unanswered questions. Clin. Infect. Dis. *27*:332–344, 1998.
60. Janda, J. M., Abbott, S. L., Khashe, S., et al.: Further studies on biochemical characteristics and serologic properties of the genus *Aeromonas*. J. Clin. Microbiol. *34*:1930–1933, 1996.
61. Janda, J. M., Bottone, E. J., and Reitano, M.: *Aeromonas* species in clinical microbiology: Significance, epidemiology and speciation. Diagn. Microbiol. Infect. Dis. *1*:221–228, 1983.
62. Jorge, M. T., Nishioka, S. de A., de Oliveira, R. B., et al.: *Aeromonas hydrophila* soft-tissue infection as a complication of snake bite: Report of three cases. Ann. Trop. Med. Parasitol. *92*:213–217, 1998.
63. Kampfer, P., Christmann, C., Swings, J., et al.: *In vitro* susceptibilities of *Aeromonas* genomic species to 69 antimicrobial agents. Syst. Appl. Microbiol. *22*:662–669, 1999.
64. Kaper, J. B., Lockman, H., and Colwell, R. R.: *Aeromonas hydrophila*: Ecology and toxigenicity of isolates from an estuary. J. Appl. Bacteriol. *50*:359–377, 1981.
65. Ketover, B. P., Young, L. S., and Armstrong, D.: Septicemia due to *Aeromonas hydrophila:* Clinical and immunologic aspects. J. Infect. Dis. *127*:284–290, 1973.
66. Khan, A. A., and Cerniglia, C. E.: Rapid and sensitive method for the detection of *Aeromonas caviae* and *Aeromonas trota* by polymerase chain reaction. Lett. Appl. Microbiol. *24*:233–239, 1997.
67. Kindschuh, M., Pickering, L. K., Cleary, T. G., et al.: Clinical and biochemical significance of toxin production by *Aeromonas hydrophila*. J. Clin. Microbiol. *25*:916–921, 1987.
68. King, G. E., Werner, S. B., and Kizer, K. W.: Epidemiology of *Aeromonas* infections in California. Clin. Infect. Dis. *15*:449–452, 1992.
69. Kirov, S. M., Barnett, T. C., Pepe, C. M., et al.: Investigation of the role of type IV *Aeromonas* pilus (Tap) in the pathogenesis of *Aeromonas* gastrointestinal infection. Infect. Immun. *68*:4040–4048, 2000.
70. Krzyminska, S., Mokracka, J., Laganowska, M., et al.: Enhancement of the virulence of *Aeromonas caviae* diarrhoeal strains by serial passages in mice. J. Med. Microbiol. *50*:303–312, 2001.
71. Kuhn, I., Albert, M. J., Ansaruzzaman, M., et al.: Characterization of *Aeromonas* spp. isolated from humans with diarrhea, from healthy controls, and from surface water in Bangladesh. J. Clin. Microbiol. *35*:369–373, 1997.
72. Kuijper, E. J., Peeters, M. F., Steigerwalt, A. G., et al.: Clinical and epidemiologic aspects of members of *Aeromonas* DNA hybridization groups isolated from human feces. J. Clin. Microbiol. *27*:1531–1537, 1989.
73. Kuijper, E. J., van Alphen, L., Leenders, E., et al.: Typing of *Aeromonas* strains by DNA restriction endonuclease analysis and polyacrylamide gel electrophoresis of cell envelopes. J. Clin. Microbiol. *27*:1280–1285, 1989.
74. Leclerc, H., and Buttiaux, R.: Fréquence des *Aeromonas* dans les eaux d'alimentation. Ann. Inst. Pasteur *103*:97–100, 1962.
75. Lee, L. R., O'Hagan, S., and Dal Pra, M.: *Aeromonas sobria* endophthalmitis. Aust. N. Z. J. Ophthalmol. *25*:299–300, 1997.
76. Ljungh, A., Eneroth, P., and Wadstrom, T.: Cytotonic enterotoxin from *Aeromonas hydrophila*. Toxicon *20*:787–794, 1982.
77. Ljungh, A., and Kronevi, T.: *Aeromonas hydrophila* toxins: Intestinal fluid accumulation and mucosal injury in animal models. Toxicon *20*:397–407, 1982.
78. Ljungh, A., and Wadstrom, T.: *Aeromonas* toxins. Pharmacol. Ther. *15*:339–354, 1982.
79. Ljungh, A., and Wadstrom, T.: *Aeromonas* and *Plesiomonas* as possible causes of diarrhea. Infection *13*:169–173, 1985.
80. Ljungh, A., and Wadstrom, T.: Toxins of *Vibrio parahaemolyticus* and *Aeromonas hydrophila*. J. Toxicol. Toxin Rev. *1*:257–307, 1982–1983.
81. Lopez, J. F., Quesada, J., and Saied, A.: Bacteremia and osteomyelitis due to *Aeromonas hydrophila:* A complication during treatment of acute leukemia. Am. J. Clin. Pathol. *50*:587–591, 1968.
82. Martinez-Murcia, A. J., Esteve, C., Garay, E., and Collins, M. D.: *Aeromonas allosaccharophila* sp. nov., a new mesophilic member of the genus *Aeromonas*. FEMS Microbiol. Lett. *91*:199–206, 1992.
83. Martinez-Silva, V. R., Guzmann-Urrego, M., and Caselitz, F. H.: Zur Frage der Bedeutung Aeromonasstammen bei Sauglingsenteritis. Z. Tropenmed. Parasitol. *12*:445–451, 1961.
84. Mattick, K. L., and Donovan, T. J.: The risk to public health of *Aeromonas* in ready-to-eat salad products. Commun. Dis. Public Health *1*:267–270, 1998.
85. McCracken, A. W., and Barkley, R.: Isolation of *Aeromonas* species from clinical sources. J. Clin. Pathol. *25*:970–975, 1972.
86. McGrath, V. A., Overman, S. B., and Overman, T. L.: Media-dependent oxidase reaction in a strain of *Aeromonas hydrophila*. J. Clin. Microbiol. *5*:112–113, 1977.
87. McNicol, L. A., Aziz, K. M. S., Huq, I., et al.: Isolation of drug-resistant *Aeromonas hydrophila* from aquatic environments. Antimicrob. Agents Chemother. *17*:477–483, 1980.
88. Meeks, M. V.: The genus *Aeromonas:* Methods for identification. Am. J. Med. Technol. *29*:361–378, 1963.
89. Mégraud, F.: Incidence and virulence of *Aeromonas* species in feces of children with diarrhea. Eur. J. Clin. Microbiol. *5*:311–316, 1986.
90. Merino, S., Camprubi, S., and Tomas, J. M.: Detection of *Aeromonas hydrophila* in food with an enzyme-linked immunosorbent assay. J. Appl. Bacteriol. *74*:149–154, 1993.
91. Mishva, S., Nair, G. B., and Bhadra, R. K.: Comparison of selective media for primary isolation of *Aeromonas* species from human and animal feces. J. Clin. Microbiol. *25*:2040–2043, 1987.
92. Morgan, D. R., Johnson, P. C., DuPont, H. L., et al.: Lack of correlation between known virulence properties of *Aeromonas hydrophila* and enteropathogenicities for humans. Infect. Immun. *50*:62–65, 1985.
93. Morita, K., Watanabe, N., Kurata, S., et al.: β-Lactam resistance of motile *Aeromonas* isolates from clinical and environmental sources. Antimicrob. Agents Chemother. *38*:353–355, 1994.
94. Motyl, M. R., and Janda, J. M.: *Aeromonas* gastroenteritis: A two-year survey. Presented at the 23rd Interscience Conference on Antimicrobial Agents and Chemotherapy, Las Vegas, October 24–26, 1983.
95. Motyl, M. R., McKinley, G., and Janda, J. M.: In vitro susceptibilities of *Aeromonas hydrophila, Aeromonas sobria,* and *Aeromonas caviae* to 22 antimicrobial agents. Antimicrob. Agents Chemother. *28*:151–153, 1985.
96. Moulsdale, M. T.: Isolation of *Aeromonas* from faeces. Lancet *1*:351, 1983.
97. Moyer, N. P.: Clinical significance of *Aeromonas* species isolated from patients with diarrhea. J. Clin. Microbiol. *25*:2044–2048, 1987.

98. Moyes, C. D., Sykes, P. A., and Rayner, J. M.: *Aeromonas hydrophila* septicaemia producing ecthyma gangrenosum in a child with leukaemia. Scand. J. Infect. Dis. *9*:151–153, 1977.
99. Nygaard, G. S., Biosett, M. L., and Wood, R. M.: Laboratory identification of aeromonads from man to other animals. Appl. Microbiol. *19*:618–620, 1970.
100. Olivier, G., Lallier, R., and Lariviere, S.: A toxigenic profile of *Aeromonas hydrophila* and *Aeromonas sobria* isolated from fish. Can. J. Microbiol. *27*:330–333, 1981.
101. Overman, T. L., and Janda, J. M.: Antimicrobial susceptibility patterns of *Aeromonas jandaei, A. schubertii, A. trota,* and *A. veronii* biotype veronii. J. Clin. Microbiol. *37*:706–708, 1999.
102. Paik, G.: Reagents, stains, and miscellaneous test procedures. *In* Lennette, E. H., Balows, A., Hausler, W. J., Jr., et al. (eds.): Manual of Clinical Microbiology. 3rd ed. Washington, D.C., American Society for Microbiology, 1980, pp. 1006–1007.
103. Pearson, T. A., Mitchell, C. A., and Hughes, W. T.: *Aeromonas hydrophila* septicemia. Am. J. Dis. Child. *123*:579–582, 1972.
104. Phillips, J. A., Bernhardt, H. E., and Rosenthal, S. G.: *Aeromonas hydrophila* infections. Pediatrics *53*:110–112, 1974.
105. Picard, B., Arlet, G., and Goullet, P.: Origin hydrique d'infections hospitalieres à *Aeromonas hydrophila*. Presse Med. *12*:700, 1983.
106. Picard, B., and Goullet, P.: Seasonal prevalence of nosocomial *Aeromonas hydrophila* infection related to *Aeromonas* in hospital water. J. Hosp. Infect. *10*:152–155, 1987.
107. Pitarangsi, C., Escheverria, P., Whitmire, R., et al.: Enteropathogenicity of *Aeromonas hydrophila* and *Plesiomonas shigelloides:* Prevalence among individuals with and without diarrhea in Thailand. Infect. Immun. *35*:666–673, 1982.
108. Pittman, M.: A study of bacteria implicated in transfusion reactions and of bacteria isolated from blood products. J. Lab. Clin. Med. *42*:273–288, 1953.
109. Popoff, M.: Genus III: *Aeromonas* Kluyver and van Niel 1936. *In* Krieg, N. R., and Holt, J. G. (eds.): Bergey's Manual of Systematic Bacteriology. Baltimore, Williams & Wilkins, 1984, p. 545.
110. Quinn, J.P.: UHL enteric bacterial disease surveillance. Lab. Hotline *28*:2, 1991.
111. Ramsey, A. M., Rosenbaum, B. J., Yarbrough, C. L., et al.: *Aeromonas hydrophila* sepsis in patient undergoing hemodialysis therapy. J. A. M. A. *239*:128–129, 1978.
112. Raszeja, S., Krynski, S., Krueger, A., et al.: Blood contamination with *Aeromonas hydrophilus* as a cause of lethal post-transfusion complications. Pol. Tyg. Lek. *28*:1159–1162, 1973.
113. Reines, H. D., and Cook, F. V.: Pneumonia and bacteremia due to *Aeromonas hydrophila*. Chest *80*:264–267, 1981.
114. Reinhardt, J. F., and George, W. L.: Comparative in vitro activities of selected antimicrobial agents against *Aeromonas* species and *Plesiomonas shigelloides*. Antimicrob. Agents Chemother. *27*:643–645, 1985.
115. Robson, W. L. M., Leung, A. K. C., and Trevenen C. L.: Haemolytic-uraemic syndrome associated with *Aeromonas hydrophila* enterocolitis. Pediatr. Nephrol. *6*:221–222, 1992.
116. Rogol, M., Sechter, I., Grinberg, L., et al.: Pril-xylose-ampicillin agar, a new selective medium for the isolation of *Aeromonas hydrophila*. J. Med. Microbiol. *12*:229–231, 1979.
117. Rose, J. M., Houston, C. W., Coppenhaver, D. H., et al.: Purification and chemical characterization of a cholera toxin–cross-reactive cytolytic enterotoxin produced by a human isolate of *Aeromonas hydrophila*. Infect. Immun. *57*:1165–1169, 1989.
118. Rosenthal, S. G., Bernhardt, H. E., and Phillips, J. A.: *Aeromonas hydrophila* wound infection. Plast. Reconstr. Surg. *53*:77–79, 1974.
119. Rosner, R.: *Aeromonas hydrophila* as the etiologic agent in a case of gastroenteritis. Am. J. Clin. Pathol. *42*:402–404, 1964.
120. San Joaquin, V. H., and Pickett, D. A.: *Aeromonas*-associated gastroenteritis in children. Pediatr. Infect. Dis. *7*:53–57, 1988.
121. San Joaquin, V. H., Pickett, D. A., Welch, D. F., et al.: *Aeromonas* species in aquaria: A reservoir of gastrointestinal infections? J. Hosp. Infect. *13*:173–177, 1989.
122. San Joaquin, V. H., Scribner, R. K., Pickett, D. A., et al.: Antimicrobial susceptibility of *Aeromonas* species isolated from patients with diarrhea. Antimicrob. Agents Chemother. *30*:794–795, 1986.
123. Sanarelli, G.: Über einem neuen Mikroorganismus des Wassers, welcher für Tieren mit veranderlichen und konstanter Temperatur Pathogen ist. Zentralbl. Bakteriol. Parasitenk. *9*:193–199, 222–228, 1891.
124. Sanyal, S. C., Singh, S. J., and Sen, P. C.: Enteropathogenicity of *Aeromonas hydrophila* and *Plesiomonas shigelloides*. J. Med. Microbiol. *8*:195–198, 1975.
125. Sasu, D., and Apostica, E.: On a strain of *Aeromonas liquefaciens* isolated from blood. Microbiologia (Bucur) *12*:437–441, 1967.
126. Sawai, T., Takahashi, I., Nakagawa, H., et al.: Immunochemical comparison between an oxacillin-hydrolyzing penicillinase of *Aeromonas hydrophila* and those mediated by R plasmids. J. Bacteriol. *135*:281–282, 1978.
127. Schubert, R. H. W.: Genus II: *Aeromonas. In* Buchanan, R., and Gibbons, N. (eds.): Bergey's Manual of Determinative Bacteriology. 8th ed. Baltimore, Williams & Wilkins, 1974, pp. 345–348.
128. Schubert, R. H. W., and Hegazi, M.: *Aeromonas eucrenophila* species nova *Aeromonas caviae:* A later and illegitimate synonym of *Aeromonas punctata*. Zentralbl. Bakteriol. Mikrobiol. Hyg. A *268*:34–39, 1988.
129. Seidler, R. J., Allen, D. A., Bockman, H., et al.: Isolation, enumeration and characterization of *Aeromonas* from polluted waters encountered in diving operations. Appl. Environ. Microbiol. *39*:1010–1018, 1980.
130. Shackelford, P. G., Ratzan, S. A., and Shearer, W. T.: Ecthyma gangrenosum produced by *Aeromonas hydrophila*. J. Pediatr. *83*:100–101, 1973.
131. Sirinavin, S., Likitnukul, S., and Lolekha, S.: *Aeromonas* septicemia in infants and children. Pediatr. Infect. Dis. *3*:122–125, 1984.
132. Skoll, P. J., Hudson, D. A., and Simpson, J. A.: *Aeromonas hydrophila* in burn patients. Burns. *24*:350–353, 1998.
133. Slotnick, I. J.: *Aeromonas* species isolates. Ann. N. Y. Acad. Sci. *174*:503–510, 1970.
134. Smith, J. A.: Ocular *Aeromonas hydrophila*. Am. J. Ophthalmol. *89*:449–451, 1980.
135. Smith, J. A.: *Aeromonas hydrophila*: Analysis of 11 cases. Can. Med. Assoc. J. *122*:1270–1272, 1980.
136. Stephens, S., Rao, K. N. A., Kumar, M. S., et al.: Human infection with *Aeromonas* species: Varied clinical manifestations. Ann. Intern. Med. *83*:368–369, 1975.
137. Teka, T., Faruque, A. S., Hossain, M. I., and Fuchs, G. J.: *Aeromonas*-associated diarrhoea in Bangladeshi children: Clinical and epidemiological characteristics. Ann. Trop. Paediatr. *19*:15–20, 1999.
138. Thelestam, M., and Ljungh, A.: Membrane-damaging and cytotoxic effects on human fibroblasts of alpha- and beta-hemolysins from *Aeromonas hydrophila*. Infect. Immun. *34*:949–956, 1981.
139. Unhanand, M., Mustafa, M. M., McCracken, G. H., Jr., et al.: Gram-negative enteric bacillary meningitis: A twenty-one-year experience. J. Pediatr. *122*:15–21, 1993.
140. von Graevenitz, A.: *Aeromonas* and *Plesiomonas*. *In* Lennette, E. H., Balows, A., Hausler, W. H., et al. (eds.): Manual of Clinical Microbiology. 3rd ed. Washington, D.C., American Society for Microbiology, 1980, pp. 220–225.
141. von Graevenitz, A., and Bucher, C.: Evaluation of differential and selective media for isolation of *Aeromonas* and *Plesiomonas* spp. from human feces. J. Clin. Microbiol. *77*:16–21, 1983.
142. Wadstrom, T., Aust-Kettis, A., Habte, D., et al.: Enterotoxin-producing bacteria and parasites in stools of Ethiopian children with diarrhoeal disease. Arch. Dis. Child. *51*:865–870, 1976.
143. Wakabongo, M., Bortey, E., Meier, F. A., et al.: Rapid identification of motile *Aeromonas*. Diagn. Microbiol. Infect. Dis. *15*:511–515, 1992.
144. Warburton, D. W., McCormick, J. K., and Bowen, B.: Survival and recovery of *Aeromonas hydrophila* in water: Development of methodology for testing bottled water in Canada. Can. J. Microbiol. *40*:145–148, 1994.
145. Washington, J. A., II: The role of *Aeromonas hydrophila* in clinical infection. *In* Holloway, W. J. (ed.): Infectious Disease Reviews. Vol. 2. Mount Kisco, NY, Futura Publishing, 1973, pp. 75–86.
146. Yadava, R., Seeler, R. A., Kalelkar, M., et al.: Fatal *Aeromonas hydrophila* sepsis and meningitis in a child with sickle cell anemia. Am. J. Dis. Child. *133*:753–754, 1979.
147. Zajc-Satler, J.: Morphological and biochemical studies of 27 strains belonging to the genus *Aeromonas* isolated from clinical sources. J. Med. Microbiol. *5*:263–265, 1972.

CHAPTER

120 Pasteurella multocida

BARBARA W. STECHENBERG

In 1878, Kitt first isolated a bacterium of the *Pasteurella* group from wild hogs during an epidemic; 2 years later, Pasteur described the organism that causes fowl cholera. Since that time, the same organism has been implicated in rabbit septicemia, swine plague, hemorrhagic septicemia, and wildseuche (a fatal disease in deer). Hueppe applied the term *hemorrhagic septicemia* to this group of infectious diseases in lower animals because of the characteristic hemorrhagic areas scattered throughout most of the viscera. Original names for the causative organisms included *Pasteurella aviseptica, boviseptica, suiseptica*, and *lepiseptica*, but these organisms now are classified under the name *Pasteurella multocida*, a small, nonmotile, gram-negative rod.[38]

Although *P. multocida* primarily is a pathogen in the animal world, recognition of its potential for infection in humans has been increasing. Brugnatelli reported the first bacteriologically proven case in a human in 1913. Schipper[34] made an extensive review of the literature from 1930 through 1947 and reported only 40 cases of infection with *P. multocida*. Since then, an increasing number of human infections with *P. multocida* have been reported.

The Organism

P. multocida generally appears as a short, ovoid, gram-negative rod; however, the form may vary from this one to coccobacilli with convex sides and rounded ends. The length ranges from 0.3 to 1.25 μm and the diameter from 0.15 to 0.25 μm. It may appear singly or in pairs, chains, or clusters. Healthy organisms stain easily with aniline dyes and are gram-negative. They may show bipolar staining, especially when smears are made directly from animal tissue or fluids. They become increasingly pleomorphic on subculture and may resemble enterics in broth. They do not grow on eosin–methylene blue agar, MacConkey, deoxycholate, or any other bile-containing agar. They are facultatively anaerobic and nonmotile. They do not require X or V factor for growth, an important differential point in distinguishing them from *Haemophilus influenzae*. Some strains require serum, and some may grow primarily on solid media because of a requirement for a low oxidation-reduction potential for primary isolation.

Colonies are nonhemolytic and translucent, usually 1 to 2 mm in diameter, and generally low, convex, and butyrous. On occasion, they may be larger and mucoid. In a study of 30 strains isolated from humans, Heddleston and Wessman[15] reported that 9 of the cultures produced watery mucoid colonies, 4 produced iridescent colonies, 10 produced blue colonies, and 3 produced a mixture of iridescent and blue colonies. Colonies on blood agar are smaller, opaque, and grayish-white. In broth cultures, turbidity, often with a flocculent sediment, is present.

Cultures tend to autoagglutinate in saline and have a peculiar odor described as musty, like semen or burning hair. They are catalase positive, usually oxidase positive, and indole positive. They usually ferment galactose, glucose, fructose, mannitol, mannose, and sucrose without production of gas. Some variability occurs in the fermentation of other sugars. They reduce nitrates but have negative urease, methyl red, and Voges-Proskauer reactions. Using fermentation reactions, Oberhofer[25] developed a biotyping system in which correlation of biotype, 61 percent A and B, was found with cat-bite isolates but not with dog-bite isolates.

The pathogenicity of the organism is variable; most mucoid and smooth colony-forming strains produce a capsule and usually are highly pathogenic for mice and rabbits. The capsule is antiphagocytic, thus resisting intracellular killing by neutrophils.

By use of the indirect hemagglutination test with capsular antigens absorbed onto human type O erythrocytes, five serotypes (A, B, C, D, and E) were selected. A and D are found most commonly in cultures of human origin. A newer capsule serogroup, serogroup F, has been isolated from turkeys.[31] Nielsen and Rosdahl[23] have developed a bacteriophage typing system for typing toxigenic and nontoxigenic strains. DNA hybridization studies have allowed a reclassification of the genus *Pasteurella*. *P. multocida* now includes three subspecies—*P. multocida* subspecies *multocida, P. multocida* subspecies *septica,* and *P. multocida* subspecies *gallicida*. Of 159 strains recovered from 46 infected humans, 95 were identified as *P. multocida* subspecies *multocida* and 21 as *P. multocida* subspecies *septica,* the remainder being divided among multiple other species.[16] The use of serology in conjunction with DNA fingerprinting can classify isolates for epidemiologic studies.[46]

Immunity to *P. multocida* can be demonstrated in many animals, and vaccines have been developed with known efficacy, especially in birds and cattle. However, the precise mechanisms involved in this immunity and, more important, in natural immunity are being elucidated. Antibodies to both somatic and capsular antigenic determinants develop within 2 weeks of clinical infection, with the capsular antibodies being longer lasting.[5] The precise role of these antibodies in human host defenses is not clear. Woolcock and Collins[47] have developed models in pathogen-free mice that may help uncover these mechanisms. The efficacy of heat-killed vaccine has been shown to be considerable when multiple doses are used. However, with the use of an aerogenic mouse model for the stimulation of respiratory spread, the protection is reduced. Local instillation of the vaccine can be used with this model to develop local antibodies, but preliminary results show protection only with modest challenge doses.[3] A footpad inoculation model may help elucidate the mechanisms in local human infections.

Transmission

The organism is found in the oral flora of many different animals. As many as 67 percent of cats may harbor this organism in their mouths or throats. Smith[35] found that *P. multocida* could be recovered from the tonsils of 54 percent and from the nose of 10 percent of dogs. Schipper[34] grew it from 14 percent of wild rats trapped in the Baltimore area.

Hansmann and Tully[14] demonstrated that *P. multocida* may remain as a commensal for prolonged periods in the mouth of a cat. They described a patient who had been bitten on two occasions 3 years apart by the same healthy pet cat; each time, an abscess caused by *P. multocida* developed. It also has been isolated from lion, tiger, panther, buffalo, mink, and opossum.[4, 17]

Although verifying the mode of transmission has been easiest when an infection has been related specifically to a pet or farm animal, many cases of infection caused by *P. multocida* have been documented despite a negative history of such exposure. Respiratory infection with this organism has been described in veterinarians, farmers, milkmen, and persons employed where animal tissues are processed. Meningitis caused by *P. multocida* has been described in a patient after undergoing brain surgery in which rabbit muscle was used for hemostasis.

The possibility of a reservoir of infection in humans with resultant interhuman transmission rarely has been considered. In a study of veterinary students, Smith[35] described 2 of 71 with positive throat isolations. The organisms were present in one for a few days and in the other for the full 4 months of the study; both patients were asymptomatic. Several other cases of isolation of the organism from the human respiratory tract, many without associated symptoms or known animal contact, have been made.

In addition, interhuman spread by nasopharyngeal excretions, feces, and urine also is a possibility because the organism has been recovered from these sites. The female genital tract is another potential source, especially for cases of septicemia and meningitis that occur during pregnancy and in the newborn period.

Investigators of an outbreak in a chronic disease hospital showed that *P. multocida* may be viable on a hand towel for up to 24 hours. Although the source in this outbreak was not proved, this finding may have implications for spread in other situations, particularly for pet owners.[19]

Epidemiology

P. multocida has been isolated from humans in all areas of North America and Europe, with some reports from other areas. In the United States, it is not a reportable organism, so incidence and prevalence data are unavailable. Lee and Buhr[22] have cited a seasonal variation in the number of reported cases related to dog bites, with the highest incidence being in the fall and winter months, possibly related to increased nasal carriage in dogs during that period. Other investigators have found no seasonal differences, however.[9, 18]

No difference in attack rate has been found between the sexes. The attack rate is higher in individuals of both sexes in the very young (0 to 4 years) and in older individuals (>55 years).

Pathogenesis and Pathology

In animals that are stressed, a benignly parasitic strain may invade the mucous membrane on which it is carried. With highly virulent strains, a picture of hemorrhagic septicemia may develop. It may be characterized by high fever, cardiac weakness, toxemia, and early death. Organisms can be cultured from the blood; autopsy findings may be minimal or include petechial hemorrhages on mucosal and serosal surfaces and in various organs. Less acute forms, such as a pneumonia with serofibrinous exudate in the interlobular septa of the lungs, a hemorrhagic gastroenteritis, and subacute and chronic infections such as otitis in the rabbit, may occur.

In humans, three major types of infection occur.[45] In the first and most common type, local infection occurs after a cat bite or scratch, a dog bite, or, rarely, the bite of another animal. Approximately 15 to 20 percent of dog-bite wounds and more than 50 percent of cat-bite wounds become infected. Many cases have been associated with non-bite exposure such as licking.[11] They usually are characterized by a rapidly progressive, acute cellulitis with lymphangitis, local lymphadenitis, or both. In the case of cat bites, they may progress to osteomyelitis of the underlying bone. This development is not because of any known predilection of *P. multocida* for the bone but because the sharp fangs of the cat deposit the organism on or under the periosteum.

The second type includes cases of chronic pulmonary infection in which the organism may be the only isolate or one of several organisms. Cases of bronchiectasis and empyema have been reported, usually in patients with underlying pulmonary disease. In a series of 28 cases of bronchiectasis in which the organism was recovered, it usually appeared as a secondary invader. It appears to have low pathogenicity in the respiratory tract until some other infection or physiologic disturbance decreases the natural resistance of the host, which enables active infection, most commonly liver disease such as cirrhosis, to occur.

Pasteurella infection also may be septicemic or occur with meningitis. The pathology and pathogenesis are not unlike those of other organisms.

Clinical Manifestations

In cases of local infection from a scratch or bite, the usual clinical pattern shows swelling, erythema, and tenderness within a few hours of the bite; most symptoms are manifest within the first 24 hours. A gray serous or sanguinopurulent discharge from the puncture sites may be present. Signs of systemic toxic effects, such as chills and fever, may or may not be present; regional lymphadenopathy often is evident. Less commonly, the infection may be lower grade and smoldering.[29] As noted, osteomyelitis and tenosynovitis most often occur after cat bites because of the sharpness of cats' teeth.

Lee and Buhr[22] found *P. multocida* to be the most common infecting organism in a report of 69 dog bites that had been cultured; 20 of the bites became grossly infected, and *P. multocida* was isolated from 10. Of 30 wounds that were sutured, 14 (47%) were infected with *P. multocida*.

Other unusual localized infections include chronic skin ulcers, secondary infection of a gouty joint, and infection of a compound fracture site and an amputation site.[41] Preexisting joint disease appears to be a risk.

Clinical manifestations of those patients having respiratory complaints are not unusual. Most of the isolates have been associated with chronic bronchitis, bronchiectasis, chronic sinusitis or otitis media, and pneumonia. Several cases of massive pulmonary abscesses, pleural effusion, and empyema also have been reported. Larsen and Holden[21] described a 14-year-old girl with chronic otitis media for 2 years who developed a *P. multocida* cerebellar abscess. A case of epiglottitis caused by this organism has been reported in an adult.[20] A child has developed Ludwig angina after a non-bite exposure.

In a report of 136 cases of *P. multocida* infection that were not related to animal bites, the most common site of infection after the respiratory tract was the abdomen; the organism was recovered from 10 patients with appendicitis.

Eight isolates were from the female reproductive tract, four from the urine, and one from a chronic sacral abscess.[18] Whether these cases are secondary to ingestion of the organism or to hematogenous spread has not been determined. Raffi and colleagues[28] described three children with appendiceal peritonitis associated with *P. multocida*.

The disseminated infections are the other major clinical group of *Pasteurella* infections. Isolated bacteremia may be present[27]; however, most of these cases have been meningitis, many of which were mistaken for *H. influenzae* or *Neisseria meningitidis* infection because of the morphologic similarities among these organisms. In a review of the subject in 1967, Controni and Jones[7] noted 14 confirmed cases of *Pasteurella* meningitis; 11 occurred in adults and 3 in children. Eight of the 14 patients had a history of accidental or surgical trauma. The mortality rate was 50 percent, but only five patients were treated with antibiotics. Evaluation of the cerebrospinal fluid showed white blood cell counts from 580 to 5200/mm^3, all with a predominance of polymorphonuclear leukocytes.

That review included one newborn infant who died of *Pasteurella* meningitis at 88 hours of age.[1] The mother had a fever in the postpartum period, but her pretreatment cultures were lost, so verification of the source was impossible.[7] Since then, a case of *Pasteurella* chorioamnionitis associated with premature delivery and neonatal sepsis and death within 1.5 hours of delivery has been reported.[37] Gingival cultures of a pet cat that had scratched a mother numerous times during pregnancy also yielded *P. multocida*. Subsequently, several young infants with septicemia and meningitis caused by this organism survived without apparent sequelae after treatment with penicillin or ampicillin and gentamicin.[2, 10, 30, 40] Another report of neonatal infection was that by Pizey[26] of a 3-week-old infant with septic arthritis. *P. multocida* infection may take a rapidly fatal course even in an older infant.[39] Clapp and associates[6] described two infants whose disease was associated with nontraumatic facial licking by pets, an avoidable exposure. In another report, a case of in utero infection at 12 weeks' gestation was described.[43]

Diagnosis and Treatment

Although *P. multocida* is one of the more likely pathogens to cause infection of cat or dog bites, its clinical manifestations are not unusual. Diagnosis of *P. multocida* infection can be made definitively only by culture. It may resemble several other organisms morphologically, but identification should not be difficult to make. The fact that it does not require X and V factors for growth should distinguish it from *H. influenzae*. Its production of indole should differentiate it from the *Neisseria* group, and its inability to grow on MacConkey or a bile salt medium should distinguish it from *Acinetobacter* spp. and the enteric organisms.

The drug of choice for *P. multocida* infection is penicillin, to which the organism is exquisitely sensitive. This feature may be used as a rapid means of distinguishing it from *H. influenzae* or the enterics. Rare strains producing β-lactamase and thus resistance to penicillins have been recovered.[32] The organism usually is sensitive to a wide variety of other antibiotics, including ampicillin, other broad-spectrum penicillins (e.g., ticarcillin, piperacillin, mezlocillin), amoxicillin—clavulanic acid,[12] tetracyclines, parenteral cephalosporins (particularly second- and third-generation),[24] cefuroxime, cefpodoxime, and chloramphenicol. Semisynthetic penicillins (e.g., nafcillin, dicloxacillin), erythromycin, some orally administered cephalosporins (cephalexin, cefaclor), clindamycin, and aminoglycosides have relatively low activity against *P. multocida*.[8, 13, 36] Azithromycin appears to have acceptable activity.[6] Trimethoprim-sulfamethoxazole may be an alternative, particularly for those unable to take a β-lactam antibiotic.[33] Surgical drainage or débridement also may be necessary. The duration of treatment depends on the primary disease process. Seven to 10 days is generally adequate for local infections.

Prognosis and Prevention

Proper cleansing and débridement of wounds caused by animal bites or scratches are important in prevention of this infection. Lee and Buhr[22] found that suturing wounds caused by dog bite was associated with a higher incidence of infection. Whether a wound is sutured often depends on site and potential cosmetic result. The use of prophylactic antibiotics to prevent infection after animal bites is controversial. Some experts recommend their use if a delay occurs in seeking medical assistance and for cat bites or for persons with immunocompromising conditions.

Limiting contact with wild and domestic animals that may harbor the organism probably is the only way to prevent infection definitely. Teaching proper handling of pets and keeping pets from licking infants and young children, particularly on the face, may help. No vaccine for human use is available.

Prognosis depends on the particular site of infection. With appropriate treatment, resolution usually occurs, but the healing process may be very slow, particularly in local infections with extension to the bone or tendons.[9, 42]

REFERENCES

1. Bates, H. A., Controni, G., Elliott, N., et al.: Septicemia and meningitis in a newborn due to *Pasteurella multocida*. Clin. Pediatr. *4*:668–670, 1965.
2. Bhave, S. A., Guy, L. M., and Rycroft, J. A.: *Pasteurella multocida* meningitis in an infant with recovery. Br. Med. J. *2*:741–742, 1977.
3. Branson, D., and Bunkfeldt, F.: *Pasteurella multocida* in animal bites of humans. Am. J. Clin. Pathol. *48*:552–555, 1967.
4. Burdge, D. R., Scheifele D., and Speart, D. P.: Serious *Pasteurella multocida* infections from lion and tiger bites. J. A. M. A. *253*:3296–3297, 1985.
5. Choudat, D., Paul, G., Legoff, C., et al.: Specific antibody responses to *Pasteurella multocida*. Scand. J. Infect. Dis. *19*:453–457, 1987.
6. Clapp, W. C., Kleiman, M. B., Reynolds, J. K., et al.: *Pasteurella multocida* meningitis in infancy. Am. J. Dis. Child. *140*:444–446, 1986.
7. Controni, G., and Jones, R. S.: *Pasteurella* meningitis: A review of the literature. Am. J. Med. Technol. *33*:379–386, 1967.
8. Fass, R. J.: Erythromycin, clarithromycin and azithromycin: Use of frequency distribution curves, scattergrams and regression analyses to compare in vitro activities and describe cross-resistance. Antimicrob. Agents Chemother. *37*:2080–2086, 1993.
9. Francis, D. P., Holmes, M. A., and Brandon, G.: *Pasteurella multocida*: Infection after domestic animal bites and scratches. J. A. M. A. *233*:42–45, 1975.
10. Frutos, A. A., Levitsky, D., Scott, E. G., et al.: A case of septicemia and meningitis in an infant due to *Pasteurella multocida*. J. Pediatr. *92*:853, 1978.
11. Goldstein, E. J. C.: Bite wounds and infection. Clin. Infect. Dis. *14*:633–640, 1991.
12. Goldstein, E. J. C., and Citron, D. M.: Comparative activities of cefuroxime, amoxicillin–clavulanic acid, ciprofloxacin, enoxacin, and ofloxacin against aerobic and anaerobic bacteria isolated from bite wounds. Antimicrob. Agents Chemother. *32*:1144–1148, 1988.
13. Goldstein, E. J. C., Citron, D. M., and Rechwald, G. A.: Lack of in vitro efficacy of oral forms of certain cephalosporins, erythromycin and oxacillin against *Pasteurella multocida*. Antimicrob. Agents Chemother. *32*:213–215, 1988.
14. Hansmann, G. H., and Tully, M.: Cat bite and scratch wounds with consequent *Pasteurella* infection of man. Am. J. Clin. Pathol. *15*:312–318, 1945.
15. Heddleston, K. L., and Wessman, G.: Characteristics of *Pasteurella multocida* of human origin. J. Clin. Microbiol. *1*:377–383, 1975.

16. Holst, E., Rollof, J., Larsson, L., et al.: Characterization and distribution of *Pasteurella* species recovered from humans. J. Clin. Microbiol. *30*:2984–2987, 1992.
17. Hubbert, W. T., and Rosen, M. N.: *Pasteurella multocida* infection due to animal bite. Am. J. Public Health *60*:1103–1108, 1970.
18. Hubbert, W. T., and Rosen, M. N.: *Pasteurella multocida* infection in man unrelated to animal bite. Am. J. Public Health *60*:1109–1117, 1970.
19. Itoh, M., Tierno, P. M., Milstoc, M., et al.: A unique outbreak of *Pasteurella multocida* in a chronic disease hospital. Am. J. Public Health *70*:1170–1173, 1980.
20. Johnson, R. H., and Rumans, L. W.: Unusual infections caused by *Pasteurella multocida*. J. A. M. A. *237*:146–147, 1977.
21. Larsen, T. E., and Holden, F. A.: Isolation of *Pasteurella multocida* from an otogenic cerebellar abscess. Can. Med. Assoc. J. *101*:629–630, 1969.
22. Lee, M. L. H., and Buhr, A. J.: Dog bites and local infection with *Pasteurella septica*. Br. Med. J. *1*:169–171, 1960.
23. Nielsen, J. P., and Rosdahl, V. T.: Development and epidemiological applications of a bacteriophage typing system for typing *Pasteurella multocida*. J. Clin. Microbiol. *28*:103–107, 1990.
24. Noel, G. T., and Teele, D. W.: In vitro activities of selected new and long-acting cephalosporins against *Pasteurella multocida*. Antimicrob. Agents Chemother. *29*:344–345, 1986.
25. Oberhofer, T. R.: Characteristics and biotypes of *Pasteurella multocida* isolated from humans. J. Clin. Microbiol. *13*:566–577, 1981.
26. Pizey, N. C. D.: Infection with *Pasteurella septica* in a child aged three weeks. Lancet *2*:324–326, 1953.
27. Raffi, F., Barrier, J., Baron, D., et al.: *Pasteurella multocida* bacteremia: Report of thirteen cases over twelve years and review of the literature. Scand. J. Infect. Dis. *19*:385–393, 1987.
28. Raffi, F., David, A., Mouzard, A., et al.: *Pasteurella multocida* appendiceal peritonitis: Report of three cases and review of the literature. Pediatr. Infect. Dis. *5*:695–698, 1986.
29. Reinert, P., Canet, J., Pesnel, G., et al.: Une cause souvent ignorée d'arthrite subaiguë chez l'enfant; la pasteurellose à *P. multocida*. Arch. Fr. Pediatr. *29*:99–104, 1972.
30. Repice, J. P., and Neter, E.: *Pasteurella multocida* meningitis in an infant with recovery. J. Pediatr. *86*:91–93, 1975.
31. Rimler, R. B., and Rhoades, K. R.: Serogroup F, a new capsule serogroup of *Pasteurella multocida*. J. Clin. Microbiol. *25*:615–618, 1987.
32. Rosenau, A., Labigne, A., Escande, F. et al.: Plasmid-mediated ROB-1 β-lactamase in *Pasteurella multocida* from a human specimen. Antimicrob. Agents Chemother. *35*:2419–2422, 1991.
33. Sands, M., Ashley, R., and Brown, R.: Trimethoprim-sulfamethoxazole therapy of *Pasteurella multocida* infection. J. Infect. Dis. *160*:353–354, 1989.
34. Schipper, G. J.: Unusual pathogenicity of *Pasteurella multocida* isolated from the throats of common wild rats. Bull. Johns Hopkins Hosp. *81*:333–356, 1947.
35. Smith, J. E.: Studies on *Pasteurella septica*. I. Occurrence in nose and tonsils of dogs. J. Comp. Pathol. *65*:239–245, 1955.
36. Stevens, D. L., Higbee, J. W., Oberhofer, T. R., et al.: Antibiotic susceptibilities of human isolates of *Pasteurella multocida*. Antimicrob. Agents Chemother. *16*:322–324, 1979.
37. Strand, C. L., and Helfman, L.: *Pasteurella multocida* chorioamnionitis associated with premature delivery and neonatal sepsis and death. Am. J. Clin. Pathol. *55*:713–716, 1971.
38. Swartz, M. N., and Kunz, L. J.: *Pasteurella multocida* infection in man. N. Engl. J. Med. *261*:889–893, 1959.
39. Tessin, I., Brorson, J. E., and Trollfors, B.: Rapidly fatal *Pasteurella multocida* septicemia in infant following cat scratch. Pediatr. Infect. Dis. *6*:425–426, 1987.
40. Thompson, C. M., Pappu, L., Levkoff, A. H., et al.: Neonatal septicemia and meningitis due to *Pasteurella multocida*. Pediatr. Infect. Dis. *3*:559–561, 1984.
41. Tindall, J. P., and Harrison, C. M.: *Pasteurella multocida* infections following animal injuries, especially cat bites. Arch. Dermatol. *105*:412–416, 1972.
42. Torphy, D. E., and Ray, C. G.: *Pasteurella multocida* in dog and cat bite infections. Pediatrics *43*:295–297, 1969.
43. Waldor, M., Roberts, D., and Kazanjian, P.: In utero infections due to *Pasteurella multocida* in the first trimester of pregnancy: Case report and news. Clin. Infect. Dis. *14*:497–500, 1992.
44. Weber, D. J., and Hausen, A. R.: Infections resulting from animal bites. Infect. Dis. Clin. North Am. *5*:663–680, 1991.
45. Weber, D. J., Wolfson, J. S., Swartz, M. N., et al.: *Pasteurella multocida* infections: Report of 34 cases and review of the literature. Medicine (Baltimore) *63*:133–154, 1984.
46. Wilson, M. A., Rimbler, R. B., and Hoffman, L. J.: Comparison of DNA fingerprints and somatic serotypes of serogroup B and E *Pasteurella multocida* isolates. J. Clin. Microbiol. *30*:1518–1524, 1992.
47. Woolcock, J. B., and Collins, F. M.: Immune mechanism in *Pasteurella multocida*-infected mice. Infect. Immun. *13*:949–958, 1976.

Cholera

BLANCA E. GONZALEZ ■ GERALD T. KEUSCH ■ JESUS G. VALLEJO

Cholera is a disease caused by infection with the gram-negative bacterium *Vibrio cholerae*. The disease is characterized by severe, watery diarrhea, which can lead rapidly to significant dehydration with a mortality rate of 50 percent if appropriate therapy is not instituted. At least 5.5 million cholera cases are reported each year worldwide. Even though rarely diagnosed in the United States and other developed countries, cholera continues to kill a significant number of children in developing countries. More than 20,000 people died of epidemic cholera in less than 4 weeks during the 1994 Rwandan refugee crisis.[34] The emergence of a new serogroup of *Vibrio cholerae,* O139 Bengal, the first serogroup of *V. cholerae* other than O1 shown to cause epidemic severe cholera, has raised concern about the ability to control this potentially deadly disease.[1, 18, 45, 93]

Microbiology

V. cholerae is a motile, gram-negative curved rod that belongs to the family *Vibrionaceae* and shares common characteristics with the family *Enterobacteriaceae.* It measures 1.4 to 2.6 μm in length and is a curved bacillus with a single polar flagellum. *V. cholerae* strains are grouped on the basis of their somatic O antigens.[59] At least 140 serogroups have been identified, but only *V. cholerae* organisms carrying the somatic antigens O1 and O139 are associated with epidemic cholera. The two serotypes of *V. cholerae* O1, termed *Ogawa* and *Inaba,* are distinguishable by agglutination in specific antisera. In addition, two biotypes known as classic and El Tor vibrios are recognized. Each biotype can express either Ogawa or Inaba antigens; hence, four distinct *V. cholerae* O1 strains exist. Biotype also is a useful marker for epidemiologic study. Although some non-O1 *V. cholerae* serogroup organisms cause diarrhea, none aside from O139 is known to produce cholera toxin (CTX), and none has caused epidemic cholera.

On Gram stain, motility cannot be observed, and the curved comma shape of the organism is not readily apparent. However, *V. cholerae* O1 or O139 can be observed easily under darkfield microscopy. The chaotic movement and the high number of bacteria seen in stool samples from patients with clinical disease are characteristic of *V. cholerae* infection.[5] A presumptive diagnosis of cholera can be made immediately by adding *Vibrio* antisera, which results in cessation of motility of only the homologous organism. Although making a rapid diagnosis is desirable, especially in epidemic situations, definitive confirmation still requires isolation of the bacteria. Specific medium is needed to optimize isolation of *V. cholerae* from stool. The two media most commonly used to isolate *V. cholerae* from stool are thiosulfate citrate bile salts sucrose agar and tellurite taurocholate gelatin agar. Selective media used routinely to differentiate enteric pathogens do not support the growth of all *V. cholerae*.

Pathogenesis

Infection with *V. cholerae* occurs after the ingestion of contaminated food or water. The infectious dose of bacteria varies with the vehicle. When water is the source, 10^3 to 10^6 bacteria are needed to cause disease. In contrast, when the vehicle is food, 10^2 to 10^4 bacteria will cause clinical symptoms. Gastric acid rapidly kills ingested vibrios, but the infectious dose can be reduced by 10,000-fold or more when an experimental inoculum is administered to adults with sodium bicarbonate or food to buffer the gastric acid.[13, 14] Conditions that reduce gastric acidity increase the risk of development of infection and predispose the patient to more severe disease. The relationship of achlorhydria and cholera susceptibility is well described.[30]

Once past the stomach, organisms must colonize the upper part of the small bowel and multiply, or they will be cleared rapidly by specific and nonspecific host defenses, including secretory antibody and peristalsis. Experimental studies suggest that a vibrio must be capable of adhering to the brush border of jejunal epithelial cell to be virulent.[29] Attachment to intestinal epithelial cells is mediated by the TcpA pilus,[90] which is synthesized in parallel with CTX because both genes are regulated at the transcriptional level by *toxR*.[55] Expression of TcpA is essential for virulence in humans, and though a poor antigen itself, TcpA increases antibody responses to other vibrio antigens.[41] Within the gut lumen, *V. cholerae* multiplies and produces the protein enterotoxin CTX. The toxin has five B subunits and one A subunit. The B subunits allow CTX to bind to a specific membrane receptor on the intestinal epithelial cell, monosialosyl G_{M1} ganglioside.[28] Activation of adenylate cyclase by the A1 component of CTX results in a net increase in cyclic adenosine monophosphate, which in turn blocks the absorption of sodium and chloride by microvilli and promotes the secretion of chloride and water by crypt cells. These physiologic changes result in the secretion of an isotonic fluid at a rate that exceeds the absorptive capacity of the colon.

Epidemiology

V. cholerae is a salt-water organism with an established niche in the marine ecosystem, where it lives in intimate association with plankton.[25, 95] Humans are infected incidentally, but the chances of becoming infected can be facilitated by seasonal increases in the number of organisms, possibly associated with changes in water temperature and algal blooms.[26] Where sanitary water and sewage systems are lacking, secondary transmission through contaminated water and food can result in explosive epidemics.

Cholera can be an endemic, an epidemic, or a pandemic disease. The epidemic and endemic characteristics of cholera are quite distinct. In newly exposed populations, both adults and children are affected equally. However, children are at greatest risk for development of infection once the disease becomes endemic.[3]

INCIDENCE AND GEOGRAPHY

The current seventh pandemic, caused by El Tor biotype, originated in the Island of Sulawesi, Indonesia, in 1961. It subsequently spread to become endemic in parts of Southeast Asia and sub-Saharan Africa. In 1991, *V. cholerae* El Tor biotype, serotype Inaba, emerged in Peru and spread rapidly through South and Central America and into Mexico (Fig. 121–1). In 1992, an epidemic in Madras, India, was caused by a different strain of *V. cholerae* designated O139 Bengal. This strain has been isolated only in Southeast Asia thus far.

Global figures of cholera are a gross underestimate of the actual number of cases and deaths. The absence of efficient surveillance systems in developing countries, as well as the fear of sanctions on commerce and tourism, results in underreporting.[15, 17] In 2001, 58 countries reported a total of 184,311 cases of cholera and 2728 deaths to the World Health Organization (WHO). Ninety-four percent of these cases came from Africa.[17] In contrast, only 535 cases were reported from the Americas, a substantial decrease from previous years.[17]

In the United States, the Gulf of Mexico has been known to be an aquatic reservoir of *V. cholerae* O1 since 1973. A handful of cases traceable to this reservoir occur annually, usually caused by the ingestion of uncooked shellfish.[10] Between 1995 and 2000, 61 cases of cholera from 18 states and two territories of the United States were reported to the Centers for Disease Control and Prevention.[89] Sixty-one percent of the cases were associated with travel, and 14 percent were acquired by the ingestion of contaminated food, especially seafood. To date, no large-scale outbreaks of cholera have occurred because of the general adequacy of environmental sanitation and chlorination of water supplies. The Gulf strain of *V. cholerae* O1, biotype El Tor, has a different ribotype than that of the strain causing the current pandemic,[98] thus enabling differentiation of imported from domestic strains.

TRANSMISSION AND RESERVOIRS

Humans and water are the two main reservoirs of *V. cholerae*. Even though it has been isolated from animals,[81] their role in the transmission of cholera remains negligible. In endemic areas, most primary infections result from the ingestion of contaminated water. Secondary cases then occur by fecal-oral spread of the organism through food or domestic water supplies.[44, 56, 61, 91] Person-to-person transmission appears to be uncommon.[60] Infection rates are highest in communities where adequate sanitation of drinking water cannot be ensured and personal and community hygiene standards are low. People traveling to such endemic areas are at risk of acquiring the infection even when they are strict about observing basic precautions regarding water and food.[8, 11, 16, 88, 101] The incubation period usually is between 1 and 3 days, with a range of a few hours to 5 days.

SEASONALITY

Cholera outbreaks tend to occur during the warm months. Recent studies suggest that an increase in ocean water temperatures as a result of global warming has had an effect on cholera epidemics.[25, 38, 66] *V. cholerae* can remain dormant in aquatic environments in a nonculturable but viable state.[43, 95] When aquatic conditions are conducive to growth,

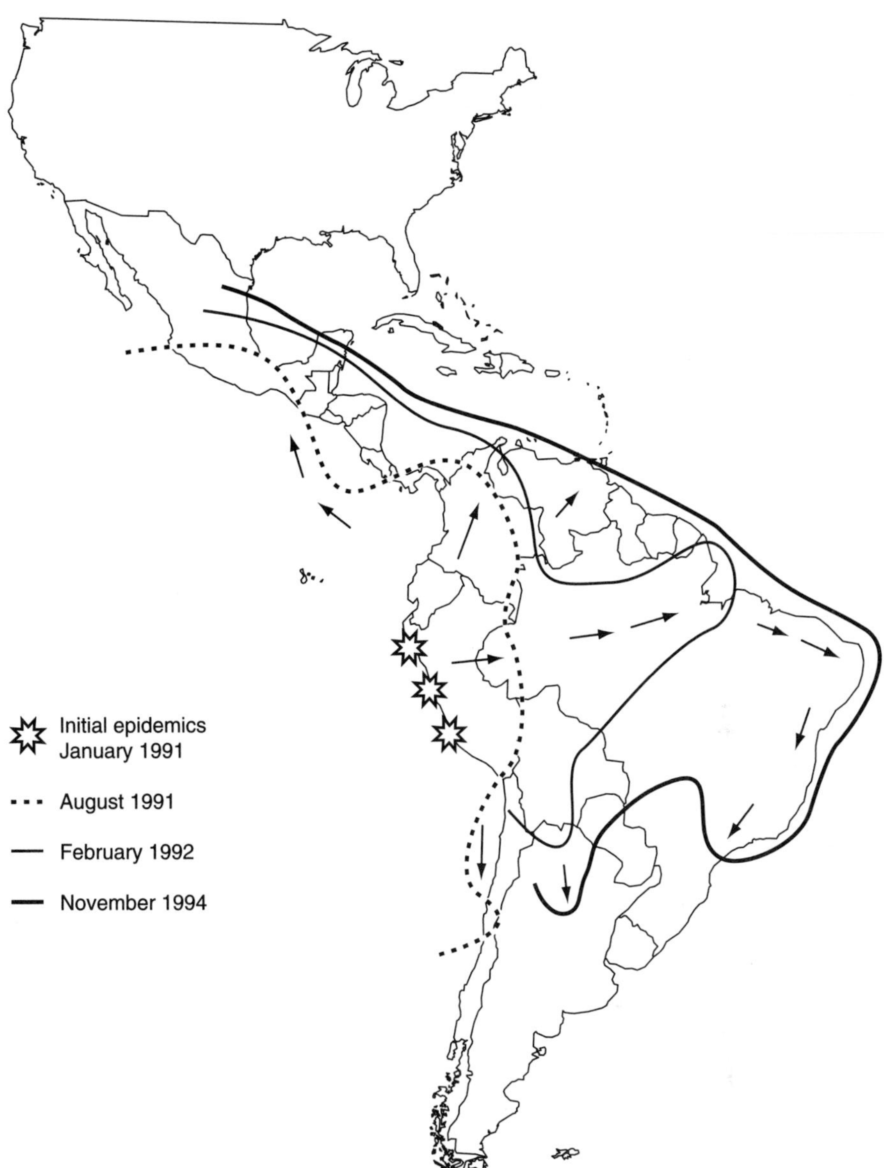

FIGURE 121–1 ■ The time course of the spread of *Vibrio cholerae* O1 in the Americas, 1991 to 1994, is shown in this map of the Western Hemisphere. (Courtesy of Dr. Robert V. Tauxe, Centers for Disease Control and Prevention, Atlanta.)

V. cholerae proliferates.[25] This reservoir plays an important role in the seasonal variations. In a 33-year observational study in Bangladesh, outbreaks were predicted by an increase in temperature and concentrations of cyanobacteria in local waters.[53]

HOST FACTORS

Gastric acidity has been shown to be important in containing *V. cholera* before it colonizes the small intestine. Therefore, patients who become achlorhydric for any reason are at higher risk of acquiring infection.[19, 30, 63] Data from Bangladesh suggested that patients with *Helicobacter pylori* infection, particularly those who lacked natural vibriocidal immunity, were at higher risk for the development of severe cholera.[19] The role of the O blood group is less certain, but in cholera-endemic areas, people with the O blood group have twice the risk of having severe cholera as do those of other blood groups.[31, 86, 92] Breast-feeding conveys protection to children during cholera outbreaks because of less exposure and because they obtain antibodies to cholera in breast milk.[21, 32]

Clinical Manifestations

The clinical characteristics of cholera are caused by massive fluid and electrolyte losses. Stool volume during cholera is greater than that of any other infectious diarrhea.[58] Patients with severe disease may have a stool volume of more than 250 mL/kg body weight in a 24-hour period.[58, 73] Although early in the course of illness the stool may contain fecal material, the characteristic cholera stool is an opaque white liquid that is not malodorous. Cholera stool often is described as having a rice-water appearance. Abdominal cramps, presumably caused by distention of loops of small bowel as a result of the large volume of intestinal secretions, are common symptoms. Vomiting is a prominent manifestation of illness in both the early[22] and later courses of illness.[6, 39] If untreated, the diarrhea and vomiting lead to isotonic dehydration and, in patients with severe disease, vascular

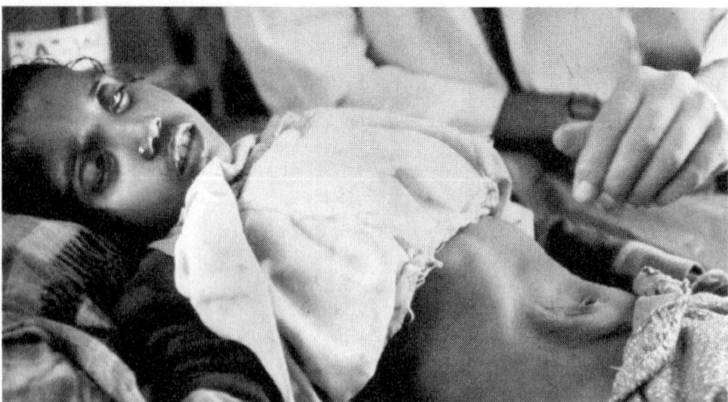

FIGURE 121–2 ■ An adolescent girl with severe dehydration from cholera. Characteristic features include obtundation, sunken eyes, and "tenting" of the abdominal skin and subcutaneous tissues after firmly pinching the abdomen.

collapse, shock, and death.[11] Dehydration can develop within hours after the onset of symptoms. Because the dehydration is isotonic, the water loss is proportional among the three body compartments, intracellular, intravascular, and interstitial.

Patients with severe dehydration have a characteristic clinical appearance that is attributable to the loss of approximately 15 percent of total-body water (approximately 10% of total-body weight). Intracellular and intravascular dehydration is manifested as decreased skin turgor (Fig. 121–2), sunken eyes, and wrinkled ("washer woman") hands, whereas decreased intravascular volume is manifested as tachycardia, peripheral pulses that are absent or barely palpable, and hypotension. Tachypnea and hypercapnia are also part of the clinical picture and are attributable to the metabolic acidosis that invariably is present in patients with cholera who are dehydrated.[6] Altered mental status is a common occurrence but usually is mild and can be manifested as somnolence, restlessness, or lethargy.

After dehydration, hypoglycemia is the most common lethal complication of cholera in children.[6] The mortality rate in children with cholera and hypoglycemia admitted to a diarrhea treatment center in Bangladesh was 15 percent, as opposed to less than 1 percent in cholera patients without hypoglycemia.[6] Hypoglycemia is a result of exhaustion of glycogen stores and defective gluconeogenesis. Acidosis in cholera is a result of bicarbonate loss in stool, accumulation of lactate because of diminished perfusion of peripheral tissues, and hyperphosphatemia.[99, 100] Severely dehydrated children invariably have serum bicarbonate concentrations less than 15 mmol/L and often less than 5 mmol/L.[73] Acidemia occurs when respiratory compensation is unable to sustain a normal blood pH.

Hypokalemia also results from potassium loss in stool, with a mean potassium concentration of approximately 30 mmol/L (Table 121–1). Because of the coexisting acidosis, however, children often have normal serum potassium concentrations when first seen, despite having severe total-body potassium depletion, and hypokalemia develops only after the acidosis is corrected and intracellular hydrogen ion is exchanged for extracellular potassium.[73, 76, 100] Hypokalemia is most severe in children with preexisting malnutrition who have diminished body stores of potassium and may be manifested as paralytic ileus. Although electrocardiographic changes associated with hypokalemia are seen frequently, severe cardiac arrhythmias rarely are observed.

Laboratory Findings and Diagnosis

The major laboratory derangements in cholera patients can be attributed to alterations in intravascular volume and electrolyte concentrations.[11, 39] Hematocrit, serum-specific gravity, and serum protein are elevated in dehydrated patients because of the resulting hemoconcentration. Serum sodium usually is 130 to 135 mmol/L as a result of the substantial loss of sodium in stool that has accompanied the loss of water.[73] As noted earlier, serum potassium usually is normal in the acute phase of illness because intracellular potassium is exchanged for extracellular hydrogen ion in an effort to correct the acidosis. The bicarbonate concentration usually is less than 15 mmol/L in severely dehydrated patients and often is undetectable.[99, 100] Blood urea nitrogen and serum creatinine are elevated as a result of the decrease in glomerular filtration. Patients generally have a leukocytosis without a left shift when first seen.

Definitive diagnosis depends on isolation of *V. cholerae* in stool. Because few laboratories in the United States perform routine culture for *V. cholerae*, clinicians should request that specimens be inoculated into appropriate media if cholera is suspected. A sensitive, immediate direct diagnostic method pioneered by the International Centre for Diarrhoeal Disease Research, Bangladesh, uses darkfield microscopy to demonstrate the characteristically motile organism in stool,[5] but virtually no laboratory outside cholera-endemic regions will have experience with this method. Latex agglutination tests

TABLE 121–1 ■ ELECTROLYTE CONCENTRATION IN CHOLERA STOOL AND IN FLUIDS USED FOR REHYDRATION AND REPLACEMENT OF STOOL LOSSES

	Electrolyte Concentration (mmol/L)				
	Na^+	*Cl^-*	*K^+*	*HCO_3*	**Osmolality**
Cholera stool					
Adults	130	100	20	44	300*
Infants and children	100	90	33	30	300*
Hydration solutions					
WHO oral rehydration	90	80	20	30†	220‡
Intravenous					
Dhaka	133	98	13	48	273
Lactated Ringer	130	109	4	28§	251
5 : 4 : 1	129	97	11	44	281

*Osmolality includes unmeasured osmotically active molecules (primarily organic acids) in addition to electrolytes.
†As citrate.
‡From electrolytes only; also contains 111 mmol/L of glucose.
§As lactate.
WHO, World Health Organization.

have been developed, but their sensitivities have not been satisfactory.[24, 85] New and simple enzyme immunoassay kits for both O1 and O139 organisms, such as the SMART test, have been created and compare very favorably with culture methods, but they are unlikely to be available in U.S. clinical microbiology laboratories, and they undoubtedly will be too expensive to use in developing countries, where cholera is endemic.[40, 70, 74] DNA-based methods, including polymerase chain reaction and oligoprobes, also have been developed.[57, 97]

Treatment

Before the development of effective regimens for replacing fluid and electrolytes, the mortality rate in severe disease was more than 50 percent.[68] With the development of effective intravenous and oral rehydration solutions, no patient who reaches a cholera treatment center alive should die of the disease.

INTRAVENOUS FLUIDS

If fluid replacement is initiated early in the course of illness, dehydration can be prevented. If it is started after dehydration has occurred, both preexisting and continuing fluid losses must be treated. The two possible routes of fluid administration are oral and parenteral. All patients with severe dehydration ideally should be rehydrated with intravenous fluids because they produce a more rapid and more predictable expansion of intracellular volume in hypovolemic patients than oral solutions do. Intravenous solutions also should be used to maintain hydration in patients who are purging heavily because oral fluids will fail to sustain hydration in most such patients.[65]

Many field facilities treating cholera patients, especially during epidemics, will not have the benefit of having staff experienced in treating severely dehydrated patients, and establishing intravenous lines in these situations will be problematic on occasion. Parenteral fluids also can be given effectively via intraosseous infusion, a method now gaining increasing acceptance in pediatric emergency units throughout the world.[33] Although the intraperitoneal route has been used, it is not recommended.[75] If intravenous fluids cannot be provided immediately, oral fluids should be administered without delay. Oral fluids can be given via nasogastric tube to severely dehydrated patients who are obtunded or unconscious.[72] Rehydration of severely dehydrated patients with intravenous fluids can be accomplished within 2 to 4 hours.[42, 73] The volume of fluid to be administered is determined by the rate of stool losses and the degree of preexisting dehydration (Table 121–2). Patients with severe dehydration initially require 100 mL/kg body weight, and

TABLE 121–2 ■ TREATMENT OF CHOLERA

	Fluid Therapy			
	Replacement Fluids		*Maintenance Fluids*	
Degree of Dehydration	**Type of Fluid to Use**	**Volume of Fluid to Administer**	**Type of Fluid to Use**	**Volume of Fluid to Administer**
Severe	Intravenous	100–120 mL/kg over 2–4 hr	Intravenous if purging >10 mL/kg body weight/hr; oral if purging ≤10 mL/kg	To match stool output and insensible loss
Some or moderate	Intravenous or oral	60–80 mL/kg over 2–4 hr	Intravenous if purging >10 mL/kg body weight/hr; oral if purging ≤10 mL/kg	To match stool output and insensible loss
None or mild	—	—	Oral	Provide frequently, with thirst and stool frequency used as a guide

Antimicrobial Therapy*

Agent	*Single Dose*	*Multiple Dose*
Doxycycline†	7 mg/kg; maximal dose, 300 mg‡	Two doses of 2 mg/kg on day 1; single dose of 2 mg/kg on days 2 and 3; maximal single dose, 100 mg
Tetracycline†	25 mg/kg; maximal dose, 1 g‡	40 mg/kg/day divided into 4 doses for 3 days; maximal dose, 2 g/day
Furazolidone	7 mg/kg; maximal dose, 300 mg‡	5 mg/kg/day divided into 4 doses for 3 days; maximal dose, 400 mg/day
Ciprofloxacin§	30 mg/kg; maximal dose, 1 g‡	30 mg/kg/day divided into 2 doses for 3 days; maximal dose, 1 g/day
Trimethoprim-sulfamethoxazole	Not evaluated	8 mg of trimethoprim, 40 mg of sulfamethoxazole/kg/day divided into 2 doses for 3 days; maximal doses, 320 mg trimethoprim and 1.6 g sulfamethoxazole daily
Ampicillin	Not evaluated	50 mg/kg/day divided into 4 doses for 3 days; maximal dose, 2 g/day
Erythromycin	Not evaluated	40 mg/kg/day erythromycin base divided into 3 doses for 3 days; maximal dose, 1 g/day

*Antimicrobial therapy is an adjunct to fluid therapy for cholera and is not an essential component. It will, however, reduce diarrhea volume and duration by approximately 50 percent. The choice of antimicrobial agent is determined by the susceptibility pattern of local strains of *Vibrio cholerae* O1 or O139. Resistance to all agents except fluoroquinolones, such as ciprofloxacin, has been reported and is commonplace in some areas.

†Both tetracycline and doxycycline can discolor the permanent teeth of children younger than 8 years. The risk is small when these drugs are used for short courses of therapy, especially if used in a single dose.

‡Single-dose therapy with these drugs has not been evaluated systematically in children, and recommendations are extrapolated from experience in adults.

§The fluoroquinolones, such as ciprofloxacin, are not approved for use in children younger than 18 years in the United States because when given in high dose to juvenile animals, they cause arthropathy. Clinical experience indicates that this risk is very small in children when used for short courses of therapy.

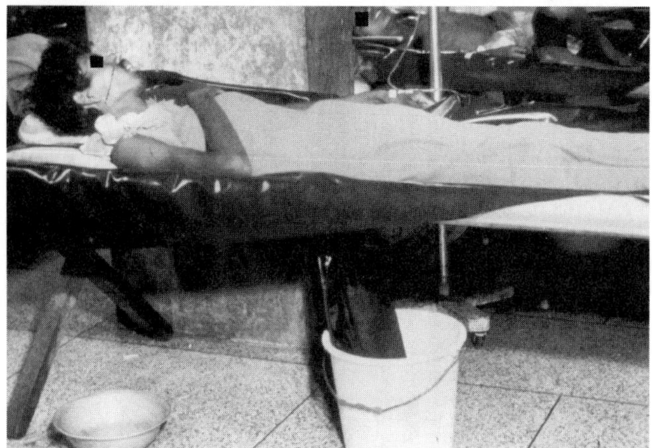

FIGURE 121–3 ■ A cholera cot: a simple folding cot covered with plastic that has a hole and bucket for collecting the stool output, as used for the care of cholera patients at the International Centre for Diarrhoeal Disease Research in Bangladesh. The bucket is calibrated, and the volume of stool (and replacement fluids required) can be calculated easily. The plastic sheet is cleaned daily and between patients.

patients with moderate dehydration require 60 to 80 mL/kg body weight.

In endemic countries, the volume of ongoing stool loss can be monitored by keeping patients on a cholera cot covered by a plastic sheet with a hole in the center to allow the stool to collect in a calibrated bucket underneath. Use of such a cot allows minimally trained health workers to calculate fluid losses and replacement needs (Fig. 121–3). The volume of stool is measured every 2 to 4 hours, and the volume of fluid administered is adjusted accordingly. In the initial phase of therapy, urine losses will account for only a small proportion of the total fluid losses, and the amount of fluid in the bucket is an adequate reflection of stool losses.[6] With rehydration, an effort to collect urine separately is useful; otherwise, a vicious circle of supplying ever greater amounts of fluid to replace urine losses will ensue. A risk of overhydration with intravenous fluids exists and usually is manifested first as puffiness around the eyes. Continued excessive administration of intravenous fluids can lead to pulmonary edema, even in children with normal cardiovascular reserve. Serum-specific gravity is an additional measure of the adequacy of rehydration.

The ideal intravenous solution for the treatment of children with cholera contains electrolytes in concentrations similar to those found in cholera stools.[42, 102] It also should contain dextrose to prevent the development of hypoglycemia. Numerous solutions that approximate these requirements are available (see Table 121–2). Although normal saline has been used to treat cholera patients, it does not correct the severe acidosis that accompanies cholera as quickly as bicarbonate-containing solutions do and does not replace potassium.[9] Because of the inevitable fall in serum potassium that accompanies the administration of bicarbonate-rich fluids in cholera patients, potassium should be included in the initial fluid regimen, even though urination might not occur for 4 or more hours.[73, 100]

ORAL THERAPY

Oral rehydration therapy was made possible by the discovery that, despite the reduction in sodium absorption across the small intestine caused by the action of CTX, the glucose-coupled sodium chloride co-transport mechanism remains intact.[27, 42, 78] Thus, solutions that contain sodium chloride and glucose or glucose-yielding carbohydrates, such as sucrose[65] or oligosaccharides derived from cereal starches,[69] can be used to replace the fluid losses that occur during cholera. Oral rehydration therapy can be provided in many different forms: as prepackaged sachets containing glucose and electrolytes, which then are dissolved in water; as ready-to-use glucose-electrolyte solutions; or as a rice polymer–based electrolyte solution.[4] Oral rehydration solution also can be prepared from home ingredients either as a solution of sucrose and salt or as a suspension of a powdered cereal (rice, wheat, maize, and sorghum all have been used successfully), water, and salt. The choice of which solution to use is entirely pragmatic because little difference in efficacy exists among preparations if they are used appropriately. Although some studies have suggested that cereal-based suspensions reduce diarrhea in children with cholera better than glucose-containing solutions do,[35] the latter remains more readily available in most cholera-endemic regions.

The electrolyte concentration of the oral solution currently recommended by the WHO for use in the treatment of cholera is shown in Table 121–1.[102] The use of solutions with lower sodium concentrations, such as solutions containing 60 mmol/L or less of sodium that are used routinely in the United States and Europe and now are being evaluated by the WHO for wider use,[62] may not be appropriate for use in cholera patients because they cannot replace adequately the high sodium loss in cholera stools. Patients treated with such solutions are at risk for development of clinically important hyponatremia. Oral rehydration solutions can have an enormous impact on the logistics of treating cholera patients, especially in epidemic conditions. The routine use of oral, rather than intravenous, solutions to maintain hydration at cholera treatment facilities can reduce requirements for intravenous solutions by up to 80 percent.[83] Sole reliance on oral solutions, however, will result in a higher mortality rate.[84]

For oral therapy to be used effectively, an adult (ideally the parents or another caretaker) must remain with the child to provide oral rehydration and encourage its intake.[4, 6] Parents need to be instructed in the appropriate use of oral rehydration solution, including the caveats that occasional vomiting is not a contraindication to beginning or continuing its use and that, if necessary, the oral rehydration solution should be offered in smaller amounts more frequently.

ANTIMICROBIAL THERAPY

The administration of effective antimicrobial agents decreases the duration and volume of diarrhea and shortens the period of excretion of *V. cholerae*.[7, 37] As such, antibiotic therapy is an important, but not essential, adjunct to fluid therapy for cholera, particularly during epidemics. Few studies have been conducted to evaluate antimicrobial treatment of pediatric cholera.[46, 47, 50, 52, 72] Hence, most of the treatments available for children are extrapolated from experience with adult patients. Tetracycline administered for 3 days or a single dose of doxycycline is the treatment of choice for cholera caused by *V. cholerae* O1 and O139 Bengal in children older than 8 years of age.[2] In younger children, tetracyclines generally are avoided because of the risk of staining the teeth; however, in cases of severe cholera, the benefits are likely to outweigh the risk. Trimethoprim-sulfamethoxazole is an alternative treatment for children younger than 8 years of age.

Almost all *V. cholerae* O139 strains are resistant to furazolidone and trimethoprim-sulfamethoxazole, but most strains have been susceptible to tetracycline.[1] Where tetracycline-resistant strains are uncommon findings, single-dose therapy with doxycycline or furazolidone probably remains the treatment of choice because of their low cost and efficacy. In addition, furazolidone is the drug of choice when treating pregnant women. In areas where tetracycline resistance is a common occurrence, ampicillin, trimethoprim-sulfamethoxazole, erythromycin, and single-dose ciprofloxacin are possible options.[7, 12, 36, 48, 49] Although concern exists about the use of fluoroquinolones in pediatric patients because of toxicity studies in juvenile animals that show damage to joint cartilage when these drugs are used in high doses, little evidence indicates that short courses of therapy in children cause this problem.[82] The use of a single dose of azithromycin was evaluated recently in a randomized double-blind trial of children 1 to 15 years of age in Bangladesh.[50] This regimen was found to be as effective as a 3-day course of erythromycin. However, the cost and availability of this drug in developing countries may preclude its widespread use. In areas where cholera is endemic and transmission rates are high, prophylactic treatment of household contacts with antibiotics may decrease transmission rates, but not without the risk of resistance developing if used indiscriminately.[54] Because secondary rates of transmission are low in the United States, prophylactic regimens are not recommended. Specific recommendations for antimicrobial therapy are shown in Table 121–2.

As a result of increasing resistance, antimicrobial susceptibility studies should be performed on all isolates when possible. Because results may not be available for 48 to 72 hours, knowledge of the resistance patterns of the *V. cholerae* strains circulating in the community is important.[7]

Prevention

Cholera vaccines have been available for more than 100 years. A better understanding of virulence factors and immunogenic antigens has led to advances in vaccine development. Currently, three vaccines are licensed for the prevention of cholera throughout the world.[79, 87] However, none is available in the United States because the manufacture and sale of them have been discontinued.

The parenteral vaccine currently available contains 10^9 phenol-inactivated *V. cholerae* O1 organisms (classic and El Tor Inaba and Ogawa serotypes). The vaccine is approximately 50 percent effective for 3 to 6 months against *V. cholerae* O1 and confers no protection against *V. cholerae* O139.[79] Revaccination every 6 months is required to produce ongoing protection. When used in endemic regions, it had higher efficacy in adults, thus suggesting a boosting effect on an already existing immune response.[17] In contrast, it conferred little, if any, protection in children, the population at highest risk in endemic regions. This finding, along with the adverse side effects experienced by most recipients of the vaccine, has limited its use.

A whole-cell B subunit (WC-BS) vaccine containing the nontoxic B subunit of cholera toxin (CtxB) and 10^{11} killed *V. cholerae* O1 organisms (classic and El Tor) is available in oral form. In the largest field trial performed in Bangladesh,[17, 79] individuals received three doses of the vaccine at 6-week intervals. During the first 6 months of the study, the vaccine provided equal protection (85%) in both young and older children. However, at 36 months, the protective effect was lowest (26%) in children 2 to 5 years of age, with 62 percent efficacy noted in children older than 5 years of age. At 3 years, the long-term efficacy of WC-BS was lower against infections caused by the El Tor biotype than against infections caused by the classic biotype.[20] Interestingly, a recent 33-year study analyzing trends in epidemic and endemic cholera in Bangladesh found no difference in the protection afforded by this vaccine against either cholera biotype.[53] A recombinant version of the CtxB component of WC-BS also is manufactured (WC-rBS). The protective efficacy of WC-rBS against cholera caused by *V. cholerae* O1 El Tor biotype in adult military personnel in Peru (86%) was similar to that induced by WC-BS in the Bangladesh study.[79,80]

A second-generation, killed, whole-cell vaccine was developed by the National Institute of Hygiene and Epidemiology in Hanoi in response to the increasing number of cases caused by the new Bengal serotype.[96, 103] This vaccine includes both the O1 and O139 serogroups (biv-WC vaccine). A recent clinical trial in Vietnamese adults and children compared WC-rBS with this new bivalent vaccine.[96] The bivalent vaccine was well tolerated and elicited a measurable immune response in most vaccinees. However, studies are needed to evaluate its protective efficacy.

The third type of vaccine available is an oral, live attenuated vaccine (CVD103-HgR). It is a derivative of the *V. cholerae* O1 classic stain and is null for the *ctxA* gene.[51, 79, 87] A single dose of this vaccine elicited an increase in vibriocidal antibody in 92 percent of North American volunteers.[17, 94] Although a large, double-blind, placebo-control study from Indonesia confirmed the immunogenicity of a single dose of the vaccine, it was not shown to protect against cholera in this area, where infection is endemic.[17, 77] As with all live vaccines, their use in immunocompromised populations and the emergence of vaccine-related cases are concerns. Data from Mali confirmed the safety of CVD103-HgR in human immunodeficiency virus (HIV)-infected patients[67]; however, an attenuated immune response was noted, particularly in patients with $CD4^+$ counts less than 500/µL. Although the effect of this live vaccine on viral load in HIV-infected patients has not been evaluated, a transient increase in viral load was observed in HIV-infected patients after vaccination with a whole-cell toxin B subunit oral cholera vaccine, thus suggesting that HIV replication may be enhanced by mucosal stimulation.[64]

Still, the role of these vaccines, other than their use in emergency situations, needs to be better defined. Therefore, adequate disposal of human feces, access to safe drinking water, and use of good food hygiene are essential to avoid or contain epidemics. Cooking food thoroughly, washing hands after defecation, and chlorination of or simply boiling water all are measures that will effectively prevent the acquisition of cholera in endemic and epidemic situations. In 1999, the WHO recommended use of the oral recombinant WC-rBS vaccine in populations that were not experiencing outbreaks but were thought to be at risk of having a cholera epidemic within 6 months.[17, 102, 103] No recommendations have been issued regarding the use of these vaccines in endemic situations. Because travelers to endemic areas are considered to be at low risk of acquiring infection and because of the brief immunity that the vaccines confer, the WHO eliminated the requirement for cholera vaccine to gain entry or leave an endemic area.[102, 103]

Advice to Travelers

For people traveling to countries where cholera is endemic, the WHO has issued the following recommendations:

- Drink only water that has been boiled or disinfected with iodine, chlorine, or other acceptable products.
- Avoid using ice unless it is made from safe water.

- Eat food that has been cooked thoroughly and is still hot when served.
- Avoid eating raw foods, especially seafood. Peel fruits and vegetables yourself.
- Avoid drinking unpasteurized milk.
- Avoid eating ice cream from unreliable sources.
- If buying food from street vendors, make sure that it is thoroughly cooked in your presence.

More information for travelers is available at *www.who.int/ith/* or *www.cdc.gov*.

REFERENCES

1. Albert, M. J.: Minireview: *Vibrio cholerae* O139 Bengal. J. Clin. Microbiol. *32*:2345–2349, 1994.
2. American Academy of Pediatrics: Vibrio infections. *In* Pickering, L. K. (ed.): 2000 Red Book: Report of the Committee on Infectious Diseases. 25th ed. Elk Grove Village, IL, American Academy of Pediatrics, 2000, pp. 638–640.
3. Barau, D., and Greenough, W. B. III (eds.): Cholera. New York, Plenum, 1992, p. 129.
4. Behrens, R. H.: Diarrhoeal disease: Current concepts and future challenges: The impact of oral rehydration and other therapies on the management of acute diarrhoea. Trans. R. Soc. Trop. Med. Hyg. *87*(Suppl. 3):35–38, 1993.
5. Benenson, A. S., Islam, M. R., and Greenough, W. B., III: Rapid identification of *Vibrio cholerae* by darkfield microscopy. Bull. World Health Organ. *30*:827–831, 1964.
6. Bennish, M. L.: Cholera: Pathophysiology, clinical features, and treatment. *In* Wachsmuth, I. K., Blake, P. A., and Olsvik, O. (eds.): *Vibrio cholerae* and Cholera: Molecular to Global Perspectives. Washington, D.C., American Society of Microbiology, 1994, pp. 229–255.
7. Bennish, M. L., and Levy, S. B.: Antimicrobial resistance of enteric pathogens. *In* Blaser, J. M., Smith, P. D., and Ravdin, J. I. (eds.): Infections of the Gastrointestinal Tract. New York, Raven Press, 1995, pp. 1499–1523.
8. Besser, R. E., Feikin, D. R., Eberhart-Phillips, J. E., et al.: Diagnosis and treatment of cholera in the United States: Are we prepared? J. A. M. A. *272*:1203–1205, 1994.
9. Biesel, W. R., Watten, R. H., Blackwell, R. Q., et al.: The role of bicarbonate pathophysiology and therapy in Asiatic cholera. Am. J. Med. *35*:58–66, 1963.
10. Blake, P. A.: Epidemiology of cholera in the Americas. Gastroenterol. Clin. North Am. *22*:639–660, 1993.
11. Boyce, T. G., Mintz, E. D., Greene, K. D., et al.: *Vibrio cholerae* O139 Bengal infections among tourists to southeast Asia: An intercontinental foodborne outbreak. J. Infect. Dis. *172*:1401–1404, 1995.
12. Burans, J. P., Podgore, J., Mansour, M. M., et al.: Comparative trial of erythromycin and sulpha-trimethoprim in the treatment of tetracycline-resistant *Vibrio cholerae* O1. Trans. R. Soc. Trop. Med. Hyg. *83*:836–838, 1989.
13. Cash, R. A., Music, S. I., Libonati, J. P., et al.: Response of man to infection with *Vibrio cholerae*. I. Clinical, serologic, and bacteriologic responses to a known inoculum. J. Infect. Dis. *129*:45–52, 1974.
14. Cash, R. A., Music, S. I., Libonati, J. P., et al.: Response of man to infection with *Vibrio cholerae*. II. Protection from illness afforded by previous diseases and vaccine. J. Infect. Dis. *130*:325–333, 1974.
15. Centers for Disease Control and Prevention: Cholera—worldwide, 1989. M. M. W. R. Morb. Mortal. Wkly. Rep. *39*(21):365–367, 1990.
16. Centers for Disease Control and Prevention: Cholera associated with international travel, 1992. M. M. W. R. Morb. Mortal. Wkly. Rep. *41*(36):664–667, 1992.
17. Cholera, 2001. Wkly. Epidemiol. Rec. *77*:257–264, 2002.
18. Cholera Working Group, International Centre for Diarrhoeal Disease Research, Bangladesh: Large epidemic of cholera-like disease in Bangladesh caused by *Vibrio cholerae* 0139 synonym Bengal. Lancet *342*:387–390, 1993.
19. Clemens, J., Albert, M. J., Rao, M., et al.: Impact of infection by *Helicobacter pylori* on the risk and severity of endemic cholera. J. Infect. Dis. *171*:1653–1656, 1995.
20. Clemens, J. D., Sack, D. A., Harris, J. R., et al.: Field trial of oral cholera vaccines in Bangladesh: Results from long-term follow-up. Lancet *1*:270–273, 1990.
21. Clemens, J. D., Sack, D. A., Harris, J. R., et al.: Breast feeding and the risk of severe cholera in rural Bangladeshi children. Am. J. Epidemiol. *131*:400–411, 1990.
22. Collins, B. J., Van Loon, F. P. L., Molla, A., et al.: Gastric emptying of oral rehydration solutions in acute cholera. J. Trop. Med. Hyg. *92*:290–294, 1989.
23. Colwell, R. R.: Global climate and infectious disease: The cholera paradigm. Science *274*:2025–2031, 1996.
24. Colwell, R. R., Hasan, J. A., Huq, A., et al.: Development and evaluation of a rapid, simple, sensitive, monoclonal antibody-based co-agglutination test for direct detection of *Vibrio cholerae* O1. F. E. M. S. Microbiol. Lett. *76*:215–219, 1992.
25. Colwell, R. R., and Huq, A.,: Environmental reservoir of *Vibrio cholerae:* The causative agent of cholera. Ann. N. Y. Acad. Sci. *740*:44–54, 1994.
26. Epstein, P. R.: Algal blooms in the spread and persistence of cholera. Biosystems *31*:209–221, 1993.
27. Field, M., Rao, M. C., and Chang, E. B.: Intestinal electrolyte transport and diarrheal diseases. N. Engl. J. Med. *321*:800–806, 879–883, 1989.
28. Finkelstein, R. A.: Cholera, the cholera enterotoxins, and the cholera enterotoxin-related enterotoxin family. *In* Owen, P., and Foster, T. J. (eds.): Immunochemical and Molecular Genetic Analysis of Bacterial Pathogens. New York, Elsevier, 1988, pp. 85–102.
29. Finkelstein, R. A., Boesman-Finkelstein, M., Chang, Y., et al.: *Vibrio cholerae* hemagglutinin-protease, colonial variation, virulence, and detachment. Infect. Immun. *60*:472–478, 1992.
30. Gitelson, S.: Gastrectomy, achlorhydria and cholera. Isr. J. Med. Sci. *7*:663–667, 1971.
31. Glass, R. I., Holmgren, J., Haley, C. E., et al.: Predisposition for cholera of individuals with O blood group: Possible evolutionary significance. Am. J. Epidemiol. *121*:791–796, 1985.
32. Glass, R. I., Svennerholm, A.-M., Stoll, B. J., et al.: Protection against cholera in breast-fed children by antibodies in breast milk. N. Engl. J. Med. *308*:1389–1392, 1983.
33. Goldstein, B., Doody, D., and Briggs, S.: Emergency intraosseous infusion in severely burned children. Pediatr. Emerg. Care *6*:195–197, 1990.
34. Goma Epidemiology Group: Public health impact of Rwandan refugee crisis: What happened in Goma, Zaire, in July, 1994? Lancet *345*:339–344, 1995.
35. Gore, S. M., Fontaine, O., and Pierce, N. F.: Impact of rice-based oral rehydration solution on stool output and duration of diarrhoea: Meta-analysis of 13 clinical trials. B. M. J. *304*:287–291, 1992.
36. Gottuzo, E., Seas, C., Echevarria, J., et al.: Ciprofloxacin for the treatment of cholera: A randomized, double-blind, controlled clinical trial of a single daily dose in Peruvian adults. Clin. Infect. Dis. *20*:1485–1490, 1995.
37. Greenough, W. B., III, Gordon, R. S., Rosenberg, I. S., et al.: Tetracycline in the treatment of cholera. Lancet *1*:355–357, 1964.
38. Harvell, C. D., Mitchell, C. E., Ward, J. R., et al.: Climate warming and disease risks for terrestrial and marine biota. Science *296*:2158–2162, 2002.
39. Harvey, R. M., Enson, Y., Lewis, M. L., et al.: Hemodynamic studies on cholera: Effects of hypovolemia and acidosis. Circulation *37*:709–728, 1968.
40. Hasan, J. A., Huq, A., Tamplin, M. L., et al.: A novel kit for rapid detection of *Vibrio cholerae* O1. J. Clin. Microbiol. *32*:249–252, 1994.
41. Herrington, D. A., Hall, R. H., Losonsky, G. A., et al.: Toxin, toxin-coregulated pili and the *tox*R regulon are essential for *Vibrio cholerae* pathogenesis in humans. J. Exp. Med. *168*:1487–1492, 1988.
42. Hirschhorn, N.: The treatment of acute diarrhea in children: An historical and physiological perspective. Am. J. Clin. Nutr. *33*:637–663, 1980.
43. Huq, A., Colwell, R. R., Rahman, R., et al.: Detection of *Vibrio cholerae* O1 in the aquatic environment by fluorescent-monoclonal antibody and culture methods. Appl. Environ. Microbiol. *56*:2370–2373, 1990.
44. Islam, M. S., Hasan, M. K., Miah, M. A., et al.: Isolation of *Vibrio cholerae* O139 synonym Bengal from the aquatic environment in Bangladesh: Implications for disease transmission. Appl. Environ. Microbiol. *60*:1684–1686, 1994.
45. Jesudason, M. V., and John, T. J.: The appearance and spread of *Vibrio cholerae* O139 in India. Ind. J. Med. Res. *99*:97–100, 1994.
46. Kabir, I., Khan, W. A., Haider, R., et al.: Erythromycin and trimethoprim-sulphamethoxazole in the treatment of cholera in children. J. Diarrhoeal Dis. Res. *14*:243–247, 1996.
47. Karchmer, A. W., Curlin, G. T., Huq, M. I., and Hirschhorn, N.: Furazolidone in paediatric cholera. Bull. World Health Organ. *43*:373–378, 1970.
48. Khan, W. A., Begum, M., Salam, M. A., et al.: Comparative trial of five antimicrobial compounds in the treatment of cholera in adults. Trans. R. Soc. Trop. Med. Hyg. *89*:103–106, 1995.
49. Khan, W. A., Bennish, M. L., Seas, C., et al.: Randomised, controlled comparison of single-dose ciprofloxacin and doxycycline for cholera caused by *Vibrio cholerae* O1 or O139. Lancet *348*:296–300, 1996.
50. Khan, W. A., Saha, D., Rahman, A. , et al.: Comparison of single-dose azithromycin and 12-dose, 3-day erythromycin for childhood cholera: A randomised, double-blind trial. Lancet *360*:1722–1727, 2002.
51. Levine, M. M., Kaper, J. B., Herrington, D., et al.: Safety, immunogenicity, and efficacy of recombinant live oral cholera vaccines, CVD 103 and CVD 103-HgR. Lancet *2*:467–470, 1988.
52. Lindenbaum, J., Greenough, W. B., and Islam, M. R.: Antibiotic therapy of cholera in children. Bull. World Health Organ. *37*:529–538, 1967.
53. Longini, I. M., Jr., Yunus, M., Zaman, K. et al.: Epidemic and endemic cholera trends over a 33-year period in Bangladesh. J. Infect. Dis. *186*:246–251, 2002.
54. McCormack, W. M., Chowdhury, A. M., Jahangir, N., et al.: Tetracycline prophylaxis in families of cholera patients. Bull. World Health Organ. *38*:787–792, 1968.

55. Mekalanos, J. J., Swartz, D. J., Pearson, G. D. N., et al.: Cholera toxin genes: Nucleotide sequence, deletion analysis, and vaccine development. Nature *306*:551–557, 1983.
56. Miller, C. J., Feachem, R. G., and Drasar, B. S.: Cholera epidemiology in developed and developing countries: New thoughts on transmission, seasonality, and control. Lancet *1*:261–263, 1985.
57. Miyagi, K., Matsumoto, Y., Hayashi, K., et al.: Successful application of enzyme-labeled oligonucleotide probe for rapid and accurate cholera diagnosis in a clinical laboratory. Microbiol. Immunol. *38*:301–304, 1994.
58. Molla, A. M., Rahman, M., Sarker, S. A., et al.: Stool electrolyte content and purging rates in diarrhea caused by rotavirus, enterotoxigenic *E. coli*, and *V. cholerae* in children. J. Pediatr. *98*:825–838, 1981.
59. Morris, J. G., Jr.: Non-O group 1 *Vibrio cholerae* strains not associated with epidemic disease. *In* Wachsmuth, I. K., Blake, P. A., and Olsvik, O. (eds.): *Vibrio cholerae* and Cholera: Molecular to Global Perspectives. Washington, D.C., American Society of Microbiology, 1994, pp. 103–115.
60. Mosley, W. H., Alvero, M. G., Joseph, P. R., et al.: Studies of cholera El Tor in the Philippines. 4. Transmission of infection among neighborhood and community contacts of cholera patients. Bull. World Health Organ. *33*:651–660, 1965.
61. Mujica, O. J., Quick, R. E., Palacios, A. M., et al.: Epidemic cholera in the Amazon: The role of produce in disease risk and prevention. J. Infect. Dis. *169*:1381–1384, 1994.
62. Multicentre evaluation of reduced-osmolarity oral rehydration salts solution: International Study Group on reduced-osmolarity ORS solutions. Lancet *345*:282–285, 1995.
63. Nalin, D. R., Levine, M. M., Rhead, J., et al.: Cannabis, hypochlorhydria, and cholera. Lancet *2*:859–862, 1978.
64. Ortigao-de-Sampaio, M. B., Shattock, R. J., Hayes, P., et al.: Increase in plasma viral load after oral cholera immunization of HIV-infected subjects. A. I. D. S. 12:F145–F150, 1998.
65. Palmer, D. L., Koster, F. T., Islam, A. F. M. R., et al.: Comparison of sucrose and glucose in the oral electrolyte therapy of cholera and other severe diarrheas. N. Engl. J. Med. *297*:1107–1110, 1977.
66. Pascual, M., Rodo, X., Ellner, S. P., et al.: Cholera dynamics and El Nino–Southern Oscillation. Science *289*:1766–1769, 2000.
67. Perry, R. T., Plowe, C. V., Koumare, B., et al.: A single dose of live oral cholera vaccine CVD 103-HgR is safe and immunogenic in HIV-infected and HIV-noninfected adults in Mali. Bull. World Health Organ. *76*:63–71, 1998.
68. Phillips, R. A.: Twenty years of cholera research. J. A. M. A. *202*:610–613, 1967.
69. Pizzaro, D., Posada, G., Sandi, L., et al.: Rice-based oral electrolyte solutions for the management of infantile diarrhea. N. Engl. J. Med. *324*:517–521, 1991.
70. Qadri, F., Hasan, J. A., Hossain, J., et al.: Evaluation of the monoclonal antibody–based kit Bengal SMART for rapid detection of *Vibrio cholerae* O139 synonym Bengal in stool samples. J. Clin. Microbiol. *33*:732–734, 1995.
71. Rabbani, G. H., Butler, T., Knight, J., et al.: Randomized, controlled trial of berberine sulfate therapy for diarrhea due to enterotoxigenic *Escherichia coli* and *Vibrio cholerae.* J. Infect. Dis. *155*:979–984, 1987.
72. Rabbani, G. H., Butler, T., Shahrier, M., et al.: Efficacy of single dose of furazolidone for treatment of cholera in children. Antimicrob. Agents Chemother. *35*:1864–1867, 1991.
73. Rahman, O., Bennish, M. L., Alam, A. N., et al.: Rapid intravenous rehydration by means of a single polyelectrolyte solution with or without dextrose. J. Pediatr. *113*:654–660, 1988.
74. Ramamurthy, T. S., Bhattacharya, S. K., Uesaka, Y., et al.: Evaluation of the bead enzyme-linked immunosorbent assay for detection of cholera toxin directly from stool specimens. J. Clin. Microbiol. *30*:1783–1786, 1992.
75. Ransome-Kuti, O., Elebute, O., Agusto-Odutola, T., et al.: Intraperitoneal fluid infusion in children with gastroenteritis. B. M. J. *3*:500–503, 1969.
76. Rapoport, S. M., Dodd, M., Clark, M., et al.: Postacidotic state of infantile diarrhea: Symptoms and chemical data: Postacidotic hypocalcemia and associated decreases in levels of potassium, phosphorus, and phosphatase in the plasma. Am. J. Dis. Child. *73*:391–441, 1947.
77. Richie, E. E., Punjabi, N. H., Sidharta, Y. Y., et al.: Efficacy trial of single-dose live oral cholera vaccine CVD 103-HgR in North Jakarta, Indonesia, a cholera-endemic area. Vaccine *18*:2399–2410, 2000.
78. Ruxin, J. N.: Magic bullet: The history of oral rehydration therapy. Med. Hist. *38*:363–397, 1994.
79. Ryan, E. T., and Calderwood, S. B.: Cholera vaccines. Clin. Infect. Dis. *31*:561–565, 2000.
80. Sanchez, J. L., Vasquez, B., Begue, R. E., et al.: Protective efficacy of oral whole-cell/recombinant-B-subunit cholera vaccine in Peruvian military recruits. Lancet *344*:1273–1276, 1994.
81. Sanyal, S. C., Singh, S. J., Tiwari, I. C., et al.: Role of household animals in maintenance of cholera infection in a community. J. Infect. Dis. *130*:575–579, 1974.
82. Schaad, U. B., Salam, M. A., Aujard, Y., et al.: Use of fluoroquinolones in pediatrics: Consensus report of an International Society of Chemotherapy commission. Pediatr. Infect. Dis. J. *14*:1–9, 1995.
83. Siddique, A. K., Mutsuddy, P., Islam, Q., et al.: Makeshift treatment centre during a cholera epidemic in Bangladesh. Trop. Doct. *20*:83–85, 1990.
84. Siddique, A. K., Salam, A., Islam, M. S., et al.: Why treatment centres failed to prevent cholera deaths among Rwandan refugees in Goma, Zaire. Lancet *345*:359–361, 1995.
85. Shaffer, N., Silva do Santos, E., Andreason, P. A., et al.: Rapid laboratory diagnosis of cholera in the field. Trans. R. Soc. Trop. Med. Hyg. *83*: 119–120, 1989.
86. Shahinian, M. L., Passaro, D. J., Swerdlow, D. L., et al.: *Helicobacter pylori* and epidemic *Vibrio cholerae* O1 infection in Peru. Lancet *355*:377–378, 2000.
87. Shears, P.: Recent developments in cholera. Curr. Opin. Infect. Dis. *14*:553–558, 2001.
88. Snyder, J. D., and Blake, P. A.: Is cholera a problem for US travelers? J. A. M. A. *247*:2268–2269, 1982.
89. Steinberg, E. B., Greene, K. D., Bopp, C. A., et al.: Cholera in the United States, 1995–2000: Trends at the end of the twentieth century. J. Infect. Dis. *184*:799–802, 2001.
90. Sun, D., Mekalanos, J. J., and Taylor, R. K.: Antibodies directed against the toxin-coregulated pilus isolated from *Vibrio cholerae* provide protection in the infant mouse experimental cholera model. J. Infect. Dis. *161*:1231–1236, 1990
91. Swerdlow, D. L., Mintz, E. D., Rodriguez, M., et al.: Waterborne transmission of epidemic cholera in Trujillo, Peru: Lessons for a continent at risk. Lancet *340*:28–33, 1992.
92. Swerdlow, D. L., Mintz, E. D., Rodriguez, M., et al.: Severe life-threatening cholera associated with blood group O in Peru: Implications for the Latin American epidemic. J. Infect. Dis. *170*:468–472, 1994.
93. Swerdlow, D. L., and Ries, A. A.: *Vibrio cholerae* non-01: The eighth pandemic? Lancet *342*:382–383, 1993.
94. Tacket, C. O., Cohen, M. B., Wasserman, S. S., et al.: Randomized, double-blind, placebo-controlled, multicentered trial of the efficacy of a single dose of live oral cholera vaccine CVD 103-HgR in preventing cholera following challenge with *Vibrio cholerae* O1 El Tor Inaba three months after vaccination. Infect. Immun. *67*:6341–6345, 1999.
95. Tamplin, M. L., Gauzens, A. L., Huq, A., et al.: Attachment of *Vibrio cholerae* serogroup O1 to zooplankton and phytoplankton of Bangladesh waters. Appl. Environ. Microbiol. *56*:1977–1980, 1990.
96. Trach, D. D., Cam, P. D., Ke, N. T., et al.: Investigations into the safety and immunogenicity of a killed oral cholera vaccine developed in Viet Nam. Bull. World Health Organ. *80*:2–8, 2002.
97. Varela, P., Pollevick, G. D., Rivas, M., et al.: Direct detection of *Vibrio cholerae* in stool samples. J. Clin. Microbiol. *32*:1246–1248, 1994.
98. Wachsmuth, I. K., Evins, G. M., Fields, P. I., et al.: The molecular epidemiology of cholera in Latin America. J. Infect. Dis. *167*:621–626, 1993.
99. Wang, F., Butler, T., Rabbani, G. H., et al.: The acidosis of cholera: Contributions of hyperproteinemia, lactic acidemia, and hyperphosphatemia to an increased anion gap. N. Engl. J. Med. *315*:1591–1595, 1986.
100. Watten, R. H., Morgan, F. M., Songkhla, Y. N., et al.: Water and electrolyte studies in cholera. J. Clin. Invest. *38*:1879–1889, 1959.
101. Weber, J. T., Levine, W. C., Hopkins, D. P., et al.: Cholera in the United States, 1965–1991: Risks at home and abroad. Arch. Intern. Med. *154*:551–556, 1994.
102. World Health Organization: Programme for Control of Diarrhoeal Disease: Guidelines for Cholera Control. Geneva, World Health Organization, 1991.
103. World Health Organization. Department of Communicable Disease Surveillance and Response: Potential use of oral cholera vaccines in emergency situations. Report of a WHO meeting. Geneva, May 12–13, 1999, pp. 1–13.

CHAPTER 122

Vibrio parahaemolyticus

THOMAS G. CLEARY

Vibrio parahaemolyticus is recognized worldwide as a cause of food-borne disease associated with consumption of seafood, in particular crustaceans and mollusks, and occasionally as a cause of wound infections and sepsis in immunocompromised hosts.

Not surprisingly, the first association of *V. parahaemolyticus* seafood-related diarrhea was reported in Japan; 40 to 60 percent of food-borne outbreaks in Japan are caused by this pathogen.[32] Almost 10 years after the first description, the organism was classified correctly in the genus *Vibrio,*[7] and its distribution in coastal waters and estuaries of temperate climates around the world was recognized. The regional differences in the incidence of this disease clearly are related to patterns of consumption of marine products and practices of food preparation. In Japan, fish and shellfish are a major source of dietary protein and customarily are eaten raw; in the United States, where sporadic outbreaks have been reported,[4, 5, 15, 16, 47] seafood more typically is cooked.[12] Nevertheless, the potential risk for development of infectious and toxic syndromes from marine products exists in the United States.[23]

Bacteriology

V. parahaemolyticus belongs to the group of 12 species of the genus *Vibrio* that are human pathogens and have brackish water as their natural habitat. Vibrios are gram-negative, non–spore-forming, straight or curved rods with rounded ends that possess a polar flagellum.[39] When grown on solid media, *V. parahaemolyticus* has additional shorter lateral peritrichous flagella. It is a facultative anaerobe with both respiratory and fermentative metabolisms. Like most vibrios, it is an oxidase-positive nonfermenter of lactose.[6] It is arginine dihydrolase negative and ornithine decarboxylase positive. The requirement of sodium and enhancement of growth in a specific range of concentration differentiate it from *Vibrio cholerae* and *Vibrio mimicus*. The optimal sodium concentration range is 2 to 4 percent; a concentration higher than 8 percent inhibits its growth.[62]

V. parahaemolyticus produces round, blue-green colonies on the widely used *Vibrio*-selective thiosulfate citrate bile salts sucrose. This medium inhibits most fecal flora by the presence of bile salts and a highly alkaline pH. Direct plating on thiosulfate citrate bile salts sucrose may be used for feces and other clinical specimens, but food samples that are not heavily contaminated require enrichment either in alkaline peptone water supplemented with 3 percent sodium chloride or in a strongly selective medium, such as glucose salt teepol broth.[62] The optimal pH for growth is in the neutral range, but *V. parahaemolyticus* can survive in alkaline media. It may survive storage at 5° C. Growth beyond 44° C is inhibited, and inactivation is greater with increased temperatures; for example, a million-fold decline occurs in viable bacteria in shrimp homogenate kept at 100° C for only 1 minute.[60] Growth is remarkable in conventional media and foodstuff, with generation times as low as 8 minutes[32]; thus, a significant number of organisms can be found after a short period of inappropriate storage.

V. parahaemolyticus can be grouped serologically into 11 O and 71 K serotypes. K antigens associate with specific somatic antigens[12]; so, for example, serotypes K3 and K28 associate with the O2 group. Environmental and clinical isolates do not differ in biochemical characteristics or in the presence of plasmids.[35] Plasmid carriage appears to be sporadic and not related to virulence but can be associated with resistance to multiple antibiotics.[31] Although many serotypes infect humans, the O3:K6 strains currently are causing pandemic disease, with outbreaks reported from Southeast Asia, Japan, and North America.[43]

Epidemiology

In the United States, *V. parahaemolyticus* is found along the East, West, and Gulf coasts.[18, 32] Water, sediments, suspended particulates, plankton, fish, and shellfish have been shown to harbor the organism.[3, 41] The organisms are present in highest numbers in water between 17° C and 35° C containing 0.5 to 2.5 percent salinity.[31] Marked seasonal and geographic variation occurs, with maximal mean concentrations occurring during late summer and spring along the Gulf Coast.[18] The seasonal distribution correlates with outbreaks predominantly between June and October.[2]

Finfish and all types of shellfish products, including oysters, clams, crabs, and shrimp, may be involved in the transmission of the infection[31] (Table 122–1). The risk of acquiring infection is highest with seafood able to concentrate contaminants,[31] and in general, shellfish are more contaminated than are finfish.[3, 24] The density of *V. parahaemolyticus* may be 100 times greater in oysters than in water.[18] No association exists with water pollution, aerobic plate count, or fecal coliform density.[18] The levels of contamination of seafood generally are low in freshly collected oysters, with the highest mean density of only 160 bacteria/g found in the United States.[18] In market shellfish, higher counts (up to 10^3 to 10^4/g) have been reported in Japan.[12] The minimum infective dose is thought to be in the range of 10^5 to 10^7 organisms, based on volunteer feeding studies.[22] However, recent outbreaks of illness caused by oysters that met bacteriologic safety standards have raised questions about current recommendations.[16]

During the period 1973 to 1987, only 23 of 1869 food-borne disease outbreaks with known bacterial etiology reported to the Centers for Disease Control and Prevention (CDC) were caused by *V. parahaemolyticus*[4]; they accounted for 535 cases and represented less than 1 percent of the total cases. In 18 of these outbreaks, a shellfish was recognized as the food vehicle; only 1 outbreak was related to finfish. No fatal cases were reported. Contributing factors included inadequate cooking (92%), improper holding temperature (75%), and food acquired from an unsafe source (75%).[4, 5] Attack rates ranged from 24 to 86 percent, with a median of 51 percent in 13 outbreaks in the United States.[2] Most of the affected people were adults, and no patterns of unusual susceptibility by age group or gender were noted. No evidence of secondary spread was found among family members.

TABLE 122–1 ■ SELECTED OUTBREAKS OF *VIBRIO PARAHAEMOLYTICUS* INFECTION

Setting	Persons Ill/ Exposed	Symptoms	Incubation	Resolution	Medical Attention/ Hospitalization	Vehicle	Risk Factor
Picnic[14]	351/631 (56%)	D (95%), C (82%), N (68%), V (61%), HA (41%), F (27%)	16 hr (4–42 hr)	4 d (<1–10 d)	60%/2%	Steamed crab	Cross-contamination, unrefrigerated food
Chronic hospital[14]	24/100 (24%)	D (100%), C (89%), N (72%), V (44%), HA (56%), F (33%)	18 hr (4–60 hr)	3 d (<1–7 d)	No data available	Crab salad	No data available
Shrimp boil[49]	ca. 600/1200 (50%)	D, C, V, HA, F	23 hr (5–92 hr)	(few hr–1 wk)	1%/0%	Boiled shrimp	Storage temperature
International flight[43]	12/134 (9%)	D, C, V	(8–20 hr)	No data available	40%/25%	Cooked crab	Cross-contamination
Parish dinner[11]	ca. 1000/1700 (59%)	D (95%), C (92%), N (72%), HA (47%), F (47%), V (12%)	16 hr (3–76 hr)	4.6 d (<1–8 d)	26%/7.4%	Shrimp	Cross-contimination, storage temperature
Pacific Northwest[47]	209 ill	D (99%), C (88%), N (52%), V (39%), F (33%)	15 hr (4–96 hr)	3 d mean	2 hospitalized 1 death	Raw oysters	Uncooked oysters

D, diarrhea; C, cramps; N, nausea; V, vomiting; HA, headache; F, fever.

Vibrio surveillance in four Gulf Coast states (Alabama, Florida, Louisiana, and Texas) found that 67 percent of patients with primary *Vibrio* septicemia and 74 percent with gastroenteritis had eaten raw oysters in the week before illness began.[38] Between 1988 and 1997, 345 sporadic cases were reported to the CDC. The vast majority of infections were related to eating raw oysters. Most of these infections (59%) were gastroenteritis.[17]

Pathogenesis

The ability of certain strains to produce beta-hemolysis on Wagatsuma agar containing human red blood cells is related to the virulence of the bacteria; this so-called Kanagawa phenomenon is produced by a thermostable direct hemolysin (TDH).[40] This substance, unlike other hemolysins produced by *V. parahaemolyticus,* is not inactivated by heating at 100° C for 10 minutes. The hemolytic activity is not enhanced by the addition of lecithin, indicating a direct action on erythrocytes.[21, 58] The biologic activities include hemolysis of erythrocytes from various species, cytotoxicity, lethality to small experimental animals, and increased vascular permeability in rabbit skin.[58]

TDH causes an increase in intracellular calcium concentrations that triggers secretion of chloride by intestinal cells.[51, 56, 57] The association of TDH and virulence was based first on epidemiologic grounds. Kanagawa phenomenon is observed in 88 to 96 percent of strains from clinical specimens and in 1 to 2 percent of strains from environmental sources.[22, 32, 59] After the epidemiologic association was made, Kanagawa phenomenon–positive strains were found to cause accumulation of fluid in rabbit ileal loop assays, adherence to epithelial cells in tissue cultures, and invasion of intestinal mucosa.[14, 61] TDH has a molecular weight of 42,000, consisting of two subunits of 21,000.[41] It can be inactivated by trypsin or pepsin. The hemolytic activity is inhibited by neuraminidase-sensitive gangliosides, especially GT_1. Cultured mouse heart cells show abnormal conduction, suggesting cardiotoxic activity in TDH and a possible explanation for changes in electrocardiograms of humans with intestinal infection.[32, 58]

Reports of outbreaks produced by Kanagawa phenomenon–negative organisms[28] and contradictory studies of highly concentrated culture filtrates containing TDH[52] have caused doubts about the significance of Kanagawa phenomenon. The inability of antiserum to TDH to eliminate the accumulation of fluid in the rabbit ileal loop assay and the requirement of unusually high doses of purified TDH to produce pathologic results have raised questions about the role of TDH.[12] A TDH-related hemolysin (TRH) immunologically and structurally similar to TDH is present in some Kanagawa phenomenon–negative strains.[29, 54] Likewise, some variants closely related to the original TDH by molecular analysis (Vp TDH/I and Vp TDH/II) have been isolated from Kanagawa phenomenon–negative strains.[42]

After the *tdh* gene had been cloned and sequenced, researchers realized that certain strains possess the genetic material but are phenotypically incomplete. Eighty-six percent of strains with weak hemolysis in Wagatsuma agar carry the *tdh* gene but in only one copy; a smaller proportion of Kanagawa phenomenon–negative strains contains both copies.[46] Low-level expression of the *tdh* genes may be the reason for the Kanagawa phenomenon–negative phenotype.[45] Fewer than 50 percent of *trh* gene–positive strains produce TRH when examined by enzyme-linked immunosorbent assay.[54] Gene probe hybridization analysis indicates that most of the environmental Kanagawa phenomenon–negative strains do not carry DNA encoding TDH.[34] The expression of the *tdh* genes is controlled by the Vp-*toxRS* operon. The basal production of mRNA and the degree of transcriptional activation seem to be related to differences in the nucleotide sequences and strength of the promoter region.[45] The *tdh* genes are chromosomal, but some variants are found on plasmids.[42] Isogeneic *tdh* gene–negative mutants lose the ability to produce accumulation of fluid in the rabbit ileal loop assay.[44] Thermostable direct hemolysin may induce intestinal chloride secretion using GT_{1b} as a receptor and calcium as a second messenger.[50]

Some studies suggest virulence mechanisms in addition to TDH.[61] *V. parahaemolyticus* requires intestinal colonization factors to cause disease. A variety of pili and other potential colonization factors are present, but the evidence is too poor to implicate any of the candidate adhesins in virulence.[12] Adherence of *V. parahaemolyticus* to intestinal epithelial cells of rabbits[13] and human small intestine[26, 63] appears to require binding to complex carbohydrates or hemagglutinins of the host.

The occurrence of cases with grossly bloody stools[30, 47] is indirect evidence of either invasiveness or production of cytotoxin. Invasion of Caco-2 cells in culture has been demonstrated in approximately 20 percent of strains.[1] Both Kanagawa phenomenon–positive and Kanagawa phenomenon–negative strains from clinical specimens can invade and colonize the mucosal cells of the rabbit ileum, producing acute inflammation, degeneration, and erosion of the villi.[6] Vibrios can be cultured from tissue specimens of spleen, liver, and heart in experimental animals, indicating spread through the lymphatic or circulatory systems.[9]

Clinical Manifestations

The spectrum of disease varies from a mild gastroenteritis to a full-blown dysenteric syndrome. The incubation period typically is 15 hours to 24 hours, with extremes of 4 hours to 96 hours[2, 55]; the variability presumably is related to the number of organisms ingested. Resolution is expected to occur in approximately 3 days,[41] but it varies from several hours to more than 10 days.[2, 10] Fatigue may persist for a few days. Diarrhea (96%) and crampy abdominal pain (95%) are the most frequent and earliest symptoms, accompanied by nausea, vomiting, and headache in 40 to 70 percent of cases. Chills and moderate fever are less frequent (20%) occurrences.[2, 15] The diarrhea is watery and explosive,[11] with patients having as many as 15 stools during the first day. Shock caused by loss of fluid is an exceptional event.[18] Mucus is observed frequently, but grossly bloody stool is uncommon.[7, 30, 38] Small superficial ulcerations on sigmoidoscopy may be present.[7] No difference in symptoms exists in cases associated with Kanagawa phenomenon–negative strains.[28]

Extraintestinal infections occur. During the *Vibrio* Surveillance Program that started in 1989 in four Gulf Coast states, 18 to 34 percent of *V. parahaemolyticus* isolates were found to come from wound infections and 3 to 5 percent were found to be associated with septicemia.[16, 38] Wound infection occurs after contamination of skin lacerations with seawater or after direct trauma with pieces of shellfish, fishhooks, or utensils contaminated with seawater.[8] Superficial infection can extend to deeper soft tissue and may require radical surgical débridement. Septicemia is a concern in immunocompromised patients, particularly patients with leukemia[20] and those with liver disease.[19, 27] Bacteremia may occur after either wound infections[8, 20] or ingestion of seafood.[27, 49] Skin bullae,[27] intravascular hemolysis,[20] and disseminated intravascular coagulation[27] may complicate both wound and bacteremic infections.

Complications

The acute diarrheal episode requires medical attention in as many as 25 to 50 percent of cases during an outbreak but infrequently requires hospitalization.[10, 15, 38, 55] Usually, no long-term sequelae occur. Severe dehydration, shock,[30, 48] and even death (0.04% of cases in Japan) can occur.[6, 62] On the other hand, primary septicemia,[36, 38, 49] septicemia secondary to wound infection,[8, 20, 36] or septicemia secondary to gastroenteritis[27, 36] in immunosuppressed patients or in those with liver diseases may cause death.[8]

Diagnosis

Epidemiologic data are the basis for the presumptive diagnosis. In a patient with compatible symptoms, a history of recent consumption of seafood should suggest this diagnosis. Leukocytosis and fecal leukocytes may be found.[7, 30] A positive stool culture on selective media, such as thiosulfate citrate bile salts sucrose, can confirm the clinical impression. Routine use of thiosulfate citrate bile salts sucrose is not cost-effective, even in coastal areas, unless an appropriate clinical setting is available.[8, 38, 39] The use of a transport medium, such as Cary-Blair, is necessary if a delay in processing the sample is expected. Isolation of more than 10^5 *V. parahaemolyticus* from epidemiologically implicated food supports the diagnosis and identifies the vehicle.[39] A correlation between the serotype of the food and isolates from patients is not always present because multiple strains can contaminate a single food.[2] Adding an enrichment broth to the processing increases the yield of isolation.

For testing blood specimens, use of routine culture media followed by selective media is appropriate.[27, 49] Immunoassays (enzyme-linked immunosorbent assay, immunoprecipitation in agar medium, reversed passive latex agglutination) are available in research laboratories and commercially in Japan (KAP-RPLA, Denka Seiken, Tokyo; BT test, Nissui Pharmaceutical, Tokyo) to detect the TDH. Strains producing TRH may be detected by cross-reactions.[64] Serologic methods (slide agglutination) can detect H antigens in lateral flagella.[53] Gene probe hybridization[46] and polymerase chain reaction with a sequence of a highly conserved DNA fragment[37] or targeting the *tdh* gene can be used to detect low numbers of the organism in environmental and clinical specimens.

Treatment

Only supportive therapy and careful control of the fluid and electrolyte balances are required for the management of gastroenteritis. Oral rehydration usually is appropriate, although intravenous fluids may be required if massive losses of fluid occur.[7, 30, 48] Antibiotic therapy is unnecessary for this short-lived disease. In the unusual protracted episode, tetracycline or a fluoroquinolone may be of benefit for adults and older children.[6, 7, 32]

For wound infections and septicemia, antibiotics always are indicated. *V. parahaemolyticus* usually is susceptible to tetracycline. In addition, only a few strains are resistant to chloramphenicol, trimethoprim-sulfamethoxazole, third-generation cephalosporins, aztreonam, imipenem, fluoroquinolones, and aminoglycosides.[8, 20, 25, 27] Penicillins are ineffective because of the presence of β-lactamases in as many as 50 percent of isolates.[25, 33] The older cephalosporins also have poor activity.[33]

Prevention and Control

Although ensuring the lack of contamination of seafood is impossible, avoiding food-handling errors should diminish the risk of infection. A recommendation for an acceptable upper limit of 100 colony-forming units per gram of *V. parahaemolyticus* in raw shrimp has been made by the International Commission on Microbiological Specification for Foods.[31] Thorough cooking eliminates the organism.[60] Heating seafood to 60° C for 15 minutes[22] or boiling for 7 minutes[10] appears to be adequate to reduce the risk of infection. When undercooked or raw seafood is consumed, adequate prior refrigeration to preclude multiplication of organisms is important. During the preparation of seafood, special attention should be paid to possible cross-contamination. Use of the same utensils, board surfaces, or containers for fresh and recently cooked seafood should be avoided.[48, 60]

Raw seafood consumption should be discouraged, particularly for individuals at high risk for development of septicemia.[19, 36, 38]

REFERENCES

1. Akeda, Y., Nagayama, K., Yamamoto, K., and Honda, T.: Invasive phenotype of *Vibrio parahaemolyticus*. J. Infect. Dis. *176*:822–824, 1997.
2. Barker, W. H., Jr.: *Vibrio parahaemolyticus* outbreaks in the United States. Lancet *1*:551–554, 1974.
3. Baross, J., and Liston, J.: Occurrence of *Vibrio parahaemolyticus* and related hemolytic vibrios in marine environments of Washington State. Appl. Microbiol. *20*:179–186, 1970.
4. Bean, N. H., and Griffin, P. M.: Foodborne disease outbreaks in the United States, 1973–1987: Pathogens, vehicles and trends. J. Food Protect. *53*:804–817, 1990.
5. Bean, N. H., Griffin, P. M., Goulding, J. S., et al.: Foodborne disease outbreaks, 5-year summary, 1983–1987. M. M. W. R. CDC Surveill. Summ. *39*:15–57, 1990.
6. Blake, P. A.: Disease of humans (other than cholera) caused by vibrios. Annu. Rev. Microbiol. *34*:341–367, 1980.
7. Bolen, J. L., Zamiska, S. A., and Greenough, W. B.: Clinical features in enteritis due to *Vibrio parahaemolyticus*. Am. J. Med. *57*:638–641, 1974.
8. Bonner, J. R., Coker, A. S., Berryman, C. R., et al.: Spectrum of *Vibrio* infections in a Gulf Coast community. Ann. Intern. Med. *99*:464–469, 1983.
9. Boutin, B. K., Townsend, S. F., Scarpino, P. V., et al.: Demonstration of invasiveness of *Vibrio parahaemolyticus* in adult rabbits by immunofluorescence. Appl. Environ. Microbiol. *37*:647–653, 1979.
10. Caraway, C. T., Gregg, J., and McFarland, L.: *Vibrio parahaemolyticus* foodborne outbreak, Louisiana. M. M. W. R. *27*:345–346, 1978.
11. Carpenter, C. J.: More pathogenic vibrios. N. Engl. J. Med. *300*:39–41, 1979.
12. Chai, T. J., and Pace, J.: *Vibrio parahaemolyticus*. *In* Hui, Y., Gorham, J. R., and Murrel, K. D. (eds.): Foodborne Disease Handbook. New York, Marcel Dekker, 1994, pp. 395–425.
13. Chakrabarti, M. K., Sinha, A. K., and Biswas, T.: Adherence of *Vibrio parahaemolyticus* to rabbit intestinal epithelial cells *in vitro*. FEMS Microbiol. Lett. *84*:113–118, 1991.
14. Chatterjee, B. D., Mukherjee, A., and Sanyal, S. N.: Enteroinvasive model of *Vibrio parahaemolyticus*. Indian J. Med. Res. *79*:151–158, 1984.
15. Dadisman, T. A., Nelson, R., Molenda, J. R., et al.: *Vibrio parahaemolyticus* gastroenteritis in Maryland. I. Clinical and epidemiological aspects. Am. J. Epidemiol. *96*:414–426, 1973.
16. Daniels, N. A., MacKinnon, L., Bishop, R., et al.: *Vibrio parahaemolyticus* infections in the United States, 1973–1998. J. Infect. Dis. *181*:1661–1666, 2000.
17. Daniels, N. A., Ray, B., Easton, A., et al.: Emergence of a new *Vibrio parahaemolyticus* serotype in raw oysters: A prevention quandary. J. A. M. A. *284*:1541–1545, 2000.
18. DePaola, A., Hopkins, L. H., Peeler, J. T., et al.: Incidence of *Vibrio parahaemolyticus* in U. S. coastal waters and oysters. Appl. Environ. Microbiol. *56*:2299–2302, 1990.
19. Desenclos, J. A., Klontz, K. C., Wolfe, L. E., et al.: The risk of *Vibrio* illness in the Florida raw oyster eating population, 1981–1988. Am. J. Epidemiol. *134*:290–297, 1991.
20. Dobroszycki, J., Sklarin, N. T., Szilagy, G., et al.: *Vibrio parahaemolyticus* septicemia in a patient with neutropenic leukemia. Clin. Infect. Dis. *15*:738–739, 1992.
21. Douet, J. P., Castroviejo, M., Dodin, A., et al.: Purification and characterization of Kanagawa hemolysin from *Vibrio parahaemolyticus*. Res. Microbiol. *143*:569–577, 1992.
22. Doyle, M. P.: Pathogenic *Escherichia coli, Yersinia enterocolitica,* and *Vibrio parahaemolyticus*. Lancet *336*:1111–1115, 1990.
23. Eastaugh, J., and Shepherd, S.: Infectious and toxic syndromes from fish and shellfish consumption. Arch. Intern. Med. *149*:1735–1740, 1989.
24. Franca, S. M., Gibbs, D. L., Samuels, P., et al.: *Vibrio parahaemolyticus* in Brazilian coastal waters. J. A. M. A. *244*:587–588, 1980.
25. French, G. L., Woo, M. L., Hui, Y. W., et al.: Antimicrobial susceptibilities of halophilic vibrios. J. Antimicrob. Chemother. *24*:183–194, 1989.
26. Gingras, S. P., and Howard, L. V.: Adherence of *Vibrio parahaemolyticus* to human epithelial cell lines. Appl. Environ. Microbiol. *39*:369–371, 1980.
27. Hally, R. J., Rubin, R. A., Fraimow, H. S., et al.: Fatal *Vibrio parahaemolyticus* septicemia in a patient with cirrhosis. Dig. Dis. Sci. *40*:1257–1260, 1995.
28. Honda, S. I., Goto, I., Minematsu, I., et al.: Gastroenteritis due to Kanagawa negative *Vibrio parahaemolyticus*. Lancet *1*:331–332, 1987.
29. Honda, T., Ni, Y., and Miwatani, T.: Purification and characterization of a hemolysin produced by a clinical isolate of Kanagawa phenomenon–negative *Vibrio parahaemolyticus* and related to the thermostable direct hemolysin. Infect. Immun. *56*:961–965, 1988.
30. Hughes, J. M., Boyce, J. M., Aleem, A. R., et al.: *Vibrio parahaemolyticus* enterocolitis in Bangladesh: Report of an outbreak. Am. J. Trop. Med. Hyg. *27*:106–112, 1978.
31. Janda, J. M., Powers, C., Bryant, R. G., et al.: Current perspective on the epidemiology and pathogenesis of clinically significant *Vibrio* spp. Clin. Microbiol. Rev. *1*:245–267, 1988.
32. Joseph, S. W., Colwell, R. R., and Kaper, J. B.: *Vibrio parahaemolyticus* and related halophilic vibrios. Crit. Rev. Microbiol. *10*:77–124, 1983.
33. Joseph, S. W., DeBell, R. M., and Brown, W. P.: *In vitro* response to chloramphenicol, tetracycline, ampicillin, gentamicin and beta-lactamase production by halophilic vibrios from human and environmental sources. Antimicrob. Agents Chemother. *13*:244–248, 1978.
34. Kaper, J. B., Campen, R. K., Seidler, R. J., et al.: Cloning of the thermostable direct or Kanagawa phenomenon–associated hemolysin of *Vibrio parahaemolyticus*. Infect. Immun. *45*:290–292, 1984.
35. Kelly, M. T., and Dan Stroh, E. M.: Urease-positive, Kanagawa-negative *Vibrio parahaemolyticus* from patients and the environment in the Pacific Northwest. J. Clin. Microbiol. *27*:2820–2822, 1989.
36. Klontz, K. C.: Fatalities associated with *Vibrio parahaemolyticus* and *Vibrio cholerae* non-O1 infections in Florida (1981 to 1988). South. Med. J. *83*:500–502, 1990.
37. Lee, C. Y., Pan, S. F., and Chen, C. H.: Sequence of a cloned pR72H fragment and its use for detection of *Vibrio parahaemolyticus* in shellfish with the PCR. Appl. Environ. Microbiol. *61*:1311–1317, 1995.
38. Levine, W. C., and Griffin, P. M.: *Vibrio* infections on the Gulf Coast: Results of first year of regional surveillance. J. Infect. Dis. *167*:479–483, 1993.
39. McLaughlin, J. C.: *Vibrio*. *In* Murray, P. R., Baron, E. J., and Pfaller, M. A. (eds.): Manual of Clinical Microbiology. 6th ed. Washington, D.C., American Society for Microbiology, 1995, pp. 465–476.
40. Miyamoto, Y., Kato, T., Obara, Y., et al.: In vitro hemolytic characteristic of *Vibrio parahaemolyticus*: Its close correlation with human pathogenicity. J. Bacteriol. *100*:1147–1149, 1969.
41. Morris, J. G., Jr., and Black, R. E.: Cholera and other vibrios in the United States. N. Engl. J. Med. *312*:343–350, 1985.
42. Nagayama, K., Yamamoto, K., Mitawani, T., et al.: Characterization of a haemolysin related to Vp-TDH produced by a Kanagawa phenomenon–negative clinical isolate of *Vibrio parahaemolyticus*. J. Med. Microbiol. *42*:83–90, 1995.
43. Nasu, H., Iida, T., Sugahara, T., et al.: A filamentous phage associated with recent pandemic *Vibrio parahaemolyticus* O3:K6 strains. J. Clin. Microbiol. *38*:2156–2161, 2000.
44. Nishibuchi, M., Fasano, A., Russell, R. G., et al.: Enterotoxigenicity of *Vibrio parahaemolyticus* with and without genes encoding thermostable direct hemolysin. Infect. Immun. *60*:3539–3545, 1992.
45. Nishibuchi, M., and Kaper, J. B.: Thermostable direct hemolysin gene of *Vibrio parahaemolyticus*: A virulence gene acquired by a marine bacterium. Infect. Immun. *63*:2093–2099, 1995.
46. Nishibuchi, M., Ishibashi, M., Takeda, Y., et al.: Detection of the thermostable direct hemolysin gene and related DNA sequences in *Vibrio parahaemolyticus* and other *Vibrio* species by the DNA colony hybridization test. Infect. Immun. *49*:481–486, 1985.
47. Outbreak of *Vibrio parahaemolyticus* infections associated with eating raw oysters—Pacific Northwest, 1997. M. M. W. R. Morb. Mortal. Wkly. Rep. *47*:457–462, 1998.
48. Peffers, A. S., Bailey, J., Barrow, G. I., et al.: *Vibrio parahaemolyticus* gastroenteritis and international air travel. Lancet *1*:143–145, 1973.
49. Rabinowitch, B. L., Nam, M. H., Levy, C. S., et al.: *Vibrio parahaemolyticus* septicemia associated with water skiing. Clin. Infect. Dis. *16*:339–340, 1993.
50. Raimondi, F., Kao, J. P., Kaper, J. B., et al.: Calcium-dependent intestinal chloride secretion by *Vibrio parahaemolyticus* thermostable direct hemolysin in a rabbit model. Gastroenterology *109*:381–386, 1995.
51. Raimondi, F., Kao, J. P., Fiorentini, C., et al.: Enterotoxicity and cytotoxicity of *Vibrio parahaemolyticus* thermostable direct hemolysin in in vitro systems. Infect. Immun. *68*:3180–3185, 2000.
52. Sakasaki, R., Tamura, K., Nakamura, A., et al.: Studies on enteropathogenic activity of *Vibrio parahaemolyticus* using ligated gut loop model in rabbits. Jpn. J. Med. Sci. Biol. *27*:35–43, 1974.
53. Shinoda, S., Nakahara, N., Ninomiya, Y., et al.: Serological method for identification of *Vibrio parahaemolyticus* from marine samples. Appl. Environ. Microbiol. *45*:148–152, 1983.
54. Shirai, H., Ito, H., Hirayama, T., et al.: Molecular epidemiologic evidence for association of thermostable direct hemolysin (TDH) and TDH-related hemolysin of *Vibrio parahaemolyticus* with gastroenteritis. Infect. Immun. *58*:3568–3573, 1990.
55. Spearman, J. G., Tronca, E. L., Nichlos, E. M., et al.: Epidemiologic notes and reports, *Vibrio parahaemolyticus*, Louisiana. M. M. W. R. Morb. Mortal. Wkly. Rep. *21*:341–343, 1972.
56. Takahashi, A., Kenjyo, N., Imura, K., et al.: Cl^- secretion in colonic epithelial cells induced by the *Vibrio parahaemolyticus* hemolytic toxin related to thermostable direct hemolysin. Infect. Immun. *68*:5435–5438, 2000.
57. Takahashi, A., Sato, Y., Shiomi, Y., et al.: Mechanisms of chloride secretion induced by thermostable direct haemolysin of *Vibrio parahaemolyticus* in human colonic tissue and a human intestinal epithelial cell line. J. Med. Microbiol. *49*:801–810, 2000.
58. Takea, Y.: Thermostable direct hemolysin of *Vibrio parahaemolyticus*. Pharmacol. Ther. *19*:123–146, 1983.

59. Thompson, C. A., and Vanderzant, C.: Serological and hemolytic characteristics of *Vibrio parahaemolyticus* from marine sources. J. Food Sci. *41*:204–205, 1976.
60. Twedt, R. M.: *Vibrio parahaemolyticus. In* Doyle, M. P. (ed.): Foodborne Bacterial Pathogens. New York, Marcel Dekker, 1989, pp. 543–568.
61. Twedt, R. M., Peerler, J. T., and Spaulding, P. L.: Effective ileal loop dose of Kanagawa-positive *Vibrio parahaemolyticus*. Appl. Environ. Microbiol. *40*:1012–1016, 1980.
62. Varmam, A. H.: *Vibrio. In* Varmam, A. H., and Evans, M. G. (eds.): Foodborne Pathogens. London, Wolfe Publishing, 1991, pp. 157–183.
63. Yamamoto, T., and Yokota, T.: Adherence targets of *Vibrio parahaemolyticus* in human small intestines. Infect. Immun. *57*:2410–2419, 1989.
64. Yoh, M., Kawakami, N., Funakoshi, Y., et al.: Evaluation of two assay kits for thermostable direct hemolysin (TDH) as an indicator of TDH-related hemolysin (TRH) produced by *Vibrio parahaemolyticus*. Microbiol. Immunol. *39*:157–159, 1995.

Vibrio vulnificus

RANDALL G. FISHER ■ THOMAS G. BOYCE ■ WILLIAM C. GRUBER

Bacteriology

Vibrio vulnificus is a small, curvilinear, gram-negative rod of the family Vibrionaceae.[6] This facultative anaerobe is oxidase- and lysine-positive, like other species of the genus *Vibrio*. Its major difference is that it ferments lactose, a feature that accounts for its original name, Lac + *Vibrio*. *V. vulnificus* is arginine-negative and ornithine-variable. This halophilic (salt-loving) organism grows in sodium chloride concentrations of 1 to 8 percent and seems to grow best at about 3 percent.[29]

Epidemiology

V. vulnificus, like *Vibrio parahaemolyticus*, is a marine organism that is a common inhabitant of off-shore waters, especially estuarial waters.[41] It has been isolated from sediment, plankton, water, finfish, crabs, and oysters, with peak recovery in the summer and early fall.[14] This increased prevalence may due be to the fact that at higher water temperatures, *V. vulnificus* is released and rises to the surface waters. There it attaches to plankton and shore fish and then is taken up and concentrated by filter-feeding mollusks and crustaceans.

V. vulnificus has been isolated from both wild and commercial oysters all over the world. It is especially prevalent in warm coastal waters. Reports about the survival of the organism in oysters stored at low temperature are conflicting.[40] However, Nilsson and associates[39] revealed that even if *V. vulnificus* is rendered nonculturable by storage at low temperature, it can be "resuscitated" by allowing the oysters to come to room temperature; this cycle could be carried out twice without any reduction in bacterial count. Because of the ubiquity of the organism in the marine environment and its ability to thrive under even the most careful conditions of sanitation, storage, and transport,[13, 25, 27] ensuring that commercial shellfish do not contain viable *V. vulnificus* is very difficult. However, so-called heat shock shucking, during which the internal meat temperature exceeds 50° C for 1 to 4 minutes, reduces *V. vulnificus* and total bacterial levels in oysters 10- to 10,000-fold in comparison to conventional processing.[19] A separate study has confirmed that low-temperature pasteurization, which brings oyster temperatures to 50° C for 10 to 15 minutes, reduces colony counts from greater than 100,000 per gram of oyster meat to undetectable levels.[2]

Disease in humans is initiated by contact with the organism either through marine contamination of a wound or through the gastrointestinal tract after ingestion of the organism in raw shellfish, most commonly oysters.[6]

Pathophysiology

V. vulnificus causes distinct diseases in humans: wound infection and gastrointestinal infection, which may be self-limited or progress to septicemia. Local infection occurs after a wound is exposed to contaminated sea water. Wound infections with *V. vulnificus* are marked by rapid spread, formation of bullae, and necrosis of involved tissues.[6] Marked edema and vascular thromboses occur in both experimental and natural infection. *V. vulnificus* elaborates a cytolysin,[17, 18, 29] a collagenase,[46] and a protease,[37] which enhance its rapid spread in tissues. The protease activates the plasma kallikrein-kinin system to produce bradykinin,[36] and histamine also is released locally. These factors account for the intense inflammatory reaction that occurs in these lesions. In otherwise healthy individuals, a mild, self-limited gastrointestinal illness similar to that caused by *V. parahaemolyticus* has been described.[28] However, the most serious infection produced by *V. vulnificus* is primary septicemia, which occurs most commonly in patients with liver disease after ingestion of the organism in raw shellfish.[6, 42, 43]

For patients with hepatic disease, the risk of acquiring septicemia is 40 to 80 times greater and the case-fatality rate is 2.5 times higher than those for otherwise healthy individuals.[20] *V. vulnificus*, like many other gram-negative organisms, requires iron for growth and grows better in an excess of iron.[54] It is able to extract iron from hemoglobin, even if the iron is completely complexed to haptoglobin.[54, 57] Liver damage, excess iron, and deferoxamine therapy all have been shown to decrease the median lethal dose (LD_{50}) of *V. vulnificus* in experimental animals. Deferoxamine alone decreased the LD_{50} by 4 orders of magnitude.[9] Iron overload almost certainly underlies *V. vulnificus* septicemia in patients who require repeated transfusions and deferoxamine therapy for anemia.[24, 56] Some evidence indicates that alcoholism, even in the absence of demonstrable liver disease, is a risk factor for development of sepsis.[42] Fatal septicemia likewise has been reported in patients with other chronic diseases such as diabetes mellitus and lymphoma.[43]

Virulence factors of the organism also have been described.[55] Virulent strains are resistant to the bactericidal activity of human serum,[30] probably because of the presence of a polysaccharide capsule.[1] Poor uptake of virulent strains into phagocytes[49] and opaqueness of the colony on agar have been correlated with the presence of a capsule.[45, 55] No difference exists in the lipopolysaccharide of virulent versus avirulent strains.[5]

The production of recalcitrant shock in patients with septicemia is secondary to toxins, loss of vascular tone, capillary leak, and possibly negative inotropy, as in other forms of gram-negative sepsis.

Clinical Manifestations

Patients commonly seek medical attention for wound infection or primary septicemia. Wound infection occurs after injury in sea water or after contamination of a recently acquired wound with sea water. Often, the wound is caused by the shell of a crustacean or mollusk. Many patients with wound infections work in shellfish-related industries. Cellulitis may develop and spread rapidly, and the overlying skin frequently is covered with tense bullae. At débridement, the extent of necrosis may exceed presurgical expectations.[53] Primary wound infection may progress to systemic infection; for this reason, wound infection with *V. vulnificus* carries a mortality rate of 7 percent[7] to 24 percent.[28]

Patients with primary septicemia will generally give a history of recent (6 to 72 hours) consumption of raw seafood. Illness is marked by the rapid onset of fever, hypotension, and septic shock. Prodromal symptoms such as malaise, chills, and fever are common findings. Vomiting and diarrhea occur in approximately 20 percent of patients.[7] The shock progresses quickly and is difficult to reverse. Secondary skin lesions develop in approximately 50 percent of patients[6] and may be bullous, petechial, or maculopapular. Frequently, *V. vulnificus* can be isolated from cultures of secondary lesions, thereby providing evidence of septicemic spread to those sites.[6] Mortality rates from primary septicemia have been reported to be 46 percent[7] to 79 percent.[42]

In addition to causing the aforementioned two syndromes, *V. vulnificus* has been reported as a cause of corneal ulcer,[15] myositis,[26] adult epiglottitis,[34] osteomyelitis,[51] endocarditis,[50] peritonitis,[22] and meningitis.[24, 42] A case of fatal septicemia in which the initial symptom was a compartment syndrome of the forearm has been described.[23]

Ninety percent of reported patients are 40 years of age or older.[6, 42] Childhood cases of septicemia have been associated with thalassemia major,[24] for which frequent transfusions and deferoxamine therapy are required. Wound infections in previously healthy children and adolescents have been reported. *V. vulnificus* also has been isolated from a premature baby's stool sample obtained on the infant's first day of life; the baby's mother worked as an oyster shucker.[4]

Diagnosis

The diagnosis of *V. vulnificus* infection is made by isolating the organism from blood or tissue culture. It also may be recovered from stool specimens.[4, 43] Agar designed specifically to aid in the growth and identification of *V. vulnificus* has been developed; cellobiose-colistin agar outperforms thiosulfate citrate bile salts sucrose agar for recovery of *V. vulnificus* from environmental samples.[21] From a practical standpoint, however, most hospital microbiology laboratories do not stock cellobiose-colistin agar. Of the commercially available media, *V. vulnificus* tends to grow best in thiosulfate citrate bile salts sucrose agar,[6] but it also may be recovered from ordinary blood agar[3, 44] or MacConkey plates.[6]

A very sensitive nested polymerase chain reaction technique that is capable of detecting as little as 1 pg of bacterial DNA and one colony-forming unit of *V. vulnificus* has been described; it was positive in 94 percent of clinical samples that grew the bacteria in culture and also was positive in 42 percent of culture-negative samples from patients with suspected *V. vulnificus* infection.[32] An enzyme immunoassay also has been developed.[49] Both these methods are experimental and not available routinely for clinical use.

The diagnosis of *V. vulnificus* wound infection or septicemia can be suspected on clinical grounds and appropriate therapy initiated while awaiting culture results. A history of ingestion of raw shellfish or of wound contamination with either sea water or brackish inland water[47] should be sought. *V. vulnificus* infection should be given high consideration in patients with hemosiderosis, anemia with transfusion therapy, liver disease, or other chronic diseases.

Treatment

In severe wound infections, rapid performance of surgical therapy is of paramount importance. In primary septicemia, supporting the patient's airway, along with providing aggressive pressor support and other adjunctive therapies for severe septic shock, is a primary concern. Secondarily, appropriate antibiotic treatment of *V. vulnificus* should be started as early as possible. In vitro, the organism is susceptible to many antibiotics, including ampicillin, third-generation cephalosporins, tetracycline, chloramphenicol, and gentamicin.[6] Bowdre and associates[8] reported that in mice, the minimal inhibitory concentrations (MICs) obtained in the laboratory did not seem to correspond with response to therapy. In particular, the organism appeared to be exquisitely sensitive to cefotaxime in vitro (MIC of 0.06 μg/mL); however, 9 of 10 mice treated with cefotaxime succumbed to overwhelming infection. Anecdotal evidence indicates that this puzzling phenomenon may occur in humans as well: four of five patients reported by Chuang and associates[11] died despite receiving therapy with third-generation cephalosporins at appropriate dosage. Similarly, although the organism almost universally is sensitive to gentamicin in the laboratory, case reports show a lack of response to this antibiotic.

Of all the antibiotics to which the organism was sensitive in vitro, only tetracycline led to mouse survival in Bowdre and colleagues' study; all 12 of the mice treated with tetracycline survived the infection.[8] Case reports also show favorable outcomes in patients treated with tetracycline or doxycycline,[11] as well as chloramphenicol[11] and ciprofloxacin.[33] More recently, the combination of minocycline and cefotaxime has been shown to be synergistic in vitro, with the combination reducing the growth of *V. vulnificus* by 6 orders of magnitude when compared with either drug alone.[10] Enhanced survival of mice infected with *V. vulnificus* and treated with minocycline plus cefotaxime provides an in vivo correlate of the in vitro results.[12] Unfortunately, no data comparing the activity of minocycline with that of tetracycline are available; nevertheless, the evidence just presented is strong enough to suggest that either tetracycline[16] or minocycline together with cefotaxime should be the treatment of choice for known or suspected *V. vulnificus* infection.

The addition of modified Dakin solution (0.025% sodium hypochlorite) may have some utility in the treatment of skin and wound infections. An in vitro study of eight different topical antibiotic preparations showed that *V. vulnificus* was most sensitive to modified Dakin solution.[35] Although no controlled trial has been performed, a series of 10 patients with culture-proven *V. vulnificus* wound infections treated with doxycycline and topical modified Dakin solution has been reported; none of them experienced progression of infection or required surgical débridement.[52]

Prevention

Patients with severe anemia, liver disease, hemosiderosis, or other debilitating chronic diseases and those receiving deferoxamine therapy should be advised against eating raw seafood of any kind. Patients with open wounds probably should avoid contact with sea water or brackish inland water.

REFERENCES

1. Amako, K., Okada, K., and Miake, S.: Evidence for the presence of a capsule in *Vibrio vulnificus*. J. Gen. Microbiol. *130*:2741–2743, 1984.
2. Andrews, L. S., Park, D. L, and Chen, Y. P.: Low temperature pasteurization to reduce the risk of vibrio infections from raw shell-stock oysters. Food Addit. Contam. *17*:787–791, 2000.
3. Armstrong, C. W., Lake, J. L., and Miller, G. B., Jr.: Extraintestinal infections due to halophilic vibrios. South. Med. J. *76*:571–574, 1983.
4. Bachman, B., Boyd, W. P., Jr., Lieb, S., et al.: Marine noncholera *Vibrio* infections in Florida. South. Med. J. *76*:296–299, 1983.
5. Bahrani, K., and Oliver, J. D.: Studies on the lipopolysaccharide of a virulent and an avirulent strain of *Vibrio vulnificus*. Biochem. Cell. Biol. *68*:547–551, 1990.
6. Blake, P. A., Merson, M. H., Weaver, R. E., et al.: Disease caused by a marine *Vibrio:* Clinical characteristics and epidemiology. N. Engl. J. Med. *300*:1–5, 1979.
7. Blake, P. A., Weaver, R. E., and Hollis, D. G.: Disease of humans (other than cholera) caused by vibrios. Annu. Rev. Microbiol. *34*:341–367, 1980.
8. Bowdre, J. H., Hull, J. H., and Cocchetto, D. M.: Antibiotic efficacy against *Vibrio vulnificus* in the mouse: Superiority of tetracycline. J. Pharmacol. Exp. Ther. *225*:595–598, 1983.
9. Brennaman, B., Soucy, D., and Howard, R. J.: Effect of iron and liver injury on the pathogenesis of *Vibrio vulnificus*. J. Surg. Res. *43*:527–531, 1987.
10. Chuang, Y. C., Liu, J. W., Ko, W. C, et al.: In vitro synergism between cefotaxime and minocycline against *Vibrio vulnificus*. Antimicrob. Agents Chemother. *41*:2214–2217, 1997.
11. Chuang, Y. C., Yuan, C. Y., Lin, C. Y., et al.: *Vibrio vulnificus* infection in Taiwan: Report of 28 cases and review of clinical manifestations and treatment. Clin. Infect. Dis. *115*:271–276, 1992.
12. Chuang, Y. W., Ko, W. C., Wang, S. T., et al.: Minocycline and cefotaxime in the treatment of experimental murine *Vibrio vulnificus* infection. Antimicrob. Agents Chemother. *42*:1319–1322, 1998.
13. Cook, D. W.: Effect of time and temperature on multiplication of *Vibrio vulnificus* in postharvest Gulf Coast shellstock oysters. Appl. Environ. Microbiol. *60*:3483–3484, 1994.
14. DePaola, A., Capers, G. M., and Alexander, D.: Densities of *Vibrio vulnificus* in the intestines of fish from the U. S. Gulf Coast. Appl. Environ. Microbiol. *60*:984–988, 1994.
15. DiGaetano, M., Ball, S. F., and Straus, J. G.: *Vibrio vulnificus* corneal ulcer: Case reports. Arch. Ophthalmol. *107*:323–324, 1989.
16. Fang, F. C.: Use of tetracycline for treatment of *Vibrio vulnificus* infections. Clin. Infect. Dis. *15*:1071–1072, 1992.
17. Gray, L. D., and Kreger, A. S.: Purification and characterization of an extracellular cytolysin produced by *Vibrio vulnificus*. Infect. Immun. *48*:62–72, 1985.
18. Gray, L. D., and Kreger, A. S.: Mouse skin damage caused by cytolysin from *Vibrio vulnificus* and by *Vibrio vulnificus* infection. J. Infect. Dis. *155*:236–241, 1987.
19. Hesselman, D. M., Motes, M. L., and Lewis, J. P.: Effects of a commercial heat-shock process on *Vibrio vulnificus* in the American oyster, *Crassostrea virginica,* harvested from the Gulf Coast. J. Food Prot. *62*:1266–1269, 1999.
20. Hlady, W. G., Mullen, R. C., and Hopkin, R. S.: *Vibrio vulnificus* from raw oysters: Leading cause of reported deaths from foodborne illness in Florida. J. Fla. Med. Assoc. *80*:536–538, 1993.
21. Hoi, L., Dalsgaard, I., and Dalsgaard, A.: Improved isolation of *Vibrio vulnificus* from seawater and sediment with cellobiose-colistin agar. Appl. Environ. Microbiol. *64*:1721–1724, 1998.
22. Holcombe, D. J.: *Vibrio vulnificus* peritonitis: A unique case. J. La. State Med. Soc. *143*:27–28, 1991.
23. Hui, K. C., Zhang, F., Komorowska-Timek, E., et al.: Compartment syndrome of the forearm as the initial symptom of systemic *Vibrio vulnificus* infection. J. Hand Surg. [Am.] *24*:715–717, 1999.
24. Katz, B. Z.: *Vibrio vulnificus* meningitis in a boy with thalassemia after eating raw oysters. Pediatrics *82*:784–786, 1988.
25. Kaysner, C. A., Tamplin, M. L., Wekell, M. M., et al.: Survival of *Vibrio vulnificus* in shellstock and shucked oysters *(Crassostrea gigas* and *Crassostrea virginica)* and effects of isolation medium on recovery. Appl. Environ. Microbiol. *55*:3072–3079, 1989.
26. Kelly, M. T., and McCormick, W. F.: Acute bacterial myositis caused by *Vibrio vulnificus*. J. A. M. A. *246*:72–73, 1981.
27. Kizer, K. W.: *Vibrio vulnificus* hazard in patients with liver disease. West. J. Med. *161*:64–65, 1994.
28. Klontz, K. C., Lieb, S., Schreiber, M., et al.: Syndromes of *Vibrio vulnificus* infections: Clinical and epidemiologic features in Florida cases, 1981–1987. Ann. Intern. Med. *109*:318–323, 1988.
29. Koga, T., and Kawata, T.: Composition of the major outer membrane proteins of *Vibrio vulnificus* isolates: Effect of different growth media and iron deficiency. Microbiol. Immunol. *30*:193–201, 1986.
30. Kreger, A., DeChatelet, L., and Shirley, P.: Interaction of *Vibrio vulnificus* with human polymorphonuclear leukocytes: Association of virulence with resistance to phagocytosis. J. Infect. Dis. *144*:244–248, 1981.
31. Kreger, A. S., Kothary, M. H., and Gray, L. D.: Cytolytic toxins of *Vibrio vulnificus* and *Vibrio damsela*. Methods Enzymol. *165*:176–189, 1988.
32. Lee, S. E., Kim, S. Y., Kim, S. J., et al.: Direct identification of *Vibrio vulnificus* in clinical specimens by nested PCR. J. Clin. Microbiol. *36*:2887–2892, 1998.
33. Meadors, M. C., and Pankey, G. A.: *Vibrio vulnificus* wound infection treated successfully with oral ciprofloxacin. J. Infect. *20*:88–89, 1990.
34. Mehtar, S., Bangham, L., Kalmanovitch, D., et al.: Adult epiglottitis due to *Vibrio vulnificus*. B. M. J. *296*:827–828, 1988.
35. Milner, S. M., and Heggers, J. P.: The use of a modified Dakin's solution (sodium hypochlorite) in the treatment of *Vibrio vulnificus* infection. Wilderness Environ. Med. *10*:10–12, 1999.
36. Miyoshi, N., Miyoshi, S., Sugiyama, K., et al.: Activation of the plasma kallikrein-kinin system by *Vibrio vulnificus* protease. Infect. Immun. *55*:1936–1939, 1987.
37. Miyoshi, S., and Shinoda, S.: Role of the protease in the permeability enhancement by *Vibrio vulnificus*. Microbiol. Immunol. *32*:1025–1032, 1988.
38. Morris, J. G., Jr., and Tenney, J.: Antibiotic therapy for *Vibrio vulnificus* infection. J. A. M. A. *253*:1121–1122, 1985.
39. Nilsson, L., Oliver, J. D., and Kjelleberg, S.: Resuscitation of *Vibrio vulnificus* from the viable but nonculturable state. J. Bacteriol. *173*:5054–5059, 1991.
40. Oliver, J. D.: Lethal cold stress of *Vibrio vulnificus* in oysters. Appl. Environ. Microbiol. *41*:710–717, 1981.
41. Oliver, J. D., Warner, R. A., and Cleland, D. R.: Distribution of *Vibrio vulnificus* and other lactose-fermenting vibrios in the marine environment. Appl. Environ. Microbiol. *45*:985–998, 1983.
42. Park, S. D., Shon, H. S., and Joh N. J.: *Vibrio vulnificus* septicemia in Korea: Clinical and epidemiologic findings in seventy patients. J. Am. Acad. Dermatol. *24*:397–403, 1991.
43. Pollak, S. J., Parrish, E. F., III, Barrett, T. J., et al.: *Vibrio vulnificus* septicemia: Isolation of organism from stool and demonstration of antibodies by indirect immunofluorescence. Arch. Intern. Med. *143*:837–838, 1983.
44. Saraswathi, K., Barve, S. M., and Deodhar, L. P.: Septicaemia due to *Vibrio vulnificus*. Trans. R. Soc. Trop. Med. Hyg. *83*:714, 1989.
45. Simpson, L. M., White, V. K., Zane, S. F., et al.: Correlation between virulence and colony morphology in *Vibrio vulnificus*. Infect. Immun. *55*:269–272, 1987.
46. Smith, G. C., and Merkel, J. R.: Collagenolytic activity of *Vibrio vulnificus:* Potential contribution to its invasiveness. Infect. Immun. *35*:1155–1156, 1982.
47. Tacket, C. O., Barrett, T. J., Mann, J. M., et al.: Wound infections caused by *Vibrio vulnificus,* a marine *Vibrio,* in inland areas of the United States. J. Clin. Microbiol. *19*:197–199, 1984.
48. Tamplin, M. L., Martin, A. L., Ruple, A. D., et al.: Enzyme immunoassay for identification of *Vibrio vulnificus* in seawater, sediment, and oysters. Appl. Environ. Microbiol. *57*:1235–1240, 1991.
49. Tamplin, M. L., Specter, S., Rodrick, G. E., et al.: *Vibrio vulnificus* resists phagocytosis in the absence of serum opsonins. Infect. Immun. *49*:715–718, 1985.
50. Truwit, J. D., Badesch, D. B., Savage, A. M., et al.: *Vibrio vulnificus* bacteremia with endocarditis. South. Med. J. *80*:1457–1459, 1987.
51. Vartian, C. V., and Septimus, E. J.: Osteomyelitis caused by *Vibrio vulnificus*. J. Infect. Dis. *161*:363, 1990.
52. Wilhelmi, B. J., Calianos, T. A., 2nd, Appelt, E. A., et al.: Modified Dakin's solution for cutaneous vibrio infections. Ann. Plast. Surg. *43*:386–389, 1999.
53. Woo, M. L., Patrick, W. G., Simon, M. T., et al.: Necrotising fasciitis caused by *Vibrio vulnificus*. J. Clin. Pathol. *37*:1301–1304, 1984.

54. Wright, A. C., Simpson, L. M., and Oliver, J. D.: Role of iron in the pathogenesis of *Vibrio vulnificus* infections. Infect. Immun. *34*:503–507, 1981.
55. Yoshida, S., Ogawa, M., and Mizuguchi, Y.: Relation of capsular materials and colony opacity to virulence of *Vibrio vulnificus*. Infect. Immun. *47*:446–451, 1985.
56. Yoshida, S., Tanabe, T., Chiba, S., et al.: Fatal *Vibrio vulnificus* infection in a patient with aplastic anemia. Sangyo Ika Daigaku Zasshi *5*:95–100, 1983.
57. Zakaria-Meehan, Z., Massad, G., Simpson, L. M., et al.: Ability of *Vibrio vulnificus* to obtain iron from hemoglobin-haptoglobin complexes. Infect. Immun. *56*:275–277, 1988.

CHAPTER 124 Miscellaneous Non-Enterobacteriaceae Fermentative Bacilli

RANDALL G. FISHER ■ WILLIAM C. GRUBER ■ THOMAS G. BOYCE

This chapter discusses fermentative bacilli that are not of the family Enterobacteriaceae. Specifically, *Chromobacterium violaceum*, *Plesiomonas shigelloides*, and *Pasteurella* organisms other than *Pasteurella multocida* are examined.

Chromobacterium violaceum

C. violaceum is a facultatively anaerobic, gram-negative rod that is a saprophyte of soil and water, especially in tropical and subtropical climates. It causes occasional illness in animals and, rarely, in humans. Infection with *C. violaceum*, when it does occur, is a serious disease with a high mortality rate.

BACTERIOLOGY

C. violaceum is a long, motile, gram-negative bacillus that appears singly or in pairs on Gram stain. It has a polar flagellum and one to four subpolar or lateral flagella that are antigenically distinct from the polar flagellum.[53] Most isolates produce an insoluble pigment, violacein. This pigment is intense and makes colonies appear dark purple to black, especially on blood agar. Violacein induces apoptotic death in certain cell types in vitro, including leukemia and lymphoma cells.[40] The therapeutic potential of violacein is being explored. *C. violaceum* grows readily on standard agar (any medium that contains tryptophan supports growth). The colonies are low convex, violet, smooth, and not gelatinous. Colonies produce hydrogen cyanide, so a faint almond odor may be present.[53]

C. violaceum is catalase- and oxidase-positive, although the latter may be difficult to interpret because of the production of pigment. Growing the organism anaerobically inhibits pigment formation.[29] Pigment also may be lost on subculture[47] or as effective treatment is initiated. *C. violaceum* mounts a fermentative, not oxidative, attack on carbohydrates.

C. violaceum produces antimicrobial agents that have been shown to have activity against bacteria and trypanosomes.

EPIDEMIOLOGY

C. violaceum commonly is found in the soil and water of areas with tropical or subtropical weather patterns. It also has been recovered from soil as far north as New Jersey.[9]

Ten of the first 12 cases reported in the United States occurred in Florida; the other 2 were in Louisiana. Subsequently, one case from New Jersey[44] and one from Ohio[55] have been reported, along with more from southeastern states. All but one case occurred during the summer months.[47] Patients tend to be young, with a median age of 14 years.[47]

PATHOPHYSIOLOGY

Although *C. violaceum* is a common inhabitant of soil and water, human infection is a relatively rare occurrence. Disorders of neutrophil function are important risk factors, and a disproportionately high number of *C. violaceum* infections have been in patients with chronic granulomatous disease.[35] A case of a child with another disorder of neutrophil function, polymorphonuclear leukocyte glucose-6-phosphate dehydrogenase deficiency, also has been reported.[36] Organisms may demonstrate variable virulence, and differences in endotoxin activity, resistance to phagocytosis, and production of catalase and hydrogen peroxide have been observed in clinical and soil isolates.[41] The organism's elastase activity, expressed through the entire life cycle and produced by a zinc metalloproteinase, may account for the propensity of *C. violaceum* to cause abscesses.[62]

The organism usually gains entrance into the body through cuts or abrasions that come in contact with contaminated soil or water. After entrance, a localized infection usually develops at or around the site of entry and commonly is followed by dissemination of infection via the bloodstream to distant sites. Rapid débridement and appropriate antibiotic therapy may arrest the infection at the wound stage.[31] Two cases of systemic infection occurred in near-drowning victims. One case report describes fulminant infection and death in an immunocompetent host from *C. violaceum* sepsis that began as conjunctivitis after a fall that splattered mud into the patient's eye.[13]

Numerous microabscesses are found in multiple organs, especially the liver, lungs, and kidneys. Spread to bone, joints, and the central nervous system also has been described.

CLINICAL MANIFESTATIONS

The pattern of illness in all reported patients is fairly similar, with a contaminated inoculation site, localized disease, regional lymphadenopathy, and then hematogenous spread to visceral organs. Progression of symptoms tends to be rapid after a varying incubation period.

Most patients have cutaneous lesions[35] that are described as being nodular or pustular and sometimes with surrounding cellulitis.[59] They may progress to suppuration and drainage or ulceration. Regional lymphadenopathy is a common occurrence; some of the nodes suppurate and require surgical drainage or removal.

Severe disease is heralded by high fever (39° C to 41° C), confusion or lethargy, abdominal pain, headaches, nausea and vomiting, and sometimes myalgias. Patients with systemic illness are toxic in appearance. Hepatosplenomegaly occurs frequently, and jaundice may be present. Progression from high fever and moderate toxicity to septic shock with disseminated intravascular coagulation and multisystem organ failure is precipitous. After the liver, the lung is the most common site of dissemination of infection, and evidence of pneumonia often is found. Adult respiratory distress syndrome is a rare complication,[32] and brain and liver abscesses have been noted.[42] The overall mortality rate is 65 percent.[35] Rarely, recurrence that can prove fatal may occur.[29, 47]

DIAGNOSIS

The diagnosis is made by recovery of the organism from blood, lymph nodes, skin lesions, or abscesses. Gram-negative bacilli occasionally can be seen in smears of material from skin lesions. Laboratory values reveal either very low or very high white blood cell counts with a marked left shift. Mild to moderate anemia is a common finding. The patient may have elevated liver enzymes, and evidence of early renal failure sometimes is present. The organism grows readily and is easy to identify if it produces the characteristic violet pigment. Nonpigmented forms exist in soil and have similar virulence in mice[52] but are recovered only rarely from clinical specimens.[55] Other cases may have been missed, however, because the nonpigmented forms often are misidentified as *Aeromonas hydrophila* or pseudomonads.[52] Reports that *C. violaceum* infection causes a melioidosis-like illness probably were due to misidentification of *Burkholderia pseudomallei* by the API 20NE system.[23] A clinical history of contamination of a wound with water or soil, especially in the southeastern part of the United States or in Southeast Asia, with subsequent local infection, lymph node suppuration, and lack of response to conventional antibiotic therapy should arouse suspicion of infection with *C. violaceum*. The clinician should be particularly aware of the possibility of infection with *C. violaceum* in patients with chronic granulomatous disease.

TREATMENT

C. violaceum is sensitive in vitro to chloramphenicol, gentamicin, fluorinated quinolones, tetracyclines, imipenem, trimethoprim-sulfamethoxazole, and semisynthetic penicillins. It often is resistant to cephalosporins, penicillin, ampicillin, and the antistaphylococcal penicillins. All isolates are resistant to vancomycin and rifampin.[3] Some strains have been shown to elaborate a β-lactamase that is chromosomal and inducible in vitro.[12] At least one case report gives in vivo evidence of inducible resistance to ceftazidime.[59] Laboratory evidence of susceptibility to erythromycin is not reliable. Fluorinated quinolones have the highest activity in vitro,[3] but clinical experience with the fluoroquinolones in *C. violaceum* infection is scarce; an impressive case of a 4-month-old infant with severe, disseminated infection with *C. violaceum* who survived after receiving therapy with trimethoprim-sulfamethoxazole and ciprofloxacin has been reported.[42]

Because infection with *C. violaceum* is rare and often rapidly fatal, the optimal antimicrobial therapy is not known. Most survivors have been treated with chloramphenicol, gentamicin, or both. The duration of therapy also is not known, but because of late recurrences, some authors recommend 3 to 4 weeks of intravenous therapy, followed by a month or more of oral trimethoprim-sulfamethoxazole.[47]

Plesiomonas shigelloides

The genus *Plesiomonas* has only one species: *P. shigelloides*. These organisms are facultatively anaerobic, motile, gram-negative rods that are common inhabitants of surface water and fish. They have been implicated in gastrointestinal infections and rarely have been recovered from extraintestinal sites.

BACTERIOLOGY

These facultatively anaerobic, gram-negative rods are members of the family Vibrionaceae, although some authorities suggest that they are more closely related to the Enterobacteriaceae.[34] They are motile by means of a polar flagellum. *Plesiomonas* organisms are lysine-, ornithine-, and arginine decarboxylase–positive. They can be distinguished from Enterobacteriaceae by oxidase positivity. They also are catalase- and indole-positive. *Plesiomonas* grows well on MacConkey agar but not on thiosulfate citrate bile salts sucrose. Growth may be enhanced by the use of selective media such as trypticase soy broth with ampicillin[48] and inositol brilliant green bile salts agar. Growth is maximal at 40° C to 44° C and completely inhibited at 8° C. One- to 1.5-mm grayish, shiny, opaque colonies with a slightly raised center and a smooth surface are usually visible within 24 hours. A few isolates of *P. shigelloides* share a common O antigen with *Shigella sonnei*.

EPIDEMIOLOGY

The organism is a ubiquitous fresh-water inhabitant at temperatures higher than 8° C. It sometimes is found in estuarial waters in temperate or tropical climates and can exist in sea water during the summer months. It has been cultured from finfish, shellfish, pigs, birds, and dogs.[61] Although infection with *P. shigelloides* has been associated with the ingestion of raw or improperly cooked fish (especially oysters), what role, if any, other animals play in the ecology of the organism is not known.

Asymptomatic carriage of *P. shigelloides* rarely occurs in developed countries[50] but may be as high as 15 percent in some parts of China.[61]

PATHOPHYSIOLOGY

Despite the ubiquity of the organism in nature, human infection is a relatively uncommon occurrence and has been recognized only recently. Most often, infection is associated with gastroenteritis. Evidence for the role of *P. shigelloides* in the production of gastrointestinal symptoms is that (1) it has been isolated much more frequently from patients with diarrhea than from healthy controls[21]; (2) some outbreaks have occurred, especially in Japan; (3) it often is the only organism detected in the stool of patients with gastroenteritis[39]; and (4) patients who have *P. shigelloides* growing from a stool culture recover more quickly with antibiotic therapy than without it.[26] Acquisition of disease has been linked specifically to the consumption of raw seafood or untreated water and to foreign travel, especially to Mexico.[20, 38]

The mechanism by which the organism produces disease, however, has been somewhat elusive. It is not enteroinvasive by laboratory tests, most investigators fail to find either a Shiga toxin or an enterotoxin,[1, 20] no animal model of gastrointestinal disease exists,[6] patients in the recovery phase do not show serologic evidence of infection, and inoculation of volunteers fails to produce illness.[20] In a suckling gnotobiotic piglet model in which the animals became septic, histologic examination of the gastrointestinal tract showed neither destruction of cells nor invasion of tissues.[20] Neonatal BALB/c mice became chronically infected with *P. shigelloides*, however, and the histopathologic findings included some cases of necrosis of the mucosal surface of the ileum and colon.[60] Some potential virulence factors (i.e., a cholera-like toxin, a weak cytolysin, serum resistance, and a large [>150 kDa] plasmid) have been described, but their exact roles in pathogenesis are uncertain; attempts to correlate these features with virulence have been fruitless.[1] Recently, transmission electron microscopy has provided investigators with the first definitive proof that *P. shigelloides* can adhere to and invade eukaryotic intestinal cells. Organisms were attached to microvilli and plasma membranes of the cells; they also were seen within vacuoles in the cell cytoplasm, thus suggesting a phagocytotic entry mechanism.[57]

P. shigelloides rarely but more clearly is a pathogen in extraintestinal sites. Osteomyelitis, endophthalmitis, cholecystitis, pseudoappendicitis, spontaneous peritonitis,[2] meningitis,[56] and septicemia have been reported sporadically.[6] Most patients with septicemia have been immunocompromised hosts, but the organism has been isolated from blood cultures in otherwise healthy persons.[24, 46] The mode of infection in extraintestinal sites is not clear. The case of a newborn with *P. shigelloides* meningitis, septicemia, and endophthalmitis who was born to a mother who reported severe diarrhea after eating raw oysters 2 weeks before delivery raises the possibility of transplacental transmission.[37]

CLINICAL MANIFESTATIONS

Patients with *P. shigelloides* gastroenteritis complain of diarrhea, crampy abdominal pain, nausea and vomiting, headache, and fever. Symptoms usually begin 24 hours to 4 days after contact with the organism.[21] The diarrhea tends to be secretory, although some patients have symptoms more consistent with colitis.[26] Passage of blood, mucus, or both in the stool is not uncommon, nor is the presence of white blood cells by Wright stain.[21] Patients with *P. shigelloides* gastroenteritis tend to have disease that is more acute, associated with more severe abdominal pain, and of longer duration than do patients with disease caused by other enteropathogens.[26] In one case-control study, 76 percent of patients were sick for longer than 2 weeks and 32 percent for more than a month.[26] In contrast, a large Japanese study of returning travelers suggested that for most patients, the symptoms abated within approximately 3 days.[51] Migratory polyarthritis developed in one child during an otherwise typical case of culture-proven gastrointestinal infection. All symptoms and signs of arthritis disappeared when the gastrointestinal infection was treated with antibiotics.[18]

Localized extraintestinal infections have been reported but are rare. Two cases of severe polymicrobial endophthalmitis resulting from fishhook trauma both progressed to enucleation.[7]

Septicemia, meningitis, or both usually occur in immunocompromised hosts. Most of the reported cases of *P. shigelloides* meningitis occur in newborns, in whom the mortality rate is 80 percent.[1] Septicemia also has a high mortality rate in adults, although otherwise well patients may recover with appropriate antimicrobial therapy.

DIAGNOSIS

A clinical history of foreign travel or ingestion of raw seafood or untreated water should raise suspicion of possible *P. shigelloides* infection, especially when the clinical illness matches the description just mentioned. Oxidase tests should be performed on any predominant or solitary organisms to distinguish them from Enterobacteriaceae.[21] They can be shown to not be aeromonads or pseudomonads by the production of ornithine decarboxylase and fermentation of inositol. A selective medium can be used if the index of suspicion is high.

TREATMENT

Most strains of *P. shigelloides* produce a β-lactamase[49] that seems to be specific for the penicillins. In one study, all isolates were resistant to ampicillin, ticarcillin, carbenicillin, and piperacillin.[27] *P. shigelloides* is susceptible universally to trimethoprim-sulfamethoxazole, the fluoroquinolones, most cephalosporins, and chloramphenicol. It is variably susceptible to the aminoglycosides and mostly resistant to erythromycin.

P. shigelloides gastroenteritis resolves without therapy, but the illness may be prolonged. Treatment seems to shorten the course.[26]

Extraintestinal infections carry a poor prognosis and should be treated aggressively. For meningitis, the cephalosporins have good penetration in cerebrospinal fluid and are effective therapy against most isolates.

Other *Pasteurella* Organisms

The genus *Pasteurella* consists of a group of pleomorphic, gram-negative coccobacilli that are part of the normal flora of many animals. These organisms are frequent animal pathogens. *P. multocida* is not an uncommon human pathogen and is discussed elsewhere (see Chapter 120). The other species of the genus *Pasteurella* are rare, but occasionally serious, causes of infection in humans.

BACTERIOLOGY

These organisms, like *P. multocida*, grow readily on most common laboratory media, including blood agar. Most of the species do not grow on MacConkey. They are non–spore-forming, nonmotile, aerobic, and facultatively anaerobic. These glucose-fermenting organisms are all oxidase-positive. Most are nitrate- and catalase-positive, and all except *Pasteurella gallinarum* produce indole. They are small, coccoid or rod-shaped bacilli that may show prominent bipolar staining on Gram stain. Colonies are small, translucent, and gray, and they may be smooth or rough. A browning discoloration may develop around them. Colonies are nonhemolytic and have a distinctive musty or "mushroom" odor.[8]

The taxonomy of these organisms is confusing and continues to be revised. *Pasteurella ureae* and *Pasteurella pneumotropica* have been moved to the genus *Actinobacillus*. *Pasteurella haemolytica* recently was reclassified into a new genus, *Mannheimia*.[5] *Pasteurella dagmatis* is the name now given to what formerly was called *Pasteurella* new species or *Pasteurella* gas.[43] Clinically recovered species other than *P. multocida* include *Actinobacillus ureae*, *Mannheimia haemolytica*, *Actinobacillus pneumotropica*, *P. dagmatis*, *Pasteurella canis*, *Pasteurella aerogenes*, *Pasteurella bettyae*, *Pasteurella "SP"* group, and *Pasteurella stomatis*. *Pasteurella caballi* has caused wound infections after horse bites.[10] *P. gallinarum* is an extremely rare pathogen in humans.

PATHOPHYSIOLOGY

Infections with *Pasteurella* spp. have been divided clinically into three types: (1) infection from animal bites, (2) infection from animal contact, and (3) infection without known animal contact.[15] Infection from animal bites includes cellulitis, abscesses, tenosynovitis, and bone and joint infection, but the infection can become generalized, especially in patients with compromised immune systems. Infection caused by animal contact can be similar to that described earlier and results from animals licking broken skin or wounds. Pulmonary infections sometimes occur, possibly related to aerosolization of organisms. Cases without a history of known animal contact comprise 3 percent[22] to 30 percent[25] of all cases.

Infection usually occurs when the organisms are inoculated into deeper tissues either on animal teeth that break the skin or in animal saliva that comes in contact with nonintact skin. Bite wound infections often are polymicrobial. Infection in cases without known animal contact is harder to explain, but some species such as *A. ureae* may be an occasional commensal of the human respiratory tract.[28] Most serious infections occur in patients with underlying diseases such as diabetes mellitus, chronic alcoholism, and other types of liver disease.[45] Infection of the central nervous system with these organisms has occurred after head trauma or neurosurgery in 10 of 11 reported cases.[28] One intrauterine death of the fetus of a 20-year-old individual who worked at a pig farm has been attributed to *P. aerogenes*.[58]

CLINICAL MANIFESTATIONS

Pasteurella infections produce pain, swelling, pus, and sometimes an abscess at the site of inoculation, beginning within 24 to 36 hours. Clinically, these infections are not distinguishable from wound infections with *Staphylococcus aureus* or other gram-positive organisms. Gram stain may show the characteristic pleomorphic bacilli with bipolar staining. Growth on standard agar is rapid.

Patients with peritonitis,[45] meningitis,[28] osteomyelitis,[16] or infectious endocarditis[4] have symptoms typical of these conditions. Risk factors such as exposure to household pets, animal contact, and animal bites should heighten suspicion of possible *Pasteurella* infection.

DIAGNOSIS

The diagnosis of *Pasteurella* infection can be difficult to make, not because the organism is fastidious or slow growing, but because it often is misidentified. Other organisms of the same family (i.e., *Actinobacillus* and *Haemophilus* spp.) have similar biochemical profiles and can be misidentified by commonly used systems such as API. Lester and associates[33] reported that of 30 species firmly identified as *Pasteurella* by biochemical means, only 3 were correctly identified by the API 20E system. *Haemophilus aphrophilus* and *Actinobacillus actinomycetemcomitans* occasionally are misidentified as *P. gallinarum* by commercial systems.[14] Additionally, Hamilton-Miller[19] reported that four strains of *Haemophilus influenzae* and three strains of *Haemophilus parainfluenzae* were falsely identified as *Pasteurella* spp. by API and suggested that if the clinical history renders *Pasteurella* infection unlikely, tests for X and V factor requirements should be performed (see Chapter 139). Clinical case reports corroborate these laboratory observations.[11, 45, 54] Notifying the bacteriology laboratory of suspected *Pasteurella* infection is helpful.

TREATMENT

Penicillin has been considered the drug of choice for *Pasteurella* infection in the past and, despite some reports of penicillin resistance, is still effective against most strains. *Pasteurella* spp. also are susceptible to ampicillin, β-lactamase inhibitor combination drugs, tetracycline, and chloramphenicol. Truncated, but fully functional tetracycline resistance genes have been identified in isolates from animal sources.[30] The aminoglycosides erythromycin, clindamycin, cefadroxil, and cefaclor are not recommended. Dicloxacillin and cephalexin, two drugs prescribed very commonly for wound infections, have poor activity against *Pasteurella* spp. and should not be used as monotherapy for animal bite wounds.[17]

REFERENCES

1. Abbott, S. L., Kokka, R. P., and Janda, J. M.: Laboratory investigations on the low pathogenic potential of *Plesiomonas shigelloides*. J. Clin. Microbiol. *29*:148–153, 1991.
2. Alcaniz, J. P., de Cuenca Moron, B., Gomez Rubio, M., et al.: Spontaneous bacterial peritonitis due to *Plesiomonas shigelloides*. Am. J. Gastroenterol. *90*:1529–1530, 1995.
3. Aldridge, K. E., Valainis, G. T., and Sanders, C. V.: Comparison of the in vitro activity of ciprofloxacin and twenty-four other antimicrobial agents against clinical strains of *Chromobacterium violaceum*. Diagn. Microbiol. Infect. Dis. *10*:31–38, 1988.
4. al-Fadel Saleh, M., al-Madan, M. S., Erwa, H. H., et al.: First case of human infection caused by *Pasteurella gallinarum* causing infective endocarditis in an adolescent ten years after surgical correction for truncus arteriosus. Pediatrics *95*:944–948, 1995.
5. Angen, O., Mutters, R., Caugant, D. A., et al.: Taxonomic relationships of the *[Pasteurella] haemolytica* complex as evaluated by DNA-DNA hybridizations and 16S rRNA sequencing with proposal of *Mannheimia haemolytica* gen. Nov., comb. Nov., *Mannheimia granulomatis* comb. Nov., *Mannheimia glucosida* sp. Nov., *Mannheimia ruminalis* sp. Nov. and *Mannheimia varigena* sp. Nov. Int. J. Syst. Bacteriol. *49*:67–86, 1999.
6. Brendan, R. A., Miller, M. A., and Janda, J. M.: Clinical disease spectrum and pathogenic factors associated with *Plesiomonas shigelloides* infections in humans. Rev. Infect. Dis. *10*:303–316, 1988.
7. Butt, A. A., Figueroa, J., and Martin, D. H.: Ocular infection caused by three unusual marine organisms. Clin. Infect. Dis. *24*:740–741, 1997.
8. Citron, D. M., Edelstein, M. A., Garcia, L. S., et al.: Gram-negative facultatively anaerobic bacilli and aerobic coccobacilli. *In* Forbes, B. A., Sahm, D. F., and Weissfeld, A. S. (eds.): Bailey and Scott's Diagnostic Microbiology. 11th ed. St. Louis, C. V. Mosby, 2002.
9. Duma, R. J.: Aztreonam, the first monobactam. Ann. Intern. Med. *106*:766, 1987.
10. Escande, F., Vallee, E., and Aubart, F.: *Pasteurella caballi* infection following a horse bite. Zentralbl. Bakteriol. *285*:440–444, 1997.
11. Fajfar-Whetsone, C. J. T., Coleman, L., Biggs, D. R., et al.: *Pasteurella multocida* septicemia and subsequent *Pasteurella dagmatis* septicemia in a diabetic patient. J. Clin. Microbiol. *33*:202–204, 1995.
12. Farrar, W. E., Jr., and O'Dell, N. M.: Beta-lactamase activity in *Chromobacterium violaceum*. J. Infect. Dis. *134*:290–293, 1976.

13. Feldman, R. B., Stern, G. A., and Hood, I.: *Chromobacterium violaceum* infection of the eye. Arch. Ophthalmol. *102*:711–713, 1984.
14. Fredericksen, W., and Tonning, B.: Possible misidentification of *Haemophilus aphrophilus* as *Pasteurella gallinarum*. Clin. Infect. Dis. *32*:987–988, 2001.
15. Furie, R. A., Cohen, R. P., Hartman, B. J., et al.: *Pasteurella multocida* infection: Report in urban setting and review of spectrum of human disease. N. Y. State Med. J. *80*:1597–1602, 1980.
16. Gadberry, J. L., Zipper, R., Taylor, J. A., et al.: *Pasteurella pneumotropica* isolated from bone and joint infections. J. Clin. Microbiol. *19*:926–927, 1984.
17. Goldstein, E. J. C., and Citron, D. M.: Comparative activities of cefuroxime, amoxicillin—clavulanic acid, ciprofloxacin, enoxacin, and ofloxacin against aerobic and anaerobic bacteria isolated from bite wounds. Antimicrob. Agents Chemother. *32*:1143–1148, 1988.
18. Gupta, S.: Migratory polyarthritis associated with *Plesiomonas shigelloides* infection. Scand. J. Rheumatol. *24*:323–325, 1995.
19. Hamilton-Miller, J. M.: A possible pitfall in the identification of *Pasteurella* spp. with the API system. J. Med. Microbiol. *39*:78–79, 1993.
20. Herrington, D. A., Tzipori, S., Robins-Browne, R. M., et al.: In vitro and in vivo pathogenicity of *Plesiomonas shigelloides*. Infect. Immun. *55*: 979–985, 1987.
21. Holmberg, S. D., Wachsmuth, K., Hickman-Brenner, F. W., et al.: *Plesiomonas* enteric infections in the United States. Ann. Intern. Med. *105*: 690–694, 1986.
22. Holst, E., Rollof, J., Larsson, L., et al.: Characterization and distribution of *Pasteurella* species recovered from infected humans. J. Clin. Microbiol. *30*:2984–2987, 1992.
23. Inglis, T. J., Chiang, D., Lee, G. S., and Chor-Kiang, L.: Potential misidentification of *Burkholderia pseudomallei* by API 20NE. Pathology *30*:62–64, 1998.
24. Ingram, C. W., Morrison, A. J., Jr., and Levitz, R. E.: Gastroenteritis, sepsis, and osteomyelitis caused by *Plesiomonas shigelloides* in an immunocompetent host: Case report and review of the literature. J. Clin. Microbiol. *25*:1791–1793, 1987.
25. Jones, F. L., Jr., and Smull, C. E.: Infections in man due to *Pasteurella multocida*: Importance of human carrier. Pa. Med. J. *76*:41–44, 1985.
26. Kain, K. C., and Kelly, M. T.: Clinical features, epidemiology, and treatment of *Plesiomonas shigelloides* diarrhea. J. Clin. Microbiol. *27*: 998–1001, 1989.
27. Kain, K. C., and Kelly, M. T.: Antimicrobial susceptibilities of *Plesiomonas shigelloides* from patients with diarrhea. Antimicrob. Agents Chemother. *33*:1609–1610, 1989.
28. Kaka, S., Lunz, R., and Klugman, K. P.: *Actinobacillus (Pasteurella) ureae* meningitis in an HIV-positive patient. Diagn. Microbiol. Infect. Dis. *20*:105–107, 1994.
29. Kaufman, S. C., Ceraso, D., and Schugurensky, A.: First case report from Argentina of fatal septicemia caused by *Chromobacterium violaceum*. J. Clin. Microbiol. *23*:956–958, 1986.
30. Kehrenberg, C., and Schwartz, S.: Identification of a truncated, but functionally active tet(H) tetracycline resistance gene in *Pasteurella aerogenes* and *Pasteurella multocida*. FEMS Microbiol. Lett. *188*:191–195, 2000.
31. Lee, J., Kim, J. S., Nahm, C. H., et al.: Two cases of *Chromobacterium violaceum* infection after injury in a subtropical region. J. Clin. Microbiol. *37*:2068–2070, 1999.
32. Leet, S., and Wright, B. D.: Fulminating chromobacterial septicemia presenting as respiratory distress syndrome. Thorax *36*:557–559, 1981.
33. Lester, A., Jarlov, J. O., Westh H., et al.: *Pasteurella haemolytica* diagnosis questioned. J. Infect. *25*:334–335, 1992.
34. MacDonell, M. T., and Colwell, R. R.: Phylogeny of the Vibrionaceae, and recommendation for two new genera, *Listonella* and *Shewanella*. Syst. Appl. Microbiol. *6*:171–182, 1985.
35. Macher, A. M., Casale, T. B., and Fauci, A. S.: Chronic granulomatous disease of childhood and *Chromobacterium violaceum* infections in the southeastern United States. Ann. Intern. Med. *97*:51–55, 1982.
36. Mamlok, R. J., Mamlok, V., Mills, G. C., et al.: Glucose-6-phosphate dehydrogenase deficiency, neutrophil dysfunction, and *Chromobacterium violaceum* sepsis. J. Pediatr. *111*:852–854, 1987.
37. Marshman, W. E., and Lyons, C. J.: Congenital endophthalmitis following maternal shellfish ingestion. Aust. N. Z. J. Ophthalmol. *26*:161–163, 1998.
38. Martin, D. L., and Gustafson, T. L.: *Plesiomonas* gastroenteritis in Texas. J. A. M. A. *15*:2063, 1985.
39. McNeely, D., Ivy, P., Craft, J. C., et al.: *Plesiomonas*: Biology of the organism and disease in children. Pediatr. Infect. Dis. *3*:176–181, 1984.
40. Melo, P. S., Maria, S. S., Vidal, B. C., et al.: Violacein cytotoxicity and induction of apoptosis in V79 cells. In Vitro Cell. Dev. Biol. Anim. *36*: 539–543, 2000.
41. Miller, D. P., Blevins, W. T., Steele, D. B., et al.: A comparative study of virulent and avirulent strains of *Chromobacterium violaceum*. Can. J. Microbiol. *32*:249–255, 1988.
42. Moore, C. C., Lane, J. E., and Stephens, J. L.: Successful treatment of an infant with *Chromobacterium violaceum* sepsis. Clin Infect Dis. *32*(6): e107–e110, 2001.
43. Mutters, R., Ihm, P., Pohl, S., et al.: Reclassification of the genus *Pasteurella* Trivisan 1887 on the basis of deoxyribonucleic acid homology, with proposals for the new species *Pasteurella dagmatis, Pasteurella canis, Pasteurella stomatis, Pasteurella anatis,* and *Pasteurella langaa.* Int. J. Syst. Bacteriol. *35*:309, 1985.
44. Myers, J., Ragasa, D. A., and Eisole, C.: *Chromobacterium violaceum* septicemia in New Jersey. J. Med. Soc. N. J. *79*:213–214, 1982.
45. Noble, R. C., Marek, B. J., and Overman, S. B.: Spontaneous bacterial peritonitis caused by *Pasteurella ureae*. J. Clin. Microbiol. *25*:442–444, 1987.
46. Paul, R., Siitonen, A., Karkkainen, P.: *Plesiomonas shigelloides* bacteremia in a healthy girl with mild gastroenteritis. J. Clin. Microbiol. *28*:1445–1446, 1990.
47. Ponte, R., and Jenkins, S. G.: Fatal *Chromobacterium violaceum* infections associated with exposure to stagnant waters. Pediatr. Infect. Dis. J. *11*:583–586, 1992.
48. Rahim, Z., and Kay, B. A.: Enrichment for *Plesiomonas shigelloides* from stools. J. Clin. Microbiol. *26*:789–790, 1988.
49. Reinhardt, J. F., and George, W. L.: Comparative in vitro activities of selected antimicrobial agents against *Aeromonas* species and *Plesiomonas shigelloides*. Antimicrob. Agents Chemother. *27*:643–645, 1985.
50. Rolston, K. V. I., and Hopfer, R. L.: Diarrhea due to *Plesiomonas shigelloides* in cancer patients. J. Clin. Microbiol. *20*:597–598, 1984.
51. Shigematsu, M., Kaufmann, M. E., Charlett, A., et al.: An epidemiologic study of *Plesiomonas shigelloides* diarrhea among Japanese travellers. Epidemiol. Infect. *125*:523–530, 2000.
52. Sivendra, R., and Tan, S. H.: Pathogenicity of unpigmented cultures of *Chromobacterium violaceum*. J. Clin. Microbiol. *5*:514–516, 1977.
53. Sneath, P. H. A. Genus *Chromobacterium*. *In* Krieg, N. R., and Holt, J. G. (eds.): Bergey's Manual of Systematic Bacteriology. Baltimore, Williams & Wilkins, 1984, pp. 580–582.
54. Sorbello, A. F., O'Donnell, J., Kaiser-Smith, J., et al.: Infective endocarditis due to *Pasteurella dagmatis:* Case report and review. Clin. Infect. Dis. *18*:336–338, 1994.
55. Sorenson, R. U., Jacobs, M. R., and Shurin, S. B.: *Chromobacterium violaceum* adenitis acquired in the northern United States as a complication of chronic granulomatous disease. Pediatr. Infect. Dis. J. *4*:701–702, 1985.
56. Terpeluk, C., Goldman, A., Bartmann, P., et al.: *Plesiomonas shigelloides* sepsis and meningoencephalitis in a neonate. Eur. J. Pediatr. *151*: 499–501, 1992.
57. Theodoropoulos, C., Wong, T. H., O'Brien, M., and Stenzel, D.: *Plesiomonas shigelloides* enters polarized human intestinal Caco-2 cells in an in vitro model system. Infect. Immun. *69*:2260–2269, 2001.
58. Thorsen, P., Moller, B. R., Arpi, M., et al.: *Pasteurella aerogenes* isolated from stillbirth and mother. Lancet *343*:485–486, 1994.
59. Ti, T. Y., Tan, W. C., Chong, A. P. Y., et al.: Nonfatal and fatal infections caused by *Chromobacterium violaceum*. Clin. Infect. Dis. *17*:505–507, 1993.
60. Vitovec, J., Aldova, E., Vladik, P., and Krovacek, K.: Enteropathogenicity of *Plesiomonas shigelloides* and *Aeromonas* spp. in experimental mono- and coinfection with *Cryptosporidium parvum* in the intestine of neonatal BALB/c mice. Comp. Immunol. Microbiol. Infect. Dis. *24*:39–55, 2001.
61. Wang, S.: A study of the ecology of *Plesiomonas shigelloides*. (Chinese.) Zhonghua Liu Xing Bing Xue Za Zhi *12*:295–298, 1991.
62. Zims, M. M., Zimprich, C. A., Petermann, S. R., and Rust, L.: Expression and partial characterization of an elastase from *Chromobacterium violaceum*. Vet. Microbiol. *80*:63–74, 2001.

CHAPTER

125 Acinetobacter

ARMANDO G. CORREA

First recognized as a human pathogen in 1908,[62] the ubiquitous organism *Acinetobacter* has emerged as a rather common cause of nosocomial infections in immunocompromised hosts.[6] Some of the confusion regarding this organism may be attributed to the many changes in nomenclature that the members of this genus have undergone over the years. Names that have been used in the past to identify this genus include *Herrella, Bacterium, Mima, Achromobacter, Alcaligenes, Neisseria, Micrococcus, Diplococcus, Moraxella,* and *Cytophaga.* Treatment of infection caused by *Acinetobacter* is complicated by its widespread multidrug resistance and the difficulty in eradicating the organism.

The Organism

The genus *Acinetobacter* belongs to the family Neisseriaceae, which also includes the *Neisseria, Moraxella,* and *Kingella* genera. *Acinetobacter* is a gram-negative bacterium that typically appears as a rod 0.9 to 1.6 μm in diameter and 1.5 to 2.5 μm in length, but it may become spherical in the stationary phase of growth. It frequently occurs in pairs or short chains. Many strains are encapsulated. The organism has a strictly aerobic respiratory metabolism and does not grow under anaerobic conditions. It does not form spores or exhibit swimming mobility. *Acinetobacter* grows well in all common complex media between 20 and 30° C, with optimal growth occurring between 33 and 35° C, and it has no growth factor requirements.

Convex, grayish-white colonies 1 to 2.5 mm in diameter are typical findings. The colonies may appear mucoid if the strain is encapsulated. *Acinetobacter* is catalase-positive and may be differentiated readily from other closely related genera by virtue of its negative reaction to oxidase.

Until recently, the genus *Acinetobacter* contained the single species *Acinetobacter calcoaceticus* subdivided into two subspecies or biovars: *anitratus* and *lwoffii.*[29] However, in 1986 the taxonomy of the genus *Acinetobacter* was changed extensively on the basis of DNA hybridization studies,[9] and seven species now are recognized: *Acinetobacter baumannii, A. calcoaceticus, Acinetobacter haemolyticus, Acinetobacter johnsonii, Acinetobacter junii, Acinetobacter lwoffii,* and *Acinetobacter radioresistens.* Several unnamed genospecies also have been identified.[15] These species may be differentiated in the clinical laboratory on the basis of their growth characteristics and biochemical activity. Under the new classification, most *A. baumannii* strains represent organisms that were classified formerly as biovar *anitratus,* whereas *A. junii* and *A. lwoffii* previously were listed under the biovar *lwoffii.*

Epidemiology

Acinetobacter strains are distributed widely in nature and can be found in soil, fresh water, and sewage.[8, 27] *Acinetobacter* also can be isolated from many animals, fresh meats, poultry, contaminated milk, and frozen foods.[8, 27] The organism can be part of the bacterial flora of the skin in healthy individuals,[8, 11] and the skin frequently becomes a reservoir for *Acinetobacter* in hospitalized patients and the health care staff.[6, 8] It occasionally forms part of the normal flora of the oral cavity and the upper respiratory, genital, and lower gastrointestinal tracts.[8, 11] Colonization by *Acinetobacter* is particularly common in patients who have undergone a tracheostomy.[49] The organism frequently can be found in the hospital environment, particularly in moist areas, such as in humidifiers, water sinks, and ventilators.[8] Nosocomial outbreaks have been linked to colonized medical equipment such as ventilator tubing and other respiratory equipment,[1, 25] intravenous catheters,[8] gloves,[44] and mattresses.[55]

The frequency of occurrence of nosocomial infections by *Acinetobacter* is not easy to assess because the pathogenic role of this organism often has been underestimated. However, a national surveillance study conducted from 1974 to 1977 identified *Acinetobacter* as a pathogen in 0.76 percent of nosocomial infections.[47] The estimated rate of nosocomial infections caused by this organism was 3.11 per 10,000 patients discharged, and approximately 15 percent of 1372 reported episodes occurred in the pediatric age group.[47] By 1978, this rate increased by 14 percent and accounted for 1 percent of the bacterial isolates associated with nosocomial infections.[11] Of interest, an unusual seasonal pattern was observed, with most infections occurring in late summer.[11, 47] The cause for this increase is unknown. Pneumonia, tracheobronchitis, and infections of the urinary tract and surgical wounds were the entities observed most frequently.[47] In a national survey of U.S. hospitals from 1995 through 1998, *Acinetobacter* spp. accounted for 1.5 percent of all nosocomial bloodstream infections.[66] Data from SENTRY, an international surveillance program that monitors the frequency of occurrence and antimicrobial susceptibility of bacterial pathogens, has revealed a significantly greater frequency of *Acinetobacter* infections in Latin America than in all other regions.[21] A higher prevalence rate of *Acinetobacter* infections has been noted from birth to the age of 10 years.[21] In the pediatric age group, neonates appear to be particularly susceptible to nosocomial infection with this organism[40] (Table 125–1).

Pathogenesis

Limited information is available regarding the pathogenesis of *Acinetobacter* infections, and specific virulence factors have not been identified. Except for the presence of lipopolysaccharide, a normal constituent of the outer membrane of gram-negative bacteria capable of eliciting multiple pathogenic host responses, no cytotoxic products have been identified. In animal models, *Acinetobacter* can enhance the virulence of other bacteria in mixed infections, perhaps by slime-induced inhibition of neutrophils.[42] Researchers have speculated that the ability to grow in an acidic pH at lower temperatures may enhance its ability to invade devitalized tissue.[2] The organism also may survive in a dry environment for as long as a week.[13]

TABLE 125–1 ■ NOSOCOMIAL CLUSTERS OF *ACINETOBACTER* INFECTION IN PEDIATRIC PATIENTS

Country	Year	Type of Unit	Infected Children	Colonized Children	Presentation	Mortality (%)	Suspected Source
United Kingdom[40]	1981	NICU	4	0	Meningitis	0	None identified
United Kingdom[57]	1983	NICU	9	1	Pulmonary infection	22	Ambu bag
Japan[60]	1983–1986	NICU	19	52	Sepsis	11	Multiple sources
India[30]	1988	Oncology	8	N/A	Meningitis	38	Intrathecal needle
Germany[52]	1988	NICU	3	41	Sepsis	100	Humidifier
Israel[46]	1988–1990	NICU	9	N/A	Sepsis	44	None identified
United Kingdom[41]	1989	NICU	7	N/A	Sepsis	0	Intravenous fluids
Bahamas[38]	1996	NICU	8	1	Sepsis	37	Air conditioner
South Africa[45]	1997	NICU	9	N/A	Sepsis	22	Suction catheters
India[39]	1995	NICU	79	N/A	Sepsis	14	None identified
India[12]	1986–1990	NICU	26	N/A	Sepsis	42	None identified

N/A, data not available; NICU, neonatal intensive care unit.

Clinical Manifestations

Acinetobacter can cause suppurative infection of virtually any organ, and the clinical manifestations typically are similar to those seen with other bacterial infections because no unique features are suggestive of *Acinetobacter* infection. The clinical manifestations also may depend on the underlying immune status of compromised hosts. Infections caused by *Acinetobacter* are rare occurrences in normal children.[17]

INTRACRANIAL INFECTION

Most cases of *Acinetobacter* meningitis are the result of a penetrating injury or occur after a neurosurgical procedure, although sporadic cases of meningitis have been reported in the absence of these factors. A cluster of eight children in whom *Acinetobacter* meningitis developed after the administration of intrathecal methotrexate has been reported.[30] All patients had fever, headache, nausea, and vomiting, and lumbar puncture revealed cerebrospinal fluid (CSF) pleocytosis.

The earlier literature contains several reports of *Acinetobacter* meningitis developing in apparently normal children.[14, 16, 28, 59, 63] CSF pleocytosis with a predominance of segmented forms occurred commonly.[16] Because as many as 30 percent of these patients had a petechial rash and gram-negative diplococci on CSF smears, the diagnosis of meningococcal meningitis was made erroneously in most of these cases, thereby leading to a delay in the institution of appropriate therapy and possibly contributing to a mortality rate as high as 27 percent.[16]

Siegman-Igra and associates,[56] in a review of 25 cases of *Acinetobacter* meningitis secondary to invasive procedures that included some children, found that fever, leukocytosis, and neck stiffness, along with other clinical signs of central nervous system infection, were common features. The CSF in these patients showed pleocytosis with a predominance of polymorphonuclear leukocytes, elevated protein concentration, and a low glucose level. Most of the infections were associated with indwelling ventriculostomy tubes or a fistula into the CSF space. Filka and colleagues[19] reported 10 cases of *Acinetobacter* meningitis that occurred over the course of a 7-year period in children who had undergone ventriculoperitoneal shunt insertion.

Researchers have suggested that an inherited or acquired complement deficiency may be associated with meningitis caused by *Acinetobacter*[18] because it is seen with *Neisseria meningitidis* and other related species. Treatment of central nervous system infections caused by *Acinetobacter* requires a minimum of 3 weeks of parenteral antibiotics.

BACTEREMIA

Acinetobacter bacteremia may occur as an isolated event or be secondary to a primary infected site, such as the respiratory or urinary tract or a wound. Primary bacteremia appears to occur more commonly in immunocompromised neonates, and its clinical manifestations can vary from an absence of clinical signs of infection to fulminant septic shock and disseminated intravascular coagulation.[31, 52] Thrombocytopenia has been reported to be a prominent feature in these neonates.[41, 46] Pneumonia has been seen more commonly in early-onset sepsis.[39] Predisposing factors include low birth weight,[50, 52] previous antibiotic therapy,[46, 50, 52] and the presence of indwelling catheters.[38, 50]

Acinetobacter bacteremia in children with malignancies also has been noted to occur rarely. Fuchs and colleagues[20] reported 29 episodes of sepsis caused by this organism over the course of a 12-year period in an oncology center. All these children were febrile and appeared ill at the time of diagnosis, and a high association of *Acinetobacter* sepsis with the presence of intravascular catheters was noted. Surprisingly, no connection was found with the level of neutropenia.[20]

RESPIRATORY TRACT

Because *Acinetobacter* may be a transient colonizer of the pharynx in 7 percent of healthy children[5] and adults[22] and this rate is increased in hospitalized patients, the relative importance of *Acinetobacter* in comparison to other potential pathogens isolated from sputum is difficult to ascertain. The tracheobronchitis and pneumonia attributed to *Acinetobacter* are mostly nosocomial infections associated with the presence of an endotracheal tube or tracheostomy.[22] Pneumonias frequently are multilobar and occasionally may lead to cavitary destruction or pleural empyema.[22]

Community-acquired pneumonia caused by *A. baumannii* has been reported to occur in adults in the Northern Territory of Australia and other tropical regions.[4] This entity generally is seen in patients with diminished host defenses caused by alcoholism, cigarette smoking, or underlying pulmonary disease and is characterized by the rapid onset of fever, dyspnea, pleuritic chest pain, and purulent sputum. The mortality rate has been as high as 53 to 64 percent.[4]

MISCELLANEOUS

Urinary tract infections occur almost exclusively in patients with indwelling bladder catheters, usually are limited to the bladder, and generally are mild in nature.[22] Burns, as well as traumatic and surgical wounds, frequently become colonized by *Acinetobacter* as a result of its ability to thrive on compromised tissue and foreign material.[22] Bacteremia may occur as a consequence of this colonization, which is often polymicrobial. *Acinetobacter* is a prominent cause of peritonitis in children undergoing peritoneal dialysis when gram-negative organisms are involved.[64]

Other rare infections caused by *Acinetobacter* that have been reported include suppurative otitis media,[48, 59] cellulitis (frequently in association with trauma, a foreign body, or an animal bite),[22, 48] synergistic necrotizing fasciitis,[3] native- and prosthetic-value endocarditis,[24] septic arthritis,[48] osteomyelitis,[59] and liver abscesses.[22] Ocular infections also have been documented.[36] A case of osteomyelitis occurring after a hamster bite in a child has been described.[37]

Diagnosis

The diagnosis of *Acinetobacter* infection is made by culture of appropriate body fluids or tissue specimens. No serologic or antigen-detection tests are available. A selective medium containing MacConkey agar with cephaloridine has been used to culture skin specimens during investigation of outbreaks[57] because of its ability to inhibit most of the skin flora but not *Acinetobacter.*

Biotyping, phage typing, electrophoretic analysis of isoenzyme and cell wall proteins, plasmid analysis, polymerase chain reaction–based DNA fingerprinting, and restriction endonuclease digestion of DNA have been used for investigation of nosocomial outbreaks.[7] Antibiogram typing no longer is considered an effective method in the investigation of *Acinetobacter* epidemics because the susceptibility pattern may change rapidly within the same outbreak.[7, 10]

Treatment

As with many other opportunistic gram-negative organisms, treatment of infections caused by *Acinetobacter* spp., particularly *A. baumannii,*[53, 61] has become more complicated by the rapid increase in resistance to the antibiotics used commonly in hospitals. Selection of an antibiotic regimen should be based on in vitro susceptibility testing and ideally should include both a β-lactam and an aminoglycoside, which may have synergistic activity[22] and prevent the emergence of resistance.[6]

In recent years, *A. baumannii* has shown decreased susceptibility to ampicillin, broad-spectrum penicillins, cephalosporins, aminoglycosides, and ciprofloxacin.[21, 53] Resistance to extended-spectrum cephalosporins may be the result of the presence of cephalosporinases, broad-spectrum β-lactamases, or changes in the outer-membrane porins and penicillin-binding proteins.[43] Resistance to aminoglycosides is mediated by aminoglycoside-modifying enzymes.[61] The carbapenems imipenem and meropenem appear to be the most active agents against *A. baumannii,*[56, 61] but recent reports have found more than 10 percent of such strains to be resistant to these antibiotics in some areas,[21, 35] and an increasing number of nosocomial outbreaks of carbapenem-resistant *Acinetobacter* infections have been reported.[23, 60, 68] The incidence of carbapenem-resistant *Acinetobacter* strains has been particularly high in Latin America (11.4% of all isolates versus 4.8% in the United States).[21] Resistance to the carbapenems has been associated with the presence of carbapenem-hydrolyzing β-lactamases. Caution should be exercised when using imipenem at high dosage in children for the treatment of meningitis (i.e., 100 mg/kg/day) because of an unusually high rate of seizures.[67] Ertapenem, a new carbapenem antibiotic, has poor in vitro activity against *Acinetobacter*[33] and should not be used for the treatment of these infections. Combinations of a β-lactam antibiotic with a β-lactamase inhibitor, such as ampicillin-sulbactam, piperacillin-tazobactam, or ticarcillin-clavulanate, have been used for infections caused by carbapenem-resistant strains.[60, 68]

Though not approved for use in children younger than 16 years of age because of the theoretic concern for damage to growth cartilage, the fluoroquinolones, in particular ciprofloxacin, have been used successfully to treat infections caused by multidrug-resistant *Acinetobacter* in children[39, 45] and adults. Of the current available quinolones, gatifloxacin exhibits the best in vitro activity against *A. baumannii,* followed by levofloxacin and trovafloxacin.[26] Although 76 to 86 percent of sporadic isolates of *A. baumannii* are susceptible to the fluoroquinolones, only 32 to 55 percent of outbreak-related strains remain susceptible to this antibiotic class.[26] In some cases, the polymyxin drugs polymyxin B and colistin are the only therapeutic option for the treatment of multidrug-resistant *Acinetobacter* infection.[23, 32]

Imipenem, meropenem, amikacin, ciprofloxacin, ceftazidime, and ceftriaxone have exhibited good in vitro activity against isolates identified as species other than *A. baumannii.*[53] In addition to antimicrobial therapy, prompt drainage of focal suppurative sites and removal of infected indwelling catheters are essential. Intraventricular administration of amikacin has been used in the treatment of central nervous system infections caused by this organism.[65]

Prognosis

Because *Acinetobacter* strains often are resistant to the antibiotics used commonly, prompt recognition of the specific etiology and institution of effective antibiotic therapy are critical to a successful outcome. The reported mortality rate in series of pediatric patients has ranged from 0 percent to more than 50 percent (see Table 125–1), and the outcome appears to correlate more closely with the underlying condition than with other factors such as polymicrobial bacteremia.[58] In a series of 58 infections caused by this organism that occurred over the course of a 2-year period from 1973 through 1974 at the Massachusetts General Hospital, the mortality rate was 23 percent.[22] A 1999 prospective study in the Slovak Republic revealed that the case-fatality rate for 157 episodes of *A. baumannii* bacteremia was significantly higher in adults than children (34 versus 12%).[31]

The nosocomial acquisition of multiresistant *A. baumannii* has been associated with high mortality rates and prolonged hospitalization in adult patients in intensive care units,[34, 51] in contrast to the more benign clinical outcome that usually is seen with other species of *Acinetobacter.*[54]

Prevention

Nosocomial acquisition of *Acinetobacter* by high-risk, compromised hosts can be prevented by placing emphasis on the control measures routinely used for endemic infections, such as careful handwashing by personnel, limitation of the frequency and duration of use of devices, proper isolation of colonized and infected patients, application of strict techniques for invasive procedures, and restricted use of antibiotics.[13, 34, 56]

REFERENCES

1. Ahmed, J., Brutus, A., D'Amato, R. F., et al.: *Acinetobacter calcoaceticus anitratus* outbreak in the intensive care unit traced to a peak flow meter. Am. J. Infect. Control *22*:319–321, 1994.
2. Allen, D. M., and Hartman, B. J.: *Acinetobacter* species. *In* Mandell, G. L., Bennett, J. E., and Dolin, R. (eds.): Mandell, Douglas and Bennett's Principles and Practice of Infectious Diseases. 4th ed. New York, Churchill Livingstone, 1995, pp. 2009–2013.
3. Amsel, M. B., and Horrilleno, E.: Synergistic necrotizing fasciitis: A case of polymicrobial infection with *Acinetobacter calcoaceticus*. Curr. Surg. *42*:370–372, 1985.
4. Anstey, N. M., Currie, B. J., and Withnall, K. M.: Community-acquired *Acinetobacter* pneumonia in the Northern Territory of Australia. Clin. Infect. Dis. *14*:83–91, 1992.
5. Baltimore, R. S., Duncan, R. L., Shapiro, E. D., et al.: Epidemiology of pharyngeal colonization of infants with aerobic gram-negative rod bacteria. J. Clin. Microbiol. *27*:91–95, 1989.
6. Bergogne-Berezin, E.: *Acinetobacter* spp., saprophytic organisms of increasing pathogenic importance. Zentrabl. Bakteriol. *81*:389–405, 1994.
7. Bergogne-Berezin, E., and Joly-Guillou, M. L.: Hospital infection with *Acinetobacter* spp.: An increasing problem. J. Hosp. Infect. *18*(Suppl. A):250–255, 1991.
8. Bergogne-Berezin, E., Joly-Guillou, M. L., and Vieu, J. F.: Epidemiology of nosocomial infections due to *Acinetobacter calcoaceticus*. J. Hosp. Infect. *10*:105–113, 1987.
9. Bouvet, P. J. M., and Grimont, P. A. D.: Taxonomy of the genus *Acinetobacter* with the recognition of *Acinetobacter baumannii* sp. nov., *Acinetobacter haemolyticus* sp. nov., *Acinetobacter johnsonii* sp. nov., and *Acinetobacter junii* sp. nov. and the emended descriptions of *Acinetobacter calcoaceticus* and *Acinetobacter lwoffii*. Int. J. Syst. Bacteriol. *36*:228–240, 1986.
10. Carlquist, J. F., Conti, M., and Burke, J. P.: Progressive resistance in a single strain of *Acinetobacter calcoaceticus* recovered during a nosocomial outbreak. Am. J. Infect. Control *10*:43–48, 1982.
11. Centers for Disease Control and Prevention: Nosocomial infections caused by *Acinetobacter calcoaceticus*—United States, 1978. M. M. W. R. Morb. Mortal Wkly. Rep. *28*:177–179, 1979.
12. Christo, G. G., Shenoy, V., Matthai, J., et al.: *Acinetobacter* sepsis in neonates. Indian Pediatr. *30*:1413–1416, 1993.
13. Crombach, W. H. J., Dijkshoorn, L., van Noort-Klaassen, M., et al.: Control of an epidemic spread of a multi-resistant strain of *Acinetobacter calcoaceticus* in a hospital. Intensive Care Med. *15*:166–170, 1989.
14. DeBord, G. G.: *Mima polymorpha* in meningitis. J. Bacteriol. *55*:764–765, 1948.
15. Dijkshoorn, L., and van der Toorn, J.: *Acinetobacter* species: Which do we mean? Clin. Infect. Dis. *15*:748–749, 1992.
16. Donald, W. D., and Doak, W. M.: Mimeae meningitis and sepsis. J. A. M. A. *200*:111–113, 1967.
17. Feigin, R. D., and Shearer, W. T.: Opportunistic infection in children: III. In the normal host. J. Pediatr. *87*:852–866, 1975.
18. Fijen, C. A. P., Kuijper, E. J., Tjia, H. G., et al.: Complement deficiency predisposes for meningitis due to nongroupable meningococci and *Neisseria*-related bacteria. Clin. Infect. Dis. *18*:780–784, 1994.
19. Filka, J., Huttova, M., Schwartzova, D., et al.: Nosocomial meningitis due to *Acinetobacter calcoaceticus* in 10 children after ventriculoperitoneal shunt insertion. J. Hosp. Infect. *44*:76–77, 2000.
20. Fuchs, G. J., Jaffe, N., and Pickering, L. K.: *Acinetobacter calcoaceticus* sepsis in children with malignancies. Pediatr. Infect. Dis. *5*:545–549, 1986.
21. Gales, A. C., Jones, R. N., Forward, K. R., et al.: Emerging importance of multidrug-resistant *Acinetobacter* species and *Stenotrophomonas maltophilia* as pathogens in seriously ill patients: Geographic patterns, epidemiological features, and trends in the SENTRY antimicrobial surveillance program (1997–1999). Clin. Infect. Dis. *32*(Suppl. 2): 104–113, 2001.
22. Glew, R. H., Moellering R. C., and Kunz L. J.: Infections with *Acinetobacter calcoaceticus (Herrella vaginicola)*: Clinical and laboratory studies. Medicine (Baltimore) *56*:79–97, 1977.
23. Go, E. S., Urban, C., Burns, J., et al.: Clinical and molecular epidemiology of *Acinetobacter* infections sensitive only to polymyxin B and sulbactam. Lancet *344*:1329–1332, 1994.
24. Gradon, J. D., Chapnick, E. K., and Lutwick, L. I.: Infective endocarditis of a native valve due to *Acinetobacter:* Case report and review. Clin. Infect. Dis. *14*:1145–1148, 1992.
25. Hartstein, A. I., Rashad, A. L., Liebler, J. M., et al.: Multiple intensive care unit outbreak of *Acinetobacter calcoaceticus* subspecies *anitratus* respiratory infection and colonization associated with contaminated, reusable ventilator circuits and resuscitation bags. Am. J. Med. *85*:624–631, 1988.
26. Heinemann, B., Wisplinghoff, H., Edmond, M., and Seifert, H.: Comparative activities of ciprofloxacin, clinafloxacin, gatifloxacin, gemifloxacin, levofloxacin, moxifloxacin, and trovafloxacin against epidemiologically defined *Acinetobacter baumanii* strains. Antimicrob. Agents Chemother. *44*:2211–2213, 2000.
27. Henriksen, S. D.: *Moraxella, Acinetobacter,* and the Mimeae. Bacteriol. Rev. *37*:522–561, 1973.
28. Hermann, G., and Melnick, T.: *Mima polymorpha* meningitis in the young. Am. J. Dis. Child. *110*:315–318, 1965.
29. Juni, E.: *Acinetobacter*. *In* Krieg, N. R. (ed.): Bergey's Manual of Systematic Bacteriology. Baltimore, Williams & Wilkins, 1984, pp. 303–306.
30. Kelkar, R., Gordon, S. M., Giri, N., et al.: Epidemic iatrogenic *Acinetobacter* spp. meningitis following administration of intrathecal methotrexate. J. Hosp. Infect. *14*:233–243, 1989.
31. Koprnova, J., Svetlansky, I., Bilikova, E., et al.: *Acinetobacter baumanii* bacteremia in children. Pediatr. Infect. Dis. J. *20*:1183, 2001.
32. Levin, A. S., Barone, A. A., Penco, J., et al.: Intravenous colistin as therapy for nosocomial infections caused by multidrug-resistant *Pseudomonas aeruginosa* and *Acinetobacter baumanii.* Clin. Infect. Dis. *28*:1008–1011, 1999.
33. Livermore, D. M., Carter, M. W., Bagel, S., et al.: In vitro activity of ertapenem (MK-0826) against recent clinical bacteria collected in Europe and Australia. Antimicrob. Agents Chemother. *45*:1860–1867, 2001.
34. Lortholary, O., Fagon, J. Y., Hoi, A. B., et al.: Nosocomial acquisition of multiresistant *Acinetobacter baumannii:* Risk factors and prognosis. Clin. Infect. Dis. *20*:790–796, 1995.
35. Manikal, V. M., Landman, D., Saurina, G., et al.: Endemic carbapenem-resistant *Acinetobacter* species in Brooklyn, New York: Citywide prevalence, interinstitutional spread, and relation to antibiotic usage. Clin. Infect. Dis. *31*:101–106, 2000.
36. Marcovich, A., and Levartovsky, S.: *Acinetobacter* exposure keratitis. Br. J. Ophthalmol. *78*:489–490, 1994.
37. Martin, R. W., Martin, D. L., and Levy, C. S.: *Acinetobacter* osteomyelitis from a hamster bite. Pediatr. Infect. Dis. J. *5*:364–365, 1988.
38. McDonald, L. C., Walker, M., Carson, L., et al.: Outbreak of *Acinetobacter* spp. bloodstream infections in a nursery associated with contaminated aerosols and air conditioners. Pediatr. Infect. Dis. J. *17*:716–722, 1998.
39. Mishra, A., Mishra, S., Jaganath, G., et al.: *Acinetobacter* sepsis in newborns. Indian Pediatr. *35*:2732, 1998.
40. Morgan, M. E. I., and Hart, C. A.: *Acinetobacter* meningitis: Acquired infection in a neonatal intensive care unit. Arch. Dis. Child. *657*:557–559, 1982.
41. Ng, P. C., Herrington, R. A., Beane, C. A., et al.: An outbreak of *Acinetobacter* septicaemia in a neonatal intensive care unit. J. Hosp. Infect. *14*:363–368, 1989.
42. Obana, Y.: Pathogenic significance of *Acinetobacter calcoaceticus:* Analysis of experimental infection in mice. Microbiol. Immunol. *30*:645–657, 1986.
43. Obara, M., and Nakae, T.: Mechanisms of resistance to β-lactam antibiotics in *Acinetobacter calcoaceticus*. J. Antimicrob. Chemother. *28*: 791–800, 1991.
44. Patterson, J. E., Vecchio, J., Pantelick, E. L., et al.: Association of contaminated gloves with transmission of *Acinetobacter calcoaceticus* var. *anitratus* in an intensive care unit. Am. J. Med. *91*:479–483, 1991.
45. Pillay, T., Pillay, D. G., Adhikari, M., and Sturm, A. W.: An outbreak of neonatal infection with *Acinetobacter* linked to contaminated suction catheters. J. Hosp. Infect. *43*:299–304, 1999.
46. Regev, R., Dolfin, T., Zelig, I., et al.: *Acinetobacter* septicemia: A threat to neonates? Special aspects in a neonatal intensive care unit. Infection *21*:394–396, 1993.
47. Retailliau, H. F., Hightower, A. W., Dixon, R. E., et al.: *Acinetobacter calcoaceticus:* A nosocomial pathogen with an unusual seasonal pattern. J. Infect. Dis. *139*:371–375, 1979.
48. Reynolds, R. C., and Cluff, L. E.: Infection of men with Mimeae. Ann. Intern. Med. *58*:759–767, 1963.
49. Rosenthal, S. L.: Sources of *Pseudomonas* and *Acinetobacter* species found in human culture materials. Am. J. Clin. Pathol. *62*:807–811, 1974.
50. Sakata, H., Fujita, K., Maruyama, S., et al.: *Acinetobacter calcoaceticus* biovar *anitratus* septicaemia in a neonatal intensive care unit: Epidemiology and control. J. Hosp. Infect. *14*:15–22, 1989.
51. Scerpella, E. G., Wanger, A. R., Armitige, L., et al.: Nosocomial outbreak caused by a multiresistant clone of *Acinetobacter baumannii:* Results of the case-control and molecular epidemiologic investigations. Infect. Control Hosp. Epidemiol. *16*:92–97, 1995.
52. Schloesser, R. L., Laufkoetter, E. A., Lehners, T., et al.: An outbreak of *Acinetobacter calcoaceticus* infection in a neonatal care unit. Infection *18*:230–233, 1990.
53. Seifert, H., Baginski, R., Schulze, A., et al.: Antimicrobial susceptibility of *Acinetobacter* species. Antimicrob. Agents Chemother. *37*:750–753, 1993.
54. Seifert, H., Strate, A., Schulze, A., et al.: Bacteremia due to *Acinetobacter* species other than *Acinetobacter baumannii.* Infection *22*:379–385, 1994.

55. Sherertz, R. J., and Sullivan, M. L.: An outbreak of infections with *Acinetobacter calcoaceticus* in burn patients: Contamination of patients' mattresses. J. Infect. Dis. *151*:252–258, 1985.
56. Siegman-Igra, Y., Bar-Yosef, S., Gorea, A., et al.: Nosocomial *Acinetobacter* meningitis secondary to invasive procedures: Report of 25 cases and review. Clin. Infect. Dis. *17*:843–849, 1993.
57. Stone, J. W., and Das, B. C.: Investigation of an outbreak of infection with *Acinetobacter calcoaceticus* in a special care baby unit. J. Hosp. Infect. *6*:42–48, 1985.
58. Tilley, P. A. G., and Roberts, F. J.: Bacteremia with *Acinetobacter* species: Risk factors and prognosis in different clinical settings. Clin. Infect. Dis. *18*:896–900, 1994.
59. Torregrosa, M. V., and Ortiz, A.: Severe infections in children due to rare gram-negative bacilli *(Mima polymorpha* and *Bacillus anitratum).* J. Pediatr. *59*:35–41, 1961.
60. Urban, C., Go, E., Mariano, N., et al.: Effect of sulbactam on infections caused by imipenem-resistant *Acinetobacter calcoaceticus* biotype *anitratus*. *167*:448–451, 1993.
61. Vila, J., Marcos, A., Marco, F., et al.: In vitro antimicrobial production of β-lactamases, aminoglycoside-modifying enzymes, and chloramphenicol acetyltransferase by and susceptibility of clinical isolates of *Acinetobacter baumannii.* Antimicrob. Agents Chemother. *37*:138–141, 1993.
62. Von Lingelsheim, W.: Beitrage zur Aetiologie der epidemischen Genickstarre nach den Ergebnissen der letzten Jahre. Z. Hyg. Infektionskrankheiten *59*:457–460, 1908.
63. Waite, C. L., and Kline, A. H.: *Mima polymorpha* meningitis. Am. J. Dis. Child. *98*:121–126, 1959.
64. Warady, B. A., Campoy, S. F., Gross, S. P., et al.: Peritonitis with continuous ambulatory peritoneal dialysis and continuous cycling peritoneal dialysis. J. Pediatr. *105*:726–729, 1984.
65. Wirt, T. C., McGee, Z. A., Oldfield, E. H., et al.: Intraventricular administration of amikacin for complicated gram-negative meningitis and ventriculitis. J. Neurosurg. *50*:95–99, 1979.
66. Wisplinghoff, H., Edmond, M. B., Pfaller, M. A., et al.: Nosocomial bloodstream infections caused by *Acinetobacter* species in United States hospitals: Clinical features, molecular epidemiology, and antimicrobial susceptibility. Clin. Infect. Dis. *31*:690–697, 2000.
67. Wong, V. K., Wright, H. T., Ross, L. A., et al.: Imipenem/cilastatin treatment of bacterial meningitis in children. Pediatr. Infect. Dis. J. *10*: 122–125, 1991.
68. Wood, C. A., and Reboli, A. C.: Infections caused by imipenem-resistant *Acinetobacter calcoaceticus* biotype *anitratus*. J. Infect. Dis. *168*: 1602–1603, 1993.

Achromobacter (Alcaligenes)

RANDALL G. FISHER ■ WILLIAM C. GRUBER ■ THOMAS G. BOYCE

Organisms of the genus *Achromobacter* are gram-negative bacilli that live in aqueous environments. Originally considered commensals, they are being recognized increasingly as important, though rare, hospital pathogens. *Achromobacter* can be especially problematic in immunocompromised patients and in neonates, in whom infection can be life-threatening. They have been isolated from such diverse clinical specimens as sputum, urine, feces, blood, cerebrospinal fluid, cornea, and peritoneal and pleural fluid.

Bacteriology

Achromobacter spp. are gram-negative, motile, indole-negative, obligate aerobes that are oxidase- and catalase-positive. They are considered to be nonfermenters because of their extremely limited action on carbohydrates. Most ferment xylose, and some ferment glucose. All reduce nitrate to nitrite. They are urease-, lysine-, and ornithine-negative. *Achromobacter* spp. grow well on both blood and MacConkey agar and produce colonies that are smooth and glistening and have a distinct edge. They alkalinize organic salts and amides, which led to the designation *Alcaligenes*, a name meaning alkali producing. *Alcaligenes faecalis* has a distinct, sweet odor that has been described as resembling that of green apples.[21]

Bacteriologically, they may be confused with other nonfermenting gram-negative organisms, especially *Pseudomonas* spp. Morphologically, however, they can be distinguished easily from pseudomonads by the presence of peritrichous flagella. *Pseudomonas* spp. have polar flagella.[17]

The taxonomy of these organisms is confusing and undergoes frequent change. They were classified as *Achromobacter* and then reclassified as *Alcaligenes;* recently, however, they were reassigned the name *Achromobacter*. The genera *Achromobacter* and *Alcaligenes* are closely related and include many species, but clinically important ones are as follows: (1) *Achromobacter xylosoxidans*, which has two subspecies: *xylosoxidans* and *dentrificans;* the former is the most common cause of clinically recognizable infection; (2) *A. faecalis*, which is a less common pathogen but has a distinct antimicrobial susceptibility pattern[2]; and (3) *Achromobacter piechaudii*, which has been isolated from clinical specimens[28] but is of doubtful significance. In the discussion that follows, the abbreviation *A. xylosoxidans* refers to *A. xylosoxidans* subspecies *xylosoxidans*.

Epidemiology

Like *Pseudomonas, Achromobacter* spp. are water organisms and prefer aqueous environments and moist soil. They do not survive long on porous surfaces or fomites or if they become desiccated.[31] They also may be part of the normal flora of the gastrointestinal and respiratory tracts of some people. These organisms establish a niche within the hospital environment and have been recovered from ventilators, humidifiers, "sterile" saline, intravenous fluids, and irrigation and dialysis solutions. *Achromobacter* spp. also have been recovered from infant formula,[12] children's soap bubbles,[26] well water,[34] and swimming pools.[19] Organisms likewise survive many disinfectants and have been cultured from chlorhexidine,[33] 1 percent eosin,[3] and alcohol- or quaternary amine–containing compounds.[31, 33] Shigeta and associates[33] reported an outbreak of *A. xylosoxidans* ventriculitis secondary to contaminated chlorhexidine used on a surgical ward. Foley and colleagues[14] reported an outbreak accompanied by deaths in a neonatal intensive care unit secondary to contamination of saline used as an eyewash. Boukadida and coworkers[3] reported a neonatal death caused by meningitis contracted by dissemination after treatment of a diaper rash with 1 percent eosin. An outbreak of 37 cases (with 2 fatalities) described by Reverdy and associates[29] was caused by bacterial contamination of deionized water in a hemodialysis system. Surgical wound infection also has occurred; the infection was suspected to be secondary to contaminated irrigation fluid used in surgery.[37] Two different kinds of pseudo-outbreaks have been described: in one, seven patients in a pediatric hospital were infected with *A. xylosoxidans*, but restriction fragment length polymorphism analysis proved that they all were genetically unrelated[1]; in another, *A. xylosoxidans* was isolated from three different clinical specimens but was later proved to be a contaminant of the saline used in their processing.[16]

During the last several years, studies have documented that colonization of cystic fibrosis patients with *A. xylosoxidans* is on the rise. In one large study, *A. xylosoxidans* was isolated from the sputum culture of 52 of 595 patients (8.7%).[4] Unlike *Burkholderia cepacia,* isolates of *A. xylosoxidans* at a single cystic fibrosis center are not genetically related, thus implying no common source of infection and little or no patient-to-patient spread within the center.[36] In at least one study, colonization with *A. xylosoxidans* was associated with exacerbation of disease.[10]

Pathophysiology

Achromobacter spp. are weakly virulent bacteria. Medical care commonly provides the conduit through which organisms are introduced into their host by way of indwelling catheters, endotracheal tubes, and the like. The bacteria may take advantage of a weakened immune system and disseminate, with subsequent development of sepsis, meningitis, and death. Preterm or small-for-gestational-age term infants are at particular risk for acquiring such severe *Achromobacter* infections.[14] Although most neonatal infections are considered to be nosocomial, vertical transmission from mother to baby may occur.[17] An increased incidence of infection has been reported in patients with neoplasms[22] and those receiving chronic steroid therapy.[20] Sporadic cases of *Achromobacter* infection in patients with idiopathic immunoglobulin M deficiency,[11] Waldenström macroglobulinemia,[35] and systemic lupus erythematosus also have been reported.[30] We have seen one boy with hyper-IgM syndrome in whom 14 separate episodes of *Achromobacter* bacteremia occurred; an exhaustive environmental search for a source was fruitless. The source eventually proved to be deep infection of a cervical lymph node, and the episodes ceased when the node was removed.[38] *Achromobacter* infections occur in patients with acquired immunodeficiency syndrome,[5, 15] but whether this syndrome is an independent risk factor for development of infection is unclear.

In unusual circumstances, *Achromobacter* infection will develop in patients with neither overt underlying disease nor obvious immune deficiency. Most of these cases involve penetrating trauma.

Clinical Manifestations

Signs of sepsis or meningitis caused by *A. xylosoxidans* in the newborn are difficult to differentiate from other causes of bacterial sepsis. However, a distinctive rash consisting of 1- to 2-cm, sharply demarcated red patches, especially in the head and neck region, may develop in some babies in association with this infection. This rash was noted in 29 of 33 newborns with *A. xylosoxidans* infection reported by Doxiadis and associates in 1960[8] and was seen again in a case reported in 1993.[3] *A. xylosoxidans* sepsis/meningitis tends to occur later in life than do infections with the usual vertically acquired pathogens and may have a more insidious onset.[24] In some cases, cerebrospinal fluid profiles may resemble those usually associated with viral meningitis, and patients may have white blood cell counts in the hundreds with a monocytic predominance.[32] Neonatal *Achromobacter* sepsis or meningitis has an extremely poor prognosis; one series noted a mortality rate that approached 75 percent, and 36 percent of survivors had severe neurologic deficits.[14] The incidence of intracranial hemorrhage also was high.

A review of all reported cases of bloodstream infection with *A. xylosoxidans* revealed that 70 percent were nosocomial and 36 percent occurred in association with an identified outbreak or point source.[9] Approximately one third of affected patients had an underlying malignancy, one fifth had cardiac disease, and one fourth were immunosuppressed. Catheter-associated bacteremia was the most common diagnosis and had by far the best prognosis, with a 3 percent case-fatality rate. Sixty-five percent of patients who had pneumonia, meningitis, or endocarditis did not survive the infection.

One child developed *A. xylosoxidans* osteomyelitis after stepping on a nail through old sneakers (a clinical situation classically associated with *Pseudomonas* infection)[18, 19]; another became infected with *Achromobacter* as a consequence of a gunshot wound.[6, 7] *A. xylosoxidans* endocarditis has been described in the setting of a patient with an artificial heart valve.[27] In older patients, *A. xylosoxidans* infection usually is not suspected on clinical grounds but rather in the context of a common source outbreak or because of microbiologic clues. *A. faecalis* infection occurs less commonly and is usually part of a polymicrobial process.

Diagnosis and Treatment

Diagnosis of *Achromobacter* infection rests on recovery of the organism from clinical samples. These organisms often are mistaken for pseudomonads, and the clinician should suspect *A. xylosoxidans* when the laboratory reports an organism as a *Pseudomonas* spp. that is resistant to all aminoglycosides.[31] Key differentiation features include the antibiogram and the morphology of the organism, with its distinctive peritrichous flagella.

Achromobacter spp. typically are resistant to a large number of antibiotics, including ampicillin, aztreonam, aminoglycosides, first- and second-generation cephalosporins, tetracyclines, and rifampin. They are variably resistant to chloramphenicol, fluoroquinolones, macrolides, ureidopenicillins, and β-lactamase combination drugs.[2] *Achromobacter* spp. have been shown to produce β-lactamases, some of which are chromosomal, constitutive, and inducible[7] and some of which are located on plasmids.[23] Some isolates overproduce β-lactamase,[7] which can stoichiometrically render β-lactamase inhibitors useless. In addition, their porins are small, thus rendering antibiotic entry difficult. Although no antibiotic exists to which all isolates have been shown to be sensitive,[27] most are sensitive in vitro to trimethoprim-sulfamethoxazole, imipenem, ceftazidime, and cefoperazone. Two case reports have described treatment failures with ceftazidime[25] and piperacillin[7] in clinical isolates that were sensitive at the time of isolation but resistance developed during the course of therapy.

Because resistance patterns vary from isolate to isolate, the combination of a third-generation cephalosporin, piperacillin, or imipenem with trimethoprim-sulfamethoxazole is reasonable empiric therapy for suspected *Achromobacter* infection, pending susceptibility results. In general, in vitro susceptibility seems to correlate well with in vivo results,[22] but the risk of development of inducible resistance to β-lactam antibiotics should be acknowledged. One report describes synergy in microbial killing with an aminoglycoside, despite the fact that the isolate was resistant to the same aminoglycoside when it was tested alone.[5] This phenomenon has been confirmed by two-disk Kirby-Bauer approximation methods involving 11 clinical blood culture isolates; all were resistant to gentamicin, but 10 of 11 were synergistically inhibited when gentamicin was added to ticarcillin-clavulanate, and 9 of 11 displayed synergy when gentamicin was added to piperacillin or ceftazidime.[9]

Removal of infected catheters may speed recovery, although some patients have been treated successfully through indwelling lines.[5] Because of a high recurrence rate, experts in caring for patients with renal failure who are undergoing continuous ambulatory peritoneal dialysis recommend removal of the peritoneal catheter in those in whom *A. xylosoxidans* peritonitis develops.[13]

REFERENCES

1. Benaoudia, F., and Bengen, E.: Evidence for the genetic unrelatedness of nosocomial *Alcaligenes xylosoxidans* strains in a pediatric hospital. Infect. Control Hosp. Epidemiol. *18*:132–134, 1997.
2. Bizet, C., Tekaia, F., and Phillipon, A.: In vitro susceptibility of *Alcaligenes faecalis* compared with those of other *Alcaligenes* spp. to antimicrobial agents including seven beta-lactams. J. Antimicrob. Chemother. *32*:907–910, 1993.
3. Boukadida, J., Monastiri, K., Snoussi, N., et al.: Nosocomial neonatal meningitis by *Alcaligenes xylosoxidans* transmitted by aqueous eosin. Pediatr. Infect. Dis. J. *12*:696–697, 1993.
4. Burns, J. L., Emerson, J., Stapp, J. R., et al: Microbiology of sputum from patients at cystic fibrosis centers in the United States. Clin. Infect. Dis. *27*:158–163, 1998.
5. Cieslak, T. J., and Raszka, W. V.: Catheter-associated sepsis due to *Alcaligenes xylosoxidans* in a child with AIDS. Clin. Infect. Dis. *16*:592–593, 1993.
6. D'Amato, R. F., Salemi, M., Mathews, A., et al.: *Achromobacter xylosoxidans (Alcaligenes xylosoxidans* subsp. *xylosoxidans)* meningitis associated with a gunshot wound. J. Clin. Microbiol. *26*:2425–2426, 1988.
7. Decre, D., Arlet, G., Danglot, C., et al.: A beta-lactamase overproducing strain of *Alcaligenes dentrificans* subsp. *xylosoxidans* isolated from a case of meningitis. J. Antimicrob. Chemother. *30*:769–779, 1992.
8. Doxiadis, S. A., Pavlatou, M., and Chryssostomidou, O.: *Bacillus foecalis alcaligenes* septicemia in the newborn. J. Pediatr. *56*:648–654, 1960.
9. Duggan, J. M., Goldstein, S. J., Chenoweth, C. E., et al.: *Achromobacter xylosoxidans* bacteremia: Report of four cases and review of the literature. Clin. Infect. Dis. *23*:569–576, 1996.
10. Dunne, W. M., Jr., and Maisch, S.: Epidemiological investigation of infections due to *Alcaligenes* spp. in children and patients with cystic fibrosis: Use of repetitive-element-sequence polymerase chain reaction. Clin. Infect. Dis. *20*:836–41, 1995.
11. Dworzack, D. L., Murray, C. M., Hodges, G. R., et al.: Community acquired bacteremic *Achromobacter xylosoxidans* type IIIa: Pneumonia in a patient with idiopathic IgM deficiency. Am. J. Clin. Pathol. *70*:712–717, 1978.
12. Edwards, L. D., Tan-Gatue, L. G., Levin, S., et al.: The problem of bacteriologically contaminated infant formulas in a newborn nursery. Clin. Pediatr. (Phila.) *13*:63–65, 1974.
13. El-Shahawy, M. A., Kim, D., and Gadallah, M. F.: Peritoneal dialysis–associated peritonitis caused by *Alcaligenes xylosoxidans*. Am. J. Nephrol. *18*:452–455, 1998.
14. Foley, J. F., Gravelle, C. R., Englehard, W. E., et al.: *Achromobacter* septicemia fatalities in prematures. Am. J. Dis. Child. *101*:279–288, 1961.
15. Gradon, J. D., Mayrev, A. R., and Hayes, J.: Pulmonary abscess associated with *Alcaligenes xylosoxidans* in a patient with AIDS. Clin. Infect. Dis. *17*:1071–1072, 1993.
16. Granowitz, E. V., and Keenholtz, S. L.: A pseudoepidemic of *Alcaligenes xylosoxidans* attributable to contaminated saline. Am. J. Infect. Control *26*:146–148, 1998.
17. Hearn, Y. R., and Gander, R. M.: *Achromobacter xylosoxidans*: An unusual neonatal pathogen. Am. J. Clin. Pathol. *96*:211–214, 1991.
18. Hoddy, D. M., and Barton, L. L.: Puncture wound–induced *Achromobacter xylosoxidans* osteomyelitis of the foot. Am. J. Dis. Child. *145*:599–600, 1991.
19. Holmes, B., Snell, J. J. S., and Lapage, S. P.: Strains of *Achromobacter xylosoxidans* from clinical material. J. Clin. Pathol. *30*:595–601, 1977.
20. Igra-Siegman, Y., Chmel, H., and Cobbs, C.: Clinical and laboratory characteristics of *Achromobacter xylosoxidans* infection. J. Clin. Microbiol. *11*:141–145, 1980.
21. Kersters, K., and DeLey, J.: Genus *Alcaligenes*. *In* Krieg, N. R., and Holt, J. G. (eds.): Bergey's Manual of Systematic Bacteriology. Baltimore, Williams & Wilkins, 1984, pp. 361–373.
22. Legrand, C., and Anqissie, E.: Bacteremia due to *Achromobacter xylosoxidans* in patients with cancer. Clin. Infect. Dis. *14*:479–484, 1992.
23. Levesque, R., Royu, P. H., Letarte, R., et al.: A plasmid-mediated cephalosporinase from *Achromobacter* species. J. Infect. Dis. *145*: 753–761, 1982.
24. Mandell, W. F., Garvey, G. J., and Neu, H. C.: *Achromobacter xylosoxidans* bacteremia. Rev. Infect. Dis. *9*:1001–1005, 1987.
25. Manjra, A. I., Moosa, A., and Bhamjee, A.: Fatal neonatal meningitis and ventriculitis caused by multi-resistant *Achromobacter xylosoxidans:* A case report. S. Afr. Med. J. *76*:571–573, 1989.
26. McGarrity, G. J., and Coriell, L. L.: Bacterial contamination of children's soap bubbles. Am. J. Dis. Child. *125*:224–226, 1973.
27. Olson, D. A., and Hoeprich, P. D.: Postoperative infection of an aortic prosthesis with *Achromobacter xylosoxidans*. West. J. Med. *136*:153–157, 1982.
28. Peel, M. M., Hibberd, A. J., King, B. M., et al.: *Alcaligenes piechaudii* from chronic ear discharge. J. Clin. Microbiol. *26*:1580–1581, 1988.
29. Reverdy, M. E., Freney, J., Fleurette, J., et al.: Nosocomial colonization and infection by *Achromobacter xylosoxidans*. J. Clin. Microbiol. *19*:140–143, 1984.
30. San-Miguel, V. V., Lavery, J. P., York, J. C., et al.: *Achromobacter xylosoxidans* septic arthritis in a patient with systemic lupus erythematosus. Arthritis Rheum. *34*:1484–1485, 1991.
31. Schoch, P. E., and Cunha, B. A.: Nosocomial *Achromobacter xylosoxidans* infections. Infect. Control Hosp. Epidemiol. *9*:84–87, 1988.
32. Sepkowitz, D. V., Bostic, D. E., and Maslow, M. J.: *Achromobacter xylosoxidans* meningitis: Case report and review of the literature. Clin. Pediatr. (Phila.) *26*:483–485, 1987.
33. Shigeta, S., Yasunaga, Y., Honsumi, K., et al.: Cerebral ventriculitis associated with *Achromobacter xylosoxidans*. J. Clin. Pathol. *70*:712–717, 1978.
34. Spear, J. B., Fuhrer, J., and Kirby, B. D.: *Achromobacter xylosoxidans (Alcaligenes xylosoxidans* subsp. *xylosoxidans)* bacteremia associated with well-water source: Case report and review of the literature. J. Clin. Microbiol. *26*:598–599, 1988.
35. Taylor, P., and Fischbein, L.: Prosthetic knee infection due to *Achromobacter xylosoxidans*. J. Rheumatol. *19*:992–993, 1992.
36. Vu-Thien, H., Moissenet, D., Valcin, M., et al.: Molecular epidemiology of *Burkholderia cepacia, Stenotrophomonas maltophilia,* and *Alcaligenes xylosoxidans* in a cystic fibrosis center. Eur. J. Clin. Microbiol. Infect. Dis. *15*:876–879, 1996.
37. Walsh, R. D., Klein, N. C., and Cunha, B. A.: *Achromobacter xylosoxidans* osteomyelitis. Clin. Infect. Dis. *16*:176–178, 1993.
38. Weitkamp, J. H., Tang, Y. W., Haas, D. W., et al.: Recurrent *Achromobacter xylosoxidans* bacteremia associated with persistent lymph node infection in a patient with hyper-immunoglobulin M syndrome. Clin. Infect. Dis. *31*:1183–1187, 2000.

CHAPTER 127 Eikenella corrodens

RANDALL G. FISHER ■ WILLIAM C. GRUBER ■ THOMAS G. BOYCE

Eikenella corrodens is a facultatively anaerobic, fastidious gram-negative rod that is part of the normal flora of the mouth and gastrointestinal and genitourinary tracts. Long regarded as a commensal, its pathogenicity is no longer in doubt. It frequently is a pathogen of periodontitis in both adults and children and is a common isolate from wounds that have been contaminated by oral secretions. It also has been recovered from pleuropulmonary infections, central nervous system infections, orbital cellulitis, peritonsillar abscesses, abdominal infections, osteomyelitis, and bloodstream infections, including endocarditis.

Bacteriology

In 1948, Hendriksen[16] described the organism and called it the corroding bacillus because it pitted the agar. It was more fully characterized in 1958 by Eiken,[10] who named it *Bacteroides corrodens.* In 1972, Jackson and Goodman[17] separated two species of corroding bacteria; the strict anaerobe kept the name *B. corrodens* (now called *Bacteroides ureolyticus),* and the facultative anaerobe was classified as *Eikenella.* It is a small, straight, nonmotile gram-negative rod that occasionally is coccobacillary. It is oxidase-positive and catalase-negative. Most strains are lysine- and ornithine decarboxylase–positive. The organism is nonfermentative, reduces nitrate to nitrite, and is urease- and indole-negative. *E. corrodens* cell surface components vary from isolate to isolate; these differences probably relate to virulence.[6]

E. corrodens will grow either aerobically or anaerobically, but its growth is not rapid. Growth can be enhanced by 3 to 10 percent carbon dioxide. It grows on blood and chocolate agar but poorly or not at all on MacConkey agar. Selective media that contain clindamycin may increase the yield. Colonies are small and grayish. They look slightly yellow when they are old. Although *E. corrodens* is nonhemolytic, a faint green appearance may be present on blood agar. Approximately 50 percent produce the characteristic pitting. They elaborate an odor that resembles that of bleach or hypochlorite.[18]

E. corrodens is a member of the so-called HACEK family of organisms, which have the following features in common: (1) slow growth, (2) a requirement for carbon dioxide, and (3) a predilection for infecting heart valves. The other members of the family are *Haemophilus aphrophilus, Actinobacillus actinomycetemcomitans, Cardiobacterium hominis,* and *Kingella kingae.*

Epidemiology

Infection with *E. corrodens* occurs when mucosal or skin barriers are disrupted and the organism gains access to deeper tissues. Puncture of the skin with forks[28] or toothpicks[34] may result in deep-seated infection. One case of vertebral osteomyelitis that occurred after a woman accidentally inoculated the organism into the paravertebral space by penetration of a fish bone through the posterior pharynx has been reported.[25] Infection commonly occurs after clenched-fist injury as a result of fistfighting.[13] Intravenous drug abusers are at risk for development of abscesses at the injection site and in soft tissue,[14] bacteremia, and endocarditis.[9, 27] The elderly and people with advanced carcinoma are the other high-risk groups. However, that children are at particularly high risk for development of serious *E. corrodens* infections now is recognized.[33] Cases of thyroid abscess[7, 42] and purulent thyroiditis[32] in children have been reported. In one review,[21] more than 20 percent of *E. corrodens* pleuropulmonary infections occurred in children younger than 14 years of age, and more than 50 percent of abdominal infections were reported in patients younger than 25 years of age.[8] *E. corrodens* orbital cellulitis,[15] empyema,[39] peritonsillar abscess,[22] paronychia,[1] and osteomyelitis[30, 36] have been observed in children. A review of 54 cases of *E. corrodens* infection in children and adolescents revealed that 41 percent of pediatric infections occurred in the head and neck. The most common single site was the thyroid gland.[28]

Pathophysiology

E. corrodens infections often are polymicrobial[40] and may include other anaerobes or gram-negative rods. However, *E. corrodens* is accompanied most frequently by recovery of alpha-hemolytic streptococci. In most reports, the streptococci are not further speciated, but Jacobs and associates[19] made a case for the *Streptococcus anginosus* group because of similarities (e.g., both are found in the mouth and gastrointestinal tract, both produce local suppurative infection, and both thrive in carbon dioxide–rich, oxygen-poor environments) between the two organisms. Brooks and colleagues[4] also reported synergy of the two organisms in a rabbit model of skin infection. In vitro studies of *E. corrodens* cocultivated with members of the *S. anginosus* group show that a significant degree of coaggregation occurs. Additionally, exponential growth of *Streptococcus constellatus* and *Streptococcus intermedius* occurs 6 hours into incubation when these species are grown in the presence of *E. corrodens;* in its absence, exponential growth does not occur until 25 hours after inoculation.[43]

E. corrodens has a propensity toward abscess formation in any location, whether alone or in concert with other organisms. Abscess formation is a hallmark of central nervous system infection.[3] Of patients with intra-abdominal infections reported by Danziger and associates,[8] 15 of 19 had abscesses. In two patients with orbital cellulitis reported by Hemady and coworkers,[15] both had subperiosteal abscesses. Deep or superficial skin abscesses in drug addicts[14] or in clenched-fist injury from fistfighting[13] often recur, even after presumed adequate drainage.[31]

Clinical Manifestations

Infections with *E. corrodens* are indolent. The time from inoculation to the onset of symptoms generally is 1 week or longer.[4] Many patients show initial improvement with therapy but relapse days later, even with appropriate therapy.[15, 22, 29, 33]

Infection of periodontal sites may be associated with rapid progression and bone resorption thought to be secondary to surface-associated material of *E. corrodens* and other organisms of periodontitis.[26] Craniofacial and neck infections tend to be associated with prolonged morbidity; many require repeated drainage procedures and long courses of antimicrobial agents.[33] Central nervous system infections often are preceded by sinus infections, but they also have been seen in children with congenital heart disease.[2, 41]

Pleuropulmonary infections are marked by fever, cough, and chest pain. Necrotizing pneumonia with multiple abscesses occasionally is seen. Effusions or empyema are noted in 30 percent of patients, and cavitation is seen in 8 percent. Children with a predisposition to aspiration may be at higher risk.[21]

Endocarditis is associated with large, friable vegetations and frequent emboli and often requires valve replacement.[11] Intravenous drug use has been implicated in approximately half of reported cases.

Abdominal *E. corrodens* infections are seen most commonly as complications of ruptured appendicitis but also have been associated with abdominal trauma and surgery. The clinical course is protracted.[8]

Chorioamnionitis leading to premature delivery has been documented infrequently.[20, 38]

Soft tissue infections tend to be severe, and many require wide débridement and skin grafting. Infection of underlying joints, tendons, or bones is not an infrequent occurrence and can be necrotizing and even lead to amputation.[31]

Diagnosis

Definitive diagnosis rests on recovery of *E. corrodens* in culture. This task can be difficult to achieve, however, because of the organism's slow growth. *Eikenella* tends to be overgrown by hardier species when it is part of a polymicrobial process and may be missed, especially if it does not pit the agar. All the HACEK organisms can pit agar,[5] though not with the regularity of *E. corrodens*.

Many bacteriology laboratories have difficulty identifying and separating catalase-negative, oxidase-positive, gram-negative rods. Not surprisingly, one report noted that of 100 isolates of *E. corrodens* identified by the National Collection of Type Cultures, only 21 were sent in as probable *E. corrodens*.[5] Organisms with which *E. corrodens* may be mistaken include the other HACEK organisms, *Haemophilus paraphrophilus*, *Moraxella atlantae*, and *Actinobacillus ureae*.

Treatment

E. corrodens has a very unusual antimicrobial susceptibility pattern in that although most isolates are sensitive to penicillin and ampicillin, they are resistant to semisynthetic penicillins such as methicillin and nafcillin.[37] Additionally, they are uniformly resistant to clindamycin and metronidazole,[18] drugs commonly used to treat anaerobic infections. They also are variably resistant to aminoglycosides.

Most isolates are sensitive to ticarcillin, second- and third-generation cephalosporins, carbapenems, and tetracycline. Although penicillin often is cited as the drug of choice, some strains produce β-lactamases, in which case ampicillin-sulbactam should be effective. One report associates the β-lactamase with a transposon[23] and another with a plasmid[35]; still another has found a chromosomal enzyme that is not inducible.[24] In addition, cases of intermediate resistance to penicillin have been reported, even in isolates that do not produce a β-lactamase.[12]

Incision and drainage of abscesses and débridement of necrotic tissue are essential to recovery from these infections. Therapy should be prolonged after patients appear to have recovered because early cessation of antibiotic therapy tends to be associated with relapse. If patients continue to have fever or other signs of infection days after appropriate therapy has been started, reimaging of the infected area may be prudent to detect early reaccumulation of purulence.

REFERENCES

1. Barton, L. L., and Anderson, L. E.: Paronychia caused by HB-1 organisms. Pediatrics *54*:372–373, 1974.
2. Brill, C. B., Pearlstein, L. S., Kaplan, M., et al.: Central nervous system infections caused by *Eikenella corrodens*. Arch. Neurol. *39*:431–432, 1982.
3. Bronitsky, R., Heim, C. R., and McGee, Z. A.: Multifocal brain abscesses: Combined medical and neurosurgical therapy. South. Med. J. *75*: 1261–1263, 1982.
4. Brooks, G. F., O'Donoghue, J. M., and Rissing, J. P.: *Eikenella corrodens:* A recently recognized pathogen: Infections in medical-surgical patients and in association with methylphenidate abuse. Medicine (Baltimore) *53*:325–342, 1974.
5. Chadwick, P. R., Malnick, H., and Ebizie, A. O.: *Haemophilus paraphrophilus* infection: A pitfall in laboratory diagnosis. J. Infect. *30*:67–69, 1995.
6. Chen, C.-K. C., and Wilson, M. E.: Outer membrane protein and lipopolysaccharide heterogeneity among *Eikenella corrodens* isolates. J. Infect. Dis. *162*:664–671, 1990.
7. Cheng, A. F., Man, D. W. K., and French, G. L.: Thyroid abscess caused by *Eikenella corrodens*. J. Infect. *16*:181–185, 1988.
8. Danziger, L. H., Schoonover, L. L., Kale, P., et al.: *Eikenella corrodens* as an intra-abdominal pathogen. Am. Surg. *60*:296–299, 1994.
9. Decker, M. D., Graham, B. S., Hunter, E. B., et al.: Endocarditis and infections of intravascular devices due to *Eikenella corrodens*. Am. J. Med. Sci. *292*:209–212, 1986.
10. Eiken, M.: Studies on an anaerobic, rod-shaped, gram-negative microorganism: *Bacteroides corrodens*. Acta Pathol. Microbiol. Scand. *43*: 391–406, 1958.
11. Ellner, J. J., Rosenthal, M. S., Lerner, P. I., et al.: Infectious endocarditis caused by slow-growing, fastidious, gram negative bacteria. Medicine (Baltimore) *58*:145–158, 1979.
12. Goldstein, E. J. C., and Citron, D. M.: Sensitivity of *Eikenella corrodens* to penicillin, apalcillin, and twelve new cephalosporins. Antimicrob. Agents Chemother. *26*:947–948, 1984.
13. Goldstein, E. J. C., Miller, T. A., Citron, D. M., et al.: Infections following clenched-fist injury: A new perspective. J. Hand Surg. [Am.] *3*:455–457, 1978.
14. Gonzalez, M. H., Garst, J., Nourbush, P., et al.: Abscesses of the upper extremities from drug abuse by injection. J. Hand Surg. [Am.] *18*:868–870, 1993.
15. Hemady, R., Zimmerman, A., Katzen, B. W., et al.: Orbital cellulitis caused by *Eikenella corrodens*. Am. J. Ophthalmol. *114*:584–588, 1992.
16. Hendriksen, S. D.: Studies in gram-negative anaerobes. II. Gram-negative anaerobic rods with spreading colonies. Acta Pathol. Microbiol. Scand. *25*:368–375, 1948.
17. Jackson, F. L., and Goodman, Y. E.: Transfer of the facultatively anaerobic organism *Bacteroides corrodens Eiken* to a new genus, *Eikenella*. Int. J. Syst. Bacteriol. *22*:73–77, 1972.
18. Jackson, F. L., and Goodman, Y.: Genus *Eikenella*. *In* Krieg, N. R., and Holt, J. G. (eds.): Bergey's Manual of Systematic Bacteriology. Baltimore, Williams & Wilkins, 1984, pp. 591–597.
19. Jacobs, J. A., Algie, G. D., Cie, G. H., et al.: Association between *Eikenella corrodens* and streptococci. Clin. Infect. Dis. *16*:173, 1993.
20. Jeppson, K. G., and Reimer, L. G.: *Eikenella corrodens* amnionitis. Obstet. Gynecol. *78*:503–505, 1991.
21. Joshi, N., O'Bryan, T., and Appelbaum, P. C.: Pleuropulmonary infections caused by *Eikenella corrodens*. Rev. Infect. Dis. *13*:1207–1212, 1991.
22. Knudsen, T. D., and Simke, E. J.: *Eikenella corrodens:* An unexpected pathogen causing a persistent peritonsillar abscess. Ear Nose Throat J. *74*:114–117, 1995.
23. Lacroix, J.-M., and Walker, C. B.: Identification of a streptomycin resistance gene and a partial Tn3 transposon coding for a beta-lactamase in a periodontal strain of *Eikenella corrodens*. Antimicrob. Agents Chemother. *36*:740–743, 1992.

24. Lacroix, J.-M., and Wallar, C.: Characteristics of a beta-lactamase found in *Eikenella corrodens*. Antimicrob. Agents Chemother. *35*:886–891, 1991.
25. Lehman, C. R., Deckey, J. E., Hu, S. S.: *Eikenella corrodens* vertebral osteomyelitis secondary to direct inoculation: A case report. Spine *25*:1185–1187, 2000.
26. Meghji, S., Wilson, M., Barber, P., et al.: Bone resorbing activity of surface-associated material from *Actinobacillus actinomycetemcomitans* and *Eikenella corrodens*. J. Med. Microbiol. *41*:197–203, 1994.
27. Patrick, W. D., Brown, W. D., Bowmer, M. I., et al.: Infectious endocarditis due to *Eikenella corrodens:* Case report and review of the literature. Can. J. Infect. Dis. *1*:139–142, 1990.
28. Paul, K., and Patel, S. S.: *Eikenella corrodens* infections in children and adolescents: Case reports and review of the literature. Clin. Infect. Dis. *33*:54–61, 2001.
29. Perez-Pomata, M. T., Dominguez, J., Hercajo, P., et al.: Spleen abscess caused by *Eikenella corrodens*. Eur. J. Clin. Microbiol. Infect. Dis. *11*:162–163, 1992.
30. Polin, K., and Shulman, S. T.: *Eikenella corrodens* osteomyelitis. Pediatrics *70*:462–463, 1982.
31. Pollner, J. H., Khan, A., and Tuazon, C. U.: Severe soft tissue infection caused by *Eikenella corrodens*. Clin. Infect. Dis. *15*:740–741, 1992.
32. Queen, J. S., Clegg, H. W., Council, J. C., et al.: Acute suppurative thyroiditis caused by *Eikenella corrodens*. J. Pediatr. Surg. *23*:359–361, 1988.
33. Raffensperger, J. G.: *Eikenella corrodens* infections in children. J. Pediatr. Surg. *21*:644–646, 1986.
34. Robinson, L. G., and Kourtis, A. P.: Tale of a toothpick: *Eikenella corrodens* osteomyelitis. Infection *28*:332–333, 2000.
35. Rotger, R. E., Garcia-Valdes, E., and Trallero, E. P.: Characterization of a beta-lactamase–specifying plasmid isolated from *Eikenella corrodens* and its relationship to a commensal *Neisseria* plasmid. Antimicrob. Agents Chemother. *30*:508–509, 1986.
36. Sagerman, S. D., and Lourie, G. M.: *Eikenella* osteomyelitis in a chronic nail biter: A case report. J. Hand Surg. *20*:71–72, 1995.
37. Sofianou, D., and Kolokotronis, A.: Susceptibility of *Eikenella corrodens* to antimicrobial agents. J. Chemother. *2*:156–158, 1990.
38. Sporken, J. M. J., Muyfjens, H. L., and Vemer, H. M.: Intrauterine infection due to *Eikenella corrodens*. Acta Obstet. Gynecol. Scand. *64*:683–684, 1985.
39. St. John, A., Belda, A. A., Matlow, A., et al.: *Eikenella corrodens* empyema in children. Am. J. Dis. Child. *135*:415–417, 1981.
40. Suwanagool, S., Rothkopf, M. M., Smith, S. M., et al.: Pathogenicity of *Eikenella corrodens* in humans. Arch. Intern. Med. *143*:2265–2268, 1983.
41. Swanston, W. H., Cameron, E. S., and Ramchaunder, V.: *Eikenella corrodens* brain abscess in a child with congenital heart disease. W. Indian Med. J. *37*:243–245, 1988.
42. Vichyanond, P., Howard, C. P., and Olson, L. C. *Eikenella corrodens* as a cause of thyroid abscess. Am. J. Dis. Child. *137*:971–973, 1983.
43. Young, K. A., Allaker, R. P., Hardie, J. M., et al.: Interactions between *Eikenella corrodens* and "*Streptococcus milleri*–group" organisms: Possible mechanisms of pathogenicity in mixed infections. Antonie Van Leeuwenhoek *69*:371–373, 1996.

CHAPTER 128 Chryseobacterium (Flavobacterium)

WILLIAM C. GRUBER ■ RANDALL G. FISHER ■ THOMAS G. BOYCE

Members of the genus *Chryseobacterium* (formerly *Flavobacterium*) are associated uncommonly with human infection, with most diseases occurring after exposure to a contaminated environmental source. In 1944, Shulmann and Johnson[42] reported a case of meningitis caused by a previously unidentified, gram-negative bacillus isolated from a 9-day-old premature infant. The term *"Flavobacterium meningosepticum"* was proposed for this organism by King[27] in 1959 based on her studies of bacterial isolates primarily associated with neonatal meningitis and septicemia. Although neonatal meningitis is the most common manifestation of human disease caused by this genus,[14, 47] chryseobacteria-associated sepsis,[13, 21, 35, 44] endocarditis, pneumonia,[46] and skin infection[18] occur in individuals beyond the newborn period.[3]

Bacteriology

All but one of the clinically relevant species of the genus *Flavobacterium* have been reclassified to the new genus *Chryseobacterium*.[51] The former *Flavobacterium odoratum*, rarely responsible for human disease, has been divided into two species (*odoratus* and *odoratimumus*) and reclassified as a member of the genus *Myroides*.[50] *Chryseobacterium indologenes* is the species most frequently isolated from human specimens, but usually it is not associated with significant disease.[26] Therefore, this chapter will focus mainly on *Chryseobacterium meningosepticum*, which can cause severe infections, especially in newborns. These organisms are long, thin, catalase-positive, gram-negative rods with slightly swollen ends; they are nonmotile, oxidase-positive, weakly fermentative, and proteolytic and grow on solid agar as 1- to 2-mm, convex glistening colonies of buttery consistency.[27] Yellow pigmentation occasionally is seen. Colonies do not demonstrate hemolysis on blood agar but may produce a lavender-green color in the surrounding media as a result of extensive proteolytic enzyme activity. *Chryseobacterium* is unable to grow on *Salmonella-Shigella* agar or Simmons citrate and lacks motility. These characteristics distinguish *Chryseobacterium* from *Pseudomonas,* with which it often is confused.[14] Similarly, utilization of glucose in an open tube of oxidation-fermentation medium distinguishes *Chryseobacterium* from *Achromobacter faecalis*.[14] The clinically relevant species *C. meningosepticum* (also referred to interchangeably in the current literature by its old name, *F. meningosepticum*) and *Flavobacterium* IIB (renamed *Chryseobacterium balustinum*) are differentiated by the former's consistent liquefaction of gelatin and early utilization of mannitol and maltose and the latter's lack of these abilities.[27] *Myroides odoratus* and *Myroides odoratimimus* (*F. odoratum*), which most commonly have been identified as saprophytes in skin wounds,[25] characteristically are nonsaccharolytic and produce a fruity odor when grown on standard media.

Epidemiology

Chryseobacteria are distributed widely as saprophytes in fresh and salt water. *C. meningosepticum* has been identified as a pathogen in birds.[49] In hospitals, chryseobacteria have been found to be ubiquitous colonizers of the patient's environment and have been isolated from flower vases,[46] ice machines,[44] vials of intravenous drugs,[36] and nebulizers.[15] In addition, tap water,[15] eyewashes,[37] tube feedings,[15] sink traps,[8] and hand cultures of hospital personnel[15] have yielded this organism. In some instances, these reservoirs of chryseobacteria have been implicated in nosocomial outbreaks of patient colonization and invasive disease.

Neonatal infection caused by *C. meningosepticum* has been reported frequently in the literature, often in association with nursery epidemics.[2, 7, 39] As with other neonatal pathogens, infants who are premature and small for gestational age seem to be at particular risk, and more than 50 percent of infected infants weigh less than 2500 g. Almost all cases occur within 3 weeks of birth, with more than 50 percent becoming infected before reaching 7 days of age.[14]

Nosocomial epidemics have occurred sporadically since the nursery outbreak reported by Brody and colleagues in 1958.[2, 5, 7, 8] Cabrera and Davis[8] reported such an outbreak in detail in 1961. During a 3-month period, the bacteria were isolated from a total of 44 infants, 14 of whom had overt infection. Most colonized infants had organisms isolated from the nasopharynx. The only reservoir of infectious bacteria discovered was a faulty sink trap, beneath which cleaning materials for the nursery were stored. Repair of the defective trap and thorough cleansing and repainting of the nursery coincided with termination of the epidemic. Recently, a cluster of neonatal and adult systemic infections caused by atypical strains of *C. meningosepticum* were reported from Taiwan. These strains first were identified erroneously as *Aeromonas salmonicida.*[11]

Nursery outbreaks of *C. meningosepticum* have been traced to the saline used to flush infants' eyes after administration of silver nitrate,[37] and organisms have been recovered from washbasins, sinks, disinfectants, and suction devices in other epidemics.[8] Colonization of patients in a surgical intensive care unit has been associated with tap water, sinks, ice machines, and washbasins yielding the bacteria.[15] Ribotyping and random amplified polymorphic DNA fingerprinting (RAPD) offer promise for more precise characterization of epidemics.[11, 12]

Pathophysiology

Chryseobacteria generally are of low virulence. Rabbits administered 1-mL intravenous injections of 24-hour-old broth cultures demonstrated no mortality or morbidity, and death rates were less than 30 percent in mice intracerebrally inoculated with "barely turbid" preparations.[27]

Most cases of invasive human disease are thought to be caused by environmental contamination with high numbers of *C. meningosepticum* and then spread to a compromised newborn or debilitated older patient. Some neonatal infections may be caused by colonization of the infant during passage through the birth canal of a colonized mother.[12] Intrapartum infection is supported by the occurrence of symptoms as early as 10 hours after birth.[14] However, only 0.3 percent of genital swabs submitted from patients with suspected sexually transmitted disease yielded the organism.[36] Continuing reports of chryseobacteria as a cause of neonatal infection in underdeveloped countries have been speculated to be related to the use of contaminated groundwater for bathing newborn infants and for feminine genital hygiene.[14] The propensity for this organism to produce meningitis in the newborn is not understood, but infection may occur in association with heavy nasopharyngeal colonization and subsequently lead to bacteremia and seeding of the meninges.

In older individuals, chryseobacteria primarily play the role of opportunists.[33] Heavy nosocomial colonization combined with a blunted immune response probably accounts for the poor capacity of immunocompromised patients to handle these otherwise noninvasive bacteria.

Clinical Manifestations

Neonatal sepsis and meningitis caused by *C. meningosepticum* share signs and symptoms in common with other forms of neonatal bacterial infection. However, the development of meningitis may be insidious, and several days of illness often pass before medical attention is sought,[14, 39] consistent with the low virulence of *C. meningosepticum* in comparison to other agents of neonatal sepsis. The prognosis is extremely poor, and mortality rates may exceed 60 percent.[28] Significant neurologic complications, often in association with hydrocephalus, develop in 50 percent of survivors.[29]

Chryseobacteria are uncommon pathogens in adults, and childhood disease beyond the newborn period is an extremely rare occurrence. Among the 24 initial isolates of *C. meningosepticum* identified by King,[27] organisms were found in a throat culture from an adult patient and in cerebrospinal fluid (CSF) from an 8-month-old infant. Bacteria formerly classified as *Flavobacterium* IIB (now known as *C. balustinum*) were isolated from the blood and CSF of several adult patients without clinical information.[24] Since their initial identification in 1959, chryseobacteria have been implicated as agents of meningitis,[33, 39] postoperative bacteremia,[3, 36] bacterial endocarditis,[52] pneumonia,[45, 46] and skin infection.[18] *C. meningosepticum* is the clinically relevant species most commonly isolated, but *C. balustinum, M. odoratus, M. odoratimimus (F. odoratum),* and other *Chryseobacterium* spp. have been implicated in human disease. *Chryseobacterium* spp. accounted for 0.25 percent of infections in a large consecutive series of patients infected with human immunodeficiency virus. Risk factors included low CD4 counts and leukopenia.[32]

C. meningosepticum meningitis developing in patients beyond the neonatal period typically occurs in immunocompromised patients. Adults with preexisting leukemia,[39] glomerulonephritis,[33] and squamous cell carcinoma[21] have been reported as having meningitis caused by this organism. In a 56-year-old woman, *C. meningosepticum* meningitis developed after she underwent trans-sphenoidal hypophysectomy[9]; in an 8-month-old boy with preceding severe neurologic damage, meningitis was caused by bacteria designated by the Centers for Disease Control and Prevention as *Chryseobacterium*-like organisms (IIE). In a 6-week-old infant, *C. meningosepticum* bacteremia and meningitis developed in association with a strangulated hernia.[14]

Chryseobacterium spp. were isolated commonly from the tracheal aspirates of intensive care patients during a 70-month observation period; during that time, however, none of more than 2000 critically ill individuals contracted pneumonia attributable to these microbes.[15] However, *Chryseobacterium* respiratory tract infection has been identified in an intubated pediatric patient and in adults receiving aerosolized medications.[6, 46]

Sporadic cases of bacteremia have been reported in adult patients.[21, 30] Infection in immunocompromised patients can occur as a complication of relatively benign invasive procedures or as a localized infection.[30, 43] Endocarditis has been documented in intravenous drug abusers and dialysis patients.[17, 52] Postoperative bacteremia in eight adult patients has been linked to chryseobacteria-contaminated intravenous medications infused during anesthesia.[35] Contaminated arterial catheters were implicated in an epidemic of *Chryseobacterium* bacteremia.[44] Four patients, including a 7-year-old boy, became bacteremic in an outbreak associated with *Chryseobacterium* contamination at the time they underwent intracardiac surgery.[3] This organism also has been associated with bacteremia in pediatric burn patients.[41]

Chryseobacterium spp. have been isolated from infected skin lesions such as papules, sheetlike lesions, plaques, and deep panniculitis.[18] Infection may have been related to wound contamination during repair of an orthopedic injury. Chryseobacteria also have been isolated from amputation stumps, but they may have been playing a largely saprophytic role at these sites.[25]

Diagnosis

Rapid identification of *Chryseobacterium* infection is urgent, not only to ensure proper therapy for the patient but also to hasten institution of appropriate infection control measures to forestall epidemic outbreaks. Identification of *C. meningosepticum* is hindered by the characteristically long periods required for oxidation of carbohydrates and weak or delayed indole production. Cultures may be misidentified as species of *Achromobacter* or *Pseudomonas.*[14] Clinical isolation of an unidentified gram-negative rod that is catalase- and oxidase-positive and shows multiple antibiotic resistance should raise suspicion of *C. meningosepticum* infection. Cultures should be kept for several days to observe for typical carbohydrate reactions, which confirm the diagnosis.[14, 38] Pulsed-field gel electrophoresis of DNA has been used successfully to identify recurrence of intravenous catheter–associated infection in a 6-year-old boy with non-Hodgkin lymphoma.[5, 40]

Treatment

Unfortunately, treatment of *C. meningosepticum* meningitis is an especially difficult challenge for the physician. Delay in making a specific identification of the organism is a common occurrence and often leads to prolonged periods of suboptimal therapy because the recommended empiric antimicrobial treatment of gram-negative neonatal meningitis usually consists of a third-generation cephalosporin or ampicillin and an aminoglycoside, drugs to which *C. meningosepticum* almost uniformly is resistant. Moreover, antimicrobial susceptibility determined by disk diffusion must be interpreted with caution. Aber and associates[1] found clinical isolates in which specific strains were sensitive to gentamicin and rifampin by disk diffusion but were resistant by agar gel dilution susceptibility testing. Therefore, more direct methods of measuring the minimal inhibitory concentration than disk diffusion sensitivity should be used to determine the optimal microbial agents for therapy.

Probably as a consequence of difficulties encountered in providing rapid and effective antibacterial therapy, persistence of organisms for prolonged periods in CSF occurs commonly. The average persistence of *Chryseobacterium* in CSF is 19 days,[14] in contrast to the 3.9 days described by McCracken[34] for most cases of gram-negative neonatal bacterial meningitis.

Recent studies of in vitro susceptibility data have forced a reappraisal of the idea that vancomycin is a good first-line choice for the treatment of chryseobacterial infection. In one report, a literature review showed that only 65 percent of historic isolates were susceptible to vancomycin[4]; in another, a thorough search for a susceptible organism among 58 clinical isolates met with utter failure.[19] Ninety-seven percent of *C. meningosepticum* isolates were susceptible to rifampin. Clinically, drugs that have been used alone or in combination with some success have included erythromycin, vancomycin, trimethoprim-sulfamethoxazole, and rifampin.[48] Some of these agents have the potential disadvantage of poor penetration in CSF. Combined use of many of these drugs renders interpreting therapeutic response difficult. The 3 survivors in the 12 patients reported by George and associates[20] all received vancomycin intravenously, intrathecally, or both as part of their regimen. Hawley and Gump[22] reported a case of *C. meningosepticum* meningitis in a neonate who responded to systemic vancomycin after being treated unsuccessfully with multiple antibiotics, including erythromycin.

Intraventricular erythromycin[16, 39] or rifampin[10, 28, 29, 39] has been used in conjunction with systemic administration of these drugs. In particular, Lee and associates[29] reported no deaths in seven infants with *C. meningosepticum* meningitis treated with intraventricular rifampin through an Ommaya reservoir at a dose of 2 to 5 mg every 24 hours combined with 40 mg/kg/day administered intravenously. Intraventricular administration continued until the CSF was sterile. However, colonization of the Ommaya reservoir occurred commonly, and formation of a porencephalic cyst occurred in one patient. Chandrika and Adler[10] reported sterilization of the ventricles in one afflicted neonate within 48 hours after institution of therapy with intraventricular and intravenous rifampin. Erythromycin has been used intraventricularly with limited success at 5 to 10 mg/day.[16, 39] Rios and colleagues[39] reported the successful addition of intraventricular rifampin to a failing regimen of intravenous and intraventricular erythromycin. Development of resistance while patients are undergoing therapy has been demonstrated with erythromycin and rifampin[16, 39]; persistence of organisms in the CSF despite presumably adequate therapy should alert the physician to test for this possibility. The addition of trimethoprim-sulfamethoxazole may be of benefit with such an occurrence; this agent effected a bacteriologic cure in eight of nine infants with meningitis.[31] However, trimethoprim-sulfamethoxazole usually is not recommended in the neonatal period because of possible displacement of bilirubin from albumin-binding sites. Bacterial eradication was achieved in 48 hours in two meningitis patients treated with clindamycin, rifampin, and cefotaxime systemically and rifampin intraventricularly.[7]

As with other types of gram-negative meningitis, antimicrobial therapy should be continued for at least 2 weeks after sterilization of ventricular fluid. Complications of hydrocephalus and the potential use of intraventricular therapy render the neurosurgeon an essential part of the management team. Historically, mortality rates have been in excess of 70 percent, no doubt in part because of delays in identifying the organism and the limited antibiotic spectrum available for effective therapy. More recent series of patients, though small, suggest some improvement in this statistic, but the morbidity rates of hydrocephalus and neurologic deficits remain high.

Recovery has been the rule in immunocompetent older individuals infected with contaminated material, often despite treatment with antibiotics to which *Chryseobacterium* is insensitive.[33] However, significant mortality and morbidity often occur in immunocompromised individuals with bacteremia or meningitis. The use of chloramphenicol, vancomycin, ciprofloxacin, erythromycin, or rifampin has shown some success in these individuals, but selection of antibiotics should be based on a detailed examination of the organism's susceptibility.[23, 41]

REFERENCES

1. Aber, R. C., Wennersten, C., and Moellering, R. C., Jr.: Antimicrobial susceptibility of flavobacteria. Antimicrob. Agents Chemother. *14*:483–487, 1978.
2. Abrahamsen, T. G., Finne, P. H., and Lingaas, E.: *Flavobacterium meningosepticum* infections in a neonatal intensive care unit. Acta Paediatr. Scand. *78*:51–55, 1989.
3. Berry, W. B., Morrow, A. G., Harrison, D. C., et al.: *Flavobacterium* septicemia following intracardiac operations. J. Thorac. Cardiovasc. Surg. *45*:476–481, 1963.
4. Bloch, K. C., Nadarajah, R., and Jacobs, R.: *Chryseobacterium meningosepticum*: An emerging pathogen among immunocompromised adults. Medicine (Baltimore) *76*:30–41, 1997.
5. Brody, J. A., Moore, H., and King, E. O.: Meningitis caused by an unclassified gram-negative bacterium in newborn infants. Am. J. Dis. Child. *96*:1–5, 1958.
6. Brown, R. B., Phillips, D., Barker, M. J., et al.: Outbreak of nosocomial *Flavobacterium meningosepticum* respiratory infections associated with use of aerosolized polymyxin B. Am. J. Infect. Control *17*:121–125, 1989.
7. Bruun, B., Jensen, E. T., Lundstrom, K., et al.: *Flavobacterium meningosepticum* infection in a neonatal ward. Eur. J. Clin. Microbiol. Infect. Dis. *8*:509–514, 1989.
8. Cabrera, H. A., and Davis, G. H.: Epidemic meningitis of the newborn caused by flavobacteria. I. Epidemiology and bacteriology. Am. J. Dis. Child. *101*:289–295, 1961.
9. Chan, K. H., Chau, P. Y., Wang, R. Y. C., et al.: Meningitis caused by *Flavobacterium meningosepticum* after transsphenoidal hypophysectomy with recovery. Surg. Neurol. *20*:294–296, 1983.
10. Chandrika, T., and Adler, S. P.: A case of neonatal meningitis due to *Flavobacterium meningosepticum* successfully treated with rifampin. Pediatr. Infect. Dis. *1*:40–41, 1982.
11. Chiu, C. H., Waddingdon, M., Greenberg, D., et al.: Atypical *Chryseobacterium meningosepticum* and meningitis and sepsis in newborns and the immunocompromised, Taiwan. Emerg. Infect. Dis. *6*:481–486, 2000.
12. Colding, H., Bangsborg, J., Fiehn, N. E., et al.: Ribotyping for differentiating *Flavobacterium meningosepticum* isolates from clinical and environmental sources. J. Clin. Microbiol. *32*:501–505, 1994.
13. Coyle-Gilchrist, M. M., Crew, P., and Roberts, G.: *Flavobacterium meningosepticum* in the hospital environment. J. Clin. Pathol. *29*:824–826, 1976.
14. Dooley, J. R., Nims, L. J., Lipp, V. H., et al.: Meningitis of infants caused by *Flavobacterium meningosepticum*. J. Trop. Pediatr. *26*:24–30, 1980.
15. du Moulin, G. C.: Airway colonization by *Flavobacterium* in an intensive care unit. J. Clin. Microbiol. *10*:155–160, 1979.
16. Ferlauto, J. J., and Wells, D. H.: *Flavobacterium meningosepticum* in the neonatal period. South. Med. J. *74*:757–759, 1981.
17. Ferrer, C., Jakob, E., Pastorino, G., et al.: Right-sided bacterial endocarditis due to *Flavobacterium odoratum* in a patient on chronic hemodialysis. Am. J. Nephrol. *15*:82–84, 1995.
18. Findlay, G. H., Hull, P. R., Smith, H. E., et al.: Cutaneous flavobacteriosis: Polymorphous skin granulomas from *Flavobacterium capsulatum*. S. Afr. Med. J. *64*:247–250, 1983.
19. Fraser, S. L, and Jorgensen, J. H.: Reappraisal of the antimicrobial susceptibilities of *Chryseobacterium* and *Flavobacterium* species and methods for reliable susceptibility testing. Antimicrob. Agents Chemother. *41*:2738–2741, 1997.
20. George, R. M., Cochran, C. P., and Wheeler, W. E: Epidemic meningitis of the newborn caused by flavobacteria. II. Clinical manifestations and treatment. Am. J. Dis. Child. *101*:296–304, 1961.
21. Harrington, S. P., and Perlino, C. A.: *Flavobacterium meningosepticum* sepsis: Disease due to bacteria with unusual antibiotic susceptibility. South. Med. J. *74*:764–766, 1981.
22. Hawley, H. B., and Gump, D. W.: Vancomycin therapy of bacterial meningitis. Am. J. Dis. Child. *126*:261–264, 1973.
23. Hirsh, B. E., Wong, B., Kiehn, T. E., et al.: *Flavobacterium meningosepticum* bacteremia in an adult with acute leukemia: Use of rifampin to clear persistent infection. Diagn. Microbiol. Infect. Dis. *4*:65–69, 1986.
24. Holmes, B., Owen, R. J., and McMeekin, T. A.: Genus *Flavobacterium*. *In* Krieg, N. R., and Holt, J. G. (eds.): Bergey's Manual of Systematic Bacteriology. Vol. 1. Baltimore, Williams & Wilkins, 1984, pp. 353–360.
25. Holmes, B., Snell, J. J. S., and Lapage, S. P.: *Flavobacterium odoratum:* A species resistant to a wide range of antimicrobial agents. J. Clin. Pathol. *32*:73–77, 1979.
26. Hsueh, P. R., Hsiue, T. R., Wu, J. J., et al.: *Flavobacterium indologenes* bacteremia: Clinical and microbiological characteristics. Clin. Infect. Dis. *23*:550–555, 1996.
27. King, E. O.: Studies on a group of previously unclassified bacteria associated with meningitis in infants. Am. J. Clin. Pathol. *31*:241–247, 1959.
28. Lee, E. L., Robinson, M. J., Thong, M. L., et al.: Rifamycin in neonatal flavobacteria meningitis. Arch. Dis. Child. *51*:209–213, 1976.
29. Lee, E. L., Robinson, M. J., Thong, M. L., et al.: Intraventricular chemotherapy in neonatal meningitis. J. Pediatr. *91*:991–995, 1977.
30. Lee, M., and Munoz, J.: Septicemia occurring after colonoscopic polypectomy in a splenectomized patient taking corticosteroids. Am. J. Gastroenterol. *89*:2245–2246, 1994.
31. Linder, N., Korman, S. H., Eyal, F., et al.: Trimethoprim-sulphamethoxazole in neonatal *Flavobacterium meningosepticum* infection. Arch. Dis. Child. *59*:582–584, 1984.
32. Manfredi, R., Nanetti, A., Ferri, M., et al.: *Flavobacterium* spp. organisms as opportunistic bacterial pathogens during advanced HIV disease. J. Infect. *39*:146–152, 1999.
33. Mani, R. M., Kuruvila, K. C., Batliwala, P. M., et al. *Flavobacterium meningosepticum* as an opportunist. J. Clin. Pathol. *31*:220–222, 1978.
34. McCracken, G. H., Jr.: New developments in the management of children with bacterial meningitis. Pediatr. Infect. Dis. *3*(Suppl.):32–34, 1984.
35. Olsen, H., Frederiksen, W. C., and Siboni, K. E.: *Flavobacterium meningosepticum* in 8 non-fatal cases of postoperative bacteraemia. Lancet *1*:1294–1296, 1965.
36. Olsen, H., and Raun, T.: *Flavobacterium meningosepticum* isolated from the genitals. Acta Pathol. Microbiol. Immunol. Scand. *79*:102–106, 1971.
37. Plotkin, S. A., and McKitrick, J. C.: Nosocomial meningitis of the newborn caused by *Flavobacterium*. J. A. M. A. *198*:662–664, 1966.
38. Ratner, H.: *Flavobacterium meningosepticum*. Infect. Control *5*:237–239, 1984.
39. Rios, I., Klimek, J. J., Maderazo, E., et al.: *Flavobacterium meningosepticum* meningitis: Report of selected aspects. Antimicrob. Agents Chemother. *14*:444–447, 1978.
40. Sader, H. S., Jones, R. N., Pfaller, M. A.: Relapse of catheter-related *Flavobacterium meningosepticum* bacteremia demonstrated by DNA macrorestriction analysis. Clin. Infect. Dis. *21*:997–1000, 1995.
41. Sheridan, R. L., Ryan, C. M., Pasternack, M. S., et al.: Flavobacterial sepsis in massively burned pediatric patients. Clin. Infect. Dis. *17*:185–187, 1993.
42. Shulmann, B. H., and Johnson, M. S.: A case of meningitis in a premature infant due to a proteolytic gram-negative bacillus. J. Lab. Clin. Med. *29*:500–507, 1944.
43. Skapek, S. X., Jones, W. S., Hoffman, K. M., et al.: Sinusitis and bacteremia caused by *Flavobacterium meningosepticum* in a sixteen-year-old with Shwachman Diamond syndrome. Pediatr. Infect. Dis. *11*:411–413, 1992.
44. Stamm, W. F., Colella, J. J., Anderson, R. L., et al.: Indwelling arterial catheters as a source of nosocomial bacteremia. N. Engl. J. Med. *292*:1099–1102, 1975.
45. Sundin, D., Gold, B. D., Berkowitz, F. E., et al.: Community-acquired *Flavobacterium meningosepticum* meningitis, pneumonia and septicemia in a normal infant. Pediatr. Infect. Dis. *10*:73–76, 1991.
46. Teres, D.: ICU-acquired pneumonia due to *Flavobacterium meningosepticum*. J. A. M. A. *228*:732, 1974.
47. Thong, W. L., Puthucheary, S. D., and Lee, E. L.: *Flavobacterium meningosepticum* infection: An epidemiological study in a newborn nursery. J. Clin. Pathol. *34*:429–433, 1981.
48. Tizer, K. B., Cervia, J. S., Dunn, A. M., et al.: Successful combination vancomycin and rifampin therapy in a newborn with community-acquired *Flavobacterium meningosepticum* neonatal meningitis. Pediatr. Infect. Dis. J. *14*:916–917, 1995.
49. Vancanneyt, M., Segers, P., Hauben, L., et al.: *Flavobacterium meningosepticum,* a pathogen in birds. J. Clin. Microbiol. *32*:2398–2403, 1994.
50. Vancanneyt, M., Segers, P, Torck, U., et al.: Reclassification of *Flavobacterium odoratum* (Stutzer 1929) strains to a new genus, *Myroides*, as *Myroides odoratus* comb. nov. and *Myroides odoratimumus* sp. nov. Int. J. Syst. Bacteriol. *46*:926–932, 1996.
51. Vandamme, P., Bernardet, J.-F., Segers, P., et al.: New perspectives in the classification of the flavobacteria: Description of *Chryseobacterium* gen. nov., *Bergeyella* gen. nov., and *Empedobacter* nom. rev. Int. J. Syst. Bacteriol. *44*:474–481, 1994.
52. Werthamer, S., and Weiner, M.: Subacute bacterial endocarditis due to *Flavobacterium meningosepticum*. Am. J. Clin. Pathol. *57*:410–412, 1972.

CHAPTER 129 *Pseudomonas* and Related Genera

MICHAEL T. BRADY

The original classification of the genus *Pseudomonas* described a wide variety of aerobic gram-negative rods divided into five rRNA homology groups (homology groups I to V). The genus since has undergone extensive revision, with four of the five homology groups reclassified into separate genera[65] (Table 129–1). This reclassification was accomplished by using DNA-rRNA hybridization, DNA-DNA hybridization, and 16S rRNA sequencing techniques.

Pseudomonas and related genera are aerobic, motile, non–spore-forming, nonfermentative, gram-negative bacilli that live in soil, in water, and on plants and animals. Most organisms of these genera are ubiquitous and rarely pathogenic in humans. Although the pseudomonads may produce disease in any individual, they usually are opportunists that more commonly cause disease in patients with burns, cystic fibrosis, malignancies, and immunodeficiency conditions; in recipients of immunosuppressive therapy; or in malnourished persons. The most important of the opportunistic pseudomonads is *Pseudomonas aeruginosa*. However, numerous other pseudomonads cause specific clinical syndromes in children.

Etiology

Pseudomonas spp. usually are gram-negative obligate aerobes (oxygen as the terminal electron acceptor), but they can grow anaerobically in the presence of nitrates or arginine (terminal electron acceptors). They lack the phosphoenolpyruvate-hexose-phosphotransferase system and catabolize carbohydrates by the Entner-Doudoroff pathway. Because pseudomonads can use a wide variety of carbon sources (simple and complex carbohydrates, alcohols, and amino acids), they can survive and multiply in almost any moist environment containing minimal amounts of organic compounds.

P. aeruginosa is the most clinically important species of the genus *Pseudomonas*. It is an oxidase-positive, gram-negative rod varying in size from 0.5 to 0.8 μm × 1.5 to 3.0 μm. Most strains are motile by one or more polar, monotrichous flagella and display fine projections (pili or fimbriae). *P. aeruginosa* grows readily on standard laboratory media. It grows optimally at 37° C but not at 4° C. Clinical *Pseudomonas* isolates are oxidase-positive (except for *Pseudomonas luteola* and *Pseudomonas oryzhabitans*) and catalase-positive. On MacConkey agar, *Pseudomonas* spp. are identified as non–lactase fermenters. They do not ferment carbohydrates but do oxidize monosaccharides such as glucose and xylose, but not maltose. Strains from clinical specimens may produce beta-hemolysis on blood agar. More than 90 percent of *P. aeruginosa* organisms produce a bluish-green phenazine pigment (pyocyanin-blue pus), as well as fluorescein, a yellow-green fluorescent pigment. Occasional *Pseudomonas* strains also produce dark red (pyorubin) or black (pyomelanin) pigment. These pigments diffuse into and color the medium surrounding

TABLE 129–1 ■ RECENT TOXIGNOMIC CHANGES AND RECLASSIFICATION OF *PSEUDOMONAS* HOMOLOGY GROUPS I TO V THAT CAUSE DISEASE IN HUMANS

Pseudomonas Homology Group	Previous Designation	Current Designation
I		*Pseudomonas aeruginosa*
		Pseudomonas fluorescens
		Pseudomonas putida
		Pseudomonas stutzeri
		Pseudomonas mendocina
		Pseudomonas pseudoalcaligenes
		Pseudomonas alcaligenes
		Pseudomonas (CDC group 1)
	Chryseomonas luteola	*Pseudomonas luteola*
	Flavimonas oryzhabitans	*Pseudomonas oryzhabitans*
II	*Pseudomonas cepacia*	*Burkholderia cepacia*
	Pseudomonas gladioli	*Burkholderia gladioli*
	Pseudomonas mallei	*Burkholderia mallei*
	Pseudomonas pickettii	*Ralstonia pickettii*
	Pseudomonas pseudomallei	*Burkholderia pseudomallei*
III	*Pseudomonas acidovorans*	*Delftia acidovorans*
	Pseudomonas testosteroni	*Comamonas testosteroni*
	Pseudomonas delafieldii	*Acidovorax delafieldii*
	Hydrogenomonas facilis	*Acidovorax facilis*
IV	*Pseudomonas diminuta*	*Brevundimonas diminuta*
	Pseudomonas vesicularis	*Brevundimonas vesicularis*
V	*Xanthomonas maltophilia*	*Stenotrophomonas maltophilia*
		Stenotrophomonas africana

CDC, Centers for Disease Control and Prevention.
Data from Gilligan, P. H., and Whitler, S.: *Burkholderia, Stenotrophomonas, Ralstonia, Brevundimonas, Comamonas, and Acidovorax. In* Murray, P. R., Baron, J., Pfaller, M. A., et al. (eds.): Manual of Clinical Microbiology. 7th ed. Washington, DC, ASM Press, 1999, pp. 526–538.

the colonies. Strains of *P. aeruginosa* can be differentiated from one another for epidemiologic purposes by serologic typing, phage typing, ribotyping, and pyocin (bacteriocin) typing.

Epidemiology

P. aeruginosa is a ubiquitous environmental organism found in soil, in water, and on vegetation, including the surface of many raw fruits and vegetables. Its minimal nutritional requirements and ability to grow in a wide variety of physical environments enhance the organism's ability to survive in numerous ecologic niches. *P. aeruginosa* is found infrequently as normal microflora of healthy humans. The gastrointestinal (GI) tract is the most frequent site of human colonization. As many as 5 to 30 percent of normal persons have *P. aeruginosa* in their GI tract, although it is rarely the predominant organism. The large intestine is the most frequent site of transient colonization after ingestion. Other moist body sites that may become colonized include the throat, nasal mucosa, axillae, perineum, and the respiratory tract of patients who have been hospitalized for extended periods, have foreign bodies in place (endotracheal tubes or tracheostomies), have poor mucociliary clearance, and have received broad-spectrum antibiotics or chemotherapy. In general, *P. aeruginosa* is an opportunistic and not a frank pathogen. Despite the ability to colonize skin and mucosal surfaces, it rarely results in persistent colonization, it does not produce specific toxic factors that damage host tissues, and it is not capable of invading normal skin or mucosa. *P. aeruginosa* proves most effective as a pathogen in situations in which the host's immune defenses are diminished or lacking (e.g., poor mucociliary clearance in children with cystic fibrosis, neutropenia in children receiving chemotherapy for cancer, damaged skin barriers in burn patients). *P. aeruginosa* frequently enters the hospital environment on the clothes, skin, respiratory tract, or shoes of patients or hospital personnel; colonization of any moist environment ensues. Thus, these organisms may be found growing in distilled water, hospital kitchens and laundries, mops, shower heads, whirlpools, antiseptic solutions, eyedrops, irrigation fluid, dialysis fluid, and equipment used for dialysis and respiratory care or inhalation therapy. *P. aeruginosa* commonly is found on the surface of many types of raw fruits and vegetables. Consumption of these foods by profoundly immunosuppressed children can result in GI colonization and potentially can lead to invasive disease. Transmission of *P. aeruginosa* from patient to patient or from hospital personnel to patient often is assumed but rarely is documented.[42, 196] In hospitalized patients, the likelihood of *Pseudomonas* colonization increases with the duration of hospitalization. Sources of *Pseudomonas* outside the hospital that may result in colonization with subsequent infection include swimming pools, water slides, hot tubs, contact lens solutions, cosmetics, illicit injectable drugs, and the inner soles of sneakers.

The environmental distribution of most of the other *Pseudomonas* spp. and related genera is similar to that of *P. aeruginosa*. *Pseudomonas pseudoalcaligenes* has one of the more unusual habitats. This organism has been identified in metalworking fluid (a mixture of water and petroleum products) at concentrations as high as 10^8 organisms per milliliter or higher. Metalworkers are exposed to aerosols containing high concentrations (10^5 organisms per milliliter) of *P. pseudoalcaligenes*.[110] Despite the development of high antibody levels to *P. pseudoalcaligenes*, these metalworkers with long-term exposure do not have clinical evidence of any acute or chronic respiratory or systemic disease.

Burkholderia, formerly *Pseudomonas, cepacia* is a plant pathogen that is ubiquitous in nature and can be found in water, soil, and decaying organic matter.[100] *Burkholderia cepacia* is an obligate aerobic, gram-negative rod that is intrinsically resistant to a wide range of antimicrobial agents, including aminoglycosides and carboxypenicillins (e.g., ticarcillin, azlocillin, and carbenicillin). Historically, it was regarded as an organism with low pathogenicity. However, *B. cepacia* increasingly has been identified as a cause of sporadic nosocomial outbreaks of infection in medical intensive care units. Outbreaks are far less common than with *P. aeruginosa*. When they occur, they have been traced to contaminated automated peritoneal dialysis machines, blood gas analyzers, povidone-iodine, and chlorhexidine.[16, 17, 69, 173] *B. cepacia* can survive for extended periods in moist environments and even in the presence of disinfectants, including povidone-iodine.[5] Colonization of the respiratory tract, sometimes associated with endobronchial infection in patients with cystic fibrosis, is becoming a more common occurrence and is associated with increased morbidity and mortality. This organism also has become more important as a cause of infection and complications in patients with chronic granulomatous disease[177] and sickle-cell hemoglobinopathies.[18]

Stenotrophomonas maltophilia (formerly *Xanthomonas maltophilia*) is an aerobic gram-negative rod that grows readily on most bacteriologic media. *S. maltophilia* is being isolated with increasing frequency in hospitalized patients. Colonization of nonsterile sites such as the respiratory tract and wounds in the absence of clinical disease occurs commonly in hospitalized patients receiving long-term or broad-spectrum antibiotics. However, clinical illnesses such as pneumonia, urinary tract infections, endocarditis, bacteremia, meningitis, and peritonitis have been reported.[12, 46, 56, 120, 188] Isolation of *S. maltophilia* from the respiratory tract of patients with cystic fibrosis is increasing; in some centers, it is the second most frequent gram-negative bacterium isolated from sputum.[10, 93]

Burkholderia pseudomallei is most prevalent in the tropical and subtropical areas of Southeast Asia and northern Australia. *B. pseudomallei* has been recovered frequently from rice paddy surface water in rice-growing areas of northern Thailand.[37, 174]

Pathogenesis

The pathogenesis of *Pseudomonas* infections is multifactorial.[13, 106] Although *P. aeruginosa* is not uncommonly a human saprophyte, it usually causes disease as an opportunistic pathogen. *P. aeruginosa* is a significant cause of infection in compromised hosts. Its ability to adapt to a variety of environments, its minimal nutritional requirements, and its propensity for the development of antibiotic resistance allow *P. aeruginosa* to survive in compromised patients. The requirement of oxygen for growth may account for the lack of invasiveness of these organisms after they have colonized and even infected the skin. *P. aeruginosa* possesses a variety of virulence factors, including an endotoxin, an enterotoxin, and numerous extracellular enzymes. *P. aeruginosa* endotoxin is not as potent as are the endotoxins produced by other gram-negative organisms (2 to 3 mg is needed to kill a 20-g mouse). This endotoxin may produce a diarrheal syndrome. A *Pseudomonas* enterotoxin also has been described, but its role in causing diarrhea in humans remains unclear.

The extracellular enzymes of *P. aeruginosa* include lecithinase, collagenase, lipase, elastase (LasA and LasB), caseinase, gelatinase, fibrinolysin, hemolysin, phospholipase C, exoenzyme S, and exotoxin A. The proteolytic enzymes may be responsible for localized necrosis of the skin or lung and for corneal ulceration. Exotoxin A is an adenosine-5′-diphosphate ribosyltransferase enzyme that inhibits the synthesis of eukaryotic cell protein (same mechanism as diphtheria toxin). Specific exotoxin A–deficient mutants of *P. aeruginosa* have reduced virulence in producing infection of the cornea or lung in mice and rats.[128, 198] Exotoxin A also diminishes the activity of host phagocytes. Passive or active immunization against exotoxin A significantly protects against experimental infection with exotoxin-producing strains of *P. aeruginosa*. Phospholipase C degrades phospholipids, which are plentiful in eukaryotic but not prokaryotic cell membranes. The hemolysis produced by *P. aeruginosa* may be caused by heat-labile phospholipase C and by a heat-stable moiety. Exoenzyme S is another virulence factor. In burn patients, *P. aeruginosa* growing in the burned area produces exoenzyme S; *P. aeruginosa* on intact skin does not.[158] In burn patients in whom *Pseudomonas* sepsis develops, exoenzyme S can be found in the blood before the bacteria can be detected. *P. aeruginosa* strains that lack exoenzyme S production are less able to cause invasive disease.[158]

The various proteases also can degrade numerous plasma proteins such as complement and coagulation factors.[199] Solubilization and destruction of lecithin (surfactant) may play a role in the atelectasis seen in pulmonary infections caused by *P. aeruginosa*. A leukocidin also has been described that may in part be capsular material. The purified slime from *Pseudomonas* is nontoxic. Pigments produced by *P. aeruginosa* also are nontoxic.

Surface structures such as pili and fimbriae are involved in attachment of *P. aeruginosa* to the epithelial cells of mucosal surfaces. *P. aeruginosa* preferentially binds to normal respiratory mucin, in contrast to some members of the family Enterobacteriaceae.[189] Fibronectin may protect epithelial cells from bacterial attachment, but the ability to do so is reduced in patients with cystic fibrosis (high levels of protease in respiratory secretions) and after cellular injury (trauma after intubation and viral infection of the lower respiratory tract, especially influenza virus). The glycocalyx (extracellular slime layer) is important in allowing *P. aeruginosa* organisms to adhere to each other and form microcolonies, which impair phagocytosis and antibody and antibiotic activity.

The pathogenicity of *P. aeruginosa* also depends on its ability to resist phagocytosis. Fick and Reynolds[52] noted that in patients with cystic fibrosis, the opsonic function of IgG was reduced as a result of a molecular change in the Fc portion of the IgG molecule. This deficit was magnified in the lungs of patients with cystic fibrosis infected with *P. aeruginosa* because bacterial proteases can fragment IgG and further impair its opsonic activity, which already may be marginal. The persistent presence of *P. aeruginosa* in the lungs of patients with cystic fibrosis also may be related to the presence of one or more factors in their sputum that interfere with the bactericidal activity of fresh normal human serum against *P. aeruginosa*. These blocking factors have been shown to be IgG antibody that blocks the normal bactericidal IgM activity of human sera.[134, 163]

Concentrations of IgG subclass immunoglobulins have been studied in patients with cystic fibrosis and compared with values obtained in age-matched healthy children and adults. Pressler and associates[139] noted that in 52 percent of patients with cystic fibrosis, at least one of the four IgG subclasses had an elevated serum concentration in comparison to controls. A significant correlation of elevated serum concentrations of IgG2 (and to a lesser extent, IgG3) with decreased forced expiratory volume at 1 second was noted. Moss[118] found that patients with cystic fibrosis who are infected with *P. aeruginosa* have markedly elevated serum concentrations of IgG antibodies to the opsonic immunodeterminant, type-specific lipopolysaccharide. This elevation was distributed among all four IgG subclasses, with a significant shift toward IgG3. Sera from cystic fibrosis patients who were colonized with *P. aeruginosa* had diminished opsonic capacity, but complement-dependent human neutrophil phagocytosis was not impaired. Serum concentrations of IgG4 but not IgG1, IgG2, or IgG3 are correlated inversely with opsonic capacity. On the basis of these data, Moss[118] suggested that high levels of IgG4 antibody to opsonic immunodeterminants may inhibit normal pulmonary clearance of *P. aeruginosa* by pulmonary macrophages in vivo.

P. aeruginosa produces two elastolytic enzymes: LasA and LasB. These enzymes are virulence factors produced during infection. They probably cause direct damage to lung tissue (elastin accounts for 30% of the protein of lung tissue) and interfere with immune clearance of *P. aeruginosa* from the lungs. Berger and associates[14] noted that elastase treatment of isolated polymorphonuclear leukocytes severely impaired their ability to kill opsonized *P. aeruginosa*. They demonstrated proteolytic degradation of C3b receptors and suggested that it may contribute to the inability of patients with cystic fibrosis to eradicate *P. aeruginosa* from their lungs. Because several cell types, including macrophages, monocytes, B lymphocytes, and some T lymphocytes, all carry the same C3b receptor, the proteolytic activity may cleave this molecule from all these cells, thereby decreasing the phagocytic activity of monocytes and macrophages in these patients. Berger and colleagues[14] demonstrated that optimal interaction between the complement-derived opsonic ligands C3b and iC3b and their respective receptors does not occur in the milieu of the lungs of patients with cystic fibrosis who are infected with *Pseudomonas*. They suggested that both *Pseudomonas* and host proteases may contribute to the initiation of a cycle of events in which neutrophils entering the infected lung actually impair phagocytosis rather than eradicate the source of these infections. Breakdown of elastin in the walls of blood vessels might be responsible for the intrapulmonary hemorrhage noted in individuals with cystic fibrosis.

The mucoid strains of *P. aeruginosa* isolated from the respiratory secretions of patients with cystic fibrosis produce large quantities of alginate (composed of acetylated D-mannuronic acid and L-glucuronic acid).[30, 178] This polysaccharide polymer not only gives *P. aeruginosa* a mucoid appearance on agar but also has antiphagocytic activity. Alginate also can elicit a significant inflammatory immune response in the lungs of patients with cystic fibrosis, which may contribute to the lung damage that is present after chronic *P. aeruginosa* lung infection.[112] Because of its viscous nature, alginate contributes to the thick bronchial secretions in the lungs of children with cystic fibrosis; these secretions obstruct small airways and impair mucociliary clearance and movement of phagocytic cells. Production of alginate by *P. aeruginosa* is regulated and inducible. Mucoid *P. aeruginosa* loses the mucoid trait when serially cultured on laboratory media. Nonmucoid isolates convert to the mucoid (alginate-producing) phenotype when inoculated into the lung in a rat model.[158]

The role of lipopolysaccharide in the virulence of *P. aeruginosa* also has been studied. The virulence of several strains of *P. aeruginosa* in burned mice was found to be related directly to lipopolysaccharide integrity.[34] Deficiency of the O side chain of lipopolysaccharide reduced virulence markedly.

S. maltophilia and *B. cepacia* are opportunistic organisms whose virulence factors include intrinsic resistance to many antimicrobials effective in treating infection with *Pseudomonas* spp., an ability to adhere to plastic materials,[87] and elaboration of exoenzymes such as elastase and gelatinase.[122] *B. cepacia* also resists nonoxidative neutrophil killing.[177] For both *S. maltophilia* and *B. cepacia*, the following factors increase the risk of colonization with these organisms, as well as progression from colonization to infection: (1) prolonged hospitalization, especially in intensive care settings[109]; (2) administration of broad-spectrum antibiotics[179]; (3) malignancy, particularly if associated with immunosuppressive therapy and neutropenia[88, 179]; and (4) breaks in mucocutaneous defense barriers, chiefly by instrumentation or the use of invasive devices.[88]

Clinical Manifestations

P. aeruginosa can produce disease in healthy, normal children.[49] Generally, when disease occurs, the organism has been introduced into a minor wound contaminated with water or soil; this contamination is followed by the development of cellulitis as a localized abscess that exudes green or blue pus. The skin lesions (whether caused by direct inoculation or secondary to septicemia) may begin as pink macules that progress to small cutaneous hemorrhagic nodules and eventually to areas of necrosis with eschar formation surrounded by an intense red areola (ecthyma gangrenosum, Fig. 129–1). Bacteria multiply locally, and rarely (in normal children), *P. aeruginosa* causes septicemia, endocarditis, corneal infection, otitis externa, mastitis, mastoiditis, meningitis, pneumonia, peritonitis, and urinary tract infections. *Pseudomonas* osteomyelitis may develop after puncture wounds, particularly in the foot.[78]

Outbreaks of dermatitis (folliculitis), plantar nodules ("*Pseudomonas* hot-foot syndrome"), otitis externa, mastitis, and urinary tract infections caused by *P. aeruginosa* have been reported in normal, healthy children after the use of community swimming pools, water slides, recreational whirlpools, or family-owned hot tubs.[48, 49, 54, 67, 157, 172, 191] Pruritic or painful skin lesions (5 to 30 mm) develop several hours to 5 days or longer (mean, 48 hours) after contact with these water sources. Skin lesions may be erythematous, macular, or pustular. In some cases, very tender nodules have been observed.[54] Illness may vary from a few scattered lesions in some patients to extensive truncal involvement in others. The rash is most severe in areas occluded by snug-fitting bathing suits. In some children, malaise, fever, otitis externa, vomiting, sore throat, conjunctivitis, rhinitis, pyuria, abdominal cramps, and swollen breasts may be associated with the dermal lesions.

Multiple serotypes of *P. aeruginosa* have been associated with these outbreaks. The use of whirlpool baths usually involves soaking in water for variable periods. Superhydration of skin and exposure to *P. aeruginosa* result in primary cutaneous infection.[72] Whirlpool water is heated to temperatures above 37.8° C (100° F) and frequently is not filtered, thereby allowing for the persistence of desquamated skin. Both these factors are conducive to growth of *P. aeruginosa*.

Otitis externa caused by *P. aeruginosa* has been reported in healthy competitive swimmers who swim repetitively in a pool contaminated with *P. aeruginosa*.[144] The organism also has been associated with a more malignant form of otitis externa manifested as high fever, necrosis of portions of the external ear, facial nerve paralysis, mastoiditis, and osteomyelitis of the temporal bone and basilar skull.[75, 123] Rarely, *P. aeruginosa* meningitis results from progression of this infection.[137] Malignant otitis externa usually is associated with predisposing factors such as malnutrition, leukopenia (a disorder of leukocyte function), malignancy, or diabetes mellitus. Successful management of this condition requires aggressive surgical débridement in addition to appropriate systemic antibiotic therapy.

P. aeruginosa is a common agent of chronic suppurative otitis media (with or without cholesteatoma) and chronic mastoiditis.[85] Chronic suppurative otitis media is a complication of inadequately treated acute otitis media and is manifested as a perforated tympanic membrane with persistent otorrhea. Chronic suppurative otitis media also occurs in children with surgically induced perforations of the tympanic membrane by tympanostomy tubes and incompletely or inadequately treated otitis media. Outpatient therapy with oral antibiotics frequently is unsuccessful because of a lack of oral antimicrobial agents with antipseudomonal activity. Intravenous antibiotics targeting the bacterial agents isolated from middle ear aspirates usually can cure chronic suppurative otitis media. This therapy may preclude the necessity of performing tympanomastoid surgery, which becomes essential in those with extensive granulation tissue and osteitis in the mastoid.

P. aeruginosa infection of the eye usually occurs after trauma or deposition of a large inoculum. Using contaminated contact lens solution, using tap water during contact lens care, and endotracheal suctioning without covering the eyes of sedated or comatose patients have been implicated.[71, 74] Infection of the cornea can result in ulceration, which may progress to more invasive disease, including endophthalmitis. Loss of vision may result, even if appropriate antimicrobial therapy is administered promptly.

P. aeruginosa may produce serious infections during the neonatal period. Septicemia may be noted in the earliest hours of life and is associated with high morbidity and mortality. In utero acquisition of the organism has been described.[154] The clinical course is similar to that of any other form of gram-negative septicemia, with hypotension, respiratory distress, and skin lesions being the predominant manifestations. Late-onset neonatal *P. aeruginosa* infection usually occurs as a nosocomial infection (bacteremia, urinary tract infection, and pneumonia) associated with a foreign body (e.g., indwelling urinary or vascular catheter or endotracheal tube) in hospitalized infants. However, maternal colonization after the use of a hot tub for relaxation during labor was responsible for *P. aeruginosa* meningitis and bacteremia in an 11-day-old infant.[190]

Other pseudomonads (except *B. pseudomallei*) rarely cause disease in healthy persons. Reports in normal, healthy children, particularly when these children have been hospitalized in an intensive care unit,[20, 164] include pneumonia, keratitis,[104] and abscesses caused by *B. cepacia*; otitis media caused by *Shewanella putrefaciens*; abscesses caused by *Pseudomonas fluorescens*; otitis media, pneumonia, and osteomyelitis[27, 152] caused by *Pseudomonas stutzeri*; post-traumatic leg ulcers[133] and brain abscess[185] caused by *Sphingomonas paucimobilis*; and cellulitis, pneumonia, septicemia, endocarditis, peritonitis, and meningitis caused by *S. maltophilia*. *S. maltophilia* septicemia and endocarditis have been associated with intravenous abuse of illicit drugs.[203]

Peritonitis and septicemia caused by *B. cepacia*, *S. putrefaciens,* and *S. paucimobilis* have been associated with contamination of equipment used for peritoneal dialysis.[8, 16, 36, 66]

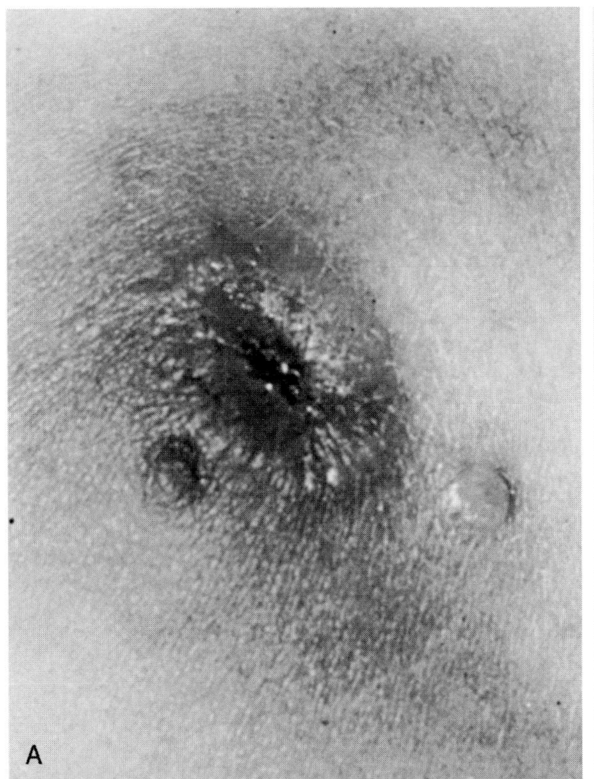

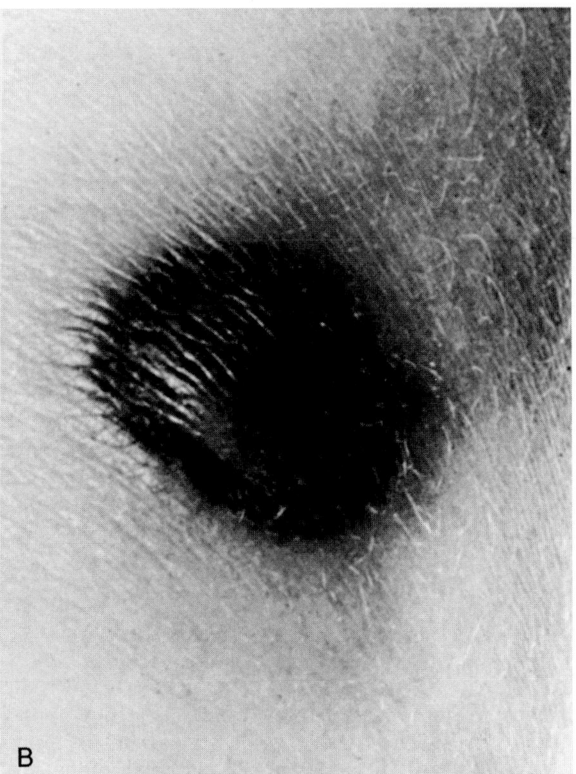

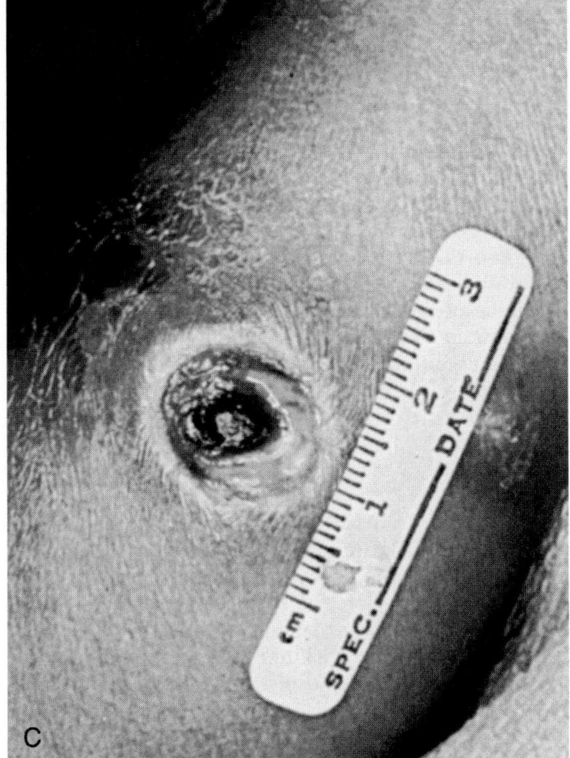

FIGURE 129–1 ■ *A,* Skin lesion caused by septicemic *Pseudomonas aeruginosa* infection. A large macule has begun to undergo central necrosis and is surrounded by two smaller macules. *B,* Small cutaneous nodule representing the skin lesion of septicemic *P. aeruginosa. C,* A final stage of ecthyma gangrenosum in which a cutaneous hemorrhagic nodule has undergone central necrosis and eschar formation.

BURNS AND WOUND INFECTION

The surface of wounds or burns frequently is populated by pseudomonads and other gram-negative organisms.[49] Colonization does not imply infection necessarily, but it is a necessary prerequisite to development of invasive disease. Septicemia with *P. aeruginosa* is a major problem in burn patients, with the mortality attributed to *Pseudomonas*-associated burn wound sepsis approaching 78 percent.[113] Systemic involvement may be related to the multiplication of organisms in devitalized surface areas, followed by invasion, or it can be associated with the prolonged intravenous or urinary catheterization required for the care of these persons. Antibiotics may diminish the susceptible microbiologic flora but permit more resistant selected strains of *P. aeruginosa* to flourish. In addition, the hydrotherapy that is commonly provided to burn patients promotes colonization of the burned area, as well as other sites.[186]

In burn patients, abnormalities in neutrophil function that precede the onset of septicemia have been described.[3] Killing of *Pseudomonas* by neutrophils is impaired. Burn injury is also associated with abnormal responses to antigens, delayed rejection of homografts, abnormal vascular responses, impaired delayed hypersensitivity responses, diminished uptake of particles by the reticuloendothelial system, and altered antimicrobial pharmacokinetics. Contamination of wounds with high concentrations of bacteria ($>10^5$ colony-forming units [CFUs] per gram of tissue) impedes contraction and healing of the wound.[131] In addition, *P. aeruginosa* produces numerous substances that can further inhibit the natural healing process of burns and wounds. Secretion of exogenous plasminogen activators and proteases breaks down proteins such as fibrin and halts the contraction process.[136] *P. aeruginosa* exotoxin A, a protein synthesis inhibitor, is also a potent cause of retardation of wound healing.[68]

BONE AND JOINT INFECTIONS

P. aeruginosa is the most common cause of osteomyelitis after puncture wounds of the foot and is responsible for more than 90 percent of cases.[22, 47, 115] The calcaneus or metatarsal bones commonly are affected.[33] Symptoms may be present for 2 to 40 days (mean, 9 days) before diagnosis is made and hospitalization is needed.[33] Pain and swelling are the most common symptoms; fever and wound drainage rarely are noted. Leukocytosis (white blood cell count $>10{,}000/mm^3$) and an elevated erythrocyte sedimentation rate are present in most patients. Radiographs of the affected foot usually show evidence of osteomyelitis at some time during the period of evaluation and treatment. Bone scan results almost universally are abnormal and frequently yield evidence of osteomyelitis before positive findings on radiographs. The inner pad of sneakers has been implicated as a possible source of *P. aeruginosa* in these patients.[55] However, *P. aeruginosa* osteomyelitis of the foot bones has developed when the puncture occurred through other types of footwear or while the child was barefoot.

Other *P. aeruginosa* infections of bones and joints are uncommon findings in children. When they do occur, they are the result of hematogenous spread of *P. aeruginosa* in patients who are intravenous drug abusers or who have urinary tract or pelvic infections. Although any bone or joint may be affected as a result of *P. aeruginosa* bacteremia, *P. aeruginosa* has a unique predilection for the vertebrae, sternoarticular joints, pelvis, and symphysis pubis. The clinical course of *P. aeruginosa* osteomyelitis or septic arthritis is more indolent than that occurring after infection with *Staphylococcus aureus*. Contiguous spread can occur after penetrating trauma, surgery, or overlying soft tissue infections, especially decubitus ulcers.

CYSTIC FIBROSIS

Cystic fibrosis is one of the most common lethal inherited diseases of children.[49] It is a generalized disorder of salt and water transport that affects the exocrine glands, and it is caused by mutations in the cystic fibrosis transmembrane conductance regulator gene.[94, 151] The course and prognosis are determined largely by chronic infections of the airways with opportunistic bacteria. Death usually results from chronic obstructive pulmonary disease. *P. aeruginosa* can be recovered from cultures in most children with cystic fibrosis. Recovery of *P. aeruginosa* from the sputum of a child with cystic fibrosis does not imply infection necessarily and the destructive pneumonitis related to this organism. Mucociliary clearance is impeded in patients with cystic fibrosis, and as a consequence they fail to cleanse the bronchopulmonary epithelium of inhaled particles, including bacteria.[94, 117] Colonization of the sputum of patients with cystic fibrosis may reflect the use of mist tents, inhalation therapy, and continuous broad-spectrum antibiotic therapy.[202] Colonization of the respiratory tract of patients with cystic fibrosis by mucoid strains of *P. aeruginosa* can be correlated with the patient's age, clinical score, extent of pulmonary function abnormalities, severity of changes on chest radiographs, and serum immunoglobulin levels.[51, 53] Once *P. aeruginosa* is in the respiratory tract, it rarely is eradicated by antibiotic therapy.

Some observations, however, suggest that the relationship between *Pseudomonas* and patients with cystic fibrosis is more specific. Patients with cystic fibrosis almost always harbor an unusual mucoid *P. aeruginosa* phenotype that produces an excessive amount of capsular slime.[145] The tracheobronchial tree of 70 to 80 percent of these patients is colonized chronically, and the organism infrequently is eradicated either spontaneously or by antibiotic therapy.[62, 170] The peculiar lung environment of a patient with cystic fibrosis is believed to trigger a switch to a cluster of genes that code for abundant production of the mucoid polysaccharide (alginate), thereby giving rise to the mucoid phenotype.[30, 178] In contrast, mucoid strains of *P. aeruginosa* are recovered from only 0.5 to 1.7 percent of patients without cystic fibrosis.

Persistence of *P. aeruginosa* within the respiratory tract is aided by growth of the organism in microcolonies embedded in a biofilm of alginate.[73, 132] This biofilm allows nutrients to pass while protecting the organism from host defense mechanisms, antibodies, and probably antibiotics.[94] In addition, investigators have noted that rabbit alveolar macrophages fail to phagocytize and kill the organism in the presence of serum from patients with cystic fibrosis. This phenomenon suggests that these patients have a specific, local defect in pulmonary resistance to *P. aeruginosa*.

A clustering of *P. aeruginosa* serotypes also occurs in isolates obtained from patients with cystic fibrosis. Homma type 8 strains may be recovered from 50 to 93 percent of patients with cystic fibrosis.

Bacterial infection in patients with cystic fibrosis is limited almost entirely to the respiratory tract, and pulmonary exacerbations with endobronchial disease are a common finding. Infection of the pulmonary parenchyma rarely occurs. Rather, the epithelium of the airways and the submucosa are edematous and contain infiltrates of chronic inflammatory cells. Documentation of a pulmonary exacerbation in cystic fibrosis relies heavily on clinical impression (e.g., increase in the frequency of productive cough; increase in volume or a change in characteristics of the sputum; increase in the respiratory rate or dyspnea; and decrease in appetite, activity, or exercise tolerance). Fever and leukocytosis are present in a minority of patients and are associated with poorer pulmonary function test results and a worse prognostic score.[171] Concentrations of *P. aeruginosa*, DNA (derived from polymorphonuclear leukocytes and to a lesser extent from respiratory epithelial cells), and total protein in sputum are increased during pulmonary exacerbations and decrease significantly after antimicrobial therapy.[171] Pulmonary infection in patients with cystic fibrosis generally is chronic. Bronchitis, bronchiolitis, and bronchiectasis can occur. Eventually, local necrotizing pneumonitis may be noted, in contrast to the overwhelming generalized necrotizing pneumonitis seen in immunosuppressed patients. Septicemia is a rare occurrence. However, bacteremia may develop in patients with indwelling venous catheters.

B. cepacia also has emerged as an increasingly frequent agent of asymptomatic colonization, pneumonia, and septicemia in patients with cystic fibrosis. Rates of colonization have been as high as 40 percent in some centers.[156] The increased frequency of colonization of the respiratory tract with *B. cepacia* in patients with cystic fibrosis has been associated with increased morbidity and mortality rates in some cystic fibrosis centers since the 1980s. The risk of colonization with *B. cepacia* increases with the severity of underlying disease and increasing age.[183] The source or mode of transmission of the organism has not been defined adequately.[105, 184] However, more recent information supports person-to-person transmission.[81] Nosocomial transmission (patient to patient and contaminated inhalation therapy equipment) within cystic fibrosis centers and social contact, particularly at summer camps, appear to be important in the acquisition of new infection with *B. cepacia*. Once colonization with *B. cepacia* has been identified in patients with cystic fibrosis, three distinct clinical patterns have been noted: (1) chronic asymptomatic carriage (usually in association with *P. aeruginosa*); (2) progressive deterioration over many months, with recurrent acute pulmonary exacerbations accompanied by fever, progressive weight loss, leukocytosis, and an elevated erythrocyte sedimentation rate; and (3) rapid, usually fatal deterioration in pulmonary function associated with necrotizing pneumonia and, at times, bacteremia.[77] The last complication can occur even in patients who were affected only mildly before acquiring *B. cepacia* infection.

B. cepacia has numerous important virulence factors, some of which may play a specific role in the clinical syndromes seen in patients with cystic fibrosis. *P. aeruginosa* enhances subsequent adhesion to epithelial surfaces by *B. cepacia*,[155] which may suggest a synergistic relationship between the two bacterial pathogens, particularly in patients with cystic fibrosis.[176] Additionally, *B. cepacia* strains from cystic fibrosis patients with the most severe progression bind most avidly to mucin.[156]

S. maltophilia was reported first in respiratory cultures of patients with cystic fibrosis in 1975.[59] Since that time, the prevalence of isolation of *S. maltophilia* from patients with cystic fibrosis has been increasing; rates in the United States range from 1.8 to 8.7 percent,[40, 119] and many European centers report higher rates. One center in Spain reported a prevalence rate of 30 percent.[9] The prognostic significance of *S. maltophilia* colonization in patients with cystic fibrosis is not certain. In general, new acquisition of *S. maltophilia* does not seem to be associated with an adverse clinical outcome.[40] However, prolonged colonization with *S. maltophilia*, particularly with high bacterial counts in excess of 10^5 to 10^6 CFUs/mL of sputum, may be associated with progressive deterioration in pulmonary function.[9, 83]

MALIGNANCY

Children with leukemia, particularly those receiving immunosuppressive therapy and those who are neutropenic, are extremely susceptible to septicemia caused by *P. aeruginosa* and other pseudomonads.[49] Most pseudomonads, including *Pseudomonas putida*, have been reported as causes of septicemia in children with malignancy.[4] Generally, infection results from invasion of the bloodstream by a colonizing *Pseudomonas* organism (e.g., from the GI tract). Anorexia, malaise, nausea, vomiting, diarrhea, and fever may be noted. Generalized vasculitis develops, and hemorrhagic necrotic lesions can be found in all organs, including the skin, where they appear as purple nodules or ecchymotic areas that become gangrenous.[143] Hemorrhagic or gangrenous perirectal cellulitis or abscess may be present, as may ileus and profound hypotension.

Children undergoing treatment of malignancies are particularly vulnerable to bacterial infection. Chemotherapy and radiation therapy can disrupt mucocutaneous barriers and result in moderate to severe immunosuppression. Fergie and associates[50] described 98 children and adolescents with cancer in whom *P. aeruginosa* bacteremia developed; the rate of bacteremia was highest in patients with leukemia. Most cases occurred when patients had absolute neutrophil counts of less than $100/mm^3$. Mortality associated with *P. aeruginosa* bacteremia was higher in patients with solid tumors, an absolute neutrophil count of less than $100/mm^3$, perineal skin lesions, and bacteremia during remission or induction therapy rather than during a relapse.

The single most important factor that predisposes children with cancer to infection is granulocytopenia. The bactericidal capacity of children with leukemia and other neoplasm also may be impaired. Heat-stable opsonins specific for *P. aeruginosa* likewise may fall precipitously in children with acute leukemia who are receiving intensive combination chemotherapy. Fatal infections with *P. aeruginosa* may be related in part to deficiency of this specific opsonin.

IMMUNOSUPPRESSION

Immunosuppressive agents may be used in the management of malignancies, transplantation, or collagen vascular disease. The location of the infectious process and the type of causative organisms depend somewhat on the underlying disease. Infection by *P. aeruginosa*, particularly pneumonia and septicemia, occurs more commonly in children receiving immunosuppressive therapy than in the normal, healthy population.

OTHER CONDITIONS THAT PREDISPOSE TO *PSEUDOMONAS* INFECTION

P. aeruginosa is a major cause of hospital-acquired infections in children. It is the leading cause of nosocomial respiratory tract infection in children undergoing mechanical ventilation or receiving inhalation therapy. Asymptomatic colonization of the upper and lower airways occurs commonly and should be distinguished from respiratory tract disease, tracheitis, and pneumonia. A predominance of gram-negative bacilli with an abundance of polymorphonuclear leukocytes on Gram stain of lower respiratory tract secretions, in conjunction with a positive culture for *P. aeruginosa,* strongly supports the role of *P. aeruginosa* as the causative agent for the lower respiratory tract infection. Absence of *P. aeruginosa* from lower respiratory tract secretions markedly reduces the likelihood that *P. aeruginosa* is in the lower respiratory tract.

P. aeruginosa septicemia occurs with increased frequency in children with indwelling vascular or urinary catheters.[181] In addition, septicemia may occur in children with congenital or acquired neutropenia or in persons with a functional deficit in polymorphonuclear leukocyte function. Urinary tract infections also have been associated with cystoscopic examination. *Pseudomonas* is a common cause of abscesses and meningitis in children with dermoid sinus tracts or dermoids extending down to or communicating with the meninges or neural tissue and in children with meningomyeloceles. *P. aeruginosa* may produce acute or subacute endocarditis in children with congenital cardiac lesions before or after cardiac surgery and in adolescents who inject illicit drugs intravenously. *P. aeruginosa* supraglottitis has been reported in a 6-month-old child with severe combined immunodeficiency syndrome.[99]

Severe *P. aeruginosa* infections have been reported in children infected with human immunodeficiency virus (HIV), primarily after severe immunodeficiency has occurred.[57, 150] Risks for acquiring *P. aeruginosa* infection in HIV-infected individuals include hospital exposure, declining $CD4^+$ cell count, and the use of dapsone or trimethoprim-sulfamethoxazole; azithromycin use was protective.[175] Bacteremia may occur with or without the presence of an indwelling vascular catheter. Fever, hypotension, skin lesions (papules or ecthyma gangrenosum), and pneumonia are common manifestations.[57] Mortality rates can be high, particularly when empiric antimicrobial therapy is inadequate for the treatment of severe, invasive *Pseudomonas* infection.

P. aeruginosa causes endocarditis on both native and prosthetic heart valves. Fortunately, it is an uncommon occurrence in children because its usual setting is in intravenous drug users. Obviously, *P. aeruginosa* needs to be considered in adolescents, particularly those with a history of intravenous drug use or at risk for acquiring HIV infection, and in infants, children, and adolescents with prosthetic valves or other intracardiac synthetic material. Tricuspid valve involvement occurs most commonly, but involvement of multiple valves is possible with *P. aeruginosa*; the manifestations are typical of subacute endocarditis. If the left side of the heart is involved (aortic or mitral valves), the patient has acute and more fulminant disease. Fever and heart murmur are almost universal findings.

DISEASE CAUSED BY OTHER PSEUDOMONADS

In addition to causing respiratory tract infection in patients with cystic fibrosis, *B. cepacia* can result in other infections, primarily in hospitalized or immunocompromised patients. Nosocomial pneumonia in ventilated patients, bacteremia, wound infections, urinary tract infections, meningitis, endocarditis, and skin lesions may be caused by *B. cepacia*. Fortunately, all of these infections are uncommon findings in children.

S. maltophilia has been reported with an ever-expanding spectrum of clinical manifestations, most notably bacteremia, endocarditis, lower respiratory tract infection, urinary tract infection, wound infection, meningitis, conjunctivitis, keratitis, dacryocystitis, otitis media, and bone and joint infections. Lower respiratory tract colonization, at times associated with symptomatic disease, is the most common manifestation in children. In addition to its occurrence in children with cystic fibrosis, *S. maltophilia* may be isolated from the respiratory tract of hospitalized children, especially those with endotracheal tubes or tracheostomies. Although colonization usually is asymptomatic, occasionally, lower respiratory tract infection with *S. maltophilia* can result in respiratory deterioration, pneumonitis, and an increased risk of mortality.[95, 116]

Bacteremia with *S. maltophilia* usually results from the presence of an intravascular device or an infection of the respiratory, GI, or urinary tracts. Pseudobacteremia with *S. maltophilia* arising from contamination of blood cultures that were performed with blood used to fill nonsterile tubes designed for coagulation studies has been reported.[79] Other infections with *S. maltophilia* in children occur primarily after trauma they experience or instrumentation they undergo.

Melioidosis is a rare disease of Southeast Asia and northern Australia that increased in frequency in the United States when Americans returned from Vietnam or, rarely, after immigration by Southeast Asians.[37, 129] The causative agent is *B. pseudomallei*, an environmental saprophyte of soil and water in the tropics, particularly in rice paddies. *B. pseudomallei* is a small, motile, pleomorphic gram-negative rod without a capsule that exhibits bipolar staining. It is an obligate aerobe that grows best at pH 7 and 37.0° C (98.6° F). Infection occurs after contact of abrasions or wounds with contaminated soil or water, inhalation of contaminated dust, or ingestion of contaminated water. Patients with poorly controlled diabetes, renal disease, or immunocompromised conditions caused by collagen vascular disease, hematologic malignancies, or immunosuppressive therapy appear to have an increased risk for development of disease after infection with *B. pseudomallei*.

Transmission from animals to humans has not been reported. The rat flea and the *Aedes aegypti* mosquito have been reported to infect animals with *B. pseudomallei*, but this route of infection has not been documented in human cases.[130] Human-to-human transmission has occurred during sexual or prolonged close contact.[97] An outbreak of melioidosis in Australia was traced to a potable water source from a water treatment plant that had irregularities in purification.[76]

Most infections with *B. pseudomallei* remain subclinical. Melioidosis can have a broad spectrum of clinical signs, and symptoms may be latent for months or years before the disease becomes clinically apparent. The initial clinical finding may be a single primary skin lesion (vesicle, pustule, bulla, urticaria) in a patient with no underlying disease. Septicemia occasionally occurs, and multiple abscesses may be noted in every organ of the body. The mortality rate associated with fulminant sepsis approaches 90 percent.[97] Meningitis, encephalitis, arthritis, nodular pulmonary densities, and endophthalmitis have been observed in both normal and compromised hosts after or concomitant with an episode of septicemia. The acute septicemic illness is indistinguishable from other types of septicemia caused by gram-negative organisms.

B. pseudomallei can cause myocarditis, pericarditis, endocarditis, intestinal abscess, cholecystitis, acute gastroenteritis, urinary tract infection, septic arthritis, paraspinal abscess, osteomyelitis, hilar lymphadenopathy, and cervical lymphadenopathy. Parotitis was documented in 38 percent of 126 children with melioidosis in Thailand.[38] None of the 126 children with melioidosis had any apparent predisposition to infection.

Subacute melioidosis generally is characterized by an illness lasting weeks to months. Pulmonary infection in this form of disease is a common occurrence and may mimic tuberculosis. The disease can vary from mild bronchitis to severe, fulminant pneumonitis.[97] Consolidation and cavitation occur frequently.

Neonatal melioidosis has been reported in Thailand.[107] Infants with neonatal septicemia, meningitis, or both caused by *B. pseudomallei* have been described. The mode of transmission of this organism to these newborn infants is not always clear. A clear case of mother-to-child transmission of *B. pseudomallei* has been reported.[1] The mother had acute melioidosis treated with ofloxacin at 32 weeks' gestation. Consolidation of the right lung of the infant occurred, and an abscess eventually developed. Postpartum cultures of the mother's cervix yielded *B. pseudomallei*.

Chronic melioidosis occurs more frequently in whites than in Asians.[111] Chronic melioidosis may involve every organ in the body, including the brain.[97] Melioidosis may become dormant, with exacerbations occurring years after primary infection when host defenses are impaired as a result of steroid use, burns, diabetes mellitus, or other processes. The longest latent period (24 years) was reported by Kingston.[91]

Melioidosis should be considered in any person who has been to Southeast Asia or northern Australia at any time and has fever of unknown origin, overwhelming sepsis, single or multiple abscesses, or any tuberculosis-like illness. The diagnosis is established by culture of blood, skin lesions, or purulent material from an abscess cavity or from other sites of infection.[101] The organism grows in media commonly used for isolation of gram-negative bacteria. On solid media, the colonies develop slowly (over a week) and have a characteristic daisy head appearance. Alpha-hemolysis is noted on sheep blood agar. A selective medium ("Ashdown medium") can increase the recovery rate of *B. pseudomallei* from clinical specimens containing mixed bacterial flora, such as throat, rectal, and sputum specimens.[6] *B. pseudomallei* produces a dry, wrinkled, and violet-purple colony with a pungent, earthy odor on Ashdown medium.[63]

Serologic tests are more useful in establishing the diagnosis of melioidosis in latent or asymptomatic forms of this disease.[2, 108, 125] Hemagglutination (HA), indirect HA, complement-fixation (CF) tests, and an enzyme-linked immunosorbent assay (ELISA) are available. Diagnostic titers are 1:40 or greater for the HA test and 1:10 or greater for the CF test. Because the sensitivity of these serologic tests varies, both should be performed. HA antibodies generally are present within 7 to 14 days after onset of the illness; the CF test yields positive results in 4 to 6 weeks. Maximal titers for both tests are reached in 4 to 6 months. Both HA and CF antibodies persist for 9 months to 2 years after the onset of disease. The indirect HA test is used by the Centers for Disease Control and Prevention for the diagnosis of melioidosis. An ELISA that detects specific IgG and IgM antibody to *B. pseudomallei* has been developed.[7] This assay proved more suitable than was an IgG indirect fluorescent antibody test in screening for melioidosis and also was more sensitive than was the indirect HA test for melioidosis. Gold blot detection of IgM- and IgG-specific antibodies has been developed[98] and allows serodiagnosis of melioidosis to be made more rapidly. *B. pseudomallei* can be detected in serum by an ELISA method.[197]

Diagnosis and Differential Diagnosis

The diagnosis of *Pseudomonas* infection depends on recovery of the organism from blood, cerebrospinal fluid (CSF), and urine obtained in a manner that avoids contamination by cutaneous flora (suprapubic aspiration or urethral catheterization is usually required for young children) and from joint fluid, peritoneal dialysis fluid, or purulent material obtained by aspiration of subcutaneous abscesses or areas of cellulitis. A diagnosis of *Pseudomonas* pneumonia can be made by needle aspiration of the lung and, less convincingly, by recovery of the organism from sputum obtained by postural drainage of a child with cystic fibrosis. Recovery of the organism from the surface of the skin or the throat, a tracheal aspirate, or bronchial secretions may reflect colonization and is not necessarily diagnostic of infection. The validity of a positive culture is enhanced when it is associated with a typical clinical syndrome (e.g., *P. aeruginosa* recovered from a skin lesion typical of "whirlpool" folliculitis). Isolation of *P. aeruginosa* from the respiratory tract, particularly when obtained from an endotracheal tube in an intubated patient, is not an unusual occurrence. Differentiating colonization from infection is clinically important. Gram stain of respiratory secretions obtained by endotracheal suction typically reveals abundant gram-negative rods and polymorphonuclear leukocytes in the setting of a true lower respiratory tract infection caused by *P. aeruginosa* (tracheitis or pneumonitis). An absence of gram-negative rods or the presence of squamous epithelial cells rather than polymorphonuclear leukocytes indicates that either the patient does not have a lower respiratory tract infection or, if an infection is present, the etiologic agent is not likely to be *P. aeruginosa*.

Isolation of *Pseudomonas* spp. other than *P. aeruginosa* from clinical specimens occurs far less frequently. Recovery of these *Pseudomonas* spp. from sites that normally are sterile, such as blood or blood product containers, always should be considered clinically significant unless proved otherwise.

Pseudomonas and *Burkholderia* are nutritionally versatile and grow well on most standard laboratory media (such as 5% sheep blood or chocolate agar). They grow optimally at 37° C and also at 42° C, but not at 4° C. All members of both genera grow in broth blood culture systems.[63] Isolation of *Pseudomonas* and *Burkholderia* from specimens with mixed bacterial flora is enhanced by using selective media such as MacConkey agar. Cetrimide, acetamide, nitrofurantoin, and 9-chloro-9[4-(diethylamino)phenyl]-9,10-dihydro-10-phenylacridine hydrochloride (C390) can be used for the isolation of *P. aeruginosa* from clinical as well as environmental specimens. Two media, PC (for *P. cepacia*)[63] and OFPBL (for oxidative-fermentative base–polymyxin B–bacitracin–lactose)[193] agar, inhibit *P. aeruginosa* and are useful for recovery of *B. cepacia* from the sputum of patients with cystic fibrosis.

P. aeruginosa usually is recognized easily on laboratory media by its characteristic colony morphology, diffusible pigment (when present), and odor (sweet grapelike or corn taco–like). Colonies generally are spreading (sometimes overrunning other organisms in mixed infections) and flat. They usually have a metallic sheen. However, patients with cystic fibrosis typically have *P. aeruginosa* isolates with mucoid colony formation. *P. aeruginosa* can be identified reasonably by the presence of the following: (1) positive oxidase test, (2) triple sugar iron agar reaction of alkaline over no charge, (3) growth at 42° C, and (4) production of a bright blue to blue-green (and to a lesser extent, red or brown) diffusible pigment on non–dye-containing agar such as Mueller-Hinton. Many laboratories rely on commercial systems for identifying *P. aeruginosa*. For pigmented *P. aeruginosa*, these systems are accurate 70 to 100 percent of the time (average, >90%).[60, 147, 149] The accuracy with nonpigmented *P. aeruginosa* is significantly less.[92]

The bluish, nodular skin lesions and the ulcers with ecchymotic and gangrenous centers and bright areolae (ecthyma gangrenosum) have been considered to be virtually pathognomonic of *P. aeruginosa* infection. Rarely, skin lesions that are clinically indistinguishable from those caused by *P. aeruginosa* develop after septicemia secondary to *Aeromonas hydrophila*.[168] Cutaneous or disseminated infections with *Aspergillus* and *Fusarium* in immunocompromised patients can also cause the necrotic skin lesions of ecthyma gangrenosum.

Immunoglobulin antibodies to *P. aeruginosa* surface antigens in serum have been detected reliably by ELISA.[23] Detection of specific IgG and IgA antibodies is not clinically useful for the diagnosis of acute *P. aeruginosa* infection. However, antibody titer increases were associated with active disease caused by *P. aeruginosa* in patients with cystic fibrosis. Antibody titers returned to baseline when *Pseudomonas* infection was controlled by effective antimicrobial therapy. Thus, this assay appears to help in differentiating between early infection and colonization. Antibodies to *P. aeruginosa* may also be detected by immunoblotting (Western blotting).[169] These methods may be sensitive and useful for determining the onset of *P. aeruginosa* infection in patients with cystic fibrosis.

Treatment

Systemic infections with *Pseudomonas* should be promptly treated with antibiotics to which the organism is susceptible in vitro.[19, 146] Community-acquired *P. aeruginosa* is typically sensitive to antipseudomonal penicillins, aminoglycosides, ciprofloxacin, ceftazidime, meropenem, and imipenem. Susceptibility is less predictable for aztreonam, a monobactam. Nosocomially acquired *P. aeruginosa* is more likely to be antibiotic-resistant than community-acquired strains are. Response to treatment may be impaired, and prolonged treatment may be required when systemic infection occurs in an immunocompromised host.

Table 129–2 provides dosages of some of the more commonly prescribed antipseudomonal antibiotics.[121] These dosages are only guidelines because the doses of some of these antibiotics may vary with different clinical situations and patient populations. Once-daily administration of aminoglycoside is being evaluated as a way to decrease nephrotoxicity and improve clinical efficacy. Aminoglycoside doses must be decreased, preferably by increasing the dosing interval, in patients with diminished creatinine clearance (e.g., renal impairment, neonates). Significantly higher doses (e.g., 7 to 12 mg/kg/day for gentamicin or tobramycin) may be required for patients with increased total plasma clearance, such as those with cystic fibrosis and burns. Therefore, aminoglycoside therapy must be individualized and doses guided by pharmacokinetic information.

Invasive infections, including septicemia caused by proven or suspected *P. aeruginosa* infection, should be treated with an aminoglycoside (gentamicin, tobramycin, netilmicin, or amikacin) combined with a β-lactam antibiotic (antipseudomonal penicillin, third- or fourth-generation cephalosporin, or carbapenem).[86] The combination of an aminoglycoside and a β-lactam antibiotic may be synergistic against the organism. Rifampin (synergistic in vitro with anti-*Pseudomonas* penicillins and aminoglycosides) may be added to the combination therapy if the clinical response is not adequate. Monotherapy with the cell wall–active β-lactam antibiotics, as well as the fluoroquinolones, frequently leads to the development of antibiotic resistance during therapy as a result of a mutation.[11, 165]

P. aeruginosa may be responsible for lower respiratory tract infections in neonates, infants, and children. Involvement of the airways in patients with cystic fibrosis and nosocomial tracheitis or pneumonitis in intubated patients are the most common manifestations. In both patients with cystic fibrosis and critically ill intubated patients, previous use of antimicrobial therapy results in a high frequency of antibiotic-resistant *P. aeruginosa*. Combination therapy with a β-lactam antibiotic and an aminoglycoside is synergistic in vitro and has superior clinical efficacy when compared with monotherapy.[70] Quinolones do not appear to be synergistic with either β-lactam antibiotics or aminoglycosides.[84] However, in postpubertal children, quinolones could be used in combination therapy when antibiotic resistance reduces the potential benefit of either the β-lactam antibiotic or the aminoglycoside.

For empiric treatment of *P. aeruginosa* lower respiratory tract disease before antibiotic susceptibility test results are available, the choice of which β-lactam antibiotic and which aminoglycoside will be used should be based on the patient's previous antibiotic experience and knowledge of the usual pattern of antibiotic susceptibility and resistance in the patient's clinical environment. Once susceptibility

TABLE 129–2 ■ DOSAGES OF COMMONLY PRESCRIBED ANTIPSEUDOMONAL ANTIBIOTICS

Generic Name	Dosage (mg/kg/day)	Route	Interval	Pediatric Precautions
Antipseudomonal penicillins				
Carbenicillin indanyl sodium	30–50	PO	q6h	SNE
Ticarcillin disodium	200–300	IV	q4–6h	
Piperacillin	200–300	IV	q4–6h	PDNE
Cephalosporins				
Ceftazidime	200–300	IV	q8h	
Aminoglycosides				
Gentamicin sulfate	3–7.5	IV, IM	q8–24h	
Tobramycin sulfate	3–7.5	IV, IM	q8–24h	
Netilmicin sulfate	3–7.5	IV, IM	q8–24h	
Amikacin sulfate	15–22.5	IV, IM	q8–24h	
Quinolones				
Ciprofloxacin	20–30	PO	q12h	>18 yr*
	10–15	IV	q12h	>18 yr*
Monobactams				
Aztreonam	90–120	IV, IM	q6h	SNE
Carbapenems				
Imipenem-cilastatin sodium	60–100	IV	q6h	SNE
Meropenem	60 (meningitis: 120)	IV	q8h	

*Safety in children younger than 18 years is not established, and use is not recommended unless no safe alternatives are available.
PDNE, pediatric dose not yet established; SNE, safety in children not yet established.
Data from Nelson, J. D., Bradley, J. S.: Pocketbook of Pediatric Antimicrobial Therapy. 15th ed. Baltimore, Williams & Wilkins, 2002–2003, pp. 80–99.

testing has been completed, at least two effective antibiotics should be included in the patient's regimen. The dose and pharmacotherapeutics of the chosen antibiotics should be optimized. If the patient fails to respond to therapy or if clinical deterioration is noted, acquisition of antibiotic resistance should be anticipated. If antibiotic failure is likely, more than one new antibiotic should be substituted. Selection of the new antibiotic should be guided by previous susceptibility testing and the probable changes that resulted in antibiotic resistance.

The route of administration also may be important with aminoglycoside antibiotics. Penetration of aminoglycosides from blood into respiratory secretions is poor.[15] Topical application of aminoglycosides by aerosolization, particularly through an endotracheal tube, provides much higher concentrations in respiratory secretions. This approach results in more rapid bacteriologic eradication, but clinical efficacy has varied in different studies.[24] Administration of aerosolized aminoglycosides to patients with cystic fibrosis resulted in improvement in pulmonary function tests, decreased concentrations of *P. aeruginosa* in sputum, and no significant apparent toxicity. This aerosol treatment did not increase the isolation of *B. cepacia*, *S. maltophilia*, or *Alcaligenes xylosoxidans*; however, isolation of the fungi *Candida albicans* and *Aspergillus* did increase.[25]

Aztreonam, a monobactam antibiotic, and the fluoroquinolones are antibiotics with excellent antipseudomonal activity but are not approved for use in pediatric patients. Polymyxin B and colistin (polymyxin E), used previously, have been superseded largely by less toxic agents, but they may be useful in selected patients who are infected with strains resistant to the other agents. However, all *Burkholderia* spp. are resistant to polymyxin B.

Ciprofloxacin and the other quinolones have been evaluated for the treatment of acute and chronic *P. aeruginosa* infection in teenage children and adults with cystic fibrosis.[80, 153, 180, 182] These antibiotics, which may be given orally or intravenously, proved to be effective, as judged by clinical scores and results of pulmonary function tests. In the United States, quinolone (ciprofloxacin, ofloxacin, norfloxacin, enoxacin, levofloxacin, lomefloxacin, sparfloxacin, and trovafloxacin) use is restricted until after puberty because these antibiotics may bind cartilage and produce growth arrest. The information available from clinical trials in Europe suggests that ciprofloxacin and the other quinolones may not be as harmful in children as they are in other juvenile animal species.[31, 160, 161] However, pefloxacin, a fluoroquinolone that had been used extensively in France, does cause arthropathy in children and adults. In addition, two other quinolones, alatrofloxacin and trovafloxacin, cause acute liver failure, and some cases resulted in patients' deaths. Ciprofloxacin may be considered in selected children when the risks associated with the use of this antibiotic are outweighed by the potential benefits associated with its clinical efficacy (e.g., multiresistant strains of *Pseudomonas*, substitution of an oral quinolone to avoid long-term intravenous therapy requiring an indwelling catheter). If ciprofloxacin is used in a patient younger than 18 years of age, the balance of the risks and benefits of administering ciprofloxacin and alternatives should be explained to the patient and parents/guardians. Ciprofloxacin may be administered in a dosage of 15 mg/kg every 12 hours orally or 10 to 15 mg/ kg twice a day intravenously. The oral dosage should not exceed 1000 mg/day in patients who weigh less than 40 kg or 1500 mg/day in patients who weigh more than 40 kg.

Determining the optimal antibiotic therapy for patients with cystic fibrosis may be very problematic. Respiratory cultures may yield *P. aeruginosa* with many different colony morphotypes. These different morphotypes may have significantly different antibiograms. The accuracy of susceptibility testing is improved when different morphotypes are tested individually. However, it is labor intensive and expensive.

After years of antibiotic exposure, patients with cystic fibrosis commonly are infected with *P. aeruginosa* that is resistant in vitro to all available antimicrobial agents. For these patients, aerosolized tobramycin may be used to yield tobramycin concentrations in the range of 100 to 200 µg/mL of respiratory secretion. Some of these pan-resistant *P. aeruginosa* strains may be susceptible in vivo when concentrations of tobramycin reach these high levels in respiratory secretions. Susceptibility testing of these pan-resistant organisms should be performed by either determining minimal inhibitory concentrations or performing an E-test to ascertain whether the organism is susceptible at these higher levels, 100 to 200 µg/mL.[64] In addition to management of resistant *P. aeruginosa*, aerosolized tobramycin given over a prolonged period (≥1 year) may have the potential to eradicate *P. aeruginosa* temporarily from cystic fibrosis patients who have newly acquired this organism.[142] Confirmation of the efficacy of prolonged antibiotic aerosol therapy may prove valuable because recent data indicate a poor outcome in children with cystic fibrosis who acquire *P. aeruginosa* by the age of 7 years.[126]

P. aeruginosa endocarditis requires aggressive medical and surgical therapy. Despite combination therapy with maximal β-lactam and aminoglycoside antibiotics, valve replacement (native and prosthetic) frequently is required for cure. When gentamicin or tobramycin is administered in three divided doses per day, peak concentrations should be maintained at 12 to 15 µg/mL. Quinolones should be reserved for patients intolerant of aminoglycosides or whose bacteria are resistant to aminoglycosides or for long-term suppression of *P. aeruginosa* prosthetic valve endocarditis.

Though fortunately uncommon, *P. aeruginosa* infection of the eye can be serious and sight threatening. *P. aeruginosa* corneal ulcerations or keratitis may be seen in contact lens wearers or in intubated, sedated patients in intensive care units. Topical therapy with ticarcillin, piperacillin, tobramycin, gentamicin, amikacin, ciprofloxacin, or ofloxacin may be used and is effective. Clinical efficacy is improved by frequently clearing inflammatory debris and topical application of antibiotics. Initially, antibiotic solutions should be administered every 15 to 30 minutes. The frequency can be decreased gradually to four to six times a day when clinical improvement is apparent.

P. aeruginosa endophthalmitis frequently occurs after invasive eye surgery or penetrating injuries. Systemic, topical, and intraocular (anterior chamber and vitreous cavity) routes all are required. Even with aggressive medical intervention, return of retinal function is not a common occurrence. The prognosis is worse when initiation of therapy is delayed. Ceftazidime, imipenem, and ciprofloxacin have greater intraocular penetration than do the aminoglycosides.[201]

P. aeruginosa meningitis or brain abscess should be treated with ceftazidime (200 mg/kg/day in four divided doses every 6 hours) and an aminoglycoside given intravenously. The initial empiric choice of the aminoglycoside should be guided by local susceptibility patterns. Concomitant intraventricular or intrathecal treatment with gentamicin may be required if initial intravenous therapy fails to sterilize the CSF. Gentamicin can be placed into the ventricular or lumbar CSF in a total dose of 1 to 5 mg once each day (the dose is independent of body weight). Meropenem has good penetration into CSF and can be used when the *P. aeruginosa* is ceftazidime-resistant. Meropenem is the preferred carbapenem because the high doses of imipenem required to treat central nervous system (CNS) infections may be associated with CNS toxicity. Fluoroquinolones such as parenteral ciprofloxacin or pefloxacin and aztreonam are possible alternatives in the treatment of *P. aeruginosa* CNS infections if more conventional therapy has failed. However, experience with these agents for CNS infections is limited.[89, 103, 127, 167]

Skin abscesses or abscesses in other locations caused by *P. aeruginosa* should be incised and drained.[143] Failure to do so may result in a poor response despite prolonged systemic antibiotic treatment. Osteomyelitis of foot bones requires surgical débridement in every case. Ten to 14 days of appropriate antibiotics appears to be adequate if surgery has removed the infected tissue effectively.[78] The adequacy of surgical débridement and clinical improvement can be monitored by serial sedimentation rates.[33] *P. aeruginosa* infection of foreign bodies (vascular, peritoneal, and CNS catheters) may require removal of the foreign material to cure the infection, particularly if a tunnel or exit-site infection exists.

Pseudomonas folliculitis and plantar nodules generally are self-limited and do not usually require specific antimicrobial therapy. More severe cases can be treated by the topical application of any of the following: 2.5 percent acetic acid compresses (vinegar is 5% acetic acid), gentamicin ointment, topical 0.1 percent polymyxin B, or silver sulfadiazine (Silvadene).

The β-lactam antibiotics (antipseudomonal penicillins, cephalosporins, carbapenems), monobactams, and ciprofloxacin are rapidly bactericidal to *P. aeruginosa*.[58] The combination of an aminoglycoside with any of these antibiotics is unlikely to have a significant effect on the initial clinical response rate. However, a reduction in the emergence of drug-resistant *P. aeruginosa* clones is the major benefit of combination therapy that includes an aminoglycoside. Combination therapy with two β-lactam antibiotics is inappropriate for serious *Pseudomonas* infections because the induction of β-lactamase may result in resistance to both antibiotics.

Antibiotic resistance is an important factor in patients with serious *Pseudomonas* infections that do not respond to antibiotic therapy. As the quintessential opportunist, *Pseudomonas* has acquired various means to resist the activity of antibiotics. *P. aeruginosa* produces numerous different β-lactamase enzymes. Plasmid-mediated β-lactamases are responsible for resistance to antipseudomonal penicillins but not to the cephalosporins or carbapenems.[32] The most clinically relevant β-lactamases produced by *P. aeruginosa* are encoded primarily chromosomally rather than located on plasmids. Cephalosporinases, classified as class I β-lactamases,[148] produced by *P. aeruginosa* increase on exposure to any of the β-lactam antibiotics (derepression of the β-lactamase gene).[159] However, the propensity to induce β-lactamase varies among the β-lactam antibiotics.[35] Imipenem and cefoxitin are strong inducers of β-lactamase.[43] All antipseudomonal penicillins, cephalosporins, and aztreonam are susceptible to the class I β-lactamase produced by *P. aeruginosa*.[124]

Clavulanate and tazobactam are β-lactamase inhibitors effective against plasmid-encoded class III and class V β-lactamases and the chromosomally encoded class II β-lactamases found in *P. aeruginosa* and some other gram-negative bacteria. However, these β-lactamase inhibitors are not only ineffective against the common class I β-lactamase of *Pseudomonas* but also are potent inducers of the β-lactamase gene. Use of these β-lactamase inhibitors will not enhance the activity of ticarcillin (Timentin) or piperacillin (Zosyn) against *Pseudomonas* and might actually increase the likelihood of emergence of resistant strains.

Pseudomonas strains with chromosomally encoded class I β-lactamase may not produce detectable β-lactamase until they are exposed to β-lactam antibiotics. These β-lactamase–encoded strains may appear sensitive to β-lactam antibiotics on in vitro sensitivity testing before antibiotic use. However, administration of β-lactam antibiotics to patients colonized or infected with these strains results in the induction of β-lactamase production and emergence of resistance. For this reason, repeat in vitro sensitivity testing of clinical isolates of *Pseudomonas* a few days after the administration of β-lactam antibiotics might reveal reduced sensitivity to β-lactams.

Whereas imipenem and meropenem resist the β-lactamases commonly produced by *Pseudomonas*, resistance to carbapenems can result through the loss of an outer-membrane porin that allows carbapenems to enter *Pseudomonas*.[26] The permeability of other β-lactam antibiotics also may be reduced when this outer-membrane porin is lost. Though chemically distinct from imipenem or meropenem, fluoroquinolones such as ciprofloxacin may induce decreased permeability to both antibiotics.[141] Plasmid-mediated metallo-β-lactamases that confer resistance to imipenem have been described.[114, 166, 192] Fortunately, these metallo-β-lactamases are identified only rarely in *P. aeruginosa*. Continued use of carbapenems might pressure an increase in these β-lactamases in the future. *S. maltophilia* is resistant innately to imipenem.

Tobramycin is the most active aminoglycoside against *P. aeruginosa*, whereas amikacin induces the lowest frequency of resistant strains. Resistance to aminoglycosides usually results from enzyme-mediated antibiotic modification.[41] The various aminoglycoside-modifying enzymes have different substrate affinities. Therefore, resistance to one aminoglycoside through aminoglycoside-modifying enzymes does not predict resistance to others necessarily. Resistance is less common to amikacin than to other aminoglycosides.[61, 200] Aminoglycoside-modifying enzymes usually are coded by plasmid-mediated genes, but they occasionally can be coded by genes on the bacterial chromosome.[41] Plasmid-encoded resistance supports rapid transference among strains within an institution. *P. aeruginosa* also can become resistant to aminoglycosides by decreasing the intracellular uptake of aminoglycosides or by modification of intracellular ribosomal attachment.[39, 43] These mechanisms of resistance generally cause cross-resistance for all aminoglycosides.

Ciprofloxacin, a bacterial DNA gyrase inhibitor, is the most effective of the quinolones against *P. aeruginosa*. Alteration of the binding site of DNA gyrase and decreased penetration of ciprofloxacin through the *Pseudomonas* cell membrane can result in resistant strains.[43, 102]

Multidrug resistance is not an unusual occurrence in *P. aeruginosa*, and it may arise after treatment with a single antibiotic. The induction and production of β-lactamase may act synergistically with diminished outer-membrane permeability.[201] In addition, facilitation of energy-dependent efflux of antibiotics by *P. aeruginosa* can result in simultaneous resistance to quinolones, β-lactams, tetracycline, and chloramphenicol.[138, 201]

In addition to antibiotic resistance, other clinical factors can adversely affect aminoglycoside activity against *Pseudomonas*. The acidic environment in tissue infected with *P. aeruginosa* can inactivate aminoglycosides.[21] Aminoglycosides may fail to reach therapeutic tissue levels because of poor penetration into bronchial secretions and lung tissue.[15] For patients with tracheitis (e.g., intubated patients) or endobronchial disease (e.g., cystic fibrosis), aminoglycosides and, less frequently, colistin have been administered by aerosol.[162] This route of delivery allows for greater availability of the antibiotic at the site of the infection, with enhanced safety because of negligible absorption into the systemic circulation. Doses of gentamicin and tobramycin of 2.5 to 8 mg/kg can be given safely by aerosol three times a day, with a maximum of 300 mg/dose. Resistance may emerge after prolonged courses.

Antibiotic therapy for *B. cepacia* infection is very challenging and should be guided by results of in vitro susceptibility testing. Unfortunately, *B. cepacia* is frequently resistant to many commonly used antipseudomonal antibiotic agents, particularly the aminoglycosides. Antibiotics that may have activity against *B. cepacia* include ceftazidime, cefoperazone, ureidopenicillins, quinolones, trimethoprim-sulfamethoxazole, and chloramphenicol. Susceptibility to carbapenems and minocycline varies; meropenem has greater in vitro activity against *B. cepacia* than imipenem does.[44] Typically, *B. cepacia* isolates from patients with cystic fibrosis are more antibiotic-resistant than are isolates from other patient populations. Combination therapy with two or three antibiotics may be required to achieve a clinical response. Combinations of β-lactam agents with aminoglycosides might provide synergy clinically, even when the *B. cepacia* strain isolated is aminoglycoside-resistant. *B. cepacia* may be sensitive to minocycline.[96] Minocycline may be considered to have an adjunctive role in the management of *B. cepacia* infection in patients with cystic fibrosis. However, resistance to minocycline commonly develops with prolonged therapy (3 to 13 months).[96]

S. maltophilia also exhibits significant antibiotic resistance to the common antipseudomonal agents. Trimethoprim-sulfamethoxazole, chloramphenicol, moxalactam, ceftazidime, cefoperazone, ticarcillin plus clavulanic acid, and ciprofloxacin may be active against this organism alone or in combinations. *S. maltophilia* is resistant to antipseudomonal penicillins, imipenem, and aminoglycosides. A combination of trimethoprim-sulfamethoxazole and ticarcillin-clavulanate has been recommended as the most appropriate initial therapy for serious infections that are suspected or known to be caused by *S. maltophilia*.[187] For patients with catheter-related infections, removal of the catheter offers the greatest opportunity for cure.[46]

The most active antibiotics against *B. pseudomallei* are imipenem, piperacillin-tazobactam, piperacillin, ceftazidime, ticarcillin-clavulanate, ampicillin-sulbactam, tetracycline, and chloramphenicol.[174] Piperacillin, ceftazidime, and imipenem are not bactericidal in vitro.[174] Ciprofloxacin seems to be of limited value because of a high rate of resistance.

Chronic melioidosis can be treated with chloramphenicol over a period of many months or with tetracycline. Trimethoprim-sulfamethoxazole was recommended previously, but most strains currently are resistant.

For acute systemic melioidosis, ceftazidime (120 mg/kg/day) or chloramphenicol (50 to 75 mg/kg/day) plus an aminoglycoside (kanamycin, 20 to 30 mg/kg/day, or amikacin, 15 to 20 mg/kg/day) and sulfisoxazole (120 to 150 mg/kg/day) should be administered for a period of 4 weeks. When third-generation cephalosporins have been used, cefoperazone and ceftazidime have shown greater activity against *B. pseudomallei* than have other third-generation cephalosporin agents. Ceftazidime was compared with chloramphenicol, doxycycline, and trimethoprim plus sulfamethoxazole for the treatment of severe melioidosis.[195] Ceftazidime in a dosage of 120 mg/kg/day intravenously in three divided doses every 8 hours was associated with a 50 percent lower overall mortality rate when compared with other forms of therapy. These results suggest that ceftazidime combined with an aminoglycoside and sulfisoxazole now should be considered the treatment of choice for severe melioidosis. Soft tissue infections should be treated for 4 to 6 months with tetracycline (in children older than 8 years) provided in a dosage of 50 mg/kg/day in four divided doses. In younger children, trimethoprim-sulfamethoxazole (8 mg/kg/day of trimethoprim and 40 mg/kg/day of sulfamethoxazole) in two divided doses may be used. Most penicillins are ineffective.[45, 174] The duration of therapy must be guided by clinical and laboratory findings; therapy for 4 weeks to many months may be required in patients with osteomyelitis. Relapses are common occurrences and should be treated as one would treat the first episode.[29]

Prevention

Prevention of infection with pseudomonads depends in part on a continuous surveillance program of the hospital environment that is designed to identify and subsequently eradicate sources of pseudomonads as quickly as possible. Pseudomonads can grow to a concentration of 10^6 organisms per milliliter in distilled water that appears to be perfectly clear. Growth of pseudomonads in distilled water, disinfectants, and medications is the factor most commonly incriminated in single-source outbreaks of *Pseudomonas* infection in hospitals. Prevention of the follicular dermatitis caused by *P. aeruginosa* contamination of whirlpools or hot tubs should be possible by maintaining the pool water at a pH of 7.2 to 7.8 and free allowable chlorine concentrations at 0.4 to 1.5 ppm.[28]

Outbreaks of *Pseudomonas* infection in newborn nurseries have been reported.[20] Generally, infection has been transmitted by the hands of personnel from washbasin surfaces and suction catheter rinse solution to the newborn infants. Strict attention to handwashing, particularly with a liquid iodophor handwashing agent before and between contact with newborn infants, may prevent or interdict epidemic disease. Growth of *Pseudomonas* on suction catheters can be prevented by rinsing the catheter in an acetic acid solution.

Daily replacement of all apparatus used for intravenous administration greatly reduces the hazard of extrinsic contamination by *Pseudomonas* and other gram-negative organisms. When intravenous administration is indicated, a small metal needle is preferable to a plastic catheter because these needles have been associated with a lower rate of septicemia and phlebitis.

Meticulous care is required in the preparation of solutions for total parenteral alimentation and in the insertion and care of catheters.

The risk of developing *Pseudomonas* infection in a burn patient also can be minimized by careful protective isolation and by the topical application of silver nitrate (0.5%) solution or 10 percent mafenide acetate cream. Débridement for removal of devitalized tissue is also imperative.

Pseudomonas infection of dermal abnormalities that communicate with the cerebrospinal axis can be prevented by careful evaluation and early surgical repair. Providing antibiotic prophylaxis of *Pseudomonas* urinary tract infection is difficult without a suitable oral antipseudomonal antibiotic for children. Identification and surgical correction of obstructive lesions of the urinary tract minimize or prevent the development of *Pseudomonas* infection of the urinary tract.

Cohorting plus isolation of patients with cystic fibrosis who are colonized with multiresistant strains of *P. aeruginosa* or *B. cepacia* has been suggested as a means of reducing nosocomial transmission of these organisms. However, the proper manner of handling patients with these organisms has not been established. Any attempt to reduce transmission should be based on measures with proven efficacy and must also consider the potential consequences of strict isolation or segregation on this population, which spends so much time at health care facilities.

In patients with cystic fibrosis and certain immunocompromised patients, high rates of *P. aeruginosa* colonization and infection and ever-increasing antibiotic resistance render active or passive immunization (or both) against *P. aeruginosa* desirable. In the last 2 decades, an understanding of the human immune response to *P. aeruginosa* and the immune responses that may provide protection against infection or disease has increased considerably. Naturally occurring immunity generally is ineffective. Certain naturally generated antibodies may even be detrimental.[194] These antibodies may form antigen-antibody complexes that increase pulmonary inflammation and direct lung damage. Even if neutralizing antibodies could be administered passively or developed after vaccine administration, the large quantities of mucoid exopolysaccharide produced by *P. aeruginosa* may mask many of the antigens targeted for antibody neutralization or opsonization.

Despite the aforementioned difficulties, numerous investigations of candidates for *P. aeruginosa* vaccines are ongoing. Purified bacterial proteins, including flagellar antigen, lipopolysaccharide-O, several inactivated bacterial toxins, high-molecular-weight polysaccharide antigen and glycoconjugate, and killed whole-cell vaccine preparations, have been tested. Many of the candidate vaccines have been shown to be safe, immunogenic, and capable of generating protective immunity in various animal systems.[140] To date, evidence of protective efficacy in humans has not been established definitively for any of these vaccines. Some studies have demonstrated the efficacy of active immunization of burned patients with specific strains of *Pseudomonas* or the administration of hyperimmune globulin in the prevention of *Pseudomonas* septicemia.[3, 82] *P. aeruginosa* vaccine also has been suggested as a possible method for preventing this disease in patients with acute leukemia or cystic fibrosis.[135]

The route of vaccine delivery may be important in creating the optimal immune response. Data from experimental animals suggest that vaccine antigens administered parenterally stimulate IgG and IgM antibodies; antigens administered orally induce IgA and IgG at mucosal surfaces. For patients whose disease occurs after mucosal colonization (e.g., cystic fibrosis), oral administration of a *P. aeruginosa* vaccine might be the preferred route of administration to develop the optimal immune response at the site of *P. aeruginosa* infection.

Purified bacterial proteins and lipopolysaccharide from *B. cepacia* are in the initial vaccine research and development stages. Whether these *B. cepacia* vaccine candidates will enter preclinical or phase I clinical trials is yet to be determined.

Prognosis

The prognosis depends largely on the nature of the underlying disease process. Septicemia is the leading cause of death in children with leukemia; *Pseudomonas* is responsible for half of these deaths. Four variables independently influence the outcome of *Pseudomonas* septicemia: (1) the development of septic shock, (2) inappropriate antibiotic therapy, (3) granulocyte counts less than 500/mm^3, and (4) the development of septic metastases.[13] Most deaths in children with cystic fibrosis are caused by pulmonary insufficiency. *Pseudomonas* can be recovered from the lungs of almost every one of these patients and, in many, has been responsible for their deaths.

REFERENCES

1. Abbink, F. C., Orendi, J. M., and DeBeaufort, A. J.: Mother-to-child transmission of *Burkholderia pseudomallei*. N. Engl. J. Med. *344*:1171, 2001.
2. Alexander, A. D., Huxsoll, D. L., Warner, A. R., et al.: Serological diagnosis of human melioidosis with indirect hemagglutination and complement fixation titers. Appl. Microbiol. *20*:825–833, 1970.
3. Alexander, J. W., and Fisher, M. W.: Immunization against *Pseudomonas* in infection after thermal injury. J. Infect. Dis. *130*(Suppl.):152–158, 1974.
4. Anaissie, E., Fainstein, V., Miller, P., et al.: *Pseudomonas putida*: Newly recognized pathogen in patients with cancer. Am. J. Med. *82*:1191–1194, 1987.
5. Anderson, R. L., Vess, R. W., Carr, J. H., et al.: Investigations of intrinsic *Pseudomonas cepacia* contamination in commercially manufactured povidone-iodine. Infect. Control Hosp. Epidemiol. *12*:297–302, 1991.
6. Ashdown, L. R.: An improved screening technique for isolation of *Pseudomonas pseudomallei* from clinical specimens. Pathology *1*: 293–297, 1979.
7. Ashdown, L. R., Johnson, R. W., Koehler, J. M., et al.: Enzyme-linked immunosorbent assay for the diagnosis of clinical and subclinical melioidosis. J. Infect. Dis. *160*:253–260, 1989.
8. Baddour, L. M., Kraus, A. P., Jr., and Smalley, D. L.: Peritonitis due to *Pseudomonas paucimobilis* during ambulatory peritoneal dialysis. South. Med. J. *78*:336, 1985.
9. Ballestero, S., Virseda, I., Escobar, H., et al.: *Stenotrophomonas maltophilia* in cystic fibrosis patients. Eur. J. Clin. Microbiol. Infect. *14*:728–729, 1995.
10. Bauernfeind, A., Bertele, R. M., Harms, K., et al.: Qualitative and quantitative microbiological analysis of sputa of 102 patients with cystic fibrosis. Infection *15*:270–277, 1987.
11. Bell, S. M., Pham, J. M., and Lanzarone, J. Y. M.: Mutation of *Pseudomonas aeruginosa* to piperacillin resistance mediated by β-lactamase production. J. Antimicrob. Chemother. *15*:665–670, 1985.
12. Berbari, N., Johnson, D. H., and Cunha, B. A.: *Xanthomonas maltophilia* peritonitis in a patient undergoing peritoneal dialysis. Heart Lung *22*:282–283, 1993.
13. Bergan, T.: Pathogenetic factors of *Pseudomonas aeruginosa*. Scand. J. Infect. Dis. *29*(Suppl.):7–12, 1981.
14. Berger, M., Sorensen, R. U., Tosi, M. F., et al.: Complement receptor expression on neutrophils at an inflammatory site, the *Pseudomonas*-infected lung in cystic fibrosis. J. Clin. Invest. *84*:1302–1313, 1989.
15. Bergogne-Berezin, E.: Pharmacokinetics of antibiotics in respiratory secretions. *In* Pennington, J. E. (ed.): Respiratory Infection: Diagnosis and Management. 2nd ed. New York, Raven, 1988, p. 608.
16. Berkelman, R. L., Godley, J., Weber, J. A., et al.: *Pseudomonas cepacia* peritonitis associated with contamination of automatic peritoneal dialysis machines. Ann. Intern. Med. *96*:456–458, 1982.
17. Berkelman, R. L., Lewis, S., Allen, J. R., et al.: Pseudobacteremia attributed to contamination of povidone-iodine with *Pseudomonas cepacia*. Ann. Intern. Med. *95*:32–36, 1981.
18. Berry, M. D., Asmar, B. I.: *Pseudomonas cepacia* bacteremia in children with sickle cell hemoglobinopathies. Pediatr. Infect. Dis. J. *10*:696–699, 1991.
19. Bisbe, J., Gatell, J. M., Puig, J., et al.: *Pseudomonas aeruginosa* bacteremia: Univariate and multivariate analyses in 133 episodes. Rev. Infect. Dis. *10*:629–635, 1988.
20. Bobo, R. A., Newton, E. J., Jones, L. F., et al.: Nursery outbreak of *Pseudomonas aeruginosa*: Epidemiologic conclusions from five different typing methods. Appl. Microbiol. *25*:414–420, 1973.
21. Bodem, C. R., Lampton, L. M., Miller, D. P., et al.: Relevance to aminoglycoside activity in gram-negative bacillary pneumonia. Am. Rev. Respir. Dis. *127*:39–41, 1983.
22. Brand, R. A., and Black, H.: *Pseudomonas* osteomyelitis following puncture wounds in children. J. Bone Joint Surg. Am. *56*:1637–1642, 1974.
23. Brett, M. M., Ghoneim, A. T. M., and Littlewood, J. M.: Prediction and diagnosis of early *Pseudomonas aeruginosa* infection in cystic fibrosis: A follow-up study. J. Clin. Microbiol. *26*:1565–1570, 1988.
24. Brown, R. B., Kruse, J. A., Counts, G. W. A., et al.: Double-blind study of endotracheal tobramycin in treatment of gram-negative bacterial pneumonia. Antimicrob. Agents Chemother. *34*:269–272, 1990.
25. Burns, J. L., Van Dalfsen, J. M., Shawar, R. M., et al.: Effect of chronic intermittent administration of inhaled tobramycin on respiratory microbiologic flora in patients with cystic fibrosis. J. Infect. Dis. *179*:1190–1196, 1999.
26. Buscher, K. H., Cullman, W., Dick, W., et al.: Imipenem resistance in *Pseudomonas aeruginosa* resulting from diminished expression of an outer membrane protein. Antimicrob. Agents Chemother. *31*:703–708, 1987.

27. Carratala, J., Salazar, A., Mascaro, J., et al.: Community-acquired pneumonia due to *Pseudomonas stutzeri*. Clin. Infect. Dis. *14*:792, 1992.
28. Centers for Disease Control: Swimming Pools: Safety and Disease Control through Proper Design and Operation [D. H. H. S. Publication Number (C. D. C.) 98–411]. Washington, DC, U. S. Government Printing Office, 1979.
29. Chaowagul, W., Suputtamongkol, Y., Dance, D. A. B., et al.: Relapse in melioidosis: Incidence and risk factors. J. Infect. Dis. *168*:1181–1185, 1993.
30. Chitnis, C. E., and Ohman, D. E.: Genetic analysis of the alginate biosynthetic gene cluster of *Pseudomonas aeruginosa* shows evidence of an operonic structure. Mol. Microbiol. *8*:583–590, 1993.
31. Chysky, V., Kapila, K., Hullmann, R., et al.: Safety of ciprofloxacin in children: Worldwide clinical experiences based on compassionate use: Emphasis on joint evaluation. Infection *19*:289–296, 1991.
32. Craig, W. A., Ebert, S. C.: Antimicrobial therapy in *Pseudomonas aeruginosa* infections. *In* Baltch, A. L., and Smith, R. P. (eds): *Pseudomonas aeruginosa* Infections and Treatment. New York, Marcel Dekker, 1994, pp. 441–518.
33. Crosby, L. A., and Powell, D. A.: The potential value of the sedimentation rate in monitoring treatment outcome in puncture-wound-related *Pseudomonas* osteomyelitis. Clin. Orthop. *188*:172–176, 1984.
34. Cryz, S. J., Jr., Pitt, T. L., Furer, E., et al.: Role of lipopolysaccharides in virulence of *Pseudomonas aeruginosa*. Infect. Immun. *44*:508–513, 1984.
35. Cullman, W., Buscher, K. H., and Dick, W.: Selection and properties of *Pseudomonas aeruginosa* variants resistant to beta-lactam antibiotics. Eur. J. Clin. Microbiol. *6*:467–473, 1987.
36. Dan, M., Gutman, R., and Biro, A.: Peritonitis caused by *Pseudomonas putrefaciens* in patients undergoing continuous ambulatory peritoneal dialysis. Clin. Infect. Dis. *14*:359–360, 1992.
37. Dance, D. A.: Melioidosis: The tip of the iceberg? Clin. Microbiol. Rev. *4*:52–60, 1991.
38. Dance, D. A., Davis, T. M. E., Wattanagoon, Y., et al.: Acute suppurative parotitis caused by *Pseudomonas pseudomallei* in children. J. Infect. Dis. *159*:654–660, 1989.
39. Davis, B. D.: Mechanism of bactericidal action of aminoglycosides. Microbiol. Rev. *51*:341–350, 1987.
40. Demko, C., Doershuk, C., and Stern, R.: Thirteen year experience with *Xanthomonas maltophilia* in patients with cystic fibrosis. Pediatr. Pulmonol. *25*:304–308, 1998.
41. Dever, L. A., and Dermody, T. S.: Mechanisms of bacterial resistance to antibiotics. Arch. Intern. Med. *151*:886–895, 1991.
42. Doring, G., Herz, M., Ortelt, J., et al.: Molecular epidemiology of *Pseudomonas aeruginosa* in an intensive care unit. Epidemiol. Infect. *110*:427–436, 1993.
43. Dunn, M., and Wunderink, R. G.: Ventilator-associated pneumonia caused by *Pseudomonas* infection. Clin. Chest Med. *16*:95–109, 1995.
44. Edwards, J. R., Turner, P. J.: Laboratory data which differentiates meropenem and imipenem. Scand. J. Infect. Dis. *96*(Suppl.):5–10, 1995.
45. Eickhoff, T. C., Bennett, J. V., and Hayes, P. J.: *Pseudomonas pseudomallei*: Susceptibility to chemotherapeutic agents. J. Infect. Dis. *121*:95–102, 1970.
46. Elting, L. S., and Bodey, G. P.: Septicemia due to *Xanthomonas* species and non-*aeruginosa Pseudomonas* species: Incidence of catheter-related infections. Medicine (Baltimore) *69*:296–306, 1990.
47. Faden, H., and Grossi, M.: Acute osteomyelitis in children: Reassessment of etiologic agents and their clinical characteristics. Am. J. Dis. Child. *145*:65–69, 1991.
48. Feder, H. M., Jr., Grant-Kels, J. M., and Tilton, R. C.: *Pseudomonas* whirlpool dermatitis. Clin. Pediatr. (Phila.) *22*:638–642, 1983.
49. Feigin, R. D., and Shearer, W. T.: Opportunistic infection in children: Parts I, II, and III. J. Pediatr. *87*:507–514, 677–694, 852–866, 1975.
50. Fergie, J. E., Sherma, S. J., Lott, L., et al.: *Pseudomonas aeruginosa* bacteremia in immunocompromised children: Analysis of factors associated with a poor outcome. Clin. Infect. Dis. *18*:390–394, 1994.
51. Fick, R. B., Jr.: Pathogenetic mechanisms in cystic fibrosis lung disease: A paradigm for inflammatory airways disease. J. Lab. Clin. Med. *121*:632–634, 1993.
52. Fick, R. B., and Reynolds, H. Y.: *Pseudomonas* respiratory infection in cystic fibrosis: A possible defect in opsonic IgG antibody? Bull. Eur. Physiopathol. Respir. *19*:151–161, 1983.
53. Fick, R. B., Jr., Sonoda, F., and Hornick, D. B.: Emergence and persistence of *Pseudomonas aeruginosa* in the cystic fibrosis airway. Semin. Respir. Infect. 7:168–178, 1992.
54. Fiorillo, L., Zucker, M., Sawyer, D., and Lin, A. N.: The *Pseudomonas* hot-foot syndrome. N. Engl. J. Med. *345*:335–338, 2001.
55. Fisher, M. C., Goldsmith, J. F., and Gilligan, P. H.: Sneakers as a source of *Pseudomonas aeruginosa* in children with osteomyelitis following puncture wounds. J. Pediatr. *106*:607–609, 1985.
56. Fisher, M. C., Long, S. S., Roberts, E. M., et al.: *Pseudomonas maltophilia* bacteremia in children undergoing open heart surgery. J. A. M. A. *246*:1571–1574, 1981.
57. Flores, G., Stavola, J. J., and Noel, G. J.: Bacteremia due to *Pseudomonas aeruginosa* in children with AIDS. Clin. Infect. Dis. *16*:706–708, 1993.
58. Fox, R. C., Williams, G. J., Wunderink, R. G., et al.: Followup bronchoscopy predicts therapeutic outcome in ventilated patients with nosocomial pneumonia. Abstract. Am. Rev. Respir. Dis. *143*:109, 1991.
59. Fredrekson, B.: *Stenotrophomonas (Xanthomonas) maltophilia* at the Danish Cystic Fibrosis Centre 1974–1993. Abstract. Pediatr. Pulmonol. *20* (Suppl. 12):287, 1995.
60. Geiss, H. R., and Geiss, M.: Evaluation of a new commercial system for the identification of Enterobacteriaceae and non-fermentative bacteria. Eur. J. Clin. Microbiol. Infect. Dis. *11*:610–616, 1992.
61. Gerding, D. N., and Larson, T. A.: Aminoglycoside resistance in gram-negative bacilli during increased amikacin use. Am. J. Med. *79*:1–7, 1985.
62. Gilligan, P. H.: Microbiology of airway disease in patients with cystic fibrosis. Clin. Microbiol. Rev. *4*:35–51, 1991.
63. Gilligan, P. H.: *Pseudomonas* and *Burkholderia*. *In* Murray, P. R., Baron, E. J., Pfaller, M. A., et al. (eds.): Manual of Clinical Microbiology. 6th ed. Washington D.C., ASM Press, 1995, pp. 509–519.
64. Gilligan, P. H.: Report on the consensus document for microbiology and infectious diseases in cystic fibrosis. Clin. Microbiol. Newsl. *18*:83–87, 1996.
65. Gilligan, P. H., and Whittier, S.: *Burkholderia, Stenotrophomonas, Ralstonia, Brevundimonas, Comamonas,* and *Acidovorax*. *In* Murray, P. R., Baron, E. J., Pfaller, M. A., et al. (eds.): Manual of Clinical Microbiology, 7th ed. Washington, DC, ASM Press, 1999, pp. 526–538.
66. Glupczynski, Y., Hansen, W., Dratwa, M., et al.: *Pseudomonas paucimobilis* peritonitis in patients treated by peritoneal dialysis. J. Clin. Microbiol. *20*:1225–1226, 1984.
67. Gustafson, T. L., Band, J. D., Hutcheson, R. H., Jr., et al.: *Pseudomonas* folliculitis: An outbreak and review. Rev. Infect. Dis. *5*:1–8, 1983.
68. Heggers, J. P., Haydon, S., Ko, F., et al.: *Pseudomonas aeruginosa* exotoxin A: Its role in retardation of wound healing: The 1992 Lindberg Award. J. Burn Care Rehabil. *13*:512–518, 1992.
69. Henderson, D. K., Baptiste, R., Parillo, J., et al.: Indolent epidemic of *Pseudomonas cepacia* bacteremia and pseudobacteremia in an intensive care unit traced to a contaminated blood gas analyzer. Am. J. Med. *84*:75–81, 1988.
70. Hilf, M., Yu, V. L., Sharp, J., et al.: Antibiotic therapy for *Pseudomonas aeruginosa* bacteremia: Outcome correlation in a prospective study of 200 patients. Am. J. Med. *87*:540–556, 1989.
71. Hilton, E., Adams, A. A., Uliss, A., et al.: Nosocomial bacterial eye infections in intensive-care units. Lancet *1*:1318–1320, 1983.
72. Hioyo-Tomoka, M. T., Marples, R. R., and Klingman, A. M.: *Pseudomonas* infection in superhydrated skin. Arch. Dermatol. *107*:723–727, 1973.
73. Hoiby, N., and Koch, C.: *Pseudomonas aeruginosa* infection in cystic fibrosis and its management. Thorax *45*:881–884, 1990.
74. Holland, S. P., Pulido, J. S., Shires, T. K., et al.: *Pseudomonas aeruginosa* ocular infections. In Fick, R. B., Jr. (ed.): *Pseudomonas aeruginosa*: The Opportunist. Boca Raton, FL, CRC Press, 1993, pp. 159–176.
75. Horn, K. L., and Gherini, S.: Malignant external otitis of childhood. Ann. J. Otol. *2*:402–404, 1981.
76. Inglis, T. J. J., Garrow, S. C., Henderson, M., et al.: *Burkholderia pseudomallei* traced to water treatment plant in Australia. Emerg. Infect. Dis. *6*:56–59, 2000.
77. Isles, A., Maclusky, I., Corey, M., et al.: *Pseudomonas cepacia* infection in cystic fibrosis: An emerging problem. J. Pediatr. *104*:206–210, 1984.
78. Jacobs, R. F., McCarthy, R. E., and Elser, J. M.: *Pseudomonas* osteochondritis complicating puncture wounds of the foot in children: A 10-year evaluation. J. Infect. Dis. *160*:657–661, 1989.
79. Jang, T.-N., Wang, F.-D., Wang, L.-H., et al.: *Xanthomonas maltophilia* bacteremia: An analysis of 32 cases. J. Formos. Med. Assoc. *91*:1170–1176, 1992.
80. Jensen, T., Pedersen, S. S., Nielsen, C. H., et al.: The efficacy and safety of ciprofloxacin and ofloxacin in chronic *Pseudomonas aeruginosa* infection in cystic fibrosis. J. Antimicrob. Chemother. *20*:585–594, 1987.
81. John, M., Ecclestone, E., Hunter, E., et al.: Epidemiology of *Pseudomonas cepacia* colonization among patients with cystic fibrosis. Pediatr. Pulmonol. *18*:108–113, 1994.
82. Jones, C. E., Alexander, J. W., and Fisher, M. W.: Clinical evaluation of *Pseudomonas* hyperimmune globulin. J. Surg. Res. *14*:87–96, 1973.
83. Kavpati, F., Malmborg, A. S., Alfredsson, H., et al.: Bacterial colonization with *Xanthomonas maltophilia*—a retrospective study in a cystic fibrosis patient population. Infection *22*:258–263, 1994.
84. Kemmerich, B., Small, G., and Pennington, J. E.: Comparative evaluation of ciprofloxacin, enoxacin, and ofloxacin in experimental *Pseudomonas aeruginosa* infections. Antimicrob. Chemother. *29*:395–399, 1986.
85. Kenna, M. A., Bluestone, C. D., Reilly, J. S., et al.: Medical management of chronic suppurative otitis media without cholesteatoma in children. Laryngoscope *96*:146–151, 1986.
86. Kercsmar, C. M., Stern, R. C., Reed, M. D., et al.: Ceftazidime in cystic fibrosis: Pharmacokinetics and therapeutic response. J. Antimicrob. Chemother. *12*(Suppl. A):289–295, 1983.
87. Kerr, K. G., Anson, J. J., Patmore, R., Snith, G.: Intravenous line infections. J. Hosp. Infect. *26*:73–75, 1994.
88. Khardori, N., Elting, L., Wong, E., et al.: Nosocomial infections due to *Xanthomonas maltophilia (Pseudomonas maltophilia)* in patients with cancer. Rev. Infect. Dis. *12*:997–1003, 1990.

89. Kilpatrick, M., Girgis, N., Farid, Z., et al.: Aztreonam for treating meningitis caused by gram-negative rods. Scand. J. Infect. Dis. *23*:125–126, 1991.
90. Kingston, C. W.: Chronic or latent melioidosis. Med. J. Aust. 2:618–621, 1971.
91. Kiska, D. L., Gilligan, P. H.: *Pseudomonas*. *In* Murray, P. R., Baron, E. J., Pfaller, M. A., et al. (eds.): Manual of Clinical Microbiology, 7th ed. Washington, DC, ASM Press, 1999, pp. 517–525.
92. Kiska, D. L., Kerr, A., Jones, M. C., et al.: Accuracy of four commercial systems for identification of *Burkholderia cepacia* and other gram-negative non-fermenting bacilli recovered from patients with cystic fibrosis. J. Clin. Microbiol. *34*:886–891, 1996.
93. Klinger, J. D., and Thomassen, M. J.: Occurrence and antimicrobial susceptibility of gram-negative nonfermentative bacilli in cystic fibrosis patients. Diagn. Microbiol. Infect. Dis. *3*:149–158, 1985.
94. Kock, C., and Koiby, N.: Pathogenesis of cystic fibrosis. Lancet *341*:1065–1069, 1993.
95. Kollef, M., Silver, H. P., Murphy, M., Trouillon, E.: The effect of late-onset ventilator pneumonia in determining patient mortality. Chest *108*:1655–1662, 1995.
96. Kurlandsky, L. E., and Fader, R. C.: In vitro activity of minocycline against respiratory pathogens from patients with cystic fibrosis. Pediatr. Pulmonol. *29*:210–212, 2000.
97. Kurukularathe, C., and Barzaga, R.: Melioidosis. Infect. Dis. Pract. Clinicians *24*:37–40, 2000.
98. Kynakorn, M., Petchlai, B., Khupulsup, K., et al.: Gold blot for detection of immunoglobulin M (IgM)-specific antibodies for rapid serodiagnosis of melioidosis. J. Clin. Microbiol. *29*:2065–2067, 1991.
99. Lacroix, J., Gauthier, M., Lapointe, N., et al.: *Pseudomonas aeruginosa* supraglottitis in a six-month-old child with severe combined immunodeficiency syndrome. Pediatr. Infect. Dis. J. *7*:739–741, 1988.
100. Laing, F. P., Ramotar, K., Read, R. R., et al.: Molecular epidemiology of *Xanthomonas maltophilia* colonization and infection in the hospital environment. J. Clin. Microbiol. *33*:513–518, 1995.
101. Leelarasamee, A., and Bovornkitti, S.: Melioidosis: Review and update. Rev. Infect. Dis. *11*:413–425, 1989.
102. Legakis, N. J., Tzouvelekis, L. S., Makris, A., et al.: Outer membrane alterations in multiresistant mutants of *Pseudomonas aeruginosa*. Antimicrob. Agents Chemother. *33*:124–127, 1989.
103. Lentnek, A. L., and Williams, R. R.: Aztreonam in the treatment of gram-negative bacterial meningitis. Rev. Infect. Dis. *13*(Suppl. 7): 586–590, 1991.
104. Levy, J. H., and Katz, H. R.: *Pseudomonas cepacia* keratitis. Cornea *8*:67–71, 1989.
105. LiPuma, J. J., Mortensen, J. E., Dasen, S. E., et al.: Ribotype analysis of *Pseudomonas cepacia* from cystic fibrosis treatment centers. J. Pediatr. *113*:859–862, 1988.
106. Liu, P. V.: Biology of *Pseudomonas aeruginosa*. Hosp. Pract. *82*:139–147, 1976.
107. Lumbiganon, P., Pengsaa, K., Puapermpoonsiri, S., et al.: Neonatal melioidosis: A report of 5 cases. Pediatr. Infect. Dis. J. *7*:634–636, 1988.
108. Malizia, W. F., West, G. A., Brundage, W. G., et al.: Melioidosis: Laboratory studies. Health Lab. Sci. *6*:27–39, 1969.
109. Marshall, W. F., Keating, M. R., Anhalt, J. P., and Steckelberg, J. M.: *Xanthomonas maltophilia*: An emerging nosocomial pathogen. Mayo Clin. Proc. *64*:1097–1104, 1989.
110. Mattsby-Baltzer, I., Edebo, L., Jarvholm, B., and Lavenius, B.: Serum antibodies to *Pseudomonas pseudoalcaligenes* in metal workers exposed to infected metal-working fluids. Int. Arch. Allergy Appl. Immunol. *88*:304–311, 1989.
111. Mayer, J. H., and Finnlayson, M. H.: Chronic melioidosis: A case with bone and pulmonary lesions. S. Afr. Med. J. *18*:109, 1944.
112. McCubbin, M., and Fick, R. B., Jr.: Pathogenesis of *Pseudomonas* lung disease in cystic fibrosis. In Fick, R. B., Jr. (ed.): *Pseudomonas aeruginosa:* The Opportunist. Boca Raton, FL, CRC Press, 1993, pp. 189–211.
113. McManus, A. J., Mason, A. D., Jr., McManus, W. F., and Pruitt, B. A., Jr.: Twenty-five year review of *Pseudomonas aeruginosa* bacteremia in a burn center. Eur. J. Clin. Microbiol. *4*:219–223, 1985.
114. Minami, S., Akama, M., Araki, H., et al.: Imipenem and cephem resistant *Pseudomonas aeruginosa* carrying plasmid coding for class B beta-lactamase. J. Antimicrob. Chemother. *37*:433–444, 1996.
115. Minnefor, A. B., Olson, M. I., and Cawer, D. H.: *Pseudomonas* osteomyelitis following puncture wounds of the foot. Pediatrics *47*:598–601, 1971.
116. Morrison, A. J., Jr., Hoffmann, K. K., and Wenzel, R. P.: Associated mortality and clinical characteristics of nosocomial *Pseudomonas maltophilia* in a university hospital. J. Clin. Microbiol. *24*:52–55, 1986.
117. Mortensen, J., Hansen, A., Falk, M., et al.: Reduced effect of inhaled beta-2-adrenergic agonists on lung mucociliary clearance in patients with cystic fibrosis. Chest *103*:805–811, 1993.
118. Moss, R. B.: The role of IgG subclass antibodies in chronic infection: The case of cystic fibrosis. N. Engl. Reg. Allergy Proc. *9*:57–61, 1988.
119. Moss, R. B.: Cystic fibrosis: Pathogenesis, pulmonary function and treatment. Clin. Infect. Dis. *21*:839–851, 1995.
120. Muder, R. R., Yu, V. L., Dummer, J. S., et al.: Infections caused by *Pseudomonas maltophilia*: Expanding clinical spectrum. Arch. Intern. Med. *147*:1672–1674, 1987.
121. Nelson, J. D., Bradley, J. S.: Pocketbook of Pediatric Antimicrobial Therapy. 12th ed. Baltimore, Williams & Wilkins, 2000–2001, pp. 68–86.
122. Nelson, J. W., Butler, S. L., Kreig, D., and Govan, J. R.: Virulence factors of *Burkholderia cepacia*. FEMS Immunol. Med. Microbiol. *8*:89–97, 1994.
123. Neu, H. C.: The role of *Pseudomonas aeruginosa* in infections. J. Antimicrob. Chemother. *11*(Suppl. B):1–13, 1983.
124. Neu, H. C.: Carbapenems: Special properties contributing to their activity. Am. J. Med. *78*(6A):33–40, 1985.
125. Niggs, C., and Johnston, M. M.: Complement fixation test in experimental clinical and subclinical melioidosis. J. Bacteriol. *82*:159–168, 1961.
126. Nixon, G. M., Armstrong, D. S., Carzino, R., et al.: Clinical outcome after early *Pseudomonas aeruginosa* infection in cystic fibrosis. J. Pediatr. *138*:699–704, 2001.
127. Norby, S. R.: 4-Quinolones in the treatment of infections of the central nervous system. Rev. Infect. Dis. *10*(Suppl. 1):253–255, 1988.
128. Ohman, D. E., Burns, R. P., and Iglewski, B. H.: Corneal infections in mice with toxin A and elastase mutants of *Pseudomonas aeruginosa*. J. Infect. Dis. *142*:547–555, 1980.
129. Patamasucon, P., Pitchyangkura, C., and Fischer, G. W.: Melioidosis in childhood. J. Pediatr. *87*:133–136, 1975.
130. Patamasucon, P., Schaad, U. B., and Nelson, J. D.: Melioidosis. J. Pediatr. *100*:175–182, 1982.
131. Peacock, E. E.: Wound Repair. 3rd ed. Philadelphia, W. B. Saunders, 1984, pp. 38–55.
132. Pedersen, S. S.: Lung infection with alginate-producing, mucoid *Pseudomonas aeruginosa* in cystic fibrosis. A. P. M. I. S. Suppl. 28:1–79, 1992.
133. Peel, M. M., Davis, J. M., Armstrong, W. L. H., et al.: *Pseudomonas paucimobilis* from a leg ulcer on a Japanese seaman. J. Clin. Microbiol. *9*:561–564, 1979.
134. Penketh, A. R., Pitt, T. L., Hodson, M. E., et al.: Bactericidal activity of serum from cystic fibrosis patients for *Pseudomonas aeruginosa*. J. Med. Microbiol. *16*:401–408, 1983.
135. Pennington, J. E., Reynolds, H. Y., Wood, R. E., et al.: Use of *Pseudomonas aeruginosa* vaccine in patients with acute leukemia and cystic fibrosis. Am. J. Med. *58*:629–636, 1975.
136. Perry, A. W., Sutkin, H. S., Gottlieb, L. D., et al.: Skin graft survival: The bacterial answer. Ann. Plast. Surg. *22*:479–483, 1989.
137. Pollack, M.: *Pseudomonas aeruginosa*. *In* Mandell, G. L., Douglas, R. G., Jr., and Bennett, J. E. (eds.): Principles and Practice of Infectious Diseases. 3rd ed. New York, Churchill Livingstone, 1990, pp. 1673–1691.
138. Poore, K.: Bacterial multidrug resistance—emphasis on efflux mechanisms and *Pseudomonas aeruginosa*. J. Antimicrob. Chemother. *34*:453–456, 1994.
139. Pressler, T., Mansa, B., Jensen, T., et al.: Increased IgG2 and IgG3 concentration is associated with advanced *Pseudomonas aeruginosa* infection and poor pulmonary function in cystic fibrosis. Acta Pediatr. Scand. *77*:576–582, 1988.
140. *Pseudomonas aeruginosa*. *In* Gerber, M. A. (ed.): The Jordan Report 2000: Accelerated Development of Vaccines. Bethesda, MD, Division of Microbiology and Infectious Diseases, National Institute of Allergy and Infectious Diseases, National Institutes of Health, 2000, pp. 60–62.
141. Radberg, G., Nilsson, L. E., and Svensson, S.: Development of quinolone-imipenem cross resistance in *Pseudomonas aeruginosa* during exposure to ciprofloxacin. Antimicrob. Agents Chemother. *34*:2142–2147, 1990.
142. Ratjen, F., Doring, G., Nikolaizik, W. H.: Effect of inhaled tobramycin in early *Pseudomonas aeruginosa* colonisation in patients with cystic fibrosis. Lancet *358*:983–984, 2001.
143. Reed, R. K., Larter, W. E., Sieber, O. F., Jr., et al.: Peripheral nodular lesions in *Pseudomonas* sepsis: The importance of incision and drainage. J. Pediatr. *88*:977–979, 1976.
144. Reid, T. M. S., and Porter, I. A.: An outbreak of otitis externa in competitive swimmers due to *Pseudomonas aeruginosa*. J. Hyg. (Camb.) *86*:357–362, 1981.
145. Reynolds, H. Y., DiSant'Agnese, P. A., and Zierdt, C. H.: Mucoid *Pseudomonas aeruginosa*. J. A. M. A. *236*:2190–2192, 1976.
146. Reynolds, H. Y., Levine, A. S., Wood, R. E., et al.: *Pseudomonas aeruginosa* infections: Persisting problems and current research to find new therapies. Ann. Intern. Med. *82*:819–831, 1975.
147. Rhoads, S., Marinelli, L., Imperative, C. A., and Machamkin, I.: Comparison of the MicroScan Walkaway System and Vitek System for identification of gram-negative bacteria. J. Clin. Microbiol. *33*:3044–3046, 1995.
148. Richmond, H. M., and Sykes, R. B.: The β-lactamases of gram-negative bacilli and their possible physiologic role. Adv. Microb. Physiol. *9*:31–88, 1973.
149. Robinson, A., McCarter, Y. S., Tetreault, J.: Comparison of crystal enteric/non-fermenter system, API 20E system and Vitek Automicrobic System for identification of gram-negative bacilli. J. Clin. Microbiol. *33*:364–370, 1995.
150. Roiliders, E., Butler, K. M., Husson, R. N., et al.: *Pseudomonas* infections in children with human immunodeficiency virus infection. Pediatr. Infect. Dis. J. *11*:547–553, 1992.

151. Romling, V., Fiedler, B., Bosshammer, J., et al.: Epidemiology of chronic *Pseudomonas aeruginosa* in cystic fibrosis. J. Infect. Dis. *170*:616–621, 1994.
152. Rowley, A. H., Dias, L. D., Chadwick, E. G., et al.: *Pseudomonas stutzeri*: An unusual cause of calcaneal *Pseudomonas* osteomyelitis. Pediatr. Infect. Dis. J. *6*:296–297, 1987.
153. Rubio, T. T.: Ciprofloxacin: Comparative data in cystic fibrosis. Am. J. Med. *82*(Suppl. 4A):185–188, 1987.
154. Ruvalo, C., and Bauer, C. R.: Intrauterinely acquired *Pseudomonas* infection in the neonate. Clin. Pediatr. (Phila.) *21*:664–667, 1982.
155. Saiman, L., Cacalano, G., Prince, A.: *Pseudomonas cepacia* adherence to respiratory epithelial cells is enhanced by *Pseudomonas aeruginosa*. Infect. Immun. *58*:2578–2584, 1990.
156. Sajjan, U. S., Karmali, M. A., and Forstner, J. F.: Binding of *Pseudomonas cepacia* to normal human intestinal mucin and respiratory mucin for patients with cystic fibrosis. J. Clin. Invest. *89*:648–656, 1992.
157. Salmen, P., Dwyer, D. M., Vorse, H., et al.: Whirlpool-associated *Pseudomonas aeruginosa* urinary tract infections. J. A. M. A. *15*: 2025–2026, 1983.
158. Salyers, A. A., Whitt, D. D.: *Pseudomonas aeruginosa*. In Salyers, A. A., and Whitt, D. D. (eds.): Bacterial Pathogenesis: A Molecular Approach. Washington, D.C., American Society for Microbiology Press, 1994, pp. 260–272.
159. Sanders, C. C., and Sanders, W. E.: Type I β-lactamases of gram-negative bacteria: Interactions with β-lactam antibiotics. J. Infect. Dis. *154*:792–800, 1986.
160. Schaad, U. B., Sander, E., Wedgwood, J., et al.: Morphologic studies for skeletal toxicity after prolonged ciprofloxacin therapy in two juvenile cystic fibrosis patients. Pediatr. Infect. Dis. J. *11*:1047–1049, 1992.
161. Schaad, U. B., Stoupis, C., Wedgwood, J., et al.: Clinical, radiologic and magnetic resonance monitoring for skeletal toxicity in pediatric patients with cystic fibrosis receiving a three-month course of ciprofloxacin. Pediatr. Infect. Dis. J. *10*:723–729, 1991.
162. Schaad, U. B., Wedgwood-Krucko, J., Suter, S., et al.: Efficacy of inhaled amikacin as adjunct to intravenous combination therapy (ceftazidime and amikacin) in cystic fibrosis. J. Pediatr. *111*:599–605, 1987.
163. Schiller, N. L., and Millard, R. L.: *Pseudomonas*-infected cystic fibrosis patient sputum inhibits the bactericidal activity of normal human sputum. Pediatr. Res. *17*:747–752, 1983.
164. Schoch, P. E., and Cunha, B. A.: *Pseudomonas maltophilia*. Infect. Control *8*:169–172, 1987.
165. Scully, B. E., Parry, M. F., Nev, H. C., et al.: Oral ciprofloxacin therapy of infections due to *Pseudomonas aeruginosa*. Lancet *1*:819–822, 1986.
166. Senda, C. C., Arakawa, Y., Nakashina, K., et al.: Multifocal outbreaks of metallo-beta-lactamase producing *Pseudomonas aeruginosa* resistant to broad spectrum beta-lactams, including carbapenem. Antimicrob. Agents Chemother. *40*:349–353, 1996.
167. Sesev, S., Rosen, N., Joseph, G., et al.: Pefloxacin efficacy in gram-negative bacillary meningitis. J. Antimicrob. Chemother. 26(Suppl. B):187–192, 1990.
168. Shackelford, P. G., Ratzan, S. A., and Shearer, W. T.: Ecthyma gangrenosum produced by *Aeromonas hydrophila*. J. Pediatr. *83*:100–101, 1973.
169. Shand, G. H., Pedersen, S. S., Tilling, R., et al.: Use of immunoblot detection of serum antibodies in the diagnosis of chronic *Pseudomonas aeruginosa* lung infection in cystic fibrosis. J. Med. Microbiol. *27*:169–177, 1988.
170. Sharma, G. D., Tosi, M. F., Stern, R. C., et al.: Progression of pulmonary disease after disappearance of *Pseudomonas* in cystic fibrosis. Am. J. Respir. Crit. Care Med. *152*:169–173, 1995.
171. Smith, A. L., Redding, G., Doershuk, C., et al.: Sputum changes associated with therapy for endobronchial exacerbation in cystic fibrosis. J. Pediatr. *112*:547–554, 1988.
172. Smith, G. L.: Methods for preventing *Pseudomonas* folliculitis. Cutis *29*:378–381, 1982.
173. Sobel, J. D., Hashman, N., Reinherz, G., et al.: Nosocomial *Pseudomonas cepacia* infection associated with chlorhexidine contamination. Am. J. Med. *73*:183–186, 1982.
174. Sookpranee, T., Sookpranee, M., Mellencamp, M. A., et al.: *Pseudomonas pseudomallei*, a common pathogen in Thailand that is resistant to bactericidal effects of many antibiotics. Antimicrob. Agents Chemother. *35*:484–489, 1991.
175. Sorvillo, F., Beall, G., Turner, P. A., et al.: Incidence and determinants of *Pseudomonas aeruginosa* infection among persons with HIV: Association with hospital exposure. Am. J. Infect. Control *29*:79–84, 2001.
176. Speert, D. P.: Understanding *Burkholderia cepacia*: Epidemiology, genomovars and virulence. Infect. Med. *18*:49–56, 2001.
177. Speert, D. P., Bond, M., Woodman, R. C., and Curnutte, J. J.: Infection with *Pseudomonas cepacia* in chronic granulomatous disease. Role of nonoxidative killing by neutrophils in host defense. J. Infect. Dis. *170*:1524–1531, 1994.
178. Speert, D. P., Farmer, S. W., Campbell, M. E., et al.: Conversion of *Pseudomonas aeruginosa* to the phenotype characteristic of strains from patients with cystic fibrosis. J. Clin. Microbiol. *28*:188–194, 1990.
179. Spencer, R. C.: The emergence of epidemic, multiple-antibiotic–resistant *Stenotrophomonas (Xanthomonas) maltophilia* and *Burkholderia (Pseudomonas) cepacia*. J. Hosp. Infect. *30*(Suppl.):453–465, 1995.
180. Steen, H. J., Scott, E. M., Stevenson, M. I., et al.: Clinical and pharmacokinetic aspects of ciprofloxacin in the treatment of acute exacerbations of *Pseudomonas* infection in cystic fibrosis patients. J. Antimicrob. Chemother. *24*:787–795, 1989.
181. Strand, C. L., Bryant, J. K., Morgan, J. W., et al.: Nosocomial *Pseudomonas aeruginosa* urinary tract infections. J. A. M. A. *248*:1615–1618, 1982.
182. Strandvik, B., Hjelte, L., Lindblad, A., et al.: Comparison of efficacy and tolerance of intravenously and orally administered ciprofloxacin in cystic fibrosis patients with acute exacerbations of lung infection. Scand. J. Infect. Dis. *60*(Suppl.):84–88, 1989.
183. Tablan, O. C., Martone, W. J., Doershuk, C. F., et al.: Colonization of the respiratory tract with *Pseudomonas cepacia* in cystic fibrosis: Risk factors and outcomes. Chest 9:527–532, 1987.
184. Tablan, O. C., Martone, W. J., and Jarvis, W. R.: The epidemiology of *Pseudomonas cepacia* in patients with cystic fibrosis. Eur. J. Epidemiol. *3*:336–342, 1987.
185. Tiffany, K. K., and Kline, M. W.: Mixed flora brain abscess with *Pseudomonas paucimobilis* after a penetrating lawn dart injury. Pediatr. Infect. Dis. J. *7*:667–669, 1988.
186. Tredget, E. E., Shankowsky, H. A., Joffe, A. M., et al.: Epidemiology of infections with *Pseudomonas aeruginosa* in burn patients: The role of hydrotherapy. Clin. Infect. Dis. *15*:941–949, 1992.
187. Vartivarian, S., and Anaissie, E.: *Stenotrophomonas maltophilia* and *Burkholderia cepacia. In* Mandell, G. L., Bennett, J. E., and Dolin, R. (eds.): Principles and Practice of Infectious Diseases, 5th ed. Philadelphia, Churchill Livingstone, 2000, pp. 2235–2237.
188. Victo, M. A., Arpi, M., Bruun, B., et al.: *Xanthomonas maltophilia* bacteremia in immunocompromised hematologic patients. Scand. J. Infect. Dis. *26*:163–170, 1994.
189. Vishwanath, S., and Ramphal, R.: Adherence of *Pseudomonas aeruginosa* to human tracheobronchial mucin. Infect. Immun. *45*:197–202, 1984.
190. Vochem, M., Vogt, M., and Doring, G.: Sepsis in a newborn due to *Pseudomonas aeruginosa* from a contaminated tub bath. N. Engl. J. Med. *345*:378, 2001.
191. Vogt, R., LaRue, D., Parry, M. F., et al.: *Pseudomonas aeruginosa* skin infections in persons using a whirlpool in Vermont. J. Clin. Microbiol. *15*:571–574, 1982.
192. Watanabe, M., Iyobe, S., Inoue, M., and Mitsuhashi, S.: Transferable imipenem resistance in *Pseudomonas aeruginosa*. Antimicrob. Chemother. *35*:147–151, 1991.
193. Welch, D. F., Muszynski, M. J., Pai, C. H., et al.: Selective and differential medium for recovery of *Pseudomonas cepacia* from the respiratory tracts of patients with cystic fibrosis. J. Clin. Microbiol. *25*:1730–1734, 1987.
194. Wheeler, W. B., Williams, R. N., Matthew, W. J., and Colten, H. R.: Progression of cystic fibrosis lung disease as a function of serum immunoglobulin G levels: A 5-year longitudinal study. J. Pediatr. *104*:695–699, 1984.
195. White, N. J., Dance, D. A., Chaowagul, W., et al.: Halving of mortality of severe melioidosis by ceftazidime. Lancet *2*:697–701, 1989.
196. Widmer, A. F., Wenzel, R. P., Trilla, A., et al.: Outbreak of *Pseudomonas aeruginosa* infections in a surgical intensive care unit: Probable transmission via hands of a health care worker. Clin. Infect. Dis. *16*:372–376, 1993.
197. Wongratanacheewin, S., Tattawasart, U., and Lulitanond, V.: An avidin-biotin enzyme-linked immunosorbent assay for the detection of *Pseudomonas pseudomallei* antigens. Trans. R. Trop. Med. Hyg. *84*:429–430, 1990.
198. Woods, D. E., Cryz, S. J., Friedman, R. L., et al.: Contribution of toxin A and elastase to virulence of *Pseudomonas aeruginosa* in chronic lung infections of rats. Infect. Immun. *36*:1223–1228, 1982.
199. Wretlind, B., and Pavlovskis, O. R.: The role of proteases and exotoxin A in the pathogenicity of *Pseudomonas aeruginosa* infections. Scand. J. Infect. Dis. Suppl. *29*:13–19, 1981.
200. Young, E. J., Sewell, M. C., Koza, M. A., et al.: Antibiotic resistance patterns during aminoglycoside restriction. Am. J. Med. *290*:223–227, 1985.
201. Yu, V. L., Paterson, D. L.: *Pseudomonas aeruginosa*. In Yu, V. L., Merigan, T. C., and Barriere, S. L. (eds.): Antimicrobial Therapy and Vaccines, Baltimore, Williams & Wilkins, 1999, pp. 348–358.
202. Zimakoff, J., Hoiby, N., Rosendal, K., et al.: Epidemiology of *Pseudomonas aeruginosa* infection and the role of contamination of the environment in a cystic fibrosis clinic. J. Hosp. Infect. *4*:31–40, 1983.
203. Zuravleff, J. J., and Yu, V. L.: Infections caused by *Pseudomonas maltophilia* with emphasis on bacteremia: Case reports and review of the literature. Rev. Infect. Dis. *4*:1236–1246, 1982.

Stenotrophomonas (Xanthomonas) maltophilia

CARLOS A. SATTLER

Stenotrophomonas maltophilia is a gram-negative bacillus that previously belonged to the *Pseudomonas* and subsequently the *Xanthomonas* genus. In 1993, the new genus *Stenotrophomonas* was proposed, resulting in the most recent reclassification of this bacterium.[45] *S. maltophilia* is an opportunistic pathogen that has emerged as a significant cause of nosocomially acquired infection. It is rarely a cause of infection in healthy, immunocompetent children.

Bacteriology

S. maltophilia is an aerobic, nonfermentative, gram-negative bacillus that is oxidase-negative and lysine decarboxylase–positive. In addition, key features that allow identification of *S. maltophilia* include oxidation of glucose and maltose, as well as a positive DNase reaction.[25] Optimal growth occurs at 35° C, and on sheep blood agar, colonies appear rough and lavender-green and have a distinct ammonia-like odor. Morphologically, the organism is a straight bacillus, 0.7 to 1.8 μm long, that is motile by means of multiple polar flagella. It grows well on standard culture media, including blood agar and chocolate agar, as well as in broth blood culture systems, within the standard 5-day incubation period. Because of the hardy nature of this organism, standard collection, transport, and storage procedures are sufficient. The use of selective media such as MacConkey agar allows for isolation of *S. maltophilia* from polymicrobial specimens, although for highly contaminated samples such as feces, the addition of antibiotics such as imipenem, vancomycin, and amphotericin B to the media should be considered.[33]

Epidemiology

S. maltophilia is a free-living, ubiquitous organism, the natural habitats for which include water, soil, and plants. The ability to survive in an aqueous milieu has allowed *S. maltophilia* to occupy a niche in the hospital environment. It has been cultured from dialysis fluids,[5] ventilators and other respiratory equipment,[34] and preoperative surgical brushes.[44] Several reports have linked nosocomial outbreaks of *S. maltophilia* to contamination of hospital water sources such as faucet aerators,[62] taps, and sinks,[34] as well as disinfectant solutions.[65] In addition, cases of "pseudoinfection" caused by contamination of blood collection tubes have been described.[52]

Infection with *S. maltophilia* generally is hospital acquired.[23, 51] Predisposing factors associated with colonization and infection by *S. maltophilia* include the presence of a severe, debilitating underlying illness, particularly malignancy, immune suppression, broad-spectrum antibiotic exposure, the presence of a central venous catheter, neutropenia, intensive care unit stay, tracheostomy, mechanical ventilation, or a combination of these factors.[7, 20, 56, 61] Among children, predisposing factors are similar to those found in adults.[51] *S. maltophilia* is being isolated from clinical samples with increasing frequency.[19, 35, 37, 39, 51] This increase probably is related to advances in medical care that allow for a rise in the survival rate of severely ill patients, who are at highest risk for acquiring infection with this organism and who require more frequent use of invasive medical equipment, including indwelling lines, as well as broad-spectrum antimicrobials to which the organism is not susceptible.

Pathophysiology

Like many pseudomonads, *S. maltophilia* is an organism with low virulence and limited invasiveness. An intact host immune system is an important deterrent to acquisition of a severe and even life-threatening infection; cases of septicemia and death occur in patients with underlying debilitating illnesses. *S. maltophilia* elaborates a wide range of extracellular enzymes, including DNase, RNase, fibrinolysin, lipase, hyaluronidase, protease, and elastase, which may play a role in the pathogenesis of disease processes associated with *S. maltophilia*.[14] In addition, *S. maltophilia* has been found to adhere to plastic materials, including intravenous catheters, and to produce biofilm, properties that may account for the relatively high incidence of catheter-related bloodstream infections caused by this organism.[14, 21] *S. maltophilia* is inherently resistant to several classes of antibiotics. Colonization with *S. maltophilia,* especially in the respiratory tract, is not an uncommon finding. In debilitated patients, exposure to broad-spectrum antimicrobials, many of which are ineffective against this bacterium, may allow overgrowth of colonizing organisms, which subsequently gain access to sterile body sites and cause infection. Portals of infection include indwelling devices such as central venous catheters, peritoneal dialysis or urinary tract catheters, the respiratory tract, and the gastrointestinal tract.

Clinical Manifestations

S. maltophilia once was regarded as a microorganism with very limited pathogenicity that was unlikely to cause infection except in the most debilitated patients.[23] However, not only the incidence but also the severity of infection and the spectrum of clinical manifestations caused by this bacterium have increased. The most common site of isolation of *S. maltophilia* is the respiratory tract, particularly in hospitalized, mechanically ventilated patients. Attributing a causative role to *S. maltophilia* occasionally is difficult when the organism is isolated only from respiratory secretions, particularly as part of a mixed culture. Most critically ill, mechanically ventilated patients have abnormal chest radiographs, and differentiating infectious from noninfectious infiltrates may be very difficult. Nevertheless, *S. maltophilia* has unequivocally been associated with pneumonia, which may be severe.[22] Occasionally, it may be associated with massive, fatal pulmonary hemorrhage in adult patients with malignancy[18] and is a cause of ventilator-associated pneumonia.[36] In adults with pneumonia, the development of secondary bacteremia signals a grave prognosis.[19]

S. maltophilia bloodstream infections usually are catheter-associated.[34, 40, 60] In a series of 32 episodes of bacteremia in children, all were related to the presence of a central venous catheter, although in 10 episodes, the primary source was not the catheter.[51] Frequently, *S. maltophilia* is isolated as part of a polymicrobial bloodstream infection. In children, the severity of illness appears to be similar regardless of whether *S. maltophilia* is isolated in a monomicrobial or mixed blood culture.[51] Malignancy is the most common underlying illness in patients with bacteremia, and many will have concomitant neutropenia. Bloodstream infections caused by *S. maltophilia* can be severe. In a pediatric series, 31 percent of the patients initially were seen in septic shock, and the attributable mortality rate was 6.3 percent.[51] The death rate associated with *S. maltophilia* bloodstream infection is, in general, higher in adults.[34, 35, 38, 40]

S. maltophilia endocarditis is a rare occurrence. It has been associated with intravenous drug abuse and frequently occurs after replacement of a prosthetic valve.[2, 27, 41, 66] Surgical therapy often is required, although cure with medical treatment alone has been reported. No cases of endocarditis caused by this organism in children have been reported.

Urinary tract infections caused by *S. maltophilia* almost invariably occur in patients with structural abnormalities of the urinary tract, indwelling urinary catheters, or underlying illnesses. Infection may be severe and associated with sepsis and septic shock.[58]

Skin and soft tissue infections caused by *S. maltophilia* have occurred after having work-related injuries and wounds contaminated with soil and plant material, such as in lawn mower injuries.[11, 17, 26] In the hospital setting, *S. maltophilia* frequently is cultured from wounds and surgical sites, although in children, determining the clinical significance of this organism, particularly when isolated in mixed culture, often is difficult.[51] In adult cancer patients, tender, erythematous nodular skin lesions have been described in association with *S. maltophilia* bacteremia and probably represent metastatic infectious foci.[59]

S. maltophilia has been implicated as a cause of conjunctivitis and keratitis in the setting of ocular surface compromise resulting from trauma, the use of soft contact lenses, or previous infection with human herpes simplex.[49] Endophthalmitis occurring after ophthalmologic surgical interventions also has been described.[9, 29, 30]

Meningitis caused by *S. maltophilia* is an extremely rare occurrence and usually is nosocomial and associated with neurosurgical procedures and infection of intraventricular devices.[48] However, spontaneous meningitis in three infants has been reported.[43, 50]

S. maltophilia is the fourth most common organism isolated from the bronchial secretions of patients with cystic fibrosis, after *Pseudomonas aeruginosa*, *Staphylococcus aureus*, and *Haemophilus influenzae*.[55] The incidence and prevalence of *S. maltophilia* isolated from the respiratory secretions of patients with cystic fibrosis are increasing,[32, 54] although they are not uniform across all cystic fibrosis centers.[13] The origin of the bacterium is uncertain, with evidence suggesting that it may be acquired both in the hospital and in the community.[13] Colonization may be transient or persistent, with chronic colonization occurring more frequently in older patients.[55] Case-control studies have identified greater exposure to antipseudomonal antibiotics, oral ciprofloxacin, inhaled aminoglycosides, and oral corticosteroids, as well as more hospitalization days, as risk factors for colonization with *S. maltophilia*.[16, 54] Unlike *Burkholderia cepacia,* no evidence of patient-to-patient transmission of *S. maltophilia* has been found, and it does not appear to be associated with rapid deterioration of pulmonary function in patients with cystic fibrosis.[15] Cases of *S. maltophilia* bacteremia have not been reported in patients with cystic fibrosis, with the exception of one patient who died of sepsis caused by this bacterium on the first day after undergoing lung transplantation.[31] The clinical significance of isolation of *S. maltophilia* from the sputum of patients with cystic fibrosis and its role in the deterioration in lung function is uncertain. Its presence may represent more a marker of severe disease than causally related respiratory deterioration.[13]

Other infections caused by *S. maltophilia* include peritoneal catheter exit-site infections and peritonitis in patients undergoing peritoneal dialysis,[12, 53] as well as cholangitis,[46] osteochondritis,[3] mastoiditis,[28] and bursitis.[47]

Diagnosis

The diagnosis of infection is established by isolating the organism from normally sterile sites in the presence of a compatible clinical picture. However, growth of *S. maltophilia* from normally sterile samples actually may represent an episode of "pseudo-infection" caused by the ability of this organism to contaminate and survive in hospital equipment such as blood collection tubes and antiseptic solutions. Because *S. maltophilia* is a common colonizer of hospitalized patients, isolation from nonsterile sites such as sputum or wounds is more difficult to interpret, particularly when isolated in mixed culture. Because nosocomial outbreaks have been reported, isolation of *S. maltophilia* from other patients in a hospital setting should alert the physician to the possibility of *Stenotrophomonas* infection. Infection control should be notified after isolation of the organism.

Occasionally, *B. cepacia* is misidentified as *S. maltophilia*, especially in patients with cystic fibrosis.[6] *S. maltophilia* is oxidase-negative and DNase-positive. These tests should be repeated in cases in which identification of the organism is in doubt. Because of the serious clinical implications of misidentification in this group of patients, molecular analysis of the isolates should be considered if results remain uncertain.[64]

Treatment

Providing antibiotic therapy for *S. maltophilia* is difficult for several reasons. It is a multidrug-resistant organism and is particularly resistant to β-lactam antibiotic agents. Mechanisms of resistance include the production of two chromosomally encoded, inducible β-lactamases designated L1 and L2. The former is a β-lactamase inhibitor–resistant metalloenzyme that hydrolyzes a broad range of β-lactam antibiotics, including carbapenems such as imipenem and meropenem. L2 is a cephalosporinase and, unlike L1, is susceptible to β-lactamase inhibitors. Other mechanisms of resistance include reduced antibiotic uptake, the main mechanism providing aminoglycoside resistance, as well as a recently characterized antibiotic efflux pump that confers multidrug resistance.[1]

In addition, in vitro antibiotic susceptibility testing is plagued by numerous methodologic problems. Several factors, including the time of incubation and the composition of the medium, affect the interpretation of test results. Furthermore, poor reproducibility among different testing methods has been described.[8] The National Committee for Clinical Laboratory Standards currently recommends testing by broth or agar dilution.[42] Moreover, no controlled clinical studies have determined the most effective antibiotic regimen or length of treatment.

Antibiotic susceptibility studies and clinical observation suggest that the most active antibiotic against *S. maltophilia* is trimethoprim-sulfamethoxazole, and most authorities agree that it is the drug of choice. It is, however, bacteriostatic, which may have clinical implications in immunosuppressed patients. In addition, resistant strains are being identified with increasing frequency.[38, 57] Other antibiotics that have shown good in vitro activity include ticarcillin-clavulanate, doxycycline, and minocycline, although clinical experience with the latter two is very limited.[14] The activity of early fluoroquinolones such as ciprofloxacin and ofloxacin varies widely, and emergence of resistance during treatment has been reported.[10] Newer quinolones appear to have better activity in vitro against *S. maltophilia,*[63] but their activity decreases against multiresistant strains.[4]

Bloodstream infections can be severe, particularly in immunosuppressed patients. Combination antibiotic therapy with trimethoprim-sulfamethoxazole and ticarcillin-clavulanate for bloodstream infections by isolates that are susceptible has been advocated by some authorities.[40, 57] Other combinations have shown varying efficacy and correlation between in vitro and in vivo findings, which have not always been consistent.[14] In cases of catheter-related bloodstream infection, removal of the catheter has been associated with improved outcome, irrespective of the appropriateness of antibiotic therapy.[19, 51] Nonetheless, successful treatment without removal of the catheter,[40] as well as an association of inappropriate antibiotic therapy and death,[38] has been described. In cases of serious infection such as bacteremia or severe pneumonia, combination antibiotic therapy should be considered when in vitro and in vivo evidence suggest that rapid emergence of resistance may occur during treatment.[24]

Appropriate management of patients from whom *S. maltophilia* is isolated from nonsterile sites, particularly in mixed culture, is not always clear because some isolates may represent colonization or contamination of the sample. In a pediatric study describing nonrespiratory infections in children, 6 of 16 patients with *S. maltophilia* cultured from sites other than the bloodstream were treated with antibiotics not active in vitro, and 5 of these children were "cured."[51] Nevertheless, in adults, *S. maltophilia* has been unquestionably associated with severe infection at sites other than the bloodstream.

REFERENCES

1. Alonso, A., and Martinez, J. L.: Expression of multidrug efflux pump SmeDEF by clinical isolates of *Stenotrophomonas maltophilia.* Antimicrob. Agents Chemother. *45*:1879–1881, 2001.
2. Aydin, K., Koksal, I., Kaygusuz, S., et al.: Endocarditis caused by *Stenotrophomonas maltophilia.* Scand. J. Infect. Dis. *32*:427–30, 2000.
3. Baltimore, R. S., and Jenson, H. B.: Puncture wound osteochondritis of the foot caused by *Pseudomonas maltophilia.* Pediatr. Infect. Dis. J. *9*:143–144, 1990.
4. Bellido, J. L., Hernandez, F. J., Zufiaurre, M. N., and Garcia-Rodriguez, J. A.: In vitro activity of newer fluoroquinolones against *Stenotrophomonas maltophilia.* J. Antimicrob. Chemother. *46*:334–335, 2000.
5. Berbari, N., Johnson, D. H., Cunha, B. A.: *Xanthomonas maltophilia* peritonitis in a patient undergoing peritoneal dialysis. Heart Lung *22*:282–283, 1993.
6. Burdge, D. R., Noble, M. A., Campbell, M. E., et al.: *Xanthomonas maltophilia* misidentified as *Pseudomonas cepacia* in cultures of sputum from patients with cystic fibrosis: A diagnostic pitfall with major clinical implications. Clin. Infect. Dis. *20*:445–448, 1995.
7. Carmeli, Y., and Samore, M. H.: Comparison of treatment with imipenem vs. ceftazidime as a predisposing factor for nosocomial acquisition of *Stenotrophomonas maltophilia:* A historical cohort study. Clin. Infect. Dis. *24*:1131–1134, 1997.
8. Carroll, K. C., Cohen, S., Nelson, R., et al.: Comparison of various in vitro susceptibility methods for testing *Stenotrophomonas maltophilia.* Diagn. Microbiol. Infect. Dis. *32*:229–235, 1998.
9. Chen, S., Stroh, E. M., Wald, K., and Jalkh, A.: *Xanthomonas maltophilia* endophthalmitis after implantation of sustained-release ganciclovir. Am. J. Ophthalmol. *114*:772–773, 1992.
10. Cheng, A. F., Li, M. K., Ling, T. K., and French, G. L.: Emergence of ofloxacin-resistant *Citrobacter freundii* and *Pseudomonas maltophilia* after ofloxacin therapy. J. Antimicrob. Chemother. *20*:283–285, 1987.
11. Daley, A. J., and McIntyre, P. B.: *Stenotrophomonas maltophilia* and lawn mower injuries in children. J. Trauma *48*:536–537, 2000.
12. Dapena, F., Selgas, R., Garcia-Perea, A., et al.: Clinical significance of exit-site infections due to *Xanthomonas* in CAPD patients: A comparison with *Pseudomonas* infection. Nephrol. Dial. Transplant. *9*:1774–1777, 1994.
13. Demko, C. A., Stern, R. C., and Doershuk, C. F.: *Stenotrophomonas maltophilia* in cystic fibrosis: Incidence and prevalence. Pediatr. Pulmonol. *25*:304–308, 1998.
14. Denton, M., and Kerr, K. G.: Microbiological and clinical aspects of infection associated with *Stenotrophomonas maltophilia.* Clin. Microbiol. Rev. *11*:57–80, 1998.
15. Denton, M., Todd, N. J., Kerr, K. G., et al.: Molecular epidemiology of *Stenotrophomonas maltophilia* isolated from clinical specimens from patients with cystic fibrosis and associated environmental samples. J. Clin. Microbiol. *36*:1953–1958, 1998.
16. Denton, M., Todd, N. J., and Littlewood, J. M.: Role of anti-pseudomonal antibiotics in the emergence of *Stenotrophomonas maltophilia* in cystic fibrosis patients. Eur. J. Clin. Microbiol. Infect. Dis. *15*:402–405, 1996.
17. Dyte, P. H., and Gillians, J. A.: *Pseudomonas maltophilia* infection in an abattoir worker. Med. J. Aust. *1*:444–445, 1977.
18. Elsner, H. A., Duhrsen, U., Hollwitz, B., et al.: Fatal pulmonary hemorrhage in patients with acute leukemia and fulminant pneumonia caused by *Stenotrophomonas maltophilia.* Ann. Hematol. *74*:155–161, 1997.
19. Elting, L. S., and Bodey, G. P.: Septicemia due to *Xanthomonas* species and non-*aeruginosa Pseudomonas* species: Increasing incidence of catheter-related infections. Medicine (Baltimore) *69*:296–306, 1990.
20. Elting, L. S., Khardori, N., Bodey, G. P., and Fainstein, V.: Nosocomial infection caused by *Xanthomonas maltophilia*: A case-control study of predisposing factors. Infect. Control Hosp. Epidemiol. *11*:134–138, 1990.
21. Elvers, K. T., Leeming, K., Moore, C. P., and Lappin-Scott, H. M.: Bacterial-fungal biofilms in flowing water photo-processing tanks. J. Appl. Microbiol. *84*:607–618, 1998.
22. Fujita, J., Yamadori, I., Xu, G., et al.: Clinical features of *Stenotrophomonas maltophilia* pneumonia in immunocompromised patients. Respir. Med. *90*:35–38, 1996.
23. Gardner, P., Griffin, W. B., Swartz, M. N., et al.: Nonfermentative gram negative bacilli of nosocomial interest. Am. J. Med. *48*:735–749, 1970.
24. Garrison, M. W., Anderson, D. E., Campbell, D. M., et al.: *Stenotrophomonas maltophilia*: Emergence of multidrug-resistant strains during therapy and in an in vitro pharmacodynamic chamber model. Antimicrob. Agents Chemother. *40*:2859–2864, 1996.
25. Gilligan, P. H., and Whittier, S.: *Burkholderia, Stenotrophomonas, Ralstonia, Brevundimonas, Comamonas, Acidovorax. In* Murray, P. R., Baron, E. J., Pfaller, M. A., et al. (eds.): Manual of Clinical Microbiology, 7th ed. Washington, D.C., American Society for Microbiology, 1999, pp. 526–538.
26. Gordon, G., Indeck, M., Bross, J., et al.: Injury from silage wagon accident complicated by mucormycosis. J. Trauma *28*:866–867, 1988.
27. Gutierrez Rodero, F., Masia, M. M., Cortes, J., et al.: Endocarditis caused by *Stenotrophomonas maltophilia:* Case report and review. Clin. Infect. Dis. *23*:1261–1265, 1996.
28. Harlowe, H. D.: Acute mastoiditis following *Pseudomonas maltophilia* infection: Case report. Laryngoscope *82*:882–883, 1972.
29. Horio, N., Horiguchi, M., Murakami, K., et al.: *Stenotrophomonas maltophilia* endophthalmitis after intraocular lens implantation. Graefes Arch. Clin. Exp. Ophthalmol. *238*:299–301, 2000.
30. Kaiser, G. M., Tso, P. C., Morris, R., and McCurdy, D.: *Xanthomonas maltophilia* endophthalmitis after cataract extraction. Am. J. Ophthalmol. *123*:410–411, 1997.
31. Kanj, S. S., Tapson, V., Davis, R. D., et al.: Infections in patients with cystic fibrosis following lung transplantation. Chest *112*:924–930, 1997.
32. Karpati, F., Malmborg, A. S., Alfredsson, H., et al.: Bacterial colonisation with *Xanthomonas maltophilia*—a retrospective study in a cystic fibrosis patient population. Infection *22*:258–263, 1994.

33. Kerr, K. G., Denton, M., Todd, N., et al.: A new selective differential medium for isolation of *Stenotrophomonas maltophilia*. Eur. J. Clin. Microbiol. Infect. Dis. *15*:607–610, 1996.
34. Khardori, N., Elting, L., Wong, E., et al.: Nosocomial infections due to *Xanthomonas maltophilia (Pseudomonas maltophilia)* in patients with cancer. Rev. Infect. Dis. *12*:997–1003, 1990.
35. Krcmery, V., Jr., Pichna, P., Oravcova, E., et al.: *Stenotrophomonas maltophilia* bacteraemia in cancer patients: Report on 31 cases. J. Hosp. Infect. *34*:75–77, 1996.
36. Maningo, E., and Watanakunakorn, C.: *Xanthomonas maltophilia* and *Pseudomonas cepacia* in lower respiratory tracts of patients in critical care units. J. Infect. *31*:89–92, 1995.
37. Marshall, W. F., Keating, M. R., Anhalt, J. P., and Steckelberg, J. M.: *Xanthomonas maltophilia:* An emerging nosocomial pathogen. Mayo Clin. Proc. *64*:1097–1104, 1989.
38. Micozzi, A., Venditti, M., Monaco, M., et al.: Bacteremia due to *Stenotrophomonas maltophilia* in patients with hematologic malignancies. Clin. Infect. Dis. *31*:705–711, 2000.
39. Morrison, A. J., Jr., Hoffmann, K. K., and Wenzel, R. P.: Associated mortality and clinical characteristics of nosocomial *Pseudomonas maltophilia* in a university hospital. J. Clin. Microbiol. *24*:52–55, 1986.
40. Muder, R. R., Harris, A. P., Muller, S., et al.: Bacteremia due to *Stenotrophomonas (Xanthomonas) maltophilia*: A prospective, multicenter study of 91 episodes. Clin. Infect. Dis. *22*:508–512, 1996.
41. Munter, R. G., Yinnon, A. M., Schlesinger, Y., and Hershko, C.: Infective endocarditis due to *Stenotrophomonas (Xanthomonas) maltophilia*. Eur. J. Clin. Microbiol. Infect. Dis. *17*:353–356, 1998.
42. National Committee for Clinical Laboratory Standards: Performance Standards for Antimicrobial Susceptibility Testing: Eleventh Informational Supplement. NCCLS Document M100–S11. Wayne, PA, NCCLS, 2001.
43. Nguyen, M. H., and Muder, R. R.: Meningitis due to *Xanthomonas maltophilia*: Case report and review. Clin. Infect. Dis. *19*:325–326, 1994.
44. Oie, S., and Kamiya, A.: Microbial contamination of brushes used for preoperative shaving. J. Hosp. Infect. *21*:103–110, 1992.
45. Palleroni, N. J., and Bradbury, J. F.: *Stenotrophomonas,* a new bacterial genus for *Xanthomonas maltophilia* (Hugh 1980) Swings et al. 1983. Int. J. Syst. Bacteriol. *43*:606–609, 1993.
46. Papadakis, K. A., Vartivarian, S. E., Vassilaki, M. E., and Anaissie, E. J.: *Stenotrophomonas maltophilia:* An unusual cause of biliary sepsis. Clin. Infect. Dis. *21*:1032–1034, 1995.
47. Papadakis, K. A., Vartivarian, S. E., Vassilaki, M. E., and Anaissie, E. J.: Septic prepatellar bursitis caused by *Stenotrophomonas (Xanthomonas) maltophilia*. Clin. Infect. Dis. *22*:388–389, 1996.
48. Papadakis, K. A., Vartivarian, S. E., Vassilaki, M. E., and Anaissie, E. J.: *Stenotrophomonas maltophilia* meningitis. Report of two cases and review of the literature. J. Neurosurg. *87*:106–108, 1997.
49. Penland, R. L., and Wilhelmus, K. R.: *Stenotrophomonas maltophilia* ocular infections. Arch. Ophthalmol. *114*:433–436, 1996.
50. Sarvamangala Devi, J. N., Venkatesh, A., and Shivananda, P. G.: Neonatal infections due to *Pseudomonas maltophilia*. Indian Pediatr. *21*:72–74, 1984.
51. Sattler, C. A., Mason, E. O., Jr., and Kaplan, S. L.: Nonrespiratory *Stenotrophomonas maltophilia* infection at a children's hospital. Clin. Infect. Dis. *31*:1321–1330, 2000.
52. Semel, J. D., Trenholme, G. M., Harris, A. A., et al.: *Pseudomonas maltophilia* pseudosepticemia. Am. J. Med. *64*:403–406, 1978.
53. Szeto, C. C., Li, P. K., Leung, C. B., et al.: *Xanthomonas maltophilia* peritonitis in uremic patients receiving continuous ambulatory peritoneal dialysis. Am. J. Kidney Dis. *29*:91–95, 1997.
54. Talmaciu, I., Varlotta, L., Mortensen, J., and Schidlow, D. V.: Risk factors for emergence of *Stenotrophomonas maltophilia* in cystic fibrosis. Pediatr. Pulmonol. *30*:10–15, 2000.
55. Valdezate, S., Vindel, A., Maiz, L., et al.: Persistence and variability of *Stenotrophomonas maltophilia* in cystic fibrosis patients, Madrid, 1991–1998. Emerg. Infect. Dis. *7*:113–122, 2001.
56. VanCouwenberghe, C. J., Farver, T. B., and Cohen, S. H.: Risk factors associated with isolation of *Stenotrophomonas (Xanthomonas) maltophilia* in clinical specimens. Infect. Control Hosp. Epidemiol. *18*:316–321, 1997.
57. Vartivarian, S., Anaissie, E., Bodey, G., et al.: A changing pattern of susceptibility *of Xanthomonas maltophilia* to antimicrobial agents: Implications for therapy. Antimicrob. Agents Chemother. *38*:624–627, 1994.
58. Vartivarian, S. E., Papadakis, K. A., and Anaissie, E. J.: *Stenotrophomonas (Xanthomonas) maltophilia* urinary tract infection. A disease that is usually severe and complicated. Arch. Intern. Med. *156*:433–435, 1996.
59. Vartivarian, S. E., Papadakis, K. A., Palacios, J. A., et al.: Mucocutaneous and soft tissue infections caused by *Xanthomonas maltophilia*. A new spectrum. Ann. Intern. Med. *121*:969–973, 1994.
60. Victor, M. A., Arpi, M., Bruun, B., et al.: *Xanthomonas maltophilia* bacteremia in immunocompromised hematological patients. Scand. J. Infect. Dis. *26*:163–170, 1994.
61. Villarino, M. E., Stevens, L. E., Schable, B., et al.: Risk factors for epidemic *Xanthomonas maltophilia* infection/colonization in intensive care unit patients. Infect. Control Hosp. Epidemiol. *13*:201–206, 1992.
62. Weber, D. J., Rutala, W. A., Blanchet, C. N., et al.: Faucet aerators: A source of patient colonization with *Stenotrophomonas maltophilia*. Am. J. Infect. Control *27*:59–63, 1999.
63. Weiss, K., Restieri, C., De Carolis, E., et al.: Comparative activity of new quinolones against 326 clinical isolates of *Stenotrophomonas maltophilia*. J. Antimicrob. Chemother. *45*:363–365, 2000.
64. Whitby, P. W., Carter, K. B., Burns, J. L., et al.: Identification and detection of *Stenotrophomonas maltophilia* by rRNA-directed PCR. J. Clin. Microbiol. *38*:4305–4309, 2000.
65. Wishart, M. M., and Riley, T. V.: Infection with *Pseudomonas maltophilia* hospital outbreak due to contaminated disinfectant. Med. J. Aust. *2*:710–712, 1976.
66. Yu, V. L., Rumans, L. W., Wing, E. J., et al.: *Pseudomonas maltophilia* causing heroin-associated infective endocarditis. Arch. Intern. Med. *138*:1667–1671, 1978.

GRAM-NEGATIVE COCCOBACILLI

CHAPTER 131 *Actinobacillus actinomycetemcomitans*

SUZANNE WHITWORTH ■ RICHARD F. JACOBS

Actinobacillus actinomycetemcomitans is a fastidious, gram-negative rod that frequently complicates actinomycosis caused by *Actinomyces israelii*. In addition to being associated with actinomycosis, it has been implicated as a pathogen in periodontal disease and is part of the oral flora. This organism is characterized by slow growth in culture and a requirement for incubation in an atmosphere enhanced with carbon dioxide.[1] Other bacterial species concomitantly isolated in human actinomycosis are *Eikenella corrodens, Fusobacterium, Bacteroides, Capnocytophaga, Staphylococcus, Streptococcus*, and members of Enterobacteriaceae.

A. actinomycetemcomitans is a pathogen in at least 30 percent of actinomycotic infections[1] (see Chapter 155). Failure to recognize this organism and treat it adequately has resulted in clinical relapse and deterioration in patients infected with actinomycosis.[2, 6] Severe forms of periodontitis, particularly localized juvenile periodontitis, also are associated with this pathogen, and studies have shown that it is related strongly to children in the 10- to 19-year-old age group.[4] *A. actinomycetemcomitans* also is an important pathogen in Papillon-Lefèvre syndrome, an autosomal recessive disorder characterized by prepubertal periodontitis and palmar-plantar hyperkeratosis.[3] Additionally, it is one of the HACEK (HACEK also includes *Haemophilus aphrophilus, Cardiobacterium hominis, E. corrodens*, and *Kingella kingae*) organisms that have a propensity for infecting heart valves. The endocarditis caused by this organism usually is insidious, with fever occurring in less than 50 percent of cases.[1] This organism also has been reported to cause pericarditis, meningitis, brain abscess, parotitis, synovitis, osteomyelitis, urinary tract infection, pneumonia, and empyema.[1]

A. actinomycetemcomitans can be cultured on blood and chocolate agar but grows poorly on MacConkey agar. Cultures require incubation in an enhanced carbon dioxide atmosphere. Growth of the organism in a blood culture may take as long as 9 days in patients with endocarditis, and thus cultures should be held longer. On Gram stain, the organism appears coccoid to coccobacillary. Molecular techniques based on nonamplification nucleic acid probes or on polymerase chain reaction can provide rapid and accurate identification of *A. actinomycetemcomitans*.[5] Because of the frequency of co-infection with this organism in cases of actinomycosis, attempts always should be made to isolate this organism in these patients.

Because co-infection with *A. actinomycetemcomitans* does occur regularly, consideration of covering this organism empirically is important, especially in critically ill patients. It is susceptible to the newer cephalosporins, rifampin, trimethoprim-sulfamethoxazole, aminoglycosides, ciprofloxacin, tetracycline, azithromycin, and chloramphenicol. It is susceptible also to penicillin and ampicillin in vitro, but test results do not necessarily correlate with clinical outcome. Vancomycin, erythromycin, and clindamycin have very little activity against this organism. In some patients with periodontitis associated with this organism, the combination of mechanical periodontal treatment with metronidazole plus amoxicillin is effective for subgingival suppression.[1]

REFERENCES

1. McGowan, J. E., and Steinberg, J. P.: Other gram-negative bacilli. *In* Mandell, G. L., Bennett, J. E., and Dolin, R. (eds.): Principles and Practices of Infectious Disease. New York, Churchill Livingstone, 1995, pp. 2106–2107.
2. Morris, J. F., and Sewell, D. L.: Necrotizing pneumonia caused by mixed infection with *Actinobacillus actinomycetemcomitans* and *Actinomyces israelii:* Case report and review. Clin. Infect. Dis. *18*:450–452, 1994.
3. Rudiger, S., Petersilka, G., and Flemmig, T. F.: Combined systemic and local antimicrobial therapy of periodontal disease in Papillon-Lefevre syndrome. J. Clin. Periodontol. *26*:847–854, 1999.
4. Savitt, E. D., and Kent, R. L.: Distribution of *Actinobacillus actinomycetemcomitans* and *Porphyromonas gingivalis*. J. Periodontol. *62*:490–494, 1991.
5. Slots, J.: *Actinobacillus actinomycetemcomitans* and *Porphyromonas gingivalis* in periodontal disease: Introduction. Periodontol. 2000 *20*:7–13, 1999.
6. Tyrrell, J., Noone, P., and Prichard, J. S.: Thoracic actinomycosis complicated by *Actinobacillus actinomycetemcomitans:* Case report and review of literature. Respir. Med. *86*:341–343, 1992.

CHAPTER 132

Bartonellosis

BARBARA W. STECHENBERG

Bartonellosis is a term that has been used to describe a geographically distinct disease caused by *Bartonella bacilliformis.* Recent advances in molecular biology have led to the reclassification of several bacterial pathogens, and the family Bartonellaceae, genus *Bartonella,* has expanded from 1 species, *B. bacilliformis,* to include 16 validated species, 8 of which have been known to be pathogenic in humans. Of the members of the genus *Rochalimaea* that have been reclassified as *Bartonella* spp., *Bartonella henselae* is the cause of cat-scratch disease (see Chapter 145). Other manifestations of *Bartonella* infection other than classic bartonellosis seldom occur in children and are discussed briefly.

Bartonellosis (Carrión Disease)

Bartonellosis is a disease unusual in its manifestations and rich in its history. The organism, *B. bacilliformis,* causes two illnesses that are both clinically and temporally distinctive. Besides producing subclinical asymptomatic infection, this organism can cause Oroya fever, a disease characterized by severe febrile hemolytic anemia, or verruga peruana, an eruption of hemangioma-like lesions. The eponym Carrión disease is used to designate the two forms collectively. The disease is restricted in its distribution to an area in South America that includes parts of Peru, Ecuador, and Colombia.

The origin of this disease in the history of the region probably considerably precedes the first written documentation of the disorder. The first written account of bartonellosis is attributed to Gago de Vadillo, who published a treatise on the subject in 1630, a century after the arrival of the first Spaniards. In 1764, Cosme Bueno first described the vector of this disease and of cutaneous leishmaniasis as the uta or sand fly.[11] The era of the mid-1800s was a period of increasing wealth in Peru because of a new industry, the mining of guano, or bird manure. With this increase came the building of a railroad from Callao to Oroya and nearly 10,000 workers from Chile, Bolivia, and China, none of whom had previously had contact with or immunity to Carrión disease.[15] An epidemic that took the lives of hundreds of workers ensued. A cavalry unit of black soldiers sent to round up deserters quickly fell ill with the disease. A physician caring for them was so impressed with the rapidity and the profound anemia of the disease that he said, “It turned the blacks to whites,” a remark henceforth frequently associated with the disease.[26]

In 1885, a Peruvian medical student (Carrión) was collecting data on the geographic distribution and clinical features of verruga peruana. Because of concern about the difficulty in diagnosing the pre-eruption period of verruga, he inoculated himself with material taken from a patient with verruga. He experienced his first symptoms 21 days after inoculation and then went on to exhibit the classic signs and symptoms of Oroya fever. He realized the significance of his experiment 3 days before he died; he had proved the unitary etiology of the two illnesses.

In 1905, Alberto Barton, a Peruvian physician, described the etiologic agent *(B. bacilliformis),* but several years passed before this organism was accepted as the cause of Oroya fever and named in his honor.

THE ORGANISM

B. bacilliformis is small, 0.2 to 1.0 μm wide by 0.3 to 2.0 μm long. It stains easily with Giemsa (purple) and is gram-negative and motile, with a brush of 10 or more unipolar flagella. On electron microscopy, the contrast between *B. bacilliformis* and other members of the genus *Bartonella* is striking. Cultured *B. bacilliformis* organisms show the retracted cytoplasm and cell walls typical of bacteria.[19] They are rod shaped in young culture and become mostly coccoid in older culture. These organisms are obligate aerobes that grow best at 28° C in semisolid nutrient agar with 10 percent rabbit serum and 0.5 percent rabbit hemoglobin. Growth is subsurface, usually in 7 to 10 days. The organism is pathogenic only for human beings and other primates, and only one antigenic type exists. Analysis of 16S rRNA sequences shows that *B. bacilliformis* is in the alpha$_2$ subgroup of proteobacteria and that its closest relatives are *Bartonella quintana* and *Brucella abortus*.[5]

EPIDEMIOLOGY

The distribution of the disease historically has been restricted to the mountain valleys of the Andes Mountains in Peru, Ecuador, and Colombia. Within these regions, it usually is seen only between the altitudes of 500 and 3200 meters above sea level and primarily in valleys that are at right angles to the prevailing wind. This interesting geographic distribution reflects the habits of the sand fly vectors, which are seen only at these altitudes. One usually acquires the disease at twilight or soon thereafter because of the feeding habits of the insects. Within the region, the disease is endemic, with sporadic epidemic outbreaks that continue to occur.[10] Recent outbreaks have occurred in nonendemic populations in the surrounding area.[14] Several isolated reports of anemia with *Bartonella*-like organisms have been reported: three cases from Thailand in 1966 and one case from the Sudan in 1969.

PATHOPHYSIOLOGY

After inoculation by the sand fly, *Bartonella* organisms enter the endothelial cells of the blood vessels, where they proliferate during the incubation period. Microscopically, masses of organisms may be noted within the cytoplasm of the cells lining the blood vessels and lymph channels, which causes them to bulge into the lumen of the vessel. The organisms may be found within reticuloendothelial cells, particularly in the lymph nodes, but also in the liver, spleen, bone marrow, kidneys, adrenals, pancreas, and, more rarely, the skin, heart, and lungs.

The organisms then re-enter the bloodstream and parasitize erythrocytes. Binding of *B. bacilliformis* to erythrocytes causes indentations and deformation of the membrane, membrane fusion is induced, and the organisms then enter into intracellular vacuoles, where they replicate.[4] The resulting anemia is caused primarily by destruction of these parasitized cells. Because as many as 90 percent of cells may be infected, profound, rapid anemia is a common symptom; the life span of infected red blood cells (RBCs) is markedly shortened, particularly in the first few days. All parasitized cells are not destroyed, and no hemolysins or agglutinins have been recovered.[22] *B. bacilliformis* can be demonstrated easily with Giemsa stain. In earlier studies, considerable controversy ensued regarding whether the parasites were within or on the surface of RBCs; Cuadra and Takano[8] have shown that they are located predominantly within the cells.

In the recovery phase of the anemia, the rod-shaped organisms change to a more coccoid form and rapidly disappear from the blood.

A patient who survives the acute phase of Oroya fever may or may not experience cutaneous manifestations of the disease, which appear as nodular, hemangiomatous lesions ranging in size from a few millimeters to several centimeters. Light microscopy reveals angioblastic and histiocytic hyperplasia of the dermis. Numerous newly formed small vessels with endothelial cell proliferation are found. Mast cells, lymphocytes, and macrophages are present.[1] Electron microscopy demonstrates that the bacterial organisms are located in the verruga, extracellular in the fine fibrous interstitium. Two types of histiocytic cells are found in the verruga: a more numerous one, clear and with many lysosomes, ribosomes, mitochondria, and cytoplasm, and a darker one, with numerous lamellar membranous structures in the cytoplasm.[21] Studies have substantiated the presence of an activity in *B. bacilliformis* that stimulates endothelial cells in vitro and is angiogenic in vivo. This finding may explain the similar pathogenesis of the verruca and the bacillary angiomatosis produced by other *Bartonella* spp.[9]

CLINICAL MANIFESTATIONS

The incubation period varies from 2 to 14 weeks, with a mean of 3 weeks. The difficulty in determining the duration of the incubation period is due to the variable symptoms of the disease. Some patients are totally asymptomatic, and disease is detected only by blood culture or on serologic survey.[14] Other patients are not anemic, but symptoms such as headache, malaise, and occasional fever develop, and *B. bacilliformis* is recovered from blood cultures. Still others have severe anemia (Oroya fever). Patients with hemolytic anemia are febrile, and organisms may parasitize the erythrocytes. The anemia develops rapidly. Patients are deeply apathetic and have a peculiar discoloration of their skin and sclerae secondary to the combination of slight icterus and severe anemia.[23] Tachycardia and soft hemic murmurs are noted; occasionally, peripheral vascular collapse occurs. Headache, vertigo, restlessness, tinnitus, and occasionally angina pectoris may be present. Clouding of the sensorium and delirium are rather common findings; these effects usually are mild but may progress to overt psychosis. The temperature usually fluctuates between 37.5° C and 38.5° C (99.5° F and 101.3° F); higher elevations may be caused by intercurrent infection. Physical examination discloses generalized lymphadenopathy.

The anemia is macrocytic and usually hypochromic, with anisocytosis and poikilocytosis. The erythrocyte count may drop to as low as 500,000/mm^3 in the first 2 to 4 weeks of illness. Reticulocytes may increase to 50 percent. The pathognomonic sign of the disease is the presence of *B. bacilliformis* within Giemsa-stained erythrocytes as red-violet rods. The leukocyte count may be normal, low, or elevated.

The "critical stage" of the anemia is the period of transition when the organism suddenly disappears from the RBCs.[23] During this time, *Bartonella* organisms change from the rod shape to more coccoid forms, the number of parasitized erythrocytes decreases, and the anemia decreases; accordingly, the RBC count increases and less hyperbilirubinemia is present. Clinically, the fever decreases and the patient stabilizes.[23] In some cases, the illness may become more severe, which suggests the development of intercurrent infection (usually with *Salmonella*). Although this complication may occur at any time, it does so most commonly during the transition period and may be noted in as many as 40 percent of patients.[7]

In the pre-eruptive stage, patients may complain of pain in their joints, bones, and muscles, as well as cramps and paresthesias. Inflammatory reactions such as phlebitis, parotitis, pleuritis, erythema nodosum, and encephalitis may occur. The anemia and lymphadenopathy of the invasive stage disappear.

The appearance of red cutaneous nodules, or verruga, is pathognomonic of the disease in the eruptive stage. Usually, they are present in the skin, but they may be found in mesenchymatous tissue. They vary greatly in number and size, from small nodules to disfiguring zonular (hemangioma-like) lesions. They rarely cause symptoms; however, larger ones may require surgical excision. This stage may last from several months to a year and may be the sole manifestation of the disease, particularly in school-age children in endemic areas.

DIAGNOSIS

The diagnosis is based on clinical manifestations, in conjunction with a blood smear showing typical organisms, or on blood cultures. In the pre-anemic stage or in patients without the typical anemia who reside in an endemic area, the diagnosis can be based on blood culture alone. The presence of typical verruga in patients from an endemic area is pathognomonic of the disease. IgM antibody may be present in both stages of the disease, as well as in some healthy persons.[12] Persons with typical Oroya fever treated with antibiotics may not have an antibody response.[10, 12] Recently, an indirect fluorescent antibody assay has shown promise for evaluating patients in both the acute and convalescent phases of the disease.[6] The differential diagnosis in the initial phase includes typhoid fever, malaria, tuberculosis, leptospirosis, brucellosis, and meningitis, as well as hematologic malignancy and aplastic or hemolytic anemia. The eruptive phase may resemble hemangiomata, bacillary angiomatosis, Kaposi sarcoma, and other nodular diseases.

TREATMENT

B. bacilliformis is sensitive to many antibiotics, including penicillin, tetracycline, streptomycin, and chloramphenicol. With treatment, the fever usually abates by 24 hours; the rod-shaped organisms change to more coccoid forms and soon disappear from the blood.

The choice of antibiotic may be guided by considerations other than simple eradication of *B. bacilliformis*, including the risk of developing intercurrent infection. Chloramphenicol is considered to be the drug of choice because it also is useful in the treatment of salmonellosis.[27] Blood transfusions may be helpful during the period of severe anemia, especially if blood is obtained from patients who have recently recovered from the disease.[22]

Treatment of verruga peruana usually is not necessary unless particularly large zonular lesions interfere with function; in these persons, surgery may be necessary. Oral tetracycline, rifampin, or ciprofloxacin (not approved for children) may be used to aid in healing of the cutaneous lesions.[15]

PROGNOSIS

The mortality rate in untreated bartonellosis has in the past been estimated at approximately 40 percent. However, the fatality rate recently has been approximately 9 percent in patients admitted to the hospital.[15] Intercurrent *Salmonella* infection increases the mortality rate. In a recent population-based study, the fatality rate was 0.7 percent.[14] With the use of chloramphenicol, the prognosis is much improved. Permanent immunity develops in most patients.

PREVENTION

DDT has been effective in controlling the disease by eliminating the vector *Lutzomyia verrucarum*. Persons can protect themselves by leaving endemic areas at night and using insect repellents. No vaccine of demonstrable efficacy has been developed.

Trench Fever *(Bartonella quintana)*

Trench fever was described first in Russia and was recognized as causing a severe epidemic during World War I, with more than a million troops infected.[3] The human body louse, *Pediculus humanus* variety *corporis,* is the vector, and humans are the only known reservoir.

The incubation period is extremely variable (from 4 to 35 days with an average of 22 days). Symptoms also are highly variable. Four major fever patterns have been described: (1) a single febrile episode; (2) a single febrile period lasting 4 to 5 days; (3) three to eight recurrent febrile episodes, each lasting 4 to 5 days (sometimes for a year or more); and (4) persistent fever lasting 2 to 6 weeks.[25] Associated signs and symptoms may include conjunctival injection, retro-orbital pain, myalgias, arthralgias, headache, bone pain (especially in the shins), and splenomegaly.

In a nonepidemic situation, establishing the diagnosis of trench fever is impossible because the manifestations are not distinctive. The relapsing form can mimic malaria or *Borrelia recurrentis* relapsing fever. A history of body louse infestation or association with an epidemic should heighten suspicion. *B. quintana* can be cultured from blood by using a modification that includes culturing on epithelial cells. Serologic testing is available; however, cross-reactions with *B. henselae* occur. No controlled trials of treatment have been performed, but dramatic defervescence has been noted with the use of tetracycline and chloramphenicol.[13, 25]

Bacillary Angiomatosis and Bacillary Peliosis Hepatis

Both *B. henselae* and *B. quintana* can cause disease in immunocompromised persons, primarily adults with acquired immunodeficiency syndrome (AIDS) or cancer or recipients of organ transplants.

Lesions of bacillary angiomatosis are the most easily recognized form of *Bartonella* infection in immunocompromised patients. They are seen predominantly in patients with AIDS and with very low CD4 counts.[13] The vasoproliferative lesions may be cutaneous or subcutaneous and pathologically resemble the verruga of *B. bacilliformis*. Most characteristically, they are red with a collarette of scale, but the clinical findings can be diverse. The differential diagnosis includes Kaposi sarcoma, pyogenic granuloma, and verruga peruana, and deep soft tissue masses may develop. Trauma may result in ulceration or bleeding. Osseous lesions occur in the long bones and can be very painful. A 12-year-old child with lymphocytic leukemia and bacillary angiomatosis has been reported.[16]

Bacillary peliosis hepatis was described first in 1990.[18] It is seen primarily in human immunodeficiency virus (HIV)-infected patients who have fever and abdominal pain. Vascular proliferative lesions develop, primarily in the liver and spleen. The differential diagnosis includes hepatic Kaposi sarcoma, lymphoma, extrapulmonary pneumocystosis, and infection with *Mycobacterium avium–intracellulare*.

Both these entities have been treated successfully with antimicrobial therapy, including erythromycin, newer macrolides such as azithromycin or clarithromycin, or as an alternative, doxycycline.[13, 18, 25]

Endocarditis

B. henselae, B. quintana, and *Bartonella elizabethae* all have been reported to cause bacteremia or endocarditis. The symptoms and signs are similar to those of other causes of endocarditis, although prolonged fever, night sweats, and profound weight loss may occur.[24] Many of the immunocompetent patients have been homeless. Cases also have been described in immunocompromised persons, particularly HIV-infected patients. *Bartonella* organisms may be a significant cause of culture-negative endocarditis.[2, 20, 24] Two children have been reported with central nervous system infection associated with *B. quintana.*[17]

Special culturing techniques, including the use of Isolator tubes, and prolonged incubation may be helpful. Initial treatment of culture-negative endocarditis with ceftriaxone and gentamicin is effective.

REFERENCES

1. Arias-Stella, J., Lieberman, P. H., Erlandson, R. A., et al.: Histology, immunohistochemistry and ultrastructure of the verruga in Carrión's disease. Am. J. Surg. Pathol. *10*:595–610, 1986.
2. Baorto, E., Payne, R. M., Slater, L. N., et al.: Culture-negative endocarditis caused by *Bartonella henselae*. J. Pediatr. *132*:1051–1054, 1998.
3. Bass, J. W., Vincent, J. M., and Person, D. A.: The expanding spectrum of *Bartonella* infections: I. Bartonellosis and trench fever. Pediatr. Infect. Dis. J. *16*:2–10, 1997.

4. Benson, N. A., Kar, S., McLaughlin, G., et al.: Entry of *Bartonella* into erythrocytes. Infect. Immun. *54*:347–353, 1986.
5. Brenner, D. J., O'Connor, S. P., Hollis, D. G., et al: Molecular characterization and proposal of a neotype strain for *Bartonella bacilliformis*. J. Clin. Microbiol. *29*:1299–1302, 1991.
6. Chamberlin, J., Laughlin, L., Gordon, S., et al.: Serodiagnosis of *Bartonella bacilliformis* infection by indirect fluorescence antibody assay. J. Clin. Microbiol. *38*:4269–4271, 2000.
7. Cuadra, M.: Salmonellosis complication in human bartonellosis. Tex. Rep. Biol. Med. *14*:97–113, 1956.
8. Cuadra, M., and Takano, J.: The relationship of *Bartonella* to the red blood cell as revealed by electron microscopy. Blood *33*:708–716, 1969.
9. Garcia, F. U., Wojta, J., and Hoover, R. L.: Interactions between live *Bartonella bacilliformis* and endothelial cells. J. Infect. Dis. *165*:1138–1141, 1992.
10. Gray, G. C., Johnson, A. A., Thornton, S. A., et al.: An epidemic of Oroya fever in the Peruvian Andes. Am. J. Trop. Hyg. *42*:215–221, 1990.
11. Herrer, A., and Christensen, H.: Implication of *Phlebotomus* sand flies as vectors of bartonellosis and leishmaniasis as early as 1764. Science *190*:154–155, 1975.
12. Knobloch, J., Solano, L., Alvarez, O., et al.: Antibodies to *Bartonella* as determined by fluorescence antibody test, indirect hemagglutination and ELISA. Trop. Med. Parasitol. *36*:183–185, 1985.
13. Koehler, J. E.: *Bartonella* infections. Adv. Pediatr. Infect. Dis. *11*:1–27, 1996.
14. Kosek, M., Lavarello, R., Gilman, R. H., et al.: Natural history of infection with *Bartonella bacilliformis* in a nonendemic population. J. Infect. Dis. *182*:865–872, 2000.
15. Maguiña, C., and Gotuzzo, E.: Bartonellosis new and old. Infect. Dis. Clin. North Am. *14*:1–22, 2000.
16. Myers, S. A., Prose, N. S., Barcia, J. A., et al.: Bacillary angiomatosis in a child undergoing chemotherapy. J. Pediatr. *121*:574–578, 1992.
17. Parrott, J. H., Dure, L., Sullender, W., et al.: Central nervous system infection associated with *Bartonella quintana*: A report of two cases. Pediatrics *100*:403–408, 1997.
18. Perkocha, L. A., Geaghan, S. M., Yen, T. S. B., et al.: Clinical and pathological features of bacillary peliosis hepatis in association with human immunodeficiency virus infection. N. Engl. J. Med. *323*:1581–1586, 1990.
19. Peters, D., and Wigand, R.: Bartonellaceae. Bacteriol. Rev. *19*:150–155, 1955.
20. Raoult, D., Fournier, P. E., Drancourt, M., et al.: Diagnosis of 22 new cases of *Bartonella* endocarditis. Ann. Intern. Med. *127*:249, 1997.
21. Recavarren, S., and Lumbreras, H.: Pathogenesis of the verruga of Carrión's disease. Am. J. Pathol. *66*:461–464, 1972.
22. Reynafarje, C., and Ramos, J.: The hemolytic anemia of human bartonellosis. Blood *17*:562–578, 1961.
23. Ricketts, W. E.: Clinical manifestations of Carrión's disease. Arch. Intern. Med. *84*:751–781, 1949.
24. Spach, D. H., Kanter, A. S., Dougherty, M. J., et al.: *Bartonella (Rochalimoea)* species as a cause of apparent "culture negative" endocarditis. Clin. Infect. Dis. *20*:1044–1047, 1995.
25. Spach, D. H., and Koehler, J. E.: *Bartonella*-associated infections. Infect. Dis. Clin. North Am. *12*:137–155, 1998.
26. Schultz, M. G.: A history of bartonellosis (Carrión's disease). Am. J. Trop. Med. Hyg. *17*:503–515, 1968.
27. Urteaga, O., and Payne, E.: Treatment of the acute febrile phase of Carrión's disease with chloramphenicol. Am. J. Trop. Med. *4*:507–511, 1955.

Brucellosis

EDWARD J. YOUNG

Brucellosis is an infection of domestic and wild animals (zoonosis) that is transmittable to humans. Humans are accidental hosts and play no role in maintaining the disease in nature. In the United States, a cooperative federal and state program to control bovine brucellosis has reduced dramatically the incidence of human infection. Nonetheless, brucellosis remains enzootic in many parts of the world, notably the Mediterranean basin, the Arabian peninsula, the Indian subcontinent, and parts of Mexico and Central and South America.[39] The World Health Organization has called for the eradication of brucellosis worldwide; however, because of a general lack of political conviction, achievement of this objective in the near future is unlikely.[100]

History

Brucellosis probably has existed since the time that humans first domesticated animals, and Hippocrates mentions a disease compatible with brucellosis (ca. 450 BC).[116] The first accurate description of human brucellosis is credited to J. A. Marston, an assistant surgeon in the Royal Army Medical Corps.[128] In 1863, Marston described an illness in troops stationed in Malta during the Crimean War. Marston's report includes a poignant depiction of his own suffering with brucellosis.[82] During the 19th century, brucellosis was known by various names, including Mediterranean fever, Malta fever, gastric remittent fever, and undulant fever.[44] Although the disease caused considerable morbidity and mortality in British military personnel stationed throughout the Mediterranean, the etiology was not immediately apparent. In 1886, David Bruce, another Royal Army Medical Corps surgeon, isolated a microorganism from the spleen tissue of victims of Malta fever.[24] He called the bacterium *Micrococcus* (later *Brucella*) *melitensis* and showed that it was present in the blood, urine, and feces of patients. Later, Bruce was appointed head of the Mediterranean Fever Commission (1904 to 1907), which investigated the disease in Malta. Themistocle Zammit, a Maltese physician working with the commission, identified native goats as the principal source of brucellosis in Malta. The goats were shown to shed bacteria in their milk, and when fresh goat's milk was replaced with tinned condensed milk in the military mess, the incidence of brucellosis declined dramatically. In 1897, Almroth Wright applied the newly discovered agglutination test to the serologic diagnosis of Malta fever.[130]

Unlike *B. melitensis*, which was isolated originally from human tissue, other *Brucella* spp. were recognized for the disease that they caused in animals (contagious abortion). In 1897, Bernhard Bang, a Danish veterinarian and physician, isolated the "abortion bacillus" (later called *Brucella abortus*) from the tissues of diseased cattle.[18] To this day, veterinarians refer to bovine brucellosis as Bang disease. Around 1914, Jacob Traum, a bacteriologist with the Bureau of Animal Industry, isolated an organism from an aborted swine fetus. Initially thought to be the agent of Bang disease, this bacterium later was shown to be a separate species (*Brucella suis*).[62]

The bacteriologist Alice Evans finally recognized the relatedness of these disparate microorganisms in 1918.[48] Evans' work was confirmed by others, and in 1920, K. F. Meyer and E. B. Shaw proposed the name *Brucella* for the genus to honor Bruce.[59]

Additional *Brucella* spp. were isolated from sheep (*Brucella ovis*) and from desert wood rats (*Brucella neotomae*), but to date they have not been shown to cause human illness. The most recent addition to the genus, *Brucella canis*, was isolated from dogs by Carmichael and Brunner in 1968.[27] However, this species is the least common cause of human brucellosis.[121, 125] Recently, a previously unknown species (tentatively termed *Brucella maris*) was isolated from marine mammals such as dolphins, seals, and whales. The role of this organism or organisms as potential pathogens in animals or humans is unknown.[66]

Etiology

Members of the genus *Brucella* are small, fastidious, nonmotile, non–spore-forming, gram-negative coccobacilli that lack native plasmids. Their metabolism is oxidative, and all strains are aerobic. Many species require carbon dioxide for growth, especially for primary isolation. *Brucella* strains always are catalase-positive, but oxidase activity varies. Although most strains reduce nitrate to nitrite, some do not. Production of hydrogen sulfide also varies, as does urease activity.[40] A variety of media, including serum dextrose agar, trypticase soy agar, and chocolate agar, support the growth of *Brucella*. Selective media are not required, except when one is attempting isolation from feces or other contaminated material. Growth of *Brucella* in vitro is fairly slow, and primary isolation may require prolonged incubation. When brucellosis is suspected, cultures should not be discarded before a minimum of 28 days.

Seven biovars of *B. abortus*, three biovars of *B. melitensis*, and five biovars of *B. suis* have been recognized. Identification of species and differentiation of biovars are based on the results of oxidative metabolism tests and bacteriophage lysis patterns.[37] Preliminary identification can be made with the use of cross-absorbed polyclonal antisera or monoclonal antibodies specific for the A and M epitopes of smooth *Brucella* strains or the R antigen of nonsmooth strains. Caution is advised when using automated bacterial identification schemes because some commercial products lack the profiles for *Brucella* spp.[19] Identification tests using polymerase chain reaction are being developed.[89] On the basis of DNA-DNA hybridization studies, the genus *Brucella* comprises a single species; however, the nomen-species classification is retained for taxonomic and epidemiologic purposes.[38, 41] Because of the risk of developing laboratory-acquired brucellosis, special precautions, including the use of biohazard safety cabinets, are recommended for the handling of specimens.[87]

Epidemiology

Brucellosis is found worldwide in domestic and wild animals, and nearly all human infections are directly or indirectly derived from animal sources.[39] Despite a wide range of susceptible animals, each *Brucella* spp. has a principal or preferred host: *B. abortus,* cattle; *B. melitensis,* goats; *B. suis,* swine; *B. ovis,* sheep; *B. neotomae,* desert wood rats; and *B. canis,* dogs. These associations are not absolute, and secondary hosts are numerous.[99] In the Middle East, for example, camels appear to be an important reservoir of brucellosis[90]; however, the course of infection in camels is understood poorly. Similarly, the role of wildlife in the epidemiology of brucellosis remains unclear.[45, 84]

Historically, brucellosis has been an occupational risk for farmers, ranchers, veterinarians, meat inspectors, abattoir workers, and laboratory personnel. Transmission commonly occurs by direct contact with diseased animals or their carcasses through cuts and abrasions in unprotected skin.[61] Another route of transmission is by aerosols of blood or other secretions through the respiratory tract or the conjunctival sac of the eye. This method of acquiring infection is especially common in abattoirs.[126] Veterinarians immunizing cattle with *B. abortus* strain 19 vaccine are at some risk of acquiring infection by accidental self-inoculation.[107]

The most common route of transmission of *B. melitensis* is through the ingestion of unpasteurized goat's milk or cheese.[124, 138] *Brucella* organisms can remain viable in cheese for considerable periods, depending on the time of curing, the salt content, the pH, and the presence of other bacteria.[93] Raw milk products are a particular hazard for travelers to countries in which brucellosis is enzootic, and in such places the disease can be contracted in food without direct animal contact.[17] The meat of infected animals is harmless when cooked adequately[106]; however, the custom of eating raw meat or bone marrow has been linked to outbreaks of human brucellosis.[29]

In the United States, virtual elimination of bovine brucellosis has resulted in a concomitant decline in human infection. Approximately 100 cases of human brucellosis are reported annually; however, underreporting by as much as 50 percent has been documented in Texas.[122] In addition, the epidemiology of human brucellosis has changed from a disease related to the production of livestock to one associated with the consumption of food, especially unpasteurized dairy products.[30, 123] Brucellosis has been shown to occur along the border with Mexico at a rate eight times the national rate and is linked predominantly to unpasteurized goat cheese originating from Mexico.[46, 138]

Brucellosis once was thought to be an uncommon occurrence in children, but susceptibility now is recognized in persons of all ages.[109] Conditions for transmission of the disease from animals to humans vary from country to country and from culture to culture. Where farm animals traditionally are raised in the home, contact between animals and children occurs frequently, thereby providing an opportunity for the transmission of zoonoses. Moreover, food-borne brucellosis is not limited to any age or sex and can occur without direct contact with animals.[134] Childhood brucellosis occurs more commonly in locations where brucellosis is enzootic and *B. melitensis* is the prevalent species.[50, 52] The clinical manifestations of brucellosis in children do not differ from those in adults,[58, 120] although unfamiliarity with the disease can delay making the diagnosis in children who are not occupationally exposed.[2, 31]

Human-to-human transmission of brucellosis is not thought to occur, but rare cases suggesting venereal transmission have been reported.[104, 118] Rare cases of brucellosis transmitted via bone marrow also have been documented.[47] Interestingly, few cases of brucellosis have been reported in patients with acquired immunodeficiency syndrome.[53] Brucellosis has been reported in pregnant women and can result in abortion[108]; however, evidence that brucellosis causes abortion more commonly than do other bacteremic infections is limited.[98] Pregnant women can be treated successfully for brucellosis without terminating pregnancy or impairing their ability to conceive again. Transplacental transmission of *Brucella* leading to neonatal infection has been suggested but appears to be a rare event.[75]

Pathogenesis

Brucella spp. are facultative, intracellular pathogens that can survive and replicate within phagocytic cells of the host.[22] Shortly after inoculation into a susceptible host, brucellae are ingested by polymorphonuclear leukocytes. However, neutrophils have limited ability to destroy phagocytized bacteria, and the organisms multiply within this protected environment.[137] The mechanisms by which *Brucella* evades intracellular killing are understood only partly but include inhibition of neutrophil granules and inhibition of the peroxidase–hydrogen peroxide–halide bactericidal system.[101, 110] Brucellae also localize within organs of the reticuloendothelial system (liver, spleen, bone marrow), where they multiply in macrophages and monocytes. As the disease progresses, the microbicidal activity of macrophages increases coincidentally with the development of cell-mediated immunity. Macrophage activation involves the action of cytokines (e.g., interferon, tumor necrosis factor) elaborated by specifically committed T lymphocytes.[67] Coincidental to the development of acquired cellular resistance, the host demonstrates dermal sensitivity to a variety of *Brucella* antigens.[64, 80]

The host response to infection with *B. abortus* is characterized by the development of tissue granulomata indistinguishable from sarcoidosis.[23] In contrast, infection with the more virulent species (*B. melitensis* and *B. suis*) more commonly results in visceral microabscesses.[129, 131]

Clinical Manifestations

The spectrum of human brucellosis ranges from subclinical (diagnosed serologically) to chronic disease (often manifested by recurrent symptoms over a period of many years).[136] Symptoms are nonspecific and usually occur within 2 to 3 weeks of inoculation. The onset of disease is insidious in approximately one half the cases. The disease is characterized by a multitude of somatic complaints such as fever, sweats, anorexia, fatigue, weight loss, and depression. In contrast to the multiple subjective complaints, often only a paucity of abnormal physical findings is present, of which fever and mild lymphadenopathy are the most common. Acute brucellosis is a systemic illness involving multiple organs or organ systems. Occasionally, patients feel well in the morning, with symptoms worsening as the day progresses. Brucellosis can be manifested as fever of undetermined origin,[31] and when untreated, the fever assumes an undulating pattern. Occasionally, symptoms related to a single organ predominate, in which case the disease is called localized.[36] Not unexpectedly, localization often involves organs rich in elements of the reticuloendothelial system.

Arthritis is said to be the most frequent localized complication of brucellosis,[56, 78, 92] and in children, monarticular disease of the hips, knees, and sacroiliac is a common findings.[81] Spondylitis and osteomyelitis also have been reported but occur less commonly in children than in adults.[71]

Neurobrucellosis comprises a variety of complications, including meningoencephalitis, myelitis and myelopathies, peripheral and cranial neuropathies, and psychiatric manifestations.[86] Fortunately, direct invasion of the central nervous system is a rare occurrence and is present in less than 2 percent of cases, predominantly with *B. melitensis*.[21, 91] Analysis of cerebrospinal fluid (CSF) in *Brucella* meningitis reveals elevated protein, normal or reduced glucose, and a lymphocytic pleocytosis. Brucellae rarely are isolated from CSF, but antibodies to *Brucella* are present in the serum and CSF in most cases.[11]

Brucellosis, like typhoid fever, can be an enteric infection in which systemic symptoms predominate over gastrointestinal findings. Nonetheless, 30 to 60 percent of patients with brucellosis complain of anorexia, nausea, vomiting, abdominal discomfort, and weight loss.[50, 58, 63, 88, 109] Rare cases of ileitis[95] and colitis[68, 119] caused by *B. melitensis* have been reported, as have cases of spontaneous peritonitis.[6] Because the liver is the largest organ of the reticuloendothelial system, it probably is involved in most cases of brucellosis. Liver function test values often are normal or elevated only mildly; however, hepatic involvement has been documented by liver biopsy, even when liver function test results were normal.[35] Occasionally, transaminase levels resemble those of acute viral hepatitis.[74] The histopathology of the liver in *B. abortus* infection is characterized by noncaseating granulomata indistinguishable from sarcoidosis.[117] The spectrum of hepatic lesions caused by *B. melitensis* ranges from small aggregates of mononuclear cells resembling viral hepatitis to collections of cells, including histiocytes and epithelioid cells resembling loose granulomata.[132] Infection with *B. suis* can be associated with chronic suppurative liver abscesses.[131] In spite of the extent of liver involvement, the lesions generally resolve with treatment, and cirrhosis is extremely rare.[85]

In the genitourinary tract, the testicles are the organs most frequently involved in brucellosis. Acute orchitis or epididymo-orchitis can be the initial complaint, but more often it occurs in the course of systemic infection.[51, 70]

The respiratory tract is known to be a portal of inoculation in abattoir-associated brucellosis[69]; however, pulmonary complications are relatively uncommon occurrences.[103] In a study of 1100 children and 400 adults with brucellosis in Kuwait, Lubani and associates[77] described 5 adults and 4 children with pulmonary complications. Hilar and peritracheal lymphadenopathy, pneumonia, lung nodules, pleural effusions, and empyema all have been noted in patients with brucellosis.

Despite the frequency of bacteremia in brucellosis, endocarditis, a potentially lethal complication, fortunately occurs only rarely.[7] *Brucella* usually affects previously damaged valves; however, infection with more virulent species (*B. melitensis* and *B. suis*) can involve normal valves. Delay in making the diagnosis can lead to complications such as myocardial abscesses and sinus of Valsalva fistulas. Hence, treatment with a combination of antimicrobial drugs and valve replacement surgery often is required to achieve a cure.[65] Other complications include myocarditis, pericarditis, and aneurysms of the aorta and cerebral vessels.

A variety of ocular lesions have been described in patients with brucellosis, the most common of which is uveitis.[111] The pathogenesis of such lesions is a matter of some speculation.[102]

Cutaneous lesions that have been attributed to brucellosis include contact lesions, rashes, abscesses, ulcers, and vasculitis.[20] Subcutaneous papules, from which *Brucella* has been cultured, have been reported in children[55] and adults.[16]

Diagnosis

The symptoms of brucellosis are nonspecific. Therefore, the importance of a detailed history, including occupation, avocations, travel, exposure to animals, and food habits, cannot be overemphasized.[132] Routine laboratory tests generally are not helpful in making the diagnosis of brucellosis; however, hematologic abnormalities are common findings.[3, 42] Unlike most infections, the white blood cell count in brucellosis usually is normal or depressed, rarely exceeding 10,000 cells/mm.[3, 28] Anemia is reported in 75 percent and thrombocytopenia in 40 percent of cases.[42] Pancytopenia was reported in 6 percent of children with brucellosis in one series.[4] Examination of bone marrow may reveal granulomata or erythrophagocytosis.[83, 127] The abnormalities usually are mild, and they resolve promptly with therapy; however, on rare occasion, severe thrombocytopenic purpura has been reported in patients with brucellosis.[139] This complication includes bleeding from various mucosal sites and carries a high risk of intracerebral hemorrhage.

Brucellosis is diagnosed definitively by isolating a *Brucella* spp. from blood, bone marrow, or other tissues. The rate of isolation from blood varies from 15 to 70 percent, depending on the methods used and the length of incubation. In some series, the recovery rate from bone marrow exceeded the recovery from blood.[57] The rapid isolation techniques in use in most clinical laboratories, such as BACTEC and the DuPont Isolator, are adequate when maintained for at least 30 days.[114]

In the absence of bacteriologic confirmation, a presumptive diagnosis can be made by measuring the titer of specific antibodies in serum.[133] A variety of methods have been applied to the serologic diagnosis of brucellosis. The serum agglutination test (SAT) using antigen from *B. abortus* strain 1119 remains the standard against which others are compared. The SAT detects cross-reacting antibodies against smooth species (*B. abortus*, *B. melitensis*, and *B. suis*), but it does not detect antibodies to rough species such as *B. canis*. For detection of antibodies to *B. canis*, antigen prepared from *B. canis* or *B. ovis* is required.[96, 97]

Human brucellosis is characterized by the initial production of IgM antibodies, followed by a switch to IgG antibody synthesis within the second week of infection.[49] After treatment, the IgG antibody concentration declines more rapidly than the IgM antibody concentration does, and in some patients, low titers of IgM antibodies can persist for many years in the absence of active disease.[26] The prompt decline in IgG antibody concentration is prognostic of a successful outcome of therapy,[54] whereas persistence of a high titer of IgG antibodies presages clinical relapse.[94]

The SAT measures the total quantity (IgM + IgG) of agglutinins; therefore, a method is needed to differentiate among antibody isotypes. A simple method uses treatment of serum with 0.05 mol/L of 2-mercaptoethanol, which destroys the agglutinability of IgM without affecting IgG.[25] No single SAT titer is *always* diagnostic, but most patients with active infection have titers of 1:160 or greater. False-negative SAT results can occur because of a prozone or the rare presence of so-called blocking antibodies. The prozone can be avoided by routinely diluting serum beyond 1:320, and blocking antibodies can be detected by the Coombs test. Among the newer serologic tests, enzyme-linked immunosorbent assay appears to be the most sensitive.[10] However, more experience is required before it replaces the SAT as the method of choice.

Treatment

Antimicrobial chemotherapy lessens morbidity, shortens the course of illness, and reduces the incidence of complications of brucellosis.[60, 135] A variety of drugs are active against *Brucella* spp. However, the results of sensitivity tests do not correlate always with clinical effectiveness. For example, β-lactam antibiotics are active in vitro, but treatment with these agents rarely is curative.[60, 72, 135]

Because brucellae are intracellular pathogens, penetration into cells is thought to be a prerequisite for an effective anti-*Brucella* drug. In addition, the rate of relapse is high unless prolonged treatment is given, usually for 4 to 6 weeks.[135]

The tetracyclines are among the most effective antibiotics for treating brucellosis, with a mean minimal inhibitory concentration of less than 1 μg/mL. Traditionally, tetracycline HCl (2 g/day orally for 6 weeks) in combination with streptomycin (1 g/day intramuscularly for 2 to 3 weeks) was the recommended treatment of human brucellosis in adults. With good compliance, this regimen yielded relapse rates of less than 5 percent.[60] Because of its longer half-life and fewer side effects, doxycycline (200 mg/day) has become the preferred tetracycline analogue. Streptomycin has been shown to enhance in vitro killing of *B. melitensis* by numerous antibiotics,[105] and the effectiveness of doxycycline and streptomycin has been documented well.[33, 135] Gentamicin (5 mg/kg/day intravenously or intramuscularly as a single daily dose) can be used in place of streptomycin, but the optimal duration of gentamicin administration has not been determined.[135] Gentamicin regimens as brief as 7 days have been used[76, 112, 113]; however, comparative studies with streptomycin have not been made.

In 1986, the World Health Organization recommended the combination of doxycycline (200 mg/day) plus rifampin (600 to 900 mg/day) as the treatment of choice in adults, with both drugs continued for 6 weeks. Comparative studies of doxycycline-rifampin and doxycycline-streptomycin generally have shown equivalent efficacy when given for 6 weeks, although the latter may be more effective for complications such as spondylitis.[9, 14, 15, 79]

Because tetracyclines are contraindicated in pregnant women and children younger than 9 years to avoid the risk of irreversible staining of deciduous teeth, alternative treatments have been sought. Lubani and colleagues[76] reported a 6-year multicenter study of childhood brucellosis in Kuwait. They recommended that children younger than 8 years receive trimethoprim-sulfamethoxazole (TMP-SMX) (10/50 mg/kg/day) given twice daily for 3 weeks plus gentamicin (5 mg/kg/day) twice daily for the first 5 days. In a study from Saudi Arabia involving 102 children 45 days to 14 years of age, Al-Eissa and associates[5] reported a high relapse rate (87%) when various combinations of antibiotics were given for only 3 weeks. In contrast, the rate of relapse fell to 8 percent for patients treated for at least 6 weeks. They reported no relapses in nine patients treated with TMP-SMX plus rifampin for 8 to 12 weeks. Others have found TMP-SMX to be less effective than doxycycline plus streptomycin.[12, 43]

The fluoroquinolones, especially ofloxacin, are active in vitro against *Brucella* spp. However, high relapse rates were reported when quinolones were used alone.[73] A study from Turkey reported that the results of a 6-week course of ofloxacin (400 mg) plus rifampin (600 mg) were comparable to those of doxycycline (200 mg) plus rifampin (600 mg).[1] Although these findings are encouraging, additional experience is needed to determine the role of quinolones in the treatment of brucellosis.

The optimal treatment of complications of brucellosis, such as meningitis and endocarditis, has not been defined with certainty. Doxycycline crosses the blood-brain barrier more effectively than generic tetracycline does, and it has been used in combination with rifampin and TMP-SMX for neurobrucellosis.[86, 91] Third-generation cephalosporins also achieve high concentrations in CSF, but the sensitivity of *Brucella* spp. varies, and in vitro susceptibility should be ensured for the specific isolates before they are used. Although individual cases of *Brucella* endocarditis have been cured with antibiotics alone,[32] most cases have required valve replacement as well.[8]

The vast majority of patients with brucellosis recover completely within a few weeks to months after receiving adequate treatment. Despite appropriate therapy, some patients suffer a relapse characterized by recurrence of symptoms and re-isolation of brucellae from their blood.[13] Obviously, relapse occurs more frequently when less than a full 6-week course of antibiotics is given. Of importance is recognition that continuing oral antibiotics for 6 weeks taxes the compliance of patients once their symptoms resolve. With few exceptions, relapse is *not* caused by the emergence of antibiotic-resistant strains of *Brucella*.[12]

Relapse and Chronic Brucellosis

In the pre-antibiotic era, the course of brucellosis was often unremitting, and chronic infection was common.[115] Since the advent of effective treatment, chronic brucellosis has become rare. Chronic brucellosis usually involves a focus of infection in bone or other tissues, and surgical drainage and antibiotics are needed for cure. Patients with chronic brucellosis often experience recurrent episodes of fever and other symptoms, and IgG agglutinins remain elevated.[54, 94] Scanning techniques (e.g., technetium 99m bone scan, gallium 67, computed tomography, magnetic resonance imaging) can be useful adjuncts for diagnosing an occult focus of infection.

Even with adequate treatment, convalescence is delayed in some proportion of patients with brucellosis. Such patients continue to complain of ill health despite the absence of objective evidence of active disease, a decline in the titer of agglutinins, and negative cultures for *Brucella*. These patients were thought to suffer from psychoneurosis or neurasthenia made worse by the infection.[115] Whether this phenomenon is a variant of chronic fatigue syndrome is not clear.[34] What is clear is that these patients do not benefit from repeated treatment with antibiotics.[135]

REFERENCES

1. Akova, M., Ozun, O., Akalin, H. E., et al.: Quinolones in treatment of human brucellosis: Comparative trial of ofloxacin-rifampin versus doxycycline-rifampin. Antimicrob. Agents Chemother. *37*:1831–1834, 1993.
2. Al-Eissa, Y. A.: Unusual suppurative complications of brucellosis in children. Acta Pediatr. *82*:987–992, 1993.
3. Al-Eissa, Y., and Al-Nasser, M.: Haematological manifestations of childhood brucellosis. Infection *21*:23–26, 1993.
4. Al-Eissa, Y. A., Assuhaimi, S. A., Al-Fawaz, I. M., et al.: Pancytopenia in children with brucellosis: Clinical manifestations and bone marrow findings. Acta Haematol. *89*:132–136, 1993.
5. Al-Eissa, Y. A., Kambal, A. M., Al-Nasser, M. N., et al.: Childhood brucellosis: A study of 102 cases. Pediatr. Infect. Dis. J. *9*:74–79, 1990.
6. Al Faraj, S.: Acute abdomen as atypical presentation of brucellosis: Report of two cases and review of literature. J. R. Soc. Med. *88*:91–92, 1995.
7. Al-Harthi, S. S.: The morbidity and mortality pattern of *Brucella* endocarditis. Int. J. Cardiol. *25*:321–324, 1989.
8. Al-Kasab, S., Al-Fagih, M. R., Al-Yousef, S., et al.: *Brucella* infective endocarditis: Successful combined medical and surgical therapy. J. Thorac. Surg. *95*:862–870, 1988.
9. Al-Majed, S. A., Al-Aska, A. K., Al-Mitwalli, A., et al.: Use of antibiotics in the treatment of human brucellosis. Curr. Ther. Res. *57*:175–180, 1996.
10. Araj, G. F., Lulu, A. R., Mustafa, M. Y., et al.: Evaluation of ELISA in the diagnosis of acute and chronic brucellosis. J. Hyg. *97*:457–469, 1986.
11. Araj, G. F., Lulu, A. R., Saadah, M. A., et al.: Rapid diagnosis of central nervous system brucellosis by ELISA. J. Neuroimmunol. *12*:173–182, 1986.
12. Ariza, J., Bosch, J., Gudiol, F., et al.: Relevance of in vitro antimicrobial susceptibility of *Brucella melitensis* to relapse rate in human brucellosis. Antimicrob. Agents Chemother. *30*:958–960, 1986.
13. Ariza, J., Corredoira, J., Pallares, R., et al.: Characteristics of and risk factors for relapse of brucellosis in humans. Clin. Infect. Dis. *20*:1241–1249, 1995.
14. Ariza, J., Gudiol, F., Pallares, R., et al.: Comparative trial of rifampin-doxycycline versus tetracycline-streptomycin in the therapy of human brucellosis. Antimicrob. Agents Chemother. *28*:548–551, 1985.
15. Ariza, J., Gudiol, F., Pallares, R., et al.: Treatment of human brucellosis with doxycycline plus rifampin or doxycycline plus streptomycin: A randomized, double-blind study. Ann. Intern. Med. *117*:25–30, 1992.
16. Ariza, J., Servite, O., Pallares, R., et al.: Characteristic cutaneous lesions in patients with brucellosis. Arch. Dermatol. *125*:380–383, 1989.
17. Arnow, P. M., Smaron, M., and Ormiste, V.: Brucellosis in a group of travelers to Spain. J. A. M. A. *251*:505–507, 1984.
18. Bang, B.: The etiology of epizootic abortion. J. Comp. Pathol. Ther. *10*:125, 1897.
19. Barham, W. B., Church, P., Brown, J. E., et al.: Misidentification of *Brucella* species with use of rapid bacterial identification systems. Clin. Infect. Dis. *17*:1068–1069, 1993.
20. Berger, T. G., Guill, M. A., and Gotte, D. K.: Cutaneous lesions in brucellosis. Arch. Dermatol. *117*:40–42, 1981.
21. Bouza, E., Garcia-de-la-Torre, M., Parras, F., et al.: Brucellar meningitis. Rev. Infect. Dis. *9*:810–822, 1987.
22. Braude, A. I.: Studies in the pathology and pathogenesis of experimental brucellosis. I. A comparison of the pathogenicity of *Brucella abortus*, *Brucella melitensis*, and *Brucella suis* for guinea pigs. J. Infect. Dis. *89*:76–82, 1951.
23. Braude, A. I.: Studies in the pathology and pathogenesis of experimental brucellosis. II. Formation of hepatic granuloma and its evolution. J. Infect. Dis. *89*:87–94, 1951.
24. Bruce, D.: Note on the discovery of a micro-organism in Malta fever. Practitioner *39*:161, 1887.
25. Buchanan, T. M., and Faber, L. C.: 2-Mercaptoethanol *Brucella* agglutination test: Usefulness for predicting recovery from brucellosis. J. Clin. Microbiol. *11*:691–693, 1980.
26. Buchanan, T. M., Faber, L. C., and Feldman, R. A.: Brucellosis in the United States, 1960–1972: An abattoir-associated disease. Part I. Clinical features and therapy. Medicine (Baltimore) *53*:403–413, 1974.
27. Carmichael, L. E., and Brunner, D. W.: Characteristics of a newly recognized species of *Brucella* responsible for infectious canine abortion. Cornell Vet. *58*:579–592, 1968.
28. Castaneda, M. R., and Guerrero, G.: Studies on the leukocyte picture in brucellosis. J. Infect. Dis. *78*:43–48, 1946.
29. Chan, J., Baxter, C., and Wennman, W. M.: Brucellosis in an Inuit child, probably related to caribou meat consumption. Scand. J. Infect. Dis. *21*:337–338, 1989.
30. Chomel, B. B., De Bess, E. E., Mangiamele, D. M., et al.: Changing trends in the epidemiology of human brucellosis in California from 1973 to 1992: A shift toward foodborne transmission. J. Infect. Dis. *170*:1216–1223, 1994.
31. Chusid, M. J., Perzigian, R. W., Dunne, M., et al.: Brucellosis: An unusual cause of a child's fever of unknown origin. Wisc. Med. J. *88*:11–13, 1989.
32. Cisneros, J. M., Pachon, J., Cuello, J. A., et al.: *Brucella* endocarditis cured by medical treatment. J. Infect. Dis. *160*:907, 1989.
33. Cisneros, J. M., Viciana, P., Colmenero, J., et al.: Multicenter prospective study of treatment of *Brucella melitensis* brucellosis with doxycycline for 6 weeks plus streptomycin for 2 weeks. Antimicrob. Agents Chemother. *34*:881–883, 1990.
34. Cluff, L. E.: Medical aspects of delayed convalescence. Rev. Infect. Dis. *13*(Suppl. 1):138–140, 1991.
35. Cohen, F. B., Robins, B., and Lipstein, W.: Isolation of *Brucella abortus* by percutaneous liver biopsy. N. Engl. J. Med. *257*:228–230, 1957.
36. Colmenero, J. D., Regnera, J. M., Martos, F., et al.: Complications associated with *Brucella melitensis* infection: A study of 530 cases. Medicine (Baltimore) *75*:195–211, 1996.
37. Corbel, M. J.: Brucella-phages: Advances in the development of a reliable phage typing system for smooth and non-smooth *Brucella* isolates. Ann. Inst. Pasteur Microbiol. *138*:70–75, 1987.
38. Corbel, M. J.: International committee on systematic bacteriology, subcommittee on the taxonomy of *Brucella*. Int. J. Syst. Bacteriol. *38*:450–452, 1988.
39. Corbel, M. J.: Brucellosis: Epidemiology and prevalence worldwide. *In* Young, E. J., and Corbel, M. J. (eds.): Brucellosis: Clinical and Laboratory Aspects. Boca Raton, FL, CRC Press, 1989, pp. 26–40.
40. Corbel, M. J.: Microbiology of the genus *Brucella*. *In* Young, E. J., and Corbel, M. J. (eds.): Brucellosis: Clinical and Laboratory Aspects. Boca Raton, FL, CRC Press, 1989, pp. 53–72.
41. Corbel, M. J.: Recent advances in brucellosis. J. Med. Microbiol. *46*:101–103, 1997.

42. Crosby, E., Llosa, L., Quesada, M. M., et al.: Hematologic changes in brucellosis. J. Infect. Dis. *150*:419–424, 1984.
43. Daikos, G. K., Papapolyzos, N., Marketos, N., et al.: Trimethoprim-sulfamethoxazole in brucellosis. J. Infect. Dis. *128*(Suppl.):731–733, 1973.
44. Dalrymple-Champneys, W.: *Brucella* Infection and Undulant Fever in Man. London, Oxford University Press, 1960, pp. 3–9.
45. Davis, D. S., Templeton, J. W., Ficht, T. A., et al.: *Brucella abortus* in captive bison. I. Serology, bacteriology, pathogenesis, and transmission to cattle. J. Wildl. Dis. *26*:360–371, 1990.
46. Doyle, T. J., and Bryan, R. T.: Infectious disease morbidity in the U.S. region bordering Mexico, 1990–1998. J. Infect. Dis. *182*:1503–1510, 2000.
47. Ertem, M., Kürekçi, A. E., Aysev, D., et al.: Brucellosis transmitted by bone marrow transplantation. Bone Marrow Transplant. *26*:225–226, 2000.
48. Evans, A. C.: Further studies on *Bacterium abortus* and related bacteria. II. A comparison of *Bacterium abortus* with *Bacterium bronchosepticus* and with the agent which causes Malta fever. J. Infect. Dis. *22*:580–587, 1918.
49. Farrell, J. D., Robertson, L., and Hinchliffe, P. M.: Serum antibody responses in acute brucellosis. J. Hyg. (Lond.) *74*:23–28, 1975.
50. Feiz, J., Sabbaghian, H., and Mirali, M.: Brucellosis due to *B. melitensis* in children. Clin. Pediatr. (Phila.) *12*:904–907, 1978.
51. Forbes, K. A., Lowry, E. G, Gibson, T. E., et al.: Brucellosis of the genitourinary tract: Review of the literature and report of a case in a child. Urol. Surv. *4*:391–412, 1954.
52. Galanakis, E., Bourantas, K. L., Leveidiotou, S., et al.: Childhood brucellosis in north-western Greece: A retrospective analysis. Eur. J. Pediatr. *155*:1–6, 1996.
53. Galle, C., Struelens, M., Liesnard, C., et al.: *Brucella melitensis* osteitis following craniotomy in a patient with AIDS. Clin. Infect. Dis. *24*:1012, 1997.
54. Gazapo, E., Lahoz, J. G., Subiza, J. L., et al.: Changes in IgM and IgG antibody concentrations in brucellosis over time: Importance for diagnosis and follow-up. J. Infect. Dis. *159*:219–225, 1989.
55. Gee-Law, B. M., Nicholas, E. A., Hirose, F. M., et al.: Unusual skin manifestations of brucellosis. Arch. Dermatol. *119*:56–58, 1983.
56. Gotuzzo, E., Alarcon, G. S., and Bocanegra, T. S.: Articular involvement in human brucellosis: A retrospective analysis of 304 cases. Semin. Arthritis Rheum. *12*:245–255, 1982.
57. Gotuzzo, E., Carrillo, C., Guerra, J., et al.: An evaluation of diagnostic methods for brucellosis: The value of bone marrow culture. J. Infect. Dis. *153*:122–125, 1986.
58. Hagenbusch, O. E., and Frei, C. F.: Undulant fever in children. Am. J. Clin. Pathol. *11*:497–515, 1947.
59. Hall, W. H.: History of *Brucella* as a human pathogen. *In* Young, E. J., and Corbel, M. J. (eds.): Brucellosis: Clinical and Laboratory Aspects. Boca Raton, FL, CRC Press, 1989, pp. 1–9.
60. Hall, W. H.: Modern chemotherapy for brucellosis in humans. Rev. Infect. Dis. *12*:1060–1099, 1990.
61. Hardy, A. V., Hudson, M. G., and Jordan, C. F.: The skin as a portal of entry in *B. melitensis* infections. J. Infect. Dis. *45*:271–282, 1929.
62. Hayes, F. M., and Traum, J.: Preliminary report of abortion in swine caused by *Br. abortus* (Bang). Mod. Vet. Pract. *1*:58–65, 1929.
63. Ho, H., Zuckerman, M. J., Schaeffer, L., et al.: Brucellosis: Atypical presentation with abdominal pain. Am. J. Gastroenterol. *81*:375–377, 1986.
64. Holland, J. J., and Pickett, M. J.: A cellular basis of immunity in experimental *Brucella* infection. J. Exp. Med. *108*:343–359, 1958.
65. Jacobs, F., Abramowicz, D., Vereerstraeten, P., et al.: *Brucella* endocarditis: The role of combined medical and surgical treatment. Rev. Infect. Dis. *12*:740–744, 1990.
66. Jahans, K. L., Foster, G., and Broughton, E. S.: The characterisation of *Brucella* strains isolated from marine mammals. Vet. Microbiol. *57*:373–382, 1997.
67. Jiang, X., and Baldwin, C. L.: Effects of cytokines on intracellular growth of *Brucella abortus*. Infect. Immun. *61*:124–134, 1993.
68. Jorens, P. G., Michielsen, P. P., Van den Enden, E. J., et al.: A rare cause of colitis: *Brucella melitensis*. Dis. Colon Rectum *34*:194–196, 1991.
69. Kaufmann, A. F., Fox, M. D., Boyce, J. M., et al.: Airborne spread of brucellosis. Ann. N. Y. Acad. Sci. *353*:105–114, 1989.
70. Khan, M. S., Humayoon, M. S., and Al Manee, M. S.: Epididymo-orchitis and brucellosis. Br. J. Urol. *63*:87–89, 1989.
71. Khateeb, M. I., Araj, G. F., Majeed, S. A., et al.: *Brucella* arthritis: A study of 96 cases in Kuwait. Ann. Rheum. Dis. *49*:994–998, 1990.
72. Lang, R., Dagan, R., Potasman, I., et al.: Failure of ceftriaxone in the treatment of acute brucellosis. Clin. Infect. Dis. *14*:506–509, 1992.
73. Lang, R., and Rubinstein, E.: Quinolones for the treatment of brucellosis. J. Antimicrob. Agents Chemother. *29*:357–360, 1992.
74. Losurdo, G., Timitilli, A., Tasso, L., et al.: Acute hepatitis due to *Brucella* in a 2-year-old child. Arch. Dis. Child. *71*:387, 1994.
75. Lubani, M. M., Dudin, K. I., Sharda, D. C., et al.: Neonatal brucellosis. Eur. J. Pediatr. *147*:520–522, 1988.
76. Lubani, M. M., Dudin, K. I., Sharda, D. C., et al.: A multicenter therapeutic study of 1100 children with brucellosis. Pediatr. Infect. Dis. J. *8*:75–78, 1989.
77. Lubani, M. M, Lulu, A. R., Araj, G. F., et al.: Pulmonary brucellosis. Q. J. Med. *71*:319–324, 1989.
78. Lubani, M. M., Sharda, D., and Helin, I.: *Brucella* arthritis in children. Infection *14*:233–236, 1986.
79. Luzzi, G. A., Brindle, R., Sockett, P. N., et al.: Brucellosis: Imported and laboratory-acquired cases, and an overview of treatment trials. Trans. R. Soc. Trop. Med. Hyg. *87*:138–141, 1993.
80. Mackaness, G. B.: The immunological basis of acquired cellular resistance. J. Exp. Med. *120*:105–120, 1964.
81. Madkour, M. M.: Childhood brucellosis. *In* Madkour M. M. (ed.): Madkour's Brucellosis. New York, Springer-Verlag, 2001, pp. 205–220.
82. Marston, J. A.: Report of fever (Malta). R. Army Med. Dept. Rep. *3*:520–521, 1863.
83. Martin-Moreno, S., Soto-Guzman, O., Bernaldo-de-Quiros, J., et al.: Pancytopenia due to hemophagocytosis in patients with brucellosis: A report of four cases. J. Infect. Dis. *147*:445–449, 1983.
84. McCorquodale, S. M., and DiGiacomo, R. F.: The role of wild North American ungulates in the epidemiology of bovine brucellosis: A review. J. Wildl. Dis. *21*:351–357, 1985.
85. McCullough, N. B., and Eisele, C. W.: *Brucella* hepatitis leading to cirrhosis of the liver. Arch. Intern. Med. *88*:793–802, 1951.
86. McLean, D. R., Russell, N., and Khan, M. Y.: Neurobrucellosis: Clinical and therapeutic features. Clin. Infect. Dis. *15*:582–590, 1992.
87. Miller, C. D., Songer, J. R. and Sullivan, J. F.: A twenty-four year review of laboratory-acquired human infections at the National Animal Disease Center. Am. Ind. Hyg. Assoc. J. *48*:271–275, 1987.
88. Mohamed, A. E. S., Ven, D., Madkour, M. M., et al.: Alimentary tract presentations of brucellosis. Ann. Saudi Med. *6*:27–31, 1986.
89. Morata, P., Queipo-Ortuño, M. I., Reguera, J. M., et al.: Posttreatment follow-up of brucellosis by PCR assay. J. Clin. Microbiol. *37*:4163–4166, 1999.
90. Mousa, A. R. M., Elhag, K. M., Khogali, M., et al.: The nature of brucellosis in Kuwait: Study of 379 cases. Rev. Infect. Dis. *10*:211–217, 1988.
91. Mousa, A. R. M., Koshy, T. S., Araj, G. F., et al.: *Brucella* meningitis: Presentation, diagnosis, and treatment: A prospective study of ten cases. Q. J. Med. *60*:873–885, 1986.
92. Mousa, A. R. M., Muhtaseb, S. A., Almudallal, D. S., et al.: Osteoarticular complications of brucellosis: A study of 169 cases. Rev. Infect. Dis. *9*:531–543, 1987.
93. Nicoletti, P.: Relationship between animal and human disease. *In* Young, E. J., and Corbel, M. J. (eds.): Brucellosis: Clinical and Laboratory Aspects. Boca Raton, FL, CRC Press, 1989, pp. 41–51.
94. Pellicer, T., Ariza, J., Foz, A., et al.: Specific antibodies detected during relapse of human brucellosis. J. Infect. Dis. *157*:918–924, 1988.
95. Petrella, R., and Young, E. J.: Acute *Brucella* ileitis. Am. J. Gastroenterol. *83*:80–82, 1988.
96. Polt, S. S., and Schaefer, J.: A microagglutination test for human *Brucella canis* antibodies. Am. J. Clin. Pathol. *77*:740–744, 1982.
97. Polt, S. S., Dismukes, W. E., Flint, A., et al.: Human brucellosis caused by *Brucella canis*. Ann. Intern. Med. *97*:717–719, 1982.
98. Porreco, R. P., and Haverkamp, A. D.: Brucellosis in pregnancy. Obstet. Gynecol. *44*:597–602, 1974.
99. Ray, W. C.: Brucellosis (due to *Brucella abortus* and *B. suis*). *In* Steele, J. H. (ed.): Handbook Series in Zoonoses. Vol. I. Boca Raton, FL, CRC Press, 1979, pp. 99–194.
100. Recommendations of the International Task Force for Disease Eradication. M. M. W. R. Morb. Mortal. Wkly. Rep. *42*:28, 1993.
101. Riley, L. D., and Robertson, D. C.: Brucellacidal activity of human and bovine polymorphonuclear leukocyte granule extracts against smooth and rough strains of *Brucella abortus*. Infect. Immun. *46*:231–236, 1984.
102. Rolando, I. M., Carbone, A. O., Gotuzzo, E., et al.: Circulating immune complexes in the pathogenesis of human *Brucella uveitis*. Chibret. Int. J. Ophthalmol. *3*:30–38, 1985.
103. Rowen, J. L., and Englund, J. A.: Brucellosis presenting with cough. Pediatr. Infect. Dis. J. *14*:721–722, 1995.
104. Rubin, B., Band, J. D., Wong, P., et al.: Person-to-person transmission of *Brucella melitensis*. Lancet *337*:14–15, 1991.
105. Rubinstein, E., Lang, R., Shasha, B., et al.: In vitro susceptibility of *Brucella melitensis* to antibiotics. Antimicrob. Agents Chemother. *35*:1925–1927, 1991.
106. Sadler, W. W.: Present evidence on the role of meat in the epidemiology of human brucellosis. Am. J. Public Health *50*:504–514, 1960.
107. Sadusk, J. F., Browne, A. S., and Born, J. L.: Brucellosis in man, resulting from *Brucella abortus* (strain 19) vaccine. J. A. M. A. *164*:1325–1328, 1957.
108. Sarrum, M., Feiz, J., Foruzandeh, M., et al.: Intrauterine fetal infection with *Brucella melitensis* as a possible cause of second trimester abortion. Am. J. Obstet. Gynecol. *119*:657–660, 1974.
109. Sharda, D. C., and Lubani, M.: A study of brucellosis in childhood. Clin. Pediatr. (Phila.) *25*:492–495, 1986.
110. Smith, L. D., and Ficht, T. A.: Pathogenesis of *Brucella*. Crit. Rev. Microbiol. *17*:209–230, 1990.
111. Solanes, M. P., Heatley, J., Arenas, F., et al.: Ocular complications in brucellosis. Am. J. Ophthalmol. *36*:657–689, 1953.

112. Solera, J., Espinoza, A., Martinez-Alfaro, E., et al.: Treatment of human brucellosis with doxycycline and gentamicin. Antimicrob. Agents Chemother. *41*:80–84, 1997.
113. Solera, J., Martinez-Alfaro, E., and Espinoza, A.: Recognition and optimum treatment of brucellosis. Drugs *53*:245–256, 1997.
114. Solomon, H. M., and Jackson, D.: Rapid diagnosis of *Brucella melitensis* in blood: Some operational characteristics of the BACTEC/ALERT. J. Clin. Microbiol. *30*:222–224, 1992.
115. Spink, W. W.: What is chronic brucellosis? Ann. Intern. Med. *35*:358–374, 1951.
116. Spink, W. W.: The Nature of Brucellosis. Minneapolis, University of Minnesota Press, 1956.
117. Spink, W. W., Hoffbauer, W., Walker, W. W., et al.: Histopathology of the liver in human brucellosis. J. Lab. Clin. Med. *34*:40–58, 1949.
118. Stantic-Pavlinic, M., Cec, V., and Mehk, J.: Brucellosis in spouses and the possibility of interhuman infection. Infection *11*:313–314, 1983.
119. Stermer, E., Levy, N., Potasman, I., et al.: Brucellosis as a cause of severe colitis. Am. J. Gastroenterol. *86*:917–919, 1991.
120. Street, L., Grant, W. W., and Alva, J. D.: Brucellosis in childhood. Pediatrics *55*:416–421, 1975.
121. Swenson, R. M., Carmichael, L. E., and Cundy, K. R.: Human infection with *Brucella canis*. Ann. Intern. Med. *76*:435–438, 1972.
122. Taylor, J. P., Pelosi, J., and Ray, B.: Underreporting of four infectious diseases by Texas hospitals. Texas Department of Health, Disease Prevention News *53*:1–3, 1993.
123. Taylor, P. M., and Perdue, J. N.: The changing epidemiology of human brucellosis in Texas, 1977–1986. Am. J. Epidemiol. *130*:160–165.
124. Thapar, M. K., and Young, E. J.: Urban outbreak of goat cheese brucellosis. Pediatr. Infect. Dis. J. *5*:640–643, 1986.
125. Tosi, M. F., and Nelson, T. J.: *Brucella canis* infection in a 17-month-old child successfully treated with moxalactam. J. Pediatr. *101*:725–727, 1982.
126. Trout, D., Gomez, T. M., Bernard, B. P., et al.: Outbreak of brucellosis at a United States pork packing plant. J. Occup. Environ. Med. *37*:697–703, 1995.
127. Ullrich, C. H., Fader, R., Fahner, J. B., et al.: Brucellosis presenting as prolonged fever and hemophagocytosis. Am. J. Dis. Child. *147*: 1037–1038, 1993.
128. Vassallo, D. J.: The Corps disease: Brucellosis and its historical association with the Royal Army Medical Corps. J. R. Army Med. Corps *138*:140–150, 1992.
129. Williams, R. K., and Crossley, K.: Acute and chronic hepatic involvement of brucellosis. Gastroenterology *83*:455–458, 1982.
130. Wright, A. E., and Semple, D.: On the employment of dead bacteria in the serum diagnosis of typhoid and Malta fever. B. M. J. *1*:1214–1215, 1897.
131. Young, E. J.: *Brucella melitensis* hepatitis: The absence of granulomas. Ann. Intern. Med. *91*:414–415, 1979.
132. Young, E. J.: Human brucellosis. Rev. Infect. Dis. *5*:821–842, 1983.
133. Young, E. J.: Serologic diagnosis of human brucellosis: Analysis of 214 cases by agglutination tests and review of the literature. Clin. Infect. Dis. *13*:359–372, 1991.
134. Young, E. J.: An overview of human brucellosis. Clin. Infect. Dis. *21*:283–290, 1995.
135. Young, E. J.: *Brucella* species. *In* Yu, V., Merigan, T. C., and Barriere, S. C. (eds.): Antimicrobial Therapy and Vaccines, Baltimore, William & Wilkins, 1999, pp. 71–89.
136. Young, E. J.: *Brucella* species. *In* Mandell, G. L., Bennett, J. E., and Dolin, R. (eds.): Principles and Practice of Infectious Diseases. 5th ed. New York, Churchill Livingstone, 2000, pp. 2386–2392.
137. Young, E. J., Borchert, M., Kretzer, F. L., et al.: Phagocytosis and killing of *Brucella* by human polymorphonuclear leukocytes. J. Infect. Dis. *151*:682–690, 1985.
138. Young, E. J., and Suvannoparrat, U.: Brucellosis outbreak attributed to ingestion of unpasteurized goat cheese. Arch. Intern. Med. *135*:240–243, 1975.
139. Young, E. J., Tarry, A., Genta, R. M., et al.: Thrombocytopenic purpura associated with brucellosis: Report of 2 cases and literature review. Clin. Infect. Dis. *31*:904–909, 2000.

Pertussis and Other *Bordetella* Infections

JAMES D. CHERRY ■ ULRICH HEININGER

Pertussis (whooping cough) is an acute infectious illness of the respiratory tract caused by *Bordetella pertussis* and, less frequently, by *Bordetella parapertussis*.[30, 36, 42, 123] The illness occurs worldwide and affects all age groups, but it is recognized primarily in children; it is most serious in young, unprotected infants.

Effective whole-cell pertussis vaccines became available in the 1940s, and the rate of pertussis was reduced dramatically in countries in which universal immunization of infants and children was implemented. Presently, acellular pertussis vaccines are in use in many countries throughout the world.[113, 155, 297] However, even with vaccine use, occasional local epidemics still occur, and evidence is growing for widespread, frequently atypical, and therefore unrecognized illness in children, adolescents, and adults.* *B. pertussis* is one of the major causes of cough illness.

History

Pertussis was noted as *the kink* (a Scottish term synonymous with fit or paroxysm) and *kindhoest* (a Teutonic word meaning "child's cough") in the Middle Ages.[38, 132] The clinical picture of pertussis was presented first in 1640 by Guillaume de Baillou, who described cases in an epidemic in Paris in 1578.[51] The term *pertussis* was not used until 1670. Isolation of *B. pertussis*, the main causative agent of pertussis, was reported by Bordet and Gengou in 1906,[22, 23] and *B. parapertussis* was recognized 30 years later by Eldering and Kendrick as a different species causing a similar illness in humans.[69, 70]

Vaccines consisting of killed whole *B. pertussis* organisms were developed shortly after the bacterium was isolated, and the first results of protection were reported by Madsen in 1925.[183] The mouse protection test, developed and reported by Kendrick and collaborators in 1947,[151] allowed standardization of vaccine production. Comprehensive studies conducted by the British Medical Research Council in the 1940s and 1950s demonstrated a correlation between the potency of pertussis vaccines as determined by the mouse protection test and their clinical efficacy in children.[196] As a consequence, immunization against pertussis, most commonly in combination with diphtheria and tetanus toxoids (DTP), became part of routine vaccination programs in many countries throughout the world.

Concern about a relationship existing between pertussis vaccination and temporally associated serious adverse events (e.g., sudden infant death syndrome and a variety of

*See references 20, 39, 40, 62, 98, 120, 175, 177, 178, 187, 210, 213, 263, 325.

neurologic illnesses) led to a sharp decline in vaccination rates in Japan and several European countries during the 1970s.[30, 36, 42, 155] This concern, along with well-documented high rates of unpleasant local and systemic reactions, led to the development of new acellular vaccines. These vaccines cause reactions less frequently and have been used in Japan since 1981 and in many developed countries during the present decade.[113, 155, 297, 308]

Microbiology

The genus Bordetella contains seven species: *B. pertussis, B. parapertussis, Bordetella bronchiseptica, Bordetella avium, Bordetella hinzii, Bordetella holmesii, and Bordetella trematum.*[55, 123, 152] *B. pertussis* infects exclusively humans. *B. parapertussis* also is a human pathogen, but it has been recovered from sheep as well.[242] Both *B. pertussis* and *B. parapertussis* are respiratory pathogens. *B. bronchiseptica* primarily is an animal pathogen that causes atrophic rhinitis and pneumonia in pigs, kennel cough in dogs, pneumonia in cats, and respiratory illnesses in other animals[55, 88, 285]; this organism also is the occasional cause of respiratory illness in humans.[46, 59, 97, 226, 257, 270, 285, 286, 322] *B. avium* is an important cause of respiratory illness in turkeys and other birds.[153]

Three additional species of *Bordetella* have been recognized to infect humans: *B. holmesii* and *B. hinzii* have been isolated from blood cultures, primarily in patients with underlying chronic illness.[54, 172, 287, 314] *B. holmesii* also has been isolated from the human respiratory tract, and *B. trematum* has been found in wounds and ear infections.[192, 301, 326]

The genus *Bordetella* consists of gram-negative, pleomorphic, aerobic bacilli that are grouped together on the basis of genotypic characteristics, and species are differentiated by phenotypic characteristics. *B. pertussis* and *B. parapertussis* are closely related organisms, with genetic homology of 98.5 percent.[8, 55, 300] However, they are listed as distinct species because of important differences, the most essential of which is the lack of production of pertussis toxin (PT) by *B. parapertussis.*

ETIOLOGY OF PERTUSSIS (WHOOPING COUGH)

B. pertussis and *B. parapertussis* are the etiologic agents of pertussis, but 95 percent of illnesses are caused by *B. pertussis.*[89, 123, 244] In rare instances, *B. bronchiseptica*, which normally is enzootic in pigs, dogs, cats, rodents, and other animals, has been isolated from humans with pertussis-like cough illnesses.[46, 59, 97, 226, 257, 270, 285, 286, 322] From 1995 to 1998, *B. holmesii* was isolated from the nasopharynx of 33 individuals in Massachusetts suspected of having pertussis, the great majority of them being adolescents and young adults.[192] Interestingly, in contrast to all other *Bordetella* spp., this organism is susceptible to cephalexin, an antibiotic that frequently is added to *Bordetella* culture media.[229] This addition may explain why the organism has not been noted in patients with pertussis in other laboratory studies.

Adenoviruses have been isolated from children with pertussis, and some researchers have suggested that several adenoviral types on occasion may cause a pertussis-like illness.[13, 50, 52, 223] However, the data of Nelson and associates[223] and Baraff and coworkers,[13] as well as our own observations, lead us to suggest that mixed infections are occurring and that the classic symptoms are caused by *B. pertussis* and not infection with an adenovirus. At variance with our view are recent data presented by Wirsing von König and associates.[320] They noted pertussis-like illnesses caused by viral or *Mycoplasma pneumoniae* infections in 83 patients in whom pertussis laboratory studies were performed and were negative. They serologically identified 33 adenoviral illnesses, 18 illnesses caused by parainfluenza viruses, 15 illnesses caused by *M. pneumoniae,* and 14 caused by respiratory syncytial virus. In young infants, co-infection may lead to more severe disease.[14, 166]

Physicians often suggest that *Chlamydia trachomatis* can cause a pertussis-like illness. However, in our opinion, the repetitive cough of *C. trachomatis* is distinctly different from the paroxysmal cough of *B. pertussis* infection, and thus illnesses caused by the two agents usually should not be confused clinically. Infections with *Chlamydia pneumoniae* and *M. pneumoniae* also cause long-lasting illness with cough.[58, 100, 320] Although infection with these agents in older children and adults can be confused with *B. pertussis* infection, true paroxysms typical of pertussis rarely occur.

ANTIGENIC AND BIOLOGICALLY ACTIVE COMPONENTS OF *BORDETELLA PERTUSSIS*

B. pertussis contains a variety of components that are antigenic or biologically active (Table 134–1).* With the exception of tracheal cytotoxin, all known virulence factors produced by *B. pertussis* are regulated by the single genetic locus *bvgAS.*[55] Under certain conditions, such as an environmental temperature of 37° C, *bvgAS* is active, toxins and adhesins are produced, and the organism is virulent in a mouse model (bvg^+ phase). In the bvg^- phase, a different set of genes (*vrg, vir* repressed genes) are expressed, and *B. pertussis* is avirulent in mice in this phase.[311] The switch from bvg^+ to bvg^- is a phenomenon common to all *Bordetella* spp. and is associated with a change in phenotype. Recently, an intermediate phase with reduced virulence and expression of specific proteins has been characterized. Although still speculative, the intermediate phase may have some function in transmission of the organism.[55, 276]

FIMBRIAE (PILI). Fimbriae are protein projections on the surface of *B. pertussis.*[211, 244, 250, 251] They are highly immunogenic, and antibody to them, as well as to other antigens, causes agglutination of the organism. Two fimbrial antigens (fimbriae 2 and 3) are the main agglutinogens; endotoxin and pertactin also are agglutinogens.[33, 250]

In the past, typing of *B. pertussis* strains was based on the agglutination patterns noted with specific antisera.[39, 68, 244, 250] Six specific agglutinogens were recognized, and typing was based on the presence or absence of agglutination by each specific antiserum. More recently, researchers have recognized that two of the agglutinogens (agglutinogens 2 and 3) are fimbrial in location (fimbriae 2 and 3) and that agglutinogens 4, 5, and 6 are minor antigens.[244, 250] All *B. pertussis* strains contain agglutinogen 1, and this agglutinogen may be endotoxin. Another agglutinogen is pertactin, but where it fits into the original typing scheme is unknown.

Fimbriae function as adhesins, but studies suggest that in infection they are not the primary adhesins but serve to sustain the attachment established by other attachment factors.[42, 251, 293, 312] In the mouse model system, immunization with purified fimbriae resulted in protection against infection when challenged with *B. pertussis.*[149]

*See references 7, 33, 42, 55, 56, 86, 108, 113, 124, 127–129, 152, 176, 180, 185, 190, 204, 211, 224, 258, 266, 293, 296, 307, 312, 331.

TABLE 134–1 ■ BIOLOGICALLY ACTIVE AND ANTIGENIC COMPONENTS OF *BORDETELLA PERTUSSIS*

Component	Characteristics
Fimbriae	Two serologic types (types 2 and 3). Antibody to specific types causes agglutination of the organism. Organisms may contain fimbriae 2, fimbriae 3, fimbriae 2 and 3, or neither fimbriae 2 nor fimbriae 3. Fimbriae may play a role as adhesins
Filamentous hemagglutinin (FHA)	A cell surface protein. It functions as an adhesin
Pertussis toxin (PT) (also called lymphocytosis-promoting factor)	A classic bacterial toxin with an enzymatically active A subunit and a B oligomer-binding protein. Effects in an animal model system include histamine sensitization, promotion of lymphocytosis, stimulation of insulin secretion, and adjuvant and mitogenic activity. It is an envelope protein that is an important adhesin. It adversely affects host immune cell function
Adenylate cyclase toxin	An extracytoplasmic enzyme that impairs host immune cell function and may contribute to local tissue damage in the respiratory tract. It is a hemolysin
Heat-labile toxin (also called dermonecrotic toxin)	Cytoplasmic protein that causes skin necrosis in laboratory animals. It may contribute to local tissue damage in the respiratory tract
Lipopolysaccharide (LPS) (endotoxin)	An envelope toxin with activities similar to endotoxins of other gram-negative bacteria. A significant cause of reactions to whole-cell pertussis vaccines. Antibody to LPS causes agglutination of the organism
Tracheal cytotoxin (TCT)	A disaccharide-tetrapeptide derived from peptidoglycan. Causes local tissue damage in the respiratory tract
Pertactin	A 69-kd outer-membrane protein that is an important adhesin. Antibody to pertactin causes agglutination of the organism
Tracheal colonization factor (TCF)	A proline-rich protein that functions predominantly as an adhesin in the trachea
Bordetella resistance to killing factor (Brk)	A 32-kd outer membrane protein. An adhesin that also provides resistance to the host's complement
Type III secretion system (bscN)	Several not yet specified proteins that secrete effector proteins into host cells

FILAMENTOUS HEMAGGLUTININ. Filamentous hemagglutinin (FHA) is a component of the cell wall of *B. pertussis* that in infection acts as an adhesin.[19, 42, 55, 156, 185, 293] Immunization of mice with FHA results in protection against respiratory challenge with *B. pertussis*.[258, 265]

PERTUSSIS TOXIN. PT is a classic bacterial adenosine diphosphate–ribosylating toxin with an enzymatically active A subunit (S_1) and a B oligomer (S_{2-5}) binding portion.* In animal model systems, effects of PT include histamine sensitization, promotion of lymphocytosis, stimulation of insulin secretion, and adjuvant and mitogenic activity. PT toxin is an envelope protein that is an important adhesin; its enzymatic activity adversely affects host immune cell function.

In 1979, researchers suggested that pertussis was a single-toxin disease, which led to the idea that pertussis could be prevented by a PT vaccine in a manner similar to the success achieved with diphtheria toxoid in diphtheria.[33, 240, 241] Although convincing arguments to the contrary have been presented, this idea persists.[248] The most compelling evidence that pertussis from *B. pertussis* infection is not a PT disease is that identical illness results from *B. parapertussis* infection and this organism does not express PT.[33, 123]

ADENYLATE CYCLASE TOXIN. Adenylate cyclase toxin is an extracytoplasmic enzyme that impairs host immune cell function and may contribute to local tissue damage in the respiratory tract.[42, 55, 129, 313] Mutant *B. pertussis* strains without adenylate cyclase result in avirulence in the murine respiratory infection model.[154]

HEAT-LABILE TOXIN OR DERMONECROTIC TOXIN. Heat-labile toxin was described by Bordet and Gengou in 1909.[23] It is a cytoplasmic protein that causes skin necrosis in laboratory animals,[221] and it may contribute to local tissue damage in the respiratory tract.

LIPOPOLYSACCHARIDE (ENDOTOXIN). The lipopolysaccharide (LPS) of *B. pertussis* is similar to the endotoxins of other gram-negative bacteria.[27, 42, 55] Its function in disease is unknown, but it may act as an adhesin.[59] It is a major cause of reactions to whole-cell pertussis vaccines.[12] LPS is a significant agglutinogen. Antibody to LPS reduces colonization of *B. pertussis* in the lungs and trachea of mice after aerosol challenge.[217]

TRACHEAL CYTOTOXIN. Tracheal cytotoxin (TCT) is a disaccharide-tetrapeptide monomer of peptidoglycan.[55, 86] It causes local damage to respiratory epithelium and may affect host neutrophil function adversely.[57, 86] The cytopathology caused by TCT probably is due to increases in nitric oxide.[55]

PERTACTIN. Pertactin is a 69-kDa outer-membrane protein that is an important adhesin.[19, 164, 229, 230] Antibody to pertactin has a strong protective effect in aerosol challenge studies in mice.[29, 266] Pertactin is an agglutinogen.

TRACHEAL COLONIZATION FACTOR. Tracheal colonization factor (TCF) is a proline-rich protein that functions as an adhesin.[79]

***BORDETELLA* RESISTANCE TO KILLING FACTOR.** A 32-kDa outer-membrane protein,[74] *Bordetella* resistance to killing factor (Brk) is an adhesin, and it resists the host's complement.

TYPE III SECRETION SYSTEM. The type III secretion system delivers effector proteins directly into the cytosol of host cells.[55, 327]

CULTURE, ANTIGEN DETECTION, AND SEROLOGY

A laboratory diagnosis of pertussis caused by either *B. pertussis* or *B. parapertussis* can be made by culturing the organisms on appropriate media, by identifying their presence by direct fluorescent antibody testing or polymerase chain reaction (PCR), and by demonstrating the presence of specific antibodies. *Bordetella* spp. can be recovered from nasopharyngeal specimens, with the highest rate of isolation occurring within the first 3 weeks of cough.[114, 282] Specimens for culture can be collected by swabbing the nasopharynx, by nasopharyngeal washing, or by nasopharyngeal aspiration.[42, 101] In general, nasopharyngeal aspiration gives the highest yield of positive cultures.

*See references 7, 42, 55, 83, 143, 164, 219, 240, 241, 295.

B. pertussis and *B. parapertussis* are most easily recovered by direct plating of the specimen from the patient onto selective media.[42, 134] Specific swabs (calcium alginate or Dacron) and media (Regan-Lowe or Bordet-Gengou agar and modified Stainer-Scholte broth) are required, and laboratory personnel should be experienced in isolating the organisms. If cultures cannot be inoculated directly, the use of Regan-Lowe transport medium is recommended. In classic disease, the culture or a direct fluorescent antibody study will be positive in approximately 80 percent of cases if the specimen is obtained within 2 weeks of the onset of cough and antibiotics have not been administered previously.[114, 234]

During the last 12 years, numerous PCR assays with primers derived from four different chromosomal regions have been developed for the diagnosis of *B. pertussis* and *B. parapertussis* infections, and they have been evaluated in multiple studies by comparison with culture and clinically typical pertussis.*

PCR has the advantage of having much higher sensitivity than conventional culture has. In a prospective study in which swabs for PCR and culture were obtained simultaneously from 555 subjects with cough illnesses, the use of PCR increased the identification of *B. pertussis* infection almost fourfold from 28 to 111.[259] Only a few studies have been reported in which the sensitivity plus specificity of PCR for the diagnosis of *B. pertussis* infection was determined by comparison with serologically identified cases.[118, 168, 170, 245, 303] In a study that our group performed, we compared PCR results with serologic diagnosis and found that PCR had a sensitivity of 61 percent and a specificity of 88 percent.[118] Similar findings have been noted in other studies.[168, 170, 246, 303] False-positive results are a potential problem with the use of PCR for the diagnosis of pertussis and other respiratory illnesses.[3, 194, 218] Therefore, internal and external laboratory controls are necessary.

Natural infection with *B. pertussis* is followed by a rise in serum concentrations of IgA, IgG, and IgM antibodies to specific antigens of the organism, as well as to preparations of the whole organism.[53, 81, 186, 199, 234] In contrast to natural infection, primary immunization of children induces mainly IgM and IgG antibodies. A serologic diagnosis of pertussis may be suspected by demonstration of a rise in agglutinin titer or by the use of enzyme-linked immunosorbent assay (ELISA) with demonstration of an increase in IgA or IgG antibody to PT, FHA, pertactin, fimbriae, or the sonicated whole organism.[102, 177, 178, 208, 210, 263, 328] Antibody responses to FHA and pertactin also occur with other *Bordetella* infections, so an isolated rise in titer to these antigens is not specific for *B. pertussis* infection.[92, 271] In addition, high antibody titers to FHA may be the result of *M. pneumoniae* or *C. pneumoniae* cross-acting antibodies.[145, 305] In addition, if age-specific control values for a population are determined, the diagnosis of pertussis can be established by high antibody values on single serum samples.[61, 208, 263, 272, 318, 325]

The use of a battery of serologic tests allows the diagnosis of pertussis in many patients with negative cultures for *B. pertussis*.[105, 208, 271] Conversely, measurable antibodies fail to develop in some culture-positive patients, particularly children younger than 3 months of age.[304]

An ELISA also has been developed for the detection of IgA antibody to *B. pertussis* in nasopharyngeal secretions as an indicator of recent infection.[87, 91, 328] *B. pertussis* IgA appears in nasopharyngeal secretions during the second or third week of illness and persists for at least 3 months.[87] However, the appearance of secretory IgA may be delayed in children younger than 1 year of age.[220] This antibody is not induced by primary parenteral *B. pertussis* vaccination. Detection with the use of ELISA of *B. pertussis* IgA in secretions may be a diagnostic aid in culture-negative patients whose symptoms have persisted for longer than 3 weeks.

*See references 64, 71, 73, 85, 96, 111, 118, 140, 167, 168, 170, 189, 194, 231, 245, 246, 259, 260, 302, 303, 329.

Epidemiology

Pertussis is one of the most highly communicable diseases; when it has been introduced into a susceptible population, attack rates of 100 percent in susceptible individuals have been recorded.[160] Infants and young children have the highest risk of acquiring the disease.

INCIDENCE

The incidence of pertussis and its mortality are markedly affected by the use of pertussis vaccine. In the prevaccine era in the United States, the average attack rate of reported pertussis was 157 per 100,000 population, versus 230 per 100,000 population in England and Wales[30] (Fig. 134–1). Previous studies, however, have suggested that reported cases represent only between 15 and 25 percent of cases that actually occur.[110, 146, 148, 277]

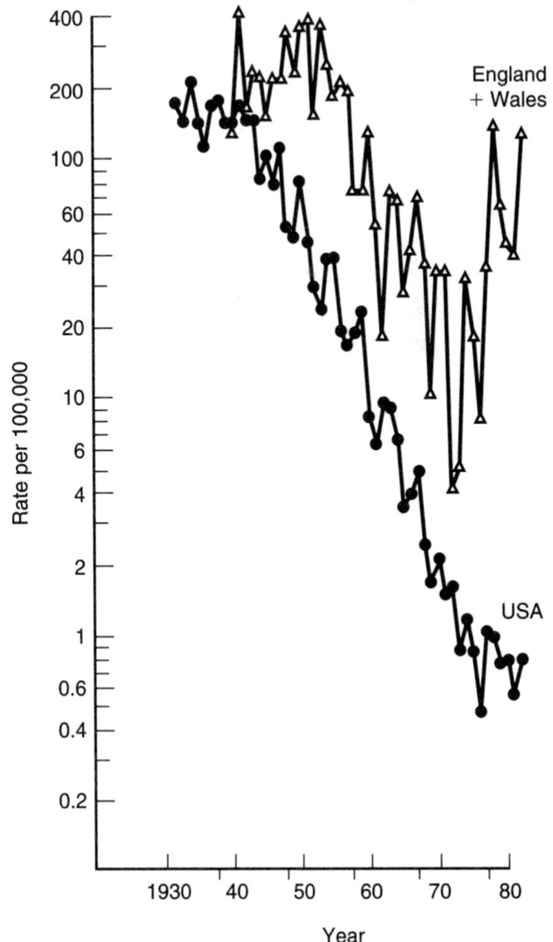

FIGURE 134–1 ■ Pertussis attack rates by year for the United States and England and Wales. (From Cherry, J. D.: The epidemiology of pertussis and pertussis immunization in the United Kingdom and the United States: A comparative study. Curr. Probl. Pediatr. *14*:1–78, 1984.)

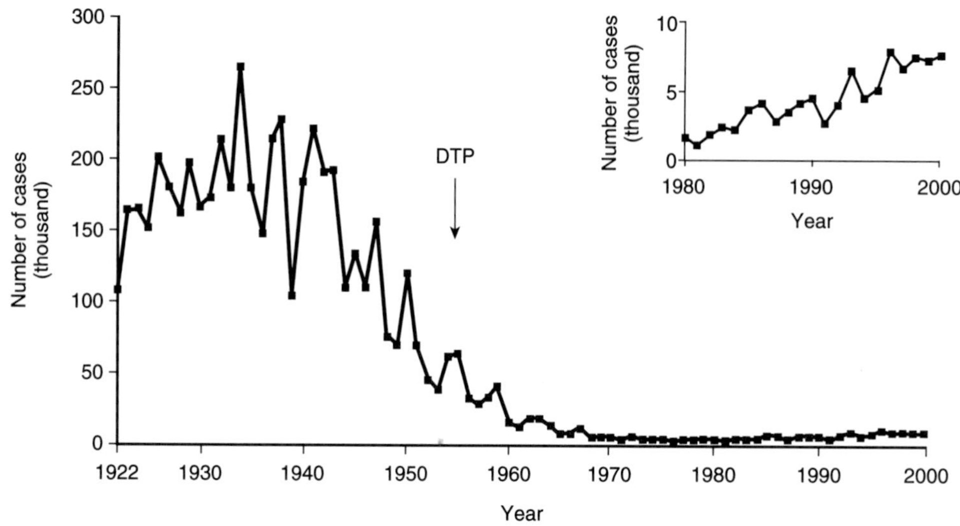

FIGURE 134–2 ■ Number of reported cases of pertussis by year, United States, 1922–2000. (Data for 2000 are provisional.) (Courtesy of Centers for Disease Control and Prevention.)

With the introduction and widespread use of pertussis vaccines, the attack rate in the United State fell approximately 150-fold from 1943 to 1976. A similar, but less pronounced, decrease in illness was noted in England and Wales. For the 7-year period 1976 to 1982, the attack rate in the United States remained between 0.5 and 1.0 per 100,000 population (Fig. 134–2). From 1982 to 2000, the attack rate curve shifted modestly upward and reached a rate of 2.9 per 100,000 in 1996.[98] The reason for this upward trend is unknown, but it is due most likely to heightened awareness of the disease (particularly in adolescents and adults) and perhaps decreased efficacy of one of the whole-cell component DTP vaccines that was used and, more recently, the universal use of diphtheria–tetanus–acellular pertussis (DTaP) vaccines, which in general are less efficacious than are most DTP vaccines.[45, 48, 93, 99]

Pertussis epidemics in the prevaccine era occurred at 2- to 5-year intervals (average, 3.2 years), and these cycles have continued in the vaccine era. As noted by Fine and Clarkson,[75, 77] this continuation of the same cycles today as in the prevaccine era indicates that although immunization has controlled disease, it has not reduced transmission of the organism in the population.[30, 35, 39]

In the prevaccine era, the following percentages of cases by age were noted in Massachusetts: younger than 1 year, 7.5 percent; 1 to 4 years, 41.1 percent; 5 to 9 years, 46.0 percent; 10 to 14 years, 4.1 percent; and 15 years and older, 0.9 percent.[30] In contrast, U.S. data from the period 1994 to 1996 revealed the following: younger than 1 year, 34 percent; 1 to 4 years, 16 percent; 5 to 9 years, 12 percent; 10 to 19 years, 22 percent; and 20 years and older, 16 percent.[98] Today, pertussis in adolescents and adults is an important source of *B. pertussis* infection in unimmunized or partially immunized children.[39, 40, 159, 174, 175, 213, 222, 298] Disease in adolescents and adults usually is not recognized as pertussis, even though the cough frequently is paroxysmal and the illness persists for weeks.[39, 243, 263]

In a study in university students, members of our group found that 26 percent of students with a cough illness of 6 days' duration or longer had *Bordetella* infections, none of which was diagnosed correctly clinically.[208] The findings in this study led to the suggestion that *B. pertussis* infections are endemic in adults and are responsible for cyclic outbreaks in susceptible children. More recent studies in the United States, Germany, and elsewhere support this hypothesis.[20, 39, 61, 63, 210, 263, 319, 325]

MORBIDITY AND MORTALITY

During the first 30 years of the 20th century, pertussis was an important cause of death in the United States.[161] The number of deaths from pertussis in the United States between 1926 and 1930 was 36,013,[89] with most of these deaths occurring in children younger than 1 year of age. The pertussis death rate curve in the United States has declined throughout this century. In infants, the mortality rate decreased approximately fivefold from 1900 to 1944. During the next 35 years, it declined more than 85-fold.[214, 215] Today, most of the deaths caused by pertussis occur in unimmunized infants younger than 6 months of age.[98] During 1990 to 1996, 57 deaths attributed to pertussis were reported in the United States.[98] Of these 57 patients, 49 were younger than 6 months. Young maternal age and preterm delivery were risk factors for fatal disease. Presently in the United States, approximately 10 deaths are reported each year.[98, 324]

Of importance is that deaths caused by pertussis frequently are misdiagnosed as deaths from other respiratory infectious illnesses.[30, 120, 227] For example, in England and Wales during the epidemic from 1977 to 1979 and at the beginning of the epidemic in 1982, 32 deaths were reported to be caused by pertussis.[30] However, when the excess deaths from other respiratory infectious illnesses were examined, approximately 362 additional deaths appeared to be caused by pertussis.

The morbidity caused by pertussis in recent years can be gleaned from numerous reports. The numbers of pertussis-related hospitalizations, complications, and deaths in the United States during 1990 to 1996 are presented in Table 134–2.[98] Of the 31,837 cases analyzed, 31.7 percent were hospitalized, 9.5 percent had pneumonia, 1.4 percent had seizures, 0.2 percent had encephalopathy, and 0.2 percent died. The most severe morbidity occurred in infants younger than 6 months of age. Of this group, 72.2 percent were hospitalized, 17.3 percent had pneumonia, 2.1 percent had seizures, 0.5 percent had encephalopathy, and 0.5 percent died.

A pertussis surveillance system was introduced in conjunction with a large pertussis vaccine efficacy trial in several regions of Germany in 1990. The initial results of this ongoing surveillance study were published in 1993.[114] Of 601 culture-proven cases, 12.3 percent occurred in infants and 86.2 percent occurred in children younger than 6 years of age. Serious complications were reported in 22 of 275 patients with follow-up. These complications included

TABLE 134–2 ■ HOSPITALIZATIONS, COMPLICATIONS, AND DEATHS IN REPORTED CASES OF PERTUSSIS IN THE UNITED STATES FROM 1990 TO 1996 BY AGE GROUP

		No. (%) of Persons				
Age	**Total No. of Persons***	*Hospitalizations*	*Pneumonia*†	*Seizures*	*Encephalopathy*	*Deaths*
<6 mo	10,093	7199 (72.2)	1516 (17.3)	205 (2.1)	44 (0.5)	49 (0.5)
6–11 mo	2282	1034 (46.0)	297 (14.8)	43 (2.0)	6 (0.3)	3 (0.1)
1–4 yr	5828	1136 (19.8)	512 (9.7)	101 (1.8)	8 (0.1)	2 (<0.1)
5–9 yr	3439	248 (7.3)	145 (4.5)	26 (0.8)	3 (0.1)	3 (0.1)
10–19 yr	5945	177 (3.0)	130 (2.3)	23 (0.4)	6 (0.1)	0
20 yr or older	4250	164 (3.9)	135 (3.4)	20 (0.5)	3 (0.1)	0
Total	31,837‡	9958§ (31.7)	2735‖ (9.5)	418¶ (1.4)	70¶ (0.2)	57¶ (0.2)

*Based on persons for whom age and clinical data were reported.
†Radiographically confirmed.
‡Excludes 28 patients whose ages were unknown.
§Excludes seven hospitalized patients whose ages were unknown. Data on hospitalization were not reported for 431 patients.
‖Excludes one patient with pneumonia whose age was unknown. Data on hospitalization were not reported for 3005 patients (9.5%).
¶Data on seizures, encephalopathy, and outcomes were not reported for 1419 patients (4.4%), 814 patients (2.6%), and 142 patients (0.005%), respectively.
Modified from Güris, D., Strebel, P. M., Bardenheier, B., et al.: Changing epidemiology of pertussis in the United States: Increasing reported incidence among adolescents and adults, 1990–1996. Clin. Infect. Dis. *28*:1230–1237, 1999.

pneumonia in 5.5 percent, apnea in 2.2 percent, and cardiorespiratory failure in 0.4 percent.

In a follow-up report of the same study, 1 of 185 culture-confirmed cases in infants was fatal.[117] In another German study from 1993 to 1996, Herzig and associates[126] noted 116 hospitalized pertussis patients with the following complications: pneumonia in 81 percent, apnea requiring assisted ventilation in 15 percent, seizures in 14 percent, encephalopathy in 5 percent, and death in 2 percent. In Canada from 1991 to 1997, Halperin and colleagues[107] analyzed the complications of pertussis in 1082 hospitalized children younger than 2 years of age and noted that 9.4 percent had pneumonia, 3 percent had atelectasis, 2.3 percent had seizures, 0.59 percent had encephalopathy, 0.8 percent had inguinal or umbilical hernias, 1.3 percent had greater than 5 percent weight loss, and 0.9 percent died.

SEASON, GEOGRAPHY, AND SEX

Pertussis occurs throughout the world.[42] Historically, epidemic pertussis had no seasonal pattern.[30] However, in the present vaccine era in North America, pertussis usually occurs in the summer and fall.[72, 90, 98, 222] In the past, the incidence of pertussis was greater in females than in males.[30, 89, 309] Between 1980 and 1996, this female preponderance was again observed, but only in older age groups.[72, 98] In the large study in Germany, 1263 (50.7%) of the 2493 subjects were females.[117]

TRANSMISSION

Transmission is thought to occur by droplets from a coughing patient that reach the upper respiratory tract of a susceptible person. Indirect spread also possibly occurs. A symptomatic patient could contaminate the environment with respiratory secretions. The hands of the new host-to-be make contact with the secretions and then may inoculate the respiratory tract.[42] Attack rates in susceptible household contacts range from 70 to 100 percent.[30, 42] Antibody studies indicate that asymptomatic infections also occur in contacts.[61, 177, 178] These asymptomatic infections are likely to be short lived and probably are not important with regard to contagion. Transmissibility is greatest early in the illness, during the catarrhal and early paroxysmal phases.

Pathology

Inflammation of the mucosal lining of the respiratory tract may be observed.[30, 42, 173] *B. pertussis* organisms multiply only in association with ciliated epithelium, with subsequent congestion and infiltration of the mucosa by lymphocytes and polymorphonuclear leukocytes. Inflammatory debris accumulates in the lumen of the bronchi. Peribronchial lymphoid hyperplasia occurs early in infection, followed by a necrotizing process that affects the midzonal and basilar layers of the bronchial epithelium. A bronchopneumonia may develop, along with necrosis and desquamation of the superficial epithelial layers of small bronchi. Bronchiolar obstruction and atelectasis are the result of accumulation of mucous secretions.

Pathologic changes in the brain and liver also have been described. Microscopic or gross cerebral hemorrhage may be noted, and cortical atrophy has been observed. These changes most likely are the result of anoxic brain damage. In some studies of pertussis encephalopathy, the findings suggested meningoencephalitis with perivascular cuffs of lymphocytes within cerebral gray matter and pleocytosis.[321] However, the studies in which inflammation was demonstrated were performed before modern virologic techniques became available. Probably, the neurologic findings in these instances were due to interactions with neurotropic viruses or other infectious agents and were not the result of *B. pertussis* infection.[42] Fatty infiltration of the liver has been noted in patients with pertussis encephalopathy.

Pathogenesis and Immunity

After the patient is exposed to *B. pertussis*, the pathogenesis of infection depends on four important steps: attachment, evasion of host defenses, local damage, and systemic disease.[42, 55, 86, 127, 217, 219, 221, 244, 312] The biologically active antigenic components of *B. pertussis* listed in Table 134–1 have various roles in pathogenesis.

Infection is initiated in the respiratory tract by the attachment of *B. pertussis* organisms to the cilia of ciliated epithelial cells.[312] Adhesins (FHA, PT, fimbriae, LPS, TCF, Brk, and pertactin) facilitate this attachment.[55, 152, 219, 244, 293, 312] Studies suggest that FHA and pertactin may act synergistically.[19, 156, 164] Because the fimbriae of some gram-negative bacteria are important for attachment, researchers have assumed that *B. pertussis* fimbriae are important in attachment. However, in one tissue culture study, fimbriae did not mediate the attachment of organisms to cells.[296] In a more recent study, investigators found that fimbriae played a role in attachment in persistent infection.[211] Furthermore, antibodies against fimbriae were shown to provide protection against colonization with *B. pertussis* in the murine respiratory tract.[316]

Both adenylate cyclase and PT adversely affect immune cell function and, therefore, allow infection, once initiated, to continue.[42, 129, 219] PT prevents migration of lymphocytes and macrophages to areas of infection and adversely affects phagocytosis and intracellular killing. Adenylate cyclase enters phagocytic cells and catalyzes excessive production of cyclic adenosine monophosphate, which results in a decrease in phagocytosis.

Tracheal cytotoxin, heat-labile toxin, and adenylate cyclase all have been implicated as contributors to local tissue damage in the respiratory tract.[42, 86, 221] Of these toxins, tracheal cytotoxin is likely to be the most important.[86] In hamster tracheal organ cultures, tracheal cytotoxin selectively destroys ciliated cells in a manner similar to that seen in *B. pertussis* infection, and the pathologic process is similar to that noted in human pertussis autopsy studies. During the last few years, several other *Bordetella* virulence factors have been described and have been characterized to some extent in mouse models[55, 74, 79, 152, 327] (see Table 134–1). Determination of their precise roles, however, requires further investigation.

Pertussis is a unique illness in that it has only one manifestation of systemic disease in uncomplicated infection: leukocytosis with lymphocytosis caused by PT.[42, 123, 141] T and B lymphocytes increase to a similar extent in the circulation.[18] In contrast with *B. pertussis* infection, lymphocytosis is not a characteristic of *B. parapertussis* infection because this organism does not liberate PT.

The most important systemic complication of pertussis is encephalopathy, the mechanism for which is not known. The most likely explanation is anoxia associated with coughing paroxysms.

Some investigators have suggested that pertussis is a toxin-mediated disease caused by PT.[240, 241] Although this idea still is entertained by some researchers,[248] little evidence supports it. Undoubtedly, PT is a fascinating protein with multiple activities in experimental animals, such as histamine sensitization, promotion of lymphocytosis, effects on glucose metabolism, and induction of adjuvant and mitogenic activity.[42, 83, 219] However, in infections in humans, the only effects that appear to be caused by PT are lymphocytosis and mild, compensated hyperinsulinemia. PT has been suggested to be the cause of the prolonged cough in pertussis. However, because persistent cough is a major manifestation of *B. bronchiseptica* infection in dogs and *B. parapertussis* infection in children and because neither organism liberates PT, this hypothesis should be refuted.[123, 229]

Cell-mediated immune function is altered by *B. pertussis* infection. In some studies, cell-mediated immunity was depressed, whereas in others it was augmented.[233]

A variety of antibodies develop after exposure of the human host to infection with *B. pertussis*. The development of agglutinins, hemagglutination-inhibiting antibodies, and bactericidal antibodies has been described.[30] ELISA techniques have demonstrated class-specific antibodies (IgA, IgE, IgG, and IgM) to many of the specific proteins of *B. pertussis*.[112, 186, 234] These antibodies develop after infection and also after immunization (except IgA). Neutralizing antibody to PT likewise develops after both infection and immunization.[103, 234] Specific IgA antibodies to PT and FHA also can be demonstrated in nasopharyngeal secretions and saliva.[91, 328]

At present, both *B. pertussis* infection and immunization with whole-cell or acellular pertussis vaccines clearly elicit protection of varying degree and duration against pertussis. The prevailing opinion throughout the last century was that immunity after *B. pertussis* infection is lifelong whereas vaccine-induced immunity is relatively short lived. Although the latter clearly is true,[77] studies by members of our research group suggest that the former opinion regarding infection-induced immunity is wrong.[36, 38, 41, 263] Proceeding from the fact that IgA antibodies to pertussis antigens (PT, FHA, and pertactin) result from infection and not primary vaccination, our group studied the prevalence of these antibodies in the sera of similarly aged young German and American men.[41] In Germany, routine childhood immunization was not carried out during the 1970s and 1980s, and pertussis was epidemic. To our surprise, the rate and mean values of IgA antibodies in the two populations were similar, thus suggesting that adult infection rates were similar. In another study in Germany, we found that *Bordetella* infections were common occurrences in adults (133 per 100,000 population), and they often occurred in those with a known history of childhood pertussis.[263]

The nature of immunity in pertussis is not known. The consensus has been that serum antibodies above some unknown concentration to one or more of the pertussis antigens are responsible for protection.[61] Antibodies to PT, FHA, and pertactin have been shown to be protective in animal model systems.[19, 56, 164, 258, 266] However, no serologic correlates of immunity had been established until recently, although several large vaccine trials were performed during the last 15 years.[1, 93, 99, 169, 268, 271, 292] In a nested household contact study, our group was able to evaluate the roles of IgG antibodies to PT, FHA, pertactin, and fimbriae 2 by determining pre-exposure imputed values in children at the time of household exposure to *B. pertussis* infection by using both classification tree and logistic regression methods.[43] The imputed geometric mean antibody values to PT, pertactin, and fimbriae 2 were higher in non-cases than cases. In the classification tree analysis, however, only antibodies against pertactin and PT contributed significantly to protection. Specifically, subjects with an imputed pertactin value of less than 7 EU/mL had a 67 percent likelihood of infection regardless of the PT value. All subjects with a pertactin value of 7 EU/mL or higher and a PT value of 66 EU/mL or higher were non-cases. In contrast, if the pertactin value was 7 EU/mL or greater and the PT value was less than 66 EU/mL, the predicted probability of being a case was 31 percent. Logistic regression analysis also found that high pertactin values were associated with prevention of illness after household exposure. In the presence of antibodies to pertactin, PT, and fimbriae 2, the additional presence of antibody to FHA did not contribute to protection. In accordance with our findings, data from a Swedish study indicate that antibody to pertactin correlates with protection and that antibodies to PT and fimbriae contribute to protection.[280]

In addition to humoral responses to several *B. pertussis* antigens, evidence exists that cell-mediated immune responses to PT, FHA, and pertactin also occur.[9, 184, 205–207, 254, 255, 291, 315, 330] Studies in a murine respiratory infection model suggest that cellular immunity plays an important role in bacterial clearance and augments the effects of antibody by predominantly T-helper-1 (T_H1) cell stimulation.[205, 206] Studies in humans demonstrate a cellular immune response shortly after natural infection with *B. pertussis,* with PT, FHA, and pertactin preferentially inducing the synthesis of T_H1 cells.[315] Immunization with a whole-cell pertussis vaccine results in a T_H1 response, whereas the response to acellular vaccines is more heterogeneous and involves both T_H1 and T_H2 cells.[315] Persistent memory T and B cells and anamnestic antibody responses are important in long-term immunity.[184]

Immunity after *B. pertussis* infection or vaccination with a whole-cell pertussis vaccine does not protect against illness caused by *B. parapertussis,* and, similarly, infection with *B. parapertussis* does not induce protection against disease caused by *B. pertussis.*[162, 288] However, in our recent vaccine efficacy trial in Germany, the results showed some evidence that the acellular pertussis multicomponent vaccine protected against *B. parapertussis* infections, whereas the whole-cell vaccine did not.[121]

Clinical Manifestations

The *clinical* manifestations of *B. pertussis* infection have considerable variation that depends on age, previous immunization or infection, the presence of passively acquired antibody, and perhaps other factors such as the degree of exposure, host genetic and acquired factors, and the genotype of the organism. The incubation period for pertussis generally varies between 6 and 20 days, with most cases having an onset 7 to 10 days after exposure. However, after household exposure, 22 percent of secondary cases were noted to have an onset more than 4 weeks after the onset of illness in the primary case.[116]

CLASSIC ILLNESS

Classic illness occurs as a primary infection in unimmunized children between 1 and 10 years of age.[38, 42, 89, 233] The illness usually lasts 6 to 8 weeks and has three stages: catarrhal, paroxysmal, and convalescent. The initial illness is characterized by rhinorrhea, lacrimation, and mild cough suggesting a common cold. Body temperature usually is normal. The severity of the cough gradually increases over a period of 1 to 2 weeks, but pertussis usually is not suspected until the cough becomes paroxysmal.

After the catarrhal period, the coughs increase in severity and number. Repetitive series of 5 to 10 or more forceful coughs during a single expiration can be noted. These paroxysms are followed by a sudden massive inspiratory effort, and a characteristic whoop may occur as air is forcefully inhaled through a narrowed glottis. Cyanosis, bulging eyes, protrusion of the tongue, salivation, lacrimation, and distention of neck veins occur during paroxysms. Several paroxysmal coughing episodes with their associated massive inspiratory effort may occur sequentially until the child succeeds in dislodging the obstructing mucus. Post-tussive vomiting is a common occurrence. Paroxysms may strike several times per hour, and they occur during both day and night.

The paroxysmal episodes are exhausting, and patients frequently appear dazed and apathetic. Weight loss may occur as a result of vomiting and because eating and drinking may be resisted because they trigger attacks. Attacks also may be triggered by yawning, sneezing, or physical exertion. Between attacks, the patient may appear normal and usually is in no distress.

Common and important complications of classic pertussis include pneumonia, otitis media, seizures, and encephalopathy. Pneumonia may be caused by *B. pertussis* or secondary bacterial invaders. Atelectasis may develop as a result of the mucus plugs. The forcefulness of the paroxysms can cause rupture of the alveoli, which produces interstitial or subcutaneous emphysema.

Otitis media is a common occurrence and frequently is caused by *Streptococcus pneumoniae.* Pertussis also has been associated with activation of latent tuberculosis. Convulsions and coma may be observed. These findings may be a reflection of cerebral hypoxia related to asphyxia. Rarely, subarachnoid and intraventricular hemorrhage may occur. Tetanic seizures may be associated with the severe alkalosis that results from the loss of gastric contents caused by persistent vomiting.

Other complications that have been noted include ulcer of the frenulum of the tongue, epistaxis, melena, subconjunctival hemorrhage, subdural hematoma, spinal epidural hematoma, rupture of the diaphragm, umbilical hernia, inguinal hernia, rectal prolapse, dehydration, meningoencephalitis, the syndrome of inappropriate antidiuretic hormone secretion, apnea, rib fracture, and nutritional disturbances.[26, 38, 144, 191, 243, 269, 310]

The convalescent stage, which usually lasts 1 to 2 weeks, is characterized by a decreasing frequency and severity of coughing episodes, whooping, and vomiting. All cases of classic pertussis caused by primary infection have leukocytosis secondary to lymphocytosis. Fever and pharyngitis are not usual manifestations in pertussis, and, therefore, a search for a secondary cause should be undertaken when they occur. Except for the observation of typical paroxysms, physical examination in pertussis usually is unrewarding. Diffuse rhonchi may be noted on auscultation.

Infection with *B. parapertussis* causes an illness that is similar to that caused by *B. pertussis,* but generally it is less severe and of shortened duration.[123]

MILD ILLNESS

Mild nonclassic illness is a common occurrence with *B. pertussis* infection.[114, 117, 259] It occurs in previously vaccinated children and also as a primary infection in nonvaccinated children. In a study in which physicians sent nasopharyngeal specimens from children with cough illness, regardless of whether the illness was typical of pertussis, to our laboratory,[114] 247 culture-positive cases were noted. Of these, 47 percent had a total cough illness duration of 28 days or less. In 26 percent, the duration of cough was less than 3 weeks. The vast majority of these cases occurred in unvaccinated children. In a 6-year, similar study involving 2592 culture-positive, previously unvaccinated children, 38 percent had a cough illness duration of 28 days or less, and in 17 percent, the duration was 21 days or less.[117] In a study in which both culture and PCR were used for the diagnosis of *B. pertussis* infection, many mild cases were found to be PCR-positive and culture-negative.[259] Of these cases, only 68 percent had a cough illness lasting 4 weeks or longer, and only 57 percent and 32 percent had paroxysmal cough and whoop, respectively.

INFANTS

Pertussis in infancy is unique. Its spectrum of clinical manifestations varies by age, immunization, and the presence or absence of transplacentally acquired antibody.[14, 30, 42, 47, 72, 120, 193, 222, 227] In the United States from 1990 to 1996, the rate of hospitalization was 67 percent; pneumonia, 15 percent; seizures, 2 percent; encephalopathy, 0.4 percent; and death, 0.4 percent.[98]

B. pertussis infection in neonates is particularly severe, with a death rate between 1 and 3 percent.[14, 47, 98, 120, 122, 136, 171, 193] A common initial finding is apnea, and typical coughing is not observed. Seizures in association with apnea occur frequently. Severe disease in young infants frequently is associated with marked leukocytosis; total white blood cell counts in the range of 30,000 to 60,000 cells/μL are seen with lymphocytosis.

Whoop is a rare manifestation of illness in infants, and other respiratory manifestations frequently are confused with those caused by respiratory viruses.[30] *B. pertussis* infection may be a cause of sudden infant death syndrome.[122, 171, 227]

ADULTS

An increased awareness of adult pertussis has occurred in recent years.* Unrecognized pertussis cases in adults often are the source from which infants and children become infected.[14, 39, 47, 120, 193, 222, 263] All adults previously have been exposed to *B. pertussis* antigens by immunization, infection, or both,[41, 61, 63] which tends to modify their illness. In a U.S. study, the following cough characteristics were noted in 31 university students with laboratory evidence of *Bordetella* infection: the median duration was 21 days before initial evaluation, 94 percent had one or more coughing episodes per hour, and 90 percent of the coughs had a staccato or paroxysmal quality.[208] Despite these findings, pertussis was not suspected in any of the students, and clinical diagnoses by the primary care providers included upper respiratory tract infection (39%), bronchitis (48%), and other diagnoses (16%). Although specific records were not available, most of these students probably were vaccinated as children and almost certainly had previous, unrecognized infections.[41, 61]

In contrast to these findings in the United States, in a study in Germany, adults were found to be more likely to have typical pertussis, even though the epidemiologic data suggested that all had a previous infection and 26 percent of 64 patients with laboratory evidence of infection recalled having had pertussis during childhood.[41, 263] Rates of clinical manifestations in the 64 laboratory-confirmed cases were as follows: paroxysms, 70 percent; whoop, 38 percent; post-tussive phlegm, 66 percent; and post-tussive vomiting, 17 percent. The clinical diagnosis in 39 percent was definite or probable pertussis; only 14 percent were thought to not have pertussis. Of note is that the clinical diagnosis was not made by primary care physicians but by a small team of specially trained central investigators with high awareness for pertussis.

In a German household contact study, similar findings were noted[243]: 80 percent of 79 adults with laboratory-confirmed *B. pertussis* infection coughed for 3 or more weeks and 63 percent had spasmodic cough for 3 or more weeks. In addition, in 53 percent of patients, coughing was followed by choking or vomiting. However, only 8 percent of the adults in this study had whoops. Complications that were observed included pneumonia, rib fracture, inguinal hernia, and severe weight loss. Unique sweating episodes are reported in approximately 5 percent of adults, and fainting can occur in association with coughing.[62, 243]

*See references 20, 39, 61, 63, 72, 98, 130, 145, 159, 208, 210, 222, 225, 243, 249, 252, 263, 290, 319, 325.

Diagnosis and Differential Diagnosis

In classic disease, the clinical diagnosis of pertussis should be made without difficulty. However, the etiology of the illness could be *B. pertussis, B. parapertussis,* or other *Bordetella* spp. A history of contact with a known case (laboratory confirmed) will help make the diagnosis in a patient with mild or atypical illness. The presence of leukocytosis with lymphocytosis in a child with a cough illness or the presence of apnea in an infant is a strong indication that the illness is caused by *B. pertussis* and not *B. parapertussis*. In a matched-control comparison, none of 11 children with culture-proven *B. parapertussis* infection versus 7 of 22 (32%) with *B. pertussis* infection had a lymphocytosis of 10,000 or more cells/μL.[123] A lymphocytosis of 10,000 or more cells/μL is observed in few other diseases.

A definitive diagnosis is made by culture or specific antibody studies. *B. pertussis* and *B. parapertussis* can be recovered from nasopharyngeal specimens and are differentiated from each other by specific agglutination reactions or by specific fluorescent antibody staining of suspicious colonies. PCR has been demonstrated to have greater sensitivity than culture has and is particularly useful in making the diagnosis in mild cases, in patients who have received antibiotics, and in patients studied late in the illness.[118, 167, 170, 246, 303] Care should be taken when assessing PCR results because false-positive results can be a problem.

Obtaining a routine laboratory diagnosis of *B. pertussis* infection in adults or in other atypical cases is hampered by the fact that medical care usually is not sought until the third or fourth week of the illness and antibiotics have frequently been administered before the possibility of pertussis was considered.[208, 263]

Serologic testing for *B. pertussis* infection in the clinical setting is neither standardized nor widely available.[42, 234] In the research setting, the use of ELISA has contributed significantly to making the diagnosis of *B. pertussis* infection in many patients with negative cultures.[63, 102, 177, 178, 208, 210, 263, 325] Most useful has been the determination of IgG and IgA antibodies to PT and FHA. The most reliable proof of acute infection is the demonstration of a significant increase in antibody values between acute- and convalescent-phase serum specimens. Frequently, because collection of acute-phase specimens is delayed and, therefore, the acute-phase values already are elevated, significant increases between first and second serum specimens cannot be demonstrated. However, a diagnosis frequently can be made on the basis of a high value or values on a single serum specimen.[61, 208, 263, 318, 325]

Because *B. parapertussis* infection induces cross-reacting antibodies to *B. pertussis* FHA, the use of this antigen alone cannot differentiate *B. pertussis* from *B. parapertussis* infection.[92, 271]

Measurement of agglutinating antibodies also is useful for the diagnosis of *B. pertussis* infection, and because the test is simple, inexpensive, and accurate, it can be used in the clinical setting.[61, 119, 208, 234, 263] Unfortunately, its sensitivity is low.

Other infectious agents that cause illnesses with cough that can be confused with pertussis are *M. pneumoniae, C. trachomatis, C. pneumoniae,* and adenoviruses and other respiratory viruses.[30, 42, 50, 52, 58, 100, 223, 320]

Spasmodic attacks of coughing may be observed in infants with bronchiolitis, bacterial pneumonia, cystic fibrosis, tuberculosis, and other diseases that cause lymphadenopathy with extrinsic compression of the trachea and bronchi. Generally, these disorders can be differentiated from infection with *B. pertussis* by the associated clinical and laboratory findings and their course. In addition, the cough associated with sinusitis can be confused with that caused by *B. pertussis* infection. Airway foreign bodies on occasion can result in confusion in diagnosis. One of the authors has seen a child with typical pertussis in whom the head and neck surgeon performed bronchoscopy because of concern that a foreign body was causing the problem.

Treatment

Several antibiotics have in vitro efficacy against *B. pertussis*.[135, 137–139] The first choice for treatment is oral erythromycin, which will ameliorate the symptoms if given early during the course of the illness and will eliminate the organism from the nasopharynx within a few days, thereby shortening the period of contagiousness.[17] The dose for children is 40 to 50 mg/kg/day given every 6 hours for 14 days; the dose for adults is 2 g/day given every 6 hours for 14 days. Recently, 7 days of erythromycin estolate was shown in a large study in Canada to be as efficacious as 14 days of treatment.[104] The newer macrolides, azithromycin (10–12 mg/kg/day in a single dose) for 5 days or clarithromycin (15–20 mg/kg/day in two divided doses) for 7 days, also can be expected to be effective.[6] The dose of azithromycin for adults is 500 mg/day for 5 days, and the adult dose of clarithromycin is 1 gm/day in two doses for 7 days. Although rare, the use of erythromycin in young infants is associated with hypertrophic pyloric stenosis, so parents need to be educated about the symptoms of this potential risk.[133] Trimethoprim-sulfamethoxazole can be used as an alternative agent in those who cannot tolerate erythromycin.[138] The first erythromycin-resistant strain of *B. pertussis* was isolated from a 2-month-old male infant in Yuma County, Arizona, in June 1994.[166] The isolate was highly resistant, with a minimal inhibitory concentration of greater than 64 µg/mL (the usual minimal inhibitory concentration of erythromycin is 0.02 to 0.1 µg/mL). More recently, two more resistant *B. pertussis* strains have been recovered from cases in California and Utah.[157, 163]

Supportive care includes avoidance of factors that provoke attacks of coughing and maintenance of hydration and nutrition. In the hospital, gentle suction to remove secretions and well-humidified oxygen may be required, particularly in infants with pneumonia and significant respiratory distress. In severe infections in neonates and young infants, assisted ventilation may be necessary.

The use of corticosteroids has received attention in the treatment of pertussis. Cortisone treatment of murine pertussis increased the mortality rate.[142] In contrast, Zoumboulakis and associates[332] found that a 7-day course of steroids and erythromycin reduced the number of coughing paroxysms and episodes of vomiting significantly, in addition to shortening the duration of symptoms. Unfortunately, this study was not controlled rigorously.

The use of salbutamol also may be of some value, but definitive studies are needed to confirm the efficacy of this mode of treatment.[24]

Prognosis

The prognosis in pertussis is related directly to the patient's age. In older children and adults, the prognosis is good, but infants have a significant risk of death and development of encephalopathy.[72, 98] In addition, long-term follow-up suggests that apnea or seizures at the time of disease may be associated with subsequent intellectual impairment.[284] The present availability of pediatric intensive care units and assisted ventilation has reduced the rate of mortality in infants who get medical care.[120] Unfortunately, many deaths occur outside the hospital. No evidence has shown that pertussis impairs ventilatory function later in life.[147]

Prevention

VACCINE EFFICACY

Whole-Cell Vaccines

The first pertussis vaccines were developed more than 75 years ago, and effective vaccines have enjoyed worldwide use for approximately 50 years.[30] In the United States, a minimal-potency standard for vaccine was established in 1949, and in 1953, a standard unit was established. Adsorbed triple vaccines (DTP) have been used widely since originally recommended in 1947. An international standard was established in 1964, at which time the recommended dose of vaccine contained at least 4 IU. The potency of vaccine in international units was ascertained by the intracerebral mouse protection test, and toxicity was assessed by the mouse weight gain test.

After World War II, extensive vaccine trials were organized by the British Medical Research Council. Five British and American vaccines were evaluated in 1951 in a series of 10 field trials that involved 3801 vaccinees and 3757 children who did not receive pertussis vaccine but who did receive an anticatarrhal vaccine (controls).[195] Overall vaccine efficacy was 78.4 percent. When secondary attack rates were examined in families, an efficacy rate of 79.2 percent was noted. The secondary attack rate in families of vaccinees was 18.2 percent, whereas it was 87.3 percent in the control group.

The results of 18 other trials conducted between 1948 and 1954 were published in 1956.[196] In 11 trials, various British vaccines were compared with vaccines produced in the United States. In these trials, 557 children were immunized; the attack rate in vaccinees exposed at home was 14 percent. In the other seven trials, various lots of British vaccines were compared. In 9794 immunized children, the attack rate of children exposed at home was 69 percent. The final report of vaccine trials in Great Britain was presented in 1959.[197] Seven different vaccines were given to 13,029 children. The potency of the various vaccines, as measured by mouse protection tests, correlated well with their clinical efficacy. The secondary attack rate for vaccinated children exposed at home was 17 percent.

The pertussis attack rate was relatively constant in the United States in the prevaccine era between 1922 and 1942 (see Fig. 134–1). From 1943 to 1976, a 150-fold reduction in the attack rate was noted in association with widespread childhood pertussis immunization.

A relationship between vaccine use and disease control also was supported by data from England and Wales. The pertussis attack rate declined between 1958 and 1973 and increased dramatically between 1977 and 1983 after a marked decrease in vaccination beginning in 1974.[30] The attack rate decreased with the widespread use of vaccine and increased when vaccine use decreased. Moreover, the attack rate after the decrease in vaccine use was increased most markedly in the newly susceptible cohort of children younger than 4 years of age. English children receive their pertussis immunization only in the first year of life, and protection is not long lasting.

In spite of the fact that a vaccine potency standard was established in 1949, no specific whole-cell vaccines used in the United States were ever studied in controlled field trials. Generic studies of vaccine efficacy have been performed in outbreak situations, however.[61, 235–238]

In one study from 1982 to 1983 involving 440 household contacts 6 months to 9 years of age, the secondary attack rate in unvaccinated contacts was compared with the rate in children who had received three or more DTP doses. Vaccine efficacy was found to be 91.4 percent. A similar study during the period 1979 to 1981 revealed an efficacy of 82.4 percent.

In a more recent study, Onorato and associates[235] noted that the calculated efficacy varied markedly according to the clinical case definition. Efficacy against any cough illness was 63 percent, whereas it was 83 percent if a cough duration of 21 or more days was required.

In contrast with the efficacy data determined in observational household contact studies in the United States, one of the two major U. S. vaccines showed poor efficacy in double-blind efficacy trials performed in Sweden and Italy.[93, 99] Specifically, the calculated efficacy against laboratory-confirmed typical pertussis after receipt of three doses in infancy was 48 percent in Sweden and 36 percent in Italy. With a similar case definition, the efficacy of the other major U. S. vaccine was noted to be 93 percent in the extensive German trial.[271]

Acellular Vaccines

Research in the 1970s showed that three *B. pertussis* antigens (PT, FHA, LPS) were liberated into the medium during culture and that these antigens could be concentrated and separated by density gradient centrifugation.[42, 127] This finding allowed for the development and production of vaccines by six manufacturers in Japan.[155, 228] All six vaccines had minimal or no endotoxin but different amounts of PT and FHA. In addition, some of the vaccines were found to contain fimbriae 2 and pertactin.

Despite limited proof of efficacy, the six vaccines were put into routine use in Japan in 1981, and they have controlled epidemic pertussis during the ensuing 20 years. However, because adequate data were not available on any single vaccine or on vaccine use in early infancy, many extensive trials have been performed subsequently in Europe, Africa, and Japan. The findings of early trials in Sweden and Japan resulted in the licensure of two acellular vaccines for fourth and fifth doses in the United States.[1, 216]

After extensive analysis of the data in the original efficacy trial in Sweden in the mid-1980s, calculated efficacy was found to vary significantly, depending on the clinical case definition and the laboratory methods.[1, 21, 102, 278, 279, 281] Therefore, researchers decided that a universal primary case definition should be developed for use in all subsequent efficacy trials so that different vaccines in different trials could be compared.

A World Health Organization (WHO) committee met in Geneva in January 1991, and a primary case definition was developed.[323] This definition, or minor variations of it, have been used in the most recent efficacy trials. The WHO case definition is as follows: (1) an illness with 21 days or more of spasmodic cough and either culture-confirmed infection with *B. pertussis* or serologic evidence of infection with *B. pertussis* as indicated by a significant rise in IgA or IgG antibody by ELISA against PT or FHA in paired sera or (2) contact with a case of culture-confirmed pertussis in the household with onset within 28 days before or after the onset of cough in the study vaccinee. Not all members of the WHO committee, including one of us (J. D. C.), agreed with this primary case definition because its use results in the elimination of many laboratory-confirmed cases from efficacy calculations.[37] With this definition, vaccines that lessen the severity of disease but are poor at preventing infection generally will be overrated.

In 1994 and 1995, seven efficacy trials with eight candidate acellular pertussis component DTP vaccines (DTaP) in four countries were completed,[93, 99, 169, 262, 268, 271, 292] and an additional trial in Sweden was completed in 1997.[232] As noted in Table 134–3, the eight vaccines are different in the number of antigens that they contain, as well as concentrations of the specific antigens. In all efficacy studies, confounding factors may affect the results. In general, double-blind studies with placebo and whole-cell vaccine controls are ideal. However, placebo control was not ethical in countries in which DTP vaccine was recommended. Therefore, studies in Germany and Senegal used various methods to obtain efficacy data in spite of the lack of a blinded diphtheria-tetanus (DT) toxoid group. Of note is that observer bias can affect the results of all studies,

TABLE 134–3 ■ PERTUSSIS ANTIGENS IN EIGHT DIPHTHERIA AND TETANUS TOXOIDS AND ACELLULAR PERTUSSIS VACCINES (DTaP) EVALUATED IN EIGHT EFFICACY TRIALS (1990–1997)

Vaccine*	Pertussis Toxin (μg/Dose)	Filamentous Hemagglutinin (μg/Dose)	Pertactin (μg/Dose)	Fimbriae (μg/Dose)
Certiva†	40			
Tripedia†	23.4	23.4		
Triavax	25	25		
SKB-2‡	25	25		
Acelluvax	5	2.5	2.5	
Infanrix†	25	25	8	
Acel-Immune†	3.5	35	2	0.8§
Daptacel (two formulations)				
Original	10	5	3	5‖
Enhanced	20	20	3	5

*Product name.
†Licensed in the United States.
‡No product name.
§Fimbriae 2.
‖Fimbriae 2 and 3.

TABLE 134–4 ■ VACCINE EFFICACY DATA FOR 10 ACELLULAR PERTUSSIS VACCINES EVALUATED IN EIGHT TRIALS CARRIED OUT IN THE 1990s AND THE EARLIER 1980s SWEDISH TRIAL

Location/References	Design	Vaccine	Schedule	Efficacy	
				Typical Pertussis	Mild and Typical Pertussis
Sweden, Stockholm*[1, 21, 278]	Double-blind prospective cohort	JNIH-6	2 doses (2–3 mo apart starting at 5–11 mo of age)	84%	42%
		JNIH-7		90%	–7%
Sweden, Göteborg†[292]	Double-blind prospective cohort	Certiva	3 doses (3, 5, 12 mo)	71%	54%
Sweden, Stockholm†[99]	Double-blind prospective cohort	SKB-2	3 doses (2, 4. 6 mo)	59%	42%
		Daptacel original		85%	78%
Italy, Rome[93]	Double-blind prospective cohort	Acelluvax	3 doses (2, 4. 6 mo)	84%	71%
		Infanrix		84%	71%
Germany, Erlangen[271]	Prospective cohort	Acel-immune	4 doses (3, 4½, 6, 15–18 mo)	83%	72%
Germany, Mainz[262]	Household contact	Infanrix	3 doses (3, 4, 5 mo)	89%	81%
Germany, Munich‡[169]	Case control	Tripedia	4 doses (2, 4, 6, 15–25 mo)	80%, 93%	—
Senegal¶[268]	Household contact	Triavax	3 doses	31%, 74%	—

*Efficacy against typical pertussis based on positive culture without serologic analysis.
†Significant observer bias occured in this trial.[37]
‡Laboratory diagnosis based on culture only; 80 percent efficacy was against cough illness of 21 or more days, and 93 percent efficacy was against the World Health Organization (WHO) case definition.
¶Thirty-one percent efficacy based on 21 days or more of cough illness; 74 percent efficacy was against the WHO case definition.

including those with double-blind control. For example, a less efficacious vaccine that prevents typical disease but not mild disease can be determined to be more efficacious than it actually is if the study observers "know pertussis" and dismiss possible cases as being other respiratory illnesses and do not obtain cultures or carry out prospective follow-up.[44]

In general, household contact studies, unless they are nested analyses in prospective cohort studies, also are subject to observer bias, and case-control studies result in significantly inflated efficacy percentages.[37, 44, 45, 76, 78, 216] In cohort studies, observer bias by parents can be reduced by frequent prospective telephone contact with study families. Finally, serologic diagnosis, as well as diagnosis by culture, increases the identification of mild cases, which are more likely to occur in vaccinees than in control subjects.

A summary of the efficacy data for 10 acellular pertussis vaccines evaluated in the eight trials performed in the 1990s and the earlier 1980s Swedish trial is presented in Table 134–4. The data in this table indicate that three- and four-component vaccines (vaccines containing pertactin and fimbriae as well as PT and FHA) have greater efficacy against *B. pertussis* illness (mild and typical) than do the PT or PT/FHA vaccines. The apparent high efficacy of the two-component vaccine in the Munich study can be explained by the type of study (case-control), significant observer bias, and the lack of serologic diagnosis. The final study done in Stockholm, Sweden, was a comparative study without a DT control group.[232] In this study, the efficacy of Daptacel (enhanced) was found to be similar to that of the whole-cell vaccine that was used in the United Kingdom and significantly more efficacious than Acelluvax (three component). Acelluvax had greater efficacy than did the two-component vaccine SKB-2.

Finally, one must point out that in general, whole-cell vaccines have greater efficacy than do all acellular vaccines except Daptacel (enhanced).[169, 262, 268, 271] The exception to this statement is the Connaught whole-cell vaccine, which was used as the DTP control in Stockholm, Sweden, and Rome, Italy.[93, 99]

ADVERSE EVENTS

Whole-Cell Vaccines

Local reactions and relatively mild systemic complaints are frequent occurrences after pertussis immunization. Less commonly, severe neurologic illness and death have been noted in temporal association with DTP immunization.

The largest study in the United States designed to assess the risk of relatively common and uncommon reactions to pertussis vaccine was performed by Baraff and associates.[10–12, 49] This study was conducted between January 1978 and December 1979. Reactions in children who received either DTP or DT immunization were compared. A total of 15,752 DTP immunizations and 784 DT immunizations were given to children between birth and 6 years of age. These children were evaluated for reactions that occurred within 48 hours of vaccine administration. All common local and systemic reactions occurred more frequently in the DTP recipients than in the DT group. Differences between the common reactions in the two groups were all highly significant ($p < .005$).

Redness at the injection site occurred in 37.4 percent of DTP recipients and 7.6 percent of DT vaccinees. Fever (≥38° C [100.4° F]) was noted in 46.5 percent of DTP recipients. A temperature of 39° C (102.2° F) or higher occurred in 6.1 percent of DTP recipients, but in only 0.7 percent of DT recipients. Drowsiness, fretfulness, vomiting, anorexia, and persistent crying were other reactions recorded in 3.1 percent (persistent crying) to 53.4 percent (fretfulness) of DTP recipients versus 0.7 percent (persistent crying) to 22.6 percent (fretfulness) of DT vaccinees. In general, rates of local reactions, but not those of systemic reactions (except fever), increase from dose to dose in an immunization series.

In addition to these reactions, 0.1 percent of DTP recipients in this study were reported by the parents to have a high-pitched, unusual cry; 0.06 percent had convulsions, and 0.06 percent had hypotonic-hyporesponsive episodes (shock, collapse). No children in the control group (DT recipients) had similar reactions; however, the control group was of modest size (784 DT recipients), so statistical significance could not be assigned to any of these relatively uncommon events.

Because convulsions in young children are the result of many different etiologic factors, the cause-and-effect relationship with pertussis vaccine is less clear. However, inasmuch as fever develops in almost one half of all DTP vaccinees and febrile convulsions are not uncommon events, a reasonable assumption is that many convulsions that occur in temporal association with DTP vaccination are in fact due to the immunization. Two studies have noted a significant association between pertussis immunization and febrile convulsions.[267, 306] Approximately 1 per 1000 vaccinees older than 6 months of age will have a first febrile seizure after receiving pertussis immunization. The concomitant use of acetaminophen (15 mg/kg per dose at the time of immunization and every 4 hours for 24 hours) and DTP vaccine has been suggested as a means of reducing the incidence of febrile convulsions in vaccinees.[165]

Neurologic disease and death occurring in temporal association with pertussis immunization have been of major concern throughout the vaccine era. During the last 55 years, several case series and individual cases of neurologic illness occurring after pertussis immunization have been reported; by 1979, more than 1000 cases of alleged neurologic damage induced by pertussis vaccine were reported.[16, 25, 28, 30, 158, 188, 317] Few of these reports had evidence of an adequate search for other possible causes of the neurologic disease, and in none were data available for rate calculations.

From 1967 to 1980, several attempts were made to determine the frequency of neurologic disease after pertussis immunization.[2, 30, 66, 67, 80, 109, 275, 283] However, because controls were not included in any of the population evaluations, all rate estimates included children with temporally related events that had other causes.

A carefully designed prospective case-control study (National Childhood Encephalopathy Study [NCES]) of all hospital admissions of children 2 to 35 months of age with acute serious neurologic disorders in England, Wales, and Scotland was undertaken between 1976 and 1979.[4, 15, 182, 200–203] The results of this study for the first time revealed an apparent statistical association between pertussis immunization and neurologic illness. Researchers found that a child who had received DTP vaccine within the previous 3 to 7 days was two to five times more likely to have neurologic disease than was a child who was not immunized during the same interval. The causal relationship between DTP immunization and neurologic illness noted in this study must be questioned, however, because both cases and controls had an equal frequency of immunization during the month preceding the index date. A more appropriate interpretation of the results is that they do not indicate cause and effect; rather, the DTP immunization calls attention to or brings out something that will occur anyway, but just moves it forward in time.[31, 32]

Infantile spasms, an identifiable seizure disorder of infancy, usually has its onset in the 6-month period from 2 to 7 months of age; therefore, that some cases occur after DTP immunization is not surprising. Simple calculations indicate that approximately 12 percent of all patients destined to have infantile spasms between 2 and 7 months of age will have an onset of illness within 7 days after DTP immunization. The temporal association between DTP immunization and infantile spasms has led many people to assume a cause-and-effect relationship. However, controlled data from the NCES in Great Britain provide strong evidence against a causative role for pertussis vaccine in infantile spasms.[15] In another study, Melchior[198] in Denmark noted that the time of onset of infantile spasms was not altered when the time of pertussis immunization was changed from 5, 6, 7, and 15 months of age to 5 weeks, 9 weeks, and 10 months of age. In both periods, 42 percent of patients had their onset during the first 4 months of life.

Data from the NCES have been reanalyzed with the exclusion of cases of infantile spasm.[201, 203] From these analyses, the risk of permanent brain damage occurring from pertussis immunization has been suggested to be 1 per 330,000 vaccine doses and the risk of any encephalopathy developing to be 1 per 140,000 vaccinations. However, a review of the NCES data by other investigators indicates that both rate estimates are incorrect. Specifically, Stephenson[274] has shown that the 1 per 140,000 rate for all encephalopathy is an artifact resulting from the inclusion of 9 children with febrile convulsions. Similarly, MacRae[181] has noted that the increased relative risk that was observed within 7 days of immunization (which was used to calculate the risk of brain damage of 1 per 330,000 immunizations) was offset by a decreased relative risk over the subsequent 3-week period. This finding, similar to the original study data and the infantile spasm data, indicates not a cause-and-effect relationship but a redistribution of events over time.

In the United States, the major neurologic illness that was noted in temporal association with DTP immunization was the first seizure of what turned out to be severe epilepsy. By chance alone, this association may occur 400 times a year in the United States. Four carefully performed studies that included approximately 330,000 children and 1 million immunizations have examined the possibility that pertussis immunization is a causative factor in epilepsy; no evidence of a causative role has been found.[32, 84, 95, 267, 306]

Similar to infantile spasms, sudden infant death syndrome also occurs in early life; therefore, that cases are noted to occur after administration of DTP immunization again is not surprising. Hoffman and associates[131] performed an extensive prospective case-control study of risk factors in sudden infant death syndrome from October 1978 through December 1979. In this study with 800 cases, they found that DTP immunization is not a risk factor for development of the syndrome. Other good, controlled studies have yielded similar results.[42, 94] No evidence has demonstrated that DTP vaccinees have an increased risk of developing asthma later in life.[125]

Acellular Vaccines

An extensive amount of reactogenicity information has been generated in phase II and phase III studies with all licensed DTaP vaccines.[60, 93, 99, 169, 247, 261, 294] Because endotoxin has been removed from all DTaP vaccines, one is not surprised that all are less reactogenic than DTP vaccines. In one double-blind study, the reactogenicity of 13 DTaP vaccines was presented and compared with the reactogenicity of a DTP vaccine.[60] This study involved 2200 infants; 113 to 217 received an acellular product, and 370 received the

TABLE 134–5 ■ SUMMARY OF REACTOGENICITY DATA FROM THE NATIONWIDE MULTICENTER ACELLULAR PERTUSSIS TRIAL

	DTaP			DTP		
Event	*1st Dose*	*2nd Dose*	*3rd Dose*	*1st Dose*	*2nd Dose*	*3rd Dose*
Local						
Redness	13.5%	17.1%	21.5%	49.4%	47.7%	47.6%
Swelling	8.7%	12.1%	13.3%	39.7%	34.1%	35.7%
Pain	3.8%	2.0%	2.1%	27.3%	18.7%	15.8%
Systemic						
Fever (Temp. ≥100.1° F)	4.2%	11.3%	15.8%	27.3%	34.1%	37.7%
Fussiness	6.6%	7.7%	6.7%	20.1%	23.5%	17.3%
Drowsiness	29.9%	17.6%	12.9%	43.5%	31.0%	24.6%
Anorexia	9.3%	8.9%	8.9%	19.5%	16.5%	14.3%
Vomiting	6.3%	4.5%	4.2%	7.0%	4.5%	5.3%
Use of antipyretic	39.3%	36.7%	36.3%	60.5%	59.8%	61.4%

DTaP, diphtheria-tetanus-acellular pertussis; DTP, diphtheria-tetanus-pertussis.
Data from Decker, M. D., Edwards, K. M., Steinhoff, M. C., et al.: Comparison of 13 acellular pertussis vaccines: Adverse reactions. Pediatrics 96:557–566, 1995.

whole-cell vaccine. Study participants received three doses of vaccine at 2, 4, and 6 months of age. Overall, all monitored reactions except vomiting occurred less frequently and were less severe in DTaP recipients than in DTP recipients. Specific results from this study are presented in Table 134–5. As can be seen, local redness and swelling and fever increased in frequency from the first to the third dose, whereas the complaint of being drowsy decreased.

In our efficacy trial in Germany with Acel-Immune, we monitored reactions in more than 8000 children after receipt of four doses of vaccine at 3, $4^1/_2$, 6, and 15 to 18 months.[264, 294] For the first three vaccine doses, the findings were similar to those noted in Table 134–5. After the fourth dose, the frequency of occurrence of local erythema and induration and fever increased considerably in comparison to their frequencies after the third dose. Ten percent of DTaP recipients had local erythema of 2.4 cm or greater, and 28 percent had temperatures of 38° C or higher. Others also have noted an increased frequency and severity of local reactions occurring after administration of the fourth and fifth doses of DTaP vaccines.[115, 239, 247, 261] Of particular concern is the observation of extensive swelling of the thigh with booster doses of some DTaP vaccines.[247, 261] Rennels and associates[247] found this event to occur more commonly after immunization with DTaP vaccines containing high amounts

TABLE 134–6 ■ RATES* OF SEVERE EVENTS AFTER DTAP VACCINES IN THE 1990s EFFICACY TRIALS

Vaccine	Persistent Crying (≥3 hr)	Hypotonic-Hyporesponsive Episodes	Seizures
Certiva	0	0	0.4
Tripedia	0.1	0.05	0.02
SKB-2	≤0.5	0	0.3
Acelluvax	0.7	0.07	0
Infanrix	0.4	0	0.07
Acel-Immune	0.2	0	0.1
Daptacel original	≤0.5	0.1	0

*Rates per 1000 doses.
Data from references 93, 99, 169, 292, 294.

of diphtheria toxoid. With Acel-Immune, a vaccine with a low diphtheria toxoid content, we noted that 15.4 percent of subjects had induration of more than 5 cm but less than 10 cm after receiving a fifth dose; entire limb swelling was not noted.[115]

In five of the 1990s efficacy trials, the occurrence of less common, more severe events (persistent crying, seizures, and hypotonic-hyporesponsive episodes) was monitored. A summary of these data is presented in Table 134–6. As can be seen, temporally related persistent crying, hypotonic-hyporesponsive episodes, and seizures were rare events after immunization with DTaP vaccines.

SCHEDULES AND CONTRAINDICATIONS

Immunization schedules with whole-cell vaccines have varied throughout the world and to great measure were determined by concern relating to true and perceived reactions.[30, 42] An immunization schedule involving only three doses at 2, 3, and 4 months of age has been quite effective in controlling pertussis morbidity and mortality in the United Kingdom.[299] However, the five-dose schedule used in the United States resulted in lower attack rates in preschool and school-age children.[30, 42]

The recommendation for the DTaP vaccine in the United States is that it be given in the same five-dose schedule as recommended for DTP vaccines.[297] However, recent follow-up data from the 1990s efficacy trials, as well as recent reactogenicity data, suggest that this "one size fits all" approach should be changed.[93, 99, 256, 261, 289, 292] Our findings with Acel-Immune suggest that the present five-dose schedule is appropriate.[179, 271] On the other hand, recent data from other trials suggest that the fourth dose of some vaccines can be postponed until the child is 4 to 6 years of age or the third dose can be moved back to the child's second year of life.[232, 256, 289, 292] These changes would not be expected to decrease efficacy but would decrease troubling local reactions with booster doses.

In addition to providing childhood immunization, the upcoming availability of adolescent and adult acellular pertussis component vaccines will allow the vaccination of adolescents and adults.[34, 35, 39, 106, 150, 253] If performed routinely, immunization of adolescents and adults might control the circulation of *B. pertussis,* as well as the disease.

Over the years, pertussis vaccine recommendations have undergone many changes. In particular, contraindications to vaccine are changing continually. An important note, however, is that few scientific data support any of the present contraindications. The primary goal of national immunization programs is to vaccinate all infants and children. If excessive contraindications or their overinterpretation leads to a large number of unimmunized children, the programs will fail and the children in greatest need of protection will get pertussis. In the United States, the most recent recommendations of the Committee on Infectious Diseases of the American Academy of Pediatrics generally should be followed. However, individual case-by-case decisions often need to be made.

ISOLATION AND PROPHYLACTIC MEASURES

Erythromycin in the index case shortens communicability of the organisms and thus limits spread of the disease. During the first few days of treatment, contact with susceptible persons should be avoided. In general, close contacts (household members, those in daycare centers, playmates) of the index case should be protected from infection. Such protection can be implemented by the prophylactic use of erythromycin[273] for 14 days and active immunization of children younger than 7 years of age who have not completed their immunization series for pertussis.[6]

The use of erythromycin prophylactically in exposed adults frequently is recommended. In the hospital setting, such use often involves many people and considerable expense. In our experience, the side effects of erythromycin are such that adult compliance is poor. Therefore, our opinion is that erythromycin should not be used prophylactically, but only for treatment at the first sign of respiratory illness in those exposed. Alternatively, because azithromycin is tolerated better by adults, its use prophylactically is reasonable.

Other *Bordetella* Infections

BORDETELLA BRONCHISEPTICA. *B. bronchiseptica* causes respiratory infections in at least 19 different mammals.[55] Most notable are atrophic rhinitis in pigs, kennel cough (rhinotracheitis) in dogs, and bronchopneumonia in rabbits and other laboratory animals. Occasional infections in humans have been noted during the last 30 years, with the majority occurring in immunocompromised adults.[5, 65] Most recent reports have noted *B. bronchiseptica* infections in patients with acquired immunodeficiency syndrome (AIDS). Respiratory infections have ranged from mild upper respiratory illnesses to pneumonia.

BORDETELLA HINZII. *B. hinzii* has been recovered from an adult patient with cystic fibrosis during pulmonary exacerbations throughout a 3-year period.[82] Bacteremia has been noted in a patient with AIDS.[54]

BORDETELLA HOLMESII. *B. holmesii* recently has been isolated from the nasopharyngeal specimens of 33 patients suspected of having pertussis.[326] Twenty-three of the cases were investigated further, and 19 (82%) were adolescents, 2 (9%) were adults, and 2 (9%) were children. All had cough, and 61 percent had paroxysms, 26 percent had post-tussive vomiting, and 9 percent had whoop. *B. holmesii* also has been isolated from a 10-month-old boy with bacteremia and from patients with septicemia, endocarditis, and respiratory failure.[212, 287]

BORDETELLA TREMATUM. *B. trematum* has been isolated from wounds and ear infections.[301]

REFERENCES

1. Ad Hoc Group for the Study of Pertussis Vaccines: Placebo-controlled trial of two acellular pertussis vaccines in Sweden: Protective efficacy and adverse events. Lancet *1*:955–960, 1988.
2. Advisory Panel of the Committee on Safety of Medicines: The collection of data relating to adverse reactions in pertussis vaccine. *In* Whooping Cough: Reports from the Committee on Safety of Medicines and the Joint Committee on Vaccination and Immunisation. London, Department of Health and Social Security, Her Majesty's Stationery Office, 1981, p. 27.
3. Aintablian, N., Walpita, P., and Sawyer, M.: Detection of *Bordetella pertussis* and respiratory syncytial virus in air samples from hospital rooms. Infect. Control Hosp. Epidemiol. *19*:918–923, 1998.
4. Alderslade, R., Bellman, M. H., Rawson, N. S. B., et al.: The National Childhood Encephalopathy Study. *In* Whooping Cough: Reports From the Committee on Safety of Medicines and the Joint Committee on Vaccination and Immunisation. London, Department of Health and Social Security, Her Majesty's Stationery Office, 1981, p. 79.
5. Amador, C., Chiner, E., Calpe, J. L., et al.: Pneumonia due to *Bordetella bronchiseptica* in a patient with AIDS. Rev. Infect. Dis. *13*:771–772, 1991.
6. American Academy of Pediatrics: Active immunization: Pertussis. *In* Pickering L. K. (ed.): 2000 Red Book: Report of the Committee on Infectious Diseases. 25th ed. Elk Grove Village, IL, American Academy of Pediatrics, 2000, pp. 1–39, 435–448.
7. Arciniega, J. L., Shahin, R. D., Burnette, W. N., et al.: Contribution of the B oligomer to the protective activity of genetically attenuated pertussis toxin. Infect. Immun. *59*:3407–3410, 1991.
8. Arico, B., and Rappuoli, R.: *Bordetella parapertussis* and *Bordetella bronchiseptica* contain transcriptionally silent pertussis toxin genes. J. Bacteriol. *169*:2847–2853, 1987.
9. Ausiello, C.M., Lande, R, Urbani, F, et al.: Cell-mediated immunity and antibody responses to *Bordetella pertussis* antigens in children with a history of pertussis infection and in recipients of an acellular pertussis vaccine. J. Infect. Dis. *181*:1989–1995, 2000.
10. Baraff, L. J., and Cherry, J. D.: Nature and rates of adverse reactions associated with pertussis immunization. *In* International Symposium on Pertussis. Bethesda, MD, U. S. Department of Health, Education and Welfare, National Institutes of Health, 1979, p. 291.
11. Baraff, L. J., Manclark, C. R., Cherry, J. D., et al.: Analyses of adverse reactions to diphtheria and tetanus toxoids and pertussis vaccine by vaccine lot, endotoxin content, pertussis vaccine potency and percentage of mouse weight gain. Pediatr. Infect. Dis. J. *8*:502–507, 1989.
12. Baraff, L. J., Cody, C. L., and Cherry, J. D.: DTP-associated reactions: An analysis by injection site, manufacturer, prior reactions, and dose. Pediatrics *73*:31–36, 1984.
13. Baraff, L. J., Wilkins, J., and Wehrle, P. F.: The role of antibiotics, immunizations and adenoviruses in pertussis. Pediatrics *61*:224–230, 1978.
14. Beiter, A., Lewis, K., Pineda, E. F., et al.: Unrecognized maternal peripartum pertussis with subsequent fatal neonatal pertussis. Obstet. Gynecol. *82*:691–693, 1993.
15. Bellman, M. H., Ross, E. M., and Miller, D. L.: Infantile spasms and pertussis immunisation. Lancet *1*:1031–1034, 1983.
16. Berg, J. M.: Neurological complications of pertussis immunization. B. M. J. *2*:24, 1958.
17. Bergquist, S., Bernander, S., Dahnsjo, H., et al.: Erythromycin in the treatment of pertussis: A study of bacteriologic and clinical effects. Pediatr. Infect. Dis. J. *6*:458–461, 1987.
18. Bernales, R., Eastman, J., and Kaplan, J.: Quantitation of circulating T and B lymphocytes in children with whooping cough. Pediatr. Res. *10*:965–967, 1976.
19. Bhargava, A., Leininger, E., Roberts, M., et al.: Filamentous hemagglutinin and the 69-kDa protein, pertactin, promote adherence of *Bordetella pertussis* to epithelial cells and macrophages. Paper presented at the 6th International Symposium on Pertussis, Bethesda, MD, September 26–28, 1990, pp. 137–138.
20. Birkebaek, N. H., Kristiansen, M., Seefeldt, T., et al.: *Bordetella pertussis* and chronic cough in adults. Clin. Infect. Dis. *29*:1239–1242, 1999.
21. Blackwelder, W. C., Storsaeter, J., Olin, P., et al.: Acellular pertussis vaccines. Am. J. Dis. Child. *145*:1285–1289, 1991.
22. Bordet, J., and Gengou, O.: Le microbe de la coqueluche. Ann. Inst. Pasteur *20*:48–68, 1906.
23. Bordet, J., and Gengou, O.: L'endotoxin coquelucheuse. Ann. Inst. Pasteur *23*:415–419, 1909.
24. Broomhall, J., and Herxheimer, A.: Treatment of whooping cough: The facts. Arch. Dis. Child. *59*:185–187, 1984.

25. Byers, R. K., and Moll, F. C.: Encephalopathies following prophylactic pertussis vaccine. Pediatrics *1*:437–457, 1948.
26. Celermajor, J. M., and Brown, J.: The neurological complications of pertussis. Med. J. Aust. *1*:1066–1069, 1966.
27. Chaby, R., and Caroff, M.: Lipopolysaccharides of *Bordetella pertussis* endotoxin. *In* Wardlaw, A. C., and Parton, R. (eds.): Pathogenesis and Immunity in Pertussis. New York, John Wiley & Sons, 1988, pp. 247–272.
28. Chakravorty, A. P.: Blindness after use of triple antigen. B. M. J. *1*:105, 1963.
29. Charles, I. G., Li, J. L., Roberts, M., et al.: Identification and characterization of a protective immunodominant B cell epitope of pertactin (P.69) from *Bordetella pertussis*. Eur. J. Immunol. *21*:1147–1153, 1991.
30. Cherry, J. D.: The epidemiology of pertussis and pertussis immunization in the United Kingdom and the United States: A comparative study. Curr. Probl. Pediatr. *14*:1–78, 1984.
31. Cherry, J. D.: Pertussis and the vaccine controversy. *In* Root, R. K., Griffiss, J. M., Warren, K. S., et al. (eds.): Immunization. New York, Churchill Livingstone, 1989, pp. 47–63.
32. Cherry, J. D.: Pertussis vaccine encephalopathy: It is time to recognize it as the myth that it is. J. A. M. A. *263*:1679–1680, 1990.
33. Cherry, J. D.: Pertussis: The trials and tribulations of old and new pertussis vaccines. Vaccine *10*:1033–1038, 1992.
34. Cherry, J. D.: Acellular pertussis vaccines: A solution to the pertussis problem. J. Infect. Dis. *168*:21–24, 1993.
35. Cherry, J. D.: Strategies for diphtheria, tetanus, and pertussis (DTP) immunization. Report of the 104th Ross Conference on Pediatric Research. Columbus, Ohio, Ross Products Division, Abbott Laboratories, 1994, pp. 218–225.
36. Cherry, J. D.: Historical review of pertussis and the classical vaccine. J. Infect. Dis. *174*(Suppl.):259–263, 1996.
37. Cherry, J. D.: Comparative efficacy of acellular pertussis vaccines: An analysis of recent trials. Pediatr. Infect. Dis. J. *16*(Suppl.):90–96, 1997.
38. Cherry, J. D.: Pertussis in the preantibiotic and prevaccine era, with emphasis on adult pertussis. Clin. Infect. Dis. *28*(Suppl. 2):107–111, 1999.
39. Cherry, J. D.: Epidemiological, clinical, and laboratory aspects of pertussis in adults. Clin. Infect. Dis. *28*(Suppl 2):112–117, 1999.
40. Cherry, J. D., Baraff, L. J., and Hewlett, E.: The past, present, and future of pertussis: The role of adults in epidemiology and future control. West. J. Med. *150*:319–328, 1989.
41. Cherry, J. D., Beer, T., Chartrand, S. A., et al.: Comparison of antibody values to *Bordetella pertussis* antigens in young German and American men. Clin. Infect. Dis. *20*:1271–1274, 1995.
42. Cherry, J. D., Brunell, P. A., Golden, G. S., et al.: Report of the Task Force on Pertussis and Pertussis Immunization: 1988. Pediatrics *81*(Suppl.):939–984, 1988.
43. Cherry, J. D., Gornbein J., Heininger, U., et al.: A search for serologic correlates of immunity to *Bordetella pertussis* cough illnesses. Vaccine *16*:1901–1906, 1998.
44. Cherry, J. D., Heininger, U., Stehr, K., et al.: The effect of investigator compliance (observer bias) on calculated efficacy in a pertussis vaccine trial. Pediatrics *102*:909–912, 1998.
45. Cherry, J. D., and Olin, P.: Commentaries: The science and fiction of pertussis vaccines. Pediatrics *104*:1381–1384, 1999.
46. Choy, K. W., Wulffraat, N. M., Wolfs, T. F. W., et al.: *Bordetella bronchiseptica* respiratory infection in a child after a bone marrow transplantation. Pediatr. Infect. Dis. J. *18*:481–482, 1999.
47. Christie, C. D. C., and Baltimore, R. S.: Pertussis in neonates. Am. J. Dis. Child. *143*:1199–1202, 1989.
48. Christie, C. D. C., Marx, M. L., Marchant, C. D., et al.: The 1993 epidemic of pertussis in Cincinnati: Resurgence of disease in a highly immunized population of children. N. Engl. J. Med. *331*:16–21, 1994.
49. Cody, C. L., Baraff, L. J., Cherry, J. D., et al.: Nature and rates of adverse reactions associated with DTP and DT immunizations in infants and children. Pediatrics *68*:650–660, 1981.
50. Collier, A. M., Connor, J. T., and Irving, W. R., Jr.: Generalized type 5 adenovirus infection associated with the pertussis syndrome. J. Pediatr. *69*:1073–1978, 1966.
51. Cone, T. E., Jr.: Whooping cough is first described as a disease *sui generis* by Baillou in 1640. Pediatrics *46*:522, 1970.
52. Connor, J. D.: Evidence for an etiological role of adenoviral infection in pertussis syndrome. N. Engl. J. Med. *283*:390–394, 1970.
53. Conway, S. P., Balfour, A. H., and Ross, H.: Serologic diagnosis of whooping cough by enzyme-linked immunosorbent assay. Pediatr. Infect. Dis. J. 7:570–574, 1988.
54. Cookson, B. T., Vandamme, P., Carlson, L. C., et al.: Bacteremia caused by a novel *Bordetella* species, "*B. hinzii*." J. Clin. Microbiol. *32*:2569–2571, 1994.
55. Cotter, P. A., Miller, J.F.: *Bordetella*. *In* Groisman, E. A. (ed.): Principles of Bacterial Pathogenesis. San Diego, CA, Academic Press, 2001, pp. 619–674.
56. Cowell, J. L., Sato, Y., Sato, H., et al.: Separation, purification and properties of the filamentous hemagglutinin and the leukocytosis promoting factor-hemagglutinin from *Bordetella pertussis*. *In* Robbins, J. B., Hill, J. C., and Sadoff, G. (eds.): Seminars in Infectious Disease. Vol. IV. Bacterial Vaccines. International Symposium on Bacterial Vaccines. New York, Thieme-Stratton, 1982, pp. 371–379.
57. Cundell, D. R., Kanthakumar, K., Taylor, G. W., et al.: Effect of tracheal cytotoxin from *Bordetella pertussis* on human neutrophil function in vitro. Infect. Immun. *62*:639–643, 1994.
58. Davis, S. F., Sutter, R. W., Strebel, P. M., et al.: Concurrent outbreaks of pertussis and *Mycoplasma pneumoniae* infection: Clinical and epidemiological characteristics of illnesses manifested by cough. Clin. Infect. Dis. *20*:621–628, 1995.
59. Decker, G. R., Lavelle, J. P., Kuman, P. N., et al.: Pneumonia due to *Bordetella bronchiseptica* in a patient with AIDS. Rev. Infect. Dis. *13*:1250–1251, 1991.
60. Decker, M. D., Edwards, K. M., Steinhoff, M. C., et al.: Comparison of 13 acellular pertussis vaccines: Adverse reactions. Pediatrics *96*:557–566, 1995.
61. Deen, J. L., Mink, C. M., Cherry, J. D., et al.: A household contact study of *Bordetella pertussis* infections in adults. Clin. Infect. Dis. *21*:1211–1219, 1995.
62. De Serres, G., Shadmani, R., Duval, B., et al.: Morbidity of pertussis in adolescents and adults. J. Infect. Dis. *182*:174–179, 2000.
63. Deville, J. G., Cherry, J. D., Christenson, P. D., et al.: Frequency of unrecognized *Bordetella pertussis* infections in adults. Clin. Infect. Dis. *21*:639–642, 1995.
64. Douglas, E., Coote, J. G., Parton, R., et al.: Identification of *Bordetella pertussis* in nasopharyngeal swabs by PCR amplification of a region of the adenylate cyclase gene. J. Med. Microbiol. *38*:140–144, 1993.
65. Dworkin, M. S., Sullivan, P. S., Buskin, S. E., et al.: *Bordetella bronchiseptica* infection in human immunodeficiency virus–infected patients. Clin. Infect. Dis. *28*:1095–1099, 1999.
66. Edsall, G.: Present status of pertussis vaccination. Practitioner *215*:310–314, 1975.
67. Edsall, G.: Comment. *In* International Symposium on Pertussis, Bilthoven, 1969. Immunobiologic Standards. Vol. 13. New York, S. Karger, 1979, p. 170.
68. Eldering, G., Hornbeck, C., and Baker, J.: Serological study of *Bordetella pertussis* and related species. J. Bacteriol. *74*:133–136, 1957.
69. Eldering, G., and Kendrick, P.: A group of cultures resembling both *Bacillus pertussis* and *Bacillus bronchisepticus* but identical with neither. J. Bacteriol. *33*:71, 1937.
70. Eldering, G., and Kendrick, P.: *Bacillus parapertussis*: A species resembling both *Bacillus pertussis* and *Bacillus bronchiseptica* but identical with neither. J. Bacteriol. *35*:561–572, 1938.
71. Erlandsson, A., Backman, A., Nygren, M., et al. Quantification of *Bordetella pertussis* in clinical samples by colorimetric detection of competitive PCR products. A. P. M. I. S. *106*:1041–1048, 1998.
72. Farizo, K. M., Cochi, S. L., Zell, E. R., et al.: Epidemiological features of pertussis in the United States, 1980–1989. Clin. Infect. Dis. *14*:708–719, 1992.
73. Farrell, D. J., McKeon, M., Daggard, G., et al.: Rapid-cycle PCR method to detect *Bordetella pertussis* that fulfills all consensus recommendations for use of PCR in diagnosis of pertussis. J. Clin. Microbiol. *38*:4499–4502, 2000.
74. Fernandez, R. C., and Weiss, A. A.: Cloning and sequencing of a *Bordetella pertussis* serum resistance locus. Infect. Immun. *62*:4727–4738, 1994.
75. Fine, P. E. M.: Epidemiological considerations for whooping cough eradication. *In* Wardlaw, A. C., and Parton, R. (eds.): Pathogenesis and Immunity in Pertussis. New York, John Wiley & Sons, 1988, pp. 451–467.
76. Fine, P. E. M.: Implications of different study designs for the evaluation of acellular pertussis vaccines. Dev. Biol. Stand. *89*:123–133, 1997.
77. Fine, P. E. M., and Clarkson, J. A.: The recurrence of whooping cough: Possible implications for assessment of vaccine efficacy. Lancet *1*:666–669, 1982.
78. Fine, P. E. M., and Clarkson, J. A.: Reflections on the efficacy of pertussis vaccines. Rev. Infect. Dis. *9*:866–883, 1987.
79. Finn, T. M., Stevens, L. A.: Tracheal colonization factor: A *Bordetella pertussis* secreted virulence determinant. Mol. Microbiol. *16*:625–634, 1995.
80. Foege, W. H.: Statement read before the Subcommittee on Investigations and General Oversight Committee on Labor and Human Resources, United States Senate, Washington, D.C., May 7, 1982.
81. Friedman, R. L.: Pertussis: The disease and new diagnostic methods. Clin. Microbiol. Rev. *1*:365–376, 1988.
82. Funke, G., Hess, T., von Graevenitz, A., et al.: Characteristics of *Bordetella hinzii* strains isolated from a cystic fibrosis patient over a 3-year period. J. Clin. Microbiol. *34*:966–969, 1996.
83. Furman, B. L., Sidey, F. M., and Smith, M.: Metabolic disturbances produced by pertussis toxin. *In* Wardlaw, A. C., and Parton, R. (eds.): Pathogenesis and Immunity in Pertussis. New York, John Wiley & Sons, 1988, pp. 147–172.
84. Gale, J. L., Thapa, P. B., Wassilak, S. G. F., et al.: Risk of serious acute neurological illness after immunization with diphtheria-tetanus-pertussis vaccine: A population-based case-control study. J. A. M. A. *271*:37–41, 1994.
85. Glare, E. M., Paton, J. C., Premier, R. R., et al.: Analysis of a repetitive DNA sequence from *Bordetella pertussis* and its application to the

diagnosis of pertussis using the polymerase chain reaction. J. Clin. Microbiol. *28*:1982–1987, 1990.

86. Goldman, W. E.: Tracheal cytotoxin of *Bordetella pertussis*. *In* Wardlaw, A. C., and Parton, R. (eds.): Pathogenesis and Immunity in Pertussis. New York, John Wiley & Sons, 1988, pp. 237–246.
87. Goodman, Y. E., Wort, A. J., and Jackson, F. L.: Enzyme-linked immunosorbent assay for detection of pertussis immunoglobulin A in nasopharyngeal secretions as an indicator of recent infection. J. Clin. Microbiol. *13*:286–292, 1981.
88. Goodnow, R. A.: Biology of *Bordetella bronchiseptica*. Microbiol. Rev. *44*:722–738, 1980.
89. Gordon, J. E., and Hood, R. I.: Whooping cough and its epidemiological anomalies. Am. J. Med. Sci. *222*:333–361, 1951.
90. Gordon, M., Davies, H. D., and Gold, R.: Clinical and microbiologic features of children presenting with pertussis to a Canadian pediatric hospital during an eleven-year period. Pediatr. Infect. Dis. J. *13*:617–622, 1994.
91. Granström, G., Askelof, P., and Granström, M.: Specific immunoglobulin A to *Bordetella pertussis* antigens in mucosal secretion for rapid diagnosis of whooping cough. J. Clin. Microbiol. *26*:869–874, 1988.
92. Granström, M., Lindberg, A. A., Askelof, P., Hederstedt, B.: Detection of antibodies in human serum against fimbrial haemagglutinin of *Bordetella pertussis* by enzyme-linked immunosorbent assay. J. Med. Microbiol. *15*:85–96, 1982.
93. Greco, D., Salmaso, S., Mastrantonio, P., et al.: A controlled trial of two acellular vaccines and one whole-cell vaccine against pertussis. N. Engl. J. Med. *334*:341–348, 1996.
94. Griffin, M. R., Ray, W. A., Livengood, J. R., et al.: Risk of sudden infant death syndrome after immunization with the diphtheria-tetanus-pertussis vaccine. N. Engl. J. Med. *319*:618–623, 1988.
95. Griffin, M. R., Ray, W. A., Mortimer, E. A., et al.: Risk of seizures and encephalopathy after immunization with the diphtheria-tetanus-pertussis vaccine. J. A. M. A. *263*:1641–1645, 1990.
96. Grimpel, E., Begue, P., Anjak, I., et al.: Comparison of polymerase chain reaction, culture and Western immunoblot serology for diagnosis of *Bordetella pertussis* infection. J. Clin. Microbiol. *31*:2745–2750, 1993.
97. Gueirard, P., Weber, C., Coustumier, A. L., et al.: Human *Bordetella bronchiseptica* infection related to contact with infected animals: Persistence of bacteria in host. J. Clin. Microbiol. *33*:2002–2006, 1995.
98. Güris, D., Strebel, P. M., Bardenheier, B., et al.: Changing epidemiology of pertussis in the United States: Increasing reported incidence among adolescents and adults, 1990–1996. Clin. Infect. Dis. *28*:1230–1237, 1999.
99. Gustafsson, L., Hallander, H. O., Olin, P., et al.: A controlled trial of a two-component acellular, a five-component acellular, and a whole-cell pertussis vaccine. N. Engl. J. Med. *334*:349–355, 1996.
100. Hallander, H. O., Gnarpe, J., Gnarpe, H., et al.: *Bordetella pertussis, Bordetella parapertussis, Mycoplasma pneumoniae, Chlamydia pneumoniae* and persistent cough in children. Scand. J. Infect. Dis. *31*:281–286, 1999.
101. Hallander, H. O., Reizenstein, I., Renemar, B., et al.: Comparison of nasopharyngeal aspirates with swabs for culture of *Bordetella pertussis*. J. Clin. Microbiol. *31*:50–52, 1993.
102. Hallander, H. O., Storsaeter, J., and Mollby, R.: Evaluation of serologic and nasopharyngeal cultures for diagnosis of pertussis in a vaccine efficacy trial. J. Infect. Dis. *163*:1046–1054, 1991.
103. Halperin, S. A., Bortolussi, R., Kasina, A., et al.: Use of a Chinese hamster ovary cell cytotoxicity assay for the rapid diagnosis of pertussis. J. Clin. Microbiol. *28*:32–38, 1990.
104. Halperin, S. A., Bortolussi, R., Langley, J. M., et al.: Seven days of erythromycin estolate is as effective as fourteen days for the treatment of *Bordetella pertussis* infections. Pediatrics *100*:65–71, 1997.
105. Halperin, S. A., Bortolussi, R., MacLean, D., et al.: Persistence of pertussis in an immunized population: Results of the Nova Scotia enhanced pertussis surveillance program. J. Pediatr. *115*:686–693, 1989.
106. Halperin, S. A., Smith, B., Russell, M., et al.: Adult formulation of a five component acellular pertussis vaccine combined with diphtheria and tetanus toxoids and inactivated poliovirus vaccine is safe and immunogenic in adolescents and adults. Pediatr. Infect. Dis. J. *19*:276–283, 2000.
107. Halperin, S. A., Wang, E. E. L., Law, B., et al.: Epidemiological features of pertussis in hospitalized patients in Canada, 1991–1997: Report of the Immunization Monitoring Program-Active (IMPACT). Clin. Infect. Dis. *28*:1238–1243, 1999.
108. Hannah, J. H., Menozzi, F. D., Renauld, G., et al.: Sulfated glycoconjugate receptors for the *Bordetella pertussis* adhesin filamentous hemagglutinin (FHA) and mapping of the heparin-binding domain on FHA. Infect. Immun. *62*:5010–5019, 1994.
109. Hannik, C. A., and Cohen, H.: Pertussis vaccine experience in the Netherlands. *In* International Symposium on Pertussis. Bethesda, MD, U. S. Department of Health, Education and Welfare, National Institutes of Health, 1979, p. 279.
110. Haward, R. A.: Scale of undernotification of infectious diseases by general practitioners. Lancet *1*:873–874, 1973.
111. He, Q., Mertsola, J., Soini, H., et al.: Sensitive and specific polymerase chain reaction assays for detection of *Bordetella pertussis* in nasopharyngeal specimens. J Pediatr. *124*:421–426, 1994.
112. Hedenskog, S., Bjorksten, B., Blennow, M., et al.: Immunoglobulin E response to pertussis toxin in whooping cough and after immunization with a whole-cell and an acellular pertussis vaccine. Int. Arch. Allergy Appl. Immunol. *89*:156–161, 1989.
113. Heininger, U.: Recent progress in clinical and basic pertussis research. Eur. J. Pediatr. *160*:203–213, 2001.
114. Heininger, U., Cherry, J. D., Eckhardt, T., et al.: Clinical and laboratory diagnosis of pertussis in the regions of a large vaccine efficacy trial in Germany. Pediatr. Infect. Dis. J. *12*:504–509, 1993.
115. Heininger, U., Cherry, J. D., Lugauer, S., et al.: Reactogenicity data following fourth and fifth doses of the Wyeth-Lederle Takeda acellular pertussis component vaccine—the Erlangen trial. Paper presented at the Acellular Pertussis Vaccine Conference, November 12–14, 2000, Bethesda, MD.
116. Heininger, U., Cherry, J. D., Stehr, K., et al.: Comparative efficacy of the Lederle/Takeda acellular pertussis component DTP (DTaP) vaccine and Lederle whole-cell component DTP vaccine in German infants following household exposure. Pediatrics *102*:546–553, 1998.
117. Heininger, U., Klich, K., Stehr, K., et al.: Clinical findings in *Bordetella pertussis* infections: Results of a prospective multicenter surveillance study. Pediatrics *100:www.pediatrics.org/cgi/content/full/100/6/e10*, 1997.
118. Heininger, U., Schläpfer, G., Cherry, J.D., et al.: Clinical validation of a polymerase chain reaction assay for the diagnosis of pertussis by comparison with serology, culture, and symptoms during a large pertussis vaccine efficacy trial. Pediatrics *105:http://www.pediatrics.org/cgi/content/full/105/3/e31*, 2000.
119. Heininger, U., Schmitt-Grohè, S., Cherry, J. D., et al.: Der Mikroagglutinationstest: Ein einfaches und sensitives Verfahren zur Serodiagnostik von Pertussis. Klin. Paediatr. *207*:277–280, 1995.
120. Heininger, U., Stehr, K., and Cherry, J. D.: Serious pertussis overlooked in infants. Eur. J. Pediatr. *151*:342–343, 1992.
121. Heininger, U., Stehr, K., Christenson, P., et al.: Evidence of efficacy of the Lederle/Takeda acellular pertussis component diphtheria and tetanus toxoids and pertussis vaccine but not the Lederle whole-cell component diphtheria and tetanus toxoids and pertussis vaccine against *Bordetella parapertussis* infection. Clin. Infect. Dis. *28*:602–604, 1999.
122. Heininger, U., Stehr, K., Schläpfer, G., et al.: *Bordetella pertussis* infections and sudden unexpected deaths in children. Eur. J. Pediatr. *155*:551–553, 1996.
123. Heininger, U., Stehr, K., Schmitt-Grohè, S., et al.: Clinical characteristics of illness caused by *Bordetella parapertussis* compared with illness caused by *Bordetella pertussis*. Pediatr. Infect. Dis. J. *13*:306–309, 1994.
124. Heiss, L. N., Lancaster, J. R., Corbett, J. A., et al.: Epithelial autotoxicity of nitric oxide: Role in the respiratory cytopathology of pertussis. Proc. Natl. Acad. Sci. U. S. A. *91*:267–270, 1994.
125. Henderson, J., North, K., Griffiths, M., et al.: Pertussis vaccination and wheezing illnesses in young children: Prospective cohort study. B. M. J. *318*:1173–1176, 1999.
126. Herzig, P., Hartmann, C., Fischer, D., et al.: Pertussis complications in Germany—3 years of hospital-based surveillance during the introduction of acellular vaccines. Infection *26*:227–231, 1998.
127. Hewlett, E. L., and Cherry, J. D.: New and improved vaccines against pertussis. *In* Woodrow, G. C., and Levine, M. M. (eds.): New Generation Vaccines. New York, Marcel Dekker, 1990, pp. 231–250.
128. Hewlett, E. L., and Cherry, J. D.: New and improved vaccines against pertussis. In Levine, M. M., Woodrow, G. C., Kaper, J. B., and Cobon, G. S. (eds.): New Generation Vaccines. New York, Marcel Dekker, 1997, pp. 387–416.
129. Hewlett, E. L., and Gordon, V. M.: Adenylate cyclase toxin of *Bordetella pertussis*. *In* Wardlaw, A. C., and Parton, R. (eds.): Pathogenesis and Immunity in Pertussis. New York, John Wiley & Sons, 1988, pp. 193–209.
130. Hodder, S. L., Cherry, J. D., Mortimer, E. A., et al.: Antibody responses to *Bordetella pertussis* antigens and clinical correlations in elderly community residents. Clin. Infect. Dis. *31*:7–14, 2000.
131. Hoffman, H. J., Hunter, J. C., Damus, K., et al.: Diphtheria-tetanus-pertussis immunization and sudden infant death: Results of the National Institute of Child Health and Human Development Cooperative Epidemiological Study of Sudden Infant Death Syndrome Risk Factors. Pediatrics *79*:598–611, 1987.
132. Holmes, W. H.: Bacillary and Rickettsial Infections: Acute and Chronic: A Textbook: Black Death to White Plague. New York, Macmillan, 1940, pp. 395–414.
133. Honein, M. A., Paulozzi, L. J., Himelright, I. M., et al.: Infantile hypertrophic pyloric stenosis after pertussis prophylaxis with erythromycin: A case review and cohort study. Lancet *354*:2101–2105, 1999.
134. Hoppe, J. E.: Methods for isolation of *Bordetella pertussis* from patients with whooping cough. Eur. J. Clin. Microbiol. Infect. Dis. *7*:616–620, 1988.
135. Hoppe, J.: State of art in antibacterial susceptibility of *Bordetella pertussis* and antibiotic treatment of pertussis. Infection *26*:242–246, 1998.
136. Hoppe, J.: Neonatal pertussis. Pediatr. Infect. Dis. J. *19*:244–247, 2000.
137. Hoppe, J., and Eichhorn, A.: Activity of new macrolides against *Bordetella pertussis* and *Bordetella parapertussis*. Eur. J. Clin. Microbiol. Infect. Dis. *8*:653–654, 1989.

138. Hoppe, J., Halm, U., Hagedorn, H., et al.: Comparison of erythromycin ethylsuccinate and co-trimoxazole for treatment of pertussis. Infection *17*:227–231, 1989.
139. Hoppe, J., and Haug, A.: Antimicrobial susceptibility of *Bordetella pertussis* (part I). Infection *16*:126–130, 1988.
140. Houard, S., Hackel, C., Herzog, A., et al.: Specific identification of *Bordetella pertussis* by the polymerase chain reaction. Res. Microbiol. *140*:477–484, 1989.
141. Hudnall, S. D., Molina, C. P.: Marked increase in L-selectin–negative T cells in neonatal pertussis. The lymphocytosis explained? Am. J. Clin. Pathol. *114*:35–40, 2000.
142. Iida, T., Kunitani, A., Komase, Y., et al.: Studies on experimental infection with *Bordetella pertussis*: Effect of cortisone on the infection and immunity in mice. Jpn. J. Exp. Med. *33*:283–295, 1983.
143. Irons, L. I., and Gorringe, A. R.: Pertussis toxin: Production, purification, molecular structure, and assay. *In* Wardlaw, A. C., and Parton, R. (eds.): Pathogenesis and Immunity in Pertussis. New York, John Wiley & Sons, 1988, pp. 95–120.
144. Jackson, F. E.: Spontaneous spinal epidural hematoma coincident with whooping cough. J. Neurosurg. *20*:715–717, 1963.
145. Jackson, L. A., Cherry, J. D., Wang, S. P, et al.: Frequency of serological evidence of *Bordetella* infections and mixed infections with other respiratory pathogens in university students with cough illnesses. Clin. Infect. Dis. *31*:3–6, 2000.
146. Jenkinson, D.: Whooping cough: What proportion of cases is notified in an epidemic? B. M. J. *287*:183–185, 1983.
147. Johnston, I. D., Strachan, D. P., Anderson, H. R., et al.: Effect of pneumonia and whooping cough in childhood on adult lung function. N. Engl. J. Med. *338*:581–587, 1998.
148. Joint Committee on Vaccination and Immunisation: The whooping cough epidemic, 1977–79. *In* Whooping Cough: Reports from the Committee on Safety in Medicine and the Joint Committee on Vaccination and Immunisation. London, Department of Health and Social Security, Her Majesty's Stationery Office, 1981, p. 170.
149. Jones, D. H., McBride, B. W., Jeffery, H., et al.: Protection of mice from *Bordetella pertussis* respiratory infection using microencapsulated pertussis fimbriae. Vaccine *13*:675–681, 1995.
150. Keitel, W. A., Muenz, L. R., Decker, M. D., et al.: A randomized clinical trial of acellular pertussis vaccines in healthy adults: Dose-response comparisons of 5 vaccines and implications for booster immunization. J. Infect. Dis. *180*:397–403, 1999.
151. Kendrick, P. L., Eldering, G., Dixon, M. K., et al.: Mouse protection tests in the study of pertussis vaccines. Am. J. Public Health *37*:803–810, 1947.
152. Kerr, J. R., and Matthews, R. C.: *Bordetella pertussis* infection: Pathogenesis, diagnosis, management, and the role of protective immunity. Eur. J. Clin. Microbiol. Infect. Dis. *19*:77–88, 2000.
153. Kersters, K., Hinz, K. H., Hertle, A., et al.: *Bordetella avium* sp. nov., isolated from the respiratory tracts of turkeys and other birds. Int. J. Syst. Bacteriol. *34*:56–70, 1984.
154. Khelef, N., Sakamoto, H., and Guiso, N.: Both adenylate cyclase and hemolytic activities are required by *Bordetella pertussis* to initiate infection. Microbiol. Pathog. *12*:227–235, 1992.
155. Kimura, M., and Kuno-Sakai, H.: Pertussis vaccines in Japan. Acta Paediatr. Jpn. *30*:143–153, 1988.
156. Kimura, A., Mountzouros, K. T., Relman, D. A., et al.: *Bordetella pertussis* filamentous hemagglutinin: Evaluation as a protective antigen and colonization factor in a mouse respiratory infection model. Infect. Immun. *58*:7–16, 1990.
157. Korgenski, E. K., Daly, J. A.: Surveillance and detection of erythromycin resistance in *Bordetella pertussis* isolates recovered from a pediatric population in the Intermountain West region of the United States. J. Clin. Microbiol. *35*:2989–2991, 1997.
158. Kulenkampff, M., Schwartzman, J. S., and Wilson, J.: Neurological complications of pertussis inoculation. Arch. Dis. Child. *49*:46, 1974.
159. Kurt, T. L., Yeager, A. S., Guenette, S., et al.: Spread of pertussis by hospital staff. J. A. M. A. *221*:264–267, 1972.
160. Lambert, H. J.: Epidemiology of a small pertussis outbreak in Kent County, Michigan. Public Health Rep. *80*:365–369, 1965.
161. Lapin, J. H.: Whooping Cough. Springfield, IL, Charles C Thomas, 1943.
162. Lautrop, H.: Observations on parapertussis in Denmark 1950–1957. Acta Pathol. Microbiol. Scand. *43*:255–266, 1958.
163. Lee, B.: Progressive respiratory distress in an infant treated for presumed pertussis. Pediatr. Infect. Dis. J. *19*:475, 492–493, 2000.
164. Leininger, E., Kenimer, J. G., and Brennan, M. J.: Surface proteins of *Bordetella pertussis*: Role in adherence. Paper presented at the 6th International Symposium on Pertussis, September 26–28, 1990, Bethesda, MD, pp. 25–26.
165. Lewis, K., Cherry, J. D., Sachs, M. H., et al.: The effect of prophylactic acetaminophen administration on reactions to DTP vaccination. Am. J. Dis. Child. *142*:62–65, 1988.
166. Lewis, K., Saubolle, M. A., Tenover, F. C., et al.: Pertussis caused by an erythromycin-resistant strain of *Bordetella pertussis*. Pediatr. Infect. Dis. J. *14*:388–391, 1995.
167. Li, A. M, Jansen, D. L., Finn, T. M., et al.: Identification of *Bordetella pertussis* infection by shared-primer PCR. J. Clin. Microbiol. *32*:783–789, 1994.
168. Lichtinghagen, R., Diedrich-Glaubitz, R., von Hörsten, B.: Identification of *B. pertussis* in nasopharyngeal swabs using the polymerase chain reaction: Evaluation of detection methods. Eur. J. Clin. Chem. Clin. Biochem. *32*:161–167, 1994.
169. Liese, J. G., Meschievitz, C. K., Harzer, E., et al.: Efficacy of a two-component acellular pertussis vaccine in infants. Pediatr. Infect. Dis. J. *16*:1038–1044, 1997.
170. Lind-Brandberg, L., Welinder-Olsson, C., Lagergard, T., et al.: Evaluation of PCR for diagnosis of *Bordetella pertussis* and *Bordetella parapertussis* infections. J. Clin. Microbiol. *36*:679–683, 1998.
171. Lindgren, C., Milerad, J., Lagercrantz, H.: Sudden infant death and prevalence of whooping cough in the Swedish and Norwegian communities. Eur. J. Pediatr. *156*:405–409, 1997.
172. Lindquist, S. W., Weber, D. J., Mangum, M. E., et al.: *Bordetella holmesii* sepsis in an asplenic adolescent. Pediatr. Infect. Dis. J. *14*:813–815, 1995.
173. Linnemann, C. C., Jr.: Host-parasite interactions in pertussis. *In* Manclark, C. R., and Hill, J. C. (eds.): International Symposium on Pertussis. Publication No. (N. I. H.) 79–1830. Washington, D.C., U. S. Dept. of Health, Education, and Welfare, U. S. Government Printing Office, 1979, pp. 3–18.
174. Linnemann, C. C., Jr., and Nasenbeny, J.: Pertussis in the adult. Annu. Rev. Med. *28*:179–185, 1977.
175. Linnemann, C. C., Jr., Ramundo, N., Perlstein, P. H., et al.: Use of pertussis vaccine in an epidemic involving hospital staff. Lancet *2*:540–543, 1975.
176. Locht, C., Bertin, P., Menozzi, F. D., et al.: The filamentous haemagglutinin, a multifaceted adhesin produced by virulent *Bordetella* spp. Mol. Microbiol. *9*:653–660, 1993.
177. Long, S., Lischner, H., Deforest, A., et al.: Serologic evidence of subclinical pertussis in immunized children. Pediatr. Infect. Dis. J. *9*:700–705, 1990.
178. Long, S., Welkon, C., and Clark, J.: Widespread silent transmission of pertussis in families: Antibody correlates of infection and symptomatology. J. Infect. Dis. *161*:480–486, 1990.
179. Lugauer, S., Heininger, U., Cherry, J. D., et al.: Long term efficacy of the Wyeth-Lederle/Takeda acellular pertussis component vaccine (DTaP) and the Lederle whole cell vaccine (DTP). Paper presented at the 39th Interscience Conference on Antimicrobial Agents and Chemotherapy, September 26–29, 1999, San Francisco, and at the Acellular Pertussis Vaccine Conference, November 12–14, 2000, Bethesda, MD.
180. Luker, K. E., Collier, J. L., Kolodziej, E. W., et al.: *Bordetella pertussis* tracheal cytotoxin and other muramyl peptides: Distinct structure-activity relationships for respiratory epithelial cytopathology. Proc. Natl. Acad. Sci. U. S. A. *90*:2365–2369, 1993.
181. MacRae, K. D.: Epidemiology, encephalopathy, and pertussis vaccine. *In* FEMS-Symposium Pertussis: Proceedings of a Conference Organized by the Society of Microbiology and Epidemiology of the GDR. Berlin, April 20–22, 1988.
182. Madge, N., Diamond, J., Miller, D., et al.: The national childhood encephalopathy study: A 10-year follow-up. Dev. Med. Child Neurol. *68*(Suppl.):1–119, 1993.
183. Madsen, T.: Whooping cough: Its bacteriology, diagnosis, prevention and treatment. Boston Med. Surg. J. *192*:50–60, 1925.
184. Mahon, B. P., Brady, M. T., and Mills, K. H. G.: Protection against *Bordetella pertussis* in mice in the absence of detectable circulating antibody: Implications for long-term immunity in children. J. Infect. Dis. *181*:2087–2091, 2000.
185. Makhov, A. M., Hannah, J. H., Brennan, M. J., et al: Filamentous hemagglutinin of *Bordetella pertussis*: A bacterial adhesin formed as a 50-nm monomeric rigid rod based on a 19-residue repeat motif rich in beta strains and turns. J. Mol. Biol. *241*:110–124, 1994.
186. Manclark, C. R., Meade, B. D., and Burstyn, D. G.: Serological response to *Bordetella pertussis*. *In* Rose, N. R., Friedman, H., and Fahey, J. L. (eds.): Manual of Clinical Laboratory Immunology. 3rd ed. Washington, D.C., American Society for Microbiology, 1986, pp. 388–394.
187. Mannerstedt, G.: Pertussis in adults. J. Pediatr. *5*:596–600, 1934.
188. Martin, G. I., and Weintraub, M. I.: Brachial neuritis and seventh nerve palsy: A rare hazard of DPT vaccination. Clin. Pediatr. (Phila.) *12*:506–507, 1973.
189. Mastrantonio, P., Stefanelli, P., Giuliano, M.: Polymerase chain reaction for the detection of *Bordetella pertussis* in clinical nasopharyngeal aspirates. J. Med. Microbiol. *44*:261–266, 1996.
190. Masure, H. R.: The adenylate cyclase toxin contributes to the survival of *Bordetella pertussis* within human macrophages. Microb. Pathog. *14*:253–260, 1993.
191. Matherne, P., Matson, J., and Marks, M. I.: Pertussis complicated by the syndrome of inappropriate antidiuretic hormone secretion. Clin. Pediatr. (Phila.) *25*:46–48, 1986.
192. Mazengia, E., Silva, E. A., Peppe, J. A., et al.: Recovery of *Bordetella holmesii* from patients with pertussis-like symptoms: Use of pulsed-field

gel electrophoresis to characterize circulating strains. J. Clin. Microbiol. *38*:2330–2333, 2000.
193. McGregor, J., Ogle, J., and Curry-Kane, G.: Perinatal pertussis. Obstet. Gynecol. *68*:582–586, 1986.
194. Meade, B. D., and Bollen, A.: Recommendations for use of the polymerase chain reaction in the diagnosis of *Bordetella pertussis* infections. J. Med. Microbiol. *41*:51–55, 1994.
195. Medical Research Council: The prevention of whooping cough by vaccination. B. M. J. *1*:1463–1471, 1951.
196. Medical Research Council: Vaccination against whooping cough: Relation between protection in children and results of laboratory tests. B. M. J. *2*:454–462, 1956.
197. Medical Research Council: Vaccination against whooping cough. B. M. J. *1*:994–1000, 1959.
198. Melchior, J. C.: Infantile spasms and early immunization against whooping cough: Danish survey from 1970 to 1975. Arch. Dis. Child. *52*:134, 1977.
199. Mertsola, J., Ruuskanen, O., Kuronen, T., et al.: Serologic diagnosis of pertussis: Evaluation of pertussis toxin and other antigens in enzyme-linked immunosorbent assay. J. Infect. Dis. *161*:966–971, 1990.
200. Miller, D., Madge, N., Diamond, J., et al.: Pertussis immunisation and serious acute neurological illnesses in children. B. M. J. *307*:1171–1176, 1993.
201. Miller, D. L., Ross, E. M., Alderslade, R., et al.: Pertussis immunisation and serious acute neurological illness in children. B. M. J. *282*:1595–1597, 1981.
202. Miller, D., Wadsworth, J., Diamond, J., et al.: Pertussis vaccine and whooping cough as risk factors in acute neurological illness and death in young children. Dev. Biol. Stand. *61*:389–394, 1985.
203. Miller, D., Wadsworth, J., and Ross, E.: Severe neurological illness: Further analyses of the British National Childhood Encephalopathy Study. Tokai J. Exp. Clin. Med. *13*(Suppl.):145–155, 1988.
204. Miller, J. J., Jr., Silverberg, R. J., Saito, T. M., et al.: An agglutinative reaction for *Hemophilus pertussis*. II. Its relation to clinical immunity. J. Pediatr. *22*:644–651, 1943.
205. Mills, K. H. G., Barnard, A., Watkins, J., et al.: Cell-mediated immunity to *Bordetella pertussis*: Role of Th1 cells in bacterial clearance in a murine respiratory infection model. Infect. Immun. *61*:399–410, 1993.
206. Mills, K. H. G., and Redhead, K.: Cellular immunity in pertussis. J. Med. Microbiol. *39*:163–164, 1993.
207. Minh, N. N. T., He, Q., Edelman, K., et al.: Cell-mediated immune responses to antigens of *Bordetella pertussis* and protection against pertussis in school children. Pediatr. Infect. Dis. J. *18*:366–370, 1999.
208. Mink, C. A. M., Cherry, J. D., Christenson, P., et al.: A search for *Bordetella pertussis* infection in university students. Clin. Infect. Dis. *14*:464–471, 1992.
209. Mink, C. M., O'Brien, C. H., Wassilak, S., et al.: Isotype and antigen specificity of pertussis agglutinins following whole-cell pertussis vaccination and infection with *Bordetella pertussis*. Infect. Immun. *62*:1118–1120, 1994.
210. Mink, C., Sirota, N. M., and Nugent, S.: Outbreak of pertussis in a fully immunized adolescent and adult population. Arch. Pediatr. Adolesc. Med. *148*:153–157, 1994.
211. Mooi, F. A., van der Heide, H. G. J., Wellems, R., et al.: *Bordetella pertussis* fimbriae: Role in pathogenesis and mechanism of phase variation. Paper presented at the 6th International Symposium on Pertussis, September 26–28, 1990, Bethesda, MD, p. 63.
212. Morris, J. T., and Myers, M.: Bacteremia due to *Bordetella holmesii*. Clin. Infect. Dis. *27*:912–913, 1998.
213. Mortimer, E. A., Jr.: Pertussis and its prevention: A family affair. J. Infect. Dis. *161*:473–479, 1990.
214. Mortimer, E. A., Jr., and Jones, P. K.: An evaluation of pertussis vaccine. Rev. Infect. Dis. *1*:927–932, 1979.
215. Mortimer, E. A., Jr., and Jones, P. K.: Pertussis vaccine in the United States: The benefit-risk ratio. *In* International Symposium on Pertussis. Bethesda, MD, U. S. Department of Health, Education and Welfare, National Institutes of Health, 1979, p. 250.
216. Mortimer, E. A., Jr., Kimura, M., Cherry, J. D., et al.: Protective efficacy of the Takeda acellular pertussis vaccine combined with diphtheria and tetanus toxoids following household exposure of Japanese children. Am. J. Dis. Child. *144*:899–904, 1990.
217. Mountzouros, K. T., Kimura, A., and Cowell, J. L.: A bactericidal monoclonal antibody specific for the lipooligosaccharide of *Bordetella pertussis* reduces colonization of the respiratory tract of mice after aerosol infection with *B. pertussis*. Infect. Immun. *60*:5316–5318, 1992.
218. Müller, F., Hoppe, J. E., and Wirsing von König, C. H.: Laboratory diagnosis of pertussis: State of the art in 1997. J. Clin. Microbiol. *135*:2435–2443, 1997.
219. Munoz, J. J.: Action of pertussigen (pertussis toxin) on the host immune system. *In* Wardlaw, A. C., and Parton, R. (eds.): Pathogenesis and Immunity in Pertussis. New York, John Wiley & Sons, 1988, pp. 173–192.
220. Nagel, J., and Poot-Scholtens, E. J.: Serum IgA antibody to *Bordetella pertussis* as an indicator of infection. J. Med. Microbiol. *16*:417–426, 1983.
221. Nakase, Y., and Endoh, M.: Heat-labile toxin of *Bordetella pertussis*. *In* Wardlaw, A. C., and Parton, R. (eds.): Pathogenesis and Immunity in Pertussis. New York, John Wiley & Sons, 1988, pp. 217–229.
222. Nelson, J. D.: The changing epidemiology of pertussis in young infants: The role of adults as reservoirs of infection. Am. J. Dis. Child. *132*:371–375, 1978.
223. Nelson, K. E., Gavitt, F., Batt, M. D., et al.: The role of adenoviruses in the pertussis syndrome. J. Pediatr. *86*:335–341, 1975.
224. Nencioni, L., Pizza, M., Volpini, G., et al.: Properties of the B oligomer of pertussis toxin. Infect. Immun. *59*:4732–4734, 1991.
225. Nennig, M. E., Shinefield, H. R., Edwards, K. M., et al.: Prevalence and incidence of adult pertussis in an urban population. J. A. M. A. *275*:1672–1674, 1996.
226. Ng, V. L., Boggs, J. M., York, M. K., et al.: Recovery of *Bordetella bronchiseptica* from patients with AIDS. Clin. Infect. Dis. *15*:376–377, 1992.
227. Nicoll, A., and Gardner, A.: Whooping cough and unrecognised postperinatal mortality. Arch. Dis. Child. *63*:41–47, 1988.
228. Noble, G. R., Bernier, R. H., Esber, E. C., et al.: Acellular and whole cell pertussis vaccines in Japan: Report of a visit by U.S. scientists. J. A. M. A. *257*:1351–1356, 1987.
229. Novotny, P.: Pathogenesis in *Bordetella* species. J. Infect. Dis. *161*:581–582, 1990.
230. Novotny, P., Chubb, A. P., Cownley, K., et al.: Biologic and protective properties of the 69-kDa outer membrane protein of *Bordetella pertussis*: A novel formulation for an acellular pertussis vaccine. J. Infect. Dis. *164*:114–122, 1991.
231. Olcen, P., Backman, A., Johansson, B., et al.: Amplification of DNA by the polymerase chain reaction for the efficient diagnosis of pertussis. Scand. J. Infect. Dis. *24*:339–345, 1992.
232. Olin, P., Rasmussen, F., Gustafsson, L., et al.: Randomised controlled trial of two-component, three-component, and five-component acellular pertussis vaccines compared with whole-cell pertussis vaccine. Lancet *350*:1569–1577, 1997.
233. Olsen, L. C.: Pertussis. Medicine (Baltimore) *54*:427–469, 1975.
234. Onorato, I. M., and Wassilak, S. G. F.: Laboratory diagnosis of pertussis: The state of the art. Pediatr. Infect. Dis. J. *6*:145–151, 1987.
235. Onorato, I. M., Wassilak, S. G., and Meade, B.: Efficacy of whole-cell pertussis vaccine in preschool children in the United States. J. A. M. A. *20*:2745–2749, 1992.
236. Pertussis—Maryland, 1982. M. M. W. R. Morb. Mortal. Wkly. Rep. *32*:297–300, 305, 1983.
237. Pertussis surveillance, 1979–1981. M. M. W. R. Morb. Mortal. Wkly. Rep. *31*:333–336, 1982.
238. Pertussis—United States, 1982 and 1983. M. M. W. R. Morb. Mortal. Wkly. Rep. *33*:573–575, 1984.
239. Pichichero, M. E., Edwards, K. M., Anderson, E. L., et al.: Safety and immunogenicity of six acellular pertussis vaccines and one whole-cell pertussis vaccine given as a fifth dose in four- to six-year-old children. Pediatrics *105:www.pediatrics.org/cgi/content/full/105/1/e11,* 2000.
240. Pittman, M.: Pertussis toxin: The cause of the harmful effects and prolonged immunity of whooping cough: A hypothesis. Rev. Infect. Dis. *1*:401–412, 1979.
241. Pittman, M.: The concept of pertussis as a toxin-mediated disease. Pediatr. Infect. Dis. *3*:467–486, 1984.
242. Porter, J. F., Connor, K., and Donachie, W.: Isolation and characterization of *Bordetella parapertussis*-like bacteria from ovine lungs. Microbiolology *140*:255–261, 1994.
243. Postels-Multani, S., Schmitt, H. J., Wirsing von König, C. H., et al.: Symptoms and complications of pertussis in adults. Infection *23*:139–142, 1995.
244. Preston, N. W.: Pertussis today. *In* Wardlaw, A. C., and Parton, R. (eds.): Pathogenesis and Immunity in Pertussis. New York, John Wiley & Sons, 1988, pp. 1–18.
245. Reizenstein, E., Johanson, B., Mardin, L., et al.: Diagnostic evaluation of polymerase chain reaction discriminative for *Bordetella pertussis*, *B. parapertussis*, and *B. bronchiseptica*. Diagn. Microbiol. Infect. Dis. *17*:185–191, 1993.
246. Reizenstein, E., Lindberg, L., Möllby, R., et al.: Validation of nested *Bordetella* PCR in a pertussis vaccine trial. J. Clin. Microbiol. *34*:810–815, 1996.
247. Rennels, M. B., Deloria, M. A., Pichichero, M. E., et al.: Extensive swelling after booster doses of acellular pertussis-tetanus-diphtheria vaccines. Pediatrics *105:www.pediatrics.org/cgi/content/full/105/1/el2,* 2000.
248. Robbins, J. B., Pittman, M., Trollfors, B., et al.: Primum non nocere: A pharmacologically inert pertussis toxoid alone should be the next pertussis vaccine. Pediatr. Infect. Dis. J. *12*:795–807, 1993.
249. Robertson, P. W., Goldberg, H., Jarvie, B. H., et al.: *Bordetella pertussis* infection: A cause of persistent cough in adults. Med. J. Aust. *146*:522–525, 1987.
250. Robinson, A., Ashworth, L. A. E., and Irons, L. I.: Serotyping *Bordetella pertussis* strains. Vaccine *7*:491–494, 1989.
251. Robinson, A., Irons, L. I., Seabrook, R. N., et al.: Structure-function studies of *Bordetella pertussis* fimbriae. *In* Manclark, C. R. (ed.): Proceedings

of the Sixth International Symposium on Pertussis. D. H. H. S. Publication No. (F. D. A.) 90. Bethesda, MD, Department of Health and Human Services, U. S. Public Health Service, 1990, pp. 126–135.
252. Rosenthal, S., Strebel, P., Cassiday, P., et al.: Pertussis infection among adults during the 1993 outbreak in Chicago. J. Infect. Dis. *171*:1650–1652, 1995.
253. Rothstein, E. P., Anderson, E. L., Decker, M. D., et al.: An acellular pertussis vaccine in healthy adults: Safety and immunogenicity. Pennridge Pediatric Associates. Vaccine *17*:2999–3006, 1999.
254. Ryan, M., Murphy, G., Gothefors, L., et al.: *Bordetella pertussis* respiratory infection in children is associated with preferential activation of type 1 T helper cells. J. Infect. Dis. *175*:1246–1250, 1997.
255. Ryan, M., Murphy, G., Ryan, E., et al.: Distinct T-cell subtypes induced with whole cell and acellular pertussis vaccines in children. Immunology *93*:1–10, 1998.
256. Salmaso, S., Mastrantonio, P., Wassilak, S. G. F., et al.: Persistence of protection through 33 months of age provided by immunization in infancy with two three-component acellular pertussis vaccines. Vaccine *13*:1270–1275, 1998.
257. Sans, M. B., Bonal, J., Bonet, J., et al.: *Bordetella bronchiseptica* septicemia in a hemodialysis patient. Nephron *59*:676, 1991.
258. Sato, H., and Sato, Y.: *Bordetella pertussis* infection in mice: Correlation of specific antibodies against two antigens, pertussis toxin, and filamentous hemagglutinin with mouse protectivity in an intracerebral or aerosol challenge system. Infect. Immun. *46*:415–421, 1984.
259. Schläpfer, G., Cherry, J. D., Heininger, U., et al.: Polymerase chain reaction identification of *Bordetella pertussis* infections in vaccinees and family members in a pertussis vaccine efficacy trial in Germany. Pediatr. Infect. Dis. J. *14*:209–214, 1995.
260. Schläpfer, G., Senn, H. P., Berger, R., et al.: Use of the polymerase chain reaction to detect *Bordetella pertussis* in patients with mild or typical symptoms of infection. Eur. J. Clin. Microbiol. Infect. Dis. *12*:459–463, 1993.
261. Schmitt, H. J., Beutel K., Schuind A, et al.: Reactogenicity and immunogenicity of a booster dose of a combined diphtheria, tetanus, and tricomponent acellular pertussis vaccine at fourteen to twenty-eight months of age. J. Pediatr. *130*:616–623, 1997.
262. Schmitt, H. J., Wirsing von König, C. H., Neiss, A., et. al.: Efficacy of acellular pertussis vaccine in early childhood after household exposure. J. A. M. A. *275*:37–41, 1996.
263. Schmitt-Grohè, S., Cherry, J. D., Heininger, U., et al.: Pertussis in German adults. Clin. Infect. Dis. *27*:860–866, 1995.
264. Schmitt-Grohè, S., Stehr, K., Cherry, J. D., et al.: Minor adverse events in a comparative efficacy trial in Germany in infants receiving either the Lederle/Takeda acellular pertussis component DTP (DTaP) vaccine, the Lederle whole-cell component DTP (DTP) or DT vaccine. Dev. Biol. Stand. *89*:113–118, 1997.
265. Shahin, R. D., Amsbaugh, D. F., and Leef, M. F.: Mucosal immunization with filamentous hemagglutinin protects against *Bordetella pertussis* respiratory infection. Infect. Immun. *60*:1482–1488, 1992.
266. Shahin, R. D., Brennan, M. J., Meade, B. D., et al.: Characterization of the protective capacity and immunogenicity of the 69-kD outer membrane protein of *Bordetella pertussis*. J. Exp. Med. *171*:63–73, 1990.
267. Shields, W. D., Nielsen, C., Buch, D., et al.: Relationship of pertussis immunization to the onset of neurologic disorders: A retrospective epidemiologic study. J. Pediatr. *113*:801–805, 1988.
268. Simonond, F., Preziosi, M. P., Yam, A., et al.: A randomized double-blind trial comparing a two-component acellular to a whole-cell pertussis vaccine in Senegal. Vaccine *15*:1606–1612, 1997.
269. Southall, D. P., Thomas, M. G., and Lambert, H. P.: Severe hypoxaemia in pertussis. Arch. Dis. Child. *63*:598–605, 1988.
270. Stefanelli, P., Mastrantonio, P., Hausman, S. Z., et al.: Molecular characterization of two *Bordetella bronchiseptica* strains isolated from children with coughs. J. Clin. Microbiol. *35*:1550–1555, 1997.
271. Stehr, K., Cherry, J. D., Heininger, U., et al.: A comparative efficacy trial in Germany in infants who received either the Lederle/Takeda acellular pertussis component DTP (DTaP) vaccine, the Lederle whole-cell component DTP vaccine or DT vaccine. Pediatrics *101*:1–11, 1998.
272. Steketee, R. W., Burstyn, D. G., Wassilak, S. G. F., et al.: A comparison of laboratory and clinical methods for diagnosing pertussis in an outbreak in a facility for the developmentally disabled. J. Infect. Dis. *157*:441–449, 1988.
273. Steketee, R. W., Wassilak, S. G. F., Adkins, W. N., Jr., et al.: Evidence for a high attack rate and efficacy of erythromycin prophylaxis in a pertussis outbreak in a facility for the developmentally disabled. J. Infect. Dis. *157*:434–440, 1988.
274. Stephenson, J. B. P.: A neurologist looks at neurological disease temporally related to DTP immunization. Tokai J. Exp. Clin. Med. *13*(Suppl.):157–164, 1988.
275. Stewart, G. T.: Vaccination against whooping-cough: Efficacy versus risks. Lancet *1*:234, 1977.
276. Stockbauer, K. E., Fuchslocher B., Miller, J. F., et al.: Identification and characterization of BipA, a *Bordetella* Bvg-intermediate phase protein. Mol. Microbiol. *39*:65–78, 2001.
277. Stocks, P.: Studies in the Population of England and Wales 1944–47. Studies on Medical and Population Subjects. No. 2. London, Her Majesty's Stationery Office, 1949.
278. Storsaeter, J., Blackwelder, W. C., and Hallander, H. O.: Pertussis antibodies, protection, and vaccine efficacy after household exposure. Am. J. Dis. Child. *146*:167–172, 1992.
279. Storsaeter, J., Hallander, H., Farrington, C. P., et al.: Secondary analyses of the efficacy of two acellular pertussis vaccines evaluated in a Swedish phase III trial. Vaccine *8*:457–461, 1990.
280. Storsaeter, J., Hallander, H. O., Gustafsson, L., et al.: Levels of anti-pertussis antibodies related to protection after household exposure to *Bordetella pertussis*. Vaccine *16*:1907–1916, 1998.
281. Storsaeter, J., and Olin, P.: Relative efficacy of two acellular pertussis vaccines during three years of passive surveillance. Vaccine *10*:142–144, 1992.
282. Strebel, P. M., Cochi, S. L., Farizo, K. M., et al.: Pertussis in Missouri: Evaluation of nasopharyngeal culture, direct fluorescent antibody testing, and clinical case definitions in the diagnosis of pertussis. Clin. Infect. Dis. *16*:276–285, 1993.
283. Ström, J.: Further experience of reactions, especially of a cerebral nature, in conjunction with triple vaccination: A study based on vaccinations in Sweden 1959–65. B. M. J. *4*:320, 1967.
284. Swansea Research Unit of the Royal College of General Practitioners: Study of intellectual performance of children in ordinary schools after certain serious complications of whooping cough. B. M. J. *295*:1044–1047, 1987.
285. Switzer, W. P., Mare, C. J., and Hubbard, E. D.: Incidence of *Bordetella bronchisepticum* in wildlife and man in Iowa. Am. J. Vet. Res. *27*:1134–1136, 1966.
286. Tamion, F., Girault, C., Chevron, V., et al.: *Bordetella bronchoseptica* pneumonia with shock in an immunocompetent patient. Scand. J. Infect. Dis. *28*:137–138, 1996.
287. Tang, Y. W., Hopkins, M. K., Kolbert, C. P., et al.: *Bordetella holmesii*–like organisms associated with septicemia, endocarditis and respiratory failure. Clin. Infect. Dis. *26*:389–392, 1998.
288. Taranger, J., Trollfors, B., Lagergard, T., et al.: Parapertussis infection followed by pertussis infection. Lancet *2*:1703, 1994.
289. Taranger, J., Trollfors, B., Lagergard, T., et al.: Unchanged efficacy of a pertussis toxoid vaccine throughout the two years after the third vaccination of infants. Pediatr. Infect. Dis. J. *16*:180–184, 1997.
290. Thomas, P. F., McIntyre, P. B., and Jalaludin, B. B.: Survey of pertussis morbidity in adults in western Sydney. Med. J. Aust. *173*:74–76, 2000.
291. Tomoda, T. Ogura, H., and Kurashige, T.: Immune responses to *Bordetella pertussis* infection and vaccination. J. Infect. Dis. *163*: 559–563, 1991.
292. Trollfors, B., Taranger, J., Lagergard, T., et al.: A placebo-controlled trial of a pertussis-toxoid vaccine. N. Engl. J. Med. *333*:1045–1050, 1995.
293. Tuomanen, E.: *Bordetella pertussis* adhesins. *In* Wardlaw, A. C., and Parton, R. (eds.): Pathogenesis and Immunity in Pertussis. New York, John Wiley & Sons, 1988, pp. 75–94.
294. Überall, M. A., Stehr, K., Cherry, J. D., et al.: Severe adverse events in a comparative efficacy trial in Germany in infants receiving either the Lederle/Takeda acellular pertussis component DTP (DTaP) vaccine, the Lederle whole-cell component DTP (DTP) or DT vaccine. Dev. Biol. Stand. *89*:83–89, 1997.
295. Ui, M.: The multiple biological activities of pertussis toxin. *In* Wardlaw, A. C., and Parton, R. (eds.): Pathogenesis and Immunity in Pertussis. New York, John Wiley & Sons, 1988, pp. 121–146.
296. Urisu, A., Cowell, J. L., and Manclark, C. R.: Filamentous hemagglutinin has a major role in mediating adherence of *Bordetella pertussis* to human WiDr cells. Infect. Immun. *52*:695–701, 1986.
297. Use of diphtheria toxoid–tetanus toxoid–acellular pertussis vaccine as a five-dose series. Supplemental recommendations of the Advisory Committee on Immunization Practices (ACIP). M. M. W. R. Recomm. Rep. *49*(RR-13):1–8, 2000.
298. Valenti, W. M., Pincus, P. H., and Messner, M. K.: Nosocomial pertussis: Possible spread by a hospital visitor. Am. J. Dis. Child. *134*:520–521, 1980.
299. Van Buynder, P. G., Owen, D., Vurdien, J. E., et al.: *Bordetella pertussis* surveillance in England and Wales: 1995–7. Epidemiol. Infect. *123*:403–411, 1999.
300. Vancanneyt, M., Vandamme, P., and Kersters, K.: Differentiation of *Bordetella pertussis*, *B. parapertussis*, and *B. bronchiseptica* by whole-cell protein electrophoresis and fatty acid analysis. Int. J. Syst. Bacteriol. *45*:843–847, 1995.
301. Vandamme, P., Heyndrickx, M., Vancanneyt, M., et al.: *Bordetella trematum* sp. nov., isolated from wounds and ear infections in humans, and reassessment of *Alcaligenes denitrificans* Rüger and Tan 1983. Int. J. Syst. Bacteriol. *46*:849–858, 1996.
302. van der Zee, A., Agterberg, C., Peeters, M., et al.: Polymerase chain reaction assay for pertussis: Simultaneous detection and discrimination of *Bordetella pertussis* and *Bordetella parapertussis*. J. Clin. Microbiol. *31*:2134–2140, 1993.
303. van der Zee, A., Agterberg, C., Peeters, M., et al.: A clinical validation of *Bordetella pertussis* and *Bordetella parapertussis* polymerase chain

reaction: Comparison with culture and serology using samples from patients with suspected whooping cough from a highly immunized population. J. Infect. Dis. *174*:89–96, 1996.

304. Viljanen, M. K., Ruuskanen, O., Granberg, C., et al.: Serological diagnosis of pertussis: IgM, IgA, and IgG antibodies against *Bordetella pertussis* measured by enzyme-linked immunosorbent assay (ELISA). Scand. J. Infect. Dis. *14*:117–122, 1982.
305. Vincent, J. M., Cherry, J. D., Nauschuetz, W. F., et al.: Prolonged afebrile nonproductive cough illnesses in American soldiers in Korea: A serological search for causation. Clin. Infect. Dis. *30*:534–539, 2000.
306. Walker, A. M., Jick, H., Perera, D. R., et al.: Neurologic events following diphtheria-tetanus-pertussis immunization. Pediatrics *81*:345–349, 1988.
307. Walker, K. E., and Weiss, A. A.: Characterization of the dermonecrotic toxin in members of the genus *Bordetella*. Infect. Immun. *62*:3817–3828, 1994.
308. Wärngård, O., Nilsson, L., Fåhraeus, C., et al.: Catch-up primary vaccination with acellular pertussis vaccines in 3–4-year-old children—reactogenicity and serological response. Vaccine *16*:480–484, 1998.
309. Washburn, T. C., Medearis, D. N., and Childs, B.: Sex differences in susceptibility to infection. Pediatrics *35*:57–67, 1965.
310. Watts, E. C., and Acosta, C.: Pertussis and bilateral subdural hematomas. Am. J. Dis. Child. *118*:518–519, 1969.
311. Weiss, A. A., and Falkow, S.: Genetic analysis of phase variation in *Bordetella pertussis*. Infect. Immun. *43*:263–269, 1984.
312. Weiss, A. A., and Hewlett, E. L.: Virulence factors of *Bordetella pertussis*. Annu. Rev. Microbiol. *40*:661–686, 1986.
313. Weiss, A. A., Hewlett, E. L., Myers, G. A., et al.: Pertussis toxin and extracytoplasmic adenylate cyclase as virulence factors of *Bordetella pertussis*. J. Infect. Dis. *2*:219–222, 1984.
314. Weyant, R. S., Hollis, D. G., Weaver, R. E., et al.: *Bordetella holmesii* sp. nov., a new gram-negative species associated with septicemia. J. Clin. Microbiol. *33*:1–7, 1995.
315. Wiertz, E. J. H., Loggen, H. G., Walvoort, H. D., et al.: In vitro induction of antigen specific antibody synthesis and proliferation of T lymphocytes with acellular pertussis vaccines, pertussis toxin and filamentous hemagglutinin in humans. J. Biol. Stand. *17*:181–190, 1989.
316. Willems, R. J. L., Kamerbeek, J., Geuijen, C. A. W., et al.: The efficacy of a whole cell pertussis vaccine and fimbriae against *Bordetella pertussis* and *Bordetella parapertussis* infections in a respiratory mouse model. Vaccine *16*:410–416, 1998.
317. Wilson, G. S.: The Hazards of Immunization. London, Althone Press, 1967.
318. Wirsing von König, C. H., Gounis, D., Laukamp, S., et al.: Evaluation of a single-sample serological technique for diagnosing pertussis in unvaccinated children. Eur. J. Clin. Microbiol. Infect. Dis. *18*:341–345, 1999.
319. Wirsing von König, C. H., Postels-Multani, S., Bock, H. L., et al.: Pertussis in adults: Frequency of transmission after household exposure. Lancet *346*:1326–1329, 1995.
320. Wirsing von König, C. H., Rott, H., Bogaerts, H., et al.: A serologic study of organisms possibly associated with pertussis-like coughing. Pediatr. Infect. Dis. J. *17*:645–649, 1998.
321. Woolf, A. L., and Caplin, H.: Whooping cough encephalitis. Arch. Dis. Child. *3*:87–91, 1956.
322. Woolfrey, B. F., and Moody, J. A.: Human infections associated with *Bordetella bronchiseptica*. Clin. Microbiol. Rev. *4*:243–255, 1991.
323. World Health Organization meeting on case definition of pertussis. Geneva, January 10–11, 1991, MIM/EPI/PERT/9.1. Geneva, W. H. O., 1991.
324. Wortis, N., Strebel, P. M., Wharton, M., et al.: Pertussis deaths: Report of 23 cases in the United States, 1992 and 1993. Pediatrics *97*:607–612, 1996.
325. Wright, S. W., Edwards, K. M., Decker, M. D., et al.: Pertussis infections in adults with persistent cough. J. A. M. A. *273*:1044–1046, 1995.
326. Yih, W. K., Silva, E. A., Ida, J., et al.: *Bordetella holmesii*–like organisms isolated from Massachusetts patients with pertussis-like symptoms. Emerg. Infect. Dis. *5*:441–443, 1999.
327. Yuk, M. H., Harvill, E. T., Miller, J. F., et al.: The BvgAS virulence control system regulates type III secretion in *Bordetella bronchiseptica*. Mol. Microbiol. *28*:945–959, 1998.
328. Zackrisson, G., Lagergard, T., Trollfors, B., et al.: Immunoglobulin A antibodies to pertussis toxin and filamentous hemagglutinin in saliva from patients with pertussis. J. Clin. Microbiol. *28*:1502–1505, 1990.
329. Zee, A., Agterberg, C., Peeters, M., et al.: Polymerase chain reaction assay for pertussis: Simultaneous detection and discrimination of *Bordetella pertussis* and *Bordetella parapertussis*. J. Clin. Microbiol. *31*:2134–2140, 1993.
330. Zepp, F., Knuf, M., Habermehl, P., et al.: Pertussis-specific cell-mediated immunity in infants after vaccination with a tricomponent acellular pertussis vaccine. Infect. Immun. *64*:4078–4084, 1996.
331. Zhang, Y. L., and Sekura, R. D.: Purification and characterization of the heat-labile toxin of *Bordetella pertussis*. Infect. Immun. *59*:3754–3759, 1991.
332. Zoumboulakis, D., Anagnostakis, D., Albams, V., et al.: Steroids in treatment of pertussis: A controlled clinical trial. Arch. Dis. Child. *48*:51–54, 1973.

Calymmatobacterium granulomatis

MARIAM R. CHACKO

Granuloma inguinale is caused by *Calymmatobacterium granulomatis*. It was described first by McLeod in 1882, and *C. granulomatis* was isolated by Donovan in 1905. This disease has been known through the years by many different names, the most common being granuloma inguinale, donovanosis, and granuloma venereum.[25]

The Organism

C. granulomatis is an encapsulated gram-negative rod measuring 1.5 × 0.7 μm. Although some of its characteristics resemble those of *Klebsiella* and *Enterobacter, C. granulomatis* is considered a unique species distinct from other related organisms belonging to the subclass Proteobacteria.[17, 25, 26] However, the biochemical and bacteriologic characteristics of the organism have not been identified.[25, 26]

Study of the organism reveals a complex cell envelope. In addition to having regular bacterial structures such as a mesosome, ribosomes, and nuclear material, the cytoplasm contains electron-dense granules, and transmission electron microscopy shows an outer membrane, middle electron-opaque layer, and an inner plasma membrane. The organisms are enclosed mainly in large histiocytic cells and occasionally in polymorphonuclear cells and plasma cells. They multiply intracellularly to approximately 30 in number and eventually cause cell rupture.[4, 25]

Epidemiology

Granuloma inguinale occurs predominantly in young and older adults and is a cause of genital ulcerative disease in tropical and subtropical regions of the world. As with all genital ulcerative diseases, granuloma inguinale has been given greater attention as a risk factor for development of human immunodeficiency virus (HIV) infection.[32] In South Africa, the prevalence of granuloma inguinale in patients with genital ulcer disease is reported to be approximately 10 percent.[29]

Granuloma inguinale is a rare occurrence in children. In the early 1950s, 4 percent of 1- to 4-year-old children in a Papua New Guinea population were found to have granuloma inguinale. The mode of transmission of the disease was thought to be via skin-to-skin contact from children sitting on the laps of infected adults,[25] but in more recent case reports, otitis media, mastoiditis, a neck mass, and cervical lymphadenopathy have been described as the initial manifestations of donovanosis in infants and children.[2, 11, 12] The modes of transmission in these cases are thought to be perinatal transmission and skin-to-skin contact.[2, 11, 12]

Granuloma inguinale has been reported since the early 1990s as being endemic in South Africa, Papua New Guinea, India, and the Aboriginal community of Australia.[24] A resurgence of the disease was reported in the late 1980s in Durban, South Africa. After the introduction of a rapid test for donovanosis in the early 1990s, the number of cases reported by the Durban Health Department in South Africa has increased substantially.[22] In 1994, after 4 decades, a case of granuloma inguinale was reported in China.[10]

Granuloma inguinale is not a common occurrence in the United States today. Until 1952, more than a thousand cases a year were reported to the Centers for Disease Control and Prevention (CDC). Since 1952, a rapid decline in the prevalence of this disease has occurred; between 1971 and 1981, 50 to 90 cases a year were reported. Except for an isolated surge of 97 cases in 1990, fewer than 50 cases a year have been reported since 1982, and in 1993, 19 cases were reported, 15 male and 4 female. In 2000, no cases were reported in the United States.[6] Granuloma inguinale was detected in a white adolescent girl in California in 1985.[13] In 1991, nongenital granuloma inguinale was diagnosed in a man with testicular carcinoma in Texas.[21] In 1992, three unrelated cases of granuloma inguinale, seen within a period of a few weeks, were reported in Toronto; two occurred in immigrants and one in a native-born Canadian. The first patient was a recent immigrant from El Salvador, and the second patient had immigrated several years previously and had sexual activity with a Jamaican who had immigrated recently. The sexual partner of the third case had come from Turkey.[15] Although the prevalence of the disease is low, this disease needs to be suspected in North America and Europe because of international travel and immigration. Granuloma inguinale usually occurs more commonly in males than females. However, in adolescents, the disease can develop more commonly in girls than boys. This ratio probably is a reflection of sexual activity between adolescent girls and adult men.[23]

The risk factors and mode of transmission of granuloma inguinale are not clear. The disease generally is considered a sexually transmitted disease. However, in many cases, granuloma inguinale cannot be detected in the sexual partners of infected persons. Nevertheless, numerous studies have reported the disease in 12 to 50 percent of marital or steady sexual partners.[25] Anal intercourse also has been associated with rectal and penile lesions of granuloma inguinale.[18] O'Farrell and associates[30] studied the patterns of sexual behavior in men and women with genital ulcer disease and found that patients with granuloma inguinale and secondary syphilis were more likely than patients with other genital ulcer diseases to have had sexual intercourse despite the presence of ulcers. Studies reported from India and South Africa have noted a preponderance of granuloma inguinale cases in uncircumcised males with poor genital hygiene.[23]

Coexistence of granuloma inguinale with other sexually transmitted diseases occurs commonly. Syphilis has been described in as many as 23 percent of patients with granuloma inguinale. In a recent report, HIV-1 antibodies were found in as many as 8 percent of males with granuloma inguinale.[23, 32]

Pathogenesis and Pathology

The primary lesion in granuloma inguinale is an indurated nodule that erodes through the skin and becomes a granulomatous heaped ulcer. Adjacent lesions form and eventually coalesce, especially in the perineal area. Secondary infection of lesions may occur and aggravate the tissue destruction and cause scarring. *C. granulomatis* organisms invade mononuclear endothelial cells. Extensive acanthosis and dense dermal infiltrates of mainly plasma cells and histiocytes have been observed in the indurated nodules. Polymorphonuclear cell infiltration also occurs, but lymphocytes are rare findings when secondary infection develops. The pathognomonic feature of granuloma inguinale is a large infected mononuclear cell, 25 to 90 μm in diameter, that contains many intracytoplasmic cysts filled with deep-staining Donovan bodies. Metastatic spread to the bones, joints, liver, and lymphatics occasionally occurs.[25]

A possible link between HLA-B57 and granuloma inguinale infection may exist; class I, class II, and DQ antigens have been detected in the genital ulcers of individuals with granuloma inguinale.[27] Circulating lymphocytes and tissue-level lymphocyte subpopulations in granuloma inguinale have been studied.[35, 36] T-lymphocyte and B-lymphocyte infiltration in tissues is almost identical, without any significant difference in ulcerogranulomatous and hypertrophic variants. Both the total leukocyte and absolute lymphocyte counts are increased in the ulcerogranulomatous variant of granuloma inguinale. Total T lymphocytes, CD4, CD8, and CD22 levels, and the CD4/CD8 ratio all are increased significantly in the ulcerogranulomatous variant. In contrast, the hypertrophic variant causes a significant elevation only in the CD4/CD8 ratio. This finding suggests a greater cell-mediated immune response in the ulcerogranulomatous variant of granuloma inguinale and is consistent with the paucity of Donovan bodies in smears obtained from patients with this variant.[35, 36]

Clinical Manifestations

The incubation period of granuloma inguinale is usually less than 2 weeks but may be as long as 3 months. The disease begins as one or more subcutaneous nodules that erode through the skin to produce clean, beefy-red, granulomatous ulcers. The lesions are sharply defined and painless, and the ulcers feel hard when palpated. The disease is characterized by large genital ulcers that bleed easily. When left untreated at this early stage, the disease progresses and causes extensive mutilating lesions[25] (see Chapter 49).

The morphology of the cutaneous lesions of granuloma inguinale can vary, depending on the stage of the disease. The exuberant or hypertrophic stage appears before secondary infection develops. It consists of large, vegetating masses with overgrowth of granulation tissue, usually in the perianal region. The ulcerative stage is accompanied by secondary infection. In this stage, large, spreading, shallow necrotic ulcers with a foul odor may be noted. The cicatricial stage results after prolonged healing and is characterized by fibrosis, scarring, depigmentation, keloid formation, elephantiasis, and stenosis of the vagina, urethra, and anus. In patients in Durban, ulcerogranulomatous lesions occurred far more commonly than did hypertrophic and necrotic lesions. Although lymphadenopathy is an unusual occurrence in granuloma inguinale, pseudobuboes and pseudo-elephantiasis may be seen. Pseudobuboes are the result of deep, inguinal granulomata; pseudo-elephantiasis is caused by cutaneous extension of lesions and inflammation.[8, 23, 25]

The genitalia are involved in 90 percent of cases, the inguinal region in 10 percent, the anal region in 5 to 10 percent, and extragenital sites in 1 to 5 percent. Extragenital sites have been reported in the mouth, chin, axillae, abdomen including the pelvic cavity, and foot.[7, 19, 21, 25, 33, 34] In males, lesions usually occur on the prepuce and also can occur on the coronal sulcus and frenulum of the penis.[25, 26] As ulcers enlarge, they can be mutilating and lead to urethral stenosis. The most common clinical manifestation in pregnant and nonpregnant women is vulvar ulceration. Genital tract bleeding is the next most common finding in nonpregnant women. Multiple sites of genital ulceration (vulva, vagina, and cervix) have been noted only in nonpregnant women.[1, 23, 25]

Hematogenous spread to the head, liver, spleen, thorax, and bones can occur. These distant sites usually are associated with a primary lesion in the genital area.[25] Lesions in the oral cavity have been described after apparently successful treatment of genital lesions.[7]

Donovanosis ulcers may take longer to heal in HIV-positive individuals, and greater destruction of tissue may be noted as well.[25, 26]

Misdiagnosis of granuloma inguinale can occur in areas where the disease is not endemic. In endemic areas, unusual manifestations of granuloma inguinale may cause confusion with a wide variety of diseases. The differential diagnosis includes carcinoma, secondary syphilis, and necrotic ulcerations of amebiasis. In addition, secondary infection can confuse the diagnosis.[25]

Diagnosis

Generally, granuloma inguinale is diagnosed on clinical grounds. The accuracy of a clinical diagnosis of granuloma inguinale can be as high as 63 percent in males and 83 percent in females. When compared with other genital ulcers, the ulcers are larger in granuloma inguinale, are painless, bleed easily to touch, and usually are not associated with inguinal lymphadenopathy.[31]

The diagnosis of granuloma inguinale can be confirmed by identification of Donovan bodies on a stained crush specimen from the lesion (see Fig. 49–22). Appropriately stained specimens from active lesions remain the most reliable diagnostic test. Light-microscopic examination of biopsy specimens that have been fixed in formalin and embedded in wax is less reliable. Donovan bodies rarely are seen by this method.[25, 31]

The common stain used to identify Donovan bodies is Wright-Giemsa blue-black stain. Sections that are formalin fixed or stained with hematoxylin and eosin are less useful for detecting Donovan bodies. If donovanosis is suspected, a swab for this condition should be taken first, before swabs for other organisms, so that an adequate amount of cellular material can be obtained.[16, 25, 28] When *C. granulomatis* organisms are likely to be scarce or when smear or crush specimens are likely to be nondiagnostic, one should consider obtaining a biopsy of the lesion. Accordingly, a biopsy specimen preferably stained with Giemsa or silver is recommended in very early, very sclerotic, or heavily superinfected specimens.[16, 25, 28]

Successful isolation of *C. granulomatis* by culture on human epithelial cell lines with a modified *Chlamydia* culture technique has been reported from South Africa and Australia.[3] Polymerase chain reaction techniques for *C. granulomatis* also have been developed and further refined into a colorimetric detection system for use in diagnostic laboratories.

Donovan bodies have been identified on Papanicolaou smears from the cervix.[5] Serologic and skin tests for granuloma inguinale are highly sensitive but not specific. A serologic test using the indirect immunofluorescence technique has been evaluated and found to have a sensitivity of 100 percent, a specificity of 98 percent, a positive predictive value of 89 percent, and a negative predictive value of 100 percent in diagnosing granuloma inguinale. In the absence of culture methods for *C. granulomatis*, this test may prove helpful in the diagnosis of established lesions and not early ulcers.[9]

Treatment

Antibiotics with good activity against *C. granulomatis* are those effective in the treatment of gram-negative bacilli or those whose lipid solubility ensures good intracellular penetration. The CDC recommends treatment with trimethoprim-sulfamethoxazole or doxycycline for a minimum of 3 weeks. The former is prescribed as one double-strength tablet, 160/800 mg orally twice a day, and the latter as 100 mg twice a day.[14] However, O'Farrell suggested that azithromycin now be the drug of choice and be prescribed at 500 mg daily for 7 days or 1 g weekly for 4 weeks.[26] Alternative CDC regimens include ciprofloxacin, 750 mg orally twice a day for a minimum of 3 weeks, or erythromycin, 500 mg four times a day for 3 weeks.[14, 25, 26] Children younger than 9 years of age can be treated with oral azithromycin suspension, 10 mg/kg daily, trimethoprim-sulfamethoxazole (10 mg/kg/day trimethoprim), or erythromycin (30 to 50 mg/kg/day).[14]

Clinical response to antibiotics should be noted within a week of treatment; the lesions should become paler and less friable. After a week of treatment, the lesions become smaller, and total healing of the area takes 3 to 5 weeks. Relapse occurs in approximately 10 percent of cases, especially if use of the antibiotic is discontinued before the primary lesion has healed completely. Donovan bodies may reappear within 7 to 10 days.[25] Treatment can fail with coexisting HIV infection.

Merianos and associates[20] reported the possible effectiveness of ceftriaxone for chronic, recurrent granuloma inguinale. Patients in this study had been suffering from the disease for 1 to 5 years and had received 4 to 19 courses of antibiotics. A single daily intramuscular injection of 1 g of ceftriaxone diluted in 2 mL of 1 percent lidocaine was administered for 7 to 26 days. Clinical improvement was dramatic in most lesions, with one third of patients recovering completely without a recurrence after receiving daily doses of ceftriaxone for 7 to 10 days. Mild recurrences responded to additional ceftriaxone or short courses of oral antibiotics.[20] Vulvectomy is reserved for infections that have not responded to antibiotic treatment or for patients with severe vulvar elephantiasis.[8]

Prognosis

Healing is complete in patients who seek treatment early in the course of the disease and comply with their medication and follow-up. O'Farrell[23] noted complete healing of lesions in 24 percent of patients who complied with follow-up. Complications of granuloma inguinale include pseudo-elephantiasis, urethral stricture, and pelvic abscess, which may require surgery. Another complication is the acquisition of HIV infection and granuloma inguinale, especially when patients with ulcerations left untreated for a prolonged period have sexual contact with an HIV-positive partner.[23, 25]

The severe mutilating complications of granuloma inguinale are primarily a result of delayed treatment or poor compliance with medication. In Durban, South Africa, almost half of the males had ulcerations for 1 to 6 months before seeking medical care, and 16 percent had ulcerations for 1 to 3 weeks. In contrast, approximately 25 percent of females had ulcerations for 1 to 6 months and 50 percent had ulcerations for 1 to 3 weeks.[23] Delayed medical attention may be related to limited education, ignorance of sexually transmitted diseases, absence of suitable medical facilities, or embarrassment in seeking treatment because of extensive genital lesions.

Prevention

Sexual partners of persons with the disease should be traced, examined, and treated. Treatment of granuloma inguinale when the nodule first appears is associated with a benign course. Thus, community-based eradication that targets males with granuloma inguinale in endemic areas should be implemented. Programs should be aimed at identification of lesions, provision of early treatment, and prevention of severe complications. Teaching the importance of personal genital hygiene, such as instruction on simple retraction of the foreskin in males and cleansing the penis with soap and water, also is effective.[23, 25]

REFERENCES

1. Bassa, A. G., Hoosen A. A., Moodley, J., et al.: Granuloma inguinale (donovanosis) in women: An analysis of 61 cases from Durban, South Africa. Sex. Transm. Dis. *20*:164–167, 1993.
2. Bowden, F. J., Bright, A., Rode, J. W., and Brewster, D.: Donovanosis causing cervical lymphadenopathy in a five-month-old boy. Pediatr. Infect. Dis. *19*:167–169, 2000.
3. Carter, J., Hutton, S., Sriprakash, K. S., et al.: Culture of the causative organism of donovanosis *(Calymmatobacterium granulomatis)* in MEP-2 cells. J. Clin. Microbiol. *35*:2915–2917, 1997.
4. Chandra, M., and Jain, A. K.: Fine structure of *Calymmatobacterium granulomatis* with particular reference to the surface structure. Indian J. Med. Res. *93*:225–231, 1991.
5. DeBoer, A., DeBoer, F., and Van Der Merwe, J.: Cytologic identification of Donovan bodies in granuloma inguinale. Acta Cytol. *28*:126–128, 1984.
6. Division of STD/HIV Prevention: Sexually Transmitted Disease Surveillance, 2000. Atlanta, U.S. Department of Health and Human Services, Public Health Service, Centers for Disease Control and Prevention, 2001, pp. 125–126.
7. Doddridge, M., and Muirhead, R.: Donovanosis of the oral cavity: Case report. Aust. Dent. J. *39*:203–205, 1994.
8. Faro, S.: Lymphogranuloma venereum, chancroid, and granuloma inguinale. Obstet. Gynecol. Clin. North Am. *16*:517–530, 1989.
9. Freinkel, A. L., Dangor, Y., Koornhof, H. J., et al.: A serological test for granuloma inguinale. Genitourin. Med. *68*:269–272, 1992.
10. Gao, Y., Ni, K., Hu, B., and Zheng, K.: Granuloma inguinale: First case reported in the last four decades in China. Int. J. Dermatol. *35*:758–759, 1996.
11. Govender, D., Hadley, G. P., and Donnellan, R.: Granuloma inguinale (donovanosis) as a neck mass in an infant. Pediatr. Surg. Int. *15*:129–131, 1999.
12. Govender, D., Naidoo, K., and Chetty, R.: Granuloma inguinale (donovanosis): An usual cause of otitis media and mastoiditis in children. Am. J. Clin. Pathol. *108*:510–514, 1997.
13. Growden, W. A., Lebherz, T. B., Moore, J. G., et al.: Granuloma inguinale in a white teenager: A diagnosis easily forgotten, poorly pursued. West. J. Med. *143*:105–108, 1985.
14. 1998 Guidelines for treatment of sexually transmitted diseases. Centers for Disease Control and Prevention. M. M. W. R. Recomm. Rep. *51*(RR-6): 17–18, 2002.
15. Hacker, P., Fisher, B. K., Dekoven, J., et al.: Granuloma inguinale: Three cases diagnosed in Toronto, Canada. Int. J. Dermatol. *31*:696–699, 1992.
16. Joseph, A. K., and Rosen, T.: Laboratory techniques used in the diagnosis of chancroid, granuloma inguinale and lymphogranuloma venereum. Dermatol. Clin. *12*:1–8, 1994.
17. Kharsany, A. B., Hoosen, A. A., Kiepala, P., et al.: Phylogenetics analysis of *Calymmatobacterium granulomatis* based on 16S sequence. J. Med. Microbiol. *48*:841–847, 1999.
18. Marmell, M.: Donovanosis of the anus in the male: An epidemiologic consideration. Br. J. Vener. Dis. *34*:213–218, 1958.
19. Mein, J., Russell, C., Know, J., et al.: Intrapelvic donovanosis presenting as a psoas abscess in two patients. Sex. Transm. Infect. *75*:75–76, 1999.
20. Merianos, A., Gilles, M., and Chuah, J.: Ceftriaxone in the treatment of chronic donovanosis in central Australia. Genitourin. Med. *70*:84–89, 1994.
21. Morris, L. F., Cohen, P. R., and Dodd, L. G.: Nongenital granuloma inguinale in an oncology patient. Am. J. Clin. Oncol. *17*:456–460, 1994.
22. O'Farrell, N.: Trends in reported cases of donovanosis in Durban, South Africa. Genitourin. Med. *68*:366–369, 1992.
23. O'Farrell, N.: Clinico-epidemiological study of donovanosis in Durban, South Africa. Genitourin. Med. *69*:108–111, 1993.
24. O'Farrell, N.: Global eradication of donovanosis: An opportunity for limiting the spread of HIV-1 infection. Genitourin. Med. *71*:27–31, 1995.
25. O'Farrell, N.: Donovanosis. *In* Holmes, K. K., Sparling, P. E., Mardh, P. A., et al. (eds.): Sexually Transmitted Disease. New York, McGraw-Hill, 1999, pp. 525–531.
26. O'Farrell, N.: Donovanosis: An update. Int. STD AIDS *12*:423–427, 2001.
27. O'Farrell, N., and Hammond, M.: HLA antigens in donovanosis (granuloma inguinale). Genitourin. Med. *67*:400–402, 1991.
28. O'Farrell, N., Hoosen, A. A., Coetzee, K. D., et al.: A rapid stain for the diagnosis of granuloma inguinale. Genitourin. Med. *66*:200–201, 1990.
29. O'Farrell, N., Hoosen, A. A., Coetzee, K. D., et al.: Genital ulcer disease in men in Durban, South Africa. Genitourin. Med. *67*:327–330, 1991.
30. O'Farrell, N., Hoosen, A. A., Coetzee, K. D., et al.: Sexual behavior in Zulu men and women with genital ulcer disease. Genitourin. Med. *68*:245–248, 1992.
31. O'Farrell, N., Hoosen, A. A., Coetzee, K. D., et al.: Genital ulcer disease: Accuracy of clinical diagnosis and strategies to improve control in Durban, South Africa. Genitourin. Med. *70*:7–11, 1994.
32. O'Farrell, N., Windsor, I., and Becker, P.: HIV-1 infection among heterosexual attenders at a sexually transmitted diseases clinic in Durban. South Afr. J. *80*:17–20, 1991.
33. Rao, M. V., Thappa, D. M., Jaisaukar, T. J., and Ratnakar, C.: Extragenital donovanosis of the foot. Sex. Transm. Infect. *74*:298–299, 1998.
34. Sanders, C. T.: Extragenital donovanosis in a patient with AIDS. Sex. Transm. Infect. *74*:142–143, 1998.
35. Sehgal, V. N., Gupta, M. M., and Jain, V. K.: Tissue level lymphocyte subpopulations in donovanosis. Int. J. Dermatol. *30*:857–859, 1991.
36. Sehgal, V. N., Sharma, H. K., and Sharma, V. K.: Characterization of circulating lymphocytes by monoclonal antibodies in donovanosis. J. Dermatol. *18*:181–183, 1991.

CHAPTER

136 Campylobacter jejuni

GLORIA P. HERESI ■ JAMES R. MURPHY ■ THOMAS G. CLEARY

Campylobacter jejuni is a frequent cause of enteritis and less often of extraintestinal infection in humans. Since it first was recognized as a common human pathogen in the 1970s, appreciation of this agent's importance as a cause of disease has been increasing steadily. *C. jejuni* is one of the most frequent bacterial causes of human enteritis in the United States and is a leading cause of bacterial food-borne diarrheal disease throughout the world.[5, 51, 139, 178]

History

The first recognition of the pathologic consequences of infection with members of the group of bacteria that includes *C. jejuni* came in 1909 from studies of abortions in sheep.[115] In 1947, the sheep abortion–associated organism *Vibrio fetus* was isolated in a blood culture from a pregnant woman who had an influenza-like illness and delivered a stillborn infant with a necrotic, infarcted placenta.[201] In 1957, King[96, 97] hypothesized that *V. fetus*–related organisms might be associated with human enteric disease. Butzler and colleagues[26] in 1972 showed that bacteria similar to *V. fetus* were present in the stools of children with diarrhea. This observation was confirmed rapidly and repeatedly.[15, 28, 56, 168, 180] Major differences in biochemical activities, growth characteristics, and DNA base nucleotide content between true vibrios and *V. fetus* led to establishment of the new genus *Campylobacter*.[200]

The Organism

C. jejuni is a gram-negative rod that may vary in width from 0.2 to 0.9 μm and in length from 0.5 to 5.0 μm.[194] The rods may be short and S-shaped or longer spirals (Fig. 136–1). *C. jejuni* possesses a lipopolysaccharide endotoxin[157] and usually is motile with either a single polar flagellum (monotrichous) or two flagella, one at each end of the rod (amphitrichous); nonmotile variants exist, and spores are not formed. Organisms obtained from stressed cultures may be coccoid or spherical. *C. jejuni* is a member of the family Campylobacteraceae, which contains two closely related genera, *Campylobacter* and *Arcobacter*.[194, 195] More than 13 species and 6 subspecies[107, 128] have been identified within the genus *Campylobacter*. The species *C. jejuni* has two subspecies: *C. jejuni jejuni* and *C. jejuni doylei*. *C. jejuni doylei* can be differentiated from *C. jejuni jejuni* by the former's failure to grow at 42°C, lack of nitrate reduction, and sensitivity to cephalothin. *C. jejuni* is differentiated routinely from *Campylobacter coli* by the capacity of *C. jejuni* to hydrolyze hippurate. Hippurate-negative *C. jejuni* organisms exist,[193] but infrequently (5%). Other pathogenic *Campylobacter*, including *Campylobacter fetus* and *Campylobacter pylori* (which has been reclassified as *Helicobacter pylori*), are addressed in other chapters. The spectrum of disease recognized as being caused by *C. jejuni*, other *Campylobacter* organisms, and related organisms is expanding.[5] In the United States, more than 99 percent of reported *Campylobacter* infections are caused by *C. jejuni*.[4]

C. jejuni has a circular chromosome of 1.64 million base pairs (30.6% guanosine + cytosine). It is predicted to encode 1654 proteins and 54 stable RNA species.[138] The genome is unusual in that it has virtually no insertion sequences or phage-associated sequences and very few repeat sequences. Despite the close phylogenetic relationship between *C. jejuni* and *H. pylori*, a comparison of genomes reveals that the similarities are confined to housekeeping genes; only 55.4 percent of *C. jejuni* genes have orthologues in *H. pylori*.[138, 190]

Because of the relative biochemical inactivity of *Campylobacter* organisms, identifying species and subspecies by conventional chemotaxonomic methods is difficult. The consequences of this difficulty in speciation include ambiguities in epidemiologic investigations and reduced resolution in studies of mechanisms of virulence and immunity. Extensive effort is being invested in devising genotyping schemes,[39, 129, 205] which hold great promise for enabling resolution of different *Campylobacter* organisms and relationships among them. Comparative knowledge of the *Campylobacter* genome should enable identification of properties that endow virulence in humans and allow tracing of the environmental origins of *Campylobacter* organisms virulent in humans.

Epidemiology

Human infection with *C. jejuni* occurs worldwide.[14] *C. jejuni* persists in zoonotic niches (Table 136–1), and most human infections are thought to arise from these zoonotic reservoirs. *C. jejuni* is a common commensal of the gastrointestinal tract of cattle, pigs, dogs, cats, and most birds used as human food.[20, 171] In the United States, *C. jejuni* infection peaks in late summer and early fall (Fig. 136–2). In the United Kingdom, water samples taken from fresh-water bathing sites have been shown to yield *Campylobacter* organisms year-round, with the highest concentrations occurring in colder months.[127] Dairy cows in the United Kingdom have higher concentrations of *Campylobacter* organisms in spring and autumn, but the concentration of *Campylobacter* organisms in beef cattle at slaughter did not change with season. Approximately 90 percent of beef cattle were stool-positive for *Campylobacter*.[175] In subtropical areas, the peak incidence of isolation of *C. jejuni* often is associated with the rainy season. In tropical climates, rates of isolation are similar year-round. Studies in volunteers have shown an incubation period of 2 to 4 days after challenges ranging from 800 to 100 million colony-forming units.[13] Fecal shedding of *C. jejuni* by humans may last a median of 2 to 3 weeks, with a range of 3 days to several months.[28, 93, 134] Studies of *C. jejuni* infections in adult volunteers show the infectious dose to be as low as 800 colony-forming units.[12] Evidence from challenges with *C. jejuni* A3249 in volunteers indicates a higher probability of illness after the ingestion of a lower number of *Campylobacter* organisms.[186]

Data on the distribution of *C. jejuni* infections within populations have been interpreted as showing a linkage to

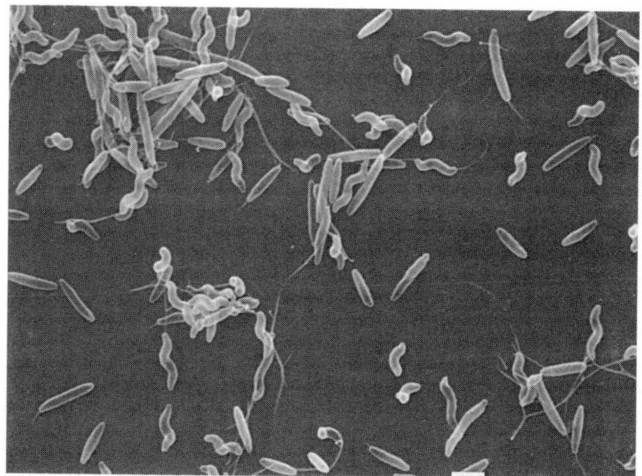

FIGURE 136–1 ■ Scanning electron microscopy of *Campylobacter jejuni* strain 20-01. (From Baqar, S., and Rice, B.: *Campylobacter jejuni* enteritis. Clin. Infect. Dis. *33*:901–905, 2001.)

the level of industrialization. In industrialized countries, *C. jejuni* infection is found often in children and adults with enteritis and seldom in healthy individuals.[178] In less industrialized areas, *C. jejuni* is isolated frequently from children, even in the absence of enteritis. However, clear examples of "industrialized" epidemiology patterns exist in less industrialized countries and vice versa (Tables 136–2 and 136–3).

In industrialized countries, *C. jejuni* has been isolated from between 1 and 13 percent of children with diarrhea, and the prevalence of infection in healthy individuals has been reported to be between 0 and 1.5 percent.[15, 26, 153, 168, 178] A 5-year, laboratory-based national surveillance of *Campylobacter* spp. performed in the United States between 1982 and 1986 showed an isolation rate of 5.5 per 100,000 person-years (with *C. jejuni* accounting for 99% of the *Campylobacter* isolates) (Fig. 136–3).[180] Population-based isolation rates of *Campylobacter* in the United States range from 28 to 1560 per 100,000 per year.[179, 180] The technical requirements for culturing *C. jejuni*, deficits in case-reporting systems, and the frequency of mild or asymptomatic *C. jejuni* infection probably combine to result in a gross underestimation of rates of infection.[5] Allos and Blaser[5] and Tauxe[178] have estimated that the actual incidence is approximately 1000 *C. jejuni* infections per 100,000 population per year. This rate is very close to the 1.1 percent annual incidence of *Campylobacter* infections reported in Great Britain.[94] Population-based studies in England, the United States, and Sweden have shown a bimodal age distribution, with a peak of illness occurring in children younger than 5 years of age and a second peak at 15 to 29 years of age.[155, 180] The highest isolation rate occurs in the first year of life (see Fig. 136–3).

In less industrialized regions, *Campylobacter* is found in association with childhood diarrhea in 8 to 45 percent of cases, but it is isolated at similar rates from healthy children[28, 32, 54]; the highest rates of *Campylobacter* isolation are in children younger than 5 years of age.[28] Cravioto and colleagues[32] showed that 75 percent of *Campylobacter* infections occurring during the first year of life were asymptomatic.

TABLE 136–1 ■ ILLUSTRATIVE STUDIES OF ISOLATION OF *CAMPYLOBACTER JEJUNI* FROM ANIMAL SOURCES

	Sample	Location	Sample Size	Positive*
Chicken	Processing plants, shops	Japan[188]	156	67.9
	Flocks on farms	England[81]	49	76.0
	Giblets	Egypt[95]	50	23.5
	Eggs from 23 farms	U.S.[9]	276	0.0
	Live birds	U.S.[9]	10	90.0
Duck	Giblets	Egypt[95]	50	19.0
	At reservoir	U.S.[132]	113	73.0
Goose	At reservoir	U.S.[132]	94	5.0
Turkey	Giblets	Egypt[95]	50	14.5
	Feces	U.K.[202]	5,000	100.0
Squab	Giblets	Egypt[95]	50	4.0
Crane	At reservoir	U.S.[132]	91	81.0
Pig	Pork at processing plants, shops	Japan[188]	94	2.1
Cow	Beef at processing plants, shops	Japan[188]	52	0.0
	Rectal swabs	U.K.[80]	668	72.0
	Farms	Canada[203]	78	13.0
	Milk cows	U.S.[40]	78	68.0
	Milk, bulk tanks	U.S.[40]	108	0.9
	Housed indoors, feces	Switzerland[24]	395	38.5
	Outdoors, feces	Switzerland[24]	395	13.3
Goat	Rectal swabs	Ghana[1]	72	33.3
Sheep	Rectal swabs	Ghana[1]	13	23.0
Cat	Domestic, rectal swabs	U.S.[55]	430	1.0
	Zoo, rectal swab (species-positive)	U.S.[55]	15	6.7
	Feces	U.S.[69]	206	1.0
Monkey	Stool	U.S.[122]	50	77.0
	Stool	Indonesia[122]	50	36.0
Dog	Rectal swabs of puppies	Denmark[65]	72	22.2
	Fecal culture of puppies	U.S.[208]	4	100.0
Birds	Feces of migrating passerines	Sweden[136]	101	3.0
Penguin	Feces	South Georgia Island[22]	100	3.0

*Percent positive. In instances in which studies reported ranges of percent positive, the highest rate is recorded.

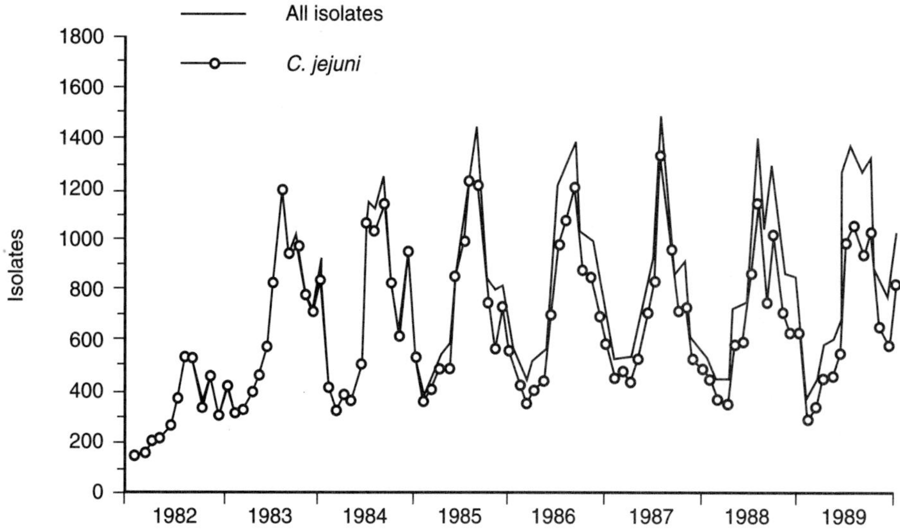

FIGURE 136–2 ■ Reported human *Campylobacter* isolates by month in the United States, 1982 to 1989. (From Tauxe, R. V.: Epidemiology of *Campylobacter jejuni* infections in the United States and other industrialized countries. *In* Nachamkin, I., Blaser, M. J., and Tompkins, L. S. [eds.]: *Campylobacter jejuni:* Current Strategy and Future Trends. Washington, D.C., American Society for Microbiology, 1992, pp. 9–19.)

Modes of transmission of *C. jejuni* differ in developed and developing countries. In industrialized regions, most sporadic cases occur because of handling, preparation, and consumption of contaminated raw or undercooked poultry.[15, 27, 34, 74, 164, 173, 180] Raw milk and contaminated water less frequently are sources.[77, 82, 118, 182, 204] *Campylobacter* organisms are present ubiquitously in the human food chain (see Table 136–1). Poor kitchen hygiene also may play a role; the risk of acquiring infection has been shown to be associated inversely with the frequency of using soap to clean cutting boards.[180] Barbecues represent a special hazard because they permit easy transfer of bacteria from raw meat to hands and other food and from there to the mouth.[28] Sporadic cases of *C. jejuni* infection occur much more frequently than do outbreaks.

Between 1978 and 1986, 57 outbreaks of *Campylobacter* infection affecting 6441 persons, including 45 food-borne outbreaks, 11 water-borne outbreaks, and 1 outbreak of unclear source in a tourist group, were reported in the United States. Of the 43 outbreaks in which a species was identified, 42 (97%) were caused by *C. jejuni*. A vehicle was implicated in 80 percent of the food-borne outbreaks; 70 percent were caused by the consumption of raw milk, 8 percent were associated with poultry, and the remaining 22 percent were related to other causes.[180] Most cases originating from cows appear to come from contamination of milk with bovine feces. However, direct excretion of *C. jejuni* into milk has been described[77, 130] and has been implicated as the source of an outbreak of disease in humans. Less frequent sources of infection include infected pets such as cats, dogs, and birds.[169] Puppies seem to be a source of infection more frequently than are older dogs.[191] Secondary person-to-person spread may occur in places where diapered children are present[139] and in the perinatal environment,[199] but otherwise, such spread occurs infrequently. *C. jejuni* has been transmitted by transfusion.[141]

In developing countries, transmission is multifactorial. The most important modes are free-roaming poultry, toddlers, unsafe water supply, and lack of adequate disposal of excreta. Chickens commonly are infected with *C. jejuni*[60] and often have free access to defecate in and outside the house. Toddlers have frequent contact with poultry feces, and the presence of live chickens in the house is a prominent risk factor for acquiring *C. jejuni* infection. Implementing personal and domestic hygiene measures such as penning chickens outside the house, preventing contact with their feces, and handwashing would probably reduce transmission further. Other species are acquired less commonly by contact with

TABLE 136–2 ■ SELECTED LONGITUDINAL STUDIES OF FREQUENCY OF *CAMPYLOBACTER JEJUNI* INFECTION IN CHILDREN

Location	No. of Children	Isolation of *C. jejuni* from Children*	
		With Diarrhea	Without Diarrhea
Guatemala[151]	321	12.1	8.1
Czechoslovakia[72]	5831	10.1	NR
Mexico[28]	179	0.4	1.7
Thailand[181]	411	0.4	1.1

*Results are reported as percent of stools positive.
NR, not reported.

TABLE 136–3 ■ SELECTED CROSS-SECTIONAL STUDIES OF FREQUENCY OF *CAMPYLOBACTER JEJUNI* INFECTION IN CHILDREN

Location	Frequency of Isolation of *C. jejuni* from Children—Percentage of Stools with *C. jejuni* (Number of Children Studied)	
	With Diarrhea	Without Diarrhea
South Africa[21]	35.0 (78)	16.0 (63)
Zaire[36]	14.4 (416)	3.0 (200)
Rwanda[35]	9.3 (150)	0.0 (58)
Zaire[25]	8.6 (70)	0.0 (30)
Cameroon[100]	7.7 (272)	3.2 (157)
Bangladesh[66]	25.5 (102)	8.6 (93)
China[210]	18.7 (48)	8.6 (105)
China[38]	11.9 (303)	4.6 (953)
Kuwait[164]	7.0 (621)	0.0 (152)
India[126]	4.0 (607)	0.9 (529)
Saudi Arabia[31]	1.0 (7369)	0.1 (1130)
Belgium[26]	5.1 (800)	1.3 (1000)
Canada[134]	4.3 (1004)	0.0 (176)
Chile[49]	10.0 (299)	6.0 (304)

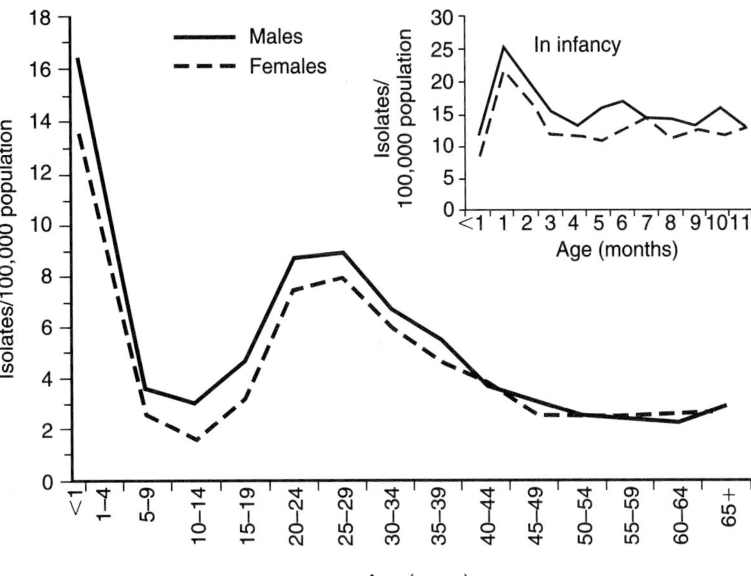

FIGURE 136–3 ■ Annual isolation rates of *Campylobacter* by age and sex, United States, 1982 to 1986. (From Tauxe, R. V., Hargrett-Bean, N., Patton, C. M., et al.: *Campylobacter* isolates in the United States, 1982–1986. Mor. Mortal. Wkly. Rep. C. D. C. Surveill Summ *37*:1–13, 1988.)

animals. *Campylobacter upsaliensis*, a rare cause of diarrhea in children, may be acquired by contact with a dog. *Campylobacter hyointestinalis*, an enteritis agent of swine, also can cause diarrhea in children. *Campylobacter lari*, a species associated with seagulls, rarely causes diarrhea in young children.

Pathology

Most *C. jejuni* infections may not be associated with illness. When illness does occur, watery diarrhea, invasive enteritis, or systemic infection may result. The spectrum of pathology reflects this range of manifestations. Acute watery diarrhea may occur in the absence of grossly visible pathology. Acute inflammation of the colon and rectum is the hallmark of *C. jejuni* invasive enteritis,[110] although hemorrhagic jejunitis and ileitis may also occur.[47, 93, 97, 168] In patients who have undergone proctoscopy, a normal mucosa is found in approximately 50 percent; in the remainder, mucosal edema, congestion, friability, and granularity are seen. The spectrum of histologic changes ranges from minimal edema with acute and chronic inflammatory cells and no vascular congestion to moderate inflammation and cryptitis to crypt abscess formation.[8] Acute appendicitis, mesenteric lymphadenitis, and ileocolitis have been reported in patients who have had appendectomies while infected with *C. jejuni*.[18, 102]

Pathogenesis

The mechanisms by which *C. jejuni* causes diarrhea and dysentery are not understood well. Evidence consistent with the production of a heat-labile enterotoxin has been presented[64, 86, 108, 157]; however, this toxic activity is not found to be universally associated with isolates from individuals who have *C. jejuni* illness. Some strains produce a cytotoxin,[87, 109] but its relevance to disease has not been established. Some *C. jejuni* can invade various cultured cell lines.[27, 48] Dogs,[150] rhesus monkeys,[50] rabbits,[174] mice,[50] and hamsters[79] have been evaluated as models of *Campylobacter* enteritis, but none faithfully reproduces the disease seen in humans. A mouse intranasal challenge model[10] has been developed for use in studies of *C. jejuni* invasiveness, and a ferret model[11] has been developed for studies of *C. jejuni*–induced diarrhea. Whether the results obtained from these models will yield information that correlates with disease in humans remains unclear.

Immunity

Evidence of protective immunity to *C. jejuni* comes mostly from studies of children in less developed countries. Such children have more frequent symptomatic infections at a younger age; with increasing age, the rate of symptomatic infection decreases.[16, 17, 19, 88–90, 112, 176, 181, 183, 206] The number of *C. jejuni* excreted per gram of stool of infected individuals also declines with increasing age,[183] as does the duration of excretion of the organism.[181] Breast feeding has been shown to protect from *C. jejuni* diarrhea.[156, 192] Further evidence of acquired immunity to *C. jejuni* comes from a study of infection in volunteers.[12] Adult volunteers who became ill after a first challenge were protected from illness after rechallenge with a homologous strain; those who were resistant to homologous rechallenge had anti–*C. jejuni* antibodies as a result of the first infection.[12] Further evidence of the importance of acquired immunity in protecting against *C. jejuni* infection is the prolonged, severe, and sometimes recurrent infections that occur in immunodeficient patients.[113, 117, 143, 145] Hypogammaglobulinemic patients have difficulty clearing *Campylobacter* organisms. Naturally acquired *C. jejuni* infection leads to the generation of antibodies that recognize *C. jejuni* antigens, and in children in developing countries, titers of these antibodies increase with age while the rate of symptomatic infection decreases.[17, 19, 88, 112, 176, 183, 187, 206] Patients with late-stage acquired immunodeficiency syndrome (AIDS) are at increased risk of acquiring severe relapsing *Campylobacter* infection; patients with early stages of human immunodeficiency virus (HIV) infection and high CD4 counts are not at risk. Immunity to disease may not protect against asymptomatic colonization. The bacterial component against which the protective immune response is directed has not been confirmed.

Very little information is available on cellular immune responses to *C. jejuni*. Cellular responses might play an important role in facilitating the formation of antibody and in clearing *C. jejuni* from eukaryotic cells.

A candidate oral vaccine consisting of a mixture of killed whole cells of *C. jejuni* in combination with heat-labile enterotoxin of *Escherichia coli* has been formulated. This vaccine was safe and induced both humoral and cellular anti–*C. jejuni* immune responses in monkeys.[10] Its efficacy in humans remains to be determined.

Clinical Manifestations

C. jejuni produces a spectrum of manifestations, the most common of which is enteritis. Bacteremia, other systemic manifestations, and perinatal infections occur infrequently.

ENTERITIS

Children with *Campylobacter* enteritis may have unformed stools, watery diarrhea, inflammatory diarrhea, or a combination of these effects.[4, 15, 18, 28, 93, 134, 168] The last manifestation can be so severe that it is misdiagnosed as inflammatory bowel disease.[168] Inflammatory diarrhea is a more common occurrence in industrialized countries, and secretory watery diarrhea more typically occurs in underdeveloped areas.

Most cases of enteric illness subside within 7 days, although 20 to 30 percent last for 2 weeks and a few (5–10%) may persist longer, with a relapsing course lasting for weeks.[93, 134] In one third to one half of patients, the initial symptoms are periumbilical cramping, intense abdominal pain, malaise, myalgia, and headache. An acute abdomen or appendicitis may be suspected at first[29] because acute abdominal pain occasionally may be the only symptom initially; pseudoappendicitis or mesenteric adenitis and terminal ileitis can be found.[142] The pain may be mild and intermittent for several weeks, and vomiting is a common occurrence. Secretory diarrhea with 10 or more profuse, watery stools per day may occur. Because this course is common in younger children, dehydration frequently (10%) is an outcome. Relapse of symptoms may occur.

The symptoms of inflammatory diarrhea are similar to those caused by *Shigella,* invasive *E. coli,* and *Salmonella* and consist of generalized malaise, fever, abdominal cramps, tenesmus, bloody stools, and the presence of fecal leukocytes on light microscopy.[110] Fever without other symptoms may develop and can be associated with febrile seizures.[209] Toxic megacolon with massive bleeding may occur.[62, 92, 163] In neonates, blood-streaked formed stools or hematochezia may be associated with the isolation of *C. jejuni.*[62, 92] The abdomen is tender, especially in the right lower quadrant. Splenomegaly occurs rarely.

EXTRAINTESTINAL INFECTIONS

Bacteremia with *C. jejuni* occurs much less commonly than does enteritis. Bacteremia was recognized first in malnourished children, patients with chronic illness or immunodeficiency, and patients at the extremes of age.[2, 63, 117, 152] Cirrhosis, cancer, immunosuppressive therapy, and HIV commonly are underlying conditions in patients with bacteremia.[147] These findings led to the view that *C. jejuni* bacteremia was a disease of the relatively immunoincompetent. However, most *C. jejuni* blood isolates actually are from healthy individuals who often have histories of recent gastrointestinal disease.[170] The average incidence of *Campylobacter* bacteremia in England and Wales is 1.5 per 1000 intestinal *Campylobacter* infections. The Centers for Disease Control and Prevention reports that only 0.4 percent of *C. jejuni* isolates in the United States are from blood cultures.[180] Most *C. jejuni* strains are susceptible to killing by serum, which perhaps explains the transient nature of the bacteremia and its tendency to resolve without specific therapy. In HIV-infected patients, *Campylobacter* bacteremia occurs more frequently and with increased morbidity and higher mortality rates.[111, 147, 184] Fatal cases have been reported in the absence of enteric disease.[111]

The main reason for the increased recognition of extraintestinal *Campylobacter* infections appears to be the growing application of appropriate microbiologic culture methods. The incidence of *C. jejuni* bacteremia probably remains underestimated. Typically, blood cultures are not performed in individuals with the primary complaint of diarrhea. Rarely, cholecystitis, urinary tract infection,[33] pancreatitis,[52] hepatitis,[99] and meningitis[41, 187] can result from *Campylobacter* infection. *C. fetus* has a predilection for vascular endothelium; fatal prosthetic valve endocarditis[140] and *C. fetus*–associated aneurysms have been described.[120]

PERINATAL INFECTIONS

Abortion or stillbirth, premature labor, neonatal sepsis, and meningitis caused by *C. jejuni* occasionally have been described.[141] *Campylobacter*-associated second-trimester abortion generally is preceded by mild gastroenteritis.[123, 166] The placenta may have areas of necrosis, infarction, microabscesses, and inflammation. The most likely route of placental/fetal infection is through the bloodstream, although a case with possible ascending spread has been reported.[37] Infected infants often are premature. Illness in neonates generally is mild or asymptomatic, but symptomatic gastroenteritis and asymptomatic bloody diarrhea caused by *C. jejuni* have been reported in newborn infants.[23, 134] Bacteremia and meningitis also may occur.[59, 146, 187] The source of the organism in these cases usually has been the mother, who may be symptomatic or asymptomatic at the time of delivery.[23, 165, 199]

IMMUNOREACTIVE COMPLICATIONS

An episode of *C. jejuni* infection may be followed by immunoreactive complications such as Guillain-Barré syndrome,[67, 68, 91, 119, 154] Reiter syndrome,[85, 144, 148] reactive arthritis,[43, 162] and erythema nodosum.

A preceding *C. jejuni* infection has been documented by serologic methods or stool culture in 12 to 60 percent of patients with Guillain-Barré syndrome.[3, 67, 68, 78, 91, 119] *C. jejuni* infection is an important causal factor for Guillain-Barré syndrome[125]; however, the risk of development of this syndrome after *C. jejuni* infection is less than 1 percent.[4] During the 2 months after a symptomatic episode of *C. jejuni* infection, the likelihood of Guillain-Barré syndrome developing is approximately 100 times (30.4 per 100,000) higher than the risk in the general population (0.3 per 100,000).[114] Guillain-Barré syndrome appears to be an age-related risk, with one study finding no cases in those younger than 20 years of age, 14 per 100,000 in patients 20 to 59 years old, and 248 per 100,000 infections in those older than 60 years of age.[114] Certain serotypes of *C. jejuni* are associated more frequently with the subsequent development of Guillain-Barré syndrome.[6, 101] Kuroki and colleagues[101] studied 46 cases of Guillain-Barré syndrome in Japan and isolated *C. jejuni* from 14, 11 of whom were Penner serogroup 19; the frequency of occurrence of that serotype among *C. jejuni* isolates was less than 2 percent. However, at least 15 different serotypes have been associated with the development of Guillain-Barré syndrome. The possible link between preceding *C. jejuni* infection and Guillain-Barré syndrome is cross-reactivity between components shared by nerve and microbe.[57, 67, 68] A positive correlation of serologic evidence of *C. jejuni* and the presence of antibody to G_{M1} has been described[61, 84]; lipopolysaccharide extracted from *C. jejuni* was found to have core oligosaccharide resembling human ganglioside G_{M1}. A pure motor neuropathy with a tendency for more distal weakness and sparing of the cranial nerves has been associated with *C. jejuni* infection in patients with anti-G_{M1} antibody.[4, 196]

Cases of Miller-Fisher syndrome, a polyneuritis variant characterized by ophthalmoplegia, areflexia, and cerebellar ataxia, also have been reported in association with *C. jejuni* infection.[83, 211] Patients with Miller-Fisher syndrome often have antibodies to ganglioside G_{Q1b}.[98] Recent studies have shown an association of *C. jejuni* with acute motor axonal neuropathy, an illness similar to Guillain-Barré syndrome that occurs primarily in northern China[116]; 76 percent of acute motor axonal neuropathy patients and 42 percent of patients with acute inflammatory demyelinization polyneuropathy were positive for anti–*C. jejuni* antibodies.[71]

Reactive arthritis may be associated with *Campylobacter* enteritis, especially in adults with HLA-B27.[43, 162] The arthritis starts a few days to several weeks after the episode of diarrhea. Involvement of joints can be monarticular or multiple, as well as migratory, and both large and small joints can be affected. Synovial fluid is sterile, and fever and leukocytosis are absent. Its duration ranges from 1 week to several months. The course is self-limited, and the prognosis is good.

Severe, persistent, and relapsing *C. jejuni* infections have been reported in patients with immune deficiencies, including congenital and acquired hypogammaglobulinemia and malnutrition.[2, 76, 117] In patients with AIDS, an increased frequency and severity of *C. jejuni* infection have been reported; severity correlates inversely with the CD4 count.[105, 143, 145]

Diagnosis

The initial characteristics of *C. jejuni* enteritis are not sufficiently unique to allow diagnosis on clinical grounds. The differential diagnosis should include *Shigella*, *Salmonella*, invasive *E. coli*, *E. coli* O157:H7, *Yersinia enterocolitica*, *Aeromonas*, and *Vibrio parahaemolyticus* infections and amebiasis. Consideration should be given to pseudomembranous colitis caused by *Clostridium difficile* if the patient has been receiving antibiotic therapy. Fecal leukocytes are found in as many as 75 percent of cases of *Campylobacter* enteritis; gross or occult fecal blood is present in 50 percent.[12, 15, 110] White blood cell counts usually are normal, although a shift to the left may occur. Mild elevations in alanine aminotransferase, alkaline phosphatase, and the sedimentation rate are observed in as many as 25 percent of patients.

Methods available for demonstration of *C. jejuni* include direct microscopy,[135, 137] bacteriologic culture, antigen detection by electroimmunoassay (EIA),[70, 189] DNA probes,[185] polymerase chain reaction (PCR),[84, 103, 131, 198] and serology.[5] Detection of antigen by EIA is nearly as sensitive and specific as is culture. PCR enables the diagnosis of some culture-negative *Campylobacter* infections.[103, 104] Serologic tests appear useful for epidemiologic investigations but are not recommended for routine diagnosis.

C. jejuni can be detected by darkfield and phase-contrast examination of fresh suspensions of stool. The distinguishing characteristic of *Campylobacter* is darting motility. Gram stain of stool showing *Vibrio* forms is said to be useful in making a presumptive diagnosis.[161] The indirect fluorescent antibody test can be used for identification of *Campylobacter* on smears; however, standardized reagents for this procedure are not available from commercial sources.

Definitive diagnosis of *C. jejuni* infection requires the demonstration of *C. jejuni* in stool or in a tissue sample. Unfortunately, not all laboratories culture for *C. jejuni*, despite its frequency. Culture of *C. jejuni* from stool requires special methods and special media. It can be accomplished with media that contain antibiotics[45] (e.g., Butzler, Skirrow, CampyBAP) to which *Campylobacter* organisms are resistant. If culturing is to be done on medium free of antibiotics, diluted stool samples should be passed through a cellulose acetate membrane filter to reduce the number of other enteric microorganisms.[58] Inoculated plates should be incubated in 5 percent oxygen and 10 percent carbon dioxide at 42° C. As long as 72 hours may be required for visible colonies to form. Identification of colonies as *C. jejuni/coli* is based on a Gram stain showing characteristic morphology and positive catalase and oxidase reactions. Hydrolysis of hippurate establishes an isolate as meeting the conventional inclusion criteria for *C. jejuni*. Routine media usually are adequate for isolation of *Campylobacter* from normally sterile body fluids and tissues.

Treatment

Most *C. jejuni* organisms are susceptible to macrolides, aminoglycosides, chloramphenicol, imipenem, and clindamycin and are resistant to cephalosporins, tetracyclines, rifampin, penicillins, trimethoprim, and vancomycin.[167, 197] Patterns of antibiotic resistance in *C. jejuni* show regional differences. A few years ago, the quinolones were used as empiric therapy for adult traveler's diarrhea because of their good microbiologic activity against *Campylobacter*, *Shigella*, and *Salmonella* strains.[4, 42, 160]

However, in recent years, *Campylobacter* strains have become resistant to fluoroquinolones all over the world (Table 136–4). The emergence of resistance has been associated with the use of quinolones such as sarafloxacin and enrofloxacin in veterinary medicine in Europe and the United States.[44, 46, 172] Patients with quinolone-resistant isolates had a longer duration of diarrhea than did patients with fluoroquinolone-sensitive isolates.[172] Fluoroquinolone resistance in *C. jejuni* appears to be related to mutations in the genes encoding subunits of DNA gyrase.[75] The frequency of erythromycin-resistant *Campylobacter* isolates is still low[160] (see Table 136–4); therefore, it remains the drug of choice in adults, as in children. Most patients with *C. jejuni* enteritis have mild symptoms and do not require antibiotic therapy. For these patients, oral rehydration plus replacement of electrolytes is sufficient. Patients who may benefit from antibiotic therapy are those with fever, bloody stool, and symptoms longer than a week in duration.[5] Patients with HIV or other immunodeficiency syndromes should be treated. Data on antibiotic treatment are controversial. Placebo-controlled studies of 5 days of erythromycin showed no effect on the course of the disease.[7, 133, 207] In contrast, early initiation of treatment with erythromycin in children with bloody diarrhea caused by *Campylobacter* shortened the duration of both diarrhea and fecal excretion of the microbe.[159] The newer macrolides azithromycin and clarithromycin may be as effective as is erythromycin and have better tolerance.

TABLE 136–4 ■ ANTIBIOTIC RESISTANCE PATTERN OF *CAMPYLOBACTER JEJUNI* ISOLATES

			Percentage of Isolates Resistant to			
Location	**Study Years**	**No. Tested**	**Erythromycin**	**Fluoroquinolones**	**Tetracycline**	**Gentamicin**
Netherlands[177]	1994-1997	1315	2	11-29	7-15	ND
Minnesota[172]	1994-1998	4953	ND	1.3-10.2	ND	ND
Spain, Barcelona[149]	1995-1998	909	5	81	72	1
Canada[53]	1995-1997	158	0	12.7	56	ND
Spain[158]	1997-1998	537	3.2	75	ND	0.4
Taiwan[106]	1994-1996	93	10	52	95	1
Thailand[73]	1995	57	ND	84	ND	ND

ND, no data.

All immunocompromised and bacteremic patients with *C. jejuni* infection should be treated with an appropriate antibiotic such as gentamicin, imipenem, or both drugs.[5]

Prevention

Tactics available for prevention of campylobacteriosis include breast feeding and avoidance of raw food and food that has been cooked under conditions that permit the survival of bacteria or that has been handled in such a way that bacterial contamination may occur. Additionally, environments contaminated with animal or human feces should be avoided. Of particular importance in urban environments is avoidance of pet feces. Daycare centers and other settings where young children may compromise hygienic standards are known risks. Researchers have demonstrated that selected microorganisms may displace *Campylobacter* from its ecologic niches. This approach may prove useful in reducing *Campylobacter* contamination of food animals.[30, 121, 124] Attempts to develop vaccines against campylobacteriosis continue, but no product is in advanced development.

REFERENCES

1. Abrahams, C. A., Agbodaze, D., Nakano, T., et al.: Prevalence and antibiogram of *Campylobacter jejuni* in domestic animals in rural Ghana. Arch. Environ. Health *45*:59–62, 1990.
2. Ahnen, D. J., and Brown, W. R.: *Campylobacter* enteritis in immune deficient patients. Ann. Intern. Med. *96*:187–188, 1982.
3. Allos, B. M.: Association between *Campylobacter* infection and Guillain-Barré syndrome. J. Infect. Dis. *176*(Suppl. 2):125–128, 1997.
4. Allos, B. M.: *Campylobacter jejuni* infections: Update on emerging issues and trends. Clin. Infect. Dis. *32*:1201–1206, 2001.
5. Allos, B. M., and Blaser, M. J.: *Campylobacter jejuni* and the expanding spectrum of related infections. Clin. Infect. Dis. *20*:1092–1099, 1995.
6. Allos, B. M., Lippy, F. T., Carson, A., et al.: *Campylobacter jejuni* strains from patients with Guillain-Barré syndrome. Emerg. Infect. Dis. *4*:263–268, 1998.
7. Anders, B. J., Lauer, B. A., Paisley, J. W., et al.: Double-blind placebo-controlled trial of erythromycin for treatment of *Campylobacter* enteritis. Lancet *1*:131–132, 1982.
8. Babakhani, F. K., Bradley, J. A., and Joens, L. A.: Newborn piglet model for campylobacteriosis. Infect. Immun. *61*:3466–3475, 1993.
9. Baker, R. C., Paredes, M. D., and Qureshi, R. A.: Prevalence of *Campylobacter jejuni* in eggs and poultry meat in New York State. Poultry Sci. *66*:766–770, 1987.
10. Baqar, S., Bourgeois, A. I., and Schultheiss, P. J., et al.: Safety and immunogenicity of a prototype oral whole-cell killed *Campylobacter* vaccine administered with a mucosal adjuvant in non-human primates. Vaccine *13*:22–28, 1995.
11. Bell, J. A., and Manning, D. D.: A domestic ferret model of immunity to *Campylobacter jejuni*–induced enteric disease. Infect. Immun. *58*: 1848–1852, 1990.
12. Black, R. E., Levine, M. M., Clements, M. L., et al.: Experimental *Campylobacter jejuni* infection in humans. J. Infect. Dis. *157*:472–479, 1988.
13. Black, R. E., Levine, M. M., Clements, M. L., et al.: Experimental *Campylobacter jejuni* infection in humans. J. Infect. Dis. *157*:472–479, 1998.
14. Blaser, M. J.: Epidemiologic and clinical features of *Campylobacter jejuni* infections. J. Infect. Dis. *176*(Suppl 2):103–105, 1997.
15. Blaser, M. E., Berkowitz, I. D., LaForce, F. M., et al.: *Campylobacter enteritis*: Clinical and epidemiologic features. Ann. Intern. Med. *91*: 179–185, 1979.
16. Blaser, M. J., and Duncan, D. J.: Human serum antibody response to *Campylobacter jejuni* infection as measured in an enzyme-linked immunosorbent assay. Infect. Immun. *44*:292–298, 1984.
17. Blaser, M. J., Duncan, D. J., Osterholm, M. T., et al.: Serologic study of two clusters of infection due to *Campylobacter jejuni*. J. Infect. Dis. *147*:820–823, 1983.
18. Blaser, M. J., Parsons, R. B., and Wang, W. L.: Acute colitis caused by *Campylobacter fetus* sp. *jejuni*. Gastroenterology *78*:448–453, 1980.
19. Blaser, M. J., Taylor, D. N., and Echeverria, P.: Immune response to *Campylobacter jejuni* in a rural community in Thailand. J. Infect. Dis. *153*:249–254, 1986.
20. Blaser, M. J., Taylor, D. N., and Feldman, R. A.: Epidemiology of *Campylobacter jejuni* infections. Epidemiol. Rev. *5*:157–176, 1983.
21. Bokkenheuser, V. D., Richardson, N. J., Bryner, J. H., et al.: Detection of enteric campylobacteriosis in children. J. Clin. Microbiol. *9*:227, 1979.
22. Broman, T., Bergstrom, S., On, S. L., et al.: Isolation and characterization of *Campylobacter jejuni* subsp. *jejuni* from macaroni penguins *(Eudyptes chrysolophus)* in the subantarctic region. Appl. Environ. Microbiol. *66*:449–452, 2000.
23. Buck, G. E., Kelly, M. T., Pichanick, A. M., et al.: *Campylobacter jejuni* in newborns: A cause of asymptomatic bloody diarrhea. Am. J. Dis. Child. *136*:744, 1982.
24. Busato, A., Hofer, D., Lentze, T., et al.: Prevalence and infection risks of zoonotic enteropathogenic bacteria in Swiss cow-calf farms. Vet. Microbiol. *69*:251–263, 1999.
25. Butzler, J. P.: Related vibrios in Africa. Lancet *2*:858, 1973.
26. Butzler, J. P., Dekeyser, P., Detrain, M., et al.: Related *Vibrio* in stools. J. Pediatr. *82*:493–495, 1973.
27. Butzler, J. P., and Skirrow, M. B.: *Campylobacter* enteritis. Clin. Gastroenterol. *8*:737–765, 1979.
28. Calva, J. J., Ruiz-Palacios, G. M., Lopez-Vidal, A. B., et al.: Cohort study of intestinal infection with *Campylobacter* in Mexican children. Lancet *1*:503–506, 1988.
29. Chan, F. T., Stringel, G., and Mackenzie, A. M.: Isolation of *Campylobacter jejuni* from an appendix. J. Clin. Microbiol. *18*:422–424, 1983.
30. Chang, M. H., and Chen, T. C.: Reduction of *Campylobacter jejuni* in a simulated chicken digestive tract by *Lactobacilli* cultures. J. Food Prot. *63*:1594–1597, 2000.
31. Chowdhury, M. N., and al-Eissa, Y. A.: *Campylobacter* gastroenteritis in children in Riyadh, Saudi Arabia. J. Trop. Pediatr. *38*:158–161, 1992.
32. Cravioto, A., Reyes, R. E., Trujillo, F., et al.: Risk of diarrhea during the first year of life associated with initial and subsequent colonization by specific enteropathogens. Am. J. Epidemiol. *131*:1886–1904, 1979.
33. Davis, J. S., and Penfold, J. B.: *Campylobacter* urinary tract infection. Lancet *1*:1091–1092, 1979.
34. Deming, M. S., Tauxe, R. V., Blake, P. A., et al.: *Campylobacter* enteritis at a university: Transmission from eating chicken and from cats. Am. J. Epidemiol. *126*:526–534, 1987.
35. De Mol, P., and Bosmans, E.: *Campylobacter* enteritis in central Africa. Lancet *1*:604, 1978.
36. De Mol, P., Brasseur, D., and Lauwers, S.: *Campylobacter:* An important enteropathogen in a tropical area. Presented at the 20th Interscience Conference on Antimicrobial Agents and Chemotherapy, September 22–24, 1980, New Orleans. Washington, D.C., American Society for Microbiology, 1980.
37. Denton, K. J., and Clarke, T.: Role of *Campylobacter jejuni* as a placental pathogen. J. Clin. Pathol. *45*:171–172, 1992.

38. Desheng, L., Zhixin, C., and Boulun, W.: Age distribution of diarrhoeal and healthy children infected with *Campylobacter jejuni*. J. Trop. Med. Hyg. *95*:218–220, 1992.
39. Dingle, K. E., Colles, F. M., Wareing, D. R., et al. Multilocus sequence typing system for *Campylobacter jejuni*. J. Clin. Microbiol. *39*:14–23, 2001.
40. Doyle, M. P., and Roman, D. J.: Prevalence and survival of *Campylobacter jejuni* in unpasteurized milk. Appl. Environ. Microbiol. *44*:1154–1158, 1982.
41. Dronda, F., Garcia-Arata, I., Navas, E., and de Rafael, L.: Meningitis in adults due to *Campylobacter fetus* subspecies *fetus*. Clin. Infect. Dis. *27*:906–907, 1998.
42. DuPont, H. L.: Use of quinolones in the treatment of gastrointestinal infections. Eur. J. Clin. Microbiol. Infect. Dis. *10*:325–329, 1991.
43. Ebright, J. R., and Ryan, L. M.: Acute erosive reactive arthritis associated with *Campylobacter jejuni*–induced colitis. Am. J. Med. *76*:321–323, 1984.
44. Endtz, H. P., Ruijs, G. J., van Klingeren, B., et al. Quinolone resistance in *Campylobacter* isolated from man and poultry following the introduction of fluoroquinolones in veterinary medicine. J. Antimicrob. Chemother. *27*:199–208, 1991.
45. Endtz, H. P., Ruijs, G. J., Zwinderman, A. H., et al.: Comparison of six media, including a semisolid agar, for the isolation of various *Campylobacter* species from stool specimens. J. Clin. Microbiol. *29*:1007–1010, 1991.
46. Engberg, J., Aarestrup, F. M., Taylor, D. E., et al.: Quinolone and macrolide resistance in *Campylobacter jejuni* and *C. coli*: Resistance mechanisms and trends in human isolates. Emerg. Infect. Dis. *7*:24–34, 2001.
47. Evans, R. G., and Dadswell, J. V.: Human vibriosis. B. M. J. *3*:240, 1967.
48. Falkow, S.: Bacterial entry into eukaryotic cells. Cell *65*:1099–1102, 1991.
49. Figueroa, G., Galeno, H., Troncoso, M., et al.: Prospective study of *Campylobacter jejuni* infection in Chilean infants evaluated by culture and serology. J. Clin. Microbiol. *27*:1040–1044, 1989.
50. Fitzgeorge, R. B., Baskerville, A., and Lander, K. P.: Experimental infection of rhesus monkeys with a human strain of *Campylobacter jejuni*. J. Hyg. *86*:343–351, 1981.
51. FoodNet Surveillance Report for 1999 (Final Report). Atlanta, Centers for Disease Control and Prevention, 2000.
52. Gallagher, P., Chadwick, P., Jones, D. M., et al.: Acute pancreatitis associated with *Campylobacter* infection. Br. J. Surg. *68*:383, 1981.
53. Gaudreau, C., and Gilbert, H.: Antimicrobial resistance of clinical strains of *Campylobacter jejuni* subsp. *jejuni* isolated from 1985 to 1997 in Quebec, Canada. Antimicrob. Agents Chemother. *42*:2106–2108, 1998.
54. Georges-Courbot, M. C., Beraud-Cassel, A. M., Gouandjika, I., et al.: Prospective study of enteric *Campylobacter* infections in children from birth to 6 months in the Central African Republic. J. Clin. Microbiol. *25*:836–839, 1987.
55. Gifford, D. H., Shane, S. M., and Smith, R. E.: Prevalence of *Campylobacter jejuni* in *felidae* in Baton Rouge, Louisiana. Int. Zoonoses *12*:67–73, 1985.
56. Glass, R. I., Stoll, B. J., Huq, M. I., et al.: Epidemiologic and clinical features of endemic *Campylobacter jejuni* infection in Bangladesh. J. Infect. Dis. *148*:292–296, 1983.
57. Goodyear, C. S., O'Hanlon, G. M., Plomp, J. J., et al.: Monoclonal antibodies raised against Guillain-Barré syndrome–associated *Campylobacter jejuni* lipopolysaccharides react with neuronal gangliosides and paralyze muscle-nerve preparations. J. Clin. Invest. *104*:697–708, 1999.
58. Goossens, H., De Boeck, M., Coignau, H., et al.: Modified selective medium for isolation of *Campylobacter* spp. from feces: Comparison with Preston medium, a blood-free medium and a filtration system. J. Clin. Microbiol. *24*:840–843, 1986.
59. Goossens, H., Henocque, G., Kremp, L., et al.: Nosocomial outbreak of *Campylobacter jejuni* meningitis in newborn infants. Lancet *2*:146–149, 1986.
60. Grados, O., Bravo, N., Black, R. E., et al.: Paediatric *Campylobacter* diarrhea from household exposure to live chickens in Lima, Peru. Bull. World Health Organ. *66*:369–374, 1988.
61. Gregson, N. A., Koblar, S., and Hughes, R. A.: Antibodies to gangliosides in Guillain-Barré syndrome: Specificity and relationship to clinical features. Q. J. Med. *86*:111–117, 1993.
62. Guandalini, S., Cucchiara, S., de Ritis, G., et al.: *Campylobacter* colitis in infants. J. Pediatr. *102*:72–74, 1983.
63. Guerrant, R. L., Lahita, R. G., Winn, W. C., Jr., et al.: Campylobacteriosis in man: Pathogenic mechanisms and review of 91 bloodstream infections. Am. J. Med. *65*:584–592, 1978.
64. Guerrant, R. L., Wanke, C. A., Pennie, R. A., et al.: Production of a unique cytotoxin by *Campylobacter jejuni*. Infect. Immun. *55*:2526–2530, 1987.
65. Hald, B., and Madsen, M.: Healthy puppies and kittens as carriers of *Campylobacter* spp., with special reference to *Campylobacter upsaliensis*. J. Clin. Microbiol. *35*:3351-3352, 1997.
66. Haq, J. A., and Rahman, K. M.: *Campylobacter jejuni* as a cause of acute diarrhoea in children: A study at an urban hospital in Bangladesh. J. Trop. Med. Hyg. *94*:50–54, 1991.
67. Hartung, H. P., Pollard, J. D., Harvey, G. K., et al.: Immunopathogenesis and treatment of the Guillain-Barré syndrome: Part I. Muscle Nerve *18*:137–153, 1995.
68. Hartung, H. P., Pollard, J. D., Harvey, G. K., et al.: Immunopathogenesis and treatment of the Guillain-Barré syndrome: Part II. Muscle Nerve *18*:154–164, 1995.
69. Hill, S. L., Cheney, J. M., Taton-Allen, G. F., et al.: Prevalence of enteric zoonotic organisms in cats. J. Am. Vet. Med. Assoc. *216*:687–692, 2000.
70. Hindiyeh, M., Jense, S., Hohmann, S., et al.: Rapid detection of *Campylobacter jejuni* in stool specimens by an enzyme immunoassay and surveillance for *Campylobacter upsaliensis* in the greater Salt Lake City area. J. Clin. Microbiol. *38*:3076–3079, 2000.
71. Ho, T. W., Mishu, B., Li, C. Y., et al.: Guillain-Barré syndrome in northern China: Relationship to *Campylobacter jejuni* infection and anti-glycolipid antibodies. Brain *118*:597–605, 1995.
72. Hofstetr, A., Dvorakova, A., Nikodymova, I., et al.: A 3-year follow-up study of the incidence of campylobacteriosis in a pediatric population. Cesk. Pediatr. *45*:651–654, 1990.
73. Hoge, C. W., Gambel, J. M., Srijan, A., et al.: Trends in antibiotic resistance among diarrheal pathogens isolated in Thailand over 15 years. Clin. Infect. Dis. *26*:341–345, 1998.
74. Hood, A. M., Pearson, A. D., and Shahamat, M.: The extent of surface contamination of retailed chickens with *Campylobacter jejuni* serogroups. Epidemiol. Infect. *100*:17–25, 1988.
75. Hooper, D. C.: Emerging mechanisms of fluoroquinolone resistance. Emerg. Infect. Dis. *7*:337–341, 2001.
76. Hossain, M. A., Kabir, I., Albert, M. J., et al.: *Campylobacter jejuni* bacteraemia in children with diarrhea in Bangladesh: Report of six cases. J. Diarrhoeal Dis. Res. *10*:101–104, 1992.
77. Hudson, P. J., Vogt, R. L., Brondum, B. J., et al.: Isolation of *Campylobacter jejuni* from milk during an outbreak of campylobacteriosis. J. Infect. Dis. *150*:789, 1984.
78. Hughes, R. A., and Rees, J. H.: Guillain-Barré syndrome. Curr. Opin. Neurol. *7*:386–392, 1994.
79. Humphrey, C. D., Montag, D. M., and Pittman, F. E.: Experimental infection of hamsters with *Campylobacter jejuni*. J. Infect. Dis. *151*:485–493, 1985.
80. Humphrey, T. J.: *Campylobacter jejuni* in dairy cows and raw milk. Epidemiol. Infect. *98*:263–269, 1987.
81. Humphrey, T. J., Henley, A., and Lanning, D. G.: The colonization of broiler chickens with *Campylobacter jejuni*: Some epidemiological investigations. Epidemiol. Infect. *110*:601–607, 1993.
82. Hutchinson, D. N., Bolton, F. J., Hinchliffe, P. M., et al.: Evidence of udder excretion of *Campylobacter jejuni* as the cause of milk-borne *Campylobacter* outbreak. J. Hyg. *94*:205–215, 1985.
83. Ichikawa, H., Sugita, K., Fukui, T., et al.: Fisher's syndrome following *Campylobacter jejuni* enteritis: A case report and review of the literature. Clin. Neurol. *35*:391–395, 1995.
84. Jacobs, B. C., van Doorn, P. A., Schmitz, P. I., et al.: *Campylobacter jejuni* infections and anti-G_{M1} antibodies in Guillain-Barré syndrome. Ann. Neurol. *40*:181–187, 1996.
85. Johnsen, K., Ostensen, M., Melbye, A. C., et al.: HLA-B27–negative arthritis related to *Campylobacter jejuni* enteritis in three children and two adults. Acta Med. Scand. *214*:165–168, 1983.
86. Johnson, W. M., and Lior, H.: Toxins produced by *Campylobacter jejuni* and *Campylobacter coli*. Lancet *1*:229–230, 1984.
87. Johnson, W. M., and Lior, H.: Cytotoxic and cytotonic factors produced by *Campylobacter jejuni*, *Campylobacter coli* and *Campylobacter laridis*. J. Clin. Microbiol. *24*:275–281, 1986.
88. Jones, D. M., Eldridge, J., and Dale, B.: Serological response to *Campylobacter jejuni/coli* infection. J. Clin. Pathol. *33*:767–769, 1980.
89. Jones, D. M., Robinson, D. A., and Eldridge, J.: Serological studies in two outbreaks of *Campylobacter jejuni* infection. J. Hyg. *87*:163–170, 1981.
90. Kaldor, J., Pritchard, H., Serpell, A., et al.: Serum antibodies in *Campylobacter* enteritis. J. Clin. Microbiol. *18*:1–4, 1983.
91. Kaldor, J., and Speed, B. R.: Guillain-Barré syndrome and *Campylobacter jejuni:* A serological study. B. M. J. Clin. Res. *288*:1867–1870, 1984.
92. Kalkay, M. N., Ayanian, Z. S., Lehaf, E. A., et al.: *Campylobacter*-induced toxic megacolon. Am. J. Gastroenterol. *78*:557–559, 1983.
93. Karmali, M. A., and Fleming, P. C.: *Campylobacter* enteritis. Can. Med. Assoc. J. *120*:1525–1532, 1979.
94. Kendall, E. J., and Tanner, E. I.: *Campylobacter* enteritis in general practice. J. Hyg. *88*:155–163, 1982.
95. Khalafalla, F. A.: *Campylobacter jejuni* in poultry giblets. Zentralbl. Veterinarmed. *37*:31–34, 1990.
96. King, E. O.: Human infections with *Vibrio fetus* and a closely related *Vibrio*. J. Infect. Dis. *101*:119–128, 1957.
97. King, E. O.: The laboratory recognition of *Vibrio fetus* and a closely related *Vibrio* isolated from cases of human vibriosis. Ann. N. Y. Acad. Sci. *98*:700–711, 1962.
98. Koba, M., Yuki, N., Takahashi, M., et al.: Close association of IgA anti-ganglioside antibodies with antecedent *Campylobacter jejuni* infection in Guillain-Barré and Fisher's syndromes. J. Neuroimmunol. *81*:138–143, 1998.

99. Korman, T. M., Varley, C. C., and Spelman, D. W.: Acute hepatitis associated with *Campylobacter jejuni* bacteraemia. Eur. J. Clin. Microbiol. Infect. Dis. *16*:678–681, 1997.
100. Koulla-Shiro, S., Loe, C., Ekoe, T.: Prevalence of *Campylobacter* enteritis in children from Yaounde (Cameroon). Cent. Afr. J. Med. *41*:91–94, 1995.
101. Kuroki, S., Saida, T., Nukina, M., et al.: *Campylobacter jejuni* strains from patients with Guillain-Barré syndrome belong mostly to Penner serogroup 19 and contain beta-*N*-acetylglucosamine residues. Ann. Neurol. *33*:243–247, 1993.
102. Lambert, M. E., Schofield, P. F., Ironside, A. G., et al.: *Campylobacter* colitis. B. M. J. *1*:857–859, 1979.
103. Lawson, A. J., Logan, J. M., O'Neill, G. L., et al.: Large-scale survey of *Campylobacter* species in human gastroenteritis by PCR and PCR–enzyme-linked immunosorbent assay. J. Clin. Microbiol. *37*: 3860–3864, 1999.
104. Lawson, A. J., Shafi, M. S., Pathak, K., and Stanley, J.: Detection of *Campylobacter* in gastroenteritis: Comparison of direct PCR assay of faecal samples with selective culture. Epidemiol. Infect. *121*:5447–5453, 1998.
105. Leyes, M., Vara, F., Reina, J., et al.: *Campylobacter* gastroenteritis in patients with human immunodeficiency virus infection. Enferm. Infecc. Microbiol. Clin. *12*:332–336, 1994.
106. Li, C., Chiu, C., Wu, J., et al.: Antimicrobial susceptibilities of *Campylobacter jejuni* and *coli* by using E-test in Taiwan. Scand. J. Infect. Dis. *30*:39–42, 1998.
107. Logan, J. M., Burnens, A., Linton, D., et al.: *Campylobacter lanienae* sp. nov., a new species isolated from workers in an abattoir. Int. J. Syst. Evol. Microbiol. *50*:865–872, 2000.
108. Madden, J. M., McCardell, B. A., and Shah, D. B.: *Campylobacter jejuni* and *Campylobacter coli* cytotonic toxin production by members of genus *Vibrio*. Lancet *2*:1217–1218, 1984.
109. Mahajan, S., and Rodgers, F. G.: Isolation, characterization and host-cell binding properties of a cytotoxin from *Campylobacter jejuni*. J. Clin. Microbiol. *28*:1314–1320, 1990.
110. Maki, M., Maki, R., and Vesikari, T.: Fecal leukocytes in *Campylobacter*-associated diarrhea in infants. Acta Paediatr. Scand. *68*:271–272, 1979.
111. Manfredi, R., Nanetti, A., Ferri, M., and Chiodo, F.: Fatal *Campylobacter jejuni* bacteraemia in patients with AIDS. J. Med. Microbiol. 48:601–603, 1999.
112. Martin, P. M., Mathiot, J., Ipero, J., et al.: Immune response to *Campylobacter jejuni* and *Campylobacter coli* in a cohort of children from birth to 2 years of age. Infect. Immun. *57*:2542–2546, 1989.
113. Martinez, R. M., Figueras, M. P., Ramos, C., et al.: *Campylobacter jejuni* and HIV infection. Enferm. Infecc. Microbiol. Clin. *12*:90–94, 1994.
114. McCarthy, N., and Giesecke, J.: Incidence of Guillain-Barré syndrome following *Campylobacter jejuni*. Am. J. Epidemiol. *153*:610–614, 2001.
115. McFadyean, F., and Stockman, S.: Report of the Departmental Committee Appointed by the Board of Agriculture and Fisheries to Inquire into Epizootic Abortion. Vol. 3. London, His Majesty's Stationery Office, 1909.
116. McKhann, G. M., Cornblath, D. R., Griffin, J. W., et al.: Acute motor axonal neuropathy: A frequent case of acute flaccid paralysis in China. Ann. Neurol. *33*:333–342, 1993.
117. Melamed, I., Bujanover, Y., Igra, Y. S., et al.: *Campylobacter* enteritis in normal and immunodeficient children. Am. J. Dis. Child. *137*:752–753, 1983.
118. Mentzing, L. O.: Waterborne outbreaks of *Campylobacter* enteritis in central Sweden. Lancet *2*:352–354, 1981.
119. Mishu, B., and Blaser, M. J.: Role of infection due to *Campylobacter jejuni* in the initiation of Guillain-Barré syndrome. Clin. Infect. Dis. *17*:104–108, 1993.
120. Montero, A., Corbella, X., Lopez, J. A., et al.: *Campylobacter fetus*–associated aneurysms: Report of a case involving the popliteal artery and review of the literature. Clin. Infect. Dis. *24*:1019–1021, 1997.
121. Morishita, T. Y., Aye, P. P., Harr, B. S., et al.: Evaluation of an avian-specific probiotic to reduce the colonization and shedding of *Campylobacter jejuni* in broilers. Avian Dis. *41*:850–855, 1997.
122. Morton, W. R., Bronsdon, M., Mickelson, G., et al.: Identification of *Campylobacter jejuni* in *Macaca fascicularis* imported from Indonesia. Lab. Anim. Sci. *33*:187–188, 1983.
123. Moscuna, M., Gross, Z., Korenblum, R., et al.: Septic abortion due to *Campylobacter jejuni*. Eur. J. Clin. Microbiol. Infect. Dis. *8*:800, 1989.
124. Moyen, E. N., Bonneville, F., and Fauchere, J. L.: Modification of intestinal colonization and translocation of *Campylobacter jejuni* by erythromycin and an extract of *Lactobacillus acidophilus* in axenic mice. Ann. Inst. Pasteur Microbiol. *137*:199–207, 1986.
125. Nachamkin, I., Allos, B. M., Ho, T.: *Campylobacter* species and Guillain-Barré syndrome. Clin. Microbiol. Rev. *11*:555–567, 1998.
126. Nath, G., Shukla, B. N., Reddy, D. C., et al.: A community study on the aetiology of childhood diarrhoea with special reference to *Campylobacter jejuni* in a semiurban slum of Varanasi, India. J. Diarrhoeal Dis. Res. *11*: 165–168, 1993.
127. Obiri-Danso, K., and Jones, K.: Distribution and seasonality of microbial indicators and thermophilic campylobacters in two freshwater bathing sites on the River Lune in northwest England. J. Appl. Microbiol. *87*:822–832, 1999.
128. On, S. L.: Identification methods for campylobacters, helicobacters, and related organisms. Clin. Microbiol. Rev. *9*:405–422, 1996.
129. On, S. L., Harrington, C. S.: Identification of taxonomic and epidemiological relationships among *Campylobacter* species by numerical analysis of AFLP profiles. FEMS Microbiol. Lett. *193*:161–169, 2000.
130. Orr, K. E., Lightfoot, N. F., Sisson, P. R., et al.: Direct milk excretion of *Campylobacter jejuni* in a dairy cow causing cases of human enteritis. Epidemiol. Infect. *114*:15, 1995.
131. Oyofo, B. A., Thornton, S. A., Burr, D. H., et al.: Specific detection of *Campylobacter jejuni* and *Campylobacter coli* by using polymerase chain reaction. J. Clin. Microbiol. *30*:2613–2619, 1992.
132. Pacha, R. E., Clark, G. W., Williams, E. A., et al.: Migratory birds of central Washington as reservoirs of *Campylobacter jejuni*. Can. J. Microbiol. *24*:80–82, 1988.
133. Pai, C. H., Gillis, F., Toumanen, E., et al.: Erythromycin in treatment of *Campylobacter* enteritis in children. Am. J. Dis. Child. *137*:286–288, 1983.
134. Pai, C. H., Sorger, S., Lackman, L., et al.: *Campylobacter* gastroenteritis in children. J. Pediatr. *94*:589–591, 1979.
135. Paisley, J. W., Mirret, S., Lauer, B. A., et al.: Dark-field microscopy of human feces for presumptive diagnosis of *Campylobacter fetus* subsp. *jejuni* enteritis. J. Clin. Microbiol. *15*:61–63, 1982.
136. Palmgren, H., Sellin, M., Bergstrom, S., and Olsen, B.: Enteropathogenic bacteria in migrating birds arriving in Sweden. Scand. J. Infect. Dis. *29*:565–568, 1997.
137. Park, C. H., Hixon, D. L., Polhemus, A. S., et al.: A rapid diagnosis of *Campylobacter* enteritis by direct smear examination. Am. J. Clin. Pathol. *80*:388–390, 1983.
138. Parkhill, J., Wren, B. W., Mungall, K., et al.: The genome sequence of the food-borne pathogen *Campylobacter jejuni* reveals hypervariable sequences. Nature *403*:665–668, 2000.
139. Pearson, A. D., and Healing, T. D.: The surveillance and control of *Campylobacter* infections. Commun. Dis. Rep. C. D. R. Rev. *2*(12): R133–R139, 1992.
140. Peetermans, W. E., De Man, F., Moerman, P., et al.: Fatal prosthetic valve endocarditis due to *Campylobacter* fetus. J. Infect. *41*:180–182, 2000.
141. Pepersack, F., Prigogyne, T., Butzler, J. P., et al.: *Campylobacter jejuni* post-transfusional septicaemia. Lancet *2*:911, 1979.
142. Perkins, D. J., and Newstead, G. L.: *Campylobacter jejuni* enterocolitis causing peritonitis, ileitis, and intestinal obstruction. Aust. N. Z. J. Surg. *64*:55–58, 1994.
143. Perlman, D. M., Ampel, N. M., Schifman, R. B., et al.: Persistent *Campylobacter jejuni* infections in patients infected with human immunodeficiency virus (HIV). Ann. Intern. Med. *108*:540–546, 1988.
144. Peterson, M. C.: Rheumatic manifestations of *Campylobacter jejuni* and *C. fetus* infections in adults. Scand. J. Rheumatol. *23*:167–170, 1994.
145. Peterson, M. C., Farr, R. W., and Castiglia, M.: Prosthetic hip infection and bacteremia due to *Campylobacter jejuni* in a patient with AIDS. Clin. Infect. Dis. *16*:439–440, 1993.
146. Pickering, L. K., Guerrant, R. L., and Cleary, T. G.: Microorganisms responsible for neonatal diarrhea. *In* Remington, J. S., and Klein, J. O. (eds.): Infectious Diseases of the Fetus and Newborn Infant. 4th ed. Philadelphia, W. B. Saunders, 1994, pp. 1142–1222.
147. Pigrau, C., Bartolome, R., Almirante, B., et al.: Bacteremia due to *Campylobacter* species: Clinical findings and antimicrobial susceptibility patterns. Clin. Infect. Dis. *25*:1414–1420, 1997.
148. Ponka, A., Martio, J., and Kosunen, T. U.: Reiter's syndrome in association with enteritis due to *Campylobacter fetus* ssp. *jejuni*. Ann. Rheumatol. Dis. *40*:414–415, 1981.
149. Prats, G., Mirelis, B., Llovet, T., et al.: Antibiotic resistance trends in enteropathogenic bacteria isolated in 1985–1987 and 1995–1998 in Barcelona. Antimicrob. Agents Chemother. *44*:1140–1145, 2000.
150. Prescott, J. F., Barker, I. K., Manninen, K. I., et al.: *Campylobacter jejuni* colitis in gnotobiotic dogs. Can. J. Comp. Med. *45*:377–383, 1981.
151. Ramiro-Cruz, J., Cano, F., Bartlett, A. V., et al.: Infection, diarrhea and dysentery caused by *Shigella* species and *Campylobacter jejuni* among Guatemalan rural children. Pediatr. Infect. Dis. J. *13*:216–223, 1994.
152. Reed, R. P., Friedland, I. R., Wegerhoff, F. O., and Khoosal, M.: *Campylobacter* bacteremia in children. Pediatr. Infect. Dis. J. *15*:345–348, 1996.
153. Rettig, P. J.: *Campylobacter* infections in human beings. J. Pediatr. *94*:855–864, 1979.
154. Rhodes, K. M., and Tattersfield, A. E.: Guillain-Barré syndrome associated with *Campylobacter* infection. B. M. J. *285*:173–174, 1982.
155. Riley, L. W., and Finch, M. J.: Results of the first year of national surveillance of *Campylobacter* infections in the United States. J. Infect. Dis. *151*:956–959, 1985.
156. Ruiz-Palacios, G. M., Calva, J. J., Pickering, L. K., et al.: Protection of breast fed infants against *Campylobacter* diarrhea by antibodies in human milk. J. Pediatr. *116*:707–713, 1990.

157. Ruiz-Palacios, G. M., Torres, J., and Escamilla, N. I.: Cholera-like enterotoxin produced by *Campylobacter jejuni:* Characterization and clinical significance. Lancet *2*:250–253, 1983.
158. Saenz, Y., Zarazaga, M., Lantero, M., et al.: Antibiotic resistance in *Campylobacter* strains isolated from animals, foods, and humans in Spain in 1997–1998. Antimicrob. Agents Chemother. *44*:267–271, 2000.
159. Salazar-Lindo, E., Sack, B., Chea-Woo, E., et al.: Early treatment with erythromycin of *Campylobacter jejuni* associated dysentery in children. J. Pediatr. *109*:355–360, 1986.
160. Sanchez, R., Fernandez-Vaca, V., Diaz, M. D., et al.: Evolution of susceptibilities of *Campylobacter* spp to quinolones and macrolides. Antimicrob. Agents Chemother. *38*:1879–1882, 1994.
161. Sazie, E. S., and Titus, A. E.: Rapid diagnosis of *Campylobacter* enteritis. Ann. Intern. Med. *96*:62–63, 1982.
162. Schaad, U. B.: Reactive arthritis associated with *Campylobacter* enteritis. Pediatr. Infect. Dis. J. *1*:328–332, 1982.
163. Schneider, A., Runzi, M., Peitgen, K., et al.: *Campylobacter jejuni*-induced severe colitis—a rare cause of toxic megacolon. Z. Gastroenterol. *38*:307–309, 2000.
164. Shanker, S., Rosenfield, J. A., Davey, G. R., et al.: *Campylobacter jejuni:* Incidence in processed broilers and biotype distribution in human and broiler isolates. Appl. Environ. Microbiol. *43*:1219–1220, 1982.
165. Simor, A. E., and Ferro, S.: *Campylobacter jejuni* infection occurring during pregnancy. Eur. J. Clin. Microbiol. Infect. Dis. *9*:142–144, 1990.
166. Simor, A. E., Karmali, M. A., Jadaviji, T., et al.: Abortion and perinatal sepsis associated with *Campylobacter* infection. Rev. Infect. Dis. *8*:397–402, 1986.
167. Sjogren, E., Kaijser, B., and Werner, M.: Antimicrobial susceptibilities of *Campylobacter jejuni* and *Campylobacter coli* isolated in Sweden: A 10-year follow-up report. Antimicrob. Agents Chemother. *36*:2847–2849, 1992.
168. Skirrow, M. B.: *Campylobacter* enteritis: A "new" disease. B. M. J. *2*: 9–11, 1977.
169. Skirrow, M. B.: *Campylobacter* enteritis in cats and dogs: A "new" zoonosis. Vet. Res. Commun. *5*:13–19, 1981.
170. Skirrow, M. B., Jones, D. M., Sutcliffe, E., et al.: *Campylobacter* bacteremia in England and Wales, 1981-91. Epidemiol. Infect. *110*:567–573, 1993.
171. Smibert, R. M.: Genus *Campylobacter*. *In* Krieg, N. R., and Holt, H. G. (eds.): Manual of Systematic Bacteriology. Vol. 1. Baltimore, Williams & Wilkins, 1984, p. 111.
172. Smith, K. E., Besser, J. M., Hedberg, C. W., et al.: Quinolone-resistant *Campylobacter jejuni* infections in Minnesota, 1992–1998. Investigation Team. N. Engl. J. Med. *340*:1525–1532, 1999.
173. Smith, M. V., and Muldoon, A. J.: *Campylobacter fetus* spp. *jejuni (Vibrio fetus)* from commercially processed poultry. Appl. Microbiol. *27*:995, 1974.
174. Spira, W. M., Sack, R. B., and Froelich, J. L.: Simple adult rabbit model for *Vibrio cholerae* and enterotoxigenic *Escherichia coli* diarrhea. Infect. Immun. *32*:739–747, 1981.
175. Stanley, K. N., Wallace, J. S., Currie, J. E., et al.: The seasonal variation of thermophilic campylobacters in beef cattle, dairy cattle and calves. J. Appl. Microbiol. *85*:472–480, 1998.
176. Svedhem, A., Gunnarsson, H., and Kaijser, B.: Diffusion-in-gel enzyme-linked immunosorbent assay for routine detection of IgG and IgM antibodies to *Campylobacter jejuni*. J. Infect. Dis. *148*:82–92, 1983.
177. Talsma, E., Goettsch, W. G., et al.: Resistance in *Campylobacter* species: Increased resistance to fluoroquinolones and seasonal variation. Clin. Infect. Dis. *29*:845–848, 1999.
178. Tauxe, R. V.: Epidemiology of *Campylobacter jejuni* infections in the United States and other industrialized countries. *In* Nachamkin, I., Blaser, M. J., and Tompkins, L. S. (eds.): *Campylobacter jejuni:* Current Strategy and Future Trends. Washington, D.C., American Society for Microbiology, 1992, pp. 9–19.
179. Tauxe, R. V., Deming, M. S., and Blake, P. A.: *Campylobacter jejuni* infections on college campuses: A national survey. Am. J. Public Health *75*:659–660, 1985.
180. Tauxe, R. V., Hargrett-Bean, N., Patton, C. M., et al.: *Campylobacter* isolates in the United States, 1982–1986. Mor. Mortal. Wkly. Rep. C. D. C. Surveill. Summ. *37*:1–13, 1988.
181. Taylor, D. N., Echeverria, P., Pitarangsi, C., et al.: Influence of strain characteristics and immunity on the epidemiology of *Campylobacter* infections in Thailand. J. Clin. Microbiol. *26*:863–868, 1988.
182. Taylor, D. N., McDermott, K. T., Little, J. R., et al.: *Campylobacter* enteritis from untreated water in the Rocky Mountains. Ann. Intern. Med. *99*:38–40, 1983.
183. Taylor, D. N., Perlman, D. N., Echeverria, P. D., et al.: *Campylobacter* immunity and quantitative excretion rates in Thai children. J. Infect. Dis. *168*:754–758, 1993.
184. Tee, W., Mijch, A.: *Campylobacter jejuni* bacteremia in human immunodeficiency virus (HIV) infected and non–HIV-infected patients: Comparison of clinical features and review. Clin. Infect. Dis. *26*:91–96, 1998.
185. Tenover, F. C., Carlson, L., Barbagallo, S. et al.: DNA probe culture confirmation assay for identification of thermophilic *Campylobacter* species. J. Clin. Microbiol. *28*:1284–1287, 1990.
186. Teunis, P. F., Nagelkerke, N. J., and Haas, C. N.: Dose response models for infectious gastroenteritis. Risk Anal. *19*:1251–1260, 1999.
187. Thomas, K., Chan, K. N., and Riberiro, C. D.: *Campylobacter jejuni/coli* meningitis in a neonate. B. M. J. *280*:1301–1302, 1980.
188. Tokumaru, M., Konuma, H., and Umesako, M.: Rates of detection of *Salmonella* and *Campylobacter* in meats in response to the sample size and the infection level of each species. Int. J. Food Microbiol. *13*:41–46, 1991.
189. Tolcin, R., LaSalvia, M. M., Kirkley, B. A., et al.: Evaluation of the Alexon-trend ProSpecT *Campylobacter* microplate assay. J. Clin. Microbiol. *38*:3853–3855, 2000.
190. Tomb, J. F., White, O., Kerlavage, A. R., et al.: The complete genome sequence of the gastric pathogen *Helicobacter pylori*. Nature *388*:539–547, 1997.
191. Torre, E., and Tello, M.: Factors influencing fecal shedding of *Campylobacter jejuni* in dogs without diarrhea. Am. J. Vet. Res. *54*:260–262, 1993.
192. Torres, O., and Cruz, J. R.: Protection against *Campylobacter* diarrhea: Role of milk IgA antibodies against bacterial surface antigens. Acta Paediatr. *82*:835–838, 1993.
193. Totten, P. A., Patton, C. M., Tenover, F. C., et al.: Prevalence and characterization of hippurate-negative *Campylobacter jejuni* in King County, Washington. J. Clin. Microbiol. *25*:1747–1752, 1987.
194. Vandamme, P., and De Ley, J.: Proposal for a new family, Campylobacteraceae. Int. J. Syst. Bacteriol. *41*:451–455, 1991.
195. Vandamme, P., Falsen, E., Rossau, R., et al.: Revision of *Campylobacter*, *Helicobacter*, and *Wolinella* taxonomy: Emendation of generic descriptions and proposal of *Arcobacter* gen. nov. Int. J. Syst. Bacteriol. *41*: 81–103, 1991.
196. Van der Meche, F. G. A., Van Doorn, P. A., Meulstee, J., et al.: Diagnostic and classification criteria for the Guillain-Barré syndrome. Eur. Neurol. *45*:133–139, 2001.
197. Vanhoof, R., Gordts, B., Dierickx, R., et al.: Bacteriostatic and bactericidal activities of 24 antimicrobial agents against *Campylobacter fetus* subsp. *jejuni*. Antimicrob. Agents Chemother. *18*:118–121, 1980.
198. Vanniasinkam, T., Lanser, J. A., and Barton, M. D.: PCR for the detection of *Campylobacter spp*. in clinical specimens. Lett. Appl. Microbiol. 28:52–56, 1999.
199. Vesikari, T., Huttunen, L., and Maki, R.: Perinatal *Campylobacter fetus* ssp *jejuni* enteritis. Acta Paediatr. Scand. *70*:261–263, 1981.
200. Vernon, M., and Chatelain, R.: Taxonomic study of the genus *Campylobacter* and designation of the neotype strain for the type species, *Campylobacter fetus*. Int. J. Syst. Bacteriol. *23*:122–134, 1973.
201. Vinzent, R., Dumas, J., and Picard, N.: Septicemia grave au cours de la grossesse due a vibrion: Avortement consecutif. Bull. Acad. Natl. Med. *131*:90–92, 1947.
202. Wallace, J. S., Stanley, K. N., and Jones, K.: The colonization of turkeys by thermophilic campylobacters. J. Appl. Microbiol. *85*:224–230, 1998.
203. Waltner-Toews, D., Martin, S. W., and Meek, A. H.: An epidemiological study of selected calf pathogens on Holstein dairy farms in southwestern Ontario. Can. J. Vet. Res. *50*:307–313, 1986.
204. Warner, D. P., Brainier, J. H., and Beran, W.: Epidemiologic study of campylobacteriosis in Iowa cattle and the possible role of unpasteurized milk as a vehicle of infection. Am. J. Vet. Res. *47*:254–258, 1986.
205. Wassenaar, T. M., and Newell, D. G.: Genotyping of *Campylobacter* spp. Appl. Environ. Microbiol. *66*:1–9, 2000.
206. Watson, K. C., Kerr, E. J. C., and McFadzean, S. M.: Serology of human *Campylobacter* infections. J. Infect. *1*:151, 1979.
207. Williams, D., Schorling, J., Barrett, L. J., et al.: Early treatment of *Campylobacter jejuni* enteritis. Antimicrob. Agents Chemother. *33*:248–250, 1989.
208. Wolfs, T. F., Duim, B., Geelen, S. P., et al.: Neonatal sepsis by *Campylobacter jejuni*: Genetically proven transmission from a household puppy. Clin. Infect. Dis. *32*:E97–E99, 2001.
209. Wright, E. P., and Seager, J.: Convulsions associated with *Campylobacter* enteritis. B. M. J. *281*:454, 1980.
210. Young, D. M., Biao, J., Zheng, Z., et al.: Isolation of *Campylobacter jejuni* in Hunan, the People's Republic of China: Epidemiology and comparison of Chinese and American methodology. Diagn. Microbiol. Infect. Dis. *5*:143–149, 1986.
211. Yuki, N., Ichikawa, H., and Doi, A.: Fisher syndrome after *Campylobacter jejuni* enteritis: Human leukocyte antigen and the bacterial serotype. J. Pediatr. *126*:55–57, 1995.

CHAPTER 137

Other *Campylobacter* Species

ROBERT J. LEGGIADRO

Although they are not isolated as frequently as are *Campylobacter jejuni* and *Campylobacter coli*, the "other" *Campylobacter* spp. are gaining recognition as human pathogens. *Campylobacter fetus*, a classic cause of perinatal infection, also is an infrequent cause of bacteremia in immunocompromised hosts. *Campylobacter upsaliensis*, *Campylobacter lari*, and *Campylobacter hyointestinalis* are associated primarily with diarrheal disease. Populations affected by these three species include normal as well as immunosuppressed hosts, especially human immunodeficiency virus (HIV)-infected persons with or without a history of animal exposure. The clinical spectrum of these organisms should expand as the special diagnostic tests needed to identify them become more widely available.

History

McFadyean and Stockman[53] first described the organisms now known as campylobacters in 1913. These *Vibrio*-like organisms were implicated as a cause of epizootic abortion in sheep, and a few years later, Smith[76] reported their association with bovine abortion as well and gave them the name *Vibrio fetus*. Although never confirmed microbiologically, these organisms are thought to have been *C. fetus* according to current nomenclature.[44] Vinzent and associates[86] first reported *Campylobacter* infection in humans in 1947. They described a pregnant woman with *V. fetus* bacteremia who subsequently aborted at 6 months' gestation. In addition to pregnancy, gastrectomy, tooth extraction, heart disease, diabetes, and cirrhosis were predisposing conditions in King's 1957 review of 15 patients with *V. fetus* bacteremia.[46]

Many reports describing "new" *Campylobacter* spp. were published in the 1980s and early 1990s. *C. upsaliensis* was reported to be a pathogen in dogs and humans.[63, 71] *C. lari*, a common isolate from healthy seagulls, was found to be a cause of gastrointestinal and extraintestinal disease in humans.[3, 81] Originally identified in the intestines of swine with proliferative ileitis, *C. hyointestinalis* was reported first as a human pathogen in a homosexual man with proctitis.[24] The hydrogen-requiring campylobacters, *Campylobacter concisus*,[85] *Campylobacter rectus*,[66] and *Campylobacter curvus*, have been associated with periodontal disease. *Campylobacter sputorum* has been identified in abscesses,[58] as well as bacteremia,[82] and *Campylobacter mucosalis* was reported in two children with diarrhea.[25]

Once called *Campylobacter*-like organisms, *Helicobacter cinaedi* and *Helicobacter fennelliae* now are classified in the *Helicobacter* genus.[60] These pathogens cause enteritis and proctocolitis in homosexual men and, on occasion, bacteremia.[62, 84] Two former *Campylobacter* spp., *Arcobacter butzleri* and *Arcobacter cryaerophilus*, are associated with abortion and enteritis in cattle and pigs, in addition to bacteremia and diarrhea in humans.[45]

Microbiology

Campylobacter is a Greek word meaning "curved rod." Members of this genus are gram-negative, curved, S-shaped or spiral, non–spore-forming rods that are 0.2 to 0.9 μm wide and 0.5 to 5 μm long.[58] Organisms are motile by means of a single polar flagellum, but some have a flagellum at each pole.[34] They are microaerophilic and have a respiratory type of metabolism.[58] Campylobacters are oxidase-positive and reduce nitrates but do not ferment or oxidize carbohydrates.[64] Although most grow at 37° C, *C. jejuni*, the *Campylobacter* sp. most commonly identified in humans, grows optimally at 42° C.[1]

Most *Campylobacter* spp. require a microaerobic atmosphere containing approximately 5 percent oxygen, 10 percent carbon dioxide, and 85 percent nitrogen for optimal recovery.[58] Some species such as *C. sputorum, C. concisus, C. mucosalis, C. curvus, C. rectus,* and *C. hyointestinalis* may require hydrogen for primary isolation and growth. Many different selective media for isolation of *Campylobacter* have been developed, but because of species differences in antibiotic resistance patterns, no single formulation isolates all species of clinical importance.[34] For example, *C. jejuni* and *C. coli* are resistant to cephalothin, whereas *C. fetus* is susceptible. A filtration method with nonselective media may be used to complement direct culture on selective media for the detection of antibiotic-susceptible *Campylobacter* spp. Because of their small size and motility, *Campylobacter* may pass through filters with pores of 0.45 to 0.65 μm, whereas other enteric flora are retained.[1, 58]

Although colonies may appear on plates within 24 to 48 hours, growth of campylobacters from stool may take as long as 72 to 96 hours. Primary isolation from blood may require 2 weeks.[1] Gram stain of young cultures reveals vibrioid forms, and longer incubation may yield spherical or coccoid bodies. *Campylobacter* spp. usually can be distinguished from one another on the basis of biochemical tests and growth characteristics (Table 137–1). Many investigators have applied molecular techniques to identify directly enteric campylobacters from stool.[8]

Epidemiology

Much needs to be learned about the epidemiology of *Campylobacter* spp. other than *C. jejuni* and *C. coli*, a group of organisms that made up only about 1 percent of *Campylobacter* spp. reported to the Centers for Disease Control and Prevention (CDC) from 1982 to 1986.[11] However, this study found that age-specific isolation rates of *C. fetus* parallel those of *C. jejuni* and *C. coli;* rates peak in infancy and increase in young adulthood, with *C. fetus* increasing substantially in the elderly. Seasonal distribution patterns of *C. jejuni, C. coli,* and *C. fetus* also were similar, with peaks in warm months. In this surveillance study, *C. jejuni* and *C. coli* isolates were predominantly from stool, whereas 54 percent of *C. fetus* isolates with a known source were from blood.[11]

C. fetus, an important cause of sporadic abortion in cattle and sheep, may be isolated from the intestines and genital tracts of these animals.[64] Contaminated food and water are the suspected sources of infection for sheep, cattle, and other animals, including goats, pigs, cats, dogs, hamsters, guinea

TABLE 137–1 ■ GROWTH AND BIOCHEMICAL CHARACTERISTICS OF SPECIES OF THE GENUS *CAMPYLOBACTER*

Species	Growth														Susceptibility	
	25° C	37° C	42° C	Anaerobically	In CO_2 Inhibitor	Glycine 1%	Bile 1%	Charcoal Casein Deoxycholate	Oxidase	Catalase	Urease	Hippurate	Nitrate	H_2S (TSI)	Nalidixic Acid	Cephalothin
C. lari	–	+	+	+	+	+	+	+	+	+	–	–	+	–	R	R
C. upsaliensis	–	+	+	+	+	–	+	+	+	(–)	–	–	+	–	S	S
C. fetus	+	+	(–)	–	+	+	–	–	+	+	–	–	+	–	R	S
C. hyointestinalis	(+)	+*	+	+	+	+	NA	NA	+	+	–	–	+	+	R	S
C. concisus	–	+	+	+	+	+	NA	NA	+	–	–	–	+	+	R	R
C. mucosalis	+	+	+	+	+	+	NA	NA	+	–	–	–	+	+	R	S
C. sputorum†	–	+	+	+	+	+	+	+	+	–	–	–	+	+	R	S

+, positive; –, negative; (+), most strains positive; (–), most strains negative; NA, data not available or found; R, resistant; S, susceptible; TSI, triple sugar iron.
*Best at 35° C.
†*C. sputorum* has three biovars with different biochemical characteristics.
Adapted from Ruiz-Palacios, G., and Pickering, L. K.: *Campylobacter* and *Helicobacter* infections. *In* Feigin, R. D., and Cherry, J. D. (eds.): Textbook of Pediatric Infectious Diseases. 3rd ed. Philadelphia, W. B. Saunders, 1992, pp. 1072–2084.

pigs, antelopes, chickens, and turkeys.[28] Although the source of *C. fetus* infection in humans generally is not apparent,[35] a 1970 review of *Vibrio fetus* infection in humans found that one third of patients had recent contact with animals or animal products and one third denied such contact, with no information available on the remaining third.[7]

C. fetus bacteremia generally occurs in immunosuppressed hosts (especially elderly men), pregnant women, and neonates.[67, 83] Predisposing conditions include alcoholism or cirrhosis, diabetes mellitus, heart disease, malignancy, splenectomy, and corticosteroid or other immunosuppressive therapy.[19, 40, 67] *C. fetus* is not considered a major cause of gastroenteritis, which may be the result of its failure to grow in stool specimens evaluated by routine laboratory methods for *C. jejuni* and *C. coli*.[11, 64]

The epidemiology of human *C. fetus* infection as a foodborne, perinatal infection was reflected in Vinzent and colleagues' original report, which described a 39-year-old pregnant woman who had a history of drinking raw milk from a cow that recently had aborted a pregnancy and contracted a flulike syndrome in the sixth month of pregnancy.[86] Two blood cultures grew *C. fetus,* and after 5 weeks of illness, a stillborn infant was delivered. In addition to raw milk,[88] raw beef liver[78] and "nutritional therapy" (raw fruit, vegetable juice, and calves' liver, along with coffee enemas) have been associated with *C. fetus* infection.[12] The latter report described nine patients with malignancy and one with systemic lupus erythematosus in whom *C. fetus* sepsis was associated with such therapy. Nine received their "nutritional therapy" in Mexico, and one died.[12]

First associated with human disease in a homosexual man with proctitis, *C. hyointestinalis* (*hyos*, hog; *intestinalis,* pertaining to the intestines) originally was isolated from the intestines of swine with proliferative ileitis.[24, 64] *C. hyointestinalis* also has been isolated from the stool of persons with nonbloody, watery diarrhea.[21] Two of these patients were homosexual men, the third was an elderly woman who had been traveling in Egypt, and the fourth was an infant from a large farm family that drank raw milk. These organisms are closer to *C. fetus* by DNA hybridization than any other catalase-positive *Campylobacter* sp. and are resistant to nalidixic acid but susceptible to cephalothin.[70]

C. lari, frequently isolated from apparently healthy seagulls, is nalidixic acid–resistant and thermophilic.[75] The name is derived from *laridis*, "of a sea bird," although seagulls do not play a direct role in its epidemiology.[81] Epidemiologically and microbiologically similar to *C. jejuni*, *C. lari* has been reported to cause enteritis in patients with and without a history of animal exposure and bacteremia in two elderly patients with multiple myeloma and permanent pacemakers.[56, 59, 74, 81] A water-borne outbreak of *C. lari*–associated gastroenteritis has also been reported.[9]

Catalase-negative or weak *Campylobacter* spp. that are hippurate-negative and thermotolerant were first isolated from dogs in 1983.[71] This *C. upsaliensis* group is associated with gastroenteritis, breast abscess, spontaneous abortion, and bacteremia in normal hosts, as well as opportunistic infections in immunocompromised persons.* Conditions predisposing to *C. upsaliensis* bacteremia include gallbladder surgery, ectopic pregnancy, kwashiorkor, and acquired immunodeficiency syndrome (AIDS).[63] Young puppies and kittens are potential transmitters of *C. upsaliensis,*[37] and an outbreak in a childcare center suggesting direct transmission between humans also has been described.[31, 36, 43] Routine selective media for *Campylobacter* may fail to detect this organism, which is slow growing and susceptible to cephalothin.[32, 50, 87] Filtration methods may improve the yield from stool cultures.[8, 32, 33, 42, 43, 52, 77]

*See references 29, 33, 36, 38, 42, 43, 50, 52, 63, 77.

Pathogenesis and Immunity

Information on the pathogenic and immune mechanisms involved in *Campylobacter* infections other than those caused by *C. jejuni* and *C. coli* is scarce. Much of what is known has been learned from animal, clinical, and epidemiologic data. The association of *Campylobacter* bacteremia with hypogammaglobulinemia, HIV infection, kwashiorkor, pregnancy, and malignancy indicates the importance of both humoral and cell-mediated immunity in host defense against this genus.[1, 15, 50, 59, 73, 90] The predilection of *C. fetus* for endovascular surfaces in adults and the central nervous system in neonates also is well documented.[20, 72]

In pregnant animals, *C. fetus* bacteremia occurs after ingestion of the organism, with subsequent infection of the placenta and fetus.[54, 61] Examination of infected animal placentas has revealed necrosis, infarction, and microabscesses, along with disruption of the placental circulation.[16] Placental changes similar to these have been described in humans after preterm maternal bacteremia, consistent with infection as a result of hematogenous rather than ascending spread.[73] Ascending infection with premature rupture of membranes and amnionitis in the absence of maternal bacteremia has resulted in stillbirth or early-onset disease.[26, 39] Contamination of the baby at the time of vaginal delivery is important in the pathogenesis of neonatal sepsis and meningitis with *C. fetus* in live-born infants.[51, 89]

Bacteremia may occur more commonly with *C. fetus* than with *C. jejuni* because the former is resistant to the bactericidal effects of human serum whereas the latter is susceptible.[5] A surface-layer protein that covers *C. fetus* functions as a capsule and appears to be an important virulence property of the organism.[4] It inhibits C3b binding, which explains both the serum resistance and the phagocytic resistance of *C. fetus*.[6]

Clinical Manifestations

The clinical spectrum of non-*jejuni* or non-*coli* *Campylobacter* infections varies with the age of the patient and the individual species involved (Table 137–2). *C. fetus* is responsible for most reported disease patterns, including prenatal, neonatal, bacteremic, and focal infections, caused by this "other *Campylobacter*" group of organisms.[83] Pregnancies complicated by maternal infection with *C. fetus* may result in abortion, stillbirth, and prematurity.[20, 65, 73] Live-born infants may suffer from sepsis and meningitis with a high case-fatality rate.

Mothers may have fever and chills with bacteremia alone or with diarrhea. Maternal blood, placenta, cervix, vaginal, and stool cultures have yielded *C. fetus* in reported perinatal cases.[20, 51, 73, 89] Maternal outcome is excellent.

Torphy and Bond[83] reviewed eight infants 12 hours to 22 days old with reported *C. fetus* disease. The initial symptoms, including fever, cough, respiratory distress, vomiting, diarrhea, cyanosis, convulsions, and jaundice, were consistent with neonatal sepsis. Meningitis developed in all eight infants, and six died. Four were premature, and three of them had an onset of illness at 2 days of age or younger and died during the first week of life. However, a subsequent review reported three additional neonatal patients who survived *C. fetus* meningitis after contracting the disease at

TABLE 137–2 ■ CLINICAL FEATURES ASSOCIATED WITH INFECTION BY "ATYPICAL" *CAMPYLOBACTER* AND RELATED SPECIES IMPLICATED AS CAUSES OF HUMAN ILLNESS

Species	Common Clinical Features	Less Common Clinical Features	Additional Information
C. fetus	Bacteremia, sepsis, meningitis, vascular infections	Diarrhea, relapsing fevers	Not usually isolated from media containing cephalothin
C. upsaliensis	Watery diarrhea, low-grade fever, abdominal pain	Bacteremia, abscesses, abortion, hemolytic-uremic syndrome	Difficult to isolate because of cephalothin susceptibility
C. lari	Abdominal pain, diarrhea	Colitis, appendicitis, bacteremia	Seagulls frequently colonized; organism often transmitted to humans via contaminated water
C. hyointestinalis	Watery or bloody diarrhea, vomiting, abdominal pain	Bacteremia	Causes proliferative enteritis in swine
C. sputorum	Pulmonary, perianal, groin, knee, and axillary abscesses	Bacteremia	Three clinically relevant biovars: *C. sputorum* subspecies *sputorum*, *C. sputorum* subspecies *bubulus*, and *C. mucosalis*
H_2-requiring *Campylobacter**	Periodontitis	Diarrhea, osteomyelitis, bacteremia	Uncertain role as human pathogen

*Includes *C. rectus*, *C. curvus*, and *C. concisus*.
Adapted from Allos, B. M., Blaser, M. J.: *Campylobacter jejuni* and the expanding spectrum of related infections. Clin. Infect. Dis. *20*:1092–1099, 1995.

1 to 3 days of age.[89] Hemorrhagic infarction and necrosis, as well as cystic degeneration of the cerebral cortex, are the cerebral lesions most commonly reported in *Campylobacter* meningitis.[89]

Descriptions of *C. fetus* infection in children outside the neonatal age group are rare.[47, 88, 90] One was a 2½-year-old child with *V. fetus* bacteremia who had low-grade fever for 3 weeks and a cervical mass on the day of admission and was treated successfully with penicillin.[88] Her past history included drinking raw cow's milk and untested well water. A 16-month-old girl from India whose father operated a dairy business was admitted for evaluation of fever lasting 10 days and seizures for 5 days before admission.[47] Her provisional diagnosis was encephalitis, and a blood culture grew *V. fetus*. No antibiotics were administered, and the patient recovered uneventfully. The authors emphasized the undulant nature of *C. fetus* infection, similar to that of brucellosis. *C. fetus* bacteremia also was detected in a nearly 5-year-old boy with agammaglobulinemia who had a 3-week history of anorexia, lethargy, fever, and more recently, hepatitis.[90] Blood culture grew *C. fetus*, and liver biopsy demonstrated hepatitis with multiple areas of severe focal necrosis, bridging necrosis, and Kupffer cell hyperplasia. He responded rapidly to ampicillin therapy.

Most reported patients with *C. fetus* infection are adult men older than 45 years of age who have bacteremia with or without focal infection.[19, 67, 83] Most of them have underlying conditions such as diabetes, malignancy, and hepatorenal or cardiovascular disease.[35, 40] Typically, illness begins with fever, malaise, and headache. Chills and night sweats are prominent, as is weight loss in prolonged illness. Diarrhea, nausea, vomiting, and abdominal pain occur in as many as 38 percent of cases, and hepatosplenomegaly or jaundice develops in two thirds.[35, 90] Pulmonary involvement is a rare finding.[7, 35]

Three patterns of invasive *C. fetus* disease have been described.[68] Clinical manifestations of the first localized infection accompanied by septicemia include meningitis,[10, 51] endocarditis,[23] pericarditis,[57] thrombophlebitis,[13] mycotic aneurysm,[69] cellulitis,[27, 40] gluteal abscess,[18] septic arthritis,[49] salpingitis,[10] and peritonitis.[80] The second form is transient asymptomatic bacteremia, which may be self-limited.[35, 67, 68] Prolonged and recurrent bacteremia with waxing and waning symptoms as spontaneous relapses and remissions occur is the third pattern of invasive *C. fetus* infection.[7, 17, 41, 68, 90]

The vascular tropism of *C. fetus*, especially in the presence of preexisting vessel damage, is well recognized.[13, 57, 90] Possible explanations for this predilection include a surface receptor on the organism with an affinity for vascular endothelium that results in endothelial damage and subsequent thrombus formation. In addition, the organism's microaerophilic growth requirements may be favored by venous oxygen tensions.[57] Previous valvular heart disease is a common finding in endocarditis.[23]

A report from the CDC reviewed clinical and epidemiologic information on 12 patients with *C. upsaliensis* isolates from 1980 to 1986.[63] Eight isolates were from blood and three from stool. Ages of the 12 patients ranged from 6 months to 83 years. Two infants with *C. upsaliensis* bacteremia that responded to amoxicillin therapy were included. One was a 10-month-old child who had fever, leukocytosis, and a history of culture-negative diarrhea, bronchiolitis, and *Klebsiella* bacteremia 3 months previously. The second was a 6½-month-old infant with fever, respiratory distress, and erythematous tympanic membranes. A 14-month-old child who lived on a farm with a private well and several household dogs and cats had a history of pica, including dirt from ground where chickens roamed. Stool culture obtained for evaluation of febrile, watery diarrhea yielded *C. upsaliensis*, and he recovered after receiving erythromycin therapy.[63]

Underlying medical problems in adults with *C. upsaliensis* bacteremia included peptic ulcer disease and partial large-bowel resection for a benign tumor, perforated gallbladder with peritonitis, AIDS, corticosteroid therapy, ruptured ectopic pregnancy, and cirrhosis with pancreatic insufficiency and partial gastrectomy.[63] One adult with a *C. upsaliensis* stool isolate was a 35-year-old woman with relapsing acute myelogenous leukemia. She was ill with fever and blood-tinged, watery diarrhea while thrombocytopenic and neutropenic. A healthy, 20-year-old student with a history of drinking raw milk and swimming in freshwater lakes and rivers was the second adult reported with a *C. upsaliensis* stool isolate. He had fever, severe cramping abdominal pain, and nonbloody, watery diarrhea of 3 weeks' duration that responded to oral erythromycin.[63]

Kwashiorkor and gastroenteritis were the predominant clinical features in a retrospective series of 16 pediatric patients with *C. upsaliensis* bacteremia from South Africa.[50] The age range was 2 to 36 months, with a mean age of 15.5 months. The authors suggested that *C. upsaliensis* bacteremia was secondary to intestinal infection with the same organism, but no confirmatory stool culture data were available.[50] A gastrointestinal source also was postulated for the *C. upsaliensis* isolated from a breast abscess in a previously healthy, 46-year-old woman.[29] Hemolytic-uremic syndrome was reported in a 14-year-old girl with *C. upsaliensis* gastroenteritis.[14]

C. upsaliensis was the only organism isolated from 83 patients in a large stool culture survey using a filtration system for *Campylobacter* in Belgium.[33] Ninety-two percent of patients had diarrhea, which was of acute onset in most cases. Vomiting (14%) and fever (7%) were uncommon occurrences, and symptoms generally abated in less than a week. Gross or occult blood was identified in 25 percent of cases, and neutrophils were seen on fecal smear in approximately 20 percent. Erythromycin (11 patients) or amoxicillin (2 patients) therapy eradicated the organism, with resolution of symptoms in all 13 patients treated with antibiotics.[33] Australian workers identified *C. upsaliensis* in 19 (0.1%) of 18,516 stool specimens from August 1992 to March 1999 at the Royal Children's Hospital in Melbourne.[43] Infection with *C. upsaliensis* was associated with milder disease than was infection with *C. jejuni*; *C. upsaliensis* patients had significantly less fever, diarrhea, and rectal bleeding.

Six clinical *C. lari* isolates were referred to the national *Campylobacter* reference laboratory at the CDC in 1982 and 1983.[81] Clinical illness associated with these isolates included enteritis in four patients, severe crampy abdominal pain in a 7-year-old girl, and terminal bacteremia in a 71-year-old man with multiple myeloma and chronic renal failure. The ages of the four patients with enteritis were 8 months, 3 years, 22 years, and 39 years. Diarrhea was watery or mucoid, and fever was an unusual occurrence. Potential exposure included consuming chicken, having contact with house pets, drinking untreated surface water, and eating raw oysters. *C. lari* colitis also developed in an HIV-infected woman.[22]

C. hyointestinalis has been isolated from the stool specimens of adult and pediatric patients experiencing nonbloody, watery diarrhea[21] and from a rectal culture of a homosexual man with proctitis.[24] The clinical features of other *Campylobacter* spp. are presented in Table 137–2.

Diagnosis

Confirmation of infection with *C. fetus* and *Campylobacter* spp. other than *C. jejuni* and *C. coli* is based on positive culture results from clinical specimens.[1] *C. fetus* has been isolated from blood, cerebrospinal fluid, joint effusions, bile, urine, and pleural and pericardial fluid in standard culture media.[35] Blood cultures generally are positive within 4 to 14 days. Isolation of *C. fetus* and "other" *Campylobacter* spp. from stool requires incubation at 37° C and media without cephalosporins. Filtration techniques also may be warranted to detect these strains in stool cultures.

Treatment

Gentamicin, erythromycin, and imipenem are bactericidal for *C. fetus*, as is ampicillin to a lesser extent.[23, 30, 55] Cefotaxime, ticarcillin, amikacin, chloramphenicol, clindamycin, tetracycline, and ciprofloxacin have variable activity against different *C. fetus* strains.[23] Reported synergistic antimicrobial combinations in vitro include ampicillin and gentamicin or cefazolin and imipenem with gentamicin.[23, 79]

Erythromycin continues to be the drug of choice for most patients with *Campylobacter* diarrhea.[1] The newer macrolide azithromycin, which has a broader spectrum of activity than does erythromycin, is effective therapy for *Campylobacter* enteritis, as well as for diarrhea caused by *Salmonella*, *Shigella*, *Vibrio cholerae*, and *Escherichia coli*, thus rendering it a useful drug in the treatment of traveler's diarrhea.[48] Increasing *Campylobacter* resistance to quinolones related to expanded use in humans and in animals used for food, especially chickens, has diminished the usefulness of quinolones such as ciprofloxacin in the treatment of *Campylobacter* gastroenteritis in adults.[1, 22, 48]

Gentamicin, imipenem, ampicillin, and cefotaxime are therapeutic options in treating *Campylobacter* bacteremia and other extraintestinal infections.[1, 2, 23, 89] Synergistic combination therapy is indicated for patients with meningitis and endocarditis, in which bactericidal activity is critical.[1, 55] Patients with *Campylobacter* in their stool who are being treated for an extraintestinal *Campylobacter* infection with gentamicin should be prescribed supplemental oral therapy because gentamicin is ineffective against *Campylobacter* in the gut.[1]

Prolonged antimicrobial therapy and follow-up blood cultures are warranted for patients with *C. fetus* bacteremia because of its relapsing nature.[57, 68] Chloramphenicol should be used with caution in treating *C. fetus* meningitis because clinical outcome and in vitro susceptibility results for this drug have been disappointing.[51, 55]

REFERENCES

1. Allos, B. M., and Blaser, M. J.: *Campylobacter jejuni* and the expanding spectrum of related infections. Clin. Infect. Dis. *20*:1092–1099, 1995.
2. American Academy of Pediatrics: *Campylobacter* infections. *In* Pickering, L. K. (ed.): 2000 Redbook: Report of the Committee on Infectious Diseases. 25th ed. Elk Grove Village, IL, American Academy of Pediatrics, 2000, pp. 196–198.
3. Benjamin, J., Leaper, S., Owen, R. J., et al.: Description of *Campylobacter laridis*, a new species comprising the nalidixic acid resistant thermophilic *Campylobacter* (NARTC) group. Curr. Microbiol. *8*:231, 1983.
4. Blaser, M. J., Smith, P. F., Hopkins, J. A., et al.: Pathogenesis of *Campylobacter fetus* infections: Serum resistance associated with high molecular weight surface proteins. J. Infect. Dis. *135*:696–706, 1987.
5. Blaser, M. J., Smith, P. F., and Kohler, P. A.: Susceptibility of *Campylobacter* isolates to the bactericidal activity in human serum. J. Infect. Dis. *151*:227–235, 1985.
6. Blaser, M. J., Smith, P. F., Repine, J. E., et al.: Pathogenesis of *Campylobacter fetus* infections: Failure of C3b to bind explains serum and phagocytosis resistance. J. Clin. Invest. *81*:1434–1444, 1988.
7. Bokkenheuser, V.: *Vibrio fetus* infection in man. I. Ten new cases and some epidemiologic observations. Am. J. Epidemiol. *91*:400–409, 1970.
8. Bourke, B., Chan, V. L., and Sherman, P.: *Campylobacter upsaliensis:* Waiting in the wings. Clin. Microbiol. Rev. *11*:440–449, 1998.
9. Broczyk, A., Thompson, S., Smith, D., and Lior, H.: Water-borne outbreak of *Campylobacter laridis*–associated gastroenteritis. Letter. Lancet *1*: 164–165, 1987.
10. Brown, W. J., and Sautter, R.: *Campylobacter fetus* septicemia with concurrent salpingitis. J. Clin. Microbiol. *6*:72–75, 1977.
11. *Campylobacter* isolates in the United States, 1982–1986. Morb. Mortal. Wkly. Rep. C. D. C. Surveill Summ *37*(SS-2):1–13, 1988.
12. *Campylobacter* sepsis associated with "nutrition therapy." M. M. W. R. Morb. Mortal. Wkly. Rep *30*:294–295, 1981.
13. Carbone, K. M., Heinrich, M. C., and Quinn. T. C.: Thrombophlebitis and cellulitis due to *Campylobacter fetus* ssp. *fetus:* Report of four cases and a review of the literature. Medicine (Baltimore) *64*:244–250, 1985.
14. Carter, J. E., and Cimolai, N.: Hemolytic-uremic syndrome associated with acute *Campylobacter upsaliensis* gastroenteritis. Nephron *74*:489, 1996.

15. Chusid, M. J., Wortman, D. W., and Dunne, W. M.: *"Campylobacter upsaliensis"* sepsis in a boy with acquired hypogammaglobulinemia. Diagn. Microbiol. Infect. Dis. *13*:367–369, 1990.
16. Coid, C. R., and Fox, H.: Short review: Campylobacters as placental pathogens. Placenta *4*:295–305, 1983.
17. Collins, H. S., Blevins, A., Benter, E.: Protracted bacteremia and meningitis due to *Vibrio fetus*. Arch. Intern. Med. *113*:361, 1964.
18. de Otero, J., Pigrau, C., Buti, M., et al.: Isolation of *Campylobacter fetus* subspecies *fetus* from a gluteal abscess. Clin. Infect. Dis. *19*:557–558, 1994.
19. Dronda, F., Garcia-Arata, I., Navas, E., and de Rafael, L.: Meningitis in adults due to *Campylobacter fetus* subspecies *fetus*. Clin. Infect. Dis. *27*:906–907, 1998.
20. Eden, A. N.: Perinatal mortality caused by *Vibrio fetus*. J. Pediatr. *68*:297, 1966.
21. Edmonds, P., Patton, C. M., Griffin, P. M., et al.: *Campylobacter hyointestinalis* associated with human gastrointestinal disease in the United States. J. Clin. Microbiol. *25*:685–691, 1987.
22. Evans, T. G., and Riley, D.: *Campylobacter laridis* colitis in a human immunodeficiency virus–positive patient treated with a quinolone. Clin. Infect. Dis. *15*:172–173, 1992.
23. Farrugia, D. C., Eykyn, S. J., and Smyth, E. G.: *Campylobacter fetus* endocarditis: Two case reports and review. Clin. Infect. Dis. *18*:443–446, 1994.
24. Fennell, C. L., Rompalo, A. M., Totten, P. A., et al.: Isolation of *Campylobacter hyointestinalis* from a human. J. Clin. Microbiol. *24*:146–148, 1986.
25. Figura, N., Guglielmetti, P., Zanchi, A., et al.: Two cases of *Campylobacter mucosalis* enteritis in children. J. Clin. Microbiol. *31*:727–728, 1993.
26. Forbes, J. D., and Scheifele, D. W.: Early onset *Campylobacter* sepsis in a neonate. Pediatr. Infect. Dis. J. *6*:494, 1987.
27. Francioli, P., Hertzstein, J., Grob, J., et al.: *Campylobacter fetus* subspecies *fetus* bacteremia. Arch. Intern. Med. *145*:289–292, 1985.
28. Franklin, B., and Ulmer, D. D.: Human infection with *Vibrio fetus*. West. J. Med. *120*:200–204, 1974.
29. Gaudreau, C., and Lamothe, F.: *Campylobacter upsaliensis* isolated from a breast abscess. J. Clin. Microbiol. *30*:1354–1356, 1992.
30. Goossens, H., Coignau, H., Vlaes, L., et al.: In vitro evaluation of antibiotic combinations against *Campylobacter fetus*. J. Antimicrob. Chemother. *24*:195–201, 1989.
31. Goossens, H., Giesendorf, A. S., Vandamme, P., et al.: Investigation of an outbreak of *Campylobacter upsaliensis* in day care centers in Brussels: Analysis of relationships among isolates by phenotypic and genotypic typing methods. J. Infect. Dis. *172*:1298–1305, 1995.
32. Goossens, H., Pot, B., Vlaes, L., et al.: Characterization and description of *Campylobacter upsaliensis* isolated from human feces. J. Clin. Microbiol. *28*:1039–1046, 1990.
33. Goossens, H., Vlaes, L., DeBoeck, M., et al.: Is "*Campylobacter upsaliensis*" an unrecognised cause of human diarrhoea? Lancet *335*:584–586, 1990.
34. Griffiths, P. L., and Park, R. W. A.: Campylobacters associated with human diarrhoeal disease. J. Appl. Bacteriol. *69*:281–301, 1990.
35. Guerrant, R. L., Lahita, R. G., Winn, W. C., et al.: Campylobacteriosis in man: Pathogenic mechanisms and review of 91 bloodstream infections. Am. J. Med. *65*:584–592, 1978.
36. Gurgani, T., and Diker, K. S.: Abortion associated with *Campylobacter upsaliensis*. J. Clin. Microbiol. *32*:3093–3094, 1994.
37. Hald, B., and Madsen, M.: Healthy puppies and kittens as carriers of *Campylobacter* spp., with special reference to *Campylobacter upsaliensis*. J. Clin. Microbiol. *35*:3351–3352, 1997.
38. Hanna, J. N., Enbom, R. M., and Murphy, D. M.: *Campylobacter upsaliensis* bacteraemia in an Aboriginal child. Med. J. Aust. *160*:655–656, 1994.
39. Hood, M., and Todd, J. M.: *Vibrio fetus*: A cause of human abortion. Am. J. Obstet. Gynecol. *80*:506, 1960.
40. Ichiyama, S., Hirai, S., Minami, T., et al.: *Campylobacter fetus* subspecies *fetus* cellulitis associated with bacteremia in debilitated hosts. Clin. Infect. Dis. *27*:252–255, 1998.
41. Jackson, J. F., Hinton, P., and Allison, F., Jr.: Human vibriosis: Report of a patient with relapsing febrile illness due to *Vibrio fetus*. Am. J. Med. *28*:986, 1960.
42. Jenkin, G. A., and Tee, W.: *Campylobacter upsaliensis*–associated diarrhea in human immunodeficiency virus–infected patients. Clin. Infect. Dis. *27*:816–821, 1998.
43. Jimenez, S. G., Heine, R. G., Ward, P. B., and Robins-Browne, R. M.: *Campylobacter upsaliensis* gastroenteritis in childhood. Pediatr. Infect. Dis. J. *18*:988–992, 1999.
44. Karmali, M. A., Allen, A. K., and Fleming, P. C.: Differentiation of catalase-positive campylobacters with special reference to morphology. Int. J. Syst. Bacteriol. *31*:64, 1981.
45. Kiehlbauch, J. A., Brenner, D. J., Nicholson, M. A., et al.: *Campylobacter butzleri* sp. nov. isolated from humans and animals with diarrheal illness. J. Clin. Microbiol. *29*:376–385, 1991.
46. King, E. O.: Human infections with *Vibrio fetus* and a closely related vibrio. J. Infect. Dis. *101*:119, 1957.
47. Koshi, G., Samuel, B. T., Malati, J., et al.: *Vibrio fetus* encephalitis with bacteremia in a child. Indian J. Med. Res. *57*:1232–1239, 1969.
48. Kuschner, R. A., Trofa, A. F., Thomas, R. J., et al.: Use of azithromycin for the treatment of *Campylobacter enteritis* in travelers to Thailand, an area where ciprofloxacin resistance is prevalent. Clin. Infect. Dis. *21*:536, 1995.
49. Kutner, L. J., and Arnold, W. D.: Septic arthritis due to *Vibrio fetus*. J. Bone Joint Surg. Am. *52*:161–164, 1970.
50. Lastovica, A. J., LeRoux, E., and Penner, J. L.: *Campylobacter upsaliensis* isolated from blood cultures of pediatric patients. J. Clin. Microbiol. *27*:657–659, 1989.
51. Lee, M. M., Welliver, R. C., and La Scolea, L. J.: *Campylobacter* meningitis in childhood. Pediatr. Infect. Dis. *4*:544–547, 1985.
52. Lindblom, G.-B., Sjogren, E., Hansson-Westerberg, J., and Kaijser, B.: *Campylobacter upsaliensis*, *C. sputorum sputorum* and *C. concisus* as common causes of diarrhea in Swedish children. Scand. J. Infect. Dis. *27*:187–188, 1995.
53. McFadyean, F., and Stockman, S.: Report of the Departmental Committee Appointed by the Board of Agriculture and Fisheries to Inquire into Epizootic Abortion, London, 1909–1913. His Majesty's Stationary Office *3*:1, 1913.
54. Miller, V. A., Jensen, R., and Gilroy, J. J.: Bacteremia in pregnant sheep following oral administration of *Vibrio fetus*. Am. J. Vet. Res. *20*:677, 1959.
55. Morooka, T., Oda, T., and Shigeoka, H.: In vitro evaluation of antibiotics for treatment of meningitis caused by *Campylobacter fetus* subspecies *fetus*. Pediatr. Infect. Dis. J. *8*:653–654, 1989.
56. Morris, C. N., Scully, B., and Garvey, G. J.: *Campylobacter lari* associated with permanent pacemaker infection and bacteremia. Clin. Infect. Dis. *27*:220–221, 1998.
57. Morrison, V. A., Lloyd, B. D., Chia, J. K. S., et al.: Cardiovascular and bacteremic manifestations of *Campylobacter fetus* infection: Case report and review. Rev. Infect. Dis. *12*:387–392, 1990.
58. Nachamkin, I.: *Campylobacter* and *Arcobacter*. *In* Murray, P. R., Baron, E. J., Pfaller, M. A., et al. (eds.): Manual of Clinical Microbiology. 6th ed. Washington, D.C., ASM Press, 1995, pp. 483–491.
59. Nachamkin, I., Stowell, C., Skalina, D., et al.: *Campylobacter laridis* causing bacteremia in an immunosuppressed patient. Ann. Intern. Med. *101*: 55–57, 1984.
60. Orlicek, S. L., Welch, D. F., and Kuhls, T. L.: Septicemia and meningitis caused by a *Helicobacter cinaedi* in a neonate. J. Clin. Microbiol. *31*:569–571, 1993.
61. Osburn, B. I., and Hoskins, R. K.: Experimentally induced *Vibrio fetus* var. *intestinalis* infection in pregnant cows. Am. J. Vet. Res. *31*: 1733–1741, 1970.
62. Pasternak, J., Bolivar, R., Hopfer, R. L., et al.: Bacteremia caused by *Campylobacter*-like organisms in two male homosexuals. Ann. Intern. Med. *101*:339–341, 1984.
63. Patton, C. M., Shaffer, N., Edmonds, P., et al.: Human disease associated with *Campylobacter upsaliensis* (catalase-negative or weakly positive *Campylobacter* species) in the United States. J. Clin. Microbiol. *27*:66–73, 1989.
64. Penner, J. L.: The genus *Campylobacter*: A decade of progress. Clin. Microbiol. Rev. *1*:157–172, 1988.
65. Premature labor and neonatal sepsis caused by *Campylobacter fetus*, subsp. *fetus*: Ontario. M. M. W. R. Morb. Mortal. Wkly. Rep. *33*:483–484, 1984.
66. Rams, T. E., Feik, D., and Slots, J.: *Campylobacter rectus* in human periodontitis. Oral Microbiol. Immunol. *8*:230–235, 1993.
67. Rettig, P. J.: *Campylobacter* infections in human beings. J. Pediatr. *94*:855–864, 1979.
68. Righter, J., Wells, W. A., Hart, G. D., et al.: Relapsing septicemia caused by *Campylobacter fetus* subsp *fetus*. Can. Med. Assoc. J. *128*:686–689, 1983.
69. Righter, J., and Woods, J. M.: *Campylobacter* and endovascular lesions. Can. J. Surg. *28*:451–452, 1985.
70. Roop, R. M., II, Smibert, R. M., Johnson, J. L., et al.: Differential characteristics of catalase positive campylobacters correlated with DNA homology groups. Can. J. Microbiol. *30*:938–951, 1984.
71. Sanstedt, K., Ursing, J., and Walder, M.: Thermotolerant *Campylobacter* with no or weak catalase activity isolated from dogs. Curr. Microbiol. *8*:209, 1983.
72. Schmidt, U., Chmel, H., Kaminski, Z., et al.: The clinical spectrum of *Campylobacter fetus* infections: Report of five cases and review of the literature. Q. J. Med. *49*:431–432, 1980.
73. Simor, A. E., Karmali, M. A., Jadavji, T., et al.: Abortion and perinatal sepsis associated with *Campylobacter* infection. Rev. Infect. Dis. *8*: 397–402, 1986.
74. Simor, A. E., and Wilcox, L.: Enteritis associated with *Campylobacter laridis*. J. Clin. Microbiol. *25*:10–12, 1987.
75. Skirrow, M. B., and Benjamin, J.: Differentiation of enteropathogenic *Campylobacter*. J. Clin. Pathol. *33*:1122, 1980.
76. Smith, T.: *Spirilla* associated with disease of the fetal membranes in cattle. J. Exp. Med. *28*:701, 1918.
77. Snijders, F., Kuijper, E. J., deWever, B., et al.: Prevalence of *Campylobacter*-associated diarrhea among patients infected with human immunodeficiency virus. Clin. Infect. Dis. *24*:1107–1113, 1997.

78. Soonattrakul, W., Andersen, B. R., and Brynor, J. H.: Raw liver as a possible source of *Vibrio fetus* septicemia in man. Am. J. Med. Sci. *261*:245, 1981.
79. Spelhaug, D. R., Gilchrist, M. J. R., and Washington, J. A., II: Bactericidal activity of antibiotics against *Campylobacter fetus* subspecies *intestinalis*. J. Infect. Dis. *143*:500, 1981.
80. Targan, S. R., Chow, A. W., and Guze, L. B.: Spontaneous peritonitis of cirrhosis due to *Campylobacter fetus*. Gastroenterology *71*:311–313, 1976.
81. Tauxe, R. V., Patton, C. M., Edmonds, P., et al.: Illness associated with *Campylobacter laridis*, a newly recognized *Campylobacter* species. J. Clin. Microbiol. *21*:222–225, 1985.
82. Tee, W., Luppino, M., and Rambaldo, S.: Bacteremia due to *Campylobacter sputorum* biovar *sputorum*. Clin. Infect. Dis. *27*:1544–1545, 1998.
83. Torphy, D. E., and Bond, W. W.: *Campylobacter fetus* infections in children. Pediatrics *64*:898–903, 1979.
84. Totten, P. A., Fennell, C. L., Tenover, F. C., et al.: *Campylobacter cinaedi* (sp. nov.) and *Campylobacter fennelliae* (sp. nov.): Two new *Campylobacter* species associated with enteric disease in homosexual men. J. Infect. Dis. *151*:131–139, 1985.
85. Vandamme, P., Falsen, E., Pot, B., et al.: Identification of EF group 22 campylobacters from gastroenteritis cases as *Campylobacter concisus*. J. Clin. Microbiol. *27*:1775–1781, 1989.
86. Vinzent, R., Dumas, J., and Picard, N.: Septicemie grave au cours de la grossesse, due a un vibrion: Avortement consecutif. Bull. Acad. Natl. Med. (Paris) *131*:90, 1947.
87. Walmsley, S. L., and Karmali, M. A.: Direct isolation of atypical thermophilic *Campylobacter* species from human feces on selective agar medium. J. Clin. Microbiol. *27*:668–670, 1989.
88. Willis, M. D., and Austin, W. J.: Human *Vibrio fetus* infection: Report of two dissimilar cases. Am. J. Dis. Child. *112*:459–462, 1966.
89. Wong, S., Tam, A. Y., and Yeun, K.: *Campylobacter* infection in the neonate: Case report and review of the literature. Pediatr. Infect. Dis. J. *9*:665, 1990.
90. Wyatt, R. A., Younoszai, K., Anuras, S., et al.: *Campylobacter fetus* septicemia and hepatitis in a child with agammaglobulinemia. J. Pediatr. *91*:441–442, 1977.

CHAPTER 138 Tularemia

RALPH D. FEIGIN ■ CHING C. LAU

Tularemia is an acute febrile illness caused by *Francisella tularensis*. Although it is primarily a disease of animals, humans also are highly susceptible hosts.

History

McCoy[62] published the first documented evidence of tularemia in 1911 when he described a plague-like disease in ground squirrels (*Citellus beecheyi*) that occurred in Tulare County, California. Within 2 years, McCoy and Chapin[63] isolated and characterized the organism *Bacterium tularense* from naturally infected ground squirrels. They also detailed the pathology produced in ground squirrels, defined the susceptibility of other animal species to *B. tularense*, and identified fleas as vectors for the plague-like disease in 1912.

The first description of tularemia in humans may be that by Hommo-Soken, a court physician in eastern Japan.[82] In 1837, he described an illness as "hare meat poisoning." Nearly a century later, Vail[103] and Wherry and Lamb[108] independently reported the first etiologically proven case of tularemia in humans in 1914. Thereafter, knowledge of the organism, susceptible hosts, modes of transmission, and clinical manifestations of disease was acquired rapidly, and retrospective information was assessed in light of this new information. Much of the current understanding of the disease in humans originated from the work of Edward Francis,[27] a U. S. Public Health Service surgeon. Intrigued by the new diseases, which were called "deer fly fever" by Pearse[75] in 1911 and "plague-like disease" by McCoy, Francis relocated to Utah in 1919 and established his laboratory in an unused coal shed.[27, 28, 30] Soon thereafter, he recognized the singular cause of these two diseases and renamed them "tularemia" because of isolation of *B. tularense* from blood.[82] He isolated the organism from humans and jackrabbits[26] and demonstrated transmission of the organism by the deer fly.[30]

For a more complete historical review, the reader is referred to the classic paper by Dr. Edward Francis,[27] "A Summary of the Present Knowledge of Tularemia." Some 7 decades later, this paper is accurate and contains most of the knowledge essential for understanding tularemia.

Etiology

The causative agent of tularemia, after having been placed in the genera *Bacterium, Bacillus, Brucella*, and *Pasteurella*, is now named *Francisella tularensis* in honor of Dr. Edward Francis. *F. tularensis* is a small (0.2 to 1.0 μm × 1 to 3 μm), nonmotile, non–spore-forming, highly pleomorphic gram-negative coccobacillus. It is a strict aerobe that infects as a facultative intracellular bacterium.[44]

Hesselbrock and Foshay[40] described the morphology as resembling that of the pleuropneumonia group of organisms, the usual coccoid form being a spheroidal cystic structure with a delicate, transparent cell wall. The morphology and mode of reproduction (chiefly budding) suggested relationships with fungi and the pleuropneumonia group and none with the genera *Pasteurella* and *Brucella*. Subsequent electron-microscopic studies confirmed the presence of a delicate, almost transparent cell wall, which Eigelsbach and associates[15] thought could explain the instability of lyophilized cultures.

The outstanding growth characteristic of these fastidious organisms is their requirement for cysteine or sulfhydryl compounds in amounts exceeding those usually present in nutrient media.[22] Although *F. tularensis* grows best on cysteine-glucose-blood agar and on coagulated egg yolk medium and less well in thioglycolate broth, it can be isolated in routine cultures and on enriched chocolate agar.[54, 65] Hornick[42] suggested that the addition of cycloheximide and penicillin facilitates isolation of the organism from the respiratory tract or skin ulcers. In one study by Johansson and colleagues,[47] an Amies agar medium with charcoal and a Thayer-Martin medium with antibiotics were equal in preserving bacterial viability for 1 week when compared with saline or Stuart medium.

F. tularensis is killed readily by heat. Exposure to a temperature of 56° C for 10 minutes is sufficient for killing.

The organisms are not destroyed by freezing and may remain viable in frozen animal carcasses for as long as 3 years. However, adequate cooking renders the meat of game birds and animals harmless. Treatment with tricresol solution (1%) for 2 minutes also kills organisms in tissue; organisms from cultures are killed in 24 hours by 0.1 percent formalin.

All strains of *F. tularensis* seem serologically identical, but individual strains may possess varying degrees of virulence. Ormsbee and associates[72] reported that the immunizing antigens seem to be concentrated in the cell wall. The purest cell wall preparations contain at least four and possibly six different antigens, but the soluble fractions did not seem to provide protection against any of these antigens when mice were immunized with these preparations.

Despite serologic homogeneity, two distinct varieties of tularemia organisms exist. The strains that are highly virulent for humans, Jellison type A (*F. tularensis* biovar *tularensis*), account for approximately 90 percent of organisms isolated in North America and have been seen in Europe as well.[36] The less virulent strains, Jellison type B (*F. tularensis* biovar *palaearctica*), are found primarily in Europe and Asia. The two strains have been found to coexist in the same ecosystem, however.[61]

F. tularensis does not produce any exotoxin, but pharmacologic tests indicate that the organism contains a lipopolysaccharide endotoxin similar to that of gram-negative bacilli.[24]

Epidemiology

Tularemia is ubiquitous in the northern hemisphere between 30 and 71 degrees north latitude.[41] It has been reported throughout the United States, in the Far East, and in Europe.[29, 68–70, 94] *F. tularensis* has been found in Canada and Mexico but has not been reported in South America or Africa. Within the United States, the disease most commonly occurs in the south central region. In 1982, four states (Arkansas, Missouri, Oklahoma, and Texas) accounted for approximately one third of reported cases.[101] From 1991 to 1992, 47 percent (165 of 352) of all cases were reported from Missouri and Arkansas.[91]

Tularemia occurs year-round. However, peaks occur in the summer and winter months, depending on the region. Tularemia occurs more commonly in the central and southern states during the summer months, when ticks are more prevalent. The incidence in the northern and eastern states peaks in the winter months during the hunting season.

In the United States, the incidence of tularemia has been recorded since 1927. The number of human cases declined steadily from 1939 (2991 cases[5]) until 1975 (129 cases). Since then, the number of reported cases has increased, and between 129 and 288 cases of tularemia have been reported annually. This range probably is a gross underestimate of the actual incidence. In 1968 in a serologic survey of 1936 subjects in California, approximately 1 percent of this population had antibody against *F. tularensis*.[20] Using skin test antigens, Casper and Phillip[9] showed that 6.6 percent of 365 persons in eastern Montana had evidence of previous infection with *F. tularensis*. Of the persons in whom skin test results were positive, 80 percent had no previous history of the disease, thus indicating a high number of subclinical or self-limited infections. The mortality rate is zero to four cases per year.

The most common sources of human infection are contact with infected animals or their carcasses and bites by ticks or tabanid flies (deer flies). Less commonly, people acquire the disease from the bite of a diseased animal or one in which the mouth has been contaminated by the ingestion of a diseased animal. Numerous outbreaks of human tularemia have occurred by water transmission,[4, 28, 50, 98, 104] the water having been contaminated by voles, beavers, lemmings, and muskrats. Infection also may occur by aerosolization of the organisms, especially in laboratory workers[51, 104] and occasionally farm workers (inhalation of dust and threshing material contaminated by voles and other rodents).[13, 41] Person-to-person transmission has not been documented.

Hopla,[41] in describing the ecology of tularemia, states that "rarely does one encounter a zoonotic disease of such complexity." Indeed, to understand the development of epizootics and transmission to humans, one must consider the role of numerous vertebrates (humans and other animals, both wild and domestic) and many invertebrates.

Approximately 100 species of wild mammals, 9 species of domestic animals, 25 species of birds, and several species of fish and amphibians have been found to be infected naturally,[71] but probably fewer than a dozen species of mammals are important in the transmission of *F. tularensis*.[41] Lagomorphs (rabbits and hares) and some rodents (muskrats, voles) are highly susceptible to *F. tularensis*; sheep and domestic rabbits are susceptible but have low sensitivity to the organism; and cats, cattle, dogs, and horses are virtually insusceptible to infection. Vertebrate animals are called reservoirs, but they rarely are true reservoirs because most of them become sick and either die or recover, with elimination of the organism. The varying hare (snowshoe rabbit) is less susceptible to *F. tularensis* and may serve as a reservoir because of its high natural resistance and carrier state.[25]

Humans act as terminal hosts of *F. tularensis* because they do not transmit it to other humans or to other mammals. Persons especially at risk are hunters, trappers, meat processors, cooks, sheep herders and shearers, muskrat farmers, and laboratory workers. The incidence of tularemia in children is less than that in adults because exposure occurs less frequently. Infection is acquired by the same routes as for adults: vector bites, animal bites, and ingestion of infected, inadequately cooked meat. In reviewing the age incidence of tularemia in Arkansas (704 cases), Washburn and Tuohy[107] found the following order of persons at risk: agricultural workers, rural housewives, and preschool and school-age children.

Many invertebrates can be infected experimentally by *F. tularensis*, but relatively few are infected naturally. In 1924, Parker and Spencer[74] first described ticks as vectors for *F. tularensis* infection in guinea pigs. However, the role of ticks in the spread of the human disease was not recognized until 1949, when Washburn and Tuohy[107] reported that 56 percent (391 of 704) of tularemia cases in Arkansas were associated with exposure to ticks. To date, ticks remain the most common vectors for *F. tularensis* in the United States and can serve as reservoirs because the organism can be transmitted from generation to generation by transovarian passage.[41]

At least 13 species of ticks have been found to be infected naturally by *F. tularensis*.[41] The species involved in transmission to humans are *Dermacentor andersoni* (wood tick), *Dermacentor variabilis* (dog tick), and *Amblyomma americanum* (Lone Star tick). A fourth tick, *Haemaphysalis leporisalustris* (rabbit tick), is important in the epidemiology of tularemia. Although this tick does not transmit tularemia directly to humans, it perpetuates the cycle of infection by acting as the sylvatic vector between rabbits.[39]

When the tick feeds on an infected animal, the organisms penetrate through the gut into the hemolymph and are disseminated throughout the body, including the salivary glands. The tick then transmits the organisms by injecting them, along with saliva, when it feeds on another animal.

In addition, transmission by tick fecal contamination also is likely. Ticks, biting flies (i.e., deer flies), and fleas probably are responsible for the continuing endemic disease in susceptible animals and for epizootic disease. Infrequently, mosquitoes and mites may transport *F. tularensis* mechanically from animal to animal or animal to human.[41]

A few cases of tularemia acquired by cat bite have been reported.[2, 8, 107] Because cats rarely are infected by *F. tularensis*, such transmission probably is due to mechanical transmission from the contaminated teeth or claws of a cat that has come into contact with or fed on an infected animal. Cat bites may be an important source of disease in children.

Pathogenesis

BACTERIAL AND HOST INTERACTIONS

Much of the knowledge regarding interactions between *F. tularensis* and the host was derived from experimental studies using live attenuated strains. During World War II, live attenuated strains of *F. tularensis* were developed in the Soviet Union in an effort to produce a vaccine.[79, 100] In 1956, a mixture of attenuated strains of *F. tularensis* was transferred from the Soviet Union to the United States. From this mixture, a strain of suitable virulence was selected, tested for safety and efficacy, and designated *F. tularensis* live vaccine strain.[16, 18, 46] This strain has been used extensively in experimental studies on the development of immunity in humans.

A single *F. tularensis* organism of a virulent strain can produce fatal infection in susceptible animals such as mice, guinea pigs, and hamsters.[110] As few as 10 organisms of a virulent strain injected intradermally or 25 organisms given by aerosol may produce systemic disease in human volunteers.[46] Tularemia is followed by effective immunospecific protection of the host; reinfection has been documented in only nine persons.[7] Studies in which the infecting bacteria were suppressed by the use of a bacteriostatic agent such as tetracycline show that protective immunity seems to be activated approximately 2 weeks after onset of the disease. When tetracycline treatment was initiated on the day of onset of tularemia and given for 10 days, early relapses were common occurrences. When tetracycline treatment was administered for 14 days, relapses occurred less frequently, thus indicating that protective immunity had begun to arise.[84]

In animals and humans, *F. tularensis* elicits both humoral and cell-mediated immune responses. Both responses reach maximal levels during the second week after infection.[10] Although the presence of IgA antibodies in nasal secretions correlates with resistance to infection by aerosolized organisms, earlier work by Bellanti and associates[3] has shown that humoral immunity plays a minor role in resistance to tularemia. However, more recent animal studies have shown that protection against tularemia live vaccine strain can be transferred by immune mouse serum and depends on host interferon-γ, interleukin-2, and $CD4^+$ T cells.[44, 81] Specific antibodies possibly are involved initially in delaying the infection, thereby allowing time for the induction of cytokine production and specific T-cell–mediated immunity. This suggestion is consistent with the observation that although neutrophils have only a minor role in resistance to infection, mice selectively depleted of neutrophils and eosinophils by treatment with a granulocyte-specific antibody are incapable of controlling infection with a sublethal inoculum of the live vaccine strain of tularensis.[87] In addition, mice depleted of $CD4^+$ T cells, $CD8^+$ T cells, or both remained capable of controlling and partly resolving a primary sublethal *F. tularensis* infection.[11]

Persistence of immunity to *F. tularensis* depends on the T-cell response to a variety of antigens; this response may not be noted for as long as 2 weeks after exposure. Poquet and associates[80] showed that virulent strains of *F. tularensis* produce high levels of phosphoantigens that cause a proliferation in gamma-delta T cells to a greater extent than does exposure to the live vaccine strain. The reduced number of this T-cell subtype in vaccinated individuals could explain the lack of complete protection seen in vaccinated laboratory workers. As with membrane proteins stimulating an alpha-beta T-cell response, heat shock protein chaperones such as DnaK and Cpn60 also create a non-immunodominant proliferation of T cells in immunized individuals.[21]

Because *F. tularensis* is described as a facultative intracellular parasite, the general consensus is that host immunity ultimately depends on cell-mediated immunity, just as in *Listeria monocytogenes* and *Mycobacterium tuberculosis*.[92, 109] It has been confirmed by several trials showing that vaccination with killed tularemia preparations, although it induces agglutinating serum antibodies, provides poor protection.[7, 46, 83] Numerous studies have shown that passive transfer of mononuclear leukocytes from infected animals to noninfected animals conferred resistance when the nonimmunized animals were challenged with a virulent strain.[87]

Denaturation of the protein or carbohydrate of a macromolecular antigen of *F. tularensis* has shown that T-cell reactivity is associated with only protein determinants, whereas human immune serum reacts mostly with carbohydrate determinants of the organism.[1, 17, 99]

INVASION AND DISEASE PRODUCTION

The organism may gain access to the human body through the skin, conjunctiva, oropharynx, respiratory tract, or gastrointestinal tract. It spreads by the lymphatics or hematogenously, and bacteremia usually develops during the first week of infection (3 to 12 days).[51] Infection commonly involves the skin, regional lymph nodes, liver, spleen, and lungs. Rarely, the gastrointestinal tract and the central nervous system also are involved.

Histopathologic examination of mammals experimentally infected with *F. tularensis* indicates that the organism disseminates and causes cellular changes in a manner typical of intracellular parasites. After the organism is introduced into a susceptible host, multiplication occurs locally, with early spread to regional lymph nodes occurring within 48 to 96 hours.[18] The developing cutaneous ulcer or soft tissue focus goes through a series of changes, with polymorphonuclear leukocytes being replaced by macrophages. In time, necrosis, epithelioid cell infiltrates, giant-cell formation, and true granulomata may develop.[37, 64, 86] Organisms are difficult to demonstrate in tissue but occasionally are found at the periphery of lesions. In addition to the development of classic necrotic and granulomatous lesions, degeneration of the parenchyma in the liver and spleen may occur, as may marked hyperplasia of the reticuloendothelial system. These granulomata can organize to form abscesses and microabscesses. The pace of the illness depends on the virulence of the strain, as well as the inoculum size, portal of entry, and immune status of the host. When organisms enter the blood circulation, typical endotoxemia may ensue, sometimes in association with acute rhabdomyolysis.[49]

Autopsies of fatal cases of tularemia in humans have confirmed the findings in experimental animals.[34, 57, 77] Lymph nodes from patients with nonfatal disease have shown follicular hyperplasia with conglomerates of macrophages and caseating granulomata.[52, 57, 59, 93] These findings are similar to those seen in miliary tuberculosis. In fact, tularemia and tuberculosis may be histopathologically distinguishable only because of the difference in timing of the development of tissue changes,[52] a difference related to the rapid replication of *F. tularensis.*

Clinical Manifestations

Regardless of the portal of entry, the mode of onset of tularemia and the general features of the disease are the same. The usual incubation period of tularemia is 3 to 4 days, with a range of 1 to 21 days. The onset of symptoms is abrupt. Symptoms include fever with a temperature usually higher than 39.4° C (103° F), chills, headache, myalgia, anorexia, vomiting, and occasionally photophobia. Fever may be continuous or biphasic with an intermittent period of defervescence. In untreated patients, fever may persist for longer than 3 weeks. Physical findings usually include lymphadenopathy, hepatosplenomegaly, pharyngitis, and skin lesions. Temperature-pulse dissociation has been described.[23, 31] A variety of skin rashes (e.g., maculopapular, vesicular, pustular, erythema nodosum, erythema multiforme) may appear during the second week of illness,[96] and subcutaneous nodules may be present.[51]

Laboratory studies, including a complete blood count, erythrocyte sedimentation rate, urinalysis, and *Proteus* OX2/OX19 titers, usually are not helpful in diagnosing tularemia. Interestingly, sterile pyuria has been reported in patients with tularemia, 22 percent in one study[23] and 32 percent in another.[76] Sterile pyuria combined with a history of fever, dysuria, or low back pain had led to an erroneous diagnosis of urinary tract infection in 11 percent of the patients reported by Evans and associates.[23] Increased liver function test values with jaundice and atypical lymphocytosis also has been reported.[32, 35]

The six clinical syndromes of tularemia can be classified by the portal of entry: ulceroglandular, glandular, oculoglandular, typhoidal, oropharyngeal, and pneumonic.

ULCEROGLANDULAR TULAREMIA

Ulceroglandular tularemia, the most common form of the disease, accounts for more than 75 percent of all cases (adults and children). The organism gains access through the skin. Approximately 2 days after the onset of general symptoms, the patient complains of tender, swollen lymph nodes, most commonly in the axillary or inguinal areas. Within 24 hours, the portal of entry may become evident when a painful swollen papule develops distal to the regional node. This papule ruptures and leaves a punched-out ulcer with raised edges. The ulcer is indolent and, in untreated cases, may persist for longer than a month. The skin over the involved nodes may be inflamed. In untreated cases, approximately 50 percent of the lymph nodes suppurate and drain. In other cases, the nodes remain firm, enlarged, and tender for several months. A mild, generalized lymphadenopathy and enlargement of the liver and spleen may be present.

GLANDULAR TULAREMIA

The glandular form of tularemia is almost identical to the ulceroglandular form, except that the portal of entry cannot be identified. The general thought is that the portal is an insignificant break in the skin. Isolated cases of cervical lymphadenopathy have been related causally to *F. tularensis* infection.

OCULOGLANDULAR TULAREMIA

With oculoglandular tularemia, the portal of entry is the conjunctival sac, which may be inoculated by rubbing with contaminated fingers, having contact with infected water, splashing of infected liquids, or inhaling infected aerosols. The eyelids may become edematous and the conjunctivae inflamed and painful. Numerous small, sharply defined, yellowish nodules and ulcers may be present on the palpebral conjunctivae. In some cases, corneal ulceration occurs. As seen in cat-scratch disease, the Parinaud complex of unilateral preauricular lymph node involvement and conjunctivitis can result.[89] The regional nodes, the preauricular nodes, and the submaxillary and cervical nodes are swollen, tender, and painful. In severe cases, the axillary nodes may be involved.[27]

TYPHOIDAL TULAREMIA

Typhoidal tularemia is manifested as a fever of unknown cause. The symptoms are those of acute septicemia with no localized skin lesions and often without lymphadenopathy. Patients are seriously ill, and shock may develop. The symptoms and signs of typhoidal tularemia are toxemia, continuous fever, myalgia, and severe headache. Patients may be delirious and may exhibit meningismus. Patients often complain of having severe pharyngeal pain, but pharyngeal lesions may not be evident. Diarrhea occurs in this form of tularemia in both adults and children. Sometimes, a dry cough and retrosternal pain are present. Pleuropulmonary involvement is a common finding in adults with typhoidal tularemia.[14] In children, typhoidal tularemia can be the result of ingestion of the causative agent, and necrotic lesions may be present throughout the bowel.[14] Inhalation of aerosolized organisms is a more common mode of acquisition in adults (laboratory workers, farmers).

OROPHARYNGEAL TULAREMIA

The oropharyngeal form resembles the ulceroglandular form. The infection is introduced into the oropharyngeal mucosa via infected, inadequately cooked meat. The organisms enter through abrasions, or aerosolization may occur during chewing. Local involvement consists of acute tonsillitis with cervical adenitis. The tonsils may be covered by an exudate or membrane that extends in all directions and may resemble a diphtheritic membrane. Complaints of sore throat are usually out of proportion to the visible pathology, but ulcers sometimes are present. The cervical nodes may suppurate. Infrequently, *F. tularensis* invades the lower portions of the gastrointestinal tract, in which case vomiting, diarrhea, and abdominal pain are prominent symptoms. Awareness of the ability of *F. tularensis* to cause oropharyngeal involvement is important for physicians caring for children.[43, 56]

PNEUMONIC TULAREMIA

The pneumonic form of the disease occurs most commonly in laboratory workers and is the most severe and lethal form.[46] Pneumonic tularemia may be acquired by the aerogenic route, or pulmonary disease may be associated with other forms of tularemia, particularly the typhoidal type. Dienst[14] and Miller and Bates[65] have published outstanding descriptions of pleuropulmonary tularemia. The latter stress that the symptoms and signs of pleuropulmonary tularemia are nonspecific and vary with the location and degree of pulmonary involvement. The variable radiographic features may be confused with those of tuberculosis, mycotic infection, common bacterial pneumonia, lymphoma, or carcinoma of the lung. In Miller and Bates' series of 29 patients, pleural effusion developed in 6. Pleural effusions have been found to contain greater than 3 g of protein per 100 mL and more than 1000 white blood cells/mm^3 with a lymphocytic predominance.[33] Because of the necrotizing nature of the pathologic process, the lung may heal with residual fibrosis or calcification. In other instances, the disease is so fulminant that death occurs before the pathologic features can progress fully.

ADDITIONAL CLINICAL MANIFESTATIONS

All large series of reported cases have patients with subcutaneous nodules resembling those seen in sporotrichosis. The nodules usually are distributed on the anterior or posterior surface of the arm and may extend from the primary lesion to the regional lymph nodes. Initially, they are firm and movable, but later they become fixed to the skin and may suppurate. They vary in size from less than a centimeter to larger than several centimeters, if they become confluent. As many as 30 single nodules may be present.

Other unusual manifestations of tularemia include pericarditis, appendicitis, peritonitis, liver abscess, cerebellitis with ataxia, meningitis, encephalitis, osteomyelitis, rhabdomyolysis, and venous thrombosis.

The incidence of these forms in children is somewhat different from that in adults. Although the pneumonic form previously was thought to be relatively rare in children,[56] more recent studies on the changing epidemiology and clinical manifestations of this disease have shown that the occurrence of pneumonic tularemia is not uncommon.[45] In a 1985 study by Jacobs and associates,[45] 14 percent of tularemia cases in children were the pneumonic form. This percentage contrasts with no pulmonary involvement in a series of 48 cases of tularemia in children reported by Levy and associates[56] in 1950. The distribution of these forms of tularemia also varies with the geographic location. In a report of 67 children with tularemia in Finland, 79 percent of the cases were of the ulceroglandular form, and 8 percent were glandular.[102] This distribution is significantly different from that in the United States. In the study by Jacobs and associates,[45] who reported on 28 cases of tularemia in children, 45 percent were ulceroglandular and 25 percent were glandular.[45] The authors of the Finnish study attribute the higher proportion of the ulceroglandular form in their study to heightened awareness of the disease and early diagnosis. In addition, the differences also could be explained by the different strains of *F. tularensis* and different vectors in the two regions.

F. tularensis also can occur in the setting of an immunocompromised host. The pneumonic form of tularemia has been reported in a patient with chronic granulomatous disease requiring lobectomy.[60] Pneumonic tularemia also has been seen in a patient who previously had undergone a peripheral blood stem cell transplant for acute myelogenous leukemia (it resulted in a solitary pulmonary nodule) and in a patient infected with human immunodeficiency virus (HIV).[35, 66] In addition, it has been noted in a patient with a ventriculoperitoneal shunt.[78] Impairment of normal immunity could prevent adequate protection from *F. tularensis* and necessitate more prolonged therapy.

Diagnosis

The diagnosis of tularemia is established by a thorough history of possible exposure, clinical manifestations, and serial serologic tests. Obtaining a careful family history often is rewarding because several family members commonly are infected simultaneously. In some instances, however, a positive history never is elicited. Tularemia has no absolute pathognomonic features. In diagnosing tularemia, the physician must account for the endemic rate of the disease in the area, the season of the year, the clinical manifestations of the disease, the precise epidemiologic setting,[90] and the unresponsiveness of the disease to antibiotics that are not effective against tularemia.

The diagnosis is confirmed by the standard agglutination test, which is available commercially and is reliable. Unfortunately, it does not provide an early diagnosis because agglutinating antibodies usually are not detectable until the second week of illness. Occasionally, seroconversion is not confirmed until the patient has experienced 4 to 6 weeks of illness. In rare cases, agglutinating antibody may never be detected. A fourfold increase in convalescent titer confirms the diagnosis, but a presumptive diagnosis should be considered with acute titers of 1:160 or greater. This titer may indicate current or past infection, but in a clinically suspicious case, it should be considered an indication for presumptive therapy. Titers of 1:1280 or greater often develop in patients with active disease as the initial manifestation of seroconversion.

The agglutination test is specific, but cross-reaction with *Brucella* and occasionally with cholera vaccine (in recent recipients) has been reported. It can easily be clarified by simultaneous testing with the individual antigens (tularemia and brucellosis). Antibiotic therapy does not prevent the development of agglutinating antibodies.

An enzyme-linked immunosorbent assay with bacterial sonicate antigen (ELISA-S) determines the presence of IgM, IgG, and IgA antibodies to *F. tularensis*.[105] This test has the advantage of confirming the diagnosis of tularemia earlier in the illness than the agglutinating test does. Like other ELISA-based methods that have been developed recently, however, the ELISA-S test is not available commercially.

Another method used for making the early diagnosis of tularemia is the whole blood lymphocyte stimulation test.[53, 95] During an epidemic in Finland in 1983, this technique was compared with the bacterial agglutination test in the diagnosis of 200 cases. The lymphocyte stimulation test yielded positive results in 21 percent of cases during the first week of illness and in 97 percent during the second week. In contrast, the bacterial agglutination test detected only 2 percent of the cases in the first week and 53 percent in the second week.

The skin test (Foshay) is an accurate method of diagnosis[6] and is positive earlier in the illness than is the agglutination test, but the skin test antigen is not available commercially.

Of the other diagnostic modalities recently evaluated, a polymerase chain reaction (PCR)-based assay holds promise for early detection of *F. tularensis* infection.[58] The PCR test has been shown to be effective in establishing the diagnosis of tularemia even when samples of a tularemic ulcer were obtained 1 to 14 days after infection.[88] When PCR and culture of the wound and blood were compared with agglutination tests, the sensitivity of PCR was 75 percent and the sensitivity of culture was 62 percent.[47] In addition to increasing the safety for laboratory personnel, the PCR method was more sensitive and could detect infection at earlier stages. This assay is not available commercially at this time.

In a Norwegian field study, a rapid immunochromatography assay has proved to be inexpensive, time efficient, and portable when compared with PCR and ELISA, but this method was less sensitive than is PCR.[4] This assay could accelerate identification and treatment decisions in clinical practice.

Gram-stained smears of patient specimens such as exudate and sputum usually do not reveal the organism. However, collecting the specimens poses no danger, and examination of direct smears helps rule out other causative agents. Specimens should not be cultured for *F. tularensis* in the usual hospital or diagnostic laboratory because isolation of these organisms in facilities other than a level P-3 laboratory is hazardous to laboratory personnel. If confirmation by culture is indicated, physicians should notify the laboratory of the potential for the specimen to contain *F. tularensis* so that appropriate laboratory precautions can be taken.

The differential diagnosis of tularemia depends on the clinical form of the disease. Ulceroglandular and glandular tularemia must be differentiated from disease caused by ordinary bacterial pathogens such as *Streptococcus* and *Staphylococcus*, from disease caused by *M. tuberculosis* and atypical mycobacteria such as *Mycobacterium marinum*, and from anthrax, HIV, and cat-scratch disease. In older patients with inguinal lymphadenopathy, lymphogranuloma venereum, granuloma inguinale, and other sexually transmitted diseases should be considered. Occasionally, sporotrichosis and infectious mononucleosis are diagnosed in these patients. Oculoglandular fever is somewhat more distinctive, but one must not rule out disease caused by common bacterial pathogens, *L. monocytogenes*, herpes zoster, inclusion conjunctivitis, and keratoconjunctivitis. Oropharyngeal tularemia must be differentiated from streptococcal tonsillopharyngitis and corynebacterial disease. Typhoidal tularemia can be confused with ordinary bacteremia and must be differentiated from the more common bacterial and enteric disease, as well as from malaria, miliary tuberculosis, brucellosis, and typhoid fever. Tularemic pneumonia must be differentiated from other bacterial as well as nonbacterial pneumonia, including tuberculosis, *Mycoplasma* infection, legionnaires' disease, psittacosis, viral pneumonia, Q fever, fungal infection, and chemical pneumonitis.

Treatment

Streptomycin traditionally is the drug of choice for the treatment of tularemia. The recommended dose is 30 to 40 mg/kg/day administered intramuscularly in two divided doses for 7 days. If a patient has mild symptoms initially or responds dramatically to therapy, an alternative streptomycin regimen of 30 to 40 mg/kg/day for 3 days followed by 15 to 20 mg/kg/day for 4 days may be given intramuscularly. In severe cases or if a child does not become afebrile and asymptomatic within a few days of therapy, extension of treatment beyond 7 days is indicated. Streptomycin-resistant strains of tularemia are reported, but they are rare.[73] Defervescence and alleviation of other signs and symptoms occur promptly, usually within several days. Response may be delayed if the lymph nodes have progressed to suppuration.

Because of the recent shortage of streptomycin in the United States,* alternative antibiotic regimens must be considered. Unfortunately, because of the lack of controlled clinical trials of the newer antibiotics for the treatment of tularemia, experience with alternative antibiotic regimens is limited. In a review of the various treatments of tularemia reported in the literature, Enderlin and associates[19] concluded that streptomycin remains the drug of choice, with a cure rate of 97 percent and no relapse. Gentamicin is an acceptable alternative to streptomycin, with a cure rate of 86 percent and a relapse incidence of 6 percent. These authors attributed some of the treatment failure with gentamicin to a delay in initiation of therapy and the short duration of therapy in some severe cases, as well as other underlying medical problems.[19] The recommended dosage of gentamicin for tularemia is 5 mg/kg/day divided into two intramuscular doses.

Bacteriostatic agents such as tetracycline and chloramphenicol also have been used to treat tularemia, with cure rates of 88 percent and 77 percent, respectively. However, these agents are considered suboptimal for the treatment of tularemia because of a high incidence of relapse after therapy is stopped (12% for tetracycline and 22% for chloramphenicol).[19]

Although in vitro susceptibility testing indicates that the third-generation cephalosporins may be effective against *F. tularensis*, one report showed treatment failure in eight children given ceftriaxone.[12] Treatment with other antibiotics reported sporadically in the literature includes one successful case with imipenem and cilastatin,[55] seven successful cases with ciprofloxacin or norfloxacin in adults,[66, 85, 97] and four isolated cases with erythromycin.[38] A recent efficacy trial in Sweden of ciprofloxacin demonstrated successful outpatient management of *F. tularensis* in 10 of 12 patients 1 to 10 years of age.[2] The dosage used was 15 to 20 mg/kg/day in two divided doses for a 10- to 14-day course of therapy. Defervescence occurred in the fourth day of treatment. Despite the lack of clear data on safety in children, this treatment has been reported as efficacious in a 17-year-old patient in the United States who developed tularemia after being bitten by a cat.[48]

Children receiving streptomycin should be monitored for ototoxicity. Hearing screening should be considered before initiation of streptomycin or gentamicin therapy. If the child has preexisting hearing loss, the alternative streptomycin regimen or gentamicin therapy can be considered, with close monitoring of serum levels in severe cases. Audiologic evaluation is indicated after therapy in these cases.

Bed rest and supportive therapy are, of course, indicated. In a severely ill patient who shows signs of endotoxic shock, appropriate monitoring and admission to an intensive care unit are indicated, and corticosteroid therapy should be considered. Suppurative nodes may require surgical drainage.

Before the advent of effective antimicrobial therapy, tularemia often was a protracted illness that lasted weeks or months. Subsequently, a long period of convalescence was necessitated by debility. Antibiotics have interrupted the natural history of the disease. When the disease is diagnosed promptly, the course generally is less than a month. As a result of administering appropriate antibiotic therapy, the mortality rate has declined from 5 to 30 percent to less than 1 percent, except in cases of fulminant pneumonic and typhoidal disease.

*As of November 1995, streptomycin is available from Pfizer Streptomycin Program, Pfizer Pharmaceuticals, New York, NY (800-254-4445).

Prevention

Prevention of human tularemia depends on prevention of exposure to either the vectors or contaminated animal tissue. Children living in areas of tick endemicity should have their skin and hair checked frequently for ticks. Ticks should be removed carefully with tweezers (not with fingernails) by pulling perpendicular to the skin where they have attached.[67] Care should be taken not to squeeze the tick between the fingers. Persons living in tick-infested areas should wear clothing with tightly fitting cuffs at the wrists and ankles when staying outdoors. Tick repellents should be used with caution on children.

Children should be cautioned against handling sick or dead rodents or rabbits. Incineration or burial should be used to dispose of rabbits caught by household pets. Rubber gloves should be worn for preparing game animals, and the meat should be cooked thoroughly before eating. Hunters, especially rabbit hunters, should take precautions against contracting tularemia.

The only tularemia vaccine available in the United States is the *F. tularensis* live vaccine strain developed in 1960. It is unlicensed and classified as an investigational product, but it is available to laboratory personnel. This vaccine appears to have reduced significantly the incidence of typhoidal tularemia and the severity of ulceroglandular disease in laboratory personnel. One lot of vaccine recently produced was found to induce an 80 percent response with IgG to the ether-extracted antigen (EEx) of the lipopolysaccharide membrane protein by day 14 and a 100 percent response by 21 days.[106] In vitro, lymphocyte responses to several antigens were noted by 14 days, in contrast to controls, in whom the EEx response appeared first.[106] The efficacy of this vaccine for prevention of naturally occurring disease in the United States is unknown.

REFERENCES

1. Allen, W. P.: Immunity against tularemia: Passive protection of mice by transfer of immune tissues. J. Exp. Med. *115*:411–420, 1962.
2. Arav-Boger, R.: Cat-bite tularemia in a seventeen-year-old girl treated with ciprofloxacin. Pediatr. Infect. Dis. J. *19*:583–584, 2000.
3. Bellanti, J. A., Buescher, E. L., Brandt, W. E., et al.: Characterization of human serum and nasal hemagglutinating antibody in *Francisella tularensis*. J. Immunol. *98*:171–178, 1967.
4. Berdal, B., Mehl, R., Haaheim, H., et al.: Field detection of *Francisella tularensis*. Scand. J. Infect. Dis. *32*:287–291, 2000.
5. Boyce, J. M.: Recent trends in the epidemiology of tularemia in the United States. J. Infect. Dis. *131*:197–199, 1914.
6. Buchanan, T. M., Brooks, G. F., and Brachman, P. S.: The tularemia skin test. Ann. Intern. Med. *74*:336–343, 1971.
7. Burke, D. S.: Immunization against tularemia: Analysis of the effectiveness of live *Francisella tularensis* vaccine in prevention of laboratory-acquired tularemia. J. Infect. Dis. *135*:55–60, 1977.
8. Callaway, G. D., Peterson, S. S., and Good, J. T.: Tularemia in southwest Missouri. Mo. Med. *51*:906–909, 1954.
9. Casper, E. A., and Phillip, R. N.: A skin test survey of tularemia in a Montana sheep-raising county. Public Health Rep. *84*:611–615, 1969.
10. Claflin, J. L., and Larson, C. L.: Infection-immunity in tularemia: Specificity of cellular immunity. Infect. Immun. *5*:311–317, 1972.
11. Conlan, J. W., Sjostedt, A., and North, R. J.: CD4^{+} and CD8^{+} T-cell-dependent and independent host defense mechanisms can operate to control and resolve primary and secondary *Francisella tularensis* LVS infection in mice. Infect. Immun. *62*:5603–5607, 1994.
12. Cross, J. T., and Jacobs, R. F.: Tularemia: Treatment failures with outpatient use of ceftriaxone. Clin. Infect. Dis. *17*:76–80, 1993.
13. Dahlstrand, S., Ringertz, O., and Zetterberg, B.: Airborne tularemia in Sweden. Scand. J. Infect. Dis. *3*:7–16, 1971.
14. Dienst, F. T., Jr.: Tularemia: A perusal of three hundred thirty-nine cases. J. La. State Med. Soc. *115*:114–127, 1963.
15. Eigelsbach, H. T., Chambers, L. A., and Coriell, L. L.: Electron microscopy of *Bacterium tularense*. J. Bacteriol. *52*:179–185, 1946.
16. Eigelsbach, H. T., Hornick, R. B., and Tulis, J. J.: Recent studies on live tularemia vaccine. Med. Ann. D. C. *36*:282–286, 1967.
17. Eigelsbach, H. T., Hunter, D. H., Janssen, W. A., et al.: Murine model for study of cell-mediated immunity: Protection against death from fully virulent *Francisella tularensis* infection. Infect. Immun. *12*:999–1005, 1915.
18. Eigelsbach, H. T., Tulis, J. J., McGavran, M. H., et al.: Live tularemia vaccine: Host-parasite relationship in monkeys vaccinated intracutaneously or aerogenically. J. Bacteriol. *84*:1020–1027, 1962.
19. Enderlin, G., Morales, L., Jacobs, R. F., et al.: Streptomycin and alternative agents for the treatment of tularemia: Review of the literature. Clin. Infect. Dis. *19*:42–47, 1994.
20. Engelfried, J. J.: Antibodies to *Pasteurella tularensis* in a selected human population. Mil. Med. *135*:723–726, 1968.
21. Ericsson, M., Golovliov, I., Sandstrom, G., et al.: Characterization of the nucleotide sequence of the groe operon encoding heat shock proteins Chaperone-60 and -10 of *F. tularensis* and determination of the T-cell response to the proteins in individuals vaccinated with *F. tularensis*. Infect. Immun. *65*:1824–1829, 1997.
22. Evans, M. E.: *Francisella tularensis*. Infect. Control *6*:381–383, 1985.
23. Evans, M. E., Gregary, D. W., Schaffner, W., et al.: Tularemia: A 30-year experience with 88 cases. Medicine (Baltimore) *64*:251–269, 1985.
24. Finegold, M. J., Pulliam, J. D., Landay, M. E., et al.: Pathological changes in rabbits injected with *Pasteurella tularensis* killed by ionizing radiation. J. Infect. Dis. *119*:635–640, 1969.
25. Foshay, L.: Tularemia. Annu. Rev. Microbiol. *4*:313–330, 1950.
26. Francis, E.: A new disease of man. J. A. M. A. *78*:1015, 1922.
27. Francis, E.: A summary of the present knowledge of tularemia. Medicine (Baltimore) *7*:411–432, 1928.
28. Francis, E.: Oculoglandular tularemia. Arch. Ophthalmol. *28*:711–741, 1942.
29. Francis, E., and Mayne, B.: Public Health Rep. *36*:1938–1946, 1921.
30. Francis, E.: Sources of infection and seasonal incidence of tularemia in man. Public Health Rep. *52*:103–113, 1937.
31. Fredricks, D., Remington, J.: Tularemia presenting as community-acquired pneumonia. Arch. Intern. Med. *156*:2137–2140, 1996.
32. Gelfand, M. S., Mehra, N., and Simmons, B. P.: Tularemia and atypical lymphocytosis. J. Tenn. Med. Assoc. *82*:417–418, 1989.
33. Gill, V., and Cunha, B.: Tularemia pneumonia. Semin. Respir. Infect. *12*:61–67, 1997.
34. Goodpasture, E. W., and House, S. J.: The pathologic anatomy of tularemia in man. Am. J. Pathol. *4*:213–216, 1928.
35. Gries, D., Fairchok, M.: Typhoidal tularemia in a human immunodeficiency virus-infected adolescent. Pediatr. Infect. Dis. J. *15*:838–839, 1996.
36. Gurycova, D.: First isolation of *F. tularensis* subsp. *tularensis* in Europe. Eur. J. Epidemiol. *14*:797–802, 1998.
37. Hall, W. C., Kovatch, R. M., and Schricker, R. L.: Tularemic pneumonia: Pathogenesis of the aerosol-induced disease in monkeys. J. Pathol. *110*:193–201, 1973.
38. Harrell, R. E., Jr., and Simmons, H. F.: Pleuropulmonary tularemia: Successful treatment with erythromycin. South. Med. J. *83*:1363–1364, 1990.
39. Harwood, R. F., and James, M. T. (eds.): Entomology in Human and Animal Health. New York, Macmillan, 1973, pp. 403–404.
40. Hesselbrock, W. B., and Foshay, L.: The morphology of *Bacterium tularense*. J. Bacteriol. *49*:209–231, 1945.
41. Hopla, C. E.: The ecology of tularemia. Adv. Vet. Sci. Comp. Med. *18*:25–53, 1974.
42. Hornick, R. B.: Tularemia. *In* Hoeprich, P. D. (ed.): Infectious Diseases. New York, Harper & Row, 1972, pp. 1043–1049.
43. Hughes, W. T., Jr., and Etteldorf, J. N.: Oropharyngeal tularemia. J. Pediatr. *51*:363–372, 1957.
44. Jacobs, R.: Tularemia. Adv. Pediatr. Infect. Dis. *12*:55–69, 1997.
45. Jacobs, R. F., Condrey, Y. M., and Yamauchi, T.: Tularemia in adults and children: A changing presentation. Pediatrics *76*:818–822, 1985.
46. Jaslaw, S., Eigelsback, H. T., Prior, J. A., et al.: Tularemia vaccine study. I. Intracutaneous challenge. Arch. Intern. Med. *107*:689–701, 1961.
47. Johansson, A., Berglund, L., Eriksson, U., et al.: Comparative analysis of PCR versus culture for diagnosis of ulceroglandular tularemia. J. Clin. Microbiol. *38*:22–26, 2000.
48. Johansson, A., Berglund, L., Gothefors, L., et al.: Ciprofloxacin for the treatment of tularemia in children. Pediatr. Infect. Dis. J. *19*:449–453, 2000.
49. Kaiser, A. B., Rieves, O., Price, A. H., et al.: Tularemia and rhabdomyolysis. J. A. M. A. *253*:241–243, 1985.
50. Karpoff, S. P., and Antonoff, N. I.: The spread of tularemia through water, as a new factor in its epidemiology. J. Bacteriol. *32*:243–258, 1936.
51. Kavanaugh, C. N.: Tularemia: A consideration of one hundred and twenty three cases with observations at autopsy in one. Arch. Intern. Med. *55*:61–85, 1935.
52. Kitamura, S., Fukada, M., Takeda, H., et al.: Pathology of tularemia. Acta Pathol. Jpn. *6*(Suppl.):719–764, 1956.
53. Koskela, P., and Merv, E.: Cell-mediated and humoral immunity induced by a live *Francisella tularensis* vaccine. Infect. Immun. *36*:983–989, 1982.
54. Larson, B. W., and Jacobson, H. J.: Tularemia with unusual laboratory characteristics in South Dakota children. S. D. J. Med. *37*:5–10, 1984.

55. Lee, H. C., Horowitz, E., and Linder, W.: Treatment of tularemia with imipenem/cilastatin sodium. South. Med. J. *84:*1277–1278, 1991.
56. Levy, H. S., Webb, C. H., and Wilkinson, J. D.: Tularemia as a pediatric problem. Pediatrics *6:*113–122, 1950.
57. Lillie, R. D., and Francis, G.: The pathology of tularemia in man (*Homo sapiens*). *In* The Pathology of Tularemia [National Institutes of Health Bulletin 167]. Washington, D.C., Public Health Service, 1936, pp. 1–81.
58. Long, G. W., Oprandy, J. J., Narayanan, R. B., et al.: Detection of *Francisella tularensis* in blood by polymerase chain reaction. J. Clin. Microbiol. *31*:152–154, 1993.
59. Ludmerer, K. M., and Kissane, J. M. (eds.): Fever, leukopenia, acute renal failure and death in a 65-year-old man. Am. J. Med. *77*:117–124, 1984.
60. Maranan, M., Schiff, D., Johnson, D., et al.: Pneumonic tularemia in a patient with chronic granulomatous disease. Clin. Infect. Dis. *25*:630–633, 1997.
61. Markwitl, L. E., Hynes, N. A., de la Cruz, P., et al.: Tick-borne tularemia: An outbreak of lymphadenopathy in children. J. A. M. A. *254*:2922–2925, 1985.
62. McCoy, G. N.: A plague-like disease in rodents. Public Health Bull. *43*:53, 1911.
63. McCoy, G. N., and Chapin, C. W.: Further observations on a plague-like disease of rodents with a preliminary note on the causative agent: *Bacterium tularense*. J. Infect. Dis. *10*:61–72, 1912.
64. McGowran, M. H., White, J. D., Eigelsbach, H. T., et al.: Morphologic and immunohistochemical studies of the pathogenesis of infection and antibody formation subsequent to vaccination of macacavirus with an attenuated strain of *Pasteurella tularensis*. I. Intracutaneous vaccination. Am. J. Pathol. *41*:259–271, 1962.
65. Miller, R. P., and Bates, J. H.: Pleuropulmonary tularemia. Am. Rev. Respir. Dis. *99*:31–41, 1969.
66. Naughton, M., Brown, R., Adkins, D., and DiPersio, J.: Tularemia—an unusual cause of a solitary pulmonary nodule in the post-transplant setting. Bone Marrow Transplant. *24*:197–199, 1999.
67. Needham, G. R.: Evaluation of five popular methods for tick removal. Pediatrics *75*:997–1002, 1985.
68. Ohara, H.: Jikken Dobutsu. Exp. Amin. *11*:508–523, 1925.
69. Ohara, H.: Kensei Igaker *12*:401–410, 1926.
70. Ohara, H.: Studies on Ohare's disease. Jpn. J. Exp. Med. *24*:69–79, 1954.
71. Olsen, P. F.: Tularemia. *In* Hubbert, W. T., McCullock, W. F., and Schnurrenberger, P. R. (eds.): Diseases Transmitted from Animals to Man. Springfield, IL, Charles C Thomas, 1975, pp. 191–223.
72. Ormsbee, R. A., Bell, J. F., and Larson, C. L.: The isolation, purification and biological activity of the antigenic preparations from *Bacterium tularense*. J. Immunol. *74*:351–359, 1955.
73. Overhold, E. L., Tigertt, W. D., Kadull, P. J., et al.: Analysis of forty-two cases of laboratory acquired tularemia: Treatment with broad spectrum antibiotics. Am. J. Med. *30*:785–806, 1961.
74. Parker, R. R., and Spencer, R. R.: Public Health Rep. *39*:1057–1073, 1924.
75. Pearse, R. A.: Insect bite. Northwest Med. *3*:81, 1911.
76. Penn, R. L., and Kinasewitz, G. T.: Factors associated with a poor outcome in tularemia. Arch. Intern. Med. *147*:265–268. 1987.
77. Permar, H. H., and Maclachlan, W. W. G.: Tularemic pneumonia. Ann. Intern. Med. *5*:687–698, 1931.
78. Pittman, T., Williams, D., Friedman, A.: A shunt infection caused by *F. tularensis*. Pediatr. Neurosurg. *24*:50–51, 1996.
79. Pollitzer, R.: History and Incidence of Tularemia in the Soviet Union: A Review. Bronx, NY, The Institute of Contemporary Russian Studies, Fordham University, 1967.
80. Poquet, Y., Kroca, M., Halary, F., et al.: Expansion of Vγ9Vδ2 T cells is triggered by *F. tularensis*-derived phosphoantigens in tularemia but not after tularemia vaccination. Infect. Immun. *66*:2107–2114, 1998.
81. Rhinehart-Jones, T. R., Fortier, A. H., and Elkins, K. L.: Transfer of immunity against lethal murine *Francisella* infection by specific antibody depends on host gamma interferon and T cells. Infect. Immun. *62*:3129–3137, 1994.
82. Rockwood, S. W.: Tularemia: What's in a name? Am. Soc. Microbiol. *49*:63–65, 1983.
83. Saslaw, S., Eigelsbach, H. T., Prior, J. A., et al.: Tularemia vaccine study. II. Respiratory challenge. Arch. Intern. Med. *107*:702–714, 1961.
84. Sawyer, W. D., Dangerfield, H. G., Hogge, A. L., et al.: Antibiotic prophylaxis and therapy of airborne tularemia. Bacteriol. Rev. *30*:542–550, 1965.
85. Scheel, O., Reiersen, R., and Hoel, T.: Treatment of tularemia with ciprofloxacin. Eur. J. Clin. Microbiol. Infect. Dis. *11*:447–448, 1992.
86. Schricker, R. L., Eigelsbach, H. T., Mitten, J. Q., et al.: Pathogenesis of tularemia in monkeys aerogenically exposed to *Francisella tularensis* 425. Infect. Immun. *5*:734–744, 1972.
86. Sjostedt, A., Conlan, J. W., and North, R. J.: Neutrophils are critical for host defense against primary infection with the facultative intracellular bacterium *Francisella tularensis* in mice and participate in defense against reinfection. Infect. Immun. *62*:2770–2783, 1994.
88. Sjostedt, A., Eriksson, U., Berglund, L., and Tarnvik, A.: Detection of *Francisella tularensis* in ulcers of patients with tularemia by PCR. J. Clin. Microbiol. *35*:1045–1048, 1997.
89. Steinmann, T., Sheikholeslami, M., Brown, H., and Bradsher, R.: Oculoglandular tularemia. Arch. Ophthalmol. *117*:132–133, 1999.
90. Stewart, S.: Tularemia: Association with hunting and farming. FEMS Immunol. Med. Microbiol. *13*:197–199, 1996.
91. Summary of notifiable diseases: United States, 1990. M. M. W. R. Morb. Mortal. Wkly. Rep. *39*:1–61, 1991.
92. Suter, E.: Passive transfer of acquired resistance to infection with *Mycobacterium tuberculosis* by means of cells. Am. Rev. Respir. Dis. *83*:535–543, 1961.
93. Sutinen, S., Syrjala, H., Anttila, S., et al.: Histopathology of human lymph node tularemia caused by *Francisella tularensis* var *palaearctica*. Acta Pathol. Lab. Med. *110*:42–46, 1986.
94. Suvorov, S. V., Volfertz, A. A., and Voronkova, M. M.: Vestn. Mikrobiol. *7*:293–299, 1928.
95. Syrjala, H., Herva, E., Ilonen, J., et al.: A whole blood lymphocyte stimulation test in human tularemia. J. Infect. Dis. *150*:912–915, 1984.
96. Syrjala, H., Karvonen, J., and Salminen, A.: Skin manifestations of tularemia: A study of 88 cases in northern Finland during 16 years (1967–1983). Acta Derm. Venereol. *64*:513–516, 1984.
97. Syrjala, H., Schildt, R., and Raijainen, S.: In vitro susceptibility of *Francisella tularensis* to fluoroquinolones and treatment of tularemia with norfloxacin and ciprofloxacin. Eur. J. Clin. Microbiol. Infect. Dis. *10*:68–70, 1991.
98. Tellison, W. L., Epler, D. C., Kunns, E., et al.: Tularemia in man from a domestic rural water supply. Public Health Rep. *65*:1219–1226, 1950.
99. Thorpe, B. D., and Marcus, S.: Phagocytosis and intracellular fate of *Pasteurella tularensis*. III. In vivo studies with passively transferred cells and sera. J. Immunol. *94*:578–585, 1965.
100. Tigertt, W. D.: Soviet viable *Pasteurella tularensis* vaccines: A review of selected articles. Bacteriol. Rev. *26*:254–373, 1962.
101. Tularemia. Annual Summary. M. M. W. R. Morb. Mortal. Wkly. Rep. *31*:89, 1982.
102. Uhari, M., Syrjala, H., and Salminen, A.: Tularemia in children caused by *Francisella tularensis* biovar *palaearctica*. Pediatr. Infect. Dis. J. *9*:80–83, 1990.
103. Vail, D. T.: Ophthalmic Res. *23*:487, 1914.
104. Van Metre, T. E., Jr., and Kadull, P. J.: Laboratory-acquired tularemia in vaccinated individuals: A report of 62 cases. Ann. Intern. Med. *50*:621–632, 1959.
105. Vilianen, M. K., Nurmi, T., and Salminen, A.: Enzyme linked immunosorbent assay (ELISA) with bacterial sonicate antigen for IgM, IgA and IgG antibodies to *Francisella tularensis*: Comparison with bacterial agglutination test and ELISA with lipopolysaccharide antigen. J. Infect. Dis. *148*:715–720, 1983.
106. Waag, D., Sandstrom, G., England, M., and Williams, J.: Immunogenicity of a new lot of *F. tularensis* live vaccine strain in human volunteers. FEMS Immunol. Med. Microbiol. *13*:205–209, 1996.
107. Washburn, A. M., and Tuohy, J. R.: The changing picture of tularemia in Arkansas. South. Med. J. *42*:60–62, 1949.
108. Wherry, W. B., and Lamb, B. H.: Infection of man with *Bacterium tularense*. J. Infect. Dis. *15*:331–340, 1914.
109. Zinkernagel, R. M.: Restriction by H-2 gene complex of transfer of cell-mediated immunity to *Listeria monocytogenes*. Nature *251*:230–233, 1974.
110. Zinsser, H.: *Francisella*. *In* Joklich, W. K., Willett, H. P., and Amos, D. B. (eds.): Zinsser Microbiology. 18th ed. E. Norwalk, CT, Appleton-Century-Crofts, 1984, pp. 649–655.

CHAPTER 139

Haemophilus influenzae

JOEL I. WARD

Relatively few species of the genus *Haemophilus* are pathogenic to humans, and nearly all that cause human disease are either encapsulated or unencapsulated strains of *Haemophilus influenzae*. These bacteria are small, gram-negative pleomorphic coccobacilli that generally are considered to be normal constituents of the microbial flora of the upper respiratory tract of humans. Strains without polysaccharide capsules often cause infections of mucosal surfaces, such as otitis media, bronchitis, conjunctivitis, sinusitis, and types of pneumonia. Encapsulated strains, especially *H. influenzae* type b (Hib), cause invasive diseases such as septicemia, meningitis, septic arthritis, cellulitis, epiglottitis, pneumonia, and empyema. Before Hib vaccines became widely available, *H. influenzae* was the leading cause of bacterial meningitis in the United States and most other countries, and it also was an important cause of other bacteremic illnesses, primarily in young children. Other *Haemophilus* spp., including *Haemophilus influenzae* (biogroup *aegyptius*), *Haemophilus ducreyi* (chancroid), *Haemophilus parainfluenzae, Haemophilus parahaemolyticus,* and *Haemophilus aphrophilus,* less commonly cause human infections.

The organism first was described in 1892 by Robert Pfeiffer, who isolated it from the lungs and sputum of patients during the 1889 to 1892 pandemic of influenza. He proposed that the organism was the cause of influenza, and it initially was known as the Pfeiffer influenza bacillus.[182] The bacteria were difficult to culture on routine media until investigators appreciated that supplementation with X (hemin) and V (nicotinamide-adenine-dinucleotide [NAD]) factors was required for its growth. By the turn of the century, the organism had been recovered from the blood and cerebrospinal fluid (CSF) of young children with meningitis. Although doubts remained about the etiologic role of the Pfeiffer bacillus as the cause of influenza, not until the influenza pandemic of 1918 was its etiologic role questioned seriously. In 1920, the organism was renamed *H. influenzae* to acknowledge its inappropriate historic association with influenza and to emphasize its requirement of blood factors for growth (from the Greek *haemophilus,* or "blood-loving").[266] In 1933, the viral etiology of influenza was discovered, which refuted any remaining confusion about the erroneous association between *H. influenzae* and influenza virus.

Key concepts relevant to the development of treatment and prevention modalities derive from the pioneering work of Margaret Pittman in the early 1930s.[185, 186] Paralleling earlier research on the pneumococcus, she defined two major categories of *H. influenzae:* encapsulated and unencapsulated strains. Among the encapsulated strains, she characterized six distinct serotypes (designated *a* through *f*), which now are known to differ biochemically in the composition of their polysaccharide capsules. She observed that Hib strains were recovered primarily from the blood and CSF of young patients with meningitis and that unencapsulated strains and other *H. influenzae* serotypes were recovered primarily from respiratory tract secretions. Furthermore, she demonstrated that antibody to Hib capsule conferred type-specific protection against lethal infection in rabbits. This observation led to the use of antiserum prepared by immunization with formalin-killed Hib as the first treatment of disease, initially in horses and later in rabbits. Before this development, Hib meningitis and other forms of invasive Hib disease almost always were fatal.[240] However, not until the late 1930s did treatment of children with meningitis with both Hib antiserum and sulfonamides substantially reduce the case-fatality rate.[3, 4]

In 1933, Fothergill and Wright[75] described the age-related risk of acquiring *H. influenzae* meningitis, which affected mostly children younger than 5 years of age. Importantly, they noted the correlation between the age-related risk of disease and the absence of bactericidal antibodies. Later researchers identified antibody to Hib capsule as the major antibody contributing to the protective activity of bactericidal serum.[116, 213] These observations suggested that naturally acquired type b anticapsular antibody is protective and that early stimulation of protective immunity with vaccines might be possible.

Unfortunately, the advent of effective antimicrobial agents focused attention away from the need for primary prevention. Even with effective antimicrobial therapies and excellent hospital care, significant mortality (approximately 5%) and neurologic morbidity (approximately 20%) remained. Ultimately, appreciation that the morbidity and mortality of the disease could never be eliminated completely by treatment gave impetus to the development of vaccines for prevention.

In the early 1970s, investigators purified and characterized the type b capsular polysaccharide (polyribosylribitol phosphate [PRP]) and proposed it as a potential vaccine candidate. Subsequently, the protective efficacy of a PRP vaccine against invasive Hib disease was demonstrated in older children in a 1974 field trial conducted in Finland.[177] This and other studies culminated in the licensure of PRP vaccine in the United States in 1985, thus rendering it the first vaccine available for the prevention of Hib disease. Unfortunately, this vaccine induced equivocal immune responses and incomplete protection in older children and provided no protection for young infants, those at greatest risk of acquiring Hib disease.[256] Improved vaccines used polysaccharide-protein conjugate techniques, and four such vaccines were licensed for use in children. Three of these vaccines were shown to protect young infants[21, 207] against Hib disease, and with the universal immunization of young infants, invasive Hib disease nearly has been eliminated in many populations.[1, 20, 178]

In this chapter, reviews of the microbiology, pathogenesis, immunology, clinical spectrum, diagnosis, epidemiology, treatment, and prevention of *H. influenzae* infection are presented. Brief discussions of disease caused by other *Haemophilus* spp. also are included.

Microbiology

GROWTH

H. influenzae is a small gram-negative coccobacillus that in clinical specimens can appear filamentous or pleomorphic, especially when obtained from patients who previously have received antibiotics. The organism is nonmotile, non–spore forming, and facultatively anaerobic and requires two supplemental factors for in vitro growth. The X factor (hemin) is a heat-stable, iron-containing protoporphyrin essential for activity of the electron transport chain, which is important for aerobic growth. The heat-labile V factor is a coenzyme, NAD. Both factors are present within erythrocytes and are released by appropriate heating or enzyme lysis of the red blood cells, which permits growth on chocolate agar. The requirement for these factors for growth remains the primary basis for the laboratory differentiation of *H. influenzae* from other *Haemophilus* spp.[12]

The growth of *H. influenzae* is fastidious, and clinical specimens need to be inoculated promptly onto appropriate media, such as chocolate agar. The organism can be grown in most enriched liquid or solid media supplemented with X and V factors. Though not mandatory for growth, 5 to 10 percent carbon dioxide makes some strains grow better. In blood or liquid media, *H. influenzae* may not grow to sufficient quantity to result in visual turbidity; therefore, to detect positive cultures, blood and CSF cultures should be assayed for release of carbon dioxide or routinely subcultured at 24 to 48 hours. After overnight incubation on solid media, colonies appear that are 0.5 to 1.5 mm in diameter and usually rough or granular in appearance. Encapsulated strains generally produce slightly larger colonies that are mucoid or glistening. Fermentation reactions and other metabolic activities are variable and, therefore, not particularly useful for identification. However, a biotyping scheme based on the metabolism of indole, urea, and ornithine decarboxylase activity has been used to subtype strains.

CAPSULAR POLYSACCHARIDE

Several surface structures of *H. influenzae* appear to be important determinants of the organism's pathogenicity. Strains can have one of six serotypic polysaccharide capsules (a, b, c, d, e, f), or they lack capsules (nontypeable strains). The Hib capsule is of particular clinical, pathogenic, and immunologic importance because Hib accounts for 95 percent of all strains that cause invasive disease (bacteremia or meningitis).[146] The Hib polysaccharide consists of a repeating polymer of ribosyl and ribitol phosphate (PRP) that has a 1-1 linkage. The genes involved in production of the Hib capsule have been cloned and consist of two repeating 17-kb DNA fragments separated by a 1-kb bridge region (hex A)[109]; 98 percent of Hib organisms tested contain this duplication. Encapsulation often is unstable, with loss of capsule production associated with loss of one 17-kb repeat. These strains produce type b capsule, but in barely detectable amounts. Of importance is that the release of Hib capsular antigen in the body fluids of infected individuals can be detected by specific immunologic techniques (i.e., latex agglutination) that are useful for rapid diagnosis. The other capsular serotypes are composed of hexose rather than pentose sugars and only occasionally result in invasive disease. Types e and f less commonly cause invasive disease.

OUTER-MEMBRANE PROTEINS

The cell envelope of gram-negative bacteria consists of a cytoplasmic membrane, a peptidoglycan layer, and an outer membrane. The outer membrane contains protein, lipopolysaccharides, and phospholipid. Electron microscopy of encapsulated and nonencapsulated strains of *H. influenzae* demonstrate a cell envelope similar to that of other gram-negative bacteria. The importance of outer-membrane proteins (OMPs) in the pathogenesis of and immunity to *H. influenzae* disease is not clear. Some membrane proteins are involved in cell transport (porins), others are adhesins, and the functions of others remain undefined. Pili or fimbriae are protein filaments that extend from the outer membrane and are thought to mediate attachment of the organism to epithelial cells.[231] Their expression appears to be reversible, but the importance of these adhesins in the pathogenesis of disease is not understood well.

Methods have been developed for differentiating isolates of Hib by differences in electrophoretic mobility patterns of the major OMPs, which has been useful for epidemiologic studies[92, 138] and for identifying potential vaccine immunogens. Although two to three dozen proteins exist, only four to six are major proteins. To date, specific OMP patterns have not been associated clearly with virulence. However, some proteins are well conserved and can be found in essentially all *H. influenzae* strains. Specifically, proteins P1 (50,000 kd), P2 (36,000 to 41,000 kd), and P6 (16,600 kd) appear to be present in all strains. They are cell surface exposed and induce bactericidal antibodies that are protective in animal challenge studies.[158, 168]

LIPOPOLYSACCHARIDES

The lipopolysaccharide (LPS) of encapsulated *H. influenzae* has been characterized partially. Although chemically different from the LPS of Enterobacteriaceae, the biologic activities of *H. influenzae* LPS appear to be similar. An Hib LPS preparation produces a dermal Shwartzman reaction, is lethal to mice, causes a febrile response in rabbits, evokes polyclonal B-cell activation, and has limulus lysate activity. Human leukocytes incubated with Hib LPS generate potent procoagulant activity,[154] which may be relevant to understanding the mechanisms responsible for intravascular coagulation in severe Hib infection. The LPS or endotoxin of Hib is important in the pathogenicity of the organism and appears to have little antigenic diversity,[263] although variability exists in LPS electrophoretic patterns after passage in vivo or in vitro. Consequently, electrophoretic characterization of endotoxin has not been useful as an epidemiologic tool.

ISOENZYMES

Multilocus enzyme electrophoresis is a method used to characterize cytoplasmic isoenzymes of the organism. This method has been used to differentiate Hib genotypes for epidemiologic purposes. Electrophoresis of numerous enzymes has disclosed isoenzyme differences that have been useful in genetic analysis of *H. influenzae* strains.[165] Population-based genetic evaluations of *H. influenzae* based on cluster analysis of multilocus enzyme electrophoretic typing have revealed that Hib strains are clonal.[164] Hib strains are distinct from nonencapsulated isolates, which are more genetically diverse.[163]

IgA PROTEASES

IgA proteases, bacterial enzymes whose only known substrate is human IgA1, cleave the heavy chain at specific sites.[127] IgA proteases are regarded as potentially important virulence factors because mucosal defense is in part IgA mediated. *H. influenzae* produces three distinct types of IgA protease that cleave different peptide bonds within the IgA1 hinge region.[187]

ANTIBIOTIC RESISTANCE

Another important microbiologic feature of *H. influenzae* has been the development of antibiotic resistance. Resistance to a wide variety of antibiotics (sulfonamides, trimethoprim-sulfamethoxazole, erythromycin, tetracycline, penicillin) has been described, but these antibiotics are not essential for therapy. Of greater importance is resistance to ampicillin, first noted in the mid-1970s,[53] because it was the primary antibiotic used for the treatment of disease. Since then, ampicillin resistance has become widespread, with between 5 and 40 percent of all isolates in various parts of the world now resistant.[35, 118] The mechanism of resistance usually involves the production of plasmid-mediated β-lactamase enzyme, and resistant strains often are characterized by their plasmid or β-lactamase enzyme content.[118] Resistance to chloramphenicol usually is mediated by the enzyme chloramphenicol acetyltransferase.[198] Although chloramphenicol-resistant strains are rare in the United States, they are more prevalent in some areas of the world, and strains resistant to both ampicillin and chloramphenicol have been reported.[38, 242] Currently, third-generation cephalosporins are the mainstays of therapy for invasive disease; concern, however, about the potential for increasing resistance to these highly effective agents further emphasizes the need for means to prevent disease.

Pathogenesis

ACQUISITION AND CARRIAGE OF ORGANISMS

Illness caused by *H. influenzae* infection results from a series of pathogenic events, beginning with exposure to the organism, acquisition of infection, and colonization of respiratory mucosal membranes. Under natural conditions, *H. influenzae* is exclusively a pathogen of humans, and it usually is transmitted asymptomatically from person to person by transfer of respiratory secretions. The incubation period is unknown because many transmission cycles may occur before a susceptible person becomes ill. Furthermore, in some individuals, the organism can be carried in the upper respiratory tract for many months before it causes disease.

Both typeable and nontypeable organisms may be part of the normal flora of the upper respiratory tract; nearly all individuals (as many as 80%) are colonized with nontypeable strains. Hib carriage rates were lowest in adults and young infants and highest in preschool-age children in the pre-vaccine era. In a prospective longitudinal study conducted at a daycare center in Dallas, Texas, where no invasive infections occurred, the average rate of colonization with Hib was 10 percent.[150] During the 18 months of the study, 71 percent of the children 18 to 35 months of age and 48 percent of the children 36 to 71 months of age were colonized at some time. Carriage rates were substantially higher in households or daycare centers in which a case occurred. For example, colonization prevalence rates among children in daycare centers where a case of invasive disease had occurred were as high as 58 to 91 percent.[94, 255] Likewise, within families in which a case of invasive disease occurred, rates of colonization of 60 to 70 percent in siblings and 20 percent in parents were observed.[33, 255] Whether the high carriage rates in these exposed semiclosed populations are the cause or the result of disease is not clear.[147, 152] Close contact among exposed susceptible individuals, as occurs within families and daycare centers, facilitated the risk of transmission and acquisition of disease.

In the pre-vaccine era, despite a low point prevalence of Hib pharyngeal carriage (1–5%), most young children became colonized with Hib during the first 2 to 5 years of life,[147, 241] and consequently, specific immunity developed in these children.[100, 213] Hib strains persisted in the nasopharynx for months[152, 159] and often were not eliminated by treatment with antimicrobial agents that did not penetrate into respiratory secretions.[218, 219] The relationship between carriage of Hib and the subsequent development of disease and immunity is not understood. Factors that influence the efficiency of transmission and the ability of the organism to establish colonization also are understood poorly. Two factors that probably potentiate the risk for acquiring infection and invasive disease are the size of the bacterial inoculum[230] and the presence of a concomitant viral infection.[129]

Inoculation of Hib organisms into the nose of infant animals results in local infection. In the animal systems used, rhinorrhea was not noted, but nasopharyngeal washings revealed numerous polymorphonuclear leukocytes and organisms that reached maximal density in approximately 24 hours. Shortly thereafter, bacteremia could be detected in the animals. With colonization of humans, Hib is found on the surface of the respiratory mucosa. Rarely, an organism can be observed by electron microscopy penetrating through a nasal mucosal epithelial cell. An acute inflammatory response to the submucosal bacteria occurs, but it is not marked. The exact mode of entrance of the organisms into the vascular compartment is unknown, but researchers assume that they enter via lymphatics, probably carried by phagocytic cells, which are found in the submucosa. In support of this hypothesis, Rubin and Moxon[201] detected early transient bacteremia (within 30 minutes) in four of eight rats after nasal inoculation.

Presumably, bacterial cell wall components, such as pili and other adhesins, promote attachment, and the capsule impedes bacterial clearance. Bacterial toxins, including LPS, impair ciliary function and damage the respiratory epithelium. *H. influenzae* also produces an IgA1 protease that degrades the predominant IgA serotype in the nasopharynx and may interfere with immunologic clearance.

PATHOGENESIS OF MUCOSAL INFECTIONS

Noninvasive or mucosal infections occur much more frequently than do invasive bacteremic infections and cause considerable morbidity and health care cost. Mucosal infections generally are caused by nontypeable *H. influenzae* strains and involve direct extension of organisms through the nasal ostia to the sinuses, up the eustachian tubes, where they cause otitis media, and down the bronchi, where they cause bronchitis and pneumonia. Bacteremia rarely is involved, and such infections generally are not life-threatening. These infections appear to be enhanced by antecedent viral infection, eustachian tube malfunction, foreign bodies, or mucosal damage from smoking or other irritants.[203]

Clinical differentiation of invasive and noninvasive disease is not absolute inasmuch as Hib strains can cause otitis media or sinusitis and non-Hib strains occasionally cause bacteremia or meningitis. A notable example of the latter is bacteremia and meningitis in neonates usually caused by nontypeable organisms that presumably are acquired from the mother's genital tract.

PATHOGENESIS OF INVASIVE DISEASE

Invasion occurs when bacteria are disseminated from the mucosa of the upper respiratory tract to the bloodstream and then elsewhere in the body. The incidence of invasive disease is a small fraction of the carrier rate. The organism appears to invade the mucosa by separating the apical tight junctions of the columnar epithelium and moving intercellularly. The resulting bacteremia initially is low in concentration but steadily increases over the course of hours.[173] The dynamics between bacterial proliferation and clearance is influenced by antibody, complement, and phagocytes, all of which have an effect on the magnitude of the bacteremia.[99, 260] The polysaccharide capsule of Hib is antiphagocytic and a major virulence factor. In the absence of anticapsular antibody, bacteremia increases steadily over a period of hours.[103] When the bacterial concentration exceeds 10^4 organisms per milliliter, metastatic seeding occurs, especially to the meninges via the choroid plexus (see later). Although meningitis is the most frequently recognized manifestation of invasive Hib disease, other potential metastatic sites include the lungs, joint synovium, pleura, peritoneum, and pericardium.

The exact pathogenesis is less well understood for pneumonia, cellulitis, and epiglottitis, even though these invasive infections are associated with bacteremia. Presumably, pneumonia occurs after the aspiration of a critical number of virulent organisms, epiglottitis involves focal infection of the epiglottis, and cellulitis occurs by secondary seeding of deep subcutaneous tissues via the bloodstream.[87] With all forms of invasive Hib disease, invasion of the bloodstream occurs as either a primary or a secondary event.

Viral interactions enhance the pathogenesis of Hib.[235] Influenza virus infection has been shown to reduce neutrophil chemotaxis, bacterial killing, systemic macrophage function, the number of circulating T cells, T-cell blastogenesis, and expression of delayed cutaneous hypersensitivity.[100] Reduced bacterial killing may be due to a defect in phagosome-lysosome fusion, a defect that is maximal 5 to 7 days after viral infection and inoculation of Hib.

BACTEREMIA

During bacteremia, organisms are cleared continually from the vascular compartment by antibody, complement, and the reticuloendothelial system. The balance of these processes determines the magnitude and duration of the bacteremia. If bacterial clearance is stopped by reticuloendothelial blockade, bacterial densities increase to a maximum and death quickly ensues, presumably because of the effects of endotoxin.

Initially, bacterial concentrations are very low (approximately 100 organisms per milliliter of blood). They then steadily increase in density over the course of the next 24 hours and reach a plateau value. In young animals, this plateau level is 10^7 organisms per milliliter of blood and usually is associated with the features of human sepsis. In older animals, the plateau value is lower: approximately 10^4 organisms per milliliter of blood. These animals have low-grade fever but a relative paucity of symptoms. This primary bacteremia leads to seeding of serous surfaces, such as the peritoneum, diarthrodial joints, pleura, pericardium, and meninges. Early in the infectious process, organisms can be obtained from all these surfaces, but without an observable inflammatory response; later in the process, an inflammatory response ensues. In experimental animals, the first evidence of an immune response is antibody directed against somatic antigens.

Strains of Hib vary in virulence potential. Furthermore, the other five capsular types or nonencapsulated strains result in only transient, low-level, or undetectable bacteremia, even with large inocula ($>10^7$ colony-forming units). Complement and the spleen are critical factors for host defense in the rat. Rats depleted of C3 and splenectomized (or with iatrogenic splenic congestion caused by hemolytic anemia) have an increased incidence and magnitude of bacteremia.[43, 269] These studies suggest the importance of the alternative pathway of complement (opsonic antibody) and reticuloendothelial phagocytes as determinants of intravascular clearance.

MENINGITIS

Bacteremia precedes the development of meningitis, except for rare situations in which direct extension of infection from adjacent sinuses or an ear infection occurs. Data from experimental studies in infant rats and infant monkeys support this hypothesis.[156] Both the magnitude and duration of bacteremia are probably the primary determinants of invasion of the central nervous system (CNS). After a critical bacterial concentration is exceeded in blood, Hib appears to enter the CNS via the choroid plexus.[224] This theory is supported by the following data: (1) the earliest histopathologic lesion seen in the CNS is choroid plexitis, (2) the choroid plexus is one of the foci seeded from the bloodstream, and (3) bacterial density early in infection is greater in the lateral cerebral ventricles than in other CSF compartments.[224] Furthermore, pulse-chase experiments using tracer strains show that organisms enter the CSF through the choroid plexus and that inflammation of the choroid plexus is a uniform feature of meningitis. Subsequently, organisms infect the CSF and the arachnoid villi of the leptomeninges and cause blockage of CSF return, thereby increasing bacterial density and CSF pressure.[201] Generally, the magnitude of CSF bacterial density correlates with the severity of clinical illness.[68, 209] Egress of CSF from the subarachnoid space is by flow through the subarachnoid villi, and bacterial density in CSF can be increased or decreased by manipulating CSF egress, which occurs in meningitis via inflammatory responses. The inflammatory response of the choroid plexus is followed by pachymeningitis, which also inhibits CSF reabsorption and increases pressure. Phlebitis of the cerebral blood vessels and thrombosis can occur. All these events contribute to decreased blood flow to the cortex. The resulting increased bacterial density, inflammation, edema, cranial nerve damage, and overall increased CSF pressure are responsible for the morbidity and mortality associated with meningitis.[67, 224] Parenchymal invasion of the brain rarely occurs.

Immunology

Resistance to Hib infection depends on successful integration of a wide variety of host defenses, including (1) mucosal factors that prevent the organism from attaching and penetrating the respiratory epithelium; (2) activation of the alternative and classical complement pathways, which leads to killing of the organism and initiation of other inflammatory responses; (3) induction of antibody formation; (4) phagocytosis and killing by macrophages and polymorphonuclear cells in tissues, the circulation, and the reticuloendothelial system; and (5) cell-mediated immunity. Assessing the role of each of these immunologic mechanisms independently or determining which mechanisms are most important in host defense is difficult. Although antibodies are not the sole defense against bacteremia, it has been the research emphasis of vaccine development. The goal has been to induce antibodies that are bactericidal, opsonophagocytic, and ultimately protective.

Although usually only antibody is measured in these studies, other immune factors are induced and probably play important roles in protection.

ANTICAPSULAR ANTIBODY

Initially, antibody activity was assessed by measuring agglutinin and bactericidal titers of serum. In 1933, Fothergill and Wright[75] suggested that bactericidal activity was responsible for immunity to Hib meningitis and that acquisition of this immunity correlated with the age of the individual. Although antibodies to several surface antigens of *H. influenzae* play roles in conferring immunity, antibody to Hib capsular polysaccharide appears to be of primary importance.[197] Newborns and young infants are at low risk for the development of infection, presumably because they have maternally acquired antibody. Young children at highest risk of acquiring disease have low or undetectable levels of antibody, whereas older children at lower risk have higher antibody levels. By 5 years of age, most children have naturally acquired anticapsular antibody that appears to provide protection,[100, 213] although natural exposure also induces antibodies to OMPs, LPS, and other surface antigens of the bacteria that contribute to natural immunity. The evidence that anticapsular antibodies protect humans from the acquisition of invasive Hib disease is considerable: they activate complement,[229, 265] are opsonophagocytic[169] and bactericidal,[75, 169] and protect animals from lethal Hib challenge.[232] Moreover, passive prophylaxis with serum preparations containing anticapsular antibody protects agammaglobulinemic patients[197] and high-risk children from the acquisition of invasive Hib disease.[205] Furthermore, in the pre-antibiotic era, immune serum was an effective therapy for Hib disease.[3, 186] However, the most compelling evidence for the protective efficacy of PRP antibody is the clinical protection achieved in older children vaccinated with purified PRP vaccine[177] and more recently in younger infants immunized with Hib conjugate vaccines. Induction of antibody to Hib polysaccharide is the immunologic basis of all Hib vaccines.

A precise minimal level of anti-PRP antibody that is protective has not been established. Data from passive protection of agammaglobulinemic children, challenge experiments in infant rats, and studies of naturally acquired antibody levels in healthy individuals of various ages suggest that the minimal serum concentration of anti-PRP antibody that provides protection ranges from 0.05 µg/mL in animals[214] to 0.15 to 1.00 µg/mL in humans.[123, 177] Such estimates are crude and do not take into account the different functional properties of different immunoglobulins or the contribution of antibodies to other Hib antigens. In addition, antibody levels decline over time, and a given peak level may not reflect levels at the time of exposure, which would predict long-term protection better.[9, 177] In a Finnish PRP vaccine trial, an antibody level greater than 1.0 µg/mL 1 month after immunization correlated with clinical protection for a minimum of 1 year.[177] However, this antibody level might not be extrapolated readily to the immunogenicity data evaluated in different studies or with different Hib conjugate vaccines.

CLASS- AND SUBCLASS-SPECIFIC ANTIBODY

Several studies have shown variable immunoglobulin class, isotype, idiotype, and IgG subclass responses to PRP polysaccharide after natural Hib exposure, disease, and immunization.[124, 214] Most individuals respond with IgG antibodies after receiving PRP immunization, although some children have predominantly IgA or IgM responses.[124] Schreiber and associates[214] showed that IgG antibody is bactericidal, opsonic for polymorphonuclear leukocytes in the presence of complement, and protective for animals. IgM antibody is equally protective and more bactericidal than IgG in the presence of complement, but it opsonizes poorly. IgA antibody is not bactericidal, opsonic, or protective for animals. Some researchers have hypothesized that IgA-specific antibody blocks the activity of other more functional antibodies and thereby may depress immunity.[164, 177]

Data from experiments in mice and humans suggest that polysaccharide antigens induce restricted IgG subclass responses.[195] The findings of increased susceptibility to Hib disease in IgG subclass–deficient patients (predominantly IgG2 and IgG4 deficiencies)[174, 215] and the low levels of IgG2 in children younger than 2 years of age [217] suggest that differences exist in the role of subclass-specific anticapsular antibodies. In adults, natural exposure or immunization with PRP vaccine results in a predominantly IgG2 subclass response.[121, 191] In children, IgG1 and IgG2 antibodies develop after PRP immunization, but IgG1 antibodies predominate after immunization with Hib conjugate vaccines.[6, 121] Human anti-PRP antibodies express predominantly kappa light chains[207] and may be grouped into a few restricted clonotypes. These clonotypes and antibody specificities have been characterized by idiotype analysis[141] and amino acid sequencing of the immunoglobulin light chain.[237] Individuals of different ages produce different proportions or repertoires of antibody. Some differences in binding specificity and affinity have been described with the different anti-PRP antibodies, but whether the antibodies have different degrees of protective potency or are substantially different in proportion in individuals given different vaccines is not clear.

The role of mucosal immunity in killing Hib or inhibiting adherence or penetration of the mucosa is understood poorly, although studies of secretory IgA antibody to the Hib capsule have been conducted.[183, 184] Moreover, Hib strains produce an IgA protease that can inactivate mucosal antibody.[157] The recent observation of reduced carriage of Hib in children given Hib conjugate vaccines[160, 234] suggests that mucosal immunity may be important in reducing transmission of the disease.

CELLULAR IMMUNE RESPONSES

Most of our understanding of the interactions of B cells, T cells, and antigen-presenting cells (macrophages) is derived from extensive research in mice.[58] Based on T-cell involvement in antibody synthesis, antigens can be classified as T-dependent (thymus-dependent) or T-independent immunogens. Most protein antigens induce helper T-cell regulation of antibody synthesis and, therefore, are considered T-dependent. These antigens first are recognized and processed by macrophages and then presented to both T and B cells. The activated T cells induce proliferation and differentiation of specific antigen-reactive B-cell subpopulations. They also retain the memory necessary for subsequent booster responses.[16] Through the release of cytokines, helper T cells appear to regulate (1) the magnitude of the immune response, especially in young infants; (2) the switch in immunoglobulin classes (IgM to IgG); (3) the functional activity of antibody; and (4) the capacity to elicit immunologic memory.

Polysaccharides consist of repeating oligosaccharide units and elicit weak immune responses involving minimal T-cell influences.[16] These T-independent antigens elicit antibody responses primarily by direct stimulation of B cells. In general, polysaccharide vaccines have the following T-independent immunologic characteristics: (1) delayed ontogeny of immune responsiveness in the young, (2) limited and variable quantitative immune responses, (3) restricted isotype (predominantly IgM) and IgG subclass responses, and (4) lack of a booster or anamnestic response with secondary antigenic challenge.

The quest for a Hib vaccine that is immunogenic and protective in young infants has involved attempts to convert the PRP antigen from a T-independent to a T-dependent antigen by using the carrier-hapten principles first defined by Landsteiner in the first half of the 20th century.[130] PRP can be considered a hapten that is linked covalently to a T-dependent immunogen, a carrier, to form a conjugate vaccine. The Hib conjugate vaccines, which demonstrate markedly enhanced immunogenicity, are described in a subsequent section.

GENETIC FACTORS

When compared with protein vaccines, the immune responses to most polysaccharide antigens are variable and may be influenced by genetic factors. Several studies have shown associations between the immune responses to PRP vaccine and genetically determined factors such as red cell antigens, human leukocyte antigen, or immunoglobulin allotypes.[5, 97, 216, 263] However, because many factors influence immunogenicity, whether these associations have relevance is not known, and establishing controls for them is difficult. In addition, whether the antibody differences, although statistically significant, are important clinically also is not known. No single genetic relationship regulating susceptibility or the immune responses to polysaccharide antigens has been demonstrated convincingly.

COMPLEMENT

The importance of complement components in host defense against Hib is substantiated by elimination of the bactericidal activity of serum via heat, by the susceptibility of complement-depleted animals to Hib disease, and by the increased susceptibility of patients with specific congenital complement deficiencies.[55, 229, 265] Hib is capable of activating both the classical and the alternative complement pathways, thereby initiating opsonophagocytosis and cell killing and eliciting other inflammatory responses. Whereas the alternative pathway probably is most important early in the course of infection in a nonimmune host, the antibody-dependent classical complement pathway is more likely to predominate as a defense mechanism at a later stage of infection.[265] Both encapsulated and unencapsulated organisms activate complement, thus underscoring the importance of noncapsular antigens in host defense. Although the Hib capsule is a poor activator of the alternative complement pathway, antibody to the capsule activates both the classical and the alternative pathways.[229] Other cell wall antigens activate the alternative pathway, and antibody to these antigens activates the classical pathway.[55, 229, 265] Thus, antibodies to both capsular and noncapsular antigens activate the complement system, primarily via the classical pathway. Activation of the terminal complement components mediates the bactericidal activity of serum.

PHAGOCYTOSIS

Opsonization leading to phagocytosis and killing of Hib also is an important determinant of host defense. Impairment of phagocytic function or a reduction in the number of phagocytes results in increased susceptibility to disease, as does loss of the spleen or impairment of its function (e.g., hemoglobinopathies).[44, 189] The opsonic activity of serum is influenced greatly by the roles of complement and antibody. Opsonization and phagocytosis of Hib appear to be dependent on (1) IgG binding, (2) antibody activation of the classical complement pathway with deposition of C3b on the bacterial surface, and (3) direct bacterial activation of the alternative complement pathway. Relatively little is known about direct cell-mediated killing of Hib.[62]

Epidemiology

Humans are the only natural host for *H. influenzae,* and asymptomatic nasopharyngeal carriage, usually by unencapsulated strains, is a common finding. Nasopharyngeal acquisition of Hib strains increases after infancy and persists for weeks to months, and most children are colonized at some time during the first 5 years of life. Colonization rates greater than 70 percent occur after recent exposure in closed populations, such as among family members or daycare center contacts of a patient with disease. Person-to-person transmission occurs via respiratory droplets, and fomites also may play a role. Because asymptomatic carriage is common, the incubation period cannot be defined accurately.

Before the development of immunization, invasive Hib disease was a leading infectious disease problem worldwide that affected primarily young children[251, 261] (Table 139–1). Hib strains are responsible for more than 95 percent of invasive infections in children. According to population-based studies, an estimated 20,000 to 25,000 persons acquired invasive Hib disease annually in the United States, 85 percent of which occurred in children younger than 5 years of age. The incidence of Hib meningitis and all invasive Hib disease was 40 to 69 and 67 to 130 cases per 100,000 children younger than 5 years, respectively. Invasive Hib disease developed in an estimated 1 in every 200 children in the United States during the first 5 years of life.[51] Hib pneumonia was estimated to cause as many as 15 percent of cases of ambulatory pneumonia in children younger than 6 years old, but the true incidence was unknown because microbiologic diagnosis is difficult. Overall, the incidence of Hib disease in the pre-vaccine era was similar to that of paralytic

TABLE 139–1 ■ WORLDWIDE INCIDENCE OF INVASIVE *HAEMOPHILUS INFLUENZAE* TYPE b (Hib) DISEASE BEFORE THE USE OF Hib VACCINES IN CHILDREN YOUNGER THAN 5 YEARS

Region	Years	Hib Meningitis*	All Hib Disease*
Australia/New Zealand	1985–1987	25–53	39–92
U.S./Canada	1959–1991	40–69	67–130
Europe	1985–1990	15–26	33–60
Israel	1985–1990	18	34
Africa	1980s	36–60	NA
South America	1989–1990	15–25	21–43
Asia	1990s	1.3–1.9	1.9–2.7

*Annual incidence per 100,000 population younger than 5 years of age.
NA, not available.
Adapted from Vadheim, C. M., and Ward, J. I.: Epidemiology in developed countries. *In* Ellis, R. W., and Granoff, D. M. (eds.): Development and Clinical Uses of *Haemophilus* b Conjugate Vaccines. New York, Marcel Dekker, 1994, pp. 231–245; and Bijlmer, H. A.: Epidemiology of *Haemophilus influenzae* invasive disease in developing countries and intervention strategies. *In* Ellis, R. W., and Granoff, D. M. (eds.): Development and Clinical Uses of *Haemophilus b* Conjugate Vaccines. New York, Marcel Dekker, 1994, pp. 247–264. By courtesy of Marcel Dekker, Inc.

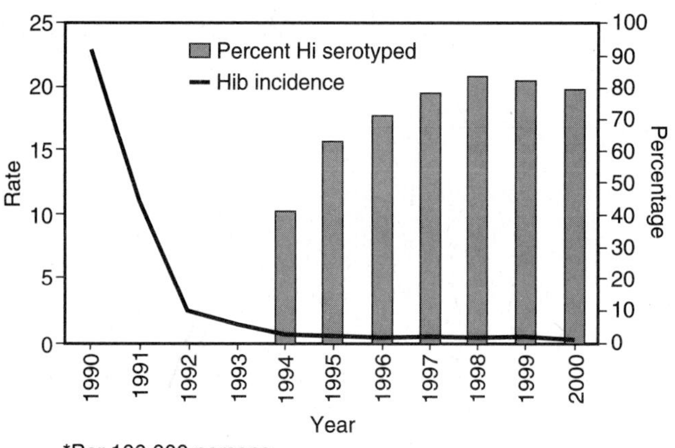

FIGURE 139–1 ■ Incidence rate* of *Haemophilus influenzae* type b (Hib) invasive disease per 100,000 persons and the percentage of *Haemophilus influenzae* (Hi) isolates serotyped in children younger than 5 years—United States, 1990–2000. (From Centers for Disease Control and Prevention: Progress towards elimination of *Haemophilus influenzae* type b invasive disease among infants and children—United States, 1998–2000. M. M. W. R. Morb. Mortal. Wkly. Rep. *51*[11]:234–237, 2002.)

poliomyelitis during its peak epidemic years before immunization. A bimodal seasonal pattern had been observed in several studies, with one peak occurring between September and December and a second peak between March and May.[192, 261] The attack rate of Hib was slightly higher in boys.[143]

The widespread use of Hib conjugate vaccines has altered the epidemiology of invasive Hib disease dramatically (Fig. 139–1). The first Hib conjugate vaccine was licensed in the United States in 1987 for use in children 18 months or older. Subsequently, decreases in the incidence of Hib disease were seen in older children and, unexpectedly, in unimmunized infants and children as well. This finding was attributed to a direct effect of vaccination on nasopharyngeal carriage, thus decreasing the environmental burden of Hib infection and, ultimately, the transmission of disease. In late 1990, Hib conjugate vaccines were approved for use in infants beginning at 2 months of age, which heralded a dramatic decline in the incidence of invasive Hib disease in all children. In populations in which immunization rates are high, the development of invasive Hib disease has been eliminated almost completely.

Some population-based studies of the incidence of *H. influenzae* disease have been conducted outside the United States, primarily in Western Europe, and they showed an incidence approximately one third to two thirds that in the United States.[179, 204, 225] The incidence of Hib disease is especially high in certain ethnic groups, including Aboriginal children in central Australia[105]; Navajo Native Americans; Native Alaskans; and Apache, Yakima, Athabascan, and Canadian Native Americans.[140, 153, 257, 268] *H. influenzae* appears to rank as a leading cause of bacterial meningitis in some developing countries as well.[32] As seen in the United States, a substantial reduction in Hib disease has occurred with the implementation of widespread vaccination programs. Studies in Asia showed a disease incidence one tenth to one thirtieth that in the United States before the introduction of vaccine, but methodologic issues exist regarding the accuracy of these disease assessments, particularly those related to antibiotic use and the validity of culture results.

Children between the ages of 6 and 18 months are at highest risk for acquiring invasive Hib disease[134]; however, the age distribution of specific clinical syndromes of the disease varies. The peak incidence of Hib meningitis occurs in children 6 to 9 months of age and declines markedly after 2 years of age.[79, 236] Hib cellulitis tended to occur during the first year of life, whereas epiglottitis generally occurred in unimmunized children older than 2 years of age. Invasive *H. influenzae* disease was seen much less frequently in adults because of the development of protective antibodies over time, but it occurred more frequently in immunocompromised patients. Nonetheless, Hib caused pneumonia and meningitis in adults,[85] and disease caused by other serotypes and nontypeable strains, especially pneumonia, otitis media, bronchitis, and sinusitis, are common findings in all age groups. Most adults in whom invasive *H. influenzae* disease develops were not immunized as children and have an underlying condition such as chronic obstructive pulmonary disease, human immunodeficiency virus (HIV) infection, alcoholism, pregnancy, or malignancy.[29, 85]

The development of invasive Hib disease in a given individual is the consequence of a complex interaction of a variety of factors, including the risk of exposure, the characteristics of the organism, and the host.[77] In populations that experienced a high incidence of disease, such as Native Americans, the age-specific incidence peaked in a younger age group (<6 months), presumably because of early or intense exposure to Hib at home or in the community. Several factors that may reflect environmental exposure to the organism, such as household size,[93, 122] crowding,[244] attendance at daycare,[52, 113] low family income,[78, 79] and low parental education level,[79, 122] have been shown to be risk factors for the acquisition of disease, whereas breast-feeding appears to be protective.[181] Several underlying medical conditions are associated with an increased risk for the acquisition of Hib disease, including HIV infection,[37, 210] sickle-cell anemia,[189] asplenia or splenectomy,[44] antibody[66] and complement deficiency syndromes,[72] and malignancy.[259]

Although the direct contagiousness of invasive Hib disease is limited, small outbreaks and direct secondary transmission of disease can occur. Numerous studies have estimated the risk of developing secondary disease in household contacts in the 30 days after the onset of disease in an index case. Overall, the attack rate for contacts of all ages in the pre-vaccine era was 0.3 percent, which represents a risk approximately 600-fold higher than the age-adjusted risk in the general population.[33, 254] However, attack rates varied inversely with age, with children younger than 4 years being at greatest risk. Among household contacts, nearly two thirds of secondary cases occurred within the first week after the onset of disease in the index patient.[236] Controversy exists about the degree of risk for the development of secondary Hib disease in daycare center contacts exposed to a child with invasive Hib disease. Such risk in unimmunized children younger than 2 years of age ranged from 0 to 3.2 percent,[14, 172] whereas for those older than 2 years, it was less than 1 percent.

Clinical Manifestations

BACTEREMIA

Occult bacteremia (i.e., not associated with a primary focus of infection) is not a common occurrence with Hib, but bacteremia does precede essentially all invasive Hib infections. In the pre-vaccine era, Hib was the second leading cause, after *Streptococcus pneumoniae,* of occult bacteremia primarily affecting children 6 to 36 months of age. Most children initially have fever and peripheral leukocytosis. Unlike *S. pneumoniae* bacteremia, the condition is not benign.

In approximately 30 to 50 percent of children with occult Hib bacteremia, a focal infection such as meningitis, pneumonia, or cellulitis develops.[54, 128]

MENINGITIS

Meningitis is the most serious manifestation of invasive Hib disease; however, no clinical feature differentiates Hib meningitis from other causes of bacterial meningitis in children. The onset of disease can be fulminant,[114] but more commonly the signs and symptoms are nonspecific (particularly in young infants) and may include irritability, fever, lethargy, poor feeding, or vomiting. Children younger than 18 months often do not have nuchal rigidity. Older children are more likely to have findings of headache, photophobia, and meningismus. With fulminant Hib meningitis, very rapid neurologic deterioration may occur with increased intracranial pressure, seizures, coma, and respiratory arrest. Ten to 20 percent of children with meningitis will have other foci of infection such as cellulitis, arthritis, or pneumonia,[13, 73] and essentially all have concomitant bacteremia.

CSF examination typically reveals a pleocytosis (mean of 4000 to 5000 white blood cells/μL) with a predominance of polymorphonuclear leukocytes. Approximately 75 percent of patients have hypoglycorrhachia, and around 90 percent have an elevated CSF protein concentration. Eighty percent of meningitis cases caused by Hib will have a positive CSF Gram stain. As with other types of bacterial meningitis, however, previous antimicrobial therapy significantly decreases the concentration of Hib organisms in the CSF and diminishes the sensitivity of Gram staining.[22] Previous treatment does not affect the total blood cell count and differential, glucose, or protein substantially, thus permitting a diagnosis of meningitis. In more than 90 percent of cases, capsular antigen can be detected in CSF or serum.[258] Anemia, leukocytosis, thrombocytosis, and thrombocytopenia also are observed frequently.[67]

Complications of Hib meningitis include seizures, cerebral edema, subdural effusions or empyema, inappropriate secretion of antidiuretic hormone, cortical infarction (often manifested by focal neurologic abnormalities), cerebritis, intracerebral abscess, hydrocephalus, and, rarely, cerebral herniation.[25, 67] Computed tomography and magnetic resonance imaging of the head should not be performed routinely for Hib meningitis, but they may be helpful if focal neurologic findings are present or if the clinical course becomes complicated. Small subdural effusions are common findings but are not usually of clinical significance.

Even with prompt intensive care, the mortality from Hib meningitis is approximately 5 percent, and significant long-term morbidity, including sensorineural hearing loss, delay in language acquisition, developmental delay, gross motor abnormalities, vision impairment, and behavior abnormalities, may occur in 15 to 30 percent of survivors.[60, 61, 67, 188, 238] A substantial proportion of such abnormalities may resolve over time, thus emphasizing the need for long-term monitoring of these patients.[67]

PNEUMONIA

Hib pneumonia is clinically indistinguishable from other bacterial pneumonias. Most patients have a preceding upper respiratory tract infection, fever, and cough accompanied by peripheral leukocytosis with a predominance of polymorphonuclear leukocytes. Radiologically, Hib pneumonia may be segmental, lobar, interstitial, or diffuse, and many cases have evidence of pleural or pericardial involvement on radiographic examination. Cavitation and pneumatoceles are rare occurrences but have been reported.[45] Computed tomography or magnetic resonance imaging can be useful adjuncts to the evaluation of complicated disease caused by Hib.[50] Blood, pleural fluid, tracheal aspirate, and lung aspirate cultures are positive in 75 to 90 percent of cases. Detection of capsular polysaccharide in pleural fluid, serum, or urine can establish the diagnosis, particularly if antimicrobial therapy had been instituted previously. Although fever may persist for several days while the patient is receiving adequate therapy, uncomplicated Hib pneumonia rarely is associated with long-term pulmonary dysfunction.

EPIGLOTTITIS (see Chapter 21)

Acute upper airway obstruction caused by Hib infection of the epiglottis and supraglottic tissues occurred in the prevaccine era primarily in children 2 to 7 years of age. Its onset usually is abrupt, with high fever, sore throat, dysphagia, and sepsis. Antecedent upper respiratory tract infection with cough occurs in approximately 50 percent of patients.[28, 139] The child may drool because of an inability to swallow oropharyngeal secretions, and progressive respiratory distress with tachypnea, stridor, cyanosis, and retractions may develop over a period of hours. The child usually is agitated and may sit forward with the chin extended to maintain an open airway. In children younger than 2 years, Hib epiglottitis may be manifested in an atypical fashion, with low-grade fever and a cough suggestive of croup.[139]

The most important aspect of the management of a child with epiglottitis is maintenance of a patent airway. Nasotracheal intubation is preferable to tracheostomy because it is equally effective, is not permanent or disfiguring, and has fewer inherent risks.[18] Seventy to 90 percent of patients with epiglottitis will have positive blood cultures; tissue for culture of the inflamed epiglottis should be obtained only after the airway has been secured. A lateral neck radiograph revealing dilatation of the hypopharynx and the "thumbprint" sign (swollen epiglottis)[27] can be helpful if the clinical findings are subtle, but in most cases, diagnostic studies should not delay intubation and direct inspection of the epiglottis in controlled surroundings. The mortality rate is 5 to 10 percent, almost always related to abrupt airway obstruction.

JOINT INFECTION

Before the routine use of Hib conjugate vaccines, Hib was the leading cause of septic arthritis in children younger than 2 years of age. It affects a single large joint at the knee, ankle, elbow, or hip in more than 90 percent of cases. Contiguous osteomyelitis occurs in 10 to 20 percent.[73, 131] No feature clearly distinguishes septic arthritis caused by Hib from that of other bacterial etiologies. Patients initially are febrile, and more than two thirds have decreased range of motion, local warmth, and swelling.[56, 73, 131] Usually, pain, swelling, and erythema of the involved joint are preceded by a nonspecific upper respiratory illness. The clinical features may be subtle, with only decreased range of motion of the joint or abnormal gait as the initial finding. Hib capsular antigen concentrations are very high in the infected joint fluid of children with septic arthritis, and rapid detection of antigen is useful diagnostically. Septic arthritis of the hip requires surgical drainage, and resolution generally is rapid, but long-term cartilage damage may result from Hib arthritis despite adequate therapy.[238]

CELLULITIS

Cellulitis is a relatively uncommon form of Hib disease and was seen in the pre-vaccine era almost exclusively in children younger than 2 years of age. Most cellulitis (74%) is located in the cheek (buccal cellulitis), the periorbital region, and the neck[56] and rarely on the extremities. Facial cellulitis occurs most commonly in infants and is manifested as acute fever and a unilateral, raised, warm, tender and indurated area that may progress to a violaceous hue, although this finding is not unique to Hib disease. Aspirate cultures of the point of maximal swelling usually yield the organism, and bacteremia is a typical finding.[74, 112] A secondary focus (including meningitis) may be present in 10 to 15 percent of patients.[63, 65] Orbital cellulitis generally is a complication of ethmoid sinusitis and, consequently, can be caused by non-Hib strains. An etiologic diagnosis can be established by blood culture or aspiration of subcutaneous tissues. Antibiotics always are indicated, but the need for surgical drainage depends on the degree of involvement of the tissues within the orbit.

PERICARDITIS

Hib pericarditis usually is a complication of adjacent pneumonia and is characterized by fever, an ill appearance, respiratory distress, and tachycardia.[42, 194] The radiographic or clinical diagnosis can be confirmed by two-dimensional echocardiography[267] and may be suggested by finding capsular polysaccharide in serum or pericardial fluid or in Gram-stained pericardial fluid. Cultures of pericardial fluid are positive in more than 70 percent of cases.[56] Early drainage is an important part of the management of this illness, and early pericardectomy or pericardiostomy is preferred over repeated pericardiocentesis.[155, 194]

NEONATAL DISEASE

H. influenzae causes 2 to 8 percent of neonatal early-onset sepsis.[34, 252] Most of these cases are caused by nontypeable strains, most of which are concordant with those isolated from the maternal genital tract. The precise pathogenesis is unknown, but neonatal disease often is associated with prematurity, low birth weight, premature rupture of membranes, and maternal chorioamnionitis; several cases have occurred after cesarean delivery, thus suggesting in utero transmission.[202] Clinical manifestations include pneumonia, bacteremia, and conjunctivitis. More than two thirds of neonatal *H. influenzae* disease occurs on the first day of life, with an overall mortality rate of 55 percent.[82]

OTHER INVASIVE INFECTIONS

Other invasive Hib infections include endophthalmitis,[239] CSF shunt infections,[133, 193] necrotizing fasciitis, pyomyositis,[167] peritonitis,[47, 81] scrotal abscess,[137] brain abscess,[70] polyserositis,[151] tenosynovitis,[166] epididymitis,[101] lung abscess,[135] periappendiceal abscess,[148] and bacterial tracheitis.[36] Invasive disease also may be characterized by fever alone, fever with petechiae, or fever of unknown origin.[30, 250]

NONTYPEABLE *H. INFLUENZAE* INFECTIONS

Respiratory tract infections associated with nontypeable *H. influenzae* are a major cause of morbidity and mortality today in both developed and nonindustrialized nations.[102, 132] Previously, invasive disease caused by nontypeable *H. influenzae* was rare and generally associated with underlying medical conditions such as prematurity, malignancy, cystic fibrosis, asthma, leakage of CSF, CNS shunts, congenital heart disease, lymphoproliferative disorders, and immunoglobulin deficiency.[15, 48, 65, 86, 175] More recently, with a decline in the rate of infections caused by Hib, other *H. influenzae* serotypes such as types f, c, d, e, and nontypeable strains have become an increasingly important cause of both mucosal infection and invasive disease.

Invasive Disease

Invasive disease caused by non–type b *H. influenzae* has become increasingly more prevalent. Urwin and associates[243] identified 91 cases of invasive *H. influenzae* type f disease in a multistate area over the course of a 6-year period. The incidence of invasive type f disease was 0.5 case per 1 million population in 1989 and 1.9 cases per 1 million population in 1994. In children, pneumonia and meningitis each accounted for 40 percent of the total cases. Overall, mortality from type f *H. influenzae* disease was 21 percent in children. Serotype f also has been reported as a cause of endocarditis[80] and septic arthritis[88] in healthy, normal children.

Invasive disease caused by nontypeable *H. influenzae* strains in normal children also has been reported.[170] Heath and associates[107] conducted an active prospective surveillance study of *H. influenzae* infections in the United Kingdom and Republic of Ireland. During the study period (October 1992 to December 1998), 102 cases of invasive disease caused by nontypeable *H. influenzae* were reported. Children with nontypeable *H. influenzae* infection were compared with those who had Hib disease. Children with nontypeable *H. influenzae* were more likely to be younger (16 versus 22 months) and more likely to have pneumonia and bacteremia ($p < .001$) than were those with Hib disease. In 1998, the incidence of non–type b *H. influenzae* disease in all children younger than 5 years of age in the United Kingdom was 1.3 per 100,000, versus 0.6 per 100,000 population for Hib disease. Most non–type b strains isolated were nontypeable. An increase in the incidence of invasive *H. influenzae* infection from non–type b strains also has been reported in native and non-native Alaskans older than 10 years.[180]

H. influenzae type a also has caused invasive disease (meningitis and bacteremia). Three of the isolates from such patients contained a gene deletion and were associated with particularly severe disease. These data support the hypothesis that a single gene deletion may identify more virulent strains of *H. influenzae*.[2]

St. Geme III[228] has documented that nontypeable *H. influenzae* organisms are capable of efficient adherence and subsequent invasion. Numerous adhesive factors exist, and each recognizes a distinct host-cell structure and influences the specificity of cellular binding. At least three invasive pathways have been identified: a pathway mediated via the platelet activating factor (PAF) receptor, a pathway involving beta-glucan receptors, and a pathway resembling micropinocytosis.[228] Selected data suggest that invasion mediated by activation of the PAF receptor is more efficient than is micropinocytosis.[233] Recent evidence indicates that the increased incidence of disease caused by non–type b encapsulated *H. influenzae* reflects the emergence of hypervirulent clones of organisms, particularly in the case of *H. influenzae* type f.[171]

Mucosal Infections

Unencapsulated or non-Hib strains usually cause a variety of mucosal infections, including otitis media, sinusitis, conjunctivitis, and bronchitis.[126] *H. influenzae* is the second leading cause of acute otitis media in adults and children[23] and has features similar to those of other causes of otitis, namely, fever and symptoms referable to the upper respiratory tract plus nonspecific symptoms such as irritability, vomiting, and diarrhea. Sinusitis may be manifested as common cold symptoms that are persistent or more severe than usual. Older children and adults are more likely to complain of headache and paranasal, dental, or facial pain. Other common symptoms are a daytime cough that may worsen at night or reactive airway disease unresponsive to therapy. Rarely, chronic otitis or sinusitis may result in the development of mastoiditis or a parameningeal abscess. Conjunctivitis usually is bilateral and purulent[24] and may occur in outbreaks. Though common, these infections rarely are life-threatening and are not associated with bacteremia.

Because noninvasive infections seldom are caused by Hib, antigen detection and blood cultures rarely are of diagnostic value. The diagnosis usually is clinical and a specific etiology is not determined, but a microbiologic diagnosis can be established for lung disease by careful Gram stain and culture of sputum, for otitis media by culture of middle ear fluid obtained by tympanocentesis, for sinusitis by culture of sinus aspirate, and for conjunctivitis by Gram stain and culture of the eye discharge. Culture of the nasopharynx to detect carriers of *H. influenzae* should not be performed for the following reasons:

1. Identifying *H. influenzae* among the many bacteria colonizing the upper respiratory tract is difficult.
2. *H. influenzae* is a normal constituent of the upper airway, and its presence or absence has little diagnostic significance.

Foxwell and associates[76] have provided a detailed review of the pathogenesis and prevention of nontypeable *H. influenzae* infection to which the reader is referred. Strategies for prevention of disease caused by nontypeable strains must be based on an understanding of the pathogenesis of diseases caused by nontypeable strains. Prevention of disease caused by nontypeable *H. influenzae* may depend on strategies that target the mucosal surface to prevent colonization and attachment of *H. influenzae* to this surface. A review of the molecular determinants of colonization of nontypeable *H. influenzae* strains and the relationship between colonization and otitis media has been provided by St. Geme III.[227] Current information suggests that some nontypeable *H. influenzae* strains possess virulence characteristics that enhance their ability to cause otitis media.

ENDOCARDITIS

H. influenzae may cause endocarditis,[57] but *H. parainfluenzae* and *H. aphrophilus* are more important causes of endocarditis and account for as many as 5 percent of such cases in adults. These species are commensal organisms of the oropharynx and, because of their fastidious growth characteristics, are included in the group of pathogens that cause "culture-negative" endocarditis, known as the HACEK group (*Haemophilus* spp., *Actinobacillus actinomycetemcomitans, Cardiobacterium hominis, Eikenella corrodens, Kingella kingae*).[264]

BRAZILIAN PURPURIC FEVER (see Chapter 140)

Brazilian purpuric fever is a fulminant infection caused by *H. influenzae* biogroup *aegyptius*. Limited primarily to Brazil, the illness afflicts children younger than 10 years, with a median age of 30 months. Illness is characterized by a purulent conjunctivitis followed 7 to 16 days later by the acute onset of high fever, vomiting, abdominal pain, purpura, vascular collapse, and death in 70 percent. Some children initially have mild fever alone. The diagnosis is confirmed by blood culture in nearly all patients,[106] and therapy with antimicrobial agents effective against other *H. influenzae* infections is adequate.

CHANCROID (see Chapter 140)

Chancroid is a sexually transmitted disease caused by *H. ducreyi*. This disease is found worldwide, especially in lower socioeconomic groups and the HIV-infected population.[104] The median incubation period is 5 to 7 days, after which tender papules develop in the inguinal or perirectal area. The lesions ulcerate, readily bleed, and are associated with tender lymphadenopathy in 25 to 50 percent of patients. Because distinguishing chancroid from other ulcerative sexually transmitted diseases is difficult, the diagnosis is confirmed by culture of the ulcer or associated bubo. Testing for concomitant syphilis infection is important.[231] Oral erythromycin or parenteral ceftriaxone is the preferred treatment.

Diagnosis

A high index of suspicion for the possibility of Hib disease must be maintained when evaluating children with appropriate clinical manifestations and findings. The primary criterion for the diagnosis of *H. influenzae* infection is Gram stain or isolation of the organism from an infected focus (e.g., CSF, pleural fluid, sputum, or blood). Because most invasive Hib disease is associated with bacteremia, blood cultures should be performed for any febrile child with potential Hib disease. The specimens need to be processed immediately because the organism is fastidious. Although most commercial blood culture media support the growth of *H. influenzae,* the inoculum should be applied, when possible, directly to chocolate agar or a semisynthetic medium containing heme and NAD.[12] In liquid medium, growth may not be sufficient to result in turbidity; therefore, for blood cultures, advanced detection systems or subcultures should be performed. In addition, selective media that suppress the growth of gram-positive organisms may increase the recovery of *H. influenzae* from upper respiratory tract specimens.[40] Identification of an isolate as *H. influenzae* relies on its dependence on heme and NAD.

Other techniques that may assist in microbiologic diagnosis include rapid antigen detection, staining techniques, and immunofluorescence. Such techniques are useful in the context of a patient whose cultures are sterile because of previous antibiotic therapy, or they can confirm the clinical diagnosis before bacterial growth occurs. The three techniques most commonly used for antigen detection are latex particle agglutination (LPA), countercurrent immunoelectrophoresis (CIE), and coagglutination (CoA).

False-positive results on CSF are rare by all three tests; however, false-positive reactions have occurred when testing serum and urine. False-positive reactions occur as a result of nonspecific agglutination (i.e., rheumatoid factors) and because of antigenic cross-reactivity with *Escherichia coli, Streptococcus pneumoniae,* staphylococci, or meningococcus. Overall, LPA appears to be more sensitive than CoA, and LPA and CoA are more sensitive than CIE in CSF, serum, urine, joint fluid, and pleural fluid.[119, 145, 150] False-positive results can occur in the urine of children with nasopharyngeal carriage of the organism or, more commonly, for several days after immunization with Hib conjugate vaccine.[226] Acridine orange is a fluorescent stain that binds to cellular nucleic acids and may be useful in situations in which smaller bacterial concentrations are present.[125] Immunofluorescent staining of purulent specimens from patients with partially treated disease also has been useful.[49] Several enzyme-linked immunosorbent assays for detection of PRP are available. These tests generally are used in the research setting and are not of substantial clinical value.

Treatment

INVASIVE DISEASE

Bacteremia plays a central role in the pathogenesis of invasive Hib disease; therefore, occult invasion of the CNS always must be considered in the context of any manifestation of Hib infection. In addition, severe Hib disease often is fatal if not treated adequately. Therefore, elimination of Hib bacteremia and its complications requires antimicrobial therapy that will (1) penetrate the blood-brain barrier to achieve bactericidal concentrations and (2) be of adequate duration to sterilize the primary and potential secondary foci. The choice of specific antibiotic therapy must take into account the local antibiotic susceptibility patterns of invasive isolates (Table 139–2). Hib resistance to several antimicrobials, including ampicillin, chloramphenicol, trimethoprim-sulfamethoxazole, rifampin, and certain second-generation cephalosporins, has been increasing in several areas of the world.[118]

For proven or suspected Hib meningitis, cefotaxime or ceftriaxone is recommended until the antibiotic susceptibility of the organism is known or an alternative diagnosis is established.[67] Both antibiotics have bactericidal activity against Hib strains, including those that produce β-lactamase, and they penetrate well into infected CSF and are well tolerated. Ceftriaxone may be useful for daily intramuscular injections, if necessary. Cefuroxime should not be used for the treatment of *H. influenzae* meningitis because delayed sterilization of CSF may be at least twofold more common than with ampicillin plus chloramphenicol or with the third-generation cephalosporins.[115, 223] Moreover, ampicillin, formerly a mainstay of therapy for this infection, should not be used empirically to treat infections caused by Hib because as many as 50 percent of Hib isolates in the United States are resistant, usually via plasmid-mediated β-lactamase production.[118] Chloramphenicol, another medication that frequently was used to treat Hib disease, now rarely is used because safer antibiotics with greater activity are available. Although adequate bactericidal blood and CNS levels of chloramphenicol can be achieved, even with oral administration,[69, 208] its use requires monitoring of drug levels. Dose-dependent, yet reversible, bone marrow toxicity may occur, particularly in neonates, in patients with liver disease, or in those who require prolonged treatment. Idiosyncratic aplastic anemia, a dose-independent complication of chloramphenicol use, is an extremely rare occurrence.

TABLE 139–2 ■ SELECTED ANTIMICROBIAL AGENTS FOR TREATMENT OF *HAEMOPHILUS INFLUENZAE* INFECTIONS

Antimicrobial Agent	Total Daily Dose (mg/kg)	Dose Frequency
Parenteral Antibiotics*		
Ampicillin†	200–400	q4–6h
Cefuroxime‡	75–150	q8h
Cefotaxime	150–200	q6–8h
Ceftriaxone	50–100	q12–24h
Oral		
Amoxicillin§	40–60	tid
Amoxicillin-clavulanate	40–60	tid/bid
Erythromycin-sulfisoxazole§	40 (erythromycin)	qid
Trimethoprim-sulfamethoxazole§	8 (trimethoprim)	bid
Clarithromycin§	15	bid
Azithromycin§	10	qd
Cefuroxime axetil	30–40	bid
Cefprozil	30	bid
Cefpodoxime	5	bid
Cefixime	8	qd

*Other parenteral agents may be used in special circumstances, but they should not be considered first line. Such agents include ureidopenicillins, carbapenems, and fluoroquinolones.
†Not to be used presumptively because of the prevalence of resistant strains.
‡Not to be used for suspected meningitis.
§Do not use these oral agents if resistance is suspected or prevalent in your area.

Cefuroxime has good activity against *H. influenzae* and is useful for empiric treatment of nonmeningitic infections such as pneumonia, periorbital cellulitis, and septic arthritis. Other parenteral agents that have activity against *H. influenzae* include imipenem-cilastatin, meropenem, ampicillin-sulbactam, aztreonam, and other third-generation cephalosporins such as ceftazidime. Imipenem-cilastatin has been associated with seizures during treatment of meningitis,[108] and its use has been supplanted by meropenem for situations in which resistance to third-generation cephalosporins is documented. In general, the spectrum of activity of these agents is too broad for routine use in pediatric infections in which Hib is an important pathogen.

Children with occult Hib bacteremia need to be re-evaluated carefully because focal disease may develop in 30 to 50 percent of such patients who are clinically well.[54, 128] The duration of therapy is determined by the site of infection and the clinical response. Children with uncomplicated Hib meningitis can be treated for 7 to 10 days. Children with Hib cellulitis can be switched to oral therapy after several days of parenteral therapy, provided that they have had a satisfactory clinical response and do not have meningitis. Patients with septic arthritis should receive at least 10 to 14 days of therapy, whereas children with pericarditis, empyema, or osteomyelitis may require longer courses of antibiotic treatment (3 to 6 weeks). These patients often can be switched to oral antibiotics after documenting susceptibility, a good therapeutic response, and adequate antimicrobial blood levels and ensuring compliance.

Equally important in the overall management of a child with invasive Hib disease is supportive care. For Hib meningitis, several studies have shown that adjunctive therapy with dexamethasone moderates the inflammatory cascade and may decrease the likelihood of hearing loss. The recommended dose is 0.6 mg/kg/day given every 6 hours for 4 days, with the first dose administered just before or concurrently with the first antibiotic dose.[190] Management of a child with meningitis requires continuing careful evaluation for complications such as the development of shock, inappropriate secretion of antidiuretic hormone, seizures, subdural empyema, and secondary foci of infection. Prolonged fever is a common occurrence, with approximately 10 percent of children remaining febrile for at least 10 days.[67] Repeat lumbar puncture to document sterility of the CSF is not necessary in uncomplicated cases.

In children with epiglottitis, protection of the airway is the most important component of therapy and should be initiated even before the administration of antimicrobials. Endotracheal intubation or tracheostomy is performed optimally in the operating room by personnel experienced with these procedures in children. Before establishing the airway, care should be taken not to precipitate laryngospasm by attempting to examine the epiglottis or by performing procedures such as venipuncture. Blood should be obtained for culture and intravenous antibiotics initiated as soon as possible after the airway has been secured.

Patients with subdural empyema, pericarditis, or pleural empyema usually require percutaneous or surgical drainage. Infected joint fluid should be aspirated from children with septic arthritis to confirm the diagnosis and reduce pressure. Repeated aspirations or placement of a surgical drain also may be needed. Infection of the hip requires surgical incision and drainage to decompress the joint; failure to do so may result in avascular necrosis of the femoral head.

NONINVASIVE DISEASE

Noninvasive *H. influenzae* infections, usually caused by nontypeable strains, include otitis media, sinusitis, conjunctivitis, bronchitis, and pneumonia. Numerous orally administered antimicrobials are available to treat these infections (see Table 139–2). Despite the increasing prevalence of β-lactamase–producing organisms, amoxicillin remains the drug of choice for empiric treatment of otitis media in most areas because of its low cost and proven safety. Several other antimicrobials with activity against *H. influenzae* are available and include amoxicillin-clavulanate; trimethoprim-sulfamethoxazole; erythromycin-sulfisoxazole; newer macrolides such as clarithromycin and azithromycin; and second- and third-generation cephalosporins such as cefuroxime axetil, cefixime, cefpodoxime, cefdinir, and cefprozil. Cefaclor is used widely but has poor activity against β-lactamase–producing organisms and causes a serum sickness–like illness in approximately 2 percent of recipients. The quinolone antibiotics, such as ciprofloxacin, also are active but are not licensed for use in children younger than 18 years because of a quinolone-induced arthropathy seen in juvenile animals. In the context of poor clinical response or isolation of β-lactamase–producing organisms, amoxicillin-clavulanate (Augmentin), cefixime, and cefpodoxime appear to be the most useful.

Most mucosal infections are treated presumptively without obtaining definitive cultures, and consequently, the duration of therapy and the need for alternative antibiotics are based on assessment of the clinical response. Otitis media usually is treated for 7 to 10 days, and sinusitis should be treated for at least 1 week beyond the resolution of symptoms. If resistance is suspected and leads to failure of treatment, an empiric change in antibiotics is indicated.

Prevention

The near elimination of invasive Hib disease in the United States and other countries is a direct result of the routine use of Hib conjugate vaccines and represents a remarkable success story. Prevention with hyperimmunoglobulin also has been shown to be effective in high-risk populations, but it is costly, of short-lived benefit, and not licensed for general use. Antimicrobial prophylaxis is effective for the prevention of secondary Hib disease, but it represents only a minor proportion of the overall disease burden.

ACTIVE IMMUNIZATION

The first Hib vaccine was the PRP polysaccharide vaccine, which is composed of purified Hib capsular polysaccharide PRP.[11, 199] In 1985, in children older than 18 months of age, it became the first vaccine to be licensed for the prevention of Hib disease. Children younger than 18 months of age had inadequate immune responses[10, 122] with PRP vaccination. PRP vaccine has immunologic properties similar to those of some other polysaccharide vaccines, which generally are considered to be T-independent immunogens. As a result, antibody responses are limited and of short duration, particularly in young children, and no booster response occurs with repeated administration of the vaccine. Furthermore, the induced antibody may have reduced functional qualities (i.e., primarily IgM, low avidity).[196, 217]

Licensure of PRP vaccine was based on the findings of a large randomized clinical trial conducted in Finland in 1974[176, 177] that suggested a protective efficacy of 90 percent for children who were immunized between 18 and 71 months of age. Subsequent to licensure of this vaccine in the United States, it became apparent that routine use of the vaccine resulted in efficacy less than that determined in the Finnish vaccine trial, between 0 and 88 percent.[256] This vaccine is mainly of historic significance because its role has been supplanted by development and licensure of the PRP-protein conjugate vaccines.

Hib conjugate vaccines were developed in an effort to enhance immune responses to the PRP antigen. Basic to all conjugate vaccines is the use of a covalently linked (conjugated) immunogenic protein carrier that confers on the PRP polysaccharide hapten recognition by T cells and macrophages and stimulation of T-dependent immunity.[130, 256] Four Hib conjugate vaccines have been developed and evaluated in infants, and all use PRP polysaccharide as the primary immunogen (Table 139–3): PRP-D (diphtheria toxoid), HbOC (mutant diphtheria toxin), PRP-OMP (major OMP of *Neisseria meningitidis* serogroup B), and PRP-T (tetanus toxoid). The immune response after administration of Hib conjugate vaccination has the following general characteristics:

1. It is quantitatively enhanced, particularly in younger infants.
2. Repeat administration of vaccine elicits booster responses.
3. Maturation of class-specific immunity with a predominance of IgG antibody and probably enhanced functional properties occurs.

The first Hib conjugate vaccine licensed was PRP-D, but it was less immunogenic than are the conjugate vaccines developed subsequently and rarely is used in the United States. In children 15 months of age or older who received PRP-D, high antibody concentrations were achieved with a single dose.[19, 110] In infants, however, antibody levels greater than 1 μg/mL develop in less than half, even after receiving

TABLE 139–3 ■ CHARACTERISTICS OF *HAEMOPHILUS INFLUENZAE* TYPE b CONJUGATE VACCINES

Vaccine	Polysaccharide Size (PS)	Protein Carrier	Linkage	Trade Name*
PRP-D	Medium	Diphtheria toxoid	Protein with 6-carbon spacer	ProHIBiT
HbOC	Small	CRM_{197} (mutant diphtheria toxin)	PS, no spacer	HibTITER
PRP-OMP	Medium	*Neisseria meningitidis* outer-membrane protein complex	Protein and PS with bigeneric spacer	PedvaxHIB
PRP-T	Large	Tetanus toxoid	PS with 6-carbon spacer	ActHIB

*HbOC, PRP-OMP, and PRP-T also are available in combination with diphtheria-tetanus-pertussis, diphtheria-tetanus–acellular pertussis, and hepatitis B vaccines.
HbOC, mutant diphtheria toxin; PRP-D, diphtheria toxoid; PRP-OMP, major outer-membrane protein of *N. meningitidis* serogroup B; PRP-T, tetanus toxoid.

three doses.[59, 121] Numerous case-control studies have demonstrated that a single dose of vaccine was at least 80 percent efficacious in preventing disease in children 18 months or older.[99, 262] In infants who received vaccine at 3, 4, 6, and 14 to 18 months of age, the protective efficacy after three doses was 94 percent in Finland.[63] In contrast, a trial conducted in Native Alaskan infants found no evidence of protection in that high-risk population.[253]

A single dose of HbOC is highly immunogenic in children older than 18 months of age,[110, 142] and after the administration of three doses in infancy, high antibody levels are achieved.[59, 200] Two prospective clinical studies have shown that two or three doses of HbOC administered in the first 6 months of life provide a high degree of protective efficacy. In the Kaiser Permanente northern California region population, HbOC was 100 percent efficacious after two doses administered in infancy.[21] The vaccine also was evaluated in Finland in infants who received vaccine at 4, 6, and 14 to 18 months of age,[64] and efficacy was 95 percent after two doses. Data from a third post-licensure study in infants in Los Angeles County also suggested a protective efficacy of 89 percent after two doses and 94 percent after three doses.[246]

PRP-OMP induces an immune response that is less age-dependent than is the response to the other Hib conjugate vaccines. Adults and children respond to a single vaccine dose with high antibody levels.[200] In infants as young as 6 to 8 weeks, a single dose of PRP-OMP induces a good antibody response.[31] In addition, the antibody levels achieved after two doses are higher than those after two doses of any of the other conjugate vaccines,[31, 59] and a third dose does not enhance the response. PRP-OMP was evaluated in a randomized, double-blind, placebo-controlled trial involving high-risk Navajo Native American infants[207] who received vaccine at 2 and 4 months of age; an overall efficacy of 95 percent was reported. Additional data from a population-based case-control study in Los Angeles County suggested a level of effectiveness similar to that seen for HbOC.[245]

PRP-T is highly immunogenic in adults and older children,[46, 212] and high concentrations of antibody are achieved in infants with a three-dose immunization series at 2, 4, and 6 months of age.[59] The protective efficacy of PRP-T was evaluated in two large prospective randomized trials that were terminated prematurely because of the licensure of other Hib conjugate vaccines for infants. More than 12,000 infants were enrolled in studies in southern California and North Carolina, and no cases of invasive Hib disease occurred in the vaccinated children versus five cases in the control groups.[83, 247] Efficacy subsequently was shown in a study in England; after three doses in infancy, the efficacy of PRP-T was estimated to be 100 percent.[26] In Finland, during the first 2 years of its general use, more than 100,000 infants were immunized, and only two cases of invasive Hib disease occurred in vaccinees, both after a single dose. In no infant who has received two or more doses of vaccine in any study has Hib disease developed.[178]

HbOC, PRP-OMP, and PRP-T are licensed for use in infants at 2, 4, 6, and 12 to 15 months of age. Any Hib conjugate vaccine can be used as the booster dose or in different sequences. Several issues, however, remain to be determined regarding the use of Hib conjugate vaccines in infancy. Direct comparisons of Hib conjugate vaccines need to be considered in the context of varying study designs, differences in vaccine lots, and different laboratory and statistical methodologies. Despite these difficulties, certain concepts are apparent:

1. All Hib conjugate vaccines are safe in infants.
2. PRP-D is the least immunogenic conjugate vaccine.
3. Only PRP-OMP induces a good immune response after one dose in young infants, but antibody levels are lower than those induced by multiple doses of HbOC and PRP-T vaccine.
4. PRP-OMP, HbOC, and PRP-T appear to be efficacious, but no direct comparison of the protective efficacy of these vaccines has been completed.

In addition, certain mixed sequences of Hib vaccines given to infants (i.e., PRP-OMP followed by HbOC or PRP-T) may enhance the antibody response.[91, 98] Furthermore, simultaneous receipt of other non-Hib vaccines and the impact of concurrent or previous receipt of the carrier protein (carrier priming)[95, 96, 136] are issues that need to be explored. Combination vaccines that include Hib (Hib plus diphtheria-tetanus-pertussis [Hib-DTP], Hib plus diphtheria and tetanus toxoids and acellular pertussis [Hib-DTaP]) currently are licensed, and several other combinations (Hib–hepatitis B, Hib plus inactivated poliovirus vaccine [Hib-IPV], Hib-DTaP/IPV) are being evaluated in infants and children.

Schmitt and associates[211] surveyed the impact and effectiveness of DTaP (IPV)-Hib combination vaccines in Germany. Although combination DTaP-Hib vaccines have been documented to elicit lower anti-Hib titers than separate vaccines do, the impact of this finding is unclear. Schmitt and colleagues[211] showed that combination vaccines were effective in reducing the incidence of Hib disease in Germany.

Although the study of Schmitt and associates[211] is encouraging, whether these findings can be extended to other populations and whether the long-term use of conjugate vaccines would be as efficacious as the use of Hib conjugate vaccines provided separately are not entirely clear. The phenomenal success of the Hib vaccination strategy has been related to the effectiveness of Hib conjugate vaccines in preventing colonization. Fernandez and associates[71] reported that the anti-Hib capsular polysaccharide antibody concentration required to prevent colonization was greater than that needed for protection against invasive disease. Whether concentrations in the range that Fernandez and associates suggested was important (>5 μg/mL) can be achieved and sustained by using conjugate vaccines in all population groups remains a subject of investigation. Studies in some high-risk population groups (Alaskan natives) have documented that invasive disease is prevented best by the use of PRP-OMP Hib vaccine,[222] at least for the first dose of vaccine, and that even the use of PRP-OMP Hib vaccine in these individuals may not eliminate carriage of the organism in the population.[84] Thus, the use of combination vaccines in this population group is unlikely to be as effective as the use of PRP-OMP Hib conjugate vaccine.

To date, essentially all *H. influenzae* vaccines are based on immunity to the Hib capsule. Antibodies to other components of the bacterium also have been shown to be bactericidal, opsonophagocytic, and protective in animal studies. Vaccines containing alternative antigens could provide supplemental protection against Hib, although this protection does not appear to be necessary based on the efficacy of the available Hib conjugate vaccines. More importantly, such alternative vaccines could provide immunity to non-Hib strains, which have substantial phenotypic and genetic variability[165] but are ubiquitous colonizers of the upper respiratory tract of humans and cause mucosal infection. The basic microbiologic problem hindering the development of such vaccines has been the diversity and instability of cell wall antigens among most *H. influenzae* strains. Studies have attempted to define OMPs, cell wall LPS, and fimbrial surface antigens of the organism.[15] Because of the variability of most of these antigens in heterologous strains and even in homologous strains over time, finding an antigen relevant to all or most strains has been difficult. Furthermore, not all bacterial antigens elicit protective immunity. The focus of most investigations has been to characterize OMPs.[168] Other efforts have focused on proteins of higher molecular weight,[248] LPS, or fimbrial antigens.[120] Immunity to these other antigens has not been consistent among heterologous strains.

Recommendations for the routine administration of *H. influenzae* conjugate vaccines to children between 2 and 6 months of age, to those whose initial immunization was delayed until 7 months of age or older, and to those whose immunization schedule may have been initiated appropriately but in whom a lapse in vaccine administration occurred are provided in Chapter 237. Recommendations also can be found in the Report of the Committee on Infectious Diseases of the American Academy of Pediatrics[8] and on the American Academy of Pediatrics website, where updates on such recommendations are maintained.

PASSIVE IMMUNIZATION

Although active immunization clearly is preferred for the control of Hib disease, passive immunization has potential utility in the following settings: (1) selected high-risk groups with a risk of acquiring disease soon after birth and too young to respond to vaccination (i.e., Eskimos or Native Americans), (2) functionally asplenic patients, (3) immunocompromised patients, and (4) prevention of secondary disease in households, daycare centers, or institutions. A human hyperimmunoglobulin from adult Hib-immunized donors called bacterial polysaccharide immunoglobulin has been prepared,[221] but it is not commercially available. Pharmacologic studies show that high levels of antibody can be achieved after intramuscular injection, and significant protective efficacy against invasive Hib disease has been demonstrated in Apache children given three doses during the first year of life.[205] The use of concurrent active immunization with bacterial polysaccharide immunoglobulin also may be an effective strategy.[134] Another possible approach in such groups would be maternal Hib immunization[89] to induce transplacental antibody, but questions remain regarding the safety and acceptability of vaccinating pregnant women and the inability to immunize women who do not receive prenatal care.

IMPACT OF *H. INFLUENZAE* TYPE b VACCINATION

The impact of widespread vaccination with Hib conjugate vaccine has been dramatic and reproduced in several areas of the United States[1, 161] and many countries throughout the world.[117, 178] Exclusively using HbOC vaccine,[20] the Kaiser Permanente northern California region has eliminated Hib disease except for a rare case in an unimmunized child and just a few cases in children with incomplete immunizations. In the Kaiser Permanente southern California region,[245] PRP-D and subsequently PRP-OMP vaccines were used in older children between 1987 and 1990. Since 1990, PRP-OMP vaccine has been administered almost exclusively. A few cases of PRP-D failure and only two cases of PRP-OMP failure occurred; disease essentially has been eliminated. Similar control of disease has been achieved with the use of PRP-OMP vaccine in Alaskan and Navajo Native American populations.[206] In Los Angeles County,[245] Minnesota, Dallas,[161] and selected other U.S. sites under surveillance by the Centers for Disease Control and Prevention, similar but less complete eradication of disease has been achieved. In these areas, both HbOC and PRP-OMP vaccines have been used in varying proportions over time, and complete immunization levels have not been achieved.

In general, the decrease in the incidence of disease has exceeded expectations given the estimated proportion of the population completely immunized. In addition, in essentially all these populations, a significant decrease in the incidence of disease was observed in infants before the licensure and recommended use of vaccines in that age group. These findings probably are explained by a reduction in Hib carriage as a result of vaccination[160, 234] and, consequently, decreased transmission from immunized children to unimmunized young children and infants.

The immunization schedules vary in different countries to parallel immunization practices for other vaccine-preventable diseases. Also the age-specific incidence of disease varies in different countries. Initially in the United Kingdom the occurrence of disease was such that physicians felt justified to use only a three-dose schedule at 2, 3, and 4 months of age, and not to provide a booster dose in the second year of life. This schedule was introduced in 1993, but in recent years the recurrence of type b disease in older children has been noted. This experience underlies the importance of giving a fourth dose when children are between 12 and 18 months of age.

CHEMOPROPHYLAXIS

Secondary disease accounts for less than 2 percent of all cases of invasive Hib disease. Chemoprophylaxis, however, can protect susceptible persons from acquiring Hib by eliminating Hib colonization in close contacts. Children younger than 4 years have a 600-fold increased risk of acquiring Hib disease after household contact with a case.[254] Risk also is increased in daycare center settings, but this risk is defined less well. In addition, adults and older children who are colonized can transmit Hib to susceptible children even though they have little risk for acquiring invasive disease themselves.

Antimicrobial agents effective for chemoprophylaxis must achieve bactericidal levels intracellularly and in mucosal secretions. Rifampin, which achieves high concentrations in respiratory secretions,[149] is the most effective antimicrobial agent for eradicating Hib from the nasopharynx. Rifampin in a dosage of 20 mg/kg once daily (maximal daily dose, 600 mg) for 4 days eradicates Hib carriage in 95 percent or more of household[14, 90] or daycare center[94] contacts of a case. Cohort studies have shown the effectiveness of rifampin prophylaxis in preventing secondary Hib disease in household and daycare center attendees.[90, 94, 144] Antimicrobials effective in the treatment of Hib disease, such as ampicillin, trimethoprim-sulfamethoxazole, erythromycin-sulfisoxazole, and cefaclor, have been shown to be ineffective for antimicrobial prophylaxis[111]; they eliminated Hib carriage in less than 70 percent of culture-positive contacts and, therefore, are not recommended.

Both the U.S. Public Health Service Advisory Committee on Immunization Practices[39] and the American Academy of Pediatrics Committee on Infectious Diseases[7] recommend rifampin prophylaxis for all household contacts, including adults, and for the index patient (therapeutic antibiotics do not eradicate Hib from the nasopharynx consistently) if the household has a contact younger than 4 years who is *not* fully immunized. Prophylaxis should be instituted as soon as possible because the risk of acquiring secondary disease is greatest during the few days after the onset of disease in the index patient and within 2 weeks of the onset of disease. With regard to the daycare center setting, no consensus exists concerning the need for chemoprophylaxis because of uncertainty about the magnitude of the risk of acquiring secondary Hib disease in this setting. Some authors recommend chemoprophylaxis if classroom contacts include those younger than 2 years of age, whereas others think that recommendations should be individualized. However, virtually all experts recommend prophylaxis if two or more cases of Hib disease have occurred among attendees within 60 days.[7, 39]

In all situations in which the potential for secondary disease exists, this risk should be explained to families, with an emphasis on the importance of seeking prompt medical attention for febrile illnesses. Clinicians should not obtain pharyngeal cultures to determine whether prophylaxis should be administered because doing so only delays the prompt administration of chemoprophylaxis.

Conclusion

The perspective on *Haemophilus* disease has changed dramatically in recent years. Before the availability of Hib conjugate vaccines, invasive Hib was one of the most important bacterial pathogens of children. It was the leading cause of bacterial meningitis and an important cause of other bacteremic illnesses. The spectrum of illness is broad, morbidity and mortality are significant, and subtleties in making an early diagnosis and instituting appropriate management exist. Currently, when one considers that most antibiotic use worldwide is for upper respiratory tract infections, including otitis media, and that *H. influenzae* causes a significant proportion of these illnesses, it still can be considered an important pediatric pathogen.

Although various aspects of disease caused by *H. influenzae* have been reviewed in this chapter, what is clear is that the most important aspect has been disease prevention by routine immunization of infants with polysaccharide-protein conjugate vaccines. This achievement is the culmination of more than 100 years of research on *H. influenzae.* Although historically many technologic problems and misunderstandings about the organism and its pathogenesis have occurred, much has been accomplished in recent years. The impact of routine infant immunizations with Hib conjugate vaccines is relatively recent and very dramatic. The public health benefits parallel the eradication of polio and the control of other vaccine-preventable childhood diseases. Widespread Hib immunization virtually has eliminated Hib disease in the United States and in many developed countries where it is used routinely. The degree of disease control exceeds all expectations and is in excess of what the known levels of immunization would have predicted. Unfortunately, Hib conjugate vaccines currently are used routinely in relatively few developing countries and only electively in some additional countries, thus leaving most of the world without the benefit of immunization. The World Health Organization recently has taken up the challenge to expand Hib immunization worldwide.

Progress also has been achieved in the development of vaccines against other *H. influenzae* serotypes and nontypeable strains. Control of infection caused by these organisms will have an important public health impact, and the use of such vaccines may have a role in adolescents and adults. The technologies that led to the development of Hib conjugate vaccines serve as a prototype for vaccines to prevent disease caused by other encapsulated bacteria, such as the pneumococcus, meningococcus, and group B *Streptococcus.* As such, the lessons learned in the quest to eliminate Hib disease will have important implications in the control of other bacterial diseases.

REFERENCES

1. Adams, W. G., Deaver, K. A., Cochi, S. L., et al.: Decline of childhood *Haemophilus influenzae* type b (Hib) disease in the Hib vaccine era. J. A. M. A. *269*:221–226, 1993.
2. Adderson, E. E., Byington, C. L., Spencer, L., et al.: Invasive serotype a *Haemophilus influenzae* infections with a virulence genotype resembling *Haemophilus influenzae* type b: Emerging pathogen in the vaccine era? Pediatrics *108*:E18, 2001.
3. Alexander, H. E., Heidelberger, M., and Leidy, G.: The protective or curative element in type b *H. influenzae* rabbit serum. Yale J. Biol. Med. *16*:425–440, 1944.
4. Alexander, H. E., Leidy, G., and MacPherson, C.: Production of types a, b, c, d, e and f *H. influenzae* antibody for diagnostic and therapeutic purposes. J. Immunol. *54*:207–211, 1946.
5. Ambrosino, D. M., Schiffman, G., Gotschlich, E. C., et al.: Correlation between G2m(n) immunoglobulin allotype and human antibody response and susceptibility to polysaccharide encapsulated bacteria. J. Clin. Invest. *75*:1935–1942, 1985.
6. Ambrosino, D. M., Sood, S. K., Lee, M. C., et al.: IgG1, IgG2 and IgM responses to two *Haemophilus influenzae* type conjugate vaccines in young infants. Pediatr. Infect. Dis. J. *11*:855–859, 1992.
7. American Academy of Pediatrics: *Haemophilus influenzae* infections. *In* Peter, G. (ed.): 1994 Red Book: Report of the Committee on Infectious Diseases. 23rd ed. Elk Grove Village, IL, American Academy of Pediatrics, 1994, pp. 203–216.
8. American Academy of Pediatrics: *Haemophilus influenzae* infections. *In* Pickering, L. K. (ed.): 2000 Red Book: Report of the Committee on Infectious Diseases. 25th ed. Elk Grove Village, IL, American Academy of Pediatrics, 2000, pp. 262–272.
9. Anderson, P.: The protective level of serum antibodies to the capsular polysaccharide of *H. influenzae* type b. J. Infect. Dis. *149*:1034, 1984.
10. Anderson, P., Smith, D. H., and Ingram, D. L.: Antibody to polyribophosphate of *H. influenzae* type b in infants and children: Effect of immunization with polyribophosphate. J. Infect. Dis. *136*(Suppl.):57–62, 1977.
11. Argaman, M., Lin, T. Y., and Robbins, J. B.: Polyribitol-phosphate: An antigen of four gram-positive bacteria cross-reactive with the capsular polysaccharide of *H. influenzae* type b. J. Immunol. *112*:649–655, 1974.
12. Artman, M., Domenech, E., and Weiner, M.: Growth of *Haemophilus influenzae* in simulated blood cultures supplemented with hemin and NAD. J. Clin. Microbiol. *18*:376–379, 1983.
13. Baker, R. C., and Bausher, J. D.: Meningitis complicating acute bacteremic facial cellulitis. Pediatr. Infect. Dis. *5*:421–423, 1986.
14. Band, J. D., Fraser, D. W., and Ajello, G.: Prevention of *H. influenzae* type b disease. J. A. M. A. *251*:2381–2386, 1984.
15. Barenkamp, S. J., Granoff, D. M., and Munson, R. S., Jr.: Outer membrane protein subtypes of *Haemophilus influenzae* type b and spread of disease in day care centers. J. Infect. Dis. *144*:210–217, 1981.
16. Barrett, D. J.: Human immune responses to polysaccharide antigens: An analysis of bacterial polysaccharide vaccines in infants. Adv. Pediatr. *32*:139–158, 1985.

17. Bartlett, A. V., Zusman, J., and Daum, R. S.: Unusual presentations of *Haemophilus influenzae* infections in immunocompromised patients. J. Pediatr. *102*:55–58, 1983.
18. Baugh, R., and Baker, S. R.: Epiglottitis in children: Review of 24 cases. Otolaryngol. Head Neck Surg. *90*:157–162, 1982.
19. Berkowitz, C. D., Ward, J. I., Meier, K., et al.: Safety and immunogenicity of *Haemophilus influenzae* type b polysaccharide and polysaccharide diphtheria toxoid conjugate vaccines in children 15 to 24 months of age. J. Pediatr. *110*:509–514, 1987.
22. Black, S. B., and Shinefield, H. R.: Immunization with oligosaccharide conjugate *Haemophilus influenzae* type b (HbOC) vaccine on a large health maintenance organization population: Extended follow-up and impact on *Haemophilus influenzae* disease epidemiology. Pediatr. Infect. Dis. J. *11*:610–613, 1992.
21. Black, S. B., Shinefield, H. R., Fireman, B., et al.: *Haemophilus influenzae* type b (HbOC) vaccine in a United States population of 61,080 children. Pediatr. Infect. Dis. J. *10*:97–104, 1991.
22. Blazer, S., Berant, M., and Alon, U.: Bacterial meningitis: Effect of antibiotic treatment on cerebrospinal fluid. Am. J. Clin. Pathol. *80*:386–387, 1983.
23. Bluestone, C. D., Stephenson, J. S., and Martin, L. M.: Ten-year review of otitis media pathogens. Pediatr. Infect. Dis. J. *11*(Suppl.):7–11, 1992.
24. Bodor, F. F.: Conjunctivitis-otitis syndrome. Pediatrics *69*:695–698, 1982.
25. Bonadio, W. A.: Cerebral herniation syndrome as the presenting sign of *Haemophilus influenzae* meningitis. Pediatr. Emerg. Care *3*:253–255, 1987.
26. Booy, R., Moxon, E. R., MacFarlane, J. A., et al.: Efficacy of *Haemophilus influenzae* type b conjugate vaccine in Oxford region. Lancet *340*:847, 1992.
27. Bottenfield, G. W., Arcinue, E. L., Sarnaik, A., et al.: Diagnosis and management of acute epiglottitis: Report of 90 consecutive cases. Laryngoscope *90*:822–825, 1980.
28. Brilli, R. J., Benzing, G., and Cotcamp, D. H.: Epiglottitis in infants less than two years of age. Pediatr. Emerg. Care *5*:16–21, 1989.
29. Broome, C. V., and Schlech, W. F., III: Recent developments in the epidemiology of bacterial meningitis. *In* Sande, M. A., Smith, A., and Root, R. D. (eds.): Bacterial Meningitis. Edinburgh, Churchill Livingstone, 1985, pp. 1–10.
30. Broughton, R. A., Edwards, M. S., Taber, L. H., et al.: Systemic *Haemophilus influenzae* type b infection presenting as fever of unknown origin. J. Pediatr. *98*:925–928, 1981.
31. Bulkow, L. R., Wainwright, R. B., Letson, G. W., et al.: Comparative immunogenicity of four *Haemophilus influenzae* type b conjugate vaccines in Alaska Native infants. Pediatr. Infect. Dis. J. *12*:484–492, 1993.
32. Cadoz, M., Prince-David, M., Mar, I. D., and Denis, F.: Epidemiologie et prognostic des meningites a *Haemophilus influenzae* en Afrique (901 cas). Pathol. Biol. *31*:128–133, 1983.
33. Campbell, L. R., Zedd, A. J., and Michaels, R. H.: Household spread of infection due to *H. influenzae* type b. Pediatrics *66*:115–117, 1980.
34. Campognone, P., and Singer, D. B.: Neonatal sepsis due to nontypable *Haemophilus influenzae*. Am. J. Dis. Child. *140*:117–121, 1986.
35. Campos, J., Garcia-Tornel, S., Gairi, J. M., and Fabregues, I.: Multiply resistant *H. influenzae* type b causing meningitis: Comparative clinical and laboratory study. J. Pediatr. *108*:897–902, 1986.
36. Cant, A. J., Gibson, P. J., and West, R. J.: Bacterial tracheitis in Down's syndrome. Arch. Dis. Child. *62*:962–963, 1987.
37. Casadevall, A., Dobroszycki, J., Small, C., and Pirofski, L.: *Haemophilus influenzae* type b bacteremia in adults with AIDS and at risk for AIDS. Am. J. Med. *92*:587–590, 1992.
38. Centers for Disease Control and Prevention: Ampicillin and chloramphenicol resistance in systemic *Haemophilus influenzae* disease. M. M. W. R. Morb. Mortal. Wkly. Rep. *33*(3):35–37, 1984.
39. Centers for Disease Control and Prevention: Recommendations for use of *Haemophilus* b conjugate vaccines and a combined diphtheria, tetanus, pertussis, and *Haemophilus* b vaccine: Recommendations of the Advisory Committee on Immunization Practices (ACIP). M. M. W. R. Recomm. Rep. *42*(RR-13):1–15, 1993.
40. Chapin, K. C., and Doern, G. V.: Selective media for recovery of *Haemophilus influenzae* from specimens contaminated with upper respiratory tract microbial flora. J. Clin. Microbiol. *17*:1163–1165, 1983.
41. Chartrand, S. A., Marks, M. I., Scribner, R. K., et al.: Moxalactam therapy of *Haemophilus influenzae* type b meningitis in children. J. Pediatr. *104*:454–459, 1984.
42. Cheatham, J. E., Jr., Grantham, R. N., Peyton, M. D., et al.: *Haemophilus influenzae* purulent pericarditis in children. J. Thorac. Cardiovasc. Surg. *79*:933–936, 1980.
43. Chen, L. T., and Moxon, E. R.: Effect of splenic congestion associated with hemolytic anemia on mortality of rats challenged with *Haemophilus influenzae* b. Am. J. Hematol. *15*:117–121, 1983.
44. Chilcote, R., Baehner, R., and Hammond, D.: Septicemia and meningitis in children splenectomized for Hodgkin's disease. N. Engl. J. Med. *295*: 798–801, 1976.
45. Chitayat, D., Diamant, S. H., Lazevnick, R., et al.: *Haemophilus influenzae* b with pneumatocele formation. Pediatr. Infect. Dis. J. *5*:276, 1986.
46. Claesson, B. A., Trollfors, B., Lagergard, T., et al.: Clinical and immunologic responses to the capsular polysaccharide of *Haemophilus influenzae* type b alone or conjugated to tetanus toxoid in 18- to 23-month-old children. J. Pediatr. *112*:695–702, 1988.
47. Clark, J. H., Fitzgerald, J. F., and Kleiman, M. B.: Spontaneous bacterial peritonitis. J. Pediatr. *104*:495–500, 1984.
48. Clarke, C. W., Hannant, C. A., Scicchitano, R., et al.: Antigen of *Haemophilus influenzae* in bronchial tissue. Thorax *36*:665–668, 1981.
49. Clausen, C. R.: Detection of bacterial pathogens in purulent clinical specimens by immunofluorescence techniques. J. Clin. Microbiol. *13*: 1119–1121, 1981.
50. Cleveland, R. H., and Foglia, R. P.: CT in the evaluation of pleural versus pulmonary disease in children. Pediatr. Radiol. *18*:14–19, 1988.
51. Cochi, S. L., and Broome, C. V.: Vaccine prevention of *H. influenzae* type b disease: Past, present and future. Pediatr. Infect. Dis. J. *5*:12–19, 1986.
52. Cochi, S. L., Fleming, D. W., and Hightower, A. W.: Primary invasive *H. influenzae* type b disease: A population-based assessment of risk factors. J. Pediatr. *108*:887–896, 1986.
53. Committee on Infectious Diseases: Ampicillin-resistant strains of *H. influenzae* type b. Pediatrics *55*:145, 1975.
54. Cortese, M. M., Goepp, J., Almeido-Hill, J., et al.: Children with *Haemophilus influenzae* bacteremia initially treated as outpatients: Outcome in 85 American Indian children. Pediatr. Infect. Dis. J. *11*:521–525, 1992.
55. Crosson, F. J., Winkelstein, J. A., and Moxon, E. R.: Participation of complement in the nonimmune host defense against experimental *H. influenzae* type b septicemia and meningitis. Infect. Immun. *14*:882–887, 1976.
56. Dajani, A. S., Asmar, B. I., and Thirumoorthi, M. C.: Systemic *H. influenzae* disease: An overview. J. Pediatr. *94*:355–364, 1979.
57. Danford, D. A., Kugler, J. D., Cheatham, J. P., et al.: *Haemophilus influenzae* endocarditis: Successful treatment with ampicillin and early valve replacement. Nebr. Med. J. *69*:88–91, 1984.
58. Davie, J. M.: Antipolysaccharide immunity in man and animals. *In* Sell, S. H., and Wright, P. F. (eds.): *Haemophilus influenzae*. New York, Elsevier Science, 1982.
59. Decker, M. D., Edwards, K. M., Bradley, R., and Palmer, P.: Comparative trial in infants of four conjugate *Haemophilus influenzae* type b vaccines. J. Pediatr. *120*:184–189, 1992.
60. Dodge, P. R., Davis, H., Feigin, R. D., et al.: Prospective evaluation of hearing impairment as a sequela of acute bacterial meningitis. N. Engl. J. Med. *311*:869–874, 1984.
61. Dodge, P. R., and Swartz, M. N.: Bacterial meningitis: A review of selected aspects. II. Special neurologic problems, post-meningitis complications and clinicopathological correlations. N. Engl. J. Med. *272*: 1003–1010, 1965.
62. Drexhage, H. A., Van de Plassche, E. M., Kokje, M., et al.: Abnormalities in cell-mediated immune functions to *H. influenzae* in chronic purulent infections of the upper respiratory tract. Clin. Immunol. Immunopathol. *28*:218–228, 1983.
63. Eskola, J., Kayhty, H., Takala, A. K., et al.: A randomized, prospective field trial of a conjugate vaccine in the protection of infants and young children against invasive *Haemophilus influenzae* type b disease. N. Engl. J. Med. *323*:1381–1387, 1990.
64. Eskola, J., Peltola, H., and Takala, A.: Protective efficacy of the *Haemophilus influenzae* type b conjugate vaccine HbOC in Finnish infants. Abstract 60. Presented at the 30th Annual Meeting of the ICAAC, 1990, Atlanta.
65. Falla, T. J., Dobson, S. R. M., Crook, D. W. M., et al.: Population-based study of non-typeable *Haemophilus influenzae* invasive disease in children and neonates. Lancet *341*:851–854, 1993.
66. Farrand, R. J.: Recurrent *Haemophilus* septicemia and immunoglobulin deficiency. Arch. Dis. Child. *45*:582–584, 1970.
67. Feigin, R. D., McCracken, G. H., Jr., and Klein, J. O.: Diagnosis and management of meningitis. Pediatr. Infect. Dis. J. *11*:785–814, 1992.
68. Feldman, W. E., Ginsburg, C. M., and McCracken, G. H.: Relation of concentrations of *H. influenzae* type b in cerebrospinal fluid to late sequelae of patients with meningitis. J. Pediatr. *100*:209–212, 1982.
69. Feldman, W. E., and Manning, N. S.: Effect of growth phase on the bactericidal action of chloramphenicol against *Haemophilus influenzae* type b and *Escherichia coli* K-1. Antimicrob. Agents Chemother. *23*: 551–554, 1983.
70. Feldman, W. E., and Schwartz, J.: *Haemophilus influenzae* type b brain abscess complicating meningitis: Case report. Pediatrics *72*:473–475, 1983.
71. Fernandez, J., Levine, O. S., Sanchez, J., et al.: Prevention of *Haemophilus influenzae* type b colonization by vaccination: Correlation with serum anti-capsular IgG concentration. J. Infect. Dis. *182*: 1553–1556, 2000.
72. Figueroa, J. E., and Densen P.: Infectious diseases associated with complement deficiencies. Clin. Microbiol. Rev. *4*:359–395, 1991.
73. Fink, C. W., and Nelson, J. D.: Septic arthritis and osteomyelitis in children. Clin. Rheum. Dis. *12*:423–435, 1986.

74. Fleisher, G., Ludwig, S., and Campos, J.: Cellulitis: Bacterial etiology, clinical features, and laboratory findings. J. Pediatr. *97*:591–592, 1980.
75. Fothergill, L. D., and Wright, J.: Influenzal meningitis: The relation of age incidence to the bactericidal power of blood against the causal organism. J. Immunol. *24*:273–284, 1933.
76. Foxwell, A. R., Kyd, J. M., and Cripps, A. W.: Nontypeable *Haemophilus influenzae*: Pathogenesis and prevention. Microbiol. Mol. Biol. Rev. *62*:294–308, 1998.
77. Fraser, D. W.: *Haemophilus influenzae* in the community and in the home. *In* Sell, S. H., and Wright, P. F. (eds.): *Haemophilus influenzae.* New York, Elsevier, 1982, pp. 11–22.
78. Fraser, D. W., Geil, C. C., and Feldman, R. A.: Bacterial meningitis in Bernalillo county, New Mexico: A comparison with three other American populations. Am. J. Epidemiol. *100*:29–34, 1974.
79. Fraser, D. W., Henke, C. E., and Feldman, R. A.: Changing patterns of bacterial meningitis in Olmsted County, Minnesota. J. Infect. Dis. *238*:300–307, 1973.
80. Frayha, H. H., Kalloghlian, A. K., and deMoor, M. M.: Endocarditis due to *Haemophilus influenzae* serotype f. Clin. Infect. Dis. *23*:401–402, 1996.
81. Freij, B. J., Votteler, T. P., and McCracken, G. H.: Primary peritonitis in previously healthy children. Am. J. Dis. Child. *138*:1058–1061, 1984.
82. Friesen, C. A., and Cho, C. T.: Characteristic features of neonatal sepsis due to *Haemophilus influenzae*. Rev. Infect. Dis. *8*:777–780, 1986.
83. Fritzell, B., and Plotkin, S. A.: Efficacy and safety of a *Haemophilus influenzae* type b capsular polysaccharide-tetanus protein conjugate vaccine. J. Pediatr. *121*:355–362, 1992.
84. Galil, K., Singleton, R., Levine, O. S., et al.: Reemergence of invasive *Haemophilus influenzae* type b disease in a well-vaccinated population in remote Alaska. J. Infect. Dis. *179*:101–106, 1999.
85. Gilsdorf, J. R.: Bacterial meningitis in southwestern Alaska. Am. J. Epidemiol. *106*:388–391, 1977.
86. Gilsdorf, J. R.: *Haemophilus influenzae* non–type b infections in children. Am. J. Dis. Child. *141*:1063–1065, 1987.
87. Ginsburg, C. M.: *Haemophilus influenzae* type b buccal cellulitis. J. Am. Acad. Dermatol. *4*:551–554, 1981.
88. Glatman-Freedman, A., and Litman, N.: Septic arthritis caused by an unusual type of *Haemophilus influenzae*. J. Infect. *32*:143–145, 1996.
89. Glezen, W. P., Englund, J. A., Siber, G. R., et al.: Maternal immunization with the capsular polysaccharide vaccine for *Haemophilus influenzae* type b. J. Infect. Dis. *165*(Suppl. 1):134–136, 1992.
90. Glode, M. P., Daum, R. S., Halsey, N. A., et al.: Rifampin alone and in combination with trimethoprim in chemoprophylaxis for infections due to *Haemophilus influenzae* type b. Rev. Infect. Dis. *5*(Suppl.):549–555, 1983.
91. Goldblatt, D., Fairley, C. K., Cartwright, K., and Miller, E.: Interchangeability of conjugated *Haemophilus influenzae* type b vaccines during primary immunisation of infants. B. M. J. *312*:817–818, 1996.
92. Granoff, D. M., Barenkamp, S. J., and Munson, R. S.: Outer membrane protein subtypes for epidemiologic investigation of *H. influenzae* type disease. *In* Sell, S. H., and Wright, P. F. (eds.): *Haemophilus influenzae*: Epidemiology, Immunology, and Prevention of Disease. New York, Elsevier, 1982, pp. 43–55.
93. Granoff, D. M., and Basden, M.: *H. influenzae* infections in Fresno County, California: A prospective study of the effects of age, race and contact with a case on incidence of disease. J. Infect. Dis. *140*:40–46, 1980.
94. Granoff, D. M., Gilsdorf, J., and Gessert, C.: *Haemophilus influenzae* type b disease in a day care center: Eradication of carrier state by rifampin. Pediatrics *63*:397–401, 1979.
95. Granoff, D. M., Holmes, S. J., Belshe, R. B., et al.: Effect of carrier protein priming on antibody responses to *Haemophilus influenzae* type b conjugate vaccines in infants. J. A. M. A. *272*:1116–1121, 1994.
96. Granoff, D. M., Rathore, M. H., Holmes, S. J., et al.: Effect of immunity to the carrier protein on antibody responses to *Haemophilus influenzae* type b conjugate vaccines. Vaccine *11*(Suppl. 1):46–51, 1993.
97. Granoff, D. M., Shackelford, P. G., Pandey, J. P., et al.: Antibody responses to *H. influenzae* type b polysaccharide vaccine in relation to Km(1) and G2, (23) immunoglobulin allotypes. J. Infect. Dis. *154*: 257–264, 1986.
98. Greenberg, D. P., Lieberman, J. M., Marcy, S. M., et al.: Enhanced antibody responses in infants given different sequences of heterogeneous *Haemophilus influenzae* type b conjugate vaccines. J. Pediatr. *126*: 206–211, 1995.
99. Greenberg, D. P., Vadheim, C. M., Bordenave, N., et al.: Protective efficacy of *Haemophilus influenzae* type b polysaccharide and conjugate vaccines in children 18 months of age and older. J. A. M. A. *265*:987–992, 1991.
100. Greenfield, S., Peter, G., and Howie, V. M.: Acquisition of type-specific antibodies to *H. influenzae* type b. J. Pediatr. *80*:204–208, 1972.
101. Greenfield, S. P.: Type b *Haemophilus influenzae* epididymo-orchitis in the prepubertal boy. J. Urol. *136*:1311–1313, 1986.
102. Greenwood, B.: Epidemiology of acute lower respiratory tract infections, especially those due to *Haemophilus influenzae* type b, in the Gambia, West Africa. J. Infect. Dis. *165*(Suppl. 1):26–28, 1992.
103. Gregorius, F. K., Johnson, B. J., Stern, W. E., and Brown, W. J.: Pathogenesis of hematogenous bacterial meningitis in rabbits. J. Neurosurg. *45*:561–567, 1976.
104. Hammond, G. W., Slutchuk, M., Scatiff, J., et al.: Epidemiologic, clinical, laboratory and therapeutic features of an urban outbreak of chancroid in North America. Rev. Infect. Dis. *2*:867–869, 1980.
105. Hansman, D., Hanna, J., and Morey, F.: High prevalence of invasive *Haemophilus influenzae* disease in central Australia, 1986. Lancet *2*:927, 1986.
106. Harrison, L. H., da Silva, G. A., Pittman, M., et al.: Epidemiology and clinical spectrum of Brazilian purpuric fever. Brazilian Purpuric Fever Study Group. J. Clin. Microbiol. *27*:599–604, 1989.
107. Heath, P. T., Booy, R., Azzopardi, H. J., et al.: Non–type b *Haemophilus influenzae* disease: Clinical and epidemiologic characteristics in the *Haemophilus influenzae* type b vaccine era. Pediatr. Infect. Dis. J. *20*: 300–305, 2001.
108. Hellinger, W. C., and Brewer, N. S.: Imipenem. Mayo Clin. Proc. *66*: 1074–1081, 1991.
109. Hoiseth, S. K., Moxon, E. A., and Silver, R. P.: Genes involved in *Haemophilus influenzae* type b expression are part of an iskilobase tandem duplication. Proc. Natl. Acad. Sci. U. S. A. *83*:1106–1110, 1986.
110. Holmes, S. J., Murphy T. V., Anderson, R. S., et al.: Immunogenicity of four *Haemophilus influenzae* type b conjugate vaccines in 17- to 19-month-old children. J. Pediatr. *118*:364–371, 1991.
111. Horner, D. B., McCracken, G. H., Ginsburg, C. M., and Zweighaft, T. C.: A comparison of three antibiotic regimens for eradication of *Haemophilus influenzae* type b from the pharynx of infants and children. Pediatrics *66*:136–138, 1980.
112. Howe, P. M., Edwardo Fajardo, J., and Orcutt, M. A.: Etiologic diagnosis of cellulitis: Comparison of aspirates obtained from the leading edge and the point of maximal inflammation. Pediatr. Infect. Dis. J. *5*: 685–686, 1987.
113. Istre, G. R., Conner, J. S., and Broome, C. V.: Risk factors for primary invasive *H. influenzae* disease: Increased risk from day care attendance and school age household members. J. Pediatr. *106*:190–195, 1985.
114. Jacobs, R. F., Hsi, S., Wilson, C. B., et al.: Apparent meningococcemia: Clinical features of disease due to *Haemophilus influenzae* and *Neisseria meningitidis.* Pediatrics *72*:469–472, 1983.
115. Jacobs, R. F., Wright, M. W., Deskin, R. L., et al.: Delayed sterilization of *Haemophilus influenzae* type b meningitis with twice-daily ceftriaxone. J. A. M. A. *259*:392–394, 1988.
116. Johnston, R. B., Anderson, P., Rosen, F. S., and Smith, D. H.: Characterization of human immunity to polyribophosphate, the capsular antigen of *H. influenzae* type b. Clin. Immunol. Immunopathol. *1*:234–240, 1973.
117. Jonsdottir, K. E., Steingrimsson, O., and Olafsson, O.: Immunisation of infants in Iceland against *Haemophilus influenzae* type b. Lancet *340*:252–253, 1992.
118. Jorgensen, J. H.: Update on mechanisms and prevalence of antimicrobial resistance in *Haemophilus influenzae*. Clin. Infect. Dis. *14*:1119–1123, 1992.
119. Kaplan, S. L.: Antigen detection in cerebrospinal fluid—Pros and cons. Am. J. Med. *75*(1B):109–118, 1983.
120. Karasic, R. B., Beste, D. J., To, S. C., et al.: Evaluation of pilus vaccines for prevention of experimental otitis media caused by nontypable *Haemophilus influenzae*. Pediatr. Infect. Dis. J. *8*(Suppl.):62–65, 1989.
121. Kayhty, H., Eskola, J., Peltola, H., et al.: Immunogenicity in infants of a vaccine composed of a *Haemophilus influenzae* type b capsular polysaccharide mixed with DPT or conjugated to diphtheria toxoid. J. Infect. Dis. *155*:100–106, 1987.
122. Kayhty, H., Karanko, V., Peltola, H., and Makela, P. H.: Serum antibodies after vaccination with *H. influenzae* type b capsular polysaccharide and responses to reimmunization: No evidence of immunologic tolerance or memory. Pediatrics *74*:857–865, 1984.
123. Kayhty, H., Peltola, H., Karanko, V., et al.: The protective level of serum antibodies to the capsular polysaccharide of *H. influenzae* type b. J. Infect. Dis. *147*:1100, 1983.
124. Kayhty, H., Schneerson, R., and Sutton, A.: Class-specific antibody response to *H. influenzae* type b capsular polysaccharide vaccine. J. Infect. Dis. *148*:767, 1983.
125. Kleiman, M. B., Reynolds, J. K., Watts, N. H., et al.: Superiority of acridine orange stain versus Gram stain in partially treated bacterial meningitis. J. Pediatr. *104*:401–404, 1984.
126. Klein, J. O.: Role of nontypeable *Haemophilus influenzae* in pediatric respiratory tract infections. Pediatr. Infect. Dis. J. *16*(2 Suppl.):5–8, 1997.
127. Koomey, J. M., and Falkow, S.: Nucleotide sequence homology between the immunoglobulin A1 protease genes of *Neisseria gonorrhoeae, Neisseria meningitidis,* and *Haemophilus influenzae.* Infect. Immun. *43*:101–107, 1984.
128. Korones, D. N., Marshall, G. S., and Shapiro, E. D.: Outcome of children with occult bacteremia caused by *Haemophilus influenzae* type b. Pediatr. Infect. Dis. J. *11*:516–520, 1992.

129. Krasinski, K., Nelson, J. D., Butler, S., et al.: Possible association of mycoplasma and viral respiratory infections with bacterial meningitis. Am. J. Epidemiol. *125*:499–508, 1987.
130. Landsteiner, K.: The Specificity of Serologic Reactions. Cambridge, Harvard University Press, 1945. Reprinted by Dover Publications, New York, 1962.
131. Lebel, M. H., and Nelson, J. D.: *Haemophilus influenzae* type b osteomyelitis in infants and children. Pediatr. Infect. Dis. J. *7*:250–254, 1988.
132. Lehmann, D.: Epidemiology of acute respiratory tract infections, especially those due to *Haemophilus influenzae,* in Papua New Guinean children. J. Infect. Dis. *165*(Suppl. 1):20–25, 1992.
133. Lerman, S. J.: *Haemophilus influenzae* infections of cerebrospinal fluid shunts. J. Neurosurg. *54*:261–263, 1981.
134. Letson, G. W., Santosham, M., Reid, R., et al.: Comparison of active and combined passive/active immunization of Navajo children against *Haemophilus influenzae* type b. Pediatr. Infect. Dis. J. *7*:747–752, 1988.
135. Lichty, E., Kleiman, M. B., Ballantine, T. V. N., et al.: Primary *Haemophilus influenzae* lung abscesses with bronchial obstruction. J. Pediatr. Surg. *17*:281–284, 1982.
136. Lieberman, J. M., Greenberg, D. P., Wong, V. K., et al. Effect of neonatal immunization with diphtheria and tetanus toxoids on antibody responses to *Haemophilus influenzae* type b conjugate vaccines. J. Pediatr. *126*:198–205, 1995.
137. Lin, Y. C., King, D. R., Birken, G. A., et al.: Acute scrotum due to *Haemophilus influenzae* type b. J. Pediatr. Surg. *23*:183–184, 1988.
138. Loeb, M. R., and Smith, D. H.: Human antibody response to individual outer membrane proteins of *Haemophilus influenzae* type b. Infect. Immun. *37*:1032–1036, 1982.
139. Losek, J. D., Dewitz-Zink, B. A., Melzer-Lange, M., et al.: Epiglottitis: Comparison of signs and symptoms in children less than 2 years old and older. Ann. Emerg. Med. *19*:55–58, 1990.
140. Losonsky, G. A., Santosham, M., Sehgal, V. M., et al.: *Haemophilus influenzae* in the White Mountain Apaches: Molecular epidemiology of a high risk population. Pediatr. Infect. Dis. J. *3*:539–547, 1984.
141. Lucas, A. H.: Expression of crossreactive idiotypes by human antibodies specific for the capsular polysaccharide of *Haemophilus influenzae* b. J. Clin. Invest. *81*:480–486, 1988.
142. Madore, D. V., Johnson, C. L., Phipps, D. C., et al.: Safety and immunogenicity of *Haemophilus influenzae* type b oligosaccharide-CRM197 conjugate vaccine in infants aged 15–23 months. Pediatrics *86*:527–534, 1990.
143. Makela, P. H., Takala, A. K., Peltola, H., and Eskola, J.: Epidemiology of invasive *Haemophilus influenzae* type b disease. J. Infect. Dis. *165*(Suppl. 1):2–6, 1992.
144. Makintubee, S., Istre, G. R., and Ward, J. I.: Transmission of invasive *Haemophilus influenzae* type b disease in day care settings. J. Pediatr. *111*:180–186, 1987.
145. Marcon, M. J., Hamoudi, A. C., and Cannon, J. H.: Comparative laboratory evaluation of three antigen detection methods for diagnosis of *Haemophilus influenzae* type b disease. J. Clin. Microbiol. *19*:333–337, 1984.
146. Mason, E. O., Kaplan, S. L., Lambeth, L. B., et al.: Serotype and ampicillin susceptibility of *Haemophilus influenzae* causing systemic infection in children: Three years of experience. J. Clin. Microbiol. *15*:543–546, 1982.
147. Masters, P. L., Brumfitt, W., Mendez, R. L., and Likar, M.: Bacterial flora of the upper respiratory tract in Paddington families. B. M. J. *1*:1200–1205, 1958.
148. McCarthy, L. G.: *Haemophilus influenzae* associated with periappendiceal abscess. Am. J. Gastroenterol. *76*:157–159, 1981.
149. McCracken, G. H., Ginsburg, C. M., Zweighaft, T. C., and Clahsen, J.: Pharmacokinetics of rifampin in infants and children: Relevance to prophylaxis against *Haemophilus influenzae* type b disease. Pediatrics *66*:17–21, 1980.
150. McGraw, T. P., and Bruckner, D. A.: Sensitivity of commercial agglutination and counterimmunoelectrophoresis methods for the detection of *Haemophilus influenzae* type b capsular polysaccharide. Am. J. Clin. Pathol. *80*:703–706, 1983.
151. Mehl, A. L.: *Haemophilus influenzae* polyserositis. J. Pediatr. *112*: 160–161, 1988.
152. Michaels, R. H., and Norden, C. W.: Pharyngeal colonization with *H. influenzae* type b: A longitudinal study of families with a child with meningitis or epiglottitis due to *H. influenzae* type b. J. Infect. Dis. *136*:222–228, 1977.
153. Michaels, R. H., and Schultz, W. F.: The frequency of *Haemophilus influenzae* infections: Analysis of racial and environmental factors. *In* Sell, S. H., and Karzon, D. T. (eds.): *Haemophilus influenzae.* Nashville, TN, Vanderbilt University Press, 1973, pp. 243–250.
154. Miragliotta, G., Colucci, M., Semeraro, N., et al.: Platelet injury and stimulation of leukocyte procoagulant activity in vitro by a lipopolysaccharide from *Haemophilus influenzae* type b. Microbiologica *4*:173–180, 1981.
155. Morgan, R. J., Stephenson, L. W., and Woolf, P. K.: Surgical treatment of purulent pericarditis in children. J. Thorac. Cardiovasc. Surg. *85*:527–531, 1983.
156. Moxon, E. R.: Experimental studies of *H. influenzae* in a rat model. *In* Sell, S. H., and Wright, P. F. (eds.): *Haemophilus influenzae:* Epidemiology, Immunology, and Prevention of Disease. New York, Elsevier, 1982.
157. Mulks, M. H., Kornfeld, S. J., Bragione, B., et al.: Relationship between the specificity of IgA proteases and serotypes in *H. influenzae.* J. Infect. Dis. *146*:266–274, 1982.
158. Munson, R., Jr., and Grass, S.: Purification, cloning, and sequence of outer membrane protein P1 of *Haemophilus influenzae* type b. Infect. Immun. *56*:2235–2242, 1988.
159. Murphy, T. V., Granoff, D., and Chrane, D. F.: Pharyngeal colonization with *Haemophilus influenzae* type b in children in a day care center without invasive disease. J. Pediatr. *106*:712–716, 1985.
160. Murphy, T. V., Pastor, P., Medley, F., et al.: Decreased *Haemophilus* colonization in children vaccinated with *Haemophilus influenzae* type b conjugate vaccine. J. Pediatr. *122*:517–523, 1993.
161. Murphy, T. V., White, K. E., Pastor, P., et al.: Declining incidence of *Haemophilus influenzae* type b disease since introduction of vaccination. J. A. M. A. *269*:246–248, 1993.
162. Musher, D. M., Goree, A., Baughn, R. E., et al.: Immunoglobulin A from bronchopulmonary secretions block bactericidal and opsonizing effects of antibody to nontypable *H. influenzae.* Infect. Immun. *45*:36–40, 1984.
163. Musser, J. M., Barenkamp, S. J., Granoff, D. M., et al.: Genetic relationships of serologically nontypable and serotype b strains of *Haemophilus influenzae.* Infect. Immun. *52*:183–191, 1986.
164. Musser, J. M., Kroll, J. S., Granoff, D. M., et al.: Global genetic structure and molecular epidemiology of encapsulated *Haemophilus influenzae.* Rev. Infect. Dis. *12*:75–111, 1990.
165. Musser, J. M., Kroll, J. S., Moxon, E. R., and Selander, R. K.: Evolutionary genetics of the encapsulated strains of *Haemophilus influenzae.* Proc. Natl. Acad. Sci. U. S. A. *85*:7758–7762, 1988.
166. Mustafa, M. M., Lebel, M. H., and McCracken, G. H., Jr.: Tenosynovitis and transient arthritis associated with *Haemophilus influenzae* type b bacteremia. Pediatr. Infect. Dis. J. *7*:517–519, 1988.
167. Mustafa, M. M., Scarvey, L., Rollins, N., et al.: Primary suppurative myositis associated with *Haemophilus influenzae* type b septicemia. Pediatr. Infect. Dis. J. *7*:815–817, 1988.
168. Nelson, M. D., Murphy, T. F., van Keulen, H., et al.: Studies on P6, an important outer-membrane protein antigen of *Haemophilus influenzae.* Rev. Infect. Dis. *10*(Suppl.):331–336, 1988.
169. Newman, S. L., Waldo, B., and Johnston R. B.: Separation of serum bactericidal and opsonizing activities for *Haemophilus influenzae* type b. Infect. Immun. *8*:488–490, 1973.
170. Nizet, V., Colina, K. F., Almquist, J. R., et al.: A virulent nonencapsulated *Haemophilus influenzae.* J. Infect. Dis *173*:180–186, 1996.
171. Omikunle, A., Takahashi, S., Ogilvie, C. L., et al.: Limited genetic diversity of recent invasive isolates of non-serotype b encapsulated *Haemophilus influenzae.* J. Clin. Microbiol. *40*:1264–1270, 2002.
172. Osterholm, M. T., Pierson, L. N., White, K. E., et al.: Risk of subsequent transmission of *Haemophilus influenzae* type b disease among children in day care. N. Engl. J. Med. *316*:1–4, 1987.
173. Ostrow, P. T., Moxon, E. R., Vernon, N., and Kapko, R.: Studies on the route of meningeal invasion following *H. influenzae* inoculation of infant rats. Lab. Invest. *40*:678–685, 1979.
174. Oxelius, V. A.: Quantitative and qualitative investigations of serum IgG subclasses in immunodeficiency diseases. Clin. Exp. Immunol. *36*:112–116, 1979.
175. Pauwels, R., Verschraegen, G., and Van Der Straeten, M.: IgE antibodies to bacteria in patients with bronchial asthma. Allergy *157*:665–669, 1980.
176. Peltola, H., Kayhty, H., and Sivonen, A.: *Haemophilus influenzae* type b capsular polysaccharide vaccine in children: A double-blind field study of 100,000 vaccinees 3 months to 5 years of age in Finland. Pediatrics *60*:730–737, 1977.
177. Peltola, H., Kayhty, H., Virtanen, M., and Makela, P. H.: Prevention of *H. influenzae* type b bacteremic infection with the capsular polysaccharide vaccine. N. Engl. J. Med. *310*:1566–1569, 1984.
178. Peltola, H., Kilpi, T., and Anttila, M.: Rapid disappearance of *Haemophilus influenzae* type b meningitis after routine childhood immunization with conjugate vaccines. Lancet *340*:592–594, 1992.
179. Peltola, H., and Virtanen, M.: Systemic *Haemophilus influenzae* infection in Finland. Clin. Pediatr. (Phila.) *5*:275–280, 1984.
180. Perdue, D. G., Bulkow, L. R., and Gellin, B. G.: Invasive H*aemophilus influenzae* disease in Alaskan residents aged 10 years and older before and after infant vaccination programs. J. A. M. A. *283*:3089–3094, 2000.
181. Peterson, G. M., Silimperi, D. R., Chiu, C. Y., and Ward, J. I.: Effects of age, breast-feeding and household structure on *Haemophilus influenzae* type b disease risk and antibody acquisition in Alaskan Eskimos. Am. J. Epidemiol. *134*:1212–1221, 1991.
182. Pfeiffer, R.: Vorlaufige mit Heilungen über die Erreger der Influenzae. Dtsch. Med. Wochenschr. *18*:28–34, 1892.
183. Pichichero, M. E., Hall, C. B., and Insel, R. A.: A mucosal antibody response following systemic *H. influenzae* type b infection in children. J. Clin. Invest. *67*:1482–1489, 1981.

184. Pichichero, M. E., and Insel, R. A.: Mucosal antibody response to parenteral vaccination with *H. influenzae* type b capsule. J. Allergy Clin. Immunol. *72*:481–486, 1983.
185. Pittman, M.: Variation and type specificity in the bacterial species: *H. influenzae*. J. Exp. Med. *53*:471–495, 1931.
186. Pittman, M.: The action of type-specific *H. influenzae* antiserum. J. Exp. Med. *58*:583–706, 1933.
187. Plaut, A. G.: The IgA1 proteases of pathogenic bacteria. Annu. Rev. Microbiol. *37*:603–622, 1983.
188. Pomeroy, S. L., Holmes, S. J., Dodge, P. R., and Feigin, R. D.: Seizures and other neurologic sequelae of bacterial meningitis in children. N. Engl. J. Med. *323*:1651–1657, 1990.
189. Powars, D., Overturf, G., and Turner, E.: Is there an increased risk of *H. influenzae* septicemia in children with sickle cell anemia? Pediatrics *71*:927–931, 1983.
190. Prober, C. G.: The role of steroids in the management of children with bacterial meningitis. Pediatrics *95*:29–31, 1995.
191. Ramada, K., Petersen, G. M., Heiner, D. C., et al.: Class and subclass antibodies of *H. influenzae* type capsule: Comparison of invasive disease and natural exposure. Infect. Immun. *53*:486–490, 1986.
192. Redmond, S. R., and Pichichero, M. E.: *Haemophilus influenzae* type b disease: An epidemiologic study with special reference to day care centers. J. A. M. A. *252*:2581–2584, 1984.
193. Rennels, M. B., and Wald, E. R.: Treatment of *Haemophilus influenzae* type b meningitis in children with cerebrospinal fluid shunts. J. Pediatr. *97*:424–426, 1980.
194. Ricketts, R. R., Ilbawi, M. N., and Idriss, F. S.: Management of *Haemophilus influenzae* pericarditis. J. Pediatr. Surg. *17*:285–289, 1982.
195. Riesen, W. F., Skavaril, F., and Braun, D. G.: Natural infection of man with group A streptococci: Levels, restriction in class, subclass, and type, and clonal appearance of polysaccharide-group specific antibodies. Scand. J. Immunol. *5*:383–390, 1976.
196. Robbins, J. B., Park, J. C., Jr., Schneerson, R., and Whisnant, J. K.: Quantitative measurement of "natural" and immunization-induced *H. influenzae* type b capsular polysaccharide antibodies. Pediatr. Res. *7*:103–110, 1973.
197. Robbins, J. B., Schneerson, R., and Pittman, M. H.: Influenzae type b infections. *In* Germanier, R. (ed.): Bacterial Vaccines. Orlando, FL, Academic Press, 1984, pp. 290–313.
198. Roberts, M. C., Swenson, C. D., Owens, I. M., and Smith, A. L.: Characterization of chloramphenicol-resistant *H. influenzae*. Antimicrob. Agents Chemother. *18*:510–515, 1980.
199. Rodrigues, L. P., Schneerson, R., and Robbins, J. B.: Immunity to *H. influenzae* type b. I. The isolation and some physiochemical, serologic and biologic properties of the capsular polysaccharide of *H. influenzae* type b. J. Immunol. *107*:1071–1080, 1971.
200. Rowe, J. E., Messinger, I. K., Schwendeman, C. A., and Popejoy, L. A.: Three-dose vaccination of infants under 8 months of age with a conjugate *Haemophilus influenzae* type b vaccine. Mil. Med. *155*:483–486, 1990.
201. Rubin, L. G., and Moxon, E. R.: Pathogenesis of bloodstream invasion with *Haemophilus influenzae* type b. Infect. Immun. *41*:280–284, 1983.
202. Rusin, P., Adam, R. D., Petersen, E. A., et al.: *Haemophilus influenzae*: An important cause of maternal and neonatal infections. Obstet. Gynecol. *77*:92–96, 1991.
203. Saez-Llorens, X.: Pathogenesis of acute otitis media. Pediatr. Infect. Dis. J. *13*:1035–1038, 1994.
204. Salwen, K. M., Vikerfors, T., and Olcen, P.: Increased incidence of childhood bacterial meningitis: A 25-year study in a defined population in Sweden. Scand. J. Infect. Dis. *19*:1–11, 1987.
205. Santosham, M., Reid, R., and Ambrosino, D. M.: Prevention of *H. influenzae* type b (Hib) infections in high-risk infants treated with bacterial polysaccharide immune globulin. N. Engl. J. Med. *317*: 923–929, 1987.
206. Santosham, M., Rivin, B., Wolff, M., et al.: Prevention of *Haemophilus influenzae* type b infections in Apache and Navajo children. J. Infect. Dis. *165*(Suppl. 1):144–151, 1992.
207. Santosham, M., Wolff, M., Reid, R., et al.: The efficacy in Navajo infants of a conjugate vaccine consisting of *Haemophilus influenzae* type b polysaccharide and *Neisseria meningitidis* outer-membrane protein complex. N. Engl. J. Med. *324*:1767–1772, 1991.
208. Schauf, V., Green, D. C., Van Der Stuyf, L., et al.: Chloramphenicol kills *Haemophilus influenzae* more rapidly than does ampicillin or cefamandole. Antimicrob. Agents Chemother. *23*:364–368, 1983.
209. Scheld, W. M., Parks, T. S., Winn, H. R., et al.: Clearance of bacteria from cerebrospinal fluid to blood in experimental meningitis. Infect. Immun. *24*:102–105, 1979.
210. Schlamm, H. T., and Yancovitz, S. R.: *Haemophilus influenzae* pneumonia in young adults with AIDS, ARC, or risk of AIDS. Am. J. Med. *86*:11–14, 1989.
211. Schmitt, H. J., von Kries, R., Hassenpflug, B., et al.: *Haemophilus influenzae* type b disease: Impact and effectiveness of diphtheria-tetanus toxoids-acellular pertussis (-inactivated poliovirus)/*H. influenzae* type b combination vaccines. Pediatr. Infect. Dis. J. *20*:767–774, 2001.
212. Schneerson, R., Robbins, J. B., and Parke, J. C.: Quantitative and qualitative analyses of serum antibodies elicited in adults by *H. influenzae* type b and pneumococcus type 6A capsular polysaccharide–tetanus toxoid conjugates. Infect. Immun. *52*:519–528, 1986.
213. Schneerson, R., Rodrigues, L. P., Parke, J. C., and Robbins, J. B.: Immunity to disease caused by *H. influenzae* type b. II. Specificity and some biological characteristics of "natural," infection acquired and immunization induced antibody to the capsular polysaccharide. J. Immunol. *107*:1081–1089, 1971.
214. Schreiber, J. R., Barrus, V., Cates, K. L., et al.: Functional characterization of human IgG, IgM, and IgA antibody directed to the capsule of *H. influenzae* type b. J. Infect. Dis. *153*:8–16, 1986.
215. Schur, P. H., Borel, H., and Gelfand, E. W.: Selective gamma-g globulin deficiencies in patients with recurrent pyogenic infections. N. Engl. J. Med. *283*:631–634, 1970.
216. Shackelford, P. G., Granoff, D. M., and Nahm, M. H.: Relation of age, race and allotype to immunoglobulin subclass concentrations. Pediatr. Res. *19*:846–849, 1985.
217. Shackelford, P. G., Granoff, D. M., Nelson, S. J., et al.: Subclass distribution of human antibodies to *Haemophilus influenzae* type b capsular polysaccharide. J. Immunol. *138*:587–592, 1987.
218. Shapiro, E. D.: Persistent pharyngeal colonization with *H. influenzae* type b after intravenous chloramphenicol therapy. Pediatrics *67*:435–437, 1981.
219. Shapiro, E. D., and Wald, E. R.: Efficacy of rifampin in eliminating pharyngeal carriage of *H. influenzae* type b. Pediatrics *66*:5–8, 1980.
220. Siber, G. R., and Ambrosino, D. M.: Heavy and light chain restriction of human antibodies to bacterial polysaccharide antigens. *In* Morell, A., and Hydegger, U. E. (eds.): Clinical Use of Intravenous Immunoglobulins. Orlando, FL, Academic Press, 1986, pp. 47–54.
221. Siber, G. R., Ambrosino, D. M., and McIver, J.: Preparation of human hyperimmune globulin to *Haemophilus influenzae* b, *Streptococcus pneumoniae*, and *Neisseria meningitidis*. Infect. Immun. *45*:248–254, 1984.
222. Singleton, R., Bulkow, L. R., Levine, O. S., et al.: Experience with the prevention of invasive *Haemophilus influenzae* type b disease by vaccination in Alaska: The impact of persistent oropharyngeal carriage. J. Pediatr. *137*:195–298, 2000.
223. Sirinavin, S., Chiemchanya, S., Visudhipan, P., et al.: Cefuroxime treatment of bacterial meningitis in infants and children. Antimicrob. Agents Chemother. *25*:273–275, 1984.
224. Smith, A. L., Daum, R. S., Scheifele, D., et al.: Pathogenesis of *H. influenzae* meningitis. *In* Sell, S. H., and Wright, P. F. (eds.): *Haemophilus influenzae:* Epidemiology, Immunology and Prevention of Disease. New York, Elsevier, 1982, pp. 89–109.
225. Spanjaard, L., Bol, P., Ekker, W., and Zanen, H. C.: The incidence of bacterial meningitis in The Netherlands: A comparison of three registration systems, 1977–1982. J. Infect. *11*:259–268, 1985.
226. Spinola, S. M., Sheaffer, C. I., Pholbrick, K. B., et al.: Antigenuria after *Haemophilus influenzae* type b polysaccharide immunization: A prospective study. J. Pediatr. *109*:835–838, 1986.
227. St. Geme, J. W., III: The pathogenesis of nontypable *Haemophilus influenzae* otitis media. Vaccine *19*(Suppl. 1):41-50, 2000.
228. St. Geme, J. W., III: Molecular and cellular determinants of non-typeable *Haemophilus influenzae* adherence and invasion. Cell Microbiol. *4*:191–200, 2002.
229. Steele, N. P., Munson, R. S., and Granoff, D. M.: Antibody-dependent alternative pathway killing of *H. influenzae* type b. Infect. Immun. *44*:452, 1984.
230. Stephens, D. S., and Farley, M. M.: Pathogenic events during infections of the human nasopharynx with *Neisseria meningitidis* and *Haemophilus influenzae*. Rev. Infect. Dis. *13*:22–33, 1991.
231. Strakosch, E. A., Kendell, H. W., Craig, R. M., et al.: Clinical and laboratory investigation of 370 cases of chancroid. J. Invest. Dermatol. *6*:95–107, 1945.
232. Stull, T. L., Jacobs, R. F., and Haas, J. E.: Human serum bactericidal activity against *H. influenzae* type b. J. Clin. Microbiol. *130*:665–672, 1984.
233. Swords, W. E., Ketterer, M. R., Campbell, C. A., et al.: Binding of the non-typeable *Haemophilus influenzae* lipooligosaccharide to the PAF receptor initiates hot cell signalling. Cell Microbiol. *3*:525–536, 2001.
234. Takala, A. K., Eskola, J., Leinonen, M., et al.: Reduction of oropharyngeal carriage of *Haemophilus influenzae* type b (Hib) in children immunized with an Hib conjugate vaccine. J. Infect. Dis. *164*:982–986, 1991.
235. Takala, A. K., Mourman, O., Kleemola, M., et al.: Preceding respiratory infection predisposing for primary and secondary invasive *Haemophilus influenzae* type b disease. Pediatr. Infect. Dis. J. *12*:189–195, 1993.
236. Tarr, P. I., and Peter, G.: Demographic factors in the epidemiology of *H. influenzae* meningitis in young children. J. Pediatr. *92*:884–888, 1978.
237. Tarrand, J. J., Scott, M. G., Takes, P. A., et al.: Clonal characterization of the human IgG antibody repertoire to *Haemophilus influenzae* type b polysaccharide: Demonstration of three types of V regions and their association with H and L chain isotypes. J. Immunol. *142*:2519–2526, 1989.

238. Taylor, H. G., Mills, E. L., Ciampi, A., et al.: The sequelae of *Haemophilus influenzae* meningitis in school-age children. N. Engl. J. Med. *323*:1657–1663, 1990.
239. Taylor, J. R. W., Cibis, G. W., and Hamtil, L. W.: Endophthalmitis complicating *Haemophilus influenzae* type b meningitis. Arch. Ophthalmol. *98*:324–326, 1980.
240. Todd, J. K., and Bruhn, F. W.: Severe *Haemophilus influenzae* infections: Spectrum of disease. Am. J. Dis. Child. *129*:607–611, 1975.
241. Turk, D. C.: Naso-pharyngeal carriage of *H. influenzae* type b. J. Hyg. *61*:247–256, 1963.
242. Uchiyama, N., Greene, G. R., Kitts, D. R., and Thrupp, L. D.: Meningitis due to *H. influenzae* type b resistant to ampicillin and chloramphenicol. J. Pediatr. *97*:421–424, 1980.
243. Urwin, G., Krohn, J. A., Deaver-Robinson, K., et al.: Invasive disease due to *Haemophilus influenzae* serotype f: Clinical and epidemiologic characteristics in the *H. influenzae* serotype b vaccine era. The *Haemophilus influenzae* Study Group. Clin. Infect. Dis. *22*:1069–1076, 1996.
244. Vadheim, C. M., Greenberg, D. P., Bordenave, N., et al.: Risk factors for invasive *Haemophilus influenzae* type b in Los Angeles County children 18–60 months of age. Am. J. Epidemiol. *136*:221–235, 1992.
245. Vadheim, C. M., Greenberg, D. P., Eriksen, E., et al.: Eradication of *Haemophilus influenzae* type b disease in Southern California. Arch. Pediatr. Adolesc. Med. *148*:51–56, 1994.
246. Vadheim, C. M., Greenberg, D. P., Eriksen, E., et al.: Protection provided by *Haemophilus influenzae* type b conjugate vaccines in Los Angeles county: A case-control study. Pediatr. Infect. Dis. J. *13*:274–280, 1994.
247. Vadheim, C. M., Greenberg, D. P., Partridge, S., et al.: Effectiveness and safety of an *Haemophilus influenzae* type b conjugate vaccine (PRP-T) in young infants. Pediatrics *92*:272–279, 1993.
248. van Alphen, L., Eijk, P., Geelen-van den Broek, L., and Dankert, J.: Immunochemical characterization of variable epitopes of outer membrane protein P2 of nontypeable *Haemophilus influenzae*. Infect. Immun. *59*:247–252, 1991.
249. Van Ham, S. M., van Alphen, L., and Mooi, F. R.: Fimbria-mediated adherence and hemagglutination of *Haemophilus influenzae*. J. Infect. Dis. *165*(Suppl. 1):97–99, 1992.
250. van Nguyen, Q., Nguyen, E. A., and Weiner, L. B.: Incidence of invasive bacterial disease in children with fever and petechiae. Pediatrics *74*:77–80, 1984.
251. Wall, R. A., Corrah, P. T., Mabey, D. C. W., and Greenwood, B. M.: The etiology of lobar pneumonia in the Gambia. Bull. World Health Organ. *64*:553–558, 1986.
252. Wallace, R. J., Baker, C. J., Quinones, F. J., et al.: Non-typeable *Haemophilus influenzae* (biotype 4) as a neonatal, maternal, and genital pathogen. Rev. Infect. Dis. *5*:123–136, 1983.
253. Ward, J. I., Brenneman, G., Letson, G. W., and Heyward, W. L.: The Alaska *H. influenzae* Vaccine Study Group: Limited efficacy of a *Haemophilus influenzae* type b conjugate vaccine in Alaska Native infants. N. Engl. J. Med. *323*:1393–1401, 1990.
254. Ward, J. I., Fraser, D. W., Baraff, L. J., and Plikaytis, B. D.: *H. influenzae* meningitis: A national study of secondary spread in household contacts. N. Engl. J. Med. *301*:122–126, 1979.
255. Ward, J. I., Gorman, G., and Phillips, C.: *Haemophilus influenzae* type b disease in a daycare center: Report of an outbreak. J. Pediatr. *92*: 713–717, 1978.
256. Ward, J. I., Lieberman, J. M., and Cochi, S. L.: *Haemophilus influenzae* vaccines. *In* Plotkin, S. A., and Mortimer, E. A. (eds.): Vaccines. Philadelphia, W. B. Saunders, 1994, pp. 337–386.
257. Ward, J. I., Lum, M. K. W., Hall, D. B., et al.: Invasive *Haemophilus influenzae* type b disease in Alaska: Background epidemiology for a vaccine efficacy trial. J. Infect. Dis. *108*:887–896, 1986.
258. Ward, J. I., Siber, G. I., Scheifele, D. W., et al.: Rapid diagnosis of *Haemophilus influenzae* type b infections by latex particle agglutination and counterimmunoelectrophoresis. J. Pediatr. *93*:37–42, 1978.
259. Weitzman, S., and Aisenberg, A. C.: Fulminant sepsis after the successful treatment of Hodgkin's disease. Am. J. Med. *62*:47–50, 1977.
260. Weller, P. F., Smith, A. L., Smith, D. H., and Anderson, P.: Role of immunity in the clearance of bacteremia due to *H. influenzae*. J. Infect. Dis. *138*:427–436, 1978.
261. Wenger, J. D., Hightower, A. W., Facklam, R. R., et al.: Bacterial meningitis in the United States, 1986: Report of a multistate surveillance study. J. Infect. Dis. *162*:1316–1323, 1990.
262. Wenger, J. D., Pierce, R., Deaver, K. A., et al.: Efficacy of *Haemophilus influenzae* type b polysaccharide–diphtheria toxoid conjugate vaccine in US children aged 18–59 months. Lancet *338*:395–398, 1991.
263. Whisnant, J. K., Mann, D. L., Rogentine, G. N., and Robbins, J. B.: Human cell-surface structures related to *H. influenzae* type b disease. Lancet *2*:895–898, 1971.
264. Wilson, W. R., Karchmer, A. W., Dajani, A. S., et al.: Antibiotic treatment of adults with infective endocarditis due to streptococci, enterococci, staphylococci, and HACEK microorganisms. J. A. M. A. *274*:1706–1713, 1995.
265. Winkelstein, J. A., and Moxon, E. R.: The role of complement in the host's defense against *Haemophilus influenzae*. J. Infect. Dis. *165*(Suppl. 1):62–65, 1992.
266. Winslow, C. E., Broadhurst, J., Buchanan, R. E., et al.: The families and genera of the bacteria: Final report of the Committee of the Society of American Bacteriologists on characterization and classification of bacterial types. J. Bacteriol. *5*:191–229, 1920.
267. Wolf, W. J.: Echocardiographic features of a purulent pericardial peel. Am. Heart J. *111*:990–992, 1986.
268. Wotton, K. A., Stiver, H. G., and Hildes, J. A.: Meningitis in the central Arctic: A 4-year experience. Can. Med. Assoc. J. *124*:887–890, 1981.
269. Zwahlen, A., Winkelstein, J. A., and Moxon, E. R.: Surface determinants of *Haemophilus influenzae* pathogenicity: Comparative virulence of capsular transformants in normal and complement-depleted rats. J. Infect. Dis. *148*:385–394, 1983.

CHAPTER 140 Other *Haemophilus* Species

STEPHEN J. BARENKAMP

Most serious pediatric infections caused by organisms of the *Haemophilus* genus are caused by *Haemophilus influenzae*. However, other *Haemophilus* spp. also can cause disease occasionally. Additional *Haemophilus* spp. that have been well documented as causes of illness in pediatric and adolescent patients include *Haemophilus aegyptius*, *Haemophilus aphrophilus*, *Haemophilus ducreyi*, and *Haemophilus parainfluenzae*. As discussed later, *H. aegyptius* has been classified as a member of the species *H. influenzae* (*H. influenzae* biogroup aegyptius), but given the unique characteristics of this organism and the distinctive illnesses with which it is associated, it is described in this chapter. Other *Haemophilus* spp., such as *Haemophilus haemolyticus* and *Haemophilus parahaemolyticus*, rarely, if ever, cause illness in the pediatric population and are not discussed here.

Members of the *Haemophilus* genus are gram-negative coccobacillary bacteria that are facultatively anaerobic. They demonstrate optimal growth when they are incubated in a humid atmosphere containing 5 to 10 percent carbon dioxide.[33, 69, 83] Most species have fastidious nutritional requirements and require special media, supplements, or both for optimal growth.[33, 83] X factor (hemin), V factor (nicotinamide adenine dinucleotide), or both are required for in vitro growth.[114] Organisms with the "para-" prefix require V factor only. The specific nutritional requirements of *Haemophilus* isolates are one characteristic used

TABLE 140–1 ■ DIFFERENTIAL CHARACTERISTICS OF *HAEMOPHILUS* SPECIES

Haemophilus Species	Factor Requirement		Hemolysis of Horse Blood	Fermentation of:				Presence of Catalase	CO_2 Enhancement of Growth
	X*	V		Glucose	Sucrose	Lactose	Mannose		
H. influenzae†	+	+	−	+	−	−	−	+	+
H. haemolyticus	+	+	+	+	−	−	−	+	−
H. ducreyi	+	−	−	−	−	−	−	−	−
H. parainfluenzae	−	+	−	+	+	−	+	D	D
H. parahaemolyticus	−	+	+	+	+	−	−	+	−
H. aphrophilus	−	−	−	+	+	+	+	−	+

*As determined by the porphyrin test.
†Includes biogroup aegyptius.
D, differences encountered.

to subclassify these organisms into the different species (Table 140–1).

Haemophilus aphrophilus

BACTERIOLOGY

H. aphrophilus was described first by Khairat[82] in 1940 in association with a fatal case of endocarditis. He suggested the species name *aphrophilus* because the organism required relatively high concentrations of carbon dioxide for isolation on the usual media. In earlier times, a well-known manifestation of carbon dioxide was the formation of bubbles of gas in fermenting wine (i.e., froth, or *aphros*).[20, 82] Although the organism originally was classified as a *Haemophilus* spp. because of the growth requirement for X factor, more recent studies suggest that it can grow independent of this factor.[83, 109, 143] Some authors have suggested that given this X-factor independence, the organism should be placed in another genus,[83, 143] but at present, it remains in the *Haemophilus* genus.

EPIDEMIOLOGY AND PATHOGENESIS

H. aphrophilus is a component of the normal oral flora. Using a selective medium, Kraut and coworkers[86] isolated the organism from gingival scrapings and interdental material of one third of the healthy adults they examined. With respect to disease pathogenesis, investigators have suggested that dental disease or manipulation predisposes to transient bacteremia, which results in seeding of distant tissue sites where localized infection subsequently develops.[20, 64, 107, 109, 128] In addition, several case reports of patients with *H. aphrophilus* disease reported an association between human infection and contact with or bites from dogs and cats.[56, 75, 107, 109, 152] However, a causal relationship has been difficult to confirm, and the human mouth and respiratory tract probably are the portals of entry for most of these infections.

CLINICAL MANIFESTATIONS

H. aphrophilus is a rare cause of infection and disease in pediatric patients, with fewer than 50 cases reported in the literature.[10, 20, 52, 56, 75, 80, 103, 157, 158] Brain abscesses and endocarditis are the pediatric infections reported most commonly with this organism.[20, 52, 56, 75, 103, 109] Other sites of infection in children include the oropharynx,[20] the abdominal cavity,[20, 80] and various superficial soft tissue sites.[109, 157, 158] Infections with *H. aphrophilus* do not appear to be associated with any distinctive clinical features, compared with infection by other organisms at the same sites. However, *H. aphrophilus* infections frequently are associated with underlying conditions predisposing the host to infection, such as congenital heart disease, trauma, and immunosuppression.[20, 54, 56, 73, 103, 109, 116, 157]

TREATMENT

Antimicrobial susceptibility testing has not been well standardized for this organism, and disk-diffusion testing, in particular, has been found to be unreliable.[20, 45, 109, 143] Tube or agar dilution testing generally is considered to be the preferred testing method. Older reports found that *H. aphrophilus* was susceptible uniformly to numerous antibiotics, including chloramphenicol and the aminoglycosides.[20, 109, 143] Susceptibility to penicillins has varied.

Even so, penicillin has been used successfully for treatment of susceptible organisms,[20, 64, 109, 152] at times in combination with aminoglycosides and other antimicrobials. Some reports document the usefulness of ceftriaxone for treatment of infection.[100, 107] Numerous different antibiotics probably can be used to treat *H. aphrophilus* infections successfully. The choice of treatment should be guided by appropriate in vitro susceptibility testing.

Haemophilus ducreyi

BACTERIOLOGY

In 1889, Ducrey[46] originally identified *H. ducreyi* in purulent material recovered from genital ulcers of patients with soft chancre or chancroid. Although unable to culture the organism in vitro, Ducrey[46] was able to establish the specificity of the infectious agent by serial cutaneous inoculations.[104] *H. ducreyi* originally was assigned to the *Haemophilus* genus because of its requirement for hemin (X factor) and a guanosine plus cytosine content within the expected range for *Haemophilus* spp.[2, 150] However, more recent studies, including genetic transformation and DNA hybridization analyses, suggest that *H. ducreyi* is not related to the true haemophili, such as *H. influenzae,* and potentially should be placed in a separate genus.[2, 150]

Significant advances have been made in the characterization of bacterial components that may contribute to disease pathogenesis. Two cytotoxins, a hemolysin and a diffusable cytolethal distending toxin, have been identified, their genes have been cloned, and their potential contributions to disease pathogenesis have been investigated.[5, 38, 111, 112] The lipooligosaccharide of *H. ducreyi* has been characterized in much greater detail, and relevant biosynthetic genes have been cloned and studied.[1, 13, 55, 99, 142] Genes encoding the major outer membrane proteins of the organism have been cloned and the corresponding proteins characterized,[84] and a novel class of pili expressed by *H. ducreyi* has been identified.[30] *H. ducreyi* requires heme for growth, and several of the critical molecules required for heme acquisition and utilization have been identified during the past several years.[48, 49, 140, 145] The knowledge gained from molecular characterization of these important bacterial components should enhance efforts to understand better the pathogenesis of disease.

EPIDEMIOLOGY

Chancroid is a genital ulcerative disease that is found throughout the world. It is reported to be seen frequently in Africa, Asia, and Latin America, where it may be a more common cause of genital ulcer disease than syphilis.[2, 17–19, 104, 150] Although generally considered a relatively uncommon cause of illness in the United States, chancroid continues to be diagnosed, particularly among patients, including adolescents, who present with genital ulcer disease in large urban areas.[22, 68, 72, 101, 102, 133] Furthermore, recent data suggest that chancroid may be more common in the United States than suspected because it can be difficult to diagnose correctly using traditional clinical and laboratory means.[44, 105, 150] Symptomatic disease among patients in the United States has been reported, most commonly among nonwhite heterosexual males.[22, 57, 68, 104] However, symptomatic disease is not restricted to men, and female prostitutes have been implicated as important sources of infection in several of the outbreaks reported in the United States.[22, 68, 104]

H. ducreyi has been the subject of renewed medical and scientific interest since the early 1980s. This interest was sparked by epidemiologic studies, primarily from Africa, demonstrating that the presence of genital ulcer disease (much of which was chancroid) was associated strongly with an increased risk for heterosexual transmission of human immunodeficiency virus (HIV) infection.[17, 76, 87, 88, 105, 117, 153] Mechanisms proposed to explain this enhanced transmission have included an increased shedding of HIV through the ulcers[88, 150] and possibly an increased number of HIV-susceptible cells (e.g., CD4 T lymphocytes) in the genital ulcers of the person being infected.[150]

PATHOGENESIS

Relatively little is known about the pathogenesis of *H. ducreyi* infection, although significant progress has been made during the past few years coincident with the renewed interest in the organism.[150] Several useful in vivo models of *H. ducreyi* infection have been developed. They include a temperature-dependent rabbit model of dermal infection,[118] a primate model of genital chancroid infection in adult pigtailed macaques,[147] and an experimental model of human infection.[6, 7, 15, 16, 113, 138] Numerous putative virulence factors have been identified, and their contributions to the pathogenesis of disease are being investigated using several in vitro and in vivo model systems. Some of the molecules and characteristics being studied include bacterial lipooligosaccharide,[14, 32, 162] pili,[8, 137] the cytolethal distending toxin,[39, 40, 62, 91, 119, 120, 141] a hemolysin,[5, 47, 110, 112, 148, 160, 163] and the ability to adhere specifically to epithelial cells of genital origin.[3, 92] The contribution of these proposed virulence factors to the pathogenesis of natural infection in humans still is being defined. However, strains deficient in expression of several of these factors are known to be attenuated in their ability to cause disease in the experimental model of human infection.[9, 26, 59] Ongoing investigations of *H. ducreyi* undoubtedly will define the virulence mechanisms of the organism more clearly and should enhance efforts to develop protective vaccines.[7, 42, 70]

CLINICAL MANIFESTATIONS

The incubation period of chancroid usually is between 4 and 7 days. It rarely is less than 3 days or more than 10 days.[104, 126, 127] Typically, the first lesion noted is a small, inflammatory papule surrounded by a zone of erythema. Within 2 or 3 days, a pustule forms that soon ruptures, leaving a sharply circumscribed ulcer with ragged undermined edges *without* induration.[104, 127] The base of the ulcer usually has a granular appearance and always is painful. In males, the most common sites of appearance of the ulcers are on the distal prepuce, on the mucosal surface of the prepuce on the frenulum, and in the coronal sulcus. In females, most lesions are at the entrance to the vagina.[104, 127] Painful, tender, inguinal adenopathy is present in as many as 50 percent of patients and usually is unilateral. The involved lymph nodes rapidly may become fluctuant and rupture, with the formation of inguinal ulcers.[104, 127]

The combination of a painful ulcer with tender inguinal adenopathy is suggestive of chancroid and, when accompanied by suppurative inguinal adenopathy, is almost pathognomonic.[35] However, a significant percentage of patients with *H. ducreyi* infection may have ulcers that can be confused with other genital ulcer diseases, such as herpes or syphilis.[61, 104, 127] Furthermore, as many as 10 percent of patients with chancroid may be co-infected with *Treponema pallidum* or herpes simplex virus.[35] Thus, establishing a definitive diagnosis by laboratory means is mandatory if one is to be confident about the diagnosis.

DIAGNOSIS

As noted earlier, diagnosing chancroid on clinical grounds alone is difficult because the clinical presentation often is not classic and many clinicians do not have a great deal of experience with the disease.[35, 150] Definitive diagnosis of chancroid requires isolation of the organism from a genital ulcer or from involved lymph nodes. However, the organism is fastidious and is difficult to isolate, even in the best circumstances.[104] To obtain specimens for culture, a swab should be used to obtain material from the purulent base of an ulcer or a fluctuant inguinal lymph node should be aspirated directly. Gram stain of purulent material may reveal gram-negative rods in the characteristic school-of-fish pattern, but this appearance probably is more characteristic of in vitro propagated organisms.[104] However, even with use of the selective media now recommended for isolation of *H. ducreyi*, the sensitivity of culture is estimated to be no higher than 80 percent.[35]

Given the low sensitivity of culture, alternative non–culture-based diagnostic tests have been evaluated. Early studies examined the utility of diagnosing chancroid serologically with an enzyme-linked immunosorbent assay using either an outer-membrane protein preparation or a lipooligosaccharide preparation of *H. ducreyi*.[4] More recent studies have employed slightly altered antigen preparations and serum preparation techniques meant to improve the sensitivity and specificity of the assay.[36] Although these modifications did lead to improvement in the performance characteristics of the assay, the ability of the modified assay to aid in the diagnosis of acute infection remains limited because many patients do not develop a serum antibody response until several weeks after onset of infection.[36, 149] Recent work has focused on the use of recombinant proteins as test antigens for a serologic test.[50] This latter assay does appear to show promise for seroprevalence studies, but its utility in the diagnosis of acute infection has yet to be demonstrated.

Nucleotide-based diagnostic methods also have been described in recent years.[36, 77, 129, 150] Perhaps most promising are techniques based on the polymerase chain reaction–based techniques. These assays demonstrate high sensitivity and appear to identify numerous patients with chancroid, from whom bacterial cultures for *H. ducreyi* are negative.[36, 150] Multiplex polymerase chain reaction assays that can amplify and subsequently detect DNA from *H. ducreyi*, *T. pallidum*, and herpes simplex virus from genital ulcer specimens simultaneously are undergoing field trials and have shown early promise.[36, 108, 150]

Even if chancroid is diagnosed definitively, patients also should be tested for HIV at the time of diagnosis. In addition, one should remember that as many as 10 percent of patients with chancroid may be co-infected with *T. pallidum* or herpes simplex virus.[35] Appropriate testing for these other pathogens should be considered strongly when a patient presents with any form of genital ulcer disease.

TREATMENT AND PREVENTION

Successful antimicrobial treatment of genital ulcers caused by *H. ducreyi* cures infection, resolves clinical symptoms, and prevents transmission to others. However, in cases of extensive ulcerative disease, scarring may result, despite successful antimicrobial therapy.[35] The Centers for Disease Control and Prevention currently recommend one of four antibiotic regimens for treatment of chancroid in adolescents and adults.[35, 134] These regimens are: (1) azithromycin, 1 g orally in a single dose, (2) ceftriaxone, 250 mg intramuscularly in a single dose, (3) ciprofloxacin, 500 mg orally twice a day for 3 days, or (4) erythromycin base, 500 mg orally four times a day for 7 days.[35, 134] All four regimens generally are effective for treatment of chancroid among patients without HIV infection.[134] A successful response to therapy usually is apparent within 48 to 72 hours, as shown by decreased ulcer tenderness and pain.[126, 134] Complete healing of ulcers may take as long as 28 days but often is achieved in 7 to 14 days.[134] Healing of fluctuant adenopathy is slower than that of the ulcers and may require needle aspiration through adjacent intact skin or incision and drainage to achieve a successful response to therapy.[53, 134]

Patients with HIV infection must be monitored closely because they may require longer courses of antimicrobial agents than the standard regimens just outlined.[35, 134] Treatment failures have been noted with several of these regimens,[25, 134, 151] and some evidence suggests that the patients who are most immunosuppressed are at the greatest risk for failure of standard regimens.[134] Some experts recommend using the erythromycin 7-day regimen for treating all HIV-infected patients because of good experience with this regimen in the HIV-infected population and limited successful experience with the alternative regimens.[134]

Identification of all sexual contacts of infected persons is critical to prevent further spread of *H. ducreyi* disease. The Centers for Disease Control and Prevention recommend that all people who have had sexual contact with a patient with proven *H. ducreyi* infection within the 10 days before onset of the patient's symptoms be examined and treated.[35] Contacts should be examined and treated even in the absence of symptoms.

In the longer term, alternative strategies for control of chancroid should be examined. If feasible, vaccination for prevention of *H. ducreyi* infection would be a worthy goal. Data generated in animal models of infection are somewhat encouraging.[42, 70] Protective immunity to both homologous and heterologous challenge has been reported after immunization of rabbits with cell surface extracts of *H. ducreyi*.[70] More recently, a purified pilus preparation also was reported to induce immunity in that same model.[42] These data suggest that prevention of chancroid by vaccination may be an achievable goal. However, recent data from the experimental human model of infection suggest that development of a protective vaccine for human use may not be straightforward.[7]

Haemophilus influenzae Biogroup Aegyptius (*Haemophilus aegyptius*)

BACTERIOLOGY

H. influenzae biogroup aegyptius (*H. aegyptius*) was described originally by Koch[85] in 1883 in Egyptian patients with conjunctivitis. A more detailed description of the organism and the clinical characteristics of disease were provided 3 years later in the work of Weeks.[155] The Koch-Weeks bacillus has continued to be an important cause of conjunctivitis since these initial reports. Because of several reportedly unique characteristics,[98] the Koch-Weeks bacillus originally was designated as a unique species of the *Haemophilus* genus (*H. aegyptius*) distinct from *H. influenzae*. However, more recent phenotypic and phylogenetic studies, including DNA-relatedness analyses, have raised questions about the validity of this separation.[29, 144] The organism is designated currently as *H. influenzae* biogroup aegyptius, but debate continues in the literature as to the appropriateness of this designation.[94]

This organism has been the subject of intense scientific study since the 1980s as a result of its association with a newly described fulminant and often fatal disease called *Brazilian purpuric fever*.[27, 28] *H. influenzae* biogroup aegyptius was isolated from nine blood cultures and one hemorrhagic cerebrospinal fluid culture from 10 clinically ill children in Serrana, Sao Paulo State, Brazil.[28] The *H. influenzae* biogroup aegyptius strains causing Brazilian purpuric fever initially were thought to be members of a single virulent clone.[29, 144] This clone was characterized by the presence of several unique features, including a 24-MDa plasmid with a characteristic restriction endonuclease pattern,[29] a unique multilocus electrophoretic enzyme typing pattern,[106] one of two rRNA gene restriction fragment-length polymorphisms,[29, 43, 144] a single sodium dodecyl sulfate-polyacrylamide gel electrophoresis profile using whole-cell lysates,[29] specific reactivity with monoclonal antibodies recognizing epitopes unique to Brazilian purpuric fever strains,[93, 144] agglutination with antisera specific for the Brazilian purpuric fever clone,[29] and conservation of certain major outer membrane proteins.[124] Although most strains of *H. influenzae* biogroup aegyptius associated with Brazilian purpuric fever appear to be members of a unique clone, a few strains with the association lack some of the defining characteristics.[144, 146] Furthermore, two cases of Brazilian purpuric fever reported from Australia were associated with strains clearly distinct from the Brazilian purpuric fever clone.[94, 144]

EPIDEMIOLOGY

In the United States, *H. influenzae* biogroup aegyptius has remained an important cause of conjunctivitis, with disease most commonly reported from the southern states.[71] The United States has not experienced any recognized cases of Brazilian purpuric fever. In Brazil, the epidemiology of Brazilian purpuric fever has been defined more clearly during the last several years.[71] The median age of patients with Brazilian purpuric fever is from 2 to 3 years, with an overall range of ages from 3 months to 10 years.[27, 28] Brazilian purpuric fever appears to occur with the onset of warmer temperatures and is less likely to occur during the Brazilian winter.[71] Furthermore, it appears to occur more commonly in small agricultural towns than in larger cities.[27, 28, 71] Case-control studies attempting to identify risk factors for development of disease identified a history of preceding conjunctivitis as being associated strongly with the development of Brazilian purpuric fever[27, 28, 71] (although many of the controls also gave a history of conjunctivitis) and suggested that attendance at a daycare center was an additional risk factor.[28]

PATHOGENESIS

Efforts to identify virulence factors of *H. influenzae* biogroup aegyptius responsible for the fulminant nature of Brazilian purpuric fever have been ongoing since the initial descriptions of the illness. Progress to date has been limited.[34] Brazilian purpuric fever clone strains express numerous novel or unique surface molecules or secreted proteins that theoretically could result in enhanced virulence.[29, 34, 93, 94, 130, 159] Distinctive lipooligosaccharide phenotypes,[34, 130] immunoglobulin A proteases,[34, 94] pili,[122, 123, 159] and secreted proteins[34] for Brazilian purpuric fever strains have been reported. However, none has been shown to have a specific role in bacterial virulence. One study suggested that the risk for acquiring Brazilian purpuric fever correlated with the lack of serum bactericidal activity against the Brazilian purpuric fever clone, but this observation needs further confirmation.[131]

Both in vitro and in vivo models have been developed for further investigating the pathogenesis of Brazilian purpuric fever.[121, 130, 156] In these model systems, strains associated with Brazilian purpuric fever demonstrated increased virulence compared with control strains not associated with Brazilian purpuric fever, but, again, the specific molecular correlates of this increased pathogenicity have yet to be identified clearly.[121, 130] During the next few years, the in vitro and in vivo models likely will prove useful in further defining specific virulence factors of the Brazilian purpuric fever strain.

CLINICAL MANIFESTATIONS

The clinical presentation of Brazilian purpuric fever is distinctive and dramatic.[27, 28, 71] The syndrome initially manifests as a purulent conjunctivitis without distinguishing characteristics. Symptoms of Brazilian purpuric fever typically appear 3 to 15 days later, after the conjunctivitis has resolved. The affected children experience the acute onset of fever, which may be associated with vomiting and abdominal pain. Death frequently ensues within 48 hours after the development of disseminated purpura, vascular collapse, and hypotensive shock. The precise pathophysiologic mechanisms responsible for progression from conjunctivitis caused by the Brazilian purpuric fever clone to full-blown Brazilian purpuric fever are unknown. The overall case-fatality rate since Brazilian purpuric fever first was recognized is estimated to be 70 percent.[71] Children may develop conjunctivitis with the Brazilian purpuric fever clone and, after recovery from the conjunctivitis, have no further problems.[71] The risk factors that predispose only some children to develop Brazilian purpuric fever are not well understood.

TREATMENT

Data from the limited number of Brazilian purpuric fever cases that have been studied suggest that early antimicrobial therapy may improve survival rates.[28] One suggested regimen is high-dose ampicillin and chloramphenicol. The small number of patients treated to date does not permit a comparison of the efficacy of different antibiotic regimens.[28]

Most of the patients who developed Brazilian purpuric fever in the Brazilian studies were treated with topical antimicrobials for conjunctivitis. Nonetheless, they still developed systemic disease,[28] suggesting that local topical therapy is ineffective in eradicating the organism from the host. One study examined the relative efficacy of oral rifampin and topical chloramphenicol in eradicating conjunctival carriage of the Brazilian purpuric fever clone.[115] Although the number of patients who actually carried the Brazilian purpuric fever clone was small, rifampin was shown to be significantly better in eradicating carriage of the Brazilian purpuric fever clone than was topical chloramphenicol.

Haemophilus parainfluenzae

BACTERIOLOGY

H. parainfluenzae was identified first as a species distinct from *H. influenzae* by Rivers in 1922.[125] Both organisms are fastidious, gram-negative coccobacilli, but with in vitro culture, *H. parainfluenzae* can be propagated on nutrient agar plates with supplemental factor V alone (thus the *para* designation), rather than with both X and V factor, which are required by *H. influenzae* isolates (see Table 140–1). Testing for hemolysis on blood-containing media differentiates *H. parainfluenzae* from hemolysis-producing species, such as *H. haemolyticus* and *H. parahaemolyticus*.[33, 83] Recovery of *H. parainfluenzae* organisms from blood cultures is enhanced by routine subculturing of all specimens. The organisms tend to grow as small colonies along the side walls of the blood bottles or in the red blood cell mass, leaving the broth clear.[69] Routine subculturing to supplemented chocolate agar and incubation with supplemental carbon dioxide should allow recovery of any *H. parainfluenzae* organisms that are present.[37, 67, 69]

EPIDEMIOLOGY AND PATHOGENESIS

H. parainfluenzae is found commonly in the oropharyngeal flora of normal children.[66, 90, 96] The organism can be recovered from oropharyngeal cultures of one fourth or more of healthy children. Of children who develop serious invasive disease caused by *H. parainfluenzae*, more than one half give histories of identifiable preceding illnesses, such as upper respiratory tract infection, otitis media, and dental infections,[11, 21, 66, 74] suggesting that local inflammation in the upper respiratory tract may predispose to transient bacteremias with this organism, which allows for seeding of other sites, such as the meninges and the heart valves. No specific virulence factors of the organism have been identified to date.

CLINICAL MANIFESTATIONS

As noted previously with *H. aphrophilus*, *H. parainfluenzae* remains an uncommon cause of infection in pediatric patients. However, an increasing number of cases have been reported since the 1970s.[21] The infection most commonly reported is meningitis.* The clinical courses of the patients described with *H. parainfluenzae* meningitis are not remarkably different from those typical of patients with acute bacterial meningitis caused by other organisms. However, the average age of affected children is 2.2 years,[21] an age significantly greater than that of the typical pediatric patient with bacterial meningitis.

The infection most commonly reported next is endocarditis.[21, 23, 24, 31, 51, 63, 95, 96, 135] *H. parainfluenzae* endocarditis has numerous unique features. The reported cases of pediatric endocarditis usually occur in adolescents and involve girls more commonly than boys.[21] The clinical presentation often is subacute and frequently is not associated with localizing signs on physical examination (i.e., pathologic murmurs), at least initially.[37, 95, 96] Another unique feature of *H. parainfluenzae* endocarditis is the high incidence of major arterial occlusion secondary to release of large emboli from the heart.[21, 37, 63, 95, 139] This high incidence of embolization is thought to be due to the particularly friable nature of the vegetations.[21, 63] Another characteristic feature noted by several authors is the relatively slow and variable response of endocarditis caused by this organism to antimicrobial therapy.[21, 37, 95, 96]

Other *H. parainfluenzae* infections reported in pediatric patients include brain abscesses,[66, 97] septic arthritis,[21] and urinary tract infection.[21]

TREATMENT

H. parainfluenzae usually is susceptible in vitro to multiple antibiotics, including chloramphenicol, aminoglycosides, trimethoprim-sulfamethoxazole, and third-generation cephalosporins.[21, 37, 78, 96] Although in the past most isolates were susceptible to penicillins, more recent studies have documented an increasing incidence of β-lactamase–producing strains resistant to penicillin and ampicillin.[21, 132] For β-lactamase–negative penicillin-susceptible organisms, administration of ampicillin with an aminoglycoside has been recommended for serious *H. parainfluenzae* infections.[37, 69] Individual case reports document successful treatment with a variety of other antimicrobials, including ampicillin alone, cephalosporins, chloramphenicol, and trimethoprim-sulfamethoxazole.[31, 37, 79, 96] At present, pending results of susceptibility testing, a reasonable approach is to initiate therapy for serious *H. parainfluenzae* infections with a third-generation cephalosporin, perhaps in combination with an aminoglycoside.

*See references 11, 12, 41, 58, 60, 65, 66, 74, 81, 89, 97, 136, 154, 161.

REFERENCES

1. Ahmed, H. J., Frisk, A., Mansson, J-E., et al.: Structurally defined epitopes of *Haemophilus ducreyi* lipooligosaccharides recognized by monoclonal antibodies. Infect. Immun. *65*:3151–3158, 1997.
2. Albritton, W. L.: Biology of *Haemophilus ducreyi*. Microbiol. Rev. *53*:377–388, 1989.
3. Alfa, M. J., DeGagne, P., and Hollyer, T.: *Haemophilus ducreyi* adheres to but does not invade cultured human foreskin cells. Infect. Immun. *61*:1735–1742, 1993.
4. Alfa, M. J., Olson, N., DeGagne, P. et al.: Humoral immune response of humans to lipooligosaccharide and outer membrane proteins of *Haemophilus ducreyi*. J. Infect. Dis. *167*:1206–1210, 1993.
5. Alfa, M. J., DeGagne, P., and Totten, P.A.: *Haemophilus ducreyi* hemolysin acts as a contact cytotoxin and damages human foreskin fibroblasts in cell culture. Infect. Immun. *64*:2349–2352, 1996.
6. Al-Tawfiq, J. A., Thornton, A. C., Katz, B. P., et al.: Standardization of the experimental model of *Haemophilus ducreyi* infection in human subjects. J. Infect. Dis. *178*:1684–1687, 1998.
7. Al-Tawfiq, J. A., Palmer, K. L., Chen, C-Y., et al.: Experimental infection of human volunteers with *Haemophilus ducreyi* does not confer protection against subsequent challenge. J. Infect. Dis. *179*:1283–1287, 1999.
8. Al-Tawfiq, J. A., Bauer, M. E., Fortney, K. R., et al.: A pilus-deficient mutant of *Haemophilus ducreyi* is virulent in the human model of experimental infection. J. Infect. Dis. *181*:1176–1179, 2000.
9. Al-Tawfiq, J. A., Fortney, K. R., Katz, B. P., et al.: An isogenic hemoglobin receptor-deficient mutant of *Haemophilus ducreyi* is attenuated in the human model of experimental infection. J. Infect. Dis. *181*:1049–1054, 2000.
10. Arneborn, P., Lindquist, B. L., Sjöberg, L.: Severe pulmonary infection by *Haemophilus aphrophilus* in a non-compromised child. Scand. J. Infect. Dis. *17*:327–329, 1985.
11. Bachman, D. S.: *Hemophilus* meningitis: Comparison of *H. influenzae* and *H. parainfluenzae*. Pediatrics *55*:526–530, 1975.
12. Barnshaw, J. A., and Phillips, C. F.: *Haemophilus parainfluenzae* meningitis in a 4-year-old boy. Pediatrics *45*:856–857, 1970.
13. Bauer, B. A., Lumbley, S. R., and Hansen, E. J.: Characterization of a WaaF (RfaF) homolog expressed by *Haemophilus ducreyi*. Infect. Immun. *67*:899–907, 1999.
14. Bauer, B. A., Stevens, M. K., and Hansen, E. J. Involvement of the *Haemophilus ducreyi gmhA* gene product in lipooligosaccharide expression and virulence. Infect. Immun. *66*:4290–4298, 1998.
15. Bauer, M., and Spinola, S. M.: Localization of *Haemophilus ducreyi* at the pustular stage of disease in the human model of infection. Infect. Immun. *68*:2309–2314, 2000.
16. Bauer, M. E., Goheen, M. P., Townsend, C. A., et al.: *Haemophilus ducreyi* associates with phagocytes, collagen, and fibrin and remains extracellular throughout infection of human volunteers. Infect. Immun. *69*:2549–2557, 2001.
17. Behets, FM-T., Liomba, G., and Lule, G.: Sexually transmitted diseases and human immunodeficiency virus control in Malawi: A field study of genital ulcer disease. J. Infect. Dis. *171*:451–455, 1995.
18. Behets, FM-T., Brathwaite, A. R., Hylton-Kong, T., et al.: Genital ulcers: Etiology, clinical diagnosis, and associated human immunodeficiency virus infection in Kingston, Jamaica. Clin. Infect. Dis. *28*:1086–1090, 1999.
19. Behets, FM-T., Andriamiadana, J., Randrianasolo, D., et al.: Chancroid, primary syphilis, genital herpes, and lymphogranuloma venereum in Antananarivo, Madagascar. J. Infect. Dis. *180*:1382–1385, 1999.
20. Bieger, R. C., Brewer, N. S., and Washington, J. A., II.: *Haemophilus aphrophilus*: A microbiologic and clinical review and report of 42 cases. Medicine (Baltimore) *57*:345–355, 1978.
21. Black, C. T., Kupferschmid, J. P., West, K. W., et al.: *Haemophilus parainfluenzae* infections in children, with the report of a unique case. Rev. Infect. Dis. *10*:342–346, 1988.
22. Blackmore, C. A., Limpakarnjanarat, K., Rigau-Perez, J. G., et al.: An outbreak of chancroid in Orange County, California: Descriptive epidemiology and disease-control measures. J. Infect. Dis. *151*:840–844, 1985.
23. Blair, D. C., Walker, W., Sodeman, T., et al.: Bacterial endocarditis due to *Haemophilus parainfluenzae*. Chest *71*:146–149, 1977.
24. Blair, D. C., and Weiner, L. B.: Prosthetic valve endocarditis due to *Haemophilus parainfluenzae* biotype II. Am. J. Dis. Child. *133*:617–618, 1979.
25. Bogaerts, J., Kestens, L., Tello, W. M., et al.: Failure of treatment for chancroid in Rwanda is not related to human immunodeficiency virus infection: In vitro resistance of *Haemophilus ducreyi* to trimethoprim-sulfamethoxazole. Clin. Infect. Dis. *20*:924–930, 1995.
26. Bong, C. T. H., Throm, R. E., Fortney, K. R., et al.: DsrA-deficient mutant of *Haemophilus ducreyi* is impaired in its ability to infect human volunteers. Infect. Immun. *69*:1488–1491, 2001.

27. Brazilian Purpuric Fever Study Group: Brazilian purpuric fever: Epidemic purpura fulminans associated with antecedent purulent conjunctivitis. Lancet *2*:757–761, 1987.
28. Brazilian Purpuric Fever Study Group: *Haemophilus aegyptius* bacteremia in Brazilian purpuric fever. Lancet *2*:761–763, 1987.
29. Brenner, D. J., Mayer, L. W., Carlone, G. M., et al.: Biochemical, genetic, and epidemiologic characterization of *Haemophilus influenzae* biogroup aegyptius (*Haemophilus aegyptius*) strains associated with Brazilian purpuric fever. J. Clin. Microbiol. *26*:1524–1534, 1988.
30. Brentjens, R. J., Ketterer, M., Apicella, M. A., and Spinola, S. M.: Fine tangled pili expressed by *Haemophilus ducreyi* are a novel class of pili. J. Bacteriol. *178*:808–816, 1996.
31. Calio, A. J., Cusumano, S., Ullman, R. F., et al.: *Haemophilus parainfluenzae* endocarditis. Heart Lung *16*:222–223, 1987.
32. Campagnari, A. A., Wild, L. M., Griffiths, G. E., et al.: Role of lipooligosaccharides in experimental dermal lesions caused by *Haemophilus ducreyi*. Infect. Immun. *59*:2601–2608, 1991.
33. Campos, J. M.: *Haemophilus*. *In* Murray, P. R., Baron, E. J., Pfaller, M. A., et al. (eds.): Manual of Clinical Microbiology. 6th ed. Washington DC, American Society for Microbiology, 1995, pp. 556–565.
34. Carlone, G. M., Gorelkin, L., Gheesling, L. L., et al.: Potential virulence-associated factors in Brazilian purpuric fever. J. Clin. Microbiol. *27*:609–614, 1989.
35. Centers for Disease Control: 1998 Guidelines for treatment of sexually transmitted diseases. M. M. W. R. Morb. Mortal. Wkly. Rep. *47* (No. RR-1):1–116, 1998.
36. Chen, C-Y., Mertz, K. J., Spinola, S. M., et al.: Comparison of enzyme immunoassays for antibodies to *Haemophilus ducreyi* in a community outbreak of chancroid in the United States. J. Infect. Dis. *175*:1390–1395, 1997.
37. Chunn, C. J., Jones, S. R., McCutchan, J. A., et al.: *Haemophilus parainfluenzae* infective endocarditis. Medicine (Baltimore) *56*:99–113, 1977.
38. Cope, L. D., Lumbley, S., Latimer, J. L., et al.: A diffusible cytotoxin of *Haemophilus ducreyi*. Proc. Natl. Acad. Sci. U. S. A. *94*:4056–4061, 1997.
39. Cortes-Bratti, X., Chaves-Olarte, E., Lagergård, T., et al.: The cytolethal distending toxin from the chancroid bacterium *Haemophilus ducreyi* induces cell-cycle arrest in the G2 phase. J. Clin. Invest. *103*:107–115, 1999.
40. Cortes-Bratti, X., Chaves-Olarte, E., Lagergård, T., et al.: Cellular internalization of cytolethal distending toxin from *Haemophilus ducreyi*. Infect. Immun. *68*:6903–6911, 2000.
41. Davis, D. J.: *Haemophilus parainfluenzae*. Pediatr. Infect. Dis. *1*:448–449, 1982.
42. Desjardins, M., Filion, L. G., Robertson, S., et al.: Inducible immunity with a pilus preparation booster vaccination in an animal model of *Haemophilus ducreyi* infection and disease. Infect. Immun. *63*: 2012–2020, 1995.
43. Dewhirst, F. E., Paster, B. J., Olsen, I., et al.: Phylogeny of 54 representative strains of species in the family *Pasteurellaceae* as determined by comparison of 16S rRNA sequences. J. Bacteriol. *174*:2002–2013, 1992.
44. DiCarlo, R. P., and Martin, D. H.: The clinical diagnosis of genital ulcer disease in men. Clin. Infect. Dis. *25*:292–298, 1997.
45. Doern, G. V.: Susceptibility tests of fastidious bacteria. *In* Murray, P. R., Baron, E. J., Pfaller, M. A., et al. (eds.): Manual of Clinical Microbiology. 6th ed. Washington DC, American Society for Microbiology, 1995, pp. 1342–1349.
46. Ducrey, A.: Experimentelle untersuchungen uber den ansteckungsstoff des weichen schankers und uber die bubonen. Monatschr. Prakt. Dermatol. *9*:387, 1889.
47. Dutro, S. M., Wood, G. E., and Totten, P. A.: Prevalence of, antibody response to, and immunity induced by *Haemophilus ducreyi* hemolysin. Infect. Immun. *67*:3317–3328, 1999.
48. Elkins, C., Chen, C. J., and Thomas, C. E.: Characterization of the *hgbA* locus of *Haemophilus ducreyi*. Infect. Immun. *63*:2194–2200, 1995.
49. Elkins, C., Totten, P. A., Olsen, B., and Thomas, C. E.: Role of the *Haemophilus ducreyi* Ton system in internalization of heme from hemoglobin. Infect. Immun. *66*:151–160, 1998.
50. Elkins, C., Yi, K., Olsen, B., et al.: Development of a serological test for *Haemophilus ducreyi* for seroprevalence studies. J. Clin. Microbiol. *38*:1520–1526, 2000.
51. Ellner, J. J., Rosenthal, M. S., Lerner, P. I., et al.: Infective endocarditis caused by slow-growing, fastidious, gram-negative bacteria. Medicine *58*:145–158, 1979.
52. Elster, S. K., Mattes, L. M., Meyers, B. R., et al.: *Haemophilus aphrophilus* endocarditis: Review of 23 cases. Am. J. Cardiol. *35*:72–79, 1975.
53. Ernst, A. A., Marvez-Valls, E., and Martin, D. H. Incision and drainage versus aspiration of fluctuant buboes in the emergency department during an epidemic of chancroid. Sex. Transm. Dis. *22*:217–220, 1995.
54. Farrington, M., Eykyn, S. J., Walker, M., et al.: Vertebral osteomyelitis due to coccobacilli of the HB group. B. M. J. *287*:1658–1660, 1983.
55. Filiatrault, M. J., Gibson, B. W., Schilling, B., et al.: Construction and characterization of *Haemophilus ducreyi* lipooligosaccharide (LOS) mutants defective in expression of heptosyltransferase III and β1, 4-glucosyltransferase: Identification of LOS glycoforms containing lactosamine repeats. Infect. Immun. *68*:3352–3361, 2000.
56. Fischbein, C. A., Beckett, K. M., and Rosenthal, A.: *Haemophilus aphrophilus* brain abscess associated with congenital heart disease. J. Pediatr. *83*:631–633, 1973.
57. Flood, J. M., Sarafian, S. K., Bolan, G. A., et al.: Multistrain outbreak of chancroid in San Francisco. 1989–1991. J. Infect. Dis. *167*:1106–1111, 1993.
58. Florman, A. L.: An acute febrile illness with rash and leucopenia due to *Haemophilus parainfluenzae*. J. Pediatr. *22*:202–204, 1943.
59. Fortney, K. R., Young, R. S., Bauer, M. E., et al.: Expression of peptidoglycan-associated lipoprotein is required for virulence in the human model of *Haemophilus ducreyi* infection. Infect. Immun. *68*:6441–6448, 2000.
60. Frazier, J. P., Cleary, T. G., and Pickering, L. K.: Meningitis due to *Haemophilus parainfluenzae*: Report of three cases and review of the literature. Pediatr. Infect. Dis. *1*:117–119, 1982.
61. Gaisin, A., and Heaton, C. L.: Chancroid: Alias the soft chancre. Int. J. Dermatol. *14*:188–197, 1975.
62. Gelfanova, V., Hansen, E. J., and Spinola, S. M.: Cytolethal distending toxin of *Haemophilus ducreyi* induces apoptotic death of Jurkat T cells. Infect. Immun. *67*:6394–6402, 1999.
63. Geraci, J. E., Wilkowske, C. J., Wilson, W. R., et al.: *Haemophilus* endocarditis: Report of 14 patients. Mayo Clin. Proc. *52*:209–215, 1977.
64. Gribble, M. J., and Hunter, T.: *Haemophilus aphrophilus* vertebral osteomyelitis: A case report and literature review. Diagn. Microbiol. Infect. Dis. *8*:189–191, 1987.
65. Gullekson, E. H., and Dumoff, M.: *Haemophilus parainfluenzae* meningitis in a newborn. J. A. M. A. *198*:1221, 1966.
66. Hable, K. A., Logan, G. B., and Washington, J. A., II: Three *Hemophilus* species: Pathogenic activity. Am. J. Dis. Child. *121*:35–37, 1971.
67. Hamed, K. A., Dormitzer, P. R., Su, C. K., et al.: *Haemophilus parainfluenzae* endocarditis: Application of a molecular approach for identification of pathogenic bacterial species. Clin. Infect. Dis. *19*:677–683, 1994.
68. Hammond, G. W., Slutchuk, M., Scatiff, J., et al.: Epidemiologic, clinical, laboratory and therapeutic features of an urban outbreak of chancroid in North America. Rev. Infect. Dis. *2*:867–879, 1980.
69. Hand, W. L.: *Haemophilus* species (including chancroid). *In* Mandell, G. L., Bennett, J. E., Dolin, R. (eds.): Mandell, Douglas, and Bennett's Principles and Practice of Infectious Diseases. 5th ed. Philadelphia, Churchill Livingstone, 2000, pp. 2378–2383.
70. Hansen, E. J., Lumbley, S. R., Richardson, J. A., et al.: Induction of protective immunity to *Haemophilus ducreyi* in the temperature-dependent rabbit model of experimental chancroid. J. Immunol. *152*:184–192, 1994.
71. Harrison, L. H., daSilva, G. A., Pittman, M., et al.: Epidemiology and clinical spectrum of Brazilian purpuric fever. J. Clin. Microbiol. *27*:599–604, 1989.
72. Haydock, A. K., Martin, D. H., Morse, S. A., et al.: Molecular characterization of *Haemophilus ducreyi* strains from Jackson, Mississippi, and New Orleans, Louisiana. J. Infect. Dis. *179*:1423–1432, 1999.
73. Ho, J. L., Soukiasian, S., Oh, W. H., et al.: *Haemophilus aphrophilus* osteomyelitis. Am. J. Med. *76*:159, 1984.
74. Holt, R. N., Taylor, C. D., Schneider, H. J., et al.: Three cases of *Hemophilus parainfluenzae* meningitis. Clin. Pediatr. *13*:666–668, 1974.
75. Isom, J. B., Gordy, P. D., Selner, J. C., et al: Brain abscess due to *Haemophilus aphrophilus*. N. Engl. J. Med. *271*:1059, 1964.
76. Jessamine, P. G., and Ronald, A. R.: Chancroid and the role of genital ulcer disease in the spread of human retrovirus. Med. Clin. North Am. *74*:1417–1431, 1990.
77. Johnson, S. R., Martin, D. H., Cammarata, C., et al.: Alterations in sample preparation increase sensitivity of PCR assay for diagnosis of chancroid. J. Clin. Microbiol. *33*:1036–1038, 1995.
78. Jorgensen, J. H., Howell, A. W., and Maher, L. A.: Antimicrobial susceptibility testing of less commonly isolated *Haemophilus* species using *Haemophilus* test medium. J. Clin. Microbiol. *28*:985–988, 1990.
79. Julander, I., Lindberg, A. A., and Svanbom, M.: *Haemophilus parainfluenzae:* An uncommon cause of septicemia and endocarditis. Scand. J. Infect. Dis. *12*:85–89, 1980.
80. Kaplan, J. M., McCracken, G. H., Jr., and Nelson, J. D.: Infections in children caused by the HB group of bacteria. J. Pediatr. *82*:398–403, 1978.
81. Kaufman, S. R., Hambly, F., Dyke, J. W., et al.: *Haemophilus parainfluenzae* meningitis: Report of two cases. Clin. Pediatr. *13*:661–663, 1974.
82. Khairat, O.: Endocarditis due to a new species of *Haemophilus*. J. Pathol. Bacteriol. *50*:497–505, 1940.
83. Kilian, M.: A taxonomic study of the genus *Haemophilus* with the proposal of a new species. J. Gen. Microbiol. *193*:9–62, 1976.
84. Klesney-Tait, J., Hiltke, T. J., Maciver, I., et al.: The major outer membrane protein of *Haemophilus ducreyi* consists of two OmpA homologs. J. Bacteriol. *179*:1764–1773, 1997.
85. Koch, R.: Bericht uber die thatigkeit der Deutschen Cholerakommission in Aegypten und Ostindien. Wein. Med. Wochenschr. *33*:1548, 1883.
86. Kraut, M. S., Attebery, H. R., Finegold, S. M., et al.: Detection of *Haemophilus aphrophilus* in the human oral flora with a selective medium. J. Infect. Dis. *126*:189–192, 1972.

87. Kreiss, J. K., Koech, D., Plummer, F. A., et al.: AIDS virus infections in Nairobi prostitutes: Spread of the epidemic to East Africa. N. Engl. J. Med. *314*:414–418, 1986.
88. Kreiss, J. K., Coombs, R., Plummer, F., et al.: Isolation of human immunodeficiency virus from genital ulcers in Nairobi prostitutes. J. Infect. Dis. *160*:380–384, 1989.
89. Krishnaswami, R., Schwartz, J., and Boodish, W.: Pathogenicity of *H. parainfluenza*. Pediatrics *50*:498–499, 1972.
90. Kuklinska, D., and Kilian, M.: Relative proportions of *Haemophilus* species in the throat of healthy children and adults. Eur. J. Clin. Microbiol. *3*:249–252, 1984.
91. Lagergard, T., and Purven, M.: Neutralizing antibodies to *Haemophilus ducreyi* cytotoxin. Infect. Immun. *61*:1589–1592, 1993.
92. Lammel, C. J., Dekker, N. P., Palefsky, J., et al.: In vitro model of *Haemophilus ducreyi* adherence to and entry into eukaryotic cells of genital origin. J. Infect. Dis. *167*:642–650, 1993.
93. Lesse, A. J., Gheesling, L. L., Bittner, W. E., et al.: Stable, conserved outer membrane epitope of strains of *Haemophilus influenzae* biogroup aegyptius associated with Brazilian purpuric fever. Infect. Immun. *60*:1351–1357, 1992.
94. Lomholt, H., and Kilian, M.: Distinct antigenic and genetic properties of the immunoglobulin A1 protease produced by *Haemophilus influenzae* biogroup aegyptius associated with Brazilian purpuric fever in Brazil. Infect. Immun. *63*:4389–4394, 1995.
95. Lutwick, L. I., Gradon, J. D., Chapnick, E. K., et al.: *Haemophilus parainfluenzae* endocarditis treated with vegetectomy and complicated by late, fatal splenic rupture. Pediatr. Infect. Dis. J. *10*:778–781, 1991.
96. Lynn, J. D., Kane, J. G., and Parker, R. H.: *Haemophilus parainfluenzae* endocarditis: A review of forty cases. Medicine *56*:115–128, 1977.
97. Maller, R., Ånséhn, S., and Frydén, A.: *Haemophilus parainfluenzae* infection of the central nervous system: A report on two infants. Scand. J. Infect. Dis. *9*:241–242, 1977.
98. Mazloum, H. A., Kilian, M., Mohamed, Z. M., et al.: Differentiation of *Haemophilus aegyptius* and *Haemophilus influenzae*. Acta Pathol. Microbiol. Immunol. Scand. *90*:109–112, 1982.
99. Melaugh, W., Campagnari, A. A., and Gibson, B. W.: The lipooligosaccharides of *Haemophilus ducreyi* are highly sialylated. J. Bacteriol. *178*:564–570, 1996.
100. Merino, D., Saavedra, J., Pujol, E., et al.: *Haemophilus aphrophilus* as a rare cause of arthritis. Clin. Infect. Dis. *19*:320–322, 1994.
101. Mertz, K. J., Weiss, J. B., Webb, R. M., et al.: An investigation of genital ulcers in Jackson, Mississippi, with use of a multiplex polymerase chain reaction assay: High prevalence of chancroid and human immunodeficiency virus infection. J. Infect. Dis. *178*:1060–1066, 1998.
102. Mertz, K. J., Trees, D., Levine, W. C., et al.: Etiology of genital ulcers and prevalence of human immunodeficiency virus. J. Infect. Dis. *178*:1795–1798, 1998.
103. Mesko, Z. G., Bauza, J., and Vinas, C.: Bacterial endocarditis due to *Haemophilus aphrophilus* with cerebral embolism. J. Pediatr. *89*:1031–1032, 1976.
104. Morse, S. A.: Chancroid and *Haemophilus ducreyi*. Clin. Microbiol. Rev. *2*:137–157, 1989.
105. Morse, S. A., Trees, D. L., Htun, Y., et al.: Comparison of clinical diagnosis and standard laboratory and molecular methods for the diagnosis of genital ulcer disease in Lesotho: Association with human immunodeficiency virus infection. J. Infect. Dis. *175*:583–589, 1997.
106. Musser, J. M., and Selander, R. K.: Brazilian purpuric fever: Evolutionary genetic relationships of the case clone of *Haemophilus influenzae* biogroup aegyptius to encapsulated strains of *Haemophilus influenzae*. J. Infect. Dis. *161*:130–133, 1990.
107. Nahass, R. G., Cook, S., and Weinstein, M. P.: Vertebral osteomyelitis due to *Haemophilus aphrophilus*: Treatment with ceftriaxone. J. Infect. Dis. *159*:811–812, 1989.
108. Orle, K. A., Gates, C. A., Martin, D. H., et al.: Simultaneous PCR detection of *Haemophilus ducreyi*, *Treponema pallidum*, and herpes simplex virus types 1 and 2 from genital ulcers. J. Clin. Microbiol. *34*:49–54, 1996.
109. Page, M. I., and King, E. O.: Infection due to *Actinobacillus actinomycetemcomitans* and *Haemophilus aphrophilus*. N. Engl. J. Med. *275*:181–188, 1966.
110. Palmer, K. L., Grass, S., and Munson, R. S., Jr.: Identification of a hemolytic activity elaborated by *Haemophilus ducreyi*. Infect. Immun. *62*:3041–3043, 1994.
111. Palmer, K. L., Goldman, W. E., and Munson, R. S., Jr.: An isogenic haemolysin-deficient mutant of *Haemophilus ducreyi* lacks the ability to produce cytopathic effects on human foreskin fibroblasts. Mol. Microbiol. *21*:13–19, 1996.
112. Palmer, K. L., Thornton, A. C., Fortney, K. R., et al.: Evaluation of an isogenic hemolysin-deficient mutant in the human model of *Haemophilus ducreyi* infection. J. Infect. Dis. *178*:191–199, 1998.
113. Palmer, K. L., Schnizlein-Bick, C. T., Orazi, A., et al.: The immune response to *Haemophilus ducreyi* resembles a delayed-type hypersensitivity reaction throughout experimental infection of human subjects. J. Infect. Dis. *178*:1688–1697, 1998.
114. Parker, R. H., and Hoeprich, P. D.: Disk method for rapid identification of *Hemophilus* species. Am. J. Clin. Pathol. *37*:319–327, 1962.
115. Perkins, B. A., Tondella, M. L. C., Bortolotto, I. M., et al.: Comparative efficacy of oral rifampin and topical chloramphenicol in eradicating conjunctival carriage of *Haemophilus influenzae* biogroup aegyptius. Pediatr. Infect. Dis. J. *11*:717–721, 1992.
116. Petty, B. G., Burrow, C. R., Robinson, R. A., et al.: *Haemophilus aphrophilus* meningitis followed by vertebral osteomyelitis and suppurative psoas abscess. Am. J. Med. *78*:159–162, 1985.
117. Plummer, F. A., Simonson, J. N., Cameron, D. W., et al.: Cofactors in male-female sexual transmissions of human immunodeficiency virus type 1. J. Infect. Dis. *163*:233–239, 1991.
118. Purcell, B. K., Richardson, J. A., Radoff, J. D., et al.: A temperature-dependent rabbit model for production of dermal lesions by *Haemophilus ducreyi*. J. Infect. Dis. *164*:359–367, 1991.
119. Purvén, M., and Lagergard, T.: *Haemophilus ducreyi*, a cytotoxin-producing bacterium. Infect. Immun. *60*:1156–1162, 1992.
120. Purvén, M., Frisk, A., Lönnroth, I., et al.: Purification and identification of *Haemophilus ducreyi* cytotoxin by use of a neutralizing monoclonal antibody. Infect. Immun. *65*:3496–3499, 1997.
121. Quinn, F. D., Weyant, R. S., Worley, M. J., et al.: Human microvascular endothelial tissue culture cell model for studying pathogenesis of Brazilian purpuric fever. Infect. Immun. *63*:2317–2322, 1995.
122. Read, T. D., Dowdell, M., Satola, S. W., et al.: Duplication of pilus gene complexes of *Haemophilus influenzae* biogroup aegyptius. J. Bacteriol. *178*:6564–6570, 1996.
123. Read, T. D., Satola, S. W., Opdyke, J. A., et al.: Copy number of pilus gene clusters in *Haemophilus influenzae* and variation in the *hifE* pilin gene. Infect. Immun. *66*:1622–1631, 1998.
124. Reed, R. B., Frost, J. B., Kort, K., et al.: DNA sequence analysis and restriction fragment length polymorphisms of the P1 gene of *Haemophilus influenzae* biogroup aegyptius associated with Brazilian purpuric fever. Infect. Immun. *64*:3666–3672, 1996.
125. Rivers, T. M.: Influenza-like bacilli: Growth of influenza-like bacilli on media containing only an autoclave-labile substance as an accessory food factor. Bull. Johns Hopkins Hosp. *33*:429–431, 1922.
126. Ronald, A. R., and Plummer, F. A.: Chancroid and *Haemophilus ducreyi*. Ann. Intern. Med. *102*:705–707, 1985.
127. Ronald, A. R., and Albritton, W.: Chancroid and *Haemophilus ducreyi*. *In* Holmes, K. K., Sparling, P. F., Mardh, P. A., et al. (eds.): Sexually transmitted diseases. 3rd ed. New York, McGraw-Hill, 1999, pp. 515–523.
128. Root, T. E., Silva, E. A., Edwards, L. D., et al.: *Haemophilus aphrophilus* endocarditis with a probable primary dental focus of infection. Chest *80*:109–110, 1981.
129. Rossau, R., Duhamel, M., James, G., et al.: The development of specific rRNA-derived oligonucleotide probes for *Haemophilus ducreyi*, the causative agent of chancroid. J. Gen. Microbiol. *137*:277–285, 1991.
130. Rubin, L. G., and St Geme, J. W., III: Role of lipooligosaccharide in virulence of the Brazilian purpuric fever clone of *Haemophilus influenzae* biogroup aegyptius for infant rats. Infect. Immun. *61*:650–655, 1993.
131. Rubin, L. G., Peters, V. B., and Ferez, M. C. C.: Bactericidal activity of human sera against a Brazilian purpuric fever (BPF) strain of *Haemophilus influenzae* biogroup aegyptius correlates with age-related occurrence of BPF. J. Infect. Dis. *167*:1262–1264, 1993.
132. Scheifele, D. W., and Fussell, S. J.: Frequency of ampicillin-resistant *Haemophilus parainfluenzae* in children. J. Infect. Dis. *143*:495–498, 1981.
133. Schmid, G. P., Sanders, L. L., Jr., Blount, J. H., et al.: Chancroid in the United States: Re-establishment of an old disease. J. A. M. A. *258*: 3265–3268, 1987.
134. Schmid, G. P.: Treatment of chancroid, 1997. Clin. Infect. Dis. *28*(Suppl. 1): S14–S20, 1999.
135. Simon, M. W., Mitchell, B. L., O'Connor, W. N., et al.: Glomerulonephritis, pulmonary hemorrhage and coagulopathy associated with *Haemophilus parainfluenzae* endocarditis. Pediatr. Infect. Dis. *4*: 183–188, 1985.
136. Smith, W. K., and Berger, H. W.: *Haemophilus parainfluenzae* meningitis: A case in an adult. Mt. Sinai. J. Med. *41*:543–548, 1974.
137. Spinola, S. M., Castellazzo, A., Shero, M., et al.: Characterization of pili expressed by *Haemophilus ducreyi*. Microb. Pathog. *9*:417–426, 1990.
138. Spinola, S. M., Wild, L. M., Apicella, M. A., et al.: Experimental human infection with *Haemophilus ducreyi*. J. Infect. Dis. *169*:1146–1150, 1994.
139. Steckelberg, J. M., Murphy, J. G., Ballard, D., et al.: Emboli in infective endocarditis: The prognostic value of echocardiography. Ann. Intern. Med. *114*:635, 1978.
140. Stevens, M. K., Porcella, S., Klesney-Tait, J., et al.: A hemoglobin-binding outer membrane protein is involved in virulence expression by *Haemophilus ducreyi* in an animal model. Infect. Immun. *64*:1724–1735, 1996.
141. Stevens, M. K., Latimer, J. L., Lumbley, S. R., et al.: Characterization of a *Haemophilus ducreyi* mutant deficient in expression of cytolethal distending toxin. Infect. Immun. *67*:3900–3908, 1999.
142. Sun, S., Schilling, B., Tarantino, L., et al.: Cloning and characterization of the lipooligosaccharide galactosyltransferase II gene of *Haemophilus ducreyi*. J. Bacteriol. *182*:2292–2298, 2000.
143. Sutter, V. L., and Finegold, S. M.: *Haemophilus aphrophilus* infections: Clinical and bacteriologic studies. Ann. N. Y. Acad. Sci. *174*:468–487, 1970.

144. Swaminathan, B., Mayer, L. W., Bibb, W. F., et al.: Microbiology of Brazilian purpuric fever and diagnostic tests. J. Clin. Microbiol. *27*: 605–608, 1989.
145. Thomas, C. E., Olsen, B., and Elkins, C.: Cloning and characterization of *tdhA*, a locus encoding a TonB-dependent heme receptor from *Haemophilus ducreyi*. Infect. Immun. *66*:4254–4262, 1998.
146. Tondella, M. L. C., Quinn, F. D., and Perkins, B. A.: Brazilian purpuric fever caused by *Haemophilus influenzae* biogroup aegyptius strains lacking the 3031 plasmid. J. Infect. Dis. *171*:209–212, 1995.
147. Totten, P. A., Morton, W. R., Knitter, G. H., et al.: A primate model of chancroid. J. Infect. Dis. *169*:1284–1290, 1994.
148. Totten, P. A., Norn, D. V., and Stamm, W. E.: Characterization of the hemolytic activity of *Haemophilus ducreyi*. Infect. Immun. *63*: 4409–4416, 1995.
149. Totten, P. A., Kuypers, J. M., Chen, C-Y., et al.: Etiology of genital ulcer disease in Dakar, Senegal, and comparison of PCR and serologic assays for detection of *Haemophilus ducreyi*. J. Clin. Microbiol. *38*:268–273, 2000.
150. Trees, D. L., and Morse, S. A.: Chancroid and *Haemophilus ducreyi*: An update. Clin. Microbiol. Rev. *8*:357–375, 1995.
151. Tyndall, M., Malisa, M., Plummer, F. A., et al.: Ceftriaxone no longer predictably cures chancroid in Kenya. J. Infect. Dis. *167*:469–471, 1993.
152. Varghese, R., Melo, J. C., Barnum, P., et al.: Endocarditis due to *Haemophilus aphrophilus*: Report of a case with possible transmission from dog to man. Chest *72*:680–682, 1977.
153. Wasserheit, J. N.: Epidemiological synergy: Interrelationships between human immunodeficiency virus infection and other sexually transmitted diseases. Sex. Transm. Dis. *19*:61–77, 1992.
154. Watson, K. C., Grimstone, J., and O'Hare, A. E.: Meningitis due to *Haemophilus parainfluenzae*. J. Infect. *3*:380–384, 1981.
155. Weeks, J. E.: The bacillus of acute conjunctival catarrh, or "pink eye." Arch. Ophthalmol. *15*:441–451, 1886.
156. Weyant, R. S., Quinn, F. D., Utt, E. A., et al.: Human microvascular endothelial cell toxicity caused by Brazilian purpuric fever-associated strains of *Haemophilus influenzae* biogroup aegyptius. J. Infect. Dis. *169*:430–433, 1994.
157. White, C. B., Lampe, R. M., Copeland, R. L., et al.: Soft tissue infection associated with *Haemophilus aphrophilus*. Pediatrics *67*:434–435, 1981.
158. White, D. R., Mukherji, S. K., Mangum, M. E., et al.: Recurrent cervical lymphadenitis caused by *Haemophilus aphrophilus*. Clin. Infect. Dis. *30*:627–629, 2000.
159. Whitney, A. M., and Farley, M. M.: Cloning and sequence analysis of the structural pilin gene of Brazilian purpuric fever-associated *Haemophilus influenzae* biogroup aegyptius. Infect. Immun. *61*:1559–1562, 1993.
160. Wood, G. E., Dutro, S. M., and Totten, P. A.: Target cell range of *Haemophilus ducreyi* hemolysin and its involvement in invasion of human epithelial cells. Infect. Immun. *67*:3740–3749, 1999.
161. Wort, A. J.: *Hemophilus parainfluenzae* meningitis. Can. Med. Assoc. J. *112*:606–607, 1975.
162. Young, R. S., Fortney, K., Haley, J. C., et al.: Expression of sialylated or paragloboside-like lipooligosaccharides is not required for pustule formation by *Haemophilus ducreyi* in human volunteers. Infect. Immun. *67*:6335–6340, 1999.
163. Young, R. S., Fortney, K. R., Gelfanova, V., et al.: Expression of cytolethal distending toxin and hemolysin is not required for pustule formation by *Haemophilus ducreyi* in human volunteers. Infect. Immun. *69*:1938–1942, 2001.

Helicobacter pylori

MARK A. GILGER

"No acid, no ulcer." Such is the dictum of modern medicine regarding peptic ulcer disease.[124] Indeed, peptic ulcers are managed successfully by acid reduction therapy. Unfortunately, the nagging problem with ulcers is their tendency to recur after treatment is completed. Most peptic ulcers are known to have an infectious cause, thus giving a plausible explanation to the chronic, recurrent nature of this disease. The discovery of *Helicobacter pylori* in 1983 by Marshall and Warren[1] as the bacterial cause of peptic ulcer disease has stimulated worldwide interest and has revolutionized the understanding, diagnosis, and treatment of peptic ulcer disease.

Background

The presence of bacteria in the gastric mucosa has been known for more than 100 years. In 1874, Bottcher[15] observed bacteria in the human stomach. Bizzozero[9] described spirochetes in the stomach of dogs in 1893, and his observations were confirmed by Solomon[129] and Kasai and Kobayashi[74] in the dog, cat, rat, and monkey. Muhlens[104] and later Luger and Neuberger[85] reported spiral organisms in ulcerating carcinomas of the stomach in humans. In 1938, Doenges[29] explored the issue of gastric spirochetes and their clinical relevance. He reported a 43 percent prevalence of spiral organisms in the human stomach in an autopsy review of 242 patients without known gastrointestinal disease. Specimen autolysis, however, rendered interpretation of the pathologic significance of the gastric spirochetes impossible. Freedburg and Barron[44] verified the findings of Doenges in 1940 when they identified spirochetes in the stomachs of 37 percent of patients after partial gastric resection for carcinoma or ulcer disease. Work on the clinical significance of gastric spiral bacteria continued until a report in 1954. In an attempt to confirm the findings of spirochetes in the gastric mucosa, Palmer[111] performed an exhaustive review of gastric fundus biopsy specimens from 1000 adult patients, 80 percent of whom were being evaluated for upper gastrointestinal complaints and 20 percent of whom were healthy control volunteers. Palmer noted, "None of the 1180 specimens was found to contain spirochetes or any structure which could reasonably be considered to be of spirochetal nature." He concluded that spirochetes are not part of the human gastric mucosa in health or illness. Palmer, a prominent researcher in gastritis, inadvertently may have curtailed further research into the role of gastric spiral bacteria.

In 1975, Steer,[130] using electron microscopy, noted curved bacteria in stomach biopsy specimens from patients with gastric ulcers. A few years later, Warren,[1] an Australian pathologist, noted the appearance of spiral bacteria overlaying inflamed gastric mucosa. Warren noted that this organism looked like a *Campylobacter*. He and Marshall began a series of culture experiments using *Campylobacter*-specific methods. The story culminates in 1983 and 1984, respectively, with their reports of the successful culture of the curved bacillus.[1, 96] In an attempt to fulfill the remainder of Koch's postulates, Marshall and associates[94] and Morris and Nicholson[103] independently ingested pure culture of

H. pylori, and both developed symptomatic acute gastritis. The organism subsequently was recovered from the gastric mucosa by endoscopy and successfully cultured, thus completing Koch's postulates.

Microbiology and Pathophysiology

H. pylori initially was named *Campylobacter pyloridis* by Marshall and Warren[1] because of its resemblance to *Campylobacter* spp. Later changed to *Campylobacter pylori*, the bacterium later was recognized as not belonging to any known genus. An entirely new genus—*Helicobacter*—was created, with "helico" describing the spiral shape and "pylori" denoting its typical location. *H. pylori* is a spiral-shaped, gram-negative bacteria with four to seven unipolar-sheathed flagella[11, 109] (Fig. 141–1). It is 0.5 μm wide and 3 to 5 μm long and has a smooth surface.[3, 99] Generally S shaped in vivo, it can take on many forms, from U shaped to cocci to rodlike.[99]

H. pylori inhabits a unique ecologic niche: the mucus layer of the gastric submucosa. Several attributes, including adherence, shape, microaerophilism, urease production, and motility, allow adaptation to the acidic gastric environment. Most *H. pylori* bacteria exist free in the mucous layer. Only a low proportion of colonizing *H. pylori* overlays the intercellular, tight junctions of epithelial cells, beneath the mucous layer. Specific adhesion molecules appear to be tropic to gastric mucus-producing cells.[79] This adherence allows the organism to maintain colonization despite the rapid gastric cell turnover.[81] The spiral shape allows the organism to corkscrew through the gastric mucus (see Fig. 141–1). This spiral movement has been demonstrated in vitro using methylcellulose solutions.[81] *H. pylori* is microaerophilic and slow growing in culture media.[11, 109] One-millimeter translucent colonies grow after 5 to 7 days on blood- or serum-supplemented media with a low concentration of oxygen and carbon dioxide at a temperature of 37° C, which promotes optimal growth. This microaerophilism is well suited to the low oxygen levels of the gastric submucosa.[79] *H. pylori* is the most potent urease producer of any known microbe, surrounding itself in a cloud of ammonia.[3, 11, 109] The urea is converted to ammonium and bicarbonate.[10, 51, 67] There is little evidence that the ammonium produced is cytotoxic to gastric epithelium.[66] The bicarbonate creates an alkaline environment in the gastric submucosa. *H. pylori* produces several other enzymes, including a mucinase,[127] lipase,[123] catalase,[84] hemolysin, and cytopathic toxin.[82] The multiple, unipolar flagella (see Fig. 141–1) provides motility that may enable the organism to escape the acid lumen of the stomach[81] and evade the host immune responses.[79]

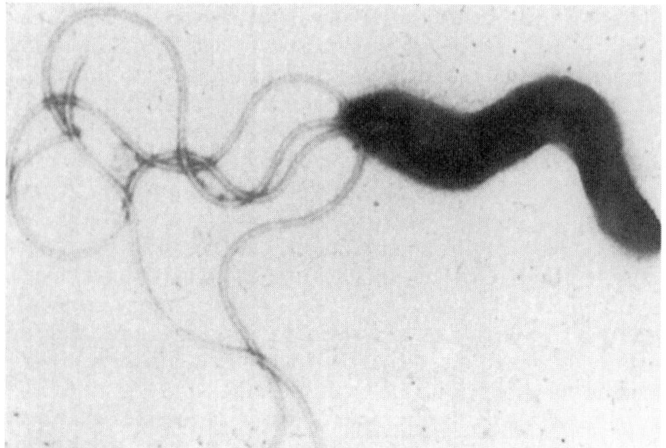

FIGURE 141–1 ■ Electron microscopy of *Helicobacter pylori* demonstrating the multipolar flagella and the typical spiral shape.

H. pylori has been suggested to be more akin to normal gastrointestinal flora because the bacterium and the host can coexist for decades without apparent problems.[57] The host immune response to *H. pylori* is a unique combination of a robust inflammatory response with antibody and a cell-mediated immune response. *H. pylori* infection produces inflammation, although in most cases, the host is asymptomatic.[11, 13] The inflammatory response is characterized by an infiltration of polymorphonuclear leukocytes, monocytes, lymphocytes, and plasma cells into the lamina propria[84] (Fig. 141–2). Despite this significant immune response, it does not clear the organism in most cases.[82] Typically, *H. pylori* produces a chronic infection that persists for decades, possibly for life.[84] This lifelong colonization is accomplished by the same features that allow survival in the gastric mucosa, namely high urease production, flagellar motility, spiral shape, microaerophilism, and adherence.[84]

Spontaneous clearance of *H. pylori* has been confirmed in children.[92, 133, 136] In fact, loss of infection as determined by seroreversion from positive to negative occurs more commonly than once realized.[78] This seroreversion may reflect the weak humoral antibody response in young children and the more frequent use of antibiotics.

Numerous potential virulence factors, such as urease, catalase, cytotoxin, lipopolysaccharide, flagellin, and the Lewis (b) oligosaccharide, have been identified, although whether any of these actually contributes to symptomatic disease is unknown. In adults, the cytotoxin-associated gene *(CagA)* has been linked to the development of more serious gastroduodenal disease. However, although it is commonly found in children with *H. pylori* infection, *CagA* does not appear to be a marker of virulence.[17, 32, 102] The urease of *H. pylori* is a potent antigen, inducing elevations of antiurease immunoglobulin G (IgG) and IgA.[84] Interestingly, the ammonia produced by the urease does not appear to have a significant role in pathogenesis.[58] Catalase, another *H. pylori* enzyme, prevents the formation of oxygen metabolites from hydrogen peroxide in neutrophils.[36] This action may provide an ability to evade host destruction. A vacuolating cytotoxin *(VacA)* has been associated with more serious gastroduodenal disease in adults. It also is found commonly in children,[36] but, like *CagA*, does not appear to be a virulence factor.[17, 32, 102] Flagellin, composed of the two genes *flaA* and *flaB*, gives the bacterium its corkscrew motility.[32, 37] *H. pylori* has a peculiar lipopolysaccharide outer membrane that expresses the Lewis antigens, which appear to mimic surface glycoproteins present in the gastric epithelium. Because these antigens are similar to the Lewis blood group antigens, they may provide yet another mechanism to allow avoidance of the host immune response and to allow colonization.[50] Unlike most gram-negative bacteria, its lipopolysaccharide coat is a significantly less potent inducer of the host complement cascade, some 1000-fold less potent than that of the Enterobacteriaceae.[84] This low biologic activity of *H. pylori*'s outer membrane may be another adaptive mechanism allowing gastric colonization.[11, 12]

Epidemiology

H. pylori may be the most common bacterial infection in humans, with an estimated 1 billion people in the world infected.[83] Transmission appears to be person to person.[80, 98, 132] The mode of transmission, whether fecal-oral, oral-oral, or other, is unknown.[131] *H. pylori* appears to be acquired in

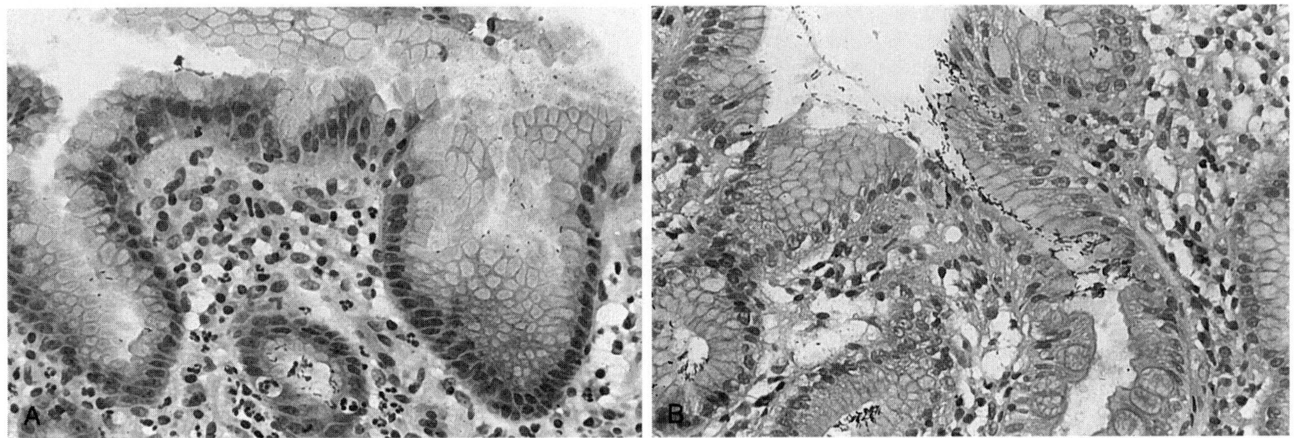

FIGURE 141–2 ■ *A,* High-power light microscopy of *Helicobacter pylori* demonstrating chronic active gastritis with small numbers of *H. pylori* seen on the epithelial surface and the mucus. An aggregate of *H. pylori* organisms is visible within the gastric pit. (Genta stain.) *B,* More *H. pylori* organisms and mild intestinal metaplasia. (*A, B,* Courtesy of Dr. Robert Genta, Baylor College of Medicine, Houston, TX.)

childhood,[25, 83] and humans appear to be a natural reservoir for infection.[60] No proven environmental sources of *H. pylori* infection have been identified, although water,[100] domestic cats,[63] and houseflies[110] have been reported.

Young children (younger than 5 years old) are important in the transmission of *H. pylori* infection, which clusters within families with children.[34, 91, 98, 107, 139] Family clustering emphasizes the role of crowding and personal hygiene in the person-to-person spread of infection. The incidence of *H. pylori* infection is estimated to be between 3 and 10 percent per year in developing countries, in contrast to approximately 1 percent in developed nations.[38] In Nigeria, for example, 58 percent of children younger than 1 year of age were infected, and 91 percent of children older than 10 years of age were infected.[69] Conversely, in the United States, only approximately 20 percent of individuals younger than 30 years of age are infected, compared with 50 percent of those older than 60 years of age.[93] Infection in young children is a rare occurrence in the United States and developed nations.[84] The phenomenon of increasing prevalence with age most likely reflects a cohort effect; that is, the high prevalence in older people simply reflects a higher childhood infection rate.[84] This cohort effect may be explained best by older people's lower standard of living during childhood. Socioeconomic status varies inversely with the prevalence of infection, with low-income individuals having the highest rates of infection.[43] A higher prevalence of infection exists in developing countries versus developed countries[98] (Fig. 141–3), and prevalence of infection varies greatly around the world. Such differences have been attributed to socioeconomic factors, hygiene, and the number of household occupants.[66] *H. pylori* is more prevalent in blacks and Hispanics than in whites in the United States, although this difference likely is only a reflection of socioeconomic status.[108, 128]

Peptic ulcer disease and gastric adenocarcinoma, both known potential consequences of *H. pylori* infection, have been declining in frequency for nearly four decades.[42, 112]

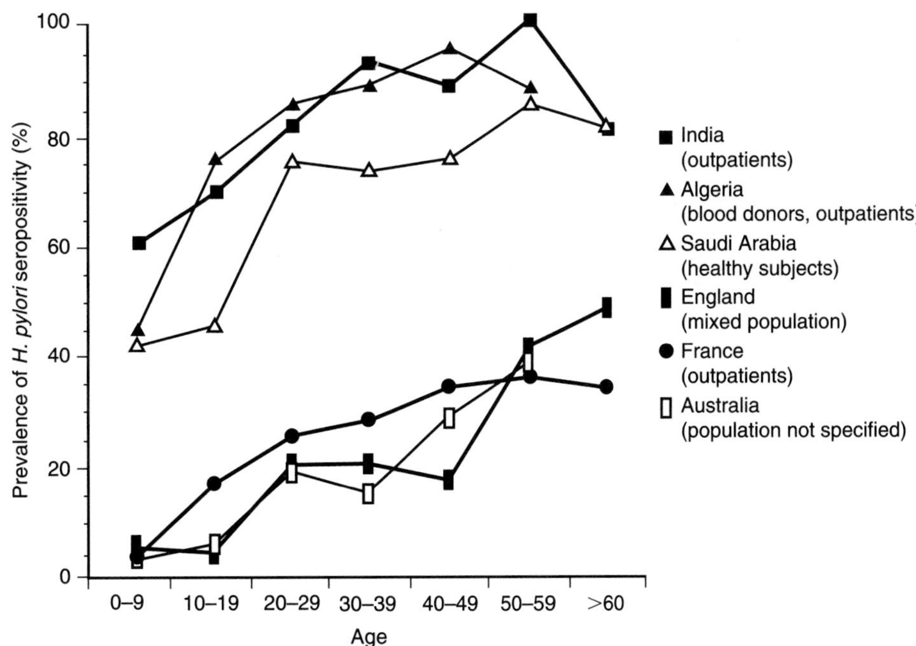

FIGURE 141–3 ■ Seroepidemiology of *Helicobacter pylori* infection demonstrating the difference in disease prevalence between developing and developed countries. (Data from Graham, D. Y., Adam, E., Reddy, G. T., et al.: Seroepidemiology of *Helicobacter pylori* infection in India: Comparison of developing and developed countries. Dig. Dis. Sci. *36*:1084–1088, 1991.)

This decline in *H. pylori*–related disease has occurred without any public health effort being made against the bacterium. This decline may accelerate naturally because of decreasing exposures of children to infected individuals. A mathematical model predicting trends in *H. pylori* infection suggests that transmissibility of *H. pylori* in the United States has decreased to values so low that, should the trend continue, the organism will disappear from the United States without specific intervention.[122] Unfortunately, this process is projected to take more than 100 years.

Clinical Manifestations

H. pylori infection in children has no specific symptoms.[49, 52, 53, 64, 89, 116, 118, 119] The presence of *H. pylori* infection alone in both adults and children usually is asymptomatic.[28, 30, 31, 44, 54, 61, 114] Symptoms such as epigastric pain, nighttime awakening with abdominal pain, hematemesis, and recurrent vomiting are suggestive, but in no way predictive, of infection.[33, 75, 105] These symptoms are typical of peptic ulcer disease, typically duodenal. Such symptoms appear to be present only if *H. pylori* infection is found with a duodenal ulcer.

H. pylori infection does not appear to be a cause of recurrent abdominal pain during childhood.[87, 88] The critical issue is whether *H. pylori* antral gastritis is a source of abdominal pain. The issue remains unresolved. A logical conclusion for the pediatrician would be that a child with active upper gastrointestinal tract complaints in whom *H. pylori* infection is found deserves either treatment for the infection or diagnostic upper endoscopy to determine the presence of ulcer disease. *H. pylori* infection also has been associated with protein-losing enteropathy,[22, 68] iron-deficiency anemia,[20] and insulin-dependent diabetes mellitus.[2, 6] The significance of these associations remains unknown.

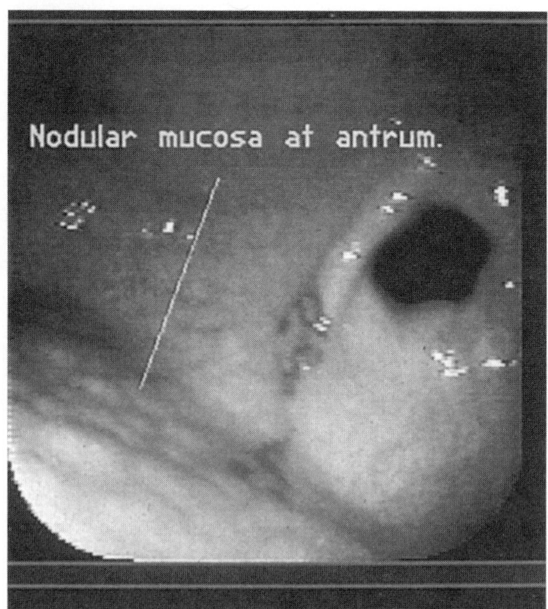

FIGURE 141–4 ■ Endoscopic view of the gastric antrum demonstrating the marked nodularity of the gastric surface.

Diagnosis

The gold standard for diagnosis of *H. pylori* infection is culture of the organism from gastric biopsies or histologic review.[1] Performing upper endoscopy is necessary to obtain such biopsy specimens. In children, upper endoscopy can be helpful, often revealing a distinct nodularity at the antrum (Fig. 141–4), but it also may appear normal. This nodularity is found in two thirds of infected children and also in adults.[16, 65, 66] Histologically, prominent lymphoid follicles are seen. Routine hematoxylin-eosin staining may be adequate but must be performed properly for the bacteria to be seen clearly. Alternative staining techniques, such as acridine orange, silver stains, and the triple stain, improve visualization.[45, 77, 90] The triple, or Genta, stain (Steiner + hematoxylin-eosin + Alcian blue) may offer some distinct advantages because it is significantly more sensitive than is hematoxylin-eosin staining and is particularly useful for the detection of small numbers of bacteria, which often is the case in children (see Fig. 141–2). Although culture and histology require the need for endoscopy, culture may be important. In cases of recurrent *H. pylori* infection in which antibiotic resistance is suspected, culture allows in vitro antibiotic sensitivities to be determined.

Because culture requires gastric biopsy, less invasive methods have been developed (Table 141–1). They include serology, various methods for detecting urease production and salivary antibody, stool antigen, polymerase chain reaction, and urine ammonia production.[70, 76, 115] Serology has been shown to be inaccurate in young children and no longer can be recommended. Urease activity detection by breath testing offers a simple, noninvasive approach to diagnosis with high accuracy. Measurement of salivary IgG antibody, like serology, has shown poor sensitivity in children younger than 5 years of age and is not recommended.[46, 86] Testing stool for the presence of *H. pylori* antigen appears to be another simple, inexpensive, and accurate diagnostic approach.[121, 141] This test detects bacterial antigen in an ongoing infection and, if absent, can predict successful treatment.

H. pylori infection induces a vigorous neutrophilic and lymphocytic response that fails to clear the infection. The humoral immune response produces IgG, IgA, and IgM antibodies that can be detected by serology. Numerous *H. pylori* antigens have been determined using bacterial cell wall sonicates, urease, or membrane extracts as the capture antigen.[23, 26, 27, 41, 125, 135] Most commercial assays have been found to have inappropriate positive and negative cutoff values for use in children.[24, 26] Although simple and widely available, serologic diagnosis does not indicate active infection and has poor sensitivity in young children. As such, it no longer can be recommended in the diagnostic evaluation of *H. pylori* infection.

H. pylori is a vigorous producer of urease. This characteristic has been used to create a variety of tests to detect the presence of urease. The urea breath test uses a labeled carbon of the urea, either radioactive carbon 14 (^{14}C)[7] or a nonradioactive, stable isotope, carbon 13 (^{13}C).[59] Patients fast 4 to 8 hours and then drink the labeled carbon accompanied by a meal to delay gastric emptying; then, the amount of labeled carbon dioxide in the breath is measured. Only those with gastric *H. pylori* present (and thus gastric urease activity to degrade the labeled urea) are identified. Urea breath testing is useful for both the initial diagnosis and determination of successful treatment because the results return rapidly to normal after eradication. The radioactive ^{14}C method does not deserve consideration for use in children, but the stable isotope ^{13}C methodology seems highly suited as a safe, noninvasive test in children. Just as with serology, urea breath testing indicates only the presence or absence of infection and does not indicate active symptoms.

TABLE 141–1 ■ SUMMARY OF METHODS FOR DETECTING *HELICOBACTER PYLORI*

Method	Sensitivity (%)	Specificity (%)	Advantages	Disadvantages
Invasive				
Histology	93–99	95–99	Widely available; detection best with special stains; can evaluate underlying mucosal damage; gold standard	Expensive; at least two biopsies required; observer error; recent antibiotics or proton pump inhibitor use can lead to false-negative results
Culture of biopsy specimens	77–92	100	In vitro antibiotic susceptibility can be determined	Expensive; organism requires special transfer and culture technique; requires up to 1 wk for results; recent antibiotics or proton pump inhibitor use can lead to false-negative results
Rapid urease test CLOtest hpFast PylorTek	89–98	93–98	Rapid results; easy to perform; less expensive than other invasive techniques	Formalin, simethicone, local anesthetic spray, recent antibiotics, bismuth, or proton pump inhibitor use can lead to false-negative results; poor technique or handling will affect results
Noninvasive				
Urea breath test ^{13}C ^{14}C	90–100	89–100	Inexpensive, represents entire mucosa (not subject to biopsy sampling bias)	Antibiotics or proton pump inhibitor use can lead to false-negative results; presence of ulcer disease not determined; can be difficult to collect in children younger than 2 yr of age
Serology (ELISA) HM-CAP Pylori.STAT Rapid serology FlexSure QuikVue	44–99	89–95	Inexpensive; good for screening or epidemiologic studies in older children but not for diagnosis	Possible cross-reactivity with similar bacteria; remains positive for a variable period after successful treatment; not accurate in children younger than 6 yr of age; currently available rapid office-based tests require serum
Stool antigen testing (HpSA)	85–94	97.7	Inexpensive, more accurate than serology; may become test of choice in children	Stool must be collected
Saliva	71–93	82–92	Easy to collect; inexpensive	Low sensitivity, especially in children younger than 2 yr of age

ELISA, enzyme-linked immunosorbent assay.
Data from Graham, D.Y.: *Helicobacter* Today. Altrincham, Cheshire, United Kingdom, Norris Communications, 1995, p. 5; Yen-Hsuan, N., Jaw-Town, L., Shui-Feng, H., et al.: Accurate diagnosis of *Helicobacter pylori* infection by stool antigen test and 6 other currently available tests in children. J. Pediatr. *136*:823–827, 2000; Rothenbacher, D., Inceoglu, J., and Brenner, H.: Acquisition of *Helicobacter pylori* infection in a high risk population occurs within the first 2 years of life. J. Pediatr. *136*:744–748; Gilger, M. A., Tolia, V., Johnson, A., *et al.*: The use of an oral fluid immunoglobulin G ELISA for the detection of *Helicobacter pylori* infection in children. Helicobacter (*in Press*); Luzza, F., Oderda, G., Maletta, M., et al.: Salivary immunoglobulin G assay to diagnose *Helicobacter pylori* infection in children. J. Clin. Microbiol. *35*:3358–3360, 1997.

The urease production of *H. pylori* can be measured directly in gastric biopsy specimens using a variety of commercial assays.[97, 103] A portion of gastric biopsy specimen is placed into urea medium, and hydrolysis of urea leads to a color change in the media from tan to pink. False-negative results have been noted in children because of low numbers of organisms.[35] Such testing is useful for a rapid diagnosis during endoscopy but requires gastric biopsy. Urease activity also can be detected by measuring another nonradioactive, stable isotope, ammonium, in the urine after oral ingestion.[73] This noninvasive test has not proved useful in children.

Treatment

Cure of *H. pylori* infection associated with peptic ulcer disease in both children and adults significantly reduces the likelihood of recurrence of ulceration.[72, 95, 117, 142] Such evidence supports a radical change in the treatment of peptic ulcer disease from the standard acid suppression therapy to antibiotic cure of *H. pylori* infection.[97]

H. pylori infection is difficult to cure. Successful treatment usually requires two or more antibiotics,[138, 140] usually administered with an acid inhibitory agent. Confirmation of successful treatment has been defined as absence of detectable organisms by tissue biopsy or urea breath test at least 1 month after completion of treatment.[8] Because tissue biopsy is invasive, urea breath testing appears to be an excellent method for determining successful treatment. Stool antigen testing may prove useful in determining successful cure, but this approach remains unproved. Serologic tests are not useful for detection of cure because of the prolonged elevation of titers, which remain elevated for 6 months to 1 year or longer after treatment.

Children with proven *H. pylori* peptic ulcer disease and gastric mucosa-associated lymphoid tissue lymphoma require treatment. Children with proven *H. pylori* gastritis that is symptomatic also deserve treatment. Currently, no other clinical scenarios of *H. pylori* infection are suggested to be treated. In particular, asymptomatic colonization, which is by far the most common type of *H. pylori* infection in both children and adults, does not require treatment by current standards. Until the natural history of untreated

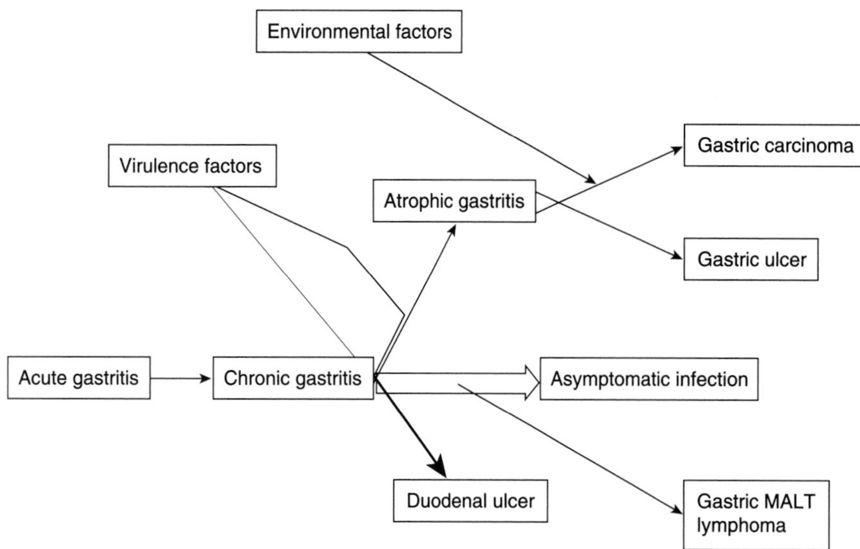

FIGURE 141–5 ■ A proposed timeline of the natural history of *Helicobacter pylori* infection. Infection begins with acute gastritis, then progresses to a variety of potential clinical scenarios. Asymptomatic infection is by far the most common clinical entity, followed by duodenal ulcer and the others. (Adapted from Graham, D. Y., and Gilger, M. A.: Treatment of *Helicobacter pylori* infection in children. Curr. Pharmaceut. Des. *6*:370–384, 2000.)

H. pylori infection in children becomes clearer, the clinician will be faced with such clinical conundrums.

Children with recurrent abdominal pain represent a particular quandary for the pediatrician. Some studies of recurrent abdominal pain in children have found that *H. pylori* infection may be a significant cause.[48, 106, 120, 132, 137] Other studies have found the opposite. Consensus conferences in Europe and Canada have argued that no compelling evidence exists to demonstrate a link between *H. pylori* infection and recurrent abdominal pain.[32, 126] As such, treatment of *H. pylori* infection in children with recurrent abdominal pain is not recommended.[32, 126]

A growing body of evidence indicates that the acquisition of *H. pylori* infection in childhood is a risk factor for the development of gastric cancers, such as adenocarcinoma and lymphoma[71, 134] (Fig. 141–5). Indeed, treatment of gastric lymphoma using antibiotics directed at *H. pylori* has resulted in tumor regression.[4, 140] Some researchers argue that this factor alone provides cause for the treatment of all children infected with *H. pylori*. Despite such provocative data and because most children with *H. pylori* infection have no clinical symptoms, no current rationale for treatment of all children exists.

In children, the most effective anti-*Helicobacter* treatment currently available is triple therapy, which includes two antibiotics and a proton pump inhibitor[32, 47, 62, 93, 126] (Table 141–2). In adults, amoxicillin often is replaced by tetracycline. This therapy is given for 2 weeks, although regimens ranging from 7 to 28 days all have been reported as being successful.[93] Efficacy rates of 85 to 95 percent have been reported for this combination. In patients allergic to penicillin, amoxicillin may be replaced with clarithromycin. Metronidazole, to which the *H. pylori* organism is highly sensitive, is a mainstay of the triple therapy. Many areas outside the United States have high rates of metronidazole resistance because of overusage for other infections.[40] Unsuccessful triple therapy, even in the United States, may be due in part to such metronidazole resistance but usually is related to incomplete therapy. No single antibiotic agent given alone is effective therapy against *H. pylori*.[19, 95, 113, 117]

TABLE 141–2 ■ SUGGESTED TREATMENT REGIMENS FOR *HELICOBACTER PYLORI* INFECTION IN CHILDREN

Medications	Dosage	Duration
Amoxicillin Clarithromycin Proton pump inhibitor* (i.e., omeprazole)	50 mg/kg/day bid (max, 1 g bid) 15 mg/kg/day bid (max, 500 mg) 1 mg/kg/day bid	2 wk
Amoxicillin Metronidazole Proton pump inhibitor* (i.e., omeprazole)	50 mg/kg/day bid (max, 1 g bid) 20 mg/kg/day bid (max, 500 mg bid) 1 mg/kg/day	2 wk
Clarithromycin Metronidazole Proton pump inhibitor* (i.e., omeprazole)	15 mg/kg/day bid (max, 500 mg bid) 20 mg/kg/day bid (max, 500 mg bid) 1 mg/kg/day (max, 20 mg bid)	2 wk
Amoxicillin Metronidazole Bismuth subsalicylate†	50 mg/kg/day bid (max, 1 g bid) 20 mg/kg/day bid (max, 500 mg bid) 15 mL (17.5 mg/mL) qid	2 wk
Amoxicillin Tetracycline‡ Proton pump inhibitor (i.e., omeprazole)	50 mg/kg/day bid (max, 1 g bid) 50 mg/kg/day bid (max, 1 g bid) 1 mg/kg/day	2 wk

*Comparable proton pump inhibitors, such as lansoperazole and rabeprazole, can be substituted at appropriate doses.
†Bismuth will produce black stools and has the potential complication of salicylate toxicity. Salicylates also pose the risk of Reye syndrome.
‡Tetracycline is not recommended in children younger than 8 years old.
From Gilger, M. A.: Treatment of *Helicobacter pylori* infection in children. Curr. Pharmaceut. Dis. *6*:370–384, 2000.

Extensive study continues to determine the optimal duration and regimen for the treatment of *H. pylori*, but, to date, triple therapy remains the accepted standard.

When cure of infection has been obtained, the long-term rates of reinfection are as low as 1 percent per year in developed countries but much higher in developing nations.[14, 113] However, reinfection may be more likely to occur in families, especially when small children are the first infected.[5] No conclusive evidence exists, however, to recommend routine treatment of the entire family.[106]

Vaccination against *H. pylori* infection is difficult because the natural immune response fails to clear the organism in most cases. Work in a mouse model has shown that oral immunization with a sonicate of *Helicobacter fetus* plus the adjuvant cholera toxin results in protection against an oral challenge.[18] Human immunization has been partially successful using an oral urease and *Escherichia coli* heat-labile enterotoxin.[101] Because heat-labile *E. coli* is not a suitable human adjuvant, this approach is not a cure. It does suggest that an effective vaccine is possible, albeit not for a long time.

Future Directions

The discovery and confirmation that *H. pylori* causes peptic ulcers has caused a dramatic reappraisal of many previous notions about ulcer disease. Although the dictum "no acid, no ulcer" still holds, many other previous considerations, such as genetic predisposition, must be re-examined. Figure 141–5 demonstrates a proposed *H. pylori* timeline. It emphasizes the acquisition of an acute infection, most likely in childhood; maintenance of an asymptomatic chronic gastritis; and the rare progression to ulcer, atrophic gastritis, and potentially gastric carcinoma and lymphoma. Future research in children will be directed toward the epidemiology of infection and vaccinology because children are a natural reservoir of infection and have the potential for developing serious long-term sequelae of *H. pylori* infection.

REFERENCES

1. Anonymous: Unidentified curved bacilli on gastric epithelium in active chronic gastritis. Lancet *1*:1273–1275, 1993.
2. Arslan, D., Kendirci, M., Kurtoglu, S., and Kula, M.: *Helicobacter pylori* infection in children with insulin dependent diabetes mellitus. J. Pediatr. Endocrinol. Metab. *5*:553–556, 2000.
3. Atonescu, C. G., and Marshall, B. J.: *Helicobacter pylori*: A potentially curable form of peptic ulcer disease. Gastroenterol. J. Club *2*:3–9, 1990.
4. Ashorn, P., Lahde, P. L., Ruuska, T., et al.: Gastric lymphoma in an 11 Y/O boy: A case report. Med. Pediatr. Oncol. *22*:66–67, 1994.
5. Bamford, K. B., Bickley, J., and Collins, J. S.: *Helicobacter pylori*: Comparison of DNA fingerprints provides evidence for intrafamilial infection. Gut *34*:1348–1350, 1993.
6. Begue, R. E., Mirza, A., Comrton, T., et al.: Helicobacter pylori infection and insulin requirement among children with type 1 diabetes mellitus. Pediatrics *103*:e83, 1999.
7. Bell, G. D., Weil, J., Garrison, G., et al.: ^{14}C-urea breath analysis: A noninvasive test for *Campylobacter pylori* in the stomach. Lancet *1*:1367–1368, 1987.
8. Bell, G. D.: Anti-*Helicobacter pylori* therapy: Clearance, elimination, or eradication? Lancet *337*:310–311, 1991.
9. Bizzozero, G.: Über die schlauchformigen drusen des magen darmkanals und die bezienhungen ihres epithels zu dem ober flachenepithel der schleimhaut. Arch. Mikr. Anast. *42*:82, 1893.
10. Blakeley, R. L., Hinds, J. A., Kunze, H. E., et al.: Jack bean urease (EC 3.5.1.5): Demonstration of a carbamoyl-transfer reaction and inhibitation by hydroxamic acids. Biochemistry *8*:1991–2000, 1969.
11. Blaser, M. J.: Gastric *Campylobacter*-like organisms, gastritis and peptic ulcer disease. Gastroenterology *96*:615–625, 1987.
12. Blaser, M. J.: *Helicobacter pylori*: Microbiology of a "slow" bacterial infection. Trends Microbiol. *1*:255–260, 1993.
13. Blaser, M. J.: The 10 most common questions about *Helicobacter pylori*. Infect. Dis. Clin. Pract. *2*:439–440, 1993.
14. Borody, T. J., Cole, P., and Noonan, S.: Recurrence of duodenal ulcer and *Campylobacter pylori* infection after eradication. Med. J. Aust. *151*: 431–435, 1989.
15. Bottcher: Dorpater Med. Z.: *5*:148, 1874.
16. Bujanover, Y., Konikoff, F., and Baratz, M.: Nodular gastritis and *Helicobacter pylori*. J. Pediatr. Gastroenterol. Nutr. *11*:41–44, 1990.
17. Celik, J., Su, B., Tiren, U., et al.: Virulence and colonization-associated properties of *Helicobacter pylori* infection isolated from children and adolescents. J. Infect. Dis. *177*:247–252, 1998.
18. Chen, M., Lee, A., Haze, S, et al.: Immunization against gastric infection with *Helicobacter* species: First step in the prophylaxis of gastric cancer. Zentralbl. Bakteriol. *290*:155–165, 1993.
19. Chiba, N., Rao, B. V., and Rademaker, J. W.: Meta-analysis of the efficacy of antibiotic therapy in eradicating *Helicobacter pylori*. Am. J. Gastroenterol. *87*:1716–1720, 1992.
20. Choe, Y. H., Kim, S. K., and Hong, Y. C.: *Helicobacter pylori* infection with iron deficiency anemia and subnormal growth at puberty. Arch. Dis. Child *82*:136–140, 2000.
21. Clayton, C., Kleanthous, H., Coates, P. J., et al.: Sensitive detection of *Helicobacter pylori* by using polymerase chain reaction. J. Clin. Microbiol. *30*:192–200, 1992.
22. Cohen, H. A., Shapiro, P., Frydman, M., et al.: Childhood protein-losing enteropathy associated with *Helicobacter pylori* infection. J. Pediatr. Gastroenterol. Nutr. *13*:201–203, 1991.
23. Correa, P., Fox, J., Fontham, E., et al.: *Helicobacter pylori* and gastric carcinoma: Serum antibody prevalence in populations with contrasting cancer risks. Cancer *66*:2569–2574, 1990.
24. Crabtree, J. E., Mahoney, M. J., Taylor, J. D., et al.: Immune responses to *Helicobacter pylori* in children with recurrent abdominal pain. J. Clin. Pathol. *44*:768–773, 1991.
25. Cullen, D. J., Collins, B. J., Christiansen, K. J., et al.: When is *Helicobacter pylori* acquired? Gut *34*:1681–1682, 1993.
26. Czinn, S. J., Carr, H. S., and Speck, W. T.: Diagnosis of gastritis caused by *Helicobacter pylori* in children by means of an ELISA. Rev. Infect. Dis. *13*(Suppl. 8):S700, 1991.
27. De Giacomo, C., Lisato, L., Negrini, R., et al.: Serum antibody response to *Helicobacter pylori* in children: Epidemiologic and clinical applications. J. Pediatr. *119*:205–210, 1991.
28. Demers, B., Karmali, M., and Sherman, P.: Seroprevalence of *Helicobacter pylori* IgG antibodies in Canadian children. Ir. J. Med. Sci. *161*(Suppl. 10):78, 1992.
29. Doenges, J. L.: Spirochetes in the gastric glands of Macacus rhesus and humans without definite history of related disease. Proc. Soc. Exp. Med. Biol. *38*:536–538, 1938.
30. Dooley, C. P., Cohen, H., Fitzgibbons, P. L., et al.: Prevalence of *Helicobacter pylori* infection and histologic gastritis in asymptomatic persons. N. Engl. J. Med. *321*:1562–1566, 1989.
31. Drumm, B.: *Helicobacter pylori* in the pediatric patient. Gastroenterol. Clin. North Am. *22*:169–182, 1991.
32. Drumm, B., Koletzko, S., and Oderda, G.: *Helicobacter pylori* infection in children: A consensus statement. Medical position paper: A report of the European Pediatric Task Force on Helicobacter pylori on a Consensus Conference. J. Pediatr. Gastroenterol. Nutr. *30*:207–213, 2000.
33. Drumm, B., O'Brien, A., Cutz, E., et al.: *Campylobacter pylori*–associated primary gastritis in children. Pediatrics *80*:192–195, 1987.
34. Drumm, B., Perez-Perez, G. L., Blaser, M. J., et al.: Intrafamilial clustering of *Helicobacter pylori* infection. N. Engl. J. Med. *322*:359–363, 1990.
35. Drumm, B., Sherman, P., Cutz, E., et al.: Rapid diagnosis of *Campylobacter pylori* infection. Lancet *1*:149, 1986.
36. Dunn, B. E.: Pathogenic mechanisms of *Helicobacter pylori*: Gastroenterol. Clin. North Am. *22*:43–57, 1993.
37. Eaton, K., Suerbaum, S., Josenhans, C., et al.: Colonization of gnotobiotic piglets by *Helicobacter pylori* deficient in two flagellin genes. Infect. Immun. *64*:2445–2448, 1996.
38. Elitsur, Y., Neace, C. Werthammer, et al.: Prevalence of CagA, VacA antibodies in symptomatic and asymptomatic children with *Helicobacter pylori* infection. Helicobacter *4*:100–105, 1999.
39. Ernst, P. B., and Gold, B. D.: *Helicobacter pylori* in childhood: New insights into the immunopathogenesis of gastric disease and implication for managing infection in children. J. Pediatr. Gastroenterol. Nutr. *28*:462–473, 1999.
40. European Study Group on Antibiotic Susceptibility of *Helicobacter pylori*: Results of a multicentre European survey in 1991 of metronidazole resistance in *Helicobacter pylori*. Eur. J. Clin. Microbiol. Infect. Dis. *11*: 777–781, 1992.
41. Evans, D. J., Evans, D. E., Graham, D. Y., et al.: A sensitive and specific serology test for detection of *Campylobacter pylori* infection. Gastroenterology *96*:1004–1008, 1989.
42. Everhart, J.: Recent developments in the epidemiology of *Helicobacter pylori*. Gastroenterol. Clin. North Am. *29*:559–578, 2000.
43. Fiedorak, S. C., Malaty, H. M., Evans, D. L., et al.: Factors influencing the epidemiology of *Helicobacter pylori* infection in children. Pediatrics *88*:578–582, 1991.
44. Freedburg, A. S., and Barron, L. E.: The presence of spirochetes in human gastric mucosa. Am. J. Dig. Dis. *7*:443–445, 1940.

45. Genta, R. M., Robason, G. O., and Graham, D. Y.: Simultaneous visualization of *Helicobacter pylori* and gastric morphology: A new stain. Hum. Pathol. *25*:221–226, 1994.
46. Gilger, M. A., Tolia, V., Johnson, A., et al.: The use of an oral fluid immunoglobulin G ELISA for the detection of *Helicobacter pylori* infection in children. Helicobacter 7:105–110, 2002.
47. Gilger, M. A.: Treatment of *Helicobacter pylori* infection in children. Curr. Pharmaceut. Des. *6*:370–384, 2000.
48. Glassman, M. S.: *Helicobacter pylori* infection in children: A clinical overview. Clin. Pediatr. *31*(Suppl.):481–487, 1992.
49. Glassman, M., Schwartz, S., Medow, M., et al.: *Campylobacter pylori*-related gastrointestinal disease in children: Incidence and clinical findings. Dig. Dis. Sci. *34*:1504–1510, 1989.
50. Go, M., and Crowe S.: Virulence and pathogenicity of *Helicobacter pylori*. Gastroenterol. Clin. North Am. *29*:649–670, 2000.
51. Gorin, G.: On the mechanism of urease action. Biochim. Biophys. Acta *34*: 268–269, 1959.
52. Gormally, S., and Drumm, B.: *Helicobacter pylori* and gastrointestinal symptoms. Arch. Dis. Child. *70*:165–166, 1994.
53. Gormally, S. M., Prakash, N., Durnin, M. T., et al.: Association of symptoms with *Helicobacter pylori* infection in children. J. Pediatr. *126*: 753–756, 1995.
54. Gormally, S., Sherman, P., and Drumm, B.: Clinical syndromes of *Helicobacter pylori* infection in children. In Goodwin, C. S. (ed.): *Helicobacter pylori*: Biology and Clinical Practice. Boca Raton, FL, CRC Press, 1993, p. 85.
55. Graham, D. Y.: *Helicobacter* today. Attrincham, Cheshire, United Kingdom, Norris Communications, 1995, p. 5.
56. Graham, D. Y., Adam, E., Reddy, G. T., et al.: Seroepidemiology of *Helicobacter pylori* infection in India: Comparison of developing and developed countries. Dig. Dis. Sci. *36*:1084–1088, 1991.
57. Graham, D. Y., Blaser, M. J., and Soll, A. H.: *Helicobacter pylori*: Pathophysiology and epdemiology. Deerfield, IL, Discovery International, 1995, p. 9.
58. Graham, D. Y., Go, M., and Evans, D., Jr.: Urease, gastric ammonium/ammonia and *Helicobacter pylori*: The past, the present, and recommendations for future research. Aliment. Pharmacol. Ther. *6*: 659–669, 1992.
59. Graham, D. Y., Klein, P. D., Evans, D. G., Jr., et al.: *Campylobacter pylori* detected noninvasively by the ^{13}C-urea breath test. Lancet 2:1174–1177, 1987.
60. Graham, D. Y., Klein, P. D., Evans, D. G., Jr., et al.: *Helicobacter pylori*: Epidemiology, relationship to gastric cancer and the role of infants in transmission. Eur. J. Gastroenterol. Hepatol. *4*(Suppl. 1):S1–S6, 1992.
61. Graham, D. Y., Malaty, H. M., Evans, D. G., et al.: Epidemiology of *Helicobacter pylori* in an asymptomatic population in the United States: Effect of age, race and socioeconomic status. Gastroenterology *100*:1495–1501, 1991.
62. Grayson, M. L., Eliopoulos, G. M., Ferraro, M. J., et al.: Effect of varying pH on the susceptibility of *Campylobacter pylori* to antimicrobial agents. Eur. J. Clin. Microbiol. Infect. Dis. *8*:888–889, 1989.
63. Handt, L. K., Fox, J. G., Dewhirst, F. E., et al.: *Helicobacter pylori* isolated from the domestic cat: Public health implications. Infect. Immun. *62*:2367–2374, 1994.
64. Hardikar, W., Davidson, P. M., Cameron, D. J., et al.: *Helicobacter pylori* infection in children. J. Gastroenterol. Hepatol. *6*:450–454, 1991.
65. Hassell, E., and Dimmick, J. E.: Unique features of *Helicobacteri pylori* disease in children. Dig. Dis. Sci. *36*:417–423, 1991.
66. Hazell, S. L.: *H. pylori* in developing countries. *In* Hunt, R. H., and Tygat, G. N. J. (eds.): *Helicobacter pylori*: Basic Mechanisms to Clinical Cure. Dordrecht, Holland, Kluwer Academic Publishers, 1994, pp. 85–94.
67. Hazell, S. L., and Lee, A.: *Campylobacter pyloridis*, urease hydrogen ion back diffusion and gastric ulcers. Lancet *2*:15–17, 1986.
68. Hill, I. D., Sinclair-Smith, C., Lastorica, A. J., et al.: Transient protein enteropathy associated with acute gastritis and *Campylobacter pylori* gastritis. Arch. Dis. Child. *62*:1215–1219, 1987.
69. Holcombe, C., Tsimuri, S., Eldridge, J., et al.: Prevalence of antibody to *Helicobacter pylori* in children in northern Nigeria. Trans. Royal Soc. Trop. Med. Hyg. *87*:19–21, 1994.
70. Husson, M. O., Gottrand, F., Truck, D., et al.: Detection of *H. pylori* in saliva using a monoclonal antibody. Zentralbl. Bakteriol. *279*:466–471, 1993.
71. Isaacson, P. G.: Gastric lymphoma and *Helicobacter pylori*. N. Engl. J. Med. *330*:1310–1311, 1994.
72. Israel, D. M., and Hassall, E.: Treatment and long-term follow up of *Helicobacter pylori*-associated duodenal ulcer disease in children. J. Pediatr. *123*:53–59, 1993.
73. Jicong, W., Guolong, L., Zhentua, Z., et al.: $^{15}NH_4^+$ excretion test: A new method for detection of *Helicobacter pylori* infection. J. Clin. Microbiol. *30*:181–184, 1992.
74. Kasai, K., and Kobayashi, R.: Stomach spirochetes occurring in mammals. J. Parasitol. *6*:1, 1919.
75. Kilbridge, P. M., Dahms, B. B., and Czinn, S. J.: *Campylobacter pylori*–associated gastritis and peptic ulcer disease in children. Am. J. Dis. Child. *142*:1149–1152, 1988.
76. Kradjen, S., Fuska, M., Anferson, J., et al.: Examination of human stomach biopsies, saliva and dental plaque for *Campylobacter pylori*. J. Clin. Microbiol. *27*:1397–1398, 1989.
77. Kradjen, S., and Sherman, P.: *Helicobacter (Campylobacter) pylori* and acid peptic disease. Can. J. Gastroenterol. *4*:237–241, 1990.
78. Kumagai, T., Malaty, H., Graham, D., et al.: Acquisition versus loss of *Helicobacter pylori* infection in Japan: Results from an 8 year birth cohort study. J. Infect. Dis. *178*:717–721, 1997.
79. Lee, A.: The microbiology and epidemiology of *Helicobacter pylori* infection. Scand. J. Gastroenterol. *29*(Suppl. 201):2–6, 1994.
80. Lee, A., Fox, J., and Hazell, S.: Pathology of *Helicobacter pylori*: A perspective. Infect. Immun. *61*:1601–1610, 1993.
81. Lee, A., and Mitchell, H.: Basic bacteriology of *H. pylori: H. pylori* colonization factors. *In* Hunt, R. H., and Tygat, G. N. J. (eds.): *Helicobacter pylori*: Basic Mechanisms to Clinical Cure. Dordrecht, Holland, Kluwer Academic Publishers, 1994, pp. 59–72.
82. Leunk, R. D., Johnson, P. T., David, B. C., et al.: Cytoxic activity in broth-culture filtrates of *Campylobacter pylori*. J. Med. Microbiol. *26*:93–99, 1988.
83. Levine, T. S., and Price, A. B.: *Helicobacter pylori*: Enough to give anyone an ulcer. Br. J. Clin. Pract. *47*:328–332, 1993.
84. Lior, H., and Johnson, W. M.: Catalase, peroxidase and superoxide dismutase activities in *Campylobacter* spp. *In* Pearson, A. D., Skirrow, M. B., Lior, H., et al. (eds.): *Campylobacter* III. London, Health Laboratory Service, 1985, pp. 226–227.
85. Luger, A., and Neuberger, H. Z.: Lin. Med. *92*:54, 1921.
86. Luzza, F., Oderda, G., Maletta, M., et al.: Salivary immunoglobulin G assay to diagnose *Helicobacter pylori* infection in children. J. Clin. Microbiol. *35*:3358–3360, 1997.
87. Macarthur, C.: *Helicobacter pylori* infection and childhood recurrent abdominal pain: Lack of evidence for a cause and effect relationship. Can. J. Gastroenterol. *13*:607–610, 1999.
88. Macarthur, C., Saunders, N., Feldman, W., et al.: *Helicobacter pylori* and childhood recurrent abdominal pain: Community based case-control study. B. M. J. *319*:822–823, 1999.
89. Macarthur, C., Saunders, N., Feldman, W., et al.: *Helicobacter pylori*, gastroduodenal disease and recurrent abdominal pain in children. J. A. M. A. *273*:729–734, 1995.
90. Maden, E., Kemp, J., Westblom, T. U., et al.: Evaluation of staining methodologies for identifying *Campylobacter pylori*. Am. J. Clin. Pathol. *90*:450–453, 1988.
91. Malaty, H., Graham, D., Klein, P., et al.: Transmission of *Helicobacter pylori* infection: Studies in families of healthy individuals. Scand. J. Gastroenterol. *26*:927–932, 1991.
92. Malaty, H. M., Graham, D. Y., Wattigney, W. A., et al.: Natural history of *Helicobacter pylori* infection in childhood: 12-year follow-up cohort in a biracial community. Clin. Infect. Dis. *28*:279–282, 1999.
93. Marshall, B. J.: Epidemiology of *H. pylori* in Western countries. *In*: Hunt, R. H., and Tygat, G. N. J. (eds.): *Helicobacter pylori*: Basic Mechanisms to Clinical Cure. Dordrecht, Holland, Kluwer Academic Publishers, 1994, pp. 75–84.
94. Marshall, B. J., Armstrong, J. A., McGechie, D. B., et al.: Attempt to fulfill Koch's postulate for pyloric *Campylobacter*. Med. J. Aust. *125*:436–444, 1985.
95. Marshall, B. J., Goodwin, C. S., and Warren, J. R.: Prospective double-blind trial of duodenal ulcer relapse after eradication of *Campylobacter pylori*. Lancet *2*:1437–1442, 1988.
96. Marshall, B. J., Royce, H., Annear, D. I., et al.: Original isolation of *Campylobacter pyloridis* from human gastric mucosa. Microbios. *25*:83–88, 1984.
97. McNutty, C. A. M., and Wise, R.: Rapid diagnosis of *Campylobacter*-associated gastritis. Lancet *1*:1443–1444, 1985.
98. Megraud, F.: Epidemiology of *Helicobacter pylori* infection. Gastroenterol. Clin. North Am. *22*:73–88, 1993.
99. Megraud, R., Bonnet, F., Garnier, M., et al.: Characterization of "*Campylobacter pyloridis*" by culture, enzymatic profile, and protein content. J. Clin. Microbiol. *22*:1007–1010, 1985.
100. Mendall, M.: Natural history and mode of transmission. *In*: Northfield, T., Mendall, M., and Goggin, P. (eds.): *Helicobacter pylori* infection: Pathophysiology, Epidemiology and Management. Boston, Kluwer Academic Publishers, 1993, pp. 21–23.
101. Michetti, P., Kreiss, C., Kotloff, K. L., et al.: Oral immunization with urease and *Escherichia coli* heat-labile enterotoxin is safe and immunogenic in *Heliocbacter pylori*-infected adults. Gastroenterology *116*:804–812, 1999.
102. Mitchell, H. M., Hazell, S. L., Bohane, T. D., et al.: The prevalence of antibody to CagA in children is not a marker for specific disease. J. Pediatr. Gastroenterol. Nutr. *28*:71–75, 1999.
103. Morris, A., and Nicholson, G.: Ingestion of *Campylobacter pyloridis* causes gastritis and raised fasting gastric pH. Am. J. Gastroenterol. *32*:192–199, 1987.
104. Muhlens, P. Z.: Vergleichende spirochätenstudien. Z. Hyg. Infekt. *57*:405–416, 1907.
105. Oderda, G., Dell'Olio, D., and Travassoli, K.: *Campylobacter pylori* gastritis and peptic ulcer disease in children. Am. J. Dis. Child. *143*:877, 1989.

106. Oderda, G., Vaira, D., and Ainley, C.: Eighteen-month follow-up of *Helicobacter pylori*-positive children treated with amoxicillin and tinidazaole. Gut *33*:1328–1330, 1992.
107. Oderda, G., Vaira, D., Holton, J., et al.: *Helicobacter pylori* in children with peptic ulcer and their families. Dig. Dis. Sci. *36*:572–576, 1991.
108. Opekun, A. R., Gilger, M. A., Denyes, S. M., et al.: *Helicobacter pylori* infection in children in Texas. J. Pediatr. Gastroenterol. Nutr. *31*: 405–410, 2000.
109. Ormand, J. E., and Talley, N. J.: *Helicobacter pylori*: Controversies and an approach to management. Mayo Clin. Proc. *65*:414–426, 1990.
110. Osato, M. S.: Houseflies are an unlikely reservoir or vector for *Helicobacter pylori* infection. J. Clin. Microbiol. *36*:2786–2788, 1998.
111. Palmer, E. D.: Investigation of the gastric mucosa spirochetes of the human. Gastroenterology *27*:218–220, 1954.
112. Parsonnet, J., Friedman, G. D., and Vandersteen, D. P.: *Helicobacter pylori* infection and the risk of gastric carcinoma. N. Engl. J. Med. *325*: 1127–1131, 1991.
113. Penston, J. G.: *Helicobacter pylori* eradication: Understandable caution but no excuse for inertia. Aliment. Pharmacol. Ther. *8*:369–389, 1994.
114. Peterson, W.: *Helicobacter pylori* and peptic ulcer disease. N. Engl. J. Med. *324*:1043–1048, 1991.
115. Pezzi, J. S., and Shiau, Y. F.: *Helicobacter pylori* and gastrointestinal disease. Am. Fam. Physician *52*:1717–1724, 1995.
116. Prieto, G., Polanco, I., Larrauri, J., et al.: *Helicobacter pylori* infection in children: Clinical endoscopic and histologic correlations. J. Pediatr. Gastroenterol. Nutr. *14*:420–425, 1992.
117. Rauws, E. A. J., and Tygat, G. N. J.: Cure of duodenal ulcer associated with eradication of *Helicobacter pylori*. Lancet *335*:1233–1239, 1990.
118. Raymond, J., Bergeret M., Benhamou, H., et al.: A two-year study of *Helicobacter pylori* in children. J. Clin. Microbiol. *32*:461–463, 1994.
119. Reifen, R., Rasooly, I., Drumm, B., et al.: *Helicobacter pylori* infection in children: Is there specific symptomatology? Dig. Dis. Sci. *39*:1488–1492, 1994.
120. Rosioru, C., Glassman, M. S., Berezin, S. H., et al.: Treatment of *Helicobacter pylori*-associated gastroduodenal disease in children: Clinical evaluation of antisecretory vs. antibacterial therapy. Dig. Dis. Sci. *38*:123–128, 1993.
121. Rothenbacher, D., Inceoglu, J., and Brenner, H.: Acquisition of *Helicobacter pylori*. J. Pediatr. *136*:744–748, 2000.
122. Rupnow, M. F. T., Shacter, R. D., Owens, D. K., et al.: A dynamic transmission model for predicting trends in *Helicobacter pylori* and associated diseases in the United States. Emerg. Infect. Dis. *6*:228–236, 2000.
123. Sarosiek, J., Slomiany, A., Van Horn, K., et al.: Lipolytic activity of *Campylobacter pylori*: Effect of sofalcone. Gastroenterology *94*:A399, 1988.
124. Schwartz, K.: Über penbtrierende magenund jejunal-geschwüre. Beltr. Ucin. Chir. *67*:96–128, 1910.
125. Sherman, P.: Peptic ulcer disease in children: Diagnosis, treatment and the implication of *Helicobacter pylori*. Gastroenterol. Clin. North Am. *23*:707–725, 1994.
126. Sherman, P., Hassall, E., Hunt, R. H., et al.: Canadian Helicobacter Study Group Consensus Conference on the Approach to *Helicobacter pylori* infection in children and adolescents. Can. J. Gastroenterol. *13*:553–559, 1999.
127. Slomiany, B. L., Bliski, J., Sarosiek, J., et al.: *Campylobacter pyloridis* degrades mucin and undermines gastric mucosal integrity. Biochem. Biophys. Res. Commun. *144*:307–314, 1987.
128. Smoak, B. L., Kelley, P. W., and Taylor D. N.: Seroprevalence of *Helicobacter pylori* infections in a cohort of U. S. Army recruits. Am. J. Epidemiol. *139*:513–519, 1994.
129. Solomon, H: Über das spirilllim des saugetiermagens und sein verhalten zu den belegzelen. Centralbl. Bakt. *19*:433, 1896.
130. Steer, H. W.: Ultrastructure of cell migration through the gastric epithelium and its relationship to bacteria. J. Clin. Pathol. *28*:639–646, 1975.
131. Talley, M. J.: Epidemiology of *Helicobacter pylori* infection. NIH Consensus Development Conference on *Helicobacter pylori* in Peptic Ulcer Disease, Bethesda, MD, February 1994, pp. 7–9.
132. Taylor, D., and Blaser, M. J.: The epidemiology of *Helicobacter pylori* infection. Epidemiol. Rev. *13*:42–59, 1991.
133. Thomas, J. E., Dale, A., Harding, M., et al.: *Helicobacter pylori* colonization in early life. Pediatr. Res. *45*:218–223, 1999.
134. Thomas, J. E., Gibson, G. R., Darboe, M. K., et al.: Isolation of *Helicobacter pylori* from human faeces. Lancet *340*:1194–1195, 1992.
135. Thomas, J. D., Whatmore, A. M., Barer, M. R., et al.: Serodiagnosis of *Helicobacter pylori* infection in childhood. J. Clin. Microbiol. *28*:2641–2645, 1990.
136. Tindberg, Y., Blennow, M., and Granstrom, M.: Clinical symptoms and social factors in a cohort of children spontaneously clearing *Helicobacter pylori* infection. Acta Pediatr. *88*:631–635, 1999.
137. Tolia, V.: *Helicobacter pylori* in pediatric nonulcer dyspepsia: Pathogen or commensal. Am. J. Gastroenterol. *90*:865–868, 1995.
138. Tygat, G. N. J.: Treatments that impact favorably upon the eradication of *Helicobacter pylori* and ulcer recurrence. Aliment. Pharmacol. Ther. *8*:359–368, 1994.
139. Vincent, P., Gottand, F., Pernes, P., et al.: High prevalence of *Helicobacter pylori* infection in cohabiting children: Epidemiology of a cluster with special emphasis on molecular typing. Gut *35*:313–316, 1994.
140. Wotherspoon, A. C., Doglioni, E., and Diss, T. C.: Regression of primary low-grade B-cell gastric lymphoma of mucosa-associated lymphoid tissue type after eradication of *Helicobacter pylori*. Lancet *342*: 575–578, 1993.
141. Yen-Hsuan, N., Jaw-Town, L., Shui-Feng, H., et al.: Accurate diagnosis of *Helicobacter pylori* infection by stool antigen test and 6 other currently available tests in children. J. Pediatr. *136*:823–827, 2000.
142. Yeung, C. K., Fu, K. H., and Yeun, K. Y.: *Helicobacter pylori* and associated duodenal ulcer. Arch. Dis. Child. *65*:1212–1215, 1990.

CHAPTER 142 *Kingella* Species

THOMAS L. KUHLS

The genus *Kingella* comprises three species: *Kingella kingae, Kingella denitrificans,* and *Kingella orale*. *K. kingae* is being recognized increasingly as an important cause of invasive infections in children. With improved methods of recovering this fastidious member of the family Neisseriaceae and increasing awareness that the microorganism is not a culture contaminant, *K. kingae* infections are being encountered almost annually by many pediatric infectious disease specialists. The assumption, however, is that most *K. kingae* infections continue to be treated empirically because the organism is difficult to isolate from clinical specimens. *K. denitrificans* rarely causes endocarditis,[4, 8, 25] empyema,[44] and chorioamnionitis[42] in adults, but it has not been reported to cause invasive disease in children. To date, *K. orale* has not been found to cause human infections.[16]

History

During the 1950s and early 1960s, Elizabeth O. King isolated gram-negative bacilli from clinical specimens that had phenotypic and growth characteristics identical to those of *Moraxella* spp., except that the organisms were beta-hemolytic and did not contain catalase.[27] In honor of King, the organism initially was named *Moraxella kingii* in 1968,[27] later renamed *Moraxella kingae* in 1974,[7] and finally reclassified as *Kingella kingae* in 1976.[28] The Centers for Disease Control and Prevention received 78 *K. kingae* isolates from 1953 to 1980, 75 percent of which were recovered from blood, bone, or joint specimens.[22] Most of the isolates were obtained from children younger than 6 years of age. During the 1980s, increasing numbers of children with *K. kingae* infection were reported because of better awareness of the microorganism and better culturing techniques for fastidious agents. Not until the 1990s did the importance of *K. kingae* in causing invasive infections in children become apparent.

Microbiology

Kingella spp. are small (0.6 to 1 μm x 1 to 3 μm), gram-negative rods that may resist Gram decolorization.[49] The organisms can appear coccoid and exist in pairs or short chains. The nonencapsulated bacilli are fastidious aerobes that grow best at 33° C to 37° C in both nutrient and blood agar. At least 4 days of incubation usually is required before *Kingella* can be detected in clinical specimens grown on agar plates, but growth can be detected earlier with newer automated detection culturing systems.[29, 40, 76, 77, 82] Two types of bacterial colonies are found on agar plates: small, smooth, and nearly translucent colonies and larger spreading colonies that appear pitted because of corrosion of the agar surface. The larger colony type, however, usually is not present after the initial colonies have been subcultured, unless the organism is cultured under anaerobic conditions. Biochemical characteristics of the genus *Kingella* include negative reactions for motility, catalase, indole, and urease and a positive reaction for oxidase. All members of the genus are able to produce trace acid from glucose.

K. kingae is the only member of the genus reported to cause invasive infections in children. It can be differentiated from *K. denitrificans, K. orale*, and *Neisseria* spp. by a distinct narrow zone of beta-hemolysis surrounding the colonies. Unlike *K. denitrificans, K. kingae* does not reduce nitrates or nitrites and produces acid from maltose. *K. kingae* can be confused easily with isolates of *Eikenella corrodens* and *Cardiobacterium hominis*, both of which can cause suppurative infections in humans. In addition, *K. kingae* can be misidentified as beta-hemolytic streptococci in Gram-stained specimens when decolorization is incomplete.

Epidemiology

Kingella spp. are a part of the normal oropharyngeal flora of children. In 1969, *K. kingae* was isolated from 1.1 percent of nose and throat swabs obtained from children and adults.[26] In this study, however, the cultures were incubated for only 24 hours and selective media were not used; thus, the prevalence rate of carriage most likely was much higher. More recently, throat and nasopharyngeal specimens from infants and children attending two daycare centers in Israel were cultured on selective media.[78, 81] Specimens were collected every 2 weeks for a duration of 11 months. Monthly prevalence rates of *K. kingae* carriage ranged from 6 to 35 percent, with the highest rates found in the months of December and April. Overall, at least one positive *K. kingae* culture was obtained in 73 percent of the children. The rate of *K. kingae* carriage in this study was similar to the previously reported rates of *Streptococcus pneumoniae* carriage in children of the same age group and much higher than the rates of *Haemophilus influenzae* type b (Hib) carriage seen in young children during the prevaccine era. Unlike these respiratory tract pathogens, *K. kingae* was isolated only from the tonsillar areas of the children and not from the nasopharynx. The investigators did not isolate *K. kingae* from 2- to 4-month-old infants attending a well-care clinic but did isolate the organism from 8 percent of healthy children older than 8 years of age who were scheduled for elective surgical procedures.[78] *K. kingae* isolates from the tonsils of daycare attendees have been shown by immunoblotting, pulsed-field electrophoresis, and ribotyping techniques to be more commonly type-specific than are isolates from unrelated individuals, thus suggesting that the organism is transmitted from person-to-person in the daycare setting.[62]

Osteoarticular *K. kingae* infections occur most commonly in children 6 months to 4 years of age,[21, 35, 77] but *K. kingae* endocarditis occurs in all age groups, including adults.[12, 21, 68, 73] In southern Israel, the annual incidence of *K. kingae* invasive infection has been estimated to be 19.2 cases per 100,000 children 24 months of age or younger and 11.9 cases per 100,000 children 48 months of age or younger.[75] The rate of invasive infection was one quarter that found for invasive Hib infection during a period when children were not receiving conjugated Hib vaccine.[77] In children with suppurative arthritis, *K. kingae* has been isolated more commonly than has Hib from joint aspirates that were cultured directly in BACTEC bottles.[76] In one more recent series of patients in whom suppurative arthritis developed after the advent of the routine use of conjugated Hib vaccine, *K. kingae* was the most common cause of infection in children younger than 36 months.[41]

Invasive *K. kingae* infection occurs as frequently in males as females in some studies,[21, 35] whereas in other series more males have been infected.[1, 41, 75] *K. kingae* infection tends to occur between the months of July and December.[12, 77] Children with *K. kingae* invasive infection often have upper respiratory tract symptoms, dental abnormalities, or evidence of stomatitis before signs of invasive illness develop.[21, 35, 77] Invasive infections have occurred in several children after or during a primary varicella infection or an episode of herpetic gingivostomatitis.[2, 36, 40, 69] In Israel, 61 percent of children with an invasive infection had evidence of a respiratory tract infection or stomatitis at the time of *K. kingae* infection.[75]

Pathogenesis

No studies have defined the mechanisms of pathogenesis of *Kingella* infection. *Kingella* spp. have type 4 pili, which may allow the organisms to adhere to oropharyngeal epithelium.[71] Because *K. kingae* normally colonizes the oropharyngeal mucosa of young children and infection frequently is associated with upper respiratory infections, dental abnormalities, and evidence of stomatitis, damage to the oropharyngeal mucosa by viruses or trauma probably allows *K. kingae* to gain access to the bloodstream. After a period of transient bacteremia, *K. kingae* can seed other tissues and cause focal infection in joints, bones, disk spaces, and heart valves.

Clinical Manifestations

K. kingae causes various infections in children (Table 142–1), with the most common invasive infection being suppurative arthritis.[21, 35, 77] Infants and young children usually have acute mon articular joint swelling and tenderness. To date, no cases of polyarticular infection in children have been reported. No features of the illness distinguish it from other bacterial causes of suppurative arthritis. Patients often have symptoms of an upper respiratory tract illness or stomatitis shortly before or at the time of illness.[2, 40, 53, 75] Eighty-six percent of children have a temperature higher than 38° C at initial evaluation.[35] The knee is the joint affected most commonly.[5, 13, 15, 17, 37, 46] However, *K. kingae* has been reported to cause infection in the hip,[6, 36, 46]

TABLE 142–1 ■ INFECTIONS IN CHILDREN CAUSED BY *KINGELLA KINGAE*

Suppurative arthritis
Osteomyelitis
Spondylodiskitis
Endocarditis
Transient bacteremia
Meningitis
Endophthalmitis
Pulmonary infections
Dactylitis
Subglottic and epiglottic infections
Soft tissue abscesses

ankle,[5, 20, 38, 46] elbow,[5, 15] wrist,[56, 77] sternoclavicular joint,[12, 13] and shoulder.[17, 77] Most children do not have an underlying illness that increases their susceptibility to infection, although *K. kingae* suppurative arthritis has developed in a child undergoing therapy for acute lymphocytic leukemia.[53]

K. kingae osteomyelitis has a more insidious onset than suppurative arthritis does, with most patients having symptoms for at least 1 week before a bone infection is diagnosed. Fever is present in only half of children with *K. kingae* osteomyelitis.[35] The proximal and distal ends of the femur are the most common sites of infection,[14, 20, 21, 61] which often occurs in an epiphysis.[6, 35, 60, 77] *K. kingae* osteomyelitis of the talus[3, 12, 68] and calcaneus[21, 36, 77, 79] also develops in young children, although unlike individuals with the more frequently encountered osteomyelitis associated with puncture wounds, these children have relatively mild symptoms and no history of trauma or penetrating injury. In fact, in a young child with osteomyelitis of the talus or calcaneus and no history of penetrating trauma, *K. kingae* infection should be highly suspected. Less commonly, *K. kingae* causes infection in the tibia,[21, 37, 60] clavicle,[57] ulna,[48] radius,[10] humerus,[5, 77] and sternum.[14, 52] In one child with *K. kingae* osteomyelitis of the neck of the femur, the histopathologic findings of the infected bone resembled those of eosinophilic granuloma.[61]

Numerous cases of *K. kingae* spondylodiskitis in children have been reported.[10, 21, 35–37, 50, 52] These children usually are younger than 5 years of age and have an insidious onset of back stiffness and tenderness, eventually leading to their refusal to walk. Fever was present in two thirds of patients, but temperatures were never higher than 39° C.[41] Various disks from T11-12 to L5-S1 have been involved, although one patient with cervical involvement has been reported.[50]

Less than one half the reported cases of *K. kingae* endocarditis have occurred in children,* and nearly three quarters of the patients have had preexisting structural cardiac defects.[21, 73] The history and physical findings of *K. kingae* endocarditis do not differ from those seen in children with subacute endocarditis of other bacterial etiologies. At least one third of patients with *K. kingae* endocarditis have oral or pharyngeal mucosal alterations before the development of systemic symptoms.[21, 73] Children usually are febrile, and they often have a new or changing heart murmur, splenomegaly, and petechial rash. Patients also can have more acute symptoms, including evidence of septic shock and cardiac failure.[12, 19, 68] *K. kingae* endocarditis occasionally has occurred in immunosuppressed persons,[12, 30, 73] including patients with acquired immunodeficiency syndrome (AIDS).[33, 66]

*See references 6, 18, 19, 21, 23, 30, 37, 38, 59, 68, 69, 72, 73.

Isolation of *K. kingae* from the blood of a febrile infant should not suggest necessarily that the child has endocarditis or an unidentified focal infection. At least 16 children with transient *K. kingae* bacteremia during infancy in whom a focal infection did not develop have been identified.[34, 46, 74, 75] A rash mimicking gonococcemia[56, 59] or meningococcemia rarely develops in bacteremic children.[65] Rarer *K. kingae* infections include meningitis,[47, 54, 65, 67, 70] endophthalmitis,[9, 21] pulmonary infections,[24, 45] dactylitis,[11, 77] subglottic[77] and epiglottic[32] infections, and soft tissue abscesses.[26, 55] A 3-year-old child with vaginitis from which *K. denitrificans* was isolated is the only reported example of other members of the *Kingella* genus causing infection during childhood.[58]

Laboratory Findings and Diagnosis

No characteristic laboratory findings suggest the presence of an invasive *K. kingae* infection. Leukocytosis (>10,000 white blood cells/mm^3) is present in only 60 percent of children with an invasive infection. However, the erythrocyte sedimentation rate almost always is elevated (>20 mm/hr) in children with bone and joint infections.[35] Interestingly, the C-reactive protein level in *K. kingae* osteoarticular infections usually is normal, thus suggesting that this test may be less helpful than is the erythrocyte sedimentation rate in diagnosing this infection.[13, 41] In children with culture-proven suppurative arthritis, the leukocyte count in synovial fluid is variable (10,000 to 161,000 white blood cells/mm^3), but neutrophils usually predominate.[77] Organisms are identified by Gram stain in less than 15 percent of clinical specimens.[21, 35] Plain radiographs demonstrate soft tissue swelling and joint effusions in one half the cases of suppurative arthritis, but lytic lesions or disk space narrowing develops in 95 percent of cases of osteomyelitis or spondylodiskitis.[21] Technetium 99m bone scans may be of assistance in diagnosing *K. kingae* osteomyelitis during the early course of disease, when plain radiographs do not yet demonstrate abnormalities.[21] In children with *K. kingae* endocarditis, large vegetations often are demonstrated by echocardiography, especially in those who have had symptoms for a long time or when evidence of embolization is present.

K. kingae infection is diagnosed by isolating the organism from an appropriate clinical specimen. The organism is isolated from blood in only 5 percent of patients with osteoarticular *K. kingae* infection.[15] The fastidious nature of the organism, the low number of organisms found in clinical specimens, and its slow growth pattern hamper recovery of *K. kingae*. Conventional cultures should be examined at least once per week for 3 weeks to detect the organism. The recovery rate of *K. kingae* can be enhanced greatly if culture material, including purulent synovial fluid, is inoculated directly into BacT/Alert, Isolator, or BACTEC culture systems.[29, 40, 76, 77, 82] In one study, 91 percent of episodes of *K. kingae* suppurative arthritis would have been missed if the specimens had not been cultured in BACTEC bottles.[76] In addition, growth of the organism can be detected within 72 hours with these culturing systems. Once growth is detected, the clinical microbiology laboratory often has difficulty in identifying it as *K. kingae*. Clinicians should suspect that a patient has a *K. kingae* infection when slow-growing, gram-negative rods that display beta-hemolysis are isolated from a normally sterile body site. In the future, broad-spectrum polymerase chain reaction amplification may be useful in diagnosing *K. kingae* infection directly from clinical specimens.[64]

Treatment and Outcome

K. kingae generally is susceptible to β-lactam antibiotics.[12, 31, 51, 80] However, three isolates obtained from children and an isolate from an adult patient with AIDS have contained β-lactamase.[5, 63] Similarly, a *K. denitrificans* isolate obtained from the bone marrow of a 39-year-old patient with AIDS contained β-lactamase.[43] A few isolates have shown in vitro resistance to antistaphylococcal β-lactams without the presence of β-lactamase.[5, 13, 23, 37] Isolates of *K. kingae* have been susceptible universally to second- and third-generation cephalosporins and aminoglycosides.[12, 31, 51] Rarely, resistance to chloramphenicol and trimethoprim-sulfamethoxazole has been reported.[5, 39, 61, 80] Many isolates, however, demonstrate at least partial resistance to erythromycin, clindamycin, and vancomycin.[5, 12, 31, 51, 80]

Children with invasive *K. kingae* infection have been treated with a variety of antibiotics, including penicillin G, ampicillin, cephalosporins, chloramphenicol, trimethoprim-sulfamethoxazole, and the antistaphylococcal β-lactams. Most infections should be treated initially with intravenous ampicillin because this antibiotic is tolerated relatively well and is inexpensive. All *K. kingae* isolates, however, should be checked for β-lactamase activity.

The duration of antibiotic treatment for *K. kingae* osteoarticular infection has ranged from 17 days to 6 months.[35] Oral therapy with an antibiotic such as amoxicillin can be considered when gastrointestinal absorption is demonstrated and compliance can be monitored. Many clinicians use normalization of the erythrocyte sedimentation rate as a guide to the duration of therapy. Surgical drainage of the bone, joint, or disk space usually is not required, except for infections in the hip and shoulder. The prognosis of patients with *K. kingae* osteoarticular infection is excellent; chronic complications from the initial infection have not been reported. However, persistent narrowing of the intervertebral disk space commonly occurs in cases of *K. kingae* spondylodiskitis.[35]

Patients with *K. kingae* endocarditis usually respond rapidly to antibiotic therapy and become afebrile in a few days. High-dose intravenous therapy usually is continued for 4 to 6 weeks. In cases in which prosthetic valves are infected, surgical excision of the valve generally is not needed for cure unless an abscess forms. Unlike osteoarticular infections, the complication rate of *K. kingae* endocarditis is high; cerebral infarction and death have been reported after embolization of vegetations.[12, 38, 39, 73]

REFERENCES

1. Abuamara, S., Louis, J. S., Guyard, M. F., et al.: Les infections osteoarticulaires a *Kingella kingae* chez l'enfant. A propos d'une serie recente de huit cas. Arch. Pediatr. 7:927–932, 2000.
2. Amir, J., and Yagupsky, P.: Invasive *Kingella kingae* infection associated with stomatitis in children. Pediatr. Infect. Dis. J. *17*:757–758, 1998.
3. Benard, M., Jean-Baptiste, A., Nelet, F., et al.: Osteomyelite a *Kingella kingae*. Arch. Fr. Pediatr. *46*:521–524, 1989.
4. Berdah, J., Feder, J. M., Bimet, F., et al.: *Kingella denitrificans* endocarditis on prosthetic aortic valve. Presse Med. *18*:1517–1518, 1989.
5. Birgisson, H., Steingrimsson, O., and Thorolfur, G.: *Kingella kingae* infections in paediatric patients: 5 cases of septic arthritis, osteomyelitis and bacteraemia. Scand. J. Infect. Dis. *29*:495–498, 1997.
6. Bosworth, D. E.: *Kingella (Moraxella) kingae* infections in children. Am. J. Dis. Child. *137*:650–653, 1983.
7. Bovre, K., Henriksen, S. D., and Jonsson, V.: Correction of the specific epithet *kingii* in the combinations *Moraxella kingii* Henriksen and Bovre 1968 and *Pseudomonas kingii* Jonsson 1970 to *kingae*. Int. J. Syst. Bacteriol. *24*:307, 1974.
8. Brown, A. M., Rothburn, M. M., Roberts, C., et al.: Septicaemia with probable endocarditis caused by *Kingella denitrificans*. J. Infect. *15*: 225–228, 1987.
9. Carden, S. M., Colville, D. J., Gonis, G., et al.: *Kingella kingae* endophthalmitis in an infant. Aust. N. Z. J. Ophthalmol. *19*:217–220, 1991.
10. Chanel, C., Tiget, F., Chapvis, P., et al.: Spondylitis and osteomyelitis caused by *Kingella kingae* in children. J. Clin. Microbiol. *25*:2407–2409, 1987.
11. Chiquito, P. E., Elliott, J., and Namnyak, S. S.: *Kingella kingae* dactylitis in an infant. J. Infect. *22*:102–103, 1991.
12. Claesson, B., Falsen, E., and Kjellman, B.: *Kingella kingae* infections: A review and a presentation of data from 10 Swedish cases. Scand. J. Infect. Dis. *17*:233–243, 1985.
13. Clement, J. L., Berard, J., Cahuzac, J. P., et al.: *Kingella kingae* osteoarthritis and osteomyelitis in children. J. Pediatr. Orthop. *8*:59–61, 1988.
14. Davis, J. M., and Peel, M. M.: Osteomyelitis and septic arthritis caused by *Kingella kingae*. J. Clin. Pathol. *35*:219–222, 1982.
15. de Groot, R., Glover, D., Clausen, C., et al.: Bone and joint infections caused by *Kingella kingae*: Six cases and review of the literature. Rev. Infect. Dis. *10*:998–1004, 1988.
16. Dewhirst, F. E., Chen, C.-K. C., Paster, B. J., et al.: Phylogeny of species in the family *Neisseriaceae* isolated from human dental plaque and description of *Kingella orale* sp. nov. Int. J. Syst. Bacteriol. *43*:490–499, 1993.
17. Dodman, T., Robson, J., and Pincus, D.: *Kingella kingae* infections in children. J. Paediatr. Child Health *36*:87–90, 2000.
18. Ferber, B., Bruckheimer, E., Schlesinger, Y., et al.: *Kingella kingae* endocarditis in a child with hair-cartilage hypoplasia. Pediatr. Cardiol. *18*:445–446, 1997.
19. Förstl, H., Ruckdeschel, G., Lang, M., et al.: Septicemia caused by *Kingella kingae*. Eur. J. Clin. Microbiol. *3*:267–269, 1984.
20. Gamble, J. G., and Rinsky, L. A.: *Kingella kingae* infection in healthy children. J. Pediatr. Orthop. *8*:445–449, 1988.
21. Goutzmanis, J. J., Gonis, G., and Gilbert, G. L.: *Kingella kingae* infection in children: Ten cases and a review of the literature. Pediatr. Infect. Dis. J. *10*:677–683, 1991.
22. Graham, D. R., Band, J. D., Thornsberry, C., et al.: Infections caused by *Moraxella, Moraxella urethralis, Moraxella*-like groups M-5 and M-6, and *Kingella kingae* in the United States, 1953–1980. Rev. Infect. Dis. *12*:423–431, 1990.
23. Grant, J. M., Bartolussi, R. A., Roy, D. L., et al.: Prosthetic valve bacterial endocarditis caused by *Kingella kingae*. Can. Med. Assoc. J. *129*:406–410, 1983.
24. Gremillion, D. H., and Crawford, G. E.: Measles pneumonia in young adults: An analysis of 106 cases. Am. J. Med. *71*:539–542, 1981.
25. Hassan, I. J., and Hayek, L.: Endocarditis caused by *Kingella denitrificans*. J. Infect. *27*:291–295, 1993.
26. Henriksen, S. D.: Corroding bacteria from the respiratory tract. Acta Pathol. Microbiol. Scand. *75*:85–90, 1969.
27. Henriksen, S. D., and Bøvre, K.: *Moraxella kingii* sp. nov., a haemolytic, saccharolytic species of the genus *Moraxella*. J. Gen. Microbiol. *51*:377–385, 1968.
28. Henriksen, S. D., and Bøvre, K.: Transfer of *Moraxella kingae* Henriksen and Bøvre to the genus *Kingella* gen. nov. in the family Neisseriaceae. Int. J. Syst. Bacteriol. *26*:447–450, 1976.
29. Host, B., Schumacher, H., Prag, J., et al.: Isolation of *Kingella kingae* from synovial fluids using four commercial blood culture bottles. Eur. J. Clin. Microbiol. Infect. Dis. *19*:608–611, 2000.
30. Huhn, P.: *Moraxella* endocarditis in a patient with systemic lupus erythematosus. W. V. A. Med. J. *129*:344–346, 1978.
31. Jensen, K. T., Schonheyder, H., and Thomsen, V. F.: In-vitro activity of β-lactam and other antimicrobial agents against *Kingella kingae*. J. Antimicrob. Chemother. *33*:635–640, 1994.
32. Kennedy, C. A., and Rosen, H.: *Kingella kingae* bacteremia and adult epiglottitis in a granulocytopenic host. Am. J. Med. *85*:701–702, 1988.
33. Kerlikowske, K., and Chambers, H. F.: *Kingella kingae* endocarditis in a patient with the acquired immunodeficiency syndrome. West. J. Med. *151*:558–560, 1989.
34. Krause, I., and Nimri, R.: *Kingella kingae* occult bacteremia in a toddler. Pediatr. Infect. Dis. J. *15*:557–558, 1996.
35. Lacour, M., Duarte, M., Beutler, A., et al.: Osteoarticular infections due to *Kingella kingae* in children. Eur. J. Pediatr. *150*:612–618, 1991.
36. La Scola, B., Iorgulescu, I., and Bollini, G.: Five cases of *Kingella kingae* skeletal infection in a French hospital. Eur. J. Clin. Microbiol. Infect. Dis. *17*:512–515, 1998.
37. LaSelve, H., Berard, J., Barbe, G., et al.: Osteoarthrites et osteomyelites a *Kingella kingae* chez l'enfant: A propos de 5 observations et revue de la litterature. Pediatrie *4*:294–304, 1986.
38. Le, C. T.: *Kingella (Moraxella) kingae* infections. Am. J. Dis. Child. *137*: 1212–1213, 1983.
39. Lee, W. L., and Dooling, E.: Acute *Kingella kingae* endocarditis with recurrent cerebral emboli in a child with mitral prolapse. Ann. Neurol. *16*:88–89, 1984.
40. Lejbkowicz, F., Cohn, L., Hashman, N., et al.: Recovery of *Kingella kingae* from blood and synovial fluid of two pediatric patients by using the BacT/Alert system. J. Clin. Microbiol. *37*:878, 1999.

41. Lundy, D. W., and Kehl, D. K.: Increasing prevalence of *Kingella kingae* in osteoarticular infections in young children. J. Pediatr. Orthop. *18*: 262–267, 1998.
42. Maccato, M., McLean, W., Riddle, G., et al.: Isolation of *Kingella denitrificans* from amniotic fluid in a woman with chorioamnionitis. J. Reprod. Med. *36*:685–687, 1991.
43. Minamoto, G. Y., and Sordillo, E. M.: *Kingella denitrificans* as a cause of granulomatous disease in a patient with AIDS. Clin. Infect. Dis. *15*:1052–1053, 1992.
44. Molina, R., Baro, T., Torne, J., et al.: Empyema caused by *Kingella denitrificans* and *Peptostreptococcus* spp. in a patient with bronchogenic carcinoma. Eur. Respir. J. *1*:870–871, 1988.
45. Morrison, V. A., and Wagner, K. F.: Clinical manifestations of *Kingella kingae* infections: Case report and review. Rev. Infect. Dis. *11*:776–782, 1989.
46. Moylett, E. H., Rossmann, S. N., Epps, H. R., et al.: Importance of *Kingella kingae* as a pediatric pathogen in the United States. Pediatr. Infect. Dis. J. *19*:263, 2000.
47. Namnyak, S. S., Quinn, R. F. M., and Ferguson, F. D. M.: *Kingella kingae* meningitis in an infant. J. Infect. *23*:104–106, 1991.
48. Noftal, F., Mersal, A., Yaschuk, Y., et al.: Osteomyelitis due to *Kingella kingae* infection. Can. J. Surg. *31*:21–22, 1988.
49. Odum, L., and Frederiksen, W.: Identification and characterization of *Kingella kingae*. Acta Pathol. Microbiol. Scand. *89*:311–315, 1981.
50. Petrus, M., Rance, F., and Clément, J. L.: Cervical spondylodiscitis due to *Kingella kingae:* A case report. Ann. Pediatr. *37*:170–172, 1990.
51. Prère, M. F., Seguy, M., Vezard, Y., et al.: Sensibilité aux antibiotiques de *Kingella kingae*. Pathol. Biol. *34*:604–607, 1986.
52. Raymond, J., Bergeret, M., Bargy, F., et al.: Isolation of two strains of *Kingella kingae* associated with septic arthritis. J. Clin. Microbiol. *24*: 1100–1101, 1986.
53. Redfield, D. C., Overturf, G. D., Ewing, N. D., et al.: Bacteria, arthritis, and skin lesions due to *Kingella kingae*. Arch. Dis. Child. *55*:411, 1980.
54. Reekmans, A., Noppen, M., Naessens, A., et al.: A rare manifestation of *Kingella kingae* infection. Eur. J. Intern. Med. *11*:343–344, 2000.
55. Rolle, U., Schille, R., Hormann, D., et al.: Soft tissue infection caused by *Kingella kingae* in a child. J. Pediatr. Surg. *36*:946–947, 2001.
56. Rosenbaum, J., Lieberman, D. H., and Katz, W. A.: Case report: *Moraxella* infectious arthritis: First report in an adult. Ann. Rheum. Dis. *39*:184–185, 1980.
57. Rotbart, H. A., Gelfand, W. M., and Glode, M. P.: *Kingella kingae* osteomyelitis of the clavicle. J. Pediatr. Orthop. *4*:500–502, 1984.
58. Salvo, S., Mazon, A., Kutz, M., et al.: Vaginitis por *Kingella denitrificans* en una paciente de 3 anos. Enferm. Infecc. Microbiol. Clin. *11*:395–396, 1993.
59. Shanson, D. C., and Gazzard, G. B.: *Kingella kingae* septicaemia with a clinical presentation resembling disseminated gonococcal infection. B. M. J. *289*:730–731, 1984.
60. Shelton, M. M., Nachtigal, M. P., Yngve, D. A., et al.: *Kingella kingae* osteomyelitis: Report of two cases involving the epiphysis. Pediatr. Infect. Dis. J. *7*:421–424, 1988.
61. Skouby, S. O., and Knudsen, F. U.: *Kingella kingae* osteomyelitis mimicking an eosinophilic granuloma. Acta Paediatr. Scand. *71*:511–512, 1982.
62. Slonim, A., Walker, E. S., Mishori, E., et al.: Person-to-person transmission of *Kingella kingae* among day care center attendees. J. Infect. Dis. *178*:1843–1846, 1998.
63. Sordillo, E. M., Rendel, M., Sood, R., et al.: Septicemia due to β-lactamase–positive *Kingella kingae*. Clin. Infect. Dis. *17*:818–819, 1993.
64. Stahelin, J., Goldenberger, D., Gnehm, H. E., et al.: Polymerase chain reaction diagnosis of *Kingella kingae* arthritis in a child. Clin. Infect. Dis. *27*:1328–1329, 1998.
65. Toshniwal, R., Draghi, T. C., Kocka, F. E., et al.: Manifestations of *Kingella kingae* infections in adults: Resemblance to neisserial infections. Diagn. Microbiol. Infect. Dis. *5*:81–85, 1986.
66. Urs, S., D'Silva, B. S. V., Jeena, C. P., et al.: *Kingella kingae* septicaemia in association with HIV disease. Trop. Doc. *24*:127, 1994.
67. Van Erps, J., Schmedding, E., Naessens, A., et al.: *Kingella kingae*, a rare cause of bacterial meningitis. Clin. Neurol. Neurosurg. *94*:173–175, 1992.
68. Verbruggen, A.-M., Hauglustaine, D., Schildermans, F., et al.: Infections caused by *Kingella kingae:* Report of four cases and review. J. Infect. *13*:133–142, 1986.
69. Waghorn, D. J., and Cheetham, C. H.: *Kingella kingae* endocarditis following chickenpox in infancy. Eur. J. Clin. Microbiol. Infect. Dis. *16*: 944–945, 1997.
70. Walterspiel, J. N.: *Kingella kingae* meningitis with bilateral infarcts of the basal ganglia. Infection *11*:307–309, 1983.
71. Weir, S., and Marrs, C. F.: Identification of type 4 pili in *Kingella denitrificans*. Infect. Immun. *60*:3437–3441, 1992.
72. Wells, L., Rutter, N., and Donald, F.: *Kingella kingae* endocarditis in a sixteen-month-old child. Pediatr. Infect. Dis. J. *20*:454–455, 2001.
73. Wolff, A. H., Ullman, R. F., Strampfer, M. J., et al.: *Kingella kingae* endocarditis: Report of a case and review of the literature. Heart Lung *16*: 579–583, 1987.
74. Yagupsky, P., Dagan, R.: *Kingella kingae* bacteremia in children. Pediatr. Infect. Dis. J. *13*:1148–1149, 1994.
75. Yagupsky, P., and Dagan, R.: Population-based study of invasive *Kingella kingae* infections. Emerg. Infect. Dis. *6*:85–87, 2000.
76. Yagupsky, P., Dagan, R., Howard, C. W., et al.: High prevalence of *Kingella kingae* in joint fluid from children with septic arthritis revealed by the BACTEC blood culture system. J. Clin. Microbiol. *30*:1278–1281, 1992.
77. Yagupsky, P., Dagan, R., Howard, C. B., et al.: Clinical features and epidemiology of invasive *Kingella kingae* infections in southern Israel. Pediatrics *92*:800–804, 1993.
78. Yagupsky, P., Dagan, R., Prajgrod, F., et al.: Respiratory carriage of *Kingella kingae* among healthy children. Pediatr. Infect. Dis. J. *14*: 673–678, 1995.
79. Yagupsky, P., Howard, C. B., Einhorn, M., et al.: *Kingella kingae* osteomyelitis of the calcaneus in young children. Pediatr. Infect. Dis. J. *12*:540–541, 1993.
80. Yagupsky, P., Katz, O., and Peled, N.: Antibiotic susceptibility of *Kingella kingae* isolates from respiratory carriers and patients with invasive infections. J. Antimicrob. Chemother. *47*:191–193, 2001.
81. Yagupsky, P., Merires, M., Bahar, J., et al.: Evaluation of novel vancomycin-containing medium for primary isolation of *Kingella kingae* from upper respiratory tract specimens. J. Clin. Microbiol. *33*:1426–1427, 1995.
82. Yagupsky, P., and Press, J.: Use of the isolator 1.5 microbial tube for culture of synovial fluid from patients with septic arthritis. J. Clin. Microbiol. *35*:2410–2412, 1997.

CHAPTER

143 Legionnaires' Disease, Pontiac Fever, and Related Illnesses

PAUL H. EDELSTEIN

Legionnaires' disease is an acute pneumonic illness caused by gram-negative bacilli of the genus *Legionella*. Pontiac fever is a febrile, nonpneumonic, systemic illness closely associated with, if not caused by, *Legionella* spp. infection.

History

Legionnaires' disease first was recognized as a distinct clinical entity when it caused an epidemic of pneumonia at an American Legion convention in Philadelphia in 1976[62]; 221 people were affected, and 34 died. Investigators were unable to determine the exact cause of the outbreak immediately; this mystery provoked considerable fear and widespread speculation about the cause. Approximately 6 months later, two investigators at the Centers for Disease Control and Prevention, Joseph McDade and Charles Shepard,[109] announced that they had discovered the etiologic agent, a fastidious gram-negative bacillus. Researchers determined subsequently that both the organism and the disease had been studied previously as long ago as the 1940s but had been forgotten.[39, 51, 141] Because of the historical association with the American Legion convention, this disease now is called legionnaires' disease, and the etiologic agents belong to the family Legionellaceae.

Etiologic Agent

Legionella is the only genus in the family Legionellaceae. Forty-one species of *Legionella* and more than 60 serogroups now are recognized (Table 143–1). *Legionella pneumophila* is the species responsible for the 1976 Philadelphia epidemic and causes most cases of legionnaires' disease.[39, 43, 51, 141] Serogroup 1 of *L. pneumophila* is estimated to cause about 70 to 90 percent of all cases of legionnaires' disease in previously healthy people.[44, 108] *Legionella* spp. and serogroups other than *L. pneumophila* serogroup 1 cause 25 to 40 percent of nosocomial outbreaks of legionnaires' disease.[81, 108]

The Legionellaceae are obligately aerobic, mesophilic, motile, gram-negative bacilli with variable oxidase and catalase reactions.[39, 141] They do not utilize carbohydrates as a source of energy but rather metabolize amino acids. They are unique in that L-cysteine is required for growth, a characteristic shared only with *Francisella tularensis*. Also, both the cellular fatty acid and ubiquinone content differ from those of other mesophilic gram-negative bacilli.

The antigenic relationships among different *Legionella* spp. and among serotypes of the same species are complex.[141] The serologic typing scheme is based on surface antigens (O antigens), which primarily are lipopolysaccharides. These surface antigens are shared by different species and, in rare cases, by other gram-negative bacilli, such as *Pseudomonas* spp. Thus, identifying an unknown strain by use of serologic methods alone occasionally leads to a false or misleading identification. Cross-reactions also may be observed in testing for human antibodies to *Legionella*. Patients with infections caused by some *Pseudomonas* spp. strains, *Campylobacter jejuni*, and other gram-negative bacilli may develop antibodies to *Legionella*.[25, 36, 39, 72, 106, 141]

Because of these complexities, definite identification of *Legionella* spp. other than *L. pneumophila* often requires the capabilities of a research laboratory. However, isolation and presumptive identification should be within the capabilities of most clinical laboratories.[39, 141]

Legionella is ubiquitous in the aqueous environment and can be found, often in high concentrations, in lake water, ponds, bathing water, hot-water tanks, hot-water plumbing, and air-conditioning cooling towers.[141] Its optimal growth temperature ranges from about 28° to 40° C (82° to 104° F). The natural hosts and probable reservoirs of environmental *Legionella* likely are freshwater amebae, such as *Acanthamoeba* and *Hartmannella*.[60, 132, 147, 148] Factors promoting growth of *Legionella* in the environment, such as the presence of other microorganisms, use of plumbing materials that promote bacterial growth (certain types of rubber gaskets), stagnation, and warm temperatures, are diverse.[141] In the home, older municipal water distribution systems, use of electric rather than gas water heaters, and use of well water all appear to promote the presence of *Legionella* in water.[1, 106] Most newly discovered *Legionella* spp. have been environmental isolates not associated with clinical illness.[39, 43, 141]

Some virulence factors responsible for initiating infection have been elucidated. They include a gene that potentiates infection of macrophages (*mip*, macrophage infectivity potentiator), a variety of iron-binding proteins, and a gene cluster inhibiting phagosomal fusion and allowing intracellular growth (*dot* and *icm* genes, defect in organelle trafficking).[10–12, 34, 35, 82, 100, 133, 146] A variety of bacterial secretory systems, including one type IV system involved in the *dot/icm* virulence complex, appear to be important for virulence.[5, 146] Whether macrophage complement receptors play a role in the uptake of the bacterium is controversial.[65, 81, 120] Elegant in vitro studies have shown that *L. pneumophila* and perhaps other species have a unique means of evading host defenses. This evasion is by growth within alveolar macrophages, the pulmonary defense cells that ordinarily ingest and then kill invading bacteria. *L. pneumophila* is not killed actively by macrophages, which, in fact, provide sustenance for the bacterium. Poor killing of *L. pneumophila* within macrophages probably is fostered by failure of both lysophagosomal fusion and phagosomal acidification.[79] These in vitro studies have been substantiated, in part, in an animal model.[41, 115] Availability of intracellular iron appears to play a key role in the growth of intracellular *L. pneumophila*. Interferon-γ, the production of which is increased during *L. pneumophila* infection of macrophages, down-regulates the number of iron-binding receptors on macrophages, which has the effect of decreasing the availability of intracellular iron and, hence, limiting intracellular growth of *L. pneumophila*.[28–30]

L. pneumophila is serum resistant.[141] High-titer antibody promotes phagocytosis but may not enhance killing.

TABLE 143–1 ■ *LEGIONELLA* SPECIES AND SEROGROUPS

Species	No. of Serogroups	Implicated in Human Disease
adelaidensis	1	No
anisa	1	Yes
birminghamensis	1	Yes
bozemanii	2	Yes
brunensis	1	No
cherrii	1	No
cincinnatiensis	1	Yes
dumoffii	1	Yes
erythra	2	No
fairfieldensis	1	No
feeleii	2	Yes
geestiana	1	No
gormanii	1	Yes
gratiana	1	No
hackeliae	2	Yes
israelensis	1	No
jamestownensis	1	No
jordanis	1	Yes
lansingensis	1	Yes
londiniensis	1	No
longbeachae	2	Yes
"lytica"	Unknown	Yes
maceachernii	1	Yes
micdadei	1	Yes
moravica	1	No
nautarum	1	No
oakridgensis	1	No
parisiensis	1	Yes
pneumophila	16	Yes
quateirensis	1	No
quinlivanii	2	No
rubrilucens	1	No
sainthelensi	2	Yes
sainticrucis	1	No
shakespearei	1	No
spiritensis	2	No
steigerwaltii	1	No
taurinensis	1	No
tucsonensis	1	Yes
wadsworthii	1	Yes
waltersii	1	No
worsleiensis	1	No

Macrophage activation factors possibly are more important than is antibody in promoting phagocytosis and bacterial killing.[79]

Both exotoxins and endotoxins are produced by *L. pneumophila*; their roles in the manifestations of disease or in organism invasiveness are unclear.[34, 39, 141]

Epidemiology

INCIDENCE AND FREQUENCY

The incidence of pediatric legionnaires' disease has been studied only by use of serosurveys, which have been used for most studies of the adult population.* Because of the less than absolute specificity of serologic testing, frequent failure to obtain appropriately timed paired serum samples, and almost uniform lack of culture confirmation of disease, these serosurveys can be used only as crude measurements of the incidence of the disease.[39, 127, 141] Regardless, pediatric legionnaires' disease rarely appears to be the cause of pneumonia in otherwise healthy children.* Fewer than 10 culture-confirmed cases of legionnaires' disease have been reported in otherwise normally healthy children, and fewer than 30 culture-confirmed cases have been reported in immunosuppressed children.†

A recent review called attention to nosocomial legionnaires' disease in neonates hospitalized in neonatal intensive care units, a special subset of immunocompromised children at presumably higher risk for acquisition of the disease.[99]

A retrospective serosurvey of 500 patients with pneumonia, 83 percent of whom did not need hospitalization, found that only 5 of the 132 patients younger than 15 years of age (26 percent of the total) had significant antibody titers against *L. pneumophila,* and none developed seroconversion.[61] The estimated incidence of legionnaires' disease in the overall population was approximately 12 per 100,000 per year. In a year-long prospective study of 191 children hospitalized with pneumonia, titers rose significantly in only 1 child (0.92 percent of cases with paired serum samples available).[118] In another prospective study of 52 children younger than 4 years of age with lower respiratory tract infections, no cases of legionnaires' disease were identified.[4] Four of 211 Iowa children (1 to 19 years of age) with atypical pneumonia demonstrated seroconversion to *L. pneumophila.*[129] In a retrospective Israeli serosurvey, titers rose in 2 of 37 children.[113] A 2-year prospective study in France found that only 2 of 278 children (0.7 percent) hospitalized for pneumonia had legionnaires' disease based on seroconversion.[37] One of these 2 children was immunosuppressed. Using these data, one could estimate that the mean frequency of legionnaires' disease as a cause of pneumonia requiring hospitalization in the normal pediatric population is approximately 1 percent. This rate is approximately the same as the 0.5 to 4 percent frequency found in the adult population.[39, 108, 141] Legionnaires' disease is not a major cause of pneumonia in either children or adults.

The frequency of legionnaires' disease in the immunosuppressed pediatric population is unknown. Several case reports document this disease in children being treated for acute leukemia, with chronic granulomatous disease, after bone marrow or solid organ transplantation, or after being treated with steroids for other reasons.‡ No large studies of this disease in the immunosuppressed pediatric population have been performed, however. One retrospective study of 55 pediatric cancer patients with atypical pneumonia found one case that had an antibody titer rise to *L. pneumophila.*[134] Immunosuppression in the pediatric population probably would result in a higher incidence of legionnaires' disease than that seen in the normal population; this is the case in adults.[51, 141] Nosocomial or community-acquired legionnaires' disease has been reported in several "immunologically normal" infants, who may have some degree of immunocompromise that predisposes them to this disease.§ As noted earlier, neonates in intensive care units may be at high risk for acquisition of nosocomial legionnaires' disease because of the immaturity of their cellular immune system and of their local defenses. In addition, the humid and warm

*See references 4, 39, 61, 75, 112, 113, 118, 127, 129, 134, 141.

*See references 3, 13, 32, 37, 42, 64, 76, 80, 96, 110, 123, 137, 140.

†See references 1, 7, 26, 31, 32, 37, 40, 55, 59, 70, 86, 93–95, 98, 99, 116, 121, 126, 145, 152.

‡See references 40, 55, 71, 77, 86, 93, 94, 97, 121, 122, 134, 136, 139, 142.

§See references 38, 58, 64, 76, 78, 88, 96, 116, 126, 152.

conditions of neonatal incubators are ideal for growth of the bacterium.

Whether atypical, mild, or asymptomatic *Legionella* infection occurs in children is unknown. Several cases of Pontiac fever in children were reported from a large outbreak of this disease at a recreation center in Scotland and from a smaller one in Denmark.[68, 102] The true frequency of Pontiac fever in children is difficult to know because the diagnosis is impossible to make with certainty in the sporadic form. Several of the serosurveys already cited have found asymptomatic elevations of *L. pneumophila* antibody in widely varying frequency. Andersen and colleagues[4] found that 27 of 52 children developed an increase in antibody titer unrelated to acute illness over a period of several years; some of these children developed significantly high titers. Muldoon and colleagues[112] found that 15 percent of 126 children sampled had antibody titers to *L. pneumophila* of 256 or greater, which was not significantly different from those seen with an adult control population. The striking finding was that the antibody titers rose with age, doubling each year until age 3 years, when the values plateaued; this finding held even when patients with pneumonia were excluded. In contrast, using a different and perhaps more specific antigen preparation, Mundel and colleagues[113] in Israel found a much lower prevalence of elevated antibody titers. That these findings may be geographic rather than methodologic is exemplified by the study of Orenstein and associates,[118] who obtained results similar to the Israeli study despite using the same type of antigen as did Andersen and colleagues.[4] The significance of these elevated titers in children without documented pneumonia is unclear, and these findings can be interpreted as cross-reactions to other colonizing or infecting bacteria, asymptomatic infection, or atypical disease.

Several investigators have examined the question of whether atypical disease caused by *Legionella* occurs in children. Unfortunately, all these studies are based exclusively on serologic testing, which, as stated before, may not be entirely specific. Italian physicians found that two children with acute, reversible cerebellar ataxia developed significant antibody titer changes to *L. pneumophila.*[117] Another Italian study found two children with pericarditis who had significant antibody changes.[138] None of 140 British infants with sudden death had measurable antibodies to *L. pneumophila,* despite suggestions that they might be linked.[149] Three studies have shown that children with cystic fibrosis have higher antibody levels to *Legionella* than do normal children, although these data especially are suspect because of known cross-reactions between *Legionella* and *Pseudomonas aeruginosa.*[36, 53, 90] Thus, despite several epidemiologic surveys, the prevalence of atypical *Legionella* infections in children is unclear.

In adults, true incidence figures are as difficult to find. Estimates based on serologic surveys range from 2 to 20 cases per 100,000 population per year.[39, 127, 141] A prospective study in Ohio found that the incidence of legionnaires' disease requiring hospitalization was approximately 6 per 100,000 per year, in what is thought to be a geographic region with an above-average frequency of the disease.[107, 124] Estimates of the proportion of adult pneumonias caused by legionnaires' disease range from 1 to 25 percent, with a reasonable mean of 3 percent.[108] Mild or atypical *Legionella* infection certainly occurs in adults, although the exact incidence is unknown. This incidence includes several outbreaks of Pontiac fever and case reports from the original Philadelphia outbreak of people with relatively mild disease.[39, 62, 66, 67, 91, 141] Asymptomatic infection may occur in adults, based on the same types of serosurveys discussed for children. Neither oropharyngeal colonization nor a carrier state has been documented. A study of a cross-section of adults showed that approximately 6 percent had oropharyngeal colonization with *L. pneumophila* on the basis of immunofluorescent studies, although none of the positive results could be confirmed by culture.[27]

DISEASE OUTBREAKS

Many epidemics of legionnaires' disease and Pontiac fever have been recognized.[26, 39, 68, 141] In the case of legionnaires' disease, most outbreaks have occurred in residents, employees, or visitors in large buildings. These include hotels, hospitals, factories, retail stores, and office buildings. Nosocomial legionnaires' disease has been reported in hospitals throughout North America and Europe. In most cases in which thorough investigations have been performed, the reservoir has been the potable water distribution system, air-conditioning cooling towers, or both.[39, 141] Outbreaks have been ended by disinfection of water and cooling tower systems by hyperchlorination or pasteurization.[39, 141] In some of these outbreaks, disease occurred for many years until effective disinfection procedures were utilized. Attack rates in legionnaires' disease epidemics consistently have been less than 5 percent overall. Incubation periods ranging from 2 to 14 days have been observed.

Pontiac fever outbreaks generally have been associated with exposure to an aerosol of warm water contaminated with *Legionella.*[67, 91, 141] Examples include whirlpool baths, an engine assembly plant using contaminated water to cool machine lathes, and a health department building in which condensate in the air-conditioning system was contaminated. The attack rates in Pontiac fever outbreaks have been high, in the range of 95 to 100 percent. The incubation period is short, approximately 12 to 36 hours.[67]

Sporadic culture-proven cases of legionnaires' disease have been well documented. In fact, 70 to 85 percent of cases of legionnaires' disease in the United States and elsewhere are neither nosocomial nor associated with an epidemic.[87, 88, 108] Some of these community-acquired cases represent undetected small case clusters, as has been shown for community-acquired cases in Glasgow, Scotland.[14–17] In that city, living close to a cooling tower was a risk factor for acquisition of legionnaires' disease. Although difficult to prove, sporadic Pontiac fever also likely occurs.[39, 141]

Risk factors for acquisition of legionnaires' disease can be divided logically into two main categories: those that increase exposure to contaminated water and those that suppress pulmonary defense mechanisms.[39, 141] Included in the former category are occupational or residential exposure to warm or stagnant water, traveling and residence in hotels, and stays in hospitals with contaminated water distribution systems; a risk factor for residential acquisition of disease is use of well water.[124] The latter category includes general anesthesia, administration of glucocorticosteroids, cigarette smoking, chronic lung disease, and diseases (including human immunodeficiency virus infection) or therapy that compromises the cellular immune system. Males are more than twice as likely as females to develop the disease, perhaps as a result of the greater male prevalence of cigarette smoking and chronic lung disease. Middle-aged and older people also are at higher risk than are younger people. Other than exposure to aerosols of contaminated water, no particular predisposing factors for the development of Pontiac fever have been identified. Exposure to patients with legionnaires' disease has not been shown to be a risk factor for acquisition of the disease.

Pathology, Pathogenesis, and Immunity

The exact mode of disease production in legionnaires' disease is unknown. Very good, but indirect, epidemiologic and pathologic evidence suggests that the initial infection results from inhalation of an aerosol rather than by the route of initial oropharyngeal colonization and subsequent aspiration.[39, 141] However, some patients undoubtedly have acquired the disease after aspiration of *Legionella*-contaminated tap water.[23, 85, 105, 144] Some investigators have speculated about the possibility of the development of a bacteremic pneumonia after ingestion and gastrointestinal tract infection, although few clinical, epidemiologic, or pathologic data support this hypothesis. Animal models for each of these modes of initial spread exist, and some investigators rightly argue that not enough is known about the initial event to exclude all possibilities effectively.[9, 45, 54, 73, 89, 125, 141]

L. pneumophila apparently does not adhere to ciliated columnar epithelial cells, a property that might not be important if the major mode of transmission is by aerosol.[9] Also, an exclusively environmental microorganism for which humans probably are accidental hosts may not have a selective advantage for such adherence traits.

In guinea pigs infected by the aerosol route, multiplication of *L. pneumophila* begins within 16 hours.[41] This multiplication most likely occurs within the alveolar macrophage, although some extracellular growth may occur. Several cell culture studies show that multiplication occurs only intracellularly and not in the extracellular tissue culture medium.[79] This intracellular location of bacteria protects them from serum factors such as antibody and complement as well as from the effects of those antimicrobials that are not concentrated intracellularly. Killing of *L. pneumophila* within macrophages in cell culture is limited by failure of phagolysosomal fusion.[79] Polymorphonuclear leukocytes do not ingest or kill the organism effectively in vitro, although Davis and colleagues[41] suggest that they may form the bulwark of initial host defenses based on in vivo studies. Their conclusions are bolstered by the experiments of Richards and colleagues,[130] which show that polymorphonuclear leukocyte depletion in hamsters enhanced the virulence of *L. pneumophila* given intratracheally. Clinical evidence suggests that leukopenic hosts without concomitant macrophage dysfunction are not high-risk candidates for legionnaires' disease, although they may be at higher risk than is the normal population.[33, 51]

The histopathologic correlate of bacterial lung invasion is intense intraalveolar inflammation.[141] Large airways are not affected, nor are small ones to the level of the terminal bronchioles. Both the terminal bronchioles and alveolar ducts may be involved in the inflammatory process. The interstitial spaces generally are uninvolved, although necrosis of alveoli may bridge the interstitial spaces. The alveoli contain a variable mixture of polymorphonuclear leukocytes, alveolar macrophages, and necrotic debris. Hemorrhage is observed, as are microabscesses. Later, fibrin formation and a histiocytic predominance occur. Pleural inflammation occurs in the presence of empyema.

Gross lung changes evolve in the classic pattern of lobar pneumonia, with first red and then gray hepatization.[141] Lymph nodes are involved occasionally. The lung segments involved often are subpleural, a finding that sometimes suggests septic or bland infarction to the clinician. The pleural space is involved variably and seemingly is more prone to infection in immunosuppressed patients. One of the most striking pulmonary findings is the usual absence of significant intrabronchial exudate.

Despite frequent signs and symptoms of extrapulmonary disease in patients with legionnaires' disease, no specific extrapulmonary pathologic findings have been identified.[141] In fatal cases, organisms often can be recovered or detected in various reticuloendothelial organs, such as the liver or spleen; however, detection of associated significant inflammation is unusual. Occasionally, patients have nonbacterial endocardial vegetations. Some patients have nonmassive hilar and paratracheal adenopathy, the result of bacterial adenitis. Patients may have metastatic foci with abscesses in almost any location, including the myocardium, pericardium, peritoneum, brain, kidney, bowel wall, perirectal region, prosthetic heart valves, and hemodialysis shunts[51, 141] (Table 143–2). Bacteremia occurs in some patients; it has been documented by positive blood cultures and is substantiated indirectly by extrapulmonary foci of infection found in some patients.[51, 141] Whether bacteremia accounts for some of the systemic clinical findings in legionnaires' disease is unproven but likely. Elaboration of toxins by *Legionella* has been postulated to account for some aspects of the systemic disease, but supporting evidence is not convincing.[141] The effect of host responses to *L. pneumophila* has not been studied as a possible explanation for these systemic manifestations. Cell culture and animal experiments show that tumor necrosis factor, interferon-γ, and other cytokines are produced during *L. pneumophila* infection; this production could account for some of the systemic manifestations of the infection.[18, 153]

Episodes of recurrent or relapsing legionnaires' disease in patients with elevated antibody titers support experimental evidence suggesting that the humoral immune system plays a minor role in this disease.[51] Also supporting this evidence is the rarity of legionnaires' disease case reports in patients with hypogammaglobulinemia or other diseases in which the humoral immune system primarily is deficient. The rise of specific antibody levels does not seem to have any clinical correlates, nor does the absolute antibody level.[51] Patients may recover from legionnaires' disease without any significant increase in antibody levels, again providing indirect evidence of the limited role of the humoral immune system.

The roles of antibody and complement in experimental models of infection vary with the model. Several studies have shown that passive or active immunization is protective

TABLE 143–2 ■ DISEASES CAUSED BY *LEGIONELLA*

- Pneumonia (legionnaires' disease)
- Associated with pneumonia
  - Hemodialysis shunt infection
  - Renal abscess
  - Brain abscess
  - Myocarditis
  - Pericarditis
  - Peritonitis
  - Perirectal abscess
  - Pleural empyema
  - Bacteremia
  - Bowel wall abscess
  - Myositis cellulitis
- Not associated with pneumonia
  - Prosthetic heart valve endocarditis
  - Sinusitis
  - Wound infection
  - Colitis
  - Pleural empyema
  - Peritonitis
  - Pontiac fever (? toxin-mediated)

against intraperitoneal and subcutaneous chamber infection in rats, mice, and guinea pigs.[6, 54, 73, 131] Preopsonization of *L. pneumophila* before intratracheal inoculation of hamsters was found to be partially protective, but several investigators have shown that active immunization fails to protect against pneumonia after intratracheal, aerosol, or intranasal inoculation of large numbers of *L. pneumophila* bacteria.[9, 45, 54, 130] Protective immunity to pulmonary challenge in the guinea pig can be achieved after sublethal infection or infection with an avirulent mutant strain and by vaccination with an *L. pneumophila*–derived metalloprotease or outer-membrane protein.[19–22, 150]

Evidence for the importance of the cellular immune system in preventing infection largely is indirect and based on the greater prevalence of legionnaires' disease in immunosuppressed patients with cellular immunodeficiencies.[51, 141] Curiously, legionnaires' disease in patients with acquired immunodeficiency syndrome (AIDS) has been reported infrequently, although an epidemiologic survey showed that patients with AIDS had a disease attack rate approximately 40 times greater than that in the normal population.[21, 22, 108, 150] Passive transfer of spleen cells from infected animals has been shown to be protective in an intratracheal model of *Legionella micdadei* infection.[115] Development of cellular immunity after infection or vaccination can be demonstrated in vitro for both humans and animals, the clinical importance of which is unclear.[141]

Vaccination for prevention of legionnaires' disease may be feasible because it has been demonstrated to be effective in an animal model.[20–22, 150] Whether vaccination in susceptible host populations would be successful is unknown, even if justified economically or on epidemiologic grounds.

The pathogenesis of Pontiac fever has not been studied. No differences have been detected between an *L. pneumophila* strain isolated from an outbreak of Pontiac fever and strains isolated from outbreaks of legionnaires' disease; these studies have included examination of virulence in an animal model, toxin production, and biochemical characteristics.[141] Detailed clinical studies of patients with Pontiac fever have not been performed, which renders producing an experimental model of this disease difficult. Because it has a short incubation time, which can be as brief as 12 hours, this disease likely does not represent widespread bacterial multiplication within the body, and more likely it represents a toxin-induced or allergic disease. In fact, the link between *Legionella* and Pontiac fever is circumstantial; entirely possible is that other microbes coexisting with *Legionella* may cause the disease.[67, 91] The clinical syndromes most like Pontiac fever are bath-water fever, humidifier fever, and extrinsic allergic alveolitis; these syndromes are thought to be caused either by the direct toxic activity of inhaled endotoxin or by an allergic reaction to microorganisms, most particularly amoebae such as *Naegleria* spp.[52, 111, 135]

Clinical Findings of Legionnaires' Disease

SIGNS AND SYMPTOMS

Legionnaires' disease usually presents as atypical pneumonia.[63] It is atypical in that usual pathogenic bacteria generally are not isolated from respiratory tract secretions or blood and patients do not respond, except fortuitously, to antimicrobial agents commonly used to treat pneumonia in adults (e.g., penicillins, cephalosporins, and aminoglycosides). Beyond these findings, considerable speculation and controversy continue over whether a distinct clinical syndrome exists. Several prospective studies of both community-acquired and nosocomial legionnaires' disease have failed to demonstrate any clinical, radiographic, or nonspecific laboratory features that distinguish legionnaires' disease from other common causes of pneumonia.[49] The classic clinical findings are reviewed because many researchers consider that they are distinctive for *Legionella* pneumonias. Whether legionnaires' disease in children mimics the clinical findings in adults is unknown because of the rare instances of well-documented pediatric cases and the possibility of spectrum bias.

The onset of pneumonia may be either insidious or abrupt. Recurrent chills, abdominal pains, myalgia, headache, malaise, anorexia, and severe fatigue are common findings. Diarrhea, consisting of loose, nonbloody stools several times a day, occurs in approximately 30 to 40 percent of cases. Fever may be low grade or absent initially. Over the course of a day to several days, these nonspecific symptoms gradually worsen, often resulting in severe debilitation. Noteworthy is the frequent absence of symptoms referable to the respiratory system. Rash, splenomegaly, adenopathy, and rhinorrhea are exceptionally uncommon findings. Physical examination early in the illness generally is remarkable for a paucity of localizing findings and the frequent impression that the patient has an influenzal or typhoidal illness.

Within a day to several days after onset, the patient usually, but not always, develops high fever. Pulse-temperature dissociation occurs in approximately one half of epidemic-associated cases. Respiratory complaints, especially dyspnea and pleuritic chest pains, may become prominent. Cough usually is not a major complaint, although it is common. The sputum almost never is frankly purulent; blood-streaked sputum or frank hemoptysis is observed in 20 to 30 percent of patients. Most patients experience confusion, cerebellar ataxia, lethargy, agitation, or some other neurologic disorder. Severe abdominal or back pain may occur, sometimes with localization. Physical examination at this time reveals a "toxic" febrile patient with apparent multisystem disease. Chest examination usually discloses findings of consolidating pneumonia, with bronchial breath sounds, increased vocal fremitus, and dullness to percussion. Depending on the stage of consolidation, rales may or may not be heard. Pleural friction rubs or signs of pleural effusion can be observed. Despite frequent symptoms of abdominal pain, signs of peritoneal irritation, such as decreased bowel sounds or rebound tenderness, seldom are detected. Signs of meningeal irritation rarely occur but have been reported.

Most normally healthy patients recover without specific therapy, usually by day 7 to 10 of illness. Those who do not recover usually die of progressive respiratory failure, along with failure of other organ systems. Empyema, pulmonary cavitation, renal failure, memory loss, fatigue, and neurologic disorders all are potential complications and may persist for weeks to months after onset of the disease.

RADIOGRAPHIC FINDINGS

The hallmark of legionnaires' disease on the chest radiograph is an acinar filling pattern with consolidation.[39, 51, 141] It has no distinctive predilection for any lung region; pleura-based consolidation and bilateral infiltrates may occur. Nodular infiltrates may be seen, as may cavitation in the areas of original consolidation. Purely interstitial infiltrates are distinctly uncommon findings in established disease but rarely occur very early in the disease process; these interstitial infiltrates rapidly progress to consolidating ones within a day or so. Pleural effusion, with or without parenchymal infiltrates, can occur. Pleural effusion has been documented as the only chest finding in patients treated early.

LABORATORY FINDINGS

General

Multiple nonspecific abnormal laboratory results can be detected in patients with legionnaires' disease.[39, 51] Hematologic abnormalities include leukocytosis or leukopenia, usually with a left shift; lymphopenia; thrombocytosis; and disseminated intravascular coagulation. Proteinuria and pyuria are common findings; myoglobinuria also may be present. Hyponatremia and hypophosphatemia commonly occur, as do elevations of aminotransferase enzymes, bilirubin, alkaline phosphatase, and creatine kinase. Severe azotemia occurs, although rarely. Arterial oxygenation usually is depressed in relation to the extent of pneumonia. Patients with severe disease also may develop severe oxygen desaturation related to either oxygen intoxication or respiratory distress syndrome. Taken together, these multiple laboratory abnormalities often suggest multisystem disease to the clinician.

Nonspecific, and occasionally confusing, laboratory abnormalities also may be seen. They include elevation of cold agglutinin titers, cold agglutinin–induced hemolytic anemia, and elevation of complement fixation titers to *Mycoplasma pneumoniae.* The elevations of *M. pneumoniae* titer probably are not caused by a cross-reaction and occur in approximately 10 percent of patients who develop seroconversion to *L. pneumophila.*[24, 69, 128, 151] This elevation possibly represents dual infection with *M. pneumoniae* and *L. pneumophila.*

Specific

Diagnosis of legionnaires' disease is accomplished best by recovery of *Legionella* from sputum or other lower respiratory tract secretions or tissues.[51, 141] Complementary to this finding is detection of *Legionella* in the same materials by immunofluorescent microscopy. Other specific diagnostic methods are detection of *L. pneumophila* antigenuria and detection of *Legionella* DNA in respiratory tract specimens using the polymerase chain reaction. Serologic diagnosis is of uncertain value in children, but it is useful in adults.

Selective media and techniques that facilitate the isolation of *Legionella* from sputum now are available.[39, 141] Sputum is pretreated with an acid solution. This material, as well as a non-pretreated sample, then is plated on buffered charcoal yeast extract medium supplemented with α-ketoglutaric acid (BCYE-α) and on BCYE supplemented with antibiotics (BMPA, or PAC, and MWY, or PAV media). *Legionella* organisms grow on these media 2 to 7 days after inoculation and incubation at 35° C in air. Culture diagnosis has a higher yield than does immunofluorescent microscopy or serology and yields no false-positive results. Blood and pleural fluid cultures generally have lower yields than do respiratory tract cultures, even when plated on proper media; the low yield of blood culture may be a result of methodologic problems.

Immunofluorescent microscopy for *L. pneumophila* is a rapid and highly specific (99.9%) technique for diagnosis.[39, 51] It can be performed in 1 to 2 hours after receipt of the specimen and, like culture, can be performed with sputum. It does have several disadvantages. The test requires considerable technical expertise in reading; if the test is performed by inexperienced technologists, its results often are erroneous. Also, one must take scrupulous care to avoid carryover from other samples and false-positive results caused by contaminated reagents.

Cross-reacting organisms are rare findings in clinical samples; they often can be detected by experienced technologists on the basis of morphologic characteristics and staining pattern. Nonetheless, some cross-reacting bacteria, such as some *Pseudomonas* spp. strains, still cause rare false-positive results. Some strains of *Bacteroides fragilis, Streptococcus pneumoniae, Bacillus* spp., and *Candida* spp. also can cross-react with diagnostic reagents, although cross-reactions caused by these organisms rarely, if ever, result in false-positive diagnosis of legionnaires' disease.[39, 141]

Patients with tularemia may have false-positive immunofluorescent stains for *Legionella.* The most specific reagent available for immunofluorescent microscopy is a monoclonal antibody to *L. pneumophila*; it reacts with all known serogroups of the species (formerly Genetic Systems, now Biorad, Hercules, CA). Polyclonal antibodies to *L. pneumophila* serogroups 1 to 4 also are highly specific and are available from a variety of sources. However, polyclonal antibodies to other *L. pneumophila* serogroups and to other *Legionella* spp. yield an unacceptable rate of false-positive results. A positive immunofluorescent test result not confirmed by culture, when performed, should be regarded as a possible false-positive result, and independent validating tests should be performed, if indicated. Finally, the sensitivity of the test is low, in the 25 to 80 percent range. The reasons for low test sensitivity are that the lowest number of detectable bacteria is in the range of 10^4 cells/mL and that more antigenic types than diagnostic serum types of *Legionella* exist.

A laboratory can increase the sensitivity of the test by screening for more than one antigenic type, but doing so increases the number of false-positive results and should be avoided in almost all situations. The best compromise is for the laboratory to screen for antigenic types common in its locale. For example, *L. pneumophila* serogroups 1 and 4 account for most of the isolates in Los Angeles; in Chicago, *L. pneumophila* serogroups 1 and 6 are found more commonly. Because of the limited sensitivity of the test, a negative result does not exclude disease.

Serologic testing is of most value in epidemiologic studies and of least value in the acute diagnosis of sporadic cases.[50] As many as 25 percent of patients with culture-documented disease fail to undergo seroconversion against the homologous serotype; this failure is not related solely to early treatment or immunosuppression, although these factors may cause failure of antibody formation. As long as 3 months may be required for antibody levels to increase after onset of illness; the median time is approximately 2 weeks. Also, as with any other means of immunologic diagnosis of this disease, the multiplicity of antigenic types renders serologic testing extremely cumbersome. Because 5 to more than 25 percent of the normal population have elevated antibody titers to *Legionella,* only a fourfold rise in titer is considered significant. Only paired samples, drawn 3 to 6 weeks apart, should be tested. Because of day-to-day variation of test results, these samples must be tested simultaneously for optimal results. For maximum yield, samples taken as long as 9 to 12 weeks after onset of the disease should be tested if earlier samples reveal no changes. As with immunofluorescent detection of bacterial antigen, a negative serologic result does not exclude disease.

The specificity of serologic diagnosis is fairly high in adults, in the range of 95 to 99 percent.[39, 141] Cross-reactive antibodies may be found in the serum of patients with leptospirosis, melioidosis, *B. fragilis* infections, *P. aeruginosa* infections, and possibly *Haemophilus influenzae* or enteric bacterial infections. However, even 99 percent specificity is not sufficient for certainty of diagnosis of a sporadic case. If the estimated 1 percent prevalence of legionnaires' disease in children is correct, fewer than one half of all seroconversions yield truly positive results (positive predictive accuracy of 45 percent). This observation, combined with the studies cited previously showing age-related elevations of anti-*Legionella* antibody in young asymptomatic children, renders serologic diagnosis of pediatric legionnaires' disease highly suspect.

Detection of soluble bacterial antigen in urine can be used to diagnose *L. pneumophila* serogroup 1 infections successfully.[39, 141] An enzyme immunoassay and immunochromatographic card kit for this procedure is available commercially (Wampole, Cranbury, NJ, and Binax, South Portland, ME, respectively). The major drawback of this test is that it preferentially detects only *L. pneumophila* serogroup 1 infections. Otherwise, it has an excellent sensitivity (90–95% versus culture) and extraordinary specificity (at least 99.9%). In some cases, the urinary antigen test yields positive results when sputum culture for *L. pneumophila* serogroup 1 is negative, especially in previously treated patients and in epidemics of legionnaires' disease.

A DNA probe test for the detection of bacterial rRNA (Gen-Probe, San Diego, CA), previously available, no longer is being made. The polymerase chain reaction test has been used to detect *L. pneumophila* in sputum, serum, and urine. The polymerase chain reaction test appears both sensitive and specific but is neither commercially available nor validated in large well-controlled studies.[74, 83, 84, 92, 101–104, 114]

None of the nonculture tests is as sensitive as is culture diagnosis under ideal circumstances. Thus, culture must be performed in every case; if desired, the other tests can be used to provide rapid answers (same day). Because none of the *Legionella*-specific tests is 100 percent sensitive, the clinician sometimes must treat for legionnaires' disease in the absence of confirmatory laboratory tests. One or 2 days of therapy with erythromycin apparently does not affect the sensitivity of the diagnostic tests; thus, therapy should not be withheld pending results of laboratory tests.

Treatment

No prospective clinical studies of antimicrobial therapy for legionnaires' disease have been performed. All recommendations regarding therapy, therefore, are based on retrospective and experimental studies.

Recent in vitro and in vivo data have resulted in a major change in the drugs of choice for the treatment of legionnaires' disease in adults. Because of the superiority of newer fluoroquinolone agents and azithromycin in experimental nonhuman studies, and on the basis of uncontrolled trials of these agents in adults with legionnaires' disease, the current recommendation is that adults with severe legionnaires' disease and immunocompromised patients with the disease be given either azithromycin or fluoroquinolone therapy, rather than the previously used erythromycin therapy. Nonhospitalized patients with mild legionnaires' disease probably will do as well with any of the specific therapies, including erythromycin, tetracycline, newer fluoroquinolones, azithromycin, or clarithromycin.[8, 46, 47] No inherent reason, other than age-specific drug toxicity, precludes these guidelines for children also.

Fluoroquinolone antimicrobial agents generally are contraindicated in children, although the evidence suggests that the risk for toxicity from short courses of therapy is low. The scope of this chapter does not allow the discussion of the use of these drugs in children, but in some cases, the benefit of using these drugs in very severe legionnaires' disease may be greater than the potential risk for development of drug side effects. Azithromycin, which is approved for use in children in the United States, probably is as active against *Legionella* bacteria as are the newer fluoroquinolone agents. Thus, azithromycin may be the preferred drug to treat severe pediatric legionnaires' disease.

Erythromycin remains the drug of choice for treatment of mild legionnaires' disease in children. Generally, it is given intravenously in four daily divided doses of 15 mg/kg. Intravenous therapy can be changed to oral therapy (30 to 50 mg/kg/day in divided doses) once clinical improvement is evident. Therapy should be given for a minimum of 18 to 21 days. Relapses may occur when intravenous erythromycin therapy is changed to the oral route and after a course of therapy that is too short. Some patients with mild illness may be treated initially with oral therapy, although generally this approach is not advisable.

Azithromycin probably is the drug of choice for more severe pediatric legionnaires' disease or for legionnaires' disease in immunocompromised children. The drug dose for children for this type of pneumonia has not been studied, but based on extrapolation from adults, a dose of 10 mg/kg (maximum, 500 mg) given once daily for 7 to 10 days should be sufficient in most cases. In fact, a 3-day course of 500 mg daily has been sufficient to treat mild legionnaires' disease in adults. Azithromycin is available in both intravenous and oral forms and is approved by the U.S. Food and Drug Administration (FDA) for use in adults with legionnaires' disease.

Newer fluoroquinolone agents, along with azithromycin, are considered to be the drugs of choice for the treatment of severe legionnaires' disease in adults. Levofloxacin is used commonly in the United States to treat this disease, in a dosage of 500 mg daily for 10 to 14 days. No dosage guidelines exist for the treatment of pediatric legionnaires' disease, because of the potential for drug toxicity in this population. Levofloxacin and gatifloxacin are the only available quinolone agents that are approved by the FDA for the treatment of legionnaires' disease in adults; note that ciprofloxacin is not approved for this indication, although it appears to be effective for this indication on the basis of case reports.

Alternative drugs to erythromycin include tetracycline or sulfamethoxazole-trimethoprim (co-trimoxazole). Neither of these agents has been approved for this use by the FDA, although limited clinical and experimental data support their effectiveness. Doxycycline, because of its high lipid solubility, may be more effective than is tetracycline, although whether it is remains conjecture. The dosage of doxycycline used in children is 2 to 4 mg/kg/day, given in one or two doses. Use of tetracyclines is associated with the risk for dental staining in children younger than 8 years of age. The daily co-trimoxazole dosage is 15 to 20 mg/kg of the trimethoprim component and 75 to 100 mg/kg of the sulfamethoxazole component in three divided doses. Duration of therapy for these drugs is the same as that for erythromycin.

Rifampin combined with erythromycin is a less favorable alternative to the use of azithromycin by itself. However, if erythromycin is a preferred therapy, then rifampin probably should be added in the case of severe disease or in immunocompromised patients. The dosage is 16 to 20 mg/kg/day, given in two divided doses for the first 3 to 7 days of therapy. This drug rapidly diminishes bacterial counts in experimental disease and has been effective in combination with other drugs in patients in whom erythromycin therapy has failed.

Use of this drug for treatment of legionnaires' disease is not approved by the FDA. No good evidence supports that combining rifampin with either azithromycin or a fluoroquinolone is of clinical benefit.

Treatment of extrapulmonary foci of infection does not appear to differ significantly from treatment of legionnaires' disease without extrapulmonary disease. The duration of therapy and indications for surgical drainage need to be assessed individually in these cases.

RESPONSE TO TREATMENT

Most patients improve dramatically within a few days after initiation of specific therapy.[39, 49, 51, 141] Response has been as rapid as 6 hours after administration of the first dose of erythromycin therapy. Patients regain their appetite, lose symptoms of myalgia and fatigue, and feel better overall. As long as a week may be required for a patient to become completely afebrile, and rarely as long as a month is required for some severely immunosuppressed patients. The chest radiograph changes slowly and even may appear to worsen despite overall clinical improvement; progressive consolidation after 3 to 4 days of intravenous antimicrobial therapy is unusual.

The mortality rate in otherwise healthy adults who are treated promptly is approximately 5 percent, whereas in treated immunosuppressed patients, it is approximately 20 percent. Untreated fatality rates range from 15 to 20 percent in normally healthy patients and upward of 80 percent in immunosuppressed patients. Even in previously healthy patients, delayed therapy and development of respiratory failure are exceptionally poor prognostic factors.[56, 119, 143]

Differential Diagnosis

Other causes of atypical, or culture-negative, pneumonia may closely resemble legionnaires' disease. *M. pneumoniae* pneumonia usually is a milder illness not requiring hospitalization. Cough is a prominent symptom in mycoplasmal pneumonia, whereas it is not in legionnaires' disease. Neither rash nor otitis is found in legionnaires' disease. Laboratory abnormalities also are found more commonly in legionnaires' disease. Serologic testing may provide positive results for both diseases, a confusing finding that can be clarified by performing sputum cultures. Fortunately, the treatment is the same for both diseases.

Psittacosis and Q fever may closely resemble legionnaires' disease. A history of bird or cattle exposure may be helpful, but its absence does not exclude either of these zoonoses. An interstitial rather than an acinar-filling infiltrate on chest radiograph would be a point against legionnaires' disease. Pathogen-specific laboratory tests help in this differential diagnosis. A tetracycline can be used successfully for all three of these diseases.

Early in their evolution, some diseases may resemble legionnaires' disease. They include typhoid fever, acute coccidioidomycosis, influenza, the typhus or spotted fevers, and leptospirosis. Distinguishing these diseases on the basis of their clinical evolution, the laboratory results, and the exposure or travel history generally is easy.

Tularemia may pose a problem in differential diagnosis because immunologic test results for legionnaires' disease can be falsely positive in tularemia and because some of the growth characteristics of *F. tularensis* closely resemble those of *Legionella*. In regions endemic for tularemia, clinicians must work closely with the laboratory to facilitate this differential diagnosis. One case record of tularemia misdiagnosed as legionnaires' disease reported that the patient responded to erythromycin therapy.

Dual infection sometimes occurs in legionnaires' disease. Coexistence of legionnaires' disease with pneumonia caused by *Mycobacterium tuberculosis*, pneumococcus, *H. influenzae*, *Neisseria meningitidis*, *Pneumocystis carinii*, *Moraxella (B.) catarrhalis*, and various viral agents has been reported. Thus, dual infection should be suspected in patients not responding to therapy for pneumonia. Pathogen-specific laboratory tests often are useful in these cases.

Clinical Syndromes Caused by Other *Legionella* Species

Relatively few cases have been reported of disease caused by the non–*L. pneumophila Legionella* spp.[57] The ones described appear to have few differences in clinical findings, diagnostic methods, or treatment. One group contends that these infections are more difficult to treat than are *L. pneumophila* infections, but whether this difficulty represents differences in host factors or reduced susceptibility of the bacteria to antibiotic therapy is unclear.[57] Whether the lower frequency of these infections reflects decreased virulence, inadequate efforts to diagnose them, rare environmental presence, or all three is unknown. They possibly cause mild disease for which major diagnostic efforts are not undertaken. The mode of spread and nosocomial reservoirs of these species are not defined as well as they are for *L. pneumophila.* These infections are less likely to be diagnosed by immunologic means because fewer laboratories routinely test for all possible species. As with *L. pneumophila,* and even more so for the non–*L. pneumophila Legionella* spp., treatment sometimes must be based solely on clinical suspicion without the benefit of confirmatory laboratory tests.

Pontiac Fever

CLINICAL SIGNS AND SYMPTOMS

Fever, myalgia, malaise, chills, and headache are the most common symptoms of Pontiac fever.[67] The symptoms may begin suddenly or have a more gradual onset for several hours. Many symptoms referable to the respiratory tract, such as dry, nonproductive cough, chest pain, and pharyngitis, also are common occurrences. Nausea is a common manifestation, but diarrhea and vomiting are less frequent. Neurologic symptoms such as dizziness, confusion, and poor coordination also have been reported. These symptoms usually are at their worst within a day after onset of illness and gradually resolve over a 2- to 7-day period. Physical examination shows only tachycardia and fever. Leukocytosis has been the only laboratory abnormality reported. Chest radiographs show no abnormalities. Pulmonary function testing has not been performed in patients with Pontiac fever. Rechallenge by return to the contaminated building in the original Pontiac outbreak produced only a mild illness compared with first exposure; the length of time between first and second exposure was not stated clearly.

SPECIFIC DIAGNOSIS

The diagnosis of Pontiac fever primarily is one of exclusion.[39, 141] Significant rises in anti-*Legionella* antibody level, combined with characteristic symptoms, and isolation of *Legionella* from an aerosol source are the diagnostic criteria. Because of the nonspecificity of the symptoms and the ubiquitous distribution of *Legionella* in our environment, rather detailed epidemiologic and environmental studies must be performed to diagnose Pontiac fever specifically. Definitive diagnosis of sporadic cases, therefore, is difficult to make.

TREATMENT

Antimicrobial therapy does not appear to be effective for either the treatment or the prophylaxis of this disease. Removal of the patient from the area of the contaminated water source, while it is being disinfected, appears to be the best means of management.

REFERENCES

1. Abernathy-Carver, K. J., Fan, L. L., Boguniewicz, M., et al. Legionella and Pneumocystis pneumonias in asthmatic children on high doses of systemic steroids. Pediatr. Pulmonol. *18*:135–138, 1994.
2. Alary, M., and Joly, J. R.: Risk factors for contamination of domestic hot water systems by legionellae. Appl. Environ. Microbiol. *57*:2360, 1991.
3. Andersen, R., Bergan, T., Halvorsen, K., et al.: Legionnaires' disease combined with erythema multiforme in a 3-year-old boy. Acta Paediatr. Scand. *70*:427, 1981.
4. Andersen, R. D., Lauer, B. A., Fraser, D. W., et al.: Infections with *Legionella pneumophila* in children. J. Infect. Dis. *143*:386, 1981.
5. Aragon, V., Kurtz, S., Flieger, A., et al. Secreted enzymatic activities of wild-type and pilD-deficient Legionella pneumophila. Infect. Immun. *68*:1855–1863, 2000.
6. Arko, R. J., Wong, K. H., and Feeley, J. C.: Immunologic factors affecting the in-vivo and in-vitro survival of the Legionnaires' disease bacterium. Ann. Intern. Med. *90*:680, 1979.
7. Aubert, G., Bornstein, N., Rayet, I., et al.: Nosocomial infection with *Legionella pneumophila* serogroup 1 and 8 in a neonate. Scand. J. Infect. Dis. *22*:367, 1990.
8. Bartlett, J.G., Dowell, S. F., Mandell, L. A., et al.: Practice guidelines for the management of community-acquired pneumonia in adults. Clin. Infect. Dis. *31*:347–382, 2000.
9. Baskerville, A., Fitzgeorge, R. B., Gibson, D. H., et al.: Pathological and bacteriological findings after aerosol *Legionella pneumophila* infection of susceptible, convalescent, and antibiotic-treated animals. *In* Thornsberry, C., Balows, A., Feeley, J. C., et al. (eds.): *Legionella*. Proceedings of the 2nd International Symposium. Washington, DC, American Society for Microbiology, 1984, pp. 131–132.
10. Berger, K. H., and Isberg, R. R.: Two distinct defects in intracellular growth complemented by a single genetic locus in *Legionella pneumophila*. Mol. Microbiol. 7:7, 1993.
11. Berger, K. H., and Isberg, R. R.: Intracellular survival by *Legionella*. Methods Cell. Biol. *45*:247, 1994.
12. Berger, K. H., Merriam, J. J., and Isberg, R. R.: Altered intracellular targeting properties associated with mutations in the *Legionella pneumophila* dotA gene. Mol. Microbiol. *14*:809, 1994.
13. Beyer, P., Kahn, D., Horbach, J., et al.: Unusual progression of a *Legionella pneumophila* infection in a young child. Eur. J. Pediatr. *141*: 173, 1984.
14. Bhopal, R.: Source of infection for sporadic Legionnaires' disease: A review. J. Infect. *30*:9, 1995.
15. Bhopal, R. S., Diggle, P., and Rowlingson, B.: Pinpointing clusters of apparently sporadic cases of Legionnaires' disease. B. M. J. *304*:1022, 1992.
16. Bhopal, R. S., and Fallon, R. J.: Variation in time and space of non-outbreak Legionnaires' disease in Scotland. Epidemiol. Infect. *106*:45, 1991.
17. Bhopal, R. S., Fallon, R. J., Buist, E. C., et al.: Proximity of the home to a cooling tower and risk of non-outbreak Legionnaires' disease. B. M. J. *302*:378, 1991.
18. Blanchard, D. K., Friedman, H., Klein, T. W., et al.: Induction of interferon-gamma and tumor necrosis factor by *Legionella pneumophila*: Augmentation of human neutrophil bactericidal activity. J. Leukoc. Biol. *45*:538, 1989.
19. Blander, S. J., Breiman, R. F., and Horwitz, M. A.: A live avirulent mutant *Legionella pneumophila* vaccine induces protective immunity against lethal aerosol challenge. J. Clin. Invest. *83*:810, 1989.
20. Blander, S. J., and Horwitz, M. A.: Vaccination with the major secretory protein of *Legionella pneumophila* induces cell-mediated and protective immunity in a guinea pig model of Legionnaires' disease. J. Exp. Med. *169*:691, 1989.
21. Blander, S. J., and Horwitz, M. A.: Vaccination with *Legionella pneumophila* membranes induces cell-mediated and protective immunity in a guinea pig model of Legionnaires' disease: Protective immunity independent of the major secretory protein of *Legionella pneumophila*. J. Clin. Invest. *87*:1054, 1991.
22. Blander, S. J., and Horwitz, M. A.: Major cytoplasmic membrane protein of *Legionella pneumophila*, a genus common antigen and member of the hsp 60 family of heat shock proteins, induces protective immunity in a guinea pig model of Legionnaires' disease. J. Clin. Invest. *91*:717, 1993.
23. Blatt, S. P., Parkinson, M. D., Pace, E., et al.: Nosocomial Legionnaires' disease: Aspiration as a primary mode of disease acquisition. Am. J. Med. *95*:16, 1993.
24. Bornstein, N., Fleurette, J., Bosshard, S., et al.: Evaluation de la frequence des reactions serologiques croisees entre *Legionella* et mycoplasma ou chlamydia. Pathol. Biol. (Paris) *32*:165, 1984.
25. Boswell, T. C., and Kudesia, G.: Serological cross-reaction between *Legionella pneumophila* and *Campylobacter* in the indirect fluorescent antibody test. Epidemiol. Infect. *109*:291, 1992.
26. Brady, M. T.: Nosocomial legionnaires' disease in a children's hospital. J. Pediatr. *115*:46, 1989.
27. Bridge, J. A., and Edelstein, P. H.: Oropharyngeal colonization with *Legionella pneumophila*. J. Clin. Microbiol. *18*:1108, 1983.
28. Byrd, T. F., and Horwitz, M. A.: Interferon gamma-activated human monocytes downregulate transferrin receptors and inhibit the intracellular multiplication of *Legionella pneumophila* by limiting the availability of iron. J. Clin. Invest. *83*:1457, 1989.
29. Byrd, T. F., and Horwitz, M. A.: Lactoferrin inhibits or promotes *Legionella pneumophila* intracellular multiplication in nonactivated and interferon gamma-activated human monocytes depending upon its degree of iron saturation: Iron-lactoferrin and nonphysiologic iron chelates reverse monocyte activation against *Legionella pneumophila*. J. Clin. Invest. *88*:1103, 1991.
30. Byrd, T. F., and Horwitz, M. A.: Chloroquine inhibits the intracellular multiplication of *Legionella pneumophila* by limiting the availability of iron: A potential new mechanism for the therapeutic effect of chloroquine against intracellular pathogens. J. Clin. Invest. *88*:351, 1991.
31. Campins, M., Ferrer, A., Callis, L., et al. Nosocomial Legionnaire's disease in a children's hospital [Review] [49 refs]. Pediatr. Infect. Dis. J. *19*: 228–234, 2000.
32. Carlson, N. C., Kuskie, M. R., Dobyns, E. L., et al.: Legionellosis in children: An expanding spectrum. Pediatr. Infect. Dis. J. *9*:133, 1990.
33. Carratala, J., Gudiol, F., Pallares, R., et al.: Risk factors for nosocomial *Legionella pneumophila* pneumonia. Am. J. Respir. Crit. Care Med. *149*: 625, 1994.
34. Cianciotto, N., Eisenstein, B. I., Engleberg, N. C., et al.: Genetics and molecular pathogenesis of *Legionella pneumophila*, an intracellular parasite of macrophages. Mol. Biol. Med. *6*:409, 1989.
35. Cianciotto, N. P., Eisenstein, B. I., Mody, C. H., et al.: A mutation in the *mip* gene results in an attenuation of *Legionella pneumophila* virulence. J. Infect. Dis. *162*:121, 1990.
36. Collins, M. T., McDonald, J., Hiby, N., et al.: Agglutinating antibody titers to members of the family Legionellaceae in cystic fibrosis patients as a result of cross-reacting antibodies to *Pseudomonas aeruginosa*. J. Clin. Microbiol. *19*:757, 1984.
37. Couvreur, J., Dournon, E., Garcia, J., et al.: La maladie des Légionnaires chez l'enfant: Enquête épidemiologique avec une nouvelle observation et revue de la littérature. Ann. Pédiatr. (Paris) *33*:379, 1986.
38. Couvreur, J., Khiati, M., Petiot, A., et al.: Pneumopathie a *Legionella pneumophila* chez un nourrisson de 4 mois et demi. Arch. Fr. Pédiatr. *40*:649, 1983.
39. Cunha, B. A. (ed.): Seminars in Respiratory Infections: Legionnaires' Disease. Vol. II. Philadelphia, Grune & Stratton, 1987.
40. Cutz, E., Thorner, P. S., Rao, C. P., et al.: Disseminated *Legionella pneumophila* infection in an infant with severe combined immunodeficiency. J. Pediatr. *100*:760, 1982.
41. Davis, G. S., Winn, W. C., Jr., Gump, D. W., et al.: The kinetics of early inflammatory events during experimental pneumonia due to *Legionella pneumophila* in guinea pigs. J. Infect. Dis. *148*:823, 1983.
42. Della Santa, L., Crimaldi, G., Pellegrini, V., et al. Pulmonary infections in children. I. Pneumonia due to Legionella pneumophila. Minerva. Pediatr. *46*:89–97, 1994.
43. Dennis, P. J., Brenner, D. J., Thacker, W. L., et al.: Five new *Legionella* species isolated from water. Int. J. Syst. Bacteriol. *43*:329, 1993.
44. Dournon, E., Bibb, W. F., Rajagopalan, P., et al.: Monoclonal antibody reactivity as a virulence marker for *Legionella pneumophila* serogroup 1 strains. J. Infect. Dis. *157*:496, 1988.
45. Drutz, D. J., Demarsh, P., Edelstein, P., et al.: *Legionella pneumophila* pneumonia in athymic nude mice. *In* Thornsberry, C., Balows, A., Feeley, J. C., et al. (eds.): *Legionella*. Proceedings of the 2nd International Symposium. Washington, DC, American Society for Microbiology, 1984, pp. 134–135.
46. Edelstein, P. H.: Antimicrobial chemotherapy for legionnaires' disease: A review. Clin. Infect. Dis. *21*:S265–S276, 1995.
47. Edelstein, P. H.: Antimicrobial chemotherapy for Legionnaires disease: Time for a change [Editorial]. Ann. Intern. Med. *129*:328–330, 1998.

48. Edelstein, P. H.: Antimicrobial therapy of Legionnaires' disease: A review. Clin. Infect. Dis. *21*(Suppl. 3):S265, 1995.
49. Edelstein, P. H.: Legionnaires' disease. Clin. Infect. Dis. *16*:741, 1993.
50. Edelstein, P. H.: Detection of antibodies to *Legionella*. *In* Rose, N. R., de Macario, E. C., Folds, J. D., et al. (eds.): Manual of Clinical Laboratory Immunology. 5th ed. Washington, DC, American Society for Microbiology, in press.
51. Edelstein, P. H., and Meyer, R. D.: Legionnaires' disease: A review. Chest *85*:114, 1984.
52. Edwards, J. H., Harbord, P., Skidmore, J. W., et al.: Humidifier fever. Thorax *32*:653, 1977.
53. Efthimiou, J., Hodson, M. E., Taylor, P., et al.: Importance of viruses and *Legionella pneumophila* in respiratory exacerbations of young adults with cystic fibrosis. Thorax *39*:150, 1984.
54. Eisenstein, T. K., Tamada, R., Meissler, J., et al.: Vaccination against *Legionella pneumophila*: Serum antibody correlates with protection induced by heat-killed or acetone-killed cells against intraperitoneal but not aerosol infection in guinea pigs. Infect. Immun. *45*:685, 1984.
55. Ephros, M., Engelhard, D., Maayan, S., et al.: *Legionella gormanii* pneumonia in a child with chronic granulomatous disease. Pediatr. Infect. Dis. J. *8*:726, 1989.
56. Falcó, V., Fernández de Sevilla, T., Alegre, J., et al.: *Legionella pneumophila*: A cause of severe community-acquired pneumonia. Chest *100*: 1007, 1991.
57. Fang, G. D., Yu, V. L., and Vickers, R. M.: Disease due to the Legionellaceae (other than *Legionella pneumophila*): Historical, microbiological, clinical, and epidemiological review. Medicine (Baltimore) *68*:116, 1989.
58. Ferrer Marcelles, A., Garcia Hernandez, F., Elcuaz Romano, R., et al.: Neumonia por *Legionella* en un recién nacido. An. Esp. Pediatr. *30*:213, 1989.
59. Ferrer, A., Elcuaz, R. I., Giménez-Pérez, M., et al.: Legionelosis infantil. Enferm. Infecc. Microbiol. Clin. *8*:278, 1990.
60. Fields, B. S., Sanden, G. N., Barbaree, J. M., et al.: Intracellular multiplication of *Legionella pneumophila* in amoebae isolated from hospital hot water tanks. Curr. Microbiol. *18*:131, 1989.
61. Foy, H. M., Broome, C. V., Hayes, P. S., et al.: Legionnaires' disease in a prepaid medical-care group in Seattle 1963–75. Lancet *1*:767, 1979.
62. Fraser, D. W., Tsai, T. R., Orenstein, W., et al.: Legionnaires' disease: Description of an epidemic of pneumonia. N. Engl. J. Med. *297*:1189, 1977.
63. Friedman, H., Widen, R., Klein, T., et al.: *Legionella pneumophila*-induced blastogenesis of murine lymphoid cells in vitro. Infect. Immun. *43*:314, 1984.
64. Fuchs, G. J., LaRocco, M., Robinson, A., et al.: Fatal Legionnaires' disease in an infant. Pediatr. Infect. Dis. *5*:377, 1986.
65. Gibson, F. C., Tzianabos, A. O., and Rodgers, F. G.: Adherence of *Legionella pneumophila* to U-937 cells, guinea-pig alveolar macrophages, and MRC-5 cells by a novel, complement-independent binding mechanism. Can. J. Microbiol. *40*:865, 1994.
66. Girod, J. C., Reichman, R. C., Winn, W. C., Jr., et al.: Pneumonic and nonpneumonic forms of legionellosis: The result of a common-source exposure to *Legionella pneumophila*. Arch. Intern. Med. *142*:545, 1982.
67. Glick, T. H., Gregg, M. B., Berman, B., et al.: Pontiac fever: An epidemic of unknown etiology in a health department. I. Clinical and epidemiologic aspects. Am. J. Epidemiol. *107*:149, 1978.
68. Goldberg, D. J., Wrench, J. G., Collier, P. W., et al.: Lochgoilhead fever: Outbreak of non-pneumonic legionellosis due to *Legionella micdadei*. Lancet *1*:316, 1989.
69. Grady, G. F., and Gilfillan, R. F.: Relation of *Mycoplasma pneumoniae* seroreactivity, immunosuppression, and chronic disease to Legionnaires' disease: A twelve-month prospective study of sporadic cases in Massachusetts. Ann. Intern. Med. *90*:607, 1979.
70. Green, M., Wald, E. R., Dashefsky, B., et al. Field inversion gel electrophoretic analysis of Legionella pneumophila strains associated with nosocomial legionellosis in children. J. Clin. Microbiol. *34*:175–176, 1996.
71. Hartemann, E., Berthier, J. C., Barrois, S., et al.: Pnemopathie grave a legionelle chez un nourrisson immunologiquement normal. Pediatrie *38*:393, 1983.
72. Harvey, C. J., and Eykyn, S. J.: Crossreactions between *Legionella* and *Campylobacter* spp.: A clinical conundrum. J. Infect. *30*:85, 1995.
73. Hedlund, K. W., McGann, V. G., Copeland, D. S., et al.: Immunologic protection against the Legionnaires' disease bacterium in the AKR/J mouse. Ann. Intern. Med. *90*:676, 1979.
74. Helbig, J. H., Engelstadter, T., Maiwald, M., et al. Diagnostic relevance of the detection of Legionella DNA in urine samples by the polymerase chain reaction. Eur. J. Clin. Microbiol. Infect. Dis. *18*:716–722, 1999.
75. Helms, C. M., Viner, J. P., Renner, E. D., et al.: Legionnaires' disease among pneumonias in Iowa (FY 1972–1978). II. Epidemiologic and clinical features of 30 sporadic cases of *L. pneumophila* infection. Am. J. Med. Sci. *281*:2, 1981.
76. Hervás, J. A., Lopez, P., de la Fuente, A., et al.: Multiple organ system failure in an infant with *Legionella* infection. Pediatr. Infect. Dis. J. *7*:671, 1988.
77. Hofflin, J. M., Potasman, I., Baldwin, J. C., et al.: Infectious complications in heart transplant recipients receiving cyclosporine and corticosteroids. Ann. Intern. Med. *106*:209, 1987.
78. Horie, H., Kawakami, H., Minoshima, K., et al.: Neonatal Legionnaires' disease: Histopathological findings in an autopsied neonate. Acta Pathol. Jpn. *42*:427, 1992.
79. Horwitz, M. A.: Interactions between macrophages and *Legionella pneumophila*. Curr. Top. Microbiol. Immunol. *181*:265, 1992.
80. Hsu, C. M., Huang, L. M., Kao, Y. F., et al. Prevalence of Legionella pneumophila infection in children and its role in pediatric community-acquired atypical pneumonia. Acta Paediatr. Sinica *37*:188–192, 1996.
81. Husmann, L. K., and Johnson, W.: Adherence of *Legionella pneumophila* to guinea pig peritoneal macrophages, J774 mouse macrophages, and undifferentiated U937 human monocytes: Role of Fc and complement receptors. Infect. Immun. *60*:5212, 1992.
82. Isberg, R. R., Rankin, S., Roy, C. R., et al.: *Legionella pneumophila*: Factors involved in the route and response to an intracellular niche. Infect. Agents Dis. *2*:220, 1993.
83. Jaulhac, B., Nowicki, M., Bornstein, N., et al.: Detection of *Legionella* spp. in bronchoalveolar lavage fluids by DNA amplification. J. Clin. Microbiol. *30*:920, 1992.
84. Jaulhac, B., Reyrolle, M., Sodahlon, Y. K., et al. Comparison of sample preparation methods for detection of Legionella pneumophila in culture-positive bronchoalveolar lavage fluids by PCR. J. Clin. Microbiol. *36*: 2120–2122, 1998.
85. Johnson, J. T., Yu, V. L., Best, M. G., et al.: Nosocomial legionellosis in surgical patients with head-and-neck cancer: Implications for epidemiological reservoir and mode of transmission. Lancet *2*:298, 1985.
86. Joly, J. R., Déry, P., Gauvreau, L., et al.: Legionnaires' disease caused by *Legionella dumoffii* in distilled water. Can. Med. Assoc. J. *135*:1274, 1986.
87. Joseph, C. A., Dedman, D., Birtles, R., et al.: Legionnaires' disease surveillance: England and Wales, 1993. Commun. Dis. Rep. C. D. R. Rev. *4*:R109, 1994.
88. Joseph, C. A., Watson, J. M., Harrison, T. G., et al.: Nosocomial Legionnaires' disease in England and Wales, 1980–92. Epidemiol. Infect. *112*:329, 1994.
89. Katz, S. M., Hammel, J. M., Matus, J. P., et al.: A self-limited febrile illness produced in guinea pigs associated with oral administration of *Legionella pneumophila*. Gastroenterology *95*:1575, 1988.
90. Katz, S. M., and Holsclaw, D. S., Jr.: Serum antibodies to *Legionella pneumophila* in patients with cystic fibrosis. J. A. M. A. *248*:2284, 1982.
91. Kaufmann, A. F., McDade, J. E., Patton, C. M., et al.: Pontiac fever: Isolation of the etiologic agent (*Legionella pneumophila*) and demonstration of its mode of transmission. Am. J. Epidemiol. *114*:337, 1981.
92. Koide, M., and Saito, A. Diagnosis of Legionella pneumophila infection by polymerase chain reaction. Clin. Infect. Dis. *21*:199–201, 1995.
93. Kovatch, A. L., Jardine, D. S., Dowling, J. N., et al.: Legionellosis in children with leukemia in relapse. Pediatrics *73*:811, 1984.
94. Kugler, J. W., Armitage, J. O., Helms, C. M. et al.: Nosocomial Legionnaires' disease: Occurrence in recipients of bone marrow transplants. Am. J. Med. *74*:281, 1983.
95. La, S., Michel, G., and Raoult, D.: Isolation of Legionella pneumophila by centrifugation of shell vial cell cultures from multiple liver and lung abscesses. J. Clin. Microbiol. *37*:785–787, 1999.
96. Lavocat, M. P., Berthier, J. C., Rousson, A., et al.: Légionellose pulmonaire chez un enfant après noyade en eau douce. Presse Med. *16*:780, 1987.
97. Lefrancois, C., Casadevall, I., Betremieux, P., et al.: Legionellose mortelle chez un nourrisson traite par ACTH. Arch. Fr. Pédiatr. *46*:591, 1989.
98. Leluc, O., Doucet, V, Petit, P., et al.: [Legionella pneumophila: Unusual lung and hepatic manifestations]. [French]. J. Radiol. *81*:241–242, 2000.
99. Levy, I., and Rubin, L. G.: Legionella pneumonia in neonates: A literature review. J. Perinatol. *18*:287–290, 1998.
100. Liles, M. R., Scheel, T. A., and Cianciotto, N. P.: Discovery of a non-classical siderophore, legiobactin, produced by strains of Legionella pneumophila. J. Bacteriol. *182*:749–757, 2000.
101. Lindsay, D. S., Abraham, W. H., and Fallon, R. J.: Detection of mip gene by PCR for diagnosis of Legionnaires' disease. J. Clin. Microbiol. *32*:3068, 1994.
102. Luttichau, H. R., Vinther, C., Uldum, S. A., et al.: An outbreak of Pontiac fever among children following use of a whirlpool. Clin. Infect. Dis. *26*:1374–1378, 1998.
103. Maiwald, M., Kissel, K., Srimuang, S., et al.: Comparison of polymerase chain reaction and conventional culture for the detection of legionellas in hospital water samples. J. Appl. Bacteriol. *76*:216, 1994.
104. Maiwald, M., Schill, M., Stockinger, C., et al.: Detection of *Legionella* DNA in human and guinea pig urine samples by the polymerase chain reaction. Eur. J. Clin. Microbiol. Infect. Dis. *14*:25, 1995.
105. Marrie, T. J., Haldane, D., MacDonald, S., et al.: Control of endemic nosocomial legionnaires' disease by using sterile potable water for high risk patients. Epidemiol. Infect. *107*:591, 1991.
106. Marshall, L. E., Boswell, T. C., and Kudesia, G.: False positive *Legionella* serology in *Campylobacter* infection: *Campylobacter*

serotypes, duration of antibody response and elimination of cross-reactions in the indirect fluorescent antibody test. Epidemiol. Infect. *112*:347, 1994.

107. Marston, B., Plouffe, J., Breiman, R., et al.: Findings of a community-based pneumonia incidence study through November 1991 [Abstract 7]. Program and Abstracts of the 1992 International Symposium on *Legionella*, January 26–29, 1992, Orlando, FL. Washington, DC, American Society for Microbiology, 1992.
108. Marston, B. J., Lipman, H. B., and Breiman, R. F.: Surveillance for Legionnaires' disease: Risk factors for morbidity and mortality. Arch. Intern. Med. *154*:2417, 1994.
109. McDade, J. E., Shepard, C. C., Fraser, D. W., et al.: Legionnaires' disease: Isolation of a bacterium and demonstration of its role in other respiratory disease. N. Engl. J. Med. *297*:1197, 1977.
110. Millunchick, E. W., Floyd, J., and Blanks, J.: Legionnaires' disease in an immunologically normal child. Am. J. Dis. Child. *135*:1065, 1981.
111. Muittari, A., Kuusisto, P., Virtanen, P., et al.: An epidemic of extrinsic allergic alveolitis caused by tap water. Clin. Allergy *10*:77, 1980.
112. Muldoon, R. L., Jaecker, D. L., and Kiefer, H. K.: Legionnaires' disease in children. Pediatrics *67*:329, 1981.
113. Mundel, G., Goldberg, A., Boldur, I., et al.: Legionnaires' disease in Israel: Serological evidence of childhood infection. Isr. J. Med. Sci. *19*: 380, 1983.
114. Murdoch, D. R., Walford, E. J., Jennings, L. C., et al.: Use of the polymerase chain-reaction to detect legionella DNA in urine and serum samples from patients with pneumonia. Clin. Infect. Dis. *23*:475–480, 1996.
115. Myerowitz, R. L., Dowling, J. N., and Pasculle, A. W.: Immunity to Pittsburgh pneumonia agent in guinea pigs [Abstract]. 20th Interscience Conference on Antimicrobial Agents and Chemotherapy, New Orleans, 1980.
116. Nĕgre, V., Chevallier, B., Dournon, E., et al.: Maladies des légionnaires noscomiale chez l'enfant: Mesures de prevention. Arch. Fr. Pédiatr. *47*:43, 1990.
117. Nigro, G., Pastoris, M. C., Fantasia, M. M., et al.: Acute cerebellar ataxia in pediatric legionellosis. Pediatrics *72*:847, 1983.
118. Orenstein, W. A., Overturf, G. D., Leedom, J. M., et al.: The frequency of *Legionella* infection prospectively determined in children hospitalized with pneumonia. J. Pediatr. *99*:403, 1981.
119. Pachon, J., Prados, M. D., Capote, F., et al.: Severe community-acquired pneumonia: Etiology, prognosis, and treatment. Am. Rev. Respir. Dis. *142*:369, 1990.
120. Payne, N. R., and Horwitz, M. A.: Phagocytosis of *Legionella pneumophila* is mediated by human monocyte complement receptors. J. Exp. Med. *166*:1377, 1987.
121. Peerless, A. G., Liebhaber, M., Anderson, S., et al.: *Legionella* pneumonia in chronic granulomatous disease. J. Pediatr. *106*:783, 1985.
122. Peeters, M., Cornu, G., and De Meyer, R.: Legionnaires' disease in an immunosuppressed child. Acta Paediatr. Belg. *33*:189, 1980.
123. Peliowski, A., and Finer, N. N.: Intractable seizures in Legionnaires disease. J. Pediatr. *109*:657, 1986.
124. Plouffe, J. F., Breiman, R. F., File, T. M., et al.: Investigation of the risk factors for sporadically occurring Legionnaires' disease. Palo Alto, Calif. Electric Power Research Institute, 1995, TR-104770s, p. i-F-2.
125. Plouffe, J. F., Para, M. F., Fuller, K. A., et al.: Oral ingestion of *Legionella pneumophila*. J. Clin. Lab. Immunol. *20*:113, 1986.
126. Quagliano, P. V., and Das Narla, L.: *Legionella* pneumonia causing multiple cavitating pulmonary nodules in a 7-month-old infant. A. J. R. Am. J. Roentgenol. *161*:367, 1993.
127. Reingold, A. L.: Role of legionellae in acute infections of the lower respiratory tract. Rev. Infect. Dis. *10*:1018, 1988.
128. Renner, E. D., Helms, C. M., Hall, N. H., et al.: Seroreactivity to *Mycoplasma pneumoniae* and *Legionella pneumophila*: Lack of a statistically significant relationship. J. Clin. Microbiol. *13*:1096, 1981.
129. Renner, E. D., Helms, C. M., Hierholzer, W. J., Jr., et al.: Legionnaires' disease in pneumonia patients in Iowa: A retrospective seroepidemiologic study, 1972–1977. Ann. Intern. Med. *90*:603, 1979.
130. Richards, S. W., Peterson, P. K., Niewoehner, D. E., et al.: *Legionella pneumophila* infection in normal and immunocompromised hamsters [Abstract]. Proceedings of the American Society Annual Meeting, 1983.
131. Rolstad, B., and Berdal, B. P.: Immune defenses against *Legionella pneumophila* in rats. Infect. Immun. *32*:805, 1981.
132. Rowbotham, T. J.: Current views on the relationships between amoebae, legionellae and man. Isr. J. Med. Sci. *22*:678, 1986.
133. Roy, C. R., and Coers, I.: Exploitation of macrophages as a replication niche by Legionella pneumophila: Response [Comment]. Trends Microbiol. *8*:49–50, 2000.
134. Ryan, M. E., Feldman, S., Pruitt, B., et al.: Legionnaires' disease in a child with cancer. Pediatrics *64*:951, 1979.
135. Rylander, R., and Haglind, P.: Airborne endotoxins and humidifier disease. Clin. Allergy *14*:109, 1984.
136. Schmid, H., Henze, G., Schwerdtfeger, R., et al.: Fractionated total body irradiation and high-dose VP-16 with purged autologous bone marrow rescue for children with high risk relapsed acute lymphoblastic leukemia. Bone Marrow Transplant. *12*:597, 1993.
137. Simpson, R. M., Cogswell, J. J., Mitchell, E. R., et al.: Legionnaires' disease in an infant. Lancet *2*:740, 1980.
138. Spanò, C., and Menozzi, M.: Legionnaire's disease in Palermo and possible involvement of *Legionella pneumophila* in cases of pericardial effusion. Infection *10*:103, 1982.
139. Sturm, R., Staneck, J. L., Myers, J. P., et al.: Pediatric Legionnaires' disease: Diagnosis by direct immunofluorescent staining of sputum. Pediatrics *68*:539, 1981.
140. Thompson, J. E.: Community acquired pneumonia in north eastern Australia: A hospital based study of aboriginal and non-aboriginal patients. Aust. N. Z. J. Med. *27*:59–61, 1997.
141. Thornsberry, C., Balows, A., Feeley, J. C., et al.: *Legionella*. Proceedings of the 2nd International Symposium. Washington, DC, American Society for Microbiology, 1984, pp. 1–371.
142. Tokunaga, Y., Concepcion, W., Berquist, W. E., et al.: Graft involvement by *Legionella* in a liver transplant recipient. Arch. Surg. *127*:475, 1992.
143. Torres, A., Serra-Batlles, J., Ferrer, A., et al.: Severe community-acquired pneumonia: Epidemiology and prognostic factors. Am. Rev. Respir. Dis. *144*:312, 1991.
144. Venezia, R. A., Agresta, M. D., Hanley, E. M., et al.: Nosocomial legionellosis associated with aspiration of nasogastric feedings diluted in tap water. Infect. Control Hosp. Epidemiol. *15*:529, 1994.
145. Visca, P., Goldoni, P., Luck, P. C., et al.: Multiple types of Legionella pneumophila serogroup 6 in a hospital heated-water system associated with sporadic infections. J. Clin. Microbiol. *37*:2189–2196, 1999.
146. Vogel, J. P., and Isberg, R. R.: Cell biology of Legionella pneumophila. Curr. Opin. Microbiol. *2*:30–34,1999.
147. Wadowsky, R. M., Butler, L. J., Cook, M. K., et al.: Growth-supporting activity for *Legionella pneumophila* in tap water cultures and implication of hartmannellid amoebae as growth factors. Appl. Environ. Microbiol. *54*:2677, 1988.
148. Wadowsky, R. M., Wilson, T. M., Kapp, N. J., et al.: Multiplication of *Legionella* spp. in tap water containing *Hartmannella vermiformis*. Appl. Environ. Microbiol. *57*:1950, 1991.
149. Watson, K. C., Bain, A. D., and Bartholomew, S. E.: Legionellosis and sudden infant death syndrome. Lancet *2*:1312, 1983.
150. Weeratna, R., Stamler, D. A., Edelstein, P. H., et al.: Human and guinea pig immune responses to *Legionella pneumophila* protein antigens OmpS and Hsp60. Infect. Immun. *62*:3454, 1994.
151. Wentworth, B. B., and Stiefel, H. E.: Studies of the specificity of *Legionella* serology. J. Clin. Microbiol. *15*:961, 1982.
152. Winn, W. C., Jr.: *Legionella* and the clinical microbiologist. Infect. Dis. Clin. North Am. *7*:377, 1993.
153. Yamamoto, Y., Retzlaff, C., He, P., et al.: Quantitative reverse transcription-PCR analysis of *Legionella pneumophila*-induced cytokine mRNA in different macrophage populations by high-performance liquid chromatography. Clin. Diagn. Lab. Immunol. *2*:18, 1995.

INDEX

Note: Page numbers followed by the letter f refer to figures; those followed by the letter t refer to tables.

B

F

G

M

Q

R

U

V

W